# GREAT BRITAIN

# BRITISH COMMONWEALTH

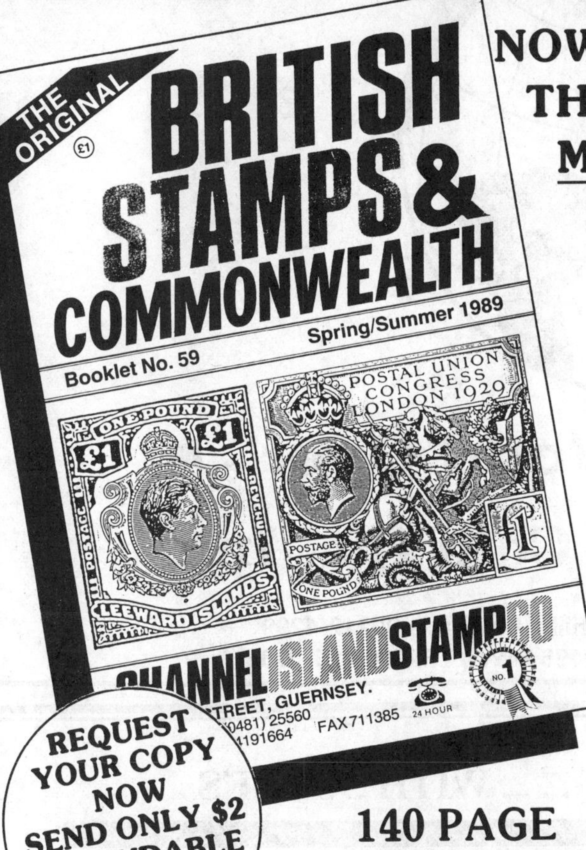


## NOW YOU CAN BU

## THE UK'S LEAD

## MAIL ORDER S

We specialize in G... ...ritain 1840-1989
Commonwealth 1935-1989

plus in depth smaller islands.

- COMPETITIVE PRICES
- VAST STOCKS
- FAST, FRIENDLY SERVICE
- CLEAR, PRECISE LISTINGS
- TOP DISCOUNTS
- INTEREST FREE CREDIT
- PAY BY U.S. OR CANADIAN CHECK — ALL MAJOR CREDIT CARDS ACCEPTED

REQUEST YOUR COPY NOW SEND ONLY $2 REFUNDABLE ON FIRST ORDER

140 PAGE ILLUSTRATED BOOKLET

**Managing Director Ian Wood and his staff of 11 experts offer you a vast stock to choose from. All goods clearly described and attractively priced. We aim to give a prompt, personal service.**

What you say:

I would like to express my sincere thanks for your most helpful and speedy service.......... D.H. Glos.

Thank you, you say that you aim to please, you have achieved your aim!.......... J.S. U.S.A.

Once again, thank you for your excellent service — truly you are No. 1.......... G.N. R.S.A.

I enjoyed the last selection 'Master Parcel' especially the unusual Q.V.'s included, the Classic Victoria was outstanding.. W.T. U.S.A.

I have recently ordered and received a 'Master Pack' from you. I would like to take this opportunity to congratulate you on an excellent package, extremely good value for money.......... M.W. G.B.

## MONTHLY MAIL POSTAL AUCTIONS

We hold a Postal Auction every month with sections covering most Commonwealth and Foreign countries, also specialised sections and rarities.

SEND FOR LATEST EDITION

$2

SATISFACTION GUARANTEED

**CHANNEL ISLAND STAMP CO**

**20 SMITH STREET, GUERNSEY, UNITED KINGDOM**

**Phone 011-44-481-25560**
**24 Hour ANSAPHONE to request a Catalogue or to place a Credit Card Order.**
**FAX 011-44-481-711385**

SCOTT®

# 1990 Standard Postage Stamp Catalogue

ONE HUNDRED AND FORTY-SIXTH EDITION IN FOUR VOLUMES

## VOLUME 1

UNITED STATES
and Affiliated Territories
UNITED NATIONS
CANADA
GREAT BRITAIN & THE BRITISH COMMONWEALTH





**Scott Publishing Co.**
911 Vandemark Road, Sidney, Ohio 45365
A division of AMOS PRESS INC., publishers of *Linn's Stamp News*, *Coin World*, *Cars & Parts* magazine and *The Sidney Daily News*.

# Table of Contents



See Volumes II, III and IV for nations of Africa, Asia, Europe, Latin America and their affiliated territories.

## Copyright Notice



## Trademark Notice



ISBN 0-89487-120-X

Library of Congress Card No. 2-3301

# Scott Publishing Co.

SCOTT®
911 VANDEMARK ROAD, SIDNEY, OHIO 45365 513-498-0802

Welcome to our 1990 Volume 1

Very quickly as you look through the pages of this volume, you will find that this truly is a new catalogue built onto an old chassis...126 years old, to be sure. We have been listening to you since Scott Publishing Co. arrived at its home in Sidney, Ohio, and we are continuing to adjust our catalogue presentation to meet your needs.

The 1990 edition of the Scott Catalogue cannot have the catalogue value of stamps within its pages compared to the values of the preceding year. Catalogue values of all stamps listed this year reflect *actual retail value* as we have found them in the marketplace.

Also, we have adjusted the grading level at which stamps are valued. Scott now values stamps at a grade of Fine-Very Fine, with an illustrated description of what we mean by that grade on the pages which follow.

The practice of purchasing stamps at a fraction of "Scott" no longer is valid. You now can expect to pay approximately the listed catalogue value when you purchase from dealer price lists, approval selections, or at stamp shows. Deep discounts will now be the exception rather than the rule.

If you purchase stamps at auction, you may need to adjust your bidding habits. Bidding at large discounts from catalogue value will decrease your chances of acquiring a lot. For best results, compare the catalogue values in this volume with recent auction realizations and place your own bids with that information in mind.

Bargains may still occur at auction sales, particularly when a specific lot is not in demand at the time of the sale. Also, when reviewing auction catalogues, be aware of the terms and conditions of that sale. Be certain of which stamp catalogue is being used as reference, and which catalogue values are being used in the text of the auction catalogue.

To determine the catalogue values used this year, we have consulted literally hundreds of dealer price lists, carefully reviewed the results of scores of public auctions, scoured the philatelic media for ads with prices, and listened to the advice of more outside experts than Scott has ever used in the past.

As an example, nearly 400 dealers — known to produce price lists — were queried for a copy. In addition, nearly 200 dealers, collectors and specialty societies were invited to provide more explicit information on stamps within their areas of expertise. Response has been tremendous, with the accompanying Acknowledgments section a testament. We continue to hear from additional persons invited to assist, so the list shown in this volume is not yet complete. Other important information that we use comes from you the user of this catalogue. We receive hundreds of letters with questions which lead to corrections and amplifications within our pages. Our thanks go out to everyone who helps in that way.

You have given us direction in more areas than only that of catalogue values. The introduction to this Volume is very different than in the past. A "mini-introduction" is designed to quickly acclimate everyone to what can be an awesome bulk of information. The pages which follow the "mini-introduction" are a completely revised approach to both our catalogue and the basics of stamp collecting in general.

By the time you complete the introduction, you should not be surprised by terms and concepts you find in the individual country listings within the text of this volume.

For the first time, some unused stamps are valued in a never-hinged state on a country-by-country basis. Previously, there were two cut-off dates used: one for British Commonwealth and the other for the remainder of the countries of the world. Where "never-hinged" is a factor in the valuing, a note appears both at the beginning of the country itself as well as just before the point in the listings where the change begins.

Not to be overlooked is the inclusion in this Volume of updated listings for the stamps of St. Kitts, which had not been revised since that island began a separate postal administration from Nevis.

Our format and size change in the 1989 edition brought about some problems in the 1989 Volume 1, i.e., some overlapping type and other similar problems, which have been corrected this year.

This catalogue continues to evolve in response to what we hear you telling us. Some years the evolution process appears to be moving more rapidly than in others, but the process continues nevertheless. That evolution is much easier with all of the support we receive from those who use the catalogue.

Sincerely,

Richard L. Sine

Richard L. Sine
Editorial Director

# Catalogue Information

## Catalogue Value

The Scott Catalogue value is a retail price, what you could expect to pay for the stamp in a grade of Fine-Very Fine. The value listed is a reference which reflects recent actual dealer selling prices.

Dealer retail price lists, public auction results, published prices in advertising, and individual solicitation of retail prices from dealers, collectors, and specialty organizations have been used in establishing the values found in this catalogue.

Use this catalogue as a guide in your own buying and selling. The actual price you pay for a stamp may be higher or lower than the catalogue value because of one or more of the following: the amount of personal service a dealer offers, increased interest in the country or topic represented by the stamp or set, whether an item is a "loss leader," part of a special sale, or otherwise is being sold for a short period of time at a lower price, or if at a public auction you are able to obtain an item inexpensively because of little interest in the item at that time.

For unused stamps, more recent issues are valued as never hinged, with the beginning point determined on a country-by-country basis. Notes to show the beginning points are prominently noted in the text.

## Grade

A stamp's grade and condition are crucial to its value. Values quoted in this catalogue are for stamps graded at Fine-Very Fine and with no faults. The accompanying illustrations show an example of a Fine-Very Fine grade between the grades immediately below and above it: Fine and Very Fine.

**FINE** stamps have the design noticeably off-center on two sides. Imperforate stamps may have small margins and earlier issues may show the design touching one edge of the stamp. Used stamps may have heavier than usual cancellations.

**FINE-VERY FINE** stamps may be somewhat off-center on one side, or only slightly off-center on two sides. Imperforate stamps will have two margins at least normal size and the design will not touch the edge. *Early issues of a country may be printed in such a way that the design naturally is very close to the edges.* Used stamps will not have a cancellation that detracts from the design. This is the grade used to establish Scott Catalogue values.

**VERY FINE** stamps may be slightly off-center on one side, with the design well clear of the edge. Imperforate stamps will have three margins at least normal size. Used stamps will have light or otherwise neat cancellations.

## Condition

The above definitions describe *grade,* which is centering and (for used stamps) cancellation. *Condition* refers to the soundness of the stamp, i.e., faults, repairs, and other factors influencing price.

Copies of a stamp which are of a lesser grade and/or condition trade at lower prices. Those of exceptional quality often command higher prices.

Factors that increase the value of a stamp include exceptionally wide margins, particularly fresh color, and the presence of selvage.

Factors other than faults that decrease the value of a stamp include missing gum or regumming, hinge remnant, foreign object adhering to gum, natural inclusion, or a straight edge.

Faults include a missing piece, tear, clipped perforation, pin or other hole, surface scuff, thin spot, crease, toning, oxidation or other form of color changeling, short or pulled perforation, stains or such man-made changes as reperforation or the chemical removal or lightening of a cancellation.

**Scott Publishing Co. recognizes that there is no formal, enforced grading scheme for postage stamps, and that the final price you pay for a stamp or obtain for a stamp you are selling will be determined by individual agreement at the time of the transaction.**

# Acknowledgments

Our appreciation and gratitude go to the following individuals and organizations who have assisted us in preparing information included in the 1990 Scott Catalogues. This list is not complete, for those who provide information for later volumes may not yet be included. Also, some helpers prefer anonymity. These individuals have generously shared their stamp knowledge with others through the medium of the Scott Catalogue.

Those who follow, provided information that is in addition to the hundreds of dealer price lists and advertisements and scores of auction catalogues and realizations which were used in producing the Catalogue Values used herein. It is from those noted here that we have been able to obtain information on items not normally seen in published lists and advertisements. Support from these people of course goes beyond data leading to Catalogue Values, for they also are key to editorial changes.

Joseph F. Albert
Simon Andrews
B.J. Ammel
Mike Armus
Joseph J. Atallah
M.S. Batchelor
Frederick Bean
Jules K. Beck
C.A. Beckwith
David Bein
Russ Bell
Ernest L. Bergman
Hank Bieniecki
Brian M. Bleckwenn
John R. Boker
Mike Bryne
Frank Buono
Roman Burkiewicz
Joseph Bush
E.J. Chamberlin
Henry Chlanda
Dr. Leonard Cohen
Howard G. DeVoe
P.J. Drossos
Bob Dumaine
Donald W. East
Norman Epstein
Stephen I. Esrati
Henry O. Feldman
Stephen I. Frater
Marvin Frey
Richard Friedberg
Earl H. Galitz
Frank Geiger
Peter Georgiadis
Brian M. Green
Horacio E. Groio
Rudolf Hamar
Ray Hanser
Leo John Harris
John B. Head
Bruce Hecht
Clifford O. Herrick
William Herzig
Jayson Hyun
Eric Jackson
Vincent E. Jay
Jack M. Jonza
H. Karen
Stanford M. Katz
Lewis S. Kaufman
Patricia Kaufmann
Jim Kerr
Stanley Kronenberg
Warren Lauzon
Steve Levine
Rosario LoGuidice
Bob Lovell
Gary J. Lyon
David MacDonnell
Donald L. MacPeek
Nick Macris
Sam Malamud
Nick Markov
Clyde E. Maxwell
Max Mayo
Mike McKillip
Hector Mena
Richard H. Muller
Victor Ostolaza
Souilen V. Panirian
Frank E. Patterson
Stanley Piller
Daniel N. Pinchot
Gilbert N. Plass
Richard Pyznar
Patrick Riggs
Peter A. Robertson
Michael Rogers
Jacques A. Schiff, Jr.
Richard Schwartz
Michael Shamilzadeh
William E. Shelton
J. Randall Shoemaker
Richard Simchak
James W. Smith
Jay Smith
Sherwood Springer
Linda Stanfield
Scott Trepel
Gary A. Van Cott
Carlos Vieiro
Jerome S. Wagshal
Daniel C. Warren
Richard A. Washburn
William R. Weiss

American Philatelic Society
P.O. Box 8000, State College, PA 16803

American Revenue Association
Bruce Miller, Suite 332, 701 S. First Ave., Arcadia, CA 91006

American Society of Netherlands Philately
Harold F. MacDonald, 2354 Roan Lane, Walnut Creek, CA 94596

Booklet Collectors Club
Larry Rosenblum, 1016 East El Camino Real, P.O. Box 107, Sunnyvale, CA 94087

Bureau Issues Association
William S. Dunn, 750 Jersey St., Denver, CO 80220

Canal Zone Study Group
Richard H. Salz, 60 27th Ave., San Francisco, CA 94121

China Stamp Society
Paul H. Gault, 140 W. 18th Ave., Columbus, OH 43210

Confederate Stamp Alliance
Brian Green, P.O. Box 1816, Kernersville, NC 27285

Costa Rica Collectors, Society of
T.C. Willoughby, 7600 Ridgemont Dr., Newburgh, IN 47630

Eire Philatelic Association
Robert C. Jones, 8 Beach St., Brockton, MA 02402

Estonian Philatelic Society
Rudolf Hamar, 243 34th St., New York, NY 10016

Ethiopian Philatelic Society
Miss Hugette Gagnon, P.O. Box F110-45, Blaine, WA 98230

Haiti Philatelic Society
Carroll L. Lloyd, 2117 Oak Lodge Road, Baltimore, MD 21228

Hellenic Philatelic Society of America
Nicholas Asimakopulos, MD, 541 Cedar Hill Ave., Wyckoff NJ 07481

International Philippine Philatelic Society
Mrs. E.C. Stanfield, P.O. Box 1936, Manila, PHILIPPINES

Korea Stamp Society
Harold L. Klein, P.O. Box 750, Lebanon, PA 17042

Latin American Philatelic Society
Piet Steen, P.O. Box 820, Hinton, AB, CANADA T0E 1B0

Mexico-Elmhurst Philatelic Society International
Robert Jones, 2350 Bunker Hill Way, Costa Mesa, CA 92626

Nepal and Tibet Philatelic Study Group
Roger D. Skinner, 1020 Covington Road, Los Altos, CA 94022

Philatelic Foundation
21 E. 40th St., New York, NY 10016

Rhodesian Study Circle
William R. Wallace, P.O. Box 16381, San Francisco, CA 94116

Rossica, Society of Russian Philately
Norman Epstein, 33 Crooke Ave., Brooklyn, NY 11226

Sarawak Specialists Society
C. Jackson Selsor, 2300 Front St., San Diego, CA 92102

Society for Hungarian Philately
P.O. Box 1162, Fairfield, CT 06432

St. Helena, Ascension & Tristan da Cunha Philatelic Society
R.V. Skavaril, 222 East Torrence Road, Columbus, OH 43214

The Spanish Main Society
Brian Moorhouse, P.O. Box 105, Peterborough, PE3 8TQ, ENGLAND

Ukrainian Philatelic/Numismatic Society
I. Kuzyck, P.O. Box 8363, Alexandria, VA 22360

# Understanding the Listings

On the opposite page is an enlarged "typical" listing from this catalogue. Following are detailed explanations of each of the highlighted parts of the listing.

**1** **Scott number** — Stamp collectors use Scott numbers to identify specific stamps when buying, selling, or trading stamps, and for ease in organizing their collections. Each stamp issued by a country has a unique number. Therefore, Germany Scott 99 can only refer to a single stamp. Although the Scott Catalogue usually lists stamps in chronological order by date of issue, when a country issues a set of stamps over a period of time the stamps within that set are kept together without regard of date of issue. This follows the normal collecting approach of keeping stamps in their natural sets.

When a country is known to be issuing a set of stamps over a period of time, a group of consecutive catalogue numbers is reserved for the stamps in that set, as issued. If that group of numbers proves to be too few, capital-letter suffixes are added to numbers to create enough catalogue numbers to cover all items in the set. Scott uses a suffix letter, i.e., "A," "b," etc., only once. If there is a Scott 16A in a set, there will not be a Scott 16a also.

There are times when the block of numbers is too large for the set, leaving some numbers unused. Such gaps in the sequence also occur when the editors move an item elsewhere in the catalogue or it is removed from the listings entirely. Scott does not attempt to account for every possible number, but rather it does attempt to assure that each stamp is assigned its own number.

Scott numbers designating regular postage normally are only numerals. Scott numbers for other types of stamps, i.e., air post, semi-postal, and so on, will have a prefix of either a capital letter or a combination of numerals and capital letters.

**2** **Illustration number** — used to identify each illustration. For most sets, the lowest face-value stamp is shown. It then serves as an example of the basic design approach for the set. Where more than one stamp in a set uses the same illustration number, that number needs to be used with the design paragraph or description line (noted below) to be certain of the exact design on each stamp within the set. Where there are both vertical and horizontal designs in a set, a single illustration may be used, with the exceptions noted in the design paragraph or description line. Illustrations normally are 75 percent of the original size of the stamp. An effort has been made to note all illustrations not at that percentage. Overprints are shown at 100 percent of the original, unless otherwise noted.

**3** **Paper color** — the color of the paper is noted in italic type when the paper used is not white.

**4** **Listing styles** — There are two principal types of catalogue listings: major and minor.

*Majors* normally are in a larger type style than minor listings. They also may be distinguished by having as their catalogue number a numeral with or without a capital-letter suffix and with or without a prefix.

*Minors* are in a smaller type style and have a small-letter suffix (or, only have the small letter itself shown if the listing is immediately beneath its major listing). These listings show a variety of the "normal," or major item. Examples include color variation or a different watermark used for that stamp only.

Examples of major numbers are 16, 28A, B97, C13A, 10N5, and 10N6A. Examples of minor numbers are 16a and C13b.

**5** **Basic information on stamp or set** — introducing each stamp issue, this section normally includes the date of issue, method of printing, perforation, watermark, and sometimes some additional information. New information on method of printing, watermark or perforation measurement appears only when that information changes. Dates of issues are as precise as Scott is able to confirm, either year only; month and year; or month, day, and year.

**6** **Denomination** — normally the face value of the stamp, i.e., the cost of the stamp at the post office at the time of issue.

**7** **Color or other description** — this line provides information to solidify identification of the stamp. Historically, when stamps normally were printed in a single color, only the color appeared here. With modern printing techniques, which include multicolor presses which mix inks on the paper, earlier methods of color identification are no longer applicable. When space permits, a description of the stamp design replaces the terms "multi" or "multicolored."

**8** **Year of issue** — in stamp sets issued over more than one year, the number in parentheses signifies the year the single stamp appeared. Stamps without a date appeared during the first year of the span. Dates are not always given for minor varieties.

**9** **Value unused and value used** — the catalogue values are based on stamps which are in a grade of Fine-Very Fine. Unused values refer to items which have not seen postal or other duty for which they were intended. For pre-1900 issue, unused stamps must have at least most of their original gum; for later issues, complete gum is expected. Stamps issued without gum are noted. Unused values are for never-hinged stamps beginning at the point immediately following a prominent notice in the actual listing. The same information also appears at the beginning of the country's information. See the section "Catalogue Values" for an explanation of the meaning of these values.

**10** **Changes in basic set information** — bold type is used to show any change in the basic data on within a set of stamps, i.e., perforation from one stamp to the next or a different paper or printing method or watermark.

**11** **Total value of set** — the total value of sets of five or more stamps, issued after 1900, are shown on a separate line. The line also notes the range of Scott numbers and total number of stamps included in the total.

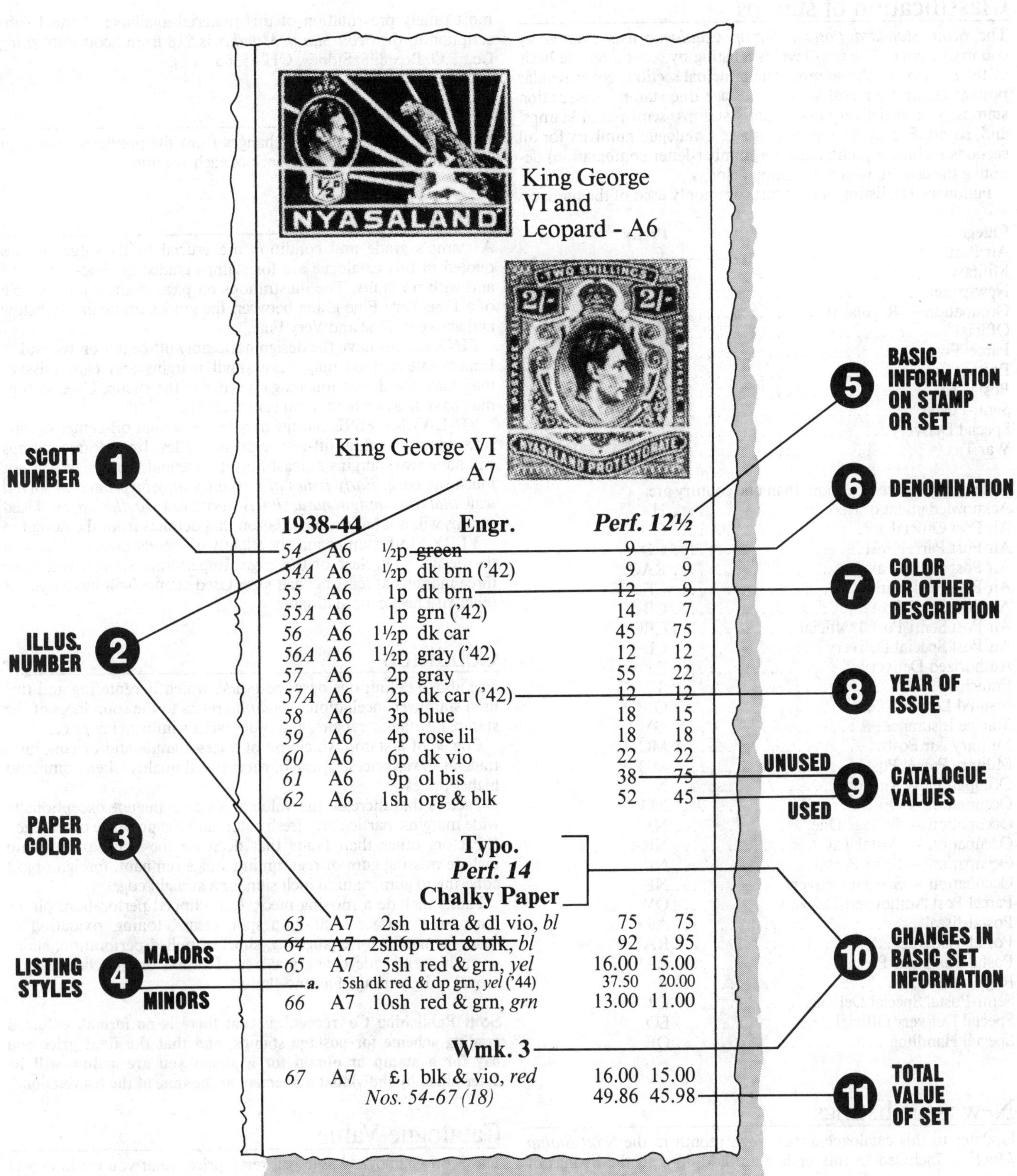
NYASALAND
King George VI and Leopard - A6
TWO SHILLINGS
2/- 2/-
POSTAGE
REVENUE
NYASALAND PROTECTORATE
King George VI
A7
1938-44 Engr. Perf. 12½
54 A6 ½p green 9 7
54A A6 ½p dk brn ('42) 9 9
55 A6 1p dk brn 12 9
55A A6 1p grn ('42) 14 7
56 A6 1½p dk car 45 75
56A A6 1½p gray ('42) 12 12
57 A6 2p gray 55 22
57A A6 2p dk car ('42) 12 12
58 A6 3p blue 18 15
59 A6 4p rose lil 18 18
60 A6 6p dk vio 22 22
61 A6 9p ol bis 38 75
62 A6 1sh org & blk 52 45
Typo.
Perf. 14
Chalky Paper
63 A7 2sh ultra & dl vio, bl 75 75
64 A7 2sh6p red & blk, bl 92 95
65 A7 5sh red & grn, yel 16.00 15.00
a. 5sh dk red & dp grn, yel ('44) 37.50 20.00
66 A7 10sh red & grn, grn 13.00 11.00
Wmk. 3
67 A7 £1 blk & vio, red 16.00 15.00
Nos. 54-67 (18) 49.86 45.98
1 SCOTT NUMBER
2 ILLUS. NUMBER
3 PAPER COLOR
4 LISTING STYLES
MAJORS
MINORS
5 BASIC INFORMATION ON STAMP OR SET
6 DENOMINATION
7 COLOR OR OTHER DESCRIPTION
8 YEAR OF ISSUE
9 CATALOGUE VALUES
UNUSED
USED
10 CHANGES IN BASIC SET INFORMATION
11 TOTAL VALUE OF SET

# Special Notices

## Classification of stamps

The *Scott Standard Postage Stamp Catalogue* lists stamps by country of issue. The next level is a listing by section on the basis of the function of the stamps. The principal sections cover regular postage stamps; air post stamps; postage due stamps, registration stamps, special delivery and express stamps, semi-postal stamps, and, so on. Except for regular postage, Catalogue numbers for all sections include a prefix letter (or number-letter combination) denoting the class to which the stamp belongs.

Following is a listing of the most commonly used of the prefixes.

| Category | Prefix |
|---|---|
| Air Post | C |
| Military | M |
| Newspaper | P |
| Occupation — Regular Issues | N |
| Official | O |
| Parcel Post | Q |
| Postage Due | J |
| Postal Tax | RA |
| Semi-Postal | B |
| Special Delivery | E |
| War Tax | MR |

Other prefixes used by more than one country are:

| | |
|---|---|
| Acknowledgment of Receipt | H |
| Air Post Official | CO |
| Air Post Parcel Post | CQ |
| Air Post Postal Tax | RAC |
| Air Post Registration | CF |
| Air Post Semi-Postal | CB |
| Air Post Semi-Postal Official | CBO |
| Air Post Special Delivery | CE |
| Authorized Delivery | EY |
| Franchise | S |
| Insured Letter | G |
| Marine Insurance | GY |
| Military Air Post | MC |
| Military Parcel Post | MQ |
| Occupation — Air Post | NC |
| Occupation — Official | NO |
| Occupation — Postage Due | NJ |
| Occupation — Postal Tax | NRA |
| Occupation — Semi-Postal | NB |
| Occupation — Special Delivery | NE |
| Parcel Post Authorized Delivery | QY |
| Postal-fiscal | AR |
| Postal Tax Due | RAJ |
| Postal Tax Semi-Postal | RAB |
| Registration | F |
| Semi-Postal Special Delivery | EB |
| Special Delivery Official | EO |
| Special Handling | QE |

## New issue listings

Updates to this catalogue appear each month in the *Scott Stamp Monthly*. Included in this update are additions to the listings of countries found in *Scott Standard Postage Stamp Catalogue* and the *Specialized Catalogue of United States Stamps*, new issues of countries not listed in the catalogues, and corrections and updates to current editions of this catalogue.

From time to time there will be changes in the listings from the *Scott Stamp Monthly* to the next edition of the catalogue, as additional information becomes available.

The catalogue update section of the *Scott Stamp Monthly* is the most timely presentation of this material available. Annual subscription to the *Scott Stamp Monthly* is $18 from Scott Publishing Co., P.O. Box 828, Sidney, OH 45365.

## Number changes

A list of catalogue number changes from the previous edition of the catalogue appears at the back of each volume.

## Grade

A stamp's grade and condition are crucial to its value. Values quoted in this catalogue are for stamps graded at Fine-Very Fine and with no faults. The illustrations on page vi show an example of a Fine-Very Fine grade between the grades immediately below and above it: Fine and Very Fine.

**FINE** stamps have the design noticeably off-center on two sides. Imperforate stamps may have small margins and earlier issues may show the design touching one edge of the stamp. Used stamps may have heavier than usual cancellations.

**FINE-VERY FINE** stamps may be somewhat off-center on one side, or only slightly off-center on two sides. Imperforate stamps will have two margins at least normal size and the design will not touch the edge. *Early issues of a country may be printed in such a way that the design naturally is very close to the edges.* Used stamps will not have a cancellation that detracts from the design.

**VERY FINE** stamps may be slightly off-center on one side, with the design well clear of the edge. Imperforate stamps will have three margins at least normal size. Used stamps will have light or otherwise neat cancellations.

## Condition

The above definitions describe *grade,* which is centering and (for used stamps) cancellation. *Condition* refers to the soundness of the stamp, i.e., faults, repairs, and other factors influencing price.

Copies of a stamp which are of a lesser grade and/or condition trade at lower prices. Those of exceptional quality often command higher prices.

Factors that increase the value of a stamp include exceptionally wide margins, particularly fresh color, and the presence of selvage.

Factors other than faults that decrease the value of a stamp include missing gum or regumming, hinge remnant, foreign object adhering to gum, natural inclusion, or a straight edge.

Faults include a missing piece, tear, clipped perforation, pin or other hole, surface scuff, thin spot, crease, toning, oxidation or other form of color changeling, short or pulled perforation, stains or such man-made changes as reperforation or the chemical removal or lightening of a cancellation.

**Scott Publishing Co. recognizes that there is no formal, enforced grading scheme for postage stamps, and that the final price you pay for a stamp or obtain for a stamp you are selling will be determined by individual agreement at the time of the transaction.**

## Catalogue Value

The Scott Catalogue value is a retail price, what you could expect to pay for the stamp in a grade of Fine-Very Fine. The value listed is a reference which reflects recent actual dealer selling prices.

Dealer retail price lists, public auction results, published prices in advertising, and individual solicitation of retail prices from dealers, collectors, and specialty organizations have been used in establishing the values found in this catalogue.

Use this catalogue as a guide in your own buying and selling. The actual price you pay for a stamp may be higher or lower than the catalogue value because of one or more of the following: the amount of personal service a dealer offers, increased interest in the country or topic represented by the stamp or set, whether an item is a "loss leader," part of a special sale, or otherwise is being sold for a short period of time at a lower price, or if at a public auction you are able to obtain an item inexpensively because of little interest in the item at that time.

For unused stamps, more recent issues are valued as never-hinged, with the beginning point determined on a country-by-country basis. Notes in the text prominently show the beginning points of these designations.

As a point of philatelic-economic fact, the lower the value shown for an item in this catalogue, the greater the percentage of that value which is attributed to dealer mark-up and profit margin. Thus, a packet of 1,000 different items — each of which has a catalogue value of five cents — normally sells for considerably less than 50 dollars!

Persons wishing to establish the specific value of a stamp or other philatelic item may wish to consult with recognized stamp experts (collectors or dealers) and review current information or recent developments which would affect stamp prices.

Scott Publishing Co. assumes no obligation to revise the values during the distribution period of this catalogue or to advise users of other facts, such as stamp availability, political and economic conditions, or collecting preferences, any of which may have an immediate positive or negative impact on values.

## Understanding valuing notations

The *absence of a value* does not necessarily suggest that a stamp is scarce or rare. In the U.S. listings, a dash in the value column means that the stamp is known in a stated form or variety, but information is lacking or insufficient for purposes of establishing a usable catalogue value.

Stamp values in *italics* generally refer to items which are difficult to value accurately. For expensive items, i.e., value at $1,000 or more, a value in italics represents an item which trades very seldom, such as a unique item. For inexpensive items, a value in italics represents a warning. One example is a "blocked" issue where the issuing postal administration controlled one stamp in a set in an attempt to make the whole set more valuable. Another example is a single item with a very low face value which sells in the marketplace, at the time of issue, at an extreme multiple of face value. Some countries have released back issues of stamps in a canceled-to-order form, sometimes covering as much as 10 years.

The Scott Catalogue values for used stamps reflect canceled-to-order material when such are found to predominate in the marketplace for the issue involved. Frequently notes appear in the stamp listings to specify items which are valued as canceled-to-order or if there is a premium for postally used examples.

Another example of a warning to collectors is a stamp that used has a value considerably higher than the unused version. Here, the collector is cautioned to be certain the used version has a readable, contemporary cancellation.

The *minimum catalogue value* of a stamp is five cents, to cover a dealer's costs and then preparing it for resale. As noted, the sum of these values does not properly represent the "value" of a packet of unsorted or unmounted stamps sold in bulk. Such large mixtures or packets generally consist of only the lower-valued stamps.

Values in the "unused" column are for stamps that have been hinged, unless there is a specific note in a listing after which unused stamps are valued as never-hinged. A similar note will appear at the beginning of the country's listings, noting exactly where the dividing point between hinged and never-hinged is for each section of the listings. Where a value for a used stamp is considerably higher than for the unused stamp, the value applies to a stamp showing a distinct contemporary postmark of origin.

Many countries sell canceled-to-order stamps at a marked reduction of face value. Countries which sell or have sold canceled-to-order stamps at *full* face value include Australia, Netherlands, France, and Switzerland. It is almost impossible to identify such stamps, if the gum has been removed, because official government canceling devices are used. Postally used copies on cover, of these items, are usually worth more than the canceled-to-order stamps with original gum.

## Abbreviations

Scott Publishing Co. uses a consistent set of abbreviations throughout this catalogue to conserve space while still providing necessary information. The first block shown here refers to color names only:

**COLOR ABBREVIATIONS**

amb............ amber
anil............ aniline
ap............ apple
aqua............ aquamarine
az............ azure
bis............ bister
bl............ blue
bld............ blood
blk............ black
bril............ brilliant
brn............ brown
brnsh............ brownish
brnz............ bronze
brt............ bright
brnt............ burnt
car............ carmine
cer............ cerise
chlky............ chalky
cham............ chamois
chnt............ chestnut
choc............ chocolate
chr............ chrome
cit............ citron
cl............ claret
cob............ cobalt
cop............ copper
crim............ crimson
cr............ cream
dk............ dark
dl............ dull
dp............ deep
db............ drab
emer............ emerald
gldn............ golden
grysh............ grayish
grn............ green
grnsh............ greenish
hel............ heliotrope
hn............ henna
ind............ indigo
int............ intense
lav............ lavender
lem............ lemon
lil............ lilac
lt............ light
mag............ magenta
man............ manila
mar............ maroon
mv............ mauve
multi............ multicolored
mlky............ milky
myr............ myrtle
ol............ olive
olvn............ olvine
org............ orange
pck............ peacock
pnksh............ pinkish
Prus............ Prussian
pur............ purple
redsh............ reddish
res............ reseda
ros............ rosine
ryl............ royal
sal............ salmon
saph............ sapphire
scar............ scarlet
sep............ sepia
sien............ sienna
sil............ silver
sl............ slate
stl............ steel
turq............ turquoise
ultra............ ultramarine
ven............ venetian
ver............ vermilion
vio............ violet
yel............ yellow
yelsh............ yellowish

When no color is given for an overprint or surcharge, black is the color used. Abbreviations for colors used for overprints and surcharges are: "(B)", "(Bk)" or "(Blk)," black; "(Bl)," blue; "(R)," red; "(G)," green; etc.

Additional abbreviations in this catalogue are shown below:

Adm........ Administration
AFL........ American Federation of Labor

Anniv. . . . . . . Anniversary
APU . . . . . . . Arab Postal Union
APS. . . . . . . . American Philatelic Society
ASEAN. . . . . Association of South East Asian Nations
ASPCA . . . . . American Society for the Prevention of Cruelty to Animals
Assoc. . . . . . . Association

b. . . . . . . . . . Born
BEP. . . . . . . . Bureau of Engraving and Printing
Bicent. . . . . . . Bicentennial
Bklt. . . . . . . . Booklet
Brit. . . . . . . . . British
btwn. . . . . . . . Between
Bur. . . . . . . . . Bureau

c. or ca. . . . . . Circa
CAR . . . . . . . Central African Republic
Cat. . . . . . . . . Catalogue
Cent. . . . . . . . Centennial, century, centenary
CEPT . . . . . . Conference Europeenne des Administrations des Postes et des Telecommunications
CIO. . . . . . . . Congress of Industrial Organizations
Conf. . . . . . . . Conference
Cong. . . . . . . . Congress
Cpl. . . . . . . . . Corporal
CTO . . . . . . . Canceled to order

d. . . . . . . . . . . Died
Dbl. . . . . . . . . Double
DDR. . . . . . . . German Democratic Republic (East Germany)

ECU . . . . . . . European currency unit
EEC. . . . . . . . European Economic Community
EKU . . . . . . . Earliest known use
Engr. . . . . . . . Engraved
Exhib. . . . . . . Exhibition
Expo. . . . . . . . Exposition

FAO . . . . . . . Food and Agricultural Organization of the United Nations
Fed. . . . . . . . . Federation
FIP . . . . . . . . Federation International de Philatelie

GB. . . . . . . . . Great Britain
Gen. . . . . . . . General
GPO . . . . . . . General post office

Horiz. . . . . . . Horizontal

ICAO . . . . . . International Civil Aviation Organization
ICY . . . . . . . . International Cooperation Year
IEY . . . . . . . . International Education Year
ILO . . . . . . . . International Labor Organization
Imperf. . . . . . Imperforate
Impt. . . . . . . . Imprint
Intl. . . . . . . . . International
Invtd. . . . . . . Inverted
IQSY . . . . . . . International Quiet Sun Year
ITU. . . . . . . . International Telecommunications Union
ITY . . . . . . . . International Tourism Year
IWY . . . . . . . International Women's Year
IYC . . . . . . . . International Year of the Child
IYD. . . . . . . . International Year of the Disabled
IYP . . . . . . . . International Year of Peace
IYSH. . . . . . . International Year of Shelter for the Homeless
IYY. . . . . . . . International Youth Year

L . . . . . . . . . . Left
Lieut. . . . . . . . Lieutenant
Litho. . . . . . . Lithographed
LL . . . . . . . . . Lower left
LR. . . . . . . . . Lower right

mm . . . . . . . . Millimeter
Ms. . . . . . . . . Manuscript

NASA . . . . . . National Aeronautics and Space Administration
Natl. . . . . . . . National
NATO. . . . . . North Atlantic Treaty Organization
No. . . . . . . . . Number
NY . . . . . . . . New York
NYC . . . . . . . New York City

OAU. . . . . . . Organization of African Unity
OPEC . . . . . . Organization of Petroleum Exporting Countries
Ovpt. . . . . . . . Overprint
Ovptd. . . . . . . Overprinted

P# . . . . . . . . . Plate number
Perf. . . . . . . . . Perforated, perforation
Phil. . . . . . . . . Philatelic
Photo. . . . . . . Photogravure
PO. . . . . . . . . Post office
Pr. . . . . . . . . . Pair
P.R. . . . . . . . . Puerto Rico
PRC . . . . . . . People's Republic of China (Mainland China)
Prec. . . . . . . . Precancel, precanceled
Pres. . . . . . . . President

Rio . . . . . . . . Rio de Janeiro
ROC . . . . . . . Republic of China (Taiwan)

SEATO. . . . . South East Asia Treaty Organization
Sgt. . . . . . . . . Sergeant
Soc. . . . . . . . . Society
Souv. . . . . . . . Souvenir
SSR. . . . . . . . Soviet Socialist Republic
St. . . . . . . . . . Saint, street
Surch. . . . . . . Surcharge

Typo. . . . . . . . Typographed

UAE . . . . . . . United Arab Emirates
UAMPT . . . . Union of African and Malagasy Posts and Telecommunications
UL. . . . . . . . . Upper left
UN . . . . . . . . United Nations
UNCTAD. . . United Nations Conference on Trade and Development
UNESCO . . . United Nations Educational, Scientific and Cultural Organization
UNICEF. . . . United Nations Children's Fund
UNPA. . . . . . United Nations Postal Administration
Unwmkd. . . . Unwatermarked
UPU . . . . . . . Universal Postal Union
UR . . . . . . . . Upper Right
US. . . . . . . . . United States
USPO . . . . . . United States Post Office Department
USPS. . . . . . . United States Postal Service
USSR . . . . . . Union of Soviet Socialist Republics

Vert. . . . . . . . Vertical
VP. . . . . . . . . Vice president

WCY....... World Communications Year
WFUNA.... World Federation of United Nations Associations
WHO ...... World Health Organization
Wmk. ...... Watermark
Wmkd...... Watermarked
WMO ...... World Meteorological Organization
WRY........ World Refugee Year
WWF ...... World Wildlife Fund
WWI....... World War I
WWII ...... World War II

YAR ....... Yemen Arab Republic
Yemen PDR Yemen People's Democratic Republic

## Examination

Scott Publishing Co. will not pass upon the genuineness, grade or condition of stamps, because of the time and responsibility involved. Rather, there are several expertizing groups which undertake this work for both collectors and dealers. Neither can Scott Publishing Co. appraise or identify philatelic material. The Company cannot take responsibility for unsolicited stamps or covers.

## How to order from your dealer

It is not necessary to write the full description of a stamp as listed in this catalogue. All that you need is the name of the country, the Scott Catalogue number and whether the item is unused or used. For example, "Japan Scott 422 unused" is sufficient to identify the stamp of Japan listed as "422 A206 5y brown."

# Basic Stamp Information

A stamp collector's knowledge of the combined elements that make a given issue of a stamp unique determines his or her ability to identify stamps. These elements include paper, watermark, method of separation, printing, design and gum. On the following pages each of these important areas is described.

## PAPER

Paper is a material composed of a compacted web of cellulose fibers formed into sheets. Paper may be manufactured in sheets, or may have been part of a roll before being cut to size. The fibers most often used for the paper on which stamps are printed are bark, wood, straw and certain grasses with linen or cotton rags added for greater strength. Grinding and bleaching these fibers reduces them to a slushy pulp. Sizing and sometimes coloring matter are added to the pulp. Thin coatings of pulp are poured onto sieve-like frames, which allow the water to run off while retaining the matted pulp. Mechanical processes convert the pulp, when it is almost dry, by passing it through smooth or engraved rollers — dandy rolls — or placed between cloth in a press then flattens and dries the product under pressure.

Stamp paper falls broadly into two types: wove and laid. The nature of the surface of the frame onto which the pulp is first fed causes the differences in appearance between the two. If the surface is smooth and even the paper will be of uniform texture throughout, showing no light and dark areas when held to a light. This is known as *wove paper.* Early paper-making machines poured the pulp onto continuously circulating web of felt, but modern machines feed the pulp onto a cloth-like screen made of closely interwoven fine wires. This paper, when held to a light, will show little dots or points very close together. The proper name for this is "wire wove," but the type is still consider wove. Any U.S. or British stamp printed after 1880 will serve as an example of wire wove paper.

Closed spaced parallel wires, with cross wires at wider intervals, make up the frames used for *laid paper.* A greater thickness of the pulp will settle between the wires. The paper, when held to a light, will show alternate light and dark lines. The spacing and the thickness of the lines may vary, but on any one sheet of paper they are all alike. See Russia Scott 31-38 for an example of laid paper.

*Batonne,* from the French word meaning "a staff," is used if the lines are spaced quite far apart, like the ruling on a writing tablet. Batonne paper may be either wove or laid. If laid, fine laid lines can be seen between the batons. The laid lines, which are a form of watermark, may be geometrical figures such as squares, diamonds, rectangles, or wavy lines.

*Quadrille* is the term used when the lines form little squares. *Oblong quadrille* is the term used when rectangles rather than squares are formed. See Mexico-Guadalajara Scott 35-37.

Paper also is classified as thick or thin, hard or soft, and by color if dye is added during manufacture. Such colors may be yellowish, greenish, bluish and reddish. Following are brief explanations of other types of paper used for stamps:

**Pelure** — A very thin, hard and often brittle paper, it is sometimes bluish or grayish. See Serbia Scott 169-170.

**Native** — A term applied to handmade papers used to produce some of the early stamps of the Indian states. Japanese paper, originally made of mulberry fibers and rice flour, is part of this group. See Japan Scott 1-18.

**Manila** — Often used to make stamped envelopes and wrappers, it is a coarse textured stock, usually smooth on one side and rough on the other. A variety of colors are known.

**Silk** — Introduced by the British in 1847 as a safeguard against counterfeiting, bits of colored silk thread are scattered throughout it. Silk-thread paper has uninterrupted threads of colored silk arranged so that one or more threads run through the stamp or postal stationery. See Great Britain Scott 5-6.

**Granite** — Filled with minute fibers of various colors and lengths, this should not be confused with either type of silk paper. See Austria Scott 172-175.

**Chalky** — A chalk-like substance coats the surface to discourage the cleaning and reuse of canceled stamps. Because the design is imprinted on the water-soluble coating of the stamp, any attempt to remove a cancellation will destroy the stamp. *Do not soak these stamps in any fluid.* To remove a stamp printed on chalky paper from an envelope, wet the paper from underneath the stamp until the gum dissolves enough to release the stamp from the paper. See St. Kitts-Nevis Scott 89-90.

**India** — Another name for this paper, originally introduced from China about 1750, is "China Paper." It is a thin, opaque paper often used for plate and die proofs by many countries.

**Double** — In philately, this has two distinct meanings. The first, used experimentally as a means to discourage reuse, is two-ply paper, usually a combination of a thick and a thin sheet, joined during manufacture. The design is printed on the thin paper. Any attempt to remove a cancellation would destroy the design. The second occurs on the rotary press, when the end of one paper roll is glued to the next roll to save time feeding the paper through the press. Stamp designs are printed over the joined paper and, if overlooked by inspectors, may get into post office stocks.

**Goldbeater's Skin** — Used for the 1866 issue of Prussia, it was made of a tough translucent paper. The design was printed in reverse on the back of the stamp, and the gum applied over the printing. It is impossible to remove stamps printed on this type of paper from the paper to which they are affixed without destroying the design.

**Ribbed** — An uneven, corrugated surface made by passing the paper through ridged roller. This type exists on some copies of U.S. Scott 163.

Various other substances have been used for stamp manufacture, including wood, aluminum, copper, silver and gold foil; plastic; and silk and cotton fabrics. Stamp collectors and dealers consider most of these as novelties designed for sale to collectors.

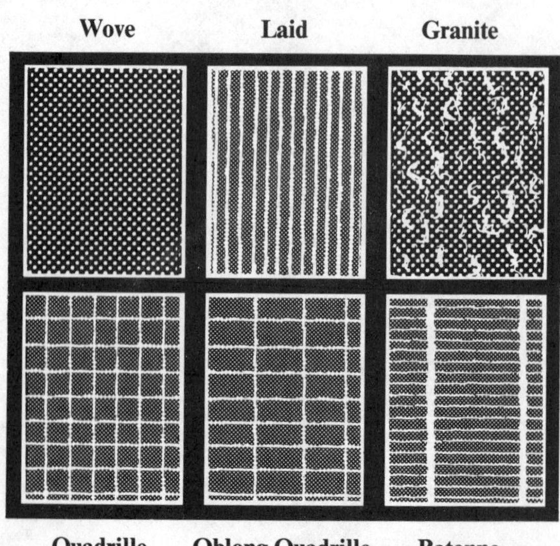

### WATERMARKS

Watermarks are an integral part of the paper, for they are formed in the process of paper manufacture. They consist of small designs formed of wire or cut from metal and soldered to the surface of the dandy roll or mold. The designs may be in the form of crowns, stars, anchors, letters, etc. These pieces of metal — known in the paper-making industry as "bits" — impress a design into the paper. The design may be seen by holding the stamp to the light. Some are more easily seen with a watermark detector. This important tool is a small black tray into which the stamp is placed face down and dampened with a watermark detection fluid that brings up the watermark in the form of dark lines against a lighter background.

**Multiple watermarks of Crown Agents and Burma**

**Watermarks of Uruguay, Vatican and Jamaica**

**WARNING:** Some inks used in the photogravure process dissolve in watermark fluids. (See section below on Soluble Printing Inks.) There also are electric watermark detectors, which come with plastic filter disks of various colors. The disks neutralize the color of the stamp, permitting the watermark to be seen more easily.

Watermarks may be found reversed, inverted, sideways or diagonal, as seen from the back of the stamp. The relationship of watermark to stamp design depends on the position of the printing plates or how paper is fed through the press. On machine-made paper, watermarks normally are read from right to left. The design is repeated closely throughout the sheet in a "multiple-watermark design." In a "sheet watermark," the design appears only once on the sheet, but extends over many stamps. Individual stamps may carry only a small fraction or none of the watermark.

"Marginal watermarks" occur in the margins of sheets or panes of stamps. They occur outside the border of paper (ostensibly outside the area where stamps are to be printed) a large row of letters may spell the name of the country or the manufacturer of the paper. Careless press feeding may cause parts of these letters to show on stamps of the outer row of a pane.

*For easier reference, Scott Publishing Co. identifies and assigns a number to watermarks. See the numerical index of watermarks at the back of this volume.*

## Soluble Printing Inks

**WARNING:** Most stamp colors are permanent. That is, they are not seriously affected by light or water. Some colors may fade from excessive exposure to light. There are stamps printed with inks which dissolve easily in water or fluids used to detect watermarks. Use of these inks is intentional to prevent the removal of cancellations. Water affects all aniline prints, those on safety paper, and some photogravure printings — known as *fugitive colors.*

## Separation

"Separation" is the general term used to describe methods of separating stamps. The earliest issues, such as the 1840 Penny Black of Great Britain (Scott 1), did not have any means provided for separating. It was expected they would be cut apart with scissors. These are imperforate stamps. Many stamps first issued imperforate were later issued perforated. Care therefore must be observed in buying imperforate stamps to be certain they were issued imperforate and are not perforated copies that have been altered by having the perforations trimmed away. Imperforate stamps sometimes are valued as singles, as within this catalogue. But, imperforate varieties of normally perforated stamps should be collected in pairs or larger pieces as indisputable evidence of their imperforate character.

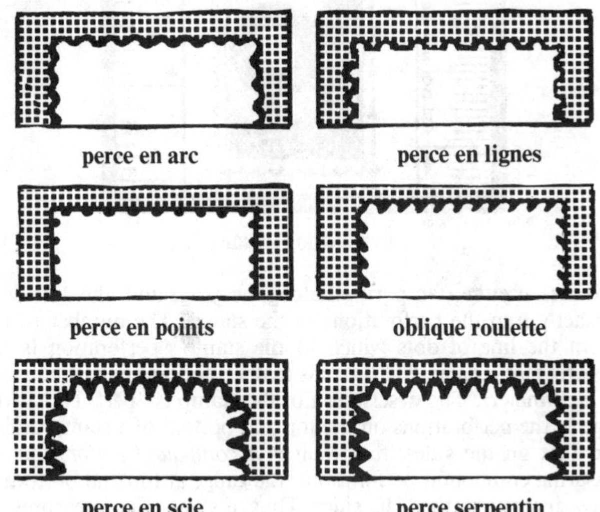


### ROULETTING

Separation is brought about by two general methods during stamp production, rouletting and perforating. In rouletting, the paper is cut partly or wholly through, with no paper removed. In perforating, a part of the paper is removed. Rouletting derives its name from the French roulette, a spur-like wheel. As the wheel is rolled over the paper, each point makes a small cut. The number of cuts made in two centimeters determines the gauge of the roulette, just as the number of perforations in two centimeters determines the gauge of the perforation (see below).

The shape and arrangement of the teeth on the wheels varies. Various roulette types generally carry French names:

*Perce en lignes* — rouletted in lines. The paper receives short, straight cuts in lines. See Mexico Scott 500.

*Perce en points* — pin-perforated. This differs from a small perforation because no paper is removed, although round, equidistant holes are pricked through the paper. See Mexico Scott 242-256.

*Perce en arc* and *perce en scie* — pierced in an arc or sawtoothed designs, forming half circles or small triangles. See Hanover (German States) Scott 25-29.

*Perce en serpentin* — serpentine roulettes. The cuts form a serpentine or wavy line. See Brunswick (German States) Scott 13-18.

### PERFORATION

The other chief style of separation of stamps, and the one which is in universal use today, is perforating. By this process, paper between the stamps is cut away in a line of holes, usually round, leaving little bridges of paper between the stamps to hold them together. These little bridges, which project from the stamp when it is torn from the pane are called the teeth of the perforation. As the size of the perforation is sometimes the only way to differentiate between two otherwise identical stamps, it is necessary to be able to measure and describe them. This is done with a perforation gauge, a ruler-like device that has dots to show how many perforations may be counted in the space of two centimeters. Two centimeters is the space universally adopted in which to measure perforations.

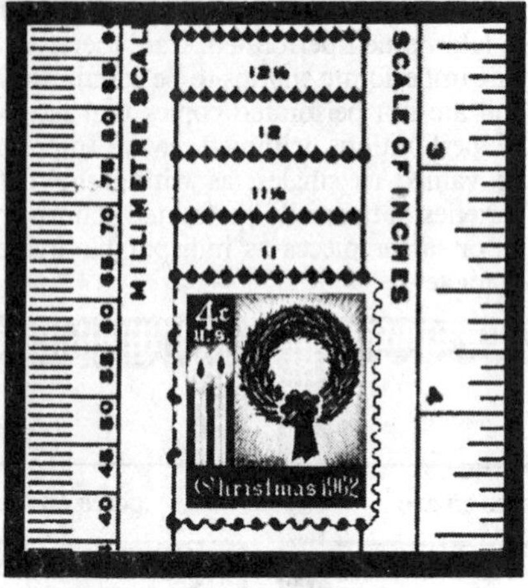


**Perforation gauge**

To measure the stamp, run it along the gauge until the dots on it fit exactly into the perforations of the stamp. The number to the side of the line of dots which fit the stamp's perforation is the measurement, i.e., an "11" means that 11 perforations fit between two centimeters. The description of the stamp is "perf. 11." If the gauge of the perforations on the top and bottom of a stamp differs from that on the sides, the result is a *compound perforation.* In measuring compound perforations, the gauge at top and bottom is always given first, then the sides. Thus, a stamp that measures 10 1/2 at top and bottom and 11 at the sides is "perf. 10 1/2 x 11." See U.S. Scott 1526.

There are stamps known with perforations different on three or all four sides. Descriptions of such items are in clockwise order, beginning with the top of the stamp.

A perforation with small holes and teeth close together is a "fine perforation." One with large holes and teeth far apart is a "coarse perforation." Holes jagged rather than clean cut, are "rough perforations." *Blind perforations* are the slight impressions left by the perforating pins if they fail to puncture the paper. Multiples of stamps showing blind perforations may command a slight premium over normally perforated stamps.

# Printing Processes

**ENGRAVING (Intaglio)**

**Master die** — The initial operation in the engraving process is making of the master die. The die is a small flat block of soft steel on which the stamp design is recess engraved in reverse.

**Master die**

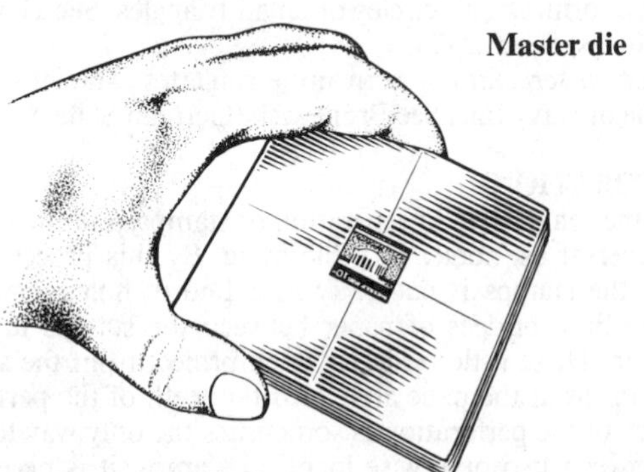

Photographic reduction of the original art is made to the appropriate size, and it serves as a tracing guide for the initial outline of the design. After completion of the engraving, the die is hardened to withstand the stress and pressures of later transfer operations.

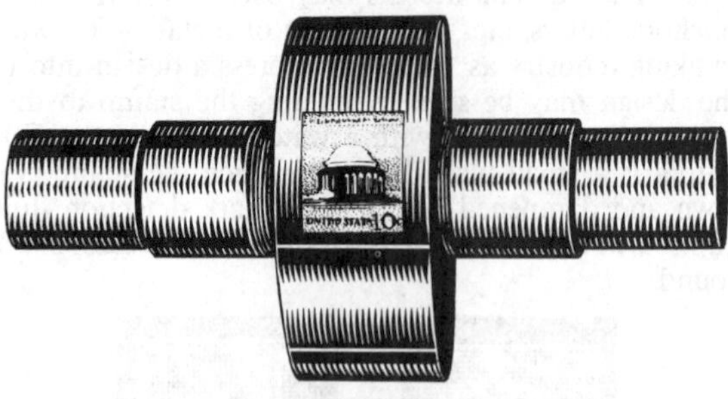

**Transfer roll**

**Transfer roll** — Next is production of the transfer roll which, as the name implies, is the medium used to transfer the subject from the die to the plate. A blank roll of soft steel, mounted on a mandrel, is placed under the bearers of the transfer press to allow it to roll freely on its axis. The hardened die is placed on the bed of the press and the face of the transfer roll is applied on the die, under pressure. The bed is then rocked back and forth under increasing pressure until the soft steel of the roll is forced into every engraved line of the die. The resulting impression on the roll is known as a "relief" or a "relief transfer." After the required number of reliefs are "rocked in," the soft steel transfer roll is also hardened.

A "relief" is the normal reproduction of the design on the die in reverse. A "defective relief" may occur during the "rocking in" process because of a minute piece of foreign material lodging on the die, or some other cause. Imperfections in the steel of the transfer roll may result in a breaking away of parts of the design. A damaged relief continued in use will transfer a repeating defect to the plate. Deliberate alterations of reliefs sometimes occur. "Broken reliefs" and "altered reliefs" designate these changed conditions.

**Plate** — The final step in the procedure is the making of the printing plate. A flat piece of soft steel replaces the die on the bed of the transfer press. One of the reliefs on the transfer roll is applied on this soft steel. "Position dots" determine the position on the plate. The dots have been lightly marked in advance. After the correct position of the relief is determined, pressure is applied. By following the same method used in making the transfer roll, a transfer is entered. This transfer reproduces the design of the relief in reverse and in detail. There are as many transfers entered on the plate as there are subjects printed on the sheet of stamps.

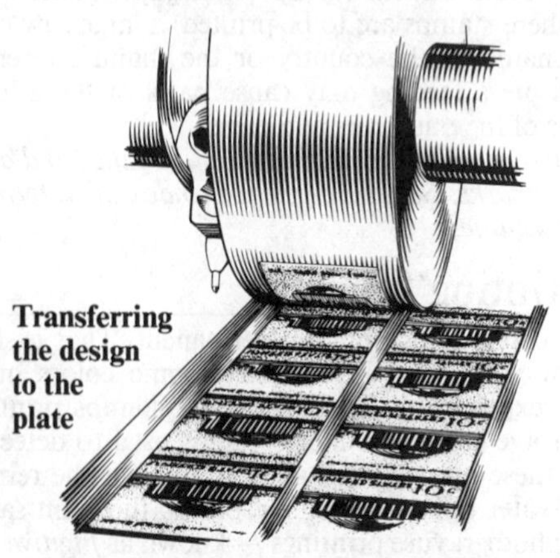

**Transferring the design to the plate**

Following the entering of the required transfers, the position dots, layout dots and lines, scratches, etc., generally are burnished out. Added at this time are any required *guide lines, plate numbers* or other *marginal markings.* A proof impression is then taken and, if approved, the plate machined for fitting to the press, hardened and sent to the plate vault ready for use.

On press, the plate is inked and the surface automatically wiped clean, leaving the ink in the depressed lines only. Paper under pressure is forced down into the engraved depressed lines, thereby receiving the ink. Thus, the ink lines on engraved stamps are slightly raised; and, conversely, slight depressions occur on the back of the stamp. Historically, paper had been dampened before inking. Newer processes do not require this procedure. Thus, there are both *wet* and *dry printings* of some stamps.

**Rotary Press** — Until 1915, only flat plates were used to print engraved stamps. Rotary press printing was introduced in 1915. After approval, *rotary press plates* require additional machining. They are curved to fit the press cylinder. "Gripper slots" are cut into the back of each plate to receive the "grippers," which hold the plate securely on the press. The plate is then hardened. Stamps printed from rotary press plates are usually longer or wider than the same stamps printed from flat press plates. The stretching of the plate during the curving process causes this enlargement.

**Re-entry** — In order to execute a re-entry, the transfer roll is reapplied to the plate, usually at some time after its first use on the press. Worn-out designs can be resharpened by carefully re-entering the transfer roll. If the transfer roll is not precisely in line with the impression of the plate, the registration will not be true and a double transfer will result. After a plate has been curved for the rotary press, it is impossible to make a re-entry.

**Double Transfer** — This is a description of the condition of a transfer on a plate that shows evidence of a duplication of all, or a portion of the design. It is usually the result of the changing of the registration between the transfer roll and the plate during the rocking-in of the original entry.

It is sometimes necessary to remove the original transfer from a plate and repeat the process a second time. If the finished re-transfer shows indications of the original impression attributable to incomplete erasure, the result is a double transfer.

**Re-engraved** — Either the die that has been used to make a plate or the plate itself may have its "temper" drawn (softened) and be re-cut. The resulting impressions from such a re-engraved die or plate may differ slightly from the original issue, and are known as "re-engraved."

**Short Transfer** — Sometimes the transfer roll is not rocked its entire length in entering a transfer onto a plate, so that the finished transfer fails to show the complete design. This is known as a "short transfer." See U.S. Scott 8.

**TYPOGRAPHY (Letterpress, Surface Printing)**

As it relates to the printing of postage stamps, typography is the reverse of engraving. Typography includes all printing where the design is above the surface area, whether it is wood, metal, or in some instances hard rubber.

The master die and the engraved die are made in much the same manner. In this instance, however, the area not used as a printing surface is cut away, leaving the surface area raised. The original die is then reproduced by stereotyping or electrotyping. The resulting electrotypes are assembled in the required number and format of the desired sheet of stamps. The plate used in printing the stamps is an electroplate of these assembled electrotypes.

Ink is applied to the raised surface and the pressure of the press transfers the ink impression to the paper. In contrast with engraving, the fine lines of typography are impressed on the surface of the stamp. When viewed from the back (as on a typewritten page), the corresponding line work will be raised slightly above the surface.

**PHOTOGRAVURE (Rotogravure, Heliogravure)**

In this process, the basic principles of photography are applied to a sensitized metal plate, as opposed to photographic paper. The design is transferred photographically to the plate through a halftone screen, breaking the reproduction into tiny dots. The plate is treated chemically and the dots form depressions of varying depths, depending on the degrees of shade in the design. Ink is lifted out of the depressions in the plate when the paper is pressed against the plate in a manner similar to that of engraved printing.

**LITHOGRAPHY**

The principle that oil and water will not mix is the basis for lithography. The stamp design is drawn by hand or transferred from engraving to the surface of a lithographic stone or metal plate in a greasy (oily) ink. The stone (or plate) is wet with an acid fluid, causing it to repel the printing ink in all areas not covered by the greasy ink.

Transfer paper is used to transfer the design from the original stone of plate. A series of duplicate transfers are grouped and, in turn, transferred to the final printing plate.

**Photolithography** — The application of photographic processes to lithography. This process allows greater flexibility of design, related to use of halftone screens combined with linework.

**Offset** — A development of the lithographic process. A rubber-covered blanket cylinder takes up the impression from the inked lithographic plate. From the "blanket" the impression is *offset* or transferred to the paper. Offset printing systems have largely displaced lithography because of its greater flexibility and speed. The term "lithography" covers both processes, and results are almost identical.

Sometimes two or even three printing methods are combined in producing stamps.

**EMBOSSED (Relief) Printing**

Embossing is a method in which the design first is sunk into the metal of the die. Printing is done against a yielding platen, such as leather or linoleum. The platen is forced into the depression of the die, thus forming the design on the paper in relief.

Embossing may be done without color (see Sardinia Scott 4-6); with color printed around the embossed area (see Great Britain Scott 5 and most U.S. envelopes); and with color in exact registration with the embossed subject (see Canada Scott 656-657).

**INK COLORS**

Inks or colored papers used in stamp printing usually are of mineral origin. The tone of any given color may be affected by many aspects: heavier pressure will cause a more intense color, slight interruptions in the ink feed will cause a lighter tint.

Hand-mixed ink formulas produced under different conditions (humidity and temperature) at different times account for notable color variations in early printings, mostly 19th century, of the same stamp (see U.S. Scott 248-250, 279B, etc.).

Papers of different quality and consistency used for the same stamp printing may affect color shade. Most pelure papers, for example, show a richer color when compared with wove or laid papers. See Russia Scott 181a.

The very nature of the printing processes can cause a variety of differences in shades or hues of the same stamp. Some of these shades are scarcer than others and are of particular interest to the advanced collector.

## Tagged Stamps

Tagging also is known as *luminescence, fluorescence,* and *phosphorescence.* Some tagged stamps have bars (Great Britain and Canada), frames (South Africa), or an overall coating of luminescent material applied after the stamps have been printed (United States). Another tagging method is to incorporate the luminescent material into some or all colors of the printing ink. See Australia Scott 366 and Netherlands Scott 478. A third is to mix the luminescent material with the pulp during the paper manufacturing process or apply it as a surface coating afterwards: "fluorescent" papers. See Switzerland Scott 510-514 and Germany Scott 848.

The treated stamps show up in specific colors when exposed to ultraviolet light. The wave length of light radiated by the luminescent material determines the colors and activates the triggering mechanism of the electronic machinery for sorting, facing or canceling letters.

Various fluorescent substances have been used as paper whiteners, but the resulting "hi-brite papers" show up differently under ultraviolet light and do not trigger the machines. The Scott Catalogue does not recognize these papers.

Many countries now use tagging in its various forms to expedite mail handling, following introduction by Great Britain, on an experimental basis, in 1959. Among these countries, and dates of their dates of introduction, are Germany, 1961; Canada and Denmark, 1962; United States, Australia, Netherlands and Switzerland, 1963; Belgium and Japan, 1966; Sweden and Norway, 1967; Italy, 1968; and Russia, 1969.

Certain stamps were issued with and without the luminescent feature. In those instances, Scott lists the "tagged" variety in the United States, Canada, Great Britain and Switzerland listings and notes the situation in some of the other countries.

## Gum

The gum on the back of a stamp may be smooth, rough, dark, white, colored or tinted. It may be either obvious or virtually invisible as on Canada Scott 453 or Rwanda Scott 287-294. Most stamp gumming adhesives use gum arabic or dextrine as a base. Certain polymers such as polyvinyl alcohol (PVA) have been used extensively since World War II.The PVA gum which the security printers Harrison & Sons of Great Britain introduced in 1968 is dull, slightly yellowish and almost invisible.

The *Scott Standard Postage Stamp Catalogue* does not list items by types of gum. The Scott *Specialized Catalogue of United States Stamps* does differentiate among some types of gum for certain issues.

Stamps having full *original gum* sell for more than those from which the gum has been removed. Reprints of stamps may have gum differing from the original issues.

Many stamps have been issued without gum and the catalogue will note this fact. See China Scott 1438-1440. Sometimes, gum may have been removed to preserve the stamp. Germany Scott B68 is valued in the catalogue with gum removed.

## Reprints and Reissues

These are impressions of stamps (usually obsolete) made from the original plates or stones. If valid for postage and from obsolete issues, they are *reissues.* If they are from current issues, they are *second, third,* etc., *printings.* If designated for a particular purpose, they are *special printings.*

Scott normally lists those reissues and reprints that are valid for postage.

When reprints are not valid for postage, but made from original dies and plates by authorized persons, they are *official reprints. Private reprints* are made from original plates and dies by private hands. *Official reproductions* or imitations are made from new dies and plates by government authorization.

For the United States' 1876 Centennial, the U.S. government made official imitations of its first postage stamps. Produced were copies of the first two stamps (listed as Scott 3-4), reprints of the demonetized pre-1861 issues and reissues of the 1861 stamps, the 1869 stamps and the then-current 1875 denominations. An example of the private reprint is that of the New Haven, Connecticut, postmaster's provisional.

Most reprints differ slightly from the original stamp in some characteristic, such as gum, paper, perforation, color or watermark. Sometimes the details are followed so meticulously that only a student of that specific stamp is able to distinguish the reprint from the original.

## Remainders and Canceled to Order

Some countries sell their stock of old stamps when a new issue replaces them. To avoid postal use, the *remainders* usually are canceled with a punch hole, a heavy line or bar, or a more-or-less regular cancellation. The most famous merchant of remainders was Nicholas F. Seebeck. In the 1880's and 1890's, he arranged printing contracts between the Hamilton Bank Note Co., of which he was a director, and several Central and South American countries. The contracts provided that the plates and all remainders of the yearly issues became the property of Hamilton. Seebeck saw to it that ample stock remained. The "Seebecks," both remainders and reprints, were standard packet fillers for decades.

Some countries also issue stamps *canceled to order (CTO),* either in sheets with original gum or stuck onto pieces of paper or envelopes and canceled. Such CTO items generally are worth less than postally used stamps. Most can be detected by the presence of gum. However, as the CTO practice goes back at least to 1885, the gum inevitably has been washed off some stamps so they could pass for postally used. The normally applied postmarks usually differ slightly and specialists are able to tell the difference. When applied individually to envelopes by philatelically minded persons, CTO material is known as *favor canceled* and generally sells at large discounts.

## Cinderellas and Facsimiles

**Cinderella** is a catchall term used by stamp collectors to describe phantoms, fantasies, bogus items, municipal issues, exhibition seals, local revenues, transportation stamps, labels, poster stamps, and so on. Some cinderella collectors include in their collections local postage issues, telegraph stamps, essays and proofs, forgeries and counterfeits.

A *fantasy* is an adhesive created for a nonexistent stamp-issuing authority. Fantasy items range from imaginary countries (Kingdom of Sedang, Principality of Trinidad, or Occusi-Ambeno), to nonexistent locals (Winans City Post), or nonexistent transportation lines (McRobish & Co.'s Acapulco-San Francisco Line).

On the other hand, if the entity exists and might have issued stamps or did issue other stamps, the items are *bogus* stamps. These would include the Mormon postage stamps of Utah, S. Allan Taylor's Guatemala and Paraguay inventions, the propaganda issues for the South Moluccas and the adhesives of the Page & Keyes local post of Boston.

*Phantoms* is another term for both fantasy and bogus issues.

*Facsimiles* are copies or imitations made to represent original stamps, but which do not pretend to be originals. A catalogue illustration is such a facsimile. Illustrations from the Moens catalogue of the last century were occasionally colored and passed off as stamps. Since the beginning of stamp collecting, facsimiles have been made for collectors as space fillers or for reference. They often carry the word "facsimile," "falsch" (German), "sanko" or "mozo" (Japanese), or "faux" (French) overprinted on the face or stamped on the back.

## Counterfeits or Forgeries

Unauthorized imitations of stamps, intended to deprive the post office of revenue, are *postal counterfeits* or *postal forgeries.* These items often command higher prices in the philatelic marketplace than the genuine stamps they imitate. Sales are illegal. Governments can, and do, prosecute those who trade in them.

The first postal forgery was of Spain's 4-cuarto carmine of 1854 (the real one is Scott 25). The forgers lithographed it, though the original was typographed. Apparently they were not satisfied and soon made an engraved forgery, which is common, unlike the scarce lithographed counterfeit. Postal forgeries quickly followed in Spain, Austria, Naples, Sardinia and the Roman States.

An infamous counterfeit to defraud is the 1-shilling Great Britain "Stock Exchange" forgery of 1872, used on telegraphs at the exchange that year. It escaped detection until a stamp dealer noticed it in 1898. Many postal counterfeits are known of U.S. stamps.

*Wartime propaganda* stamps of World War I and World War II may be classed as postal counterfeits. They were distributed by enemy governments or resistance groups.

*Philatelic forgeries* or *counterfeits* are unauthorized imitations of stamps designed to deceive and defraud stamp collectors. Such spurious items first appeared on the market around 1860 and most old-time collections contain one or more. Many are crude and easily spotted, even by the non-specialist, but some can deceive the experts.

An important supplier of these early philatelic forgeries was the Hamburg printer Gebruder Spiro. Many others with reputations in this craft were S. Allan Taylor, George Hussey, James Chute, George Forune, Benjamin & Sarpy, Julius Goldner, E. Oneglia and L.H. Mercier. Among the noted 20th century forgers were Francois Fournier, Jean Sperati, and the prolific Raoul DeThuin.

Fraudulently produced copies are known of most classic rarities, many medium-priced stamps and, in this century, cheap stamps destined for beginners' packets. Few new philatelic forgeries have appeared in recent decades, however, and virtually no new frauds of valuable classics. Successful imitation of engraved work is virtually impossible.

It has proven far easier to produce a fake by altering a genuine stamp than to duplicate a stamp completely.

## Repairs, Restoration and Fakes

Scott Publishing Co. bases its catalogue values on stamps which are free of defects and otherwise meet the standards set forth earlier in this introduction. Stamp collectors desire to have the finest copy of an item possible. Even within given grading categories there are variances. This leads to practice that is not universally defined, nor accepted, that of stamp *restoration.*

There are differences of opinion about what is "permissible" when it comes to restoration. Applying a soft erasure carefully to a stamp to remove dirt marks is one form of restoration, as is the washing of the stamp in mild soap and water. More severe forms of restoration are the pressing out of creases, or the removal of stains caused by tape. To what degree each of the above is "acceptable" is dependent on the individual situation. Further along the spectrum is the freshening of a stamp's color by removing oxide build-up or removing toning or the effects of wax paper left next to stamps shipped to the tropics.

At some point along this spectrum the concept of *repair* replaces that of "restoration." Repairs include filling in thin spots, mending tears by reweaving, adding a missing perforation tooth. Regumming stamps may have been acceptable as a restoration technique decades ago, but today it is considered a form of fakery.

Restored stamps may not sell at a discount, and it is possible that the value of individual restored items may be enhanced over that of their pre-restoration state. Specific situations will dictate the resultant value of such an item. Repaired stamps sell at substantial discounts.

When the purchaser of an item has any reason to suspect an item has been repaired, and the detection of such a repair is beyond his own ability, he should seek expert advice. There are services that specialize in such advice.

*Fakes* are genuine stamps altered in some way to make them more desirable. One student of this part of stamp collecting has estimated that by the 1950's more than 30,000 varieties of fakes were known. That number has grown. The widespread existence of fakes makes it important for stamp collectors to study their philatelic holdings and use relevant literature. Likewise, they should buy from reputable dealers who will guarantee their stamps and make full and prompt refund should a purchase be declared not genuine by some mutually agreed-upon authority. Because fakes always have some genuine characteristics, it is not always possible to obtain unanimous agreement among experts regarding specific items. These students may change their opinions as philatelic knowledge increases. More than 80 percent of all fakes on the philatelic market today are regummed, reperforated (or, perforated for the first time), or bear altered overprints, surcharges or cancellations.

Stamps can be chemically treated to alter or eliminate colors. For example, a pale rose stamp can be recolored into a blue of high market value, or a "missing color" variety can be created. Designs may be changed by "painting," or a stroke or a dot added or bleached out to turn an ordinary variety into a seemingly scarcer stamp. Part of a stamp can be bleached and reprinted in a different version, achieving an inverted center or frame. Margins can be added or repairs done so deceptively that the stamps move from the "repaired" into the "fake" category.

The fakers have not left the backs of the stamps untouched. They may create false watermarks, add fake grills or press out genuine grills. A thin India paper proof may be glued onto a thicker backing to "create" an issued stamp, or a proof printed on cardboard maybe shaved down. Silk threads are impressed into paper and stamps have been split so that a rare paper variety is "added" to an otherwise inexpensive stamp. The most common treatment to the back of a stamp, however, is regumming.

Some in the business of faking stamps openly advertise "foolproof" application of "original gum" to stamps that lack it. This is faking, not counterfeiting. It is believed that few early stamps have survived without being hinged. The large number of never-hinged examples of such earlier material offered for sale thus suggests the widespread extent of regumming activity. Regumming also may be used to hide repairs or thin spots. Dipping the stamp into watermark fluid often will reveal these flaws.

Fakers also tamper with separations. Ingenious ways to add margins are known. Perforated wide-margin stamps may be falsely represented as imperforate when trimmed. Reperforating is commonly done to create scarce coil or perforation varieties and to eliminate the straight-edge stamps found in sheet margin positions of many earlier issues. Custom has made straight edges less desirable. Fakers have obliged by perforating straight-edged stamps so that many are now uncommon, if not rare.

Another fertile field of the faker is that of the overprint, surcharge and cancellation. The forging of rare surcharges or overprints began in the 1880's or 1890's. These forgeries are sometimes difficult to detect, but the experts have identified almost all. Only occasionally are overprints or cancellations removed to create unoverprinted stamps or seemingly unused items. "SPECIMEN" overprints may be removed — scraping and repainting is one way — to create unoverprinted varieties. Fakers use inexpensive revenues or pen-canceled stamps to generate "unused" stamps for further faking by adding other markings. The quartz lamp and a high-powered magnifying glass help in detecting cancellation removal.

The bigger problem, however, is the addition of overprints, surcharges or cancellations — many with such precision that they are very difficult to ascertain. Plating of the stamps or the overprint can be an important method of detection.

Fake postmarks may range from many spurious fancy cancellations, to the host of markings applied to transatlantic covers, to adding "normal" postmarks to World War II-vintage definitives of some countries whose stamps are valued at far more used than unused. With the advance of cover collecting and the widespread interest in postal history, a fertile new field for fakers has come about. Some have tried to create entire covers. Others specialize in adding stamps, tied by fake cancellations, to genuine stampless covers, or replacing less expensive or damaged stamps with more valuable ones. Detailed study of postal rates in effect at the time of the cover in question, including the analysis of each handstamp in the period, ink analysis and similar techniques, usually will unmask the fraud.

# Terminology

**Booklets** — Many countries have issued stamps in small booklets for the convenience of users. This idea is becoming increasingly more popular today in many countries. Booklets have been issued in all sizes and forms, often with advertising on the covers, on the panes of stamps or on the interleaving.

The panes may be printed from special plates or made from regular sheets. All panes from booklets issued by the United States and many from those of other countries contain stamps that are straight edged on the bottom and both sides, but perforated between. Any stamp-like unit in the pane, either printed or blank, which is not a postage stamp, is considered a *label* in the catalogue listings.

Scott lists and values panes only. Complete booklets are listed only in a very few cases. See Grenada Scott 1055. Panes are listed only when they are not fashioned from existing sheet stamps and, therefore, are identifiable from their sheet-stamp counterparts.

Panes usually do not have a "used" value because there is little market activity in used panes, even though many exist used.

**Cancellations** — the marks or obliterations put on a stamp by the postal authorities to show that the stamp has done service and is no longer valid for postage. If made with a pen, the marking is a "pen cancellation." When the location of the post office appears in the cancellation, it is a "town cancellation." When calling attention to a cause or celebration, it is a "slogan cancellation." Many other types and styles of cancellations exist, such as duplex, numerals, targets, etc.

**Coil Stamps** — stamps issued in rolls for use in dispensers, affixing and vending machines. Those of the United States, Canada, Sweden and some other countries are perforated horizontally or vertically only, with the outer edges imperforate. Coil stamps of some countries, such as Great Britain, are perforated on all four sides.

**Covers** — envelopes, with or without adhesive postage stamps, which have passed through the mail and bear postal or other markings of philatelic interest. Before the introduction of envelopes in about 1840, people folded letters and wrote the address on the outside. Many people covered their letters with an extra sheet of paper on the outside for the address, producing the term "cover." Used air letter sheets, stamped envelopes, and other items of postal stationery also are considered covers.

**Errors** — stamps having some unintentional deviation from the normal. Errors include, but are not limited to, mistakes in color, paper, or watermark; inverted centers or frames on multicolor printing, surcharges or overprints, and double impressions. Factually wrong or misspelled information, if it appears on all examples of a stamp, even if corrected later, is not classified as a philatelic error.

**Overprinted and Surcharged Stamps** — Overprinting is a wording or design placed on stamps to alter the place of use (i.e., "Canal Zone" on U.S. stamps), to adapt them for a special purpose ("Porto" on Denmark's 1913-20 regular issues for use as postage due stamps, Scott J1-J7), or for a special occasion (Guatemala Scott 374-378).

A *surcharge* is an overprint which changes or restates the face value of the item.

Surcharges and overprints may be handstamped, typeset or, occasionally, lithographed or engraved. A few hand-written overprints and surcharges are known.

**Precancels** — stamps canceled before they are placed in the mail. Precanceling is done to expedite the handling of large mailings.

In the United States, precancellations generally identified the point of origin. That is, the city and state names or initials appeared, usually centered between parallel lines. More recently, bureau precancels retained the parallel lines, but the city and state designation was dropped. Recent coils have a "service inscription" to show the mail service paid for by the stamp. Since these stamps do not receive any further cancellation when used as intended, they fall under the general precancel umbrella.

Such items may not have parallel lines as part of the precancellation.

In France, the abbreviation *Affranchts* in a semicircle together with the word *Postes* is the general form. Belgian precancellations are usually a box in which the name of the city appears. Netherlands' precancellations have the name of the city enclosed between a large and small circle, sometimes called a "life-saver."

Precancellations of other countries usually follow these patterns, but may be any arrangement of bars, boxes and city names.

Precancels are listed in the catalogue only if the precancel changes the denomination (Belgium Scott 477-478); the precanceled stamp is different from the non-precancel version (untagged U.S. stamps); or, if the stamp only exists precanceled (France Scott 1096-1099, U.S. Scott 2265).

**Proofs and Essays** — Proofs are impressions taken from an approved die, plate or stone in which the design and color are the same as the stamp issued to the public. Trial color proofs are impressions taken from approved dies, plates or stones in varying colors. An essay is the impression of a design that differs in some way from the stamp as issued.

**Provisionals** — stamps issued on short notice and intended for temporary use pending the arrival of regular issues. They usually are issued to meet such contingencies as changes in government or currency, shortage of necessary postage values, or military occupation.

In the 1840's, postmasters in certain American cities issued stamps that were valid only at specific post offices. In 1861, postmasters of the Confederate States also issued stamps with limited validity. Both of these examples are known as "postmaster's provisionals."

**Se-Tenant** — joined, referring to an unsevered pair, strip or block of stamps differing in design, denomination or overprint. See U.S. Scott 2158a.

**Tete Beche** — A pair of stamps in which one is upside down in relation to the other. Some of these are the result of intentional sheet arrangements, i.e. Morocco Scott B10-B11. Others occurred when one or more electrotypes accidentally were placed upside down on the plate. See Colombia Scott 57a. Separation of the stamps, of course, destroys the tete beche variety.

**Specimens** — One of the regulations of the Universal Postal Union requires member nations to send samples of all stamps they put into service to the International Bureau in Switzerland. Member nations of the UPU receive these specimens as samples of what stamps are valid for postage. Many are overprinted, handstamped or initial-perforated "Specimen," "Canceled" or "Muestra." Some are marked with bars across the denominations (China-Taiwan), punched holes (Czechoslovakia) or back inscriptions (Mongolia).

Stamps distributed to government officials or for publicity purposes, and stamps submitted by private security printers for official approval, also may receive such defacements.

These markings prevent postal use, and all such items generally are known as "specimens."

# UNITED STATES

GOVT. — Republic
AREA — 3,615,211 sq. mi.
POP. — 226,545,805 (1980)
CAPITAL — Washington, D.C.

In addition to the 50 States and the District of Columbia, the Republic includes Guam, the Commonwealth of Puerto Rico, the Virgin Islands, American Samoa, Wake, Midway, and a number of small islands in the Pacific Ocean, all of which use stamps of the United States.

100 Cents = 1 Dollar

**Catalogue values for unused stamps in this country are for Never Hinged items, beginning with Scott 772 in the regular postage section, Scott C19 in the air post section, Scott E17 in the special delivery section, Scott O127 in officials section, Scott J88 in the postage due section, Scott R733 in the revenues section, Scott RW1 in the hunting permit stamps section.**

## PROVISIONAL ISSUES BY POSTMASTERS

**Values for Envelopes are for entires.**

### Alexandria, Va.

A1

Type I. 40 asterisks in circle.
Type II. 39 asterisks in circle.

**1846** **Typeset** ***Imperf.***

*1X1* A1 5c *buff*, Type I — *20,000.*
**a.** 5c *buff*, Type II *40,000.*
*1X2* A1 5c *blue*, Type I, on cover —

All known copies of Nos. 1X1-1X2 are cut to shape.

### Annapolis, Md.

**ENVELOPE**

E1

**1846**

*2XU1* E1 5c car red, *white* *45,000.*

Handstamped impressions of the circular design with "2" in blue or red exist on envelopes and letter sheets. Value $1,750.

A letter sheet exists with circular design and "5" handstamped in red. Value $2,250.

A similar circular design in blue was used as a postmark.

### Baltimore, Md.

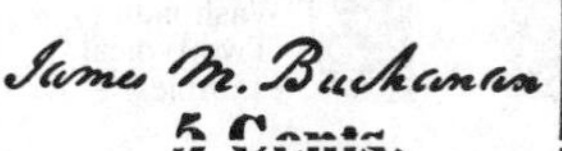


Signature of Postmaster — A1

**1845** **Engr.** ***Imperf.***

*3X1* A1 5c blk, *white* *4,000.*
*3X2* A1 10c blk, *white* — *32,500.*
*3X3* A1 5c blk, *bluish* *25,000.* *5,000.*
*3X4* A1 10c blk, *bluish* *50,000.*

Nos. 3X1-3X4 were printed from a plate of 12 (2x6) containing nine 5c and three 10c.

**ENVELOPES**

E1

The color given is that of the "PAID 5" and oval. "James M. Buchanan" is handstamped in black, blue or red. The paper is manila, buff, white, salmon or grayish.

**1845** **Handstamped**
**Various Papers**

*3XU1* E1 5c blue *3,000.*
*3XU2* E1 5c red *3,500.*
*3XU3* E1 10c blue *13,000.*
*3XU4* E1 10c red *13,500.*

On the formerly listed "5+5" envelopes, the second "5" in oval is believed not to be part of the basic prepaid marking.

### Boscawen, N. H.

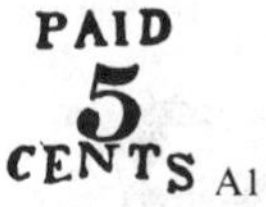


A1

**1846 (?)** **Typeset** ***Imperf.***

*4X1* A1 5c dull blue, *yellowish*, on cover *100,000.*

### Brattleboro, Vt.

Initials of Postmaster (FNP) — A1

**1846** **Engr.** ***Imperf.***

*5X1* A1 5c *buff* *15,000.* *5,000.*

Printed from plate of 10 (5x2).

### Lockport, N. Y.

A1

**Handstamped, "5" in Black Ms.**
**1846**

*6X1* A1 5c red, *buff*, on cover *100,000.*

### Millbury, Mass.

George Washington — A1

**Printed from a Woodcut**

**1846** ***Imperf.***

*7X1* A1 5c *bluish* — *17,500.*

### New Haven, Conn.

**ENVELOPES**

E1

**1845** **Handstamped**
**Signed in Blue, Black, Magenta or Red**

*8XU1* E1 5c red, *white* (Bl or M) —
*8XU2* E1 5c red, *light bluish* (Bk) *35,000.*
*8XU3* E1 5c dull blue, *buff* (Bl) *25,000.*
*8XU4* E1 5c dull blue, *white* (Bk) *25,000.*
*8XU5* E1 5c dull blue, *buff* (R) —

*Reprints were made at various times between 1871 and 1932. They differ in shade and paper from the originals.*

### New York, N. Y.

George Washington — A1

Plate of 40 (5x8)

**1845** **Engr.** ***Imperf.***

*9X1* A1 5c *bluish* 800. 325.
**a.** blue paper *6,000.* *2,000.*
**b.** Signed RHM *12,500.* *2,500.*
**c.** Signed MMJr —
**d.** Without signature 1,450. 650.

These stamps were usually initialed "ACM" in magenta ink, as a control, before being sold or passed through the mails.

*A plate of 9 (3x3) was made later from which sheets were printed in black on white and deep blue papers; also in blue, green, brown and red on white bond paper. Value about $165 each.*

### Providence, R. I.

A1

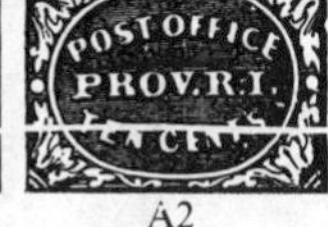


A2

**1846** **Engr.** ***Imperf.***

*10X1* A1 5c gray black 200. *1,250.*
*10X2* A2 10c gray black 1,000.
**a.** Se-tenant with 5c 1,300.

Plate of 12 (3x4) contains 11 of 5c and one 10c.

*Reprints were made in 1898. Each stamp bears one of the following letters on the back: B. O. G. E. R. T. D. U. R. B. I. N. Some reprint sheets received no back print. Value of 5c, $50; 10c, $125; sheet, $725.*

### St. Louis, Mo.

Missouri Coat of Arms
A1 A2 A3

**1845-46** **Wove Paper** **Engr.** ***Imperf.***

*11X1* A1 5c *greenish* *5,000.* *2,350.*
*11X2* A2 10c *greenish* *4,500.* *2,000.*
*11X3* A3 20c *greenish* —

Three varieties of 5c, three of 10c, two of 20c.

**1846**

*11X4* A1 5c *gray lilac* — *3,500.*
*11X5* A2 10c *gray lilac* *4,500.* *1,750.*
*11X6* A3 20c *gray lilac* *10,000.*

One variety of 5c, three of 10c, two of 20c.

**1847**

**Pelure Paper**

*11X7* A1 5c *bluish* — *5,000.*
*11X8* A2 10c *bluish* *5,000.*
**a.** Impression of 5c on back —

Three varieties of 5c, three of 10c.
Used values are for pencanceled copies.

### Tuscumbia, Ala.

**ENVELOPE**

E1

**1858** **Handstamped**

*12XU1* E1 3c dull red, *buff* *9,000.*

See Confederate States Nos. 84XU1-84XU6.

## GENERAL ISSUES

**All Issues from 1847 to 1894 are Unwatermarked.**

Benjamin Franklin
A1

George Washington
A2

**1847, July 1** **Engr.** ***Imperf.***

*1* A1 5c red brn, *bluish* 4,000. 500.00
**a** 5c dark brn, *bluish* 4,000. 500.00
**b** 5c org brown, *bluish* 4,500. 600.00
**c** 5c red org, *bluish* *10,000.* *1,850.*
Pen cancel 250.00
*2* A2 10c blk, *bluish* *17,500.* 1,400.
**a** Diagonal half used as 5c on cover *15,000.*
**b** Vertical half used as 5c on cover *21,000.*
**c** Horizontal half used as 5c on cover —
Pen cancel 800.00

## REPRODUCTIONS

Actually, official imitations made from new plates by order of the Post Office Department.

Bluish paper without gum

A3

A4

**1875**

| | | | |
|---|---|---|---|
| *3* | A3 | 5c red brown | 850.00 |
| *4* | A4 | 10c black | 1,000. |

*Reproductions. The letters R. W. H. & E. at the bottom of each stamp are less distinct on the reproductions than on the originals.*

*5c. On the originals the left side of the white shirt frill touches the oval on a level with the top of the "F" of "Five." On the reproductions it touches the oval about on a level with the top of the figure "5."*

*10c. On the reproductions, line of coat at left points to right tip of "X" and line of coat at right points to center of "S" of CENTS. On the originals, line of coat points to "T" of TEN and between "T" and "S" of CENTS. On the reproductions the eyes have a sleepy look, the line of the mouth is straighter, and in the curl of hair near the left cheek is a strong black dot, while the originals have only a faint one.*

See No. 948.

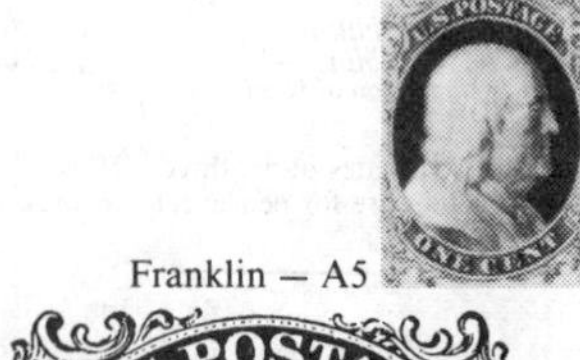
Franklin — A5

ONE CENT

Type I. Has complete curved lines outside the labels with "U.S. Postage" and "One Cent." The scrolls below the lower label are turned under, forming little balls. The ornaments at top are substantially complete.

Type Ib. Same as I but balls below the bottom label are not so clear. The plumelike scrolls at bottom are not complete.

A6

Type Ia. Same as I at bottom but top ornaments and outer line at top are partly cut away.

A7

Type II. The little balls of the bottom scrolls and the bottoms of the lower plume ornaments are missing. The side ornaments are complete.

A8

Type III. The top and bottom curved lines outside the labels are broken in the middle. The side ornaments are complete.

Type IIIa. Similar to type III with the outer line broken at top or bottom but not both.

A9

Type IV. Similar to type II, but with the curved lines outside the labels recut at top or bottom or both.

Values for types I and III are for stamps showing the marked characteristics plainly. Copies of type I showing the balls indistinctly and of type III with the lines only slightly broken, sell for much lower prices.

Washington — A10

THREE CENTS

Type I. There is an outer frame line on all four sides.

Thomas Jefferson — A11

FIVE CENTS

Type I. There are projections on all four sides.

Washington — A12

TEN CENTS

Type I. The "shells" at the lower corners are practically complete. The outer line below the label is very nearly complete. The outer lines are broken above the middle of the top label and the "X" in each upper corner.

A13

Type II. The design is complete at the top. The outer line at the bottom is broken in the middle. The shells are partly cut away.

A14

Type III. The outer lines are broken above the top label and the "X" numerals. The outer line at the bottom and the shells are partly cut away, as in Type II.

A15

Type IV. The outer lines have been recut at top or bottom or both.

Types I, II, III and IV have complete ornaments at the sides of the stamps and three pearls at each outer edge of the bottom panel.

Washington — A16

| **1851-56** | | | ***Imperf.*** | |
|---|---|---|---|---|
| *5* | A5 | 1c bl, Type I | *200,000.* | *17,500.* |
| *5A* | A5 | 1c bl, Type Ib | *7,500.* | *2,500.* |
| *6* | A6 | 1c bl, Type Ia | *20,000.* | *6,500.* |
| *7* | A7 | 1c bl, Type II | 450.00 | 85.00 |
| *8* | A8 | 1c bl, Type III | *5,500.* | 1,500. |
| *8A* | A8 | 1c bl, Type IIIa | *2,000.* | 600.00 |
| *9* | A9 | 1c bl, Type IV ('52) | 300.00 | 75.00 |
| **a.** | | Printed on both sides, reverse invtd. | | — |
| *10* | A10 | 3c org brn, Type I | 1,000. | 40.00 |
| **a.** | | Printed on both sides | | — |
| *11* | A10 | 3c dull red, Type I | 130.00 | 7.00 |
| **a** | | 3c claret, Type I | 160.00 | 10.00 |
| **c** | | Vertical half used as 1c on cover | | *6,000.* |
| **d** | | Diagonal half used as 1c on cover | | *5,500.* |
| **e** | | Double impression | | — |
| *12* | A11 | 5c red brn, Type I ('56) | *10,000.* | 1,300. |
| *13* | A12 | 10c grn, Type I ('55) | *9,000.* | 700.00 |
| *14* | A13 | 10c grn, Type II ('55) | 2,000. | 300.00 |
| *15* | A14 | 10c grn, Type III ('55) | 2,000. | 300.00 |
| *16* | A15 | 10c grn, Type IV ('55) | *11,500.* | 1,500. |
| *17* | A16 | 12c black | 2,000. | 250.00 |
| **a** | | Diagonal half used as 6c on cover | | *3,500.* |
| **b** | | Vert. half used as 6c on cover | | *8,500.* |
| **c** | | Printed on both sides | | *3,500.* |

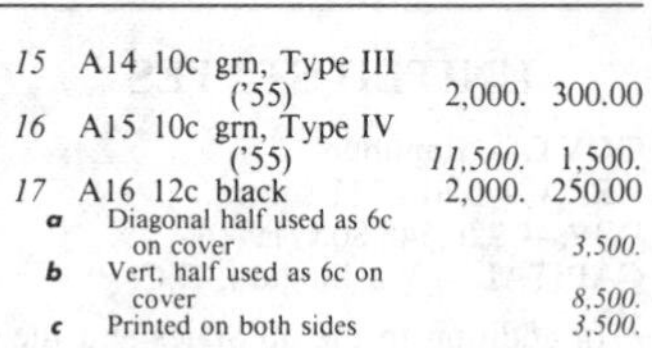

Values for No. 5A are for the less distinct positions. Best examples sell for more.

### Same Designs as 1851-56 Issues

Franklin — A20

ONE CENT

Type V. Similar to type III of 1851-56 but with side ornaments partly cut away.

Washington — A21

THREE CENTS

Type II. The outer frame line has been removed at top and bottom. The side frame lines were recut so as to be continuous from the top to the bottom of the plate.

Type IIa. The side frame lines extend only to the top and bottom of the stamp design.

Jefferson — A22

FIVE CENTS

Type II. The projections at top and bottom are partly cut away.

Washington (Two typical examples) — A23

TEN CENTS

Type V. The side ornaments are slightly cut away. Usually only one pearl remains at each end of the lower label but some copies show two or three pearls at the right side. At the bottom the outer line is complete and the shells nearly so. The outer lines at top are complete except over the right "X".

Washington
A17

Franklin
A18

Washington — A19

TWELVE CENTS Plate I. Outer frame lines complete. Plate III. Outer frame lines noticeably uneven or broken, sometimes partly missing.

**1857-61** *Perf. 15*

| No. | Type | Description | Unused | Used |
|---|---|---|---|---|
| *18* | A5 | 1c blue, Type I ('61) | 800.00 | 375.00 |
| *19* | A6 | 1c bl, Type Ia | *10,000.* | *2,500.* |
| *20* | A7 | 1c bl, Type II | 425.00 | 150.00 |
| *21* | A8 | 1c bl, Type III | 4,500. | 1,400. |
| *22* | A8 | 1c bl, Type IIIa | 700.00 | 250.00 |
| **b.** | | Horiz. pair, imperf. btwn. | | 3,500. |
| *23* | A9 | 1c bl, Type IV | 1,850. | 300.00 |
| *24* | A20 | 1c bl, Type V | 110.00 | 22.50 |
| **b** | | Laid paper | 450.00 | *250.00* |
| *25* | A10 | 3c rose, Type I | 650.00 | 27.50 |
| **b** | | Vert. pair, imperf. horiz. | | *6,000.* |
| *26* | A21 | 3c dl red, Type II | 45.00 | 2.75 |
| **a** | | 3c dull red, Type IIa | 110.00 | 20.00 |
| **b** | | Horiz. pair, imperf. vert., Type II | — | — |
| **c** | | Vert. pair, imperf. horiz., Type II | | — |
| **d** | | Horizontal pair, imperf. between, Type II | | — |
| **e** | | Dbl. impression, Type II | | — |
| *27* | A11 | 5c brick red, Type I ('58) | *8,500.* | 800.00 |
| *28* | A11 | 5c red brown, Type I | 1,350. | 250.00 |
| **b** | | bright red brown | 1,850. | 400.00 |
| *28A* | A11 | 5c Indian red, Type I ('58) | *10,000.* | 2,000. |
| *29* | A11 | 5c brn, Type I ('59) | 750.00 | 200.00 |
| *30* | A22 | 5c org brn, Type II ('61) | 750.00 | 900.00 |
| *30A* | A22 | 5c brn, Type II ('60) | 450.00 | 175.00 |
| **b** | | Printed on both sides | *3,750.* | *3,000.* |
| *31* | A12 | 10c grn, Type I | 5,250. | 525.00 |
| *32* | A13 | 10c grn, Type II | 1,750. | 185.00 |
| *33* | A14 | 10c grn, Type III | 1,750. | 185.00 |
| *34* | A15 | 10c grn, Type IV | *17,500.* | 1,750. |
| *35* | A23 | 10c grn, Type V ('59) | 175.00 | 50.00 |
| *36* | A16 | 12c blk, plate I | 325.00 | 75.00 |
| **a** | | Diagonal half used as 6c on cover (I) | | — |
| **b** | | 12c black, plate III ('59) | 250.00 | 100.00 |
| **c** | | Horizontal pair, imperf. between (I) | | — |
| *37* | A17 | 24c gray lil ('60) | 600.00 | 235.00 |
| **a** | | 24c gray | 600.00 | 235.00 |
| **b** | | 24c red lilac | 1,000. | |
| **c** | | Imperf. | *2,500.* | |
| *38* | A18 | 30c org ('60) | 775.00 | 300.00 |
| **a** | | Imperf. | *2,500.* | |
| *39* | A19 | 90c blue ('60) | 1,250. | *3,500.* |
| **a** | | Imperf. | *2,500.* | |
| | | Pen cancel | | 1,000. |

Nos. 37b, 37c, 38a and 39a probably came from trial printings and were not regularly issued.

Genuine cancellations on the 90c are rare.

## GOVERNMENT REPRINTS

White Paper
Without Gum

**1875** *Perf. 12*

| No. | Type | Description | Unused |
|---|---|---|---|
| *40* | A5 | 1c bright blue | *500.00* |
| *41* | A10 | 3c scarlet | *2,500.* |
| *42* | A22 | 5c orange brown | *1,000.* |
| *43* | A12 | 10c blue green | *2,000.* |
| *44* | A16 | 12c greenish blk | *2,250.* |
| *45* | A17 | 24c blk violet | *2,500.* |
| *46* | A18 | 30c yel orange | *2,500.* |
| *47* | A19 | 90c deep blue | *3,500.* |

Franklin — A24a

Washington — A25a

Jefferson — A26a

Washington — A27a

Washington — A28a

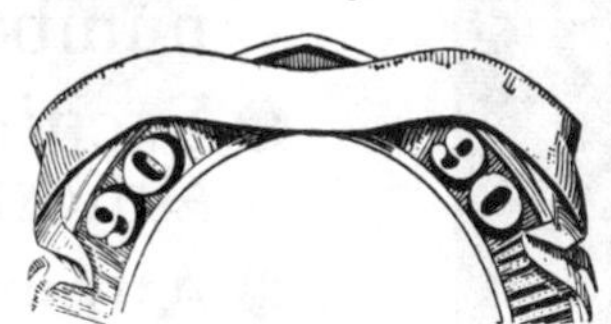
Washington — A31a

**1861** *Perf. 12*

| No. | Type | Description | Unused |
|---|---|---|---|
| *55* | A24a | 1c indigo | *20,000.* |
| *56* | A25a | 3c brown rose | 500.00 |
| **a** | | Imperf., pair | *1,750.* |
| *57* | A26a | 5c brown | *14,000.* |
| *58* | A27a | 10c dark green | *6,000.* |
| *59* | A28a | 12c black | *40,000.* |
| *60* | A29 | 24c dark violet | *6,500.* |
| *61* | A30 | 30c red orange | *17,500.* |
| *62* | A31a | 90c dull blue | *22,500.* |
| **a** | | Imperf., pair | *5,500.* |

The paper of Nos. 55-62 is thin and semi-transparent. That of the following issues is thicker and more opaque, except Nos. 62B, 70c, and 70d.

Nos. 55-62 were not regularly issued.

**1861**

| No. | Type | Description | Unused | Used |
|---|---|---|---|---|
| *62B* | A27a | 10c dark green | *6,000.* | 450.00 |

No. 62B unused cannot be distinguished from No. 58 which does not exist used.

Franklin — A24

1c. A dash has been added under the tip of the ornament at right of the numeral in upper left corner.

Washington — A25

3c. Ornaments at corners have been enlarged and end in a small ball.

Jefferson — A26

5c. A leaflet has been added to the foliated ornaments at each corner.

Washington — A27

10c. A heavy curved line has been cut below the stars and an outer line added to the ornaments above them.

Washington — A28

12c. Ovals and scrolls have been added to the corners.

Washington
A29

Franklin
A30

Washington — A31

90c. Parallel lines form an angle above the ribbon with "U. S. Postage"; between these lines a row of dashes has been added and a point of color to the apex of the lower pair.

**1861-62** *Perf. 12*

| No. | Type | Description | Unused | Used |
|---|---|---|---|---|
| *63* | A24 | 1c blue | 125.00 | 15.00 |
| **a** | | 1c ultramarine | 225.00 | 40.00 |
| **b** | | 1c dark blue | 175.00 | 25.00 |
| **c** | | Laid paper | — | 150.00 |
| **d** | | Vert. pair, imperf. horiz. | | — |
| **e** | | Printed on both sides | — | *2,500.* |
| *64* | A25 | 3c pink | 4,000. | 300.00 |
| **a** | | 3c pigeon blood pink | — | *1,350.* |
| **b** | | 3c rose pink | 260.00 | 45.00 |
| *65* | A25 | 3c rose | 65.00 | 1.00 |
| **b** | | Laid paper | *250.00* | 35.00 |
| **c** | | Imperf., pair | *450.00* | — |
| **d** | | Vert. pair, imperf. horiz. | *1,200.* | *750.00* |
| **e** | | Printed on both sides | *1,650.* | *1,000.* |
| **f** | | Double impression | | *1,200.* |
| *66* | A25 | 3c lake | 1,650. | |
| **a** | | Imperf., pair | *1,850.* | |
| *67* | A26 | 5c buff | *5,000.* | 375.00 |
| **a** | | 5c brown yellow | *5,000.* | 375.00 |
| **b** | | 5c olive yellow | *5,000.* | 375.00 |
| *68* | A27 | 10c yel green | 250.00 | 30.00 |
| **a** | | 10c dark green | 265.00 | 31.00 |
| **b** | | Vert. pair, imperf. horiz. | | *5,000.* |
| *69* | A28 | 12c black | 475.00 | 55.00 |
| *70* | A29 | 24c red lil ('62) | 575.00 | 80.00 |
| **a** | | 24c brown lilac | 475.00 | 67.50 |
| **b** | | 24c steel blue | 3,750. | 275.00 |
| **c** | | 24c violet | 3,750. | 550.00 |
| **d** | | 24c grayish lilac | 1,250. | 275.00 |
| *71* | A30 | 30c orange | 475.00 | 70.00 |
| **a** | | Printed on both sides | | — |
| *72* | A31 | 90c blue | 1,300. | 250.00 |
| **a** | | 90c pale blue | 1,300. | 250.00 |
| **b** | | 90c dark blue | 1,400. | 275.00 |

Nos. 66, 66a were not regularly issued.

Nos. 70c, 70d are on a thinner, harder and more transparent paper than Nos. 70, 70a, 70b, or the later Nos. 78, 78a, 78b and 78c.

### Designs as 1861 Issue

Andrew
Jackson
A32

Abraham
Lincoln
A33

**1861-66** *Perf. 12*

| No. | Type | Description | Unused | Used |
|---|---|---|---|---|
| *73* | A32 | 2c black ('63) | 110.00 | 22.50 |
| **a** | | Half used as 1c on cover, diagonal, vert. or horiz. | | *1,250.* |
| **d** | | Laid paper | — | — |
| **e** | | Printed on both sides | | *4,000.* |
| *74* | A25 | 3c scarlet | *4,500.* | |
| | | With 4 horiz. black pen strokes | | *1,850.* |
| **a** | | Imperf., pair | *3,750.* | |
| *75* | A26 | 5c red brn ('62) | 1,300. | 225.00 |
| *76* | A26 | 5c brown ('63) | 325.00 | 52.50 |
| **a** | | 5c dark brown | 375.00 | 65.00 |
| **b** | | Laid paper | | — |
| *77* | A33 | 15c black ('66) | 500.00 | 67.50 |
| *78* | A29 | 24c lilac ('63) | 275.00 | 50.00 |
| **a** | | 24c grayish lilac | 275.00 | 50.00 |
| **b** | | 24c gray | 275.00 | 50.00 |
| **c** | | 24c black violet | *10,000.* | *550.00* |
| **d** | | Printed on both sides | | *3,000.* |

Nos. 74 and 74a were not regularly issued.

Grill

Same as 1861-66 Issues
Embossed with grills of various sizes

**Grill with Points Up**

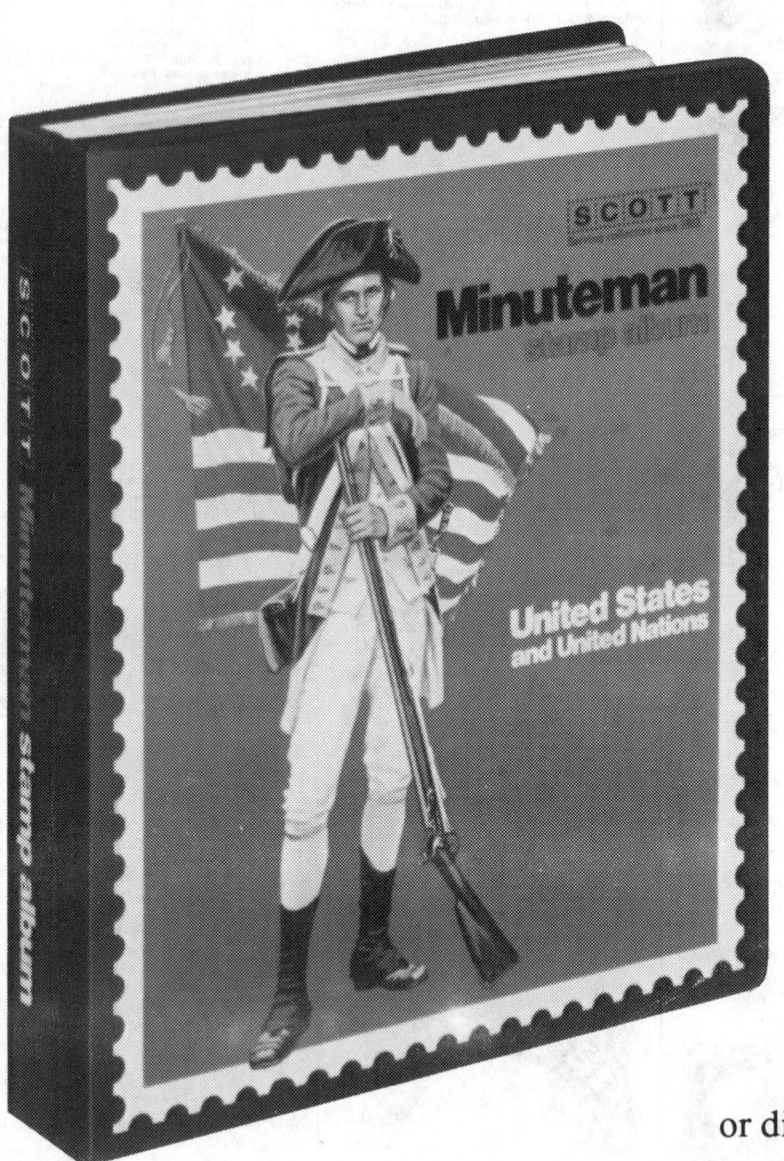

Grills A and C were made by a roller covered with ridges shaped like an inverted V. Pressing the ridges into the stamp paper forced the paper into the pyramidal pits between the ridges, causing irregular breaks in the paper.

Grill B was made by a roller with raised bosses.

### A. Grill covering the entire stamp

**1867** *Perf. 12*

| No. | Type | Description | Unused | Used |
|---|---|---|---|---|
| *79* | A25 | 3c rose | 1,750. | 425.00 |
| a | | Imperf., pair | *1,650.* | |
| b | | Printed on both sides | | — |
| *80* | A26 | 5c brown | *40,000.* | — |
| a | | 5c dark brown | | *37,500.* |
| *81* | A30 | 30c orange | | *32,500.* |

An essay which is often mistaken for No. 79 shows the points of the grill as small squares faintly impressed in the paper, but not cutting through it. On No. 79 the grill breaks through the paper. Copies free from defects are rare.

No. 79a was not regularly issued.

### B. Grill about 18x15mm (22 by 18 points)

| No. | Type | Description | Unused | Used |
|---|---|---|---|---|
| *82* | A25 | 3c rose | | *45,000.* |

### C. Grill about 13x16mm (16 to 17 by 18 to 21 points)

| No. | Type | Description | Unused | Used |
|---|---|---|---|---|
| *83* | A25 | 3c rose | 1,750. | 400.00 |
| a | | Imperf., pair | *1,650.* | |

The grilled area on each of four C grills in the sheet may total about 18x15mm when a normal C grill adjoins a fainter grill extending to the right or left edge of the stamp. This is caused by a partial erasure on the grill roller when it was changed to produce C grills instead of the all-over A grill.

No. 83a was not regularly issued.

### Grill with Points Down

The grills were produced by rollers with the surface covered by pyramidal bosses. On the Z grill the tips of the pyramids are very short horizontal ridges. On the D, E and F grills the ridges are vertical.

### D. Grill about 12x14mm (15 by 17 to 18 points)

| No. | Type | Description | Unused | Used |
|---|---|---|---|---|
| *84* | A32 | 2c black | 3,500. | 1,000. |
| *85* | A25 | 3c rose | 1,500. | 450.00 |

### Z. Grill about 11x14mm (13 to 14 by 17 to 18 points)

| No. | Type | Description | Unused | Used |
|---|---|---|---|---|
| *85A* | A24 | 1c blue | | — |
| *85B* | A32 | 2c black | 1,300. | 350.00 |
| *85C* | A25 | 3c rose | 4,000. | 950.00 |
| *85D* | A27 | 10c green | | *25,000.* |
| *85E* | A28 | 12c black | 1,650. | 575.00 |
| *85F* | A33 | 15c black | | — |

### E. Grill about 11x13mm (14 by 15 to 17 points)

| No. | Type | Description | Unused | Used |
|---|---|---|---|---|
| *86* | A24 | 1c blue | 800.00 | 250.00 |
| a | | 1c dull blue | 800.00 | 250.00 |
| *87* | A32 | 2c black | 350.00 | 70.00 |
| a | | Half used as 1c on cover, diagonal or vert. | | *2,000.* |
| *88* | A25 | 3c rose | 250.00 | 10.00 |
| a | | 3c lake red | 300.00 | 12.50 |
| *89* | A27 | 10c green | 1,300. | 175.00 |
| *90* | A28 | 12c black | 1,500. | 190.00 |
| *91* | A33 | 15c black | 3,250. | 450.00 |

### F. Grill about 9x13mm (11 to 12 by 15 to 17 points)

| No. | Type | Description | Unused | Used |
|---|---|---|---|---|
| *92* | A24 | 1c blue | 350.00 | 100.00 |
| a | | 1c pale blue | 350.00 | 100.00 |
| *93* | A32 | 2c black | 135.00 | 25.00 |
| a | | Half used as 1c on cover, diagonal, vert. or horiz. | | *1,250.* |
| *94* | A25 | 3c red | 95.00 | 2.50 |
| a | | 3c rose | 95.00 | 2.50 |
| b | | Imperf., pair | *650.00* | |
| c | | Vert. pair, imperf. horiz. | *1,000.* | |
| d | | Printed on both sides | *950.00* | |
| *95* | A26 | 5c brown | 900.00 | 225.00 |
| a | | 5c dark brown | 950.00 | 250.00 |
| *96* | A27 | 10c yel green | 700.00 | 110.00 |
| a | | 10c dark green | 700.00 | 110.00 |
| *97* | A28 | 12c black | 700.00 | 120.00 |
| *98* | A33 | 15c black | 700.00 | 135.00 |
| *99* | A29 | 24c gray lilac | 1,350. | 475.00 |
| *100* | A30 | 30c orange | 1,500. | 375.00 |
| *101* | A31 | 90c blue | 4,400. | 950.00 |

Some authorities believe that more than one size of grill probably existed on one of the grill rolls.

### Re-issue
### Without Grill

**1875** *Perf. 12*

| No. | Type | Description | Unused | Used |
|---|---|---|---|---|
| *102* | A24 | 1c blue | *500.00* | *800.00* |
| *103* | A32 | 2c black | *2,500.* | *4,000.* |
| *104* | A25 | 3c brown red | *3,250.* | *4,250.* |
| *105* | A26 | 5c brown | *1,800.* | *2,250.* |
| *106* | A27 | 10c green | *2,100.* | *3,750.* |
| *107* | A28 | 12c black | *3,000.* | *4,500.* |
| *108* | A33 | 15c black | *3,000.* | *4,750.* |
| *109* | A29 | 24c deep violet | *4,000.* | *6,000.* |
| *110* | A30 | 30c brownish org | *4,500.* | *7,000.* |
| *111* | A31 | 90c blue | *5,750.* | *18,500.* |

These stamps can be distinguished from the 1861-66 issues by the shades and the paper which is hard and very white instead of yellowish. The gum is white and crackly.

Franklin A34

Post Horse and Rider A35

Locomotive A36

Washington A37

Shield and Eagle A38

S. S. Adriatic A39

Landing of Columbus — A40

FIFTEEN CENTS

Type I. Picture unframed.

A40a

Type II. Picture framed.

Type III. Same as type I but without fringe of brown shading lines around central vignette.

"The Declaration of Independence" A41

Shield, Eagle and Flags A42

Lincoln — A43

### G. Grill measuring 9½x9mm (12 by 11 to 11½points)

**1869** *Perf. 12*

| No. | Type | Description | Unused | Used |
|---|---|---|---|---|
| *112* | A34 | 1c buff | 225.00 | 60.00 |
| b | | Without grill | *750.00* | |
| *113* | A35 | 2c brown | 160.00 | 25.00 |
| b | | Without grill | *600.00* | |
| c | | Half used as 1c on cover, diagonal, vert. or horiz. | | — |
| d | | Printed on both sides | | — |
| *114* | A36 | 3c ultramarine | 135.00 | 5.50 |
| a | | Without grill | *600.00* | — |
| b | | Vertical one third used as 1c on cover | | — |
| c | | Vertical two thirds used as 2c on cover | | — |
| d | | Double impression | | — |
| *115* | A37 | 6c ultramarine | 775.00 | 100.00 |
| b | | Vertical half used as 3c on cover | | — |
| *116* | A38 | 10c yellow | 850.00 | 95.00 |
| *117* | A39 | 12c green | 750.00 | 90.00 |
| *118* | A40 | 15c brn & blue, Type I | 1,750. | 300.00 |
| a | | Without grill | *3,500.* | |
| *119* | A40a | 15c brn & blue, Type II | 850.00 | 150.00 |
| b | | Center inverted | *145,000.* | *17,500.* |
| c | | Center dbl., one invtd. | — | |
| *120* | A41 | 24c grn & vio | 2,500. | 450.00 |
| a | | Without grill | *5,000.* | |
| b | | Center inverted | *125,000.* | *16,500.* |
| *121* | A42 | 30c blue & car | 2,250. | 225.00 |
| a | | Without grill | *3,750.* | |
| b | | Flags inverted | *120,000.* | *45,000.* |
| *122* | A43 | 90c car & black | 7,000. | 1,200. |
| a | | Without grill | *13,500.* | |

Values of varieties of Nos. 112 to 122 without grill are for copies with full original gum.

### Re-issues
### Without Grill
### Hard White Paper

**1875** *Perf. 12*

| No. | Type | Description | Unused | Used |
|---|---|---|---|---|
| *123* | A34 | 1c buff | 325.00 | 225.00 |
| *124* | A35 | 2c brown | 375.00 | 325.00 |
| *125* | A36 | 3c blue | 2,750. | *10,000.* |
| *126* | A37 | 6c blue | 850.00 | 550.00 |
| *127* | A38 | 10c yellow | 1,400. | 1,200. |
| *128* | A39 | 12c green | 1,500. | 1,200. |
| *129* | A40 | 15c brown & blue, Type III | 1,300. | 550.00 |
| a | | Imperf. horizontally, single | *1,600.* | — |
| *130* | A41 | 24c green & vio | 1,250. | 550.00 |
| *131* | A42 | 30c blue & car | 1,750. | 1,000. |
| *132* | A43 | 90c car & black | 5,500. | *6,000.* |

**1880**

### Soft Porous Paper

| No. | Type | Description | Unused | Used |
|---|---|---|---|---|
| *133* | A34 | 1c buff | 200.00 | 135.00 |
| a | | 1c brown orange | 175.00 | 120.00 |

No. 133 was issued with gum, No. 133a without gum.

### Printed by the National Bank Note Company

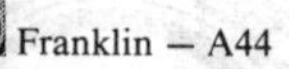

Franklin — A44

A44

Jackson — A45

A45

Washington — A46

A46

The Scott Catalogue value is a retail price, what you could expect to pay for the stamp in a grade of Fine-Very Fine. The value listed is a reference which reflects recent actual dealer selling price.

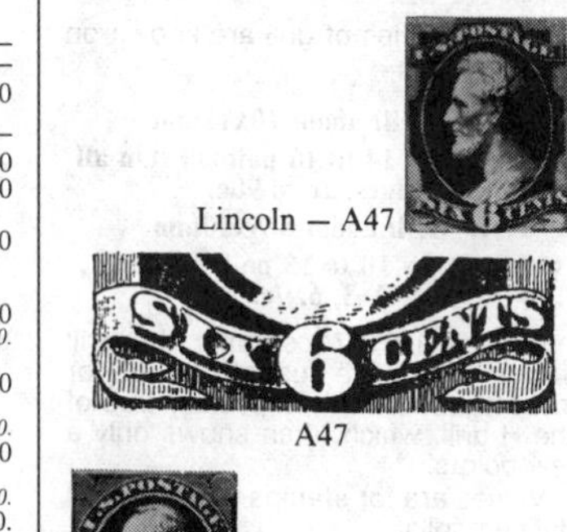

Lincoln — A47

A47

Edwin M. Stanton — A48

A48

Jefferson — A49

A49

Henry Clay — A50

A50

Daniel Webster — A51

A51

Gen. Winfield Scott A52

Alexander Hamilton A53

Commodore O. H. Perry — A54

Two varieties of grill are known on this issue.

**H. Grill about 10x12mm**

**(11 to 13 by 14 to 16 points.) On all values, 1c to 90c.**

**I. Grill about 8½x10mm**

**(10 to 11 by 10 to 13 points.) On 1, 2, 3, 6, 7c.**

On the 1870-71 stamps the grill impressions are usually faint or incomplete. This is especially true of the H grill, which often shows only a few points.

Values are for stamps showing well defined grills.

White Wove Paper

**1870-71** ***Perf. 12***

| No. | Design | Description | Unused | Used |
|---|---|---|---|---|
| *134* | A44 | 1c ultramarine | 500.00 | 57.50 |
| *135* | A45 | 2c red brown | 350.00 | 37.50 |
| *a* | | Diagonal half used as 1c on cover | | — |
| *136* | A46 | 3c green | 285.00 | 10.00 |
| *b* | | Imperf., pair | *1,200.* | |
| *137* | A47 | 6c carmine | 1,650. | 250.00 |
| *138* | A48 | 7c ver ('71) | 1,100. | 225.00 |
| *139* | A49 | 10c brown | 1,450. | 400.00 |
| *140* | A50 | 12c dull violet | *12,000.* | 1,500. |
| *141* | A51 | 15c orange | 1,850. | 700.00 |
| *142* | A52 | 24c purple | — | *9,500.* |
| *143* | A53 | 30c black | 4,500. | 825.00 |
| *144* | A54 | 90c carmine | 6,000. | 750.00 |

Without Grill

White Wove Paper

**1870-71** ***Perf. 12***

| No. | Design | Description | Unused | Used |
|---|---|---|---|---|
| *145* | A44 | 1c ultramarine | 165.00 | 6.50 |
| *146* | A45 | 2c red brown | 57.50 | 4.50 |
| *a* | | Half used as 1c on cover, diagonal or vert. | | — |
| *c* | | Double impression | — | |
| *147* | A46 | 3c green | 120.00 | 50 |
| *a* | | Printed on both sides | | *1,500.* |
| *b* | | Double impression | | *1,000.* |
| *c* | | Imperf., pair | *700.00* | |
| *148* | A47 | 6c carmine | 225.00 | 12.00 |
| *a* | | Vert. half used as 3c on cover | | — |
| *b* | | Double impression | | *1,250.* |
| *149* | A48 | 7c ver ('71) | 325.00 | 50.00 |
| *150* | A49 | 10c brown | 225.00 | 12.00 |
| *151* | A50 | 12c dull violet | 525.00 | 60.00 |
| *152* | A51 | 15c bright org | 500.00 | 60.00 |
| *153* | A52 | 24c purple | 600.00 | 80.00 |
| *154* | A53 | 30c black | 1,000. | 95.00 |
| *155* | A54 | 90c carmine | 1,350. | 175.00 |

**Printed by the Continental Bank Note Co.**

Designs of the 1870-71 Issue with secret marks on the values from 1c to 15c as described and illustrated below.

Franklin — A44a

1c. In pearl at left of numeral "1" is a small cresent.

Jackson — A45a

2c. Under the scroll at the left of "U. S." there is a small diagonal line. This mark seldom shows clearly. The stamp, No. 157, can be distinguished by its color.

Washington — A46a

3c. The under part of the upper tail of the left ribbon is heavily shaded.

Lincoln — A47a

6c. The first four vertical lines of the shading in the lower part of the left ribbon have been strengthened.

Stanton — A48a

7c. Two small semi-circles are drawn around the ends of the lines which outline the ball in the lower right hand corner.

Jefferson — A49a

10c. There is a small semi-circle in the scroll at the right end of the upper label.

Clay — A50a

12c. The balls of the figure "2" are crescent shaped.

Webster — A51a

15c. In the lower part of the triangle in the upper left corner two lines have been made heavier forming a "V". This mark can be found on some of the Continental and American (1879) printings, but not all stamps show it.

Secret marks were added to the dies of the 24c, 30c and 90c but new plates were not made from them. The various printings of these stamps can be distinguished only by the shades and paper.

White Wove Paper, thin to thick

Without Grill*

**1873** ***Perf. 12***

| No. | Design | Description | Unused | Used |
|---|---|---|---|---|
| *156* | A44a | 1c ultramarine | 55.00 | 1.75 |
| *e* | | With grill | *1,200.* | |
| *f* | | Imperf., pair | — | *500.00* |
| *157* | A45a | 2c brown | 150.00 | 7.00 |
| *c* | | With grill | *850.00* | *600.00* |
| *d* | | Double impression | | — |
| *e* | | Vertical half used as 1c on cover | | — |
| *158* | A46a | 3c green | 45.00 | 15 |
| *e* | | With grill | *175.00* | |
| *f* | | Imperf., pair, with grill | *650.00* | |
| *g* | | Imperf., pair | *750.00* | |
| *h* | | Horiz. pair, imperf. vert. | | — |
| *i* | | Horiz. pair, imperf. btwn. | | *1,300.* |
| *j* | | Double impression | | *600.00* |
| *k* | | Printed on both sides | | — |
| *159* | A47a | 6c dull pink | 200.00 | 9.00 |
| *b* | | With grill | *650.00* | |
| *160* | A48a | 7c org ver | 400.00 | 55.00 |
| *a* | | With grill | *1,350.* | |
| *161* | A49a | 10c brown | 225.00 | 10.00 |
| *c* | | With grill | *1,750.* | |
| *d* | | Horiz. pair, imperf. btwn. | | *2,500.* |
| *162* | A50a | 12c blk vio | 600.00 | 65.00 |
| *a* | | With grill | *3,000.* | |
| *163* | A51a | 15c yel org | 575.00 | 60.00 |
| *a* | | With grill | *3,000.* | |
| *165* | A53 | 30c gray black | 650.00 | 60.00 |
| *c* | | With grill | *3,000.* | |
| *166* | A54 | 90c rose car | 1,350. | 185.00 |

It is generally accepted as fact that the Continental Bank Note Co. printed and delivered a quantity of 24c stamps. They are impossible to distinguish from those printed by the National Bank Note Co.

* All values except 90c exist with experimental (J) grill, about 7x9½mm.

**Special Printing**

Hard, White Wove Paper

Without Gum

**1875** ***Perf. 12***

| No. | Design | Description | Unused | Used |
|---|---|---|---|---|
| *167* | A44a | 1c ultramarine | *7,500.* | |
| *168* | A45a | 2c dark brown | *3,500.* | |
| *169* | A46a | 3c blue green | *9,500.* | — |
| *170* | A47a | 6c dull rose | *8,500.* | |
| *171* | A48a | 7c redsh ver | *2,100.* | |
| *172* | A49a | 10c pale brown | *7,750.* | |
| *173* | A50a | 12c dark violet | *2,750.* | |
| *174* | A51a | 15c brt org | *7,750.* | |
| *175* | A52 | 24c dull purple | *1,850.* | — |
| *176* | A53 | 30c grnsh black | *7,000.* | |
| *177* | A54 | 90c vio carmine | *7,000.* | |

Although perforated, these stamps were usually cut apart with scissors. As a result, the perforations are often much mutilated and the design is frequently damaged.

These can be distinguished from the 1873 issue by the shades, also by the paper, which is very white instead of yellowish.

These and the subsequent issues listed under this heading are special printings of stamps then in current use which, together with the reprints and reissues, were made for sale to collectors. They were available for postage.

Zachary Taylor — A55

Yellowish Wove Paper

**1875, June 21** ***Perf. 12***

| No. | Design | Description | Unused | Used |
|---|---|---|---|---|
| *178* | A45a | 2c vermilion | 160.00 | 5.00 |
| *a* | | Imperf., pair | 600.00 | |
| *b* | | Half used as 1c on cover | | — |
| *c* | | With grill | *250.00* | |
| *179* | A55 | 5c blue | 175.00 | 9.00 |
| *c* | | With grill | 325.00 | |

Almost all of the stamps of the Continental Bank Note Co. printing including the Department stamps and some of the Newspaper stamps may be found upon a paper which shows more or less of the characteristics of a ribbed paper.

**Special Printing**

Hard, White Wove Paper

Without Gum

**1875**

| No. | Design | Description | Unused | Used |
|---|---|---|---|---|
| *180* | A45a | 2c carmine ver | *19,000.* | |
| *181* | A55 | 5c brt blue | *32,500.* | |

**Printed by the American Bank Note Company**

Same as 1870-75 Issues

Soft Porous Paper

Varying from Thin to Thick

**1879** ***Perf. 12***

| No. | Design | Description | Unused | Used |
|---|---|---|---|---|
| *182* | A44a | 1c dark ultra | 120.00 | 1.20 |
| *183* | A45a | 2c vermilion | 55.00 | 1.20 |
| *a* | | Double impression | — | *500.00* |
| *184* | A46a | 3c green | 42.50 | 10 |
| *a* | | Imperf., pair | 500.00 | |
| *b* | | Double impression | | — |
| *185* | A55 | 5c blue | 225.00 | 7.50 |
| *186* | A47a | 6c pink | 450.00 | 12.00 |
| *187* | A49 | 10c brown (without secret mark) | 750.00 | 14.00 |
| *188* | A49a | 10c brown (with secret mark) | 475.00 | 15.00 |
| *c* | | Vert. pair, imperf. between | | — |
| *189* | A51a | 15c red orange | 165.00 | 14.00 |
| *190* | A53 | 30c full black | 475.00 | 30.00 |
| *191* | A54 | 90c carmine | 1,000. | 150.00 |
| *b* | | Imperf., pair | *3,250.* | |

No. 191b was not regularly issued.

The ABN Co. used many Continental plates to print the postage, Departmental and Newspaper stamps. Therefore, stamps bearing the Continental imprint were not always its product.

The ABN Co. also used the National 90c plate and possibly the 30c plate.

Early printings of No. 188 were from Continental plates 302 and 303 which contained the normal secret mark of 1873. After those plates were re-entered by the ABN Co. in 1880, pairs or multiple pieces contained combinations of normal, hairline or missing marks. The pairs or other multiples usually found contain at least one hairline mark which tended to disappear as the plate wore.

ABN Co. plates 377 and 378 were made in 1881 from the National transfer roll of 1870. No. 187 from those plates has no secret mark.

**Special Printing**

Soft Porous Paper

Without Gum

**1880** ***Perf. 12***

| No. | Design | Description | Unused | Used |
|---|---|---|---|---|
| *192* | A44a | 1c dark ultra | *10,000.* | |
| *193* | A45a | 2c black brown | *6,500.* | |
| *194* | A46a | 3c blue green | *15,000.* | |
| *195* | A47a | 6c dull rose | *10,500.* | |
| *196* | A48a | 7c scar vermilion | *2,100.* | |
| *197* | A49a | 10c deep brown | *9,750.* | |
| *198* | A50a | 12c black purple | *4,500.* | |
| *199* | A51a | 15c orange | *9,250.* | |
| *200* | A52 | 24c dark violet | *3,000.* | |
| *201* | A53 | 30c grnsh black | *7,500.* | |
| *202* | A54 | 90c dull carmine | *8,500.* | |
| *203* | A45a | 2c scar ver | *18,000.* | |
| *204* | A55 | 5c deep blue | *32,500.* | |

No. 197 was printed from Continental plate 302 (or 303) after plate was re-entered, therefore stamp may show normal, hairline or missing secret mark.

James A. Garfield — A56

**1882, Apr. 10** ***Perf. 12***

| No. | Design | Description | Unused | Used |
|---|---|---|---|---|
| *205* | A56 | 5c yellow brown | 120.00 | 4.00 |

**Special Printing**

Soft Porous Paper

Without Gum

**1882**

| No. | Design | Description | Unused | Used |
|---|---|---|---|---|
| *205C* | A56 | 5c gray brown | *18,500.* | |

Designs of 1873 Re-engraved

Franklin — A44b

1c. The vertical lines in the upper part of the stamp have been so deepened that the background often appears to be solid. Lines of shading have been added to the upper arabesques.

Washington — A46b

3c. The shading at the sides of the central oval appears only about one-half the previous width. A short horizontal dash has been cut about 1mm below the "TS" of "CENTS."

Lincoln — A47b

6c. On the original stamps four vertical lines can be counted from the edge of the panel to the outside of the stamp. On the re-engraved stamps there are but three lines in the same place.

Jefferson — A49b

10c. On the original stamps there are five vertical lines between the left side of the oval and the edge of the shield. There are only four lines on the re-engraved stamps. In the lower part of the latter, also, the horizontal lines of the background have been strengthened.

| **1881-82** | | | *Perf. 12* | |
|---|---|---|---|---|
| *206* | A44b | 1c gray blue | 32.50 | 40 |
| *207* | A46b | 3c blue green | 40.00 | 12 |
| *208* | A47b | 6c rose ('82) | 225.00 | 45.00 |
| *a* | | 6c brown red | 200.00 | 55.00 |
| *209* | A49b | 10c brown ('82) | 75.00 | 2.50 |
| *b* | | 10c black brown | 125.00 | 6.75 |
| *c* | | Double impression | | — |

Washington A57

Jackson A58

| **1883, Oct. 1** | | | *Perf. 12* | |
|---|---|---|---|---|
| *210* | A57 | 2c red brown | 32.50 | 8 |
| *b* | | Imperf., pair | — | |
| *211* | A58 | 4c blue green | 140.00 | 7.50 |
| *a* | | Imperf., pair | — | |

**Special Printing**
Soft Porous Paper

| **1883** | | | | |
|---|---|---|---|---|
| *211B* | A57 | 2c pale red brn | 750.00 | — |
| *c* | | Horiz. pair, imperf. btwn. | *2,250.* | |
| *211D* | A58 | 4c deep bl grn | *15,000.* | |

No. 211D is without gum.

Franklin — A59

| **1887** | | | *Perf. 12* | |
|---|---|---|---|---|
| *212* | A59 | 1c ultramarine | 60.00 | 65 |
| *a* | | Imperf., pair | *750.00* | *325.00* |
| *213* | A57 | 2c green | 22.50 | 8 |
| *a* | | Imperf., pair | *750.00* | *325.00* |
| *b* | | Printed on both sides | | — |
| *214* | A46b | 3c vermilion | 45.00 | 37.50 |

| **1888** | | | *Perf. 12* | |
|---|---|---|---|---|
| *215* | A58 | 4c carmine | 140.00 | 11.00 |
| *216* | A56 | 5c indigo | 140.00 | 6.50 |
| *b* | | Imperf., pair | *1,000.* | |
| *217* | A53 | 30c org brown | 325.00 | 75.00 |
| *a* | | Imperf., pair | *1,350.* | |
| *218* | A54 | 90c purple | 700.00 | 130.00 |
| *a* | | Imperf., pair | — | |

Nos. 216b, 217a and 218a were not regularly issued.

Franklin A60

Washington A61

Jackson A62

Lincoln A63

Grant A64

Garfield A65

William T. Sherman A66

Daniel Webster A67

Henry Clay A68

Jefferson A69

Perry — A70

| **1890-93** | | | *Perf. 12* | |
|---|---|---|---|---|
| *219* | A60 | 1c dull blue | 18.50 | 10 |
| *c* | | Imperf., pair | 225.00 | |
| *219D* | A61 | 2c lake | 150.00 | 45 |
| *e* | | Imperf., pair | 100.00 | |
| *220* | A61 | 2c carmine | 15.00 | 5 |
| *a* | | Cap on left "2" | 35.00 | 1.00 |
| *c* | | Cap on both "2's" | 110.00 | 8.00 |
| *d* | | Imperf., pair | 100.00 | |
| | | As "d," without gum | 40.00 | |
| *221* | A62 | 3c purple | 50.00 | 4.50 |
| *a* | | Imperf., pair | 275.00 | |
| *222* | A63 | 4c dark brown | 50.00 | 1.50 |
| *a* | | Imperf., pair | 250.00 | |
| *223* | A64 | 5c chocolate | 50.00 | 1.50 |
| *b* | | Imperf., pair | 275.00 | |
| *224* | A65 | 6c brown red | 55.00 | 15.00 |
| *a* | | Imperf., pair | 275.00 | |
| *225* | A66 | 8c lilac ('93) | 40.00 | 8.50 |
| *a* | | Imperf., pair | *1,250.* | |
| *226* | A67 | 10c green | 95.00 | 1.75 |
| *a* | | Imperf., pair | 400.00 | |
| *227* | A68 | 15c indigo | 135.00 | 15.00 |
| *a* | | Imperf., pair | 750.00 | |
| *228* | A69 | 30c black | 200.00 | 20.00 |
| *a* | | Imperf., pair | *1,350.* | |
| *229* | A70 | 90c orange | 325.00 | 95.00 |
| *a* | | Imperf., pair | *2,750.* | |
| | | *Nos. 219-229 (12)* | 1,183. | 163.35 |

The imperf. stamps were not regularly issued.

The "cap on right 2" variety is due to imperfect inking, not a plate defect.

### Columbian Exposition Issue

Columbus in Sight of Land — A71

Landing of Columbus A72

Flagship of Columbus A73

Fleet of Columbus A74

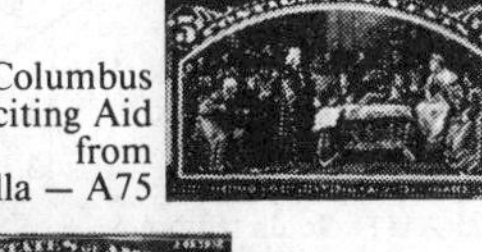
Columbus Soliciting Aid from Isabella — A75

Columbus Welcomed at Barcelona A76

Columbus Restored to Favor — A77

Columbus Presenting Natives — A78

Columbus Announcing his Discovery A79

Columbus at La Rabida — A80

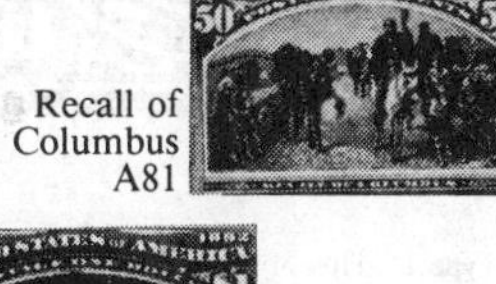
Recall of Columbus A81

Isabella Pledging her Jewels — A82

Columbus in Chains — A83

Columbus Describing his Third Voyage — A84

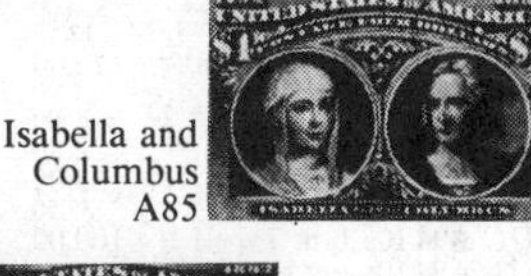
Isabella and Columbus A85

Columbus A86

| **1893** | | | *Perf. 12* | |
|---|---|---|---|---|
| *230* | A71 | 1c deep blue | 17.50 | 25 |
| *231* | A72 | 2c brn violet | 16.00 | 6 |
| *b* | | Imperf., pair | *1,200.* | |
| *232* | A73 | 3c green | 38.50 | 12.50 |
| *233* | A74 | 4c ultra | 55.00 | 5.00 |
| *a* | | 4c blue (error) | *8,000.* | *3,250.* |
| *234* | A75 | 5c chocolate | 62.50 | 6.00 |
| *235* | A76 | 6c purple | 55.00 | 16.50 |
| *a* | | 6c red violet | 55.00 | 16.50 |
| *236* | A77 | 8c magenta | 45.00 | 7.00 |
| *237* | A78 | 10c blk brown | 90.00 | 5.00 |
| *238* | A79 | 15c dark grn | 150.00 | 45.00 |
| *239* | A80 | 30c org brown | 210.00 | 65.00 |
| *240* | A81 | 50c slate blue | 300.00 | 110.00 |
| *241* | A82 | $1 salmon | 1,050. | 475.00 |
| *242* | A83 | $2 brown red | 1,150. | 400.00 |
| *243* | A84 | $3 yel green | 1,950. | 700.00 |
| *a* | | $3 olive green | 1,950. | 700.00 |
| *244* | A85 | $4 crim lake | 2,750. | 1,000. |
| *a* | | $4 rose carmine | 2,750. | 1,000. |
| *245* | A86 | $5 black | 3,000. | 1,300. |

World's Columbian Expo., Chicago, May 1-Oct. 30, 1893.

Nos. 230-245 are known imperf., but were not regularly issued. (See Scott's U. S. Specialized Catalogue.)

Condition is extremely important in evaluating Nos. 230-245. Values are for stamps free from faults and with the design well clear of the perforations. Stamps of superior quality command substantial premiums.

### Bureau Issues

Starting in 1894, the Bureau of Engraving and Printing at Washington has produced most U.S. postage stamps. Until 1965 Bureau-printed stamps were engraved except Nos. 525-536, which are offset. The combination of lithography and engraving (see No. 1253) was first used in 1964, and photogravure (see No. 1426) in 1971.

Franklin A87

Washington A88

Jackson A89

Lincoln A90

Grant A91

Garfield A92

Sherman A93

Webster A94

Clay A95

Jefferson A96

Perry A97

James Madison A98

John Marshall — A99

TWO CENTS

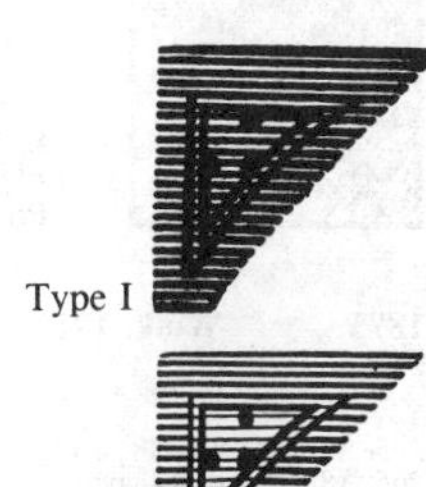
Type I

Type II

Type I. The horizontal lines of the ground work run across the triangle and are of the same thickness within it as without.

Type II. The horizontal lines cross the triangle but are thinner within it than without.

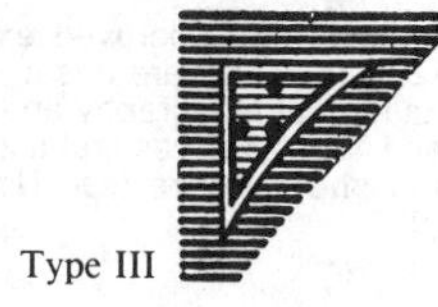
Type III

Type III. The horizontal lines do not cross the double frame lines of the triangle. The lines within the triangle are thin, as in type II.

ONE DOLLAR

Type I

Type I. The circles enclosing "$1" are broken where they meet the curved line below "One Dollar." The 15 left vert. rows of impressions from plate 76 are Type I, the balance Type II.

Type II

Type II. The circles are complete.

**1894 Unwmk. *Perf. 12***

| No. | Design | Description | Unused | Used |
|---|---|---|---|---|
| *246* | A87 | 1c ultramarine | 15.00 | 2.00 |
| *247* | A87 | 1c blue | 37.50 | 85 |
| *248* | A88 | 2c pink, Type I | 17.50 | 2.00 |
| *a* | | Vert. pair, imperf. horiz. | *2,000.* | |
| *249* | A88 | 2c car lake, Type I | 85.00 | 95 |
| *250* | A88 | 2c car, Type I | 14.00 | 15 |
| *a* | | Vert. pair, imperf. horiz. | *1,500.* | |
| *b* | | Horiz. pair, imperf. btwn. | *1,500.* | |
| *251* | A88 | 2c car, Type II | 110.00 | 1.50 |
| *252* | A88 | 2c car, Type III | 70.00 | 2.00 |
| *a* | | Horiz. pair, imperf. vert. | *1,350.* | |
| *b* | | Horiz. pair, imperf. btwn. | *1,500.* | |
| *253* | A89 | 3c purple | 55.00 | 4.25 |
| *a* | | Imperf., pair | 350.00 | |
| *254* | A90 | 4c dark brown | 60.00 | 1.75 |
| *a* | | Imperf., pair | 350.00 | |
| *255* | A91 | 5c chocolate | 52.50 | 2.50 |
| *b* | | Imperf., pair | 350.00 | |
| *c* | | Vert. pair, imperf. horiz. | *900.00* | |
| *256* | A92 | 6c dull brown | 95.00 | 12.00 |
| *a* | | Vert. pair, imperf. horiz. | *850.00* | |
| *257* | A93 | 8c vio brn ('95) | 80.00 | 8.00 |
| *258* | A94 | 10c dark green | 115.00 | 5.00 |
| *a* | | Imperf., pair | 650.00 | |
| *259* | A95 | 15c dark blue | 175.00 | 30.00 |
| *260* | A96 | 50c orange | 225.00 | 50.00 |
| *261* | A97 | $1 blk, Type I | 550.00 | 160.00 |
| *261A* | A97 | $1 blk, Type II | 1,200. | 325.00 |
| *262* | A98 | $2 bright bl | 1,400. | 400.00 |
| *263* | A99 | $5 dark green | 2,250. | 750.00 |

Nos. 248a, 253a, 254a, 255b and 258a were not regularly issued.

Note on condition and pricing after No. 245 also applies to Nos. 246-263.

Same as 1894 Issue

Wmk. 191-Double-lined "USPS" in Capitals

**1895 Wmk. 191 *Perf. 12***

| No. | Design | Description | Unused | Used |
|---|---|---|---|---|
| *264* | A87 | 1c blue | 3.50 | 10 |
| *b* | | Horiz. pair, imperf. vert. | — | |
| *c* | | Imperf., pair | 325.00 | |
| *265* | A88 | 2c car, Type I | 15.00 | 40 |
| *266* | A88 | 2c car, Type II | 13.00 | 1.75 |
| *267* | A88 | 2c car, Type III | 3.00 | 5 |
| *a* | | Imperf., pair | 300.00 | |

The three left vertical rows from plate 170 are Type II, the balance being Type III.

| No. | Design | Description | Unused | Used |
|---|---|---|---|---|
| *268* | A89 | 3c purple | 22.50 | 65 |
| *a* | | Imperf., pair | 350.00 | |
| *269* | A90 | 4c dark brn | 34.00 | 75 |
| *a* | | Imperf., pair | 350.00 | |
| *270* | A91 | 5c chocolate | 22.50 | 1.20 |
| *b* | | Imperf., pair | 350.00 | |
| *271* | A92 | 6c dull brn | 42.50 | 2.50 |
| *a* | | Wmkd. USIR | *2,250.* | 350.00 |
| *b* | | Imperf., pair | 400.00 | |
| *272* | A93 | 8c vio brn | 30.00 | 65 |
| *a* | | Wmkd. USIR | 1,100. | 110.00 |
| *b* | | Imperf., pair | 550.00 | |
| *273* | A94 | 10c dark grn | 40.00 | 80 |
| *a* | | Imperf., pair | 450.00 | |
| *274* | A95 | 15c dark bl | 110.00 | 5.50 |
| *a* | | Imperf., pair | *1,450.* | |
| *275* | A96 | 50c orange | 160.00 | 14.00 |
| *a* | | 50c red orange | 170.00 | 16.00 |
| *b* | | Imperf., pair | *1,600.* | |
| *276* | A97 | $1 blk, Type I | 375.00 | 45.00 |
| *b* | | Imperf., pair | *2,750.* | |
| *276A* | A97 | $1 blk, Type II | 825.00 | 92.50 |
| *277* | A98 | $2 bright bl | 600.00 | 200.00 |
| *a* | | $2 dark blue | 650.00 | 210.00 |
| *b* | | Imperf., pair | *3,500.* | |
| *278* | A99 | $5 dark grn | 2,000. | 425.00 |
| *a* | | Imperf., pair | *6,000.* | |

The imperforate varieties of the 1895 issue, and No. 264b, were not regularly issued.

TEN CENTS

Type I

Type I. Tips of foliate ornaments do not impinge on white curved line below "TEN CENTS".

Type II

Type II. Tips of ornaments break curved line below "E" of "TEN" and "T" of "CENTS".

**1898 Wmk. 191 *Perf. 12***

| No. | Design | Description | Unused | Used |
|---|---|---|---|---|
| *279* | A87 | 1c deep green | 6.00 | 6 |
| *279B* | A88 | 2c red, Type III | 5.50 | 5 |
| *c* | | 2c rose car, Type III | 100.00 | 30.00 |
| *d* | | 2c orange red, Type III | 6.50 | 9 |
| *e* | | Booklet pane of 6 | 350.00 | *200.00* |
| *f* | | 2c deep red, Type III | 13.50 | 50 |
| *280* | A90 | 4c rose brown | 20.00 | 45 |
| *a* | | 4c lilac brown | 20.00 | 45 |
| *b* | | 4c orange brown | 20.00 | 45 |
| *281* | A91 | 5c dark blue | 22.50 | 40 |
| *282* | A92 | 6c lake | 35.00 | 1.40 |
| *a* | | 6c purple lake | 37.50 | 1.65 |
| *282C* | A94 | 10c brn, Type I | 100.00 | 1.20 |
| *283* | A94 | 10c org brn, Type II | 60.00 | 1.00 |
| *284* | A95 | 15c olive grn | 85.00 | 4.50 |
| | | *Nos. 279-284 (8)* | 334.00 | 9.06 |

**Trans-Mississippi Exposition Issue**

Marquette on the Mississippi A100

Farming in the West — A101

Indian Hunting Buffalo A102

Fremont on the Rocky Mountains A103

Troops Guarding Train — A104

Hardships of Emigration A105

Western Mining Prospector A106

Western Cattle in Storm — A107

Mississippi River Bridge — A108

**1898, June 17 Wmk. 191 *Perf. 12***

| No. | Design | Description | Unused | Used |
|---|---|---|---|---|
| *285* | A100 | 1c dk yel grn | 20.00 | 3.75 |
| *286* | A101 | 2c cop red | 17.50 | 1.00 |
| *287* | A102 | 4c orange | 100.00 | 16.00 |
| *288* | A103 | 5c dull blue | 87.50 | 14.00 |
| *289* | A104 | 8c vio brn | 125.00 | 30.00 |
| *a* | | Vert. pair, imperf. horiz. | *12,000.* | |
| *290* | A105 | 10c gray vio | 140.00 | 17.50 |
| *291* | A106 | 50c sage grn | 500.00 | 150.00 |
| *292* | A107 | $1 black | 1,325. | 475.00 |
| *293* | A108 | $2 org brn | 1,950. | 725.00 |
| | | *Nos. 285-293 (9)* | 4,265. | 1,432. |

Trans-Mississippi Exposition, Omaha, Neb., June 1 to Nov. 1, 1898.

Note on condition and pricing after No. 245 also applies to Nos. 285-293.

**Pan-American Exposition Issue**

Fast Lake Navigation A109

"Empire State" Express A110

Electric Automobile A111

Bridge at Niagara Falls A112

Canal Locks at Sault Ste. Marie A113

Fast Ocean Navigation A114

**1901, May 1 Wmk. 191 *Perf. 12***

| No. | Design | Description | Unused | Used |
|---|---|---|---|---|
| *294* | A109 | 1c grn & blk | 13.50 | 2.50 |
| *a* | | Center inverted | *10,000.* | *4,500.* |
| *295* | A110 | 2c car & blk | 13.50 | 75 |
| *a* | | Center inverted | *45,000.* | *13,500.* |
| *296* | A111 | 4c dp red brn & blk | 70.00 | 12.50 |
| *a* | | Center inverted | *13,000.* | |
| *297* | A112 | 5c ultra & blk | 82.50 | 12.50 |
| *298* | A113 | 8c brn vio & blk | 100.00 | 50.00 |
| *299* | A114 | 10c yel brn & blk | 150.00 | 22.50 |
| | | *Nos. 294-299 (6)* | 429.50 | 100.75 |

Buffalo, N.Y., May 1 to Nov. 1, 1901.

No. 296a was not regularly issued.

Note on condition and pricing after No. 245 also applies to Nos. 294-299.

Franklin A115

Washington A116

Jackson A117

Grant A118

Lincoln A119

Garfield A120

Martha Washington A121

Webster A122

Benjamin Harrison A123

Clay A124

Jefferson A125

David G. Farragut A126

Madison A127

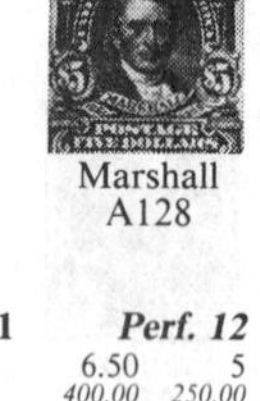
Marshall A128

**1902-03 Wmk. 191 *Perf. 12***

| No. | Design | Description | Unused | Used |
|---|---|---|---|---|
| *300* | A115 | 1c bl grn ('03) | 6.50 | 5 |
| *b* | | Booklet pane of 6 | *400.00* | *250.00* |
| *301* | A116 | 2c car ('03) | 7.50 | 5 |
| *c* | | Booklet pane of 6 | *350.00* | *250.00* |
| *302* | A117 | 3c brt vio ('03) | 30.00 | 2.00 |
| *303* | A118 | 4c brown ('03) | 30.00 | 60 |
| *304* | A119 | 5c blue ('03) | 35.00 | 65 |
| *305* | A120 | 6c claret ('03) | 37.50 | 1.50 |
| *306* | A121 | 8c vio blk | 25.00 | 1.25 |
| *307* | A122 | 10c pale red brn ('03) | 30.00 | 70 |
| *308* | A123 | 13c pur blk | 25.00 | 5.00 |
| *309* | A124 | 15c ol grn ('03) | 87.50 | 3.75 |
| *310* | A125 | 50c org ('03) | 250.00 | 17.50 |
| *311* | A126 | $1 black ('03) | 450.00 | 35.00 |
| *312* | A127 | $2 dk bl ('03) | 600.00 | 125.00 |
| *313* | A128 | $5 dk grn ('03) | 1,650. | 450.00 |
| | | *Nos. 300-313 (14)* | 3,264. | 643.05 |

For listings of designs A127 and A128 with Perf. 10, see Nos. 479 and 480.

**1906-08 *Imperf.***

| No. | Design | Description | Unused | Used |
|---|---|---|---|---|
| *314* | A115 | 1c blue grn | 16.00 | 13.00 |
| *314A* | A118 | 4c brown ('08) | *17,500.* | *9,000.* |
| *315* | A119 | 5c blue ('08) | 375.00 | 150.00 |

No. 314A was issued imperforate but all copies were privately perforated with large oblong perforations at the sides (Schermack type III).

### Coil Stamps

Imperforate stamps are being fraudulently perforated to resemble coil stamps and part perforate varieties.

**1908** ***Perf. 12 Horizontally***

*316* A115 1c bl grn, pair *50,000.* —
*317* A119 5c blue, pair *5,500.* —

***Perf. 12 Vertically***

*318* A115 1c bl grn, pair *4,250.* —

Coil stamps for use in vending and affixing machines are perforated on two sides only, either horizontally or vertically. They were first issued in 1908, using perf. 12. This was changed to 8½ in 1910, and to 10 in 1914.

Imperforate sheets of certain denominations were sold to the vending machine companies which applied a variety of private perforations and separations.

Several values of the 1902 and later issues are found on an apparently coarse ribbed paper. This is caused by worn blankets on the printing press and is not a true paper variety.

Washington — A129

Die I Die II

### Shield-Shaped Background

**1903, Nov. 12** **Wmk. 191** ***Perf. 12***

| | | | |
|---|---|---|---|
| *319* A129 2c carmine (I) | | 4.00 | 5 |
| a | 2c lake (I) | — | — |
| b | 2c carmine rose (I) | 6.00 | 20 |
| c | 2c scarlet (I) | 4.00 | 6 |
| d | Vert. pair, imperf. horiz. | *1,200.* | |
| e | Vert. pair, imperf. btwn. | *550.00* | |
| f | 2c lake (II) | 4.50 | 10 |
| g | Booklet pane of 6, car (I) | 90.00 | *20.00* |
| h | As "g" (II) | 125.00 | |
| i | 2c carmine (II) | 17.50 | — |
| j | 2c carmine rose (II) | — | |
| k | 2c scarlet (II) | — | |
| m | As "g", lake (I) | — | |
| n | As "g", car rose (I) | — | |
| p | As "g", scarlet (I) | 90.00 | |
| q | As "g", lake (II) | 125.00 | |

**1906, Oct. 2** ***Imperf.***

| | | | |
|---|---|---|---|
| *320* A129 2c carmine | | 17.50 | 11.00 |
| a | 2c lake (II) | 50.00 | 35.00 |
| b | 2c scarlet | 16.00 | 12.00 |

### Coil Stamps

**1908** ***Perf. 12 Horizontally***

*321* A129 2c car, pair *60,000.* —

***Perf. 12 Vertically.***

*322* A129 2c car, pair *5,500.* —

### Louisiana Purchase Exposition Issue

Robert R. Livingston A130

Thomas Jefferson A131

James Monroe A132

William McKinley A133

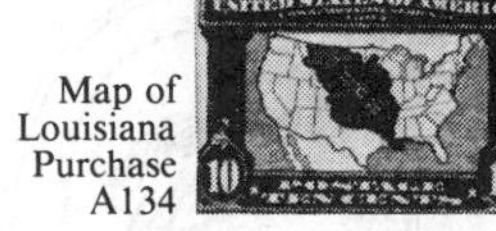
Map of Louisiana Purchase A134

**1904, Apr. 30** **Wmk. 191** ***Perf. 12***

| | | | |
|---|---|---|---|
| *323* A130 | 1c green | 17.00 | 2.75 |
| *324* A131 | 2c carmine | 15.00 | 90 |
| a | Vert. pair, imperf. horiz. | *6,000.* | |
| *325* A132 | 3c violet | 60.00 | 22.50 |
| *326* A133 | 5c dark blue | 65.00 | 14.50 |
| *327* A134 | 10c red brown | 115.00 | 20.00 |
| | *Nos. 323-327 (5)* | 272.00 | 60.65 |

Louisiana Purchase Expo., St. Louis, Mo., Apr. 30 to Dec. 1, 1904.

Note on condition and pricing after No. 245 also applies to Nos. 323-327.

### Jamestown Exposition Issue.

Captain John Smith A135

Founding of Jamestown A136

Pocahontas A137

**1907** **Wmk. 191** ***Perf. 12***

| | | | |
|---|---|---|---|
| *328* A135 | 1c green | 11.50 | 1.90 |
| *329* A136 | 2c carmine | 15.00 | 1.50 |
| *330* A137 | 5c blue | 67.50 | 15.00 |

Jamestown Expo., Hampton Roads, Va., Apr. 26 to Dec. 1.

Franklin A138

Washington A139

Washington — A140

There are several types of some of the 2c and 3c stamps of this and succeeding issues. These types are described under the dates when they first appeared. The differences between the types are usually minute and difficult to distinguish.

Illustrations of Types I-VII of the 2c (A140) and Types I-IV of the 3c (A140) are reproduced by permission of H. L. Lindquist.

TYPE I

THREE CENTS

Type I. The top line of the toga rope is weak and the rope shading lines are thin. The fifth line from the left is missing.

The line between the lips is thin.

Used on both flat plate and rotary press printings.

**1908-09** **Wmk. 191** ***Perf. 12***

| | | | |
|---|---|---|---|
| *331* A138 | 1c green | 4.50 | 5 |
| a | Booklet pane of 6 | 165.00 | *35.00* |
| *332* A139 | 2c carmine | 4.25 | 5 |
| a | Booklet pane of 6 | 100.00 | *35.00* |
| *333* A140 | 3c dp violet, Type I | 20.00 | 1.75 |
| *334* A140 | 4c org brn | 23.50 | 55 |
| *335* A140 | 5c blue | 30.00 | 1.50 |
| *336* A140 | 6c red org | 32.50 | 3.50 |
| *337* A140 | 8c olive grn | 26.00 | 1.75 |
| *338* A140 | 10c yel ('09) | 42.50 | 1.00 |
| *339* A140 | 13c bl grn ('09) | 25.00 | 14.00 |
| *340* A140 | 15c pale ultra ('09) | 40.00 | 3.75 |
| *341* A140 | 50c vio ('09) | 175.00 | 10.00 |
| *342* A140 | $1 vio brn ('09) | 300.00 | 50.00 |
| | *Nos. 331-342 (12)* | 723.25 | 87.90 |

For listing of other perforated stamps of designs A138, A139 and A140 see

| | | |
|---|---|---|
| #357-366 | Bluish Paper | |
| #374-382, 405-407 | Single line wmk. | Perf. 12 |
| #424-430 | Single line wmk. | Perf. 10 |
| #461 | Single line wmk. | Perf. 11 |
| #462-469 | Unwmkd. | Perf. 10 |
| #498-507 | Unwmkd. | Perf. 11 |
| #519 | Double line wmk. | Perf. 11 |
| #525-530, 536 | Offset printing | |
| #538-546 | Rotary press printing | |

***Imperf***

| | | | |
|---|---|---|---|
| *343* A138 | 1c green | 4.50 | 2.75 |
| *344* A139 | 2c carmine | 6.50 | 2.00 |
| *345* A140 | 3c dp violet, Type I | 12.00 | 10.00 |
| *346* A140 | 4c org brn ('09) | 21.00 | 12.00 |
| *347* A140 | 5c blue ('09) | 37.50 | 27.50 |
| | *Nos. 343-347 (5)* | 81.50 | 54.25 |

For listings of other imperforate stamps of designs A138, A139 and A140 see

| | |
|---|---|
| Nos. 383 & 384, 408 & 409, 459 | Single line wmk. |
| Nos. 481-485 | Unwmkd. |
| Nos. 531-535 | Offset printing |

### Coil Stamps

**1908-10** ***Perf. 12 Horizontally***

| | | | |
|---|---|---|---|
| *348* A138 | 1c green | 17.50 | 9.25 |
| *349* A139 | 2c car ('09) | 30.00 | 5.00 |
| *350* A140 | 4c org brn ('10) | 67.50 | 50.00 |
| *351* A140 | 5c blue ('09) | 75.00 | 67.50 |

**1909** ***Perf. 12 Vertically***

| | | | |
|---|---|---|---|
| *352* A138 | 1c green | 32.50 | 20.00 |
| *353* A139 | 2c carmine | 30.00 | 5.00 |
| *354* A140 | 4c org brn | 87.50 | 37.50 |
| *355* A140 | 5c blue | 95.00 | 55.00 |
| *356* A140 | 10c yellow | 1,300. | 400.00 |

For listings of other coil stamps of designs A138, A139 and A140 see

| | |
|---|---|
| Nos. 385-396, 410-413, 441-458 | Single line wmk. |
| Nos. 486-496 | Unwmkd. |

### Bluish Paper

This was made with 35 per cent rag stock instead of all wood pulp. The bluish color goes through the paper showing clearly on the back as well as on the face.

**1909** ***Perf. 12***

| | | | |
|---|---|---|---|
| *357* A138 | 1c green | 75.00 | 65.00 |
| *358* A139 | 2c carmine | 70.00 | 55.00 |
| *359* A140 | 3c dp violet, Type I | 1,500. | 1,250. |
| *360* A140 | 4c org brn | *17,500.* | |
| *361* A140 | 5c blue | 2,900. | 3,000. |
| *362* A140 | 6c red org | 1,150. | 750.00 |
| *363* A140 | 8c ol grn | *17,500.* | |
| *364* A140 | 10c yellow | 1,200. | 800.00 |
| *365* A140 | 13c bl grn | 2,000. | 1,100. |
| *366* A140 | 15c pale ultra | 900.00 | 600.00 |

### Lincoln Memorial Issue

Lincoln — A141

**1909, Feb. 12** **Wmk. 191** ***Perf. 12***

*367* A141 2c carmine 4.25 1.40

***Imperf***

*368* A141 2c carmine 19.50 15.00

### Bluish Paper

**1909** ***Perf. 12***

*369* A141 2c carmine 170.00 165.00

100th anniv. of the birth of Abraham Lincoln.

### Alaska-Yukon Pacific Exposition Issue

William H. Seward — A142

**1909, June 1** **Wmk. 191** ***Perf. 12***

*370* A142 2c carmine 7.00 1.10

**1909** ***Imperf.***

*371* A142 2c carmine 27.50 19.00

Seattle, Wash., June 1 to Oct. 16.

### Hudson-Fulton Celebration Issue

"Half Moon" and Steamship A143

**1909, Sept. 25** **Wmk. 191** ***Perf. 12***

*372* A143 2c carmine 9.50 3.25

***Imperf***

*373* A143 2c carmine 30.00 21.00

Tercentenary of the discovery of the Hudson River and Centenary of Robert Fulton's steamship.

### Designs of 1908-09 Issue

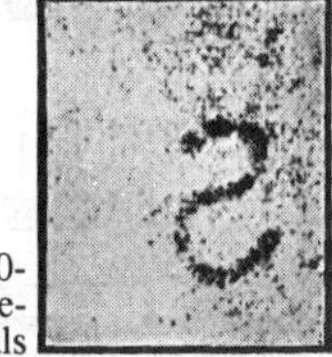
Wmk. 190- "USPS" in Single-lined Capitals

**1910-11** **Wmk. 190** ***Perf. 12***

| | | | |
|---|---|---|---|
| *374* A138 | 1c green | 5.00 | 6 |
| a | Booklet pane of 6 | 110.00 | *30.00* |
| *375* A139 | 2c carmine | 5.00 | 5 |
| a | Booklet pane of 6 | 95.00 | *25.00* |
| *376* A140 | 3c dp vio, Type I ('11) | 11.50 | 1.00 |
| *377* A140 | 4c brn ('11) | 17.50 | 30 |
| *378* A140 | 5c blue ('11) | 17.50 | 30 |
| *379* A140 | 6c red org ('11) | 24.00 | 40 |
| *380* A140 | 8c ol grn ('11) | 70.00 | 8.50 |
| *381* A140 | 10c yellow ('11) | 65.00 | 2.50 |
| *382* A140 | 15c pale ultra ('11) | 175.00 | 11.50 |
| | *Nos. 374-382 (9)* | 390.50 | 24.61 |

**1911** ***Imperf.***

| | | | |
|---|---|---|---|
| *383* A138 | 1c green | 2.25 | 2.00 |
| *384* A139 | 2c carmine | 3.50 | 1.75 |

### Coil Stamps

**1910** ***Perf. 12 Horizontally***

| | | | |
|---|---|---|---|
| *385* A138 | 1c green | 15.00 | 7.00 |
| *386* A139 | 2c carmine | 27.50 | 10.00 |

**1910-11** ***Perf. 12 Vertically***

| | | | |
|---|---|---|---|
| *387* A138 | 1c green | 40.00 | 20.00 |
| *388* A139 | 2c carmine | 400.00 | 75.00 |
| *389* A140 | 3c dp vio, Type I ('11) | *15,000.* | *6,000.* |

Stamps sold as No. 388 sometimes are fraudulently perforated copies of No. 384 or trimmed copies of No. 375.

**1910** ***Perf. 8½ Horizontally***

| | | | |
|---|---|---|---|
| *390* A138 | 1c green | 3.00 | 3.00 |
| *391* A139 | 2c carmine | 20.00 | 4.75 |

**1910-13** ***Perf. 8½ Vertically***

| No. | Design | Description | Unused | Used |
|---|---|---|---|---|
| *392* | A138 | 1c green | 12.00 | 12.00 |
| *393* | A139 | 2c carmine | 24.00 | 4.50 |
| *394* | A140 | 3c dp vio, Type I ('11) | 32.50 | 27.50 |
| *395* | A140 | 4c brn ('12) | 32.50 | 27.50 |
| *396* | A140 | 5c blue ('13) | 32.50 | 27.50 |

### Panama-Pacific Exposition Issue

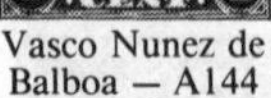

Vasco Nunez de Balboa – A144

Pedro Miguel Locks, Panama Canal – A145

Golden Gate – A146

Discovery of San Francisco Bay – A147

**1913** **Wmk. 190** ***Perf. 12***

| No. | Design | Description | Unused | Used |
|---|---|---|---|---|
| *397* | A144 | 1c green | 11.00 | 85 |
| *398* | A145 | 2c carmine | 12.50 | 28 |
| *399* | A146 | 5c blue | 47.50 | 6.50 |
| *400* | A147 | 10c org yel | 90.00 | 14.00 |
| *400A* | A147 | 10c orange | 160.00 | 10.50 |

**1914-15** ***Perf. 10***

| No. | Design | Description | Unused | Used |
|---|---|---|---|---|
| *401* | A144 | 1c green | 16.00 | 4.00 |
| *402* | A145 | 2c car ('15) | 52.50 | 1.00 |
| *403* | A146 | 5c blue ('15) | 115.00 | 11.50 |
| *404* | A147 | 10c org ('15) | 775.00 | 42.50 |

San Francisco, Cal., Feb. 20 to Dec. 4.

TYPE I

TWO CENTS

Type I. There is one shading line in the first curve of the ribbon above the left "2" and one in the second curve of the ribbon above the right "2."

The button of the toga has a faint outline.

The top line of the toga rope, from the button to the front of the throat, is also very faint.

The shading lines at the face terminate in front of the ear with little or no joining, to form a lock of hair.

Used on both flat and rotary press printings.

**1912-14** **Wmk. 190** ***Perf. 12***

| No. | Design | Description | Unused | Used |
|---|---|---|---|---|
| *405* | A140 | 1c green | 3.50 | 6 |
| *a* | | Vert. pair, imperf. horiz. | *650.00* | — |
| *b* | | Booklet pane of 6 | 50.00 | *7.50* |
| *406* | A140 | 2c car, Type I | 3.25 | 5 |
| *a* | | Booklet pane of 6 | 60.00 | *17.50* |
| *b* | | Double impression | — | |
| *407* | A140 | 7c black ('14) | 60.00 | 8.00 |

**1912** ***Imperf.***

| No. | Design | Description | Unused | Used |
|---|---|---|---|---|
| *408* | A140 | 1c green | 90 | 50 |
| *409* | A140 | 2c car, Type I | 1.00 | 50 |

### Coil Stamps

**1912** ***Perf. 8½ Horizontally***

| No. | Design | Description | Unused | Used |
|---|---|---|---|---|
| *410* | A140 | 1c green | 4.00 | 2.50 |
| *411* | A140 | 2c car, Type I | 5.00 | 2.00 |

***Perf. 8½ Vertically***

| No. | Design | Description | Unused | Used |
|---|---|---|---|---|
| *412* | A140 | 1c green | 13.00 | 3.00 |
| *413* | A140 | 2c car, Type I | 22.00 | 60 |

Franklin – A148

**1912-14** **Wmk. 190** ***Perf. 12***

| No. | Design | Description | Unused | Used |
|---|---|---|---|---|
| *414* | A148 | 8c pale ol grn | 25.00 | 85 |
| *415* | A148 | 9c sal red ('14) | 32.50 | 9.50 |
| *416* | A148 | 10c org yel | 26.00 | 25 |
| *417* | A148 | 12c cl brn ('14) | 28.50 | 3.00 |
| *418* | A148 | 15c gray | 47.50 | 2.00 |
| *419* | A148 | 20c ultra ('14) | 110.00 | 9.00 |
| *420* | A148 | 30c org red ('14) | 80.00 | 10.00 |
| *421* | A148 | 50c vio ('14) | 300.00 | 10.00 |

**1912, Feb. 12** **Wmk. 191** ***Perf. 12***

| No. | Design | Description | Unused | Used |
|---|---|---|---|---|
| *422* | A148 | 50c violet | 160.00 | 9.50 |
| *423* | A148 | $1 vio brn | 360.00 | 40.00 |

Other stamps of type A148:

| | | |
|---|---|---|
| #431-440 | Single line wmk. | Perf. 10 |
| #460 | Double line wmk. | Perf. 10 |
| #470-478 | Unwmkd. | Perf. 10 |
| #508-518 | Unwmkd. | Perf. 11 |

**1914-15** **Wmk. 190** ***Perf. 10***

| No. | Design | Description | Unused | Used |
|---|---|---|---|---|
| *424* | A140 | 1c green | 1.60 | 6 |
| *a* | | Perf. 12x10 | *300.00* | *250.00* |
| *b* | | Perf. 10x12 | | *125.00* |
| *c* | | Vert. pair, imperf. horiz. | *425.00* | *250.00* |
| *d* | | Booklet pane of 6 | 3.50 | *75* |
| *e* | | Vert. pair, imperf. btwn. | — | |
| *425* | A140 | 2c rose red, Type I | 1.50 | 5 |
| *c* | | Perf. 10x12 | | — |
| *d* | | Perf. 12x10 | | *250.00* |
| *e* | | Booklet pane of 6 | 12.50 | *3.00* |
| *426* | A140 | 3c dp violet, Type I | 8.50 | 90 |
| *427* | A140 | 4c brown | 22.00 | 28 |
| *428* | A140 | 5c blue | 18.50 | 28 |
| *a* | | Perf. 12x10 | | *400.00* |
| *429* | A140 | 6c red org | 24.00 | 90 |
| *430* | A140 | 7c black | 55.00 | 2.50 |
| *431* | A148 | 8c pale ol grn | 24.00 | 1.10 |
| *432* | A148 | 9c sal red | 32.50 | 5.00 |
| *433* | A148 | 10c org yel | 30.00 | 18 |
| *434* | A148 | 11c dk grn ('15) | 13.50 | 5.50 |
| *435* | A148 | 12c cl brn | 15.00 | 2.75 |
| *a* | | 12c copper red | 16.00 | 2.75 |
| *b* | | Vert. pair, imperf. btwn. | *650.00* | |
| *437* | A148 | 15c gray | 72.50 | 4.50 |
| *438* | A148 | 20c ultra | 140.00 | 2.50 |
| *439* | A148 | 30c org red | 190.00 | 10.00 |
| *440* | A148 | 50c vio ('15) | 500.00 | 10.00 |
| | | *Nos. 424-440 (16)* | 1,148. | 46.50 |

### Coil Stamps

**1914** ***Perf. 10 Horizontally***

| No. | Design | Description | Unused | Used |
|---|---|---|---|---|
| *441* | A140 | 1c green | 55 | 80 |
| *442* | A140 | 2c carmine, Type I | 6.00 | 4.50 |

**1914** ***Perf. 10 Vertically***

| No. | Design | Description | Unused | Used |
|---|---|---|---|---|
| *443* | A140 | 1c green | 14.00 | 4.00 |
| *444* | A140 | 2c car, Type I | 19.00 | 1.00 |
| *445* | A140 | 3c vio, Type I | 160.00 | 75.00 |
| *446* | A140 | 4c brown | 82.50 | 21.00 |
| *447* | A140 | 5c blue | 27.50 | 17.50 |

No. 443 represents stamps from coils. Part of a sheet of No. 424 is also known perf. vert. and imperf. horiz.

TYPE II

TWO CENTS

Type II. Shading lines in ribbons as on type I.

The toga button, rope, and shading lines are heavy.

The shading lines of the face at the lock of hair end in a strong vertical curved line.

Used on rotary press printings only.

TYPE III

TWO CENTS

Type III. Two lines of shading in the curves of the ribbons.

Other characteristics similar to type II.

Used on rotary press printings only.

---

Fraudulently altered copies of Type III (Nos. 455, 488, 492 and 540) have had one line of shading scraped off to make them resemble Type II (Nos. 454, 487, 491 and 539).

---

### Coil Stamps

#### Rotary Press Printing

**1915-16** ***Perf. 10 Horizontally***

| No. | Design | Description | Unused | Used |
|---|---|---|---|---|
| *448* | A140 | 1c green | 4.25 | 2.25 |
| *449* | A140 | 2c red, Type I | 1,750. | 190.00 |
| *450* | A140 | 2c car, Type III ('16) | 7.00 | 2.25 |

**1914-16** ***Perf. 10 Vertically***

| No. | Design | Description | Unused | Used |
|---|---|---|---|---|
| *452* | A140 | 1c green | 7.00 | 1.40 |
| *453* | A140 | 2c carmine rose, Type I | 72.50 | 3.25 |
| *454* | A140 | 2c red, Type II | 70.00 | 7.50 |
| *455* | A140 | 2c car, Type III | 6.50 | 75 |
| *456* | A140 | 3c vio, Type I ('16) | 190.00 | 75.00 |
| *457* | A140 | 4c brn ('16) | 18.00 | 15.00 |
| *458* | A140 | 5c blue ('16) | 22.50 | 15.00 |

**1914, June 30** ***Imperf.***

| No. | Design | Description | Unused | Used |
|---|---|---|---|---|
| *459* | A140 | 2c car, Type I | 375.00 | *600.00* |

No. 459 is a horizontal coil.

The Rotary Press stamps are printed from plates that are curved to fit around a cylinder. This curvature produces stamps that are slightly larger, either horizontally or vertically, than those printed from flat plates. Stamps from flat plates measure about 18½-19mm wide by 22mm high. When the impressions are placed sideways on the curved plates the stamps are 19½-20mm wide; when they are placed vertically the stamps are 23mm high.

#### Flat Plate Printings

**1915, Feb. 8** **Wmk. 191** ***Perf. 10***

| No. | Design | Description | Unused | Used |
|---|---|---|---|---|
| *460* | A148 | $1 vio blk | 600.00 | 55.00 |

**1915, June 17** **Wmk. 190** ***Perf. 11***

| No. | Design | Description | Unused | Used |
|---|---|---|---|---|
| *461* | A140 | 2c pale car red, Type I | 75.00 | 50.00 |

Fraudulently perforated copies of No. 409 are offered as No. 461.

---

Unwatermarked

From 1916 onward all postage stamps except Nos. 519 and 832b are on unwatermarked paper.

---

**1916-17** **Unwmk.** ***Perf. 10***

| No. | Design | Description | Unused | Used |
|---|---|---|---|---|
| *462* | A140 | 1c green | 5.00 | 15 |
| *a* | | Booklet pane of 6 | 7.50 | *1.00* |
| *463* | A140 | 2c car, Type I | 3.25 | 10 |
| *a* | | Booklet pane of 6 | 70.00 | *20.00* |
| *464* | A140 | 3c vio, Type I | 47.50 | 8.00 |
| *465* | A140 | 4c org brn | 27.50 | 1.00 |
| *466* | A140 | 5c blue | 47.50 | 1.00 |
| *467* | A140 | 5c car (error in plate of 2c, '17) | 475.00 | 500.00 |
| *468* | A140 | 6c red org | 60.00 | 5.00 |
| *469* | A140 | 7c black | 77.50 | 7.50 |
| *470* | A148 | 8c ol grn | 35.00 | 3.75 |
| *471* | A148 | 9c sal red | 37.50 | 9.50 |
| *472* | A148 | 10c org yel | 70.00 | 75 |
| *473* | A148 | 11c dk grn | 20.00 | 11.00 |
| *474* | A148 | 12c cl brn | 32.50 | 3.50 |
| *475* | A148 | 15c gray | 110.00 | 7.00 |
| *476* | A148 | 20c lt ultra | 160.00 | 7.50 |
| *476A* | A148 | 30c org red | — | — |
| *477* | A148 | 50c lt vio ('17) | 900.00 | 40.00 |
| *478* | A148 | $1 vio blk | 600.00 | 11.00 |

Types of 1903 Issue

**1917, Mar. 22** ***Perf. 10***

| No. | Design | Description | Unused | Used |
|---|---|---|---|---|
| *479* | A127 | $2 dk bl | 325.00 | 30.00 |
| *480* | A128 | $5 lt grn | 250.00 | 32.50 |

TYPE Ia

TWO CENTS

Type Ia. Design characteristics similar to type I except that all lines of design are stronger.

The toga button, toga rope and rope shading lines are heavy. The latter characteristics are those of type II, which, however, occur only on impressions from rotary plates.

Used only on flat plates 10208 and 10209.

TYPE II

THREE CENTS

Type II. The top line of the toga rope is strong and the rope shading lines are heavy and complete.

The line between the lips is heavy.

Used on both flat plate and rotary press printings.

**1916-17** ***Imperf.***

| No. | Design | Description | Unused | Used |
|---|---|---|---|---|
| *481* | A140 | 1c green | 65 | 45 |
| *482* | A140 | 2c car, Type I | 1.00 | 1.00 |
| *482A* | A140 | 2c deep rose, Type Ia | | *6,000.* |
| *483* | A140 | 3c vio, Type I ('17) | 9.50 | 6.50 |
| *484* | A140 | 3c vio, Type II | 7.00 | 3.00 |
| *485* | A140 | 5c car (error in plate of 2c) ('17) | *13,000.* | |

### Coil Stamps

#### Rotary Press Printing

**1916-19** ***Perf. 10 Horizontally***

| No. | Design | Description | Unused | Used |
|---|---|---|---|---|
| *486* | A140 | 1c green ('18) | 60 | 20 |
| *487* | A140 | 2c car, Type II | 10.00 | 2.50 |
| *488* | A140 | 2c car, Type III ('19) | 1.75 | 1.35 |
| *489* | A140 | 3c vio, Type I ('17) | 3.75 | 1.00 |

**1916-22** ***Perf. 10 Vertically***

| No. | Design | Description | Unused | Used |
|---|---|---|---|---|
| *490* | A140 | 1c green | 40 | 15 |
| *491* | A140 | 2c car, Type II | 1,450. | 225.00 |
| *492* | A140 | 2c car, Type III | 5.75 | 15 |
| *493* | A140 | 3c vio, Type I ('17) | 13.50 | 1.75 |
| *494* | A140 | 3c vio, Type II ('18) | 7.50 | 90 |
| *495* | A140 | 4c org brn ('17) | 8.00 | 3.00 |
| *496* | A140 | 5c blue ('19) | 2.75 | 90 |
| *497* | A148 | 10c org yel ('22) | 16.00 | 7.00 |

See note above No. 448 regarding Nos. 487 and 491.

Blind Perfs.

Listings of imperforate-between varieties are for examples which show no trace of "blind perfs.," traces of impressions from the perforating pins which do not cut into the paper.

Types of 1912-14 Issue

**Flat Plate Printings**

**1917-19** *Perf. 11*

| No. | Design | Description | Unused | Used |
|---|---|---|---|---|
| *498* | A140 | 1c green | 30 | 5 |
| *a* | | Vert. pair, imperf. horiz. | 175.00 | |
| *b* | | Horiz. pair, imperf. btwn. | 75.00 | |
| *c* | | Vert. pair, imperf. btwn. | *450.00* | — |
| *d* | | Double impression | 150.00 | |
| *e* | | Booklet pane of 6 | 1.75 | *35* |
| *f* | | Booklet pane of 30 | 600.00 | |
| *499* | A140 | 2c rose, Type I | 25 | 5 |
| *a* | | Vert. pair, imperf. horiz. | 150.00 | |
| *b* | | Horiz. pair, imperf. vert. | 150.00 | *100.00* |
| *c* | | Vert.l pair, imperf. btwn. | *500.00* | *225.00* |
| *e* | | Booklet pane of 6 | 2.00 | *50* |
| *f* | | Booklet pane of 30 | *10,000* | |
| *g* | | Double impression | 125.00 | — |
| *500* | A140 | 2c dp rose, Type Ia | 200.00 | 85.00 |
| *501* | A140 | 3c lt vio, Type I | 8.00 | 10 |
| *b* | | Booklet pane of 6 | 65.00 | *15.00* |
| *c* | | Vert. pair, imperf. horiz. | 300.00 | |
| *d* | | Double impression | 150.00 | |
| *502* | A140 | 3c dk vio, Type II | 11.00 | 15 |
| *b* | | Booklet pane of 6 | 50.00 | *10.00* |
| *c* | | Vert. pair, imperf. horiz. | 250.00 | 125.00 |
| *d* | | Double impression | 125.00 | |
| *503* | A140 | 4c brown | 7.50 | 12 |
| *b* | | Double impression | — | |
| *504* | A140 | 5c blue | 6.50 | 8 |
| *a* | | Horiz. pair, imperf. btwn. | *1,250.* | — |
| *505* | A140 | 5c rose (error in plate of 2c) | 350.00 | 400.00 |
| *506* | A140 | 6c red org | 9.50 | 20 |
| *507* | A140 | 7c black | 20.00 | 85 |
| *508* | A148 | 8c ol bis | 8.50 | 40 |
| *b* | | Vert. pair, imperf. btwn. | — | — |
| *509* | A148 | 9c sal red | 11.00 | 1.40 |
| *510* | A148 | 10c org yel | 12.50 | 10 |
| *511* | A148 | 11c lt grn | 6.75 | 2.00 |
| *512* | A148 | 12c cl brn | 6.50 | 30 |
| *a* | | 12c brown carmine | 7.00 | 35 |
| *513* | A148 | 13c ap grn ('19) | 8.00 | 4.75 |
| *514* | A148 | 15c gray | 30.00 | 80 |
| *515* | A148 | 20c lt ultra | 37.50 | 16 |
| *b* | | Vert. pair, imperf. btwn. | *325.00* | |
| *c* | | Double impression | *400.00* | |
| *516* | A148 | 30c org red | 30.00 | 55 |
| *517* | A148 | 50c red vio | 60.00 | 40 |
| *b* | | Vert. pair, imperf. btwn. | *1,750.* | *750.00* |
| *518* | A148 | $1 vio brn | 74.00 | 1.10 |
| *b* | | $1 deep brown | *750.00* | *250.00* |
| | | *Nos. 498-504,506-518 (20)* | 547.80 | 98.56 |

Type of 1908-09 Issue

**1917, Oct. 10 Wmk. 191** *Perf. 11*

| No. | Design | Description | Unused | Used |
|---|---|---|---|---|
| *519* | A139 | 2c carmine | 200.00 | *275.00* |

Fraudulently perforated copies of No. 344 are offered as No. 519.

Franklin — A149

**1918, Aug. 19 Unwmk.** *Perf. 11*

| No. | Design | Description | Unused | Used |
|---|---|---|---|---|
| *523* | A149 | $2 org red & blk | 675.00 | 250.00 |
| *524* | A149 | $5 dp grn & blk | 275.00 | 20.00 |

See No. 547 for $2 carmine & black.

Types of 1912-14 Issue

TYPE IV

TWO CENTS

Type IV. Top line of toga rope is broken. Shading lines in toga button are so arranged that the curving of the first and last form "DID".

Line of color in left "2" is very thin and usually broken.

Used on offset printings only.

TYPE V

TWO CENTS

Type V. Top line of toga is complete.

Five vertical shading lines in toga button.

Line of color in left "2" is very thin and usually broken.

Shading dots on the nose and lip are as indicated on the diagram.

Used on offset printings only.

TYPE Va

TWO CENTS

Type Va. Characteristics same as type V, except in shading dots of nose. Third row from bottom has 4 dots instead of 6. Overall height of type Va is ⅓mm less than type V.

Used on offset printings only.

TYPE VI

TWO CENTS

Type VI. General characteristics same as type V, except that line of color in left "2" is very heavy.

Used on offset printings only.

TYPE VII

TWO CENTS

Type VII. Line of color in left "2" is invariably continuous, clearly defined, and heavier than in type V or Va, but not as heavy as in type VI.

Additional vertical row of dots has been added to the upper lip.

Numerous additional dots have been added to hair on top of head.

Used on offset printings only.

TYPE III

THREE CENTS

Type III. The top line of the toga rope is strong but the fifth shading line is missing as in type I.

Center shading line of the toga button consists of two dashes with a central dot.

The "P" and "O" of "POSTAGE" are separated by a line of color.

The frame line at the bottom of the vignette is complete.

Used on offset printings only.

TYPE IV

THREE CENTS

Type IV. Shading lines of toga rope are complete.

Second and fourth shading lines in toga button are broken in the middle and the third line is continuous with a dot in the center.

"P" and "O" of "POSTAGE" are joined.

Frame line at bottom of vignette is broken.

Used on offset printings only.

**1918-20 Offset Printing** *Perf. 11*

| No. | Design | Description | Unused | Used |
|---|---|---|---|---|
| *525* | A140 | 1c gray green | 1.15 | 35 |
| *a* | | 1c dark green | 1.35 | 75 |
| *c* | | Horiz. pair, imperf. btwn. | 60.00 | |
| *d* | | Double impression | 15.00 | 15.00 |
| *526* | A140 | 2c car, Type IV ('20) | 19.00 | 2.75 |
| *527* | A140 | 2c car, Type V | 10.00 | 60 |
| *a* | | Double impression | 45.00 | 10.00 |
| *b* | | Vert. pair, imperf. horiz. | *600.00* | |
| *c* | | Horiz. pair, imperf. vert. | | — |
| *528* | A140 | 2c car, Type Va | 5.25 | 15 |
| *c* | | Double impression | 25.00 | |
| *g* | | Vert. pair, imperf. btwn. | — | |
| *528A* | A140 | 2c car, Type VI | 32.50 | 1.00 |
| *d* | | Double impression | 100.00 | — |
| *f* | | Vert. pair, imperf. horiz. | — | |
| *h* | | Vert. pair, imperf. btwn. | — | |
| *528B* | A140 | 2c car, Type VII | 12.50 | 12 |
| *e* | | Double impression | 45.00 | |
| *529* | A140 | 3c vio, Type III | 1.75 | 10 |
| *a* | | Double impression | 20.00 | — |
| *b* | | Printed on both sides | *350.00* | |
| *530* | A140 | 3c pur, Type IV | 50 | 6 |
| *a* | | Double impression | 12.50 | 6.00 |
| *b* | | Printed on both sides | 150.00 | |
| | | *Nos. 525-530 (8)* | 82.65 | 5.13 |

**1918-20** ***Imperf.***

| No. | Design | Description | Unused | Used |
|---|---|---|---|---|
| *531* | A140 | 1c green ('19) | 6.00 | 7.00 |
| *532* | A140 | 2c car rose, Type IV ('20) | 30.00 | 22.50 |
| *533* | A140 | 2c car, Type V | 150.00 | 55.00 |
| *534* | A140 | 2c car, Type Va | 8.50 | 6.00 |
| *534A* | A140 | 2c car, Type VI | 27.50 | 17.50 |
| *534B* | A140 | 2c car, Type VII | 1,250. | 425.00 |
| *535* | A140 | 3c vio, Type IV | 6.00 | 4.50 |
| *a* | | Double impression | 80.00 | — |

**1919, Aug. 15** ***Perf. 12½***

| No. | Design | Description | Unused | Used |
|---|---|---|---|---|
| *536* | A140 | 1c gray green | 9.00 | 11.00 |
| *a* | | Horiz. pair, imperf. vert. | *500.00* | |

**Victory Issue**

"Victory" and Flags of the Allies — A150

Flat Plate Printing

**1919, Mar. 3 Engr.** ***Perf. 11***

| No. | Design | Description | Unused | Used |
|---|---|---|---|---|
| *537* | A150 | 3c violet | 6.25 | 2.75 |
| *a* | | 3c deep red violet | 325.00 | 40.00 |
| *b* | | 3c light redish violet | 6.25 | 2.75 |
| *c* | | 3c red violet | 30.00 | 7.50 |

Victory of Allies in World War I.

**Rotary Press Printings**

**1919** ***Perf. 11x10***

**Size: 19½ to 20mm wide by 22 to 22¼mm high**

| No. | Design | Description | Unused | Used |
|---|---|---|---|---|
| *538* | A140 | 1c green | 6.50 | 6.00 |
| *a* | | Vert. pair, imperf. horiz. | 50.00 | 50.00 |
| *539* | A140 | 2c car rose, Type II | 2,500. | 750.00 |
| *540* | A140 | 2c car rose, Type III | 7.00 | 6.00 |
| *a* | | Vert. pair, imperf. horiz. | 50.00 | 50.00 |
| *b* | | Horiz. pair, imperf. vert. | *550.00* | |
| *541* | A140 | 3c vio, Type II | 22.50 | 20.00 |

The part perforate varieties of Nos. 538a and 540a were issued in sheets and may be had in blocks; similar part perforate varieties, Nos. 490 and 492, are from coils and are found only in strips.

See note over No. 448 regarding No. 539.

**Size: 19mm by 22½-22¾mm**

**1920, May 26** ***Perf. 10x11***

| No. | Design | Description | Unused | Used |
|---|---|---|---|---|
| *542* | A140 | 1c green | 6.50 | 65 |

**Size: 19x22½mm**

**1921** ***Perf. 10***

| No. | Design | Description | Unused | Used |
|---|---|---|---|---|
| *543* | A140 | 1c green | 35 | 6 |
| *a* | | Horiz. pair, imperf. between | *550.00* | |

**Size: 19x22½mm**

**1923** ***Perf. 11***

| No. | Design | Description | Unused | Used |
|---|---|---|---|---|
| *544* | A140 | 1c green | *7,500.* | *2,400.* |

**Size: 19½-20 mm by 22 mm**

**1921** ***Perf. 11***

| No. | Design | Description | Unused | Used |
|---|---|---|---|---|
| *545* | A140 | 1c green | 95.00 | 45.00 |
| *546* | A140 | 2c car rose, Type III | 60.00 | 45.00 |

**Flat Plate Printing**

**1920, Nov. 1** ***Perf. 11***

| No. | Design | Description | Unused | Used |
|---|---|---|---|---|
| *547* | A149 | $2 car & blk | 225.00 | 25.00 |

Values quoted in this catalogue are for stamps graded at Fine-Very Fine and with no faults. An illustrated guide to grade is provided in introductory material, beginning on Page V.

## Pilgrim Tercentenary Issue

"Mayflower" A151

Landing of the Pilgrims A152

Signing of the Compact — A153

| **1920, Dec. 21** | | | ***Perf. 11*** | |
|---|---|---|---|---|
| *548* | A151 | 1c green | 3.25 | 1.65 |
| *549* | A152 | 2c car rose | 5.25 | 1.25 |
| *550* | A153 | 5c deep blue | 32.50 | 10.00 |

Tercentenary of the landing of the Pilgrims at Plymouth, Mass.

Nathan Hale A154

Franklin A155

Harding A156

Washington A157

Lincoln A158

Martha Washington A159

Theodore Roosevelt A160

Garfield A161

McKinley A162

Grant A163

Jefferson A164

Monroe A165

Rutherford B. Hayes A166

Grover Cleveland A167

American Indian A168

Statue of Liberty A169

Golden Gate — A170

Niagara Falls — A171

Buffalo A172

Arlington Amphitheater A173

Lincoln Memorial A174

US Capitol A175

Head of Freedom Statue, Capitol Dome — A176

| **1922-25** | | | ***Perf. 11*** | |
|---|---|---|---|---|
| *551* | A154 | ½c ol brn ('25) | 9 | 8 |
| *552* | A155 | 1c dp grn ('23) | 1.10 | 5 |
| *a* | | Booket pane of 6 | 4.50 | *50* |
| *553* | A156 | 1½c yel brn ('25) | 1.90 | 15 |
| *554* | A157 | 2c car ('23) | 1.00 | 5 |
| *a* | | Horiz. pair, imperf. vert. | 175.00 | |
| *b* | | Vert. pair, imperf. horiz. | *500.00* | |
| *c* | | Booklet pane of 6 | 6.00 | *1.00* |
| *555* | A158 | 3c vio ('23) | 12.50 | 85 |
| *556* | A159 | 4c yel brn ('23) | 12.50 | 20 |
| *a* | | Vert. pair, imperf. horiz. | — | |
| *557* | A160 | 5c dark blue | 12.50 | 8 |
| *a* | | Imperf., pair | *700.00* | |
| *b* | | Horiz. pair, imperf. vert. | — | |
| *558* | A161 | 6c red orange | 24.00 | 75 |
| *559* | A162 | 7c black ('23) | 5.75 | 45 |
| *560* | A163 | 8c ol grn ('23) | 35.00 | 35 |
| *561* | A164 | 9c rose ('23) | 10.00 | 90 |
| *562* | A165 | 10c org ('23) | 14.00 | 10 |
| *a* | | Vert. pair, imperf. horiz. | *500.00* | |
| *b* | | Imperf., pair | *650.00* | |
| *563* | A166 | 11c light bl | 1.10 | 25 |
| *d* | | Imperf., pair | | — |
| *564* | A167 | 12c brn vio ('23) | 4.50 | 8 |
| *a* | | Horiz. pair, imperf. vert. | *650.00* | |
| *b* | | Imperf., pair | — | |
| *565* | A168 | 14c blue ('23) | 3.25 | 65 |
| *566* | A169 | 15c gray | 17.50 | 6 |
| *567* | A170 | 20c car rose ('23) | 17.50 | 6 |
| *a* | | Horiz. pair, imperf. vert. | *750.00* | |
| *568* | A171 | 25c yel grn | 15.00 | 38 |
| *b* | | Vert. pair, imperf. horiz. | *850.00* | |
| *569* | A172 | 30c ol brn ('23) | 27.50 | 30 |
| *570* | A173 | 50c lilac | 50.00 | 12 |
| *571* | A174 | $1 vio blk ('23) | 37.50 | 35 |
| *572* | A175 | $2 dp bl ('23) | 85.00 | 8.00 |
| *573* | A176 | $5 car & bl ('23) | 200.00 | 12.50 |
| | | *Nos. 551-573 (23)* | 589.19 | 26.76 |

For listings of other perforated stamps of designs A154 to A176 see

| | |
|---|---|
| Nos. 578 and 579 | Perf. 11x10 |
| Nos. 581 to 591 | Perf. 10 |
| Nos. 594 and 595 | Perf. 11 |
| Nos. 632 to 642, 653, 692 to 696 | |
| 653, 692 to 696 | Perf. 11x10½ |
| Nos. 697 to 701 | Perf. 10½x11 |

This series includes Nos. 622-623 (perf. 11).

| **1923-25** | | | ***Imperf.*** | |
|---|---|---|---|---|
| *575* | A155 | 1c green | 6.00 | 2.75 |
| *576* | A156 | 1½c yel brn ('25) | 1.25 | 1.00 |
| *577* | A157 | 2c carmine | 1.40 | 1.25 |

The 1½c A156 rotary press imperforate is listed as No. 631.

Prices of premium quality never hinged stamps will be in excess of catalogue price.

### Rotary Press Printings
***Perf. 11x10***
**Size: 19¾x22¼mm**

| | | | | |
|---|---|---|---|---|
| *578* | A155 | 1c green | 50.00 | 47.50 |
| *579* | A157 | 2c carmine | 35.00 | 35.00 |

| **1923-26** | | | ***Perf. 10*** | |
|---|---|---|---|---|
| *581* | A155 | 1c green | 6.00 | 55 |
| *582* | A156 | 1½c brown ('25) | 3.00 | 45 |
| *583* | A157 | 2c car ('24) | 1.40 | 5 |
| *a* | | Booklet pane of 6 | 75.00 | *25.00* |
| *584* | A158 | 3c vio ('25) | 17.50 | 1.75 |
| *585* | A159 | 4c yel brn ('25) | 11.00 | 30 |
| *586* | A160 | 5c blue ('25) | 11.50 | 18 |
| *a* | | Horiz. pair, imperf. btwn. | | — |
| *587* | A161 | 6c red org ('25) | 4.50 | 25 |
| *588* | A162 | 7c black ('26) | 7.00 | 4.25 |
| *589* | A163 | 8c ol grn ('26) | 17.50 | 2.75 |
| *590* | A164 | 9c rose ('26) | 3.25 | 1.90 |
| *591* | A165 | 10c org ('25) | 45.00 | 15 |
| | | *Nos. 581-591 (11)* | 127.65 | 12.58 |

***Perf. 11***

| | | | | |
|---|---|---|---|---|
| *594* | A155 | 1c green | *10,000.* | 3,500. |
| *595* | A157 | 2c carmine | 225.00 | 225.00 |

Nos. 594-595 were made from coil waste of Nos. 597 and 599, and measure approximately 19¾x22¼mm.

***Perf. 11***

| | | | |
|---|---|---|---|
| *596* | A155 | 1c green | *13,500.* |

No. 596 measures approximately 19¼x22¾mm. Most copies carry the Bureau precancel "Kansas City, Mo."

ROTARY PRESS DOUBLE PAPER

The web of paper used on rotary presses must be continuous, therefore any break in the paper must be lapped and pasted, causing the "double paper" varieties. These are no longer listed since they may occur on any rotary press stamp.

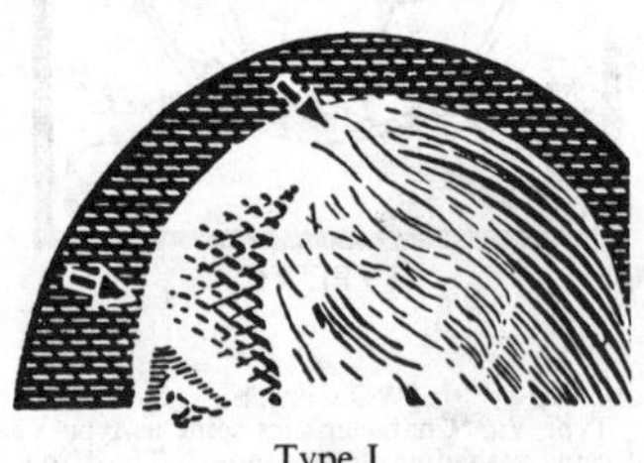
Type I

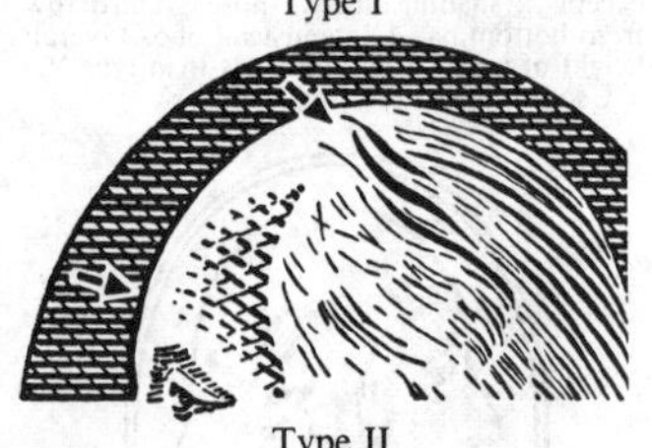
Type II

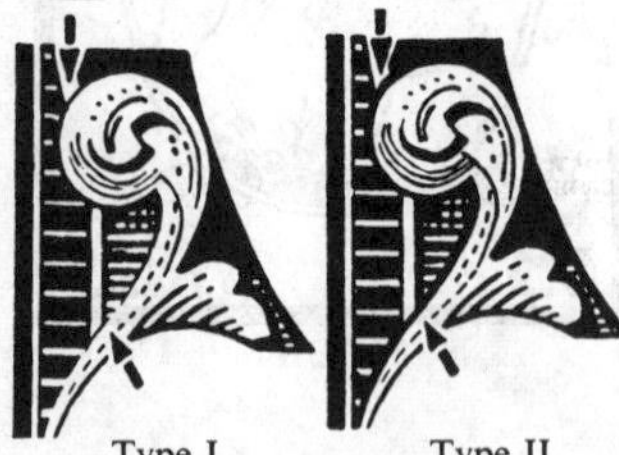
Type I Type II

Type I—No heavy hair lines at top center of head. Outline of left acanthus scroll generally faint at top and toward base at left side.

Type II—The heavy hair lines at top center of head; two being outstanding in the white area. Outline of left acanthus scroll very strong and clearly defined at top (under left edge of lettered panel) and at lower curve (above and to left of numeral oval). Type II is found only on Nos. 599A and 634A.

Coil Stamps

### Rotary Press Printing

| **1923-29** | | | ***Perf. 10 Vertically*** | |
|---|---|---|---|---|
| *597* | A155 | 1c green | 20 | 6 |
| *598* | A156 | 1½c brn ('25) | 40 | 10 |
| *599* | A157 | 2c car, Type I ('23) | 25 | 5 |
| *599A* | A157 | 2c car, Type II ('29) | 100.00 | 8.50 |
| *600* | A158 | 3c violet ('24) | 4.25 | 8 |
| *601* | A159 | 4c yellow brown | 2.50 | 30 |
| *602* | A160 | 5c dk bl ('24) | 1.10 | 14 |
| *603* | A165 | 10c org ('24) | 2.25 | 8 |

***Perf. 10 Horizontally***

| | | | | |
|---|---|---|---|---|
| *604* | A155 | 1c yellow green | 18 | 8 |
| *605* | A156 | 1½c yel brn ('25) | 18 | 15 |
| *606* | A157 | 2c carmine | 18 | 8 |
| | | *Nos. 597-599,600-606 (10)* | 11.49 | 1.12 |

## Harding Memorial Issue

Warren G. Harding — A177

Flat Plate Printing
(19¼x22¼mm)

| **1923, Sept. 1** | | | ***Perf. 11*** | |
|---|---|---|---|---|
| *610* | A177 | 2c black | 45 | 10 |
| *a* | | Horiz. pair, imperf. vert. | *800.00* | |

| **1923, Nov. 15** | | | ***Imperf.*** | |
|---|---|---|---|---|
| *611* | A177 | 2c black | 6.50 | 4.25 |

Rotary Press Printing
(19¼x22¾mm)

| **1923, Sept. 12** | | | ***Perf. 10*** | |
|---|---|---|---|---|
| *612* | A177 | 2c black | 11.00 | 1.50 |

| **1923** | | | ***Perf. 11*** |
|---|---|---|---|
| *613* | A177 | 2c black | *13.500.* |

Tribute to the memory of President Warren G. Harding, who died August 2, 1923.

## Huguenot-Walloon Tercentenary Issue

"New Netherland" A178

Landing at Fort Orange A179

Monument to Jan Ribault at Mayport, Fla. — A180

### Flat Plate Printings

| **1924, May 1** | | | ***Perf. 11*** | |
|---|---|---|---|---|
| *614* | A178 | 1c dark green | 2.25 | 3.00 |
| *615* | A179 | 2c carmine rose | 5.25 | 1.90 |
| *616* | A180 | 5c dark blue | 26.00 | 11.00 |

Tercentenary of the settling of the Walloons and in honor of the Huguenots.

## Lexington-Concord Issue

Washington at Cambridge A181

"Birth of Liberty," by Henry Sandham A182

The Minute Man, by Daniel Chester French A183

| **1925, Apr. 4** | | | ***Perf. 11*** | |
|---|---|---|---|---|
| *617* | A181 | 1c deep green | 2.50 | 2.25 |
| *618* | A182 | 2c carmine rose | 5.00 | 3.75 |
| *619* | A183 | 5c dark blue | 24.00 | 12.50 |

150th anniv. of the Battle of Lexington-Concord.

**Norse-American Issue**

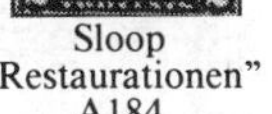

Sloop "Restaurationen" A184

Viking Ship A185

| **1925, May 18** | | | ***Perf. 11*** | |
|---|---|---|---|---|
| *620* | A184 | 2c car & blk | 4.00 | 2.75 |
| *621* | A185 | 5c dk bl & blk | 14.00 | 10.50 |

100th anniv. of the arrival in NY on Oct. 9, 1825, of the sloop "Restaurationen" with the first group of immigrants from Norway to the US.

Benjamin Harrison A186

Woodrow Wilson A187

| **1925-26** | | | ***Perf. 11*** | |
|---|---|---|---|---|
| *622* | A186 | 13c green ('26) | 11.00 | 40 |
| *623* | A187 | 17c black | 15.00 | 20 |

**Sesquicentennial Exposition Issue**

Liberty Bell — A188

| **1926, May 10** | | | ***Perf. 11.*** | |
|---|---|---|---|---|
| *627* | A188 | 2c car rose | 2.25 | 35 |

150th anniv. of the Declaration of Independence, Philadelphia, June 1-Dec. 1.

Statue of John Ericsson A189

Alexander Hamilton's Battery A190

**Ericsson Memorial Issue**

| **1926, May 29** | | | ***Perf. 11*** | |
|---|---|---|---|---|
| *628* | A189 | 5c gray lilac | 5.00 | 2.50 |

John Ericsson, builder of the "Monitor".

**Battle of White Plains Issue**

| **1926, Oct. 18** | | | ***Perf. 11*** | |
|---|---|---|---|---|
| *629* | A190 | 2c carmine rose | 1.50 | 1.25 |
| *a* | | Vert. pair, imperf. btwn. | *1,250.* | |

150th anniv. of the Battle of White Plains, NY.

An enhanced introduction to the Scott Catalogue begins on Page V. A thorough understanding of the material presented there will greatly aid your use of the catalogue itself.

**International Philatelic Exhibition**

Souvenir Sheet

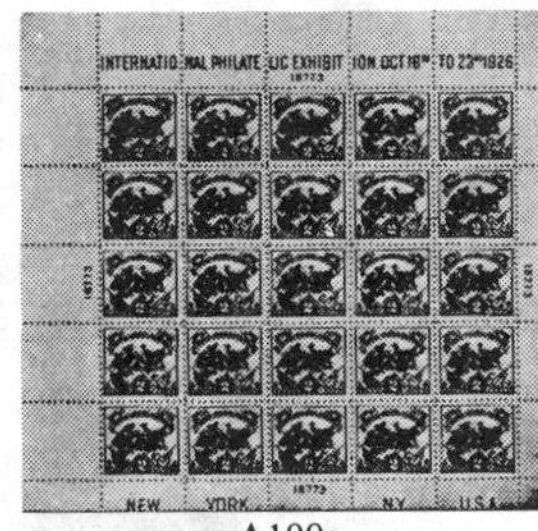

A190a

| **1926, Oct. 18** | | | ***Perf. 11*** | |
|---|---|---|---|---|
| *630* | A190a | 2c car rose, sheet of 25 | 350.00 | 300.00 |

Intl. Phil. Exhib. in NYC, Oct. 16-23. Size: 158-160¼x136-146½mm.

Types of 1922-26

**Rotary Press Printings**

| **1926, Aug. 27** | | | ***Imperf.*** | |
|---|---|---|---|---|
| *631* | A156 | 1½c yellow brown | 1.45 | 1.40 |

| **1926-34** | | | ***Perf. 11x10½*** | |
|---|---|---|---|---|
| *632* | A155 | 1c green ('27) | 12 | 5 |
| *a* | | Booklet pane of 6 | 4.50 | *25* |
| *b* | | Vert. pair, imperf. btwn. | 175.00 | *100.00* |
| *633* | A156 | 1½c yel brn ('27) | 1.25 | 8 |
| *634* | A157 | 2c car, Type I | 10 | 5 |
| *b* | | 2c carmine lake | 3.00 | 1.00 |
| *c* | | Horiz. pair, imperf. btwn. | *2,000.* | |
| *d* | | Booklet pane of 6 | 1.75 | *15* |
| *634A* | A157 | 2c car, Type II ('28) | 300.00 | 10.00 |
| *635* | A158 | 3c violet ('27) | 35 | 5 |
| *a* | | 3c bright violet ('34) | 25 | 5 |
| *636* | A159 | 4c yel brn ('27) | 1.75 | 8 |
| *637* | A160 | 5c dk bl ('27) | 1.65 | 5 |
| *638* | A161 | 6c red org ('27) | 1.75 | 5 |
| *639* | A162 | 7c black ('27) | 1.75 | 8 |
| *a* | | Vert. pair, imperf. btwn. | 125.00 | 80.00 |
| *640* | A163 | 8c ol grn ('27) | 1.75 | 5 |
| *641* | A164 | 9c org red ('31) | 1.75 | 5 |
| *642* | A165 | 10c org ('27) | 2.75 | 5 |
| | | *Nos. 632-634,635-642 (11)* | 14.97 | 64 |

For ½c, 11c-50c see Nos. 653, 692-701.

**Vermont Sesquicentennial Issue**

Green Mountain Boy — A191

**Flat Plate Printing**

| **1927, Aug. 3** | | | ***Perf. 11*** | |
|---|---|---|---|---|
| *643* | A191 | 2c carmine rose | 1.00 | 75 |

150th anniv. of the Battle of Bennington, Vt., and independence of the State of Vermont.

Surrender of Gen. John Burgoyne A192

Washington at Prayer A193

**Burgoyne Campaign Issue**

| **1927, Aug. 3** | | | ***Perf. 11*** | |
|---|---|---|---|---|
| *644* | A192 | 2c carmine rose | 2.50 | 1.90 |

| **1928, May 26** | | | ***Perf. 11*** | |
|---|---|---|---|---|
| *645* | A193 | 2c carmine rose | 70 | 35 |

150th anniv. of Washington's encampment at Valley Forge, Pa.

**Battle of Monmouth Issue**

No. 634 Overprinted **MOLLY PITCHER**

**Rotary Press Printing**

| **1928, Oct. 20** | | | ***Perf. 11x10½*** | |
|---|---|---|---|---|
| *646* | A157 | 2c carmine | 80 | 80 |

The normal space between a vertical pair of the overprints is 18 mm., but pairs are known with the space measuring 28 mm.

150th anniv. of the Battle of Monmouth, NJ, and as a memorial to Molly Pitcher, the heroine of the battle.

**Hawaii Sesquicentennial Issue**

Nos. 634 and 637 Overprinted **HAWAII 1778 - 1928**

**Rotary Press Printing**

| **1928, Aug. 13** | | | ***Perf. 11x10½*** | |
|---|---|---|---|---|
| *647* | A157 | 2c carmine | 3.00 | 3.25 |
| *648* | A160 | 5c dark blue | 10.00 | 10.00 |

150th anniv. of the discovery of the Hawaiian Islands by Captain Cook.

These stamps were on sale at post offices in the Hawaiian Islands and at the Postal Agency in Washington, DC They were not on sale at post offices in the Continental US, though they were available for postage there.

Normally the overprints were placed 18mm apart vertically, but pairs exist with a space of 28mm between the overprints.

**Aeronautics Conference Issue**

Wright Airplane A194

Globe and Airplane A195

**Flat Plate Printing**

| **1928, Dec. 12** | | | ***Perf. 11*** | |
|---|---|---|---|---|
| *649* | A194 | 2c carmine rose | 70 | 75 |
| *650* | A195 | 5c blue | 4.50 | 3.00 |

Intl. Civil Aeronautics Conf. at Washington, DC, Dec. 12-14, 1928, and of the 25th anniv. of the 1st airplane flight by the Wright brothers, Dec. 17, 1903.

**George Rogers Clark Issue**

Surrender of Fort Sackville A196

| **1929, Feb. 25** | | | ***Perf. 11*** | |
|---|---|---|---|---|
| *651* | A196 | 2c car & blk | 45 | 35 |

150th anniv. of the surrender of Fort Sackville, the present site of Vincennes, Ind., to George Rogers Clark.

Type of 1925

**Rotary Press Printing**

| **1929, May 25** | | | ***Perf. 11x10½*** | |
|---|---|---|---|---|
| *653* | A154 | ½c olive brown | 5 | 5 |

Edison's First Lamp A197

Maj. Gen. John Sullivan A198

**Electric Light Jubilee Issue**

| **1929** | | **Flat Plate Printing** | ***Perf. 11*** | |
|---|---|---|---|---|
| *654* | A197 | 2c carmine rose | 50 | 50 |

**Rotary Press Printing**

***Perf. 11x10½***

| *655* | A197 | 2c carmine rose | 45 | 15 |
|---|---|---|---|---|

**Coil Stamp (Rotary Press)**

***Perf. 10 Vertically***

| *656* | A197 | 2c carmine rose | 9.50 | 1.25 |
|---|---|---|---|---|

50th anniv. of invention of the incandescent lamp by Thomas Alva Edison, Oct. 21, 1879. Issued: No. 654, June 5. Nos. 655-656, June 11.

**Sullivan Expedition Issue**

**Flat Plate Printing**

| **1929, June 17** | | | ***Perf. 11*** | |
|---|---|---|---|---|
| *657* | A198 | 2c carmine rose | 60 | 50 |

150th anniv. of the Sullivan Expedition in NY State during the Revolutionary War.

Regular Issue of 1926-27 Overprinted **Kans.**

**Rotary Press Printing**

| **1929** | | | ***Perf. 11x10½*** | |
|---|---|---|---|---|
| *658* | A155 | 1c green | 1.40 | 1.25 |
| *a* | | Vert. pair, one without ovpt. | *300.00* | |
| *659* | A156 | 1½c brown | 1.90 | 1.75 |
| *a* | | Vert. pair, one without ovpt. | *325.00* | |
| *660* | A157 | 2c carmine | 2.50 | 70 |
| *661* | A158 | 3c violet | 11.00 | 9.00 |
| *a* | | Vert. pair, one without ovpt. | *400.00* | |
| *662* | A159 | 4c yellow brn | 11.00 | 5.50 |
| *a* | | Vert. pair, one without ovpt. | *400.00* | |
| *663* | A160 | 5c deep blue | 8.00 | 6.00 |
| *664* | A161 | 6c red org | 17.50 | 11.50 |
| *665* | A162 | 7c black | 16.00 | 17.00 |
| *a* | | Vert. pair, one without ovpt. | *400.00* | |
| *666* | A163 | 8c olive grn | 55.00 | 45.00 |
| *667* | A164 | 9c light rose | 8.00 | 7.00 |
| *668* | A165 | 10c org yel | 14.00 | 7.50 |
| | | *Nos. 658-668 (11)* | 146.30 | 112.20 |

Overprinted **Nebr.**

| | | | | |
|---|---|---|---|---|
| *669* | A155 | 1c green | 2.00 | 1.40 |
| *a* | | Vert. pair, one without ovpt. | *275.00* | |
| *670* | A156 | 1½c brown | 1.65 | 1.50 |
| *671* | A157 | 2c carmine | 1.65 | 70 |
| *672* | A158 | 3c violet | 7.00 | 6.50 |
| *a* | | Vert. pair, one without ovpt. | *400.00* | |
| *673* | A159 | 4c yel brn | 12.50 | 9.00 |
| *674* | A160 | 5c deep blue | 10.00 | 9.00 |
| *675* | A161 | 6c red org | 24.00 | 14.00 |
| *676* | A162 | 7c black | 13.00 | 11.00 |
| *677* | A163 | 8c olive grn | 17.00 | 15.00 |
| *678* | A164 | 9c light rose | 22.50 | 17.00 |
| *a* | | Vert. pair, one without ovpt. | *600.00* | |
| *679* | A165 | 10c org yel | 70.00 | 14.00 |
| | | *Nos. 669-679 (11)* | 181.30 | 99.10 |

Nos. 658-660, 669-673, 677 and 678 are known with the overprints on vertical pairs spaced 32mm. apart instead of the normal 22mm.

Gen. Anthony Wayne Memorial A199

Lock No. 5, Monongahela River A200

**Battle of Fallen Timbers Issue**

**Flat Plate Printing**

| **1929, Sept. 14** | | | ***Perf. 11*** | |
|---|---|---|---|---|
| *680* | A199 | 2c carmine rose | 60 | 65 |

General Anthony Wayne memorial and the 135th anniv. of the Battle of Fallen Timbers, Ohio.

**Ohio River Canalization Issue**

| **1929, Oct. 19** | | | ***Perf. 11*** | |
|---|---|---|---|---|
| *681* | A200 | 2c carmine rose | 45 | 50 |

Completion of the Ohio River Canalization Project between Cairo, Ill. and Pittsburgh.

### Massachusetts Bay Colony Issue

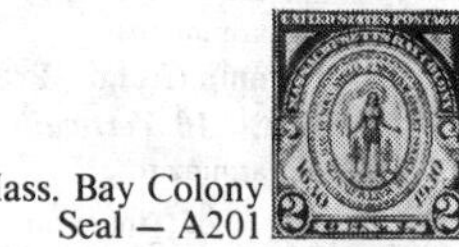

Mass. Bay Colony Seal — A201

**1930, Apr. 8** ***Perf. 11***

*682* A201 2c carmine rose 40 38

300th anniv. of the founding of the Massachusetts Bay Colony.

### Carolina-Charleston Issue

Gov. Joseph West and Chief Shadoo, a Kiawah — A202

**1930, Apr. 10** ***Perf. 11***

*683* A202 2c carmine rose 85 85

260th anniv. of the founding of the Province of Carolina, and the 250th anniv. of the City of Charleston, SC.

Warren G. Harding — A203

William H. Taft — A204

Type of 1922-26 Issue

**Rotary Press Printing**

**1930** ***Perf. 11x10½***

*684* A203 1½c brown 18 5
*685* A204 4c brown 55 6

**Coil Stamps**

***Perf. 10 Vertically***

*686* A203 1½c brown 1.25 7
*687* A204 4c brown 2.25 50

### Braddock's Field Issue

Statue of Col. George Washington — A205

**Flat Plate Printing**

**1930, July 9** ***Perf. 11***

*688* A205 2c carmine rose 65 65

175th anniv. of the Battle of Braddock's Field, otherwise the Battle of Monongahela.

General von Steuben A206

General Casimir Pulaski A207

### Von Steuben Issue

**1930, Sept. 17** ***Perf. 11***

*689* A206 2c carmine rose 38 40
*a* Imperf., pair *2,250.*

Gen. Baron Friedrich Wilhelm von Steuben (1730-1794), German soldier who served with distinction in American Revolution.

### Pulaski Issue

**1931, Jan. 16** ***Perf. 11***

*690* A207 2c carmine rose 16 10

150th anniv. (in 1929) of the death of Gen. Count Casimir Pulaski (1748-1779), Polish patriot and hero of American Revolution.

Types of 1922-26

**Rotary Press Printing**

**1931** ***Perf. 11x10½***

*692* A166 11c light blue 1.65 10
*693* A167 12c brn vio 3.25 6
*694* A186 13c yel grn 1.40 10
*695* A168 14c dark blue 2.00 22
*696* A169 15c gray 5.75 6

***Perf. 10½x11***

*697* A187 17c black 3.25 14
*698* A170 20c car rose 7.00 5
*699* A171 25c bl grn 6.75 8
*700* A172 30c brown 10.50 7
*701* A173 50c lilac 30.00 7
*Nos. 692-701 (10)* 71.55 95

"The Greatest Mother" A208

Count de Rochambeau, Washington, Count de Grasse A209

### Red Cross Issue

**Flat Plate Printing**

**1931, May 21** ***Perf. 11***

*702* A208 2c black & red 8 8

50th anniv. of the founding of the American Red Cross Society.

### Yorktown Issue

**1931, Oct. 19** ***Perf. 11***

*703* A209 2c car rose & blk 24 20
*a* 2c lake & black 3.50 50
*b* 2c dark lake & black *300.00*
*c* Horiz. pair, imperf. vert. *2,500.*

Surrender of Yorktown, sesquicentennial.

### Washington Bicentennial Issue

Various Portraits of George Washington

A210

A211

A212

A213

A214

A215

A216

A217

A218

A219

A220

A221

### Rotary Press Printings

**1932, Jan. 1** ***Perf. 11x10½***

*704* A210 ½c olive brown 9 8
*705* A211 1c green 10 5
*706* A212 1½c brown 32 8
*707* A213 2c car rose 10 5
*708* A214 3c deep vio 40 6
*709* A215 4c light brn 22 6
*710* A216 5c blue 1.40 10
*711* A217 6c red org 2.75 6
*712* A218 7c black 22 10
*713* A219 8c olive bis 2.25 50
*714* A220 9c pale red 2.00 15
*715* A221 10c org yel 8.50 10
*Nos. 704-715 (12)* 18.35 1.39

200th anniv. of the birth of Washington.

Ski Jumper A222

Boy and Girl Planting Tree A223

### Olympic Winter Games Issue

**Flat Plate Printing**

**1932, Jan. 25** ***Perf. 11***

*716* A222 2c carmine rose 35 16

Olympic Winter Games, Lake Placid, NY, Feb. 4-13.

### Arbor Day Issue

**Rotary Press Printing**

**1932, Apr. 22** ***Perf. 11x10½***

*717* A223 2c carmine rose 10 8

60th anniv. of the 1st observance of Arbor Day in Nebr., April, 1872, and the centenary birth of Julius Sterling Morton, who conceived the plan and the name "Arbor Day," while a member of the Nebr. State Board of Agriculture.

### 10th Olympic Games Issue

Runner at Starting Mark A224

Myron's Discobolus A225

**1932, June 15** ***Perf. 11x10½***

*718* A224 3c violet 1.10 8
*719* A225 5c blue 1.90 20

Los Angeles, Cal., July 30-Aug. 14.

Washington — A226

**1932, June 16** ***Perf. 11x10½***

*720* A226 3c deep violet 12 5
*b* Booklet pane of 6 22.50 *5.00*
*c* Vert. pair, imperf. btwn. 225.00

Coil Stamps

**Rotary Press Printing**

**1932, June 24** ***Perf. 10 Vertically***

*721* A226 3c deep violet 2.25 8

**1932, Oct. 12** ***Perf. 10 Horizontally***

*722* A226 3c deep violet 1.00 30

Garfield Type of 1922-26 Issue

**1932, Aug. 18** ***Perf. 10 Vertically***

*723* A161 6c deep org 7.50 25

William Penn A227

Daniel Webster A228

### William Penn Issue

**Flat Plate Printing**

**1932, Oct. 24** ***Perf. 11***

*724* A227 3c violet 22 25
*a* Vert. pair, imperf. horiz. —

250th anniv. of the arrival in America of William Penn (1644-1718), English Quaker and founder of Pennsylvania.

### Daniel Webster Issue

**1932, Oct. 24** ***Perf. 11***

*725* A228 3c violet 28 24

Daniel Webster (1782-1852), statesman.

Gen. James Edward Oglethorpe — A229

Washington's Headquarters, Newburgh, NY — A230

### Georgia Bicentennial Issue

**1933, Feb. 12** ***Perf. 11***

*726* A229 3c violet 20 18

200th anniv. of the founding of the Colony of Georgia and James Edward Oglethorpe, who landed from England, Feb. 12th, 1733, and personally supervised the establishing of the colony.

### Peace of 1783 Issue

**Rotary Press Printing**

**1933, Apr. 19** ***Perf. 10½x11***

*727* A230 3c violet 9 8

150th anniv. of the Proclamation of Peace between the US and Great Britain at the end of the Revolutionary War.

See No. 752.

### Century of Progress Issue

Restoration of Fort Dearborn A231

Federal Building at Chicago, 1933 A232

**1933, May 25** ***Perf. 10½x11***

*728* A231 1c yellow green 10 6
*729* A232 3c violet 10 5

"Century of Progress" Intl. Phil. Exhib., Chicago, 1933 and 100th anniv. of the incorporation of Chicago as a city.

### American Philatelic Society Issue

Souvenir Sheets

Without Gum

**Flat Plate Printing**

**1933, Aug. 25** ***Imperf.***

*730* sheet of 25 24.00 24.00
*a* A231 1c deep yellow green 65 35
*731* sheet of 25 22.50 22.50
*a* A232 3c deep violet 50 35

Sheets measure 134x120mm and are inscribed in the margins:

PRINTED BY THE TREASURY DEPARTMENT, BUREAU OF ENGRAVING AND PRINTING,—UNDER AUTHORITY OF JAMES A. FARLEY, POSTMASTER GENERAL, AT CENTURY OF PROGRESS,—IN COMPLIMENT TO THE AMERICAN PHILATELIC SOCIETY FOR ITS CONVENTION AND EXHIBITION—CHICAGO, ILLINOIS, AUGUST, 1933.

See Nos. 766-767.

**National Recovery Act Issue**

Group of Workers — A233

**Rotary Press Printing**

**1933, Aug. 15** *Perf. 10½x11*

*732* A233 3c violet 10 5

Issued to direct attention to and arouse support of the Nation for the NRA.

World Map on van der Grinten's Projection A234

Statue of Gen. Tadeusz Kosciuszko A235

**Byrd Antarctic Issue**

**Flat Plate Printing**

**1933, Oct. 9** *Perf. 11*

*733* A234 3c dark blue 40 48

Second Antarctic expedition of Rear Admiral Richard E. Byrd.

In addition to the 3 cents postage, letters sent by the ships of the expedition to be canceled in Little America were subject to a service charge of 50 cents each.

See Nos. 735, 753.

**Kosciuszko Issue**

**1933, Oct. 13** *Perf. 11*

*734* A235 5c blue 40 22
  *a* Horiz. pair, imperf. vert. *1,750.*

Gen. Tadeusz Kosciuszko (1746-1807), Polish soldier and statesman who served in American Revolution. 150th anniv. of grant of American citizenship.

**National Stamp Exhibition Issue**

Souvenir Sheet

Without Gum

**1934, Feb. 10** *Imperf.*

*735* Sheet of six 15.00 12.50
  *a* A235 3c dark blue 2.00 2.00

Sheets measure 87x93mm and are inscribed in the margins: "Printed by the Treasury Department, Bureau of Engraving and Printing, under authority of James A. Farley, Postmaster General in compliment to the National Stamp Exhibition of 1934, New York, N. Y., February 10-18, Plate Number 21184."

See No. 768.

**Maryland Tercentenary Issue**

"The Ark" and "The Dove" — A236

**1934, Mar. 23** *Perf. 11*

*736* A236 3c carmine rose 12 8
  *a* Horiz. pair, imperf. btwn. *1,000.*

300th anniv. of the founding of Maryland.

**Mothers of America Issue**

Adaptation of Whistler's Portrait of his Mother A237

**Rotary Press Printing**

**1934, May 2** *Perf. 11x10½*

*737* A237 3c deep violet 9 6

**Flat Plate Printing**

*Perf. 11*

*738* A237 3c deep violet 12 10

Mother's Day. See No. 754.

**Wisconsin Tercentenary Issue**

Nicolet's Landing A238

**1934, July 7** *Perf. 11*

*739* A238 3c deep violet 12 10
  *a* Vert. pair, imperf. horiz. 250.00
  *b* Horiz. pair, imperf. vert. 325.00

Tercentenary of the arrival of French explorer Jean Nicolet at Green Bay, Wis..

See No. 755.

**National Parks Issue**

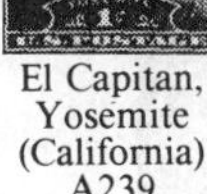

El Capitan, Yosemite (California) A239

Old Faithful, Yellowstone (Wyoming) A243

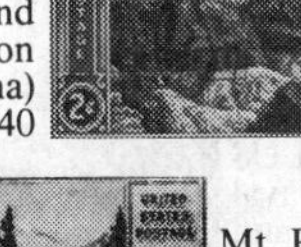

Grand Canyon (Arizona) A240

Mt. Rainier and Mirror Lake (Washington) A241

Mesa Verde (Colorado) A242

Crater Lake (Oregon) A244

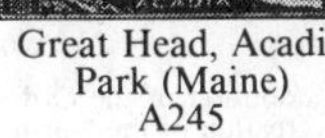

Great Head, Acadia Park (Maine) A245

Great White Throne, Zion Park (Utah) A246

Great Smoky Mountains (North Carolina) A248

Mt. Rockwell (Mt. Sinopah) and Two Medicine Lake, Glacier National Park (Montana) A247

**1934 Flat Plate Printing** *Perf. 11*

*740* A239 1c green 7 6
  *a* Vert. pair, imperf. horiz., with gum 450.00
*741* A240 2c red 9 6
  *a* Vert. pair, imperf. horiz., with gum 300.00
  *b* Horiz. pair, imperf. vert., with gum 300.00
*742* A241 3c deep vio 10 6
  *a* Vert. pair, imperf. horiz., with gum 350.00
*743* A242 4c brown 35 50
  *a* Vert. pair, imperf. horiz., with gum 500.00
*744* A243 5c blue 60 90
  *a* Horiz. pair, imperf. vert., with gum 400.00
*745* A244 6c dark blue 1.00 75
*746* A245 7c black 55 65
  *a* Horiz. pair, imperf. vert., with gum 450.00
*747* A246 8c sage grn 1.40 1.65
*748* A247 9c red org 1.50 55
*749* A248 10c gray blk 2.75 90
  *Nos. 740-749 (10)* 8.41 6.08

National Parks Year.

See Nos. 756-765, 750-751, 769-770.

**American Philatelic Society Issue**

Souvenir Sheet

**1934, Aug. 28** *Imperf.*

*750* Sheet of six 30.00 27.50
  *a* A241 3c deep violet 3.50 3.50

Sheet measures 99x97mm and is inscribed in the margins:

PRINTED BY THE TREASURY DEPARTMENT, BUREAU OF ENGRAVING AND PRINTING,—UNDER AUTHORITY OF JAMES A. FARLEY, POSTMASTER GENERAL,—IN COMPLIMENT TO THE AMERICAN PHILATELIC SOCIETY FOR ITS CONVENTION AND EXHIBITION,—ATLANTIC CITY, NEW JERSEY, AUGUST 1934. PLATE NO. 21303.

See No. 770.

**Trans-Mississippi Philatelic Exposition Issue**

Souvenir Sheet

**1934, Oct. 10** *Imperf.*

*751* Sheet of six 10.00 10.00
  *a* A239 1c green 1.40 1.40

Sheet measures 94x99mm and is inscribed in the margins:

PRINTED BY THE TREASURY DEPARTMENT, BUREAU OF ENGRAVING AND PRINTING,—UNDER AUTHORITY OF JAMES A. FARLEY, POSTMASTER GENERAL,—IN COMPLIMENT TO THE TRANS-MISSISSIPPI PHILATELIC EXPOSITION AND CONVENTION, OMAHA, NEBRASKA—OCTOBER, 1934. PLATE NO. 21341.

See No. 769.

**Special Printing (Nos. 752-771)**

"Issued for a limited time in full sheets as printed, and in blocks thereof, to meet the requirements of collectors and others who may be interested."—From Postal Bulletin, No. 16614.

Issuance of the following 20 stamps in complete sheets resulted from the protest of collectors and others at the practice of presenting, to certain government officials, complete sheets of unsevered panes, imperforate (except Nos. 752 and 753) and generally ungummed.

Without Gum.

Note. In 1940 the P.O. Department offered to and did gum full sheets of Nos. 754 to 771 sent in by owners.

Type of Peace Issue

Issued in sheets of 400

**Rotary Press Printing**

**1935, Mar. 15** *Perf. 10½x11*

*752* A230 3c violet 14 8

**Type of Byrd Issue**

**Issued in sheets of 200**

**Flat Plate Printing**

*Perf. 11*

*753* A234 3c dark blue 40 40

**Type of Mothers of America Issue**

**Issued in sheets of 200**

*Imperf*

*754* A237 3c deep violet 50 50

**Type of Wisconsin Issue**

**Issued in sheets of 200**

*Imperf*

*755* A238 3c deep violet 50 50

**Types of National Parks Issue**

Issued in sheets of 200.

*Imperf.*

*756* A239 1c green 20 20
*757* A240 2c red 22 22
*758* A241 3c dp vio 45 40
*759* A242 4c brown 90 90
*760* A243 5c blue 1.40 1.25
*761* A244 6c dk bl 2.25 2.00
*762* A245 7c black 1.40 1.25
*763* A246 8c sage grn 1.50 1.40
*764* A247 9c red org 1.75 1.50
*765* A248 10c gray blk 3.50 3.00
  *Nos. 756-765 (10)* 13.57 12.12

**Souvenir Sheets**

**Type of Century of Progress Issue**

**Issued in sheets of 9 panes of 25 stamps each**

Note. Single items from these sheets are identical with other varieties, 766 & 730, 766a & 730a, 767 & 731, 767a & 731a, 768 & 735, 768a & 735a, 769 & 756, 770 & 758. Positive identification is by blocks or pairs showing wide gutters between stamps. These wide gutters occur only on Nos. 766 to 770 and measure, horizontally, 13mm on Nos. 766-767; 16mm on No. 768, and 23mm on Nos. 769-770.

*Imperf*

*766* Pane of 25 24.00 24.00
  *a* A231 1c yellow green 65 35
*767* Pane of 25 22.50 22.50
  *a* A232 3c violet 50 35

**National Exhibition Issue**

**Type of Byrd Issue**

**Issued in sheets of 25 panes of 6 stamps each**

*Imperf*

*768* Pane of six 15.00 12.50
  *a* A234 3c dark blue 2.00 2.00

**Types of National Parks Issue**

**Issued in sheets of 20 panes of 6 stamps each**

*Imperf*

*769* Pane of six 10.00 10.00
  *a* A239 1c green 1.40 1.40
*770* Pane of six 30.00 27.50
  *a* A241 3c deep violet 3.50 3.50

**Type of Air Post Special Delivery**

Issued in sheets of 200

*Imperf.*

*771* APSD1 16c dark blue 2.00 2.00

**Catalogue values for unused stamps in this section, from this point to the end of the section, are for Never Hinged items.**

**Connecticut Tercentenary Issue**

Charter Oak — A249

**Rotary Press Printing**

**1935, Apr. 26** ***Perf. 11x10½***

*772* A249 3c violet 10 6

300th anniv. of the settlement of Conn. See No. 778a.

**California-Pacific Exposition Issue**

View of San Diego Exposition A250

**1935, May 29** ***Perf. 11x10½***

*773* A250 3c purple 9 6

California-Pacific Expo., San Diego. See No. 778b.

**Boulder Dam Issue**

Boulder Dam — A251

**Flat Plate Printing**

**1935, Sept. 30** ***Perf. 11***

*774* A251 3c purple 9 6

Dedication of Boulder Dam.

**Michigan Centenary Issue**

Michigan State Seal — A252

**Rotary Press Printing**

**1935, Nov. 1** ***Perf. 11x10½***

*775* A252 3c purple 9 6

Advance celebration of Michigan statehood centenary. Michigan was admitted to Union Jan. 26, 1837.
See No. 778c.

**Texas Centennial Issue**

Sam Houston, Stephen F. Austin and the Alamo A253

**1936, Mar. 2** ***Perf. 11x10½***

*776* A253 3c purple 9 6

Centennial of Texas independence. See No. 778d.

**Rhode Island Tercentenary Issue**

Statue of Roger Williams — A254

**1936, May 4** ***Perf. 10½x11***

*777* A254 3c purple 10 6

Settlement of Rhode Island, 1636.

**Third International Philatelic Exhibition Issue**
Souvenir Sheet

A254a

**Flat Plate Printing**

**1936, May 9** ***Imperf.***

*778* A254a Sheet of 4 1.75 1.75
*a* A249 3c violet 35 30
*b* A250 3c violet 35 30
*c* A252 3c violet 35 30
*d* A253 3c violet 35 30

Sheet measures 98x66mm and is inscribed in the margins:
"Printed by the Treasury Department, Bureau of Engraving and Printing.—Under Authority of James A. Farley, Postmaster General—In compliment to the Third International Philatelic Exhibition of 1936—New York, N. Y., May 9-17, 1936. Plate Number 21557 or 21558."

**Arkansas Centennial Issue**

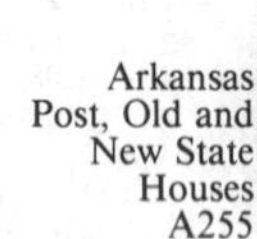

Arkansas Post, Old and New State Houses A255

**Rotary Press Printing**

**1936, June 15** ***Perf. 11x10½***

*782* A255 3c purple 9 6

Centennial of Arkansas statehood.

Map of Oregon Territory A256

Susan B. Anthony A257

**Oregon Territory Issue**

**1936, July 14** ***Perf. 11x10½***

*783* A256 3c purple 9 6

Centenary of Oregon Territory opening.

**Susan B. Anthony Issue**

**1936, Aug. 26** ***Perf. 11x10½***

*784* A257 3c dark violet 9 5

Susan Brownell Anthony (1820-1906), woman suffrage advocate, honored on 16th anniv. of ratification of 19th Amendment granting American women the right to vote.

**Army Issue**

George Washington, Nathanael Greene and Mount Vernon A258

Andrew Jackson, Winfield Scott and the Hermitage A259

Generals Sherman, Grant and Sheridan A260

Generals Robert E. Lee, "Stonewall" Jackson and Stratford Hall — A261

US Military Academy, West Point — A262

**1936-37** ***Perf. 11x10½***

*785* A258 1c green 8 6
*786* A259 2c carmine ('37) 8 6
*787* A260 3c purple ('37) 12 6
*788* A261 4c gray ('37) 30 12
*789* A262 5c ultra ('37) 60 12
*Nos. 785-789 (5)* 1.18 42

Issued in honor of the United States Army.

**Navy Issue**

John Paul Jones and John Barry — A263

Stephen Decatur and Thomas MacDonough A264

Admirals David G. Farragut and David D. Porter A265

Admirals William T. Sampson, George Dewey and Winfield S. Schley A266

Seal of US Naval Academy and Naval Cadets A267

**1936-37** ***Perf. 11x10½***

*790* A263 1c green 8 6
*791* A264 2c carmine ('37) 9 6
*792* A265 3c purple ('37) 14 6
*793* A266 4c gray ('37) 32 12
*794* A267 5c ultra ('37) 60 12
*Nos. 790-794 (5)* 1.23 42

Issued in honor of the United States Navy.

**Northwest Ordinance Sesquicentennial Issue**

Manasseh Cutler, Rufus Putnam and Map of Northwest Territory A268

**1937, July 13** ***Perf. 11x10½***

*795* A268 3c red violet 10 6

150th anniv. of the adoption of the Ordinance of 1787 and the creation of the Northwest Territory.

**Virginia Dare Issue**

Virginia Dare and Parents — A269

**Flat Plate Printing**

**1937, Aug. 18** ***Perf. 11***

*796* A269 5c gray blue 20 28

350th anniv. of the birth of Virginia Dare and the settlement at Roanoke Island. Virginia was the first child born in America of English parents (Aug. 18, 1587).

**Society of Philatelic Americans**
Souvenir Sheet

A269a

**1937, Aug. 26** ***Imperf.***

*797* A269a 10c blue green 60 40

Sheet measures 67x78mm, and is inscribed in margins: "Printed by the Treasury Department, Bureau of Engraving and Printing—Under the Authority of James A. Farley, Postmaster General—In Compliment to the 43rd Annual Convention of the Society of Philatelic Americans—Asheville, N. C. August 26-28, 1937. Plate Number 21695 (6)."

**Constitution Sesquicentennial Issue**

Signing of the Constitution A270

**Rotary Press Printing**

**1937, Sept. 17** ***Perf. 11x10½***

*798* A270 3c bright red violet 12 7

Sesquicentennial of the Signing of the Constitution, Sept. 17, 1787.

**Territorial Issues.**
**Hawaii**

Statue of Kamehameha I, Honolulu — A271

**1937, Oct. 18** ***Perf. 10½x11***

*799* A271 3c violet 10 7

**Alaska**

Landscape with Mt. McKinley A272

**1937, Nov. 12** ***Perf. 11x10½***

*800* A272 3c violet 10 7

### Puerto Rico

La Fortaleza, San Juan — A273

**1937, Nov. 25** *Perf. 11x10½*

| | | | | |
|---|---|---|---|---|
| *801* | A273 | 3c bright violet | 10 | 7 |

### Virgin Islands

Charlotte Amalie A274

**1937, Dec. 15** *Perf. 11x10½*

| | | | | |
|---|---|---|---|---|
| *802* | A274 | 3c light violet | 10 | 7 |

### Presidential Issue

Benjamin Franklin A275

George Washington A276

Martha Washington A277

John Adams A278

Thomas Jefferson A279

James Madison A280

White House A281

James Monroe A282

John Q. Adams A283

Andrew Jackson A284

Martin Van Buren A285

William H. Harrison A286

John Tyler A287

James K. Polk A288

Zachary Taylor A289

Millard Fillmore A290

Franklin Pierce A291

James Buchanan A292

Abraham Lincoln A293

Andrew Johnson A294

Ulysses S. Grant A295

Rutherford B. Hayes A296

James A. Garfield A297

Chester A. Arthur A298

Grover Cleveland A299

Benjamin Harrison A300

William McKinley A301

Theodore Roosevelt A302

William Howard Taft A303

Woodrow Wilson A304

Warren G. Harding A305

Calvin Coolidge A306

**1938-54** *Perf. 11x10½*

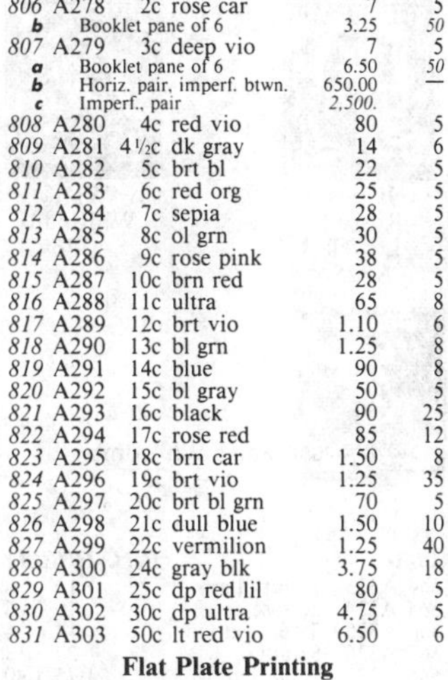

| | | | | |
|---|---|---|---|---|
| *803* | A275 | ½c dp org | 5 | 5 |
| *804* | A276 | 1c green | 5 | 5 |
| *b* | | Booklet pane of 6 | 1.50 | *20* |
| *805* | A277 | 1½c bis brn | 6 | 5 |
| *b* | | Horiz. pair, imperf. btwn. | 150.00 | 15.00 |
| *806* | A278 | 2c rose car | 7 | 5 |
| *b* | | Booklet pane of 6 | 3.25 | *50* |
| *807* | A279 | 3c deep vio | 7 | 5 |
| *a* | | Booklet pane of 6 | 6.50 | *50* |
| *b* | | Horiz. pair, imperf. btwn. | 650.00 | — |
| *c* | | Imperf., pair | *2,500.* | |
| *808* | A280 | 4c red vio | 80 | 5 |
| *809* | A281 | 4½c dk gray | 14 | 6 |
| *810* | A282 | 5c brt bl | 22 | 5 |
| *811* | A283 | 6c red org | 25 | 5 |
| *812* | A284 | 7c sepia | 28 | 5 |
| *813* | A285 | 8c ol grn | 30 | 5 |
| *814* | A286 | 9c rose pink | 38 | 5 |
| *815* | A287 | 10c brn red | 28 | 5 |
| *816* | A288 | 11c ultra | 65 | 8 |
| *817* | A289 | 12c brt vio | 1.10 | 6 |
| *818* | A290 | 13c bl grn | 1.25 | 8 |
| *819* | A291 | 14c blue | 90 | 8 |
| *820* | A292 | 15c bl gray | 50 | 5 |
| *821* | A293 | 16c black | 90 | 25 |
| *822* | A294 | 17c rose red | 85 | 12 |
| *823* | A295 | 18c brn car | 1.50 | 8 |
| *824* | A296 | 19c brt vio | 1.25 | 35 |
| *825* | A297 | 20c brt bl grn | 70 | 5 |
| *826* | A298 | 21c dull blue | 1.50 | 10 |
| *827* | A299 | 22c vermilion | 1.25 | 40 |
| *828* | A300 | 24c gray blk | 3.75 | 18 |
| *829* | A301 | 25c dp red lil | 80 | 5 |
| *830* | A302 | 30c dp ultra | 4.75 | 5 |
| *831* | A303 | 50c lt red vio | 6.50 | 6 |

**Flat Plate Printing**

*Perf. 11*

| | | | | |
|---|---|---|---|---|
| *832* | A304 | $1 pur & blk | 8.25 | 10 |
| *a* | | Vert. pair, imperf. horiz. | *1,000.* | |
| *b* | | Wmkd. USIR ('51) | 250.00 | 50.00 |
| *c* | | $1 red vio & blk ('54) | 6.75 | 15 |
| *d* | | As "c", vert. pair, imperf. horiz. | *1,000.* | |
| *e* | | Vert. pair, imperf. btwn. | *2,500.* | |
| *f* | | As "c", vert. pair, imperf. btwn. | *6,000.* | |
| *833* | A305 | $2 yel grn & blk | 21.00 | 3.75 |
| *834* | A306 | $5 car & blk | 105.00 | 3.50 |
| *a* | | $5 red brown & black | 800.00 | 175.00 |
| | | *Nos. 803-834 (32)* | 165.35 | 10.05 |

No. 832c is printed on thick white paper with smooth, colorless gum.

See Nos. 839-851.

### Constitution Ratification Issue.

Old Court House, Williamsburg, Va. — A307

**Rotary Press Printing**

**1938, June 21** *Perf. 11x10½*

| | | | | |
|---|---|---|---|---|
| *835* | A307 | 3c deep violet | 16 | 7 |

150th anniv. of the ratification of the US Constitution.

Landing of the Swedes and Finns A308

Statue Symbolizing Colonization of the West A309

### Swedish-Finnish Tercentenary Issue

**Flat Plate Printing**

**1938, June 27** *Perf. 11*

| | | | | |
|---|---|---|---|---|
| *836* | A308 | 3c red violet | 12 | 8 |

Tercentenary of the founding of the Swedish and Finnish settlement at Wilmington, Del.

### Northwest Territory Issue

**Rotary Press Printing**

**1938, July 15** *Perf. 11x10½*

| | | | | |
|---|---|---|---|---|
| *837* | A309 | 3c bright violet | 14 | 8 |

Sesquicentennial of the settlement of the Northwest Territory.

### Iowa Territory Centennial Issue

Old Capitol, Iowa City — A310

**1938, Aug. 24** *Perf. 11x10½*

| | | | | |
|---|---|---|---|---|
| *838* | A310 | 3c violet | 12 | 8 |

Centenary of Iowa Territory.

Presidential Types of 1938
Coil Stamps

**Rotary Press Printing**

**1939** *Perf. 10 Vertically*

| | | | | |
|---|---|---|---|---|
| *839* | A276 | 1c green | 20 | 6 |
| *840* | A277 | 1½c bis brn | 24 | 6 |
| *841* | A278 | 2c rose car | 24 | 5 |
| *842* | A279 | 3c dp vio | 42 | 5 |
| *843* | A280 | 4c red vio | 6.75 | 35 |
| *844* | A281 | 4½c dk gray | 42 | 35 |
| *845* | A282 | 5c brt bl | 4.75 | 30 |
| *846* | A283 | 6c red org | 1.10 | 15 |
| *847* | A287 | 10c brn red | 11.00 | 40 |

***Perf. 10 Horizontally***

| | | | | |
|---|---|---|---|---|
| *848* | A276 | 1c green | 55 | 12 |
| *849* | A277 | 1½c bis brn | 1.10 | 30 |
| *850* | A278 | 2c rose car | 2.50 | 40 |
| *851* | A279 | 3c dp vio | 2.25 | 35 |
| | | *Nos. 839-851 (13)* | 31.52 | 2.94 |

"Tower of the Sun" A311

Trylon and Perisphere A312

### Golden Gate International Exposition Issue

**Rotary Press Printing**

**1939, Feb. 18** *Perf. 10½x11*

| | | | | |
|---|---|---|---|---|
| *852* | A311 | 3c bright purple | 10 | 6 |

Golden Gate Intl. Expo., San Francisco.

### New York World's Fair Issue

**1939, Apr. 1** *Perf. 10½x11*

| | | | | |
|---|---|---|---|---|
| *853* | A312 | 3c deep purple | 10 | 6 |

NY World's Fair.

### Washington Inauguration Issue

George Washington Taking Oath of Office — A313

**Flat Plate Printing**

**1939, Apr. 30** *Perf. 11*

| | | | | |
|---|---|---|---|---|
| *854* | A313 | 3c bright red vio | 25 | 10 |

Sesquicentennial of the inauguration of George Washington as 1st president.

### Baseball Centennial Issue

Sand-lot Baseball Game — A314

**Rotary Press Printing**

**1939, June 12** *Perf. 11x10½*

| | | | | |
|---|---|---|---|---|
| *855* | A314 | 3c violet | 32 | 8 |

Centennial of baseball.

### Panama Canal Issue

Theodore Roosevelt, Gen. George W. Goethals and Gaillard Cut — A315

### Flat Plate Printing

**1939, Aug. 15** *Perf. 11*

| | | | |
|---|---|---|---|
| *856* A315 3c deep red violet | | 18 | 8 |

25th anniv. of the Panama Canal opening.

### Printing Tercentenary Issue

Stephen Daye Press — A316

### Rotary Press Printing

**1939, Sept. 25** *Perf. 10½x11*

| | | | |
|---|---|---|---|
| *857* A316 3c violet | | 9 | 8 |

300th anniv. of printing in Colonial America.

### 50th Anniversary of Statehood Issue.

Map of North and South Dakota, Montana and Washington A317

**1939, Nov. 2** *Perf. 11x10½*

| | | | |
|---|---|---|---|
| *858* A317 3c rose violet | | 9 | 8 |

50th anniv. of admission to Statehood of North Dakota, South Dakota, Montana and Washington.

### Famous Americans Issues
### Authors

Washington Irving A318

James Fenimore Cooper A319

Ralph Waldo Emerson A320

Louisa May Alcott A321

Samuel L. Clemens (Mark Twain) — A322

**1940** *Perf. 10½x11*

| No. | Design | Denom. | Color | Unused | Used |
|---|---|---|---|---|---|
| *859* | A318 | 1c | brt bl grn | 7 | 6 |
| *860* | A319 | 2c | rose car | 8 | 8 |
| *861* | A320 | 3c | brt red vio | 10 | 6 |
| *862* | A321 | 5c | ultra | 28 | 20 |
| *863* | A322 | 10c | dk brn | 1.60 | 1.35 |
| | | | *Nos. 859-863 (5)* | 2.13 | 1.75 |

### Poets

Henry W. Longfellow A323

John Greenleaf Whittier A324

James Russell Lowell A325

Walt Whitman A326

James Whitcomb Riley — A327

**1940** *Perf. 10½x11*

| No. | Design | Denom. | Color | Unused | Used |
|---|---|---|---|---|---|
| *864* | A323 | 1c | brt bl grn | 10 | 8 |
| *865* | A324 | 2c | rose car | 10 | 8 |
| *866* | A325 | 3c | brt red vio | 14 | 6 |
| *867* | A326 | 5c | ultra | 32 | 18 |
| *868* | A327 | 10c | dark brn | 1.75 | 1.40 |
| | | | *Nos. 864-868 (5)* | 2.41 | 1.80 |

### Educators

Horace Mann A328

Mark Hopkins A329

Charles W. Eliot A330

Frances E. Willard A331

Booker T. Washington — A332

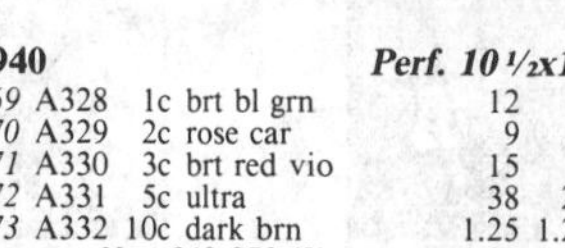

**1940** *Perf. 10½x11*

| No. | Design | Denom. | Color | Unused | Used |
|---|---|---|---|---|---|
| *869* | A328 | 1c | brt bl grn | 12 | 8 |
| *870* | A329 | 2c | rose car | 9 | 6 |
| *871* | A330 | 3c | brt red vio | 15 | 6 |
| *872* | A331 | 5c | ultra | 38 | 25 |
| *873* | A332 | 10c | dark brn | 1.25 | 1.25 |
| | | | *Nos. 869-873 (5)* | 1.99 | 1.70 |

### Scientists

John James Audubon A333

Dr. Crawford W. Long A334

Luther Burbank A335

Dr. Walter Reed A336

Jane Addams — A337

**1940** *Perf. 10½x11*

| No. | Design | Denom. | Color | Unused | Used |
|---|---|---|---|---|---|
| *874* | A333 | 1c | brt bl grn | 8 | 6 |
| *875* | A334 | 2c | rose car | 8 | 6 |
| *876* | A335 | 3c | brt red vio | 10 | 6 |
| *877* | A336 | 5c | ultra | 25 | 15 |
| *878* | A337 | 10c | dark brn | 1.05 | 95 |
| | | | *Nos. 874-878 (5)* | 1.56 | 1.28 |

### Composers

Stephen Collins Foster A338

John Philip Sousa A339

Victor Herbert A340

Edward MacDowell A341

Ethelbert Nevin — A342

**1940** *Perf. 10½x11*

| No. | Design | Denom. | Color | Unused | Used |
|---|---|---|---|---|---|
| *879* | A338 | 1c | brt bl grn | 7 | 6 |
| *880* | A339 | 2c | rose car | 9 | 6 |
| *881* | A340 | 3c | brt red vio | 10 | 6 |
| *882* | A341 | 5c | ultra | 35 | 22 |
| *883* | A342 | 10c | dark brn | 3.75 | 1.35 |
| | | | *Nos. 879-883 (5)* | 4.36 | 1.75 |

### Artists

Gilbert Charles Stuart A343

James A. McNeill Whistler A344

Augustus Saint-Gaudens A345

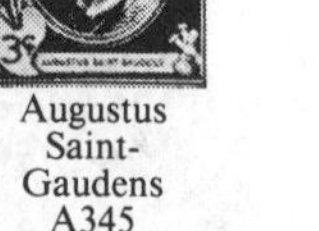

Daniel Chester French A346

Frederic Remington — A347

**1940** *Perf. 10½x11*

| No. | Design | Denom. | Color | Unused | Used |
|---|---|---|---|---|---|
| *884* | A343 | 1c | brt bl grn | 8 | 6 |
| *885* | A344 | 2c | rose car | 8 | 6 |
| *886* | A345 | 3c | brt red vio | 10 | 6 |
| *887* | A346 | 5c | ultra | 45 | 22 |
| *888* | A347 | 10c | dark brn | 1.65 | 1.40 |
| | | | *Nos. 884-888 (5)* | 2.36 | 1.80 |

### Inventors

Eli Whitney A348

Samuel F. B. Morse A349

Cyrus Hall McCormick A350

Elias Howe A351

Alexander Graham Bell — A352

**1940** *Perf. 10½x11*

| No. | Design | Denom. | Color | Unused | Used |
|---|---|---|---|---|---|
| *889* | A348 | 1c | brt bl grn | 12 | 8 |
| *890* | A349 | 2c | rose car | 12 | 6 |
| *891* | A350 | 3c | brt red vio | 25 | 6 |
| *892* | A351 | 5c | ultra | 1.00 | 32 |
| *893* | A352 | 10c | dark brn | 11.00 | 2.25 |
| | | | *Nos. 889-893 (5)* | 12.49 | 2.77 |
| | | | *Nos. 859-893 (35)* | 27.30 | 12.85 |

### Pony Express Issue

Pony Express Rider A353

**1940, Apr. 3** *Perf. 11x10½*

| | | | |
|---|---|---|---|
| *894* A353 3c henna brown | | 22 | 10 |

80th anniv. of the Pony Express.

### Pan American Union Issue

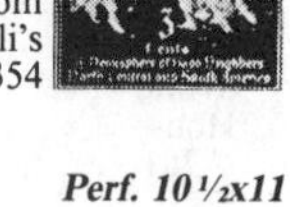

The Three Graces from Botticelli's "Spring" — A354

**1940, Apr. 14** *Perf. 10½x11*

| | | | |
|---|---|---|---|
| *895* A354 3c light violet | | 18 | 9 |

Pan American Union founding, 50th anniv.

### Idaho Statehood Issue

Idaho Capitol, Boise — A355

**1940, July 3** *Perf. 11x10½*

| | | | |
|---|---|---|---|
| *896* A355 3c bright violet | | 14 | 8 |

Idaho statehood, 50th anniv..

For unused stamps, more recent issues are valued as never hinged, with the beginning point determined on a country-by-country basis. Notes to show the beginning points are prominently placed in the text.

**Wyoming Statehood Issue**

Wyoming State Seal — A356

**1940, July 10** *Perf. 10½x11*

*897* A356 3c brown violet 14 8

Wyoming statehood, 50th anniv.

**Coronado Expedition Issue**

"Coronado and His Captains" Painted by Gerald Cassidy A357

**1940, Sept. 7** *Perf. 11x10½*

*898* A357 3c violet 14 8

400th anniv. of the Coronado Expedition.

**National Defense Issue**

Statue of Liberty — A358

90-millimeter Anti-aircraft Gun — A359

Torch of Enlightenment — A360

**1940, Oct. 16** *Perf. 11x10½*

| | | | |
|---|---|---|---|
| *899* A358 1c brt bl grn | | 5 | 5 |
| *a* | Vert. pair, imperf. btwn. | 500.00 | — |
| *b* | Horiz. pair, imperf. btwn. | 40.00 | — |
| *900* A359 2c rose carmine | | 6 | 5 |
| *a* | Horiz. pair, imperf. btwn. | 45.00 | — |
| *901* A360 3c bright violet | | 9 | 5 |
| *a* | Horiz. pair, imperf. btwn. | 25.00 | — |

**Thirteenth Amendment Issue**

"Emancipation," Statue of Lincoln and Slave, by Thomas Ball — A361

**1940, Oct. 20** *Perf. 10½x11*

*902* A361 3c deep violet 16 10

75th anniv. of the 13th Amendment to the Constitution.

**Vermont Statehood Issue**

Vermont Capitol, Montpelier A362

**1941, Mar. 4** *Perf. 11x10½*

*903* A362 3c light violet 14 8

Vermont statehood, 150th anniv.

**Kentucky Statehood Issue**

Daniel Boone and Three Frontiersmen, from Mural by Gilbert White A363

**1942, June 1** *Perf. 11x10½*

*904* A363 3c violet 10 9

Kentucky statehood, 150th anniv.

American Eagle A364

Lincoln, Sun Yat-sen and Map A365

**Win the War Issue**

**1942, July 4** *Perf. 11x10½*

| | | | |
|---|---|---|---|
| *905* A364 3c violet | | 8 | 5 |
| *b* | 3c purple | 20.00 | 8.00 |

**Chinese Resistance Issue**

**1942, July 7** *Perf. 11x10½*

*906* A365 5c bright blue 18 16

Five years' resistance of the Chinese people to Japanese aggression.

Allegory of Victory A366

Liberty Holding Torch of Freedom and Enlightenment A367

**Allied Nations Issue**

**1943, Jan. 14** *Perf. 11x10½*

*907* A366 2c rose carmine 8 5

**Four Freedoms Issue**

**1943, Feb. 12** *Perf. 11x10½*

*908* A367 1c bright bl grn 8 5

**Overrun Countries Issue**

Flag of Poland A368

Frames Engraved, Centers Offset Printing

**Flat Plate Printing**

| **1943-44** | **Unwmk.** | *Perf. 12* | |
|---|---|---|---|
| *909* A368 5c | Poland | 18 | 12 |
| *910* A368 5c | Czechoslovakia | 18 | 9 |
| *911* A368 5c | Norway | 14 | 7 |
| *912* A368 5c | Luxembourg | 14 | 7 |
| *913* A368 5c | Netherlands | 14 | 7 |
| *914* A368 5c | Belgium | 14 | 7 |
| *915* A368 5c | France | 14 | 7 |
| *916* A368 5c | Greece | 38 | 25 |
| *917* A368 5c | Yugoslavia | 28 | 15 |
| *918* A368 5c | Albania | 18 | 15 |
| *919* A368 5c | Austria | 18 | 15 |
| *920* A368 5c | Denmark | 18 | 15 |
| *921* A368 5c | Korea ('44) | 15 | 12 |
| | *Nos. 909-921 (13)* | 2.41 | 1.53 |

**Transcontinental Railroad Issue**

"Golden Spike Ceremony" Painting by John McQuarrie A369

**Engraved; Rotary Press Printing**

**1944, May 10** *Perf. 11x10½*

*922* A369 3c violet 15 5

75th anniv. of the completion of the first transcontinental railroad.

**Steamship Issue**

"Savannah" A370

**1944, May 22** *Perf. 11x10½*

*923* A370 3c violet 9 5

125th anniv. of the first steamship to cross the Atlantic Ocean.

**Telegraph Issue**

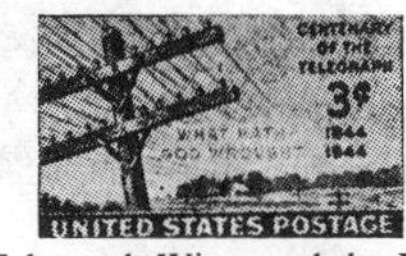


Telegraph Wires and the First Transmitted Words "What Hath God Wrought" A371

**1944, May 24** *Perf. 11x10½*

*924* A371 3c bright red violet 8 5

100th anniv. of the 1st message transmitted by telegraph.

**Philippines Issue**

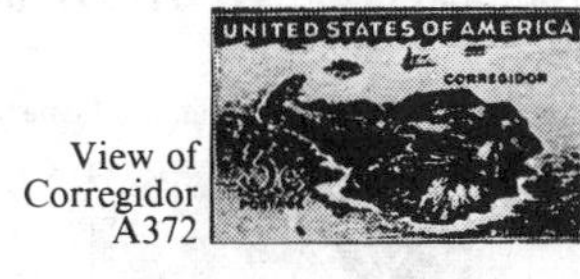


View of Corregidor A372

**1944, Sept. 27** *Perf. 11x10½*

*925* A372 3c deep violet 8 5

Final resistance of the US and Philippine defenders on Corregidor.

**Motion Picture Issue**

Motion Picture Showing for the Armed Forces in South Pacific A373

**1944, Oct. 31** *Perf. 11x10½*

*926* A373 3c deep violet 8 5

50th anniv. of motion pictures.

**Florida Statehood Issue**

Old Florida Seal, St. Augustine Gates and State Capitol A374

**1945, Mar. 3** *Perf. 11x10½*

*927* A374 3c bright red violet 8 5

Centenary of Florida statehood.

**United Nations Conference Issue**

A375

**1945, Apr. 25** *Perf. 11x10½*

*928* A375 5c ultramarine 8 5

United Nations conference, San Francisco.

**Iwo Jima (Marines) Issue**

Marines Raising the Flag on Mt. Suribachi, Iwo Jima — A376

**1945, July 11** *Perf. 10½x11*

*929* A376 3c yellow green 8 5

Achievements of the US Marines in WW II.

**Franklin D. Roosevelt Issue**

Roosevelt and Hyde Park Home — A377

Roosevelt and "Little White House," Warm Springs, Georgia A378

Roosevelt and White House A379

Roosevelt, Globe and Four Freedoms A380

**1945-46** *Perf. 11x10½*

| | | |
|---|---|---|
| *930* A377 1c blue green | 5 | 5 |
| *931* A378 2c carmine rose | 6 | 5 |
| *932* A379 3c purple | 6 | 5 |
| *933* A380 5c bright blue ('46) | 9 | 5 |

Franklin Delano Roosevelt (1882-1945).

**Army Issue**

US Troops Passing Arch of Triumph, Paris — A381

**1945, Sept. 28** *Perf. 11x10½*

*934* A381 3c olive 6 5

Achievements of the US Army in WW II.

**Navy Issue**

US Sailors A382

**1945, Oct. 27** *Perf. 11x10½*
*935* A382 3c blue 6 5

Achievements of the US Navy in WW II.

### Coast Guard Issue

Coast Guard Landing Craft and Supply Ship — A383

**1945, Nov. 10** *Perf. 11x10½*
*936* A383 3c bright bl grn 6 5

Achievements of the US Coast Guard in WW II.

Alfred E. Smith A384

US and Texas State Flags A385

### Alfred E. Smith Issue

**1945, Nov. 26** *Perf. 11x10½*
*937* A384 3c purple 6 5

Smith (1873-1944), governor of NY.

### Texas Statehood Issue

**1945, Dec. 29** *Perf. 11x10½*
*938* A385 3c dark blue 6 5

Texas statehood, 100th anniv.

Liberty Ship Unloading Cargo A386

Honorable Discharge Emblem A387

### Merchant Marine Issue

**1946, Feb. 26** *Perf. 11x10½*
*939* A386 3c blue green 6 5

Achievements of the US Merchant Marine in WW II.

### Veterans of World War II Issue

**1946, May 9** *Perf. 11x10½*
*940* A387 3c dark violet 6 5

Issued to honor all veterans of WW II.

### Tennessee Statehood Issue

Andrew Jackson, John Sevier and Tennessee Capitol A388

**1946, June 1** *Perf. 11x10½*
*941* A388 3c dark violet 6 5

Tennessee statehood, 150th anniv.

### Iowa Statehood Issue

Iowa State Flag and Map — A389

**1946, Aug. 3** *Perf. 11x10½*
*942* A389 3c deep blue 6 5

Iowa statehood, centenary.

### Smithsonian Institution Issue

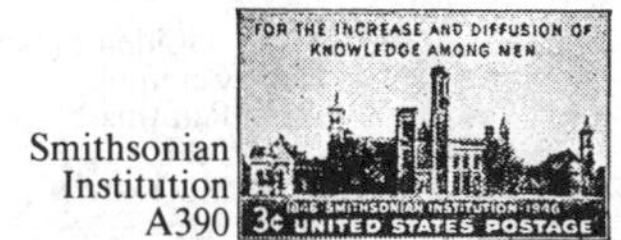


Smithsonian Institution A390

**1946, Aug. 10** *Perf. 11x10½*
*943* A390 3c violet brown 6 5

Centenary of the establishment of the Smithsonian Institution, Washington, DC.

### Kearny Expedition Issue

"Capture of Santa Fe" by Kenneth M. Chapman A391

**1946, Oct. 16** *Perf. 11x10½*
*944* A391 3c brown violet 6 5

Centenary of the entry of General Stephen Watts Kearny into Santa Fe.

### Thomas Alva Edison Issue

Thomas A. Edison, Birth Centenary — A392

**1947, Feb. 11** *Perf. 10½x11*
*945* A392 3c bright red vio 6 5

### Joseph Pulitzer Birth Centenary

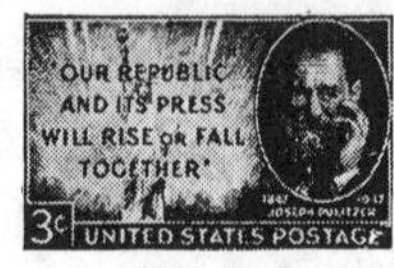


Joseph Pulitzer and Statue of Liberty A393

**1947, Apr. 10** *Perf. 11x10½*
*946* A393 3c purple 6 5

### Postage Stamp Centenary Issue

Washington and Franklin, Early and Modern Mail-carrying Vehicles A394

**1947, May 17** *Perf. 11x10½*
*947* A394 3c deep blue 6 5

Centenary of the 1st postage stamps issued by the US Government.

### Centenary International Philatelic Exhibition (CIPEX)

Souvenir Sheet

A395

### Flat Plate Printing

**1947, May 19** *Imperf.*
*948* A395 Sheet of two 65 45
*a* A1 5c blue 25 25
*b* A2 10c brown orange 30 30

Sheet inscribed below stamps: "100th Anniversary United States Postage Stamps" and in margins:

"Printed by the Treasury Department, Bureau of Engraving and Printing.—Under Authority of Robert E. Hannegan, Postmaster General.—In compliment to the Centenary International Philatelic Exhibition.—New York, N. Y., May 17-25, 1947."

Sheet size varies: 96-98x66-68mm

### Doctors Issue

"The Doctor," by Sir Luke Fildes — A396

### Rotary Press Printing

**1947, June 9** *Perf. 11x10½*
*949* A396 3c brown violet 6 5

Issued to honor the physicians of America.

### Utah Issue

Pioneers Entering the Valley of Great Salt Lake — A397

**1947, July 24** *Perf. 11x10½*
*950* A397 3c dark violet 6 5

Settlement of Utah, centenary.

### US Frigate Constitution Issue

Naval Architect's Drawing of Frigate Constitution A398

**1947, Oct. 21** *Perf. 11x10½*
*951* A398 3c blue green 6 5

150th anniv. of the launching of the US Frigate Constitution ("Old Ironsides").

Great White Heron and Map of Florida A399

Dr. George Washington Carver A400

### Everglades National Park Issue

**1947, Dec. 5** *Perf. 10½x11*
*952* A399 3c bright green 6 5

Dedication of Everglades Natl. Park, Florida, Dec. 6, 1947.

### Dr. George Washington Carver Issue

**1948, Jan. 5** *Perf. 10½x11*
*953* A400 3c bright red vio 6 5

5th anniv. of the death of Dr. George Washington Carver, scientist.

### California Gold Centennial Issue

Sutter's Mill, Coloma, California A401

**1948, Jan. 24** *Perf. 11x10½*
*954* A401 3c dark violet 6 5

Discovery of gold in California, centenary.

### Mississippi Territory Issue

Map, Seal and Gov. Winthrop Sargent A402

**1948, Apr. 7** *Perf. 11x10½*
*955* A402 3c brown violet 6 5

150th anniv. of the establishment of the Mississippi Territory.

### Four Chaplains Issue

Four Chaplains and Sinking S. S. Dorchester A403

**1948, May 28** *Perf. 11x10½*
*956* A403 3c gray black 6 5

Honoring George L. Fox, Clark V. Poling, John P. Washington and Alexander D. Goode, the four chaplains who sacrificed their lives in the sinking of the SS Dorchester, Feb. 3, 1943.

### Wisconsin Statehood Issue

Map on Scroll and State Capitol A404

**1948, May 29** *Perf. 11x10½*
*957* A404 3c dark violet 6 5

Wisconsin statehood, centenary.

### Swedish Pioneer Issue

Swedish Pioneer with Covered Wagon Moving Westward A405

**1948, June 4** *Perf. 11x10½*
*958* A405 5c deep blue 9 5

Centenary of the coming of the Swedish pioneers to the Middle West.

### Progress of Women Issue

Elizabeth Stanton, Carrie C. Catt and Lucretia Mott — A406

**1948, July 19** *Perf. 11x10½*
*959* A406 3c dark violet 6 5

Century of progress of American women.

### William Allen White Issue

William Allen White, Editor and Author — A407

**1948, July 31** *Perf. 10½x11*
*960* A407 3c bright red vio 6 6

### US-Canada Friendship Issue

Niagara Railway Suspension Bridge A408

**1948, Aug. 2** ***Perf. 11x10½***
*961* A408 3c blue 6 5

Century of friendship between the US and Canada.

### Francis Scott Key Issue

Key and American Flags of 1814 and 1948 — A409

**1948, Aug. 9** ***Perf. 11x10½***
*962* A409 3c rose pink 6 5

Francis Scott Key (1779-1843), Maryland lawyer and author of "The Star-Spangled Banner" (1813).

### Salute to Youth Issue

Girl and Boy Carrying Books — A410

**1948, Aug. 11** ***Perf. 11x10½***
*963* A410 3c deep blue 6 6

Youth of America and "Youth Month," Sept. 1948.

### Oregon Territory Issue

John McLoughlin, Jason Lee and Wagon on Oregon Trail — A411

**1948, Aug. 14** ***Perf. 11x10½***
*964* A411 3c brown red 6 5

Centenary of the establishment of Ore. Terr.

Chief Justice Harlan Fiske Stone — A412

Observatory, Palomar Mt., Cal. — A413

### Harlan Fiske Stone Issue

**1948, Aug. 25** ***Perf. 10½x11***
*965* A412 3c brt red vio 9 8

### Palomar Mountain Observatory Issue

**1948, Aug. 30** ***Perf. 10½x11***
*966* A413 3c blue 9 5
*a* Vert. pair, imperf btwn. *550.00*

### Clara Barton Issue

Clara Barton (1821-1912) and Cross — A414

**1948, Sept. 7** ***Perf. 11x10½***
*967* A414 3c rose pink 6 5

Founder of the American Red Cross (1882).

### Poultry Industry Issue

Light Brahma Rooster A415

**1948, Sept. 9** ***Perf. 11x10½***
*968* A415 3c sepia 6 5

Centenary of the establishment of the American poultry industry.

### Gold Star Mothers Issue

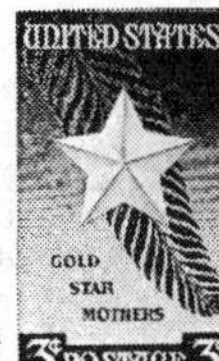


Star and Palm Frond — A416

**1948, Sept. 21** ***Perf. 10½x11***
*969* A416 3c orange yellow 6 5

Honoring mothers of deceased members of the US armed forces.

### Fort Kearny Issue

Fort Kearny and Pioneer Group A417

**1948, Sept. 22** ***Perf. 11x10½***
*970* A417 3c violet 6 5

Cent. of the establishment of Fort Kearny, Nebr.

### Volunteer Firemen Issue

Peter Stuyvesant; Early and Modern Fire Engines A418

**1948, Oct. 4** ***Perf. 11x10½***
*971* A418 3c brt rose car 6 5

300th anniv. of the organization of the 1st volunteer firemen in America by Peter Stuyvesant (1592-1672), Dutch colonial gov. of New Netherland.

### Indian Centennial Issue

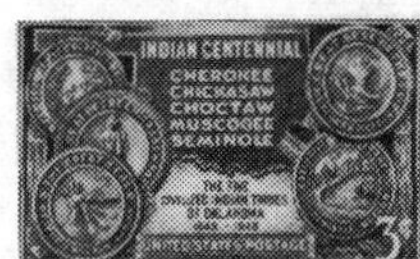


Map of Indian Territory and Seals of Five Tribes A419

**1948, Oct. 15** ***Perf. 11x10½***
*972* A419 3c dark brown 6 5

Cent. of the arrival in Indian Territory, later Okla., of the Five Civilized Indian Tribes.

### Rough Riders Issue

Statue of Capt. William O. (Bucky) O'Neill A420

**1948, Oct. 27** ***Perf. 11x10½***
*973* A420 3c violet brown 6 5

50th anniv. of the organization of the Rough Riders of the Spanish-American War.

Low and Girl Scout Emblem A421

Will Rogers A422

### Juliette Low Issue

**1948, Oct. 29** ***Perf. 11x10½***
*974* A421 3c blue green 6 5

Juliette Gordon Low (1860-1927), organizer of the Girl Scouts of America.

### Will Rogers Issue

**1948, Nov. 4** ***Perf. 10½x11***
*975* A422 3c brt red vio 6 5

Will Rogers, 1879-1935, humorist and political commentator.

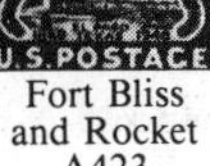


Fort Bliss and Rocket A423

Moina Michael and Poppy Plant A424

### Fort Bliss Centennial Issue

**1948, Nov. 5** ***Perf. 10½x11***
*976* A423 3c henna brown 9 5

Centenary of Fort Bliss, Texas.

### Moina Michael Issue

**1948, Nov. 9** ***Perf. 11x10½***
*977* A424 3c rose pink 6 5

Michael (1870-1944), educator who originated (1918) Flanders Field Poppy Day idea as memorial to war dead.

### Gettysburg Address Issue

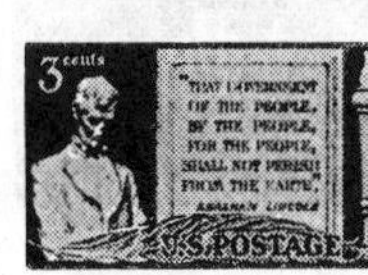


Lincoln and Quotation from Gettysburg Address A425

**1948, Nov. 19** ***Perf. 11x10½***
*978* A425 3c bright blue 6 5

85th anniv. of Abraham Lincoln's address at Gettysburg, Pa.

Torch and American Turners' Emblem A426

Joel Chandler Harris A427

### American Turners Issue

**1948, Nov. 20** ***Perf. 10½x11***
*979* A426 3c carmine 6 5

Centenary of the formation of the American Turners Society.

### Joel Chandler Harris Issue

**1948, Dec. 9** ***Perf. 10½x11***
*980* A427 3c brt red vio 6 5

Harris (1848-1908), editor and author.

### Minnesota Territory Issue

Pioneer and Red River Oxcart A428

**1949, Mar. 3** ***Perf. 11x10½***
*981* A428 3c blue green 6 5

Cent. of the establishment of Minn. Terr.

### Washington and Lee University Issue

George Washington, Robert E. Lee and University Building A429

**1949, Apr. 12** ***Perf. 11x10½***
*982* A429 3c ultramarine 6 5

200th anniv. of the founding of Washington and Lee Univ.

### Puerto Rico Election Issue.

Puerto Rican Farmer Holding Cogwheel and Ballot Box — A430

**1949, Apr. 27** ***Perf. 11x10½***
*983* A430 3c green 6 5

1st gubernatorial election in the Territory of P.R., Nov. 2, 1948.

### Annapolis Tercentenary Issue

Stoddert's 1718 Map of Regions about Annapolis, Redrawn A431

**1949, May 23** ***Perf. 11x10½***
*984* A431 3c aquamarine 6 5

300th anniv. of the founding of Annapolis, Md.

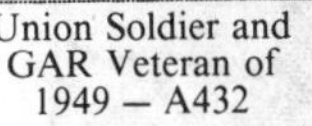


Union Soldier and GAR Veteran of 1949 — A432

Edgar Allan Poe — A433

### GAR Issue

**1949, Aug. 29** ***Perf. 11x10½***
*985* A432 3c brt rose car 6 5

Final encampment of the Grand Army of the Republic, Indianapolis, Aug. 28 to Sept. 1.

### Edgar Allan Poe Issue

**1949, Oct. 7** ***Perf. 10½x11***
*986* A433 3c brt red vio 6 5

Poe (1809-1849), writer and poet.

*United States stamps can be mounted in Scott's annually supplemented National and Minuteman Album.*

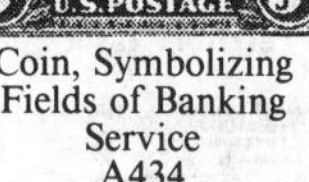

Coin, Symbolizing Fields of Banking Service
A434

Samuel Gompers
A435

### Bankers Issue

**1950, Jan. 3** ***Perf. 11x10½***
*987* A434 3c yellow green 6 5

75th anniv. of the formation of the American Bankers Assoc.

### Samuel Gompers Issue

**1950, Jan. 27** ***Perf. 10½x11***
*988* A435 3c brt red vio 6 5

Gompers (1850-1924), labor leader.

### National Capital Sesquicentennial Issue

Statue of Freedom on Capitol Dome
A436

Executive Mansion
A437

Supreme Court Building
A438

United States Capitol — A439

**1950** ***Perf. 10½x11, 11x10½***
*989* A436 3c bright blue 6 5
*990* A437 3c deep green 6 5
*991* A438 3c light violet 6 5
*992* A439 3c brt red vio 6 5

150th anniv. of the establishment of the National Capital, Washington, D.C. Issue dates: Apr. 20, June 12, Aug. 2 and Nov. 22.

### Railroad Engineers Issue

"Casey" Jones and Locomotives of 1900 and 1950 — A440

**1950, Apr. 29** ***Perf. 11x10½***
*993* A440 3c violet brown 6 5

Honoring the Railroad Engineers of America.

### Kansas City, Missouri, Issue

Kansas City Skyline, 1950 and Westport Landing, 1850 — A441

**1950, June 3** ***Perf. 11x10½***
*994* A441 3c violet 6 5

Cent. of the incorporation of Kansas City, Mo.

### Boy Scouts Issue

Three Boys, Statue of Liberty and Scout Badge — A442

**1950, June 30** ***Perf. 11x10½***
*995* A442 3c sepia 6 6

Honoring the BSA on the occasion of the 2nd Natl. Jamboree, held at Valley Forge, Pa.

### Indiana Territory Issue

Gov. William Henry Harrison and First Indiana Capitol, Vincennes
A443

**1950, July 4** ***Perf. 11x10½***
*996* A443 3c bright blue 6 5

150th anniv. of the establishment of Ind. Terr.

### California Statehood Issue

Gold Miner, Pioneers and S.S. *Oregon*
A444

**1950, Sept. 9** ***Perf. 11x10½***
*997* A444 3c yellow orange 6 5

California statehood, centenary.

### United Confederate Veterans Final Reunion Issue.

Confederate Soldier and United Confederate Veteran
A445

**1951, May 30** ***Perf. 11x10½***
*998* A445 3c gray 6 5

Final reunion of the United Confederate Veterans, Norfolk, Va, May 30, 1951.

### Nevada Centennial Issue

Carson Valley, c. 1851
A446

**1951, July 14** ***Perf. 11x10½***
*999* A446 3c light olive grn 6 5

Centenary of the settlement of Nevada.

### Landing of Cadillac Issue

Detroit Skyline and Cadillac Landing
A447

**1951, July 24** ***Perf. 11x10½***
*1000* A447 3c blue 6 5

250th anniv. of the landing of Antoine de la Mothe Cadillac at Detroit.

### Colorado Statehood Issue

Colorado Capitol and Mount of the Holy Cross — A448

**1951, Aug. 1** ***Perf. 11x10½***
*1001* A448 3c blue violet 6 5

Colorado statehood, 75th anniv. Design includes columbine and statue, "The Bronco Buster", by A. Phimister Proctor.

### American Chemical Society Issue

A. C. S. Emblem and Symbols of Chemistry
A449

**1951, Sept. 4** ***Perf. 11x10½***
*1002* A449 3c violet brown 6 5

American Chemical Soc., 75th anniv.

### Battle of Brooklyn Issue

Gen. George Washington Evacuating Army — A450

**1951, Dec. 10** ***Perf. 11x10½***
*1003* A450 3c violet 7 5

175th anniv. of the Battle of Brooklyn. Design includes Fulton Ferry House.

### Betsy Ross Issue

Betsy Ross Showing Flag to Gen. George Washington, Robert Morris and George Ross — A451

**1952, Jan. 2** ***Perf. 11x10½***
*1004* A451 3c carmine rose 7 5

200th anniv. of the birth of Betsy Ross, maker of the 1st American flag.

### 4-H Club Issue

Farm, Club Emblem, Boy and Girl — A452

**1952, Jan. 15** ***Perf. 11x10½***
*1005* A452 3c blue green 6 5

Issued to honor the 4-H Club movement.

### B. & O. Railroad Issue.

Charter and Three Stages of Rail Transportation — A453

**1952, Feb. 28** ***Perf. 11x10½***
*1006* A453 3c bright blue 7 5

125th anniv. of the granting of a charter to the Baltimore and Ohio Railroad Company by the Maryland Legislature.

### A. A. A. Issue

School Girls and Safety Patrolman, Automobiles of 1902 and 1952 — A454

**1952, Mar. 4** ***Perf. 11x10½***
*1007* A454 3c deep blue 6 5

50th anniv. of the formation of the American Automobile Association.

Torch of Liberty and Globe
A455

Spillway, Grand Coulee Dam
A456

### NATO Issue

**1952, Apr. 4** ***Perf. 11x10½***
*1008* A455 3c deep violet 6 5

3rd anniv. of the signing of the North Atlantic Treaty.

### Grand Coulee Dam Issue

**1952, May 15** ***Perf. 11x10½***
*1009* A456 3c blue green 6 5

50 years of Federal cooperation in developing the resources of rivers and streams in the West.

### Lafayette Issue

Marquis de Lafayette, Flags, Cannon and Landing Party — A457

**1952, June 13** ***Perf. 11x10½***
*1010* A457 3c bright blue 6 5

175th anniv. of the arrival of Lafayette in America.

### Mt. Rushmore Memorial Issue

Sculptured Heads on Mt. Rushmore — A458

**1952, Aug. 11** ***Perf. 10½x11***
*1011* A458 3c blue green 6 5

25th anniv. of the dedication of the Mt. Rushmore Natl. Memorial.

### Engineering Centennial Issue

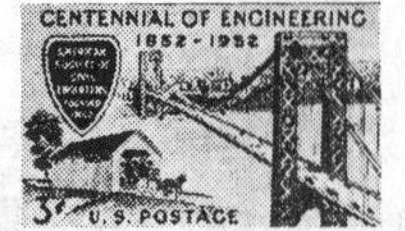

George Washington Bridge and Covered Bridge of 1850's
A459

**1952, Sept. 6** ***Perf. 11x10½***
*1012* A459 3c violet blue 6 5

Centenary of the founding of the American Soc. of Civil Engineers.

### Service Women Issue

Women of the Marine Corps, Army, Navy and Air Force — A460

**1952, Sept. 11** ***Perf. 11x10½***
*1013* A460 3c deep blue 6 5

Honoring the women in the US Armed Services.

### Gutenberg Bible Issue

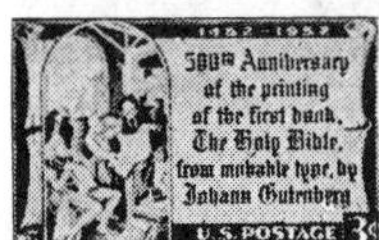


Gutenberg Showing Proof to the Elector of Mainz A461

**1952, Sept. 30** ***Perf. 11x10½***
*1014* A461 3c violet 6 5

500th anniv. of the printing of the 1st book, the Holy Bible, from movable type, by Johann Gutenberg.

### Newspaper Boys Issue.

Newspaper Boy, Torch and Group of Homes A462

**1952, Oct. 4** ***Perf. 11x10½***
*1015* A462 3c violet 6 5

Honor the newspaper boys of America.

### Red Cross Issue

Globe, Sun and Cross — A463

***Perf. 11x10½***
**1952, Nov. 21** **Cross Typo.**
*1016* A463 3c dp bl & car 6 5

Honoring the Intl. Red Cross.

### National Guard Issue

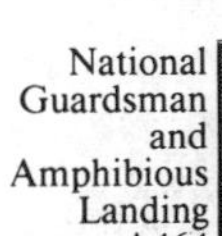

National Guardsman and Amphibious Landing A464

**1953, Feb. 23** ***Perf. 11x10½***
*1017* A464 3c bright blue 6 5

Honor the Natl. Guard of the US.

### Ohio Statehood Issue

Map and Ohio State Seal — A465

**1953, Mar. 2** ***Perf. 11x10½***
*1018* A465 3c chocolate 6 5

Ohio statehood, sesquicentennial.

### Washington Territory Issue.

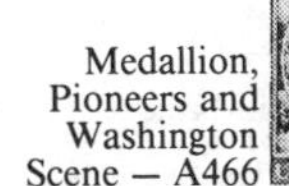

Medallion, Pioneers and Washington Scene — A466

**1953, Mar. 2** ***Perf. 11x10½***
*1019* A466 3c green 6 5

Centenary of the organization of Washington Territory.

### Louisiana Purchase Issue

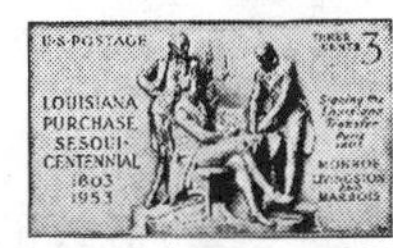


Monroe, Livingston and Barbé-Marbois — A467

**1953, Apr. 30** ***Perf. 11x10½***
*1020* A467 3c violet brown 6 5

Louisiana Purchase, 150th anniv.

### Opening of Japan Centennial Issue.

Commodore Perry and 1st Anchorage off Tokyo Bay — A468

**1953, July 14** ***Perf. 11x10½***
*1021* A468 5c green 9 5

Cent. of Commodore Matthew Calbraith Perry's negotiations with Japan, which opened her doors to foreign trade.

### American Bar Association Issue

Section of Frieze, Supreme Court Room A469

**1953, Aug. 24** ***Perf. 11x10½***
*1022* A469 3c rose violet 6 5

75th anniv. of the formation of the American Bar Assoc.

### Sagamore Hill Issue

Home of Theodore Roosevelt A470

**1953, Sept. 14** ***Perf. 11x10½***
*1023* A470 3c yellow green 6 5

Opening of Sagamore Hill, Theodore Roosevelt's home, as a national shrine.

### Future Farmers Issue

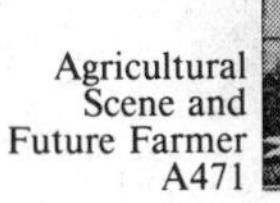

Agricultural Scene and Future Farmer A471

**1953, Oct. 13** ***Perf. 11x10½***
*1024* A471 3c deep blue 6 5

25th anniv. of the organization of Future Farmers of America.

### Trucking Industry Issue.

Truck, Farm and Distant City — A472

**1953, Oct. 27** ***Perf. 11x10½***
*1025* A472 3c violet 6 5

50th anniv. of the Trucking Industry in the US.

### General Patton Issue

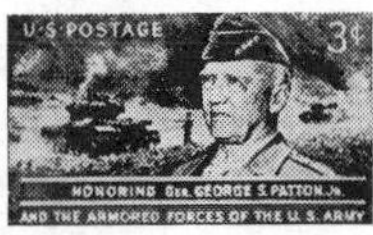


Gen. George S. Patton, Jr., and Tank in Action A473

**1953, Nov. 11** ***Perf. 11x10½***
*1026* A473 3c blue violet 7 5

Honoring Patton and the armored forces of the US army.

### New York City Issue

Dutch Ship in New Amsterdam Harbor A474

**1953, Nov. 20** ***Perf. 11x10½***
*1027* A474 3c bright red vio 6 5

300th anniv. of the founding of New York City.

### Gadsden Purchase Issue

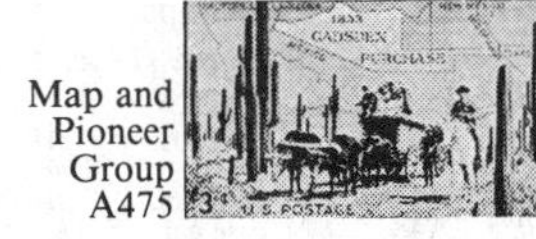

Map and Pioneer Group A475

**1953, Dec. 30** ***Perf. 11x10½***
*1028* A475 3c copper brown 7 5

Centenary of James Gadsden's purchase of territory from Mexico, to adjust US-Mexico boundary.

### Columbia University Issue

Low Memorial Library A476

**1954, Jan. 4** ***Perf. 11x10½***
*1029* A476 3c blue 6 5

Columbia Univ., 200th anniv.

---

Wet and Dry Printings

In 1953 the Bureau of Engraving and Printing began experiments in printing on "dry" paper (moisture content 5-10 per cent). In previous "wet" printings the paper had a moisture content of 13-35 per cent.

The new process required a thicker, stiffer paper, special types of inks and greater pressure to force the paper into the recessed plates. The "dry" printings show whiter paper, a higher sheen on the surface, feel thicker and stiffer, and the designs stand out more clearly than on the "wet" printings.

Nos. 832c and 1041 (flat plate) were the first "dry" printings to be issued of flat-plate, regular-issue stamps. No. 1063 was the first rotary-press stamp to be produced entirely by "dry" printing.

All postage stamps have been printed by the "dry" process since the late 1950's.

See Scott's Specialized Catalogue of United States Stamps for listings of the wet and dry printings.

---

### Liberty Issue

Franklin A477

Washington A478

Palace of the Governors, Santa Fe A478a

Mount Vernon A479

Thomas Jefferson A480

Bunker Hill Monument, Mass. Flag, 1776 A481

Statue of Liberty A482

Abraham Lincoln A483

The Hermitage A484

James Monroe A485

Theodore Roosevelt A486

Woodrow Wilson A487

Statue of Liberty
A488 A489

John J. Pershing A489a

The Alamo A490

Independence Hall — A491

Statue of Liberty A491a

Benjamin Harrison A492

John Jay A493

Monticello A494

Paul Revere A495

Robert E. Lee A496

John Marshall A497

Susan B. Anthony A498

Patrick Henry A499

Alexander Hamilton A500

***Perf. 11x10½, 10½x11***

**1954-68 Rotary Press Printing**

| | | | | |
|---|---|---|---|---|
| *1030* | A477 | ½c red org ('55) | 5 | 5 |
| *1031* | A478 | 1c dark grn | 5 | 5 |
| *1031A* | A478a | 1¼c turq ('60) | 5 | 5 |
| *1032* | A479 | 1½c brn car ('56) | 7 | 5 |
| *1033* | A480 | 2c car rose | 5 | 5 |
| *1034* | A481 | 2½c gray bl ('59) | 6 | 5 |
| *1035* | A482 | 3c deep vio | 6 | 5 |
| *a* | | Booklet pane of 6 | 3.00 | *50* |
| *b* | | Tagged ('66) | 25 | 20 |
| *c* | | Vert. pair, imperf. | *1,500.* | |
| *d* | | Horiz. pair, imperf. btwn. | *800.00* | |
| *1036* | A483 | 4c red violet | 7 | 5 |
| *a* | | Booklet pane of 6 ('58) | 2.25 | *50* |
| *b* | | Tagged ('63) | 48 | 16 |
| *1037* | A484 | 4½c bl grn ('59) | 8 | 5 |
| *1038* | A485 | 5c deep blue | 10 | 5 |
| *1039* | A486 | 6c car ('55) | 25 | 5 |
| *1040* | A487 | 7c rose car ('56) | 20 | 5 |

**Flat Plate or Rotary Press Printing**

***Perf. 11***

| | | | | |
|---|---|---|---|---|
| *1041* | A488 | 8c dk vio bl & car | 24 | 6 |
| *a* | | Carmine double impression | *750.00* | |

**Giori Press Printing**

**Redrawn Design**

| | | | | |
|---|---|---|---|---|
| *1042* | A489 | 8c dk vio bl & car rose ('58) | 25 | 5 |

**Rotary Press Printing**

***Perf. 11x10½, 10½x11***

| | | | | |
|---|---|---|---|---|
| *1042A* | A489a | 8c brown ('61) | 22 | 5 |
| *1043* | A490 | 9c rose lil ('56) | 28 | 5 |
| *1044* | A491 | 10c rose lake ('56) | 22 | 5 |
| *b* | | Tagged ('66) | 1.20 | 1.10 |

**Giori Press Printing**

***Perf. 11***

| | | | | |
|---|---|---|---|---|
| *1044A* | A491a | 11c car & dk vio bl ('61) | 30 | 6 |
| *c* | | Tagged ('67) | 1.75 | 1.25 |

**Rotary Press Printing**

***Perf. 11x10½, 10½x11***

| | | | | |
|---|---|---|---|---|
| *1045* | A492 | 12c red ('59) | 32 | 5 |
| *a* | | Tagged ('68) | 48 | 15 |
| *1046* | A493 | 15c rose lake ('58) | 95 | 5 |
| *a* | | Tagged ('66) | 80 | 22 |
| *1047* | A494 | 20c ultra ('56) | 50 | 5 |
| *1048* | A495 | 25c green ('58) | 1.50 | 5 |
| *1049* | A496 | 30c black ('55) | 1.20 | 5 |
| *1050* | A497 | 40c brn red ('55) | 1.90 | 6 |
| *1051* | A498 | 50c brt pur ('55) | 1.75 | 5 |
| *1052* | A499 | $1 pur ('55) | 5.75 | 6 |

**Flat Plate Printing**

***Perf. 11***

| | | | | |
|---|---|---|---|---|
| *1053* | A500 | $5 black ('56) | 75.00 | 6.75 |
| | | *Nos. 1030-1053 (27)* | 91.47 | 8.09 |

Luminescence

During 1963 quantities of certain issues (Nos. C64a, 1213b, 1213c and 1229a) were overprinted with phosphorescent coating, "tagged," for use in testing automated facing and canceling machines. Listings for tagged varieties of stamps previously issued without tagging start with Nos. 1035b and C59a.

The entire printings of Nos. 1238, 1278, 1280-1281, 1283B, 1286-1288, 1298-1305, 1323-1340, 1342-1362, 1364, and C69-C75 and all following listings, unless otherwise noted, were tagged.

Stamps tagged with zinc orthosilicate glow yellow green. Airmail stamps with calcium silicate overprint glow orange red. Both tagging overprints are activated only by shortwave ultraviolet light.

Coil Stamps

***Perf. 10 Vert., Horiz. (1¼c, 4½c)***

**1954-73**

| | | | | |
|---|---|---|---|---|
| *1054* | A478 | 1c dark grn | 18 | 12 |
| *b* | | Imperf., pair | *2,000.* | — |
| *1054A* | A478a | 1¼c turq ('60) | 18 | 12 |
| *1055* | A480 | 2c rose car | 8 | 5 |
| *a* | | Tagged ('68) | 5 | 5 |
| *b* | | Imperf., pair (Bureau precanceled) | | *325.00* |
| *c* | | As "a," imperf. pair | *350.00* | |
| *1056* | A481 | 2½c gray bl ('59) | 38 | 25 |
| *1057* | A482 | 3c deep vio | 10 | 5 |
| *a* | | Imperf., pair | *750.00* | — |
| *b* | | Tagged ('66) | 50 | 25 |
| *1058* | A483 | 4c red vio ('58) | 12 | 5 |
| *a* | | Imperf., pair | 95.00 | 95.00 |
| *1059* | A484 | 4½c bl grn ('59) | 1.75 | 1.20 |
| *1059A* | A495 | 25c green ('65) | 50 | 30 |
| *b* | | Tagged ('73) | 45 | 20 |
| *c* | | Imperf., pair | *55.00* | |
| | | *Nos. 1054-1059A (8)* | 3.29 | 2.14 |

**Nebraska Territory Issue.**

Mitchell Pass, Scotts Bluff and "The Sower," by Lee Lawrie A507

**1954, May 7** ***Perf. 11x10½***

*1060* A507 3c violet 6 5

Centenary of the establishment of the Nebraska Territory.

**Kansas Territory Issue**

Wheat Field and Pioneer Wagon Train A508

**1954, May 31** ***Perf. 11x10½***

*1061* A508 3c brown orange 6 5

Centenary of the establishment of the Kansas Territory.

**George Eastman Issue**

George Eastman (1854-1932), Inventor and Philanthropist — A509

**1954, July 12** ***Perf. 10½x11***

*1062* A509 3c violet brown 6 5

**Lewis and Clark Exped. Sesquicentennial**

Landing of Lewis and Clark — A510

**1954, July 28** ***Perf. 11x10½***

*1063* A510 3c violet brown 6 5

**Pennsylvania Acad. of the Fine Arts**

Charles Willson Peale in his Museum, Self-portrait — A511

**1955, Jan. 15** ***Perf. 10½x11***

*1064* A511 3c violet brown 6 5

150th anniv. of the founding of the Pa. Acad. of the Fine Arts, Philadelphia.

**Land Grant Colleges Issue.**

Open Book and Symbols of Subjects Taught A512

**1955, Feb. 12** ***Perf. 11x10½***

*1065* A512 3c green 6 5

Cent. of the founding of Mich. State College and Penn. State Univ., 1st of the land-grant institutions.

**Rotary International Issue**

Torch, Globe and Rotary Emblem A513

**1955, Feb. 23** ***Perf. 11x10½***

*1066* A513 8c deep blue 15 5

Rotary Intl., 50th anniv.

**Armed Forces Reserve Issue**

Marine, Coast Guard, Army, Navy, and Air Force Personnel A514

**1955, May 21** ***Perf. 11x10½***

*1067* A514 3c purple 6 5

Honoring the Armed Forces Reserve.

**New Hampshire Issue**

Great Stone Face — A515

**1955, June 21** ***Perf. 10½x11***

*1068* A515 3c green 6 5

Honor NH on the occasion of the sesquicentennial of the discovery of the "Old Man of the Mountains."

**Soo Locks Issue**

Map of Great Lakes and Two Steamers A516

**1955, June 28** ***Perf. 11x10½***

*1069* A516 3c blue 6 5

Centenary of the opening of the Soo Locks.

**Atoms for Peace Issue**

Atomic Energy Encircling the Hemispheres A517

**1955, July 28** ***Perf. 11x10½***

*1070* A517 3c deep blue 8 5

Promoting an Atoms for Peace policy.

**Fort Ticonderoga Issue**

Map of the Fort, Ethan Allen and Artillery A518

**1955, Sept. 18** ***Perf. 11x10½***

*1071* A518 3c light brown 6 5

Bicentenary of Fort Ticonderoga.

**Andrew W. Mellon Issue**

Andrew W. Mellon — A519

**1955, Dec. 20** ***Perf. 10½x11***

*1072* A519 3c rose carmine 6 5

Mellon, US Sec. of the Treasury (1921-32), financier and art collector.

**Benjamin Franklin Issue**

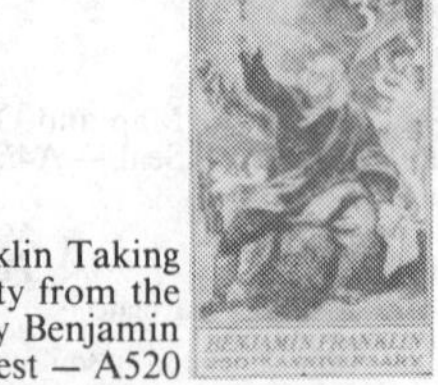
"Franklin Taking Electricity from the Sky," by Benjamin West — A520

**1956, Jan. 17** *Perf. 10½x11*
*1073* A520 3c bright carmine 6 5

250th anniv. of the birth of Franklin.

### Booker T. Washington Issue

Log Cabin — A521

**1956, Apr. 5** *Perf. 11x10½*
*1074* A521 3c deep blue 6 5

Washington (1856-1915), black educator.

### Fifth Intl. Phil. Exhib. Issues
Souvenir Sheet

A522

### Flat Plate Printing

**1956, Apr. 28** *Imperf.*
*1075* A522 Sheet of two 2.25 2.00
*a.* A482 3c deep violet 90 80
*b.* A488 8c dark violet blue & carmine 1.25 1.00

No. 1075 measures 108x73mm; Nos. 1075a and 1075b measure 24x28mm. Below the stamps appears the signature of Arthur E. Summerfield, Postmaster General of the US. Marginal inscription reads: "In compliment to 5th International Philatelic Exhibition, 1956. New York, N. Y. Apr. 28-May 6."
Inscriptions printed in dark violet blue; scrolls and stars in carmine.

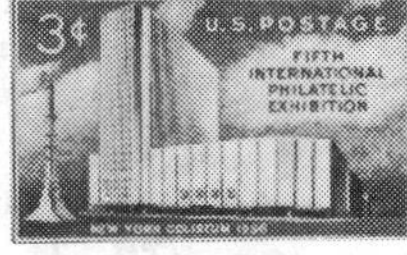

New York Coliseum and Columbus Monument A523

### Rotary Press Printing

**1956, Apr. 30** *Perf. 11x10½*
*1076* A523 3c deep violet 6 5

FIPEX, New York City, Apr. 28-May 6.

### Wildlife Conservation Issue

Wild Turkey A524

Pronghorn Antelope A525

King Salmon A526

**1956** *Perf. 11x10½*
*1077* A524 3c rose lake 6 5
*1078* A525 3c brown 6 5
*1079* A526 3c blue green 6 5

Emphasizing the importance of Wildlife conservation in America.
Issued May 5, June 22 and Nov. 9.
See Nos. 1098, 1392.

### Pure Food and Drug Laws Issue

Harvey W. Wiley — A527

**1956, June 27** *Perf. 10½x11*
*1080* A527 3c dark blue green 6 5

50th anniv. of the passage of the laws.

### Wheatland Issue

President Buchanan's Home, "Wheatland," Lancaster, Pa. — A528

**1956, Aug. 5** *Perf. 11x10½*
*1081* A528 3c black brown 6 5

### Labor Day Issue

Mosaic, AFL-CIO Headquarters — A529

**1956, Sept. 3** *Perf. 10½x11*
*1082* A529 3c deep blue 6 5

### Nassau Hall Issue

Nassau Hall, Princeton, NJ — A530

**1956, Sept. 22** *Perf. 11x10½*
*1083* A530 3c blk, *org* 6 5

200th anniv. of Nassau Hall, Princeton University.

### Devils Tower Issue

Devils Tower — A531

**1956, Sept. 24** *Perf. 10½x11*
*1084* A531 3c violet 6 5

50th anniv. of the Federal law providing for protection of American natural antiquities. Devils Tower Natl. Monument, Wyoming, is an outstanding example.

### Children's Issue

Children of the World A532

**1956, Dec. 15** *Perf. 11x10½*
*1085* A532 3c dark blue 6 5

Promoting friendship among the world's children.

### Alexander Hamilton Issue

Alexander Hamilton (1757-1804) and Federal Hall — A533

**1957, Jan. 11** *Perf. 11x10½*
*1086* A533 3c rose red 6 5

### Polio Issue

Allegory — A534

**1957, Jan. 15** *Perf. 10½x11*
*1087* A534 3c red lilac 6 5

Honoring "those who helped fight polio," and 20th anniv. of the Natl. Foundation for Infantile Paralysis and the March of Dimes.

### Coast and Geodetic Survey Issue

Flag of Coast and Geodetic Survey and Ships at Sea — A535

**1957, Feb. 11** *Perf. 11x10½*
*1088* A535 3c dark blue 6 5

150th anniv. of the establishment of the Coast and Geodetic Survey.

### Architects Issue

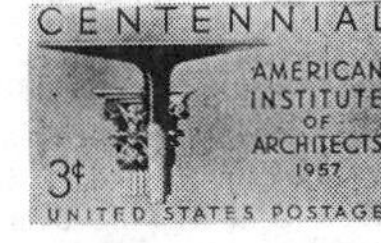

Corinthian Capital and Mushroom Type Head and Shaft — A536

**1957, Feb. 23** *Perf. 11x10½*
*1089* A536 3c red lilac 6 5

Centenary of the American Institute of Architects.

### Steel Industry Issue

American Eagle and Pouring Ladle — A537

**1957, May 22** *Perf. 10½x11*
*1090* A537 3c bright ultra 6 5

Centenary of the steel industry in America.

### International Naval Review Issue

Aircraft Carrier and Jamestown Festival Emblem A538

**1957, June 10** *Perf. 11x10½*
*1091* A538 3c blue green 6 5

Intl. Naval Review and Jamestown Festival.

### Oklahoma Statehood Issue

Map of Oklahoma, Arrow and Atom Diagram A539

**1957, June 14** *Perf. 11x10½*
*1092* A539 3c dark blue 6 5

Oklahoma statehood, 50th anniv.

### School Teachers Issue

Teacher and Pupils — A540

**1957, July 1** *Perf. 11x10½*
*1093* A540 3c rose lake 6 5

Honoring the school teachers of America.

### Flag Issue

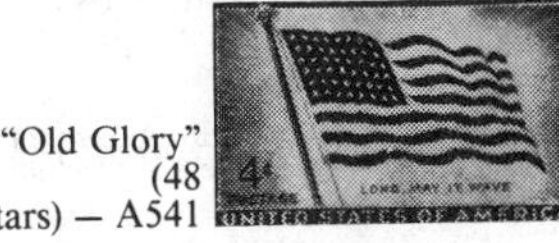

"Old Glory" (48 Stars) — A541

### Giori Press Printing

**1957, July 4** *Perf. 11*
*1094* A541 4c dk bl & dp car 7 5

"Virginia of Sagadahock" and Seal of Maine A542

Ramon Magsaysay A543

### Shipbuilding Issue
### Rotary Press Printing

**1957, Aug. 15** *Perf. 10½x11*
*1095* A542 3c deep violet 6 5

350th anniv. of shipbuilding in America.

### Champion of Liberty Issue
### Giori Press Printing

**1957, Aug. 31** *Perf. 11*
*1096* A543 8c car, ultra & ocher 15 8

Ramon Magsaysay (1907-1957), Philippines Pres..

Marquis de Lafayette A544

Whooping Cranes A545

**Lafayette Bicentenary Issue**
**Rotary Press Printing**

**1957, Sept. 6** ***Perf. 10½x11***
*1097* A544 3c rose lake 6 5

Bicentenary of the birth of Lafayette.

**Wildlife Conservation Issue**
**Giori Press Printing**

**1957, Nov. 22** ***Perf. 11***
*1098* A545 3c bl, ocher & grn 6 5

Emphasizing the importance of Wildlife Conservation in America.

Bible, Hat and Quill Pen A546

"Bountiful Earth" A547

**Religious Freedom Issue**
**Rotary Press Printing**

**1957, Dec. 27** ***Perf. 10½x11***
*1099* A546 3c black 6 5

Flushing Remonstrance, 300th anniv.

**Gardening-Horticulture Issue**

**1958, Mar. 15**
*1100* A547 3c green 6 5

Garden clubs of America and cent. of the birth of Liberty Hyde Bailey, horticulturist.

**Brussels Fair Issue**

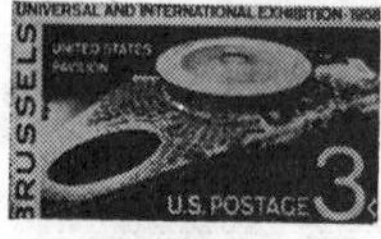

US Pavilion at Brussels A551

**Rotary Press Printing**

**1958, Apr. 17** ***Perf. 11x10½***
*1104* A551 3c deep claret 6 5

Opening of the Universal and Intl. Exhib., Brussels, Apr. 17.

**James Monroe Issue**

James Monroe, by Gilbert Stuart — A552

**1958, Apr. 28** ***Perf. 11x10½***
*1105* A552 3c purple 6 5

Monroe (1758-1831), 5th pres. of the US.

**Minnesota Statehood Issue**

Minnesota Lakes and Pines — A553

**Rotary Press Printing**

**1958, May 11**
*1106* A553 3c green 6 5

Minnesota statehood, centenary.

The Scott Catalogue value is a retail price, what you could expect to pay for the stamp in a grade of Fine-Very Fine. The value listed is a reference which reflects recent actual dealer selling price.

**Geophysical Year Issue**

Solar Disc and Hands from Michelangelo's "Creation of Adam" A554

**Giori Press Printing**

**1958, May 31** ***Perf. 11***
*1107* A554 3c blk & red org 6 5

IGY, 1957-58.

**Gunston Hall Issue**

Gunston Hall, Virginia A555

**Rotary Press Printing**

**1958, June 12** ***Perf. 11x10½***
*1108* A555 3c light green 6 5

Bicent. of Gunston Hall and honoring George Mason, author of the Constitution of Va. and the Va. Bill of Rights.

Mackinac Bridge A556

Simon Bolivar A557

**Mackinac Bridge Issue**

**1958, June 25** ***Perf. 10½x11***
*1109* A556 3c brt grnsh bl 6 5

Dedication of Mackinac Bridge, Mich.

**Champion of Liberty Issue**
**Rotary Press Printing**

**1958, July 24** ***Perf. 10½x11***
*1110* A557 4c olive bister 7 5

**Giori Press Printing**
***Perf. 11***

*1111* A557 8c car, ultra & ocher 15 8

Simon Bolivar, So. American freedom fighter.

**Atlantic Cable Centennial Issue**

Neptune, Globe and Mermaid A558

**Rotary Press Printing**

**1958, Aug. 15** ***Perf. 11x10½***
*1112* A558 4c redsh purple 8 5

Centenary of the Atlantic Cable, linking the Eastern and Western hemispheres.

**Lincoln Sesquicentennial Issue**

Lincoln, by George Healy A559

Lincoln, by Gutzon Borglum A560

Abraham Lincoln and Stephen A. Douglas Debating A561

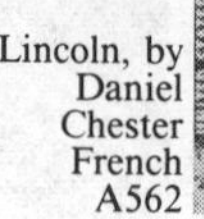

Lincoln, by Daniel Chester French A562

**1958-59** ***Perf. 10½x11, 11x10½***
*1113* A559 1c green ('59) 5 5
*1114* A560 3c purple ('59) 6 5
*1115* A561 4c sepia 8 5
*1116* A562 4c dark blue ('59) 8 5

No. 1114 also commemorates the cent. of the founding of Cooper Union, NYC. No. 1115 also commemorates the cent. of the Lincoln-Douglas debates.

Issue dates: Nos. 1113, 1114, 1116, Feb. 12, Feb. 27 and May 30. No. 1115, Aug. 27.

Lajos Kossuth, (1802-1892) A563

Early Press and Hand Holding Quill A564

**Champion of Liberty Issue**
**Rotary Press Printing**

**1958, Sept. 19** ***Perf. 10½x11***
*1117* A563 4c green 8 5

**Giori Press Printing**
***Perf. 11***

*1118* A563 8c car, ultra & ocher 16 8

Kossuth, Hungarian freedom fighter.

**Freedom of Press Issue**
**Rotary Press Printing**

**1958, Sept. 22** ***Perf. 10½x11***
*1119* A564 4c black 8 5

Honoring journalism and freedom of the press in connection with the 50th anniv. of the 1st School of Journalism at the Univ. of Mo.

**Overland Mail Issue**

Mail Coach and Map of Southwest US — A565

**1958, Oct. 10** ***Perf. 11x10½***
*1120* A565 4c crimson rose 8 5

Centenary of overland mail service.

Noah Webster A566

Forest Scene A567

**Noah Webster Issue**

**1958, Oct. 16** ***Perf. 10½x11***
*1121* A566 4c dk car rose 8 5

Webster (1758-1843), lexicographer.

**Forest Conservation Issue**
**Giori Press Printing**

**1958, Oct. 27** ***Perf. 11***
*1122* A567 4c grn, yel & brn 8 5

Publicizing forest conservation and the protection of natural resources and honoring Theodore Roosevelt, a leading forest conservationist, on the cent. of his birth.

**Fort Duquesne Issue**

Occupation of Fort Duquesne A568

**Rotary Press Printing**

**1958, Nov. 25** ***Perf. 11x10½***
*1123* A568 4c blue 8 5

Bicentennial of Fort Duquesne (Fort Pitt).

**Oregon Statehood Issue**

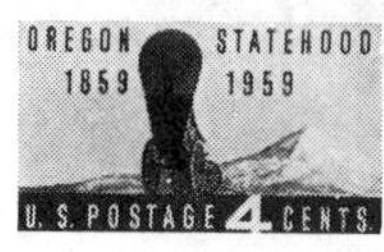

Covered Wagon and Mt. Hood — A569

**1959, Feb. 14** ***Perf. 11x10½***
*1124* A569 4c blue green 8 5

Oregon statehood, centenary.

José de San Martin — A570

NATO Emblem — A571

**Champion of Liberty Issue**
**Rotary Press Printing**

**1959, Feb. 25** ***Perf. 10½x11***
*1125* A570 4c blue 8 5
*a* Horiz. pair, imperf. btwn. *1,100.*

**Giori Press Printing**
***Perf. 11***

*1126* A570 8c car, ultra & ocher 16 8

San Martin, So. American soldier and statesman.

**NATO Issue**
**Rotary Press Printing**

**1959, Apr. 1** ***Perf. 10½x11***
*1127* A571 4c blue 8 5

10th anniv. of the No. Atlantic Treaty Organ.

**Arctic Explorations Issue**

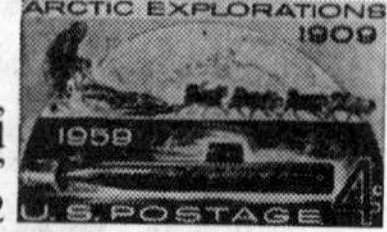

North Pole, Dog Sled and "Nautilus" A572

**1959, Apr. 6** ***Perf. 11x10½***
*1128* A572 4c brt grnsh bl 8 5

Conquest of the Arctic by land by Rear Admiral Robert Edwin Peary in 1909 and by sea by the submarine "Nautilus" in 1958.

**World Peace Through World Trade Issue**

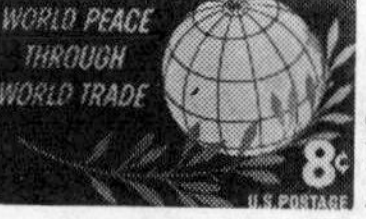

Globe and Laurel A573

**1959, Apr. 20** *Perf. 11x10½*
*1129* A573 8c rose lake 15 12

Issued in conjunction with the 17th Cong. of the Intl. Chamber of Commerce, Washington, DC, Apr. 19-25.

### Silver Centennial Issue

Henry Comstock at Mount Davidson Site — A574

**1959, June 8** *Perf. 11x10½*
*1130* A574 4c black 8 5

Cent. of the discovery of silver at the Comstock Lode, Nev.

### St. Lawrence Seaway Issue

Great Lakes, Maple Leaf and Eagle Emblems A575

### Giori Press Printing

**1959, June 26** *Perf. 11*
*1131* A575 4c red & dk bl 8 5

Opening of the St. Lawrence Seaway, June 26, 1959. See Canada No. 387.

### 49-Star Flag Issue

US Flag, 1959 — A576

**1959, July 4** *Perf. 11*
*1132* A576 4c ocher, dk bl & dp car 8 5

### Soil Conservation Issue

Modern Farm — A577

**1959, Aug. 26**
*1133* A577 4c bl, grn & ocher 8 5

Tribute to farmers and ranchers who use soil and water conservation measures.

### Petroleum Industry Issue

Oil Derrick — A578

### Rotary Press Printing

**1959, Aug. 27** *Perf. 10½x11*
*1134* A578 4c brown 8 5

Cent. of the completion of the nation's 1st oil well at Titusville, Pa.

### Dental Health Issue

Children A579

**1959, Sept. 14** *Perf. 11x10½*
*1135* A579 4c green 8 5

Publicizing dental health and cent. of the American Dental Assoc.

Ernst Reuter A580

Dr. Ephraim McDowell A581

### Champion of Liberty Issue

### Rotary Press Printing

**1959, Sept. 29** *Perf. 10½x11*
*1136* A580 4c gray 8 5

### Giori Press Printing

*Perf. 11*

*1137* A580 8c car, ultra & ocher 16 8

Ernst Reuter, mayor of Berlin 1948-53.

### Dr. Ephraim McDowell Issue

### Rotary Press Printing

**1959, Dec. 3** *Perf. 10½x11*
*1138* A581 4c rose lake 8 5
*a* Vert. pair, imperf. btwn. *500.00*
*b* Vert. pair, imperf. horiz. *350.00*

Honoring McDowell on the 150th anniv. of the 1st successful ovarian operation performed in the US.

### American Credo Issue

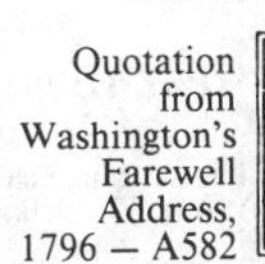

Quotation from Washington's Farewell Address, 1796 — A582

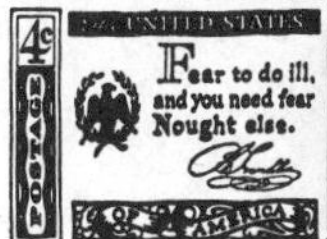


Benjamin Franklin Quotation A583

Thomas Jefferson Quotation A584

Francis Scott Key Quotation A585

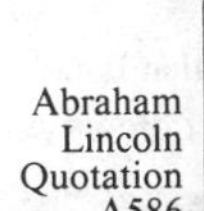
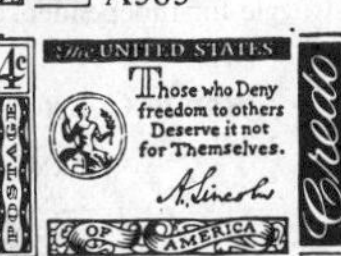


Abraham Lincoln Quotation A586

Patrick Henry Quotation A587

### Giori Press Printing

**1960-61** *Perf. 11*
*1139* A582 4c dk vio bl & car 8 5
*1140* A583 4c ol bis & grn 8 5
*1141* A584 4c gray & ver 9 5
*1142* A585 4c car & dk bl 10 5
*1143* A586 4c mag & grn 10 5
*1144* A587 4c grn & brn ('61) 12 5
*Nos. 1139-1144 (6)* 57 30

Re-emphasizing the ideals upon which America was founded and honoring those great Americans who wrote or uttered the credos.

Issue dates: Jan. 20, Mar. 31, May 18, Sept. 14, Nov. 19, and Jan. 11.

### Boy Scout Jubilee Issue

Boy Scout Giving Scout Sign — A588

### Giori Press Printing

**1960, Feb. 8** *Perf. 11*
*1145* A588 4c red, dk bl & dk bis 8 5

50th anniv. of the BSA.

Olympic Rings and Snowflake A589

Thomas G. Masaryk A590

### Olympic Winter Games Issue

### Rotary Press Printing

**1960, Feb. 18** *Perf. 10½x11*
*1146* A589 4c dull blue 8 5

Opening of the 8th Olympic Winter Games, Squaw Valley, Feb. 18-29.

### Champion of Liberty Issue

### Rotary Press Printing

**1960, Mar. 7** *Perf. 10½x11*
*1147* A590 4c blue 8 5
*a* Vert. pair, imperf. btwn. *1,600.*

### Giori Press Printing

*Perf. 11*

*1148* A590 8c car, ultra & ocher 16 8
*a* Horiz. pair, imperf. btwn. —

Masaryk, founder and pres. of Czechoslovakia (1918-35), on the 110th anniv. of his birth.

### World Refugee Year Issue

Refugee Family Walking Toward New Life — A591

### Rotary Press Printing

**1960, Apr. 7** *Perf. 11x10½*
*1149* A591 4c gray black 8 5

WRY, July 1, 1959 - June 30, 1960.

### Water Conservation Issue

Water, from Watershed to Consumer A592

### Giori Press Printing

**1960, Apr. 18** *Perf. 11*
*1150* A592 4c dk bl, brn org & grn 8 5

Stressing the importance of water conservation, and 7th Watershed Cong., Washington, DC.

### SEATO Issue

SEATO Emblem — A593

### Rotary Press Printing

**1960, May 31** *Perf. 10½x11*
*1151* A593 4c blue 8 5
*a* Vert. pair, imperf. btwn. *175.00*

South-East Asia Treaty Org. and the SEATO Conf., Washington, DC, May 31-June 3.

### American Woman Issue

Mother and Daughter A594

**1960, June 2** *Perf. 11x10½*
*1152* A594 4c deep violet 8 5

A tribute to American women and their accomplishments in civic affairs, education, arts and industry.

### 50-Star Flag Issue

US Flag, 1960 — A595

### Giori Press Printing

**1960, July 4** *Perf. 11*
*1153* A595 4c dark blue & red 8 5

### Pony Express Centennial Issue

Pony Express Rider — A596

### Rotary Press Printing

**1960, July 19** *Perf. 11x10½*
*1154* A596 4c sepia 8 5

Centenary of the Pony Express.

Man in Wheelchair Operating Drill Press — A597

5th World Forestry Congress Seal — A598

### Employ the Handicapped Issue

**1960, Aug. 28** *Perf. 10½x11*
*1155* A597 4c dark blue 8 5

Promotinge employment of the physically handicapped and publicizing the 8th World Cong. of the Intl. Soc. for the Welfare of Cripples, NYC.

### World Forestry Congress Issue

**1960, Aug. 29**
*1156* A598 4c green 8 5

5th World Forestry Cong., Seattle, Wash., Aug. 29-Sept. 10.

The lack of a price for a listed item does not necessarily indicate rarity.

**Mexican Independence Issue**

Independence Bell — A599

**Giori Press Printing**

**1960, Sept. 16** *Perf. 11*
*1157* A599 4c grn & rose red 8 5

150th anniv. of Mexican independence. See Mexico No. 910.

**US-Japan Treaty Issue**

Washington Monument and Cherry Blossoms — A600

**1960, Sept. 28** *Perf. 11*
*1158* A600 4c blue & pink 8 5

Cent. of the US-Japan Treaty of Amity and Commerce.

Ignacy Jan Paderewski A601

Robert A. Taft A602

**Champion of Liberty Issue**
**Rotary Press Printing**

**1960, Oct. 8** *Perf. 10½x11*
*1159* A601 4c blue 8 5

**Giori Press Printing**
*Perf. 11*

*1160* A601 8c car, ultra & ocher 16 8

Paderewski (1866-1941), Polish statesman and musician.

**Senator Taft Memorial Issue**
**Rotary Press Printing**

**1960, Oct. 10** *Perf. 10½x11*
*1161* A602 4c dull violet 8 5

Senator Taft (1889-1953), of Ohio.

**Wheels of Freedom Issue**

Globe and Steering Wheel with Tractor, Car and Truck — A603

**1960, Oct. 15** *Perf. 11x10½*
*1162* A603 4c dark blue 8 5

Honoring the automotive industry and in connection with the National Automobile Show, Detroit, Oct. 15-23.

Values quoted in this catalogue are for stamps graded at Fine-Very Fine and with no faults. An illustrated guide to grade is provided in introductory material, beginning on Page V.

**Boys' Clubs of America Issue**

Profile of a Boy — A604

**Giori Press Printing**

**1960, Oct. 18** *Perf. 11*
*1163* A604 4c ind, sl & rose red 8 5

Cent. of the Boys' Clubs of America movement.

**Automated Post Office Issue**

Architect's Sketch of New Post Office, Providence, RI — A605

**1960, Oct. 20** *Perf. 11*
*1164* A605 4c dk bl & car 8 5

Opening of the 1st automated PO in the US.

Baron Gustaf Emil Mannerheim A606

Camp Fire Girls Emblem A607

**Champion of Liberty Issue**
**Rotary Press Printing**

**1960, Oct. 26** *Perf. 10½x11*
*1165* A606 4c blue 8 5

**Giori Press Printing**
*Perf. 11*

*1166* A606 8c car, ultra & ocher 16 8

Mannerheim (1867-1951), marshal and pres. of Finland.

**Camp Fire Girls Issue**
**Giori Press Printing**

**1960, Nov. 1** *Perf. 11*
*1167* A607 4c dk bl & brt red 8 5

50th anniv. of the Camp Fire Girls' movement and with their Golden Jubilee Convention celebration.

Giuseppe Garibaldi (1807-1882) A608

Walter F. George (1878-1957) A609

**Champion of Liberty Issue**
**Rotary Press Printing**

**1960, Nov. 2** *Perf. 10½x11*
*1168* A608 4c green 8 5

**Giori Press Printing**
*Perf. 11*

*1169* A608 8c car, ultra & ocher 16 8

Garibaldi, Italian patriot and freedom fighter.

**Senator George Memorial Issue**
**Rotary Press Printing**

**1960, Nov. 5** *Perf. 10½x11*
*1170* A609 4c dl vio 8 5

Senator Walter F. George of Georgia.

Andrew Carnegie A610

John Foster Dulles A611

**Andrew Carnegie Issue**

**1960, Nov. 25**
*1171* A610 4c deep claret 8 5

Carnegie (1835-1919), industrialist and philanthropist.

**John Foster Dulles Memorial Issue**

**1960, Dec. 6** *Perf. 10½x11*
*1172* A611 4c dull violet 8 5

John Foster Dulles (1888-1959), Sec. of State (1953-1959).

**Echo I – Communications for Peace Issue**

Radio Waves Connecting Echo I and Earth — A612

**1960, Dec. 15** *Perf. 11x10½*
*1173* A612 4c deep violet 25 8

World's 1st communications satellite, Echo I, placed in orbit by NASA, Aug. 12, 1960.

**Champion of Liberty Issue**

Mahatma Gandhi — A613

**Rotary Press Printing**

**1961, Jan. 26** *Perf. 10½x11*
*1174* A613 4c red orange 8 5

**Giori Press Printing**
*Perf. 11*

*1175* A613 8c car, ultra & ocher 16 8

Mohandas K. Gandhi, leader in India's struggle for independence.

**Range Conservation Issue**

The Trail Boss and Modern Range A614

**Giori Press Printing**

**1961, Feb. 2** *Perf. 11*
*1176* A614 4c bl, sl & brn org 8 5

Importance of range conservation and meeting of the American Soc. of Range Management, Washington, DC. "The Trail Boss" from a drawing by Charles M. Russell is the Society's emblem.

**Horace Greeley Issue**

Horace Greeley (1811-1872), publisher and editor — A615

**Rotary Press Printing**

**1961, Feb. 3** *Perf. 10½x11*
*1177* A615 4c dull violet 8 5

**Civil War Centennial Issue**

Sea Coast Gun of 1861 — A616

Rifleman at Shiloh, 1862 — A617

Blue and Gray at Gettysburg, 1863 — A618

Battle of the Wilderness, 1864 A619

Appomattox, 1865 A620

**1961-65** *Perf. 11x10½*
*1178* A616 4c light green 12 5
*1179* A617 4c blk, *peach blossom* ('62) 10 5

**Giori Press Printing**
*Perf. 11*

*1180* A618 5c gray & bl ('63) 10 5
*1181* A619 5c dk red & blk ('64) 10 5
*1182* A620 5c Prus bl & blk ('65) 12 5
*a* Horiz. pair, imperf. vert. —
*Nos. 1178-1182 (5)* 54 25

Cent. of the firing on Fort Sumter, No. 1178; cent. of the Battle of Shiloh, No. 1179; cent. of the Battle of Gettysburg, No. 1180; cent. of the Battle of the Wilderness, No. 1181; cent. of the surrender of Gen. Robert E. Lee to Lt. Gen. Ulysses S. Grant at Appomattox Court House, No. 1182.

Issue dates of Nos. 1178-1182: Apr. 12; Apr. 7; July 1; May 5; Apr. 9.

**Kansas Statehood Issue**

Sunflower, Pioneer Couple and Stockade A621

**Giori Press Printing**

**1961, May 10** *Perf. 11*
*1183* A621 4c brn, dk red & grn, *yel* 8 5

Kansas statehood, centenary.

**Senator George W. Norris Issue**

Norris and Norris Dam, Tenn. — A622

**Rotary Press Printing**

**1961, July 11** *Perf. 11x10 ½*
*1184* A622 4c blue green 8 5

Norris (1861-1944) of Nebraska.

**Naval Aviation Issue**

Navy's First Plane (Curtiss A-1 of 1911) and Naval Air Wings A623

**1961, Aug. 20**
*1185* A623 4c blue 8 5

50th anniv. of Naval Aviation.

Scales of Justice, Factory, Worker and Family A624

Remington's "Smoke Signal" A625

**Workmen's Compensation Issue**

**1961, Sept. 4** *Perf. 10 ½x11*
*1186* A624 4c ultra, *grysh* 8 5

50th anniv. of the 1st successful Workmen's Compensation Law, enacted by the Wis. legislature.

**Frederic Remington Issue**

**Giori Press Printing**

**1961, Oct. 4** *Perf. 11*
*1187* A625 4c multicolored 8 5

Frederic Remington (1861-1909), artist of the West. The design is from an oil painting, Amon Carter Museum of Western Art, Fort Worth, Texas.

Sun Yat-sen A626

Basketball A627

**Republic of China Issue**

**Rotary Press Printing**

**1961, Oct. 10** *Perf. 10 ½x11*
*1188* A626 4c blue 8 5

50th anniv. of the Republic of China.

**Naismith-Basketball Issue**

**1961, Nov. 6** *Perf. 10 ½x11*
*1189* A627 4c brown 8 5

Honoring basketball and James A. Naismith (1861-1939), who invented the game in 1891.

**Nursing Issue**

Student Nurse Lighting Candle — A628

**Giori Press Printing**

**1961, Dec. 28** *Perf. 11*
*1190* A628 4c bl, grn, org & blk 8 5

Honoring the nursing profession.

**New Mexico Statehood Issue**

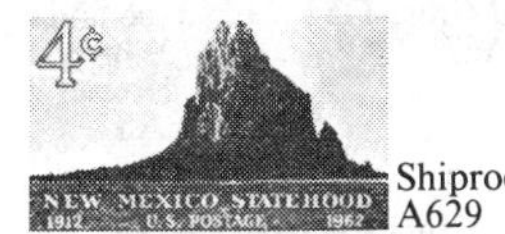

Shiprock A629

**1962, Jan. 6** *Perf. 11*
*1191* A629 4c lt bl, mar & bis 8 5

New Mex. statehood, 50th anniv.

**Arizona Statehood Issue**

Giant Saguaro Cactus — A630

**1962 Feb. 14** *Perf. 11*
*1192* A630 4c car, vio bl & grn 8 5

Arizona statehood, 50th anniv.

**Project Mercury Issue**

"Friendship 7" Capsule and Globe A631

**1962, Feb. 20** *Perf. 11*
*1193* A631 4c dk bl & yel 8 5

First orbital flight of a US astronaut, Lt. Col. John H. Glenn, Jr., Feb. 20, 1962. Imperfs. are printers waste.

**Malaria Eradication Issue**

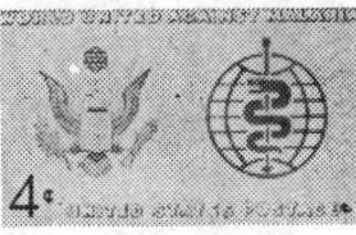
Great Seal of US and WHO Symbol A632

**1962, Mar. 30** *Perf. 11*
*1194* A632 4c blue & bister 8 5

WHO drive to eradicate malaria.

Charles Evans Hughes A633

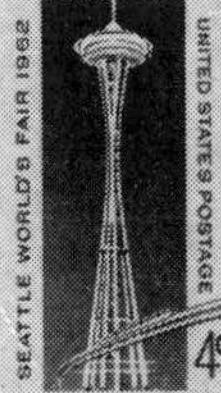

Space Needle and Monorail A634

**Charles Evans Hughes Issue**

**Rotary Press Printing**

**1962, Apr. 11** *Perf. 10 ½x11*
*1195* A633 4c black, *buff* 8 5

Hughes (1862-1948), Gov. of NY, Chief Justice of the US.

**Seattle World's Fair Issue**

**Giori Press Printing**

**1962, Apr. 25** *Perf. 11*
*1196* A634 4c red & dk bl 8 5

"Century 21" Intl. Expo., Seattle, Wash., Apr. 21-Oct. 21.

**Louisiana Statehood Issue**

Riverboat on the Mississippi A635

**1962, Apr. 30** *Perf. 11*
*1197* A635 4c bl, dk sl grn & red 8 5

Louisiana statehood, sesquicentennial.

**Homestead Act Issue**

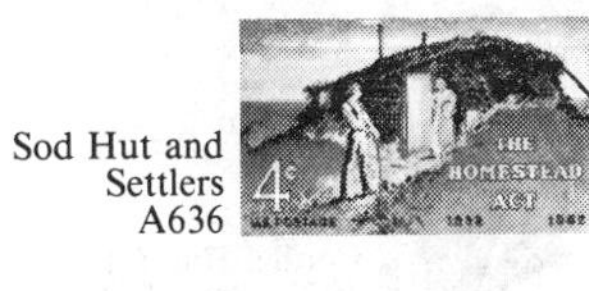

Sod Hut and Settlers A636

**Rotary Press Printing**

**1962, May 20** *Perf. 11x10 ½*
*1198* A636 4c slate 8 5

Centenary of the Homestead Act.

**Girl Scout Jubilee Issue**

Senior Girl Scout and Flag — A637

**1962, July 24** *Perf. 11x10 ½*
*1199* A637 4c rose red 8 5

50th anniv. of the Girl Scouts of America.

**Senator Brien McMahon Issue**

Brien McMahon and Atomic Diagram A638

**1962, July 28** *Perf. 11x10 ½*
*1200* A638 4c violet 8 5

Honoring Sen. McMahon, Conn., for his role in opening the way to peaceful uses of atomic energy.

**Apprenticeship Issue**

Machinist Handing Micrometer to Apprentice A639

**1962, Aug. 31** *Perf. 11x10 ½*
*1201* A639 4c blk, *yel bis* 8 5

Natl. Apprenticeship Program and 25th anniv. of the Natl. Apprenticeship Act.

**Sam Rayburn Issue**

Sam Rayburn and Capitol — A640

**Giori Press Printing**

**1962, Sept. 16** *Perf. 11*
*1202* A640 4c dk bl & red brn 8 5

Sam Rayburn (1882-1961), Speaker of the House of Representatives.

**Dag Hammarskjold Issue**

UN Headquarters and Dag Hammarskjold A641

**Giori Press Printing**

**1962, Oct. 23** *Perf. 11*
*1203* A641 4c blk, brn & yel 8 5

Dag Hammarskjold, Sec. Gen. of the UN, 1953-61.

**Hammarskjold Special Printing**

**1962, Nov. 16**
*1204* A641 4c blk, brn & yel (yel inverted) 9 6

No. 1204 was issued following discovery of No. 1203 with yellow background inverted.

Wreath and Candles A642

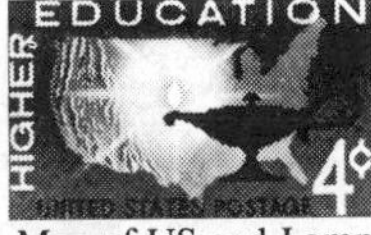

Map of US and Lamp A643

**Christmas Issue**

**Giori Press Printing**

**1962, Nov. 1** *Perf. 11*
*1205* A642 4c green & red 8 5

**Higher Education Issue**

**1962, Nov. 14** *Perf. 11*
*1206* A643 4c bl grn & blk 8 5

Higher education's role in American cultural and industrial development in connection with the centenary celebrations of the signing of the law creating land-grant colleges and universities.

**Winslow Homer Issue**

"Breezing Up" — A644

**1962, Dec. 15** *Perf. 11*
*1207* A644 4c multicolored 8 5
*a* Horiz. pair, imperf. btwn.

Winslow Homer (1836-1910), painter (showing his oil which hangs in the Natl. Gallery, Washington, DC.)

**Flag Issue**

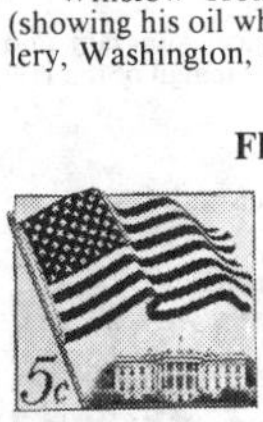

Flag over White House — A645

**1963-66** *Perf. 11*
*1208* A645 5c blue & red 10 5
*a* Tagged ('66) 16 5
*b* Horiz. pair, imperf. btwn. *1,250.*

Issue dates: No. 1208, Jan. 9. No. 1208a, Aug. 25.

The Catalogue editors cannot undertake to appraise, identify or judge the genuineness or condition of stamps.

**Regular Issue**

Andrew Jackson A646

George Washington A650

**Rotary Press Printing**

**1962-66** ***Perf. 11x10½***

*1209* A646 1c green ('63) 5 5
*a* Tagged ('66) 6 5
*1213* A650 5c dk bl gray 12 5
*a* Booklet pane 5 + label 2.25 *75*
*b* Tagged ('63) 50 22
*c* As "a," tagged ('63) 1.25 *50*

See Luminescence note after No. 1053.

Three different messages are found on the label in No. 1213a, and two messages on that of No. 1213c.

Unused catalogue numbers (1210-1212, 1214-1224, 1226-1228) were left vacant for additional denominations in this regular series which were not produced.

Coil Stamps; Rotary Press

**1962-66** ***Perf. 10 Vertically***

*1225* A646 1c green ('63) 12 5
*a* Tagged ('66) 12 5
*1229* A650 5c dk bl gray 1.25 5
*a* Tagged ('63) 1.00 6
*b* Imperf., pair *300.00*

**Carolina Charter Issue**

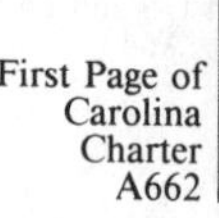

First Page of Carolina Charter A662

**Giori Press Printing**

**1963, Apr. 6** ***Perf. 11***

*1230* A662 5c dk car & brn 10 5

Carolina Charter, 1663, granting to 8 Englishmen lands, extending coast-to-coast roughly along the present border of Va. to the north and Fla. to the south. Original charter on display at Raleigh.

**Food for Peace-Freedom from Hunger**

Wheat — A663

**1963, June 4** ***Perf. 11***

*1231* A663 5c grn, buff & red 10 5

American "Food for Peace" program and "Freedom from Hunger" campaign of the UN FAO.

**West Virginia Statehood Issue**

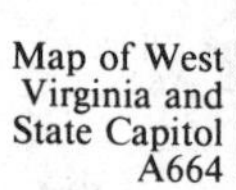

Map of West Virginia and State Capitol A664

**1963, June 20**

*1232* A664 5c grn, red & blk 10 5

West Virginia statehood, centenary.

**Emancipation Proclamation Issue**

Severed Chain — A665

**1963, Aug. 16** ***Perf. 11***

*1233* A665 5c dk bl, blk & red 10 5

Cent. of Lincoln's Emancipation Proclamation, freeing about 3,000,000 slaves in 10 southern states.

**Alliance for Progress Issue**

Alliance Emblem A666

**1963, Aug. 17**

*1234* A666 5c ultra & grn 10 5

2nd anniv. of the Alliance for Progress, which aims to stimulate economic growth and raise living standards in Latin America.

**Cordell Hull Issue**

Cordell Hull (1871-1955), Sec. of State (1933-44) — A667

**Rotary Press Printing**

**1963, Oct. 5** ***Perf. 10½x11***

*1235* A667 5c blue green 10 5

**Eleanor Roosevelt Issue**

Mrs. Franklin D. Roosevelt (1884-1962) A668

**1963, Oct. 11** ***Perf. 11x10½***

*1236* A668 5c bright purple 10 5

**Science Issue**

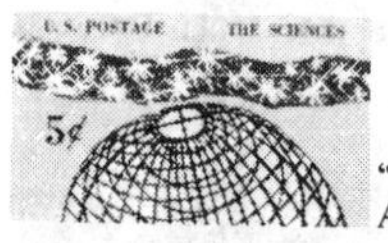


"The Universe" A669

**Giori Press Printing**

**1963, Oct. 14** ***Perf. 11***

*1237* A669 5c Prus bl & blk 10 5

Honoring the sciences and cent. of the Natl. Academy of Science.

**City Mail Delivery**

Letter Carrier, 1863 — A670

**1963, Oct. 26** **Tagged** ***Perf. 11***

*1238* A670 5c gray, dk bl & red 10 5

Cent. of free city mail delivery.

Cuban Refugees on S.S. *Morning Light* and Red Cross Flag A671

National Christmas Tree and White House A672

**Red Cross Centenary Issue**

**1963, Oct. 29** ***Perf. 11***

*1239* A671 5c bluish blk & red 10 5

International Red Cross, cent.

**Christmas Issue**

**1963, Nov. 1** ***Perf. 11***

*1240* A672 5c dk bl, bluish blk & red 10 5
*a* Tagged 65 25

See Luminescence note after No. 1053.

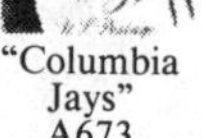


"Columbia Jays" A673

Sam Houston A674

**John James Audubon Issue**

**1963, Dec. 7** ***Perf. 11***

*1241* A673 5c dk bl & multi 10 5

James Audubon (1785-1851), ornithologist and artist. The birds pictured are actually Collie's magpie jays.

**Sam Houston Issue**

**Rotary Press Printing**

**1964, Jan. 10** ***Perf. 10½x11***

*1242* A674 5c black 10 5

Sam Houston (1793-1863), soldier, pres. of Texas, US senator.

**Charles M. Russell Issue**

"Jerked Down" A675

**Giori Press Printing**

**1964, Mar. 19** ***Perf. 11***

*1243* A675 5c ind, red brn & ol 10 5

Russell (1864-1926), painter. The design is from a painting, Thomas Gilcrease Inst. of American History and Art, Tulsa, Okla.

**New York World's Fair Issue**

Mall with Unisphere and "Rocket Thrower," by Donald De Lue — A676

**Rotary Press Printing**

**1964, Apr. 22** ***Perf. 11x10½***

*1244* A676 5c blue green 10 5

New York World's Fair, 1964-65.

**John Muir Issue**

John Muir (1838-1914), naturalist and conservationist and Redwood Forest — A677

**Giori Press Printing**

**1964, Apr. 29** ***Perf. 11***

*1245* A677 5c brn, grn, yel grn & ol 10 5

**Kennedy Memorial Issue**

Pres. John F. Kennedy (1917-63) and Eternal Flame A678

**Rotary Press Printing**

**1964, May 29** ***Perf. 11x10½***

*1246* A678 5c blue gray 10 5

**New Jersey Tercentenary Issue**

Philip Carteret Landing at Elizabethtown, and Map of New Jersey — A679

**1964, June 15** ***Perf. 10½x11***

*1247* A679 5c bright ultra 10 5

300th anniv. of English colonization of NJ. The design is from a mural by Howard Pyle in the Essex County Courthouse, Newark.

**Nevada Statehood Issue**

Virginia City and Map of Nevada A680

**Giori Press Printing**

**1964, July 22** ***Perf. 11***

*1248* A680 5c red, yel & bl 10 5

Nevada statehood, cent.

Flag A681

William Shakespeare A682

**Register and Vote Issue**

**Giori Press Printing**

**1964, Aug. 1** ***Perf. 11***

*1249* A681 5c dk bl & red 10 5

Campaign to draw more voters to the polls.

**Shakespeare Issue**

**Rotary Press Printing**

**1964, Aug. 14** ***Perf. 10½x11***

*1250* A682 5c blk brn, *tan* 10 5

400th anniv. of the birth of Shakespeare (1564-1616).

### Doctors Mayo Issue

Drs. William and Charles Mayo — A683

**1964, Sept. 11** ***Perf. 10½x11***

*1251* A683 5c green 10 5

William (1861-1939) and his brother, Charles (1865-1939), surgeons who founded the Mayo Foundation for Medical Education and Research in affiliation with the Univ. of Minn. at Rochester. From a sculpture by James Earle Fraser.

### American Music Issue

Lute, Horn, Laurel, Oak and Music Score — A684

**Giori Press Printing**

**1964, Oct. 15** ***Perf. 11***

**Gray Paper with Blue Threads**

*1252* A684 5c red, blk & bl 10 5
*a* Blue omitted *1,300.*

50th anniv. of the founding of ASCAP (American Soc. of Composers, Authors and Publishers).

### Homemakers Issue

Farm Scene Sampler A685

**Lithographed, Engraved (Giori)**

**1964, Oct. 26** ***Perf. 11***

*1253* A685 5c multicolored 10 5

Honoring American women as homemakers and 50th anniv. of the passage of the Smith-Lever Act. By providing economic experts under an extension service of the US Dept. of Agriculture, this legislation helped to improve homelife.

### Christmas Issue

Holly A686 Mistletoe A687

Poinsettia A688 Sprig of Conifer A689

**Giori Press Printing**

**1964, Nov. 9** ***Perf. 11***

*1254* A686 5c grn, car & blk 35 5
*a* Tagged 75 25
*1255* A687 5c car, grn & blk 35 5
*a* Tagged 75 25
*1256* A688 5c car, grn & blk 35 5
*a* Tagged 75 25
*1257* A689 5c blk, grn & car 35 5
*a* Tagged 75 25
*b* Block of 4, #1254-1257 1.40 75
*c* Block of 4, #1254a-1257a 3.50 1.50

Printed in panes of 100 containing 25 each of Nos. 1254-1257. The tagged stamps were issued Nov. 10.

### Verrazano-Narrows Bridge Issue

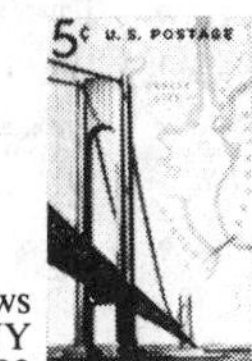


Verrazano-Narrows Bridge and Map of NY Bay — A690

**Rotary Press Printing**

**1964, Nov. 21** ***Perf. 10½x11***

*1258* A690 5c blue green 10 5

Opening of the Verrazano-Narrows Bridge connecting Staten Island and Brooklyn, NY.

### Fine Arts Issue

Abstract Design by Stuart Davis — A691

**Giori Press Printing**

**1964, Dec. 2** ***Perf. 11***

*1259* A691 5c ultra, blk & dl red 10 5

### Amateur Radio Issue

Radio Waves and Dial — A692

**Rotary Press Printing**

**1964, Dec. 15** ***Perf. 10½x11***

*1260* A692 5c red lilac 10 5

Honoring radio amateurs on the 50th anniv. of the American Radio Relay League.

### Battle of New Orleans Issue

General Andrew Jackson and Sesquicentennial Medal — A693

**Giori Press Printing**

**1965, Jan. 8** ***Perf. 11***

*1261* A693 5c dp car, vio bl & gray 10 5

Battle of New Orleans, Chalmette Plantation, Jan. 8-18, 1815, which established 150 years of peace and friendship between the US and Great Britain.

Discus Thrower A694

Microscope and Stethoscope A695

### Physical Fitness-Sokol Issue

**1965, Feb. 15** ***Perf. 11***

*1262* A694 5c mar & blk 10 5

Importance of physical fitness and cent. of the founding of the Sokol (athletic) org. in America.

### Crusade Against Cancer Issue

**1965, Apr. 1** ***Perf. 11***

*1263* A695 5c blk, pur & red org 10 5

"Crusade Against Cancer" and stressing the importance of early diagnosis.

### Churchill Memorial Issue

Winston Churchill — A696

**Rotary Press Printing**

**1965, May 13** ***Perf. 10½x11***

*1264* A696 5c black 10 5

Sir Winston Spencer Churchill (1874-1965), British statesman and WW II leader.

### Magna Carta Issue

Procession of Barons and King John's Crown A697

**Giori Press Printing**

**1965, June 15** ***Perf. 11***

*1265* A697 5c blk, yel ocher & red lil 10 5

750th anniv. of the Magna Carta, the basis of English and American common law.

### International Cooperation Year Issue

ICY Emblem A698

**1965, June 26** ***Perf. 11***

*1266* A698 5c dl bl & blk 10 5

ICY, 1965, and 20th anniv. of the UN.

A699

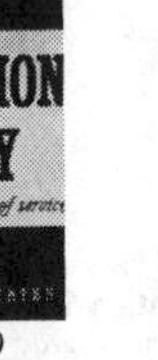

Dante — A700

### Salvation Army Issue

**1965, July 2** ***Perf. 11***

*1267* A699 5c red, blk & dk bl 10 5

Cent. of the founding of the Salvation Army in London by William Booth.

### Dante Alighieri Issue

**Rotary Press Printing**

**1965, July 17** ***Perf. 10½x11***

*1268* A700 5c maroon, *tan* 10 5

Alighieri (1265-1321), Italian poet. Design after a 16th cent. painting.

### Herbert Hoover Issue

Pres. Herbert Clark Hoover (1874-1964) — A701

**1965, Aug. 10** ***Perf. 10½x11***

*1269* A701 5c rose red 10 5

### Robert Fulton Issue

Robert Fulton and Clermont A702

**Giori Press Printing**

**1965, Aug. 19** ***Perf. 11***

*1270* A702 5c black & blue 10 5

Fulton (1765-1815), inventor of the 1st commercial steamship.

### Settlement of Florida Issue

Spanish Explorer, Royal Flag of Spain and Ships — A703

**1965, Aug. 28** **Giori Press Printing**

*1271* A703 5c red, yel & blk 10 5
*a* Yellow omitted *675.00*

400th anniv. of the settlement of Fla., and the 1st permanent European settlement in the continental US, St. Augustine, Fla. See Spain No. 1312.

### Traffic Safety Issue

Traffic Signal A704

**1965, Sept. 3** ***Perf. 11***

*1272* A704 5c emer, blk & red 10 5

Traffic safety and the prevention of traffic accidents.

### John Singleton Copley Issue

Elizabeth Clarke Copley — A705

**1965, Sept. 17**

*1273* A705 5c blk, brn & ol 10 5

Copley (1738-1815), painter. The portrait of the artist's daughter is from the oil painting "The Copley Family," which hangs in the Natl. Gallery of Art, Washington, DC.

The indexes in each volume of the Scott Catalogue contain many listings which help to identify stamps.

**International Telecommunication Union Centenary**

Gall Projection World Map and Radio Sine Wave A706

**1965, Oct. 6** ***Perf. 11***
*1274* A706 11c blk, car & bis 32 16

Adlai E. Stevenson A707

Angel with Trumpet, 1840 Weather Vane A708

**Adlai E. Stevenson Issue**

**1965, Oct. 23 Litho., Engr. (Giori)**
*1275* A707 5c pale bl, blk, car & vio bl 10 5

Stevenson (1900-65), gov. of Ill., US ambassador to the UN.

**Christmas Issue**
**Giori Press Printing**

**1965, Nov. 2** ***Perf. 11***
*1276* A708 5c car, dk ol grn & bis 10 5
*a* Tagged 65 15

**Prominent Americans Issue**

Thomas Jefferson A710

Albert Gallatin A711

Frank Lloyd Wright and Guggenheim Museum, New York A712

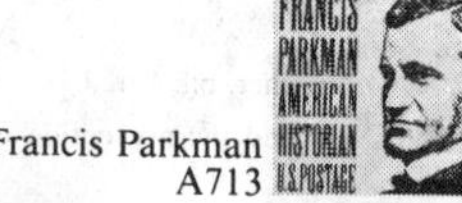

Francis Parkman A713

Lincoln A714

Washington A715

Washington (Redrawn) A715a

Franklin D. Roosevelt A716

Albert Einstein A717

Andrew Jackson A718

Henry Ford and 1909 Model T A718a

John F. Kennedy A719

Oliver Wendell Holmes A720

George Catlett Marshall A721

Frederick Douglass A722

John Dewey A723

Thomas Paine A724

Lucy Stone A725

Eugene O'Neill A726

John Bassett Moore A727

***Perf. 11x10½, 10½x11***

**1965-78 Rotary Press Printing**
*1278* A710 1c grn, tagged ('68) 5 5
*a* Booklet pane of 8 ('68) 1.00 *25*
*b* Bklt. pane of 4 + 2 labels ('71) 75 *20*
*c* Untagged (Bureau precanceled) 7
*1279* A711 1¼c lt grn ('67) 8 5
*1280* A712 2c dk bl gray, tagged ('66) 5 5
*a* Booklet pane of 5 + label ('68) 1.20 *40*
*b* Untagged (Bureau precanceled) 10
*c* Booklet pane of 6 ('71) 1.00 *35*
*1281* A713 3c vio, tagged ('67) 6 5
*a* Untagged (Bureau precanceled) 12
*1282* A714 4c black 8 5
*a* Tagged 8 5
*1283* A715 5c bl ('66) 10 5
*a* Tagged ('66) 10 5
*1283B* A715a 5c bl, tagged ('67) 10 5
*d* Untagged (Bureau precanceled) 15
*1284* A716 6c gray brn ('66) 18 5
*a* Tagged ('66) 12 5
*b* Booklet pane of 8 ('67) 1.50 *50*
*c* Booklet pane of 5 + label ('68) 1.25 *50*
*1285* A717 8c vio ('66) 20 5
*a* Tagged ('66) 16 5
*1286* A718 10c lil, tagged ('67) 22 5
*b* Untagged (Bureau precanceled) 20
*1286A* A718a 12c blk, tagged ('68) 28 5
*c* Untagged (Bureau precanceled) 25
*1287* A719 13c brn, tagged ('67) 24 5
*a* Untagged (Bureau precanceled) 25
*1288* A720 15c rose cl, tagged ('68) 30 6
*a* Untagged (Bureau precanceled) 30
*d* Type II 30 6

Type II: necktie does not touch coat at bottom.

***Perf. 10***
*1288B* A720 15c dk rose cl (from bklt. pane) ('78) 30 5
*c* Booklet pane of 8 2.40 *1.25*
*e* As "c" vert. imperf. btwn. —

***Perf. 11x10½, 10½x11***
*1289* A721 20c dp ol ('67) 42 6
*a* Tagged ('73) 40 6
*1290* A722 25c rose lake ('67) 55 5
*a* Tagged ('73) 50 5
*1291* A723 30c red lil ('68) 65 8
*a* Tagged ('73) 60 6
*1292* A724 40c bl blk ('68) 1.10 10
*a* Tagged ('73) 80 8
*1293* A725 50c rose mag ('68) 1.00 5
*a* Tagged ('73) 95 5
*1294* A726 $1 dl pur ('67) 2.50 8
*a* Tagged ('73) 2.00 8
*1295* A727 $5 gray blk ('66) 12.50 2.00
*a* Tagged ('73) 10.00 2.00
*Nos. 1278-1295 (21)* 20.96 3.13

On No. 1283B the highlights and shadows have been softened.

No. 1288B issued in booklets only. All stamps have one or two straight edges.

Issue dates (without tagging)—1965: 4c, Nov. 19. 1966: 5c, Feb. 22; 6c, Jan. 29; 8c, Mar. 14; $5, Dec. 3. 1967: 1¼c, Jan. 30; 20c, Oct. 24; 25c, Feb. 14; $1, Oct. 16. 1968: 30c, Oct. 21; 40c, Jan. 29; 50c, Aug. 13.

Dates for tagged: 1965: 4c, Dec. 1. 1966: 2c, June 8; 5c, Feb. 23; 6c, Dec. 29; 8c, July 6. 1967: 3c, Sept. 16; No. 1283B, Nov. 17; No. 1284b, Dec. 28; 10c, Mar. 15; 13c, May 29. 1968: 1c & No. 1284c, Jan. 12; No. 1280a, Jan. 8; 12c, July 30; 15c, Mar. 8. 1973: 20c, 25c, 30c, 40c, 50c, $1, $5, Apr. 3. 1978: No. 1288B, June 14.

Franklin D. Roosevelt — A727a

Coil Stamps

**Rotary Press Printing**

**1966-81 Tagged** ***Perf. 10 Horiz.***
*1297* A713 3c vio ('75) 8 5
*a* Imperf., pair *27.50*
*b* Untagged (Bureau precanceled) 12
*c* As "b," imperf. pair 10.00
*1298* A716 6c gray brn ('67) 15 5
*a* Imperf., pair *2,000.*

***Perf. 10 Vertically***
*1299* A710 1c grn ('68) 7 5
*a* Untagged (Bureau precanceled) 7
*b* Imperf., pair *35.00* —
*1303* A714 4c black 14 5
*a* Untagged (Bureau precanceled) 15
*b* Imperf., pair *450.00*
*1304* A715 5c blue 12 5
*a* Untagged (Bureau precanceled) 15
*b* Imperf., pair *200.00*
*e* As "a," imperf. pair 250.00
*1304C* A715a 5c blue ('81) 12 5
*d* Imperf., pair —
*1305* A727a 6c gray brn ('68) 15 5
*a* Imperf., pair *85.00*
*b* Untagged (Bureau precanceled) 20
*1305E* A720 15c rose cl ('78) 25 5
*f* Untagged (Bureau precancelled) 30
*g* Imperf., pair *30.00*
*h* Pair, imperf. between *200.00*
*i* Type II 25 5
*1305C* A726 $1 dl pur ('73) 1.50 20
*d* Imperf., pair *2,000.*
*Nos. 1297-1305C (9)* 2.58 60

Issued dates: 1c, Jan. 12, 1968. 3c, Nov. 4, 1975. 4c, May 28, 1966. No. 1304, Sept. 8, 1966. 6c, No. 1298, Dec. 28, 1967; No. 1305, Feb. 28, 1968. $1, Jan. 12, 1973. 15c, June 14, 1978.

See Nos. 1393-1395, 1397-1402 for more Prominent Americans.

**Migratory Bird Treaty Issue**

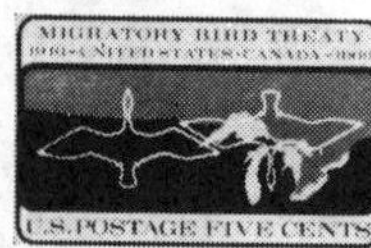

Migratory Birds over Canada-US Border A728

**Giori Press Printing**

**1966, March 16** ***Perf. 11***
*1306* A728 5c blk, crim & dk bl 10 5

50th anniv. of the Migratory Bird Treaty between the US and Canada.

**Humane Treatment of Animals Issue**

Mongrel A729

**Lithographed, Engraved (Giori)**

**1966, Apr. 9** ***Perf. 11***
*1307* A729 5c org brn & blk 10 5

Humane treatment of all animals and cent. of the ASPCA.

**Indiana Statehood Issue**

Sesquicentennial Seal; Map of Indiana with 19 Stars and Old Capitol at Corydon — A730

**1966, Apr. 16 Giori Press Printing**
*1308* A730 5c yel, ocher & vio bl 10 5

Sesquicentennial of Indiana statehood.

**American Circus Issue**

Clown — A731

**1966, May 2** ***Perf. 11***
*1309* A731 5c multicolored 10 5

Honoring the American circus on the cent. of the birth of John Ringling.

**Sixth Intl. Phil. Exhib. Issues**

Stamped Cover — A732

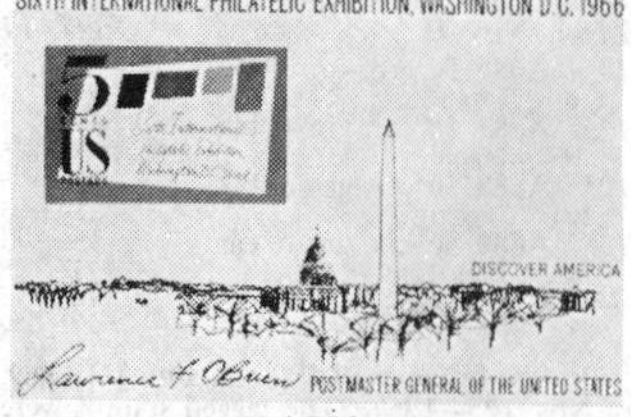

A733

**Lithographed, Engraved (Giori)**

**1966, May** *Perf. 11*

*1310* A732 5c multicolored 10 5

**Souvenir Sheet**

***Imperf***

*1311* A733 5c multicolored 15 12

SIPEX, Washington, DC, May 21-30.

No. 1311 measures 108x74mm. Below the stamp is a line drawing of the Capitol and Washington Monument, the inscription "Discover America" and the signature of Lawrence F. O'Brien, Postmaster General of the US. Top inscription reads: "Sixth International Philatelic Exhibition D.C. 1966." The drawing and inscriptions in margin are green.

Issue dates: No. 1310, May 21. No. 1311, May 23.

"Freedom" Checking "Tyranny" A734

Polish Eagle and Cross A735

**Bill of Rights Issue**

**Giori Press Printing**

**1966, July 1** *Perf. 11*

*1312* A734 5c car, dk & lt bl 10 5

175th anniv. of the Bill of Rights.

**Polish Millennium Issue**

**Rotary Press Printing**

**1966, July 30** *Perf. 10½x11*

*1313* A735 5c red 10 5

1000th anniv. of the adoption of Christianity in Poland.

Tagging Extended

During 1966 experimental use of tagged stamps was extended to the Cincinnati Postal Region covering offices in Indiana, Kentucky and Ohio. To supply these offices about 12 percent of the following nine issues (Nos. 1314-1322) were tagged.

**National Park Service Issue**

National Park Service Emblem A736

**Lithographed, Engraved (Giori)**

**1966, Aug. 25** *Perf. 11*

*1314* A736 5c yel, blk & grn 10 5
*a* Tagged 32 15

50th anniv.of the Natl. Park Service of the Interior Dept. The design "Parkscape U.S.A." identifies Natl. Park Service facilities. No. 1314a was issued Aug. 26.

**Marine Corps Reserve Issue**

Combat Marine, 1966; Frogman; WW II Flier; WW I "Devil Dog" and Marine, 1775 — A737

**Lithographed, Engraved (Giori)**

**1966, Aug. 29** *Perf. 11*

*1315* A737 5c blk, bis, red & ultra 10 5
*a* Tagged 30 15
*b* blk & bis (engr.) omitted —

50th anniv. of the founding of the US Marine Corps Reserve.

**General Federation of Women's Clubs**

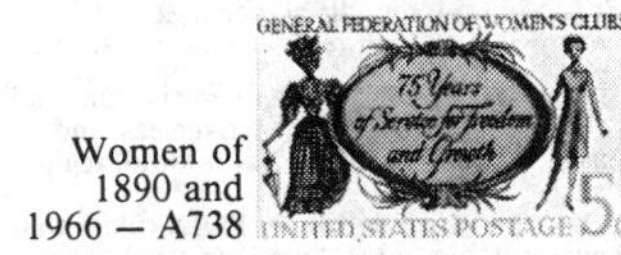

Women of 1890 and 1966 — A738

**Giori Press Printing**

**1966, Sept. 12** *Perf. 11*

*1316* A738 5c blk, pink & bl 10 5
*a* Tagged 30 15

75 years of service by the Gen. Fed. of Women's Clubs. No. 1316a was issued Sept. 13.

**American Folklore Issue**

Johnny Appleseed — A739

**1966, Sept. 24** *Perf. 11*

*1317* A739 5c grn, red & blk 10 5
*a* Tagged 30 15

Johnny Appleseed, (John Chapman, 1774-1845), who wandered over 100,000 square miles planting apple trees, and who gave away and sold seedlings to Midwest pioneers. No. 1317a was issued Sept. 26.

**Beautification of America Issue**

Jefferson Memorial, Tidal Basin and Cherry Blossoms A740

**1966, Oct. 5** *Perf. 11*

*1318* A740 5c emer, pink & blk 10 5
*a* Tagged 30 15

Pres. Johnson's "Plant for a more beautiful America" campaign.

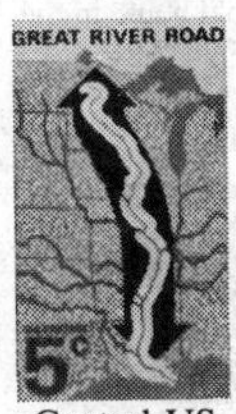

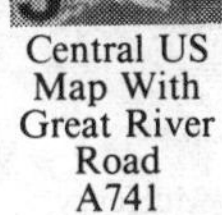

Central US Map With Great River Road A741

Statue of Liberty and "Old Glory" A742

**Great River Road Issue**

**Lithographed, Engraved (Giori)**

**1966, Oct. 21** *Perf. 11*

*1319* A741 5c ver, yel, bl & grn 10 5
*a* Tagged 30 15

5,600-mile Great River Road connecting New Orleans with Kenora, Ontario, following the Mississippi most of the way. No. 1319a was issued Oct. 22.

**Savings Bond-Servicemen Issue**

**1966, Oct. 26**

*1320* A742 5c red, dk bl, lt bl & blk 10 5
*a* Tagged 30 15
*b* Red, dk bl & blk omitted 3,500.

25th anniv. of US Savings Bonds, and to honor American servicemen. No. 1320a was issued Oct. 27.

**Christmas Issue**

Madonna and Child, by Hans Memling — A743

**Lithographed, Engraved (Giori)**

**1966, Nov. 1** *Perf. 11*

*1321* A743 5c multicolored 10 5
*a* Tagged 25 10

The design is from "Madonna and Child with Angels," by the Flemish artist Hans Memling (c. 1430-1494), National Gallery of Art, Washington, D.C. No. 1321a was issued Nov. 2. See No. 1336.

**Mary Cassatt Issue**

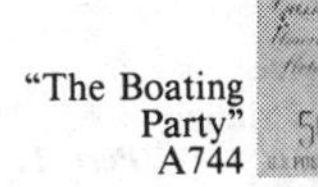

"The Boating Party" A744

**Giori Press Printing**

**1966, Nov. 17** *Perf. 11*

*1322* A744 5c multicolored 12 5
*a* Tagged 30 15

Cassatt (1844-1926), painter. The original painting is in the Natl. Gallery of Art, Washington, DC.

**National Grange Issue**

Grange Poster, 1870 — A745

**1967, Apr. 17** **Tagged** *Perf. 11*

*1323* A745 5c multicolored 10 5

Cent. of the founding of the National Grange, American farmers' organization.

Phosphor Tagging

From No. 1323 onward, all postage issues are tagged, unless otherwise noted.

Tagging Omitted

Inadvertent omissions of tagging occurred on Nos. 1238, 1278, 1281, 1298 and 1305. In addition most tagged issues from 1967 on exist with tagging unintentionally omitted.

**Canada Centenary Issue**

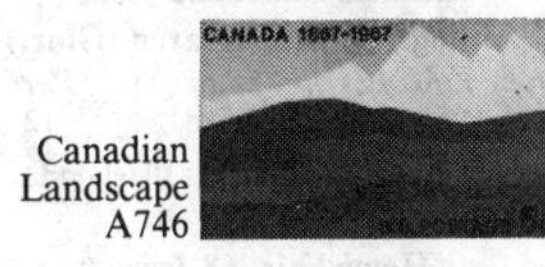

Canadian Landscape A746

**Giori Press Printing**

**1967, May 25** *Perf. 11*

*1324* A746 5c multicolored 10 5

Cent. of Canada's emergence as a nation.

**Erie Canal Issue**

Stern of Early Canal Boat — A747

**Lithographed, Engraved (Giori)**

**1967, July 4** *Perf. 11*

*1325* A747 5c multicolored 10 5

150th anniv. of the Erie Canal groundbreaking ceremony. The canal links Lake Erie and NYC.

**"Peace"—Lions Issue**

Peace Dove — A748

**Giori Press Printing**

**1967, July 5** *Perf. 11*

**Gray Paper with Blue Threads**

*1326* A748 5c bl, red & blk 10 5

Publicizing the Search for Peace. This was the theme of an essay contest for young men and women sponsored by Lions Intl. on its 50th anniv.

**Henry David Thoreau Issue**

Henry David Thoreau — A749

**1967, July 12**

*1327* A749 5c red, blk & grn 10 5

David Thoreau (1817-1862), writer.

**Nebraska Statehood Issue**

Hereford Steer and Corn — A750

**Lithographed, Engraved (Giori)**

**1967, July 29** *Perf. 11*

*1328* A750 5c dk red brn, lem & yel 10 5

Centenary of Nebraska statehood.

**Voice of America Issue**

Radio Transmission Tower and Waves — A751

**1967, Aug. 1** **Giori Press Printing**

*1329* A751 5c red, bl, blk & car 10 5

25th anniv. of the radio branch of the US Information Agency (USIA).

**American Folklore Issue**

Davy Crockett (1786-1836) and Scrub Pines — A752

**Lithographed, Engraved (Giori)**

**1967, Aug. 17** *Perf. 11*

*1330* A752 5c grn, blk & yel 10 5
*a* Vert. pair, imperf. btwn. —

Crockett, frontiersman and congressman, died in defense of the Alamo.

### Space Accomplishments Issue

Space-Walking Astronaut — A753

Gemini 4 Capsule and Earth A754

**Lithographed, Engraved (Giori)**

**1967, Sept. 29** *Perf. 11*

| | | | |
|---|---|---|---|
| *1331* A753 5c multicolored | 65 | 15 |
| ***a*** Pair, # 1331-1332 | 1.50 | 1.25 |
| *1332* A754 5c multicolored | 65 | 15 |

US accomplishments in space. Printed se-tenant in horizontal rows of 5 in panes of 50, four panes to a sheet. On the UL and LL panes No. 1331 is 1st, 3rd and 5th, No. 1332 is 2nd and 4th. This is reversed on UR and LR panes.

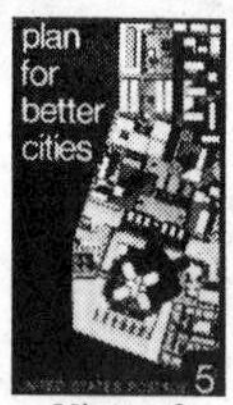


View of Model City A755

Finnish Coat of Arms A756

### Urban Planning Issue

**Lithographed, Engraved (Giori)**

**1967, Oct. 2** *Perf. 11*

*1333* A755 5c dk bl, lt bl & blk 10 5

Importance of Urban Planning and the Intl. Conf. of the American Inst. of Planners, Washington, DC, Oct. 1-6.

### Finnish Independence Issue

**Engraved (Giori)**

**1967, Oct. 6** *Perf. 11*

*1334* A756 5c blue 10 5

50th anniv. of Finland's independence.

### Thomas Eakins Issue

"The Biglin Brothers Racing" (Sculling on Schuylkill River, Philadelphia) A757

**1967, Nov. 2** **Photo.** *Perf. 12*

*1335* A757 5c gold & multi 10 5

Eakins (1844-1916), painter and sculptor. The painting is in the Natl. Gallery of Art, Washington, DC.

### Christmas Issue

Madonna and Child, by Hans Memling — A758

**Lithographed, Engraved (Giori)**

**1967, Nov. 6** *Perf. 11*

*1336* A758 5c multicolored 10 5

See note after No. 1321.

Magnolia A759

Flag and White House A760

### Mississippi Statehood Issue

**Giori Press Printing**

**1967, Dec. 11** *Perf. 11*

*1337* A759 5c brt grnsh bl, grn & red brn 10 5

150th anniv. of Mississippi statehood.

### Flag Issue

**Giori Press Printing**

**1968-71** *Perf. 11*

**Size: 19x22mm**

| | | |
|---|---|---|
| *1338* A760 6c dk bl, red & grn | 12 | 5 |
| ***k*** Vert. pair, imperf. btwn. | *400.00* | |

**Multicolor Huck Press**

***Perf. 11x10½***

**Size: 18¼x21mm**

| | | |
|---|---|---|
| *1338D* A760 6c dk bl, red & grn ('70) | 16 | 5 |
| ***e*** Horiz. pair, imperf. btwn. | *120.00* | |
| *1338F* A760 8c multi ('71) | 18 | 5 |
| ***i*** Vert. pair, imperf. | *60.00* | |
| ***j*** Horiz. pair, imperf. btwn. | *50.00* | |

Issue dates: No. 1338, Jan. 24, 1968; No. 1338D, Aug. 7, 1970; 8c, May 10, 1971.

Coil Stamps

**Multicolor Huck Press**

**1969-71** *Perf. 10 Vert.*

**Size: 18¼x21mm**

| | | |
|---|---|---|
| *1338A* A760 6c dk bl, red & grn | 14 | 5 |
| ***b*** Imperf., pair | *500.00* | |
| *1338G* A760 8c multi ('71) | 18 | 5 |
| ***h*** Imperf., pair | *50.00* | |

Issue dates: 6c, May 30; 8c, May 10.

Farm House and Fields of Ripening Grain A761

Map of North and South America A762

### Illinois Statehood Issue

**Lithographed, Engraved (Giori)**

**1968, Feb. 12** *Perf. 11*

*1339* A761 6c multicolored 12 5

150th anniv. of Illinois statehood.

### HemisFair '68 Issue

**1968, Mar. 30** *Perf. 11*

| | | |
|---|---|---|
| *1340* A762 6c bl, rose red & white | 12 | 5 |
| ***a*** White omitted | *1,350.* | |

HemisFair '68 exhib. at San Antonio, Tex., Apr. 6-Oct. 6, for the 250th anniv. of San Antonio.

### Airlift Issue

Eagle Holding Pennant A763

**Lithographed, Engraved (Giori)**

**1968, Apr. 4** **Untagged** *Perf. 11*

*1341* A763 $1 sep, dk bl, ocher & brn red 2.75 1.25

Issued to pay for airlift of parcels from and to US ports to servicemen overseas and in Alaska, Hawaii and P.R. Valid for all regular postage.

On Apr. 26, 1969, the POD ruled that henceforth No. 1341 "may be used toward paying the postage or fees for special services on airmail articles."

### "Youth"—Elks Issue

Girls and Boys — A764

**Lithographed, Engraved (Giori)**

**1968, May 1** *Perf. 11*

*1342* A764 6c ultra & org red 12 5

Support Our Youth program, and honoring the Benevolent and Protective Order of Elks, which extended its youth service program in observance of its centennial year.

Policeman and Small Boy A765

Eagle Weather Vane A766

### Law and Order Issue

**Giori Press Printing**

**1968, May 17** *Perf. 11*

*1343* A765 6c chlky bl, blk & red 12 5

The police as protector and friend and respect for law and order.

### Register and Vote Issue

**Lithographed, Engraved (Giori)**

**1968, June 27** *Perf. 11*

*1344* A766 6c blk, yel & org 12 5

Campaign to draw more voters to the polls. The weather vane is from an old house in the Russian Hill section of San Francisco.

### Historic Flag Series

Ft. Moultrie, 1776 — A767

Ft. McHenry, 1795-1818 A768

Washington's Cruisers, 1775 — A769

Bennington, 1777 — A770

Rhode Island, 1775 — A771

First Stars and Stripes, 1777 — A772

Bunker Hill, 1775 A773

Grand Union, 1776 — A774

Philadelphia Light Horse, 1775 — A775

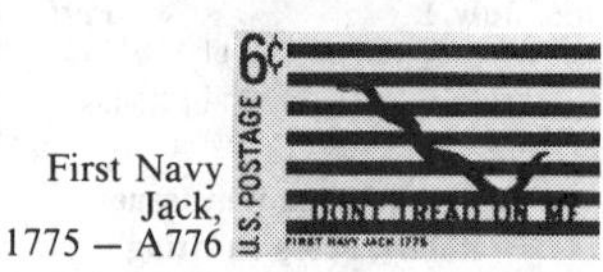


First Navy Jack, 1775 — A776

**Engraved (Giori) (#1345-1348, 1350): Engr. & Litho. (#1349, 1351-1354)**

**1968, July 4** *Perf. 11*

| | | |
|---|---|---|
| *1345* A767 6c dark blue | 50 | 25 |
| *1346* A768 6c dk bl & red | 35 | 25 |
| *1347* A769 6c dk bl & ol grn | 30 | 25 |
| *1348* A770 6c dk bl & red | 30 | 25 |
| *1349* A771 6c dk bl, yel & red | 30 | 25 |
| *1350* A772 6c dk bl & red | 30 | 25 |
| *1351* A773 6c dk bl, ol grn & red | 30 | 25 |
| *1352* A774 6c dk bl & red | 30 | 25 |
| *1353* A775 6c dk bl, yel & red | 30 | 25 |
| *1354* A776 6c dk bl, red & yel | 30 | 25 |
| ***a*** Strip of 10, Nos. 1345-1354 | 3.25 | 3.00 |

Flags carried by American colonists and by citizens of the new United States. Nos. 1345-1354 are printed se-tenant in vert. rows of 10 in panes of 50, 4 panes to a sheet. The flag sequence on the upper panes is as listed. On the lower panes the sequence is reversed with the Navy Jack in the 1st row and the Fort Moultrie flag in the 10th.

### Walt Disney Issue

Walt Disney and Children of the World — A777

**1968, Sept. 11** **Photo.** *Perf. 12*

| | | |
|---|---|---|
| *1355* A777 6c multi | 14 | 5 |
| ***a*** Ocher (Walt Disney, 6c, etc.) omitted | *750.00* | — |
| ***b*** Vert. pair, imperf. horiz. | *725.00* | |
| ***c*** Imperf., pair | *800.00* | |
| ***d*** Black omitted | *2,250.* | |
| ***e*** Horiz. pair, imperf. btwn. | *3,250.* | |
| ***f*** Blue omitted | *1,750.* | |

Walt Disney (1901-1966), cartoonist, film producer, creator of Mickey Mouse.

### Father Marquette Issue

Father Marquette and Louis Jolliet Exploring the Mississippi A778

### Giori Press Printing

**1968, Sept. 20** *Perf. 11*

*1356* A778 6c blk, ap grn & org brn 12 5

Father Jacques Marquette (1637-1675). French Jesuit missionary, who with Louis Jolliet explored the Mississippi and its tributaries.

### American Folklore Issue

Daniel Boone (1734-1820)

Pennsylvania Rifle, Powder Horn, Tomahawk Pipe and Knife — A779

### Lithographed, Engraved (Giori)

**1968, Sept. 26** *Perf. 11*

*1357* A779 6c yel, dp yel, mar & blk 12 5

Daniel Boone, frontiersman and trapper.

### Arkansas River Navigation Issue

Ship's Wheel, Power Transmission Tower and Barge — A780

**1968, Oct. 1** *Perf. 11*

*1358* A780 6c brt bl, dk bl & blk 12 5

Opening of the Arkansas River to commercial navigation.

### Leif Erikson Issue

Leif Erikson, by Stirling Calder — A781

**1968, Oct. 9** **Litho., Engr.** *Perf. 11*

*1359* A781 6c lt gray brn & blk brn 12 5

Erikson, 11th cent. Norse explorer, was the 1st European to set foot on the American continent, at a place he called Vinland. The statue by an American sculptor is in Reykjavik, Iceland.

The light gray brown ink carries the tagging element.

### Cherokee Strip Issue

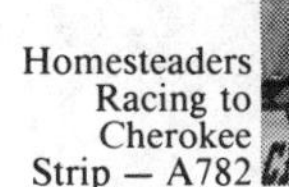

Homesteaders Racing to Cherokee Strip — A782

### Rotary Press Printing

**1968, Oct. 15** *Perf. 11x10½*

*1360* A782 6c brown 12 5

75th anniv. of the opening of the Cherokee Strip to settlers, Sept. 16, 1893.

### John Trumbull Issue

Detail from "The Battle of Bunker's Hill" — A783

### Lithographed, Engraved

**1968, Oct. 18** *Perf. 11*

*1361* A783 6c multicolored 12 5

Trumbull (1756-1843), painter. The stamp shows Lt. Thomas Grosvenor and his attendant, Peter Salem. The painting is at Yale Univ., New Haven, CT.

### Waterfowl Conservation Issue

Wood Ducks A784

### Lithographed, Engraved (Giori)

**1968, Oct. 24** *Perf. 11*

*1362* A784 6c blk & multi 14 5
- *a* Vert. pair, imperf. btwn. *700.00*
- *b* Red & dark blue omitted *1,750.*

Waterfowl conservation.

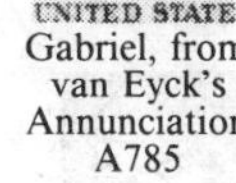


Gabriel, from van Eyck's Annunciation A785

Chief Joseph, by Cyrenius Hall A786

### Christmas Issue

### Engraved (Multicolor Huck)

**1968, Nov. 1 Tagged** *Perf. 11*

*1363* A785 6c multi 12 5
- *a* Untagged 20 5
- *b* Imperf., pair, tagged *375.00*
- *c* Light yellow omitted *200.00*
- *d* Imperf., pair, untagged *450.00*

"The Annunciation" by the 15th cent. Flemish artist Jan van Eyck is in the Natl. Gallery of Art, Washington, DC. No. 1363a was issued Nov. 2.

---

Luminescence

No. 1364 and all following postage stamps are tagged, unless otherwise noted.

---

### American Indian Issue

### Lithographed, Engraved (Giori)

**1968, Nov. 4** *Perf. 11*

*1364* A786 6c blk & multi 14 5

Honoring American Indians and the opening of the Natl. Portrait Gallery, Oct. 5, 1968. Chief Joseph (Indian name Thunder Traveling over the Mountains) a leader of the Nez Percetribe, was born c. 1840 in eastern Oregon and died at the Colesville Reservation in Washington in 1904.

### Beautification of America Issue

Capitol, Azaleas and Tulips A787

Washington Monument, Potomac River and Daffodils A788

Poppies and Lupines along Highway A789

Blooming Crabapples along Street A790

### Lithographed, Engraved (Giori)

**1969, Jan. 16** *Perf. 11*

*1365* A787 6c multicolored 48 15
*1366* A788 6c multicolored 48 15
*1367* A789 6c multicolored 48 15
*1368* A790 6c multicolored 48 15
- *a* Block of 4, #1365-1368 2.00 1.25

Natural Beauty Campaign for more beautiful cities, parks, highways and streets. Nos. 1365-1368 are printed in blocks of 4 in panes of 50, 4 panes to a sheet. On the UL and LL panes Nos. 1365, 1367 appear in 1st, 3rd and 5th place, Nos. 1366, 1368 appear in 2nd and 4th place. This arrangement is reversed on the UR and LR panes.

Eagle from Great Seal of US A791

July Fourth, by Grandma Moses A792

### American Legion Issue

### Lithographed, Engraved (Giori)

**1969, Mar. 15** *Perf. 11*

*1369* A791 6c red, bl & blk 12 5

50th anniv. of the American Legion.

### American Folklore Issue

Grandma Moses

### Lithographed, Engraved (Giori)

**1969, May 1** *Perf. 11*

*1370* A792 6c multicolored 12 5
- *a* Horiz. pair, imperf. btwn. *300.00*
- *b* Black and Prus bl omitted *950.00*

Grandma Moses (Anna Mary Robertson Moses, 1860-1961), primitive painter of American life.

### Apollo 8 Issue

Moon Surface and Earth — A793

### Giori Press Printing

**1969, May 5** *Perf. 11*

*1371* A793 6c blk, bl & ocher 14 6

Apollo 8 mission, which put the 1st men into orbit around the moon, Dec. 21-27, 1968.

### William Christopher Handy Issue

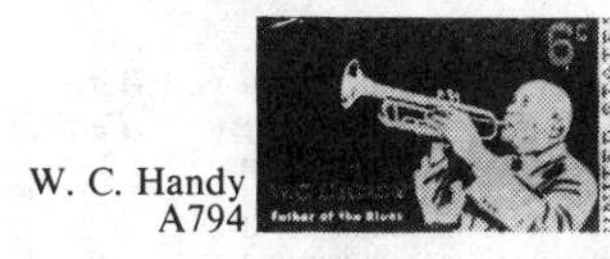


W. C. Handy A794

### Lithographed, Engraved (Giori)

**1969, May 17** *Perf. 11*

*1372* A794 6c multicolored 12 5

Handy (1873-1958), jazz musician and composer.

### California Settlement Issue

Carmel Mission Belfry — A795

**1969, July 16** *Perf. 11*

*1373* A795 6c multicolored 12 5

California sttlement, 200th anniv.

### John Wesley Powell Issue

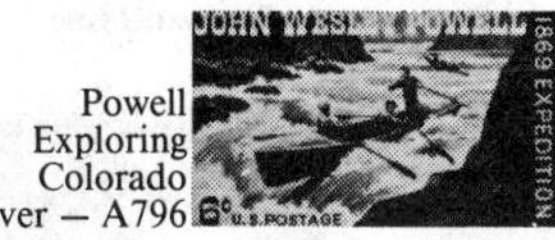


Powell Exploring Colorado River — A796

**1969, Aug. 1** *Perf. 11*

*1374* A796 6c multicolored 12 5

Powell (1834-1902), geologist and explorer of the Green and Colorado Rivers, 1869-1875.

### Alabama Statehood Issue

Camellia and Yellow-shafted Flicker — A797

**1969, Aug. 2** *Perf. 11*

*1375* A797 6c multicolored 12 5

Alabama statehood, 1819.

### Botanical Congress Issue

Douglas Fir (Northwest) A798

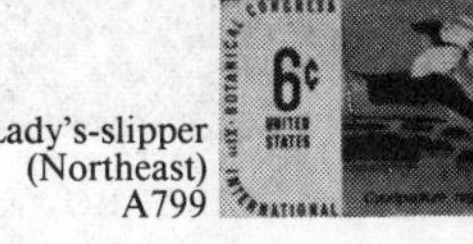


Lady's-slipper (Northeast) A799

Ocotillo (Southwest) A800

Franklinia (Southeast) A801

### Lithographed, Engraved (Giori)

**1969, Aug. 23** *Perf. 11*

*1376* A798 6c multicolored 1.10 15
*1377* A799 6c multicolored 1.10 15
*1378* A800 6c multicolored 1.10 15
*1379* A801 6c multicolored 1.10 15
- *a* Block of 4, #1376-1379 5.50 5.00

11th Intl. Botanical Cong., Seattle, Wash., Aug. 24-Sept. 2. Nos. 1376-1379 are printed in blocks of 4 in panes of 50, 4 panes to a sheet. In the UL and LL left panes Nos. 1376, 1378 appear in 1st, 3rd and 5th place; Nos. 1377, 1379 in 2nd and 4th place. This arrangement is reversed in the UR and LR panes.

**Dartmouth College Case Issue**

Daniel Webster and Dartmouth Hall — A802

**Rotary Press Printing**

**1969, Sept. 22** ***Perf. 10½x11***

*1380* A802 6c green 18 5

Sesquicentennial of the Dartmouth College case, argued by Daniel Webster before the Supreme Court, which reasserted the sanctity of contracts.

**Professional Baseball Issue**

Batter — A803

**Lithographed, Engraved (Giori)**

**1969, Sept. 24** ***Perf. 11***

*1381* A803 6c yel, red, blk & grn 25 5
**a** Black (1869-1969, United States, 6c, Professional Baseball) omitted *1,250.*

Centenary of professional baseball.

**Intercollegiate Football Issue**

Football Player and Coach A804

**1969, Sept. 26** ***Perf. 11***

*1382* A804 6c red & grn 20 5

Centenary of intercollegiate football.

**Dwight D. Eisenhower Issue**

Dwight D. Eisenhower — A805

**Giori Press Printing**

**1969, Oct. 14** ***Perf. 11***

*1383* A805 6c bl, blk & red 12 5

Gen. Eisenhower, 34th Pres. (1890-1969).

**Christmas Issue**

Winter Sunday in Norway, Maine A806

**Engraved (Multicolor Huck)**

**1969, Nov. 3** ***Perf. 11x10½***

*1384* A806 6c dk grn & multi 12 5
Precanceled 60 6
**b** Imperf., pair *1,500.*
**c** lt grn omitted *27.50*
**d** lt grn, red & yel omitted *1,100.* —
**e** yel omitted —

The precancel value applies to the experimental precancel printed in four cities with the names between lines 4½mm apart: in black or green "ATLANTA, GA" and in green only "BALTIMORE, MD", "MEMPHIS, TN" and "NEW HAVEN, CT". They were sold freely to the public and could be used on any class of mail at all post offices during the experimental program and thereafter.

Cured Child A807

"Old Models" A808

**Hope for Crippled Issue**

**Lithographed, Engraved (Giori)**

**1969, Nov. 20** ***Perf. 11***

*1385* A807 6c multicolored 12 5

Issued to encourage the rehabilitation of crippled children and adults, and to honor the Natl. Soc. for Crippled Children and Adults (Easter Seal Soc.) on its 50th anniv.

**William M. Harnett Issue**

**1969, Dec. 3** ***Perf. 11***

*1386* A808 6c multicolored 12 5

Harnett (1848-1892), painter. The painting is in the Museum of Fine Arts, Boston.

**Natural History Issue**

American Bald Eagle — A809

African Elephant Herd — A810

Tlingit Chief in Haida Ceremonial Canoe — A811

Brontosaurus, Stegosaurus and Allosaurus from Jurassic Period — A812

**Lithographed, Engraved (Giori)**

**1970, May 6** ***Perf. 11***

*1387* A809 6c multicolored 12 12
*1388* A810 6c multicolored 12 12
*1389* A811 6c multicolored 12 12
*1390* A812 6c multicolored 12 12
**a** Block of 4, #1387-1390 50 50

1969-1970 celebration of the cent. of the American Museum of Natural History in NYC. Nos. 1387-1390 are printed in blocks of 4 in panes of 32. Nos. 1387-1388 alternate in 1st row, Nos. 1389-1390 in 2nd row. This arrangement is repeated throughout the pane.

The design of No. 1390 is a detail from a mural by Rudolph Zallinger in Yale's Peabody Museum.

**Maine Statehood Issue**

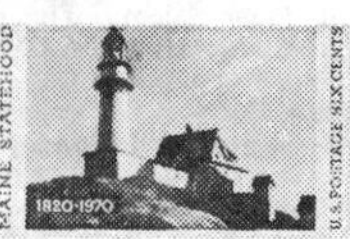


Lighthouse at Two Lights, Maine A813

**Lithographed, Engraved (Giori)**

**1970, July 9** ***Perf. 11***

*1391* A813 6c blk & multi 12 5

Sesquicentennial of Maine statehood. The painting by Edward Hopper (1882-1967) hangs in the Metropolitan Museum of Art, NYC.

**Wildlife Conservation Issue**

American Buffalo A814

**Rotary Press Printing**

**1970, July 20** ***Perf. 10½x11***

*1392* A814 6c blk, *lt brn* 12 5

**Regular Issue**

Dwight David Eisenhower

A815
Dot between "R" and "U"

A815a
No dot between "R" and "U"

Benjamin Franklin A816

USPS Emblem A817

Fiorello H. LaGuardia A817a

Ernie Pyle
Journalist
USA 16c

Ernest Taylor Pyle A818

Dr. Elizabeth Blackwell A818a

Amadeo P. Giannini A818b

**Rotary (6c, 7c, 14c, 16c, 18c, 21c, #1395); Giori (#1394); Photo. (#1396)**

***Perf. 11x10½, 10½x11; 11 (#1394)***

**1970-74**

*1393* A815 6c dk bl gray 12 5
**a** Booklet pane of 8 1.25 *50*
**b** Booklet pane of 5 + label 1.20 *35*
**c** Untagged (Bureau precanceled) 12
*1393D* A816 7c brt bl ('72) 14 5
**e** Untagged (Bureau precanceled) 14
*1394* A815a 8c blk, red & bl gray ('71) 16 5
*1395* A815 8c dp cl ('71) 16 5
**a** Booklet pane of 8 2.00 *1.25*
**b** Booklet pane of 6 1.25 *75*
**c** Booklet pane of 4 + 2 labels ('72) 1.50 *50*
**d** Booklet pane of 7 + label ('72) 1.75 *1.00*
*1396* A817 8c multi ('71) 15 5
*1397* A817a 14c gray brn ('72) 25 5
**a** Untagged (Bureau precanceled) 25
*1398* A818 16c brn ('71) 30 5
**a** Untagged (Bureau precanceled) 35
*1399* A818a 18c vio ('74) 32 6
*1400* A818b 21c grn ('73) 35 6
*Nos. 1393-1400 (9)* 1.95 47

No. 1395 was issued in booklets only. All stamps have one or two straight edges.

Issue dates: 6c, Aug. 6, 1970; 7c, Oct. 20, 1972; Nos. 1394-1395, May 10, 1971; No. 1396, July 1, 1971; 14c, Apr. 24, 1972; 16c, May 7, 1971; 18c, Jan. 23, 1974; 21c, June 27, 1973.

Coil Stamps

**1970-71 Rotary Press** ***Perf. 10 Vert.***

*1401* A815 6c dk bl gray 14 5
**a** Untagged (Bureau precanceled) 14
**b** Imperf., pair *900.00*
*1402* A815 8c dp cl ('71) 18 5
**a** Imperf., pair 50.00
**b** Untagged (Bureau precanceled) 18
**c** Pair, imperf. btwn. —

Issue dates: 6c, Aug. 6; 8c, May 10.

**Edgar Lee Masters Issue**

Edgar Lee Masters (1869-1950), poet — A819

**Lithographed, Engraved (Giori)**

**1970, Aug. 22** ***Perf. 11***

*1405* A819 6c blk & ol bis 12 5

**Woman Suffrage Issue**

Suffragettes, 1920, and Woman Voter, 1970 A820

**Giori Press Printing**

**1970, Aug. 26** ***Perf. 11***

*1406* A820 6c blue 12 5

50th anniv. of the 19th Amendment, which gave women the vote.

**South Carolina Issue**

Symbols of South Carolina A821

**Lithographed, Engraved (Giori)**

**1970, Sept. 12** ***Perf. 11***

*1407* A821 6c bis, blk & red 12 5

300th anniv. of the founding of Charles Town (Charleston), the 1st permanent settlement of SC. Against a background of pine wood the line drawings of the design represent the economic and historic development of SC: the spire of St. Phillip's Church, Capitol, state flag, a ship, 17th cent. man and woman, a Fort Sumter cannon, barrels, cotton, tobacco and yellow jessamine.

**Stone Mountain Memorial Issue**

Robert E. Lee, Jefferson Davis and "Stonewall" Jackson A822

### Giori Press Printing

**1970, Sept. 19** ***Perf. 11***

| | | | |
|---|---|---|---|
| *1408* | A822 6c gray | 12 | 5 |

Dedication of the Stone Mountain Confederate Memorial, GA, May 9, 1970.

### Fort Snelling Issue

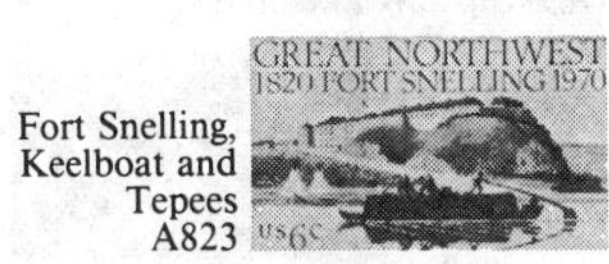

Fort Snelling, Keelboat and Tepees
A823

### Lithographed, Engraved (Giori)

**1970, Oct. 17** ***Perf. 11***

| | | | |
|---|---|---|---|
| *1409* | A823 6c yel & multi | 12 | 5 |

150th anniv. of Fort Snelling, MN, which was an important outpost for the opening of the Northwest.

### Anti-Pollution Issue

Globe and Wheat — A824

Globe and City — A825

Globe and Bluegill
A826

Globe and Seagull — A827

**1970, Oct. 28** **Photo.** ***Perf. 11x10½***

| | | | |
|---|---|---|---|
| *1410* | A824 6c multicolored | 22 | 13 |
| *1411* | A825 6c multicolored | 22 | 13 |
| *1412* | A826 6c multicolored | 22 | 13 |
| *1413* | A827 6c multicolored | 22 | 13 |
| *a* | Block of 4, #1410-1413 | 1.00 | 1.00 |

Issued to focus attention on the mounting problems of pollution. Nos. 1410-1413 are printed in blocks of 4 in panes of 50, 4 panes to a sheet. In the left panes Nos. 1410, 1412 appear in 1st, 3rd and 5th place; Nos. 1411, 1413 in 2nd and 4th place. This arrangement is reversed in right panes.

### Christmas Issue

Nativity, by Lorenzo Lotto (1480-1556)
A828

Tin and Cast-iron Locomotive
A829

Toy Horse on Wheels
A830

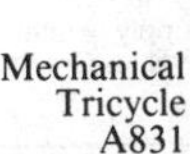

Mechanical Tricycle
A831

Doll Carriage
A832

**1970, Nov. 5** **Photo.** ***Perf. 10½x11***

| | | | |
|---|---|---|---|
| *1414* | A828 6c multicolored | 12 | 5 |
| *a* | Precanceled | 25 | 8 |
| *b* | Black omitted | *1,000.* | |
| *c* | As "a," blue omitted | *1,600.* | |

***Perf. 11x10½***

| | | | |
|---|---|---|---|
| *1415* | A829 6c multicolored | 40 | 10 |
| *a* | Precanceled | 1.00 | 15 |
| *b* | Black omitted | — | |
| *1416* | A830 6c multicolored | 40 | 10 |
| *a* | Precanceled | 1.00 | 15 |
| *b* | Black omitted | — | |
| *c* | Imperf., pair (#1416, 1418) | | — |
| *1417* | A831 6c multicolored | 40 | 10 |
| *a* | Precanceled | 1.00 | 15 |
| *b* | Black omitted | — | |
| *1418* | A832 6c multicolored | 40 | 10 |
| *a* | Precanceled | 1.00 | 15 |
| *b* | Block of 4, #1415-1418 | 1.75 | 1.25 |
| *c* | As "b," precanceled | 4.00 | 2.50 |
| *d* | Black omitted | — | |

The design of No. 1414 is from a painting in the Natl. Gallery of Art, Washington, DC; Nos. 1415-1418 are antique Christmas toys.

Nos. 1415, 1417 appear in 1st, 3rd and 5th place; Nos. 1416, 1418 in 2nd and 4th place. This arrangement is reversed in right panes.

The precanceled stamps, Nos. 1414a-1418a, were furnished to 68 cities. The plates include two straight (No. 1414a) or two wavy (Nos. 1415a-1418a) black lines that make up the precancellation. Unused values are for copies with gum and used values are for copies with an additional cancellation or without gum.

### United Nations Issue

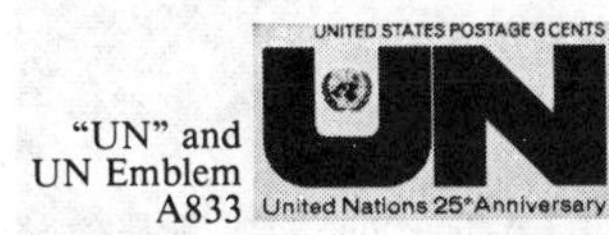

"UN" and UN Emblem
A833

### Lithographed, Engraved (Giori)

**1970, Nov. 20** ***Perf. 11***

| | | | |
|---|---|---|---|
| *1419* | A833 6c blk, ver & ultra | 12 | 5 |

25th anniv. of the UN.

### Landing of the Pilgrims Issue

Mayflower and Pilgrims — A834

### Lithographed, Engraved (Giori)

**1970, Nov. 21** ***Perf. 11***

| | | | |
|---|---|---|---|
| *1420* | A834 6c blk, org, yel, brn, mag & bl | 12 | 5 |
| *a* | Orange & yellow omitted | *1,250.* | |

Mayflower landing, 350th anniv.

### Disabled Veterans and Servicemen Issue

A835

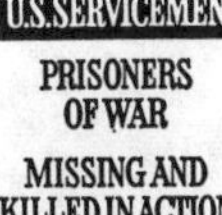

A836

### Lithographed, Engraved (Giori)

**1970, Nov. 24** ***Perf. 11***

| | | | |
|---|---|---|---|
| *1421* | A835 6c multi | 15 | 6 |
| *a* | Pair, #1421-1422 | 30 | 30 |

**Engr.**

| | | | |
|---|---|---|---|
| *1422* | A836 6c dk bl, blk & red | 15 | 6 |

50th anniv. of the Disabled Veterans of America Organization (No. 1421); honoring the contribution of servicemen, particularly those who were prisoners of war or missing in action (No. 1422). Nos. 1421-1422 are printed se-tenant in horizontal rows of 10 in panes of 50, 4 panes to a sheet.

Ewe and Lamb
A837

Douglas MacArthur
A838

### American Wool Industry Issue

### Lithographed, Engraved (Giori)

**1971, Jan. 19** ***Perf. 11***

| | | | |
|---|---|---|---|
| *1423* | A837 6c multicolored | 12 | 5 |

450th anniv. of the introduction of sheep to the No. American continent and the beginning of the American wool industry.

### Gen. Douglas MacArthur Issue

**1971, Jan. 26** **Giori Press Printing**

| | | | |
|---|---|---|---|
| *1424* | A838 6c blk, red & dk bl | 12 | 5 |

MacArthur (1880-1964), Chief of Staff, Supreme Commander for the Allied Powers in the Pacific Area during WW II and Supreme Commander in Japan after the war.

### Blood Donor Issue

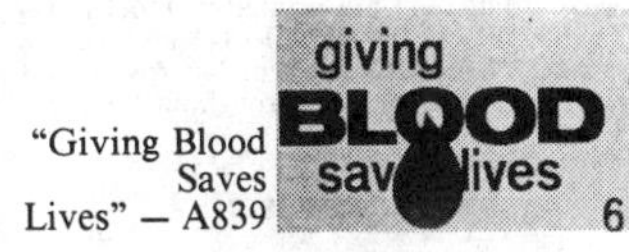

"Giving Blood Saves Lives" — A839

**1971, Mar. 12** ***Perf. 11***

| | | | |
|---|---|---|---|
| *1425* | A839 6c lt bl, scar & ind | 12 | 5 |

Salute to blood donors and spur to participation in the blood donor program.

### Missouri Sesquicentennial Issue

"Independence and the Opening of the West," Detail, by Thomas Hart Benton
A840

**1971, May 8** **Photo.** ***Perf. 11x10½***

| | | | |
|---|---|---|---|
| *1426* | A840 8c multicolored | 15 | 5 |

Sesquicentennial of Missouri's admission to the Union. The stamp design shows a Pawnee facing a hunter-trapper and a group of settlers. Original mural is at Harry S Truman Library, Independence, Mo.

### Wildlife Conservation Issue

Trout
A841

Alligator — A842

Polar Bear and Cubs
A843

California Condor — A844

### Lithographed, Engraved (Giori)

**1971, June 12** ***Perf. 11***

| | | | |
|---|---|---|---|
| *1427* | A841 8c multicolored | 14 | 8 |
| *1428* | A842 8c multicolored | 14 | 8 |
| *1429* | A843 8c multicolored | 14 | 8 |
| *1430* | A844 8c multicolored | 14 | 8 |
| *a* | Block of 4, #1427-1430 | 60 | 60 |
| *b* | As "a", light green & dark green omitted from #1427-1428 | *3,000.* | |
| *c* | As "a", red omitted from #1427, 1429-1430 | | — |

### Antarctic Treaty Issue

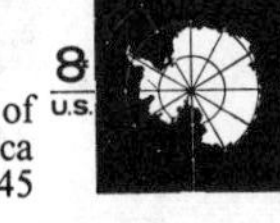

Map of Antarctica
A845

**1971, June 23** **Giori Press Printing**

| | | | |
|---|---|---|---|
| *1431* | A845 8c red & dark blue | 15 | 5 |

10th anniv. of the Antarctic Treaty pledging peaceful uses of and scientific cooperation in Antarctica.

### American Revolution Bicentennial

Bicentennial Commission Emblem — A846

### Lithographed, Engraved (Giori)

**1971, July 4** ***Perf. 11***

| | | | |
|---|---|---|---|
| *1432* | A846 8c red, bl, gray & blk | 15 | 5 |
| *a* | Gray & black omitted | *700.00* | |
| *b* | Gray ("U.S. Postage 8c") omitted | *1,250.* | |

### John Sloan Issue

The Wake of the Ferry
A847

**1971, Aug. 2** ***Perf. 11***

| | | | |
|---|---|---|---|
| *1433* | A847 8c multicolored | 15 | 5 |

Sloan (1871-1951), painter. The painting hangs in the Phillips Gallery, Washington, DC.

### Space Achievement Decade Issue

Earth, Sun, Landing Craft on Moon
A848

Lunar Rover and Astronauts A849

**Lithographed, Engraved (Giori)**

**1971, Aug. 2** *Perf. 11*

| | | | |
|---|---|---|---|
| *1434* A848 8c blk, bl, yel & red | | 15 | 10 |
| *a* | Pair, #1434-1435 | 30 | 25 |
| *b* | As "a," blue & red (litho.) omitted | *1,250.* | |
| *1435* A849 8c blk, bl, yel & red | | 15 | 10 |

A decade of space achievements. Apollo 15 moon exploration mission July 26-Aug. 7. Nos. 1434-1435 are printed se-tenant in horizontal rows of 5 in panes of 50, 4 panes to a sheet. On the UL and LL panes No. 1434 is 1st, 3rd and 5th, No. 1435 2nd and 4th. This arrangement is reversed on the UR and LR panes.

Emily Elizabeth Dickinson A850

Sentry Box, Morro Castle, San Juan A851

**Emily Dickinson Issue**

**Lithographed, Engraved (Giori)**

**1971, Aug. 28** *Perf. 11*

| | | | |
|---|---|---|---|
| *1436* A850 8c multi, *grnsh* | | 15 | 5 |
| *a* | Black & olive (engr.) omitted | *950.00* | |
| *b* | Pale rose omitted | — | |

Dickinson (1830-1886), poet.

**San Juan Issue**

**1971, Sept. 12**

*1437* A851 8c multicolored 15 5

450th anniv. of the founding of San Juan, P.R.

Young Woman Drug Addict A852

Hands Reaching for CARE A853

**Prevent Drug Abuse Issue**

**1971, Oct. 5 Photo.** *Perf. 10½x11*

*1438* A852 8c bl, dp bl & blk 15 5

Drug Abuse Prevention Week, Oct. 3-9.

**CARE Issue**

**1971, Oct. 27**

*1439* A853 8c multicolored 15 5

25th anniv. of CARE, a US-Canadian Cooperative for American Relief Everywhere.

**Historic Preservation Issue**

Decatur House, Washington, DC — A854

Whaling Ship Charles W. Morgan, Mystic, Conn. — A855

Cable Car, San Francisco — A856

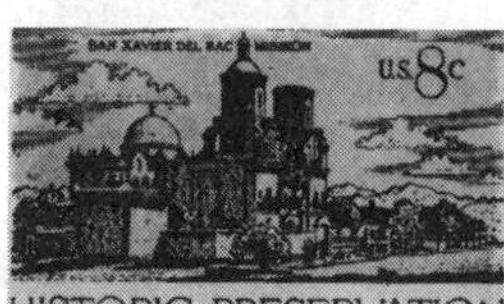

San Xavier del Bac Mission, Tucson, Ariz. — A857

**Lithographed, Engraved (Giori)**

**1971, Oct. 29 Buff Paper** *Perf. 11*

| | | | |
|---|---|---|---|
| *1440* A854 8c blk brn & ocher | | 16 | 12 |
| *1441* A855 8c blk brn & ocher | | 16 | 12 |
| *1442* A856 8c blk brn & ocher | | 16 | 12 |
| *1443* A857 8c blk brn & ocher | | 16 | 12 |
| *a* | Block of 4, #1440-1443 | 75 | 75 |
| *b* | As "a," blk brn omitted | *2,500.* | |
| *c* | As "a," ocher omitted | — | |

Nos. 1440-1443 are printed in blocks of 4 in panes of 32. Nos. 1440-1441 alternate in 1st row, Nos. 1442-1443 in 2nd row. This arrangement is repeated throughout the pane.

**Christmas Issue**

Adoration of the Shepherds, by Giorgione A858

Partridge in a Pear Tree, by Jamie Wyeth A859

**1971, Nov. 10 Photo.** *Perf. 10½x11*

| | | | |
|---|---|---|---|
| *1444* A858 8c gold & multi | | 15 | 5 |
| *a* | Gold omitted | *525.00* | |
| *1445* A859 8c dk grn, red & multi | | 15 | 5 |

No. 1444 is from a painting in the Natl. Gallery of Art, Washington, DC.

Sidney Lanier (1842-1881) A860

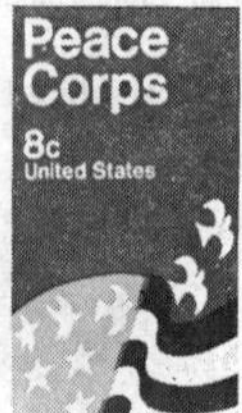

Peace Corps Poster, by David Battle A861

**Sidney Lanier Issue**

**Giori Press Printing**

**1972, Feb. 3** *Perf. 11*

*1446* A860 8c blk, brn & lt bl 15 5

Lanier, poet, musician, lawyer, educator.

**Peace Corps Issue**

**1972, Feb. 11 Photo.** *Perf. 10½x11*

*1447* A861 8c dk bl, lt bl & red 15 5

**National Parks Centennial Issue**

Hulk of Ship A862

Cape Hatteras Lighthouse A863

Laughing Gulls on Driftwood A864

Laughing Gulls and Dune A865

Wolf Trap Farm, Va. — A866

Old Faithful, Yellowstone A867

Family — A869

Mt. McKinley, Alaska A868

**Lithographed, Engraved (Giori)**

**1972** *Perf. 11*

| | | | |
|---|---|---|---|
| *1448* A862 2c blk & multi | | 5 | 5 |
| *1449* A863 2c blk & multi | | 5 | 5 |
| *1450* A864 2c blk & multi | | 5 | 5 |
| *1451* A865 2c blk & multi | | 5 | 5 |
| *a* | Block of 4, #1448-1451 | 25 | 20 |
| *b* | As "a," black (litho.) omitted | *2,000.* | |
| *1452* A866 6c blk & multi | | 12 | 8 |
| *1453* A867 8c blk, bl, brn & multi | | 16 | 5 |
| *1454* A868 15c blk & multi | | 30 | 18 |

Cent. of Yellowstone Natl. Park, the 1st Natl. Park, and of the Natl. Park System. The four 2c stamps were issued for Cape Hatteras, NC, Natl. Seashore; 6c for Wolf Trap Farm, Vienna, Va.; 8c for Yellowstone Natl. Park, Wyo. and 15c for Mt. McKinley Natl. Park, Alaska.

Issue dates: 2c, Apr. 5; 6c, June 26; 8c, Mar. 1; 15c, July 28.

See No. C84.

**Family Planning Issue**

**1972, Mar. 18**

| | | | |
|---|---|---|---|
| *1455* A869 8c blk & multi | | 15 | 5 |
| *a* | Yellow omitted | — | |

**American Bicentennial**

Colonial American Craftsmen

Glassmaker A870

Silversmith A871

Wigmaker A872

Hatter A873

**1972, July 4 Engr.** *Perf. 11x10½*

**Dull Yellow Paper**

| | | | |
|---|---|---|---|
| *1456* A870 8c deep brown | | 30 | 8 |
| *1457* A871 8c deep brown | | 30 | 8 |
| *1458* A872 8c deep brown | | 30 | 8 |
| *1459* A873 8c deep brown | | 30 | 8 |
| *a* | Block of 4, #1456-1459 | 1.25 | 1.25 |

Nos. 1456-1459 are printed in blocks of 4 in panes of 50, 4 panes to a sheet. In UL and LL panes Nos. 1456, 1458 appear in 1st, 3rd and 5th place; Nos. 1457, 1459 in 2nd and 3rd place. This arrangement is reversed in UR and LR panes.

**Olympic Games Issue**

Bicycling and Olympic Rings — A874

Bobsledding A875

Running A876

**1972, Aug. 17 Photo.** *Perf. 11x10½*

| | | |
|---|---|---|
| *1460* A874 6c multicolored | 16 | 12 |
| *1461* A875 8c multicolored | 16 | 5 |
| *1462* A876 15c multicolored | 35 | 18 |

11th Winter Olympic Games, Sapporo, Japan, Feb. 3-13, and 20th Summer Olympic Games, Munich, Germany, Aug. 26-Sept. 11.

See No. C85.

**Parent Teacher Association Issue**

Blackboard A877

**1972, Sept. 15 Photo.** *Perf. 11x10½*

*1463* A877 8c yel & blk 16 5

PTA, 75th anniv.

Demand, as well as supply, determines a stamp's market value. One is as important as the other.

## Wildlife Conservation Issue

Fur Seals A878

Cardinal — A879

Brown Pelican A880

Bighorn Sheep — A881

**Lithographed, Engraved**

**1972, Sept. 20** *Perf. 11*

*1464* A878 8c multicolored 16 8
*1465* A879 8c multicolored 16 8
*1466* A880 8c multicolored 16 8
*1467* A881 8c multicolored 16 8
a Block of 4, #1464-1467 65 60
b As "a," brown omitted *3,500.*
c As "a," grn & bl omitted —

Printed in blocks of 4 in panes of 32. Nos. 1464-1465 alternate in 1st row, Nos. 1466-1467 in 2nd row. This arrangement is repeated throughout the pane.

## Mail Order Issue

Rural Post Office Store A882

**1972, Sept. 27 Photo.** *Perf. 11x10½*

*1468* A882 8c multicolored 15 5

Cent. of mail order business, originated by Aaron Montgomery Ward, Chicago.

## Osteopathic Medicine Issue

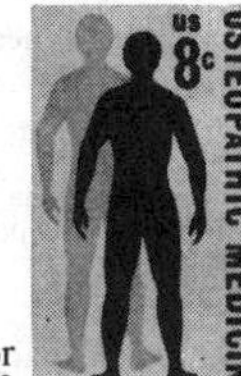

Man's Quest for Health — A883

**1972, Oct. 9 Photo.** *Perf. 10½x11*

*1469* A883 8c yel, org & dk brn 15 5

75th anniv. of the American Osteopathic Assoc., founded by Dr. Andrew T. Still.

An enhanced introduction to the Scott Catalogue begins on Page V. A thorough understanding of the material presented there will greatly aid your use of the catalogue itself.

## American Folklore Issue

Tom Sawyer, by Norman Rockwell — A884

**Lithographed, Engraved (Giori)**

**1972, Oct. 13** *Perf. 11*

*1470* A884 8c blk & multi 15 5
a Horiz. pair, imperf. btwn. *2,500.*
b Red & blk (engr.) omitted *1,250.*
c Yel & tan (litho.) omitted *1,500.*

Tom Sawyer, hero of "The Adventures of Tom Sawyer," by Mark Twain.

Angel from "Mary, Queen of Heaven" A885

Santa Claus A886

**1972, Nov. 9 Photo.** *Perf. 10½x11*

*1471* A885 8c multicolored 15 5
a Pink omitted *400.00*
b Black omitted —
*1472* A886 8c multicolored 15 5

Design of No. 1471 shows detail from a painting by the Master of the St. Lucy Legend in the Natl. Gallery of Art, Washington, DC.

## Pharmacy Issue

Mortar and Pestle, Bowl of Hygeia, 19th Century Medicine Bottles A887

**Lithographed, Engraved (Giori)**

**1972, Nov. 10** *Perf. 11*

*1473* A887 8c blk & multi 15 5
a Blue & orange omitted *1,150.*
b Blue omitted —
c Orange omitted —

Honoring American druggists, and 120th anniv. of the American Pharmaceutical Assoc.

## Stamp Collecting Issue

US No. 1 Under Magnifying Glass A888

**1972, Nov. 17** *Perf. 11*

*1474* A888 8c dk bl grn, blk & brn 15 5
a Black (litho.) omitted *950.00*

To publicize stamp collecting.

## Love Issue

"Love," by Robert Indiana A889

**1973, Jan. 26 Photo.** *Perf. 11x10½*

*1475* A889 8c red, emer & vio bl 15 5

## American Bicentennial

Communications in Colonial Times

Printer and Patriots Examining Pamphlet A890

Posting a Broadside A891

Postrider A892

Drummer A893

**1973 Giori Press Printing** *Perf. 11*

*1476* A890 8c ultra, grnsh blk & red 15 5
*1477* A891 8c blk, ver & ultra 15 5

**Lithographed, Engraved (Giori)**

*1478* A892 8c multicolored 15 5
*1479* A893 8c multicolored 15 5

Issue dates: No. 1476, Feb. 16; No. 1477, Apr. 13; No. 1478, June 22; No. 1479, Sept. 28.

## Boston Tea Party

British Merchantman A894

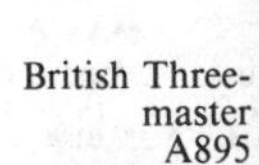

British Three-master A895

Boats and Ship's Hull — A896

Boat and Dock — A897

**Lithographed, Engraved (Giori)**

**1973, July 4** *Perf. 11*

*1480* A894 8c blk & multi 15 10
*1481* A895 8c blk & multi 15 10
*1482* A896 8c blk & multi 15 10
*1483* A897 8c blk & multi 15 10
a Block of 4, #1480-1483 60 45
b As "a," blk (engr.) omitted *2,000.*
c As "a," blk (litho.) omitted *1,700.*

Nos. 1480-1483 are printed in blocks of 4 in panes of 50, 4 panes to a sheet. In UL and LL panes Nos. 1480, 1482 appear in 1st, 3rd and 5th place, Nos. 1481, 1483 appear in 2nd and 4th place. This arrangement is reversed in UR and LR panes.

## American Arts Issue

Gershwin, Sportin' Life, Porgy and Bess A898

Robinson Jeffers, Man and Children of Carmel with Burro A899

Henry Ossawa Tanner, Palette and Rainbow A900

Willa Cather, Pioneer Family and Covered Wagon A901

**1973 Photo.** *Perf. 11*

*1484* A898 8c dp grn & multi 15 5
a Vert. pair, imperf. horiz. *300.00*
*1485* A899 8c Prus. bl & multi 15 5
a Vert. pair, imperf. horiz. *350.00*
*1486* A900 8c yel brn & multi 15 5
*1487* A901 8c dp brn & multi 15 5
a Vert. pair, imperf. horiz. *350.00*

Honoring: No. 1484, George Gershwin (1899-1937), composer. No. 1485, Robinson Jeffers (1887-1962), poet. No. 1486, Henry Ossawa Tanner (1859-1937), black painter (portrait by Thomas Eakins). No. 1487, Willa Sibert Cather (1873-1947), novelist.

Issue dates: No. 1484, Feb. 28; No. 1485, Aug. 13; No. 1486, Sept. 10; No. 1487, Sept. 20.

## Copernicus Issue

Nicolaus Copernicus (1473-1543), Polish Astronomer — A902

**Lithographed, Engraved (Giori)**

**1973, Apr. 23** *Perf. 11*

*1488* A902 8c blk & org 15 5
a Orange omitted *1,100.*
b Blk (engraved) omitted *1,750.*

The orange color can be chemically removed.

## Postal Service Employees' Issue

Stamp Counter A903

Mail Collection A904

Letter Facing on Conveyor Belt A905

Parcel Post Sorting A906

Mail Canceling A907

Manual Letter Routing A908

Electronic Letter Routing A909

Loading Mail on Truck A910

Mailman A911

Rural Mail Delivery A912

**1973, Apr. 30 Photo. *Perf. 10½x11***

| | | | | |
|---|---|---|---|---|
| *1489* | A903 | 8c multicolored | 15 | 10 |
| *1490* | A904 | 8c multicolored | 15 | 10 |
| *1491* | A905 | 8c multicolored | 15 | 10 |
| *1492* | A906 | 8c multicolored | 15 | 10 |
| *1493* | A907 | 8c multicolored | 15 | 10 |
| *1494* | A908 | 8c multicolored | 15 | 10 |
| *1495* | A909 | 8c multicolored | 15 | 10 |
| *1496* | A910 | 8c multicolored | 15 | 10 |
| *1497* | A911 | 8c multicolored | 15 | 10 |
| *1498* | A912 | 8c multicolored | 15 | 10 |
| *a* | | Strip of 10, Nos. 1489-1498 | 1.50 | 1.00 |

A tribute to USPS employees. Nos. 1489-1498 are printed se-tenant in horizontal rows of 10 in panes of 50, 4 panes to a sheet. Emerald inscription on back, printed beneath gum in water-soluble ink, includes the USPS emblem, "People Serving You" and a statement, differing for each of the 10 stamps, about some aspect of postal service.

Each stamp in top or bottom row has a tab with blue inscription enumerating various jobs in postal service.

### Harry S Truman Issue

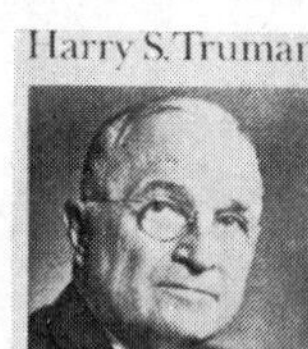

Harry S Truman, 33rd President (1884-1972) A913

**Giori Press Printing**

**1973, May 8 *Perf. 11***

| | | | | |
|---|---|---|---|---|
| *1499* | A913 | 8c car rose, blk & bl | 15 | 5 |

### Electronics Progress Issue

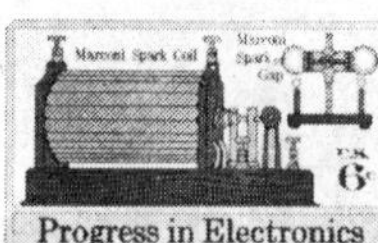

Marconi's Spark Coil and Gap — A914

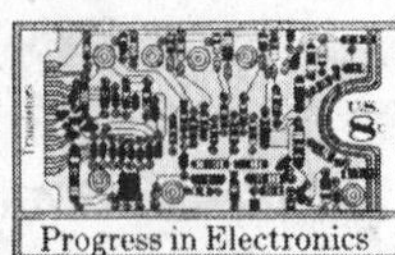

Transistors and Printed Circuit Board A915

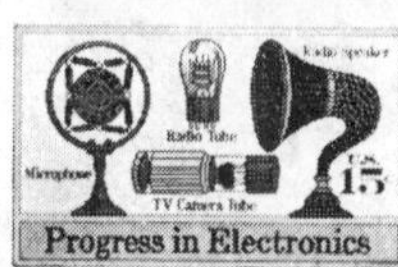

Microphone, Speaker, Vacuum Tube, TV Camera Tube A916

**Lithographed, Engraved (Giori)**

**1973, July 10 *Perf. 11***

| | | | | |
|---|---|---|---|---|
| *1500* | A914 | 6c lil & multi | 12 | 10 |
| *1501* | A915 | 8c tan & multi | 15 | 5 |
| *a* | | Black (inscriptions & "U.S. 8c") omitted | *750.00* | |
| *b* | | Tan (background) & lil omitted | *1,600.* | |
| *1502* | A916 | 15c gray grn & multi | 28 | 15 |
| *a* | | Black (inscriptions & "U.S. 15c") omitted | *1,750.* | |

### Lyndon B. Johnson Issue

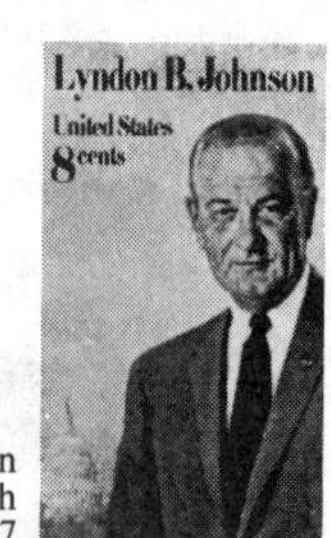

Lyndon B. Johnson (1908-1973), 36th President — A917

**1973, Aug. 27 Photo. *Perf. 11***

| | | | | |
|---|---|---|---|---|
| *1503* | A917 | 8c blk & multi | 15 | 5 |
| *a* | | Horiz. pair, imperf. vert. | *375.00* | |

### Rural America Issue

Angus and Longhorn Cattle A918

Chautauqua Tent and Buggies A919

Wheat Fields and Train A920

**Lithographed, Engraved (Giori)**

**1973-74 *Perf. 11***

| | | | | |
|---|---|---|---|---|
| *1504* | A918 | 8c multicolored | 15 | 5 |
| *a* | | Green & red brn omitted | *550.00* | |
| *1505* | A919 | 10c multi ('74) | 18 | 5 |
| *1506* | A920 | 10c multi ('74) | 28 | 5 |
| *a* | | Black & bl (engr.) omitted | *600.00* | |

Cent. of introduction of Aberdeen Angus cattle to US (No. 1504); of Chautauqua Institution (No. 1505); of introduction of hard winter wheat into Kansas by Mennonite immigrants (No. 1506).

Issue dates: No. 1504, Oct. 5, 1973. No. 1505, Aug. 6, 1974. No. 1506, Aug. 16, 1974.

### Christmas Issue

Small Cowper Madonna, by Raphael A921

Christmas Tree in Needlepoint A922

**1973, Nov. 7 Photo. *Perf. 10½x11***

| | | | | |
|---|---|---|---|---|
| *1507* | A921 | 8c tan & multi | 15 | 5 |
| *1508* | A922 | 8c grn & multi | 15 | 5 |
| *a* | | Vert. pair, imperf. btwn. | *550.00* | |

50-Star and 13-Star Flags — A923

Jefferson Memorial and Signature — A924

Mail Transport A925

Liberty Bell A926

**Multicolor Huck Press**

**1973-74 Tagged *Perf. 11x10½***

| | | | | |
|---|---|---|---|---|
| *1509* | A923 | 10c red & bl | 18 | 5 |
| *a* | | Horiz. pair, imperf. btwn. | *60.00* | — |
| *b* | | Blue omitted | *200.00* | |
| *c* | | Vert. pair, imperf. | *850.00* | |

**Rotary Press Printing**

| | | | | |
|---|---|---|---|---|
| *1510* | A924 | 10c blue | 18 | 5 |
| *a* | | Untagged (Bureau precanceled) | | 18 |
| *b* | | Bklt. pane of 5 + label | 1.50 | *30* |
| *c* | | Bklt. pane of 8 | 1.60 | *30* |
| *d* | | Bklt. pane of 6 ('74) | 3.50 | *30* |
| *e* | | Vert. pair, imperf. horiz. | *250.00* | |
| *f* | | Vert. pair, imperf. btwn. | — | |
| *1511* | A925 | 10c multi, photo | 18 | 5 |
| *a* | | Yellow omitted | *50.00* | |

The yellow can be chemically removed.

**Coil Stamps**

***Perf. 10 Vert.***

**Rotary Press Printing**

| | | | | |
|---|---|---|---|---|
| *1518* | A926 | 6.3c brick red | 12 | 7 |
| *a* | | Untagged (Bureau precanceled) | | 14 |
| *b* | | Imperf., pair | *250.00* | |
| *c* | | As "a," imperf. pair | | *125.00* |

**Multicolor Huck Press**

| | | | | |
|---|---|---|---|---|
| *1519* | A923 | 10c red & blue | 18 | 5 |
| *a* | | Imperf., pair | 30.00 | |

**Rotary Press Printing**

| | | | | |
|---|---|---|---|---|
| *1520* | A924 | 10c blue | 18 | 5 |
| *a* | | Untagged (Bureau precanceled) | | 20 |
| *b* | | Imperf., pair | *40.00* | |

Issue dates: Nos. 1509, 1519, Dec. 8, 1973; Nos. 1510, 1520, Dec. 14, 1973; No. 1511, Jan. 4, 1974; No. 1518, Oct. 1, 1974.

### Veterans of Foreign Wars Issue

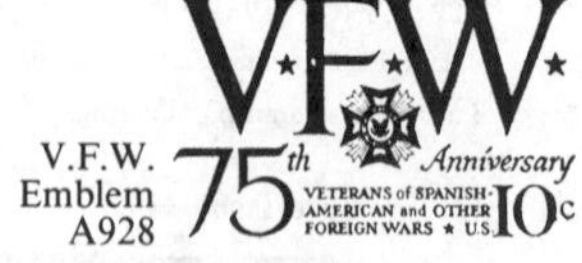

V.F.W. Emblem A928

**Giori Press Printing**

**1974, Mar. 11 *Perf. 11***

| | | | | |
|---|---|---|---|---|
| *1525* | A928 | 10c red & dk bl | 18 | 5 |

75th anniv. of Veterans of Spanish American and other Foreign Wars.

### Robert Frost Issue

Robert Frost (1874-1963), Poet — A929

**Rotary Press Printing**

**1974, Mar. 26 *Perf. 10½x11***

| | | | | |
|---|---|---|---|---|
| *1526* | A929 | 10c black | 18 | 5 |

### EXPO '74 Issue

"Cosmic Jumper" A930

**1974, Apr. 18 Photo. *Perf. 11***

| | | | | |
|---|---|---|---|---|
| *1527* | A930 | 10c multicolored | 18 | 5 |

EXPO '74, Spokane, Wash., May 4-Nov. 4. Theme, "Preserve the Environment."

### Horse Racing Issue

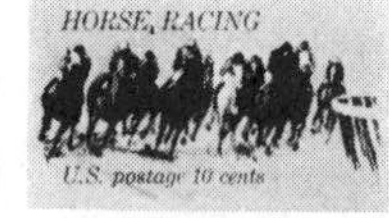

Horses Rounding Turn — A931

**1974, May 4 Photo. *Perf. 11x10½***

| | | | | |
|---|---|---|---|---|
| *1528* | A931 | 10c yel & multi | 18 | 5 |
| *a* | | Blue ("Horse Racing") omitted | *1,300.* | |
| *b* | | Red ("U.S. postage 10 cents") omitted | | — |

### Skylab Issue

Skylab A932

**Lithographed, Engraved (Giori)**

**1974, May 14 *Perf. 11***

| | | | | |
|---|---|---|---|---|
| *1529* | A932 | 10c multicolored | 18 | 5 |
| *a* | | Vert. pair, imperf. btwn. | | — |

1st anniv. of the launching of Skylab and to honor all who participated in the Skylab projects.

### Centenary of UPU Issue

Michelangelo, from "School of Athens," by Raphael — A933

"Five Feminine Virtues," by Hokusai — A934

Old Time Letter Rack, by Peto — A935

Mlle. La Vergne, by Jean Liotard — A936

Lady Writing Letter, by Gerard Terborch — A937

Inkwell and Quill, by Jean Chardin A938

Mrs. John Douglas, by Thomas Gainsborough A939

Don Antonio Noreiga, by Francisco de Goya — A940

**1974, June 6 Photo. *Perf. 11***

| | | | | |
|---|---|---|---|---|
| *1530* | A933 10c multicolored | | 20 | 15 |
| *1531* | A934 10c multicolored | | 20 | 15 |
| *1532* | A935 10c multicolored | | 20 | 15 |
| *1533* | A936 10c multicolored | | 20 | 15 |
| *1534* | A937 10c multicolored | | 20 | 15 |
| *1535* | A938 10c multicolored | | 20 | 15 |
| *1536* | A939 10c multicolored | | 20 | 15 |
| *1537* | A940 10c multicolored | | 20 | 15 |
| *a* | Block or strip of 8, #1530-1537 | | 1.60 | 1.50 |
| *b* | As "a" (block), imperf. vert. | *6,000.* | | |

**Mineral Heritage Issue**

Petrified Wood A941

Tourmaline — A942

Amethyst A943

Rhodochrosite — A944

**Lithographed, Engraved (Giori)**

**1974, June 13 *Perf. 11***

| | | | | |
|---|---|---|---|---|
| *1538* | A941 10c lt bl & multi | | 18 | 10 |
| *a* | Lt bl & yel omitted | | — | |
| *1539* | A942 10c lt bl & multi | | 18 | 10 |
| *a* | Light blue omitted | | — | |
| *b* | Black & pur omitted | | — | |
| *1540* | A943 10c lt bl & multi | | 18 | 10 |
| *a* | Lt. bl & yel omitted | | — | |
| *1541* | A944 10c lt bl & multi | | 18 | 10 |
| *a* | Block or strip of 4, #1538-1541 | | 75 | 75 |
| *b* | As "a," lt bl & yel omitted | *1,900.* | | |
| *c* | Light blue omitted | | — | |
| *d* | Black & red omitted | | — | |

Nos. 1538-1541 printed in blocks of 4 in panes of 48, four panes to a sheet.

**Kentucky Settlement Issue**

Fort Harrod — A945

**Lithographed, Engraved (Giori)**

**1974, June 15 *Perf. 11***

| | | | | |
|---|---|---|---|---|
| *1542* | A945 10c grn & multi | | 20 | 5 |
| *a* | Dull blk (litho.) omitted | *1,100.* | | |
| *b* | Grn (engr. & litho.), blk (engr. & litho.), blue omitted | *3,000.* | | |

**American Bicentennial**

First Continental Congress

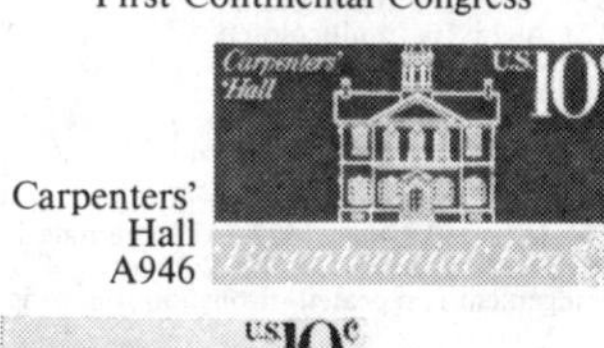

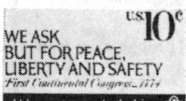

Carpenters' Hall A946

A947

A948

Independence Hall — A949

**Giori Press Printing**

**1974, July 4 *Perf. 11***

| | | | |
|---|---|---|---|
| *1543* | A946 10c dk bl & red | 20 | 10 |
| *1544* | A947 10c gray, dk bl & red | 20 | 10 |
| *1545* | A948 10c gray, dk bl & red | 20 | 10 |
| *1546* | A949 10c red & dk bl | 20 | 10 |
| *a* | Block of 4, #1543-1546 | 1.00 | 80 |

Nos. 1543-1546 are printed in blocks of 4 in panes of 50. Nos. 1543-1544 alternate in 1st row, 1545-1546 in 2nd row. This arrangement is repeated throughout the pane.

**Energy Conservation Issue**

Molecules and Drops of Gasoline and Oil — A950

**Lithographed, Engraved (Giori)**

**1974, Sept. 23 *Perf. 11***

| | | | |
|---|---|---|---|
| *1547* | A950 10c multicolored | 18 | 5 |
| *a* | Blue & orange omitted | *800.00* | |
| *b* | Orange & green omitted | *675.00* | |
| *c* | Green omitted | *700.00* | |

To publicize the importance of conserving all forms of energy.

**American Folklore Issue**

Legend of Sleepy Hollow

Headless Horseman Pursuing Ichabod Crane A951

**Lithographed, Engraved (Giori)**

**1974, Oct. 10 *Perf. 11***

| | | | |
|---|---|---|---|
| *1548* | A951 10c dk bl, blk, org & yel | 18 | 5 |

Legend of Sleepy Hollow, by Washington Irving.

**Retarded Children Issue**

Retarded Child — A952

**Giori Press Printing**

**1974, Oct. 12 *Perf. 11***

| | | | |
|---|---|---|---|
| *1549* | A952 10c brn red & dk brn | 18 | 5 |

Natl. Assoc. of Retarded Citizens.

**Christmas Issue**

Angel, from Perussis Altarpiece, 1480 — A953

"The Road-Winter," by Currier and Ives — A954

Dove Weather Vane, Mount Vernon A955

**1974 Photo. *Perf. 10½x11***

| | | | |
|---|---|---|---|
| *1550* | A953 10c multicolored | 18 | 5 |

***Perf. 11x10½***

| | | | |
|---|---|---|---|
| *1551* | A954 10c multicolored | 18 | 5 |

***Imperf., Paper Backing Rouletted***

**Self-adhesive**

**Inscribed "Precanceled"**

**Untagged**

| | | | |
|---|---|---|---|
| *1552* | A955 10c multicolored | 18 | 8 |

Issue dates: Nos. 1550-1551, Oct. 23, No. 1552, Nov. 15.

Unused value of No. 1552 is for copy on rouletted paper backing as issued. Used value is for copy on piece, with or without postmark. Most copies are becoming discolored, probably from the adhesive. The Catalogue value is for discolored copies.

Die cutting includes crossed slashes through dove, applied to prevent removal and re-use of stamp. The stamp will separate into layers if soaked.

**American Arts Issue**

Benjamin West, Self-portrait A956

Paul Laurence Dunbar A957

D. W. Griffith and Projector A958

**1975 Photo. *Perf. 10½x11***

| | | | | |
|---|---|---|---|---|
| *1553* | A956 10c multicolored | | 18 | 5 |

***Perf. 11***

| | | | | |
|---|---|---|---|---|
| *1554* | A957 10c multicolored | | 18 | 5 |
| *a* | Imperf., pair | *1,100.* | | |

**Litho., Engr. (Giori)**

| | | | | |
|---|---|---|---|---|
| *1555* | A958 10c multicolored | | 18 | 5 |
| *a* | Brown (engr.) omitted | *900.00* | | |

Honoring: Benjamin West (1738-1820), painter (No. 1553). Paul Laurence Dunbar (1872-1906), poet (No. 1554). David Lewelyn Wark Griffith (1875-1948), motion picture producer (No. 1555).

Issue dates: No. 1553, Feb. 10. No. 1554, May 1. No. 1555, May 27.

### Space Issue

Pioneer 10 Passing Jupiter A959

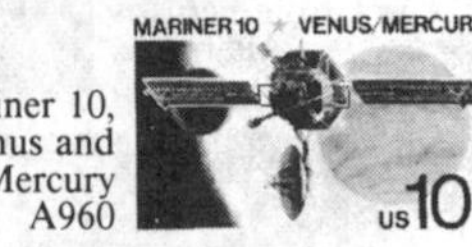


Mariner 10, Venus and Mercury A960

**Lithographed, Engraved (Giori)**

**1975** *Perf. 11*

*1556* A959 10c vio bl, yel & red 18 5
  *a* Red & yel (litho.) omitted *1,450.*
  *b* Blue omitted *1,100.*
*1557* A960 10c blk, red, ultra & bis 18 5
  *a* Red omitted *600.00*
  *b* Ultra & bister omitted *1,900.*

US unmanned accomplishments in space. Pioneer 10 passed within 81,000 miles of Jupiter, Dec. 3, 1973. Mariner 10 explored Venus and Mercury in 1974, and Mercury again in Mar. 1975.

Issue dates: No. 1556, Feb. 28; No. 1557, Apr. 4.

### Collective Bargaining Issue

"Labor and Management" A961

**1975, Mar. 13 Photo.** *Perf. 11*

*1558* A961 10c multicolored 18 5

Collective Bargaining Law, enacted 1935 with Wagner Act. Imperfs. are printers waste.

### American Bicentennial
Contributors to the Cause

Sybil Ludington A962

Salem Poor — A963

Haym Salomon A964

Peter Francisco A965

**1975, Mar. 25 Photo.** *Perf. 11x10½*

*1559* A962 8c multicolored 16 13
  *a* Back inscription omitted *200.00*
*1560* A963 10c multicolored 18 5
  *a* Back inscription omitted *325.00*
*1561* A964 10c multicolored 18 5
  *a* Back inscription omitted *300.00*
  *b* Red omitted *275.00*
*1562* A965 18c multicolored 32 20

Sybil Ludington, age 16, rallied militia Apr. 26, 1777. Salem Poor, black freeman, fought in Battle of Bunker Hill. Haym Salomon, Jewish immigrant, raised money to finance Revolutionary War. Peter Francisco, Portuguese-French immigrant, joined Continental Army at 15.

Emerald inscription on back, printed beneath gum in water-soluble ink, gives thumbnail sketch of portrayed contributor.

Lexington-Concord Battle

"Birth of Liberty," by Henry Sandham A966

**1975, Apr. 19 Photo.** *Perf. 11*

*1563* A966 10c multicolored 20 5
  *a* Vert. pair, imperf. horiz. *450.00*

Battle of Lexington and Concord, bicent.

Battle of Bunker Hill

Battle of Bunker Hill, by John Trumbull — A967

**1975, June 17** *Perf. 11*

*1564* A967 10c multicolored 20 5

Bicentenary of the Battle of Bunker Hill.

Military Uniforms

Soldier with Flintlock Musket, Uniform Button A968

Sailor with Grappling Hook, First Navy Jack, 1775 A969

Marine with Musket, Full-rigged Ship — A970

Militiaman with Musket, Powder Horn — A971

**1975, July 4** *Perf. 11*

*1565* A968 10c multicolored 18 8
*1566* A969 10c multicolored 18 8
*1567* A970 10c multicolored 18 8
*1568* A971 10c multicolored 18 8
  *a* Block of 4, #1565-1568 75 75

Bicentenary of US Military Services. Nos. 1565-1568 printed se-tenant in sheets of 50. Nos. 1565-1566 alternate in one horizontal row, Nos. 1567-1568 in the next.

### Apollo Soyuz Space Issue

Apollo and Soyuz After Docking and Earth — A972

A particular stamp may be scarce, but if few collectors want it, its market value may remain relatively low.

Spacecrafts Before Docking, Earth and Project Emblem — A973

**1975, July 15 Photo.** *Perf. 11*

*1569* A972 10c multicolored 18 10
  *a* Pair, #1569-1570 36 25
  *b* As "a," vert. pair, imperf. horiz. *900.00*
*1570* A973 10c multicolored 18 10

Apollo Soyuz space test project (Russo-American cooperation); launching, July 15; link-up, July 17. Nos. 1569-1570 are printed se-tenant in horizontal rows of 3 in panes of 24, 4 panes to a sheet. In the 1st row of the pane No. 1569 is in 1st and 3rd space, No. 1570 in 2nd space; in the 2nd row No. 1570 is in 1st and 3rd space, No. 1569 in 2nd space, etc. See Russia Nos. 4339-4340.

### International Women's Year Issue

Worldwide Equality for Women A974

**1975, Aug. 26 Photo.** *Perf. 11x10½*

*1571* A974 10c bl, org & dk bl 18 5

International Women's Year 1975.

### Postal Service Bicentennial Issue

Stagecoach and Trailer Truck A975

Old and New Locomotives — A976

Early Mail Plane and Jet — A977

Satellite for Transmission of Mailgrams — A978

**1975, Sept. 3 Photo.** *Perf. 11x10½*

*1572* A975 10c multicolored 18 8
*1573* A976 10c multicolored 18 8
*1574* A977 10c multicolored 18 8
*1575* A978 10c multicolored 18 8
  *a* Block of 4, #1572-1575 80 75
  *b* As "a," red ("10c") omitted —

Nos. 1572-1575 are printed in blocks of 4 in panes of 50. Nos. 1572-1573 alternate in 1st row, Nos. 1574-1575 in 2nd row. This arrangement is repeated throughout the pane.

### World Peace Through Law Issue

Law Book, Olive Branch and Globe A979

### Giori Press Printing

**1975, Sept. 29** *Perf. 11*

*1576* A979 10c grn, Prus bl & rose brn 18 5

A prelude to 7th World Conf. of the World Peace Through Law Center at Washington, DC, Oct. 12-17.

### Banking and Commerce Issue

Engine Turning, Indian Head Penny and Morgan Silver Dollar A980

Seated Liberty Quarter, $20 Gold (Double Eagle), Engine Turning A981

**Lithographed, Engraved (Giori)**

**1975, Oct. 6** *Perf. 11*

*1577* A980 10c multicolored 18 8
  *a* Pair, #1577-1578 36 20
  *b* Brn & bl (litho.) omitted *1,250.*
*1578* A981 10c multicolored 18 8

Banking and commerce in the US and for the Centennial Convention of the American Bankers Association. Nos. 1577-1578 are printed se-tenant in horizontal rows of 5 in panes of 40, four panes to a sheet.

### Christmas Issue

Madonna, by Domenico Ghirlandaio A982

Christmas Card, by Louis Prang, 1878 A983

**1975, Oct. 14 Photo.** *Perf. 11*

*1579* A982 (10c) multicolored 18 5
  *a* Imperf., pair *100.00*
*1580* A983 (10c) multicolored 18 5
  *a* Imperf., pair *105.00*
  *b* Perf. 10½x11 65 5

### Americana Issue

Inkwell and Quill — A984



Speaker's Stand — A985

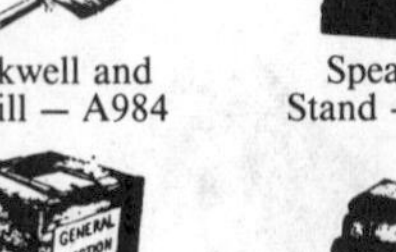

Early Ballot Box A987

Books, Bookmark, Eyeglasses A988

Dome of Capitol — A994



Contemplation of Justice — A995

Early American Printing Press — A996



Torch — A997

Liberty Bell — A998

Eagle and Shield — A999

Fort McHenry Flag — A1001

Head, Statue of Liberty — A1002

Old North Church, Boston A1003

Fort Nisqually A1004

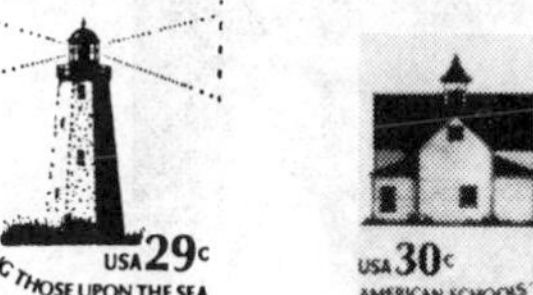


Sandy Hook Lighthouse, NJ — A1005

Morris Township School No. 2, Devils Lake, ND — A1006

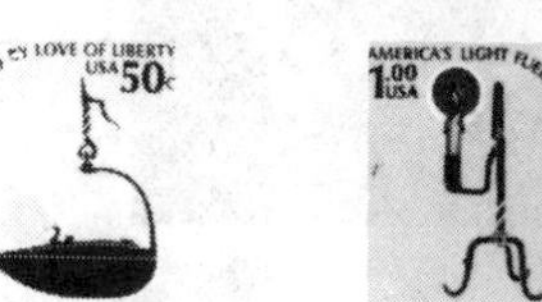


Iron "Betty" Lamp, 17th-18th Cent. — A1007

Rush Lamp and Candle Holder — A1008

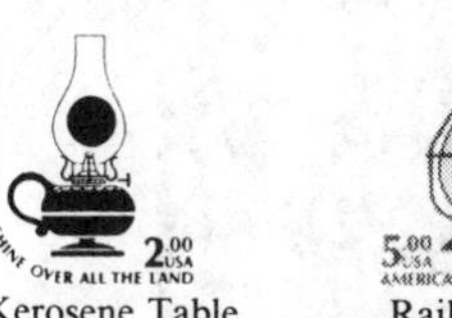


Kerosene Table Lamp — A1009

Railroad Conductor's Lantern, c. 1850 — A1010

**1975-81 Engr. *Perf. 11x10½***

| No. | Type | Description | Unused | Used |
|---|---|---|---|---|
| *1581* | A984 | 1c dk bl, *grnsh* ('77) | 5 | 5 |
| *a* | | Untagged (Bureau precanceled) | | 5 |
| *1582* | A985 | 2c red brn, *grnsh* ('77) | 5 | 5 |
| *a* | | Untagged (Bureau precanceled) | | 6 |
| *b* | | Cream paper ('81) | 5 | 5 |
| *1584* | A987 | 3c ol, *grnsh* ('77) | 6 | 5 |
| *a* | | Untagged (Bureau precanceled) | | 6 |
| *1585* | A988 | 4c rose mag, *cr* ('77) | 8 | 5 |
| *a* | | Untagged (Bureau precanceled) | | 8 |

**Size: 17½x20½mm**

| No. | Type | Description | Unused | Used |
|---|---|---|---|---|
| *1590* | A994 | 9c sl grn ('77) | 75 | 20 |
| *a* | | Perf. 10 | 17.50 | 10.00 |

**Size: 18½x22½mm**

| No. | Type | Description | Unused | Used |
|---|---|---|---|---|
| *1591* | A994 | 9c sl grn, *gray* | 16 | 5 |
| *a* | | Untagged (Bureau precanceled) | | 18 |
| *1592* | A995 | 10c vio, *gray* ('77) | 18 | 5 |
| *a* | | Untagged (Bureau precanceled) | | 25 |
| *1593* | A996 | 11c org, *gray* | 20 | 5 |
| *1594* | A997 | 12c brn red, *beige* ('81) | 22 | 5 |
| *1595* | A998 | 13c brown | 26 | 5 |
| *a* | | Booklet pane of 6 | 1.60 | *50* |
| *b* | | Booklet pane of 7 + label | 1.80 | *50* |
| *c* | | Booklet pane of 8 | 2.10 | *50* |
| *d* | | Booklet pane of 5 + label ('76) | 1.30 | *50* |
| *e* | | Vert. pair, imperf btwn. | — | |

**Photo.**

***Perf. 11***

| No. | Type | Description | Unused | Used |
|---|---|---|---|---|
| *1596* | A999 | 13c multi | 24 | 5 |
| *a* | | Imperf., pair | *45.00* | — |
| *b* | | Yellow omitted | *225.00* | |

**Engr.**

| No. | Type | Description | Unused | Used |
|---|---|---|---|---|
| *1597* | A1001 | 15c gray, dk bl & red ('78) | 28 | 5 |
| *a* | | Vert. pair, imperf. | *17.50* | |
| *b* | | Gray omitted | — | |

***Perf. 11x10½***

| No. | Type | Description | Unused | Used |
|---|---|---|---|---|
| *1598* | A1001 | 15c gray, dk bl & red ('78) | 28 | 5 |
| *a* | | Booklet pane of 8 | 3.25 | *60* |
| *1599* | A1002 | 16c blue ('78) | 32 | 5 |
| *1603* | A1003 | 24c red, *blue* | 50 | 9 |
| *1604* | A1004 | 28c brn, *blue* ('78) | 55 | 8 |
| *1605* | A1005 | 29c blue, *blue* ('78) | 55 | 8 |
| *1606* | A1006 | 30c grn, *blue* ('79) | 55 | 8 |

**Engr. & Litho.**

***Perf. 11***

| No. | Type | Description | Unused | Used |
|---|---|---|---|---|
| *1608* | A1007 | 50c tan, blk & org ('79) | 85 | 15 |
| *a* | | Black omitted | *500.00* | |
| *1610* | A1008 | $1 tan, brn, org & yel ('79) | 1.75 | 15 |
| *a* | | Brn (engraved) omitted | *525.00* | |
| *b* | | Tan, org & yel omitted | *375.00* | |
| *c* | | Brown inverted | — | |
| *1611* | A1009 | $2 tan, dk grn, org & yel ('78) | 3.75 | 35 |
| *1612* | A1010 | $5 tan, red brn, yel & org ('79) | 9.00 | 1.65 |
| | | *Nos. 1581-1612 (22)* | 20.63 | 3.48 |

Nos. 1590, 1590a, 1595, 1598 issued in booklets only. All stamps have one or two straight edges.

Guitar A1011

Saxhorns A1012

Drum A1013

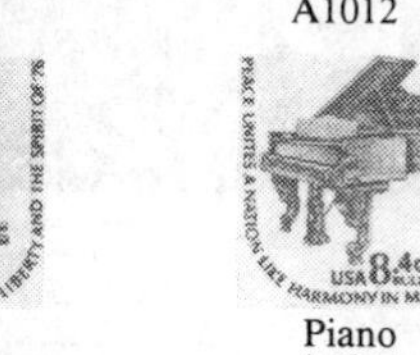


Piano A1014

Coil Stamps

**Engr.**

***Perf. 10 Vertically***

| No. | Type | Description | Unused | Used |
|---|---|---|---|---|
| *1613* | A1011 | 3.1c brn, *yel* ('79) | 9 | 5 |
| *a* | | Untagged (Bureau precanceled) | | 10 |
| *b* | | Imperf., pair | *850.00* | |
| *1614* | A1012 | 7.7c brn, *brt yel* ('76) | 16 | 8 |
| *a* | | Untagged (Bureau precanceled) | | 16 |
| *b* | | As "a," imperf., pair | | *800.00* |
| *1615* | A1013 | 7.9c car, *yel* ('76) | 18 | 8 |
| *a* | | Untagged (Bureau precanceled) | | 16 |
| *b* | | Imperf., pair | *500.00* | |
| *1615C* | A1014 | 8.4c dk bl, *yel* ('78) | 18 | 8 |
| *d* | | Untagged (Bureau precanceled) | | 16 |
| *e* | | As "d", pair, imperf. btwn. | | 60.00 |
| *f* | | As "d", imperf., pair | | 25.00 |
| *1616* | A994 | 9c sl grn, *gray* | 20 | 5 |
| *a* | | Imperf., pair | *110.00* | |
| *b* | | Untagged (Bureau precanceled) | | 18 |
| *c* | | As "b," imperf., pair | | *190.00* |
| *1617* | A995 | 10c vio, *gray* ('77) | 20 | 5 |
| *a* | | Untagged (Bureau precanceled) | | 25 |
| *b* | | Imperf., pair | *60.00* | |
| *1618* | A998 | 13c brown | 24 | 5 |
| *a* | | Untagged (Bureau precanceled) | | 25 |
| *b* | | Imperf., pair | 25.00 | |
| *1618C* | A1001 | 15c gray, dk bl & red ('78) | 25 | 5 |
| *d* | | Imperf., pair | 20.00 | |
| *e* | | Pair, imperf. between | 200.00 | |
| *f* | | Gray omitted | *50.00* | |
| *1619* | A1002 | 16c blue ('78) | 32 | 5 |
| | | *Nos. 1613-1619 (9)* | 1.82 | 54 |

No. 1619 was printed on two different presses. Huck press printings have white background without bluish tinge, are a fraction of a millimeter smaller and have block instead of overall tagging. Cottrell press printings show a joint line. See Nos. 1811, 1813, 1816.

13-Star Flag, Independence Hall A1015

Flag over Capitol A1016

**Multicolor Huck Press**

**1975-77 *Perf. 11x10½***

| No. | Type | Description | Unused | Used |
|---|---|---|---|---|
| *1622* | A1015 | 13c dk bl & red | 24 | 5 |
| *a* | | Horiz. pair, imperf. btwn. | 55.00 | |
| *b* | | Vert. pair, imperf. | — | |
| *c* | | Perf. 11 ('81) | 55 | 5 |
| *1623* | A1016 | 13c bl & red ('77) | 24 | 5 |
| *a* | | Booklet pane of 8 (1 #1590 and 7 #1623) | 2.50 | *60* |
| *b* | | Perf. 10 | 1.50 | 1.00 |
| *c* | | Booklet pane of 8 (1 #1590a + 7 #1623b) | 30.00 | — |
| *d* | | Se-tenant pair, #1590 & 1623 | 1.50 | — |
| *e* | | Se-tenant pair, #1590a & 1623a | 22.50 | — |

**Coil Stamp**

***Perf. 10 Vertically***

| No. | Type | Description | Unused | Used |
|---|---|---|---|---|
| *1625* | A1015 | 13c dk bl & red | 26 | 5 |
| *a* | | Imperf., pair | 20.00 | |

Nos. 1623 and 1623b issued in booklets only. All stamps have one or two straight edges.

**American Bicentennial – Spirit of '76**

Drummer Boy A1019

Old Drummer A1020

Fifer — A1021

Designed after painting "The Spirit of '76," by Archibald M. Willard.

**1976, Jan. 1 Photo. *Perf. 11***

| No. | Type | Description | Unused | Used |
|---|---|---|---|---|
| *1629* | A1019 | 13c multi | 24 | 8 |
| *1630* | A1020 | 13c multi | 24 | 8 |
| *1631* | A1021 | 13c multi | 24 | 8 |
| *a* | | Strip of 3, #1629-1631 | 75 | 60 |
| *b* | | As "a," imperf. | *1,500.* | |
| *c* | | Vert. pair, imperf. | *1,000.* | |

Nos. 1629-1631 printed se-tenant.

**Interphil Issue**

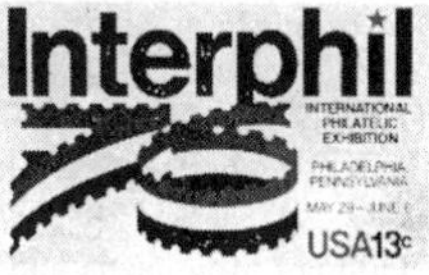


"Interphil 76" — A1022

**Lithographed, Engraved (Giori)**

**1976, Jan. 17 *Perf. 11***

| No. | Type | Description | Unused | Used |
|---|---|---|---|---|
| *1632* | A1022 | 13c dk bl, red & ultra | 26 | 5 |

Interphil 76 Intl. Phil. Exhib., Philadelphia, Pa., May 29-June 6.

State Flags — A1023-A1072

**1976, Feb. 23 Photo. *Perf. 11***

| No. | Type | Description | Unused | Used |
|---|---|---|---|---|
| *1633* | A1023 | 13c *Delaware* | 30 | 25 |
| *1634* | A1024 | 13c *Pennsylvania* | 30 | 25 |
| *1635* | A1025 | 13c *New Jersey* | 30 | 25 |
| *1636* | A1026 | 13c *Georgia* | 30 | 25 |
| *1637* | A1027 | 13c *Connecticut* | 30 | 25 |
| *1638* | A1028 | 13c *Massachusetts* | 30 | 25 |
| *1639* | A1029 | 13c *Maryland* | 30 | 25 |
| *1640* | A1030 | 13c *South Carolina* | 30 | 25 |
| *1641* | A1031 | 13c *New Hampshire* | 30 | 25 |
| *1642* | A1032 | 13c *Virginia* | 30 | 25 |
| *1643* | A1033 | 13c *New York* | 30 | 25 |
| *1644* | A1034 | 13c *North Carolina* | 30 | 25 |
| *1645* | A1035 | 13c *Rhode Island* | 30 | 25 |
| *1646* | A1036 | 13c *Vermont* | 30 | 25 |
| *1647* | A1037 | 13c *Kentucky* | 30 | 25 |
| *1648* | A1038 | 13c *Tennessee* | 30 | 25 |
| *1649* | A1039 | 13c *Ohio* | 30 | 25 |
| *1650* | A1040 | 13c *Louisiana* | 30 | 25 |
| *1651* | A1041 | 13c *Indiana* | 30 | 25 |
| *1652* | A1042 | 13c *Mississippi* | 30 | 25 |
| *1653* | A1043 | 13c *Illinois* | 30 | 25 |
| *1654* | A1044 | 13c *Alabama* | 30 | 25 |
| *1655* | A1045 | 13c *Maine* | 30 | 25 |
| *1656* | A1046 | 13c *Missouri* | 30 | 25 |
| *1657* | A1047 | 13c *Arkansas* | 30 | 25 |
| *1658* | A1048 | 13c *Michigan* | 30 | 25 |
| *1659* | A1049 | 13c *Florida* | 30 | 25 |
| *1660* | A1050 | 13c *Texas* | 30 | 25 |
| *1661* | A1051 | 13c *Iowa* | 30 | 25 |
| *1662* | A1052 | 13c *Wisconsin* | 30 | 25 |
| *1663* | A1053 | 13c *California* | 30 | 25 |
| *1664* | A1054 | 13c *Minnesota* | 30 | 25 |
| *1665* | A1055 | 13c *Oregon* | 30 | 25 |
| *1666* | A1056 | 13c *Kansas* | 30 | 25 |
| *1667* | A1057 | 13c *West Virginia* | 30 | 25 |
| *1668* | A1058 | 13c *Nevada* | 30 | 25 |
| *1669* | A1059 | 13c *Nebraska* | 30 | 25 |
| *1670* | A1060 | 13c *Colorado* | 30 | 25 |
| *1671* | A1061 | 13c *North Dakota* | 30 | 25 |
| *1672* | A1062 | 13c *South Dakota* | 30 | 25 |
| *1673* | A1063 | 13c *Montana* | 30 | 25 |
| *1674* | A1064 | 13c *Washington* | 30 | 25 |
| *1675* | A1065 | 13c *Idaho* | 30 | 25 |
| *1676* | A1066 | 13c *Wyoming* | 30 | 25 |
| *1677* | A1067 | 13c *Utah* | 30 | 25 |
| *1678* | A1068 | 13c *Oklahoma* | 30 | 25 |
| *1679* | A1069 | 13c *New Mexico* | 30 | 25 |
| *1680* | A1070 | 13c *Arizona* | 30 | 25 |
| *1681* | A1071 | 13c *Alaska* | 30 | 25 |
| *1682* | A1072 | 13c *Hawaii* | 30 | 25 |
| *a* | | Pane of 50 | 15.00 | — |

**Telephone Centenary Issue**



Bell's Telephone Patent Application A1073

**Engraved (Giori)**

**1976, Mar. 10 *Perf. 11***

| No. | Type | Description | Unused | Used |
|---|---|---|---|---|
| *1683* | A1073 | 13c blk, pur & red, *tan* | 24 | 5 |

1st telephone call by Alexander Graham Bell, Mar. 10, 1876.

For unused stamps, more recent issues are valued as never hinged, with the beginning point determined on a country-by-country basis. Notes to show the beginning points are prominently placed in the text.

**Commercial Aviation Issue**

Ford-Pullman Monoplane and Laird Swallow Biplane — A1074

**1976, Mar. 19** **Photo.** ***Perf. 11***

*1684* A1074 13c bl & multi 24 5

50th anniv. of 1st contract airmail flights: Dearborn, MI to Cleveland, OH, Feb. 15, 1926; and Pasco, WA to Elko, NV, Apr. 6, 1926.

**Chemistry Issue**

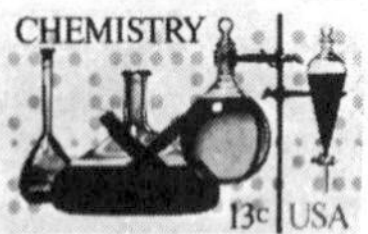


Various Flasks, Separatory Funnel, Computer Tape
A1075

**1976, Apr. 6** **Photo.** ***Perf. 11***

*1685* A1075 13c multicolored 24 5

Honoring American chemists, cent. of the American Chemical Society.

**American Bicentennial Issue**
Souvenir Sheets

Surrender of Cornwallis at Yorktown, by John Trumbull
A1076

Declaration of Independence, by John Trumbull
A1077

Washington Crossing the Delaware, by Emanuel Leutze/Eastman Johnson
A1078

Washington Reviewing Army at Valley Forge, by William T. Trego
A1079

Designs, from Left to Right, No. 1686: a. Two British officers. b. Gen. Benjamin Lincoln. c. George Washington. d. John Trumbull, Col. Cobb, von Steuben, Lafayette, Thomas Nelson. Alexander Hamilton, John Laurens, Walter Stewart (all vert.).

No. 1687: a. John Adams, Roger Sherman, Robert R. Livingston. b. Jefferson, Franklin. c. Thomas Nelson, Jr., Francis Lewis, John Witherspoon, Samuel Huntington, d. John Hancock, Charles Thomson. e. George Read, John Dickinson, Edward Rutledge (a, d, vert., b, c, e, horiz.).

No. 1688: a. Boatsman. b. Washington. c. Flag bearer. d. Men in boat. e. Men on shore (a, d, horiz., b, c, e, vert.).

No. 1689: a. Two officers. b. Washington. c. Officer, black horse. d. Officer, white horse. e. Three soldiers (a, c, e, horiz., b, d, vert.).

| **1976, May 29** | **Litho.** | ***Perf. 11*** | |
|---|---|---|---|
| *1686* A1076 | Sheet of 5 | 3.50 | — |
| a.-e | 13c multi, any single | 65 | 40 |
| f | USA 13c omitted on "b," "c" & "d," imperf., untagged | — | — |
| g | USA 13c omitted on "a" & "e" | — | — |
| h | Imperf., untagged | | — |
| i | USA 13c omitted on "b," "c" & "d" | — | |
| j | USA 13c double on "b" | — | — |
| k | USA 13c omitted on "c" & "d" | — | |
| l | USA 13c omitted on "e" | — | |
| m | USA 13c omitted, imperf., untagged | — | |
| *1687* A1077 | Sheet of 5 | 4.00 | — |
| a.-e | 18c multi, any single | 80 | 55 |
| f | Design & marginal inscriptions omitted | — | |
| g | USA 18c omitted on "a" & "c" | — | |
| h | USA 18c omitted on "b," "d" & "e" | — | |
| i | USA 18c omitted on "d" | — | |
| j | Black omitted in design | — | |
| k | USA 18c omitted, imperf., untagged | — | |
| m | USA 18c omitted on "b" & "e" | — | |
| *1688* A1078 | Sheet of 5 | 4.50 | — |
| a.-e | 24c multi, any single | 90 | 75 |
| f | USA 24c ommitted, imperf., untagged | — | |
| g | USA 24c omitted on "d" & "e" | — | — |
| h | Design & marginal inscriptions omitted | — | |
| i | USA 24c omitted on "a," "b" & "c" | — | — |
| j | Imperf., untagged | — | |
| k | USA 24c of "d" & "e" inverted | — | |
| *1689* A1079 | Sheet of 5 | 6.00 | — |
| a.-e | 31c multi, any single | 1.10 | 90 |
| f | USA 31c omitted, imperf., untagged | — | |
| g | USA 31c omitted on "a" & "c" | — | |
| h | USA 31c omitted on "b," "d" & "e" | — | — |
| i | USA 31c omitted on "e" | — | |
| j | Black omitted in design | — | |
| k | Imperf., untagged | | — |
| l | USA 31c omitted on "b" & "d" | — | |
| m | USA 31c omitted on "a" "c" & "e" | — | |
| n | As "m", imperf., untagged | — | |
| p | As "h", imperf., untagged | | — |

Nos. 1688-1689 exist with inverted perforations.

Issued in connection with Interphil 76 Intl. Phil. Exhib., Philadelphia, Pa., May 29-June 6. Size of sheets: 203x152mm; stamps: 25x39½mm, 39½x25mm.

### Benjamin Franklin Issue

Franklin and Map of North America, 1776 — A1080

| **Lithographed, Engraved (Giori)** | | | |
|---|---|---|---|
| **1976, June 1** | | ***Perf. 11*** | |
| *1690* A1080 | 13c ultra & multi | 26 | 5 |
| a | Light blue omitted | 575.00 | |

American Bicentennial; Franklin (1706-1790), deputy postmaster general for the colonies (1753-1774) and statesman.

See Canada No. 691

### American Bicentennial Issue

Declaration of Independence, by John Trumbull

A1081 A1082 A1083 A1084

| **1976, July 4** | **Photo.** | ***Perf. 11*** | |
|---|---|---|---|
| *1691* A1081 | 13c multicolored | 20 | 8 |
| *1692* A1082 | 13c multicolored | 20 | 8 |
| *1693* A1083 | 13c multicolored | 20 | 8 |
| *1694* A1084 | 13c multicolored | 20 | 8 |
| a | Strip of 4, #1691-1694 | 80 | 60 |

Nos. 1691-1694 printed se-tenant.

### Olympic Games Issue

Diving A1085 Skiing A1086

Running A1087 Skating A1088

| **1976, July 16** | **Photo.** | ***Perf. 11*** | |
|---|---|---|---|
| *1695* A1085 | 13c multicolored | 30 | 8 |
| *1696* A1086 | 13c multicolored | 30 | 8 |
| *1697* A1087 | 13c multicolored | 30 | 8 |
| *1698* A1088 | 13c multicolored | 30 | 8 |
| a | Block of 4, #1695-1698 | 1.20 | 85 |
| b | As "a," imperf. | 900.00 | |

12th Winter Olympic Games, Innsbruck, Austria, Feb. 4-15, and 21st Summer Olympic Games, Montreal, Canada, July 17-Aug. 1. Nos. 1695-1698 printed se-tenant in sheets of 50. Nos. 1695-1696 alternate in one horizontal row, Nos. 1697-1698 in next.

### Clara Maass Issue

Clara Maass, Newark German Hospital Pin — A1089

| **1976, Aug. 18** | **Photo.** | ***Perf. 11*** | |
|---|---|---|---|
| *1699* A1089 | 13c multicolored | 24 | 6 |
| a | Horiz. pair, imperf. vert. | 525.00 | |

Clara Maass (1876-1901), volunteer in fight against yellow fever, birth centenary.

### Adolph S. Ochs Issue

Adolph S. Ochs, (1858-1935) A1090

| **Giori Press Printing** | | | |
|---|---|---|---|
| **1976, Sept. 18** | | ***Perf. 11*** | |
| *1700* A1090 | 13c blk & gray | 24 | 5 |

Publisher of the NY Times, 1896-1935.

### Christmas Issue

Nativity, by John Singleton Copley A1091

"Winter Pastime," by Nathaniel Currier A1092

| **1976, Oct. 27** | **Photo.** | ***Perf. 11*** | |
|---|---|---|---|
| *1701* A1091 | 13c multicolored | 24 | 5 |
| a | Imperf., pair | 95.00 | |
| *1702* A1092 | 13c multicolored | 24 | 5 |
| a | Imperf., pair | 120.00 | |
| *1703* A1092 | 13c multicolored | 24 | 5 |
| a | Imperf., pair | 120.00 | |
| b | Vert. pair, imperf. btwn. | — | |

No. 1702 has overall tagging. Lettering at base is black and usually ½mm below design. As a rule, no "snowflaking" in sky or pond. Pane of 50 has margins on 4 sides with slogans.

No. 1703 has block tagging the size of printed area. Lettering at base is gray black and usually ¾mm below design. "Snowflaking" generally in sky and pond. Pane has margin only at right or left, and no slogans.

### American Bicentennial Issue

Washington at Princeton

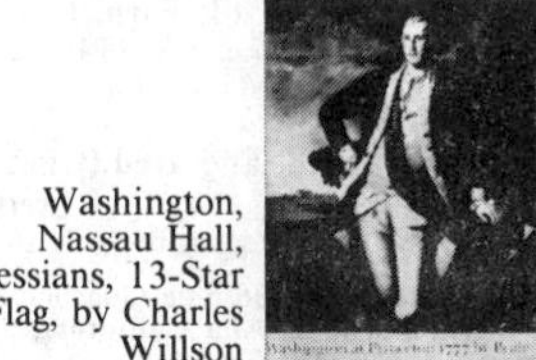

Washington, Nassau Hall, Hessians, 13-Star Flag, by Charles Willson Peale — A1093

| **1977, Jan. 3** | **Photo.** | ***Perf. 11*** | |
|---|---|---|---|
| *1704* A1093 | 13c multicolored | 24 | 5 |
| a | Horiz. pair, imperf. vert. | 450.00 | |

Washington's victory at Princeton over Lord Cornwallis, bicentennial.

### Sound Recording Issue

Tin Foil Phonograph A1094

| **Lithographed, Engraved (Giori)** | | | |
|---|---|---|---|
| **1977, Mar. 23** | | ***Perf. 11*** | |
| *1705* A1094 | 13c blk & multi | 24 | 5 |

Centenary of invention of the phonograph by Thomas Alva Edison, and development of sophisticated recording industry.

### American Folk Art Issue

Pueblo Pottery

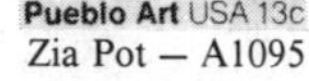

Zia Pot — A1095

San Ildefonso Pot — A1096

Hopi Pot — A1097

Acoma Pot — A1098

| **1977, Apr. 13** | **Photo.** | ***Perf. 11*** | |
|---|---|---|---|
| *1706* A1095 | 13c multicolored | 24 | 8 |
| *1707* A1096 | 13c multicolored | 24 | 8 |
| *1708* A1097 | 13c multicolored | 24 | 8 |
| *1709* A1098 | 13c multicolored | 24 | 8 |
| a | Block or strip of 4 | 1.00 | 60 |
| b | As "a", imperf. vert. | 2,500. | |

Pueblo art, 1880-1920, from museums in NM, AZ and CO. In the 1st row stamps are in sequence as listed. In the 2nd row Nos. 1708-1709 are followed by Nos. 1706-1709, 1708-1709.

### Lindbergh Flight Issue

Spirit of St. Louis A1099

| **1977, May 20** | **Photo.** | ***Perf. 11*** | |
|---|---|---|---|
| *1710* A1099 | 13c multicolored | 24 | 5 |
| a | Imperf., pair | 1,500. | |

Charles A. Lindbergh's solo transatlantic flight from NY to Paris, 50th anniv.

### Colorado Statehood Issue

Columbine and Rocky Mountains — A1100

| **1977, May 21** | **Photo.** | ***Perf. 11*** | |
|---|---|---|---|
| *1711* A1100 | 13c multicolored | 24 | 5 |
| a | Horiz. pair, imperf. btwn. | — | |
| b | Horiz. pair, imperf. vert. | — | |

Colorado became a state in 1876.

### Butterfly Issue

Swallowtail A1101

Checkerspot A1102

Dogface A1103

Orange Tip – A1104

**1977, June 6 Photo. *Perf. 11***

| | | | |
|---|---|---|---|
| *1712* A1101 13c tan & multi | 24 | 8 |
| *1713* A1102 13c tan & multi | 24 | 8 |
| *1714* A1103 13c tan & multi | 24 | 8 |
| *1715* A1104 13c tan & multi | 24 | 8 |
| *a* Block of 4, #1712-1715 | 1.00 | 60 |
| *b* As "a," imperf. horiz. | — | |

Nos. 1712-1715 are printed in blocks of 4, in panes of 50. Nos. 1712-1713 alternate in 1st row, Nos. 1714-1715 in 2nd row. This arrangement is repeated throughout the pane.

### American Bicentennial Issues
Lafayette

Marquis de Lafayette – A1105

**1977, June 13 Engr. *Perf. 11***

| | | |
|---|---|---|
| *1716* A1105 13c bl, blk & red | 24 | 5 |

200th anniv. of Lafayette's landing on the coast of SC, north of Charleston.

Skilled Hands for Independence

Seamstress A1106

Blacksmith A1107

Wheelwright A1108

Leatherworker A1109

**1977, July 4 Photo. *Perf. 11***

| | | |
|---|---|---|
| *1717* A1106 13c multicolored | 24 | 8 |
| *1718* A1107 13c multicolored | 24 | 8 |
| *1719* A1108 13c multicolored | 24 | 8 |
| *1720* A1109 13c multicolored | 24 | 8 |
| *a* Block of 4, #1717-1720 | 1.00 | 60 |

Nos. 1717-1720 are printed se-tenant in blocks of 4, in panes of 50. Nos. 1717-1718 alternate in 1st row, Nos. 1719-1720 in 2nd row. This arrangement is repeated throughout the pane.

### Peace Bridge Issue

Peace Bridge and Dove – A1110

**1977, Aug. 4 Engr. *Perf. 11x10½***

| | | |
|---|---|---|
| *1721* A1110 13c blue | 24 | 5 |

50th anniv. of the Peace Bridge, connecting Buffalo, NY with Fort Erie, Ontario.

### American Bicentennial Issue
Battle of Oriskany

Herkimer at Oriskany, by Frederick Yohn A1111

**1977, Aug. 6 Photo. *Perf. 11***

| | | |
|---|---|---|
| *1722* A1111 13c multicolored | 24 | 5 |

200th anniv. of Battle of Oriskany, American Militia led by Brig. Gen. Nicholas Herkimer (1728-1777).

### Energy Issue

Energy Conservation A1112

Energy Development A1113

**1977, Oct. 20 Photo. *Perf. 11***

| | | |
|---|---|---|
| *1723* A1112 13c multicolored | 24 | 8 |
| *a* Pair, #1723-1724 | 50 | 35 |
| *1724* A1113 13c multicolored | 24 | 8 |

Conservation and development of nation's energy resources. Nos. 1723-1724 printed setenant vertically in sheets of 40.

### Alta California Issue

Farm Houses A1114

**Lithographed, Engraved (Giori)**

**1977, Sept. 9 *Perf. 11***

| | | |
|---|---|---|
| *1725* A1114 13c blk & multi | 24 | 5 |

El Pueblo de San José de Guadalupe, 1st civil settlement in Alta California, 200th anniv.



### American Bicentennial Issue
Articles of Confederation

Members of Continental Congress in Conference A1115

**Engraved (Giori)**

**1977, Sept. 30 *Perf. 11***

| | | |
|---|---|---|
| *1726* A1115 13c red & brn, *cr* | 24 | 5 |

200th anniv. of drafting the Articles of Confederation, York Town, Pa.

### Talking Picture Issue

Movie Projector and Phonograph A1116

**Lithographed, Engraved (Giori)**

**1977, Oct. 6 *Perf. 11***

| | | |
|---|---|---|
| *1727* A1116 13c multicolored | 24 | 5 |

50th anniv. of talking pictures.

### American Bicentennial Issue
Surrender at Saratoga

Surrender of Burgoyne, by John Trumbull A1117

**1977, Oct. 7 Photo. *Perf. 11***

| | | |
|---|---|---|
| *1728* A1117 13c multicolored | 24 | 5 |

200th anniv. of Gen. John Burgoyne's surrender at Saratoga.

### Christmas Issue

Washington at Valley Forge A1118

Rural Mailbox A1119

**1977, Oct. 21 Photo. *Perf. 11***

| | | |
|---|---|---|
| *1729* A1118 13c multicolored | 24 | 5 |
| *a* Imperf., pair | *70.00* | |
| *1730* A1119 13c multicolored | 24 | 5 |
| *a* Imperf., pair | *250.00* | |

### Carl Sandburg Issue

Carl Sandburg, by William A. Smith, 1952 – A1120

**Engraved (Giori)**

**1978, Jan. 6 *Perf. 11***

| | | |
|---|---|---|
| *1731* A1120 13c blk & brn | 24 | 5 |

Sandburg (1878-1967), poet, biographer and collector of American folk songs.

### Captain Cook Issue

Capt. Cook, by Nathaniel Dance, 1776 A1121

"Resolution" and "Discovery," by John Webber A1122

**Giori Press Printing**

**1978, Jan. 20 *Perf. 11***

| | | |
|---|---|---|
| *1732* A1121 13c dark blue | 24 | 8 |
| *a* Pair, #1732-1733 | 50 | 30 |
| *b* As "a," imperf. btwn. | — | |
| *1733* A1122 13c green | 24 | 8 |
| *a* Vert. pair, imperf. horiz. | — | |

Capt. James Cook, 200th anniv. of his arrival in Hawaii, at Waimea, Kauai, Jan. 20, 1778, and of his anchorage in Cook Inlet, near Anchorage, Alaska, June 1, 1778. Nos. 1732-1733 issued in panes of 50, containing 25 each of Nos. 1732-1733 including 5 No. 1732a. Design of No. 1733 is after etching "A View of Karakekooa in Owyhee."

Indian Head Penny, 1877 A1123

Eagle A1124

Roses – A1126

**Engraved (Giori)**

**1978, Jan. 11 *Perf. 11***

| | | |
|---|---|---|
| *1734* A1123 13c brn & bl grn, *bis* | 24 | 10 |
| *a* Horiz. pair, imperf. vert. | *325.00* | |

**1978, May 22 Photo. *Perf. 11***

| | | |
|---|---|---|
| *1735* A1124 (15c) orange | 24 | 5 |
| *a* Imperf., vert. pair | *65.00* | |
| *b* Vert. pair, imperf. horiz. | *300.00* | |

**Engr. *Perf. 11x10½***

| | | |
|---|---|---|
| *1736* A1124 (15c) orange | 24 | 5 |
| *a* Booklet pane of 8 | 2.25 | *60* |

See No. 1743

**1978, July 11 Engr. *Perf. 10***

| | | |
|---|---|---|
| *1737* A1126 15c multicolored | 24 | 6 |
| *a* Booklet pane of 8 | 2.40 | *60* |
| *b* As "a," imperf. | — | |

Nos. 1736, 1737 issued in booklets only. All stamps have 1 or 2 straight edges.

Robertson Windmill, Williamsburg A1127

Old Windmill, Portsmouth A1128

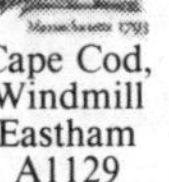

Cape Cod, Windmill Eastham A1129

Dutch Mill, Batavia A1130

Southwestern Windmill — A1131

**1980, Feb. 7 Engr. *Perf. 11***

| | | | |
|---|---|---|---|
| *1738* | A1127 15c sepia, *yel* | 30 | 5 |
| *1739* | A1128 15c sepia, *yel* | 30 | 5 |
| *1740* | A1129 15c sepia, *yel* | 30 | 5 |
| *1741* | A1130 15c sepia, *yel* | 30 | 5 |
| *1742* | A1131 15c sepia, *yel* | 30 | 5 |
| *a* | Booklet pane of 10 | 3.25 | *60* |
| | *Nos. 1738-1742 (5)* | 1.50 | 25 |

Nos. 1738-1742 issued in booklets only; pane of 10 contains 2 each of #1738-1742.

Coil Stamp

**1978, May 22 Engr. *Perf. 10 Vert.***

| | | | |
|---|---|---|---|
| *1743* | A1124 (15c) orange | 24 | 5 |
| *a* | Imperf., pair | *110.00* | |

### Black Heritage Issue

Harriet Tubman (1820-1913), Cart Carrying Slaves — A1133

**1978, Feb. 1 Photo. *Perf. 10½x11***

| | | | |
|---|---|---|---|
| *1744* | A1133 13c multicolored | 24 | 5 |

Tubman, born a slave, helped more than 300 slaves escape to freedom.

### American Folk Art Issue

American Quilts, Basket Design

A1134 A1135

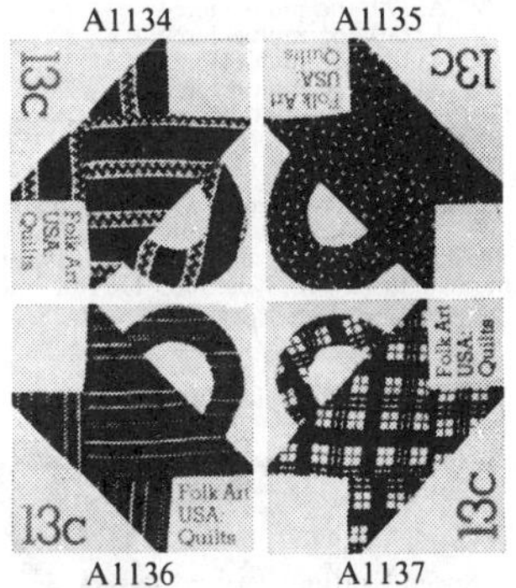

A1136 A1137

**1978, Mar. 8 Photo. *Perf. 11***

| | | | |
|---|---|---|---|
| *1745* | A1134 13c multicolored | 24 | 8 |
| *1746* | A1135 13c multicolored | 24 | 8 |
| *1747* | A1136 13c multicolored | 24 | 8 |
| *1748* | A1137 13c multicolored | 24 | 8 |
| *a* | Block of 4, #1745-1748 | 1.00 | 60 |

Nos. 1745-1748 printed in blocks of 4 in panes of 48, four panes to a sheet.

### American Dance Issue

Ballet A1138

Theater A1139

Folk Dance A1140

Modern Dance A1141

**1978, Apr. 26 Photo. *Perf. 11***

| | | | |
|---|---|---|---|
| *1749* | A1138 13c multicolored | 24 | 8 |
| *1750* | A1139 13c multicolored | 24 | 8 |
| *1751* | A1140 13c multicolored | 24 | 8 |
| *1752* | A1141 13c multicolored | 24 | 8 |
| *a* | Block of 4, #1749-1752 | 1.00 | 60 |

Printed in blocks of 4 in panes of 48.

### American Bicentennial Issue

French Alliance

Louis XVI and Franklin, Porcelain Sculpture by C. G. Sauvage — A1142

### Giori Press Printing

**1978, May 4 *Perf. 11***

| | | | |
|---|---|---|---|
| *1753* | A1142 13c bl, blk & red | 24 | 5 |

Bicent. of French Alliance, signed in Paris, Feb. 6, 1778, and ratified by Continental Cong., May 4.

### Early Cancer Detection Issue

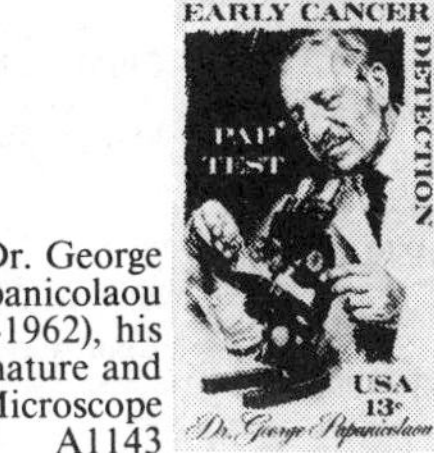

Dr. George Papanicolaou (1883-1962), his Signature and Microscope A1143

**1978, May 18 Engr. *Perf. 10½x11***

| | | | |
|---|---|---|---|
| *1754* | A1143 13c brown | 24 | 5 |

Papanicolaou, developer of Pap Test, early cancer detection in women.

### The Scott Catalogue value

The Scott Catalogue value is a retail price, what you could expect to pay for the stamp in a grade of Fine-Very Fine. The value listed is a reference which reflects recent actual dealer selling price.

### Performing Arts Issues

Jimmie Rodgers and Locomotive A1144

George M. Cohan, "Yankee Doodle Dandy" and Stars A1145

**1978 Photo. *Perf. 11***

| | | | |
|---|---|---|---|
| *1755* | A1144 13c multicolored | 24 | 5 |
| *1756* | A1145 13c multicolored | 24 | 5 |

Rodgers (1897-1933), the "Singing Brakeman, Father of Country Music," and Cohan (1878-1942), actor and playwright.

Issue dates: No. 1755, May 24; No. 1756, July 3.

### CAPEX Issue

Wildlife from Canadian-US Border — A1146

**Lithographed, Engraved (Giori)**

**1978, June 10 *Perf. 11***

| | | | |
|---|---|---|---|
| *1757* | A1146 Block of 8 | 2.10 | 1.75 |
| *a* | 13c *Cardinal* | 25 | 10 |
| *b* | 13c *Mallard* | 25 | 10 |
| *c* | 13c *Canada goose* | 25 | 10 |
| *d* | 13c *Blue jay* | 25 | 10 |
| *e* | 13c *Moose* | 25 | 10 |
| *f* | 13c *Chipmunk* | 25 | 10 |
| *g* | 13c *Red fox* | 25 | 10 |
| *h* | 13c *Raccoon* | 25 | 10 |
| *i* | Yel, grn, red, brn, bl, blk (litho.) omitted | — | |

CAPEX, Canadian Intl. Phil. Exhib., Toronto, Ont., June 9-18. No. 1757 has black inscriptions on green panel: "Canadian International Exhibition, Toronto" and in French and English "This tribute features wildlife that share the Canadian-United States Border." Signature of Postmaster General William F. Bolger. Size: 108x74mm.

### Photography Issue

Photographic Equipment A1147

**1978, June 26 Photo. *Perf. 11***

| | | | |
|---|---|---|---|
| *1758* | A1147 15c multicolored | 26 | 5 |

### Viking Missions to Mars Issue

Viking 1 Lander Scooping Up Soil on Mars A1148

**Lithographed, Engraved**

**1978, July 20**

| | | | |
|---|---|---|---|
| *1759* | A1148 15c multicolored | 28 | 5 |

2nd anniv. of landing of Viking 1 on Mars.

### American Owls Issue

Great Gray Owl A1149 Saw-whet Owl A1150

Barred Owl A1151 Great Horned Owl A1152

**1978, Aug. 26 Engr. *Perf. 11***

| | | | |
|---|---|---|---|
| *1760* | A1149 15c multicolored | 28 | 8 |
| *1761* | A1150 15c multicolored | 28 | 8 |
| *1762* | A1151 15c multicolored | 28 | 8 |
| *1763* | A1152 15c multicolored | 28 | 8 |
| *a* | Block of 4, #1760-1763 | 1.20 | 85 |

Nos. 1760-1763 printed se-tenant in sheets of 50. Nos. 1760-1761 alternate in one horizontal row, Nos. 1762-1763 in the next.

### American Trees Issue

Giant Sequoia A1153

White Pine A1154

White Oak A1155

Gray Birch A1156

**1978, Oct. 9 Photo. *Perf. 11***

| | | | |
|---|---|---|---|
| *1764* | A1153 15c multicolored | 28 | 8 |
| *1765* | A1154 15c multicolored | 28 | 8 |
| *1766* | A1155 15c multicolored | 28 | 8 |
| *1767* | A1156 15c multicolored | 28 | 8 |
| *a* | Block of 4, #1764-1767 | 1.20 | 85 |
| *b* | As "a," imperf. horiz. | — | |

Nos. 1764-1767 printed se-tenant in sheets of 40. Nos. 1764-1765 alternate in one horizontal row, Nos. 1766-1767 in the next.

### Christmas Issue

Madonna and Child with Cherubim, by Andrea della Robbia — A1157

Child on Hobby-horse and Christmas Trees — A1158

**1978, Oct. 18 Photo. *Perf. 11***

| | | | |
|---|---|---|---|
| *1768* | A1157 15c bl & multi | 28 | 5 |
| *a* | Imperf., pair | *100.00* | |
| *1769* | A1158 15c red & multi | 28 | 5 |
| *a* | Imperf., pair | *100.00* | |
| *b* | Vert. pair, imperf. horiz. | — | |

### Robert F. Kennedy Issue

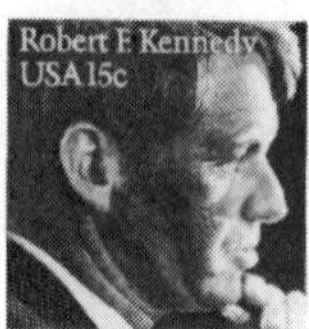
Robert F. Kennedy (1925-68), US Attorney General — A1159

**1979, Jan. 12 Engr. *Perf. 11***

| | | | |
|---|---|---|---|
| *1770* | A1159 15c blue | 28 | 5 |

### Black Heritage Issue

Dr. Martin Luther King, Jr. (1929-68), and Civil Rights Marchers — A1160

**1979, Jan. 13 Photo. *Perf. 11***

| | | | |
|---|---|---|---|
| *1771* | A1160 15c multicolored | 28 | 5 |
| *a* | Imperf., pair | — | |

Civil rights leader.

### Year of the Child Issue

Children A1161

**1979, Feb. 15 Engr. *Perf. 11***

| | | | |
|---|---|---|---|
| *1772* | A1161 15c orange red | 28 | 5 |

International Year of the Child.

John Steinbeck A1162

Albert Einstein A1163

### John Steinbeck Issue

**1979, Feb. 27 Engr. *Perf. 10½x11***

| | | | |
|---|---|---|---|
| *1773* | A1162 15c dark blue | 28 | 5 |

John Ernst Steinbeck (1902-68), novelist.

### Albert Einstein Issue

**1979, Mar. 4 Engr. *Perf. 10½x11***

| | | | |
|---|---|---|---|
| *1774* | A1163 15c chocolate | 28 | 5 |

Einstein (1879-1955), theoretical physicist.

### American Folk Art Issue

Pennsylvania Toleware

Coffeepot A1164

Tea Caddy A1165

Sugar Bowl A1166

Coffeepot A1167

**1979, Apr. 19 Photo. *Perf. 11***

| | | | |
|---|---|---|---|
| *1775* | A1164 15c multicolored | 28 | 8 |
| *1776* | A1165 15c multicolored | 28 | 8 |
| *1777* | A1166 15c multicolored | 28 | 8 |
| *1778* | A1167 15c multicolored | 28 | 8 |
| *a* | Block of 4, #1775-1778 | 1.20 | 85 |
| *b* | As "a," imperf. horiz. | — | |

Nos. 1775-1778 are printed se-tenant.

### American Architecture Issue

Virginia Rotunda, by Thomas Jefferson A1168

Baltimore Cathedral, by Benjamin Latrobe A1169

Boston State House, by Charles Bulfinch A1170

Philadelphia Exchange, by William Strickland A1171

**1979, June 4 Engr. *Perf. 11***

| | | | |
|---|---|---|---|
| *1779* | A1168 15c blk & brick red | 28 | 8 |
| *1780* | A1169 15c blk & brick red | 28 | 8 |
| *1781* | A1170 15c blk & brick red | 28 | 8 |
| *1782* | A1171 15c blk & brick red | 28 | 8 |
| *a* | Block of 4, #1779-1782 | 1.20 | 85 |

Printed se-tenant in panes of 48.

The only foreign revenue stamps listed in this Catalogue are those authorized for prepayment of postage.

### Endangered Flora Issue

Persistent Trillium A1172

Hawaiian Wild Broadbean A1173

Contra Costa Wallflower A1174

Antioch Dunes Evening Primrose A1175

**1979, June 7 Photo. *Perf. 11***

| | | | |
|---|---|---|---|
| *1783* | A1172 15c multicolored | 28 | 8 |
| *1784* | A1173 15c multicolored | 28 | 8 |
| *1785* | A1174 15c multicolored | 28 | 8 |
| *1786* | A1175 15c multicolored | 28 | 8 |
| *a* | Block of 4, #1783-1786 | 1.20 | 85 |
| *b* | As "a", imperf. | *900.00* | |

Printed se-tenant in panes of 50.

### Seeing Eye Dogs Issue

German Shepherd Leading Man — A1176

**1979, June 15**

| | | | |
|---|---|---|---|
| *1787* | A1176 15c multicolored | 28 | 5 |
| *a* | Imperf., pair | *500.00* | |

### Special Olympics Issue

Child Holding Winner's Medal — A1177

**1979, Aug. 9 *Perf. 11***

| | | | |
|---|---|---|---|
| *1788* | A1177 15c multicolored | 28 | 5 |

Special Olympics for special children, Brockport, NY, Aug. 8-13.

### John Paul Jones Issue

John Paul Jones, by Charles Willson Peale — A1178

**1979, Sept. 23 Photo. *Perf. 11x12***

| | | | |
|---|---|---|---|
| *1789* | A1178 15c multicolored | 28 | 5 |
| *a* | Perf. 11 | 28 | 6 |
| *b* | Perf. 12 | — | |
| *c* | Vert. pair, imperf horiz. | *200.00* | |
| *d* | As "a", vert. pair, imperf horiz. | *150.00* | |

John Paul Jones (1747-1792), Naval Commander, American Revolution.

Imperfs., perf. or imperf. gutter pairs and blocks exist from printer's waste.

### Olympic Games Issue

Decathlon, Javelin A1179

Running A1180

Swimming, Women's A1181

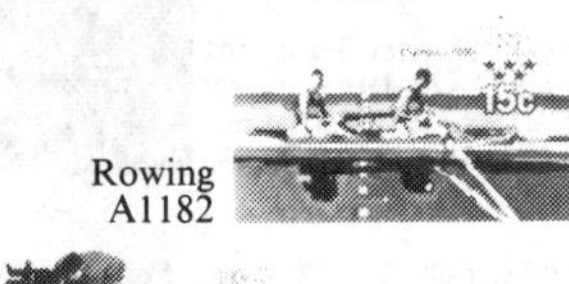
Rowing A1182

Equestrian A1183

**1979 Photo. *Perf. 11***

| | | | |
|---|---|---|---|
| *1790* | A1179 10c multicolored | 20 | 22 |
| *1791* | A1180 15c multicolored | 28 | 8 |
| *1792* | A1181 15c multicolored | 28 | 8 |
| *1793* | A1182 15c multicolored | 28 | 8 |
| *1794* | A1183 15c multicolored | 28 | 8 |
| *a* | Block of 4, #1791-1794 | 1.20 | 85 |
| *b* | As "a", imperf. | *1,850.* | |

22nd Summer Olympic Games, Moscow, July 19-Aug. 3, 1980. Printed se-tenant in blocks of 4, in panes of 50. Nos. 1791-1792 alternate in 1st row, Nos. 1793-1794 in 2nd.

Issue dates: 10c, Sept. 5; 15c, Sept. 28.

### Winter Olympic Games Issue

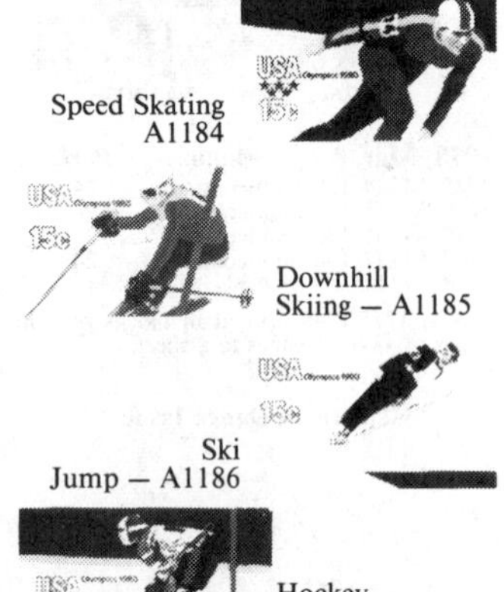
Speed Skating A1184

Downhill Skiing — A1185

Ski Jump — A1186

Hockey Goaltender A1187

**1980, Feb. 1 Photo. *Perf. 11x10½***

| | | | |
|---|---|---|---|
| *1795* | A1184 15c multicolored | 35 | 8 |
| *a* | Perf.11 | 1.10 | — |
| *1796* | A1185 15c multicolored | 35 | 8 |
| *a* | Perf.11 | 1.10 | — |
| *1797* | A1186 15c multicolored | 35 | 8 |
| *a* | Perf.11 | 1.10 | — |
| *1798* | A1187 15c multicolored | 35 | 8 |
| *a* | Perf.11 | 1.10 | — |
| *b* | Block of 4, #1795-1798 | 1.50 | 1.00 |
| *c* | Block of 4, #1795a-1798a | 4.50 | — |

13th Winter Olympic Games, Lake Placid, NY, Feb. 12-24. Printed se-tenant in blocks of 4, in panes of 50. Nos. 1795-1796 alternate in one row, Nos. 1797-1798 in next.

### Christmas Issue

Virgin and Child, by Gerard David A1188

Santa Claus, Christmas Tree Ornament A1189

**1979, Oct. 18 Photo. *Perf. 11***

| | | | | |
|---|---|---|---|---|
| *1799* | A1188 | 15c multicolored | 28 | 5 |
| *a* | | Imperf., pair | *100.00* | |
| *b* | | Vert. pair, imperf. horiz. | *1,000.* | |
| *c* | | Vert. pair, imperf. btwn. | — | |
| *1800* | A1189 | 15c multicolored | 28 | 5 |
| *a* | | Grn & yel omitted | *750.00* | |
| *b* | | Grn, yel & tan omitted | *800.00* | |

### Performing Arts Issue

Will Rogers (1879-1935), Actor and Humorist — A1190

**1979, Nov. 4 Photo. *Perf. 11***

| | | | | |
|---|---|---|---|---|
| *1801* | A1190 | 15c multicolored | 28 | 5 |
| *a* | | Imperf., pair | *250.00* | |

### Viet Nam Veterans Issue

Ribbon for Viet Nam Service Medal A1191

**1979, Nov. 11 Photo. *Perf. 11***

| | | | | |
|---|---|---|---|---|
| *1802* | A1191 | 15c multicolored | 28 | 5 |

A tribute to veterans of the Viet Nam War.

### Performing Arts Issue

W.C. Fields (1880-1946), actor and comedian — A1192

**1980, Jan. 29 Photo. *Perf. 11***

| | | | | |
|---|---|---|---|---|
| *1803* | A1192 | 15c multicolored | 28 | 5 |

### Black Heritage

Benjamin Banneker (1731-1806), Astronomer and Mathematician, Transverse — A1193

**1980, Feb. 15 Photo. *Perf. 11***

| | | | | |
|---|---|---|---|---|
| *1804* | A1193 | 15c multicolored | 28 | 5 |
| *a* | | Horiz. pair, imperf. vert. | — | |

Imperfs. exist from printer's waste.

### Letter Writing

Letters Preserve Memories A1194

P.S. Write Soon A1195

Letters Lift Spirits A1196

Letters Shape Opinions A1197

**1980, Feb. 25**

| | | | | |
|---|---|---|---|---|
| *1805* | A1194 | 15c multicolored | 30 | 8 |
| *1806* | A1195 | 15c cl & multi | 30 | 8 |
| *1807* | A1196 | 15c multicolored | 30 | 8 |
| *1808* | A1195 | 15c grn & multi | 30 | 8 |
| *1809* | A1197 | 15c multicolored | 30 | 8 |
| *1810* | A1195 | 15c red & multi | 30 | 8 |
| *a* | | Strip of 6 #1805-1810 | 1.90 | 1.50 |
| | | *Nos. 1805-1810 (6)* | 1.80 | 48 |

Natl. Letter Writing Week, Feb. 24-Mar. 1. Printed vertically se-tenant in panes of 60 (10x6), four panes to a sheet.

### Americana Type

Weaver Violins — A1199

Coil Stamps

**1980 Engr. *Perf. 10 Vert.***

| | | | | |
|---|---|---|---|---|
| *1811* | A984 | 1c dk bl, *grnsh* | 5 | 5 |
| *a* | | Imperf., pair | *200.00* | |
| *1813* | A1199 | 3.5c pur, *yel* | 9 | 5 |
| *a* | | Untagged (Bureau precanceled, lines only) | | 10 |
| *b* | | Imperf., pair | *275.00* | |
| *1816* | A997 | 12c brn red, *beige* ('81) | 20 | 5 |
| *a* | | Untagged (Bureau precanceled) | | 25 |
| *b* | | Imperf., pair | *200.00* | |

A1207

**1981, Mar. 15 Photo. *Perf. 11x10½***

| | | | | |
|---|---|---|---|---|
| *1818* | A1207 | (18c) violet | 30 | 5 |

**Engr. *Perf. 10***

| | | | | |
|---|---|---|---|---|
| *1819* | A1207 | (18c) vio, from bklt. pane | 38 | 5 |
| *a* | | Booklet pane of 8 | 4.50 | *1.50* |

**Coil Stamp**

***Perf. 10 Vert.***

| | | | | |
|---|---|---|---|---|
| *1820* | A1207 | (18c) violet | 35 | 5 |
| *a* | | Imperf., pair | *90.00* | |

### Frances Perkins

A1208

**1980, Apr. 10 *Perf. 10½x11***

| | | | | |
|---|---|---|---|---|
| *1821* | A1208 | 15c Prus bl | 28 | 5 |

Frances Perkins (1882-1965), Sec. of Labor, 1933-45 (1st woman cabinet member).

### Dolley Madison

Dolley Madison (1768-1849), First Lady, 1809-1817 — A1209

**1980, May 20 *Perf. 11***

| | | | | |
|---|---|---|---|---|
| *1822* | A1209 | 15c red brn & sep | 28 | 5 |

### Emily Bissell

Emily Bissell (1861-1948), Social Worker; Introduced Christmas seals in US — A1210

**1980, May 31**

| | | | | |
|---|---|---|---|---|
| *1823* | A1210 | 15c blk & red | 28 | 5 |
| *a* | | Vert. pair, imperf. horiz. | *300.00* | |

### Helen Keller

Helen Keller and Anne Sullivan — A1211

**Lithographed, Engraved**

**1980, June 27 *Perf. 11***

| | | | | |
|---|---|---|---|---|
| *1824* | A1211 | 15c multicolored | 28 | 5 |

Keller (1880-1968), blind and deaf writer and lecturer taught by Sullivan (1867-1936).



Veterans Administration Emblem A1212

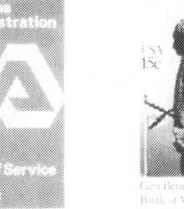

Gen. Bernardo de Galvez A1213

### Veterans Administration

**1980, July 21 Photo.**

| | | | | |
|---|---|---|---|---|
| *1825* | A1212 | 15c car & vio bl | 28 | 5 |
| *a* | | Horiz. pair, imperf. vert. | *500.00* | |

### General Bernardo de Galvez

**1980, July 23 Engr. *Perf. 11***

| | | | | |
|---|---|---|---|---|
| *1826* | A1213 | 15c multicolored | 28 | 5 |
| *a* | | Red, brn & bl (engr.) omitted | *750.00* | |
| *b* | | Red, brn, bl (engr.) & yel (litho.) omitted | *1,300.* | |

Galvez (1746-1786), helped defeat British in Battle of Mobile, 1780.

### Coral Reefs

Brain Coral, Beaugregory Fish A1214

Elkhorn Coral, Porkfish A1215

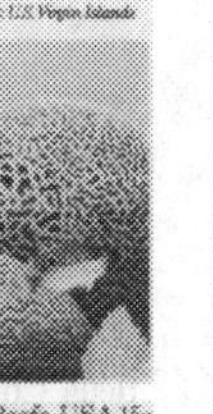


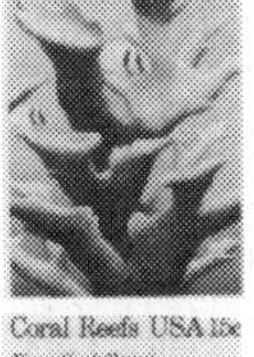

Chalice Coral, Moorish Idol Fish A1216

Finger Coral, Sabertooth Blenny Fish A1217

**1980, Aug. 26 Photo. *Perf. 11***

| | | | | |
|---|---|---|---|---|
| *1827* | A1214 | 15c multicolored | 28 | 8 |
| *1828* | A1215 | 15c multicolored | 28 | 8 |
| *1829* | A1216 | 15c multicolored | 28 | 8 |
| *1830* | A1217 | 15c multicolored | 28 | 8 |
| *a* | | Block of 4 (#1827-1830) | 1.10 | 85 |
| *b* | | As "a," imperf. | *1,500.* | |
| *c* | | As "a," imperf. btwn., vert. | | — |
| *d* | | As "a," imperf. vert. | | — |

American Bald Eagle A1218

Edith Wharton A1219

### Organized Labor

**1980, Sept. 1 Photo. *Perf. 11***

| | | | | |
|---|---|---|---|---|
| *1831* | A1218 | 15c multicolored | 28 | 5 |
| *a* | | Imperf., pair | *450.00* | |

### Edith Wharton

**1980, Sept. 5 Engr. *Perf. 10½x11***

| | | | | |
|---|---|---|---|---|
| *1832* | A1219 | 15c purple | 28 | 5 |

Edith Wharton (1862-1937), writer.

### American Education

"Homage to the Square: Glow," by Josef Albers — A1220

**1980, Sept. 12 Photo. *Perf. 11***

| | | | | |
|---|---|---|---|---|
| *1833* | A1220 | 15c multicolored | 28 | 5 |
| *a* | | Horiz. pair, imperf. btwn. | *300.00* | |

### American Folk Art
Pacific Northwest Indian Masks

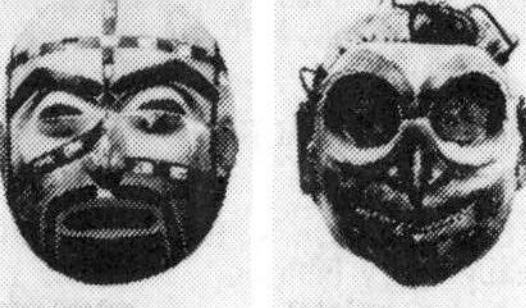


Heiltsuk, Bella Bella Tribe A1221 — Chilkat Tlingit Tribe A1222

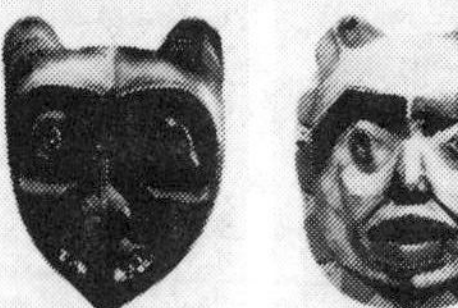


Tlingit Tribe A1223 — Bella Coola Tribe A1224

**1980, Sept. 25**

| | | | | |
|---|---|---|---|---|
| *1834* | A1221 | 15c multicolored | 28 | 8 |
| *1835* | A1222 | 15c multicolored | 28 | 8 |
| *1836* | A1223 | 15c multicolored | 28 | 8 |
| *1837* | A1224 | 15c multicolored | 28 | 8 |
| *a* | | Block of 4, #1834-1837 | 1.10 | 85 |

Nos. 1834-1837 printed in blocks of 4 in panes of 40, four panes to a sheet.

### American Architecture

Smithsonian Institution, by James Renwick – A1225

Trinity Church, Boston, by Henry Hobson Richardson A1226

Pennsylvania Academy of Fine Arts, by Frank Furness – A1227

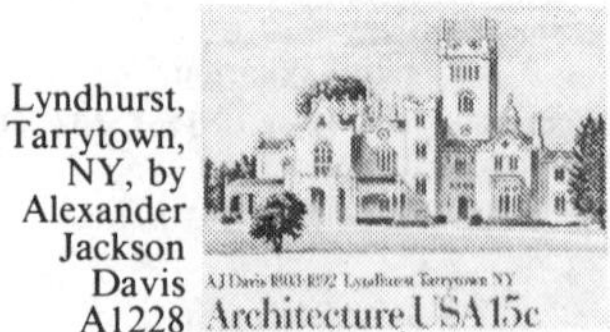


Lyndhurst, Tarrytown, NY, by Alexander Jackson Davis A1228

**1980, Oct. 9 Engr. *Perf. 11***

| | | | | |
|---|---|---|---|---|
| *1838* | A1225 | 15c blk & brick red | 28 | 8 |
| *1839* | A1226 | 15c blk & brick red | 28 | 8 |
| *1840* | A1227 | 15c blk & brick red | 28 | 8 |
| *1841* | A1228 | 15c blk & brick red | 28 | 8 |
| *a* | | Block of 4, #1838-1841 | 1.10 | 85 |

Printed se-tenant in panes of 40.



### Christmas

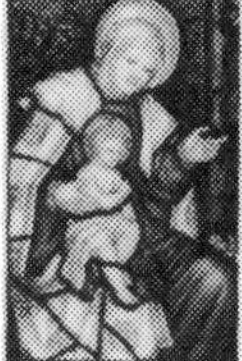


Madonna and Child A1229

Wreath, Toys on Windowsill A1230

**1980, Oct. 31 Photo. *Perf. 11***

| | | | | |
|---|---|---|---|---|
| *1842* | A1229 | 15c multicolored | 28 | 5 |
| *a* | | Imperf., pair | *100.00* | |
| *1843* | A1230 | 15c multicolored | 28 | 5 |
| *a* | | Imperf., pair | *100.00* | |

### Great Americans

A1231 A1232 A1233 A1234

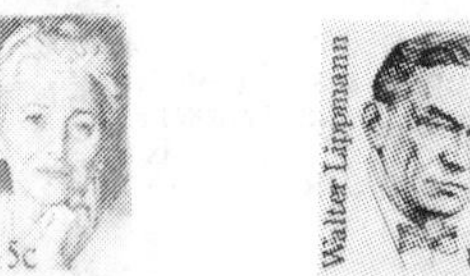


A1235 A1236

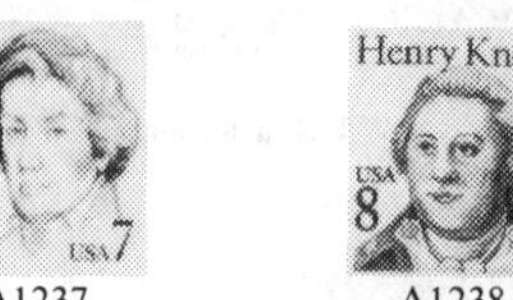


A1237 A1238

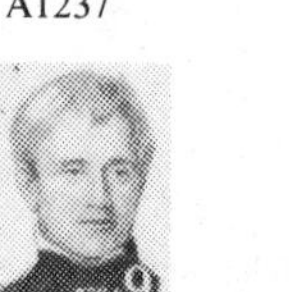


A1239 A1240

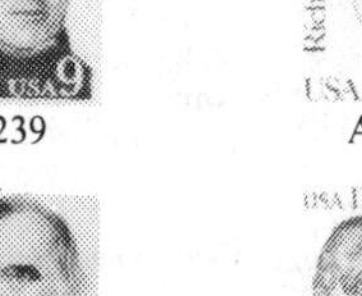


A1241 A1242

A1243

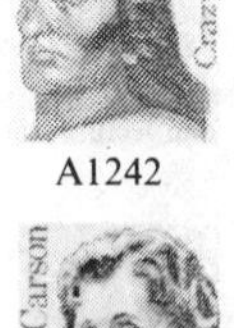


A1244

A1245

A1246

A1247 A1248

A1249 A1250

A1251 A1252

A1253 A1254

A1255 A1256

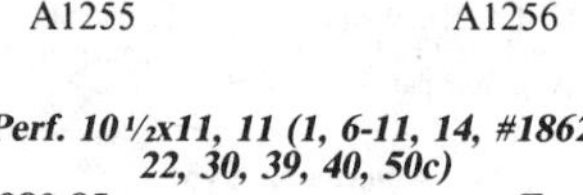

***Perf. 10½x11, 11 (1, 6-11, 14, #1862, 22, 30, 39, 40, 50c)***

**1980-85 Engr.**

| | | | | |
|---|---|---|---|---|
| *1844* | A1231 | 1c blk ('83) | 5 | 5 |
| *a* | | Imperf. pair | *300.00* | |
| *b.* | | Vert. pair, imperf. btwn. | — | |
| *1845* | A1232 | 2c brn blk ('82) | 5 | 5 |
| *1846* | A1233 | 3c ol grn ('83) | 6 | 5 |
| *1847* | A1234 | 4c vio ('83) | 7 | 5 |
| *1848* | A1235 | 5c hn brn ('83) | 9 | 5 |
| *1849* | A1236 | 6c org ver ('85) | 12 | 5 |
| *a* | | Vert. pair, imperf. horiz. | — | |
| *1850* | A1237 | 7c brt car ('85) | 12 | 5 |
| *1851* | A1238 | 8c ol blk ('85) | 14 | 5 |
| *1852* | A1239 | 9c dk grn ('85) | 16 | 5 |
| *1853* | A1240 | 10c Prus bl ('84) | 18 | 5 |
| *a.* | | Vert. pair, imperf. btwn. | — | |
| *1854* | A1241 | 11c dk bl ('85) | 20 | 5 |
| *1855* | A1242 | 13c lt mar ('82) | 22 | 5 |
| *1856* | A1243 | 14c sl grn ('85) | 25 | 5 |
| *a* | | Vert. pair, imperf. horiz. | *175.00* | |
| *b* | | Horiz. pair, imperf. btwn. | 12.50 | |
| *c* | | Vert. pair, imperf. btwn. | *1,500.* | |
| *1857* | A1244 | 17c grn ('81) | 30 | 5 |
| *1858* | A1245 | 18c dk bl ('81) | 32 | 5 |
| *1859* | A1246 | 19c brown | 35 | 7 |
| *1860* | A1247 | 20c cl ('82) | 38 | 5 |
| *1861* | A1248 | 20c grn ('83) | 38 | 5 |
| *1862* | A1249 | 20c blk ('84) | 38 | 5 |
| *1863* | A1250 | 22c dk chalky bl ('85) | 40 | 5 |
| *a.* | | Vert. pair, imperf. btwn. | — | |
| *1864* | A1251 | 30c ol gray ('84) | 52 | 8 |
| *1865* | A1252 | 35c gray ('81) | 60 | 8 |
| *1866* | A1253 | 37c blue ('82) | 70 | 5 |
| *1867* | A1254 | 39c rose lil ('85) | 70 | 8 |
| *a* | | Vert. pair, imperf. horiz. | *700.00* | |
| *b* | | Vert. pair, imperf. btwn. | *1,100.* | |
| *1868* | A1255 | 40c dk grn ('84) | 70 | 10 |
| *1869* | A1256 | 50c brown ('85) | 85 | 10 |
| | | *Nos. 1844-1869 (26)* | 8.29 | 1.51 |

### Everett Dirksen

Everett Dirksen (1896-1969), Senate Minority Leader, 1960-69 – A1261

**1981, Jan. 4 *Perf. 11***

| | | | | |
|---|---|---|---|---|
| *1874* | A1261 | 15c gray | 28 | 5 |

### Black Heritage

Whitney Moore Young (1921-1971), Civil Rights Leader – A1262

**1981, Jan. 30 Photo. *Perf. 11***

| | | | | |
|---|---|---|---|---|
| *1875* | A1262 | 15c multi | 28 | 5 |

### Flowers

A1263 A1264

A1265 A1266

**1981, Apr. 23 *Perf. 11***

| | | | | |
|---|---|---|---|---|
| *1876* | A1263 | 18c multicolored | 32 | 8 |
| *1877* | A1264 | 18c multicolored | 32 | 8 |
| *1878* | A1265 | 18c multicolored | 32 | 8 |
| *1879* | A1266 | 18c multicolored | 32 | 8 |
| *a* | | Block of 4, #1876-1879 | 1.30 | 85 |

A1267-A1276

**1981, May 14 Engr. *Perf. 11***

| | | | | |
|---|---|---|---|---|
| *1880* | A1267 | 18c *Bighorn* | 32 | 5 |
| *1881* | A1268 | 18c *Puma* | 32 | 5 |
| *1882* | A1269 | 18c *Harbor seal* | 32 | 5 |
| *1883* | A1270 | 18c *Bison* | 32 | 5 |
| *1884* | A1271 | 18c *Brown bear* | 32 | 5 |
| *1885* | A1272 | 18c *Polar bear* | 32 | 5 |
| *1886* | A1273 | 18c *Elk (wapiti)* | 32 | 5 |
| *1887* | A1274 | 18c *Moose* | 32 | 5 |
| *1888* | A1275 | 18c *White-tailed deer* | 32 | 5 |
| *1889* | A1276 | 18c *Pronghorn* | 32 | 5 |
| *a* | | Booklet pane of 10 | 7.00 | — |

Nos. 1880-1889 issued in booklet only. All stamps have one or two straight edges.

See No. 1949.

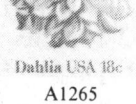

A1277

A1278

A1279

A1280

### Multicolor Huck Press

**1981, Apr. 24** *Perf. 11*

*1890* A1277 18c multicolored 32 5
  *a* Imperf., pair 100.00

**Coil Stamp**

*Perf. 10 Vert.*

*1891* A1278 18c multicolored 32 5
  *a* Imperf., pair 20.00

**Booklet Stamps**

*Perf. 11*

*1892* A1279 6c multicolored 55 10
*1893* A1280 18c multicolored 32 5
  *a* Booklet pane of 8 (2 #1892, 6 #1893) 3.00 —
  *b* As "a," vert. imperf. btwn. *75.00*

A1281

**1981, Dec. 17** *Perf. 11*

*1894* A1281 20c blk, dk bl & red 35 5
  *a* Vert. pair, imperf. 25.00
  *b* Vert. pair, imperf. horiz. *650.00*
  *c* Dk bl omitted *250.00*
  *d* Blk omitted *400.00*

**Coil Stamp**

*Perf. 10 Vert.*

*1895* A1281 20c blk, dk bl & red 35 5
  *a* Imperf., pair 6.00
  *b* Blk omitted 65.00
  *c* Dk bl omitted —
  *d* Pair, imperf. btwn. —
  *e* Untagged (Bureau precanceled) 40

**Booklet Stamp**

*Perf. 11x10½*

*1896* A1281 20c blk, dk bl & red 35 5
  *a* Booklet pane of 6 2.50 —
  *b* Booklet pane of 10 4.00 —

### Transportation Coils

A1282 A1283

A1284

A1285

A1286

A1287

A1288

A1289

A1290

A1291

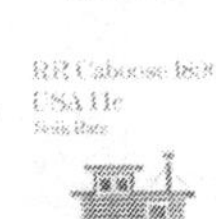
A1292


A1293

A1294

A1295

**1981-84** **Engr.** *Perf. 10 Vert.*

*1897* A1282 1c vio ('83) 5 5
  *b* Imperf., pair *525.00*
*1897A* A1283 2c black ('82) 10 5
  *e* Imperf., pair *70.00*
*1898* A1284 3c dk grn ('83) 9 5
*1898A* A1285 4c redsh brn ('82) 9 5
  *b* Untagged (Bureau precanceled) 9
  *c* As "b," imperf., pair *600.00*
*1899* A1286 5c gray grn ('83) 12 5
  *a* Imperf., pair —
*1900* A1287 5.2c car ('83) 12 5
  *a* Untagged (Bureau precanceled) 12
*1901* A1288 5.9c blue ('82) 18 5
  *a* Untagged (Bureau precanceled, lines only) 18
  *b* As "a," imperf., pair *250.00*
*1902* A1289 7.4c brown 18 8
  *a* Untagged (Bureau precanceled) 18
*1903* A1290 9.3c car rose 22 8
  *a* Untagged (Bureau precanceled, lines only) 22
  *b* As "a," imperf., pair *125.00*
*1904* A1291 10.9c pur ('82) 24 5
  *a* Untagged (Bureau precanceled, lines only) 24
  *b* As "a," imperf., pair *200.00*
*1905* A1292 11c red ('84) 24 8
  *a* Untagged (Bureau precanceled, lines only) 24
*1906* A1293 17c ultra 32 5
  *a* Untagged (Bureau precanceled, Presorted First Class) 35
  *b* Imperf., pair *175.00*
  *c* As "a," imperf., pair *500.00*
*1907* A1294 18c dark brown 34 5
  *a* Imperf., pair *125.00*
*1908* A1295 20c vermilion 32 5
  *a* Imperf., pair *110.00*
*Nos. 1897-1908 (14)* 2.61 79

See Nos. 2123-2136, 2225-2231, 2252-2266.

A1296

**1983, Aug. 12** **Photo.** *Perf. 10 Vert.*

*1909* A1296 $9.35 multi 26.00 7.50
  *a* Booklet pane of 3 80.00 —

A1297

A1298

### American Red Cross Centennial

**1981, May 1** *Perf. 10½x11*

*1910* A1297 18c multicolored 32 5

### Savings & Loan Sesquicentennial

**1981, May 8** *Perf. 11*

*1911* A1298 18c multicolored 32 5

### Space Achievement

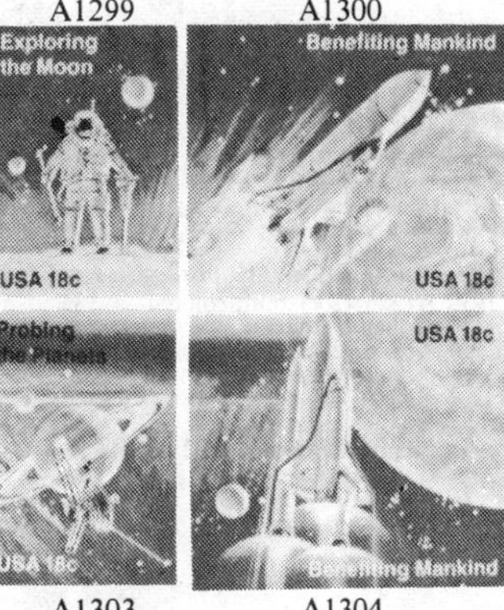

A1299 A1300
A1303 A1304

A1301 A1302
A1305 A1306

**1981, May 21** *Perf. 11*

*1912* A1299 18c multicolored 32 10
*1913* A1300 18c multicolored 32 10
*1914* A1301 18c multicolored 32 10
*1915* A1302 18c multicolored 32 10
*1916* A1303 18c multicolored 32 10
*1917* A1304 18c multicolored 32 10
*1918* A1305 18c multicolored 32 10
*1919* A1306 18c multicolored 32 10
  *a* Block of 8, #1912-1919 3.00 2.75
  *b* As "a," imperf. —

### Professional Management

Joseph Wharton A1307

**1981, June 18**

*1920* A1307 18c blue & black 32 5

A little time given to the study of the arrangement of the Scott Catalogue can make it easier to use effectively.

### Preservation of Wildlife Habitats

A1308 A1309

Save Wetland Habitats / Save Grassland Habitats

Save Mountain Habitats / Save Woodland Habitats

A1310 A1311

**1981, June 26**

*1921* A1308 18c multicolored 32 8
*1922* A1309 18c multicolored 32 8
*1923* A1310 18c multicolored 32 8
*1924* A1311 18c multicolored 32 8
  *a* Block of 4, #1921-1924 1.40 1.00

Printed se-tenant in panes of 50.

### International Year of the Disabled

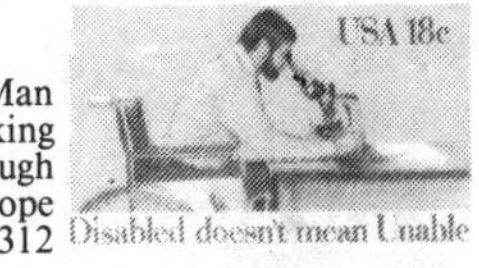

Man Looking through Microscope A1312

**1981, June 29** **Photo.** *Perf. 11*

*1925* A1312 18c multicolored 32 5
  *a* Vert. pair, imperf. horiz. *2,000.*

### Edna St. Vincent Millay, 1892-1950

A1313

**Lithographed, Engraved**

**1981, July 10** *Perf. 11*

*1926* A1313 18c multicolored 32 5
  *a* Black (engr., inscriptions) omitted *600.00*

### Alcoholism

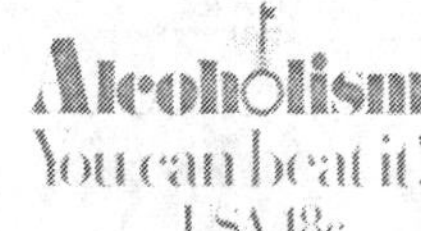

A1314

**1981, Aug. 19** **Engr.** *Perf. 11*

*1927* A1314 18c blue & black 42 5
  *a* Imperf., pair *300.00*

### American Architecture

New York University Library by Sanford White A1315

Biltmore House by Richard Morris Hunt A1316

Palace of the Arts by Bernard Maybeck A1317

National Farmer's Bank by Louis Sullivan A1318

**1981, Aug. 28 Engr. *Perf. 11***

*1928* A1315 18c blk & red 32 8
*1929* A1316 18c blk & red 32 8
*1930* A1317 18c blk & red 32 8
*1931* A1318 18c blk & red 32 8
*a* Block of 4, #1928-1931 1.40 1.00

**Athletes**

Mildred Didrikson Zaharias A1319

Robert Tyre Jones A1320

**1981, Sept. 22 Engr. *Perf. 10½x11***

*1932* A1319 18c purple 32 5
*1933* A1320 18c green 32 5

**Frederic Remington, 1861-1909**

Coming Through the Rye — A1321

**1981, Oct. 9 *Perf. 11***

*1934* A1321 18c gray, grn & brn 32 5
*a* Vert. pair, imperf. btwn. *250.00*
*b* Brown omitted *500.00*

**James Hoban, 1762?-1831**

Irish-American Architect of White House — A1322

**1981, Oct. 13 Photo. *Perf. 11***

*1935* A1322 18c multicolored 32 25
*1936* A1322 20c multicolored 35 5

See Ireland No. 504.

**American Bicentennial**

Battle of Yorktown A1323

Battle of Virginia Capes A1324

**Lithographed, Engraved**

**1981, Oct. 16 *Perf. 11***

*1937* A1323 18c multicolored 32 6
*1938* A1324 18c multicolored 32 6
*a* Pair, #1937-1938 70 15
*b* As "a," black (engr., inscriptions) omitted *600.00*

**Christmas**

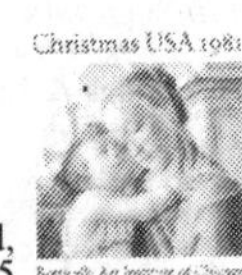

Madonna and Child, Botticelli — A1325

Felt Bear on Sled A1326

**1981, Oct. 28 Photo. *Perf. 11***

*1939* A1325 (20c) multicolored 35 5
*a* Imperf., pair *115.00*
*1940* A1326 (20c) multicolored 35 5
*a* Imperf., pair *225.00*
*b* Vert. pair, imperf. horiz. —

**John Hanson, 1721-1783**

First President of Continental Congress — A1327

**1981, Nov. 5 Photo. *Perf. 11***

*1941* A1327 20c multicolored 35 5

**Desert Plants**

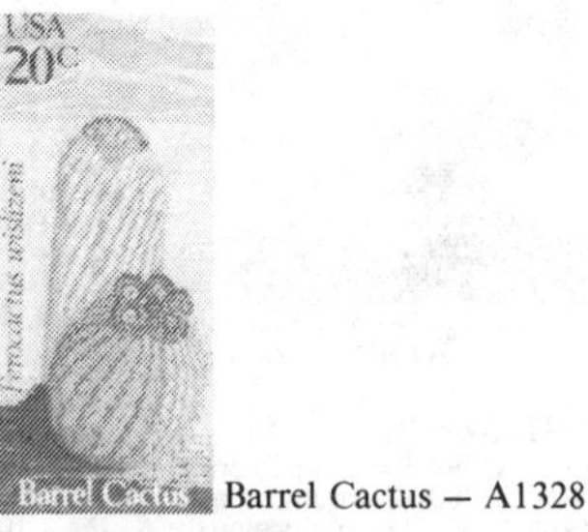

Barrel Cactus — A1328

Agave — A1329

Beavertail Cactus — A1330

The first price column gives the catalogue value of an unused stamp, the second that of a used stamp.

Saguaro — A1331

**Lithographed, Engraved**

**1981, Dec. 11**

*1942* A1328 20c multicolored 35 6
*1943* A1329 20c multicolored 35 6
*1944* A1330 20c multicolored 35 6
*1945* A1331 20c multicolored 35 6
*a* Block of 4, #1942-1945 1.40 85

A1332

A1333

**1981, Oct. 11 Photo. *Perf. 11x10½***

*1946* A1332 (20c) brown 35 5

**Coil Stamp**

***Perf. 10 Vert.***

*1947* A1332 (20c) brown 38 5
*a* Imperf., pair *1,250.*

**Booklet Stamp**

***Perf. 11x10½***

*1948* A1333 (20c) brown 38 5
*a* Booklet pane of 10 4.00 —

A1334

**1982, Jan. 8 Engr. *Perf. 11***

*1949* A1334 20c dk bl (from bklt. pane) 42 5
*a* Booklet pane of 10 4.75 —
*b* As "a," vert. imperf. btwn. *85.00*

See No. 1880.

**Franklin Delano Roosevelt**

A1335

**1982, Jan. 30 Engr. *Perf. 11***

*1950* A1335 20c blue 38 5

A1336

**1982, Feb. 1 Photo. *Perf. 11x10½***

*1951* A1336 20c multicolored 42 5
*a* Perf. 11 48 5
*b* Imperf., pair *250.00*
*c* Blue omitted *150.00*

**George Washington**

A1337

**1982, Feb. 22 Photo. *Perf. 11***

*1952* A1337 20c multicolored 38 5

**State Birds & Flowers**

A1338-A1387

**1982, Apr. 14 Photo. *Perf. 10½x11***

*1953* A1338 20c *Alabama* 38 20
*1954* A1339 20c *Alaska* 38 20
*1955* A1340 20c *Arizona* 38 20
*1956* A1341 20c *Arkansas* 38 20
*1957* A1342 20c *California* 38 20
*1958* A1343 20c *Colorado* 38 20
*1959* A1344 20c *Connecticut* 38 20
*1960* A1345 20c *Delaware* 38 20
*1961* A1346 20c *Florida* 38 20
*1962* A1347 20c *Georgia* 38 20
*1963* A1348 20c *Hawaii* 38 20
*1964* A1349 20c *Idaho* 38 20
*1965* A1350 20c *Illinois* 38 20
*1966* A1351 20c *Indiana* 38 20
*1967* A1352 20c *Iowa* 38 20
*1968* A1353 20c *Kansas* 38 20
*1969* A1354 20c *Kentucky* 38 20
*1970* A1355 20c *Louisiana* 38 20
*1971* A1356 20c *Maine* 38 20
*1972* A1357 20c *Maryland* 38 20
*1973* A1358 20c *Massachusetts* 38 20
*1974* A1359 20c *Michigan* 38 20
*1975* A1360 20c *Minnesota* 38 20
*1976* A1361 20c *Mississippi* 38 20
*1977* A1362 20c *Missouri* 38 20
*1978* A1363 20c *Montana* 38 20
*1979* A1364 20c *Nebraska* 38 20
*1980* A1365 20c *Nevada* 38 20
*1981* A1366 20c *New Hampshire* 38 20
*1982* A1367 20c *New Jersey* 38 20
*1983* A1368 20c *New Mexico* 38 20
*1984* A1369 20c *New York* 38 20
*1985* A1370 20c *North Carolina* 38 20
*1986* A1371 20c *North Dakota* 38 20
*1987* A1372 20c *Ohio* 38 20
*1988* A1373 20c *Oklahoma* 38 20
*1989* A1374 20c *Oregon* 38 20
*1990* A1375 20c *Pennsylvania* 38 20
*1991* A1376 20c *Rhode Island* 38 20
*1992* A1377 20c *South Carolina* 38 20
*1993* A1378 20c *South Dakota* 38 20
*1994* A1379 20c *Tennessee* 38 20
*1995* A1380 20c *Texas* 38 20
*1996* A1381 20c *Utah* 38 20
*1997* A1382 20c *Vermont* 38 20
*1998* A1383 20c *Virginia* 38 20
*1999* A1384 20c *Washington* 38 20
*2000* A1385 20c *West Virginia* 38 20
*2001* A1386 20c *Wisconsin* 38 20
*2002* A1387 20c *Wyoming* 38 20
*a* #1953a-2002a, any single, perf. 11 50 30
*b* Pane of 50, perf. 10½x11 19.00 —
*c* Pane of 50, perf. 11 25.00 —
*d* Pane of 50, imperf. —

**US-Netherlands**

200th Anniv. of Diplomatic Recognition by the Netherlands A1388

**1982, Apr. 20 Photo. *Perf. 11***

*2003* A1388 20c ver, brt bl & gray blk 38 5
*a* Imperf., pair *450.00*

See Netherlands Nos. 640-641.

### Library of Congress

A1389

**1982, Apr. 21 Engr. *Perf. 11***
*2004* A1389 20c red & blk 38 5

### Consumer Education

A1390

Coil Stamp

**1982, Apr. 27 Engr. *Perf. 10 Vert.***
*2005* A1390 20c sky blue 50 5
*a* Imperf., pair *110.00*

### Knoxville World's Fair

A1391

A1392

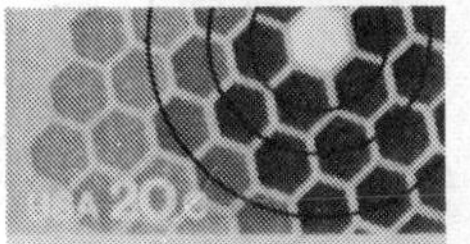

A1393

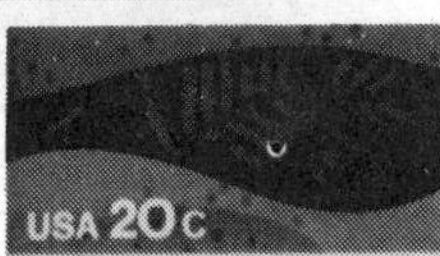

A1394

**1982, Apr. 29 Photo. *Perf. 11***
*2006* A1391 20c multicolored 38 8
*2007* A1392 20c multicolored 38 8
*2008* A1393 20c multicolored 38 8
*2009* A1394 20c multicolored 38 8
*a* Block of 4, #2006-2009 1.60 1.00

### American Author, 1832-1899

Frontispiece from "Ragged Dick" — A1395

**1982, Apr. 30 Engr. *Perf. 11***
*2010* A1395 20c red & blk, *tan* 38 5

### Aging Together

A1396

**1982, May 21 *Perf. 11***
*2011* A1396 20c brown 38 5

Actors John, Ethel & Lionel Barrymore — A1397

### Performing Arts

**1982, June 8 Photo. *Perf. 11***
*2012* A1397 20c multicolored 38 5

### Dr. Mary E. Walker, 1832-1919

A1398

**1982, June 10 Photo. *Perf. 11***
*2013* A1398 20c multicolored 38 5

### International Peace Garden

A1399

**1982, June 30 Photo. *Perf. 11***
*2014* A1399 20c multicolored 38 5
*a* Blk, grn & brn (engr.) omitted *425.00*

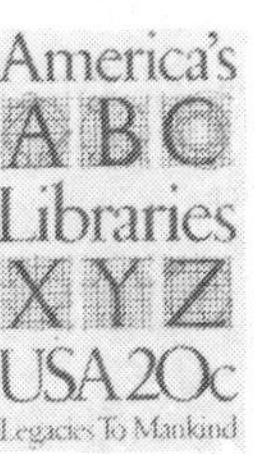

A1400

A1401

### America's Libraries

**1982, July 13 Engr. *Perf. 11***
*2015* A1400 20c red & blk 38 5
*a* Vert. pair, imperf. horiz. *350.00*

### Jackie Robinson, 1919-1972

**1982, Aug. 2 Photo. *Perf. 10½x11***
*2016* A1401 20c multicolored 38 5

### Touro Synagogue

A1402

### Photogravure, Engraved

**1982, Aug. 22 *Perf. 11***
*2017* A1402 20c multicolored 38 5
*a* Imperf., pair *650.00*

### Wolf Trap Farm Park

A1403

**1982, Sept. 1 Photo. *Perf. 11***
*2018* A1403 20c multicolored 38 5

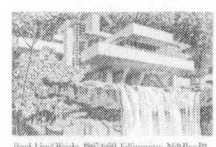

### American Architecture

Fallingwater, Mill Run, Pa., by Frank Lloyd Wright — A1404

Illinois Institute of Technology by Ludwig Mies van der Rohe A1405

Gropius House, Lincoln, Mass., by Walter Gropius A1406

Dulles Airport, by Eero Saarinen A1407

**1982, Sept. 30 Engr. *Perf. 11***
*2019* A1404 20c blk & brn 38 8
*2020* A1405 20c blk & brn 38 8
*2021* A1406 20c blk & brn 38 8
*2022* A1407 20c blk & brn 38 8
*a* Block of 4, #2019-2022 1.60 1.00

### St. Francis of Assisi, 1182-1226

A1408

**1982, Oct. 7 Photo. *Perf. 11***
*2023* A1408 20c multicolored 38 5

### Ponce de Leon, 1527-1591

A1409

**1982, Oct. 12 Photo. *Perf. 11***
*2024* A1409 20c multicolored 38 5
*a* Imperf., pair *800.00*

### Christmas

A1410

A1411

A1412

A1413

A1414

A1415

**1982, Nov. 3 Photo. *Perf. 11***
*2025* A1410 13c multi 24 5
*a* Imperf., pair *500.00*

**1982, Oct. 28**
*2026* A1411 20c multi 38 5
*a* Imperf., pair *150.00*
*b* Horiz. pair, imperf. vert. —
*2027* A1412 20c multi 38 5
*2028* A1413 20c multi 38 5
*2029* A1414 20c multi 38 5
*2030* A1415 20c multi 38 5
*a* Block of 4, #2027-2030 1.60 1.00
*b* As "a," imperf. —
*c* As "a," imperf. horiz. —

### Science & Industry

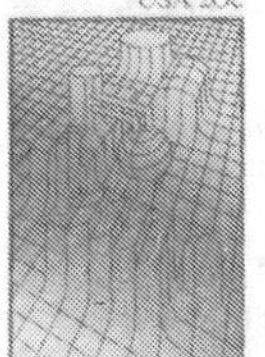

A1416

### Lithographed, Engraved

**1983, Jan. 19 *Perf. 11***
*2031* A1416 20c multi 38 5
*a* Blk (engr.) omitted *1,000.*

### Balloons

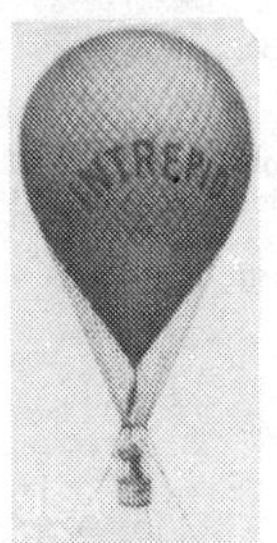

A1417

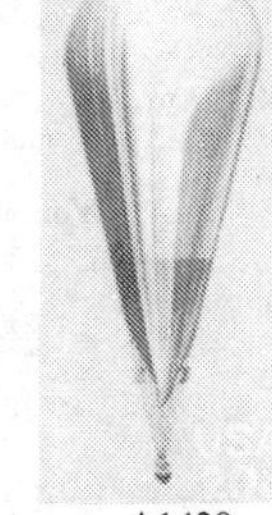
A1420

Values quoted in this catalogue are for stamps graded at Fine-Very Fine and with no faults. An illustrated guide to grade is provided in introductory material, beginning on Page V.

A1418

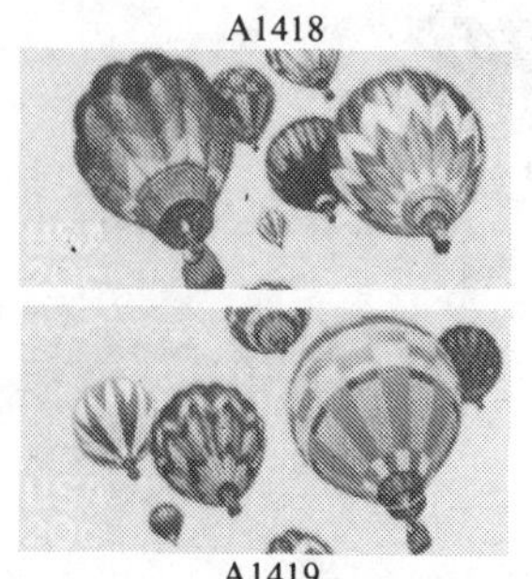

A1419

**Lithographed, Engraved**

**1983, Mar. 31** *Perf. 11*

| | | | |
|---|---|---|---|
| *2032* A1417 20c multicolored | 38 | 8 |
| *2033* A1418 20c multicolored | 38 | 8 |
| *2034* A1419 20c multicolored | 38 | 8 |
| *2035* A1420 20c multicolored | 38 | 8 |
| *a* Block of 4, #2032-2035 | 1.60 | 1.00 |
| *b* As "a," imperf. | *2,500.* | |

**US-Sweden**

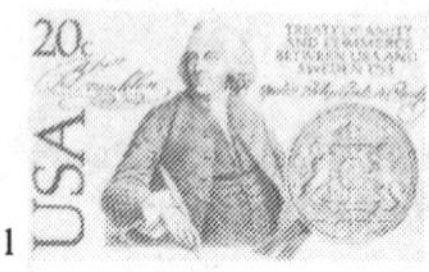


A1421

**1983, Mar. 24** **Engr.** *Perf. 11*
*2036* A1421 20c multicolored 38 5

**Civilian Conservation Corps**

A1422

**1983, Apr. 5** **Photo.** *Perf. 11*
*2037* A1422 20c multicolored 38 5
*a* Imperf., pair *2,250.*

**Joseph Priestley, 1733-1804**

A1423

**1983, Apr. 13** **Photo.** *Perf. 11*
*2038* A1423 20c multicolored 38 5

**Voluntarism**

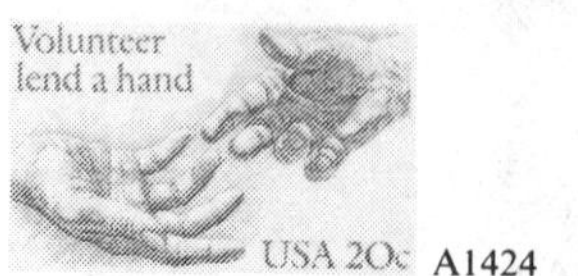


A1424

**1983, Apr. 20** **Engr.** *Perf. 11*
*2039* A1424 20c red & blk 38 5
*a* Imperf., pair *1,000.*

**US-Germany**

Concord, 1683
A1425

**1983, Apr. 29** *Perf. 11*
*2040* A1425 20c brown 38 5

**Brooklyn Bridge**

A1426

**1983, May 17** **Engr.** *Perf. 11*
*2041* A1426 20c blue 38 5

**T.V.A.**

A1427

**Photogravure, Engraved**

**1983, May 18** *Perf. 11*
*2042* A1427 20c multicolored 38 5

**Physical Fitness**

A1428

**1983, May 14** *Perf. 11*
*2043* A1428 20c multicolored 38 5

**Scott Joplin, 1868-1917**

A1429

**1983, June 9** **Photo.**
*2044* A1429 20c multicolored 38 5
*a* Imperf., pair *500.00*

**Medal of Honor**

A1430

**Litho. & Engr.**

**1983, June 7** *Perf. 11*
*2045* A1430 20c multi 38 5
*a* Red omitted *350.00*

A1431 A1432

**George Herman Ruth, 1895-1948**

**1983, July 6** **Engr.** *Perf. 10½x11*
*2046* A1431 20c blue 38 5

**Nathaniel Hawthorne, 1804-1864**

**1983, July 8** **Photo.** *Perf. 11*
*2047* A1432 20c multicolored 38 5

**1984 Los Angeles Olympics**

A1433

A1434

A1435

A1436

**1983, July 28** **Photo.** *Perf. 11*

| | | |
|---|---|---|
| *2048* A1433 13c multicolored | 24 | 5 |
| *2049* A1434 13c multicolored | 24 | 5 |
| *2050* A1435 13c multicolored | 24 | 5 |
| *2051* A1436 13c multicolored | 24 | 5 |
| *a* Block of 4, #2048-2051 | 1.00 | 80 |

**Signing of Treaty of Paris**

John Adams, Franklin, John Jay, David Hartley
A1437

**1983, Sept. 2** **Photo.** *Perf. 11*
*2052* A1437 20c multicolored 38 5

**Civil Service**

A1438

**1983, Sept. 9** **Photo. & Engr.**
*2053* A1438 20c buff, bl & red 38 5

**Metropolitan Opera**

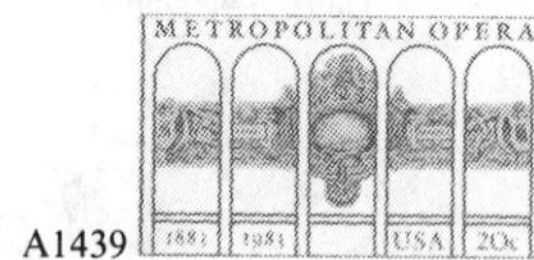


A1439

**1983, Sept. 14** **Litho. & Engr.**
*2054* A1439 20c yel & mar 38 5

**American Inventors**

A1440

A1441

A1442

A1443

**1983, Sept. 21** **Litho.& Engr**

| | | |
|---|---|---|
| *2055* A1440 20c multi | 38 | 8 |
| *2056* A1441 20c multi | 38 | 8 |
| *2057* A1442 20c multi | 38 | 8 |
| *2058* A1443 20c multi | 38 | 8 |
| *a* Block of 4, #2055-2058 | 1.60 | 1.00 |
| *b* As "a," black omitted | *500.00* | |

**Streetcars**

A1444

A1445

A1446

A1447

**1983, Oct. 8** **Photo. & Engr.**

| | | |
|---|---|---|
| *2059* A1444 20c multi | 38 | 8 |
| *2060* A1445 20c multi | 38 | 8 |
| *2061* A1446 20c multi | 38 | 8 |
| *2062* A1447 20c multi | 38 | 8 |
| *a* Block of 4, #2059-2062 | 1.60 | 1.00 |
| *b* As "a," black omitted | *525.00* | |

**Christmas**

A1448

A1449

**1983, Oct. 28** **Photo.** *Perf. 11*
*2063* A1448 20c multi 38 5
*2064* A1449 20c multi 38 5
*a* Imperf., pair *150.00*

A1450

Caribou and Alaska Pipeline — A1451

**Martin Luther, 1483-1546**

**1983, Nov. 11 Photo. *Perf. 11***
*2065* A1450 20c multicolored 38 5

**25th Anniv. of Alaska Statehood**

**1984, Jan. 3 Photo. *Perf. 11***
*2066* A1451 20c multicolored 38 5

**Winter Olympic Games**

Ice Dancing A1452 Downhill Skiing A1453

Cross-country Skiing A1454 Hockey A1455

**1984, Jan. 6 *Perf. 10½x11***
*2067* A1452 20c multicolored 38 8
*2068* A1453 20c multicolored 38 8
*2069* A1454 20c multicolored 38 8
*2070* A1455 20c multicolored 38 8
*a* Block of 4, #2067-2070 1.60 1.00

14th Winter Olympic Games, Sarajevo, Jugoslavia, Feb. 8-19. No. 2067-2070 printed se-tenant. Nos. 2067-2068 alternate in one horizontal row, Nos. 2069-2070 in next.

A1456

LOVE
LOVE
LOVE
LOVE
LOVE
USA 20c
A1457

**Federal Deposit Insurance Corp., 50th Anniv.**

**1984, Jan. 12 *Perf. 11***
*2071* A1456 20c multicolored 38 5

**Love**

**1984, Jan. 31 Photo. & Engr.**
*2072* A1457 20c multicolored 38 5
*a* Horiz. pair, imperf. vert. *250.00*

Carter G. Woodson (1875-1950), Writer — A1458

A1459

**Black Heritage Issue**

**1984, Feb. 1 Photo.**
*2073* A1458 20c multicolored 38 5
*a* Horiz. pair, imperf. vert. —

**Soil and Water Conservation**

**1984, Feb. 6**
*2074* A1459 20c multicolored 38 5

**50th Anniv. of Credit Union Act**

Dollar Sign, Coin — A1460

**1984, Feb. 10 Photo. *Perf. 11***
*2075* A1460 20c multicolored 38 5

**Orchids**

A1461 A1462

A1463 A1464

**1984, Mar. 5**
*2076* A1461 20c Wild pink 38 8
*2077* A1462 20c Yellow lady's-slipper 38 8
*2078* A1463 20c Spreading pogonia 38 8
*2079* A1464 20c Pacific calypso 38 8
*a* Block of 4, #2076-2079 1.60 1.00

**25th Anniv. of Hawaii Statehood**

Eastern Polynesian Canoe, Golden Plover, Mauna Loa Volcano A1465

**1984, Mar. 12 Photo. *Perf. 11***
*2080* A1465 20c multicolored 38 5

Canceled-to-order stamps are often from remainders. Most collectors of canceled stamps prefer postally used specimens.

**National Archives**

Abraham Lincoln, George Washington — A1466

**1984, Apr. 16 Photo. *Perf. 11***
*2081* A1466 20c multicolored 38 5

**1984 Los Angeles Olympics**

Diving A1467 Long Jump A1468

Wrestling A1469 Kayak A1470

**1984, May 4 *Perf. 11***
*2082* A1467 20c multicolored 38 8
*2083* A1468 20c multicolored 38 8
*2084* A1469 20c multicolored 38 8
*2085* A1470 20c multicolored 38 8
*a* Block of 4, #2082-2085 1.60 1.00

**New Orleans World Exposition**

River Wildlife A1471

**1984, May 11 *Perf. 11***
*2086* A1471 20c multicolored 38 5

**Health Research**

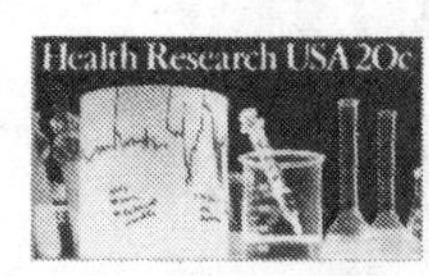

Lab Equipment A1472

**1984, May 17 *Perf. 11***
*2087* A1472 20c multicolored 38 5

Actor Douglas Fairbanks (1883-1939) A1473

A1474

**Performing Arts**

**1984, May 23 Photo. & Engr.**
*2088* A1473 20c multicolored 38 5

**Jim Thorpe, 1888-1953**

**1984, May 24 Engr. *Perf. 11***
*2089* A1474 20c dark brown 38 5

**Performing Arts**

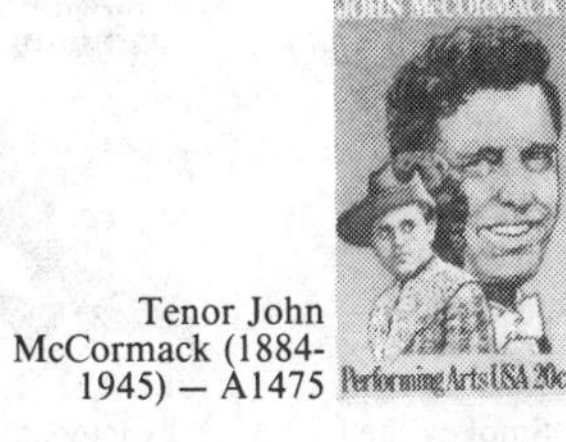

Tenor John McCormack (1884-1945) — A1475

**1984, June 6 Photo. *Perf. 11***
*2090* A1475 20c multicolored 38 5

**25th Anniv. of St. Lawrence Seaway**

Aerial View of Seaway, Freighters A1476

**1984, June 26 Photo. *Perf. 11***
*2091* A1476 20c multicolored 38 5

**50th Anniv. of Waterfowl Preservation Act**

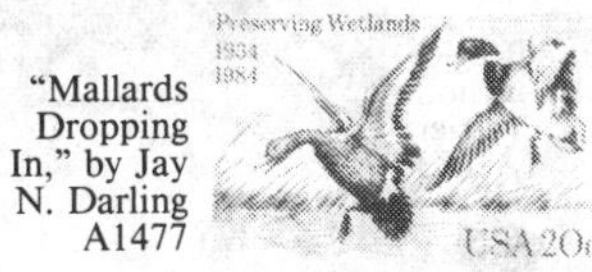

"Mallards Dropping In," by Jay N. Darling A1477

**1984, July 2 Engr. *Perf. 11***
*2092* A1477 20c multi 38 5
*a* Horiz. pair, imperf. vert. *500.00*

See No. RW1.

A1478

Author — A1479

**Roanoke Voyages**

**1984, July 13 Photo. *Perf. 11***
*2093* A1478 20c multicolored 38 5

**Herman Melville (1819-1891)**

**1984, Aug. 1** **Engr.** ***Perf. 11***

| | | | | |
|---|---|---|---|---|
| *2094* | A1479 20c sage green | 38 | 5 |

**Horace Moses (1862-1947)**

Junior Achievement Founder — A1480

**1984, Aug. 6** **Photo. & Engr.**

| | | | |
|---|---|---|---|
| *2095* | A1480 20c org & dk brn | 38 | 5 |

Smokey the Bear — A1481

Clemente, Puerto Rican Flag — A1482

**1984, Aug. 13** **Litho. & Engr.**

| | | | |
|---|---|---|---|
| *2096* | A1481 20c multicolored | 38 | 5 |
| *a* | Horiz. pair, imperf. btwn. | *400.00* | |
| *b* | Vert. pair, imperf. btwn. | *275.00* | |
| *c* | Block of 4, imperf. btwn, vert. and horiz. | *3,500.* | |

**Roberto Clemente (1934-1972)**

**1984, Aug. 17** **Photo.** ***Perf. 11***

| | | | |
|---|---|---|---|
| *2097* | A1482 20c multicolored | 38 | 5 |
| *a* | Horiz. pair, imperf. vert. | *1,250.* | |

**Dogs**

Beagle, Boston Terrier A1483

Chesapeake Bay Retriever, Cocker Spaniel A1484

Alaskan Malamute, Collie A1485

Black & Tan Coonhound, American Foxhound — A1486

**1984, Sept. 7** **Photo.** ***Perf. 11***

| | | | |
|---|---|---|---|
| *2098* | A1483 20c multicolored | 38 | 8 |
| *2099* | A1484 20c multicolored | 38 | 8 |
| *2100* | A1485 20c multicolored | 38 | 8 |
| *2101* | A1486 20c multicolored | 38 | 8 |
| *a* | Block of 4, #2098-2101 | 1.60 | 1.00 |

**Crime Prevention**

McGruff, The Crime Dog — A1487

**1984, Sept. 26** **Photo.** ***Perf. 11***

| | | | |
|---|---|---|---|
| *2102* | A1487 20c multicolored | 38 | 5 |

**Hispanic Americans**

A1488

**1984, Oct. 31** **Photo.** ***Perf. 11***

| | | | |
|---|---|---|---|
| *2103* | A1488 20c multicolored | 38 | 5 |
| *a* | Vert. pair, imperf. horiz. | — | |

**Family Unity**

A1489

**1984, Oct. 1** **Photo. & Engr.**

| | | | |
|---|---|---|---|
| *2104* | A1489 20c multicolored | 38 | 5 |
| *a* | Horiz. pair, imperf. vert. | *550.00* | |

**Eleanor Roosevelt**

A1490

**1984, Oct. 11** **Engr.** ***Perf. 11***

| | | | |
|---|---|---|---|
| *2105* | A1490 20c deep blue | 38 | 5 |

**Nation of Readers**

Lincoln, Son Tad — A1491

**1984, Oct. 16** **Engr.** ***Perf. 11***

| | | | |
|---|---|---|---|
| *2106* | A1491 20c brn & mar | 38 | 5 |

**Christmas**

Madonna and Child by Fra Filippo Lippi — A1492

Santa Claus — A1493

**1984, Oct. 30** **Photo.** ***Perf. 11***

| | | | |
|---|---|---|---|
| *2107* | A1492 20c multicolored | 38 | 5 |
| *2108* | A1493 20c multicolored | 38 | 5 |
| *a* | Horiz. pair, imperf. vert. | — | |

**Vietnam Veterans Memorial**

Memorial Wall — A1494

**1984, Nov. 10** **Engr.** ***Perf. 10½***

| | | | |
|---|---|---|---|
| *2109* | A1494 20c multicolored | 38 | 5 |

**Performing Arts**

Composer Jerome Kern (1885-1945) — A1495

**1985, Jan. 23** **Photo.** ***Perf. 11***

| | | | |
|---|---|---|---|
| *2110* | A1495 22c multicolored | 40 | 5 |

A1496

A1497

**1985, Feb. 1** **Photo.** ***Perf. 11***

| | | | |
|---|---|---|---|
| *2111* | A1496 (22c) green | 40 | 5 |
| *a* | Vert. pair, imperf. | *50.00* | |
| *b* | Vert. pair, imperf. horiz. | — | |

**Coil Stamp**

***Perf. 10 Vert.***

| | | | |
|---|---|---|---|
| *2112* | A1496 (22c) green | 40 | 5 |
| *a* | Imperf., pair | 45.00 | |

**Booklet Stamp**

***Perf. 11***

| | | | |
|---|---|---|---|
| *2113* | A1497 (22c) green | 40 | 5 |
| *a* | Booklet pane of 10 | 4.50 | |

A1498

Flag over Capitol Dome A1499

**1985, Mar. 29** **Engr.** ***Perf. 11***

| | | | |
|---|---|---|---|
| *2114* | A1498 22c bl, red & blk | 40 | 5 |

**Coil Stamp**

***Perf. 10 Vert.***

| | | | |
|---|---|---|---|
| *2115* | A1498 22c bl, red & blk | 40 | 5 |
| *a* | Imperf., pair | 12.50 | |
| *b* | Inscribed "T" at bottom ('87) | 40 | 8 |

**Booklet Stamp**

***Perf. 10 Horiz.***

| | | | |
|---|---|---|---|
| *2116* | A1499 22c bl, red & blk | 40 | 5 |
| *a* | Booklet pane of 5 | 2.20 | — |

**Seashells**

Frilled Dogwinkle A1500

Reticulated Helmet A1501

New England Neptune A1502

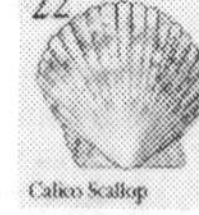

Calico Scallop A1503

Lightning Whelk — A1504

**1985, Apr. 4** **Engr.** ***Perf. 10***

| | | | |
|---|---|---|---|
| *2117* | A1500 22c blk & brn | 40 | 5 |
| *2118* | A1501 22c multicolored | 40 | 5 |
| *2119* | A1502 22c blk & brn | 40 | 5 |
| *2120* | A1503 22c blk & vio | 40 | 5 |
| *2121* | A1504 22c multicolored | 40 | 5 |
| *a.* | Booklet pane of 10 | 4.00 | — |
| *b.* | As "a," violet omitted | — | |
| *c.* | As "a," vert. imperf. btwn. | *800.00* | |
| *d.* | As "a," imperf. | | — |
| *e.* | Strip of 5, Nos. 2117-2121 | 2.00 | — |

Issued in booklets only.

Eagle and Half Moon A1505

**1985, Apr. 29** **Photo.** ***Perf. 10 Vert.***

| | | | |
|---|---|---|---|
| *2122* | A1505 $10.75 multi | 19.00 | — |
| *a* | Booklet pane of 3 | 57.50 | — |

Issued in booklets only.

**Transportation Coils**

A1506

A1507

A1508

A1509

A1510 A1511

A1512 A1513

A1514 A1515

A1516 A1517

A1518 A1519

**1985-87 Engr. *Perf. 10 Vert.***

*2123* A1506 3.4c dk bluish grn 7 5
a Untagged (Bureau Precancel) 15
*2124* A1507 4.9c brn blk 10 5
a Untagged (Bureau Precancel) 10
*2125* A1508 5.5c dp mag ('86) 11 5
a Untagged (Bureau precancel) 11
*2126* A1509 6c red brown 12 5
a Untagged (Bureau Precancel) 12
b As "a," imperf., pair —
*2127* A1510 7.1c lake ('87) 15 5
a Untagged (Bureau Precancel) 15
*2128* A1511 8.3c green 18 5
a Untagged (Bureau Precancel) 16
*2129* A1512 8.5c dk Prus grn ('87) 18 5
a Untagged (Bureau Precancel) 18
*2130* A1513 10.1c sl bl 22 5
a Untagged (Bureau Precancel) 22
b As "a," imperf., pair *175.00*
*2131* A1514 11c dark green 22 5
*2132* A1515 12c dark blue 24 5
a Untagged (Bureau Precancel) 24
*2133* A1516 12.5c ol grn 25 5
a Untagged (Bureau Precancel) 25
b As "a," imperf., pair 60.00
*2134* A1517 14c sky blue 28 5
a Imperf., pair 85.00
*2135* A1518 17c sky bl ('86) 34 5
a Imperf., pair —
*2136* A1519 25c org brn ('86) 45 5
a. Imperf., pair 15.00
*Nos. 2123-2136 (14)* 2.91 70

See Nos. 1897-1908, 2225-2231, 2252-2266.

### Black Heritage Issue

Mary McLeod Bethune (1875-1955), Educator — A1520

**1985, Mar. 5 Photo. *Perf. 11***

*2137* A1520 22c multicolored 40 5

### Duck Decoys

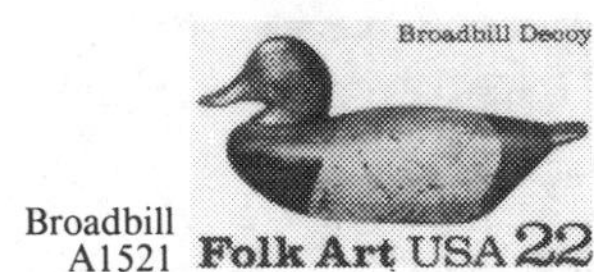


Broadbill A1521

Mallard A1522

Canvasback A1523

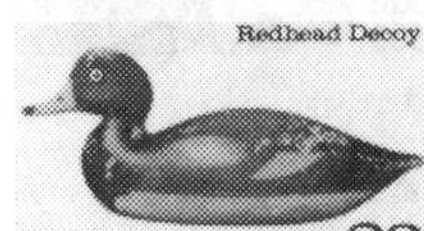


Redhead A1524

**1985, Mar. 22 Photo. *Perf. 11***

*2138* A1521 22c multicolored 40 8
*2139* A1522 22c multicolored 40 8
*2140* A1523 22c multicolored 40 8
*2141* A1524 22c multicolored 40 8
a Block of 4, #2138-2141 1.60 1.00

### Winter Special Olympics

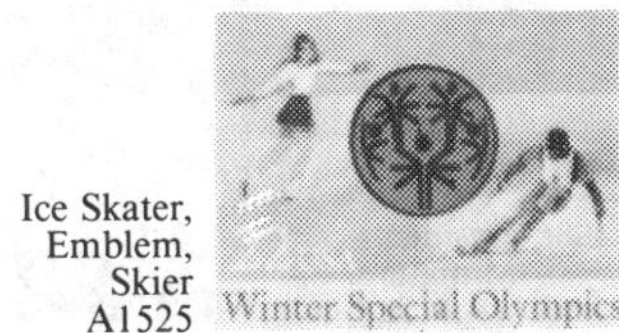


Ice Skater, Emblem, Skier A1525

**1985, Mar. 25 Photo. *Perf. 11***

*2142* A1525 22c multi 40 5
a Vert. pair, imperf. horiz. *850.00*

### Love

A1526

**1985, Apr. 17 Photo.**

*2143* A1526 22c multicolored 40 5
a. Imperf., pair —

### Rural Electrification Administration

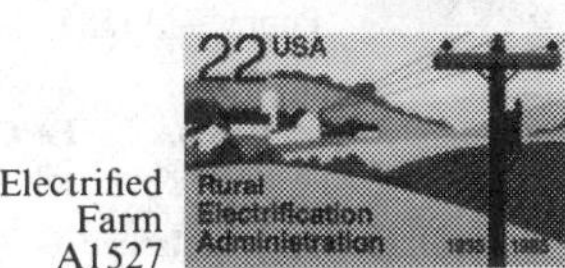


Electrified Farm A1527

**1985, May 11 Photo. & Engr.**

*2144* A1527 22c multicolored 40 5

### AMERIPEX '86

US No. 134 — A1528

**1985, May 25 Litho. & Engr.**

*2145* A1528 22c multi 40 5
a Red, blk & bl omitted *275.00*

### US First Lady

Abigail Adams (1744-1818) — A1529

**1985, June 14 Litho. *Perf. 11***

*2146* A1529 22c multi 40 5
a Imperf., pair *400.00*

### Architect, Sculptor

F A Bartholdi, Statue of Liberty Sculptor

Frederic Auguste Bartholdi (1834-1904), Statue of Liberty A1530

**1985, July 18 Litho. & Engr.**

*2147* A1530 22c multicolored 40 5

George Washington, Washington Monument A1532

Envelopes A1533

### COIL STAMPS

**1985 Photo. *Perf. 10 Vert.***

*2149* A1532 18c multi 32 8
a Untagged (Bureau Precancel) 32
b Imperf., pair *1,250.*
c As "a," imperf., pair 900.00
*2150* A1533 21.1c multi 42 8
a Untagged (Bureau Precancel) 42

Issue dates: 18c, Nov. 6. 21.1c, Oct. 22.
Precancellations on Nos. 2149a, 2150a do not have lines.

### Korean War Veterans

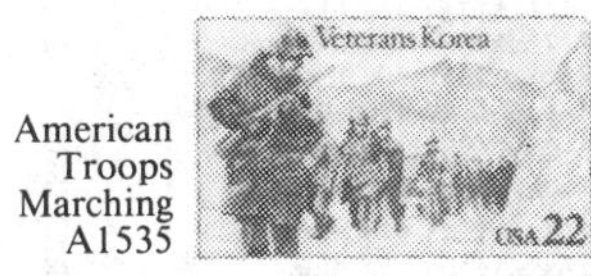


American Troops Marching A1535

**1985, July 26 Engr. *Perf. 11***

*2152* A1535 22c gray grn & rose red 40 5

### Social Security Act, 50th Anniv.

Men, Women, Children, Corinthian Columns A1536

**1985, Aug. 14 Photo. *Perf. 11***

*2153* A1536 22c dp bl & lt bl 40 5

Prices of premium quality never hinged stamps will be in excess of catalogue price.

### World War I Veterans

The Battle of Marne, France, by Harvey Dunn A1537

**1985, Aug. 26 Engr. *Perf. 11***

*2154* A1537 22c gray grn & rose red 40 5

### Horses

Quarter Horse A1538

Morgan A1539

Saddlebred A1540

Appaloosa A1541

**1985, Sept. 25 Photo. *Perf. 11***

*2155* A1538 22c multicolored 40 8
*2156* A1539 22c multicolored 40 8
*2157* A1540 22c multicolored 40 8
*2158* A1541 22c multicolored 40 8
a Block of 4, #2155-2158 1.60 1.00

### Public Education in America

Quill Pen, Apple, Spectacles, Penmanship Quiz — A1542

**1985, Oct. 1 Photo. *Perf. 11***

*2159* A1542 22c multicolored 40 5

### International Youth Year

YMCA Youth Camping, Cent. A1543

Boy Scouts, 75th Anniv. A1544

Big Brothers/Big Sisters Fed., 40th Anniv. — A1545

Camp Fire, Inc., 75th Anniv. A1546

**1985, Oct. 7 Photo. *Perf. 11***

| | | | | |
|---|---|---|---|---|
| *2160* | A1543 | 22c multicolored | 40 | 8 |
| *2161* | A1544 | 22c multicolored | 40 | 8 |
| *2162* | A1545 | 22c multicolored | 40 | 8 |
| *2163* | A1546 | 22c multicolored | 40 | 8 |
| *a* | | Block of 4, #2160-2163 | 1.60 | 1.00 |

### Help End Hunger

Youths and the Elderly Suffering from Malnutrition A1547

**1985, Oct. 15 Photo.**

| | | | | |
|---|---|---|---|---|
| *2164* | A1547 | 22c multicolored | 40 | 5 |

### Christmas

Genoa Madonna, Enameled Terra-Cotta by Luca Della Robbia (1400-1482) — A1548

Poinsettia Plants A1549

**1985, Oct. 30 Photo.**

| | | | | |
|---|---|---|---|---|
| *2165* | A1548 | 22c multi | 40 | 5 |
| *a* | | Imperf., pair | *130.00* | |
| *2166* | A1549 | 22c multi | 40 | 5 |
| *a* | | Imperf., pair | *150.00* | |

### Arkansas Statehood, 150th Anniv.

Old State House, Little Rock A1550

**1986, Jan. 3 Photo. *Perf. 11***

| | | | | |
|---|---|---|---|---|
| *2167* | A1550 | 22c multicolored | 40 | 5 |
| *a* | | Vert. pair, imperf. horiz. | — | |

### Great Americans

A1551

A1552

A1553

A1554

A1555

A1559

A1560

A1561

A1562

A1563

A1565

A1566

A1571

A1574

A1575

A1577

A1578

A1579

**1986-88 Engr. *Perf. 11***

| | | | | |
|---|---|---|---|---|
| *2168* | A1551 | 1c brnsh ver | 5 | 5 |
| *2169* | A1552 | 2c bright blue ('87) | 5 | 5 |
| *2170* | A1553 | 3c bright blue | 6 | 5 |
| *2171* | A1554 | 4c bl vio | 7 | 5 |
| *2172* | A1555 | 5c dk ol grn | 9 | 5 |
| *2176* | A1559 | 10c lake ('87) | 16 | 5 |
| *2177* | A1560 | 14c crimson ('87) | 24 | 5 |
| *2178* | A1561 | 15c claret ('88) | 25 | 5 |
| *2179* | A1562 | 17c dl bl grn | 28 | 6 |
| *2180* | A1563 | 21c ('88) | 32 | 5 |
| *2182* | A1565 | 23c ('88) | 35 | 5 |
| *2183* | A1566 | 25c blue | 38 | 6 |
| *a* | | Bklt. pane of 10 ('88) | 4.00 | |
| *2188* | A1571 | 45c brt blue ('88) | 70 | 5 |
| *2191* | A1574 | 56c scarlet | 80 | 8 |
| *2192* | A1575 | 65c ('88) | 95 | 18 |
| *2194* | A1577 | $1 dk Prus grn | 1.40 | 50 |
| *2195* | A1578 | $2 brt vio | 3.00 | 50 |
| *2196* | A1579 | $5 cop red ('87) | 7.00 | 1.00 |
| | | *Nos. 2168-2196 (18)* | 16.15 | 2.93 |

**Booklet Stamp**

***Perf. 10 on 2 or 3 sides***

| | | | | |
|---|---|---|---|---|
| *2197* | A1566 | 25c blue ('88) | 50 | 5 |
| *a* | | Bklt. pane of 6 | 3.00 | |

This is an expanding set. Numbers will change if necessary.

### Stamp Collecting

Handstamped Cover, No. 213, Philatelic Memorabilia A1581

Boy Examining Stamp Collection A1582

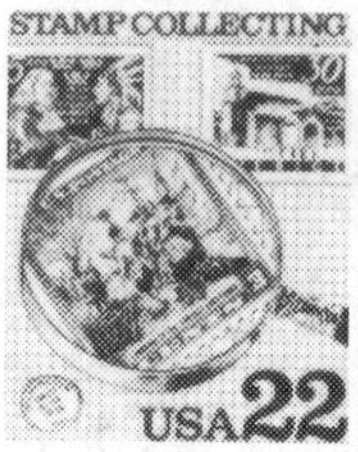


No. 836 Under Magnifying Glass, Sweden Nos. 268, 271 — A1583

1986 Presidents Miniature Sheet — A1584

***Perf. 10 Vert. on 1 or 2 Sides***

**1986, Jan. 23 Litho. & Engr.**

| | | | | |
|---|---|---|---|---|
| *2198* | A1581 | 22c multi | 40 | 5 |
| *2199* | A1582 | 22c multi | 40 | 5 |
| *2200* | A1583 | 22c multi | 40 | 5 |
| *2201* | A1584 | 22c multi | 40 | 5 |
| *a.* | | Bklt. pane of 4, #2198-2201 | 1.70 | |
| *b.* | | As "a," blk omitted on #2198, 2201 | 50.00 | |
| *c.* | | As "a," blue (litho.) omitted on Nos. 2198-2200 | — | |
| *d.* | | As "a," buff (litho.) omitted | — | |

See Sweden Nos. 1585-1588.

### Love

Puppy — A1585

**1986, Jan. 30 Photo. *Perf. 11***

| | | | | |
|---|---|---|---|---|
| *2202* | A1585 | 22c multicolored | 40 | 5 |

### Black Heritage Issue

Sojourner Truth (c. 1797-1883), Abolitionist — A1586

**1986, Feb. 4 Photo. *Perf. 11***

| | | | | |
|---|---|---|---|---|
| *2203* | A1586 | 22c multicolored | 40 | 5 |

### Republic of Texas, 150th Anniv.

Texas State Flag and Silver Spur — A1587

**1986, Mar. 2 Photo.**

| | | | | |
|---|---|---|---|---|
| *2204* | A1587 | 22c dk bl, dk red & grysh blk | 40 | 5 |
| *a* | | Horiz. pair, imperf. vert. | *950.00* | |

### Fish

Muskellunge — A1588

Atlantic Cod A1589

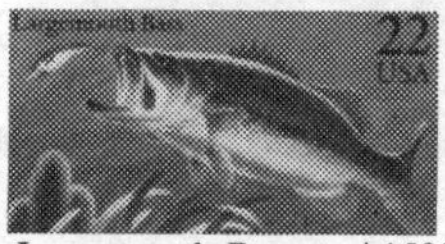


Largemouth Bass — A1590

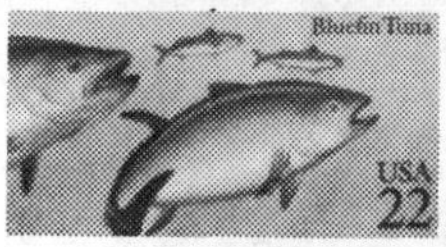


Bluefin Tuna A1591

Catfish A1592

***Perf. 10 Horiz.***

**1986, Mar. 21 Photo.**

| | | | | |
|---|---|---|---|---|
| *2205* | A1588 | 22c multicolored | 40 | 5 |
| *2206* | A1589 | 22c multicolored | 40 | 5 |
| *2207* | A1590 | 22c multicolored | 40 | 5 |
| *2208* | A1591 | 22c multicolored | 40 | 5 |
| *2209* | A1592 | 22c multicolored | 40 | 5 |
| *a* | | Bklt. pane of 5, #2205-2209 | 2.25 | |

Issued in booklets only.

### Public Hospitals

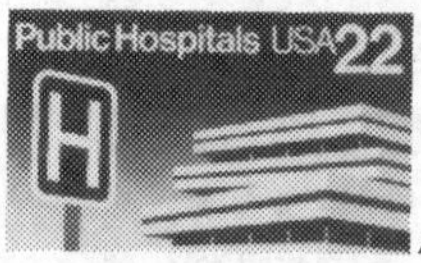


A1593

**1986, Apr. 11 Photo. *Perf. 11***

| | | | | |
|---|---|---|---|---|
| *2210* | A1593 | 22c multicolored | 40 | 5 |
| *a.* | | Vert. pair, imperf. horiz. | *425.00* | |
| *b.* | | Horiz. pair, imperf. vert. | — | |

### Performing Arts

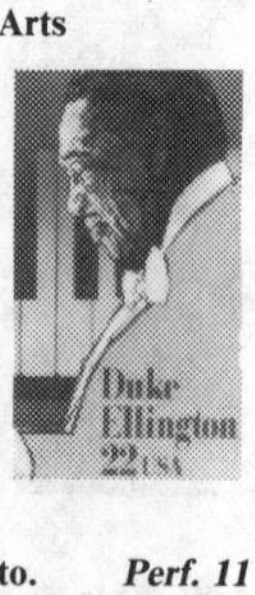


Edward Kennedy "Duke" Ellington (1899-1974), Jazz Composer — A1594

**1986, Apr. 29 Photo. *Perf. 11***

| | | | | |
|---|---|---|---|---|
| *2211* | A1594 | 22c multicolored | 40 | 5 |
| *a* | | Vert. pair, imperf. horiz. | — | |

### Miniature Sheets

35 Presidents — A1599

No. 2216: a., Washington. b., John Adams. c., Jefferson. d., Madison. e., Monroe. f., John Quincy Adams. g., Jackson. h., Van Buren. i., Harrison.
No. 2217; a., Tyler. b., Polk. c., Taylor. d., Fillmore. e., Pierce. f., Buchanan. g., Lincoln. h., Andrew Johnson. i., Grant.
No. 2218: a., Hayes. b., Garfield. c., Arthur. d., Cleveland. e., Harrison. f., McKinley. g., Theodore Roosevelt. h., Taft. i., Wilson.
No. 2219: a., Harding. b., Coolidge. c., Hoover. d., Franklin Delano Roosevelt. e., White House. f., Truman. g., Eisenhower. h., Kennedy. i., Lyndon B. Johnson.

**1986, May 22** **Litho. & Engr.**

| | | | |
|---|---|---|---|
| *2216* | Sheet of 9 | 3.75 | |
| *a.-i* | A1599 22c, any single | 40 | 20 |
| *j* | Blue omitted | — | |
| *2217* | Sheet of 9 | 3.75 | |
| *a.-i* | A1599 22c, any single | 40 | 20 |
| *2218* | Sheet of 9 | 3.75 | |
| *a.-i* | A1599 22c, any single | 40 | 20 |
| *j* | Brown omitted | — | |
| *2219* | Sheet of 9 | 3.75 | |
| *a.-i* | A1599 22c, any single | 40 | 20 |

Issued at AMERIPEX '86 Intl. Phil. Exhib., Chicago, IL, May 22-June 1.

### Polar Explorers

Elisha Kent Kane A1600

Adolphus W. Greely A1601

Vilhjalmur Stefansson — A1602

Robert E. Peary and Matthew Alexander Henson A1603

**1986, May 28** **Photo.** ***Perf. 11***

| | | | | |
|---|---|---|---|---|
| *2220* | A1600 | 22c multicolored | 40 | 5 |
| *2221* | A1601 | 22c multicolored | 40 | 5 |
| *2222* | A1602 | 22c multicolored | 40 | 5 |
| *2223* | A1603 | 22c multicolored | 40 | 5 |
| *a* | | Block of 4, #2220-2223 | 1.60 | 1.00 |
| *b* | | As "a," black (engr.) omitted | — | |

Statue of Liberty, Cent. — A1604

**1986, July 4** **Engr.** ***Perf. 11***

| | | | | |
|---|---|---|---|---|
| *2224* | A1604 | 22c scar & dk blue | 40 | 5 |

See France No. 2014.

### Transportation Coils

A1604a

A1604b

**1986-87** **Engr.** ***Perf. 10 Vert.***

| | | | | |
|---|---|---|---|---|
| *2225* | A1604a | 1c violet | 5 | 5 |
| *2226* | A1604b | 2c black ('87) | 5 | 5 |
| *2228* | A1285 | 4c redsh brn | 8 | 5 |
| *2231* | A1511 | 8.3c green (Bureau precancel) | | 16 |

Issue dates: 1c, Nov. 26. 2c, Mar. 6. Earliest known usage of 4c, Aug. 15, 1986. 8.3c, Aug. 29.
On No. 2228 "Stagecoach 1890s" is 17mm long, on No. 1898A 19½mm long. On No. 2231 "Ambulance 1860s" is 18mm long.
No. 2226 inscribed "2 USA;" No. 1897A inscribed "USA 2c."
This is an expanding set. Numbers will change if necessary.

### Navajo Art

A1605 A1606

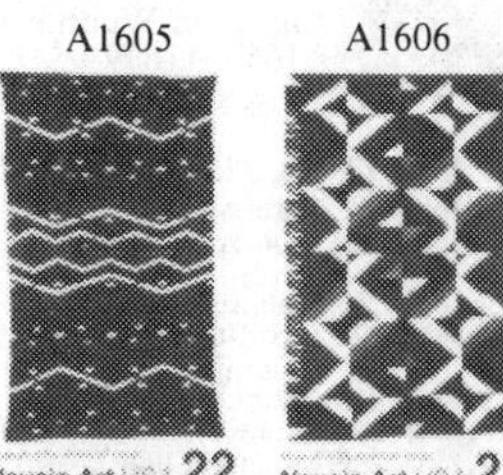


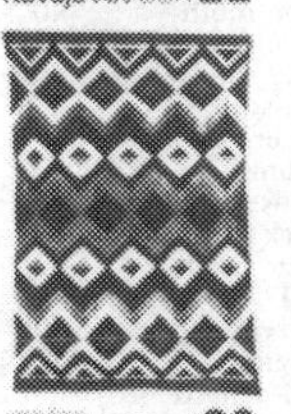

A1607 A1608

Blankets in the Museum of the American Indian and Lowe Art Museum.

**Lithographed, Engraved**

**1986, Sept. 4** ***Perf. 11***

| | | | | |
|---|---|---|---|---|
| *2235* | A1605 | 22c multi | 40 | 8 |
| *2236* | A1606 | 22c multi | 40 | 8 |
| *2237* | A1607 | 22c multi | 40 | 8 |
| *2238* | A1608 | 22c multi | 40 | 8 |
| *a* | | Block of 4, #2235-2238 | 1.60 | 1.00 |
| *b* | | As "a," black (engr.) omitted | *475.00* | |

### Literary Arts

T. S. Eliot (1888-1965), Poet — A1609

**1986, Sept. 26** **Engr.** ***Perf. 11***

| | | | | |
|---|---|---|---|---|
| *2239* | A1609 | 22c copper red | 40 | 5 |

An enhanced introduction to the Scott Catalogue begins on Page V. A thorough understanding of the material presented there will greatly aid your use of the catalogue itself.

### Woodcarved Figurines

Highlander Figure A1610 Ship Figurehead A1611

Nautical Figure A1612 Cigar Store Figure A1613

**1986, Oct. 1** **Photo.** ***Perf. 11***

| | | | | |
|---|---|---|---|---|
| *2240* | A1610 | 22c multicolored | 40 | 8 |
| *2241* | A1611 | 22c multicolored | 40 | 8 |
| *2242* | A1612 | 22c multicolored | 40 | 8 |
| *2243* | A1613 | 22c multicolored | 40 | 8 |
| *a* | | Block of 4, #2240-2243 | 1.60 | 1.00 |
| *b* | | As "a," imperf. vert. | — | |

### Christmas

Madonna, National Gallery, by Perugino (c. 1450-1523) A1614

Village Scene A1615

**1986, Oct. 24** ***Perf. 11***

| | | | | |
|---|---|---|---|---|
| *2244* | A1614 | 22c multicolored | 40 | 5 |
| *2245* | A1615 | 22c multicolored | 40 | 5 |

### Michigan Statehood Sesquicent.

White Pine — A1616

**1987, Jan. 26** **Photo.** ***Perf. 11***

| | | | | |
|---|---|---|---|---|
| *2246* | A1616 | 22c multicolored | 40 | 5 |

### Pan American Games, Indianapolis, August 7-25

Runner in Full Stride A1617

**1987, Jan. 29** ***Perf. 11***

| | | | | |
|---|---|---|---|---|
| *2247* | A1617 | 22c multicolored | 40 | 5 |
| *a.* | | Silver omitted | — | |

### Love

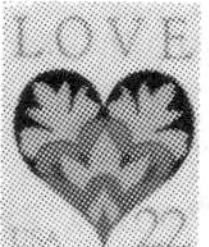


A1618

**1987, Jan. 30** **Photo.** ***Perf. 11½x11***

| | | | | |
|---|---|---|---|---|
| *2248* | A1618 | 22c multicolored | 40 | 5 |

### Black Heritage

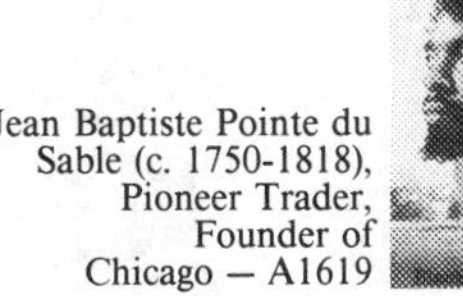

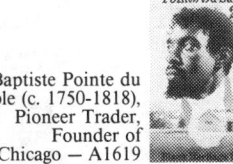


Jean Baptiste Pointe du Sable (c. 1750-1818), Pioneer Trader, Founder of Chicago — A1619

**1987, Feb. 20** **Photo.** ***Perf. 11***

| | | | | |
|---|---|---|---|---|
| *2249* | A1619 | 22c multicolored | 40 | 5 |

### Performing Arts

Enrico Caruso (1873-1921), Opera Tenor — A1620

**1987, Feb. 27** ***Perf. 11***

| | | | | |
|---|---|---|---|---|
| *2250* | A1620 | 22c multicolored | 40 | 5 |
| *a* | | Black omitted | — | |

### Girl Scouts, 75th Anniv.

Fourteen Achievement Badges — A1621

**Lithographed, Engraved**

**1987, Mar. 12** ***Perf. 11***

| | | | | |
|---|---|---|---|---|
| *2251* | A1621 | 22c multicolored | 40 | 5 |

### Transportation Coils

A1622

A1623

A1624

A1625 A1627 A1629

A1626

A1628

A1630

A1631

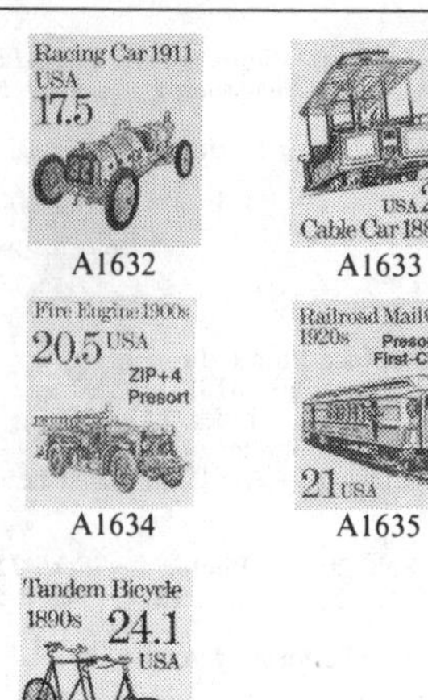


A1632 A1633

A1634 A1635

A1636

| 1987-88 | | Engr. | *Perf. 10 Vert.* | |
|---|---|---|---|---|
| *2252* | A1622 | 3c claret ('88) | 6 | 5 |
| *2253* | A1623 | 5c black | 9 | 5 |
| *2254* | A1624 | 5.3c black (Bureau precancel in scarlet) ('88) | | 10 |
| *2255* | A1625 | 7.6c brown (Bureau precancel in scarlet) ('88) | | 14 |
| *2256* | A1626 | 8.4c deep claret (Bureau precancel in red) ('88) | | 15 |
| *2257* | A1627 | 10c sky blue | 18 | 5 |
| *2258* | A1628 | 13c black (Bureau precancel in red) ('88) | | 22 |
| *2259* | A1629 | 13.2c slate green (Bureau precancel in red) ('88) | | 22 |
| *a.* | | Imperf., pair | | — |
| *2260* | A1630 | 15c violet ('88) | 24 | 5 |
| *2261* | A1631 | 16.7c rose (Bureau precancel in black) | | 28 |
| *2262* | A1632 | 17.5c dark vio | 30 | 5 |
| *a.* | | Untagged (Bureau precancel) | | 30 |
| *b.* | | Imperf., pair | — | |
| *2263* | A1633 | 20c blue vio ('88) | 35 | 5 |
| *2264* | A1634 | 20.5c (Bureau precancel in black) ('88) | | 38 |
| *2265* | A1635 | 21c olive green (Bureau precancel in red) ('88) | | 38 |
| *a.* | | Imperf., pair | | — |
| *2266* | A1636 | 24.1c deep ultra (Bureau precancel) ('88) | | 42 |

The 5.3c, 7.6c, 8.4c, 13.2c, 16.7c, 20.5c, 21c and 24.1c are only available precanceled and are untagged.

See Nos. 1897-1908, 2123-2136, 2225-2231.

**Special Occasions**

Booklet Stamps

A1637

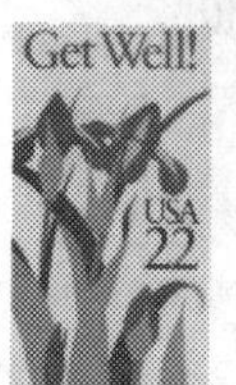

A1638 A1639

A1640

A1641

A1642

A1643

A1644

*Perf. 10 on 1, 2, or 3 sides*

| 1987, Apr. 20 | | | Photo. | |
|---|---|---|---|---|
| *2267* | A1637 | 22c multicolored | 40 | 5 |
| *2268* | A1638 | 22c multicolored | 40 | 5 |
| *2269* | A1639 | 22c multicolored | 40 | 5 |
| *2270* | A1640 | 22c multicolored | 40 | 5 |
| *2271* | A1641 | 22c multicolored | 40 | 5 |
| *2272* | A1642 | 22c multicolored | 40 | 5 |
| *2273* | A1643 | 22c multicolored | 40 | 5 |
| *2274* | A1644 | 22c multicolored | 40 | 5 |
| *a.* | | Bklt. pane of 10 (#2268-2271, 2273-2274, and 2 each #2267, 2272) | 4.00 | |

**United Way Centenary**

Six Profiles
A1645

**Lithographed, Engraved**

| 1987, Apr. 28 | | | *Perf. 11* | |
|---|---|---|---|---|
| *2275* | A1645 | 22c multicolored | 40 | 5 |

A1646

A1647

A1648

A1649

Pheasant
A1649a

Grosbeak
A1649b

Owl
A1649c

Honeybee
A1649d

**Photo., Engr. (No. 2280), Litho. & Engr. (No. 2281)**

| 1987-88 | | | *Perf. 11* | |
|---|---|---|---|---|
| *2276* | A1646 | 22c multi | 40 | 5 |
| *a.* | | Booklet pane of 20 | 8.00 | |
| *2277* | A1647 | (25c) multi ('88) | 40 | 5 |
| *2278* | A1648 | 25c multi ('88) | 40 | 5 |

**Coil Stamps**

*Perf. 10 Vert.*

| | | | | |
|---|---|---|---|---|
| *2279* | A1647 | (25c) multi ('88) | 40 | 5 |
| *a.* | | Imperf., pair | — | |
| *2280* | A1649 | 25c multi ('88) | 40 | 5 |
| *a.* | | Imperf., pair | — | |
| *2281* | A1649d | 25c multi ('88) | 40 | 5 |
| *a.* | | Imperf., pair | — | |

**Booklet Stamps**

***Perf. 10 on 2 or 3 Sides, 11 on 2 or 3 sides (#2283)***

| | | | | |
|---|---|---|---|---|
| *2282* | A1647 | (25c) multi ('88) | 40 | 5 |
| *a.* | | Bklt. pane of 10 | 4.00 | |
| *2283* | A1649a | 25c multi ('88) | 40 | 5 |
| *a.* | | Bklt. pane of 10 | 4.00 | |

Imperfs. are printer's waste.

| | | | | |
|---|---|---|---|---|
| *2284* | A1649b | 25c multi ('88) | 40 | 5 |
| *2285* | A1649c | 25c multi ('88) | 40 | 5 |
| *b.* | | Bklt. pane of 10, 5 each Nos. 2284-2285 | 4.00 | |
| *2285A* | A1648 | 25c multi ('88) | 40 | 5 |
| *c.* | | Booklet pane of 6 | 2.50 | |

Issue dates: No. 2276, May 9; Nos. 2277, 2279, 2282, Mar. 22; No. 2278, May 6; No. 2280, May 20; No. 2281, Sept. 2; No. 2283, Apr. 29; Nos. 2284-2285, May 28. Nos. 2285A, July 5.

American Wildlife
A1650-A1699

| 1987, June 13 | | Photo. | *Perf. 11* | |
|---|---|---|---|---|
| *2286* | A1650 | 22c Barn swallow | 40 | 5 |
| *2287* | A1651 | 22c Monarch butterfly | 40 | 5 |
| *2288* | A1652 | 22c Bighorn sheep | 40 | 5 |
| *2289* | A1653 | 22c Broad-tailed hummingbird | 40 | 5 |
| *2290* | A1654 | 22c Cottontail | 40 | 5 |
| *2291* | A1655 | 22c Osprey | 40 | 5 |
| *2292* | A1656 | 22c Mountain lion | 40 | 5 |
| *2293* | A1657 | 22c Luna moth | 40 | 5 |
| *2294* | A1658 | 22c Mule deer | 40 | 5 |
| *2295* | A1659 | 22c Gray squirrel | 40 | 5 |
| *2296* | A1660 | 22c Armadillo | 40 | 5 |
| *2297* | A1661 | 22c Eastern chipmunk | 40 | 5 |
| *2298* | A1662 | 22c Moose | 40 | 5 |
| *2299* | A1663 | 22c Black bear | 40 | 5 |
| *2300* | A1664 | 22c Tiger swallowtail | 40 | 5 |
| *2301* | A1665 | 22c Bobwhite | 40 | 5 |
| *2302* | A1666 | 22c Ringtail | 40 | 5 |
| *2303* | A1667 | 22c Red-winged blackbird | 40 | 5 |
| *2304* | A1668 | 22c American lobster | 40 | 5 |
| *2305* | A1669 | 22c Black-tailed jack rabbit | 40 | 5 |
| *2306* | A1670 | 22c Scarlet tanager | 40 | 5 |
| *2307* | A1671 | 22c Woodchuck | 40 | 5 |
| *2308* | A1672 | 22c Roseate spoonbill | 40 | 5 |
| *2309* | A1673 | 22c Bald eagle | 40 | 5 |
| *2310* | A1674 | 22c Alaskan brown bear | 40 | 5 |
| *2311* | A1675 | 22c Iiwi | 40 | 5 |
| *2312* | A1676 | 22c Badger | 40 | 5 |
| *2313* | A1677 | 22c Pronghorn | 40 | 5 |
| *2314* | A1678 | 22c River otter | 40 | 5 |
| *2315* | A1679 | 22c Ladybug | 40 | 5 |
| *2316* | A1680 | 22c Beaver | 40 | 5 |
| *2317* | A1681 | 22c White-tailed deer | 40 | 5 |
| *2318* | A1682 | 22c Blue jay | 40 | 5 |
| *2319* | A1683 | 22c Pika | 40 | 5 |
| *2320* | A1684 | 22c Bison | 40 | 5 |
| *2321* | A1685 | 22c Snowy egret | 40 | 5 |
| *2322* | A1686 | 22c Gray wolf | 40 | 5 |
| *2323* | A1687 | 22c Mountain goat | 40 | 5 |
| *2324* | A1688 | 22c Deer mouse | 40 | 5 |
| *2325* | A1689 | 22c Black-tailed prairie dog | 40 | 5 |
| *2326* | A1690 | 22c Box turtle | 40 | 5 |
| *2327* | A1691 | 22c Wolverine | 40 | 5 |
| *2328* | A1692 | 22c American elk | 40 | 5 |
| *2329* | A1693 | 22c California sea lion | 40 | 5 |
| *2330* | A1694 | 22c Mockingbird | 40 | 5 |
| *2331* | A1695 | 22c Raccoon | 40 | 5 |
| *2332* | A1696 | 22c Bobcat | 40 | 5 |
| *2333* | A1697 | 22c Black-footed ferret | 40 | 5 |
| *2334* | A1698 | 22c Canada goose | 40 | 5 |
| *2335* | A1699 | 22c Red fox | 40 | 5 |
| *a.* | | Pane of 50, #2286-2335 | 20.00 | |

**Ratification of the Constitution**

A1700



A1701

A1702

A1703

A1704

A1705

A1706

A1707

A1708

A1709

A1710

**Litho. & Engr., Photo. (#2337, 2343-2344)**

| 1987-88 | | | *Perf. 11* | |
|---|---|---|---|---|
| *2336* | A1700 | 22c multi | 40 | 5 |
| *2337* | A1701 | 22c multi | 40 | 5 |
| *2338* | A1702 | 22c multi | 40 | 5 |
| *2339* | A1703 | 22c multi | 40 | 5 |
| *2340* | A1704 | 22c multi | 40 | 5 |
| *2341* | A1705 | 22c dk bl & dk red ('88) | 40 | 5 |
| *2342* | A1706 | 22c multi ('88) | 40 | 5 |
| *2343* | A1707 | 25c multi ('88) | 40 | 5 |
| *2344* | A1708 | 25c multi ('88) | 40 | 5 |
| *2345* | A1709 | 25c multi ('88) | 40 | 5 |
| *2346* | A1710 | 25c multi ('88) | 40 | 5 |
| | | *Nos. 2336-2346 (11)* | 4.40 | 55 |

Issue dates: No. 2336, July 4. No. 2337, Aug. 26. No. 2238, Sept. 11. No. 2339, Jan. 6. No. 2340, Jan. 9. No. 2341, Feb. 6. No. 2342, Feb. 15. No. 2343, May 23; No. 2344, June 21; No. 2345, June 25. No. 2346, July 26.

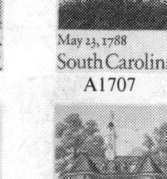

## US-Morocco Diplomatic Relations Bicentennial

Arabesque, Dar Batha Palace, Fez — A1713

**Litho. & Engr.**

**1987, July 18** *Perf. 11*

*2349* A1713 22c scar & blk 40 5
*a.* Black (engr.) omitted *450.00*

See Morocco No. 642.

## Literary Arts

William Cuthbert Faulkner (1897-1962), Novelist — A1714

**1987, Aug. 3** **Engr.** *Perf. 11*

*2350* A1714 22c bright green 40 5

## Folk Art Issue

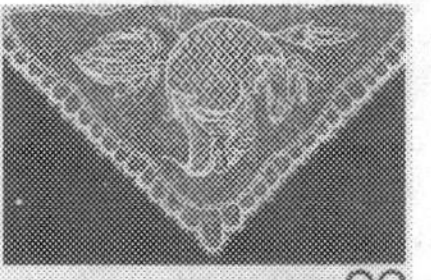


A1715

A1716

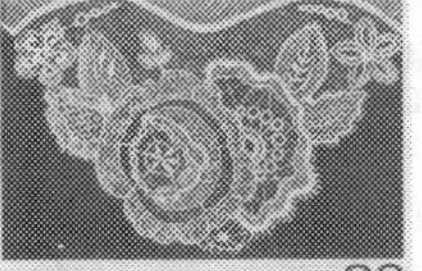


A1717

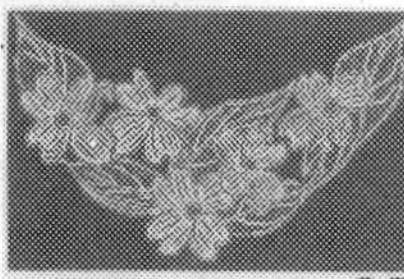


A1718

**Litho. & Engr.**

**1987, Aug. 14** *Perf. 11*

*2351* A1715 22c ultra & wht 40 8
*2352* A1716 22c ultra & wht 40 8
*2353* A1717 22c ultra & wht 40 8
*2354* A1718 22c ultra & wht 40 8
*a.* Block of 4, Nos. 2351-2354 1.60 1.00
*b.* As "a," white omitted —

## Drafting of the Constitution Bicentennial

A1719

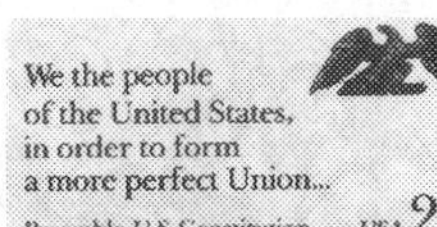


A1720

A1721

A1722

A1723

Booklet Stamps

***Perf. 10 Horiz.***

**1987, Aug. 28** **Photo.**

*2355* A1719 22c multicolored 40 8
*2356* A1720 22c multicolored 40 8
*2357* A1721 22c multicolored 40 8
*2358* A1722 22c multicolored 40 8
*2359* A1723 22c multicolored 40 8
*a.* Booklet pane of 5, Nos. 2355-2359 2.00

## Signing of the Constitution

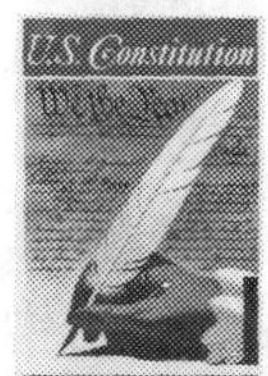


A1724

**Litho. & Engr.**

**1987, Sept. 17** *Perf. 11*

*2360* A1724 22c multicolored 40 5

## Certified Public Accounting

A1725

**1987, Sept. 21** **Litho. & Engr.**

*2361* A1725 22c multicolored 40 5
*a.* Black (engr.) omitted —

## Locomotives

Booklet Stamps

Stourbridge Lion, 1829 A1726

Best Friend of Charleston A1727

John Bull, 1831 A1728

Brother Johnathan, 1832 A1729

Gowan & Marx, 1839 A1730

**1987, Oct. 1** ***Perf. 10 Horiz.***

*2362* A1726 22c multicolored 40 8
*2363* A1727 22c multicolored 40 8
*2364* A1728 22c multicolored 40 8
*2365* A1729 22c multicolored 40 8
*2366* A1730 22c multicolored 40 8
*a.* Booklet pane of 5, Nos. 2362-2366 2.00

## Christmas 1987

Moroni Madonna A1731

Christmas Ornaments A1732

**1987, Oct. 23** **Photo.** *Perf. 11*

*2367* A1731 22c multicolored 40 5
*2368* A1732 22c multicolored 40 5

## 1988 Winter Olympics, Calgary

Skiing — A1733

**1988, Jan. 10** **Photo.** *Perf. 11*

*2369* A1733 22c multicolored 40 5

## Australia Bicentennial

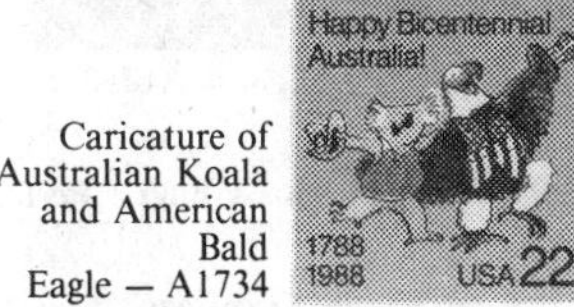


Caricature of Australian Koala and American Bald Eagle — A1734

**1988, Jan. 10** **Photo.** *Perf. 11*

*2370* A1734 22c multicolored 40 5

See Australia No. 1052.

## Black Heritage

James Weldon Johnson, 1871-1938, Author, Lyricist — A1735

**1988, Feb. 2** **Photo.** *Perf. 11*

*2371* A1735 22c multicolored 40 5

Siamese, Exotic Shorthair A1736

Abyssinian, Himalayan A1737

Maine Coon, Burmese A1738

American Shorthair, Persian A1739

**1988, Feb. 5** *Perf. 11*

*2372* A1736 22c multicolored 40 5
*2373* A1737 22c multicolored 40 5
*2374* A1738 22c multicolored 40 5
*2375* A1739 22c multicolored 40 5
*a.* Block of 4, Nos. 2372-2375 1.60 1.00

Knute Kenneth Rockne (1888-1931), Notre Dame Football Coach — A1740

**1988, Mar. 9** **Litho. & Engr.**

*2376* A1740 22c multicolored 40 5

## American Sports Issue

Francis Ouimet (1893-1967), 1st Amateur Golfer to Win the US Open Championship A1741

**1988, June 13** **Photo.** *Perf. 11*

*2377* A1741 25c multicolored 40 8

## Love Issue

Rose — A1742

Scott's editorial staff cannot undertake to identify, authenticate or appraise stamps and postal markings.

A1743

**1988** Photo. *Perf. 11*
*2378* A1742 25c multicolored 40 5
*2379* A1743 45c multicolored 65 5

Issue dates: 25c, July 4; 45c, Aug. 8.

**1988 Summer Olympics, Seoul**

A1744

**1988, Aug. 19** Photo. *Perf. 11*
*2380* A1744 25c multicolored 40 8

**Classic Automobiles**

1928 Locomobile A1745

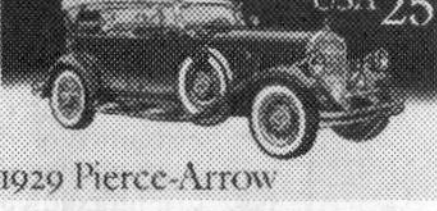

1929 Pierce-Arrow A1746

1931 Cord A1747

1932 Packard A1748

1935 Duesenberg A1749

Booklet Stamps
***Perf. 10 Horiz.***

**1988, Aug. 25** Litho. & Engr.
*2381* A1745 25c multicolored 40 8
*2382* A1746 25c multicolored 40 8
*2383* A1747 25c multicolored 40 8
*2384* A1748 25c multicolored 40 8
*2385* A1749 25c multicolored 40 8
*a.* Bklt. pane of 5, Nos. 2381-2385 2.00

**Antarctic Explorers**

Nathaniel Palmer (1799-1877) A1750

Lt. Charles Wilkes (1798-1877) A1751

Richard E. Byrd (1888-1957) A1752

Lincoln Ellsworth (1880-1951) A1753

**1988, Sept. 14** Photo. *Perf. 11*
*2386* A1750 25c multi 50 8
*2387* A1751 25c multi 50 8
*2388* A1752 25c multi 50 8
*2389* A1753 25c multi 50 8
*a.* Block of 4, Nos. 2386-2389 2.00 32
*b.* Blk (engr.) omitted —

**Folk Art Issue**
Carousel Animals

Deer A1754

Horse A1755

Camel A1756

Goat A1757

**1988, Oct. 1** Litho. & Engr. *Perf. 11*
*2390* A1754 25c multi 50 8
*2391* A1755 25c multi 50 8
*2392* A1756 25c multi 50 8
*2393* A1757 25c multi 50 8
*a.* Block of 4, Nos. 2390-2393 2.00 1.25

**Express Mail**

Eagle in Flight — A1758

**1988, Oct. 4** Litho. & Engr. *Perf. 11*
*2394* A1758 $8.75 multi 17.50 —

**Special Occasions**

Happy Birthday — A1759

Best Wishes A1760

Thinking of You — A1761

Love You A1762

Booklet Stamps
***Perf. 11 on 2 sides***

**1988, Oct. 22** Photo.
*2395* A1759 25c multi 50 5
*2396* A1760 25c multi 50 5
*a.* Bklt. pane of 6, 3 #2395 + 3 #2396 with gutter btwn. 3.00
*2397* A1761 25c multi 50 5
*2398* A1762 25c multi 50 5
*a.* Bklt. pane of 6, 3 #2397 + 3 #2398 with gutter btwn. 3.00

Madonna and Child, by Botticelli A1763

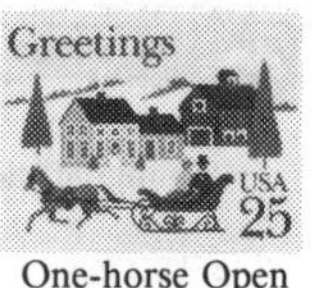

One-horse Open Sleigh and Village Scene A1764

**Litho. & Engr., Photo. (No. 2400)**
**1988, Oct. 20** *Perf. 11½*
*2399* A1763 25c multi 50 5
*a.* Gold omitted —
*2400* A1764 25c multi 50 5

**Montana Statehood Centennial**

*C.M. Russell and Friends,* by Charles M. Russell (1865-1926) A1765

**Litho. & Engr.**
**1989, Jan. 15** *Perf. 11*
*2401* A1765 25c multi 50 5

**BLACK HERITAGE SERIES**

Asa Philip Randolph (1889-1979), Labor and Civil Rights Leader — A1766

**1989, Feb. 3** Photo. *Perf. 11*
*2402* A1766 25c multi 50 5

**North Dakota Statehood Centennial**

A1767

**1989, Feb. 21** *Perf. 11*
*2403* A1767 25c multi 50 5

**Washington Statehood Centennial**

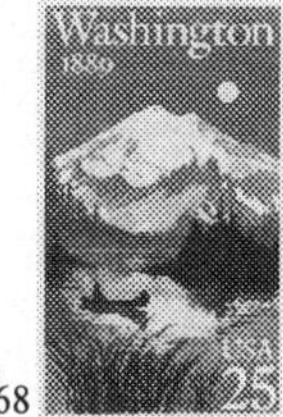

A1768

**1989, Feb. 22** *Perf. 11*
*2404* A1768 25c multi 50 5

**STEAMBOATS**

*Experiment,* 1788-1790 — A1769

*Phoenix,* 1809 A1770

*New Orleans,* 1812 A1771

*Washington,* 1816 — A1772

*Walk in the Water,* 1818 A1773

**1989, Mar. 3** Litho. & Engr.
***Perf. 10 horiz. on 1 or 2 sides***
*2405* A1769 25c multi 50 8
*2406* A1770 25c multi 50 8
*2407* A1771 25c multi 50 8
*2408* A1772 25c multi 50 8
*2409* A1773 25c multi 50 8
*a.* Bklt. pane of 5, Nos. 2405-2409 2.50

**WORLD STAMP EXPO '89**
Nov. 17-Dec. 3, Washington, DC

No. 122 — A1774

**1989, Mar.16** Litho. & Engr. *Perf. 11*
*2410* A1774 25c 50 5

**PERFORMING ARTS**

Arturo Toscanini (1867-1975), Italian Conductor — A1775

**1989, Mar. 25** Photo. *Perf.*
*2411* A1775 25c multi 50 5

# Index of United States Commemorative Issues

## AIR POST STAMPS

For prepayment of postage on all mailable matter sent by airmail.

Curtiss Jenny — AP1

**Engraved (Flat Plate Printing)**

**1918 Unwmk. *Perf. 11***

| | | | |
|---|---|---|---|
| *C1* AP1 6c orange | | 70.00 | 30.00 |
| *C2* AP1 16c green | | 100.00 | 32.50 |
| *C3* AP1 24c car rose & bl | | 100.00 | 35.00 |
| *a* Center inverted | | *135,000.* | |

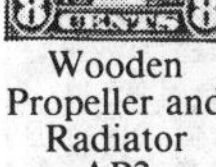

Wooden Propeller and Radiator AP2

Emblem of Air Service AP3

De Havilland Biplane — AP4

**1923**

| | | |
|---|---|---|
| *C4* AP2 8c dark green | 25.00 | 11.00 |
| *C5* AP3 16c dark blue | 95.00 | 30.00 |
| *C6* AP4 24c carmine | 100.00 | 25.00 |

Map of US and Two Mail Planes AP5

**1926-27**

| | | |
|---|---|---|
| *C7* AP5 10c dark blue | 2.25 | 25 |
| *C8* AP5 15c olive brown | 2.50 | 1.65 |
| *C9* AP5 20c yellow grn ('27) | 8.00 | 1.25 |

Lindbergh's Airplane "Spirit of St. Louis" — AP6

**1927, June 18**

| | | |
|---|---|---|
| *C10* AP6 10c dark blue | 6.00 | 1.50 |
| *a* Booklet pane of 3 | 110.00 | *60.00* |

Singles from No. C10a are imperf. at sides or imperf. at sides and bottom.

Nos. C1-C10 were available for ordinary postage.

Beacon on Rocky Mountains AP7

**1928, July 25 *Perf. 11***

| | | |
|---|---|---|
| *C11* AP7 5c carmine & blue | 3.00 | 25 |
| *a* Vertical pair, imperf. btwn. | *5,500.* | |

Winged Globe AP8

**1930, Feb. 10 *Perf. 11***

**Size: 46½x19mm**

| | | |
|---|---|---|
| *C12* AP8 5c violet | 8.00 | 22 |
| *a* Horiz. pair, imperf. btwn. | *4,500.* | |

See Nos. C16-C17, C19.

**Graf Zeppelin Issue**

Zeppelin over Atlantic Ocean — AP9

Zeppelin between Continents — AP10

Zeppelin Passing Globe — AP11

**1930, Apr. 19 *Perf. 11***

| | | |
|---|---|---|
| *C13* AP9 65c green | 250.00 | 175.00 |
| *C14* AP10 $1.30 brown | 700.00 | 485.00 |
| *C15* AP11 $2.60 blue | 1,050. | 550.00 |

Issued for use on mail carried on first Europe-Pan-America round-trip flight of Graf Zeppelin, May, 1930.

Type of 1930 Issue

**Rotary Press Printing**

**1931-32 *Perf. 10½x11***

**Size: 47½x19mm**

| | | |
|---|---|---|
| *C16* AP8 5c violet | 4.75 | 30 |
| *C17* AP8 8c olive bister ('32) | 1.90 | 20 |

**Century of Progress Issue**

Airship "Graf Zeppelin" — AP12

**Flat Plate Printing**

**1933, Oct. 2 *Perf. 11***

| | | |
|---|---|---|
| *C18* AP12 50c green | 90.00 | 75.00 |

Flight of the "Graf Zeppelin" in Oct. 1933, to Miami, Akron and Chicago, and from the last city to Europe.

**Catalogue values for unused stamps in this section, from this point to the end of the section, are for Never Hinged items.**

Type of 1930 Issue

**Rotary Press Printing**

**1934, July 1 *Perf. 10½x11***

| | | |
|---|---|---|
| *C19* AP8 6c dull orange | 2.25 | 12 |

**Transpacific Issues**

The "China Clipper" over the Pacific AP13

**Flat Plate Printing**

**1935, Nov. 22 *Perf. 11***

| | | |
|---|---|---|
| *C20* AP13 25c blue | 1.10 | 75 |

Issued to pay postage on mail carried on the Transpacific air post service inaugurated Nov. 22, 1935.

The "China Clipper" over the Pacific AP14

**1937, Feb. 15 *Perf. 11***

| | | |
|---|---|---|
| *C21* AP14 20c green | 8.00 | 1.25 |
| *C22* AP14 50c carmine | 7.75 | 3.25 |

Eagle Holding Shield, Olive Branch and Arrows AP15

**1938, May 14 *Perf. 11***

| | | |
|---|---|---|
| *C23* AP15 6c dark bl & car | 50 | 6 |
| *a* Vert. pair, imperf. horiz. | 275.00 | |
| *b* Horiz. pair, imperf. vert | *8,500.* | |
| *c* 6c ultramarine & carmine | 150.00 | |

**Transatlantic Issue**

Winged Globe AP16

**1939, May 16 *Perf. 11***

| | | |
|---|---|---|
| *C24* AP16 30c dull blue | 6.00 | 1.25 |

Twin-Motored Transport Plane — AP17

**Rotary Press Printing**

**1941-44** *Perf. 11x10½*

*C25* AP17 6c carmine 12 5
*a* Booklet pane of 3 ('43) 6.50 *1.00*
*b* Horiz. pair, imperf. between *1,800.*
*C26* AP17 8c olive grn ('44) 16 5
*C27* AP17 10c violet 1.10 20
*C28* AP17 15c brown carmine 2.25 35
*C29* AP17 20c bright green 1.65 30
*C30* AP17 30c blue 2.00 30
*C31* AP17 50c orange 10.00 4.00
*Nos. C25-C31 (7)* 17.28 5.25

Singles from No. C25a are imperf. at sides or imperf. at sides and bottom.

DC-4 Skymaster AP18

**1946, Sept. 25** *Perf. 11x10½*

*C32* AP18 5c carmine 10 5

DC-4 Skymaster — AP19

**1947, Mar. 26** *Perf. 10½x11*

*C33* AP19 5c carmine 10 5

See Nos. C37, C39, C41.

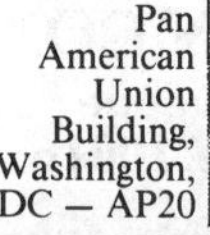

Pan American Union Building, Washington, DC — AP20

Statue of Liberty and New York Skyline AP21

Plane over San Francisco-Oakland Bay Bridge — AP22

**1947** *Perf. 11x10½*

*C34* AP20 10c black 20 6
*C35* AP21 15c bright blue grn 30 5
*a* Horiz. pair, imperf. between *1,500.*
*C36* AP22 25c blue 75 12

Coil Stamp

**1948, Jan. 15** *Perf. 10 Horiz.*

*C37* AP19 5c carmine 80 75

**New York City Issue**

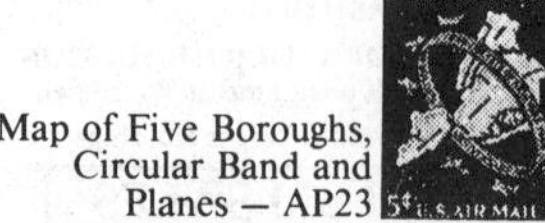


Map of Five Boroughs, Circular Band and Planes — AP23

**1948, July 31** *Perf. 11x10½*

*C38* AP23 5c bright carmine 10 10

50th anniv. of the consolidation of the 5 boroughs of NYC.

Type of 1947

**1949, Jan. 18** *Perf. 10½x11*

*C39* AP19 6c carmine 12 5
*a* Booklet pane of 6 12.00 *5.00*

The lack of a price for a listed item does not necessarily indicate rarity.

**Alexandria Bicentennial Issue**

Home of John Carlyle, Alexandria Seal and Gadsby's Tavern AP24

**Rotary Press Printing**

**1949, May 11** *Perf. 11x10½*

*C40* AP24 6c carmine 12 10

200th anniv. of the founding of Alexandria, Va.

Type of 1947
Coil Stamp

**1949, Aug. 25** *Perf. 10 Horiz.*

*C41* AP19 6c carmine 2.75 5

**Universal Postal Union Issue**

Post Office Department Building AP25

Globe and Doves Carrying Messages AP26

Boeing Stratocruiser and Globe — AP27

**1949** **Unwmk.** *Perf. 11x10½*

*C42* AP25 10c violet 20 20
*C43* AP26 15c ultramarine 28 28
*C44* AP27 25c rose carmine 48 48

75th anniv. of the UPU.

**Wright Brothers Issue**

Wilbur and Orville Wright and their Plane — AP28

**1949, Dec. 17** *Perf. 11x10½*

*C45* AP28 6c magenta 14 10

46th anniv. of the Wright Brothers' 1st flight, Dec. 17, 1903.

Diamond Head, Honolulu, Hawaii AP29

**1952, Mar. 26** *Perf. 11x10½*

*C46* AP29 80c bright red vio 6.00 1.50

First Plane and Modern Plane AP30

Eagle in Flight AP31

**Powered Flight Issue**

**1953, May 29** *Perf. 11x10½*

*C47* AP30 6c carmine 14 10

50th anniversary of powered flight.

For Domestic Post Cards

**1954, Sept. 3** *Perf. 11x10½*

*C48* AP31 4c bright blue 8 8

See No. C50.

**Air Force Issue**

B-52 Stratofortress and F-104 Starfighters AP32

**Rotary Press Printing**

**1957, Aug. 1** *Perf. 11x10½*

*C49* AP32 6c blue 12 10

50th anniv. of US Air Force.

Flying Eagle Type of 1954
For Domestic Post Cards

**1958, July 31** *Perf. 11x10½*

*C50* AP31 5c rose red 14 12

Silhouette of Jet Airliner — AP33

**1958, July 31** *Perf. 10½x11*

*C51* AP33 7c blue 14 5
*a* Booklet pane of 6 15.00 *6.50*

**Coil Stamp**

***Perf. 10 Horizontally***

*C52* AP33 7c blue 2.00 10

See Nos. C60-C61.

**Alaska Statehood Issue**

Big Dipper, North Star and Map of Alaska AP34

**Rotary Press Printing**

**1959, Jan. 3** *Perf. 11x10½*

*C53* AP34 7c dark blue 15 12

Alaska's admission to statehood.

**Balloon Jupiter Issue**

Balloon and Crowd — AP35

**Giori Press Printing**

**1959, Aug. 17** *Perf. 11*

*C54* AP35 7c dark bl & red 15 12

Cent. of the carrying of mail by the balloon Jupiter from Lafayette to Crawfordsville, Ind.

**Hawaii Statehood Issue**

Alii Warrior, Map of Hawaii and Star of Statehood AP36

**Rotary Press Printing**

**1959, Aug. 21** *Perf. 11x10½.*

*C55* AP36 7c rose red 15 12

Hawaii's admission to statehood.

**Pan American Games Issue**

Runner Holding Torch — AP37

**Giori Press Printing**

**1959, Aug. 27** *Perf. 11*

*C56* AP37 10c vio bl & brt red 30 30

3rd Pan American Games, Chicago, Aug. 27-Sept. 7.

Liberty Bell — AP38

Statue of Liberty AP39

Abraham Lincoln AP40

**Giori Press Printing**

**1959-66** *Perf. 11*

*C57* AP38 10c blk & grn ('60) 1.50 1.00
*C58* AP39 15c black & orange 40 6
*C59* AP40 25c blk & mar ('60) 50 6
*a* Tagged ('66) 50 15

Luminescence

See note following No. 1053. "Tagged" varieties of untagged air-mail stamps start with No. C59a and end with No. C67a.

Airmail stamps starting with No. C69 are tagged unless otherwise noted.

Type of 1958
**Rotary Press Printing**

**1960, Aug. 12** *Perf. 10½x11*

*C60* AP33 7c carmine 14 5
*a* Booklet pane of 6 20.00 *7.00*

Type of 1958
Coil Stamp
***Perf. 10 Horiz.***

**1960, Oct. 22** **Unwmk.**

*C61* AP33 7c carmine 3.75 25

Type of 1959-60 and

Statue of Liberty AP41

**Giori Press Printing**

**1961-67** *Perf. 11*

*C62* AP38 13c black & red 35 10
*a* Tagged ('67) 1.00 25
*C63* AP41 15c black & orange 30 8
*a* Tagged ('67) 35 12
*b* As "a," horiz. pair, imperf. vert. *15,000.*

No. C63 has a gutter between the two parts of the design; No. C58 has none.

Jet Airliner Over Capitol — AP42

**Rotary Press Printing**

**1962, Dec. 5** *Perf. 10½x11*
*C64* AP42 8c carmine 18 5
*a* Tagged ('63) 22 5
*b* Booklet pane 5 + label 7.50 *1.25*
*c* As "b," tagged ('64) 2.25 *50*

Three different messages are found on the label in No. C64b, and one on No. C64c.

**Coil Stamp**

***Perf. 10 Horizontally***

*C65* AP42 8c carmine 35 8
*a* Tagged ('65) 40 10

The 1st luminescent tagged US issue was No. C64a issued Aug. 1, 1963, at Dayton, OH. Initial experiments there used tagged stamps and an automated facer-canceler to extract airmail as an aid to dispatch.

Montgomery Blair AP43

Bald Eagle AP44

**Montgomery Blair Issue**

**Giori Press Printing**

**1963, May 3 Unwmk.** *Perf. 11*
*C66* AP43 15c car, dp cl & bl 52 50

Blair (1813-1883), Postmaster Gen. (1861-64), who called the 1st Intl. Postal Conf., Paris, 1863, forerunner of the UPU.

For Domestic Post Cards

**Rotary Press Printing**

**1963, July 12** *Perf. 11x10½*
*C67* AP44 6c red 12 10
*a* Tagged ('67) 2.50 50

**Amelia Earhart Issue**

Amelia Earhart and Lockheed Electra — AP45

**Giori Press Printing**

**1963, July 24** *Perf. 11*
*C68* AP45 8c car & maroon 20 15

Earhart (1898-1937), 1st woman to fly across the Atlantic.

**Dr. Robert H. Goddard Issue**

Robert H. Goddard, Atlas Rocket and Launching Tower, Cape Kennedy AP46

**1964, Oct. 5 Unwmk. Tagged**
*C69* AP46 8c bl, red & bister 40 15

Goddard (1882-1945), physicist and pioneer rocket researcher.

United States Booklet Panes can be mounted in Scott's U.S. Booklet Panes Album.

Tlingit Totem, Southern Alaska AP47

"Columbia Jays," by Audubon AP48

**Alaska Purchase Issue**

**Giori Press Printing**

**1967, Mar. 30** *Perf. 11*
*C70* AP47 8c brown 20 20

Cent. of the Alaska Purchase. The Tlingit totem is from the Alaska State Museum, Juneau.

**1967, Apr. 26** *Perf. 11*
*C71* AP48 20c multicolored 80 15

See note after No. 1241.

50-Star Runway — AP49

**Rotary Press Printing**

**1968, Jan. 5 Unwmk.** *Perf. 11x10½*
*C72* AP49 10c carmine 22 5
*b* Booklet pane of 8 4.00 75
*c* Booklet pane of 5 + label 2.50 75

**Coil Stamp**

***Perf. 10 Vertically***

*C73* AP49 10c carmine 32 5
*a* Imperf., pair 600.00

The $1 Air Lift stamp is listed as No. 1341.

**Air Mail Service Issue**

Curtiss Jenny AP50

**Lithographed, Engraved (Giori)**

**1968, May 15** *Perf. 11*
*C74* AP50 10c bl, blk & red 25 15
*a* Red (tail stripe) omitted —

50th anniv. of regularly scheduled US air mail service.

USA and Jet — AP51

**1968, Nov. 22** *Perf. 11*
*C75* AP51 20c red, blue & blk 50 6

See No. C81.

**Moon Landing Issue**

First Man on the Moon — AP52

**Lithographed, Engraved (Giori)**

**1969, Sept. 9** *Perf. 11*
*C76* AP52 10c multicolored 20 15
*a* Rose red (litho.) omitted 350.00 —

Man's 1st landing on the moon, July 20, 1969. US astronauts Neil A. Armstrong and Col. Edwin E. Aldrin, Jr., with Lieut. Col. Michael Collins piloting Apollo 11.

On No. C76a, the litho. rose red is missing from the entire vignette—the dots on top of the yellow areas as well as the flag shoulder patch.

Silhouette of Delta Wing Plane AP53

Silhouette of Jet Airliner AP54

Winged Airmail Envelope AP55

Statue of Liberty AP56

Design: 21c, "USA" and jet (as C75).

**Rotary Press Printing**

**1971-73** *Perf. 10½x11*
*C77* AP53 9c red 16 15

***Perf. 11x10½***

*C78* AP54 11c carmine 22 5
*a* Booklet pane of 4 + 2 labels 1.50 *40*
*b* Untagged (Bureau precanceled) 25
*C79* AP55 13c carmine ('73) 22 10
*a* Booklet pane of 5 + label ('73) 1.35 *70*
*b* Untagged (Bureau precanceled) 30

**Giori Press Printing**

***Perf. 11***

*C80* AP56 17c bluish black, red & dark green 35 15

**Lithographed, Engraved (Giori)**

***Perf. 11***

*C81* AP51 21c red, bl & blk 38 10

Issue dates: 9c, May 15; 11c, May 7; 17c, July 13; 21c, May 21, 1971; 13c, Nov. 16, 1973.

The 9c was for use on domestic post cards.

No. C78b is precanceled "WASHINGTON D.C." (or "DC") and No. C79b "WASHINGTON DC" for the use of Congressmen and the public.

Coil Stamps

**Rotary Press Printing**

**1971-73** *Perf. 10 Vertically*
*C82* AP54 11c carmine 25 6
*a* Imperf., pair 200.00
*C83* AP55 13c carmine ('73) 28 10
*a* Imperf., pair 90.00

Issue dates: 11c, May 7; 13c, Dec. 27.

**National Parks Centennial Issue**

Kii Statue and Temple, City of Refuge, Hawaii — AP57

**Lithographed, Engraved (Giori)**

**1972, May 3** *Perf. 11*
*C84* AP57 11c org & multi 20 15
*a* Blue & green (litho) omitted *1,750.*

Cent. of the Natl. Parks system. No. C84 shows view of the City of Refuge Natl. Historical Park at Honaunau.

**Olympic Games Issue**

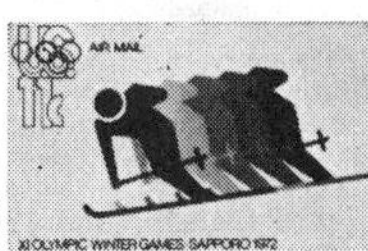

Skiing and Olympic Rings — AP58

**Photogravure (Andreotti)**

**1972, Aug. 17** *Perf. 11x10½*
*C85* AP58 11c multi 22 15

11th Winter Olympic Games, Sapporo, Japan, Feb. 3-13, and 20th Summer Olympic Games, Munich, Germany, Aug. 26-Sept. 11.

**Electronics Progress Issue**

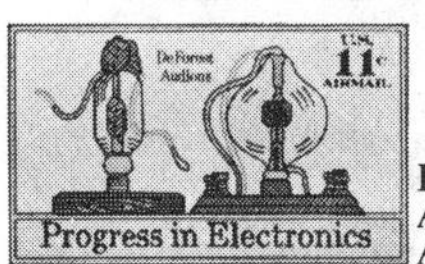

De Forest Audions AP59

**Lithographed, Engraved (Giori)**

**1973, July 10** *Perf. 11*
*C86* AP59 11c rose lil & multi 20 15
*a* Vermilion & olive (litho.) omitted *2,000.*

Statue of Liberty AP60


Mt. Rushmore National Memorial AP61

**1974 Giori Press Printing** *Perf. 11*
*C87* AP60 18c car, blk & ultra 35 35
*C88* AP61 26c ultra, blk & car 45 15

Issue dates: 18c, Jan. 11; 26c, Jan. 2.

Plane and Globes AP62

Plane, Globes and Flag — AP63

**Giori Press Printing**

**1976, Jan. 2** *Perf. 11*
*C89* AP62 25c ultra, red & blk 45 18
*C90* AP63 31c ultra, red & blk 55 10

**Wright Brothers Issue**

Orville and Wilbur Wright and Flyer A — AP64

Wright Brothers, Flyer A and Shed — AP65

**Lithographed, Engraved**

**1978, Sept. 23** *Perf. 11*
*C91* AP64 31c ultra & multi 65 15
*C92* AP65 31c ultra & multi 65 15
*a* Pair, #C91-C92 1.40 1.25
*b* As "a", ultramarine & black (engr.) omitted *1,500.*
*c* As "a," black (engr.) omitted —

*d.* As "a.," black, yellow, magenta, blue & brown (litho.) omitted —

75th anniv. of 1st powered flight, Kill Devil Hill, NC, Dec. 17, 1903. Nos. C91-C92 printed se-tenant vertically in sheets of 100.

### Octave Chanute Issue

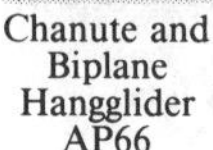

Chanute and Biplane Hangglider AP66

Biplane Hanggliders and Chanute AP67

**Lithographed, Engraved**

| **1979, Mar. 29** | | **Perf. 11** |
|---|---|---|
| *C93* AP66 21c ultra & multi | 85 | 32 |
| *C94* AP67 21c ultra & multi | 85 | 32 |
| *a* Pair, #C93-C94 | 1.75 | 75 |
| *b* As "a", ultramarine & black (engr.) omitted | *3,000.* | |

Octave Chanute (1832-1910), civil engineer and aviation pioneer. Nos. C93-C94 printed se-tenant vertically in sheets of 100.

### Wiley Post Issue

Wiley Post and "Winnie Mae" — AP68

NR-105 W, Post in Pressurized Suit, Portrait — AP69

**Lithographed, Engraved**

| **1979, Nov. 20** | | **Perf. 11** |
|---|---|---|
| *C95* AP68 25c ultra & multi | 1.15 | 35 |
| *C96* AP69 25c ultra & multi | 1.15 | 35 |
| *a* Pair, #C95-C96 | 2.50 | 85 |

Post (1899-1935), 1st man to fly around the world alone and high-altitude flying pioneer. Printed se-tenant vertically.

### Olympic Games Issue

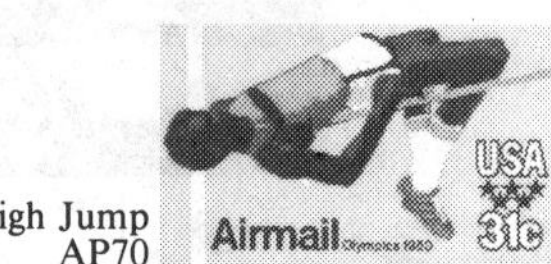

High Jump AP70

| **1979, Nov. 1** **Photo.** | | **Perf. 11** |
|---|---|---|
| *C97* AP70 31c multicolored | 70 | 30 |

22nd Olympic Games, Moscow, July 19-Aug. 3, 1980.

Philip Mazzei (1730-1816), Italian-born Political Writer — AP71

| **1980, Oct. 13** **Photo.** | | **Perf. 11** |
|---|---|---|
| *C98* AP71 40c multicolored | 75 | 30 |
| *a* Perf. 10½x11 | 2.00 | — |
| *b* Imperf., pair | *2,250.* | |

Blanche Stuart Scott (1886-1970) AP72

Glenn Curtiss (1878-1930) AP73

| **1980, Dec. 30** | | |
|---|---|---|
| *C99* AP72 28c multicolored | 55 | 15 |
| *C100* AP73 35c multicolored | 65 | 15 |

Scott, 1st woman pilot, and Curtiss, aviation pioneer and aircraft designer.

### 1984 Olympic Games

AP81

| **1983, June 17** | | **Perf. 11** |
|---|---|---|
| *C101* AP81 28c Gymnast | 56 | 28 |
| *C102* AP81 28c Hurdler | 56 | 28 |
| *C103* AP81 28c Basketball | 56 | 28 |
| *C104* AP81 28c Soccer | 56 | 28 |
| *a* Block of 4, #C101-C104 | 2.75 | 1.75 |
| *b* As "a," imperf. vert. | — | |

Nos. C101-C104 are vertical.

| **1983, Apr. 8** | | |
|---|---|---|
| *C105* AP81 40c Shot put | 80 | 40 |
| *C106* AP81 40c Gymnast | 80 | 40 |
| *C107* AP81 40c Swimmer | 80 | 40 |
| *C108* AP81 40c Weightlifting | 80 | 40 |
| *a.* Block of 4, #C105-C108 | 3.75 | 2.00 |
| *b.* As "a", imperf. | *1,100.* | |
| *c.* Perf. 11x10½ | 90 | 45 |
| *d.* As "a," perf. 11x10½ | 4.00 | — |

| **1983, Nov. 4** | | |
|---|---|---|
| *C109* AP81 35c Women's fencing | 70 | 35 |
| *C110* AP81 35c Cycling | 70 | 35 |
| *C111* AP81 35c Women's volleyball | 70 | 35 |
| *C112* AP81 35c Pole vaulting | 70 | 35 |
| *a* Block of 4, #C109-C112 | 3.25 | 1.85 |

Alfred V. Verville AP86

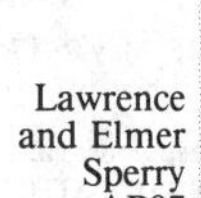

Lawrence and Elmer Sperry AP87

| **1985, Feb. 13** | | **Photo.** |
|---|---|---|
| *C113* AP86 33c multicolored | 66 | 20 |
| *a* Imperf., pair | *900.00* | |
| *C114* AP87 39c multicolored | 78 | 20 |
| *a* Imperf., pair | — | |

Alfred V. Verville (1890-1970), aircraft designer, Lawrence Sperry (1892-1931), designer and pilot, and Elmer Sperry (1860-1930), inventor.

Transpacific Airmail AP88

| **1985, Feb. 15** | | **Photo.** |
|---|---|---|
| *C115* AP88 44c multicolored | 88 | 20 |
| *a* Imperf., pair | *1,000.* | |

**Fr. Junipero Serra (1713-84)**
California Missionary

Outline Map of Southern California, Portrait, San Gabriel Mission AP89

| **1985, Aug. 22** **Photo.** | | **Perf. 11** |
|---|---|---|
| *C116* AP89 44c multicolored | 1.00 | 20 |
| *a* Imperf., pair | — | |

Settling of New Sweden, 350th Anniv. AP90

Design: 17th Cent. European settler negotiating with two American Indians, map of New Sweden, the Swedish ships *Kalmar Nyckel* and *Fogel Grip*, based on an 18th cent. illustration from a Swedish book about the Colonies.

| **1988, Mar. 29** **Litho. & Engr.** | | |
|---|---|---|
| *C117* AP90 44c multicolored | 88 | 20 |

See Finland No. 768 and Sweden No. 1672.

**Samuel Pierpont Langley (1834-1906), Astronomer, Aviation Pioneer and Inventor**

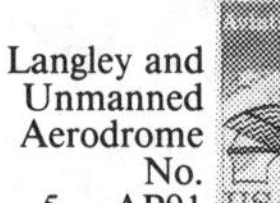

Langley and Unmanned Aerodrome No. 5 — AP91

**Litho. & Engr.**

| **1988, May 14** | | **Perf. 11** |
|---|---|---|
| *C118* AP91 45c multicolored | 90 | 20 |

**Igor Sikorsky (1889-1972), Aeronautic Engineer**

Sikorsky and VS300 Helicopter, 1939 AP92

| **1988, June 23** **Photo.** | | **Perf. 11** |
|---|---|---|
| *C119* AP92 36c multicolored | 72 | 20 |

---

## AIR POST SPECIAL DELIVERY STAMPS

To provide for the payment of both the postage and the special delivery fee in one stamp.

Great Seal of United States APSD1

**Flat Plate Printing**

| **1934** **Unwmk.** | | **Perf. 11** |
|---|---|---|
| *CE1* APSD1 16c dark blue | 65 | 85 |

For imperforate variety see No. 771.

| **1936** | | |
|---|---|---|
| *CE2* APSD1 16c red & blue | 40 | 25 |
| *a.* Horiz. pair, imperf. vert. | *3,250.* | |

---

## SPECIAL DELIVERY STAMPS

When affixed to any letter or article of mailable matter, secure immediate delivery, between 7 A. M. and midnight, at any post office.

Messenger Running SD1

**Flat Plate Printing**

| **1885** **Unwmk.** | | **Perf. 12** |
|---|---|---|
| *E1* SD1 10c blue | 175.00 | 20.00 |

Messenger Running SD2

| **1888** | | |
|---|---|---|
| *E2* SD2 10c blue | 175.00 | 5.00 |
| **1893** | | |
| *E3* SD2 10c orange | 110.00 | 11.00 |

Messenger Running SD3

Line under "Ten Cents"

| **1894** | | |
|---|---|---|
| *E4* SD3 10c blue | 450.00 | 12.50 |
| *a.* Imperf., pair | *5,500.* | |

| **1895** | | **Wmk. 191** |
|---|---|---|
| *E5* SD3 10c blue | 85.00 | 1.50 |
| *a.* Imperf., pair | *4,500.* | |
| *b.* Printed on both sides | *1,250.* | |

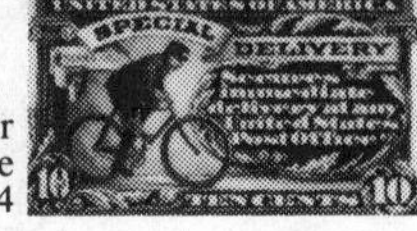

Messenger on Bicycle SD4

| **1902** | | |
|---|---|---|
| *E6* SD4 10c ultramarine | 52.50 | 1.50 |

Helmet of Mercury and Olive Branch — SD5

| **1908** | | |
|---|---|---|
| *E7* SD5 10c green | 57.50 | 21.00 |

| **1911** **Wmk. 190** | | **Perf. 12** |
|---|---|---|
| *E8* SD4 10c ultramarine | 55.00 | 2.25 |
| *b.* 10c violet blue | 55.00 | 2.25 |

| **1914** | | **Perf. 10** |
|---|---|---|
| *E9* SD4 10c ultramarine | 110.00 | 2.50 |

| **1916** **Unwmk.** | | **Perf. 10** |
|---|---|---|
| *E10* SD4 10c pale ultra | 200.00 | 12.50 |

| **1917** | | **Perf. 11** |
|---|---|---|
| *E11* SD4 10c ultramarine | 10.00 | 20 |
| *b.* 10c gray violet | 10.00 | 20 |
| *c.* 10c blue | 20.00 | 50 |

Postman and Motorcycle SD6

**1922**

| | | |
|---|---|---|
| *E12* SD6 10c gray violet | 18.00 | 15 |
| *a.* 10c deep ultramarine | 25.00 | 20 |

Motorcycle Type of 1922 and

Post Office Truck — SD7

**1925**

| | | |
|---|---|---|
| *E13* SD6 15c deep orange | 15.00 | 40 |
| *E14* SD7 20c black | 1.90 | 85 |

No. E13 measures 36½x21½mm.
No. E16 measures 36¾x22¼mm.
No. E14 measures 35½x21½mm.
No. E19 measures 36¼x22mm.

**Type of 1922 Issue**

**Rotary Press Printing**

**1927** ***Perf. 11x10½***

| | | |
|---|---|---|
| *E15* SD6 10c gray violet | 60 | 5 |
| *a.* 10c red lilac | 60 | 5 |
| *b.* 10c gray lilac | 60 | 5 |
| *c.* Horiz. pair, imperf. btwn. | 275.00 | |

No. E15 measures 36½x21¾mm. Stamps from the flat plates measure 36x21½mm.

Type of 1922 Issue

**1931**

| | | |
|---|---|---|
| *E16* SD6 15c orange | 70 | 8 |

**Catalogue values for unused stamps in this section, from this point to the end of the section, are for Never Hinged items.**

Type of 1922 Issue

**1944**

| | | |
|---|---|---|
| *E17* SD6 13c blue | 60 | 6 |
| *E18* SD6 17c orange yellow | 2.75 | 1.25 |

Type of 1925 Issue

**1951**

| | | |
|---|---|---|
| *E19* SD7 20c black | 1.50 | 12 |

Special Delivery Letter, Hand to Hand — SD8

**1954-57** ***Perf. 11x10½***

| | | |
|---|---|---|
| *E20* SD8 20c deep blue | 38 | 8 |
| *E21* SD8 30c lake ('57) | 48 | 5 |

Arrows SD9

**Giori Press Printing**

**1969-71** ***Perf. 11***

| | | |
|---|---|---|
| *E22* SD9 45c carmine & vio bl | 90 | 12 |
| *E23* SD9 60c vio bl & car ('71) | 85 | 10 |

Issue dates: 45c, Nov. 21; 60c, May 10.

## REGISTRATION STAMP

Issued for the prepayment of registry fees; not usable for postage.

Eagle — RS1

**1911 Engr. Wmk. 190** ***Perf. 12***

| | | |
|---|---|---|
| *F1* RS1 10c ultramarine | 55.00 | 2.25 |

## CERTIFIED MAIL STAMP

For use on first-class mail for which no indemnity value is claimed, but for which proof of mailing and proof of delivery are available at less cost than registered mail.

Letter Carrier — CM1

**Rotary Press Printing**

**1955 Unwmk.** ***Perf. 10½x11***

| | | |
|---|---|---|
| *FA1* CM1 15c red | 28 | 20 |

## POSTAGE DUE STAMPS

For affixing, by a postal clerk to any piece of mailable matter, to denote the amount to be collected from the addressee because of insufficient prepayment of postage.

Unused Values for Nos. J1-J14 are for stamps with full original gum

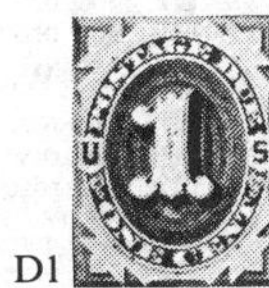

D1

Printed by the American Bank Note Company

**1879 Unwmk. Engraved** ***Perf. 12***

| | | |
|---|---|---|
| *J1* D1 1c brown | 30.00 | 5.00 |
| *J2* D1 2c brown | 200.00 | 4.00 |
| *J3* D1 3c brown | 25.00 | 2.50 |
| *J4* D1 5c brown | 300.00 | 25.00 |
| *J5* D1 10c brown | 350.00 | 12.50 |
| *a.* Imperf., pair | *1,600.* | |
| *J6* D1 30c brown | 175.00 | 20.00 |
| *J7* D1 50c brown | 225.00 | 30.00 |

Special Printing

**1879**

| | |
|---|---|
| *J8* D1 1c deep brown | *5,750.* |
| *J9* D1 2c deep brown | *3,750.* |
| *J10* D1 3c deep brown | *3,500.* |
| *J11* D1 5c deep brown | *3,000.* |
| *J12* D1 10c deep brown | *1,850.* |
| *J13* D1 30c deep brown | *1,850.* |
| *J14* D1 50c deep brown | *2,000.* |

Regular Issue

**1884-89**

| | | |
|---|---|---|
| *J15* D1 1c red brown | 30.00 | 2.50 |
| *J16* D1 2c red brown | 37.50 | 2.50 |
| *J17* D1 3c red brown | 500.00 | 100.00 |
| *J18* D1 5c red brown | 250.00 | 12.50 |
| *J19* D1 10c red brn ('87) | 225.00 | 7.00 |
| *J20* D1 30c red brown | 110.00 | 22.50 |
| *J21* D1 50c red brown | 1,000. | 125.00 |

**1891-93**

| | | |
|---|---|---|
| *J22* D1 1c brt claret | 12.50 | 50 |
| *a.* Imperf., pair | 450.00 | |
| *J23* D1 2c brt claret | 15.00 | 45 |
| *a.* Imperf., pair | 450.00 | |
| *J24* D1 3c brt claret | 27.50 | 4.00 |
| *a.* Imperf., pair | 450.00 | |
| *J25* D1 5c brt claret | 35.00 | 4.00 |
| *a.* Imperf., pair | 450.00 | |
| *J26* D1 10c brt claret | 70.00 | 10.00 |
| *a.* Imperf., pair | 450.00 | |
| *J27* D1 30c brt claret | 250.00 | 85.00 |
| *a.* Imperf., pair | 525.00 | |
| *J28* D1 50c brt clzret | 275.00 | 85.00 |
| *a.* Imperf., pair | 525.00 | |
| *Nos. J22-J28 (7)* | 685.00 | 188.95 |

The imperforate varieties, Nos. J22a-J28a, were not regularly issued.

D2

Printed by the Bureau of Engraving and Printing

**1894**

| | | |
|---|---|---|
| *J29* D2 1c vermilion | 575.00 | 100.00 |
| *J30* D2 2c vermilion | 250.00 | 50.00 |

**1894**

| | | |
|---|---|---|
| *J31* D2 1c dp claret | 20.00 | 3.00 |
| *a.* Imperf., pair | 225.00 | |
| *b.* Vert. pair, imperf. horiz. | — | |
| *J32* D2 2c dp claret | 15.00 | 1.75 |
| *J33* D2 3c dp claret | 75.00 | 20.00 |
| *J34* D2 5c dp claret | 100.00 | 22.50 |
| *J35* D2 10c dp claret | 85.00 | 17.50 |
| *J36* D2 30c dp claret | 225.00 | 50.00 |
| *a.* 30c carmine | 225.00 | 45.00 |
| *b.* 30c pale rose | 210.00 | 45.00 |
| *J37* D2 50c dp claret | 500.00 | 120.00 |
| *a.* 50c pale rose | 450.00 | 100.00 |

Shades are numerous in the 1894 and later issues.

**1895** **Wmk. 191**

| | | |
|---|---|---|
| *J38* D2 1c dp claret | 5.00 | 30 |
| *J39* D2 2c dp claret | 5.00 | 20 |
| *J40* D2 3c dp claret | 35.00 | 1.00 |
| *J41* D2 5c dp claret | 37.50 | 1.00 |
| *J42* D2 10c dp claret | 40.00 | 2.00 |
| *J43* D2 30c dp claret | 300.00 | 22.50 |
| *J44* D2 50c dp claret | 190.00 | 20.00 |
| *Nos. J38-J44 (7)* | 612.50 | 47.00 |

**1910-12** **Wmk. 190**

| | | |
|---|---|---|
| *J45* D2 1c dp claret | 20.00 | 2.00 |
| *a.* 1c rose carmine | 17.50 | 1.75 |
| *J46* D2 2c dp claret | 20.00 | 15 |
| *a.* 2c rose carmine | 17.50 | 15 |
| *J47* D2 3c dp claret | 350.00 | 17.50 |
| *J48* D2 5c dp claret | 60.00 | 3.50 |
| *a.* 5c rose carmine | — | — |
| *J49* D2 10c dp claret | 75.00 | 7.50 |
| *a.* 10c rose carmine | — | — |
| *J50* D2 50c dp claret ('12) | 600.00 | 75.00 |

**1914-15** ***Perf. 10***

| | | |
|---|---|---|
| *J52* D2 1c carmine lake | 40.00 | 7.50 |
| *a.* 1c dull rose | 40.00 | 7.50 |
| *J53* D2 2c carmine lake | 32.50 | 20 |
| *a.* 2c dull rose | 32.50 | 20 |
| *b.* 2c vermilion | 32.50 | 20 |
| *J54* D2 3c carmine lake | 425.00 | 20.00 |
| *a.* 3c dull rose | 425.00 | 17.50 |
| *J55* D2 5c carmine lake | 25.00 | 1.50 |
| *a.* 5c dull rose | 25.00 | 1.50 |
| *J56* D2 10c carmine lake | 40.00 | 1.00 |
| *a.* 10c dull rose | 40.00 | 1.00 |
| *J57* D2 30c carmine lake | 140.00 | 12.00 |
| *J58* D2 50c carmine lake | *5,500.* | 375.00 |

**1916 Unwmk.** ***Perf. 10***

| | | |
|---|---|---|
| *J59* D2 1c rose | 1,100. | 175.00 |
| *J60* D2 2c rose | 85.00 | 10.00 |

**1917** ***Perf. 11***

| | | |
|---|---|---|
| *J61* D2 1c carmine rose | 1.75 | 8 |
| *a.* 1c rose red | 1.75 | 15 |
| *b.* 1c deep claret | 1.75 | 8 |
| *J62* D2 2c carmine rose | 1.50 | 5 |
| *a.* 2c rose red | 1.50 | 5 |
| *b.* 2c deep claret | 1.50 | 5 |
| *J63* D2 3c carmine rose | 8.50 | 8 |
| *a.* 3c rose red | 8.50 | 7 |
| *b.* 3c deep claret | 8.50 | 25 |
| *J64* D2 5c carmine | 8.50 | 8 |
| *a.* 5c rose red | 8.50 | 8 |
| *b.* 5c deep claret | 8.50 | 5 |
| *J65* D2 10c car rose | 12.50 | 20 |
| *a.* 10c rose red | 12.50 | 6 |
| *b.* 10c deep claret | 12.50 | 6 |
| *J66* D2 30c carmine rose | 55.00 | 40 |
| *a.* 30c deep claret | 55.00 | 40 |
| *J67* D2 50c carmine rose | 75.00 | 12 |
| *a.* 50c rose red | 75.00 | 12 |
| *b.* 50c deep claret | 75.00 | 15 |

**1925**

| | | |
|---|---|---|
| *J68* D2 ½c dull red | 65 | 6 |

D3

D4

**1930** ***Perf. 11***

| | | |
|---|---|---|
| *J69* D3 ½c carmine | 2.00 | 70 |
| *J70* D3 1c carmine | 2.50 | 15 |
| *J71* D3 2c carmine | 2.00 | 15 |
| *J72* D3 3c carmine | 12.50 | 1.00 |
| *J73* D3 5c carmine | 13.00 | 1.50 |
| *J74* D3 10c carmine | 30.00 | 50 |
| *J75* D3 30c carmine | 85.00 | 1.00 |
| *J76* D3 50c carmine | 100.00 | 30 |
| *J77* D4 $1 carmine | 20.00 | 6 |
| *a.* $1 scarlet | 15.00 | 6 |
| *J78* D4 $5 carmine | 27.50 | 12 |
| *a.* $5 scarlet | 22.50 | 12 |

**Rotary Press Printing**

**1931-56** ***Perf. 11x10½***

| | | |
|---|---|---|
| *J79* D3 ½c dull carmine | 1.00 | 8 |
| *a.* ½c scarlet | 1.00 | 8 |
| *J80* D3 1c dull carmine | 15 | 5 |
| *a.* 1c scarlet | 15 | 5 |
| *J81* D3 2c dull carmine | 15 | 5 |
| *a.* 2c scarlet | 15 | 5 |
| *J82* D3 3c dull carmine | 25 | 5 |
| *a.* 3c scarlet | 25 | 5 |
| *J83* D3 5c dull carmine | 35 | 5 |
| *a.* 5c scarlet | 35 | 5 |
| *J84* D3 10c dull carmine | 1.10 | 5 |
| *a.* 10c scarlet | 1.10 | 5 |
| *J85* D3 30c dull carmine | 8.50 | 8 |
| *a.* 30c scarlet | 8.50 | 8 |
| *J86* D3 50c dull carmine | 9.50 | 6 |
| *a.* 50c scarlet | 9.50 | 6 |

***Perf. 10½x11***

| | | |
|---|---|---|
| *J87* D4 $1 scarlet ('56) | 40.00 | 20 |
| *Nos. J79-J87 (9)* | 61.00 | 67 |
| *Nos. J79a-J86a (8)* | 21.00 | 47 |

**Catalogue values for unused stamps in this section, from this point to the end of the section, are for Never Hinged items.**

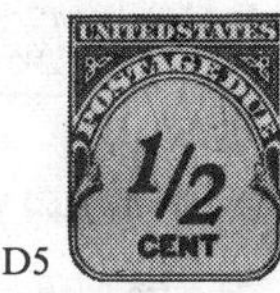

D5

Denominations added by rubber plates in an operation similar to precanceling.

**Rotary Press Printing**

***Perf. 11x10½***

**1959, June 19** **Unwmk.**

**Denomination in Black**

| | | |
|---|---|---|
| *J88* D5 ½c carmine rose | 1.25 | 85 |
| *J89* D5 1c carmine rose | 5 | 5 |
| *a.* "1 CENT" omitted | *375.00* | |
| *b.* Pair, one without "1 CENT" | — | |
| *J90* D5 2c carmine rose | 6 | 5 |
| *J91* D5 3c carmine rose | 7 | 5 |
| *a.* Pair, one without "3 CENTS" | *575.00* | |
| *J92* D5 4c carmine rose | 8 | 5 |
| *J93* D5 5c carmine rose | 10 | 5 |
| *a.* Pair, one without "5 CENTS" | — | |
| *J94* D5 6c carmine rose | 12 | 5 |
| *a.* Pair, one without "6 CENTS" | *625.00* | |
| *J95* D5 7c carmine rose | 14 | 6 |
| *J96* D5 8c carmine rose | 16 | 5 |
| *a.* Pair, one without "8 CENTS" | *625.00* | |
| *J97* D5 10c carmine rose | 20 | 5 |
| *J98* D5 30c carmine rose | 70 | 5 |
| *J99* D5 50c carmine rose | 1.10 | 5 |

**Straight Numeral Outlined in Black**

| | | |
|---|---|---|
| *J100* D5 $1 carmine rose | 2.00 | 5 |
| *J101* D5 $5 carmine rose | 8.00 | 15 |
| *Nos. J88-J101 (14)* | 14.03 | 1.61 |

**1978-85**

**Denomination in Black**

| | | |
|---|---|---|
| *J102* D5 11c carmine rose | 22 | 5 |
| *J103* D5 13c carmine rose | 26 | 5 |
| *J104* D5 17c carmine rose ('85) | 34 | 5 |

Issue dates: Jan. 2, 1978, June 10, 1985.

## UNITED STATES OFFICES IN CHINA

Issued for sale by the postal agency at Shanghai, at their surcharged value in local currency. Valid to the amount of their original values for the prepayment of postage on mail dispatched from the US postal agency at Shanghai to addresses in the US.

Nos. 498-499, 502-504, 506-510, 512, 514-518 Surcharged

**SHANGHAI**
**2¢**
**CHINA**

**1919 Unwmk. *Perf. 11***

*K1* A140 2c on 1c green 20.00 22.50
*K2* A140 4c on 2c rose, Type I 20.00 22.50
*K3* A140 6c on 3c vio, Type II 37.50 50.00
*K4* A140 8c on 4c brown 45.00 50.00
*K5* A140 10c on 5c blue 50.00 57.50
*K6* A140 12c on 6c red org 60.00 72.50
*K7* A140 14c on 7c black 65.00 80.00
*K8* A148 16c on 8c ol bis 50.00 55.00
*a.* 16c on 8c olive green 45.00 47.50
*K9* A148 18c on 9c sal red 50.00 60.00
*K10* A148 20c on 10c org yel 45.00 52.50
*K11* A148 24c on 12c brown carmine 52.50 62.50
*a.* 24c on 12c claret brn 67.50 77.50
*K12* A148 30c on 15c gray 65.00 80.00
*K13* A148 40c on 20c deep ultra 100.00 125.00
*K14* A148 60c on 30c org red 90.00 110.00
*K15* A148 $1 on 50c lt vio 600.00 500.00
*K16* A148 $2 on $1 vio brn 425.00 425.00
*a.* Double surcharge *2,500. 2,250.*
*Nos. K1-K16 (16)* 1,775. 1,825.

Nos. 498 and 528B Surcharged

**SHANGHAI**
**2 Cts.**
**CHINA**

**1922, July 3**

*K17* A140 2c on 1c green 90.00 75.00
*K18* A140 4c on 2c carmine, Type VII 80.00 70.00

## OFFICIAL STAMPS

The franking privilege having been abolished, as of July 1, 1873, these stamps were provided for each of the departments of Government for the prepayment of postage on official matter.

These stamps were supplanted on May 1, 1879, by penalty envelopes and on July 5, 1884, were declared obsolete.

Designs, except Post Office, resemble those illustrated but are not identical. Each bears the name of Department. Portraits are as follows: 1c, Franklin; 2c, Jackson; 3c, Washington; 6c, Lincoln; 7c, Stanton; 10c, Jefferson; 12c, Clay; 15c, Webster; 24c, Scott; 30c, Hamilton; 90c, Perry.

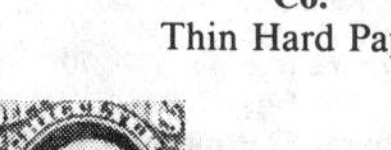

**Printed by the Continental Bank Note Co.**

Thin Hard Paper

O1

**1873 Unwmk. Engr. *Perf. 12***

**Dept. of Agriculture**

*O1* O1 1c yellow 65.00 30.00
*O2* O1 2c yellow 45.00 13.50
*O3* O1 3c yellow 40.00 3.50
*O4* O1 6c yellow 50.00 12.50
*O5* O1 10c yellow 110.00 47.50
*O6* O1 12c yellow 140.00 70.00
*O7* O1 15c yellow 110.00 47.50
*O8* O1 24c yellow 125.00 55.00
*O9* O1 30c yellow 165.00 85.00

**Executive Dept.**

*O10* O1 1c carmine 250.00 85.00
*O11* O1 2c carmine 165.00 70.00
*O12* O1 3c carmine 190.00 65.00
*a* 3c violet rose 165.00 65.00
*O13* O1 6c carmine 300.00 140.00
*O14* O1 10c carmine 275.00 150.00

**Dept. of the Interior**

*O15* O1 1c vermilion 17.50 3.50
*O16* O1 2c vermilion 15.00 2.00
*O17* O1 3c vermilion 22.50 2.00
*O18* O1 6c vermilion 17.50 2.00
*O19* O1 10c vermilion 16.00 5.00
*O20* O1 12c vermilion 25.00 4.00
*O21* O1 15c vermilion 40.00 10.00
*O22* O1 24c vermilion 30.00 7.00
*O23* O1 30c vermilion 40.00 8.00
*O24* O1 90c vermilion 90.00 15.00

**Dept. of Justice**

*O25* O1 1c purple 40.00 17.50
*O26* O1 2c purple 65.00 20.00
*O27* O1 3c purple 65.00 8.00
*O28* O1 6c purple 60.00 11.00
*O29* O1 10c purple 70.00 25.00
*O30* O1 12c purple 50.00 14.00
*O31* O1 15c purple 110.00 47.50
*O32* O1 24c purple 300.00 120.00
*O33* O1 30c purple 275.00 85.00
*O34* O1 90c purple 400.00 175.00

**Navy Dept.**

*O35* O1 1c ultramarine 35.00 10.00
*a* 1c dull blue 42.50 12.00
*O36* O1 2c ultramarine 25.00 9.00
*a* 2c dull blue 32.50 11.00
*O37* O1 3c ultramarine 27.50 4.00
*a* 3c dull blue 32.50 5.50
*O38* O1 6c ultramarine 25.00 6.00
*a* 6c dull blue 32.50 7.50
*O39* O1 7c ultramarine 165.00 65.00
*a* 7c dull blue 185.00 75.00
*O40* O1 10c ultramarine 35.00 11.00
*a* 10c dull blue 40.00 13.00
*O41* O1 12c ultramarine 45.00 10.00
*O42* O1 15c ultramarine 75.00 25.00
*O43* O1 24c ultramarine 75.00 30.00
*a* 24c dull blue 85.00 —
*O44* O1 30c ultramarine 65.00 15.00
*O45* O1 90c ultramarine 300.00 80.00
*a* Double impression *2,000.*

O6

**Post Office Dept**

*O47* O6 1c black 7.25 3.00
*O48* O6 2c black 7.00 2.50
*a* Double impression 300.00
*O49* O6 3c black 2.50 75
*O50* O6 6c black 8.00 1.65
*a* Diagonal half used as 3c on cover *2,750.*
*O51* O6 10c black 40.00 16.50
*O52* O6 12c black 22.50 5.00
*O53* O6 15c black 25.00 8.50
*a* Imperf., pair *600.00*
*O54* O6 24c black 32.50 10.00
*O55* O6 30c black 32.50 9.00
*O56* O6 90c black 47.50 12.50

Stamps of the POD are often on paper with a gray surface. This is due to insufficient wiping of the plates during printing.

Seward — O8

**Dept. of State**

*O57* O1 1c dark green 42.50 13.00
*O58* O1 2c dark green 85.00 25.00
*O59* O1 3c bright grn 35.00 9.00
*O60* O1 6c bright grn 32.50 9.00
*O61* O1 7c dark green 60.00 18.50
*O62* O1 10c dark green 50.00 15.00
*O63* O1 12c dark green 75.00 27.50
*O64* O1 15c dark green 70.00 20.00
*O65* O1 24c dark green 175.00 75.00
*O66* O1 30c dark green 160.00 60.00
*O67* O1 90c dark green 300.00 125.00
*O68* O8 $2 grn & blk 550.00 250.00
*O69* O8 $5 grn & blk 4,250. 2,000.
*O70* O8 $10 grn & blk 2,750. 1,300.
*O71* O8 $20 grn & blk 2,250. 1,100.

**Treasury Dept.**

*O72* O1 1c brown 17.50 1.75
*O73* O1 2c brown 20.00 1.75
*O74* O1 3c brown 12.50 1.00
*O75* O1 6c brown 17.50 1.00
*O76* O1 7c brown 42.50 12.50
*O77* O1 10c brown 42.50 4.50
*O78* O1 12c brown 42.50 3.00
*O79* O1 15c brown 37.50 4.50
*O80* O1 24c brown 185.00 60.00
*O81* O1 30c brown 62.00 5.00
*O82* O1 90c brown 67.50 5.00

**War Dept.**

*O83* O1 1c rose 60.00 4.00
*O84* O1 2c rose 55.00 6.00
*O85* O1 3c rose 50.00 1.50
*O86* O1 6c rose 240.00 4.00
*O87* O1 7c rose 52.50 30.00
*O88* O1 10c rose 19.00 5.00
*O89* O1 12c rose 52.50 4.00
*O90* O1 15c rose 15.00 2.50
*O91* O1 24c rose 15.00 3.00
*O92* O1 30c rose 17.50 2.50
*O93* O1 90c rose 40.00 12.50

SPECIAL PRINTING. In 1875 a Special Printing of the Official stamps was made along with those of the regular issues. These stamps were overprinted "SPECIMEN".

**Printed by the American Bank Note Co.**

**1879 Soft Porous Paper**

**Dept. of Agriculture**

*O94* O1 1c yellow 1,350.
*O95* O1 3c yellow 175.00 37.50

**Dept. of the Interior**

*O96* O1 1c vermilion 125.00 65.00
*O97* O1 2c vermilion 2.50 75
*O98* O1 3c vermilion 2.00 60
*O99* O1 6c vermilion 3.00 1.00
*O100* O1 10c vermilion 32.50 17.50
*O101* O1 12c vermilion 65.00 30.00
*O102* O1 15c vermilion 150.00 70.00
*O103* O1 24c vermilion 1,200.

**Dept. of Justice**

*O106* O1 3c bluish purple 50.00 17.50
*O107* O1 6c bluish purple 110.00 60.00

**Post Office Dept.**

*O108* O6 3c black 7.50 1.40

**Treasury Dept.**

*O109* O1 3c brown 27.50 3.50
*O110* O1 6c brown 50.00 17.50
*O111* O1 10c brown 65.00 15.00
*O112* O1 30c brown 750.00 135.00
*O113* O1 90c brown 775.00 135.00

**War Dept.**

*O114* O1 1c rose red 2.00 75
*O115* O1 2c rose red 3.00 1.00
*O116* O1 3c rose red 3.00 65
*a* Imperf., pair *800.00*
*b* Double impression 500.00
*O117* O1 6c rose red 2.50 70
*O118* O1 10c rose red 20.00 6.00
*O119* O1 12c rose red 15.00 3.00
*O120* O1 30c rose red 47.50 25.00

**Official Postal Savings Mail**

These stamps were used to prepay postage on official correspondence of the Postal Savings Division of the POD. Discontinued Sept. 23, 1914.

O11

**1911 Wmk. 191**

*O121* O11 2c black 9.00 1.10
*O122* O11 50c dark grn 110.00 32.50
*O123* O11 $1 ultra 100.00 9.50

**Wmk. 190**

*O124* O11 1c dark vio 4.00 1.00
*O125* O11 2c black 30.00 3.50
*O126* O11 10c carmine 8.50 1.00

**Catalogue values for unused stamps in this section, from this point to the end of the section, are for Never Hinged items.**

**Official Mail**

O12

O13

Type O13 has frame line completely around blue design.

**1983-85 *Perf. 11***

*O127* O12 1c red, bl & blk 5 —
*O128* O12 4c red, bl & blk 8 —
*O129* O12 13c red, bl & blk 26 —
*O129A* O12 14c red, bl & blk ('85) 28 —
*O130* O12 17c red, bl & blk 34 —
*O132* O12 $1 red, bl & blk 1.75 —
*O133* O12 $5 red, bl & blk 9.00 —
*Nos. O127-O133 (7)* 11.76

**Coil Stamp**

***Perf. 10 Vert.***

*O135* O12 20c red, bl & blk 2.00 40
*a* Imperf., pair —
*O136* O12 22c red, bl & blk ('85) 44 —

No. O129A does not have a "c" after the "14."

Inscribed: Postal Card Rate D

**1985, Feb. 4 *Perf. 11***

*O138* O12 (14c) red, bl & blk 3.00 —

Coil Stamps

Inscribed: No. O139, Domestic Letter Rate D. No. O140, Domestic Mail E.

**1985-88 *Perf. 10 Vert.***

*O138A* O13 15c red, blue & blk('88) 30 —
*O138B* O13 20c red, blue & blk ('88) 40 —
*O139* O12 (22c) red, bl & blk 3.00 —
*O140* O13 (25c) red, blue & blk('88) 50 —
*O141* O13 25c red, blue & blk ('88) 50 —

Issue dates: 15c, June 11; 20c, May 19; E, Mar. 22; 25c, June 11.

## NEWSPAPER STAMPS

For the prepayment of postage on bulk shipments of newspapers and periodicals. From 1875 on, the stamps were affixed

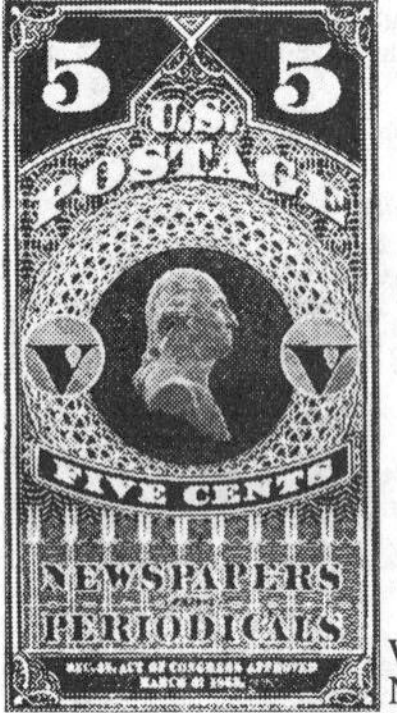


Washington
N1

Franklin
N2

For unused stamps, more recent issues are valued as never hinged, with the beginning point determined on a country-by-country basis. Notes to show the beginning points are prominently placed in the text.

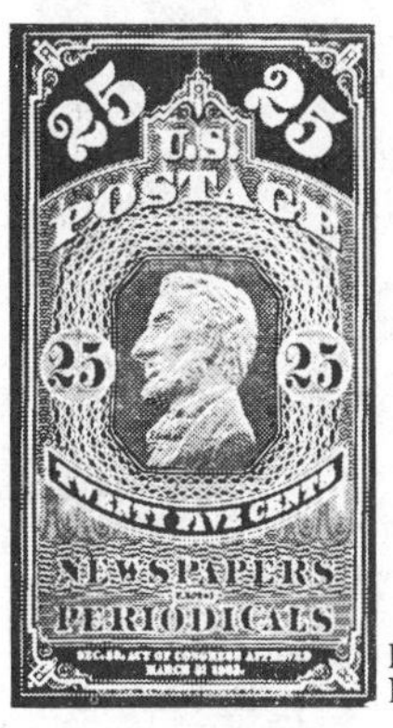
Lincoln N3

**Printed by the National Bank Note Co.**

Thin Hard Paper, No Gum

**1865 Unwmk. Typo.** ***Perf. 12***

**Size: 51x95mm**

**Colored Border**

| | | | | |
|---|---|---|---|---|
| *PR1* | N1 | 5c dark blue | 150.00 | — |
| *a.* | | 5c light blue | 165.00 | — |
| *PR2* | N2 | 10c blue green | 70.00 | — |
| *a.* | | 10c green | 70.00 | — |
| *b.* | | Pelure paper | 75.00 | — |
| *PR3* | N3 | 25c org red | 70.00 | — |
| *a.* | | 25c carmine red | 70.00 | — |
| *b.* | | Pelure paper | 75.00 | |

**White Border**

**Yellowish Paper**

| | | | | |
|---|---|---|---|---|
| *PR4* | N1 | 5c light blue | 35.00 | 30.00 |
| *a.* | | 5c dark blue | 25.00 | 30.00 |
| *b.* | | Pelure paper | 40.00 | — |

**Reprints**

**Printed by the Continental Bank Note Co.**

Hard White Paper, No Gum

**1875**

| | | | | |
|---|---|---|---|---|
| *PR5* | N1 | 5c dull blue | 60.00 | |
| *a.* | | Printed on both sides | — | |
| *PR6* | N2 | 10c dk bluish grn | 37.50 | |
| *a.* | | Printed on both sides | *1,500.* | |
| *PR7* | N3 | 25c dark carmine | 65.00 | |

The 5c has white border, 10c and 25c have colored borders.

**Printed by the American Bank Note Co.**

Soft Porous Paper

**1880**

**White Border**

| | | | |
|---|---|---|---|
| *PR8* | N1 | 5c dark blue | 110.00 |

Statue of Freedom N4

"Justice" N5

Ceres N6

"Victory" N7

Clio — N8

Minerva — N9

Vesta N10

"Peace" N11

"Commerce" N12

Hebe N13

Indian Maiden — N14

**Printed by the Continental Bank Note Co.**

**Engraved Thin Hard Paper**

**1875 Size: 24x35mm**

| | | | | |
|---|---|---|---|---|
| *PR9* | N4 | 2c black | 12.50 | 11.00 |
| *PR10* | N4 | 3c black | 16.00 | 14.00 |
| *PR11* | N4 | 4c black | 14.00 | 12.50 |
| *PR12* | N4 | 6c black | 18.00 | 17.00 |
| *PR13* | N4 | 8c black | 25.00 | 22.50 |
| *PR14* | N4 | 9c black | 55.00 | 50.00 |
| *PR15* | N4 | 10c black | 25.00 | 20.00 |
| *PR16* | N5 | 12c rose | 55.00 | 40.00 |
| *PR17* | N5 | 24c rose | 67.50 | 45.00 |
| *PR18* | N5 | 36c rose | 72.50 | 50.00 |
| *PR19* | N5 | 48c rose | 135.00 | 85.00 |
| *PR20* | N5 | 60c rose | 65.00 | 45.00 |
| *PR21* | N5 | 72c rose | 165.00 | 110.00 |
| *PR22* | N5 | 84c rose | 250.00 | 135.00 |
| *PR23* | N5 | 96c rose | 135.00 | 100.00 |
| *PR24* | N6 | $1.92 dark brn | 185.00 | 125.00 |
| *PR25* | N7 | $3 vermilion | 240.00 | 135.00 |
| *PR26* | N8 | $6 ultra | 400.00 | 165.00 |
| *PR27* | N9 | $9 yellow | 525.00 | 225.00 |
| *PR28* | N10 | $12 blue grn | 650.00 | 300.00 |
| *PR29* | N11 | $24 dk gray vio | 650.00 | 325.00 |
| *PR30* | N12 | $36 brn rose | 675.00 | 375.00 |
| *PR31* | N13 | $48 red brn | 875.00 | 500.00 |
| *PR32* | N14 | $60 violet | 875.00 | 450.00 |

**Special Printing**

**Hard White Paper**

**Without Gum**

| | | | |
|---|---|---|---|
| *PR33* | N4 | 2c gray blk | 70.00 |
| *PR34* | N4 | 3c gray blk | 75.00 |
| *PR35* | N4 | 4c gray blk | 90.00 |
| *PR36* | N4 | 6c gray blk | 120.00 |
| *PR37* | N4 | 8c gray blk | 140.00 |
| *PR38* | N4 | 9c gray blk | 165.00 |
| *PR39* | N4 | 10c gray blk | 200.00 |
| *PR40* | N5 | 12c pale rose | 225.00 |
| *PR41* | N5 | 24c pale rose | 300.00 |
| *PR42* | N5 | 36c pale rose | 425.00 |
| *PR43* | N5 | 48c pale rose | 475.00 |
| *PR44* | N5 | 60c pale rose | 550.00 |
| *PR45* | N5 | 72c pale rose | 700.00 |
| *PR46* | N5 | 84c pale rose | 725.00 |
| *PR47* | N5 | 96c pale rose | 875.00 |
| *PR48* | N6 | $1.92 dk brn | *2,750.* |
| *PR49* | N7 | $3 vermilion | *5,750.* |
| *PR50* | N8 | $6 ultra | *6,750.* |
| *PR51* | N9 | $9 yellow | *13,000.* |
| *PR52* | N10 | $12 bl grn | *12,500.* |
| *PR53* | N11 | $24 dk gray vio | — |
| *PR54* | N12 | $36 brn rose | — |
| *PR55* | N13 | $48 red brn | — |
| *PR56* | N14 | $60 violet | — |

Nos. PR33 to PR56 exist imperf. but were not regularly issued. (See Scott's US Specialized Catalogue.)

**Printed by the American Bank Note Co.**

**1879**

**Soft Porous Paper**

| | | | | |
|---|---|---|---|---|
| *PR57* | N4 | 2c black | 6.00 | 4.50 |
| *PR58* | N4 | 3c black | 7.50 | 5.00 |
| *PR59* | N4 | 4c black | 7.50 | 5.00 |
| *PR60* | N4 | 6c black | 15.00 | 11.00 |
| *PR61* | N4 | 8c black | 15.00 | 11.00 |
| *PR62* | N4 | 10c black | 15.00 | 11.00 |
| *PR63* | N5 | 12c red | 45.00 | 25.00 |
| *PR64* | N5 | 24c red | 45.00 | 22.50 |
| *PR65* | N5 | 36c red | 150.00 | 95.00 |
| *PR66* | N5 | 48c red | 115.00 | 60.00 |
| *PR67* | N5 | 60c red | 85.00 | 60.00 |
| *a.* | | Imperf., pair | *600.00* | |
| *PR68* | N5 | 72c red | 185.00 | 115.00 |
| *PR69* | N5 | 84c red | 140.00 | 85.00 |
| *PR70* | N5 | 96c red | 100.00 | 60.00 |
| *PR71* | N6 | $1.92 pale brn | 80.00 | 55.00 |
| *PR72* | N7 | $3 red ver | 80.00 | 55.00 |
| *PR73* | N8 | $6 blue | 140.00 | 90.00 |
| *PR74* | N9 | $9 orange | 95.00 | 60.00 |
| *PR75* | N10 | $12 yel grn | 140.00 | 85.00 |
| *PR76* | N11 | $24 dk vio | 185.00 | 110.00 |
| *PR77* | N12 | $36 indian red | 225.00 | 135.00 |
| *PR78* | N13 | $48 yel brn | 300.00 | 165.00 |
| *PR79* | N14 | $60 purple | 325.00 | 165.00 |

Nos. PR57-PR62, PR71-PR79 exist imperforate but were not regularly issued.

Special Printing

**1883**

| | | | |
|---|---|---|---|
| *PR80* | N4 | 2c intense blk | 175.00 |

Regular Issue

**1885**

| | | | | |
|---|---|---|---|---|
| *PR81* | N4 | 1c black | 8.50 | 5.00 |
| *PR82* | N5 | 12c carmine | 27.50 | 12.50 |
| *PR83* | N5 | 24c carmine | 30.00 | 15.00 |
| *PR84* | N5 | 36c carmine | 42.50 | 17.50 |
| *PR85* | N5 | 48c carmine | 60.00 | 30.00 |
| *PR86* | N5 | 60c carmine | 85.00 | 40.00 |
| *PR87* | N5 | 72c carmine | 95.00 | 45.00 |
| *PR88* | N5 | 84c carmine | 200.00 | 110.00 |
| *PR89* | N5 | 96c carmine | 140.00 | 85.00 |

Nos. PR81-PR89 exist imperforate but were not regularly issued.

**Printed by the Bureau of Engraving and Printing**

**1894 Soft Wove Paper**

| | | | | |
|---|---|---|---|---|
| *PR90* | N4 | 1c int blk | 42.50 | |
| *PR91* | N4 | 2c int blk | 42.50 | |
| *PR92* | N4 | 4c int blk | 60.00 | |
| *PR93* | N4 | 6c int blk | 850.00 | |
| *PR94* | N4 | 10c int blk | 110.00 | |
| *PR95* | N5 | 12c pink | 500.00 | — |
| *PR96* | N5 | 24c pink | 400.00 | |
| *PR97* | N5 | 36c pink | *2,750.* | |
| *PR98* | N5 | 60c pink | *2,750.* | — |
| *PR99* | N5 | 96c pink | *4,000.* | |
| *PR100* | N7 | $3 scarlet | *5,500.* | |
| *PR101* | N8 | $6 pale blue | *6,250.* | *3,000.* |

Statue of Freedom N15

"Justice" N16

"Victory" N17

Clio N18

Vesta — N19

"Peace" — N20

"Commerce" N21

Indian Maiden N22

**1895 Unwmk.**

**Sizes: 1c to 50c, 21x34mm, $2 to $100, 24x35mm**

| | | | | |
|---|---|---|---|---|
| *PR102* | N15 | 1c black | 25.00 | 7.50 |
| *PR103* | N15 | 2c black | 25.00 | 7.50 |
| *PR104* | N15 | 5c black | 35.00 | 12.50 |
| *PR105* | N15 | 10c black | 75.00 | 32.50 |
| *PR106* | N16 | 25c carmine | 100.00 | 35.00 |
| *PR107* | N16 | 50c carmine | 235.00 | 95.00 |
| *PR108* | N17 | $2 scarlet | 275.00 | 65.00 |
| *PR109* | N18 | $5 ultra | 375.00 | 150.00 |
| *PR110* | N19 | $10 green | 350.00 | 165.00 |
| *PR111* | N20 | $20 slate | 675.00 | 300.00 |
| *PR112* | N21 | $50 dull rose | 700.00 | 300.00 |
| *PR113* | N22 | $100 purple | 775.00 | 350.00 |

**1895-97 Wmk. 191**

| | | | | |
|---|---|---|---|---|
| *PR114* | N15 | 1c black ('96) | 3.50 | 2.00 |
| *PR115* | N15 | 2c black | 4.00 | 1.50 |
| *PR116* | N15 | 5c black ('96) | 6.00 | 3.00 |
| *PR117* | N15 | 10c black | 4.00 | 2.00 |
| *PR118* | N16 | 25c carmine | 8.00 | 3.75 |
| *PR119* | N16 | 50c carmine | 10.00 | 3.50 |
| *PR120* | N17 | $2 scar ('97) | 12.00 | 11.50 |
| *PR121* | N18 | $5 dk bl ('96) | 20.00 | 25.00 |
| *a.* | | $5 light blue | 100.00 | 45.00 |
| *PR122* | N19 | $10 green ('96) | 18.00 | 25.00 |
| *PR123* | N20 | $20 slate ('96) | 20.00 | 27.50 |
| *PR124* | N21 | $50 dl rose ('97) | 25.00 | 30.00 |
| *PR125* | N22 | $100 pur ('96) | 30.00 | 37.50 |
| | | *Nos. PR114-PR125 (12)* | 160.50 | 172.25 |

*In 1899 the Government sold 26,989 sets of these stamps, but, as the stock of the high values was not sufficient to make up the required number, the $5, $10, $20, $50 and $100 were reprinted. These are virtually indistinguishable from earlier printings.*

## PARCEL POST STAMPS

Issued for the prepayment of postage on parcel post packages only.

Post Office Clerk — PP1

City Carrier PP2

Railway Postal Clerk — PP3

Rural Carrier PP4

Mail Train — PP5

Steamship and Mail Tender PP6

Automobile Service PP7

Airplane Carrying Mail — PP8

Manufacturing — PP9

Dairying PP10

Harvesting PP11

Fruit Growing PP12

**1912-13 Engr. Wmk. 190 *Perf. 12***

| | | | | |
|---|---|---|---|---|
| *Q1* | PP1 | 1c car rose | 2.75 | 90 |
| *Q2* | PP2 | 2c car rose | 3.25 | 70 |
| *Q3* | PP3 | 3c car ('13) | 6.50 | 5.00 |
| *Q4* | PP4 | 4c car rose | 17.50 | 2.00 |
| *Q5* | PP5 | 5c car rose | 13.50 | 1.25 |
| *Q6* | PP6 | 10c car rose | 25.00 | 1.75 |
| *Q7* | PP7 | 15c car rose | 40.00 | 9.00 |
| *Q8* | PP8 | 20c car rose | 90.00 | 17.50 |
| *Q9* | PP9 | 25c car rose | 40.00 | 4.50 |
| *Q10* | PP10 | 50c car rose ('13) | 175.00 | 35.00 |
| *Q11* | PP11 | 75c car rose | 55.00 | 30.00 |
| *Q12* | PP12 | $1 car rose ('13) | 300.00 | 20.00 |
| | | *Nos. Q1-Q12 (12)* | 768.50 | 127.60 |

## SPECIAL HANDLING STAMPS

For use on parcel post packages to secure the same expeditious handling accorded to first class mail matter.

PP13

**1925-29 Unwmk. Engr. *Perf. 11***

| | | | | |
|---|---|---|---|---|
| *QE1* | PP13 | 10c yel grn ('28) | 1.25 | 90 |
| *QE2* | PP13 | 15c yel grn ('28) | 1.40 | 90 |
| *QE3* | PP13 | 20c yel grn ('28) | 2.25 | 1.75 |
| *QE4* | PP13 | 25c yel grn ('29) | 15.00 | 7.50 |
| *a.* | | 25c dp grn ('25) | 25.00 | 4.50 |

## PARCEL POST POSTAGE DUE STAMPS

For affixing by a postal clerk, to any parcel post package, to denote the amount to be collected from the addressee because of insufficient prepayment of postage.

PPD1

**1912 Engr. Wmk. 190 *Perf. 12***

| | | | | |
|---|---|---|---|---|
| *JQ1* | PPD1 | 1c dark green | 5.00 | 3.00 |
| *JQ2* | PPD1 | 2c dark green | 40.00 | 15.00 |
| *JQ3* | PPD1 | 5c dark green | 6.00 | 3.50 |
| *JQ4* | PPD1 | 10c dark green | 110.00 | 35.00 |
| *JQ5* | PPD1 | 25c dark green | 50.00 | 3.50 |
| | | *Nos. JQ1-JQ5 (5)* | 211.00 | 60.00 |

## CARRIERS' STAMPS

### OFFICIAL ISSUES

Issued by the US Government to facilitate payment of fees for delivering and collecting letters.

Franklin OC1

Eagle OC2

**1851 Unwmk. Engr. *Imperf.***

| | | | | |
|---|---|---|---|---|
| *LO1* | OC1 | (1c) dull bl, *rose* | *1,500.* | *2,000.* |
| *LO2* | OC2 | 1c blue | 20.00 | 20.00 |

*Reprints of the Franklin Carrier are printed in dark blue, instead of the dull blue or deep blue of the originals. The reprints of the Eagle carrier are on hard white paper, ungummed and sometimes perforated, and also on a coarse wove paper. Originals are on yellowish paper with brown gum.*

### GOVERNMENT REPRINTS

**1875**

**Without Gum**

| | | | |
|---|---|---|---|
| *LO3* | OC1 | (1c) bl, *rose*, imperf. | 40.00 |
| *LO4* | OC1 | (1c) blue, perf. 12 | *2,500.* |
| *LO5* | OC2 | 1c blue, imperf. | 20.00 |
| *LO6* | OC2 | 1c blue, perf. 12 | 120.00 |

The perforated stamps, Nos. LO4 and LO6, are a Special Printing, possibly made in 1875.

### SEMI-OFFICIAL ISSUES

Issued by officials or employees of the US Government for the purpose of securing or indicating payment of carriers' fees.

**Baltimore, Md.**

C1

**1850-55 Typo. *Imperf.***

| | | | | |
|---|---|---|---|---|
| *1LB1* | C1 | 1c red, *bluish* | 100.00 | 60.00 |
| *1LB2* | C1 | 1c blue, *bluish* | 125.00 | 90.00 |
| *a.* | | Bluish laid paper | — | — |
| *1LB3* | C1 | 1c blue | 75.00 | 50.00 |
| *a.* | | Laid paper | 150.00 | 100.00 |
| *1LB4* | C1 | 1c green | — | 600.00 |
| *1LB5* | C1 | 1c red | 350.00 | 275.00 |

Ten varieties.

C2

C3

**1856 Typo.**

| | | | | |
|---|---|---|---|---|
| *1LB6* | C2 | 1c blue | 90.00 | 60.00 |
| *1LB7* | C2 | 1c red | 65.00 | 40.00 |

Shades exist of Nos. 1LB6-1LB7.

**1857**

| | | | | |
|---|---|---|---|---|
| *1LB8* | C3 | 1c black | 25.00 | 20.00 |
| *a.* | | "SENT" | 35.00 | 25.00 |
| *b.* | | Short rays | 35.00 | 25.00 |
| *1LB9* | C3 | 1c red | 40.00 | 30.00 |
| *a.* | | "SENT" | 50.00 | 40.00 |
| *b.* | | Short rays | 50.00 | 40.00 |

Ten varieties of C3.

**Boston, Mass.**

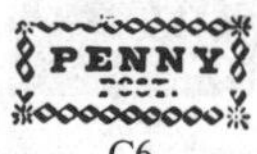

C6

C7

**1849-50 Typeset**

| | | | | |
|---|---|---|---|---|
| *3LB1* | C6 | 1c blue | 120.00 | 75.00 |
| *3LB2* | C7 | 1c blue, *grayish* | 135.00 | 65.00 |
| *3LB3* | C7 | 1c blue, *bluish* | 125.00 | 65.00 |

**Charleston, S. C.**

C8

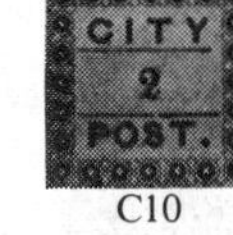

C10

**1849 Typo.**

| | | | | |
|---|---|---|---|---|
| *4LB1* | C8 | 2c *brown rose* | *1,300.* | *1,300.* |
| *4LB2* | C8 | 2c *yellow* | | *1,300.* |

**1854 Typeset**

| | | | |
|---|---|---|---|
| *4LB3* | C10 | 2c black | *650.00* |

C11

**1849-50 Typeset**

| | | | | |
|---|---|---|---|---|
| *4LB5* | C11 | 2c *bluish*, pelure | *400.00* | *300.00* |
| *4LB7* | C11 | 2c *yellow* | *400.00* | *400.00* |

Several varieties of C11.

C13

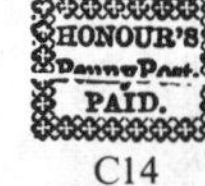

C14

C15

**1851-58 Typeset**

| | | | | |
|---|---|---|---|---|
| *4LB8* | C13 | 2c *bluish* | 175.00 | 100.00 |
| *a.* | | Period after "Paid" | 350.00 | 150.00 |
| *b.* | | "Cens" | | *700.00* |
| *c.* | | "Conours" and "Bents" | | — |
| *4LB9* | C13 | 2c *bluish*, pelure | *375.00* | *425.00* |
| *4LB11* | C14 | (2c) *bluish* | — | *250.00* |
| *4LB12* | C14 | (2c) *bluish*, pelure | — | *250.00* |
| *4LB13* | C15 | (2c) *bluish* ('58) | 250.00 | 125.00 |
| *a.* | | Comma after "PAID" | 300.00 | |
| *b.* | | No period after "Post" | 300.00 | |

Several varieties of C13.

C16

C17

**1851-58 Typeset**

| | | | | |
|---|---|---|---|---|
| *4LB14* | C16 | 2c *bluish* | *450.00* | *450.00* |
| *4LB15* | C17 | 2c *bluish* | *500.00* | *500.00* |

Several varieties of each.

C18

**1858 Typeset**

| | | | |
|---|---|---|---|
| *4LB16* | C18 | 2c *bluish* | *2,750.* |

Several varieties.

Same as C19, but Inscribed "Beckmann's City Post"

**1860**

| | | | |
|---|---|---|---|
| *4LB17* | C19 | 2c black | — |

One copy exists, on cover.

C19

C20

**1859 Typeset**

| | | | | |
|---|---|---|---|---|
| *4LB18* | C19 | 2c *bluish* | *2,500.* | |
| *4LB19* | C20 | 2c *bluish* | *1,500.* | — |
| *4LB20* | C20 | 2c *pink* | *100.00* | — |
| *4LB21* | C20 | 2c *yellow* | 85.00 | |

**Cincinnati, Ohio**

C20a

**1854 Litho. Wove Paper**

| | | | | |
|---|---|---|---|---|
| *9LB1* | C20a | 2c brown | *500.00* | 500.00 |

**Cleveland, Ohio**

C20b

C20c

**1854 Wove Paper Litho.**

| | | | | |
|---|---|---|---|---|
| *10LB1* | C20b | blue | *400.00* | *400.00* |

**Vertically Laid Paper**

| | | | | |
|---|---|---|---|---|
| *10LB2* | C20c | 2c *bluish* | *400.00* | *400.00* |

**Louisville, Ky.**

C21

C22

**1857-58 Litho.**

| | | | | |
|---|---|---|---|---|
| *5LB1* | C21 | (2c) bluish grn | *35.00* | |
| *5LB2* | C22 | (2c) blue ('58) | 100.00 | 150.00 |
| *5LB3* | C22 | (2c) black ('58) | *600.00* | *1,750.* |

### New York, N.Y.

C23

**1842** **Engr.**

| | | | | |
|---|---|---|---|---|
| *6LB1* | C23 | 3c | *grayish* | *750.00* |

Used copies are Carriers' stamps only when canceled with the regular government cancellation "U.S." in octagonal frame (see illustration). When canceled "FREE" in frame they were used as local stamps (see No. 40L1 in Scott's Specialized Catalogue of United States Stamps).

C24

**1842-45** **Engr.**

**Unsurfaced Paper, Colored Through**

| | | | | | |
|---|---|---|---|---|---|
| *6LB2* | C24 | 3c | *rosy buff* | *550.00* | |
| *6LB3* | C24 | 3c | *light blue* | *300.00* | 200.00 |
| *6LB4* | C24 | 3c | *green* | *2,000.* | |

Some authorities consider No. 6LB2 to be an essay, and No. 6LB4 to be a color changeling.

**Glazed Paper, Surface Colored**

| | | | | | |
|---|---|---|---|---|---|
| *6LB5* | C24 | 3c | *dark blue* | 100.00 | 75.00 |
| *a.* | | | Double impression | | *500.00* |
| *6LB6* | C24 | 3c | *bluish green* | 125.00 | 75.00 |
| *a.* | | | Double impression | | *550.00* |

No. 6LB6 Surcharged in Red — C25

**1846**

| | | | | |
|---|---|---|---|---|
| *6LB7* | C25 | 2c on 3c | *bluish green*, on cover | *5,000.* |

The City Despatch 2c red is listed in Scott's United States Specialized Catalogue as a Local stamp.

C27

**1849-50** **Typo.**

| | | | | | |
|---|---|---|---|---|---|
| *6LB9* | C27 | 1c | *rose* | 50.00 | 25.00 |
| *6LB10* | C27 | 1c | *yellow* | 45.00 | 25.00 |
| *6LB11* | C27 | 1c | *buff* | 40.00 | 25.00 |
| *a.* | | | Pair, one stamp sideways | *1,000.* | |

### Philadelphia, Pa.

C28

C29

**1849-50** **Typeset**

| | | | | |
|---|---|---|---|---|
| *7LB1* | C28 | 1c | *rose* (with letters L.P.) | 175.00 |
| *7LB2* | C28 | 1c | *rose* (with letter S) | *500.00* |
| *7LB3* | C28 | 1c | *rose* (with letter H) | 175.00 |
| *7LB4* | C28 | 1c | *rose* (with letters L.S.) | 175.00 |
| *7LB5* | C28 | 1c | *rose* (with letters J.J.) | *2,000.* |
| *7LB6* | C29 | 1c | *rose* | 150.00 125.00 |
| *7LB7* | C29 | 1c | *blue*, glazed | *600.00* |
| *7LB8* | C29 | 1c | *ver*, glazed | *600.00* |
| *7LB9* | C29 | 1c | *yel*, glazed | *1,350.* |

Several varieties of each.

Nos. 7LB1-7LB9 normally received no cancellation.

The 1c black on buff (unglazed), type C29, is believed to be a color changeling.

C30

C31

C32

**1850-52** **Litho.**

| | | | | | |
|---|---|---|---|---|---|
| *7LB11* | C30 | 1c | gold, *blk*, glazed | 60.00 | 55.00 |
| *7LB12* | C30 | 1c | blue | 200.00 | 100.00 |
| *7LB13* | C30 | 1c | black | — | *500.00* |

25 varieties of C30.

**Handstamped**

| | | | | | |
|---|---|---|---|---|---|
| *7LB14* | C31 | 1c | blue, *buff* | *1,000.* | |
| *7LB16* | C31 | 1c | black | | *1,650.* |

**1856(?)**

| | | | | | |
|---|---|---|---|---|---|
| *7LB18* | C32 | 1c | black | *1,200.* | *1,300.* |

P. O. PAID
1 Cent.

P. O. PAID,
One Cent.

The authenticity of stamps of these designs is in doubt.

### St. Louis, Mo.

C36

(Actual size) — C37

Several varieties.

**1849** **Litho.**

| | | | | | |
|---|---|---|---|---|---|
| *8LB1* | C36 | 2c | black | *2,000.* | *2,750.* |

**1857** **Litho.**

| | | | | | |
|---|---|---|---|---|---|
| *8LB2* | C37 | 2c | blue | | *2,500.* |

Carrier stamps Nos. 9LB1, 10LB1-10LB2 are listed following No. 4LB21.

## STAMPED ENVELOPES AND WRAPPERS

Values are for cut square specimens with good margins on all sides. (Entire envelopes and wrappers are listed in Scott's U.S. Specialized Catalogue.)

Wrappers are listed with envelopes of corresponding designs, and indicated by prefix letter "W" instead of "U."

Envelopes with the stamp printed by error in colorless embossing from an uninked die, are "albinos." They are worth more than normal, inked impressions. Albinos of earlier issues, canceled while current, are scarce.

The papers of these issues vary greatly in texture, and in color from yellowish to bluish white and from amber to dark buff.

"+" Some authorities claim that Nos. U37, U48, U49, U110, U124, U125, U130, U133A, U137A, U137B, U137C, W138, U145, U162, U178A, U185, U220, U285, U286, U298, U299, UO3, UO32, UO38, UO45 and UO45A (each with "+" before number) were not regularly issued and are not known to have been used.

Washington
U1 U2

U1 -- "THREE" in short label with curved ends; 13mm wide at top.

U2 -- "THREE" in short label with straight ends; 15½mm wide at top.

U3

"THREE" in short label with octagon ends.

U4

"THREE" in wide label with straight ends; 20mm wide at top.

U5

"THREE" in medium wide label with curved ends; 14½mm wide at top.

U6 U7

"TEN" in short label; 15⅓mm wide at top.

U8

"TEN" in wide label 20mm wide at top.

**1853-55** **On Diagonally Laid Paper**

| | | | | | |
|---|---|---|---|---|---|
| *U1* | U1 | 3c | red | 175.00 | 15.00 |
| *U2* | U1 | 3c | red, *buff* | 65.00 | 6.00 |
| *U3* | U2 | 3c | red | 600.00 | 30.00 |
| *U4* | U2 | 3c | red, *buff* | 180.00 | 12.00 |
| *U5* | U3 | 3c | red ('54) | 3,000. | 375.00 |
| *U6* | U3 | 3c | red, *buff* ('54) | 125.00 | 25.00 |
| *U7* | U4 | 3c | red | 525.00 | 60.00 |
| *U8* | U4 | 3c | red, *buff* | 1,000. | 85.00 |
| *U9* | U5 | 3c | red ('54) | 15.00 | 1.50 |
| *U10* | U5 | 3c | red, *buff* ('54) | 9.50 | 1.00 |
| *U11* | U6 | 6c | red | 125.00 | 60.00 |
| *U12* | U6 | 6c | red, *buff* | 85.00 | 50.00 |
| *U13* | U6 | 6c | green | 165.00 | 85.00 |
| *U14* | U6 | 6c | grn, *buff* | 165.00 | 60.00 |
| *U15* | U7 | 10c | green ('55) | 125.00 | 50.00 |
| *U16* | U7 | 10c | grn, *buff* ('55) | 55.00 | 40.00 |
| *a.* | | 10c | pale green, *buff* | 55.00 | 40.00 |
| *U17* | U8 | 10c | green ('55) | 175.00 | 90.00 |
| *a.* | | 10c | pale green | 140.00 | 70.00 |
| *U18* | U8 | 10c | grn, *buff* ('55) | 90.00 | 50.00 |
| *a.* | | 10c | pale green, *buff* | 90.00 | 50.00 |

*Nos. U9, U10, U11, U12, U13, U14, U17 and U18 have been reprinted on white and buff papers, vertically laid. The originals are on diagonally laid paper. Value of 8 reprints, $120.*

Period after "POSTAGE."
U9

Franklin
U10

U10--Bust touches inner frame-line at front and back.

No period after "POSTAGE"
U11

Washington
U12

Envelopes are on diagonally laid paper. Wrappers on vertically or horizontally laid paper.

**1860-61**

| | | | | | |
|---|---|---|---|---|---|
| *U19* | U9 | 1c | bl, *buff* | 22.50 | 10.00 |
| *W20* | U9 | 1c | bl, *buff* ('61) | 50.00 | 45.00 |
| *W21* | U9 | 1c | bl, *man* ('61) | 35.00 | 35.00 |
| *W22* | U9 | 1c | bl, *org* ('61) | 1,250. | |
| *U23* | U10 | 1c | bl, *org* | 400.00 | 400.00 |
| *U24* | U11 | 1c | bl, *buff* | 180.00 | 90.00 |
| *W25* | U11 | 1c | bl, *man* ('61) | 1,200. | 950.00 |
| *U26* | U12 | 3c | red | 17.50 | 10.00 |
| *U27* | U12 | 3c | red, *buff* | 15.00 | 9.00 |
| *U28* | U12+9 | 3c + 1c | red & blue | 350.00 | 250.00 |
| *U29* | U12+9 | 3c + 1c | red & bl, *buff* | 250.00 | 200.00 |
| *U30* | U12 | 6c | red | 2,250. | 1,250. |
| *U31* | U12 | 6c | red, *buff* | 1,500. | 900.00 |
| *U32* | U12 | 10c | green | 800.00 | 275.00 |
| *U33* | U12 | 10c | grn, *buff* | 750.00 | 225.00 |

*Nos. U26, U27, U30 to U33 have been reprinted on the same papers as the reprints of the 1853-55 issue. Value for set of six, $150.*

Washington — U13

U14

U15

U16

Envelopes are on diagonally laid paper.

**1861**

| | | | | |
|---|---|---|---|---|
| *U34* | U13 | 3c pink | 14.00 | 4.00 |
| *U35* | U13 | 3c pink, *buff* | 12.50 | 4.00 |
| *U36* | U13 | 3c pink, *bl* (letter sheet) | 65.00 | 45.00 |
| +*U37* | U13 | 3c pink, *org* | 2,250. | |
| *U38* | U14 | 6c pink | 90.00 | 75.00 |
| *U39* | U14 | 6c pink, *buff* | 55.00 | 55.00 |
| *U40* | U15 | 10c yellow green | 25.00 | 22.50 |
| a | | 10c blue green | 25.00 | 25.00 |
| *U41* | U15 | 10c yel grn, *buff* | 22.50 | 19.00 |
| a | | 10c blue green, *buff* | 20.00 | 20.00 |
| *U42* | U16 | 12c red & brn, *buff* | 175.00 | 140.00 |
| a | | 12c lake & brown, *buff* | *800.00* | |
| *U43* | U16 | 20c red & bl, *buff* | 150.00 | 140.00 |
| *U44* | U16 | 24c red & grn, *buff* | 150.00 | 140.00 |
| a | | 24c lake & green, *sal* | 140.00 | 150.00 |
| *U45* | U16 | 40c blk & red, *buff* | 225.00 | 275.00 |

*Nos. U38 and U39 have been reprinted on the same papers as the reprints of the 1853-55 issue and are not known entire. Value of two reprints, $35.*

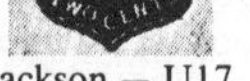
Jackson — U17 Jackson — U18

U17--"U. S. POSTAGE" above. The downstroke and tail of the "2" unite near the point.

U18--"U. S. POSTAGE" above. The downstroke and tail of the "2" touch but do not merge.

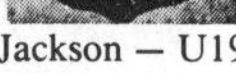
Jackson — U19

Jackson — U20

U19--"U.S. POST" above. Stamp measures 24 to 25mm in width.

U20--"U.S. POST" above. Stamp measures 25½to 26¼mm in width.

Envelopes are on diagonally laid paper. Wrappers on vertically or horizontally laid paper.

**1863-64**

| | | | | |
|---|---|---|---|---|
| *U46* | U17 | 2c blk, *buff* | 25.00 | 12.00 |
| *W47* | U17 | 2c blk, *dk man* | 35.00 | 30.00 |
| +*U48* | U18 | 2c blk, *buff* | 1,500. | |
| +*U49* | U18 | 2c blk, *orange* | 950.00 | |
| *U50* | U19 | 2c blk, *buff* ('64) | 8.00 | 7.00 |
| *W51* | U19 | 2c blk, *buff* ('64) | 140.00 | 140.00 |
| *U52* | U19 | 2c blk, *org* ('64) | 9.50 | 6.00 |
| *W53* | U19 | 2c blk, *dk man* ('64) | 25.00 | 17.50 |
| *U54* | U20 | 2c blk, *buff* ('64) | 9.50 | 8.00 |
| *W55* | U20 | 2c blk, *buff* ('64) | 65.00 | 40.00 |
| *U56* | U20 | 2c blk, *org* ('64) | 7.50 | 6.00 |
| *W57* | U20 | 2c blk, *lt man* ('64) | 10.00 | 8.00 |

Washington U21

Washington U22

**1864-65**

| | | | | |
|---|---|---|---|---|
| *U58* | U21 | 3c pink | 5.00 | 1.25 |
| *U59* | U21 | 3c pink, *buff* | 3.50 | 80 |
| *U60* | U21 | 3c brown ('65) | 35.00 | 20.00 |
| *U61* | U21 | 3c brn, *buff* ('65) | 35.00 | 20.00 |
| *U62* | U21 | 6c pink | 40.00 | 25.00 |
| *U63* | U21 | 6c pink, *buff* | 27.50 | 20.00 |
| *U64* | U21 | 6c purple ('65) | 35.00 | 20.00 |
| *U65* | U21 | 6c pur, *buff* ('65) | 30.00 | 17.50 |
| *U66* | U22 | 9c lem, *buff* ('65) | 300.00 | 200.00 |
| *U67* | U22 | 9c org, *buff* ('65) | 75.00 | 70.00 |
| a | | 9c orange yellow, *buff* | 85.00 | 80.00 |
| *U68* | U22 | 12c brn, *buff* ('65) | 300.00 | 190.00 |
| *U69* | U22 | 12c red brn, *buff* ('65) | 75.00 | 50.00 |
| *U70* | U22 | 18c red, *buff* ('65) | 75.00 | 75.00 |
| *U71* | U22 | 24c bl, *buff* ('65) | 70.00 | 70.00 |
| *U72* | U22 | 30c grn, *buff* ('65) | 50.00 | 50.00 |
| a | | 30c yellow green, *buff* | 50.00 | 60.00 |
| *U73* | U22 | 40c rose, *buff* ('65) | 60.00 | *200.00* |

## Reay Issue

The engravings in this issue are finely executed.

Franklin — U23

Jackson — U24

U23--Bust points to the end of the "N" of "ONE".

U24--Bust narrow at back. Small, thick figures of value.

Washington U25

Lincoln U26

U25--Queue projects below bust.

U26--Neck very long at the back.

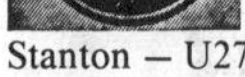
Stanton — U27

Jefferson — U28

U27--Bust pointed at the back, figures "7" are normal.

U28--Queue forms straight line with the bust.

Clay — U29

Webster — U30

U29--Ear partly concealed by hair, mouth large, chin prominent.

U30--Has side whiskers.

Scott — U31

Hamilton — U32

U31--Straggling locks of hair at top of head; ornaments around the inner oval end in squares.

U33--Back of bust very narrow, chin almost straight; labels containing figures of value are exactly parallel.

Perry — U33

U34--Front of bust very narrow and pointed; inner lines of shields project very slightly beyond the oval.

**1870-71**

| | | | | |
|---|---|---|---|---|
| *U74* | U23 | 1c blue | 25.00 | 20.00 |
| a | | 1c ultramarine | 50.00 | 25.00 |
| *U75* | U23 | 1c bl, *amber* | 25.00 | 20.00 |
| a | | 1c ultramarine, *amb* | 40.00 | 25.00 |
| *U76* | U23 | 1c blue, *org* | 12.00 | 9.00 |
| *W77* | U23 | 1c bl, *man* | 35.00 | 25.00 |
| *U78* | U24 | 2c brown | 30.00 | 12.00 |
| *U79* | U24 | 2c brn, *amb* | 13.00 | 6.00 |
| *U80* | U24 | 2c brn, *org* | 7.00 | 4.50 |
| *W81* | U24 | 2c brn, *man* | 17.50 | 15.00 |
| *U82* | U25 | 3c green | 5.00 | 60 |
| *U83* | U25 | 3c grn, *amb* | 3.50 | 1.50 |
| *U84* | U25 | 3c grn, *cr* | 6.50 | 2.50 |
| *U85* | U26 | 6c dark red | 14.00 | 10.00 |
| a | | 6c vermilion | 12.00 | 12.00 |
| *U86* | U26 | 6c dk red, *amb* | 16.00 | 12.00 |
| a | | 6c vermilion, *amb* | 16.00 | 12.00 |
| *U87* | U26 | 6c dk red, *cr* | 20.00 | 12.00 |
| a | | 6c vermilion, *cr* | 22.50 | 12.00 |
| *U88* | U27 | 7c ver, *amb* ('71) | 35.00 | *165.00* |
| *U89* | U28 | 10c olive black | 300.00 | 300.00 |
| *U90* | U28 | 10c ol blk, *amb* | 300.00 | 300.00 |
| *U91* | U28 | 10c brown | 45.00 | 60.00 |
| *U92* | U28 | 10c brn, *amb* | 60.00 | 45.00 |
| a | | 10c dark brown, *amb* | 60.00 | 50.00 |
| *U93* | U29 | 12c plum | 85.00 | 60.00 |
| *U94* | U29 | 12c plum, *amb* | 90.00 | 90.00 |
| *U95* | U29 | 12c plum, *cr* | 200.00 | 190.00 |
| *U96* | U30 | 15c red orange | 50.00 | 65.00 |
| a | | 15c orange | 50.00 | |
| *U97* | U30 | 15c red org, *amb* | 140.00 | 175.00 |
| a | | 15c orange, *amb* | 140.00 | |
| *U98* | U30 | 15c red org, *cr* | 200.00 | 200.00 |
| a | | 15c orange, *cr* | 200.00 | |
| *U99* | U31 | 24c purple | 110.00 | 75.00 |
| *U100* | U31 | 24c pur, *amb* | 160.00 | 275.00 |
| *U101* | U31 | 24c pur, *cream* | 160.00 | 275.00 |
| *U102* | U32 | 30c black | 65.00 | 80.00 |
| *U103* | U32 | 30c blk, *amb* | 155.00 | 225.00 |
| *U104* | U32 | 30c blk, *cream* | 200.00 | 350.00 |
| *U105* | U33 | 90c carmine | 125.00 | 200.00 |
| *U106* | U33 | 90c car, *amb* | 275.00 | 350.00 |
| *U107* | U33 | 90c car, *cream* | 300.00 | 450.00 |

## Plimpton Issue

The profiles in this issue are inferior to the fine engraving of the Reay issue.

U34

U35

U34--Bust forms an angle at the back near the frame. Lettering poorly executed. Distinct circle in "O" of "POSTAGE".

U35--Lower part of bust points to the end of the "E" in "ONE." Head inclined downward.

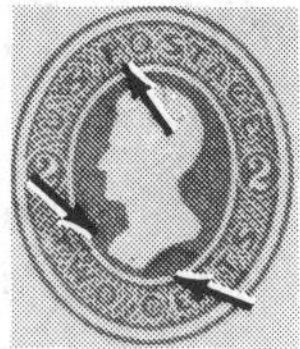
U36

U37

U36--Bust narrow at back. Thin figures of value. The head of the "P" in "POSTAGE" is very narrow. The bust at front is broad and ends in sharp corners.

U37--Bust broad. Figures of value in long ovals.

U38

U39

U38--Similar to die 2 but the figure "2" at the left touches the oval.

U39--Similar to die 2 but the "O" of "TWO" has the center netted instead of plain. The "G" of "POSTAGE" and the "C" of "CENTS" have diagonal crossline.

U40

U41

U40--Bust broad; numerals in ovals short and thick.

U41--Similar to die 5 but the ovals containing the numerals are much heavier. A diagonal line runs from the upper part of the "U" to the white frame-line.

U42

U43

U42--Similar to die 5 but the middle stroke of "N" in "CENTS" is as thin as the vertical strokes.

U43--Bottom of bust cut almost semi-circularly.

U44

U45

U44--Thin lettering, long thin figures of value.

U45--Thick lettering, well-formed figures of value, queue does not project below bust.

U46

U46--Top of head egg-shaped; knot of queue well marked and projects triangularly.

Taylor — U47

Die 1

Die 2

Die 1--Figures of value with thick curved tops.

Die 2--Figures of value with long, thin tops.

U48

U49

U48--Neck very short at the back.

U49--Figures of value turned up at the ends.

U50

U51

U50--Very large head.

U51--Knot of queue stands out prominently.

U52

U53

U52--Ear prominent, chin receding.

U53--No side whiskers, forelock projects above head.

U54

U55

U54--Hair does not project; ornaments around the inner oval end in points.

U55--Back of bust rather broad, chin slopes considerably; labels containing figures of value are not exactly parallel.

U56

Front of bust sloping; inner lines of shields project considerably into the inner oval.

**1874-86**

**U34**

| *U108* | 1c dark blue | 70.00 | 35.00 |
|---|---|---|---|
| a | 1c light blue | | |
| *U109* | 1c dk bl, *amb* | 85.00 | 55.00 |
| +*U110* | 1c dk bl, *cr* | 600.00 | |
| *U111* | 1c dk bl, *org* | 15.00 | 12.50 |
| a | 1c light bl, *org* | 17.00 | 8.00 |
| *W112* | 1c dk bl, *man* | 35.00 | 27.50 |

**U35**

| *U113* | 1c light blue | 1.00 | 60 |
|---|---|---|---|
| a | 1c dark blue | 5.50 | 4.00 |
| *U114* | 1c lt bl, *amb* | 3.00 | 2.50 |
| a | 1c dark bl, *amb* | 11.00 | 8.00 |
| *U115* | 1c bl, *cr* | 3.00 | 3.00 |
| a | 1c dark bl, *cr* | 14.00 | 4.00 |
| *U116* | 1c lt bl, *org* | 40 | 30 |
| a | 1c dark bl, *org* | 1.50 | 85 |
| *U117* | 1c lt bl, *bl* ('80) | 4.00 | 3.00 |
| *U118* | 1c lt bl, *fawn* ('79) | 4.00 | 3.00 |
| *U119* | 1c lt bl, *man* ('86) | 4.00 | 2.50 |
| *W120* | 1c lt bl, *man* | 1.00 | 80 |
| a | 1c dark bl, *man* | 3.50 | 2.00 |
| *U121* | 1c lt bl, *amb man* ('86) | 8.00 | 7.50 |

**U36**

| *U122* | 2c brown | 75.00 | 30.00 |
|---|---|---|---|
| *U123* | 2c brn, *amb* | 40.00 | 30.00 |
| +*U124* | 2c brn, *cr* | 500.00 | |
| +*U125* | 2c brn, *org* | *6,500.* | |
| *W126* | 2c brn, *man* | 75.00 | 35.00 |
| *W127* | 2c ver, *man* | 1,000. | 275.00 |

**U37**

| *U128* | 2c brown | 35.00 | 22.50 |
|---|---|---|---|
| *U129* | 2c brn, *amb* | 50.00 | 30.00 |
| +*U130* | 2c brn, *cr* | *18,500.* | |
| *W131* | 2c brn, *man* | 12.00 | 12.00 |

**U38**

| *U132* | 2c brown | 50.00 | 20.00 |
|---|---|---|---|
| *U133* | 2c brn, *amb* | 175.00 | 55.00 |
| +*U133A* | 2c brn, *cr* | | — |

**U39**

| *U134* | 2c brown | 600.00 | 100.00 |
|---|---|---|---|
| *U135* | 2c brn, *amb* | 37.00 | 100.00 |
| *U136* | 2c brn, *org* | 27.50 | 25.00 |
| *W137* | 2c brn, *man* | 45.00 | 27.50 |
| +*U137A* | 2c vermilion | *17,500.* | |
| +*U137B* | 2c ver, *amb* | *17,500.* | |
| +*U137C* | 2c ver, *org* | *17,500.* | |
| +*W138* | 2c ver, *man* | *6,000.* | |

**U40**

| *U139* | 2c brown ('75) | 35.00 | 30.00 |
|---|---|---|---|
| *U140* | 2c brn, *amb* ('75) | 60.00 | 50.00 |
| *W141* | 2c brn, *man* ('75) | 30.00 | 20.00 |
| *U142* | 2c ver ('75) | 4.00 | 2.00 |
| a | 2c pink | 7.00 | 5.00 |
| *U143* | 2c ver, *amb* ('75) | 4.00 | 2.00 |
| *U144* | 2c ver, *cr* ('75) | 9.00 | 4.00 |
| +*U145* | 2c ver, *org* ('75) | *8,000.* | |
| *U146* | 2c ver, *bl* ('80) | 110.00 | 27.50 |
| *U147* | 2c ver, *fawn* ('75) | 5.00 | 3.50 |
| *W148* | 2c ver, *man* ('75) | 2.50 | 2.50 |

**U41**

| *U149* | 2c ver ('78) | 30.00 | 20.00 |
|---|---|---|---|
| a | 2c pink | 30.00 | 20.00 |
| *U150* | 2c ver, *amb* ('78) | 17.00 | 12.00 |
| *U151* | 2c ver, *bl* ('80) | 7.00 | 6.00 |
| a | 2c pink, *bl* | 7.00 | 6.00 |
| *U152* | 2c ver, *fawn* ('78) | 7.50 | 3.00 |

**U42**

| *U153* | 2c ver ('76) | 40.00 | 25.00 |
|---|---|---|---|
| *U154* | 2c ver, *amb* ('76) | 250.00 | 70.00 |
| *W155* | 2c ver, *man* ('76) | 12.00 | 7.00 |

**U43**

| *U156* | 2c ver ('81) | 600.00 | 110.00 |
|---|---|---|---|
| *U157* | 2c ver, *amb* ('81) | *14,000.* | *14,000.* |
| *W158* | 2c ver, *man* ('81) | 60.00 | 50.00 |

**U44**

| *U159* | 3c green | 16.00 | 4.00 |
|---|---|---|---|
| *U160* | 3c grn, *amb* | 18.00 | 7.50 |
| *U161* | 3c grn, *cr* | 30.00 | 8.00 |
| +*U162* | 3c grn, *bl* | | — |

**U45**

| *U163* | 3c green | 75 | 25 |
|---|---|---|---|
| *U164* | 3c grn, *amb* | 1.00 | 40 |
| *U165* | 3c grn, *cr* | 4.50 | 4.00 |
| *U166* | 3c grn, *bl* | 5.00 | 3.00 |
| *U167* | 3c grn, *fawn* ('75) | 3.00 | 2.00 |

**U46**

| *U168* | 3c grn ('81) | 400.00 | 30.00 |
|---|---|---|---|
| *U169* | 3c grn, *amb* ('81) | 175.00 | 90.00 |
| *U170* | 3c grn, *bl* ('81) | *7,000.* | *1,500.* |
| *U171* | 3c grn, *fawn* ('81) | *24,000.* | *1,250.* |

**U47**

| *U172* | 5c bl, die 1 ('75) | 7.00 | 6.00 |
|---|---|---|---|
| *U173* | 5c bl, die 1, *amb* ('75) | 7.50 | 6.50 |
| *U174* | 5c bl, die 1, *cr* ('75) | 75.00 | 37.50 |
| *U175* | 5c bl, die 1, *bl* ('75) | 12.50 | 12.50 |
| *U176* | 5c bl, die 1, *fawn* ('75) | 90.00 | 50.00 |
| *U177* | 5c bl, die 2 ('75) | 4.75 | 4.75 |
| *U178* | 5c bl, die 2, *amb* ('75) | 5.50 | 5.00 |
| +*U178A* | 5c bl, die 2, *cr* ('76) | *1,500.* | |
| *U179* | 5c bl, die 2, *bl* ('75) | 10.00 | 6.00 |
| *U180* | 5c bl, die 2, *fawn* ('75) | 70.00 | 40.00 |

**U48**

| *U181* | 6c red | 4.00 | 4.00 |
|---|---|---|---|
| a | 6c vermilion | 4.00 | 4.00 |
| *U182* | 6c red, *amb* | 4.00 | 4.00 |
| a | 6c vermilion, *amb* | 7.00 | 4.00 |
| *U183* | 6c red, *cr* | 14.00 | 9.00 |
| a | 6c vermilion, *cr* | 14.00 | 10.00 |
| *U184* | 6c red, *fawn* ('75) | 14.00 | 9.00 |

**U49**

| +*U185* | 7c ver | *1,000.* | |
|---|---|---|---|
| *U186* | 7c ver, *amb* | 75.00 | 55.00 |

**U50**

| *U187* | 10c brown | 25.00 | 15.00 |
|---|---|---|---|
| *U188* | 10c brn, *amb* | 50.00 | 25.00 |

**U51**

| *U189* | 10c choc ('75) | 4.00 | 2.50 |
|---|---|---|---|
| a | 10c bister brown | 5.00 | 3.00 |
| b | 10c yellow ocher | 1,000. | |
| *U190* | 10c choc, *amb* ('75) | 5.50 | 5.00 |
| a | 10c bis brn, *amb* | 5.50 | 5.00 |
| b | 10c yel ocher, *amb* | 1,000. | |
| *U191* | 10c brn, *oriental buff* ('86) | 7.00 | 6.00 |
| *U192* | 10c brn, *bl* ('86) | 8.00 | 6.00 |
| a | 10c gray blk, *bl* | 8.00 | 6.00 |
| b | 10c red brn, *bl* | 8.00 | 6.00 |
| *U193* | 10c brn, *man* ('86) | 8.50 | 6.00 |
| a | 10c red brn, *man* | 9.00 | 6.00 |
| *U194* | 10c brn, *amb man* ('86) | 10.00 | 5.00 |
| a | 10c red brn, *amb man* | 10.00 | 5.00 |

**U52**

| *U195* | 12c plum | 150.00 | 75.00 |
|---|---|---|---|
| *U196* | 12c plum, *amb* | 140.00 | 140.00 |
| *U197* | 12c plum, *cr* | 175.00 | 150.00 |

**U53**

| *U198* | 15c orange | 30.00 | 25.00 |
|---|---|---|---|
| *U199* | 15c org, *amb* | 110.00 | 90.00 |
| *U200* | 15c org, *cr* | 350.00 | 350.00 |

**U54**

| *U201* | 24c purple | 150.00 | 100.00 |
|---|---|---|---|
| *U202* | 24c pur, *amb* | 155.00 | 100.00 |
| *U203* | 24c pur, *cr* | 150.00 | 110.00 |

**U55**

| *U204* | 30c black | 50.00 | 25.00 |
|---|---|---|---|
| *U205* | 30c blk, *amb* | 55.00 | 50.00 |
| *U206* | 30c blk, *cr* | 400.00 | 375.00 |
| *U207* | 30c blk, *oriental buff* ('86) | 80.00 | 70.00 |
| *U208* | 30c blk, *bl* ('86) | 85.00 | 70.00 |
| *U209* | 30c blk, *man* ('86) | 75.00 | 70.00 |
| *U210* | 30c blk, *amb man* ('86) | 100.00 | 70.00 |

**U56**

| *U211* | 90c car ('75) | 100.00 | 70.00 |
|---|---|---|---|
| *U212* | 90c car, *amb* ('75) | 150.00 | 200.00 |
| *U213* | 90c car, *cr* ('75) | 1,250. | |
| *U214* | 90c car, *oriental buff* ('86) | 175.00 | 250.00 |
| *U215* | 90c car, *bl* ('86) | 150.00 | 200.00 |
| *U216* | 90c car, *man* ('86) | 100.00 | 200.00 |
| *U217* | 90c car, *amb man* ('86) | 100.00 | 175.00 |

See Nos. U336-U347.

**United States Centennial Issue**

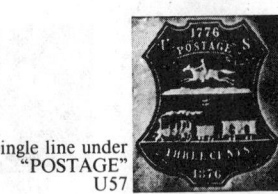

Single line under "POSTAGE" U57

Double line under "POSTAGE" U58

**1876**

| *U218* | U57 | 3c red | 60.00 | 20.00 |
|---|---|---|---|---|
| *U219* | U57 | 3c green | 45.00 | 12.50 |
| +*U220* | U58 | 3c red | *20,000.* | |
| *U221* | U58 | 3c green | 55.00 | 15.00 |

Cent. of the US, and the World's Fair at Philadelphia.

See No. U582.

Garfield U59

Washington U60

**1882-86**

| *U222* | U59 | 5c brown | 2.75 | 1.50 |
|---|---|---|---|---|
| *U223* | U59 | 5c brown, *amb* | 3.00 | 1.75 |
| *U224* | U59 | 5c brn, *oriental buff* ('86) | 85.00 | 45.00 |
| *U225* | U59 | 5c brown, *bl* | 40.00 | 30.00 |
| *U226* | U59 | 5c brown, *fawn* | 200.00 | |

**1883, Oct.**

| *U227* | U60 | 2c red | 2.75 | 1.25 |
|---|---|---|---|---|
| a | | 2c brn (error), entire | *2,000.* | |
| *U228* | U60 | 2c red, *amber* | 3.50 | 1.50 |
| *U229* | U60 | 2c red, *blue* | 5.00 | 3.50 |
| *U230* | U60 | 2c red, *fawn* | 4.50 | 2.00 |

Wavy lines fine and clear — U61

Wavy lines thick and blurred — U62

Four Wavy Lines in Oval.

**1883, Nov.**

| *U231* | U61 | 2c red | 2.00 | 1.00 |
|---|---|---|---|---|
| *U232* | U61 | 2c red, *amber* | 2.50 | 1.25 |
| *U233* | U61 | 2c red, *blue* | 5.00 | 3.50 |
| *U234* | U61 | 2c red, *fawn* | 3.00 | 2.00 |
| *W235* | U61 | 2c red, *manila* | 6.00 | 3.00 |

**1884, June**

| *U236* | U62 | 2c red | 4.00 | 2.00 |
|---|---|---|---|---|
| *U237* | U62 | 2c red, *amber* | 7.50 | 5.50 |
| *U238* | U62 | 2c red, *blue* | 10.00 | 5.50 |
| *U239* | U62 | 2c red, *fawn* | 7.50 | 5.00 |

See Nos. U260-W269.

3½ links over left "2" — U63

2 links below right "2" — U64

Round "O" in "TWO" — U65

| | | | | |
|---|---|---|---|---|
| *U240* | U63 | 2c red | 35.00 | 25.00 |
| *U241* | U63 | 2c red, *amber* | 550.00 | 275.00 |
| *U242* | U63 | 2c red, *fawn* | | *6,250.* |
| *U243* | U64 | 2c red | 50.00 | 35.00 |
| *U244* | U64 | 2c red, *amber* | 100.00 | 60.00 |
| *U245* | U64 | 2c red, *blue* | 250.00 | 95.00 |
| *U246* | U64 | 2c red, *fawn* | 250.00 | 100.00 |
| *U247* | U65 | 2c red | 800.00 | 225.00 |
| *U248* | U65 | 2c red, *amber* | 1,500. | 600.00 |
| *U249* | U65 | 2c red, *fawn* | 450.00 | 275.00 |

See Nos. U270-U276.

Jackson — U66

Die 1-- Numeral at left is 2¾mm wide

Die 2-- Numeral at left is 3¼mm wide

**1883-86**

| | | | | |
|---|---|---|---|---|
| *U250* | U66 | 4c grn, die 1 | 2.00 | 2.00 |
| *U251* | U66 | 4c grn, die 1, *amb* | 3.00 | 2.00 |
| *U252* | U66 | 4c grn, die 1, *oriental buff* ('86) | 5.00 | 5.00 |
| *U253* | U66 | 4c grn, die 1, *bl* ('86) | 5.00 | 3.50 |
| *U254* | U66 | 4c grn, die 1, *man* ('86) | 6.00 | 3.50 |
| *U255* | U66 | 4c grn, die 1, *amb man* ('86) | 15.00 | 7.50 |
| *U256* | U66 | 4c grn, die 2 | 3.00 | 2.75 |
| *U257* | U66 | 4c grn, die 2, *amb* | 7.00 | 4.00 |
| *U258* | U66 | 4c grn, die 2, *man* ('86) | 6.00 | 4.00 |
| *U259* | U66 | 4c grn, die 2, *amb man* ('86) | 6.00 | 4.00 |

**1884, May**

| | | | | |
|---|---|---|---|---|
| *U260* | U61 | 2c brown | 9.00 | 3.00 |
| *U261* | U61 | 2c brn, *amber* | 8.00 | 3.50 |
| *U262* | U61 | 2c brn, *blue* | 8.50 | 4.00 |
| *U263* | U61 | 2c brn, *fawn* | 7.50 | 4.00 |
| *W264* | U61 | 2c brn, *manila* | 10.00 | 7.00 |

**1884, June** **Retouched Die**

| | | | | |
|---|---|---|---|---|
| *U265* | U62 | 2c brown | 10.00 | 3.00 |
| *U266* | U62 | 2c brn, *amber* | 40.00 | 16.00 |
| *U267* | U62 | 2c brn, *blue* | 7.00 | 4.00 |
| *U268* | U62 | 2c brn, *fawn* | 8.00 | 6.50 |
| *W269* | U62 | 2c brn, *manila* | 15.00 | 10.00 |

**2 Links Below Right "2"**

| | | | | |
|---|---|---|---|---|
| *U270* | U64 | 2c brown | 60.00 | 35.00 |
| *U271* | U64 | 2c brn, *amber* | 165.00 | 85.00 |
| *U272* | U64 | 2c brn, *fawn* | *2,100.* | 1,000. |

**Round "O" in "Two"**

| | | | | |
|---|---|---|---|---|
| *U273* | U65 | 2c brown | 110.00 | 60.00 |
| *U274* | U65 | 2c brn, *amber* | 125.00 | 60.00 |
| *U275* | U65 | 2c brn, *blue* | | *4,500.* |
| *U276* | U65 | 2c brn, *fawn* | 850.00 | 600.00 |

Washington — U67

U68

U67--Extremity of bust below the queue forms a point.

U68--Extremity of bust is rounded.

Similar to U61
Two wavy lines in oval

**1884-86**

| | | | | |
|---|---|---|---|---|
| *U277* | U67 | 2c brown | 25 | 15 |
| *a* | | 2c brown lake | 17.50 | 10.00 |
| *U278* | U67 | 2c brn, *amb* | 40 | 30 |
| *a* | | 2c brown lake, *amb* | 30.00 | 10.00 |
| *U279* | U67 | 2c brn, *oriental buff* ('86) | 2.00 | 1.25 |
| *U280* | U67 | 2c brn, *blue* | 1.50 | 1.00 |
| *U281* | U67 | 2c brn, *fawn* | 2.00 | 1.25 |
| *U282* | U67 | 2c brn, *man* ('86) | 7.00 | 2.50 |
| *W283* | U67 | 2c brn, *man* | 4.00 | 3.50 |
| *U284* | U67 | 2c brn, *amb man* ('86) | 4.00 | 4.00 |
| *+U285* | U67 | 2c red | 500.00 | |
| *+U286* | U67 | 2c red, *blue* | 200.00 | |
| *W287* | U67 | 2c red, *man* | 90.00 | |
| *U288* | U68 | 2c brown | 150.00 | 30.00 |
| *U289* | U68 | 2c brn, *amb* | 10.00 | 9.00 |
| *U290* | U68 | 2c brn, *blue* | 675.00 | 125.00 |
| *U291* | U68 | 2c brn, *fawn* | 17.00 | 14.00 |
| *W292* | U68 | 2c brn, *man* | 17.00 | 14.00 |

Grant — US1

**1886** **Letter Sheet**

| | | | | |
|---|---|---|---|---|
| *U293* | US1 | 2c green entire | 20.00 | 8.50 |

Franklin
U69

Washington
U70

U70--Bust points between 3rd and 4th notches of inner oval; "G" of "POSTAGE" has no bar.

U71

U72

U71--Bust points between second and third notches of inner oval; "G" of "POSTAGE" has a bar; ear is indicated by one heavy line; one vertical line at corner of mouth.

U72--Frame same as die 2; upper part of head more rounded; ear indicated by two curved lines with two locks of hair in front; two vertical lines at corner of mouth.

Jackson — U73

Grant — U74

U75

U74--There is a space between the beard and the collar of the coat. A button is on the collar.

U75--The collar touches the beard and there is no button.

**1887-94**

| | | | | |
|---|---|---|---|---|
| *U294* | U69 | 1c blue | 40 | 20 |
| *U295* | U69 | 1c dk bl ('94) | 5.50 | 2.00 |
| *U296* | U69 | 1c bl, *amb* ('94) | 2.00 | 1.00 |
| *U297* | U69 | 1c dk bl, *amb* ('94) | 35.00 | 17.50 |
| *+U298* | U69 | 1c bl, *oriental buff* ('94) | *2,200.* | |
| *+U299* | U69 | 1c bl, *bl* ('94) | *3,000.* | |
| *U300* | U69 | 1c bl, *man* ('94) | 50 | 25 |
| *W301* | U69 | 1c bl, *man* ('94) | 30 | 25 |
| *U302* | U69 | 1c dk bl, *man* ('94) | 17.50 | 7.00 |
| *W303* | U69 | 1c dk bl, *man* ('94) | 10.00 | 8.50 |
| *U304* | U69 | 1c bl, *amb man* | 3.00 | 2.25 |
| *U305* | U70 | 2c green | 7.00 | 6.00 |
| *U306* | U70 | 2c grn, *amb* | 16.00 | 10.50 |
| *U307* | U70 | 2c grn, *oriental buff* | 55.00 | 25.00 |
| *U308* | U70 | 2c grn, *bl* | *2,750.* | 650.00 |
| *U309* | U70 | 2c grn, *man* | 1,700. | 400.00 |
| *U310* | U70 | 2c grn, *amb man* | 1,500. | 500.00 |
| *U311* | U71 | 2c green | 25 | 10 |
| *U312* | U71 | 2c grn, *amb* | 30 | 10 |
| *U313* | U71 | 2c grn, *oriental buff* | 40 | 20 |
| *U314* | U71 | 2c grn, *bl* | 40 | 20 |
| *U315* | U71 | 2c grn, *man* | 75 | 35 |
| *W316* | U71 | 2c grn, *man* | 1.90 | 1.65 |
| *U317* | U71 | 2c grn, *amb man* | 1.50 | 1.25 |
| *U318* | U72 | 2c green | 90.00 | 10.00 |
| *U319* | U72 | 2c grn, *amb* | 115.00 | 15.00 |
| *U320* | U72 | 2c grn, *oriental buff* | 125.00 | 30.00 |
| *U321* | U72 | 2c grn, *bl* | 140.00 | 40.00 |
| *U322* | U72 | 2c grn, *man* | 125.00 | 60.00 |
| *U323* | U72 | 2c grn, *amb man* | 300.00 | 75.00 |
| *U324* | U73 | 4c carmine | 1.10 | 95 |
| *a* | | 4c lake | 1.50 | 90 |
| *b* | | 4c scarlet ('94) | 1.50 | 90 |
| *U325* | U73 | 4c car, *amb* | 1.75 | 1.50 |
| *a* | | 4c lake, *amber* | 1.75 | 1.50 |
| *b* | | 4c scar, *amber* ('94) | 1.75 | 2.00 |
| *U326* | U73 | 4c car, *oriental buff* | 4.00 | 2.00 |
| *a* | | 4c lake, *oriental buff* | 4.00 | 2.00 |
| *U327* | U73 | 4c car, *blue* | 3.00 | 3.00 |
| *a* | | 4c lake, *blue* | 3.50 | 3.00 |
| *U328* | U73 | 4c car, *man* | 5.00 | 4.00 |
| *a* | | 4c lake, *manila* | 5.00 | 4.00 |
| *b* | | 4c pink, *manila* | 6.00 | 3.00 |
| *U329* | U73 | 4c car, *amb man* | 3.00 | 2.00 |
| *a* | | 4c lake, *amb man* | 3.00 | 2.00 |
| *b* | | 4c pink, *amb man* | 4.00 | 2.00 |
| *U330* | U74 | 5c blue | 2.50 | 2.25 |
| *U331* | U74 | 5c bl, *amber* | 3.00 | 1.50 |
| *U332* | U74 | 5c bl, *oriental buff* | 3.00 | 2.50 |
| *U333* | U74 | 5c bl, *blue* | 4.00 | 3.00 |
| *U334* | U75 | 5c blue ('94) | 7.00 | 4.00 |
| *U335* | U75 | 5c bl, *amb* ('94) | 7.50 | 4.00 |
| *U336* | U55 | 30c red brn | 30.00 | 35.00 |
| *a* | | 30c yel brn | 40.00 | 27.50 |
| *b* | | 30c chocolate | 40.00 | 45.00 |
| *U337* | U55 | 30c red brn, *amb* | 35.00 | 50.00 |
| *a* | | 30c yel brn, *amber* | 40.00 | 40.00 |
| *b* | | 30c choc, *amber* | 40.00 | 40.00 |
| *U338* | U55 | 30c red brn, *oriental buff* | 30.00 | 40.00 |
| *a* | | 30c yel brn, *oriental buff* | 30.00 | 40.00 |
| *U339* | U55 | 30c red brn, *bl* | 30.00 | 40.00 |
| *a* | | 30c yellow brn, *blue* | 30.00 | 25.00 |
| *U340* | U55 | 30c red brn, *manila* | 35.00 | 35.00 |
| *a* | | 30c brown, *manila* | 35.00 | 35 00 |
| *U341* | U55 | 30c red brown, *amb man* | 40.00 | 25.00 |
| *a* | | 30c yel brn, *amb man* | 40.00 | 25.00 |
| *U342* | U56 | 90c purple | 50.00 | 60.00 |
| *U343* | U56 | 90c pur, *amb* | 60.00 | 60.00 |
| *U344* | U56 | 90c pur, *oriental buff* | 60.00 | 65.00 |
| *U345* | U56 | 90c pur, *blue* | 65.00 | 70.00 |
| *U346* | U56 | 90c pur, *man* | 65.00 | 70.00 |
| *U347* | U56 | 90c pur, *amb manila* | 65.00 | 70.00 |

**Columbian Exposition Issue**

Columbus and Liberty
U76

**1893**

| | | | | |
|---|---|---|---|---|
| *U348* | U76 | 1c deep blue | 1.75 | 75 |
| *U349* | U76 | 2c violet | 1.50 | 40 |
| *a* | | 2c dark slate (error) | *1,000.* | |
| *U350* | U76 | 5c chocolate | 7.50 | 6.50 |
| *a* | | 5c slate brown (error) | 600.00 | 600.00 |
| *U351* | U76 | 10c slate brown | 35.00 | 25.00 |

Franklin
U77

Washington
U78

U78- Bust points to first notch of inner oval and is only slightly concave below.

U79

U80

U79--Bust points to middle of second notch of inner oval and is quite hollow below. Queue has ribbon around it.

U80--Same as die 2 but hair flowing and no ribbon around queue.

Lincoln — U81

Pointed but not draped.

U82

U83

U82--Bust broad and draped.

U83--Head larger, inner oval has no notches.

Grant — U84

Similar to designs of 1887-95 but smaller

**1899**

| | | | | |
|---|---|---|---|---|
| *U352* | U77 | 1c green | 40 | 20 |
| *U353* | U77 | 1c grn, *amb* | 3.50 | 1.25 |
| *U354* | U77 | 1c grn, *oriental buff* | 7.00 | 2.00 |
| *U355* | U77 | 1c grn, *bl* | 7.50 | 2.00 |
| *U356* | U77 | 1c grn, *man* | 1.50 | 75 |
| *W357* | U77 | 1c grn, *man* | 1.50 | 75 |
| *U358* | U78 | 2c carmine | 1.65 | 75 |
| *U359* | U78 | 2c car, *amb* | 13.00 | 9.00 |
| *U360* | U78 | 2c car, *oriental buff* | 13.00 | 7.50 |
| *U361* | U78 | 2c car, *blue* | 45.00 | 22.50 |
| *U362* | U79 | 2c carmine | 25 | 20 |
| *a* | | 2c dark lake | 25.00 | 30.00 |
| *U363* | U79 | 2c car, *amb* | 75 | 15 |
| *U364* | U79 | 2c car, *oriental buff* | 75 | 15 |
| *U365* | U79 | 2c car, *blue* | 95 | 45 |
| *W366* | U79 | 2c car, *man* | 3.50 | 2.25 |
| *U367* | U80 | 2c carmine | 3.00 | 1.50 |

| | | | | |
|---|---|---|---|---|
| U368 | U80 | 2c car, *amb* | 6.00 | 4.50 |
| U369 | U80 | 2c car, *oriental buff* | 18.00 | 9.00 |
| U370 | U80 | 2c car, *blue* | 8.00 | 6.00 |
| U371 | U81 | 4c brown | 13.00 | 9.00 |
| U372 | U81 | 4c brn, *amb* | 13.00 | 9.00 |
| U373 | U82 | 4c brown | 3,500. | 350.00 |
| U374 | U83 | 4c brown | 7.50 | 5.00 |
| U375 | U83 | 4c brn, *amb* | 32.50 | 10.00 |
| W376 | U83 | 4c brn, *man* | 12.00 | 6.00 |
| U377 | U84 | 5c blue | 7.50 | 7.00 |
| U378 | U84 | 5c blue, *amb* | 10.00 | 8.50 |

Franklin U85

Washington U86

U86--One short and two long vertical lines at right of "CENTS".

Grant — U87

Lincoln — U88

**1903**

| | | | | |
|---|---|---|---|---|
| U379 | U85 | 1c green | 50 | 10 |
| U380 | U85 | 1c green, *amb* | 10.00 | 1.75 |
| U381 | U85 | 1c grn, *oriental buff* | 8.00 | 1.65 |
| U382 | U85 | 1c green, *blue* | 10.00 | 1.75 |
| U383 | U85 | 1c grn, *manila* | 2.00 | 75 |
| W384 | U85 | 1c grn, *manila* | 80 | 30 |
| U385 | U86 | 2c carmine | 30 | 15 |
| U386 | U86 | 2c carmine, *amb* | 1.25 | 20 |
| U387 | U86 | 2c car, *oriental buff* | 1.25 | 30 |
| U388 | U86 | 2c carmine, *blue* | 1.00 | 50 |
| W389 | U86 | 2c car, *manila* | 12.00 | 6.00 |
| U390 | U87 | 4c chocolate | 14.00 | 8.00 |
| U391 | U87 | 4c choc, *amber* | 14.00 | 8.50 |
| W392 | U87 | 4c choc, *manila* | 14.00 | 9.50 |
| U393 | U88 | 5c blue | 14.00 | 7.50 |
| U394 | U88 | 5c blue, *amber* | 14.00 | 8.00 |

U89

The three lines at the right of "CENTS" and at the left of "TWO" are usually all short; the lettering is heavier and the ends of the ribbons slightly changed.

**1904** **Re-cut Die**

| | | | | |
|---|---|---|---|---|
| U395 | U89 | 2c carmine | 35 | 15 |
| U396 | U89 | 2c car, *amber* | 6.00 | 45 |
| U397 | U89 | 2c car, *oriental buff* | 4.00 | 1.00 |
| U398 | U89 | 2c carmine, *blue* | 2.50 | 75 |
| W399 | U89 | 2c car, *manila* | 9.50 | 5.50 |

Franklin — U90

Die 1

Die 2

Die 3

Die 4

Die 1. Wide "D" in "UNITED".
Die 2. Narrow "D" in "UNITED".
Die 3. Wide "S-S" in "STATES" (1910).
Die 4. Sharp angle at back of bust, "N" and "E" of "ONE" are parallel (1912).

**1907-16** **Die 1**

| | | | | |
|---|---|---|---|---|
| U400 | U90 | 1c green | 25 | 10 |
| *a* | | Die 2 | 40 | 15 |
| *b* | | Die 3 | 50 | 25 |
| *c* | | Die 4 | 50 | 20 |
| U401 | U90 | 1c green, *amber* | 60 | 40 |
| *a* | | Die 2 | 75 | 50 |
| *b* | | Die 3 | 75 | 50 |
| *c* | | Die 4 | 70 | 45 |
| U402 | U90 | 1c grn, *oriental buff* | 2.50 | 1.00 |
| *a* | | Die 2 | 2.50 | 1.00 |
| *b* | | Die 3 | 4.00 | 1.50 |
| *c* | | Die 4 | 3.00 | 1.25 |
| U403 | U90 | 1c green, *blue* | 3.00 | 1.25 |
| *a* | | Die 2 | 3.00 | 1.00 |
| *b* | | Die 3 | 3.00 | 1.50 |
| *c* | | Die 4 | 2.75 | 75 |
| U404 | U90 | 1c grn, *manila* | 2.25 | 1.75 |
| *a* | | Die 3 | 2.50 | 2.00 |
| W405 | U90 | 1c grn, *manila* | 40 | 25 |
| *a* | | Die 2 | 30.00 | 20.00 |
| *b* | | Die 3 | 3.50 | 2.00 |
| *c* | | Die 4 | 25.00 | 20.00 |

Washington — U91

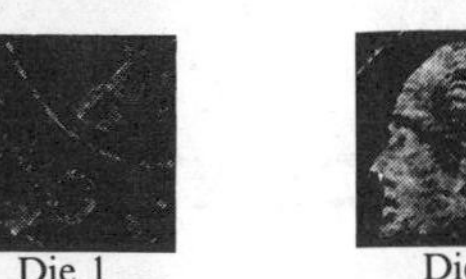
Die 1 Die 2

Die 3 Die 4

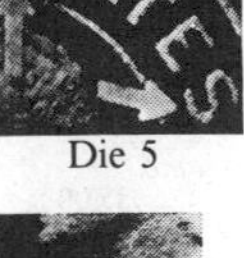
Die 5 Die 6

Die 7

Die 8

Die 1. Oval "O" in "TWO" and "C" in "CENTS", front of bust broad.
Die 2. Similar to 1 but hair in two distinct locks at top of head.
Die 3. Round "O" in "TWO" and "C" in "CENTS", coarse lettering.
Die 4. Similar to 3 but lettering fine and clear, hair lines clearly embossed. Inner oval thin and clear.
Die 5. All "S's" wide (1910).
Die 6. Similar to 1 but front of bust narrow (1913).
Die 7. Similar to 6 but upper corner of front of bust cut away (1916).
Die 8. Similar to 7 but lower stroke of "S" in "CENTS" is a straight line. Hair as in Die 2 (1916).

**Die I**

| | | | | |
|---|---|---|---|---|
| U406 | U91 | 2c brn red | 35 | 15 |
| *a* | | Die 2 | 20.00 | 7.50 |
| *b* | | Die 3 | 30 | 20 |
| U407 | U91 | 2c brn red, *amb* | 4.00 | 2.00 |
| *a* | | Die 2 | 85.00 | 40.00 |
| *b* | | Die 3 | 1.75 | 60 |
| U408 | U91 | 2c brown red, *oriental buff* | 5.50 | 1.25 |
| *a* | | Die 2 | 110.00 | 50.00 |
| *b* | | Die 3 | 4.50 | 2.00 |
| U409 | U91 | 2c brn red, *blue* | 3.00 | 1.50 |
| *a* | | Die 2 | 110.00 | 80.00 |
| *b* | | Die 3 | 3.50 | 1.50 |
| W410 | U91 | 2c brn red, *man* | 35.00 | 22.50 |
| U411 | U91 | 2c carmine | 20 | 15 |
| *a* | | Die 2 | 20 | 8 |
| *b* | | Die 3 | 40 | 25 |
| *c* | | Die 4 | 20 | 15 |
| *d* | | Die 5 | 30 | 20 |
| *e* | | Die 6 | 20 | 8 |
| *f* | | Die 7 | 11.00 | 9.00 |
| *g* | | Die 8 | 11.00 | 9.00 |
| *h* | | Die 1, with added impression of 1c grn (#U400), entire | 225.00 | |
| *i* | | Die 1, with added impression of 4c blk (#U416a), entire | 175.00 | |
| U412 | U91 | 2c carmine, *amb* | 20 | 10 |
| *a* | | Die 2 | 12 | 10 |
| *b* | | Die 3 | 1.00 | 30 |
| *c* | | Die 4 | 20 | 15 |
| *d* | | Die 5 | 35 | 20 |
| *e* | | Die 6 | 15 | 10 |
| *f* | | Die 7 | 9.00 | 7.00 |
| U413 | U91 | 2c car, *oriental buff* | 40 | 20 |
| *a* | | Die 2 | 45 | 45 |
| *b* | | Die 3 | 5.00 | 2.50 |
| *c* | | Die 4 | 10 | 10 |
| *d* | | Die 5 | 35 | 25 |
| *e* | | Die 6 | 30 | 25 |
| *f* | | Die 7 | 30.00 | 15.00 |
| *g* | | Die 8 | 9.00 | 7.00 |
| U414 | U91 | 2c car, *blue* | 30 | 10 |
| *a* | | Die 2 | 25 | 20 |
| *b* | | Die 3 | 50 | 35 |
| *c* | | Die 4 | 10 | 8 |
| *d* | | Die 5 | 50 | 30 |
| *e* | | Die 6 | 25 | 15 |
| *f* | | Die 7 | 10.00 | 6.00 |
| *g* | | Die 8 | 10.00 | 6.00 |
| W415 | U91 | 2c car, *manila* | 3.00 | 1.75 |
| *a* | | Die 2 | 2.00 | 90 |
| *b* | | Die 5 | 2.00 | 90 |
| *c* | | Die 7 | 35.00 | 30.00 |

"F" 1mm from left "4" — Die 1

"F" 1¾mm from left "4" — Die 2

| | | | | |
|---|---|---|---|---|
| U416 | U90 | 4c blk, die 2 | 2.75 | 1.50 |
| *a* | | Die 1 | 3.75 | 2.75 |
| U417 | U90 | 4c blk, *amb*, die 2 | 4.00 | 2.00 |
| *a* | | Die 1 | 4.00 | 2.00 |

Die 1-Tall "F" in "FIVE"

Die 2-Short "F" in "FIVE"

| | | | | |
|---|---|---|---|---|
| U418 | U91 | 5c bl, die 2 | 5.00 | 1.75 |
| *a* | | Die 1 | 5.00 | 1.75 |
| *b* | | 5c bl, *buff*, die 2 (error) | *700.00* | |
| *c* | | 5c bl, *blue*, die 2 (error) | *700.00* | |
| *d* | | 5c bl, *blue*, die 1 (error) | *800.00* | |
| U419 | U91 | 5c bl, *amb*, die 2 | 10.00 | 9.00 |
| *a* | | Die 1 | 10.00 | 9.00 |

Franklin U92

Washington U93

Die 1

Die 2

Die 3

Die 4

Die 5

(The 1c and 4c dies are the same except for figures of value.)
Die 1. UNITED nearer inner circle than outer circle.
Die 2. Large U; large NT closely spaced.
Die 3. Knob of hair at back of neck. Large NT widely spaced.
Die 4. UNITED nearer outer circle than inner circle.
Die 5. Narrow oval C, (also O and G).

Some of the engraved dies of this series represent printing methods now obsolete, others are still in service. Some are best distinguished in the entire envelope. Many electrotypes were used.

**1916-32** **Die 1**

| | | | | |
|---|---|---|---|---|
| U420 | U92 | 1c green | 6 | 5 |
| *a* | | Die 2 | 60.00 | 45.00 |
| *b* | | Die 3 | 8 | 5 |
| *c* | | Die 4 | 12 | 10 |
| *d* | | Die 5 | 12 | 10 |
| U421 | U92 | 1c grn, *amber* | 30 | 30 |
| *a* | | Die 2 | 250.00 | 150.00 |
| *b* | | Die 3 | 1.00 | 50 |
| *c* | | Die 4 | 1.00 | 40 |
| *d* | | Die 5 | 80 | 30 |
| U422 | U92 | 1c grn, *oriental buff* | 1.25 | 75 |
| *a* | | Die 4 | 3.00 | 1.00 |
| U423 | U92 | 1c green, *blue* | 35 | 8 |
| *a* | | Die 3 | 60 | 40 |
| *b* | | Die 4 | 1.00 | 40 |
| *c* | | Die 5 | 60 | 30 |
| U424 | U92 | 1c grn, (unglazed) *man* | 5.00 | 3.00 |
| W425 | U92 | 1c grn, (unglazed) *man* | 8 | 6 |
| *a* | | Die 3 | 125.00 | 110.00 |
| U426 | U92 | 1c grn, (glazed) *brn* ('20) | 20.00 | 12.50 |
| W427 | U92 | 1c grn, (glazed) *brn* ('20) | 60.00 | |
| U428 | U92 | 1c grn, (unglazed) *brn* ('20) | 6.00 | 6.00 |

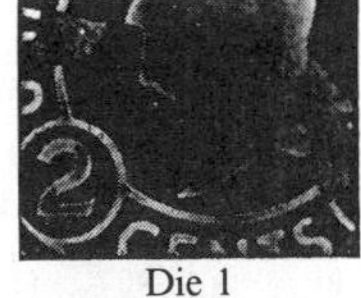
Die 1 Die 2

Die 3

Die 4

Die 5 Die 6

Die 7

Die 8

Die 9

(The 1½c, 2c, 3c, 5c, and 6c are the same except for figures of value.)
Die 1. Letters broad. Numerals vertical. Large head (9¼mm.) from tip of nose to back of neck. E closer to inner circle than N of cents.
Die 2. Similar to 1; but U far from left circle.
Die 3. Similar to 2; but all inner circles very thin (Rejected Die).
Die 4. Similar to 1; but very close to left circle.
Die 5. Small head (8¾mm) from tip of nose to back of neck. T and S of CENTS close at bottom.
Die 6. Similar to 5; but T and S of CENTS far apart at bottom. Left numeral slopes to right.
Die 7. Large head. Both numerals slope to right.

Clean cut lettering. All letters T have short top strokes.
Die 8. Similar to 7; but all letters T have long top strokes.
Die 9. Narrow oval C, (also O and G).

**Die 1**

U429 U93 2c car 5 5
a Die 2 7.00 5.00
b Die 3 25.00 20.00
c Die 4 7.00 6.00
d Die 5 25 15
e Die 6 25 15
f Die 7 30 15
g Die 8 25 10
h Die 9 15 6
i 2c green, error, die 1, entire 4,250.
j 2c car, die 1 with added impression of 1c grn (#U420), die 1, entire 550.00
k Die 1, with added impression of 4c blk (#U416a), entire 500.00
l Die 1, with added impression of 1c grn (#U400), die 1, entire 400.00
U430 U93 2c car, *amber* 12 6
a Die 2 8.50 6.00
b Die 4 17.50 9.00
c Die 5 25 25
d Die 6 45 15
e Die 7 35 20
f Die 8 35 20
g Die 9 25 8
U431 U93 2c car, *oriental buff* 1.25 35
a Die 2 80.00 30.00
b Die 4 25.00 25.00
c Die 5 2.00 1.00
d Die 6 2.50 1.10
e Die 7 2.50 1.10
U432 U93 2c car, *blue* 10 5
b Die 2 20.00 15.00
c Die 3 85.00 75.00
d Die 4 20.00 20.00
e Die 5 30 10
f Die 6 20 16
g Die 7 30 15
h Die 8 35 20
i Die 9 30 20
U432A U93 2c car, *manila*, die 7, entire —
W433 U93 2c car, *manila* 20 15
W434 U93 2c car, (glazed) *brn* ('20) 75.00 50.00
W435 U93 2c carmine, (unglazed) *brn* ('20) 75.00 50.00
U436 U93 3c dk vio 40 15
a 3c purple ('32), die 1 25 15
b 3c dark violet, die 5 1.00 10
c 3c dark violet, die 6 1.25 25
d 3c dark violet, die 7 1.00 10
e 3c pur ('32), die 7 30 10
f 3c pur ('32), die 9 10 5
g 3c car (error), die 1 25.00 25.00
h 3c car (error), die 5 25.00 25.00
i 3c dk vio, die 1, with added impression of 1c grn (#U420), die 1, entire 500.00
j 3c dk violet, die 1, with added impression of 2c car (#U429), die 1, entire 600.00 —
U437 U93 3c dk vio, *amb* 1.90 75
a 3c pur ('32), die 1 15 5
b 3c dark vio, die 5 4.00 1.25
c 3c dark vio, die 6 4.50 1.25
d 3c dark vio, die 7 3.25 80
e 3c pur ('32), die 7 50 10
f 3c pur ('32), die 9 35 10
g 3c car (error), die 5 300.00 225.00
h 3c blk (error), die 1 140.00 —
U438 U93 3c dk vio, *oriental buff* 18.00 1.00
a Die 5 18.00 75
b Die 6 20.00 1.25
c Die 7 30.00 3.00
U439 U93 3c dk vio, *bl* 5.25 1.00
a 3c pur ('32), die 1 18 5
b 3c dark vio, die 5 5.00 2.00
c 3c dark vio, die 6 4.50 2.50
d 3c dark vio, die 7 7.50 2.75
e 3c pur ('32), die 7 30 20
f 3c pur ('32), die 9 30 10
g 3c car (error), die 5 275.00 275.00
U440 U92 4c blk 60 35
a 4c blk with added impression of 2c car (#U429), die 1, entire 225.00
U441 U92 4c blk, *amb* 2.00 55
U442 U92 4c blk, *bl* ('21) 2.00 40
U443 U93 5c blue 2.00 50
U444 U93 5c bl, *amber* 2.50 75
U445 U93 5c bl, *blue* ('21) 2.75 75

See Nos. U529-U531.

Listings of double or triple surcharges of 1920-25 are for specimens with the surcharges directly or partly upon the stamp.

Surcharged Type 1

**1920-21**

U446 U93 2c on 3c dk vio (U436) 8.50 9.00
a Die 5 8.50 9.00

Surcharged Type 2

**Rose Surcharge**

U447 U93 2c on 3c dk vio (U436) 4.75 5.00
b Die 6 4.75 5.00

**Black Surcharge**

U447A U93 2c on 2c car (U429) 1,500.
U447C U93 2c on 2c car, *amb* (U430) —
U448 U93 2c on 3c dk vio (U436) 1.75 1.75
U449 U93 2c on 3c dk vio, *amb* (U437) 4.00 4.00
U450 U93 2c on 3c dk vio, *oriental buff* (U438) 12.00 12.00
U451 U93 2c on 3c dk vio, *blue* (U439) 9.50 10.00

Surcharged Type 3

2

**Bars 2mm apart**

U451A U90 2c on 1c grn (U400) 1,500.
U452 U92 2c on 1c grn (U420) 750.00
a Dbl. surch., Type 3 850.00
U453 U91 2c on 2c car (U411) 750.00
a Die 4 750.00
U453B U91 2c on 2c car, *bl* (U414e) 625.00
U453C U91 2c on 2c car, *oriental buff* (U413e) 650.00 600.00
d Die 1 650.00
U454 U93 2c on 2c car (U429) 75.00
U455 U93 2c on 2c car, *amb* (U430) 850.00
U456 U93 2c on 2c car, *oriental buff* (U431) 150.00
a Dbl. surch., Type 3 225.00
U457 U93 2c on 2c car, *bl* (U432) 175.00
U458 U93 2c on 3c dk vio (U436) 30 30
a Double surcharge 12.00 6.00
b Triple surcharge 27.50
c Dbl. surch., one in mag 55.00
d Dbl. surcharge, Types 2 & 3 85.00
U459 U93 2c on 3c dk vio, *amb* (U437) 2.00 75
a Dbl. surch., Type 3 15.00
b Double surcharge, Types 2 & 3 67.50
U460 U93 2c on 3c dk vio, *oriental buff* (U438) 2.00 75
a Double surcharge 9.00
b Triple surcharge 22.50
U461 U93 2c on 3c dk vio, *bl* (U439) 3.25 75
a Double surcharge 12.00
U462 U87 2c on 4c choc (U390) 300.00 150.00
U463 U87 2c on 4c choc, *amb* (U391) 300.00 75.00
U463A U90 2c on 4c blk (U416) 650.00 375.00
U464 U93 2c on 5c bl (U443) 800.00

Surcharged Type 4

2

Similar to Type 3, but bars 1½mm apart.

U465 U92 2c on 1c grn (U420) 750.00
U466 U91 2c on 2c car (U411e) *2,750.*
U466A U93 2c on 2c car (U429) 190.00
c Die 5 350.00
U466B U93 2c on 2c car, *amb* (U430) 1,500.
U467 U45 2c on 3c grn (U163) 210.00
U468 U93 2c on 3c dk vio (U436) 45 30
a Double surcharge 12.00
b Triple surcharge 15.00
c Inverted surcharge 60.00
d Dbl. surch., Types 2 & 4 60.00
e 2c on 3c car (error) (U436h) 375.00
U469 U93 2c on 3c dk vio, *amb* (U437) 2.50 1.50
a Dbl. surch., Types 2 & 4 50.00
U470 U93 2c on 3c dk vio, *oriental buff* (U438) 3.50 2.00
a Double surcharge, Type 4 15.00
b Dbl. surch., Types 2 & 4 50.00
U471 U93 2c on 3c dk vio, *bl* (U439) 3.00 1.00
a Double surcharge, Type 4 15.00
b Dbl. surch., Types 2 & 4 125.00
U472 U87 2c on 4c choc (U390) 9.50 8.00
a Double surcharge 30.00
U473 U87 2c on 4c choc, *amb* (U391) 11.00 7.50

1 CENT

Dbl. Surch., Type 4 and as above

U474 U93 2c on 1c on 3c dk vio (U436) 200.00
U475 U93 2c on 1c on 3c dk vio, *amb* (U437) 200.00

Surcharged Type 5

2

U476 U93 2c on 3c dk vio, *amb* (U437 85.00
a Double surcharge —

Surcharged Type 6

2

U477 U93 2c on 3c dk vio (U436) 85.00
U478 U93 2c on 3c dk vio, *amb* (U437) 175.00

Handstamped Surcharge in Black or Violet — Type 7

2

U479 U93 2c on 3c dk vio (Bk) (U436) 275.00
U480 U93 2c on 3c dk vio (V) (U436d) 1,000.

Type of 1916-32 Issue

**1925-34**

U481 U93 1½c brn, die 1 10 6
a Die 8 15 10
b 1½c pur, die 1 (error) ('34) 75.00
U482 U93 1½c brn, die 1, *amb* 75 20
a Die 8 85 35
U483 U93 1½c brn, die 1, *bl* 1.25 60
a Die 8 1.40 65
U484 U93 1½c brn, die 1, *man* 5.00 2.00
W485 U93 1½c brn, die 1, *man* 60 10
a With added impression of W433 100.00

Surcharged Type 8

1½

**1925**

U486 U71 1½c on 2c grn (U311) 575.00
U487 U71 1½c on 2c grn, *amb* (U312) 675.00
U488 U77 1½c on 1c grn (U352) 500.00
U489 U77 1½c on 1c grn, *amb* (U353) 75.00 70.00
U490 U90 1½c on 1c grn (U400) 3.00 3.00
a Die 2 10.00 8.00
b Die 4 5.00 2.00
U491 U90 1½c on 1c grn, *amb* (U401) 6.00 2.00
a Die 2 60.00 60.00
b Die 4 3.50 1.75
U492 U90 1½c on 1c grn, *oriental buff* (U402a) 175.00 75.00
a Die 4 175.00 75.00
U493 U90 1½c on 1c grn, *bl* (U403c) 75.00 55.00
a Die 2 75.00 55.00
U494 U90 1½c on 1c grn, *man* (U404) 190.00 75.00
U495 U92 1½c on 1c grn (U420) 25 15
a Die 3 1.10 50
b Die 4 1.50 50
c Double surcharge 3.00 1.50
U496 U92 1½c on 1c grn, *amb* (U421) 12.00 12.00
U497 U92 1½c on 1c grn, *oriental buff* (U422) 2.50 1.50
U498 U92 1½c on 1c grn, *bl* (U423) 75 50
U499 U92 1½c on 1c grn, *man* (U424) 9.00 6.00
U500 U92 1½c on 1c grn, *brn* (unglazed) (U428) 50.00 30.00
U501 U93 1½c on 1c grn, *brn* (glazed) (U426) 50.00 25.00
U502 U93 1½c on 2c car (U429) 225.00 —
U503 U93 1½c on 2c car, *oriental buff* (U431) 250.00 —
a Double surcharge —
U504 U93 1½c on 2c car, *bl* (U432) 225.00 —

**On Envelopes of 1925**

U505 U93 1½c on 1½c brn (U481) 375.00
a Die 8 450.00
U506 U93 1½c on 1½c brn, *bl* (U483) 300.00

The paper of No. U500 is not glazed and appears to be the same as that used for wrappers of 1920.

Surcharged Type 9

1½

**Black Surcharge**

U507 U69 1½c on 1c bl (U294) 1,000.
U508 U77 1½c on 1c grn, *amb* (U353) 45.00
U508A U85 1½c on 1c grn (U379) 1,150.
U509 U85 1½c on 1c grn, *amb* (U380) 10.00 10.00
a Double surcharge 20.00
U509B U85 1½c on 1c grn, *oriental buff* (U381) 45.00 40.00
U510 U90 1½c on 1c grn (U400) 1.50 1.00
a Double surcharge 5.00
b Die 2 5.00 3.00
c Die 3 14.00 7.00
d Die 4 2.50 1.00
U511 U90 1½c on 1c grn, *amb* (U401) 150.00 75.00
U512 U90 1½c on 1c grn, *oriental buff* (U402) 5.00 3.00
a Die 4 15.00 12.00
U513 U90 1½c on 1c grn, *bl* (U403) 4.00 2.00
a Die 4 4.00 3.00
U514 U90 1½c on 1c grn, *man* (U404) 15.00 7.50
a Die 3 50.00 50.00

*U515* U92 1½c on 1c grn (U420) 25 15
- *a* Double surcharge 5.00
- *b* Inverted surcharge 7.50
- *c* Triple surcharge 8.50

*U516* U92 1½c on 1c grn, *amb* (U421) 35.00 25.00

*U517* U92 1½c on 1c grn, *oriental buff* (U422) 3.50 1.00

*U518* U92 1½c on 1c grn, *bl* (U423) 3.50 1.00
- *a* Double surcharge 7.00

*U519* U92 1½c on 1c grn, *man* (U424) 15.00 10.00
- *a* Double surcharge 20.00

*U520* U93 1½c on 2c car (U429) 150.00 —

### Magenta Surcharge

*U521* U92 1½c on 1c grn (U420) 3.50 3.00
- *a* Double surcharge 20.00

### Sesquicentennial Exposition Issue

Liberty Bell — U94

Die 1. The center bar of "E" of "POSTAGE" is shorter than top bar.
Die 2. The center bar of "E" of "POSTAGE" is of same length as top bar.

**1926**

*U522* U94 2c carmine, die 1 1.50 50
- *a* Die 2 8.50 6.00

See note below No. 627.

### Washington Bicentennial Issue

Mount Vernon U95

2 cent:
Die 1. "S" of "POSTAGE" normal.
Die 2. "S" of "POSTAGE" raised.

**1932**

*U523* U95 1c olive green 1.75 1.25
*U524* U95 1½c chocolate 3.50 1.75
*U525* U95 2c car, die 1 40 5
- *a* Die 2 90.00 15.00
- *b* Die 1, *blue*, entire (error) *10,000.*

*U526* U95 3c violet 3.50 35
*U527* U95 4c black 25.00 15.00
*U528* U95 5c dark blue 5.00 4.00
*Nos. U523-U528 (6)* 39.15 22.40

Bicen. of the birth of Washington.

**1932** **Die 7**

*U529* U93 6c orange 4.50 2.75
*U530* U93 6c orange, *amber* 10.00 7.50
*U531* U93 6c orange, *blue* 10.00 7.50

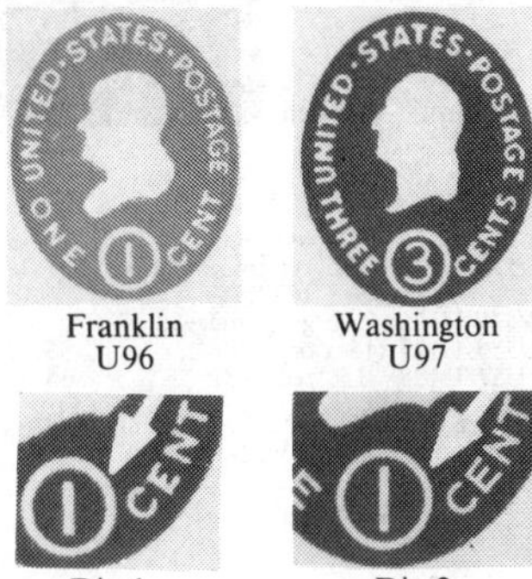

Franklin U96 — Washington U97

Die 1 — Die 2

Die 3

Die 1. Short (3½mm) and thick "1" in thick circle.
Die 2. Tall (4½mm) and thin "1" in thin circle; upper and lower bars of E in ONE long and 1mm from circle.
Die 3. As in Die 2, but E normal and 1½mm from circle.

**1950**

*U532* U96 1c green, die 1 5.00 1.75
- *a* Die 2 5.00 3.00
- *b* Die 3 5.00 3.00
- Die 3, precanceled 60

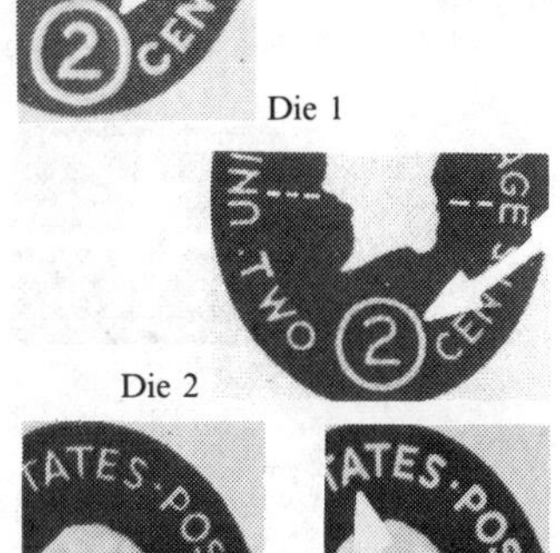

Die 1 — Die 2

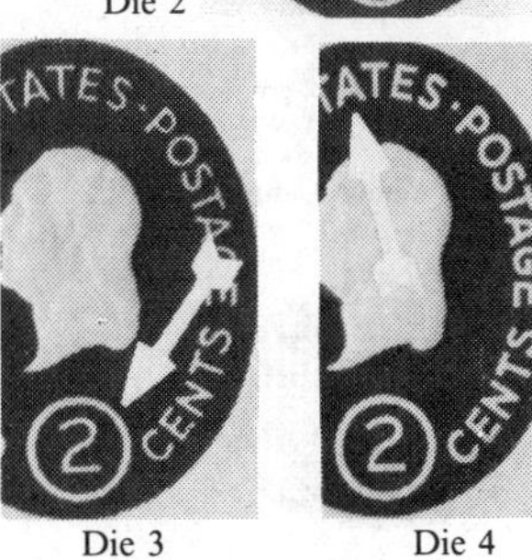

Die 3 — Die 4

Die 1. Thick "2" in circle; toe of "2" is an acute angle.
Die 2. Thin "2" in thin circle; toe of "2" is almost right angle; line through stand of "E" in POSTAGE goes considerably below tip of chin; "N" of UNITED is tall; "O" of TWO is high.
Die 3. Thin "2" in thin circle; toe of "2" is almost right angle; short UN in UNITED: thin crossbar in A of STATES.
Die 4. Tall UN in UNITED; thick crossbar in A of STATES; otherwise like Die 3.

*U533* U97 2c carmine, die 3 65 8
- *a* Die 1 75 25
- *b* Die 2 1.30 80
- *c* Die 4 1.20 50

Die 1

Die 2

Die 3

Die 4

Die 5

Die 1. Thick and tall (4½mm) "3" in thick circle; long top bars and short stems in T's of STATES.
Die 2. Thin and tall (4½mm) "3" in medium circle; short top bars and long stems in T's of STATES.
Die 3. Thin and short (4mm) "3" in thin circle; lettering wider than Dies 1 and 2; line from left stand of N to stand of E is distinctly below tip of chin.
Die 4. Figure and letters as in Die 3. Line hits tip of chin; short N in UNITED and thin crossbar in A of STATES.
Die 5. Figure, letter and chin line as in Die 4; but tall N in UNITED and thick crossbar in A of STATES.

*U534* U97 3c dk violet, die 4 35 10
- *a* Die 1 1.25 30
- *b* Die 2 65 25
- *c* Die 3 50 25
- *d* Die 5 50 30

Washington — U98

**1952**

*U535* U98 1½c brown 4.50 3.50
- Precanceled 35

Die 1

Die 2

Die 3

Die 1. Head high in oval (2mm below T of STATES). Circle near (1mm) bottom of colored oval.
Die 2. Head low in oval (3mm). Circle 1½mm. from edge of oval. Right leg of A of POSTAGE shorter than left. Short leg on P.
Die 3. Head centered in oval (2½mm). Circle as in Die 2. Legs of A of POSTAGE about equal. Long leg on P.

**1958**

*U536* U96 4c red violet, die 1 75 10
- *a* Die 2 1.00 10
- *b* Die 3 1.00 10

Nos. U429, U429f, U429h, U533, U533a-U533c Surcharged in Red at Left of Stamp — b

**1958**

*U537* U93 2c + 2c car, die 1 3.00 1.50
- *a* 2c + 2c carmine, die 7 10.00 7.00
- *b* 2c + 2c carmine, die 9 5.00 4.00

*U538* U97 2c + 2c car, die 1 75 18
- *a* 2c + 2c carmine, die 2 1.00 —
- *b* 2c + 2c carmine, die 3 80 15
- *c* 2c + 2c carmine, die 4 80 —

Nos. U436a, U436e-U436f, U534a-U534d Surcharged in Green at Left of Stamp — a

*U539* U93 3c + 1c pur, die 1 14.00 11.50
- *a* 3c + 1c purple, die 7 12.00 10.00
- *b* 3c + 1c purple, die 9 30.00 16.00

*U540* U97 3c + 1c dk vio, die 3 50 10
- *a* 3c + 1c dk vio, die 2, entire *900.00* —
- *b* 3c + 1c dark violet, die 4 75 10
- *c* 3c + 1c dark violet, die 5 75 10

See No. U545.

Franklin U99

Washington U100

Die 1 — Die 2

Dies of 1¼c
Die 1. The "4" is 3mm high. Upper leaf in left cluster 2mm from "U."
Die 2. The "4" is 3½mm high. Leaf clusters are larger. Upper leaf at left is 1mm from "U."

**1960**

*U541* U99 1¼c turq, die 1 70 50
- Die 1, precanceled 5
- *a* Die 2, precanceled 2.00

*U542* U100 2½c dull blue 80 50
- Precanceled 10

### Pony Express Centennial Issue

Pony Express Rider U101

Envelope White Outside, Blue Inside

**1960, July 19**

*U543* U101 4c brown 60 30

Abraham Lincoln — U102

Die 1

Die 2

Die 3

Die 1. Center bar of E of POSTAGE is above the middle. Center bar of E of STATES slants slightly upward. Nose sharper, more pointed. No offset ink specks inside envelope on back of die impression.
Die 2. Center bar of E in POSTAGE in middle. P of POSTAGE has short stem. Ink specks on back of die impression.
Die 3. FI of FIVE closer than Die 1 or 2. Second T of STATES seems taller than ES. Ink specks on back of die impression.

**1962, Nov. 19**

*U544* U102 5c dark bl, die 2 80 20
*a* Die 1 85 25
*b* Die 3 90 30
*c* Die 2 with albino impression of 4c (#U536) 45.00 —
*d* Die 3 with albino impression of 4c (#U536) 67.50 —

### No. U536 Surcharged Type "a" in Green at Left of Stamp

Two types of surcharge "a":
Type I. "U.S. POSTAGE" 18½mm high. Serifs on cross of T both diagonal. Two lines of shading in C of CENT.
Type II. "U.S. POSTAGE" 17½mm high. Right serif on cross of T is vertical. Three shading lines in C.

**1962, Nov.**

*U545* U96 4c + 1c red vio, Type I 1.30 50
*a* Type II 1.30 50

### New York World's Fair (1964-65)

Globe with Satellite Orbit U103

**1964, Apr. 22**

*U546* U103 5c carmine rose 60 40

Liberty Bell U104

Old Ironsides U105

Eagle — U106

Head of Statue of Liberty — U107

**1965-69 Tagged (6c)**

*U547* U104 1¼c brown 15
*U548* U104 1⁴⁄₁₀c brown ('68) 10
*U548A* U104 1⁶⁄₁₀c orange ('69) 10
*U549* U105 4c bright bl 75 10
*U550* U106 5c bright pur 75 5
*a* Tagged ('67) 60 5
*U551* U107 6c lt grn ('68) 70 5

Issue dates: 5c, Jan. 5; 1¼c, Jan. 6; 6c, Jan. 4; 1⁴⁄₁₀c, Mar. 26; 1⁶⁄₁₀c, June 16.
No. U550a has a luminescent panel 9x29mm at left of stamp. It glows yellow green under ultraviolet light.

### Nos. U549-U550 Surcharged Types "b" and "a" in Red or Green at Left of Stamp

**1968, Feb. 5**

*U552* U105 4c + 2c brt blue (R) 3.75 1.50
*U553* U106 5c + 1c brt pur (G) 3.50 2.50
*a* Tagged 3.50 2.50

**Tagging**
Envelopes from No. U554 onward are tagged, with the tagging element in the ink unless otherwise noted.

### Herman Melville Issue

Moby Dick — U108

**1970, Mar. 7**

*U554* U108 6c light blue 50 15

Herman Melville (1819-91), writer, and the whaling industry.

### Youth Conference Issue

Youth Conference Emblem U109

**1971, Feb. 24**

*U555* U109 6c light blue 75 15

White House Conference on Youth, Estes Park, Colo., Apr. 18-22.

Bell Type of 1965-69 and

Eagle — U110

**1971 Untagged (1⁷⁄₁₀c)**

*U556* U104 1⁷⁄₁₀c deep lilac 8
*U557* U110 8c brt ultra 40 5

Issue dates: 1⁷⁄₁₀c, May 10; 8c, May 6.

Nos. U551 and U555 Surcharged in Green at Left of Stamp

**1971, May 16**

*U561* U107 6c + (2c) light grn 1.00 30
*U562* U109 6c + (2c) light bl 2.50 1.00

### Bowling Issue

Bowling Ball and Pin — U111

**1971, Aug. 21**

*U563* U111 8c rose red 50 15

Salute to bowling and 7th World Tournament of the Intl. Bowling Fed., Milwaukee, WI.

### Aging Conference Issue

Conference Symbol — U112

**1971, Nov. 5**

*U564* U112 8c light blue 50 15

White House Conference on Aging, Washington, DC, Nov. 28-Dec. 2, 1971.

### International Transportation Exhibition Issue

Transportation Exhibition Emblem — U113

(Illustration ⅔ actual size.)

**1972, May 2**

*U565* U113 8c ultra & rose red 50 5

US Intl. Transportation Exhib., Dulles Intl. Airport, Washington, May 27-June 4.

### No. U557 Surcharged Type "b" in Ultramarine at Left of Stamp

**1973, Dec. 1**

*U566* U110 8c + 2c bright ultra 40 5

Liberty Bell — U114

**1973, Dec. 5**

*U567* U114 10c emerald 35 5

"Volunteer Yourself" — U115

**1974, Aug. 23**

*U568* U115 1⁸⁄₁₀c bl grn, untagged 8

### US Tennis Centenary Issue

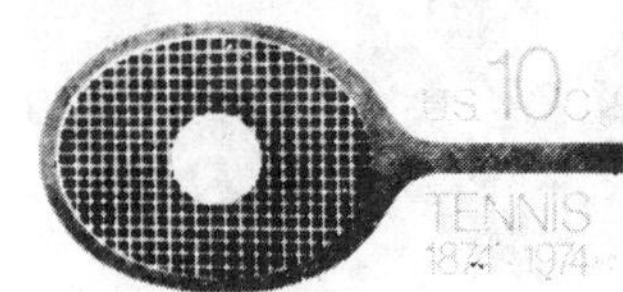


Tennis Racquet — U116

**1974, Aug. 31**

*U569* U116 10c yel, brt bl & lt grn 24 15

### Bicentennial Era Issue

The Seafaring Tradition--Compass Rose — U118

The American Homemaker--Quilt Pattern — U119

The American Farmer--Sheaf of Wheat — U120

The American Doctor — U121

The American Craftsman--Tools, c. 1750 — U122

Designs (in brown on left side of envelope): 10c, Norwegian sloop Restaurationen. No. U572, Spinning wheel. No. U573, Plow. No. U574, Colonial era medical instruments and bottle. No. U575, Shaker rocking chair.

### Light Brown Diagonally Laid Paper

**1975-76**

*U571* U118 10c brn & bl 24 15
*a* Brown ("10c/USA") omitted, entire 125.00
*U572* U119 13c brn & bl grn 30 15
*a* Brown ("13c/USA") omitted, entire 125.00
*U573* U120 13c brn & brt grn 30 15
*a* Brown ("13c/USA") omitted, entire —
*U574* U121 13c brn & org 30 15
*U575* U122 13c brn & car 30 13
*a* Brown ("13c/USA") omitted, entire —

Issue dates: 10c, Oct. 13, 1975. No. U572, Feb. 2, 1976. No. U573, Mar. 15, 1976. No. 574, June 30, 1976. No. U575, Aug. 6, 1976.

Liberty Tree, Boston, 1646 — U123

**1975, Nov. 8**

*U576* U123 13c orange brown 30 13

Star and Pinwheel — U124

U125

U126

Eagle — U127

"Uncle Sam" — U128

**1976-78**

*U577* U124 2c red, untagged ('76) 5
*U578* U125 2.1c yel grn, untagged ('77) 5
*U579* U126 2.7c grn, untagged ('78) 5
*U580* U127 (15c) org ('78) 35 15
*U581* U128 15c red ('78) 35 15

Issue dates; 2c, Sept. 10. 2.1c June 3. 2.7c, July 5. A, May 22. 15c, June 3.

### Bicentennial Issue

Centennial Envelope, 1876 — U129

**1976, Oct. 15**

*U582* U129 13c emerald 30 13

See Nos. U218-U221.

### Golf Issue

Golf Club in Motion and Golf Ball — U130

**1977, Apr. 7**

*U583* U130 13c blk, bl & yel grn 30 13
- *a* Black omitted, entire —
- *b* Black & blue omitted, entire —

### Energy Issue

Energy Conservation U131

Energy Development U132

**1977, Oct. 20**

*U584* U131 13c blk, red & yel 30 13
- *a* Red & yel omitted, entire —
- *b* Yellow omitted, entire —
- *c* Black omitted, entire —
- *d* Black & red omitted, entire —

*U585* U132 13c blk, red & yel 30 13

Nos. U584-U585 have a luminescent panel at left of stamp.

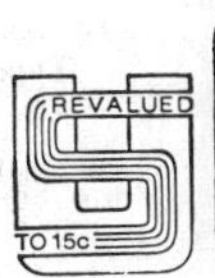

Olive Branch and Star — U133

**1978, July 28**

*U586* U133 15c on 16c blue 35 15
- *a* Surcharge omitted, entire — —
- *b* Surch. on #U581, entire — —

### Auto Racing Issue

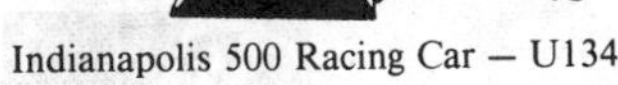

Indianapolis 500 Racing Car — U134

**1978, Sept. 2**

*U587* U134 15c red, bl & blk 35 15
- *a* Black omitted, entire 200.00
- *b* Black & bl omitted, entire —
- *c* Red omitted, entire —

No. U576 Surcharged at left of Stamp Like No. U586

**1978, Nov. 28** **Embossed**

*U588* U123 15c on 13c org brn 35 15

U135

Weaver Violins — U136

U137

Eagle — U138

Star — U139

Eagle U140

**1979-82** **Untagged (3.1c, 3.5c)**

| | | | | |
|---|---|---|---|---|
| *U589* | U135 | 3.1c ultramarine | | 5 |
| *U590* | U136 | 3.5c purple | | 8 |
| *U591* | U137 | 5.9c brown | | 8 |
| *U592* | U138 | (18c) violet | 45 | 18 |
| *U593* | U139 | 18c dark blue | 45 | 18 |
| *U594* | U140 | (20c) brown | 40 | 10 |

Issue dates: 3.1c, May 18; 3.5c, June 23; 5.9c, Feb. 17, 1982. #U592, Mar. 15, 1981; #U593, Apr. 2, 1981; #U594, Oct. 11, 1981.

### Veterinary Medicine Issue

Seal of Veterinarians U141

Design on left side of envelope shows 5 animals and a bird in brown and "Veterinary Medicine" in gray.

**1979, July 24**

*U595* U141 15c brown & gray 35 15

### Olympic Games Issue

U142

Design (multicolored on left side of envelope) shows two soccer players with ball.

**1979, Dec. 10**

*U596* U142 15c red, grn & blk 60 15
- *a* Red & grn omitted, untagged, entire 200.00
- *b* Black omitted, untagged, entire 200.00
- *c* Black & grn omitted, entire 200.00

22nd Olympic Games, Moscow, July 19-Aug. 3, 1980.

### Bicycling Issue

Highwheeler Bicycle — U143

Design (on left side of envelope) shows racing bicycle.

**1980, May 16**

*U597* U143 15c bl & rose claret 35 15
- *a* Blue ("15c USA") omitted —

### America's Cup Yacht Races Issue

Racing Yacht — U144 AMERICA'S CUP

**1980, Sept. 15**

*U598* U144 15c light blue 35 15

Italian Honeybee and Orange Blossoms U145

**Bee & Petals Colorless Embossed**

**1980, Oct. 10**

*U599* U145 15c multicolor 35 15
- *a* Brown ("USA 15c") omitted, entire —

U146

Design: Hand and braille colorless embossed

**1981, Oct. 11**

*U600* U146 18c blue & red 45 18

Capitol Dome U147

**1981, Nov. 13**

*U601* U147 20c deep magenta 45 10

U148

Illustration reduced.

**1982, June 15**

*U602* U148 20c dk bl, blk & mag 45 10
- *a* Dark blue omitted, entire —

U149

**1982, Aug. 6**

*U603* U149 20c purple & black 45 10

U150

**1983, Mar. 21**

*U604* U150 5.2c orange 10

U151

**1983, Aug. 3**

*U605* U151 20c red, bl & blk 45 10

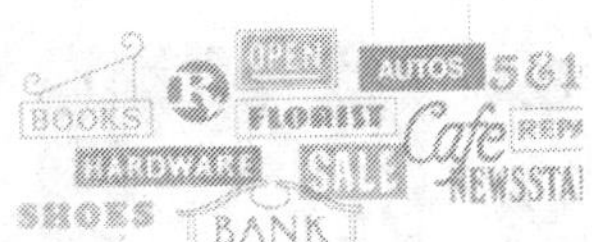

Small Business USA 20c

U152

Design shows storefronts at lower left. Stamp and design continue on back of envelope.

**1984, May 7** **Photo.**

*U606* U152 20c multicolor 50 10

U153

**1985, Feb. 1** **Embossed**

*U607* U153 (22c) deep green 55 12

Bison
U154

**1985, Feb. 25** **Embossed**
*U608* U154 22c violet brown 55 12
*a* Untagged, precanceled with 3 blue lines 15

Frigate U.S.S. Constitution, "Old Ironsides" — U155

**1985, May 3** **Embossed**
*U609* U155 6c green blue 5

Mayflower — U156

Precanceled
**1986, Dec. 4** **Embossed**
**Untagged**
*U610* U156 8.5c blk & gray 5

Stars — U157

**1988, Mar. 26** **Embossed & Typo.**
*U611* U157 25c dark blue & dark red 60 14

Sea Gulls, Frigate USS Constellation — U158

**1988, Apr. 12** **Embossed & Typo.**
*U612* U158 8.4c blk & brt blue 28 6

Snowflake — U159

"Holiday Greetings!" inscribed at lower left.

**1988, Sept. 8** **Typo.**
*U613* U159 25c dark red & green 50 25

## AIR POST STAMPED ENVELOPES AND AIR LETTER SHEETS

UC1 UC2

UC1--Vertical rudder is not semi-circular but slopes down to the left. The tail of the plane projects into the G of POSTAGE.

UC2--Vertical rudder is semi-circular. The tail of the plane touches but does not project into the G of POSTAGE.

6c: Same as UC2 except 3 types of numeral.
Die 2a. Numeral "6" 6½mm wide.
Die 2b. Numeral "6" 6mm wide.
Die 2c. Numeral "6" 5½mm wide.
Die 3: Vertical rudder leans forward. S closer to O than to T of POSTAGE. E of POSTAGE has short center bar.

**1929-44** **Embossed**
*UC1* UC1 5c blue 3.00 1.75
*UC2* UC2 5c blue 12.50 5.00
*UC3* UC2 6c org, die 2a ('34) 1.25 25
*a.* No. UC3 with added impression of 3c pur (#U436a), entire without border *3,000.*
*UC4* UC2 6c org, die 2b ('42) 2.00 1.25
*UC5* UC2 6c org, die 2c ('44) 75 30
*UC6* UC2 6c org, die 3 ('42) 1.00 35
*a.* 6c orange, *blue* (error), die 3, entire *3,500. 2,250.*
*UC7* UC2 8c ol grn ('32) 12.50 3.00

Surcharged in black on envelopes indicated by numbers in brackets.

AIR 6¢ MAIL

**1945**
*UC8* U93 6c on 2c (U429) 1.00 55
*a.* 6c on 1c grn, error, (U420) *1,750.*
*b.* 6c on 3c pur, error, (U436a) *1,750.*
*c.* 6c on 3c pur, error, *amb* (U437a) *3,000.*
*d.* 6c on 3c vio, error, (U526) *3,000.*
*UC9* U95 6c on 2c (U525) 75.00 40.00

Nos. UC8a-UC8d are known only entire.

Surcharged in Black on 6c Orange Air Post Envelopes without borders

REVALUED
5¢
P.O. DEPT.

**1946**
*UC10* UC2 5c on 6c die 2a 2.50 1.25
*a.* Double surcharge 60.00
*UC11* UC2 5c on 6c die 2b 9.00 5.00
*UC12* UC2 5c on 6c die 2c 75 50
*a.* Double surcharge 60.00 60.00
*UC13* UC2 5c on 6c die 3 80 60
*a.* Double surcharge 60.00

The 6c borderless envelopes and the revalued envelopes were issued primarily for use to and from members of the armed forces. The 5c rate came into effect Oct. 1, 1946.

DC-4 Skymaster UC3

Die 1. The end of the wing at the right is a smooth curve. The juncture of the front end of the plane and the engine forms an acute angle. The first T of STATES and the E's of UNITED STATES lean to the left.
Die 2. The end of the wing at the right is a straight line. The juncture of the front end of the plane and the engine is wide open. The first T of STATES and the E's of UNITED STATES lean to the right.

**1946** **Embossed**
*UC14* UC3 5c carmine, die 1 75 20
*UC15* UC3 5c carmine, die 2 85 25

See Nos. UC18, UC26.

DC-4 Skymaster — UC4

Letter Sheet for Foreign Postage

"Air Letter" on face, 2-line inscription on back.

**1947, Apr. 29** **Typo.**
*UC16* UC4 10c brt red, *pale bl,* entire 7.50 6.00
*a.* "Air Letter" on face, 4-line inscription on back ('51), entire 12.50 10.00
*b.* As "a", 10c choc, *pale bl,* entire 400.00
*c.* "Air Letter" and "Aerogramme" on face, 4-line inscription on back ('53), entire 55.00 10.00
*d.* "Air Letter" and "Aerogramme" on face, 3-line inscription on back ('55), entire 8.00 8.00

Washington and Franklin, Early and Modern Mail-carrying Vehicles — UC5

**Embossed, Rotary Press Printing**
**1947, May 21**
*UC17* UC5 5c car, (22¼mm high) 40 25
*a.* Flat plate printing (21¾mm high) 50 30

Cent. of the 1st postage stamps issued by the US Government.

Type of 1946

Type I. 6's lean to right.
Type II. 6's upright.

**1950, Sept. 22**
*UC18* UC3 6c carmine, Type I 25 8
*a.* Type II 75 25

Several other types differ slightly from the two listed.

Nos. UC14, UC15, UC18 Surcharged in Red at Left of Stamp

**1951**
*UC19* UC3 6c on 5c car, die 1 85 50
*UC20* UC3 6c on 5c car, die 2 80 50
*a.* 6c on 6c car, error, entire *1,500.*
*b.* 6c on 5c, double surcharge *250.00* —

Nos. UC14, UC15 and UC17 Surcharged in Red at Left of Stamp

REVALUED
6¢
P.O. DEPT.

**1952**
*UC21* UC3 6c on 5c car, die 1 30.00 15.00
*UC22* UC3 6c on 5c car, die 2 3.50 2.50
*a.* Double surcharge 75.00
*UC23* UC5 6c on 5c car, entire 1,000.

The 6c on 4c black (No. U440) is believed to be a favor printing.

Eagle in Flight — UC6

**1956, May 2** **Embossed**
*UC25* UC6 6c red 75 50

FIPEX, NYC, Apr. 28-May 6. Two types exist, differing mainly in the clouds at top.

Skymaster Type of 1946

**1958, July 31**
*UC26* UC3 7c blue 65 50

Nos. UC3-UC5, UC18 and UC25 Surcharged in Green at Left of Stamp

**1958**
*UC27* UC2 6c + 1c org, die 2a 175.00 200.00
*UC28* UC2 6c + 1c org, die 2b 60.00 75.00
*UC29* UC2 6c + 1c org, die 2c 35.00 50.00
*UC30* UC3 6c + 1c car, Type I 1.00 50
*a.* Type II 1.00 50
*UC31* UC6 6c + 1c red 1.00 50

Jet Airliner — UC7

Letter Sheet for Foreign Postage.

Two types:
I. Back inscription in 3 lines.
II. Back inscription in 2 lines.

**1958-59** **Typo.**
*UC32* UC7 10c bl & red, *bl,* II ('59), entire 6.00 5.00
*a.* Type I ('58), entire 10.00 5.00
*b.* Red omitted, II, entire —
*c.* Blue omitted, II, entire *850.00*

Silhouette of Jet Airliner — UC8

**1958, Nov. 21** **Embossed**
*UC33* UC8 7c blue 60 12

**1960, Aug. 18**
*UC34* UC8 7c carmine 60 12

Jet Plane and Globe — UC9

Letter Sheet for Foreign Postage

**1961, Nov. 16** **Typo.**
*UC35* UC9 11c red & bl, *bl,* entire 2.25 1.50
*a.* Red omitted, entire *850.00*
*b.* Blue omitted, entire *850.00*

UC10

UC11

**1962, Nov. 17** **Embossed**
*UC36* UC10 8c red 50 8

**1965, Jan. 7**
*UC37* UC11 8c red 35 6
*a.* Tagged ('67) 85 30

No. UC37a has a luminescent panel ⅜x1 inches at left of stamp. It glows orange red under ultraviolet light.

Pres. John F. Kennedy and Jet Plane UC12

Letter Sheets for Foreign Postage

**1965-67** **Typo.**
*UC38* UC12 11c red & dk bl, *blue*, entire 3.25 1.00
*UC39* UC12 13c red & dk bl, *blue*, entire 3.00 75
*a.* Red omitted 500.00
*b.* Dark blue omitted 500.00

Issue dates: 11c, May 29, 1965. 13c, May 29, 1967.

UC13

**1968, Jan. 8** **Tagged** **Embossed**
*UC40* UC13 10c red 50 6

No. UC37 Surcharged in Red at Left of Stamp

**1968, Feb. 5**
*UC41* UC11 8c + 2c red 55 15

---

Tagging
Envelopes and Letter Sheets from No. UC42 onward are tagged unless otherwise noted.

---

Globes and Flock of Birds — UC14

Letter Sheet for Foreign Postage

**1968, Dec. 3** **Photo.**
*UC42* UC14 13c gray, brn, org & blk, *blue*, entire 7.50 2.00
*a.* Orange omitted, entire —
*b.* Brown omitted, entire —
*c.* Black omitted, entire —

Intl. Human Rights Year, and 20th anniv. of the UN Declaration of Human Rights.

UC15

**1971, May 6** **Embossed**
*UC43* UC15 11c red & blue 50 10

Birds in Flight and "usa" — UC16

Letter Sheet for Foreign Postage
"postage 15c" in Gray

**1971, May 28** **Photo.**
*UC44* UC16 15c gray, red, white & blue, *blue*, entire 1.50 90
*a.* "AEROGRAMME" added, entire 1.50 90

Folding instructions (2 steps) in capitals on No. UC44; (4 steps) in upper and lower case on No. UC44a. No. UC44a issued Dec. 13. See No. UC46.

No. UC40 Surcharged in Green at Left of Stamp

**1971, June 28** **Embossed**
*UC45* UC13 10c + (1c) red 1.50 20

Letter Sheet for Foreign Postage
"usa" Type of 1971

Design: Three balloons and cloud at left in address section; no birds beside stamp.

"postage 15c" in Blue

**1973, Feb. 10** **Photo.**
*UC46* UC16 15c red, white & bl, *blue*, entire 75 40

Hot Air Ballooning World Championships, Albuquerque, NM, Feb. 10-17. Folding instructions as on No. UC44a, with "INTERNATIONAL HOT AIR BALLOONING" added to inscription.

Bird in Flight — UC17

**1973, Dec. 1** **Embossed**
*UC47* UC17 13c rose red 28 10

---

Beginning with No. UC48 all letter sheets are for Foreign Postage unless noted otherwise.

---

UC18

**1974, Jan. 4** **Photo.**
*UC48* UC18 18c red & blue, *blue*, entire 70 30
*a.* Red omitted, entire —

UC19

Design: "NATO" and NATO emblem in multicolor at left in address section.

**1974, Apr. 4** **Photo.**
*UC49* UC19 18c red & blue, *blue*, entire 70 25

25th anniv. of NATO.

usa/22c
UC20

**1976, Jan. 16** **Photo.**
*UC50* UC20 22c red & blue, *blue*, entire 70 25

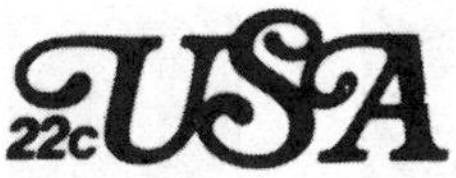

22c USA
UC21

**1978, Nov. 3** **Photo.**
*UC51* UC21 22c bl, *bl*, entire 70 25

UC22

Design (multicolored in bottom left corner) shows discus thrower.

**1979, Dec. 5** **Photo.**
*UC52* UC22 22c red, blk & grn, *bluish*, entire 1.50 22

22nd Olympic Games, Moscow, July 19-Aug. 3, 1980.

UC23

Design shows Statue of Liberty at lower left. Inscribed "Tour the United States," folding area shows tourist attractions.

**1980-81** **Photo.**
*UC53* UC23 30c bl, red & brn, *bl*, entire 60 30
*a.* Red ("30c") omitted, entire —
*UC54* UC23 30c yel, mag, bl & blk, *bl*, entire ('81) 60 30

Issue dates: Dec. 29. Sept. 21, 1981.

UC24

"Made in USA . . . world's best buys."

**1982, Sept. 16** **Photo.**
*UC55* UC24 30c multi, *bl*, entire 60 30

**World Communications Year Issue**

World Map Showing Locations of Satellite Tracking Stations — UC25

**1983, Jan. 7** **Photo.**
*UC56* UC25 30c multi, *bl*, entire 60 30

**1984 Olympics**

Olympics 84
USA
30c
UC26

**1983, Oct. 14** **Photo.**
*UC57* UC26 30c multi, *bl*, entire 60 30

UC27

Design: Satellite over Earth at lower left, with Landsat photographs on folding area. Inscribed: Landsat views the Earth.

**1985, Feb. 14** **Photo.**
*UC58* UC27 36c multi, *bl*, entire 72 36

**National Tourism Week**

Urban Skyline UC28

**1985, May 21** **Photo.**
*UC59* UC28 36c multi, *bl*, entire 72 36

**Mark Twain (1835-1910) and Halley's Comet**

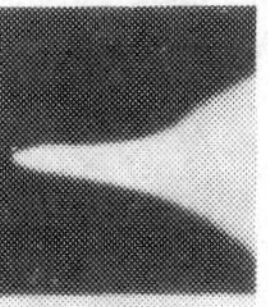

Comet Tail Viewed from Space — UC29

**1985, Dec. 4** **Photo.**
*UC60* UC29 36c multi, entire 72 36

The Scott Catalogue value is a retail price, what you could expect to pay for the stamp in a grade of Fine-Very Fine. The value listed is a reference which reflects recent actual dealer selling price.

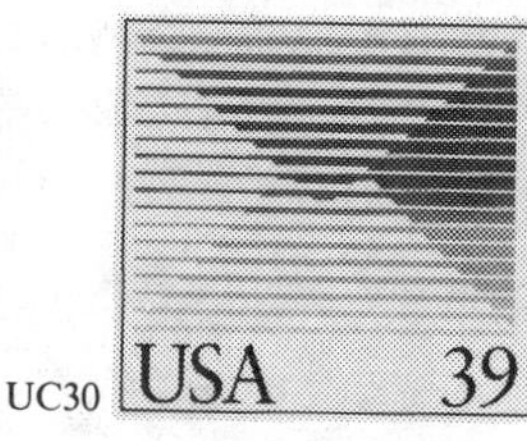

UC30

**1988, May 9** **Litho.**

| | | | | |
|---|---|---|---|---|
| *UC61* | UC30 | 39c multi, entire | 78 | 39 |

POSTAL CARDS
"R.F." CONTROL OVERPRINT
STAMPED ENVELOPES
are listed in Scott's Specialized Catalogue of United States Stamps.
NEWSPAPER WRAPPERS
Included in listings of Stamped Envelopes with prefix "W" instead of "U"
LETTER SHEETS Included with Stamped Envelopes

## OFFICIAL STAMPED ENVELOPES

### Post Office Department

"2" 9mm high — UO1

"3" 9mm high — UO2

"6" 9½mm high — UO3

**1873**

| | | | | |
|---|---|---|---|---|
| *UO1* | UO1 | 2c blk, *lem* | 9.00 | 5.00 |
| *UO2* | UO2 | 3c blk, *lem* | 3.00 | 3.00 |
| *+UO3* | UO2 | 3c black | *6,000.* | |
| *UO4* | UO3 | 6c blk, *lem* | 9.00 | 8.00 |

"2" 9¼mm high — UO4

"3" 9¼mm high — UO5

"6" 10½mm. high — UO6

**1874-79**

| | | | | |
|---|---|---|---|---|
| *UO5* | UO4 | 2c blk, *lem* | 3.00 | 2.50 |
| *UO6* | UO4 | 2c black | 45.00 | 30.00 |
| *UO7* | UO5 | 3c blk, *lem* | 2.00 | 50 |
| *UO8* | UO5 | 3c black | 700.00 | 750.00 |
| *UO9* | UO5 | 3c blk, *amb* | 35.00 | 25.00 |
| *UO10* | UO5 | 3c blk, *bl* | *15,000.* | |
| *UO11* | UO5 | 3c blue, *bl* | *14,000.* | |
| *UO12* | UO6 | 6c blk, *lem* | 3.00 | 2.00 |
| *UO13* | UO6 | 6c black | 525.00 | |

### Postal Service

UO7

**1877**

| | | | | |
|---|---|---|---|---|
| *UO14* | UO7 | black | 3.00 | 2.50 |
| *UO15* | UO7 | blk, *amb* | 20.00 | 15.00 |
| *UO16* | UO7 | blue, *amb* | 25.00 | 16.00 |
| *UO17* | UO7 | blue, *blue* | 4.00 | 4.00 |

### War Department

Franklin — UO8

Jackson — UO9

UO8--Bust points to the end of "N" of "ONE".

UO9--Bust narrow at the back.

Washington UO10

Lincoln UO11

UO10--Queue projects below the bust.

UO11--Neck very long at the back

Jefferson UO12

Clay UO13

UO12--Queue forms straight line with bust.

UO13--Ear partly concealed by hair, mouth large, chin prominent.

Webster UO14

Scott UO15

UO14--Has side whiskers.

Hamilton — UO16

Back of bust very narrow, chin almost straight; the labels containing the letters "U S" are exactly parallel.

**1873**

#### Reay Issue

| | | | | |
|---|---|---|---|---|
| *UO18* | UO8 | 1c dk red | 500.00 | 225.00 |
| *UO19* | UO9 | 2c dk red | 550.00 | 275.00 |
| *UO20* | UO10 | 3c dk red | 45.00 | 30.00 |
| *UO21* | UO10 | 3c dk red, *amb* | *9,000.* | |
| *UO22* | UO10 | 3c dk red, *cr* | 350.00 | 150.00 |
| *UO23* | UO11 | 6c dk red | 150.00 | 50.00 |
| *UO24* | UO11 | 6c dk red, *cr* | 1,250. | 300.00 |
| *UO25* | UO12 | 10c dk red | 2,250. | 250.00 |
| *UO26* | UO13 | 12c dk red | 95.00 | 35.00 |
| *UO27* | UO14 | 15c dk red | 95.00 | 40.00 |
| *UO28* | UO15 | 24c dk red | 100.00 | 30.00 |
| *UO29* | UO16 | 30c dk red | 325.00 | 90.00 |
| *UO30* | UO8 | 1c ver | 135.00 | |
| *WO31* | UO8 | 1c ver, *man* | 6.00 | 2.50 |
| *+UO32* | UO9 | 2c ver | 200.00 | |
| *WO33* | UO9 | 2c ver, *man* | 150.00 | |
| *UO34* | UO10 | 3c ver | 60.00 | 30.00 |
| *UO35* | UO10 | 3c ver, *amb* | 75.00 | |
| *UO36* | UO10 | 3c ver, *cr* | 9.00 | 2.75 |
| *UO37* | UO11 | 6c ver | 65.00 | |
| *UO38* | UO11 | 6c ver, *cr* | 300.00 | |
| *UO39* | UO12 | 10c ver | 175.00 | |
| *UO40* | UO13 | 12c ver | 110.00 | |
| *UO41* | UO14 | 15c ver | 175.00 | |
| *UO42* | UO15 | 24c ver | 300.00 | |
| *UO43* | UO16 | 30c ver | 350.00 | |

UO17

UO18

UO17--Bottom serif on "S" is thick and short, bust at bottom below hair forms sharp point.

UO18--Bottom serif on "S" is thick and short front part of bust is rounded.

UO19

UO20

UO19--Bottom serif on "S" is short, queue does not project below bust.

UO20--Neck very short at the back.

UO21

UO22

UO21--Knot of queue stands out prominently.

UO22--Ear prominent, chin receding.

UO23 UO24

UO23--Has no side whiskers, forelock projects above head.

UO24--Back of bust rather broad; chin slopes considerably; the labels containing letters "U S" are not exactly parallel.

**1875**

#### Plimpton Issue

| | | | | |
|---|---|---|---|---|
| *UO44* | UO17 | 1c red | 90.00 | 75.00 |
| *+UO45* | UO17 | 1c red, *amb* | 600.00 | |
| *+UO45A* | UO17 | 1c red, *org* | *17,500.* | |
| *WO46* | UO17 | 1c red, *man* | 2.00 | 75 |
| *UO47* | UO18 | 2c red | 75.00 | |
| *UO48* | UO18 | 2c red, *amb* | 20.00 | 6.00 |
| *UO49* | UO18 | 2c red, *org* | 30.00 | 10.00 |
| *WO50* | UO18 | 2c red, *man* | 60.00 | 45.00 |
| *UO51* | UO19 | 3c red | 8.00 | 5.00 |
| *UO52* | UO19 | 3c red, *amb* | 9.00 | 5.00 |
| *UO53* | UO19 | 3c red, *cr* | 4.00 | 2.00 |
| *UO54* | UO19 | 3c red, *bl* | 2.00 | 1.50 |
| *UO55* | UO19 | 3c red, *fawn* | 3.00 | 50 |
| *UO56* | UO20 | 6c red | 27.50 | 17.50 |
| *UO57* | UO20 | 6c red, *amb* | 60.00 | 20.00 |
| *UO58* | UO20 | 6c red, *cr* | 150.00 | 60.00 |
| *UO59* | UO21 | 10c red | 110.00 | 75.00 |
| *UO60* | UO21 | 10c red, *amb* | 1,000. | |
| *UO61* | UO22 | 12c red | 30.00 | 30.00 |
| *UO62* | UO22 | 12c red, *amb* | 600.00 | |
| *UO63* | UO22 | 12c red, *cr* | 500.00 | |
| *UO64* | UO23 | 15c red | 125.00 | 90.00 |
| *UO65* | UO23 | 15c red, *amb* | 600.00 | |
| *UO66* | UO23 | 15c red, *cr* | 550.00 | |
| *UO67* | UO24 | 30c red | 125.00 | 90.00 |
| *UO68* | UO24 | 30c red, *amb* | 850.00 | |
| *UO69* | UO24 | 30c red, *cr* | 850.00 | |

## POSTAL SAVINGS STAMPED ENVELOPES

UO25

**1911**

| | | | | |
|---|---|---|---|---|
| *UO70* | UO25 | 1c green | 50.00 | 7.50 |
| *UO71* | UO25 | 1c grn, *oriental buff* | 145.00 | 45.00 |
| *UO72* | UO25 | 2c carmine | 6.00 | 1.50 |
| *a.* | | 2c car, *manila* (error) | *1,400.* | |

## OFFICIAL MAIL

UO26

**1983, Jan. 12**

| | | | | |
|---|---|---|---|---|
| *UO73* | UO26 | 20c blue, entire | 50 | — |

UO27

**1984, Feb. 26**

| | | | | |
|---|---|---|---|---|
| *UO74* | UO27 | 22c blue, entire | 55 | — |

UO28

**1987, Mar. 2** **Typo.**

| | | | | |
|---|---|---|---|---|
| *UO75* | UO28 | 22c blue, entire | 55 | — |

Used exclusively to mail US Savings Bonds.

UO29

**1988, Mar. 22** **Typo.**

| | | | | |
|---|---|---|---|---|
| *UO76* | UO29 | (25c) blk & blue, entire | 60 | — |

Used exclusively to mail US Saving Bonds.

UO30

**1988, Apr. 11 Embossed & Typo.**
*UO77* UO30 25c blk & blue, entire 60 —

UO31

**1988, Apr. 11 Typo.**
*UO78* UO31 25c blk & blue, entire 60 —

Used exclusively to mail US Saving Bonds.

OFFICIAL WRAPPERS
Included in listings of Official Stamped Envelopes with prefix letters "WO" instead of "UO"

## REVENUE STAMPS

Nos. R1-R102 were used to pay taxes on documents and proprietary articles including playing cards. Until Dec. 25, 1862, the law stated that a revenue stamp could be used only for payment of the tax upon the particular instrument or article specified on its face. After that date stamps, except the Proprietary, could be used indiscriminately.

### General Issue

First Issue. Head of Washington in Oval. Various Frames as Illustrated.

**Old Paper**

**Imperf. or Perf. 12**

Nos. R1b to R42b, part perforate, occur perforated sometimes at sides only and sometimes at top and bottom only. The higher values, part perforate, are perforated at sides only. Imperforate and part perforate revenues often bring much more in pairs or blocks than as single copies.

The experimental silk paper is a variety of the old paper and has only a very few minute fragments of fiber.

Some of the stamps were in use eight years and were printed several times. Many color variations occurred, particularly when unstable pigments were used and the color was intended to be purple or violet, such as the 4c Proprietary, 30c and $2.50 stamps. Before 1868 dull colors predominate on these and the early red stamps. In later printings of the 4c Proprietary, 30c and $2.50 stamps, red predominates in the mixture, and on the dollar values the red is brighter. The early $1.90 stamp is dull purple, imperf. or perforated. In a later printing, perforated only, the purple is darker.

R1

R2

R3

R4

R5

**1862-71 Engr.**

*R1* R1 1c Express, red 1.00
a. Imperf. 50.00
b. Part perf. 35.00
d. Silk paper 50.00
*R2* R1 1c Playing Cards, red 125.00
a. Imperf. 800.00
b. Part perf. 400.00
*R3* R1 1c Proprietary, red 35
a. Imperf. 500.00
b. Part perf. 100.00
d. Silk paper 6.00
*R4* R1 1c Telegraph, red 8.00
a. Imperf. 275.00
*R5* R2 2c Bank Check, bl 6
a. Imperf. 75
b. Part perf. 90
e. Vertical pair, imperf. between, old paper —
*R6* R2 2c Bank Check, org 5
b. Part perf. 75.00
d. Silk paper 150.00
e. Old paper, *green* 325.00
*R7* R2 2c Certificate, bl 21.00
a. Imperf. 10.00
*R8* R2 2c Certificate, org 20.00
*R9* R2 2c Express, blue 25
a. Imperf. 10.00
b. Part perf. 12.00
*R10* R2 2c Express, org 6.00
d. Silk paper 30.00
*R11* R2 2c Playing Cards, bl 3.00
b. Part perf. 130.00
*R12* R2 2c Playing Cards, org 25.00
*R13* R2 2c Proprietary, bl 35
b. Part perf. 120.00
d. Silk paper 12.50
e. Ultramarine 150.00
*R14* R3 2c Proprietary, org 30.00
*R15* R3 2c U.S. Int. Rev., org ('64) 5
d. Silk paper 12
e. Old paper, *green* 350.00
*R16* R3 3c For. Exch., grn 2.50
b. Part perf. 150.00
d. Silk paper 17.50
*R17* R3 3c Playing Cards, grn ('63) 100.00
a. Imperf. *6,750.*
*R18* R3 3c Proprietary, grn 1.75
b. Part perf. 175.00
d. Silk paper 15.00
e. Printed on both sides, old paper —
*R19* R3 3c Telegraph, grn 2.25
a. Imperf. 45.00
b. Part perf. 16.00
d. Silk paper —
*R20* R3 4c Inland Exch., brown ('63) 1.50
d. Silk paper 17.50
*R21* R3 4c Playing Cards, slate ('63) 350.00
*R22* R3 4c Proprietary, pur 2.50
b. Part perf. 200.00
d. Silk paper 22.50

Many shade and color variations of No. R22. See foreword, "Revenue Stamps."

*R23* R3 5c Agreement, red 20
d. Silk paper 1.00
*R24* R3 5c Certificate, red 10
a. Imperf. 2.00
b. Part perf. 8.00
d. Silk paper 30
*R25* R3 5c Express, red 25
a. Imperf. 3.50
b. Part perf. 4.00
*R26* R3 5c Foreign Exchange, red 25
b. Part perf. —
d. Silk paper 100.00
*R27* R3 5c Inland Exch., red 10
a. Imperf. 3.50
b. Part perf. 3.00
d. Silk paper 7.00
*R28* R3 5c Playing Cards, red ('63) 12.00
*R29* R3 5c Proprietary, red ('64) 16.00
d. Silk paper 40.00
*R30* R3 6c Inland Exch., orange ('63) 90
d. Silk paper 25.00
*R31* R3 6c Proprietary, org ('71) *1,250.*

Nearly all copies of No. R31 are faulty or repaired and poorly centered.

The Catalogue value is for a fine centered copy with minor faults which do not detract from its appearance.

*R32* R3 10c Bill of Lading, bl 85
a. Imperf. 45.00
b. Part perf. 150.00
*R33* R3 10c Certificate, blue 20
a. Imperf. 90.00
b. Part perf. 95.00
d. Silk paper 3.00
*R34* R3 10c Contract, blue 20
b. Part perf. 100.00
d. Silk paper 2.00
e. Ultramarine, part perf. 225.00
f. Ultramarine, old paper 50
*R35* R3 10c For. Exch., blue 3.00
d. Silk paper —
e. ultra, old paper 6.50
*R36* R3 10c Inland Exch., bl 15
a. Imperf. 120.00
b. Part perf. 3.00
d. Silk paper 15.00
*R37* R3 10c Power of Attorney, blue 25
a. Imperf. 300.00
b. Part perf. 17.00
*R38* R3 10c Proprietary, blue ('64) 13.00
*R39* R3 15c For. Exch., brown ('63) 12.00
*R40* R3 15c Inland Exch., brown 1.00
a. Imperf. 25.00
b. Part perf. 10.00
*R41* R3 20c For. Exch., red 30.00
a. Imperf. 40.00
*R42* R3 20c Inland Exch., red 30
a. Imperf. 12.00
b. Part perf. 16.00
d. Silk paper —

**Old Paper**

*R43* R4 25c Bond, red 1.75
a. Imperf. 80.00
b. Part perf. 5.00
*R44* R4 25c Certificate, red 10
a. Imperf. 5.00
b. Part perf. 5.00
d. Silk paper 2.00
e. Printed on both sides, old paper —
f. Impression of No. R48 on back, old paper —
*R45* R4 25c Entry of Goods, red 40
a. Imperf. 15.00
b. Part perf. 30.00
d. Silk paper 8.00
*R46* R4 25c Insurance, red 20
a. Imperf. 8.00
b. Part perf. 9.00
d. Silk paper 3.00
*R47* R4 25c Life Insurance, red 5.00
a. Imperf. 30.00
b. Part perf. 100.00
*R48* R4 25c Power of Attorney, red 25
a. Imperf. 5.00
b. Part perf. 15.00
*R49* R4 25c Protest, red 6.00
a. Imperf. 20.00
b. Part perf. 125.00
*R50* R4 25c Warehouse Receipt, red 21.00
a. Imperf. 35.00
b. Part perf. 125.00
*R51* R4 30c For. Exch., lilac 35.00
a. Imperf. 60.00
b. Part perf. 350.00
d. Silk paper —
*R52* R4 30c Inland Exch., lil 2.25
a. Imperf. 35.00
b. Part perf. 40.00

Many shade and color variations of Nos. R51-R52. See foreword, "Revenue Stamps."

*R53* R4 40c Inland Exch., brown 2.25
a. Imperf. 425.00
b. Part perf. 3.50
d. Silk paper —

*R54* R5 50c Conveyance, bl 10
a. Imperf. 10.00
b. Part perf. 1.00
d. Silk paper 2.75
e. Ultramarine, old paper 20
f. Ultramarine, silk paper —
*R55* R5 50c Entry of Goods, blue 20
b. Part perf. 10.00
d. Silk paper 12.00
*R56* R5 50c For. Exch., bl 4.50
a. Imperf. 35.00
b. Part perf. 30.00
*R57* R5 50c Lease, blue 6.50
a. Imperf. 20.00
b. Part perf. 50.00
*R58* R5 50c Life Insurance, blue 60
a. Imperf. 25.00
b. Part perf. 50.00
*R59* R5 50c Mortgage, blue 30
a. Imperf. 10.00
b. Part perf. 1.50
d. Silk paper 25.00
*R60* R5 50c Original Process, blue 25
a. Imperf. 2.50
d. Silk paper 1.50
*R61* R5 50c Passage Ticket, blue 50
a. Imperf. 60.00
b. Part perf. 100.00
*R62* R5 50c Probate of Will, blue 15.00
a. Imperf. 30.00
b. Part perf. 40.00
*R63* R5 50c Surety Bond, bl 15
a. Imperf. 120.00
b. Part perf. 2.00
e. Ultramarine, old paper 80
*R64* R5 60c Inland Exch., org 5.00
a. Imperf. 75.00
b. Part perf. 40.00
d. Silk paper 22.50
*R65* R5 70c For. Exch., grn 5.00
a. Imperf. 300.00
b. Part perf. 80.00
d. Silk paper 22.50
e. Vert. pair, imperf. btwn., old paper —

R6

R7

R8

R9

R10

(Illustration sideways) – R11

### Old Paper

*R66* R6 $1 Conveyance, red 2.00
a. Imperf. 10.00
b. Part perf. 250.00
d. Silk paper 27.50
*R67* R6 $1 Entry of Goods, red 1.25
a. Imperf. 25.00
d. Silk paper 22.50
*R68* R6 $1 For. Exch., red 50
a. Imperf. 45.00
d. Silk paper 12.50
*R69* R6 $1 Inland Exch., red 35
a. Imperf. 10.00
b. Part perf. 225.00
d. Silk paper 2.00
*R70* R6 $1 Lease, red 1.50
a. Imperf. 30.00
*R71* R6 $1 Life Insurance, red 4.50
a. Imperf. 130.00
d. Silk paper —
*R72* R6 $1 Manifest, red 21.00
a. Imperf. 50.00
*R73* R6 $1 Mortgage, red 125.00
a. Imperf. 18.00
*R74* R6 $1 Passage Ticket, red 125.00
a. Imperf. 150.00
*R75* R6 $1 Power of Attorney, red 1.50
a. Imperf. 60.00
*R76* R6 $1 Probate of Will, red 30.00
a. Imperf. 55.00
*R77* R7 $1.30 For. Exch., org ('63) 45.00
a. Imperf. *2,000.*
*R78* R7 $1.50 Inland Exch., blue 2.75
a. Imperf. 20.00
*R79* R7 $1.60 For. Exch., grn ('63) 85.00
a. Imperf. 600.00
*R80* R7 $1.90 For. Exch., purple ('63) 60.00
a. Imperf. *1,900.*
d. Silk paper 125.00

Many shade and color variations of No. R80. See foreword, "Revenue Stamps."

*R81* R8 $2 Conveyance, red 1.50
a. Imperf. 85.00
b. Part perf. 800.00
d. Silk paper 12.00
*R82* R8 $2 Mortgage, red 2.50
a. Imperf. 75.00
d. Silk paper 27.50
*R83* R8 $2 Probate of Will, red ('63) 40.00
a. Imperf. *2,100.*
*R84* R8 $2.50 Inland Exch., pur ('63) 3.00
a. Imperf. 850.00
d. Silk paper 12.50
*R85* R8 $3 Charter Party, grn 3.00
a. Imperf. 90.00
d. Silk paper 30.00
e. Printed on both sides *2,000.*
g. Impression of #RS208 on back *4,000.*

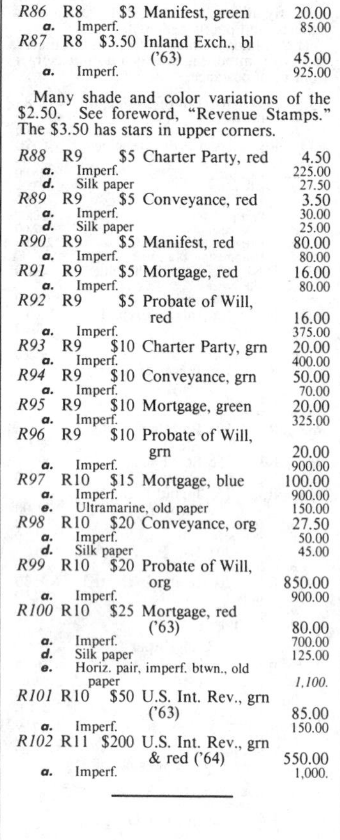

*R86* R8 $3 Manifest, green 20.00
a. Imperf. 85.00
*R87* R8 $3.50 Inland Exch., bl ('63) 45.00
a. Imperf. 925.00

Many shade and color variations of the $2.50. See foreword, "Revenue Stamps." The $3.50 has stars in upper corners.

*R88* R9 $5 Charter Party, red 4.50
a. Imperf. 225.00
d. Silk paper 27.50
*R89* R9 $5 Conveyance, red 3.50
a. Imperf. 30.00
d. Silk paper 25.00
*R90* R9 $5 Manifest, red 80.00
a. Imperf. 80.00
*R91* R9 $5 Mortgage, red 16.00
a. Imperf. 80.00
*R92* R9 $5 Probate of Will, red 16.00
a. Imperf. 375.00
*R93* R9 $10 Charter Party, grn 20.00
a. Imperf. 400.00
*R94* R9 $10 Conveyance, grn 50.00
a. Imperf. 70.00
*R95* R9 $10 Mortgage, green 20.00
a. Imperf. 325.00
*R96* R9 $10 Probate of Will, grn 20.00
a. Imperf. 900.00
*R97* R10 $15 Mortgage, blue 100.00
a. Imperf. 900.00
e. Ultramarine, old paper 150.00
*R98* R10 $20 Conveyance, org 27.50
a. Imperf. 50.00
d. Silk paper 45.00
*R99* R10 $20 Probate of Will, org 850.00
a. Imperf. 900.00
*R100* R10 $25 Mortgage, red ('63) 80.00
a. Imperf. 700.00
d. Silk paper 125.00
e. Horiz. pair, imperf. btwn., old paper *1,100.*
*R101* R10 $50 U.S. Int. Rev., grn ('63) 85.00
a. Imperf. 150.00
*R102* R11 $200 U.S. Int. Rev., grn & red ('64) 550.00
a. Imperf. 1,000.

## DOCUMENTARY STAMPS

### Second Issue

After release of the First Issue revenue stamps, the Bureau of Internal Revenue received many reports of fraudulent cleaning and re-use. The Bureau ordered a Second Issue with new designs and colors, using a patented "chameleon" paper which is usually slightly violet or pinkish, with silk fibers.

R12

R12a

R13a

R13

R13b

Head of Washington in Black within Octagon. Various Frames and Numeral Arrangements.

**1871** ***Perf. 12***
*R103* R12 1c blue & blk 25.00
a. Inverted center *1,300.*
*R104* R12 2c blue & blk 1.00
a. Inverted center *4,500.*
*R105* R12a 3c blue & blk 12.00
*R106* R12a 4c blue & blk 45.00
*R107* R12a 5c blue & blk 1.00
a. Inverted center *1,850.*
*R108* R12a 6c blue & blk 65.00
*R109* R12a 10c blue & blk 75
a. Inverted center *1,650.*
*R110* R12a 15c blue & blk 20.00
*R111* R12a 20c blue & blk 4.00
a. Inverted center *7,500.*

### Head of Washington in Black within Circle. Various Frames

*R112* R13 25c blue & blk 50
a. Inverted center *9,500.*
b. Sewing machine perf. 90.00
c. Perf. 8 250.00
*R113* R13 30c blue & blk 45.00
*R114* R13 40c blue & blk 27.50
*R115* R13a 50c blue & blk 50
a. Sewing machine perf. 90.00
b. Inverted center 650.00
Inverted center, punch cancellation 200.00
*R116* R13a 60c blue & blk 60.00
*R117* R13a 70c blue & blk 25.00
a. Inverted center *3,000.*
*R118* R13b $1 blue & blk 2.50
a. Inverted center *5,250.*
Invtd. center, punch cancel *1,000.*
*R119* R13b $1.30 blue & blk 225.00
*R120* R13b $1.50 blue & blk 10.00
a. Sewing machine perf. 350.00
*R121* R13b $1.60 blue & blk 325.00
*R122* R13b $1.90 blue & blk 150.00
*R123* R13b $2 blue & blk 10.00
*R124* R13b $2.50 blue & blk 18.00
*R125* R13b $3 blue & blk 30.00
*R126* R13b $3.50 blue & blk 110.00
*R127* R13b $5 blue & blk 15.00
a. Inverted center *2,150.*
Invtd. center, punch cancel *600.00*
*R128* R13b $10 blue & blk 100.00
*R129* R13b $20 blue & blk 300.00
*R130* R13b $25 blue & blk 300.00
*R131* R13b $50 blue & blk 325.00
*R132* R13b $200 blue, blk & red *5,250.*
*R133* R13b $500 blk, grn & red *15,000.*

Fraudulently produced inverted centers exist, some excellently made.

### Third Issue

Violet "Chameleon" Paper with Silk Fibers Various Frames and Numeral Arrangements.

**1871-72** ***Perf. 12***
*R134* R12 1c cl & blk ('72) 20.00
*R135* R12 2c orange & blk 5
a. 2c vermilion & blk (error) *400.00*
b. Inverted center 250.00
*R136* R12a 4c brn & blk ('72) 27.50
*R137* R12a 5c orange & blk 20
a. Inverted center *3,500.*
*R138* R12a 6c org & blk ('72) 30.00
*R139* R12a 15c brn & blk ('72) 7.50
a. Inverted center *8,000.*
*R140* R13 30c org & blk ('72) 11.00
a. Inverted center *1,350.*
*R141* R13 40c brn & blk ('72) 20.00
*R142* R13 60c org & blk ('72) 45.00
*R143* R13 70c grn & blk ('72) 30.00
*R144* R13b $1 grn & blk ('72) 1.00
a. Inverted center *7,000.*
*R145* R13b $2 ver & blk ('72) 18.00
*R146* R13b $2.50 cl & blk ('72) 30.00
a. Inverted center *15,000.*
*R147* R13b $3 grn & blk ('72) 30.00
*R148* R13b $5 ver & blk ('72) 17.50
*R149* R13b $10 grn & blk ('72) 85.00
*R150* R13b $20 org & blk ('72) 375.00
a. $20 vermilion & blk (error) 525.00

**1874** ***Perf. 12***
*R151* R12 2c org & blk, *green* 6
a. Inverted center 325.00

Liberty – R14

**1875-78**
*R152* R14 2c bl, *blue*, silk paper 6
b. Wmk. 191R 6
c. Wmk. 191R, rouletted 32.50
d. Vert. pair, imperf. horiz. 100.00
e. As "b," imperf., pair *250.00*

Postage Stamps 1895-98 Overprinted in Red or Blue

**I. R.** a  **I. R.** b

**1898** **Wmk. 191** ***Perf. 12***
*R153* A87 (a) 1c green (R) 1.25 1.25
*R154* A87 (b) 1c green (R) 12 10
a. Overprint inverted 10.00 7.50
b. Overprint on back instead of face, inverted —
c. Pair, one without ovpt. —
*R155* A88 (b) 2c carmine (Bl) 15 6
a. Overprint inverted 1.25 1.00
b. Pair, one without ovpt. *400.00*
c. Overprinted on back instead of face, inverted *400.00*

### Handstamped Type "b"

*R156* A93 8c *vio brn* *2,000.*
*R157* A94 10c *dk grn* *2,250.*
*R158* A95 15c *dk bl* *2,750.*

Nos. R156-R158 were emergency provisionals, privately prepared, not officially issued.

Privately Prepared Provisionals

No. 285 Overprinted in Red **I. R.** L. H. C.

**1898** **Wmk. 191** ***Perf. 12***
*R158A* A100 1c dark yel grn — *3,500.*

### Same Overprinted "I.R./P.I.D. & Son" in Red

*R158B* A100 1c dark yel grn — *6,000.*

Nos. R158A-R158B were overprinted with federal government permission by the Purvis Printing Co. upon order of Capt. L.H. Chapman of the Chapman Steamboat Line. Both the Chapman line and P.I. Daprix & Son operated freight-carrying steamboats on the Erie Canal. The Chapman Line touched at Syracuse, Utica, Little Falls and Fort Plain; the Daprix boat ran between Utica and Rome. 250 of each stamp were overprinted.

Dr. Kilmer & Co. provisional overprints are listed in Scott's Specialized Catalogue of United States Stamps under Private Die Medicine Stamps, Nos. RS307-RS315.

Newspaper Stamp No. PR121 Surcharged Vertically in Red **INT. REV. $5. DOCUMENTARY.**

**1898** **Wmk. 191** ***Perf. 12***

### Reading Down

*R159* N18 $5 on $5 dk bl 150.00 125.00
a. OCUMENTARY 300.00 200.00

### Reading Up

*R160* N18 $5 on $5 dk bl 80.00 55.00
a. OCUMENTARY 300.00 200.00

Battleship R15

### Inscribed: "Series of 1898" and "Documentary."

**1898** **Wmk. 191R** ***Rouletted 5½***
*R161* R15 ½c orange 1.50 5.00
*R162* R15 ½c dark gray 15 10
a. Vert. pair, imperf. horiz. 40.00
*R163* R15 1c pale blue 8 5
a. Vert. pair, imperf. horiz. 7.50
*R164* R15 2c carmine rose 10 5
a. Vert. pair, imperf. horiz. 30.00
b. Imperf., pair 125.00
c. Horiz. pair, imperf. vert. —

*R165* R15 3c dark blue 70 12
*R166* R15 4c pale rose 25 10
**a.** Vert. pair, imperf. horiz. 75.00
*R167* R15 5c lilac 15 6
**a.** Pair, imperf. horiz. or vert. 125.00 75.00
*R168* R15 10c dark brown 20 6
**a.** Vert. pair, imperf. horiz. 20.00 20.00
**b.** Horiz. pair, imperf. vert. —
*R169* R15 25c purple brn 20 10
*R170* R15 40c blue lilac 30.00 1.00
Cut cancellation 15
*R171* R15 50c slate vio 2.75 12
**a.** Imperf., pair 300.00
*R172* R15 80c bister 17.50 25
Cut cancellation 8

### *Hyphen Hole Perf. 7*

*R163p* 1c 25 15
*R164p* 2c 30 10
*R165p* 3c 2.00 25
*R166p* 4c 60 25
*R167p* 5c 40 15
*R168p* 10c 40 15
*R169p* 25c 50 20
*R170p* 40c 40.00 10.00
*R171p* 50c 4.50 20
**b.** Horiz. pair, imperf. btwn. —
*R172p* 80c 45.00 15.00

Commerce R16

**1898** ***Rouletted 5½***

*R173* R16 $1 dark green 3.50 10
**a.** Vert. pair, imperf. horiz. —
**b.** Horiz. pair, imperf. vert. — 250.00
**p.** Hyphen hole perf. 7 — 50
*R174* R16 $3 dark brown 6.00 20
Cut cancellation 12
**a.** Horiz. pair, imperf. vert. 325.00
**p.** Hyphen hole perf. 7 — 1.25
*R175* R16 $5 orange red — 1.00
Cut cancellation 18
*R176* R16 $10 black 27.50 2.50
Cut cancellation 50
**a.** Horiz. pair, imperf. vert. —
*R177* R16 $30 red 110.00 70.00
Cut cancellation 25.00
*R178* R16 $50 gray brown 45.00 2.75
Cut cancellation 1.25

There are 2 styles of rouletting for the 1898 proprietary and documentary stamps, an ordinary roulette 5½ and one where small rectangles of the paper are cut out, called hyphen hole perf. 7. Except for Nos. R161, R162 and R175-R178, all the stamps of the 2 series exist with both roulettes.

See Nos. R182-R183.

John Marshall R17

Alexander Hamilton R18

James Madison R19

### Inscribed "Series of 1898"

**1899** **Without Gum** ***Imperf.***

*R179* R17 $100 yel brn & black 50.00 27.50
Cut cancellation 13.00
*R180* R18 $500 car lake & black — 400.00
Cut cancellation 175.00
*R181* R19 $1000 grn & blk 400.00 300.00
Cut cancellation 90.00

See Nos. R224-R227, R246-R252, R282-R286.

### Type of 1898

**1900** ***Hyphen-Hole Perf. 7***

*R182* R16 $1 carmine 5.50 50
Cut cancellation 10
*R183* R16 $3 lake 55.00 40.00
Cut cancellation 7.00

### Surcharged in Black

a

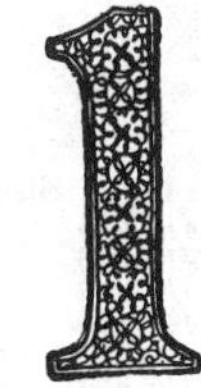
b

### Surcharged type "a"

**1900**

*R184* R16 $1 gray 3.75 12
Cut cancellation 6
**a.** Horiz. pair, imperf. vert. —
**b.** Surcharge omitted 125.00
As "b", cut cancellation 80.00
*R185* R16 $2 gray 3.00 12
Cut cancellation 6
*R186* R16 $3 gray 25.00 11.00
Cut cancellation 2.00
*R187* R16 $5 gray 15.00 4.50
Cut cancellation 25
*R188* R16 $10 gray 35.00 10.00
Cut cancellation 3.00
*R189* R16 $50 gray 500.00 350.00
Cut cancellation 70.00

### Surcharged type "b"

**1902**

*R190* R16 $1 green 6.00 2.25
Cut cancellation 20
**a.** Inverted surcharge 150.00
*R191* R16 $2 green 5.50 1.00
Cut cancellation 20
**a.** Surcharged as #R185 75.00 75.00
**b.** Surch. as #R185, in vio — —
**c.** Dbl. surch. 100.00
*R192* R16 $5 green 30.00 12.50
Cut cancellation 1.75
**a.** Surcharge omitted 50.00
**b.** Pair, one without surch. 300.00
*R193* R16 $10 green 200.00 125.00
Cut cancellation 25.00
*R194* R16 $50 green 900.00 700.00
Cut cancellation 225.00

Warning: If Nos. R190-R194 are soaked, the center part of the surcharged numeral may wash off. Before surcharging, a square of soluble varnish was applied to the middle of some stamps.

R20

Liberty – R21

### Inscribed "Series of 1914"

### Offset Printing

**1914** **Wmk. 190** ***Perf. 10***

*R195* R20 ½c rose 5.00 2.50
*R196* R20 1c rose 1.25 12
*R197* R20 2c rose 1.25 10
*R198* R20 3c rose 27.50 20.00
*R199* R20 4c rose 6.50 1.00
*R200* R20 5c rose 2.50 12
*R201* R20 10c rose 2.25 8
*R202* R20 25c rose 12.50 40
*R203* R20 40c rose 7.50 50
*R204* R20 50c rose 3.50 10
*R205* R20 80c rose 40.00 6.00
*Nos. R195-R205 (11)* 109.75 30.92

### Wmk. 191R

*R206* R20 ½c rose 1.25 45
*R207* R20 1c rose 12 5
*R208* R20 2c rose 15 5
*R209* R20 3c rose 1.25 20
*R210* R20 4c rose 2.25 30
*R211* R20 5c rose 1.25 10
*R212* R20 10c rose 40 6
*R213* R20 25c rose 3.50 60
*R214* R20 40c rose 35.00 7.00
Cut cancellation 45
*R215* R20 50c rose 7.50 12
*R216* R20 80c rose 40.00 7.50
Cut cancellation 1.00
*Nos. R206-R216 (11)* 92.67 16.43

### Engr.

*R217* R21 $1 green 12.50 15
**a.** $1 yellow grn — 12
Cut cancellation 5
*R218* R21 $2 carmine 25.00 20
Cut cancellation 6
*R219* R21 $3 purple 35.00 1.25
Cut cancellation 20
*R220* R21 $5 blue 30.00 2.00
Cut cancellation 50
*R221* R21 $10 orange 57.50 4.50
Cut cancellation 75
*R222* R21 $30 vermilion 100.00 10.00
Cut cancellation 2.00
*R223* R21 $50 violet 800.00 600.00
Cut cancellation 250.00

See Nos. R240-R245, R257-R259, R276-R281.

### Portrait Types of 1899 Inscribed "Series of 1915" (#R224), or "Series of 1914"

**1914-15** **Without Gum** ***Perf. 12***

*R224* R19 $60 brn *(Lincoln)* — 100.00
Cut cancellation 45.00
*R225* R17 $100 grn *(Washington)* — 40.00
Cut cancellation 15.00
*R226* R18 $500 blue — 450.00
Cut cancellation 200.00
*R227* R19 $1000 orange — 450.00
Cut cancellation 200.00

The stamps of types R17, R18 and R19 in this and subsequent issues are issued in vert. strips of 4 which are imperf. at the top, bottom and right side; therefore, single copies are always imperf. on 1 or 2 sides.

R22

### Offset Printing

**1917** **Wmk. 191R** ***Perf. 11***

**Size: 21x18mm**

*R228* R22 1c carmine rose 12 8
*R229* R22 2c carmine rose 8 5
*R230* R22 3c carmine rose 25 15
*R231* R22 4c carmine rose 12 5
*R232* R22 5c carmine rose 15 5
*R233* R22 8c carmine rose 1.50 12
*R234* R22 10c carmine rose 15 5
*R235* R22 20c carmine rose 30 5
*R236* R22 25c carmine rose 60 5
*R237* R22 40c carmine rose 1.00 8
*R238* R22 50c carmine rose 1.25 5
*R239* R22 80c carmine rose 3.00 8
*Nos. R228-R239 (12)* 8.52 86

### Type of 1914 without "Series 1914"

**1917-33** **Engr.**

**Size: 18½x27½mm**

*R240* R21 $1 yellow green 4.00 5
**a.** $1 green 4.50 5
*R241* R21 $2 rose 8.50 8
*R242* R21 $3 violet 20.00 40
Cut cancellation 8
*R243* R21 $4 yel brn ('33) 11.00 1.00
Cut cancellation 12
*R244* R21 $5 dark blue 9.00 15
Cut cancellation 6
*R245* R21 $10 orange 17.50 50
Cut cancellation 12

### Portrait Types of 1899-1915 without "Series of" and Date

Portraits: $30, Grant. $100, Washington.

**1917** **Without Gum** ***Perf. 12***

*R246* R17 $30 dp org, grn numerals 25.00 2.00
Cut cancellation 55
**a.** Imperf., pair —
**b.** Numerals in blue — 1.75
As "b", cut cancellation 90
*R247* R19 $60 brown 30.00 7.00
Cut cancellation 80
*R248* R17 $100 green 20.00 75
Cut cancellation 35
*R249* R18 $500 blue, red numerals — 30.00
Cut cancellation 7.00
**a.** Numerals in orange — 70.00
*R250* R19 $1000 orange 80.00 11.00
Cut cancellation 4.00
**a.** Imperf., pair —

See note after No. R227.

**1928-29** **Offset Printing** ***Perf. 10***

*R251* R22 1c carmine rose 2.00 1.10
*R252* R22 2c carmine rose 60 20
*R253* R22 4c carmine rose 5.50 3.75
*R254* R22 5c carmine rose 1.10 35
*R255* R22 10c carmine rose 1.75 1.00
*R256* R22 20c carmine rose 5.50 4.50
*Nos. R251-R256 (6)* 16.45 10.90

### Engr.

*R257* R21 $1 green 45.00 25.00
Cut cancellation 5.00
*R258* R21 $2 rose 15.00 2.00
*R259* R21 $10 orange 70.00 32.50
Cut cancellation 20.00

**1929** **Offset Printing** ***Perf. 11x10***

*R260* R22 2c carmine rose 2.75 2.25
*R261* R22 5c carmine rose 2.00 1.75
*R262* R22 10c carmine rose 7.50 6.50
*R263* R22 20c carmine rose 15.00 9.00

Used values for Nos. R264-R734 are for copies which are neither cut nor perforated with initials. Copies with cut cancellations or perforated initials are valued in Scott's U. S. Specialized Catalogue.

Types of 1917-33 Overprinted in Black **SERIES 1940**

**1940** **Offset Printing** ***Perf. 11***

*R264* R22 1c rose pink 1.75 1.25
*R265* R22 2c rose pink 1.75 1.25
*R266* R22 3c rose pink 5.00 3.00
*R267* R22 4c rose pink 2.00 35
*R268* R22 5c rose pink 2.25 60
*R269* R22 8c rose pink 12.00 11.00
*R270* R22 10c rose pink 1.00 25
*R271* R22 20c rose pink 1.50 30
*R272* R22 25c rose pink 2.75 40
*R273* R22 40c rose pink 3.00 40
*R274* R22 50c rose pink 3.50 30
*R275* R22 80c rose pink 5.00 50
*Nos. R264-R275 (12)* 41.50 19.60

### Engr.

*R276* R21 $1 green 14.00 30
*R277* R21 $2 rose 14.00 60
*R278* R21 $3 violet 15.00 12.00
*R279* R21 $4 yellow brn 35.00 17.50
*R280* R21 $5 dark blue 20.00 5.00
*R281* R21 $10 orange 45.00 15.00

Types of 1917 Handstamped in Green **SERIES 1940**

### *Perf. 12*

### Without Gum

*R282* R17 $30 vermilion 425.00
*R283* R19 $60 brown 600.00
**a.** As #R285a, cut cancel —
*R284* R17 $100 green 900.00
*R285* R18 $500 blue 1,200.
**a.** With black 2-line handstamp in larger type 1,600.
**b.** Blue handstamp, double transfer —
*R286* R19 $1000 orange 550.00

Values quoted in this catalogue are for stamps graded at Fine-Very Fine and with no faults. An illustrated guide to grade is provided in introductory material, beginning on Page V.

Alexander Hamilton — R23

Levi Woodbury — R24

Thomas Corwin R25

Portraits: 2c, Oliver Wolcott, Jr. 3c, Samuel Dexter. 4c, Albert Gallatin. 5c, George Washington Campbell. 8c, Alexander Dallas. 10c, William H. Crawford. 20c, Richard Rush. 25c, Samuel D. Ingham. 40c, Louis McLane. 50c, William J. Duane. 80c, Roger B. Taney. $2, Thomas Ewing. $3, Walter Forward. $4, John Canfield Spencer. $5, George M. Bibb. $10, Robert J. Walker. $20, William M. Meredith. $50, James Guthrie. $60, Howell Cobb. $100, P. F. Thomas. $500, John Adams Dix. $1,000, Salmon P. Chase.

Overprinted in Black **SERIES 1940**

**1940 Size: 19x22mm** ***Perf. 11***

**Various Portraits**

| No. | Type | Denomination | Unused | Used |
|---|---|---|---|---|
| *R288* | R23 | 1c carmine | 3.00 | 2.25 |
| *R289* | R23 | 2c carmine | 3.25 | 2.25 |
| *R290* | R23 | 3c carmine | 12.50 | 5.50 |
| *R291* | R23 | 4c carmine | 27.50 | 12000 |
| *R292* | R23 | 5c carmine | 2.75 | 60 |
| *R293* | R23 | 8c carmine | 37.50 | 32.50 |
| *R294* | R23 | 10c carmine | 1.75 | 30 |
| *R295* | R23 | 20c carmine | 2.25 | 1.75 |
| *R296* | R23 | 25c carmine | 2.00 | 20 |
| *R297* | R23 | 40c carmine | 20.00 | 12.00 |
| *R298* | R23 | 50c carmine | 3.00 | 20 |
| *R299* | R23 | 80c carmine | 50.00 | 45.00 |
| *Nos. R288-R299 (12)* | | | 165.50 | 222.55 |

**Size: 21½x36¼mm**

| No. | Type | Denomination | Unused | Used |
|---|---|---|---|---|
| *R300* | R24 | $1 carmine | — | 15 |
| *R301* | R24 | $2 carmine | — | 25 |
| *R302* | R24 | $3 carmine | — | 50.00 |
| *R303* | R24 | $4 carmine | — | 20.00 |
| *R304* | R24 | $5 carmine | — | 80 |
| *R305* | R24 | $10 carmine | — | 3.00 |
| *R305A* | R24 | $20 carmine | 600.00 | 500.00 |
| **b.** | | Imperf., pair | 750.00 | |

**Size: 28½x42mm**

**Various Frame Designs**

***Perf. 12***

**Without Gum**

| No. | Type | Denomination | Unused | Used |
|---|---|---|---|---|
| *R306* | R25 | $30 carmine | 75.00 | 35.00 |
| *R306A* | R25 | $50 carmine | — | 800.00 |
| *R307* | R25 | $60 carmine | — | 40.00 |
| **a.** | | Vert. pair, imperf. btwn. | | — |
| *R308* | R25 | $100 carmine | — | 37.50 |
| *R309* | R25 | $500 carmine | — | 500.00 |
| *R310* | R25 | $1000 carmine | — | 250.00 |

The $30 to $1,000 denominations in this and following similar issues, and the $2,500, $5,000 and $10,000 stamps of 1952-58 have straight edges on one or two sides. They were issued without gum through No. R723.

Documentary Stamps of 1940 Overprinted in Black

**SERIES 1941**

**1941 Size: 19x22mm** ***Perf. 11***

| No. | Type | Denomination | Unused | Used |
|---|---|---|---|---|
| *R311* | R23 | 1c carmine | 2.00 | 1.75 |
| *R312* | R23 | 2c carmine | 2.00 | 75 |
| *R313* | R23 | 3c carmine | 5.00 | 3.00 |
| *R314* | R23 | 4c carmine | 3.00 | 75 |
| *R315* | R23 | 5c carmine | 75 | 15 |
| *R316* | R23 | 8c carmine | 12.00 | 5.00 |
| *R317* | R23 | 10c carmine | 1.00 | 20 |
| *R318* | R23 | 20c carmine | 2.25 | 40 |
| *R319* | R23 | 25c carmine | 1.25 | 10 |
| *R320* | R23 | 40c carmine | 7.00 | 2.00 |
| *R321* | R23 | 50c carmine | 2.00 | 10 |
| *R322* | R23 | 80c carmine | 32.50 | 6.00 |
| *Nos. R311-R322 (12)* | | | 70.75 | 20.20 |

**Size: 21½x36¼mm**

| No. | Type | Denomination | Unused | Used |
|---|---|---|---|---|
| *R323* | R24 | $1 carmine | 5.00 | 10 |
| *R324* | R24 | $2 carmine | 6.00 | 12 |
| *R325* | R24 | $3 carmine | 10.00 | 1.75 |
| *R326* | R24 | $4 carmine | 15.00 | 8.00 |
| *R327* | R24 | $5 carmine | 20.00 | 30 |
| *R328* | R24 | $10 carmine | 30.00 | 2.00 |
| *R329* | R24 | $20 carmine | 100.00 | 80.00 |

**Size: 28½x42 mm**

***Perf. 12***

**Without Gum**

| No. | Type | Denomination | Unused | Used |
|---|---|---|---|---|
| *R330* | R25 | $30 carmine | — | 16.00 |
| *R331* | R25 | $50 carmine | 100.00 | 80.00 |
| *R332* | R25 | $60 carmine | — | 30.00 |
| *R333* | R25 | $100 carmine | — | 13.00 |
| *R334* | R25 | $500 carmine | — | 135.00 |
| *R335* | R25 | $1000 carmine | — | 100.00 |

Documentary Stamps of 1940 Overprinted in Black

**SERIES 1942**

**1942 Size: 19x22mm** ***Perf. 11***

| No. | Type | Denomination | Unused | Used |
|---|---|---|---|---|
| *R336* | R23 | 1c carmine | 30 | 25 |
| *R337* | R23 | 2c carmine | 30 | 25 |
| *R338* | R23 | 3c carmine | 50 | 35 |
| *R339* | R23 | 4c carmine | 80 | 40 |
| *R340* | R23 | 5c carmine | 35 | 10 |
| *R341* | R23 | 8c carmine | 3.50 | 2.25 |
| *R342* | R23 | 10c carmine | 70 | 10 |
| *R343* | R23 | 20c carmine | 95 | 25 |
| *R344* | R23 | 25c carmine | 1.25 | 15 |
| *R345* | R23 | 40c carmine | 3.50 | 75 |
| *R346* | R23 | 50c carmine | 2.25 | 10 |
| *R347* | R23 | 80c carmine | 8.50 | 6.00 |
| *Nos. R336-R347 (12)* | | | 22.90 | 10.95 |

**Size: 21½x36¼mm**

| No. | Type | Denomination | Unused | Used |
|---|---|---|---|---|
| *R348* | R24 | $1 carmine | 4.50 | 10 |
| *R349* | R24 | $2 carmine | 5.50 | 10 |
| *R350* | R24 | $3 carmine | 9.00 | 1.50 |
| *R351* | R24 | $4 carmine | 11.00 | 3.25 |
| *R352* | R24 | $5 carmine | 18.00 | 50 |
| *R353* | R24 | $10 carmine | 30.00 | 1.75 |
| *R354* | R24 | $20 carmine | 50.00 | 25.00 |

**Size: 28½x42mm**

***Perf. 12***

**Without Gum**

| No. | Type | Denomination | Unused | Used |
|---|---|---|---|---|
| *R355* | R25 | $30 carmine | — | 18.00 |
| *R356* | R25 | $50 carmine | 150.00 | 110.00 |
| *R357* | R25 | $60 carmine | 160.00 | 135.00 |
| *R358* | R25 | $100 carmine | — | 50.00 |
| *R359* | R25 | $500 carmine | — | 150.00 |
| *R360* | R25 | $1000 carmine | — | 100.00 |

Documentary Stamps of 1940 Overprinted in Black

**SERIES 1943**

**1943 Size: 19x22mm** ***Perf. 11***

| No. | Type | Denomination | Unused | Used |
|---|---|---|---|---|
| *R361* | R23 | 1c carmine | 50 | 25 |
| *R362* | R23 | 2c carmine | 40 | 20 |
| *R363* | R23 | 3c carmine | 1.75 | 1.50 |
| *R364* | R23 | 4c carmine | 80 | 50 |
| *R365* | R23 | 5c carmine | 35 | 20 |
| *R366* | R23 | 8c carmine | 3.00 | 2.50 |
| *R367* | R23 | 10c carmine | 40 | 15 |
| *R368* | R23 | 20c carmine | 1.25 | 40 |
| *R369* | R23 | 25c carmine | 1.00 | 20 |
| *R370* | R23 | 40c carmine | 4.00 | 1.50 |
| *R371* | R23 | 50c carmine | 1.10 | 10 |
| *R372* | R23 | 80c carmine | 7.00 | 4.50 |
| *Nos. R361-R372 (12)* | | | 21.55 | 12.00 |

**Size: 21½x36¼mm**

| No. | Type | Denomination | Unused | Used |
|---|---|---|---|---|
| *R373* | R24 | $1 carmine | 3.75 | 8 |
| *R374* | R24 | $2 carmine | 5.50 | 10 |
| *R375* | R24 | $3 carmine | 9.00 | 1.75 |
| *R376* | R24 | $4 carmine | 11.00 | 2.50 |
| *R377* | R24 | $5 carmine | 16.00 | 40 |
| *R378* | R24 | $10 carmine | 25.00 | 2.00 |
| *R379* | R24 | $20 carmine | 45.00 | 10.00 |

**Size: 28½x42mm**

***Perf. 12***

**Without Gum**

| No. | Type | Denomination | Unused | Used |
|---|---|---|---|---|
| *R380* | R25 | $30 carmine | — | 15.00 |
| *R381* | R25 | $50 carmine | — | 22.00 |
| *R382* | R25 | $60 carmine | — | 35.00 |
| *R383* | R25 | $100 carmine | — | 10.00 |
| *R384* | R25 | $500 carmine | — | 110.00 |
| *R385* | R25 | $1000 carmine | — | 140.00 |

Documentary Stamps of 1940 Overprinted in Black

**Series 1944**

**1944 Size: 19x22mm** ***Perf. 11***

| No. | Type | Denomination | Unused | Used |
|---|---|---|---|---|
| *R386* | R23 | 1c carmine | 25 | 20 |
| *R387* | R23 | 2c carmine | 25 | 20 |
| *R388* | R23 | 3c carmine | 35 | 20 |
| *R389* | R23 | 4c carmine | 40 | 35 |
| *R390* | R23 | 5c carmine | 30 | 10 |
| *R391* | R23 | 8c carmine | 1.25 | 75 |
| *R392* | R23 | 10c carmine | 40 | 6 |
| *R393* | R23 | 20c carmine | 65 | 20 |
| *R394* | R23 | 25c carmine | 1.10 | 10 |
| *R395* | R23 | 40c carmine | 2.25 | 30 |
| *R396* | R23 | 50c carmine | 2.25 | 10 |
| *R397* | R23 | 80c carmine | 7.00 | 3.50 |
| *Nos. R386-R397 (12)* | | | 16.45 | 6.06 |

**Size: 21½x36¼mm**

| No. | Type | Denomination | Unused | Used |
|---|---|---|---|---|
| *R398* | R24 | $1 carmine | 3.75 | 8 |
| *R399* | R24 | $2 carmine | 5.00 | 10 |
| *R400* | R24 | $3 carmine | 7.50 | 1.50 |
| *R401* | R24 | $4 carmine | 12.00 | 8.00 |
| *R402* | R24 | $5 carmine | 12.00 | 25 |
| *R403* | R24 | $10 carmine | 25.00 | 90 |
| *R404* | R24 | $20 carmine | 45.00 | 12.50 |

**Size: 28½x42mm**

***Perf. 12***

**Without Gum**

| No. | Type | Denomination | Unused | Used |
|---|---|---|---|---|
| *R405* | R25 | $30 carmine | 50.00 | 20.00 |
| *R406* | R25 | $50 carmine | 20.00 | 7.50 |
| *R407* | R25 | $60 carmine | 90.00 | 35.00 |
| *R408* | R25 | $100 carmine | — | 8.00 |
| *R409* | R25 | $500 carmine | — | 450.00 |
| *R410* | R25 | $1000 carmine | — | 125.00 |

Documentary Stamps of 1940 Overprinted in Black

**Series 1945**

**1945 Size: 19x22mm** ***Perf. 11***

| No. | Type | Denomination | Unused | Used |
|---|---|---|---|---|
| *R411* | R23 | 1c carmine | 15 | 10 |
| *R412* | R23 | 2c carmine | 15 | 10 |
| *R413* | R23 | 3c carmine | 40 | 30 |
| *R414* | R23 | 4c carmine | 25 | 15 |
| *R415* | R23 | 5c carmine | 25 | 6 |
| *R416* | R23 | 8c carmine | 3.00 | 1.25 |
| *R417* | R23 | 10c carmine | 50 | 10 |
| *R418* | R23 | 20c carmine | 3.50 | 75 |
| *R419* | R23 | 25c carmine | 90 | 15 |
| *R420* | R23 | 40c carmine | 3.00 | 75 |
| *R421* | R23 | 50c carmine | 2.00 | 10 |
| *R422* | R23 | 80c carmine | 11.00 | 6.00 |
| *Nos. R411-R422 (12)* | | | 25.10 | 9.81 |

**Size: 21½x36¼mm**

| No. | Type | Denomination | Unused | Used |
|---|---|---|---|---|
| *R423* | R24 | $1 carmine | 3.75 | 10 |
| *R424* | R24 | $2 carmine | 5.00 | 15 |
| *R425* | R24 | $3 carmine | 7.50 | 2.25 |
| *R426* | R24 | $4 carmine | 11.00 | 2.50 |
| *R427* | R24 | $5 carmine | 12.00 | 30 |
| *R428* | R24 | $10 carmine | 25.00 | 1.10 |
| *R429* | R24 | $20 carmine | 40.00 | 8.00 |

**Size: 28½x42mm**

**Without Gum**

***Perf. 12***

| No. | Type | Denomination | Unused | Used |
|---|---|---|---|---|
| *R430* | R25 | $30 carmine | — | 17.50 |
| *R431* | R25 | $50 carmine | — | 20.00 |
| *R432* | R25 | $60 carmine | 75.00 | 30.00 |
| *R433* | R25 | $100 carmine | — | 10.00 |
| *R434* | R25 | $500 carmine | 150.00 | 110.00 |
| *R435* | R25 | $1000 carmine | 100.00 | 70.00 |

Documentary Stamps of 1940 Overprinted in Black

**Series 1946**

**1946 Wmk. 191R** ***Perf. 11***

**Size: 19x22mm**

| No. | Type | Denomination | Unused | Used |
|---|---|---|---|---|
| *R436* | R23 | 1c carmine | 15 | 10 |
| *R437* | R23 | 2c carmine | 20 | 18 |
| *R438* | R23 | 3c carmine | 25 | 15 |
| *R439* | R23 | 4c carmine | 35 | 30 |
| *R440* | R23 | 5c carmine | 25 | 8 |
| *R441* | R23 | 8c carmine | 90 | 75 |
| *R442* | R23 | 10c carmine | 60 | 8 |
| *R443* | R23 | 20c carmine | 1.00 | 40 |
| *R444* | R23 | 25c carmine | 1.00 | 15 |
| *R445* | R23 | 40c carmine | 1.25 | 70 |
| *R446* | R23 | 50c carmine | 2.50 | 10 |
| *R447* | R23 | 80c carmine | 5.50 | 3.25 |
| *Nos. R436-R447 (12)* | | | 13.95 | 6.24 |

**Size: 21½x36¼mm**

| No. | Type | Denomination | Unused | Used |
|---|---|---|---|---|
| *R448* | R24 | $1 carmine | 3.75 | 15 |
| *R449* | R24 | $2 carmine | 5.50 | 20 |
| *R450* | R24 | $3 carmine | 8.00 | 4.50 |
| *R451* | R24 | $4 carmine | 10.00 | 8.00 |
| *R452* | R24 | $5 carmine | 11.00 | 40 |
| *R453* | R24 | $10 carmine | 22.00 | 1.25 |
| *R454* | R24 | $20 carmine | 40.00 | 7.50 |

**Size: 28½x42mm**

**Without Gum**

***Perf. 12***

| No. | Type | Denomination | Unused | Used |
|---|---|---|---|---|
| *R455* | R25 | $30 carmine | 40.00 | 10.00 |
| *R456* | R25 | $50 carmine | 20.00 | 8.00 |
| *R457* | R25 | $60 carmine | 40.00 | 12.00 |
| *R458* | R25 | $100 carmine | — | 8.00 |
| *R459* | R25 | $500 carmine | — | 75.00 |
| *R460* | R25 | $1000 carmine | — | 70.00 |

Documentary Stamps of 1940 Overprinted in Black

**Series 1947**

**1947 Wmk. 191R** ***Perf. 11***

**Size: 19x22mm**

| No. | Type | Denomination | Unused | Used |
|---|---|---|---|---|
| *R461* | R23 | 1c carmine | 40 | 25 |
| *R462* | R23 | 2c carmine | 35 | 25 |
| *R463* | R23 | 3c carmine | 40 | 25 |
| *R464* | R23 | 4c carmine | 40 | 35 |
| *R465* | R23 | 5c carmine | 30 | 15 |
| *R466* | R23 | 8c carmine | 75 | 35 |
| *R467* | R23 | 10c carmine | 70 | 15 |
| *R468* | R23 | 20c carmine | 1.00 | 35 |
| *R469* | R23 | 25c carmine | 1.25 | 35 |
| *R470* | R23 | 40c carmine | 2.25 | 60 |
| *R471* | R23 | 50c carmine | 2.00 | 15 |
| *R472* | R23 | 80c carmine | 4.00 | 3.50 |
| *Nos. R461-R472 (12)* | | | 13.80 | 6.70 |

**Size: 21½x36¼mm**

| No. | Type | Denomination | Unused | Used |
|---|---|---|---|---|
| *R473* | R24 | $1 carmine | 3.75 | 20 |
| *R474* | R24 | $2 carmine | 5.00 | 20 |
| *R475* | R24 | $3 carmine | 6.75 | 4.00 |
| *R476* | R24 | $4 carmine | 8.00 | 3.50 |
| *R477* | R24 | $5 carmine | 11.00 | 40 |
| *R478* | R24 | $10 carmine | 25.00 | 2.00 |
| *R479* | R24 | $20 carmine | 40.00 | 7.50 |

**Size: 28½x42mm**

***Perf. 12***

**Without Gum**

| No. | Type | Denomination | Unused | Used |
|---|---|---|---|---|
| *R480* | R25 | $30 carmine | 60.00 | 17.50 |
| *R481* | R25 | $50 carmine | 30.00 | 9.00 |
| *R482* | R25 | $60 carmine | — | 22.50 |
| *R483* | R25 | $100 carmine | 30.00 | 8.00 |
| *R484* | R25 | $500 carmine | — | 100.00 |
| *R485* | R25 | $1000 carmine | — | 70.00 |

Documentary Stamps of 1940 Overprinted in Black

**Series 1948**

**1948 Wmk. 191R** ***Perf. 11***

**Size: 19x22mm**

| No. | Type | Denomination | Unused | Used |
|---|---|---|---|---|
| *R486* | R23 | 1c carmine | 15 | 12 |
| *R487* | R23 | 2c carmine | 18 | 15 |
| *R488* | R23 | 3c carmine | 30 | 25 |
| *R489* | R23 | 4c carmine | 25 | 25 |
| *R490* | R23 | 5c carmine | 25 | 10 |
| *R491* | R23 | 8c carmine | 50 | 30 |
| *R492* | R23 | 10c carmine | 50 | 10 |
| *R493* | R23 | 20c carmine | 1.00 | 30 |
| *R494* | R23 | 25c carmine | 1.00 | 15 |
| *R495* | R23 | 40c carmine | 2.25 | 1.00 |
| *R496* | R23 | 50c carmine | 2.00 | 12 |
| *R497* | R23 | 80c carmine | 4.50 | 3.50 |
| *Nos. R486-R497 (12)* | | | 12.88 | 6.34 |

**Size: 21½x36¼mm**

| No. | Type | Denomination | Unused | Used |
|---|---|---|---|---|
| *R498* | R24 | $1 carmine | 3.75 | 20 |
| *R499* | R24 | $2 carmine | 5.00 | 15 |
| *R500* | R24 | $3 carmine | 7.00 | 2.00 |
| *R501* | R24 | $4 carmine | 10.00 | 2.50 |
| *R502* | R24 | $5 carmine | 11.00 | 50 |
| *R503* | R24 | $10 carmine | 20.00 | 1.00 |
| **a.** | | Pair, one dated "1946" | | — |
| *R504* | R24 | $20 carmine | 40.00 | 7.50 |

**Size: 28½x42mm**

***Perf. 12***

**Without Gum**

| No. | Type | Denomination | Unused | Used |
|---|---|---|---|---|
| *R505* | R25 | $30 carmine | 40.00 | 15.00 |
| *R506* | R25 | $50 carmine | 40.00 | 12.50 |
| **a.** | | Vert. pair, imperf. btwn. | — | |
| *R507* | R25 | $60 carmine | 50.00 | 17.50 |
| **a.** | | Vert. pair, imperf. btwn. | — | |
| *R508* | R25 | $100 carmine | — | 10.00 |
| **a.** | | Vert. pair, imperf. btwn. | 350.00 | |
| *R509* | R25 | $500 carmine | 125.00 | 75.00 |
| *R510* | R25 | $1000 carmine | 80.00 | 50.00 |

Documentary Stamps of 1940 Overprinted in Black

**Series 1949**

**1949 Wmk. 191R** ***Perf. 11***

**Size: 19x22mm**

| No. | Type | Denomination | Unused | Used |
|---|---|---|---|---|
| *R511* | R23 | 1c carmine | 10 | 10 |
| *R512* | R23 | 2c carmine | 20 | 15 |
| *R513* | R23 | 3c carmine | 20 | 15 |
| *R514* | R23 | 4c carmine | 30 | 25 |
| *R515* | R23 | 5c carmine | 30 | 15 |
| *R516* | R23 | 8c carmine | 50 | 30 |
| *R517* | R23 | 10c carmine | 35 | 20 |
| *R518* | R23 | 20c carmine | 50 | 40 |

| | | | | |
|---|---|---|---|---|
| *R519* | R23 | 25c carmine | 75 | 45 |
| *R520* | R23 | 40c carmine | 2.25 | 1.25 |
| *R521* | R23 | 50c carmine | 2.00 | 25 |
| *R522* | R23 | 80c carmine | 3.75 | 3.00 |
| | | *Nos. R511-R522 (12)* | 11.20 | 6.65 |

**Size: 21½x36¼mm**

| | | | | |
|---|---|---|---|---|
| *R523* | R24 | $1 carmine | 3.75 | 30 |
| *R524* | R24 | $2 carmine | 4.50 | 1.25 |
| *R525* | R24 | $3 carmine | 7.50 | 5.00 |
| *R526* | R24 | $4 carmine | 7.50 | 4.75 |
| *R527* | R24 | $5 carmine | 10.00 | 1.75 |
| *R528* | R24 | $10 carmine | 20.00 | 2.50 |
| *R529* | R24 | $20 carmine | 40.00 | 6.00 |

**Size: 28½x42mm**

***Perf. 12***

**Without Gum**

| | | | | |
|---|---|---|---|---|
| *R530* | R25 | $30 carmine | 50.00 | 18.00 |
| *R531* | R25 | $50 carmine | — | 30.00 |
| *R532* | R25 | $60 carmine | — | 35.00 |
| *R533* | R25 | $100 carmine | — | 15.00 |
| *R534* | R25 | $500 carmine | — | 140.00 |
| *R535* | R25 | $1000 carmine | — | 80.00 |

Documentary Stamps of 1940 Overprinted in Black

Series 1950

**1950 Wmk. 191R *Perf. 11***

**Size: 19x22mm**

| | | | | |
|---|---|---|---|---|
| *R536* | R23 | 1c carmine | 10 | 6 |
| *R537* | R23 | 2c carmine | 20 | 10 |
| *R538* | R23 | 3c carmine | 20 | 15 |
| *R539* | R23 | 4c carmine | 25 | 20 |
| *R540* | R23 | 5c carmine | 25 | 12 |
| *R541* | R23 | 8c carmine | 50 | 30 |
| *R542* | R23 | 10c carmine | 60 | 15 |
| *R543* | R23 | 20c carmine | 75 | 35 |
| *R544* | R23 | 25c carmine | 1.10 | 35 |
| *R545* | R23 | 40c carmine | 2.50 | 1.25 |
| *R546* | R23 | 50c carmine | 3.00 | 20 |
| *R547* | R23 | 80c carmine | 4.00 | 3.50 |
| | | *Nos. R536-R547 (12)* | 13.45 | 6.73 |

**Size: 21½x36¼mm**

| | | | | |
|---|---|---|---|---|
| *R548* | R24 | $1 carmine | 3.50 | 20 |
| *R549* | R24 | $2 carmine | 4.00 | 2.00 |
| *R550* | R24 | $3 carmine | 5.50 | 3.00 |
| *R551* | R24 | $4 carmine | 8.00 | 4.00 |
| *R552* | R24 | $5 carmine | 10.00 | 75 |
| *R553* | R24 | $10 carmine | 20.00 | 6.50 |
| *R554* | R24 | $20 carmine | 40.00 | 7.00 |

**Size: 28½x42mm**

***Perf. 12***

**Without Gum**

| | | | | |
|---|---|---|---|---|
| *R555* | R25 | $30 carmine | — | 30.00 |
| *R556* | R25 | $50 carmine | — | 11.00 |
| *a.* | | Vert. pair, imperf. horiz. | | — |
| *R557* | R25 | $60 carmine | — | 40.00 |
| *R558* | R25 | $100 carmine | — | 17.50 |
| *R559* | R25 | $500 carmine | — | 100.00 |
| *R560* | R25 | $1000 carmine | — | 60.00 |

Documentary Stamps of 1940 Overprinted in Black

**Series 1951**

**1951 Wmk. 191R *Perf. 11***

**Size: 19x22mm**

| | | | | |
|---|---|---|---|---|
| *R561* | R23 | 1c carmine | 10 | 10 |
| *R562* | R23 | 2c carmine | 20 | 10 |
| *R563* | R23 | 3c carmine | 15 | 15 |
| *R564* | R23 | 4c carmine | 20 | 15 |
| *R565* | R23 | 5c carmine | 30 | 15 |
| *R566* | R23 | 8c carmine | 50 | 30 |
| *R567* | R23 | 10c carmine | 55 | 15 |
| *R568* | R23 | 20c carmine | 1.00 | 35 |
| *R569* | R23 | 25c carmine | 1.00 | 35 |
| *R570* | R23 | 40c carmine | 2.00 | 70 |
| *R571* | R23 | 50c carmine | 2.00 | 30 |
| *R572* | R23 | 80c carmine | 2.75 | 2.25 |
| | | *Nos. R561-R572 (12)* | 10.75 | 5.05 |

**Size: 21½x36¼mm**

| | | | | |
|---|---|---|---|---|
| *R573* | R24 | $1 carmine | 3.50 | 20 |
| *R574* | R24 | $2 carmine | 4.00 | 25 |
| *R575* | R24 | $3 carmine | 7.00 | 3.50 |
| *R576* | R24 | $4 carmine | 9.00 | 4.50 |
| *R577* | R24 | $5 carmine | 9.00 | 40 |
| *R578* | R24 | $10 carmine | 20.00 | 2.25 |
| *R579* | R24 | $20 carmine | 40.00 | 6.50 |

**Size: 28½x42mm**

***Perf. 12***

**Without Gum**

| | | | | |
|---|---|---|---|---|
| *R580* | R25 | $30 carmine | — | 10.00 |
| *a.* | | Imperf., pair | | *750.00* |
| *R581* | R25 | $50 carmine | — | 12.50 |
| *R582* | R25 | $60 carmine | — | 30.00 |
| *R583* | R25 | $100 carmine | — | 12.50 |
| *R584* | R25 | $500 carmine | 125.00 | 70.00 |
| *R585* | R25 | $1000 carmine | — | 75.00 |

Documentary Stamps and Types of 1940 Overprinted in Black

Series 1952

Designs: 55c, $1.10, $1.65, $2.20, $2.75, $3.30, L. J. Gage; $2500, William Windom; $5000, C. J. Folger; $10,000, W. Q. Gresham.

**1952 Wmk. 191R *Perf. 11***

**Size: 19x22mm**

| | | | | |
|---|---|---|---|---|
| *R586* | R23 | 1c carmine | 10 | 6 |
| *R587* | R23 | 2c carmine | 20 | 10 |
| *R588* | R23 | 3c carmine | 15 | 15 |
| *R589* | R23 | 4c carmine | 15 | 15 |
| *R590* | R23 | 5c carmine | 20 | 10 |
| *R591* | R23 | 8c carmine | 40 | 30 |
| *R592* | R23 | 10c carmine | 35 | 15 |
| *R593* | R23 | 20c carmine | 60 | 35 |
| *R594* | R23 | 25c carmine | 1.00 | 40 |
| *R595* | R23 | 40c carmine | 1.75 | 80 |
| *R596* | R23 | 50c carmine | 2.00 | 20 |
| *R597* | R23 | 55c carmine | 10.00 | 5.00 |
| *R598* | R23 | 80c carmine | 4.50 | 2.25 |
| | | *Nos. R586-R598 (13)* | 21.40 | 10.01 |

**Size: 21½x36¼mm**

| | | | | |
|---|---|---|---|---|
| *R599* | R24 | $1 carmine | 3.00 | 1.50 |
| *R600* | R24 | $1.10 carmine | 18.00 | 12.50 |
| *R601* | R24 | $1.65 carmine | 75.00 | 40.00 |
| *R602* | R24 | $2 carmine | 5.00 | 40 |
| *R603* | R24 | $2.20 carmine | 55.00 | 45.00 |
| *R604* | R24 | $2.75 carmine | 75.00 | 40.00 |
| *R605* | R24 | $3 carmine | 8.00 | 3.50 |
| *a.* | | Horiz. pair, imperf. btwn. | — | |
| *R606* | R24 | $3.30 carmine | 55.00 | 40.00 |
| *R607* | R24 | $4 carmine | 10.00 | 3.50 |
| *R608* | R24 | $5 carmine | 10.00 | 1.25 |
| *R609* | R24 | $10 carmine | 22.00 | 1.25 |
| *R610* | R24 | $20 carmine | 35.00 | 8.00 |

**Size: 28½x 42mm**

***Perf. 12***

**Without Gum**

| | | | | |
|---|---|---|---|---|
| *R611* | R25 | $30 carmine | — | 12.00 |
| *R612* | R25 | $50 carmine | — | 12.00 |
| *R613* | R25 | $60 carmine | — | 30.00 |
| *R614* | R25 | $100 carmine | — | 8.00 |
| *R615* | R25 | $500 carmine | — | 75.00 |
| *R616* | R25 | $1000 carmine | — | 30.00 |

Documentary Stamps and Types of 1940 Overprinted in Black

**Series 1953**

**1953 Wmk. 191R *Perf. 11***

**Size: 19x22mm**

| | | | | |
|---|---|---|---|---|
| *R620* | R23 | 1c carmine | 15 | 10 |
| *R621* | R23 | 2c carmine | 15 | 10 |
| *R622* | R23 | 3c carmine | 15 | 10 |
| *R623* | R23 | 4c carmine | 15 | 10 |
| *R624* | R23 | 5c carmine | 15 | 10 |
| *R625* | R23 | 8c carmine | 35 | 20 |
| *R626* | R23 | 10c carmine | 40 | 18 |
| *R627* | R23 | 20c carmine | 50 | 40 |
| *R628* | R23 | 25c carmine | 75 | 50 |
| *R629* | R23 | 40c carmine | 1.50 | 75 |
| *R630* | R23 | 50c carmine | 1.65 | 15 |
| *R631* | R23 | 55c carmine | 2.25 | 1.50 |
| *a.* | | Horiz. pair, imperf. vert. | *275.00* | |
| *R632* | R23 | 80c carmine | 2.75 | 1.65 |
| | | *Nos. R620-R632 (13)* | 10.90 | 5.83 |

**Size: 21½x36¼mm**

| | | | | |
|---|---|---|---|---|
| *R633* | R24 | $1 carmine | 2.75 | 25 |
| *R634* | R24 | $1.10 carmine | 4.00 | 2.50 |
| *a.* | | Horiz. pair, imperf. vert. | *300.00* | |
| *b.* | | Imperf., pair | *450.00* | |
| *R635* | R24 | $1.65 carmine | 5.00 | 3.50 |
| *R636* | R24 | $2 carmine | 4.50 | 50 |
| *R637* | R24 | $2.20 carmine | 6.00 | 5.00 |
| *R638* | R24 | $2.75 carmine | 8.00 | 6.00 |
| *R639* | R24 | $3 carmine | 6.00 | 3.00 |
| *R640* | R24 | $3.30 carmine | 12.00 | 7.00 |
| *R641* | R24 | $4 carmine | 8.00 | 5.50 |
| *R642* | R24 | $5 carmine | 10.00 | 75 |
| *R643* | R24 | $10 carmine | 20.00 | 1.75 |
| *R644* | R24 | $20 carmine | 40.00 | 15.00 |

**Size: 28½x42mm**

***Perf. 12***

**Without Gum**

| | | | | |
|---|---|---|---|---|
| *R645* | R25 | $30 carmine | — | 12.00 |
| *R646* | R25 | $50 carmine | — | 20.00 |
| *R647* | R25 | $60 carmine | — | 45.00 |
| *R648* | R25 | $100 carmine | 35.00 | 12.00 |
| *R649* | R25 | $500 carmine | — | 90.00 |
| *R650* | R25 | $1000 carmine | 100.00 | 50.00 |
| *R651* | R25 | $2500 carmine | 400.00 | 300.00 |
| *R652* | R25 | $5000 carmine | — | 850.00 |
| *R653* | R25 | $10,000 carmine | — | *600.00* |

Types of 1940 without Overprint

**1954 Wmk. 191R *Perf. 11***

**Size: 19 x 22 mm.**

| | | | | |
|---|---|---|---|---|
| *R654* | R23 | 1c carmine | 6 | 5 |
| *a.* | | horiz. pair, imperf. vert. | — | |
| *R655* | R23 | 2c carmine | 8 | 6 |
| *R656* | R23 | 3c carmine | 12 | 10 |
| *R657* | R23 | 4c carmine | 12 | 10 |
| *R658* | R23 | 5c carmine | 13 | 8 |
| *R659* | R23 | 8c carmine | 25 | 20 |
| *R660* | R23 | 10c carmine | 25 | 15 |
| *R661* | R23 | 20c carmine | 50 | 35 |
| *R662* | R23 | 25c carmine | 60 | 40 |
| *R663* | R23 | 40c carmine | 90 | 60 |
| *R664* | R23 | 50c carmine | 1.00 | 15 |
| *a.* | | Horiz. pair, imperf. vert | 200.00 | |
| *R665* | R23 | 55c carmine | 1.15 | 1.10 |
| *R666* | R23 | 80c carmine | 1.75 | 1.65 |
| | | *Nos. R654-R666 (13)* | 6.91 | 4.99 |

**Size: 21½x36¼mm**

| | | | | |
|---|---|---|---|---|
| *R667* | R24 | $1 carmine | 1.00 | 20 |
| *R668* | R24 | $1.10 carmine | 2.75 | 2.35 |
| *R669* | R24 | $1.65 carmine | 100.00 | 75.00 |
| *R670* | R24 | $2 carmine | 1.75 | 45 |
| *R671* | R24 | $2.20 carmine | 4.50 | 3.75 |
| *R672* | R24 | $2.75 carmine | 100.00 | 75.00 |
| *R673* | R24 | $3 carmine | 3.00 | 2.00 |
| *R674* | R24 | $3.30 carmine | 6.50 | 5.00 |
| *R675* | R24 | $4 carmine | 4.50 | 3.50 |
| *R676* | R24 | $5 carmine | 10.00 | 50 |
| *R677* | R24 | $10 carmine | 20.00 | 1.50 |
| *R678* | R24 | $20 carmine | 40.00 | 6.00 |

Documentary Stamps and Type of 1940 Overprinted in Black

**Series 1954**

***Perf. 12***

***Size: 28½x42mm***

**Without Gum**

| | | | | |
|---|---|---|---|---|
| *R679* | R25 | $30 carmine | — | 12.00 |
| *R680* | R25 | $50 carmine | — | 15.00 |
| *R681* | R25 | $60 carmine | — | 17.50 |
| *R682* | R25 | $100 carmine | — | 7.00 |
| *R683* | R25 | $500 carmine | — | 60.00 |
| *R684* | R25 | $1000 carmine | — | 40.00 |
| *R685* | R25 | $2500 carmine | — | 125.00 |
| *R686* | R25 | $5000 carmine | — | 400.00 |
| *R687* | R25 | $10,000 carmine | — | 350.00 |

Documentary Stamps and Type of 1940 Overprinted in Black

**Series 1955**

Without Gum

**1955 Wmk. 191R *Perf. 12***

**Size: 28½x42mm**

| | | | | |
|---|---|---|---|---|
| *R688* | R25 | $30 carmine | — | 9.00 |
| *R689* | R25 | $50 carmine | — | 13.50 |
| *R690* | R25 | $60 carmine | — | 16.50 |
| *R691* | R25 | $100 carmine | — | 7.00 |
| *R692* | R25 | $500 carmine | — | 90.00 |
| *R693* | R25 | $1000 carmine | — | 35.00 |
| *R694* | R25 | $2500 carmine | — | 100.00 |
| *R695* | R25 | $5000 carmine | — | 550.00 |
| *R696* | R25 | $10,000 carmine | — | 300.00 |

Documentary Stamps and Type of 1940 Overprinted in Black "Series 1956"

Without Gum

**1956 Size: 28½x42mm**

| | | | | |
|---|---|---|---|---|
| *R697* | R25 | $30 carmine | — | 13.50 |
| *R698* | R25 | $50 carmine | — | 15.00 |
| *R699* | R25 | $60 carmine | — | 30.00 |
| *R700* | R25 | $100 carmine | — | 10.00 |
| *R701* | R25 | $500 carmine | — | 62.50 |
| *R702* | R25 | $1000 carmine | — | 50.00 |
| *R703* | R25 | $2500 carmine | — | 200.00 |
| *R704* | R25 | $5000 carmine | — | 1,050. |
| *R705* | R25 | $10,000 carmine | — | 350.00 |

Documentary Stamps and Type of 1940 Overprinted in Black "Series 1957"

Without Gum

**1957 Size: 28½x42mm**

| | | | | |
|---|---|---|---|---|
| *R706* | R25 | $30 carmine | — | 27.50 |
| *R707* | R25 | $50 carmine | — | 15.00 |
| *R708* | R25 | $60 carmine | — | 85.00 |
| *R709* | R25 | $100 carmine | — | 12.50 |
| *R710* | R25 | $500 carmine | 175.00 | 75.00 |
| *R711* | R25 | $1000 carmine | — | 65.00 |
| *R712* | R25 | $2500 carmine | — | 450.00 |
| *R713* | R25 | $5000 carmine | — | 450.00 |
| *R714* | R25 | $10,000 carmine | — | 350.00 |

Documentary Stamps and Type of 1940 Overprinted in Black "Series 1958"

Without Gum

**1958 Size: 28½x42mm**

| | | | | |
|---|---|---|---|---|
| *R715* | R25 | $30 carmine | — | 15.00 |
| *R716* | R25 | $50 carmine | — | 16.00 |
| *R717* | R25 | $60 carmine | — | 25.00 |
| *R718* | R25 | $100 carmine | — | 10.00 |
| *R719* | R25 | $500 carmine | 100.00 | 45.00 |
| *R720* | R25 | $1000 carmine | — | 55.00 |
| *R721* | R25 | $2500 carmine | — | 600.00 |
| *R722* | R25 | $5000 carmine | — | 1,250. |
| *R723* | R25 | $10,000 carmine | — | 650.00 |

Documentary Stamps and Type of 1940 Without Overprint

With Gum

**1958 Size: 28½x42mm**

| | | | | |
|---|---|---|---|---|
| *R724* | R25 | $30 carmine | 35.00 | 6.00 |
| *a.* | | Vert. pair, imperf. horiz. | | — |
| *R725* | R25 | $50 carmine | 35.00 | 5.00 |
| *a.* | | Vert. pair, imperf. horiz. | | — |
| *R726* | R25 | $60 carmine | — | 20.00 |
| *R727* | R25 | $100 carmine | 17.50 | 4.75 |
| *R728* | R25 | $500 carmine | 80.00 | 25.00 |
| *R729* | R25 | $1000 carmine | 50.00 | 20.00 |
| *a.* | | Vert. pair, imperf. horiz. | | — |
| *R730* | R25 | $2500 carmine | — | 125.00 |
| *R731* | R25 | $5000 carmine | — | 125.00 |
| *R732* | R25 | $10,000 carmine | — | 100.00 |

**Catalogue values for unused stamps in this section, from this point to the end of the section, are for Never Hinged items.**

Internal Revenue Building, Washington, DC — R26

**Giori Press Printing**

**1962, July 1 Unwmk. *Perf. 11***

| | | | | |
|---|---|---|---|---|
| *R733* | R26 | 10c vio bl & brt grn | 1.00 | 20 |

Centenary of Internal Revenue Service.

"Established 1862" Removed

**1963**

| | | | | |
|---|---|---|---|---|
| *R734* | R26 | 10c vio bl & brt grn | 3.00 | 10 |

Documentary revenue stamps were no longer required after Dec. 31, 1967.

## PROPRIETARY STAMPS

Stamps for use on proprietary articles were included in the first general issue of 1862-71. They are Nos. R3, R13, R14, R18, R22, R29, R31 and R38.

Washington — RB1

Various Frames and Sizes
Violet or Green Paper with Silk Threads

**1871-74 Engr. *Perf. 12***

**a. left column = Violet Paper (1871)**

**b. right column = Green Paper (1874)**

| | | | | |
|---|---|---|---|---|
| *RB1* | RB1 | 1c grn & blk | 4.00 | 6.00 |
| *c.* | | Imperf. | 100.00 | |
| *d.* | | Inverted center | *2,500.* | |
| *RB2* | RB1 | 2c grn & blk | 4.50 | 13.00 |
| *c.* | | Inverted center | *40,000.* | *9,500.* |
| *RB3* | RB1 | 3c grn & blk | 12.00 | 35.00 |
| *c.* | | Sewing machine perf. | 125.00 | |
| *d.* | | Inverted center | *15,000.* | |
| *RB4* | RB1 | 4c grn & blk | 7.00 | 12.50 |
| *c.* | | Inverted center | *16,500.* | |
| *RB5* | RB1 | 5c grn & blk | 90.00 | 95.00 |
| *c.* | | Inverted center | *40,000.* | |
| *RB6* | RB1 | 6c grn & blk | 27.50 | 70.00 |
| *RB7* | RB1 | 10c grn & blk ('73) | 125.00 | 35.00 |
| *RB8* | RB1 | 50c grn & blk ('73) | 550.00 | 800.00 |
| *RB9* | RB1 | $1 grn & blk ('73) | *1,200.* | *3,000.* |
| *RB10* | RB1 | $5 grn & blk ('73) | *2,500.* | — |

Washington — RB2

Various Frames and Sizes
Green Paper
**Wmk. 191R, Unwmkd. (Silk Paper)**
**1875-81**
**b. left column = Perf.**
**c. right column = Rouletted 6**

*RB11* RB2 1c green 35 30.00
*a.* Silk paper 1.50
*d.* Vert. pair, imperf btwn. 250.00
*RB12* RB2 2c brown 1.25 45.00
*a.* Silk paper 2.00
*RB13* RB2 3c orange 2.25 45.00
*a.* Silk paper 9.00
*d.* Horiz. pair, imperf. btwn. —
*RB14* RB2 4c red brown 4.00
*a.* Silk paper 4.50
*RB15* RB2 4c red 3.50 45.00
*RB16* RB2 5c black 70.00 725.00
*a.* Silk paper 80.00
*RB17* RB2 6c vio blue 13.00 125.00
*a.* Silk paper 20.00
*RB18* RB2 6c violet 20.00 150.00
*RB19* RB2 10c blue ('81) 175.00

Battleship RB3

***Rouletted 5½***
**1898 Wmk. 191R Engr.**

*RB20* RB3 ⅛c yel green 6 6
*a.* Vert. pair, imperf. horiz. —
*RB21* RB3 ¼c brown 6 6
*a.* ¼c red brown 6 6
*b.* ¼c yellow brown 6 6
*c.* ¼c orange brown 6 6
*d.* ¼c bister 6 6
*e.* Vert. pair, imperf. horiz. — —
*f.* Printed on both sides —
*RB22* RB3 ⅜c deep org 12 8
*a.* Horiz. pair, imperf. vert. 9.00
*b.* Vert. pair, imperf. horiz. —
*RB23* RB3 ⅝c deep ultra 12 10
*a.* Vert. pair, imperf. horiz. 50.00
*b.* Horiz. pair, imperf. vert. 200.00
*RB24* RB3 1c dark grn 30 15
*a.* Vert. pair, imperf. horiz. —
*RB25* RB3 1¼c violet 10 8
*a.* 1¼c brown violet 12 10
*b.* Vert. pair, imperf. btwn. —
*RB26* RB3 1⅞c dull blue 2.00 65
*RB27* RB3 2c vio brown 35 18
*a.* Horiz. pair, imperf. vert. 25.00
*RB28* RB3 2½c lake 40 12
*a.* Vert. pair, imperf. horiz. 30.00
*RB29* RB3 3¾c olive gray 5.00 2.50
*RB30* RB3 4c purple 2.00 75
*RB31* RB3 5c brn org 2.00 75
*a.* Vert. pair, imperf. horiz. — 225.00
*b.* Horiz. pair, imperf. vert. —
*Nos. RB20-RB31 (12)* 12.51 5.48

***Hyphen Hole Perf. 7***

| | | | |
|---|---|---|---|
| *RB20p* | ⅛c | 12 | 10 |
| *RB21p* | ¼c | 12 | 10 |
| *RB22p* | ⅜c | 25 | 15 |
| *RB23p* | ⅝c | 25 | 15 |
| *RB24p* | 1c | 12.00 | 5.00 |
| *RB25p* | 1¼c | 20 | 12 |
| *RB26p* | 1⅞c | 7.50 | — |
| *RB27p* | 2c | 75 | 25 |
| *RB28p* | 2½c | 50 | 20 |
| *RB29p* | 3¾c | 10.00 | 5.00 |
| *RB30p* | 4c | — | — |
| *RB31p* | 5c | 10.00 | 6.00 |

See note following No. R178.

RB4

**Offset Printing**
**1914 Wmk. 190 *Perf. 10***

*RB32* RB4 ⅛c black 20 15
*RB33* RB4 ¼c black 1.25 1.00
*RB34* RB4 ⅜c black 20 15
*RB35* RB4 ⅝c black 2.50 1.75
*RB36* RB4 1¼c black 1.75 80
*RB37* RB4 1⅞c black 25.00 15.00
*RB38* RB4 2½c black 3.50 2.50
*RB39* RB4 3⅛c black 70.00 50.00
*RB40* RB4 3¾c black 25.00 19.00
*RB41* RB4 4c black 45.00 27.50
*RB42* RB4 4⅜c black 900.00 —
*RB43* RB4 5c black 90.00 65.00
*Nos. RB32-RB41,RB43 (11)* 264.40 182.85

**Wmk. 191R**

*RB44* RB4 ⅛c black 15 10
*RB45* RB4 ¼c black 15 10
*RB46* RB4 ⅜c black 60 30
*RB47* RB4 ½c black 2.75 2.00
*RB48* RB4 ⅝c black 15 10
*RB49* RB4 1c black 3.50 2.75
*RB50* RB4 1¼c black 35 25
*RB51* RB4 1½c black 3.00 2.25
*RB52* RB4 1⅞c black 1.00 60
*RB53* RB4 2c black 5.00 4.00
*RB54* RB4 2½c black 1.25 1.00
*RB55* RB4 3c black 3.50 2.75
*RB56* RB4 3⅛c black 4.50 3.00
*RB57* RB4 3¾c black 9.00 7.50
*RB58* RB4 4c black 30 20
*RB59* RB4 4⅜c black 11.00 7.50
*RB60* RB4 5c black 2.75 2.50
*RB61* RB4 6c black 45.00 37.50
*RB62* RB4 8c black 13.50 11.00
*RB63* RB4 10c black 9.00 7.00
*RB64* RB4 20c black 17.50 15.00
*Nos. RB44-RB64 (21)* 133.95 107.40

RB5

**1919 *Perf. 11***

*RB65* RB5 1c dark blue 10 8
*RB66* RB5 2c dark blue 12 8
*RB67* RB5 3c dark blue 1.00 60
*RB68* RB5 4c dark blue 1.00 50
*RB69* RB5 5c dark blue 1.25 60
*RB70* RB5 8c dark blue 11.00 9.00
*RB71* RB5 10c dark blue 2.25 1.75
*RB72* RB5 20c dark blue 4.00 3.00
*RB73* RB5 40c dark blue 22.50 8.00
*Nos. RB65-RB73 (9)* 43.22 23.61

## FUTURE DELIVERY STAMPS

Issued to facilitate the collection of a tax upon each sale, agreement of sale or agreement to sell any products or merchandise at any exchange or board of trade, or other similar place for future delivery.

Documentary Stamps Nos. R228 to R250 Overprinted in Black or Red

**FUTURE**
**DELIVERY**

**Offset Printing**
**1918-34 Wmk. 191R *Perf. 11***
**Overprint Horizontal (Lines 8mm apart)**

*RC1* R22 2c car rose 1.25 10
*RC2* R22 3c car rose ('34) 25.00 22.50
Cut cancellation 12.50
*RC3* R22 4c car rose 1.25 10
*RC3A* R22 5c car rose ('33) — 3.00
*RC4* R22 10c car rose 2.50 15
*a.* Double overprint — 5.00
*b.* "FUTURE" omitted —
*c.* "DELIVERY FUTURE" 35.00
*RC5* R22 20c car rose 2.75 10
*a.* Double overprint 20.00
*RC6* R22 25c car rose 10.00 40
Cut cancellation 6
*RC7* R22 40c car rose 10.00 75
Cut cancellation 6
*RC8* R22 50c car rose 3.00 12
*a.* "DELIVERY" omitted —
*RC9* R22 80c car rose 20.00 7.50
Cut cancellation 1.00
*a.* Double overprint 25.00
Cut cancellation 6.00
*Nos. RC1-RC9 (10)* 75.75 34.72

**Overprint Vertical, Reading Up (Lines 2mm apart)**
**Engr.**

*RC10* R21 $1 green (R) — 25
Cut cancellation 5
*a.* Overprint reading down 275.00
*b.* Black overprint —
Cut cancellation 125.00
*RC11* R21 $2 rose — 25
Cut cancellation 5
*RC12* R21 $3 violet (R) — 1.25
Cut cancellation 12
*a.* Overprint reading down — 50.00
*RC13* R21 $5 dark bl (R) — 35
Cut cancellation 8
*RC14* R21 $10 orange — 60
Cut cancellation 15
*a.* "DELIVERY FUTURE" —
*RC15* R21 $20 olive bis — 3.75
Cut cancellation 50
*Nos. RC10-RC15 (6)* 6.45

***Perf. 12***
**Overprint Horiz. (Lines 11½mm apart)**
**Without Gum**

*RC16* R17 $30 ver, green numerals — 3.00
Cut cancellation 1.25
*a.* Numerals in blue 50.00 3.00
Cut cancellation 1.50
*b.* As "a," imperf. —
*RC17* R19 $50 ol grn — 1.00
Cut cancellation 40
*a.* $50 olive bister — 1.00
Cut cancellation 40
*RC18* R19 $60 brown — 2.00
Cut cancellation 75
*a.* Vert. pair, imperf. horiz. 400.00
*RC19* R17 $100 yel grn ('34) 55.00 22.50
Cut cancellation 6.00
*RC20* R18 $500 blue, red numerals (R) 50.00 10.00
Cut cancellation 4.50
*a.* Numerals in orange — 60.00
Cut cancellation 10.00
*RC21* R19 $1000orange — 4.00
Cut cancellation 1.50
*a.* Vert. pair, imperf. horiz. 500.00
*Nos. RC16-RC21 (6)* 42.50

See note after No. R227.

**1923-24 Offset Printing *Perf. 11***
**Overprint Horiz. (Lines 2mm apart)**

*RC22* R22 1c carmine rose 75 15
*RC23* R22 80c carmine rose — 1.75
Cut cancellation 25

Documentary Stamps of 1917 Overprinted in Red or Black

**FUTURE**
**DELIVERY**

**1925-34 Engr.**

*RC25* R21 $1 green (R) 8.00 60
Cut cancellation 6
*RC26* R21 $10 org (Bk) ('34) — 12.00
Cut cancellation 7.00

Overprinted like Nos. RC1-RC9

**1928-29 Offset Printing *Perf. 10***

*RC27* R22 10c carmine rose 850.00
*RC28* R22 20c carmine rose 850.00

## STOCK TRANSFER STAMPS

Issued to facilitate the collection of a tax on all sales or agreements to sell, or memoranda of sales or delivery of, or transfers of legal title to shares or certificates of stock.

Documentary Stamps Nos. R228 to R259 Overprinted in Black or Red

**STOCK**
**TRANSFER**

**Offset Printing**
**1918-29 Wmk. 191R *Perf. 11***
**Overprint Horiz. (Lines 8mm apart)**

*RD1* R22 1c car rose 30 10
*a.* Double overprint — —
*RD2* R22 2c car rose 15 5
*a.* Double overprint — 5.00
Cut cancellation 2.50
*RD3* R22 4c car rose 12 5
*a.* Double overprint — 4.00
Cut cancellation 2.00
*b.* "STOCK" omitted 10.00
*d.* Ovpt. lines 10 mm apart —
*RD4* R22 5c car rose 20 5
*RD5* R22 10c car rose 12 5
*a.* Double overprint — 5.00
Cut cancellation 2.50
*b.* "STOCK" omitted —
*RD6* R22 20c car rose 20 5
*a.* Double overprint — 6.00
*b.* "STOCK" double —
*RD7* R22 25c car rose 75 10
Cut cancellation 5
*RD8* R22 40c car rose ('22) 65 6
*RD9* R22 50c car rose 25 5
*a.* Double overprint —
*RD10* R22 80c car rose 90 25
Cut cancellation 5
*Nos. RD1-RD10 (10)* 3.64 81

**Overprint Vertical, Reading Up (Lines 2mm apart)**
**Engr.**

*RD11* R21 $1 grn (R) 30.00 7.75
Cut cancellation 45
*a.* Ovpt. reading down — 11.00
Cut cancellation 4.00
*RD12* R21 $1 grn (Bk) 1.50 5
*a.* Pair, one without overprint —
*b.* Ovptd. on back instead of face, invtd. — —
*c.* Overprint reading down — 5.00
*d.* $1 yellow green — 6
*RD13* R21 $2 rose 1.50 5
*a.* Overprint reading down 10.00
Cut cancellation 1.50
*b.* Vert. pair, imperf. horiz. 500.00
*c.* "TRANSFER STOCK" —
*RD14* R21 $3 vio (R) 5.50 1.00
Cut cancellation 20
*RD15* R21 $4 yel brn 4.00 5
Cut cancellation 5
*RD16* R21 $5 dk bl (R) 2.25 5
Cut cancellation 5
*a.* Ovpt. reading down — 75
Cut cancellation 15
*RD17* R21 $10 orange 3.25 12
Cut cancellation 5
*a.* "TRANSFER STOCK" —
*b.* "TRANSFER" omitted —
*RD18* R21 $20 ol bis ('21) 30.00 15.00
Cut cancellation 3.00
*Nos. RD11-RD18 (8)* 78.00 24.07

**1918 Without Gum *Perf. 12***
**Overprint Horizontal (Lines 11½mm apart)**

*RD19* R17 $30 ver, green numerals 12.50 4.00
Cut cancellation 1.00
*a.* Numerals in blue 50.00
*RD20* R19 $50 ol grn, *(Cleveland)* 75.00 50.00
Cut cancellation 10.00
*RD21* R19 $60 brown 50.00 16.00
Cut cancellation 6.00
*RD22* R17 $100 green 15.00 5.00
Cut cancellation 2.00
*RD23* R18 $500 blue (R) — 100.00
Cut cancellation 45.00
*a.* Numerals in orange 125.00
*RD24* R19 $1000 orange — 65.00
Cut cancellation 22.50

See note after No. R227.

**1928-32 Offset Printing *Perf. 10***
**Overprint Horiz. (Lines 8mm apart)**

*RD25* R22 2c car rose 50 5
*RD26* R22 4c car rose 45 5
*RD27* R22 10c car rose 50 6
*a.* Invtd. ovpt. 1,000.
*RD28* R22 20c car rose 60 6
*RD29* R22 50c car rose 1.25 10

**Overprint Vertical, Reading Up. (Lines 2mm. apart)**
**Engr.**

*RD30* R21 $1 green 2.00 5
*a.* $1 yellow green — —
*RD31* R21 $2 car rose 2.00 5
*a.* Pair, one without overprint 150.00
*RD32* R21 $10 orange 8.00 15
Cut cancellation 5
*Nos. RD25-RD32 (8)* 15.30 57

Overprinted Horiz. in Black

**STOCK**
**TRANSFER**

**1920-28 Offset Printing *Perf. 11***

*RD33* R22 2c car rose 3.00 50
*RD34* R22 10c car rose 50 5
*a.* "TRANSFER STOCK" 40.00
*RD35* R22 20c car rose 60 5
*a.* Pair, one without overprint 175.00 —
*b.* "TRANSFER STOCK" 75.00
*c.* "TRANSFER" omitted 65.00
*RD36* R22 50c car rose 1.25 8

**Engr.**

*RD37* R21 $1 green 12.50 6.50
Cut cancellation 25
*RD38* R21 $2 rose 10.00 6.00
Cut cancellation 25
*Nos. RD33-RD38 (6)* 27.85 13.18

***Perf. 10***
**Offset Printing**

*RD39* R22 2c car rose 2.75 35
*RD40* R22 10c car rose 90 10
*RD41* R22 20c car rose 1.25 6

Used values for Nos. RD42-RD372 are for copies which are neither cut nor perforated with initials. Copies with cut cancellations or perforated initials are valued in Scott's U.S. Specialized Catalogue.

SERIES 1940

Documentary Stamps of 1917-33 Overprinted in Black **STOCK TRANSFER**

**1940** *Perf. 11*

*RD42* R22 1c rose pink 1.75 45
*a.* "Series 1940" inverted — 225.00
*RD43* R22 2c rose pink 1.10 50
*RD45* R22 4c rose pink 1.10 10
*RD46* R22 5c rose pink 1.25 10
*RD48* R22 10c rose pink 1.75 10
*RD49* R22 20c rose pink 5.00 15
*RD50* R22 25c rose pink 5.00 35
*RD51* R22 40c rose pink 2.50 60
*RD52* R22 50c rose pink 3.50 15
*RD53* R22 80c rose pink 45.00 25.00
*Nos. RD42-RD53 (10)* 67.95 27.50

**Engr.**

*RD54* R21 $1 green 9.00 25
*RD55* R21 $2 rose 9.00 25
*RD56* R21 $3 violet — 2.00
*RD57* R21 $4 yel brn 10.00 30
*RD58* R21 $5 dark blue 12.00 30
*RD59* R21 $10 orange 30.00 3.50
*RD60* R21 $20 olive bis 55.00 17.50
*Nos. RD54-RD60 (6)* 125.00

Stock Transfer Stamps of 1918 Handstamped in Blue "Series 1940"

**1940** **Without Gum** *Perf. 12*

*RD61* R17 $30 vermilion 350.00
*RD62* R19 $50 olive grn 450.00
*a.* Double ovpt. (perf. initials canc.) 325.00
*RD63* R19 $60 brown 400.00
*RD64* R17 $100 green 350.00
*RD65* R18 $500 blue 1,250.
*RD66* R19 $1000 orange 1,750.

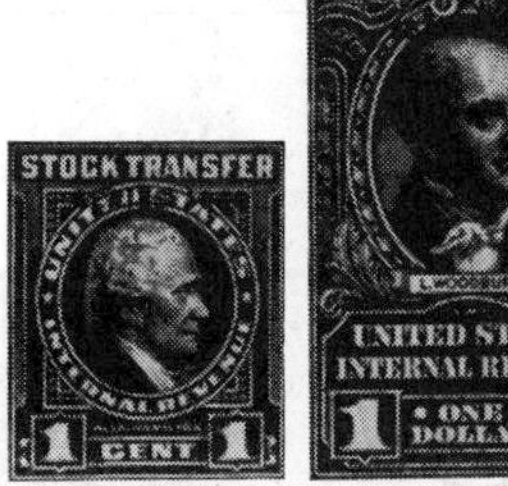

Alexander Hamilton — ST1 Levi Woodbury — ST2

Thomas Corwin ST3

Portraits (see R23-R25): 2c, Wolcott. 4c, Gallatin. 5c, Campbell. 10c, Crawford. 20c, Rush. 25c, Ingham. 40c, McLane. 50c, Duane. 80c, Taney. $2, Ewing. $3, Forward. $4, Spencer. $5, Bibb. $10, Walker. $20, Meredith. $50, Guthrie. $60, Cobb. $100, Thomas. $500, Dix. $1,000, Chase.

Overprinted in Black SERIES 1940

**1940** **Wmk. 191R** *Perf. 11*
**Various Portraits**
**Size: 19x22mm**

*RD67* ST1 1c brt grn 4.75 1.75
*RD68* ST1 2c brt grn 2.00 75
*RD70* ST1 4c brt grn 4.50 2.25
*RD71* ST1 5c brt grn 3.00 1.00
*a.* Without ovpt. (cut canc.) —
*RD73* ST1 10c brt grn 4.00 90
*RD74* ST1 20c brt grn 4.00 75
*RD75* ST1 25c brt grn 15.00 4.50
*RD76* ST1 40c brt grn 30.00 21.00
*RD77* ST1 50c brt grn 4.00 90
*RD78* ST1 80c brt grn 40.00 25.00
*Nos. RD67-RD78 (10)* 111.25 58.80

**Size: 21½x36¼mm**

*RD79* ST2 $1 brt grn 7.00 1.25
*a.* Without overprint (perf. initials canc.) 150.00
*RD80* ST2 $2 brt grn 8.00 3.50
*RD81* ST2 $3 brt grn 16.00 5.00
*RD82* ST2 $4 brt grn — 100.00
*RD83* ST2 $5 brt grn 16.00 7.00
*RD84* ST2 $10 brt grn — 16.00
*RD85* ST2 $20 brt grn — 22.50

*Perf. 12*
**Without Gum**
**Size: 28½x42mm**
**Various Frame Designs**

*RD86* ST3 $30 brt grn — 80.00
*RD87* ST3 $50 brt grn — 100.00
*RD88* ST3 $60 brt grn — 140.00
*RD89* ST3 $100 brt grn — 110.00
*RD90* ST3 $500 brt grn — 375.00
*RD91* ST3 $1000 brt grn — 275.00

Stock Transfer Stamps of 1940 Overprinted in Black SERIES 1941

**1941** **Size: 19x22mm** *Perf. 11*

*RD92* ST1 1c brt grn 50 25
*RD93* ST1 2c brt grn 25 8
*RD95* ST1 4c brt grn 25 6
*RD96* ST1 5c brt grn 25 6
*RD98* ST1 10c brt grn 35 6
*RD99* ST1 20c brt grn 80 6
*RD100* ST1 25c brt grn 1.00 20
*RD101* ST1 40c brt grn 1.10 25
*RD102* ST1 50c brt grn 2.25 15
*RD103* ST1 80c brt grn 9.00 3.75
*Nos. RD92-RD103 (10)* 15.75 4.92

**Size: 21½x36¼mm**

*RD104* ST2 $1 brt grn 5.00 10
*RD105* ST2 $2 brt grn 6.00 15
*RD106* ST2 $3 brt grn 8.00 1.00
*RD107* ST2 $4 brt grn 15.00 4.50
*RD108* ST2 $5 brt grn 18.00 40
*RD109* ST2 $10 brt grn 40.00 2.50
*RD110* ST2 $20 brt grn — 27.50
*Nos. RD104-RD110 (6)* 92.00

*Perf. 12*
**Without Gum**
**Size: 28½x42mm**

*RD111* ST3 $30 brt grn 85.00 70.00
*RD112* ST3 $50 brt grn — 75.00
*RD113* ST3 $60 brt grn 160.00 100.00
*RD114* ST3 $100 brt grn — 45.00
*RD115* ST3 $500 brt grn — 325.00
*RD116* ST3 $1000 brt grn — 275.00

Stock Transfer Stamps of 1940 Overprinted in Black SERIES 1942

**1942** **Size: 19x22mm** *Perf. 11*

*RD117* ST1 1c brt grn 35 15
*RD118* ST1 2c brt grn 20 15
*RD119* ST1 4c brt grn 2.25 70
*RD120* ST1 5c brt grn 30 10
*a.* Ovpt. invtd. (cut cancel) 225.00
*RD121* ST1 10c brt grn 75 10
*RD122* ST1 20c brt grn 1.10 10
*RD123* ST1 25c brt grn 1.25 10
*RD124* ST1 40c brt grn 2.25 25
*RD125* ST1 50c brt grn 3.00 10
*RD126* ST1 80c brt grn 7.00 3.50
*Nos. RD117-RD126 (10)* 18.45 5.25

**Size: 21½x36¼mm**

*RD127* ST2 $1 brt grn 5.50 10
*RD128* ST2 $2 brt grn 9.50 15
*RD129* ST2 $3 brt grn 11.00 55
*RD130* ST2 $4 brt grn 17.50 11.00
*RD131* ST2 $5 brt grn 13.00 25
*a.* Dbl. ovpt. (perf. initials cancel) —
*RD132* ST2 $10 brt grn 27.50 4.50
*RD133* ST2 $20 brt grn 55.00 21.00
*Nos. RD127-RD133 (7)* 139.00 37.55

*Perf. 12*
**Without Gum**
**Size: 28½x42mm**

*RD134* ST3 $30 brt grn — 35.00
*RD135* ST3 $50 brt grn — 55.00
*RD136* ST3 $60 brt grn — 75.00
*RD137* ST3 $100 brt grn — 60.00
*RD138* ST3 $500 brt grn — —
*RD139* ST3 $1000 brt grn — 200.00

Stock Transfer Stamps of 1940 Overprinted in Black SERIES 1943

**1943** **Size: 19x22mm** *Perf. 11*

*RD140* ST1 1c brt grn 30 20
*RD141* ST1 2c brt grn 40 20
*RD142* ST1 4c brt grn 1.10 10
*RD143* ST1 5c brt grn 40 10
*RD144* ST1 10c brt grn 45 10
*RD145* ST1 20c brt grn 1.00 10
*RD146* ST1 25c brt grn 2.25 25
*RD147* ST1 40c brt grn 2.25 25
*RD148* ST1 50c brt grn 2.25 10
*RD149* ST1 80c brt grn 6.00 2.50
*Nos. RD140-RD149 (10)* 16.40 3.90

**Size: 21½x36¼mm**

*RD150* ST2 $1 brt grn 4.50 10
*RD151* ST2 $2 brt grn 7.00 20
*RD152* ST2 $3 brt grn 7.50 75
*RD153* ST2 $4 brt grn 16.00 10.00
*RD154* ST2 $5 brt grn 26.00 35
*RD155* ST2 $10 brt grn 27.50 3.00
*RD156* ST2 $20 brt grn 45.00 22.50
*Nos. RD150-RD156 (7)* 133.50 36.90

*Perf. 12*
**Without Gum**
**Size: 28½x42mm**

*RD157* ST3 $30 brt grn 175.00 75.00
*RD158* ST3 $50 brt grn — 75.00
*RD159* ST3 $60 brt grn — 90.00
*RD160* ST3 $100 brt grn — 45.00
*RD161* ST3 $500 brt grn — 175.00
*RD162* ST3 $1000 brt grn — 165.00

Stock Transfer Stamps and Types of 1940 Overprinted in Black **Series 1944**

Portraits: $2,500, William Windom. $5,000, C. J. Folger. $10,000, Walter Q. Gresham.

**1944** **Wmk. 191R** *Perf. 11*
**Size: 19x22mm**

*RD163* ST1 1c brt grn 50 40
*RD164* ST1 2c brt grn 35 15
*RD165* ST1 4c brt grn 50 20
*RD166* ST1 5c brt grn 40 10
*RD167* ST1 10c brt grn 40 10
*RD168* ST1 20c brt grn 60 15
*RD169* ST1 25c brt grn 1.25 30
*RD170* ST1 40c brt grn 4.50 3.75
*RD171* ST1 50c brt grn 2.50 15
*RD172* ST1 80c brt grn 4.00 3.00
*Nos. RD163-RD172 (10)* 15.00 8.30

**Size: 21½x36¼mm**

*RD173* ST2 $1 brt grn 3.50 30
*RD174* ST2 $2 brt grn — 35
*RD175* ST2 $3 brt grn 9.00 75
*RD176* ST2 $4 brt grn 13.00 3.50
*RD177* ST2 $5 brt grn 11.00 60
*RD178* ST2 $10 brt grn 25.00 3.00
*RD179* ST2 $20 brt grn 50.00 5.50
*Nos. RD173-RD179 (6)* 111.50

*Perf. 12*
**Without Gum**
**Size: 28½x42mm**
**Bright Green**

*RD180* ST3 $30 50.00 35.00
*RD181* ST3 $50 50.00 30.00
*RD182* ST3 $60 125.00 75.00
*RD183* ST3 $100 — 35.00
*RD184* ST3 $500 — 300.00
*RD185* ST3 $1000 (cut canc.) — 175.00
*RD185A* ST3 $2500 — —
*RD185B* ST3 $5000 — —
*RD185C* ST3 $10,000 (cut cancel) 800.00

Stock Transfer Stamps of 1940-44 Overprinted in Black **Series 1945**

**1945** **Wmk. 191R** *Perf. 11*
**Size: 19x22mm**

*RD186* ST1 1c brt grn 12 10
*RD187* ST1 2c brt grn 20 15
*RD188* ST1 4c brt grn 15 10
*RD189* ST1 5c brt grn 18 10
*RD190* ST1 10c brt grn 40 30
*RD191* ST1 20c brt grn 60 25
*RD192* ST1 25c brt grn 1.00 35
*RD193* ST1 40c brt grn 1.65 20
*RD194* ST1 50c brt grn 1.75 20
*RD195* ST1 80c brt grn 2.75 2.00
*Nos. RD186-RD195 (10)* 8.80 3.75

**Size: 21½x36¼mm**

*RD196* ST2 $1 brt grn 6.00 20
*RD197* ST2 $2 brt grn 8.50 25
*RD198* ST2 $3 brt grn 12.00 50
*RD199* ST2 $4 brt grn 12.00 1.25
*RD200* ST2 $5 brt grn 10.00 30
*RD201* ST2 $10 brt grn 20.00 3.75
*RD202* ST2 $20 brt grn 35.00 4.25

*United States Hunting Permit stamps can be mounted in Scott's Federal and State Duck Album.*

*Perf. 12*
**Without Gum**
**Size: 28½x42mm**
**Bright green**

*RD203* ST3 $30 60.00 30.00
*RD204* ST3 $50 40.00 10.00
*RD205* ST3 $60 100.00 65.00
*RD206* ST3 $100 — 20.00
*RD207* ST3 $500 — 200.00
*RD208* ST3 $1000 — 225.00
*RD208A* ST3 $2500 — —
*RD208B* ST3 $5000 — —
*RD208C* ST3 $10,000 (cut canc.) — 800.00

Stock Transfer Stamps of 1940-44 Overprinted in Black **Series 1946**

**1946** **Wmk. 191R** *Perf. 11*
**Size: 19x22mm**

*RD209* ST1 1c brt grn 15 10
*a.* Pair, one dated "1945" 375.00
*RD210* ST1 2c brt grn 20 10
*RD211* ST1 4c brt grn 15 10
*RD212* ST1 5c brt grn 30 10
*RD213* ST1 10c brt grn 40 10
*RD214* ST1 20c brt grn 90 15
*RD215* ST1 25c brt grn 85 20
*RD216* ST1 40c brt grn 1.50 40
*RD217* ST1 50c brt grn 1.75 20
*RD218* ST1 80c brt grn 3.00 2.75
*Nos. RD209-RD218 (10)* 9.20 4.20

**Size: 21½x36¼mm**

*RD219* ST2 $1 brt grn 3.00 30
*RD220* ST2 $2 brt grn 4.00 30
*RD221* ST2 $3 brt grn 7.00 75
*RD222* ST2 $4 brt grn 7.50 3.00
*RD223* ST2 $5 brt grn 11.00 50
*RD224* ST2 $10 brt grn 20.00 1.00
*RD225* ST2 $20 brt grn 35.00 21.00
*Nos. RD219-RD225 (7)* 87.50 26.85

*Perf. 12*
**Without Gum**
**Size: 28½x42mm**

*RD226* ST3 $30 brt grn 45.00 25.00
*RD227* ST3 $50 brt grn 45.00 25.00
*RD228* ST3 $60 brt grn 100.00 60.00
*RD229* ST3 $100 brt grn 60.00 30.00
*RD230* ST3 $500 brt grn — 125.00
*RD231* ST3 $1000 brt grn — 110.00
*RD232* ST3 $2500 brt grn — —
*RD233* ST3 $5000 brt grn — —
*RD234* ST3 $10,000 brt grn (cut cancel) 800.00

Stock Transfer Stamps of 1940-44 Overprinted in Black **Series 1947**

**1947** **Wmk. 191R** *Perf. 11*
**Size: 19x22mm**

*RD235* ST1 1c brt grn 50 40
*RD236* ST1 2c brt grn 40 25
*RD237* ST1 4c brt grn 30 25
*RD238* ST1 5c brt grn 25 20
*RD239* ST1 10c brt grn 40 25
*RD240* ST1 20c brt grn 60 30
*RD241* ST1 25c brt grn 90 35
*RD242* ST1 40c brt grn 1.25 45
*RD243* ST1 50c brt grn 1.65 15
*RD244* ST1 80c brt grn 7.50 5.50
*Nos. RD235-RD244 (10)* 13.75 8.10

**Size: 21½x36¼mm**

*RD245* ST2 $1 brt grn 3.00 35
*RD246* ST2 $2 brt grn 4.50 50
*RD247* ST2 $3 brt grn 7.00 90
*RD248* ST2 $4 brt grn 15.00 3.75
*RD249* ST2 $5 brt grn 10.00 90
*RD250* ST2 $10 brt grn 17.50 3.00
*RD251* ST2 $20 brt grn 35.00 17.50
*Nos. RD245-RD251 (7)* 92.00 26.90

*Perf. 12*
**Without Gum**
**Size: 28½x42mm**

*RD252* ST3 $30 brt grn 50.00 22.50
*RD253* ST3 $50 brt grn 100.00 70.00
*RD254* ST3 $60 brt grn 100.00 75.00
*RD255* ST3 $100 brt grn — 21.00
*RD256* ST3 $500 brt grn — 175.00
*RD257* ST3 $1000 brt grn — 75.00
*RD258* ST3 $2500 brt grn (cut canc.) — 300.00
*RD259* ST3 $5000 brt grn (cut canc.) — 350.00
*RD260* ST3 $10,000 brt grn (cut canc.) — 65.00
*a.* Horiz. pair, imperf. vert. (cut canc.) —

Stock Transfer Stamps of 1940-44 Overprinted in Black **Series 1948**

**1948** **Wmk. 191R** *Perf. 11*

**Size: 19x22mm**

| No. | Type | Description | Unused | Used |
|---|---|---|---|---|
| *RD261* | ST1 | 1c brt grn | 15 | 15 |
| *RD262* | ST1 | 2c brt grn | 15 | 15 |
| *RD263* | ST1 | 4c brt grn | 25 | 20 |
| *RD264* | ST1 | 5c brt grn | 20 | 15 |
| *RD265* | ST1 | 10c brt grn | 25 | 15 |
| *RD266* | ST1 | 20c brt grn | 65 | 25 |
| *RD267* | ST1 | 25c brt grn | 75 | 30 |
| *RD268* | ST1 | 40c brt grn | 1.10 | 40 |
| *RD269* | ST1 | 50c brt grn | 2.00 | 20 |
| *RD270* | ST1 | 80c brt grn | 6.00 | 5.00 |
| *Nos. RD261-RD270 (10)* | | | 11.50 | 6.95 |

**Size: 21 1/2x36 1/4mm**

| No. | Type | Description | Unused | Used |
|---|---|---|---|---|
| *RD271* | ST2 | $1 brt grn | 3.50 | 30 |
| *RD272* | ST2 | $2 brt grn | 6.00 | 40 |
| *RD273* | ST2 | $3 brt grn | 7.00 | 2.50 |
| *RD274* | ST2 | $4 brt grn | 8.00 | 6.00 |
| *RD275* | ST2 | $5 brt grn | 12.00 | 1.25 |
| *RD276* | ST2 | $10 brt grn | 18.00 | 3.00 |
| *RD277* | ST2 | $20 brt grn | 35.00 | 12.00 |
| *Nos. RD271-RD277 (7)* | | | 89.50 | 25.45 |

*Perf. 12*

**Without Gum**

**Size: 28 1/2x42mm**

| No. | Type | Description | Unused | Used |
|---|---|---|---|---|
| *RD278* | ST3 | $30 brt grn | 50.00 | 25.00 |
| *RD279* | ST3 | $50 brt grn | 40.00 | 25.00 |
| *RD280* | ST3 | $60 brt grn | 75.00 | 55.00 |
| *RD281* | ST3 | $100 brt grn | — | 12.00 |
| *RD282* | ST3 | $500 brt grn | — | 125.00 |
| *RD283* | ST3 | $1000 brt grn | — | 75.00 |
| *RD284* | ST3 | $2500 brt grn | 250.00 | 200.00 |
| *RD285* | ST3 | $5000 brt grn | — | 200.00 |
| *RD286* | ST3 | $10,000 brt grn (cut canc.) | — | 60.00 |

Stock Transfer Stamps of 1940-44 Overprinted in Black **Series 1949**

**1949** **Wmk. 191R** *Perf. 11*

**Size: 19x22mm**

| No. | Type | Description | Unused | Used |
|---|---|---|---|---|
| *RD287* | ST1 | 1c brt grn | 25 | 20 |
| *RD288* | ST1 | 2c brt grn | 25 | 20 |
| *RD289* | ST1 | 4c brt grn | 30 | 25 |
| *RD290* | ST1 | 5c brt grn | 30 | 25 |
| *RD291* | ST1 | 10c brt grn | 50 | 25 |
| *RD292* | ST1 | 20c brt grn | 1.00 | 30 |
| *RD293* | ST1 | 25c brt grn | 1.25 | 50 |
| *RD294* | ST1 | 40c brt grn | 2.50 | 90 |
| *RD295* | ST1 | 50c brt grn | 2.50 | 25 |
| *RD296* | ST1 | 80c brt grn | 5.00 | 3.50 |
| *Nos. RD287-RD296 (10)* | | | 13.85 | 6.60 |

**Size: 21 1/2x36 1/4mm**

| No. | Type | Description | Unused | Used |
|---|---|---|---|---|
| *RD297* | ST2 | $1 brt grn | 3.50 | 40 |
| *RD298* | ST2 | $2 brt grn | 6.00 | 60 |
| *RD299* | ST2 | $3 brt grn | 10.00 | 3.50 |
| *RD300* | ST2 | $4 brt grn | 12.00 | 6.00 |
| *RD301* | ST2 | $5 brt grn | 17.50 | 1.75 |
| *RD302* | ST2 | $10 brt grn | 25.00 | 3.00 |
| *RD303* | ST2 | $20 brt grn | 50.00 | 12.00 |
| *Nos. RD297-RD303 (7)* | | | 124.00 | 27.25 |

*Perf. 12*

**Without Gum**

**Size: 28 1/2x42mm**

| No. | Type | Description | Unused | Used |
|---|---|---|---|---|
| *RD304* | ST3 | $30 brt grn | — | 35.00 |
| *RD305* | ST3 | $50 brt grn | — | 35.00 |
| *RD306* | ST3 | $60 brt grn | 125.00 | 70.00 |
| *RD307* | ST3 | $100 brt grn | — | 35.00 |
| *RD308* | ST3 | $500 brt grn | — | 110.00 |
| *RD309* | ST3 | $1000 brt grn | — | 60.00 |
| *RD310* | ST3 | $2500 brt grn (cut canc.) | — | *325.00* |
| *RD311* | ST3 | $5000 brt grn (cut canc.) | — | *300.00* |
| *RD312* | ST3 | $10,000 brt grn (cut canc.) | — | 30.00 |
| *a.* | | Pair, one without overprint (cut cancel) | | — |

Stock Transfer Stamps of 1940-44 Overprinted in Black **Series 1950**

**1950** **Wmk. 191R** *Perf. 11*

**Size: 19x22mm**

| No. | Type | Description | Unused | Used |
|---|---|---|---|---|
| *RD313* | ST1 | 1c brt grn | 25 | 20 |
| *RD314* | ST1 | 2c brt grn | 25 | 20 |
| *RD315* | ST1 | 4c brt grn | 25 | 20 |
| *RD316* | ST1 | 5c brt grn | 30 | 15 |
| *RD317* | ST1 | 10c brt grn | 1.00 | 20 |
| *RD318* | ST1 | 20c brt grn | 1.25 | 30 |
| *RD319* | ST1 | 25c brt grn | 2.25 | 40 |
| *RD320* | ST1 | 40c brt grn | 2.50 | 60 |
| *RD321* | ST1 | 50c brt grn | 4.00 | 30 |
| *RD322* | ST1 | 80c brt grn | 3.50 | 3.50 |
| *Nos. RD313-RD322 (10)* | | | 15.55 | 6.05 |

**Size: 21 1/2x36 1/4mm**

| No. | Type | Description | Unused | Used |
|---|---|---|---|---|
| *RD323* | ST2 | $1 brt grn | 4.00 | 35 |
| *RD324* | ST2 | $2 brt grn | 7.50 | 50 |
| *RD325* | ST2 | $3 brt grn | 11.00 | 3.00 |
| *RD326* | ST2 | $4 brt grn | 12.50 | 7.50 |
| *RD327* | ST2 | $5 brt grn | 17.50 | 1.25 |
| *RD328* | ST2 | $10 brt grn | 30.00 | 4.00 |
| *RD329* | ST2 | $20 brt grn | 40.00 | 14.00 |
| *Nos. RD323-RD329 (7)* | | | 122.50 | 30.60 |

*Perf. 12*

**Without Gum**

**Size: 28 1/2x42mm**

| No. | Type | Description | Unused | Used |
|---|---|---|---|---|
| *RD330* | ST3 | $30 brt grn | 60.00 | 35.00 |
| *RD331* | ST3 | $50 brt grn | 70.00 | 50.00 |
| *RD332* | ST3 | $60 brt grn | — | 75.00 |
| *RD333* | ST3 | $100 brt grn | — | 30.00 |
| *RD334* | ST3 | $500 brt grn | — | 100.00 |
| *RD335* | ST3 | $1000 brt grn | — | 65.00 |
| *RD336* | ST3 | $2500 brt grn (cut canc.) | — | 425.00 |
| *RD337* | ST3 | $5000 brt grn | — | 350.00 |
| *RD338* | ST3 | $10,000 brt grn (cut canc.) | — | 60.00 |

Stock Transfer Stamps of 1940-44 Overprinted in Black **Series 1951**

**1951** **Wmk. 191R** *Perf. 11*

**Size: 19x22mm**

| No. | Type | Description | Unused | Used |
|---|---|---|---|---|
| *RD339* | ST1 | 1c brt grn | 30 | 25 |
| *RD340* | ST1 | 2c brt grn | 30 | 25 |
| *RD341* | ST1 | 4c brt grn | 40 | 30 |
| *RD342* | ST1 | 5c brt grn | 40 | 25 |
| *RD343* | ST1 | 10c brt grn | 50 | 25 |
| *RD344* | ST1 | 20c brt grn | 1.25 | 50 |
| *RD345* | ST1 | 25c brt grn | 1.75 | 50 |
| *RD346* | ST1 | 40c brt grn | 3.00 | 2.75 |
| *RD347* | ST1 | 50c brt grn | 3.00 | 50 |
| *RD348* | ST1 | 80c brt grn | 4.50 | 3.50 |
| *Nos. RD339-RD348 (10)* | | | 15.40 | 9.05 |

**Size: 21 1/2x36 1/4mm**

| No. | Type | Description | Unused | Used |
|---|---|---|---|---|
| *RD349* | ST2 | $1 brt grn | 6.00 | 50 |
| *RD350* | ST2 | $2 brt grn | 7.00 | 75 |
| *RD351* | ST2 | $3 brt grn | 11.00 | 5.50 |
| *RD352* | ST2 | $4 brt grn | 13.00 | 7.50 |
| *RD353* | ST2 | $5 brt grn | 18.00 | 2.00 |
| *RD354* | ST2 | $10 brt grn | 30.00 | 7.50 |
| *RD355* | ST2 | $20 brt grn | 45.00 | 12.50 |
| *Nos. RD349-RD355 (7)* | | | 130.00 | 36.25 |

*Perf. 12*

**Without Gum**

**Size: 28 1/2x42mm**

| No. | Type | Description | Unused | Used |
|---|---|---|---|---|
| *RD356* | ST3 | $30 brt grn | — | 27.50 |
| *RD357* | ST3 | $50 brt grn | — | 25.00 |
| *RD358* | ST3 | $60 brt grn | — | *150.00* |
| *RD359* | ST3 | $100 brt grn | — | 20.00 |
| *RD360* | ST3 | $500 brt grn | — | 90.00 |
| *RD361* | ST3 | $1000 brt grn | — | 50.00 |
| *RD362* | ST3 | $2500 brt grn | — | *500.00* |
| *RD363* | ST3 | $5000 brt grn | — | *500.00* |
| *RD364* | ST3 | $10,000 brt grn | — | 100.00 |

Stock Transfer Stamps of 1940 Overprinted in Black **Series 1952**

**1952** **Wmk. 191R** *Perf. 11*

**Size: 19x22mm**

| No. | Type | Description | Unused | Used |
|---|---|---|---|---|
| *RD365* | ST1 | 1c brt grn | 20.00 | 10.00 |
| *RD366* | ST1 | 10c brt grn | 15.00 | 7.50 |
| *RD367* | ST1 | 20c brt grn | 350.00 | — |
| *RD368* | ST1 | 25c brt grn | 475.00 | — |
| *RD369* | ST1 | 40c brt grn | 40.00 | 15.00 |

**Size: 21 1/2x36 1/4mm**

| No. | Type | Description | Unused | Used |
|---|---|---|---|---|
| *RD370* | ST2 | $4 brt grn | 750.00 | 350.00 |
| *RD371* | ST2 | $10 brt grn | 1,500. | — |
| *RD372* | ST2 | $20 brt grn | 2,000. | — |

Stock Transfer stamps were discontinued in 1952.

---

## HUNTING PERMIT STAMPS

The receipts of the sales of these "Migratory Bird Hunting" stamps help to maintain waterfowl life in the United States.

**Catalogue values for unused stamps in this section are for Never Hinged items.**

**Department of Agriculture**

HP1

Various Designs
Inscribed "U. S. Department of Agriculture"

**Engraved; Flat Plate Printing**

**1934 Unwmk. *Perf. 11***

**"Void after June 30, 1935"**

*RW1* HP1 $1 blue 350.00 60.00
*a.* Imperf., pair 4,000.
*b.* Vert. pair, imperf. horiz. —

**1935 "Void after June 30, 1936"**
*RW2* $1 *Canvasback Ducks Taking to Flight* 400.00 100.00

**1936 "Void after June 30, 1937"**
*RW3* $1 *Canada Geese in Flight* 200.00 50.00

**1937 "Void after June 30, 1938"**
*RW4* $1 *Scaup Ducks Taking to Flight* 160.00 25.00

**1938 "Void after June 30, 1939"**
*RW5* $1 *Pintail Drake and Duck Alighting* 160.00 30.00

**Department of the Interior**

Green-Winged Teal — HP2

Various Designs
Inscribed: "U. S. Department of the Interior"

**1939 "Void after June 30, 1940"**
*RW6* HP2 $1 chocolate 115.00 15.00

**1940 "Void after June 30, 1941"**
*RW7* $1 *Black Mallards* 110.00 15.00

**1941 "Void after June 30, 1942"**
*RW8* $1 *Family of Ruddy Ducks* 110.00 15.00

**1942 "Void after June 30, 1943"**
*RW9* $1 *Baldpates* 110.00 15.00

**1943 "Void after June 30, 1944"**
*RW10* $1 *Wood Ducks* 47.50 15.00

**1944 "Void after June 30, 1945"**
*RW11* $1 *White-fronted Geese* 50.00 14.00

**1945 "Void after June 30, 1946"**
*RW12* $1 *Shoveller Ducks in Flight* 35.00 10.00

**1946 "Void after June 30, 1947"**
*RW13* $1 *Redhead Ducks* 32.50 9.00

**1947 "Void after June 30, 1948"**
*RW14* $1 *Snow Geese* 35.00 9.00

**1948 "Void after June 30, 1949"**
*RW15* $1 *Bufflehead Ducks in Flight* 32.50 9.00

Goldeneye Ducks HP3

**1949 "Void after June 30, 1950"**
*RW16* HP3 $2 bright green 32.50 8.00

**1950 "Void after June 30, 1951"**
*RW17* $2 *Trumpeter Swans in Flight* 45.00 7.00

**1951 "Void after June 30, 1952"**
*RW18* $2 *Gadwall Ducks* 45.00 5.00

**1952 "Void after June 30, 1953"**
*RW19* $2 *Harlequin Ducks* 45.00 5.00

**1953 "Void after June 30, 1954"**
*RW20* $2 *Blue-winged Teal* 45.00 5.00

**1954 "Void after June 30, 1955"**
*RW21* $2 *Ring-necked Ducks* 45.00 4.75

**1955 "Void after June 30, 1956"**
*RW22* $2 *Blue Geese* 45.00 4.75

**1956 "Void after June 30, 1957"**
*RW23* $2 *American Merganser* 45.00 4.75

**1957 "Void after June 30, 1958"**
*RW24* $2 *American Eider* 45.00 4.75

**1958 "Void after June 30, 1959"**
*RW25* $2 *Canada Geese* 45.00 5.00

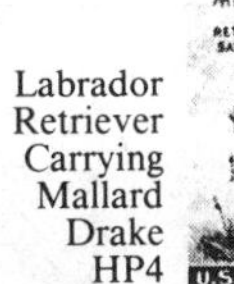

Labrador Retriever Carrying Mallard Drake HP4

**1959 Giori Press Printing**

**"Void after June 30, 1960"**
*RW26* HP4 $3 bl, ocher & blk 65.00 5.00

Redhead Ducks HP5

**1960 "Void after June 30, 1961"**
*RW27* HP5 $3 red brn, dk bl & bister 65.00 4.00

**1961 "Void after June 30, 1962"**
*RW28* $3 *Mallard Hen and Ducklings* 70.00 4.00

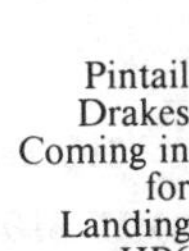

Pintail Drakes Coming in for Landing HP6

**1962 "Void after June 30, 1963"**
*RW29* HP6 $3 dk bl, dk red brn & black 80.00 5.50

**1963 "Void after June 30, 1964"**
*RW30* $3 *Pair of Brant landing* 75.00 5.50

**1964 "Void after June 30, 1965"**
*RW31* $3 *Hawaiian Nene Geese* 75.00 5.50

**1965 "Void after June 30, 1966"**
*RW32* $3 *3 Canvasback Drakes* 75.00 5.50

Whistling Swans HP7

**1966 "Void after June 30, 1967"**
*RW33* HP7 $3 ultra, sl grn & blk 75.00 5.00

**1967 "Void after June 30, 1968"**
*RW34* $3 *Old Squaw Ducks* 72.50 5.00

**1968 "Void after June 30, 1969"**
*RW35* $3 *Hooded Mergansers* 45.00 5.50

White-winged Scoters — HP8

**1969 "Void after June 30, 1970"**
*RW36* HP8 $3 gray, brn, indigo & brn red 45.00 4.50

**1970 Engraved & Lithographed**

**"Void after June 30, 1971"**
*RW37* $3 *Ross' Geese* 40.00 4.00

**1971 "Void after June 30, 1972"**
*RW38* $3 *3 Cinnamon Teal* 27.50 3.75

**1972 "Void after June 30, 1973"**
*RW39* $5 *Emperor Geese* 17.00 3.75

**1973 "Void after June 30, 1974"**
*RW40* $5 *Steller's Eiders* 17.00 3.75

**1974 "Void after June 30, 1975"**
*RW41* $5 *Wood ducks* 14.00 3.75

**1975 "Void after June 30, 1976"**
*RW42* $5 *Weathered canvasback duck decoy and flying ducks* 12.00 3.75

**1976 "Void after June 30, 1977"**
*RW43* $5 *Family of Canada Geese* 9.50 3.75

**1977 "Void after June 30, 1978"**
*RW44* $5 *Ross' Geese, pair* 9.50 3.75

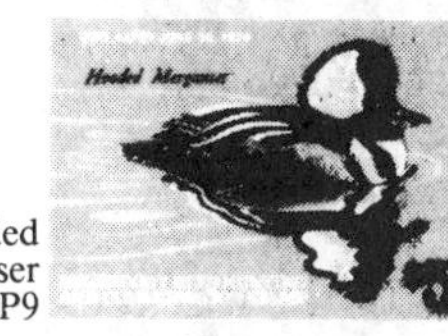

Hooded Merganser HP9

**1978 "Void after June 30, 1979"**
*RW45* HP9 $5 multicolor 9.50 3.75

**1979 "Void after June 30, 1980"**
*RW46* $7.50 *Green-winged teal* 13.00 4.00

**1980 "Void after June 30, 1981"**
*RW47* $7.50 *Mallards* 13.00 4.00

**1981 "Void after June 30, 1982"**
*RW48* $7.50 *Ruddy Ducks* 13.00 4.00

**1982 "Void after June 30, 1983"**
*RW49* $7.50 *Canvas backs* 13.00 4.00

**1983 "Void after June 30, 1984"**
*RW50* $7.50 *Pintails* 13.00 4.00

**1984 "Void after June 30, 1985"**
*RW51* $7.50 *Wigeon* 13.00 4.00

**1985 "Void after June 30, 1986"**
*RW52* $7.50 *Cinnamon teal* 13.00 4.00

**1986 "Void after June 30, 1987"**
*RW53* $7.50 *Fulvous whistling duck* 13.00 4.00
*a.* Black omitted —

**1987 "Void after June 30, 1988"**
*RW54* $10 *Redheads* 15.00 4.00

**1988 "Void after June 30, 1989"**
*RW55* $10 *Snow goose* 15.00 4.00

## CONFEDERATE STATES

### PROVISIONAL ISSUES

These stamps and envelopes were issued by individual postmasters generally during the interim between June 1, 1861, when the use of US stamps stopped in the Confederacy, and Oct. 16, 1861, when the 1st Confederate Government stamps were issued. They were occasionally issued at later periods, especially in Texas, when regular issues of Government stamps were unavailable.

Canceling stamps of the post offices were often used to produce envelopes, some of which were supplied in advance by private citizens. These envelopes and other stationery therefore may be found in a wide variety of papers, colors, sizes and shapes, including patriotic and semi-official types. It is often difficult to determine whether the impression made by the canceling stamp indicates provisional usage or merely postage paid at the time the letter was deposited in the post office. Occasionally the same mark was used for both purposes.

The *press-printed* provisional envelopes are in a different category. They were produced in quantity, using envelopes procured in advance by the postmaster, such as those of Charleston, Lynchburg, Memphis, etc. *The press-printed envelopes are listed and valued on all known papers.*

*The handstamped provisional envelopes are listed and valued according to type and variety of handstamp, but not according to paper. Many exist on such a variety of papers that they defy accurate, complete listing. The value of a handstamped provisional envelope is determined primarily by the clarity of the markings and its overall condition and attractiveness, rather than the type of paper. All handstamped provisional envelopes, when used, should also show the postmark of the town of issue.*

*Most handstamps are impressed at top right, although they exist from some towns in other positions.*

Illustrations in this section are reduced in size.

XU numbers are envelope entires.

### Aberdeen, Miss.

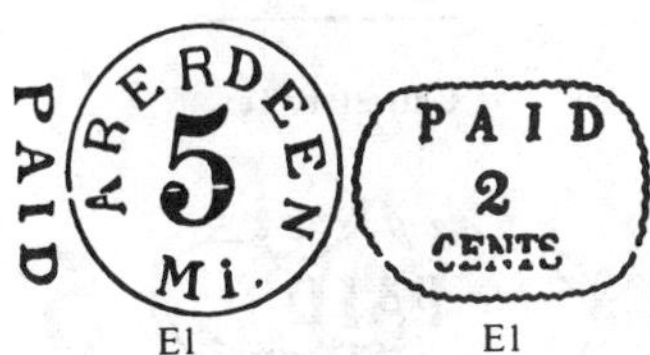


E1 E1

Handstamped

| | | | |
|---|---|---|---|
| *1XU1* | E1 | 5c black | *2,000.* |
| *1XU2* | E1 | 10c (ms.) on 5c black | — |

### Abingdon, Va.

Handstamped

| | | | |
|---|---|---|---|
| *2XU1* | E1 | 2c black | *11,000.* |
| *2XU2* | E1 | 5c black | 900. |
| *2XU3* | E1 | 10c black | *2,500.* |

No. 2XU1 is unique.

### Albany, Ga.

E1

E2

Handstamped

| | | | |
|---|---|---|---|
| *3XU1* | E1 | 5c greenish blue | 750. |
| *3XU2* | E1 | 10c greenish blue | 1,250. |
| *3XU3* | E1 | 10c on 5c grnsh bl | 1,750. |
| *3XU5* | E2 | 5c greenish blue | — |
| *3XU6* | E2 | 10c greenish blue | 1,350. |

### Anderson Court House, S.C.

E1

Two varieties — A1

Handstamped

| | | | | |
|---|---|---|---|---|
| *4XU1* | E1 | 5c black | | 1,000. |
| *4XU2* | E1 | 10c (ms.) black | 700. | *3,000.* |

### Athens, Ga.

Typo.

| | | | | |
|---|---|---|---|---|
| *5X1* | A1 | 5c purple (shades) | 750. | 800. |
| *a.* | | Vertical tete beche pair | | *4,000.* |
| *5X2* | A1 | 5c red | — | 2,500. |

### Atlanta, Ga.

E1

E2

E3

Handstamped

| | | | | |
|---|---|---|---|---|
| *6XU1* | E1 | 5c red | | 2,000. |
| *6XU2* | E1 | 5c black | 150. | 750. |
| *6XU3* | E1 | 10c on 5c black | | 1,500. |
| *6XU4* | E2 | 2c black | | *3,500.* |
| *6XU5* | E2 | 5c black | | 800. |
| *6XU6* | E2 | 10c black | | 700. |
| *6XU7* | E2 | 10c on 5c blk | | 2,500. |
| *6XU8* | E3 | 5c black | | 3,250. |
| *6XU9* | E3 | 10c blk ("10" upright) | | 2,250. |

### Augusta, Ga.

E1

Handstamped

| | | | |
|---|---|---|---|
| *7XU1* | E1 | 5c black | — |

Provisional status questioned.

### Austin, Miss.

E1

E1

Typo.

| | | | |
|---|---|---|---|
| *8XU1* | E1 | 5c red, *amber* | *14,500.* |

No. 8XU1 is unique.

### Austin, Texas

Handstamped

| | | | |
|---|---|---|---|
| *9XU1* | E1 | 10c black | 1,350. |

### Autaugaville, Ala.

E1

E2

Handstamped

| | | | |
|---|---|---|---|
| *10XU1* | E1 | 5c black | *8,000.* |
| *10XU2* | E2 | 5c black | *5,000.* |

### Baton Rouge, La.

A1

A2

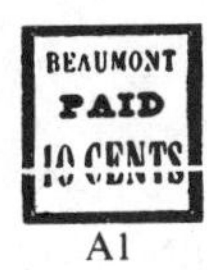

A3

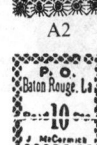

A4

Typeset

Ten varieties each of A1, A2 and A3

| | | | | |
|---|---|---|---|---|
| *11X1* | A1 | 2c green | *5,000.* | *3,500.* |
| *a.* | | "McCcrmick" | *8,000.* | *7,500.* |
| *11X2* | A2 | 5c grn & car | 1,100. | 800. |
| *a.* | | "McCcrmick" | — | 2,000. |
| *11X3* | A3 | 5c grn & car | *3,000.* | *1,750.* |
| *a.* | | "McCcrmick" | | *3,250.* |
| *11X4* | A4 | 10c blue | | *15,000.* |

### Beaumont, Tex.

A1

A2

Typeset

Several varieties of A1

| | | | | |
|---|---|---|---|---|
| *12X1* | A1 | 10c *yellow* | — | *4,500.* |
| *12X2* | A1 | 10c *pink* | — | *4,000.* |
| *12X3* | A2 | 10c *yellow*, on cover | | *135,000.* |

### Bridgeville, Ala.



A1



E1

Handstamped

| | | | |
|---|---|---|---|
| *13X1* | A1 | 5c black & red | *20,000.* |

### Canton, Miss.

Handstamped

| | | | |
|---|---|---|---|
| *14XU1* | E1 | 5c black | 1,850. |
| *14XU2* | E1 | 10c (ms.) on 5c black | 3,500. |

### Carolina City, N.C.

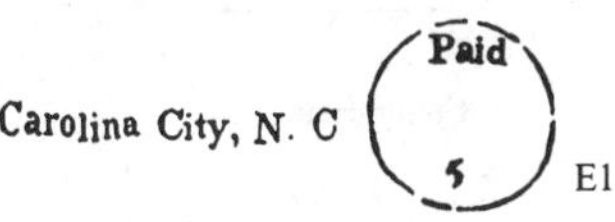


E1

Handstamped

| | | | |
|---|---|---|---|
| *118XU1* | E1 | 5c black | — |

### Chapel Hill, N.C.

E1

Handstamped

| | | | |
|---|---|---|---|
| *15XU1* | E1 | 5c black | 1,750. |

### Charleston, S.C.

A1

E1



E2

Litho.

| | | | | |
|---|---|---|---|---|
| *16X1* | A1 | 5c blue | 550.00 | 500.00 |

Typographed from Woodcut

| | | | |
|---|---|---|---|
| *16XU1* | E1 | 5c blue | 1,000. |
| *16XU2* | E1 | 5c blue, *amb* | 1,000. |
| *16XU3* | E1 | 5c blue, *org* | 1,000. |
| *16XU4* | E1 | 5c blue, *buff* | 1,000. |
| *16XU5* | E1 | 5c blue, *blue* | 1,000. |
| *16XU6* | E2 | 10cblue, *org* | *16,500.* |

Handstamped

| | | | |
|---|---|---|---|
| *16X7* | E2 | 10cblack | *3,000.* |

### Chattanooga, Tenn.

E1

Handstamped

| | | | |
|---|---|---|---|
| *17XU2* | E1 | 5c black | 1,750. |
| *17XU3* | E1 | 5c on 2c black | — |

### Christiansburg, Va.

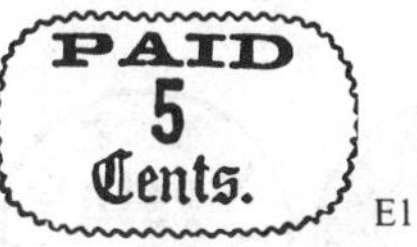


E1

Typeset. Impressed at top right.

| | | | |
|---|---|---|---|
| *99XU1* | E1 | 5c blk, *blue* | 1,250. |
| *99XU2* | E1 | 5c blue | 1,250. |
| *99XU3* | E1 | 5c blk, *org* | 1,250. |

*99XU4* E1 5c grn on U.S. envelope No. U27 — 4,500.
*99XU5* E1 10c black, *blue* — —

**Colaparchee, Ga.**

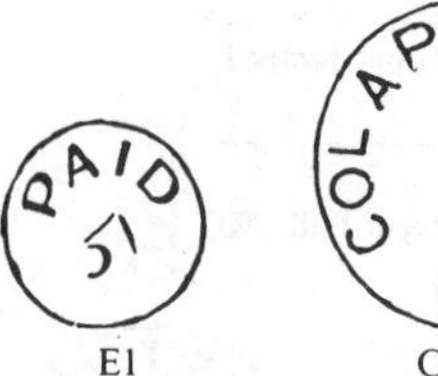


E1  Control

**Handstamped**

*119XU1* E1 5c black —

**Columbia, S.C.**

E1

PAID POST OFFICE COLUMBIA

E2

Handstamped

*18XU1* E1 5c blue 135. 750.
*18XU2* E1 5c black 235. 750.
*18XU3* E1 10c on 5c blue —
*18XU4* E2 5c blue (seal on front) 1,000.
*a.* Seal on back 900.
*18XU5* E2 10c blue (seal on back) 1,400.

**Circular Seal similar to E2, 27mm diameter**

*18XU6* E2 5c bl (seal on back) 1,000.

**Columbia, Tenn.**

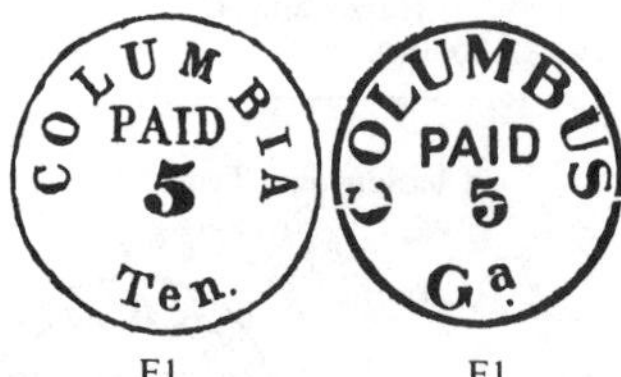


E1 E1

**Handstamped**

*113XU1* E1 5c red 2,250.

**Columbus, Ga.**

*19XU1* E1 5c blue 1,000.
*19XU2* E1 10c red 2,500.

**Courtland, Ala.**

E1 E1

Handstamped from Woodcut

*103XU1* E1 5c black —
*103XU2* E1 5c red 10,000.

Provisional status of No. 103XU1 questioned.

**Dalton, Ga.**

**Handstamped**

*20XU1* E1 5c black 500.
*20XU2* E1 10c black 700.
*20XU3* E1 10c (ms.) on 5c black 1,000.

**Danville, Va.**

A1

SOUTHERN CONFEDERACY, Danville, Va. PAID W. B. PAYNE, P.M. 5

Design measures 60x37mm — E1

E2

E3

Wove Paper

**Typeset**

*21X1* A1 5c red 5,500.
Cut to shape 4,000.

**Laid Paper**

*21X2* A1 5c red 6,500.

Two types: "SOUTHERN" in straight or curved line.

**Typo.**

*21XU1* E1 5c black 5,500.
*21XU2* E1 5c black, *amber* 5,500.
*21XU3* E1 5c blk, *dark buff* 4,750.

**Handstamped**

*21XU4* E2 10cblack 1,250.
*21XU5* E2 10cblue 1,250.
*21XU6* E3 10cblack 1,400.

**Demopolis, Ala.**

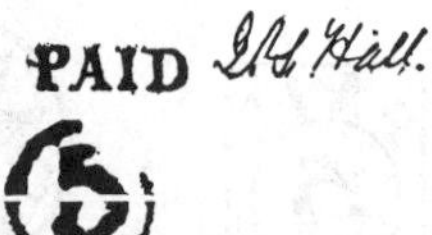


E1

Handstamped. Signature in ms.

*22XU1* E1 5c blk ("Jno. Y. Hall") 1,250.
*22XU2* E1 5c blk ("J. Y. Hall") 1,250.
*22XU3* E1 5c (ms.) black ("J. Y. Hall") 1,000.

*United States Booklet Panes can be mounted in Scott's U.S. Booklet Panes Album.*

**Eatonton, Ga.**

E1

**Handstamped**

*23XU1* E1 5c black 3,000.
*23XU2* E1 5c + 5c black 1,250.

**Emory, Va.**

A1

E1

PAID EMORY 10

E2

***Perf. 15 on Three Sides***

**Handstamped on sheet margins of U.S. 1857 1c stamps.**

*24X1* A1 5c blue — 4,000.

No. 24X1 exists with "5" above or below "PAID".

**Handstamped**

*24XU1* E1 5c blue 1,000.
*24XU2* E2 10cblue 2,000.

**Fincastle, Va.**

E1

**Typeset**

*104XU1* E1 10c black —

No. 104XU1 is unique.

**Forsyth, Ga.**

E1

**Handstamped**

*120XU1* E1 10c black 450.

**Franklin, N.C.**

E1

FREDERICKSB'G. R. T. THOM 10 POST OFFICE, VA.

A1

**Typo.**

*25XU1* E1 5c blue, *buff* 30,000.

No. 25XU1 is unique.

**Fredericksburg, Va.**

Typeset. Ten varieties.
Thin Bluish Paper

*26X1* A1 5c blue, *bluish* 200. 600.
*26X2* A1 10c red (shades), *bluish* 650.

**Gainesville, Ala.**

E1  E2

**Handstamped**

*27XU1* E1 5c black 1,500.
*27XU2* E2 10c black 7,500.

**Galveston, Tex.**

E1

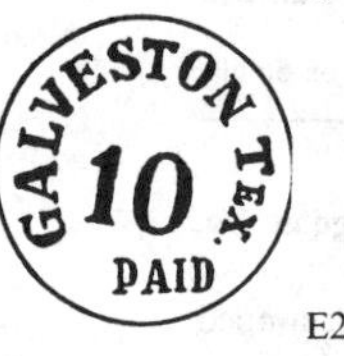


E2

**Handstamped**

*98XU1* E1 5c black 500. 2,000.
*98XU2* E1 10c black 2,250.
*98XU3* E2 10c black 550. 1,000.
*98XU4* E2 20c black 3,500.

**Georgetown, S.C.**

E1 Control

**Handstamped**

*28XU1* E1 5c black 750.

**Goliad, Tex.**

Goliad 10 POSTAGE. — GOLIAD 10 POSTAGE

A1  A2

Typeset
Several varieties of A1 and A2

*29X1* A1 5c black 5,000.
*29X2* A1 5c *gray* 4,500.
*29X3* A1 5c *rose* 5,000.
*29X4* A1 10c black — 5,000.
*29X5* A1 10c *rose* 5,000.

Type A1 stamps bear ms. control: "Clarke P.M."

*29X6* A2 5c *gray* 5,000.
*a.* "Goilad" 5,500.
*29X7* A2 10c *gray* 5,000.
*a.* "Goilad" 5,500.
*29X8* A2 5c *dark blue* 6,000.
*29X9* A2 10c *dark blue* 6,500.

**Gonzales, Tex.**

A1

*30X1* A1 (5c) gold, *dark blue* 7,500.

No. 30X1 must bear double circle town cancel as validating control. All items of type A1 without this control are book labels.

**Greensboro, Ala.**

E1

E2

**Handstamped**

*31XU1* E1 5c black 1,000.
*31XU2* E1 10c black 1,000.
*31XU3* E2 10c black 1,250.

**Greensboro, N.C.**

E1

**Handstamped**

*32XU1* E1 10c red 1,500.

**Greenville, Ala.**

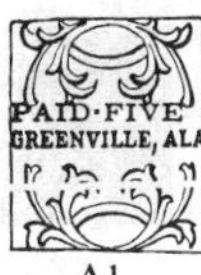

A1

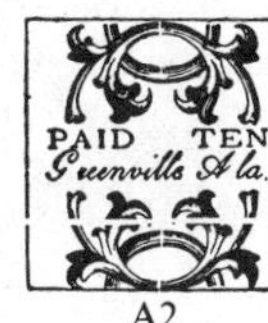

A2

Typeset

Type I- "Greenville, Ala." in Roman.
Type II- "Greenville, Ala." in script.

*33X1* A1 5c red & bl, Type I 4,500.
*a.* Type II 4,500.
*33X2* A2 10c red & blue 5,000.

**Greenville Court House, S.C.**

E1 PAID 5

Control

Handstamped. Several Types.

*34XU1* E1 5c black 800.
*34XU2* E1 10c black 900.
*34XU3* E1 20c (ms.) on 10c blk 1,000.

Envelopes usually bear the black circle control on the back.

**Greenwood Depot, Va.**

A1

"PAID" Handstamped; value and signature ms.
Laid Paper

*35X1* A1 10c blk, *gray blue* 4,500. —

**Griffin, Ga.**

E1

**Handstamped**

*102XU1* E1 5c black 1,350.

**Grove Hill, Ala.**

A1

A1

**Typo.**

*36X1* A1 5c black —

**Hallettsville, Tex.**

Handstamped
Ruled Letter Paper

*37X1* A1 10c black, *gray blue* 15,000.

**Hamburgh, S.C.**

E1

**Handstamped**

*112XU1* E1 5c black 1,000.

**Helena, Tex.**

A1

A1

Typeset
Several varieties

*38X1* A1 5c black, *buff* 7,500. 5,000.
*38X2* A1 10c black, *gray* 5,000.

**Hillsboro, N.C.**

Handstamped

*39X1* A1 5c black, on cover 15,000.

**Houston, Tex.**

E1

**Handstamped**

*40XU1* E1 5c red 600.
*40XU2* E1 10c red 1,000.
*40XU3* E1 10c black 750.
*40XU4* E1 5c + 10c red 1,500.
*40XU5* E1 10c + 10c red 1,500.
*40XU6* E1 10c (ms.) on 5c red 3,000.

**Huntsville, Tex.**

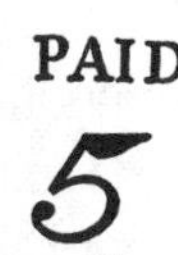

E1

Control

**Handstamped**

*92XU1* E1 5c black 1,350.

No. 92XU1 exists with "5" outside or within control circle.

**Independence, Tex.**

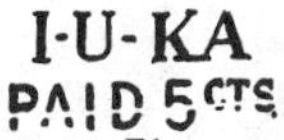

A1

I-U-KA
PAID 5 CTS
E1

**Handstamped**

*41X1* A1 10c blk, *buff* 3,250.
*41X2* A1 10c blk, *dl rose* 3,500.
*41X3* A1 10c blk, *buff* (small "10", "Pd" in ms.) 4,000.

No. 41X3 is known only cut to shape.

**Iuka, Miss.**

**Typeset**

*42XU1* E1 5c black 2,000.

**Jackson, Miss.**

E1

E1

**Handstamped**

*43XU1* E1 5c black 500.
*43XU2* E1 10c black 2,750.
*43XU3* E1 10c on 5c black 1,350.
*43XU4* E1 10c on 5c blue 1,350.

The 5c also exists on a lettersheet.

**Jacksonville, Ala.**

**Handstamped**

*110XU1* E1 5c black — 1,500.

**Jetersville, Va.**

A1

E1

Typeset ("5"); ms. ("AHA.")
Laid Paper

*44X1* A1 5c black —

**Jonesboro, Tenn.**

**Handstamped**

*45XU1* E1 5c black 4,000.
*45XU2* E1 5c dark blue 4,250.

**Kingston, Ga.**

PAID
5
CENTS
E1

PAID
c 5 s
CENTS
E2

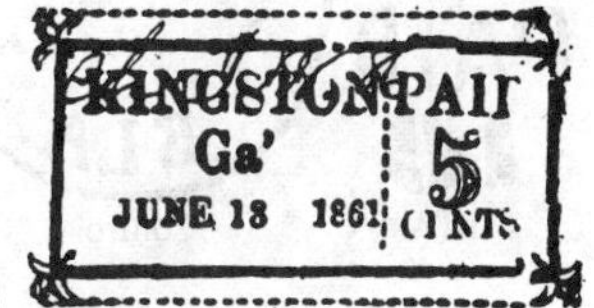

E3

E4

**Typo. (E1-E3); Handstamped (E4)**

*46XU1* E1 5c black 800.
*46XU2* E2 5c black — 1,500.
*46XU3* E2 5c blk, *amber* 1,500.
*46XU4* E3 5c black —
*46XU5* E4 5c black 5,000.

**Knoxville, Tenn.**

A1

Grayish White Laid Paper

*47X1* A1 5c brick red 1,000. 550.
*47X2* A1 5c carmine 1,500. 1,000.
*47X3* A1 10c green

*The 5c has been reprinted in red, brown and chocolate on white and bluish wove and laid paper.*

E1 E2

**Typo.**

*47XU1* E1 5c blue 500. 1,500.
*47XU2* E1 5c blue, *org* 500. 1,500.
*47XU3* E1 10c red (cut to shape) 1,000.
*47XU4* E1 10c red, *org* (cut to shape) 1,000.

**Handstamped**

*47XU5* E2 5c black 500. 2,000.
*47XU6* E2 10c on 5c blk *3,500.*

Type E2 exists with "5" above or below "PAID".

---

### La Grange, Tex.

E1

**Handstamped**

*48XU1* E1 5c black — 1,250.
*48XU2* E1 10c black 1,500.

---

### Lake City, Fla.

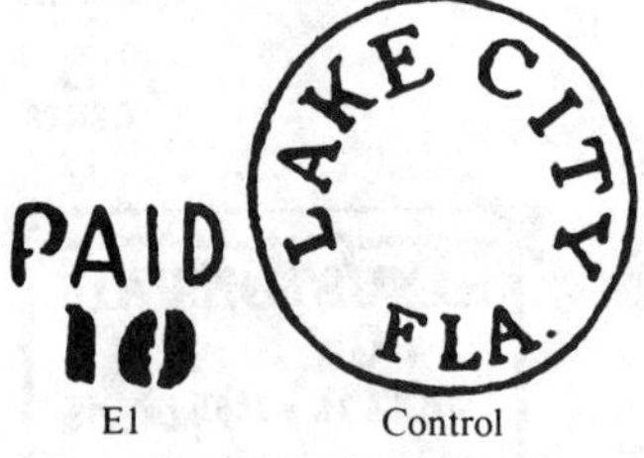

E1 Control

**Handstamped**

*96XU1* E1 10c black *3,500.*

Envelopes have black circle control mark, or printed name of E.R. Ives, postmaster, on face or back.

---

### Laurens Court House, S.C.

E1

**Handstamped**

*116XU1* E1 5c black —

---

### Lenoir, N.C.

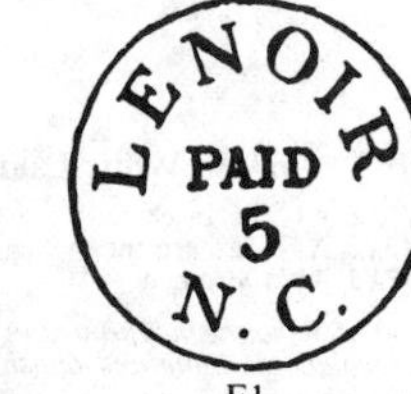

A1 E1

**Handstamped from Woodcut**
Paper has ruled lines in orange

*49X1* A1 5c blue *3,250. 3,000.*

**Handstamped**

*49XU1* A1 5c black —
*49XU2* A1 10c(5c + 5c) bl —
*49XU3* E1 5c blue *3,500.*
*49XU4* E1 5c black 900.

---

### Lexington, Miss.

E1

**Handstamped**

*50XU1* E1 5c black *3,000.*
*50XU2* E1 10c black *4,000.*

---

### Liberty, Va.

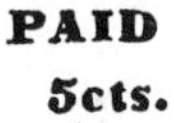

PAID
5cts.
A1

A1

Typeset. Laid Paper

*74X1* A1 5c black —

A cover with Salem, Va., postmark is known.

---

### Limestone Springs, S.C.

**Handstamped**

*121X1* A1 5c black, on cover 4,000.

Stamps are round, square or rectangular. Covers are not postmarked.

---

### Livingston, Ala.

A1

**Litho.**

*51X1* A1 5c blue *7,000.*

---

### Lynchburg, Va.

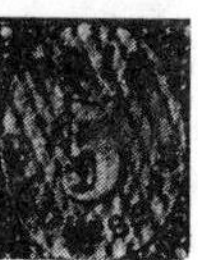

A1 E1

Stereotype from Woodcut

*52X1* A1 5c blue (shades) 500. 650.

**Typo.**

*52XU1* E1 5c black *1,500.*
*52XU2* E1 5c blk, *amb* 650. *1,500.*
*52XU3* E1 5c blk, *buff* *1,500.*
*52XU4* E1 5c blk, *brown* 900. *1,500.*

---

### Macon, Ga.

A1 A2 A3

A4

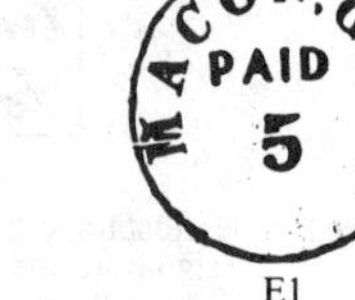

E1

Typeset. Wove Paper.
Several varieties of each. Ten of A2.

*53X1* A1 5c *light bl grn* (shades) 800. 600.
*53X3* A2 5c *yellow* 2,250. 750.
*53X4* A3 5c *yel* (shades) 2,250. 1,000.
  *a.* Vertical tete beche pair *12,000.*
*53X5* A4 2c *gray green* *6,500.*

**Laid Paper**

*53X6* A2 5c *yellow* *3,000. 3,500.*
*53X7* A3 5c *yellow* *6,000.*
*53X8* A1 5c *light bl grn* 1,750. *2,000.*

Handstamped
Two types of "PAID" and "5"

*53XU1* E1 5c black 250. 500.

---

### Marietta, Ga.

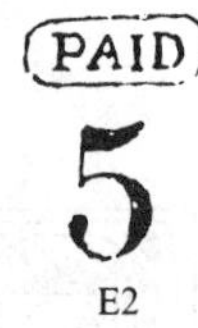

E1 E2

Handstamped
Two types of "PAID" and numerals

*54XU1* E1 5c black 400.
*54XU2* E1 10c on 5c black 1,200.
*54XU3* E1 10c black 750.
*54XU4* E2 5c black 450.

---

### Marion, Va.

A1

Handstamped Numeral within
Typeset Frame
Wove Paper

*55X1* A1 5c black *5,000.*
*55X2* A1 10c black *16,500. 8,000.*

**Bluish Laid Paper**

*55X3* A1 5c black —

The 2c, 3c, 15c and 20c are believed to be bogus.

---

### Memphis Tenn.

A1 A2

Stereotype from Woodcut

*56X1* A1 2c blue (shades) 75. *750.*
*56X2* A2 5c red (shades) 150. 200.
  *a.* Tete beche pair 1,500.
  *b.* Pair, one sideways 750.
  *c.* Pelure paper — —

**Typo.**

*56XU1* A2 5c red 2,500.
*56XU2* A2 5c red, *amber* 2,500.
*56XU3* A2 5c red, *orange* 2,750.

---

### Micanopy, Fla.

E1

**Handstamped**

*105XU1* E1 5c black *11,500.*

---

### Milledgeville, Ga.

E1

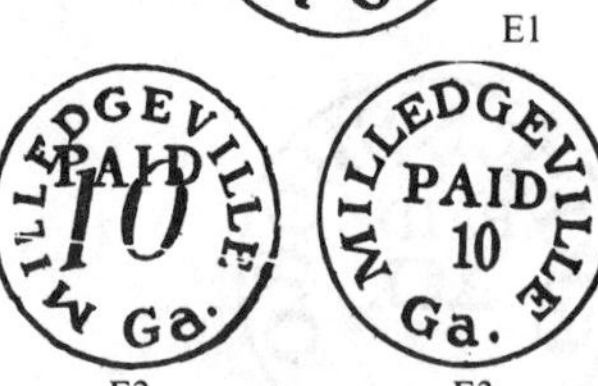

E2 E3

**Handstamped**

*57XU1* E1 5c black 300.
*57XU2* E1 5c blue 400.
*57XU3* E1 10c on 5c black 850.
*57XU4* E2 10c black 225. 750.
*57XU5* E3 10c black 750.

---

### Mobile, Ala.

A1

**Litho.**

*58X1* A1 2c black 1,250. 700.
*58X2* A1 5c blue 250. 150.

---

### Montgomery, Ala.

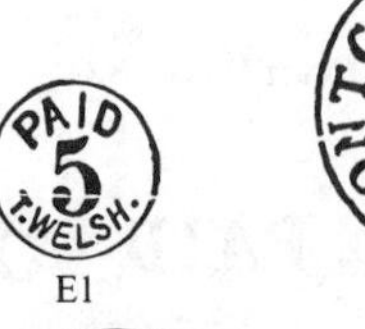

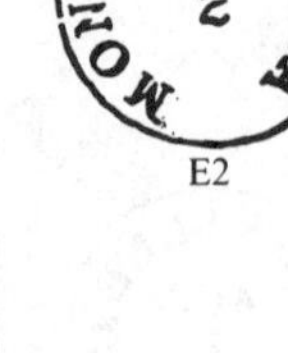

E1 E2

E3

### Handstamped

| No. | Type | Description | Unused | Used |
|---|---|---|---|---|
| 59XU1 | E1 | 5c red | | 1,000. |
| 59XU2 | E1 | 5c blue | 400. | 1,200. |
| 59XU3 | E1 | 10c red | | 1,000. |
| 59XU4 | E1 | 10c blue | | 1,250. |
| 59XU5 | E1 | 10c black | | 1,000. |
| 59XU6 | E1 | 10c on 5c red | | *2,000.* |

The 10c design is larger than the 5c.

| No. | Type | Description | Unused | Used |
|---|---|---|---|---|
| 59XU7 | E2 | 2c red | | — |
| 59XU7A | E2 | 2c blue | | 3,000. |
| 59XU8 | E2 | 5c black | | 1,000. |
| 59XU9 | E3 | 10c black | | 1,500. |
| 59XU10 | E3 | 10c red | | 1,500. |

## Mt. Lebanon, La.

A1

### Woodcut, Design Reversed

| No. | Type | Description | Unused | Used |
|---|---|---|---|---|
| 60X1 | A1 | 5c red brown | | — |

No. 60X1 is unique.

## Nashville, Tenn.

A1

A2

E1

### Typeset (5 varieties of 3c)

| No. | Type | Description | Unused | Used |
|---|---|---|---|---|
| 61X1 | A1 | 3c carmine | 125. | |

No. 61X1 was not placed in use.

### Stereotype from Woodcut
### Gray Blue Ribbed Paper

| No. | Type | Description | Unused | Used |
|---|---|---|---|---|
| 61X2 | A2 | 5c car (shades) | 700. | 400. |
| a. | | Vertical tete beche pair | | *2,000.* |
| 61X3 | A2 | 5c brick red | 700. | 400. |
| 61X4 | A2 | 5c gray (shades) | 700. | 500. |
| 61X5 | A2 | 5c vio brown | 600. | 400. |
| a. | | Vertical tete beche pair | *4,000.* | *5,000.* |
| 61X6 | A2 | 10c green | *3,000.* | *2,250.* |

### Handstamped

| No. | Type | Description | Unused | Used |
|---|---|---|---|---|
| 61XU1 | E1 | 5c blue | | 900. |
| 61XU2 | E1 | 5c + 10c blue | | 1,500. |

## New Orleans, La.

A1

A2

J.L.RIDDELL,P.M.
PD 5 CTS
N O.P.O
E1

### Stereotype from Woodcut

| No. | Type | Description | Unused | Used |
|---|---|---|---|---|
| 62X1 | A1 | 2c blue | 100. | 400. |
| a. | | Printed on both sides | | — |
| 62X2 | A1 | 2c red (shades) | 100. | *650.* |
| 62X3 | A2 | 5c brn, *white* | 200. | 125. |
| a. | | Printed on both sides | | 1,000. |
| b. | | 5c ocher | 500. | 350. |
| 62X4 | A2 | 5c red brn, *bluish* | 225. | 95. |
| a. | | Printed on both sides | | *1,050.* |
| 62X5 | A2 | 5c yellow brn, *off-white* | 90. | 200. |
| 62X6 | A2 | 5c red | — | *7,500.* |
| 62X7 | A2 | 5c red, *blue* | | *10,000.* |

### Handstamped

| No. | Type | Description | Unused | Used |
|---|---|---|---|---|
| 62XU1 | E1 | 5c black | | 3,500. |
| 62XU2 | E1 | 10cblack | | *5,000.* |

"J L. RIDDELL, P.M." omitted

| No. | Type | Description | Unused | Used |
|---|---|---|---|---|
| 62XU3 | E1 | 2c black | | *7,500.* |

## New Smyrna, Fla.

A1

A1

### Handstamped

| No. | Type | Description | Unused | Used |
|---|---|---|---|---|
| 63X1 | A1 | 10c ("01") on 5c blk | | *50,000.* |

No. 63X1 is unique.

## Oakway, S.C.

### Handstamped

| No. | Type | Description | Unused | Used |
|---|---|---|---|---|
| 115X1 | A1 | 5c blk, on cover | — | *12,000.* |

## Pensacola, Fla.

E1

A1

### Handstamped

| No. | Type | Description | Unused | Used |
|---|---|---|---|---|
| 106XU1 | E1 | 5c black | | *4,000.* |
| 106XU2 | E1 | 10c (ms.) on 5c blk | | *4,250.* |

## Petersburg, Va.

### Typeset (10 varieties)

| No. | Type | Description | Unused | Used |
|---|---|---|---|---|
| 65X1 | A1 | 5c red (shades) | *600.* | 400. |

## Pittsylvania Court House, Va.

A1

A1

### Typeset
### Wove Paper

| No. | Type | Description | Unused | Used |
|---|---|---|---|---|
| 66X1 | A1 | 5c red | *6,000.* | *5,000.* |
| | | Octagonally cut | | *4,000.* |

### Laid Paper

| No. | Type | Description | Unused | Used |
|---|---|---|---|---|
| 66X2 | A1 | 5c red | | *6,500.* |
| | | Octagonally cut | | *5,500.* |

## Pleasant Shade, Va.

### Typeset (5 varieties)

| No. | Type | Description | Unused | Used |
|---|---|---|---|---|
| 67X1 | A1 | 5c blue | *2,500.* | *4,500.* |

## Port Lavaca, Tex.

A1

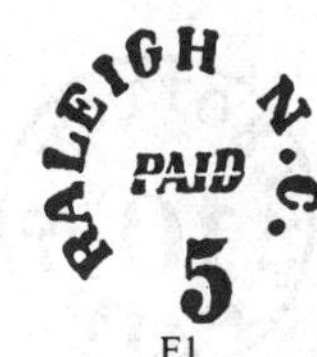

E1

### Typeset

| No. | Type | Description | Unused | Used |
|---|---|---|---|---|
| 107X1 | A1 | 10c black | | — |

No. 107X1 is unique.

## Raleigh, N.C.

### Handstamped

| No. | Type | Description | Unused | Used |
|---|---|---|---|---|
| 68XU1 | E1 | 5c red | | 425. |
| 68XU2 | E1 | 5c blue | | 1,000. |

## Rheatown, Tenn.

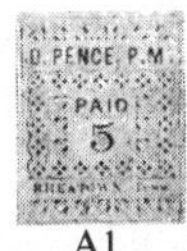
A1

E1

### Typeset. Three varieties.

| No. | Type | Description | Unused | Used |
|---|---|---|---|---|
| 69X1 | A1 | 5c red | 2,000. | *2,750.* |
| | | Pen canceled | | *2,000.* |

## Richmond, Tex.

### Handstamped

| No. | Type | Description | Unused | Used |
|---|---|---|---|---|
| 70XU1 | E1 | 5c red | | 2,500. |
| 70XU2 | E1 | 10c red | | 2,500. |
| 70XU3 | E1 | 10c on 5c red | | 5,000. |
| 70XU4 | E1 | 15c (ms.) on 10c red | | — |

## Ringgold, Ga.

E1 E1

### Handstamped

| No. | Type | Description | Unused | Used |
|---|---|---|---|---|
| 71XU1 | E1 | 5c blue black | | *4,000.* |

## Rutherfordton, N.C.

### Handstamped; "Paid 5cts" in ms.

| No. | Type | Description | Unused | Used |
|---|---|---|---|---|
| 72X1 | E1 | 5c black, cut round | | *24,000.* |

No. 72X1 is on cover, uncanceled and probably unique.

## Salem, N.C.

"Paid 5" in Ms.
E1

"Paid 5" Handstamped
E2

### Handstamped

| No. | Type | Description | Unused | Used |
|---|---|---|---|---|
| 73XU1 | E1 | 5c black | | 750. |
| 73XU2 | E1 | 10c black | | 850. |
| 73XU3 | E2 | 5c black | | 750. |
| 73XU4 | E2 | 10c on 5c black | | 1,600. |

*Reprints exist on various papers. They either lack the "Paid" and value or have them counterfeited.*

## Salisbury, N.C.

SALISBURY
N. C.
POSTAGE
FIVE CENTS
P.M. E1

### Typo.
### Impressed at top left

| No. | Type | Description | Unused | Used |
|---|---|---|---|---|
| 75XU1 | E1 | 5c blk, *greenish* | | — |

One example known with part of envelope torn away, leaving part of design missing. Illustration E1 partly suppositional.

## San Antonio, Tex.

E1 E2

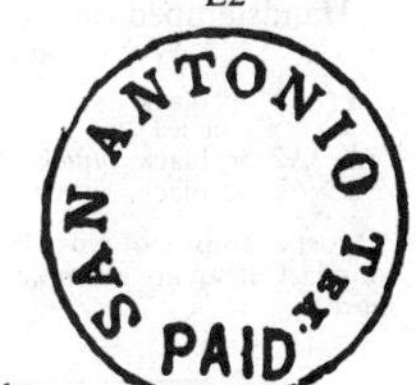

Control

### Handstamped

| No. | Type | Description | Unused | Used |
|---|---|---|---|---|
| 76XU1 | E1 | 10c black | 275. | 1,100. |
| 76XU2 | E2 | 10c black | | 1,250. |

Black circle control mark is on front or back.

## Savannah, Ga.

E1

Control

PAID 10 E2

### Handstamped

| No. | Type | Description | Unused | Used |
|---|---|---|---|---|
| 101XU1 | E1 | 5c black | | 300. |
| 101XU2 | E2 | 5c black | | 450. |
| 101XU3 | E1 | 10c black | | 500. |
| 101XU4 | E2 | 10c black | | 500. |
| 101XU5 | E1 | 10c on 5c black | | 1,500. |
| 101XU6 | E2 | 20c on 5c black | | 3,000. |

Envelope must bear octagonal control mark.

### Selma, Ala.

E1 E1

**Handstamped; Signature in ms.**

*77XU1* E1 5c black *1,500.*
*77XU2* E1 10c black *2,500.*
*77XU3* E1 10c on 5c black *3,000.*

### Sparta, Ga.

**Handstamped**

*93XU1* E1 5c red — 750.
*93XU2* E1 10c red 1,000.

### Spartanburg, S.C.

A1

A2

Handstamped on Ruled or Plain Wove Paper

*78X1* A1 5c black *2,500.*
*a.* "5" omitted —
*78X2* A2 5c black, *bluish* *3,000.*
*78X3* A2 5c black, *brown* *3,000.*

Most examples of Nos. 78X1-78X3 are cut round. Cut square examples are worth much more.

### Statesville, N.C.

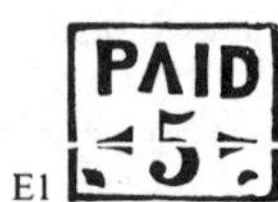

E1

**Handstamped**

*79XU1* E1 5c black 135. 700.
*79XU2* E1 10c on 5c black 1,500.

### Sumter, S.C.

E1

**Handstamped**

*80XU1* E1 5c black 150.
*80XU2* E1 10c black 100.
*80XU3* E1 10c on 5c black 175.
*80XU4* E1 2c (ms.) on 10c blk 800.

Used examples of Nos. 80XU1-80XU2 are indistinguishable from handstamped "Paid" covers.

### Talbotton, Ga.

E1

A1

**Handstamped**

*94XU1* E1 5c black 750.
*94XU2* E1 10c black 500.
*94XU3* E1 10c on 5c blk 1,000.

### Tellico Plains, Tenn.

**Typeset** **Laid Paper**

*81X1* A1 5c red 800.
*81X2* A1 10c red 1,500.

### Thomasville, Ga.

E1

Control

E2

**Handstamped**

*82XU1* E1 5c black 1,000.
*82XU2* E2 5c black 900.

### Tullahoma, Tenn.

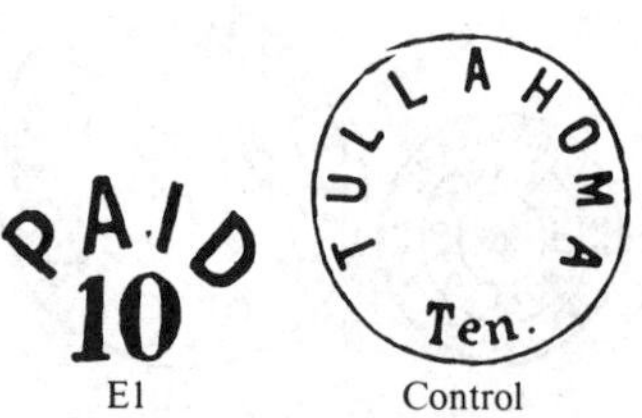

E1 Control

**Handstamped**

*111XU1* E1 10c black *3,000.*

### Tuscaloosa, Ala.

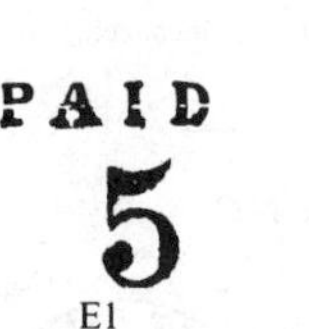

E1

E1

**Handstamped**

*83XU1* E1 5c black 250.
*83XU2* E1 10c black 250.

Used examples of Nos. 83XU1-83XU2 are indistinguishable from handstamped "Paid" covers.

### Tuscumbia, Ala.

**Handstamped**

*84XU1* E1 5c black 1,900.
*84XU2* E1 5c red 2,100.
*84XU3* E1 10c black 3,500.

See US Postmasters' Provisional No. 12XU1.

### Union City, Tenn.

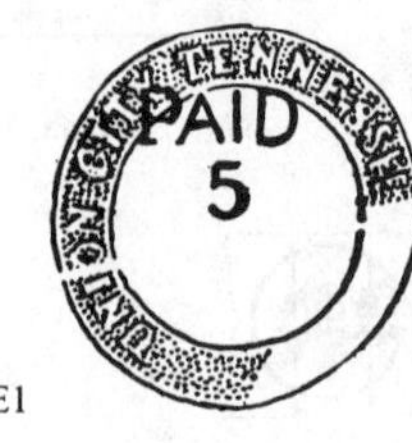

E1

The use of E1 to produce provisional envelopes is doubtful.

### Uniontown, Ala.

A1

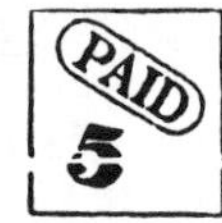

A1

Typeset in settings of four (2x2)
Four varieties of each value
Laid Paper

*86X1* A1 2c dk bl, *gray bl* *9,500.* —
*86X2* A1 2c dark blue *5,500.*
*86X3* A1 5c grn, *gray bl* *2,750.* *2,000.*
*86X4* A1 5c green *2,750.* *2,000.*
*86X5* A1 10c red, *gray bl* *8,000.* *5,000.*

### Unionville, S.C.

Handstamped
Wove Paper with Blue Ruled Lines

*87X1* A1 5c black, *grayish* *13,500.*

### Valdosta, Ga.

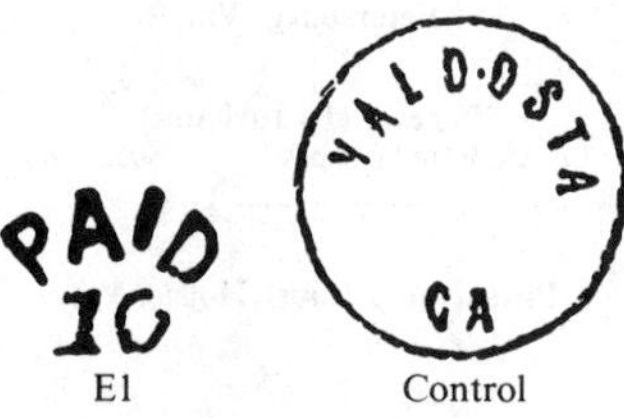

E1 Control

**Handstamped**

*100XU1* E1 10c black 800.

The black control is usually on back of envelope.

### Victoria, Tex.

A1

E1

**Typeset**

*88X1* A1 5c red brn, *grn* *4,000.*
*88X2* A1 10c red brn, *grn* *4,250.* *4,500.*

**Pelure Paper**

*88X3* A1 10c red brn, *grn* ("10" in bold face type) *5,500.* *5,250.*

### Walterborough, S.C.

**Typeset**

*108XU1* E1 10c black, *buff* *2,000.*
*108XU2* E1 10c carmine *4,000.*

### Warrenton, Ga.

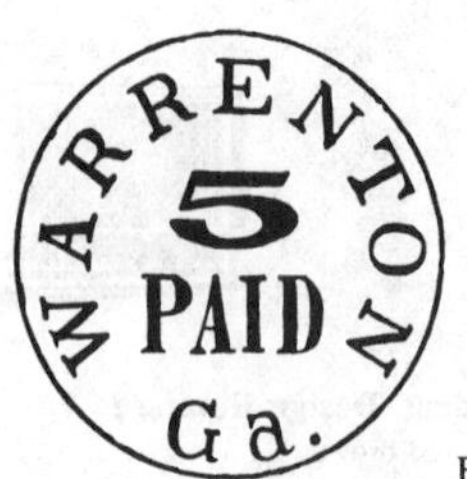

E1

**Handstamped**

*89XU1* E1 5c black 1,250.
*89XU2* E1 10c (ms.) on 5c blk 1,000.

### Washington, Ga.

E1

E1

**Handstamped**

*117XU1* E1 10c black 1,500.

### Weatherford, Tex.

Woodcut with "PAID" inserted in type.
Handstamped

*109XU1* E1 5c black *2,000.*
*109XU2* E1 5c + 5c black *16,000.*

### Winnsborough, S.C.

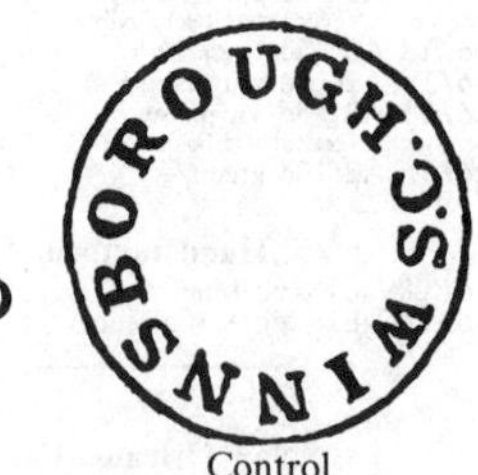

E1 Control

**Handstamped**

*97XU1* E1 5c black *1,000.*
*97XU2* E1 10c black *1,000.*

Envelopes must bear black circle control on front or back.

### Wytheville, Va.

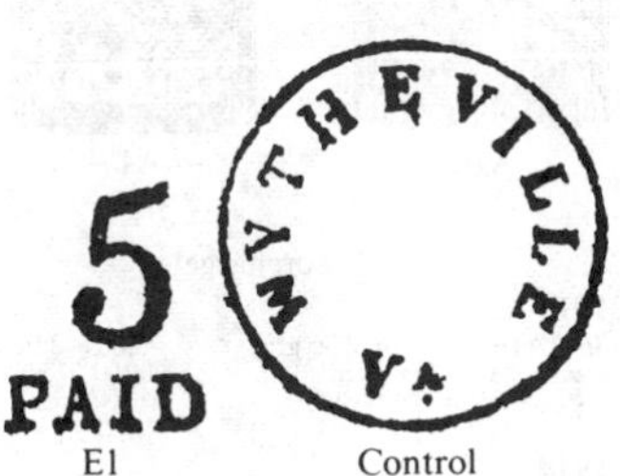


E1 Control

**Handstamped**

*114XU1* E1 5c black 900.

For later additions, listed out of numerical sequence, see:

| | |
|---|---|
| *No. 74X1,* | Liberty, Va. |
| *No. 92XU1,* | Huntsville, Tex. |
| *No. 93XU1,* | Sparta, Ga. |
| *No. 94XU1,* | Talbotton, Ga. |
| *No. 96XU1,* | Lake City, Fla. |
| *No. 97XU1,* | Winnsborough, S.C. |
| *No. 98XU1,* | Galveston, Tex. |
| *No. 99XU1,* | Christiansburg, Va. |
| *No. 100XU1,* | Valdosta, Ga. |
| *No. 101XU1,* | Savannah, Ga. |
| *No. 102XU1,* | Griffin, Ga. |
| *No. 103XU1,* | Courtland, Ala. |
| *No. 104XU1,* | Fincastle, Va. |
| *No. 105XU1,* | Micanopy, Fla. |
| *No. 106XU1,* | Pensacola, Fla. |
| *No. 107X1,* | Port Lavaca, Tex. |
| *No. 108XU1,* | Walterborough, S.C. |
| *No. 109XU1,* | Weatherford, Tex. |
| *No. 110XU1,* | Jacksonville, Ala. |
| *No. 111XU1,* | Tullahoma, Tenn. |
| *No. 112XU1,* | Hamburgh, S.C. |
| *No. 113XU1,* | Columbia, Tenn. |
| *No. 114XU1,* | Wytheville, Va. |
| *No. 115X1,* | Oakway, S.C. |
| *No. 116XU1,* | Laurens Court House, S.C. |
| *No. 117XU1,* | Washington, Ga. |
| *No. 118XU1,* | Carolina City, N.C. |
| *No. 119XU1,* | Colaparchee, Ga. |
| *No. 120XU1,* | Forsyth, Ga. |
| *No. 121XU1,* | Limestone Springs, S.C. |

### GENERAL ISSUES

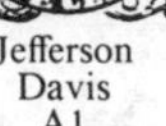

Jefferson Davis A1

Thomas Jefferson A2

**1861 Unwmk. Litho. *Imperf.***

| | | | |
|---|---|---|---|
| *1* | A1 5c green | 140.00 | 100.00 |
| *a.* | 5c light green | 140.00 | 100.00 |
| *b.* | 5c dark green | 145.00 | 110.00 |
| *c.* | 5c olive green | 150.00 | 120.00 |
| *2* | A2 10c blue | 180.00 | 140.00 |
| *a.* | 10c light blue | 180.00 | 140.00 |
| *b.* | 10c dark blue | 225.00 | 130.00 |
| *c.* | 10c indigo | — | — |
| *d.* | Printed on both sides | — | — |
| *e.* | 10c greenish blue | 275.00 | 225.00 |

The earliest printings of No. 2 were made by Hoyer & Ludwig, the later ones by J. T. Paterson & Co. Stamps of the later printings usually have a small colored dash below the lowest point of the upper left spandrel.

Andrew Jackson A3

Jefferson Davis A4

**1862**

| | | | |
|---|---|---|---|
| *3* | A3 2c green | 400.00 | 450.00 |
| *a.* | 2c bright yellow green | *1,200.* | *1,600.* |
| *4* | A1 5c blue | 100.00 | 80.00 |
| *a.* | 5c dark blue | 120.00 | 100.00 |
| *b.* | 5c light milky bl | 120.00 | 100.00 |
| *5* | A2 10c rose | 650.00 | 400.00 |
| *a.* | 10c carmine | — | 850.00 |

**Typo.**

| | | | |
|---|---|---|---|
| *6* | A4 5c lt bl (London print) | 8.00 | 16.00 |
| *7* | A4 5c bl (local print) | 10.00 | 8.00 |
| *a.* | 5c deep blue | 10.00 | 8.00 |
| *b.* | Printed on both sides | 1,000. | 700.00 |

No. 6 has fine, clear impression. No. 7 has coarser impression and the color is duller and often blurred.

Both 2c and 10c stamps, types A4 and A10, were privately printed in various colors.

Andrew Jackson — A5

**1863 Engr.**

| | | | |
|---|---|---|---|
| *8* | A5 2c brown red | 40.00 | *200.00* |
| *a.* | 2c pale red | 50.00 | *255.00* |

Jefferson Davis

A6 A6a

**Thick or Thin Paper**

| | | | |
|---|---|---|---|
| *9* | A6 10c blue | 600.00 | 400.00 |
| *a.* | 10c milky blue | 650.00 | 450.00 |
| *b.* | 10c gray blue | 600.00 | 400.00 |
| *10* | A6a 10c bl (with frame line) | 2,250. | 1,000. |
| *a.* | 10c milky blue | 2,400. | 1,250. |
| *b.* | 10c greenish blue | 2,250. | 1,000. |
| *c.* | 10c dark blue | 2,250. | 1,000. |

Values of Nos. 10, 10a, 10b and 10c are for copies showing parts of lines on at least three sides.

A7

A8

There are many slight differences between A7 and A8, the most noticeable being the additional line outside the ornaments at the corners of A8.

| | | | |
|---|---|---|---|
| *11* | A7 10c blue | 8.00 | 12.50 |
| *a.* | 10c milky blue | 20.00 | 25.00 |
| *b.* | 10c dark blue | 8.00 | 12.50 |
| *c.* | 10c greenish blue | 8.00 | 12.50 |
| *d.* | 10c green | 27.50 | 37.50 |
| *e.* | Perforated | 120.00 | 135.00 |
| *12* | A8 10c blue | 9.00 | 12.50 |
| *a.* | 10c milky blue | 20.00 | 25.00 |
| *b.* | 10c light blue | 9.00 | 12.50 |
| *c.* | 10c greenish blue | 9.00 | 12.50 |
| *d.* | 10c dark blue | 9.00 | 12.50 |
| *e.* | 10c green | 27.50 | 37.50 |
| *f.* | Perforated | 150.00 | 165.00 |

The paper of Nos. 11 and 12 varies from thin hard to thick soft. The so-called laid paper is probably due to thick streaky gum.

*Canal Zone stamps can be mounted in Scott's U.S. Possessions Album.*

George Washington A9

John C. Calhoun A10

| | | | |
|---|---|---|---|
| *13* | A9 20c green | 30.00 | *350.00* |
| *a.* | 20c yellow green | 30.00 | *350.00* |
| *b.* | 20c dark green | 30.00 | *400.00* |
| *c.* | Diagonal half used as 10c on cover | | *4,000.* |
| *d.* | Horiz. half used as 10c on cover | | *4,500.* |

**1862 Typo.**

| | | |
|---|---|---|
| *14* | A10 1c orange | 60.00 |
| *a.* | 1c deep orange | 80.00 |

The 1c was never put in use.

## CANAL ZONE

LOCATION — A strip of land 10 miles wide, extending through the Republic of Panama, between the Atlantic and Pacific Oceans.

GOVT. — From 1904-79 a US Government Reservation; from 1979 under control of the Republic of Panama.

AREA — 552.8 sq. mi.

POP. — 41,800 (est. 1976)

The Canal Zone, site of the Panama Canal, was leased in perpetuity to the United States for a cash payment of $10,000,000 and a yearly rental. Treaties between the two countries provided for transfer of control of this area to Panama in 1979, including the postal service.

100 Centavos = 1 Peso
100 Centesimos = 1 Balboa
100 Cents = 1 Dollar

**Catalogue values for unused stamps in this country are for Never Hinged items, beginning with Scott 118 in the regular postage section and Scott C6 in the air post section.**

Map Of Panama — A1

Violet to Violet-blue Handstamp, "CANAL ZONE," on Panama Nos. 72, 72c, 78 and 79

**1904 Unwmk. *Perf. 12***

| | | | |
|---|---|---|---|
| *1* | A1 2c rose, both "PANAMA" up or down | 400.00 | 375.00 |
| *a.* | "CANAL ZONE" inverted | 675.00 | 675.00 |
| *b.* | "CANAL ZONE" double | 1,850. | 1,850. |
| *c.* | "CANAL ZONE" double, both inverted | *3,500.* | |
| *d.* | "PANAMA" reading down and up | 500.00 | 500.00 |
| *e.* | As "d", "CANAL ZONE" inverted | 3,500. | 3,500. |
| *f.* | Vert. pair, "Panama" reading up on top 2c, down on other | 1,100. | 1,100. |
| *2* | A1 5c blue | 275.00 | 225.00 |
| *a.* | "CANAL ZONE" inverted | 450.00 | 450.00 |
| *b.* | "CANAL ZONE" double | 900.00 | 900.00 |
| *c.* | Pair, one without "CANAL ZONE" | 2,250. | 2,250. |
| *d.* | "CANAL ZONE" diagonal, running down to right | 500.00 | 500.00 |
| *3* | A1 10c yellow | 300.00 | 275.00 |
| *a.* | "CANAL ZONE" inverted | 500.00 | 500.00 |
| *b.* | "CANAL ZONE" double | | 3,000. |
| *c.* | Pair, one without "CANAL ZONE" | 2,750. | 2,750. |

On the 2c stamp "PANAMA" is about 13mm; on the 5c and 10c about 15mm.

Varieties of "PANAMA" overprint exist on the 2c with inverted "V" for "A", accent on "A", inverted "N", etc.

Conterfeit "CANAL ZONE" overprints exist.

US Nos. 300, 319, 304, 306 and 307 Overprinted in Black

CANAL ZONE

PANAMA

**1904 Wmk. 191**

| | | | |
|---|---|---|---|
| *4* | A115 1c blue green | 27.50 | 22.50 |
| *5* | A129 2c carmine | 22.50 | 20.00 |
| *a.* | 2c scarlet | 27.50 | 22.50 |
| *6* | A119 5c blue | 100.00 | 70.00 |
| *7* | A121 8c violet blk | 150.00 | 130.00 |
| *8* | A122 10c pale red brn | 175.00 | 130.00 |
| | *Nos. 4-8 (5)* | 475.00 | 372.50 |

A2

A3

CANAL ZONE — Regular Type

CANAL ZONE — Antique Type

Black Overprint on Stamps of Panama

**1904-06 Unwmk.**

| | | | |
|---|---|---|---|
| *9* | A2 1c green | 2.25 | 1.75 |
| *a.* | "CANAL" in antique type | 125.00 | 125.00 |
| *b.* | "ZONE" in antique type | 75.00 | 75.00 |
| *c.* | Inverted overprint | — | *2,000.* |
| *d.* | Double overprint | *1,200.* | *800.00* |
| *10* | A2 2c rose | 5.00 | 3.00 |
| *a.* | Inverted overprint | 250.00 | 250.00 |
| *b.* | "L" of "CANAL" sideways | 1,100. | 1,100. |

**Overprinted "CANAL ZONE" Black, "PANAMA" and Bar in Red on Panama Nos. 77-79. "PANAMA" 15mm long**

| | | | |
|---|---|---|---|
| *11* | A3 2c rose | 6.50 | 4.50 |
| *a.* | "ZONE" in antique type | 125.00 | 125.00 |
| *b.* | "PANAMA" invtd., bar at bottom | 350.00 | 350.00 |

| No. | Type | Description | Unused | Used |
|---|---|---|---|---|
| 12 | A3 | 5c blue | 8.50 | 4.25 |
| a. | | "CANAL" in antique type | 75.00 | 75.00 |
| b. | | "ZONE" in antigue type | 75.00 | 75.00 |
| c. | | "CANAL ZONE" double | 500.00 | 500.00 |
| d. | | "PANAMA" ovpt. dbl. | 650.00 | 650.00 |
| e. | | "PANAMA" invtd., bar at bottom | 950.00 | 950.00 |
| 13 | A3 | 10cyellow | 20.00 | 15.00 |
| a. | | "CANAL" in antigue type | 200.00 | 200.00 |
| b. | | "ZONE" in antigue type | 175.00 | 175.00 |
| c. | | "PANAMA" ovpt. dbl. | 600.00 | 600.00 |
| d. | | "PANAMA" overprint in red brown | 25.00 | 25.00 |

With Additional Surcharge in Red on Panama No. 81

**8 cts**

| No. | Type | Description | Unused | Used |
|---|---|---|---|---|
| 14 | A3 | 3c on 50c bis brn | 35.00 | 25.00 |
| a. | | "ZONE" in antique type | 750.00 | 700.00 |
| b. | | "CANAL ZONE" invtd. | 325.00 | 325.00 |
| c. | | Rose brn overprint | 37.50 | 37.50 |
| d | | As "c" "CANAL" in antique type | 1,500. | |
| e | | As "c" "ZONE" in antique type | 1,500. | |
| f | | As "c" "8 cts" double | 700.00 | |
| g | | As "c" "8" omitted | 4,000. | |

Panama No. 74 Overprinted "CANAL ZONE" in Regular Type in Black and Surch. Like No. 14 in Red. Both "PANAMA" Reading Up. "PANAMA" 13mm long.

**1905**

| No. | Type | Description | Unused | Used |
|---|---|---|---|---|
| 15 | A3 | 8c on 50c bis brn | 2,400. | 2,400. |
| a | | "PANAMA" reading down and up | 3,300. | 3,300. |

Panama Nos. 19 and 21 Surcharged in Black:

a — PANAMA CANAL ZONE 1 ct. PANAMA

b — PANAMA CANAL ZONE 1 ct. PANAMA

c — PANAMA CANAL ZONE 1 ct. PANAMA

d — PANAMA CANAL ZONE 2 cts. PANAMA

e — PANAMA CANAL ZONE 2 cts. PANAMA

f — PANAMA CANAL ZONE 2 cts. PANAMA

There were 3 printings of each denomination differing mainly in the relative position of the various parts of the surcharges. Varieties occur with invtd. "v" for the 3rd "a" in "Panama", "CA" spaced, "ZO" spaced, "2c" spaced, accents in various positions, and with bars shifted so that 2 bars appear on top or bottom of the stamp) either with or without the corresponding bar on top or bottom) and sometimes with only 1 bar at top or bottom.

**1906**

| No. | Type | Description | Unused | Used |
|---|---|---|---|---|
| 16 | A4 | 1c on 20c vio, type a | 1.75 | 1.20 |
| a. | | Surcharge type b | 1.75 | 1.20 |
| b. | | Surcharge type c | 1.50 | 1.20 |
| 17 | A4 | 2c on 1p lake, type d | 2.50 | 1.75 |
| a. | | Surcharge type e | 2.50 | 1.75 |
| b. | | Surcharge type f | 22.50 | 22.50 |

Panama No. 74 Overprinted "CANAL ZONE" in Regular Type in Black and Surcharged in Red

8 cts. (b) — 8 cts (c)

Both "Panama" reading up

**1905-06**

| No. | Type | Description | Unused | Used |
|---|---|---|---|---|
| 18 | A3 | 8c on 50c bis brn (b) | 70.00 | 70.00 |
| a. | | "ZONE" in antique type | 200.00 | 200.00 |
| b. | | "PANAMA" down & up | 125.00 | 125.00 |
| 19 | A3 | 8c on 50c bister brn (c) ('06) | 70.00 | 65.00 |
| a. | | "CANAL" in antique type | 175.00 | 175.00 |
| b. | | "ZONE" in antique type | 175.00 | 175.00 |
| c. | | "8" cts. "double" | 1,000. | 1,000. |
| d. | | "PANAMA" down & up | 100.00 | 100.00 |

Panama No. 81 Overprinted "CANAL ZONE" in Regular Type in Black and Surcharged in Red Type "c" plus Period. "Panama" reading up and down

| No. | Type | Description | Unused | Used |
|---|---|---|---|---|
| 20 | A3 | 8c on 50c bis brn | 60.00 | 50.00 |
| a. | | "CANAL" in antique type | 175.00 | 175.00 |
| b. | | "ZONE" in antique type | 175.00 | 175.00 |
| c. | | "8" cts omitted | 700.00 | 700.00 |
| d. | | "8" cts double | 1,250. | |

Numerous minor varieties of all these surcharges exist. Nos. 14, 18, 19 and 20 exist without CANAL ZONE overprint but were not regularly issued.

Vasco Nunez de Balboa A5

Francisco Hernandez de Cordoba A6

Justo Arosemena A7

Manuel J. Hurtado A8

Jose de Obaldia — A9

Stamps of Panama Ovptd. in Black

**1906-07**

**Overprint Reading Up**

| No. | Type | Description | Unused | Used |
|---|---|---|---|---|
| 21 | A6 | 2c red & black | 35.00 | 30.00 |
| a. | | "Canal" only | 4,500. | |

**Overprint Reading Down**

| No. | Type | Description | Unused | Used |
|---|---|---|---|---|
| 22 | A5 | 1c grn & blk | 2.25 | 1.25 |
| a. | | Horiz. pair, imperf. btwn. | 900.00 | 900.00 |
| b. | | Vert. pair, imperf. btwn. | 1,500. | 1,500. |
| c. | | Vert. pair, imperf. horiz. | 1,500. | 1,500. |
| d. | | Invtd. ovpt., reading up | 300.00 | 300.00 |
| e. | | Double overprint | 225.00 | 225.00 |
| f. | | Dbl. ovpt., one reading up | 1,100. | 1,100. |
| g. | | Inverted center, and ovpt reading up | 2,250. | 2,250. |
| 23 | A6 | 2c red & blk | 2.75 | 1.25 |
| a. | | Horiz. pair, imperf. btwn. | 1,000. | 1,000. |
| b. | | Vertical pair, one without overprint | 1,500. | 1,500. |
| c. | | Double overprint | 400.00 | 400.00 |
| d. | | Dbl. ovpt., one diagonal | 550.00 | 550.00 |
| e. | | Double overprint, one diagonal in pair with normal | 1,300. | |
| f. | | 2c carmine red & black | 6.00 | 4.00 |
| g. | | As "f", inverted center and overprint reading up | | 5,500. |
| h. | | As "d", one "ZONE CANAL" | 2,250. | |
| i. | | "CANAL" double | 2,750. | |
| 24 | A7 | 5c ultra & black | 7.25 | 2.75 |
| a. | | 5c dull blue & black | 7.25 | 2.75 |
| b. | | 5c light blue & black | 6.00 | 2.25 |
| c. | | Double overprint | 350.00 | 250.00 |
| d. | | "CANAL" only | 1,750. | |
| e. | | "ZONE CANAL" | 3,000. | |
| 25 | A8 | 8c purple & blk | 27.50 | 12.50 |
| a. | | Horizontal pair, imperf. between and at left margin | 700.00 | 700.00 |
| 26 | A9 | 10c violet & blk | 27.50 | 10.00 |
| a. | | Dbl. ovpt., one reading up | 2,000. | |
| b. | | Overprint reading up | 2,250. | |
| | | *Nos. 22-26 (5)* | 67.25 | 27.75 |

Nos. 22 to 25 occur with "CA" spaced.

Cordoba A11

Arosemena A12

Hurtado A13

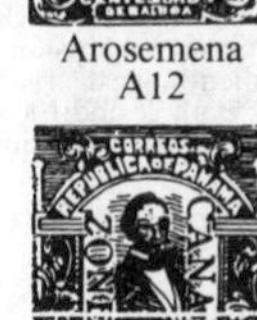

Jose de Obaldia A14

Overprint Reading Down

**1909**

| No. | Type | Description | Unused | Used |
|---|---|---|---|---|
| 27 | A11 | 2c vermilion & blk | 17.50 | 9.00 |
| a. | | Horiz. pair, one without ovpt. | 2,250. | |
| b. | | Vert. pair, one without ovpt. | 2,400. | |
| 28 | A12 | 5c dp bl & blk | 62.50 | 14.00 |
| 29 | A13 | 8c violet & blk | 55.00 | 12.50 |
| 30 | A14 | 10c violet & blk | 55.00 | 15.00 |
| a. | | Horiz. pair, one without ovpt. | 3,250. | |
| b. | | Vert. pair, one without ovpt. | 3,750. | |

Nos. 27 to 30 occur with "CA" spaced.

Vasco Nunez de Balboa — A15

Type I — CANAL ZONE

Smaller Black Overprint, Reading Up

Type I Overprint: "C" with serifs both top and bottom. "L" "Z" and "E" with slanting serif.

Illustrations of Types I to V are considerably enlarged and do not show actual spacing between lines of overprint.

**1909-10**

| No. | Type | Description | Unused | Used |
|---|---|---|---|---|
| 31 | A15 | 1c dark grn & blk | 3.50 | 2.00 |
| a. | | Inverted center and overprint reading down | | 12,000. |
| c. | | Bklt. pane of 6 handmade, perf. margins | 550.00 | |
| 32 | A11 | 2c ver & blk | 4.25 | 2.00 |
| a. | | Vert. pair, imperf. horiz | 700.00 | 700.00 |
| c. | | Bklt. paine of 6 bandmade, perf. margins | 700.00 | |
| 33 | A12 | 5c dp bl & blk | 13.00 | 4.50 |
| a. | | Double overprint | 275.00 | 275.00 |
| 34 | A13 | 8c vio & blk ('10) | 9.50 | 5.00 |
| a. | | Vert. pair, one without ovpt. | 1,750 | |
| 35 | A14 | 10c vio & blk | 65.00 | 25.00 |
| | | *Nos. 31-35 (5)* | 95.25 | 38.50 |

A16

A17

Black Surcharge

**1911**

| No. | Type | Description | Unused | Used |
|---|---|---|---|---|
| 36 | A16 | 10c on 13c gray | 5.00 | 2.00 |
| a. | | "10cts" inverted | 300.00 | 225.00 |
| b. | | "10cts" omitted | 250.00 | — |

**1914**

| No. | Type | Description | Unused | Used |
|---|---|---|---|---|
| 37 | A17 | 10c gray | 50.00 | 12.00 |

Type II: "C" with serif at top only. "L" and "E" with vertical serifs. Inner oval of "O" tilts to left — CANAL ZONE

**1912-16**

| No. | Type | Description | Unused | Used |
|---|---|---|---|---|
| 38 | A15 | 1c grn & blk ('13) | 12.00 | 2.75 |
| a. | | Vert. pair, one without ovpt. | 1,250. | 1,250. |
| b. | | Booklet pane of 6 | 525.00 | |
| c. | | As "b" handmade, perf. margins | 900.00 | |
| 39 | A11 | 2c ver & blk | 7.00 | 1.25 |
| a. | | Horiz. pair, one without ovpt. | 700.00 | |
| b. | | "CANAL" only | | 1,000. |
| c. | | Booklet pane of 6 | 500.00 | |
| d. | | Overprint reading down | 150.00 | |
| e. | | As "d", inverted center | 750.00 | 750.00 |
| f. | | As "e", booklet pane of 6 handmade, perf. margins | 5,000. | |
| g. | | As "c", handmade, perf. margins | 850.00 | |
| 40 | A12 | 5c dp bl & blk | 25.00 | 2.75 |
| a. | | With portrait of 2c | | 7,000. |
| 41 | A14 | 10c vio & blk ('16) | 50.00 | 10.00 |

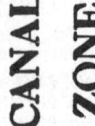

Map of Panama Canal — A18

Balboa Takes Possession of the Pacifc Ocean — A19

Gatun Lock — A20

Culebra Cut — A21

Blue Overprint, Type II

**1915**

| No. | Type | Description | Unused | Used |
|---|---|---|---|---|
| 42 | A18 | 1c dark grn & blk | 8.25 | 5.00 |
| 43 | A19 | 2c carmine & blk | 10.00 | 5.50 |
| 44 | A20 | 5c blue & black | 10.00 | 5.50 |
| 45 | A21 | 10 orange & blk | 22.50 | 15.00 |

Type III: Similar to Type I but letters appear thinner, particularly the lower bar of "L", "Z" and "E". Impressions are often light, rough and irregular — CANAL ZONE

**1915-20**

| No. | Type | Description | Unused | Used |
|---|---|---|---|---|
| 46 | A15 | 1c green & blk | 200.00 | 120.00 |
| a. | | Overprint reading down | 350.00 | |
| b. | | Double overprint | 375.00 | |
| c | | "ZONE" double | 3,250. | |
| d. | | Double overprint, one "ZONE CANAL" | 1,000. | |
| 47 | A11 | 2c org ver & blk | 2,500. | 100.00 |
| 48 | A12 | 5c deep bl & blk | 700.00 | 200.00 |

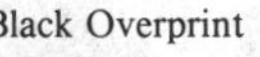

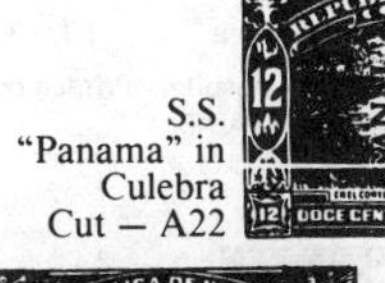

S.S. "Panama" in Culebra Cut — A22

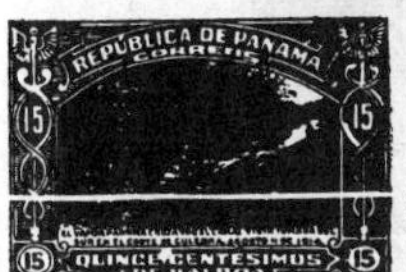

S.S. "Panama" in Culebra Cut — A23

S.S. "Cristobal" in Gatun Locks — A24

Blue Overprint, Type II

**1917**

| No. | Type | Description | Unused | Used |
|---|---|---|---|---|
| *49* | A22 | 12c purple & blk | 20.00 | 7.00 |
| *50* | A23 | 15c bright bl & blk | 55.00 | 35.00 |
| *51* | A24 | 24c yel brn & blk | 50.00 | 17.50 |

Type IV: "C" thick at bottom, "E" with center bar same length as top and bottom bars

CANAL ZONE

Black Overprint, Reading Up

**1918-20**

| No. | Type | Description | Unused | Used |
|---|---|---|---|---|
| *52* | A15 | 1c green & blk | 37.50 | 6.50 |
| ***a.*** | | Overprint reading down | 125.00 | |
| ***b.*** | | Booklet pane of 6 | 600.00 | |
| ***c.*** | | Bklt. pane of 6, left vert. row of 3 without ovpt. | *2,250.* | |
| ***d.*** | | Bklt. pane of 6, right vert. row of 3 with dbl. ovpt. | *2,250.* | |
| ***e.*** | | Pair, one without overprint | *850.00* | |
| *53* | A11 | 2c ver & blk | 150.00 | 10.00 |
| ***a.*** | | Overprint reading down | 140.00 | 140.00 |
| ***b.*** | | Horizontal pair, one without overprint | 1,250. | |
| ***c.*** | | Booklet pane of 6 | 700.00 | |
| ***d.*** | | Bklt. pane of 6, left vert. row of 3 without ovpt. | *2,250.* | |
| *54* | A12 | 5c dp bl & blk ('20) | 250.00 | 45.00 |

Normal spacing between words of overprint on Nos. 52 and 53 is 9¼mm. On No. 54 and the booklet printings of Nos. 52 and 53, the normal spacing is 9mm. Minor spacing varieties are known.

Type V: Smaller block type 1¾mm high. "A" with flat top

CANAL ZONE

Black Overprint, Reading Up

**1920-21**

| No. | Type | Description | Unused | Used |
|---|---|---|---|---|
| *55* | A15 | 1c lt grn & blk | 25.00 | 4.50 |
| ***a.*** | | Overprint reading down | 140.00 | 140.00 |
| ***b.*** | | Pair, one without overprint | 800.00 | |
| ***c.*** | | "CANAL" double | *1,100* | |
| ***d.*** | | "ZONE" only | *2,250.* | |
| ***e.*** | | Booklet pane of 6 | *2,750.* | |
| *56* | A11 | 2c org ver & blk | 9.00 | 3.00 |
| ***a.*** | | Double overprint | 350.00 | |
| ***b.*** | | Double overprint, one reading down | 350.00 | |
| ***c.*** | | Horiz. pair, one without overprint | 800.00 | |
| ***d.*** | | Vertical pair, one without overprint | 1,750. | |
| ***e.*** | | "CANAL" double | 900.00 | |
| ***f.*** | | "ZONE" double | 1,000. | |
| ***g.*** | | Booklet pane of 6 | 850.00 | |
| *57* | A12 | 5c dp bl & blk | 325.00 | 50.00 |
| ***a.*** | | Horiz. pair, one without overprint | 1,200. | |

Drydock at Balboa — A25

Ship in Pedro Miguel Locks — A26

Black Overprint, Type V

**1920**

| No. | Type | Description | Unused | Used |
|---|---|---|---|---|
| *58* | A25 | 50c orange & blk | 350.00 | 200.00 |
| *59* | A26 | 1b dk vio & blk | 180.00 | 75.00 |

Jose Vallarino A27

The "Land Gate" A28

Bolivar's Tribute — A29

Municipal Building in 1821 and 1921 — A30

Statue of Balboa A31

Tomas Gerrera A32

Jose de Fabrega — A33

Black or Red Overprint, Type V

**1921**

| No. | Type | Description | Unused | Used |
|---|---|---|---|---|
| *60* | A27 | 1c green | 3.50 | 1.50 |
| ***a.*** | | "CANAL" double | *1,200.* | |
| ***b.*** | | Booklet pane of 6 | *750.00* | |
| *61* | A28 | 2c carmine | 2.50 | 1.40 |
| ***a.*** | | Overprint reading down | 175.00 | 175.00 |
| ***b.*** | | Double overprint | 650.00 | |
| ***c.*** | | Vertical pair, one without overprint | *3,500.* | |
| ***d.*** | | "CANAL" double | *1,750.* | |
| ***e.*** | | "ZONE" only | *3,500.* | |
| ***f.*** | | Booklet pane of 6 | *1,200.* | |
| *62* | A29 | 5c blue (R) | 10.00 | 4.00 |
| ***a.*** | | Overprint reading down (R) | 80.00 | |
| *63* | A30 | 10c violet | 17.50 | 7.50 |
| ***a.*** | | Overprint reading down | 100.00 | |
| *64* | A31 | 15c light blue | 60.00 | 17.50 |
| *65* | A32 | 24c blk brown | 70.00 | 27.50 |
| *66* | A33 | 50c black | 150.00 | 110.00 |
| | | *Nos. 60-66 (7)* | 313.50 | 169.40 |

Experts question the status of the 5c blue with a small type V overprint in red or black.

Type III Ovpt. in Black, Reading Up

**1924**

| No. | Type | Description | Unused | Used |
|---|---|---|---|---|
| *67* | A27 | 1c green | 475.00 | 200.00 |
| ***a.*** | | "ZONE CANAL" reading down | 750.00 | |
| ***b.*** | | "ZONE" reading down | *1,500.* | |

Coat of Arms — A34

Black Overprint

**1924**

| No. | Type | Description | Unused | Used |
|---|---|---|---|---|
| *68* | A34 | 1c dark green | 12.50 | 4.00 |
| *69* | A34 | 2c carmine | 10.00 | 3.50 |

The 5c to 1b values were prepared but never issued. See listing in Scott's U.S. Specialized Catalogue.

US Nos. 551-554, 557, 562, 564-566, and 569-571 Overprinted in Red or Black

Type A

CANAL

ZONE

Letters "A" with Flat Tops

**Flat Plate Printing**

**1924-25** ***Perf. 11***

| No. | Type | Description | Unused | Used |
|---|---|---|---|---|
| *70* | A154 | ½c ol brn (R) | 1.00 | 1.00 |
| *71* | A155 | 1c deep green | 1.75 | 80 |
| ***a.*** | | Inverted overprint | 500.00 | 500.00 |
| ***b.*** | | "ZONE" inverted | 350.00 | 325.00 |
| ***c.*** | | "CANAL" only | 1,000. | |
| ***d.*** | | "ZONE CANAL" | 300.00 | |
| ***e.*** | | Booklet pane of 6 | 125.00 | |
| *72* | A156 | 1½c yel brn | 2.25 | 1.25 |
| *73* | A157 | 2c carmine | 10.00 | 1.50 |
| ***a.*** | | Booklet pane of 6 | 150.00 | |
| *74* | A160 | 5c dark bl | 22.50 | 9.00 |
| *75* | A165 | 10c orange | 45.00 | 20.00 |
| *76* | A167 | 12c brn vio | 40.00 | 22.50 |
| ***a.*** | | "ZONE" inverted | *3,000.* | *2,000.* |
| *77* | A168 | 14c dark bl | 25.00 | 17.50 |
| *78* | A169 | 15c gray | 55.00 | 30.00 |
| *79* | A172 | 30c olive brn | 30.00 | 20.00 |
| *80* | A173 | 50c lilac | 65.00 | 40.00 |
| *81* | A174 | $1 vio brn | 350.00 | 180.00 |
| | | *Nos. 70-81 (12)* | 647.50 | 343.55 |

The space between the two lines of the overprint, on both type A and B, varies to accord with the dimensions of the stamps.

US Nos. 554, 555, 557, 562, 564-567, 569-571 and 623 Overprinted in Black or Red

Type B

CANAL

ZONE

Letters "A" with Sharp Pointed Tops

**1925-26**

| No. | Type | Description | Unused | Used |
|---|---|---|---|---|
| *84* | A157 | 2c carmine | 35.00 | 8.50 |
| ***a.*** | | "CANAL" ONLY | 1,000. | |
| ***b.*** | | "ZONE CANAL" | 300.00 | |
| ***c.*** | | Horiz. pair, one without overprint | *2,750.* | |
| ***d.*** | | Booklet pane of 6 | 200.00 | |
| *85* | A158 | 3c violet | 4.75 | 2.50 |
| ***a.*** | | "ZONE ZONE" | 500.00 | 500.00 |
| *86* | A160 | 5c dark blue | 4.50 | 2.50 |
| ***a.*** | | "ZONE ZONE" | 900.00 | |
| ***b.*** | | "CANAL" inverted | 900.00 | |
| ***c.*** | | Inverted overprint | 450.00 | |
| ***d.*** | | Pair, one without overprint | *3,250.* | |
| ***e.*** | | "ZONE CANAL" | 325.00 | |
| ***f.*** | | "ZONE" only | *2,000.* | |
| ***g.*** | | Pair, one without ovpt., other ovpt. invtd. | *2,000.* | |
| ***h.*** | | "CANAL" only | *2,000.* | |
| *87* | A165 | 10c orange | 40.00 | 10.00 |
| ***a.*** | | "ZONE ZONE" | *3,250.* | |
| ***b.*** | | "ZONE" only | *3,500.* | |
| *88* | A167 | 12c brn vio | 30.00 | 15.00 |
| ***a.*** | | "ZONE ZONE" | *3,250.* | |
| *89* | A168 | 14c dark blue | 22.50 | 18.00 |
| *90* | A169 | 15c gray | 7.75 | 2.75 |
| ***a.*** | | "ZONE ZONE" | *3,500.* | |
| *91* | A187 | 17c black (R) | 4.25 | 2.00 |
| ***a.*** | | "ZONE" only | 1,100. | |
| ***b.*** | | "CANAL" only | 1,400. | |
| ***c.*** | | "ZONE CANAL" | 200.00 | |
| *92* | A170 | 20c car rose | 9.00 | 4.25 |
| ***a.*** | | "CANAL" inverted | *3,500.* | |
| ***b.*** | | "ZONE" inverted | *3,500.* | |
| ***c.*** | | "ZONE CANAL" | *3,500.* | |
| *93* | A172 | 30c olive brn | 7.00 | 3.75 |
| *94* | A173 | 50c lilac | 300.00 | 130.00 |
| *95* | A174 | $1 vio brn | 150.00 | 55.00 |
| | | *Nos. 84-95 (12)* | 614.75 | 254.25 |

Overprint Type B on US Sesquicentennial Stamp No. 627

**1926**

| No. | Type | Description | Unused | Used |
|---|---|---|---|---|
| *96* | A188 | 2c carmine rose | 5.00 | 4.50 |

On this stamp there is a space of 5mm (instead of 9mm) between the two words of the overprint.

Overprint Type B on US Nos. 583, 584 and 591.

**Rotary Press Printings**

**1927** ***Perf. 10***

| No. | Type | Description | Unused | Used |
|---|---|---|---|---|
| *97* | A157 | 2c carmine | 65.00 | 10.00 |
| ***a.*** | | Pair, one without overprint | *2,000.* | |
| ***b.*** | | Booklet pane of 6 | 650.00 | |
| ***c.*** | | "CANAL" only | *1,400.* | |
| ***d.*** | | "ZONE" only | *2,500.* | |
| *98* | A158 | 3c violet | 8.50 | 4.00 |
| *99* | A165 | 10c orange | 14.00 | 6.50 |

Overprint Type B on US Nos. 632, 634, 635, 637 and 642

**Rotary Press Printings**

**1927-31** ***Perf. 11x10½***

| No. | Type | Description | Unused | Used |
|---|---|---|---|---|
| *100* | A155 | 1c green | 2.00 | 1.50 |
| ***a.*** | | Pair, one without overprint | *2,000.* | |
| *101* | A157 | 2c carmine | 2.25 | 80 |
| ***a.*** | | Booklet pane of 6 | 190.00 | |
| *102* | A158 | 3c violet | 4.50 | 1.75 |
| ***a.*** | | Booklet pane of 6, handmade, perf. margins | *2,500.* | |
| *103* | A160 | 5c dark blue | 27.50 | 15.00 |
| *104* | A165 | 10c orange | 20.00 | 8.00 |
| | | *Nos. 100-104 (5)* | 56.25 | 27.05 |

Gen. William Crawford — A35

Gen. George Washington Goethals — A36

Gaillard Cut A37

Harry Foote Hodges A38

Col. David D. Gaillard — A39

Gen. William L. Sibert — A40

Jackson Smith — A41

Admiral Harry H. Rousseau — A42

Col. Sydney B. Williamson A43

J.C.S. Blackburn A44

**Flat Plate Printing**

**1928-40** ***Perf. 11***

| No. | Type | Description | Unused | Used |
|---|---|---|---|---|
| *105* | A35 | 1c green | 10 | 8 |
| *106* | A36 | 2c carmine | 20 | 10 |
| ***a.*** | | Booklet pane of 6 | 17.50 | *7.50* |
| *107* | A37 | 5c blue ('29) | 1.50 | 60 |
| *108* | A38 | 10c orange ('32) | 30 | 15 |
| *109* | A39 | 12c vio brn ('29) | 1.00 | 60 |
| *110* | A40 | 14c blue ('37) | 1.10 | 85 |
| *111* | A41 | 15c gray ('32) | 50 | 35 |
| *112* | A42 | 20c olive brn ('32) | 75 | 20 |
| *113* | A43 | 30c brown blk ('40) | 1.00 | 70 |
| *114* | A44 | 50c lilac ('29) | 2.00 | 65 |
| | | *Nos. 105-114 (10)* | 8.45 | 4.28 |

Wet and Dry Printings

Canal Zone stamps printed by both the "wet" and "dry" process are Nos.105, 108-109, 111-114, 117, 138-140, C21-C24, C26, J25, J27. Starting with Nos. 147 and C27, the Bureau of Engraving and Printing used the "dry" method exclusively. See note following US No. 1029.

United States Nos. 720 and 695
Overprinted type B

**Rotary Press Printing**

**1933** ***Perf. 11x10½***

*115* A226 3c deep violet 3.00 25
**b.** "CANAL" only *3,000.*
**c.** Bklt. pane of 6, handmade, perf. margins 325.00
*116* A168 14c dark blue 7.00 3.50
**a.** "ZONE CANAL" *1,250.*

Gen. George Washington Goethals — A45

**Flat Plate Printing**

**1934, Aug. 15** ***Perf. 11***

*117* A45 3c deep violet 10 6
**a.** Booklet pane of 6 45.00 *20.00*
**b.** As "a", handmade, perf. margins 250.00 —

20th anniv. of the Panama Canal opening. See No. 153.

**Catalogue values for unused stamps in this section, from this point to the end of the section, are for Never Hinged items.**

US Nos. 803 and 805 Overprinted in Black

**CANAL ZONE**

**Rotary Press Printing**

**1939** ***Perf. 11x10½***

*118* A275 ½c deep orange 15 10
*119* A277 1½c bister brown 20 20

**Panama Canal Anniversary Issue.**

Balboa-Before A46

Balboa-After A47

Gaillard Cut-Before A48

Gaillard Cut-After A49

Bas Obispo-Before A50

Bas Obispo-After A51

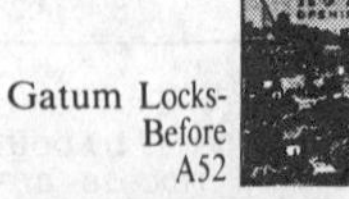

Gatum Locks-Before A52

Gatun Locks-After A53

Canal Channel-Before — A54

Canal Channel-After A55

Gamboa-Before — A56

Gamboa-After A57

Pedro Miguel Locks-Before A58

Pedro Miguel Locks-After A59

Gatun Spillway-Before — A60

Gatun Spillway-After A61

**Flat Plate Printing**

**1939, Aug. 15** ***Perf. 11***

*120* A46 1c yellow green 40 30
*121* A47 2c rose carmine 50 35
*122* A48 3c purple 40 15
*123* A49 5c dark blue 1.00 90
*124* A50 6c red orange 2.25 1.50
*125* A51 7c black 2.25 1.50
*126* A52 8c green 3.25 2.25
*127* A53 10c ultramarine 3.25 2.00
*128* A54 11c blue green 7.50 6.00
*129* A55 12c brn carmine 6.00 5.00
*130* A56 14c dark violet 6.75 4.50
*131* A57 15c olive green 11.00 3.75
*132* A58 18c rose pink 9.00 6.00
*133* A59 20c brown 13.00 3.00
*134* A60 25c orange 20.00 9.00
*135* A61 50c violet brn 22.50 3.50
*Nos. 120-135 (16)* 109.05 49.70

25th anniv. of the Panama Canal.

Maj. Gen. George W. Davis — A62

Gov. Charles E. Magoon — A63

Theodore Roosevelt — A64

John F. Stevens — A65

John F. Wallace — A66

**1946-49 Size: 19x22mm** ***Perf. 11***

*136* A62 ½c bright red ('48) 35 15
*137* A63 1½c choc ('48) 35 15
*138* A64 2c rose car ('49) 10 5
*139* A65 5c deep blue 40 10
*140* A66 25c yel grn ('48) 2.25 1.00
*Nos. 136-140 (5)* 3.45 1.45

See Nos. 155, 162, 164.

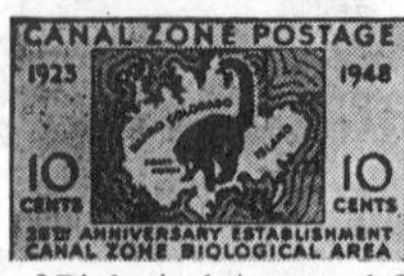
Map of Biological Area and Coati-Mundi — A67

**1948, Apr. 17** ***Perf. 11***

*141* A67 10c black 1.75 1.35

25th anniv. of the establishment of the Canal Zone Biological Area on Barro Colorado Is.

"Forty-niners" Arriving at Chagres — A68

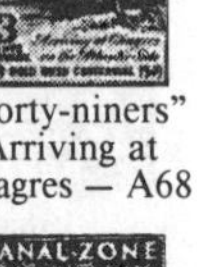
Journey to "Bungo" to Las Cruces — A69

Las Cruces Trail to Panama — A70

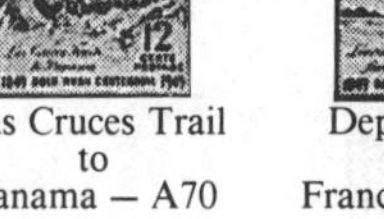
Departure for San Francisco — A71

**1949, June 1** ***Perf. 11***

*142* A68 3c blue 85 35
*143* A69 6c violet 90 45
*144* A70 12c bright grn 2.50 1.40
*145* A71 18c deep red lil 3.25 2.00

Centenary of the California Gold Rush.

Workers in Culebra Cut — A72

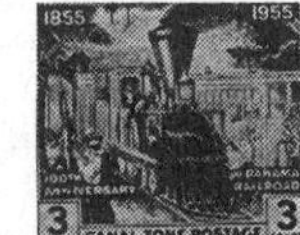
Early Railroad Scene — A73

**1951, Aug. 15**

*146* A72 10c carmine 4.00 1.65

Contribution of West Indian laborers in the construction of the Canal.

**1955, Jan. 28** ***Perf. 11***

*147* A73 3c violet 1.10 50

Cent. of the completion of the Panama Railroad and the 1st transcontinental railroad trip in Americas.

Gorgas Hospital and Ancon Hill — A74

**1957, Nov. 17**

*148* A74 3c blk, *blue green* 60 35

75th anniv. of Gorgas Hospital. Printed on two shades of blue green paper.

S.S. Ancon A75

**1958, Aug. 30 Engr. Unwmk.**

*149* A75 4c greenish blue 45 20

Roosevelt Medal and Map — A76

**1958, Nov. 15** ***Perf. 11***

*150* A76 4c brown 60 30

Theodore Roosevelt (1858-1919).

Boy Scout Badge A77

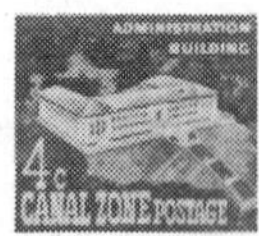
Administration Building A78

**Giori Press Printing**

**1960, Feb. 8** ***Perf. 11***

*151* A77 4c dk bl, red & bis 75 40

Boy Scouts of America, 50th anniv.

**1960, Nov. 1 Engr.** ***Perf. 11***

*152* A78 4c rose lilac 20 12

Types of 1934, 1960 and 1946
Coil Stamps

**1960** ***Perf. 10 Vert.***

*153* A45 3c deep violet 15 12

***Perf. 10 Horiz.***

*154* A78 4c deep rose lilac 20 12

**1962, Feb. 10** ***Perf. 10 Vert.***

*155* A65 5c deep blue 30 20

Girl Scout Badge and Camp at Gatun Lake — A79

**Giori Press Printing**

**1962, Mar. 12** ***Perf. 11***

*156* A79 4c bl, dk grn & bis 40 30

50th anniv. of Girl Scouts.

Thatcher Ferry Bridge and Map of Western Hemisphere A80

**1962, Oct. 12**

*157* A80 4c black & silver 35 25
**a.** Silver (bridge) omitted *7,500.*

Opening of the Thatcher Ferry Bridge, spanning the Panama Canal.

Goethals Memorial, Balboa — A81

Fort San Lorenzo — A82

**Giori Press Printing**

**1968-71** *Perf. 11*
*158* A81 6c green & ultra 40 30
*159* A82 8c multicolor 45 25

Issue dates: 6c, Mar. 15, 1968; 8c, July 14, 1971.

Portrait Type of 1928-48
Coil Stamps

**1975, Feb. 14 Engr.** *Perf. 10 Vert.*
*160* A35 1c green 20 10
*161* A38 10c orange 85 25
*162* A66 25c yellow green 4.00 1.00

Dredge Cascadas A83

**Giori Press Printing**

**1976, Feb. 23** *Perf. 11*
*163* A83 13c multicolor 40 20
*a.* Booklet pane of 4 3.00 —

Stevens Type of 1946

**Rotary Press Printing**

**1977** *Perf. 11x10½*

**Size: 19x22½mm**

*164* A65 5c deep blue 60 25

Towing Locomotive, Ship in Lock — A84

**1978, Oct. 25 Engr.** *Perf. 11*
*165* A84 15c dp grn & bl grn 40 20

---

## AIR POST STAMPS

**AIR MAIL**

Nos. 105-106 Surcharged in Dark Blue

**25 CENTS 25**

Type I. Flag of "5" pointing up **15**

Type II. Flag of "5" curved **15**

**Flat Plat Printing**

**1929 Unwmk.** *Perf. 11*
*C1* A35 15c on 1c green, I 10.00 6.50
*C2* A35 15c on 1c green, II 135.00 85.00
*C3* A36 25c on 2c carmine 4.00 2.25

**AIR MAIL**

Nos. 114 and 106 Surcharged

**≡10c**

**1929, Dec. 31**
*C4* A44 10c on 50c lilac 10.00 9.00
*C5* A36 20c on 2c carmine 7.00 2.00
*a.* Dropped "2" in surcharge 100.00 —

**Catalogue values for unused stamps in this section, from this point to the end of the section, are for Never Hinged items.**

Gaillard Cut — AP1

**1931-49** **Engr.**
*C6* AP1 4c red vil ('49) 75 60
*C7* AP1 5c yellow grn 50 30
*C8* AP1 6c yel brn ('46) 70 30
*C9* AP1 10c orange 85 30
*C10* AP1 15c blue 1.00 25
*C11* AP1 20c red violet 2.00 25
*C12* AP1 30c rose lake ('41) 3.50 1.00
*C13* AP1 40c yellow 3.00 1.00
*C14* AP1 $1 black 10.00 2.25
*Nos. C6-C14 (9)* 22.30 6.25

Douglas Plane over Sosa Hill — AP2

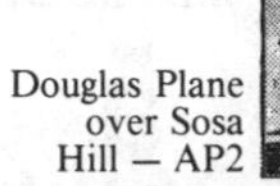

Planes and Map of Central America AP3

Pan American Clipper and Scene near Fort Amador AP4

Pan American Clipper at Cristobal Harbor AP5

Pan American Clipper over Gaillard Cut — AP6

Pan American Clipper Landing AP7

**1939, July 15**
*C15* AP2 5c greenish blk 3.75 3.25
*C16* AP3 10c dull vio 3.75 3.00
*C17* AP4 15c light brn 4.00 1.25
*C18* AP5 25c blue 17.50 11.00
*C19* AP6 30c rose carmine 12.50 8.00
*C20* AP7 $1 green 42.50 35.00
*Nos. C15-C20 (6)* 84.00 61.50

10th anniv. of Air Mail service and the 25th anniv. of the opening of the Panama Canal.

Globe and Wing — AP8

**1951, July 16 Unwmk.** *Perf. 11*
*C21* AP8 4c red violet 80 30
*C22* AP8 6c brown 65 25
*C23* AP8 10c red orange 1.10 40
*C24* AP8 21c blue 9.50 3.50
*C25* AP8 31c cerise 9.00 3.25
*a.* Horiz. pair, imperf. vert. 750.00 —
*C26* AP8 80c gray black 6.50 1.25
*Nos. C21-C26 (6)* 27.55 8.95

**1958, Aug. 16**
*C27* AP8 5c yellow grn 1.50 50
*C28* AP8 7c olive 1.40 40
*C29* AP8 15c brn violet 6.00 1.50
*C30* AP8 25c orange yel 13.00 2.00
*C31* AP8 35c dark blue 11.50 2.00
*Nos. C27-C31 (5)* 33.40 6.40
*Nos. C21-C31 (11)* 60.95 15.35

See No. C34.

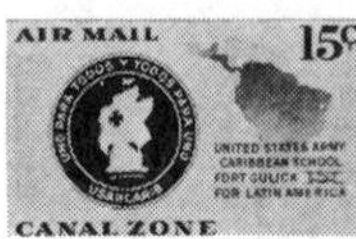

Emblem of US Army Caribbean School — AP9

**Giori Press Printing**

**1961, Nov. 21** *Perf. 11*
*C32* AP9 15c red & dark bl 2.00 1.25

Malaria Eradication Emblem and Mosquito AP10

**1962, Sept. 24 Unwmk.** *Perf. 11*
*C33* AP10 7c yellow & black 75 50

WHO drive to eradicate malaria.

Type of 1951

**Rotary Press Printing**

**1963, Jan. 7** *Perf. 10½x11*
*C34* AP8 8c carmine 75 30

Alliance Emblem AP11

**Giori Press Printing**

**1963, Aug. 17 Unwmk.** *Perf. 11*
*C35* AP11 15c gray, grn & dark ultramarine 1.50 1.00

2nd anniv. of the Alliance for Progress, which aims to stimulate economic growth and raise living standards in Latin America.

Jet over Cristobal AP12

Designs: 8c, Gatun Locks. 15c, Madden Dam. 20c, Gaillard Cut. 30c, Miraflores Locks. 80c, Balboa.

**1964, Aug. 15** *Perf. 11*
*C36* AP12 6c green & blk 60 35
*C37* AP12 8c rose red & blk 70 35
*C38* AP12 15c blue & blk 1.65 50
*C39* AP12 20c rose lil & blk 2.75 85
*C40* AP12 30c redsh brn & blk 4.00 2.00
*C41* AP12 80c ol bis & blk 7.00 3.00
*Nos. C36-C41 (6)* 16.70 7.05

50th anniv. of the Panama Canal.

Seal and Jet Plane — AP13

**1965, July 15 Unwmk.** *Perf. 11*
*C42* AP13 6c green & black 45 20
*C43* AP13 8c rose red & blk 35 10
*C44* AP13 15c blue & black 45 20
*C45* AP13 20c lilac & blk 75 30
*C46* AP13 30c redsh brn & blk 1.00 35
*C47* AP13 80c bister & blk 3.25 90
*Nos. C42-C47 (6)* 6.25 2.05

**1968-76**
*C48* AP13 10c dl org & blk 35 15
*a.* Booklet pane of 4 ('70) 4.25 —
*C49* AP13 11c gray ol & blk 40 18
*a.* Booklet pane of 4 3.50 —
*C50* AP13 13c emer & blk 1.10 30
*a.* Booklet pane of 4 6.00 —
*C51* AP13 22c violet & blk 1.25 50
*C52* AP13 25c pale yel grn & blk 1.10 35
*C53* AP13 35c salmon & blk 2.00 60
*Nos. C48-C53 (6)* 6.20 2.08

The 10c and 25c were issued Mar. 15, 1968; 11c, Sept. 24, 1971; 13c, Feb. 11, 1974; 22c, 35c, May 10, 1976.

---

## AIR POST OFFICIAL STAMPS

Nos. C7, C9-C14 Overprinted in Black

**OFFICIAL**

**PANAMA CANAL**

Two Types of Overprint

**1941-42 Unwmk.** *Perf. 11*

**"PANAMA CANAL" 19-20mm**

*CO1* AP1 5c yellow grn 4.25 1.50
*CO2* AP1 10c orange 9.00 2.00
*CO3* AP1 15c blue 11.00 2.75
*CO4* AP1 20c red violet 16.00 4.50
*CO5* AP1 30c rose lake ('42) 20.00 4.50
*CO6* AP1 40c yellow 22.50 7.00
*CO7* AP1 $1 black 30.00 10.00
*Nos. CO1-CO7 (7)* 112.75 32.25

Overprint varieties occur on Nos. CO1-CO7 and CO14: "O" over "N" of "PANAMA" (entire 3rd row). "O" broken at top (pos. 31). "O" over 2nd "A" of "PANAMA" (pos. 45). 1st "F" of "OFFICIAL" over 2nd "A" of "PANAMA" (pos. 50).

**1941**

**"PANAMA CANAL" 17mm long**

*CO8* AP1 5c light grn — 200.00
*CO9* AP1 10c orange — 250.00
*CO10* AP1 20c red violet — 200.00
*CO11* AP1 30c rose lake — 60.00
*CO12* AP1 40c yellow — 200.00
*Nos. CO8-CO12 (5)* 910.00

Same Overprint on No. C8

**1947, Nov.**

**"PANAMA CANAL" 19-20mm long**

*CO14* AP1 6c yellow brown 11.00 3.50
*a.* Inverted overprint 1,200.

---

## POSTAGE DUE STAMPS

Postage Due Stamps of the US Nos. J45a, J46a and J49a Overprinted in Black

**CANAL ZONE**

**1914, Mar. Wmk. 190** *Perf. 12*
*J1* D2 1c rose carmine 80.00 17.00
*J2* D2 2c rose carmine 250.00 50.00
*J3* D2 10c rose carmine 700.00 50.00

Castle Gate (See footnote) D1

Statue of Columbus D2

Pedro J. Sosa — D3

Blue Overprint, Type II, on Postage Due Stamps of Panama

**1915** **Unwmk.**

*J4* D1 1c olive brown 10.00 4.25
*J5* D2 2c olive brown 140.00 22.50
*J6* D3 10c olive brown 40.00 11.00

The 1c was intended to show a gate of San Lorenzo Castle, Chagres. By error the stamp actually shows the main gate of San Geronimo Castle, Portobelo.

Experts believe that the 1c with overprint type V, reading up or down, is bogus.

Surcharged in Red — CANAL 2 ZONE

*J7* D1 1c on 1c ol brn 110.00 20.00
*J8* D2 2c on 2c ol brn 25.00 7.50
*J9* D3 10c on 10c ol brn 22.50 4.50

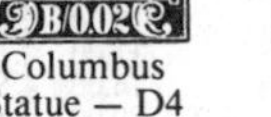

Columbus Statue — D4

Capitol, Panama City — D5

Carmine Surcharge

**1919**

*J10* D4 2c on 2c olive brn 27.50 11.00
*J11* D5 4c on 4c olive brn 35.00 15.00
  ***a.*** "ZONE" omitted *3,250.*
  ***b.*** "4" omitted *2,750.*

US Postage Due Stamps Nos. J61, J62b and J65b Overprinted in Black

Type A — **CANAL ZONE**

Letters "A" with Flat Tops

**1924** ***Perf. 11***

*J12* D2 1c car rose 140.00 30.00
*J13* D2 2c dp claret 85.00 15.00
*J14* D2 10c dp claret 325.00 50.00

US Postage Stamps Nos. 552, 554 and 562 Overprinted Type A and additional Overprint in Red or Blue — POSTAGE DUE

**1925**

*J15* A155 1c green (R) 100.00 17.50
*J16* A157 2c carmine (Bl) 27.50 7.00
*J17* A165 10c orange (R) 55.00 11.00
  ***a.*** "POSTAGE DUE" double 400.00
  ***b.*** "E" of "POSTAGE" missing 350.00
  ***c.*** As "a" and "b", double overprint *2,750.*

"CANAL ZONE" Type B Overprinted on US Nos. J61, J62, J65, J65a

Letters "A" with Sharp Pointed Tops

**1925**

*J18* D2 1c carmine rose 9.00 3.00
  ***a.*** "ZONE ZONE" 1,400.
*J19* D2 2c carmine rose 20.00 5.00
  ***a.*** "ZONE ZONE" 1,400.
*J20* D2 10c carmine rose 130.00 20.00
  ***a.*** Pair, one without overprint *1,750.*
  ***b.*** 10c rose red 165.00 70.00
  ***c.*** As "b", double overprint 325.00

No. 107 Surcharged in Black

**POSTAGE DUE**

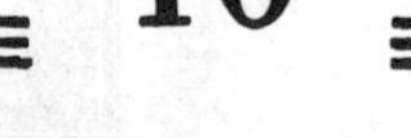

**1929-30**

*J21* A37 1c on 5c blue 3.00 1.75
  ***a.*** "POSTAGE DUE" omitted *2,250.*
*J22* A37 2c on 5c blue 5.00 2.50
*J23* A37 5c on 5c blue 5.00 2.75
*J24* A37 10c on 5c blue 4.50 2.75

On No. J23 the horizontal bars in the lower corners of the surcharge are omitted.

Canal Zone Seal — D6

**1932-41**

*J25* D6 1c claret 10 10
*J26* D6 2c claret 15 10
*J27* D6 5c claret 35 20
*J28* D6 10c claret 1.40 1.25
*J29* D6 15c claret ('41) 1.10 90
  *Nos. J25-J29 (5)* 3.10 2.55

The 1c and 5c are found in both "wet" and "dry" printings. (See note after US No. 1029.) The dry printings are in red violet.

---

## OFFICIAL STAMPS

Regular Issues of 1928-34 Overprinted in Black:

OFFICIAL PANAMA CANAL — Type 1

OFFICIAL PANAMA CANAL — Type 2

Type 1: "PANAMA" 10 mm long.
Type 1A: "PANAMA" 9 mm long.

**1941** **Unwmk.** ***Perf. 11***

*O1* A35 1c yel grn (1) 2.00 35
*O2* A45 3c deep vio (1) 3.75 70
*O3* A37 5c blue (2) — 40.00
*O4* A38 10c orange (1) 5.75 1.75
*O5* A41 15c gray (1) 12.00 2.00
*O6* A42 20c ol brn (1) 15.00 2.50
*O7* A44 50c lilac (1) 50.00 7.50
*O8* A44 50c rose lil (1A) 650.00

Same Overprint on No. 139

**1947**

*O9* A65 5c deep blue (1) 7.50 3.00

---

## CUBA

LOCATION — The largest island of the West Indies; south of Florida.

GOVT. — socialist; under US military governor 1899-1902 and US provisional governor 1906-1909.

AREA — 44,206 sq. mi.

POP. — 9,710,000 (1981)

CAPITAL — Havana

Formerly a Spanish possession, Cuba's attempts to gain freedom led to US intervention in 1898. Under Treaty of Paris of that year, Spain relinquished the island to US trust. In 1902, a republic was established and Cuban Congress took over government from US military authorities.

100 Cents = 1 Dollar

King Alfonso XIII

A19 N2

Cuba stamps can be mounted in Scott's U.S. Possessions Album.

**United States Administration**

**Puerto Principe Issue**

Issues of Cuba of 1898 and 1896 Surcharged:

HABILITADO 1 cent. — a
HABILITADO 1 cents. — b
HABILITADO 2 cents. — c
HABILITADO 2 cents. — d
HABILITADO 3 cents. — e
HABILITADO 3 cents. — f
HABILITADO 5 cents. — g
HABILITADO 5 cents. — h
HABILITADO 5 cents. — i
HABILITADO 5 cents. — j
HABILITADO 3 cents. — k
HABILITADO 3 cents. — l
HABILITADO 10 cents. — m

Types a, c, d, e, f, g and h are 17½mm high, the others are 19½mm high.

**Black Surch. on Nos. 156-158, 160**

**1898-99**

*176* (a) 1c on 1m org brn 55.00 37.50
*177* (b) 1c on 1m org brn 45.00 30.00
  ***a.*** Broken figure "1" 75.00 60.00
  ***b.*** Inverted surcharge 200.00
  ***d.*** Same as "a", inverted *250.00*
*178* (c) 2c on 2m org brn 22.50 15.00
  ***a.*** Inverted surcharge 250.00 50.00
*179* (d) 2c on 2m org brn 40.00 25.00
  ***a.*** Inverted surcharge 350.00 100.00
*179B* (k) 3c on 1m org brn 450.00 150.00
  ***c.*** Double surcharge 1,500. 750.00
*179D* (l) 3c on 1m org brn *1,500.* *600.00*
  ***e.*** Double surcharge — —
*179F* (e) 3c on 2m org brn *2,000.*
*179G* (f) 3c on 2m org brn — *2,500.*
*180* (e) 3c on 3m org brn 27.50 22.50
  ***a.*** Inverted surcharge 100.00
*181* (f) 3c on 3m org brn 75.00 50.00
  ***a.*** Inverted surcharge *300.00*
*182* (g) 5c on 1m org brn 700.00 175.00
  ***a.*** Inverted surcharge *500.00*
*183* (h) 5c on 1m org brn *1,500.* *400.00*
  ***a.*** Inverted surcharge *700.00*
*184* (g) 5c on 2m org brn 750.00 200.00
*185* (h) 5c on 2m org brn 1,500. 400.00
*186* (g) 5c on 3m org brn 165.00
  ***a.*** Inverted surcharge 700.00
*187* (h) 5c on 3m org brn 400.00
  ***a.*** Inverted surcharge 1,000.
*188* (g) 5c on 5m org brn 70.00 55.00
  ***a.*** Inverted surcharge 400.00 175.00
  ***b.*** Double surcharge — —
*189* (h) 5c on 5m org brn 350.00 225.00
  ***a.*** Inverted surcharge 400.00
  ***b.*** Double surcharge — —
*189C* (i) 5c on 5m org brn *8,000.*

**Black Surcharge on No. P25**

*190* (g) 5c on ½m bl grn 250.00 75.00
  ***a.*** Inverted surcharge 500.00 150.00
  ***b.*** Pair, one without surch. 700.00
*191* (h) 5c on ½m bl grn 300.00 90.00
  ***a.*** Inverted surcharge 200.00
*192* (i) 5c on ½m bl grn 550.00 200.00
  ***a.*** Dbl. surch., one diagonal *6,000.*
*193* (j) 5c on ½m bl grn 700.00 300.00

**Red Surcharge on No. 161**

*196* (k) 3c on 1c blk vio 60.00 25.00
  ***a.*** Inverted surcharge 200.00
*197* (l) 3c on 1c blk vio 125.00 45.00
  ***a.*** Inverted surcharge 300.00
*198* (i) 5c on 1c blk vio 20.00 20.00
  ***a.*** Inverted surcharge 100.00
  ***b.*** Vertical surcharge *2,000.*
  ***c.*** Double surcharge *400.00* *600.00*
  ***d.*** Dbl. invtd. surch. —
*199* (j) 5c on 1c blk vio 50.00 40.00
  ***a.*** Inverted surcharge 250.00
  ***b.*** Vertical surcharge *2,000.*
  ***c.*** Double surcharge 1,000. 600.00
*200* (m) 10c on 1c blk vio 20.00 *50.00*
  ***a.*** Broken figure "1" 40.00 *100.00*

**Black Surcharge on Nos. P26-P30**

*201* (k) 3c on 1m bl grn 300.00 200.00
  ***a.*** Inverted surcharge 400.00
  ***b.*** "EENTS" 550.00 400.00
  ***c.*** Same as "b", inverted 850.00
*202* (l) 3c on 1m bl grn 500.00 400.00
  ***a.*** Inverted surcharge 850.00
*203* (k) 3c on 2m bl grn 850.00 250.00
  ***a.*** "EENTS" 1,250. 450.00
  ***b.*** Inverted surcharge 600.00
  ***c.*** Same as "a" inverted 750.00
*204* (l) 3c on 2m bl grn 1,000. 450.00
  ***a.*** Inverted surcharge 750.00
*205* (k) 3c on 3m bl grn 900.00 250.00
  ***a.*** Inverted surcharge 500.00
  ***b.*** "EENTS" 1,250. 375.00
  ***c.*** Same as "b" inverted 700.00
*206* (l) 3c on 3m bl grn 1,200. 375.00
  ***a.*** Inverted surcharge 700.00
*211* (i) 5c on 1m bl grn 2,000.
  ***a.*** "EENTS" — 2,500.
*212* (j) 5c on 1m bl grn 2,500.
*213* (i) 5c on 2m bl grn 1,500.
  ***a.*** "EENTS" — 2,000.
*214* (j) 5c on 2m bl grn 1,750.
*215* (i) 5c on 3m bl grn 500.00
  ***a.*** "EENTS" 1,000.
*216* (j) 5c on 3m bl grn — 1,000.
*217* (i) 5c on 4m bl grn *2,500.* 700.00
  ***a.*** "EENTS" *3,000.* 1,500.
  ***b.*** Inverted surcharge 1,400.
  ***c.*** Same as "a", inverted 2,000.
*218* (j) 5c on 4m bl grn *1,500.*
  ***a.*** Inverted surcharge *2,000.*
*219* (i) 5c on 8m bl grn *3,000.* 1,000.
  ***a.*** Inverted surcharge 1,500.
  ***b.*** "EENTS" — 2,000.
  ***c.*** Same as "b", inverted 2,500.
*220* (j) 5c on 8m bl grn 2,000.
  ***a.*** Inverted surcharge 2,500.

CUBA 1 c. de PESO.

US Nos. 279, 267, 279B, 268, 281, 282C and 283 Surcharged in Black

**1899** **Wmk. 191** ***Perf. 12***

*221* A87 1c on 1c yel grn 4.25 60
*222* A88 2c on 2c car 4.25 50
  ***a.*** 2c on 2c red 5.00 40
  ***b.*** "CUPA" 135.00 120.00
  ***c.*** Inverted surcharge. *3,000.* *3,000.*
*223* A88 2½c on 2c red 3.00 60
  ***a.*** 2½c on 2c car 3.50 2.00
*224* A89 3c on 3c pur 8.50 1.25
  ***a.*** Period btwn. "B" and "A" 27.50 27.50
*225* A91 5c on 5c bl 8.50 1.25
  ***a.*** "CUPA" 75.00 50.00
*226* A94 10c on 10c brn, type I 22.50 8.00
  ***b.*** "CUBA" omitted *3,500.* *3,500.*
*226A* A94 10c on 10c brn, type II *5,000.*
  *Nos. 221-226 (6)* 51.00 12.20

The 2½c was sold and used as a 2c stamp.

Excellent counterfeits of this and the preceding issue exist, especially inverted and double surcharges.

### Issues of the Republic under US Military Rule

Statue of Columbus A20

Royal Palms A21

"Cuba" A22

Ocean Liner A23

Cane Field — A24

**Wmk. U S-C (191C)**

**1899** **Engr.** ***Perf. 12***

| | | | | |
|---|---|---|---|---|
| *227* | A20 | 1c yel grn | 3.00 | 15 |
| *228* | A21 | 2c carmine | 3.00 | 15 |
| ***a.*** | | scar | 3.00 | 15 |
| ***b.*** | | Booklet pane of 6 | *1,750.* | |
| *229* | A22 | 3c purple | 3.00 | 25 |
| *230* | A23 | 5c blue | 4.50 | 30 |
| *231* | A24 | 10c brown | 10.00 | 75 |
| | | *Nos. 227-231 (5)* | 23.50 | 1.60 |

### SPECIAL DELIVERY STAMPS

**United States Administration**

US No. E5 Surcharged in Red

CUBA.
10c.
de PESO

**1899** **Wmk. 191** ***Perf. 12***

| | | | | |
|---|---|---|---|---|
| *E1* | SD3 | 10c on 10c bl | 120.00 | 80.00 |
| ***a.*** | | No period after "CUBA" | 350.00 | 400.00 |

**Issues of the Republic under US Military Rule**

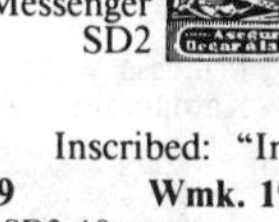
Special Delivery Messenger SD2

Inscribed: "Immediata"

**1899** **Wmk. 191C** **Engr.**

| | | | | |
|---|---|---|---|---|
| *E2* | SD2 | 10c orange | 45.00 | 12.00 |

### POSTAGE DUE STAMPS

**United States Administration**

Postage Due Stamps of the US Nos. J38, J39, J41 and J42 Surcharged in Black Like Nos. 221-226A

**1899** **Wmk. 191** ***Perf. 12***

| | | | | |
|---|---|---|---|---|
| *J1* | D2 | 1c on 1c deep cl | 25.00 | 3.50 |
| *J2* | D2 | 2c on 2c deep cl | 22.50 | 3.50 |
| ***a.*** | | Inverted surcharge | | *2,000.* |
| *J3* | | 5c on 5c deep cl | 25.00 | 3.50 |
| ***a.*** | | "CUPA" | 175.00 | 160.00 |
| *J4* | D2 | 10c on 10c deep cl | 22.50 | 1.25 |

## DANISH WEST INDIES

LOCATION — A group of islands in the West Indies, lying east of Puerto Rico.

GOVT. — A former Danish colony.

AREA — 132 sq. mi.

POP. — 27,086 (1911)

CAPITAL — Charlotte Amalie

The US bought these islands in 1917 and they became the US Virgin Islands, using US stamps and currency.

100 Cents = 1 Dollar
100 Bit = 1 Franc (1905)

Coat of Arms — A1

Wmk. 111- Small Crown

Yellowish Paper

Yellow Wavy-line Burelage, UL to LR

**1856** **Wmk. 111** **Typo.** ***Imperf.***

| | | | | |
|---|---|---|---|---|
| *1* | A1 | 3c dk car, brn gum | 175.00 | 200.00 |
| ***a.*** | | 3c dk car, yellow gum | 225.00 | 210.00 |
| ***b.*** | | 3c carmine, white gum | 2,250. | |

*No. 1 reprints 1981, carmine, back-printed across two stamps ("Reprint by Dansk Post og Telegrafmuseum 1978"), value, pair, $7.*

White Paper

Yellow Wavy-line Burelage, UR to LL

**1866**

| | | | | |
|---|---|---|---|---|
| *2* | A1 | 3c rose | 80.00 | 70.00 |

*No. 2 reprints unwatermarked: 1930 carmine, value $120. 1942 rose carmine, back-printed across each row ("Nytryk 1942 G. A. Hagemann Danmark og Dansk Vestindiens Friemaerker Bind 2"), value $60.*

**1872** ***Perf. 12½***

| | | | | |
|---|---|---|---|---|
| *3* | A1 | 3c rose | 160.00 | 170.00 |

**1873**

**Without Burelage**

| | | | | |
|---|---|---|---|---|
| *4* | A1 | 4c dull blue | 300.00 | 350.00 |
| ***a.*** | | Imperf., pair | 950.00 | 1,200. |
| ***b.*** | | Horiz. pair, imperf. vert. | 750.00 | 900.00 |

*No. 4 reprints, unwatermarked, imperf.: 1930, ultramarine, value $120. 1942, blue back-printed like 1942 reprint of No. 2, value $60.*

Numeral of Value — A2

NORMAL FRAME

INVERTED FRAME

The arabesques in the corners have a main stem and a branch. When the frame is in normal position, in the upper left corner the branch leaves the main stem half way between two little leaflets. In the lower right corner the branch starts at the foot of the second leaflet. When the frame is inverted the corner designs are, of course, transposed.

Wmk. 112- Crown

White Wove Paper, Varying from Thin to Thick

**1874-79** **Wmk. 112** ***Perf. 14x13½***

| | | | | |
|---|---|---|---|---|
| *5* | A2 | 1c grn & brn red | 25.00 | 20.00 |
| ***a.*** | | 1c green & rose lilac | 37.50 | 37.50 |
| ***b.*** | | 1c green & red violet | 37.50 | 37.50 |
| ***c.*** | | 1c green & violet | 80.00 | 110.00 |
| ***e.*** | | Inverted frame | 25.00 | 25.00 |
| *6* | A2 | 3c blue & car | 27.50 | 17.00 |
| ***d.*** | | Imperf., pair | 600.00 | |
| ***e.*** | | Inverted frame | 27.50 | 16.00 |
| *7* | A2 | 4c brn & dl bl | 17.00 | 17.00 |
| ***b.*** | | 4c brown & ultramarine | 250.00 | 175.00 |
| ***c.*** | | Diagonal half used as 2c on cover | | 225.00 |
| ***d.*** | | Inverted frame | 1,000. | 1,000. |
| *8* | A2 | 5c green & gray ('76) | 30.00 | 22.50 |
| ***b.*** | | Inverted frame | 30.00 | 22.50 |
| *9* | A2 | 7c lilac & org | 27.50 | *60.00* |
| ***a.*** | | 7c lilac & yellow | 70.00 | 90.00 |
| ***b.*** | | Inverted frame | 65.00 | 100.00 |
| *10* | A2 | 10c blue & brn ('76) | 30.00 | 18.00 |
| ***b.*** | | Period btwn. t & s of "cents" | 45.00 | 35.00 |
| ***c.*** | | Inverted frame | 30.00 | 20.00 |
| *11* | A2 | 12c red lil & yel grn ('77) | 35.00 | 47.50 |
| ***a.*** | | 12c lilac & deep green | 100.00 | 70.00 |
| *12* | A2 | 14c lilac & grn | 700.00 | 825.00 |
| ***a.*** | | Inverted frame | 2,000. | 2,750. |
| *13* | A2 | 50c violet ('79) | 120.00 | 130.00 |
| ***a.*** | | 50c gray violet | 160.00 | 200.00 |

See Nos. 16-20.

Nos. 9 and 13 Surcharged in Black

1 CENT

10
CENTS
1895

**1887-95**

| | | | | |
|---|---|---|---|---|
| *14* | A2 | 1c on 7c lil & org | 75.00 | 90.00 |
| ***a.*** | | 1c on 7c lilac & yellow | 120.00 | 175.00 |
| ***b.*** | | Double surcharge | 250.00 | 350.00 |
| ***c.*** | | Inverted frame | 115.00 | 135.00 |
| *15* | A2 | 10c on 50c vio ('95) | 35.00 | 40.00 |

Type of 1873

**1896-1901** ***Perf. 13***

| | | | | |
|---|---|---|---|---|
| *16* | A2 | 1c grn & red vio ('98) | 15.00 | 15.00 |
| ***a.*** | | Normal frame | 300.00 | 350.00 |
| *17* | A2 | 3c bl & lake ('98) | 13.00 | 13.00 |
| ***a.*** | | Normal frame | 260.00 | 300.00 |
| *18* | A2 | 4c bis & dl bl ('01) | 13.00 | 13.00 |
| ***a.*** | | Diagonal half used as 2c on cover | | 45.00 |
| ***b.*** | | Inverted frame | 60.00 | 60.00 |
| *19* | A2 | 5c grn & gray | 37.50 | 32.50 |
| ***a.*** | | Normal frame | 750.00 | 750.00 |
| *20* | A2 | 10c bl & brn ('01) | 85.00 | 100.00 |
| ***a.*** | | Inverted frame | 1,100. | 1,600. |
| ***b.*** | | Period between "t" and "s" of "cents" | 85.00 | 100.00 |
| | | *Nos. 16-20 (5)* | 163.50 | 173.50 |

Arms — A5

**1900**

| | | | | |
|---|---|---|---|---|
| *21* | A5 | 1c light green | 2.50 | 2.50 |
| *22* | A5 | 5c light blue | 13.00 | 13.00 |

See Nos. 29-30.

Nos. 6, 17, 20 Surcharged:

2
CENTS
1902
c

8
Cents
1902
d

**Surcharge "c" in Black**

**1902** ***Perf. 14x13½***

| | | | | |
|---|---|---|---|---|
| *23* | A2 | 2c on 3c bl & car | 500.00 | 650.00 |
| ***a.*** | | "2" in date with straight tail | 525.00 | 675.00 |
| ***b.*** | | Normal frame | 1,500. | — |

***Perf. 13***

| | | | | |
|---|---|---|---|---|
| *24* | A2 | 2c on 3c bl & lake | 8.00 | 10.00 |
| ***a.*** | | "2" in date with straight tail | 9.00 | 11.00 |
| ***b.*** | | Dated "1901" | 450.00 | 500.00 |
| ***c.*** | | Normal frame | 225.00 | 275.00 |
| ***d.*** | | Dark green surcharge | 1,600. | |
| ***e.*** | | As "d" & "a" | 1,700. | |
| ***f.*** | | As "d" & "c" | *3,000.* | |
| *25* | A2 | 8c on 10c bl & brn | 25.00 | 35.00 |
| ***a.*** | | "2" with straight tail | 27.50 | 37.50 |
| ***b.*** | | On No. 20b | 42.50 | 52.50 |
| ***c.*** | | Inverted frame | 350.00 | 350.00 |

**Surcharge "d" in Black**

| | | | | |
|---|---|---|---|---|
| *27* | A2 | 2c on 3c bl & lake | 12.50 | 25.00 |
| ***a.*** | | Normal frame | 275.00 | 300.00 |
| *28* | A2 | 8c on 10c bl & brn | 11.00 | 11.00 |
| ***a.*** | | On No. 20b | 20.00 | 20.00 |
| ***b.*** | | Inverted frame | 275.00 | 275.00 |

Wmk. 113- Crown

**1903** **Wmk. 113**

| | | | | |
|---|---|---|---|---|
| *29* | A5 | 2c carmine | 13.00 | 13.00 |
| *30* | A5 | 8c brown | 27.50 | 27.50 |

King Christian IX A8

St. Thomas Harbor A9

**1905** **Typo.** ***Perf. 13***

| | | | | |
|---|---|---|---|---|
| *31* | A8 | 5b green | 7.50 | 4.00 |
| *32* | A8 | 10b red | 7.50 | 4.00 |
| *33* | A8 | 20b green & blue | 13.00 | 13.00 |
| *34* | A8 | 25b ultramarine | 13.00 | 13.00 |
| *35* | A8 | 40b red & gray | 12.50 | 12.50 |
| *36* | A8 | 50b yellow & gray | 11.00 | 13.00 |

**Frame Typo., Center Engr.**

**Wmk. Two Crowns (113)**

***Perf. 12***

| | | | | |
|---|---|---|---|---|
| *37* | A9 | 1fr green & blue | 20.00 | 30.00 |
| *38* | A9 | 2fr org red & brn | 42.50 | 75.00 |
| *39* | A9 | 5fr yellow & brn | 110.00 | 250.00 |
| | | *Nos. 31-39 (9)* | 237.00 | 414.50 |

Nos. 18, 22, 30 Surcharged in Black

5
BIT
1905

**1905** **Wmk. 112** ***Perf. 13***

| | | | | |
|---|---|---|---|---|
| *40* | A2 | 5b on 4c bis & dl bl | 22.50 | 45.00 |
| ***a.*** | | Inverted frame | 42.50 | 75.00 |
| *41* | A5 | 5b on 5c light blue | 15.00 | 27.50 |

**Wmk. 113**

| | | | | |
|---|---|---|---|---|
| *42* | A5 | 5b on 8c brown | 14.00 | 30.00 |

King Frederik VIII — A10

**Frame Typo., Center Engr.**

**1907-08** **Wmk. 113** ***Perf. 13***

| | | | | |
|---|---|---|---|---|
| *43* | A10 | 5b green | 2.50 | 1.50 |
| *44* | A10 | 10b red | 2.50 | 1.50 |
| *45* | A10 | 15b vio & brn | 6.00 | 6.00 |
| *46* | A10 | 20b grn & blue | 47.50 | 20.00 |
| *47* | A10 | 25b bl & dk bl | 3.25 | 2.00 |
| *48* | A10 | 30b cl & slate | 70.00 | 30.00 |
| *49* | A10 | 40b ver & gray | 6.50 | 10.00 |
| *50* | A10 | 50b yel & brn | 7.00 | 10.00 |
| | | *Nos. 43-50 (8)* | 145.25 | 81.00 |

King Christian X — A11

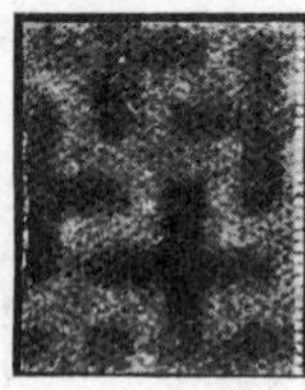

Wmk. 114-
Multiple Crosses

**1915 Wmk. 114 *Perf. 14x14½***

| No. | Type | Description | Unused | Used |
|---|---|---|---|---|
| *51* | A11 | 5b yel grn | 3.00 | *7.00* |
| *52* | A11 | 10b red | 3.00 | *60.00* |
| *53* | A11 | 15b lil & red brn | 3.00 | *60.00* |
| *54* | A11 | 20b grn & bl | 3.00 | *60.00* |
| *55* | A11 | 25b bl & dk bl | 3.00 | *15.00* |
| *56* | A11 | 30b cl & blk | 3.00 | *60.00* |
| *57* | A11 | 40b org & blk | 3.00 | *60.00* |
| *58* | A11 | 50b yel & brn | 3.00 | *60.00* |
| | | *Nos. 51-58 (8)* | 24.00 | 382.00 |

Forged and favor cancellations exist.

## POSTAGE DUE STAMPS

Royal Cipher,
"Christian 9 Rex"
D1

**1902 Unwmk. Litho. *Perf. 11½***

| No. | Type | Description | Unused | Used |
|---|---|---|---|---|
| *J1* | D1 | 1c dark blue | 10.00 | 15.00 |
| *J2* | D1 | 4c dark blue | 14.00 | 20.00 |
| *J3* | D1 | 6c dark blue | 35.00 | 60.00 |
| *J4* | D1 | 10c dark blue | 25.00 | 35.00 |

There are five types of each value. On the 4c they may be distinguished by differences in the figures "4"; on the other values the differences are minute.

Used values of Nos. J1-J8 are for canceled copies. Uncanceled examples without gum have probably been used. Value 60% of unused.

Counterfeits of Nos. J1-J4 exist.

D2

**1905-13 *Perf. 13***

| No. | Type | Description | Unused | Used |
|---|---|---|---|---|
| *J5* | D2 | 5b red & gray | 7.00 | 9.00 |
| *J6* | D2 | 20b red & gray | 14.00 | 20.00 |
| *J7* | D2 | 30b red & gray | 8.50 | 13.00 |
| *J8* | D2 | 50b red & gray | 12.50 | 20.00 |
| ***a.*** | | Perf. 14x14½ ('13) | 25.00 | 125.00 |
| ***b.*** | | Perf. 11½ | 325.00 | |

All values of this issue are known imperforate, but were not regularly issued.

Counterfeits of Nos. J5-J8 exist.

Danish West Indies stamps were replaced by those of the US in 1917, after the US bought the islands.

# GUAM

LOCATION – One of the Mariana Islands in the Pacific Ocean, about 1450 miles east of the Philippines.
GOVT. – United States Possession
AREA – 206 sq. mi.
POP. – 9,000 (est. 1899)
CAPITAL – Agana

Formerly a Spanish possession, Guam was ceded to the United States in 1898 following the Spanish-American War. Stamps overprinted "Guam" were superseded by the regular postage stamps of the United States in 1901.

100 Cents = 1 Dollar

United States Stamps Nos. 279, 267, 279c, 268, 280a, 281a, 282, 272, 282C, 283a, 284, 275, 275a, 276 and 276A Overprinted

**GUAM**

**1899 Wmk. 191 *Perf. 12***

**Black Overprint**

| No. | Type | Description | Unused | Used |
|---|---|---|---|---|
| *1* | A87 | 1c dp grn | 27.50 | *35.00* |
| ***a.*** | | Inverted overprint | | — |
| *2* | A88 | 2c carmine | 25.00 | *35.00* |
| ***a.*** | | 2c rose car | 30.00 | *40.00* |
| *3* | A89 | 3c purple | 125.00 | *175.00* |
| *4* | A90 | 4c lil brn | 125.00 | *175.00* |
| *5* | A91 | 5c blue | 35.00 | *45.00* |
| *6* | A92 | 6c lake | 125.00 | *175.00* |
| *7* | 93 | 8c vio brn | 125.00 | *175.00* |
| *8* | A94 | 10c brn, type I | 55.00 | *70.00* |
| *9* | A94 | 10c brn, type II | *5,000.* | |
| *10* | A95 | 15c ol grn | 135.00 | *175.00* |
| *11* | A96 | 50c orange | 250.00 | *350.00* |
| ***a.*** | | 50c red org | 300.00 | — |

**Red Overprint**

| No. | Type | Description | Unused | Used |
|---|---|---|---|---|
| *12* | A97 | $1 blk, type I | 400.00 | *550.00* |
| *13* | A97 | $1 blk, type II | *3,000.* | |
| | | *Nos. 1-8,10-12 (11)* | 1,427. | 1,960. |

## SPECIAL DELIVERY STAMP

United States No. E5 Overprinted in Red **GUAM**

**1899 Wmk. 191 *Perf. 12***

| No. | Type | Description | Unused | Used |
|---|---|---|---|---|
| *E1* | SD3 | 10c blue | 150.00 | *200.00* |

Guam Guard Mail stamps of 1930 are listed in Scott's Specialized United States Catalogue.

# HAWAII

LOCATION – A group of 20 islands in the Pacific Ocean, about 2,000 miles southwest of San Francisco.
GOVT. – Former Kingdom and Republic.
AREA – 6,435 sq. mi.
POP. – 150,000 (est. 1899)
CAPITAL – Honolulu

Until 1893 an independent kingdom, from 1893 to 1898 a republic, the Hawaiian Islands were annexed to the US in 1898 at the request of the inhabitants. The Territory of Hawaii achieved statehood in 1959.

100 Cents = 1 Dollar

> Values of early Hawaii stamps vary according to condition. Quotations for Nos. 1-18 are for fine to very fine copies. Very fine to superb specimens sell at much higher prices, and inferior or poor copies sell at reduced prices, depending on the condition of the individual specimen.

A1

A2

A3

**Pelure Paper**

**1851-52 Unwmk. Typeset *Imperf.***

| No. | Type | Description | Unused | Used |
|---|---|---|---|---|
| *1* | A1 | 2c blue | *350,000.* | *250,000.* |
| *2* | A1 | 5c blue | *35,000.* | *15,000.* |
| *3* | A2 | 13c blue | *17,500.* | *9,000.* |
| *4* | A3 | 13c blue | *45,000.* | *21,000.* |

Two varieties of each.

King Kamehameha III
A4 A5

**Thick White Wove Paper**

**1853 Engr.**

| No. | Type | Description | Unused | Used |
|---|---|---|---|---|
| *5* | A4 | 5c blue | 650.00 | 450.00 |
| *6* | A5 | 13c dark red | 325.00 | 350.00 |

A6

**1857**

| No. | Type | Description | Unused | Used |
|---|---|---|---|---|
| *7* | A6 | 5c on 13c dark red | *4,500.* | *5,500.* |

**1857**

**Thin White Wove Paper**

| No. | Type | Description | Unused | Used |
|---|---|---|---|---|
| *8* | A4 | 5c blue | 250.00 | 250.00 |
| ***a.*** | | Double impression | *2,000.* | — |

**1861**

**Thin Bluish Wove Paper**

| No. | Type | Description | Unused | Used |
|---|---|---|---|---|
| *9* | A4 | 5c blue | 110.00 | 110.00 |
| ***a.*** | | Double impression | | — |

**1868**

**Ordinary White Wove Paper**

| No. | Type | Description | Unused | Used |
|---|---|---|---|---|
| *10* | A4 | 5c blue | 25.00 | |
| *11* | A5 | 13c dull rose | 225.00 | |

Nos. 10 and 11 were never placed in use.

*Reprints:*

*5c. Originals have two small dots near the left side of the square in the upper right corner. These dots are missing in the reprints.*

*13c. The bottom of the 3 of 13 in the upper left corner is flattened in the originals and rounded in the reprints. The "t" of "Cts" on the left side is as tall as the "C" in the reprints, but shorter in the originals.*

*On August 19, 1892, the remaining supply of reprints was overprinted in black "REPRINT". The reprints (both with and without overprint) were sold at face value.*

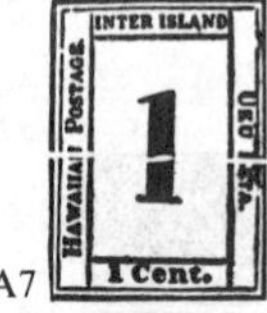


A7

A8

A9

**1859-62 Typeset**

| No. | Type | Description | Unused | Used |
|---|---|---|---|---|
| *12* | A7 | 1c lt bl, *bluish white* | *2,750.* | *3,000.* |
| ***a.*** | | "1 Ce" omitted | | — |
| *13* | A7 | 2c lt bl, *bluish white* | *2,250.* | *1,250.* |
| ***a.*** | | 2c dark blue, *grysh white* | | — |
| ***b.*** | | Comma after "Cents" | | — |
| *14* | A7 | 2c blk, *grnsh bl* ('62) | *3,250.* | *1,250.* |
| ***a.*** | | "2-Cents." | | — |

**1863**

| No. | Type | Description | Unused | Used |
|---|---|---|---|---|
| *15* | A7 | 1c blk, *grayish* | 225.00 | 275.00 |
| ***a.*** | | Tete beche pair | *3,500.* | |
| ***b.*** | | "NTER" | — | |
| *16* | A7 | 2c blk, *grayish* | 375.00 | 325.00 |
| ***a.*** | | "2" at top of rectangle | *1,800.* | *1,800.* |
| ***b.*** | | Printed on both sides | | — |
| ***c.*** | | "NTER" | 1,400. | 1,400. |
| ***d.*** | | 2c black, *grayish white* | 375.00 | 325.00 |
| ***e.*** | | Period omitted after "Cents" | | — |
| ***f.*** | | Double impression | | — |
| ***g.*** | | "tage." | | — |
| *17* | A7 | 2c dk bl, *bluish* | *3,500.* | 1,600. |
| *18* | A7 | 2c blk, *blue gray* | 700.00 | 1,100. |

**1864-65**

| No. | Type | Description | Unused | Used |
|---|---|---|---|---|
| *19* | A7 | 1c black | 275.00 | 425.00 |
| *20* | A7 | 2c black | 325.00 | 425.00 |
| *21* | A8 | 5c blue, *blue* ('65) | 275.00 | 275.00 |
| ***a.*** | | Tete beche pair | *4,500* | |
| ***b.*** | | 5c black, *grysh white* | | — |
| *22* | A9 | 5c blue, *blue* ('65) | 225.00 | 250.00 |
| ***a.*** | | Tete beche pair | *3,500.* | |
| ***b.*** | | 5c blue, *grayish white* | | — |

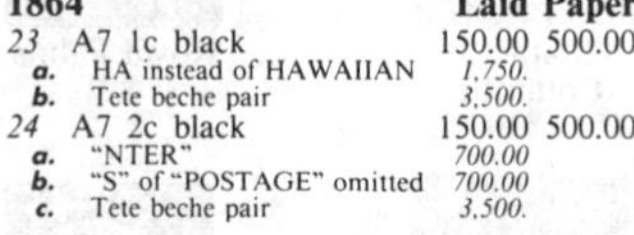

**1864 Laid Paper**

| No. | Type | Description | Unused | Used |
|---|---|---|---|---|
| *23* | A7 | 1c black | 150.00 | 500.00 |
| ***a.*** | | HA instead of HAWAIIAN | *1,750.* | |
| ***b.*** | | Tete beche pair | *3,500.* | |
| *24* | A7 | 2c black | 150.00 | 500.00 |
| ***a.*** | | "NTER" | *700.00* | |
| ***b.*** | | "S" of "POSTAGE" omitted | *700.00* | |
| ***c.*** | | Tete beche pair | *3,500.* | |

A10

**1865 Wove Paper**

| No. | Type | Description | Unused | Used |
|---|---|---|---|---|
| *25* | A10 | 1c dark blue | 150.00 | |
| *26* | A10 | 2c dark blue | 125.00 | |

Nos. 12 to 26 were typeset and were printed in settings of ten, each stamp differing from the others.

King Kamehameha IV
A11

**1861-63 Litho.**

**Horizontally Laid Paper**

| No. | Type | Description | Unused | Used |
|---|---|---|---|---|
| *27* | A11 | 2c pale rose | 175.00 | 110.00 |
| ***a.*** | | 2c carmine rose ('63) | 600.00 | 500.00 |

**Vertically Laid Paper**

| No. | Type | Description | Unused | Used |
|---|---|---|---|---|
| *28* | A11 | 2c pale rose | 175.00 | 110.00 |
| ***a.*** | | 2c carmine rose ('63) | 135.00 | 135.00 |

**1869 Engr. Thin Wove Paper**

| No. | Type | Description | Unused | Used |
|---|---|---|---|---|
| *29* | A11 | 2c red | 50.00 | — |

No. 29 is a re-issue. It was not issued for postal purposes although canceled copies are known. It was sold only at the Honolulu post office, at first without overprint and later with overprint "CANCELLED".

See Nos. 50-51 and note following No. 51.

Princess Victoria
Kamamalu – A12

King
Kamehameha
IV – A13

King
Kamehameha
V – A14

Kamehameha
V – A15

Mataio
Kekuanaoa – A16

**1864-71 Wove Paper *Perf. 12***

*30* A12 1c purple ('71) 7.50 6.00
*a.* 1c violet 7.50 6.00
*31* A13 2c rose ver 11.00 7.00
*a.* 2c vermilion 11.00 7.00
*b.* Half used as 1c on cover —
*32* A14 5c blue ('66) 50.00 19.00
*33* A15 6c green ('71) 17.50 6.00
*a.* 6c yellow green 17.50 6.00
*34* A16 18c dl rose ('71) 85.00 14.00
Without gum 17.50
*Nos. 30-34 (5)* 171.00 52.00

No. 32 has traces of rectangular frame lines surrounding the design. Nos. 39 and 52C have no such frame lines.

King David Kalakaua A17

Prince William Pitt Leleiohoku A18

**1875**

*35* A17 2c brown 6.00 2.25
*36* A18 12c black 40.00 20.00

See Nos. 38, 43, 46.

Princess Likelike — A19

King David Kalakaua — A20

Queen Kapiolani — A21

Statue of King Kamehameha I — A22

King William Lunalilo A23

Queen Emma Kaleleonalani A24

**1882**

*37* A19 1c blue 4.00 7.50
*38* A17 2c lilac rose 90.00 30.00
*a.* Half used as 1c on cover 1,250.
*39* A14 5c ultramarine 12.00 2.25
*a.* Vert. pair, imperf. horiz. 3,500.
*40* A20 10c black 22.50 15.00
*41* A21 15c red brown 40.00 22.50
*Nos. 37-41 (5)* 168.50 77.25

**1883-86**

*42* A19 1c green 2.25 1.50
*43* A17 2c rose ('86) 3.50 75
*44* A20 10c red brn ('84) 17.50 7.00
*45* A20 10c vermilion 20.00 12.50
*46* A18 12c red lilac 60.00 30.00
*47* A22 25c dark vio 85.00 42.50
*48* A23 50c red 135.00 75.00
*49* A24 $1 rose red 200.00 85.00
Maltese cross cancellation 25.00
*Nos. 42-49 (8)* 523.25 254.25

Reproduction and Reprint
Yellowish Wove Paper

**1886-89 *Imperf.***

*50* A11 2c orange ver 150.00
*51* A11 2c carmine ('89) 25.00

In 1885 the Postmaster General wished to have on sale complete sets of Hawaii's stamps as far back as type A11, but was unable to find either the stone from which Nos. 27 and 28, or the plate from which No. 29 was printed. He therefore sent a copy of No. 29 to the American Bank Note Co., with an order to engrave a new plate and print 10,000 stamps, of which 5000 were overprinted "Specimen" in blue.

The original No. 29 was printed in sheet of 15 (5x3), but the plate of these "Official Imitations" was made up of 50 stamps (10x5). Later, in 1887, the original die for No. 29 was discovered, and after retouching, a new plate was made and 37,500 stamps were printed. These, like the originals, were printed in sheets of 15. They were delivered during 1889 and 1890. In 1892 all remaining unsold in the Post Office were overprinted "Reprint".

No. 29 is red in color, and printed on very thin white wove paper. No. 50 is orange vermilion in color, on medium, white to buff paper. In No. 50 the vertical line on the left side of the portrait touches the horizontal line over the label "Elua Keneta", while in the other two varieties, Nos. 29 and 51, it does not touch the horizontal line by half a millimeter. In No. 51 there are three parallel lines on the left side of the King's nose, while in No. 29 and No. 50 there are no such lines. No. 51 is carmine in color and printed on thick, yellowish to buff wove paper.

It is claimed that both Nos. 50 and 51 were available for postage, although not made to fill a postal requirement.

Queen Liliuokalani — A25

**1890-91 *Perf. 12***

*52* A25 2c dull vio ('91) 6.50 1.25
*a.* Vert. pair, imperf. horiz. 2,750.
*52C* A14 5c deep indigo 110.00 75.00

Stamps of 1864-91 Overprinted in Red

**Provisional GOVT. 1893**

**1893**

*53* A12 1c purple 4.00 3.50
*a.* "189" instead of "1893" 225.00
*b.* No period after "GOVT" 35.00
*c.* Double overprint 300.00
*54* A19 1c blue 4.00 6.50
*a.* Double overprint 175.00
*b.* No period after "GOVT" 35.00
*55* A19 1c green 1.50 3.00
*a.* Pair, one without ovpt. 1,250.
*b.* Double overprint 400.00 150.00
*56* A17 2c brown 5.00 10.00
*a.* No period after "GOVT" 100.00
*b.* Double overprint —
*57* A25 2c dull vio 1.50 1.25
*a.* Inverted overprint 1,000. 1,000.
*b.* Double overprint 350.00 250.00
*c.* "18 3" instead of "1893" 125.00 90.00
*58* A14 5c dp indigo 9.00 17.50
*a.* No period after "GOVT" 100.00
*b.* Double overprint 1,400. —
*59* A14 5c ultra 5.00 2.50
*a.* Inverted overprint 900.00 700.00
*b.* Double overprint 1,200.
*60* A15 6c green 10.00 17.50
*a.* Double overprint 650.00
*61* A20 10c black 7.00 10.00
*a.* Double overprint 900.00 800.00
*61B* A20 10c red brn 16,500. 17,500.
*62* A18 12c black 7.50 12.00
*a.* Double overprint 750.00
*63* A18 12c red lilac 125.00 160.00
*64* A22 25c dark vio 20.00 22.50
*a.* No period after "GOVT" 165.00
*b.* Double overprint 1,000.
*Nos. 53-61,62-64 (12)* 199.50 266.25

**Overprinted in Black**

*65* A13 2c rose ver 50.00 55.00
*a.* No period after "GOVT" 200.00 175.00
*66* A17 2c rose 1.25 2.25
*a.* Double overprint 1,100.
*b.* No period after "GOVT" 50.00 45.00
*66C* A15 6c green 16,500. —
*67* A20 10c vermilion 11.00 20.00
*a.* Double overprint 1,100.
*68* A20 10c red brn 6.00 10.00
*a.* Double overprint —
*69* A18 12c red lilac 225.00 275.00
*70* A21 15c red brn 17.50 30.00
*a.* Double overprint 800.00
*71* A16 18c dull rose 22.50 35.00
*a.* Double overprint 175.00
*b.* Pair, one without ovpt. 1,000.
*c.* No period after "GOVT" 125.00 125.00
*72* A23 50c red 55.00 85.00
*a.* Double overprint 650.00
*b.* No period after "GOVT" 750.00
*73* A24 $1 rose red 100.00 140.00
*a.* No period after "GOVT" 350.00 450.00
*Nos. 65-66,67-73 (9)* 488.25 652.25

*Hawaii stamps can be mounted in Scott's U.S. Possessions Album.*

Coat of Arms — A26

View of Honolulu — A27

Statue of Kamehameha I — A28

Stars and Palms — A29

S. S. "Arawa" — A30

Pres. Sanford Ballard Dole — A31

Statue of King Kamehameha I — A32

**1894**

*74* A26 1c yellow 1.85 1.25
*75* A27 2c brown 2.00 60
*76* A28 5c rose lake 3.75 1.50
*77* A29 10c yellow green 5.00 4.50
*78* A30 12c blue 10.00 12.00
*79* A31 25c deep blue 10.00 12.00
*Nos. 74-79 (6)* 32.60 31.85

**1899**

*80* A26 1c dark green 1.50 1.25
*81* A27 2c rose 1.35 1.00
*a.* 2c salmon 1.50 1.25
*b.* Vert. pair, imperf. horiz. 2,750.
*82* A32 5c blue 5.00 3.00

## OFFICIAL STAMPS

Lorrin Andrews Thurston — O1

**1896 Unwmk. Engr. *Perf. 12***

*O1* O1 2c green 27.50 17.50
*O2* O1 5c black brown 27.50 17.50
*O3* O1 6c deep ultra 27.50 17.50
*O4* O1 10c bright rose 27.50 17.50
*O5* O1 12c orange 27.50 17.50
*O6* O1 25c gray violet 27.50 17.50
*Nos. O1-O6 (6)* 165.00 105.00

The stamps of Hawaii were replaced by those of the United States.

# MARSHALL ISLANDS, REPUBLIC OF THE

LOCATION — Two chains of islands in the West Pacific Ocean, about 2,500 miles southeast of Tokyo.
GOVT. — Trust Territ
LOCATION — Two chains of islands in the West Pacific Ocean, about 2,500 miles southeast of Tokyo.
GOVT. — Trust Territ
LOCATION — Two chains of islands in the West Pacific Ocean, about 2,500 miles southeast of Tokyo.
GOVT. — Trust Territory, constitutional.
AREA — 70 sq. mi.
POP. — 31,042 (1980)
CAPITAL — Majuro

A German possession fro 1914, stamps numbered 1-27 are listed in Volume III of this catalogue. Seized by Japan in 1914, the islands were taken by the US in WW II and they became part of the US Trust Territory of the Pacific in 1947. By agreement with the USPS, the islands began issuing their own stamps in 1984, with the USPS continuing to carry the mail to and from the islands.

100 Cents = 1 Dollar

**Catalogue values for all unused stamps in this country are for Never Hinged items.**

Inauguration of Postal Service — A5

**1984, May 2 Litho. *Perf. 14x13½***

*31* A5 20c Outrigger canoe 40 40
*32* A5 20c Fishnet 40 40
*33* A5 20c Navigational stick chart 40 40
*34* A5 20c Islet 40 40
*a.* Block of 4, Nos. 31-34 1.60 1.60

Mili Atoll, Astrolabe — A6

Maps and Navigational Instruments.

**1984-85 Litho. *Perf. 15x14***

*35* A6 1c shown 5 5
*36* A6 3c Likiep, Azimuth compass 6 6
*37* A6 5c Ebon, 16th cent. compass 10 10
*38* A6 10c Jaluit, anchor buoys 20 20
*39* A6 13c Ailinginae, Nocturnal 26 26
*a* Booklet pane of 10 2.60
*40* A6 14c Wotho Atoll, navigational stick chart 28 28
*a* Booklet pane of 10 2.80
*41* A6 20c Kwajalein and Ebeye, stick chart 40 40
*a* Booklet pane of 10 4.00
*b* Bklt. pane of 5 each, 13c, 20c 3.30
*42* A6 22c Enewetak, 18th cent. lode stone storage case 44 44
*a* Booklet pane of 10 4.40
*b* Bklt. pane of 5 each, 14c, 22c 3.60
*43* A6 28c Ailinglaplap, printed compass 56 56
*44* A6 30c Majuro, navigational stick-chart 60 60
*45* A6 33c Namu, stick chart 66 66
*46* A6 37c Rongelap, quadrant 74 74
*47* A6 39c Taka, map compass, 16th cent. sea chart 78 78
*48* A6 44c Ujelang, chronograph 88 88
*49* A6 50c Maloelap and Aur, nocturlabe 1.00 1.00
*49A* A6 $1 Arno, 16th cent. sector compass 2.00 2.00
*Nos. 35-49A (16)* 9.01 9.01

Issue dates: 1c, 3c, 10c, 30c and $1, June 12. 13c, 20c, 28c and 37c. Dec. 19, 1984. 14c, 22c, 33c, 39c, 44c and 50c, June 5, 1985.
See Nos. 107-109.

No. 7 — A7

**1984, June 19** *Perf. 14½x15*

*50* A7 40c shown 60 60
*51* A7 40c No. 13 60 60
*52* A7 40c No. 4 60 60
*53* A7 40c No. 25 60 60
*a* Block of 4, Nos. 50-53 2.40 2.40

Philatelic Salon, 19th UPU Congress, Hamburg, June 19-26.

Ausipex '84 — A8

Dolphins.

**1984, Sept. 5** **Litho.** *Perf. 14*

*54* A8 20c Common 35 35
*55* A8 20c Risso's 35 35
*56* A8 20c Spotter 35 35
*57* A8 20c Bottlenose 35 35
*a* Block of 4, Nos. 54-57 1.40 1.40

Christmas 1984 — A9

Illustration reduced.

**1984, Nov. 7** **Litho.** *Perf. 14*

*58* Strip of 4 1.60 1.60
*a.-d.* A9 20c, any single 40 40

Printed in sheets of 16; background shows text from Marshallese New Testament, giving each stamp on the sheet a different background.

Marshall Islands Constitution, 5th Anniv. — A10

**1984, Dec. 19** **Litho.** *Perf. 14*

*59* A10 20c Traditional chief 35 35
*60* A10 20c Amata Kabua 35 35
*61* A10 20c Chester Nimitz 35 35
*62* A10 20c Trygve Lie 35 35
*a* Block of 4, Nos. 59-62 1.40 1.40

Audubon Bicentenary — A11

**1985, Feb. 15** **Litho.** *Perf. 14*

*63* A11 22c Forked-tailed Petrel 40 40
*64* A11 22c Pectoral Sandpiper 40 40
*a* Pair, Nos. 63-64 80 80

See Nos. C1-C2.

Sea Shells — A12

**1985, Apr. 17** **Litho.** *Perf. 14*

*65* A12 22c Cymatium lotorium 35 35
*66* A12 22c Chicoreus cornucervi 35 35
*67* A12 22c Strombus aurisdanae 35 35
*68* A12 22c Turbo marmoratus 35 35
*69* A12 22c Chicoreus palmarosae 35 35
*a* Strip of 5, Nos. 65-69 1.75 1.75
*Nos. 65-69 (5)* 1.75 1.75

See Nos. 119-123, 152-156.

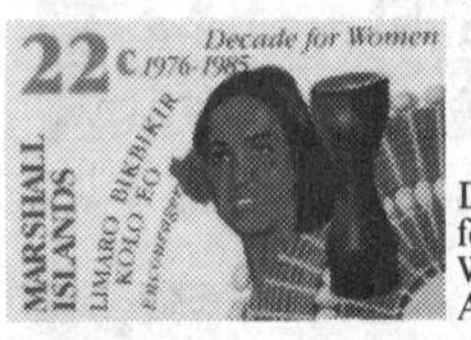


Decade for Women A13

**1985, June 5** **Litho.** *Perf. 14*

*70* A13 22c Native drum 35 35
*71* A13 22c Palm branches 35 35
*72* A13 22c Pounding stone 35 35
*73* A13 22c Ak bird 35 35
*a* Block of 4, Nos. 70-73 1.40 1.40

Reef and Lagoon Fish A14

**1985, July 15** **Litho.** *Perf. 14*

*74* A14 22c Acanthurus dussumieri 35 35
*75* A14 22c Adioryx caudimaculatus 35 35
*76* A14 22c Ostracion meleacaris 35 35
*77* A14 22c Chaetodon ephippium 35 35
*a* Block of 4, Nos. 74-77 1.40 1.40

Intl. Youth Year A15

IYY and Alele Nautical Museum emblems and: No. 78, Marshallese youths and Peace Corps volunteers playing basketball. No. 79, Legend teller reciting local history, girl listening to recording. No. 80, Islander explaining navigational stick charts. No. 81, Jabwa stick dance.

**1985, Aug. 31** **Litho.** *Perf. 14*

*78* A15 22c multicolor 35 35
*79* A15 22c multicolor 35 35
*80* A15 22c multicolor 35 35
*81* A15 22c multicolor 35 35
*a* Block of 4, Nos. 78-81 1.40 1.40

1856 American Board of Commissions Stock Certificate for Foreign Missions — A16

Missionary ship Morning Star I: 22c, Launch, Jothan Stetson Shipyard, Chelsea, MA, Aug. 7, 1857. 33c, First voyage, Honolulu to the Marshalls, 1857. 44c, Marshall islanders pulling Morning Star I into Ebon Lagoon, 1857.

**1985, Oct. 21** **Litho.** *Perf. 14*

*82* A16 14c multicolor 20 20
*83* A16 22c multicolor 35 35
*84* A16 33c multicolor 55 55
*85* A16 44c multicolor 75 75

Christmas 1985.

US Space Shuttle, Astro Telescope, Halley's Comet — A17

Comet tail and research spacecraft: No. 87, Planet A Space Probe, Japan. No. 88, Giotto spacecraft, European Space Agency. No. 89, INTERCOSMOS Project Vega spacecraft, Russia, France, etc. No. 90, US naval tracking ship, NASA observational aircraft, cameo portrait of Edmond Halley (1656-1742), astronomer. Se-tenant in continuous design.

**1985, Nov. 21**

*86* A17 22c multicolor 75 75
*87* A17 22c multicolor 75 75
*88* A17 22c multicolor 75 75
*89* A17 22c multicolor 75 75
*90* A17 22c multicolor 75 75
*a* Strip of 5, Nos. 86-90 3.75 3.75

Medicinal Plants A18

**1985, Dec. 31** **Litho.** *Perf. 14*

*91* A18 22c Sida fallax 35 35
*92* A18 22c Scaevola frutescens 35 35
*93* A18 22c Guettarda speciosa 35 35
*94* A18 22c Cassytha filiformis 35 35
*a* Block of 4, Nos. 91-94 1.40 1.40

Maps Type of 1984

**1986-87** *Perf. 15x14, 14 ($10)*

*107* A6 $2 Wotje and Erikub, terrestrial globe, 1571 3.00 3.00
*108* A6 $5 Bikini, Stick chart 8.00 8.00

**Size: 31x31mm**

*109* A6 $10 Stick chart of the atolls 15.00 15.00

Issue dates: $2, $5, Mar 7, 1986. $10, Mar. 31, 1987.

Marine Invertebrates — A19

**1986, Mar. 31** **Litho.** *Perf. 14½x14*

*110* A19 14c Triton's trumpet 28 28
*111* A19 14c Giant clam 28 28
*112* A19 14c Small giant clam 28 28
*113* A19 14c Coconut crab 28 28
*a* Block of 4, Nos. 110-113 1.15 1.15

**Souvenir Sheet**

AMERIPEX '86, Chicago, May 22-June 1 — A20

**1986, May 22** **Litho.** *Perf. 14*

*114* A20 $1 Douglas C-54 Globester 2.00 2.00

1st Around-the-world scheduled flight, 40th anniv. No. 114 has multicolored margin continuing the design and picturing US Air Transport Command Base, Kwajalein Atoll and souvenir card. Size: 89x63mm.

See Nos. C3-C6.

Operation Crossroads, Atomic Bomb Tests, 40th Anniv. — A21

Designs: No. 115, King Juda, Bikinians sailing tibinal canoe. No. 116, USS Sumner, amphibious DUKW, advance landing. No. 117, Evacuating Bikinians. No. 118, Land reclamation, 1986.

**1986, July 1** **Litho.** *Perf. 14*

*115* A21 22c multicolor 35 35
*116* A21 22c multicolor 35 35
*117* A21 22c multicolor 35 35
*118* A21 22c multicolor 35 35
*a* Block of 4, Nos. 115-118 1.40 1.40

See No. C7.

Seashells Type of 1985

**1986, Aug. 1** **Litho.** *Perf. 14*

*119* A12 22c Ramose murex 35 35
*120* A12 22c Orange spider 35 35
*121* A12 22c Red-mouth frog shell 35 35
*122* A12 22c Laciniate conch 35 35
*123* A12 22c Giant frog shell 35 35
*a* Strip of 5, Nos. 119-123 1.75 1.75
*Nos. 119-123 (5)* 1.75 1.75

Game Fish A22

**1986, Sept. 10** **Litho.**

*124* A22 22c Blue marlin 35 35
*125* A22 22c Wahoo 35 35
*126* A22 22c Dolphin fish 35 35
*127* A22 22c Yellowfin tuna 35 35
*a* Block of 4, Nos. 124-127 1.40 1.40

Christmas 1986, Intl. Peace Year — A23

**1986, Oct. 28** **Litho.** *Perf. 14*

*128* A23 22c United Nations UR 35 35
*129* A23 22c United Nations UL 35 35
*130* A23 22c United Nations LR 35 35
*131* A23 22c United Nations LL 35 35
*a* Block of 4, Nos. 128-131 1.40 1.40

See No. C8.

US Whaling Ships A24

**1987, Feb. 20** **Litho.** *Perf. 14*

*132* A24 22c James Arnold, 1854 35 35
*133* A24 22c General Scott, 1859 35 35
*134* A24 22c Charles W. Morgan, 1865 35 35
*135* A24 22c Lucretia, 1884 35 35
*a* Block of 4, Nos. 132-135 1.40 1.40

*Marshall Islands stamps can be mounted in Scott's annually supplemented Trust Territories Album.*

Historic and Military Flights A25

Designs: No. 136, Charles Lindbergh commemorative medal, Spirit of St. Louis crossing the Atlantic, 1927. No. 137, Lindbergh flying in the Battle of the Marshalls, 1944. No. 138, William Bridgeman flying in the Battle of Kwajalein, 1944. No. 139, Bridgeman testing the Douglas Skyrocket, 1951. No. 140, John Glenn flying in the Battle of the Marshalls. No. 141, Glenn, the first American to orbit the Earth, 1962.

**1987, Mar. 12 Litho. *Perf. 14½***

*136* A25 33c multicolor 60 60
*137* A25 33c multicolor 60 60
*a* Pair, Nos. 136-137 1.20 1.20
*138* A25 39c multicolor 65 65
*139* A25 39c multicolor 65 65
*a* Pair, Nos. 138-139 1.30 1.30
*140* A25 44c multicolor 70 70
*141* A25 44c multicolor 70 70
*a* Pair, Nos. 140-141 1.40 1.40
*Nos. 136-141 (6)* 3.90 3.90

**Souvenir Sheet**

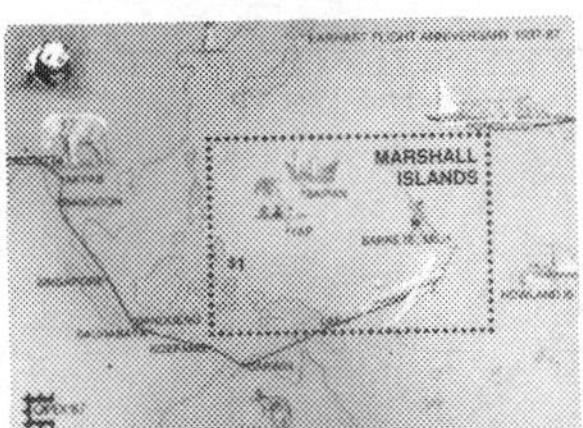

CAPEX '87 — A26

**1987, June 15 Litho. *Perf. 14***

*142* A26 $1 Map of flight 1.75 1.75

Amelia Earhart (1897-1937), American aviator who died during attempted round-the-world flight, 50th anniv. No. 142 has multicolored margin picturing Earhart's flight pattern from Calcutta, India, to the crash site near Barre Is., Marshall Isls. Size: 88x63mm.

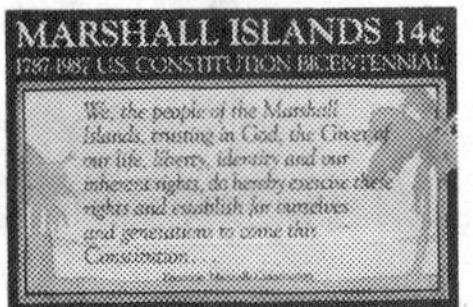

US Constitution Bicentennial — A27

Excerpts from the Marshall Islands and US Constitutions.

**1987, July 16 Litho. *Perf. 14***

*143* A27 14c We.... Marshall 25 25
*144* A27 14c National seals 25 25
*145* A27 14c We.... United States 25 25
*a* Triptych, Nos. 143-145 75 75
*146* A27 22c All we have... 35 35
*147* A27 22c Flags 35 35
*148* A27 22c to establish... 35 35
*a* Triptych, Nos. 146-148 1.05 1.05
*149* A27 44c With this Constitution... 70 70
*150* A27 44c Stick chart, Liberty Bell 70 70
*151* A27 44c to promote... 70 70
*a* Triptych, Nos. 149-151 2.10 2.10
*Nos. 143-151 (9)* 3.90 3.90

Triptychs printed in continuous designs.

Seashells Type of 1985

**1987, Sept. 1 Litho. *Perf. 14***

*152* A12 22c Magnificent cone 35 35
*153* A12 22c Partridge tun 35 35
*154* A12 22c Scorpion spider conch 35 35
*155* A12 22c Hairy triton 35 35
*156* A12 22c Chiragra spider conch 35 35
*a* Strip of 5, Nos. 152-156 1.75 1.75
*Nos. 152-156 (5)* 1.75 1.75

Copra Industry A28

Contest-winning crayon drawings by Amram Enox; design contest sponsored by the Tobular Copra Processing Co.

**1987, Dec. 10 Litho. *Perf. 14***

*157* A28 44c Planting coconut 75 75
*158* A28 44c Making copra 75 75
*159* A28 44c Bottling coconut oil 75 75
*a* Triptych, Nos. 157-159 2.25

Biblical Verses — A29

**1987, Dec. 10**

*160* A29 14c Matthew 2:1 25 25
*161* A29 22c Luke 2:14 35 35
*162* A29 33c Psalms 33:3 55 55
*163* A29 44c Pslams 150:5 70 70

Christmas 1987.

Marine Birds — A30

**1988, Jan. 27**

*164* A30 44c Pacific reef herons 75 75
*165* A30 44c Bar-tailed godwit 75 75
*166* A30 44c Masked booby 75 75
*167* A30 44c Northern shoveler 75 75

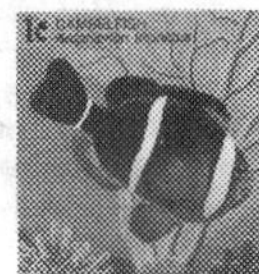

Fish — A31

**1988, Mar. 17 Litho. *Perf. 14½x14***

*168* A31 1c Damselfish 5 5
*169* A31 3c Blackface butterflyfish 6 6
*170* A31 14c Hawkfish 28 28
*a* Bklt. pane of 10 2.80
*171* A31 17c Trunk fish 34 34
*172* A31 22c Lyretail wrasse 44 44
*a* Bklt. pane of 10 4.40
*b* Bklt. pane of 10 (5 each 14c, 22c) 3.60
*173* A31 33c White-spotted boxfish 66 66
*174* A31 39c Surgeonfish 78 78
*175* A31 44c Long-snouted butterflyfish 88 88
*176* A31 56c Sharp-nosed puffer 1.12 1.12
*177* A31 $1 Seahorse 2.00 2.00
*178* A31 $2 Ghost pipefish 4.00 4.00
*179* A31 $5 Big-spotted triggerfish 10.00 10.00

Booklets issued Mar. 31.

**1988, July 19**

*180* A31 15c Balloonfish 30 30
*181* A31 25c Parrotfish 50 50
*182* A31 36c Spotted boxfish 72 72
*183* A31 45c Trumpetfish 90 90
*Nos. 168-183 (15)* 22.73 22.73

A32

1988 Summer Olympics, Seoul — A33

Athletes in motion: 15c, Javelin thrower (Nos. 188a-188e as shown). 25c, Runner (Nos. 189a-189e as shown). Illustrations reduced.

**1988, June 30 Litho. *Perf. 14***

*188* Strip of 5 1.50 1.50
*a.-e.* A32 15c any single 30 30
*189* Strip of 5 2.50 2.50
*a.-e.* A33 25c any single 50 50

Souvenir Sheet

Pacific Voyages of Robert Louis Stevenson — A34

Stick chart of the Marshalls and: No. 190a, *Casco* sailing through the Golden Gate. No. 190b, At the Needles of Ua-Pu, Marquesas. No. 190c, *Equator* departing from Honolulu and Kaiulani, an Hawaian princess. No. 190d, Chief's canoe, Majuro Lagoon. No. 190e, Bronze medallion, 1887, by Augustus St. Gaudens in the Tate Gallery, London. No. 190f, Outrigger canoe and S.S. *Janet Nicoll* in Majuro Lagoon. No. 190g, View of Apemama, Gilbert Is. No. 190h, Samoan outrigger canoe, Apia Harbor. No. 190i, Stevenson riding horse Jack at his estate, Vallima, Samoa.

**1988, July 19 Litho. *Perf. 14***

*190* Sheet of 9 4.50 4.50
*a.-i.* A34 25c any single 50 50

Robert Louis Stevenson (1850-1894), Scottish novelist, poet and essayist. No. 190 has multicolored decorative margin. Size: 215x152mm.

Colonial Ships and Flags A35

Designs: No. 191, Galleon *Santa Maria de La Victoria*, 1526, and Spanish "Ragged Cross" ensign in use from 1516 to 1785. No. 192, Transport ships *Charlotte* and *Scarborough*, 1788, and British red ensign, 1707-1800. No. 193, Schooner *Flying Fish*, sloop-of-war *Peacock*, 1841, and U.S. flag, 1837-1845. No. 194, Steamer *Planet*, 1909, and German flag, 1867-1919.

**1988, Sept. 2 Litho. *Perf. 14***

*191* A35 25c multi 50 50
*192* A35 25c multi 50 50
*193* A35 25c multi 50 50
*194* A35 25c multi 50 50
*a.* Block of 4, Nos. 191-194 2.00 2.00

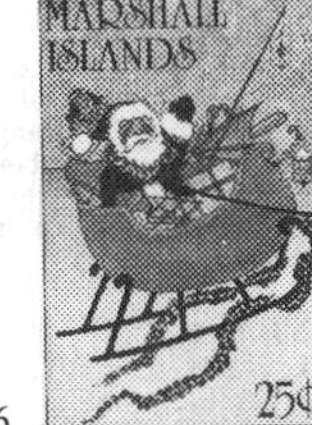

Christmas — A36

Designs: No. 195, Santa Claus riding in sleigh. No. 196, Reindeer, hut and palm trees. No. 197, Reindeer and palm trees. No. 198, Reindeer, palm tree, fish. No. 199, Reindeer and outrigger canoe.

**1988, Nov. 7 Litho. *Perf. 14***

*195* A36 25c multi 50 50
*196* A36 25c multi 50 50
*197* A36 25c multi 50 50
*198* A36 25c multi 50 50
*199* A36 25c multi 50 50
*a.* Strip of 5, Nos. 195-199 2.50 2.50
*Nos. 195-199 (5)* 2.50 2.50

Nos. 195-199 printed se-tenant in a continuous design.

Tribute to John F. Kennedy — A37

**1988, Nov. 22 Litho. *Perf. 14***

*200* A37 25c Nuclear threat diminished 50 50
*201* A37 25c Signing the Test Ban Treaty 50 50
*202* A37 25c Portrait 50 50
*203* A37 25c US-USSR Hotline 50 50
*204* A37 25c Peace Corps enactment 50 50
*a.* Strip of 5, Nos. 200-204 2.50 2.50

Se-tenant in a continuous design. Printed in sheets containing 3 No. 204a; decorative margin pictures the declaration signed by Pres. Kennedy and Secretary of State Dean Rusk, ratifying the Test Ban Treaty. Size: 240x177mm.

US Space Shuttle Program and Kwajalein — A38

Designs: No. 205, Launch of *Prime* from Vandenberg Air Force Base downrange to the Kwajalein Missile Range. No. 206, *Prime* X023A/SV-5D lifting body reentering atmosphere. No. 207, Parachute landing and craft recovery off Kwajalein Is. No. 208, Shuttle over island.

**1988, Dec. 23** **Litho.** ***Perf. 14***

*205* A38 25c multi 50 50
*206* A38 25c multi 50 50
*207* A38 25c multi 50 50
*208* A38 25c multi 50 50
*a.* Strip of 4, Nos. 205-208 2.00 2.00

NASA 30th anniv. and 25th anniv. of the Project PRIME wind tunnel tests.

See No. C21.

Links to Japan A39

Designs: No. 209, Typhoon Monument, Majuro, 1918. No. 210, Seaplane base and railway depot, Djarrej Islet, c. 1940. No. 211, Fishing boats. No. 212, Japanese honeymooners scuba diving, 1988.

**1989, Jan. 19** **Litho.** ***Perf. 14***

*209* A39 45c multi 90 90
*210* A39 45c multi 90 90
*211* A39 45c multi 90 90
*212* A39 45c multi 90 90
*a.* Block of 4, Nos. 209-212 3.60 3.60

## AIR POST STAMPS

Audubon Type of 1985

**1985, Feb. 15** **Litho.** ***Perf. 14***

*C1* A11 44c Booby Gannet, vert. 80 80
*C2* A11 44c Esquimaux Curlew, vert. 80 80
*a.* Pair, No. C1-C2 1.60 1.60

AMERIPEX Type of 1986

Designs: No. C3, consolidated PBY-5A Catalin Amphibian. No. C4, Grumman SA-16 Albatross. No. C5, McDonnell Douglas DC-6B Super Cloudmaster. No. C6, Boeing &27-100.

**1986, May 22** **Litho.** ***Perf. 14***

*C3* A20 44c multicolored 88 88
*C4* A20 44c multicolored 88 88
*C5* A20 44c multicolored 88 88
*C6* A20 44c multicolored 88 88
*a.* Block of 4, #C3-C6 3.60 3.60

Operation Crossroads Type of 1986
**Souvenir Sheet**

**1986, July 1** **Litho.** ***Perf. 14***

*C7* A21 44c USS Saratoga 88 88

No. C7 has multicolored margin inscribed "Baker Day Atomic Bomb Test, 25 July 1946," and picturing mushroom cloud. Size: 106x72mm.

Statue of Liberty Cent., Intl. Peace Year — AP1

**1986, Oct. 28** **Litho.**

*C8* AP1 44c multicolored 70 70

Natl. Girl Scout Movement, 20th Anniv. — AP2

**1986, Dec. 8** **Litho.**

*C9* AP2 44c Community service 70 70
*C10* AP2 44c Salute 70 70
*C11* AP2 44c Health care 70 70
*C12* AP2 44c Learning skills 70 70
*a.* Block of 4, #C9-C12 3.00 3.00

Girl Scout Movement in the US, 75th anniv. (1912-1987).

Marine Birds AP3

**1987, Jan. 12** **Litho.** ***Perf. 14***

*C13* AP3 44c Wedge-tailed shearwater 70 70
*C14* AP3 44c Red-footed booby 70 70
*C15* AP3 44c Red-tailed tropicbird 70 70
*C16* AP3 44c Great frigatebird 70 70
*a.* Block of 4, #C13-C16 3.00 3.00

CAPEX '87 AP4

Last flight of Amelia Earhart: No. C17, Take-off at Lae, New Guinea, July 2, 1937. No. C18, USCG Itasca cutter at Howland Is. No. C19, Purported crash landing of the Electra at Mili Atoll. No. C20, Recovery of the Electra by the Koshu, a Japanese survey ship.

**1987, June 15** **Litho.** ***Perf. 14***

*C17* AP4 44c multicolored 70 70
*C18* AP4 44c multicolored 70 70
*C19* AP4 44c multicolored 70 70
*C20* AP4 44c multicolored 70 70
*a.* Block of 4, Nos. C17-C20 3.00 3.00

Space Shuttle Type of 1988

**1988, Dec. 23** **Litho.** ***Perf. 14***

*C21* A38 45c Astronaut, shuttle over Rongelap 90 90

# MICRONESIA, FEDERATED STATES OF

LOCATION — A group of over 600 islands in the West Pacific Ocean, north of the Equator.
GOVT. — US Trust Territory, constitutional
AREA — 271 sq. miles
POP. — 73,755 (1980)
CAPITAL — Kolonia

These islands, also known as the Caroline Islands, were bought by Germany from Spain in 1899. Caroline Islands stamps issued as a German territory are listed in Vol. II of this Catalogue. Seized by Japan in 1914, they were taken by the US in WWII and became part of the US Trust Territory of the Pacific in 1947. By agreement with the USPS, the islands began issuing their own stamps in 1984, with the USPS continuing to carry the mail to and from the islands.

100 Cents = 1 Dollar

**Catalogue values for all unused stamps in this country are for Never Hinged items.**

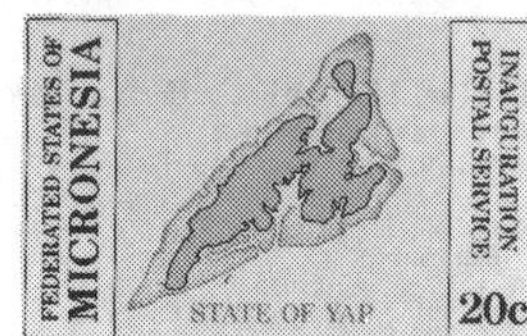


Postal Service Inauguration — A1

**1984, July 12** **Litho.** ***Perf. 14***

*1* A1 20c Yap 35 40
*2* A1 20c Truk 35 40
*3* A1 20c Pohnpei 35 40
*4* A1 20c Kosrae 35 40
*a.* Block of 4, Nos. 1-4 1.40 1.40

See Nos. 48-51.

Fernandez de Quiros A2

Men's House, Yap A3

Designs: 1c, 19c, Pedro Fernandez de Quiros, Spanish explorer, first discovered Pohnpei, 1595. 2c, 20c, Louis Duperrey, French explorer. 3c, 30c, Fyedor Lutke, Russian explorer. 4c, 37c, Dumont d'Urville. 10c, Sleeping Lady, Kosrae. 13c, Liduduhriap Waterfall, Pohnpei. 17c, Tonachau Peak, Truk. 50c, Devil mask, Truk. $1, Sokeh's Rock, Pohnpei. $2, Canoes, Kosrae. $5, Stone money, Yap.

**1984, July 12** ***Perf. 13½x13***

*5* A2 1c Prussian blue 5 5
*6* A2 2c deep claret 5 5
*7* A2 3c dark blue 5 5
*8* A2 4c green 7 7
*9* A3 5c yellow brown 8 8
*10* A3 10c dark violet 16 16
*11* A3 13c dark blue 20 20
*12* A3 17c brown lake 25 25
*13* A2 19c dark violet 28 28
*14* A2 20c olive green 30 30
*15* A2 30c rose lake 45 45
*16* A2 37c deep violet 55 55
*17* A3 50c brown 75 75
*18* A3 $1 olive 1.50 1.50
*19* A3 $2 Prussian blue 3.00 3.00
*20* A3 $5 brown lake 7.00 7.00
*Nos. 5-20 (16)* 14.74 14.74

See Nos. 33-40.

Ausipex '84 A4

**1984, Sept. 21** **Litho.** ***Perf. 13½***

*21* A4 20c Truk Post Office 35 35

See Nos. C4-C6.

Christmas 1984 — A5

Child's drawing.

**1984, Dec. 20**

*22* A5 20c Child in manger 35 35

See Nos. C7-C9.

Ships — A6

**1985, Aug. 19**

*23* A6 22c U.S.S. Jamestown 35 35

See Nos. C10-C12.

Christmas 1985 — A7

**1985, Oct. 15** **Litho.** ***Perf. 13½***

*24* A7 22c Lelu Protestant Church, Kosrae 35 35

See Nos. C13-C14.

Audubon Birth Bicentenary — A8

**1985, Oct. 30** ***Perf. 14½***

*25* A8 22c Noddy tern 35 35
*26* A8 22c Turnstone 35 35
*27* A8 22c Golden plover 35 35

*28* A8 22c Black-bellied plover 35 35
*a.* Block of 4, Nos. 25-28 1.40 1.40

See No. C15.

Birds — A8a

Tall Ship Senyavin A9 — Natl. Seal A10

***Perf. 13½ (A8a), 13½x13***

**1985-88** **Litho.**

*30* A8a 3c Long-billed white-eye 6 6
*32* A8a 14c Truk monarch 28 28
*33* A3 15c Liduduhriap Waterfall, Pohnpei 30 30
*a.* Bklt. pane of 10 3.00
*34* A9 22c brt bl grn 35 35
*35* A8a 22c Pohnpei mountain starling 44 44
*36* A3 25c Tonachau Peak, Truk 50 50
*a.* Bklt. pane of 10 5.00
*b.* Bklt. pane of 10, 5 15c + 5 25c 4.00
*39* A9 36c ultramarine 72 72
*40* A3 45c Sleeping Lady, Kosrae 90 90
*42* A10 $10 brt ultra 14.00 14.00
*Nos. 30-42 (9)* 17.55 17.55

Issue dates: $10, Oct. 15. No. 34, Apr. 14, 1986. 3c, 14c, No. 35, Aug. 1, 1988. 15c, 25c, 36c, 45c, Sept. 1, 1988.

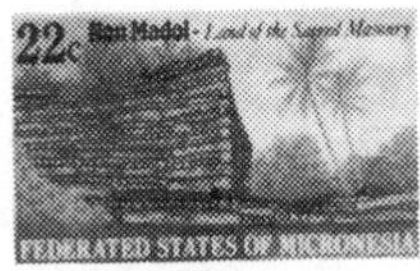

Nan Madol Ruins, Pohnpei A16

**1985, Dec.** **Litho.** ***Perf. 13½***
*45* A16 22c Land of the Sacred Masonry 35 35

See Nos. C16-C18.

Intl. Peace Year — A17

**1986, May 16**
*46* A17 22c multicolor 35 35

Nos. 1-4 Surcharged

**1986, May 19** **Litho.** ***Perf. 14***
*48* A1 22c on 20c No. 1 35 35
*49* A1 22c on 20c No. 2 35 35
*50* A1 22c on 20c No. 3 35 35
*51* A1 22c on 20c No. 4 35 35
*a.* Block of 4, Nos. 48-51 1.40 1.40

AMERIPEX '86 A18

Bully Hayes (1829-1877), Buccaneer.

**1986, May 22** ***Perf. 13½***
*52* A18 22c At ship's helm 35 35
*Nos. 52,C21-C24 (5)* 3.35 3.35

First Passport A19

**1986, Nov. 4** **Litho.** ***Perf. 13½***
*53* A19 22c multicolor 35 35

Christmas 1986 — A20

Virgin and child paintings: 5c, Italy, 18th cent. 22c, Germany, 19th cent.

**1986, Oct. 15** **Litho.** ***Perf. 14½***
*54* A20 5c multicolor 8 8
*55* A20 22c multicolor 35 35

See Nos. C26-C27.

Anniversaries and Events — A21

**1987, June 13** **Litho.** ***Perf. 14½***
*56* A21 22c Intl. Year of Shelter for the Homeless 35 35

**Souvenir Sheet**

*57* A21 $1 CAPEX '87 2.00 2.00

See Nos. C28-C30. No. 57 has inscribed multicolored margin picturing Toronto landmarks. Size: 85x55mm.

Christmas 1987 — A22

Design: 22c, Archangel Gabriel appearing before Mary.

**1987, Nov. 16** **Litho.** ***Perf. 14½***
*58* A22 22c multicolor 35 35

See. Nos. C31-C33.

*Micronesia stamps can be mounted in Scott's annually supplemented Trust Territories Album.*

Colonial Eras — A23

**1988, July 20** **Litho.** ***Perf. 13x13½***
*59* A23 22c German 44 44
*60* A23 22c Spanish 44 44
*61* A23 22c Japanese 44 44
*62* A23 22c US Trust Territory 44 44
*a.* Block of 4, Nos. 59-62 1.80 1.80
*Nos. 59-62,C37-C38 (6)* 3.52 3.52

Printed se-tenant in sheets of 28 plus 4 center labels picturing flags of Spain (UL), Germany (UR), Japan (LL) and the US (LR).

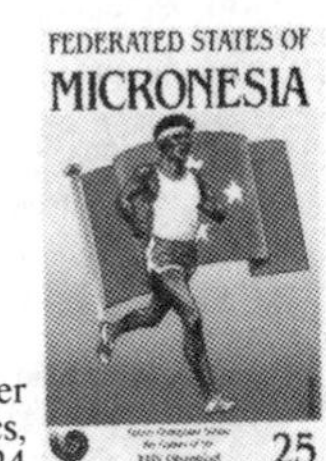

1988 Summer Olympics, Seoul — A24

**1988, Sept. 1** **Litho.** ***Perf. 14***
*63* A24 25c Running 50 50
*64* A24 25c Women's hurdles 50 50
*a.* Pair, Nos. 63-64 1.00 1.00
*65* A24 45c Basketball 90 90
*66* A24 45c Women's volleyball 90 90
*a.* Pair, Nos. 65-66 1.80 1.80

Christmas A25

Children decorating tree: No. 67, Two girls, UL of tree. No. 68, Boy, girl, dove, UR of tree. No. 69, Boy, girl, LL of tree. No. 70, Boy, girl, LR of tree. Se-tenant in a continuous design.

**1988, Oct. 28** **Litho.** ***Perf. 14***
*67* A25 25c multi 50 50
*68* A25 25c multi 50 50
*69* A25 25c multi 50 50
*70* A25 25c multi 50 50
*a.* Block of 4, Nos. 67-70 2.00 2.00

Miniature Sheet

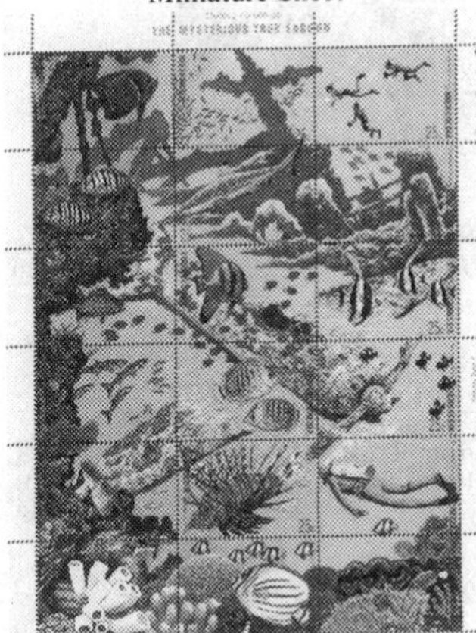
Truk Lagoon State Monument — A26

Designs: a, Sun and stars angelfish. b, School of fish. c, 3 divers. d, Goldenjack. e, Blacktip reef shark. f, 2 schools of fish. g, Squirrelfish. h, Batfish. i, Moorish idols. j, Barracudas. k, Spot banded butterflyfish. l, Three-spotted damselfish. m, Foxface. n, Lionfish. o, Diver. p, Coral. q, Butterflyfish. r, Bivalve, fish, coral.

**1988, Dec. 19 Litho. *Perf. 14***
*71* Sheet of 18 9.00 9.00
*a.-r.* A26 25c any single 50 50

Size: 154x199mm.

## AIR POST STAMPS

Boeing 727, 1968 – AP1

**1984, July 12 Litho. *Perf. 13½***
*C1* AP1 28c shown 45 45
*C2* AP1 35c SA-16 Albatross, 1960 55 55
*C3* AP1 40c PBY-5A Catalina, 1951 60 60

Ausipex Type of 1984

Ausipex '84 emblem and: 28c, Caroline Islands No. 4. 35c, No. 7. 40c, No. 19.

**1984, Sept. 21 Litho. *Perf. 13½***
*C4* A4 28c multicolor 50 50
*C5* A4 35c multicolor 60 60
*C6* A4 40c multicolor 65 65

Christmas Type of 1984

Children's drawings.

**1984, Dec. 20**
*C7* A5 28c Illustrated Christmas text 50 50
*C8* A5 35c Decorated palm tree 60 60
*C9* A5 40c Feast preparation 65 65

Ships Type of 1985

**1985, Aug. 19**
*C10* A6 33c L'Astrolabe 55 55
*C11* A6 39c La Coquille 65 65
*C12* A6 44c Shenandoah 70 70

Christmas Type of 1985

**1985, Oct. 15 Litho. *Perf. 13½***
*C13* A7 33c Dublon Protestant Church 55 55
*C14* A7 44c Pohnpei Catholic Church 70 70

Audubon Type of 1985

**1985, Oct. 31 *Perf. 14½***
*C15* A8 44c Sooty tern 70 70

Ruins Type of 1985

**1985, Dec. Litho. *Perf. 13½***
*C16* A16 33c Nan Tauas inner courtyard 55 55
*C17* A16 39c Outer wall 65 65
*C18* A16 44c Tomb 70 70

Halley's Comet AP2

**1986, May 16**
*C19* AP2 44c dark bl, bl & blk 70 70

Return of Nauruans from Truk, 40th Anniv. AP3

**1986, May 16**
*C20* AP3 44c Ship in port 70 70

AMERIPEX '86 Type of 1986

Bully Hayes (1829-1877), buccanneer.

**1986, May 22**
*C21* A18 33c Hawaii No. 5 55 55
*C22* A18 39c Sinking of the Leonora, Kosrae 65 65
*C23* A18 44c Hayes escapes capture 70 70
*C24* A18 75c Biography, by Louis Becke 1.10 1.10

**Souvenir Sheet**

*C25* A18 $1 Hayes ransoming chief 2.00 2.00

No. C25 has multicolored inscribed margin continuing the design and picturing exhibition emblem. Size: 128x71mm.

Christmas Type of 1986

Virgin and child paintings: 33c, Austria, 19th cent. 44c, Italy, 18th cent., diff.

**1986, Oct. 15 Litho. *Perf. 14½***
*C26* A20 33c multicolor 55 55
*C27* A20 44c multicolor 70 70

Anniversaries and Events Type of 1987

**1987, June 13 Litho. *Perf. 14½***
*C28* A21 33c US currency, bicent. 55 55
*C29* A21 39c 1st American in orbit, 25th anniv. 65 65
*C30* A21 44c US Constitution, bicent. 70 70

Christmas Type of 1987

**1987, Nov. 16 Litho. *Perf. 14½***
*C31* A22 33c Holy Family 55 55
*C32* A22 39c Shepherds 65 65
*C33* A22 44c Three Wise Men 70 70

Bird Type of 1988

**1988, Aug. 1 Litho. *Perf. 13½***
*C34* A11 33c Great truk white-eye 66 66
*C35* A11 44c Blue-faced parrotfinch 88 88
*C36* A11 $1 Yap monarch 2.00 2.00

Colonial Era Type of 1988

**1988, July 20 *Perf. 13x13½***
*C37* A23 44c Traditional skills (boat-building) 88 88
*C38* A23 44c Modern Micronesia (tourism) 88 88
*a.* Pair, Nos. C37-C38 1.80 1.80

Printed se-tenant in sheets of 28 plus 4 center labels picturing flags of Kosrae (UL), Truk (UR), Pohnpei (LL) and Yap ((LR).

Flags of the Federated States of Micronesia AP4

**1989, Jan. 19 Litho. *Perf.***
*C39* AP4 45c Pohnpei 90 90
*C40* AP4 45c Truk 90 90
*C41* AP4 45c Kosrae 90 90
*C42* AP4 45c Yap 90 90
*a.* Block of 4, Nos. C39-C42 3.60 3.60

## PALAU, REPUBLIC OF

LOCATION – A group of 100 islands in the West Pacific Ocean about 1,000 miles southeast of Manila.
GOVT. – U.S. Trust Territory, constitutional.
AREA – 179 sq. mi.
POP. – 16,000 (est. 1983)
CAPITAL – Koror (Headquarters)

Palau, the western section of the Caroline Islands (Micronesia), is part of the US Trust Territory of the Pacific, established in 1947. By agreement with the USPS, the republic began issuing its own stamps in 1984, with the USPS continuing to carry the mail to and from the islands.

100 Cents = 1 Dollar

**Catalogue values for all unused stamps in this country are for Never Hinged items.**

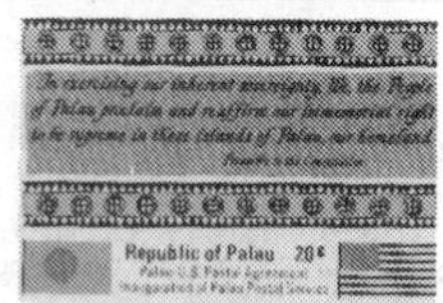


Inauguration of Postal Service – A1

**1983, Mar. 10 Litho. *Perf. 14***
*1* A1 20c Constitution preamble 50 50
*2* A1 20c Hunters 50 50
*3* A1 20c Fish 50 50
*4* A1 20c Preamble, diff. 50 50
*a.* Block of 4, Nos. 1-4 2.00 2.00

Palau Fruit Dove – A2

**1983, May 16 *Perf. 15***
*5* A2 20c shown 35 35
*6* A2 20c Palau morningbird 35 35
*7* A2 20c Giant white-eye 35 35
*8* A2 20c Palau fantail 35 35
*a.* Block of 4, Nos. 5-8 1.40 1.40

Sea Fan – A3

**1983-84 Litho. *Perf. 13½x14***
*9* A3 1c shown 5 5
*10* A3 3c Map cowrie 5 5
*11* A3 5c Jellyfish 8 8
*12* A3 10c Hawksbill turtle 16 16
*13* A3 13c Giant Clam 20 20
*a.* Booklet pane of 10 2.00
*b.* Bklt. pane of 10 (5 #13, 5 #14) 2.75
*14* A3 20c Parrotfish 35 35
*b.* Booklet pane of 10 3.50
*15* A3 28c Chambered Nautilus 45 45
*16* A3 30c Dappled sea cucumber 50 50
*17* A3 37c Sea Urchin 55 55
*18* A3 50c Starfish 85 85
*19* A3 $1 Squid 1.60 1.60

***Perf. 15x14***

*20* A3 $2 Dugong 3.25 3.25
*21* A3 $5 Pink sponge 8.00 8.00
*Nos. 9-21 (13)* 16.09 16.09

See Nos. 75-85

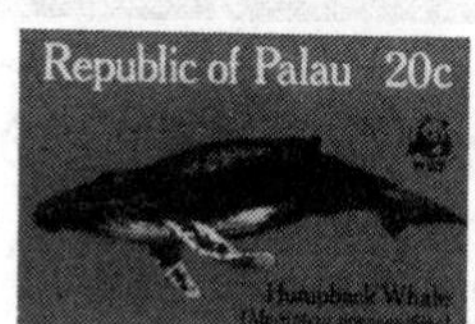


Humpback Whale, World Wildlife Emblem – A4

**1983, Sept. 21 *Perf. 14***
*24* A4 20c shown 35 35
*25* A4 20c Blue whale 35 35
*26* A4 20c Fin whale 35 35
*27* A4 20c Great sperm whale 35 35
*a.* Block of 4, Nos. 24-27 1.40 1.40

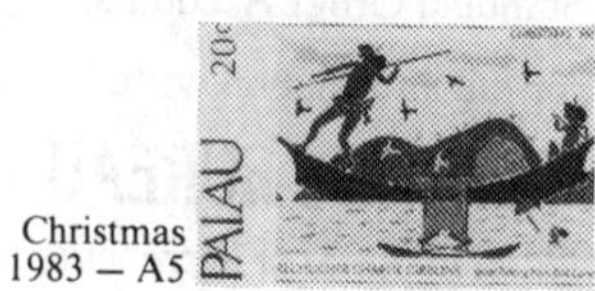


Christmas 1983 – A5

Paintings by Charlie Gibbons, 1971.

**1983, Oct. Litho. *Perf. 14½***
*28* A5 20c First Child ceremony 40 40
*29* A5 20c Spearfishing from Red Canoe 40 40
*30* A5 20c Traditional feast at the Bai 40 40
*31* A5 20c Taro gardening 40 40
*32* A5 20c Spearfishing at New Moon 40 40
*a.* Strip of 5, Nos. 28-32 2.00 2.00
*Nos. 28-32 (5)* 2.00 2.00

A6

Capt. Wilson's Voyage, Bicentennial – A7

**1983, Dec. 14 *Perf. 14x15***
*33* A6 20c Capt. Henry Wilson 40 40
*34* A7 20c Approaching Pelew 40 40
*35* A7 20c Englishman's Camp on Ulong 40 40
*36* A6 20c Prince Lee Boo 40 40
*37* A6 20c King Abba Thulle 40 40
*38* A7 20c Mooring in Koror 40 40
*39* A7 20c Village scene of Pelew Islands 40 40
*40* A6 20c Ludee 40 40
*a.* Block or strip of 8, Nos. 33-40 3.20 3.20
*Nos. 33-40 (8)* 3.20 3.20

Local Seashells – A8

Shell paintings (dorsal and ventral) by Deborah Dudley Max.

**1984, Mar. 15 Litho. *Perf. 14***
*41* A8 20c Triton trumpet, d. 35 35
*42* A8 20c Horned helmet, d. 35 35
*43* A8 20c Giant clam, d. 35 35
*44* A8 20c Laciniate conch, d. 35 35
*45* A8 20c Royal cloak scallop, d. 35 35
*46* A8 20c Triton trumpet, v. 35 35
*47* A8 20c Horned helmet, v. 35 35
*48* A8 20c Giant clam, v. 35 35
*49* A8 20c Laciniate conch, v. 35 35
*50* A8 20c Royal cloak scallop, v. 35 35
*a.* Block of 10, Nos. 41-50 3.50 3.50
*Nos. 41-50 (10)* 3.50 3.50

Explorer Ships A9

**1984, June 19 Litho. *Perf. 14***
*51* A9 40c Oroolong, 1783 70 70
*52* A9 40c Duff, 1797 70 70
*53* A9 40c Peiho, 1908 70 70
*54* A9 40c Albatross, 1885 70 70
*a.* Block of 4, Nos. 51-54 2.80 2.80

UPU Congress.

Ausipex '84 — A10

Fishing Methods.

**1984, Sept. 6 Litho. *Perf. 14***

*55* A10 20c Throw spear fishing 35 35
*56* A10 20c Kite fishing 35 35
*57* A10 20c Underwater spear fishing 35 35
*58* A10 20c Net fishing 35 35
***a.*** Block of 4, Nos. 55-58 1.40 1.40

Christmas Flowers — A11

**1984, Nov. 28 Litho. *Perf. 14***

*59* A11 20c Mountain Apple 35 35
*60* A11 20c Beach Morning Glory 35 35
*61* A11 20c Turmeric 35 35
*62* A11 20c Plumeria 35 35
***a.*** Block of 4, Nos. 59-62 1.40 1.40

Audubon Bicentenary — A12

**1985, Feb. 6 Litho. *Perf. 14***

*63* A12 22c Shearwater chick 44 44
*64* A12 22c Shearwater's head 44 44
*65* A12 22c Shearwater in flight 44 44
*66* A12 22c Swimming 44 44
***a.*** Block of 4, Nos. 63-66 1.80 1.80

See No. C5.

Canoes and Rafts A13

**1985, Mar. 27 Litho.**

*67* A13 22c Cargo canoe 35 35
*68* A13 22c War canoe 35 35
*69* A13 22c Bamboo raft 35 35
*70* A13 22c Racing/sailing canoe 35 35
***a.*** Block of 4, Nos. 67-70 1.40 1.40

Marine Life Type of 1983

**1985, June 11 Litho. *Perf. 14½x14***

*75* A3 14c Trumpet triton 20 20
***a.*** Booklet pane of 10 2.00
*76* A3 22c Bumphead parrotfish 35 35
***a.*** Booklet pane of 10 3.50
***b.*** Bklt. pane of 10 (5 14c, 5 22c) 2.75
*77* A3 25c Soft coral, damsel fish 40 40
*79* A3 33c Sea anemone, clownfish 55 55
*80* A3 39c Green sea turtle 65 65
*81* A3 44c Pacific sailfish 70 70

***Perf. 15x14***

*85* A3 $10 Spinner dolphins 15.00 15.00
*Nos. 75-85 (7)* 17.85 17.85

Intl. Youth Year — A14

IYY emblem and children of all nationalities joined in a circle.

**1985, July 15 Litho. *Perf. 14***

*86* A14 44c multicolor 70 70
*87* A14 44c multicolor 70 70
*88* A14 44c multicolor 70 70
*89* A14 44c multicolor 70 70
***a.*** Block of 4, Nos. 86-89 2.80 2.80

Nos. 86-89 se-tenant in continuous design.

Christmas 1985 — A15

Island mothers and children.

**1985, Oct. 21 Litho. *Perf. 14***

*90* A15 14c multicolor 25 25
*91* A15 22c multicolor 40 40
*92* A15 33c multicolor 60 60
*93* A15 44c multicolor 75 75

**Souvenir Sheet**

Pan American Airways Martin M-130 China Clipper A16

**1985, Nov. 21 Litho. *Perf. 14***

*94* A16 $1 multicolor 2.00 2.00

1st Trans-Pacific Mail Flight, Nov. 22, 1935. No. 94 has multicolored decorative margin continuing the design and picturing the S.S. North Haven support ship at sea, the flight map and China Clipper emblem. Size: 96x70mm.

See Nos. C10-C13.

Return of Halley's Comet A17

Fictitious local sightings.

**1985, Dec. 21 Litho. *Perf. 14***

*95* A17 44c Kaeb canoe, 1758 70 70
*96* A17 44c U.S.S. Vincennes, 1835 70 70
*97* A17 44c S.M.S. Scharnhorst, 1910 70 70
*98* A17 44c Yacht, 1986 70 70
***a.*** Block of 4, Nos. 95-98 2.80 2.80

*Palau stamps can be mounted in Scott's annually supplemented Trust Territories Album.*

Songbirds — A18

**1986, Feb. 24 Litho. *Perf. 14***

*99* A18 44c Mangrove flycatcher 70 70
*100* A18 44c Cardinal honeyeater 70 70
*101* A18 44c Blue-faced parrotfinch 70 70
*102* A18 44c Dusky and bridled white-eyes 70 70
***a.*** Block of 4, Nos. 99-102 2.80 2.80

World of Sea and Reef — A19

**1986, May 22 Litho. *Perf. 15x14***

*103* Sheet of 40 *50.00*
***a.*** A19 14c, any single 30 30

AMERIPEX '86, Chicago, May 22-June 1

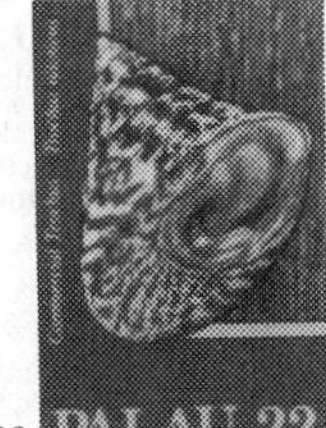

Seashells — A20

**1986, Aug. 1 Litho. *Perf. 14***

*104* A20 22c Commercial trochus 35 35
*105* A20 22c Marble cone 35 35
*106* A20 22c Fluted giant clam 35 35
*107* A20 22c Bullmouth helmet 35 35
*108* A20 22c Golden cowrie 35 35
***a.*** Strip of 5, Nos. 104-108 1.75 1.75
*Nos. 104-108 (5)* 1.75 1.75

See Nos. 150-154, 191-195.

Intl. Peace Year A21

**1986, Sept. 19 Litho.**

*109* A21 22c Soldier's helmet 35 35
*110* A21 22c Plane wreckage 35 35
*111* A21 22c Woman playing guitar 35 35
*112* A21 22c Airai vista 35 35
***a.*** Block of 4, Nos. 109-112 1.40 1.40
*Nos. 109-112,C17 (5)* 2.10 2.10

Reptiles — A22

**1986, Oct. 28 Litho. *Perf. 14***

*113* A22 22c Gecko 35 35
*114* A22 22c Emerald tree skink 35 35
*115* A22 22c Estuarine crocodile 35 35
*116* A22 22c Leatherback turtle 35 35
***a.*** Block of 4, Nos. 113-116 1.40 1.40

Christmas — A23

Joy to the World, carol by Isaac Watts and Handel: No. 117, Girl playing guitar, boys, goat. No. 118, Girl carrying bouquet, boys singing. No. 119, Palauan mother and child. No. 120, Children, baskets of fruit. No. 121, Girl, fairy tern. Nos. 117-121 printed in a continuous design.

**1986, Nov. 26 Litho.**

*117* A23 22c multicolor 35 35
*118* A23 22c multicolor 35 35
*119* A23 22c multicolor 35 35
*120* A23 22c multicolor 35 35
*121* A23 22c multicolor 35 35
***a.*** Strip of 5, Nos. 117-121 1.75 1.75

Butterflies — A23a

**1987, Jan. 5 Litho. *Perf. 14***

*121B* A23a 44c Tangadik, soursop 70 70
*121C* A23a 44c Dira amartal, sweet orange 70 70
*121D* A23a 44c Ilhuochel, swamp cabbage 70 70
*121E* A23a 44c Bauosech, fig 70 70
***f.*** Block of 4, Nos. 121B-121E 2.80 2.80

See Nos. 183-186.

Fruit Bats — A24

**1987, Feb. 23 Litho.**

*122* A24 44c In flight 70 70
*123* A24 44c Hanging 70 70
*124* A24 44c Eating 70 70
*125* A24 44c Head 70 70
***a.*** Block of 4, #122-125 2.80 2.80

Indigenous Flowers — A25

**1987-88 Litho. *Perf. 14***

*126* A25 1c Ixora casei 5 5
*127* A25 3c Lumnitzera littorea 5 5
*128* A25 5c Sonneratia alba 8 8
*129* A25 10c Tristellateria australasiae 16 16
*130* A25 14c Bikkia palauensis 20 20
***a.*** Bklt. pane of 10 2.00
*131* A25 15c Limnophila aromatica ('88) 25 25
***a.*** Bklt. pane of 10 ('88) 2.50
*132* A25 22c Bruguiera gymnorhiza 35 35
***a.*** Bklt. pane of 10 3.50
***b.*** Bklt. pane of 10 (5 14c, 5 22c) 2.75
*133* A25 25c Fagraea ksid ('88) 42 42
***a.*** Bklt. pane of 10 ('88) 4.25
***b.*** Bklt. pane of 10 (5 each 15c, 25c) ('88) 3.50

*137* A25 36c Ophiorrhiza palauensis ('88) 58 58
*138* A25 39c Cerbera manghas 60 60
*140* A25 44c Sandera indica 70 70
*141* A25 45c Maesa canfieldiae ('88) 72 72
*142* A25 50c Dolichandrone spathacea 85 85
*143* A25 $1 Barringtonia racemosa 1.60 1.60
*144* A25 $2 Nepenthes mirabilis 3.25 3.25
*145* A25 $5 Dendrobium palawense 8.00 8.00

**Size: 49x28mm**

*145A* A25 $10 Bouquet ('88) 18.00 18.00
*Nos. 126-145A (17)* 35.86 35.86

Issue dates: Mar. 12. $10, Mar. 17. 15c, 25c, 36c, 45c, July 1. Nos. 131a, 133a-133b, July 5.

CAPEX '87 — A26

**1987, June 15 Litho. *Perf. 14***

*146* A26 22c Babeldaob Is. 35 35
*147* A26 22c Floating Garden Isls. 35 35
*148* A26 22c Rock Is. 35 35
*149* A26 22c Koror 35 35
*a.* Block of 4, Nos. 146-149 1.40 1.40

Seashells Type of 1986

**1987, Aug. 25 Litho. *Perf. 14***

*150* A20 22c Black-striped triton 35 35
*151* A20 22c Tapestry turban 35 35
*152* A20 22c Adusta murex 35 35
*153* A20 22c Little fox miter 35 35
*154* A20 22c Cardinal miter 35 35
*a.* Strip of 5, Nos. 150-154 1.75 1.75
*Nos. 150-154 (5)* 1.75 1.75

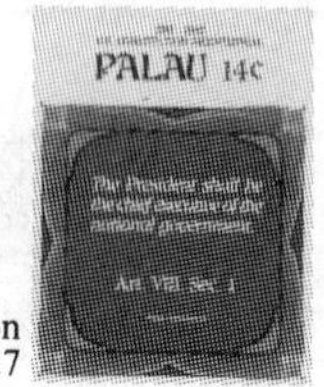

US Constitution Bicentennial — A27

Excerpts from Articles of the Palau and US Constitutions and Seals.

**1987, Sept. 17 Litho. *Perf. 14***

*155* A27 14c Art. VIII, Sec. 1, Palau 20 20
*156* A27 14c Presidential seals 20 20
*157* A27 14c Art. II, Sec. 1, US 20 20
*a.* Triptych + label, Nos. 155-157 60 60
*158* A27 22c Art. IX, Sec. 1, Palau 35 35
*159* A27 22c Legislative seals 35 35
*160* A27 22c Art. I, Sec. 1, US 35 35
*a.* Triptych + label, Nos. 158-160 1.05 1.05

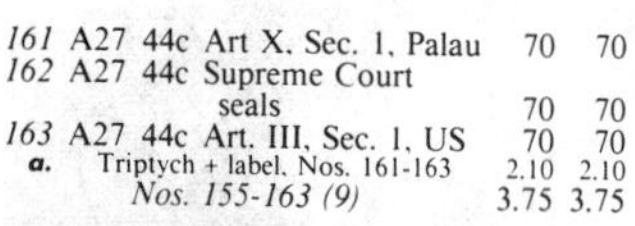

*161* A27 44c Art X, Sec. 1, Palau 70 70
*162* A27 44c Supreme Court seals 70 70
*163* A27 44c Art. III, Sec. 1, US 70 70
*a.* Triptych + label, Nos. 161-163 2.10 2.10
*Nos. 155-163 (9)* 3.75 3.75

Triptychs printed se-tenant with inscribed label picturing national flags.

Japanese Links to Palau — A28

Japanese stamps, period cancellations and installations: 14c, No. 257 and 1937 Datsun sedan used as mobile post office, near Ngerchelechuus Mountain. 22c, No. 347 and phosphate mine at Angaur. 33c, No. B1 and Japan Airways DC-2 over stone monuments at Badrulchau. 44c, No. 201 and Japanese post office, Koror. $1, Aviator's Grave, Japanese Cemetary, Peleliu, vert.

**1987, Oct. 16 Litho. *Perf. 14x13½***

*164* A28 14c multicolor 20 20
*165* A28 22c multicolor 35 35
*166* A28 33c multicolor 55 55
*167* A28 44c multicolor 70 70

**Souvenir Sheet**

***Perf. 13½x14***

*168* A28 $1 multicolor 2.00 2.00

No. 168 has multicolored margin continuing the design and picturing Japan Nos. 547 and B7. Size: 81x94mm.

Christmas — A30

Verses from carol "I Saw Three Ships," Biblical characters, landscape and Palauans in outrigger canoes.

**1987, Nov. 24 Litho. *Perf. 14***

*173* A30 22c I saw... 35 35
*174* A30 22c And what was... 35 35
*175* A30 22c 'Twas Joseph... 35 35
*176* A30 22c Saint Michael... 35 35
*177* A30 22c And all the bells... 35 35
*a.* Strip of 5, Nos. 173-177 1.75 1.75

Symbiotic Marine Species — A31

Designs: No. 178, Snapping shrimp, goby. No. 179, Mauve vase sponge, sponge crab. No. 180, Pope's damselfish, cleaner wrasse. No. 181, Clown anemone fish, sea anemone. No. 182, Four-color nudibranch, banded coral shrimp.

**1987, Dec. 15**

*178* A31 22c multicolor 35 35
*179* A31 22c multicolor 35 35
*180* A31 22c multicolor 35 35
*181* A31 22c multicolor 35 35
*182* A31 22c multicolor 35 35
*a.* Strip of 5, Nos. 178-182 1.75 1.75

Butterflies and Flowers Type of 1987

Designs: No. 183, Dannaus plexippus, Tournefotia argentia. No. 184, Papilio machaon, Citrus reticulata. No. 185, Captopsilia, Crataeva speciosa. No. 186, Colias philodice, Crataeva speciosa.

**1988, Jan. 25**

*183* A23a 44c multicolor 70 70
*184* A23a 44c multicolor 70 70
*185* A23a 44c multicolor 70 70
*186* A23a 44c multicolor 70 70
*a.* Block of 4, Nos. 183-186 2.80 2.80

Ground-dwelling Birds — A32

**1988, Feb. 29 Litho. *Perf. 14***

*187* A32 44c Whimbrel 88 88
*188* A32 44c Yellow bittern 88 88
*189* A32 44c Rufous night-heron 88 88
*190* A32 44c Banded rail 88 88
*a.* Block of 4, Nos. 187-190 3.55 3.55

Seashells Type of 1986

**1988, May 11 Litho. *Perf. 14***

*191* A20 25c Striped engina 50 50
*192* A20 25c Ivory cone 50 50
*193* A20 25c Plaited miter 50 50
*194* A20 25c Episcopal miter 50 50
*195* A20 25c Isabelle cowrie 50 50
*a.* Strip of 5, Nos. 191-195 2.50 2.50
*Nos. 191-195 (5)* 2.50 2.50

Souvenir Sheet

Postal Independence, 5th Anniv. — A33

Designs: a. Kaep (pre-European outrigger sailboat). b. Spanish colonial cruiser. c. German colonial cruiser SMS Cormoran, c. 1885. d. Japanese mailbox, WWII machine gun, Koror Museum. e. US Trust Territory ship, Malakal Harbor. f. Koror post office.

**1988, June 8 Litho. *Perf. 14***

*196* Souv. sheet of 6 3.00 3.00
*a.-f.* A33 25c multi 50 50

FINLANDIA '88. No. 196 has multicolored inscribed margin picturing Palau flag and exhibition emblem. Size: 150x97mm.

Souvenir Sheet

US Possessions Phil. Soc., 10th Anniv. — A34

Designs: a. "Collect Palau Stamps," original artwork for No. 196f and head of a man. b. Soc. emblem. c. Nos. 1-4. d. China Clipper original artwork and covers. e. Man and boy studying covers. f. Girl at show cancel booth.

**1988, Aug. 26 Litho. *Perf. 14***

*197* A34 Sheet of 6 5.40 5.40
*a.-f.* 45c any single 90 90

PRAGA '88. No. 197 has multicolored inscribed margin picturing exhibition and FIP emblems. Size: 149x97mm.

Christmas — A35

*Hark! The Herald Angels Sing:* No. 198, Angels playing the violin, singing and sitting. No. 199, 3 angels and 3 children. No. 200, Nativity. No. 201, 2 angels, birds. No. 202, 3 children and 2 angels playing horns. Se-tenant in a continuous design.

**1988, Nov. 7 Litho. *Perf. 14***

*198* A35 25c multi 50 50
*199* A35 25c multi 50 50
*200* A35 25c multi 50 50
*201* A35 25c multi 50 50
*202* A35 25c multi 50 50
*a.* Strip of 5, Nos. 199-202 2.50 2.50
*Nos. 198-202 (5)* 2.50 2.50

Miniature Sheet

Chambered Nautilus — A36

Designs: a, Fossil and cross section. b, Palauan *bai* symbols for the nautilus. c, Specimens trapped for scientific study. d, *Nautilus belauensis, pompilius, macromphalus, stenomphalus* and *scrobiculatus*. e, Release of a tagged nautilus.

**1988, Dec. 23 Litho. *Perf. 14***

*203* A36 Sheet of 5 2.50 2.50
*a.-e.* 25c multi 50 50

No. 203 has multicolored inscribed margin picturing *Nautilus belauensis* and a verse from *The Chambered Nautilus*, a poem by Oliver Wendell Holmes.

An enhanced introduction to the Scott Catalogue begins on Page V. A thorough understanding of the material presented there will greatly aid your use of the catalogue itself.

### SEMI-POSTAL STAMPS

Olympic Sports SP1

**1988, Aug. 8 Litho. *Perf. 14***

*B1* SP1 25c +5c Baseball glove, player 60 60
*B2* SP1 25c +5c Running shoe, athlete 60 60
*a.* Pair, Nos. B1-B2 1.20 1.20
*B3* SP1 45c +5c Goggles, swimmer 1.00 1.00
*B4* SP1 45c +5c Gold medal, diver 1.00 1.00
*a.* Pair, Nos. B3-B4 2.00 2.00

### AIR POST STAMPS

White-tailed Tropicbird — AP1

**1984, June 12 Litho. *Perf. 14***

*C1* AP1 40c shown 65 65
*C2* AP1 40c Fairy tern 65 65
*C3* AP1 40c Black noddy 65 65
*C4* AP1 40c Black-naped tern 65 65
*a.* Block of 4, Nos. C1-C4 2.60 2.60

Audubon Type of 1985

**1985, Feb. 6 Litho. *Perf. 14***

*C5* A12 44c Audubon's Shearwater 70 70

Palau-Germany Political, Economic & Cultural Exchange Cent. — AP2

Germany Nos. 40, 65, Caroline Islands Nos. 19, 13 and: No. C6, German flag-raising at Palau, 1885. No. C7, Early German trading post in Angaur. No. C8, Abai architecture recorded by Prof. & Frau Kramer, 1908-1910. No. C9, S.M.S. Cormoran.

**1985, Sept. 19 Litho. *Perf. 14x13½***

*C6* AP2 44c multicolor 70 70
*C7* AP2 44c multicolor 70 70
*C8* AP2 44c multicolor 70 70
*C9* AP2 44c multicolor 70 70
*a.* Block of 4, Nos. C6-C9 2.80 2.80

Trans-Pacific Airmail Anniv. Type of 1985

Aircraft: No. C10, 1951 Trans-Ocean Airways PBY-5A Catalina Amphibian. No. C11, 1968 Air Micronesia DC-6B Super Cloudmaster. No. C12, 1960 Trust Territory Airline SA-16 Albatross. No. C13, 1967 Pan American Douglas DC-4.

**1985, Nov. 21 Litho. *Perf. 14***

*C10* A16 44c multicolor 70 70
*C11* A16 44c multicolor 70 70
*C12* A16 44c multicolor 70 70
*C13* A16 44c multicolor 70 70
*a.* Block of 4, Nos. C10-C13 2.80 2.80

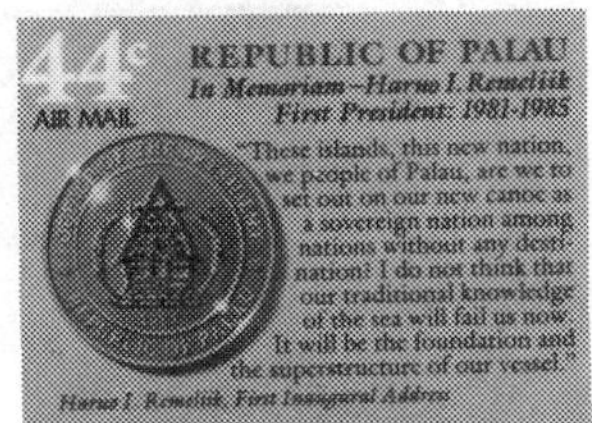


Haruo I. Remeliik (1933-1985), 1st President — AP3

Designs: No. C14, Presidential seal, excerpt from 1st inaugural address. No. C15, War canoe, address excerpt, diff. No. C16, Remeliik, US Pres. Reagan, excerpt from Reagan's speech, Pacific Basin Conference, Guam, 1984.

**1986, June 30 Litho. *Perf. 14***

*C14* AP3 44c multicolor 65 65
*C15* AP3 44c multicolor 65 65
*C16* AP3 44c multicolor 65 65
*a.* Strip of 3, Nos. C14-C16 1.95 1.95

Intl. Peace Year, Statue of Liberty Cent. — AP4

**1986, Sept. 19 Litho.**

*C17* AP4 44c multicolor 70 70

## PHILIPPINES

LOCATION — A group of 7,100 islands and islets in the Malay Archipelago, north of Borneo, in the North Pacific Ocean.
GOVT. — US Admin., 1898-1946.
AREA — 115,748 sq. mi.
POP. — 16,971,100 (est. 1941)
CAPITAL — Quezon City

The islands were ceded to the US by Spain in 1898. On Nov. 15, 1935, they were given their independence, subject to a transition period which ended July 4, 1946. On that date the Commonwealth became the "Republic of the Philippines."

100 Cents = 1 Dollar (1899)
100 Centavos = 1 Peso (1906)

### Issued under US Administration

Issues of the US Overprinted in Black

On No. 260

**1899-1900 Unwmk. *Perf. 12***

*212* A96 50c orange 425.00 250.00

On Nos. 279, 279d, 267, 268, 281, 282C, 283, 284, 275 and 275a.

**Wmk. 191**

*213* A87 1c yellow grn 3.75 90
*214* A88 2c orange red, type III 1.75 60
*a.* 2c carmine, type III 2.50 1.00
*b.* Booklet pane of 6 ('00) 325.00 *175.00*
*215* A89 3c purple 6.50 1.75
*216* A91 5c blue 6.50 1.50
*a.* Inverted overprint *3,000.*
*217* A94 10c brown, type I 20.00 5.00
*217A* A94 10c orange brn, type II 250.00 50.00
*218* A95 15c olive grn 35.00 8.75
*a.* 15c light olive grn 45.00 12.50
*219* A96 50c orange 125.00 50.00
*a.* 50c red orange 250.00
*Nos. 213-219 (8)* 448.50 118.50

On Nos. 280b, 282 and 272

**1901**

*220* A90 4c orange brn 22.50 6.00
*221* A92 6c lake 27.50 8.00
*222* A93 8c violet brn 30.00 8.00

**On Nos. 276, 276A, 277a and 278**

**Red Overprint**

*223* A97 $1 blk, type I 475.00 275.00
*223A* A97 $1 blk, type II 2,750. 1,350.
*224* A98 $2 dark blue 700.00 350.00
*225* A99 $5 dark green 1,650. 1,100.

On Nos. 300-313 and shades
Black Overprint

**1903-04**

*226* A115 1c blue grn 4.50 50
*227* A116 2c carmine 7.50 1.75
*228* A117 3c brt vio 85.00 20.00
*229* A118 4c brown ('04) 90.00 30.00
*a.* 4c orange brown 90.00 25.00
*230* A119 5c blue 12.00 1.25
*231* A120 6c brownish lake ('04) 95.00 25.00
*232* A121 8c vio blk ('04) 40.00 15.00
*233* A122 10c pale red brn ('04) 22.50 3.50
*a.* 10c red brown 27.50 5.00
*b.* Pair, one without ovpt. *1,350.*
*234* A123 13c pur blk 35.00 17.50
*a.* 13c brown violet 35.00 17.50
*235* A124 15c olive grn 60.00 13.00
*236* A125 50c orange 175.00 55.00
*Nos. 226-236 (11)* 626.50 182.50

**Red Overprint**

*237* A126 $1 black 650.00 300.00
*238* A127 $2 dark bl ('04) 2,000. 1,200.
*239* A128 $5 dk grn ('04) 2,400. 1,400.

On Nos. 319, 319c in Black

**1904**

*240* A129 2c carmine 5.50 2.50
*a.* Booklet pane of 6 *1,200.*
*b.* Scarlet 6.50 2.75

Jose Rizal — A40

Arms of Manila — A41

Wmk. 191PI-Double-lined PIPS

Designs: 4c, McKinley. 6c, Magellan. 8c, Miguel Lopez de Legaspi. 10c, Gen. Henry W. Lawton. 12c, Lincoln. 16c, Adm. William T. Sampson. 20c, Washington. 26c, Francisco Carriedo. 30c, Franklin.

Each Inscribed "Philippine Islands/United States of America"

**1906, Sept. 8 Engr. Wmk. 191PI**

*241* A40 2c deep green 30 6
*a.* 2c yellow green ('10) 50 6
*b.* Booklet pane of 6 225.00
*242* A40 4c carmine 40 6
*a.* 4c carmine lake ('10) 75 6
*b.* Booklet pane of 6 225.00
*243* A40 6c violet 1.25 15
*244* A40 8c brown 2.25 75
*245* A40 10c blue 1.65 10
*246* A40 12c brown lake 5.00 2.25
*247* A40 16c violet blk 3.25 25
*248* A40 20c orange brn 3.75 40
*249* A40 26c violet brn 6.00 2.50
*250* A40 30c olive grn 4.50 1.60
*251* A41 1p orange 25.00 11.00
*252* A41 2p black 35.00 1.50
*253* A41 4p dark blue 100.00 17.50
*254* A41 10p dark grn 200.00 85.00
*Nos. 241-254 (14)* 388.35 123.12

Change of Colors

**1909-13 *Perf. 12***

*255* A40 12c red orange 8.00 3.00
*256* A40 16c olive green 2.00 50
*257* A40 20c yellow 7.50 1.50
*258* A40 26c blue green 1.50 80
*259* A40 30c ultramarine 10.00 4.00
*260* A41 1p pale violet 30.00 6.00
*260A* A41 2p vio brn ('13) 80.00 3.00
*Nos. 255-260A (7)* 139.00 18.80

Wmk. 190PI-Single-lined PIPS

**1911 Wmk. 190PI *Perf. 12***

*261* A40 2c green 60 10
*a.* Booklet pane of 6 200.00
*262* A40 4c carmine lake 3.00 12
*a.* 4c carmine —
*b.* Booklet pane of 6 200.00
*263* A40 6c deep vio 1.75 10
*264* A40 8c brown 8.00 50
*265* A40 10c blue 3.00 10
*266* A40 12c orange 2.00 50
*267* A40 16c olive grn 2.25 20
*268* A40 20c yellow 2.00 15
*a.* 20c orange 2.00 15
*269* A40 26c blue grn 2.75 30
*270* A40 30c ultramarine 3.25 50
*271* A41 1p pale vio 20.00 50
*272* A41 2p vio brn 25.00 1.00
*273* A41 4p deep blue 650.00 60.00
*274* A41 10p deep grn 200.00 22.50
*Nos. 261-274 (14)* 923.60 86.57

**1914**

*275* A40 30c gray 10.00 65

**1914-23 *Perf. 10***

*276* A40 2c green 1.50 12
*a.* Booklet pane of 6 200.00
*277* A40 4c carmine 1.50 15
*a.* Booklet pane of 6 200.00
*278* A40 6c light violet 35.00 15.00
*a.* 6c deep violet 37.50 7.00
*279* A40 8c brown 35.00 12.50
*280* A40 10c dark blue 22.50 25
*281* A40 16c olive grn 70.00 5.00
*282* A40 20c orange 20.00 1.00
*283* A40 30c gray 50.00 3.50
*284* A41 1p pale violet 110.00 4.00
*Nos. 276-284 (9)* 345.50 41.52

**1918-26 *Perf. 11***

*285* A40 2c green 20.00 5.00
*a.* Booklet pane of 6 *600.00*
*286* A40 4c carmine 27.50 3.00
*a.* Booklet pane of 6 *600.00*
*287* A40 6c deep vio 37.50 2.00
*287A* A40 8c light brn 225.00 40.00
*288* A40 10c dark blue 50.00 1.75
*289* A40 16c olive grn 100.00 8.00
*289A* A40 20c orange 55.00 10.00
*289C* A40 30c gray 50.00 17.50
*289D* A41 1p pale violet 60.00 15.00
*Nos. 285-289D (9)* 625.00 102.25

**1917-25 Unwmk. *Perf. 11***

*290* A40 2c yellow green 10 5
*a.* 2c dark green 12 5
*b.* Vert. pair, imperf. horiz. *1,000.* —
*c.* Horiz. pair, imperf. btwn. *1,200.*
*d.* Vert. pair, imperf. btwn. *1,850.*
*e.* Booklet pane of 6 25.00
*291* A40 4c carmine 10 5
*a.* 4c light rose 25 5
*b.* Booklet pane of 6 17.50 —
*292* A40 6c deep violet 30 8
*a.* 6c lilac 40 8
*b.* 6c red violet 40 10
*c.* Booklet pane of 6 250.00
*293* A40 8c yellow brn 20 12
*a.* 8c orange brown 20 12
*294* A40 10c deep blue 20 8
*295* A40 12c red orange 40 15
*296* A40 16c light ol grn 50.00 25
*a.* 16c olive bister 50.00 50
*297* A40 20c orange yel 35 10
*298* A40 26c green 55 65
*a.* 26c blue green 70 40
*299* A40 30c gray 50 10
*300* A41 1p pale violet 32.50 1.25
*a.* 1p red lilac 32.50 1.25
*b.* 1p pale rose lilac 32.50 1.50
*301* A41 2p violet brn 30.00 75
*302* A41 4p blue 21.00 50
*a.* 4p dark blue 21.00 50
*Nos. 290-302 (13)* 136.20 4.13

**1923-26**

Design: 16c, Adm. George Dewey.

*303* A40 16c olive bister 75 20
*a.* 16c olive green 1.35 20
*304* A41 10p deep green ('26) 60.00 8.00

See Nos. 326-353.

Legislative Palace — A42

**1926, Dec. 20 Unwmk. *Perf. 12***

*319* A42 2c green & blk 50 30
*a.* Horiz. pair, imperf. between *275.00*
*b.* Vert. pair, imperf. between *425.00*
*320* A42 4c car & blk 50 40
*a.* Horiz. pair, imperf. between *275.00*
*b.* Vert. pair, imperf. between *350.00*
*321* A42 16c ol grn & blk 1.00 85
*a.* Horiz. pair, imperf. between *325.00*
*b.* Vert. pair, imperf. between *425.00*
*c.* Double impression of center *550.00*
*322* A42 18c lt brn & blk 1.25 75
*a.* Double impression of center *550.00*
*b.* Vert. pair, imperf. between *425.00*
*323* A42 20c orange & blk 1.75 1.25
*a.* 20c orange & brown *400.00* —
*b.* Imperf., pair *450.00* *450.00*
*c.* As "a," imperf., pair *375.00*
*d.* Vert. pair, imperf. between *425.00*
*324* A42 24c gray & blk 1.50 1.00
*a.* Vert. pair, imperf. between *425.00*
*325* A42 1p rose lil & blk 70.00 35.00
*a.* Vert. pair, imperf. between *475.00*
*Nos. 319-325 (7)* 76.50 39.55

Opening of the Legislative Palace.

Coil Stamp
Rizal Type of 1906

**1928 *Perf. 11 Vertically***

*326* A40 2c green 8.50 10.00

Types of 1906-23

**1925-31 Unwmk. *Imperf.***

*340* A40 2c yel grn ('31) 12 12
*341* A40 4c car rose ('31) 20 20
*342* A40 6c violet ('31) 2.00 2.00
*343* A40 8c brown ('31) 1.75 1.75
*344* A40 10c blue ('31) 2.00 2.00
*345* A40 12c dp org ('31) 3.00 3.00
*346* A40 16c ol grn *(Dewey)* ('31) 2.25 2.25
*347* A40 20c org yel ('31) 2.25 2.25
*348* A40 26c green ('31) 2.25 2.25
*349* A40 30c lt gray ('31) 2.50 2.50
*350* A41 1p lt vio ('31) 8.00 8.00
*351* A41 2p brn vio ('31) 20.00 20.00
*352* A41 4p blue ('31) 60.00 60.00
*353* A41 10p green ('31) 175.00 175.00
*Nos. 340-353 (14)* 281.32 281.32

Two imperforate issues were made, in 1925 and 1931. They differ in shade.

Mount Mayon, Luzon — A43

Post Office, Manila — A44

Pier No. 7, Manila Bay A45

(See footnote) A46

Rice Planting A47

Rice Terraces A48

Baguio Zigzag — A49

**1932, May 3 *Perf. 11***

*354* A43 2c yellow green 75 35
*355* A44 4c rose carmine 50 35
*356* A45 12c orange 75 75
*357* A46 18c red orange 25.00 12.50
*358* A47 20c yellow 1.00 80
*359* A48 24c deep violet 1.50 1.00
*360* A49 32c olive brown 1.50 1.15
*Nos. 354-360 (7)* 31.00 16.90

The 18c vignette was intended to show Pagsanjan Falls in Laguna, central Luzon, and is so labeled. Through error the stamp pictures Vernal Falls in Yosemite Natl. Park, CA.

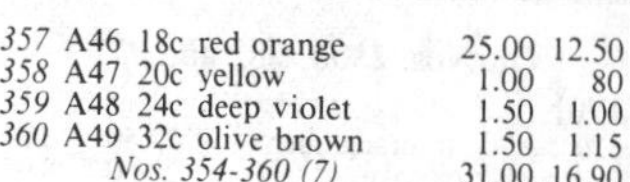

Nos. 302, 302a Surcharged in Orange or Red

**1932**

*368* A41 1p on 4p blue (O) 2.50 50
*a.* 1p on 4p dark blue (O) 3.50 1.50
*369* A41 2p on 4p dark blue (R) 4.50 1.00
*a.* 2p on 4p blue (R) 4.50 1.00

Baseball — A50

Tennis — A51

Basketball — A52

**1934, Apr. 14 Typo. *Perf. 11½***

*380* A50 2c yellow brown 20 20
*381* A51 6c ultramarine 40 35
*a.* Vert. pair, imperf. between *900.00*
*382* A52 16c violet brown 90 90
*a.* Vert. pair, imperf. horiz. *900.00*

Tenth Far Eastern Championship Games.

Jose Rizal A53

Woman and Carabao A54

La Filipina A55

Pearl Fishing A56

Fort Santiago — A57

Salt Spring — A58

Magellan's Landing, 1521 A59

"Juan de la Cruz" A60

Rice Terraces — A61

"Blood Compact," 1565 — A62

Barasoain Church, Malolos A63

Battle of Manila Bay, 1898 — A64

Montalban Gorge — A65

George Washington — A66

**1935, Feb. 15 Engr. *Perf. 11***

*383* A53 2c rose 5 5
*384* A54 4c yellow green 5 5
*385* A55 6c dark brown 9 6
*386* A56 8c violet 12 12
*387* A57 10c rose carmine 25 20
*388* A58 12c black 18 15
*389* A59 16c dark blue 18 12
*390* A60 20c light olive grn 25 6
*391* A61 26c indigo 35 35
*392* A62 30c orange red 35 35
*393* A63 1p red org & blk 2.50 1.85
*394* A64 2p bis brn & blk 5.00 1.75
*395* A65 4p blue & blk 5.00 3.75
*396* A66 5p green & blk 10.00 2.25
*Nos. 383-396 (14)* 24.37 11.11

**Commonwealth Issues**

The Temples of Human Progress — A67

**1935, Nov. 15**

*397* A67 2c carmine rose 15 10
*398* A67 6c deep violet 20 15
*399* A67 16c blue 30 20
*400* A67 36c yellow green 50 45
*401* A67 50c brown 80 80
*Nos. 397-401 (5)* 1.95 1.70

Inauguration of the Philippine Commonwealth, Nov. 15th, 1935.

Jose Rizal — A68

President Manuel L. Quezon — A69

**1936, June 19 *Perf. 12***

*402* A68 2c yellow brown 10 10
*403* A68 6c slate blue 15 10
*a.* Horizx. pair, imperf. vert. *800.00*
*404* A68 36c red brown 75 70

75th anniv. of the birth of Jose Rizal.

**1936, Nov. 15 *Perf. 11***

*408* A69 2c orange brown 6 6
*409* A69 6c yellow green 12 10
*410* A69 12c ultramarine 18 15

1st anniv. of the Commonwealth.

Nos. 383-396 Overprinted in Black

COMMON-
WEALTH
a

COMMONWEALTH
b

**1936-37 *Perf. 11***

*411* A53 (a) 2c rose 6 5
*a.* Booklet pane of 6 5.00 *1.00*
*412* A54 (b) 4c yel grn ('37) 75 40
*413* A55 (a) 6c dark brn 25 10
*414* A56 (b) 8c vio ('37) 35 30
*415* A57 (b) 10c rose car 20 6
*a.* "Commonwealt" —
*416* A58 (b) 12c black ('37) 20 8
*417* A59 (b) 16c dark blue 25 20
*418* A60 (a) 20c lt ol grn ('37) 75 50
*419* A61 (b) 26c indigo ('37) 65 45
*420* A62 (b) 30c orange red 30 15
*421* A63 (b) 1p red org & blk 1.00 30
*422* A64 (b) 2p bister brown & blk ('37) 7.00 3.00
*423* A65 (b) 4p bl & blk ('37) 25.00 4.00
*424* A66 (b) 5p grn & blk ('37) 2.50 1.65
*Nos. 411-424 (14)* 39.26 11.24

Map of Philippines A70

Arms of Manila A71

**1937, Feb. 3**

*425* A70 2c yellow green 10 6
*426* A70 6c light brown 18 10
*427* A70 12c sapphire 20 10
*428* A70 20c deep orange 35 5
*429* A70 36c deep violet 60 50
*430* A70 50c carmine 70 35
*Nos. 425-430 (6)* 2.13 1.16

33rd Eucharistic Congress.

**1937, Aug. 27 *Perf. 11***

*431* A71 10p gray 6.50 3.00
*432* A71 20p henna brown 3.50 2.00

Nos. 383-396 Overprinted in Black

COMMON-
WEALTH
a

COMMONWEALTH
b

**1938-40 *Perf. 11***

*433* A53 (a) 2c rose ('39) 8 5
*a.* Booklet pane of 6 5.00 *1.00*
*b.* "WEALTH COMMON-" *3,000.*
*c.* Hyphen omitted — —
*434* A54 (b) 4c yel grn ('40) 60 50
*435* A55 (a) 6c dk brn ('39) 8 8
*a.* 6c golden brown 15 8
*436* A56 (b) 8c vio ('39) 10 10
*a.* "Commonwealt" 100.00
*437* A57 (b) 10c rose car ('39) 10 6
*438* A58 (b) 12c black ('40) 10 9
*439* A59 (b) 16c dark blue 18 10
*440* A60 (a) 20c lt ol grn ('39) 20 10
*441* A61 (b) 26c indigo ('40) 30 30
*442* A62 (b) 30c org red ('39) 1.60 85
*443* A63 (b) 1p red org & blk 60 25
*444* A64 (b) 2p bis brn & blk 4.00 1.00
*445* A65 (b) 4p bl & blk ('40) 65.00 65.00

*446* A66 (b) 5p green & blk ('40) 7.00 4.00
*Nos. 433-446 (14)* 79.94 72.48

Overprint "b" measures 18½x1¾mm. No. 433b occurs in booklet pane, No. 433a, position 5: all copies are straight-edged, left and bottom.

Stamps of 1917-37 Surcharged in Red, Violet or Black

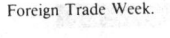

FIRST FOREIGN
a

TRADE WEEK 2 CENTAVOS MAY 21-27,1939

FIRST FOREIGN TRADE WEEK 50CENTAVOS50

MAY 21-27, 1939 6CENTAVOS6
b

FIRST FOREIGN TRADE WEEK MAY 21-27,1939
c

**1939, July 5**

*449* A54 (a) 2c on 4c yel grn (R) 10 8
*450* A40 (b) 6c on 26c blue grn (V) 20 20
*a.* 6c on 26c green 1.00 45
*451* A71 (c) 50c on 20p henna brn (Bk) 1.25 1.25

Foreign Trade Week.

Triumphal Arch — A72

Malacanan Palace — A73

**1939, Nov. 15** *Perf. 11*

*452* A72 2c yellow green 10 8
*453* A72 6c carmine 15 10
*454* A72 12c bright blue 25 10

**1939, Nov. 15**

*455* A73 2c green 10 6
*456* A73 6c orange 15 10
*457* A73 12c carmine 25 8

Nos. 452-457 commemorate the 4th anniversary of the Commonwealth.

Quezon Taking Oath of Office A74

Jose Rizal A75

**1940, Feb. 8**

*458* A74 2c dark orange 10 8
*459* A74 6c dark green 15 12
*460* A74 12c purple 30 15

4th anniversary of Commonwealth.

**Rotary Press Printing**
**Size: 19x22½mm**

**1941, Apr. 14** *Perf. 11x10½*

*461* A75 2c apple green 5 5

**Flat Plate Printing**
**Size: 18¾x22mm**

**1941-43** *Perf. 11*

*462* A75 2c apple grn ('43) 12 6
*a.* 2c pale apple green 25 6
*b.* Bklt. pane of 6 (apple green, '43) 1.50 *1.50*
*c.* Bklt. pane of 6 (pale apple grn) 4.00 *3.50*

No. 462 was issued only in booklet panes and all copies have straight edges.

Further printings were made in 1942 and 1943 in different shades from the first supply of stamps sent to the islands.

Philippine Stamps of 1935-41, Handstamped in Violet

VICTORY

**1944** *Perf. 11, 11x10½*

*463* A53 2c rose (On 411) *225.00 125.00*
*a.* Booklet pane of 6 *1,850.*
*463B* A53 2c rose (On 433) *1,450. 1,450.*
*464* A75 2c apple grn (On 461) 2.50 2.50
*465* A54 4c yellow grn (On 384) *25.00 25.00*
*466* A55 6c dark brn (On 385) *1,350. 750.00*
*467* A69 6c yellow grn (On 409) *100.00 85.00*
*468* A55 6c dark brn (On 413) *550.00 300.00*
*469* A72 6c car (On 453) *125.00 100.00*
*470* A73 6c org (On 456) *500.00 300.00*
*471* A74 6c dark grn (On 459) *150.00 90.00*
*472* A56 8c vio (On 436) 12.50 15.00
*473* A57 10c rose car (On 415) *100.00 60.00*
*474* A57 10c rose car (On 437) *125.00 80.00*
*475* A69 12c ultra (On 410) *300.00 110.00*
*476* A72 12c bright bl (On 454) *3,500. 1,400.*
*477* A74 12c pur (On 460) *175.00 100.00*
*478* A59 16c dark blue (On 389) *700.00*
*479* A59 16c dark blue (On 417) *350.00 120.00*
*480* A59 16c dark blue (On 439) *130.00 100.00*
*481* A60 20c lt olive grn (On 440) 27.50 27.50
*482* A62 30c orange red (On 420) *200.00 125.00*
*483* A62 30c orange red (On 442) *275.00 135.00*
*484* A63 1p red org & blk (On 443) *7,000. 4,500.*

Types of 1935-37 Overprinted

VICTORY
COMMON-WEALTH
a

VICTORY
COMMONWEALTH
b

**1945** *Perf. 11*

*485* A53 (a) 2c rose 10 6
*486* A54 (b) 4c yellow green 12 8
*487* A55 (a) 6c golden brn 15 10
*488* A56 (b) 8c violet 20 18
*489* A57 (b) 10c rose car 20 15
*490* A58 (b) 12c black 30 18
*491* A59 (b) 16c dark blue 40 15
*492* A60 (a) 20c lt olive grn 45 12
*493* A62 (b) 30c orange red 60 50
*494* A63 (b) 1p red org & blk 1.75 40
*Nos. 485-494 (10)* 4.27 1.92

Nos. 431-432 Overprinted in Black

VICTORY

*495* A71 10p gray 60.00 20.00
*496* A71 20p henna brown 50.00 22.50

Jose Rizal — A76

**Rotary Press Printing**

**1946, May 28** *Perf. 11x10½*

*497* A76 2c sepia 10 6

---

**Succeeding issues, released by the Philippine Republic on and after July 4, 1946, are listed in Vol. IV.**

---

*Philippines stamps can be mounted in Scott's U.S. Possessions Album.*

## AIR POST STAMPS

### Madrid-Manila Flight Issue

Regular Issue of 1917-26 Overprinted in Red or Violet

1926 MADRID-MANILA

**1926, May 13** **Unwmk.** *Perf. 11*

*C1* A40 2c green (R) 5.00 4.00
*C2* A40 4c carmine (V) 6.50 4.50
*a.* Inverted overprint *1,200.* —
*C3* A40 6c lilac (R) 35.00 12.00
*C4* A40 8c org brn (V) 35.00 12.00
*C5* A40 10c deep bl (R) 35.00 12.00
*C6* A40 12c red org (V) 40.00 17.50
*C7* A40 16c lt olive grn *(Sampson)* (V) *1,350. 1,000.*
*C8* A40 16c ol bis *(Sampson)* (R) *2,000. 1,650.*
*C9* A40 16c ol grn *(Dewey)* (V) 40.00 17.50
*C10* A40 20c org yel (V) 40.00 17.50
*C11* A40 26c blue grn (V) 40.00 17.50
*C12* A40 30c gray (V) 40.00 17.50
*C13* A41 2p vio brn (R) 350.00 250.00
*C14* A41 4p dark bl (R) 600.00 350.00
*C15* A41 10p dp grn (V) 900.00 600.00

**Same Overprint on No. 269**
**Wmk. 190PI**
***Perf. 12***

*C16* A40 26c blue grn (V) *2,000.*

**Same Overprint on No. 284**
***Perf. 10***

*C17* A41 1p pale vio (V) 120.00 85.00

Flight of Spanish aviators Gallarza and Loriga from Madrid to Manila.

### London-Orient Flight Issue

Regular Issue of 1917-25 Overprinted in Red

L.O.F. 1928

**1928, Nov. 9** **Unwmk.** *Perf. 11*

*C18* A40 2c green 60 40
*C19* A40 4c carmine 60 50
*C20* A40 6c violet 2.25 1.75
*C21* A40 8c orange brn 2.50 2.25
*C22* A40 10c deep blue 2.50 2.25
*C23* A40 12c red orange 3.50 3.00
*C24* A40 16c ol grn *(Dewey)* 2.75 2.25
*C25* A40 20c orange yel 3.50 3.00
*C26* A40 26c blue green 10.00 7.50
*C27* A40 30c gray 10.00 7.50

**Same Overprint on No. 271**
**Wmk. 190PI**
***Perf. 12***

*C28* A41 1p pale violet 35.00 35.00
*Nos. C18-C28 (11)* 73.20 65.40

Flight from London to Manila.

Nos. 354-360 Overprinted

**1932, Sept. 27** **Unwmk.** *Perf. 11*

*C29* A43 2c yellow green 45 45
*C30* A44 4c rose carmine 50 50
*C31* A45 12c orange 80 80
*C32* A46 18c red orange 4.00 4.00
*C33* A47 20c yellow 2.25 2.25
*C34* A48 24c deep violet 2.25 2.25
*C35* A49 32c olive brown 2.25 2.25
*Nos. C29-C35 (7)* 12.50 12.50

Visit of Capt. Wolfgang von Gronau on his round-the-world flight.

Regular Issue of 1917-25 Overprinted

F.REIN MADRID-MANILA FLIGHT-1933

**1933, Apr. 11**

*C36* A40 2c green 45 45
*C37* A40 4c carmine 50 50
*C38* A40 6c deep violet 80 80
*C39* A40 8c orange brn 1.75 1.65
*C40* A40 10c dark blue 1.50 1.25
*C41* A40 12c orange 1.25 1.25
*C42* A40 16c ol grn *(Dewey)* 1.25 1.25
*C43* A40 20c yellow 1.25 1.25
*C44* A40 26c green 1.50 1.50
*a.* 26c blue green 2.50 2.50
*C45* A40 30c gray 2.00 1.85
*Nos. C36-C45 (10)* 12.25 11.75

Flight from Madrid to Manila of aviator Fernando Rein y Loring.

Stamp of 1917 Overprinted

**1933, May 26** **Unwmk.** *Perf. 11*

*C46* A40 2c green 65 50

Regular Issue of 1932 Overprinted

*C47* A44 4c rose carmine 10 8
*C48* A45 12c orange 50 18
*C49* A47 20c yellow 50 30
*C50* A48 24c deep violet 50 35
*C51* A49 32c olive brown 75 45
*Nos. C46-C51 (6)* 3.00 1.86

Nos. 387 and 392 Overprinted in Gold

**1935, Dec. 2**

*C52* A57 10c rose carmine 25 25
*C53* A62 30c orange red 50 50

China Clipper flight from Manila to San Francisco, Dec. 2-5, 1935.

Regular Issue of 1917-25 Surcharged in Various Colors

MANILA-MADRID ARNACAL FLIGHT-1936 2CENTAVOS2

**1936, Sept. 6** *Perf. 11*

*C54* A40 2c on 4c car (Bl) 8 6
*C55* A40 6c on 12c red org (V) 15 12
*C56* A40 16c on 26c bl grn (Bk) 30 30
*a.* 16c on 26c green (Bk) 1.50 1.00

Manila-Madrid flight by aviators Antonio Arnaiz and Juan Calvo.

Regular Issue of 1917-37 Surcharged in Black or Red

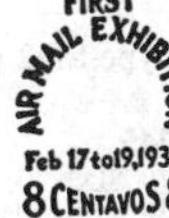


**1939, Feb. 17**

*C57* A40 8c on 26c bl grn (Bk) 1.00 55
*a.* 8c on 26c green (Bk) 2.00 75
*C58* A71 1p on 10p gray (R) 3.00 2.50

1st Air Mail Exhib., Feb. 17-19, 1939.

Moro Vinta and Clipper — AP1

**1941, June 30**

*C59* AP1 8c carmine 1.10 70
*C60* AP1 20c ultramarine 1.40 55
*C61* AP1 60c blue green 2.00 1.00
*C62* AP1 1p sepia 1.00 65

No. C47 Handstamped in Violet VICTORY

**1944, Dec. 3 Unwmk. *Perf. 11.***

*C63* A44 4c rose carmine *1,650. 1,000.*

### SPECIAL DELIVERY STAMPS

US No. E5 Overprinted in Red PHILIPPINES

**1901, Oct. 15 Wmk. 191 *Perf. 12***

*E1* SD3 10c dark blue 110.00 125.00

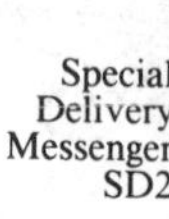

Special Delivery Messenger SD2

**1906 Engr. Wmk. 191PI**

*E2* SD2 20c ultramarine 30.00 8.00
*b.* 20c pale ultramarine 30.00 10.00

**Special Printing**

Overprinted in Red as No. E1 on US No. E6

**1907**

*E2A* SD4 10c ultramarine *1,600.*

**1911 Wmk. 190PI**

*E3* SD2 20c deep ultramarine 20.00 2.00

**1916 *Perf. 10***

*E4* SD2 20c deep ultramarine 165.00 40.00

**1919 Unwmk. *Perf. 11***

*E5* SD2 20c ultramarine 60 25
*a.* 20c pale blue 1.00 25
*b.* 20c dull violet 60 25

Type of 1906 Issue

**1925-31 *Imperf.***

*E6* SD2 20c dull vio ('31) 20.00 *25.00*

Type of 1919 Overprinted in Black COMMONWEALTH

**1939 *Perf. 11***

*E7* SD2 20c blue violet 30 30

Nos. E5b and E7, Handstamped in Violet VICTORY

**1944 *Perf. 11***

*E8* SD2 20c dull violet (On E5b) *400.00 300.00*
*E9* SD2 20c bl vio (On E7) *200.00 165.00*

Type SD2 Overprinted "VICTORY" As No. 486

**1945**

*E10* SD2 20c blue violet 85 85
*a.* "IC" close together 3.50 3.50

### SPECIAL DELIVERY OFFICIAL STAMP

Type of 1906 Issue Overprinted O. B.

**1931 Unwmk. *Perf. 11***

*EO1* SD2 20c dull violet 85 65
*a.* No period after "B" 25.00 20.00
*b.* Double overprint —

### POSTAGE DUE STAMPS

Postage Due Stamps of the US Nos. J38-J44 Overprinted in Black

**1899, Aug. 16 Wmk. 191 *Perf. 12***

*J1* D2 1c dp claret 5.00 2.00
*J2* D2 2c dp claret 5.00 1.75
*J3* D2 5c dp claret 11.00 3.75
*J4* D2 10c dp claret 15.00 7.00
*J5* D2 50c dp claret 165.00 100.00
*Nos. J1-J5 (5)* 201.00 114.50

No. J1 was used to pay regular postage Sept. 5-19, 1902.

**1901, Aug. 31**

*J6* D2 3c dp claret 15.00 10.00
*J7* D2 30c dp claret 225.00 100.00

Post Office Clerk — D3

**Unwmk.**

**1928, Aug. 21 Engr. *Perf. 11***

*J8* D3 4c brown red 15 15
*J9* D3 6c brown red 15 15
*J10* D3 8c brown red 15 15
*J11* D3 10c brown red 20 20
*J12* D3 12c brown red 20 20
*J13* D3 16c brown red 25 25
*J14* D3 20c brown red 20 20
*Nos. J8-J14 (7)* 1.30 1.30

No. J8 Surcharged in Blue 3 CVOS. 3

**1937**

*J15* D3 3c on 4c brown red 25 15

Nos. J8 to J14 Handstamped in Violet VICTORY

**1944**

*J16* D3 4c brown red *130.00* —
*J17* D3 6c brown red *90.00* —
*J18* D3 8c brown red *100.00* —
*J19* D3 10c brown red *90.00* —
*J20* D3 12c brown red *90.00* —
*J21* D3 16c brown red *100.00* —
*J22* D3 20c brown red *100.00* —

### OFFICIAL STAMPS

**Official Handstamped Overprints**

"Officers purchasing stamps for government business may, if they so desire, overprint them with the letters "O.B." either in writing with black ink or by rubber stamps but in such a manner as not to obliterate the stamp that postmasters will be unable to determine whether the stamps have been previously used". C. M. Cotterman, Director of Posts, Dec. 26, 1905.

Beginning with Jan. 1, 1906, all branches of the Insular Government used postage stamps to prepay postage instead of franking them as before. Some officials used manuscript, some utilized typewriting machines, some made press-printed overprints, but by far the larger number provided themselves with rubber stamps. The majority of these read "O.B." but other forms were: "OFFICIAL BUSINESS" or "OFFICIAL MAIL" in 2 lines, with variations on many of these.

These "O.B." overprints are known on US 1899-1901 stamps; on 1903-06 stamps in red and blue; on 1906 stamps in red, blue, black, yellow and green.

"O.B." overprints were also made on the centavo and peso stamps of the Philippines, per order of May 25, 1907.

Beginning in 1926 the stamps were overprinted and issued by the Government, but some post offices continued to handstamp "O.B."

Regular Issue of 1926 Overprinted in Red OFFICIAL

**1926, Dec. 20 Unwmk. *Perf. 12***

*O1* A42 2c green & blk 2.50 1.75
*O2* A42 4c carmine & blk 2.50 1.60
*a.* Vertical pair, imperf. between 375.00
*O3* A42 18c light brn & blk 7.00 6.00
*O4* A42 20c orange & blk 6.00 2.00

Opening of the Legislative Palace.

Regular Issue of 1917-26 Overprinted O. B.

**1931 *Perf. 11***

*O5* A40 2c green 6 5
*a.* No period after "B" 10.00 5.00
*b.* No period after "O" —
*O6* A40 4c carmine 8 5
*a.* No period after "B" 10.00 5.00
*O7* A40 6c deep violet 10 8
*O8* A40 8c yellow brn 10 8
*O9* A40 10c deep blue 40 12
*O10* A40 12c red orange 25 15
*a.* No period after "B" 30.00
*O11* A40 16c lt ol grn *(Dewey)* 25 10
*a.* 16c olive bister 1.50 30
*O12* A40 20c orange yel 30 10
*a.* No period after "B" 15.00 15.00
*O13* A40 26c green 45 45
*a.* 26c blue green 1.25 1.00
*O14* A40 30c gray 40 35
*Nos. O5-O14 (10)* 2.39 1.53

Same Overprint on Nos. 383-392

**1935**

*O15* A53 2c rose 6 5
*a.* No period after "B" 10.00 5.00
*O16* A54 4c yellow green 6 5
*a.* No period after "B" 10.00 7.50
*O17* A55 6c dark brown 10 6
*a.* No period after "B" 17.50 17.50
*O18* A56 8c violet 12 12
*O19* A57 10c rose carmine 15 6
*O20* A58 12c black 20 15
*O21* A59 16c dark blue 20 15
*O22* A60 20c lt olive grn 20 15
*O23* A61 26c indigo 40 35
*O24* A62 30c orange red 45 40
*Nos. O15-O24 (10)* 1.94 1.54

Same Overprint on Nos. 411 and 418

**1937-38 *Perf. 11***

*O25* A53 2c rose 8 5
*a.* No period after "B" 6.50 3.50
*O26* A60 20c lt ol grn ('38) 1.00 75

Nos. 383-392 Overprinted in Black:

O. B.

COMMON-WEALTH O. B.

a b

**1938-40**

*O27* A53 (a) 2c rose 8 5
*a.* Hyphen omitted 17.50 15.00
*b.* No period after "B" 20.00 15.00
*O28* A54 (b) 4c yellow grn 10 8
*O29* A55 (a) 6c dark brown 15 6
*O30* A56 (b) 8c violet 15 10
*O31* A57 (b) 10c rose car 17 10
*a.* No period after "O" 25.00 25.00
*O32* A58 (b) 12c black 18 18
*O33* A59 (b) 16c dark blue 25 12
*O34* A60 (a) 20c lt ol grn ('40) 35 35
*O35* A61 (b) 26c indigo 45 45
*O36* A62 (b) 30c orange red 40 40
*Nos. O27-O36 (10)* 2.28 1.89

No. 461 Overprinted in Black O. B.

***Perf. 11x10½***

**1941, Apr. 14 Unwmk.**

*O37* A75 2c apple green 6 6

Official Stamps Handstamped in Violet VICTORY

**1944 *Perf. 11, 11x10½***

*O38* A53 2c rose (On O27) *130.00 85.00*
*O39* A75 2c ap grn (On O37) 5.00 3.00
*O40* A54 4c yellow grn (On O16) *25.00 20.00*
*O40A* A55 6c dark brown (On O29) *3,000.* —
*O41* A57 10c rose carmine (On O31) *100.00*
*O42* A60 20c lt olive grn (On O22) *3,500.*
*O43* A60 20c lt olive grn (On O26) *1,400.*

No. 497 Overprinted Like No. O37 in Black

***Perf. 11x10½***

**1946, June 19 Unwmk.**

*O44* A76 2c sepia 6 5

### OCCUPATION STAMPS

**Issued under Japanese Occupation**

Nos. 461, 438 and 439 Overprinted with Bars in Black

**1942-43 Unwmk. *Perf. 11x10½, 11***

*N1* A75 2c apple green 6 6
*a.* Pair, one without overprint —
*N2* A58 12c black ('43) 15 15
*N3* A59 16c dark blue 4.50 3.50

Nos. 435, 442, 443 and 423 Surcharged in Black

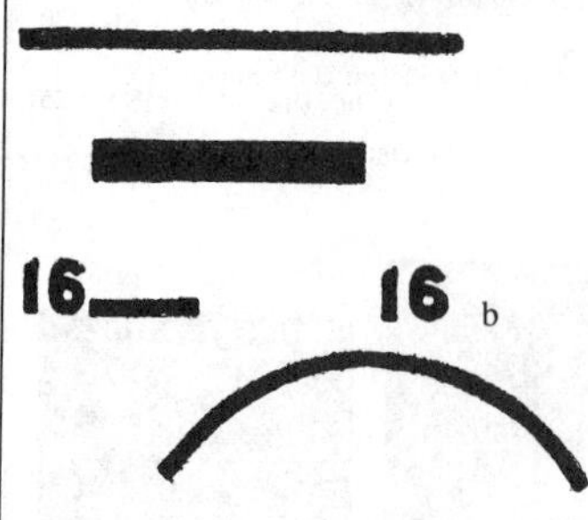


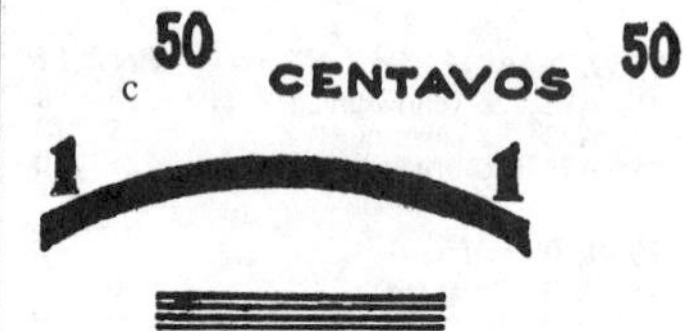

***Perf. 11***

*N4* A55 5c on 6c golden brn 10 10
*a.* Top bar shorter, thinner 20 20
*b.* 5c on 6c dark brown 20 20
*c.* As "b" and "a" 20 20
*N5* A62 16c on 30c org red ('43) 20 20
*N6* A63 50c on 1p red org & blk ('43) 60 60
*a.* Double surcharge *250.00*
*N7* A65 1p on 4p blue & blk ('43) 67.50 52.50

On Nos. N4 and N4b, the top bar measures 1½x22½mm. On Nos. N4a and N4c, the top bar measures 1x21mm and the "5" is smaller and thinner.

No. 384 Surcharged in Black

CONGRATULATIONS
FALL OF
BATAAN AND
CORREGIDOR
1942
2

**1942, May 18**

*N8* A54 2c on 4c yellow grn 2.50 2.00

Japan's capture of Bataan and Corregidor. The American-Filipino forces finally surrendered May 7, 1942.

No. 384 Surcharged in Black

ダイトーアセンソー
イッシューネンキネン
12-8-1942 5

**1942, Dec. 8**

| | | | | |
|---|---|---|---|---|
| *N9* | A54 | 5c on 4c yellow green | 45 | 30 |

1st anniv. of the "Greater East Asia War".

Nos. C59 and C62 Surcharged in Black

ヒトー ギョーセイフ
イッシューネン キネン
1-23-43
2

**1943, Jan. 23**

| | | | | |
|---|---|---|---|---|
| *N10* | AP1 | 2(c) on 8c carmine | 20 | 20 |
| *N11* | AP1 | 5c on 1p sepia | 40 | 40 |

1st anniv. of the Philippine Executive Commission.

Nipa Hut — OS1

Rice Planting — OS2

Mt. Mayon and Mt. Fuji OS3

Moro Vinta OS4

Wmk. 257- Curved Wavy Lines

**Engr., Typo. (2, 6, 25c)**

**1943-44 Wmk. 257 Perf. 13**

| | | | | |
|---|---|---|---|---|
| *N12* | OS1 | 1c deep orange | 5 | 5 |
| *N13* | OS2 | 2c bright green | 5 | 5 |
| *N14* | OS1 | 4c slate green | 5 | 5 |
| *N15* | OS3 | 5c orange brown | 5 | 5 |
| *N16* | OS2 | 6c red | 8 | 8 |
| *N17* | OS3 | 10c blue green | 6 | 6 |
| *N18* | OS4 | 12c steel blue | 75 | 75 |
| *N19* | OS4 | 16c dark brown | 6 | 6 |
| *N20* | OS1 | 20c rose violet | 85 | 85 |
| *N21* | OS3 | 21c violet | 15 | 15 |
| *N22* | OS2 | 25c pale brown | 6 | 5 |
| *N23* | OS3 | 1p deep car | 18 | 15 |
| *N24* | OS4 | 2p dull violet | 1.75 | 1.50 |
| *N25* | OS4 | 5p dark olive | 6.00 | 5.00 |
| | | *Nos. N12-N25 (14)* | 10.14 | 8.85 |

Map of Manila Bay Showing Bataan and Corregidor OS5

**1943, May 7 Photo. Unwmk.**

| | | | | |
|---|---|---|---|---|
| *N26* | OS5 | 2c carmine red | 12 | 12 |
| *N27* | OS5 | 5c bright green | 18 | 18 |

1st anniv. of the fall of Bataan and Corregidor.

No. 440 Surcharged in Black

Limbagan
1593 - 1943
12 12

**1943, June 20 Engr. Perf. 11**

| | | | | |
|---|---|---|---|---|
| *N28* | A60 | 12c on 20c lt ol grn | 25 | 20 |
| *a.* | | Double surcharge | | |

350th anniv. of the printing press in the Philippines. "Limbagan" is Tagalog for "printing press."

Rizal Monument, Filipina and Philippine Flag — OS6

**1943, Oct. 14 Photo. Perf. 12**

| | | | | |
|---|---|---|---|---|
| *N29* | OS6 | 5c light blue | 10 | 10 |
| *a.* | | Imperf. | 12 | 12 |
| *N30* | OS6 | 12c orange | 14 | 14 |
| *a.* | | Imperf. | 16 | 16 |
| *N31* | OS6 | 17c rose pink | 16 | 16 |
| *a.* | | Imperf. | 22 | 22 |

"Independence of the Philippines." Japan granted "independence" Oct. 14, 1943, when the puppet republic was founded.

The imperforate stamps were issued without gum.

Jose Rizal OS7

Rev. Jose Burgos OS8

Apolinario Mabini — OS9

**1944, Feb. 17 Litho. Perf. 12**

| | | | | |
|---|---|---|---|---|
| *N32* | OS7 | 5c blue | 22 | 22 |
| *a.* | | Imperf. | 22 | 22 |
| *N33* | OS8 | 12c carmine | 12 | 12 |
| *a.* | | Imperf. | 12 | 12 |
| *N34* | OS9 | 17c deep orange | 16 | 16 |
| *a.* | | Imperf. | 16 | 16 |

Nos. C60 and C61 Surcharged in Black

REPÚBLIKA
NG PILIPINAS
5-7-44
5

**1944, May 7 Perf. 11**

| | | | | |
|---|---|---|---|---|
| *N35* | AP1 | 5c on 20c ultra | 50 | 50 |
| *N36* | AP1 | 12c on 60c blue grn | 1.00 | 1.00 |

Fall of Bataan and Corregidor, 2nd anniv.

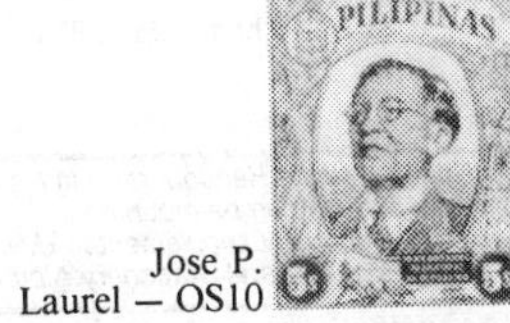

Jose P. Laurel — OS10

Without Gum

**1945, Jan. 12 Litho. Imperf.**

| | | | | |
|---|---|---|---|---|
| *N37* | OS10 | 5c dull vio brown | 7 | 6 |
| *N38* | OS10 | 7c blue green | 10 | 8 |
| *N39* | OS10 | 20c chalky blue | 15 | 12 |

1st anniv. of the puppet Philippine Republic (Oct. 14, 1944). "S" stands for "sentimos".

## OCCUPATION SEMI-POSTAL STAMPS

Woman, Farming and Cannery — OSP1

Unwmk.

**1942, Nov. 12 Litho. Perf. 12**

| | | | | |
|---|---|---|---|---|
| *NB1* | OSP1 | 2c + 1c pale vio | 15 | 15 |
| *NB2* | OSP1 | 5c + 1c brt grn | 10 | 10 |
| *NB3* | OSP1 | 16c + 2c orange | 13.00 | 10.00 |

Campaign to produce and conserve food. The surtax aided the Red Cross.

Souvenir Sheet

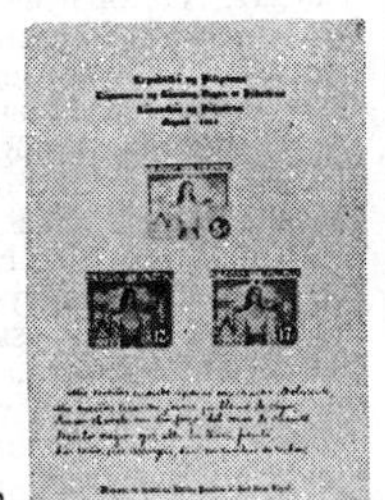

OSP2

Without Gum

**1943, Oct. 14 Imperf.**

| | | | | |
|---|---|---|---|---|
| *NB4* | OSP2 | Sheet of 3 | 35.00 | *2.00* |

"Independence of the Philippines."

No. NB4 contains Nos. N29a-N31a. Lower inscription from Rizal's "Last Farewell." Size: 127x177mm. Sold for 2.50p.

Nos. N18, N20 and N21 Surcharged in Black

BAHÂ
1943
+21

**1943, Dec. 8 Wmk. 257 Perf. 13**

| | | | | |
|---|---|---|---|---|
| *NB5* | OS4 | 12c + 21c steel blue | 15 | 15 |
| *NB6* | OS1 | 20c + 36c rose violet | 12 | 12 |
| *NB7* | OS3 | 21c + 40c violet | 15 | 15 |

The surtax was for the benefit of victims of a Luzon flood. "Baha" is Tagalog for "flood."

Souvenir Sheet

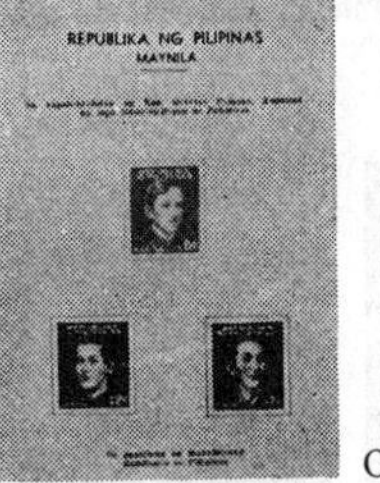

OSP3

Without Gum

Unwmk.

**1944, Feb. 9 Litho. Imperf.**

| | | | | |
|---|---|---|---|---|
| *NB8* | OSP3 | Sheet of 3 | 2.00 | *2.50* |

No. NB8 contains Nos. N32a-N34a.

Sheet sold for 1p. surtax going to a fund for the care of heroes' monuments. Size: 101x143mm.

## OCCUPATION POSTAGE DUE STAMP

No. J15 Ovptd. with Bar in Blue

**1942, Oct. 14 Unwmk. Perf. 11**

| | | | | |
|---|---|---|---|---|
| *NJ1* | D3 | 3c on 4c brown red | 27.50 | 12.00 |

On copies of No. J15, two lines were drawn in India ink with a ruling pen across "United States of America" by employees of the Short Paid Section of the Manila Post Office to make a provisional 3c postage due stamp which was used from Sept. 1, 1942, (when the letter rate was raised from 2c to 5c) until Oct. 14 when No. NJ1 went on sale.

## OCCUPATION OFFICIAL STAMPS

Nos. 461, 413, 435, 435a and 442 Overprinted or Surcharged in Black with Bars and 公用 (K.P.)

**1943-44 Unwmk. Perf. 11x10½, 11**

| | | | | |
|---|---|---|---|---|
| *NO1* | A75 | 2c apple green | 8 | 8 |
| *a.* | | Double overprint | | |
| *NO2* | A55 | 5c on 6c dk brn (#413, '44) | 20.00 | 20.00 |
| *NO3* | A55 | 5c on 6c gldn brn (No. 435a) | 15 | 15 |
| *a.* | | Narrower spacing btwn. bars | 20 | 20 |
| *b.* | | 5c on 6c dk brn (#435) | 15 | 12 |
| *c.* | | As "b", narrower spacing between bars | 20 | 20 |
| *NO4* | A62 | 16c on 30c org red | 45 | 45 |
| *a.* | | Wider spacing between bars | 45 | 45 |

On Nos. NO3 and NO3b, the bar deleting "United States of America" is 9¾-10mm above the bar deleting "Common-". On Nos. NO3a and NO3c, the spacing is 8-8½mm.

On No. NO4 the center bar is 19mm long, 3½mm below the top bar and 6mm above the Japanese characters. On No. NO4a, the center bar is 20½mm long, 9mm below the top bar and 1mm above the Japanese characters.

"K. P." (Kagamitang Pampamahalaan) is Tagalog for "Official Business."

Nos. 435 and 435a Surcharged in Black

5

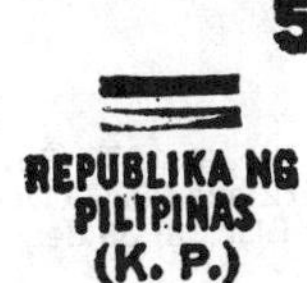


**1944 Perf. 11**

| | | | | |
|---|---|---|---|---|
| *NO5* | A55 | 5c on 6c golden brn | 10 | 10 |
| *a.* | | 5c on 6c dark brown | 10 | 10 |

Nos. O34 and C62 Overprinted in Black

a

REPUBLIKA NG PILIPINAS

(K. P.)

b

| | | | | |
|---|---|---|---|---|
| *NO6* | A60 (a) | 20c lt olive grn | 35 | 35 |
| *NO7* | AP1 (b) | 1p sepia | 1.00 | 1.00 |

## PUERTO RICO

### (Porto Rico)

LOCATION — A large island in the West Indies, east of Hispaniola.
GOVT. — Former Spanish possession
AREA — 3,435 sq. mi.
POP. — 953,243 (1899)
CAPITAL — San Juan

The island was ceded to the US by the Treaty of 1898.

Spanish issues of 1855-73 used in both Puerto Rico and Cuba are listed as Cuba Nos. 1-4, 9-14, 18-21, 32-34, 35A-37, 39-41, 43-45, 47-49, 51-53, 55-57.

Spanish issues of 1873-1898 for Puerto Rico only are listed in Vol. IV of this Catalogue.

100 Cents = 1 Dollar (1898)

**Issued under US Administration**

**Ponce Issue**

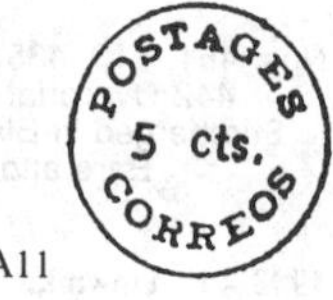


A11

| **1898** | **Unwmk.** | ***Imperf.*** | |
|---|---|---|---|
| *200* A11 5c vio, *yellowish* | | 6,500. | — |

Counterfeits exist of Nos. 200-201.

**Coamo Issue**

CORREOS
5 CTS.
COAMO

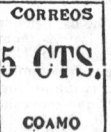

A12

| **1898** | **Unwmk.** | ***Imperf.*** | |
|---|---|---|---|
| *201* A12 5c black | | 425.00 | 425.00 |

There are ten varieties in the setting (see the Scott United States Specialized Catalogue). The stamps bear the control mark "F. Santiago" in violet.

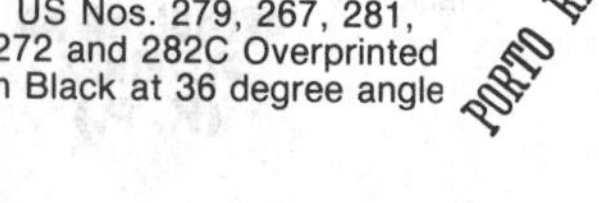


US Nos. 279, 267, 281, 272 and 282C Overprinted in Black at 36 degree angle

| **1899** | **Wmk. 191** | ***Perf. 12*** | |
|---|---|---|---|
| *210* A87 1c yellow grn | | 6.50 | 1.75 |
| *a.* Ovpt. at 25 degree angle | | 9.00 | 2.50 |
| *211* A88 2c car, type III | | 6.00 | 1.50 |
| *a.* Ovpt. at 25 degree angle | | 7.50 | 2.00 |
| *212* A91 5c blue | | 9.00 | 2.25 |
| *213* A93 8c violet brn | | 30.00 | 17.50 |
| *a.* Ovpt. at 25 degree angle | | 37.50 | 20.00 |
| *c.* "PORTO RIC" | | 125.00 | 125.00 |
| *214* A94 10c brn, type I | | 21.00 | 6.00 |
| *Nos. 210-214 (5)* | | 72.50 | 29.00 |

Misspellings of the overprint, actually broken letters (PORTO RICU, PORTU RICO, FORTO RICO), are found on 1c, 2c, 8c and 10c.

US Nos. 279 and 267 Overprinted Diagonally in Black

| **1900** | | |
|---|---|---|
| *215* A87 1c yellow green | 6.50 | 1.75 |
| *216* A88 2c carmine | 6.00 | 1.25 |
| *a.* 2c orange red | 6.50 | 1.25 |
| *b.* Invertd overprint | | 4,500. |

**POSTAGE DUE STAMPS**

US Nos. J38, J39 and J42 Overprinted in Black at 36 degree angle

| **1899** | **Wmk. 191** | ***Perf. 12*** | |
|---|---|---|---|
| *J1* D2 1c deep claret | | 22.00 | 8.00 |
| *a.* Overprint at 25 degree angle | | 27.50 | 10.00 |
| *J2* D2 2c deep claret | | 15.00 | 7.50 |
| *a.* Overprint at 25 degree angle | | 20.00 | 8.50 |
| *J3* D2 10c deep claret | | 150.00 | 55.00 |
| *a.* Overprint at 25 degree angle | | 185.00 | 65.00 |

Stamps of Puerto Rico were replaced by those of the US.

*Puerto Rico stamps can be mounted in Scott's U.S. Possessions Album.*

## UNITED NATIONS

LOCATION — Headquarters in New York City.

United Nations stamps are used on UN official mail sent from UN Headquarters, NY, or from the UN Offices in Geneva, Switzerland, and Vienna, Austria to points throughout the world. They may be used on private correspondence sent through the UN post offices, and are valid only at the individual UN post offices.

UN mail is carried by the US, Swiss and Austrian postal systems.

The UN stamps issued for use in Geneva and Vienna are listed in separate sections at the end of the NY issues. They are denominated in centimes and francs, and are valid only in Geneva or Vienna. The UN stamps issued for use in New York, denominated in cents and dollars, are valid only in New York.

Letters bearing Nos. 170-174 provide an exception as they were carried by the Canadian postal system.

See Switzerland Nos. 7O1-7O39 in Volume IV for stamps issued by the Swiss Government for official use of the UN European Office in Geneva.

The 1962 UN Temporary Executive Authority (UNTEA) overprints on stamps of Netherlands New Guinea are listed under West Irian in Volume IV.

**Catalogue values for all unused stamps in this country are for Never Hinged items.**

Peoples of the World — A1

UN Headquarters Building — A2

"Peace, Justice, Security" — A3

UN Flag — A4

UN Children's Fund — A5

World Unity — A6

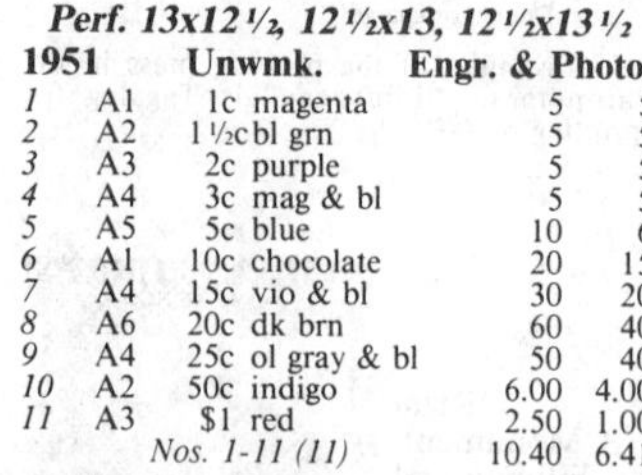

***Perf. 13x12½, 12½x13, 12½x13½***

| **1951** | **Unwmk.** | **Engr. & Photo.** | | |
|---|---|---|---|---|
| *1* | A1 | 1c magenta | 5 | 5 |
| *2* | A2 | 1½c bl grn | 5 | 5 |
| *3* | A3 | 2c purple | 5 | 5 |
| *4* | A4 | 3c mag & bl | 5 | 5 |
| *5* | A5 | 5c blue | 10 | 6 |
| *6* | A1 | 10c chocolate | 20 | 15 |
| *7* | A4 | 15c vio & bl | 30 | 20 |
| *8* | A6 | 20c dk brn | 60 | 40 |
| *9* | A4 | 25c ol gray & bl | 50 | 40 |
| *10* | A2 | 50c indigo | 6.00 | 4.00 |
| *11* | A3 | $1 red | 2.50 | 1.00 |
| | | *Nos. 1-11 (11)* | 10.40 | 6.41 |

The 2c and 5c are perf. 12½x13½. Other denominations are perf. 13x12½ or 12½x13. See Offices in Geneva Nos. 4, 14.

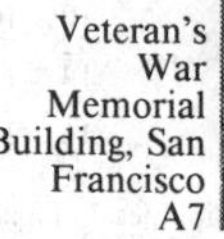

Veteran's War Memorial Building, San Francisco A7

| **1952, Oct. 24** | **Engr.** | ***Perf. 12*** | |
|---|---|---|---|
| *12* A7 5c blue | | 30 | 15 |

7th anniv. of the signing of the UN charter.

Globe and Encircled Flame A8

| **1952, Dec. 10** | ***Perf. 13½x14*** | | |
|---|---|---|---|
| *13* A8 3c dp grn | | 10 | 10 |
| *14* A8 5c blue | | 60 | 20 |

Fourth anniv. of the adoption of the Universal Declaration of Human Rights.

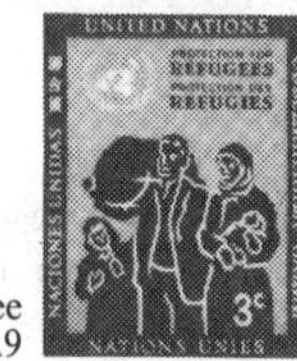

Refugee Family — A9

| **1953, Apr. 24** | ***Perf. 12½x13*** | | |
|---|---|---|---|
| *15* A9 3c dk red brn & rose brn | | 25 | 10 |
| *16* A9 5c ind & bl | | 1.00 | 50 |

Issued to publicize "Protection for Refugees."

Envelope, UN Emblem and Map — A10

| **1953, June 12** | **Unwmk.** | ***Perf. 13*** | |
|---|---|---|---|
| *17* A10 3c blk brn | | 25 | 12 |
| *18* A10 5c dk bl | | 1.25 | 60 |

Issued to honor the UPU.

*United Nations Headquarters in New York stamps can be mounted in Scott's annually supplemented U.N. Singles and Postal Stationery Album.*

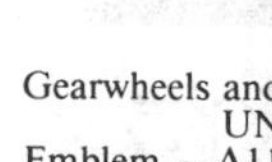

Gearwheels and UN Emblem — A11

| **1953, Oct. 24** | ***Perf. 13x12½*** | | |
|---|---|---|---|
| *19* A11 3c dk gray | | 10 | 12 |
| *20* A11 5c dk grn | | 90 | 50 |

UN activities in the field of technical assistance.

Hands Reaching Toward Flame — A12

Ear of Wheat — A13

| **1953, Dec. 10** | ***Perf. 12½x13*** | | |
|---|---|---|---|
| *21* A12 3c brt bl | | 25 | 12 |
| *22* A12 5c rose red | | 1.75 | 50 |

Human Rights Day.

| **1954, Feb. 11** | | | |
|---|---|---|---|
| *23* A13 3c dk grn & yel | | 50 | 10 |
| *24* A13 8c ind & yel | | 1.00 | 60 |

Issued to honor the FAO.

UN Emblem and Anvil — A14

Design: 8c, Same inscribed "OIT."

| **1954, May 10** | ***Perf. 12½x13*** | | |
|---|---|---|---|
| *25* A14 3c brown | | 15 | 15 |
| *26* A14 8c magenta | | 3.50 | 75 |

Honoring the International Labor Organization.

UN European Office, Geneva A15

| **1954, Oct. 25** | ***Perf. 14*** | | |
|---|---|---|---|
| *27* A15 3c dk bl vio | | 3.75 | 1.25 |
| *28* A15 8c red | | 20 | 25 |

UN Day.

Mother and Child — A16

| **1954, Dec. 10** | ***Perf. 14*** | | |
|---|---|---|---|
| *29* A16 3c red org | | 9.50 | 2.75 |
| *30* A16 8c ol grn | | 35 | 25 |

Human Rights Day.

Symbol of Flight
A17

Design: 8c, inscribed "OACI."

**1955, Feb. 9** *Perf. 13½x14*

*31* A17 3c blue 3.00 50
*32* A17 8c rose car 1.00 1.25

International Civil Aviation Organization.

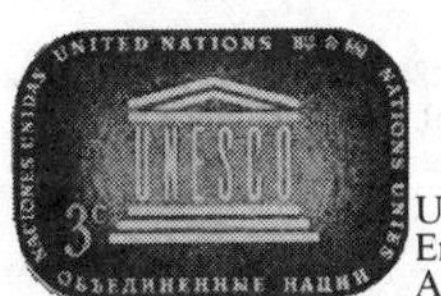


UNESCO Emblem
A18

**1955, May 11** *Perf. 13½x14*

*33* A18 3c lil rose 1.30 50
*34* A18 8c lt bl 20 25

Honoring the UN Educational, Scientific and Cultural Organization.

UN Charter
A19

Inscriptions: 4c, Spanish. 8c, French.

**1955, Oct. 24** *Perf. 13½x14*

*35* A19 3c dp plum 3.00 75
*36* A19 4c dl grn 20 10
*37* A19 8c bluish blk 30 15

10th anniv. of the UN.

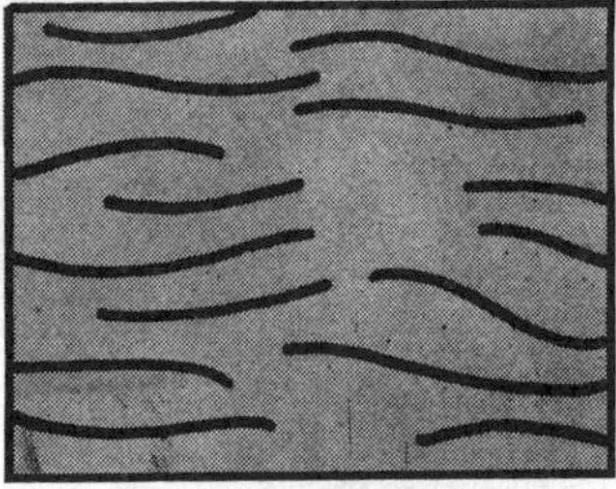

Wmk. 309- Wavy Lines

Souvenir Sheet

**Wmk. 309** *Imperf.*

*38* A19 Sheet of three 180.00 45.00
*a* 3c dp plum 10.00 5.00
*b* 4c dl grn 10.00 5.00
*c* 8c bluish blk 10.00 5.00

No. 38 has marginal inscriptions in deep plum. Size: 108x83mm.

Two printings were made of No. 38. The first may be distinguished by the broken line of background shading on the 8c. It leaves a small white spot below the left leg of the "n" of "Unies." For the second printing, the broken line was retouched, eliminating the white spot.

Hand Holding Torch — A20

**1955, Dec. 9 Unwmk.** *Perf. 14x13½*

*39* A20 3c ultra 10 10
*40* A20 8c green 1.00 50

Human Rights Day, Dec. 10.

Symbols of Telecommunication — A21

Design: 8c, inscribed "UIT."

**1956, Feb. 17** *Perf. 14*

*41* A21 3c turq bl 30 15
*42* A21 8c dp car 80 45

Honoring the International Telecommunication Union.

Globe and Caduceus — A22

Design: 8c, inscribed "OMS."

**1956, Apr. 6** *Perf. 14*

*43* A22 3c brt grnsh bl 10 10
*44* A22 8c gldn brn 1.00 50

Honoring the World Health Organization.

General Assembly
A23

Design: 8c, French inscription.

**1956, Oct. 24** *Perf. 14*

*45* A23 3c dk bl 5 5
*46* A23 8c gray ol 12 10

UN Day, Oct. 24.

Flame and Globe — A24

**1956, Dec. 10** *Perf. 14*

*47* A24 3c plum 5 5
*48* A24 8c dk bl 12 10

Human Rights Day.

Weather Balloon — A25

Design: 8c, agency name in French.

**1957, Jan. 28** *Perf. 14*

*49* A25 3c vio bl 5 5
*50* A25 8c dk car rose 12 10

Honoring the World Meteorological Organization.

Badge of UN Emergency Force — A26

UN Emblem and Globe — A27

**1957, Apr. 8** *Perf. 14x12½*

*51* A26 3c lt bl 5 5
*52* A26 8c rose car 12 10

UN Emergency Force.

Re-engraved

**1957, April-May**

*53* A26 3c blue 6 6
*54* A26 8c rose car 15 12

On Nos. 53-54 the background within and around the circles is shaded lightly, giving a halo effect. The letters are more distinct with a line around each letter.

**1957, Oct. 24 Engr.** *Perf. 12½x13*

*55* A27 3c org brn 5 5
*56* A27 8c dk bl grn 12 10

Honoring the Security Council. French inscription on No. 56.

Flaming Torch
A28

**1957, Dec. 10** *Perf. 14*

*57* A28 3c red brn 5 5
*58* A28 8c black 12 10

Human Rights Day.

Atom and UN Emblem
A29

Central Hall, Westminster
A30

**1958, Feb. 10** *Perf. 12*

*59* A29 3c olive 5 5
*60* A29 8c blue 12 10

Honoring the International Atomic Energy Agency. French inscription on No. 60.

**1958, Apr. 14** *Perf. 12*

*61* A30 3c vio bl 5 5
*62* A30 8c rose cl 12 10

Central Hall, Westminster, London, was the site of the first session of the UN General Assembly 1946.

French inscription on No. 62.

UN Seal
A31

Gearwheels
A32

**1958** *Perf. 13½x14*
63 A31 4c red org 6 6
*Perf. 13x14*
64 A31 8c brt bl 12 10

Issue dates: 4c, Oct. 24; 8c, June 2.

**1958, Oct. 24** **Engr.** *Perf. 12*
65 A32 4c dk bl grn 6 6
66 A32 8c vermilion 12 10

Honoring the Economic and Social Council. French inscription on No. 66.

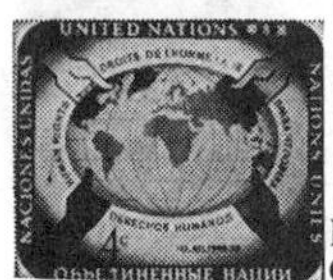

Hands Upholding Globe — A33

**1958, Dec. 10** **Unwmk.**
67 A33 4c yel grn 6 6
68 A33 8c red brn 12 10

Human Rights Day and the 10th anniv. of the signing of the Universal Declaration of Human Rights.

New York City Building, Flushing Meadows A34

**1959, Mar. 30** *Perf. 12*
69 A34 4c lt lil rose 6 6
70 A34 8c aqua 12 10

Site of many General Assembly meetings, 1946-50. French inscription on No. 70.

UN Emblems and Symbols of Agriculture, Industry and Trade — A35

Figure Adapted from Rodin's "Age of Bronze" — A36

**1959, May 18** *Perf. 12*
71 A35 4c blue 8 5
72 A35 8c red org 16 12

Honoring the UN Economic Commission for Europe.

**1959, Oct. 23** **Engr.** *Perf. 12*
73 A36 4c brt red 6 6
74 A36 8c dk ol grn 12 10

Honor the Trusteeship Council. French inscription on No. 74.

World Refugee Year Emblem — A37

**1959, Dec. 10** **Unwmk.**
75 A37 4c ol & red 8 6
76 A37 8c ol & brt grnsh bl 16 12

World Refugee Year, July 1, 1959-June 30, 1960. French inscription on No. 76.

Chaillot Palace, Paris — A38

**1960, Feb. 29** *Perf. 14*
77 A38 4c rose lil & bl 6 6
78 A38 8c dl grn & brn 12 10

Chaillot Palace in Paris was the site of General Assembly meetings in 1948 and 1951. French inscription on No. 78.

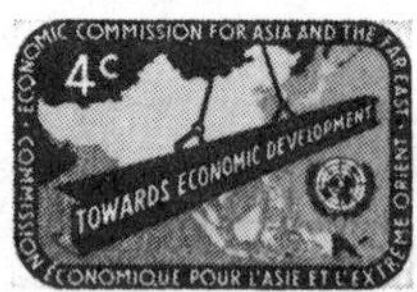

Map of Far East and Steel Beam A39

**1960, Apr. 11** **Photo.** *Perf. 13x13½*
79 A39 4c dp cl, bl grn & dl yel 6 6
80 A39 8c ol grn, bl & rose 12 10

Honoring the Economic Commission for Asia and the Far East (ECAFE). French inscription on No. 80.

Tree, FAO and UN Emblems — A40

**1960, Aug. 29** *Perf. 13½*
81 A40 4c grn, dk bl & org 6 6
*a* Imperf., pair —
82 A40 8c yel grn, blk & org 12 10

5th World Forestry Congress, Seattle, Wash., Aug. 29-Sept. 10. French inscription on No. 82.

UN Headquarters and Preamble to UN Charter — A41

**1960, Oct. 24** **Engr.** *Perf. 11*
83 A41 4c blue 6 6
84 A41 8c gray 12 10

**Souvenir Sheet**
***Imperf***
85 A41 Sheet of two 1.35 1.35
*a* 4c bl 25 15
*b* 8c gray 25 15

15th anniv. of the UN. French inscription on No. 84.
No. 85 has gray marginal inscription. Size: 92x71mm.

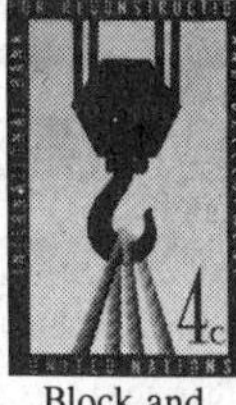

Block and Tackle — A42

Scales of Justice — A43

**1960, Dec. 9** **Photo.** *Perf. 13½x13*
86 A42 4c multi 6 6
87 A42 8c multi 12 10
*a* Imperf., pair —

Honoring the International Bank for Reconstruction and Development. French inscription on No. 87.
No. 86 exists imperf.

**1961, Feb. 13** **Unwmk.**
88 A43 4c yel, org brn & blk 6 6
89 A43 8c yel, grn & blk 12 10

Honoring the International Court of Justice. The design was taken from Raphael's "Stanze." French inscription on No. 89.
Nos. 88-89 exist imperf.

Seal of International Monetary Fund — A44

**1961, Apr. 17** *Perf. 13x13½*
90 A44 4c brt bluish grn 6 6
91 A44 7c fawn & yel 12 10

Honoring the International Monetary Fund. French inscription on No. 91.
No. 90 exists imperf.

Abstract Group of Flags — A45

**1961, June 5** *Perf. 11½*
92 A45 30c multi 35 15

See Offices in Geneva No. 10.

Cogwheel and Map of Latin America — A46

**1961, Sept. 18** *Perf. 13½*
93 A46 4c bl, red & cit 10 10
94 A46 11c grn, lil & org ver 30 20

Honoring the Economic Commission for Latin America. Spanish inscription on No. 94.

Africa House, Addis Ababa, and Map — A47

**1961, Oct. 24** **Photo.** *Perf. 11½*
95 A47 4c ultra, org, yel & brn 6 5
96 A47 11c emer, org, yel & brn 16 12

Honoring the Economic Commission for Africa. English inscription on No. 96.

Mother Bird Feeding Young and UNICEF Seal — A48

**1961, Dec. 4** **Unwmk.** *Perf. 11½*
97 A48 3c brn, gold, org & yel 6 5
98 A48 4c brn, gold, bl & emer 8 6
99 A48 13c dp grn, gold, pur & pink 26 20

15th anniv. of the UN Children's Fund. Spanish inscription on No. 97. French inscription on No. 99.

Family and Symbolic Buildings A49

**1962, Feb. 28** **Photo.** *Perf. 14½x14*
**Central design multicolored**
100 A49 4c brt bl 8 6
*a* Black omitted —
*b* Yellow omitted —
*c* Brown omitted —
101 A49 7c org brn 14 10
*a* Red omitted —

UN program for housing and urban development. French inscription, "Services Collectifs," on No. 101.

"The World Against Malaria" — A50

**1962, Mar. 30** *Perf. 14x14½*
**Word frame in gray**
102 A50 4c org, yel, grn & blk 8 6
103 A50 11c grn, yel, brn & ind 22 12

Honoring the WHO and to call attention to the international campaign to eradicate malaria from the world.

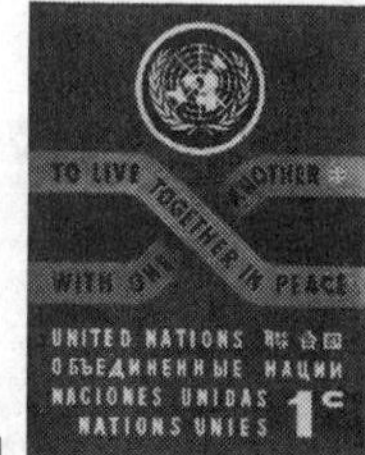

"Peace" — A51

UN Flag — A52

Hands Combining "UN" and Globe A53

UN Emblem over Globe — A54

**Photogravure; Engraved (5c)**
**1962, May 25** *Perf. 14x14½*
104 A51 1c ver, bl, blk & gray 5 5
105 A52 3c lt grn, Prus bl, yel & gray 6 5
*Perf. 12*
**Size: 36½x23½mm.**
106 A53 5c dk car rose 15 10

***Perf. 12½***

*107* A54 11c dk & lt bl & gold 18 18

See No. 167 and UN Offices in Geneva Nos. 2 and 6.

Flag at Half-mast and UN Headquarters A55

World Map Showing Congo A56

**1962, Sept. 17 Unwmk. *Perf. 11½***

| | | | |
|---|---|---|---|
| *108* A55 | 5c blk, lt bl & bl | 15 | 10 |
| *109* A55 | 15c blk, gray ol & bl | 55 | 20 |

1st anniv. of the death of Dag Hammarskjold, Secretary General of the UN 1953-61, in memory of those who died in the service of the UN.

**1962, Oct. 24**

| | | | |
|---|---|---|---|
| *110* A56 | 4c ol, org, blk & yel | 15 | 10 |
| *111* A56 | 11c bl grn, org, blk & yel | 50 | 20 |

UN Operation in the Congo. French inscription on No. 111.

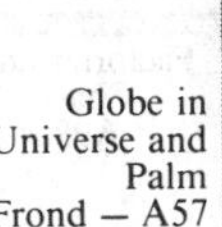

Globe in Universe and Palm Frond — A57

**1962, Dec. 3 Engr. *Perf. 14x13½***

| | | | |
|---|---|---|---|
| *112* A57 | 4c vio bl | 6 | 5 |
| *113* A57 | 11c rose cl | 16 | 12 |

Honoring the Committee on Peaceful Uses of Outer Space. English inscription on No. 112.

Development Decade Emblem — A58

***Perf. 11½***

**1963, Feb. 4 Unwmk. Photo.**

| | | | |
|---|---|---|---|
| *114* A58 | 5c pale grn, mar, dk bl & Prus bl | 8 | 6 |
| *115* A58 | 11c yel, mar, dk bl & Prus bl | 18 | 10 |

UN Development Decade and the UN Conference on the Application of Science and Technology for the Benefit of the Less Developed Areas, Geneva, Feb. 4-20. French inscription on No. 115.

Stalks of Wheat — A59

**1963, Mar. 22 *Perf. 11½***

| | | | |
|---|---|---|---|
| *116* A59 | 5c ver, grn & yel | 8 | 6 |
| *117* A59 | 11c ver, dp cl & yel | 18 | 10 |

"Freedom from Hunger" campaign of the FAO. French inscription on No. 117.

Bridge over Map of New Guinea — A60

**1963, Oct. 1 Unwmk. *Perf. 11½***

| | | | |
|---|---|---|---|
| *118* A60 | 25c bl, grn & gray | 38 | 20 |

1st anniv. of the UN Temporary Executive Authority (UNTEA) in West New Guinea (West Irian).

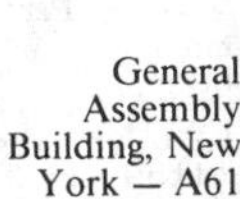

General Assembly Building, New York — A61

**1963, Nov. 4 Photo. *Perf. 13***

| | | | |
|---|---|---|---|
| *119* A61 | 5c vio bl & multi | 8 | 6 |
| *120* A61 | 11c grn & multi | 18 | 10 |

Since Oct. 1955 all sessions of the General Assembly have been held in the General Assembly Hall, UN Headquarters, N.Y. French inscription on No. 120.

UN Postal Stationery is listed in Scott's Specialized United States Catalogue.

Flame — A62

**1963, Dec. 10 *Perf. 13***

| | | | |
|---|---|---|---|
| *121* A62 | 5c grn, gold, red & yel | 8 | 6 |
| *122* A62 | 11c car, gold, bl & yel | 18 | 10 |

15th anniv. of the signing of the Universal Declaration of Human Rights. No. 122 inscribed "15e ANNIVERSAIRE."

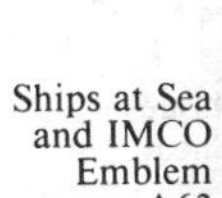

Ships at Sea and IMCO Emblem A63

Design: 11c, inscribed "OMCI."

**1964, Jan. 13 *Perf. 11½***

| | | | |
|---|---|---|---|
| *123* A63 | 5c bl, ol, ocher & yel | 8 | 6 |
| *124* A63 | 11c bl, dk grn, emer & yel | 18 | 10 |

Honoring the Intergovernmental Maritime Consultative Organization.

Map of the World — A64

UN Emblem A65

Three Men United Before Globe A66

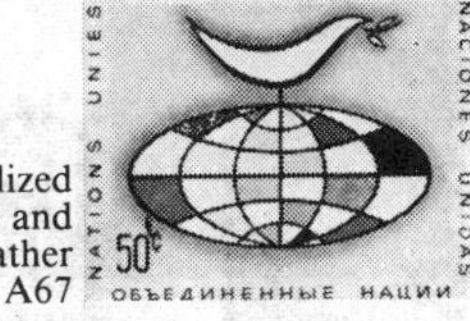

Stylized Globe and Weather Vane — A67

**1964-71 Unwmk. Photo. *Perf. 14***

| | | | |
|---|---|---|---|
| *125* A64 | 2c lt & dk bl, org & yel grn | 5 | 5 |
| *a* | Perf. 13x13½ ('71) | 6 | 6 |

***Perf. 11½***

| | | | |
|---|---|---|---|
| *126* A65 | 7c dk bl, org brn & blk | 10 | 8 |
| *127* A66 | 10c bl grn, ol grn & blk | 15 | 10 |
| *128* A67 | 50c multi | 75 | 40 |

Dates of issue: 2c, 7c, 10c, May 29; 50c, Mar. 6, 1964. See UN Offices in Geneva Nos. 3, 12.

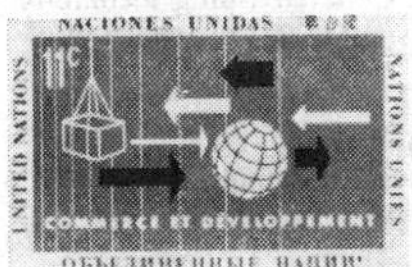

Arrows Showing Global Flow of Trade A68

**1964, June 15 *Perf. 13***

| | | | |
|---|---|---|---|
| *129* A68 | 5c blk, red & yel | 8 | 6 |
| *130* A68 | 11c blk, ol & yel | 18 | 10 |

UN Conference on Trade and Development, Geneva, Mar. 23-June 15. English inscription on No. 129.

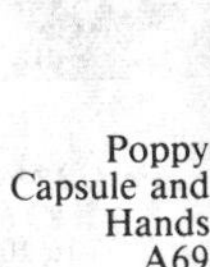

Poppy Capsule and Hands A69

**1964, Sept. 21 Engr. *Perf. 12***

| | | | |
|---|---|---|---|
| *131* A69 | 5c rose red & blk | 8 | 6 |
| *132* A69 | 11c emer & blk | 18 | 10 |

International efforts and achievements in the control of narcotics. French inscription on No. 132.

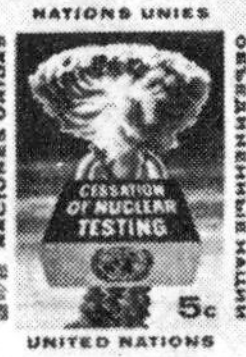

Padlocked Atomic Blast — A70

"Education for Progress" — A71

**Photogravure and Engraved**

**1964, Oct. 23 *Perf. 11x11½***

| | | | |
|---|---|---|---|
| *133* A70 | 5c dk red & dk brn | 8 | 5 |

Signing of the nuclear test ban treaty pledging an end to nuclear explosions in the atmosphere, outer space and under water.

**1964, Dec. 7 Photo. *Perf. 12½***

| | | | |
|---|---|---|---|
| *134* A71 | 4c multi | 6 | 5 |
| *135* A71 | 5c multi | 8 | 5 |
| *136* A71 | 11c multi | 16 | 10 |

UNESCO world campaign for universal literacy and for free compulsory primary education. French inscription on No. 136.

Progress Chart of Special Fund, Key and Globe A72

Leaves and View of Cyprus A73

***Perf. 13½x13***

**1965, Jan. 25 Unwmk.**

| | | | |
|---|---|---|---|
| *137* A72 | 5c multi | 8 | 5 |
| *138* A72 | 11c multi | 16 | 10 |
| *a* | Black omitted (UN emblem on key) | — | |

Special Fund Program, which aims to speed economic growth and social advancement in low-income countries. French inscription on No. 138.

**1965, Mar. 4 Photo. *Perf. 11½***

| | | | |
|---|---|---|---|
| *139* A73 | 5c org, ol & blk | 8 | 5 |
| *140* A73 | 11c yel grn, bl grn & blk | 16 | 10 |

UN Peace-keeping Force on Cyprus. French inscription on No. 140.

"From Semaphore to Satellite" A74

**1965, May 17 Unwmk. *Perf. 11½***

| | | | |
|---|---|---|---|
| *141* A74 | 5c multi | 8 | 5 |
| *142* A74 | 11c multi | 16 | 10 |

Centenary of the International Telecommunication Union. French inscription on No. 142.

ICY Emblem — A75

**1965, June 26 Engr. *Perf. 14x13½***

| | | | |
|---|---|---|---|
| *143* A75 | 5c dk bl | 8 | 5 |
| *144* A75 | 15c lil rose | 24 | 10 |

**Souvenir Sheet**

| | | | |
|---|---|---|---|
| *145* A75 | Sheet of two | 50 | 40 |

20th anniv. of the UN and International Cooperation Year. French inscription on No. 144.

No. 145 contains one each of Nos. 143-144, with dark blue and ocher marginal inscription and ocher edging. Size: 92x70mm.

"Peace" — A76

Opening Words, UN Charter — A77

UN Headquarters and Emblem — A78

UN Emblem — A79

UN Emblem — A80

**1965-66 Photo. *Perf. 13½***

*146* A76 1c ver, bl, blk & gray 5 5

***Perf. 14***

*147* A77 15c ol bis, dl yel, blk & dp cl 24 12

***Perf. 12***

*148* A78 20c dk bl, bl, red & yel 30 15
*a* Yellow omitted —

**Lithographed and Embossed**

***Perf. 14***

*149* A79 25c lt & dk bl 40 20

**Photo.**

***Perf. 11½***

*150* A80 $1 saph & aqua 1.50 75
*Nos. 146-150 (5)* 2.49 1.27

Issue dates: 1c, 25c, Sept. 20, 1965. 15c, 20c, Oct. 25, 1965. $1, Mar. 25, 1966.
See UN Offices in Geneva Nos. 5, 9 and 11.

Fields and People A81

Globe and Flags of UN Members A82

**1965, Nov. 29 Photo. *Perf. 12***

*151* A81 4c multi 6 5
*152* A81 5c multi 8 5
*153* A81 11c multi 16 10

Emphasize the importance of the world's population growth and its problems and to call attention to population trends and developments. French inscription on No. 153.

**1966, Jan. 31 Photo. *Perf. 11½***

*154* A82 5c multi 8 5
*155* A82 15c multi 22 12

World Federation of UN Associations. French inscription on No. 155.

WHO Headquarters, Geneva — A83

**1966, May 26 Photo. *Perf. 12½x12***
**Granite Paper**

*156* A83 5c multi 8 5
*157* A83 11c multi 16 10

WHO Headquarters, Geneva. French inscription on No. 157.

Coffee — A84

**1966, Sept. 19 *Perf. 13½x13***

*158* A84 5c multi 8 5
*159* A84 11c multi 16 10

International Coffee Agreement of 1962. Spanish inscription on No. 159.

UN Observer A85

Children of Various Races A86

**1966, Oct. 24 Photo. *Perf. 11½***
**Granite Paper**

*160* A85 15c multi 22 12

Peace Keeping UN Observers.

**1966, Nov. 28 Litho. *Perf. 13x13½***

Designs: 5c, Children riding locomotive and tender. 11c, Children in open railroad car playing medical team (French inscription).

*161* A86 4c pink & multi 6 5
*162* A86 5c pale grn & multi 8 6
*a* Yellow omitted — —
*163* A86 11c ultra & multi 16 10
*a* Imperf., pair —
*b* Dark blue omitted —

20th anniv. of the UN Children's Fund (UNICEF).

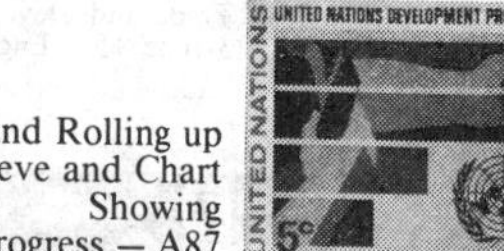

Hand Rolling up Sleeve and Chart Showing Progress — A87

**1967, Jan. 23 Photo. *Perf. 12½***

*164* A87 5c multi 8 6
*165* A87 11c multi 16 10

UN Development Program. French inscription on No. 165.

Type of 1962 and

UN Headquarters, New York and World Map — A88

**1967 Photo. *Perf. 11½***

*166* A88 1½c ultra, blk, org & ocher 5 5

**Size: 33x23mm**

*167* A53 5c red brn, brn & org yel 8 8

Issue dates: 1½c, Mar. 17; 5c, Jan. 23. See UN Offices in Geneva No. 1.

Fireworks — A89

**1967, Mar. 17 *Perf. 14x14½***

*168* A89 5c dk bl & multi 8 6
*169* A89 11c brn lake & multi 16 10

Honoring all nations which gained independence since 1945. French inscription on No. 169.

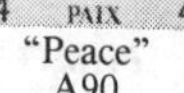

"Peace" A90

UN Pavilion, EXPO '67 A91

Designs: 5c, Justice. 10c, Fraternity. 15c, Truth.

**Litho. & Engr.; Litho. (8c)**

**1967, Apr. 28 *Perf. 11***

*170* A90 4c red & red brn 7 7
*171* A90 5c bl & red brn 9 9
*172* A91 8c multi 15 15
*173* A90 10c grn & red brn 18 18
*174* A90 15c dk brn & red brn 28 28
*Nos. 170-174 (5)* 77 77

Montreal World's Fair, EXPO '67, Apr. 28-Oct. 27. Under special agreement with the Canadian Government Nos. 170-174 were valid for postage only on mail posted at the UN pavilion during the fair. The denominations are expressed in Canadian currency.

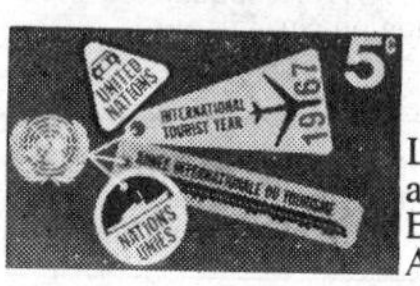

Luggage Tags and UN Emblem A92

**Unwmk.**

**1967, June 19 Litho. *Perf. 14***

*175* A92 5c multi 8 5
*176* A92 15c multi 22 12

International Tourist Year, 1967.

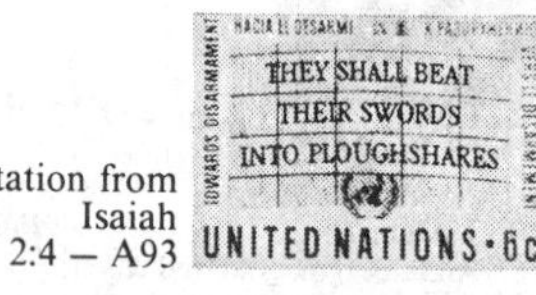

Quotation from Isaiah 2:4 — A93

**1967, Oct. 24 Photo.**

*177* A93 6c multi 9 5
*178* A93 13c multi 18 12

UN General Assembly's resolutions on general and complete disarmament and for suspension of nuclear and thermonuclear tests. French inscription on No. 178.

**Art at UN Issue**
**Miniature Sheet**

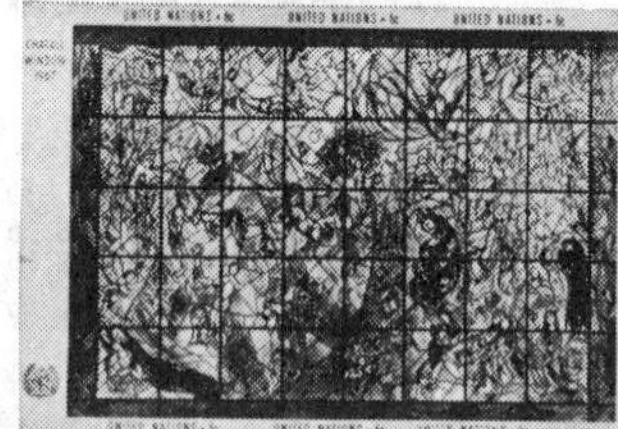
Memorial Window, by Marc Chagall — A94

"The Kiss of Peace" by Marc Chagall — A95

**1967, Nov. 17 Litho. *Rouletted 9***

*179* A94 Sheet of six 55 30
*a* 6c multi, 41x46mm 9 5
*b* 6c multi, 24x46mm 9 5
*c* 6c multi, 41x33½mm 9 5
*d* 6c multi, 36x33½mm 9 5
*e* 6c multi, 29x33½mm 9 5
*f* 6c multi, 41½x47mm 9 5

***Perf. 12½x13½***

*180* A95 6c multi 9 5

No. 179 is divisible into six 6c stamps, each rouletted on 3 sides, imperf. on fourth side. Size: 124x80mm. On Nos. 179a-179c, "United Nations . 6c" appears at top; on Nos. 179d-179f, at bottom. No. 179f includes name "Marc Chagall."

Globe and Major UN Organs — A96

**1968, Jan. 16 Photo. *Perf. 11½***

*181* A96 6c multi 9 5
*182* A96 13c multi 18 12

Honoring the UN Secretariat. French inscription on No. 182.

Statue by Henrik Starcke A97

Factories and Chart A98

**Art at UN Issue**

**1968, Mar. 1 Photo. *Perf. 11½***

*183* A97 6c bl & multi 9 6
*184* A97 75c rose lake & multi 1.50 75

The 6c is part of the "Art at UN" series. The 75c belongs to the definitive series. The 6c exists imperforate.

The Starcke statue represents mankind's search for freedom and happiness.

See UN Offices in Geneva No. 13.

**1968, Apr. 18 Litho. *Perf. 12***

Design: 13c, inscribed "ONUDI."

*185* A98 6c multi 9 5
*186* A98 13c multi 18 12

UN Industrial Development Organization. French inscription on No. 186.

UN Headquarters — A99

**1968, May 31 Litho. *Perf. 13½***

*187* A99 6c multi 9 6

Radarscope and Globes A100

**1968, Sept. 19 Photo. *Perf. 13x13½***

*188* A100 6c grn & multi 9 6
*189* A100 20c lil & multi 30 20

World Weather Watch, a new weather system directed by the World Meterological Organization. French inscription on No. 189.

Human Rights Flame A101

Books and UN Emblem A102

**Photogravure; Foil Embossed**

**1968, Nov. 22** ***Perf. 12½***

*190* A101 6c brt bl, dp ultra & gold 9 6
*191* A101 13c rose red, dk red & gold 20 12

International Human Rights Year. French inscription on No. 191.

**1969, Feb. 10 Litho. *Perf. 13½***

Design: 13c, French inscription in center, denomination panel at bottom.

*192* A102 6c yel grn & multi 9 6
*193* A102 13c bluish lil & multi 18 12

UN Institute for Training and Research (UNITAR).

UN Building, Santiago, Chile A103

**1969, Mar. 14 Litho. *Perf. 14***

*194* A103 6c lt bl, vio bl & lt grn 9 6
*195* A103 15c pink, cr & red brn 22 15

The UN Building in Santiago, Chile is the seat of the UN Economic Commission for Latin America and of the Latin American Institute for Economic and Social Planning. Spanish inscription on No. 195.

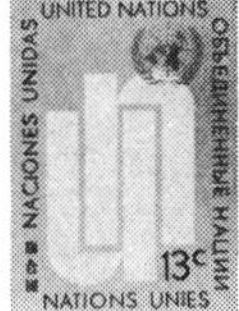
"UN" and UN Emblem A104

UN Emblem and Scales of Justice A105

**1969, Mar. 14 Photo. *Perf. 13½***

*196* A104 13c brt bl, blk & gold 18 12

See UN Offices in Geneva No. 7.

**1969, Apr. 21 Photo. *Perf. 11½***
**Granite Paper**

*197* A105 6c brt grn, ultra & gold 9 6
*198* A105 13c crim, lil & gold 18 12

20th anniv. session of the UN International Law Commission. French inscription on No. 198.

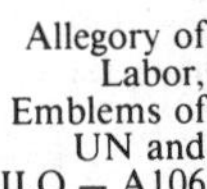

Allegory of Labor, Emblems of UN and ILO — A106

**1969, June 5 Photo. *Perf. 13***

*199* A106 6c bl, dp bl, yel & gold 9 6
*200* A106 20c org ver, mag, yel & gold 30 20

"Labor and Development" and the 50th anniv. of the ILO. French inscription on No. 200.

**Art at UN Issue**

Ostrich, Tunisian Mosaic, 3rd Century — A107

Design: 13c, Pheasant; French inscription.

**1969, Nov. 21 Photo. *Perf. 14***

*201* A107 6c bl & multi 9 6
*202* A107 13c red & multi 18 12

**Art at UN Issue**

Peace Bell, Gift of Japanese A108

**1970, Mar. 13 Photo. *Perf. 13½x13***

*203* A108 6c vio bl & multi 9 6
*204* A108 25c cl & multi 38 25

French inscription on No. 204.

Mekong River, Power Lines and Map of Delta — A109

**1970, Mar. 13 *Perf. 14***

*205* A109 6c dk bl & multi 9 6
*206* A109 13c dp plum & multi 18 12

Lower Mekong Basin, Viet Nam, Development project under UN auspices. French inscription on No. 206.

"Fight Cancer" — A110

**1970, May 22 Litho. *Perf. 14***

*207* A110 6c bl & blk 9 6
*208* A110 13c ol & blk 18 12

Fight against cancer in connection with the 10th Intl. Cancer Congress of the International Union Against Cancer, Houston, Texas, May 22-29. French inscription on No. 208.

UN Emblem and Olive Branch A111

UN Emblem A112

**1970, June 26 Photo. *Perf. 11½***

*209* A111 6c red, gold, dk & lt bl 9 6
*210* A111 13c dk bl, gold, grn & red 18 12

***Perf. 12½***

*211* A112 25c dk bl, gold & lt bl 38 25

**Souvenir Sheet**
***Imperf***

| | | | |
|---|---|---|---|
| *212* | Sheet of 3 | 65 | 45 |
| *a* | A111 6c multi | 9 | 6 |
| *b* | A111 13c multi | 18 | 12 |
| *c* | A112 25c multi | 38 | 25 |

25th anniv. of the UN. No. 212 has gold border and violet blue marginal inscription. Size: 94½x78mm. French inscription on Nos. 210 and 212b.

Scales, Olive Branch, Progress Symbol A113

Sea Bed, Fish, Underwater Research A114

**1970, Nov. 20 Photo. *Perf. 13½***

*213* A113 6c gold & multi 9 6
*214* A113 13c sil & multi 18 12

Issued to publicize "Peace, Justice and Progress" in connection with the 25th anniv. of the UN. French inscription on No. 214.

**Photogravure and Engraved**

**1971, Jan. 25 *Perf. 13***

*215* A114 6c bl & multi 9 6

Peaceful uses of the sea bed. See Offices in Geneva No. 15.

Refugees, Sculpture by Kaare K. Nygaard — A115

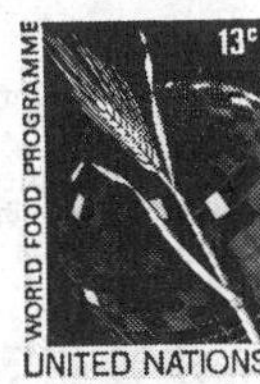
Wheat and Globe — A116

**1971, Mar. 12 Litho. *Perf. 13x12½***

*216* A115 6c brn, ocher & blk 9 6
*217* A115 13c ultra, grnsh bl & blk 18 12

International support for refugees. See Offices in Geneva No. 16.

**1971, Apr. 13 Photo. *Perf. 14***

*218* A116 13c brn red, gold & grn 18 12

Publicizing the UN World Food Program. See Offices in Geneva No. 17.

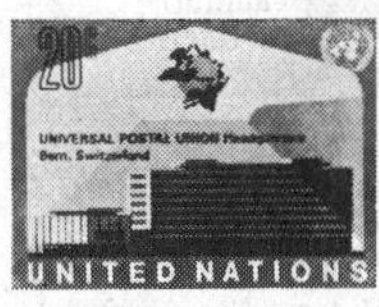
UPU Headquarters, Bern — A117

**1971, May 28 Photo. *Perf. 11½***

*219* A117 20c brn org & multi 30 20

Opening of new UPU Headquarters, Bern. See Offices in Geneva No. 18.

"Eliminate Racial Discrimination" A118

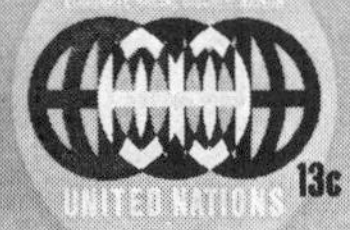
A119

**1971, Sept. 21 Photo. *Perf. 13½***

*220* A118 8c yel grn & multi 12 8
*221* A119 13c bl & multi 18 12

International Year Against Racial Discrimination. See Offices in Geneva Nos. 19-20.

UN Headquarters, New York — A120

UN Emblem and Symbolic Flags A121

**1971, Oct. 22 *Perf. 13½; 13 (60c)***

*222* A120 8c vio bl & multi 12 8
*223* A121 60c ultra & multi 90 60

Maia by Pablo Picasso — A122

**1971, Nov. 19 Photo. *Perf. 11½***

*224* A122 8c ol & multi 12 8
*225* A122 21c ultra & multi 32 20

UN International School. See Offices in Geneva No. 21.

Letter Changing Hands A123

**1972, Jan. 5 Litho. *Perf. 14***

*226* A123 95c bl & multi 1.90 1.50

"No More Nuclear Weapons" A124

**1972, Feb. 14 Photo. *Perf. 13½x14***

*227* A124 8c dl rose, blk, bl & gray 12 8

To promote non-proliferation of nuclear weapons. See Offices in Geneva No. 23.

Proportions of Man (c. 1509), by Leonardo da Vinci A125

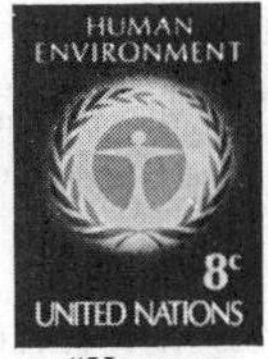
"Human Environment" A126

**Lithographed and Engraved**

**1972, Apr. 7** ***Perf. 13x13½***
*228* A125 15c black & multi 22 15

World Health Day, Apr. 7. See Offices in Geneva No. 24.

**Lithographed and Embossed**

**1972, June 5** ***Perf. 12½x14***
*229* A126 8c multi 12 8
*230* A126 15c multi 22 15

UN Conference on Human Environment, Stockholm, June 5-16, 1972.
See Offices in Geneva Nos. 25-26.

"Europe" and UN Emblem A127

The Five Continents, by Jose Maria Sert A128

**1972, Sept. 11** **Litho.** ***Perf. 13x13½***
*231* A127 21c yel brn & multi 32 20

Economic Commission for Europe, 25th anniv.
See Offices in Geneva No. 27.

**Art at UN Issue**

**1972, Nov. 17** **Photo.** ***Perf. 12x12½***
*232* A128 8c gold, brn & gldn brn 12 8
*233* A128 15c gold, brn & bl grn 22 15

See Offices in Geneva Nos. 28-29.

Olive Branch and Broken Sword — A129

**1973, Mar. 9** **Litho.** ***Perf. 13½x13***
*234* A129 8c bl & multi 12 8
*235* A129 15c lil rose & multi 22 15

Disarmament Decade, 1970-79.
Nos. 234-235 exist imperf. See Offices in Geneva Nos. 30-31.

Poppy Capsule and Skull — A130

Honeycomb — A131

**1973, Apr. 13** **Photo.** ***Perf. 13½***
*236* A130 8c multi 15 8
*237* A130 15c multi 30 15

Fight against drug abuse. See Offices in Geneva No. 32.

**1973, May 25** **Photo.** ***Perf. 14***
*238* A131 8c ol bis & multi 12 8
*239* A131 21c gray bl & multi 32 20

5th anniv. of the UN Volunteer Program. See UN Offices in Geneva No. 33.

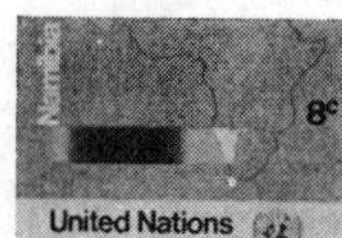


Map of Africa with Namibia A132

**1973, Oct. 1** **Photo.** ***Perf. 13½***
*240* A132 8c emer & multi 12 8
*241* A132 15c brt rose & multi 32 20

To publicize Namibia (South-West Africa), for which the UN General Assembly ended the mandate of South Africa and established the UN Council for Namibia to administer the territory until independence. See Offices in Geneva No. 34.

UN Emblem, Human Rights Flame — A133

**1973, Nov. 16** **Photo.** ***Perf. 13½***
*242* A133 8c dp car & multi 12 8
*243* A133 21c bl grn & multi 32 20

25th anniv. of the adoption and proclamation of the Universal Declaration of Human Rights. See Offices in Geneva Nos. 35-36.

ILO Headquarters, Geneva A134

**1974, Jan. 11** **Photo.** ***Perf. 14***
*244* A134 10c ultra & multi 15 10
*245* A134 21c bl grn & multi 32 20

New Headquarters of Intl. Labor Organization. See Offices in Geneva Nos. 37-38.

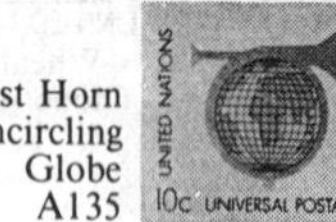


Post Horn Encircling Globe A135

**1974, Mar. 22** **Photo.** ***Perf. 14***
*246* A135 10c multi 15 10

Centenary of UPU. See Offices in Geneva Nos. 39-40.

**Art at UN Issue**

Peace Mural, by Candido Portinari A136

**1974, May 6** **Photo.** ***Perf. 14***
*247* A136 10c gold & multi 15 10
*248* A136 18c ultra & multi 28 18

See Offices in Geneva Nos. 41-42.

Dove and UN Emblem A137

UN Headquarters A138

Globe, UN Emblem, Flags — A139

**1974, June 10** **Photo.** ***Perf. 14***
*249* A137 2c dk & lt bl 5 5
*250* A138 10c multi 15 10
*251* A139 18c multi 28 18

Children of the World — A140

Law of the Sea — A141

**1974, Oct. 18** **Photo.** ***Perf. 14***
*252* A140 10c lt bl & multi 15 10
*253* A140 18c lil & multi 28 18

World Population Year. See Offices in Geneva Nos. 43-44.

**1974, Nov. 22** **Photo.** ***Perf. 14***
*254* A141 10c grn & multi 15 10
*255* A141 26c multi 40 25

UN General Assembly declared the sea bed common heritage of mankind, exempt from arms race. See Offices in Geneva No. 45.

Satellite and Globe A142

**1975, Mar. 14** **Litho.** ***Perf. 13***
*256* A142 10c multi 15 10
*257* A142 26c multi 40 25

Peaceful uses of outer space (meteorology, industry, fishing, communications).
See Offices in Geneva Nos. 46-47.

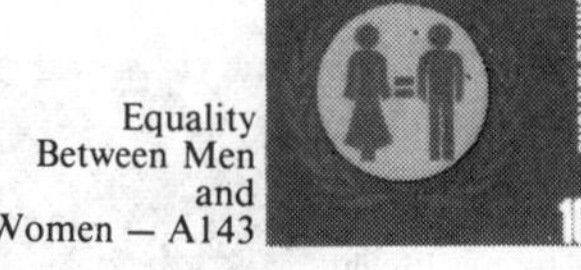


Equality Between Men and Women — A143

**1975, May 9** **Litho.** ***Perf. 15***
*258* A143 10c multi 15 10
*259* A143 18c multi 28 18

International Women's Year 1975. See Offices in Geneva Nos. 48-49.

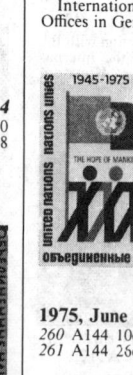

UN Flag and "XXX" — A144

**1975, June 26** **Litho.** ***Perf. 13***
*260* A144 10c multi 15 10
*261* A144 26c pur & multi 40 25

**Souvenir Sheet**

***Imperf***

*262* A144 Sheet of 2 80 60
*a.* 10c ol bis & multi 15 10
*b.* 26c pur & multi 40 28

30th anniv. of the UN. No. 262 has blue and bister margin with inscription and U.N. emblem. Size: 92x70mm. See Offices in Geneva Nos. 50-52.

Hand Reaching up over Map of Africa and Namibia A145

Wild Rose Growing from Barbed Wire A146

**1975, Sept. 22** **Photo.** ***Perf. 13½***
*263* A145 10c multi 15 10
*264* A145 18c multl 28 18

"Namibia—United Nations direct responsibility." See note after No. 241. See Offices in Geneva Nos. 53-54.

**1975, Nov. 21** **Engr.** ***Perf. 12½***
*265* A146 13c ultra 18 12
*266* A146 26c rose car 40 25

UN Peace-keeping Operations. See Offices in Geneva Nos. 55-56.

Symbolic Flags Forming Dove — A147

People of All Races A148

UN Emblem A149

UN Flag A150

Dove and Rainbow — A151

***Perf. 13x13½, 13½x13, 14 (9c)***

**Lithograph; Photogravure (9c)**

**1976**

*267* A147 3c multi 5 5
*268* A148 4c multi 6 6
*269* A149 9c multi 14 8
*270* A150 30c bl, emer & blk 45 30
*271* A151 50c multi 75 50
*Nos. 267-271 (5)* 1.45 99

Issue dates: 9c, Nov. 19. Others, Jan. 9.
See Offices in Vienna No. 8.

Interlocking Bands — A152

**1976, Mar. 12 Photo. *Perf. 14***

*272* A152 13c bl, grn & blk 18 12
*273* A152 26c grn & multi 40 25

World Federation of UN Association. See Offices in Geneva No. 57.

Cargo, Globe and Graph — A153

Houses Around Globe — A154

**1976, Apr. 23 Photo. *Perf. 11½***

*274* A153 13c multi 18 12
*275* A153 31c multi 45 30

UN Conference on Trade and Development (UNCTAD), Nairobi, Kenya, May 1976. See Offices in Geneva No. 58.

**1976, May 28 Photo. *Perf. 14***

*276* A154 13c multi 18 12
*277* A154 25c grn & multi 40 25

Habitat, UN Conference on Human Settlements, Vancouver, Canada, May 31-June 11. See Offices in Geneva Nos. 59-60.

Magnifying Glass, Sheet of Stamps, UN Emblem — A155

Grain — A156

**1976, Oct. 8 Photo. *Perf. 11½***

*278* A155 13c bl & multi 30 15
*279* A155 31c grn & multi 3.50 2.00

UN Postal Administration, 25th anniv. Sheets of 20. See Offices in Geneva Nos. 61-62.

**1976, Nov. 19 Litho. *Perf. 14½***

*280* A156 13c multi 18 12

World Food Council. See Offices in Geneva No. 63.

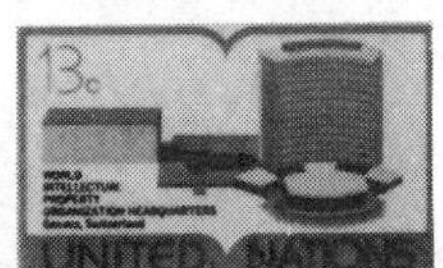

WIPO Headquarters, Geneva — A157

**1977, Mar. 11 Photo. *Perf. 14***

*281* A157 13c cit & multi 18 12
*282* A157 31c brt grn & multi 45 30

World Intellectual Property Organization. See Geneva No. 64.

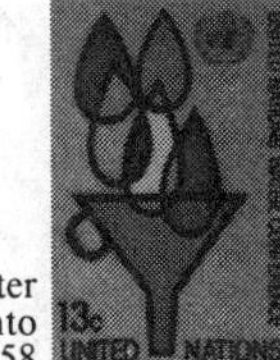

Drops of Water Falling into Funnel — A158

**1977, Apr. 22 Photo. *Perf. 13½x13***

*283* A158 13c yel & multi 18 12
*284* A158 25c sal & multi 40 25

UN Water Conference, Mar del Plata, Argentina, Mar. 14-25. See Offices in Geneva Nos. 65-66.

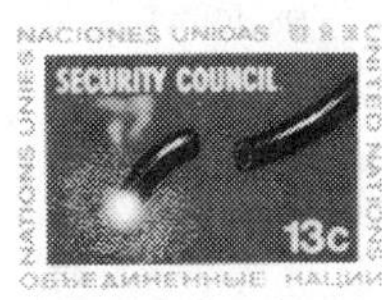

Burning Fuse Severed A159

**1977, May 27 Photo. *Perf. 14***

*285* A159 13c pur & multi 18 12
*286* A159 31c dk bl & multi 45 30

UN Security Council. See Geneva Nos. 67-68.

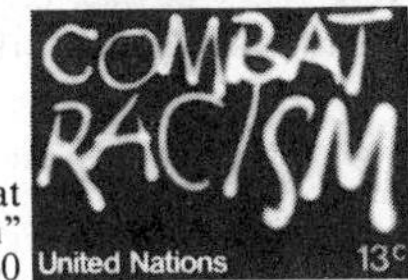

"Combat Racism" A160

**1977, Sept. 19 Litho. *Perf. 13½x13***

*287* A160 13c blk & yel 18 12
*288* A160 25c blk & ver 40 25

Fight against racial discrimination. See Geneva Nos. 69-70.

Atom, Grain, Fruit and Factory — A161

**1977, Nov. 18 Photo.**

*289* A161 13c yel bis & multi 18 12
*290* A161 18c dl grn & multi 28 18

Peaceful uses of atomic energy. See Geneva Nos. 71-72.

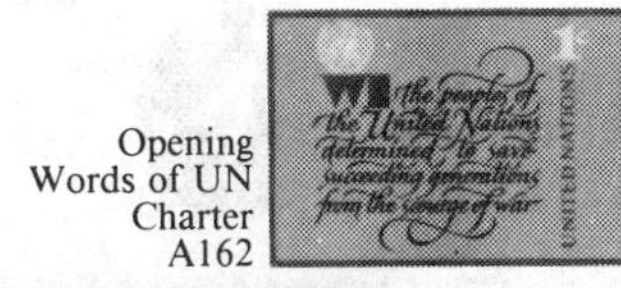
Opening Words of UN Charter A162

"Live Together in Peace" A163

People of the World — A164

**1978, Jan. 27 Litho. *Perf. 14½***

*291* A162 1c gold, brn & red 5 5
*292* A163 25c multi 40 25
*293* A164 $1 multi 1.50 1.00

See Offices in Geneva No. 73.

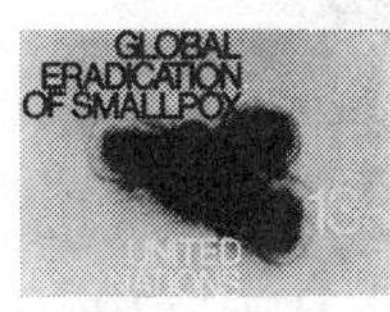

Smallpox Virus — A165

**1978, Mar. 31 Photo. *Perf. 12x11½***

*294* A165 13c rose & blk 18 12
*295* A165 31c bl & blk 45 30

Global eradication of smallpox. See Offices in Geneva Nos. 74-75.

Open Handcuff A166

Multicolored Bands and Clouds A167

**1978, May 5 Photo. *Perf. 12***

*296* A166 13c multi 18 12
*297* A166 18c multi 28 18

Liberation, justice and cooperation for Namibia. See Offices in Geneva No. 76.

**1978, June 12 Photo. *Perf. 14***

*298* A167 13c multi 18 12
*299* A167 25c multi 40 25

International Civil Aviation Organization for "Safety in the Air." See Offices in Geneva Nos. 77-78.

General Assembly A168

**1978, Sept. 15 Photo. *Perf. 13½***

*300* A168 13c multi 18 12
*301* A168 18c multi 28 18

See Offices in Geneva Nos. 79-80.

Hemispheres as Cogwheels A169

**1978, Nov. 17 Photo. *Perf. 14***

*302* A169 13c multi 18 12
*303* A169 31c multi 45 30

Technical Cooperation Among Developing Countries Conference, Buenos Aires, Argentina, Sept. 1978. See Offices in Geneva No. 81.

For unused stamps, more recent issues are valued as never hinged, with the beginning point determined on a country-by-country basis. Notes to show the beginning points are prominently placed in the text.

Hand Holding Olive Branch — A170

Tree of Various Races — A171

Globe, Dove with Olive Branch — A172

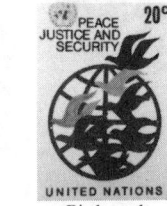

Birds and Globe — A173

**1979, Jan. 19 Photo. *Perf. 14***

*304* A170 5c multi 8 5
*305* A171 14c multi 20 14
*306* A172 15c multi 28 15
*307* A173 20c multi 30 20

UNDRO Against Fire and Water — A174

**1979, Mar. 9 Photo. *Perf. 14***

*308* A174 15c multi 22 15
*309* A174 20c multi 30 20

Office of the UN Disaster Relief Coordinator. See Offices in Geneva Nos. 82-83.

Child and ICY Emblem A175

**1979, May 4 Photo. *Perf. 14***

*310* A175 15c multi 45 15
*311* A175 31c multi 90 30

International Year of the Child. See Offices in Geneva Nos. 84-85.

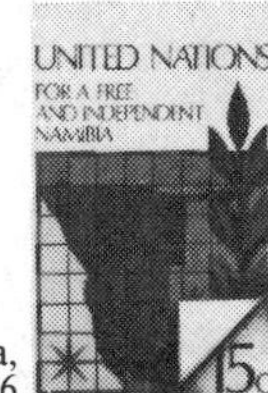

Map of Namibia, Olive Branch — A176

**1979, Oct. 5 Litho. *Perf. 13½***

*312* A176 15c multi 22 15
*313* A176 31c multi 45 30

For a free and independent Namibia. See Offices in Geneva No. 86.

Scales and Sword of Justice — A177

**1979, Nov. 9** **Litho.** ***Perf. 13x13½***

*314* A177 15c multi 22 15
*315* A177 20c multi 30 20

International Court of Justice, The Hague, Netherlands. See Offices in Geneva Nos. 87-88.

Graph of Economic Trends A178

Key A179

**1980, Jan. 11** ***Perf. 15x14½***

*316* A178 15c multi 22 15
*317* A179 31c multi 45 30

New International Economic Order. See Offices in Geneva No. 89; Vienna No. 7.

Women's Year Emblems A180

**1980, Mar. 7** **Litho.** ***Perf. 14½x15***

*318* A180 15c multi 22 15
*319* A180 20c multi 30 20

UN Decade for Women. See Offices in Geneva Nos. 90-91; Offices in Vienna Nos. 9-10.

UN Emblem and "UN" on Helmet A181

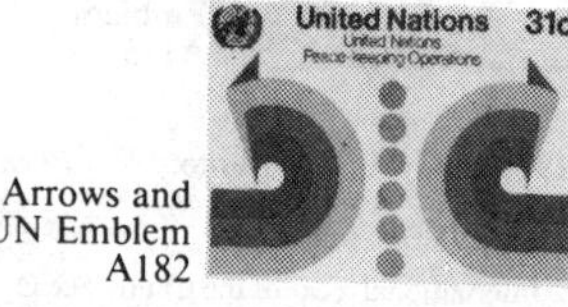


Arrows and UN Emblem A182

**1980, May 16** **Litho.** ***Perf. 14x13***

*320* A181 15c blk & brt bl 25 15
*321* A182 31c multi 50 30

UN Peace-keeping Operations. See Offices in Geneva No. 92; Vienna No. 11.

"35" and Flags — A183

Globe and Laurel — A184

**1980, June 26** **Litho.** ***Perf. 13***

*322* A183 15c multi 22 15
*323* A184 31c multi 45 30

**Souvenir Sheet**

***Imperf***

*324* Sheet of 2 70 70
*a* A183 15c multi 22
*b* A184 31c multi 45

35th anniv. of the UN. No. 324 has multicolored margin with inscription and UN emblem. Size: 92x73mm. See Offices in Geneva Nos. 93-95; Vienna Nos. 12-14.

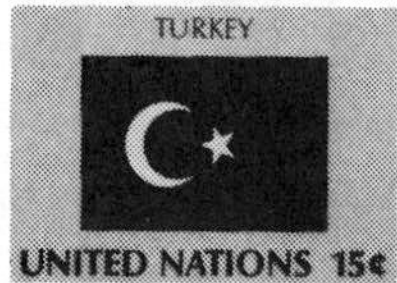


Flag of Turkey A185

**1980, Sept. 26** **Litho.** ***Perf. 12***

*325* A185 15c *shown* 25 20
*326* A185 15c *Luxembourg* 25 20
*327* A185 15c *Fiji* 25 20
*328* A185 15c *Viet Nam* 25 20
*329* A185 15c *Guinea* 25 20
*330* A185 15c *Surinam* 25 20
*331* A185 15c *Bangladesh* 25 20
*332* A185 15c *Mali* 25 20
*333* A185 15c *Jugoslavia* 25 20
*334* A185 15c *France* 25 20
*335* A185 15c *Venezuela* 25 20
*336* A185 15c *El Salvador* 25 20
*337* A185 15c *Madagascar* 25 20
*338* A185 15c *Cameroon* 25 20
*339* A185 15c *Rwanda* 25 20
*340* A185 15c *Hungary* 25 20
*Nos. 325-340 (16)* 4.00 3.20

Issued in 4 sheets of 16. Each sheet contains 4 blocks of 4 (Nos. 325-328, 329-332, 333-336, 337-340). A se-tenant block of 4 designs centers each sheet. See Nos. 350-365, 374-389, 399-414, 425-440, 450-465, 477-492, 499-514, 528-543.

Symbolic Flowers A186

Symbols of Progress A187

**1980, Nov. 21** **Litho.** ***Perf. 13½x13***

*341* A186 15c multi 35 20
*342* A187 20c multi 50 30

Economic and Social Council (ECOSOC). See Offices in Geneva Nos. 96-97; Vienna Nos. 15-16.

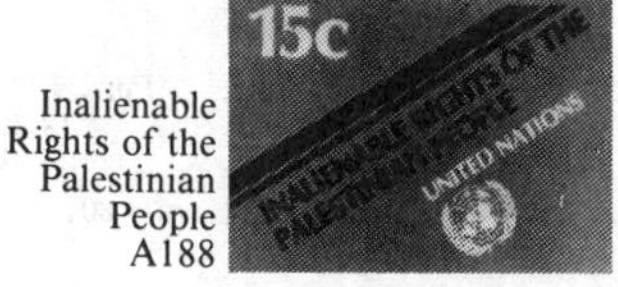


Inalienable Rights of the Palestinian People A188

**1981, Jan. 30** **Photo.**

*343* A188 15c multi 40 25

See Offices in Geneva No. 98; Vienna No. 17.

Interlocking Puzzle Pieces — A189

Stylized Person — A190

**1981, Mar. 6** **Photo.**

*344* A189 20c multi 50 30
*345* A190 35c multi 85 50

International Year of the Disabled. See Offices in Geneva Nos. 99-100; Vienna Nos. 18-19.

Divislava and Sebastocrator Kaloyan, Bulgarian Mural, 1259, Boyana Church, Sofia — A191

**1981, Apr. 15** **Photo.** ***Perf. 11½***

**Granite Paper**

*346* A191 20c multi 40 30
*347* A191 31c multi 65 45

See Offices in Geneva No. 101; Vienna No. 20.

Solar Energy A192

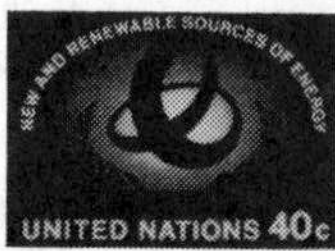


Conference Emblem A193

**1981, May 29** **Litho.** ***Perf. 13***

*348* A192 20c multi 40 30
*349* A193 40c multi 80 60

Conference on New and Renewable Sources of Energy, Nairobi, Aug. 10-21. See Offices in Geneva No. 102; Vienna No. 21.

Flag Type of 1980

**1981, Sept. 25** **Litho.**

*350* A185 20c Djibouti 30 25
*351* A185 20c Sri Lanka 30 25
*352* A185 20c Bolivia 30 25
*353* A185 20c Equatorial Guinea 30 25
*354* A185 20c Malta 30 25
*355* A185 20c Czechoslovakia 30 25
*356* A185 20c Thailand 30 25
*357* A185 20c Trinidad & Tobago 30 25
*358* A185 20c Ukrainian SSR 30 25
*359* A185 20c Kuwait 30 25
*360* A185 20c Sudan 30 25
*361* A185 20c Egypt 30 25
*362* A185 20c US 30 25
*363* A185 20c Singapore 30 25
*364* A185 20c Panama 30 25
*365* A185 20c Costa Rica 30 25
*Nos. 350-365 (16)* 4.80 4.00

Issued in 4 sheets of 16. Each sheet contains 4 blocks of 4 (Nos. 350-353, 354-357, 358-361, 362-365). A se-tenant block of 4 designs centers each sheet.

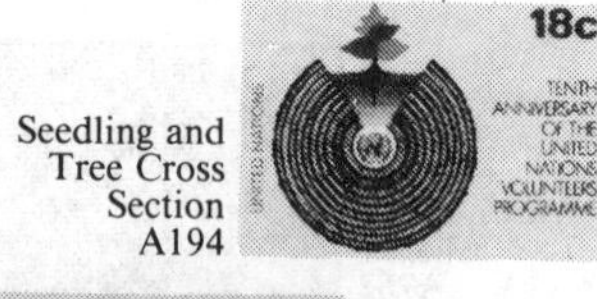


Seedling and Tree Cross Section A194

"10" and Symbols of Progress A195

**1981, Nov. 13** **Litho.**

*366* A194 18c multi 40 30
*367* A195 28c multi 60 45

UN Volunteers Program, 10th anniv. See Offices in Geneva Nos. 103-104; Vienna Nos. 22-23.

Respect for Human Rights — A196

Independence of Colonial Countries and People — A197

Second Disarmament Decade — A198

**1982, Jan. 22** ***Perf. 11½x12***

*368* A196 17c multi 35 15
*369* A197 28c multi 56 25
*370* A198 40c multi 80 40

10th Anniv. of UN Environment Program A199 A200

**1982, Mar. 19** **Litho.** ***Perf. 13½x13***

*371* A199 20c multi 50 35
*372* A200 40c multi 1.00 70

UN Emblem and Olive Branch in Outer Space — A201

***Perf. 13 x 13½***

**1982, June 11** **Litho.**

*373* A201 20c multi 50 35

Exploration and Peaceful Uses of Outer Space. See Offices in Geneva Nos. 109-110; Vienna No. 27.

Flag Type of 1980

**1982, Sept. 24** **Litho.** ***Perf. 12***

*374* A185 20c Austria 40 25
*375* A185 20c Malaysia 40 25
*376* A185 20c Seychelles 40 25
*377* A185 20c Ireland 40 25
*378* A185 20c Mozambique 40 25
*379* A185 20c Albania 40 25
*380* A185 20c Dominica 40 25
*381* A185 20c Solomon Islands 40 25
*382* A185 20c Philippines 40 25
*383* A185 20c Swaziland 40 25
*384* A185 20c Nicaragua 40 25
*385* A185 20c Burma 40 25
*386* A185 20c Cape Verde 40 25
*387* A185 20c Guyana 40 25
*388* A185 20c Belgium 40 25
*389* A185 20c Nigeria 40 25
*Nos. 374-389 (16)* 6.40 4.00

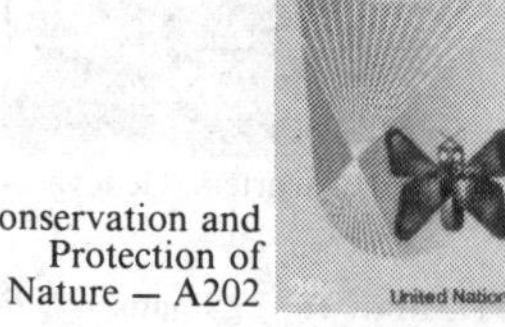


Conservation and Protection of Nature — A202

**1982, Nov. 19 Photo. *Perf. 14***

*390* A202 20c Leaf 50 30
*391* A202 28c Butterfly 70 45

See Offices in Geneva Nos. 111-112; Vienna Nos. 28-29.

A203

World Communications Year — A204

**1983, Jan. 28 Litho. *Perf. 13***

*392* A203 20c multi 40 20
*393* A204 40c multi 80 40

See Offices in Geneva No. 113; Vienna No. 30.

Safety at Sea
A205 A206

**1983, Mar. 18 Litho. *Perf. 14½***

*394* A205 20c multi 40 20
*395* A206 37c multi 75 38

See Offices in Geneva Nos. 114-115; Vienna Nos. 31-32.

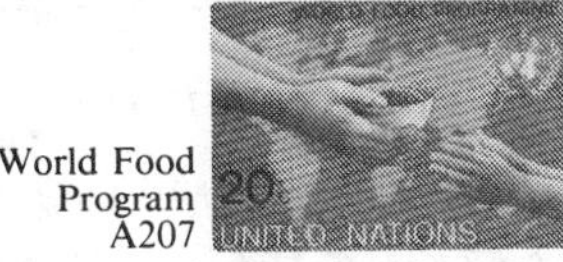

World Food Program
A207

**1983, Apr. 22 Engr. *Perf. 13½***

*396* A207 20c rose lake 40 20

See Offices in Geneva Nos. 116; Vienna Nos. 33-34.

Trade and Development
A208 A209

**1983, June 6 Litho. *Perf. 14***

*397* A208 20c multi 50 20
*398* A209 28c multi 75 28

See Offices in Geneva Nos. 117-118; Vienna Nos. 35-36.

Flag Type of 1980

**1983, Sept. 23 Photo. *Perf. 12***

*399* A185 20c Great Britain 40 20
*400* A185 20c Barbados 40 20
*401* A185 20c Nepal 40 20
*402* A185 20c Israel 40 20
*403* A185 20c Malawi 40 20
*404* A185 20c Byelorussian SSR 40 20
*405* A185 20c Jamaica 40 20
*406* A185 20c Kenya 40 20
*407* A185 20c People's Republic of China 40 20
*408* A185 20c Peru 40 20
*409* A185 20c Bulgaria 40 20
*410* A185 20c Canada 40 20
*411* A185 20c Somalia 40 20
*412* A185 20c Senegal 40 20
*413* A185 20c Brazil 40 20
*414* A185 20c Sweden 40 20
*Nos. 399-414 (16)* 6.40 3.20

35th Anniv. of the Universal Declaration of Human Rights
A210 A211

**Photogravure and Engraved**

**1983, Dec. 9 *Perf. 13½***

*415* A210 20c Window Right 60 20
*416* A211 40c Peace Treaty with Nature 1.20 40

See Offices in Geneva Nos. 119-120, Vienna Nos. 37-38.

Intl. Population Conference
A212

**1984, Feb. 3 Litho. *Perf. 14***

*417* A212 20c multi 60 20
*418* A212 40c multi 1.50 40

See Offices in Geneva No. 121; Vienna No. 39.

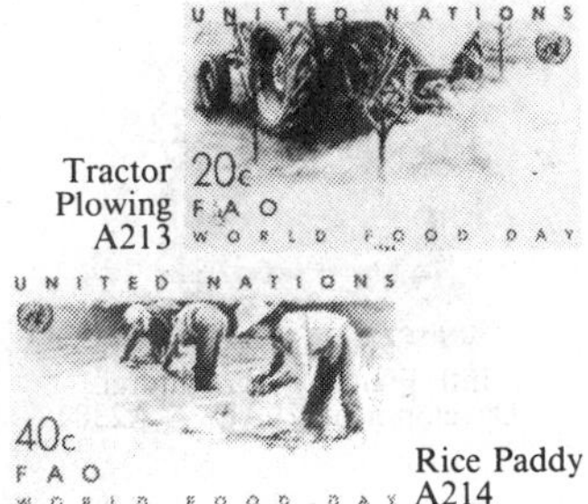

Tractor Plowing
A213

Rice Paddy
A214

**1984, Mar. 15 Litho. *Perf. 14½***

*419* A213 20c multi 75 20
*420* A214 40c multi 1.60 40

World Food Day, Oct. 16. See Offices in Geneva Nos. 122-123; Vienna Nos. 40-41.

Grand Canyon
A215

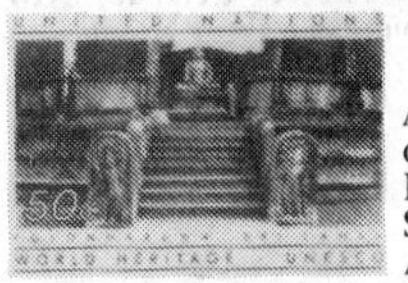

Ancient City of Polonnaruwa, Sri Lanka
A216

**1984, Apr. 18 Litho. *Perf. 14***

*421* A215 20c multi 80 20
*422* A216 50c multi 2.00 50

World Heritage (protection of world cultural and natural sites). See Offices in Geneva Nos. 124-125; Vienna Nos. 42-43.

A217

A218

**1984, May 29 Photo. *Perf. 11½***

*423* A217 20c multi 60 20
*424* A218 50c multi 1.50 50

Future for Refugees. See Offices in Geneva Nos. 126-127; Vienna Nos. 44-45.

Flag Type of 1980

**1984, Sept. 21 Photo. *Perf. 12***

*425* A185 20c Burundi 65 20
*426* A185 20c Pakistan 65 20
*427* A185 20c Benin 65 20
*428* A185 20c Italy 65 20
*429* A185 20c Tanzania 65 20
*430* A185 20c United Arab Emirates 65 20
*431* A185 20c Ecuador 65 20
*432* A185 20c Bahamas 65 20
*433* A185 20c Poland 65 20
*434* A185 20c Papua New Guinea 65 20
*435* A185 20c Uruguay 65 20
*436* A185 20c Chile 65 20
*437* A185 20c Paraguay 65 20
*438* A185 20c Bhutan 65 20
*439* A185 20c Central African Republic 65 20
*440* A185 20c Australia 65 20
*Nos. 425-440 (16)* 10.40 3.20

International Youth Year — A219

**1984, Nov. 15 Litho. *Perf. 13½***

*441* A219 20c multi 75 20
*442* A219 35c multi 1.50 35

See Offices in Geneva No. 128; Vienna Nos. 46-47.

ILO Turin Center — A220

**1985, Feb. 1 Engr.**

*443* A220 23c Turin Center emblem 60 24

See Offices in Geneva Nos. 129-130; Vienna No. 48.

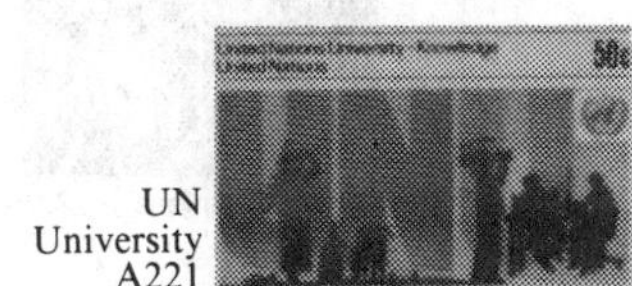

UN University
A221

**1985, Mar. 15 Photo. *Perf. 13½***

*444* A221 50c multi 1.10 50

See Offices in Geneva Nos. 131-132; Vienna No. 49.

The Catalogue editors cannot undertake to appraise, identify or judge the genuineness or condition of stamps.

Peoples of the World — A222

Painting UN Emblem
A223

**1985, May 10 Litho. *Perf. 14***

*445* A222 22c multi 50 22
*446* A223 $3 multi 6.50 3.00

See Offices in Geneva Nos. 133-134; Vienna Nos. 50-51.

The Corner
A224

Alvaro Raking Hay
A225

Oil paintings (details) by American artist Andrew Wyeth.

**1985, June 26 Photo. *Perf. 12x11½***

*447* A224 22c multi 50 22
*448* A225 45c multi 1.00 45

**Souvenir Sheet**

***Imperf***

*449* Sheet of 2 2.00 2.00
*a* A224 22c multi 50
*b* A225 45c multi 1.00

40th anniv. of the UN. No. 449 has multicolored margin with inscription and UN emblem. Size: 75x83mm. See Offices in Geneva Nos. 135-137; Vienna Nos. 52-54.

Flag Type of 1980

**1985, Sept. 20 Photo. *Perf. 12***

*450* A185 22c Grenada 44 22
*451* A185 22c Federal Republic of Germany 44 22
*452* A185 22c Saudi Arabia 44 22
*453* A185 22c Mexico 44 22
*454* A185 22c Uganda 44 22
*455* A185 22c St. Thomas & Prince 44 22
*456* A185 22c USSR 44 22
*457* A185 22c India 44 22
*458* A185 22c Liberia 44 22
*459* A185 22c Mauritius 44 22
*460* A185 22c Chad 44 22
*461* A185 22c Dominican Republic 44 22
*462* A185 22c Sultanate of Oman 44 22
*463* A185 22c Ghana 44 22
*464* A185 22c Sierra Leone 44 22
*465* A185 22c Finland 44 22
*Nos. 450-465 (16)* 7.04 3.52

Issued in 4 sheets of 16. Each sheet contains 4 blocks of 4 (Nos. 450-453, 454-457, 458-461, 462-465). A se-tenant block of 4 designs is at the center of each sheet.

UNICEF Child Survival Campaign — A226

**Photoravure and Engraved**

**1985, Nov. 22 *Perf. 13½***

*466* A226 22c Asian child 44 22
*467* A226 33c Breastfeeding 66 33

See Offices in Geneva Nos. 138-139; Vienna Nos. 55-56.

Abstract Painting by Wosene Kosrof — A227

**1986, Jan. 31 Photo. Perf. 11 1/2**

*468* A227 22c multi 50 22

Africa in Crisis, campaign against hunger. See Offices in Geneva No. 140; Vienna No. 57.

Water Resources A228

**1986, Mar. 14 Photo. Perf. 13 1/2**

| | | | |
|---|---|---|---|
| *469* | A228 22c Dam | 50 | 22 |
| *470* | A228 22c Irrigation | 50 | 22 |
| *471* | A228 22c Hygiene | 50 | 22 |
| *472* | A228 22c Well | 50 | 22 |
| *a* | Block of 4, #469-472 | 2.00 | 88 |

UN Development program. Nos. 469-472 printed se-tenant in continuous design. See Offices in Geneva Nos. 141-144; Vienna Nos. 58-61.

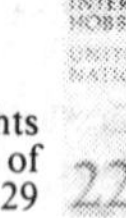

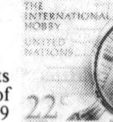

Human Rights Stamp of 1954 — A229

Stamp collecting: 44c, Engraver.

**1986, May 22 Engr. Perf. 12 1/2**

| | | | |
|---|---|---|---|
| *473* | A229 22c dk vio & brt bl | 44 | 22 |
| *474* | A229 44c brn & emer grn | 88 | 44 |

See Offices in Geneva Nos. 146-147; Vienna Nos. 62-63.

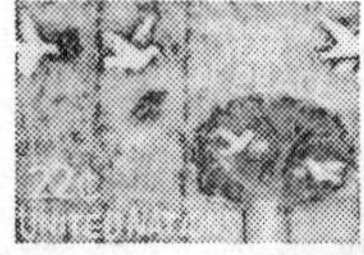

Birds Nest in Tree — A230

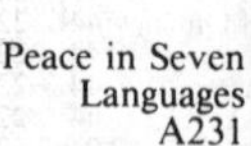

Peace in Seven Languages A231

**Photo. & Embossed**

**1986, June 20 Perf. 13 1/2**

| | | | |
|---|---|---|---|
| *475* | A230 22c multi | 44 | 22 |
| *476* | A231 33c multi | 66 | 35 |

Intl. Peace Year. See Offices in Geneva Nos. 148-149; Vienna Nos. 64-65.

Flag Type of 1980

**1986, Sept. 19 Photo. Perf. 12**

| | | | |
|---|---|---|---|
| *477* | A185 22c New Zealand | 40 | 22 |
| *478* | A185 22c Lao PDR | 40 | 22 |
| *479* | A185 22c Burkina Faso | 40 | 22 |
| *480* | A185 22c Gambia | 40 | 22 |
| *481* | A185 22c Maldives | 40 | 22 |
| *482* | A185 22c Ethiopia | 40 | 22 |
| *483* | A185 22c Jordan | 40 | 22 |
| *484* | A185 22c Zambia | 40 | 22 |
| *485* | A185 22c Iceland | 40 | 22 |
| *486* | A185 22c Antigua & Barbuda | 40 | 22 |
| *487* | A185 22c Angola | 40 | 22 |
| *488* | A185 22c Botswana | 40 | 22 |
| *489* | A185 22c Romania | 40 | 22 |
| *490* | A185 22c Togo | 40 | 22 |
| *491* | A185 22c Mauritania | 40 | 22 |
| *492* | A185 22c Colombia | 40 | 22 |
| | *Nos. 477-492 (16)* | 6.40 | 3.52 |

Issued in 4 sheets of 16. Each sheet contains 4 blocks of 4 (Nos. 477-480, 481-484, 485-488, 489-492). A se-tenant block of 4 designs is at the center of each sheet.

Souvenir Sheet

World Federation of UN Associations, 40th Anniv. — A232

Designs: 22c, Mother Earth, by Edna Hibel, US. 33c, Watercolor by Salvador Dali (b. 1904), Spain. 39c, New Dawn, by Dong Kingman, US. 44c, Watercolor by Chaim Gross, US.

**1986, Nov. 14 Litho. Perf. 13x13 1/2**

| | | | |
|---|---|---|---|
| *493* | Sheet of 4 | 2.50 | 2.50 |
| *a* | A232 22c multi | 40 | |
| *b* | A232 33c multi | 60 | |
| *c* | A232 39c multi | 70 | |
| *d* | A232 44c multi | 80 | |

See Offices in Geneva No. 150; Vienna No. 66. No. 493 has inscribed margin picturing UN and WFUNA emblems.

Trygve Halvdan Lie (1896-1968), 1st Secretary-General A233

**Photogravure and Engraved**

**1987, Jan. 30 Perf. 13 1/2**

*494* A233 22c multi 35 22

See Offices in Geneva No. 151; Vienna No. 67.

Intl. Year of Shelter for the Homeless A234

**Perf. 13 1/2x12 1/2**

**1987, Mar. 13 Litho.**

| | | | |
|---|---|---|---|
| *495* | A234 22c Surveying, blueprint | 35 | 22 |
| *496* | A234 44c Cutting lumber | 70 | 44 |

See Offices in Geneva No. 154-155; Vienna No. 68-69.

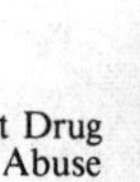

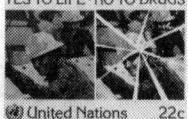

Fight Drug Abuse A235

**1987, June 12 Litho. Perf. 14 1/2x15**

| | | | |
|---|---|---|---|
| *497* | A235 22c Construction | 40 | 22 |
| *498* | A235 33c Education | 60 | 35 |

See Offices in Geneva Nos. 156-157; Vienna Nos. 70-71.

Flag Type of 1980

**1987, Sept. 18 Photo. Perf. 12**

| | | | |
|---|---|---|---|
| *499* | A185 22c Comoros | 40 | 22 |
| *500* | A185 22c Yemen PDR | 40 | 22 |
| *501* | A185 22c Mongolia | 40 | 22 |
| *502* | A185 22c Vanuatu | 40 | 22 |
| *503* | A185 22c Japan | 40 | 22 |
| *504* | A185 22c Gabon | 40 | 22 |
| *505* | A185 22c Zimbabwe | 40 | 22 |
| *506* | A185 22c Iraq | 40 | 22 |
| *507* | A185 22c Argentina | 40 | 22 |
| *508* | A185 22c Congo | 40 | 22 |
| *509* | A185 22c Niger | 40 | 22 |
| *510* | A185 22c St. Lucia | 40 | 22 |
| *511* | A185 22c Bahrain | 40 | 22 |
| *512* | A185 22c Haiti | 40 | 22 |
| *513* | A185 22c Afghanistan | 40 | 22 |
| *514* | A185 22c Greece | 40 | 22 |
| | *Nos. 499-514 (16)* | 6.40 | 3.52 |

Issued in 4 sheets of 16. Each sheet contains 4 blocks of 4 (Nos. 499-502, 503-506, 507-510, 511-514). A se-tenant block of 4 designs is at the center of each sheet.

UN Day — A236

Designs: Multinational people in various occupations.

**1987, Oct. 23 Litho. Perf. 14 1/2x15**

| | | | |
|---|---|---|---|
| *515* | A236 22c multi | 44 | 22 |
| *516* | A236 39c multi | 78 | 40 |

See Offices in Geneva Nos. 158-159; Vienna Nos. 74-75.

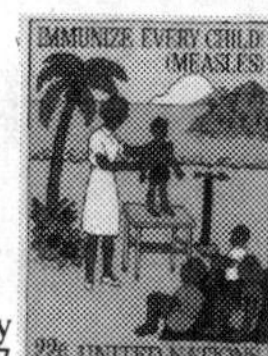

Immunize Every Child — A237

**1987, Nov. 20 Litho. Perf. 15x14 1/2**

| | | | |
|---|---|---|---|
| *517* | A237 22c Measles | 44 | 22 |
| *518* | A237 44c Tetanus | 88 | 44 |

See Offices in Geneva Nos. 160-161; Vienna Nos. 76-77.

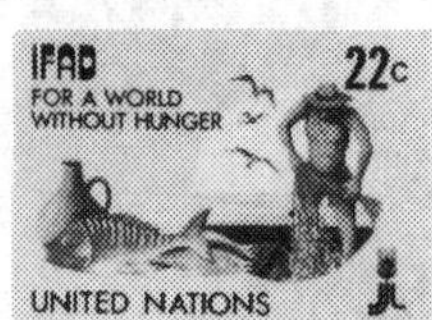

Intl. Fund for Agricultural Development (IFAD) — A238

**1988, Jan. 29 Litho. Perf. 13 1/2**

| | | | |
|---|---|---|---|
| *519* | A238 22c Fishing | 44 | 32 |
| *520* | A238 33c Farming | 66 | 35 |

See Offices in Geneva Nos. 162-163; Vienna Nos. 78-79.

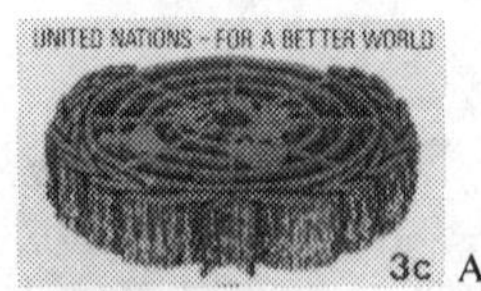

A239

**1988, Jan. 29 Photo. Perf. 13 1/2x14**

*521* A239 3c multi ('88) 6 5

Survival of the Forests A240

**1988, Mar. 18 Litho. Perf. 14x15**

| | | | |
|---|---|---|---|
| *522* | A240 25c multicolored | 50 | 38 |
| *523* | A240 44c multicolored | 88 | 65 |

Nos. 522-523 printed in a continuous design. See Offices in Geneva Nos. 165-166; Vienna Nos. 80-81.

Intl. Volunteer Day — A241

**1988, May 6 Perf. 13x14, 14x13**

| | | | |
|---|---|---|---|
| *524* | A241 25c Education, vert. | 50 | 38 |
| *525* | A241 50c Vocational training | 1.00 | 75 |

See Offices in Geneva Nos. 167-168; Vienna Nos. 82-83.

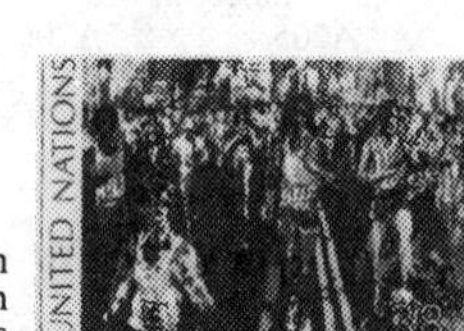

Health in Sports A242

**Perf. 13 1/2x13, 13x13 1/2**

**1988, June 17 Litho.**

| | | | |
|---|---|---|---|
| *526* | A242 25c Cycling, vert. | 50 | 38 |
| *527* | A242 38c Marathon | 76 | 58 |

See Offices in Geneva Nos. 169-170; Vienna Nos. 84-85.

Flag Type of 1980

**1988, Sept. 16 Photo. Perf. 12**

| | | | |
|---|---|---|---|
| *528* | A185 25c Spain | 50 | 25 |
| *529* | A185 25c St. Vincent & Grenadines | 50 | 25 |
| *530* | A185 25c Ivory Coast | 50 | 25 |
| *531* | A185 25c Lebanon | 50 | 25 |
| *532* | A185 25c Yemen (Arab Republic) | 50 | 25 |
| *533* | A185 25c Cuba | 50 | 25 |
| *534* | A185 25c Denmark | 50 | 25 |
| *535* | A185 25c Libya | 50 | 25 |
| *536* | A185 25c Qatar | 50 | 25 |
| *537* | A185 25c Zaire | 50 | 25 |
| *538* | A185 25c Norway | 50 | 25 |
| *539* | A185 25c German Democratic Republic | 50 | 25 |
| *540* | A185 25c Iran | 50 | 25 |
| *541* | A185 25c Tunisia | 50 | 25 |
| *542* | A185 25c Samoa | 50 | 25 |
| *543* | A185 25c Belize | 50 | 25 |
| | *Nos. 528-543 (16)* | 8.00 | 4.00 |

Issued in sheets of 16. Each sheet contains 4 blocks of 4 (Nos. 528-531, 532-535, 536-539 and 540-543). A se-tenant block of 4 designs is at the center of each sheet.

Universal Declaration of Human Rights, 40th Anniv. — A243

**1988, Dec. 9 Photo. & Engr. Perf.**
*544* A243 25c multi 50 25

**Souvenir Sheet**

*545* A243 $1 multi 2.00 2.00

See Offices in Geneva Nos. 171-172; Vienna Nos. 86-87.

No. 545 has multicolored decorative margin picturing the preamble to the Universal Declaration of Human Rights (inscribed in English). Size:

World Bank — A244

**1989, Jan. 27 Litho. Perf.**
*546* A244 25c Energy and nature 50 25
*547* A244 45c Agriculture 90 45

See Offices in Geneva Nos. 173-174; Vienna Nos. 88-89.

## AIR POST STAMPS

Plane and Gull — AP1

Swallows and UN Emblem AP2

***Perf. 14.***
**1951, Dec. 14 Unwmk. Engr.**
*C1* AP1 6c hn brn 12 12
*C2* AP1 10c brt bl grn 20 20
*C3* AP2 15c dp ultra 45 25
*C4* AP2 25c gray blk 2.00 1.25

The 6c, 15c and 25c exist imperforate.

Airplane Wing and Globe — AP3

**1957, May 27 *Perf. 12½x14***
*C5* AP3 4c maroon 6 6

**1959, Feb. 9 *Perf. 12½x13½***
*C6* AP3 5c rose red 8 8

UN Flag and Plane AP4

**1959, Feb. 9 *Perf. 13½x14***
*C7* AP4 7c ultra 12 10

Outer Space — AP5

UN Emblem — AP6

"Flight Across Globe" — AP8

Bird of Laurel Leaves — AP7

Jet Plane and Envelope AP9

**1963-64 Photo. *Perf. 11½***
*C8* AP5 6c blk, bl & yel grn 9 8
*C9* AP6 8c yel, ol grn & red 12 10

***Perf. 12½x12***
*C10* AP7 13c ultra, aqua, gray & car 18 15

***Perf. 11½x12, 12x11½***
*C11* AP8 15c vio, buff, gray & pale grn ('64) 35 20
*a.* Gray omitted —
*C12* AP9 25c yel, org, gray, bl & red ('64) 65 30
*Nos. C8-C12 (5)* 1.39 83

Dates of issue: 6c, 8c, 13c, June 17, 1963; 15c, 25c, May 1, 1964. See UN Offices in Geneva No. 8.

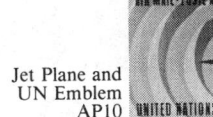

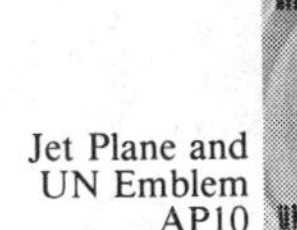
Jet Plane and UN Emblem AP10

**1968, Apr. 18 Litho. *Perf. 13***
*C13* AP10 20c multi 30 25

Wings, Envelopes and UN Emblem — AP11

**1969, Apr. 21 Litho.**
*C14* AP11 10c org ver, org, yel & blk 20 15

UN Emblem and Stylized Wing — AP12

Birds in Flight — AP13

Clouds AP14

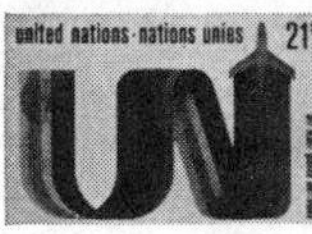
"UN" and Plane — AP15

**Lithographed and Engraved**
**1972, May 1 *Perf. 13x13½***
*C15* AP12 9c lt bl, dk red & vio bl 12 10

**Photo. *Perf. 14x13½***
*C16* AP13 11c bl & multi 16 10

***Perf. 13½x14***
*C17* AP14 17c yel, red & org 25 18

***Perf. 13***
*C18* AP15 21c sil & multi 30 22

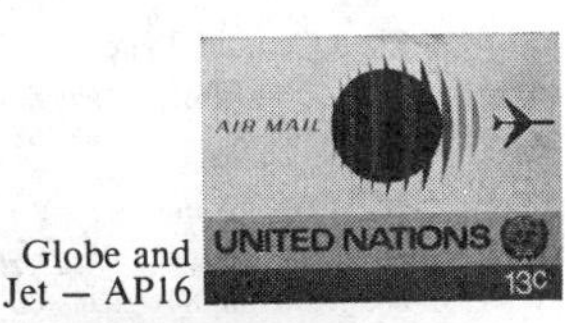
Globe and Jet — AP16

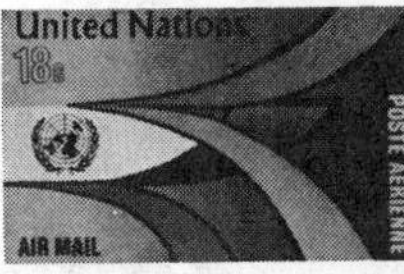
Pathways Radiating from UN Emblem AP17

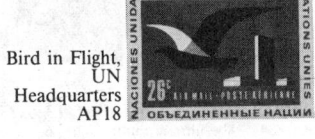

Bird in Flight, UN Headquarters AP18

***Perf. 13, 12½x13 (18c)***
**1974, Sept. 16 Litho.**
*C19* AP16 13c multi 18 14
*C20* AP17 18c multi 28 20
*C21* AP18 26c bl & multi 40 30

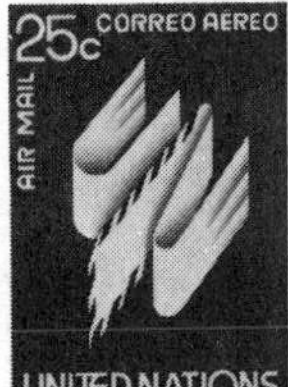
Winged Airmail Letter — AP19

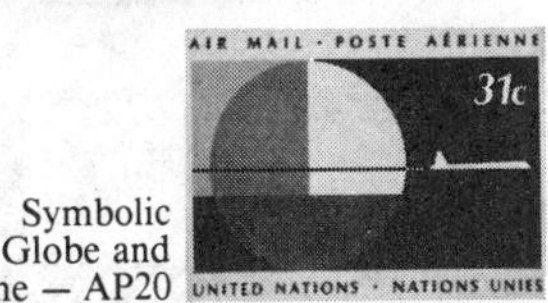
Symbolic Globe and Plane — AP20

**1977, June 27 Photo. *Perf. 14***
*C22* AP19 25c grnsh bl & multi 38 25
*C23* AP20 31c magenta 45 30

## OFFICES IN GENEVA, SWITZERLAND

For use only on mail posted at the Palais des Nations (UN European Office), Geneva. Inscribed in French unless otherwise stated.

100 Centimes = 1 Franc

Types of UN Issues 1961-69 and

UN European Office, Geneva — G1

Designs: 5c, UN Headquarters, New York, and world map. 10c, UN flag. 20c, Three men united before globe. 50c, Opening words of UN Charter. 60c, UN emblem over globe. 70c, "UN" and UN emblem. 75c, "Flight Across Globe." 80c, UN Headquarters and emblem. 90c, Abstract group of flags. 1fr, UN Emblem. 2fr, Stylized globe and weather vane. 3fr, Statue by Henrik Starcke. 10fr, "Peace, Justice, Security."

***Perf. 13 (5c, 70c, 90c); Perf. 12½x12 (10c); Perf. 11½ (20c-60c, 3fr); Perf. 11 ½x12 (75c); Perf. 13½x14 (80c); Perf. 14 (1fr); Perf. 12x11½ (2fr); Perf. 12 (10fr).***

**Photogravure; Lithographed & Embossed (1fr); Engraved (10fr).**

**1969-70 Unwmk.**
*1* A88 5c pur & multi 5 5
*a.* Green omitted 250.00
*2* A52 10c sal & multi 5 5
*3* A66 20c blk & multi 10 10
*4* G1 30c dk bl & multi 15 15
*5* A77 50c ultra & multi 25 25
*6* A54 60c dk brn, sal & gold ('70) 30 30
*7* A104 70c red, blk & gold ('70) 35 35
*8* AP8 75c car rose & multi 40 40
*9* A78 80c bl grn, red & yel ('70) 40 40
*10* A45 90c bl & multi ('70) 45 45
*11* A79 1fr lt & dk grn 50 50
*12* A67 2fr bl & multi ('70) 1.00 1.00
*13* A97 3fr ol & multi 1.50 1.50
*14* A3 10fr dp bl ('70) 5.00 5.00
*Nos. 1-14 (14)* 10.50 10.50

The 20c, 80c and 90c are inscribed in French. The 75c and 10fr carry French inscription at top, English at bottom.

Issue dates: 60c and 10fr, Apr. 17, 1970; 70c, 80c, 90c, 2fr, Sept. 22, 1970. Others, Oct. 4, 1969.

**Sea Bed Type**
**Photogravure and Engraved**
**1971, Jan. 25 *Perf. 13***
*15* A114 30c grn & multi 25 20

**Refugee Type**
**1971, Mar. 12 Litho. *Perf. 13x12½***
*16* A115 50c dp car, dp org & blk 40 30

**Food Program Type**
**1971, Apr. 13 Photo. *Perf. 14***
*17* A116 50c dk pur, gold & grn 50 35

**UPU Headquarters Type**
**1971, May 28 Photo. *Perf. 11½***
*18* A117 75c grn & multi 1.00 75

**Eliminate Discrimination Types**
**1971, Sept. 21 Photo. *Perf. 13½***
*19* A118 30c bl & multi 30 25
*20* A119 50c multi 50 40

**Picasso Type**
**1971, Nov. 19 Photo. *Perf. 11½***
*21* A122 1.10fr car & multi 1.25 90

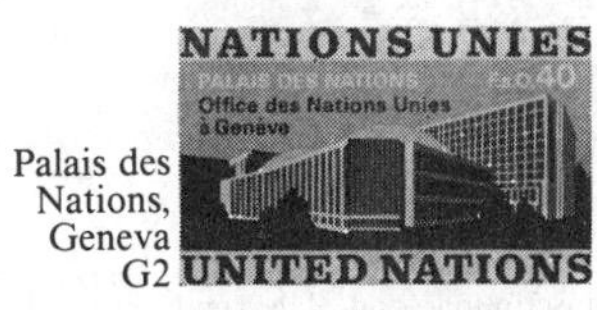
Palais des Nations, Geneva G2

**1972, Jan. 5 Photo. *Perf. 11½***
*22* G2 40c ol & multi 30 25

**Nuclear Weapons Type**
**1972, Feb. 14 Photo. *Perf. 13½x14***
*23* A124 40c yel grn, blk, rose & gray 70 45

**World Health Day Type**
**Lithographed and Engraved**
**1972, Apr. 7 *Perf. 13x13½***
*24* A125 80c blk & multi 85 65

**Environment Type**
**Lithographed and Embossed**
**1972, June 5 *Perf. 12½x14***
*25* A126 40c multi 55 40
*26* A126 80c multi 1.10 80

**ECE Type**

**1972, Sept. 11 Litho.** ***Perf. 13x13½***
*27* A127 1.10fr red & multi 1.50 1.10

**Art at UN Type**

**1972, Nov. 17 Photo.** ***Perf. 12x12½***
*28* A128 40c gold, brn & red 55 40
*29* A128 80c gold, brn & ol 1.10 80

**Disarmament Type**

**1973, Mar. 9 Litho.** ***Perf. 13½x13***
*30* A129 60c vio & multi 60 45
*31* A129 1.10fr ol & multi 1.10 85

Nos. 30-31 exist imperf.

**Drug Abuse Type**

**1973, Apr. 13 Photo.** ***Perf. 13½***
*32* A130 60c bl & multi 60 55

**Volunteers Type**

**1973, May 25 Photo.** ***Perf. 14***
*33* A131 80c multi 80 70

**Namibia Type**

**1973, Oct. 1 Photo.** ***Perf. 13½***
*34* A132 60c red & multi 60 55

**Human Rights Type**

**1973, Nov. 16 Photo.** ***Perf. 13½***
*35* A133 40c ultra & multi 30 30
*36* A133 80c ol & multi 60 60

**ILO Headquarters Type**

**1974, Jan. 11 Photo.** ***Perf. 14***
*37* A134 60c vio & multi 45 45
*38* A134 80c brn & multi 60 60

**UPU Type**

**1974, Mar. 22 Photo.** ***Perf. 14***
*39* A135 30c multi 25 25
*40* A135 60c multi 45 45

**Art at UN Type**

**1974, May 6 Photo.** ***Perf. 14***
*41* A136 60c dk red & multi 45 45
*42* A136 1fr grn & multi 80 80

**WPY Type**

**1974, Oct. 18 Photo.** ***Perf. 14***
*43* A140 60c brt grn & multi 45 45
*44* A140 80c brn & multi 60 60

**Law of the Sea Type**

**1974, Nov. 22 Photo.** ***Perf. 14***
*45* A141 1.30fr bl & multi 95 95

**Outer Space Type**

**1975, Mar. 14 Litho.** ***Perf. 13***
*46* A142 60c multi 45 45
*47* A142 90c multi 70 70

**IWY Type**

**1975, May 9 Litho.** ***Perf. 15***
*48* A143 60c multi 50 45
*49* A143 90c multi 75 70

**30th Anniv. Type**

**1975, June 26 Litho.** ***Perf. 13***
*50* A144 60c grn & multi 45 40
*51* A144 90c vio & multi 70 60

**Souvenir Sheet**

***Imperf***

*52* A144 Sheet of 2 1.10 1.10
*a.* 60c grn & multi 40 40
*b.* 90c vio & multi 60 60

No. 52 has blue and bister margin with inscription and UN emblem. Size: 92x70mm.

**Namibia Type**

**1975, Sept. 22 Photo.** ***Perf. 13½***
*53* A145 50c multi 40 40
*54* A145 1.30fr multi 1.00 1.00

**Peace-keeping Operations Type**

**1975, Nov. 21 Engr.** ***Perf. 12½***
*55* A146 60c grnsh bl 45 45
*56* A146 70c brt vio 55 55

**WFUNA Type**

**1976, Mar. 12 Photo.** ***Perf. 14***
*57* A152 90c multi 70 65

**UNCTAD Type**

**1976, Apr. 23 Photo.** ***Perf. 11½***
*58* A153 1.10fr multi 80 80

**Habitat Type**

**1976, May 28 Photo.** ***Perf. 14***
*59* A154 40c multi 30 30
*60* A154 1.50fr vio & multi 1.10 1.10

UN Emblem, Post Horn and Rainbow — G3

**1976, Oct. 8 Photo.** ***Perf. 11½***
*61* G3 80c tan & multi 1.25 1.00
*62* G3 1.10fr lt grn & multi 4.00 3.00

Sheets of 20.

**Food Council Type**

**1976, Nov. 19 Litho.** ***Perf. 14½***
*63* A156 70c multi 55 55

**WIPO Type**

**1977, Mar. 11 Photo.** ***Perf. 14***
*64* A157 80c red & multi 60 60

Drop of Water and Globe — G4

**1977, Apr. 22 Photo.** ***Perf. 13½x13***
*65* G4 80c ultra & multi 60 60
*66* G4 1.10fr dk car & multi 85 85

UN Water Conference, Mar del Plata, Argentina, Mar. 14-25.

Hands Protecting UN Emblem — G5

**1977, May 24 Photo.** ***Perf. 14***
*67* G5 80c blue & multi 60 60
*68* G5 1.10fr emer & multi 85 85

UN Security Council.

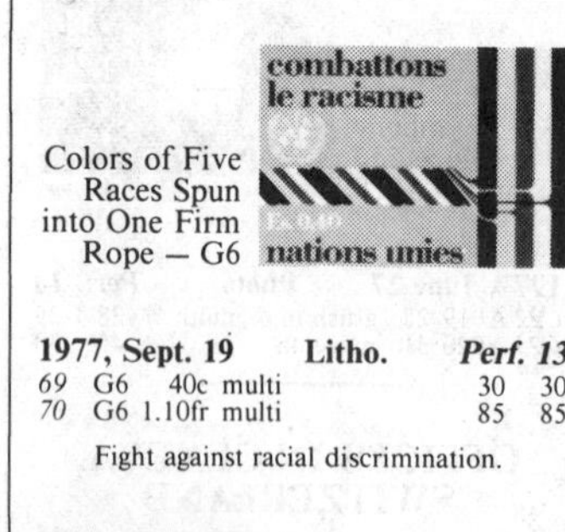


Colors of Five Races Spun into One Firm Rope — G6

**1977, Sept. 19 Litho.** ***Perf. 13***
*69* G6 40c multi 30 30
*70* G6 1.10fr multi 85 85

Fight against racial discrimination.

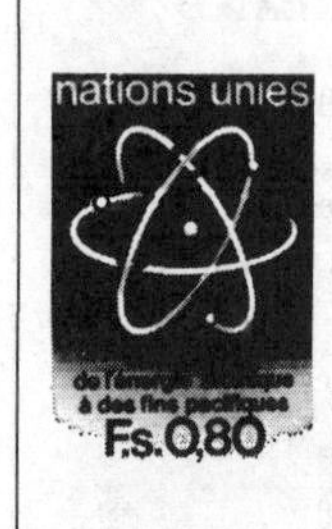


Atomic Energy Turning Partly into Olive Branch — G7

**1977, Nov. 18** **Photo.**
*71* G7 80c dk car & multi 60 60
*72* G7 1.10fr Prus bl & multi 85 85

Peaceful uses of atomic energy.

"Tree" of Doves — G8

**1978, Jan. 27 Litho.** ***Perf. 14½***
*73* G8 35c multi 30 20

Globes with Smallpox Distribution G9

**1978, Mar. 31 Photo.** ***Perf. 12x11½***
*74* G9 80c yel & multi 60 60
*75* G9 1.10fr lt grn & multi 85 85

Global eradication of smallpox.

**Namibia Type**

**1978, May 5 Photo.** ***Perf. 12***
*76* A166 80c multi 60 60

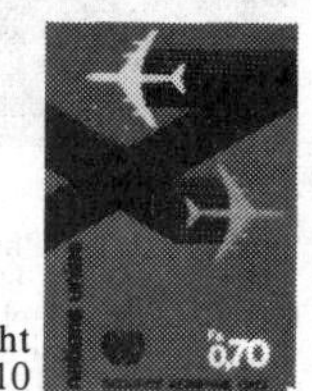

Jets and Flight Patterns — G10

**1978, June 12 Photo.** ***Perf. 14***
*77* G10 70c multi 55 55
*78* G10 80c multi 60 60

International Civil Aviation Organization for "Safety in the Air."

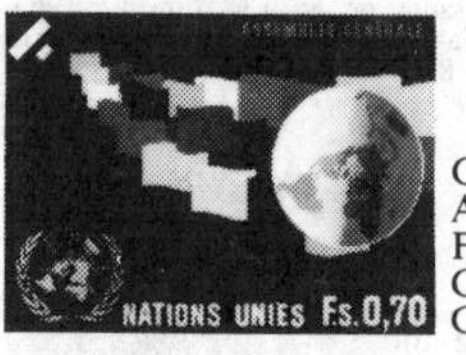


General Assembly, Flags and Globe G11

**1978, Sept. 15 Photo.** ***Perf. 13½***
*79* G11 70c multi 60 55
*80* G11 1.10fr multi 70 60

**Technical Cooperation Type**

**1978, Nov. 17 Photo.** ***Perf. 14***
*81* A169 80c multi 60 60

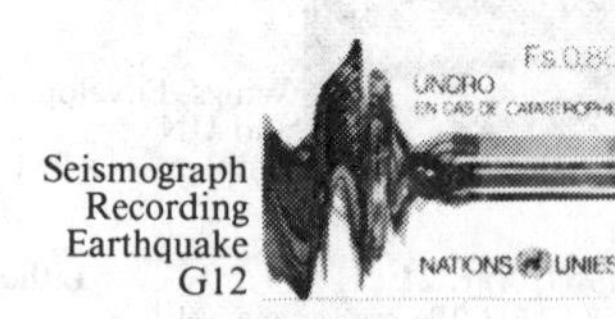


Seismograph Recording Earthquake G12

**1979, Mar. 9 Photo.** ***Perf. 14***
*82* G12 80c multi 60 60
*83* G12 1.50fr multi 1.10 1.10

Office of the UN Disaster Relief Coordinator (UNDRO).

Children and Rainbow G13

**1979, May 4 Photo.** ***Perf. 14***
*84* G13 80c multi 60 60
*85* G13 1.10fr multi 1.00 1.00

International Year of the Child.

**Namibia Type**

**1979, Oct. 5 Litho.** ***Perf. 13½***
*86* A176 1.10fr multi 85 85

International Court of Justice, Scales — G14

**1979, Nov. 9 Litho.** ***Perf. 13x13½***
*87* G14 80c multi 60 60
*88* G14 1.10fr multi 85 85

International Court of Justice, The Hague, Netherlands.

**Economic Order Type**

**1980, Jan. 11** ***Perf. 15x14½***
*89* A179 80c multi 60 60

Women's Year Emblem G15

**1980, Mar. 7 Litho.** ***Perf. 14½x15***
*90* G15 40c multi 30 30
*91* G15 70c multi 55 55

UN Decade for Women.

**Peace-keeping Operations Type**

**1980, May 16 Litho.** ***Perf. 14x13***
*92* A181 1.10fr bl & grn 85 85

35th Anniv. Type and

Dove and "35" — G16

**1980, June 26 Litho.** ***Perf. 13***
*93* G16 40c multi 30 30
*94* A183 70c multi 55 55

**Souvenir Sheet**

***Imperf***

*95* Sheet of 2 1.10 1.10
*a.* G16 40c multi 30
*b.* A183 70c multi 55

35th anniv. of the UN. No. 95 has multicolored margin with inscription and UN emblem. Size: 92x73mm.

ECOSOC Type and

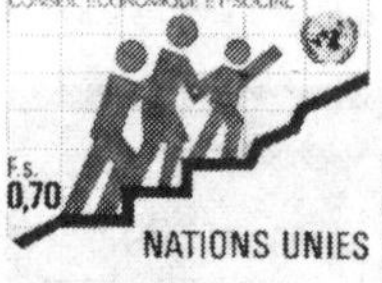


Family Climbing Line Graph — G17

**1980, Nov. 21 Litho.** ***Perf. 13½x13***
*96* A186 40c multi 30 30
*97* G17 70c multi 55 55

**Palestinian Rights Type**

**1981, Jan. 30** **Photo.**
*98* A188 80c multi 60 60

**Disabled Type of UN, Vienna**

**1981, Mar. 6** **Photo.**
*99* A190 40c multi 30 30
*100* V4 1.50fr multi 1.10 1.10

**Art Type**

**1981, Apr. 15 Photo. *Perf. 11½***
*101* A191 80c multi 60 60

**Energy Type**

**1981, May 29 Litho. *Perf. 13***
*102* A192 1.10fr multi 95 85

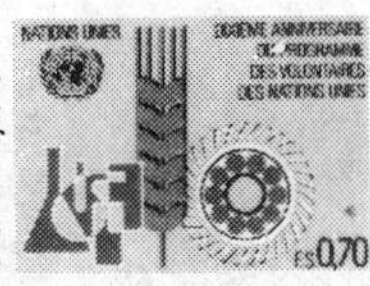
Volunteers Program Type and Symbols of Science, Agriculture and Industry — G18

**1981, Nov. 13 Litho. *Perf. 13½x13***
*103* A194 40c multi 35 30
*104* G18 70c multi 60 55

Fight Against Apartheid G19

Flower of Flags G20

**1982, Jan. 22 Photo. *Perf. 11½x12***
*105* G19 30c multi 20 10
*106* G20 1fr multi 80 35

Human Environment — G21

**1982, Mar. 19 Litho. *Perf. 13½x13***
*107* G21 40c multi 35 30
*108* A199 1.20fr multi 1.10 90

**Outer Space Type of U.N. and**

Satellite Applications of Space Technology G22

***Perf. 13 x 13½***

**1982, June 11 Litho.**
*109* A201 80c multi 75 60
*110* G22 1fr multi 90 75

**Conservation and Protection of Nature**

**1982, Nov. 19 Photo. *Perf. 14***
*111* A202 40c Bird 40 30
*112* A202 1.50fr Reptile 1.50 1.10

**World Communications Year Type**

**1983, Jan. 28 Litho. *Perf. 13***
*113* A204 1.20fr multi 1.40 1.15

**Safety at Sea Type and**

Life Preserver and Radar — G23

**1983, Mar. 18 Litho. *Perf. 14½***
*114* A205 40c multi 38 38
*115* G23 80c multi 75 75

**World Food Program Type**

**1983, Apr. 22 Engr. *Perf. 13½***
*116* A207 1.50fr blue 1.50 1.50

Type of UN and

G24

**1983, June 6 Litho. *Perf. 14***
*117* A208 80c multi 75 75
*118* G24 1.10fr multi 1.00 1.00

35th Anniv. of the Universal Declaration of Human Rights
G25 G26

***Perf. 13½***

**1983, Dec. 9 Photo. Engr.**
*119* G25 40c Homo Humus Humanitas 50 38
*120* G26 1.20fr Right to Create 1.40 70

**Intl. Population Conference Type**

**1984, Feb. 3 Litho. *Perf. 14***
*121* A212 1.20fr multi 1.20 70

**World Food Day**

Fishing G27

Women Farm Workers, Africa G28

**1984, Mar. 15 Litho. *Perf. 14½***
*122* G27 50c multi 50 25
*123* G28 80c multi 80 40

**World Heritage**

Valletta, Malta — G29

Los Glaciares Natl. Park, Argentina G30

**1984, Apr. 18 Litho. *Perf. 14***
*124* G29 50c multi 50 25
*125* G30 70c multi 70 35

G31

G32

**1984, May 29 Photo. *Perf. 11½***
*126* G31 35c multi 35 18
*127* G32 1.50fr multi 1.50 75

International Youth Year — G33

**1984, Nov. 15 Litho. *Perf. 13½***
*128* G33 1.20fr multi 1.00 45

ILO Type of UN and

Turin Center — G34

**1985, Feb. 1 Engr.**
*129* A220 80c Turin Center emblem 80 45
*130* G34 1.20fr U Thant Pavilion 1.20 70

**UN University Type**

**1985, Mar. 15 Photo. *Perf. 13½***
*131* A221 50c Farmer, discussion group 45 28
*132* A221 80c As above 70 45

Postman G35

Doves — G36

**1985, May 10 Litho. *Perf. 14***
*133* G35 20c multi 20 8
*134* G36 1.20fr multi 1.20 50

**40th Anniv. Type**

**1985, June 26 Photo. *Perf. 12x11½***
*135* A224 50c multi 50 20
*136* A225 70c multi 70 28

**Souvenir Sheet**

***Imperf***

*137* Sheet of 2 1.50 1.50
*a.* A224 50c multi 60
*b.* A225 70c multi 85

No. 137 has multicolored margin with inscription and UN emblem. Size: 75x83mm.

**UNICEF Child Survival Campaign**

**Photo. & Engr.**

**1985, Nov. 22 *Perf. 13½***
*138* A226 50c Three girls *1.00* 20
*139* A226 1.20fr Infant drinking *2.50* 50

**Africa in Crisis Type**

Abstract painting by Alemayehou Gabremedhin.

**1986, Jan. 31 Photo. *Perf. 11½***
*140* A227 1.40fr Mother, hungry children 1.25 62

**UN Development Program Type**

**1986, Mar. 14 Photo. *Perf. 13½***
*141* A228 35c Erosion control 50 15
*142* A228 35c Logging 50 15
*143* A228 35c Lumber transport 50 15
*144* A228 35c Nursery 50 15
*a.* Block of 4, Nos. 141-144 2.00 60

Nos. 141-144 printed se-tenant in continuous design.

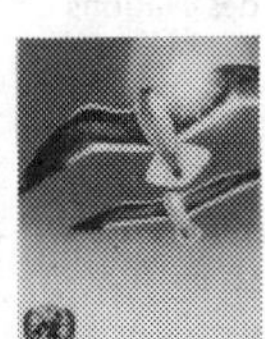
Doves and Sun — G37

**1986, Mar. 14 Litho. *Perf. 15x14½***
*145* G37 5c multi 10 5

**UN Stamp Collecting Type**

Designs: 50c, UN Human Rights stamp. 80c, UN stamps.

**1986, May 22 Engr. *Perf. 12½***
*146* A229 50c dk grn & hn brn 50 25
*147* A229 80c dk grn & yel org 80 42

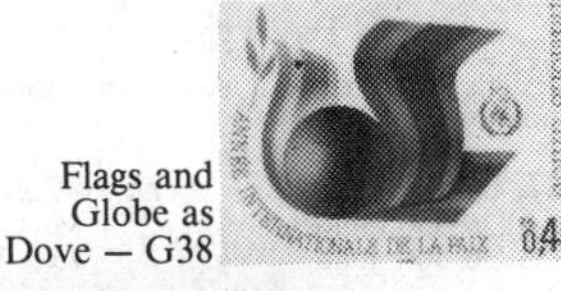
Flags and Globe as Dove — G38

Peace in French — G39

**Photo. & Embossed**

**1986, June 20 *Perf. 13½***
*148* G38 45c multi 60 25
*149* G39 1.40fr multi 1.75 80

Intl. Peace Year.

**WFUNA Anniv. Type**

**Souvenir Sheet**

Designs: 35c, Abstract by Benigno Gomez, Honduras. 45c, Abstract by Alexander Calder (1898-1976), US. 50c, Abstract by Joan Miro (b. 1893), Spain. 70c, Sextet with Dove, by Ole Hamann, Denmark.

**1986, Nov. 14 Litho. *Perf. 13x13½***
*150* Sheet of 4 2.45 2.45
*a.* A232 35c multi 42
*b.* A232 45c multi 55
*c.* A232 50c multi 62
*d.* A232 70c multi 85

No. 150 has inscribed margin picturing UN and WFUNA emblems.

**Trygve Lie Type**

**Photo. & Engr.**

**1987, Jan. 30 *Perf. 13½***
*151* A233 1.40fr multi 1.40 90

Sheaf of Colored Bands, by Georges Mathieu
G40

Armillary Sphere, Palais des Nations
G41

**Photo., Photo. & Engr. (No. 153)**
***Perf. 11½x12, 13½ (No. 153)***

**1987, Jan. 30**
*152* G40 90c multi 90 60
*153* G41 1.40fr multi 1.40 90

***Perf. 13½x12½***

**1987, Mar. 13** **Litho.**
*154* A234 50c Construction 70 35
*155* A234 90c Finishing interior 1.20 60

**Fight Drug Abuse Type**

**1987, June 12** **Litho.** ***Perf. 14½***
*156* A235 80c Mother and child 80 55
*157* A235 1.20fr Workers in rice paddy 1.20 80

**UN Day Type**

Designs: Multinational people in various occupations.

**1987, Oct. 23** **Litho.** ***Perf. 14½x15***
*158* A236 35c multi 55 25
*159* A236 50c multi 75 35

**Immunize Every Child Type**

**1987, Nov. 20** **Litho.** ***Perf. 15x14½***
*160* A237 90c Whooping cough 1.00 60
*161* A237 1.70fr Tuberculosis 2.00 1.15

**IFAD Type**

**1988, Jan. 29** **Litho.** ***Perf. 13½***
*162* A238 35c Flocks 45 25
*163* A238 1.40fr Fruit 1.80 1.10

G42

**1988, Jan. 29** **Photo.** ***Perf. 14***
*164* A42 50c multi 65 40

**Survival of the Forests Type**

**1988, Mar. 18** **Litho.** ***Perf. 14x15***
*165* A240 50c Pine forest 1.50 40
*166* A240 1.10fr as 50c 3.50 90

Nos. 165-166 printed se-tenant in a continuous design.

Intl. Volunteer Day Type
***Perf. 13x14, 14x13***

**1988, May 6** **Litho.**
*167* A241 80c Agriculture, vert. 1.20 60
*168* A241 90c Veterinary medicine 1.35 68

Health in Sports Type
***Perf. 13½x13, 13x13½***

**1988, June 17** **Litho.**
*169* A242 50c Soccer, vert. 70 35
*170* A242 1.40fr Swimming 2.00 1.00

Human Rights Declaration Anniv. Type

**1988, Dec. 9** **Photo. & Engr.** ***Perf.***
*171* A243 90c multi 1.20 60

**Souvenir Sheet**

*172* A243 2fr multi 2.60 2.60

No. 172 has multicolored decorative margin picturing the preamble to the Universal Declaration of Human Rights (inscribed in French). Size:

World Bank Type

**1989, Jan. 27** **Litho.** ***Perf.***
*173* A244 80c Telecommunications 1.15 1.05
*174* A244 1.40fr Industry 2.00 1.00

## OFFICES IN VIENNA, AUSTRIA

For use only on mail posted at the Vienna International Center for the UN and the International Atomic Energy Agency.

100 Groschen = 1 Schilling

Type of Geneva 1978, UN Types of 1961-72 and

Donaupark, Vienna — V1

Aerial View — V2

***Perf. 11½***

**1979, Aug. 24** **Photo.** **Unwmk.**
**Granite Paper**
*1* G8 50g multi 5 5
*2* A52 1s multi 10 8
*3* V1 4s multi 40 25
*4* AP13 5s multi 50 35
*5* V2 6s multi 60 45
*6* A45 10s multi 1.00 70
*Nos. 1-6 (6)* 2.65 1.88

No. 6 has no frame.

**Economic Order Type**

**1980, Jan. 11** **Litho.** ***Perf. 15x14½***
*7* A178 4s multi 2.00 1.35

**Dove Type**

**1980, Jan. 11** **Litho.** ***Perf. 13x13½***
*8* A147 2.50s multi 30 15

Women's Year Emblem on World Map — V3

**1980, Mar. 7** **Litho.** ***Perf. 14½x15***
*9* V3 4s lt grn & dk grn 55 35
*10* V3 6s bis brn 85 50

UN Decade for Women.

**Peace-keeping Operations Type**

**1980, May 16** **Litho.** ***Perf. 14x13***
*11* A182 6s multi 75 50

**35th Anniv. Types of Geneva and UN**

**1980, June 26** **Litho.** ***Perf. 13***
*12* G16 4s multi 50 35
*13* A184 6s multi 75 50

**Souvenir Sheet**
***Imperf***

*14* Sheet of 2 1.40 1.00
*a.* G16 4s multi 50
*b.* A184 6s multi 75

35th anniv. of the UN. No. 14 has multicolored margin with inscription and UN emblem. Size: 92x73mm.

**ECOSOC Types of UN and Geneva**

**1980, Nov. 21** **Litho.** ***Perf. 13½x13***
*15* A187 4s multi 45 35
*16* G17 6s multi 70 50

**Palestinian Rights Type**

**1981, Jan. 30** **Photo.**
*17* A188 4s multi 55 35

Disabled Type of UN and

Interlocking Stitches — V4

**1981, Mar. 6** **Photo.**
*18* A189 4s multi 40 35
*19* V4 6s multi 60 50

**Art Type**

**1981, Apr. 15** **Photo.** ***Perf. 11½***
*20* A191 6s multi 65 50

**Energy Type**

**1981, May 29** **Litho.** ***Perf. 13***
*21* A193 7.50s multi 90 65

**Volunteers Program Types of UN and Geneva**

**1981, Nov. 13** **Litho.** ***Perf. 13½x13***
*22* A195 5s multi 60 40
*23* G18 7s multi 80 60

"For a Better World" — V5

**1982, Jan. 22** **Photo.** ***Perf. 11½x12***
*24* V5 3s multi 40 20

**Human Environment Types of UN and Geneva**

**1982, Mar. 19** **Litho.** ***Perf. 13½x13***
*25* A200 5s multi 60 40
*26* G21 7s multi 80 86

**Outer Space Type of Geneva**

**1982, June 11** **Litho.** ***Perf. 13x13½***
*27* G22 5s multi 60 40

**Conservation and Protection of Nature Type**

**1982, Nov. 19** **Photo.** ***Perf. 14***
*28* A202 5s Fish 60 40
*29* A202 7s Animal 80 60

**World Communications Year Type**

**1983, Jan. 28** **Litho.** ***Perf. 13***
*30* A203 4s multi 65 42

**Safety at Sea Type of Geneva and UN**

**1983, Mar. 18** **Litho.** ***Perf. 14½***
*31* G23 4s multi 65 42
*32* A206 6s multi 95 62

**World Food Program Type**

**1983, Apr. 22** **Engr.** ***Perf. 13½***
*33* A207 5s green 75 50
*34* A207 7s brown 1.05 70

**Trade and Development Types of Geneva and UN**

**1983, June 6** **Litho.** ***Perf. 14***
*35* G24 4s multi 65 42
*36* A209 8.50s multi 1.40 1.00

35th Anniv. of the Universal Declaration of Human Rights
V6 V7

**Photogravure and Engraved**

**1983, Dec. 9** ***Perf. 13½***
*37* V6 5s The Second Skin 75 50
*38* V7 7s Right to Think 1.05 70

**Intl. Population Conference Type**

**1984, Feb. 3** **Litho.** ***Perf. 14***
*39* A212 7s multi 75 50

**World Food Day**

Field Irrigation
V8

Pest Control
V9

**1984, Mar. 15** **Litho.** ***Perf. 14½***
*40* V8 4.50s multi 70 25
*41* V9 6s multi 90 40

**World Heritage**

Serengeti Park, Tanzania
V10

Ancient City of Shiban, People's Democratic Rep. of Yemen — V11

**1984, Apr. 18** **Litho.** ***Perf. 14***
*42* V10 3.50s multi 70 25
*43* V11 15s multi 2.50 90

**Refugees**

V12

V13

**1984, May 29** **Photo.** ***Perf. 11½***
*44* V12 4.50s multi 60 25
*45* V13 8.50s multi 1.35 50

*United Nations Offices in Vienna stamps can be mounted in Scott's annually supplemented U.N. Singles and Postal Stationery Album.*

International Youth Year — V14

**1984, Nov. 15 Litho. *Perf. 13½***

*46* V14 3.50s multi 50 20
*47* V14 6.50s multi 90 40

### ILO Type of Geneva

**1985, Feb. 1 Engr. *Perf. 13½***

*48* G33 7.50s U Thant Pavilion 1.50 45

### UN University Type

**1985, Mar. 15 Photo. *Perf. 13½***

*49* A221 8.50s Rural scene, scientist 1.75 50

Ship of Peace V15

Sharing Umbrella V16

**1985, May 10 Litho. *Perf. 14***

*50* V15 4.50s multi 60 25
*51* V16 15s multi 2.50 90

### 40th Anniv. Type

**1985, June 26 Photo. *Perf. 12x11½***

*52* A224 6.50s multi 1.00 36
*53* A225 8.50s multi 1.40 48

### Souvenir Sheet
### *Imperf*

*54* Sheet of 2 2.50 1.50
*a.* A224 6.50s multi 1.00
*b.* A225 8.50s multi 1.40

No. 54 has multicolored margin with inscription and UN emblem. Size: 75x83mm.

### UNICEF Child Survival Campaign
### Photogravure and Engraved

**1985, Nov. 22 *Perf. 13½***

*55* A226 4s Spoonfeeding children 70 20
*56* A226 6s Mother hugging infant 1.10 30

### Africa in Crisis Type

Abstract painting by Tesfaye Tessema.

**1986, Jan. 31 Photo. *Perf. 11½***

*57* A227 8s multi 1.25 45

### UN Development Program Type

**1986, Mar. 14 Photo. *Perf. 13½***

*58* A228 4.50s Developing corp strains 75 22
*59* A228 4.50s Animal husbandry 75 22
*60* A228 4.50s Technical instruction 75 22
*61* A228 4.50s Nutrition education 75 22
*a.* Block of 4, Nos. 58-61 3.00 88

Nos. 58-61 printed se-tenant in continuous design.

### UN Stamp Collecting Type

Designs: 3.50s, UN stamps. 6.50s, Engraver.

**1986, May 22 Engr. *Perf. 12½***

*62* A229 3.50s dk ultra & dk brn 45 22
*63* A229 6.50s int bl & brt rose 80 40

Olive Branch, Rainbow, Earth — V17

### Photogravure and Embossed

**1986, June 20 *Perf. 13½***

*64* V17 5s shown 75 32
*65* V17 6s Doves, UN emblem 95 40

Intl. Peace Year.

### WFUNA Anniv. Type
### Souvenir Sheet

Designs: 4c, White Stallion, by Elisabeth von Janota-Bzowski, Germany. 5s, Surrealistic landscape by Ernst Fuchs, Austria. 6s, Geometric abstract by Victor Vasarely (b. 1908), France. 7s, Mythological abstract by Wolfgang Hutter (b. 1928), Austria.

**1986, Nov. 14 Litho. *Perf. 13x13½***

*66* Sheet of 4 3.15 3.15
*a.* A232 4s multi 58 30
*b.* A232 5s multi 72 35
*c.* A232 6s multi 85 42
*d.* A232 7s multi 1.00 50

No. 66 has inscribed margin picturing UN and WFUNA emblems.

### Trygve Lie Type
### Photogravure and Engraved

**1987, Jan. 30 *Perf. 13½***

*67* A233 8s multi 1.00 62

### Shelter for the Homeless Type
### *Perf. 13½x12½*

**1987, Mar. 13 Litho.**

*68* A234 4s Family, homes 55 32
*69* A234 9.50s Entering home 1.20 75

### Fight Drug Abuse Type

**1987, June 12 Litho. *Perf. 14½x15***

*70* A235 5s Soccer players 60 40
*71* A235 8s Family 1.00 65

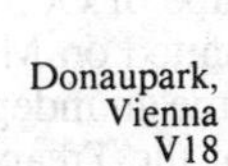

Donaupark, Vienna V18

Peace Embracing the Earth — V19

**1987, June 12 *Perf. 14½x15***

*72* V18 2s multi 30 16
*73* V19 17s multi 2.00 1.40

### UN Day Type

**1987, Oct. 23 Litho. *Perf. 14½x15***

*74* A236 5s multi 80 40
*75* A236 6s multi 95 48

### Immunize Every Child Type

**1987, Nov. 20 *Perf. 15x14½***

*76* A237 4s Polio 65 32
*77* A237 9.50s Diphtheria 1.50 75

### IFAD Type

**1988, Jan. 29 Litho. *Perf. 13½***

*78* A238 4s Grains 72 5
*79* A238 6s Vegetables 1.00 50

### Survival of the Forests Type

Deciduous forest in fall.

**1988, Mar. 18 Litho. *Perf. 14x15***

*80* A240 4s multicolored 78 40
*81* A240 5s multicolored 95 48

Nos. 80-81 printed se-tenant in a continuous design.

### Intl. Volunteer Day Type
### *Perf. 13x14, 14x13*

**1988, May 6 Litho.**

*82* A241 6s Medical care, vert. 1.05 52
*83* A241 7.50s Construction 1.30 65

### Health in Sports Type
### *Perf. 13½x13, 13x13½*

**1988, June 17 Litho.**

*84* A242 6s Skiing, vert. 1.00 50
*85* A242 8s Tennis 1.35 68

### Human Rights Declaration Anniv. Type

**1988, Dec. 9 Photo. & Engr. *Perf.***

*86* A243 5s multi 78 52

### Souvenir Sheet

*87* A243 11s multi 1.70 1.70

No. 87 has multicolored decorative margin picturing preamble to the Universal Declaration of Human Rights (inscribed in German). Size:

### World Bank Type

**1989, Jan. 27 Litho. *Perf.***

*88* A244 5.50s Transportation 92 62
*89* A244 8s Health care, education 1.35 90

# British Commonwealth of Nations

## Dominions, Colonies, Territories, Offices and Independent Members

Comprising stamps of the British Commonwealth and associated nations.

A strict observance of technicalities would bar some or all of the stamps listed under Burma, Iraq, Ireland, Jordan, Kuwait, Nepal, New Republic, Orange Free State, Samoa, South Africa, South-West Africa, Stellaland, Sudan, Swaziland, the two Transvaal Republics and others but these are included for the convenience of collectors.

## 1. Great Britain

Great Britain: Including England, Scotland, Wales and Northern Ireland.

## 2. The Dominions, Present and Past

**AUSTRALIA**

The Commonwealth of Australia was proclaimed on January 1, 1901. It consists of six former colonies as follows:

| | |
|---|---|
| New South Wales | Tasmania |
| Queensland | Victoria |
| South Australia | Western Australia |

Territories belonging to, or administered by Australia: Australian Antarctic Territory, Christmas Island, Cocos (Keeling) Islands, Nauru, New Guinea, Norfolk Island, Papua New Guinea.

**CANADA**

The Dominion of Canada was created by the British North America Act in 1867. The following provinces were former separate colonies and issued postage stamps:

| | |
|---|---|
| British Columbia and Vancouver Island | Newfoundland |
| | Nova Scotia |
| New Brunswick | Prince Edward Island |

**FIJI**

The colony of Fiji became an independent nation with dominion status on Oct. 10, 1970.

**GHANA**

This state came into existence Mar. 6, 1957, with dominion status. It consists of the former colony of the Gold Coast and the Trusteeship Territory of Togoland. Ghana became a republic July 1, 1960.

**INDIA**

The Republic of India was inaugurated on January 26, 1950. It succeeded the Dominion of India which was proclaimed August 15, 1947, when the former Empire of India was divided into Pakistan and the Union of India. The Republic is composed of about 40 predominantly Hindu states of three classes: governor's provinces, chief commissioner's provinces and princely states. India also has various territories, such as the Andaman and Nicobar Islands.

The old Empire of India was a federation of British India and the native states. The more important princely states were autonomous. Of the more than 700 Indian states, these 43 are familiar names to philatelists because of their postage stamps.

**CONVENTION STATES**

| | | |
|---|---|---|
| Chamba | Gwalior | Nabha |
| Faridkot | Jhind | Patiala |

**NATIVE FEUDATORY STATES**

| | | |
|---|---|---|
| Alwar | Duttia | Kishangarh |
| Bahawalpur | Faridkot (1879-85) | Las Bela |
| Bamra | Hyderabad | Morvi |
| Barwani | Idar | Nandgaon |
| Bhopal | Indore | Nowanuggur |
| Bhor | Jaipur | Orchha |
| Bijawar | Jammu | Poonch |
| Bundi | Jammu and Kashmir | Rajpeepla |
| Bussahir | Jasdan | Sirmur |
| Charkhari | Jhalawar | Soruth |
| Cochin | Jhind (1875-76) | Travancore |
| Dhar | Kashmir | Wadhwan |

**NEW ZEALAND**

Became a dominion on September 26, 1907. The following islands and territories are, or have been, administered by New Zealand:

| | |
|---|---|
| Aitutaki | Ross Dependency |
| Cook Islands (Rarotonga) | Samoa (Western Samoa) |
| Niue | Tokelau Islands |
| Penrhyn | |

**PAKISTAN**

The Republic of Pakistan was proclaimed March 23, 1956. It succeeded the Dominion which was proclaimed August 15, 1947. It is made up of all or part of several Moslem provinces and various districts of the former Empire of India, including Bahawalpur and Las Bela. Pakistan withdrew from the Commonwealth in 1972.

**SOUTH AFRICA**

Under the terms of the South African Act (1909) the self-governing colonies of Cape of Good Hope, Natal, Orange River Colony and Transvaal united on May 31, 1910, to form the Union of South Africa. It became an independent republic May 3, 1961.

Under the terms of the Treaty of Versailles, South-West Africa, formerly German South-West Africa, was mandated to the Union of South Africa.

**SRI LANKA (CEYLON)**

The Dominion of Ceylon was proclaimed February 4, 1948. The island had been a Crown Colony from 1802 until then. On May 22, 1972, Ceylon became the Republic of Sri Lanka.

## 3. Colonies, Past and Present; Controlled Territory and Independent Members of the Commonwealth

| | |
|---|---|
| Abu Dhabi | Botswana |
| Aden | British Antarctic Territory |
| Aitutaki | British Central Africa |
| Ajman | British Columbia & Vancouver Island |
| Antigua | |
| Ascension | British East Africa |
| Bahamas | British Guiana |
| Bahrain | British Honduras |
| Bangladesh | British Indian Ocean Territory |
| Barbados | British New Guinea |
| Barbuda | British Solomon Islands |
| Basutoland | British Somaliland |
| Batum | Brunei |
| Bechuanaland | Burma |
| Bechuanaland Prot. | Bushire |
| Belize | Cameroons |
| Bermuda | Cape of Good Hope |

Cayman Islands
Christmas Island
Cocos (Keeling) Islands
Cook Islands
Crete,
  British Administration
Cyprus
Dominica
Dubai
East Africa & Uganda
  Protectorates
Egypt (see Vol. II)
Falkland Islands
Fiji
Fujeira
Gambia
German East Africa
Gibraltar
Gilbert Islands
Gilbert & Ellice Islands
Gold Coast
Grenada
Griqualand West
Guernsey
Guyana
Heligoland
Hong Kong
Indian Native States
  (see India)
Ionian Islands
Iraq
Jamaica
Jersey
Kenya
Kenya, Uganda & Tanzania
Kuwait
Labuan
Lagos
Leeward Islands
Lesotho
Madagascar

Malawi
Malaya
  Federated Malay States
  Johore
  Kedah
  Kelantan
  Malacca
  Negri Sembilan
  Pahang
  Penang
  Perak
  Perlis
  Selangor
  Singapore
  Sungei Ujong
  Trengganu
Malaysia
Maldive Islands
Malta
Man, Isle of
Mauritius
Mesopotamia
Montserrat
Muscat
Natal
Nauru
Nevis
New Britain
New Brunswick
Newfoundland
New Guinea
New Hebrides
New Republic
New South Wales
Niger Coast Protectorate
Nigeria
Niue
Norfolk Island
North Borneo
Northern Nigeria
Northern Rhodesia

North West Pacific Islands
Nova Scotia
Nyasaland Protectorate
Oman
Orange River Colony
Palestine
Papua New Guinea
Penrhyn Island
Pitcairn Islands
Prince Edward Island
Qatar
Queensland
Ras al Khaima
Rhodesia
Rhodesia & Nyasaland
Ross Dependency
Sabah
St. Christopher
St. Helena
St. Kitts
St. Kitts-Nevis-Anguilla
St. Lucia
St. Vincent
Samoa
Sarawak
Seychelles
Sharjah & Dependencies
Sierra Leone
Solomon Islands
Somaliland Protectorate
South Arabia
South Australia
South Georgia

Southern Nigeria
Southern Rhodesia
South-West Africa
Stellaland
Straits Settlements
Sudan
Swaziland
Tanganyika
Tanganyika and Zanzibar
Tanzania
Tasmania
Tobago
Togo
Tokelau Islands
Tonga
Trans-Jordan (see Jordan)
Transvaal
Trinidad
Trinidad and Tobago
Tristan da Cunha
Trucial States
Turks and Caicos
Turks Islands
Tuvalu
Uganda
Umm al Qiwain
United Arab Emirates
Victoria
Virgin Islands
Western Australia
Zambia
Zanzibar
Zululand

**POST OFFICES IN FOREIGN COUNTRIES**

Africa
  East Africa Forces
  Middle East Forces
Bangkok
China
Morocco
Turkish Empire

# Common Design Types

Pictured in this section are issues where one illustration has been used for a number of countries in the Catalogue. Not included in this section are overprinted stamps or those issues which are illustrated in each country.

## EUROPA

### Europa Issue, 1956

The design symbolizing the cooperation among the six countries comprising the Coal and Steel Community is illustrated in each country.

Belgium 496-497
France 805-806
Germany 748-749
Italy 715-716
Luxembourg 318-320
Netherlands 368-369

### Europa Issue, 1958

"E" and Dove
CD1

European Postal Union at the service of European integration.

**1958, Sept. 13**

Belgium 527-528
France 889-890
Germany 790-791
Italy 750-751
Luxembourg 341-343
Netherlands 375-376
Saar 317-318

### Europa Issue, 1959

6-Link Endless Chain
CD2

**1959, Sept. 19**

Belgium 536-537
France 929-930
Germany 805-806
Italy 791-792
Luxembourg 354-355
Netherlands 379-380

### Europa Issue, 1960

19-Spoke Wheel
CD3

First anniverary of the establishment of C.E.P.T. (Conference Europeenne des Administrations des Postes et des Telecommunications.)

The spokes symbolize the 19 founding members of the Conference.

**1960, Sept.**

Belgium 553-554
Denmark 379
Finland 376-377
France 970-971
Germany 818-820
Great Britain 377-378
Greece 688
Iceland 327-328
Ireland 175-176
Italy 809-810
Luxembourg 374-375
Netherlands 385-386
Norway 387
Portugal 866-867
Spain 941-942
Sweden 562-563
Switzerland 400-401
Turkey 1493-1494

### Europa Issue, 1961

19 Doves Flying as One
CD4

The 19 doves represent the 19 members of the Conference of European Postal and Telecommunications Administrations C.E.P.T.

**1961-62**

Belgium 572-573
Cyprus 201-203
France 1005-1006
Germany 844-845
Great Britain 383-384
Greece 718-719
Iceland 340-341
Italy 845-846
Luxembourg 382-383
Netherlands 387-388
Spain 1010-1011
Switzerland 410-411
Turkey 1518-1520

### Europa Issue 1962

Young Tree with 19 Leaves
CD5

The 19 leaves represent the 19 original members of C.E.P.T.

**1962-63**

Belgium 582-583
Cyprus 219-221
France 1045-1046
Germany 852-853
Greece 739-740
Iceland 348-349
Ireland 184-185
Italy 860-861
Luxembourg 386-387
Netherlands 394-395
Norway 414-415
Switzerland 416-417
Turkey 1553-1555

### Europa Issue, 1963

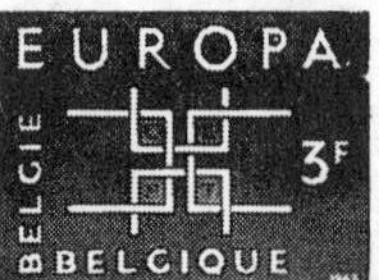


Stylized Links, Symbolizing Unity
CD6

**1963, Sept.**

Belgium 598-599
Cyprus 229-231
Finland 419
France 1074-1075
Germany 867-868
Greece 768-769
Iceland 357-358
Ireland 188-189
Italy 880-881
Luxembourg 403-404
Netherlands 416-417
Norway 441-442
Switzerland 429
Turkey 1602-1603

### Europa Issue, 1964

Symbolic Daisy
CD7

5th anniversary of the establishment of C.E.P.T. The 22 petals of the flower symbolize the 22 members of the Conference.

**1964, Sept.**

Austria 738
Belgium 614-615
Cyprus 244-246
France 1109-1110
Germany 897-898
Greece 801-802
Iceland 367-368
Ireland 196-197
Italy 894-895
Luxembourg 411-412
Monaco 590-591
Netherlands 428-429
Norway 458
Portugal 931-933
Spain 1262-1263
Switzerland 438-439
Turkey 1628-1629

### Europa Issue, 1965

Leaves and "Fruit"
CD8

**1965**

Belgium 636-637
Cyprus 262-264
Finland 437
France 1131-1132
Germany 934-935
Greece 833-834
Iceland 375-376
Ireland 204-205
Italy 915-916
Luxembourg 432-433
Monaco 616-617
Netherlands 438-439
Norway 475-476
Portugal 958-960
Switzerland 469
Turkey 1665-1666

### Europa Issue, 1966

Symbolic Sailboat
CD9

**1966, Sept.**

Andorra, French 172
Belgium 675-676
Cyprus 275-277
France 1163-1164
Germany 963-964
Greece 862-863
Iceland 384-385
Ireland 216-217
Italy 942-943
Liechtenstein 415
Luxembourg 440-441
Monaco 639-640
Netherlands 441-442
Norway 496-497
Portugal 980-982
Switzerland 477-478
Turkey 1718-1719

### Europa Issue, 1967

Cogwheels
CD10

**1967**

Andorra, French 174-175
Belgium 688-689
Cyprus 297-299
France 1178-1179
Greece 891-892
Germany 969-970
Iceland 389-390
Ireland 232-233
Italy 951-952
Liechtenstein 420
Luxembourg 449-450
Monaco 669-670
Netherlands 444-447
Norway 504-505
Portugal 994-996
Spain 1465-1466
Switzerland 482
Turkey B120-B121

### Europa Issue, 1968

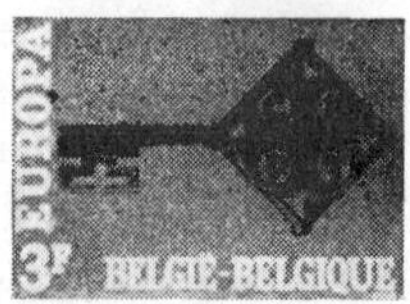


Golden Key with C.E.P.T. Emblem
CD11

**1968**

Andorra, French 182-183
Belgium 705-706
Cyprus 314-316
France 1209-1210
Germany 983-984
Greece 916-917
Iceland 395-396
Ireland 242-243
Italy 979-980
Liechtenstein 442
Luxembourg 466-467
Monaco 689-691
Netherlands 452-453
Portugal 1019-1021
San Marino 687
Spain 1526
Turkey 1775-1776

### Europa Issue, 1969

"EUROPA" and "CEPT"
CD12

Tenth anniversary of C.E.P.T.

**1969**

Andorra, French 188-189
Austria 837
Belgium 718-719
Cyprus 326-328
Denmark 458
Finland 483
France 1245-1246
Germany 996-997
Great Britain 585

Greece 947-948
Iceland 406-407
Ireland 270-271
Italy 1000-1001
Jugoslavia 1003-1004
Liechtenstein 453
Luxembourg 474-475
Monaco 722-724
Netherlands 475-476
Norway 533-534
Portugal 1038-1040
San Marino 701-702
Spain 1567
Sweden 814-816
Switzerland 500-501
Turkey 1799-1800
Vatican 470-472

### Europa Issue, 1970

Interwoven Threads CD13

**1970**

Andorra, French 196-197
Belgium 741-742
Cyprus 340-342
France 1271-1272
Germany 1018-1019
Greece 985, 987
Iceland 420-421
Ireland 279-281
Italy 1013-1014
Jugoslavia 1024-1025
Liechtenstein 470
Luxembourg 489-490
Monaco 768-770
Netherlands 483-484
Portugal 1060-1062
San Marino 729-730
Spain 1607
Switzerland 515-516
Turkey 1848-1849

### Europa Issue, 1971

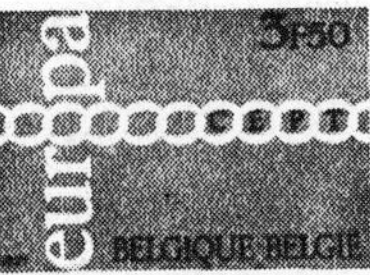


"Fraternity, Cooperation, Common Effort"—CD14

**1971**

Andorra, French 205-206
Belgium 803-804
Cyprus 365-367
Finland 504
France 1304
Germany 1064-1065
Greece 1029-1030
Iceland 429-430
Ireland 305-306
Italy 1038-1039
Jugoslavia 1052-1053
Liechtenstein 485
Luxembourg 500-501
Malta 425-427
Monaco 797-799
Netherlands 488-489
Portugal 1094-1096
San Marino 749-750
Spain 1675-1676
Switzerland 531-532
Turkey 1876-1877

### Europa Issue, 1972

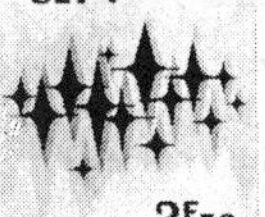


Sparkles, Symbolic of Communications CD15

**1972**

Andorra, French 210-211
Andorra, Spanish 62
Belgium 825-826
Cyprus 380-382
Finland 512-513
France 1341
Germany 1089-1090
Greece 1049-1050
Iceland 439-440
Ireland 316-317
Italy 1065-1066
Jugoslavia 1100-1101
Liechtenstein 504
Luxembourg 512-513
Malta 450-453
Monaco 831-832
Netherlands 494-495
Portugal 1141-1143
San Marino 771-772
Spain 1718
Switzerland 544-545
Turkey 1907-1908

### Europa Issue, 1973

Post Horn and Arrows CD16

**1973**

Andorra, French 319-320
Andorra, Spanish 76
Belgium 839-840
Cyprus 396-398
Finland 526
France 1367
Germany 1114-1115
Greece 1090-1092
Iceland 447-448
Ireland 329-330
Italy 1108-1109
Jugoslavia 1138-1139
Liechtenstein 528-529
Luxembourg 523-524
Malta 469-471
Monaco 866-867
Netherlands 504-505
Norway 604-605
Portugal 1170-1172
San Marino 802-803
Spain 1753
Switzerland 580-581
Turkey 1935-1936

## BRITISH COMMONWEALTH OF NATIONS

The listings follow established trade practices when these issues are offered as units by dealers. The Peace issue, for example, includes only one stamp from the Indian state of Hyderabad. The U.P.U. issue lacks the Jordan set and includes the Egypt set (see Vol. II). Pairs are included for those varieties issues with bilingual designs setenant.

The first seven issue totals (through the 1953 Coronation) include the stamps of Great Britain, Offices and Dominions. Thereafter the totals include the same-design issues for colonies and territories.

### Silver Jubilee Issue

Windsor Castle and King George V CD301

25th anniversary of the reign of King George V.

**1935**

Antigua 77-80
Ascension 33-36
Bahamas 92-95
Barbados 186-189
Basutoland 11-14
Bechuanaland Protectorate 117-120
Bermuda 100-103
British Guiana 223-226
British Honduras 108-111
Cayman Islands 81-84
Ceylon 260-263
Cyprus 136-139
Dominica 90-93
Falkland Islands 77-80
Fiji 110-113
Gambia 125-128
Gibraltar 100-103
Gilbert & Ellice Islands 33-36
Gold Coast 108-111
Grenada 124-127
Hong Kong 147-150
Jamaica 109-112
Kenya, Uganda, Tanganyika 42-45
Leeward Islands 96-99
Malta 184-187
Mauritius 204-207
Montserrat 85-88
Newfoundland 226-229
Nigeria 34-37
Northern Rhodesia 18-21
Nyasaland Protectorate 47-50
St. Helena 111-114
St. Kitts-Nevis 72-75
St. Lucia 91-94
St. Vincent 134-137
Seychelles 118-121
Sierra Leone 166-169
Solomon Islands 60-63
Somaliland Protectorate 77-80
Straits Settlements 213-216
Swaziland 20-23
Trinidad & Tobago 43-46
Turks & Caicos Islands 71-74
Virgin Islands 69-72

The following have different designs but are included in the omnibus set:

Great Britain 226-229
Offices in Morocco 67-70, 226-229, 422-425, 508-510
Australia 152-154
Canada 211-216
Cook Islands 98-100
India 142-148
Nauru 31-34
New Guinea 46-47
New Zealand 199-201
Niue 67-69
Papua 114-117
Samoa 163-165
South Africa 68a-71a
Southern Rhodesia 33-36
South-West Africa 121-124
249 stamps

### Coronation Issue

Queen Elizabeth and King George VI CD302

**1937**

Aden 13-15
Antigua 81-83
Ascension 37-39
Bahamas 97-99
Barbados 190-192
Basutoland 15-17
Bechuanaland Protectorate 121-123
Bermuda 115-117
British Guiana 227-229
British Honduras 112-114
Cayman Islands 97-99
Ceylon 275-277
Cyprus 140-142
Dominica 94-96
Falkland Islands 81-83
Fiji 114-116
Gambia 129-131
Gibraltar 104-106
Gilbert & Ellice Islands 37-39
Gold Coast 112-114
Grenada 128-130
Hong Kong 151-153
Jamaica 113-115
Kenya, Uganda, Tanganyika 60-62
Leeward Islands 100-102
Malta 188-190
Mauritius 208-210
Montserrat 89-91
Newfoundland 230-232
Nigeria 50-52
Northern Rhodesia 22-24
Nyasaland Protectorate 51-53
St. Helena 115-117
St. Kitts-Nevis 76-78
St. Lucia 107-109
St. Vincent 138-140
Seychelles 122-124
Sierra Leone 170-172
Solomon Islands 64-66
Somaliland Protectorate 81-83
Straits Settlements 235-237
Swaziland 24-26
Trinidad & Tobago 47-49
Turks & Caicos Islands 75-77
Virgin Islands 73-75

The following have different designs but are included in the omnibus set:

Great Britain 234
Offices in Morocco 82, 439, 514
Canada 237
Cook Islands 109-111
Nauru 35-38
Newfoundland 233-243
New Guinea 48-51
New Zealand 223-225
Niue 70-72
Papua 118-121
South Africa 74a-78a
Southern Rhodesia 38-41
South-West Africa 125a-132a
202 stamps

### Peace Issue

King George VI and Parliament Buildings, London CD303

Return to peace at the close of World War II.

**1945-46**

Aden 28-29
Antigua 96-97
Ascension 50-51
Bahamas 130-131
Barbados 207-208
Bermuda 131-132
British Guiana 242-243
British Honduras 127-128
Cayman Islands 112-113
Ceylon 293-294
Cyprus 156-157
Dominica 112-113
Falkland Islands 97-98
Falkland Islands Dep. 1L9-1L10
Fiji 137-138
Gambia 144-145
Gibraltar 119-120
Gilbert & Ellice Islands 52-53
Gold Coast 128-129
Grenada 143-144
Jamaica 136-137
Kenya, Uganda, Tanganyika 84-85
Leeward Islands 116-117
Malta 206-207
Mauritius 223-224
Montserrat 104-105
Nigeria 71-72
Northern Rhodesia 46-47
Nyasaland Protectorate 82-83
Pitcairn Island 9-10
St. Helena 128-129
St. Kitts-Nevis 91-92
St. Lucia 127-128
St. Vincent 152-153
Seychelles 149-150
Sierra Leone 186-187
Solomon Islands 80-81
Somaliland Protectorate 108-109
Trinidad & Tobago 62-63
Turks & Caicos Islands 90-91
Virgin Islands 88-89

The following have different designs but are included in the omnibus set:

Great Britain 264-265
Offices in Morocco 523-524
Aden
Kathiri State of Seiyun 12-13
Qu'aiti State of Shihr and Mukalla 12-13
Australia 200-202
Basutoland 29a-31a
Bechuanaland Protectorate 137a-139a
Burma 66-69
Cook Islands 127-130
Hong Kong 174-175
India 195-198
Hyderabad 51
New Zealand 247-257
Niue 90-93
Pakistan-Bahawalpur O16
Samoa 191-194
South Africa 100a-102a
Southern Rhodesia 67-70
South-West Africa 153a-155a
Swaziland 38a-40a
Zanzibar 222-223
164 stamps

### Silver Wedding Issue

King George VI and Queen Elizabeth CD304 CD305

**1948-49**

Aden 30-31
Kathiri State of Seiyun 14-15
Qu'aiti State of Shihr and Mukalla 14-15
Antigua 98-99
Ascension 52-53
Bahamas 148-149
Barbados 210-211
Basutoland 39-40
Bechuanaland Protectorate 147-148
Bermuda 133-134
British Guiana 244-245
British Honduras 129-130
Cayman Islands 116-117
Cyprus 158-159
Dominica 114-115
Falkland Islands 99-100
Falkland Islands Dep. 1L11-1L12
Fiji 139-140
Gambia 146-147
Gibraltar 121-122
Gilbert & Ellice Islands 54-55
Gold Coast 142-143
Grenada 145-146
Hong Kong 178-179
Jamaica 138-139

Kenya, Uganda, Tanganyika ..... 86-87
Leeward Islands ..... 118-119
Malaya
Johore ..... 128-129
Kedah ..... 55-56
Kelantan ..... 44-45
Malacca ..... 1-2
Negri Sembilan ..... 36-37
Pahang ..... 44-45
Penang ..... 1-2
Perak ..... 99-100
Perlis ..... 1-2
Selangor ..... 74-75
Trengganu ..... 47-48
Malta ..... 223-224
Mauritius ..... 229-230
Montserrat ..... 106-107
Nigeria ..... 73-74
North Borneo ..... 238-239
Northern Rhodesia ..... 48-49
Nyasaland Protectorate ..... 85-86
Pitcairn Island ..... 11-12
St. Helena ..... 130-131
St. Kitts-Nevis ..... 93-94
St. Lucia ..... 129-130
St. Vincent ..... 154-155
Sarawak ..... 174-175
Seychelles ..... 151-152
Sierra Leone ..... 188-189
Singapore ..... 21-22
Solomon Islands ..... 82-83
Somaliland Protectorate ..... 110-111
Swaziland ..... 48-49
Trinidad & Tobago ..... 64-65
Turks & Caicos Islands ..... 92-93
Virgin Islands ..... 90-91
Zanzibar ..... 224-225

The following have different designs but are included in the omnibus set:

Great Britain ..... 267-268
Offices in Morocco ... 93-94, 525-526
Bahrain ..... 62-63
Kuwait ..... 82-83
Oman ..... 25-26
South Africa ..... 106a
South-West Africa ..... 159a
138 stamps

### U.P.U. Issue

Mercury and Symbols of Communications
CD306

Plane, Ship and Hemispheres
CD307

Mercury Scattering Letters over Globe
CD308

U.P.U. Monument, Bern
CD309

Universal Postal Union, 75th anniversary.

**1949**

Aden ..... 32-35
Kathiri State of Seiyun ..... 16-19
Qu'aiti State of Shihr and Mukalla ..... 16-19
Antigua ..... 100-103
Ascension ..... 57-60
Bahamas ..... 150-153
Barbados ..... 212-215
Basutoland ..... 41-44
Bechuanaland Protectorate ..... 149-152
Bermuda ..... 138-141
British Guiana ..... 246-249
British Honduras ..... 137-140
Brunei ..... 79-82
Cayman Islands ..... 118-121
Cyprus ..... 160-163
Dominica ..... 116-119
Falkland Islands ..... 103-106
Falkland Islands Dep. ..... 1L14-1L17
Fiji ..... 141-144
Gambia ..... 148-151
Gibraltar ..... 123-126
Gilbert & Ellice Islands ..... 56-59
Gold Coast ..... 144-147
Grenada ..... 147-150
Hong Kong ..... 180-183
Jamaica ..... 142-145
Kenya, Uganda, Tanganyika ..... 90-93
Leeward Islands ..... 126-129
Malaya
Johore ..... 151-154
Kedah ..... 57-60
Kelantan ..... 46-49
Malacca ..... 18-21
Negri Sembilan ..... 59-62
Pahang ..... 46-49
Penang ..... 23-26
Perak ..... 101-104
Perlis ..... 3-6
Selangor ..... 76-79
Trengganu ..... 49-52
Malta ..... 225-228
Mauritius ..... 231-234
Montserrat ..... 108-111
New Hebrides ..... 62-65
Nigeria ..... 75-78
North Borneo ..... 240-243
Northern Rhodesia ..... 50-53
Nyasaland Protectorate ..... 87-90
Pitcairn Islands ..... 13-16
St. Helena ..... 132-135
St. Kitts-Nevis ..... 95-98
St. Lucia ..... 131-134
St. Vincent ..... 170-173
Sarawak ..... 176-179
Seychelles ..... 153-156
Sierra Leone ..... 190-193
Singapore ..... 23-26
Solomon Islands ..... 84-87
Somaliland Protectorate ..... 112-115
Southern Rhodesia ..... 71-72
Swaziland ..... 50-53
Tonga ..... 87-90
Trinidad & Tobago ..... 66-69
Turks & Caicos Islands ..... 101-104
Virgin Islands ..... 92-95
Zanzibar ..... 226-229

The following have different designs but are included in the omnibus set:

Great Britain ..... 276-279
Offices in Morocco ..... 546-549
Australia ..... 223
Bahrain ..... 68-71
Burma ..... 116-121
Ceylon ..... 304-306
Egypt ..... 281-283
India ..... 223-226
Kuwait ..... 89-92
Oman ..... 31-34
Pakistan-Bahawalpur .. 26-29, O25-O28
South Africa ..... 109a-111a
South-West Africa ..... 160a-162a
315 stamps

### University Issue

Arms of University College
CD310

Alice, Princess of Athlone
CD311

Issued to commemorate the 1948 opening of University College of the West Indies at Jamaica.

**1951**

Antigua ..... 104-105
Barbados ..... 228-229
British Guiana ..... 250-251
British Honduras ..... 141-142
Dominica ..... 120-121
Grenada ..... 164-165
Jamaica ..... 146-147
Leeward Islands ..... 130-131
Montserrat ..... 112-113
St. Kitts-Nevis ..... 105-106
St. Lucia ..... 149-150
St. Vincent ..... 174-175
Trinidad & Tobago ..... 70-71
Virgin Islands ..... 96-97
28 stamps

### Coronation Issue

Queen Elizabeth II
CD312

**1953**

Aden ..... 47
Kathiri State of Seiyun ..... 28
Qu'aiti State of Shihr and Mukalla ..... 28
Antigua ..... 106
Ascension ..... 61
Bahamas ..... 157
Barbados ..... 234
Basutoland ..... 45
Bechuanaland Protectorate ..... 153
Bermuda ..... 142
British Guiana ..... 252
British Honduras ..... 143
Cayman Islands ..... 150
Cyprus ..... 167
Dominica ..... 141
Falkland Islands ..... 121
Falkland Islands Dependencies ... 1L18
Fiji ..... 145
Gambia ..... 152
Gibraltar ..... 131
Gilbert & Ellice Islands ..... 60
Gold Coast ..... 160
Grenada ..... 170
Hong Kong ..... 184
Jamaica ..... 153
Kenya, Uganda, Tanganyika ..... 101
Leeward Islands ..... 132
Malaya
Johore ..... 155
Kedah ..... 82
Kelantan ..... 71
Malacca ..... 27
Negri Sembilan ..... 63
Pahang ..... 71
Penang ..... 27
Perak ..... 126
Perlis ..... 28
Selangor ..... 101
Trengganu ..... 74
Malta ..... 241
Mauritius ..... 250
Montserrat ..... 127
New Hebrides ..... 77
Nigeria ..... 79
North Borneo ..... 260
Northern Rhodesia ..... 60
Nyasaland Protectorate ..... 96
Pitcairn ..... 19
St. Helena ..... 139
St. Kitts-Nevis ..... 119
St. Lucia ..... 156
St. Vincent ..... 185
Sarawak ..... 196
Seychelles ..... 172
Sierra Leone ..... 194
Singapore ..... 27
Solomon Islands ..... 88
Somaliland Protectorate ..... 127
Swaziland ..... 54
Trinidad & Tobago ..... 84
Tristan da Cunha ..... 13
Turks & Caicos Islands ..... 118
Virgin Islands ..... 114

The following have different designs but are included in the omnibus set:

Great Britain ..... 313-316
Offices in Morocco ..... 579-582
Australia ..... 259-261
Bahrain ..... 92-95
Canada ..... 330
Ceylon ..... 317
Cook Islands ..... 145-146
Kuwait ..... 113-116
New Zealand ..... 280-284
Niue ..... 104-105
Oman ..... 52-55
Samoa ..... 214-215
South Africa ..... 192
Southern Rhodesia ..... 80
South-West Africa ..... 244-248
Tokelau Islands ..... 4
106 stamps

### Royal Visit 1953

Separate designs for each country for the visit of Queen Elizabeth II and the Duke of Edinburgh.

**1953**

Aden ..... 62
Australia ..... 267-269
Bermuda ..... 163
Ceylon ..... 318
Fiji ..... 146
Gibraltar ..... 146
Jamaica ..... 154
Kenya, Uganda, Tanganyika ..... 102
Malta ..... 242
New Zealand ..... 286-287
13 stamps

### West Indies Federation

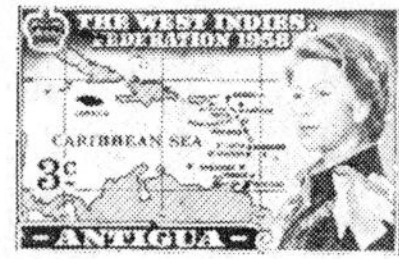


Map of the Caribbean
CD313

Federation of the West Indies, April 22, 1958.

**1958**

Antigua ..... 122-124
Barbados ..... 248-250
Dominica ..... 161-163
Grenada ..... 184-186
Jamaica ..... 175-177
Montserrat ..... 143-145
St. Kitts-Nevis ..... 136-138
St. Lucia ..... 170-172
St. Vincent ..... 198-200
Trinidad & Tobago ..... 86-88
30 stamps

### Freedom from Hunger Issue

Protein Food
CD314

United Nations Food and Agricultural Organization's "Freedom from Hunger" campaign.

**1963**

Aden ..... 65
Antigua ..... 133
Ascension ..... 89
Bahamas ..... 180
Basutoland ..... 83
Bechuanaland Protectorate ..... 194
Bermuda ..... 192
British Guiana ..... 271
British Honduras ..... 179
Brunei ..... 100
Cayman Islands ..... 168
Dominica ..... 181
Falkland Islands ..... 146
Fiji ..... 198
Gambia ..... 172
Gibraltar ..... 161
Gilbert & Ellice Islands ..... 76
Grenada ..... 190
Hong Kong ..... 218
Malta ..... 291
Mauritius ..... 270
Montserrat ..... 150
New Hebrides ..... 93
North Borneo ..... 296
Pitcairn ..... 35
St. Helena ..... 173
St. Lucia ..... 179
St. Vincent ..... 201
Sarawak ..... 212
Seychelles ..... 213
Solomon Islands ..... 109
Swaziland ..... 108
Tonga ..... 127
Tristan da Cunha ..... 68
Turks & Caicos Islands ..... 138
Virgin Islands ..... 140
Zanzibar ..... 280
37 stamps

### Red Cross Centenary Issue

Red Cross and Elizabeth II
CD315

Centenary of the International Red Cross.

**1963**

Antigua ..... 134-135
Ascension ..... 90-91
Bahamas ..... 183-184
Basutoland ..... 84-85
Bechuanaland Protectorate ..... 195-196
Bermuda ..... 193-194
British Guiana ..... 272-273
British Honduras ..... 180-181
Cayman Islands ..... 169-170
Dominica ..... 182-183
Falkland Islands ..... 147-148
Fiji ..... 203-204
Gambia ..... 173-174
Gibraltar ..... 162-163
Gilbert & Ellice Islands ..... 77-78
Grenada ..... 191-192
Hong Kong ..... 219-220
Jamaica ..... 203-204

Malta 292-293
Mauritius 271-272
Montserrat 151-152
New Hebrides 94-95
Pitcairn Islands 36-37
St. Helena 174-175
St. Kitts-Nevis 143-144
St. Lucia 180-181
St. Vincent 202-203
Seychelles 214-215
Solomon Islands 110-111
South Arabia 1-2
Swaziland 109-110
Tonga 134-135
Tristan da Cunha 69-70
Turks & Caicos Islands 139-140
Virgin Islands 141-142
70 stamps

### Shakespeare Issue

Shakespeare Memorial Theatre, Stratford-on-Avon
CD316

400th anniversary of the birth of William Shakespeare.

**1964**

Antigua 151
Bahamas 201
Bechuanaland Protectorate 197
Cayman Islands 171
Dominica 184
Falkland Islands 149
Gambia 192
Gibraltar 164
Montserrat 153
St. Lucia 196
Turks & Caicos Islands 141
Virgin Islands 143
12 stamps

### ITU ISSUE

ITU Emblem
CD317

Centenary of the International Telecommunication Union.

**1965**

Antigua 153-154
Ascension 92-93
Bahamas 219-220
Barbados 265-266
Basutoland 101-102
Bechuanaland Protectorate 202-203
Bermuda 196-197
British Guiana 293-294
British Honduras 187-188
Brunei 116-117
Cayman Islands 172-173
Dominica 185-186
Falkland Islands 154-155
Fiji 211-212
Gibraltar 167-168
Gilbert & Ellice Islands 87-88
Grenada 205-206
Hong Kong 221-222
Mauritius 291-292
Montserrat 157-158
New Hebrides 108-109
Pitcairn Islands 52-53
St. Helena 180-181
St. Kitts-Nevis 163-164
St. Lucia 197-198
St. Vincent 224-225
Seychelles 218-219
Solomon Islands 126-127
Swaziland 115-116
Tristan da Cunha 85-86
Turks & Caicos Islands 142-143
Virgin Islands 159-160
64 stamps

### Intl. Cooperation Year Issue

ICY Emblem—CD318

International Cooperation Year, 1965.

**1965**

Antigua 155-156
Ascension 94-95
Bahamas 222-223
Basutoland 103-104
Bechuanaland Protectorate 204-205
Bermuda 199-200
British Guiana 295-296
British Honduras 189-190
Brunei 118-119
Cayman Islands 174-175
Dominica 187-188
Falkland Islands 156-157
Fiji 213-214
Gibraltar 169-170
Gilbert & Ellice Islands 104-105
Grenada 207-208
Hong Kong 223-224
Mauritius 293-294
Montserrat 176-177
New Hebrides 110-111
Pitcairn Islands 54-55
St. Helena 182-183
St. Kitts-Nevis 165-166
St. Lucia 199-200
Seychelles 220-221
Solomon Islands 143-144
South Arabia 17-18
Swaziland 117-118
Tristan da Cunha 87-88
Turks & Caicos Islands 144-145
Virgin Islands 161-162
62 stamps

### Churchill Memorial Issue

Winston Churchill and St. Paul's, London, During Air Attack
CD319

Sir Winston Leonard Spencer Churchill (1874-1965), statesman and World War II leader.

**1966**

Antigua 157-160
Ascension 96-99
Bahamas 224-227
Barbados 281-284
Basutoland 105-108
Bechuanaland Protectorate 206-209
Bermuda 201-204
British Antarctic Territory 16-19
British Honduras 191-194
Brunei 120-123
Cayman Islands 176-179
Dominica 189-192
Falkland Islands 158-161
Fiji 215-218
Gibraltar 171-174
Gilbert & Ellice Islands 106-109
Grenada 209-212
Hong Kong 225-228
Mauritius 295-298
Montserrat 178-181
New Hebrides 112-115
Pitcairn Islands 56-59
St. Helena 184-187
St. Kitts-Nevis 167-170
St. Lucia 201-204
St. Vincent 241-244
Seychelles 222-225
Solomon Islands 145-148
South Arabia 19-22
Swaziland 119-122
Tristan da Cunha 89-92
Turks & Caicos Islands 146-149
Virgin Islands 163-166
132 stamps

### Royal Visit Issue, 1966

Queen Elizabeth II and Prince Philip
CD320

Visit to the Caribbean, Feb. 4-March 6, 1966.

**1966**

Antigua 161-162
Bahamas 228-229
Barbados 285-286
British Guiana 299-300
Cayman Islands 180-181
Dominica 193-194
Grenada 213-214
Montserrat 182-183
St. Kitts-Nevis 171-172
St. Lucia 205-206
St. Vincent 245-246
Turks & Caicos Islands 150-151
Virgin Islands 167-168
26 stamps

### World Cup Soccer Issue

Soccer Player and Jules Rimet Cup
CD321

Issued to publicize the World Cup Soccer Championship, Wembley, England, July 11-30.

**1966**

Antigua 163-164
Ascension 100-101
Bahamas 245-246
Bermuda 205-206
Brunei 124-125
Cayman Islands 182-183
Dominica 195-196
Fiji 219-220
Gibraltar 175-176
Gilbert & Ellice Islands 125-126
Grenada 230-231
New Hebrides 116-117
Pitcairn Islands 60-61
St. Helena 188-189
St. Kitts-Nevis 173-174
St. Lucia 207-208
Seychelles 226-227
Solomon Islands 167-168
South Arabia 23-24
Tristan da Cunha 93-94
40 stamps

### WHO Headquarters Issue

World Health Organization Headquarters, Geneva
CD322

**1966**

Antigua 165-166
Ascension 102-103
Bahamas 247-248
Brunei 126-127
Cayman Islands 184-185
Dominica 197-198
Fiji 224-225
Gibraltar 180-181
Gilbert & Ellice Islands 127-128
Grenada 232-233
Hong Kong 229-230
Montserrat 184-185
New Hebrides 118-119
Pitcairn Islands 62-63
St. Helena 190-191
St. Kitts-Nevis 177-178
St. Lucia 209-210
St. Vincent 247-248
Seychelles 228-229
Solomon Islands 169-170
South Arabia 25-26
Tristan da Cunha 99-100
44 stamps

### UNESCO Anniversary Issue

"Education"
CD323

Designs: "Science" (Wheat ears and flask enclosing globe). "Culture" (lyre and columns).

20th anniversary of the United Nations Educational, Scientific and Cultural Organization.

**1966-67**

Antigua 183-185
Ascension 108-110
Bahamas 249-251
Barbados 287-289
Bermuda 207-209
Brunei 128-130
Cayman Islands 186-188
Dominica 199-201
Gibraltar 183-185
Gilbert & Ellice Islands 129-131
Grenada 234-236
Hong Kong 231-233
Mauritius 299-301
Montserrat 186-188
New Hebrides 120-122
Pitcairn Islands 64-66
St. Helena 192-194
St. Kitts-Nevis 179-181
St. Lucia 211-213
St. Vincent 249-251
Seychelles 230-232
Solomon Islands 171-173
South Arabia 27-29
Swaziland 123-125
Tristan da Cunha 101-103
Turks & Caicos Islands 155-157
Virgin Islands 176-178
81 stamps

### Silver Wedding Issue, 1972

Queen Elizabeth II and Prince Philip—CD324

Designs: borders differ for each country.

**1972**

Anguilla 161-162
Antigua 295-296
Ascension 164-165
Bahamas 344-345
Bermuda 296-297
British Antarctic Territory 43-44
British Honduras 306-307
British Indian Ocean Territory 48-49
Brunei 186-187
Cayman Islands 304-305
Dominica 352-353
Falkland Islands 223-224
Fiji 328-329
Gibraltar 292-293
Gilbert & Ellice Islands 206-207
Grenada 466-467
Hong Kong 271-272
Montserrat 286-287
New Hebrides 169-170
Pitcairn Islands 127-128
St. Helena 271-272
St. Kitts-Nevis 257-258
St. Lucia 328-329
St.Vincent 344-345
Seychelles 309-310
Solomon Islands 248-249
South Georgia 35-36
Tristan da Cunha 178-179
Turks & Caicos Islands 257-258
Virgin Islands 241-242
60 stamps

### Princess Anne's Wedding Issue

Princess Anne and Mark Phillips
CD325

Wedding of Princess Anne and Mark Phillips, Nov. 14, 1973.

**1973**

Anguilla 179-180
Ascension 177-178
Belize 325-326
Bermuda 302-303
British Antarctic Territory 60-61
Cayman Islands 320-321
Falkland Islands 225-226
Gibraltar 305-306
Gilbert & Ellice Islands 216-217
Hong Kong 289-290
Montserrat 300-301
Pitcairn Island 135-136
St. Helena 277-278
St. Kitts-Nevis 274-275
St. Lucia 349-350
St. Vincent 358-359
Seychelles 311-312
Solomon Islands 259-260
South Georgia 37-38
Tristan da Cunha 189-190
Turks & Caicos Islands 286-287
Virgin Islands 260-261
44 stamps

The indexes in each volume of the Scott Catalogue contain many listings which help to identify stamps.

### Elizabeth II Coronation Anniversary Issue

Lion of England CD326

Queen Elizabeth II CD327

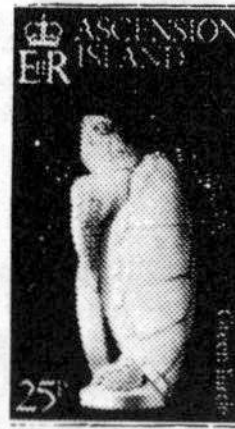


Green Turtle CD328

Designs: Royal and local beasts in heraldic form and simulated stonework. Portrait of Elizabeth II by Peter Grugeon.

25th anniversary of coronation of Queen Elizabeth II.

**1978**

| | |
|---|---|
| Ascension | 229 |
| Barbados | 474 |
| Belize | 397 |
| British Antarctic Territory | 71 |
| Cayman Islands | 404 |
| Christmas Island | 87 |
| Falkland Islands | 275 |
| Fiji | 384 |
| Gambia | 380 |
| Gilbert Islands | 312 |
| Mauritius | 464 |
| New Hebrides | 258 |
| St. Helena | 317 |
| St. Kitts-Nevis | 354 |
| Samoa | 472 |
| Solomon Islands | 368 |
| South Georgia | 51 |
| Swaziland | 302 |
| Tristan da Cunha | 238 |
| Virgin Islands | 337 |

20 sheets

### Queen Mother Elizabeth's 80th Birthday

CD330

Designs: Photographs of Queen Mother Elizabeth. Falkland Islds. issued in sheets of 50; others in sheets of 9.

**1980**

| | |
|---|---|
| Ascension | 261 |
| Bermuda | 401 |
| Cayman Islands | 443 |
| Falkland Islands | 305 |
| Gambia | 412 |
| Gibraltar | 393 |
| Hong Kong | 364 |
| Pitcairn Islands | 193 |
| St. Helena | 341 |
| Samoa | 532 |
| Solomon Islands | 426 |
| Tristan da Cunha | 277 |

12 stamps

### Royal Wedding Issue, 1981

Prince Charles and Lady Diana CD331

**1981**

Wedding of Charles, Prince of Wales, and Lady Diana Spencer, St. Paul's Cathedral, London, July 29, 1981.

| | |
|---|---|
| Antigua | 623-625 |
| Ascension | 294-296 |
| Barbados | 547-549 |
| Bermuda | 412-414 |
| Brunei | 268-270 |
| Cayman Islands | 471-473 |
| Dominica | 701-703 |
| Falkland Islands | 324-326 |
| Falkland Islands Dep. | 1L59-1L61 |
| Fiji | 442-444 |
| Gambia | 426-428 |
| Ghana | 759-761 |
| Grenada | 1051-1053 |
| Hong Kong | 373-375 |
| Jamaica | 500-503 |
| Lesotho | 335-337 |
| Maldive Islands | 906-908 |
| Mauritius | 520-522 |
| Norfolk Island | 280-282 |
| Pitcairn Islands | 206-208 |
| St. Helena | 353-355 |
| St. Lucia | 543-545 |
| Samoa | 558-560 |
| Sierra Leone | 509-517 |
| Solomon Islands | 450-452 |
| Swaziland | 382-384 |
| Tristan da Cunha | 294-296 |
| Turks & Caicos Islands | 486-488 |
| Uganda | 314-316 |
| Vanuatu | 308-310 |
| Virgin Islands | 406-408 |

### Princess Diana

CD332 CD333

Designs: Photographs and portrait of Princess Diana, wedding or honeymoon photographs, royal residences, arms of issuing country. Portrait photograph by Clive Friend. Souvenir sheet margins show family tree, various people related to the princess. 21st birthday of Princess Diana of Wales, July 1.

**1982**

| | |
|---|---|
| Antigua | 663-666 |
| Ascension | 313-316 |
| Bahamas | 510-513 |
| Barbados | 585-588 |
| British Antarctic Territory | 92-95 |
| Cayman Islands | 486-489 |
| Dominica | 773-776 |
| Falkland Islands | 348-351 |
| Falkland Islands Dep. | 1L72-1L75 |
| Fiji | 470-473 |
| Gambia | 447-450 |
| Grenada | 1102-1105 |
| Lesotho | 372-375 |
| Maldive Islands | 952-955 |
| Mauritius | 548-551 |
| Pitcairn Islands | 213-216 |
| St. Helena | 372-375 |
| St. Lucia | 591-594 |
| Sierra Leone | 531-534 |
| Solomon Islands | 471-474 |
| Swaziland | 406-409 |
| Tristan da Cunha | 310-313 |
| Turks and Caicos Islands | 530A-534 |
| Virgin Islands | 430-433 |

96 stamps

### Commonwealth Day

CD334

Annual event started in 1982 to increase awareness of Commonwealth and its goals. Designs: Local scenes, maps, flags, Queen Elizabeth II.

**1983**

| | |
|---|---|
| Antigua | 694-697 |
| Bahamas | 528-531 |
| Bangladesh | 216-219 |
| Barbados | 598-601 |
| Botswana | 325-328 |
| Brunei | 290-293 |
| Cayman Islands | 510-513 |
| Cyprus | 591-594 |
| Dominica | 796-799 |
| Falkland Islands | 371-374 |
| Fiji | 485-488 |
| Gambia | 459-462 |
| Ghana | 822-825 |
| Gibraltar | 443-446 |
| Grenada | 1150-1153 |
| Hong Kong | 411-414 |
| Jamaica | 552-555 |
| Kenya | 243-246 |
| Kiribati | 418-421 |
| Malawi | 410-413 |
| Mauritius | 558-561 |
| New Zealand | 776-779 |
| Pitcairn Islands | 221-224 |
| St. Kitts | 106-107 |
| St. Lucia | 599-602 |
| St. Vincent | 670-673 |
| Sierra Leone | 581-584 |
| Swaziland | 423-426 |
| Tanzania | 217-220 |
| Tonga | 537-540 |
| Turks and Caicos Islands | 555-558 |
| Uganda | 360-363 |
| Vanuatu | 349-352 |
| Zambia | 276-279 |

250th anniv. of first edition of Lloyd's List (shipping news publication) and of Lloyd's marine insurance.

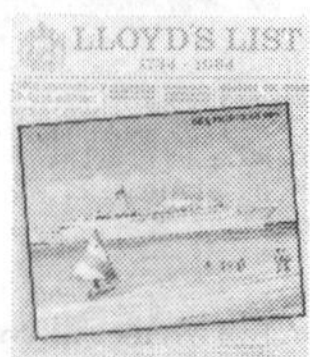


CD335

Designs: First page of early edition of the list; historical ships, modern transportation or harbor scenes.

**1984**

| | |
|---|---|
| Ascension | 351-354 |
| Bahamas | 555-558 |
| Barbados | 627-630 |
| Cayman Islands | 522-525 |
| Falkland Islands | 404-407 |
| Fiji | 509-512 |
| Gambia | 519-522 |
| Mauritius | 587-590 |
| Nauru | 280-283 |
| St. Helena | 412-415 |
| Samoa | 624-627 |
| Seychelles | 538-541 |
| Solomon Islands | 521-524 |
| Vanuatu | 368-371 |
| Virgin Islands | 466-469 |

### Queen Mother 85th Birthday

On Holiday with the Duke of York, Balmoral, 1924—CD336

Designs: Photographs tracing the life of the Queen Mother, Elizabeth. The high value in each set pictures the same photograph taken of the Queen Mother holding the infant Prince Henry.

**1985**

| | |
|---|---|
| Ascension | 372-376 |
| Bahamas | 580-584 |
| Barbados | 660-664 |
| Bermuda | 469-473 |
| Falkland Islands | 420-424 |
| Falkland Islands Dep. | 1L92-1L96 |
| Fiji | 531-535 |
| Hong Kong | 447-450 |
| Jamaica | 599-603 |
| Mauritius | 604-608 |
| Norfolk Island | 364-368 |
| Pitcairn Islands | 253-257 |
| St. Helena | 428-432 |
| Samoa | 649-653 |
| Seychelles | 567-571 |
| Solomon Islands | 543-547 |
| Swaziland | 476-480 |
| Tristan da Cunha | 372-376 |
| Vanuatu | 392-396 |

### Queen Elizabeth II, 60th Birthday

CD337

**1986, April 21**

| | |
|---|---|
| Ascension | 389-393 |
| Bahamas | 592-596 |
| Barbados | 675-679 |
| Bermuda | 499-503 |
| Cayman Islands | 555-559 |
| Falkland Islands | 441-445 |
| Falkland Islands Dep. | 1L101-1L105 |
| Fiji | 544-548 |
| Hong Kong | 465-469 |
| Jamaica | 620-624 |
| Kiribati | 470-474 |
| Mauritius | 629-633 |
| Papua New Guinea | 640-644 |
| Pitcairn Islands | 270-274 |
| St. Helena | 451-455 |
| Samoa | 670-674 |
| Seychelles | 592-596 |
| Solomon Islands | 562-566 |
| Swaziland | 490-494 |
| Tristan da Cunha | 388-392 |
| Vanuatu | 414-418 |
| Zambia | 343-347 |

### Royal Wedding

CD338

Marriage of Prince Andrew and Sarah Ferguson

**1986, July 23**

| | |
|---|---|
| Ascension | 399-400 |
| Bahamas | 602-603 |
| Barbados | 687-688 |
| Cayman Islands | 560-561 |
| Jamaica | 629-630 |
| Pitcairn Islands | 275-276 |
| St. Helena | 460-461 |
| St. Kitts | 181-182 |
| Seychelles | 602-603 |
| Solomon Islands | 567-568 |
| Tristan da Cunha | 397-398 |
| Zambia | 348-349 |

### Queen Elizabeth II, 60th Birthday

Queen Elizabeth II Inspecting Guard, 1946—CD339

Designs: Photographs tracing the life of Queen Elizabeth II.

**1986**

| | |
|---|---|
| Anguilla | 674-677 |
| Antigua | 925-928 |
| Dominica | 950-953 |
| Gambia | 611-614 |
| Grenada | 1371-1374 |
| Lesotho | 531-534 |
| Maldive Islands | 1172-1175 |
| Sierra Leone | 760-763 |
| Uganda | 495-498 |

### Royal Wedding Issue, 1986

Engagement of Prince Andrew and Sarah Ferguson—CD340

Designs: Photographs of Prince Andrew and Sarah Ferguson during courtship, engagement and marriage.

**1986**

| | |
|---|---|
| Antigua | 939-942 |
| Dominica | 970-973 |
| Gambia | 635-638 |
| Grenada | 1385-1388 |
| Lesotho | 545-548 |
| Maldive Islands | 1181-1184 |
| Sierra Leone | 769-772 |
| Uganda | 510-513 |

**Lloyds of London, 300th Anniv.**

CD341

Designs: 17th century aspects of Lloyds, representations of each country's individual connections with Lloyds and publicized disasters insured by the organization.

**1986**

| | |
|---|---|
| Ascension | 450-453 |
| Bahamas | 655-658 |
| Barbados | 731-734 |
| Bermuda | 541-544 |
| Falkland Islands | 481-484 |
| Liberia | 1101-1104 |
| Malawi | 534-537 |
| St. Helena | 497-500 |
| St. Lucia | 923-926 |
| Seychelles | 649-652 |
| Solomon Islands | 627-630 |
| Trinidad & Tobago | 484-487 |
| Tristan da Cunha | 439-442 |
| Vanuatu | 485-488 |

# Historical Footnotes

**Scouting Year:** 75th anniversary of scouting and 125th birth anniversary of its founder, Lord Baden-Powell (1857-1941).

**Robert Koch:** Centenary of tuberculosis bacillus discovery by Robert Koch (1843-1910), German physician. Awarded 1905 Nobel Prize for physiology and medicine; also discovered cholera bacillus, 1883.

**George Washington:** 250th birth anniversary of George Washington (1732-1799), first U.S. president.

**Charles Darwin:** Death centenary of Charles Darwin (1809-1882), British naturalist. Traveled through South America and Australasia, 1831-1836, aboard the Beagle developing his theory of evolution. Published findings in *On the Origin of Species,* 1859.

**Norman Rockwell** (1894-1978): American illustrator who is best known for his paintings of people in everyday situations. Many of his works have been on the covers of *The Saturday Evening Post, Boy's Life, American Boy* and *St. Nicholas.*

**Lewis B. Carroll** (1832-1898): English author of the childhood classics *Alice in Wonderland* and *Through the Looking Glass.* He also wrote many works on mathematics under his real name, Charles Lutwidge Dodgson.

**World Cup Soccer:** The 12th World Cup Soccer Championship was held in Spain from June 13th to July 11th. The series, held every 4 years, opened in Barcelona with Belgium over Argentina before a crowd of 95,000. The 52 games were held in 17 stadiums in 14 cities with 24 participating teams. The final game was played in Madrid with Italy defeating Germany by a score of 3 to 1.

**Olympic Games:** The 14th Winter Olympic Games were held in Sarajevo, Jugoslavia, Feb. 7-18, 1984. Russia captured 25 medals, though East Germany won the most gold, with 9. The United States Received 4 gold and 4 silver medals, primarily on the surprisingly strong showing of the ski team.

The 23rd Olympic Games were held in Los Angeles, July 28-August 12, 1984, marred by a boycott by Russia and other eastern bloc nations. The boycott was viewed as a retaliatory action against the U.S. led boycott of the 1980 Moscow Olympics. The U.S. gathered 174 medals, 83 of them gold, to lead all participants.

**Universal Postal Union Congress:** The 19th Universal Postal Union Congress was held in Hamburg, Germany, July 18-July 27, 1984. It was attended by approximately 750 delegates from 166 member countries.

**International Stamp Exhibition:**
AUSIPEX '84 Melbourne, Australia, Sept. 21-30, 1984.
PHILATELIA '84 Stuttgart, Germany, Oct. 5-7, 1984.
FILACENTO '84 The Hague, Netherlands, Sept. 6-9, 1984.
ITALIA '85 Rome, Italy, Oct. 25-Nov. 3, 1985.

# Numerical Index of Vol. 1 Watermark Illustrations

| Wmk. | Country | Page |
|---|---|---|
| 1,2,3,4, 4a, 314, 373, 384 | British Colonies | 1117 |
| 1a,1b, | Ceylon | 368 |
| 5 | Antigua | 220 |
| | Natal | 742 |
| | St. Lucia | 900 |
| | St. Vincent | 911 |
| | Turks Islands | 1063 |
| 5-6 | Barbados | 279 |
| | Grenada | 472 |
| | Queensland | 879 |
| 6 | Ceylon | 367 |
| | New Zealand | 774 |
| | St. Helena | 886 |
| | South Australia | 984 |
| | Tasmania | 1027 |
| | Victoria | 1094 |
| 7 | Grenada | 473 |
| | South Australia | 984 |
| 8-11 | Australia | 239-240 |
| 12-13 | Australia | 259 |
| | New South Wales | 773 |
| | Queensland | 880 |
| 13 | Papua New Guinea | 851 |
| | Tasmania | 1028 |
| | Victoria | 1095 |
| | Western Australia | 1105 |
| 14 | Bechuanaland | 290 |
| 15-16 | Cape of Good Hope | 360 |
| 17 | Fiji | 428 |
| 18-29 | Great Britain | 151-154 |
| 29 | Bechuanaland | 290 |
| 30-35 | Great Britain | 154-158 |
| 33 | Palestine | 850 |
| 36-39 | India | 508-509 |
| 40 | India | 540 |
| 41 | Cochin | 552 |
| 42 | Hyderabad | 554 |
| 43 | Cochin | 552 |
| | Travancore | 563 |
| 44 | Ireland | 589 |
| 45 | Jamaica | 602 |
| 46 | Labuan | 656 |
| 47 | Johore | 678 |
| | Maldive Islands | 698 |
| | Papua New Guinea | 851 |
| | Sarawak | 933 |
| | South Africa | 972 |
| | Zanzibar | 1111 |
| 48 | Mesopotamia | 733 |
| 49-52 | Tasmania | 1027 |
| 49-50 | Victoria | 1094 |
| 49-54 | New South Wales | 771 |
| 55-58 | New South Wales | 772 |
| 55 | Australia | 259 |
| 59-63 | New Zealand | 774-775 |
| 61 | Aitutaki | 205 |
| | Niue | 803 |
| 61-62 | Cook Islands | 380 |
| 62 | Samoa | 923 |
| | Tonga | 1031 |
| 64 | New Zealand | 793 |
| 65-70 | Queensland | 879-880 |
| 70 | New South Wales | 773 |
| | South Australia | 984 |
| | Tasmania | 1028 |
| | Victoria | 1094 |
| | Western Australia | 1105 |
| 71 | Johore | 678 |
| | Sarawak | 933 |
| | Sudan | 1008 |
| | Zanzibar | 1111 |
| 72-74 | South Australia | 984 |
| 74 | Papua New Guinea | 851 |
| | South Australia | 985 |
| | Western Australia | 1105 |
| 75 | Victoria | 1094 |
| 75-78 | Tasmania | 1027-1028 |
| 79 | Tonga | 1031 |
| 80, 80a, 81 | Victoria | 1094 |
| 82, 83 | Western Australia | 1104 |
| 111-114 | Danish West Indies | 111-112 |
| 125 | Cameroons | 330 |
| | Togo | 1028 |
| 138-139 | Ionian Islands | 565 |
| 139 | Victoria | 1094 |
| 161 | Bushire | 330 |
| 177 | South Africa | 972 |
| 179 | Sudan | 1008 |
| 190-191 | United States | 10, 11 |
| | Philippines | 121 |
| 196 | India | 510 |
| 199 | New South Wales | 773 |
| 201 | South Africa | 972 |
| | Southern Rhodesia | 987 |
| 203 | Australia | 240 |
| 211 | Hyderabad | 555 |
| 214 | Sudan | 1008 |
| 219 | Great Britain | 158 |
| 224 | Newfoundland | 763 |
| 228 | Australia | 240 |
| | Papua New Guinea | 851 |
| 231 | Sarawak | 933 |
| 233 | Maldive Islands | 698 |
| 250-251 | Great Britain | 159 |
| 253 | Cook Islands | 381 |
| | New Zealand | 777 |
| | Niue | 804 |
| | Samoa | 924 |
| | Tokelau Islands | 1029 |
| 254 | Burma | 325 |
| 257 | Burma | 329 |
| | Philippines | 125 |
| 259 | Great Britain | 159 |
| 262 | Ireland | 590 |
| 274 | Bahawalpur | 849 |
| 290 | Ceylon | 370 |
| 294 | Cochin | 552 |
| 298 | Great Britain | 160 |
| 305 | Jordan | 615 |
| 308 | Great Britain | 160 |
| 309 | United Nations | 127 |
| 314 | British Colonies | 1117 |
| 322 | Great Britain | 161 |
| 324 | India | 512 |
| 325 | Ghana | 446 |
| 328 | Jordan | 615 |
| 330 | South Africa | 974 |
| 335 | Nigeria | 796 |
| 336 | Sierra Leone | 945 |
| 338 | Malaya (Selangor) | 687 |
| 344 | Cyprus | 395 |
| 345 | Sudan | 1009 |
| 348 | South Africa | 975 |
| 351 | Pakistan | 833 |
| 352 | Jamaica | 605 |
| 354 | Malta | 715 |
| 355 | Samoa | 925 |
| 357 | Malawi | 669 |
| 359 | South Africa | 976 |
| 360 | India | 541 |
| 362 | Lesotho | 660 |
| 364 | Guyana | 493 |
| 366 | Singapore | 957 |
| 373 | British Colonies | 1117 |
| 378 | Malaysia | 692 |
| 379 | Nigeria | 799 |
| 384 | British Colonies | 1117 |

## GREAT BRITAIN

### (United Kingdom)

LOCATION — Northwest of the continent of Europe and separated from it by the English Channel.
GOVT. — Constitutional monarchy.
AREA — 94,511 sq. mi.
POP. — 55,767,387 (1981)
CAPITAL — London

12 Pence = 1 Shilling
20 Shillings = 1 Pound
100 Pence = 1 Pound (1970)

Cancellations on Great Britain stamps are usually heavy. Values for used copies are for average cancellations. Lightly canceled specimens bring more than the quoted values.

The letters in the corners of the early postage issues indicate position in the horizontal and vertical rows in which that particular specimen was placed.

In the case of illustration A1, this stamp came from the 14th horizontal row (N) and was the 12th stamp (L) from the left in that row. The left corner refers to the horizontal row and the right corner to the vertical row. Thus no two stamps on the plate bore the same combination of letters.

When four corner letters are used (starting in 1858), the lower ones indicate the stamp's position in the sheet and the top ones are the same letters reversed.

**Catalogue values for unused stamps in this country are for Never Hinged items, beginning with Scott 264 in the regular postage section, Scott J34 in the postage due section, Scott 10 in British Offices -- East Africa Forces, and Scott 93, Scott 246 and Scott 523 in British Offices in Morocco. All of the listings in British Offices -- for Use in Eritrea and for Use in Tripolitania are valued as never-hinged.**

Queen Victoria
A1 A2

Wmk. 18 - Small Crown

**1840, May Wmk. 18 Engr. *Imperf.***
**White Paper**

1 A1 1p black 2,000. 140.00
2 A1 2p blue 6,000. 300.00
*a.* 2p pale blue 7,500. 350.00

No. 1 was printed from 11 plates; No. 2 from 2 plates. The 1p plates 1, 2, 5, 6, 8 and 9 can be found in two or more states.

Issue dates: 1p, May 6; 2p, May 8.

**1841 Bluish Paper**

3 A1 1p red brown 65.00 1.50
*a.* 1p orange brown 150.00 17.50
*b.* 1p lake red 250.00 150.00
*c.* Rouletted 12 4,000.
*d.* "A" missing in lower right corner (position BA, P77) 5,500.

4 A2 2p blue 950. 27.50
*a.* 2p pale blue 1,050. 30.00

No. 3 exists on silk thread paper, but was not regularly issued.

No. 4 was printed from two plates.

A3 A4

With Vertical Silk Threads

**1847 Embossed Unwmk.**

5 A3 1sh green 2,250. 200.00
*a.* 1sh pale green 2,250. 200.00
*b.* Double impression 2,250.
Cut to shape 5.00

Die numbers (on base of bust): 1 and 2.

**1848**

6 A3 10p red brown 2,250. 450.00
*a.* Double impression
Cut to shape 5.00

Die numbers (on base of bust): 1, 2, 3, 4; also without die number.

Wmk. 19 - V.R.

**1854 Wmk. 19**

7 A4 6p red vio 2,500. 225.00
*a.* 6p dl vio 2,500. 225.00
*b.* 6p dp vio 2,500. 225.00
Cut to shape 2.50
*c.* Double impression

**1854-55 Wmk. 18 Engr. *Perf. 16***
**Bluish Paper**

8 A1 1p red brn 100.00 1.25
*a.* 1p yel brn 110.00 4.00
9 A1 1p red brn, re-engraved ('55) 110.00 12.50
*a.* Imperf. 800.
10 A2 2p blue 1,200. 25.00
*a.* 2p pale bl 1,500. 40.00

In the re-engraved 1p stamps, the lines of the features are deeper and stronger, the fillet behind the ear more distinct, the shading about the eye heavier, the line of the nostril is turned downward at right and an indentation of color appears between lower lip and chin.

***Perf. 14***

11 A1 1p red brn ('55) 300.00 17.50
*a.* Imperf.
12 A1 1p red brn, re-engraved ('55) 175.00 20.00
*a.* 1p org brn, re-engraved 425.00 75.00
13 A2 2p bl ('55) 1,650. 150.00
*a.* Imperf. (P5)

Wmk. 20 - Large Crown

Wmk. 20 exists in two types. The first includes two vertical prongs, rising from the top of the crown's headband and extending into each of the two balancing midsections. The second type (illustrated), introduced in 1861, omits these prongs.

**1855 Wmk. 20 *Perf. 16***
**Bluish Paper**

14 A1 1p red brn, re-engraved 350.00 30.00
15 A2 2p blue 2,250. 150.00
*a.* Imperf. (P5) 1,750.

**1855 Bluish Paper *Perf. 14***

16 A1 1p red brn, re-engraved 90.00 75
*a.* 1p org brn, re-engraved 200.00 15.00
*b.* 1p brn rose, re-engraved 110.00 8.00
*c.* Imperf. 625.00 625.00
17 A2 2p blue 650. 17.50

**1856-58 White Paper *Perf. 16***

18 A1 1p rose red, re-engraved ('57) 425.00 27.50
19 A2 2p bl, thin lines ('58) 2,750. 100.00

***Perf. 14***

20 A1 1p rose red, re-engraved ('56) 35.00 30
*a.* Imperf. 400.00 400.00
*b.* 1p red brn, re-engraved 200.00 15.00
21 A2 2p bl, thin lines ('57) 750. 27.50

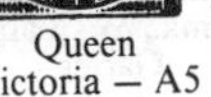

Queen Victoria — A5

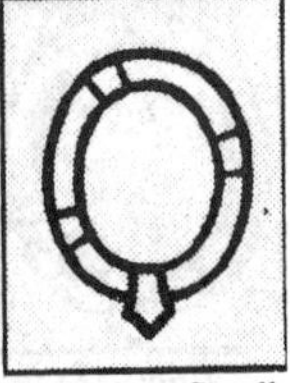

Wmk. 21 - Small Garter

**1855 Typo. Wmk. 21**

22 A5 4p rose, *bluish* 1,800. 125.00
23 A5 4p rose, *white* 2,800. 250.00

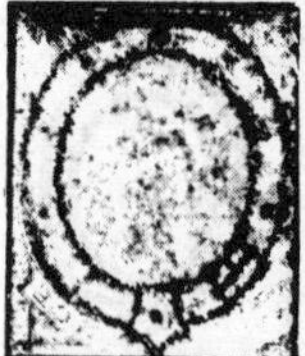

Wmk. 22 - Medium Garter

Wmk. 23 - Large Garter

**1856** **Wmk. 22**

*24* A5 4p rose, *bluish* 2,750. 165.00
*25* A5 4p rose, *white* 1,300. 150.00

**1857** **Wmk. 23**

*26* A5 4p rose, *white* 550.00 15.00

A6

A7

Wmk. 24 - Heraldic Emblems

**1856** **Wmk. 24**

*27* A6 6p lilac 450.00 35.00
*a.* 6p dp lil 500.00 60.00
*28* A7 1sh green 600.00 75.00
*a.* 1sh pale grn 575.00 80.00

Queen Victoria
A8 A9

**1858-69 Engr. Wmk. 20** ***Perf. 14***

*29* A8 2p dp bl (P9) 150.00 2.25
*a.* 2p bl 140.00 2.25
*b.* Imperf. (P9) *3,500.*
Plate 7, 8 375.00 14.00
Plate 12 650.00 25.00

**Lines Above and Below Head Thinner**

*30* A8 2p bl ('69) (P13) 125.00 2.75
*a.* Imperf. (P13) *1,150.*
Plate 14, 15 140.00 6.00

**1860-70**

*31* A9 1½p lil rose, *bluish* (P1) ('60) 2,000.
*a.* Lettered "OP-PC" *15,000.*
*32* A9 1½p dl rose ('70) (P3) 125.00 8.75
*a.* 1½p lake red 125.00 8.75
*b.* Lettered "OP-PC" *4,250.* 650.00
*c.* Imperf.
Plate 1 225.00 17.50

The 1½p stamps from Plate 1 carry no plate number. The Plate 3 number is in the border at each side above the lower corner letters.

No. 31 was prepared but not issued.

Queen Victoria — A10

**1864**

*33* A10 1p rose red 7.50 40
*a.* 1p brick red 7.50 40
*b.* 1p lake red 7.50 40
*c.* Imperf. (P116) 900.00 750.00
Plate 71 18.00 1.00
Plate 72 22.50 1.00
Plate 73 18.00 1.00
Plate 74 18.00 40
Plate 76 25.00 40
Plate 77 *65,000.* *65,000.*
Plate 78 50.00 40
Plate 79 18.00 40
Plate 80 16.00 55
Plate 81 40.00 55
Plate 82 150.00 1.50
Plate 83 165.00 3.50
Plate 84 40.00 60
Plate 85 15.00 60
Plate 86 30.00 1.00
Plate 87 9.25 40
Plate 88 200.00 4.75
Plate 89 18.00 40
Plate 90 22.50 40
Plate 91 25.00 2.00
Plate 92 13.00 50
Plate 93 25.00 50
Plate 94 22.50 1.50
Plate 95 18.00 50
Plate 96 24.00 40
Plate 97 15.00 1.00
Plate 98 15.00 2.00
Plate 99 18.00 1.65
Plate 100 18.00 60
Plate 101 30.00 2.50
Plate 102 15.00 40
Plate 103 16.00 60
Plate 104 24.00 1.75
Plate 105 57.50 3.50
Plate 106 18.00 50
Plate 107 25.00 1.75
Plate 108 37.50 90
Plate 109 90.00 85
Plate 110 15.00 2.25
Plate 111 22.50 60
Plate 112 37.50 60
Plate 113 13.00 3.00
Plate 114 375.00 4.00
Plate 115 90.00 65
Plate 116 62.50 3.50
Plate 117 5.75 40
Plate 118 15.00 40
Plate 119 9.25 40
Plate 120 7.50 40
Plate 121 40.00 4.00
Plate 122 7.50 40
Plate 123-124 8.75 60
Plate 125 10.50 85
Plate 127 32.50 85
Plate 129 10.50 1.75
Plate 130 11.00 60
Plate 131 67.50 10.00
Plate 132 110.00 15.00
Plate 133 100.00 4.50
Plate 134 7.50 60
Plate 135 90.00 20.00
Plate 136 90.00 15.00
Plate 137 11.00 60
Plate 138 9.25 60
Plate 139 11.00 4.00
Plate 140 7.50 40
Plate 141 100.00 1.50
Plate 142 37.50 6.00
Plate 143 18.00 6.00
Plate 144 67.50 7.50
Plate 145 7.50 60
Plate 146 7.50 1.75
Plate 147 11.00 85
Plate 148 11.00 1.00
Plate 149 11.00 1.25
Plate 150 9.25 40
Plate 151 16.00 3.00
Plate 152 11.00 1.50
Plate 153 55.00 1.50
Plate 154 11.00 40
Plate 155 11.00 50
Plate 156-157 11.00 40
Plate 158-159 9.25 40
Plate 160 7.75 40
Plate 161 40.00 2.00
Plate 162 11.00 1.50
Plate 163-164 11.00 90
Plate 165 11.00 40
Plate 166 11.00 2.00
Plate 167 7.50 40
Plate 168 10.50 1.50
Plate 169 18.00 1.75
Plate 170 10.50 40
Plate 171 7.50 40
Plate 172 10.50 60
Plate 173 32.50 3.00
Plate 174 7.50 40
Plate 175 18.00 1.25
Plate 176 15.00 75
Plate 177 7.50 40
Plate 178 15.00 1.00
Plate 179 15.00 60
Plate 180 16.00 1.25
Plate 181 11.00 40
Plate 182 55.00 1.25
Plate 183 15.00 85
Plate 184 7.50 60
Plate 185 11.00 85
Plate 186 18.00 75
Plate 187 11.00 40
Plate 188 15.00 4.50
Plate 189 22.50 1.75
Plate 190 7.50 1.75
Plate 191 7.50 3.00
Plate 192 22.50 40
Plate 193 7.50 40
Plate 194 11.00 2.25
Plate 195 13.00 2.50
Plate 196 9.25 1.50
Plate 197 15.00 7.00
Plate 198 9.25 2.00
Plate 199 11.00 2.00
Plate 200 11.00 40
Plate 201 7.50 1.75
Plate 202 9.25 2.00
Plate 203 9.25 4.00
Plate 204 11.00 40
Plate 205 11.00 90
Plate 206 11.00 2.25
Plate 207 13.00 2.50
Plate 208 11.00 3.00
Plate 209 15.00 2.50
Plate 210 16.00 7.50
Plate 211 42.50 8.00
Plate 212-213 11.00 6.00
Plate 214 15.00 5.00
Plate 215 15.00 10.00
Plate 216 15.00 10.00
Plate 217 15.00 2.50
Plate 218 11.00 2.25
Plate 219 57.50 30.00
Plate 220 8.25 2.25
Plate 221 27.50 7.50
Plate 222 25.00 17.50
Plate 223 37.50 30.00
Plate 224 57.50 30.00
Plate 225 2,000. 325.00

Plate numbers are contained in the scroll work at the sides of the stamp.

Thirty-nine plate numbers besides Plate 116 (No. 33c) are also known imperforate. Values for used copies start at $450.

A11

**1862 Typo. Wmk. 23**

*34* A11 4p vermilion 525.00 15.00
*a.* Hair lines 500.00 15.00
*b.* Imperf. (P4) 850.

Hair lines on stamps 34a, 39b and 40b are fine colorless lines drawn diagonally across the corners of the stamp.

A12

A13

A14

A15

**1862** **Wmk. 24**

*37* A12 3p pale rose 425.00 60.00
*a.* 3p dp rose 1,150. 125.00
*b.* With white dots under side ornaments *3,000.*
*c.* Wmk. error, 3 roses and shamrock
*39* A13 6p lilac 525.00 15.00
*a.* 6p dp lil 575.00 45.00
*b.* Hair lines 600.00 60.00
*c.* Same as b, imperf. (P4) 750.
*40* A14 9p straw 1,000. 80.00
*a.* 9p bis 1,150. 80.00
*b.* Hair lines *10,000.* *2,750.*
*42* A15 1sh green 850. 50.00
*a.* 1sh dp grn 900. 75.00
*b.* As "a," imperf. 1,500.

A16

**1865** **Wmk. 23**

*43* A16 4p ver (P12) 175.00 12.00
*a.* 4p dl ver 175.00 12.00
*b.* Imperf. (P11,12) 450.00
Plate 7 250.00 15.00
Plate 8 200.00 15.00
Plate 9 200.00 12.00
Plate 10 325.00 30.00
Plate 11 200.00 12.00
Plate 13 200.00 15.00
Plate 14 275.00 27.50

A17

(Hyphen after SIX) – A18

A19 A20

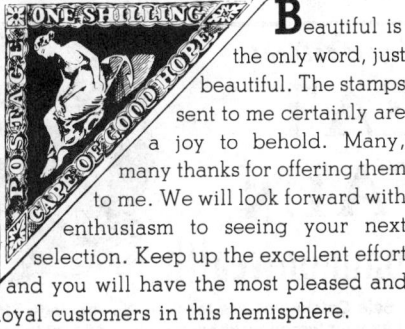

A21

**1865** **Wmk. 24**

*44* A17 3p rose (P4) 425.00 22.50
 *a.* Wmk. error, 3 roses and shamrock 1,250. 275.00
*45* A18 6p lil (P5) 350.00 15.00
 *a.* 6p dp lil 425.00 22.50
 *b.* Double impression 6,000.
 *c.* Wmk. error, 3 roses and shamrock 300.00
 Plate 6 1,350. 45.00
*46* A19 9p straw (P4) 1,000. 130.00
 *a.* Wmk. error, 3 roses and shamrock (P4) 2,500. 425.00
 Plate 5 12,500.
*47* A20 10p red brn (P1) 21,500.
*48* A21 1sh grn (P4) 600.00 25.00
 *b.* Wmk. error, 3 roses and shamrock 400.00
 *c.* Vertical pair, imperf. between 6,250.

(No hyphen after SIX) — A22

A23

Wmk. 25 - Spray of Rose

**1867-80** **Wmk. 25**

*49* A17 3p rose (P6) 200.00 10.00
 *a.* 3p dp rose 225.00 10.00
 *b.* Imperf. (P5,6,8,9) 425.00
 Plate 4 350.00 55.00
 Plate 5 200.00 12.50
 Plate 7,8 250.00 12.50
 Plate 9 250.00 15.00
 Plate 10 275.00 25.00
*50* A18 6p dl vio (P6) 475.00 20.00
 *a.* brt vio (P6) 475.00 20.00
*51* A22 6p brt vio ('69) (P9) 300.00 15.00
 *a.* 6p red vio 300.00 15.00
 *b.* Imperf. (P8, 9) 550.00 400.00
 Plate 8 300.00 17.50
 Plate 10 20,000.
*52* A19 9p bis (P4) ('67) 725.00 65.00
 *a* Imperf. (P4) 2,250.
*53* A20 10p red brn (P1) 1,150. 100.00
 *a.* 10p dp red brn 1,200. 95.00
 *b.* Imperf. (P1) 1,600.
 Plate 2 20,000. 4,000.
*54* A21 1sh grn (P4) 350.00 10.00
 *a.* 1sh dp grn 475.00 10.00
 *b.* Imperf. (P4) 1,150. 750.
 Plate 5 400.00 5.50
 Plate 6 725.00 5.50
 Plate 7 725.00 30.00
*55* A23 2sh bl (P1) 1,000. 60.00
 *a.* 2sh pale bl 1,300. 75.00
 *b.* Imperf. (P1) 2,000.
 Plate 3 4,500.
*56* A23 2sh pale brn (P1) ('80) 6,000. 1,400.

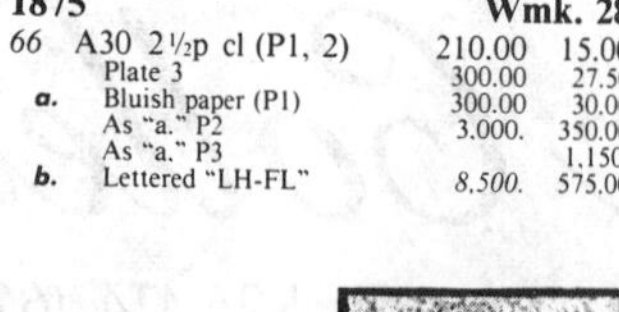
A24 Wmk. 26 - Maltese Cross

**1867** **Wmk. 26** ***Perf. 15½x15***

*57* A24 5sh rose (P1) 2,500. 145.00
 *a.* 5sh pale rose 3,250. 200.00
 *b.* Imperf. (P1) 4,250.
 Plate 2 3,250. 135.00

A25

Wmk. 27 - "Half Penny" in Script

**1870** **Engr.** **Wmk. 27** ***Perf. 14***

*58* A25 ½p rose (P4-6, 10-14) 35.00 3.00
 Plate 1 75.00 27.50
 Plate 3 42.50 5.00
 Plate 8 85.00 22.50
 Plate 9 1,500. 275.00
 Plate 15 42.50 5.00
 Plate 19 60.00 9.00
 Plate 20 72.50 12.50

Plates 1, 4, 5, 6, 8 and 14 are known imperf.

A26

A27

A28

A29

**1872-73** **Wmk. 25** **Typo.**

*59* A26 6p brn (P11) 275.00 14.00
 *a.* 6p dp brn 350.00 14.00
 Plate 12 625.00 45.00
*60* A26 6p gray (P12) ('73) 500.00 25.00
 *a.* Imperf. 1,300.

**1873-80**

*61* A27 3p rose (P11, 16) 200.00 10.00
 *a.* 3p dp rose 200.00 10.00
 Plate 12 225.00 11.00
 Plate 14 250.00 12.50
 Plate 15 200.00 12.50
 Plate 17 225.00 10.00
 Plate 18 225.00 12.50
 Plate 19 200.00 12.50
 Plate 20 225.00 22.50
*62* A28 6p gray (P15, 16) 180.00 11.00
 Plate 13, 14 180.00 12.50
 Plate 17 275.00 25.00
*63* A28 6p buff (P13) 10,000.
*64* A29 1sh pale grn (P12, 13) 180.00 15.00
 *a.* 1sh dp grn 250.00 17.50
 Plate 8, 9, 10, 11 275.00 20.00
 Plate 14 15,000.
*65* A29 1sh sal (P13) ('80) 900. 160.00

A30

Wmk. 28 - Anchor

**1875** **Wmk. 28**

*66* A30 2½p cl (P1, 2) 210.00 15.00
 Plate 3 300.00 27.50
 *a.* Bluish paper (P1) 300.00 30.00
 As "a." P2 3,000. 350.00
 As "a." P3 1,150.
 *b.* Lettered "LH-FL" 8,500. 575.00

Wmk. 29 - Orb

**1876-80** **Wmk. 29**

*67* A30 2½p cl (P4, 6-9, 11, 14-16) 200.00 6.00
 Plate 3 400.00 27.50
 Plate 5 200.00 7.50
 Plate 10 250.00 8.75
 Plate 12, 13 200.00 8.75
 Plate 17 550.00 75.00
*68* A30 2½p ultra ('80) (P19, 20) 150.00 4.50
 Plate 17 150.00 15.00
 Plate 18 175.00 6.50

A31

A32

**1876-80** **Wmk. 23**

*69* A31 4p ver (P15) 600.00 150.00
 Plate 16 20,000.
*70* A31 4p pale ol grn ('77) (P15, 16) 450.00 55.00
 *a.* Imperf. (P15) 625.00
 Plate 17 10,000.
*71* A31 4p gray brn (P17) ('80) 625.00 100.00
*72* A32 8p brn lil (P1) ('76) 4,500.
*73* A32 8p org (P1) ('76) 625.00 100.00
 *a.* Imperf.

No. 72 was never placed in use.

A33 A34

**1878** **Wmk. 26** ***Perf. 15½x15***

*74* A33 10sh sl (P1) 20,000. 800.
*75* A34 £1 brn lil (P1) 27,500. 1,600.

A35

A36

A37

A38

A39

A40

Wmk. 30 - Imperial Crown

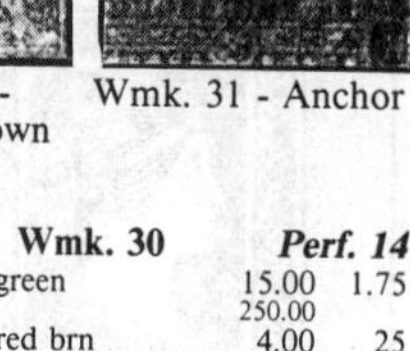
Wmk. 31 - Anchor

**1880-81** **Wmk. 30** ***Perf. 14***

*78* A35 ½p green 15.00 1.75
 *a.* Imperf. 250.00
*79* A36 1p red brn 4.00 25
 *a.* Imperf. 250.00
 *b.* Wmk. 29, error
*80* A37 1½p red brn 85.00 12.50
*81* A38 2p lil rose 100.00 17.50

82 A30 2½p ultra ('81) (P22, 23) 175.00 2.75
a. Imperf. (P23)
Plate 21 250.00 4.50
83 A27 3p rose ('81) (P21) 175.00 10.00
Plate 20 275.00 25.00
84 A31 4p gray brn (P17, 18) 175.00 8.50
85 A39 5p dp ind ('81) 400.00 30.00
86 A28 6p gray (P17, 18) 175.00 8.00
87 A29 1sh sal (P13, 14) ('81) 250.00 35.00
a. Imperf. (P14)

**1881**

88 A40 1p lil (14 dots in each angle) 100.00 15.00
89 A40 1p lil (16 dots in each angle) 75 10
a. Printed on both sides 525.00
b. Imperf., pair 725.00
c. Unwmk. 275.00
d. Bluish paper 1,275.

**1882-83** **Wmk. 31**

90 A24 5sh rose, *bluish* (P4) 6,750. 850.00
a. White paper 6,750. 850.00
91 A33 10sh sl, *bluish* (P1) 22,500. 1,000.
a. White paper 25,000. 1,000.
92 A34 £1 brn lil, *bluish* (P1) 30,000. 2,500.
a. White paper 32,500. 2,500.

A41

**1882** **Wmk. Two Anchors (31)**

93 A41 £5 brt org (P1) 4,000. 1,250.
a. £5 pale dl org, *bluish* 17,500. 2,500.
b. £5 brt org, *bluish* 11,000. 2,500.

The paper of No. 93b is less bluish than that of No. 93a, and it is a later printing.

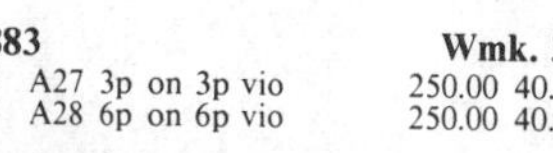
Types of 1873-80 Surcharged in Carmine 3d

**1883** **Wmk. 30**

94 A27 3p on 3p vio 250.00 40.00
95 A28 6p on 6p vio 250.00 40.00

A44

**1883** **Wmk. 31**

96 A44 2sh6p lilac 250.00 35.00
a. Bluish paper 1,500. 150.00

A45

A46

A47

A48

A49

A50

**1883-84** **Wmk. 30**

98 A35 ½p sl bl ('84) 8.00 1.00
99 A45 1½p lil ('84) 55.00 10.00
100 A46 2p lil ('84) 75.00 14.00
101 A47 2½p lil ('84) 40.00 2.25
102 A48 3p lil ('84) 100.00 14.00
103 A49 4p grn ('84) 180.00 50.00
104 A45 5p grn ('84) 150.00 50.00
105 A46 6p grn ('84) 200.00 55.00
106 A50 9p green 475.00 190.00
107 A48 1sh grn ('84) 350.00 80.00

Values are for copies of good color. Faded copies sell for much less.

No. 104 with line instead of period under "d" was not regularly issued.

Nos. 98-105 and 107 exist imperf. Values from $300 to $600 each.

A51

A52

**1884** **Wmk. 31**

108 A51 5sh car rose 350.00 60.00
a. Bluish paper 4,500. 475.00
109 A52 10sh ultra 575.00 180.00
a. 10sh cob 15,000. 3,000.
b. Bluish paper 12,500. 1,500.
c. As "a", bluish paper 13,000. 3,000.

A53

**1884** **Wmk. 30**

110 A53 £1 brn vio 8,000. 1,150.

**Queen Victoria Jubilee Issue**

A54

A55

A56

A57

A58

A59

A60

A61

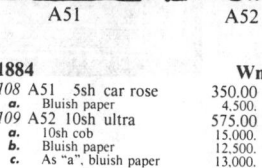

A62

A63

A64

A65

Two types of 5p:
I - Squarish dots beside "d".
II - Tiny vertical dashes beside "d".

**1887-92** **Wmk. 30**

| No. | Type | Description | Unused | Used |
|---|---|---|---|---|
| *111* | A54 | ½p vermilion | 75 | 10 |
| *a.* | | Printed on both sides | | |
| *b.* | | Double impression | *1,250.* | |
| *112* | A55 | 1½p vio & grn | 8.00 | 50 |
| *113* | A56 | 2p grn & car rose | 12.50 | 1.00 |
| *a.* | | 2p grn & ver | 200.00 | 55.00 |
| *114* | A57 | 2½p vio, *bl* | 6.00 | 15 |
| *115* | A58 | 3p vio, *yel* | 14.00 | 50 |
| *a.* | | vio, *org* | 325.00 | 75.00 |
| *116* | A59 | 4p brn & grn | 15.00 | 3.00 |
| *117* | A60 | 4½p car rose & grn ('92) | 3.25 | 6.75 |
| *118* | A61 | 5p lil & bl, II | 24.00 | 2.25 |
| *a.* | | Type I | 350.00 | 27.50 |
| *119* | A62 | 6p vio, *rose* | 17.00 | 2.25 |
| *120* | A63 | 9p bl & lil | 40.00 | 15.00 |
| *121* | A64 | 10p car rose & lil ('90) | 35.00 | 15.00 |
| *122* | A65 | 1sh green | 70.00 | 20.00 |
| | | *Nos. 111-122 (12)* | 245.50 | 66.50 |

**1888** **Wmk. Three Orbs (29)**

| No. | Type | Description | Unused | Used |
|---|---|---|---|---|
| *123* | A53 | £1 brn vio | 22,500. | 1,500. |

**Wmk. Three Imperial Crowns (30)**

**1891**

| No. | Type | Description | Unused | Used |
|---|---|---|---|---|
| *124* | A53 | £1 green | 2,000. | 250.00 |

**1900** **Wmk. 30**

| No. | Type | Description | Unused | Used |
|---|---|---|---|---|
| *125* | A54 | ½p bl grn | 50 | 10 |
| *126* | A65 | 1sh car rose & grn | 35.00 | 25.00 |

No. 125 in bright blue is a color changeling.

King Edward VII
A66 A67

A68

A69

A70 A71

A72

A73

*Great Britain stamps can be mounted in Scott's annually supplemented Great Britain Album.*

A74

A75

A76

A77

A78

**1902-11** **Wmk. 30** ***Perf. 14***

| No. | Type | Description | Unused | Used |
|---|---|---|---|---|
| *127* | A66 | ½p gray grn | 52 | 10 |
| *128* | A66 | 1p carmine | 24 | 5 |
| *a.* | | 1p anil rose ('11) | 225.00 | 70.00 |
| *b.* | | Bklt. pane of 6 | 35.00 | |
| *c.* | | Double impression | | |
| *d.* | | Unwmk. | 90.00 | 90.00 |
| *e.* | | Imperf., pair | *3,250.* | |
| *129* | A67 | 1½p vio & grn | 8.75 | 1.50 |
| *130* | A68 | 2p grn & car | 7.75 | 1.75 |
| *a.* | | 2p grn & red | 7.75 | 2.00 |
| *131* | A66 | 2½p ultra | 3.50 | 60 |
| *132* | A69 | 3p vio, *yel* | 8.75 | 90 |
| *133* | A70 | 4p brn & grn | 21.00 | 3.50 |
| *134* | A71 | 5p lil & ultra | 8.75 | 2.00 |
| *135* | A66 | 6p dl vio | 8.75 | 1.90 |
| *a.* | | 6p red vio | 8.75 | 1.90 |
| *b.* | | 6p vio | 8.75 | 1.90 |
| *c.* | | 6p blk vio | 10.50 | 2.00 |
| *136* | A72 | 9p ultra & vio | 30.00 | 15.00 |
| *137* | A73 | 10p car rose & vio | 27.50 | 10.00 |
| *a.* | | 10p scar & vio | 32.50 | 10.00 |
| *138* | A74 | 1sh car rose & grn | 27.50 | 3.00 |

**Wmk. 31**

| No. | Type | Description | Unused | Used |
|---|---|---|---|---|
| *139* | A75 | 2sh6p dl vio | 150.00 | 25.00 |
| *a.* | | 2sh6p dk vio | 175.00 | 25.00 |
| *140* | A76 | 5sh car rose | 225.00 | 40.00 |
| *a.* | | 5sh car | 275.00 | 40.00 |
| *141* | A77 | 10sh ultra | 500.00 | 100.00 |

**Wmk. Three Imperial Crowns (30)**

| No. | Type | Description | Unused | Used |
|---|---|---|---|---|
| *142* | A78 | £1 green | 1,000. | 225.00 |
| | | *Nos. 127-138 (12)* | 153.01 | 40.30 |

Nos. 129, 130 and 132 to 139 inclusive exist on both ordinary and chalky paper.

**1904** **Wmk. 30**

| No. | Type | Description | Unused | Used |
|---|---|---|---|---|
| *143* | A66 | ½p pale yel grn | 35 | 5 |
| *a.* | | Bklt. pane of 6 | 25.00 | |
| *b.* | | Booklet pane of 5 + label | 175.00 | |
| *c.* | | Double impression | *3,250.* | |
| *d.* | | Imperf., pair | *2,500.* | |

Edward VII — A79

**1909-10**

| No. | Type | Description | Unused | Used |
|---|---|---|---|---|
| *144* | A70 | 4p org ('10) | 7.50 | 3.00 |
| *145* | A79 | 7p gray ('10) | 2.50 | 2.50 |

**1911** ***Perf. 15x14***

| No. | Type | Description | Unused | Used |
|---|---|---|---|---|
| *146* | A66 | ½p yel grn | 24.00 | 15.00 |
| *147* | A66 | 1p carmine | 4.50 | 2.00 |
| *148* | A66 | 2½p ultra | 12.00 | 1.75 |
| *149* | A69 | 3p vio, *yel* | 13.00 | 1.25 |
| *a.* | | 3p gray, *lem* | *4,500.* | |
| *150* | A70 | 4p orange | 12.00 | 3.00 |
| | | *Nos. 146-150 (5)* | 65.50 | 23.00 |

King George V
A80 A81

**1911 Wmk. 30 *Perf. 15x14***

| No. | Type | Description | Unused | Used |
|---|---|---|---|---|
| *151* | A80 | ½p yel grn | 2.50 | 50 |
| **a.** | | Booklet pane of 6 | 55.00 | |
| **b.** | | Perf. 14 (error) | *4,000.* | 250.00 |
| *152* | A81 | 1p carmine | 3.25 | 30 |
| **a.** | | Booklet pane of 6 | 55.00 | |
| **b.** | | Perf. 14 (error) | *4,750.* | |

**1912 Re-engraved**

| No. | Type | Description | Unused | Used |
|---|---|---|---|---|
| *153* | A80 | ½p yel grn | 2.75 | 20 |
| *154* | A81 | 1p scarlet | 1.40 | 20 |
| **a.** | | 1p anil scar | 125.00 | 45.00 |

In the re-engraved stamps the lines of the hair and beard are clearer. The re-engraved ½p has 3 lines of shading instead of 4 between the point of neck and frame; in the 1p the body of the lion is nearly covered by lines of shading.

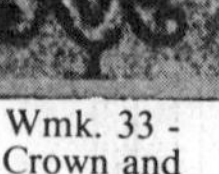

Wmk. 33 - Crown and GvR

Wmk. 32 - Crown and GvR Multiple

In the normal watermark (sometimes termed the "repeated" watermark) the letters "GvR" are extended. The royal cyphers are placed one above the other and usually two appear on each stamp. In the multiple watermark the letters "GvR" are condensed, the cyphers are smaller and are so placed that those in each succeeding row are below the spaces between the cyphers in the row above.



**Wmk. 33 *Perf. 15x14***
**Die I (Before Re-engraving)**

| No. | Type | Description | Unused | Used |
|---|---|---|---|---|
| *155* | A80 | ½p yel grn | 7.50 | 4.50 |
| **a.** | | Bklt. pane of 6 | 125.00 | |
| *156* | A81 | 1p scarlet | 7.00 | 4.50 |
| **a.** | | Bklt. pane of 6 | 100.00 | |

**Die II (Re-engraved)**

| No. | Type | Description | Unused | Used |
|---|---|---|---|---|
| *157* | A80 | ½p yel grn | 1.90 | 20 |
| *158* | A81 | 1p scarlet | 1.65 | 20 |

**Wmk. 32**

| No. | Type | Description | Unused | Used |
|---|---|---|---|---|
| *158A* | A80 | ½p yel grn | 1.90 | 1.00 |
| **c.** | | Imperf., pair | 175.00 | |
| *158B* | A81 | 1p scarlet | 6.25 | 2.25 |
| **d.** | | Imperf., pair | 150.00 | |

A82

A83

A84

A85

A86

A87

A88

A89

King George V — A90

"Britannia Rules the Waves"
A91

TWO PENCE

Die I. Four horizontal lines above head. Heavy colored lines above and below bottom tablet.

Die II. Three lines above head. Thinner lines above and below bottom tablet.

**1912-13 Wmk. 33 *Perf. 15x14***

| No. | Type | Description | Unused | Used |
|---|---|---|---|---|
| *159* | A82 | ½p green | 10 | 5 |
| **a.** | | Double impression | *3,000.* | |
| **b.** | | Bklt. pane of 6 | 9.00 | |
| *160* | A83 | 1p scarlet | 10 | 5 |
| **a.** | | Bklt. pane of 6 | 7.50 | |
| **b.** | | Tete beche pair | | |
| *161* | A84 | 1½p red brn | 20 | 5 |
| **a.** | | 1½p org brn | 1.25 | 5 |
| **b.** | | "PENCF." | 125.00 | 45.00 |
| **c.** | | Unwmkd. | 125.00 | |
| **d.** | | Bklt. pane of 6 | 17.50 | |
| **e.** | | Booklet pane of 4 + 2 labels | 350.00 | |
| *162* | A85 | 2p dp org (I) | 45 | 5 |
| **a.** | | 2p dp org (II) | 2.50 | 60 |
| **b.** | | Booklet pane of 6 (I) | 45.00 | |
| **c.** | | Booklet pane of 6(II) | 75.00 | |
| *163* | A86 | 2½p ultra | 3.50 | 14 |
| *164* | A87 | 3p bluish vio | 2.00 | 14 |
| *165* | A88 | 4p sl grn | 2.00 | 30 |
| *166* | A89 | 5p yel brn | 4.25 | 90 |
| **a.** | | Unwmkd. | 450.00 | |
| *167* | A89 | 6p rose lil | 3.25 | 28 |
| **a.** | | 6p dl vio | 8.50 | 3.00 |
| **b.** | | Perf. 14 | 50.00 | 37.50 |
| *168* | A89 | 7p ol grn | 8.75 | 2.00 |
| *169* | A89 | 8p *yellow* | 21.00 | 4.25 |
| *170* | A90 | 9p blk brn | 7.00 | 1.75 |
| *171* | A90 | 10p lt bl | 8.75 | 3.50 |
| *172* | A90 | 1sh bister | 5.25 | 35 |
| | | *Nos. 159-172 (14)* | 66.60 | 13.81 |

No. 167 is on chalky paper.

Wmk. 34 - Large Crown and GvR

***Perf. 11x12***
**1913-18 Engr. Wmk. 34**

| No. | Type | Description | Unused | Used |
|---|---|---|---|---|
| *173* | A91 | 2sh6p lt brn | 150.00 | 32.50 |
| **a.** | | 2sh 6p blk brn | 135.00 | 30.00 |
| *174* | A91 | 5sh carmine | 300.00 | 90.00 |
| **a.** | | 5sh rose car | 200.00 | 80.00 |
| *175* | A91 | 10sh lt bl | 1,250. | 175.00 |
| **a.** | | 10sh ind bl | 400.00 | 175.00 |
| *176* | A91 | £1 green | 1,300. | 550.00 |

Nos. 173a, 174a, 175a and 176 were printed in 1913 by Waterlow Bros. & Layton; Nos. 173, 174 and 175 were printed in 1915-18 by Thomas De La Rue & Co.

**1913 Wmk. 32 Typo. *Perf. 15x14***
**Coil Stamps**

| No. | Type | Description | Unused | Used |
|---|---|---|---|---|
| *177* | A82 | ½p green | 95.00 | 80.00 |
| *178* | A83 | 1p scarlet | 200.00 | 160.00 |

Type of 1913-18 Retouched

**1919 Engr. Wmk. 34 *Perf. 11x12***

| No. | Type | Description | Unused | Used |
|---|---|---|---|---|
| *179* | A91 | 2sh6p gray brn | 70.00 | 8.00 |
| *180* | A91 | 5sh car rose | 125.00 | 14.00 |
| *181* | A91 | 10sh blue | 275.00 | 60.00 |

The retouched stamps usually have a dot above the middle of the top frame. They are 22¾mm. high, whereas Nos. 173-176 are 22mm. high.

Nos. 179-181 were printed by Bradbury, Wilkinson & Co. See also Nos. 222-224.

Type of 1912-13

**1922 Typo. Wmk. 33 *Perf. 15x14***

| No. | Type | Description | Unused | Used |
|---|---|---|---|---|
| *183* | A90 | 9p ol grn | 65.00 | 9.50 |

**British Empire Exhibition Issue**

British Lion and King George V — A92

Wmk. 35 - Crown and Block GvR Multiple

**Wmk. 35**
**1924, Apr. 23 Engr. *Perf. 14***

| No. | Type | Description | Unused | Used |
|---|---|---|---|---|
| *185* | A92 | 1p vermilion | 9.00 | 6.25 |
| *186* | A92 | 1½p dk brn | 11.50 | 5.25 |

See Nos. 203-204.

Types of 1912-13 Issue

**1924 Typo. *Perf. 15x14***

| No. | Type | Description | Unused | Used |
|---|---|---|---|---|
| *187* | A82 | ½p green | 12 | 5 |
| **a.** | | Wmkd. sideways | 5.25 | 3.25 |
| **b.** | | Booklet pane of 6 | 3.50 | |
| **c.** | | Double impression | *3,750.* | |
| *188* | A83 | 1p scarlet | 24 | 5 |
| **a.** | | Wmkd. sideways | 12.00 | 8.75 |
| **b.** | | Booklet pane of 6 | 5.25 | |
| *189* | A84 | 1½p red brn | 32 | 5 |
| **a.** | | Tete beche pair | 150.00 | 125.00 |
| **b.** | | Wmkd. sideways | 3.50 | 2.00 |
| **c.** | | Booklet pane of 6 | 6.00 | |
| **d.** | | Booklet pane of 4 + 2 labels | 52.50 | |
| *190* | A85 | 2p dp org (II) | 80 | 5 |
| **a.** | | Wmkd. sideways | 100.00 | 62.50 |
| **b.** | | Unwmkd. | 350.00 | |
| *191* | A86 | 2½p ultra | 2.50 | 10 |
| **a.** | | Unwmkd. | 500.00 | |
| *192* | A87 | 3p violet | 3.25 | 5 |
| *193* | A88 | 4p sl grn | 4.00 | 10 |
| *194* | A89 | 5p yel brn | 6.25 | 45 |
| *195* | A89 | 6p dl vio | 2.00 | 50 |
| *198* | A90 | 9p ol grn | 8.00 | 75 |
| *199* | A90 | 10p dl bl | 16.00 | 10.00 |
| *200* | A90 | 1sh bister | 12.00 | 50 |
| | | *Nos. 187-200 (12)* | 55.48 | 12.65 |

Nos. 187a, 188a, 189b and 190a were issued in coils.

Inverted watermarks on the three lowest values are usually from booklet panes.

Nos. 188-189 were issued also on experimental paper with variety of Wmk. 35: closer spacing; letters shorter, rounder.

**British Empire Exhibition Issue**
Type of 1924, Dated "1925"

**1925, May 9 Engr. *Perf. 14***

| No. | Type | Description | Unused | Used |
|---|---|---|---|---|
| *203* | A92 | 1p vermilion | 16.00 | 4.00 |
| *204* | A92 | 1½p brown | 32.50 | 14.00 |

A93

A94

A95

St. George Slaying the Dragon
A96

Wmk. 219 - Large Crown and GvR

**1929, May 10 Typo. *Perf. 15x14***

| No. | Type | Description | Unused | Used |
|---|---|---|---|---|
| *205* | A93 | ½p green | 1.50 | 25 |
| **a.** | | Wmkd. sideways | 32.50 | 25.00 |
| **b.** | | Bklt. pane of 6 | 22.50 | |
| *206* | A94 | 1p scarlet | 2.25 | 75 |
| **a.** | | Wmkd. sideways | 55.00 | 30.00 |
| **b.** | | Bklt. pane of 6 | 22.50 | |
| *207* | A94 | 1½p dk brn | 1.40 | 30 |
| **a.** | | Wmkd. sideways | 32.50 | 27.50 |
| **b.** | | Bklt. pane of 6 | 16.00 | |
| **c.** | | Booklet pane of 4 + 2 labels | 150.00 | |
| *208* | A95 | 2½p dp bl | 10.00 | 6.00 |

Nos. 205a, 206a and 207a were issued in coils.

**Wmk. 219**
**Engr. *Perf. 12***

| No. | Type | Description | Unused | Used |
|---|---|---|---|---|
| *209* | A96 | £1 black | *525.00* | *375.00* |

Universal Postal Union, 9th Congress.

Types of 1924 and

A97

The backgrounds appear to be solid, but under a magnifying glass show the photoengraving screen.

***Perf. 14½x14***
**1934-36 Photo. Wmk. 35**

| No. | Type | Description | Unused | Used |
|---|---|---|---|---|
| *210* | A82 | ½p dk grn | 15 | 5 |
| **a.** | | Wmkd. sideways | 6.75 | 1.50 |
| **b.** | | Bklt. pane of 6 | 11.00 | |
| *211* | A97 | 1p carmine | 15 | 5 |
| **a.** | | Wmkd. sideways | 11.00 | 4.75 |
| **b.** | | Bklt. pane of 6 | 11.00 | |
| **c.** | | Imperf., pair | *850.* | |

| | | | | |
|---|---|---|---|---|
| *212* | A84 | 1½p red brn | 20 | 5 |
| *a.* | | Imperf., pair | 300.00 | |
| *b.* | | Wmkd. sideways | 11.00 | 3.75 |
| *c.* | | Booklet pane of 6 | 5.50 | |
| *d.* | | Booklet pane of 4 + 2 labels | 30.00 | |
| *213* | A85 | 2p red org ('35) | 40 | 10 |
| *a.* | | Imperf., pair | *1,000.* | |
| *b.* | | Wmkd. sideways | 125.00 | 62.50 |
| *214* | A97 | 2½p ultra ('35) | 60 | 15 |
| *215* | A87 | 3p dk vio ('35) | 65 | 15 |
| *216* | A88 | 4p dk sl grn ('35) | 65 | 20 |
| *217* | A89 | 5p yel brn ('36) | 1.65 | 35 |
| *218* | A90 | 9p dk ol grn ('35) | 6.50 | 50 |
| *219* | A90 | 10p Prus bl ('36) | 9.25 | 1.00 |
| *220* | A90 | 1sh bis brn ('36) | 11.50 | 35 |
| | | *Nos. 210-220 (11)* | 31.70 | 2.95 |

Nos. 210a, 211a, 212b and 213b were issued in coils.

### Britannia Type of 1913-18

**1934 Engr. Wmk. 34 *Perf. 11x12***

| | | | | |
|---|---|---|---|---|
| *222* | A91 | 2sh6p brown | 37.50 | 4.00 |
| *223* | A91 | 5sh carmine | 90.00 | 20.00 |
| *224* | A91 | 10sh dk bl | 200.00 | 30.00 |

Waterlow & Sons. Can be distinguished by the crossed lines in background of portrait. Previous issues have horizontal lines only.

### Silver Jubilee Issue

A98

***Perf. 14½x14***

**1935, May 7 Photo. Wmk. 35**

| | | | | |
|---|---|---|---|---|
| *226* | A98 | ½p dk grn | 15 | 5 |
| *a.* | | Booklet pane of 4 | 13.00 | |
| *227* | A98 | 1p carmine | 50 | 40 |
| *a.* | | Booklet pane of 4 | 13.00 | |
| *228* | A98 | 1½p red brn | 40 | 5 |
| *a.* | | Booklet pane of 4 | 6.50 | |
| *229* | A98 | 2½p ultra | 2.50 | 1.75 |
| *a.* | | 2½p Prus bl | 3,750. | 2,750. |

25th anniv. of the reign of George V. Device at right differs on 1½p and 2½p.

King Edward VIII — A99

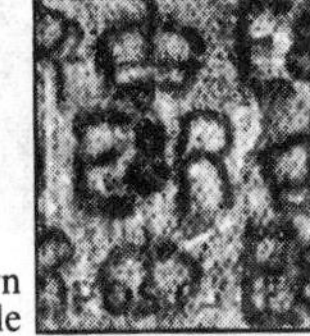
Wmk. 250 - Crown and E8R Multiple

**1936 Wmk. 250**

| | | | | |
|---|---|---|---|---|
| *230* | A99 | ½p dk grn | 5 | 5 |
| *a.* | | Booklet pane of 6 | 1.75 | |
| *231* | A99 | 1p crimson | 15 | 5 |
| *a.* | | Booklet pane of 6 | 1.75 | |
| *232* | A99 | 1½p red brn | 18 | 5 |
| *a.* | | Booklet pane of 6 | 1.75 | |
| *b.* | | Booklet pane of 4 + 2 labels | 15.00 | |
| *c.* | | Booklet pane of 2 | 2.00 | |
| *233* | A99 | 2½p brt ultra | 20 | 20 |

King George VI and Queen Elizabeth A100

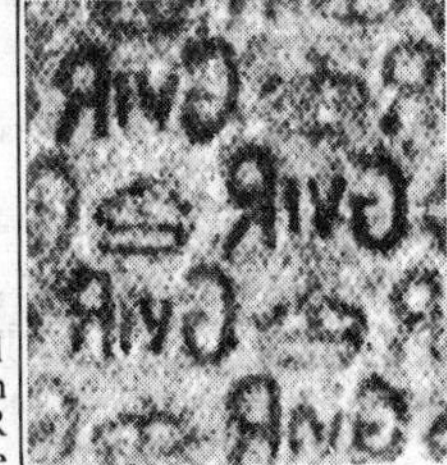
Wmk. 251 - Crown and GviR Multiple

***Perf. 14½x14***

**1937, May 13 Wmk. 251**

| | | | | |
|---|---|---|---|---|
| *234* | A100 | 1½p pur brn | 10 | 5 |

Coronation of King George VI and Queen Elizabeth.

A101

A102

King George VI — A103

Nos. 235-240 show face and neck highlighted, background solid.

**1937-39**

| | | | | |
|---|---|---|---|---|
| *235* | A101 | ½p dp grn | 10 | 5 |
| *a.* | | Wmkd. sideways | 65 | 38 |
| *b.* | | Booklet pane of 6 | 2.75 | |
| *c.* | | Bklt. pane of 4 | 20.00 | 20.00 |
| *d.* | | Booklet pane of 2 | 4.50 | |
| *236* | A101 | 1p scarlet | 20 | 5 |
| *a.* | | Wmkd. sideways | 7.50 | 1.90 |
| *b.* | | Bklt. pane of 6 | 6.00 | |
| *c.* | | Bklt. pane of 4 | 60.00 | 42.50 |
| *d.* | | Booklet pane of 2 | 4.50 | |
| *237* | A101 | 1½p red brn | 20 | 5 |
| *a.* | | Wmkd. sideways | 1.65 | 45 |
| *b.* | | Booklet pane of 6 | 4.50 | |
| *c.* | | Booklet pane of 4 + 2 labels | 35.00 | |
| *d.* | | Booklet pane of 2 | 2.75 | |
| *238* | A101 | 2p org ('38) | 54 | 5 |
| *a.* | | Wmkd. sideways | 45.00 | 27.50 |
| *b.* | | Booklet pane of 6 | 22.50 | |
| *239* | A101 | 2½p brt ultra | 54 | 5 |
| *a.* | | Wmkd. sideways | 57.50 | 15.00 |
| *b.* | | Booklet pane of 6 | 20.00 | |
| *c.* | | Tete beche pair | | |
| *240* | A101 | 3p dk pur ('38) | 2.75 | 10 |
| *241* | A102 | 4p gray grn ('38) | 80 | 10 |
| *a.* | | Imperf., pair | *800.00* | |
| *242* | A102 | 5p lt brn ('38) | 1.40 | 15 |
| *a.* | | Imperf., pair | *900.00* | |
| *243* | A102 | 6p rose lil ('39) | 1.40 | 6 |
| *244* | A103 | 7p emer ('39) | 2.75 | 15 |
| *a.* | | Imperf., pair | *650.00* | |
| *245* | A103 | 8p brt rose ('39) | 4.00 | 25 |
| *246* | A103 | 9p dp ol grn ('39) | 2.75 | 20 |
| *247* | A103 | 10p ryl bl ('39) | 2.75 | 25 |
| *a.* | | Imperf., pair | | |
| *248* | A103 | 1sh brn ('39) | 2.75 | 5 |
| | | *Nos. 235-248 (14)* | 22.93 | 1.56 |

Nos. 235a, 236a, 237a, 238a and 239a were issued in coils.

Nos. 235c and 236c are watermarked sideways.

The 1½p, 1p, 1½p, 2p and 2½p with watermark inverted are from booklet panes.

See Nos. 258-263, 266, 280-285.

### Oman Surcharges

Various definitive and commemorative stamps between Nos. 243 and 372 were surcharged in annas (a), new paisa (np) and rupees (r) for use in Oman. The surcharges do not indicate where the stamps were used.

King George VI and Royal Arms A104

King George VI A105

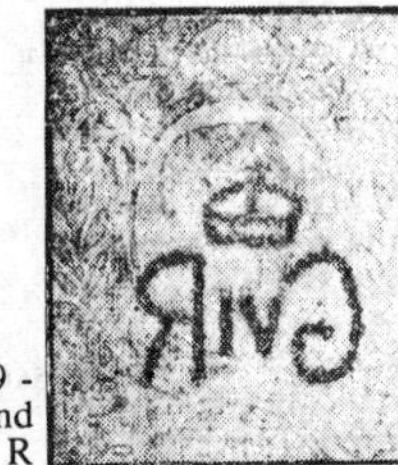
Wmk. 259 - Crown and Large G VI R

**1939-42 Engr. Wmk. 259 *Perf. 14***

| | | | | |
|---|---|---|---|---|
| *249* | A104 | 2sh6p chestnut | 32.50 | 3.25 |
| *249A* | A104 | 2sh6p yel grn ('42) | 3.75 | 12 |
| *250* | A104 | 5sh dl red | 7.50 | 50 |
| *251* | A105 | 10sh indigo | 130.00 | 10.00 |
| *251A* | A105 | 10sh ultra ('42) | 13.00 | 85 |

See No. 275.

Victoria and George VI A106

***Perf. 14½x14***

**1940, May 6 Photo. Wmk. 251**

| | | | | |
|---|---|---|---|---|
| *252* | A106 | ½p dp grn | 14 | 6 |
| *253* | A106 | 1p scarlet | 24 | 10 |
| *254* | A106 | 1½p red brn | 40 | 20 |
| *255* | A106 | 2p orange | 40 | 25 |
| *256* | A106 | 2½p brt ultra | 60 | 12 |
| *257* | A106 | 3p dk pur | 2.25 | 1.50 |
| | | *Nos. 252-257 (6)* | 4.03 | 2.23 |

Centenary of the postage stamp.

### Type of 1937-39, with Background Lightened

**1941-42**

| | | | | |
|---|---|---|---|---|
| *258* | A101 | ½p green | 18 | 5 |
| *a.* | | Booklet pane of 6 | 3.25 | |
| *b.* | | Booklet pane of 2 | 1.10 | |
| *c.* | | Imperf., pair | *850.* | |
| *d.* | | Tete beche pair | *1,150.* | |
| *259* | A101 | 1p vermilion | 25 | 5 |
| *a.* | | Wmkd. sideways ('42) | 3.50 | 2.75 |
| *b.* | | Booklet pane of 2 | 1.10 | |
| *c.* | | Imperf., pair | *800.00* | |
| *260* | A101 | 1½p lt red brn ('42) | 60 | 25 |
| *a.* | | Booklet pane of 2 | 3.00 | |
| *261* | A101 | 2p lt org | 50 | 5 |
| *a.* | | Wmkd. sideways ('42) | 9.00 | 9.00 |
| *b.* | | Booklet pane of 6 | 7.00 | |
| *c.* | | Imperf., pair | *1,250.* | |
| *d.* | | Tete beche pair | 1,500. | |
| *262* | A101 | 2½p ultra | 25 | 8 |
| *a.* | | Wmkd. sideways ('42) | 8.00 | 5.00 |
| *b.* | | Booklet pane of 6 | 3.75 | |
| *c.* | | Imperf., pair | *675.00* | |
| *d.* | | Tete beche pair | 1,150. | |
| *263* | A101 | 3p violet | 1.25 | 8 |
| | | *Nos. 258-263 (6)* | 3.03 | 56 |

Nos. 259a, 261a and 262a were issued in coils.

**Catalogue values for unused stamps in this section, from this point to the end of the section, are for Never Hinged items.**

### Peace Issue

A107

King George VI and Symbols of Peace and Industry A108

***Perf. 14½x14***

**1946, June 11 Photo. Wmk. 251**

| | | | | |
|---|---|---|---|---|
| *264* | A107 | 2½p brt ultra | 15 | 6 |
| *265* | A108 | 3p violet | 25 | 12 |

Return to peace at the close of World War II.

### George VI Type of 1939

**1947, Dec. 29**

| | | | | |
|---|---|---|---|---|
| *266* | A103 | 11p vio brn | 3.00 | 60 |

The indexes in each volume of the Scott Catalogue contain many listings which help to identify stamps.

A109

King George VI and Queen Elizabeth — A110

***Perf. 14½x14, 14x14½***

**1948, Apr. 26**

| | | | | |
|---|---|---|---|---|
| *267* | A109 | 2½p brt ultra | 10 | 5 |
| *268* | A110 | £1 dp chlky bl | 60.00 | 30.00 |

25th anniversary of the marriage of King George VI and Queen Elizabeth.

A111

Vraicking (Gathering Seaweed) A112

**1948, May 10 *Perf. 14½x14***

| | | | | |
|---|---|---|---|---|
| *269* | A111 | 1p red | 18 | 12 |
| *270* | A112 | 2½p brt ultra | 22 | 18 |

Third anniversary of the liberation of the Channel Islands from German occupation.

Sold at post offices in the Channel Islands, but valid for postage throughout Great Britain.

A113

A114

A115

A116

**1948, July 29**

| | | | | |
|---|---|---|---|---|
| *271* | A113 | 2½p brt ultra | 12 | 5 |
| *272* | A114 | 3p dp vio | 28 | 18 |
| *273* | A115 | 6p red vio | 55 | 35 |
| *274* | A116 | 1sh dk brn | 90 | 60 |

1948 Olympic Games held at Wembley during July and August.

### George VI Type of 1939

**Wmk. 259**

**1948, Oct. 1 Engr. *Perf. 14***

| | | | | |
|---|---|---|---|---|
| *275* | A105 | £1 red brn | 21.00 | 9.00 |

A117

A118

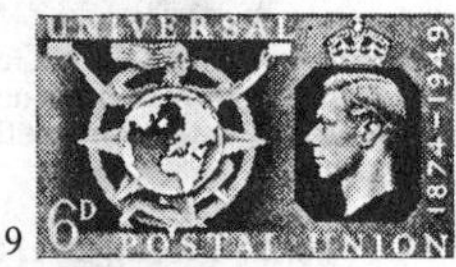

A119

A120

*Perf. 14½x14*

**1949, Oct. 10 Photo. Wmk. 251**

*276* A117 2½p brt ultra 10 6
*277* A118 3p brt vio 25 15
*278* A119 6p red vio 60 52
*279* A120 1sh brown 1.10 1.00

UPU, 75th anniversary.

Types of 1937

**1950-51 Wmk. 251 *Perf. 14½x14***

*280* A101 ½p lt org 15 5
**a.** Booklet pane of 2 1.00
**b.** Booklet pane of 4 1.75
**c.** Booklet pane of 6 2.50
**d.** Imperf., pair *750.00*
**e.** Tete beche pair *2,200.*
*281* A101 1p ultra 18 5
**a.** Wmkd. sideways 60 20
**b.** Booklet pane of 2 1.20
**c.** Booklet pane of 4 1.75
**d.** Booklet pane of 6 2.50
**e.** Booklet pane of 3 + 3 labels 12.00
**f.** Imperf., pair *675.00*
*282* A101 1½p green 35 8
**a.** Wmkd. sideways 85 50
**b.** Booklet pane of 2 1.50
**c.** Booklet pane of 4 3.00
**d.** Booklet pane of 6 3.75
*283* A101 2p lt red brn 45 8
**a.** Wmkd. sideways 1.00 40
**b.** Booklet pane of 6 7.00
**c.** Tete beche pair *1,900.*
*284* A101 2½p vermilion 30 5
**a.** Wmkd. sideways 1.75 60
**b.** Booklet pane of 6 3.25
**c.** Tete beche pair
*285* A102 4p ultra ('50) 1.25 30
*Nos. 280-285 (6)* 2.68 61

Nos. 281a, 282a, 283a and 284a were issued in coils.

H.M.S. Victory A121

St. George Slaying the Dragon A122

Royal Arms A123

Design: 5sh, White Cliffs, Dover.

*Perf. 11x12*

**1951, May 3 Engr. Wmk. 259**

*286* A121 2sh6p green 7.50 65
*287* A121 5sh dl red 19.00 1.10
*288* A122 10sh ultra 11.50 7.50
*289* A123 £1 lt red brn 37.50 11.50

Britannia, Symbols of Commerce and Prosperity, King George VI – A124

Festival Symbol A125

*Perf. 14½x14*

**1951, May 3 Photo. Wmk. 251**

*290* A124 2½p scarlet 15 8
*291* A125 4p brt ultra 45 45

Festival of Britain, 1951.

Queen Elizabeth
A126 A127

A128

A129

A130

A131

A132

Wmk. 298- Tudor Crown and E 2 R Multiple

Type I

Type II

*Perf. 12½x14*

**1952-54 Photo. Wmk. 298**

*292* A126 ½p red org ('53) 9 5
**a.** Booklet pane of 2 70
**b.** Booklet pane of 4 1.25
**c.** Booklet pane of 6 1.50
*293* A126 1p ultra ('53) 12 5
**a.** Booklet pane of 2 90
**b.** Booklet pane of 4 1.75
**c.** Booklet pane of 6 2.25
**d.** Bklt. pane 3 + 3 labels 35.00
*294* A126 1½p grn ('52) 9 5
**a.** Booklet pane of 2 70
**b.** Booklet. pane of 4 1.25
**c.** Booklet pane of 6 ('53) 1.50
**d.** Wmk. sideways 30 25
**e.** As "c," imperf. (error) *750.00*
*295* A126 2p red brn ('53) 60 5
**a.** Booklet pane of 6 5.00
**b.** Wmk. sideways 1.40 90
*296* A127 2½p scar, Type I ('52) 22 5
**a.** Booklet pane of 6, Type II ('53) 7.00
**b.** Wmk. sideways, Type I ('54) 13.00 10.00
**c.** Type II 60 52
*297* A127 3p dk pur 60 20
*298* A128 4p ultra ('53) 1.50 80
*299* A129 5p lt brn ('53) 1.25 80
*300* A129 6p lil rose 1.65 28
*301* A129 7p emerald 3.75 1.65
*302* A130 8p brt rose ('53) 1.65 80
*303* A130 9p dp ol grn 17.00 1.40
*304* A130 10p ryl bl 14.00 1.40
*305* A130 11p vio brn 32.50 10.00
*306* A131 1sh brn ('53) 1.50 28
*307* A132 1sh3pdk grn ('53) 4.00 65
*308* A131 1sh6pdk bl ('53) 27.50 80
*Nos. 292-308 (17)* 108.02 19.31

Nos. 294d, 295b and 296b were issued in coils.

Nos. 292-296 with watermark inverted are from booklets.

Type II stamps of No. 296 come only from booklet panes.

See Nos. 317-333, 353-369.

Carrickfergus Castle, Ireland – A133

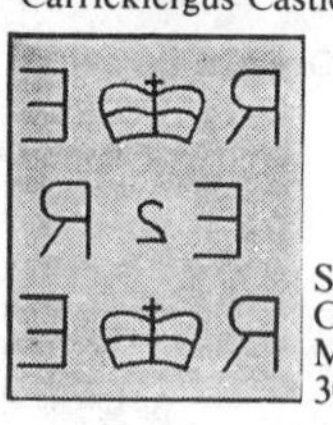
St. Edward's Crown and E 2 R Multiple – Wmk. 308

Designs (Castles): 5sh, Caernarvon, Wales. 10sh, Edinburgh, Scotland. £1, Windsor, England.

**1955 Engr. Wmk. 308 *Perf. 11x12***

*309* A133 2sh6pdk brn 11.50 52
*310* A133 5sh crimson 25.00 1.40
*311* A133 10sh brt ultra 62.50 4.50
*312* A133 £1 int blk 115.00 5.50

See Nos. 371-374, 525-528.

A134

A135

A136

A137

*Perf. 14½x14*

**1953, June 3 Photo. Wmk. 298**

*313* A134 2½p scarlet 60 5
*314* A135 4p ultra 2.00 60
*315* A136 1sh3pdark grn 7.25 2.25
*316* A137 1sh6pdark blue 7.50 2.50

Types of 1952-54

**1955-57 Wmk. 308 *Perf. 14½x14***

*317* A126 ½p red org ('56) 10 5
**a.** Booklet pane of 6 1.50
**b.** Booklet pane of 4 1.25
**d.** Booklet pane of 2 60
*318* A126 1p ultra ('56) 15 5
**a.** Booklet pane of 3 + 3 labels 20.00
**b.** Booklet pane of 6 1.75
**c.** Booklet pane of 4 1.25
**e.** Tete Beche pr. 300.00
**f.** Booklet pane of 2 70
*319* A126 1½p grn ('56) 15 5
**a.** Booklet pane of 6 6.50
**b.** Booklet pane of 4 5.00
**c.** Wmk. sideways ('56) 25 25
**e.** Tete beche pair *700.00*
**f.** Booklet pane of 2 1.10
*320* A126 2p red brn ('56) 20 5
**a.** Wmk. sideways ('56) 28 25
**b.** Booklet pane of 6 2.50
**d.** Tete beche pair *250.00*
**e.** Vert. pair, imperf. between *750.00*
**f.** As "a", horiz. pair, imperf. between *750.00*
**h.** Imperf., pair 250.00
*321* A127 2½p scar, Type I ('56) 16 15
**a.** Booklet pane of 6, Type II 4.00
**b.** Wmk. sideways, Type I ('56) 1.50 1.00
**d.** Type II 30 25
**e.** Tete beche pair 100.00
**f.** Imperf., pair
*322* A127 3p dk pur ('56) 16 5
**a.** Booklet pane of 6 4.00
**b.** Booklet pane of 4 5.50
**c.** Wmk. sideways 11.00 9.00
**e.** Tete beche pair *350.00*
*323* A128 4p ultra 1.25 45
*324* A129 5p lt brn ('56) 2.50 1.50
*325* A129 6p lil rose ('56) 2.00 45
*326* A129 7p emerald 30.00 7.00
*327* A130 8p brt rose ('56) 5.00 90
*328* A130 9p dp ol grn ('56) 15.00 90
*329* A130 10p ryl bl ('56) 10.50 90
*330* A130 11p vio brn 90 90
*331* A131 1sh brown 8.50 30
*332* A132 1sh3pdk grn ('56) 21.00 75
*333* A131 1sh6pdk bl 27.50 75
*Nos. 317-333 (17)* 125.07 15.20

Nos. 319c, 320a, 321b and 322c were issued in coils.

Nos. 317-322 with watermark inverted are from booklets. See Nos. 353-369.

Black Graphite Lines on Back

**1957-59 Wmk. 308**

*317c* A126 ½p red org 16 16
**p.** Phosphor. ('59) 6.00 5.00
*318d* A126 1p ultra 30 30
**p.** Phosphor. ('59) 7.50 5.00
*319d* a126 1½p green 85 60
**p.** Phosphor. ('59) 3.75 2.75
*320c* A126 2p red brn 2.00 1.25
**p.** Phosphor. ('59) 225.00 150.00
*321c* A127 2½p scar (II) 7.00 4.25
*322d* A127 3p dk pur 1.65 60
*Nos. 317c-322d (6)* 11.96 7.16

The vertical black graphite lines were applied to facilitate mail sorting by an electronic machine. The 2p has one line (at right, seen from back), the others two.

---

Phosphorescent bands were overprinted vertically in Nov. 1959 on the face of the preceding ½p, 1p, 1½p and 2p graphite-lined stamps, plus the 2p, 2½p, 3p, 4p and 4½p graphite-lined stamps with Wmk. 322, in a letter-sorting experiment. These faint bands can be seen best with an ultraviolet lamp; without it they can be seen best on unused stamps.

---

Scout Emblem and Rolling Hitch Knot A138

Designs: 4p, Swallows. 1sh 3p, Globe encircled by compass.

*Perf. 14½x14*

**1957, Aug. 1 Wmk. 308**

*334* A138 2½p scarlet 22 10
*335* A138 4p ultra 1.40 1.00
*336* A138 1sh3pdk grn 6.75 6.25

50th anniv. of the Boy Scout movement and the World Scout Jubilee Jamboree, Sutton Coldfield, Aug. 1-12.

A139

**1957, Sept. 12 Photo.**

*337* A139 4p ultra 1.10 1.10

46th Conf. of the Inter-Parliamentary Union, London, Sept. 12-19.

The Scott Catalogue value is a retail price, what you could expect to pay for the stamp in a grade of Fine-Very Fine. The value listed is a retail price which reflects recent actual dealer selling price.

Welsh Dragon
A140

Designs: 6p, Flag with British Empire and Commonwealth Games Emblem. 1sh3p, Welsh dragon holding laurel.

**1958, July 18** ***Perf. 14½x14***

*338* A140 3p dk pur 16 10
*339* A140 6p red lil 55 52
*340* A140 1sh3p green 2.75 1.40

6th British Empire and Commonwealth Games, Cardiff, July 18-26.

Regional Issues of Great Britain for Guernsey, Jersey, Isle of Man, Northern Ireland, Scotland and Wales-Monmouthshire are listed in separate sections following Great Britain Envelopes.

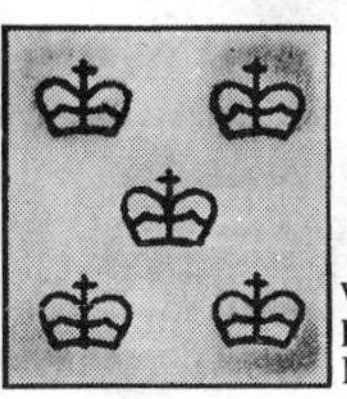

Wmk. 322- St. Edward's Crown Multiple

Types of 1952-55

***Perf. 14½x14***

**1958-65 Photo. Wmk. 322**

*353* A126 ½p red org 8 5
**a.** Booklet pane of 6 70
**b.** Booklet pane of 4 55
**e.** Booklet pane of 4 (3 No. 353 + No. 357) ('63) 7.50 7.50
**f.** Tete beche pair *850.00*
**g.** Booklet pane of 4 (2 Nos. 353 + 2 No. 357) ('64) 2.25 2.25
*354* A126 1p ultra ('59) 10 5
**a.** Booklet pane of 6 ('59) 1.00
**b.** Booklet pane of 4 75
**e.** Imperf., pair
**f.** Booklet pane of 4 ('65) (2 No. 354 + 2 No. 258) 2.25 2.25
*355* A126 1½p green 8 5
**a.** Booklet pane of 6 1.00
**b.** Booklet pane of 4 75
*365* A126 2p red brn 10 5
**a.** Wmk. sideways 30 20
**b.** Booklet pane of 6 6.00
*357* A127 2½p scar, type II ('59) 10 5
**a.** Type I ('61) 75 45
**b.** Wmk. sideways, type I 28 25
**c.** Booklet pane of 6, Type II ('59) 1.00
**f.** Tete beche pair, type II
**g.** Booklet pane of 4, type II ('64) 2.50
**h.** Imperf., pair
*358* A127 3p dk pur 12 6
**a.** Booklet pane of 6 1.75
**b.** Booklet pane of 4 1.25
**e.** Imperf., pair 90.00
**g.** Wmk. sideways 14 10
*359* A128 4p ultra 16 6
**b.** Booklet pane of 6 ('65) 3.00
**c.** Booklet pane of 4 ('65) 1.50
**d.** Wmk. sideways 60 50
*360* A128 4½p henna brn 15 15
*361* A129 5p lt brn 40 18
*362* A129 6p lil rose ('59) 32 12
*363* A129 7p emerald 65 22
*364* A130 8p brt rose ('60) 55 18
*365* A130 9p dp ol grn ('59) 65 12
*366* A130 10p royal bl 55 22
*367* A131 1sh brown 40 12
*368* A132 1sh 3p dk grn ('59) 48 12
*369* A131 1sh 6p dark blue 4.00 22
*Nos. 353-369 (17)* 8.89 2.02

Nos. 356a and 357b were issued in coils. The 3p and 4p watermarked sideways may be from a coil or booklet pane of 4.

Booklet panes of this issue have watermarks normal, inverted or sideways.

Part perf. booklet panes exist of No. 353a and No. 354a.

Black Graphite Lines on Back

**1958-59 Wmk. 322**

*353c* A126 ½p red org ('59) 2.50 2.75
**d.** Booklet pane of 6 25.00
*354c* A126 1p ultra 1.25 1.25
**d.** Booklet pane of 6 12.50
*355c* A126 1½p grn ('59) 85.00 37.50
**d.** Booklet pane of 6 550.00
*356c* A126 2p red brn 7.75 4.00
**cp.** Phosphor. ('59) 6.50 5.00
*357d* A127 2½p scar (II) ('59) 17.50 11.50
**dp.** Phosphor. ('59) 21.50 20.00
**e.** Booklet pane of 6 165.00
*358c* A127 3p dk pur 1.00 75
**cp.** Phosphor. ('59) 17.50 10.00
**d.** Booklet pane of 6 7.00
*359a* A128 4p Ultra ('59) 8.50 6.75
**ap.** Phosphor. ('59) 10.00 7.00
*360a* A128 4½p hn brn ('59) 9.00 3.75
**ap.** Phosphor. ('59) 42.50 30.00
*Nos. 353c-360a (8)* 132.50 68.25

The vertical black graphite lines were applied to facilitate mail sorting by an electronic machine. The 2p has one line; the others two. Missing or misplaced lines occur on 1p, 3p and 4p.

Nos. 353c and 354c were issued only in booklets or coils; No. 355c only in booklets.

Phosphorescent Stamps of 1958-65

**1960-67 Wmk. 322**

*353p* A126 ½p red org 6 5
*354p* A126 1p ultra 6 5
*355p* A126 1½p green 6 5
*356p* A126 2p red brn 6 5
**ap.** Watermark sideways 15 9
*357p* A127 2½p scar (II) 12 18
**ap.** Type I ('61) 45.00 30.00
*358p* A127 3p dk pur 32 22
**gp.** Watermark sideways 1.25 50
*359p* A128 4p ultra 20 12
**dp.** Watermark sideways 18 10
*360p* A128 4½p hn brn ('61) 24 22
*361p* A129 5p lt brn ('67) 24 22
*362p* A129 6p lil rose 24 12
*363p* A129 7p emer ('67) 38 45
*364p* A130 8p brt rose ('67) 38 38
*365p* A130 9p dp ol grn ('67) 65 30
*366p* A130 10p ryl bl ('67) 75 45
*367p* A131 1sh brn ('67) 38 18
*368p* A132 1sh3p dk grn 3.00 45
*369p* A131 1sh6p dk bl ('66) 2.00 65
*Nos. 353p-369p (17)* 9.14 4.14

The 2p, 2½p (II) and 3p were issued with both one and two phosphorescent bands. The less expensive is valued here.

Watermarked sidewas, the 2p is from a coil; the 3p and 4p from booklet pane of coil; the ½p, 1p and 1½p from booklet panes (hence unlisted in this state).

Booklet panes of 4 with phosphorescent bands: ½p, 1p, 1½p, 3p (2 bands), 4p, and 1p se-tenant with 3p (1 or 2 bands). Booklet panes of 6 with phosphorescent bands: ½p, 1p, 1½p, 2½p (II) (1 or 2 bands), 3p (1 or 2 bands), 4p.

**1959 Engr. Wmk. 322** ***Perf. 11x12***

*371* A133 2sh6p dk brn 80 15
*372* A133 5sh crimson 2.00 50
*373* A133 10sh brt ultra 6.25 1.00
*374* A133 £1 int blk 8.00 3.25

Postboy on Horsebac
A147

Queen Elizabeth II, Oak Leaves and 1660 Post Horn — A148

***Perf. 14½x14, 14x14½***

**1960, July 7 Photo. Wmk. 322**

*375* A147 3p brt vio 75 8
*376* A148 1sh3p dk grn 5.50 1.75

Tercentenary of the act establishing the General Letter Office (General Post Office).

Symbolic Wheel
CD3

***Perf. 14½x14***

**1960, Sept. 19 Wmk. 322**

*377* CD3 6p red lil & grn 1.25 8
*378* CD3 1sh6p dk bl & red brn 5.75 2.00

1st anniv. of the establishment of CEPT.

Symbolic Thrift Plant — A150

Nut Tree, Nest, Squirrel, Owl
A151

Thrift Plant
A152

***Perf. 14x14½, 14½x14***

**1961, Aug. 28 Photo. Wmk. 322**

*379* A150 2½p scar & blk 18 9
**a.** Black omitted *10,000.*
*380* A151 3p pur & org 24 8
**a.** Orange omitted 150.00 75.00
*381* A152 1sh6p dk bl & ver 3.00 2.00

Centenary of Post Office Savings Bank.

CEPT Emblem
A153

Nineteen Doves Flying as One — CD4

Design: 10p, Queen at right.

**1961, Sept. 18** ***Perf. 14½x14***

*382* A153 2p red brn, yel & rose 8 5
*383* CD4 4p ultra, pink & buff 18 18
*384* CD4 10p dk bl, yel grn & Prus bl 60 55
**a.** Yel grn omitted *5,000.*
**b.** Dark blue omitted *5,000.*

Hammer Beam Roof of Westminster Hall — A155

Parliament — A156

***Perf. 14½x14, 14x14½***

**1961, Sept. 25 Wmk. 322**

*385* A155 6p red lil & gold 55 22
**a.** Gold omitted *850.00*
*386* A156 1sh3p grn & slate 3.25 1.75
**a.** sl (Queen's head) omitted *5,000.*

the 7th Commonwealth Parliamentary Conference.

National Productivity Symbol — A157

Designs: 3p, Two arrows and map of the British Isles. 1sh3p, Five arrows pointing up.

***Perf. 14½x14***

**1962, Nov. 14 Photo. Wmk. 322**

*387* A157 2½p car rose & dk grn 16 6
**p.** Phosphor 1.65 1.25
*388* A157 3p vio & bl 28 6
**a.** Queen's head omitted *1,000*
**p.** Phosphor 3.50 2.50
*389* A157 1sh3p dk grn, car rose & bl 2.75 1.90
**a.** Queen's head omitted *3,500.*
**p.** Phosphor 32.50 13.00

National Productivity Year. The watermark on Nos. 387-388 is inverted.

Phosphorescent Commemoratives
Commemorative stamps between Nos. 387-493 were issued both with and without phosphorescence on the front unless otherwise noted with the issue.
Starting with No. 514, commemorative stamps were issued only with phosphorescence on the front unless otherwise noted.
Phosphorescent Regulars Starting in 1967, all small stamps (lower values) of the regular series were issued only with phosphorescence.

Wheat Emblem and People
A158

Design: 1sh3p, Caucasian, Negro and Mongol boys.

**1963, Mar. 21 Wmk. 322**

*390* A158 2½p pink & dp car 24 10
**p.** Phosphor. 2.00 1.50
*391* A158 1sh3p yel & brn 3.00 2.00
**p.** Phosphor. 32.50 21.00

"Freedom from Hunger" campaign of the UNFAO.

Paris Postal Conference
A159

**1963, May 7 Wmk. 322**

*392* A159 6p pur & grn 80 65
**a.** grn omitted *2,500.*
**p.** Phosphor 9.00 3.00

Cent. of the 1st Intl. Postal Conf., Paris, 1863, and to publicize the Paris Postal Conf., May 7-9, 1963.

Buttercups, Daisies and Bee
A160

Design: 4½p, Badger, Fawn, woodpecker, lark, titmouse, butterfly, mouse and wild plants.

**1963, May 16** ***Perf. 14½x14***

*393* A160 3p buff, sep, yel & grn 15 7
**p.** Phosphor 1.10 90

*394* A160 4½p dk red, yel, blk, bl & rose 65 50
p. Phosphor 5.00 2.75

Publicizing National Nature Week, May 18-25, and the importance of wildlife conservation.

Helicopter Lifting Man from Lifeboat A161

Lifeboat Men A162

Design: 4p, 19th century lifeboat under sail.

**1963, May 31** **Photo.**
*395* A161 2½p red, bl & blk 28 10
p. Phosphor 80 40
*396* A161 4p bl, ocher, brn, blk & car 1.10 85
p. Phosphor 1.50 1.50
*397* A162 1sh6p dk bl, yel, brn & blk 4.50 3.25
p. Phosphor 40.00 27.50

Ninth Intl. Life-Boat Conf., Edinburgh, June 3-5.

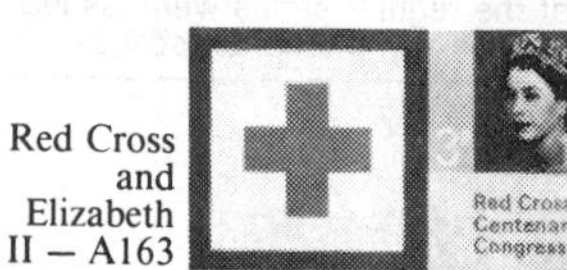

Red Cross and Elizabeth II — A163

Designs: 1sh3p, Cross at upper left. 1sh6p, Cross in center.

**1963, Aug. 15** **Wmk. 322**

**Cross in Red**

*398* A163 3p purple 15 8
a. Red cross omitted *3,500.*
p. Phosphor 2.00 1.50
*399* A163 1sh3p gray & bl 3.50 2.75
p. Phosphor 52.50 32.50
*400* A163 1sh6p dl bl & ol bis 4.00 3.25
p. Phosphor 45.00 30.00

Red Cross Cent. Cong., Geneva, Sept. 2.

Cable Around World and Under Sea — A164

**1963, Dec. 3** ***Perf. 14½x14***
*401* A164 1sh6p bl & blk 4.50 4.00
a. Blk. omitted *3,500.*
p. Phosphor 27.50 16.00

Opening of the Commonwealth Pacific (telephone) cable service, COMPAC.

Puck and Bottom from "A Midsummer Night's Dream," Shakespeare A165

Hamlet Holding Yorick's Skull A166

First Folio Portrait of Shakespeare and: 6p, Feste the Clown, from "Twelfth Night." 1sh3p, Romeo and Juliet. 1sh6p, Henry V praying at Agincourt.

***Perf. 14½x14***

**1964, Apr. 23** **Photo.** **Wmk. 322**
*402* A165 3p vio, blk & bis 15 8
p. Phosphor. 50 32
*403* A165 6p ol, blk, yel & org 38 38
p. Phosphor. 1.00 1.00
*404* A165 1sh3p brn, blk, car & brt grn 80 95
p. Phosphor. 8.25 6.50
*405* A165 1sh6p dk bl, blk, grnsh bl & vio 1.50 1.25
p. Phosphor. 13.00 10.00

***Perf. 11x12***

**Engr.**

*406* A166 2sh6p dark gray 2.25 1.90
*Nos. 402-406 (5)* 5.08 4.56

400th anniv. of the birth of William Shakespeare. No. 406 was not issued with phosphorescence.

Apartment Buildings, London — A170

Designs: 4p, Shipyards, Belfast. 8p, Beddgelert Forest Park, Snowdonia. 1sh6p, Dounreay nuclear reactor and sheaves of wheat.

**1964, July 1** **Photo.** ***Perf. 14½x14***
*410* A170 2½p gray, blk, bl grn & yel 15 10
p. Phosphor. 38 32
*411* A170 4p blk, vio, pink & ocher 50 40
a. Violet ("4d") omitted *175.00*
b. Ocher omitted *275.00*
c. Violet & ocher omitted *200.00*
p. Phosphor. 1.10 85
*412* A170 8p grn, blk, lt brn & emer 1.25 1.00
a. Green omitted *2,000.*
p. Phosphor. 9.25 5.75
*413* A170 1sh6p pale rose, blk, brn & ocher 3.50 2.00
p. Phosphor. 25.00 13.00

20th International Geographical Congress, London, July 20-28.

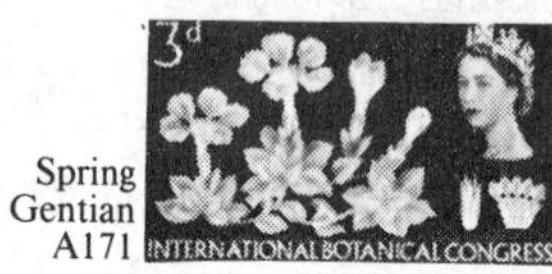

Spring Gentian A171

Designs: 6p, Dog rose. 9p, Honeysuckle. 1sh3p, Fringed water lily.

**1964, Aug. 5** **Wmk. 322**
*414* A171 3p dk pur, bl, yel & lt yel grn 15 8
a. Blue omitted *5,500.*
p. Phosphor. 40 28
*415* A171 6p dp grn, pink, yel & red 38 30
p. Phosphor. 2.00 1.65
*416* A171 9p red, yel, lt grn & crim 2.25 1.90
a. Light green omitted *5,500.*
p. Phosphor. 10.00 9.00
*417* A171 1sh3p sl grn, yel, yel grn & pink 3.00 1.10
p. Phosphor. 22.50 15.00

10th Intl. Botanical Congress, Edinburgh, Aug. 3-12.

Forth Road Bridge A172

Design: 6p, Bridge and railroad bridge.

**1964, Sept. 4** ***Perf. 14½x14***
*418* A172 3p blk, lil & bl 15 6
p. Phosphor. 1.00 1.00
*419* A172 6p vio blk, grnsh bl & car lake 65 45
a. Greenish blue omitted *2,750.* *1,500.*
p. Phosphor. 5.25 5.25

Opening of Forth Road Bridge, Scotland.

Winston Churchill A173

Design: 1sh3p, Large portrait.

**1965, July 8** **Photo.** **Wmk. 322**
*420* A173 4p dk brn & blk 15 6
p. Phosphor. 48 38
*421* A173 1sh3p gray & blk 65 50
p. Phosphor. 4.00 3.50

Sir Winston Spencer Churchill (1874-1965), statesman and WWII leader.

Seal of Simon de Montfort A174

St. Stephen's Hall, Westminster Hall and Abbey, Engraving by Wenceslaus Hollar, 1647 — A175

**1965, July 19** ***Perf. 14½x14***
*422* A174 6p dk ol 14 10
p. Phosphor. 1.40 1.25
*423* A175 2sh6p brn blk 1.25 1.25

700th anniv. of Parliament. No. 423 was not issued with phosphorescence; size: 58x21mm.

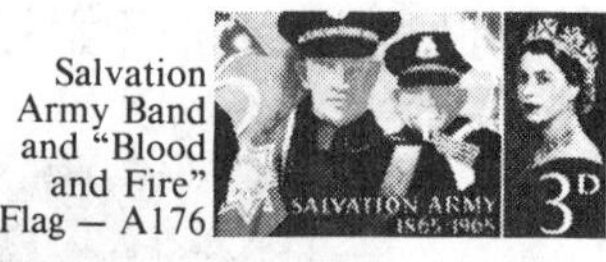

Salvation Army Band and "Blood and Fire" Flag — A176

Design: 1sh6p, Salvation Army officers and flag.

**1965, Aug. 9**
*424* A176 3p dk bl, yel & brt car 15 6
p. Phosphor. 45 38
*425* A176 1sh6p red, yel & brt bl 1.40 1.10
p. Phosphor. 4.50 4.25

Centenary of the Salvation Army.

Lister's Carbolic Spray A177

Design: 1sh, Joseph Lister and carbolic acid formula.

**1965, Sept. 1**
*426* A177 4p gray, bluish blk & red brn 15 6
a. Red brown (tubing) omitted *300.00*
b. Bluish black omitted *1,750.*
p. Phosphor. 16 10
*427* A177 1sh blk, bl & pur 1.10 95
p. Phosphor. 1.50 1.40

Introduction of antiseptic surgery by Joseph Lister, cent.

Common Design Types are pictured in section before Great Britain.

Trinidad Folk Dancers, Shrove Monday Carnival A178

Design: 1sh6p, French Canadian folk dancers, Les Feux Follets.

***Perf. 14½x14***

**1965, Sept. 1** **Photo.** **Wmk. 322**
*428* A178 6p org & blk 32 25
p. Phosphor. 40 30
*429* A178 1sh6p brt vio & blk 1.50 1.25
p. Phosphor. 2.50 2.25

First Commonwealth Arts Festival, Sept. 16-Oct. 2.

Supermarine Spitfire Fighters — A179

Anti-Aircraft Gun Battery in Action — A180

Designs: No. 431, Pilot in cockpit of Hawker Hurricane fighter. No. 432, Wing tips of Messerschmitt ME-109 and Spitfire. No. 433, Two Spitfires attacking Heinkel HE-111 bomber. No. 434, Hurricane attacking Junkers JU-187B Stuka dive bomber. No. 435, Hurricanes returning over wreckage of Dornier DO-17 Z bomber. 1sh3p, Vapor trails over St. Paul's Cathedral, London.

***Perf. 14½x14***

**1965, Sept. 13** **Photo.** **Wmk. 322**
*430* A179 4p sl & dk ol 40 22
*431* A179 4p sl & dk ol 40 22
*432* A179 4p sl, dk ol, brt bl & red 40 22
*433* A179 4p sl & dk ol 40 22
*434* A179 4p sl & dk ol 40 22
*435* A179 4p sl, dk ol & brt bl 48 25
a. Bright blue omitted
*436* A180 9p vio bl, org & vio blk 2.75 1.75
*437* A180 1sh3p brt bl, sl & grnsh gray 2.75 2.50
*Nos. 430-437 (8)* 7.98 5.60

**Phosphorescent**

*430p* A179 4p sl & dk ol 50 35
*431p* A179 4p sl & dk ol 50 35
*432p* A179 4p sl, dk ol, brt bl & red 50 35
*433p* A179 4p sl & dk ol 50 35
*434p* A179 4p sl & dk ol 50 35
*435p* A179 4p sl, dk ol & brt bl 50 35
*436p* A180 9p vio bl, org & vio blk 4.50 3.25
*437p* A180 1sh3p brt bl, sl & grnsh gray 4.00 3.25
*Nos. 430p-437p (8)* 11.50 8.60

25th anniv. of the Battle of Britain. Nos. 430-435 printed in blocks of 6 (3x2) in sheets of 120.

Post Office Tower and Georgian Buildings — A181

Design: 1sh3p, Post Office Tower and Nash Terrace, Regents Park (horiz.).

**1965, Oct. 8** ***Perf. 14x14½, 14½x14***

*438* A181 3p brt bl, lem & ol grn — 6 5
*a.* Lemon (tower) omitted — 950.
*p.* Phosphor. — 6 5
*439* A181 1sh3p grn, ol grn & bl — 65 60
*p.* Phosphor. — 75 75

Opening of the Post Office Tower, London.

UN Emblem A182

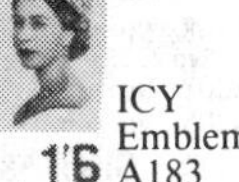

ICY Emblem A183

**1965, Oct. 25** ***Perf. 14½x14***

*440* A182 3p multi — 10 5
*p.* Phosphor. — 10 8
*441* A183 1sh6p multi — 1.00 1.00
*p.* Phosphor. — 1.10 1.10

20th anniv. of the UN and Intl. Cooperation Year, 1965.

"World Telecommunication Stations" — A184

Design: 1sh6p, "Radio waves and switchboard."

**1965, Nov. 15** **Photo.** **Wmk. 322**

*442* A184 9p multi — 38 32
*p.* Phosphor. — 1.65 1.65
*443* A184 1sh6p bl, red, blk, ind & pink — 1.00 90
*a.* Pink omitted — 500.00
*p.* Phosphor. — 6.50 5.25

ITU, cent.

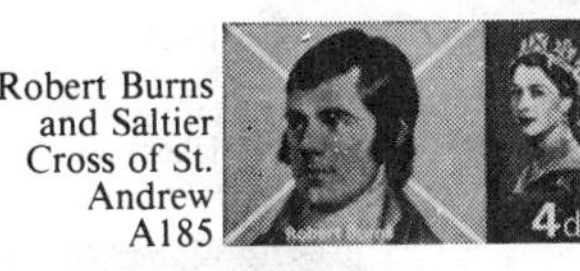

Robert Burns and Saltier Cross of St. Andrew A185

Design: 1sh3p, Alexander Nasmyth portrait of Burns, his signature and symbols of his life. Portrait of Burns on 4p stamp is adaptation of Archibald Skirvings', chalk drawing, 1798.

**1966, Jan. 25** ***Perf. 14½x14***

*444* A185 4p bl, blk & dk sl — 8 6
*p.* Phosphor. — 14 10
*445* A185 1sh3p org, blk & Prus bl — 55 50
*p.* Phosphor. — 1.00 1.00

Robert Burns (1759-1796), Scottish national poet.

Westminster Abbey — A186

Fan Vaulting, Chapel of Henry VII A187

**1966, Feb. 28** **Photo.** ***Perf. 14½x14***

*452* A186 3p bl, blk, & red brn — 8 8
*p.* Phosphor. — 25 25

***Perf. 11x12***

**Engr.**

*453* A187 2sh6p black — 1.10 1.00

900th anniv. of Westminster Abbey. No. 453 was issued only without phosphorescence.

Landscape near Hassock, Sussex A188

Views: 6p, Antrim, Northern Ireland. 1sh3p, Harlech Castle, Wales. 1sh6p, The Cairngorms (mountains), Scotland.

***Perf. 14½x14***

**1966, May 2** **Photo.** **Wmk. 322**

*454* A188 4p multi — 6 5
*p.* Phosphor. — 10 8
*455* A188 6p multi — 14 12
*p.* Phosphor. — 22 20
*456* A188 1sh3p multi — 30 30
*p.* Phosphor. — 45 45
*457* A188 1sh6p multi — 40 35
*p.* Phosphor. — 55 55

Soccer Players — A189

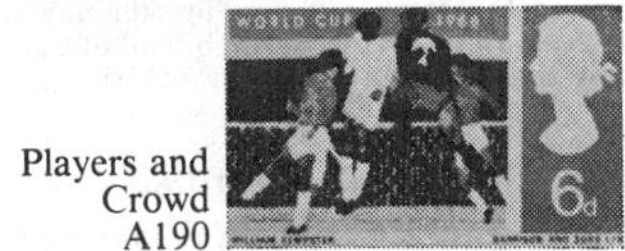

Players and Crowd A190

Design: 1sh3p, Goalkeeper and two players.

***Perf. 14x14½, 14½x14***

**1966, June 1** **Photo.** **Wmk. 322**

*458* A189 4p multi — 5 5
*p.* Phosphor. — 8 8
*459* A190 6p bl, sep, red, yel grn & blk — 12 10
*a.* Black omitted — 65.00
*b.* Yellow green omitted — 1,000.
*c.* Red omitted — 1,000.
*p.* Phosphor. — 22 22
*460* A190 1sh3p blk, red, yel, bl & cit — 30 30
*a.* Blue omitted — 200.00
*p.* Phosphor. — 50 50

Final games of the 1965-66 World Soccer Championship for the Jules Rimet Cup, Wembley, July 11-30.

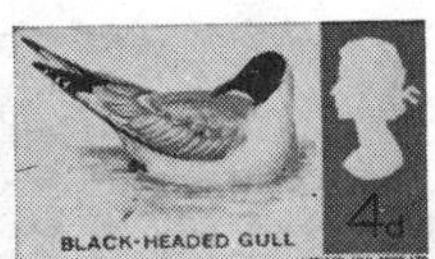

Blackheaded Gull — A191

Birds: No. 462, Blue tit. No. 463, European robin. No. 464, European blackbird.

***Perf. 14½x14***

**1966, Aug. 8** **Photo.** **Wmk. 322**

**Birds in Natural Colors**

*461* A191 4p gray & blk — 22 10
*p.* Phosphor. — 22 18
*462* A191 4p gray & blk — 22 10
*p.* Phosphor. — 22 18
*463* A191 4p gray & blk — 22 10
*p.* Phosphor. — 22 18
*464* A191 4p gray & blk — 22 10
*p.* Phosphor. — 22 18

Nos. 461-464 were printed in blocks of 4 in sheets of 120 (6x20).

Seven colors have been found omitted (singly or in combinations) on Nos. 461-464; green, red, ultramarine, brown, red brown, yellow and black.

No. 458 Inscribed: "ENGLAND WINNERS"

**1966, Aug. 18** ***Perf. 14x14½***

*465* A189 4p multi — 10 20

England's victory in the World Soccer Cup Championship.

Jodrell Bank Radio Telescope A192

Designs: 6p, Automobiles (Jaguar and 3 Mini-Minors). 1sh3p, SR N6 Hovercraft. 1sh6p, Windscale atomic reactor.

**1966, Sept. 19** ***Perf. 14½x14***

*466* A192 4p yel & blk — 5 5
*p.* Phosphor. — 8 8
*467* A192 6p org, red & dk bl — 10 9
*a.* Red (Mini-Minors) omitted — 3,000.
*b.* Dark blue (Jaguar & imprint) omitted — 3,500.
*p.* Phosphor. — 12 10
*468* A192 1sh3p sl, blk, org & bl — 28 28
*p.* Phosphor. — 35 35
*469* A192 1sh6p multi — 35 35
*p.* Phosphor. — 45 45

British technology.

Battle of Hastings A193

Battle of Hastings from Bayeux Tapestry: No. 471, Two knights on horseback, one killed, one attacking. No. 472, Slain Harold on horseback and knight with shield. No. 473, Knight with shield and axe fighting horseman. No. 474, Knight on foot killing man, and horseman attacking with lance. No. 475, Four knights and two horses in battle scene. 6p, Norman ship. 1sh3p, King Harold's housecarls (body guard) battling Normans.

**Photo.; Gold Impressed on 6p, 1sh3p**

***Perf. 14½x14***

**1966, Oct. 14** **Wmk. 322**

**Size: 38½x22mm.**

*470* A193 4p multi — 12 7
*471* A193 4p multi — 12 7
*472* A193 4p multi — 12 7
*473* A193 4p multi — 12 7
*474* A193 4p multi — 12 7
*475* A193 4p multi — 12 7
*476* A193 6p multi & gold — 32 28

**Size: 58x22mm.**

*477* A193 1sh3p multi & gold — 75 65
*Nos. 470-477 (8)* — 1.79 1.35

**Phosphorescent**

*470p* A193 4p multi — 12 15
*471p* A193 4p multi — 12 15
*472p* A193 4p multi — 12 15
*473p* A193 4p multi — 12 15
*474p* A193 4p multi — 12 15
*475p* A193 4p multi — 12 15
*476p* A193 6p multi & gold — 30 30
*477p* A193 1sh3p multi & gold — 85 85
*Nos. 470p-477p (8)* — 1.87 2.05

900th anniv. of the Battle of Hastings. Nos. 470-475 printed se-tenant in strips of six in sheets of 60 (6x10).

Eight colors have been found omitted (singly or in pair) on Nos. 470-475 and 470p-477p: gray, orange, blue, dark blue, bright green, olive green, brown and magenta. Also violet on 1sh3p.

**Gold Omitted**

The variety "Gold (Queen's head) omitted" can be counterfeited by chemically removing the gold.

King — A194

Design: 1sh6p, Snowman.

**Photo.; Gold Impressed**

**1966, Dec. 1** ***Perf. 14x14½***

*478* A194 3p multi & gold — 10 6
*b.* Green omitted — 250.00
*p.* Phosphor. — 10 6
*479* A194 1sh6p multi & gold — 50 50
*b.* Pink omitted — 1,000.
*p.* Phosphor. — 55 55

Christmas.

Loading Ship at Dock and Train A195

Design: 1sh6p, Loading plane from trucks and flags of EFTA members.

***Perf. 14½x14***

**1967, Feb. 20** **Photo.** **Wmk. 322**

*480* A195 9p bl & multi — 15 10
*p.* Phosphor. — 12 12
*481* A195 1sh6p vio & multi — 20 20
*p.* Phosphor. — 18 18

European Free Trade Assoc. Tariffs were abolished Dec. 31, 1966, among EFTA members (Austria, Denmark, Finland, Great Britain, Norway, Portugal, Sweden, Switzerland).

Colors omitted include: 9p—yellow, brown, light blue, light violet and green singly; black, brown, light blue and yellow simultaneously. 1sh6p—dark blue, bister, yellow, red, ultramarine and gray. Value range for one-color omissions, $17.50 to $35.

Hawthorn and Wild Blackberry A196

Flowers: No. 489, Morning-glory and viper's bugloss. No. 490, Ox-eye daisy, coltsfoot and buttercup. No. 491, Bluebell, red campion and wood anemone. 9p, Dog violet. 1sh9p, Primrose.

***Perf. 14½x14***

**1967, Apr. 24** **Photo.** **Wmk. 322**

*488* A196 4p multi — 10 7
*489* A196 4p multi — 10 7
*490* A196 4p multi — 10 7
*491* A196 4p multi — 10 7
*492* A196 9p multi — 30 25
*493* A196 1sh9p multi — 38 35
*Nos. 488-493 (6)* — 1.08 88

**Phosphorescent**

*488p* A196 4p multi — 10 8
*489p* A196 4p multi — 10 8
*490p* A196 4p multi — 10 8
*491p* A196 4p multi — 10 8
*492p* A196 9p multi — 25 25
*493p* A196 1sh9p multi — 35 35
*Nos. 488p-493p (6)* — 1.00 92

Nos. 488-491 were printed in blocks of 4 in sheets of 120 (6x20).

Four colors have been found omitted on Nos. 488-491 and three on 488p-491p: dark brown, red, violet and dull purple.

A197

Type I

Type II

Two types of 2p:
Type I - Head off-center to right. Foot of "2" 1mm. from left margin.
Type II - Head centered. Foot of "2" ½mm. from margin.

**1967-69 Unwmk. *Perf. 15x14***
**Size: 17½x21½mm**

*494* A197 ½p brn org ('68) 10 5
*495* A197 1p ol ('68) 10 5
*a.* Booklet pane of 6 ('68) 1.00
*b.* Bklt. pane of 4 (2 No. 495, 2 No. 497) ('68) 2.00
*c.* Bklt. pane of 6 (4 No. 495, 2 No. 498) ('68) 4.00
*d.* Coil strip of 5 (1 each Nos. 495, 497, 499; 2 No. 496a) ('69) 3.00 1.25
*e.* Bklt. pane of 6 (4 No. 495, 2 No. 499) ('69) 3.75
*f.* Bklt. pane of 15 (6 No. 495, 6 No. 499, 3 No. 500 + recipe) ('69) 14.00
*496* A197 2p mar (I) ('68) 15 5
*a.* Type II ('69) 20 5
*497* A197 3p dk vio 10 5
*a.* Booklet pane of 6 ('68) 12.00
*b.* Imperf., pair 700.00
*498* A197 4p brn blk 12 5
*a.* Booklet pane of 4 ('68) 1.00
*b.* Booklet pane of 6 ('68) 1.50
*c.* Bklt. pane of 2 + 2 labels ('68) 1.00
*d.* Imperf., pair
*499* A197 4p brt red ('69) 12 5
*a.* Booklet pane of 4 ('69) 1.00
*b.* Booklet pane of 6 ('69) 1.00
*c.* Bklt. pane of 2 + 2 labels ('69) 1.00
*d.* Bklt. pane of 15 + recipe ('69) 5.00
*500* A197 5p dk bl ('68) 12 5
*a.* Booklet pane of 6 ('68) 1.50
*b.* Bklt. pane of 15 + recipe ('69) 5.00
*501* A197 6p magenta ('68) 25 10
*502* A197 7p brt grn ('68) 50 8
*503* A197 8p scarlet ('68) 15 5
*504* A197 8p lt grnsh bl ('69) 55 20
*505* A197 9p dp grn 50 5
*506* A197 10p gray ('68) 60 20
*507* A197 1sh lt vio 55 5
*508* A197 1sh6p ind & grnsh bl 70 8
*a.* Grnsh bl omitted 110.00
*509* A197 1sh9p blk & org 55 10

***Perf. 12***
**Engr.**
**Size: 27x31mm**

*510* A197 2sh6p brown ('69) 1.10 14
*511* A197 5sh dk car (& '69) 3.25 50
*512* A197 10sh ultramarine ('69) 10.00 2.75
*513* A197 £1 bluish blk ('69) 4.00 85
*Nos. 494-513 (20)* 23.51 5.50

No. 513 resembles No. 638 on which "£1" is redrawn. On No. 513, "£" has loop at bottom and numeral is a figure "1". On No. 638, "£" lacks loop and numeral is roman like a capital "I".
Most of Nos. 494-509 exist with phosphor bands omitted in error.
See Nos. 622-638, 762-775, 887A-900, 969-982, 1071-1087B.

Master Lambton, by Thomas Lawrence — A198

Mares and Foals, by George Stubbs A199

Design: 1sh6p, Children Coming out of School, by Laurence Stephen Lowry.

**Photo.; Gold Impressed on 4p, 1sh6p**
***Perf. 14x14½, 14½x14***

**1967, July 10 Unwmk.**
*514* A198 4p multi 10 5
*a.* Gold (Queen's head & value) omitted 125.00
*515* A199 9p multi 12 12
*a.* Black (Queen's head & value) omitted 750.00
*b.* yel omitted 1,000.
*516* A199 1sh6p multi 22 22
*a.* Blue omitted 150.00
*b.* Gray omitted 50.00
*c.* Gold (Queen's head) omitted 1,250.

See Nos. 568-571.

Gipsy Moth IV — A200

**1967, July 24 Photo. *Perf. 14½x14***
*517* A200 1sh9p multi 18 14

Sir Francis Chichester's one-man voyage around the world, Aug. 27, 1966-May 28, 1967.

Radar Screen A201

Designs: 1sh, Penicillin mold. 1sh6p, Vickers 10 twin jet engines. 1sh9p, Television camera (vert.).

***Perf. 14½x14, 14x14½***
**1967, Sept. 19 Photo. Wmk. 322**
*518* A201 4p red, yel & blk 6 5
*519* A201 1sh vio bl, gray & grnsh bl 10 10
*520* A201 1sh6p multi 18 18
*521* A201 1sh9p multi 22 22
*a.* Gray omitted 250.00

British discoveries.

Madonna and Child, by Murillo — A202

Adoration of the Shepherds, by Le Nain A203

Christmas 1967: 3p, Adoration of the Shepherds, ascribed to School of Seville.

***Perf. 14x14½, 14½x14***
**Photo.; Gold Impressed**
**1967 Unwmk.**
*522* A202 3p multi 8 5
*a.* Gold (Queen's head & value) omitted 55.00
*b.* Pink omitted 675.00
*523* A202 4p multi 10 5
*a.* Gold (Queen's head & value) omitted 60.00
*524* A203 1sh6p multi 20 20
*a.* Gold (Queen's head & value) omitted
*b.* Blue omitted 500.00

Issue dates: 4p, Oct. 18; 3p, 1sh6p, Nov. 27.

Castle Type of 1955

**1967-68 Engr. Unwmk. *Perf. 11x12***
*525* A133 2sh6p dk brn ('68) 38 18
*526* A133 5sh crimson ('68) 85 30
*527* A133 10sh brt ultra ('68) 7.00 85
*528* A133 £1 int blk 3.75 1.25

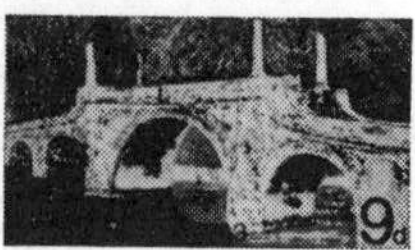
Aberfeldy Bridge, Perthshire A204

Designs: 4p, Prehistoric Tarr Steps, Exmoor. 1sh6p, Menai Bridge, North Wales, 1826. 1sh9p, Viaduct, Highway M4.

***Perf. 14½x14***
**1968, Apr. 29 Photo. Unwmk.**
*560* A204 4p gold & multi 6 6
*561* A204 9p gold & multi 10 10
*a.* Blue omitted
*b.* Gold (Queen's head) omitted 125.00
*562* A204 1sh6p gold & multi 15 15
*a.* Gold (Queen's head) omitted 125.00
*b.* Red omitted
*563* A204 1sh9p gold & multi 25 25
*a.* Gold (Queen's head) omitted 150.00

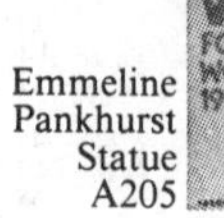

Emmeline Pankhurst Statue A205

Designs: 4p, Letters "TUC" and faces. 1sh, Sopwith Camel 1914-1918 fighter plane and formation of Lightning jets. 1sh9p, Capt. Cook's "Endeavour" and signature.

**1968, May 29**
*564* A205 4p brt grn, blk, ol & bl 8 5
*565* A205 9p gray, vio & blk 10 10
*566* A205 1sh gray, ol, red, bl & blk 15 15
*567* A205 1sh9p blk & bis 25 25

Cent. of Trades Union Congress (4p); 50th anniv. of women's suffrage (9p); 50th anniv. of the Royal Air Force (1sh); bicent. of Captain Cook's first discovery voyage (1sh9p).

Paintings Types of 1967

Paintings: 4p, Elizabeth I, c. 1575, artist unknown. 1sh, Pinkie (Miss Sarah Moulton-Barrett) by Sir Thomas Lawrence. 1sh6p, St. Mary le Port, by John Piper. 1sh9p, The Hay Wain (landscape), by John Constable.

***Perf. 14x14½, 14½x14***
**Photo.; Gold Impressed**
**1968, Aug. 12**
*568* A198 4p multi 8 5
*a.* Gold (Queen's head & value) omitted 100.00
*569* A198 1sh multi 10 9
*a.* Gold (Queen's head & value) omitted 100.00
*570* A198 1sh6p multi 18 16
*a.* Gold (Queen's head & value) omitted 125.00
*571* A199 1sh9p multi 22 20
*a.* Gold (Queen's head & value) omitted 250.00

Sizes: 4p, 27x37½mm; 1sh, 25½x37½mm; 1sh6p, 31x37½mm; 1sh9p, 38x28mm.

Boy and Girl with Rocking Horse A206

Girl Playing with Dolls and Dollhouse A207

Design: 1sh6p, Boy with toy train and building blocks.

***Perf. 14½x14, 14x14½***
**1968, Nov. 25 Photo.**
*572* A206 4p gold & multi 8 5
*a.* Gold omitted 2,500.
*573* A207 9p gold & multi 10 8
*a.* Yellow omitted 60.00
*574* A207 1sh6p gold & multi 15 15

Christmas.

Elizabethan Galleon A208

British Ships: 5p, R.M.S. Queen Elizabeth 2. No. 577, East Indiaman. No. 578, Cutty Sark. No. 579, S.S. Great Britain. No. 580, R.M.S. Mauretania.

**1969, Jan. 15 *Perf. 14½x14***
**Size: 58x22mm**
*575* A208 5p multi 8 5
*a.* Black omitted 1,350.
*b.* Gray omitted 100.00
*c.* Red omitted 37.50

**Size: 38½x22mm**
*576* A208 9p multi 20 20
*a.* Red & blue omitted 2,000.
*577* A208 9p multi 20 20
*578* A208 9p multi 20 20

**Size: 58x22mm**
*579* A208 1sh multi 32 32
*580* A208 1sh multi 32 32
*Nos. 575-580 (6)* 1.32 1.29

British seamen and shipbuilders.
Nos. 576-578 are printed se-tenant, as are Nos. 579-580.

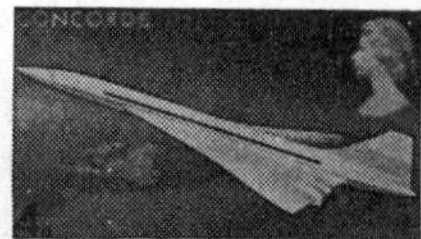
Concorde over Great Britain and France A209

Designs: 9p, Concorde seen from above and from side, flags of France and Great Britain. 1sh6p, Outlines of plane's nose and tail superimposed.

**1969, Mar. 3 Photo. *Perf. 14½x14***
*581* A209 4p multi 10 5
*a.* Violet omitted 500.00
*b.* Orange omitted 125.00
*582* A209 9p red, ultra, emer & ind 14 10
*583* A209 1sh6p dk bl, bl & sil 30 25
*a.* Silver omitted 225.00

First flight of the prototype Concorde plane at Toulouse, France, March 1, 1969.

Alcock, Brown, Daily Mail and Vickers Vimy Plane — A210

"EUROPA" and "CEPT" CD11

Hand Holding Wrench A212

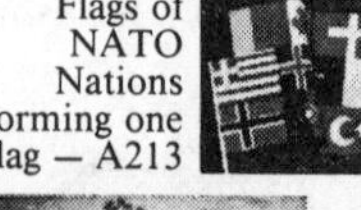
Flags of NATO Nations Forming one Flag — A213

Vickers-Vimy Plane and Globe — A214

**1969, Apr. 2**
*584* A210 5p multi 8 8
*585* CD11 9p multi 14 14
*586* A212 1sh multi 18 18
*587* A213 1sh6p multi 22 22
*a.* Black omitted 50.00
*b.* Green omitted 50.00
*588* A214 1sh9p multi 28 28
*Nos. 584-588 (5)* 90 90

50th anniv. of the 1st non-stop Atlantic flight from Newfoundland to Ireland of Capt. John Alcock and Lt. Arthur Whitten Brown; 10th anniv. of the Conference of European

Postal and Telecommunications Administrations: 50th anniv. of the ILO (1sh); 20th anniv. of NATO; 50th anniv. of the first England to Australia flight (1sh9p).

Durham Cathedral A215

British Cathedrals: No. 590, York Minster. No. 591, St. Giles', Edinburgh. No. 592, Canterbury. 9p, St. Paul's. 1sh6p, Liverpool Metropolitan.

***Perf. 14½x14***

**1969, May 28 Photo. Unwmk.**

*589* A215 5p multi 8 6
*590* A215 5p multi 8 6
*591* A215 5p multi 8 6
*592* A215 5p multi 8 6
*593* A215 9p multi 32 28
**a.** Black (9d) omitted 80.00
*594* A215 1sh6p multi 50 40
*Nos. 589-594 (6)* 1.14 92

Nos. 589-592 were printed in blocks of 4 in sheets of 72.

King's Gate, Caernarvon Castle, Wales A216

Celtic Cross, Margam Abbey, Glamorgan A217

Prince of Wales — A218

Designs: No. 596, Eagle Tower, Caernarvon Castle (2 flags). No. 597, Queen Eleanor's Gate, Caernarvon Castle.

***Perf. 14x14½***

**1969, July 1 Photo. Unwmk.**

*595* A216 5p sil & multi 7 5
*596* A216 5p sil & multi 7 5
*597* A216 5p sil & multi 7 5
*598* A217 9p gold, gray & blk 14 14
*599* A218 1sh blk & gold 16 16
*Nos. 595-599 (5)* 51 45

Investiture of Prince Charles as Prince of Wales, July 1. Nos. 595-597 are printed se-tenant in sheets of 72.

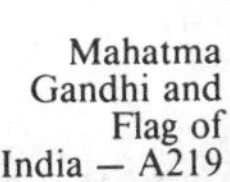

Mahatma Gandhi and Flag of India — A219

**1969, Aug. 13 *Perf. 14½x14***

*600* A219 1sh6p org, blk & grn 24 24

Mohandas K. Gandhi (1869-1948), leader in India's fight for independence, birth centenary.

Emblem of Post Office Bank — A220

International Subscriber Dialing A221

Automatic Letter Sorting A222

Design: 1sh, Telecommunications (pulse code modulation graph).

***Perf. 13½x14***

**1969, Oct. 1 Litho. Unwmk.**

*601* A220 5p bl & multi 6 6
*602* A221 9p ultra & multi 10 10
*603* A221 1sh grn & multi 14 14
*604* A222 1sh6p multi 22 22

Technological advancements of the British Post Office, transfer of responsibility from the government to the Post Office Corporation.

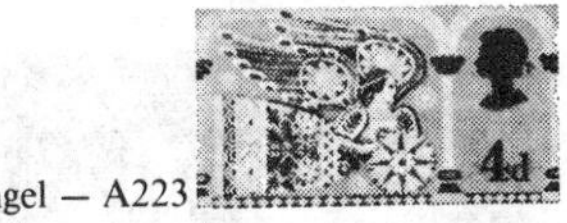

Angel — A223

Designs: 5p, Three shepherds. 1sh6p, The Three Kings.

**Photo.; Gold Embossed**

**1969, Nov. 26 *Perf. 14x15***

*605* A223 4p multi 5 5
*606* A223 5p multi 6 5
*607* A223 1sh6p multi 20 18

Christmas.

Fife Harling House, Scotland A224

British Rural Architecture: 9p, Cotswold limestone house, Gloucestershire, England. 1sh, Aberaeron town house, Wales. 1sh6p, Irish cottage with Ulster thatching.

***Perf. 14x15***

**1970, Feb. 11 Photo. Unwmk.**

**Size: 38½x22mm.**

*608* A224 5p multi 6 6
*609* A224 9p multi 14 14

**Size: 38½x27mm.**

*610* A224 1sh multi 18 18
*611* A224 1sh6p multi 32 32

Mayflower Leaving Plymouth, England A225

Designs: 5p, Signing of the Declaration of Arbroath. 9p, Florence Nightingale and soldiers in Scutari Hospital. 1sh, Earl Grey, Great Britain; Charles Robert, France; Victor Bohmert, Germany; De Keussler, Russia, and document in 4 languages. 1sh9p, Sir William Herschel, Francis Bailey, Sir John Herschel and telescope.

**Photo.; Gold Embossed**

**1970, Apr. 1 *Perf. 14x15***

*612* A225 5p red & multi 6 6
*613* A225 9p bl & multi 16 10
*614* A225 1sh lt bl & multi 20 14
*615* A225 1sh6p ol & multi 35 20
*616* A225 1sh9p brt pink & multi 40 25
*Nos. 612-616 (5)* 1.17 75

650th anniv. of the Declaration of Arbroath (5p); sesquicentennial of the birth of Florence Nightingale (1820-1910), nurse and hospital reformer (9p); 75th anniv. of the International Cooperative Alliance (1st); 350th anniv. of Mayflower sailing (1sh6p); sesquicentennial of the Royal Astronomical Soc. (1sh9p).

Missing colors or embossing occur on each denomination.

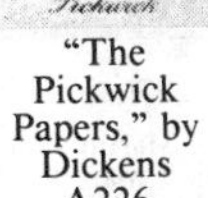

"The Pickwick Papers," by Dickens A226

Wordsworth's Grasmere, Lake District A227

Designs: No. 618, Mr. and Mrs. Micawber ("David Copperfield"). No. 619, David Copperfield and Betsy Trotwood ("David Copperfield"). No. 620, "Oliver Twist."

***Perf. 14x14½***

**1970, June 3 Photo. Unwmk.**

*617* A226 5p org & multi 10 7
*618* A226 5p lil rose & multi 10 7
*619* A226 5p grnsh bl & multi 10 7
*620* A226 5p lem & multi 10 7
*621* A227 1sh6p cit & multi 50 50
*Nos. 617-621 (5)* 90 78

Death cent. of Charles Dickens (1812-1870),novelist, Nos. 617-620; printed se-tenant in blocks of 4 within sheet. Birth bicent.of William Wordsworth (1770-1850), poet, No. 621.

**Decimal Currency Issue**

Queen Elizabeth Type of 1967-69

"P" instead of "D"

TYPE II- Numerals are narrower than originally. Look more upright. "1" and "2" of ½ are aligned vertically.

***Perf. 15x14***

**1970-88 Photo. Unwmk.**

**Size: 17½x21½mm**

*622* A197 ½p grnsh bl ('71) 5 5
**c.** Coil strip of 5 (2 each #622-623,1 #625) 60
**f.** Coil strip of 5 (2 #622, 1 each #623, 625, 631) ('75) 60
**j.** Coil strip of 5 (2 #622, 2 #623, 1 #631B) ('78) 60
*623* A197 1p mag ('71) 5 5
**c.** Strip of 3 + 2 labels (2 #623, 632A) 60
**e.** Type II ('84) 5 5
*624* A197 1½p blk ('71) 8 5
*625* A197 2p grn ('71) 8 5
**f.** Type II ('88) 8 5
*626* A197 2½p brt pink ('71) 15 5
*627* A197 3p ultra ('71) 15 5
*628* A197 3½p gray grn ('71) 25 5
*629* A197 4p ol bis ('71) 20 5
**c.** Imperf., pair
*629A* A197 4½p grysh bl ('73) 25 5
*630* A197 5p bluish lil ('71) 20 5
*630A* A197 5½p dk vio ('73) 35 5
*631* A197 6p lt emer ('71) 25 5
*631A* A197 6½p Prus bl ('74) 30 5
*631B* A197 7p red brn ('75) 30 5
*632* A197 7½p lt red brn ('71) 35 5
*632A* A197 8p red ('73) 30 5
*632B* A197 8½p yel grn ('75) 30 5
*633* A197 9p blk & ocher ('71) 60 5
*634* A197 10p org brn & lt org brn ('71) 35 10

**Engr.**

***Perf. 12***

**Size: 27x31mm**

*635* A197 10p car rose 3.50 10
*636* A197 20p olive 1.25 10
*637* A197 50p ultra 1.75 60
**p.** Phosphor ('73) 5.25 60
*638* A197 £1 bluish blk ('72) 3.25 1.25
*Nos. 622-638 (23)* 14.31 3.05

On No. 638, "£1" is redrawn. The "£" has no loop at bottom and the numeral "I" is roman. On No. 513, "£" has a loop and the numeral is a "1".

Booklet Panes

**1970-80**

*622a* Pane of 4 (2 #622, 2 #625) 4.00
*622b* Pane of 5 + label 4.50
*622d* Pane of 6 (4 #622, 2 #626) ('72) 70.00
*622e* Pane of 12 (3 #622, 9 #626) ('72) 25.00
*622g* Pane of 6 (2 #622, 3 #623, 1 #631) ('76) 1.00
*622h* Pane of 10 (2 #622, 2 #623, 2 #631A, 4 #632B) ('76) 5.25
*622i* Pane of 5 + label (2 #622, 2 #623, 1 #631B) ('78) 75
*623a* Pane of 4 (2 #623, 2 #624) 2.00
*623b* Pane of 8 (2 #623, 3 #631B, 3 #762) ('77) 2.50
*623d* Pane of 3 + label (2 #623, 632A) 50
*625a* Pane of 7 + label (3 #625, 2 #764, 2 #893) ('80) 2.00
*625b* Pane of 7 + label (2 #625, 2 #632A, 3 #764 2.00
*625c* Pane of 6 + printed margin 1.00
*626a* Pane of 4 + 2 labels 5.50
*626b* Pane of 5 + label 5.50
*626c* Pane of 6 (2 #626, 4 #627) 8.00
*626d* Pane of 12 (6 #626, 6 #627) ('72) 18.00
*627a* Pane of 5 + label 5.00
*627b* Pane of 6 5.00
*627c* Pane of 12 ('72) 10.00
*628a* Pane of 5 + label ('73) 6.00
*629Ab* Pane of 5 + label ('74) 6.00
*631Be* Pane of 20 (10 #631B, 10 #762) ('78) 4.00
*632Ad* Pane of 20 (10 #632A, 10 #764) 5.00

Nos. 622h and 623b issued with stamps in two arrangements.

Nos. 622d, 622e, 626d and 627c have a large side margin with inscription about Wedgwood or postal rates.

Athletics A228

**1970, July 15 Litho. *Perf. 14x14½***

*639* A228 5p shown 10 5
*640* A228 1sh6p Swimming 40 40
*641* A228 1sh9p Bicycling 40 40

9th British Commonwealth Games, Edinburgh, July 16-25.

Penny Black — A229

Designs: 9p, One-shilling stamp of 1847, No. 5. 1sh6p, Four-pence stamp of 1855, No. 22.

**1970, Sept. 18 Photo. *Perf. 14x14½***

*642* A229 5p multicolored 6 6
*643* A229 9p multicolored 30 24
*644* A229 1sh6p multicolored 52 50

Philympia, London Philatelic Exhibition, Sept. 18-26.

Angel and Shepherds — A230

Designs (Illuminations from 14th Century de Lisle Psalter): 5p, Nativity. 1sh6p, Adoration of the Kings.

**1970, Nov. 25 Photo. *Perf. 14x14½***

*645* A230 4p red & multi 5 5
*646* A230 5p vio & multi 6 5
**a.** Imperf., pair 375.00
*647* A230 1sh6p olive & multi 40 40

Christmas.

Mountain Road, by T.P. Flanagan A231

Paintings from Northern Ireland: 7½p, Deer's Meadow, by Thomas Carr. 9p, Tollymore Forest Park, by Colin Middleton.

**1971, June 16 Photo. *Perf. 14½x14***

| | | | | |
|---|---|---|---|---|
| *648* A231 | 3p | multicolored | 16 | 5 |
| *649* A231 | 7½p | multicolored | 1.40 | 1.00 |
| *650* A231 | 9p | multicolored | 1.40 | 1.00 |

Ulster '71 Festival, Belfast, May-Oct.

John Keats A232

Writers and their signatures: 5p, Thomas Gray. 7½p, Sir Walter Scott.

**1971, July 28 Photo. *Perf. 14½x14***

| | | | | |
|---|---|---|---|---|
| *651* A232 | 3p | dl bl, blk & gold | 14 | 5 |
| *652* A232 | 5p | ol, blk & gold | 45 | 35 |
| *653* A232 | 7½p | yel brn, blk & gold | 1.25 | 1.00 |

John Keats (1795-1821), death sesquicentennial; Thomas Gray (1716-1771), death bicent.; and Sir Walter Scott (1771-1832), birth bicent.

Soldier, Sailor, Airman, Nurse, 1921, and Poppy A233

Designs: 7½p, Roman centurion on horseback, York Castle and coat of arms. 9p, Rugby players 100 years ago, and rose.

**1971, Aug. 25**

| | | | | |
|---|---|---|---|---|
| *654* A233 | 3p | ultra & multi | 10 | 4 |
| *655* A233 | 7½p | ocher & multi | 1.00 | 65 |
| *656* A233 | 9p | olive & multi | 1.50 | 1.25 |

50th anniv. of the British Legion (3p); 1900th anniv. of the founding of York (7½p); cent. of the Rugby Football Union (9p).

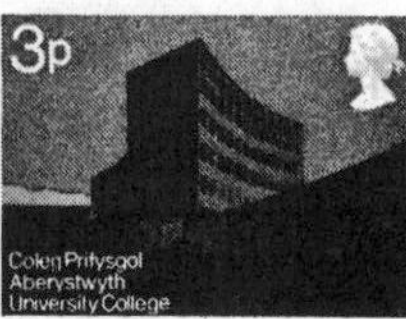

Physical Sciences Building, University College of Wales, Aberystwyth — A234

Modern University Buildings: 5p, Faraday Building, Engineering Faculty, University of Southampton. 7½p, Engineering Building, University of Leicester. 9p, Hexagon Restaurant, University of Essex.

**1971, Sept. 22 Photo. *Perf. 14½x14***

| | | | | |
|---|---|---|---|---|
| *657* A234 | 3p | cit & multi | 14 | 6 |
| *658* A234 | 5p | rose vio & multi | 45 | 32 |
| *659* A234 | 7½p | dp brn & multi | 1.25 | 70 |
| *660* A234 | 9p | dk bl & multi | 1.40 | 1.25 |

Dream of the Kings A235

Designs (from Stained Glass Windows, Canterbury Cathedral): 3p, Adoration of the Kings. 7½p, Journey of the Kings.

**1971, Oct. 13**

| | | | | |
|---|---|---|---|---|
| *661* A235 | 2½p | scar & multi | 8 | 5 |
| *662* A235 | 3p | ultra & multi | 12 | 6 |
| *663* A235 | 7½p | green & multi | 1.40 | 90 |

Christmas.

James Clark Ross (1800-1862) and Map of South Polar Sea — A236

British Polar Explorers: 5p, Martin Frobisher (1535-1594), and Desceliers map, 1550. 7½p, Henry Hudson (c. 1560-1611) and Petrus Plancius map, 1592. 9p, Robert Falcon Scott (1868-1912) and map of Antarctica.

**1972, Feb. 16 *Perf. 14x14½***

| | | | | |
|---|---|---|---|---|
| *664* A236 | 3p | dp bis & multi | 10 | 5 |
| *665* A236 | 5p | brick red & multi | 35 | 28 |
| *666* A236 | 7½p | vio & multi | 80 | 60 |
| *667* A236 | 9p | blue & multi | 1.25 | 60 |

See Nos. 689-693.

Head of Tutankhamen as Fisherman — A237

Coast Guard A238

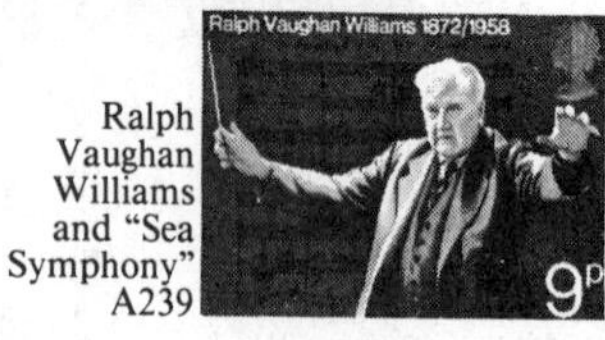

Ralph Vaughan Williams and "Sea Symphony" A239

**1972, Apr. 26 Photo. *Perf. 14½x14***

| | | | | |
|---|---|---|---|---|
| *668* A237 | 3p | gold & multi | 14 | 6 |

**Photo.; Queen's Head Gold Embossed**

| | | | | |
|---|---|---|---|---|
| *669* A238 | 7½p | blue & multi | 55 | 55 |
| *670* A239 | 9p | multicolored | 80 | 80 |

50th anniv. of the discovery of the tomb of Tutankhamen by Howard Carter and Lord Carnarvon (3p); sesquicentennial of the British Coast guard (7½p); Ralph Vaughan Williams (1872-1958), composer, birth cent. (9p).

St. Andrew's, Greensted-Juxta-Ongar — A240

Old Village Churches: 4p, All Saints, Earls Barton. 5p, St. Andrew's, Letheringsett. 7½p, St. Andrew's, Helpringham. 9p, St. Mary the Virgin, Huish Episcopi.

**Photo.; Queen's Head Gold Embossed**

**1972, June 21 *Perf. 14x14½***

| | | | | |
|---|---|---|---|---|
| *671* A240 | 3p | dl bl & multi | 10 | 5 |
| *672* A240 | 4p | olive & multi | 35 | 22 |
| *673* A240 | 5p | dp grn & multi | 45 | 35 |
| *674* A240 | 7½p | red & multi | 1.50 | 1.10 |
| *675* A240 | 9p | blue & multi | 1.75 | 1.40 |
| | | *Nos. 671-675 (5)* | 4.15 | 3.12 |

Old village churches.

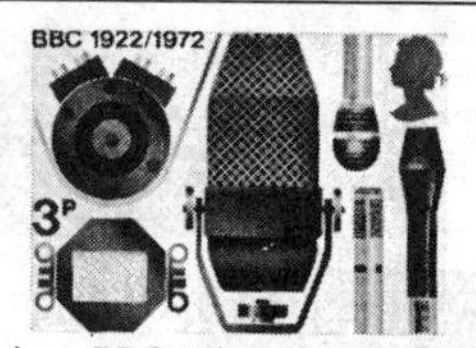

Various BBC Microphones — A241

Designs: 5p, Wooden horn loudspeaker 1925. 7½p, Color TV camera, 1972, 9p. Marconi's oscillator and spark transmitter, 1897.

**1972, Sept. 13 Photo. *Perf. 14½x14***

| | | | | |
|---|---|---|---|---|
| *676* A241 | 3p | blk, brn & yel | 12 | 6 |
| *677* A241 | 5p | hn brn & blk | 38 | 25 |
| *678* A241 | 7½p | blk & mag | 75 | 60 |
| *679* A241 | 9p | blk & yel | 1.10 | 1.00 |

50th anniv. of daily broadcasting in the United Kingdom (British Broadcasting Corporation)(Nos. 676-678), 75th anniv. of the Marconi-Kemp experiments resulting in the first radio transmission across water (No. 679).

Angel with Trumpet — A242

Queen Elizabeth II, Prince Philip — A243

**Photo.; Gold Embossed**

**1972, Oct. 18 *Perf. 14x14½***

| | | | | |
|---|---|---|---|---|
| *680* A242 | 2½p | shown | 8 | 7 |
| *681* A242 | 3p | Angel with lute | 10 | 7 |
| *682* A242 | 7½p | Angel with harp | 50 | 50 |

Christmas.

**1972, Nov. 20 Photo. *Perf. 14x14½***

| | | | | |
|---|---|---|---|---|
| *683* A243 | 3p | dk bl, sep & sil | 14 | 7 |
| *684* A243 | 20p | dk pur, sep & sil | 80 | 80 |

25th anniv. of the marriage of Queen Elizabeth II and Prince Philip. No. 684 is without phosphor.

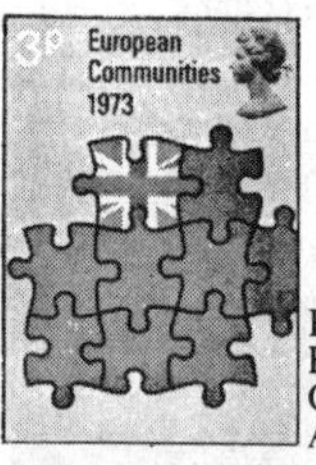

Britain as Part of European Community A244

**1973, Jan. 3**

| | | | | |
|---|---|---|---|---|
| *685* A244 | 3p | brn org & multi | 35 | 12 |
| *686* A244 | 5p | blue & multi | 70 | 40 |
| *687* A244 | 5p | emerald & multi | 70 | 40 |

Britain's entry into the European Community.

Nos. 686-687 are printed se-tenant in sheets of 100.

Oak A245

**1973, Feb. 28 Photo. *Perf. 14½x14***

| | | | | |
|---|---|---|---|---|
| *688* A245 | 9p | multicolored | 60 | 60 |

Tree Planting Year.

Explorer Type of 1972

Designs: No. 689, David Livingstone and map of Africa. No. 690, Henry Stanley and map of Africa. 5p, Sir Francis Drake and world map. 7½p, Sir Walter Raleigh and world map. 9p, Charles Sturt and map of Australia.

**1973, Apr. 8 Photo. *Perf. 14x14½***

| | | | | |
|---|---|---|---|---|
| *689* A236 | 3p | multicolored | 9 | 6 |
| *690* A236 | 3p | multicolored | 9 | 6 |
| *691* A236 | 5p | multicolored | 50 | 38 |
| *692* A236 | 7½p | multicolored | 1.10 | 85 |
| *693* A236 | 9p | multicolored | 1.50 | 1.40 |
| | | *Nos. 689-693 (5)* | 3.28 | 2.75 |

British explorers. Nos. 689-690 printed se-tenant in sheets of 100.

William Gilbert Grace A246

Sir Joshua Reynolds, Self-portrait A247

**1973, May 16 Photo. *Perf. 14x14½***

Designs: Caricatures of William Gilbert Grace, the Great Cricketer, by Harry Furniss.

| | | | | |
|---|---|---|---|---|
| *694* A246 | 3p | brown & black | 20 | 10 |
| *695* A246 | 7½p | green & black | 1.40 | 80 |
| *696* A246 | 9p | blue & black | 1.40 | 1.00 |

Centenary of British County Cricket.

**1973, July 4 Photo. *Perf. 14x14½***

Paintings: 5p, Sir Henry Raeburn, self-portrait. 7½p, Nelly O'Brien, by Reynolds. 9p, Rev. R. Walker (The Skater), by Raeburn.

| | | | | |
|---|---|---|---|---|
| *697* A247 | 3p | multicolored | 12 | 8 |
| *698* A247 | 5p | multicolored | 35 | 20 |
| *699* A247 | 7½p | multicolored | 60 | 42 |
| *700* A247 | 9p | gray & multi | 65 | 48 |

250th birth anniv. of Sir Joshua Reynolds (1723-1792), and 150th death anniv. of Sir Henry Raeburn (1756-1823), painters.

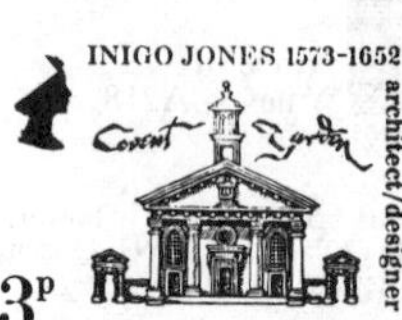


Tuscan Portico, St. Paul's Church, Covent Garden A248

Designs: No. 701, Costumes for Oberon and Titania. No. 703, Prince's Lodging, Newmarket. No. 704, Stage scenery for Oberon.

**Litho. and Typo.**

**1973, Aug. 15 *Perf. 14½x14***

| | | | | |
|---|---|---|---|---|
| *701* A248 | 3p | blk, pur & gold | 30 | 12 |
| *702* A248 | 3p | gold, brn & blk | 30 | 12 |
| *703* A248 | 5p | blk, bl & gold | 1.00 | 70 |
| *704* A248 | 5p | gold, ol & blk | 1.00 | 70 |

400th birth anniv. of Inigo Jones (1573-1652), architect and designer. Nos. 701-702 and 703-704 printed se-tenant.

Parliament, from Whitehall A249

Design: 10p, Parliament from Millbank.

**1973, Sept. 12 Engr. and Typo.**

| | | | | |
|---|---|---|---|---|
| *705* A249 | 8p | buff, gray & blk | 38 | 38 |
| *706* A249 | 10p | black & gold | 50 | 45 |

Opening by the Queen of the 19th Commonwealth Parliamentary Assoc. Conf., Westminster Hall.

Princess Anne and Mark Phillips A250

**1973, Nov. 14 Photo. *Perf. 14½x14***
*707* A250 3½p violet & silver 12 13
*708* A250 20p brown & silver 1.40 85

Wedding of Princess Anne and Captain Mark Phillips, Nov. 14, 1973.

Good King Wenceslas A251

Designs: Illustrations for Christmas carol "Good King Wenceslas."

**1973, Nov. 28**
*709* A251 3p shown 55 30
*710* A251 3p King, page looking out of window 55 30
*711* A251 3p King, page leaving castle 55 30
*712* A251 3p King, page in storm 55 30
*713* A251 3p King, page bringing gifts 55 30
*714* A251 3½p King, page and peasant 55 30
*Nos. 709-714 (6)* 3.30 1.80

Christmas. Nos. 709-713 printed se-tenant in sheets of 100.

Horse Chestnut A252

**1974, Feb. 27 Photo. *Perf. 14½x14***
*715* A252 10p green & multi 50 50

Fire Engine, 1766 A253

Designs: 3½p, First motorized fire engine, 1904. 5½p, Prize winning Sutherland fire engine, 1863. 8p, First steam engine, 1830.

**1974, Apr. 24**
*716* A253 3½p multicolored 15 9
*717* A253 5½p multicolored 20 20
*718* A253 8p multicolored 60 55
*719* A253 10p multicolored 75 70

Bicent. of the Fire Prevention (Metropolis) Act.

Packet "Peninsular," 1888, and "Southampton Packet Letter" Postmark — A254

Development of Overseas Mail Transport: 5½p, Farnham Biplane and "Aerial Post" postmark. 8p, Truck and pillar box for air-mail and "London F.S. Air Mail" postmark. 10p, Imperial Airways flying boat and "Southampton Airport" postmark.

**1974, June 12 *Perf. 14½x14***
*720* A254 3½p multicolored 14 8
*721* A254 5½p multicolored 20 20
*722* A254 8p multicolored 45 45
*723* A254 10p multicolored 60 60

UPU, Cent.

Robert the Bruce A255

Designs: "Great Britons" on caparisoned chargers.

**1974, July 10 *Perf. 14½x14***
*724* A255 4½p shown 10 7
*725* A255 5½p Owain Glyndwr 45 35
*726* A255 8p King Henry V 1.10 80
*727* A255 10p Black Prince 1.40 1.10

Churchill, Lord Warden of the Cinque Ports, 1942 — A256

Designs (Churchill): 5½p, with bowler and cigar, 1940. 8p, with top hat, as Secretary of War and Air, 1919. 10p, in uniform of South African Light Horse Regiment, 1899.

**1974, Oct. 9 Photo. *Perf. 14x14½***
*728* A256 4½p silver & multi 15 9
*729* A256 5½p silver & multi 45 45
*730* A256 8p silver & multi 35 35
*731* A256 10p silver & multi 40 40

Birth cent. of Sir Winston Spencer Churchill (1874-1965).

Adoration of the Kings, York Minster, c.1355 A257

Designs (Roof Bosses): 4½p, Nativity, St. Helen's, Norwich, c. 1480. 8p, Virgin and Child, Church of Ottery St. Mary, Devonshire, c. 1350. 10p, Virgin and Child, Lady Chapel, Worcester Cathedral, c. 1224.

**1974, Nov. 27 *Perf. 14½x14***
*732* A257 3½p gold & multi 9 7
*733* A257 4½p gold & multi 14 10
*734* A257 8p gold & multi 35 28
*735* A257 10p gold & multi 45 35

Christmas.

"Peace-Burial at Sea," by Turner — A258

Paintings: 5½p, "Snowstorm-Steamer off a Harbour's Mouth." 8p, "Arsenal, Venice." 10p, "View of St. Laurent."

**1975, Feb. 19 Photo. *Perf. 14½x14***
*736* A258 4½p multicolored 15 9
*737* A258 5½p multicolored 18 10
*738* A258 8p multicolored 25 15
*739* A258 10p multicolored 32 20

Birth bicent. of Joseph Mallord William Turner (1775-1851), painter.

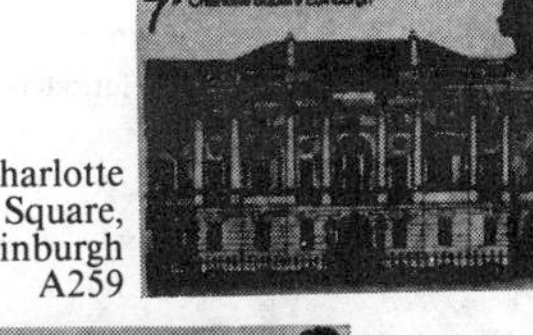

Charlotte Square, Edinburgh A259

National Theater, London A260

Designs: No. 740, The Rows, Chester (double-storied medieval shopping streets). 8p, Sir Christopher Wren's Flamsteed House, Royal Observatory, Greenwich. 10p, St. George's Chapel, Windsor.

**1975, Apr. 23 *Perf. 14½x14***
*740* A259 7p multicolored 18 12
*741* A259 7p multicolored 18 12
*742* A259 8p multicolored 20 12
*743* A259 10p multicolored 40 35
*744* A260 12p multicolored 50 42
*Nos. 740-744 (5)* 1.46 1.13

European Architectural Heritage Year 1975. Nos. 740-741 printed se-tenant in sheets of 100. 300th anniv. of Royal Observatory, (No. 742) and 500th anniv. of St. George's Chapel (No. 743).

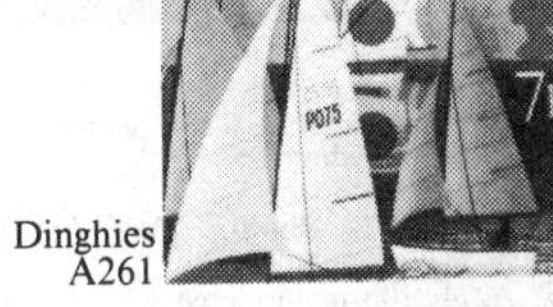

Dinghies A261

**1975, June 11 Photo. & Engr.**
*745* A261 7p shown 12 10
*746* A261 8p Racing keelboats 15 15
*747* A261 10p Cruising yachts 20 20
*748* A261 12p Multihulls 60 60

Royal Thames Yacht Club bicent. and other sailing club anniversaries.

Stephenson's Locomotion, 1825 — A262

Locomotives: 8p, Abbotsford, Waverley Class, 1876. 10p, Caerphilly Castle, 1923. 12p, High-speed train, 1975.

**1975, Aug. 13 Photo. *Perf. 14½x14***
*749* A262 7p multicolored 24 15
*750* A262 8p multicolored 25 22
*751* A262 10p multicolored 50 45
*752* A262 12p multicolored 60 55

Sesquicentennial of public railroads in Great Britain.

Parliament A263

**1975, Sept. 3**
*753* A263 12p multicolored 45 40

62nd Inter-Parliamentary Conference, London, Sept. 1975.

Emma and Mr. Woodhouse from "Emma" — A264

Designs (Illustrations by Barbara Brown of Characters from Jane Austen's Novels): 10p, Catherine Morland from "Northanger Abbey." 11p, Mr. Darcy from "Pride and Prejudice." 13p, Mary and Henry Crawford from "Mansfield Park."

**1975, Oct. 22 Photo. *Perf. 14x14½***
*754* A264 8½p multicolored 28 15
*755* A264 10p multicolored 32 32
*756* A264 11p multicolored 35 35
*757* A264 13p multicolored 42 42

Jane Austen (1775-1817), novelist.

Angels with Lute and Harp A265

Designs: 8½p, Angel with mandolin. 11p, Angel with horn. 13p, Angel with trumpet.

**1975, Nov. 26 Photo. *Perf. 14½x14***
*758* A265 6½p violet & multi 18 14
*759* A265 8½p multicolored 24 18
*760* A265 11p multicolored 48 42
*761* A265 13p ocher & multi 55 48

Christmas.

### Redrawn Queen Type of 1970

**1976-79 Photo. *Perf. 15x14***
**Size: 17½x21½mm**
*762* A197 9p violet blue 32 5
*763* A197 9½p bright lilac 40 5
*764* A197 10p salmon 40 5
**a.** Bklt. pane of 9 + printed margin ('80) 4.00
**b.** Type II ('84) 40 5
*765* A197 10½p yellow 40 5
*766* A197 10½p steel blue ('78) 52 5
*767* A197 11p pink 45 5
*768* A197 11½p olive bis ('79) 45 5
*769* A197 13p gray green ('79) 60 6
*770* A197 15p deep ultra ('79) 60 10
*771* A197 20p sepia 80 15
*772* A197 50p bis brown ('77) 1.50 35

***Perf. 14x15***
**Size: 27x38mm**
*773* A197 £1 ol grn & yel ('77) 2.75 60
*774* A197 £2 mar & lt grn ('77) 4.75 1.50
*775* A197 £5 dk bl & pink ('77) 14.00 4.00
*Nos. 762-775 (14)* 27.94 7.11

Woman Making Social Call — A266

Designs: 10p, Policeman making emergency call. 11p, District nurse making social welfare call. 13p, Refinery worker making field call.

**1976, Mar. 10 Photo. *Perf. 14½x14***
*777* A266 8½p multicolored 18 15
*778* A266 10p multicolored 30 30
*779* A266 11p multicolored 32 32
*780* A266 13p multicolored 45 45

First telephone call by Alexander Graham Bell, March 10, 1876, cent..

Coal Miner's Hands (Thomas Hepburn) A267

Designs: 10p, Child's hands, textile mill (Robert Owen). 11p, Boy's hand sweeping chimney (Lord Shaftesbury). 13p, Woman's hands holding prison bars (Elizabeth Frey).

**1976, Apr. 28 Photo. *Perf. 14½x14***

| | | | | | |
|---|---|---|---|---|---|
| *781* | A267 | 8½p | gray & black | 18 | 15 |
| *782* | A267 | 10p | multicolored | 28 | 28 |
| *783* | A267 | 11p | multicolored | 38 | 38 |
| *784* | A267 | 13p | multicolored | 50 | 45 |

19th century industrial and social reformers: Thomas Hepburn formed first miners' union in 1831; Robert Owen, improved working conditions in his mill and established schools; Lord Shaftesbury, philanthropist and sponsor of reform work laws; Elizabeth Frey, pioneer of women's prison reforms.

Benjamin Franklin, by Jean-Jacques Caffieri — A268

Elizabeth of Glamis Rose — A269

**1976, June 2 *Perf. 14x14½***

| | | | | | |
|---|---|---|---|---|---|
| *785* | A268 | 11p | multicolored | 45 | 45 |

American Bicentennial.

**1976, June 30 Photo. *Perf. 14x14½***

Roses Painted by Kristin Rosenberg: 10p, Grandpa Dickson. 11p, Rosa Mundi. 13p, Sweet Briar.

| | | | | | |
|---|---|---|---|---|---|
| *786* | A269 | 8½p | multicolored | 18 | 15 |
| *787* | A269 | 10p | multicolored | 30 | 30 |
| *788* | A269 | 11p | multicolored | 40 | 32 |
| *789* | A269 | 13p | multicolored | 50 | 40 |

Royal National Rose Society, centenary.

Archdruid, Eisteddfod A270

Morris Dancing A271

Designs: 11p, Piper and dancers, Highland gathering. 13p, Woman playing Welsh harp (telyn), Eisteddfod.

**1976, Aug. 4 Photo. *Perf. 14x14½***

| | | | | | |
|---|---|---|---|---|---|
| *790* | A270 | 8½p | multicolored | 18 | 15 |
| *791* | A271 | 10p | multicolored | 32 | 28 |
| *792* | A271 | 11p | multicolored | 38 | 35 |
| *793* | A270 | 13p | multicolored | 50 | 40 |

British cultural traditions.

Squire, from Canterbury Tales — A272

Designs: 10p, Page from Tretyse of Love, c. 1493, set in Caxton typeface. 11p, Philosopher, from The Game and Playe of Chesse, c. 1483. 13p, Printing press and printers, early 16th century woodcut.

**Photo.; Queen's Head Gold Embossed**
**1976, Sept. 29 *Perf. 14x14½***

| | | | | | |
|---|---|---|---|---|---|
| *794* | A272 | 8½p | blue & indigo | 20 | 18 |
| *795* | A272 | 10p | olive & dk grn | 35 | 30 |
| *796* | A272 | 11p | gray & black | 40 | 40 |
| *797* | A272 | 13p | ocher & red brn | 48 | 48 |

500 years of British printing, introduced by William Caxton (1422-1491).

Virgin and Child, Clare Chasuble A273

English medieval embroideries: 8½p, Angel with crown. 11p, Angel appearing to the shepherds. 13p, Three Kings bringing gifts, Butler-Bowden cope.

**1976, Nov. 24 Photo. *Perf. 14½x14***

| | | | | | |
|---|---|---|---|---|---|
| *798* | A273 | 6½p | multicolored | 15 | 12 |
| *799* | A273 | 8½p | multicolored | 24 | 24 |
| *800* | A273 | 11p | multicolored | 40 | 32 |
| *801* | A273 | 13p | multicolored | 55 | 45 |

Christmas.

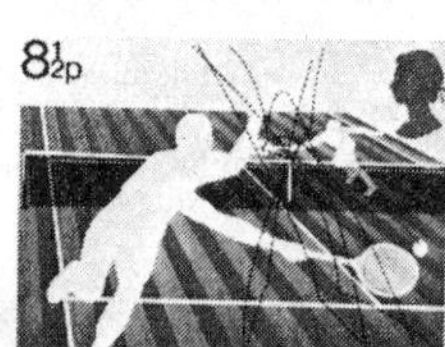

Tennis A274

Racket Sports: 10p, Table tennis. 11p, Squash. 13p, Badminton.

**1977, Jan. 12 Photo. *Perf. 14½x14***

| | | | | | |
|---|---|---|---|---|---|
| *802* | A274 | 8½p | multicolored | 22 | 20 |
| *803* | A274 | 10p | multicolored | 25 | 25 |
| *804* | A274 | 11p | multicolored | 35 | 35 |
| *805* | A274 | 13p | multicolored | 40 | 40 |

Wimbledon Tennis Championships, cent. and 1977 World Table Tennis Championships, Birmingham.

Steroids Conformational Analysis — A275

Designs: 10p, Vitamin C synthesis (formula and orange). 11p, Starch chromatography. 13p, Salt crystallography.

**1977, Mar. 2 Photo. *Perf. 14½x14***

| | | | | | |
|---|---|---|---|---|---|
| *806* | A275 | 8½p | multicolored | 24 | 16 |
| *807* | A275 | 10p | multicolored | 30 | 30 |
| *808* | A275 | 11p | multicolored | 35 | 35 |
| *809* | A275 | 13p | multicolored | 42 | 42 |

British chemists who won Nobel prize. Derek Barton, 1969 (8½p); Walter Norman Haworth, 1937 (10p); Archer J. P. Martin and Richard L. M. Synge, 1952 (11p); William and Lawrence Bragg, 1915 (13p).

Queen Elizabeth II — A276

**1977 Photo. *Perf. 14½x14***

| | | | | | |
|---|---|---|---|---|---|
| *810* | A276 | 8½p | silver & multi | 24 | 20 |
| *811* | A276 | 9p | silver & multi | 32 | 24 |
| *812* | A276 | 10p | silver & multi | 28 | 28 |
| *813* | A276 | 11p | silver & multi | 35 | 35 |
| *814* | A276 | 13p | silver & multi | 45 | 45 |
| | | | *Nos. 810-814 (5)* | 1.64 | 1.52 |

25th anniv. of the reign of Queen Elizabeth II.

Issue dates: 9p, June 15. Others, May 11.

Pentagons, Symbolic of Continents and Nations — A277

**1977, June 8 Photo. *Perf. 14x14½***

| | | | | | |
|---|---|---|---|---|---|
| *815* | A277 | 13p | multicolored | 45 | 45 |

Summit Conference of Commonwealth Heads of Government, London, June 1977.

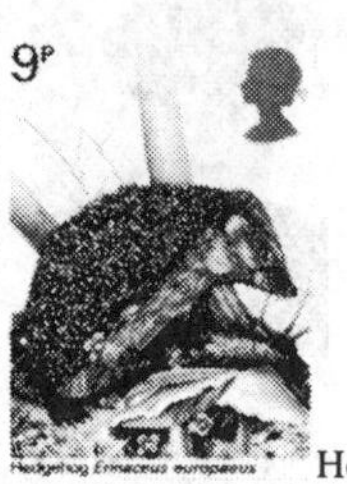

Hedgehog — A278

**1977, Oct. 5 Photo. *Perf. 14x14½***

| | | | | | |
|---|---|---|---|---|---|
| *816* | A278 | 9p | shown | 35 | 25 |
| *817* | A278 | 9p | Brown hare | 40 | 25 |
| *818* | A278 | 9p | Red squirrel | 50 | 25 |
| *819* | A278 | 9p | Otter | 35 | 25 |
| *820* | A278 | 9p | Badger | 35 | 25 |
| | | | *Nos. 816-820 (5)* | 1.95 | 1.25 |

Wildlife protection. Nos. 816-820 printed se-tenant in sheets of 100.

"Two Turtle Doves, Three French Hens. . ." — A279

The Twelve Days of Christmas: No. 822, 4 colly birds, 5 gold rings, 6 geese a-laying. No. 823, 7 swans a-swimming, 8 maids a-milking. No. 824, 9 drummers drumming, 10 pipers piping. No. 825, 11 ladies dancing, 12 lords a-leaping. 9p, A partridge in a pear tree.

**1977, Nov. 23 Photo. *Perf. 14½x14***

| | | | | | |
|---|---|---|---|---|---|
| *821* | A279 | 7p | multicolored | 20 | 10 |
| *822* | A279 | 7p | multicolored | 20 | 10 |
| *823* | A279 | 7p | multicolored | 20 | 10 |
| *824* | A279 | 7p | multicolored | 20 | 10 |
| *825* | A279 | 7p | multicolored | 20 | 10 |
| *826* | A279 | 9p | multicolored | 24 | 16 |
| | | | *Nos. 821-826 (6)* | 1.24 | 66 |

Christmas. Nos. 821-825 printed se-tenant in sheets of 100.

Oil Production Platform, North Sea — A280

Designs: 10½p, Coal, pithead. 11p, Natural gas, flame. 13p, Electricity-producing nuclear power plant and uranium atom diagram.

**1978, Jan. 25 Photo. *Perf. 14x14½***

| | | | | | |
|---|---|---|---|---|---|
| *827* | A280 | 9p | multicolored | 30 | 18 |
| *828* | A280 | 10½p | multicolored | 36 | 20 |
| *829* | A280 | 11p | multicolored | 38 | 22 |
| *830* | A280 | 13p | multicolored | 45 | 25 |

Great Britain's wealth of energy resources.

Tower of London A281

British Architecture: 10½p, Abbey and Palace, Holyrood House, Edinburgh. 11p, Caernarvon Castle, Wales. 13p, Hampton Court Palace, London.

**1978, Mar. 1 Photo. *Perf. 14½x14***

| | | | | | |
|---|---|---|---|---|---|
| *831* | A281 | 9p | multicolored | 24 | 14 |
| *832* | A281 | 10½p | multicolored | 32 | 16 |
| *833* | A281 | 11p | multicolored | 35 | 18 |
| *834* | A281 | 13p | multicolored | 45 | 20 |
| ***a.*** | | | Souvenir sheet of 4 | 2.00 | |

No. 834a issued to publicize London 1980 International Stamp Exhibition; it contains one each of Nos. 831-834; gray and buff margin with black inscription. Size: 121x89mm. Sold for 53½p, of which 10p went to exhibition fund.

Gold State Coach — A282

Designs: 10½p, St. Edward's crown. 11p, Orb. 13p, Imperial State crown.

**1978, May 31 Photo. *Perf. 14x14½***

| | | | | | |
|---|---|---|---|---|---|
| *835* | A282 | 9p | vio blue & gold | 24 | 14 |
| *836* | A282 | 10½p | car lake & gold | 28 | 16 |
| *837* | A282 | 11p | dp green & gold | 30 | 18 |
| *838* | A282 | 13p | purple & gold | 35 | 20 |

25th anniv. of coronation of Queen Elizabeth II.

Shire Horse A283

British Horses: 10½p, Shetland pony. 11p, Merlyn Cymreig Welsh pony. 13p, Thoroughbred.

**1978, July 5 Photo. *Perf. 14½x14***

| | | | | | |
|---|---|---|---|---|---|
| *839* | A283 | 9p | multicolored | 25 | 15 |
| *840* | A283 | 10½p | multicolored | 30 | 16 |
| *841* | A283 | 11p | multicolored | 38 | 20 |
| *842* | A283 | 13p | multicolored | 45 | 22 |

"Penny-farthing," 19th Century — A284

British bicycles: 10½p, 1920 touring bicycles. 11p, Modern small-wheel bicycles. 13p, Road racers.

**1978, Aug. 2 Photo. *Perf. 14½x14***

*843* A284 9p multicolored 30 18
*844* A284 10½p multicolored 36 20
*845* A284 11p multicolored 40 22
*846* A284 13p multicolored 45 25

Centenary of first national cycling organizations: British Cycling Federation and Cyclists Touring Club.

Carolers Around Christmas Tree A285

Christmas: 9p, Christmas waits (watchmen). 11p, 18th century carolers. 13p, Boar's head carol.

**1978, Nov. 22 Photo. *Perf. 14½x14***

*847* A285 7p multicolored 20 14
*848* A285 9p multicolored 25 15
*849* A285 11p multicolored 35 18
*850* A285 13p multicolored 42 20

Old English Sheepdog A286

British dogs: 10½p, Welsh springer spaniel. 11p, West Highland white terrier. 13p, Irish setter.

**1979, Feb. 7 Photo. *Perf. 14½x14***

*851* A286 9p multicolored 24 14
*852* A286 10½p multicolored 28 15
*853* A286 11p multicolored 30 16
*854* A286 13p multicolored 35 18

Primroses — A287

British wild flowers: 10½p, Daffodils. 11p, Bluebells. 13p, Snowdrops.

**1979, Mar. 21 Photo. *Perf. 14x14½***

*855* A287 9p multicolored 24 14
*856* A287 10½p multicolored 28 15
*857* A287 11p multicolored 30 16
*858* A287 13p multicolored 35 18

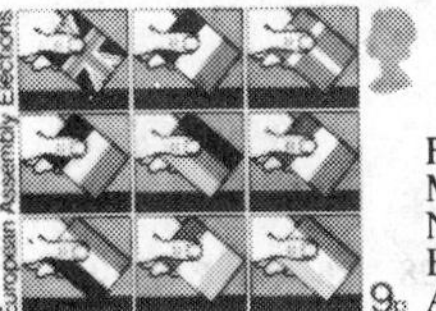


Flags of Member Nations as Ballots A288

Flags of European Community Members: United Kingdom, Italy, Denmark, Belgium, Fed. Rep. of Germany, France, Netherlands, Ireland, Luxembourg. Positions of hands and flags different on each denomination.

**1979, May 9 Photo. *Perf. 14½x14***

*859* A288 9p multicolored 24 14
*860* A288 10½p multicolored 28 15
*861* A288 11p multicolored 30 16
*862* A288 13p multicolored 35 18

European Parliament, first direct elections, June 7-10.

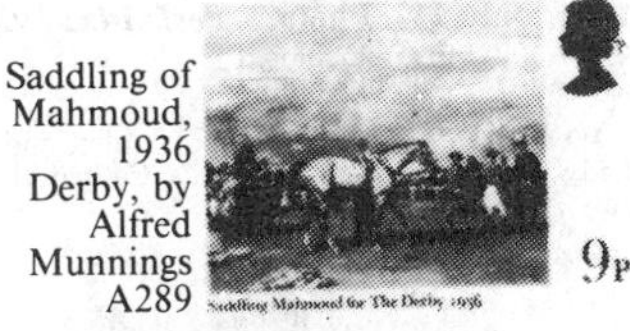

Saddling of Mahmoud, 1936 Derby, by Alfred Munnings A289

Designs: 10½p, Liverpool Great National Steeple Chase, 1839, aquatint by F. C. Turner. 11p, First Spring Meeting, Newmarket, 1793, by J. N. Sartorius. 13p, Charles II watching racing at Dorsett Ferry, Windsor, 1684, by Francis Barlow.

**1979, June 6 Photo. *Perf. 14½x14***

*863* A289 9p multicolored 24 14
*864* A289 10½p multicolored 28 15
*865* A289 11p multicolored 30 16
*866* A289 13p multicolored 35 18

200th anniv. of the Derby.

Peter Rabbit — A290 Rowland Hill — A291

Children's books: 10½p, The Wind in the Willows. 11p, Winnie-the-Pooh. 13p, Alice's Adventures in Wonderland.

**1979, July 11 Photo. *Perf. 14x14½***

*867* A290 9p multicolored 32 18
*868* A290 10½p multicolored 38 20
*869* A290 11p multicolored 40 22
*870* A290 13p multicolored 48 25

International Year of the Child.

**1979, Aug. 22 Photo. *Perf. 14x14½***

Designs: 11½p, Bellman, early 19th century. 13p, London post office and mailman, early 19th century. 15p, Victorian woman and child mailing letter.

*871* A291 10p multicolored 25 14
*872* A291 11½p multicolored 30 15
*873* A291 13p multicolored 32 18
*874* A291 15p multicolored 40 22
***a.*** Souvenir sheet of 4 1.40 90

Sir Rowland Hill (1795-1879), originator of penny postage.

No. 874a issued to publicize London 1980 International Stamp Exhibition. It contains one each of Nos. 871-874; blue and black margin with black inscription. Sold for 59½p, of which 10p went to exhibition fund. Size: 89½x122½mm.

Police Constable and Children A292

Designs: 11½p, Police constable directing traffic. 13p, Police woman on horseback. 15p, River patrol boat.

**1979, Sept. 26 Photo. *Perf. 14½x14***

*875* A292 10p multicolored 30 15
*876* A292 11½p multicolored 35 18
*877* A292 13p multicolored 38 18
*878* A292 15p multicolored 45 25

150th anniversary of London Metropolitan Police.

*Great Britain stamps can be mounted in Scott's annually supplemented Great Britain Album.*

Three Kings Following Star A293

Christmas: 10p, Angel appearing before the shepherds. 11½p, Nativity. 13p, Joseph and Mary traveling to Bethlehem. 15p, Annunciation.

**1979, Nov. 21 Photo. *Perf. 14½x14***

*879* A293 8p multicolored 22 12
*880* A293 10p multicolored 28 14
*881* A293 11½p multicolored 30 15
*882* A293 13p multicolored 35 18
*883* A293 15p multicolored 45 20
*Nos. 879-883 (5)* 1.60 79

Kingfisher — A294

**1980, Jan. 16 Photo. *Perf. 14x14½***

*884* A294 10p shown 30 15
*885* A294 11½p Dipper 35 16
*886* A294 13p Moorhen 38 18
*887* A294 15p Yellow wagtail 45 22

Redrawn Queen Type of 1970

**1980-86 Photo. *Perf. 15x14***

*887A* A197 2p grn, perf. 13½x14 ('80) 8 5
***b.*** Perf. 15x14 ('84) 8 5
***c.*** Litho., perf. 15x14, type II ('88) 8 5
*888* A197 2½p org ver ('81) 10 5
*889* A197 3p dp lil rose 12 6
***a.*** Coil strip of 4 (#888, 3 #889) 50 35
***b.*** Bklt. pane of 9 + label (#889,2 #969,6 #972) 3.00
*890* A197 4p Prus blue, perf. 13½x14 25 8
***a.*** Perf. 15x14, Photo. ('81) 25 8
***b.*** Coil strip of 4 (#622, 3 #890a) 50 35
***c.*** Photo., perf. 15x14, type II ('84) 25 8
***e.*** Litho., perf. 15x14, type II ('86) 25 8
***f.*** Dk turq, photo., perf. 15x14, type II ('88) 25 8
*891* A197 5p pale lil, litho., perf. 13½x14 ('80) 25 5
*892* A197 11½p dl brn ('81) 50 22
***a.*** Bklt. pane of 6 (#622, #623, 3 #892, #895) 2.25
***b.*** Bklt. pane of 8 (3 #888, 2 #890, 3 #892) 2.50
*893* A197 12p yellow green 48 24
***a.*** Bklt. pane, 10 #893, 10 #764 7.00
***b.*** Bklt. pane of 9 + printed margin (#625, #764, 4 #893) 2.50
***c.*** Bklt. pane of 9 + printed margin ('80) 4.50
*894* A197 13½p brown 70 28
*895* A197 14p gray bl ('81) 55 28
***a.*** Bklt. pane, 10 #895, 10 #892 8.00
***b.*** Bklt. pane, 6 #895, 4 #892 4.50
*896* A197 15½p lt vio ('81) 55 32
***a.*** Bklt. pane of 6 + printed margin ('82) 3.50
***b.*** Bklt. pane of 9 + printed margin ('82) 5.25
*897* A197 17p light green 70 34
*898* A197 17½p lt red brn 80 35
*899* A197 18p vio bl ('81) 72 35
*900* A197 20p sepia, perf. 13½x14 ('80) 80 40
***a.*** Litho., perf. 15x14, type II ('86) 70 40
*901* A197 22p dark blue 88 45
*902* A197 25p lilac ('81) 1.00 50
*903* A197 75p black, litho., perf. 13½x14 2.50 1.25
***a.*** Litho., Perf. 15x14 ('84) 2.50 30
***b.*** Litho., perf. 15x14, type II ('88) 2.50 30
***c.*** Photo., perf. 15x14, type II ('88) 2.50 30
*Nos. 887A-903 (17)* 10.98 5.27

"Rocket" Locomotive — A295

**1980, Mar. 12 Photo. *Perf. 14½x14***

*904* A295 12p shown 35 15
*905* A295 12p 1st, 2nd class cars 35 15
*906* A295 12p 3rd class and sheep cars 35 15
*907* A295 12p Flat cars 35 15
*908* A295 12p Flat car, mail coach 35 15
*Nos. 904-908 (5)* 1.75 75

Liverpool-Manchester Railroad, 150th anniversary. Nos. 904-908 printed se-tenant in continuous design.

London View A296

**1980, Apr. 9 Engr. *Perf. 14½***

*909* A296 50p multicolored 1.40 70
***a.*** Souvenir sheet 1.65 95

London 1980, International Stamp Exhibition, May 6-14. No. 909a contains one stamp, multicolored decorative margin and inscription; sold for 75p. Size: 90x122mm; issued May 7.

Buckingham Palace — A297

**1980, May 7 Photo. *Perf. 14x14½***

*910* A297 10½p shown 28 14
*911* A297 12p Albert Memorial 32 15
*912* A297 13½p Royal Opera House 38 18
*913* A297 15p Hampton Court 45 20
*914* A297 17½p Kensington Palace 50 24
*Nos. 910-914 (5)* 1.93 91

Emily Bronte and "Wuthering Heights" — A298

Victorian novelists and scenes from their novels: 12p, Charlotte Bronte, "Jane Eyre." 13½p, George Eliot, "The Mill on the Floss." 17½p, Mrs. Gaskell, "North and South." 12p and 13½p show CEPT (Europa) emblem.

**1980, July 9 Photo. *Perf. 15x14***

*915* A298 12p multicolored 32 15
*916* A298 13½p multicolored 38 18
*917* A298 15p multicolored 45 20
*918* A298 17½p multicolored 50 24

Queen Mother Elizabeth, 80th Birthday — A299

**1980, Aug. 4 Photo. *Perf. 14x14½***
*919* A299 12p multicolored 42 20

Henry Wood, (1869-1944) Conductor A300

English conductors: 13½p, Thomas Beecham (1879-1961). 15p, Malcolm Sargent (1895-1967). 17½p, John Barbirolli (1899-1970).

**1980, Sept. 10**
*920* A300 12p multicolored 32 15
*921* A300 13½p multicolored 38 18
*922* A300 15p multicolored 45 20
*923* A300 17½p multicolored 50 24

Running A301

Designs: 13½p, Rugby. 15p, Boxing. 17½p, Cricket.

**1980, Oct. 10 Litho. *Perf. 14x14½***
*924* A301 12p multicolored 32 15
*925* A301 13½p multicolored 38 18
*926* A301 15p multicolored 45 20
*927* A301 17½p multicolored 50 24

Centenaries: Amateur Athletics Association; Welsh Rugby Union; Amateur Boxing Association; first cricket test match against Australia.

Christmas Tree with Candles A302

Christmas (Traditional Decorations): 12p, Candles, ivy, ribbons. 13½p, Mistletoe, apples. 15p, Paper chain and bell. 17½p, Holly wreath.

**1980, Nov. 19 Photo. *Perf. 14½x14***
*928* A302 10p multicolored 28 14
*929* A302 12p multicolored 32 15
*930* A302 13½p multicolored 38 18
*931* A302 15p multicolored 45 20
*932* A302 17½ multicolored 50 24
*Nos. 928-932 (5)* 1.93 91

Values quoted in this catalogue are for stamps graded at Fine-Very Fine and with no faults. An illustrated guide to grade is provided in introductory material, beginning on Page V.

Lovebirds, Angels and Heart (Valentine's Day) — A303

Folklore: 18p, Morris Dancers, 16th century window, Shropshire. 22p, Wheat, fruit, farm couple dancing (Lammastide). 25p, Medieval mummers, 14th century manuscript illustration. 14p and 18p show CEPT (Europa) emblem.

**1981, Feb. 6 Photo. *Perf. 14½x14***
*933* A303 14p multicolored 45 24
*934* A303 18p multicolored 55 28
*935* A303 22p multicolored 70 35
*936* A303 25p multicolored 80 40

Guide Dog Leading Blind Man A304

**1981, Mar. 25 Photo.**
*937* A304 14p shown 38 18
*938* A304 18p Sign language 50 24
*939* A304 22p Man in wheelchair 60 30
*940* A304 25p Foot painting 70 35

International Year of the Disabled.

Small Tortoiseshell A305

**1981, May 13 *Perf. 14x14½***
*941* A305 14p shown 45 24
*942* A305 18p Large blue 55 28
*943* A305 22p Peacock 70 35
*944* A305 25p Checkered skipper 80 40

Glenfinnan, Highlands, Scotland A306

50th anniv. of National Trust for Scotland: 18p, Derwentwater, Lake District, England. 20p, Stackpole Head, Dyfed, Wales. 22p, Giant's Causeway, County Antrim, Northern Ireland. 25p, St. Kilda, Scotland.

**1981, June 24 Photo. *Perf. 14½x14***
*945* A306 14p multicolored 40 20
*946* A306 18p multicolored 52 25
*947* A306 20p multicolored 60 30
*948* A306 22p multicolored 65 35
*949* A306 25p multicolored 75 38
*Nos. 945-949 (5)* 2.92 1.48

Prince Charles and Lady Diana — A307

**1981, July 22 Photo. *Perf. 14x14½***
*950* A307 14p multicolored 45 24
*951* A307 25p multicolored 85 42

Wedding of Charles, Prince of Wales, and Lady Diana Spencer, St. Paul's Cathedral, July 29.

Hikers Reading Map A308

**1981, Aug. 12 Litho. *Perf. 14***
*952* A308 14p shown 45 22
*953* A308 18p Girl at potter's wheel 55 28
*954* A308 22p Woman administering artificial respiration 70 35
*955* A308 25p Hurdler 80 40

The Duke of Edinburgh's Awards (expeditions, skills, service, recreation), 25th anniv.

Cockle Dredging — A309

**1981, Sept. 23 Photo. *Perf. 14½x14***
*956* A309 14p shown 40 20
*957* A309 18p Hauling trawl net 52 25
*958* A309 22p Lobster potting 65 35
*959* A309 25p Hauling seine net 75 38

Fishermen's Year and Royal Natl. Mission to Deep Sea Fishermen centenary.

Joseph and Mary Arriving at Bethlehem A310

Christmas: Children's Drawings.

**1981, Nov. 18 Photo.**
*960* A310 11½p Santa Claus 35 16
*961* A310 14p Jesus 40 20
*962* A310 18p Angel 52 25
*963* A310 22p shown 65 35
*964* A310 25p Three Kings 75 38
*Nos. 960-964 (5)* 2.67 1.34

Death Centenary of Charles Darwin (1809-1882) — A311

**1982, Feb. 10 Photo.**
*965* A311 15½p Giant tortoises 45 22
*966* A311 19½p Iguanas 55 28
*967* A311 26p Darwin's finches 80 38
*968* A311 29p Skulls 85 42

Redrawn Queen Type of 1970

**1982-87 Photo. *Perf. 15x14***
*969* A197 3½p vio brown, type II ('83) 15 5
*970* A197 5p pink, litho., perf. 13½x14 20 10
*a.* Litho., perf. 15x14 ('84) 20 5
*b.* Photo., perf. 15x14, type II ('86) 20 5
*971* A197 12½p emerald 50 25
*b.* Bklt. pane of 10 (4 #971, 6 #896) 6.00
*c.* Bklt. pane (10 #971, 10 #896) 11.50
*d.* Bklt. pane of 8 (#622, 4 #889, 3 #971) 2.00
*e.* Bklt. pane of 8 (3 #969, 971, 2 #623) 2.00
*f.* Bklt. pane of 6 + printed margin 3.00
*g.* Bklt. pane of 9 + printed margin (#625, #889, 7 #971) 4.00
*972* A197 16p dull brown ('83) 55 25
*a.* Booklet pane of 10 5.50
*b.* Bklt. pane of 10 (4 #971, 6 #972) 5.50
*c.* Bklt. pane of 9 + printed margin 5.00
*973* A197 16½p fawn 68 34
*974* A197 17p blue gray, type II ('83) 52 26
*a.* Bklt. pane of 3 + label 1.60
*b.* Bklt. pane of 9 + printed margin 4.75
*c.* Bklt. pane of 9 + printed margin (#764b, 7 #974, #1073) ('84) 4.50
*975* A197 19½p olive green 2.75 40
*976* A197 20½p ultra, type II ('83) 75 32
*977* A197 23p org ver, type II ('83) 80 36
*978* A197 26p red 85 52
*a.* Type II ('87) 85 52
*b.* Bklt. pane of 4, No. 978a ('87) 3.50
*979* A197 28p deep violet, type II ('83) 90 42
*980* A197 29p brown olive 2.75 60
*981* A197 31p brt rose lil, type II ('83) 95 48

***Perf. 14x15***

**Size: 27x38mm**

*982* A197 £1.30 sl bl & buff 8.00 1.90
*Nos. 969-982 (14)* 20.35 6.25

See description of type II before Nos. 622-638.

Bklt. of ten 16p sold at 15p discount. Stamps have blue "D" on back.

No. 978b has margins on four sides. No. 974b comes with different margins.

Youth Organizations A312

**1982, Mar. 24 Photo. *Perf. 14x14½***
*983* A312 15½p Boy's Brigade 50 24
*984* A312 19½p Girl's Brigade 65 32
*985* A312 26p Boy Scouts 85 42
*986* A312 29p Girl Guides 1.00 48

75th anniv. of scouting and 125th birth anniv. of founder Robert Baden-Powell (26p).

Performing Arts — A313

**1982, Apr. 28 Photo. *Perf. 14x14½***
*987* A313 15½p Ballet 50 24
*988* A313 19½p Pantomime 65 32
*989* A313 26p Shakespearean drama 85 42
*990* A313 29p Opera 1.00 48

Nos. 987-990 show CEPT (Europa) emblem.

King Henry VIII and the Mary Rose A314

**1982, June 16** ***Perf. 14½x14***
*991* A314 15½p shown 50 24
*992* A314 19½p Admiral Blake, Triumph 65 32
*993* A314 24p Lord Nelson, Victory 75 35
*994* A314 26p Lord Fisher, Dreadnought 85 42
*995* A314 29p Viscount Cunningham, Warspite 1.00 48
*Nos. 991-995 (5)* 3.75 1.81

Textile Designs — A315

**1982, July 23** **Photo.** ***Perf. 14x14½***
*996* A315 15½p Strawberry Thief, 1883 45 22
*997* A315 19½p Tulips, 1906 60 30
*998* A315 26p Cherry Orchard, 1930 80 38
*999* A315 29p Chevron, 1973 95 45

Information Technology — A316

**1982, Sept. 8** **Photo.**
*1000* A316 15½p Hieroglyphics, library, word processor 50 24
*1001* A316 26p Viewdata set, satellite, laser pen 85 42

Austin's Seven (1922) and Metro A317

Cars: 19½p, Ford Model T (1913) and Escort. 26p, Jaguar SS (1931) and XJ6 (1967). 29p, Rolls-Royce Silver Ghost (1907) and Silver Spirit (1982).

**1982, Oct. 13** **Litho.** ***Perf. 14½x14***
*1002* A317 15½p multicolored 75 38
*1003* A317 19½p multicolored 1.00 50
*1004* A317 26p multicolored 1.25 65
*1005* A317 29p multicolored 1.50 75

Christmas 1982 A318

Designs: Christmas carols.

**1982, Nov. 17** **Photo.**
*1006* A318 12½p While Shepherds Watched 38 18
*1007* A318 15½p The Holly and the Ivy 45 22
*1008* A318 19½p I Saw Three Ships 60 30
*1009* A318 26p We Three Kings 80 38
*1010* A318 29p Good King Wenceslas 95 45
*Nos. 1006-1010 (5)* 3.18 1.53

River Fish A319

**1983, Jan. 26** **Photo.** ***Perf. 15x14***
*1011* A319 15½p Salmon 50 25
*1012* A319 19½p Pike 70 35
*1013* A319 26p Trout 85 45
*1014* A319 29p Perch 1.10 50

Commonwealth Day — A320

Landscapes by Donald Hamilton Fraser.

**1983, Mar. 9** **Photo.** ***Perf. 14x14½***
*1015* A320 15½p Tropical island 55 28
*1016* A320 19½p Desert 70 35
*1017* A320 26p Farmland 95 48
*1018* A320 29p Mountains 1.00 55

Engineering Achievements (Europa) — A321

**1983, May 25** **Photo.** ***Perf. 15x14***
*1019* A321 16p Humber Bridge 1.00 38
*1020* A321 20½p Thames Flood Barrier 1.00 42
*1021* A321 28p Emergency oil rig support vessel Lolair 1.50 58

The Royal Scots (Royal Regiment) — A322

**1983, July 6** ***Perf. 14x14½***
*1022* A322 16p shown 55 28
*1023* A322 20½p Royal Welsh Fusiliers 40 35
*1024* A322 26p Royal Green Jackets 90 45
*1025* A322 28p Irish Guards 95 48
*1026* A322 31p Parachute Regiment 1.10 52
*Nos. 1022-1026 (5)* 3.90 2.08

20th Cent. Garden, Sissinghurst A323

**1983, Aug. 24** **Litho.** ***Perf. 14***
*1027* A323 16p shown 55 28
*1028* A323 20½p Biddulph Grange, 19th cent. 70 35
*1029* A323 28p Blenheim, 18th cent. 95 48
*1030* A323 31p Pitmeeden, 17th cent. 1.10 50

British Fairs A324

**1983, Oct. 5** **Photo.** ***Perf. 14½x14***
*1031* A324 16p Merry-go-round 55 28
*1032* A324 20½p Animals, rides 70 35
*1033* A324 28p Games 95 48
*1034* A324 31p Ancient market fair 1.00 50

850th anniv. of St. Bartholomew's Fair.

Christmas A325

**1983, Nov. 16** **Photo.**
*1035* A325 12½p Birds mailing cards 45 24
*1036* A325 16p Three Kings chimney pots 60 28
*1037* A325 20½p Birds under umbrella 70 35
*1038* A325 28p Birds under street lamp 1.00 48
*1039* A325 31p Topiary dove 1.10 52
*Nos. 1035-1039 (5)* 3.85 1.87

Heraldry A326

Designs: 16p, Arms of The College of Arms. 20½p, Arms of Richard III, founder. 28p, Arms of The Earl Marshal. 31p, Arms of The City of London.

**1984, Jan. 17** **Photo.** ***Perf. 14½***
*1040* A326 16p multicolored 55 28
*1041* A326 20½p multicolored 70 35
*1042* A326 28p multicolored 95 48
*1043* A326 31p multicolored 1.00 50

National Cattle Breeders' Association A327

**1984, Mar. 6** **Litho.** ***Perf. 15x14½***
*1044* A327 16p Highland Cow 50 25
*1045* A327 20½p Chillingham Wild Bull 62 30
*1046* A327 26p Hereford Bull 80 40
*1047* A327 28p Welsh Black Bull 85 42
*1048* A327 31p Irish Moiled Cow 95 45
*Nos. 1044-1048 (5)* 3.72 1.82

Common Design Types are pictured in section before Great Britain.

Royal Institute of British Architects Sesquicentennial — A328

Urban renewal projects and plans.

**1984, Apr. 3** **Photo.**
*1049* A328 16p Liverpool 55 28
*1050* A328 20½p Durham 70 35
*1051* A328 28p Bristol 95 48
*1052* A328 31p Perth 1.10 50

Europa (1959-1984) A329

**1984, May 9** **Photo.** ***Perf. 14½x14***
*1053* A329 16p Bridge 60 30
*1054* A329 16p Abduction of Europa 60 30
*1055* A329 20½p like No. 1053 75 38
*1056* A329 20½p like No. 1054 75 38

Nos. 1054, 1056 also for 2nd Election of the European Parliament.

London Economic Summit, June 7-9 — A330

**1984, June 5** **Photo.** ***Perf. 14x15***
*1057* A330 31p Lancaster House 1.00 50

Greenwich Meridian Centenary — A331

**1984, June 26** **Litho.** ***Perf. 14x14½***
*1058* A331 16p View from Apollo 11 55 28
*1059* A331 20½p English Channel map 70 35
*1060* A331 28p Greenwich Observatory 95 48
*1061* A331 31p Airy's transit telescope, 1850 1.10 55

Bath-Bristol-London Mail Coach Bicentenary — A332

18th century drawings by James Pollard: Nos. 1062-1066 se-tenant.

**Photo. & Engr.**
**1984, July 31** ***Perf. 14½x14***
*1062* A332 16p Bath, 1784 50 25
*1063* A332 16p Exeter, 1816 50 25
*1064* A332 16p Norwich, 1827 50 25

*1065* A332 16p Holyhead & Liverpool 50 25
*1066* A332 16p Edinburgh, 1831 50 25
*Nos. 1062-1066 (5)* 2.50 1.25

50th Anniv. of British Council A333

**1984, Sept. 25** **Photo.**
*1067* A333 17p Education for development 60 30
*1068* A333 22p Promoting the arts 80 38
*1069* A333 31p Technical training 1.10 55
*1070* A333 34p Language & libraries 1.10 60

Redrawn Queen Type of 1970
Type II

**1984-88** **Photo.** ***Perf. 15x14***
*1071* A197 7p hn brn ('85) 28 6
*1072* A197 12p brt grn ('85) 48 8
- *a.* Bklt. pane of 9 + printed margin 4.50
- *b.* Bklt. pane of 10 (6 #974, 4 #1072) 5.50
- *c.* Bklt. pane of 9 + printed margin (6 #1072, 2 #974, #981) 4.00
- *d.* Bklt. pane of 6 (2 #623d, 4 #1072) 1.50

*1073* A197 13p lt red brown 32 16
- *a.* Booklet pane of 10 3.25
- *b.* Bklt. pane of 10 (6 #974, 4 #1073) 3.80
- *c.* Bklt. pane of 8 (3 #623d, 2 #890, 3 #1073) 1.25
- *d.* Bklt. pane of 6 ( #623d, 2 #970b, 3 #1073) 1.35
- *e.* Bklt. pane of 6 + printed margin 2.00
- *f.* Bklt. pane of 9 + printed margin 3.00
- *g.* Bklt. pane of 6 (#623d, 2 #970b, 3 #1073)('87) 1.20
- *h.* Booklet pane of 4 ('87) 1.30
- *i.* Litho. ('88) 32 16
- *j.* Bklt. pane of 9 + printed margin (2 #890c, 2 #974, 4 #1073, #1083) ('85) 4.00
- *k.* As "e," litho. ('88) 2.00
- *l.* Bklt. pane of 9 + printed margin (6 #1073i, #1075h, #1078a, #1084a) 4.00

*1074* A197 14p dark blue ('88) 52 25
- *a.* Bklt. pane of 4 2.15
- *b.* As "a," imperf. edges 2.15
- *c.* Bklt. pane of 10 5.50
- *d.* As "c," imperf. edges 5.50
- *e.* Litho. 52 25
- *f.* Bklt. pane of 10 #1074e 5.25

*1075* A197 18p olive green 60 22
- *a.* Bklt. pane of 4 (#623d, #1073, 2 #1075) 1.50
- *b.* Bklt. pane of 6 (#1073, 5 #1075) 3.50
- *c.* Bklt. pane of 9 + printed margins 5.50
- *d.* Bklt. pane of 9 + printed margins (#623, #978, 2 #1073, 5 #1075) 4.50
- *e.* Bklt. pane of 4 ('87) 2.50
- *f.* Bklt. pane of 6 (#1073, 5 #1075) ('87) 3.50
- *g.* Booklet pane of 10 ('87) 6.00
- *h.* Litho. ('88) 60 22
- *i.* Bklt. pane of 6 #1075h + printed margin ('88) 3.75
- *j.* As "c," litho. ('88) 4.25

*1076* A197 19p brt org ('88) 70 35
- *a.* Bklt. pane of 3 + label (#1074, 2 #1076)('88) 2.00
- *b.* Bklt. pane of 6 (2 #1074, 4 #1076) ('88) 4.00
- *c.* Bklt. pane of 4 3.00
- *d.* As "c," imperf. edges 3.00
- *e.* Bklt. pane of 10 7.50
- *f.* As "e," imperf. edges 7.50
- *g.* Litho. 70 35
- *h.* Bklt. pane of 10 #1076g 7.50

*1077* A197 20p g[illegible] blue ('88) 75 38
*1078* A197 22p yellow green 55 28
- *a.* Litho. ('88) 55 28

*1079* A197 23p brt yel grn ('88) 85 42
*1080* A197 24p violet 60 30
*1081* A197 27p brown ('88) 98 50
- *a.* Bklt. pane of 4 4.00
- *b.* As "a," imperf. edges 4.00

*1082* A197 28p dark olive bister ('88) 1.00 50
*1083* A197 32p Prus blue ('88) 1.15 58
*1084* A197 34p deep bister 85 42
- *a.* Litho. ('88) 85 42

*1085* A197 35p dark brn ('88) 1.25 62

**Size: 27x38mm**

***Perf. 14x15***
*1086* A197 £1.33 blk & pale rose lil 6.00 1.25
*1087* A197 £1.41 ind & buff ('85) 5.00 1.50
*1087A* A197 £1.50 blk & lt pk ('86) 4.75 2.50
*1087B* A197 £1.60 indigo & buff ('87) 5.50 2.00

Nos. 1073a, 1073h, 1074a, 1074c, 1075e, 1075g, 1076c, 1076e and 1081a have margins on four sides. Nos. 1073g, 1074b, 1074d, 1075f, 1076d, 1076f and 1081b are straight-edged at left and right or top and bottom.

Christmas 1984 — A334

Crayon Sketches by Yvonne Gilbert.

**1984, Nov. 20** **Photo.** ***Perf. 15x14***
*1088* A334 13p Holy Family 42 20
*1089* A334 17p Arrival in Bethlehem 55 25
*1090* A334 22p Shephard and Lamb 70 35
*1091* A334 31p Virgin and child 1.00 50
*1092* A334 34p Offering Frankincense 1.10 55
*Nos. 1088-1092 (5)* 3.77 1.85

Bklt. of 20 13p sold at 30p discount. Stamps have blue stars printed on the back.

Great Western Railway Sesquicentennial — A335

**1985, Jan. 22** **Photo.** ***Perf. 15x14***
*1093* A335 17p Flying Scotsman 95 40
*1094* A335 22p Golden Arrow 1.10 55
*1095* A335 29p Cheltenham Flyer 1.25 65
*1096* A335 31p Royal Scot 1.65 75
*1097* A335 34p Cornish Riviera 1.75 95
*Nos. 1093-1097 (5)* 6.70 3.30

Insects — A336

**1985, Mar. 12** **Photo.** ***Perf. 15x14½***
*1098* A336 17p Buff tailed bumble bee 65 30
*1099* A336 22p Seven spotted ladybird 80 42
*1100* A336 29p Wart-biter bush-cricket 1.00 48
*1101* A336 31p Stag beetle 1.10 48
*1102* A336 34p Emperor dragonfly 1.25 60
*Nos. 1098-1102 (5)* 4.80 2.28

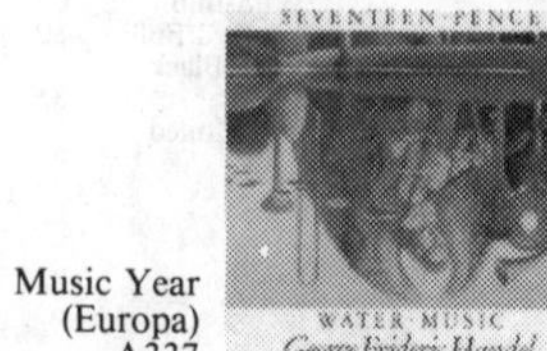

Music Year (Europa) A337

British Composers: 17p, Water Music, by George Frideric Handel. 22p, The Planets Suite, by Gustav Holst. 31p, The First Cockoo, by Frederick Delius. 34p, Sea Pictures, by Edward Elgar.

**1985, May 14** ***Perf. 14½***
*1103* A337 17p Reflections in pool 60 30
*1104* A337 22p View of planets 75 38
*1105* A337 31p Roosting cuckoo 1.00 52
*1106* A337 34p Waves, wing 1.10 60

Safety at Sea A338

**1985, June 18** **Litho.** ***Perf. 14***
*1107* A338 17p Lifeboat 60 30
*1108* A338 22p Beachy Head Lighthouse, chart 80 42
*1109* A338 31p Marecs-A satellite 1.10 60
*1110* A338 34p Signal buoy, yacht 1.25 65

Royal Mail Service, 350th Anniv. — A339

Designs: 17p, Royal Mail Datapost motorcyclist and plane. 22p, Postbus on country road. 31p, Parcel service delivery. 34p, Postman delivering mail.

**1985, July 30** **Photo.** ***Perf. 14x14½***
*1111* A339 17p multicolored 60 30
*1112* A339 22p multicolored 80 35
*1113* A339 31p multicolored 1.00 42
*1114* A339 34p multicolored 1.25 55

Arthurian Legends A340

Designs: 17p, Arthur consulting with Merlin. 22p, The Lady of the Lake with the sword "Excalibur." 31p, Guinevere and Lancelot fleeing from Camelot. 34p, Sir Galahad praying during his quest for the Holy Grail.

**1985, Sept. 3** **Photo.** ***Perf. 15x14***
*1115* A340 17p multicolored 52 25
*1116* A340 22p multicolored 70 35
*1117* A340 31p multicolored 1.00 50
*1118* A340 34p multicolored 1.10 55

500th anniv. of William Caxton's edition of Le Morte D'Arthur, by Sir Thomas Mallory.

20th Cent. Stars and Directors of Film — A341

Photographs: 17p, Peter Sellers (1925-80). 22p, David Niven (1910-83). 29p, Charlie Chaplin (1889-1977). 31p, Vivien Leigh (1913-67). 34p, Sir Alfred Hitchcock (1899-1980), director.

**1985, Oct. 8** **Photo.** ***Perf. 14½***
*1119* A341 17p multicolored 52 25
*1120* A341 22p multicolored 70 35
*1121* A341 29p multicolored 95 48
*1122* A341 31p multicolored 1.00 50
*1123* A341 34p multicolored 1.10 55
*Nos. 1119-1123 (5)* 4.27 2.13

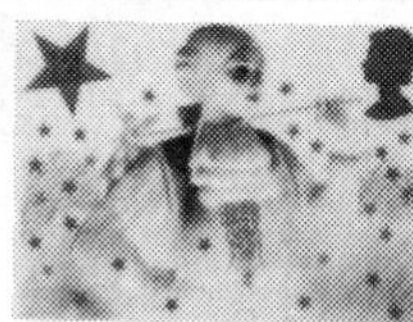
Christmas Pantomime A342

**1985, Nov. 19** **Photo.** ***Perf. 15x14½***
*1124* A342 12p Principal boy 35 18
- *a.* Bklt. pane of 20 7.00

*1125* A342 17p Genie 50 25
*1126* A342 22p Grande dame 65 32
*1127* A342 31p Good fairy 90 45
*1128* A342 34p Cat 1.00 50
*Nos. 1124-1128 (5)* 3.40 1.70

No. 1124a has random star design printed on back.

Industry Year — A343

**1986, Jan. 14** **Litho.** ***Perf. 15x14***
*1129* A343 17p North Sea oil rig, light bulb 55 28
*1130* A343 22p Medical research lab, thermometer 70 35
*1131* A343 31p Steel mill, garden hoe 1.00 50
*1132* A343 34p Cornfield, bread 1.10 55

Halley's Comet A344

Designs: 17p, Caricature, Edmond Halley (1656-1742), astronomer. 22p, European Space Agency Giotto spacecraft pursuing comet. 31p, Comet and legend, Maybe Twice in a Lifetime. 34p, Comet orbiting sun.

**1986, Feb. 18** **Photo.**
*1133* A344 17p multicolored 55 28
*1134* A344 22p multicolored 70 35
*1135* A344 31p multicolored 1.00 50
*1136* A344 34p multicolored 1.10 55

A345

Queen Elizabeth II, 60th Birthday A346

**1986, Apr. 21** **Photo.**
*1137* A345 17p multicolored 60 30
*1138* A346 17p multicolored 60 30
- *a.* Pair, #1137-1138 1.25 60

*1139* A345 34p multicolored 1.25 60
*1140* A346 34p multicolored 1.25 60
- *a.* Pair, #1139-1140 2.50 1.25

Europa A347

**1986, May 20 Photo. *Perf. 14½***

| | | | | | |
|---|---|---|---|---|---|
| *1141* | A347 | 17p | Barn owl | 60 | 30 |
| *1142* | A347 | 22p | Pine marten | 75 | 35 |
| *1143* | A347 | 31p | Wild cat | 1.10 | 55 |
| *1144* | A347 | 34p | Natterjack toad | 1.25 | 60 |

Domesday Book, 900th Anniv. A348

**1986, June 17 Photo.**

| | | | | | |
|---|---|---|---|---|---|
| *1145* | A348 | 17p | Peasant | 40 | 32 |
| *1146* | A348 | 22p | Freeman | 80 | 40 |
| *1147* | A348 | 31p | Knight | 1.10 | 60 |
| *1148* | A348 | 34p | Lord | 1.25 | 65 |

Domesday Book, first nationwide survey in British history.

Sports A349

**1986, July 15 Photo. *Perf. 15x14***

| | | | | | |
|---|---|---|---|---|---|
| *1149* | A349 | 17p | Track and field | 52 | 25 |
| *1150* | A349 | 22p | Rowing | 68 | 35 |
| *1151* | A349 | 29p | Weight lifting | 90 | 45 |
| *1152* | A349 | 31p | Shooting | 95 | 48 |
| *1153* | A349 | 34p | Field hockey | 1.05 | 52 |
| | | | *Nos. 1149-1153 (5)* | 4.10 | 2.05 |

1986 Commonwealth Games, Edinburgh. World Hockey Cup, London.

Wedding of Prince Andrew and Sarah Ferguson — A350

**1986, July 22 *Perf. 14x15***

| | | | | | |
|---|---|---|---|---|---|
| *1154* | A350 | 12p | multicolored | 42 | 22 |
| *1155* | A350 | 17p | multicolored | 60 | 28 |

Commonwealth Parliamentary Assoc. Conference, London, Sept. — A351

**1986, Aug. 19 Litho. *Perf. 14x14½***

| | | | | | |
|---|---|---|---|---|---|
| *1156* | A351 | 34p | multicolored | 1.05 | 52 |

Royal Air Force Commanders and Aircraft A352

Designs: 17p, Lord Dowding (1882-1970), Hurricane. 22p, Lord Tedder (1890-1967), Hawker Typhoon. 29p, Lord Trenchard (1873-1956), De Havilland 9A World War I bomber. 31p, Sir Arthur Harris (1892-1984), Avro Lancaster. 34p, Lord Portal (1893-1971), De Havilland Mosquito.

**1986, Sept. 16 Photo. *Perf. 14½***

| | | | | | |
|---|---|---|---|---|---|
| *1157* | A352 | 17p | multicolored | 52 | 25 |
| *1158* | A352 | 22p | multicolored | 68 | 35 |
| *1159* | A352 | 29p | multicolored | 90 | 45 |
| *1160* | A352 | 31p | multicolored | 95 | 48 |
| *1161* | A352 | 34p | multicolored | 1.05 | 52 |
| | | | *Nos. 1157-1161 (5)* | 4.10 | 2.05 |

Christmas A353

Customs: 12p, 13p, Glastonbury Thorn. 18p, Tanad Valley Plygain. 22p, Hebrides Tribute. 31p, Dewsbury Church Knell. 34p, Hereford Boy Bishop.

**1986, Nov. 18 Photo. *Perf. 15x14½***

| | | | | | |
|---|---|---|---|---|---|
| *1162* | A353 | 12p | multicolored | 35 | 18 |
| *1163* | A353 | 13p | multicolored | 38 | 20 |
| *a.* | | | Pane of 36 | 13.75 | |
| *1164* | A353 | 18p | multicolored | 55 | 28 |
| *1165* | A353 | 22p | multicolored | 65 | 32 |
| *1166* | A353 | 31p | multicolored | 90 | 45 |
| *1167* | A353 | 34p | multicolored | 1.00 | 50 |
| | | | *Nos. 1162-1167 (6)* | 3.83 | 1.93 |

No. 1163a printed in two panes of 18 with gutter between, stars on back; folded and sold in discount booklet for £4.30.

Flora — A354

Photographs by Alfred Lammer.

**1987, Jan. 20 Photo. *Perf. 14½***

| | | | | | |
|---|---|---|---|---|---|
| *1168* | A354 | 18p | Gaillardia | 52 | 25 |
| *1169* | A354 | 22p | Echinops | 65 | 32 |
| *1170* | A354 | 31p | Echeveria | 90 | 45 |
| *1171* | A354 | 34p | Colchicum | 1.00 | 50 |

Sir Isaac Newton (1642-1727), Physicist, Mathematician — A355

Manuscripts and principles: 18p, Philosophiae Naturalis Principia Mathematica, 1687. 22p, Motion of bodies in ellipses. 31p, Opticks Treatise of the Refraction, Reflections and Colors of Light. 34p, The System of the World.

**1987, Mar. 24 Photo. *Perf. 14***

| | | | | | |
|---|---|---|---|---|---|
| *1172* | A355 | 18p | multicolored | 60 | 30 |
| *1173* | A355 | 22p | multicolored | 75 | 40 |
| *1174* | A355 | 31p | multicolored | 1.10 | 48 |
| *1175* | A355 | 34p | multicolored | 1.25 | 60 |

Europa A356

Modern architecture: 18p, Willis Faber & Dumas Building, Ipswich, designed by Norman Foster. 22p, Pompidou Centre, Paris, designed by Richard Rogers and Renzo Piano. 31p, Staatsgalerie, Stuttgart, designed by James Stirling and Michael Wilford. 34p, European Investment Bank, Luxembourg, designed by Sir Denys Lasdun.

**1987, May 12 Photo. *Perf. 15x14***

| | | | | | |
|---|---|---|---|---|---|
| *1176* | A356 | 18p | multicolored | 60 | 30 |
| *1177* | A356 | 22p | multicolored | 75 | 38 |
| *1178* | A356 | 31p | multicolored | 1.05 | 52 |
| *1179* | A356 | 34p | multicolored | 1.15 | 58 |

St. John Ambulance, Cent. — A357

First aid.

**1987, June 16 Litho. *Perf. 14x14½***

| | | | | | |
|---|---|---|---|---|---|
| *1180* | A357 | 18p | Ambulance, 1887 | 62 | 30 |
| *1181* | A357 | 22p | War victims, 1940 | 75 | 38 |
| *1182* | A357 | 31p | Public event, 1965 | 1.05 | 52 |
| *1183* | A357 | 34p | Transplant organ flight, 1987 | 1.15 | 58 |

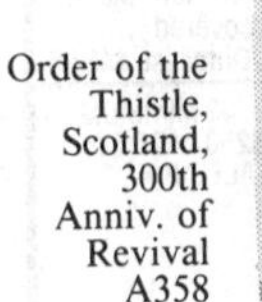

Order of the Thistle, Scotland, 300th Anniv. of Revival A358

Coats of arms: 18p, Lord Lyon, King of Arms, 1687. 22p, Duke of Rothesay, bestowed on Prince Charles in 1974. 31p, Royal Scottish Academy of Painting, Sculpture & Architecture, 1826. 34p, The Royal Society of Edinburgh, 1783.

**1987, July 21 Photo. *Perf. 14½***

| | | | | | |
|---|---|---|---|---|---|
| *1184* | A358 | 18p | multicolored | 60 | 30 |
| *1185* | A358 | 22p | multicolored | 75 | 38 |
| *1186* | A358 | 31p | multicolored | 1.00 | 50 |
| *1187* | A358 | 34p | multicolored | 1.15 | 58 |

Accession of Queen Victoria, 150th Anniv. A359

Portraits of Victoria and: 18p, Great Exhibition (1851) at the Crystal Palace, Grace Darling's rescue (1838) of the Forfashire's survivors, and Monarch of the Glen, by Sir Edwin Henry Landseer. 22p, Launching of Brunel's ship Great Eastern, portrait of Prince Consort Albert, Mrs. Beeton's Book of Household Management (1889). 31p, The Albert Memorial, Prime Minister Disraeli and 1st ballot box. 34p, The Boer War, Guglielmo Marconi's wireless telegraph communications linking Paris and London (1898 ), and diamond jubilee emblem.

**Photo. & Engr.**

**1987, Sept. 8 *Perf. 15x14***

| | | | | | |
|---|---|---|---|---|---|
| *1188* | A359 | 18p | multicolored | 60 | 30 |
| *1189* | A359 | 22p | multicolored | 75 | 38 |
| *1190* | A359 | 31p | multicolored | 1.05 | 52 |
| *1191* | A359 | 34p | multicolored | 1.15 | 58 |

Studio Pottery A360

**1987, Oct. 13 Photo. *Perf. 14½***

| | | | | | |
|---|---|---|---|---|---|
| *1192* | A360 | 18p | Bernard Leach | 60 | 30 |
| *1193* | A360 | 26p | Elizabeth Fritsch | 85 | 42 |
| *1194* | A360 | 31p | Lucie Rie | 1.05 | 52 |
| *1195* | A360 | 34p | Hans Coper | 1.15 | 58 |

Christmas — A361

Childhood memories: 13p, Decorating tree. 18p, Looking out window, Christmas eve. 26p, Sweet dreams. 31p, Reading new book to toys, Christmas morning. 34p, Playing horn, snowman.

**1987, Nov. 17 Photo. *Perf. 15x14***

| | | | | | |
|---|---|---|---|---|---|
| *1196* | A361 | 13p | multicolored | 45 | 22 |
| *a.* | | | Pane of 36 | 16.25 | |
| *1197* | A361 | 18p | multicolored | 60 | 30 |
| *1198* | A361 | 26p | multicolored | 88 | 45 |
| *1199* | A361 | 31p | multicolored | 1.05 | 52 |
| *1200* | A361 | 34p | multicolored | 1.15 | 58 |
| | | | *Nos. 1196-1200 (5)* | 4.13 | 2.07 |

No. 1196a printed in two panes of 18 with gutter between, stars on back; folded and sold in discount booklets for £4.30.

Linnean Society of London, 200th Anniv. A362

**1988, Jan. 19 *Perf. 15x14½***

| | | | | | |
|---|---|---|---|---|---|
| *1201* | A362 | 18p | Bull-rout fish | 68 | 35 |
| *1202* | A362 | 26p | Yellow waterlily | 98 | 45 |
| *1203* | A362 | 31p | Bewick's swan | 1.15 | 58 |
| *1204* | A362 | 34p | Morel | 1.25 | 62 |

Linnaeus (Carl von Linne, 1707-1778), inventor of system of taxonomic nomenclature.

Welsh Bible, 400th Anniv. A363

**1988, Mar. 1 Photo. *Perf. 14½***

| | | | | | |
|---|---|---|---|---|---|
| *1205* | A363 | 18p | William Morgan | 68 | 35 |
| *1206* | A363 | 26p | William Salesbury | 98 | 50 |
| *1207* | A363 | 31p | Richard Davies | 1.15 | 58 |
| *1208* | A363 | 34p | Richard Parry | 1.30 | 65 |

*Great Britain stamps can be mounted in Scott's annually supplemented Great Britain Album.*

Sports
A364

**1988, Mar. 22** **Photo.** ***Perf. 14½***

| | | | | |
|---|---|---|---|---|
| *1209* | A364 | 18p Balance beam | 65 | 32 |
| *1210* | A364 | 26p Downhill skiing | 95 | 48 |
| *1211* | A364 | 31p Tennis | 1.15 | 58 |
| *1212* | A364 | 34p Soccer | 1.25 | 62 |

Ski Club of Great Britain and centenaries of the British Amateur Gymnastics Assoc., Lawn Tennis Assoc. and the Soccer League.

Europa 1988 A365

Transportation and communication, 1938.

**1988, May 10** ***Perf. 15x14***

| | | | | |
|---|---|---|---|---|
| *1213* | A365 | 18p Mallard locomotive | 68 | 35 |
| *1214* | A365 | 26p Queen Elizabeth ocean liner | 98 | 50 |
| *1215* | A365 | 31p Tram No. 1173, Glasgow | 1.15 | 58 |
| *1216* | A365 | 34p Handley Page aircraft, Croydon Airport | 1.25 | 62 |

Defeat of the Spanish Armada by the Royal Navy, 400th Anniv. A366

Designs: No. 1217, Armada approaching The Lizard, July 19, 1588. No. 1218, Royal Navy vessels sailing from Plymouth to engage Spaniards in battle, July 21. No. 1219, Battle scene off the Isle of Wight, July 25. No. 1220, Battle scene off Calais, France, July 28-29. No. 1221, Spanish ships foundering in the North Sea storms, July 29-Aug. 2. Printed se-tenant in a continuous design.

**1988, July 19**

| | | | | |
|---|---|---|---|---|
| *1217* | A366 18p multi | | 60 | 30 |
| *1218* | A366 18p multi | | 60 | 30 |
| *1219* | A366 18p multi | | 60 | 30 |
| *1220* | A366 18p multi | | 60 | 30 |
| *1221* | A366 18p multi | | 60 | 30 |
| *a.* | Strip of 5, Nos. 1217-1221 | | 3.00 | 1.50 |
| | *Nos. 1217-1221 (5)* | | 3.00 | 1.50 |

Australia Bicentennial A367

Designs: No. 1222, Colonist, First Fleet vessel. No. 1223, British and Australian parliaments, Queen Elizabeth II. No. 1224, Cricketer W.G. Grace. No. 1225, John Lennon (1940-1980), William Shakespeare (1564-1616) and Sydney Opera House. Stamps of the same denomination printed se-tenant in a continuous design picturing flag of Australia.

**1988, June 21 Litho. *Perf. 14½***

| | | | |
|---|---|---|---|
| *1222* | A367 18p multi | 70 | 35 |
| *1223* | A367 18p multi | 70 | 35 |
| *1224* | A367 34p multi | 1.30 | 65 |
| *1225* | A367 34p multi | 1.30 | 65 |

See Australia Nos. 1082-1085.

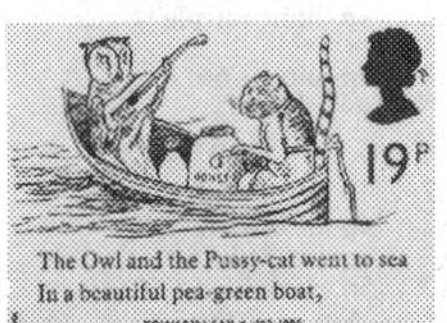


Nonsensical Drawings by Edward Lear (1812-1888) — A368

Illustrations and text: 19p, *The Owl and the Pussycat*, 1867. 27p, Self-portrait as a bird, pen-and-ink sketch from a letter. 32p, "C" is for Cat, alphabet book character. 35p, Girl, birds and part of a limerick.

**1988, Sept. 6 Photo. *Perf. 15x14***

| | | | |
|---|---|---|---|
| *1226* | A368 19p multi | 68 | 35 |
| *1227* | A368 27p multi | 95 | 48 |
| *1228* | A368 32p multi | 1.15 | 68 |
| *1229* | A368 35p multi | 1.25 | 62 |
| *a.* | Souv. sheet of 4, Nos. 1226-1229 | 4.75 | |

No. 1229a has decorative inscribed margin picturing Stamp World London '90 emblem and Lear's signature. Sold for £1.35 to benefit the stamp exhibition.

An enhanced introduction to the Scott Catalogue begins on Page V. A thorough understanding of the material presented there will greatly aid your use of the catalogue itself.

Photographs of Castles by Prince Andrew — A369

**1988, Oct 18 Engr.**

| | | | | |
|---|---|---|---|---|
| *1230* | A369 | £1 Carrickfergus | 3.50 | 1.75 |
| *1231* | A369 | £1.50 Caernarfon | 5.25 | 2.65 |
| *1232* | A369 | £2 Edinburgh | 7.00 | 3.50 |
| *1233* | A369 | £5 Windsor | 17.50 | 8.75 |

Christmas Cards A370

**1988, Nov. 15 Photo. *Perf. 15x14½***

| | | | |
|---|---|---|---|
| *1234* | A370 14p Journey to Bethlehem | 50 | 25 |
| *a.* | Bklt. pane of 36 | | |
| *1235* | A370 19p Shepherds see star | 70 | 35 |
| *1236* | A370 27p Magi follow star | 98 | 50 |
| *1237* | A370 32p Nativity | 1.15 | 58 |
| *1238* | A370 35p The Annunciation | 1.25 | 62 |
| | *Nos. 1234-1238 (5)* | 4.58 | 2.30 |

No. 1234a printed in two panes of 18 with gutter between, stars on back; folded and sold in discount booklets.

Birds — A371

**1989, Jan. 17 *Perf.***

| | | | |
|---|---|---|---|
| *1239* | A371 19p Puffin | 70 | 35 |
| *1240* | A371 27p Avocet | 98 | 50 |
| *1241* | A371 32p Oystercatcher | 1.15 | 58 |
| *1242* | A371 35p Gannet | 1.25 | 62 |

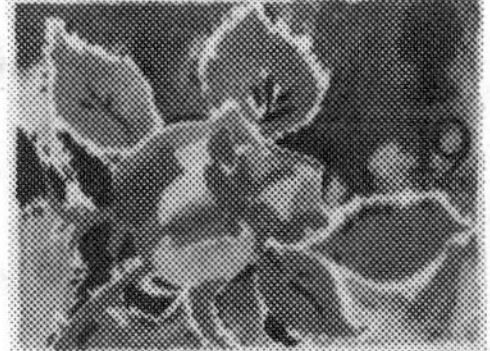

Special Occasions — A372

**1989, Jan. 31 Photo. *Perf.***
**Booklet Stamps**

| | | | |
|---|---|---|---|
| *1243* | A372 19p Rose | 72 | 35 |
| *1244* | A372 19p Cupid | 72 | 35 |
| *1245* | A372 19p Ships | 72 | 35 |
| *1246* | A372 19p Fruit bowl | 72 | 35 |
| *1247* | A372 19p Teddy Bear | 72 | 35 |
| *a.* | Bklt. pane of 10 (2 each Nos. 1243-1247) +12 labels | 7.25 | |
| | *Nos. 1243-1247 (5)* | 3.60 | 1.75 |

Labels inscribed "CONGRATULATIONS," "BEST WISHES," "HAPPY BIRTHDAY," "HAPPY ANNIVERSARY," "WITH LOVE," or "THANK YOU."

Food and Farming Year A373

Foods and tile mosaics in agricultural motifs.

**1989, Mar. 7 Photo. *Perf.***

| | | | |
|---|---|---|---|
| *1248* | A373 19p Fruit and vegetables | 70 | 35 |
| *1249* | A373 27p Meat, fish, fruit | 1.00 | 50 |
| *1250* | A373 32p Dairy products | 1.20 | 60 |
| *1251* | A373 35p Breads, cake, cereal | 1.30 | 65 |

## SEMI-POSTAL STAMPS

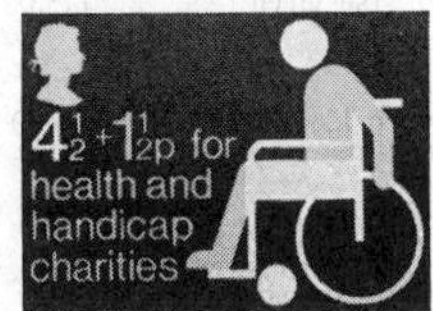


Handicapped Person — SP1

***Perf. 14½x14***

**1975, Jan. 22 Photo. Unwmk.**

| | | | |
|---|---|---|---|
| *B1* | SP1 4½p + 1½p bl & lt bl | 25 | 30 |

For the benefit of health and handicap charities. No. B1 is phosphorescent.

## POSTAGE DUE STAMPS

D1

D2

***Perf. 14x14½***

**1914-22 Typo. Wmk. 33**

| | | | | |
|---|---|---|---|---|
| *J1* | D1 | ½p emerald | 45 | 22 |
| *J2* | D1 | 1p rose | 52 | 9 |
| *J3* | D1 | 1½p red brn ('22) | 45.00 | 15.00 |
| *J4* | D1 | 2p brown black | 95 | 20 |
| *J5* | D1 | 3p violet ('18) | 2.50 | 95 |
| *J6* | D1 | 4p gray green ('21) | 5.50 | 55 |
| *J7* | D1 | 5p org brown | 3.25 | 55 |
| *J8* | D1 | 1sh blue | 25.00 | 2.25 |
| | | *Nos. J1-J8 (8)* | 83.17 | 19.81 |

**1924-30 Wmk. 35**

| | | | | |
|---|---|---|---|---|
| *J9* | D1 | ½p emerald | 52 | 15 |
| *J10* | D1 | 1p car rose | 52 | 9 |
| *J11* | D1 | 1½p red brown | 32.50 | 15.00 |
| *J12* | D1 | 2p blk brown | 2.00 | 12 |
| *J13* | D1 | 3p violet | 3.00 | 18 |
| *a.* | | Experimental wmk. | 42.50 | 37.50 |
| *J14* | D1 | 4p deep green | 9.00 | 75 |
| *J15* | D1 | 5p org brn ('30) | 24.00 | 20.00 |
| *J16* | D1 | 1sh blue | 4.75 | 55 |
| *J17* | D2 | 2sh6p brn, *yel* | 40.00 | 95 |
| | | *Nos. J9-J17 (9)* | 116.29 | 37.79 |

The experimental watermark of No. J13a resembles Wmk. 35 but is spaced more closely, with letters short and rounded, crown with flat arch and sides high, lines thicker.

**1936-37 Wmk. 250**

| | | | | |
|---|---|---|---|---|
| *J18* | D1 | ½p emerald ('37) | 1.90 | 1.90 |
| *J19* | D1 | 1p car rose ('37) | 1.00 | 90 |
| *J20* | D1 | 2p blk brown ('37) | 2.50 | 2.00 |
| *J21* | D1 | 3p violet ('37) | 1.25 | 90 |
| *J22* | D1 | 4p slate green | 4.25 | 5.25 |
| *J23* | D1 | 5p bister | 5.25 | 4.50 |
| *a.* | | 5p orange brown ('37) | 25.00 | 17.50 |
| *J24* | D1 | 1sh blue ('36) | 3.75 | 4.25 |
| *J25* | D2 | 2sh6p brn, *yel* ('37) | 100.00 | 14.00 |
| | | *Nos. J18-J25 (8)* | 119.90 | 33.70 |

**1938-39 Wmk. 251**

| | | | | |
|---|---|---|---|---|
| *J26* | D1 | ½p emerald | 2.75 | 2.25 |
| *J27* | D1 | 1p carmine rose | 1.00 | 40 |
| *J28* | D1 | 2p black brown | 1.00 | 60 |
| *J29* | D1 | 3p violet | 1.10 | 20 |
| *J30* | D1 | 4p slate green | 27.50 | 6.50 |
| *J31* | D1 | 5p bister ('39) | 3.25 | 35 |
| *J32* | D1 | 1sh blue | 11.50 | 1.00 |
| *J33* | D2 | 2sh6p brn, *yel* ('39) | 32.50 | 2.00 |
| | | *Nos. J26-J33 (8)* | 80.60 | 13.30 |

**Catalogue values for unused stamps in this section, from this point to the end of the section, are for Never Hinged items.**

**1951-52**

| | | | | |
|---|---|---|---|---|
| *J34* | D1 | ½p orange | 1.25 | 1.25 |
| *J35* | D1 | 1p violet blue | 2.75 | 52 |
| *J36* | D1 | 1½p green ('52) | 2.75 | 2.00 |
| *J37* | D1 | 4p bright blue | 13.00 | 6.50 |
| *J38* | D1 | 1sh olive bister | 35.00 | 6.50 |
| | | *Nos. J34-J38 (5)* | 54.75 | 16.77 |

**1954-55 Wmk. 298**

| | | | | |
|---|---|---|---|---|
| *J39* | D1 | ½p orange ('55) | 3.75 | 3.75 |
| *J40* | D1 | 2p brn black ('55) | 3.75 | 1.50 |
| *J41* | D1 | 3p purple ('55) | 62.50 | 21.00 |
| *J42* | D1 | 4p brt blue ('55) | 19.00 | 8.50 |
| *a.* | | Imperf., pair | 250.00 | |
| *J43* | D1 | 5p bister brn ('55) | 17.50 | 10.00 |
| *J44* | D2 | 2sh6p dk pur brn, *yel* | 125.00 | 8.00 |
| | | *Nos. J39-J44 (6)* | 231.50 | 52.75 |

**1955-57 Wmk. 308 *Perf. 14x14½***

| | | | | |
|---|---|---|---|---|
| *J45* | D1 | ½p orange ('56) | 5.75 | 2.75 |
| *J46* | D1 | 1p ultra ('56) | 4.75 | 85 |
| *J47* | D1 | 1½p green ('56) | 9.25 | 2.00 |
| *J48* | D1 | 2p brn blk ('56) | 17.00 | 5.75 |
| *J49* | D1 | 3p purple ('56) | 5.75 | 2.00 |
| *J50* | D1 | 4p brt bl ('56) | 22.50 | 4.75 |
| *J51* | D1 | 5p bis brn ('56) | 22.50 | 2.75 |
| *J52* | D1 | 1sh dp olive bis | 22.00 | 2.75 |
| *J53* | D2 | 2sh6p dk red brn, *yel* ('57) | 200.00 | 9.50 |
| *J54* | D2 | 5sh red, *yellow* | 85.00 | 14.00 |
| | | *Nos. J45-J54 (10)* | 394.50 | 47.10 |

**1959-63 Wmk. 322 *Perf. 14x14½***

| | | | | |
|---|---|---|---|---|
| *J55* | D1 | ½p orange ('61) | 22 | 16 |
| *J56* | D1 | 1p ultra ('60) | 16 | 6 |
| *J57* | D1 | 1½p green ('60) | 1.65 | 1.65 |
| *J58* | D1 | 2p brown black | 85 | 22 |
| *J59* | D1 | 3p purple | 60 | 8 |
| *J60* | D1 | 4p brt blue ('60) | 60 | 12 |
| *J61* | D1 | 5p bis brown ('62) | 85 | 16 |
| *J62* | D1 | 6p deep mag ('62) | 85 | 10 |
| *J63* | D1 | 1sh dp ol bis ('60) | 1.10 | 22 |
| *J64* | D2 | 2sh6p dark red brown, *yellow* ('61) | 2.00 | 42 |
| *J65* | D2 | 5sh red, *yel* ('61) | 2.50 | 60 |
| *J66* | D2 | 10sh ultra, *yel* ('63) | 12.50 | 2.00 |
| *J67* | D2 | £1 *yellow* ('63) | 42.50 | 2.75 |
| | | *Nos. J55-J67 (13)* | 66.38 | 8.54 |

Nos. J1-J67 are watermarked sideways.

***Perf. 14x14½***

**1968-69 Unwmk. Typo.**

| | | | | |
|---|---|---|---|---|
| *J68* | D1 | 2p greenish black | 1.00 | 25 |
| *J69* | D1 | 3p purple | 75 | 15 |
| *J70* | D1 | 4p bright blue | 90 | 25 |
| *J71* | D1 | 5p brown org ('69) | 8.00 | 8.00 |
| *J72* | D1 | 6p deep magenta | 1.50 | 40 |
| *J73* | D1 | 1sh bister ('69) | 2.00 | 35 |
| | | *Nos. J68-J73 (6)* | 14.15 | 9.40 |

**1968-69 Photo.**

| | | | | |
|---|---|---|---|---|
| *J74* | D1 | 4p bright blue ('69) | 6.50 | 2.50 |
| *J75* | D1 | 8p bright red | 1.75 | 40 |

D3

D4

***Perf. 14x14½***

**1970-75 Photo. Unwmk.**

| | | | | |
|---|---|---|---|---|
| *J79* | D3 | ½p grnsh bl ('71) | 5 | 5 |
| *J80* | D3 | 1p magenta ('71) | 5 | 5 |
| *J81* | D3 | 2p green ('71) | 7 | 8 |
| *J82* | D3 | 3p ultra ('71) | 8 | 8 |
| *J83* | D3 | 4p olive bis ('71) | 12 | 10 |
| *J84* | D3 | 5p bluish lil ('71) | 14 | 12 |
| *J85* | D3 | 7p brown red ('74) | 20 | 18 |
| *J86* | D4 | 10p carmine rose | 28 | 12 |
| *J87* | D4 | 11p slate ('75) | 32 | 12 |
| *J88* | D4 | 20p olive | 55 | 25 |
| *J89* | D4 | 50p ultramarine | 1.50 | 55 |
| *J90* | D4 | £1 black | 3.00 | 1.10 |
| *J91* | D4 | £5 org & blk ('73) | 15.00 | 5.00 |
| | | *Nos. J79-J91 (13)* | 21.36 | 7.80 |

D5

**1982, June 9 Photo. *Perf. 14x14½***

| | | | | |
|---|---|---|---|---|
| *J92* | D5 | 1p rose carmine | 5 | 5 |
| *J93* | D5 | 2p ultramarine | 8 | 5 |
| *J94* | D5 | 3p deep rose lil | 10 | 6 |
| *J95* | D5 | 4p dark blue | 12 | 8 |
| *J96* | D5 | 5p sepia | 16 | 8 |
| *J97* | D5 | 10p brown | 32 | 16 |
| *J98* | D5 | 20p dark ol green | 48 | 32 |
| *J99* | D5 | 25p slate blue | 70 | 40 |
| *J100* | D5 | 50p black | 1.40 | 80 |
| *J101* | D5 | £1 vermilion | 2.50 | 1.50 |
| *J102* | D5 | £2 greenish blue | 4.75 | 3.25 |
| *J103* | D5 | £5 yellow bister | 12.00 | 6.25 |
| | | *Nos. J92-J103 (12)* | 22.66 | 13.00 |

## OFFICIAL STAMPS

Type of Regular Issue of 1840
"V R" in Upper Corners

**1840 Wmk. 18 *Imperf.***

*O1* A1 1p black *7,000.*

No. O1 was never placed in use.

Postage stamps perforated with a crown and initials "H.M.O.W.," "O.W.," "B.T." or "S.O.," or with only the initials "H.M.S.O." or "D.S.I.R.," were used for official purposes.

Counterfeits exist of Nos. O2-O83.

### Inland Revenue

Regular Issues Overprinted in Black:

I.R. OFFICIAL — a
I. R. OFFICIAL — b

Type "a" is overprinted on the stamps of ½ penny to 1 shilling inclusive, type "b" on the higher values.

**1882-85 Wmk. 30 *Perf. 14***

| | | | | |
|---|---|---|---|---|
| *O2* | A35 | ½p green | 9.00 | 85 |
| *O3* | A35 | ½p slate bl ('85) | 14.00 | 85 |
| *O4* | A40 | 1p lilac | 1.00 | 15 |
| *a.* | | "OFFICIAL" omitted | | *3,750.* |
| *b.* | | Ovpt. lines transposed | | |
| *O5* | A47 | 2½p lilac ('85) | 55.00 | 17.50 |
| *O6* | A28 | 6p gray | 100.00 | 10.00 |
| *O7* | A48 | 1sh green ('85) | *3,000.* | 425.00 |

**Wmk. 31**

| | | | | |
|---|---|---|---|---|
| *O8* | A51 | 5sh car rose ('85) | 1,500. | 300.00 |
| *a.* | | Bluish paper ('85) | *2,750.* | *450.00* |
| *O9* | A52 | 10sh ultramarine | *2,500.* | 465.00 |
| *a.* | | 10sh cobalt | *5,000.* | *750.* |
| *b.* | | Bluish paper | *6,000.* | *1,500.* |

**Wmk. Three Imperial Crowns (30)**

*O10* A53 £1 brown violet *20,000.* *4,000.*

**1888-89 Wmk. 30**

| | | | | |
|---|---|---|---|---|
| *O11* | A54 | ½p vermilion | 1.10 | 18 |
| *a.* | | "I.R." omitted | *2,250.* | |
| *O12* | A65 | 1sh green ('89) | 145.00 | 15.00 |

**1890 Wmk. Three Orbs (29)**

*O13* A53 £1 brn vio *20,000.* *4,000.*

**1891 Wmk. 30**

*O14* A57 2½p violet, *blue* 55.00 1.75

**Wmk. Three Imperial Crowns (30)**

**1892**

| | | | | |
|---|---|---|---|---|
| *O15* | A53 | £1 green | *3,750.* | 400.00 |
| *a.* | | No period after "R" | *9,000.* | *1,000.* |

**1901 Wmk. 30**

| | | | | |
|---|---|---|---|---|
| *O16* | A54 | ½p blue green | 4.00 | 50 |
| *O17* | A62 | 6p violet, *rose* | 100.00 | 7.50 |
| *O18* | A65 | 1sh car rose & grn | 525.00 | 75.00 |

**1902-04**

| | | | | |
|---|---|---|---|---|
| *O19* | A66 | ½p gray green | 5.00 | 75 |
| *O20* | A66 | 1p carmine | 3.50 | 25 |
| *O21* | A66 | 2½p ultra | 550.00 | 65.00 |
| *O22* | A66 | 6p dl vio ('04) | *80,000.* | |
| *O23* | A74 | 1sh car rose & grn | 475.00 | 75.00 |

**Wmk. 31**

| | | | | |
|---|---|---|---|---|
| *O24* | A76 | 5sh car rose | *4,500.* | *1,750.* |
| *O25* | A77 | 10sh ultra | *22,500.* | *15,000.* |

**Wmk. Three Imperial Crowns. (30)**

*O26* A78 £1 green *17,500.* *6,500.*

Nos. O4, O8, O9 and O15 also exist with overprint in blue black.

### Government Parcels

Overprinted GOVT PARCELS

**1883-86 Wmk. 30**

| | | | | |
|---|---|---|---|---|
| *O27* | A45 | 1½p lilac ('86) | 80.00 | 18.00 |
| *O28* | A46 | 6p green ('86) | 350.00 | 52.50 |
| *O29* | A50 | 9p green | 550. | 150.00 |
| *O30* | A29 | 1sh salmon (P13) | 425.00 | 57.50 |
| | | Plate 14 | 750. | 85.00 |

**1887-92**

| | | | | |
|---|---|---|---|---|
| *O31* | A55 | 1½p violet & grn | 15.00 | 1.00 |
| *O32* | A56 | 2p green & carmine rose ('91) | 60.00 | 2.25 |
| *O33* | A60 | 4½p carmine rose & green ('92) | 85.00 | 47.50 |
| *O34* | A62 | 6p violet, *rose* | 42.50 | 3.75 |
| *O35* | A63 | 9p bl & lil ('88) | 80.00 | 8.25 |
| *O36* | A65 | 1sh green | 175.00 | 32.50 |

**1897**

| | | | | |
|---|---|---|---|---|
| *O37* | A40 | 1p lilac | 6.00 | 30 |
| *a.* | | Inverted ovpt. | 900. | 425.00 |

**1900**

| | | | | |
|---|---|---|---|---|
| *O38* | A65 | 1sh car rose & grn | 160.00 | 35.00 |
| *a.* | | Inverted overprint | | *6,000.* |

**1902**

| | | | | |
|---|---|---|---|---|
| *O39* | A66 | 1p carmine | 10.00 | 5.00 |
| *O40* | A68 | 2p green & car | 67.50 | 11.00 |
| *O41* | A66 | 6p dull violet | 150.00 | 7.00 |
| *O42* | A72 | 9p ultra & violet | 250.00 | 32.50 |
| *O43* | A74 | 1sh car rose & grn | 400.00 | 62.50 |

### Office of Works

Overprinted O.W. OFFICIAL

**1896**

| | | | | |
|---|---|---|---|---|
| *O44* | A54 | ½p vermilion | 40.00 | 10.00 |
| *O45* | A40 | 1p lilac | 45.00 | 7.00 |

**1901-02**

| | | | | |
|---|---|---|---|---|
| *O46* | A54 | ½p blue green | 47.50 | 25.00 |
| *O47* | A61 | 5p lilac & ultra | 650. | 175.00 |
| *O48* | A64 | 10p car rose & lil | 900. | 375.00 |

**1902**

| | | | | |
|---|---|---|---|---|
| *O49* | A66 | ½p gray green | 100.00 | 65.00 |
| *O50* | A66 | 1p carmine | 150.00 | 42.50 |
| *O51* | A68 | 2p grn & carmine | 400.00 | 100.00 |
| *O52* | A66 | 2½p ultramarine | 750. | 125.00 |
| *O53* | A73 | 10p car rose & vio | *4,000.* | 900. |

### Army

Overprinted:

ARMY OFFICIAL — a
ARMY OFFICIAL — b

**1896**

| | | | | |
|---|---|---|---|---|
| *O54* | A54(a) | ½p vermilion | 1.50 | 50 |
| *a.* | | "OFFICIAI" | 30.00 | 16.00 |
| *O55* | A40(a) | 1p lilac | 1.25 | 18 |
| *a.* | | "OFFICIAI" | 30.00 | 15.00 |
| *O56* | A57(b) | 2½p violet, *bl* | 5.00 | 1.25 |

**1900**

*O57* A54(a) ½p blue green 1.50 30

**1901**

*O58* A62(b) 6p violet, *rose* 12.50 4.75

**1902**

| | | | | |
|---|---|---|---|---|
| *O59* | A66(a) | ½p gray green | 1.10 | 18 |
| *O60* | A66(a) | 1p carmine | 1.10 | 15 |
| *a.* | | "ARMY" omitted | | |
| *O61* | A66(a) | 6p dl violet | 50.00 | 21.00 |

Overprinted ARMY OFFICIAL

**1903**

*O62* A66 6p dull violet 1,600. 500.00

### Royal Household

Overprinted R.H. OFFICIAL

**1902**

| | | | | |
|---|---|---|---|---|
| *O63* | A66 | ½p gray green | 125.00 | 110.00 |
| *O64* | A66 | 1p carmine | 110.00 | 90.00 |

### Board of Education

Overprinted BOARD OF EDUCATION

**1902**

| | | | | |
|---|---|---|---|---|
| *O65* | A61 | 5p lilac & ultra | 500.00 | 75.00 |
| *O66* | A65 | 1sh car rose & grn | 1,300. | 400.00 |

**1902-04**

| | | | | |
|---|---|---|---|---|
| *O67* | A66 | ½p gray green | 21.00 | 2.50 |
| *O68* | A66 | 1p carmine | 18.00 | 2.50 |
| *O69* | A66 | 2½p ultramarine | 400.00 | 60.00 |
| *O70* | A71 | 5p lilac & ultra ('04) | 1,750. | 425.00 |
| *O71* | A74 | 1sh carmine rose & green | *30,000.* | *15,000.* |

### Admiralty

Overprinted ADMIRALTY OFFICIAL

**1903**

| | | | | |
|---|---|---|---|---|
| *O72* | A66 | ½p gray green | 10.50 | 2.25 |
| *O73* | A66 | 1p carmine | 6.50 | 1.25 |
| *O74* | A67 | 1½p vio & green | 65.00 | 30.00 |
| *O75* | A68 | 2p green & car | 80.00 | 35.00 |
| *O76* | A66 | 2½p ultra | 70.00 | 35.00 |
| *O77* | A69 | 3p vio, *yel* | 110.00 | 30.00 |

Overprinted ADMIRALTY OFFICIAL

**1903**

| | | | | |
|---|---|---|---|---|
| *O78* | A66 | ½p gray green | 10.00 | 2.50 |
| *O79* | A66 | 1p carmine | 6.50 | 2.50 |
| *O80* | A67 | 1½p vio & green | 225.00 | 50.00 |
| *O81* | A68 | 2p green & car | 450.00 | 150.00 |
| *O82* | A66 | 2½p ultramarine | 900. | 300.00 |
| *O83* | A69 | 3p violet, *yel* | 450.00 | 50.00 |

The two types of the "Admiralty Official" overprint differ principally in the shape of the letter "M".

*Great Britain Regional Issues can be mounted in Scott's Great Britain Album.*

## ENVELOPES

Britannia Sending Letters to World (William Mulready, Designer) — E1

**1840**

| | | | | |
|---|---|---|---|---|
| *U1* | E1 | 1p black | 90.00 | 100.00 |
| *U2* | E1 | 2p blue | 145.00 | 375.00 |

## LETTER SHEETS

| | | | | |
|---|---|---|---|---|
| *U3* | E1 | 1p black | 90.00 | 95.00 |
| *U4* | E1 | 2p blue | 145.00 | 350.00 |

## REGIONAL ISSUES

Sold only at post offices within the respective regions, but valid for postage throughout Great Britain. Issues for Guernsey and Jersey were withdrawn Sept. 30, 1970.

Starting in 1967, all Regional stamps were issued only with phosphorescence.

### Guernsey

Guernsey Lily and Crown of William the Conqueror
A1 A2

***Perf. 14½x14***

**1958-69 Photo. Wmk. 322**

| | | | | |
|---|---|---|---|---|
| *1* | A1 | 2½p rose red ('64) | 35 | 25 |
| *2* | A2 | 3p light purple | 35 | 12 |
| *p.* | | Phosphor. ('67) | 15 | 10 |
| *3* | A2 | 4p ultra ('66) | 35 | 12 |
| *p.* | | Phosphor. ('67) | 18 | 10 |

**Unwmk.**

| | | | | |
|---|---|---|---|---|
| *4* | A2 | 4p ultra ('68) | 18 | 8 |
| *5* | A2 | 4p ol brown ('68) | 18 | 8 |
| *6* | A2 | 4p brt red ('69) | 20 | 8 |
| *7* | A2 | 5p dark blue ('68) | 20 | 10 |
| | | *Nos. 1-7 (7)* | 1.81 | 83 |

Nos. 4-7 are phosphorescent.

Issues of the Guernsey independent postal administration are listed after the Wales and Monmouthshire Regional Issues.

### Jersey

Royal Mace and Arms of Jersey
A1 A2

***Perf. 14½x14***

**1958-69 Photo. Wmk. 322**

| | | | | |
|---|---|---|---|---|
| *1* | A1 | 2½p rose red ('64) | 35 | 25 |
| *2* | A2 | 3p light purple | 35 | 12 |
| *p.* | | Phosphor. ('67) | 15 | 8 |
| *3* | A2 | 4p ultra ('66) | 35 | 10 |
| *p.* | | Phosphor. ('67) | 18 | 8 |

**Unwmk.**

| | | | | |
|---|---|---|---|---|
| *4* | A2 | 4p ol brown ('68) | 18 | 8 |
| *5* | A2 | 4p brt red ('69) | 20 | 6 |
| *6* | A2 | 5p dark blue ('68) | 20 | 6 |
| | | *Nos. 1-6 (6)* | 1.63 | 67 |

Nos. 4-6 are phosphorescent.

Issues of the Jersey independent postal administration are listed after the Guernsey independent issues which follow the Wales and Monmouthshire Regional Issues.

## Man, Isle of

Manx Emblem
A1 A2 A3

*Perf. 14½x14*

**1958-69 Photo. Wmk. 322**
1 A1 2½p rose red ('64) 55 40
2 A2 3p purple 15 8
p. Phosphor. ('68) 15 10
3 A2 4p ultra ('66) 1.25 22
p. Phosphor. ('67) 18 10

**Unwmk.**
4 A2 4p ultra ('68) 15 8
5 A2 4p ol brown ('68) 15 10
6 A2 4p brt red ('69) 60 25
7 A2 5p dark bl ('68) 60 16
*Nos. 1-7 (7)* 3.45 1.29

Nos. 4-7 are phosphorescent.
A 1963 printing of No. 2 is on chalky paper.

**1971, July 7 Photo. Unwmk.**
8 A3 2½p bright pink 35 10
9 A3 3p ultramarine 38 15
10 A3 5p bluish lilac 48 55
11 A3 7½p light red brn 65 65

Issues of the independent Isle of Man postal administration are listed after the Jersey independent issues.

## Northern Ireland

Flax and Red Hand of Ulster
A1 A2

Designs: 6p, 9p, Flax plant and Red Right Hand of Ulster. 1sh3p, 1sh6p, Flax plant, Red Right Hand of Ulster and Ulster field gate.

*Perf. 14½x14*

**1958-67 Photo. Wmk. 322**
1 A1 3p dark purple 15 6
p. Phosphor. ('67) 15 5
2 A1 4p ultra ('66) 15 8
p. Phosphor. ('67) 15 6
3 A1 6p rose lilac 30 8
4 A1 9p dk grn ('67) 35 8
5 A1 1sh3p dark green 32 12
6 A1 1sh6p dark blue ('67) 35 15
*Nos. 1-6 (6)* 1.62 57

Nos. 4, 6 and following are phosphorescent.

**1968-69 Unwmk.**

Design: 1sh6p, Flax plant, Red Right Hand of Ulster and Ulster field gate.

7 A1 4p ultramarine 18 8
8 A1 4p olive brown 15 8
9 A1 4p brt red ('69) 32 8
10 A1 5p dark blue 20 8
11 A1 1sh6p dk blue ('69) 3.50 1.65
*Nos. 7-11 (5)* 4.35 1.97

**1971-80 Photo. *Perf. 14½x14***
12 A2 2½p bright pink 1.25 20
13 A2 3p ultramarine 60 6
14 A2 3½p dk ol grn ('74) 30 10
15 A2 4½p dark blue ('74) 30 14
16 A2 5p bluish lilac 2.25 80
17 A2 5½p dark vio ('74) 32 15
18 A2 6½p Prus blue ('76) 32 15
19 A2 7p red brown ('78) 32 15
20 A2 7½p light red brown 3.25 1.40
21 A2 8p red ('74) 35 25
22 A2 8½p yel green ('76) 32 25
23 A2 9p violet bl ('78) 38 25
24 A2 10p org brown ('76) 42 30
25 A2 10½p steel blue ('78) 42 30
26 A2 11p red ('76) 48 35
27 A2 12p yel green ('80) 50 24
28 A2 13½p dk red brn ('80) 75 28
29 A2 15p ultra ('80) 60 30
*Nos. 12-29 (18)* 13.13 5.67

The 5½p with two phosphorescent bands was issued in 1974; with one center band in 1975.

**1981, Apr. 8 Photo. *Perf. 14***
30 A2 11½p olive gray 60 22
31 A2 14p gray violet 65 24
32 A2 18p blue violet 75 35
33 A2 22p dark blue 1.00 45

**1982, Feb. 24 Litho. *Perf. 14***
34 A2 12½p emerald 55 25
35 A2 15½p light violet 80 35
36 A2 19½p olive green 2.00 40
37 A2 26p red 95 52
a. Perf. 15x14 ('87) 95 52

**1983, Mar. 30 Litho. *Perf. 14***
38 A2 16p dull brown 85 25
39 A2 20½p ultramarine 90 32
40 A2 28p deep violet 1.00 42
a. Perf. 15x14 ('87) 1.00 42

**1984, Oct. 23 Litho. *Perf. 15x14***
41 A2 13p pale salmon 48 15
42 A2 17p light bl gray 60 20
43 A2 22p yellow green 70 25
44 A2 31p deep magenta 1.00 35

**1986, Jan. 7 Litho. *Perf. 15x14***
45 A2 12p green 38 18

## Scotland

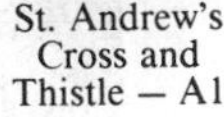

St. Andrew's Cross and Thistle — A1

Scottish Lion Rampant — A2

Designs: 6p, 9p, Thistle in each upper corner. 1sh3p, 1sh6p, Unicorns holding flags with lion rampant and St. Andrew's Cross.

*Perf. 14½x14*

**1958-67 Photo. Wmk. 322**
1 A1 3p dark purple 15 6
p. Phosphor. 15 5
2 A1 4p ultra ('66) 15 8
p. Phosphor. ('67) 15 8
3 A1 6p rose lilac 22 6
p. Phosphor. ('63) 25 10
4 A1 9p dark grn ('67) 32 14
5 A1 1sh3p dark green 32 15
p. Phosphor. ('63) 32 15
6 A1 1sh6p dark blue ('67) 32 22
*Nos. 1-6 (6)* 1.48 71

The 3p with two phosphorescent bands was issued in 1963; with one side band in 1965, and one center band in 1967. The value of No. 1p is for one center band. Nos. 4, 6 and following are phosphorescent.

**1967-70 Unwmk.**

Designs: 9p, Thistle in each upper corner. 1sh6p, Unicorns holding flags with lion rampant and St. Andrew's Cross.

7 A1 3p purple ('68) 15 6
8 A1 4p ultramarine 18 7
9 A1 4p ol brown ('68) 18 7
10 A1 4p brt red ('69) 18 7
11 A1 5p dark blue ('68) 28 7
12 A1 9p dark grn ('70) 7.50 4.25
13 A1 1sh6p dark blue ('68) 1.40 85
*Nos. 7-13 (7)* 9.87 5.44

**1971-80 Photo. *Perf. 14½x14***
14 A2 2½p bright pink 32 5
15 A2 3p ultramarine 42 6
16 A2 3½p dk ol grn ('74) 32 10
17 A2 4½p dark blue ('74) 32 14
18 A2 5p bluish lilac 2.25 80
19 A2 5½p dark vio ('74) 32 15
20 A2 6½p Prus blue ('76) 32 15
21 A2 7p red brown ('78) 32 15
22 A2 7½p light red brown 2.50 1.10
23 A2 8p red ('74) 48 25
24 A2 8½p yel green ('76) 48 25
25 A2 9p violet bl ('78) 48 25
26 A2 10p orange brn ('76) 48 20
27 A2 10½p steel blue ('78) 48 30
28 A2 11p red ('76) 48 32
29 A2 12p yel green ('80) 48 24
30 A2 13½p dk red brn ('80) 75 28
31 A2 15p ultra ('80) 60 30
*Nos. 14-31 (18)* 11.80 5.09

The 5½p with two phosphorescent bands was issued in 1974; with one center band in 1975.

**1981, Apr. 8 Photo. *Perf. 14***
32 A2 11½p olive gray 60 22
33 A2 14p gray violet 60 24
34 A2 18p blue violet 72 35
35 A2 22p dark blue 1.00 45

**1981, Feb. 24 Litho. *Perf. 14***
36 A2 12½p emerald 60 25
37 A2 15½p light violet 80 35
38 A2 19½p olive green 2.25 40
39 A2 26p red 95 52
a. Perf. 15x14 ('87) 95 52

**1983, Mar. 30 Litho. *Perf. 14***
40 A2 16p dull brown 60 25
41 A2 20½p ultramarine 90 32
42 A2 28p deep violet 95 42
a. Perf. 15x14 ('87) 95 42

**1984, Oct. 23 Litho. *Perf. 14***
43 A2 13p pale salmon 50 15
44 A2 17p lt blue gray 70 20
a. Perf. 15x14 ('86) 70 20
45 A2 22p yellow green 75 25
a. Perf. 15x14 ('87) 90 45
46 A2 31p deep magenta 1.00 35
a. Perf. 15x14 ('86) 1.00 35

**1986, Jan. 7 Litho. *Perf. 14***
47 A2 12p green 52 18
a. Perf. 15x14 52 18

Issue date of Nos. 44a, 46a, 47a, Apr. 29.

## Wales and Monmouthshire

Welsh Dragon
A1 A2

Designs: 6p, 9p, Dragon in rectangular panel at bottom. 1sh3p, 1sh6p, Dragon and leek.

*Perf. 14½x14*

**1958-67 Photo. Wmk. 322**
1 A1 3p dark purple 15 6
p. Phosphor. band ('67) 15 12
2 A1 4p ultra ('66) 18 12
p. Phosphor. bands ('67) 18 8
3 A1 6p rose lilac 40 30
4 A1 9p dark grn ('67) 32 15
5 A1 1sh3p dark green 32 15
6 A1 1sh6p dark blue ('67) 32 20
*Nos. 1-6 (6)* 1.69 98

Nos. 4, 6 and following are phosphorescent.

**1967-69 Unwmk.**
7 A1 3p dark purple 15 6
8 A1 4p ultra ('68) 15 6
9 A1 4p ol brown ('68) 15 6
10 A1 4p brt red ('69) 18 6
11 A1 5p dark bl ('68) 22 6
12 A1 1sh6p dark bl ('69) 3.25 2.50
*Nos. 7-12 (6)* 4.10 2.80

**1971-80 Photo. *Perf. 14½x14***
13 A2 2½p bright pink 18 5
14 A2 3p ultramarine 32 6
15 A2 3½p dk ol grn ('74) 28 10
16 A2 4½p dark blue ('74) 28 14
17 A2 5p bluish lilac 2.00 65
18 A2 5½p dk violet ('74) 32 15
19 A2 6½p Prus blue ('76) 32 15
20 A2 7p red brown ('78) 32 15
21 A2 7½p light red brown 2.75 1.40
22 A2 8p red ('74) 40 25
23 A2 8½p yel green ('76) 40 25
24 A2 9p violet bl ('78) 42 25
25 A2 10p org brown ('76) 42 30
26 A2 10½p steel blue ('78) 42 30
27 A2 11p red ('76) 48 32
28 A2 12p yel green ('80) 48 24
29 A2 13½p dk red brn ('80) 70 28
30 A2 15p ultra ('80) 60 30
*Nos. 13-30 (18)* 11.09 5.34

The 5½p with two phosphorescent bands was issued in 1974; with one center band in 1975.

**1981, Apr. 8 Photo. *Perf. 14***
31 A2 11½p olive gray 60 22
32 A2 14p gray violet 65 24
33 A2 18p blue violet 72 35
34 A2 22p dark blue 1.00 45

**1982, Feb. 24 Litho. *Perf. 14***
35 A2 12½p emerald 55 25
a. Perf. 15x14 55 25
36 A2 15½p light violet 80 35
37 A2 19½p olive green 2.25 40
38 A2 26p red 95 52
a. Perf. 15x14 ('87) 95 52

**1983, Mar. 30 Litho. *Perf. 14***
39 A2 16p dull brown 90 25
a. Perf. 15x14 90 25
40 A2 20½p ultramarine 95 32
41 A2 28p deep violet 1.00 42
a. Perf. 15x14 ('87) 1.00 42

**1984, Oct. 23 Litho. *Perf. 15x14***
42 A2 13p pale salmon 48 15
43 A2 17p lt blue gray 55 20
44 A2 22p yellow green 70 25
45 A2 31p deep magenta 95 35

**1986, Jan. 7 Litho. *Perf. 15x14***
46 A2 12p green 38 18

# GUERNSEY

LOCATION — A group of islands in the English Channel.
GOVT. — Dependent territory (bailiwick) of the British Crown.
AREA — 30 sq. mi.
POP. — 53,313 (1981)
CAPITAL — St. Peter Port

The bailiwick includes the islands of Guernsey, Alderney, Sark, Herm, Jethou and Lithou.

Following the establishment of the British General Post Office as a public corporation on October 1, 1969, the post office of the Bailiwick of Guernsey became a separate entity and British postage stamps ceased to be valid.

Between 1958-69, Great Britain issued seven stamps that were sold only in Guernsey and intended for use there. These are listed under "Regional Issues" following Envelopes and Letter Sheets in the Great Britain section.

William the Conqueror, Queen Elizabeth II and Map of Bailiwick — A3

Creux Harbor, Sark
A4

Designs (Queen Elizabeth II and): ½p, Castle Cornet and Edward the Confessor. 1½p, Martello Tower and Henry II. 2p, Arms of Sark and King John. 3p, Arms of Alderney and Edward III. 4p, Guernsey lily and Henry V. 5p, Arms of Guernsey and Queen Elizabeth I. 6p, Arms of Alderney and Charles II. 9p, Arms of Sark and George III. 1sh, Arms of Guernsey and Queen Victoria. 1sh6p, Map of Bailiwick and William I. 1sh9p, Guernsey lily and Queen Elizabeth I. 2sh6p, Martello Tower and King John. 10sh, Braye Harbor, Alderney. £1, St. Peter Port, Guernsey.

*Perf. 14½x14*

**1969, Oct. 1 Photo. Unwmk.**
8 A3 ½p mag & blk 12 12
9 A3 1p ultra & blk 12 12
10 A3 1½p bis & blk 12 12
11 A3 2p dk bl & multi 12 12
12 A3 3p dp org & multi 16 16

## ISLE OF MAN

Unwatermarked

1973-75

No. 12

No. 13

No. 14

No. 15

No. 16

No. 17

No. 18

No. 19

*13* A3 4p yel grn & multi 16 16
*a* Booklet pane of 1 40 40
*14* A3 5p vio bl & multi 24 24
*a* Booklet pane of 1 80 80
*15* A3 6p ol grn & multi 28 28
*16* A3 9p plum & multi 48 48
*17* A3 1sh dk ol & multi 80 80
*18* A3 1sh6p bl grn & blk 2.00 2.00
*19* A3 1sh9p mag & multi 3.00 2.00
*20* A3 2sh6p pur & blk 8.00 3.25

***Perf. 12½***

*21* A4 5sh multi 5.50 4.00
*22* A4 10sh multi 32.50 27.50
*a* Perf. 13½x13 90.00 80.00
*23* A4 £1 multi 11.00 10.00
*a* Perf. 13½x13 3.25 3.25
*Nos. 8-23 (16)* 64.60 51.35

See Nos. 28-29, 41-55.

Seven denominations of the 1969 regular series were re-issued in 1970 with phosphorescence: 2p, 3p, 6p, 9p, 1sh, 1sh9p and 2sh6p.

Col. Isaac Brock — A5

Designs: 5p, Sir Isaac Brock as major general. 1sh9p, as ensign, flags of 1789 and 1969. 2sh6p, Regimental coat of arms and flags (horiz.).

***Perf. 14x13½, 13½x14***

**1969, Dec. 1 Litho. Unwmk.**

*24* A5 4p multi 35 18
*25* A5 5p blk & multi 38 18
*26* A5 1sh9p dp bl & multi 2.25 2.00
*27* A5 2sh6p pur & multi 2.50 2.50

Sir Isaac Brock (1769-1812), born on Guernsey, commander of Quebec garrison.

**Map Type of 1969 Redrawn**

**1969-70 Photo. *Perf. 14½x14***

*28* A3 1p ultra & blk ("49o 30'N") 16 14
*a* Booklet pane of 1 28 28
*29* A3 1sh6p bl, grn & blk ("49o 30'N") 8.50 2.75

Nos. 28-29 were issued Feb. 4, 1970. No. 28a was issued Dec. 12, 1969, in booklets containing also Nos. 13 and 14 in panes of 1.

Nos. 9 and 18 are inscribed "40o 30' N".

Destroyer "Bulldog" near Castle Cornet — A6

Designs: 5p, Liberation fleet in roadsteads between Guernsey, Herm and Jethou. 1sh6p, Brigadier A. E. Snow reading proclamation of King George VI on steps of Elizabeth College in Guernsey (vert.).

**1970, May 9 Photo. *Perf. 11½***

*30* A6 4p vio bl & lt bl 65 32
*31* A6 5p dp plum & gray 85 40
*32* A6 1sh6p dk brn & bis 4.00 4.00

25th anniv. of Guernsey's liberation from the Germans.

Guernsey Cow — A7

**1970, Aug. 12 Photo. *Perf. 11½***

*33* A7 4p Tomatoes 1.50 60
*34* A7 5p shown 1.50 90
*35* A7 9p Guernsey bull 15.00 10.50
*36* A7 1sh6p Freesias 22.50 11.50

**Christmas Issue**

St. Anne, Alderney — A8

Designs (Churches): 5p, St. Peter, Town Church, Guernsey. 9p, St. Peter, Sark (vert.). 1sh6p, St. Tugual Chapel, Herm (vert.).

**1970, Nov. 11 Photo. *Perf. 11½***

*37* A8 4p bl, gold & brn 55 22
*38* A8 5p brt grn, gold & brn 65 25
*39* A8 9p rose red, gold & brn 1.90 1.65
*40* A8 1sh6p brt pur, gold & brn 3.50 2.50

**Decimal Currency Issue**
**Types of 1969**
**"p" instead of "d"**

Designs: ½p, Castle Cornet and Edward the Confessor. 1p, 5p, Map of Bailiwick and William the Conqueror. 1½p, Martello Tower and Henry II. 2p, Guernsey lily and Henry V. 2½p, Arms of Guernsey and Elizabeth I. 3p, Arms of Alderney and Edward III. 3½p, Guernsey lily and Elizabeth I. 4p, Arms of Sark and King John. 6p, Arms of Alderney and Charles II. 7½p, Arms of Guernsey and Queen Victoria. 9p, Arms of Sark and George III. 10p, Martello Tower and King John. 20p, Creux Harbor. 50p, Braye Harbor.

**1971 Photo. *Perf. 14½x14***

*41* A3 ½p mag & blk 5 5
*a* Booklet pane of 1 5
*42* 1p ultra & blk 6 6
*43* A3 1½p bis & blk 10 10
*44* A3 2p yel grn & multi 12 12
*a* Booklet pane of 1 12
*45* A3 2½p vio bl & multi 15 15
*a* Booklet pane of 1 15
*46* A3 3p dp org & multi 20 20
*47* A3 3½p mag & multi 22 22
*48* A3 4p dk bl & multi 25 25
*49* A3 5p brt grn & multi 32 32
*50* A3 6p dk grn & multi 40 40
*51* A3 7½p brn ol & multi 50 50
*52* A3 9p plum & multi 1.25 1.25
*53* A3 10p pur & blk 1.25 1.25

***Perf. 13***

*54* A4 20p dk red & multi 1.00 1.00
*55* A4 50p multi 2.75 2.75
*Nos. 41-55 (15)* 8.62 8.62

Issue dates: Nos. 53-55, Jan. 6; others Feb. 15.

Thomas de la Rue, Hong Kong No. 1 — A9

Thomas de la Rue and: 2½p, GB No. 22. 4p, Italy No. 26. 7½p, US Confederate States No. 6.

**1971, June 2 Engr. *Perf. 14x13½***

*56* A9 2p brown 45 25
*57* A9 2½p carmine 52 32
*58* A9 4p dk grn 5.00 2.25
*59* A9 7½p vio bl 6.50 3.25

Thomas de la Rue (1793-1866), founder of Thomas de la Rue & Co., Ltd., security printers.

Ebenezer Methodist Church — A10

Historic Churches of Guernsey: 2½p, St. Pierre du Bois. 5p, St. Joseph's (vert.). 7½p, St. Philippe de Torteval (vert.).

**1971, Oct. 27 Photo. *Perf. 11½***

*60* A10 2p grn, sil & blk 80 45
*61* A10 2½p bl, sil & blk 90 55
*62* A10 5p pur, sil & blk 3.25 2.25
*63* A10 7½p red, sil & blk 5.50 4.50

Christmas 1971.

Mail Boat, Earl of Chesterfield, 1794 — A11

**1972, Feb. 10 Photo. *Perf. 11½***

*64* A11 2p *shown* 18 18
*65* A11 2½p *Dasher, 1827* 20 20
*66* A11 7½p *Ibex, 1891* 90 90
*67* A11 9p *Alberta, 1900* 1.50 1.50

See Nos. 77-80.

Guernsey Bull — A12

**1972, May 22 Photo. *Perf. 11½***

*68* A12 5p brn & multi 1.25 90

Guernsey Breeders, 2nd World Conf.

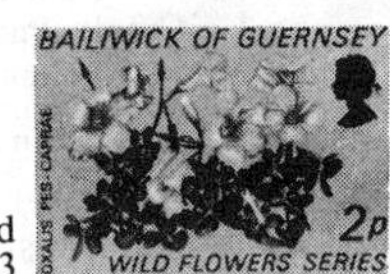

Wild Flowers — A13

**1972, May 24**

*69* A13 2p Sorrel 15 9
*70* A13 2½p Orchis maculata, vert. 18 12
*71* A13 7½p Carpobrotus edulis 90 85
*72* A13 9p Pimpernel, vert. 1.10 90

Angels, St. Martin's Church — A14

Stained Glass Windows from Guernsey Churches: 2½p, Virgin and Child, St. Andre's. 7½p, Virgin Mary, St. Sampson's. 9p, Christ Victorious, St. Pierre's.

**1972, Nov. 20 Photo. *Perf. 11½***

*73* A14 2p brick red & multi 8 8
*74* A14 2½p lt vio & multi 14 14
*75* A14 7½p yel & multi 55 55
*76* A14 9p lt grn & multi 75 75

Christmas 1972 and for the 25th anniv. of the marriage of Queen Elizabeth II and Prince Philip.

**Mail Boat Type of 1972**

**1973, Mar. 9 Photo. *Perf. 11½***

*77* A11 2½p *St. Julien, 1925* 10 10
*78* A11 3p *Isle of Sark, 1932* 14 14
*79* A11 7½p *St. Patrick, 1947* 65 65
*80* A11 9p *Sarnia, 1961* 65 65

No. 78 is incorrectly inscribed "Isle of Guernsey 1930".

Supermarine Sea Eagle — A15

Airplanes: 3p, Westland Wessex. 5p, De Havilland Rapide. 7½p, Douglas Dakota. 9p, Vickers Viscount.

**1973, July 4 Photo. *Perf. 11½***

*81* A15 2½p multi 8 8
*82* A15 3p multi 10 10
*83* A15 5p multi 22 22
*84* A15 7½p multi 45 45
*85* A15 9p multi 55 55
*Nos. 81-85 (5)* 1.40 1.40

50th anniversary of air service to Guernsey.

The Good Shepherd, St. Michel du Valle — A16

Stained-glass Windows from Guernsey Churches: 3p, Jesus preaching, St. Marie du Castel. 7½p, St. Dominic, Notre Dame du Rosaire. 20p, Virgin and Child, St. Sauveur.

**1973, Oct. 24 Photo. *Perf. 11½***

*86* A16 2½p sal & multi 7 7
*87* A16 3p bl & multi 9 9
*88* A16 7½p yel & multi 22 22
*89* A16 20p multi 55 55

Christmas 1973.

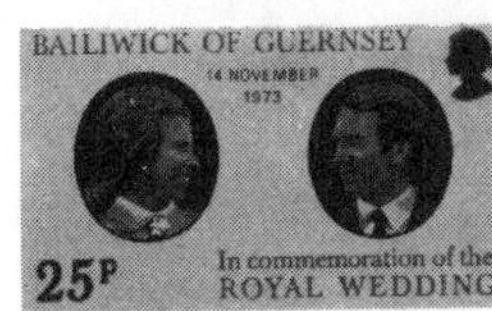

Princess Anne and Mark Phillips — A17

**1973, Nov. 14**

*90* A17 25p bl & multi 80 80

Wedding of Princess Anne and Capt. Mark Phillips, Nov. 14, 1973.

"John Lockett," 1875 — A18

Guernsey Lifeboats: 3p, "Arthur Lionel," 1875. 8p, "Euphrosyne Kendal," 1954. 10p, "Arum," 1972.

**1974, Jan. 15 Photo. *Perf. 11½***
**Granite Paper**

*91* A18 2½p multi 10 10
*92* A18 3p multi 15 15
*93* A18 8p multi 52 52
*94* A18 10p multi 65 65

Sesqui. of Royal Natl. Lifeboat Institution.

Militia, 1815 — A19

Militia, 1814 — A20

**1974-76 Photo. Perf. 11½**
**Granite Paper (Nos. 95-107)**

95 A19 ½p *shown* 5 5
a. Bklt. pane of 8 (5 #95, 3 #99) 40
b. Booklet pane of 16 (4 #95, 6 #99 and 6 #100) 1.25
96 A19 1p *Militia 1825* 5 5
a. Bklt. pane of 8 (4 #96, #100, 2 #102, #102A) ('77) 75
b. Bklt. pane of 4 (#96, 2 #98, #102A) ('78) 36
97 A19 1½p *Militia 1787* 5 5
98 A19 2p *Militia 1815* 7 7
99 A19 2½p *Royal Militia 1868* 8 8
100 A19 3p *Royal Militia 1895* 10 10
101 A19 3½p *Royal Militia 1867* 12 12
102 A19 4p *Militia 1822* 14 14
102A A19 5p *Royal Militia 1895* 35 35
103 A19 5½p *Royal Militia 1833* 18 18
104 A19 6p *Royal Militia 1832* 20 20
104A A19 7p *Militia 1822* 40 40
105 A19 8p *Royal Militia 1868* 25 25
106 A19 9p *Militia 1785* 28 28
107 A19 10p *Militia 1824* 30 30

**Perf. 13x13½, 13½x13**

108 A20 20p *Royal Militia, 1848, vert.* 55 55
109 A20 50p *Royal Militia, 1868, vert.* 1.25 1.25
110 A20 £1 *shown* 2.50 2.50
*Nos. 95-110 (18)* 6.92 6.92

Issue dates: Nos. 95-107, Apr. 2, 1974. Nos. 108-110, Apr. 1, 1975. Nos. 102A, 104A, May 29, 1976.
Stamps in booklet panes are from special sheets of 80 (two 8x5 panes) which were sold separately.

Bailiwick Seal and UPU Emblem — A21

Centenary of Universal Postal Union (UPU Emblem and): 3p, Map of Guernsey. 8p, UPU Headquarters, Bern, flag of Guernsey. 10p, Legislative Chamber, Parliament.

**1974, June 11 Photo. Perf. 11½**
**Granite Paper**

111 A21 2½p multi 8 8
112 A21 3p ultra & multi 10 10
113 A21 8p multi 28 28
114 A21 10p multi 35 35

Cradle Rock, by Renoir A22

Paintings by Renoir: 5½p, Moulin-Huet Bay. 8p, Woman at the Shore (vert.). 10p, Self-portrait (vert.).

**1974, Sept. 21 Photo. Perf. 13**

115 A22 3p multi 8 8
116 A22 5½p multi 14 14
117 A22 8p multi 22 20
118 A22 10p multi 35 32

Pierre Auguste Renoir (1841-1919), who painted pictures shown on Nos. 115-117 while visiting Guernsey.

Guernsey Spleenwort — A23

Designs: Guernsey ferns.

**1975, Jan. 7 Photo. Perf. 11½**

119 A23 3½p *shown* 10 10
120 A23 4p *Sand quillwort* 12 12
121 A23 8p *Guernsey fern* 24 24
122 A23 10p *Least adder's tongue* 30 30

Hauteville, Hugo's House A24

Victor Hugo Statue, Candie Gardens — A25

Designs: 8p, United Europe Oak, Hauteville (planted by Hugo). 10p, Departure for the Hunt, Aubusson tapestry, Hauteville.

**1975, June 6 Photo. Perf. 11½**
**Granite Paper**

123 A24 3½p dl yel & multi 9 9
124 A25 4p lt bl & multi 10 10
125 A25 8p yel grn & multi 22 22
126 A24 10p multi 30 30
a. Souv. sheet of 4, #123-126 1.00 1.00

Victor Hugo (1802-85), French writer, political exile in Guernsey (1855-70). No. 126a has gray marginal inscription. Size: 113½x142mm.

Arms and Map of Guernsey — A26

Designs (Globe with Map of Bailiwick): 6p, Flag of Guernsey. 10p, Flag of Guernsey and arms of Alderney (horiz.). 12p, Flag of Guernsey and arms of Sark (horiz.).

**1975, Oct. 7 Photo. Perf. 13½**

127 A26 4p ol grn & multi 10 10
128 A26 6p rose lil & multi 15 15
129 A26 10p brt grn & multi 30 30
130 A26 12p org & multi 32 32

Christmas 1975.

Lighthouses — A27

**1976, Feb. 10 Photo. Perf. 11½**
**Granite Paper**

131 A27 4p Les Hanois 12 12
132 A27 6p Les Casquets 16 16
133 A27 11p Quesnard, Alderney 35 35
134 A27 13p Point Robert, Sark 45 45

**Europa Issue 1976**

Guernsey Milk Can — A28

Design: 25p, Silver christening cup.

**1976, May 29 Photo. Perf. 11½**
**Granite Paper**

135 A28 10p multi 55 45
136 A28 25p multi 1.00 90

Sheets of 9.

Pine Forest, Guernsey — A29

Guernsey Views: 7p, Herm Harbor and Jethou. 11p, Grande Grave Bay, Sark Cliffs (vert.). 13p, Trois Vaux Bay, Alderney Cliffs (vert.).

**1976, Aug. 3 Photo. Perf. 11½**
**Granite Paper**

137 A29 5p multi 15 15
138 A29 7p multi 20 20
139 A29 11p multi 32 32
140 A29 13p multi 40 40

Royal Court House, Guernsey — A30

Buildings in the Bailiwick: 7p, Elizabeth College, Guernsey. 11p, La Seigneurie, Sark. 13p, Island Hall, Alderney.

**1976, Oct. 14 Photo. Perf. 11½**
**Granite Paper**

141 A30 5p multi 15 15
142 A30 7p multi 18 18
143 A30 11p multi 32 32
144 A30 13p multi 40 40

Christmas 1976.

Elizabeth II with Order of the Garter — A31

Design: 7p, Queen Elizabeth II.

**1977, Feb. 8 Photo. Perf. 12x11½**

145 A31 7p bl & multi 20 20
146 A31 35p pur & multi 90 90

25th anniv. of the reign of Elizabeth II.

Talbots Valley — A32

Design: 25p, Fields and hedges, Talbots Valley.

**1977, May 17 Photo. Perf. 11½**
**Granite Paper**

147 A32 7p multi 15 15
148 A32 25p multi 65 65

Megalithic Tomb, Le Catioroc — A33

Prehistoric monuments: 5p, Menhir (statue), Castel (vert.). 11p, Cist (tomb), Alderney. 13p, Menhir, St. Martin (vert.).

**1977, Aug. 2 Photo. Perf. 11½**

149 A33 5p multi 15 15
150 A33 7p multi 18 18
151 A33 11p multi 30 30
152 A33 13p multi 35 35

Mobile First Aid Unit A34

Designs: 7p, Mobile radar and rescue coordination unit, for ships in distress. 11p, Marine ambulance "Flying Christine II" (vert.). 13p, Cliff rescue (vert.).

**1977, Oct. 25 Photo. Perf. 11½**

153 A34 5p multi 15 15
154 A34 7p multi 18 18
155 A34 11p multi 30 30
156 A34 13p multi 35 35

St. John Ambulance Assoc. cent. (in GB).

View from Clifton, c. 1830 — A35

19th Century Prints, Guernsey: 7p, Market Square, c. 1838. 11p, Petit-Bo Bay, c. 1839. 13p, The Quay, c. 1830.

**1978, Feb. 7 Litho. Perf. 14x13½**

157 A35 5p pale grn & blk 15 15
158 A35 7p buff & blk 22 22
159 A35 11p pink & blk 42 42
160 A35 13p lt vio & blk 42 42

See Nos. 236-239.

**Europa Issue 1978**

Memorial to Seamen of Ship Prosperity; Sank 1974 — A36

Design: 7p, Victoria monument (vert.).

**1978, May 2 Litho. Perf. 14½**

161 A36 5p multi 16 16
162 A36 7p multi 25 25

Elizabeth II — A37

**1978, May 2** **Photo.** ***Perf. 11½***

*163* A37 20p ultra & blk 60 60

25th anniv. of coronation of Elizabeth II.

Inscribed: "VISIT OF/H.M. THE QUEEN AND/H.R.H. THE DUKE OF EDINBURGH/JUNE 28-29, 1978"

**1978, June 28**

*164* A37 7p emer & blk 32 32

Gannet
A38

Birds: 7p, Firecrest. 11p, Dartford warbler. 13p, Spotted redshank.

**1978, Aug. 29** **Photo.** ***Perf. 11½***

| | | | | |
|---|---|---|---|---|
| *165* | A38 | 5p multi | 15 | 15 |
| *166* | A38 | 7p multi | 20 | 20 |
| *167* | A38 | 11p multi | 35 | 35 |
| *168* | A38 | 13p multi | 38 | 38 |

Solanum — A39

Christmas: 7p, Christmas rose. 11p, Holly (vert.). 13p, Mistletoe (vert.).

**1978, Oct. 31** **Photo.** ***Perf. 11½***

| | | | | |
|---|---|---|---|---|
| *169* | A39 | 5p multi | 15 | 15 |
| *170* | A39 | 7p multi | 20 | 20 |
| *171* | A39 | 11p multi | 35 | 35 |
| *172* | A39 | 13p multi | 38 | 38 |

1 Double, 1930 — A40

**1979, Feb. 13**

**Granite Paper**

| | | | | | |
|---|---|---|---|---|---|
| *173* | A40 | ½p | 1 double, 1930 | 5 | 5 |
| *174* | A40 | 1p | 2 doubles, 1899 | 5 | 5 |
| *175* | A40 | 2p | 4 doubles, 1902 | 8 | 8 |
| *176* | A40 | 4p | 8 doubles, 1959 | 10 | 10 |
| *177* | A40 | 5p | 3 pence, 1956 | 12 | 12 |
| *178* | A40 | 6p | 5 new pence, 1968 | 15 | 15 |
| *179* | A40 | 7p | 50 new pence, 1969 | 18 | 18 |
| *180* | A40 | 8p | 10 new pence, 1970 | 20 | 20 |
| *181* | A40 | 9p | ½ new penny, 1971 | 22 | 22 |
| *182* | A40 | 10p | 1 new penny, 1971 | 25 | 25 |
| *183* | A40 | 11p | 2 new pence, 1971 | 30 | 30 |
| *184* | A40 | 12p | 1 penny, 1977 | 30 | 30 |
| *185* | A40 | 13p | 2 pence, 1977 | 32 | 32 |
| *186* | A40 | 14p | 5 pence, 1977 | 35 | 35 |
| *187* | A40 | 15p | 10 pence, 1977 | 40 | 40 |
| *188* | A40 | 20p | 25 pence, 1977 | 52 | 52 |
| | | | *Nos. 173-188 (16)* | 3.59 | 3.59 |

See Nos. 199-203A.

Booklets containing 5 each #176, 181, 185 and 2 #176, 3 #181, 5 #185 exist produced from sheets of 30 (two 3x5 panes) and 20 (two 2x5 panes).

**Europa Issue 1979**

Oldest Pillar Box, 1853 Cancel, Truck — A41

Design: 8p, Telephone, 1897, and telex machine.

**1979, May 8** **Photo.** ***Perf. 11½***

| | | | | |
|---|---|---|---|---|
| *189* | A41 | 6p multi | 22 | 22 |
| *190* | A41 | 8p multi | 25 | 25 |

Steam Tram, 1879
A42

Public Transportation: 8p, Electric tram, 1896. 11p, Autobus, 1911. 13p, Autobus, 1979.

**1979, Aug. 7** **Photo.** ***Perf. 11½***

| | | | | |
|---|---|---|---|---|
| *191* | A42 | 6p multi | 15 | 15 |
| *192* | A42 | 8p multi | 24 | 24 |
| *193* | A42 | 11p multi | 30 | 30 |
| *194* | A42 | 13p multi | 38 | 38 |

Centenary of public transportation.

Postal Bureau and Headquarters — A43

Designs: 8p, Mail and telegram deliverymen. 13p, Parcel trucks. 15p, Post Office philatelic room.

**1979, Oct. 1** **Photo.** ***Perf. 11½***

| | | | | |
|---|---|---|---|---|
| *195* | A43 | 6p multi | 14 | 14 |
| *196* | A43 | 8p multi | 18 | 18 |
| *197* | A43 | 13p multi | 30 | 30 |
| *198* | A43 | 15p multi | 35 | 35 |
| *a.* | | Souv. sheet of 4, Nos. 195-198 | 1.10 | 1.10 |

Guernsey PO, 10th anniv.; Christmas 1979. No. 198a has black marginal inscription. Size: 120x80mm.

**Coin Type of 1979**

Designs: 10p, like No. 182. 11½p, ½pence, 1979. 50p, Battle of Hastings coin, 1966. £1, Queen Elizabeth II 25th anniv., 1977 (horiz.) £2, Queen Elizabeth II 25th wedding anniv., 1972 (horiz.). £5, 5-pound note.

**1980, Feb. 5** **Photo.** ***Perf. 11½***

**Granite Paper**

| | | | | |
|---|---|---|---|---|
| *199* | A40 | 10p org & brnz | 30 | 30 |
| *200* | A40 | 11½p red & brnz | 35 | 35 |

**Size: 26x45, 45x26mm**

| | | | | |
|---|---|---|---|---|
| *201* | A40 | 50p red org & sil | 1.50 | 1.50 |
| *202* | A40 | £1 grn & sil | 2.25 | 2.25 |
| *203* | A40 | £2 bl & sil | 4.50 | 4.50 |

**1981, May 22**

**Granite Paper**

| | | | | |
|---|---|---|---|---|
| *203A* | A40 | £5 multi ('81) | 12.50 | 12.50 |
| | | *Nos. 199-203A (6)* | 21.40 | 21.40 |

A particular stamp may be scarce, but if few collectors want it, its market value may remain relatively low.

Policewoman Helping Child — A44

Guernsey Police Force, 60th Anniv.: 15p, Policeman on motorcycle. 17½p, Police dog and officer.

**1980, May 6** **Litho.** ***Perf. 14***

| | | | | |
|---|---|---|---|---|
| *204* | A44 | 7p multi | 18 | 18 |
| *205* | A44 | 15p multi | 40 | 40 |
| *206* | A44 | 17½p multi | 45 | 45 |

**Europa Issue 1980**

Major Gen. John Gaspard Le Marchant — A45

Design: 13½p, Admiral James Lord de Saumarez (1757-1836).

**1980, May 6** **Photo.** ***Perf. 11½***

**Granite Paper**

| | | | | |
|---|---|---|---|---|
| *207* | A45 | 10p multi | 25 | 25 |
| *208* | A45 | 13½p multi | 35 | 35 |

Guernsey Golden Goat — A46

Designs: Various Guernsey golden goats.

**1980, Aug. 5** **Photo.** ***Perf. 13***

| | | | | |
|---|---|---|---|---|
| *209* | A46 | 7p multi | 20 | 20 |
| *210* | A46 | 10p multi | 30 | 30 |
| *211* | A46 | 15p multi | 45 | 45 |
| *212* | A46 | 17½p multi | 52 | 52 |

Sark Cottage, by Peter Le Lievre, 1847 — A47

Christmas 1980 (Le Lievre Paintings): 10p, Moulin Huet, 1850. 13½p, Boats at Sea, 1850. 15p, Cow Lane, 1852 (vert.). 17½p, Portrait, by Le Lievre's sister (vert.).

**1980, Nov. 15** **Photo.** ***Perf. 12***

**Granite Paper**

| | | | | |
|---|---|---|---|---|
| *213* | A47 | 7p multi | 18 | 18 |
| *214* | A47 | 10p multi | 25 | 25 |
| *215* | A47 | 13½p multi | 35 | 35 |
| *216* | A47 | 15p multi | 40 | 40 |
| *217* | A47 | 17½p multi | 45 | 45 |
| | | *Nos. 213-217 (5)* | 1.63 | 1.63 |

Common Blue — A48

**1981, Feb. 24** **Photo.** ***Perf. 14½***

| | | | | |
|---|---|---|---|---|
| *218* | A48 | 8p shown | 24 | 24 |
| *219* | A48 | 12p Red Admiral | 35 | 35 |
| *220* | A48 | 22p Small Tortoiseshell | 65 | 65 |
| *221* | A48 | 25p Wall Brown | 75 | 75 |

**Europa Issue 1981**

Le Petit Bonhomme Andriou (Head-shaped Rock) — A49

**1981, May 22** **Litho.** ***Perf. 14½***

| | | | | |
|---|---|---|---|---|
| *222* | A49 | 12p shown | 35 | 35 |
| *223* | A49 | 18p Guernsey lily | 50 | 50 |

Prince Charles and Lady Diana — A50

**1981, July 29** **Litho.** ***Perf. 14½***

| | | | |
|---|---|---|---|
| *224* | Strip of 3 | 75 | 75 |
| *a* | A50 8p Charles | 25 | 25 |
| *b* | A50 8p shown | 25 | 25 |
| *c* | A50 8p Diana | 25 | 25 |
| *225* | Strip of 3 | 1.10 | 1.10 |
| *a* | A50 12p Charles | 35 | 35 |
| *b* | A50 12p Couple | 35 | 35 |
| *c* | A50 12p Diana | 35 | 35 |

**Size: 49x32mm**

| | | | |
|---|---|---|---|
| *226* | A50 25p Royal family | 75 | 75 |
| *a* | Souv. sheet of 3, Nos. 224-226 | 3.00 | 3.00 |

Royal Wedding. No. 226a has gray and gold decorative margin. Size: 105x127mm.

Sark Launch — A51

Designs: Interisland transportation.

**1981, Aug. 25** **Photo.** ***Perf. 11½***

**Granite Paper**

| | | | | |
|---|---|---|---|---|
| *227* | A51 | 8p shown | 20 | 20 |
| *228* | A51 | 12p Trislander plane | 32 | 32 |
| *229* | A51 | 18p Hydrofoil | 48 | 48 |
| *230* | A51 | 22p Herm catamaran | 60 | 60 |
| *231* | A51 | 25p Alderney coaster | 65 | 65 |
| | | *Nos. 227-231 (5)* | 2.25 | 2.25 |

Rifle-shooting Competition
A52

**1981, Nov. 17** **Litho.** ***Perf. 14***

| | | | | |
|---|---|---|---|---|
| *232* | A52 | 8p shown | 22 | 22 |
| *233* | A52 | 12p Riding | 35 | 35 |
| *234* | A52 | 22p Swimming | 60 | 60 |
| *235* | A52 | 25p Electronics workers | 70 | 70 |

Intl. Year of the Disabled.

**Print Type of 1978**

**Litho. & Engr.**

**1982, Feb. 2** ***Perf. 14***

| | | | | |
|---|---|---|---|---|
| *236* | A35 | 8p Jethou | 22 | 22 |
| *237* | A35 | 12p Fermain Bay | 35 | 35 |
| *238* | A35 | 22p The Terres | 60 | 60 |
| *239* | A35 | 25p St. Pierre Port | 70 | 70 |

La Societe Guernesiaise Centenary
A53

Society Emblem and Activities: 8p, Sir Edgar MacCulloch, founding president. 13p, William the Conqueror's fleet, Battle at Hastings (history). 20p, Sir James Saumarez's Crescent rescued from French fleet (history). 24p, Dragonfly (entomology). 26p, Vale Parish Church bird sanctuary (ornithology). 29p, Samian bowl, King's Road excavation (archaeology). 13p and 20p show CEPT (Europa) emblem.

**1982, Apr. 28 Photo. *Perf. 11½***
**Granite Paper**

*240* A53 8p multi 24 24
*241* A53 13p multi 40 40
*242* A53 20p multi 60 60
*243* A53 24p multi 75 75
*244* A53 26p multi 75 75
*245* A53 29p multi 80 80
*Nos. 240-245 (6)* 3.54 3.54

Scouting Year — A54

**1982, July 13 Litho. *Perf. 14½***

*246* A54 8p Sea scouts, Castle Cornet, St. Peter Port 24 24
*247* A54 13p Boy scouts building bridge 40 40
*248* A54 26p Cub scouts parading 75 75
*249* A54 29p Air scouts reading chart 95 95

Christmas 1982 — A55

**1982, Oct. 12 Photo. *Perf. 14½***

*250* A55 8p Midnight mass, St. Peter Port Church 20 20
*251* A55 13p Exchanging presents 32 32
*252* A55 24p Dinner 60 60
*253* A55 26p Exchanging cards 65 65
*254* A55 29p Watching Queen's TV greeting 85 85
*Nos. 250-254 (5)* 2.62 2.62

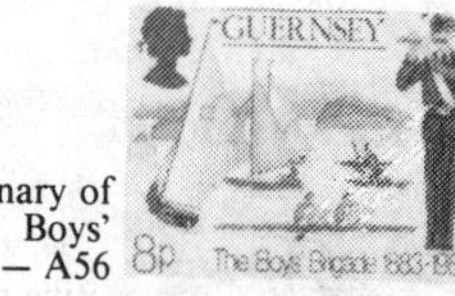

Centenary of Boys' Brigade — A56

Designs: Various brigade activities.

**1983, Jan. 18 *Perf. 14***

*255* A56 8p multi 28 28
*256* A56 13p multi 45 45
*257* A56 24p multi 80 80
*258* A56 26p multi 85 85
*259* A56 29p multi 1.10 1.10
*Nos. 255-259 (5)* 3.48 3.48

Europa 1983 — A57

Views of St. Peter Port Harbor. Stamps of same denomination se-tenant.

**1983, Mar. 14 Photo. *Perf. 11½***
**Granite Paper**

*260* A57 13p multi 40 40
*261* A57 13p multi 40 40
*262* A57 20p multi 60 60
*263* A57 20p multi 60 60

View at Guernsey, by Renoir — A58

Centenary of Renoir's Visit: 13p, Children at the Seashore (26x39mm.). 26p, Marine Guernsey. 28p, Moulin Huet Bay through the Trees. 31p, Fog in Guernsey.

***Perf. 12, 11½x12 (13p)***
**1983, Sept. 6 Photo.**
**Granite Paper**

*264* A58 9p multi 28 28
*265* A58 13p multi 40 40
*266* A58 26p multi 80 80
*267* A58 28p multi 85 85
*268* A58 31p multi 95 95
*Nos. 264-268 (5)* 3.28 3.28

Star of the West, 1869 Merchant Ship, Capt. J.G. Lenfestey
A59

**1983, Nov. 15 Photo. *Perf. 14½***

*269* A59 9p Launching 28 28
*270* A59 13p Launching St. Peter Port 40 40
*271* A59 26p Rio Grande Bar 80 80
*272* A59 28p St. Lucia 85 85
*273* A59 31p Voyage Map 95 95
*Nos. 269-273 (5)* 3.28 3.28

Dame of Sark (Sibyl Hathaway, 1884-1974) — A60

Biographical Scenes: 9p, Portrait, La Seigneurie (residence). 13p, German occupation, 1940-45. 26p, Royal visit, 1957. 28p, Chief Pleas (parliament). 31p, Dame of Sark rose.

**1984, Feb. 7 Litho. *Perf. 14½***

*274* A60 9p multi 28 28
*275* A60 13p multi 40 40
*276* A60 26p multi 80 80
*277* A60 28p multi 85 85
*278* A60 31p multi 95 95
*Nos. 274-278 (5)* 3.28 3.28

Links with the Commonwealth — A61

Designs: 9p, Flag of Guernsey, Royal Court. 31p, Union Jack, Castle Cornet.

**1984, Apr. 10 Litho. *Perf. 14½***

*279* A61 9p multi 28 28
*280* A61 31p multi 95 95

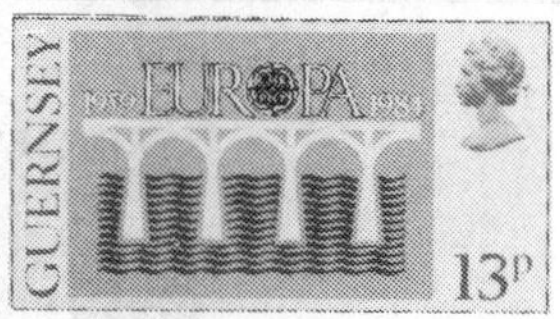

Europa (1959-84) — A62

**1984, Apr. 10 *Perf. 15***

*281* A62 13p multi 40 40
*282* A62 20½p multi 62 62

Petit Port — A63

***Perf. 15x14½, 14½x15***
**1984-85 Litho.**

*283* A63 1p Little Chapel, vert. ('85) 5 5
*284* A63 2p Ft. Grey ('85) 6 6
*285* A63 3p St. Apolline Chapel, vert. 8 8
*286* A63 4p shown 10 10
*287* A63 5p Little Russel ('85) 12 12
*288* A63 6p The Harbour, Herm ('85) 15 15
*289* A63 7p Saints ('85) 16 16
*290* A63 8p St. Saviour, vert. ('85) 20 20
*291* A63 9p Cambridge Berth 22 22
*292* A63 10p Belvoir, Herm 25 25
**a.** Miniature sheet (2 2p, 4 4p, 2 5p, 2 10p) 1.00 1.00
*293* A63 11p La Seigneurie, Sark ('85) 25 25
*294* A63 13p St. Saviour's Reservoir 32 32
**a.** Miniature sheet of 10 (2 4p, 3 9p, 5 13p) ('86) 2.50
**b.** Miniature sheet of 15 5 each 4p, 9p, 13p) ('86) 3.25
*295* A63 14p St. Peter Port, vert. 35 35
**a.** Miniature sheet of 10 (4 9p, 6 14p) 3.00 3.00
**b.** Miniature sheet of 10 (2 9p, 8 14p) 3.50 3.50
*296* A63 15p Havelet, vert. ('85) 38 38
**a.** Miniature sheet of 10 (3p, 2 4p, 4 11p, 3 15p) 2.75 2.75
**b.** Miniature sheet of 10 (5 each 11p, 15p) 3.25 3.25
*297* A63 20p La Coupee, Sark 52 52
*298* A63 30p Grandes Rocques ('85) 75 75
*299* A63 40p St. Torteval Church, vert. 1.10 1.10
*300* A63 50p Bordeaux 1.25 1.25
*301* A63 £1 Albecq 2.50 2.50
*302* A63 £2 L'Ancresse ('85) 4.75 4.75
*Nos. 283-302 (20)* 13.56 13.56

Issue dates: 1p, 2p, 5p, 6p, 7p, 8p, 11p, 15p, 30p, £2, July 23. 3p, 4p, 9p, 10p, 13p, 14p, 20p, 40p, 50p, £1, Sept. 18. No. 292a, Dec. 2. Nos. 295a-295b, Mar. 19.

Miniature sheets sold folded and unattached in booklet covers.

See Nos. 372-380.

Lieutenant-General John Doyle (1756-1834) — A64

Designs: 13p, Portrait by James Ramsey, 1817 (vert.). 29p, American War of Independence battle. 31p, Land fill, Grand Havre Bay. 39p, Ship approaching Casquets Reef, 1811.

**1984, Nov. 20 Photo. *Perf. 11½***

*303* A64 13p multi 40 40
*304* A64 29p multi 95 95
*305* A64 31p multi 1.05 1.05
*306* A64 34p multi 1.10 1.10

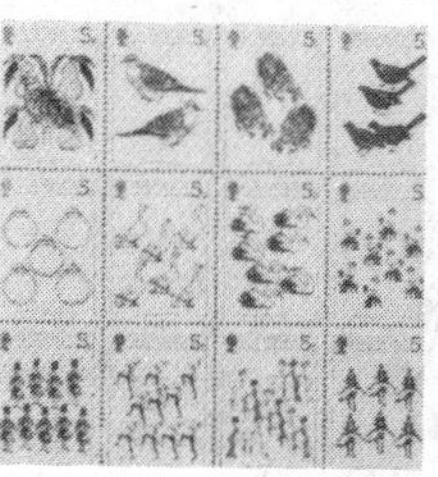
Christmas 1984
A65

Twelve Days of Christmas: a. Partridge in a Pear Tree. b. Two Turtle Doves. c. Three French Hens. d. Four Colling Birds. e. Five Golden Rings. f. Six Geese-a-Laying. g. Seven Swans a-Swimming. h. Eight Maids a-Milking. i. Nine Drummers Drumming. j. Ten Pipers Piping. k. Eleven Ladies Dancing. l. Twelve Lords a-Leaping. Illustration reduced.

**1984, Nov. 20 Litho. *Perf. 14½***

*307* A65 Sheet of 12 1.75 1.75
**a.-l.** 5p. any single 14 14

Indigenous Fish
A66

**1985, Jan. 22 Photo. *Perf. 12***

*308* A66 9p Cockoo Wrasse 25 25
*309* A66 13p Red Gurnard 35 35
*310* A66 29p Red Mullet 80 80
*311* A66 31p Mackerel 85 85
*312* A66 34p Sunfish 95 95
*Nos. 308-312 (5)* 3.20 3.20

Liberation from German Forces, 40th Anniv.
A67

**1985, May 9 Litho. *Perf. 14x14½***

*313* A67 22p Peace dove 70 70

Celebrating the D-Day landings of June, 1944.

Europa 1985 — A68

Designs: 14p, Musical staff, flags of Great Britain, Netherlands, Germany, Italy, Cross of St. George. 22p, Music, cello, French horn.

**1985, May 14 Litho. *Perf. 14½***

*314* A68 14p multi 40 40
*315* A68 22p multi 65 65

Intl. Youth Year — A69

Girl Guides, 75th Anniv. — A70

**1985, May 14 Litho. *Perf. 14***

*316* A69 9p IYY emblem, circle of children 22 22
*317* A69 31p Girl Guides in camp 70 70

Children's drawings.

**1985, May 14 Litho. *Perf. 14***

*318* A70 34p Leader, guide and brownie 90 90

Child's drawing.

Christmas 1985 — A71

Religious and folk figures: a, Santa Claus. b, Lussibruden. c, Balthasar. d, St. Nicholas. e, La Befana. f, Julenisse. g, Christkind. h, King Wenceslas. i, Shepherd of Les Baux. j, Caspar. k, Baboushka. l, Melchior.

**1985, Nov. 19 Litho. *Perf. 12½***
**Granite Paper**

*319* Sheet of 12 1.65 1.65
***a.-l.*** A71 5p, any single 14 14

No. 319 has silver and black inscribed margin. Size: 121x118mm.

Watercolors by Paul Jacob Naftel — A72

**1985, Nov. 19 *Perf. 15x14½***

*320* A72 9p Vraicing 22 22
*321* A72 14p Castle Cornet 35 35
*322* A72 22p Rocquaine Bay 55 55
*323* A72 31p Little Russel 80 80
*324* A72 34p Seaweed Gatherers 90 90
*Nos. 320-324 (5)* 2.82 2.82

Adm. Lord De Saumarez, 150th Death Anniv. — A73

Designs: 9p, Squadron off Nargue Is., 1809. 14p, Battle of the Nile, 1798. 29p, Battle of St. Vincent, 1797. 31p, HMS Crescent off Cherbourg, 1793. 34p, Battle of the Saints, 1782.

**1986, Feb. 4 Litho. *Perf. 12x11½***
**Granite Paper**

*325* A73 9p multi 25 25
*326* A73 14p multi 40 40
*327* A73 29p multi 80 80
*328* A73 31p multi 85 85
*329* A73 34p multi 95 95
*Nos. 325-329 (5)* 3.25 3.25

Queen Elizabeth II, 60th Birthday — A74

**1986, Apr. 21 *Perf. 14***

*330* A74 60p pale gray grn, dk bl & gold 1.85 1.85

Europa 1986 — A75

**1986, May 22 *Perf. 11½***
**Granite Paper**

*331* A75 10p Operation Gannet 30 30
*332* A75 14p Whitsun orchid 42 42
*333* A75 22p Guernsey elm 68 68

Wedding of Prince Andrew and Sarah Ferguson — A76

**1986, July 23 Litho. *Perf. 14***

*334* A76 14p Couple 35 35

**Size: 48x32mm**

*335* A76 34p Couple, diff. 90 90

Sports A77

**1986, July 24 *Perf. 14½***

*336* A77 10p Lawn bowling 28 28
*337* A77 14p Cricket 38 38
*338* A77 22p Badminton 60 60
*339* A77 29p Field hockey 80 80
*340* A77 31p Swimming, horiz. 85 85
*341* A77 34p Rifle shooting, horiz. 95 95
*Nos. 336-341 (6)* 3.86 3.86

Museums A78

**1986, Nov. 18 Litho. *Perf. 14½***

*342* A78 14p Guernsey Museum and Art Gallery 32 32
*343* A78 29p Ft. Grey Maritime Museum 65 65
*344* A78 31p Castle Cornet 70 70
*345* A78 34p Natl. Trust of Guernsey Folk Museum 80 80

**Miniature Sheet**

Christmas — A79

Carols: a, "While Shepherds Watched Their Flocks by Night." b, "In the Bleak Mid-Winter." c, "O Little Town of Bethlehem." d, "The Holly and the Ivy." e, "O Little Christmas Tree." f, "Away in a Manger." g, "Good King Wenceslas." h, "We Three Kings of Orient Are." i, "Hark the Herald Angels Sing." j, "I Saw Three Ships." k, "Little Donkey." l, "Jingle Bells."

**1986, Nov. 18 *Perf. 12½***

*346* Sheet of 12 2.00 2.00
***a.-l.*** A79 6p, any single 16 16

**Souvenir Sheet**

Duke of Richmond, 18th Century Map Detail — A80

**1987, Feb. 10 Litho. *Perf. 14½***

*347* Sheet of 4 3.35 3.35
***a.*** A80 14p shown 45 45
***b.*** A80 29p North 90 90
***c.*** A80 31p Southwest 95 95
***d.*** A80 34p Southeast 1.05 1.05

Duke of Richmond's survey of Guernsey, bicent. No. 347 has multicolored inscribed margin.

Europa 1987 — A81

Modern architecture.

**1987, May 5 Litho. *Perf. 13x13½***

*348* A81 15p Postal headquarters 50 50
*349* A81 15p Headquarters, schematic view 50 50
*350* A81 22p Grammar school entrance 75 75
*351* A81 22p School, schematic view 75 75

Stamps of the same denomination printed se-tenant.

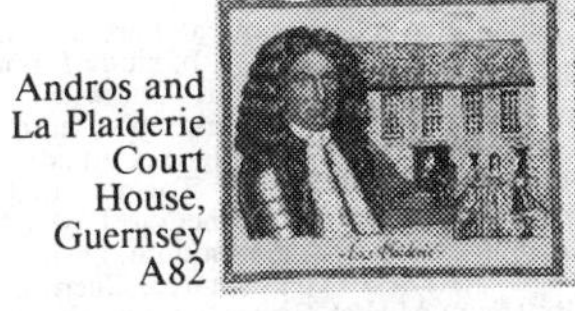

Andros and La Plaiderie Court House, Guernsey A82

Andros and: 29p, Governor's Palace, Virginia. 31p, "Governor Andros and the Boston People," print fron Harper's New Monthly Magazine. 34p, Map of New Amsterdam (New York City).

**1987, July 7 *Perf. 12***
**Granite Paper**

*352* A82 15p multi 50 50
*353* A82 29p multi 95 95
*354* A82 31p multi 1.05 1.05
*355* A82 34p multi 1.15 1.15

Sir Edmund Andros (1637-1714), lieutenant-governor of Guernsey (1704-1706) and statesman of Colonial America (1672-1710).

William the Conqueror (c. 1028-1087), King of England (1066-1087) — A83

Designs: 11p, Jester warning young William of a plot to murder him. No. 357, Battle of Hastings. No. 358, King William, his banner at the Battle of Hastings. No. 359, William the Conqueror. No. 360, Abbey at Caen and Queen Matilda of Flanders (d. 1083). 34p, Halley's Comet and regalia of William I.

**1987, Sept. 9 *Perf. 13½x14***

*356* A83 11p multi 35 35
*357* A83 15p multi 48 48
*358* A83 15p multi 48 48
*359* A83 22p multi 70 70
*360* A83 22p multi 70 70
*361* A83 34p multi 1.10 1.10
*Nos. 356-361 (6)* 3.81 3.81

Stamps of the same denomination printed se-tenant.

Visit of John Wesley (1703-1791), Religious Reformer, Bicent. — A84

Designs: 7p, Preaching at the quay, Alderney. 15p, Preaching at Mon Plaisir. 29p, Preaching at Assembly Rooms, St. Peter Port. 31p, Wesley and La Ville Baudu, an early Methodist meeting place, Vale Parish. 34p, Wesley and Ebenezer Methodist Church, first Methodist chapel, Union Street, 1816.

**1987, Nov. 17 Litho. *Perf. 14½***

*362* A84 7p multi 25 25
*363* A84 15p multi 55 55
*364* A84 29p multi 1.05 1.05
*365* A84 31p multi 1.15 1.15
*366* A84 34p multi 1.25 1.25
*Nos. 362-366 (5)* 4.25 4.25

Voyage of the Golden Spur, Apr. 12, 1872-Jan. 4, 1874 — A85

Designs: 11p, Off St. Sampson's Harbor. 15p, Entering Hong Kong Harbor. 29p, Anchored off Macao. 31p, In China Tea Race. 34p, Golden Spur, map of voyage.

**1988, Feb. 9 Litho. *Perf. 13½x14***

*367* A85 11p multi 40 40
*368* A85 15p multi 55 55
*369* A85 29p multi 1.05 1.05
*370* A85 31p multi 1.15 1.15
*371* A85 34p multi 1.25 1.25
*Nos. 367-371 (5)* 4.40 4.40

Guernsey's Golden Age of Shipping: largest vessel built on Guernsey, the Golden Spur, launched Oct. 15, 1864, wrecked at Haiphong on Feb. 27, 1879.

Landscape Type of 1984

**1988, Mar. 28 Litho. *Perf.***

*372* A63 12p Petit Bot beach, vert. 45 45
*373* A63 16p St. John's Hostel for the Aged 58 58
***a.*** Miniature sheet of 10 (5 each 12p, 16p) 5.15
***b.*** Miniature sheet of 8 (4 4p, 3 12p, 16p) 2.50

Nos. 373a-373b sold folded and unattached in booklet covers.

Coil Stamps

**1988 Litho.**
**Sizes: 21½x12½mm, 12½x21½mm**
***Perf. 14x14½, 14½x14***

*376* A63 11p La Seigneurie, Sark 40 40
*377* A63 12p Petit Bot beach 45 45
*377A* A63 15p Havelet, vert. 52 52
*378* A63 16p St. John's Hostel for the Aged 60 60

Issue dates: 11p, 15p, May 15. 12p, 16p, Mar. 28.

The Scott Catalogue value is a retail price, what you could expect to pay for the stamp in a grade of Fine-Very Fine. The value listed is a reference which reflects recent actual dealer selling price.

Europa 1988 A86

Communication and transportation: No. 381, Bedford Rascal postal van, Lihou Is. rowboat. No. 382, Rowboat, Viscount plane. No. 383, Horse and buggy, front wheel of bicycle. No. 384, Back wheel of bicycle, No. 4 coach.

**1988, May 10 Litho. Perf. 14½**
*381* A86 16p multi 58 58
*382* A86 16p multi 58 58
*383* A86 22p multi 80 80
*384* A86 22p multi 80 80

Nos. 381-382 and 383-384 printed se-tenant in continuous designs.

Frederick Corbin Lukis (1788-1871), Archaeologist A87

Designs: 12p, Entrance to Lukis House, St. Peter Port, and portrait. 16p, Bound manuscript containing illustrations painted by Lukis's daughter Mary Anne (born 1822). 29p, Lukis supervising excavation of Le Creux es Faies dolmen at L'Eree, Guernsey. 31p, Rear of Lukis House and garden. 34p, Artifacts recovered by Lukis and preserved as part of the museum collection.

**1988, July 12 Photo. Perf. 12½**
**Granite Paper**
*385* A87 12p multi 42 42
*386* A87 16p multi 55 55
*387* A87 29p multi 1.00 1.00
*388* A87 31p multi 1.10 1.10
*389* A87 34p multi 1.20 1.20
*Nos. 385-389 (5)* 4.27 4.27

1988 World Offshore Powerboat Championships — A88

Designs: 16p, Racing boats, Royal Navy helicopter. 30p, Boats racing through Gouliot Passage (separating Sark from Brecqhou). 32p, Boats, helicopter, St. John's Ambulance rescue ship, vert. 35p, Race course marked in red on Admiralty Chart, vert.

**1988, Sept. 6 Perf. 12**
**Granite Paper**
*390* A88 16p multi 58 58
*391* A88 30p multi 1.05 1.05
*392* A88 32p multi 1.10 1.10
*393* A88 35p multi 1.20 1.20

Publication of *Flora Sarniensis,* Bicent. — A89

Designs: 12p, Joshua Gosselin (1739-1813), botanist, and herbarium made by Rollo Sherwill in 1976. No. 395, *Lagurus ovatus* (pressed specimen). No. 396, *Lagurus ovatus,* diff. No. 397, *Silene gallica quinquevulnera* (pressed specimen). No. 398, *Silene gallica quinquevulnera,* diff. 35p, *Limonium binervosum sarniense serquense.*

**1988, Nov. 15 Litho. Perf. 14**
*394* A89 12p shown 42 42
*395* A89 16p multi 55 55
*396* A89 16p multi 55 55
*397* A89 23p multi 80 80
*398* A89 23p multi 80 80
*399* A89 35p multi 1.20 1.20
*Nos. 394-399 (6)* 4.32 4.32

Miniature Sheet

Ecclesiastical Links to France and Great Britain — A90

Church interiors, exteriors and artifacts: a, Coutances Cathedral, France. b, Notre Dame du Rosaire Church interior, Guernsey. c, Stained-glass window, St. Sampson's Church, Guernsey. d, Dol-de-Bretagne Cathedral, France. e, Bishop's Throne, Town Church, Guernsey. f, Winchester Cathedral, England. g, St. John's Cathedral, Portsmouth, England. h, High Altar, St. Joseph's Church, Guernsey. i, Mont Saint-Michel, France. j, Chancel, Vale Church, Guernsey. k, Lich gate, Forest Church, Guernsey. l, Marmoutier Abbey, France.

**1988, Nov. 15 Perf. 14½x15**
*400* Sheet of 12 3.40 3.40
*a.-l.* A90 8p any single 28 28

Christmas 1988. No. 400 has inscribed margin picturing bells. Size:

Europa 1989 A91

Traditional children's toys and games.

**1989, Feb. 28 Litho. Perf.**
*401* A91 12p Tip cat (Le Cat) 45 45
*402* A91 16p Girl, Cobo Alice doll 58 58
*403* A91 23p Hopscotch (Le Colimachaon) 85 85

## POSTAGE DUE STAMPS

Castle Cornet and St. Peter Port — D1

**Perf. 12½x12**
**1969, Oct. 1 Photo. Unwmk.**
**Black Numeral**
*J1* D1 1p dp mag 1.10 85
*J2* D1 2p yel grn 2.25 2.00
*J3* D1 3p red 3.00 2.25
*J4* D1 4p ultra 4.25 2.50
*J5* D1 5p yel bis 6.25 4.25
*J6* D1 6p grnsh bl 8.50 5.25
*J7* D1 1sh red brn 21.00 15.00
*Nos. J1-J7 (7)* 46.35 32.10

**Type of 1969**
**"p" instead of "d"**

**1971-76**
**Black Numeral**
*J8* D1 ½p dp mag 5 5
*J9* D1 1p yel grn 5 5
*J10* D1 2p red 10 10
*J11* D1 3p ultra 15 15
*J12* D1 4p yel bis 20 20
*J13* D1 5p grnsh bl 25 25
*J14* D1 6p pur ('76) 20 20
*J15* D1 8p org ('75) 28 28
*J16* D1 10p red brn 50 50
*J17* D1 15p gray ('76) 52 52
*Nos. J8-J17 (10)* 2.30 2.30

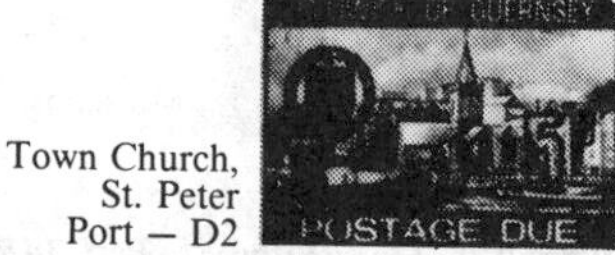
Town Church, St. Peter Port — D2

**1977-80 Photo. Perf. 13½x13**
**Arms and Denomination in Black**
*J18* D2 ½p red brn 5 5
*J19* D2 1p lil rose 5 5
*J20* D2 2p orange 8 8
*J21* D2 3p red 10 10
*J22* D2 4p grnsh bl 12 12
*J23* D2 5p ol grn 15 15
*J24* D2 6p grnsh bl 18 18
*J25* D2 8p ocher 25 25
*J26* D2 10p dk bl 30 30
*J27* D2 14p grn ('80) 45 45
*J28* D2 15p purple 42 42
*J29* D2 16p sal rose ('80) 55 55
*Nos. J18-J29 (12)* 2.70 2.70

Woman Milking Cow — D3

**1982, July 13 Litho. Perf. 14½**
*J30* D3 1p shown 5 5
*J31* D3 2p Vale Mill 8 8
*J32* D3 3p Sark cottage 10 10
*J33* D3 4p St. Peter Port 14 14
*J34* D3 5p Well, Moulin Huet 16 16
*J35* D3 16p Seaweed gathering 55 55
*J36* D3 18p Upper Walk, White Rock 60 60
*J37* D3 20p Cobo Bay 70 70
*J38* D3 25p Saints' Bay 85 85
*J39* D3 30p La Coupee, Sark 1.10 1.10
*J40* D3 50p Old Harbor, St. Peter Port 1.65 1.65
*J41* D3 £1 Greenhouses, Victoria Tower 3.50 3.50
*Nos. J30-J41 (12)* 9.48 9.48

## ALDERNEY

LOCATION — Northernmost of the Channel Islands in the Guernsey Bailiwick.
GOVT. — Dependent territory under Bailiwick of Guernsey.
AREA — 3 sq. mi.
POP. — 2086 (est. 1981)
CAPITAL — St. Anne

Part of the Bailiwick of Guernsey, this island began issuing its own stamps.

Map of Alderney, Arms — A1

**1983, June 14 Litho. Perf. 12**
*1* A1 1p shown 5 5
*2* A1 4p Hanging Rock 12 12
*3* A1 9p States Building 25 25
*4* A1 10p St. Anne's Church 28 28
*5* A1 11p Yachts, Braye Bay 30 30
*6* A1 12p Victoria St., St. Anne 32 32
*7* A1 13p Map, arms 35 35
*8* A1 14p Ft. Clonque 40 40
*9* A1 15p Corblets Bay Port 42 42
*10* A1 16p Old Tower, St. Anne 45 45
*11* A1 17p Essex Castle Golf Course 48 48
*12* A1 18p Ships in Old Harbor 50 50
*Nos. 1-12 (12)* 3.92 3.92

Oystercatcher, Telegraph Bay — A2

**1984, June 12 Perf. 14½**
*13* A2 9p shown 1.00 1.00
*14* A2 13p Turnstone, Corblets Bay 1.65 1.65
*15* A2 26p Ringed plover, Corblets Bay 2.75 2.75
*16* A2 28p Dunlin, Arch Bay 2.75 2.75
*17* A2 31p Curlew, Old Harbor 3.50 3.50
*Nos. 13-17 (5)* 11.65 11.65

Alderney Airport, 50th Anniv. A3

Aircraft: 9p, Wessex helicopter of the Queen's Flight, 1984. 13p, Aurigny Air Joey Britten-Norman Trislander, 1981. 29p, Morton Air Services DeHavilland Heron, 1946. 31p, DeHavilland Dragon Rapide, c. 1930. 34p, Saunders-Roe Saro Windhover, 1935.

**1985, Mar. 19 Perf. 12x11½**
*18* A3 9p multi 1.00 1.00
*19* A3 13p multi 1.40 1.40
*20* A3 29p multi 3.25 3.25
*21* A3 31p multi 3.25 3.25
*22* A3 34p multi 3.75 3.75
*Nos. 18-22 (5)* 12.65 12.65

*Alderney stamps can be mounted in Scott's Channel Islands Album.*

Regimental Uniforms, Alderney Garrison — A4

| 1985, Sept. 24 | | | Perf. 14½ | |
|---|---|---|---|---|
| 23 | A4 | 9p Royal Engineers, 1890 | 1.00 | 1.00 |
| 24 | A4 | 14p Duke of Albany's Own Highlanders, 1856 | 1.50 | 1.50 |
| 25 | A4 | 29p Royal Artillery, 1855 | 3.25 | 3.25 |
| 26 | A4 | 31p South Hampshire Regiment, 1810 | 3.50 | 3.50 |
| 27 | A4 | 34p Royal Irish Regiment, 1782 | 3.75 | 3.75 |
| | | *Nos. 23-27 (5)* | 13.00 | 13.00 |

Forts — A5

| 1986, Sept. 23 | Litho. | | Perf. 13x13½ | |
|---|---|---|---|---|
| 28 | A5 | 10p Grosnez | 75 | 75 |
| 29 | A5 | 14p Tourgis | 95 | 95 |
| 30 | A5 | 31p Clonque | 2.00 | 2.00 |
| 31 | A5 | 34p Albert | 2.25 | 2.25 |

Shipwrecks A6

| 1987, May 5 | Litho. | | Perf. 14½ | |
|---|---|---|---|---|
| 32 | A6 | 11p Liverpool, 1902 | 38 | 38 |
| 33 | A6 | 15p Petit Raymond, 1906 | 50 | 50 |
| 34 | A6 | 29p Maina, 1910 | 1.00 | 1.00 |
| 35 | A6 | 31p Burton, 1911 | 1.05 | 1.05 |
| 36 | A6 | 34p Point Law, 1975 | 1.15 | 1.15 |
| | | *Nos. 32-36 (5)* | 4.08 | 4.08 |

## JERSEY

LOCATION — Island in the English Channel.
GOVT. — Dependent territory (bailiwick) of the British Crown.
AREA — 45 sq. mi.
POP. — 76,100 (1980)
CAPITAL — St. Helier

Following the establishment of the British General Post Office as a public corporation on October 1, 1969, the post office of the Bailiwick of Jersey became a separate entity and British postage stamps ceased to be valid.

Between 1958-69 Great Britain issued six stamps that were sold only in Jersey and intended for use there. They are listed under "Regional Issues" following Envelopes and Letter Sheets in the Great Britain section.

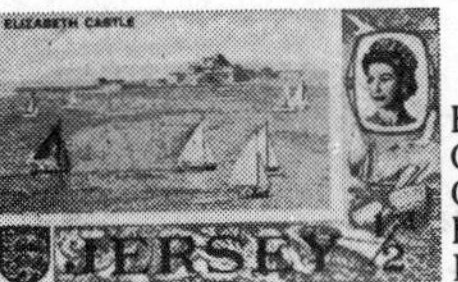
Elizabeth Castle and Queen Elizabeth II — A3

Queen Elizabeth II — A4

Designs (Queen Elizabeth II and): 1p, La Hougue Bie (prehistoric tomb). 2p, Portelet Bay. 3p, La Corbiere Lighthouse. 4p, Mont Orgueil by night. 5p, Arms of Jersey and Royal Mace. 6p, Jersey cow. 9p, 1sh6p, Map of English Channel with Jersey. 1sh, Mont Orgueil. 2sh6p, Airport. 5sh, Legislative Chamber. 10sh, Royal Court. £1, Queen Elizabeth II, photograph by Cecil Beaton.

*Perf. 14½*

| 1969, Oct. 1 | Photo. | | Unwmk. | |
|---|---|---|---|---|
| 7 | A3 | ½p ocher & multi | 32 | 32 |
| 8 | A3 | 1p brn & multi | 12 | 12 |
| a. | | Bklt. pane of 1 | 40 | |
| b. | | Bklt. pane of 2 | 1.00 | |
| 9 | A3 | 2p multi | 15 | 15 |
| 10 | A3 | 3p dp bl & multi | 15 | 15 |
| 11 | A3 | 4p multi | 20 | 20 |
| a. | | Bklt. pane of 1 | 65 | |
| b. | | Bklt. pane of 2 | 1.25 | |
| 12 | A3 | 5p multi | 22 | 22 |
| a. | | Bklt. pane of 2 | 2.00 | |
| 13 | A3 | 6p multi | 32 | 32 |
| 14 | A3 | 9p multi | 45 | 45 |
| 15 | A3 | 1sh lil & multi | 1.00 | 1.00 |
| 16 | A3 | 1sh6p grn & multi | 2.00 | 2.00 |
| | | ***Perf. 12*** | | |
| 17 | A4 | 1sh9p multi | 1.65 | 1.65 |
| 18 | A3 | 2sh6p multi | 6.50 | 4.50 |
| 19 | A3 | 5sh multi | 13.00 | 9.25 |
| 20 | A3 | 10sh gray & multi | 27.50 | 16.00 |
| a. | | 10sh grn & multi (error) | *4,250.* | |
| 21 | A4 | £1 tan & multi | 3.25 | 3.25 |
| | | *Nos. 7-21 (15)* | 56.83 | 39.58 |

See Nos. 34-48, 107-109.

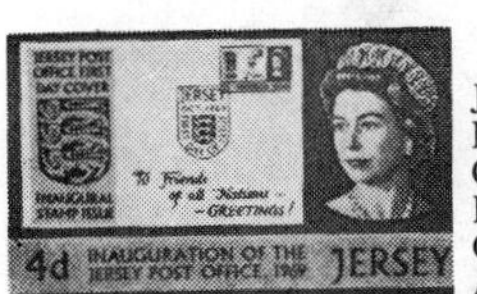
Jersey Post Office First Day Cover A5

| 1969, Oct. 1 | | | Perf. 14½ | |
|---|---|---|---|---|
| 22 | A5 | 4p multi | *25* | *20* |
| 23 | A5 | 5p bl & multi | *32* | *22* |
| 24 | A5 | 1sh6p brn & multi | *2.25* | *2.00* |
| 25 | A5 | 1sh9p emer & multi | *2.75* | *2.25* |

Inauguration of independent postal service.

Jersey Woman Reaching for Royal Mace, Flags of USSR, US and Great Britain — A6

Designs: 4p, Lord Coutanche, Bailiff of Jersey, by James Gunn (vert.). 5p, Sir Winston Churchill, by D. Van Praag (vert.). 1sh9p, Swedish Red Cross ship "Vega."

| 1970, May 9 | Photo. | | Perf. 11½ | |
|---|---|---|---|---|
| 26 | A6 | 4p gold & multi | *25* | *20* |
| 27 | A6 | 5p gold & multi | *32* | *22* |
| 28 | A6 | 1sh6p gold & multi | *2.25* | *1.65* |
| 29 | A6 | 1sh9p gold & multi | *2.75* | *1.65* |

25th anniv. of Jersey's liberation from the Germans.

*Jersey stamps can be mounted in Scott's annually supplemented Channel Islands Album.*

"Rags to Riches" Cinderella — A7

Designs (Parade Floats Made of Flowers): 4p, "A Tribute to Enid Blyton," author of children's books. 1sh6p, "Gourmet's Delight." 1sh9p, "We're the Greatest" (ostriches and trees).

| 1970, July 28 | Photo. | | Perf. 11½ | |
|---|---|---|---|---|
| 30 | A7 | 4p gold & multi | *48* | *40* |
| 31 | A7 | 5p gold & multi | *60* | *48* |
| 32 | A7 | 1sh6p gold & multi | 12.00 | *4.75* |
| 33 | A7 | 1sh9p gold & multi | 14.00 | *6.25* |

"Battle of Flowers" annual parade.

### Decimal Currency Issue
### Types of 1969
### "p" instead of "d"

Designs: ½p, Elizabeth Castle. 1p, La Corbiere Lighthouse. 1½p, Jersey cow. 2p, Mont Orgueil by night. 2½p, Arms of Jersey and Royal Mace. 3p, La Hougue Bie. 3½p, Portelet Bay. 4p, 7½p, Map of English Channel and Jersey. 5p, Mont Orgueil by day. 6p, Martello Tower at Archirondel. 9p, Queen Elizabeth II, by Cecil Beaton. 10p, Airport. 20p, Legislative Chamber. 50p, Royal Court.

| 1970-75 | Photo. | | Perf. 14½ | |
|---|---|---|---|---|
| 34 | A3 | ½p ocher & multi ('71) | 5 | 5 |
| a. | | Booklet pane of 1 | 12 | |
| 35 | A3 | 1p multi ('71) | 5 | 5 |
| a. | | Booklet pane of 2 ('75) | 15 | |
| b. | | Booklet pane of 4 ('75) | 30 | |
| 36 | A3 | 1½p multi ('71) | 6 | 6 |
| 37 | A3 | 2p multi ('71) | 10 | 10 |
| a. | | Booklet pane of 1 | 15 | |
| b. | | Booklet pane of 2 | 30 | |
| 38 | A3 | 2½p multi ('71) | 12 | 12 |
| a. | | Booklet pane of 1 | 30 | |
| b. | | Booklet pane of 2 | 40 | |
| 39 | A3 | 3p brn & multi ('71) | 15 | 15 |
| a. | | Booklet pane of 1 ('72) | 30 | |
| b. | | Booklet pane of 2 ('72) | 45 | |
| 40 | A3 | 3½p multi ('71) | 16 | 16 |
| a. | | Booklet pane of 1 | 30 | |
| b. | | Booklet pane of 2 | 50 | |
| 41 | A3 | 4p multi ('71) | 20 | 20 |
| a | | Booklet pane of 2 ('75) | 50 | |
| b. | | Booklet pane of 4 ('75) | 80 | |
| 42 | A3 | 5p lil & multi ('71) | 24 | 24 |
| a. | | Booklet pane of 2 ('75) | 60 | |
| b. | | Booklet pane of 4 ('75) | 96 | |
| 43 | A3 | 6p green & multi ('71) | 30 | 30 |
| 44 | A3 | 7½p multi ('71) | 34 | 34 |
| 45 | A4 | 9p multi ('71) | 45 | 45 |
| | | ***Perf. 12*** | | |
| 46 | A3 | 10p multi | 48 | 48 |
| 47 | A3 | 20p multi | 75 | 75 |
| 48 | A3 | 50p multi | 1.75 | 1.75 |
| | | *Nos. 34-48 (15)* | 5.20 | 5.20 |

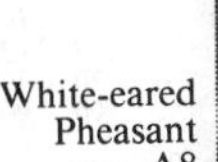

White-eared Pheasant A8

Designs: 2½p, Thick-billed parrots (vert.). 7½p, Ursine colobus monkeys (vert.). 9p, Ring-tailed lemurs.

| 1971, Mar. 9 | Photo. | | Perf. 11½ | |
|---|---|---|---|---|
| 49 | A8 | 2p dp plum & multi | *75* | *25* |
| 50 | A8 | 2½p dk gray & multi | *75* | *30* |
| 51 | A8 | 7½p ol & multi | *11.00* | *4.00* |
| 52 | A8 | 9p vio bl & multi | *13.00* | *5.75* |

Jersey Wildlife Preservation Trust.
See Nos. 65-68.

British Legion Emblem A9

Designs: 2½p, Poppy field and poppy emblem. 7½p, Jack Counter (1899-1970) and

Victoria Cross. 9p, Flags of France and Great Britain.

**1971, June 15 Litho. Perf. 14½**

| | | | | |
|---|---|---|---|---|
| 53 | A9 | 2p multi | 28 | 18 |
| 54 | A9 | 2½p multi | 32 | 20 |
| 55 | A9 | 7½p multi | 3.00 | 1.90 |
| 56 | A9 | 9p multi | 3.50 | 2.50 |

50th anniversary of the British Legion.

English Fleet in Channel, by Peter Monamy A10

Paintings by Jersey Artists: 2p, Tante Elizabeth (women in farm kitchen), by Edmund Blampied (vert.). 7½p, Boyhood of Raleigh (man and boys at seashore), by Sir John Millais. 9p, The Blind Beggar (old man and girl), by W. W. Ouless (vert.).

**1971, Oct. 5 Photo. Perf. 11½**

| | | | | |
|---|---|---|---|---|
| 57 | A10 | 2p gold & multi | 40 | 28 |
| 58 | A10 | 2½p gold & multi | 48 | 32 |
| 59 | A10 | 7½p gold & multi | 2.75 | 2.50 |
| 60 | A10 | 9p gold & multi | 3.50 | 3.25 |

Jersey Fern — A11

Jersey Royal Artillery Shako — A12

Jersey Wild Flowers: 5 p, Thrift. 7½p, Orchid (laxiflora). 9p, Viper's bugloss.

**1972, Jan. 18**

**Flowers in Natural Colors**

| | | | | |
|---|---|---|---|---|
| 61 | A11 | 3p brn & blk | 28 | 14 |
| 62 | A11 | 5p lt bl & blk | 90 | 60 |
| 63 | A11 | 7½p lil & blk | 2.75 | 2.00 |
| 64 | A11 | 9p grn & blk | 3.50 | 2.75 |

**Wildlife Type of 1971**

Designs: 2½p, Cheetahs. 3p, Rothschild's mynahs (vert.). 7½p, Spectacled bear. 9p, Tuatara lizards.

**1972, March 17 Photo. Perf. 11½**

**Queen's Head in Gold**

| | | | | |
|---|---|---|---|---|
| 65 | A8 | 2½p Prus bl & multi | 35 | 32 |
| 66 | A8 | 3p dk pur & multi | 45 | 40 |
| 67 | A8 | 7½p yel bis & multi | 1.75 | 1.50 |
| 68 | A8 | 9p multi | 2.50 | 2.25 |

Jersey Wildlife Preservation Trust.

**1972, June 27**

| | | | | |
|---|---|---|---|---|
| 69 | A12 | 2½p *shown* | 14 | 10 |
| 70 | A12 | 3p *2nd North Regiment* | 22 | 18 |
| 71 | A12 | 7½p *South West Regiment* | 1.10 | 1.00 |
| 72 | A12 | 9p *3rd (South) Light Infantry* | 1.40 | 1.25 |

Royal Jersey Militia shakos of 19th century.

Princess Anne — A13

Designs: 3p, Queen Elizabeth II and Prince Philip (horiz.). 7½p, Prince Charles. 20p, Queen Elizabeth II and family (horiz.).

**1972, Nov. 1 Photo. Perf. 11½**

| | | | | |
|---|---|---|---|---|
| 73 | A13 | 2½p cit & multi | 8 | 8 |
| 74 | A13 | 3p rose & multi | 10 | 10 |
| 75 | A13 | 7½p bl & multi | 38 | 38 |
| 76 | A13 | 20p gray & multi | 65 | 65 |

25th anniversary of the marriage of Queen Elizabeth II and Prince Philip.

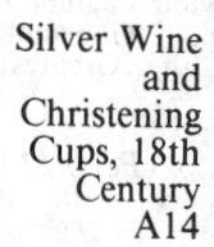

Silver Wine and Christening Cups, 18th Century A14

Designs: 3p, Gold torque, Bronze Age (vert.). 7½p, Seal of Charles II, 1659 (vert.). 9p, Armorican (Brittany) coins, c. 55 B.C.

**1973, Jan. 23 Photo. Perf. 11½**

| | | | | |
|---|---|---|---|---|
| 77 | A14 | 2½p ultra & multi | 6 | 6 |
| 78 | A14 | 3p dp car & multi | 8 | 8 |
| 79 | A14 | 7½p org & multi | 30 | 30 |
| 80 | A14 | 9p bl & multi | 50 | 50 |

Cent. of the Jersey Soc. Designs are from exhibits in the Soc. museum in St. Helier.

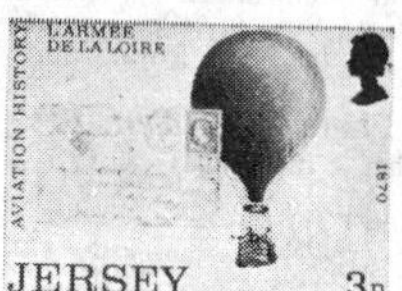



Balloon, Letter to Jersey from Siege of Paris, 1870 — A15

Designs: 5p, Astra seaplane, 1912. 7½p, Supermarine Sea Eagle, 1923. 9p, De Havilland DH86, 1933.

**1973, May 16 Photo. Perf. 11½**

| | | | | |
|---|---|---|---|---|
| 81 | A15 | 3p brt bl & multi | 8 | 8 |
| 82 | A15 | 5p bl grn & multi | 25 | 25 |
| 83 | A15 | 7½p ultra & multi | 60 | 60 |
| 84 | A15 | 9p vio bl & multi | 1.10 | 1.10 |

Aviation history connected with Jersey before 1939.

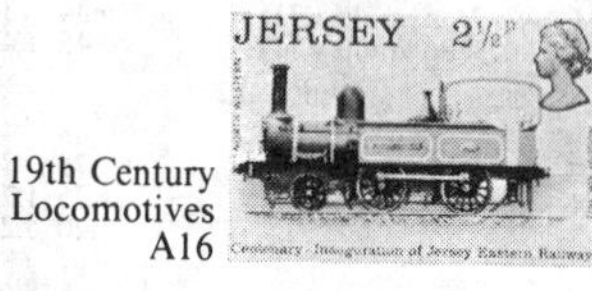



19th Century Locomotives A16

**1973, Aug. 6 Photo. Perf. 11½**

| | | | | |
|---|---|---|---|---|
| 85 | A16 | 2½p *North Western* | 10 | 10 |
| 86 | A16 | 3p *Calvados* | 12 | 12 |
| 87 | A16 | 7½p *Carteret* | 70 | 70 |
| 88 | A16 | 9p *Caesarea* | 90 | 90 |

Centenary of Jersey Eastern Railroad.

Princess Anne and Mark Phillips A17

**1973, Nov. 14 Photo. Perf. 11½**

| | | | | |
|---|---|---|---|---|
| 89 | A17 | 3p lt bl & multi | 18 | 18 |
| 90 | A17 | 20p pink & multi | 1.10 | 1.10 |

Wedding of Princess Anne and Capt. Mark Phillips, Nov. 14, 1973.

Spider Crab — A18

**1973, Nov. 15 Photo. Perf. 11½**

| | | | | |
|---|---|---|---|---|
| 91 | A18 | 2½p *shown* | 10 | 10 |
| 92 | A18 | 3p *Conger eel* | 12 | 12 |
| 93 | A18 | 7½p *Lobster* | 28 | 28 |
| 94 | A18 | 20p *Ormer* | 70 | 70 |

Jersey Spring Flowers — A19

**1974, Feb. 13 Photo. Perf. 12x11½**

| | | | | |
|---|---|---|---|---|
| 95 | A19 | 3p *Freesias* | 10 | 10 |
| 96 | A19 | 5½p *Anemones* | 20 | 20 |
| 97 | A19 | 8p *Carnations and gladioli* | 28 | 28 |
| 98 | A19 | 10p *Daffodils and iris* | 35 | 35 |

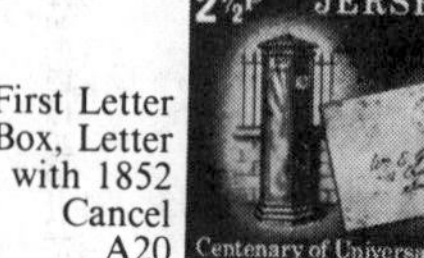

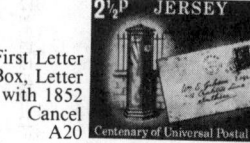

First Letter Box, Letter with 1852 Cancel A20

UPU Cent.: 3p, Postmen, 1862 and 1969. 5½p, Contemporary pillar box and first day cover of No. 101. 20p, BAC 111 and paddle steamer "Aquila," 1874.

**1974, June 7 Photo. Perf. 11½**

| | | | | |
|---|---|---|---|---|
| 99 | A20 | 2½p multi | 12 | 12 |
| 100 | A20 | 3p ultra & multi | 15 | 15 |
| 101 | A20 | 5½p ol & multi | 30 | 30 |
| 102 | A20 | 20p gray & multi | 1.10 | 1.10 |

John Wesley — A21

**Lithographed and Engraved**

**1974, July 31 Perf. 13½x14**

| | | | | |
|---|---|---|---|---|
| 103 | A21 | 3p shown | 10 | 10 |
| 104 | A21 | 3½p Hillary | 12 | 12 |
| 105 | A21 | 8p Wace | 25 | 25 |
| 106 | A21 | 20p Churchill | 65 | 65 |

Anniversaries: Methodism in Jersey, bicen.; John Wesley, theologian, founder of Methodism. Sesquicentennial of Royal Natl .Lifeboat Institution, Lt. Col. Sir William Hillary, founder. 800th death anniv. of Canon Wace, poet and chronicler. Sir Winston Churchill.

**Type of 1969**

**1974, Oct. 31 Photo. Perf. 14½**

Designs: 4½p, Arms of Jersey and Royal Mace. 5½p, Jersey cow. 8p, Mont Orgueil by night.

| | | | | |
|---|---|---|---|---|
| 107 | A3 | 4½p ol & multi | 18 | 18 |
| 108 | A3 | 5½p mag & multi | 24 | 24 |
| 109 | A3 | 8p yel & multi | 30 | 30 |

English Yacht, 1660, by Peter Monamy — A22

Designs: Marine paintings by Peter Monamy (d. 1749): 5½p, French ship. 8p, Dutch ship (horiz.). 25p, Naval battle, 1662.

**1974, Nov. 22 Photo. Perf. 11½**

**Size: 31x38, 38x31mm**

| | | | | |
|---|---|---|---|---|
| 116 | A22 | 3½p gold & multi | 10 | 10 |
| 117 | A22 | 5½p gold & multi | 18 | 18 |
| 118 | A22 | 8p gold & multi | 22 | 22 |

**Size: 54x25mm**

| | | | | |
|---|---|---|---|---|
| 119 | A22 | 25p gold & multi | 70 | 70 |

Potato Digger — A23

19th century farming tools: 3½p, Cider apple crusher. 8p, Six-horse plow. 10p, Hay cart.

**1975, Feb. 25 Photo. Perf. 11½**

| | | | | |
|---|---|---|---|---|
| 120 | A23 | 3p multi | 14 | 14 |
| 121 | A23 | 3½p multi | 15 | 15 |
| 122 | A23 | 8p multi | 35 | 35 |
| 123 | A23 | 10p multi | 42 | 42 |

Shell Design as Letter "J" — A24

Designs (Posters): 8p, Beach umbrella. 10p, Beach chair. 12p, Sand castle with Union Jacks and Jersey flag.

**1975, June 8 Photo. Perf. 11½**

| | | | | |
|---|---|---|---|---|
| 124 | A24 | 5p multi | 14 | 14 |
| 125 | A24 | 8p multi | 20 | 20 |
| 126 | A24 | 10p multi | 25 | 25 |
| 127 | A24 | 12p multi | 32 | 32 |
| *a.* | | Souvenir sheet of 4 | 1.00 | 1.00 |

Tourist publicity. No. 127a Nos. 124-127 in continuous design extending into margin; multicolored margin shows Corbiere Lighthouse; inscribed "Welcome to Jersey" in six languages. Size: 146x68½mm.

Queen Mother Elizabeth — A25

**1975, May 30 Photo. Perf. 11½**

| | | | | |
|---|---|---|---|---|
| 128 | A25 | 20p multi | 50 | 50 |

Visit of Queen Mother Elizabeth to Jersey.

Common Tern — A26

**1975, July 28 Photo. Perf. 11½**

| | | | | |
|---|---|---|---|---|
| 129 | A26 | 4p *shown* | 16 | 16 |
| 130 | A26 | 5p *Storm petrel* | 20 | 20 |
| 131 | A26 | 8p *Brent geese* | 32 | 32 |
| 132 | A26 | 25p *Shag* | 1.00 | 1.00 |

Demand, as well as supply, determines a stamp's market value. One is as important as the other.

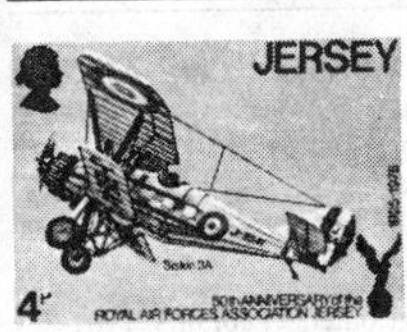

Siskin 3A, 1925 — A27

R.A.F. Planes: 5p, Southampton 1, 1925. 10p, Spitfire 1, 1931. 25p, Gnat T.1, 1962.

**1975, Oct. 30 Photo. *Perf. 11½***

| | | | | |
|---|---|---|---|---|
| *133* | A27 | 4p bl & multi | 12 | 12 |
| *134* | A27 | 5p lt grn & multi | 14 | 14 |
| *135* | A27 | 10p yel & multi | 28 | 28 |
| *136* | A27 | 25p ultra & multi | 70 | 70 |

Royal Air Force Assoc., Jersey Branch, 50th anniv.

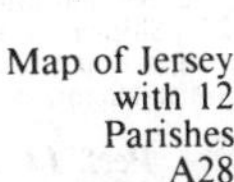

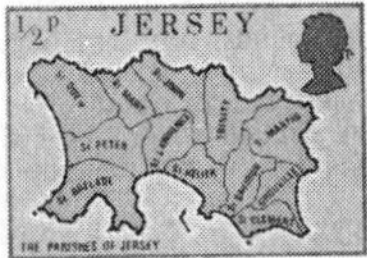

Map of Jersey with 12 Parishes A28

Arms of Trinity and Zoo — A29

Queen Elizabeth II — A30

Arms and scene: 5p, Church of St. Mary. 6p, Grouville, Seymour Tower. 7p, St. Brelade, La Corbiere Lighthouse. 8p, Church of St. Saviour. 9p, St. Helier, Elizabeth Castle. 10p, St. Martin, Gorey Harbor. 11p, St. Peter, Jersey Airport. 12p, St. Ouen, Grosnez Castle. 13p, St. John, Bonne Nuit Harbor. 14p, St. Clement and Le Hocq Tower. 15p, St. Lawrence, Morel Farm. 20p, 12 Parishes, view of harbor. 30p, Jersey flag, map of Island. 40p, Postal Administration emblem, PO Headquarters. 50p, Jersey, Parliament and Royal Court. £1, Flag of Lt.-Governor, Government House.

**1976-77 Litho. *Perf. 14½***

**Size: 33x23mm**

| | | | | |
|---|---|---|---|---|
| *137* | A28 | ½p lt bl & multi | 5 | 5 |
| *138* | A29 | 1p bis & multi | 5 | 5 |
| *a.* | | Bklt. pane of 2 + 2 labels ('77) | 15 | |
| *b.* | | Bklt. pane of 4 ('77) | 25 | |
| *139* | A29 | 5p rose & multi | 16 | 16 |
| *a.* | | Bklt. pane of 4 ('77) | 75 | |
| *140* | A29 | 6p vio bl & multi | 20 | 20 |
| *a.* | | Bklt. pane of 4 ('78) | 80 | |
| *141* | A29 | 7p fawn & multi | 24 | 24 |
| *a.* | | Bklt. pane of 4 ('77) | 1.00 | |
| *142* | A29 | 8p yel grn & multi | 28 | 28 |
| *a.* | | Bklt. pane of 4 ('78) | 1.12 | |
| *143* | A29 | 9p lil rose & multi | 32 | 32 |
| *144* | A29 | 10p ol bis & multi | 34 | 34 |
| *145* | A29 | 11p bl grn & multi | 38 | 38 |
| *146* | A29 | 12p org & multi | 42 | 42 |
| *147* | A29 | 13p bl & multi | 45 | 45 |
| *148* | A29 | 14p yel org & multi | 48 | 48 |
| *149* | A29 | 15p vio & multi | 52 | 52 |

**Photo.**

***Perf. 12***

**Size: 41x26mm, 26x41mm**

| | | | | |
|---|---|---|---|---|
| *150* | A29 | 20p gold & multi | 68 | 68 |
| *151* | A28 | 30p gold & multi | 1.00 | 1.00 |
| *152* | A29 | 40p gold & multi | 1.30 | 1.30 |
| *153* | A29 | 50p gold & multi | 1.70 | 1.70 |
| *154* | A29 | £1 gold & multi | 2.50 | 2.50 |
| *155* | A30 | £2 multi ('77) | 5.00 | 5.00 |
| | | *Nos. 137-155 (19)* | 16.07 | 16.07 |

Issue dates: Nos. 137-149, Jan. 29; Nos. 150-154, Aug. 20. No. 155, Nov. 16.

Sir Walter Raleigh and Old Map of Virginia — A31

American Bicentennial: 7p, Sir George Carteret and old map of New Jersey. 11p, Philippe Dauvergne and ships landing on Long Island. 13p, John Singleton Copley and his "Death of Major Pierson."

**1976, May 29 Photo. *Perf. 11½***

| | | | | |
|---|---|---|---|---|
| *160* | A31 | 5p multi | 20 | 14 |
| *161* | A31 | 7p multi | 20 | 20 |
| *162* | A31 | 11p multi | 30 | 30 |
| *163* | A31 | 13p multi | 35 | 35 |

Dr. Grandin, Central and Southern China Map A32

Designs: 7p, Yangtze River journey. 11p, On horseback to Chaotung. 13p, Dr. Grandin holding infant.

**1976, Nov. 25 Photo. *Perf. 11½***

| | | | | |
|---|---|---|---|---|
| *164* | A32 | 5p multi | 14 | 14 |
| *165* | A32 | 7p multi | 20 | 20 |
| *166* | A32 | 11p multi | 30 | 30 |
| *167* | A32 | 13p multi | 35 | 35 |

Lilian Mary Grandin (1876-1924), Jersey-born missionary doctor in China.

Queen Wearing St. Edward's Crown — A33

Designs: 7p, Queen with Jersey Bailiff Sir Alexander Coutanche, 1957. 25p, Portrait, 1976.

**1977, Feb. 7 Photo. *Perf. 11½***

| | | | | |
|---|---|---|---|---|
| *168* | A33 | 5p multi | 12 | 12 |
| *169* | A33 | 7p multi | 15 | 15 |
| *170* | A33 | 25p multi | 85 | 85 |

25th anniv. of the reign of Queen Elizabeth II.

1/13th sh, 1871 and 1/12th sh, 1877 A34

Coins: 7p, 1/12th sh, 1949. 11p, Silver crown, 1966. 13p, Silver £2, 1972.

**1977, Mar. 25 Litho. *Perf. 14***

| | | | | |
|---|---|---|---|---|
| *171* | A34 | 5p multi | 14 | 14 |
| *172* | A34 | 7p multi | 20 | 20 |
| *173* | A34 | 11p multi | 30 | 30 |
| *174* | A34 | 13p multi | 35 | 35 |

Centenary of Jersey's currency reform.

Sir William Weston and Santa Anna, 1530 — A35

Designs: 7p, Sir William Drogo and horse-drawn ambulance, 1877. 11p, Duke of Connaught and Jersey ambulance, 1917. 13p, Richard, Duke of Gloucester and ambulance team, 1977.

**1977, June 24 Litho. *Perf. 14x13½***

| | | | | |
|---|---|---|---|---|
| *175* | A35 | 5p multi | 14 | 14 |
| *176* | A35 | 7p multi | 20 | 20 |
| *177* | A35 | 11p multi | 30 | 30 |
| *178* | A35 | 13p multi | 35 | 35 |

St. John Ambulance Assoc. cent. (in GB).

Victoria and Albert Arriving in Jersey, 1846 A36

Designs: 10½p, Victoria College, 1852. 11p, Statue of Sir Galahad near college gate (vert.). 13p, College Hall, interior (vert.).

**1977, Sept. 29 Litho. *Perf. 14½***

| | | | | |
|---|---|---|---|---|
| *179* | A36 | 7p multi | 18 | 18 |
| *180* | A36 | 10½p multi | 28 | 28 |
| *181* | A36 | 11p multi | 32 | 32 |
| *182* | A36 | 13p multi | 40 | 40 |

Jersey Victoria College, 125th anniv.

Harry Vardon Statuette, Layout of Golf Course A37

Designs: 8p, Golf grip and swing perfected by Vardon. 11p, Vardon's putting grip and stance. 13p, Vardon's British and US Open Golf trophies, his book "The Complete Golfer" and biography.

**1978, Feb. 28 Litho. *Perf. 14***

| | | | | |
|---|---|---|---|---|
| *183* | A37 | 6p multi | 18 | 18 |
| *184* | A37 | 8p multi | 28 | 28 |
| *185* | A37 | 11p multi | 32 | 32 |
| *186* | A37 | 13p multi | 40 | 40 |

Cent. of Royal Jersey Golf Club and to honor Vardon (1870-1937), Jersey-born golfer.

**Europa Issue 1978**

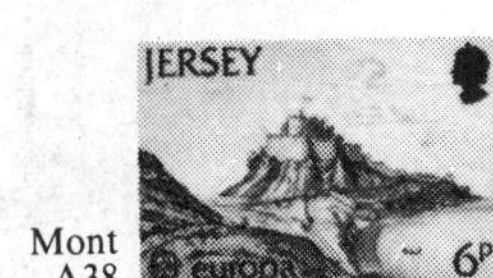

Mont Orgueil — A38

Designs: 8p, St. Aubin's Fort. 10½p, Elizabeth Castle.

**1978, May 1 Photo. *Perf. 11½***

| | | | | |
|---|---|---|---|---|
| *187* | A38 | 6p multi | 16 | 16 |
| *188* | A38 | 8p multi | 24 | 24 |
| *189* | A38 | 10½p multi | 32 | 32 |

Gaspe Basin, by P. J. Ouless — A39

Designs: 8p, Early map of Gaspe Peninsula, after Capt. Cook. 10½p, Sailing ship Century. 11p, Early map of Jersey. 13p, St. Aubin's Bay Town and Harbor.

**1978, June 9 Litho. *Perf. 14x15***

| | | | | |
|---|---|---|---|---|
| *190* | A39 | 6p multi | 15 | 15 |
| *191* | A39 | 8p multi | 22 | 22 |
| *192* | A39 | 10½p multi | 25 | 25 |
| *193* | A39 | 11p multi | 30 | 30 |
| *194* | A39 | 13p multi | 38 | 38 |
| | | *Nos. 190-194 (5)* | 1.30 | 1.30 |

Jersey's links with Canada and for CAPEX, Canadian Intl. Phil. Exhib., Toronto, Ont., June 9-18.

Elizabeth II, Portraits 1953 and 1977 — A40

Design: 8p, Elizabeth II and Prince Philip.

**1978, June 27 Photo. *Perf. 11½***

| | | | | |
|---|---|---|---|---|
| *195* | A40 | 8p car, sil & blk | 20 | 20 |
| *196* | A40 | 25p bl, sil & blk | 70 | 70 |

25th anniv. of coronation of Queen Elizabeth II and for Royal visit, June 27.

Mail Cutter — A41

Packets: 8p, Flamer, paddle vessel. 10½p, Diana, screw steamer. 11p, Ibex, steamer. 13p, Caesarea, mini-liner.

**1978, Oct. 18 Litho. *Perf. 14½x14***

| | | | | |
|---|---|---|---|---|
| *197* | A41 | 6p multi | 18 | 18 |
| *198* | A41 | 8p multi | 22 | 22 |
| *199* | A41 | 10½p multi | 30 | 30 |
| *200* | A41 | 11p multi | 35 | 35 |
| *201* | A41 | 13p multi | 38 | 38 |
| | | *Nos. 197-201 (5)* | 1.43 | 1.43 |

First Government packet between Britain and Jersey, bicentenary.

Jersey Pillar Box, 1860 — A42

Soft-colored Jersey Heifer — A43

Designs: No. 203, Mailman emptying 1979 mailbox. No. 204, Telephone switchboard, c. 1900. No. 205, Operator working on contemporary telecommunications system.

**Europa Issue 1979**

***Perf. 14, 14½x15***

**1979, Mar. 1 Litho.**

| | | | | |
|---|---|---|---|---|
| *202* | A42 | 8p yel & blk | 16 | 16 |
| *203* | A42 | 8p car & blk | 16 | 16 |
| *204* | A42 | 10½p vio & blk | 38 | 38 |
| *205* | A42 | 10½p bl & blk | 38 | 38 |

Stamps of same denomination printed se-tenant in continuous design in sheets of 20 (4x5).

**1979, Mar. 1**

Design: 25p, Milk-laden Jersey cow with First Prize ribbon.

**Size: 31x31mm**

| | | | | |
|---|---|---|---|---|
| *206* | A43 | 6p multi | 18 | 18 |

**Size: 48x31mm**

*207* A43 25p multi 75 75

30th anniv. of 1st Intl. Conf. of Jersey Breed Societies and 9th Conf. of the World Jersey Cattle Bureau.

Percival Mew Gull — A44

Planes: 8p, De Havilland Chipmunk. 10½p, Druine D-31 Turbulent. 11p, De Havilland Tiger Moth. 13p, North American Harvard Mk. 4.

**1979, Apr. 24 Photo. *Perf. 11½***

*208* A44 6p multi 18 18
*209* A44 8p multi 22 22
*210* A44 10½p multi 32 32
*211* A44 11p multi 35 35
*212* A44 13p multi 38 38
*Nos. 208-212 (5)* 1.45 1.45

25th International Air Rally.

My First Sermon, by Millais — A45

Paintings by Millais: 10½p, Orphan. 11p, The Princes in the Tower. 25p, Jesus in the Home of His Parents (horiz.).

**1979, Aug. 13 Photo. *Perf. 11½***

**Size: 25x35mm**

*213* A45 8p multi 22 22
*214* A45 10½p multi 28 28
*215* A45 11p multi 30 30

**Size: 49x30mm**

*216* A45 25p multi 70 70

IYC and for John Everett Millais (1829-96).

Waldrapp Ibis A46

**1979, Nov. 8 Photo. *Perf. 11½***

*217* A46 6p *Pink pigeons* 15 15
*218* A46 8p *Orangutans* 20 20
*219* A46 11½p *shown* 30 30
*220* A46 13p *Lowland gorillas* 32 32
*221* A46 15p *Rodrigues fruit bats* 40 40
*Nos. 217-221 (5)* 1.37 1.37

Nos. 217-218, 220-221 vertical.

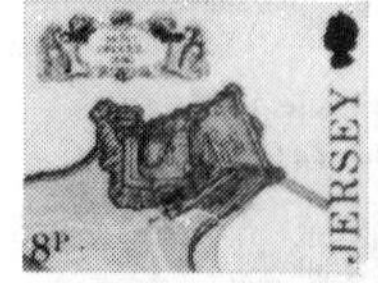

Mont Orgueil Fortress — A47

Fortresses, 300th Anniversary: 11½p, St. Aubin Tower. 13p, Elizabeth. 25p, Map of Jersey showing fortress locations.

**1980, Feb. 5 Litho. *Perf. 14½x13½***

*222* A47 8p multi 20 20
*223* A47 11½p multi 30 30
*224* A47 13p multi 32 32

***Perf. 13½x14***

**Size 37½x26mm**

*225* A47 25p multi 65 65

Potato Harvest — A48

Royal Jersey Potato Cent.: 7p, Planting potatoes. 17½p, Loading dock, Weighbridge.

**1980, May 6 Litho. *Perf. 14***

*226* A48 7p multi 18 18
*227* A48 15p multi 40 40
*228* A48 17½p multi 45 45

**Europa Issue 1980**

Sir Walter Raleigh and Paul Ivy
A49 A50

Wax Figures from Mont Orgveil and Elizabeth Castles: No. 230, Charles II and Sir George Carteret, Lady Carteret. Pairs in continuous design.

**1980, May 6**

*229* Pair 50 50
*a.* A49 9p multi 25 25
*b.* A50 9p multi 25 25
*230* Pair 75 75
*a.* A49 13½p multi 32 32
*b.* A50 13½p multi 32 32

Three-lap Motorcycle Race — A51

**1980, July 24 Litho. *Perf. 12***

**Granite Paper**

*231* A51 7p *shown* 18 18
*232* A51 9p *Intl. road race* 25 25
*233* A51 13½p *Motorcycle scrambling* 38 38
*234* A51 15p *Sand racing, saloon cars* 45 45
*235* A51 17½p *Natl. Hill climb* 50 50
*Nos. 231-235 (5)* 1.76 1.76

Jersey Motorcycle and Light Car Club, 60th anniv.

"Eye of the Wind" Leaving St. Helier — A52

Designs: 9p, Medical research, Cuna Indians, Panama. 13½p, Exploration, Papua New Guinea. 14p, Capt. Scott's ship, Antarctica. 15p, Conservation, Sulawesi. 17½p, Marine studies.

**1980, Oct. 1 Litho. *Perf. 14½***

*236* A52 7p multi 18 18
*237* A52 9p multi 22 22
*238* A52 13½ multi 35 35
*239* A52 14p multi 35 35
*240* A52 15p multi 40 40
*241* A52 17½p multi 45 45
*Nos. 236-241 (6)* 1.95 1.95

Operation Drake, a two-year, round-the-world scientific expedition in tribute to Royal Geographic Society sesquicentennial.

Armed Soldiers and Wounded Drummer A53

Designs: Details from The Death of Major Peirson, by John Singleton Copley.

**1981, Jan. 6 Photo. *Perf. 12½***

**Granite Paper**

*242* A53 7p multi 20 20
*243* A53 10p multi 30 30
*244* A53 15p multi 45 45
*245* A53 17½p multi 52 52
*a.* Souvenir sheet of 4 1.50 1.50

Battle of Jersey bicentenary. No. 245a contains Nos. 242-245; multicolored margin shows entire painting. Size: 145x97mm.

De Bagot Family Arms A54

Jersey, Channel Map A54a

Queen Elizabeth II, by Norman Hepple — A54b

**1981-82 Litho. *Perf. 14***

*246* A54 ½p shown 5 5
*247* A54 1p De Carteret 5 5
*a.* Bklt. pane of 6 30
*b.* Perf. 15x14 ('88) 5 5
*248* A54 2p La Cloche 8 8
*a.* Bklt. pane of 6 48
*b.* Bklt. pane of 6, perf. 15x14 ('86) 48
*c.* Perf. 15x14 ('88) 8 8
*249* A54 3p Dumaresq 10 10
*a.* Bklt. pane of 6 60
*b.* Bklt. pane of 6, perf. 15x14 ('84) 60
*250* A54 4p Payn 12 12
*a.* Bklt. pane of 6, perf. 15x14 ('87) 1.00
*b.* Perf. 15x14 ('88) 12 12
*251* A54 5p Janvrin 16 16
*252* A54 6p Poingdestre 18 18
*253* A54 7p Pipon 20 20
*a.* Bklt. pane of 6 1.25
*254* A54 8p Marett 24 24
*a.* Bklt. pane of 6 ('83) 1.50
*255* A54 9p Le Breton 25 25
*a.* Bklt. pane of 6, perf. 15x14 ('84) 1.50
*256* A54 10p Le Maistre 30 30
*a.* Bklt. pane of 6 1.80
*b.* Bklt. pane of 6, perf. 15x14 ('86) 1.80
*257* A54 11p Bisson 35 35
*a.* Bklt. pane of 6, perf. 15x14 ('87) 2.25
*b.* Bklt. pane of 6 ('83) 2.25
*258* A54 12p Robin 35 35
*a.* Bklt. pane of 6, perf. 15x14 ('84) 2.25
*b.* Perf. 15x14 ('88) 35 35
*259* A54 13p Herault 38 38
*260* A54 14p Messervy 40 40
*a.* Bklt. pane of 6, perf. 15x14 ('86) 2.50
*261* A54 15p Fiott 45 45
*a.* Perf. 15x14 ('87) 38 38
*b.* Bklt. pane of 6, perf. 15x14 ('87) 2.75
*262* A54 20p Badier 60 60
*263* A54 25p L'Arbalestier 75 75
*264* A54 30p Journeaulx 95 95
*265* A54 40p Lempriere 1.10 1.10
*a.* Perf. 15x14 ('87) 1.00 1.00
*266* A54 50p D'Auvergne 1.25 1.25
*a.* Perf. 15x14 ('87) 1.25 1.25
*267* A54a £1 shown 1.90 1.90

**1983, Nov. 17 Photo. *Perf. 12½x12***

*268* A54b £5 multi 9.75 9.75
*Nos. 246-268 (23)* 19.96 19.96

Issue dates: Nos. 246-256, Feb. 24. Nos. 257-262, July 28. Nos. 263-267, Feb. 23, 1982. £5, Nov. 17, 1983.

See Nos. 381-388.

Nos. 247a-248a dated "Febraury 1981" or "April 1983"; Nos. 253a, 256a dated "February 1981" or "December 1981."

**Europa Issue 1981**

Knight of Hamby Killing the Dragon A55

Legends, 10p, La Hougue Bie. 18p, Easter Voyage of St. Brelade. No. 272, Servant killing Knight of Hamby. No. 273, Shipwreck of St. Brelade. No. 274, Fish, ships' departure. Stamps of same denomination se-tenant.

**1981, Apr. 7 *Perf. 14½***

*271* A55 10p multi 30 30
*272* A55 10p multi 30 30
*273* A55 18p multi 52 52
*274* A55 18p multi 52 52

Royal Square by Gaslight A56

**1981, May 22 Photo. *Perf. 12***

**Granite Paper**

*275* A56 7p The Harbor 18 18
*276* A56 10p The Quay 28 28
*277* A56 18p shown 50 50
*278* A56 22p Halkett Place 60 60
*279* A56 25p Central Market 70 70
*Nos. 275-279 (5)* 2.26 2.26

Gas light sesquicentennial.

Prince Charles and Lady Diana A57

**1981, July 28 Photo. *Perf. 12***

**Granite Paper**

*280* A57 10p multi 45 45
*281* A57 25p multi 1.10 1.10

Royal Wedding.

Christmas Tree, Royal Square, St. Helier — A58

**1981, Sept. 29 Litho. *Perf. 14½***

*282* A58 7p shown 24 24
*283* A58 10p East window, St. Helier's Church, choir 35 35
*284* A58 18p Boxing Day, Jersey Drag Hunt 60 60

Christmas 1981.

Europa 1982 — A59

Designs: Maps showing formation of Channel Islands resulting from rise in sea level.

**1982, Apr. 20 Litho. *Perf. 14½***

*285* A59 11p 16,000 BC 30 30
*286* A59 11p 10,000 BC, vert. 30 30
*287* A59 19½p 7,000 BC, vert. 52 52
*288* A59 19½p 4,000 BC 52 52

Rollon Duke of Normandy, William the Conqueror, Clameur de Haro (Plea of Injunction) — A60

Links with France: No. 290, Kings John and Philippe Auguste, Siege of Rouen. No. 291, Jean Martxell (1694-1753), brandy merchant. No. 292, Victor Hugo. No. 293, Pierre Teilhard de Chardin (1881-1955), theologian. No. 294, Charles Rey (1897-1981), meteorologist. Stamps of same denomination se-tenant.

**1982, June 11 Litho. *Perf. 14***

*289* A60 8p multi 25 25
*290* A60 8p multi 25 25
*291* A60 11p multi 35 35
*292* A60 11p multi 35 35
*293* A60 19½p multi 65 65
*294* A60 19½p multi 65 65
*Nos. 289-294 (6)* 2.50 2.50

Scouting Year A61

Designs: 8p, Sir William Smith (Boys Brigade founder). 11p, Liberation parade, 1945 (vert.). 24p, Boys Brigade annual display, 1903. 26p, The Baden-Powells, 1924 (vert.). 29p, Scouts.

**1982, Nov. 18 Photo. *Perf. 12***
**Granite Paper**

*295* A61 8p multi 24 24
*296* A61 11p multi 35 35
*297* A61 24p multi 75 75
*298* A61 26p multi 80 85
*299* A61 29p multi 95 95
*Nos. 295-299 (5)* 3.09 3.14

Port Egmont A62

250th Birth Anniv. of Capt. Philippe de Carteret (1733-97): 18th cent. engravings.

**1983, Feb. 15 Litho. *Perf. 14¼***

*300* A62 8p shown 22 22
*301* A62 11p Dolphin, Swallow 30 30
*302* A62 19½p Discovering Pitcairn Isld. 55 55
*303* A62 24p English Cove, New Ireland 70 70
*304* A62 26p Sinking pirate ship 75 75
*305* A62 29p Endymion 90 90
*Nos. 300-305 (6)* 3.42 3.42

**Europa 1983**

No. 19 A63

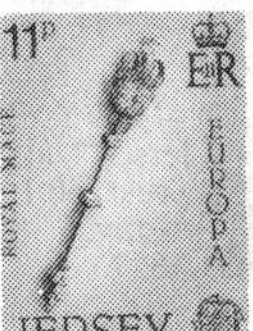

Royal Mace — A64

**1983, Apr. 19 Litho.**

*306* A63 11p shown 38 38
*307* A64 11p shown 38 38
*308* A63 19½p No. 20 70 70
*309* A64 19½p Bailiff's seal 70 70

Stamps of same denomination se-tenant.

World Communications Year — A65

1st Postmaster Charles William LeGeyt (1733-1827): 8p, Commanding Grenadier Co., 25th Foot, Battle of Minden, 1759. 11p, London-Weymouth mail coach. 24p, PO Mail Packet attacked by French privateer. 25p, Hue St. PO. 29p, St. Helier Harbor.

**1983, June 21 Litho. *Perf. 14***

*310* A65 8p multi 24 24
*311* A65 11p multi 35 35
*312* A65 24p multi 75 75
*313* A65 26p multi 80 80
*314* A65 29p multi 95 95
*Nos. 310-314 (5)* 3.09 3.09

Intl. Assoc. of French-Speaking Parliamentarians 1983 General Assembly — A66

**1983, June 21 *Perf. 15***

*315* A66 19½p multi 60 60

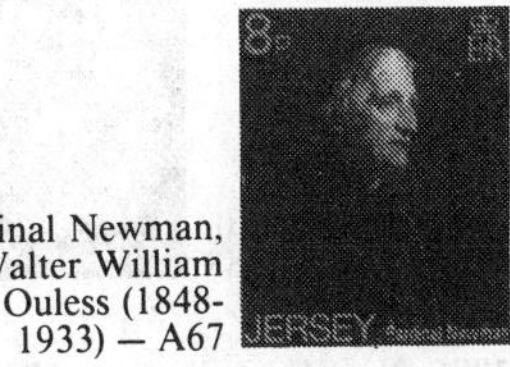

Cardinal Newman, by Walter William Ouless (1848-1933) — A67

**1983, Sept. 20 Photo. *Perf. 11½***

*316* A67 8p shown 25 25
*317* A67 11p M. De Cazotte and his Daughter 35 35
*318* A67 20½p Thomas Hardy 62 62

**Size: 41x34mm**

*319* A67 31p David with the Head of Goliath 95 95

Jersey Wildlife Preservation Trust — A68

**1984, Jan. 17 Litho. *Perf. 14***

*320* A68 9p Golden Lion Tamarin 28 28
*321* A68 12p Snow Leopard 36 36
*322* A68 20½p Jamaican Boa 62 62
*323* A68 26p Round Island Gecko 78 78
*324* A68 28p Coscoroba Swan 85 85
*325* A68 31p St. Lucia Parrot 95 95
*Nos. 320-325 (6)* 3.84 3.84

Europa 1984 (25th Anniv.) A69

**1984, Mar. 12 *Perf. 14½x15***

*326* A69 9p multi 28 28
*327* A69 12p multi 36 36
*328* A69 20½p multi 62 62

**Souvenir Sheet**

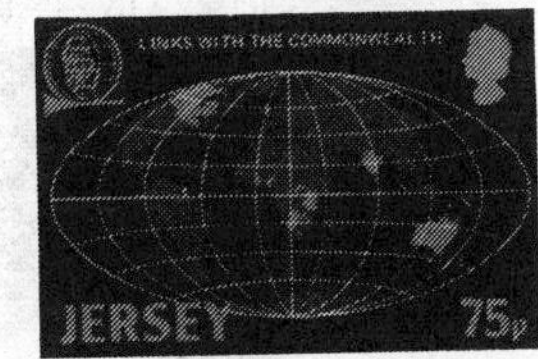

Jersey Links with the Commonwealth — A70

**1984, Mar. 12 *Perf. 15x14½***

*329* A70 75p multi 2.75 2.75

Commonwealth Postal Administrations Conf. Multicolored margin shows flags of member countries; marginal inscription.

Royal Natl. Lifeboat Institution Centenary A71

Rescue Scenes (Lifeboats and Ships).

**1984, June 1 Litho. *Perf. 14½***

*330* A71 9p Sarah Brooshoft, Demie de Pas Light 32 32
*331* A71 9p Hearts of Oak, Maurice Georges 32 32
*332* A71 12p Elizabeth Rippon, Hanna 42 42
*333* A71 12p Elizabeth Rippon, Santa Maria 42 42
*334* A71 20½p Elizabeth Rippon, Bacchus 75 75
*335* A71 20½p Thomas James King, Cythara 75 75
*Nos. 330-335 (6)* 2.98 2.98

40th Anniv. of Intl. Civil Aviation Org. A72

**1984, July 24 Litho. *Perf. 14***
**Granite Paper**

*336* A72 9p Bristol Type 170 35 35
*337* A72 12p Airspeed AS-57 Ambassador 2 45 45
*338* A72 26p De Havilland Heron 1B 95 95
*339* A72 31p DH-89A Dragon Rapide 1.25 1.25

Foreign postal stationery (stamped envelopes, postal cards and air letter sheets) lies beyond the scope of this Catalogue, which is limited to adhesive postage stamps.

Robinson Crusoe, by John Alexander Gilfillan (1793-1864) — A73

Gilfillan Paintings.

**1984, Sept. 21 Photo. *Perf. 11½***

*340* A73 9p shown 25 25
*341* A73 12p Edinburgh Castle 34 34
*342* A73 20½p Maori Village 56 56
*343* A73 26p Australian Landscape 72 72
*344* A73 28p Waterhouse's Corner, Adelaide 78 78
*345* A73 31p Capt. Cook at Botany Bay 85 85
*Nos. 340-345 (6)* 3.50 3.50

Christmas 1984 — A74

**1984, Nov. 15 Photo. *Perf. 12x11½***

*346* A74 9p St. Helier orchid 25 25
*347* A74 12p Mt. Bingham orchid 34 34

Ship Paintings by Philip John Ouless (1817-85) A75

**1985, Feb. 26 Photo. *Perf. 14x14½***

*348* A75 9p Hebe, 1874 22 22
*349* A75 12p Gaspe 28 28
*350* A75 22p London, 1856 55 55
*351* A75 31p Rambler 78 78
*352* A75 34p Elizabeth Castle 85 85
*Nos. 348-352 (5)* 2.68 2.68

Europa 1985 A76

Performing Arts: 10p, John Ireland, composer (1879-1962). 13p, Ivy St. Helier, actress (1886-1971). 22p, Claude Debussy, composer.

**1985, Apr. 23 Litho. *Perf. 14***

*353* A76 10p multi 30 30
*354* A76 13p multi 38 38
*355* A76 22p multi 65 65

Intl. Youth Year — A77

**1985, May 30 Litho. *Perf. 14½***

*356* A77 10p Girls' Brigade 25 25
*357* A77 13p Girl Guides 32 32
*358* A77 29p Jersey Youth Service 72 72
*359* A77 31p Sea Cadet Corps 78 78
*360* A77 34p Air Training Corps 85 85
*Nos. 356-360 (5)* 2.92 2.92

Railway History A78

**1985, July 16 Photo. *Perf. 12x11½***

| | | | | |
|---|---|---|---|---|
| *361* A78 | 10p | Duke of Normandy, Cheapside | 32 | 32 |
| *362* A78 | 13p | Saddletank, First Tower | 40 | 40 |
| *363* A78 | 22p | La Moye, Millbrook | 70 | 70 |
| *364* A78 | 29p | St. Helier's, St. Aubin | 90 | 90 |
| *365* A78 | 34p | St. Aubyns, Corbiere | 1.10 | 1.10 |
| | | *Nos. 361-365 (5)* | 3.42 | 3.42 |

Centenary of Jersey's first train from St. Helier to Corbiere.

Huguenot Heritage A79

300th anniv. of revocation of the Edict of Nantes (religious tolerance) by King Louis XIV of France: No. 366, James Hemery (1814-1849), Dean of Jersey, Rector of St. Helier. No. 367, Francis Henry Jeune, Baron St. Helier, law lord and junior counsel in the Tichbourne case. No. 368, Francois Voisin, merchant. No. 369, Pierre Amiraux, silversmith. No. 370, George Henry Ingouville, Victoria Cross recipient. No. 371, Robert Brohier, co-founder of Schweppes soft-drink company.

**1985, Sept. 10 Litho. *Perf. 14***

| | | | | |
|---|---|---|---|---|
| *366* A79 | 10p | Memorial window, St. Helier Town Church | 28 | 28 |
| *a.* | | Bklt. pane of 4 | 1.15 | |
| *367* A79 | 10p | Houses of Parliament, Westminster | 28 | 28 |
| *a.* | | Bklt. pane of 4 | 1.15 | |
| *368* A79 | 13p | Great Fair, Nijni-Novgorod, Russia | 34 | 34 |
| *a.* | | Bklt. pane of 4 | 1.40 | |
| *369* A79 | 13p | Silver coffee pot, pitcher | 34 | 34 |
| *a.* | | Bklt. pane of 4 | 1.40 | |
| *370* A79 | 22p | Naval Battle of Viborg | 58 | 58 |
| *a.* | | Bklt. pane of 4 | 2.35 | |
| *371* A79 | 22p | Glass bottles, carbonated water commercial patent | 58 | 58 |
| *a.* | | Bklt. pane of 4 | 2.35 | |
| | | *Nos. 366-371 (6)* | 2.40 | 2.40 |

Thomas Benjamin Frederick Davis (1867-1942), Shipping Magnate, Philanthropist A80

Portrait and endowments: 10p, Howard Davis Hall, Victoria College. 13p, Yacht, racing schooner Westward. 31p, Howard Davis Park, St. Helier. 34p, Howard Davis Agricultural Development Farm, Trinity.

**1985, Oct. 25 *Perf. 13½***

| | | | | |
|---|---|---|---|---|
| *372* A80 | 10p | multi | 28 | 28 |
| *373* A80 | 13p | multi | 34 | 34 |
| *374* A80 | 31p | multi | 85 | 85 |
| *375* A80 | 34p | multi | 90 | 90 |

50th anniv. of Howard Davis Hall, Victoria College, donated by Davis in memory of his son.

Arms Type of 1981-82

**1985-88 Litho. *Perf. 15x14***

| | | | | |
|---|---|---|---|---|
| *381* A54 | 16p | Malet | 48 | 48 |
| *a.* | | Bklt. pane of 6 ('88) | 2.90 | |
| *382* A54 | 17p | Mabon | 50 | 50 |
| *383* A54 | 18p | De St. Martin ('88) | 68 | 68 |
| *384* A54 | 19p | Hamptonne ('88) | 72 | 72 |
| *386* A54 | 26p | De Bagot ('88) | 98 | 98 |
| *388* A54 | 75p | Remon ('87) | 2.50 | 2.50 |
| | | *Nos. 381-388 (6)* | 5.86 | 5.86 |

Issue dates: 16p, 17p, Oct. 25. 75p, Apr. 23. 18p, 19p, 26p, Apr. 26.

No. 381a inscribed "May 1988".

Elizabeth II, 60th Birthday — A80a

**1986, Apr. 21 Litho. *Perf. 11½x12***

| | | | | |
|---|---|---|---|---|
| *389* A80a | £1 | multi | 2.50 | 2.50 |

Jersey Lily — A81

Lillie Langtry, by Sir John Millais — A82

**1986, Jan. 28 Litho. *Perf. 15x14½***

| | | | | |
|---|---|---|---|---|
| *391* A81 | 13p | multi | 38 | 38 |
| *392* A82 | 34p | multi | 1.00 | 1.00 |
| *a.* | | Souvenir sheet of 5 (4 13p, 34p) | 3.00 | 3.00 |

Intl. Flower Gala, June 10-14. No. 392a has multicolored inscribed margin picturing Langtry's signature, the Lalee and the White Ladye.

Halley's Comet Sightings A83

Comet and coinciding historic events: 10p, Conquest of England, Bayeux Tapestry, A.D. 912 and 1066 sightings. 22p, Lady Carteret signing New Jersey over to William Penn, 1301. Edmond Halley observing the comet, 1682. 31p, Giotto spacecraft and technology developed in 1910, 1986. Caesarea maiden voyage.

**1986, Mar. 4 *Perf. 13½x13***

| | | | | |
|---|---|---|---|---|
| *393* A83 | 10p | multi | 30 | 30 |
| *394* A83 | 22p | multi | 65 | 65 |
| *395* A83 | 31p | multi | 90 | 90 |

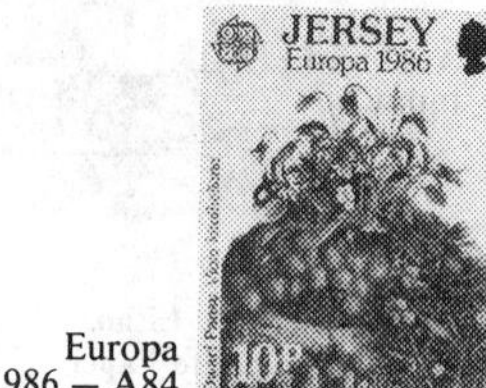


Europa 1986 — A84

**1986, Apr. 21 *Perf. 14½***

| | | | | |
|---|---|---|---|---|
| *396* A84 | 10p | Viola kitaibeliana | 30 | 30 |
| *397* A84 | 14p | Matthiola sinuata | 42 | 42 |
| *398* A84 | 22p | Romulea columnae | 65 | 65 |

Environmental conservation.

Jersey Natl. Trust, 50th Anniv. A85

**1986, June 17 Litho. *Perf. 13½x13***

| | | | | |
|---|---|---|---|---|
| *399* A85 | 10p | Le Rat cottage | 24 | 24 |
| *400* A85 | 14p | The Elms, headquarters | 32 | 32 |
| *401* A85 | 22p | Morel Farm entrance | 52 | 52 |
| *402* A85 | 29p | Quetivel Mill | 70 | 70 |
| *403* A85 | 31p | La Vallette | 75 | 75 |
| | | *Nos. 399-403 (5)* | 2.53 | 2.53 |

Wedding of Prince Andrew and Sarah Ferguson — A86

**1986, July 23 *Perf. 13½***

| | | | | |
|---|---|---|---|---|
| *404* A86 | 14p | multi | 42 | 42 |
| *405* A86 | 40p | multi | 1.25 | 1.25 |

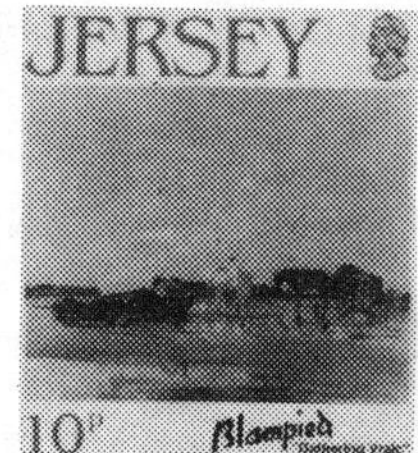


Paintings by Edmund Blampied (1886-1966), Artist — A87

**1986, Aug. 28 Litho. *Perf. 14***

| | | | | |
|---|---|---|---|---|
| *406* A87 | 10p | Gathering Vraic | 24 | 24 |
| *407* A87 | 14p | Driving Home in the Rain | 32 | 32 |
| *408* A87 | 29p | The Miller | 70 | 70 |
| *409* A87 | 31p | The Joy Ride | 75 | 75 |
| *410* A87 | 34p | Tante Elizabeth | 85 | 85 |
| | | *Nos. 406-410 (5)* | 2.86 | 2.86 |

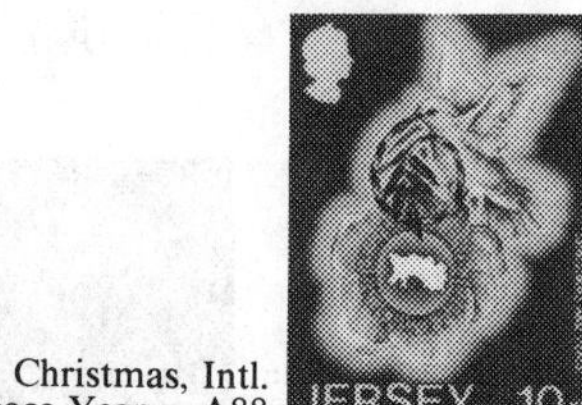


Christmas, Intl. Peace Year — A88

**1986, Nov. 4 *Perf. 14½***

| | | | | |
|---|---|---|---|---|
| *411* A88 | 10p | Dove, map, flower | 25 | 25 |
| *412* A88 | 14p | Lovebirds | 35 | 35 |
| *413* A88 | 34p | Dove, noise-maker | 85 | 85 |

Racing Schooner Westward A89

**1987, Jan. 15 Litho. *Perf. 13½***

| | | | | |
|---|---|---|---|---|
| *414* A89 | 10p | Under full sail | 28 | 28 |
| *415* A89 | 14p | T.B. Davis, owner | 35 | 35 |
| *416* A89 | 31p | Overhauling Britannia | 80 | 80 |
| *417* A89 | 34p | Dry dock, St. Helier | 90 | 90 |

Jersey Airport, 50th Anniv. A90

**1987, Mar. 3 Litho. *Perf. 14***

| | | | | |
|---|---|---|---|---|
| *418* A90 | 10p | DH86 Belcroute Bay | 28 | 28 |
| *419* A90 | 14p | Boeing 757, Douglas DC-9 | 35 | 35 |
| *420* A90 | 22p | Britten Norman Trislander, Islander | 60 | 60 |
| *421* A90 | 29p | Short SD330, Vickers Viscount | 75 | 75 |
| *422* A90 | 31p | BAC1-11, HPR.7 Dart Herald | 80 | 80 |
| | | *Nos. 418-422 (5)* | 2.78 | 2.78 |

Europa 1987 A91

Modern architecture.

**1987, Apr. 23 *Perf. 15x14***

| | | | | |
|---|---|---|---|---|
| *423* A91 | 11p | St. Mary and St. Peter's Church | 32 | 32 |
| *424* A91 | 15p | Villa Devereux | 42 | 42 |

**Size: 61x31mm**

| | | | | |
|---|---|---|---|---|
| *425* A91 | 22p | Fort Regent, St. Helier | 60 | 60 |

Adm. Philippe D'Auvergne (1754-1816) — A92

Ships: 11p, Racehorse trapped in the Arctic. 15p, Alarm burned at Rhode Island. 29p, Arethusa wrecked off Ushant, France. 31p, Rattlesnake stranded on Trinidad. 34p, Mount Orgueil Castle.

**1987, July 9 *Perf. 14***

| | | | | |
|---|---|---|---|---|
| *426* A92 | 11p | multi | 30 | 30 |
| *427* A92 | 15p | multi | 40 | 40 |
| *428* A92 | 29p | multi | 80 | 80 |
| *429* A92 | 31p | multi | 85 | 85 |
| *430* A92 | 34p | multi | 90 | 90 |
| | | *Nos. 426-430 (5)* | 3.25 | 3.25 |

William the Conqueror (c. 1028-87), King of England (1066-87) A93

Designs in the style of the Bayeux Tapestry: 11p, King Charles negotiating peace with the Vikings, 911, and cession of Jersey to Rollo's son William, 933. 15p, Duke Robert I and King Edward ashore Jersey after storm, 1030; Edward's succession to the throne of England, 1042. 22p, William the Conqueror's coronation, 1066, and succession of William II, 1087. 29p, Death of King William Rufus, and Henry defeating Duke Robert to unite England and Normandy, 1106. 31p, Death of Henry, battle for the throne and succession of King Stephen, 1135. 34p, Successions of Henry II, 1154, and John Lackland, 1189.

**1987 *Perf. 13½***

| | | | | |
|---|---|---|---|---|
| *431* A93 | 11p | multi | 35 | 35 |
| *a.* | | Bklt. pane of 4 + label | 1.40 | |
| *432* A93 | 15p | multi | 48 | 48 |
| *a.* | | Bklt. pane of 4 + label | 1.95 | |
| *433* A93 | 22p | multi | 70 | 70 |
| *a.* | | Bklt. pane of 4 + label | 2.80 | |

*434* A93 29p multi 95 95
*a.* Bklt. pane of 4 + label 3.80
*435* A93 31p multi 1.00 1.00
*a.* Bklt. pane of 4 + label 4.00
*436* A93 34p multi 1.10 1.10
*a.* Bklt. pane of 4 + label 4.40
*Nos. 431-436 (6)* 4.58 4.58

Paintings by John Le Capelain (1812-1848) — A94

**1987, Nov. 3 Photo. *Perf. 12x11½***

*437* A94 11p Grosnez Castle 25 25
*438* A94 15p St. Aubin's Bay 38 38
*439* A94 22p Mt. Orgueil Castle 52 52
*440* A94 31p Town Fort and Harbor, St. Helier 75 75
*441* A94 34p The Hermitage 80 80
*Nos. 437-441 (5)* 2.70 2.70

Christmas.

Hybrids, Eric Young Orchid Foundation, Trinity — A95

**1988, Jan. 12 Litho. *Perf. 14***

*442* A95 11p Cymbidium pontac 38 38
*443* A95 15p Odontioda Eric Young 52 52
*444* A95 29p Lycaste auburn Seaford and Ditchling 1.00 1.00
*445* A95 31p Odontoglossum St. Brelade 1.10 1.10
*446* A95 34p Cymbidium mavourneen Jester 1.20 1.20
*Nos. 442-446 (5)* 4.20 4.20

Jersey Dog Club, Cent. A96

**1988, Mar. 2**

*447* A96 11p Labrador retriever 42 42
*448* A96 15p Wire-haired dachshund 58 58
*449* A96 22p Pekingese 82 82
*450* A96 31p Cavalier King Charles spaniel 1.20 1.20
*451* A96 34p Dalmatian 1.30 1.30
*Nos. 447-451 (5)* 4.32 4.32

Europa 1988 A97

Transport and communication.

**1988, Apr. 26 Litho. *Perf. 14x13½***

*452* A97 16p Air transport 60 60
*453* A97 16p Air communication 60 60
*454* A97 22p Sea transport 82 82
*455* A97 22p Sea communication 82 82

Nos. 453 and 455 vert.

Wildlife Preservation Trust, 25th Anniv. — A98

**1988, July 6 Litho.**

*456* A98 12p Rodrigues fody, vert. 40 40
*457* A98 16p Volcano rabbit 52 52
*458* A98 29p White-faced marmoset, vert. 95 95
*459* A98 31p Ploughshare tortoise 1.00 1.00
*460* A98 34p Mauritius kestrel, vert. 1.10 1.10
*Nos. 456-460 (5)* 3.97 3.97

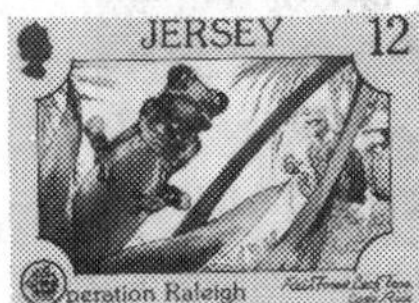


Operation Raleigh A99

Activities: 12p, Rain Forest Leaf Frog, Costa Rica. 16p, Archaeological Survey, Peru. 22p, Glacier Climbing, Chile. 29p, Medical Assistance, Solomon Isls. 31p, Underwater Exploration, Australia. 34p, *Zebu* returns to St. Helier, Jersey.

**1988, Sept. 27 Photo. *Perf. 12***

*461* A99 12p multi 42 42
*462* A99 16p multi 55 55
*463* A99 22p multi 78 78
*464* A99 29p multi 1.00 1.00
*465* A99 31p multi 1.10 1.10
*466* A99 34p multi 1.20 1.20
*Nos. 461-466 (6)* 5.05 5.05

Operation Raleigh: voyage of the *Zebu*, on which youths were trained with the aim of remotivating them and helping them to earn new self-respect.

WHO 40th anniv. (29p).

Parish Churches A100

**1988, Nov. 15 Litho. *Perf.***

*467* A100 12p St. Clement 42 42
*468* A100 16p St. Ouen 55 55
*469* A100 31p St. Brelade 1.10 1.10
*470* A100 34p St. Lawrence 1.20 1.20

Christmas.

Classic Cars A101

Designs: 12p, 1912 Talbot Tourer, seaweed harvest at Le Hocq. 16p, 1920 De Dion Bouton, Grosnez Castle ruins. 23p, 1926 Austin Chummy, brick kiln at Mont a l'Abbe. 30p, 1926 Ford Model T, harvest of the Jersey royal potato crop. 32p, 1930 Bentley 8-Litre, Guard House and Gate at Government House. 35p, 1931 Cadillac V16 Fleetwood Sports Phaeton, St. Ouen's Manor.

**1989, Jan. 31 Litho. *Perf.***

*471* A101 12p multi 45 45
*472* A101 16p multi 58 58
*473* A101 23p multi 85 85
*474* A101 30p multi 1.10 1.10
*475* A101 32p multi 1.15 1.15
*476* A101 35p multi 1.25 1.25
*Nos. 471-476 (6)* 5.38 5.38

Scenic Views — A102

**1989, Mar. 21 Litho. *Perf.***

*477* A102 1p Belcroute Bay 5 5
*478* A102 2p High St., St. Aubin 8 8
*480* A102 4p Royal Jersey Golf Course 15 15
*481* A102 5p Portelet Bay 18 18
*485* A102 10p Les Charrieres D'Anneport 38 38
*486* A102 13p St. Helier Marina 48 48
*487* A102 14p St. Ouen's Bay 52 52
*488* A102 15p Rozel Harbor 55 55
*489* A102 16p St. Aubin's Harbor 58 58
*490* A102 17p Jersey Airport 62 62
*491* A102 18p Corbiere Lighthouse 66 66
*492* A102 19p Val de la Mare 70 70
*493* A102 20p Elizabeth Castle 75 75
*Nos. 477-493 (13)* 5.70 5.70

## POSTAGE DUE STAMPS

Numeral — D1

Map of Jersey — D2

**Unwmk.**

**1969, Oct. 1 Litho. *Perf. 14***

*J1* D1 1p vio bl 1.75 1.50
*J2* D1 2p sepia 1.75 1.50
*J3* D1 3p brt car 5.00 3.50
*J4* D2 1sh emerald 15.00 12.50
*J5* D2 2sh 6p gray grn 25.00 22.50
*J6* D2 5sh red org 45.00 40.00
*Nos. J1-J6 (6)* 93.50 81.50

**Type of 1969**
**Decimal Currency**

**1971-75 Litho. *Perf. 14***

*J7* D2 ½p black 5 5
*J8* D2 1p pale vio 5 5
*J9* D2 2p brown 7 7
*J10* D2 3p brt pink 8 8
*J11* D2 4p orange 12 12
*J12* D2 5p emerald 14 14
*J13* D2 6p org ('74) 16 16
*J14* D2 7p brt yel ('74) 20 20
*J15* D2 8p grnsh bl ('75) 22 22
*J16* D2 10p gray 28 28
*J17* D2 11p bis ('75) 32 32
*J18* D2 14p lilac 40 40
*J19* D2 25p dl grn ('74) 80 80
*J20* D2 50p plum ('75) 1.50 1.50
*Nos. J7-J20 (14)* 4.39 4.39

St. Clement Arms, Dovecote, Samares — D3

Arms and Scenes from Jersey Parishes: 2p, St. Lawrence and Handois Reservoir. 3p, St. John and Sorel Point. 4p, St. Ouen and Pinnacle Rock. 5p, St. Peter and Quetivel Mill. 10p, St. Martin and St. Catherine's Breakwater. 12p, St. Helier and St. Helier Harbor. 14p, St. Saviour and Highlands College. 15p, St. Brelade and Beauport Bay. 20p, Grouville and La Hougue Bie. 50p, St. Mary and Perry Farm. £1, Trinity and Bouley Bay.

**1978, Jan. 17 Litho. *Perf. 14***

*J21* D3 1p brt grn & blk 5 5
*J22* D3 2p org & blk 7 7
*J23* D3 3p mar & blk 8 8
*J24* D3 4p ver & blk 12 12
*J25* D3 5p dp ultra & blk 14 14
*J26* D3 10p ol & blk 28 28
*J27* D3 12p bl & blk 32 32
*J28* D3 14p red org & blk 38 38
*J29* D3 15p lil rose & blk 40 50
*J30* D3 20p yel grn & blk 55 55
*J31* D3 50p brn & blk 1.40 1.40
*J32* D3 £1 vio & blk 2.75 2.75
*Nos. J21-J32 (12)* 6.54 6.64

St. Brelade — D4

**1982, Sept. 4 Litho. *Perf. 13½x14***

*J33* D4 1p shown 5 5
*J34* D4 2p St. Aubin 8 8
*J35* D4 3p Rozel 10 10
*J36* D4 4p Greve de Lecq 14 14
*J37* D4 5p Bouley Bay 18 18
*J38* D4 6p St. Catherine 22 22
*J39* D4 7p Gorey 25 25
*J40* D4 8p Bonne Nuit 30 30
*J41* D4 9p La Rocque 32 32
*J42* D4 10p St. Helier 35 35
*J43* D4 20p Ronez 70 70
*J44* D4 30p La Collette 1.00 1.00
*J45* D4 40p Elizabeth Castle 1.25 1.25
*J46* D4 £1 Upper Harbor Marina 3.00 3.00
*Nos. J33-J46 (14)* 7.94 7.94

# MAN, ISLE OF

LOCATION — In the Irish Sea, off Northwest coast of England.
GOVT. — Semi-autonomous within the British Commonwealth.
AREA — 221 sq. mi.
POP. — 64,679 (1981)
CAPITAL — Douglas

Between 1958-71 Great Britain issued 11 stamps that were sold only on the Isle of Man and intended for use there. They are listed under "Regional Issues" following Envelopes and Letter Sheets in the Great Britain section.

Castletown and Manx Emblem A4

Manx Cat — A5

***Perf. 11½***

**1973, July 5 Photo. Unwmk.**

*12* A4 ½p *shown* 5 5
*a* Booklet pane of 2 2.75
*b* Booklet pane of 4 ('74) 90
*13* A4 1p *Port Erin* 6 6
*14* A4 1½p *Mt. Snaefell* 6 6
*15* A4 2p *Laxey Village* 6 6
*a* Booklet pane of 2 2.75
*16* A4 2½p *Tynwald Hill* 8 8
*a* Booklet pane of 2 75
*17* A4 3p *Douglas Promenade* 10 10
*a* Booklet pane of 2 70
*b* Booklet pane of 4 ('74) 90
*18* A4 3½p *Port St. Mary* 12 12
*a* Booklet pane of 4 ('74) 1.40
*19* A4 4p *Fairy Bridge* 14 14
*20* A4 5p *Peel, Castle and shore* 16 16
*21* A4 6p *Cregneish Village* 20 20
*22* A4 7½p *Ramsey Bay* 28 28
*23* A4 9p *Douglas Bay* 30 30
*24* A5 10p *shown* 35 35
*25* A5 20p *Manx ram* 70 70
*26* A5 50p *Manx shearwaters* 1.50 1.50
*27* A5 £1 *Viking longship* 2.75 2.75
*Nos. 12-27 (16)* 6.91 6.91

See Nos. 52-59.

The only foreign revenue stamps listed in this Catalogue are those authorized for prepayment of postage.

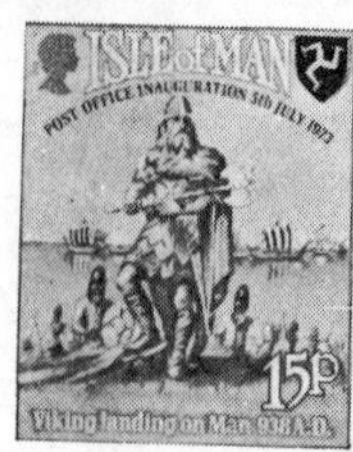

Vikings Landing on Man, 938 — A6

**1973, July 5** *Perf. 14*

*28* A6 15p multi *1.40 1.40*

Inauguration of postal independence.

Engine No. 1, Sutherland, 1873 — A7

**1973, Aug. 4** *Perf. 14½x14*

*29* A7 2½p *shown* *12 12*
*30* A7 3p *Caledonia, 1885* *18 18*
*31* A7 7½p *Kissack, 1910* *1.25 1.25*
*32* A7 9p *Pender, 1873* *1.50 1.50*

Centenary of Manx steam railroad.

Leslie Randles, 1923 Winner A8

Design: 3½p, Alan Holmes, 1957 double winner.

**1973, Sept. 4** **Litho.** *Perf. 14*

*33* A8 3p multi *30 30*
*34* A8 3½p multi *30 30*

Manx Grand Prix Motorcycle Race, 50th anniversary.

Princess Anne and Mark Phillips — A9

**Lithographed and Engraved**

**1973 Nov. 14** *Perf. 14x13½*

*35* A9 25p lt bl & multi *1.25 1.25*

Wedding of Princess Anne and Capt. Mark Phillips, Nov. 14, 1973.

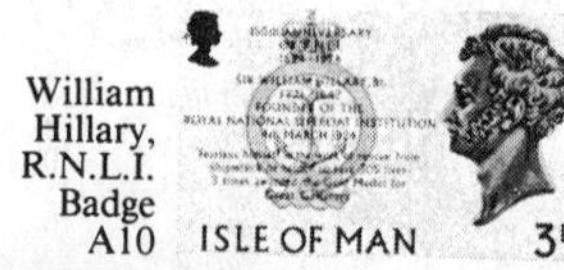

William Hillary, R.N.L.I. Badge A10

Wreck of "St. George" A11

Designs: 8p, Tower of Refuge and lifeboat "Manchester & Salford." 10p, "Osman Gabriel" at Port Erin. 3½p and 8p are from paintings.

**1974, Mar. 4** **Photo.** *Perf. 11½*

*36* A10 3p blk & multi *12 12*
*37* A11 3½p blk & multi *15 15*
*38* A11 8p blk & multi *55 55*
*39* A11 10p blk & multi *65 65*

Sesqui. of the founding of the Royal Natl. Lifeboat Institution by Sir William Hillary.

Stanley Woods on Moto Guzzi Motorcycle — A12

Designs: 3½p, Freddie Frith on Norton. 8p, Max Deubel on BMW with sidecar. 10p, Mike Hailwood on Honda.

**1974, May 29** **Litho.** *Perf. 13*

*40* A12 3p yel grn & multi 8 8
*41* A12 3½p crim & multi 12 12
*42* A12 8p yel & multi 32 28
*43* A12 10p ultra & multi 40 32

Tourist Trophy Motorcycle Races on the Isle of Man.

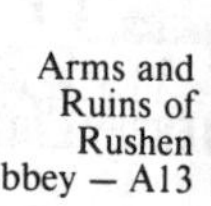

Arms and Ruins of Rushen Abbey — A13

Designs: 4½p, King Edgar of England visiting Chester in boat rowed by 8 kings including King Magnus Haraldson. 8p, Fleet under King Magnus' command and arms he gave to Isle of Man. 10p, Bridge at Avignon, Bishop's mitre and Three Legs of Man.

**1974, Sept. 18** **Litho.** *Perf. 14*

*44* A13 3½p multi 12 12
*45* A13 4½p multi 15 15
*46* A13 8p multi 32 32
*47* A13 10p multi 40 40

1,000th death anniv. of Magnus Haraldson, King of Many Islands (Nos. 45-46), and 600th death anniv. of William Russell, Bishop of Sodor and Mann (Nos. 44, 47).

Churchill and "Bugler Dunne at Colenso, 1899" — A14

Sir Winston Churchill: 4½p, Government Buildings, Douglas, and Warrant of Appointment. 8p, Manx A.A. Regiment in action. 20p, Freedom of Douglas Scroll, and casket.

**1974, Nov. 22** **Photo.** *Perf. 11½*

*48* A14 3½p multi 12 12
*49* A14 4½p multi 14 14
*50* A14 8p multi 24 24
*51* A14 20p multi 60 60
*a* Souvenir sheet of 4 1.25 1.25

No. 51a contains one each of Nos. 48-51, black marginal inscription. Size: 120x91mm.

Type of 1973

**1975** **Unwmk.** *Perf. 11½*

*52* A4 4½p *Tynwald Hill* 20 20
*53* A4 5½p *Douglas Promenade* 20 20
*54* A4 7p *Laxey Village* 40 40
*55* A4 8p *Ramsey Bay* 40 40
*58* A4 11p *Monk's Bridge* 45 45
*59* A4 13p *Derbyhaven* 55 55
*Nos. 52-59 (6)* 2.20 2.20

Issue dates: Nos. 52, 55, Jan. 8; Nos. 53-54, May 28; Nos. 58-59, Oct. 29.

Log Cabin School, Cleveland Medal, Names of Settlers A15

Designs: 5½p, Terminal Tower Building, Cleveland, John Gill and Robert Carran. 8p, Clague House Museum, Margaret and Robert Clague. 10p, Thomas Quayle and S. S. William T. Graves.

**1975, Mar. 14** **Photo.** *Perf. 11½*

*62* A15 4½p multi 15 15
*63* A15 5½p multi 20 20
*64* A15 8p multi 30 30
*65* A15 10p multi 35 35

Sesquicentennial of arrival of Manx settlers in Cleveland, Ohio, area.

Tom Sheard and "Douglas" — A16

Designs: 7p, Walter L. Handley and "Rex-Acme." 10p, Geoffrey Duke and "Gilera." 12p, Peter Williams and "Norton."

**1975, May 28** **Litho.** *Perf. 13½*

*66* A16 5½p bis & multi 15 15
*67* A16 7p sal & multi 22 22
*68* A16 10p lt grn & multi 32 32
*69* A16 12p ultra & multi 42 42

Tourist Trophy Motorcycle races on Isle of Man.

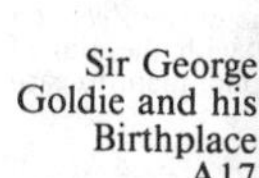

Sir George Goldie and his Birthplace A17

Designs (Sir George Goldie and): 7p, Map of Africa with Niger River basin (vert.). 10p, Goldie as president of Royal Geographical Society and Society emblem (vert.). 12p, River boats: trading hulk, native canoe, sternwheeler.

**1975, Sept. 9** **Photo.** *Perf. 11½*

*70* A17 5½p multi 15 15
*71* A17 7p multi 22 22
*72* A17 10p multi 32 32
*73* A17 12p multi 42 42

Sir George Dashwood Goldie-Taubman (1846-1925), founder of Royal Niger Company.

Manx Bible — A18

Bicentenary of Manx Bible and Christmas 1975: 7p, Rev. Philip Moore and Old Ballaugh Church. 11p, Bishop Mark Hildesley and Bishops Court. 13p, Shipwreck off Cumberland Coast with John Kelly holding manuscript above water.

**1975, Oct. 29** **Litho.** *Perf. 14*

*74* A18 5½p multi 14 14
*75* A18 7p multi 20 20
*76* A18 11p multi 30 30
*77* A18 13p multi 32 32

William Christian Listening to Patrick Henry — A19

Designs: 7p, Christian carrying Fincastle Resolutions to Williamsburg. 13p, Col. Patrick Henry and Lt. Col. William Christian of 1st Virginia Regiment. 20p, Christian as frontiersman and Indians.

**1976, Mar. 12** **Litho.** *Perf. 13½*

*78* A19 5½p multi 14 14
*79* A19 7p multi 20 20
*80* A19 13p multi 32 32
*81* A19 20p multi 52 52
*a* Souvenir sheet of 4 3.00 3.00

American Bicentennial. William Christian (1743-1786), patriot, son of a Manx-man and Patrick Henry's brother-in-law. No. 81a contains one each of Nos. 78-81, perf. 14; multicolored margin with Manx arms and flag, Union Jack and American Bicentennial emblem. Size: 152x89mm

First Double-decker Tram Car — A20

Designs: 7p, Toast-rack tram, 1890. 11p, Horse bus, 1895. 13p, Decorated tram with Queen Elizabeth II and Prince Philip.

**1976, May 26** **Photo.** *Perf. 11½*

*82* A20 5½p multi 14 14
*83* A20 7p multi 18 18
*84* A20 11p multi 28 28
*85* A20 13p multi 30 30

Douglas Horse Trams, centenary.

Barroose Beaker, Bronze Age — A21

Virgin and Child, on Sodor and Man Banner — A22

**Europa Issue 1976**

Manx Ceramic Art: No. 87, Souvenir teapot (3-legged man), 19th century. No. 88, Laxey jug, 1854. No. 89, Cronk Aust food vessel, early Bronze Age. No. 90, Sansbury bowl, 1851. No. 91, Knox urn, 20th century. Nos. 89-91 horiz.

**1976, July 28** **Photo.** *Perf. 11½*

*86* A21 5p multi 90 90
*87* A21 5p multi 90 90
*88* A21 5p multi 90 90
*89* A21 10p multi 90 90
*90* A21 10p multi 90 90
*91* A21 10p multi 90 90
*Nos. 86-91 (6)* 5.40 5.40

Stamps of same denomination printed se-tenant in sheets of 9 (3x3).

**1976, Oct. 14** **Litho.** *Perf. 14x14½*

Virgin and Child on Embroidered Church Banners: 7p, St. Peter's, Onchan, Mothers' Union. 11p, Castletown. 13p, St. Olav's, Ramsey.

*92* A22 6p multi 15 15
*93* A22 7p multi 18 18
*94* A22 11p multi 28 28
*95* A22 13p multi 35 35

Christmas 1976 and centenary of Mothers' Union.

Elizabeth II and Arms of Man — A23

Designs: 7p, Queen Elizabeth II and Prince Philip (vert.). 25p, Queen, 1976 portrait.

**Lithographed and Engraved**

**1977, Mar. 1** ***Perf. 13½x14, 14x13½***

*96* A23 6p multi 20 20
*97* A23 7p multi 20 20
*98* A23 25p multi 70 70

25th anniv. of the reign of Elizabeth II.

**Europa Issue 1977**

Carrick Bay from Tom-the-Dipper's — A24

Design: 10p, Looking south from Mooragh Park, Ramsey.

**1977, May 25** **Litho.** ***Perf. 14***

*99* A24 6p multi 20 20
*100* A24 10p multi 32 32

"Pa" Applebee at Ballig Bridge, 1912 — A25

Designs: 7p, Hairpin curve at Governor's Bridge and ambulance attendants. 11p, Boy Scouts tending scoreboards. 13p, John Willams at Windy Corner on Snaefell Mountain, winner of 1976 Open Classic Race.

**1977, May 25** ***Perf. 13½***

*101* A25 6p multi 20 20
*102* A25 7p multi 22 22
*103* A25 11p multi 35 35
*104* A25 13p multi 42 42

Tourist Trophy Motorcycle Races, and Boy Scouts, 70th anniv.; St. John Ambulance Assoc. cent. (in GB).

Meeting House, Mt. Morrison A26

Designs: 7p, John Wesley preaching at Castletown, 1777. 11p, Wesley preaching outside Braddan Church. 13p, Methodist Church on Douglas Promenade, 1976.

**1977, Oct. 19** **Photo.** ***Perf. 11½***

**Size: 30x24mm**

*105* A26 6p multi 18 18

**Size: 37½x24mm**

*106* A26 7p multi 18 18
*107* A26 11p multi 30 30

**Size: 30x24mm**

*108* A26 13p multi 38 38

Bicentenary of John Wesley's first visit to the Isle of Man.

Seaplane and Carrier Ben My Chree — A27

Designs: 7p, Bristol Scout and carrier Vindex, 1915. 11p, Boulton Paul Defiant over Douglas Bay, 1941. 13p, RAF Jaguar over Ramsey, 1977.

**1978, Feb. 28** **Litho.** ***Perf. 13½x14***

*109* A27 6p multi 22 22
*110* A27 7p multi 22 22
*111* A27 11p multi 35 35
*112* A27 13p multi 42 42

Royal Air Force, 60th anniversary.

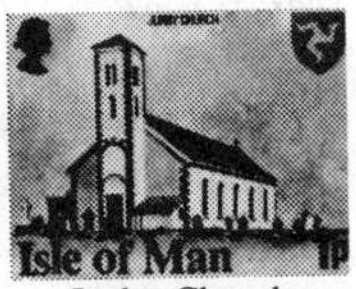

Watch Tower, Langness A28

Jurby Church A29

Fuchsia — A30

Landmarks: 6p, Government buildings. 7p, Tynwald Hill. 8p, Milner's Tower. 9p, Laxey Wheel. 10p, Castle Rushen. 11p, St. Ninian's Church. 12p, Tower of Refuge. 13p, St. German's Cathedral. 14p, Point of Ayre Lighthouse. 15p, Corrin's Tower. 16p, Douglas Head Lighthouse. 25p, Manx cat. 50p, Chough (crows). £1, Viking warrior.

**1978** **Litho.** ***Perf. 14; 14½***

*113* A28 ½p multi 5 5
*114* A29 1p multi 5 5
*115* A28 6p multi 15 15
*116* A29 7p multi 18 18
*117* A28 8p multi 20 20
*118* A28 9p multi 22 22
*119* A29 10p multi 25 25
*120* A28 11p multi 28 28
*121* A29 12p multi 30 30
*122* A29 13p multi 35 35
*123* A29 14p multi 35 35
*124* A29 15p multi 38 38
*125* A29 16p multi 40 40

**Photo.**

***Perf. 11½***

*126* A30 20p multi 60 60
*127* A30 25p multi 75 75
*128* A30 50p multi 1.50 1.50
*129* A30 £1 multi 3.00 3.00
*Nos. 113-129 (17)* 9.01 9.01

Issue dates: Nos. 113-125, Feb. 28; Nos. 126-129, Oct. 18.

Elizabeth II — A31

Keeil Chiggyrt Stone — A32

**1978, May 24** **Litho.** ***Perf. 14½x14***

*130* A31 25p bl & multi 70 70

25th anniv. of coronation of Elizabeth II.

**Europa Issue 1978**

**1978, May 24** ***Perf. 11½***

Carved Gravestones: No. 132, Wheel-headed cross slab. No. 133, Celtic Wheel cross. No. 134, Thor cross. No. 135, Olaf Liotulfson cross. No. 136, Odd's and Thorleif's crosses.

*131* A32 6p multi 12 12
*132* A32 6p multi 12 12
*133* A32 6p multi 12 12
*134* A32 11p multi 24 24
*135* A32 11p multi 24 24
*136* A32 11p multi 24 24
*Nos. 131-136 (6)* 1.08 1.08

Stamps of same denomination printed se-tenant in sheets of 9 (3x3).

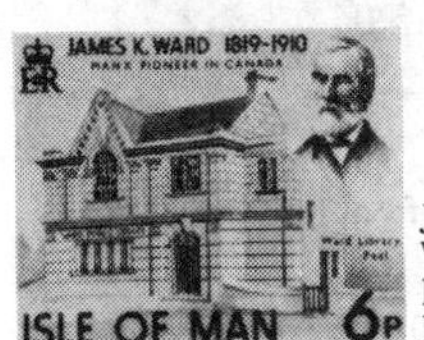


J. K. Ward, Ward Library, Peel — A33

Design: 13p, Lumber camp at Three Rivers and J. K. Ward.

**1978, June 10** **Litho.** ***Perf. 13½***

*137* A33 6p multi 15 15
*138* A33 13p multi 30 30

James K. Ward (1819-1910), Manx pioneer in Canada.

Athletes, Games' Emblem and Manx Arms A34

Eagle, Manx Arms, Maple Leaf A35

**1978, June 10**

*139* A34 7p multi 15 15
*140* A35 11p multi 28 28

11th Commonwealth Games, Edmonton, Aug. 3-12 (7p); No. American Manx Soc., 50th anniv. (11p).

"Hunt the Wren" — A36

**1978, Oct. 18** **Litho.** ***Perf. 13***

*141* A36 5p multi 60 40

Christmas 1978.

Philip M. C. Kermode and Nassa Kermodei A37

Designs: 7p, Peregrine falcons. 11p, Fulmars. 13p, Asilid fly.

**1979, Feb. 27** **Litho.** ***Perf. 14***

*142* A37 6p multi 18 18
*143* A37 7p multi 20 20
*144* A37 11p multi 35 35
*145* A37 13p multi 42 42

Isle of Man Natural History and Antiquarian Society.

Viking Ship — A38

A39

Viking Raid at Garwick A40

Designs (Tynwald Emblem and): 7p, 10th century meeting at Tynwald. 11p, Tynwald Hill and St. John's Church. 13p, Contemporary Tynwald Day parade.

**1979, May 16** **Litho.** ***Perf. 14***

*146* A38 3p *Insularem* 8 8
**a** Bklt. pane of 6 (4 #146, 2 #147) 60
**b** *Insularum* ("1980") 8 8
*147* A39 4p multi 12 12
*148* A40 6p multi 15 15
*149* A40 7p multi 18 18
*150* A40 11p multi 30 30
*151* A40 13p multi 35 35
*Nos. 146-151 (6)* 1.18 1.18

Millennium of Tynwald, Legislative Council. Nos. 146-147 printed se-tenant in sheets of 80.

**Europa Issue 1979**

19th Century Mailman — A41

Design: 11p, Contemporary mailman.

**1979, May 16**

*152* A41 6p multi 15 15
*153* A41 11p multi 30 30

Ceremony on Tynwald Hill — A42

Design: 13p, Procession from St. John's Church to Tynwald Hill.

**1979, July 5 Litho. *Perf. 14½***

| | | | | |
|---|---|---|---|---|
| *154* | A42 | 7p multi | 22 | 22 |
| *155* | A42 | 13p multi | 40 | 40 |

Visit of Queen Elizabeth II for the celebration of millennium of Tynwald.

Girl Holding Teddy Bear — A43

Christmas and IYC: 7p, Children with Santa.

**1979, Oct. 19 Litho. *Perf. 13***

| | | | | |
|---|---|---|---|---|
| *156* | A43 | 5p multi | 16 | 16 |
| *157* | A43 | 7p multi | 25 | 25 |

Capt. John Quilliam and Spencer A44

Capt. Quilliam: 6p, Seized by press gang. 8p, Battle of Trafalgar. 15p, Castle Rushen.

**1979, Oct. 19 *Perf. 14***

| | | | | |
|---|---|---|---|---|
| *158* | A44 | 6p multi | 14 | 14 |
| *159* | A44 | 8p multi | 20 | 20 |
| *160* | A44 | 13p multi | 32 | 32 |
| *161* | A44 | 15p multi | 40 | 40 |

Capt. John Quilliam (1771-1829), British naval hero and member of House of Keys.

"Odin's Raven" A45

**1979, Oct. 19 *Perf. 14x14½***

| | | | | |
|---|---|---|---|---|
| *162* | A45 | 15p multi | 42 | 42 |

Voyage of replica Viking longboat across North Sea (Trondheim to Peel), May 27-July 4.

Conglomerate Arch and Emblem — A46

Langness Emblem and: 8p, Braaid Circle. 12p, Cashtal yn Ard (Neolithic burial ground). 13p, Volcanic rocks, Scarlett. 15, Sugar-loaf Rock.

**1980, Feb. 5 Litho. *Perf. 14½***

| | | | | |
|---|---|---|---|---|
| *163* | A46 | 7p multi | 25 | 25 |
| *164* | A46 | 8p multi | 30 | 30 |
| *165* | A46 | 12p multi | 35 | 35 |
| *166* | A46 | 13p multi | 40 | 40 |
| *167* | A46 | 15p multi | 45 | 45 |
| | | *Nos. 163-167 (5)* | 1.75 | 1.75 |

Royal Geographical Soc., 150th anniv.

"Mona's Isle I" A47

**1980, May 6 Photo. *Perf. 11½***
**Granite Paper**

| | | | | |
|---|---|---|---|---|
| *168* | A47 | 7p *shown* | 22 | 22 |
| *169* | A47 | 8p *"Douglas I"* | 25 | 25 |
| *170* | A47 | 11½p *"Mona's Queen II," sinking U-boat* | 32 | 32 |
| *171* | A47 | 12p *"King Orry III"* | 35 | 35 |
| *172* | A47 | 13p *"Ben-My-Chree IV"* | 38 | 38 |
| *173* | A47 | 15p *"Lady of Mann II"* | 45 | 45 |
| *a* | | Souvenir sheet of 6 | 2.00 | 2.00 |
| | | *Nos. 168-173 (6)* | 1.97 | 1.97 |

Isle of Man Steam Packet Company sesqui.; London 80 Intl. Stamp Exhib., May 6-14. No. 173a contains Nos. 168-173; multicolored margin shows London 80 and Manx PO emblems, statue of Eros, London, Steam Packet flag. Size: 180x125mm.

**Europa Issue 1980**

Thomas Edward Brown and Characters from his Poems — A48

Brown (1830-1897), Poet and Scholar: 13½p, Cricket game, Clifton College Bristol.

**1980, May 6**

| | | | | |
|---|---|---|---|---|
| *174* | A48 | 7p multi | 18 | 18 |
| *175* | A48 | 13½p multi | 35 | 35 |

Visit of King Olav V of Norway A49

**1980, June 13 Litho. *Perf. 14½***

| | | | | |
|---|---|---|---|---|
| *176* | A49 | 12p multi | 38 | 38 |
| *a* | | Souvenir sheet of 2 | 1.10 | 1.10 |

Visit of King Olav V of Norway, Aug. 2-7, 1979, and NORWEX 80 stamp exhibition, Oslo, June 13-22.

No. 176a contains Nos. 162, 176. Multicolored margin shows map and arms. Size: 125½x157mm.

William Kermode and "Robert Quayle" — A50

Kermode Family (First Manx Pioneers in Tasmania): 9p, First homestead, Mona Vale, Merino sheep, 1834. 13½p, Ross Bridge, W. Kermode. 15p, Calendar House, 1868. 17½p, Parliament Buildings, Hobart, Robert Quayle Kermode.

**1980, Sept. 29 Litho.**

| | | | | |
|---|---|---|---|---|
| *177* | A50 | 7p multi | 22 | 22 |
| *178* | A50 | 9p multi | 28 | 28 |
| *179* | A50 | 13½p multi | 45 | 45 |
| *180* | A50 | 15p multi | 48 | 48 |
| *181* | A50 | 17½p multi | 55 | 55 |
| | | *Nos. 177-181 (5)* | 1.98 | 1.98 |

Wren A51

**1980, Sept. 29 Litho. *Perf. 13½x14***

| | | | | |
|---|---|---|---|---|
| *182* | A51 | 6p *shown* | 20 | 20 |
| *183* | A51 | 8p *Robin* | 28 | 28 |

Wildlife conservation and Christmas 1980.

Luggers, Red Pier, Douglas — A52

**1981, Feb. 24 Litho.**

| | | | | |
|---|---|---|---|---|
| *184* | A52 | 8p *shown* | 24 | 24 |
| *185* | A52 | 9p *Wanderer saving Lusitania Survivors* | 25 | 25 |
| *186* | A52 | 18p *Nickey, Port St. Mary* | 52 | 52 |
| *187* | A52 | 20p *Nobby, Ramsey Harbor* | 60 | 60 |
| *188* | A52 | 22p *Sunbeam and Zebra, Port Erin* | 65 | 65 |
| | | *Nos. 184-188 (5)* | 2.26 | 2.26 |

Royal National Mission to Deep Sea Fishermen centenary.

Peregrine Falcon — A53

**1980, Sept. 29 Litho. *Perf. 14½x14***

| | | | | |
|---|---|---|---|---|
| *189* | A53 | 1p shown | 5 | 5 |
| *190* | A53 | 5p Loaghtyn ram | 20 | 20 |
| *a* | | Bklt. pane of 6 (2 each #147, 189, 190) | 85 | |

Issued in booklets only.

**Europa Issue 1981**

Crosh Cuirn (Cross of Mountain Ash Twigs, Harvest Charm) — A54

Design: 18p, Bollan fish cross-bone (fishermen's charm)

**1981, May 22 Litho.**

| | | | | |
|---|---|---|---|---|
| *191* | A54 | 8p multi | 25 | 25 |
| *192* | A54 | 18p multi | 55 | 55 |

Col. Mark Wilks, Peel Castle A55

**1981, May 22 *Perf. 14***

| | | | | |
|---|---|---|---|---|
| *193* | A55 | 8p shown | 25 | 25 |
| *194* | A55 | 20p Wilks, Fort. St. George, Madras | 52 | 52 |
| *195* | A55 | 22p Wilks, Napoleon | 60 | 60 |
| *196* | A55 | 25p Wilks at Kirby estate | 65 | 65 |

Wilks (d. 1831), governor of St. Helena.

Suffragettes Emmeline Goulden Pankhurst and Sophia Jane Goulden A56

**1981, May 22 *Perf. 14***

| | | | | |
|---|---|---|---|---|
| *197* | A56 | 9p multi | 28 | 28 |

Centenary of women's suffrage and of House of Keys Election Act (granting widows and unmarried women voting rights).

Prince Charles and Lady Diana A57

**1981, July 29 Litho. *Perf. 14***

| | | | | |
|---|---|---|---|---|
| *198* | A57 | 9p multi | 30 | 30 |
| *199* | A57 | 25p multi | 85 | 85 |
| *a* | | Souvenir sheet of 4 | 2.50 | 2.50 |

Royal Wedding. No. 199a contains 2 each Nos. 198-199, multicolored margin shows St. Paul's Cathedral. Size: 133x182mm.

Queen Elizabeth II — A58

**1981, Sept. 29 Photo. *Perf. 11½***
**Granite paper**

| | | | | |
|---|---|---|---|---|
| *200* | A58 | £2 multi | 5.75 | 5.75 |

Douglas War Memorial, Poppies, Quote from Laurence Binyon's For the Fallen — A59

**1981, Sept. 29**
**Granite Paper**

| | | | | |
|---|---|---|---|---|
| *201* | A59 | 8p shown | 22 | 22 |
| *202* | A59 | 10p Maj. R.H. Cain, Battle of Arnhem, 1944 | 28 | 28 |
| *203* | A59 | 18p Festival of Remembrance | 50 | 50 |
| *204* | A59 | 20p Tynwald and Spitfire, Dunkirk, 1940 | 55 | 55 |

Royal British Legion, 60th anniv.

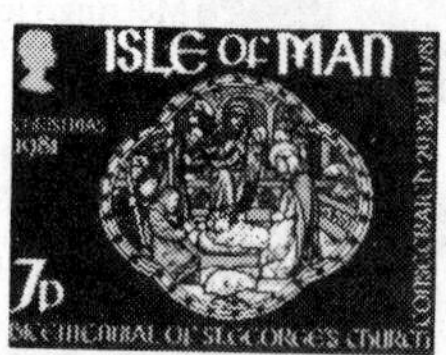

Nativity Stained-glass Window, 1865, St. George's Church, Douglas — A60

Design: Christmas pageant, Glencrutchery Special School, Douglas.

**1981, Sept. 29 Litho. *Perf. 14½x14***

**Plain paper**

*205* A60 7p multi 24 24

**Size: 47x28mm**

*206* A60 9p multi 32 32

Christmas and St. George's Church bicen. (7p), IYD (9p).

Scouting Year — A61

Designs: 9p, Cunningham House (Man Scout Headquarters). 10p, Baden-Powell's visit, 1911. 19½p, Portrait (32x41mm., Perf. 14½). 24p, Baden-Powell with scouts, message. 29p, Sign, handshake, globe, emblem.

**1982, Feb. 23 Litho. *Perf. 13½x14***

| | | | | |
|---|---|---|---|---|
| *207* | A61 | 9p multi | 30 | 30 |
| *208* | A61 | 10p multi | 32 | 32 |
| *209* | A61 | 19½p multi | 65 | 65 |
| *210* | A61 | 24p multi | 80 | 80 |
| *211* | A61 | 29p multi | 1.00 | 1.00 |
| | | *Nos. 207-211 (5)* | 3.07 | 3.07 |

Europa 1982 A62

Designs: 9p, Bishop Thomas Wilson (1663-1755) and his "The Principles and Duties of Christianity," first book printed in Manx, 1707. 19½p, Visit of Thomas, 2nd Earl of Derby, 1507.

**1982, June 1 Photo. *Perf. 12½***

**Granite Paper**

| | | | | |
|---|---|---|---|---|
| *212* | A62 | 9p multi | 22 | 22 |
| *213* | A62 | 19½p multi | 52 | 52 |

75th Anniv. of Tourist Trophy Motorcycle Races — A63

Designs: Winners on their bikes.

**1982, June 1 Litho. *Perf. 14***

| | | | | |
|---|---|---|---|---|
| *214* | A63 | 9p Charlie Collier, 431 Matchless, 1907 | 25 | 25 |
| *215* | A63 | 10p Freddie Dixon, Douglas, 1923 | 30 | 30 |
| *216* | A63 | 24p Jimmie Simpson, Norton, 1932 | 75 | 75 |
| *217* | A63 | 26p Mike Hailwood, Norton, 1961 | 80 | 80 |
| *218* | A63 | 29p Jock Taylor, 700 Fowler Yamaha, '80 | 95 | 95 |
| | | *Nos. 214-218 (5)* | 3.05 | 3.05 |

Isle of Man Steam Packet Co. Mail Contract Sesquicentennial — A64

**1982, Oct. 5 Litho. *Perf. 13½x14***

| | | | | |
|---|---|---|---|---|
| *219* | A64 | 12p Mona I | 40 | 40 |
| *220* | A64 | 19½p Manx Maid II | 65 | 65 |

Christmas 1982 — A65

**1982, Oct. 5 *Perf. 13x13½***

| | | | | |
|---|---|---|---|---|
| *221* | A65 | 8p Three Kings | 32 | 32 |
| *222* | A65 | 11p Robin, Christmas tree, vert. | 45 | 45 |

Souvenir Sheet

Princess Diana and Prince William — A66

**1982, Oct. 12**

*223* A66 50p multi 2.25 2.25

Birth of Prince William of Wales (June 21) and 21st birthday of Princess Diana (July 1). Size: 100x84mm.

Marine Birds — A67

**1983, Feb. 15 Litho. *Perf. 14½***

| | | | | |
|---|---|---|---|---|
| *224* | A67 | 1p Puffins, Cranstal | 5 | 5 |
| *225* | A67 | 2p Gannets, Point of Ayre | 8 | 8 |
| *226* | A67 | 5p Lesser black-backed gulls, Santon | 15 | 15 |
| *227* | A67 | 8p Cormorants, Maughold Head | 24 | 24 |
| *228* | A67 | 10p Kittiwakes, White Strand | 30 | 30 |
| *229* | A67 | 11p Shags, Calf of Man | 35 | 35 |
| *230* | A67 | 12p Herons, Douglas Foreshore | 35 | 35 |
| *231* | A67 | 13p Herring gulls, Peel | 38 | 38 |
| *232* | A67 | 14p Razorbills, Calf of Man | 40 | 40 |
| *233* | A67 | 15p Great black-backed gulls, Calf of Man | 45 | 45 |
| *234* | A67 | 16p Shelducks, Poyll Vaaish | 48 | 48 |
| *235* | A67 | 18p Oystercatchers, Langness | 52 | 52 |

**1983, Sept. 14 Litho. *Perf. 14***

**Size: 39x25mm**

| | | | | |
|---|---|---|---|---|
| *236* | A67 | 20p Arctic terns, Blue Point | 45 | 45 |
| *237* | A67 | 25p Guillemots, Calf of Man | 75 | 75 |
| *238* | A67 | 50p Redshanks, Langness | 1.25 | 1.25 |
| *239* | A67 | £1 Mute swans, Port St. Mary Bay | 2.50 | 2.50 |
| | | *Nos. 224-239 (16)* | 8.70 | 8.70 |

Centenary of Salvation Army in Isle of Man — A68

Designs: 10p, Citadel opening ceremony, 1932, T.H. Cannell. 12p, Founder William Booth, early meeting place (former Unitarian Church, Douglas). 19½p, Band, Bandmaster Gordon Cowley, 1981. 26p, Lt.-Col. Thomas Bridson, treating lepers in Dutch East Indies.

**1983, Feb. 15 Photo. *Perf. 11½***

**Granite Paper**

| | | | | |
|---|---|---|---|---|
| *240* | A68 | 10p multi | 32 | 32 |
| *241* | A68 | 12p multi | 38 | 38 |
| *242* | A68 | 19½ multi | 65 | 65 |
| *243* | A68 | 26p multi | 85 | 85 |

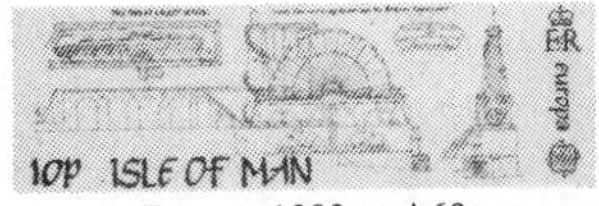


Europa 1983 — A69

**1983, May 18 *Perf. 14***

| | | | | |
|---|---|---|---|---|
| *244* | A69 | 10p Laxey Wheel | 35 | 35 |
| *245* | A69 | 20½p Designer Robert Casement | 70 | 70 |

King William's College Sesquicentennial — A70

Graduates: 10p, Nick Keig, Yachtsman. 12p, College, arms. 28p, William Bragg, 1915 Nobel Prize winner in physics, ionization spectrometer. 31p, Gen. George Stuart White, Defense of Ladysmith, Boer War.

**1983, May 18 Photo. *Perf. 11½***

**Granite Paper**

| | | | | |
|---|---|---|---|---|
| *246* | A70 | 10p multi | 32 | 32 |
| *247* | A70 | 12p multi | 38 | 38 |
| *248* | A70 | 28p multi | 95 | 95 |
| *249* | A70 | 31p multi | 1.00 | 1.00 |

World Communications Year and 10th Anniv. of Post Office — A71

**1983, July 5 Litho. *Perf. 15***

| | | | | |
|---|---|---|---|---|
| *250* | A71 | 10p New P.O. Headquarters | 35 | 35 |
| *251* | A71 | 15p Viking landing, 938 | 55 | 55 |

Christmas 1983 A72

**1983, Sept. 14 Litho. *Perf. 13x13½***

| | | | | |
|---|---|---|---|---|
| *252* | A72 | 9p Shepherds | 35 | 35 |
| *253* | A72 | 12p Three Kings | 45 | 45 |

Karran Fleet A73

Links with Falkland Islands A74

**1984, Feb. 14 Litho. *Perf. 14***

| | | | | |
|---|---|---|---|---|
| *254* | A73 | 10p Manx King, 1884 | 35 | 35 |
| *255* | A73 | 13p Hope, 1858 | 45 | 45 |
| *256* | A73 | 20½p Rio Grande, 1868 | 70 | 70 |
| *257* | A73 | 28p Lady Elizabeth, 1879 | 1.00 | 1.00 |
| *258* | A73 | 31p Sumatra, 1858 | 1.25 | 1.25 |
| | | *Nos. 254-258 (5)* | 3.75 | 3.75 |

**1984, Feb. 14**

| | | | |
|---|---|---|---|
| *259* | Sheet of 2 | 3.00 | 3.00 |
| *a* | A74 31p multi | 1.50 | 1.50 |

No. 259 contains Nos. 257 and 259a. Margin shows maps and arms.

Europa (1959-1984) A75

**1984, Apr. 27 Photo. *Perf. 11½***

| | | | | |
|---|---|---|---|---|
| *260* | A75 | 10p dk yel org, dk brn & buff | 30 | 30 |
| *261* | A75 | 20½p bl, dk bl & lt bl | 62 | 62 |

DH-48, Ronaldsway Airport — A76

**1984, Apr. 27 Litho. *Perf. 14***

| | | | | |
|---|---|---|---|---|
| *262* | A76 | 11p shown | 34 | 34 |
| *263* | A76 | 13p DH-86, Calf of Man | 40 | 40 |
| *264* | A76 | 26p DC-3, Ronaldsway Airport | 80 | 80 |
| *265* | A76 | 28p Vickers Viscount, Douglas | 85 | 85 |
| *266* | A76 | 31p Islander, Ronaldsway Airport | 95 | 95 |
| | | *Nos. 262-266 (5)* | 3.34 | 3.34 |

50th Anniv. of official airmail service and 40th anniv. of Intl. Civil Aviation Org.

William Cain as Mayor of Melbourne, 1886-87 — A77

**1984, Sept. 21 Litho. *Perf. 14½***

| | | | | |
|---|---|---|---|---|
| *267* | A77 | 11p Ballasalla (birthplace) | 34 | 34 |
| *268* | A77 | 22p Voyage to Australia | 68 | 68 |
| *269* | A77 | 28p Railway, Victoria | 85 | 85 |
| *270* | A77 | 30p shown | 90 | 90 |
| *271* | A77 | 33p Royal Exhibition Buildings, Melbourne | 1.00 | 1.00 |
| | | *Nos. 267-271 (5)* | 3.77 | 3.77 |

William Cain (1831-1914), building contractor and public servant in Australia.



Queen Elizabeth II, CPA Emblem A78

**1984, Sept. 21 *Perf. 14***

| | | | | |
|---|---|---|---|---|
| *272* | A78 | 14p shown | 42 | 42 |
| *273* | A78 | 33p Arms, Elizabeth II | 1.00 | 1.00 |

30th Conference of Commonwealth Parliamentary Assoc., Sept. 28-Oct. 5.

*Isle of Man stamps can be mounted in Scott's annually supplemented Channel Islands Album.*

Christmas — A79

Stained-glass windows.

**1984, Sept. 21**

*274* A79 10p Birds, Glencrutchery House 30 30
*275* A79 13p Arms, Lonan Old Church 40 40

75th Anniv. of Girl Guides — A80

Designs: 11p, Cunningham House (headquarters), Mrs. W. and J. Cunningham (early Island Commissioners). 14p, Princess Margaret (president), color guard. 29p, Lady Olave Baden-Powell, headquarters opening. 31p, Uniforms, 1910-85. 34p, Sign, handclasp, trefoil.

**1985, Jan. 31 Photo. *Perf. 12***

*276* A80 11p multi 28 28
*277* A80 14p multi 38 38
*278* A80 29p multi 70 70
*279* A80 31p multi 85 85
*280* A80 34p multi 95 95
*Nos. 276-280 (5)* 3.16 3.16

Queen Elizabeth II — A81

**1985, Jan. 31 Litho. *Perf. 14***

*281* A81 £5 multi 13.00 13.00

Europa 1985 — A82

Manx composers and excerpts from their works: No. 282a, "O'Land of our Birth." No. 282b, William H. Gill (1839-1922). No. 283a, Hymn "Crofton;" No. 283b, Dr. John Clague (1842-1908).

**1985, Apr. 24 Photo. *Perf. 12***

*282* Pair 95 95
*a.-b.* A82 12p. Any single 45 45
*283* Pair 90 90
*a.-b.* A82 22p. Any single 45 45

Motoring A83

Motor races and winning vehicles: No. 284a, 1906 Tourist Trophy Race. No. 284b, 1922 Tourist Trophy Race. No. 285a, 1950 British Empire Trophy Race. No. 285b, 1934 Manin Moar Race. No. 286a, 1984 Tourist Trophy Motorcycle Race (official car). No. 286b, 1981 Rothmans Manx Intl. Rally.

**1985, May 25 Litho. *Perf. 14***

*284* Pair 64 64
*a.-b* A83 12p. Any single 32 32
*285* Pair 76 76
*a.-b* A83 14p. Any single 38 38
*286* Pair 1.65 1.65
*a.-b* A83 31p. Any single 82 82

H.R.H. Alexandra (1885-1925), Princess of Wales — A84

SSA presidents: 15p, Queen Mary (1925-1953). 29p, Earl Mountbatten of Burma (1953-1979). 34p, Prince Michael of Kent (1982-).

**1985, Sept. 4 Litho. *Perf. 14***

*287* A84 12p multi 32 32
*288* A84 15p multi 42 42
*289* A84 29p multi 80 80
*290* A84 34p multi 95 95

Soldier's, Sailors' & Airmen's Families Assoc., cent.

Lt.-Gen. Sir Mark Cubbon, K.C.B. (1785-1861), Commissioner of Mysore — A85

**1985, Oct. 2 Litho. *Perf. 14***

*291* A85 12p Kirk Maughold Parish Church, 14th century 35 35
*292* A85 22p Portrait, vert. 60 60
*293* A85 45p Equestrian monument, 1866 Bangalore, India, vert. 1.25 1.25

Christmas 1985 A86

**1985, Oct. 2 Litho. *Perf. 13½***

*294* A86 11p Onchan Parish Church, 1833 30 30
*295* A86 14p St. John's Church 40 40
*296* A86 31p Bride Parish Church, 1876 90 90

1986 Commonwealth Games, Edinburgh — A87

**1986, Feb. 5 Litho. *Perf. 14***

*297* A87 12p Women's swimming 28 28
*298* A87 15p Walking 35 35
*299* A87 31p Rifle shooting 70 70
*300* A87 34p Bicycling 80 80

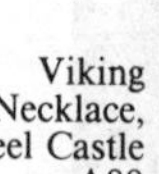

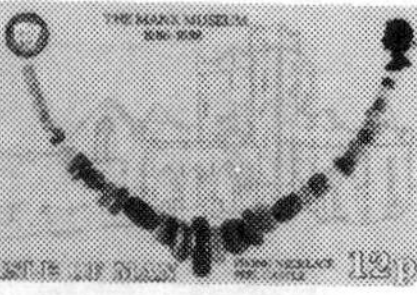


Viking Necklace, Peel Castle A88

Artifacts, architecture: 15p, Meayll Circle burial ground, Rushen. 22p, Prehistoric Cervus giganteus skeleton, Glose-y-Garey, vert. 26p, Norwegian viking longship, vert. 29p, Open-air Museum, Cregneash.

**1986, Feb. 5 *Perf. 14½x14, 14x14½***

*301* A88 12p multi 32 32
*302* A88 15p multi 40 40
*303* A88 22p multi 55 55
*304* A88 26p multi 65 65
*305* A88 29p multi 75 75
*Nos. 301-305 (5)* 2.67 2.67

Centenaries of Manx Museum and Ancient Monuments Act.

Europa 1986, Manx National Trust — A89

Designs: No. 306a, Bridge, the Ayres. No. 306b, Calf of Man. No. 307a, Eary Cushlin. No. 307b, St. Michael's Isle.

**1986, Apr. 10 Litho. *Perf. 12***

*306* Pair 60 60
*a.-b* A89 12p, any single 30 30
*307* Pair 1.10 1.10
*a.-b* A89 22p, any single 55 55

Settling of Plymouth — A90

Designs: 12p, Ellanbane, Isle of Man, Myles Standish's home, 15p, The Mayflower. 31p, Pilgrims landing, 1620. 34p, Capt. Myles Standish (c.1584-1656).

**1986, May 22 *Perf. 13½***

*308* A90 12p multi 32 32
*309* A90 15p multi 40 40
*310* A90 31p multi 85 85
*311* A90 34p multi 90 90
*a* Souvenir sheet of 2, #310-311, perf. 13x12½ 1.75 1.75

AMERIPEX '86, Chicago, May 22-June 1. No. 311 has multicolored margin picturing exhibition and World Manx Assoc. emblems. Size: 100x75mm.

Heritage Year — A91

**1986, Apr. 10 Litho. *Perf. 15x14***

*312* A91 2p Viking longship bow 8 8
*a* Bklt. pane of 6, 2 #312, 4 #313 1.50
*313* A91 10p Celtic cross 32 32
*a* Bklt. pane of 3 + 3 labels 1.00

Issued in booklets only.

Wedding of Prince Andrew and Sarah Ferguson A92

**1986, July 23**

*314* A92 15p Wedding date 38 38
*315* A92 40p Engagement date 1.00 1.00

Royal Birthdays — A93

Designs: No. 316a, Prince Philip, 65. No. 316b, Elizabeth II, 60. No. 317 is the same size as No. 316.

**1986, Aug. 28 *Perf. 11½***

*316* Pair 80 80
*a.-b* A93 15p, any single 40 40
*317* A93 34p Royal couple 85 85

STOCKHOLMIA '86, Swedish Post Office 350th anniv. Stamps issued in sheets of 6.

Intl. Peace Year — A94

**1986, Sept. 25 Litho. *Perf. 14***

*318* A94 11p Robins, globe, Braille 30 30
*319* A94 14p Hands, dove 35 35
*320* A94 31p Hand-holding, sign language 75 75

Accession of Queen Victoria to the British Throne, 150th Anniv. A95

Photographs of Victorian Douglas, by John Miller Nicholson.

**1987, Jan. 21 Litho. *Perf. 14½***

*321* A95 2p North Quay 6 6
*322* A95 3p The Old Fish Market 8 8
*323* A95 10p Breakwater 25 25
*a* Bklt. pane of 8 (2 2p, 2 3p, 4 10p) ('87) 1.40
*324* A95 15p Jubilee Clock 38 38
*a* Bklt. pane of 8 (2 2p, 2 3p, 2 10p, 2 15p) ('87) 1.65
*325* A95 31p Loch Promenade 80 80
*326* A95 34p Beach 90 90
*Nos. 321-326 (6)* 2.47 2.47

19th Century Paintings by John Miller Nicholson (1840-1913) — A96

Harbor scenes: 12p, The Old Fish Market and Harbor, Douglas. 26p, Red Sails at Douglas. 29p, The Double Corner. 34p, Peel Harbor.

**1987, Feb. 18 *Perf. 13½***

*327* A96 12p multi 30 30
*328* A96 26p multi 65 65
*329* A96 29p multi 70 70
*330* A96 34p multi 85 85

Promenade, Douglas — A97

**1987, Apr. 29 Litho. Perf. 13½**

*331* A97 12p Sea Terminal, 1965 32 32
*332* A97 12p Tower of Refuge, 1832 32 32
*333* A97 22p Gaiety Theater, c. 1900 60 60
*334* A97 22p Villa Marina 60 60

Europa 1987. Stamps of the same denomination printed se-tenant in sheets of 10.

Tourist Trophy Motorcycle Races, 80th Anniv. — A98

**1987, May 27 Perf. 13½x13**

*335* A98 12p 1939 Supercharged BMW 500CC 32 32
*336* A98 15p 1953 Manx "Kneeler" Norton 350CC 40 40
*337* A98 29p 1956 MV Agusta 500CC 4 80 80
*338* A98 31p 1957 Guzzi 500CC V8 85 85
*339* A98 34p 1967 Honda 250CC 6 95 95
***a*** Souv. sheet of 5 (Nos. 335-339) + 7 labels 3.50 3.50
*Nos. 335-339 (5)* 3.32 3.32

No. 339a has inscribed margin picturing CAPEX '87 emblem; labels picture map of race course. Size: 151x141mm.

Wildflowers A99

Christmas A100

**1987, Sept. 9 Litho. Perf. 14½x13½**

*340* A99 16p Fuchsia, wild roses 50 50
*341* A99 29p Field scabius, ragwort 90 90
*342* A99 31p Wood anemone, celandine 95 95
*343* A99 34p Violets, primroses 1.00 1.00

**1987, Oct. 16 Perf. 14**

Victorian family scenes based on drawings by Alfred Hunt for The Illustrated London News, c. 1870-1890.

*344* A100 12p Stirring the pudding 28 28
*345* A100 15p Christmas tree selection 35 35
*346* A100 31p Decorating tree 75 75

Railways & Tramways A101

Designs: 1p, Horse-drawn "Toast Rack" tram, Douglas Bay, 1884. 2p, No. 5 electric tram, Snaefell Mountain Railway, 1895. 3p, No. 3 open-top double-deck electric tram, Marine Drive-Port Soderick line, Douglas Southern Electric Tramway, 1896. 5p, Tower of Refuge and open tram, Douglas Head Incline Railway. 10p, Electric tram at Maughold Head, 1893, Douglas and Laxey Coast Electric Tramway. 13p, Douglas Cable Car No. 72, 1896. 14p, Manx Northern Railway No. 4 Caledonia, a Dubs 0-6-0T, 1885, at Gob-y-Deigan. 15p, Great Laxey Mine Railway Lewin steam engine Ant pulling coal cars. 16p, Henry B. Loch, first locomotive on the island, Port Erin Breakwater Railway, 1864. 17p, Locomotive No. 1, Ramsey Harbor Tramway. 18p, Engine No. 7 Tynwald, 1880, Foxdale Railway. 19p, Douglas Corp. engine, Baldwin Reservoir Railway. 20p, "Kissack" leaving St. John's for Peel. 25p, "Hutchinson" leaving Douglas Station. 50p, "Polar Bear" of Groudle Glen Railway. £1, The Royal Train.

**1988, Feb. 10 Litho. Perf. 13½**

*347* A101 1p multi 5 5
*348* A101 2p multi 8 8
*349* A101 3p multi 12 12
*350* A101 5p multi 18 18
*351* A101 10p multi 35 35
*352* A101 13p multi 48 48
*353* A101 14p multi 52 52
*354* A101 15p multi 55 55
*355* A101 16p multi 58 58
***a.*** Bklt. pane of 5 (2 3p, 13p, 2 16p) 1.90
***b.*** Bklt. pane of 10 (2 No. 355a) 4.00
*356* A101 17p multi 62 62
*357* A101 18p multi 65 65
*358* A101 19p multi 68 68

**Perf. 15**

*358A* A101 20p multi 70 70
*358B* A101 25p multi 88 88
*358C* A101 50p multi 1.75 1.75
*358D* A101 £1 multi 3.50 3.50
*Nos. 347-358 (12)* 4.86 4.86

Issue dates: 1p-19p, Feb. 10. Nos. 355a-355b, Mar. 16. 20p-£1, Sept. 21.

Car Racing — A102

Winning automobiles, drivers: 13p, Vauxhall Opel, Russell Brookes, 1985. 26p, Ford Escort, Ari Vatanen of Finland, 1976. 31p, Repco March 761, Terry Smith, 1980. 34p, Williams/Honda Nigel Mansell, 1986-87.

**1988, Feb. 10 Perf. 13½x14½**

*359* A102 13p multi 48 48
*360* A102 26p multi 95 95
*361* A102 31p multi 1.15 1.15
*362* A102 34p multi 1.25 1.25

Europa 1988 A103

Telecommunications: No. 363, IOM-UK optical fiber cable-laying plow. No. 364, Cable-laying ship. No. 365, 1st IOM Earth station, Braddan, established by Manx Telecom. No. 366, Intelsat V satellite.

**1988, Apr. 14 Litho. Perf. 14x13½**

*363* A103 13p multi 48 48
*364* A103 13p multi 48 48
*365* A103 22p multi 80 80
*366* A103 22p multi 80 80

Submarine cable linking the Isle of Man and Silecroft in Cumbria, 1987 (13p). Stamps of the same denomination printed se-tenant in continuous designs.

Historic Ships Built on the Isle A104

Isle of Man flag, Australia bicen. emblem or US flag and: 16p, Euterpe, 1863, built in Ramsey. 29p, Vixen leaving Peel for Australia, 1853. 31p, Ramsey, an immigrant ship in Brisbane, 1870. 34p, Star of India (renamed in 1906, was the Euterpe), restored 1960-1976, Maritime Museum at San Diego.

**1988, May 11 Litho. Perf. 14**

*367* A104 16p multi 60 60
*368* A104 29p multi 1.10 1.10
*369* A104 31p multi 1.15 1.15
*370* A104 34p multi 1.25 1.25
***a.*** Souv. sheet of 2 (16p, 34p) 1.85 1.85

No. 370a has multicolored inscribed margin picturing the emblem of the Maritime Museum, San Diego, and the Star of India in full sail. Size: 111x85mm.

Fuchsia Blossoms — A105

**1988, Sept. 21 Litho. Perf. 13½x14**

*371* A105 13p Magellanica 45 45
*372* A105 16p Pink cloud 55 55
*373* A105 22p Leonora 78 78
*374* A105 29p Satellite 1.05 1.05
*375* A105 31p Preston Guild 1.10 1.10
*376* A105 34p Thalia 1.20 1.20
*Nos. 371-376 (6)* 5.13 5.13

British Fuchsia Society, 50th anniv.

Christmas A106

**1988, Oct. 12 Perf. 14**

*377* A106 12p Long-earred owl 42 42
*378* A106 15p Robin 52 52
*379* A106 31p Partridge 1.10 1.10

Manx Cats A107

Various cats.

**1989, Feb. 8 Litho. Perf.**

*380* A107 16p multi 60 60
*381* A107 27p multi 1.00 1.00
*382* A107 30p multi 1.15 1.15
*383* A107 40p multi 1.50 1.50

## POSTAGE DUE STAMPS

D1

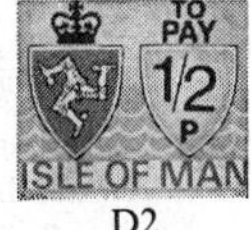

D2

Imprint: "1973 Questa"

**Perf. 13½**

**1973, July 5 Litho. Unwmk.**

**Inscriptions and Coat of Arms in Black and Red**

*J1* D1 ½p yellow 28 28
*J2* D1 1p buff 65 45
*J3* D1 2p lt yel grn 1.40 1.40
*J4* D1 3p gray 2.25 2.25
*J5* D1 4p dl rose 3.75 3.75
*J6* D1 5p light bl 4.00 4.00
*J7* D1 10p light vio 9.00 9.00
*J8* D1 20p lt grnsh bl 20.00 20.00
*Nos. J1-J8 (8)* 41.33 41.13

Imprint: "1973 A Questa"

**1973, Sept.**

**Colors as Before**

*J1a* D1 ½p 4.00 3.50
*J2a* D1 1p 2.25 1.00
*J3a* D1 2p 40 20
*J4a* D1 3p 45 25
*J5a* D1 4p 50 35
*J6a* D1 5p 50 40
*J7a* D1 10p 1.00 75
*J8a* D1 20p 2.25 1.50
*Nos. J1a-J8a (8)* 11.35 7.95

**1975, Jan. 8 Litho. Perf. 14**

**Inscriptions and Coat of Arms in Black and Red**

*J9* D2 ½p yellow 5 5
*J10* D2 1p buff 5 5
*J11* D2 4p lil rose 16 16
*J12* D2 7p blue 28 28
*J13* D2 9p sepia 35 35
*J14* D2 10p lilac 38 38
*J15* D2 50p orange 1.40 1.40
*J16* D2 £1 brt grn 2.50 2.50
*Nos. J9-J16 (8)* 5.17 5.17

Manx Emblem — D3

**1982, Oct. 5 Litho. Perf. 15x14**

*J17* D3 1p lt grn 5 5
*J18* D3 2p brt pink 8 8
*J19* D3 5p grnsh bl 20 20
*J20* D3 10p brt lil 40 40
*J21* D3 20p gray 80 80
*J22* D3 50p dl yel 2.00 2.00
*J23* D3 £1 brick red 3.00 3.00
*J24* D3 £2 blue 6.50 6.50
*Nos. J17-J24 (8)* 13.03 13.03

## BRITISH OFFICES ABROAD

### OFFICES IN AFRICA
### MIDDLE EAST FORCES

For use in Ethiopia, Cyrenaica, Eritrea, the Dodecanese and Somalia

Stamps of Great Britain, 1937-42 Overprinted in Black or Blue Black

**M.E.F.**

**1942-43 Wmk. 251 *Perf. 14½x14***

*1* A101 1p scarlet 7 7
*2* A101 2p orange 9 9
*3* A101 2½p brt ultra 12 12
*4* A101 3p dark purple 15 15
*a.* Double ovpt.
*5* A102 5p lt brn (Bl Blk) ('43) 15 15
*a.* Black ovpt. 15 15
*6* A102 6p rose lilac ('43) 24 24
*7* A103 9p dp ol grn ('43) 30 30
*8* A103 1sh brn ('43) 30 30

**Wmk. 259**
***Perf. 14***

*9* A104 2sh6p yel grn ('43) 2.00 2.00
*Nos. 1-9 (9)* 3.42 3.42

Same Overprint in Blue Black on Nos. 259, 261, 262 and 263

**1943, Jan. 1 Wmk. 251**

*10* A101 1p vermilion 8 8
*11* A101 2p lt orange 9 9
*12* A101 2½p ultramarine 9 9
*13* A101 3p violet 12 12

There were two printings of Nos. 1-4 and 5a, both issued Mar. 2, 1942, and both black. The Cairo printing measures 13½mm., the London printing 14mm.

Nos. 5 and 6-13 compose a third printing, also made in London. On these stamps, issued Jan. 1, 1943, the overprint is 13½mm. wide. The 2sh6p overprint is black, the others blue black.

Same Overprint in Black on Nos. 250 and 251A

**1947 Wmk. 259 *Perf. 14***

*14* A104 5sh dull red 7.50 6.25
*15* A105 10sh ultramarine 17.50 15.00

In 1950 Nos. 1-15 were declared valid for use in Great Britain. Used values are for copies postmarked in territory of issue. Others sell for about 25 percent less.

---

### POSTAGE DUE STAMPS

Postage Due Stamps of Great Britain Overprinted in Blue **M.E.F.**

**1942 Wmk. 251 *Perf. 14x14½***

*J1* D1 ½p emerald 30 *45*
*J2* D1 1p carmine rose 35 *60*
*J3* D1 2p black brown 60 1.25
*J4* D1 3p violet 1.50 2.50
*J5* D1 1sh blue 4.75 19.00
*Nos. J1-J5 (5)* 7.50 *23.80*

No. J1 to J5 were used in Eritrea.

---

### FOR USE IN ERITREA

**Catalogue values for unused stamps in this section, from this point to the end of the section, are for Never Hinged items.**

100 Cents = 1 Shilling

Stamps of Great Britain 1937-42 Surcharged in Black

**B. M. A.**
**ERITREA**

a

**5**
**CENTS**

**1948, June Wmk. 251 *Perf. 14½x14***

*1* A101 5c on ½p green (II) 10 10
*2* A101 10c on 1p vermilion (II) 15 15
*3* A101 20c on 2p light org (II) 20 20
*4* A101 25c on 2½p ultra (II) 65 65
*5* A101 30c on 3p violet (II) 20 20
*6* A101 40c on 5p light brown 25 25
*7* A101 50c on 6p rose lilac 30 30
*8* A103 75c on 9p deep ol green 50 50
*9* A103 1sh on 1sh brown 50 50

"B. M. A." stands for British Military Administration.

Great Britain Nos. 249A, 250 and 251A Surcharged in Black

**B. M. A.**
**ERITREA**

**2 SH. 50 CTS.**

**1948, June Wmk. 259 *Perf. 14***

*10* A104 2sh50c on 2sh 6p yel grn 6.50 *8.25*
*11* A104 5sh on 5sh dl red 10.00 *13.00*
*12* A105 10sh on 10sh ultra 18.00 *21.50*

Great Britain No. 245 Surcharged Type "a"

**1949 Wmk. 251 *Perf. 14½x14***

*13* A103 65c on 8p brt rose 1.00 2.00
*Nos. 1-13 (13)* 38.35 *47.60*

Stamps of Great Britain 1937-42 Surcharged in Black

**B. A.**
**ERITREA**

c

**5**
**CENTS**

**1950, Feb. 6**

*14* A101 5c on ½p green (II) 6 6
*15* A101 10c on 1p ver (II) 10 10
*16* A101 20c on 2p lt orange (II) 12 12
*17* A101 25c on 2½p ultra (II) 15 15
*18* A101 30c on 3p violet (II) 20 20
*19* A102 40c on 5p light brown 30 30
*20* A102 50c on 6p rose lilac 30 30
*21* A103 65c on 8p bright rose 30 30
*22* A103 75c on 9p deep ol green 40 40
*23* A103 1sh on 1sh brown 45 45

Great Britain Nos. 249A, 250, 251A Surcharged

**B. A.**
**ERITREA**

**2 SH. 50 CTS.**

**Wmk. 259 *Perf. 14***

*24* A104 2sh50c on 2sh6p yel grn 5.00 *6.50*
*25* A104 5sh on 5sh dl red 11.50 *13.00*
*26* A105 10sh on 10sh ultra 25.00 *27.50*
*Nos. 14-26 (13)* 43.88 *49.38*

Great Britain Nos. 280, 281, 283 and 284 Surcharged Type "c"

***Perf. 14½x14***

**1951, May 3 Wmk. 251**

*27* A101 5c on ½p lt org 8 8
*28* A101 10c on 1p ultra 10 10
*29* A101 20c on 2p lt red brn 15 15
*30* A101 25c on 2½p ver 22 22

Great Britain Nos. 286-288 Surcharged

**B.A.**
**ERITREA**

**2 SH. 50 CTS.**

***Perf. 11x12***

**1951, May 31 Wmk. 259**

*31* A121 2sh50c on 2sh6p grn 3.25 3.25
*32* A121 5sh on 5sh dl red 10.00 8.25
*33* A122 10sh on 10sh ultra 16.00 20.00
*Nos. 27-33 (7)* 29.80 32.05

The surcharge is arranged to fit the design on No. 33.

### POSTAGE DUE STAMPS

Great Britain Nos. J26 to J29 and J32 Surcharged

**B. M. A.**
**ERITREA**
**5 CENTS**

**1948 Wmk. 251 *Perf. 14x14½***

*J1* D1 5c on ½p emer 10.00 *20.00*
*J2* D1 10c on 1p car rose 10.00 *20.00*
*J3* D1 20c on 2p blk brn 8.00 *15.00*
*J4* D1 30c on 3p violet 12.50 *25.00*
*J5* D1 1sh on 1sh blue 20.00 *35.00*
*Nos. J1-J5 (5)* 60.50 115.00

Great Britain Nos. J26 to J29 and J32 Surcharged in Black

**B. A.**
**ERITREA**
**5 CENTS**

**1950, Feb. 6**

*J6* D1 5c on ½p emer 11.00 *12.00*
*J7* D1 10c on 1p car rose 9.25 *9.00*
*a.* "C" of CENTS omitted *1,000.*
*J8* D1 20c on 2p blk brn 11.00 *10.50*
*J9* D1 30c on 3p violet 11.00 *12.00*
*J10* D1 1sh on 1sh blue 18.00 *20.00*
*Nos. J6-J10 (5)* 60.25 *63.50*

---

## EAST AFRICA FORCES

**For use in Somalia (Italian Somaliland)**

12 Pence = 1 Shilling
100 Cents = 1 Shilling

Stamps of Great Britain 1938-42 Overprinted in Blue **E.A.F.**

***Perf. 14½x14***

**1943, Jan. 15 Wmk. 251**

*1* A101 1p vermilion 7 7
*2* A101 2p light orange 10 10
*3* A101 2½p ultramarine 15 15
*4* A101 3p violet 15 15
*5* A101 5p light brown 18 18
*6* A101 6p rose lilac 28 28
*7* A103 9p deep ol grn 30 30
*8* A103 1sh brown 32 32

On Great Britain No. 249A

**1946 Wmk. 259 *Perf. 14***

*9* A104 2sh6p yellow grn 3.50 3.50
*Nos. 1-9 (9)* 5.05 5.05

**Catalogue values for unused stamps in this section, from this point to the end of the section, are for Never Hinged items.**

Stamps of Great Britain, 1937-42 Surcharged in Black

**B. M. A.**
**SOMALIA**

**25**
**CENTS**

***Perf. 14½x14***

**1948, May 27 Wmk. 251**

*10* A101 5c on ½p grn (II) 12 12
*11* A101 15c on 1½p lt red brn (II) 90 90
*12* A101 20c on 2p lt org (II) 22 22
*13* A101 25c on 2½p ultra (II) 18 18
*14* A101 30c on 3p vio (II) 1.65 *4.50*
*15* A102 40c on 5p lt brown 35 35
*16* A102 50c on 6p rose lilac 28 28
*17* A103 75c on 9p dp ol grn 1.40 2.75
*18* A103 1sh on 1sh brown 1.65 *5.50*

Great Britain Nos. 249A and 250 Surcharged in Black

**B. M. A.**
**SOMALIA**

**2 SH. 50 CTS.**

**Wmk. 259 *Perf. 14***

*19* A104 2sh50c on 2sh6p yel grn 6.00 9.00
*20* A104 5sh on 5sh dl red 11.50 13.00
*Nos. 10-20 (11)* 24.25 *36.80*

Stamps of Great Britain 1937-42 Surcharged in Black

**B. A.**
**SOMALIA**

**25**
**CENTS**

***Perf. 14½x14***

**1950, Jan. 2 Wmk. 251**

*21* A101 5c on ½p grn (II) 16 16
*22* A101 15c on 1½p lt red brn (II) 65 1.25
*23* A101 20c on 2p lt org (II) 60 60
*24* A101 25c on 2½p ultra (II) 24 24
*25* A101 30c on 3p violet (II) 80 *2.00*
*26* A101 40c on 5p light brn 45 45
*27* A102 50c on 6p rose lilac 45 *80*
*28* A103 75c on 9p deep ol grn 80 *2.00*
*29* A103 1sh on 1sh brown 48 *80*

Great Britain Nos. 249A and 250 Surcharged in Black

**B. A.**
**SOMALIA**

**2 SH. 50 CTS.**

**Wmk. 259 *Perf. 14***

*30* A104 2sh50c on 2sh 6p yel grn 8.00 *12.00*
*31* A104 5sh on 5sh dl red 12.00 *20.00*
*Nos. 21-31 (11)* 24.63 *40.30*

---

### For Use in Tripolitania

**Catalogue values for unused stamps in this section, from this point to the end of the section, are for Never Hinged items.**

Stamps of Great Britain, 1937-42, Surcharged in Black

**B. M. A.**
**TRIPOLITANIA**

**5**
**M.A.L.**

M.A.L.=Military Authority Lire

***Perf. 14½x14***

**1948, July 1 Wmk. 251**

*1* A101 1 l on ½p green (II) 18 18
*2* A101 2 l on 1p ver (II) 12 12
*3* A101 3 l on 1½p lt red brn (II) 16 16
*4* A101 4 l on 2p lt org (II) 12 12
*5* A101 5 l on 2½p ultra (II) 18 18
*6* A101 6 l on 3p violet (II) 22 22
*7* A102 10 l on 5p lt brown 22 22
*8* A102 12 l on 6p rose lilac 30 30
*9* A103 18 l on 9p dp ol grn 60 *1.40*
*10* A103 24 l on 1sh brown 90 *1.75*

*Great Britain Offices Abroad stamps can be mounted in Scott's Great Britain Album.*

Great Britain Nos. 249A, 250 and 251A Surcharged in Black

B.M.A.
TRIPOLITANIA
60 M.A.L.

**Wmk. 259** *Perf. 14*

*11* A104 60 l on 2sh6p yel grn 2.25 *11.50*
*12* A104 120 l on 5sh dl red 11.50 *27.50*
*13* A105 240 l on 10sh ultra 20.00 *55.00*
*Nos. 1-13 (13)* 36.75 *98.65*

Stamps of Great Britain 1937-42 Surcharged in Black

B. A.
TRIPOLITANIA
5
M.A.L.

*Perf. 14½x14*

**1950, Feb. 6** **Wmk. 251**

*14* A101 1 l on ½p green (II) 16 *1.75*
*15* A101 2 l on 1p ver (II) 7 7
*16* A101 3 l on 1½p lt red brn (II) 20 *1.40*
*17* A101 4 l on 2p lt org (II) 14 70
*18* A101 5 l on 2½p ultra (II) 16 *1.00*
*19* A101 6 l on 3p violet (II) 16 70
*20* A102 10 l on 5p lt brown 20 20
*21* A102 12 l on 6p rose lilac 35 35
*22* A103 18 l on 9p dp ol grn 55 55
*23* A103 24 l on 1sh brown 55 55

Great Britain Nos. 249A, 250 and 251A Surcharged in Black

B. A.
TRIPOLITANIA
60 M.A.L.

**Wmk. 259** *Perf. 14*

*24* A104 60 l on 2sh6p yel grn 5.25 *10.50*
*25* A104 120 l on 5sh dl red 10.50 *17.50*
*26* A105 240 l on 10sh ultra 19.00 *27.50*
*Nos. 14-26 (13)* 37.29 *62.77*

Great Britain Nos. 280-284 Surcharged like Nos. 14-23

*Perf. 14½x14*

**1951, May 3** **Wmk. 251**

*27* A101 1 l on ½p light org 16 *80*
*28* A101 2 l on 1p ultra 16 *80*
*29* A101 3 l on 1½p green 35 *1.50*
*30* A101 4 l on 2p lt red brown 24 *80*
*31* A101 5 l on 2½p ver 20 *1.25*

Great Britain Nos. 286-288 Surcharged in Black

B.A.
TRIPOLITANIA
60 M.A.L.

**1951, May 3** **Wmk. 259** *Perf. 11x12*

*32* A121 60 l on 2sh6p grn 8.00 *12.00*
*33* A121 120 l on 5sh dl red 10.00 *18.00*
*34* A122 240 l on 10sh ultra 22.50 *32.50*
*Nos. 27-34 (8)* 41.61 *67.65*

The surcharge is arranged to fit the design on No. 34.

## POSTAGE DUE STAMPS

Great Britain Nos. J26 to J29 and J32, Surcharged in Black

B. M. A
TRIPOLITANIA
1 M.A.L.

**1948** **Wmk. 251** *Perf. 14x14½*

*J1* D1 1 l on ½p emer 3.25 *10.00*
*J2* D1 2 l on 1p car rose 3.25 *10.00*
*J3* D1 4 l on 2p blk brn 4.00 *13.00*
*J4* D1 6 l on 3p violet 6.50 *20.00*
*J5* D1 24 l on 1sh blue 20.00 *40.00*
*Nos. J1-J5 (5)* 37.00 *93.00*

Great Britain Nos. J26 to J29 and J32 Surcharged in Black

B. A
TRIPOLITANIA
1 M.A.L.

**1950, Feb. 6**

*J6* D1 1 l on ½p emer 5.25 *13.00*
*J7* D1 2 l on 1p car rose 5.00 *10.00*
*J8* D1 4 l on 2p blk brn 5.00 *10.00*
*J9* D1 6 l on 3p violet 8.25 *22.50*
*J10* D1 24 l on 1sh blue 25.00 *40.00*
*Nos. J6-J10 (5)* 48.50 *95.50*

# OFF. IN CHINA

100 CENTS = 1 DOLLAR

Stamps of Hong Kong, 1912-14, Overprinted CHINA

**1917** **Wmk. 3** *Perf. 14*

**Ordinary Paper**

*1* A11 1c brown 22 22
*2* A11 2c deep green 35 10
*3* A12 4c scarlet 65 8
*4* A13 6c orange 1.25 22
*5* A12 8c gray 80 25
*6* A11 10c ultramarine 1.00 15

**Chalky Paper**

*7* A14 12c violet, *yel* 2.75 75
*8* A14 20c ol green & vio 2.25 45
*9* A15 25c red vio & dl vio (on No. 117) 2.75 2.25
*10* A13 30c org & violet 5.75 75
*11* A14 50c *emerald* 3.75 1.90
**a.** 50c *blue green*, ol back 5.75 1.25
**b.** 50c *emerald*, ol back 10.00 1.90
*12* A11 $1 blue & vio, *bl* 12.00 95
*13* A14 $2 black & red 75.00 37.50
*14* A13 $3 violet & grn 100.00 95.00
*15* A14 $5 red & grn, *bl grn*, ol back 100.00 100.00
*16* A13 $10 blk & vio, *red* 325.00 250.00
*Nos. 1-16 (16)* 633.52 490.57

Stamps of Hong Kong, 1921-26, Overprinted CHINA

**1922-27** **Wmk. 4**

**Ordinary Paper**

*17* A11 1c brown 35 52
*18* A11 2c green 24 24
*19* A12 4c scarlet 35 52
*20* A13 6c orange 52 1.40
*21* A12 8c gray 70 75
*22* A11 10c ultramarine 90 90

**Chalky Paper**

*23* A14 20c ol grn & vio 1.75 1.75
*24* A15 25c red violet & dull vio 2.00 *3.50*
*25* A14 50c *emerald* ('27) 5.25 *10.50*
*26* A11 $1 ultra & vio, *bl* 10.50 8.75
*27* A14 $2 black & red 87.50 77.50
*Nos. 17-27 (11)* 110.06 106.33

# OFF. IN MOROCCO

100 Centimos = 1 Peseta
12 Pence = 1 Shilling
20 Shillings = 1 Pound
100 Centimes = 1 Franc

These stamps were issued for various purposes:

a. For general use at the British Post Offices throughout Morocco.

b. For use in the Spanish Zone of Northern Morocco.

c. For use in the French Zone of Southern Morocco.

d. For use in the International Zone of Tangier.

For convenience these stamps are listed in four groups according to the coinage expressed or surcharged on the stamps, namely:

1. Value expressed in Spanish currency.
2. Value in British currency.
3. Value in French currency.
4. Stamps overprinted "Tangier".

## Spanish Currency

Gibraltar Stamps of 1889-95 Overprinted

Morocco
Agencies

**1898** **Wmk. 2** *Perf. 14*

**Black Overprint**

*1* A11 5c green 24 15
**a.** Inverted "V" for "A" 19.00 24.00
*2* A11 10c carmine rose 24 15
**a.** Inverted "V" for "A" 310.00 375.00
**b.** Double ovpt. 525.00
*3* A11 20c olive green 48 52
**a.** Inverted "V" for "A" 32.50 37.50
*4* A11 25c ultramarine 48 42
**a.** Inverted "V" for "A" 100.00 125.00
*5* A11 40c orange brown 2.50 2.75
**a.** Inverted "V" for "A" 175.00 200.00
*6* A11 50c violet 24.00 *27.50*
**a.** Inverted "V" for "A" 275.00 350.00
*7* A11 1pe bister & blue 4.75 *13.00*
**a.** Inverted "V" for "A" 185.00 250.00
*8* A11 2pe blk & car rose 4.50 *10.00*
**a.** Inverted "V" for "A" 225.00 300.00
*Nos. 1-8 (8)* 37.19 *54.49*

**Dark Blue Overprint**

*9* A11 40c orange brown *50.00 50.00*
*10* A11 50c violet 8.00 12.00
*11* A11 1pe bister & blue *300.00 325.00*

Overprinted in Black

Morocco
Agencies

(Narrower "M," ear of "g" horiz.)

**1899**

*12* A11 5c green 30 30
**a.** "M" with long serif 3.00 *3.75*
*13* A11 10c carmine rose 75 16
**a.** "M" with long serif 3.75 *5.00*
*14* A11 20c olive green 2.25 70
**a.** "M" with long serif 16.00 *17.50*
*15* A11 25c ultramarine 3.00 55
**a.** "M" with long serif 16.00 *17.50*
*16* A11 40c orange brown 5.00 4.25
**a.** "M" with long serif 62.50 *67.50*
*17* A11 50c violet 4.75 2.75
**a.** "M" with long serif 90.00 *110.00*
*18* A11 1pe bister & blue 7.00 *14.00*
**a.** "M" with long serif *110.00* 125.00
*19* A11 2pe blk & car rose 14.00 *17.50*
**a.** "M" with long serif 250.00 *275.00*
*Nos. 12-19 (8)* 37.05 *40.21*

Type of Gibraltar, 1903, with Value in Spanish Currency, Overprinted in Black

**1903-05**

*20* A12 5c gray grn & bl grn 1.65 32
**a.** "M" with long serif 24.00 24.00
*21* A12 10c violet, *red* 3.00 40
**a.** "M" with long serif 32.50 32.50
*22* A12 20c gray grn & car rose ('04) 2.50 2.50
**a.** "M" with long serif 52.50 57.50
*23* A12 25c vio & blk, *bl* 1.25 28
**a.** "M" with long serif 32.50 37.50
*24* A12 50c violet 42.50 *50.00*
**a.** "M" with long serif 275.00 300.00
*25* A12 1pe blk & car rose 42.50 *47.50*
**a.** "M" with long serif 250.00 275.00
*26* A12 2pe black & ultra 45.00 *55.00*
**a.** "M" with long serif 275.00 300.00
*Nos. 20-26 (7)* 138.40 *156.00*

**1905-06** **Wmk. 3** **Chalky Paper**

*27* A12 5c gray grn & bl grn 55 50
**a.** "M" with long serif 19.00 19.00
*28* A12 10c violet, *red* 55 20
**a.** "M" with long serif 19.00 19.00
*29* A12 20c gray grn & car rose ('06) 2.00 *7.50*
**a.** "M" with long serif 37.50 *42.50*
*30* A12 25c violet & blk, *bl* ('06) 27.50 6.00
**a.** "M" with long serif 110.00 125.00
*31* A12 50c violet 6.00 *9.00*
**a.** "M" with long serif 140.00 150.00
*32* A12 1pe blk & car rose 27.50 *45.00*
**a.** "M" with long serif 225.00 250.00
*33* A12 2pe black & ultra 15.00 *27.50*
**a.** "M" with long serif 225.00 *275.00*
*Nos. 27-33 (7)* 79.10 *95.70*

No. 29 is on ordinary paper. Nos. 27 and 28 are on both ordinary and chalky paper.

Numerous other minor overprint varieties exist of Nos. 1-33.

British Stamps of 1902-10 Surcharged in Spanish Currency:

MOROCCO AGENCIES
5 CENTIMOS
a

MOROCCO AGENCIES
3 PESETAS
b

**1907-10** **Wmk. 30**

*34* A66(a) 5c on ½p pale grn 42 12
*35* A66(a) 10c on 1p car 45 9
*36* A67(a) 15c on 1½p vio & grn 65 35
**a.** "1" of "15" omitted 3,750.
*37* A68(a) 20c on 2p grn & car55 55 35
*38* A66(a) 25c on 2½p ultra 1.50 75
*39* A70(a) 40c on 4p brn & grn 1.10 *2.00*
*40* A70(a) 40c on 4p orange ('10) 45 90
*41* A71(a) 50c on 5p lil & ultra 1.75 1.75
*42* A73(a) 1pe on 10p car rose & vio 5.50 *7.50*

**Wmk. 31**

*43* A75(b) 3pe on 2sh6p vio 21.00 21.00
*44* A76(b) 6pe on 5sh car rose 37.50 37.50
*45* A77(b) 12pe on 10sh ultra 60.00 60.00
*Nos. 34-45 (12)* 130.87 132.31

Nos. 36-37, 39-43 are on chalky paper.

Great Britain Nos. 153, 154 and 148 Surcharged Type "a"

**1912** **Wmk. 30** *Perf. 15x14*

*46* A80 5c on ½p yel grn 24 7
*47* A81 10c on 1p scarlet 45 7
*48* A66 25c on 2½p ultra 12.00 13.00

British Stamps of 1912-18 Surcharged in Black or Carmine:

MOROCCO AGENCIES
15 CENTIMOS
c

MOROCCO AGENCIES
10 CENTIMOS
d

MOROCCO AGENCIES
6 PESETAS
e

**1914-18** **Wmk. 33**

*49* A82(a) 5c on ½p grn 10 6
*50* A83(d) 10c on 1p scar 15 67
*51* A84(c) 15c on 1½p red brn ('15) 20 12
*52* A85(d) 20c on 2p org (I) 20 20
*53* A86(d) 25c on 2½p ultra 55 55
*54* A90(d) 1pe on 10p lt bl 90 1.10

**Wmk. 34**

*Perf. 11x12*

*55* A91(e) 3pe on 2sh6p lt brn 24.00 30.00
**a.** 3pe on 2sh6p dk brn 24.00 30.00
*56* A91(e) 6pe on 5sh car 24.00 30.00
**a.** 6pe on 5sh lt car 125.00
*57* A91(e) 12pe on 10sh dk bl (C) 85.00 85.00
**a.** 12pe on 10sh bl 85.00 *105.00*
*Nos. 49-57 (9)* 135.10 147.70

Great Britain Nos. 159, 165 Surcharged in Spanish Currency

MOROCCO AGENCIES 3 CENTIMOS
f

MOROCCO AGENCIES 40 CENTIMOS
g

**1917-23 Wmk. 33 *Perf. 15x14***

*58* A82(f) 3c on ½p grn 2850 3260
*59* A88(g) 40c on 4p sl grn 6.75 *8.25*

Great Britain Nos. 189, 191, 179 Surcharged in Spanish Currency

**1926 Wmk. 35**

*60* A84(c) 15c on 1½p red brn 9.75 *11.00*
*61* A86(d) 25c on 2½p ultra 1.10 1.40

**Wmk. 34**
***Perf. 11x12***

*62* A91(e) 3pe on 2sh6p brn 16.00 15.00

British Stamps of 1924 Surcharged in Spanish Currency

**1929-31 Wmk. 35 *Perf. 15x14***

*63* A82(a) 5c on ½p grn ('31) 50 70
*64* A83(d) 10c on 1p scar 80 1.40
*65* A85(d) 20c on 2p org (II) ('31) 4.00 4.75
*66* A88(g) 40c on 4p sl grn ('30) 28 50

**Silver Jubilee Issue**

Great Britain Nos. 226-229 Surcharged in Blue or Red

MOROCCO AGENCIES 5 CENTIMOS

**1935, May 8 *Perf. 14½x14***

*67* A98 5c on ½p dk grn 28 32
*68* A98 10c on 1p car 2.25 2.25
*a.* Pair, one reading "CENTIMES" 1,850.
*69* A98 15c on 1½p red brn 40 50
*70* A98 25c on 2½p ultra (R) 3.00 3.00

Issued in commemoration of the 25th anniversary of the reign of King George V.

Great Britain Nos. 210-214, 216, 219 Surcharged in Spanish Currency

**1935-37 Photo.**

*71* A82(a) 5c on ½p dk grn ('36) 9 15
*72* A97(d) 10c on 1p car 18 20
*73* A84(c) 15c on 1½p red brn 3.00 3.75
*74* A85(d) 20c on 2p red org ('36) 12 18
*75* A97(d) 25c on 2½p ultra ('36) 1.50 1.75
*76* A88(d) 40c on 4p dk sl grn ('37) 15 30
*77* A90(d) 1pe on 10p Prus bl ('37) 22 30
*Nos. 71-77 (7)* 5.26 6.63

Great Britain Nos. 230-233 Surcharged in Black

MOROCCO 5 AGENCIES CENTIMOS

"MOROCCO" 14mm.

**1936 Wmk. 250**

*78* A99 5c on ½p dk grn 8 8
*79* A99 10c on 1p crim 8 8
*a.* "Morocco" 15mm long 25 25
*80* A99 15c on 1½p red brn 12 12
*81* A99 25c on 2½p brt ultra 15 15

Great Britain No. 234 Surcharged in Blue

MOROCCO 15 CENTIMOS AGENCIES

***Perf. 14½x14***

**1937, May 13 Wmk. 251**

*82* A100 15c on 1½p pur brn 10 10

Coronation of King George VI and Queen Elizabeth.

Great Britain Nos. 235-237, 239, 241, 244 Surcharged in Blue or Black

MOROCCO AGENCIES 25 CENTIMOS
h

**1937-40**

*83* A101 5c on ½p dp grn (Bl) 6 6
*84* A101 10c on 1p scarlet 8 9
*85* A101 15c on 1½p red brown (Bl) 8 12
*86* A101 25c on 2½p brt ultra 9 12
*87* A102 40c on 4p gray green ('40) 35 40
*88* A103 70c on 7p emer ('40) 55 55
*Nos. 83-88 (6)* 1.21 1.34

Great Britain Nos. 252-254, 256 Surcharged in Blue or Black

MOROCCO AGENCIES 5 CENTIMOS

**1940, May 6**

*89* A106 5c on ½p deep grn (Bl) 18 18
*90* A106 10c on 1p scarlet 30 30
*91* A106 15c on 1½p red brn (Bl) 45 45
*92* A106 25c on 2½p brt ultra 50 50

Centenary of the postage stamp.

**Catalogue values for unused stamps in this section, from this point to the end of the section, are for Never Hinged items.**

Great Britain Nos. 267 and 268 Surcharged in Black:

25 CENTIMOS
i

MOROCCO AGENCIES 45 PESETAS MOROCCO AGENCIES
j

***Perf. 14½x14, 14x14½***

**1948, Apr. 26 Wmk. 251**

*93* A109(i) 25c on 2½p brt ultra 10 10
*94* A110(j) 45pe on £1 dp chlky bl 25.00 27.50

25th anniversary of the marriage of King George VI and Queen Elizabeth.

Great Britain Nos. 271-274 Surcharged "MOROCCO AGENCIES" and New Value in Black

**1948, July 29 *Perf. 14½x14***

*95* A113 25c on 2½p brt ultra 15 15
*96* A114 30c on 3p dp vio 18 18
*97* A115 60c on 6p red vio 30 30
*98* A116 1.20pe on 1sh dk brn 60 60
*a.* Double surcharge 600.00

1948 Olympic Games, Wembley, July-Aug.
A square of dots obliterates the original denomination on No. 98.

Great Britain Nos. 280-282, 284-285, 247 Surcharged Type "h" in Black

**1951-52 Wmk. 251 *Perf. 14½x14.***

*99* A101 5c on ½p light org 12 12
*100* A101 10c on 1p ultra 15 15
*101* A101 15c on 1½p green 15 15
*102* A101 25c on 2½p ver 25 25
*103* A102 40c on 4p ultra ('52) 25 25
*104* A103 1pe on 10p ryl bl ('52) 40 40
*Nos. 99-104 (6)* 1.32 1.32

Great Britain Nos. 292-293 Surcharged Type "h"

**1954-55 Wmk. 298**

*105* A126 5c on ½p red org 10 10
*106* A126 10c on 1p ultra ('55) 20 20

Great Britain Nos. 317 and 323 Surcharged Type "h" in Black

**1956 Wmk. 308 *Perf. 14x14½***

*107* A126 5c on ½p red org 10 10
*108* A128 40c on 4p ultra 1.00 1.00

---

**BRITISH CURRENCY**

British Stamps of 1902-11 Overprinted

MOROCCO AGENCIES
a

MOROCCO AGENCIES
b

Overprint "a" 14½ mm. long

**1907-12 Wmk. 30 *Perf. 14***

**Ordinary Paper**

*201* A66 ½p pale yel grn 35 55
*202* A66 1p carmine 1.10 1.10

**Chalky Paper**

*203* A68 2p grn & car 1.10 1.10
*204* A70 4p brn & grn 12.00 1.75
*205* A70 4p org ('12) 1.75 *3.00*
*a.* Perf. 15x14 7.50 *9.00*
*206* A66 6p dl vio 4.50 3.00
*207* A74 1sh car rose & grn 9.00 10.50

**Overprinted Type "b"**
**Wmk. 31**

*208* A75 2sh6p violet 35.00 47.50
*Nos. 201-208 (8)* 64.80 *68.50*

British Stamps of 1912-18 Overprinted Type "a"

***Perf. 14½x14, 15x14***

**1914-21 Wmk. 33**

*209* A82 ½p green ('18) 18 18
*210* A83 1p scarlet ('17) 55 7
*211* A84 1½p red brn ('21) 1.65 1.90
*212* A85 2p orange ('18) 80 20
*213* A87 3p violet ('21) 1.75 28
*214* A88 4p sl green ('21) 70 50
*215* A89 6p dull vio ('21) 4.75 5.50
*216* A90 1sh bister ('17) 8.25 1.65

MOROCCO AGENCIES
c

**Wmk. 34 *Perf. 11x12***

*217* A91 2sh6p lt brown 30.00 22.50
*a.* 2sh6p brn 30.00 22.50
*b.* 2sh6p blk brn 30.00 22.50
*c.* Dbl. ovpt. 2,250. 1,400.
*Nos. 209-217 (9)* 48.63 32.78

Same Overprint on Great Britain Nos. 179-180

**1925-31**

*218* A91 2sh6p gray brown 32.50 18.00
*219* A91 5sh car rose ('31) 45.00 47.50

British Stamps of 1924 Overprinted Type "a" (14½mm. long)

**1925-31 Wmk. 35 *Perf. 15x14***

*220* A82 ½p green 70 55
*221* A84 1½p red brn ('31) 8.25 11.00
*222* A85 2p dp org (Die II) 1.10 1.10
*223* A86 2½p ultra 1.25 *2.75*
*224* A89 6p red vio ('31) 4.50 *5.50*
*225* A90 1sh bister 12.50 4.00
*Nos. 220-225 (6)* 28.30 *24.90*

**Silver Jubilee Issue**

Great Britain Nos. 226-229 Overprinted in Blue or Red

MOROCCO AGENCIES

**1935, May 8 *Perf. 14½x14***

*226* A98 ½p dark green (Bl) 38 45
*227* A98 1p carmine (Bl) 45 55
*228* A98 1½p red brown (Bl) 1.65 *3.75*
*229* A98 2½p ultramarine (R) 2.25 2.50

25th anniversary of the reign of King George V.

British Stamps of 1924 Overprinted Type "a" (15½mm. long)

**1935-36**

*230* A82 ½p green 3.25 *6.50*
*231* A86 2½p ultra *145.00* 27.50
*232* A88 4p sl green 5.50 *16.00*
*233* A89 6p red vio 55 80
*234* A90 1sh bister 50.00 45.00
*Nos. 230-234 (5)* *204.30* *95.80*

British Stamps of 1934-36 Overprinted "MOROCCO AGENCIES"

**1935-36**

*235* A97 1p carmine 18 24
*236* A84 1½p red brn ('36) 75 1.10
*237* A85 2p red org ('36) 15 18
*238* A97 2½p ultra ('36) 80 1.00
*239* A87 3p dk vio ('36) 18 18
*240* A88 4p dk sl grn ('36) 18 18
*241* A90 1sh bis brn ('36) 55 60

**Overprinted Type "c"**
**Wmk. 34**
***Perf. 11x12***

*242* A91 2sh6p brown 42.50 24.00
*243* A91 5sh car ('37) 27.50 30.00
*Nos. 235-243 (9)* 72.79 57.48

Great Britain Nos. 231, 233 Overprinted in Black

MOROCCO AGENCIES

"MOROCCO" 14mm.

**1936 Wmk. 250 *Perf. 14½x14***

*244* A99 1p crimson 7 7
*a.* "Morocco" 15mm long 75 75
*245* A99 2½p brt ultra 20 20
*a.* "Morocco" 15mm long 75 75

**Catalogue values for unused stamps in this section, from this point to the end of the section, are for Never Hinged items.**

Great Britain Nos. 258-263, 241-248, 266, 249A-250 Overprinted "MOROCCO AGENCIES" (14½mm. long)

**1949, Aug. 16 Wmk. 251**

*246* A101 ½p green 16 16
*247* A101 1p vermilion 28 28
*248* A101 1½p lt red brown 38 38
*249* A101 2p lt orange 38 38
*250* A101 2½p ultra 38 38
*251* A101 3p violet 38 38
*252* A102 4p gray green 50 50
*253* A102 5p lt brown 75 75
*254* A102 6p rose lilac 65 65
*255* A103 7p emerald 85 85
*256* A103 8p brt rose 1.10 1.10
*257* A103 9p dp ol grn 90 90
*258* A103 10p royal blue 1.00 1.00
*259* A103 11p violet brn 1.25 1.25
*260* A103 1sh brown 1.25 1.25

**"MOROCCO AGENCIES" 17½mm. long**

**Wmk. 259**

***Perf. 14***

| No. | Type | Description | Unused | Used |
|---|---|---|---|---|
| 261 | A104 | 2sh6p yel green | 8.25 | 8.25 |
| 262 | A104 | 5sh dull red | 16.00 | 16.00 |
| | | *Nos. 246-262 (17)* | 34.46 | 34.46 |

Stamps of Morocco Agencies were accepted for postage in Great Britain, starting in mid-1950.

Great Britain Nos. 280-284, 286-287 Overprinted "MOROCCO AGENCIES" (14½mm. long).

***Perf. 14½x14***

**1951, May 3** **Wmk. 251**

| No. | Type | Description | Unused | Used |
|---|---|---|---|---|
| 263 | A101 | ½p lt org | 14 | 14 |
| 264 | A101 | 1p ultra | 16 | 16 |
| 265 | A101 | 1½p green | 32 | 32 |
| 266 | A101 | 2p lt red brn | 32 | 32 |
| 267 | A101 | 2½p vermilion | 45 | 45 |

**"MOROCCO AGENCIES" 17½mm. long**

**Wmk. 259**

***Perf. 11x12***

| No. | Type | Description | Unused | Used |
|---|---|---|---|---|
| 268 | A121 | 2sh6p green | 11.00 | 14.00 |
| 269 | A121 | 5sh dl red | 16.00 | 20.00 |
| | | *Nos. 263-269 (7)* | 28.39 | 35.39 |

Great Britain Nos. 292-296, 299, 302 and 306 Overprinted "MOROCCO AGENCIES" (14½mm. long)

**1952-55** **Wmk. 298** ***Perf. 14½x14***

| No. | Type | Description | Unused | Used |
|---|---|---|---|---|
| 270 | A126 | ½p red orange | 6 | 6 |
| 271 | A126 | 1p ultramarine | 10 | 10 |
| 272 | A126 | 1½p green ('52) | 14 | 14 |
| 273 | A126 | 2p red brown | 20 | 20 |
| 274 | A127 | 2½p scarlet ('52) | 28 | 28 |
| 275 | A128 | 4p ultra ('55) | 50 | 50 |
| 276 | A129 | 5p light brown | 60 | 60 |
| 277 | A129 | 6p lil rose ('55) | 65 | 65 |
| 278 | A130 | 8p bright rose | 1.40 | 1.40 |
| 279 | A131 | 1sh brown | 1.10 | 1.10 |
| | | *Nos. 270-279 (10)* | 5.03 | 5.03 |

Same Overprint on Great Britain No. 321

**1956** **Wmk. 308** ***Perf. 14½x14***

| No. | Type | Description | Unused | Used |
|---|---|---|---|---|
| 280 | A127 | 2½p scarlet | 1.00 | 1.00 |

**French Currency**

British Stamps of 1912-22 Surcharged in French Currency in Red or Black:

MOROCCO AGENCIES 3 CENTIMES h

MOROCCO AGENCIES 1 FRANC i

***Perf. 14½x14, 15x14***

**1917-24** **Wmk. 33**

| No. | Type | Description | Unused | Used |
|---|---|---|---|---|
| 401 | A82(h) | 3c on ½p grn (R) | 6 | 6 |
| 402 | A82(h) | 5c on ½p green | 6 | 6 |
| 403 | A83(h) | 10c on 1p scarlet | 14 | 6 |
| 404 | A84(h) | 15c on 1½p red brn | 50 | 38 |
| 405 | A86(h) | 25c on 2½p ultra | 14 | 6 |
| 406 | A88(h) | 40c on 4p sl green | 50 | 18 |
| 407 | A89(h) | 50c on 5p yellow brown ('23) | 1.50 | 70 |
| 408 | A90(h) | 75c on 9p olive green ('24) | 40 | 40 |
| 409 | A90(i) | 1fr on 10p lt blue | 1.65 | 55 |
| | | *Nos. 401-409 (9)* | 4.95 | 2.45 |

Great Britain No. 179 Surcharged:

MOROCCO AGENCIES k 3 FRANCS

**1924** **Wmk. 34** ***Perf. 11x12***

| No. | Type | Description | Unused | Used |
|---|---|---|---|---|
| 410 | A91(k) | 3fr on 2sh6p brn | 13.00 | 4.00 |

British Stamps of 1924 Surcharged in French Currency as in 1917-24

**1925-26** **Wmk. 35** ***Perf. 15x14***

| No. | Type | Description | Unused | Used |
|---|---|---|---|---|
| 411 | A82(h) | 5c on ½p green | 12 | 22 |
| 412 | A83(h) | 10c on 1p scarlet | 10 | 14 |
| 413 | A84(h) | 15c on 1½p red brn | 32 | 32 |
| 414 | A86(h) | 25c on 2½p ultra | 18 | 18 |
| 415 | A88(h) | 40c on 4p sl green | 20 | 18 |
| 416 | A89(h) | 50c on 5p yel brown | 35 | 22 |
| 417 | A90(h) | 75c on 9p ol green | 80 | 45 |
| 418 | A90(i) | 1fr on 10p dl blue | 35 | 32 |
| | | *Nos. 411-418 (8)* | 2.42 | 2.03 |

Great Britain No. 180 Surcharged type "k"

**1932** **Wmk. 34** ***Perf. 11x12***

| No. | Type | Description | Unused | Used |
|---|---|---|---|---|
| 419 | A91 | 6fr on 5sh car rose | 42.50 | 27.50 |

Great Britain Nos. 198 and 200 Surcharged Type "h"

**1934** **Wmk. 35** ***Perf. 14½x14***

| No. | Type | Description | Unused | Used |
|---|---|---|---|---|
| 420 | A90 | 90c on 9p ol grn | 2.50 | 2.75 |
| 421 | A90 | 1.50fr on 1sh bister | 90 | 1.25 |

**Silver Jubilee Issue**

Great Britain Nos. 226-229 Surcharged in Blue or Red

MOROCCO AGENCIES 5 CENTIMES

**1935, May 8** ***Perf. 14½x14***

| No. | Type | Description | Unused | Used |
|---|---|---|---|---|
| 422 | A98 | 5c on ½p dk grn | 15 | 15 |
| 423 | A98 | 10c on 1p carmine | 1.25 | 1.50 |
| 424 | A98 | 15c on 1½p red brn | 50 | 50 |
| 425 | A98 | 25c on 2½p ultra (R) | 50 | 50 |

25th anniv. of the reign of King George V.

British Stamps of 1934-36 Surcharged Types "h" or "k"

***Perf. 14½x14***

**1935-37** **Photo.** **Wmk. 35**

| No. | Type | Description | Unused | Used |
|---|---|---|---|---|
| 426 | A82(h) | 5c on ½p dk grn | 8 | 8 |
| 427 | A97(h) | 10c on 1p car ('36) | 8 | 8 |
| 428 | A84(h) | 15c on 1½p red brn | 60 | 60 |
| 429 | A97(h) | 25c on 2½p ultra | 15 | 15 |
| 430 | A88(h) | 40c on 4p dk sl grn | 12 | 15 |
| 431 | A89(h) | 50c on 5p yel brn | 20 | 20 |
| 432 | A90(h) | 90c on 9p dk ol grn | 20 | 20 |
| 433 | A90(k) | 1fr on 10p Prus bl | 20 | 20 |
| 434 | A90(h) | 1.50fr on 1sh bister brn ('37) | 30 | 40 |

**Waterlow Printing**

**Wmk. 34**

***Perf. 11x12***

| No. | Type | Description | Unused | Used |
|---|---|---|---|---|
| 435 | A91(k) | 3fr on 2sh6p brn | 11.50 | 8.25 |
| 436 | A91(k) | 6fr on 5sh carmine ('36) | 22.50 | 18.00 |
| | | *Nos. 426-436 (11)* | 35.93 | 28.31 |

Great Britain Nos. 230, 232 Surcharged in Black

MOROCCO 5 AGENCIES CENTIMES

**1936** **Wmk. 250** ***Perf. 14½x14***

| No. | Type | Description | Unused | Used |
|---|---|---|---|---|
| 437 | A99 | 5c on ½p dk grn | 7 | 7 |
| 438 | A99 | 15c on 1½p red brn | 8 | 8 |

Great Britain No. 234 Surcharged in Blue

MOROCCO 15 CENTIMES AGENCIES

**1937, May 13** **Wmk. 251**

| No. | Type | Description | Unused | Used |
|---|---|---|---|---|
| 439 | A100 | 15c on 1½p pur brn | 10 | 10 |

Coronation of King George VI and Queen Elizabeth.

MOROCCO AGENCIES 5 CENTIMES

Great Britain No. 235 Surcharged in Blue

**1937**

| No. | Type | Description | Unused | Used |
|---|---|---|---|---|
| 440 | A101 | 5c on ½p dp grn | 12 | 12 |

**For Use in the International Zone of Tangier**

Great Britain Nos. 187-190 Overprinted in Black

a TANGIER

**1927** **Wmk. 35** ***Perf. 15x14***

| No. | Type | Description | Unused | Used |
|---|---|---|---|---|
| 501 | A82 | ½p green | 70 | 80 |
| 502 | A83 | 1p scarlet | 70 | 14 |
| 503 | A84 | 1½p red brown | 2.25 | 1.65 |
| 504 | A85 | 2p orange (II) | 1.65 | 18 |

Same Overprint in Black on Great Britain Nos. 210-212

**1934-35** **Photo.** ***Perf. 14½x14***

| No. | Type | Description | Unused | Used |
|---|---|---|---|---|
| 505 | A82 | ½p dark green | 38 | 38 |
| 506 | A97 | 1p carmine | 1.10 | 1.25 |
| 507 | A84 | 1½p red brown | 38 | 38 |

**Silver Jubilee Issue**

Great Britain Nos. 226-228 Overprinted in Blue

b TANGIER TANGIER

**1935, May 8**

| No. | Type | Description | Unused | Used |
|---|---|---|---|---|
| 508 | A98 | ½p dark green | 75 | 75 |
| 509 | A98 | 1p carmine | 1.65 | 1.65 |
| 510 | A98 | 1½p red brown | 65 | 65 |

25th anniv. of the reign of King George V.

Great Britain Nos. 230-232 Overprinted Type "a" in Black

**1936** **Wmk. 250**

| No. | Type | Description | Unused | Used |
|---|---|---|---|---|
| 511 | A99 | ½p dark green | 7 | 7 |
| 512 | A99 | 1p crimson | 12 | 12 |
| 513 | A99 | 1½p red brown | 15 | 15 |

Great Britain No. 234 Overprinted Type "b" in Blue

**1937, May 13** **Wmk. 251**

| No. | Type | Description | Unused | Used |
|---|---|---|---|---|
| 514 | A100 | 1½p purple brown | 10 | 10 |

Issued in commemoration of the Coronation of King George VI and Queen Elizabeth.

Great Britain Nos. 235-237 Overprinted in Blue or Black

c TANGIER

**1937** ***Perf. 14½x14***

| No. | Type | Description | Unused | Used |
|---|---|---|---|---|
| 515 | A101 | ½p deep green (Bl) | 8 | 8 |
| 516 | A101 | 1p scarlet (Bk) | 10 | 10 |
| 517 | A101 | 1½p red brown (Bl) | 12 | 12 |

Great Britain Nos. 252-254 Overprinted Type "a" in Blue or Black

**1940, May 6**

| No. | Type | Description | Unused | Used |
|---|---|---|---|---|
| 518 | A106 | ½p deep green (Bl) | 15 | 15 |
| 519 | A106 | 1p scarlet (Bk) | 25 | 25 |
| 520 | A106 | 1½p red brown (Bl) | 35 | 35 |

Centenary of the postage stamp.

Great Britain Nos. 258 and 259 Overprinted Type "c" in Blue or Black

**1944-45**

| No. | Type | Description | Unused | Used |
|---|---|---|---|---|
| 521 | A101 | ½p green (Bl) | 10 | 10 |
| 522 | A101 | 1p ver (Bk) ('45) | 15 | 15 |

**Catalogue values for unused stamps in this section, from this point to the end of the section, are for Never Hinged items.**

Great Britain Nos. 264-265 Overprinted in Black:

d TANGIER

e TANGIER

**1946, June 11**

| No. | Type | Description | Unused | Used |
|---|---|---|---|---|
| 523 | A107(d) | 2½p bright ultra | 20 | 20 |
| 524 | A108(e) | 3p violet | 25 | 25 |

Return to peace at close of World War II.

Great Britain Nos. 267 and 268 Overprinted Type "a" in Black

***Perf. 14½x14, 14x14½***

**1948, Apr. 26**

| No. | Type | Description | Unused | Used |
|---|---|---|---|---|
| 525 | A109 | 2½p bright ultra | 15 | 15 |
| *a.* | | Pair, one without overprint | *1,750.* | |
| 526 | A110 | £1 dp chalky bl | 27.50 | 32.50 |

25th anniv. of the marriage of King George VI and Queen Elizabeth.

Great Britain Nos. 271 to 274 Overprinted Type "a" in Black

**1948, July 29** ***Perf. 14½x14***

| No. | Type | Description | Unused | Used |
|---|---|---|---|---|
| 527 | A113 | 2½p bright ultra | 20 | 16 |
| 528 | A114 | 3p deep violet | 28 | 24 |
| 529 | A115 | 6p red violet | 40 | 32 |
| 530 | A116 | 1sh dark brown | 80 | 70 |

1948 Olympic Games, Wembley, July-Aug.

Stamps of Great Britain, 1937-47, and Nos. 249A, 250 and 251A Overprinted Type "c" in Black

**1949, Jan. 1**

| No. | Type | Description | Unused | Used |
|---|---|---|---|---|
| 531 | A101 | 2p lt org (II) | 15 | 15 |
| 532 | A101 | 2½p ultra (II) | 14 | 14 |
| 533 | A101 | 3p violet (II) | 14 | 14 |
| 534 | A102 | 4p gray green | 55 | 55 |
| 535 | A102 | 5p light brown | 52 | 52 |
| 536 | A102 | 6p rose lilac | 35 | 35 |
| 537 | A103 | 7p emerald | 45 | 45 |
| 538 | A103 | 8p bright rose | 60 | 60 |
| 539 | A103 | 9p deep ol grn | 60 | 60 |
| 540 | A103 | 10p royal blue | 80 | 80 |
| 541 | A103 | 11p violet brn | 95 | 95 |
| 542 | A103 | 1sh brown | 55 | 55 |

**Wmk. 259**

***Perf. 14***

| No. | Type | Description | Unused | Used |
|---|---|---|---|---|
| 543 | A104 | 2sh6p yellow grn | 4.50 | 4.50 |
| 544 | A104 | 5sh dull red | 9.25 | 9.25 |
| 545 | A105 | 10sh ultra | 22.50 | 22.50 |
| | | *Nos. 531-545 (15)* | 42.05 | 42.05 |

Great Britain Nos. 276 to 279 Overprinted Type "a" in Black

***Perf. 14½x14***

**1949, Oct. 10** **Wmk. 251**

| No. | Type | Description | Unused | Used |
|---|---|---|---|---|
| 546 | A117 | 2½p bright ultra | 14 | 14 |
| 547 | A118 | 3p bright violet | 25 | 22 |
| 548 | A119 | 6p red violet | 30 | 30 |
| 549 | A120 | 1sh brown | 60 | 60 |

Great Britain Nos. 280-288 Overprinted Type "c" or "a" (Shilling Values)

**1950-51**

| No. | Type | Description | Unused | Used |
|---|---|---|---|---|
| 550 | A101 | ½p lt org | 6 | 6 |
| 551 | A101 | 1p ultra | 9 | 9 |
| 552 | A101 | 1½p green | 22 | 22 |
| 553 | A101 | 2p lt red brn | 22 | 22 |
| 554 | A101 | 2½p vermilion | 18 | 18 |
| 555 | A102 | 4p ultra ('50) | 52 | 52 |

**Wmk. 259**

***Perf. 11x12***

| No. | Type | Description | Unused | Used |
|---|---|---|---|---|
| 556 | A121 | 2sh6p green | 2.50 | 2.50 |
| 557 | A121 | 5sh dl red | 5.25 | 5.25 |
| 558 | A122 | 10sh ultra | 10.50 | 10.50 |
| | | *Nos. 550-558 (9)* | 19.54 | 19.54 |

Great Britain Nos. 292-308 Overprinted Type "c" in Black

**1952-54** **Wmk. 298** ***Perf. 14½x14***

| No. | Type | Description | Unused | Used |
|---|---|---|---|---|
| 559 | A126 | ½p red org ('53) | 5 | 5 |
| 560 | A126 | 1p ultra ('53) | 8 | 6 |
| 561 | A126 | 1½p green ('52) | 8 | 6 |
| 562 | A126 | 2p red brn ('53) | 15 | 9 |
| 563 | A127 | 2½p scarlet ('52) | 12 | 8 |
| 564 | A127 | 3p dk pur (Dk Bl) | 22 | 15 |
| 565 | A128 | 4p ultra ('53) | 60 | 45 |
| 566 | A129 | 5p lt brn ('53) | 1.25 | 95 |
| 567 | A129 | 6p lilac rose | 60 | 45 |
| 568 | A129 | 7p emerald | 1.10 | 95 |
| 569 | A130 | 8p brt rose ('53) | 1.10 | 95 |
| 570 | A130 | 9p deep ol grn | 1.10 | 95 |
| 571 | A130 | 10p royal blue | 1.50 | 1.10 |
| 572 | A130 | 11p violet brn | 1.50 | 1.10 |
| 573 | A131 | 1sh brown ('53) | 75 | 60 |

*574* A132 1sh3p dk grn ('53) 1.10 95
*575* A131 1sh6p dk blue ('53) 1.50 1.10
*Nos. 559-575 (17)* 12.80 10.04

Stamp and Type of Great Britain 1955 Overprinted Type "a" in Black

***Perf. 11x12***

**1955, Sept. 23 Engr. Wmk. 308**
*576* A133 2sh6p dark brn 2.50 2.50
*577* A133 5sh crimson 7.50 7.50
*578* A133 10sh brt ultra 15.00 15.00

**Coronation Issue**

Great Britain Nos. 313-316 Overprinted Type "a" in Black

**1953, June 3 Photo. Wmk. 298**
*579* A134 2½p scarlet 30 30
*580* A135 4p brt ultra 52 52
*581* A136 1sh3p dark grn 1.50 1.50
*582* A137 1sh6p dark blue 1.75 1.75

Great Britain Nos. 317, 323, 325 and 332 Overprinted Type "c" in Black

**1956 Wmk. 308 *Perf. 14½x14***
*583* A126 ½p red orange 10 10
*584* A126 1p ultra 28 20
*585* A126 1½p green 55 50
*586* A126 2p red brown 90 90
*587* A127 2½p scarlet 70 70
*588* A127 3p dark pur 70 70
*589* A128 4p ultra 1.40 1.40
*590* A129 6p lilac rose 90 90
*591* A132 1sh3p dark green 1.00 1.00
*Nos. 583-591 (9)* 6.53 6.40

Great Britain Nos. 317-333 and 309-311 Overprinted "1857-1957 TANGIER"

**1957, Apr. 1 Photo. Wmk. 308**
*592* A126 ½p red orange 5 5
*593* A126 1p ultra 5 5
*594* A126 1½p green 8 6
*595* A126 2p red brown 10 9
*596* A127 2½p scarlet 14 10
*597* A127 3p dark pur 15 12
*598* A128 4p ultra 22 15
*599* A129 5p lt brown 22 15
*600* A129 6p lilac rose 30 20
*601* A129 7p emerald 40 25
*602* A130 8p brt rose 40 25
*603* A130 9p dp ol grn 40 25
*a.* "TANGIER" omitted 5,500.
*604* A130 10p royal blue 42 30
*605* A130 11p violet brn 60 40
*606* A131 1sh brown 30 32
*607* A132 1sh3p dark green 60 40
*608* A131 1sh6p dark blue 85 50

**Engr.**

***Perf. 11x12***
*609* A133 2sh6p dark brown 2.00 1.25
*610* A133 5sh crimson 3.25 2.75
*611* A133 10sh ultra 6.50 5.25
*Nos. 592-611 (20)* 17.03 12.89

Centenary of British P.O. in Tangier.

Nos. 609-611 are found with hyphen omitted (one stamp in sheet of 40).

British stamps overprinted "Tangier" were discontinued Apr. 30, 1957.

## OFF. IN THE TURKISH EMPIRE

40 Paras = 1 Piastre
12 Pence = 1 Shilling (1905)

Great Britain Nos. 101, 104, 96 Surcharged:

40 PARAS (a) 80 PARAS (b)
12 PIASTRES (c) 40 PARAS (d)

**1885, Apr. 1 Wmk. 30 *Perf. 14***
*1* A47(a) 40pa on 2½p lil 24.00 1.75
*2* A45(b) 80pa on 5p grn 100.00 6.75

**Wmk. 31**
*3* A44(c) 12pi on 2sh6p lil 32.50 7.50
*a.* Bluish paper 250.00 125.00

Great Britain Nos. 114, 118 Surcharged

**1887 Wmk. 30**
*4* A57(a) 40pa on 2½p vio, *bl* 1.50 15
*a.* Double surcharge 3,000. 4,000.
*5* A61(b) 80pa on 5p lil & bl 6.25 75
*a.* Small "0" in "80" 85.00 55.00

Great Britain No. 111 Handstamp Surcharged

**1893, Feb. 25**
*6* A54(d) 40pa on ½p ver *600.00 150.00*

No. 6 was a provisional, made and used at Constantinople for five days. Excellent forgeries are known.

Great Britain No. 121 Surcharged

4 PIASTRES (e)

**1896**
*7* A64(e) 4pi on 10p car rose & lil 7.50 6.00

British Stamps of 1902 Surcharged

**1902-05 Wmk. 30**
*8* A66(a) 40pa on 2½p ultra 3.50 10
*9* A71(b) 80pa on 5p lil & bl 4.75 1.10
*a.* Small "0" in "80" 150.00 100.00
*10* A73(e) 4pi on 10p car rose & vio 2.50 2.25

**Wmk. 31**
*11* A75(c) 12pi on 2sh6p vio ('03) 24.00 27.50
*12* A76(c) 24pi on 5sh car rose ('05) 47.50 *60.00*
*Nos. 8-12 (5)* 82.25 *90.95*

Great Britain Nos. 131, 134 Surcharged

1 PIASTRE (f)

**1906 Wmk. 30**
*13* A66(f) 1pi on 2½p ultra 1.80 18
*14* A71(f) 2pi on 5p lil & ultra 2.75 1.75

Nos. 10, 11, 14 are on both ordinary and chalky paper.

Great Britain Nos. 127-135, 138 Overprinted

LEVANT (g)

**1905**
*15* A66 ½p pale green 90 14
*16* A66 1p carmine 90 22
*17* A67 1½p violet & grn 6.00 *5.75*
*18* A68 2p green & car 1.75 *3.75*
*19* A66 2½p ultra 7.75 *16.50*
*20* A69 3p violet, *yel* 7.75 *13.00*
*21* A70 4p brown & grn 6.50 11.00
*22* A71 5p lilac & ultra 12.00 *18.00*
*23* A66 6p dull violet 9.00 *18.00*
*24* A74 1sh car rose & grn 21.00 *30.00*
*Nos. 15-24 (10)* 73.55 *116.36*

Nos. 17, 18 and 24 are on both ordinary and chalky paper.

No. 18 Surcharged 1 Piastre

**1906, July 2**
*25* A68 1pi on 2p grn & car 2,000. 950.00

British Stamps of 1902-09 Surcharged:

30 PARAS (j) 1 PIASTRE 10 PARAS (k)

**1909**
*26* A67(j) 30pa on 1½p vio & grn 52 52
*27* A69(k) 1pi10pa on 3p vio, *yel* 4.50 5.25
*28* A70(k) 1pi30pa on 4p brn & grn 4.50 5.00
*29* A70(k) 1pi30pa on 4p org 5.75 5.25
*30* A66(k) 2pi20pa on 6p dl violet 9.25 9.25
*31* A74(k) 5pi on 1sh car rose & grn 3.00 3.00
*Nos. 26-31 (6)* 27.52 28.27

No. 29 is on ordinary paper, the others are on chalky paper.

Great Britain Nos. 132, 144, 135 Surcharged:

1¼ PIASTRE (m) 2½ PIASTRES (n)

**1910**
*32* A69(m) 1¼pi on 3p vio, *yel* 35 35
*33* A70(m) 1¾pi on 4p orange 45 48
*34* A66(n) 2½pi on 6p dl vio 80 80

There are three different varieties of "4" in the fraction of the 1¾ piastre.

Great Britain Nos. 151-154 Overprinted Type "g"

**1911-12 *Perf. 15x14***
*35* A80 ½p yellow green 50 60
*36* A81 1p carmine 75 90

**Re-engraved**
*37* A80 ½p yel grn ('12) 20 20
*38* A81 1p scarlet ('12) 25 25

Great Britain No. 148 Surcharged

1 PIASTRE (o)

*39* A66(o) 1pi on 2½p ultra 1.75 90

The surcharge on No. 39 exists in two types with the letters 2½ and 3mm. high respectively. The stamp also differs from No. 13 in the perforation.

British Stamps of 1912-13 Surcharged with New Values

**1913-14 Wmk. 33**
*40* A84(j) 30pa on 1½p red brown 1.80 2.50
*41* A86(o) 1pi on 2½p ultra 40 40
*42* A87(m) 1¼pi on 3p vio 1.50 2.10
*43* A88(m) 1¾pi on 4p sl grn 1.20 1.30
*44* A90(o) 4pi on 10p lt bl 7.50 10.00
*45* A90(o) 5pi on 1sh bis 12.50 12.50
*Nos. 40-45 (6)* 24.90 28.80

British Stamps of 1912-19 Overprinted Type "g"

**1913-21**
*46* A82 ½p green 30 18
*47* A83 1p scarlet 30 30
*48* A85 2p orange ('21) 2.00 *5.00*
*49* A87 3p violet ('21) 2.10 1.25
*50* A88 4p sl grn ('21) 1.80 2.50
*51* A89 5p yel brn ('21) 3.50 4.00
*52* A89 6p dl vio ('21) 2.75 2.75
*53* A90 1sh bister ('21) 4.00 2.75

**Wmk. 34**

***Perf. 11x12***
*54* A91 2sh6p brn ('21) 30.00 *40.00*
*Nos. 46-54 (9)* 46.75 *58.73*

British Stamps of 1912-19 Surcharged as in 1909-10 and

1½ PIASTRES (p) 45 PIASTRES (q)

**1921 Wmk. 33 *Perf. 14½x14***
*55* A82(j) 30pa on ½p grn 6 6
*a.* Inverted surcharge 100.00
*56* A83(p) 1½pi on 1p scar 8 8
*57* A86(p) 3¾pi on 2½p ultra 10 9
*58* A87(p) 4½pi on 3p vio 12 15
*59* A89(p) 7½pi on 5p yel brn 18 10
*60* A90(p) 15pi on 10p lt bl 45 35
*61* A90(p) 18¾pi on 1sh bis 4.25 3.00

**Wmk. 34**

***Perf. 11x12***
*62* A91(q) 45pi on 2sh6p brown 17.50 *24.00*
*63* A91(q) 90pi on 5sh car rose 30.00 32.50
*64* A91(q) 180pi on 10sh blue 45.00 35.00
*Nos. 55-64 (10)* 97.74 *95.33*

## ABU DHABI

LOCATION — Arabia, on Persian Gulf.
GOVT. — Sheikdom under British protection.
POP. — 25,000 (estimated).
CAPITAL — Abu Dhabi.

Abu Dhabi is one of six Persian Gulf sheikdoms to join the United Arab Emirates, which proclaimed its independence Dec. 2, 1971. See United Arab Emirates.

100 Naye Paise = 1 Rupee
1000 Fils = 1 Dinar (1966)

**Catalogue values for all unused stamps in this country are for Never Hinged items.**

Sheik Shakbut bin Sultan — A1

Palace — A2

Designs: 40np, 50np, 75np, Gazelle. 5r, 10r, Oil rig and camels.

***Perf. 14½***

**1964, Mar. 30 Photo. Unwmk.**
*1* A1 5np brt yel grn 8 7
*2* A1 15np brown 22 16
*3* A1 20np brt ultra 28 20
*4* A1 30np red org 35 25
*5* A1 40np brt vio 45 32
*6* A1 50np brn ol 55 35
*7* A1 75np gray 80 55

**Engr. *Perf. 13x13½***
*8* A2 1r lt grn 1.10 75
*9* A2 2r black 2.75 1.75
*10* A2 5r car rose 7.00 4.75
*11* A2 10r dk bl 16.00 12.00
*Nos. 1-11 (11)* 29.58 21.15

Falcon Perched on Wrist — A3

Designs: 40np, Falcon facing left. 2r, Falcon facing right.

**1965, Mar. 30 Photo. *Perf. 14½***
*12* A3 20np chlky bl & brn 1.25 50
*13* A3 40np ultra & brn 2.50 1.75
*14* A3 2r brt bl grn & gray brn 11.50 11.50

Nos. 1-11 Surcharged

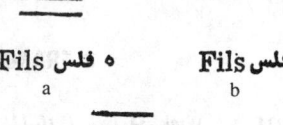

5Fils ٥ فلس (a) Fils فلس (b)

100 Fils ١٠٠ فلس (c)

**1966, Oct. 1 Photo. *Perf. 14½***

*15* A1 (a) 5f on 5np brt yel grn 10 10
*16* A1 (a) 15f on 15np brn 40 35
*17* A1 (a) 20f on 20np brt ultra 45 45
*18* A1 (a) 30f on 30np red org 70 60
*19* A1 (b) 40f on 40np brt vio 1.10 85
*20* A1 (b) 50f on 50np brn ol 5.50 8.25
*21* A1 (b) 75f on 75np gray 6.75 8.25

**Engr.**

*22* A2 (c) 100f on 1r lt grn 6.75 5.50
*23* A2 (c) 200f on 2r blk 15.00 11.00
*24* A2 (c) 500f on 5r car rose 32.50 40.00
*25* A2 (c) 1d on 10r dk bl 65.00 92.50
*Nos. 15-25 (11)* 134.25 167.85

The overprint on No. 25 has "1 Dinar" on one line and 3 bars through old denomination.

Sheik Zaid bin Sultan al Nahayan
A4 A6

Dorcas Gazelle — A5

Designs: 5f, 15f, 20f, 35f, Crossed flags of Abu Dhabi. 200f, Falcon. 500f, 1d, Palace.

**Engr.; Flags Litho.**

**1967, Apr. 1 *Perf. 13x13½***

*26* A4 5f dl grn & red 15 10
*27* A4 15f dk brn & red 28 20
*28* A4 20f dk bl & red 35 25
*29* A4 35f pur & red 60 45

**Engr.**

*30* A4 40f green 70 55
*31* A4 50f brown 90 70
*32* A4 60f blue 1.25 80
*33* A4 100f car rose 2.00 1.50

**Litho.**

*34* A5 125f grn & brn ol 2.50 1.90
*35* A5 200f sky bl & brn 4.00 3.00
*36* A5 500f org & brt pur 11.00 7.50
*37* A5 1d grn & vio bl 22.50 15.00
*Nos. 26-37 (12)* 46.23 31.95

In 1969, the 15f was surcharged "25" in Arabic in black with a numbering machine.

**1967, Aug. 6 Photo. *Perf. 14½x14***

*38* A6 40f Prus grn 1.10 1.10
*39* A6 50f brown 1.10 75
*40* A6 60f blue 1.90 1.00
*41* A6 100f car rose 3.50 1.90

Human Rights Flame and Sheik Zaid A6a

***Perf. 14½x14***

**1968, Apr. 1 Photo. Unwmk.**

**Emblem in Red and Green**

*42* A6a 35f pck bl & gold 90 60
*43* A6a 60f dk bl & gold 1.50 75
*44* A6a 150f dk brn & gold 3.50 1.75

International Human Rights Year.

Sheik Zaid and Coat of Arms A7

***Perf. 14x14½***

**1968, Aug. 6 Photo. Unwmk.**

*45* A7 5f grn, sil, red & blk 35 12
*46* A7 10f brn org, sil, red & blk 50 22
*47* A7 100f lil, gold, red & blk 3.25 1.50
*48* A7 125f lt bl, gold, red & blk 4.50 2.25

Accession of Sheik Zaid, 2nd anniversary.

Abu Dhabi Airport — A8

Designs: 5f, Buildings under construction and earth-moving equipment. 35f, New bridge and falcon. Each stamp shows different portrait of Sheik Zaid.

***Perf. 12, 12½x13 (10f)***

**1969, Mar. 28 Litho.**

**Size: 59x34mm.**

*49* A8 5f multi 85 25

**Size: 46½x34mm.**

*50* A8 10f multi 1.25 60

**Size: 59x34mm.**

*51* A8 35f multi 5.00 2.50

Issued to publicize progress made in Abu Dhabi during preceding 2 years.

Sheik Zaid and Abu Dhabi Petroleum Co. — A9

Designs: 60f, Abu Dhabi Marine Areas drilling platform and helicopter. 125f, Zakum Field separator at night. 200f, Tank farm.

**1969, Aug. 6 Litho. *Perf. 14x13½***

*52* A9 35f ol grn & multi 55 25
*53* A9 60f yel brn & multi 1.00 55
*54* A9 125f multi 2.25 1.10
*55* A9 200f red brn & multi 4.00 2.00

Accession of Sheik Zaid, 3rd anniversary.

Sheik Zaid — A10

Sheik Zaid and Stallion A11

Designs: 5f, 25f, 60f, 90f, Oval frame around portrait. 150f, Gazelle and Sheik. 500f, Fort Jahili and Sheik. 1d, Grand Mosque and Sheik.

**1970-71 Litho. *Perf. 14***

*56* A10 5f lt grn & multi 12 5
*57* A10 10f bis & multi 20 8
*58* A10 25f lil & multi 40 18
*59* A10 35f vio & multi 60 25
*60* A10 50f sep & multi 85 35
*61* A10 60f vio & multi 1.10 40
*62* A10 70f rose red & multi 1.40 50
*63* A10 90f car rose & multi 1.50 60
*64* A11 125f multi ('71) 2.00 85
*65* A11 150f multi ('71) 2.50 1.00
*66* A11 500f multi ('71) 8.00 3.50
*67* A11 1d multi ('71) 16.00 6.50
*Nos. 56-67 (12)* 34.67 14.26

Sheik Zaid and Mt. Fuji — A12

**1970, Aug. Litho. *Perf. 13½x13***

*68* A12 25f multi 1.50 1.00
*69* A12 35f multi 2.00 1.50
*70* A12 60f multi 3.50 2.00

Issued to publicize EXPO '70 International Exhibition, Osaka, Japan, Mar. 15-Sept. 13.

Abu Dhabi Airport A13

Designs: 60f, Airport entrance. 150f, Aerial view of Abu Dhabi Town (vert.).

***Perf. 14x13½, 13½x14***

**1970, Sept. 22 Litho.**

*71* A13 25f multi 1.00 50
*72* A13 60f multi 3.50 1.25
*73* A13 150f multi 6.00 3.00

Accession of Sheik Zaid, 4th anniversary.

Gamal Abdel Nasser — A14

**1971, May 3 Litho. *Perf. 14***

*74* A14 25f dp rose & blk 1.50 1.00
*75* A14 35f rose vio & blk 2.25 1.25

In memory of Gamal Abdel Nasser (1918-1970), President of U.A.R.

Scout Cars A15

Designs: 60f, Patrol boat. 125f, Armored car in desert. 150f, Meteor jet fighters.

**1971, Aug. 6 Litho. *Perf. 13***

*76* A15 35f multi 1.10 50
*77* A15 60f multi 1.50 75
*78* A15 125f multi 2.25 1.10
*79* A15 150f multi 2.50 1.50

Accession of Sheik Zaid, 5th anniversary.

٥ فلوس

No. 60 Surcharged in Green

**5 Fils**

**1971, Dec. 8 *Perf. 14***

*80* A10 5f on 50f multi *35.00 30.00*

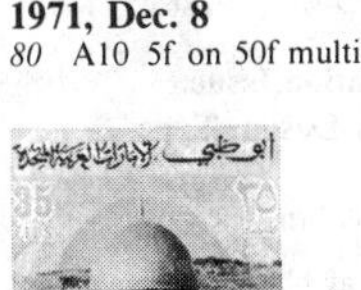


Dome of the Rock, Jerusalem — A16

Designs: Different views of Dome of the Rock.

**1972, June 3 *Perf. 13***

*81* A16 35f lt vio & multi 3.75 1.90
*82* A16 60f lt vio & multi 5.50 2.50
*83* A16 125f lil & multi 11.00 5.25

Nos. 80-83 were issued after Abu Dhabi joined the United Arab Emirates Dec. 2, 1971. Stamps of U.A.E. replaced those of Abu Dhabi. U.A.E. Nos. 1-12 were used only in Abu Dhabi except the 10f and 25f which were issued later in Dubai and Sharjah.

## ADEN

LOCATION — Southern Arabia.
GOVT. — Former British colony and protectorate.
AREA — 112,075 sq. mi.
POP. — 220,000 (est. 1964).
CAPITAL — Aden.

Aden used India stamps before 1937. In January, 1963, the colony of Aden (the port) and the sheikdoms and emirates of the Western Aden Protectorate formed the Federation of South Arabia. This did not include the Eastern Aden Protectorate with Kathiri and Qu'aiti States. Stamps of Aden, except those of Kathiri and Qu'aiti States, were replaced Apr. 1, 1965, by those of the Federation of South Arabia. See South Arabia, Vol. I, and People's Democratic Republic of Yemen, Vol. IV.

12 Pies = 1 Anna
16 Annas = 1 Rupee
100 Cents = 1 Shilling (1951)

**Catalogue values for unused stamps in this country are for Never Hinged items, beginning with Scott 28 in the regular postage section and for all of the items in the states' sections.**

Dhow — A1

Common Design Types are pictured in section before Great Britain.

*Perf. 13x11½*

**1937, Apr. 1 Engr. Wmk. 4**

| | | | | |
|---|---|---|---|---|
| *1* | A1 | ½a lt grn | 25 | 25 |
| *2* | A1 | 9p dk grn | 40 | 40 |
| *3* | A1 | 1a blk brn | 40 | 32 |
| *4* | A1 | 2a red | 70 | 70 |
| *5* | A1 | 2½a blue | 90 | 75 |
| *6* | A1 | 3a car rose | 1.65 | 2.25 |
| *7* | A1 | 3½a gray bl | 1.40 | 1.40 |
| *8* | A1 | 8a rose lil | 2.25 | 2.75 |
| *9* | A1 | 1r brown | 5.00 | 4.75 |
| *10* | A1 | 2r org yel | 8.50 | 8.00 |
| *11* | A1 | 5r rose vio | 40.00 | 40.00 |
| *12* | A1 | 10r ol grn | 125.00 | 125.00 |
| | | *Nos. 1-12 (12)* | 186.45 | 186.57 |

**Coronation Issue.**

Common Design Type

**1937, May 12** ***Perf. 13½x14***

| | | | | |
|---|---|---|---|---|
| *13* | CD302 | 1a blk brn | 9 | 9 |
| *14* | CD302 | 2½a blue | 28 | 28 |
| *15* | CD302 | 3½a gray bl | 50 | 50 |

Aidrus Mosque — A2

Designs: ¾a, 5r, Camel Corpsman. 1a, 2r, Aden Harbor. 1½a, 1r, Adenese dhow. 2½a, 8a, Mukalla. 3a, 14a, 10r, Capture of Aden, 1839.

**1939-45 Engr. Wmk. 4** ***Perf. 12½***

| | | | | |
|---|---|---|---|---|
| *16* | A2 | ½a green | 6 | 6 |
| *17* | A2 | ¾a brn vio | 9 | 9 |
| *18* | A2 | 1a lt bl | 10 | 10 |
| *19* | A2 | 1½a red | 22 | 14 |
| *20* | A2 | 2a dk brn | 15 | 12 |
| *21* | A2 | 2½a brt ultra | 22 | 14 |
| *22* | A2 | 3a rose car & dk brn | 18 | 12 |
| *23* | A2 | 8a orange | 38 | 14 |
| *23A* | A2 | 14a lt bl & brn blk ('45) | 38 | 38 |
| *24* | A2 | 1r brt grn | 42 | 42 |
| *25* | A2 | 2r rose vio & ind | 1.65 | 75 |
| *26* | A2 | 5r ol grn & red brn | 4.50 | 2.75 |
| *27* | A2 | 10r dk pur & vio brn | 5.50 | 5.50 |
| | | *Nos. 16-27 (13)* | 13.85 | 10.71 |

**Catalogue values for unused stamps in this section, from this point to the end of the section, are for Never Hinged items.**

**Peace Issue.**

Common Design Type

*Perf. 13½x14*

**1946, Oct. 15 Engr. Wmk. 4**

| | | | | |
|---|---|---|---|---|
| *28* | CD303 | 1½a carmine | 14 | 14 |
| *29* | CD303 | 2½a dp bl | 28 | 28 |

Return to peace at end of World War II.

**Silver Wedding Issue.**

Common Design Types

**1949, Jan. 17 Photo.** ***Perf. 14x14½***

| | | | | |
|---|---|---|---|---|
| *30* | CD304 | 1½a scarlet | 20 | 20 |

**Engraved; Name Typographed**

***Perf. 11½x11.***

| | | | | |
|---|---|---|---|---|
| *31* | CD305 | 10r purple | 20.00 | 20.00 |

25th anniv. of the marriage of King George VI and Queen Elizabeth.

**UPU Issue**

Common Design Types

Surcharged with New Values in Annas and Rupees.

**Engr.; Name typo. on Nos. 33-34**

**1949, Oct. 10** ***Perf. 13½, 11x11½***

| | | | | |
|---|---|---|---|---|
| *32* | CD306 | 2½a on 20c dp ultra | 32 | 32 |
| *33* | CD307 | 3a on 30c dp car | 45 | 45 |
| *34* | CD308 | 8a on 50c org | 1.65 | 1.65 |
| *35* | CD309 | 1r on 1sh bl | 2.75 | 2.75 |

75th anniv. of the formation of the UPU.

Common Design Types pictured in section before Great Britain.

Nos. 18 and 20 to 27 Surcharged with New Values in Black or Carmine.

**1951, Oct. 1 Wmk. 4** ***Perf. 12½***

| | | | | |
|---|---|---|---|---|
| *36* | A2 | 5c on 1a lt bl | 20 | 20 |
| *37* | A2 | 10c on 2a dk brn | 26 | 26 |
| *38* | A2 | 15c on 2½a brt ultra | 35 | 35 |
| *a.* | | Double surcharge | 600.00 | |
| *39* | A2 | 20c on 3a rose car & dk brn | 65 | 65 |
| *40* | A2 | 30c on 8a org (C) | 65 | 65 |
| *41* | A2 | 50c on 8a org | 65 | 52 |
| *42* | A2 | 70c on 14a lt bl & brn blk | 90 | 90 |
| *43* | A2 | 1sh on 1r brt grn | 1.00 | 90 |
| *44* | A2 | 2sh on 2r rose vio & ind | 4.00 | 3.50 |
| *45* | A2 | 5sh on 5r ol grn & red brn | 6.25 | 6.25 |
| *46* | A2 | 10sh on 10r dk pur & vio brn | 12.50 | 12.50 |
| | | *Nos. 36-46 (11)* | 27.41 | 26.68 |

Surcharge on No. 40 includes 2 bars.

**Coronation Issue.**

Common Design Type

**1953, June 2 Engr.** ***Perf. 13½x13***

| | | | | |
|---|---|---|---|---|
| *47* | CD312 | 15c dk grn & blk | 35 | 35 |

Minaret A10

Camel Transport A11

Designs: 15c, Crater. 25c, Mosque. 35c, Dhow. 50c, Map. 70c, Salt works. 1sh, Dhow building. 1sh, 25c, Colony Badge. 2sh, Aden Protectorate levy. 5sh, Crater Pass. 10sh, Tribesman. 20sh, Aden in 1572.

***Perf. 12, 12x13½ ('56)***

**1953-58 Engr. Wmk. 4**

**Size: 29x23, 23x29mm**

| | | | | |
|---|---|---|---|---|
| *48* | A10 | 5c grn, perf. 12x13½ ('56) | 5 | 5 |
| *a.* | | Perf. 12 | 5 | 5 |
| *49* | A11 | 10c orange | 6 | 6 |
| *50* | A11 | 15c bl grn | 9 | 9 |
| *51* | A11 | 25c carmine | 15 | 10 |
| *52* | A10 | 35c dp bl, perf. 12x13½ ('58) | 40 | 30 |
| *a.* | | 35c ultra, perf. 12 | 45 | 30 |
| *53* | A10 | 50c bl, perf. 12x13½ ('56) | 25 | 22 |
| *a.* | | Perf. 12 | 35 | 32 |
| *54* | A10 | 70c gray, perf. 12x13½ ('56) | 25 | 25 |
| *a.* | | Perf. 12 | 55 | 55 |
| *55* | A11 | 1sh pur & sep | 55 | 45 |
| *55A* | A11 | 1sh vio & blk ('55) | 35 | 32 |
| *56* | A10 | 1sh25c blk & lt bl ('56) | 55 | 42 |
| *57* | A10 | 2sh car rose & sep | 1.50 | 1.40 |
| *57A* | A10 | 2sh car & blk ('56) | 2.25 | 55 |
| *58* | A10 | 5sh bl & sep | 3.75 | 3.75 |
| *58A* | A10 | 5sh dk bl & blk ('56) | 2.00 | 1.50 |
| *59* | A10 | 10sh ol & sep | 5.75 | 7.25 |
| *60* | A10 | 10sh ol gray & blk ('54) | 4.50 | 3.25 |

**Size: 36½x27mm**

***Perf. 13½x13***

| | | | | |
|---|---|---|---|---|
| *61* | A11 | 20sh rose vio & dk brn | 11.00 | 9.50 |
| *61A* | A11 | 20sh lt vio & blk ('57) | 7.25 | 6.25 |
| | | *Nos. 48-61A (18)* | 40.70 | 35.71 |

Various shades from two or more printings exist. No. 60 has heavier shading on tribesman's lower garment than No. 59.

See Nos. 66-75.

Type of 1953

Inscribed: "Royal Visit 1954."

**1954, Apr. 27** ***Perf. 12***

| | | | | |
|---|---|---|---|---|
| *62* | A11 | 1sh pur & sep | 38 | 38 |

Nos. 50 and 56 Overprinted in Red

تعديل
الدستور
١٩٥٩
a

REVISED
CONSTITUTION
1959
b

**1959, Jan. 26** ***Perf. 12, 12x13½***

| | | | | |
|---|---|---|---|---|
| *63* | A11(a) | 15c dk bl grn | 24 | 24 |
| *64* | A10(b) | 1sh25c blk & lt bl | 70 | 70 |

Introduction of a revised constitution.

**Freedom from Hunger Issue**

Common Design Type

***Perf. 14x14½***

**1963, June 4 Photo. Wmk. 314**

| | | | | |
|---|---|---|---|---|
| *65* | CD314 | 1sh25c green | 85 | 65 |

Types of 1953-57

***Perf. 12, 12x13½***

**1964-65 Engr. Wmk. 314**

| | | | | |
|---|---|---|---|---|
| *66* | A10 | 5c grn ('65) | 18 | 20 |
| *67* | A11 | 10c orange | 20 | 14 |
| *68* | A11 | 15c Prus grn | 24 | 20 |
| *69* | A11 | 25c carmine | 42 | 18 |
| *70* | A10 | 35c dk bl | 70 | 42 |
| *71* | A10 | 50c dl bl | 70 | 38 |
| *72* | A10 | 70c gray | 75 | 52 |
| *73* | A11 | 1sh vio & blk | 75 | 52 |
| *74* | A10 | 1sh25c blk & lt bl | 1.50 | 1.40 |
| *75* | A10 | 2sh car & blk ('65) | 2.75 | 3.50 |
| | | *Nos. 66-75 (10)* | 8.19 | 7.46 |

## KATHIRI STATE OF SEIYUN

LOCATION — In Eastern Aden Protectorate.

GOVT. — Sultanate

CAPITAL — Seiyun

**Catalogue values for unused stamps in this section, from this point to the end of the section, are for Never Hinged items.**

Sultan Ja'far bin Mansur al Kathiri A1

Seiyun A2

Minaret at Tarim — A3

Designs: 2½a, Mosque at Seiyun. 3a, Palace at Tarim. 8a, Mosque at Seiyun (horiz.). 1r, South Gate, Tarim. 2r, Kathiri House. 5r, Mosque at Tarim.

**1942 Engr. Wmk. 4** ***Perf. 14***

| | | | | |
|---|---|---|---|---|
| *1* | A1 | ½a dk grn | 14 | 14 |
| *2* | A1 | ¾a cop brn | 14 | 14 |
| *3* | A1 | 1a dp bl | 18 | 18 |

***Perf. 13x11½, 11½x13***

| | | | | |
|---|---|---|---|---|
| *4* | A2 | 1½a dk car rose | 20 | 20 |
| *5* | A3 | 2a blk brn | 20 | 20 |
| *6* | A3 | 2½a dp bl | 20 | 20 |
| *7* | A2 | 3a dk car rose & dl brn | 25 | 25 |
| *8* | A2 | 8a org red | 55 | 55 |
| *9* | A3 | 1r green | 85 | 85 |
| *10* | A2 | 2r rose vio & dk bl | 3.00 | 4.00 |
| *11* | A3 | 5r gray grn & fawn | 4.25 | 6.50 |
| | | *Nos. 1-11 (11)* | 9.96 | 13.21 |

Nos. 4 and 6 Overprinted in Black or Red:

VICTORY
ISSUE
8TH JUNE 1946
a

VICTORY
ISSUE
8TH JUNE
1946
b

***Perf. 13x11½, 11½x13.***

**1946, Oct. 15 Wmk. 4**

| | | | | |
|---|---|---|---|---|
| *12* | A2 (a) | 1½a dk car rose | 18 | 18 |
| *13* | A3 (b) | 2½a dp bl (R) | 22 | 22 |
| *a.* | | Inverted overprint | 400.00 | |

Victory of the Allied Nations in WWII.

**Silver Wedding Issue.**

Common Design Types

**1949, Jan. 17 Photo.** ***Perf. 14x14½***

| | | | | |
|---|---|---|---|---|
| *14* | CD304 | 1½a scarlet | 22 | 22 |

**Engraved; Name Typographed.**

***Perf. 11½x11***

| | | | | |
|---|---|---|---|---|
| *15* | CD305 | 5r green | 7.00 | 12.5 |

Issued to commemorate the 25th anniversary of the marriage of King George VI and Queen Elizabeth.

**U. P. U. Issue.**

Common Design Types

Surcharged with New Values in Annas and Rupees.

**Engr.; Name Typo. on Nos. 17-18**

**1949, Oct. 10** ***Perf. 13½, 11x11½***

| | | | | |
|---|---|---|---|---|
| *16* | CD306 | 2½a on 20c dp ultra | 15 | 15 |
| *17* | CD307 | 3a on 30c dp car | 25 | 25 |
| *18* | CD308 | 8a on 50c org | 90 | 90 |
| *19* | CD309 | 1r on 1sh bl | 1.75 | 1.75 |

75th anniv. of the formation of the UPU.

Nos. 3 and 5 to 11 Surcharged with New Values in Carmine or Black.

***Perf. 14, 13x11½, 11½x13***

**1951, Oct. 1 Engr. Wmk. 4**

| | | | | |
|---|---|---|---|---|
| *20* | A1 | 5c on 1a dp bl (C) | 12 | 12 |
| *21* | A3 | 10c on 2a dk brn | 16 | 16 |
| *22* | A3 | 15c on 2½a dp bl | 55 | 55 |
| *23* | A2 | 20c on 3a dk car rose & dl brn | 24 | 24 |
| *24* | A2 | 50c on 8a org red | 32 | 32 |
| *25* | A3 | 1sh on 1r grn | 80 | 80 |
| *26* | A2 | 2sh on 2r rose vio & dk bl | 1.75 | 1.75 |
| *27* | A3 | 5sh on 5r gray grn & fawn | 4.00 | 4.00 |
| | | *Nos. 20-27 (8)* | 7.94 | 7.94 |

**Coronation Issue.**

Common Design Type

**1953, June 2** ***Perf. 13½x13***

| | | | | |
|---|---|---|---|---|
| *28* | CD312 | 15c dk grn & blk | 40 | 40 |

Sultan Hussein A10

Qarn Adh Dhabi A11

Designs: 15c, Seiyun scene (horiz.). 25c, Minaret at Tarim. 35c, Mosque at Seiyun. 50c, Palace at Tarim (horiz.). 1sh, Mosque at Seiyun (horiz.). 2sh, South Gate, Tarim. 5sh, Kathiri house (horiz.). 10sh, Mosque entrance, Tarim.

**1954, Jan. 15 Engr.** ***Perf. 12½***

| | | | | |
|---|---|---|---|---|
| *29* | A10 | 5c dk brn | 5 | 5 |
| *30* | A10 | 10c dp bl | 5 | 5 |

***Perf. 13x11½, 11½x13***

| | | | | |
|---|---|---|---|---|
| *31* | A11 | 15c dk bl grn | 7 | 7 |
| *32* | A11 | 25c dk car rose | 9 | 9 |
| *33* | A11 | 35c dp bl | 12 | 12 |
| *34* | A11 | 50c dk car rose & dk brn | 14 | 14 |
| *35* | A11 | 1sh dp org | 28 | 28 |
| *36* | A11 | 2sh gray grn | 70 | 70 |
| *37* | A11 | 5sh vio & dk bl | 1.90 | 2.75 |
| *38* | A11 | 10sh vio & yel brn | 3.75 | 5.50 |
| | | *Nos. 29-38 (10)* | 7.15 | 9.75 |

***Perf. 11½x13, 13x11½***

**1964, July 1 Wmk. 314**

Designs: 1sh25c, Seiyun (horiz.). 1sh50c, View of Gheil Omer (horiz.).

| | | | | |
|---|---|---|---|---|
| *39* | A11 | 70c black | 38 | 38 |
| *40* | A11 | 1sh25c brt grn | 60 | 60 |
| *41* | A11 | 1sh50c purple | 80 | 80 |

## QUAITI STATE OF SHIRH AND MUKALLA.

LOCATION — In Eastern Aden Protectorate.
GOVT. — Sultanate
CAPITAL — Mukalla

**Catalogue values for unused stamps in this section, from this point to the end of the section, are for Never Hinged items.**

Sultan Sir Saleh bin Ghalib al Qu'aiti
A1

Mukalla Harbor
A2

Buildings at Shibam — A3

Designs: 2a. Gateway of Shihr. 3a. Outpost of Mukalla. 8a. View of 'Einat. 1r. Governor's Castle, Du'an. 3r. Mosque in Hureidha. 5r. Meshhed.

**1942 Engr. Wmk. 4 Perf. 14**

*1* A1 ½a dk grn 10 10
*2* A1 ¾a cop brn 10 10
*3* A1 1a dp bl 10 10

***Perf. 13x11½, 11½x13***

*4* A2 1½a dk car rose 12 12
*5* A2 2a blk brn 12 12
*6* A3 2½a dp bl 12 12
*7* A2 3a dk car rose & dl brn 16 16
*8* A3 8a org red 32 32
*9* A2 1r green 48 48
*10* A3 2r rose vio & dk bl 2.00 2.00
*11* A3 5r gray grn & fawn 3.75 3.25
*Nos. 1-11 (11)* 7.37 6.87

Nos. 4 and 6 Overprinted in Black or Carmine:

VICTORY
ISSUE
8TH JUNE
1946
a

VICTORY
ISSUE
8TH JUNE 1946
b

***Perf. 11½x13, 13x11½***

**1946, Oct. 15**

*12* A2 (a) 1½a dk car rose 15 15
*13* A3 (b) 2½a dp bl (C) 25 25

Issued to commemorate the victory of the Allied Nations in World War II.

**Silver Wedding Issue.**
Common Design Types

**1949, Jan. 17 Photo. Perf. 14x14½**

*14* CD304 1½a scarlet 22 22

**Engraved; Name Typographed**
***Perf. 11½x11.***

*15* CD305 5r green 7.00 *12.50*

Issued to commemorate the 25th anniversary of the marriage of King George VI and Queen Elizabeth.

**U. P. U. Issue.**
Common Design Types
Surcharged with New Values in Annas and Rupees.
**Engraved; Name Typographed on Nos. 17 and 18.**

**1949, Oct. 10 Perf. 13½, 11x11½**

*16* CD306 2½a on 20c dp ultra 18 18
*17* CD307 3a on 30c dp car 42 42
*18* CD308 8a on 50c org 1.10 1.10
*19* CD309 1r on 1sh bl 3.00 3.00
*a.* Surcharge omitted *1,200.*

Issued to commemorate the 75th anniversary of the formation of the Universal Postal Union.

Nos. 3 and 5 to 11 Surcharged with New Values in Carmine or Black.

***Perf. 14, 13x11½, 11½x13***

**1951, Oct. 1 Engr. Wmk. 4**

*20* A1 5c on 1a dp bl (C) 12 12
*21* A2 10c on 2a bl brn 22 22
*22* A3 15c on 2½a dp bl 22 22
*23* A2 20c on 3a dk car rose & dl brn 22 22
*24* A3 50c on 8a org red 35 35
*25* A2 1sh on 1r grn 60 60
*26* A3 2sh on 2r rose vio & dk bl 1.25 2.00
*27* A3 5sh on 5r gray grn & fawn 4.25 5.50
*Nos. 20-27 (8)* 7.23 9.23

**Coronation Issue.**
Common Design Type

**1953, June 2 Engr. Perf. 13½x13**

*28* CD312 15c dk bl & blk 40 40

**Qu'aiti State in Hadhramaut**

Metal Work — A10

Fisheries
A11

Designs: 10c, Mat making. 15c, Weaving. 25c, Pottery. 35c, Building. 50c, Date cultivation. 90c, Agriculture. 1sh 25c, 10sh, Lime burning. 2sh, Dhow building. 5sh, Agriculture.

***Perf. 11½x13, 13½x14***

**1955, Sept. 1 Engr. Wmk. 4**

*29* A10 5c grnsh bl 5 5
*30* A10 10c black 5 5
*31* A10 15c dk grn 8 8
*32* A10 25c carmine 8 8
*33* A10 35c ultra 14 14
*34* A10 50c red org 22 22
*35* A10 90c brown 30 30
*36* A11 1sh pur & blk 32 32
*37* A11 1sh25c red org & blk 38 38
*38* A11 2sh dk bl & blk 65 65
*39* A11 5sh grn & blk 1.65 1.65
*40* A11 10sh car & blk 3.25 3.25
*Nos. 29-40 (12)* 7.17 7.17

Types of 1955 with Portrait of Sultan Awadh Bin Saleh El-Qu'aiti.
Designs as Before

Design: 70c, Agriculture.

**1963, Oct. 20 Wmk. 314**

*41* A10 5c grnsh bl 5 5
*42* A10 10c black 5 5
*43* A10 15c dk grn 5 5
*44* A10 25c carmine 8 8
*45* A10 35c ultra 12 12
*46* A10 50c red org 16 16
*47* A10 70c brown 24 24
*48* A11 1sh pur & blk 35 35
*49* A11 1sh25c red org & blk 45 45
*50* A11 2sh dk bl & blk 75 1.00
*51* A11 5sh grn & blk 1.75 2.50
*52* A11 10sh car & blk 4.00 4.75
*Nos. 41-52 (12)* 8.05 9.80

## AITUTAKI

LOCATION — One of the larger Cook Islands, in the South Pacific Ocean northeast of New Zealand.
GOVT. — A dependency of the British dominion of New Zealand.
AREA — 7 sq. mi.
POP. — 2,335 (1981).

The Cook Islands were attached to New Zealand in 1901. Stamps of Cook Islands were used in 1932-72.

Aitutaki acquired its own postal service in August 1972, though remaining part of Cook Islands.

12 Pence = 1 Shilling
100 Cents = 1 Dollar (1972)

**Catalogue values for unused stamps in this country are for Never Hinged items, beginning with Scott 37.**

Stamps of New Zealand Surcharged in Red or Blue:

AITUTAKI. / Ava Pene. — a
AITUTAKI. / Tai Pene. — b

**Wmk. Single-lined N. Z. and Star Close Together. (61)**

**1903 Engr. Perf. 14**

*1* A18 (a) ½p grn (R) 2.75 *5.00*
*2* A35 (b) 1p rose (Bl) 3.00 *6.25*

AITUTAKI. / Rua Pene Ma Te Ava. — c
AITUTAKI. / Toru Pene. — d
AITUTAKI. / Ono Pene. — e
AITUTAKI. / Tai Tiringi. — f

***Perf. 11.***

*3* A22 (c) 2½p bl (R) 3.00 *7.50*
*4* A23 (d) 3p yel brn (Bl) 4.25 *10.00*
*5* A26 (e) 6p red (Bl) 10.00 *24.00*
*6* A29 (f) 1sh scar (Bl) 42.50 *45.00*
*a.* 1sh org red (Bl) 42.50 *67.50*

**1912 Typo. Perf. 14, 14x15**

*7* A41 (a) ½p yel grn (R) 65 *2.00*

**Engr.**

*9* A22 (c) 2½p dp bl (R) 4.00 *6.00*

AITUTAKI. / Ono Pene. — g
AITUTAKI. / Tai Tiringi. — h

**1913-16 Typo.**

*10* A42 (b) 1p rose (Bl) 1.25 *2.50*

**Engr.**

*12* A41 (g) 6p car rose (Bl) ('16) 27.50 *42.50*
*13* A41 (h) 1sh ver (Bl) ('14) 40.00 *62.50*

**1916-17 Perf. 14x13½, 14x14½.**

*17* A45 (g) 6p car rose (Bl) 9.00 *17.50*
*18* A45 (h) 1sh ver (Bl) ('17) 25.00 *42.50*

New Zealand Stamps of 1909-19 Overprinted in Red or Dark Blue — AITUTAKI.

**1917-20 Typo. Perf. 14x15**

*19* A43 ½p yel grn ('20) 50 *1.75*
*20* A42 1p car (Bl) ('20) 75 *2.00*
*21* A47 1½p gray blk 1.50 *5.00*
*22* A47 1½p brn org ('19) 1.10 *4.25*
*23* A43 3p choc (Bl) ('19) 3.00 *6.00*

***Perf. 14x13½, 14x14½***
**Engr.**

*24* A44 2½p dl bl ('18) 1.10 *5.00*
*25* A45 3p vio brn (Bl) ('18) 1.50 *6.50*
*26* A45 6p car rose (Bl) 3.00 *10.00*
*27* A45 1sh ver (Bl) 8.00 *17.50*
*Nos. 19-27 (9)* 20.45 58.00

Landing of Capt. Cook
A15

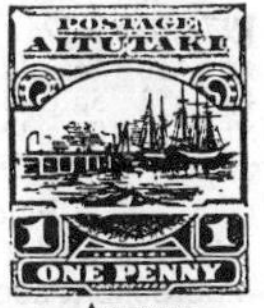

Avarua Waterfront
A16

Capt. James Cook — A17

Palm — A18

Houses at Arorangi — A19

Avarua Harbor — A20

**1920 Engr. Unwmk. Perf. 14**

*28* A15 ½p grn & blk 65 1.75
*29* A16 1p car & blk 85 2.50
*30* A17 1½p brn & blk 1.40 *4.00*
*31* A18 3p dp bl & blk 1.40 *5.00*
*32* A19 6p sl & red brn 4.25 10.00
*a.* Center inverted *600.00*
*33* A20 1sh cl & blk 5.50 *17.50*
*a.* Double frame *300.00*
*Nos. 28-33 (6)* 14.05 40.75

Wmk. 61- Single-lined N Z and Star Close Together

Rarotongan Chief (Te Po) — A21

**1926-27 Wmk. 61 Perf. 14**

*34* A15 ½p grn & blk ('27) 1.10 1.25
*35* A16 1p car & blk 1.10 1.25
*36* A21 2½p bl & blk ('27) 4.50 5.00

**Catalogue values for unused stamps in this section, from this point to the end of the section, are for Never Hinged items.**

Cook Islands Nos. 199-200, 202, 205-206, 210, 212-213, 215-217 Overprinted

**1972 Photo. Unwmk. Perf. 14x13½**

*37* A34 ½c gold & multi 80 1.00
*38* A34 1c gold & multi 1.50 2.00
*39* A34 2½c gold & multi 6.75 8.00
*40* A34 4c gold & multi 1.50 1.50
*41* A34 5c gold & multi 10.00 12.00

| | | | | |
|---|---|---|---|---|
| *42* | A34 | 10c gold & multi | 8.00 | 8.75 |
| *43* | A34 | 20c gold & multi | 1.50 | 1.50 |
| *44* | A34 | 25c gold & multi | 1.50 | 1.50 |
| *45* | A34 | 50c gold & multi | 10.50 | 10.50 |
| *46* | A35 | $1 gold & multi | 20.00 | 20.00 |
| *47* | A35 | $2 gold & multi | 6.00 | 6.00 |
| | | *Nos. 37-47 (11)* | 68.05 | 72.75 |

Overprint horizontal on Nos. 46-47. On $2. overprint is in capitals of different font; size: 21x3mm.

Issue dates: Nos. 37-46, Aug. 9; No. 47, Nov. 24.

### Same Overprint Horizontal in Silver On Cook Islands Nos. 330-332.

**1972, Oct. 27** ***Perf. 13½***

| | | | | |
|---|---|---|---|---|
| *48* | A53 | 1c gold & multi | 5 | 5 |
| *49* | A53 | 5c gold & multi | 40 | 40 |
| *50* | A53 | 10c gold & multi | 65 | 65 |

### Fluorescence

Starting in 1972, stamps carry a "fluorescent security underprinting" in a multiple pattern of New Zealand's coat of arms with "Aitutaki" above, "Cook Islands" below and two stars at each side.

### Silver Wedding Type of Cook Islands

**1972, Nov. 20 Photo.** ***Perf. 13½***

**Size: 29x40mm.**

| | | | | |
|---|---|---|---|---|
| *51* | A54 | 5c sil & multi | 5.00 | 3.75 |

**Size: 66x40mm.**

| | | | | |
|---|---|---|---|---|
| *52* | A54 | 15c sil & multi | 2.25 | 1.75 |

25th anniversary of the marriage of Queen Elizabeth II and Prince Philip. Nos. 51-52 printed in sheets of 5 stamps and one label.

### Flower Issue of Cook Islands Overprinted

**1972, Dec. 11 Photo.** ***Perf. 14x13½***

**Gold & Multicolored**

| | | | | |
|---|---|---|---|---|
| *53* | A34 | ½c (#199) | 5 | 5 |
| *54* | A34 | 1c (#200) | 5 | 5 |
| *55* | A34 | 2½c (#202) | 10 | 10 |
| *56* | A34 | 4c (#205) | 12 | 12 |
| *57* | A34 | 5c (#206) | 16 | 16 |
| *58* | A34 | 10c (#210) | 30 | 30 |
| *59* | A34 | 20c (#212) | 70 | 70 |
| *60* | A34 | 25c (#213) | 90 | 90 |
| *61* | A34 | 50c (#215) | 1.75 | 1.75 |
| *62* | A35 | $1 (#216) | 3.75 | 3.75 |
| | | *Nos. 53-62 (10)* | 7.88 | 7.88 |

The Passion of Christ, by Mathias Grunewald — A22

Paintings: No. 63b, St. Veronica, by Rogier van der Weyden. No. 63c, Crucifixion, by Raphael. No. 63d, Resurrection, by della Francesca. No. 64a, Last Supper, by Master of Amiens. No. 64b, Condemnation of Christ, by Hans Holbein, the Elder. No. 64c, Crucifixion, by Rubens. No. 64d, Resurrection, by El Greco. No. 65a, Passion of Christ, by El Greco. No. 65b, St. Veronica, by Jakob Cornelisz. No. 65c, Crucifixion, by Rubens. No. 65d, Resurrection, by Dierik Bouts.

***Perf. 13½***

**1973, Apr. 6 Photo. Unwmk.**

| | | | | |
|---|---|---|---|---|
| *63* | A22 | Block of four | 20 | 20 |
| **a.-d.** | | 1c any single | 5 | 5 |
| *64* | A22 | Block of four | 65 | 65 |
| **a.-d.** | | 5c any single | 15 | 15 |
| *65* | A22 | Block of four | 1.50 | 1.50 |
| **a.-d.** | | 10c any single | 35 | 35 |

Easter 1973. Printed in blocks of 4 in sheets of 40. Design descriptions in top and bottom margins.

### Coin Type of Cook Islands

Queen Elizabeth II Coins: 1c, Taro leaf. 2c, Pineapples. 5c, Hibiscus. 10c, Oranges. 20c, Fairy terns. 50c, Bonito. $1, Tangaroa, Polynesian god of creation (vert.).

**1973, May 14** ***Perf. 13x13½***

**Size: 37x24mm.**

| | | | | |
|---|---|---|---|---|
| *66* | A55 | 1c dp car & multi | 5 | 5 |
| *67* | A55 | 2c bl & multi | 8 | 8 |
| *68* | A55 | 5c grn & multi | 14 | 14 |

**Size: 46x30mm.**

| | | | | |
|---|---|---|---|---|
| *69* | A55 | 10c vio bl & multi | 30 | 30 |
| *70* | A55 | 20c grn & multi | 60 | 60 |
| *71* | A55 | 50c dp car & multi | 1.40 | 1.40 |

**Size: 32x54½mm.**

| | | | | |
|---|---|---|---|---|
| *72* | A55 | $1 bl, blk & sil | 2.75 | 2.75 |
| | | *Nos. 66-72 (7)* | 5.32 | 5.32 |

Cook Islands coinage commemorating silver wedding anniversary of Queen Elizabeth II.

Printed in sheets of 20 stamps and label showing Westminster Abbey.

### Cook Islands Nos. 208, 210, 212 and 215 Overprinted Like Nos. 53-62 and: "TENTH ANNIVERSARY/ CESSATION/ OF/ NUCLEAR TESTING/ TREATY"

**1973, July Photo.** ***Perf. 14x13½***

| | | | | |
|---|---|---|---|---|
| *73* | A34 | 8c gold & multi | 32 | 32 |
| *74* | A34 | 10c gold & multi | 48 | 48 |
| *75* | A34 | 20c gold & multi | 1.00 | 1.00 |
| *76* | A34 | 50c gold & multi | 2.25 | 2.25 |

Nuclear Test Ban Treaty, 10th anniversary, and as protest against French nuclear testing on Mururoa Atoll.

Princess Anne, Hibiscus A23

Design: 30c, Mark Phillips and hibiscus.

**1973, Nov. 14 Photo.** ***Perf. 13½x14***

| | | | | |
|---|---|---|---|---|
| *77* | A23 | 25c gold & multi | 65 | 65 |
| *78* | A23 | 30c gold & multi | 85 | 85 |
| **a.** | | Souvenir sheet of 2 | 1.65 | 1.65 |

Wedding of Princess Anne and Capt. Mark Phillips. No. 78a contains one each of Nos. 77-78. Gold inscription and border. Size: 113x65mm.

Virgin and Child, by Il Perugino — A24

Paintings of the Virgin and Child by various masters.

**1973, Dec. Photo.** ***Perf. 13***

| | | | | |
|---|---|---|---|---|
| *79* | A24 | Block of four | 20 | 20 |
| **a.** | | 1c *Van Dyck* | 5 | 5 |
| **b.** | | 1c *Bartolommeo Montagna* | 5 | 5 |
| **c.** | | 1c *Carlo Crivelli* | 5 | 5 |
| **d.** | | 1c *Il Perugino* | 5 | 5 |
| *80* | A24 | Block of four | 60 | 60 |
| **a.** | | 5c *Cima da Conegliano* | 14 | 14 |
| **b.** | | 5c *Memling* | 14 | 14 |
| **c.** | | 5c *Veronese* | 14 | 14 |
| **d.** | | 5c *Veronese* | 14 | 14 |
| *81* | A24 | Block of four | 1.50 | 1.50 |
| **a.** | | 10c *Raphael* | 35 | 35 |
| **b.** | | 10c *Lorenzo Lotto* | 35 | 35 |
| **c.** | | 10c *Del Colle* | 35 | 35 |
| **d.** | | 10c *Memling* | 35 | 35 |

Christmas 1973. Printed in blocks of 4 in sheets of 48. Design descriptions in margins.

Murex Ramosus A25

Terebra Maculata — A26

Pacific Shells: 1c, Nautilus macromphalus. 2c, Harpa major. 3c, Phalium strigatum. 4c, Cypraea talpa. 5c, Mitra stictica. 8c, Charonia tritonis. 10c, Murex triremis. 20c, Oliva sericea. 25c, Tritonalia rubeta. 60c, Strombus latissimus. $1, Biplex perca. $5, Cypraea hesitata.

**1974-75 Photo.** ***Perf. 13***

| | | | | |
|---|---|---|---|---|
| *82* | A25 | ½c sil & multi | 5 | 5 |
| *83* | A25 | 1c sil & multi | 5 | 5 |
| *84* | A25 | 2c sil & multi | 5 | 5 |
| *85* | A25 | 3c sil & multi | 8 | 7 |
| *86* | A25 | 4c sil & multi | 9 | 6 |
| *87* | A25 | 5c sil & multi | 12 | 8 |
| *88* | A25 | 8c sil & multi | 18 | 12 |
| *89* | A25 | 10c sil & multi | 22 | 15 |
| *90* | A25 | 20c sil & multi | 45 | 30 |
| *91* | A25 | 25c sil & multi | 55 | 40 |
| *92* | A25 | 60c sil & multi | 1.50 | 90 |
| *93* | A25 | $1 sil & multi | 3.00 | 1.75 |

***Perf. 14***

| | | | | |
|---|---|---|---|---|
| *94* | A26 | $2 sil & multi ('75) | 3.75 | 3.75 |
| *95* | A26 | $5 sil & multi ('75) | 9.00 | 9.00 |
| | | *Nos. 82-95 (14)* | 19.09 | 16.73 |

Issue dates: Nos. 82-93, Jan. 31, 1974; $2, Jan. 20, 1975; $5, Feb. 28, 1975.

William Bligh and "Bounty" A27

**1974, Apr. 11 Photo.** ***Perf. 13***

**Size: 38x22mm.**

| | | | | |
|---|---|---|---|---|
| *96* | A27 | 1c *shown* | 5 | 5 |
| *97* | A27 | 1c *"Bounty" at sea* | 5 | 5 |
| *98* | A27 | 5c *Bligh and "Bounty" off Aitutaki* | 32 | 32 |
| *99* | A27 | 5c *Chart of Aitutaki, 1856* | 32 | 32 |
| *100* | A27 | 8c *James Cook and "Resolution"* | 65 | 65 |
| *101* | A27 | 8c *Maps of Aitutaki and Pacific Ocean* | 65 | 65 |
| | | *Nos. 96-101,C1-C6 (12)* | 5.64 | 5.64 |

Capt. William Bligh (1754-1817), European discoverer of Aitutaki, Apr. 11, 1789. Stamps of same denomination printed se-tenant in sheets of 32.

Aitutaki Nos. 1 & 2 Map and UPU Emblem A28

Design: 50c, Aitutaki Nos. 4 and 28, map of Aitutaki and UPU emblem.

**1974, July 15 Photo.** ***Perf. 13½***

| | | | | |
|---|---|---|---|---|
| *102* | A28 | 25c bl & multi | 80 | 80 |
| *103* | A28 | 50c bl & multi | 1.60 | 1.60 |
| **a.** | | Souvenir sheet of 2 | 2.50 | 2.50 |

Centenary of Universal Postal Union. Printed in sheets of 5 plus label showing UPU emblem. No. 103a contains one each of Nos. 102-103. Multicolored margin. Size: 67½x74mm.

*Aitutaki stamps can be mounted in Scott's annual New Zealand Dependencies Supplement.*

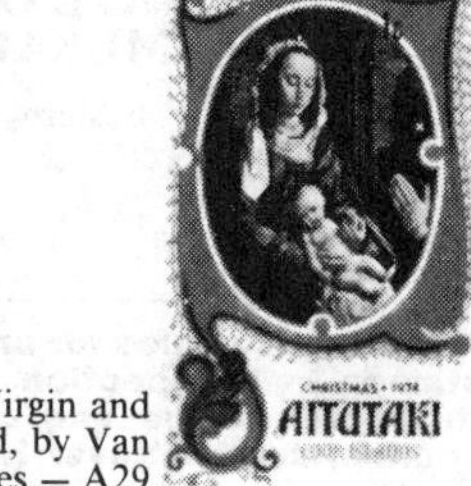

Virgin and Child, by Van der Goes — A29

Designs: Paintings of the Virgin and Child.

**1974, Oct. 11 Photo.** ***Perf. 13½***

| | | | | |
|---|---|---|---|---|
| *104* | A29 | 1c *shown* | 5 | 5 |
| *105* | A29 | 5c *Giovanni Bellini* | 12 | 12 |
| *106* | A29 | 8c *Gerard David* | 20 | 20 |
| *107* | A29 | 10c *Antonello da Messina* | 25 | 25 |
| *108* | A29 | 25c *Joos van Cleve* | 70 | 70 |
| *109* | A29 | 30c *Maitre de St. Catherine* | 80 | 80 |
| **a.** | | Souvenir sheet of 6 | 3.25 | 3.25 |
| | | *Nos. 104-109 (6)* | 2.12 | 2.12 |

Christmas 1974. Nos. 104-109 printed in sheets of 15 stamps and corner label. No. 109a contains one each of Nos. 104-109, gold and multicolored margin. Size: 127x135mm. See Nos. B1-B6.

Churchill, Dublin, Age 5 — A30

Designs: Churchill portraits.

**1974, Nov. 29 Photo.** ***Perf. 14***

| | | | | |
|---|---|---|---|---|
| *110* | A30 | 10c *shown* | 25 | 15 |
| *111* | A30 | 25c *As young man* | 60 | 40 |
| *112* | A30 | 30c *Inspecting troops, WWII* | 75 | 50 |
| *113* | A30 | 50c *Painting* | 1.50 | 90 |
| *114* | A30 | $1 *Giving V sign* | 3.00 | 1.75 |
| **a.** | | Souvenir sheet of 5 | 6.00 | 5.00 |
| | | *Nos. 110-114 (5)* | 6.10 | 3.70 |

Sir Winston Churchill (1874-1965), birth centenary. Nos. 110-114 printed in sheets of 5 stamps and corner label. No. 114a contains one each of Nos. 110-114, perf. 13½, and label showing Blenheim Palace; brown and gold margin. Size: 115x108mm.

Emblem US & USSR Flags A31

Design: 50c, Icarus and Apollo Soyuz spacecraft.

**1975, July 24 Photo.** ***Perf. 13x14½***

| | | | | |
|---|---|---|---|---|
| *115* | A31 | 25c multi | 75 | 75 |
| *116* | A31 | 50c multi | 1.75 | 1.75 |
| **a.** | | Souvenir sheet of 2 | 2.50 | 2.50 |

Apollo Soyuz space test project (Russo-American cooperation), launching July 15; link-up July 17. Nos. 115 and 116 each printed in sheets of 5 stamps and one label showing area of Apollo splash-downs. No. 116a contains one each of Nos. 115-116 with gold and black border and inscription. Size: 122x62mm.

Madonna and Child, by Pietro Lorenzetti — A32

Paintings: 7c, Adoration of the Kings, by Rogier van der Weyden. 15c, Madonna and Child, by Bartolommeo Montagna. 20c, Adoration of the Shepherds.

**1975, Nov. 24 Photo. *Perf. 14x13½***

*117* A32 Strip of 3 45 45
**a.** 6c *St. Francis* 12 12
**b.** 6c *Madonna and Child* 12 12
**c.** 6c *St. John the Evangelist* 12 12
*118* A32 Strip of 3 52 52
**a.** 7c *One King* 15 15
**b.** 7c *Madonna and Child* 15 15
**c.** 7c *Two Kings* 15 15
*119* A32 Strip of 3 1.25 1.25
**a.** 15c *St. Joseph* 40 40
**b.** 15c *Madonna and Child* 40 40
**c.** 15c *St. John the Baptist* 40 40
*120* A32 Strip of 3 1.90 1.90
**a.** 20c *One Shepherd* 60 60
**b.** 20c *Madonna and Child* 60 60
**c.** 20c *Two Shepherds* 60 60
**d.** Souvenir sheet of 12 (3x4) 5.50 5.50

Christmas 1975. Nos. 117-120 printed in sheets of 30 (10 strips of 3). No. 120d contains one each of Nos. 117-120, perf. 13½; multicolored margin. Size: 103x200mm.

Descent from the Cross, detail — A33

Designs (Painting, Flemish School, 16th Century): 30c, Virgin Mary, disciple and body of Jesus. 35c, Mary Magdalene and disciple.

**1976, Apr. 5 Photo. *Perf. 13½***

*121* A33 15c gold & multi 30 430
*122* A33 30c gold & multi 75 75
*123* A33 35c gold & multi 85 85
**a.** Souvenir sheet of 3 2.25 2.25

Easter 1976. No. 123a contains 3 stamps similar to Nos. 121-123, perf. 13, in continuous design without gold frames and white margins. Sheet has gold border and inscription. Size: 87x67mm.

Declaration of Independence — A34

Paintings by John Trumbull: 35c, Surrender of Cornwallis at Yorktown. 50c, Washington's Farewell Address.

**1976, June 1 Photo. *Perf. 13½***

*124* A34 Strip of 3 1.75 1.75
**a.** 30c *"1976 BICENTENARY"* 55 55
**b.** 30c *"UNITED STATES"* 55 55
**c.** 30c *"INDEPENDENCE 1776"* 55 55
*125* A34 Strip of 3 2.50 2.50
**a.** 35c *"1976 BICENTENARY"* 80 80
**b.** 35c *"UNITED STATES"* 80 80
**c.** 35c *"INDEPENDENCE 1776"* 80 80
*126* A34 Strip of 3 3.25 3.25
**a.** 50c *"1976 BICENTENARY"* 1.00 1.00
**b.** 50c *"UNITED STATES"* 1.00 1.00
**c.** 50c *"INDEPENDENCE 1776"* 1.00 1.00
**d.** Souvenir sheet of 9 (3x3) 8.00 8.00

American Bicentennial. Nos. 124-126 printed in sheets of 5 strips of 3 and 3-part corner label showing portrait of John Trumbull, commemorative inscription and portraits of Washington (30c), John Adams (35c) and Jefferson (50c). No. 126d contains 3 strips similar to Nos. 124-126; multicolored margin with Bicentennial emblem, Trumbull portrait and inscription. Size: 133x120mm.

Bicycling A35

Designs (Montreal Olympic Games Emblem and): 35c, Sailing. 60c, Field hockey. 70c, Running.

**1976, July 15 Photo. *Perf. 13x14***

*127* A35 15c multi 30 30
*128* A35 35c multi 70 70
*129* A35 60c multi 1.10 1.10
*130* A35 70c multi 1.40 1.40
**a.** Souvenir sheet of 4 4.00 4.00

21st Olympic Games, Montreal, Canada, July 17-Aug. 1. Nos. 127-130 printed in sheets of 5 stamps and label showing coat of Arms and Montreal Olympic Games emblem. No. 130a contains 4 stamps similar to Nos. 127-130 with gold margin around each stamp. Sheet has multicolored margin with Queen's head, inscription, Canadian maple leaf and Olympic emblem. Size: 107x97mm.

Nos. 127-130a Overprinted Diagonally: "ROYAL VISIT JULY 1976"

**1976, July 30**

*131* A35 15c multi 30 30
*132* A35 35c multi 75 75
*133* A35 60c multi 1.10 1.10
*134* A35 70c multi 1.50 1.50
**a.** Souvenir sheet of 4 5.00 5.00

Visit of Queen Elizabeth II to Montreal and official opening of the Games. Each stamp of No. 134a has diagonal overprint. Sheet margin has additional overprint: "ROYAL VISIT OF H.M. QUEEN ELIZABETH II/OFFICIALLY OPENED 17 JULY 1976".

Annunciation
A36 A37

Designs: Nos. 137-138, Angel appearing to the shepherds. Nos. 139-140, Nativity. Nos. 141-142, Three Kings.

**1976, Oct. 18 *Perf. 13½x13***

*135* A36 6c dk grn & gold 15 15
*136* A37 6c dk grn & gold 15 15
*137* A36 7c dk brn & gold 18 18
*138* A37 7c dk brn & gold 18 18
*139* A36 15c dk bl & gold 45 45
*140* A37 15c dk bl & gold 45 45
*141* A36 20c pur & gold 55 55
*142* A37 20c pur & gold 55 55
**a.** Souvenir sheet of 8 3.25 3.25
*Nos. 135-142 (8)* 2.66 2.66

Christmas 1976. Stamps of same denomination printed se-tenant in sheets of 50. No. 142a contains 8 stamps similar to Nos. 135-142 with white margin around each pair of stamps; gold decorative margin. Size: 127x96mm.

A. G. Bell and 1876 Telephone — A38

Design: 70c, Satellite and radar.

**1977, Mar. 3 Photo. *Perf. 13½x13***

*143* A38 25c rose & multi 45 45
*144* A38 70c vio & multi 1.50 1.50
**a.** Souvenir sheet of 2 2.00 2.00

Centenary of first telephone call by Alexander Graham Bell, Mar. 10, 1876. No. 144a contains a 25c in colors of 70c and 70c in colors of 25c. Gold and violet border. Size: 116x59mm.

Calvary (detail), by Rubens A39

Paintings by Rubens: 20c, Lamentation. 35c, Descent from the Cross.

**1977, Mar. 31 Photo. *Perf. 13½x14***

*145* A39 15c gold & multi 38 38
*146* A39 20c gold & multi 45 45
*147* A39 35c gold & multi 65 65
**a.** Souvenir sheet of 3 1.75 1.75

Easter 1977, and 400th birth anniversary of Peter Paul Rubens (1577-1640), Flemish painter. No. 147a contains one each of Nos. 145-147, perf. 13. Gold and dark brown margin. Size: 152x57mm.

Capt. Bligh, "Bounty" and George III — A40

Designs: 35c, Rev. John Williams, George IV, First Christian Church. 50c, British flag, map of Aitutaki, Queen Victoria. $1, Elizabeth II and family on balcony after coronation.

**1977, Apr. 21 *Perf. 13½***

*148* A40 25c gold & multi 75 75
*149* A40 35c gold & multi 1.40 1.40
*150* A40 50c gold & multi 1.90 1.90
*151* A40 $1 gold & multi 4.00 4.00
**a.** Souv. sheet of 4, #148-151 10.00 10.00

25th anniversary of the reign of Queen Elizabeth II. No. 151a contains one each of Nos. 148-151; gold and purple margin. Size: 13x87mm.

Annunciation
A41 A42

Designs: No. 154, Virgin, Child and ox. No. 155, Joseph and donkey (Nativity). No. 156, Three Kings. No. 157, Virgin and Child. No. 158, Joseph. No. 159, Virgin, Child and donkey (Flight into Egypt).

**1977, Oct. 14 Photo. *Perf. 13½x14***

*152* A41 6c multi 18 18
*153* A42 6c multi 18 18
*154* A41 7c multi 18 18
*155* A42 7c multi 18 18
*156* A41 15c multi 38 38
*157* A42 15c multi 38 38
*158* A41 20c multi 55 55
*159* A42 20c multi 55 55
**a.** Souvenir sheet of 8 3.00 3.00
*Nos. 152-159 (8)* 2.58 2.58

Christmas 1977. Stamps of same denomination printed se-tenant in sheets of 32. No. 159a contains one each of Nos. 152-159; green, yellow and blue margin. Size: 130x95mm.

Hawaiian Wood Figurine — A43

Designs: 50c, Talbot hunting dog, figurehead of "Resolution" (horiz.). $1, Temple figure.

**1978, Jan. 19 Litho. *Perf. 13½***

*160* A43 35c multi 60 60
*161* A43 50c multi 80 80
*162* A43 $1 multi 1.50 1.50
**a.** Souvenir sheet of 3 3.50 3.50

Bicentenary of Capt. Cook's arrival in Hawaii. Nos. 160-162 issued in sheets of 6. No. 162a contains one each of Nos. 160-162; multicolored margin. Size: 168x75mm.

Avignon Pieta, 15th Century A44

Paintings: 15c, Jesus Carrying Cross, by Simone di Martini. 35c, Christ at Emmaus, by Rembrandt.

**1978, Mar. 17 Photo. *Perf. 13½x14***

*163* A44 15c gold & multi 25 25
*164* A44 20c gold & multi 40 40
*165* A44 35c gold & multi 60 60
**a.** Souvenir sheet of 3 1.50 1.50

Easter 1978. No. 165a contains one each of Nos. 163-165, perf. 13½, and label showing Louvre, Paris; green and gold margin. Size: 108x84mm.

Elizabeth II — A45

Virgin and Child, by Dürer — A46

Souvenir Sheets

**1978, June 15 Photo. *Perf. 13½x13***

*166* Sheet of 6 12.00 12.00
**a.** A45 $1 *Yale of Beaufort* 1.90 1.90
**b.** A45 $1 *shown* 1.90 1.90
**c.** A45 $1 *Ancestral statue* 1.90 1.90
**d.** Souvenir sheet of 6 12.00 12.00

25th anniversary of coronation of Queen Elizabeth II. No. 166 contains 2 each of Nos. 166a-166c, silver marginal inscription and coats of arms. Size: 95x109mm. No. 166d contains 2 strips of Nos. 166a-166c separated by horizontal slate green gutter showing Royal family on balcony, silver marginal inscription. Size: 87x127mm.

**1978, Dec. 4 Photo. *Perf. 14½x13***

Designs: Various paintings of the Virgin and Child by Albrecht Dürer.

*167* A46 15c multi 22 22
*168* A46 17c multi 30 30
*169* A46 30c multi 55 55
*170* A46 35c multi 70 70

Christmas 1978 and 450th death anniversary of Albrecht Dürer (1471-1528), German painter. Nos. 167-170 issued in sheets of 5 stamps and corner label.

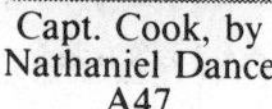

Capt. Cook, by Nathaniel Dance A47

Boy Holding Hibiscus, IYC Emblem A48

Design: 75c, "Resolution" and "Adventure," by William Hodges.

**1979, July 20 Photo. *Perf. 14x13 ½***

| No. | Type | Description | Unused | Used |
|---|---|---|---|---|
| *171* | A47 | 50c multi | 1.10 | 1.10 |
| *172* | A47 | 75c multi | 1.50 | 1.50 |
| ***a.*** | | Souvenir sheet of 2 | 3.25 | 3.25 |

Capt. James Cook (1728-1779), explorer, death bicentenary. No. 172a contains Nos. 171-172; multicolored margin with Cook's coat of arms. Size: 95x58mm.

**1979, Oct. 1 Photo. *Perf. 14x13 ½***

IYC Emblem and: 35c, Boy playing guitar. 65c, Boys in outrigger canoe.

| No. | Type | Description | Unused | Used |
|---|---|---|---|---|
| *173* | A48 | 30c multi | 50 | 50 |
| *174* | A48 | 35c multi | 55 | 55 |
| *175* | A48 | 65c multi | 1.10 | 1.10 |

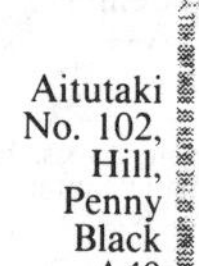

Aitutaki No. 102, Hill, Penny Black A49

Designs: Nos. 176, 178-179, 181, paintings of letter writers, Flemish School, 17th century.

**1979, Nov. 14 Photo. *Perf. 13***

| No. | Type | Description | Unused | Used |
|---|---|---|---|---|
| *176* | A49 | 50c *Gabriel Metsu* | 75 | 75 |
| *177* | A49 | 50c *shown* | 75 | 75 |
| *178* | A49 | 50c *Jan Vermeer* | 75 | 75 |
| *179* | A49 | 65c *Gerard Terborch* | 90 | 90 |
| *180* | A49 | 65c *No. 103 (like No. 177)* | 90 | 90 |
| *181* | A49 | 65c *Jan Vermeer* | 90 | 90 |
| | | *Nos. 176-181 (6)* | 4.95 | 4.95 |

**Souvenir Sheet**

| No. | Type | Description | Unused | Used |
|---|---|---|---|---|
| *182* | A49 | Sheet of 6 | 3.25 | 3.25 |
| ***a.*** | | 30c like No. 176 | 45 | 45 |
| ***b.*** | | 30c like No. 177 | 45 | 45 |
| ***c.*** | | 30c like No. 178 | 45 | 45 |
| ***d.*** | | 30c like No. 179 | 45 | 45 |
| ***e.*** | | 30c like No. 180 | 45 | 45 |
| ***f.*** | | 30c like No. 181 | 45 | 45 |

Sir Rowland Hill (1795-1879), originator of penny postage. Nos. 176-178 and 179-181 printed se-tenant in sheets of 9 (3x3). No. 182 has brown lilac margin with gold inscription. Size: 151 ½x86mm.

Descent from the Cross, Detail — A50

Easter 1980: 30c, 35c, Descent from the Cross, by Quentin Metsys (details).

**1980, Apr. 3 Photo. *Perf. 13x13 ½***

| No. | Type | Description | Unused | Used |
|---|---|---|---|---|
| *183* | A50 | 20c multi | 30 | 30 |
| *184* | A50 | 30c multi | 45 | 45 |
| *185* | A50 | 35c multi | 55 | 55 |

Albert Einstein — A51

**1980, July 21 Photo. *Perf. 14***

| No. | Type | Description | Unused | Used |
|---|---|---|---|---|
| *186* | A51 | 12c *shown* | 22 | 22 |
| *187* | A51 | 12c *Formula, atom structure* | 22 | 22 |
| *188* | A51 | 15c *Portrait, diff.* | 25 | 25 |
| *189* | A51 | 15c *Atomic blast* | 25 | 25 |
| *190* | A51 | 20c *Portrait, diff.* | 35 | 35 |
| *191* | A51 | 20c *Atomic blast, trees* | 35 | 35 |
| ***a.*** | | Souvenir sheet of 6, perf. 13 | 1.75 | 1.75 |
| | | *Nos. 186-191 (6)* | 1.64 | 1.64 |

Albert Einstein (1879-1955), theoretical physicist. Stamps of same denomination se-tenant. No. 191a contains Nos. 186-191; multicolored margin shows atom nucleus. Size: 114x118mm.

Ancestral Figure, Aitutaki — A52

**1980, Sept. 26 Photo. *Perf. 14***

| No. | Type | Description | Unused | Used |
|---|---|---|---|---|
| *192* | A52 | 6c *shown* | 9 | 9 |
| *193* | A52 | 6c *God image staff, Rarotonga* | 9 | 9 |
| *194* | A52 | 6c *Trade adze, Mangaia* | 9 | 9 |
| *195* | A52 | 6c *Tangaroa carving, Rarotonga* | 9 | 9 |
| *196* | A52 | 12c *Wooden image, Aitutaki* | 18 | 18 |
| *197* | A52 | 12c *Hand club, Rarotonga* | 18 | 18 |
| *198* | A52 | 12c *Carved mace, Mangaia* | 18 | 18 |
| *199* | A52 | 12c *Fisherman's god, Rarotonga* | 18 | 18 |
| *200* | A52 | 15c *Ti'i image, Aitutaki* | 22 | 22 |
| *201* | A52 | 15c *Fisherman's god, diff.* | 22 | 22 |
| *202* | A52 | 15c *Carved mace, Cook Islands* | 22 | 22 |
| *203* | A52 | 15c *Tangaroa, diff.* | 22 | 22 |
| *204* | A52 | 20c *Chief's headdress, Aitutaki* | 30 | 30 |
| *205* | A52 | 20c *Carved mace, diff.* | 30 | 30 |
| *206* | A52 | 20c *God image staff, diff.* | 30 | 30 |
| *207* | A52 | 20c *like #195* | 30 | 30 |
| ***a.*** | | Souvenir sheet of 16 | 3.50 | |
| | | *Nos. 192-207 (16)* | 3.16 | 3.16 |

Third South Pacific Arts Festival, Port Moresby, Papua New Guinea. No. 207a contains Nos. 192-207; multicolored decorative margin. Size: 134x195mm. Stamps of same denomination se-tenant.

Virgin and Child, 13th Century Sculpture — A53

Christmas 1980: Virgin and Child Sculptures, 14th Century (20c), 15th Century (25c,35c).

**1980, Nov. 21 Photo. *Perf. 13x13 ½***

| No. | Type | Description | Unused | Used |
|---|---|---|---|---|
| *208* | A53 | 15c multi | 22 | 22 |
| *209* | A53 | 20c multi | 30 | 30 |
| *210* | A53 | 25c multi | 38 | 38 |
| *211* | A53 | 35c multi | 55 | 55 |

Mourning Virgin, by Pedro Roldan — A54

Sturnus Vulgaris — A55

Easter 1981 (Roldan Sculptures): 40c, Christ. 50c, Mourning St. John.

**1981, Mar. 31 Photo. *Perf. 14***

| No. | Type | Description | Unused | Used |
|---|---|---|---|---|
| *212* | A54 | 30c grn & gold | 45 | 45 |
| *213* | A54 | 40c brt pur & gold | 55 | 55 |
| *214* | A54 | 50c dk bl & gold | 70 | 70 |

**1981-82 *Perf. 14x13 ½, 13 ½x14***

| No. | Type | Description | Unused | Used |
|---|---|---|---|---|
| *215* | A55 | 1c shown | 5 | 5 |
| *216* | A55 | 1c Poephila gouldiae | 5 | 5 |
| *217* | A55 | 2c Petroica multicolor | 5 | 5 |
| *218* | A55 | 2c Pachycephala pectoralis | 5 | 5 |
| *219* | A55 | 3c Falco peregrinus | 5 | 5 |
| *220* | A55 | 3c Rhipidura rufifrous | 5 | 5 |
| *221* | A55 | 4c Tyto alba | 7 | 7 |
| *222* | A55 | 4c Padda oryzivora | 7 | 7 |
| *223* | A55 | 5c Artamus leucorhynchus | 9 | 9 |
| *224* | A55 | 5c Vini peruviana | 9 | 9 |
| *225* | A55 | 6c Columba livia | 10 | 10 |
| *226* | A55 | 6c Porphyrio porphyria | 10 | 10 |
| *227* | A55 | 10c Geopelia striata | 18 | 18 |
| *228* | A55 | 10c Lonchura castaneothorax | 18 | 18 |
| *229* | A55 | 12c Acridotheres tristis | 20 | 20 |
| *230* | A55 | 12c Egretta sacra | 20 | 20 |
| *231* | A55 | 15c Diomeda melanophris | 25 | 25 |
| *232* | A55 | 15c Numenius phaeopus | 25 | 25 |
| *233* | A55 | 20c Gygis alba | 35 | 35 |
| *234* | A55 | 20c Pluvialis dominica | 35 | 35 |
| *235* | A55 | 25c Sula leucogaster | 45 | 45 |
| *236* | A55 | 25c Anas superciliosa | 45 | 45 |
| *237* | A55 | 30c Anas acuta | 50 | 50 |
| *238* | A55 | 30c Fregata minor | 50 | 50 |
| *239* | A55 | 35c Stercorarius pomarinus | 60 | 60 |
| *240* | A55 | 35c Conopoderas caffra | 60 | 60 |
| *241* | A55 | 40c Lalage maculosa | 70 | 70 |
| *242* | A55 | 40c Gallirallus philippensis | 70 | 70 |
| *243* | A55 | 50c Vini stepheni | 85 | 85 |
| *244* | A55 | 50c Diomedea epomophora | 85 | 85 |
| *245* | A55 | 70c Ptilinopus victor | 1.25 | 1.25 |
| *246* | A55 | 70c Erythrura cyaneovirens | 1.25 | 1.25 |

**Photo. *Perf. 13 ½***

**Size: 35x47mm.**

| No. | Type | Description | Unused | Used |
|---|---|---|---|---|
| *246A* | A55 | $1 Myiagra azureocapilla | 1.75 | 1.75 |
| *246B* | A55 | $2 Myiagra vanikorensis | 3.50 | 3.50 |
| *246C* | A55 | $4 Strawberry finch | 6.75 | 6.75 |
| *246D* | A55 | $5 Flat-billed kingfisher | 8.50 | 8.50 |
| | | *Nos. 215-246D (36)* | 31.98 | 31.98 |

Issue dates: Nos. 215-230, Apr. 6; Nos. 231-238, May 8; Nos. 239-246, Jan. 14, 1982; Nos. 246A-246B, Feb. 15, 1982. Stamps of same denomination se-tenant. Nos. 231-246 horiz.

Prince Charles and Lady Diana — A56

***Perf. 13x13 ½, 13 ½x13***

**1981, June 10 Photo.**

| No. | Type | Description | Unused | Used |
|---|---|---|---|---|
| *247* | A56 | 60c Charles, vert. | 1.10 | 1.10 |
| *248* | A56 | 80c Lady Diana, vert. | 1.40 | 1.40 |
| *249* | A56 | $1.40 Shown | 2.25 | 2.25 |

Royal Wedding. Issued in sheets of 4.

1982 World Cup Soccer — A57

Designs: Various soccer players.

**1981, Nov. 30 Photo. *Perf. 14***

| No. | Type | Description | Unused | Used |
|---|---|---|---|---|
| *250* | | Pair | 40 | 40 |
| ***a.-b.*** | A57 | 12c multi | 20 | 20 |
| *251* | | Pair | 48 | 48 |
| ***a.-b.*** | A57 | 15c multi | 24 | 24 |
| *252* | | Pair | 65 | 65 |
| ***a.-b.*** | A57 | 20c multi | 32 | 32 |
| *253* | | Pair | 80 | 80 |
| ***a.-b.*** | A57 | 25c multi | 40 | 40 |

Christmas 1981 A58

Rembrandt Etchings: 15c, Holy Family, 1632 (vert.). 30c, Virgin with Child, 1634 (vert.). 40c, Adoration of the Shepherds, 1654. 50c, Holy Family with Cat, 1644.

**1981, Dec. 10 *Perf. 14***

| No. | Type | Description | Unused | Used |
|---|---|---|---|---|
| *254* | A58 | 15c gold & dk brn | 22 | 22 |
| *255* | A58 | 30c gold & dk brn | 45 | 45 |
| *256* | A58 | 40c gold & dk brn | 60 | 60 |
| *257* | A58 | 50c gold & dk brn | 75 | 75 |

**Souvenir Sheets**

| No. | Type | Description | Unused | Used |
|---|---|---|---|---|
| *258* | A58 | 80 + 5c like #254 | 1.10 | 1.10 |
| *259* | A58 | 80 + 5c like #255 | 1.10 | 1.10 |
| *260* | A58 | 80 + 5c like #256 | 1.10 | 1.10 |
| *261* | A58 | 80 + 5c like #257 | 1.10 | 1.10 |

Nos. 258-261 have multicolored margins showing entire etching. Size: 66x82mm. Surtax on Nos. 258-261 was for local charities.

21st Birthday of Princess Diana — A59

**1982, June 24 Photo. *Perf. 14***

| No. | Type | Description | Unused | Used |
|---|---|---|---|---|
| *262* | A59 | 70c shown | 85 | 85 |
| *263* | A59 | $1 Wedding portrait | 1.10 | 1.10 |
| *264* | A59 | $2 Diana, diff. | 2.50 | 2.50 |
| ***a.*** | | Souvenir sheet of 3 | 5.00 | 5.00 |

No. 264a contains Nos. 262-264; multicolored margin shows arms of Prince of Wales. Size: 82x92mm.

Nos. 247-249 Overprinted: "21 June 1982 PRINCE WILLIAM OF WALES" or "COMMEMORATING THE ROYAL BIRTH"

**1982, July 13 *Perf. 13x13 ½, 13 ½x13***

| No. | Type | Description | Unused | Used |
|---|---|---|---|---|
| *265* | A56 | 60c multi | 90 | 90 |
| *266* | A56 | 80c multi | 1.25 | 1.25 |
| *267* | A56 | $1.40 multi | 2.00 | 2.00 |

Nos. 262-264a Overprinted: "ROYAL BIRTH 21 JUNE 1982 PRINCE WILLIAM OF WALES"

**1982, Aug. 5 *Perf. 14***

| No. | Type | Description | Unused | Used |
|---|---|---|---|---|
| *268* | A59 | 70c multi | 1.10 | 1.10 |
| *269* | A59 | $1 multi | 1.50 | 1.50 |
| *270* | A59 | $2 multi | 3.00 | 3.00 |
| ***a.*** | | Souvenir sheet of 3 | 5.25 | 5.25 |

Christmas 1982 — A60

Madonna and Child Sculptures, 12th-15th Cent.

**1982, Dec. 10 Photo. *Perf. 13***
*271* A60 18c multi 25 25
*272* A60 36c multi 55 55
*273* A60 48c multi 75 75
*274* A60 60c multi 90 90

**Souvenir Sheet**

*275* Sheet of 4 2.75 2.75
**a.** A60 18 + 2c like 18c 30 30
**b.** A60 36 + 2c like 36c 55 55
**c.** A60 48 + 2c like 48c 75 75
**d.** A60 60 + 2c like 60c 90 90

No. 275 has multicolored margin showing Princess Diana and Prince William. Size: 100x115mm. Surtax was for children's charities.

Commonwealth Day — A61

**1983, Mar. 14 Photo. *Perf. 13x13½***
*276* A61 48c Bananas 75 75
*277* A61 48c Ti'i statuette 75 75
*278* A61 48c Boys canoeing 75 75
*279* A61 48c Capt. William Bligh, Bounty 75 75

Nos. 276-279 se-tenant.

Scouting Year A62

**1983, Apr. 18 Photo. *Perf. 14***
*280* A62 36c Campfire 55 55
*281* A62 48c Salute 75 75
*282* A62 60c Hiking 90 90

**Souvenir Sheet**

***Perf. 13½***

*283* Sheet of 3 3.00 3.00
**a.** A62 36c + 3c like #280 75 75
**b.** A62 48c + 3c like #281 90 90
**c.** A62 60c + 3c like #282 1.20 1.20

Size of No. 283: 78x108mm. Surtax was for benefit of Scouting.

Nos. 280-283 Overprinted: "15th WORLD SCOUT JAMBOREE"

**1983, July 11 Photo. *Perf. 14***
*284* A62 36c multi 55 55
*285* A62 48c multi 75 75
*286* A62 60c multi 90 90

**Souvenir Sheet**

*287* Sheet of 3 3.00 3.00
**a.** A62 36c + 3c like #284 75 75
**b.** A62 48c + 3c like #285 90 90
**c.** A62 60c + 3c like #286 1.20 1.20

Manned Flight Bicentenary — A63

Modern sport balloons.

A little time given to the study of the arrangement of the Scott Catalogue can make it easier to use effectively.

**1983, July 22 Photo. *Perf. 14x13***
*288* A63 18c multi 25 25
*289* A63 36c multi 55 55
*290* A63 48c multi 75 75
*291* A63 60c multi 90 90

**Souvenir Sheet**

*292* A63 $2.50 multi 3.75 3.75

No. 292 contains one stamp (32x50mm.); multicolored margin continues design. Size: 64x81mm.

Nos. 233-246, 246D, 248-249, 263-264 Surcharged

***Perf. 13½x14, 14½x14, 13x13½, 14, 13½***

**1983, Sept. 22 Photo.**
*293* A55 18c on 20c, #233 36 36
*294* A55 18c on 20c, #234 36 36
*295* A55 36c on 25c, #235 72 72
*296* A55 36c on 25c, #236 72 72
*297* A55 36c on 30c, #237 72 72
*298* A55 36c on 30c, #238 72 72
*299* A55 36c on 35c, #239 72 72
*300* A55 36c on 35c, #240 72 72
*301* A55 48c on 40c, #241 95 95
*302* A55 48c on 40c, #242 95 95
*303* A55 48c on 50c, #243 95 95
*304* A55 48c on 50c, #244 95 95
*305* A55 72c on 70c, #245 1.45 1.45
*306* A55 72c on 70c, #246 1.45 1.45
*307* A56 96c on 80c, #248 1.90 1.90
*308* A59 96c on $1, #263 1.90 1.90
*309* A56 $1.20 on $1.40, #249 2.40 2.40
*310* A59 $1.20 on $2, #264 2.40 2.40

**Size: 35x47mm.**

*311* A55 $5.60 on $5, #246D 11.00 11.00
*Nos. 293-311 (19)* 31.34 31.34

Nos. 293-306 printed in se-tenant pairs. Nos. 307-308, 310-311 vert.

World Communications Year — A64

**1983, Sept. 29 Photo. *Perf. 14***
*312* A64 48c shown 70 70
*313* A64 60c Communications satellite 90 90
*314* A64 96c Global coverage 1.50 1.50
**a.** Souvenir sheet of 3 3.00 3.00

No. 314a contains Nos. 312-314, marginal inscription and emblem.

Christmas 1983 A65

Raphael Paintings.

**1983, Nov. 21 Photo. *Perf. 13½x14***
*315* A65 36c Madonna of the Chair 55 55
*316* A65 48c Alba Madonna 75 75
*317* A65 60c Connestabile Madonna 90 90

**Souvenir Sheet**

*318* Sheet of 3 2.50 2.50
**a.** A65 36c + 3c like #315 60 60
**b.** A65 48c + 3c like #316 75 75
**c.** A65 60c + 3c like #317 90 90

**1983, Dec. 15**

**Size: 46x46mm. Imperf.**

*319* A65 85c + 5c like #315 1.25 1.25
*320* A65 85c + 5c like #316 1.25 1.25
*321* A65 85c + 5c like #317 1.25 1.25

No. 318 has olive green and gold margin showing angel. Size: 96x108mm. Surtax was for children's charities.

Local Birds — A66

**1984 Photo. *Perf. 14***
*322* A66 2c Gouldian finch 5 5
*323* A66 3c Common starling 5 5
*324* A66 5c Scarlet robin 9 9
*325* A66 10c Golden whistler 14 14
*326* A66 12c Long-tailed fantails 18 18
*327* A66 18c Peregrine falcon 25 25
*328* A66 24c Barn owl 35 35
*329* A66 30c Java sparrow 42 42
*330* A66 36c White-breasted wood swallow 50 50
*331* A66 48c Pacific lorikeet 70 70
*332* A66 50c Rock dove 50 50
*333* A66 60c Purple swamp hen 65 65
*334* A66 72c Peaceful dove 80 80
*335* A66 96c Chestnut-breasted finch 1.10 1.10
*336* A66 $1.20 Common mynah 1.25 1.25
*337* A66 $2.10 Reef heron 2.25 2.25
*338* A66 $3 Blue-crested broadbill 3.25 3.25
*339* A66 $4.20 Vanikoro broadbill 3.75 3.75
*340* A66 $5.60 Strawberry finch 4.25 4.25
*341* A66 $9.60 Flat-billed kingfisher 7.25 7.25
*Nos. 322-341 (20)* 27.78 27.78

1984 Summer Olympics — A67

**1984, July 24 Photo. *Perf. 13x13½***
*342* A67 36c Javelin 32 32
*343* A67 48c Shot put 45 45
*344* A67 60c Hurdles 55 55
*345* A67 $2 Handball 1.75 1.75

**Souvenir Sheet**

*346* Sheet of 4 3.50 3.50
**a.** A67 36c + 5c like #342 38 38
**b.** A67 48c + 5c like #343 50 50
**c.** A67 60c + 5c like #344 60 60
**d.** A67 $2 + 5c like #345 1.75 1.75

Surtax was for benefit of local sports. Size: 90x119mm.

Nos. 342-345 Overprinted in Gold on Black with Winners' Names, Event, Nationality.

**1984, Aug. 21 Photo. *Perf. 13x13½***
*347* A67 36c multi 32 32
*348* A67 48c multi 45 45
*349* A67 60c multi 55 55
*350* A67 $2 multi 1.75 1.75

Ausipex '84 A68

**1984, Sept. 14 Photo. *Perf. 14***
*351* A68 60c William Bligh, map 55 55
*352* A68 96c Bounty, map 85 85
*353* A68 $1.40 Stamps, map 1.25 1.25

**Souvenir Sheet**

*354* Sheet of 3 3.25 3.25
**a.** A68 60c + 5c like #351 65 65
**b.** A68 96c + 5c like #352 1.00 1.00
**c.** A68 $1.40 + 5c like #353 1.40 1.40

Size of No. 354: 85x113mm.

No. 247 Surcharged with Black Bar and New Value in Gold and: "15.9.84 Birth/Prince Henry"

**1984, Oct. 10 Photo. *Perf. 13x13½***
*355* A56 $3 multi 3.00 3.00

Issued in sheets of 4.

Christmas 1984 — A69

**1984, Nov. 16 Photo. *Perf. 13***
*356* A69 36c Annunciation 32 32
*357* A69 48c Nativity 45 45
*358* A69 60c Epiphany 55 55
*359* A69 96c Flight into Egypt 90 90

**Souvenir Sheets**

**Size: 45x53mm.**

***Imperf***

*360* A69 90c + 7c like #356 90 90
*361* A69 90c + 7c like #357 90 90
*362* A69 90c + 7c like #358 90 90
*363* A69 90c + 7c like #359 90 90

Christmas 1984, Birth of Prince Henry, Sept. 15 — A70

**1984, Dec. 10 Photo. *Perf. 13½x14***
*364* A70 48c Diana, Henry 45 45
*365* A70 60c William, Henry 55 55
*366* A70 $2.10 Family 1.75 1.75

**Souvenir Sheet**

*367* Sheet of 3 3.00 3.00
**a.** A70 96c + 7c like #364 90 90
**b.** A70 96c + 7c like #365 90 90
**c.** A70 96c + 7c like #366 90 90

Surtax was for benefit of local children's charities. Size: 113x65mm.

Audubon Birth Bicentenary A71

Illustrations of bird species by John J. Audubon.

**1985, Mar. 22 Litho. *Perf. 13***
*368* A71 55c Gray kingbird 40 40
*369* A71 65c Bohemian waxwing 45 45
*370* A71 75c Summer tanager 55 55
*371* A71 95c Cardinal 70 70

| | | |
|---|---|---|
| 372 A71 $1.15 White-winged crossbill | 85 | 85 |
| Nos. 368-372 (5) | 2.95 | 2.95 |

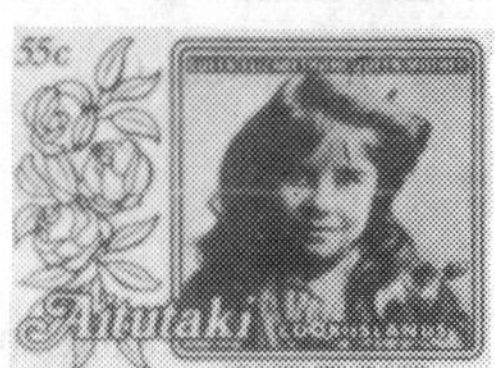

Queen Mother, 85th Birthday — A72

Photographs: 55c, Lady Elizabeth Bowes-Lyon, age 7. 65c, Engaged to the Duke of York. 75c, Duchess of York with daughter, Elizabeth. $1.30, Holding the infant Prince Charles. $3, Portrait taken on 63rd birthday.

**1985, June 14** **Perf. 13½x13**

| | | |
|---|---|---|
| 373 A72 55c multi | 50 | 50 |
| 374 A72 65c multi | 60 | 60 |
| 375 A72 75c multi | 70 | 70 |
| 376 A72 $1.30 multi | 1.20 | 1.20 |
| a. Souvenir sheet of 4, #373-376 | 3.25 | 3.25 |

**Souvenir Sheet**

| | | |
|---|---|---|
| 377 A72 $3 multi | 2.25 | 2.25 |

Nos. 373-376 printed in sheets of 4.

No. 377 has decorative margin picturing the 1937 coronation crown. Size: 76x50mm.

No. 376a issued Aug. 4, 1986, for Queen Mother 86th birthday; multicolored decorative margin pictures crown. Size: 133x82mm.

Intl. Youth Year A73

Designs: 75c, The Calmady Children, by Thomas Lawrence (1769-1830). 90c, Madame Charpentier's Children, by Renoir (1841-1919). $1.40, Young Girls at Piano, by Renoir.

**1985, Sept. 16** **Photo.** **Perf. 13**

| | | |
|---|---|---|
| 378 A73 75c multi | 65 | 65 |
| 379 A73 90c multi | 75 | 75 |
| 380 A73 $1.40 multi | 1.25 | 1.25 |

**Souvenir Sheet**

| | | |
|---|---|---|
| 381 Sheet of 3 | 3.75 | 3.75 |
| a. A73 75c + 10c like #378 | 95 | 95 |
| b. A73 90c + 10c like #379 | 1.10 | 1.10 |
| c. A73 $1.40 + 10c like #380 | 1.70 | 1.70 |

Surcharged for children's activities. No. 381 has decorative margin picturing Herbert Adams' (1858-1945) bas-relief, Singing boys, and IYY emblem. Size: 103x104mm.

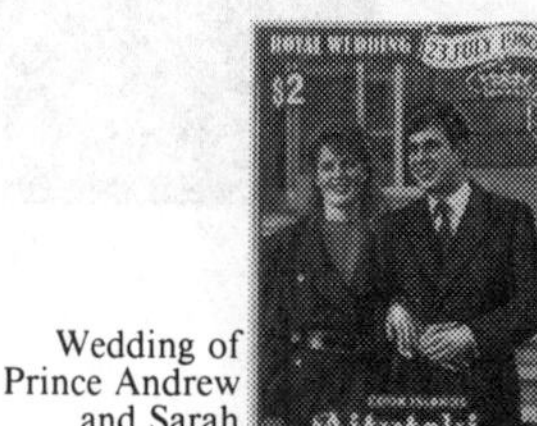

Adoration of the Magi, by Giotto di Bondone (1276-1337) — A74

**1985, Nov. 15** **Photo.** **Perf. 13½x13**

| | | |
|---|---|---|
| 382 A74 95c multi | 1.10 | 1.10 |
| 383 A74 95c multi | 1.10 | 1.10 |
| 384 A74 $1.15 multi | 1.40 | 1.40 |
| 385 A74 $1.15 multi | 1.40 | 1.40 |

**Souvenir Sheet**

***Imperf***

| | | |
|---|---|---|
| 386 A74 $6.40 multi | 6.50 | 6.50 |

Christmas 1985, return of Halley's Comet, 1985-1986. Stamps of the same denomination se-tenant. No. 386 has multicolored decorative margin. Size: 52x55mm.

Halley's Comet A75

Designs: 90c, Halley's Comet, A.D. 684, wood engraving, Nuremberg Chronicles. $1.25, Sighting of 1066, Bayeux Tapestry, detail, c. 1092, France. $1.75, The Comet Inflicting Untold Disasters, 1456, Lucerne Chronicles, by Diebolt Schilling. $4.20, Melancolia I, engraving by Durer.

**1986, Feb. 25** **Photo.** **Perf. 13½x13**

| | | |
|---|---|---|
| 387 A75 90c multi | 1.00 | 1.00 |
| 388 A75 $1.25 multi | 1.40 | 1.40 |
| 389 A75 $1.75 multi | 2.00 | 2.00 |

**Souvenir Sheets**

| | | |
|---|---|---|
| 390 Sheet of 3 + label | 3.30 | 3.30 |
| a. A75 95c, like #387 | 1.10 | 1.10 |
| b. A75 95c, like #388 | 1.10 | 1.10 |
| c. A75 95c, like #389 | 1.10 | 1.10 |

***Imperf***

| | | |
|---|---|---|
| 391 A75 $4.20 multi | 4.75 | 4.75 |

Nos. 390-391 have multicolored decorative margins. Sizes: 107x81mm, 65x80mm (No. 391).

Elizabeth II, 60th Birthday — A76

**1986, Apr. 21** **Perf. 14**

| | | |
|---|---|---|
| 392 A76 95c Coronation portrait | 1.15 | 1.15 |

**Souvenir Sheet**

***Perf. 13½***

| | | |
|---|---|---|
| 393 A76 $4.20 Portrait, diff. | 5.00 | 5.00 |

No. 392 printed in sheets of 5 with label picturing U.K. flag and Queen's flag for New Zealand. No. 393 has multicolored margin continuing the design. Size: 58x68mm.

Statue of Liberty, Cent. A77

**1986, June 27** **Photo.** **Perf. 14**

| | | |
|---|---|---|
| 394 A77 $1 Liberty head | 1.15 | 1.15 |
| 395 A77 $2.75 Statue | 3.10 | 3.10 |

**Souvenir Sheet**

***Perf. 13½***

| | | |
|---|---|---|
| 396 Sheet of 2 | 2.80 | 2.80 |
| a. A77 $1.25 like $1 | 1.40 | 1.40 |
| b. A77 $1.25 like $2.75 | 1.40 | 1.40 |

No. 396 has multicolored margin picturing statue under restoration. Size: 91x78mm.

Wedding of Prince Andrew and Sarah Ferguson — A78

**1986, July 23** **Perf. 14**

| | | |
|---|---|---|
| 397 A78 $2 multi | 2.30 | 2.30 |

**Souvenir Sheet**

***Perf. 13½***

| | | |
|---|---|---|
| 398 A78 $5 multi | 5.75 | 5.75 |

No. 397 printed in sheets of 5 plus label picturing Westminster Abbey. No. 398 has multicolored margin picturing abbey. Size: 85x70mm.

### No. 354 Ovptd. with Gold Circle over AUSIPEX Emblem, Black and Gold STAMPEX '86 Emblem.

**1986, Aug. 4** **Photo.** **Perf. 14**

| | | |
|---|---|---|
| 399 Sheet of 3 | 3.35 | 3.35 |
| a. A68 60c + 5c like #351 | 70 | 70 |
| b. A68 96c + 5c like #352 | 1.10 | 1.10 |
| c. A68 $1.40 + 5c like #353 | 1.55 | 1.55 |

STAMPEX '86, Adelaide, Aug. 4-10.

Christmas A79

Paintings by Albrecht Durer: 75c, No. 404a, St. Anne with Virgin and Child. $1.35, No. 404b, Virgin and Child. $1.95, No. 404c, Adoration of the Magi. $2.75, No. 404d, Rosary Festivity.

**1986, Nov. 21** **Litho.** **Perf. 13½**

| | | |
|---|---|---|
| 400 A79 75c multi | 80 | 80 |
| 401 A79 $1.35 multi | 1.45 | 1.45 |
| 402 A79 $1.95 multi | 2.10 | 2.10 |
| 403 A79 $2.75 multi | 2.95 | 2.95 |

**Souvenir Sheet**

| | | |
|---|---|---|
| 404 Sheet of 4 | 7.00 | 7.00 |
| a.-d. A79 $1.65, any single | 1.75 | 1.75 |

No. 404 has multicolored decorative margin. Size: 89x125mm.

### Nos. 247-249 Surcharged in Gold and Black

**1987, Nov. 20** **Photo.** **Perf. 13x12½**

| | | |
|---|---|---|
| 405 A56 $2.50 on 60c No. 247 | 3.00 | 3.00 |
| 406 A56 $2.50 on 80c No. 248 | 3.00 | 3.00 |
| 407 A56 $2.50 on $1.40 No. 249 | 3.00 | 3.00 |

Issued in sheets of 4 with margin inscriptions overprinted with gold bar and "40th Anniversary of the Royal Wedding / 1947-1987" in black; "OVERPRINTED BY NEW ZEALAND GOVERNMENT PRINTER, / WELLINGTON, NOVEMBER 1987" at left.

A80

For unused stamps, more recent issues are valued as never hinged, with the beginning point determined on a country-by-country basis. Notes to show the beginning points are prominently placed in the text.

The Virgin with Garland, by Rubens — A81

Painting details.

**1987, Dec. 10** **Photo.** **Perf. 13x13½**

| | | |
|---|---|---|
| 408 A80 70c UL | 90 | 90 |
| 409 A80 85c UR | 1.10 | 1.10 |
| 410 A80 $1.50 LL | 1.95 | 1.95 |
| 411 A80 $1.85 LR | 2.35 | 2.35 |

**Souvenir Sheets**

| | | |
|---|---|---|
| 412 Sheet of 4 | 5.00 | 5.00 |
| a. A80 95c like No. 408 | 1.25 | 1.25 |
| b. A80 95c like No. 409 | 1.25 | 1.25 |
| c. A80 95c like No. 410 | 1.25 | 1.25 |
| d. A80 95c like No. 411 | 1.25 | 1.25 |

***Perf. 13***

| | | |
|---|---|---|
| 413 A81 $6 multi | 7.75 | 7.75 |

Christmas. No. 412 has intense blue and gold decorative margin. Size: 92x120mm. No. 413 has multicolored margin continuing the painting. Size: 96x85mm.

1988 Summer Olympics, Seoul — A82

Flags of Korea, Aitutaki, ancient and modern events, and Seoul Games emblem or $50 silver coin issued to commemorate the participation of Aitutaki athletes in the Olympics for the 1st time: 70c, No. 418a, Obverse of silver coin, chariot race, running. 85c, Emblem, running, soccer. 95c, Emblem, boxing, handball. $1.40, No. 418b, Reverse of coin, spearmen, women's tennis.

**1988, Aug. 22** **Photo.** **Perf. 14½x15**

| | | |
|---|---|---|
| 414 A82 70c multi | 95 | 95 |
| 415 A82 85c multi | 1.15 | 1.15 |
| 416 A82 95c multi | 1.30 | 1.30 |
| 417 A82 $1.40 multi | 1.90 | 1.90 |

**Souvenir Sheet**

| | | |
|---|---|---|
| 418 Sheet of 2 | 5.50 | 5.50 |
| a.-b. A82 $2 any single | 2.75 | 2.75 |

No. 418 has multicolored inscribed margin picturing Games emblem. Size: 104x102mm.

### Nos. 414-417 Ovptd. with Names of 1988 Olympic Gold Medalists

*a.* "FLORENCE GRIFFTH JOYNER / UNITED STATES / 100 M AND 200 M"
*b.* "GELINDO BORDIN / ITALY / MARATHON"
*c.* "HITOSHI SAITO / JAPAN / JUDO"
*d.* "STEFFI GRAF / WEST GERMANY / WOMEN'S TENNIS"

**1988, Oct. 10** **Litho.** **Perf. 14½x15**

| | | |
|---|---|---|
| 419 A82(a) 70c on No. 414 | 95 | 95 |
| 420 A82(b) 85c on No. 415 | 1.15 | 1.15 |
| 421 A82(c) 95c on No. 416 | 1.30 | 1.30 |
| 422 A82(d) $1.40 on No. 417 | 1.90 | 1.90 |

Griffith is spelled incorrectly on No. 419.

Christmas A83

Paintings by Rembrandt: 55c, *Adoration of the Shepherds* (detail), National Gallery, London. 70c, *Holy Family*, Alte Pinakothek, Munich. 85c, *Presentation in the Temple*, Kunsthalle, Hamburg. 95c, *The Holy Family*, Louvre, Paris. $1.15, *Presentation in the Temple*, diff., Mauritshuis, The Hague. $4.50, *Adoration of the Shepherds* (entire painting).

**1988, Nov. 2 Photo. *Perf. 13½***

*423* A83 55c multi 70 70
*424* A83 70c multi 90 90
*425* A83 85c multi 1.10 1.10
*426* A83 95c multi 1.20 1.20
*427* A83 $1.15 multi 1.50 1.50
*Nos. 423-427 (5)* 5.40 5.40

**Souvenir Sheet**

***Perf. 14***

*428* A83 $4.50 multi 5.75 5.75

No. 428 contains one stamp (size: 52x34mm): multicolored margin continues the painting. Size: 86x101mm.

## SEMI-POSTAL STAMPS

Christmas Type of 1974

Designs: 1c+1c, like No. 104. 5c+1c, like No. 105. 8c+1c, like No. 106. 10c+1c, like No. 107. 25c+1c, like No. 108. 30c+1c, like No. 109.

**1974, Dec. 2 Photo. *Perf. 13½***

*B1* A29 1c + 1c multi 5 5
*B2* A29 5c + 1c multi 20 20
*B3* A29 8c + 1c multi 28 28
*B4* A29 10c + 1c multi 40 40
*B5* A29 25c + 1c multi 90 90
*B6* A29 30c + 1c multi 1.00 1.00
*Nos. B1-B6 (6)* 2.83 2.83

Surtax was for child welfare.

Nos. 117-120 Surcharged in Silver

**1975, Dec. 19 Photo. *Perf. 14x13½***

*B7* A32 Strip of 3 45 45
***a.-c.*** 6c + 1c any single 14 14
*B8* A32 Strip of 3 52 52
***a.-c.*** 7c + 1c any single 16 16
*B9* A32 Strip of 3 1.25 1.25
***a.-c.*** 15c + 1c any single 40 40
*B10* A32 Strip of 3 1.90 1.90
***a.-c.*** 20c + 1c any single 50 50

Christmas 1975. The surtax was for children's activities during holiday season.

Nos. 135-142a Surcharged in Silver

**1976, Nov. 19 Photo. *Perf. 13½x13***

*B11* A36 6c + 1c multi 15 15
*B12* A37 6c + 1c multi 15 15
*B13* A36 7c + 1c multi 15 15
*B14* A37 7c + 1c multi 15 15
*B15* A36 15c + 1c multi 35 35
*B16* A37 15c + 1c multi 35 35
*B17* A36 20c + 1c multi 50 50
*B18* A37 20c + 1c multi 50 50
***a.*** Souvenir sheet of 8 3.50 3.50
*Nos. B11-B18 (8)* 2.30 2.30

Surtax was for child welfare. Stamps of No. B18a each surcharged 2c.

Nos. 152-159a Surcharged in Black

**1977, Nov. 15 *Perf. 13½x14***

*B19* A41 6c + 1c multi 15 15
*B20* A42 6c + 1c multi 15 15
*B21* A41 7c + 1c multi 15 15
*B22* A42 7c + 1c multi 15 15
*B23* A41 15c + 1c multi 35 35
*B24* A42 15c + 1c multi 35 35
*B25* A41 20c + 1c multi 50 50
*B26* A42 20c + 1c multi 50 50
***a.*** Souvenir sheet of 8 3.25 3.25
*Nos. B19-B26 (8)* 2.30 2.30

Surtax was for child welfare. Stamps of No. B26a each surcharged 2c.

Souvenir Sheets

Easter Type of 1978

Paintings: No. B27, like No. 163. No. B28, like No. 164. No. B29, like No. 165.

**1978, Mar. 17 Photo. *Perf. 14***

*B27* A44 50c + 5c multi 90 90
*B28* A44 50c + 5c multi 90 90
*B29* A44 50c + 5c multi 90 90

Easter 1978. Nos. B27-B29 contain one stamp each (33x25mm.); multicolored margin shows entire paintings. Size: 75x58mm.

Souvenir Sheet

Christmas Type of 1978

Designs like Nos. 167-170.

**1978, Dec. 4 Photo. *Perf. 14½x13***

*B30* Sheet of 4 2.00 2.00
***a.*** A46 15c + 2c multi 28 28
***b.*** A46 17c + 2c multi 30 30
***c.*** A46 30c + 2c multi 52 52
***d.*** A46 35c + 2c multi 60 60

Christmas 1978. No. B30 has grayish blue and silver margin showing Nativity. Size: 101x108mm.

Souvenir Sheet

Year of the Child Type

Designs like Nos. 173-175.

**1979, Oct. 1 Photo. *Perf. 14x13½***

*B31* Sheet of 3 2.50 2.50
***a.*** A48 30c + 3c multi 55 55
***b.*** A48 35c + 3c multi 60 60
***c.*** A48 65c + 3c multi 1.10 1.10

International Year of the Child. No. B31 has multicolored margin showing flowers, IYC emblem. Size: 105x80mm.

Souvenir Sheet

Easter Type of 1980

Designs: No. B32 shows entire painting in continuous design. Nos. B32a-B32c similar to Nos. B183-185. Size of Nos. B32a-B32c: 25x50mm.

**1980, Apr. 3 Photo. *Perf. 13x13½***

*B32* Sheet of 3 1.50 1.50
***a.*** A50 20c + 2c multi 35 35
***b.*** A50 30c + 2c multi 50 50
***c.*** A50 35c + 2c multi 60 60

No. B32 has gold and black decorative margin. Size: 93x72mm.

Souvenir Sheet

Christmas Type of 1980

**1980, Nov. 21 Photo. *Perf. 13x13½***

*B33* Sheet of 4 1.75 1.75
***a.*** A53 15c + 2c *like #208* 28 28
***b.*** A53 20c + 2c *like #209* 35 35
***c.*** A53 25c + 2c *like #210* 45 45
***d.*** A53 35c + 2c *like #211* 60 60

No. B33 has gold and green decorative margin. Size: 82½x121mm.

Souvenir Sheet

Easter Type of 1981

**1981, Mar. 31 Photo. *Perf. 13½***

*B34* Sheet of 3 2.25 2.25
***a.*** A54 30c + 2c like #212 50 50
***b.*** A54 40c + 2c like #213 70 70
***c.*** A54 50c + 2c like #214 90 90

No. B34 has gold and lilac decorative margin. Size: 108x60mm.

Royal Wedding Type of 1981

Nos. 247-249 Surcharged.

**1981, Nov. 23 Photo. *Perf. 13x13½***

*B35* A56 60 + 5c multi 1.00 1.00
*B36* A56 80 + 5c multi 1.25 1.25
*B37* A56 $1.40 + 5c multi 2.25 2.25

Intl. Year of the Disabled. Surtax was for the handicapped.

Souvenir Sheet

Soccer Type of 1981

**1981, Nov. 30 *Perf. 14***

*B38* A57 Sheet of 8 multi 2.50 2.50

No. B38 contains Nos. 250-253; gold and black margin. Size: 100x137 mm. Surtax was for local sports.

Nos. 400-404 Surcharged "NOVEMBER/21-24 1986/FIRST VISIT TO SOUTH/PACIFIC" and 10c in Silver.

**1986, Nov. 25 Litho. *Perf. 13½***

*B39* A79 75c + 10c multi 70 70
*B40* A79 $1.35 + 10c multi 1.10 1.10
*B41* A79 $1.95 + 10c multi 1.75 1.75
*B42* A79 $2.75 + 10c multi 2.25 2.25

**Souvenir Sheet**

*B43* Sheet of 4 6.00 6.00
***a.-d.*** A79 $1.65 + 10c on Nos. 404a-404d 1.50 1.50

State visit of Pope John Paul II.

Nos. 394-395, 397 and 400-403 Surcharged "HURRICANE RELIEF / + 50c" in Silver or Black.

**1987, Apr. 29 Litho. *Perf. 13½, 14***

*B44* A79 75c + 50c No. 400 1.50 1.50
*B45* A77 $1 + 50c No. 394 (B) 1.75 1.75
*B46* A79 $1.35 + 50c No. 401 2.25 2.25
*B47* A79 $1.95 + 50c No. 402 3.00 3.00
*B48* A78 $2 + 50c No. 397 3.00 3.00
*B49* A77 $2.75 + 50c No. 395 (B) 4.00 4.00
*B50* A79 $2.75 + 50c No. 403 4.00 4.00
*Nos. B44-B50 (7)* 19.50 19.50

Nos. B39-B42 Surcharged "HURRICANE RELIEF / +50c" in Silver.

**1987, Apr. 29 Litho. *Perf. 13½***

*B51* A79 75c +50c No. B39 1.80 1.80
*B52* A79 $1.35 +50c No. B40 2.60 2.60
*B53* A79 $1.95 +50c No. B41 3.40 3.40
*B54* A79 $2.75 +50c No. B42 4.40 4.40

## AIR POST STAMPS

Capt. Bligh Type of 1974

**1974, Sept. 9 Litho. *Perf. 13***

**Size: 46x26mm.**

*C1* A27 10c *Bligh and "Bounty"* 30 30
*C2* A27 10c *"Bounty" at sea* 30 30
*C3* A27 25c *Bligh and "Bounty"* 65 65
*C4* A27 25c *Chart, 1856* 65 65
*C5* A27 30c *Cook and "Resolution"* 85 85
*C6* A27 30c *Maps* 85 85
*Nos. C1-C6 (6)* 3.60 3.60

Stamps of same denomination printed se-tenant in sheets of 20. See note after No. 101.

## OFFICIAL STAMPS

Nos. 83-90, 92-95, 150-151 Overprinted or Surcharged in Black, Silver or Gold **O.H.M.S.**

**1978-79 Photo. *Perf. 13x13½***

*O1* A25 1c multi 5 5
*O2* A25 2c multi 5 5
*O3* A25 3c multi 5 5
*O4* A25 4c multi (G) 7 7
*O5* A25 5c multi 8 8
*O6* A25 8c multi 14 14
*O7* A25 10c multi 16 16
*O8* A25 15c on 60c multi 25 25
*O9* A25 18c on 60c multi 30 30
*O10* A25 20c multi (G) 35 35
*O11* A40 50c multi 80 80
*O12* A25 60c multi 1.00 1.00
*O13* A25 $1 multi 1.50 1.50
*O14* A26 $2 multi 3.25 3.25
*O15* A40 $4 on $1 multi (S) 6.50 6.50
*O16* A26 $5 multi 8.00 8.00
*Nos. O1-O16 (16)* 22.55 22.55

Overprint on 4c, 20c, $1 diagonal.
Issue dates: Nos. O14-O16, Feb. 20, 1979. Others, Nov. 3, 1978.

Stamps of 1983-84 Ovptd. or Surcharged "O.H.M.S." in Green or Gold (#O29-O32).

***Perf. 14, 13x13½***

**1985, Aug. 9 Litho.**

*O17* A66 2c No. 322 5 5
*O18* A66 5c No. 324 6 6
*O19* A66 10c No. 325 12 12
*O20* A66 12c No. 326 14 14
*O21* A66 18c No. 327 20 20
*O22* A66 20c on 24c No. 328 22 22
*O23* A66 30c No. 329 35 35
*O24* A66 40c on 36c No. 330 45 45
*O25* A66 50c No. 332 55 55
*O26* A66 55c on 48c No. 331 62 62
*O27* A66 60c No. 333 68 68
*O28* A66 65c on 72c No. 334 72 72
*O29* A66 75c on 48c No. 276 85 85
*O30* A66 75c on 48c No. 277 85 85
*O31* A66 75c on 48c No. 278 85 85
*O32* A66 75c on 48c No. 279 85 85
*O33* A66 80c on 96c No. 335 90 90
*Nos. O17-O33 (17)* 8.46 8.46

Nos. O29-O32 se-tenant in block of 4.

Nos. 338-341 Ovptd. "O.H.M.S." in Metallic Green.

**1986, Oct. 1 Litho. *Perf. 14***

*O34* A66 $3 multi 3.10 3.10
*O35* A66 $4.20 multi 4.35 4.35
*O36* A66 $5.60 multi 5.80 5.80
*O37* A66 $9.60 multi 10.00 10.00

Nos. 336-337 Ovptd. and 246C Surcharged "O.H.M.S." in Metallic Green or Blue.

***Perf. 14, 13½ ($14)***

**1988, June 15 Photo.**

*O38* A66 $1.20 No. 336 1.65 1.65
*O39* A66 $2.10 No. 337 2.85 2.85
*O40* A55 $14 on $4 No. 246C (B) 19.00 19.00

# AJMAN

LOCATION — Oman Peninsula, Arabia, on Persian Gulf.
GOVT. — Sheikdom under British Protection.
AREA — 100 sq. mi.
POP. — 4,400.
CAPITAL — Ajman.

Ajman is one of six Persian Gulf sheikdoms to join the United Arab Emirates, which proclaimed its independence Dec. 2, 1971. See United Arab Emirates.

100 Naye Paise = 1 Rupee

**Catalogue values for all unused stamps in this country are for Never Hinged items.**

Sheik Rashid bin Humaid al Naimi and Arab Stallion A1

Designs: 2np, 50np, Regal angelfish. 3np, 70np, Camel. 4np, 1r, Angelfish. 5np, 1.50r, Green turtle. 10np, 2r, Jewelfish. 15np, 3r, White storks. 20np, 5r, White-eyed gulls. 30np, 10r, Lanner falcon. 40np as 1np.

**Photo. & Litho.**

**1964 Unwmk. *Perf. 14***

**Size: 35x22mm.**

*1* A1 1np gold & multi 5 5
*2* A1 2np gold & multi 5 5
*3* A1 3np gold & multi 5 5
*4* A1 4np gold & multi 5 5
*5* A1 5np gold & multi 5 5
*6* A1 10np gold & multi 5 5
*7* A1 15np gold & multi 5 5
*8* A1 20np gold & multi 5 5
*9* A1 30np gold & multi 8 5

**Size: 42x27mm.**

*10* A1 40np gold & multi 10 5
*11* A1 50np gold & multi 10 5
*12* A1 70np gold & multi 14 5
*13* A1 1r gold & multi 24 7
*14* A1 1.50r gold & multi 32 10
*15* A1 2r gold & multi 45 14

**Size: 53x33½mm.**

*16* A1 3r gold & multi 75 20
*17* A1 5r gold & multi 1.10 32
*18* A1 10r gold & multi 2.75 70
*Nos. 1-18 (18)* 6.43 2.13

Dates of issue: Nos. 1-9, June 20; Nos. 10-15, Sept. 7; Nos. 16-18, Nov. 4.

Pres. and Mrs. John F. Kennedy with Caroline — A2

Designs (Pres. Kennedy): 10np, As a boy in football uniform. 15np, Diving. 50np, As navy lieutenant, receiving Navy and Marine Corps Medal from Capt. Frederic L. Conklin. 1r, Sailing with Jacqueline Kennedy. 2r, With Eleanor Roosevelt. 5r, With Lyndon B. Johnson and Hubert H. Humphrey. 10r, Portrait.

**1964, Dec. 15 Photo. *Perf. 13½x14***

| | | | | |
|---|---|---|---|---|
| *19* | A2 | 10np grn & red lil | 5 | 5 |
| *20* | A2 | 15np Prus bl & vio | 5 | 5 |
| *21* | A2 | 50np org brn & dk bl | 14 | 5 |
| *22* | A2 | 1r brn & Prus grn | 26 | 7 |
| *23* | A2 | 2r red lil & dp ol | 55 | 14 |
| *24* | A2 | 3r grn & red brn | 80 | 20 |
| *25* | A2 | 5r vio & brn | 1.40 | 32 |
| *26* | A2 | 10r dk bl & red brn | 2.75 | 70 |
| | | *Nos. 19-26 (8)* | 6.00 | 1.58 |

Issued in memory of John F. Kennedy (1917-63). A souvenir sheet contains one each of Nos. 23-26. Dark green border and inscription. Size: 105x140mm.

Runners at Start — A3

Designs: 10np, 1.50r, Boxing. 25np, 2r, Judo. 50np, 5r, Gymnast on vaulting horse. 1r, 3r, Sailing yacht.

**1965, Jan. 12 Photo. *Perf. 13½x14***

| | | | | |
|---|---|---|---|---|
| *27* | A3 | 5np red brn, brt pink & Prus grn | 5 | 5 |
| *28* | A3 | 10np dk ol grn, bl gray & red brn | 5 | 5 |
| *29* | A3 | 15np dk vio, grn & sep | 5 | 5 |
| *30* | A3 | 25np bl sal pink & blk | 7 | 5 |
| *31* | A3 | 50np mar, bl & ind | 14 | 5 |
| *32* | A3 | 1r dk grn, lil & ultra | 26 | 10 |
| *33* | A3 | 1.50r lil, grn & brn | 40 | 16 |
| *34* | A3 | 2r red org, bis & dk bl | 55 | 20 |
| *35* | A3 | 3r dk brn, grnsh bl & lil | 80 | 26 |
| *36* | A3 | 5r grn, yel & red brn | 1.40 | 40 |
| | | *Nos. 27-36 (10)* | 3.77 | 1.37 |

Issued to commemorate the 18th Olympic Games, Tokyo, Oct. 10-25, 1964. A souvenir sheet contains four stamps similar to Nos. 33-36 in changed colors. Maroon marginal inscription. Size: 120x100mm.

Stanley Gibbons Catalogue, 1865, and U.S. No. 1X2 A4

Designs: 10np, Austria, Scarlet Mercury 1856. 15np, British Guiana 1c, 1856. 25np, Canada 12p, 1851. 50np, Hawaii 2c, 1851. 1r, Mauritius 2p, 1847. 3r, Switzerland, Geneva 10c, 1843. 5r, Tuscany 31, 1860. 5np, 15np, 50np and 3r show first edition of Stanley Gibbons Catalogue; 10np, 25np, 1r and 5r show 1965 Elizabethan Catalogue.

**1965, May 6 Unwmk. *Perf. 13***

| | | | | |
|---|---|---|---|---|
| *37* | A4 | 5np gold, blk, buff & bl | 5 | 5 |
| *38* | A4 | 10np gold, blk, Prus grn & org | 5 | 5 |
| *39* | A4 | 15np gold, blk, ol & dp car | 5 | 5 |
| *40* | A4 | 25np gold, blk & Prus grn | 6 | 5 |
| *41* | A4 | 50np gold, blk, buff, car & bl | 14 | 7 |
| *42* | A4 | 1r gold, blk, buff, ocher & bl | 26 | 10 |
| *43* | A4 | 3r gold, blk, buff, car & yel grn | 80 | 26 |
| *a.* | | Souv. sheet of four | 1.25 | |
| *44* | A4 | 5r gold, blk, brn & ocher | 1.40 | 40 |
| *a.* | | Souv. sheet of four | 1.65 | |
| | | *Nos. 37-44 (8)* | 2.81 | 1.03 |

Issued to commemorate the Gibbons Catalogue Centenary Exhibition, London, Feb. 17-20. Nos. 43a and 44a commemorate the 125th anniversary of the first postage stamp. No. 43a contains one each of Nos. 38-39 and 42-43 and has pale green margin; No. 44a contains one each of Nos. 37, 40-41 and 44 and has pale lilac margin. Marginal inscriptions on both sheets are in black, gold and carmine rose, and margins contain pictures of Sir Rowland Hill and the Penny Black. Sheets exist imperf. Size: 125x99mm.

Stamps of Ajman were replaced in 1972 by those of United Arab Emirates.

### AIR POST STAMPS

Type of Regular Issue, 1964

Designs: 15np, Arab stallion. 25np, Regal angelfish. 35np, Camel. 50np, Angelfish. 75np, Green turtle. 1r, Jewelfish. 2r, White storks. 3r, White-eyed gulls. 5r, Lanner falcon.

**Photo. & Litho.**

**1965 Unwmk. *Perf. 14***

**Size: 42x25½mm.**

| | | | | |
|---|---|---|---|---|
| *C1* | A1 | 15np sil & multi | 5 | 5 |
| *C2* | A1 | 25np sil & multi | 7 | 5 |
| *C3* | A1 | 35np sil & multi | 10 | 5 |
| *C4* | A1 | 50np sil & multi | 14 | 5 |
| *C5* | A1 | 75np sil & multi | 16 | 7 |
| *C6* | A1 | 1r sil & multi | 24 | 5 |

**Size: 53x33½mm.**

| | | | | |
|---|---|---|---|---|
| *C7* | A1 | 2r sil & multi | 48 | 14 |
| *C8* | A1 | 3r sil & multi | 70 | 20 |
| *C9* | A1 | 5r sil & multi | 1.10 | 32 |
| | | *Nos. C1-C9 (9)* | 3.04 | 98 |

Issue dates: Nos. C1-C9, Dec 18.

### AIR POST OFFICIAL STAMPS

Type of Regular Issue, 1964

Designs: 75np, Jewelfish. 2r, White storks. 3r, White-eyed gulls. 5r, Lanner falcon.

**Photo. & Litho.**

**1965, Dec. 18 Unwmk. *Perf. 14***

**Size: 42x25½mm.**

| | | | | |
|---|---|---|---|---|
| *CO1* | A1 | 75np gold & multi | 18 | 5 |

**Size: 53x33½mm.**

| | | | | |
|---|---|---|---|---|
| *CO2* | A1 | 2r gold & multi | 50 | 14 |
| *CO3* | A1 | 3r gold & multi | 75 | 20 |
| *CO4* | A1 | 5r gold & multi | 1.25 | 32 |

### OFFICIAL STAMPS

Type of Regular Issue, 1964

Designs: 25np, Arab stallion. 40np, Regal angelfish. 50np, Camel. 75np, Angelfish. 1r, Green turtle.

**Photo. & Litho.**

**1965, Dec. 1 Unwmk. *Perf. 14***

**Size: 42x25½mm.**

| | | | | |
|---|---|---|---|---|
| *O1* | A1 | 25np gold & multi | 7 | 5 |
| *O2* | A1 | 40np gold & multi | 10 | 5 |
| *O3* | A1 | 50np gold & multi | 14 | 5 |
| *O4* | A1 | 75np gold & multi | 20 | 5 |
| *O5* | A1 | 1r gold & multi | 26 | 7 |
| | | *Nos. O1-O5 (5)* | 77 | 27 |

## ANGUILLA

LOCATION — In the West Indies southeast of Puerto Rico.
GOVT. — British territory.
AREA — 60 sq. mi.
POP. — 6,500 (est. 1980).
CAPITAL — The Valley.

Anguilla separated unilaterally from the Associated State of St. Kitts-Nevis-Anguilla in 1967, formalized in 1980 following direct United Kingdom intervention some years before. A British Commissioner exercises executive authority.

100 Cents = 1 Dollar

**Catalogue values for all unused stamps in this country are for Never Hinged items.**

St. Kitts-Nevis Nos. 145-160 Overprinted

On Type A14

Independent Anguilla

On Type A15

Independent Anguilla

**Wmk. 314**

**1967, Sept. 4 Photo. *Perf. 14***

| | | | | |
|---|---|---|---|---|
| *1* | A14 | ½c bl & dk brn | 12.50 | 12.50 |
| *2* | A15 | 1c multi | 10.00 | 7.50 |
| *3* | A14 | 2c multi | 11.50 | 6.00 |
| *4* | A14 | 3c multi | 12.00 | 9.00 |
| *5* | A15 | 4c multi | 12.50 | 8.00 |
| *6* | A15 | 5c multi | 50.00 | 22.50 |
| *7* | A15 | 6c multi | 20.00 | 10.00 |
| *8* | A15 | 10c multi | 12.50 | 9.00 |
| *9* | A14 | 15c multi | 27.50 | 9.50 |
| *10* | A15 | 20c multi | 45.00 | 15.00 |
| *11* | A14 | 25c multi | 37.50 | 17.50 |
| *12* | A15 | 50c multi | *750.00* | *300.00* |
| *13* | A14 | 60c multi | *2,500.* | *1,125.* |
| *14* | A14 | $1 multi | *850.00* | *300.00* |
| *15* | A15 | $2.50 multi | *675.00* | *225.00* |
| *16* | A14 | $5 multi | *625.00* | *210.00* |
| | | *Nos. 1-16 (16)* | 5,651. | 2,286. |

Mahogany Tree, The Quarter — A1

Designs: 2c, Sombrero Lighthouse. 3c, St. Mary's Church. 4c, Valley Police Station. 5c, Old Plantation House, Mt. Fortune. 6c, Valley Post Office. 10c, Methodist Church, West End. 15c, Wall-Blake Airport. 20c, Plane over Sandy Ground. 25c, Island Harbor. 40c, Map of Anguilla. 60c, Hermit crab and starfish. $1, Hibiscus. $2.50, Coconut harvest. $5, Spiny lobster.

***Perf. 12½x13***

**1967-68 Litho. Unwmk.**

| | | | | |
|---|---|---|---|---|
| *17* | A1 | 1c org & multi | 5 | 5 |
| *18* | A1 | 2c gray grn & blk | 6 | 6 |
| *19* | A1 | 3c emer & blk | 5 | 5 |
| *20* | A1 | 4c brt bl & blk | 6 | 6 |
| *21* | A1 | 5c lt bl & multi | 8 | 8 |
| *22* | A1 | 6c ver & blk | 12 | 12 |
| *23* | A1 | 10c multi | 18 | 18 |
| *24* | A1 | 15c multi | 22 | 22 |
| *25* | A1 | 20c multi | 30 | 30 |
| *26* | A1 | 25c multi | 38 | 38 |
| *27* | A1 | 40c bl & multi | 60 | 60 |
| *28* | A1 | 60c yel & multi | 90 | 90 |
| *29* | A1 | $1 lt grn & multi | 1.75 | 1.75 |
| *30* | A1 | $2.50 multi | 4.25 | 4.25 |
| *31* | A1 | $5 multi | 8.00 | 8.00 |
| | | *Nos. 17-31 (15)* | 17.00 | 17.00 |

Issue dates: 1c, 5c, 10c, 20c, 25c, 40c, Nov. 27, 1967; 3c, 4c, 15c, 60c, $1, $5, Feb. 10, 1968; 2c, 6c, $2.50, Mar. 21, 1968.

Sailboats A2

Designs: 15c, Boat building. 25c, Schoone Warspite. 40c, Yacht Atlantic Star.

**1968, May 11 *Perf. 1***

| | | | | |
|---|---|---|---|---|
| *32* | A2 | 10c rose & multi | 35 | 3 |
| *33* | A2 | 15c ol & multi | 60 | 6 |
| *34* | A2 | 25c lil rose & multi | 90 | 9 |
| *35* | A2 | 40c dl bl & multi | 1.50 | 1.5 |

Purple-throated Carib — A3

Girl Guide Badge — A4

Anguillan Birds: 15c, Bananaquit. 25c, Black-necked stilt (horiz.). 40c, Royal tern (horiz.).

**1968, July 8**

| | | | | |
|---|---|---|---|---|
| *36* | A3 | 10c dl yel & multi | 35 | 25 |
| *37* | A3 | 15c yel grn & multi | 50 | 38 |
| *38* | A3 | 25c multi | 1.50 | 85 |
| *39* | A3 | 40c multi | 1.65 | 1.50 |

***Perf. 13x13½, 13½x13***

**1968, Oct. 14**

Designs: 10c, Girl Guide badge (horiz.). 25c, Badge and Headquarters (horiz.). 40c, Merit Badges.

| | | | | |
|---|---|---|---|---|
| *40* | A4 | 10c lt grn & multi | 20 | 20 |
| *41* | A4 | 15c lt bl & multi | 30 | 30 |
| *42* | A4 | 25c multi | 60 | 60 |
| *43* | A4 | 40c multi | 85 | 85 |

Anguillan Girl Guides, 35th anniversary.

Three Kings A5

Designs: 10c, Three Kings seeing Star (vert.). 15c, Holy Family (vert.). 40c, Shepherds seeing Star. 50c, Holy Family and donkey.

**1968, Nov. 18**

| | | | | |
|---|---|---|---|---|
| *44* | A5 | 1c lil rose & blk | 8 | 8 |
| *45* | A5 | 10c bl & blk | 22 | 22 |
| *46* | A5 | 15c brn & blk | 48 | 48 |
| *47* | A5 | 40c brt ultra & blk | 1.10 | 1.10 |
| *48* | A5 | 50c grn & blk | 1.60 | 1.60 |
| | | *Nos. 44-48 (5)* | 3.48 | 3.48 |

Christmas 1968.

Bagging Salt — A6

Salt Industry: 15c, Packing salt. 40c, Salt pond. 50c, Loading salt.

**1969, Jan. 4 *Perf. 13***

| | | | | |
|---|---|---|---|---|
| *49* | A6 | 10c red & multi | 16 | 16 |
| *50* | A6 | 15c lt bl & multi | 28 | 28 |
| *51* | A6 | 40c emer & multi | 75 | 75 |
| *52* | A6 | 50c pur & multi | 90 | 90 |

Nos. 17-31 Overprinted: "INDEPENDENCE/JANUARY, 1969"

**1969, Jan. 9 *Perf. 12½x13***

| | | | | |
|---|---|---|---|---|
| *53* | A1 | 1c org & multi | 5 | 5 |
| *54* | A1 | 2c gray grn & blk | 5 | 5 |
| *55* | A1 | 3c emer & blk | 5 | 5 |
| *56* | A1 | 4c brt bl & blk | 7 | 7 |
| *57* | A1 | 5c lt bl & multi | 8 | 8 |
| *58* | A1 | 6c ver & blk | 10 | 10 |
| *59* | A1 | 10c multi | 16 | 16 |
| *60* | A1 | 15c multi | 25 | 25 |
| *61* | A1 | 20c multi | 32 | 32 |
| *62* | A1 | 25c multi | 40 | 40 |

63 A1 40c bl & multi 55 55
64 A1 60c yel & multi 80 80
65 A1 $1 lt grn & multi 1.40 1.40
66 A1 $2.50 multi 3.50 3.50
67 A1 $5 multi 7.00 7.00
*Nos. 53-67 (15)* 14.78 14.78

Crucifixion, School of Quentin Massays — A7

Painting: 40c, The Last Supper, ascribed to Roberti.

**1969, Mar. 31** **Litho.** ***Perf. 13½***
68 A7 25c multi 50 50
69 A7 40c multi 90 90

Easter 1969.

Amaryllis A8

**1969, June 10** ***Perf. 14***
70 A8 10c *shown* 20 20
71 A8 15c *Bougainvillea* 35 35
72 A8 40c *Hibiscus* 80 80
73 A8 50c *Cattleya orchid* 1.10 1.10

Turban and Star Shells A9

Sea Shells: 15c, Spiny oysters. 40c, Scotch, royal and smooth bonnets. 50c, Triton trumpet.

**1969, Sept. 22**
74 A9 10c multi 35 35
75 A9 15c multi 50 50
76 A9 40c multi 1.10 1.10
77 A9 50c multi 1.50 1.50

Nos. 17, 25-28 Overprinted "CHRISTMAS 1969" and Various Christmas Designs.

**1969, Oct. 27** ***Perf. 12½x13***
78 A1 1c org & multi 18 8
79 A1 20c multi 70 45
80 A1 25c multi 90 75
81 A1 40c bl & multi 1.75 1.40
82 A1 60c yel & multi 3.75 2.75
*Nos. 78-82 (5)* 7.28 5.43

Christmas 1969.

Red Goatfish A10

Designs: 15c, Blue-striped grunts. 40c, Mutton grouper. 50c, Banded butterfly-fish.

**1969, Dec. 1** ***Perf. 14***
83 A10 10c multi 28 28
84 A10 15c multi 40 40
85 A10 40c multi 1.40 1.40
86 A10 50c multi 1.65 1.65

Morning Glory — A11

Flowers: 15c, Blue petrea. 40c, Hibiscus. 50c, Flamboyant.

**1970, Feb. 23**
87 A11 10c multi 25 25
88 A11 15c multi 40 40
89 A11 40c multi 1.40 1.40
90 A11 50c multi 1.75 1.75

The Way to Calvary, by Tiepolo — A12

Paintings: 20c, Crucifixion, by Masaccio (vert.). 40c, Descent from the Cross, by Rosso Fiorentino (vert.). 60c, Jesus Carrying the Cross, by Murillo.

**1970, Mar. 26** ***Perf. 13½***
91 A12 10c multi 20 20
92 A12 20c multi 35 35
93 A12 40c multi 75 75
94 A12 60c multi 1.10 1.10

Easter 1970.

Anguilla Map, Scout Badge A13

Designs: 15c, Cub Scouts practicing first aid. 40c, Monkey bridge. 50c, Scout Headquarters, The Valley, and Lord Baden-Powell.

**1970, Aug. 10** ***Perf. 13***
95 A13 10c multi 25 25
96 A13 15c multi 40 40
97 A13 40c multi 1.00 1.00
98 A13 50c multi 1.25 1.25

Anguilla Boy Scouts, 40th anniversary.

Boat Building A14

Designs: 2c, Road construction. 3c, Blowing Point dock. 4c, Radio announcer. 5c, Cottage Hospital extension. 6c, Valley secondary school. 10c, Hotel extension. 15c, Sandy Ground. 20c, Supermarket and movie house. 25c, Bananas and mangoes. 40c, Wall-Blake airport. 60c, Sandy Ground jetty. $1, Administration building. $2.50, Cow and calf. $5, Sandy Hill Bay.

**1970, Nov. 23** **Litho.** ***Perf. 14***
99 A14 1c multi 5 5
100 A14 2c multi 5 5
101 A14 3c multi 5 5
102 A14 4c multi 6 6
103 A14 5c multi 8 8
104 A14 6c multi 12 12
105 A14 10c multi 22 22
106 A14 15c multi 30 30
107 A14 20c multi 35 35
108 A14 25c multi 42 42
109 A14 40c multi 75 75
110 A14 60c multi 1.10 1.10
111 A14 $1 multi 1.75 1.75
112 A14 $2.50 multi 4.50 4.50
113 A14 $5 multi 9.00 9.00
*Nos. 99-113 (15)* 18.80 18.80

Adoration of the Shepherds, by Guido Reni — A15

Paintings: 20c, Virgin and Child, by Benozzo Gozzoli. 25c, Nativity, by Botticelli. 40c, Santa Margherita Madonna, by Mazzola. 50c, Adoration of the Kings, by Tiepolo.

**1970, Dec. 11** ***Perf. 13½***
114 A15 1c multi 5 5
115 A15 20c multi 35 35
116 A15 25c multi 40 40
117 A15 40c multi 60 60
118 A15 50c multi 65 65
*Nos. 114-118 (5)* 2.05 2.05

Christmas 1970.

Angels Weeping over the Dead Christ, by Guercino — A16

Paintings: 10c, Ecce Homo, by Correggio (vert.). 15c, Christ Appearing to St. Peter, by Carracci (vert.). 50c, The Supper at Emmaus, by Caravaggio.

**1971, Mar. 29**
119 A16 10c pink & multi 18 18
120 A16 15c lt bl & multi 30 30
121 A16 40c yel grn & multi 75 75
122 A16 50c vio & multi 90 90

Easter 1971.

Hypolimnas Misippus A17

Butterflies: 15c, Junonia lavinia. 40c, Agraulis vanillae. 50c, Danaus plexippus.

**1971, June 21** ***Perf. 14x14½***
123 A17 10c multi 70 70
124 A17 15c multi 90 90
125 A17 40c multi 1.75 1.75
126 A17 50c multi 2.25 2.25

Magnanime and Aimable in Battle — A18

Ships: 15c, HMS Duke and Agamemnon against Glorieux. 25c, HMS Formidable and Namur against Ville de Paris. 40c, HMS Canada. 50c, HMS St. Albans and wreck of Hector.

**1971, Aug. 30** **Litho.** ***Perf. 14***
127 A18 10c multi 35 35
128 A18 15c multi 60 60
129 A18 25c multi 1.25 1.25
130 A18 40c multi 2.00 2.00
131 A18 50c multi 2.75 2.75
Strip of 5 7.25 7.25

West Indies sea battles. Nos. 127-131 printed se-tenant.

Ansidei Madonna, by Raphael — A19

Paintings: 25c, Mystic Nativity, by Botticelli. 40c, Virgin and Child, School of Seville, inscribed Murillo. 50c, Madonna of the Iris, ascribed to Dürer.

**1971, Nov. 29** ***Perf. 14x13½***
132 A19 20c grn & multi 40 40
133 A19 25c bl & multi 55 55
134 A19 40c lil rose & multi 90 90
135 A19 50c vio & multi 1.10 1.10

Christmas 1971.

Map of Anguilla and St. Maarten, by Jefferys, 1775 A20

Jesus Buffeted, Stained-glass Window A21

Maps of Anguilla by: 15c, Samuel Fahlberg, 1814. 40c, Thomas Jefferys, 1775 (horiz.). 50c, Capt. E. Barnett, 1847 (horiz.).

***Perf. 14x13½, 13½x14***

**1972, Jan. 24**
136 A20 10c lt bl & multi 22 22
137 A20 15c lt grn & multi 35 35
138 A20 40c lt grn & multi 90 90
139 A20 50c lt ultra & multi 1.10 1.10

**1972, Mar. 14** ***Perf. 14x13½***

Stained-glass Windows (19th Century), Bray Church: 15c, Jesus Carrying the Cross. 25c, Crucifixion. 40c, Descent from the Cross. 50c, Burial.

140 A21 10c multi 25 25
141 A21 15c multi 42 42
142 A21 25c multi 60 60
143 A21 40c multi 1.10 1.10
144 A21 50c multi 1.25 1.25
Strip of 5 3.75 3.75

Easter 1972. Nos. 140-144 printed se-tenant.

Spear Fishing A22

Sandy Ground A23

**1972-75** *Perf. 13½*

| No. | Type | Value | Design | Unused | Used |
|---|---|---|---|---|---|
| 145 | A22 | 1c | *shown* | 5 | 5 |
| 146 | A23 | 2c | *Loblolly tree* (vert.) | 5 | 5 |
| 147 | A23 | 3c | *shown* | 5 | 5 |
| 148 | A23 | 4c | *Ferry, Blowing Point* (vert.) | 6 | 6 |
| 149 | A23 | 5c | *Agriculture* | 7 | 7 |
| 150 | A23 | 6c | *St. Mary's Church* (vert.) | 8 | 8 |
| 151 | A23 | 10c | *St. Gerard's Church* | 16 | 16 |
| 152 | A22 | 15c | *Cottage Hospital* | 25 | 25 |
| 153 | A23 | 20c | *Public Library* | 28 | 28 |
| 154 | A23 | 25c | *Sunset, Blowing Point* | 40 | 40 |
| 155 | A22 | 40c | *Boat building* | 60 | 60 |
| 156 | A22 | 60c | *Hibiscus* | 1.00 | 1.00 |
| 157 | A23 | $1 | *Man-o-war bird* | 1.90 | 1.90 |
| 158 | A23 | $2.50 | *Frangipani* | 4.50 | 4.50 |
| 159 | A23 | $5 | *Brown pelican* | 9.00 | 9.00 |
| 160 | A22 | $10 | *Green-back turtle* | 22.50 | 22.50 |
| | | | *Nos. 145-160 (16)* | 40.95 | 40.95 |

Issue dates: $10, May 20, 1975; others Oct. 30, 1972.

Common Design Types pictured in section before Great Britain.

### Silver Wedding Issue, 1972
Common Design Type

Design: Queen Elizabeth II, Prince Philip, schooner and dolphin.

*Perf. 14x14½*

**1972, Nov. 20** **Photo.** **Wmk. 314**

| No. | Type | Value | Design | Unused | Used |
|---|---|---|---|---|---|
| 161 | CD324 | 25c | ol & multi | 2.00 | 2.00 |
| 162 | CD324 | 40c | mar & multi | 2.50 | 2.50 |

Flight into Egypt — A24

*Perf. 13½*

**1972, Dec. 4** **Litho.** **Unwmk.**

| No. | Type | Value | Design | Unused | Used |
|---|---|---|---|---|---|
| 163 | A24 | 1c | *shown* | 5 | 5 |
| 164 | A24 | 20c | *Star of Bethlehem* | 35 | 35 |
| 165 | A24 | 25c | *Nativity* | 40 | 40 |
| 166 | A24 | 40c | *Three Kings* | 70 | 70 |
| 167 | A24 | 50c | *Adoration of the Kings* | 1.00 | 1.00 |
| | | | Strip of 4 | 2.75 | 2.75 |
| | | | *Nos. 163-167 (5)* | 2.50 | 2.50 |

Christmas 1972. Nos. 164-167 printed vertically se-tenant.

Betrayal of Jesus — A25

**1973, Mar. 26**
**Multicolored, Black Bottom Panel**

| No. | Type | Value | Design | Unused | Used |
|---|---|---|---|---|---|
| 168 | A25 | 1c | *shown* | 5 | 5 |
| 169 | A25 | 10c | *Man of Sorrow* | 18 | 18 |
| 170 | A25 | 20c | *Jesus Carrying Cross* | 35 | 35 |
| 171 | A25 | 25c | *Crucifixion* | 40 | 40 |
| 172 | A25 | 40c | *Descent from Cross* | 70 | 70 |
| 173 | A25 | 50c | *Resurrection* | 90 | 90 |
| | | a | Souvenir sheet of 6 | 2.75 | 2.75 |
| | | | Strip of 5 | 2.75 | 2.75 |
| | | | *Nos. 168-173 (6)* | 2.58 | 2.58 |

Easter 1973. Nos. 169-173 printed vertically se-tenant. No. 173a contains 6 stamps similar to Nos. 168-173 with bottom panel in lilac rose. Gray and green margin showing various churches, black inscription. Size: 140x140mm.

Santa Maria A26

**1973, Sept. 10**

| No. | Type | Value | Design | Unused | Used |
|---|---|---|---|---|---|
| 174 | A26 | 1c | *shown* | 5 | 5 |
| 175 | A26 | 20c | *Old West Indies map* | 45 | 45 |
| 176 | A26 | 40c | *Map of voyages* | 1.10 | 1.10 |
| 177 | A26 | 70c | *Sighting land* | 1.75 | 1.75 |
| 178 | A26 | $1.20 | *Columbus landing* | 3.75 | 3.75 |
| | | a | Souvenir sheet of 5 | 7.50 | 7.50 |
| | | | Strip of 4 | 7.50 | 7.50 |
| | | | *Nos. 174-178 (5)* | 7.10 | 7.10 |

Discovery of West Indies by Christopher Columbus. Nos. 175-178 printed horizontally se-tenant. No. 178a contains one each of Nos. 174-178 and label giving design description; gray decorative margin. Size: 193x92mm.

### Princess Anne's Wedding Issue
Common Design Type

**1973, Nov. 14** **Wmk. 314** *Perf. 13½*

| No. | Type | Value | Design | Unused | Used |
|---|---|---|---|---|---|
| 179 | CD325 | 60c | bl grn & multi | 45 | 45 |
| 180 | CD325 | $1.20 | lil & multi | 90 | 90 |

Wedding of Princess Anne and Capt. Mark Phillips, Nov. 14, 1973.

Adoration of the Shepherds, by Guido Reni — A27

Paintings: 10c, Virgin and Child, by Filippino Lippi. 20c, Nativity, by Meester Van de Brunswijkse Diptiek. 25c, Madonna of the Meadow, by Bellini. 40c, Virgin and Child, by Cima. 50c, Adoration of the Kings, by Geertgen Tot Sint Jans.

**1973, Dec. 2** **Unwmk.**

| No. | Type | Value | Design | Unused | Used |
|---|---|---|---|---|---|
| 181 | A27 | 1c | multi | 5 | 5 |
| 182 | A27 | 10c | multi | 20 | 20 |
| 183 | A27 | 20c | multi | 35 | 35 |
| 184 | A27 | 25c | multi | 40 | 40 |
| 185 | A27 | 40c | multi | 70 | 70 |
| 186 | A27 | 50c | multi | 90 | 90 |
| | | a | Souvenir sheet of 6 | 2.75 | 2.75 |
| | | | Strip of 5 | 2.75 | 2.75 |
| | | | *Nos. 181-186 (6)* | 2.60 | 2.60 |

Christmas 1973. Nos. 182-186 printed horizontally se-tenant. No. 186a contains one each of Nos. 181-186; multicolored decorative margin. Size: 148x148mm.

*Anguilla stamps can be mounted in Scott's annually supplemented British Leeward Islands Album.*

Crucifixion, by Raphael — A28

Details from Crucifixion by Raphael: 15c, Virgin Mary and St. John. 20c, The Two Marys. 25c, Left Angel. 40c, Right Angel. $1, Christ on the Cross.

**1974, Mar. 30**

| No. | Type | Value | Design | Unused | Used |
|---|---|---|---|---|---|
| 187 | A28 | 1c | lil & multi | 5 | 5 |
| 188 | A28 | 15c | gray & multi | 20 | 20 |
| 189 | A28 | 20c | sal & multi | 28 | 28 |
| 190 | A28 | 25c | yel grn & multi | 35 | 35 |
| 191 | A28 | 40c | org & multi | 48 | 48 |
| 192 | A28 | $1 | lt bl & multi | 1.25 | 1.25 |
| | | a | Souvenir sheet of 6 | 2.75 | 2.75 |
| | | | Strip of 5 | 2.75 | 2.75 |
| | | | *Nos. 187-192 (6)* | 2.61 | 2.61 |

Easter 1974. Nos. 188-192 printed vertically se-tenant. No. 192a contains one each of Nos. 187-192; light gray margin with white inscription. Size: 123x140mm.

Churchill Making Victory Sign — A29

Designs: 20c, Roosevelt, Churchill, American and British flags. 25c, Churchill broadcasting during the war. 40c, Blenheim Palace. 60c, Churchill Statue and Parliament. $1.20, Chartwell.

**1974, June 24**

| No. | Type | Value | Design | Unused | Used |
|---|---|---|---|---|---|
| 193 | A29 | 1c | multi | 5 | 5 |
| 194 | A29 | 20c | multi | 20 | 20 |
| 195 | A29 | 25c | multi | 25 | 25 |
| 196 | A29 | 40c | multi | 40 | 40 |
| 197 | A29 | 60c | multi | 60 | 60 |
| 198 | A29 | $1.20 | multi | 1.25 | 1.25 |
| | | a | Souvenir sheet of 6 | 3.00 | 3.00 |
| | | | Strip of 5 | 2.75 | 2.75 |
| | | | *Nos. 193-198 (6)* | 2.75 | 2.75 |

Centenary of birth of Sir Winston Spencer Churchill (1874-1965). Nos. 194-198 printed horizontally se-tenant. No. 198a contains one each of Nos. 193-198; black marginal inscription and decoration. Size: 192x95mm.

UPU Emblem, Map of Anguilla — A30

**1974, Aug. 27**

| No. | Type | Value | Design | Unused | Used |
|---|---|---|---|---|---|
| 199 | A30 | 1c | blk & ultra | 5 | 5 |
| 200 | A30 | 20c | blk & org | 22 | 22 |
| 201 | A30 | 25c | blk & yel | 25 | 25 |
| 202 | A30 | 40c | blk & brt lil | 50 | 50 |
| 203 | A30 | 60c | blk & lt grn | 70 | 70 |
| 204 | A30 | $1.20 | blk & bl | 1.25 | 1.25 |
| | | a | Souvenir sheet of 6 | 3.50 | 3.50 |
| | | | Strip of 5 | 3.25 | 3.25 |
| | | | *Nos. 199-204 (6)* | 2.97 | 2.97 |

Centenary of Universal Postal Union. Nos. 200-204 printed horizontally se-tenant. No. 204a contains one each of Nos. 199-204 with second row (40c, 60c, $1.20) perf. 15 at bottom. Light green margin with black inscription. Size: 195x95mm.

Fishermen Seeing Star — A31

Designs: 20c, Nativity. 25c, King offering gift. 40c, Star over map of Anguilla. 60c, Family looking at star. $1.20, Two angels with star and "Peace."

**1974, Dec. 16** **Litho.** *Perf. 14½*

| No. | Type | Value | Design | Unused | Used |
|---|---|---|---|---|---|
| 205 | A31 | 1c | brt bl & multi | 5 | 5 |
| 206 | A31 | 20c | dl grn & multi | 22 | 22 |
| 207 | A31 | 25c | gray & multi | 25 | 25 |
| 208 | A31 | 40c | car & multi | 50 | 50 |
| 209 | A31 | 60c | dp bl & multi | 70 | 70 |
| 210 | A31 | $1.20 | ultra & multi | 1.25 | 1.25 |
| | | a | Souvenir sheet of 6 | 3.50 | 3.50 |
| | | | Strip of 5 | 3.25 | 3.25 |
| | | | *Nos. 205-210 (6)* | 2.97 | 2.97 |

Christmas 1974. Nos. 206-210 printed horizontally se-tenant. No. 210a contains one each of Nos. 205-210; blue and yellow decorative margin. Size: 175x83mm.

Virgin Mary, St. John, Mary Magdalene — A32

Paintings from Isenheim Altar, by Matthias Grunewald: 10c, Crucifixion. 15c, John the Baptist. 20c, St. Sebastian and Angels. $1, Burial of Christ (horiz.). $1.50, St. Anthony, the Hermit.

**1975, Mar. 25** *Perf. 13½*

| No. | Type | Value | Design | Unused | Used |
|---|---|---|---|---|---|
| 211 | A32 | 1c | multi | 5 | 5 |
| 212 | A32 | 10c | multi | 10 | 10 |
| 213 | A32 | 15c | multi | 14 | 14 |
| 214 | A32 | 20c | multi | 22 | 22 |
| 215 | A32 | $1 | multi | 90 | 90 |
| 216 | A32 | $1.50 | multi | 1.40 | 1.40 |
| | | a | Souvenir sheet of 6 | 3.25 | 3.25 |
| | | | Strip of 5 | 3.00 | 3.00 |
| | | | *Nos. 211-216 (6)* | 2.81 | 2.81 |

Easter 1975. Nos. 212-216 printed horizontally se-tenant. No. 216a contains 6 stamps similar to Nos. 211-216 with simulated perforations; deep blue margin with black inscription and ornaments. Size: 133x126mm.

Statue of Liberty, N.Y. Skyline — A33

Designs: 10c, Capitol, Washington, D.C. 15c, Congress voting independence. 20c, Washington, map and his battles. $1, Boston Tea Party. $1.50, Bicentennial emblem, historic U.S. flags.

**1975, Nov. 10**

| No. | Type | Value | Design | Unused | Used |
|---|---|---|---|---|---|
| 217 | A33 | 1c | multi | 5 | 5 |
| 218 | A33 | 10c | multi | 10 | 10 |
| 219 | A33 | 15c | multi | 15 | 15 |
| 220 | A33 | 20c | multi | 22 | 22 |
| 221 | A33 | $1 | multi | 1.00 | 1.00 |
| 222 | A33 | $1.50 | multi | 1.50 | 1.50 |
| | | a | Souvenir sheet of 6 | 3.50 | 3.50 |
| | | | Strip of 5 | 3.25 | 3.25 |
| | | | *Nos. 217-222 (6)* | 3.02 | 3.02 |

American Bicentennial. Nos. 218-222 printed horizontally se-tenant. No. 222a contains one each of Nos. 217-222 with second row (20c, $1, $1.50) perf. 15 at bottom; blue and red margin with flags and inscription. Size: 199x97mm.

Virgin and Child with St. John, by Raphael — A34

Paintings. Virgin and Child by: 10c, Cima. 15c, Dolci. 20c, Durer. $1, Bellini. $1.50, Botticelli.

**1975, Dec. 8** *Perf. 14x13½*

*223* A34 1c ultra & multi 5 5
*224* A34 10c Prus bl & multi 12 12
*225* A34 15c plum & multi 14 14
*226* A34 20c car rose & multi 20 20
*227* A34 $1 brt grn & multi 1.00 1.00
*228* A34 $1.50 bl grn & multi 1.40 1.40
*a* Souvenir sheet of 6 3.25 3.25
Strip of 5 3.25 3.25
*Nos. 223-228 (6)* 2.91 2.91

Christmas 1975. Nos. 224-228 printed horizontally se-tenant. No. 228a contains one each of Nos. 223-228; multicolored margin. Size: 129x146mm.

### Nos. 145-146, 148, 150-160 Overprinted "NEW CONSTITUTION 1976"

**1976** **Litho.** *Perf. 13½*

*229* A22 1c (#145) 5 5
*230* A22 2c on 1c (#145) 5 5
*231* A23 2c (#146) 70 70
*232* A22 3c on 40c (#155) 5 5
*233* A23 4c (#148) 5 5
*234* A22 5c on 40c (#155) 5 5
*235* A23 6c (#150) 6 6
*236* A23 10c on 20c (#153) 10 10
*237* A23 10c (#151) 90 90
*238* A22 15c (#152) 15 15
*239* A23 20c (#153) 20 20
*240* A23 25c (#154) 25 25
*241* A22 40c (#155) 35 35
*242* A22 60c (#156) 55 55
*243* A23 $1 (#157) 90 90
*244* A23 $2.50 (#158) 2.25 2.25
*245* A23 $5 (#159) 4.50 4.50
*246* A22 $10 (#160) 10.50 10.50
*Nos. 229-246 (18)* 21.66 21.66

Almond Tree — A35

Flowering Trees: 10c, Clusia rosea. 15c, Calabash. 20c, Cordia. $1, Papaya. $1.50, Flamboyant.

**1976, Feb. 16** *Perf. 13½x14*

*247* A35 1c rose & multi 5 5
*248* A35 10c yel & multi 15 15
*249* A35 15c lt vio & multi 20 20
*250* A35 20c sal & multi 22 22
*251* A35 $1 lt bl & multi 1.00 1.00
*252* A35 $1.50 yel & multi 1.40 1.40
*a* Souvenir sheet of 6 3.25 3.25
Strip of 5 3.25 3.25
*Nos. 247-252 (6)* 3.02 3.02

Nos. 248-252 printed horizontally se-tenant. No. 252a contains one each of Nos. 247-252; multicolored decorative margin. Size: 193x99mm.

The Three Marys — A36

Designs: 10c, Crucifixion. 15c, Two soldiers. 20c, Annunciation. $1, Altar tapestry, 1470, Monastery of Rheinau, Switzerland (horiz.). $1.50, "Noli me Tangere" (Jesus and Mary Magdalene). Designs of vertical stamps show details from tapestry shown on $1 stamp.

**1976, Apr. 5** *Perf. 14x13½, 13½x14*

*253* A36 1c multi 5 5
*254* A36 10c multi 14 14
*255* A36 15c multi 18 18
*256* A36 20c multi 20 20
*257* A36 $1 multi 90 90
*258* A36 $1.50 multi 1.25 1.25
*a* Souvenir sheet of 6 2.75 2.75
Strip of 5 2.75 2.75
*Nos. 253-258 (6)* 2.72 2.72

Easter 1976. Nos. 254-258 printed horizontally se-tenant. No. 258a contains 6 stamps similar to Nos. 253-258 with simulated perforations, multicolored decorative margin. Size: 138x132mm.

Le Desius and La Vaillante Approaching Anguilla — A37

Sailing Ships: 3c, Sailboat leaving Anguilla for Antigua to get help. 15c, HMS Lapwing in battle with frigate Le Desius and brig La Vaillante. 25c, La Vaillante aground off St. Maarten. $1, Lapwing. $1.50, Le Desius burning.

**1976, Nov. 8** **Litho.** *Perf. 13½x14*

*259* A37 1c multi 5 5
*260* A37 3c multi 5 5
*261* A37 15c multi 20 20
*262* A37 25c multi 35 35
*263* A37 $1 multi 1.40 1.40
*264* A37 $1.50 multi 2.25 2.25
*a* Souvenir sheet of 6 5.25 5.25
Strip of 5 4.50 4.50
*Nos. 259-264 (6)* 4.30 4.30

Bicentenary of Battle of Anguilla between French and British ships. Nos. 260-264 printed se-tenant. No. 264a contains one each of Nos. 259-264; multicolored margin. Size: 206x104mm.

Christmas Carnival — A38

Children's Paintings: 3c, 3 children dreaming of Christmas gifts. 15c, Caroling. 25c, Candlelight procession. $1, Going to Church on Christmas Eve. $1.50, Airport, coming home for Christmas.

**1976, Nov. 22**

*265* A38 1c multi 5 5
*266* A38 3c multi 6 5
*267* A38 15c multi 18 15
*268* A38 25c multi 22 18
*269* A38 $1 multi 90 80
*270* A38 $1.50 multi 1.25 90
*a* Souvenir sheet of 6 2.75 2.00
Strip of 5 2.75 2.25
*Nos. 265-270 (6)* 2.66 2.13

Christmas 1976. Nos. 266-270 printed se-tenant. No. 270a contains one each of Nos. 265-270; blue and black margin shows church goers; black inscription with names and schools of children. Size: 230x146mm.

Prince Charles and HMS Minerva, 1973 — A39

Designs: 40c, Prince Philip landing at Road Bay, 1964. $1.20, Hommage to Queen at Coronation. $2.50, Coronation regalia and map of Anguilla.

**1977, Feb. 9**

*271* A39 25c multi 18 18
*272* A39 40c multi 30 30
*273* A39 $1.20 multi 90 90
*274* A39 $2.50 multi 1.75 1.75
*a* Souvenir sheet of 4 3.50 3.50

25th anniversary of reign of Queen Elizabeth II. No. 274a contains one each of Nos. 271-274; black marginal inscription and regalia. Size: 145x96mm.

Nos. 271-274 each exist in a booklet pane of 2.

Yellow-crowned Night Heron — A40

Designs: 2c, Great barracuda. 3c, Queen conch. 4c, Spanish bayonet (Yucca). 5c, Trunkfish. 6c, Cable and telegraph building. 10c, American sparrow hawk. 15c, Ground orchids. 20c, Parlorfish. 22c, Lobster fishing boat. 35c, Boat race. 50c Sea bean (flowers). $1, Sandy Island with palms. $2.50, Manchineel (fruit). $5, Ground lizard. $10, Red-billed tropic bird.

**1977-78** **Litho.** *Perf. 13½*

*275* A40 1c multi 5 5
*276* A40 2c multi 5 5
*277* A40 3c multi 5 5
*278* A40 4c multi 5 5
*279* A40 5c multi 5 5
*280* A40 6c multi 6 6
*281* A40 10c multi 10 10
*282* A40 15c multi 15 15
*283* A40 20c multi 20 20
*284* A40 22c multi 22 22
*285* A40 35c multi 35 35
*286* A40 50c multi 50 50
*287* A40 $1 multi 1.00 1.00
*288* A40 $2.50 multi 2.50 2.50
*289* A40 $5 multi 5.00 5.00
*290* A40 $10 multi 10.00 10.00
*Nos. 275-290 (16)* 20.33 20.33

Issue dates: Nos. 275-280, 290 Apr. 18, 1977. Others Feb. 20, 1978.

Crucifixion, by Quentin Massys — A41

Paintings: 3c, Betrayal of Christ, by Ugolino. 22c, Way to Calvary, by Ugolino. 30c, The Deposition, by Ugolino. $1, Resurrection, by Ugolino. $1.50, Crucifixion, by Andrea del Castagno.

**1977, Apr. 25**

*291* A41 1c multi 5 5
*292* A41 3c multi 5 5
*293* A41 22c multi 18 18
*294* A41 30c multi 22 22
*295* A41 $1 multi 90 90
*296* A41 $1.50 multi 1.25 1.25
*a* Souvenir sheet of 6 2.50 2.50
Strip of 5 2.75 2.75
*Nos. 291-296 (6)* 2.65 2.65

Easter 1977. Nos. 292-296 printed se-tenant. No. 296a contains one each of Nos. 291-296; black marginal inscription. Size: 193x127mm.

### Nos. 271-274, 274b Overprinted: "ROYAL VISIT/TO WEST INDIES"

**1977, Oct.** **Litho.** *Perf. 13½x14*

*297* A39 25c multi 18 18
*298* A39 40c multi 28 28
*299* A39 $1.20 multi 75 75
*300* A39 $2.50 multi 1.50 1.50
*a* Souvenir sheet of 4 3.00 3.00

Visit of Queen Elizabeth II to West Indies.

Suzanne Fourment in Velvet Hat, by Rubens — A42

Rubens Paintings: 40c, Helena Fourment with her Children. $1.20, Rubens with his wife. $2.50, Marchesa Brigida Spinola-Doria.

**1977, Nov. 1** *Perf. 14x13½*

*301* A42 25c blk & multi 18 18
*302* A42 40c blk & multi 25 25
*303* A42 $1.20 multi 90 90
*304* A42 $2.50 blk & multi 1.75 1.75
*a* Souvenir sheet of 4 3.25 3.25

Peter Paul Rubens, 400th birth anniv. Nos. 301-304 printed in sheets of 5 stamps and blue label with Rubens' portrait. No. 304a contains one each of Nos. 301-304; black marginal design. Size: 92x134mm.

### Nos. 265-270a Overprinted 1977 and Surcharged

**1977, Nov. 7** *Perf. 13½x14*

*305* A38 1c multi 5 5
*306* A38 5c on 3c multi 5 5
*307* A38 12c on 15c multi 7 7
*308* A38 18c on 25c multi 12 12
*309* A38 $1 multi 65 65
*310* A38 $2.50 on $1.50 multi 1.75 1.75
*a* Souvenir sheet of 6 3.25 1.75
Strip of 5 3.00 3.00
*Nos. 305-310 (6)* 2.69 2.69

Christmas 1977. Nos. 306-310 printed se-tenant. No. 310a contains one each of Nos. 305-310. Stamps and souvenir sheet have "1976" and old denominations obliterated with variously shaped rectangles.

### Nos. 301-304a Ovptd. in Gold: "EASTER 1978"

**1978, Mar. 6** *Perf. 14x13½*

*311* A42 25c blk & multi 18 18
*312* A42 40c blk & multi 28 28
*313* A42 $1.20 blk & multi 80 80
*314* A42 $2.50 blk & multi 1.75 1.75
*a* Souv. sheet of 4 3.25 3.25

Easter 1978. No. 314a contains one each of Nos. 311-314. Size: 92x134mm.

Buckingham Palace — A43

Designs: 50c, Coronation procession. $1.50, Royal family on balcony. $2.50, Royal coat of arms.

**1978, Apr. 6** *Perf. 14*

*315* A43 22c multi 12 12
*316* A43 50c multi 25 25
*317* A43 $1.50 multi 75 75
*318* A43 $2.50 multi 1.25 1.25
*a* Souvenir sheet of 4 3.25 3.25

25th anniversary of coronation of Queen Elizabeth II. No. 318a contains one each of Nos. 315-318; black marginal inscription. Size: 138x92mm.

Nos. 315-318 each exist in a booklet pane of 2.

### Nos. 284-285 and 288 Ovptd. and Surcharged: "VALLEY / SECONDARY / SCHOOL / 1953-1978."

**1978, Aug. 14** **Litho.** *Perf. 13½*

*319* A40 22c multi 35 35
*320* A40 35c multi 50 50
*321* A40 $1.50 on $2.50 multi 2.25 2.25

Valley Secondary School, 25th anniversary. Surcharge on No. 321 includes heavy bar over old denomination.

Nos. 286-C287, 289 Ovptd. and Surcharged: "ROAD / METHODIST / CHURCH / 1878-1978."

**1978, Aug. 14**

| | | | | |
|---|---|---|---|---|
| *322* | A40 | 50c multi | 65 | 65 |
| *323* | A40 | $1 multi | 1.30 | 1.30 |
| *324* | A40 | $1.20 on $5 multi | 1.75 | 1.75 |

Road Methodist Church, centenary. Surcharge on No. 324 includes heavy bar over old denomination.

Mother and Child — A44

Design: 12c, Christmas masquerade. 18c, Christmas dinner. 22c, Serenade. $1, Star over manger. $2.50, Family going to church.

**1978, Dec. 11 Litho. *Perf. 13½***

| | | | | |
|---|---|---|---|---|
| *325* | A44 | 5c multi | 6 | 5 |
| *326* | A44 | 12c multi | 8 | 8 |
| *327* | A44 | 18c multi | 12 | 9 |
| *328* | A44 | 22c multi | 14 | 12 |
| *329* | A44 | $1 multi | 75 | 55 |
| *330* | A44 | $2.50 multi | 1.75 | 1.50 |
| *a* | | Souvenir sheet of 6 | 3.00 | 2.25 |
| | | *Nos. 325-330 (6)* | 2.90 | 2.39 |

Christmas 1978 No. 330a contains Nos. 325-330; light blue and black margin showing Christmas scenes. Size: 192x100mm.

Type A44 in Changed Colors with IYC Emblem and Inscription.

**1979, Jan. 15 Litho. *Perf. 13½***

| | | | | |
|---|---|---|---|---|
| *331* | A44 | 5c multi | 5 | 5 |
| *332* | A44 | 12c multi | 10 | 10 |
| *333* | A44 | 18c multi | 15 | 15 |
| *334* | A44 | 22c multi | 18 | 18 |
| *335* | A44 | $1 multi | 85 | 85 |
| *336* | A44 | $2.50 multi | 1.75 | 1.75 |
| *a* | | Souvenir sheet of 4 | 2.75 | 2.75 |
| | | *Nos. 331-336 (6)* | 3.08 | 3.08 |

International Year of the Child. No. 336a contains Nos. 331-336, yellow and black margin shows children. Size: 205x113mm.

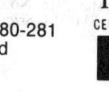

Nos. 275-278, 280-281 Surcharged

**1979, Feb. 8 Litho. *Perf. 13½***

| | | | | |
|---|---|---|---|---|
| *337* | A40 | 12c on 2c multi | *45* | *45* |
| *338* | A40 | 14c on 4c multi | *50* | *50* |
| *339* | A40 | 18c on 3c multi | *75* | *75* |
| *340* | A40 | 25c on 6c multi | *1.25* | *1.25* |
| *341* | A40 | 38c on 10c multi | *1.75* | *1.75* |
| *342* | A40 | 40c on 1c multi | *2.00* | *2.00* |
| | | *Nos. 337-342 (6)* | *6.70* | *6.70* |

Valley Methodist Church A45

Church Interiors: 12c, St. Mary's Anglican Church, The Valley. 18c, St. Gerard's Roman Catholic Church, The Valley. 22c, Road Methodist Church. $1.50, St. Augustine's Anglican Church, East End. $2.50, West End Methodist Church.

**1979, Mar. 30 Litho. *Perf. 14***

| | | | | |
|---|---|---|---|---|
| *343* | A45 | 5c multi | 5 | 5 |
| *344* | A45 | 12c multi | 8 | 8 |
| *345* | A45 | 18c multi | 12 | 12 |
| *346* | A45 | 22c multi | 15 | 15 |
| *347* | A45 | $1.50 multi | 1.00 | 1.00 |
| *348* | A45 | $2.50 multi | 1.60 | 1.60 |
| *a* | | Souvenir sheet of 6 | 3.25 | 3.25 |
| | | *Nos. 343-348 (6)* | 3.00 | 3.00 |

Easter 1979. Nos. 343-348 printed se-tenant in strips of 6. No. 348a contains Nos. 343-348 in 2 horizontal rows of 3. View of churches in black in margin. Size: 190x105mm.

1c

U.S. No. C3a — A46

Designs: No. 350, Cape of Good Hope No. 1. No. 351, Penny Black. No. 352, Germany No. C36. No. 353, US No. 245. No. 354, Great Britain No. 93

**1979, Apr. 23 Litho. *Perf. 14***

| | | | | |
|---|---|---|---|---|
| *349* | A46 | 1c multi | 5 | 5 |
| *350* | A46 | 1c multi | 5 | 5 |
| *351* | A46 | 22c multi | 15 | 15 |
| *352* | A46 | 35c multi | 20 | 20 |
| *353* | A46 | $1.50 multi | 1.00 | 1.00 |
| *354* | A46 | $2.50 multi | 1.75 | 1.75 |
| *a* | | Souvenir sheet of 6 | 3.25 | 3.25 |
| | | *Nos. 349-354 (6)* | 3.20 | 3.20 |

Sir Rowland Hill (1795-1879), originator of penny postage. No. 354a contains Nos. 349-354, black and white margin shows Mulready envelope. Size: 183x124mm.

Nos. 349-354 were also issued in booklet panes of 2.

Wright's Flyer A — A47

History of Aviation: 12c, Louis Bleriot landing at Dover, 1909. 18c, Vickers Vimy, 1919. 22c, Spirit of St. Louis, 1927. $1.50, LZ127 Graf Zeppelin, 1928. $2.50, Concorde, 1979.

**1979, May 21 Litho. *Perf. 14***

| | | | | |
|---|---|---|---|---|
| *355* | A47 | 5c multi | 5 | 5 |
| *356* | A47 | 12c multi | 8 | 8 |
| *357* | A47 | 18c multi | 12 | 12 |
| *358* | A47 | 22c multi | 15 | 15 |
| *359* | A47 | $1.50 multi | 1.00 | 1.00 |
| *360* | A47 | $2.50 multi | 1.50 | 1.50 |
| *a* | | Souvenir sheet of 6 | 3.00 | 3.00 |
| | | *Nos. 355-360 (6)* | 2.90 | 2.90 |

No. 360a contains Nos. 355-360; light blue margin shows various aircraft. Size: 202x115mm.

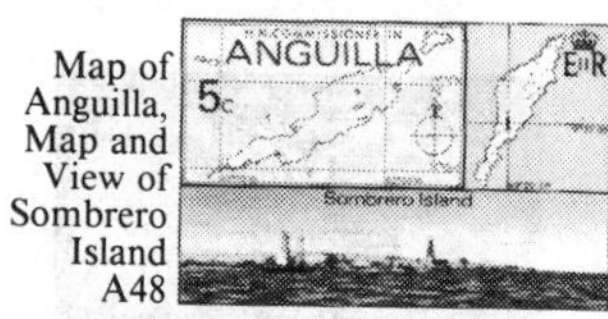

Map of Anguilla, Map and View of Sombrero Island A48

Map of Anguilla, Map and View of: 12c, Anguillita Island. 18c, Sandy Island. 25c, Prickly Pear Cays. $1, Dog Island. $2.50, Scrub Island.

**1979 Litho. *Perf. 14***

| | | | | |
|---|---|---|---|---|
| *361* | A48 | 5c multi | 5 | 5 |
| *362* | A48 | 12c multi | 8 | 8 |
| *363* | A48 | 18c multi | 12 | 12 |
| *364* | A48 | 25c multi | 18 | 18 |
| *365* | A48 | $1 multi | 65 | 65 |
| *366* | A48 | $2.50 multi | 1.75 | 1.75 |
| *a* | | Souvenir sheet of 6 | 3.00 | 3.00 |
| | | *Nos. 361-366 (6)* | 2.83 | 2.83 |

Anguilla's Outer Islands. No. 366a contains Nos. 361-366; bluish green and black margin shows maps and views of islands. Size: 181x92mm.

The first price column gives the catalogue value of an unused stamp, the second that of a used stamp.

Red Poinsettia — A49

**1979, Oct. 22 Litho. *Perf. 14½***

| | | | | |
|---|---|---|---|---|
| *367* | A49 | 22c *shown* | 15 | 12 |
| *368* | A49 | 35c *Kalanchoe* | 25 | 20 |
| *369* | A49 | $1.50 *Cream poinsettia* | 1.10 | 90 |
| *370* | A49 | $2.50 *White poinsettia* | 2.00 | 1.50 |
| *a* | | Souvenir sheet of 4 | 3.75 | 2.75 |

Christmas 1979. No. 370a contains Nos. 367-370 multicolored margin shows various Christmas symbols. Size: 147x164mm.

Booths and Frames A50

Designs: 50c, Earls Court Exhibition Hall. $1.50, Penny Black, Gt. Britain No. 2. $2.50, Exhibition emblem.

**1979, Dec. 10 Litho. *Perf. 13, 14½***

| | | | | |
|---|---|---|---|---|
| *371* | A50 | 35c multi | 20 | 20 |
| *372* | A50 | 50c multi | 30 | 30 |
| *373* | A50 | $1.50 multi | 1.00 | 1.00 |
| *374* | A50 | $2.50 multi | 1.50 | 1.50 |
| *a* | | Souvenir sheet of 4 | 3.00 | 3.00 |

London 1980, International Stamp Exhibition, May 6-14, 1980. No. 374a contains Nos. 371-374; margin shows London buildings and monuments. Size: 150x94mm.

Lake Placid and Olympic Rings — A51

Olympic Rings and: 18c, Ice Hockey. 35c, Figure skating. 50c, Bobsledding. $1, Ski jump. $2.50, Luge.

**1980, Jan. Litho. *Perf. 13½, 14½***

| | | | | |
|---|---|---|---|---|
| *375* | A51 | 5c multi | 5 | 5 |
| *376* | A51 | 18c multi | 10 | 10 |
| *377* | A51 | 35c multi | 18 | 18 |
| *378* | A51 | 50c multi | 28 | 28 |
| *379* | A51 | $1 multi | 55 | 55 |
| *380* | A51 | $2.50 multi | 1.40 | 1.40 |
| *a* | | Souvenir sheet of 6 | 3.00 | 3.00 |
| | | *Nos. 375-380 (6)* | 2.56 | 2.56 |

13th Winter Olympic Games, Lake Placid, N.Y., Feb. 12-24. No. 380a contains Nos. 375-380; blue margin shows various Olympic sports. Size: 136x127½mm.

Salt Field A52

**1980, Apr. 14 Litho. *Perf. 14***

| | | | | |
|---|---|---|---|---|
| *381* | A52 | 5c *shown* | 5 | 5 |
| *382* | A52 | 12c *Tallying salt* | 7 | 7 |
| *383* | A52 | 18c *Unloading salt flats* | 10 | 10 |
| *384* | A52 | 22c *Storage pile* | 12 | 12 |
| *385* | A52 | $1 *Bagging and grinding* | 60 | 60 |
| *386* | A52 | $2.50 *Loading onto boats* | 1.40 | 1.40 |
| *a* | | Souvenir sheet of 6 | 2.50 | 2.50 |
| | | *Nos. 381-386 (6)* | 2.34 | 2.34 |

Salt industry. No. 386a contains Nos. 381-386; light blue and black margin shows designs of Nos. 382, 384, palm trees. Size: 181x92mm.

Nos. 281, 288 Overprinted: "50th Anniversary / Scouting 1980"

**1980, Apr. 16 *Perf. 13½***

| | | | | |
|---|---|---|---|---|
| *387* | A40 | 10c multi | 8 | 8 |
| *388* | A40 | $2.50 multi | 2.00 | 2.00 |

Nos. 283, 289 Overprinted: "75th Anniversary / Rotary 1980" and Rotary Emblem

**1980, Apr. 16 *Perf. 14***

| | | | | |
|---|---|---|---|---|
| *389* | A40 | 20c multi | 14 | 14 |
| *390* | A40 | $5 multi | 3.50 | 3.50 |

Rotary International, 75th anniversary.

Big Ben, Gt. Britain No. 643, London 1980 Emblem — A53

Designs: $1.50, Canada No. 756. $2.50, Statue of Liberty, U.S. No. 1632.

**1980, May**

| | | | | |
|---|---|---|---|---|
| *391* | A53 | 50c multi | 25 | 25 |
| *392* | A53 | $1.50 multi | 85 | 85 |
| *393* | A53 | $2.50 multi | 1.40 | 1.40 |
| *a* | | Souvenir sheet of 3 | 3.00 | 3.00 |

London 1980 International Stamp Exhibition, May 6-14. No. 393a contains Nos. 391-393; blue and black margin shows London 1980 emblem, beefeater, London buildings. Size: 156½x130½mm.

Queen Mother Elizabeth, 80th Birthday — A54

**1980, Aug. 4 Litho. *Perf. 14***

| | | | | |
|---|---|---|---|---|
| *394* | A54 | 35c multi | 18 | 18 |
| *395* | A54 | 50c multi | 30 | 30 |
| *396* | A54 | $1.50 multi | 90 | 90 |
| *397* | A54 | $3 multi | 1.75 | 1.75 |
| *a* | | Souvenir sheet of 4 | 3.00 | 3.00 |

No. 397a contains Nos. 394-397, light and dark blue margin shows castles. Size: 160x110½mm.

Pelicans — A55

**1980, Nov. 10 Litho. *Perf. 14***

| | | | | |
|---|---|---|---|---|
| *398* | A55 | 5c *shown* | 5 | 5 |
| *399* | A55 | 22c *Great gray herons* | 15 | 15 |
| *400* | A55 | $1.50 *Swallows* | 1.00 | 1.00 |

*401* A55 $3 *Hummingbirds* 2.00 2.00
*a* Souvenir sheet of 4 3.25 3.25

Christmas 1980. No. 401a contains Nos. 398-401; black margin shows birds and trees. Size: 127½x159½mm.

Nos. 275, 278, 280-290, 334, 400-401 Overprinted: "SEPARATION 1980"

***Perf. 13½, 14 (A55)***

**1980, Dec. 18** **Litho.**

*402* A40 1c (#275) 5 5
*403* A40 2c on 4c (#278) 5 5
*404* A40 5c on 15c (#282) 5 5
*405* A55 5c on $1.50 (#400) 5 5
*406* A55 5c on $3 (#401) 5 5
*407* A40 10c (#281) 8 8
*408* A40 12c on $1 (#287) 10 10
*409* A40 14c on $2.50 (#288) 12 12
*410* A40 15c (#282) 14 14
*411* A40 18c on $5 (#289) 15 15
*412* A40 20c (#283) 18 18
*413* A40 22c (#284) 20 20
*414* A40 25c on 15c (#282) 22 22
*415* A40 35c (#285) 30 30
*416* A40 38c on 22c (#334) 32 32
*417* A40 40c on 1c (#275) 35 35
*418* A40 50c (#286) 42 42
*419* A40 $1 ($287) 75 75
*420* A40 $2.50 (#288) 1.75 1.75
*421* A40 $5 (#289) 3.50 3.50
*422* A40 $10 (#290) 7.25 7.25
*423* A40 $10 on 6c (#280) 7.25 7.25
*Nos. 402-423 (22)* 23.33 23.33

Petition for Separation, 1825 — A56

**1980, Dec. 18** ***Perf. 14***

*424* A56 18c shown 12 12
*425* A56 22c Referendum ballot, 1967 15 15
*426* A56 35c Airport blockade, 1967 25 25
*427* A56 50c Anguilla flag 35 35
*428* A56 $1 Separation celebration, 1980 65 65
*a* Souvenir sheet of 5 1.60 1.60
*Nos. 424-428 (5)* 1.52 1.52

Separation from St. Kitts-Nevis. No. 428a contains Nos. 424-428; light blue and black margin shows historic scenes. Size: 179x92mm.

Nelson's Dockyard, by R. Granger Barrett A57

Ship Paintings: 35c, Agamemnon, Vanguard, Elephant, Captain and Victory, by Nicholas Pocock. 50c, Victory, by Monamy Swaine. $3, Battle of Trafalgar, by Clarkson Stanfield. $5, Lord Nelson, by L.F. Abbott and Nelson's arms.

**1981, Mar. 2** **Litho.** ***Perf. 14***

*429* A57 22c multi 14 14
*430* A57 35c multi 22 22
*431* A57 50c multi 32 32
*432* A57 $3 multi 1.75 1.75

**Souvenir Sheet**

*433* A57 $5 multi 2.75 2.75

Lord Horatio Nelson (1758-1805), 175th death anniversary (1980). No. 433 has black margin showing flags and cannons. Size: 83x63mm.

Minnie Mouse — A58

Designs: Various Disney characters in Easter outfits.

**1981, Mar. 30** **Litho.** ***Perf. 13½***

*434* A58 1c multi 5 5
*435* A58 2c multi 5 5
*436* A58 3c multi 5 5
*437* A58 5c multi 5 5
*438* A58 7c multi 6 6
*439* A58 9c multi 8 8
*440* A58 10c multi 8 8
*441* A58 $2 multi 1.75 1.75
*442* A58 $3 multi 2.50 2.50
*Nos. 434-442 (9)* 4.67 4.67

**Souvenir Sheet**

*443* A58 $5 multi 4.25 4.25

Easter 1981. No. 443 has multicolored margin showing Donald Duck. Size: 133½x108½mm.

Prince Charles, Lady Diana, St. Paul's Cathedral A59

**1981, June 15** **Litho.** ***Perf. 14***

*444* A59 50c shown 32 32
*a* Souvenir sheet of 2 65 65
*445* A59 $2.50 Althorp 1.60 1.60
*a* Souvenir sheet of 2 3.25 3.25
*446* A59 $3 Windsor Castle 2.00 2.00
*a* Souvenir sheet of 2 4.00 4.00

**Souvenir Sheet**

*447* A59 $5 Buckingham Palace 3.25 3.25

Royal Wedding. No. 447 has black decorative margin. Size: 90x72mm.

Nos. 444a-446a contain stamps in different colors. Size 95x139mm

Boys Climbing Tree A60

**1981, July 31** **Litho.** ***Perf. 14***

*448* A60 5c shown 5 5
*449* A60 10c Boys sailing boats 8 8
*450* A60 15c Children playing instruments 12 12
*451* A60 $3 Children with animals 2.25 2.25

**Souvenir Sheet**

*452* A60 $4 Boys playing soccer, vert. 3.00 3.00

UNICEF, 35th anniv. No. 452 has multicolored margin showing boys playing soccer, UNICEF emblem. Size: 77x116mm.

"The Children were Nestled all Snug in their Beds" — A61

Christmas 1981: Scenes from Walt Disney's The Night Before Christmas.

**1981, Nov. 2** **Litho.** ***Perf. 13½***

*453* A61 1c multi 5 5
*454* A61 2c multi 5 5
*455* A61 3c multi 5 5
*456* A61 5c multi 5 5
*457* A61 7c multi 7 7
*458* A61 10c multi 8 8
*459* A61 12c multi 10 10
*460* A61 $2 multi 1.60 1.60
*461* A61 $3 multi 2.50 2.50
*Nos. 453-461 (9)* 4.55 4.55

**Souvenir Sheet**

*462* A61 $5 multi 4.25 4.25

No. 462 has multicolored margin continuing design. Size: 130x104mm.

Red Grouper — A62

**1982, Jan. 1** **Litho.** ***Perf. 14***

*463* A62 1c shown 5 5
*464* A62 5c Ferries, Blowing Point 5 5
*465* A62 10 Racing boats 7 7
*466* A62 15c Majorettes 10 10
*467* A62 20c Launching boat, Sandy Hill 12 12
*468* A62 25c Coral 15 15
*469* A62 30c Little Bay cliffs 18 18
*470* A62 35c Fountain Cave 20 20
*471* A62 40c Sandy Isld. 25 25
*472* A62 45c Landing, Sombrero 28 28
*473* A62 50c on 45c, #472 30 30
*474* A62 60c Seine fishing 35 35
*475* A62 75c Boat race, Sandy Ground 40 40
*476* A62 $1 Bagging lobster, Island Harbor 65 65
*477* A62 $5 Pelicans 2.75 2.75
*478* A62 $7.50 Hibiscus 4.25 4.25
*479* A62 $10 Queen triggerfish 6.00 6.00
*Nos. 463-479 (17)* 16.15 16.15

Easter 1982 — A63

Princess Diana, 21st Birthday — A64

Designs: Butterflies on flowers.

**1982, Apr. 5**

*480* A63 10c Zebra, anthurium 10 10
*481* A63 35c Caribbean buckeye 35 35
*482* A63 75c Monarch, allamanda 75 75
*483* A63 $3 Red rim, orchid 3.00 3.00

**Souvenir Sheet**

*484* A63 $5 Flambeau, amaryllis 3.50 3.50

No. 484 has multicolored margin showing butterflies and flowers. Size: 65x79mm.

**1982, May 17**

Designs: Portraits, 1961-1981.

*485* A64 10c 1961 7 7
*486* A64 30c 1968 20 20
*487* A64 40c 1970 25 25
*488* A64 60c 1974 40 40
*489* A64 $2 1981 1.40 1.40
*490* A64 $3 1981 2.00 2.00
*a* Souv. sheet of 6, #485-490 4.50 4.50
*Nos. 485-490 (6)* 4.32 4.32

**Souvenir Sheet**

*491* A64 $5 1981 3.75 3.75

No. 491 has multicolored decorative margin. Size: 72x91mm.

Common Design Types are pictured in section before Great Britain.

1982 World Cup — A65

Designs: Various Disney characters playing soccer.

**1982, Aug. 3** **Litho.** ***Perf. 11***

*492* A65 1c multi 5 5
*493* A65 3c multi 5 5
*494* A65 4c multi 5 5
*495* A65 5c multi 5 5
*496* A65 7c multi 6 6
*497* A65 9c multi 8 8
*498* A65 10c multi 8 8
*499* A65 $2.50 multi 1.90 1.90
*500* A65 $3 multi 2.25 2.25
*Nos. 492-500 (9)* 4.57 4.57

**Souvenir Sheet**

***Perf. 14***

*501* A65 $5 multi 4.00 4.00

No. 501 has multicolored margin continuing design. Size: 127x102mm.

Scouting Year A66

**1982, July 5**

*502* A66 10c Pitching tent 8 8
*503* A66 35c Marching band 30 30
*504* A66 75c Sailing 65 65
*505* A66 $3 Flag bearers 2.50 2.50

**Souvenir Sheet**

*506* A66 $5 Camping 4.00 4.00

No. 506 has black and yellow green margin showing scouting activities. Size: 90x72mm.

Nos. 465, 474-475, 477 Overprinted: "COMMONWEALTH / GAMES 1982."

**1982, Oct. 18** **Litho.** ***Perf. 14***

*507* A62 10c multi 8 8
*508* A62 60c multi 45 45
*509* A62 75c multi 55 55
*510* A62 $5 multi 3.75 3.75

12th Commonwealth Games, Brisbane, Australia, Sept. 30-Oct. 9.

Christmas 1982 — A67

Designs: Scenes from Walt Disney's Winnie the Pooh.

**1982, Nov. 29**

*511* A67 1c multi 5 5
*512* A67 2c multi 5 5
*513* A67 3c multi 5 5
*514* A67 5c multi 5 5
*515* A67 7c multi 7 7
*516* A67 10c multi 8 8
*517* A67 12c multi 10 10
*518* A67 20c multi 15 15
*519* A67 $5 multi 4.00 4.00
*Nos. 511-519 (9)* 4.60 4.60

**Souvenir Sheet**

*520* A67 $5 multi 4.25 4.25

No. 520 has multicolored margin continuing design.

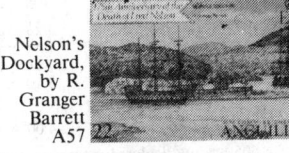

Commonwealth Day (Mar. 14) — A68

**1983, Feb. 28 Litho. *Perf. 14***

*521* A68 10c Carnival procession 8 8
*522* A68 35c Flags 30 30
*523* A68 75c Economic cooperation 65 65
*524* A68 $2.50 Salt pond 2.00 2.00

**Souvenir Sheet**

*525* A68 $5 Map showing Commonwealth 4.00 4.00

Size of No. 525: 77x61mm.

Easter 1983 — A69

Ten Commandments.

**1983, Mar. 31 Litho. *Perf. 14***

*526* A69 1c multi 5 5
*527* A69 2c multi 5 5
*528* A69 3c multi 5 5
*529* A69 10c multi 8 8
*530* A69 35c multi 25 25
*531* A69 60c multi 45 45
*532* A69 75c multi 55 55
*533* A69 $2 multi 1.50 1.50
*534* A69 $2.50 multi 1.75 1.75
*535* A69 $5 multi 3.75 3.75
*Nos. 526-535 (10)* 8.48 8.48

**Souvenir Sheet**

*536* A69 $5 Moses Taking Tablets 4.00 4.00

No. 536 has multicolored margin showing entire 16th cent. woodcut. Size: 128x102mm.

Local Turtles and World Wildlife Fund Emblem — A70

**1983, Aug. 10 Litho. *Perf. 13½***

*537* A70 10c Leatherback 10 10
*538* A70 35c Hawksbill 35 35
*539* A70 75c Green 75 75
*540* A70 $1 Loggerhead 1.00 1.00

**Souvenir Sheet**

*541* A70 $5 Leatherback, diff. 4.00 4.00

Size of No. 541: 93x72mm.

Manned Flight Bicentenary — A71

**1983, Aug. 22 *Perf. 14***

*542* A71 10c Montgolfiere, 1783 8 8
*543* A71 60c Blanchard & Jeffries, 1785 45 45
*544* A71 $1 Giffard's airship, 1852 75 75
*545* A71 $2.50 Lilienthal's glider, 1890 1.75 1.75

**Souvenir Sheet**

*546* A71 $5 Wright Brothers' plane, 1909 3.75 3.75

Size of No. 546: 72x90mm.

Nos. 465, 471, 476-477 Overprinted: 150TH ANNIVERSARY / ABOLITION OF SLAVERY ACT

**1983, Oct. Litho. *Perf. 14***

*546A* A62 10c Racing boats 8 8
*546B* A62 40c Sandy Isld 32 32
*546C* A62 $1 Bagging lobster, Island Harbor 80 80
*546D* A62 $5 Pelicans 4.00 4.00

Jiminy Cricket A72

Designs: Various Disney productions.

**1983, Nov. *Perf. 13½***

*547* A72 1c shown 5 5
*548* A72 2c Jiminy Cricket, kettle 5 5
*549* A72 3c Jiminy Cricket, toys 5 5
*550* A72 4c Mickey and Morty 5 5
*551* A72 5c Scrooge McDuck 5 5
*552* A72 6c Minnie and Goofy 5 5
*553* A72 10c Goofy and Elf 10 10
*554* A72 $2 Scrooge McDuck, diff. 2.00 2.00
*555* A72 $3 Disney characters 3.00 3.00
*Nos. 547-555 (9)* 5.40 5.40

**Souvenir Sheet**

*556* A72 $5 Scrooge McDuck 4.25 4.25

No. 556 has multicolored margin showing Donald Duck and Ludwig Von Drake. Size: 130x114mm.

Boys' Brigade Centenary — A73

**1983, Sept. 12 Litho. *Perf. 14***

*557* A73 10c Anguilla company, banner 8 8
*558* A73 $5 Marching with drummer 3.75 3.75
*a* Souvenir sheet of 2 3.85 3.85

No. 558a has margin showing Boys' Brigade members and emblem. Size: 97x115mm.

1984 Olympics, Los Angeles — A74

Mickey Mouse Competing in Decathlon.

**1984, Feb. Litho. *Perf. 14***

*559* A74 1c 100-meter run 5 5
*560* A74 2c Long jump 5 5
*561* A74 3c Shot put 5 5
*562* A74 4c High jump 5 5
*563* A74 5c 400-meter run 5 5
*564* A74 6c Hurdles 5 5
*565* A74 10c Discus 8 8
*566* A74 $1 Pole vault 80 80
*567* A74 $4 Javelin 3.25 3.25
*Nos. 559-567 (9)* 4.43 4.43

**Souvenir Sheet**

*568* A74 $5 1500-meter run 4.25 4.25

No. 568 has multicolored margin continuing design.

**1984 Litho.**

*559a* Perf. 12½x12 5 5
*560a* Perf. 12½x12 5 5
*561a* Perf. 12½x12 5 5
*562a* Perf. 12½x12 5 5
*563a* Perf. 12½x12 5 5
*564a* Perf. 12½x12 5 5
*565a* Perf. 12½x12 8 8
*566a* Perf. 12½x12 80 80
*567a* Perf. 12½x12 3.25 3.25

**Souvenir Sheet**

*568a* With Olympic rings emblem 4.25 4.25

Nos. 559a-567a inscribed with Olympic rings emblem. Printed in sheets of 5 plus label.

Easter 1984 — A75

Ceiling and Wall Frescoes, La Stanze della Segnatura, by Raphael (details).

**1984, Apr. 24 Litho. *Perf. 13½x14***

*569* A75 10c Justice 8 8
*570* A75 25c Poetry 18 18
*571* A75 35c Philosophy 25 25
*572* A75 40c Theology 30 30
*573* A75 $1 Abraham & Paul 75 75
*574* A75 $2 Moses & Matthew 1.50 1.50
*575* A75 $3 John & David 2.25 2.25
*576* A75 $4 Peter & Adam 3.00 3.00
*Nos. 569-576 (8)* 8.31 8.31

**Souvenir Sheet**

*577* A75 $5 Astronomy 3.75 3.75

No. 577 has multicolored margin continuing design. Size: 83x110mm.

Nos. 463, 469, 477-479 Surcharged.

**1984, July Litho. *Perf. 14***

*578* A62 25c on $7.50 #478 20 20
*579* A62 35c on 30c #469 28 28
*580* A62 60c on 1c #463 48 48
*581* A62 $2.50 on $5 #477 2.00 2.00
*582* A62 $2.50 on $10 #479 2.00 2.00
*Nos. 578-582 (5)* 4.96 4.96

Ausipex '84 — A76

Australian stamps.

**1984, July 16 Litho. *Perf. 13½***

*583* A76 10c No. 2 8 8
*584* A76 75c No. 18 55 55
*585* A76 $1 No. 130 80 80
*586* A76 $2.50 No. 178 2.00 2.00

**Souvenir Sheet**

*587* A76 $5 Nos. 378, 379 3.75 3.75

No. 587 has multicolored margin showing map of Australia, show emblem. Size: 106x88mm.

Slavery Abolition Sesquicentennial — A77

Abolitionists and Vignettes: 10c, Thomas Fowell Buxton, planting sugar cane. 25c, Abraham Lincoln, cotton field. 35c, Henri Christophe, armed slave revolt. 60c, Thomas Clarkson, addressing Anti-Slavery Society. 75c, William Wilberforce, Slave auction. $1, Olaudah Equiano, slave raid on Benin coast. $2.50, General Gordon, slave convoy in Sudan. $5, Granville Sharp, restraining ship captain from boarding slave.

**1984, Aug. 1 *Perf. 12***

*588* A77 10c multi 8 8
*589* A77 25c multi 18 18
*590* A77 35c multi 25 25
*591* A77 60c multi 42 42
*592* A77 75c multi 50 50
*593* A77 $1 multi 72 72
*594* A77 $2.50 multi 1.75 1.75
*595* A77 $5 multi 3.50 3.50
*a* Miniature sheet of 8 7.75 7.75
*Nos. 588-595 (8)* 7.40 7.40

No. 595a contains Nos. 588-595. Size: 122x151mm.

Christmas 1984 — A78

Various Disney characters and celebrations.

**1984, Nov. Litho. *Perf. 14***

*596* A78 1c multi 5 5
*597* A78 2c multi 5 5
*598* A78 3c multi 5 5
*599* A78 4c multi 5 5
*600* A78 5c multi 5 5
*601* A78 10c multi 7 7
*602* A78 $1 multi 68 68
*603* A78 $2 multi 1.35 1.35
*604* A78 $4 multi 2.75 2.75
*Nos. 596-604 (9)* 5.10 5.10

**Souvenir Sheet**

*605* A78 $5 multi 4.00 4.00

No. 605 has multicolored margin continuing design. Size: 127x102mm. No. 603, perf. 12½x12.

Nos. 464-465, 477 Overprinted or Overprinted and Surcharged: "U.P.U. CONGRESS / HAMBURG 1984"

**1984, Aug. 13**

*606* A62 5c #464 5 5
*607* A62 20c on 10c #465 16 16
*608* A62 $5 #477 4.00 4.00

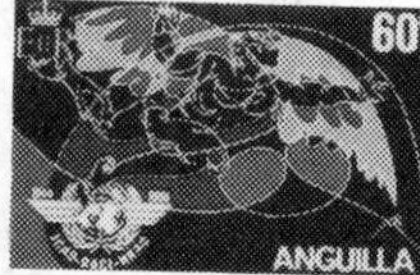

Intl. Civil Aviation Org., 40th Anniv. A79

**1984, Dec. 3 Litho. *Perf. 14***

*609* A79 60c Icarus, by Hans Erni 45 45
*610* A79 75c Sun Princess, by Sadiou Diouf 55 55
*611* A79 $2.50 Anniv. emblem, vert. 1.75 1.75

**Souvenir Sheet**

*612* A79 $5 Map of the Caribbean 3.75 3.75

No. 612 has multicolored margin continuing design and picturing air routes to the island. Size: 66x49mm.

Audubon Birth Bicentenary — A80

Illustrations by artist/naturalist J. J. Audubon (1785-1851).

**1985, Apr. 30 Litho. *Perf. 14***

| | | | |
|---|---|---|---|
| *613* | A80 10c Hirundo rustica | 8 | 8 |
| *614* | A80 60c Mycteria americana | 45 | 45 |
| *615* | A80 75c Sterna dougallii | 55 | 55 |
| *616* | A80 $5 Pandion haliaetus | 3.75 | 3.75 |

**Souvenir Sheets**

| | | | |
|---|---|---|---|
| *617* | A80 $4 Vireo solitarus, horiz. | 3.00 | 3.00 |
| *618* | A80 $4 Piranga ludoviciana, horiz. | 3.00 | 3.00 |

Nos. 617-618 have decorative margins continuing the designs. Sizes: 73x104mm.

Queen Mother 85th Birthday — A81

Photographs: 10c, Visiting the children's ward at King's College Hospital. $2, Inspecting Royal Marine Volunteer Cadets at Deal. $3, Outside Clarence House in London. $5, In an open carriage at Ascot.

**1985, July 2**

| | | | |
|---|---|---|---|
| *619* | A81 10c multi | 8 | 8 |
| *620* | A81 $2 multi | 1.50 | 1.50 |
| *621* | A81 $3 multi | 2.25 | 2.25 |

**Souvenir Sheet**

| | | | |
|---|---|---|---|
| *622* | A81 $5 multi | 3.75 | 3.75 |

Nos. 619-621 printed in sheetlets of 5.
No. 622 has decorative margin continuing the design. Size: 52x85mm.

Birds A82

**1985 Litho. *Perf. 13½x14***

| | | | | |
|---|---|---|---|---|
| *623* | A82 | 5c Brown pelican | 5 | 5 |
| *624* | A82 | 10c Turtle dove | 8 | 8 |
| *625* | A82 | 15c Man-o-war | 12 | 12 |
| *626* | A82 | 20c Antillean crested hummingbird | 15 | 15 |
| *627* | A82 | 25c White-tailed tropicbird | 20 | 20 |
| *628* | A82 | 30c Caribbean elaenia | 22 | 22 |
| *629* | A82 | 35c Black-whiskered vireo | 25 | 25 |
| *629A* | A82 | 35c Lesser Antillean bullfinch ('86) | 28 | 28 |
| *630* | A82 | 40c Yellow-crowned night heron | 30 | 30 |
| *631* | A82 | 45c Pearly-eyed thrasher | 35 | 35 |
| *632* | A82 | 50c Laughing bird | 38 | 38 |
| *633* | A82 | 65c Brown booby | 48 | 48 |
| *634* | A82 | 80c Gray kingbird | 60 | 60 |
| *635* | A82 | $1 Audubon's shearwater | 75 | 75 |
| *636* | A82 | $1.35 Roseate tern | 1.00 | 1.00 |
| *637* | A82 | $2.50 Bananaquit | 1.85 | 1.85 |
| *638* | A82 | $5 Belted kingfisher | 3.75 | 3.75 |
| *639* | A82 | $10 Green heron | 7.50 | 7.50 |

Nos. 485-490 Ovptd. "PRINCE HENRY / BIRTH 15.9.84."

**1985, Oct. Litho. *Perf. 14***

| | | | |
|---|---|---|---|
| *639A* | A64 10c multi | 8 | 8 |
| *639B* | A64 30c multi | 22 | 22 |
| *639C* | A64 40c multi | 30 | 30 |
| *639D* | A64 60c multi | 45 | 45 |
| *639E* | A64 $2 multi | 1.50 | 1.50 |
| *639F* | A64 $3 multi | 2.25 | 2.25 |
| ***h*** | Souvenir sheet of 6, #639A-639F | 4.80 | 4.80 |
| *639G* | A64 $5 multi | 3.75 | 3.75 |
| | *Nos. 639A-639G (7)* | 8.55 | 8.55 |

Nos. 464, 469 and 477 Ovptd. with Anniversary Emblem and "GIRL GUIDES 75th ANNIVERSARY / 1910-1985."

**1985, Oct. 14 Litho. *Perf. 14***

| | | | |
|---|---|---|---|
| *640* | A62 5c multi | 5 | 5 |
| *641* | A62 30c multi | 22 | 22 |
| *642* | A62 75c multi | 55 | 55 |
| *643* | A62 $5 multi | 3.75 | 3.75 |

Organization Emblem and "80th ANNIVERSARY ROTARY 1985."

**1985, Nov.**

| | | | |
|---|---|---|---|
| *644* | A62 10c multi | 8 | 8 |
| *645* | A62 35c multi | 25 | 25 |

Nos. 476, 469 Surcharged or Ovptd. with Emblem, Text and "INTERNATIONAL YOUTH YEAR."

**1985, Nov.**

| | | | |
|---|---|---|---|
| *646* | A62 $1 multi | 75 | 75 |
| *647* | A62 $5 multi | 3.75 | 3.75 |

Brothers Grimm — A83

Disney characters in Hansel and Gretel.

**1985, Nov. 11 Litho. *Perf. 14***

| | | | |
|---|---|---|---|
| *648* | A83 5c multi | 5 | 5 |
| *649* | A83 50c multi | 42 | 42 |
| *650* | A83 90c multi | 70 | 70 |
| *651* | A83 $4 multi | 3.25 | 3.25 |

**Souvenir Sheet**

| | | | |
|---|---|---|---|
| *652* | A83 $5 multi | 4.00 | 4.00 |

Christmas 1985. No. 652 has multicolored margin continuing the design. Size: 129x104mm.

Mark Twain (1835-1910), Author — A84

Disney characters in Huckleberry Finn.

**1985, Nov. 11**

| | | | |
|---|---|---|---|
| *653* | A84 10c multi | 8 | 8 |
| *654* | A84 60c multi | 50 | 50 |
| *654A* | A84 $1 Goofy | 80 | 80 |
| *655* | A84 $3 multi | 2.50 | 2.50 |

**Souvenir Sheet**

| | | | |
|---|---|---|---|
| *656* | A84 $5 multi | 4.00 | 4.00 |

Christmas 1985. No. 656 has multicolored margin continuing the design. Size: 127x101mm.
No. 654 printed in sheets of 8.

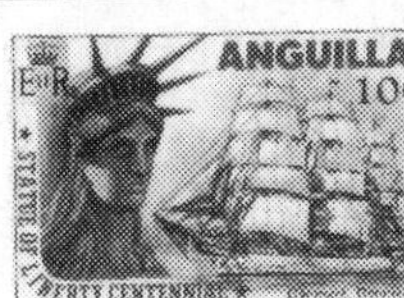


Operation SAIL, 1976 A85

**1985 Nov. 25**

| | | | |
|---|---|---|---|
| *657* | A85 10c Danmark, Denmark | 8 | 8 |
| *658* | A85 20c Eagle, USA | 18 | 18 |
| *659* | A85 60c Amerigo Vespucci, Italy | 50 | 50 |
| *660* | A85 75c Sir Winston Churchill, Great Britain | 60 | 60 |
| *661* | A85 $2 Nippon Maru, Japan | 1.65 | 1.65 |
| *662* | A85 $2.50 Gorch Germany | 1.90 | 1.90 |

**Souvenir Sheet**

| | | | |
|---|---|---|---|
| *663* | A85 $5 Statue of Liberty, vert. | 3.75 | 3.75 |

Statue of Liberty, cent. No. 663 has multicolored margin continuing design and picturing the Tawau Eagle and Gorch Fock. Size: 96x70mm.

Easter — A86

Stained glass windows.

**1986, Mar. Litho. *Perf. 14***

| | | | |
|---|---|---|---|
| *664* | A86 10c multi | 8 | 8 |
| *665* | A86 25c multi | 20 | 20 |
| *666* | A86 45c multi | 35 | 35 |
| *667* | A86 $4 multi | 3.00 | 3.00 |

**Souvenir Sheet**

| | | | |
|---|---|---|---|
| *668* | A86 $5 multi, horiz. | 3.75 | 3.75 |

No. 668 has red decorative margin. Size: 94x75mm.

A87

Halley's Comet A88

Designs: 5c, Johannes Hevelius (1611-1687), Mayan temple observatory. 10c, US Viking probe landing on Mars, 1976. 60c, Theatri Cosmicum (detail), 1668. $4, Sighting, 1835. $5, Comet over Anguilla.

**1986, Mar. 24**

| | | | |
|---|---|---|---|
| *669* | A87 5c multi | 5 | 5 |
| *670* | A87 10c multi | 8 | 8 |
| *671* | A87 60c multi | 45 | 45 |
| *672* | A87 $4 multi | 3.00 | 3.00 |

**Souvenir Sheet**

| | | | |
|---|---|---|---|
| *673* | A88 $5 multi | 3.75 | 3.75 |

No. 673 has multicolored margin showing plane and rowboat. Size: 102x70mm.

**Queen Elizabeth II, 60th Birthday**
Common Design Type

**1986, Apr. 21**

| | | | |
|---|---|---|---|
| *674* | CD339 20c Inspecting guards, 1946 | 15 | 15 |
| *675* | CD339 $2 Garter Ceremony, 1985 | 1.50 | 1.50 |
| *676* | CD339 $3 Trooping the color | 2.25 | 2.25 |

**Souvenir Sheet**

| | | | |
|---|---|---|---|
| *677* | CD339 $5 Christening, 1926 | 3.75 | 3.75 |

No. 677 has beige and gray inscribed margin. Size: 120x85mm.

Nos. 623, 631, 635, 637 and 639 Ovptd. "AMERIPEX 1986."

**1986, May 22 *Perf. 13½x14***

| | | | |
|---|---|---|---|
| *678* | A82 5c multi | 5 | 5 |
| *679* | A82 45c multi | 35 | 35 |
| *680* | A82 $1 multi | 75 | 75 |
| *681* | A82 $2.50 multi | 1.85 | 1.85 |
| *682* | A82 $10 multi | 7.50 | 7.50 |
| | *Nos. 678-682 (5)* | 10.50 | 10.50 |

Wedding of Prince Andrew and Sarah Ferguson — A89

**1986, July 23 Litho. *Perf. 14***

| | | | |
|---|---|---|---|
| *683* | A89 10c Couple | 8 | 8 |
| *684* | A89 35c Andrew | 25 | 25 |
| *685* | A89 $2 Sarah | 1.50 | 1.50 |
| *686* | A89 $3 Couple, diff. | 2.25 | 2.25 |

**Souvenir Sheet**

| | | | |
|---|---|---|---|
| *687* | A89 $6 Westminster Abbey | 4.50 | 4.50 |

No. 687 has multicolored margin picturing abbey. Size: 119x91mm.

Nos. 588-595 Ovptd. "INTERNATIONAL / YEAR OF / PEACE."

**1986 Litho. *Perf. 12***

| | | | |
|---|---|---|---|
| *688* | A77 10c multi | 8 | 8 |
| *689* | A77 25c multi | 20 | 20 |
| *690* | A77 35c multi | 28 | 28 |
| *691* | A77 60c multi | 48 | 48 |
| *692* | A77 75c multi | 60 | 60 |
| *693* | A77 $1 multi | 80 | 80 |
| *694* | A77 $2.50 multi | 1.75 | 1.75 |
| *695* | A77 $5 multi | 3.50 | 3.50 |
| ***a*** | Miniature sheet of 8 | 7.75 | 7.75 |
| | *Nos. 688-695 (8)* | 7.69 | 7.69 |

Ships A90

**1986, Nov. 29 Litho. *Perf. 14***

| | | | |
|---|---|---|---|
| *696* | A90 10c Trading Sloop | 8 | 8 |
| *697* | A90 45c Lady Rodney | 35 | 35 |
| *698* | A90 80c West Derby | 65 | 65 |
| *699* | A90 $3 Warspite | 2.40 | 2.40 |

**Souvenir Sheet**

| | | | |
|---|---|---|---|
| *700* | A90 $6 Boat Race Day, vert. | 4.50 | 4.50 |

Christmas 1986. No. 700 has multicolored margin continuing the design. Size: 130x100mm.

Discovery of America, 500th Anniv. (in 1992) — A91

Dragon Tree — A92

Designs: 5c, Christopher Columbus, astrolabe. 10c, Aboard ship. 35c, Santa Maria. 80c, Ferdinand, Isabella, horiz. $4, Indians. No. 707, Caribbean manatee, horiz.

**1986, Dec. 22**

*701* A91 5c multi 5 5
*702* A91 10c multi 8 8
*703* A91 35c multi 28 28
*704* A91 80c multi 65 65
*705* A91 $4 multi 3.20 3.20
*Nos. 701-705 (5)* 4.26 4.26

**Souvenir Sheets**

*706* A92 $5 shown 4.00 4.00
*707* A92 $5 multi 4.00 4.00

Nos. 706-707 have multicolored margins picturing maps of Columbus's landfall in America and the site of the Santa Maria's wreckage, 1492. Sizes: 97x67mm, 96x67mm (#707).

Butterflies A93

**1987, Apr. 14 Litho. *Perf. 14***

*708* A93 10c Monarch 8 8
*709* A93 80c White peacock 65 65
*710* A93 $1 Zebra 80 80
*711* A93 $2 Caribbean buckeye 1.60 1.60

**Souvenir Sheet**

*712* A93 $6 Flambeau 4.50 4.50

Easter 1987. No. 712 has multicolored margin picturing a Monarch caterpillar and butterfly. Size: 91x69mm.

Nos. 629A, 631, 634 and 639 Ovptd. with CAPEX '87 Emblem in Red

**1987, May 25 Litho. *Perf. 13½x14***

*713* A82 35c on No. 629A 28 28
*714* A82 45c on No. 631 35 35
*715* A82 80c on No. 634 60 60
*716* A82 $10 on No. 639 7.50 7.50

Separation from St. Kitts and Nevis, 20th Anniv. — A94

Designs: 10c, Old goose iron, electric iron. 35c, Old East End School, Albena Lake-Hodge Comprehensive College. 45c, Old market place, People's Market. 80c, Old ferries and modern ferry at Blowing Point. $1, Old and new cable and wireless offices. $2, Public meeting at Burrowes Park, House of Assembly.

**1987, May 25 *Perf. 14***

*717* A94 10c multi 8 8
*718* A94 35c multi 22 22
*719* A94 45c multi 35 35
*720* A94 80c multi 60 60
*721* A94 $1 multi 75 75
*722* A94 $2 multi 1.50 1.50
*a.* Souv. sheet of 6, Nos. 717-722 3.50 3.50
*Nos. 717-722 (6)* 3.50 3.50

No. 722a has inscribed margin. Size: 160x128mm.

Nos. 623, 625-628, 629A-639 Ovptd. "20 YEARS OF PROGRESS / 1967-1987" in Red. No. 625 also Surcharged in Black.

**1987, Sept. 4 Litho. *Perf. 13½x14***

*723* A82 5c No. 623 5 5
*724* A82 10c on 15c No. 625 8 8
*725* A82 15c No. 625 10 10
*726* A82 20c No. 626 14 14
*727* A82 25c No. 627 18 18
*728* A82 30c No. 628 20 20
*729* A82 35c No. 629A 22 22
*730* A82 40c No. 630 28 28
*731* A82 45c No. 631 32 32
*732* A82 50c No. 632 35 35
*733* A82 65c No. 633 45 45
*734* A82 80c No. 634 55 55
*735* A82 $1 No. 635 70 70
*736* A82 $1.35 No. 636 90 90
*737* A82 $2.50 No. 637 1.75 1.75
*738* A82 $5 No. 638 3.50 3.50
*739* A82 $10 No. 639 6.75 6.75
*Nos. 723-739 (17)* 16.52 16.52

Cricket World Cup A95

Various action scenes.

**1987, Oct. 5 *Perf. 14***

*740* A95 10c multi 8 8
*741* A95 35c multi 28 28
*742* A95 45c multi 38 38
*743* A95 $2.50 multi 2.00 2.00

**Souvenir Sheet**

*744* A95 $6 multi 4.50 4.50

No. 744 has multicolored margin picturing batsman on field. Size: 101x75mm.

Sea Shells, Crabs A96

**1987, Nov. 2**

*745* A96 10c West Indian top shell 8 8
*746* A96 35c Ghost crab 28 28
*747* A96 50c Spiny Caribbean vase 42 42
*748* A96 $2 Great land crab 1.60 1.60

**Souvenir Sheet**

*749* A96 $6 Queen conch 4.75 4.75

Christmas 1987. No. 749 has multicolored margin picturing reticulated cowrie-helmet. Size: 101x75mm.

Nos. 629A, 635-636 and 639 Ovptd. "40TH WEDDING ANNIVERSARY / H.M. QUEEN ELIZABETH II / H.R.H. THE DUKE OF EDINBURGH" in Scarlet

**1987, Dec. 14 Litho. *Perf. 13½x14***

*750* A82 35c multi 32 32
*751* A82 $1 multi 90 90
*752* A82 $1.35 multi 1.20 1.20
*753* A82 $10 multi 8.75 8.75

Lilies — A97

**1988, Mar. 28 Litho. *Perf. 14***

*754* A97 30c Crinum erubescens 28 28
*755* A97 45c Hymenocallis caribaea 40 40
*756* A97 $1 Crinum macowanii 88 88
*757* A97 $2.50 Hemerocallis fulva 2.20 2.20

**Souvenir Sheet**

*758* A97 $6 Lilium longiflorum 5.25 5.25

Easter 1988. No. 758 has multicolored inscribed margin picturing Easter lily. Size: 100x74mm.

1988 Summer Olympics, Seoul — A98

**1988, July 25 Litho. *Perf. 14***

*759* A98 35c 4x100-Meter relay 28 28
*760* A98 45c Windsurfing 35 35
*761* A98 50c Tennis 38 38
*762* A98 80c Basketball 60 60

**Souvenir Sheet**

*763* A98 $6 Women's 200 meters 4.50 4.50

No. 763 has multicolored decorative margin picturing Olympic flame and map of Korea. Size: 104x78mm.

Nos. 629A, 634-635 and 637 Ovptd. "H.R.H. PRINCESS / ALEXANDRA'S / VISIT NOVEMBER 1988."

**1988, Nov. Litho. *Perf. 13½x14***

*764* A82 35c multi 28 28
*765* A82 80c multi 60 60
*766* A82 $1 multi 75 75
*767* A82 $2.50 multi 1.90 1.90

## ANTIGUA

LOCATION — In the West Indies, southeast of Puerto Rico.
GOVT. — Independent state
AREA — 171 sq. mi.
POP. — 74,000 (est. 1981)
CAPITAL — St. John's.

Antigua was one of the presidencies of the former Leeward Islands colony until becoming a Crown Colony in 1956. It became an Associated State of the United Kingdom in 1967 and an independent nation on November 1, 1981, taking the name of Antigua and Barbuda.

Antigua stamps were discontinued in 1890 and resumed in 1903. In the interim, stamps of Leeward Islands were used. Between 1903-1956, stamps of Antigua and Leeward Islands were used concurrently.

12 Pence = 1 Shilling
20 Shillings = 1 Pound
100 Cents = 1 Dollars (1951)

**Catalogue values for unused stamps in this country are for Never Hinged items, beginning with Scott 96.**

Queen Victoria
A1 A2

**1862 Engr. Unwmk. *Perf. 14 to 16***

*1* A1 6p bl grn 750.00 400.00
*a.* Perf. 11 to 13 *6,000.*
*b.* Perf. 11 to 13x14 to 16 *3,750.*

There is a question whether Nos. 1a and 1b ever did postal duty.

Wmk.5

**1863 Wmk. Star. (5)**

*2* A1 1p lil rose 77.50 16.50
*a.* Imperf., pair *1,750.*
*3* A1 1p vermilion 55.00 15.00
*a.* Imperf. vert., pair *12,000.*
*4* A1 6p bl grn 140.00 19.00
*a.* 6p yel grn *3,750.* 42.50
*b.* Imperf., pair *1,125.*

**1873 Wmk. 1 *Perf. 12½.***

*5* A1 1p lake 65.00 27.50
*6* A1 1p vermilion 75.00 32.50
*7* A1 6p blue green 400.00 10.00

**1873-79 *Perf. 14***

*8* A1 1p rose 34.00 15.00
*a.* Half used as ½p on cover *1,500.*

**Typo.**

*9* A2 2½p red brn ('79) 350.00 150.00
*10* A2 4p bl ('79) 225.00 17.50

**Engr.**

*11* A1 6p bl grn ('76) 135.00 13.00

**1882-86 Typo. Wmk. 2**

*12* A2 ½p green 3.00 6.00
*13* A2 2½p red brn 105.00 32.50
*14* A2 2½p ultra ('86) 8.50 9.00
*15* A2 4p blue 150.00 20.00
*16* A2 4p brn org ('86) 2.50 4.00
*17* A2 1sh vio ('86) 135.00 60.00

**Engr.**

*18* A1 1p rose ('84) 1.00 *2.00*
*19* A1 6p dp grn 40.00 62.50

No. 18 was used for a time in St. Christopher.

**1884 *Perf. 12***

*20* A1 1p rose red 50.00 14.50

Seal of the Colony — A3

King Edward VII — A4

**Wmk. Crown and C. C. (1)**

**1903 Typo. *Perf. 14***

*21* A3 ½p bl grn & blk 1.00 1.35
*22* A3 1p car & blk 3.00 1.00
*a.* Bluish paper 45.00 45.00
*23* A3 2p org brn & vio 5.00 *10.00*
*24* A3 2½p ultra & blk 6.75 6.00
*25* A3 3p ocher & gray grn 4.50 7.00
*26* A3 6p blk & red vio 17.00 20.00
*27* A3 1sh vio & ultra 16.00 20.00
*28* A3 2sh pur & gray grn 22.00 25.00
*29* A3 2sh6p red vio & blk 21.00 30.00
*30* A4 5sh pur & gray grn 62.00 80.00
*Nos. 21-30 (10)* 158.25 200.35

The 2½p, 1sh and 5sh exist on both ordinary and chalky paper.

**1908-15 Wmk. 3**

*31* A3 ½p green 1.00 1.00
*32* A3 1p carmine 1.00 1.00
*a.* 1p scar ('15) 1.25 1.25
*33* A3 2p org brn & dl vio ('12) 3.25 5.00
*34* A3 2½p ultra 4.00 5.00
*35* A3 3p ocher & grn ('12) 3.75 6.00
*36* A3 6p blk & red vio ('11) 8.00 12.50
*37* A3 1sh vio & ultra 7.00 15.75
*38* A3 2sh vio & grn ('12) 45.00 55.00
*Nos. 31-38 (8)* 73.00 101.25

Nos. 33, 35 to 38 are on chalky paper.

King George V — A6

St. John's Harbor — A7

**1913**

41 A6 5sh vio & grn 42.50 *60.00*

**1921-29** **Wmk. 4**

42 A7 ½p green 50 20
43 A7 1p rose red 40 12
44 A7 1p dp vio ('23) 2.00 50
45 A7 1½p org ('22) 3.50 5.75
46 A7 1½p rose red ('26) 1.10 1.00
47 A7 1½p fawn ('29) 1.50 1.00
48 A7 2p gray 75 40
49 A7 2½p ultra 1.00 1.00
50 A7 2½p org ('23) 1.10 *3.00*

**Chalky Paper**

51 A7 3p vio, *yel* ('25) 2.75 4.00
52 A7 6p vio & red vio 2.25 3.25
53 A7 1sh *emer* ('29) 5.75 *9.00*
54 A7 2sh vio & ultra, *bl* ('27) 10.00 *15.00*
55 A7 2sh6p blk & red, *bl* ('27) 11.00 *15.00*
56 A7 3sh grn & vio ('22) 18.00 *24.00*
57 A7 4sh blk & red ('22) 32.50 *35.00*
*Nos. 42-57 (16)* 94.10 118.22

**Wmk. Multiple Crown and C. A. (3)**

**Chalky Paper.**

58 A7 3p vio, *yel* 2.50 *5.00*
59 A7 4p blk & red, *yel* ('22) 1.00 *4.00*
60 A7 1sh *emerald* 3.00 *6.00*
61 A7 2sh vio & ultra, *bl* 5.00 *9.00*
62 A7 2sh6p blk & red, *bl* 5.75 *12.00*
63 A7 5sh grn & red, *yel* ('22) 13.00 *22.50*
64 A7 £1 vio & blk, *red* ('22) 190.00 *260.00*
*Nos. 58-64 (7)* 220.25 318.50

Old Dockyard, English Harbour — A8

Govt. House, St. John's — A9

Nelson's "Victory," 1805 — A10

Sir Thomas Warner's Ship, 1632 — A11

**1932, Jan. 27** **Engr.** ***Perf. 12½***

67 A8 ½p green 1.00 1.00
68 A8 1p scarlet 1.00 1.00
69 A8 1½p lt brn 2.50 2.60
70 A9 2p gray 3.25 3.50
71 A9 2½p ultra 3.75 3.75
72 A9 3p orange 5.75 6.00
73 A10 6p violet 10.00 *14.00*
74 A10 1sh ol grn 12.00 *16.00*
75 A10 2sh6p claret 45.00 57.50
76 A11 5sh red brn & blk 120.00 140.00
*Nos. 67-76 (10)* 204.25 245.35

Tercentenary of the colony.

**Silver Jubilee Issue.**

Common Design Type

**1935, May 6** ***Perf. 13½x14***

77 CD301 1p car & bl 75 75
78 CD301 1½p gray blk & ultra 1.00 1.00
79 CD301 2½p bl & brn 3.25 *3.50*
80 CD301 1sh brt vio & ind 8.00 *8.75*

**Coronation Issue.**

Common Design Type

**1937, May 12** ***Perf. 11x11½***

81 CD302 1p carmine 20 20
82 CD302 1½p brown 22 22
83 CD302 2½p dp ultra 65 65

English Harbour A14

Nelson's Dockyard A15

Fort James — A16

St. John's Harbor — A17

**1938-48** **Engr.** ***Perf. 12½***

84 A14 ½p green 6 6
85 A15 1p red 8 8
86 A15 1½p brn vio 8 8
87 A14 2p dk gray 10 8
88 A15 2½p dp ultra 12 8
89 A16 3p orange 12 10
90 A17 6p purple 14 15
91 A17 1sh red brn & blk 30 30
92 A16 2sh6p dp cl 65 65
93 A17 5sh ol grn 1.50 1.75
94 A15 10sh red vio ('48) 8.25 11.00
95 A16 £1 Prus bl ('48) 9.50 17.50
*Nos. 84-95 (12)* 20.90 31.83

**Catalogue values for unused stamps in this section, from this point to the end of the section, are for Never Hinged items.**

**Peace Issue.**

Common Design Type

**1946, Nov. 1** **Wmk. 4** ***Perf. 13½x14***

96 CD303 1½p brown 20 20
97 CD303 3p dp org 25 25

**Silver Wedding Issue.**

Common Design Types

**1949, Jan. 3** **Photo.** ***Perf. 14x14½***

98 CD304 2½p brt ultra 15 15

**Engraved; Name Typographed**

***Perf. 11½x11***

99 CD305 5sh dk brn ol 5.00 *10.00*

**UPU Issue**

Common Design Types

**Engr.; Name Typo. on 3p and 6p**

***Perf. 13½, 11x11½***

**1949, Oct. 10** **Wmk. 4**

100 CD306 2½p dp ultra 25 25
101 CD307 3p orange 1.10 1.10
102 CD308 6p purple 2.25 2.25
103 CD309 1sh red brn 2.50 2.50

**University Issue**

Common Design Types

***Perf. 14x14½***

**1951, Feb. 16** **Engr.** **Wmk. 4**

104 CD310 3c choc & blk 25 25
105 CD311 12c pur & blk 65 65

Common Design Types pictured in section before Great Britain.

**Coronation Issue.**

Common Design Type

**1953, June 2** ***Perf. 13½x13***

106 CD312 2c dk grn & blk 75 75

Types of 1938 with Portrait of Queen Elizabeth II

Martello Tower — A24

***Perf. 13x13½, 13½x13***

**1953-56** **Wmk. 4**

107 A16 ½c dk red brn ('56) 8 6
108 A14 1c gray 8 6
109 A15 2c dp grn 8 5
110 A15 3c yel & blk 16 10
111 A14 4c rose red (shades) 16 10
112 A15 5c dl vio & blk 16 10
113 A16 6c orange 25 12
114 A24 8c dp bl 35 25
115 A17 12c violet 35 18
116 A17 24c choc & blk 50 22
117 A24 48c dp bl & rose lil 1.25 1.10
118 A16 60c claret 1.75 1.40
119 A17 $1.20 ol grn 1.75 1.40
120 A15 $2.40 magenta 6.00 *7.00*
121 A16 $4.80 grnsh bl 12.00 *12.50*
*Nos. 107-121 (15)* 24.92 24.64

See Nos. 138-145.

**West Indies Federation**

Common Design Type

***Perf. 11½x11***

**1958, Apr. 22** **Engr.** **Wmk. 314**

122 CD313 3c green 16 15
123 CD313 6c blue 35 28
124 CD313 12c car rose 75 65

Nos. 110 and 115 Overprinted in Red or Black: "Commemoration Antigua Constitution 1960"

***Perf. 13x13½, 13½x13***

**1960, Jan. 1** **Wmk. 4**

125 A15 3c yel & blk (R) 22 22
126 A17 12c violet 50 50

Issued to commemorate constitutional reforms effective Jan. 1, 1960.

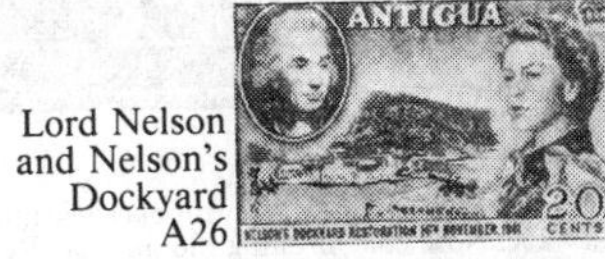

Lord Nelson and Nelson's Dockyard A26

***Perf. 11½x11***

**1961, Nov. 14** **Wmk. 314**

127 A26 20c brn & lil 50 40
128 A26 30c dk bl & grn 80 60

Issued to commemorate the completion of the restoration of Lord Nelson's headquarters, English Harbour.

Stamp of 1862 and Royal Mail Steam Packet in English Harbour A27

**1962, Aug. 1** **Engr.** ***Perf. 13***

129 A27 3c dl grn & pur 10 10
130 A27 10c dl grn & ultra 20 20
131 A27 12c dl grn & blk 28 28
132 A27 50c dl grn & brn org 1.40 1.40

Centenary of first Antigua postage stamp.

**Freedom from Hunger Issue**

Common Design Type

***Perf. 14x14½***

**1963, June 4** **Photo.** **Wmk. 314**

133 CD314 12c green 90 90

**Red Cross Centenary Issue**

Common Design Type

**1963, Sept. 2** **Litho.** ***Perf. 13***

134 CD315 3c blk & red 35 35
135 CD315 12c ultra & red 2.25 2.25

Types of 1938-53 with Portrait of Queen Elizabeth II

***Perf. 13x13½, 13½x13***

**1963-65** **Engr.** **Wmk. 314**

136 A16 ½c brn ('65) 28 28
137 A14 1c gray ('65) 28 28
138 A15 2c dp grn 16 16
139 A15 3c org yel & blk 22 22
140 A14 4c brn red 35 35
141 A15 5c dl vio & blk 35 35
142 A16 6c orange 38 38
143 A24 8c dp bl 45 45
144 A17 12c violet 85 85
145 A17 24c choc & blk 1.75 1.75
*Nos. 136-145 (10)* 5.07 5.07

**Shakespeare Issue**

Common Design Type

***Perf. 14x14½***

**1964, Apr. 23** **Photo.** **Wmk. 314**

151 CD316 12c red brn 75 75

No. 144 Surcharged with New Value and Bars

***Perf. 13½x13***

**1965, Apr. 1** **Engr.** **Wmk. 314**

152 A17 15c on 12c vio 50 50

**International Telecommunication Union Issue**

Common Design Type

***Perf. 11x11½***

**1965, May 17** **Litho.** **Wmk. 314**

153 CD317 2c bl & ver 15 15
154 CD317 50c org & vio bl 2.25 2.25

**Intl. Cooperation Year Issue**

Common Design Type

**1965, Oct. 25** ***Perf. 14½***

155 CD318 4c bl grn & cl 15 15
156 CD318 15c lt vio & grn 70 70

**Churchill Memorial Issue**

Common Design Type

**1966, Jan. 24** **Photo.** ***Perf. 14***

**Design in Black, Gold and Carmine Rose**

157 CD319 ½c brt bl 8 8
158 CD319 4c green 25 25
159 CD319 25c brown 1.10 90
160 CD319 35c violet 1.75 1.50

**Royal Visit Issue**

Common Design Type

**1966, Feb. 4** **Litho.** ***Perf. 11x12***

**Portraits in Black**

161 CD320 6c vio bl 1.10 90
162 CD320 15c dk car rose 1.75 1.10

**World Cup Soccer Issue**

Common Design Type

**1966, July 1** **Wmk. 314** ***Perf. 14***

163 CD321 6c multi 20 20
164 CD321 35c multi 80 80

**WHO Headquarters Issue**

Common Design Type

**1966, Sept. 20** ***Perf. 14***

165 CD322 2c multi 12 12
166 CD322 15c multi 75 75

Nelson's Dockyard A35

Designs: 1c, Old post office, St. John's. 2c, Health Center. 3c, Teachers' Training College. 4c, Martello Tower, Barbuda. 5c, Ruins of officers quarters, Shirley Heights. 6c, Government House, Barbuda. 10c, Princess Margaret School. 15c, Air terminal. 25c, General post office. 35c, Clarence House. 50c, Government House. 75c, Administration building. $1, Court House, St. John's. $2.50, Magistrates' Court. $5, St. John's Cathedral.

***Perf. 11½x11***

**1966, Nov. 1** **Engr.** **Wmk. 314**

167 A35 ½c grn & bl 5 5
168 A35 1c pur & rose 5 5
169 A35 2c sl & org 5 5
170 A35 3c rose red & blk 6 6
171 A35 4c dl vio & brn 7 7
172 A35 5c vio bl & ol 8 8
*a.* Bklt pane of 4 ('68) 40

| No. | Type | Value | Description | Unused | Used |
|---|---|---|---|---|---|
| 173 | A35 | 6c | dp org & pur | 15 | 15 |
| 174 | A35 | 10c | brt grn & rose red | 22 | 22 |
| a. | | | Bklt pane of 4 ('68) | 1.10 | |
| 175 | A35 | 15c | brn & bl | 30 | 30 |
| a. | | | Bklt pane of 4 ('68) | 1.50 | |
| 176 | A35 | 25c | sl & brn | 48 | 48 |
| 177 | A35 | 35c | dp rose & sep | 70 | 70 |
| 178 | A35 | 50c | grn & blk | 1.00 | 1.00 |
| 179 | A35 | 75c | Prus bl & vio bl | 1.25 | 1.25 |
| 180 | A35 | $1 | dp rose & ol | 1.75 | 1.75 |
| 181 | A35 | $2.50 | blk & rose | 4.25 | 4.25 |
| 182 | A35 | $5 | ol grn & dl vio | 9.00 | 9.00 |
| | | | *Nos. 167-182 (16)* | 19.46 | 19.46 |

**1969** *Perf. 13½*

**Colors as Before**

| No. | Type | Value | Unused | Used |
|---|---|---|---|---|
| 167a | A35 | ½c | 5 | 5 |
| 168a | A35 | 1c | 6 | 6 |
| 169a | A35 | 2c | 7 | 7 |
| 170a | A35 | 3c | 8 | 8 |
| 171a | A35 | 4c | 9 | 9 |
| 172b | A35 | 5c | 12 | 12 |
| 173a | A35 | 6c | 15 | 15 |
| 174b | A35 | 10c | 20 | 20 |
| 175b | A35 | 15c | 30 | 30 |
| 176a | A35 | 25c | 45 | 45 |
| 177a | A35 | 35c | 60 | 60 |
| 178a | A35 | 50c | 90 | 90 |
| 180a | A35 | $1 | 2.50 | 2.50 |
| 181a | A35 | $2.50 | 6.00 | 6.00 |
| 182a | A35 | $5 | 20.00 | 20.00 |
| | | *Nos. 167a-182a (15)* | 31.57 | 31.57 |

**UNESCO Anniversary Issue**

Common Design Type

Designs: 4c, "Education", (Pen and blocks). 25c, "Science," (Wheat ears and flask enclosing globe). $1, "Culture," (Lyre and columns).

**1966, Dec. 1** **Litho.** *Perf. 14*

| No. | Type | Value | Description | Unused | Used |
|---|---|---|---|---|---|
| 183 | CD323 | 4c | dp org, yel & dl vio | 18 | 18 |
| 184 | CD323 | 25c | vio, dk ol grn & yel | 50 | 50 |
| 185 | CD323 | $1 | yel, mag & blk | 2.50 | 2.50 |

**Independent State**

Flag of Antigua, Spiny Lobster, Maps of Antigua and Barbuda
A37

Designs: 15c, 35c, Flag of Antigua. 25c, Flag and Premier's Office Building.

**1967, Feb. 27** **Photo.** *Perf. 14*

| No. | Type | Value | Description | Unused | Used |
|---|---|---|---|---|---|
| 186 | A37 | 4c | multi | 6 | 6 |
| 187 | A37 | 15c | multi | 25 | 25 |
| 188 | A37 | 25c | multi | 40 | 40 |
| 189 | A37 | 35c | multi | 50 | 50 |

Antigua's independence, Feb. 27, 1967.

Gilbert Memorial Church, Antigua — A38

Designs: 25c, Nathaniel Gilbert's House. 35c, Map of the Caribbean and Central America.

*Perf. 14x13½*

**1967, May 18** **Photo.** **Wmk. 314**

| No. | Type | Value | Description | Unused | Used |
|---|---|---|---|---|---|
| 190 | A38 | 4c | brt red & blk | 7 | 7 |
| 191 | A38 | 25c | emer & blk | 40 | 40 |
| 192 | A38 | 35c | ultra & blk | 55 | 55 |

Issued to commemorate the attainment of autonomy by the Methodist Church in the Caribbean and the Americas, and the opening of headquarters near St. John's, Antigua, May 1967.

Antiguan and British Royal Arms — A39

**1967, July 21** *Perf. 14½x14*

| No. | Type | Value | Description | Unused | Used |
|---|---|---|---|---|---|
| 193 | A39 | 15c | dk grn & multi | 20 | 20 |
| 194 | A39 | 35c | dp bl & multi | 45 | 45 |

Issued to commemorate the granting of a new coat of arms to the State of Antigua and the 300th anniversary of the Treaty of Breda.

Sailing Ship, 17th Century
A40

Design: 6c, 35c, Map of Barbuda from Jan Blaeu's Atlas, 1665.

*Perf. 11½x11*

**1967, Dec. 14** **Engr.** **Wmk. 314**

| No. | Type | Value | Description | Unused | Used |
|---|---|---|---|---|---|
| 195 | A40 | 4c | dk bl | 8 | 8 |
| 196 | A40 | 6c | dp plum | 12 | 12 |
| 197 | A40 | 25c | green | 30 | 30 |
| 198 | A40 | 35c | black | 50 | 50 |

Issued to commemorate the 300th anniversary of the resettlement of Barbuda.

Dow Hill Antenna — A41

Designs: 15c, Antenna and rocket blasting off. 25c, Nose cone orbiting moon. 50c, Reentry of space capsule.

*Perf. 14½x14*

**1968, Mar. 29** **Photo.** **Wmk. 314**

| No. | Type | Value | Description | Unused | Used |
|---|---|---|---|---|---|
| 199 | A41 | 4c | dk bl, org & blk | 6 | 6 |
| 200 | A41 | 15c | dk bl, org & blk | 25 | 25 |
| 201 | A41 | 25c | dk bl, org & blk | 35 | 35 |
| 202 | A41 | 50c | dk bl, org & blk | 65 | 65 |

Issued to commemorate the dedication of the Dow Hill tracking station in Antigua for the NASA (National Space Administration) Apollo project.

Beach and Sailfish
A42

Designs: ½c, 50c, Limbo dancer, flames and dancing girls. 15c, Three girls on a beach and water skier. 35c, Woman scuba diver, corals and fish.

**1968, July 1** **Photo.** *Perf. 14*

| No. | Type | Value | Description | Unused | Used |
|---|---|---|---|---|---|
| 203 | A42 | ½c | red & multi | 5 | 5 |
| 204 | A42 | 15c | sky bl & multi | 25 | 25 |
| 205 | A42 | 25c | bl & multi | 35 | 35 |
| 206 | A42 | 35c | brt bl & multi | 45 | 45 |
| 207 | A42 | 50c | multi | 75 | 75 |
| | | | *Nos. 203-207 (5)* | 1.85 | 1.85 |

Issued for tourist publicity.

St. John's Harbor, 1768
A43

St. John's Harbor: 15c, 1829. 25c, Map of deep-sea harbor, 1968. 35c, Dock, 1968. 2c, Like $1.

**Engr. & Litho.; Engr. ($1)**

**1968, Oct. 31** **Wmk. 314** *Perf. 13*

| No. | Type | Value | Description | Unused | Used |
|---|---|---|---|---|---|
| 208 | A43 | 2c | dp car & lt bl | 7 | 7 |
| 209 | A43 | 15c | sep & yel grn | 25 | 25 |
| 210 | A43 | 25c | dk bl & yel | 40 | 40 |
| 211 | A43 | 35c | dp grn & sal | 45 | 45 |
| 212 | A43 | $1 | black | 1.40 | 1.40 |
| | | | *Nos. 208-212 (5)* | 2.57 | 2.57 |

Opening of St. John's deep-sea harbor.

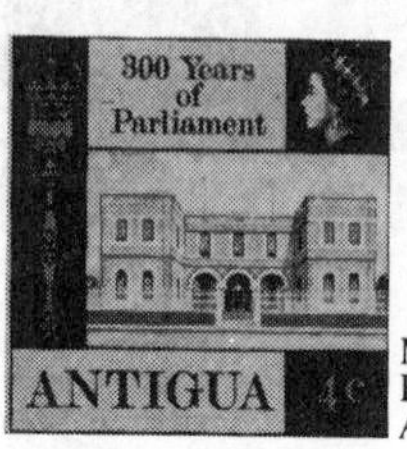


Mace and Parliament
A44

Designs (Mace and): 15c, Mace bearer. 25c, House of Representatives, interior. 50c, Antigua coat of arms and great seal.

**1969, Feb. 3** **Photo.** *Perf. 12½*

| No. | Type | Value | Description | Unused | Used |
|---|---|---|---|---|---|
| 213 | A44 | 4c | crim & multi | 6 | 6 |
| 214 | A44 | 15c | crim & multi | 20 | 20 |
| 215 | A44 | 25c | crim & multi | 30 | 30 |
| 216 | A44 | 50c | crim & multi | 65 | 65 |

300th anniversary of Antigua Parliament.

CARIFTA Cargo — A45

Design: 4c, 15c, Ship, plane and trucks (horiz.).

*Perf. 13½x13, 13x13½*

**1969, Apr. 14** **Litho.** **Wmk. 314**

| No. | Type | Value | Description | Unused | Used |
|---|---|---|---|---|---|
| 217 | A45 | 4c | blk & brt lil rose | 6 | 6 |
| 218 | A45 | 15c | blk & brt grnsh bl | 25 | 25 |
| 219 | A45 | 25c | bis & blk | 30 | 30 |
| 220 | A45 | 35c | tan & blk | 45 | 45 |

Issued to commemorate the 1st anniversary of CARIFTA (Caribbean Free Trade Area).

Map of Redonda Island
A46

Design: 25c, View of Redonda from the sea and seagulls.

*Perf. 13x13½*

**1969, Aug. 1** **Photo.** **Wmk. 314**

| No. | Type | Value | Description | Unused | Used |
|---|---|---|---|---|---|
| 221 | A46 | 15c | ultra & multi | 30 | 30 |
| 222 | A46 | 25c | multi | 45 | 45 |
| 223 | A46 | 50c | sal & multi | 1.25 | 1.25 |

Centenary of Redonda phosphate industry.

Adoration of the Kings, by Gugliemo Marcillat
A47

Design: 10c, 50c, Holy Family, by anonymous German artist, 15th century.

**1969, Oct. 15** **Litho.** *Perf. 13x14*

| No. | Type | Value | Description | Unused | Used |
|---|---|---|---|---|---|
| 224 | A47 | 6c | bis brn & multi | 15 | 15 |
| 225 | A47 | 10c | fawn & multi | 20 | 20 |
| 226 | A47 | 35c | gray ol & multi | 50 | 50 |
| 227 | A47 | 50c | gray bl & multi | 90 | 90 |

Christmas 1969.

Arms of Antigua — A48

**Coil Stamps**

*Perf. 14½x14*

**1970, Jan. 30** **Photo.** **Wmk. 314**

| No. | Type | Value | Description | Unused | Used |
|---|---|---|---|---|---|
| 228 | A48 | 5c | brt bl | 15 | 15 |
| 229 | A48 | 10c | brt grn | 20 | 20 |
| 230 | A48 | 25c | dp mag | 45 | 45 |

No. 176 Surcharged

*Perf. 11½x11*

**1970, Jan. 2** **Engr.** **Wmk. 314**

| No. | Type | Value | Description | Unused | Used |
|---|---|---|---|---|---|
| 231 | A35 | 20c | on 25c sl & brn | 35 | 35 |

Sikorsky S-38
A49

Aircraft: 20c, Dornier DO-X. 35c, Hawker Siddeley 748. 50c, Douglas C-124C Globemaster II. 75c, Vickers VC 10.

**1970, Feb. 16** **Litho.** *Perf. 14½*

| No. | Type | Value | Description | Unused | Used |
|---|---|---|---|---|---|
| 232 | A49 | 5c | brt grn & multi | 12 | 12 |
| 233 | A49 | 20c | ultra & multi | 35 | 35 |
| 234 | A49 | 35c | bl grn & multi | 60 | 60 |
| 235 | A49 | 50c | bl & multi | 90 | 90 |
| 236 | A49 | 75c | vio bl & multi | 1.50 | 1.50 |
| | | | *Nos. 232-236 (5)* | 3.47 | 3.47 |

40th anniversary of air service.

Dickens and Scene from "Pickwick Papers"
A50

Designs (Charles Dickens and Scene from): 5c, "Nicholas Nickleby." 35c, "Oliver Twist." $1, "David Copperfield."

**Wmk. 314**

**1970, May 19** **Litho.** *Perf. 14*

| No. | Type | Value | Description | Unused | Used |
|---|---|---|---|---|---|
| 237 | A50 | 5c | ol & sep | 10 | 10 |
| 238 | A50 | 20c | aqua & sep | 35 | 35 |
| 239 | A50 | 35c | vio & sep | 40 | 40 |
| 240 | A50 | $1 | scar & sep | 1.25 | 1.25 |

Issued to commemorate the centenary of the death of Charles Dickens (1812-1870), English novelist.

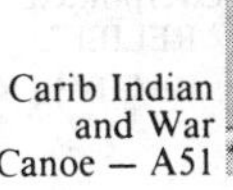

Carib Indian and War Canoe — A51

Designs (Ships): 1c, Columbus and "Nina." 2c, Sir Thomas Warner's arms and sailing ship. 3c, Viscount Hood and "Barfleur." 4c, Sir George Rodney and "Formidable." 5c, Capt. Horatio Nelson and "Boreas." 6c, King William IV and "Pegasus." 10c, Blackbeard (Edward Teach) and pirate ketch. 15c, Capt. Cuthbert Collingwood and "Pelican." 20c, Admiral Nelson and "Victoria." 25c, Paddle steamer "Solent" and Steam Packet Company emblem. 35c, King George V and corvette "Canada." 50c, Cruiser "Renown" and royal badge. 75c, S.S. "Federal Maple" and maple leaf. $1, Racing yacht "Sol-Quest" and Gallant 53 class emblem. $2.50, Missile destroyer "London" and her emblem. $5, Tug "Pathfinder" and arms of Antigua.

**Wmk. 314 Sideways**

**1970, Aug. 19 Litho. *Perf. 14***

*241* A51 ½c ocher & multi 9 6
*242* A51 1c Prus bl & multi 9 6
*243* A51 2c yel grn & multi 10 7
*244* A51 3c ol bis & multi 12 8
*245* A51 4c bl gray & multi 14 8
*246* A51 5c fawn & multi 16 10
*247* A51 6c rose lil & multi 18 12
*248* A51 10c brn org & multi 22 14
*249* A51 15c ultra & multi 35 22
*250* A51 20c ol grn & multi 28 16
*251* A51 25c ol & multi 32 20
*252* A51 35c dl red brn & multi 60 35
*253* A51 50c lt brn & multi 80 55
*254* A51 75c beige & multi 1.10 75
*255* A51 $1 Prus grn & multi 1.60 1.10
*256* A51 $2.50 gray & multi 4.50 2.75
*257* A51 $5 yel & multi 10.50 7.00
*Nos. 241-257 (17)* 21.15 13.79

**1972-74 Wmk. 314 Upright**

**Colors as Before**

*241a* A51 ½c 5 5
*242a* A51 1c 5 5
*244a* A51 3c 7 7
*245a* A51 4c 7 7
*246a* A51 5c 10 10
*247a* A51 6c 12 12
*248a* A51 10c 20 20
*249a* A51 15c 1.60 28
*254a* A51 75c 3.25 1.25
*255a* A51 $1 3.60 1.60
*256a* A51 $2.50 6.00 *7.50*
*257a* A51 $5 6.75 *10.50*
*Nos. 241a-257a (12)* 21.86 21.79

**1975, Jan. 21 Wmk. 373**

*257b* A51 $5 yel & multi 14.50 14.50

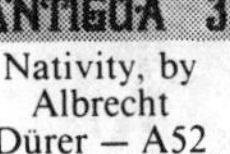
Nativity, by Albrecht Dürer — A52

Private, 4th West India Regiment, 1804 — A53

Designs: 10c, 50c, Adoration of the Magi, by Albrecht Dürer.

**Engr. & Litho.**

**1970, Oct. 28 *Perf. 13½x14***

*258* A52 3c brt grnsh bl & blk 8 8
*259* A52 10c pink & plum 20 20
*260* A52 35c brick red & blk 50 50
*261* A52 50c lil & vio 90 90

Christmas 1970.

***Perf. 14x13½***

**1970, Dec. 1 Litho. Wmk. 314**

Military Uniforms: ½c, Drummer Boy, 4th King's Own Regiment, 1759. 20c, Grenadier Company Officer, 60th Regiment, The Royal American, 1809. 35c, Light Company Officer, 93rd Regiment, The Sutherland Highlanders, 1826-1834. 75c, Private, 3rd West India Regiment, 1851.

*262* A53 ½c lake & multi 5 5
*263* A53 10c brn org & multi 45 45
*264* A53 20c Prus grn & multi 75 75
*265* A53 35c dl pur & multi 1.50 1.50
*266* A53 75c dk ol grn & multi 4.00 4.00
*a.* Souvenir sheet of 5 10.00 10.00
*Nos. 262-266 (5)* 6.75 6.75

No. 266a contains one each of Nos. 262-266, and label with date and guns. Decorative margin with inscription. Size: 125x143½mm.

See also Nos. 274-278, 283-287, 307-311, 329-333.

Market Woman Voting — A54

Designs (Voting by): 20c, Businessman. 35c, Mother (and child). 50c, Workman.

***Perf. 14½x14***

**1971, Feb. 1 Photo. Wmk. 314**

*267* A54 5c brown 6 6
*268* A54 20c ol blk 20 20
*269* A54 35c rose mag 35 35
*270* A54 50c vio bl 60 60

Adult suffrage, 20th anniversary.

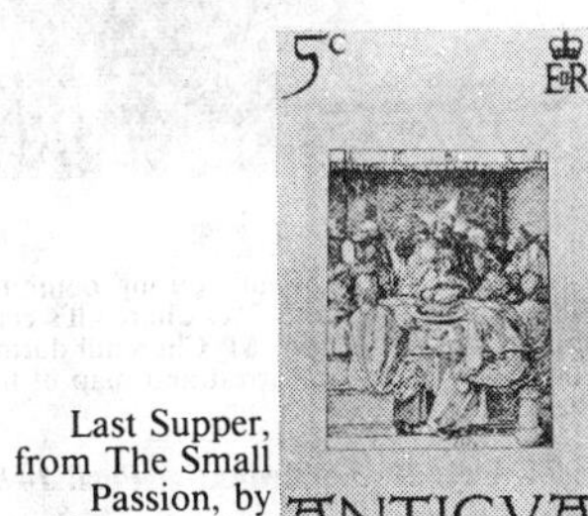

Last Supper, from The Small Passion, by Dürer — A55

Woodcuts by Albrecht Dürer: 35c, Crucifixion from Eichstaff Missal. 75c, Resurrection from The Great Passion.

***Perf. 14x13½***

**1971, Apr. 7 Litho. Wmk. 314**

*271* A55 5c gray, red & blk 8 8
*272* A55 35c gray, vio & blk 40 40
*273* A55 75c gray, gold & blk 90 90

Easter 1971.

Military Uniform Type of 1970

Military Uniforms: ½c, Private, Suffolk Regiment, 1704. 10c, Grenadier, South Staffordshire, 1751. 20c, Fusilier, Royal Northumberland, 1778. 35c, Private, Northamptonshire, 1793. 75c, Private, East Yorkshire, 1805.

**1971, July 12 Litho. Wmk. 314**

*274* A53 ½c gray grn & multi 5 5
*275* A53 10c bluish blk & multi 30 30
*276* A53 20c dk pur & multi 50 50
*277* A53 35c dk ol & multi 1.10 1.10
*278* A53 75c brn & multi 2.50 2.50
*a.* Souvenir sheet of 5 7.25 7.50
*Nos. 274-278 (5)* 4.45 4.45

No. 278a contains one each of Nos. 274-278 and label with date and crossed swords. Decorative margin with magenta inscription. Size: 117x144mm.

Values quoted in this catalogue are for stamps graded at Fine-Very Fine and with no faults. An illustrated guide to grade is provided in introductory material, beginning on Page V.

Virgin and Child, by Veronese — A56

Designs: 5c, 50c, Adoration of the Shepherds, by Bonifazio Veronese.

**1971, Oct. 4 *Perf. 14x13½***

*279* A56 3c multi 6 6
*280* A56 5c multi 12 12
*281* A56 35c multi 55 55
*282* A56 50c multi 90 90

Christmas 1971.

Uniform Type of 1970

Military Uniforms: ½c, Officer, King's Own Borderers Regiment, 1815. 10c, Sergeant, Buckinghamshire Regiment, 1837. 20c, Private, South Hampshire Regiment, 1853. 35c, Officer, Royal Artillery, 1854. 75c, Private, Worcestershire Regiment, 1870.

**1972, July 1**

*283* A53 ½c ol brn & multi 5 5
*284* A53 10c dp grn & multi 40 40
*285* A53 20c brt vio & multi 80 80
*286* A53 35c mar & multi 1.50 1.50
*287* A53 75c dk vio bl & multi 3.25 3.25
*a.* Souvenir sheet of 5 9.00 9.25
*Nos. 283-287 (5)* 6.00 6.00

No. 287a contains one each of Nos. 283-287 and label with coat of arms and date. Blue marginal inscription and ornament. Size: 126x144mm.

Reticulated Helmet Cowrie — A57

Sea Shells: 5c, Measled cowrie. 35c, West Indian fighting conch. 50c, Hawkwing conch.

**1972, Aug. 1 *Perf. 14½x14***

*288* A57 3c multi 15 15
*289* A57 5c ver & multi 35 35
*290* A57 35c lt vio & multi 1.40 1.40
*291* A57 50c rose red & multi 2.00 2.00

St. John's Cathedral, 1745-1843 A58

Designs: 50c, Interior of St. John's. 75c, St. John's rebuilt.

**1972, Nov. 6 Litho. *Perf. 14***

*292* A58 35c org brn & multi 45 45
*293* A58 50c vio & multi 85 85
*294* A58 75c multi 1.40 1.40
*a.* Souvenir sheet of 4 3.50 5.00

Christmas 1972. No. 294a contains one each of Nos. 292-294, perf. 15. Blue and silver margin. Size: 136x102mm.

**Silver Wedding Issue, 1972**

Common Design Type

**1972, Nov. 20 Photo. *Perf. 14x14½***

*295* CD324 20c ultra & multi 30 30
*296* CD324 35c stl bl & multi 50 50

25th anniversary of the marriage of Queen Elizabeth II and Prince Philip.

Map of Antigua, Batsman Driving Ball — A60

Designs: 35c, Batsman and wicketkeeper. $1, Emblem of Rising Sun Cricket Club.

**1972, Dec. 15 *Perf. 13½x14***

*297* A60 5c multi 25 25
*298* A60 35c multi 1.25 1.25
*299* A60 $1 multi 3.00 3.00
*a.* Souvenir sheet of 3 5.00 6.50

50th anniversary of the Rising Sun Cricket Club, St. John's. No. 299a contains one each of Nos. 297-299. Light green margin with black inscription. Size: 87½x130mm.

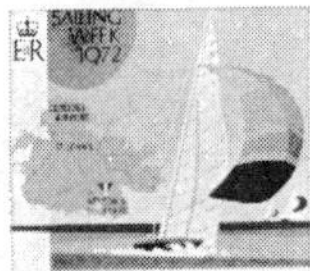

Map of Antigua and Yacht — A61

**1972, Dec. 29 *Perf. 14½***

*300* A61 35c *shown* 35 35
*301* A61 50c *Racing yachts* 40 40
*302* A61 75c *St. John's G.P.O.* 70 70
*303* A61 $1 *Statue of Liberty* 1.10 1.10
*a.* Souvenir sheet of 2 2.50 3.00

Opening of Antigua and Barbuda Information Office in New York City. No. 303a contains one each of Nos. 301 and 303. Light brown and yellow margin with black inscription and flags of Antigua. Size: 98½x92mm.

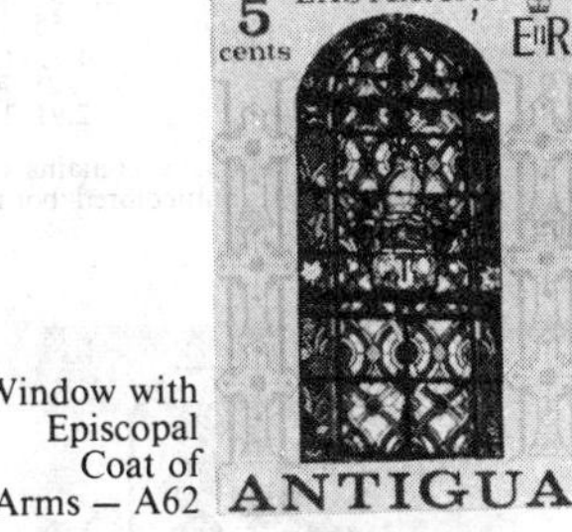

Window with Episcopal Coat of Arms — A62

Designs (stained glass windows from Cathedral of St. John): 35c, Crucifixion. 75c, Arm of Rt. Rev. D.G. Davis, 1st bishop of Antigua.

**1973, Apr. 16 Litho. *Perf. 13½***

*304* A62 5c yel & multi 6 6
*305* A62 35c brt lil & multi 40 40
*306* A62 75c bl & multi 80 80

Easter 1973.

Uniform Type of 1970

Military Uniforms: ½c, Private, Col. Zacharia Tiffin's Regiment, 1701. 10c, Private, 63rd Regiment, 1759. 20c, Officer, 35th Sussex Regiment, 1828. 35c, Private, 2nd West India Regiment, 1853. 75c, Sergeant, Princess of Wales Regiment, Hertfordshire, 1858.

***Perf. 14x13½***

**1973, July 1 Wmk. 314**

*307* A53 ½c dp ultra & multi 5 5
*308* A53 10c rose lil & multi 25 25
*309* A53 20c gray & multi 45 45
*310* A53 35c multi 80 80
*311* A53 75c multi 2.00 2.00
*a.* Souvenir sheet of 5 4.00 5.00
*Nos. 307-311 (5)* 3.55 3.55

No. 311a contains one each of Nos. 307-311 and label with coat of arms and date. Rose lilac marginal inscription and ornament. Size: 126x144mm.

Butterfly Costumes — A63

Designs: 20c, Carnival revelers. 35c, Costumed group. 75c, Carnival Queen.

*Perf. 13½x14*

**1973, July 30** **Unwmk.**

| | | | | |
|---|---|---|---|---|
| *312* | A63 | 5c multi | 10 | 10 |
| *313* | A63 | 20c multi | 30 | 30 |
| *314* | A63 | 35c multi | 50 | 50 |
| *315* | A63 | 75c multi | 1.25 | 1.25 |
| *a.* | | Souvenir sheet of 4 | 2.50 | 4.00 |

Carnival, July 29-Aug. 7. No. 315a contains one each of Nos. 312-315. Multicolored margin. Size: 133x95mm.

Virgin of the Porridge, by David — A64

Paintings: 5c, Adoration of the Kings, by Stomer. 20c, Virgin of the Grand Duke, by Raphael. 35c, Nativity with God the Father and Holy Ghost, by Tiepolo. $1, Madonna and Child, by Murillo.

*Perf. 14½*

**1973, Oct. 15** **Photo.** **Unwmk.**

| | | | | |
|---|---|---|---|---|
| *316* | A64 | 3c brt bl & multi | 6 | 6 |
| *317* | A64 | 5c emer & multi | 10 | 10 |
| *318* | A64 | 20c gold & multi | 35 | 35 |
| *319* | A64 | 35c vio & multi | 65 | 65 |
| *320* | A64 | $1 red & multi | 1.75 | 1.75 |
| *a.* | | Souvenir sheet of 5 | 3.25 | 4.00 |
| | | *Nos. 316-320 (5)* | 2.91 | 2.91 |

Christmas 1973. No. 320a contains one each of Nos. 316-320; multicolored border. Size: 130x128mm.

Princess Anne and Mark Phillips — A65

Design: $2, different border.

**1973, Nov. 14** **Litho.** ***Perf. 13½***

| | | | | |
|---|---|---|---|---|
| *321* | A65 | 35c dl ultra & multi | 20 | 20 |
| *322* | A65 | $2 yel grn & multi | 1.10 | 1.10 |
| *a.* | | Souvenir sheet of 2 | 1.40 | 1.40 |

Wedding of Princess Anne and Capt. Mark Phillips.

Nos. 321-322 were issued in sheets of 5 plus label, with multicolored, inscribed margins.

No. 322a contains one each of Nos. 321-322; multicolored margins with commemorative inscriptions. Size: 78x99mm.

### Nos. 321-322 and 322a Overprinted Vertically: "HONEYMOON / VISIT / DECEMBER 16th / 1973"

**1973, Dec. 15** **Litho.** ***Perf. 13½***

| | | | | |
|---|---|---|---|---|
| *323* | A65 | 35c multi | 25 | 25 |
| *324* | A65 | $2 multi | 1.25 | 1.25 |
| *a.* | | Souvenir sheet of 2 | 1.60 | 1.60 |

Visit of Princess Anne and Mark Phillips to Antigua, Dec. 16. Same overprint in sheet margins of Nos. 323-324 and 324a.

Arms of Antigua and U.W.I. A66

Designs: 20c, Dancers. 35c, Antigua campus. 75c, Chancellor Sir Hugh Wooding.

**1974, Feb. 18** **Wmk. 314**

| | | | | |
|---|---|---|---|---|
| *325* | A66 | 5c multi | 6 | 6 |
| *326* | A66 | 20c multi | 25 | 25 |
| *327* | A66 | 35c multi | 40 | 40 |
| *328* | A66 | 75c multi | 80 | 80 |

24th anniversary of the University of the West Indies.

### Uniform Type of 1970

Military Uniforms: ½c, Officer, 59th Foot, 1797. 10c, Gunner, Royal Artillery, 1800. 20c, Private, 1st West India Regiment, 1830. 35c, Officer, Gordon Highlanders, 1843. 75c, Private, Royal Welsh Fusiliers, 1846.

**1974, May 1** ***Perf. 14x13½***

| | | | | |
|---|---|---|---|---|
| *329* | A53 | ½c dl grn & multi | 5 | 5 |
| *330* | A53 | 10c ocher & multi | 15 | 15 |
| *331* | A53 | 20c multi | 30 | 30 |
| *332* | A53 | 35c gray bl & multi | 50 | 50 |
| *333* | A53 | 75c dk gray & multi | 1.10 | 1.10 |
| *a.* | | Souvenir sheet of 5 | 2.75 | 3.00 |
| | | *Nos. 329-333 (5)* | 2.10 | 2.10 |

No. 333a contains one each of Nos. 329-333. Margin with inscription, ornament and arms in slate green. Size: 126x145mm.

English Mailman and Coach, Helicopter — A67

Designs (UPU Emblem and): 1c, English beliman, 1846; Orinoco mailboat, 1851; telecommunications satellite. 2c, English mail-train guard, 1852; Swiss post passenger bus, 1906; Italian hydrofoil. 5c, Swiss messenger, 16th century; Wells Fargo coach, 1800; Concorde. 20c, German position, 1820; Japanese mailmen, 19th century; carrier pigeon. 35c, Contemporary Antiguan mailman; radar station; aquaplane. $1, Medieval French courier; American train, 1884; British Airways jet.

**1974, July 15** **Litho.** ***Perf. 14½***

| | | | | |
|---|---|---|---|---|
| *334* | A67 | ½c multi | 5 | 5 |
| *335* | A67 | 1c multi | 5 | 5 |
| *336* | A67 | 2c multi | 6 | 5 |
| *337* | A67 | 5c multi | 7 | 6 |
| *338* | A67 | 20c multi | 25 | 20 |
| *339* | A67 | 35c multi | 60 | 45 |
| *340* | A67 | $1 multi | 1.40 | 1.10 |
| *a.* | | Souvenir sheet of 7 | 2.25 | 2.50 |
| | | *Nos. 334-340 (7)* | 2.48 | 1.96 |

Centenary of Universal Postal Union. No. 340a contains one each of Nos. 334-340, perf. 13, and label with commemorative inscription. Multicolored margin with airmail labels from various countries. Size: 141x163mm.

Traditional Steel Band — A68

Designs (Steel Bands): 5c, Traditional players (vert.). 35c, Modern steel band. 75c, Modern players (vert.).

**1974, Aug. 1,** **Wmk. 314** ***Perf. 14***

| | | | | |
|---|---|---|---|---|
| *341* | A68 | 5c rose red, dk red & blk | 6 | 6 |
| *342* | A68 | 20c ocher, brn & blk | 25 | 25 |
| *343* | A68 | 35c yel grn, grn & blk | 40 | 40 |
| *344* | A68 | 75c dl bl, dk bl & blk | 75 | 75 |
| *a.* | | Souvenir sheet of 4 | 1.75 | 2.00 |

Carnival 1974. No. 344a contains one each of Nos. 341-344; black marginal inscription and multicolored design. Size: 115x107½mm.

Soccer — A69

Designs: Games' emblem and soccer.

**1974, Sept. 23** **Unwmk.** ***Perf. 14½***

| | | | | |
|---|---|---|---|---|
| *345* | A69 | 5c multi | 8 | 8 |
| *346* | A69 | 35c multi | 40 | 40 |
| *347* | A69 | 75c multi | 80 | 80 |
| *348* | A69 | $1 multi | 1.10 | 1.10 |
| *a.* | | Souvenir sheet of 4 | 2.25 | 2.75 |

World Cup Soccer Championship, Munich, June 13-July 7. Nos. 345-348 issued in sheets of 5 plus label showing Soccer Cup. No. 348a contains one each of Nos. 345-348, perf. 13½, and 2 labels; multicolored margin with flags of participating nations. Size: 133½x129mm.

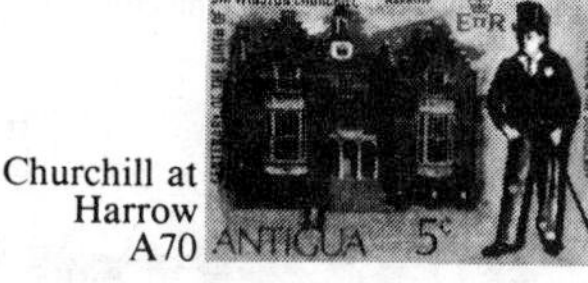


Churchill at Harrow A70

Designs: 35c, St. Paul's during bombing and Churchill portrait. 75c, Churchill's coat of arms and catafalque. $1, Churchill during Boer war, warrant for arrest and map of his escape route.

**1974, Oct. 20** **Unwmk.** ***Perf. 14½***

| | | | | |
|---|---|---|---|---|
| *349* | A70 | 5c multi | 8 | 8 |
| *350* | A70 | 35c multi | 30 | 30 |
| *351* | A70 | 75c multi | 75 | 75 |
| *352* | A70 | $1 multi | 90 | 90 |
| *a.* | | Souvenir sheet of 4 | 1.75 | 2.00 |

Birth centenary of Winston Churchill (1874-1965). No. 352a contains one each of Nos. 349-352; margin in colors and design of Union Jack. Size: 107x82mm.

Virgin and Child, by Giovanni Bellini — A71

Designs: Paintings of the Virgin and Child.

**1974, Nov. 18** **Litho.** ***Perf. 14½***

| | | | | |
|---|---|---|---|---|
| *353* | A71 | ½c *shown* | 5 | 5 |
| *354* | A71 | 1c *Raphael* | 5 | 5 |
| *355* | A71 | 2c *Van der Weyden* | 6 | 6 |
| *356* | A71 | 3c *Giorgione* | 6 | 6 |
| *357* | A71 | 5c *Andrea Mantegna* | 7 | 7 |
| *358* | A71 | 20c *Alvise Vivarini* | 25 | 25 |
| *359* | A71 | 35c *Bartolommeo Montagna* | 40 | 40 |
| *360* | A71 | 75c *Lorenzo Costa* | 85 | 85 |
| *a.* | | Souvenir sheet of 4 | 1.60 | 1.60 |
| | | *Nos. 353-360 (8)* | 1.79 | 1.79 |

Christmas 1974. No. 360a contains one each of Nos. 357-360, perf. 13½. Multicolored decorative margin. Size: 138x125mm.

### Nos. 346-348 Overprinted and No. 344 Surcharged and Overprinted: "EARTHQUAKE / RELIEF"

**1974, Oct. 16** **Litho.** ***Perf. 14½, 14***

| | | | | |
|---|---|---|---|---|
| *361* | A69 | 35c multi | 25 | 20 |
| *362* | A69 | 75c multi | 70 | 60 |
| *363* | A69 | $1 multi | 90 | 75 |
| *364* | A68 | $5 on 75c multi | 4.50 | 4.00 |

Earthquake of Oct. 8, 1974.

### Nos. 338-340 and 254a Surcharged with New Value and Two Bars

**1974-75** **Wmk. 314** ***Perf. 14½***

| | | | | |
|---|---|---|---|---|
| *365* | A67 | 50c on 20c | 55 | 55 |
| *366* | A67 | $2.50 on 35c | 2.75 | 2.75 |
| *367* | A67 | $5 on $1 | 5.25 | 5.25 |

*Perf. 14*

| | | | | |
|---|---|---|---|---|
| *368* | A51 | $10 on 75c | 10.50 | 10.50 |

Carib War Canoe, English Harbour A72

Designs (Nelson's Dockyard): 15c, Raising ship, 1770. 35c, Lord Nelson and "Boreas." 50c, Yachts arriving for Sailing Week, 1974. $1, "Anchorage" in Old Dockyard, 1970.

**1975, Mar. 17** **Unwmk.** ***Perf. 14½***

| | | | | |
|---|---|---|---|---|
| *369* | A72 | 5c multi | 10 | 10 |
| *370* | A72 | 15c multi | 32 | 32 |
| *371* | A72 | 35c multi | 60 | 60 |
| *372* | A72 | 50c multi | 90 | 90 |
| *373* | A72 | $1 multi | 1.75 | 1.75 |
| *a.* | | Souvenir sheet of 5 | 4.50 | 5.25 |
| | | *Nos. 369-373 (5)* | 3.67 | 3.67 |

No. 373a contains one each of Nos. 369-373, perf. 13½, and one label. Multicolored margin with nautical design. Size: 130x133mm.

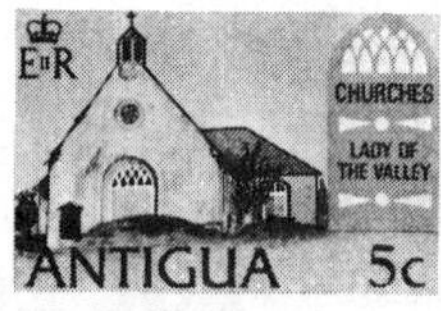


Lady of the Valley Church A73

Churches of Antigua: 20c, Gilbert Memorial. 35c, Grace Hill Moravian. 50c, St. Philip's. $1, Ebenezer Methodist.

**1975, May 19** **Litho.** ***Perf. 14½***

| | | | | |
|---|---|---|---|---|
| *374* | A73 | 5c multi | 8 | 8 |
| *375* | A73 | 20c multi | 25 | 25 |
| *376* | A73 | 35c multi | 45 | 45 |
| *377* | A73 | 50c multi | 75 | 75 |
| *378* | A73 | $1 multi | 1.25 | 1.25 |
| *a.* | | Souvenir sheet of 3 | 2.75 | 3.50 |
| | | *Nos. 374-378 (5)* | 2.78 | 2.78 |

No. 378a contains one each of Nos. 376-378, perf. 13½; multicolored margin showing altar. Size: 91x101mm.

Antigua, Senex's Atlas, 1721, and Hevelius Sextant, 1640 A74

Designs (Maps of Antigua): 20c, Jeffery's Atlas, 1775, and 18th century engraving of ship. 35c, Barbuda and Antigua, 1775 and 1975. $1, St. John's and English Harbour, 1973.

**1975, July 21** **Wmk. 314**

| | | | | |
|---|---|---|---|---|
| *379* | A74 | 5c multi | 8 | 8 |
| *380* | A74 | 20c multi | 35 | 35 |
| *381* | A74 | 35c multi | 60 | 60 |
| *382* | A74 | $1 multi | 1.75 | 1.75 |
| *a.* | | Souvenir sheet of 4 | 3.00 | 3.50 |

No. 382a contains one each of Nos. 379-382; multicolored margin showing ancient navigational and astrological instruments. Size: 130x88mm.

Bugler and Sunset A75

Designs (Nordjamb 75 Emblem and): 20c, Black and white Scouts, tents and flags. 35c, Lord Baden-Powell and tents. $2, Dahomey dancers.

**Unwmk.**

**1975, Aug. 26 Litho. *Perf. 14***

| | | | | |
|---|---|---|---|---|
| *383* | A75 | 15c multi | 30 | 30 |
| *384* | A75 | 20c multi | 40 | 40 |
| *384* | A75 | 35c multi | 60 | 60 |
| *386* | A75 | $2 multi | 2.75 | 2.75 |
| *a.* | | Souvenir sheet of 4 | 4.50 | 5.50 |

Nordjamb 75, 14th Boy Scout Jamboree, Lillehammer, Norway, July 29-Aug. 7. No. 386a contains one each of Nos. 383-386; light green and multicolored margin black inscription and multicolored Scout emblems. Size: 143x106½mm.

Eurema Elathea A76

Butterflies: 1c, Danaus plexippus. 2c, Phoebis philea. 5c, Marpesia petreus thetys. 20c, Eurema proterpia. 35c, Papilio polydamas. $2, Vanessa cardui.

**1975, Oct. 30 Litho. *Perf. 14***

| | | | | |
|---|---|---|---|---|
| *387* | A76 | ½c multi | 5 | 5 |
| *388* | A76 | 1c multi | 5 | 5 |
| *389* | A76 | 2c multi | 7 | 5 |
| *390* | A76 | 5c multi | 14 | 10 |
| *391* | A76 | 20c multi | 50 | 40 |
| *392* | A76 | 35c multi | 90 | 75 |
| *393* | A76 | $2 multi | 4.50 | 3.50 |
| *a.* | | Miniature sheet of 4 | 6.75 | 7.25 |
| | | *Nos. 387-393 (7)* | 6.21 | 4.90 |

No. 393a contains one each of Nos. 390-393, multicolored margin shows butterflies and lepidopterists. Size: 146x92mm.

Virgin and Child, by Correggio — A77

Designs: Virgin and Child paintings.

**1975, Nov. 17 Unwmk.**

| | | | | |
|---|---|---|---|---|
| *394* | A77 | ½c *shown* | 5 | 5 |
| *395* | A77 | 1c *El Greco* | 5 | 5 |
| *396* | A77 | 2c *Durer* | 5 | 5 |
| *397* | A77 | 3c *Antonello* | 5 | 5 |
| *398* | A77 | 5c *Bellini* | 10 | 10 |
| *399* | A77 | 10c *Durer* | 20 | 20 |
| *400* | A77 | 35c *Bellini* | 70 | 70 |
| *401* | A77 | $2 *Durer* | 2.75 | 2.75 |
| *a.* | | Souvenir sheet of 4 | 3.75 | 3.75 |
| | | *Nos. 394-401 (8)* | 3.95 | 3.95 |

Christmas 1975. No. 401a contains one each of Nos. 398-401; multicolored margin with stained glass window design. Size: 137x118mm.

West Indies Team A78

Designs: 5c, Batsman I.V.A. Richards and cup (vert.). 35c, Bowler A.M.E. Roberts and cup (vert.).

**1975, Dec. 15 Litho. *Perf. 13½***

| | | | | |
|---|---|---|---|---|
| *402* | A78 | 5c multi | 20 | 12 |
| *403* | A78 | 35c multi | 90 | 75 |
| *404* | A78 | $2 multi | 3.50 | 3.50 |

World Cricket Cup, victory of West Indies team.

Antillean Crested Hummingbird — A79

Irrigation System, Diamond Estate — A80

Designs: 1c, Imperial parrot. 2c, Zenaida dove. 3c, Loggerhead kingbird. 4c, Red-necked pigeon. 5c, Rufous-throated solitaire. 6c, Orchid tree. 10c, Bougainvillea. 15c, Geiger tree. 20c, Flamboyant. 25c, Hibiscus. 35c, Flame of the Woods. 50c, Cannon at Fort James. 75c, Premier's Office. $1, Potworks Dam. $5, Government House. $10, Coolidge International Airport.

**1976, Jan. 19 Litho. *Perf. 14½***

| | | | | |
|---|---|---|---|---|
| *405* | A79 | ½c multi | 8 | 8 |
| *406* | A79 | 1c multi | 8 | 8 |
| *407* | A79 | 2c multi | 8 | 8 |
| *408* | A79 | 3c multi | 8 | 8 |
| *409* | A79 | 4c multi | 8 | 8 |
| *410* | A79 | 5c multi | 8 | 8 |
| *411* | A79 | 6c multi | 8 | 8 |
| *412* | A79 | 10c multi | 8 | 8 |
| *413* | A79 | 15c multi | 12 | 12 |
| *414* | A79 | 20c multi | 15 | 15 |
| *415* | A79 | 25c multi | 20 | 20 |
| *416* | A79 | 35c multi | 30 | 30 |
| *417* | A79 | 50c multi | 40 | 40 |
| *418* | A79 | 75c multi | 60 | 60 |
| *419* | A79 | $1 multi | 80 | 80 |

***Perf. 13½x14***

| | | | | |
|---|---|---|---|---|
| *420* | A80 | $2.50 rose & multi | 1.75 | 1.75 |
| *421* | A80 | $5 lil & multi | 3.75 | 3.75 |
| *422* | A80 | $10 multi | 7.50 | 7.50 |
| | | *Nos. 405-422 (18)* | 16.21 | 16.21 |

In 1978 Nos. 405-422 were reissued with "1978" centered below design.

Privates, Clark's Illinois Regiment — A81

Designs: 1c, Riflemen, Pennsylvania Militia. 2c, Decorated American powder horn. 5c, Water bottle of Maryland troops. 35c, "Liberty Tree" and "Rattlesnake" flags. $1, American privateer Montgomery. $2.50, Congress Flag. $5, Continental Navy sloop Ranger.

**1976, Mar. 17 Litho. *Perf. 14½***

| | | | | |
|---|---|---|---|---|
| *423* | A81 | ½c multi | 5 | 5 |
| *424* | A81 | 1c multi | 5 | 5 |
| *425* | A81 | 2c multi | 5 | 5 |
| *426* | A81 | 5c multi | 8 | 8 |
| *427* | A81 | 35c multi | 40 | 40 |
| *428* | A81 | $1 multi | 1.25 | 1.25 |
| *429* | A81 | $5 multi | 5.00 | 5.00 |
| | | *Nos. 423-429 (7)* | 6.88 | 6.88 |

Souvenir Sheet

*Perf. 13*

| | | | | |
|---|---|---|---|---|
| *430* | A81 | $2.50 multi | 3.75 | 3.75 |

American Bicentennial. No. 430 has multicolored margin showing "A sketch of the action between the British Forces and the American Provincials on the Heights of the Peninsula of Charlestown." Size: 71x84mm.

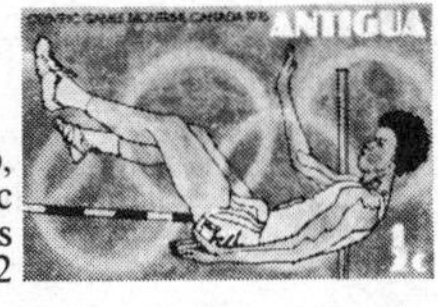

High Jump, Olympic Rings A82

Designs (Olympic Rings and): 1c, Boxing. 2c, Pole vault. 15c, Swimming. 30c, Running. $1, Bicycling. $2, Shot put.

**1976, July 12 Litho. *Perf. 14½***

| | | | | |
|---|---|---|---|---|
| *431* | A82 | ½c yel & multi | 5 | 5 |
| *432* | A82 | 1c pur & multi | 5 | 5 |
| *433* | A82 | 2c emer & multi | 5 | 5 |
| *434* | A82 | 15c brt bl & multi | 15 | 15 |
| *435* | A82 | 30c ol & multi | 40 | 40 |
| *436* | A82 | $1 org & multi | 1.00 | 1.00 |
| *437* | A82 | $2 red & multi | 2.00 | 2.00 |
| *a.* | | Souvenir sheet of 4 | 3.50 | 5.00 |
| | | *Nos. 431-437 (7)* | 3.70 | 3.70 |

21st Olympic Games, Montreal, Canada, July 17-Aug. 1. No. 437a contains one each of Nos. 434-437, perf. 13½; black marginal inscription. Size: 89x137mm.

Water Skiing A83

Water Sports: 1c, Sailfish sailing. 2c, Snorkeling. 20c, Deep-sea fishing. 50c, Scuba diving. $2, Swimming.

**1976, Aug. 26 *Perf. 14***

| | | | | |
|---|---|---|---|---|
| *438* | A83 | ½c yel grn & multi | 5 | 5 |
| *439* | A83 | 1c sep & multi | 5 | 5 |
| *440* | A83 | 2c gray & multi | 5 | 5 |
| *441* | A83 | 20c multi | 15 | 15 |
| *442* | A83 | 50c brt vio & multi | 40 | 40 |
| *443* | A83 | $2 lt gray & multi | 1.25 | 1.25 |
| *a.* | | Souvenir sheet of 3 | 2.50 | 3.50 |
| | | *Nos. 438-443 (6)* | 1.95 | 1.95 |

No. 443a contains one each of Nos. 441-443; multicolored margin shows beach scene. Size: 89x113½mm.

French Angelfish — A84

**1976, Oct. 4 Litho. *Perf. 13½x14***

| | | | | |
|---|---|---|---|---|
| *444* | A84 | 15c *shown* | 20 | 20 |
| *445* | A84 | 30c *Yellowfish grouper* | 35 | 35 |
| *446* | A84 | 50c *Yellowtail snappers* | 65 | 65 |
| *447* | A84 | 90c *Shy hamlet* | 1.10 | 1.10 |

The Annunciation A85

Designs: 10c, Flight into Egypt. 15c, Three Kings. 50c, Shepherds and star. $1, Kings presenting gifts to Christ Child.

**1976, Nov. 15 Litho. *Perf. 14***

| | | | | |
|---|---|---|---|---|
| *448* | A85 | 8c multi | 10 | 10 |
| *449* | A85 | 10c multi | 15 | 15 |
| *450* | A85 | 15c multi | 20 | 20 |
| *451* | A85 | 50c multi | 50 | 50 |
| *452* | A85 | $1 multi | 1.00 | 1.00 |
| | | *Nos. 448-452 (5)* | 1.95 | 1.95 |

Christmas 1976.

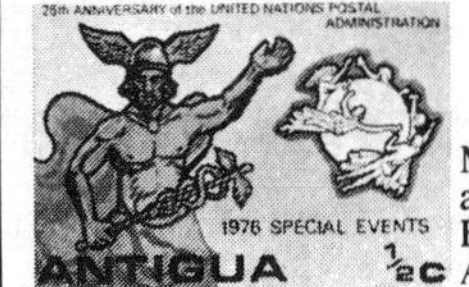

Mercury and UPU Emblem A86

Designs: 1c, Alfred Nobel, symbols of prize categories. 10c, Viking spacecraft. 50c, Vivi Richards (batsman) and Andy Roberts (bowler). $1, Alexander G. Bell, telephones, 1876 and 1976. $2, Schooner Freelance.

**1976, Dec. 28 Litho. *Perf. 14***

| | | | | |
|---|---|---|---|---|
| *453* | A86 | ½c multi | 5 | 5 |
| *454* | A86 | 1c multi | 5 | 5 |
| *455* | A86 | 10c multi | 15 | 15 |
| *456* | A86 | 50c multi | 65 | 65 |
| *457* | A86 | $1 multi | 1.00 | 1.00 |
| *458* | A86 | $2 multi | 1.75 | 1.75 |
| *a.* | | Souvenir sheet of 4 | 4.25 | 6.00 |
| | | *Nos. 453-458 (6)* | 3.65 | 3.65 |

Special 1976 Events: U.N. Postal Administration, 25th anniversary (½c); Nobel Prize, 75th anniversary (1c); Viking Space Mission to Mars (10c); World Cricket Cup victory (50c); Telephone centenary ($1); Operation Sail, American Bicentenary ($2).

No. 458a contains one each of Nos. 455-458, yellow and black decorative margin. Size: 128x101mm.

Royal Family — A87

Designs: 30c, Elizabeth II and Prince Philip touring Antigua. 50c, Queen enthroned. 90c, Queen wearing crown. $2.50, Queen and Prince Charles. $5, Queen and Prince Philip.

**1977, Feb. 7 *Perf. 13½x14, 12***

| | | | | |
|---|---|---|---|---|
| *459* | A87 | 10c multi | 8 | 8 |
| *460* | A87 | 30c multi | 18 | 18 |
| *461* | A87 | 50c multi | 30 | 30 |
| *462* | A87 | 90c multi | 60 | 60 |
| *463* | A87 | $2.50 multi | 1.50 | 1.50 |
| | | *Nos. 459-463 (5)* | 2.66 | 2.66 |

**Souvenir Sheet**

| | | | | |
|---|---|---|---|---|
| *464* | A87 | $5 multi | 4.00 | 4.00 |

25th anniversary of the reign of Queen Elizabeth II.

No. 464 has dull orange margin with black inscription. Size: 116x78mm.

Nos. 459-463 were printed in sheets of 40 (10x4), perf. 13½x14, and sheets of 5 plus label, perf. 12.

A booklet of self-adhesive stamps contains one pane of six 50c stamps in design of 90c, and one pane of one $5. Stamps have changed colors. Panes have marginal inscriptions.

Scouts Camping A88

Designs (Boy Scout Emblem and): 1c, Scouts on hike. 2c, Rock climbing. 10c, Cutting logs. 30c, Map and compass reading. 50c, First aid. $2, Scouts on raft.

**1977, May 23 Litho. *Perf. 14***

| | | | | |
|---|---|---|---|---|
| *465* | A88 | ½c multi | 5 | 5 |
| *466* | A88 | 1c multi | 5 | 5 |
| *467* | A88 | 2c multi | 5 | 5 |
| *468* | A88 | 10c multi | 12 | 12 |
| *469* | A88 | 30c multi | 30 | 30 |

| | | | | |
|---|---|---|---|---|
| *470* | A88 | 50c multi | 50 | 50 |
| *471* | A88 | $2 multi | 1.90 | 1.90 |
| *a.* | | Souvenir sheet of 3 | 2.50 | 3.50 |
| | | *Nos. 465-471 (7)* | 2.97 | 2.97 |

Caribbean Boy Scout Jamboree, Jamaica. No. 471a contains one each of Nos. 469-471; multicolored margin shows 3 Scouts. Size: 127x112mm.

Carnival Queen Holding Horseshoe — A89

Designs: 30c, Carnival Queen in feather costume. 50c, Butterfly costume. 90c, Carnival Queen with ornaments. $1, Carnival King and Queen.

**1977, July 18 Litho. *Perf. 14***

| | | | | |
|---|---|---|---|---|
| *472* | A89 | 10c multi | 10 | 10 |
| *473* | A89 | 30c multi | 20 | 20 |
| *474* | A89 | 50c multi | 35 | 35 |
| *475* | A89 | 90c multi | 60 | 60 |
| *476* | A89 | $1 multi | 65 | 65 |
| *a.* | | Souvenir sheet of 4 | 2.00 | 3.00 |
| | | *Nos. 472-476 (5)* | 1.90 | 1.90 |

21st Summer Carnival. No. 476a contains one each of Nos. 473-476; multicolored decorative margin. Size: 140x120mm.

Nos. 459-464 Overprinted: "ROYAL VISIT / 28th OCTOBER 1977"

***Perf. 13½x14, 12***

**1977, Oct. 17 Litho.**

| | | | | |
|---|---|---|---|---|
| *477* | A87 | 10c multi | 8 | 8 |
| *478* | A87 | 30c multi | 20 | 20 |
| *479* | A87 | 50c multi | 35 | 35 |
| *480* | A87 | 90c multi | 60 | 60 |
| *481* | A87 | $2.50 multi | 1.75 | 1.75 |
| | | *Nos. 477-481 (5)* | 2.98 | 2.98 |

**Souvenir Sheet**

| | | | | |
|---|---|---|---|---|
| *482* | A87 | $5 multi | 3.25 | 3.25 |

Visit of Queen Elizabeth II, Oct. 28.

Virgin and Child, by Cosimo Tura — A90

Virgin and Child by: 1c, $2, Carlo Crivelli (different). 2c, 25c, Lorenzo Lotto (different). 8c, Jacopo da Pontormo. 10c, Tura.

**1977, Nov. 15 Litho. *Perf. 14***

| | | | | |
|---|---|---|---|---|
| *483* | A90 | ½c multi | 5 | 5 |
| *484* | A90 | 1c multi | 5 | 5 |
| *485* | A90 | 2c multi | 5 | 5 |
| *486* | A90 | 8c multi | 8 | 8 |
| *487* | A90 | 10c multi | 10 | 10 |
| *488* | A90 | 25c multi | 22 | 22 |
| *489* | A90 | $2 multi | 1.75 | 1.75 |
| *a.* | | Souvenir sheet of 4 | 2.25 | 3.00 |
| | | *Nos. 483-489 (7)* | 2.30 | 2.30 |

Christmas 1977. No. 489a contains one each of Nos. 486-489; multicolored margin shows Christmas tree, candles and angel. Size: 143x117½mm.

Pineapple — A91

Designs: 15c, Flag of Antigua. 50c, Police band. 90c, Prime Minister V. C. Bird. $2, Coat of Arms.

**1977, Dec. 28 Litho. *Perf. 13x13½***

| | | | | |
|---|---|---|---|---|
| *490* | A91 | 10c multi | 8 | 8 |
| *491* | A91 | 15c multi | 12 | 12 |
| *492* | A91 | 50c multi | 40 | 40 |
| *493* | A91 | 90c multi | 75 | 75 |
| *494* | A91 | $2 multi | 1.60 | 1.60 |
| *a.* | | Souvenir sheet of 4 | 2.75 | 3.50 |
| | | *Nos. 490-494 (5)* | 2.95 | 2.95 |

10th anniversary of Statehood. No. 494a contains one each of Nos. 491-494; multicolored decorative margin. Size: 125x98mm.

Wright Glider III, 1902 A92

Designs: 1c, Flyer I in air, 1903. 2c, Weight and derrick launch system and Wright engine, 1903. 10c, Orville Wright (vert.). 50c, Flyer III, 1905. 90c, Wilbur Wright (vert.). $2, Wright Model B, 1910. $2.50, Flyer I, 1903, on ground.

**1978, Mar. 28 *Perf. 14***

| | | | | |
|---|---|---|---|---|
| *495* | A92 | ½c multi | 5 | 5 |
| *496* | A92 | 1c multi | 5 | 5 |
| *497* | A92 | 2c multi | 5 | 5 |
| *498* | A92 | 10c multi | 8 | 8 |
| *499* | A92 | 50c multi | 35 | 35 |
| *500* | A92 | 90c multi | 60 | 60 |
| *501* | A92 | $2 multi | 1.40 | 1.40 |
| | | *Nos. 495-501 (7)* | 2.58 | 2.58 |

**Souvenir Sheet**

| | | | | |
|---|---|---|---|---|
| *502* | A92 | $2.50 multi | 2.00 | 2.00 |

75th anniversary of first powered flight by Wright brothers. No. 502 has lilac and black margin showing plane and aviator at controls. Size: 90x75mm.

Sunfish Regatta A93

Designs: 50c, Fishing and work boat race. 90c, Curtain Bluff race. $2, Powerboat rally. $2.50, Guadeloupe-Antigua race.

**1978, Apr. 29 Litho. *Perf. 14½***

| | | | | |
|---|---|---|---|---|
| *503* | A93 | 10c multi | 8 | 8 |
| *504* | A93 | 50c multi | 40 | 40 |
| *505* | A93 | 90c multi | 75 | 75 |
| *506* | A93 | $2 multi | 1.60 | 1.60 |

**Souvenir Sheet**

| | | | | |
|---|---|---|---|---|
| *507* | A93 | $2.50 multi | 2.40 | 2.40 |

Sailing Week 1978. No. 507 has blue and multicolored margin showing route of race from Des Hayes, Guadeloupe, to English Harbour, Antigua. Size: 110x77mm.

Elizabeth II and Prince Philip — A94

Designs: 30c, Coronation. 50c, State coach. 90c, Elizabth II and Archbishop. $2.50, Elizabeth II. $5, Elizabeth II, Prince Philip, Prince Charles and Princess Anne as children.

**1978, June 2 Litho. *Perf. 14, 12***

| | | | | |
|---|---|---|---|---|
| *508* | A94 | 10c multi | 8 | 8 |
| *509* | A94 | 30c multi | 20 | 20 |
| *510* | A94 | 50c multi | 35 | 35 |
| *511* | A94 | 90c multi | 60 | 60 |
| *512* | A94 | $2.50 multi | 1.75 | 1.75 |
| | | *Nos. 508-512 (5)* | 2.98 | 2.98 |

**Souvenir Sheet**

| | | | | |
|---|---|---|---|---|
| *513* | A94 | $5 multi | 3.50 | 3.50 |

25th anniversary of coronation of Queen Elizabeth II. No. 513 has lilac rose and black margin showing palace gate. Size: 113x103mm.

Nos. 508-512 were printed in sheets of 50 (2 panes of 25), perf. 14, and in sheets of 3 plus label, perf. 12, with frames in changed colors.

Glass Coach A95

Royal Coaches: 50c, Irish state coach. $5, Coronation coach.

**1978, June 2 Litho. *Imperf.***

**Self-adhesive.**

| | | | |
|---|---|---|---|
| *514* | | Souvenir booklet, multi | 5.75 |
| *a.* | A95 | Bklt pane of (6 (3 each 25c and 50c) | 1.75 |
| *b.* | A95 | Bklt pane of 1 ($5) | 3.75 |

25th anniversary of coronation of Queen Elizabeth II. No. 514 contains 2 booklet panes printed on peelable paper backing showing royal processions. Size of panes: 156x93mm.

Soccer — A96

Purple Wreath — A97

Designs: Various soccer scenes. Stamps in souvenir sheet horizontal.

**1978, Aug. 18 Litho. *Perf. 14½***

| | | | | |
|---|---|---|---|---|
| *515* | A96 | 10c multi | 10 | 10 |
| *516* | A96 | 15c multi | 15 | 15 |
| *517* | A96 | $3 multi | 3.00 | 3.00 |

**Souvenir Sheet**

| | | | | |
|---|---|---|---|---|
| *518* | | Sheet of 4 | 3.25 | 3.25 |
| *a.* | A96 | 25c multi | 25 | 25 |
| *b.* | A96 | 30c multi | 30 | 30 |
| *c.* | A96 | 50c multi | 50 | 50 |
| *d.* | A96 | $2 multi | 2.00 | 2.00 |

11th World Cup Soccer Championship, Argentina, June 1-25. No. 518 has multicolored margin showing Jules Rimet Cup. Size: 126x89mm.

**1978, Oct. Litho. *Perf. 14***

Flowers: 50c, Sunflowers. 90c, Frangipani. $2, Passionflower. $2.50, Red hibiscus.

| | | | | |
|---|---|---|---|---|
| *519* | A97 | 25c multi | 22 | 22 |
| *520* | A97 | 50c multi | 45 | 45 |
| *521* | A97 | 90c multi | 80 | 80 |
| *522* | A97 | $2 multi | 1.75 | 1.75 |

**Souvenir Sheet**

| | | | | |
|---|---|---|---|---|
| *523* | A97 | $2.50 multi | 2.50 | 2.50 |

No. 523 has red, blue and black margin showing flowers. Size: 118x85mm.

St. Ildefonso Receiving Chasuble, by Rubens — A98

Paintings: 25c, Flight of St. Barbara, by Rubens. $2, Holy Family, by Sebastiano del Piombo. $4, Annunciation, by Rubens.

**1978, Oct. 30 Litho. *Perf. 14***

| | | | | |
|---|---|---|---|---|
| *524* | A98 | 8c multi | 7 | 7 |
| *525* | A98 | 25c multi | 20 | 20 |
| *526* | A98 | $2 multi | 1.90 | 1.90 |

**Souvenir Sheet**

| | | | | |
|---|---|---|---|---|
| *527* | A98 | $4 multi | 5.00 | 5.00 |

Christmas 1978. No. 527 has multicolored margin showing Rubens portrait. Size: 170x113mm.

Antigua No. 2 — A99

Crucifixion, by Dürer — A100

Designs: 50c, Great Britain Penny Black, 1840. $1, Woman posting letter in pillar box, and coach. $2, Mail train, ship, plane and Concorde. $2.50, Rowland Hill.

**1979, Feb. 12 Litho. *Perf. 14***

| | | | | |
|---|---|---|---|---|
| *528* | A99 | 25c multi | 20 | 20 |
| *529* | A99 | 50c multi | 40 | 40 |
| *530* | A99 | $1 multi | 75 | 75 |
| *531* | A99 | $2 multi | 1.65 | 1.65 |

**Souvenir Sheet**

| | | | | |
|---|---|---|---|---|
| *532* | A99 | $2.50 multi | 2.25 | 2.25 |

Sir Rowland Hill (1795-1879), originator of penny postage. No. 532 has multicolored margin showing Penny Black and ancient means of postal service. Size: 108x83mm.

Nos. 528-531 were printed in sheets of 50 (2 panes of 25), perf. 14, and in sheets of 5 plus label, perf. 12, with frames in changed colors.

**1979, Mar. 15**

Designs (after Dürer): 10c, Deposition. $2.50, Crucifixion. $4, Man of Sorrows.

| | | | | |
|---|---|---|---|---|
| *533* | A100 | 10c multi | 8 | 8 |
| *534* | A100 | 50c multi | 40 | 40 |
| *535* | A100 | $4 multi | 3.00 | 3.00 |

**Souvenir Sheet**

| | | | | |
|---|---|---|---|---|
| *536* | A100 | $2.50 multi | 2.25 | 2.25 |

Easter 1979. No. 536 has light blue and ultramarine margin showing head of Jesus. Size: 113x101mm.

Child Playing with Ship — A101

Designs (IYC emblem, child's hand holding toy): 50c, Rocket. 90c, Automobile. $2, Train. $5, Plane.

**1979, Apr. 9 Litho. *Perf. 14***

| | | | | |
|---|---|---|---|---|
| *537* | A101 | 25c multi | 20 | 20 |
| *538* | A101 | 50c multi | 40 | 40 |
| *539* | A101 | 90c multi | 75 | 75 |
| *540* | A101 | $2 multi | 1.65 | 1.65 |

**Souvenir Sheet**

| | | | | |
|---|---|---|---|---|
| *541* | A101 | $5 multi | 4.00 | 4.00 |

International Year of the Child. Margin of No. 541 has picture of boy. Size: 80x111mm.

Yellowjacks — A102

Sport Fish: 50c, Bluefin tunas. 90c, Sailfish. $2.50, Barracuda. $3, Wahoos.

**1979, May Litho. Perf. 14½**

542 A102 30c multi 25 25
543 A102 50c multi 40 40
544 A102 90c multi 70 70
545 A102 $3 multi 2.25 2.25

**Souvenir Sheet**

546 A102 $2.50 multi 2.00 2.00

No. 546 has multicolored margin showing harbor and boats. Size: 123x75mm.

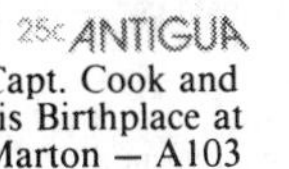


Capt. Cook and his Birthplace at Marton — A103

Holy Family — A104

Designs (Capt. Cook and): 50c, HMS Endeavour. 90c, Marine timekeeper. $2.50, HMS Resolution. $3, Landing at Botany Bay.

**1979, July 2 Litho. Perf. 14**

547 A103 25c multi 20 20
548 A103 50c multi 35 35
549 A103 90c multi 60 60
550 A103 $3 multi 2.00 2.00

**Souvenir Sheet**

551 A103 $2.50 multi 2.25 2.25

200th death anniversary of Capt. James Cook (1728-1779). No. 551 has multicolored margin showing Whitby Harbor and ships. Size: 111x86mm.

**1979, Oct. 1 Litho. Perf. 14**

Stained-glass Windows: 25c, Flight into Egypt. 50c, Shepherd and star. $3, Angel with trumpet. $4, Three Kings offering gifts.

552 A104 8c multi 8 8
553 A104 25c multi 20 20
554 A104 50c multi 40 40
555 A104 $4 multi 3.00 3.00

**Souvenir Sheet**

556 A104 $3 multi 2.25 2.25

Christmas 1979. No. 556 has multicolored margin showing kings and shepherds under Star of Bethlehem. Size: 114x94½mm.

Javelin, Olympic Rings — A105

**1980, Feb. 7 Litho. Perf. 14**

557 A105 10c *shown* 8 8
558 A105 25c *Running* 20 20
559 A105 $1 *Pole vault* 65 65
560 A105 $2 *Hurdles* 1.40 1.40

**Souvenir Sheet**

561 A105 $3 *Boxing*, horiz. 2.00 2.00

22nd Summer Olympic Games, Moscow, July 19-Aug. 3. No. 561 has multicolored margin showing boxing ring and audience. Size: 128x96mm.

Disney Characters and IYC Emblem A105a

Designs: Transportation scenes.

**1980, Mar. 24 Litho. Perf. 11**

562 A105a ½c *Mickey Mouse, plane*, horiz. 5 5
563 A105a 1c *Donald Duck, car* 5 5
564 A105a 2c *Goofy driving taxi*, horiz. 5 5
565 A105a 3c *Mickey and Minnie in sidecar*, horiz. 5 5
566 A105a 4c *Huey, Dewey and Louie*, horiz. 5 5
567 A105a 5c *Grandma Duck*, horiz. 5 5
568 A105a 10c *Mickey Mouse in jeep* 10 10
569 A105a $1 *Chip and Dale sailing*, horiz. 1.00 1.00
570 A105a $4 *Donald Duck on train* 4.00 4.00
*Nos. 562-570 (9)* 5.40 5.40

**Souvenir Sheet**

571 A105a $2.50 *Goofy in glider*, horiz. 5.00 5.00

No. 571 has multicolored margin showing Disney characters on hillside. Size: 101x127mm.

Nos. 528-531 Overprinted "LONDON 1980"

**1980, May 6 Litho. Perf. 12**

571A A99 25c multi 20 20
571B A99 50c multi 35 35
571C A99 $1 multi 60 60
571D A99 $2 multi 1.40 1.40

London '80 Intl. Stamp Exhib., May 6-14.

Birth of Venus, by Botticelli — A106

Designs: 10c, David, by Donatello (vert.). 50c, Reclining Couple, sarcophagus, Cerveteri. 90c, The Garden of Earthly Delights, by Hieronymus Bosch. $1, Portinari Altarpiece, by Hugo van der Goes. $4, Eleanora of Toledo and her Son Giovanni de Medici, by Bronzino (vert.). $5, The Holy Family, by Rembrandt.

***Perf. 13½x14, 14x13½***

**1980, June 23 Litho.**

572 A106 10c multi 8 8
573 A106 30c multi 20 20
574 A106 50c multi 35 35
575 A106 90c multi 60 60
576 A106 $1 multi 65 65
577 A106 $4 multi 3.75 3.75
*Nos. 572-577 (6)* 5.63 5.63

**Souvenir Sheet**

578 A106 $5 multi 3.75 3.75

No. 578 has multicolored margin showing entire painting. Size: 99½x125mm.

Anniversary Emblem, Intl. Headquarters, Evanston, Ill — A107

**1980, July 21 Litho. Perf. 14**

579 A107 3c *shown* 20 20
580 A107 50c *Antigua club banner* 35 35
581 A107 90c *Map of Antigua* 60 60
582 A107 $3 *Paul. P. Harris, emblem* 2.00 2.00

**Souvenir Sheet**

583 A107 $5 *Emblems, Antigua flags* 3.25 3.25

Rotary International, 75th anniversary. No. 583 has multicolored margin showing anniversary emblem. Size: 103x78mm.

Queen Mother Elizabeth, 80th Birthday — A108

**1980, Sept. 15**

584 A108 10c multi 8 8
585 A108 $2.50 multi 1.75 1.75

**Souvenir Sheet**

***Perf. 12***

586 A108 $3 multi 2.00 2.00

Size of No. 586: 68x90mm.

Ringed Kingfisher — A109

**1980, Nov. 3 Litho. Perf. 14**

587 A109 10c *shown* 10 10
588 A109 30c *Plain pigeon* 30 30
589 A109 $1 *Green-throated carib* 75 75
590 A109 $2 *Black-necked stilt* 1.75 1.75

**Souvenir Sheet**

591 A109 $2.50 *Roseate tern* 3.00 3.00

No. 592 has multicolored margin showing tern on beach. Size: 73x73mm.

Sleeping Beauty and the Prince — A110

Christmas 1980. Various scenes from Walt Disney's Sleeping Beauty. $4 vert.

**1980, Dec. 23 *Perf. 11, 13½x14 ($4)***

592 A110 ½c multi 5 5
593 A110 1c multi 5 5
594 A110 2c multi 5 5
595 A110 4c multi 5 5
596 A110 8c multi 7 7
597 A110 10c multi 8 8
598 A110 25c multi 22 22
599 A110 $2 multi 1.75 1.75
600 A110 $2.50 multi 2.25 2.25
*Nos. 592-600 (9)* 4.57 4.57

**Souvenir Sheet**

601 A110 54 multi 3.25 3.25

No. 601 has multicolored margin showing Sleeping Beauty in forest. Size: 127x102mm.

Sugar-cane Railway Diesel Locomotive No. 15 — A111

**1981, Jan. 12 Perf. 14**

602 A111 25c *shown* 15 15
603 A111 50c *Narrow-gauge steam locomotive* 35 35
604 A111 90c *Diesels #1, #10* 60 60
605 A111 $3 *Hauling sugar-cane* 2.00 2.00

**Souvenir Sheet**

606 A111 $2.50 *Sugar factory, train yard* 1.75 1.75

No. 606 has multicolored margin showing locomotive and tracks. Size: 82½x111½mm.

Nos. 411-412, 414-422 Overprinted: "INDEPENDENCE 1981"

**1981, Mar. 31 Litho. Perf. 14½**

607 A79 6c multi 6 6
608 A79 10c multi 8 8
609 A79 20c multi 15 15
610 A79 25c multi 20 20
611 A79 35c multi 25 25
612 A79 50c multi 40 40
613 A79 75c multi 60 60
614 A79 $1 multi 75 75
615 A79 $2.50 multi 1.75 1.75
616 A79 $5 multi 3.75 3.75
617 A79 $10 multi 7.50 7.50
*Nos. 607-617 (11)* 15.49 15.49

Pipes of Pan, by Picasso — A112

Picasso Paintings: 50c, Seated Harlequin. 90c, Paulo as Harlequin. $4, Mother and Child. $5, Three Musicians.

**1981, May 5 Litho. Perf. 14**

618 A112 10c multi 8 8
619 A112 50c multi 40 40
620 A112 90c multi 75 75
621 A112 $4 multi 3.00 3.00

**Souvenir Sheet**

622 A112 $5 multi 3.25 3.25

Pablo Picasso (1881-1973). No. 622 has multicolored margin showing entire painting. Size: 116x141mm.

**Royal Wedding Issue**

Common Design Type

**1981, June 16 Litho. Perf. 14**

623 CD331 25c Couple 15 15
624 CD331 50c Glamis Castle 35 35
625 CD331 $4 Charles 2.75 2.75

**Souvenir Sheet**

626 CD331 $5 Glass coach 3.50 3.50
627 CD331 Booklet 10.00
a. Pane of 6 (2x25c, 2x$1, 2x$2), Charles 5.50
b. Pane of 1, $5, Couple 4.50

No. 626 has light green and black margin showing heraldic designs. Size: 96x81mm. No. 627 contains imperf., self-adhesive stamps.

Nos. 623-625 also printed in sheets of 5 plus label, perf. 12 in changed colors.

Campfire Sing A113

**1981, Oct. 28 Litho. *Perf. 15***

*628* A113 10c Irene Joshua 8 8
*629* A113 50c shown 35 35
*630* A113 90c Sailing 60 60
*631* A113 $2.50 Milking cow 1.75 1.75

**Souvenir Sheet**

*632* A113 $5 Flag raising 3.75 3.75

Girl Guides, 50th anniv. No. 632 has multicolored margin continuing design. Size: 110x85mm.

Independence A114

**1981, Nov. 1 Litho. *Perf. 15***

*633* A114 10c Arms 8 8
*634* A114 50c Flag 35 35
*635* A114 90c Prime Minister Bird 60 60
*636* A114 $2.50 St. John's Cathedral, horiz. 1.75 1.75

**Souvenir Sheet**

*637* A114 $5 Map 3.25 3.25

No. 637 contains one stamp (41x41mm.); multicolored margin. Size: 105x80mm.

Holy Night, by Jacques Stella (1596-1657) — A115

Christmas 1981 (Virgin and Child Paintings by): 30c Julius Schnorr von Carolfeld (1794-1872). $1, Alonso Cano (1601-1667). $3, Lorenzo de Credi (1459-1537). $5, Holy Family, by Pieter von Avoni (1600-1652).

**1981, Nov. 16**

*638* A115 8c multi 8 8
*639* A115 30c multi 20 20
*640* A115 $1 multi 65 65
*641* A115 $3 multi 2.00 2.00

**Souvenir Sheet**

*642* A115 $5 multi 3.25 3.25

No. 642 has multicolored margin showing entire painting. Size: 78x112mm.

Intl. Year of the Disabled A116

**1981, Dec. 1 Litho. *Perf. 15***

*643* A116 10c Swimming 8 8
*644* A116 50c Discus 35 35
*645* A116 90c Archery 60 60
*646* A116 $2 Baseball 1.40 1.40

**Souvenir Sheet**

*647* A116 $4 Basketball 3.00 3.00

No. 647 has multicolored margin continuing design. Size: 110x85mm.

1982 World Cup Soccer A117

Designs: Various soccer players.

**1982, Apr. 15 Litho. *Perf. 14***

*648* A117 10c multi 8 8
*649* A117 50c multi 35 35
*650* A117 90c multi 60 60
*651* A117 $4 multi 2.75 2.75

**Souvenir Sheet**

*652* A117 $5 multi 3.75 3.75

No. 652 has multicolored margin continuing design. Size: 75x93mm.

Also issued in sheetlets of 5 + label in changed colors, perf. 12.

Coolidge Intl. Airport Opening — A118

**1982, June 17 Litho. *Perf. 14½***

*653* A118 10c A-300 Airbus 8 8
*654* A118 50c Hawker-Siddeley 748 40 40
*655* A118 90c De Havilland Twin Otter DCH6 70 70
*656* A118 $2.50 Britten-Norman Islander 1.75 1.75

**Souvenir Sheet**

*657* A118 $5 Jet, horiz. 3.50 3.50

No. 657 has multicolored margin continuing design. Size: 99x73mm.

Charles Darwin's Death Centenary — A119

**1982, June 28 Litho. *Perf. 14½***

*658* A119 10c Cordia, vert. 8 8
*659* A119 50c Golden spotted mongoose 40 40
*660* A119 90c Corallita, vert. 70 70
*661* A119 $3 Bulldog bats 2.25 2.25

**Souvenir Sheet**

*662* A119 $5 Caribbean monk seals 3.75 3.75

No. 662 has multicolored margin showing wildlife. Size: 108x85mm.

**Princess Diana Issue**

Common Design Type

**1982, July 1 Litho. *Perf. 14½x14***

*663* CD332 90c Greenwich Palace 70 70
*664* CD332 $1 Wedding 75 75
*665* CD332 $4 Diana 3.00 3.00

**Souvenir Sheet**

*666* CD332 $5 Diana, diff. 3.75 3.75

No. 666 has multicolored margin showing family tree, Admiral Hugh Seymour. Size: 103x77mm.

Scouting Year A120

Designs: Independence Day celebration.

**1982, July 15 *Perf. 14***

*667* A120 10c Decorating buildings 8 8
*668* A120 50c Helping woman 40 40
*669* A120 90c Princess Margaret 70 70
*670* A120 $2.20 Cub Scout giving directions 1.75 1.75

**Souvenir Sheet**

*671* A120 $5 Baden-Powell 3.75 3.75

No. 671 has multicolored margin showing scouts saluting. Size: 102x72mm.

Nos. 663-666 Overprinted: "ROYAL BABY / 21.6.82"

**1982, Aug. 30 Litho. *Perf. 14½x14***

*672* CD332 90c multi 70 70
*673* CD332 $1 multi 75 75
*674* CD332 $4 multi 3.00 3.00

**Souvenir Sheet**

*675* CD332 $5 multi 3.50 3.50

Roosevelt Driving by "The Little White House" A121

**1982, Sept. 20 *Perf. 14½***

*676* A121 10c shown 8 8
*677* A121 25c Washington as blacksmith 18 18
*678* A121 45c Churchill, Roosevelt, Stalin 35 35
*679* A121 60c Washington crossing Delaware, vert. 45 45
*680* A121 $1 Roosevelt on train, vert. 75 75
*681* A121 $3 Roosevelt, vert. 2.25 2.25
*Nos. 676-681 (6)* 4.06 4.06

**Souvenir Sheets**

*682* A121 $4 Washington, vert. 3.00 3.00
*683* A121 $4 Eleanor and Franklin 3.00 3.00

George Washington's 250th birth anniv. and Franklin D. Roosevelt's birth centenary. Nos. 682-683 have multicolored margins. Size: 93x88mm.

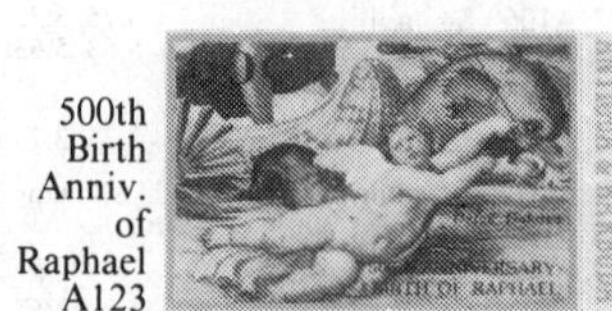


Christmas 1982 — A122

Raphael Paintings.

**1982, Nov. Litho. *Perf. 14x13½***

*684* A122 10c Annunciation 8 8
*685* A122 30c Adoration of the Magi 22 22
*686* A122 $1 Presentation at the Temple 75 75
*687* A122 $4 Coronation of the Virgin 3.00 3.00

**Souvenir Sheet**

*688* A122 $5 Marriage of the Virgin 3.50 3.50

No. 688 has multicolored margin showing entire painting. Size: 95x125mm.

500th Birth Anniv. of Raphael A123

**1983, Jan. 28. Litho. *Perf. 14½***

*689* A123 45c Galatea taking Reins of Dolphins, vert. 35 35
*690* A123 50c Sea Nymphs carried by Tritons, vert. 40 40
*691* A123 60c Winged Angel Steering Dolphins 45 45
*692* A123 $4 Cupids Shooting Arrows 3.00 3.00

**Souvenir Sheet**

*693* A123 $5 Galatea 3.75 3.75

No. 693 shows entire painting. Size: 101x127mm.

**Commonwealth Day**

Common Design Type

**1983, Mar. 14 *Perf. 14***

*694* CD334 25c Pineapple crop 20 20
*695* CD334 45c Carnival 30 30
*696* CD334 60c Tourists, sailboat 40 40
*697* CD334 $3 Control Tower 2.00 2.00

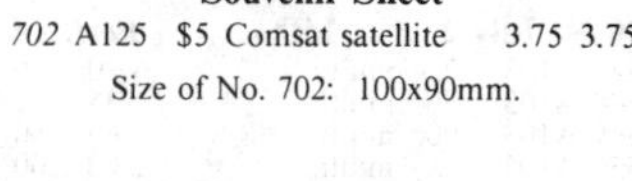


World Communications Year — A125

**1983, Apr. 5 Litho. *Perf. 14***

*698* A125 15c TV screen, camera 12 12
*699* A125 50c Police radio, car 40 40
*700* A125 60c Long distance phone call 45 45
*701* A125 $3 Dish antenna, planets 2.25 2.25

**Souvenir Sheet**

*702* A125 $5 Comsat satellite 3.75 3.75

Size of No. 702: 100x90mm.

Bottlenose Dolphin — A126

**1983, May 9 Litho. *Perf. 15***

*703* A126 15c shown 10 10
*704* A126 50c Finback whale 35 35
*705* A126 60c Bowhead whale 40 40
*706* A126 $3 Spectacled porpoise 2.00 2.00

**Souvenir Sheet**

*707* A126 $5 Unicorn whale 3.50 3.50

No. 707 has multicolored margin showing whale tail. Size: 123x102mm.

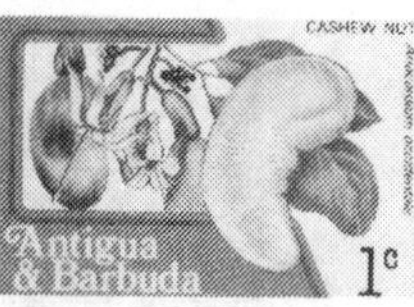


Cashew Nut A127

**1983, June *Perf. 14***

*708* A127 1c shown 5 5
*709* A127 2c Passion fruit 5 5
*710* A127 3c Mango 5 5
*711* A127 5c Grapefruit 5 5
*712* A127 10c Pawpaw 8 8
*713* A127 15c Breadfruit 12 12
*714* A127 20c Coconut 15 15
*715* A127 25c Oleander 18 18
*716* A127 30c Banana 22 22
*717* A127 40c Pineapple 30 30
*718* A127 45c Cordcia 35 35
*719* A127 50c Cassia 40 40
*720* A127 60c Poui 45 45
*721* A127 $1 Frangipani 75 75
*722* A127 $2 Flamboyant 1.50 1.50
*a.* Perf. 12½x12 ('85) 1.10 1.10
*723* A127 $2.50 Lemon 1.75 1.75
*a.* Perf. 12½x12 ('85) 1.25 1.25
*724* A127 $5 Lignum vitae 3.75 3.75
*a.* Perf. 12½x12 ('85) 2.75 2.75
*725* A127 $10 Arms 7.50 7.50
*Nos. 708-725 (18)* 17.70 17.70

Manned Flight Bicentenary A128

**1983, Aug. 15** *Perf. 15*

*726* A128 30c Dornier DoX 20 20
*727* A128 50c Supermarine S-6B 35 35
*728* A128 60c Curtiss F9C, USS Akron 40 40
*729* A128 $4 Pro Juventute balloon 2.75 2.75

**Souvenir Sheet**

*730* A128 $5 Graf Zeppelin 3.25 3.25

Christmas 1983 — A129

Raphael Paintings: 10c, 30c, $1, $4, Sybils and Angels details. $5, Vision of Ezekiel.

**1983, Oct. 4** **Litho.** *Perf. 13½*

*731* A129 10c Angel flying with scroll 10 10
*732* A129 30c Angel, diff. 30 30
*733* A129 $1 Inscribing tablet 30 30
*734* A129 $4 Angel showing tablet 3.25 3.25

**Souvenir Sheet**

*735* A129 $5 multi 3.75 3.75

Size: 102x131mm.

Methodist Church, Anniv. — A130

Designs: 15c, John Wesley founder of Methodism. 50c, Nathaniel Gilbert, Antiguan founder. 60c, St. John's Methodist Church Steeple. $3, Ebenezer Methodist Church.

**1983, Nov.** **Litho.** *Perf. 14*

*736* A130 15c multi 12 12
*737* A130 50c multi 40 40
*738* A130 60c multi 45 45
*739* A130 $3 multi 2.25 2.25

1984 Olympics, Los Angeles — A131

**1984, Jan.** **Litho.** *Perf. 15*

*740* A131 25c Discus 18 18
*741* A131 50c Gymnastics 40 40
*742* A131 90c Hurdling 70 70
*743* A131 $3 Bicycling 2.25 2.25

**Souvenir Sheet**

*744* A131 $5 Volleyball, horiz. 3.75 3.75

Multicolored margin continues design. Size: 82x67mm.

Booker Vanguard A132

**1984, June 4** **Litho.** *Perf. 14½*

*745* A132 45c shown 35 35
*746* A132 50c Canberra 40 40
*747* A132 60c Yachts 45 45
*748* A132 $4 Fairwind 3.00 3.00

**Souvenir Sheet**

*749* A132 $5 Man-of-war, vert. 3.75 3.75

No. 749 has multicolored margin continuing design.

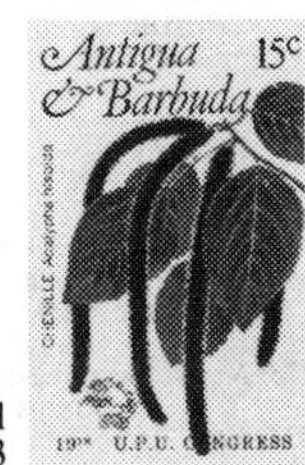

Local Flowers — A133

**1984, June 25** **Litho.** *Perf. 14½*

*755* A133 15c multi 12 12
*756* A133 50c multi 38 38
*757* A133 60c multi 45 45
*758* A133 $3 multi 2.25 2.25

**Souvenir Sheet**

*759* A133 $5 multi 3.75 3.75

US Presidents — A134

**1984, July 18** **Litho.** *Perf. 14*

*760* A134 10c Lincoln 8 8
*761* A134 20c Truman 15 15
*762* A134 30c Eisenhower 22 22
*763* A134 40c Reagan 30 30
*764* A134 90c Lincoln, diff. 68 68
*765* A134 $1.10 Truman, diff. 85 85
*766* A134 $1.50 Eisenhower, diff. 1.15 1.15
*767* A134 $2 Reagan, diff. 1.50 1.50
*Nos. 760-767 (8)* 4.93 4.93

Slavery Abolition Sesquicentennial — A135

**1984, Aug. 1**

*768* A135 40c Moravian Mission 30 30
*769* A135 50c Antigua Courthouse, 1823 38 38
*770* A135 60c Sugar cane planting 45 45
*771* A135 $3 Boiling House, Delaps' Estate 2.25 2.25

**Souvenir Sheet**

*772* A135 $5 Willoughby Bay 3.75 3.75

Song Birds — A136

**1984, Aug. 15** *Perf. 14½*

*773* A136 40c Rufous-sided towhee 30 30
*774* A136 50c Parula warbler 38 38
*775* A136 60c House wren 45 45
*776* A136 $2 Ruby-crowned kinglet 1.50 1.50
*777* A136 $3 Yellow-shafted flicker 2.25 2.25
*Nos. 773-777 (5)* 4.88 4.88

**Souvenir Sheet**

*778* A136 $5 Yellow-breasted chat 3.75 3.75

Size of No. 778: 77x77mm.

AUSIPEX '84 — A137

**1984, Sept. 21** *Perf. 15*

*779* A137 $1 Grass skiing 75 75
*780* A137 $5 Soccer game 3.75 3.75

**Souvenir Sheet**

*781* A137 $5 Boomerang 3.75 3.75

No. 781 has multicolored margin continuing design. Size: 110x78mm.

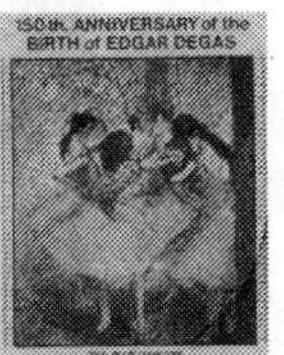

The Blue Dancers, by Edgar Degas — A137a

Paintings by Correggio: 25c, Virgin and Infant with Angels and Cherubs. 60c, The Four Saints. 90c, Saint Catherine. $3, The Campori Madonna. No. 790, St. John the Baptist. Paintings by Degas: 50c, The Pink Dancers. 70c, Two Dancers. $4, Dancers at the Bar. No. 791, Folk Dancers.

**1984, Oct.** **Litho.** *Perf. 15*

*782* A137a 15c multi 12 12
*783* A137a 25c multi 20 20
*784* A137a 50c multi 38 38
*785* A137a 60c multi 45 45
*786* A137a 70c multi 50 50
*787* A137a 90c multi 68 68
*788* A137a $3 multi 2.25 2.25
*789* A137a $4 multi 3.00 3.00
*Nos. 782-789 (8)* 7.58 7.58

**Souvenir Sheets**

*790* A137a $5 multi 3.75 3.75
*791* A137a $5 multi horiz. 3.75 3.75

Nos. 790 and 791 each have multicolored margins continuing design. Size: 91x61mm.

**Nos. 623-626, 663-666, 672-675, 694-697 Surcharged in Black or Gold.**

**1984, June** *Perf. 14, 14½x14*

*792* CD331 $2 on 25c #623 1.50 1.50
*793* CD334 $2 on 25c #694 1.50 1.50
*794* CD334 $2 on 45c #695 1.50 1.50
*795* CD331 $2 on 50c #624 1.50 1.50
*796* CD334 $2 on 60c #696 1.50 1.50
*797* CD332 $2 on 90c #663 (G) 1.50 1.50
*798* CD332 $2 on 90c #672 (G) 1.50 1.50
*799* CD332 $2 on $1 #664 (G) 1.50 1.50
*800* CD332 $2 on $1 #673 (G) 1.50 1.50
*801* CD334 $2 on $3 #697 1.50 1.50
*802* CD331 $2 on $4 #625 1.50 1.50
*803* CD332 $2 on $4 #665 (G) 1.50 1.50
*804* CD332 $2 on $4 #674 (G) 1.50 1.50
*Nos. 792-804 (13)* 19.50 19.50

**Souvenir Sheets**

*805* CD331 $2 on $5 #626 1.50 1.50
*806* CD332 $2 on $5 #666 1.50 1.50
*807* CD332 $2 on $5 #675 1.50 1.50

Nos. 797-800,803-804 exist with silver surcharge.

Canceled-to-order stamps are often from remainders. Most collectors of canceled stamps prefer postally used specimens.

Christmas 1984 and 50th Anniv. of Donald Duck — A138

Scenes from various Donald Duck comics.

**1984, Nov.** **Litho.** *Perf. 11*

*808* A138 1c multi 5 5
*809* A138 2c multi 5 5
*810* A138 3c multi 5 5
*811* A138 4c multi 5 5
*812* A138 5c multi 5 5
*813* A138 10c multi 10 10
*814* A138 $1 multi 85 85
*815* A138 $2 multi 1.65 1.65
*816* A138 $5 multi 4.00 4.00
*Nos. 808-816 (9)* 6.85 6.85

**Souvenir Sheets**
***Perf. 14***

*817* A138 $5 multi, horiz. 4.00 4.00
*818* A138 $5 Donald in desk chair 4.00 4.00

20th Century Leaders A139

**1984, Nov. 19** **Litho.** *Perf. 15*

*819* A139 60c John F. Kennedy (1917-1963), vert. 45 45
*820* A139 60c Winston Churchill (1874-1965), vert. 45 45
*821* A139 60c Mahatma Gandhi (1869-1948), vert. 45 45
*822* A139 60c Mao Tse-Tung (1883-1976), vert. 45 45
*823* A139 $1 Kennedy in Berlin 75 75
*824* A139 $1 Churchill in Paris 75 75
*825* A139 $1 Gandhi in Great Britain 75 75
*826* A139 $1 Mao in Peking 75 75

**Souvenir Sheet**

*827* A139 $5 Flags of Great Britain, India, China, USA 3.75 3.75

No. 827 has multicolored margin showing portraits of the leaders. Size 114x81mm.

Statue of Liberty Centennial A140

**1985, Jan. 7**

*828* A140 25c Torch on display, 1885 15 15
*829* A140 30c Restoration, 1984-1986, vert. 20 20
*830* A140 50c Bartholdi supervising construction, 1876 32 32
*831* A140 90c Statue on Liberty Island 60 60
*832* A140 $1 Dedication Ceremony, 1886, vert. 65 65
*833* A140 $3 Operation Sail, 1976, vert. 1.90 1.90

**Souvenir Sheet**

*834* A140 $5 Port of New York 3.25 3.25

No. 834 has multicolored margin continuing design. Size: 112x82mm.

Traditional Scenes A141

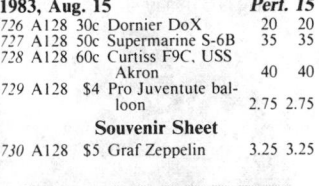

**1985, Jan. 21**

| | | | | | |
|---|---|---|---|---|---|
| *835* | A141 | 15c | Ceramics, Arawak pot shard | 12 | 12 |
| *836* | A141 | 50c | Tatooing, body design | 38 | 38 |
| *837* | A141 | 60c | Harvesting Manioc, god Yocahu | 45 | 45 |
| *838* | A141 | $3 | Caribs in battle, war club | 2.25 | 2.25 |

**Souvenir Sheet**

| | | | | | |
|---|---|---|---|---|---|
| *839* | A141 | $5 | Tainos worshiping | 3.75 | 3.75 |

Scott No. 839 has multicolored margin continuing design. Size: 98x69mm.

Invention of the Motorcycle, Cent. A142

**1985, Mar. 7** *Perf. 14*

| | | | | | |
|---|---|---|---|---|---|
| *840* | A142 | 10c | Triumph 2HP Jap, 1903 | 8 | 8 |
| *841* | A142 | 30c | Indian Arrow, 1949 | 22 | 22 |
| *842* | A142 | 60c | BMW R100RS, 1976 | 45 | 45 |
| *843* | A142 | $4 | Harley Davidson Model II, 1916 | 3.00 | 3.00 |

**Souvenir Sheet**

| | | | | | |
|---|---|---|---|---|---|
| *844* | A142 | $5 | Laverda Jota, 1975 | 3.75 | 3.75 |

No. 844 has a multicolored margin showing the front axle of the motorcycle. Size 91x93mm.

John J. Audubon A143

**1985, Mar. 25** *Perf. 15*

| | | | | | |
|---|---|---|---|---|---|
| *845* | A143 | 90c | Horned grebe | 68 | 68 |
| *846* | A143 | $1 | Least petrel | 75 | 75 |
| *847* | A143 | $1.50 | Great blue heron | 1.15 | 1.15 |
| *848* | A143 | $3 | Double-crested cormorant | 2.25 | 2.25 |

**Souvenir Sheet**

| | | | | | |
|---|---|---|---|---|---|
| *849* | A143 | $5 | White-tailed tropic bird, vert. | 3.75 | 3.75 |

No. 849 has a multicolored margin continuing design. Size: 104x73mm.

Butterflies A144

**1985, Apr. 16** *Perf. 14*

| | | | | | |
|---|---|---|---|---|---|
| *850* | A144 | 25c | Polygrapha cyanea | 15 | 15 |
| *851* | A144 | 60c | Leodonta dysoni | 35 | 35 |
| *852* | A144 | 95c | Junea doraete | 60 | 60 |
| *853* | A144 | $4 | Prepona xenagoras | 2.50 | 2.50 |

**Souvenir Sheet**

| | | | | | |
|---|---|---|---|---|---|
| *854* | A144 | $5 | Caerois gerdrudtus | 3.25 | 3.25 |

No. 854 has a multicolored margin showing various butterflies. Size: 133x106mm.

Cessna 172 — A145

**1985, Apr. 30**

| | | | | | |
|---|---|---|---|---|---|
| *855* | A145 | 30c | shown | 20 | 20 |
| *856* | A145 | 90c | Fokker DVII | 60 | 60 |
| *857* | A145 | $1.50 | Spad VII | 1.00 | 1.00 |
| *858* | A145 | $3 | Boeing 747 | 1.90 | 1.90 |

**Souvenir Sheet**

| | | | | | |
|---|---|---|---|---|---|
| *859* | A145 | $5 | Twin Otter, Coolidge Intl. Airport | 3.25 | 3.25 |

40th anniv. of the Intl. Civil Aviation Org. Nos. 855, 858-859 show the ICAO and UN emblems. No. 859 has multicolored margin continuing design. Size 99x83mm.

Maimonides (ne Moses Ben Maimon, 1135-1204), Judaic Philosopher and Physician — A146

**1985, June 17** **Litho.** *Perf. 14*

| | | | | | |
|---|---|---|---|---|---|
| *860* | A146 | $2 | yel grn | 1.50 | 1.50 |

**Souvenir Sheet**

| | | | | | |
|---|---|---|---|---|---|
| *861* | A146 | $5 | dp brn | 3.25 | 3.25 |

Intl. Youth Year A147

**1985, July 1**

| | | | | | |
|---|---|---|---|---|---|
| *862* | A147 | 25c | Agriculture | 15 | 15 |
| *863* | A147 | 50c | Hotel management | 28 | 28 |
| *864* | A147 | 60c | Environmental studies | 35 | 35 |
| *865* | A147 | $3 | Windsurfing | 1.90 | 1.90 |

**Souvenir Sheet**

| | | | | | |
|---|---|---|---|---|---|
| *866* | A147 | $5 | Youths, national flag | 3.50 | 3.50 |

No. 866 has multicolored margin continuing the design. Size: 102x73mm.

Queen Mother, 85th Birthday — A148

Designs: $1, Attending a church service. $1.50, Touring the London Gardens, children in a sandpit. $2.50, Photograph (1979). $5, With Prince Edward at the wedding of Prince Charles and Lady Diana Spencer.

**1985, July 15**

| | | | | | |
|---|---|---|---|---|---|
| *866A* | A148 | 90c | like #867 ('86) | 65 | 65 |
| *867* | A148 | $1 | multi | 75 | 75 |
| *867A* | A148 | $1 | like #868 ('86) | 75 | 75 |
| *868* | A148 | $1.50 | multi | 1.10 | 1.10 |
| *869* | A148 | $2.50 | multi | 1.85 | 1.85 |
| *869A* | A148 | $3 | like #869 ('86) | 2.25 | 2.25 |

**Souvenir Sheet**

| | | | | | |
|---|---|---|---|---|---|
| *870* | A148 | $5 | multi | 3.25 | 3.25 |

85th birthday of the Queen Mother. No. 870 has multicolored margin continuing the design. Size: 57x85mm.

Nos. 866A, 867A, 869A issued in sheets of 5 plus label.

Common Design Types are pictured in section before Great Britain.

Marine Life — A149

Johann Sebastian Bach — A150

**1985, Aug. 1** *Perf. 14*

| | | | | | |
|---|---|---|---|---|---|
| *871* | A149 | 15c | Fregata magnificens | 8 | 8 |
| *872* | A149 | 45c | Diploria labyrinthi-formis | 30 | 30 |
| *873* | A149 | 60c | Oreaster reticulatus | 40 | 40 |
| *874* | A149 | $3 | Gymnothorax moringa | 2.00 | 2.00 |

**Souvenir Sheet**

| | | | | | |
|---|---|---|---|---|---|
| *875* | A149 | $5 | Acropora palmata | 3.25 | 3.25 |

No. 875 has multicolored margin continuing the design. Size: 110x81mm.

**1985, Aug. 26** **Litho.** *Perf. 14*

| | | | | | |
|---|---|---|---|---|---|
| *876* | A150 | 25c | Bass trombone | 15 | 15 |
| *877* | A150 | 50c | English horn | 30 | 30 |
| *878* | A150 | $1 | Violino piccolo | 65 | 65 |
| *879* | A150 | $3 | Bass racket | 1.90 | 1.90 |

**Souvenir Sheet**

| | | | | | |
|---|---|---|---|---|---|
| *880* | A150 | $5 | Portrait | 3.25 | 3.25 |

Nos. 876-880 bear the same portrait of Bach, his signature and music from Invention No. 15 in B Minor. No. 880 has decorative margin picturing a portrait of the Bach family by Toby E. Rosenthal. Size: 105x72mm.

Girl Guides, 75th Anniv. A151

Public service and growth-oriented activities.

**1985, Sept. 10**

| | | | | | |
|---|---|---|---|---|---|
| *881* | A151 | 15c | Public service | 8 | 8 |
| *882* | A151 | 45c | Guides meeting | 30 | 30 |
| *883* | A151 | 60c | Lord and Lady Baden-Powell | 40 | 40 |
| *884* | A151 | $3 | Nature study | 2.00 | 2.00 |

**Souvenir Sheet**

| | | | | | |
|---|---|---|---|---|---|
| *885* | A151 | $5 | Barn swallow | 3.25 | 3.25 |

No. 885 has multicolored decorative margin picturing three guides bird-watching. Size: 68x97mm.

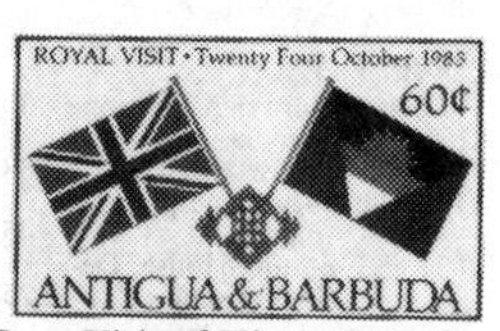

State Visit of Elizabeth II, Oct. 24 — A152

**1985, Oct. 24** **Litho.** *Perf. 14½*

| | | | | | |
|---|---|---|---|---|---|
| *886* | A152 | 60c | Natl. flags | 35 | 35 |
| *887* | A152 | $1 | Elizabeth II, vert. | 60 | 60 |
| *888* | A152 | $4 | HMY Britannia | 2.25 | 2.25 |

**Souvenir Sheet**

| | | | | | |
|---|---|---|---|---|---|
| *889* | A152 | $5 | Map of Antigua | 3.25 | 3.25 |

No. 889 has multicolored margin continuing design and picturing the Britannia and map of the Caribbean. Size: 111x83mm.

Mark Twain — A153

Disney characters in Roughing It.

**1985, Nov. 4** *Perf. 14*

| | | | | | |
|---|---|---|---|---|---|
| *890* | A153 | 25c | Cowboys and Indians | 18 | 18 |
| *891* | A153 | 50c | Canoeing | 38 | 38 |
| *892* | A153 | $1.10 | Pony Express | 80 | 80 |
| *893* | A153 | $1.50 | Buffalo hunt in Missouri | 1.10 | 1.10 |
| *894* | A153 | $2 | Nevada silver mine | 1.50 | 1.50 |
| | | | *Nos. 890-894 (5)* | 3.96 | 3.96 |

**Souvenir Sheet**

| | | | | | |
|---|---|---|---|---|---|
| *895* | A153 | $5 | Stagecoach on Kansas plains | 4.00 | 4.00 |

No. 895 has multicolored margin continuing design and picturing a cameo portrait of Twain and IYY emblem. Size: 126x101mm.

Jacob and Wilhelm Grimm, Fabulists and Philologists — A154

Disney characters in Spindle, Shuttle and Needle.

**1985, Nov. 11**

| | | | | |
|---|---|---|---|---|
| *896* | A154 | 30c multi | 22 | 22 |
| *897* | A154 | 60c multi | 45 | 45 |
| *898* | A154 | 70c multi | 52 | 52 |
| *899* | A154 | $1 multi | 75 | 75 |
| *900* | A154 | $3 multi | 2.25 | 2.25 |

**Souvenir Sheet**

| | | | | |
|---|---|---|---|---|
| *900A* | A154 | $5 multi | 3.75 | 3.75 |

No. 900A has multicolored margin continuing the design. Size: 127x101mm.

UN 40th Anniv. A155

Stamps of UN and portraits: 40c, No. 18 and Benjamin Franklin. $1, No. 391 and George Washington Carver, agricultural chemist. $3, No. 299 and Charles Lindbergh. $5, Marc Chagall, artist, vert.

**1985, Nov. 18**

| | | | | |
|---|---|---|---|---|
| *901* | A155 | 40c multi | 30 | 30 |
| *902* | A155 | $1 multi | 75 | 75 |
| *903* | A155 | $3 multi | 2.25 | 2.25 |

**Souvenir Sheet**

| | | | | |
|---|---|---|---|---|
| *904* | A155 | $5 multi | 3.75 | 3.75 |

No. 904 has multicolored margin picturing the UN emblem and UN No. 179, The Kiss of Peace, stained glass window by Chagall. Size: 101x76mm.

Christmas 1985 — A156

Religious paintings. 10c, Madonna and Child, by De Landi. 25c, Madonna and Child, by Bonaventura Berlingheiri (d.1244). 60c, The Nativity, by Fra Angelico (1400-1455). $4, Presentation in the Temple, by Giovanni di Paolo Grazia (c.1403-1482). $5, The Nativity, by Antoniazzo Romano.

**1985, Dec. 30** ***Perf. 15***

*905* A156 10c multi 8 8
*906* A156 25c multi 18 18
*907* A156 60c multi 45 45
*908* A156 $4 multi 3.00 3.00

**Souvenir Sheet**

*909* A156 $5 multi 3.75 3.75

No. 909 has multicolored margin continuing the painting. Size: 113x81mm.

Audubon Type of 1985

Illustrations of North American ducks.

**1986, Jan. 6** ***Perf. 12½x12***

*910* A143 60c Mallard 45 45
*911* A143 90c Dusky duck 65 65
*912* A143 $1.50 Common pintail 1.10 1.10
*913* A143 $3 Wigeon 2.25 2.25

**Souvenir Sheet**

***Perf. 14***

*914* A143 $5 Common eider 3.75 3.75

No. 914 has multicolored margin continuing the design. Size: 103x73mm.

1986 World Cup Soccer Championships, Mexico — A157

**1986, Mar. 17** **Litho.** ***Perf. 14***

*915* A157 30c shown 22 22
*916* A157 60c Heading the ball 45 45
*917* A157 $1 Referee 75 75
*918* A157 $4 Goal 3.00 3.00

**Souvenir Sheet**

*919* A157 $5 Action 3.75 3.75

Nos. 916-917 vert. No. 919 has multicolored inscribed margin continuing the design. Size: 87x76mm.

A158

Halley's Comet A159

Designs: 5c, Edmond Halley, Greenwich Observatory. 10c, Me 163B Komet, German WWII fighter plane. 60c, Montezuma sighting comet, 1517. $4, Pocahontas saving Capt. John Smith's life, 1607 sighting as sign for Powhatan Indians to raid Jamestown. $5, Comet over Antigua.

**1986, Mar. 24**

*920* A158 5c multi 5 5
*921* A158 10c multi 8 8
*922* A158 60c multi 45 45
*923* A158 $4 multi 3.00 3.00

**Souvenir Sheet**

*924* A159 $5 multi 3.75 3.75

No. 924 has multicolored margin showing English Harbor. Size: 102x70mm.

**Queen Elizabeth II, 60th Birthday**

Common Design Type

**1986, Apr. 21**

*925* CD339 60c Wedding, 1947 45 45
*926* CD339 $1 Trooping the color 75 75
*927* CD339 $4 Visiting Scotland 3.00 3.00

**Souvenir Sheet**

*928* CD339 $5 Held by Queen Mary, 1927 3.75 3.75

No. 928 has beige and gray inscribed margin. Size: 120x85mm.

Boats — A160

**1986, May 15**

*929* A160 30c Tugboat 22 22
*930* A160 60c Fishing boat 45 45
*931* A160 $1 Sailboat 2056 75 75
*932* A160 $4 Lateen-rigged sailboat 3.00 3.00

**Souvenir Sheet**

*933* A160 $5 Boatbuilding 3.75 3.75

No. 933 has multicolored margin continuing the design. Size: 108x78mm.

AMERIPEX '86 — A161

Famous American trains.

**1986, May 22** ***Perf. 15***

*934* A161 25c Hiawatha 20 20
*935* A161 50c Grand Canyon 38 38
*936* A161 $1 Powhattan Arrow 75 75
*937* A161 $3 Empire State 2.25 2.25

**Souvenir Sheet**

*938* A161 $5 Daylight 3.75 3.75

No. 938 has multicolored margin continuing the design. Size: 117x87mm.

**Wedding of Prince Andrew and Sarah Ferguson**

Common Design Type

**1986, July 23** ***Perf. 14***

*939* CD340 45c Couple 35 35
*940* CD340 60c Prince Andrew 45 45
*941* CD340 $4 Princes Andrew, Philip 3.00 3.00

**Souvenir Sheet**

*942* CD340 $5 Couple, diff. 3.75 3.75

No. 942 has multicolored margin continuing the design. Size: 88x88mm.

Conch Shells — A162

**1986, Aug. 6** **Litho.** ***Perf. 15***

*943* A162 15c Say fly-specked cerith 12 12
*944* A162 45c Gmelin smooth scotch bonnet 35 35
*945* A162 60c Linne West Indian crown conch 45 45
*946* A162 $3 Murex ciboney 2.25 2.25

**Souvenir Sheet**

*947* A162 $5 Atlantic natica 3.75 3.75

No. 947 has multicolored margin picturing marine life. Size: 110x75mm.

Flowers A163

**1986, Aug. 25** **Litho.** ***Perf. 15***

*948* A163 10c Water lily 5 5
*949* A163 15c Queen of the night 12 12
*950* A163 50c Cup of gold 38 38
*951* A163 60c Beach morning glory 45 45
*952* A163 70c Golden trumpet 55 55
*953* A163 $1 Air plant 75 75
*954* A163 $3 Purple wreath 2.25 2.25
*955* A163 $4 Zephyr lily 3.00 3.00
*Nos. 948-955 (8)* 7.55 7.55

**Souvenir Sheets**

*956* A163 $4 Dozakie 3.00 3.00
*957* A163 $5 Four o'clock 3.75 3.75

Nos. 956-957 have multicolored margins continuing the designs. Sizes: 102x73mm.

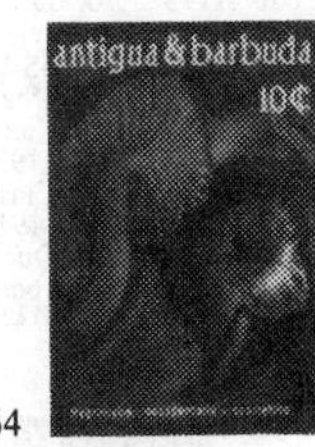


Fungi — A164

**1986, Sept. 15**

*958* A164 10c Hygrocybe occidentalis scarletina 5 5
*959* A164 50c Trogia buccinalis 38 38
*960* A164 $1 Collybia subpruinosa 75 75
*961* A164 $4 Leucocoprinus brebissonii 3.00 3.00

**Souvenir Sheet**

*962* A164 $5 Pyrrhoglossum pyrrhum 3.75 3.75

No. 962 has multicolored margin continuing the design. Size: 102x83mm.

Nos. 915-919 Ovptd. "WINNERS Argentina 3 W. Germany 2" in Gold in 2 or 3 lines.

**1986, Sept. 15** ***Perf. 14***

*963* A157 30c multi 22 22
*964* A157 60c multi 45 45
*965* A157 $1 multi 75 75
*966* A157 $4 multi 3.00 3.00

**Souvenir Sheet**

*967* A157 $5 multi 3.75 3.75

Automobile, Cent. — A165

Carl Benz and classic automobiles.

**1986, Oct. 20**

*968* A165 10c 1933 Auburn Speedster 5 5
*968A* A165 15c 1986 Mercury Sable 12 12
*969* A165 50c 1959 Cadillac 38 38
*970* A165 60c 1950 Studebaker 45 45
*970A* A165 70c 1939 Lagonda V-12 52 52
*970B* A165 $1 1930 Adler Standard 75 75
*970C* A165 $3 1956 DKW 2.25 2.25
*971* A165 $4 1936 Mercedes 500K 3.00 3.00
*Nos. 968-971 (8)* 7.52 7.52

**Souvenir Sheet**

*972* A165 $5 1921 Mercedes Knight 3.75 3.75
*972A* A165 $5 1896 Daimler 3.75 3.75

No. 972 has multicolored margin picturing manufacturers' emblems. Size: 99x70mm.

No. 972A has multicolored margin picturing internal combustion engine. Size: 99x70mm.

Nos. 920-924 Ovptd. with Halley's Comet Emblem in Black or Silver.

**1986, Oct. 22** **Litho.** ***Perf. 14***

*973* A158 5c multi 5 5
*974* A158 10c multi 8 8
*975* A158 60c multi 45 45
*976* A158 $4 multi 3.00 3.00

**Souvenir Sheet**

*977* A159 $5 multi (S) 3.75 3.75

Christmas — A166

Disney characters as children.

**1986, Nov. 4** ***Perf. 11***

*978* A166 25c Mickey 20 20
*979* A166 30c Mickey, Minnie 22 22
*980* A166 40c Aunt Matilda, Goofy 30 30
*981* A166 60c Goofy, Pluto 45 45
*982* A166 70c Pluto, Donald, Daisy 55 55
*983* A166 $1.50 Stringing popcorn 1.15 1.15
*984* A166 $3 Grandma Duck, Minnie 2.30 2.30
*985* A166 $4 Donald, Pete 3.05 3.05
*Nos. 978-985 (8)* 8.22 8.22

**Souvenir Sheets**

***Perf. 14***

*986* A166 $5 Playing with presents 3.80 3.80
*987* A166 $5 Reindeer 3.80 3.80

Nos. 985 printed in sheets of 8. Nos. 986-987 have multicolored margins continuing the designs. Sizes: 127x102mm.

Coat of Arms — A167

Natl. Flag — A168

**1986, Nov. 25** **Litho.** ***Perf. 14x14½***

*988* A167 10c brt bl 8 8
*989* A168 25c orange 20 20

Marc Chagall (1887-1985), Artist A169

Designs: No. 990, The Profile, 1957. No. 991, Portrait of the Artist's Sister, 1910. No. 992, Bride with Fan, 1911. No. 993, David in

Profile, 1914. No. 994, Fiancee with Bouquet, 1977. No. 995, Self-portrait with Brushes, 1909. No. 996, The Walk, 1973. No. 997, Candles, 1938. No. 998, Fall of Icarus, 1975. No. 999, Myth of Orpheus, 1977.

**1987, Mar. 30 Litho.** ***Perf. 13½x14***

| | | | | |
|---|---|---|---|---|
| *990* | A169 | 10c multi | 8 | 8 |
| *991* | A169 | 30c multi | 24 | 24 |
| *992* | A169 | 40c multi | 32 | 32 |
| *993* | A169 | 60c multi | 48 | 48 |
| *994* | A169 | 90c multi | 72 | 72 |
| *995* | A169 | $1 multi | 80 | 80 |
| *996* | A169 | $3 multi | 2.40 | 2.40 |
| *997* | A169 | $4 multi | 3.20 | 3.20 |

**Size: 110x95mm.**

***Imperf***

| | | | | |
|---|---|---|---|---|
| *998* | A169 | $5 multi | 4.00 | 4.00 |
| *999* | A169 | $5 multi | 4.00 | 4.00 |
| | | *Nos. 990-999 (10)* | 16.24 | 16.24 |

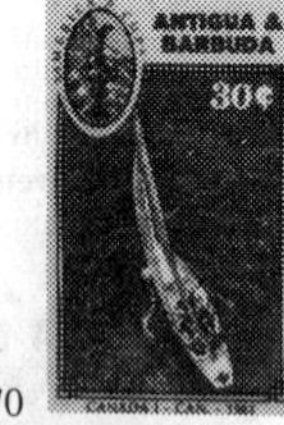

A170

America's Cup A171

**1987, Feb. 5** ***Perf. 15***

| | | | | |
|---|---|---|---|---|
| *1000* | A170 | 30c Canada I, 1981 | 24 | 24 |
| *1001* | A170 | 60c Gretel II, 1970 | 45 | 45 |
| *1002* | A170 | $1 Sceptre, 1958 | 75 | 75 |
| *1003* | A170 | $3 Vigilant, 1893 | 2.25 | 2.25 |

**Souvenir Sheet**

| | | | | |
|---|---|---|---|---|
| *1004* | A171 | $5 Australia II, Liberty, 1983 | 3.75 | 3.75 |

No. 1004 has multicolored margin continuing the design and picturing flag of Australia and America's cup. Size: 113x84mm.

Fish, World Wildlife Fund A172

Marine Birds A173

**1987, Feb. 23 Litho.** ***Perf. 14***

| | | | | |
|---|---|---|---|---|
| *1005* | A172 | 15c Bridled burrfish | 12 | 12 |
| *1006* | A173 | 30c Brown noddy | 24 | 24 |
| *1007* | A172 | 40c Nassau grouper | 32 | 32 |
| *1008* | A173 | 50c Laughing gull | 40 | 40 |
| *1009* | A172 | 60c French angelfish | 48 | 48 |
| *1010* | A172 | $1 Porkfish | 80 | 80 |
| *1011* | A173 | $2 Royal tern | 1.60 | 1.60 |
| *1012* | A173 | $3 Sooty tern | 2.40 | 2.40 |
| | | *Nos. 1005-1012 (8)* | 6.36 | 6.36 |

**Souvenir Sheets**

| | | | | |
|---|---|---|---|---|
| *1013* | A172 | $5 Banded butterfly fish | 4.00 | 4.00 |
| *1014* | A173 | $5 Brown booby | 4.00 | 4.00 |

Nos. 1013-1014 have multicolored margins continuing the designs. Sizes: 121x94mm (No. 1013), 120x94mm (No. 1014). No. 1013 does not picture the WWF emblem.

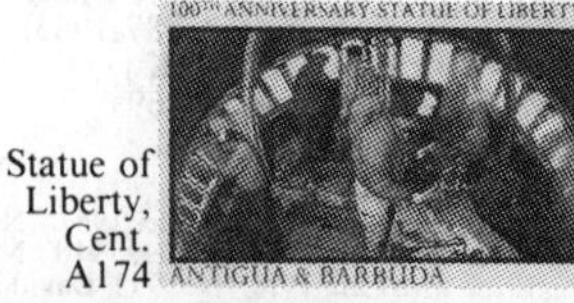

Statue of Liberty, Cent. A174

Photographs by Peter B. Kaplan.

**1987, Apr. 20** ***Perf. 14***

| | | | | |
|---|---|---|---|---|
| *1015* | A174 | 15c Lee Iacocca | 12 | 12 |
| *1016* | A174 | 30c Statue at dusk | 24 | 24 |
| *1017* | A174 | 45c Crown, head | 35 | 35 |
| *1018* | A174 | 50c Iacocca, torch | 40 | 40 |
| *1019* | A174 | 60c Crown observatory | 48 | 48 |
| *1020* | A174 | 90c Interior restoration | 70 | 70 |
| *1021* | A174 | $1 Head | 80 | 80 |
| *1022* | A174 | $2 Statue at sunset | 1.60 | 1.60 |
| *1023* | A174 | $3 Men on scaffold, flag | 2.40 | 2.40 |
| *1024* | A174 | $5 Statue at night | 4.00 | 4.00 |
| | | *Nos. 1015-1024 (10)* | 11.09 | 11.09 |

Nos. 1015-1018, 1021-1022, 1024 vert.

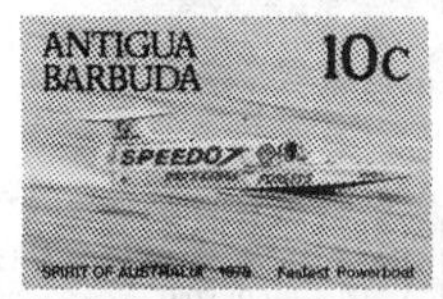

Transportation Innovations — A175

**1987, Apr. 19** ***Perf. 15***

| | | | | |
|---|---|---|---|---|
| *1025* | A175 | 10c Spirit of Australia, 1978 | 8 | 8 |
| *1026* | A175 | 15c Siemen's Electric locomotive, 1879 | 12 | 12 |
| *1027* | A175 | 30c USS Triton, 1960 | 24 | 24 |
| *1028* | A175 | 50c Trevithick, 1801 | 38 | 38 |
| *1029* | A175 | 60c USS New Jersey, 1942 | 48 | 48 |
| *1030* | A175 | 70c Draisine bicycle, 1818 | 52 | 52 |
| *1031* | A175 | 90c SS United States, 1952 | 68 | 68 |
| *1032* | A175 | $1.50 Cierva C-4, 1923 | 1.15 | 1.15 |
| *1033* | A175 | $2 Curtiss NC-4, 1919 | 1.50 | 1.50 |
| *1034* | A175 | $3 Queen Elizabeth II, 1969 | 2.25 | 2.25 |
| | | *Nos. 1025-1034 (10)* | 7.40 | 7.40 |

Reptiles and Amphibians — A176

**1987, June 15** ***Perf. 14***

| | | | | |
|---|---|---|---|---|
| *1035* | A176 | 30c Eleutherodactylus martinicensis | 24 | 24 |
| *1036* | A176 | 60c Thecadactylus bapicauda | 48 | 48 |
| *1037* | A176 | $1 Anolis bimaculatus leachi | 75 | 75 |
| *1038* | A176 | $3 Geochelone carbonaria | 2.25 | 2.25 |

**Souvenir Sheet**

| | | | | |
|---|---|---|---|---|
| *1039* | A176 | $5 Ameiva griswoldi | 3.75 | 3.75 |

No. 1029 has multicolored margin continuing the design. Size: 107x76mm.

Entertainers A177

**1987, May 11**

| | | | | |
|---|---|---|---|---|
| *1040* | A177 | 15c Grace Kelly | 12 | 12 |
| *1041* | A177 | 30c Marilyn Monroe | 22 | 22 |
| *1042* | A177 | 45c Orson Welles | 35 | 35 |
| *1043* | A177 | 50c Judy Garland | 38 | 38 |
| *1044* | A177 | 60c John Lennon | 45 | 45 |
| *1045* | A177 | $1 Rock Hudson | 75 | 75 |
| *1046* | A177 | $2 John Wayne | 1.50 | 1.50 |
| *1047* | A177 | $3 Elvis Presley | 2.25 | 2.25 |
| | | *Nos. 1040-1047 (8)* | 6.02 | 6.02 |

No. 1047 Overprinted

**1987, Sept. 9 Litho.** ***Perf. 14***

| | | | | |
|---|---|---|---|---|
| *1047A* | A177 | $3 multi | 2.25 | 2.25 |

1988 Summer Olympics, Seoul A178

**1987, Mar. 23**

| | | | | |
|---|---|---|---|---|
| *1048* | A178 | 10c Basketball | 8 | 8 |
| *1049* | A178 | 60c Fencing | 48 | 48 |
| *1050* | A178 | $1 Women's gymnastics | 75 | 75 |
| *1051* | A178 | $3 Soccer | 2.25 | 2.25 |

**Souvenir Sheet**

| | | | | |
|---|---|---|---|---|
| *1052* | A178 | $5 Boxing glove | 3.75 | 3.75 |

No. 1052 has multicolored decorative margin picturing boxers in ring. Size: 100x71mm.

16th World Scout Jamboree, Australia, 1987-88 A179

**1987, Nov. 2 Litho.** ***Perf. 15***

| | | | | |
|---|---|---|---|---|
| *1053* | A179 | 10c Campfire, red kangaroo | 8 | 8 |
| *1054* | A179 | 60c Kayaking, blue-winged kookaburra | 45 | 45 |
| *1055* | A179 | $1 Obstacle course, ring-tailed rock wallaby | 75 | 75 |
| *1056* | A179 | $3 Field kitchen, koalas | 2.25 | 2.25 |

**Souvenir Sheet**

| | | | | |
|---|---|---|---|---|
| *1057* | A179 | $5 Flags | 3.75 | 3.75 |

No. 1057 has multicolored margin picturing jamboree emblem and map of Barbuda, Antigua and Austalia. Size: 104x78mm.

U.S. Constitution Bicent. — A180

Designs: 15c, Virginia House of Burgesses exercising right of freedom of speech. 45c, Connecticut state seal. 60c, Delaware state seal. $4, Gouverneur Morris (1752-1816), principal writer of the Constitution, vert. $5, Roger Sherman (1721-1793), jurist and statesman, vert.

**1987, Nov. 16 Litho.** ***Perf. 14***

| | | | | |
|---|---|---|---|---|
| *1058* | A180 | 15c multi | 12 | 12 |
| *1059* | A180 | 45c multi | 35 | 35 |
| *1060* | A180 | 60c multi | 48 | 48 |
| *1061* | A180 | $4 multi | 3.05 | 3.05 |

**Souvenir Sheet**

| | | | | |
|---|---|---|---|---|
| *1062* | A180 | $5 multi | 3.80 | 3.80 |

No. 1062 has multicolored inscribed margin picturing Independence Hall and "We the People..." Size: 105x76mm.

The lack of a price for a listed item does not necessarily indicate rarity.

Christmas — A181

Paintings: 45c, Madonna and Child, by Bernardo Daddi (1290-1355). 60c, Joseph, detail from The Nativity, by Sano Di Pietro (1406-1481). $1, Mary, detail from Di Pietro's The Nativity. $4, Music-making Angel, by Melozzo Da Forli (1438-1494). $5, The Flight into Egypt, by Di Pietro.

**1987, Dec. 1**

| | | | | |
|---|---|---|---|---|
| *1063* | A181 | 45c multi | 32 | 32 |
| *1064* | A181 | 60c multi | 45 | 45 |
| *1065* | A181 | $1 multi | 75 | 75 |
| *1066* | A181 | $4 multi | 2.95 | 2.95 |

**Souvenir Sheet**

| | | | | |
|---|---|---|---|---|
| *1067* | A181 | $5 multi | 3.80 | 3.80 |

No. 1067 has multicolored margin continuing the design. Size: 100x70mm.

40th Wedding Anniv. of Queen Elizabeth II and Prince Philip — A182

**1988, Feb. 8 Litho.** ***Perf. 14***

| | | | | |
|---|---|---|---|---|
| *1068* | A182 | 25c Wedding portrait | 15 | 15 |
| *1069* | A182 | 60c Elizabeth II, c. 1970 | 45 | 45 |
| *1070* | A182 | $2 Christening of Charles, 1948 | 1.50 | 1.50 |
| *1071* | A182 | $3 Elizabeth II, c. 1980 | 2.25 | 2.25 |

**Souvenir Sheet**

| | | | | |
|---|---|---|---|---|
| *1072* | A182 | $5 Royal family, c. 1951 | 3.75 | 3.75 |

No. 1072 has multicolored inscribed margin picturing wedding at Westminster Abbey. Size: 103x77mm.

Tropical Birds A183

**1988, Mar. 1**

| | | | | |
|---|---|---|---|---|
| *1073* | A183 | 10c Great blue heron, vert. | 8 | 8 |
| *1074* | A183 | 15c Ringed kingfisher | 12 | 12 |
| *1075* | A183 | 50c Bananaquit | 38 | 38 |
| *1076* | A183 | 60c Purple gallinule | 45 | 45 |
| *1077* | A183 | 70c Blue-hooded euphonia | 55 | 55 |
| *1078* | A183 | $1 Caribbean parakeet, vert. | 75 | 75 |
| *1079* | A183 | $3 Troupial | 2.30 | 2.30 |
| *1080* | A183 | $4 Hummingbird | 3.00 | 3.00 |
| | | *Nos. 1073-1080 (8)* | 7.63 | 7.63 |

**Souvenir Sheets**

| | | | | |
|---|---|---|---|---|
| *1081* | A183 | $5 Roseate flamingo, vert. | 3.75 | 3.75 |
| *1082* | A183 | $5 Brown pelicans, vert. | 3.75 | 3.75 |

Nos. 1081-1082 have multicolored margins continuing the designs. Sizes: 116x86mm.

Salvation Army — A184

**1988, Mar. 7**

*1083* A184 25c Day-care, Antigua 20 20
*1084* A184 30c Penicillin inoculation, Indonesia 22 22
*1085* A184 40c Day-care Center, Bolivia 30 30
*1086* A184 45c Rehabilitation, India 35 35
*1087* A184 50c Training the blind, Kenya 38 38
*1088* A184 60c Infant care, Ghana 45 45
*1089* A184 $1 Job training, Zambia 78 78
*1090* A184 $2 Food distribution, Sri Lanka 1.50 1.50
*Nos. 1083-1090 (8)* 4.18 4.18

**Souvenir Sheet**

*1091* A184 $5 General Eva Burrows 3.75 3.75

No. 1091 has multicolored margin picturing emblems and flags of Antigua and the Salvation Army. Size: 153x83mm.

A185

Discovery of America, 500th Anniv. (in 1992) A186

Anniv. emblem and: 10c, Fleet. 30c, View of fleet in harbor from Paino Indian village. 45c, Caravel anchored in harbor, Paino village. 60c, Columbus, 3 Indians in canoe. 90c, Indian, parrot, Columbus. $1, Columbus in longboat. $3, Spanish guard, fleet in harbor. $4, Ships under full sail. No. 1100, Stone cross given to Columbus by Queen Isabella. No. 1101, Gold exelente.

**1988, Mar. 14 Litho. *Perf. 14***

*1092* A185 10c multi 8 8
*1093* A185 30c multi 22 22
*1094* A185 45c multi 35 35
*1095* A185 60c multi 45 45
*1096* A185 90c multi 68 68
*1097* A185 $1 multi 75 75
*1098* A185 $3 multi 2.25 2.25
*1099* A185 $4 multi 3.00 3.00
*Nos. 1092-1099 (8)* 7.78 7.78

**Souvenir Sheets**

*1100* A186 $5 multi 3.75 3.75
*1101* A186 $5 multi 3.75 3.75

Nos. 1100-1101 have multicolored inscribed margins picturing coat of arms bestowed on Columbus, admiral of the seas, by Ferdinand and Isabella on May 20, 1493, (No. 1100), and map showing routes of four voyages to the New World (No. 1101). Sizes: 110x80mm.

Paintings by Titian A187

Details: 30c, Bust of Christ. 40c, Scourging of Christ. 45c, Madonna in Glory with Saints. 50c, The Averoldi Polyptych. $1, Christ Crowned with Thorns. $2, Christ Mocked. $3, Christ and Simon of Cyrene. $4, Crucifixion with Virgin and Saints. No. 1110, Ecce Homo. No. 1111, Noli Me Tangere.

**1988, Apr. 11 Litho. *Perf. 13½x14***

*1102* A187 30c shown 22 22
*1103* A187 40c multi 30 30
*1104* A187 45c multi 35 35
*1105* A187 50c multi 38 38
*1106* A187 $1 multi 78 78
*1107* A187 $2 multi 1.50 1.50
*1108* A187 $3 multi 2.25 2.25
*1109* A187 $4 multi 3.00 3.00
*Nos. 1102-1109 (8)* 8.78 8.78

**Souvenir Sheets**

*1110* A187 $5 multi 3.75 3.75
*1111* A187 $5 multi 3.75 3.75

Nos. 1110-1111 have multicolored margins continuing the paintings. Sizes: 110x95mm.

Sailing Week A188

**1988, Apr. 18 *Perf. 15***

*1112* A188 30c "Canada I," 1980 22 22
*1113* A188 60c "Gretal II," Australia, 1970 48 48
*1114* A188 $1 "Sceptre," GB, 1958 78 78
*1115* A188 $3 "Vigilant," US, 1893 2.25 2.25

**Souvenir Sheet**

*1116* A188 $5 "Australia II," 1983 3.75 3.75

No. 1116 has multicolored margin picturing race. Size: 104x93mm.

Walt Disney Animated Characters and Epcot Center, Walt Disney World — A189

**1988, May 3 *Perf. 14x13½, 13½x14***

*1116A* A189 1c like 25c 5 5
*1116B* A189 2c like 30c 5 5
*1116C* A189 3c like 40c 5 5
*1116D* A189 4c like 60c 5 5
*1116E* A189 5c like 70c 5 5
*1116F* A189 10c like $1.50 8 8
*1117* A189 25c The Living Seas 18 18
*1118* A189 30c World of Motion 22 22
*1119* A189 40c Spaceship Earth 30 30
*1120* A189 60c Universe of Energy 45 45
*1121* A189 70c Journey to Imagination 55 55
*1122* A189 $1.50 The Land 1.15 1.15
*1123* A189 $3 Communicore 2.25 2.25
*1124* A189 $4 Horizons 3.00 3.00
*Nos. 1116a-1124 (14)* 8.43 8.43

**Souvenir Sheets**

*1125* A189 $5 Epcot Center 3.75 3.75
*1126* A189 $5 The Contemporary Resort Hotel 3.75 3.75

30c, 40c, $1.50, $3 and No. 1126 are vert. Nos. 1125-1126 have multicolored decorative margins continuing the designs. Sizes: 126x100mm.

The Scott Catalogue value is a retail price, what you could expect to pay for the stamp in a grade of Fine-Very Fine. The value listed is a reference which reflects recent actual dealer selling price.

A190

Flowering Trees — A191

**1988, May 16 *Perf. 14***

*1127* A190 10c Jacaranda 8 8
*1128* A190 30c Cordia 22 22
*1129* A190 50c Orchid tree 38 38
*1130* A190 90c Flamboyant 70 70
*1131* A190 $1 African tulip tree 75 75
*1132* A190 $2 Potato tree 1.50 1.50
*1133* A190 $3 Crepe myrtle 2.25 2.25
*1134* A190 $4 Pitch apple 3.00 3.00
*Nos. 1127-1134 (8)* 8.88 8.88

**Souvenir Sheets**

*1135* A191 $5 Cassia 3.75 3.75
*1136* A191 $5 Chinaberry 3.75 3.75

Nos. 1135-1136 have multicolored margins continuing the designs. Sizes: 107x76mm.

Nos. 1011-1012, 1014 and 1013 Ovptd. in Black for Philatelic Exhibitions

a 

b 

c 

d 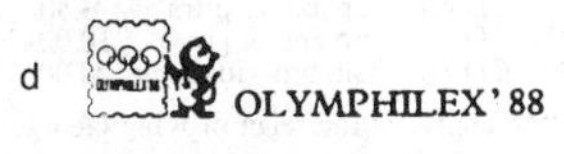


**1988, May 9 Litho. *Perf. 14***

*1137* A173 (a) $2 multi 1.50 1.50
*1138* A173 (b) $3 multi 2.25 2.25

**Souvenir Sheets**

*1139* A173 (c) $5 multi 3.75 3.75
*1139A* A172 (d) $5 multi 3.75 3.75

PRAGA '88 ($2), INDEPENDENCE 40 ($3), FINLANDIA '88 (No. 1139) and OLYMPHILEX '88 (No. 1139A).

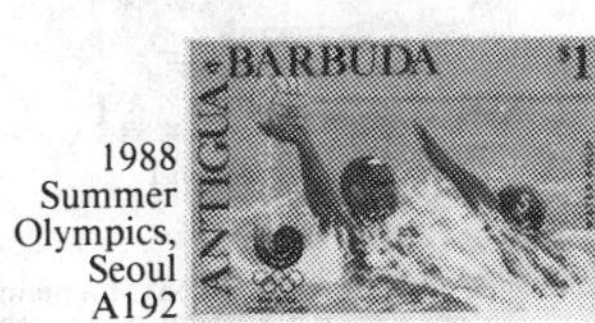

1988 Summer Olympics, Seoul A192

**1988, June 10**

*1140* A192 40c Gymnastic rings, vert. 30 30
*1141* A192 60c Weight lifting, vert. 45 45
*1142* A192 $1 Water polo 75 75
*1143* A192 $3 Boxing 2.25 2.25

**Souvenir Sheet**

*1144* A192 $5 Torch-bearer, vert. 3.75 3.75

No. 1144 has multicolored margin picturing Seoul Games and five-ring Olympic emblems. Size: 114x80mm.

Butterflies A193

**1988, Aug. 29 Litho. *Perf. 14***

*1145* A193 1c Monarch 5 5
*1146* A193 2c Jamaican clearwing 5 5
*1147* A193 3c Yellow-barred ringlet 5 5
*1148* A193 5c Cracker 5 5
*1149* A193 10c Jamaican mestra 8 8
*1150* A193 15c Mimic 12 12
*1151* A193 20c Silver spot 15 15
*1152* A193 25c Zebra 18 18
*1153* A193 30c Fiery sulphur 22 22
*1154* A193 40c Androgeus swallowtail 30 30
*1155* A193 45c Giant brimstone 35 35
*1156* A193 50c Orbed sulphur 38 38
*1157* A193 60c Blue-backed skipper 45 45
*1158* A193 $1 Common white skipper 75 75
*1159* A193 $2 Baracoa skipper 1.50 1.50
*1160* A193 $2.50 Mangrove skipper 1.90 1.90
*1161* A193 $5 Silver king 3.75 3.75
*1162* A193 $10 Pygmy skipper 7.50 7.50
*Nos. 1145-1162 (18)* 17.83 17.83

John F. Kennedy A194

**1988, Nov. 22 Litho. *Perf. 14***

*1162A* A194 1c like 30c 5 5
*1162B* A194 2c like $4 5 5
*1162C* A194 3c like $1 5 5
*1162D* A194 4c like 60c 5 5
*1163* A194 30c First family 22 22
*1164* A194 60c Motorcade, Mexico 45 45
*1165* A194 $1 Funeral procession 75 75
*1166* A194 $4 Aboard PT109 3.00 3.00

**Souvenir Sheet**

*1167* A194 $5 Taking Oath of Office 3.75 3.75

No. 1167 has multicolored margin picturing Kennedy walking on Hyannis Port beach. Size: 105x75mm.

Miniature Sheet

Christmas, Mickey Mouse 60th Anniv. — A195

Walt Disney characters: No. 1168a, Morty and Ferdie. No. 1168b, Goofy. No. 1168c, Chip-n-Dale. No. 1168d, Huey and Dewey. No. 1168e, Minnie Mouse. No. 1168f, Pluto. No. 1168g, Mickey Mouse. No. 1168h, Donald Duck and Louie. No. 1169, Goofy driving Mickey and Minnie in a horse-drawn carriage. No. 1170, Characters on roller skates, caroling.

**1988, Dec. 1 *Perf. 13½x14, 14x13½***

*1168* A195 Sheet of 8 6.00 6.00
*a.-h.* $1 any single 75 75

**Souvenir Sheets**

*1169* A195 $7 multi 5.25 5.25
*1170* A195 $7 multi, horiz. 5.25 5.25

Nos. 1169-1170 have multicolored margins continuing the designs. Sizes: 128x102mm.

Disney Christmas Type of 1988

**1988, Dec. 1 Litho. *Perf.***

| | | | | |
|---|---|---|---|---|
| *1171* | A195 | 10c like No. 1168e | 8 | 8 |
| *1172* | A195 | 25c like No. 1168f | 18 | 18 |
| *1173* | A195 | 30c like No. 1168g | 22 | 22 |
| *1174* | A195 | 70c like No. 1168h | 52 | 52 |

### WAR TAX STAMPS

No. 31 and Type A3 Overprinted in Black or Red **WAR STAMP**

**1916-18 Wmk. 3 *Perf. 14***

| | | | | |
|---|---|---|---|---|
| *MR1* | A3 | ½p green | 30 | 30 |
| *MR2* | A3 | ½p grn (R) ('17) | 35 | 35 |
| *MR3* | A3 | 1½p orange ('18) | 40 | 40 |

## ASCENSION

LOCATION — An island in the South Atlantic Ocean, 900 miles from Liberia.
GOVT. — A part of the British Crown Colony of St. Helena.
AREA — 34 sq. mi.
POP. — 1,625 (1982).

In 1922 Ascension was placed under the administration of the Colonial Office and annexed to the British Crown Colony of St. Helena. The only post office is at Georgetown.

12 Pence = 1 Shilling
20 Shillings = 1 Pound
100 Pence = 1 Pound (1971)

**Catalogue values for unused stamps in this country are for Never Hinged items, beginning with Scott 50.**

Stamps and Types of St. Helena, 1912-22 Overprinted in Black or Red

**ASCENSION**

**1922 Wmk. 4 *Perf. 14***

| | | | | |
|---|---|---|---|---|
| *1* | A9 | ½p grn & blk | 1.75 | *5.50* |
| *2* | A10 | 1p green | 2.00 | *5.50* |
| *3* | A10 | 1½p rose red | 4.25 | *11.00* |
| *4* | A9 | 2p gray & blk | 4.00 | *8.50* |
| *5* | A9 | 3p ultra | 4.00 | *9.00* |
| *6* | A10 | 8p dl vio & blk | 10.00 | *18.00* |
| *7* | A10 | 2sh ultra & blk, *blue* | 57.50 | *75.00* |
| *8* | A10 | 3sh vio & blk | 95.50 | *130.00* |

**Wmk. 3**

| | | | | |
|---|---|---|---|---|
| *9* | A9 | 1sh *gray green* (R) | 16.00 | *20.00* |
| | | *Nos. 1-9 (9)* | 195.00 | *282.50* |

Seal of Colony — A3

**1924-27 Typo. Wmk. 4 *Perf. 14***
**Chalky Paper**

| | | | | |
|---|---|---|---|---|
| *10* | A3 | ½p black & gray | 85 | 1.00 |
| *11* | A3 | 1p green & blk | 1.00 | 1.10 |
| *12* | A3 | 1½p rose red | 2.00 | 2.25 |
| *13* | A3 | 2p bluish gray & gray | 2.25 | 2.50 |
| *14* | A3 | 3p ultra | 2.25 | 3.00 |
| *15* | A3 | 4p blk & gray, *yel* | 14.00 | *22.50* |
| *16* | A3 | 5p ol & lil ('27) | 8.50 | *11.50* |
| *17* | A3 | 6p rose lil & gray | 30.00 | *45.00* |
| *18* | A3 | 8p violet & gray | 10.00 | *12.50* |
| *19* | A3 | 1sh brown & gray | 11.50 | *17.00* |
| *20* | A3 | 2sh ultra & gray, *blue* | 42.50 | *57.50* |
| *21* | A3 | 3sh blk & gray, *blue* | 75.00 | *85.00* |
| | | *Nos. 10-21 (12)* | 199.85 | *260.85* |

View of Georgetown — A4

Map of Ascension — A5

Sooty Tern Breeding Colony A9

Designs: 1½p, Pier at Georgetown. 3p, Long Beach. 5p, Three Sisters. 5sh, Green Mountain.

**1934, July 2 Engr.**

| | | | | |
|---|---|---|---|---|
| *23* | A4 | ½p violet & blk | 20 | 55 |
| *24* | A5 | 1p lt grn & blk | 65 | 65 |
| *25* | A4 | 1½p red & black | 80 | 80 |
| *26* | A5 | 2p org & black | 1.65 | 1.65 |
| *27* | A4 | 3p ultra & blk | 95 | 95 |
| *28* | A4 | 5p blue & black | 1.00 | 1.40 |
| *29* | A5 | 8p dk brn & blk | 3.25 | *8.00* |
| *30* | A9 | 1sh carmine & blk | 5.75 | *11.00* |
| *31* | A5 | 2sh6p violet & blk | 32.50 | *50.00* |
| *32* | A4 | 5sh brown & blk | 62.50 | *65.00* |
| | | *Nos. 23-32 (10)* | 109.25 | *140.00* |

**Silver Jubilee Issue**
Common Design Type

**1935, May 6 *Perf. 11x12***

| | | | | |
|---|---|---|---|---|
| *33* | CD301 | 1½p carmine & dk bl | 1.75 | *5.00* |
| *34* | CD301 | 2p blk & ultra | 3.50 | *7.00* |
| *35* | CD301 | 5p ind & grn | 10.00 | *20.00* |
| *36* | CD301 | 1sh brn vio & ind | 20.00 | *37.50* |

25th anniv. of the reign of King George V.

**Coronation Issue**
Common Design Type

**1937, May 19 *Perf. 13½x14***

| | | | | |
|---|---|---|---|---|
| *37* | CD302 | 1p deep green | 14 | 14 |
| *38* | CD302 | 2p deep orange | 55 | 55 |
| *39* | CD302 | 3p bright ultra | 95 | 95 |

Georgetown — A11

Designs: 1p, 2p, 4p, Green Mountain. 1½p, 2sh 6p, Pier at Georgetown. 3p, 5sh, Long Beach. 6p, 10sh, Three Sisters.

**1938-49 *Perf. 13½***
**Center in Black**

| | | | | |
|---|---|---|---|---|
| *40* | A11 | ½p violet | 6 | 6 |
| *a* | | Perf. 13 ('44) | 6 | 6 |
| *41* | A11 | 1p green | 13.00 | 7.50 |
| *41A* | A11 | 1p org yellow, perf. 13 ('42) | 8 | 8 |
| *b* | | Perf. 14 ('49) | 70 | 70 |
| *c* | | Perf. 13½ | 1.50 | 1.50 |
| *42* | A11 | 1½p red | 18 | 18 |
| *a* | | Perf. 14 ('49) | 1.75 | 2.25 |
| *b* | | Perf. 13 ('44) | 18 | 18 |
| *43* | A11 | 2p orange | 14 | 14 |
| *a* | | Perf. 14 ('49) | 5.50 | *13.00* |
| *b* | | Perf. 13 ('44) | 15 | 15 |
| *44* | A11 | 3p ultra | 32.50 | 20.00 |
| *44A* | A11 | 3p black ('40) | 32 | 32 |
| *c* | | Perf. 13 ('44) | 32 | 32 |
| *44B* | A11 | 4p ultra, perf. 13 ('44) | 32 | 32 |
| *d* | | Perf. 13½ | 32 | 32 |
| *45* | A11 | 6p gray blue | 38 | 38 |
| *a* | | Perf. 13 ('44) | 55 | 55 |

***Perf. 13***

| | | | | |
|---|---|---|---|---|
| *46* | A11 | 1sh dk brn ('44) | 65 | 65 |
| *a* | | Perf. 13½ | 85 | 85 |
| *47* | A11 | 2sh6p car ('44) | 3.50 | 3.50 |
| *a* | | Perf. 13½ | 4.50 | 4.50 |
| *48* | A11 | 5sh yel brn ('44) | 7.50 | 7.50 |
| *a* | | Perf. 13½ | 8.75 | 8.75 |
| *49* | A11 | 10sh red vio ('44) | 12.00 | 12.00 |
| *a* | | Perf. 13½ | 14.00 | 14.00 |
| | | *Nos. 40-49 (13)* | 70.63 | 52.63 |

See Nos. 54-56.

**Catalogue values for unused stamps in this section, from this point to the end of the section, are for Never Hinged items.**

**Peace Issue**
Common Design Type

***Perf. 13½x14***

**1946, Oct. 21 Engr. Wmk. 4**

| | | | | |
|---|---|---|---|---|
| *50* | CD303 | 2p deep orange | 24 | 24 |
| *51* | CD303 | 4p deep blue | 30 | 30 |

Return to peace at the close of WWII.

**Silver Wedding Issue**
Common Design Types

**1948, Oct. 20 Photo. *Perf. 14x14½***

| | | | | |
|---|---|---|---|---|
| *52* | CD304 | 3p black | 35 | 35 |

**Engraved; Name Typographed**
***Perf. 11½x11***

| | | | | |
|---|---|---|---|---|
| *53* | CD305 | 10sh red vio | 35.00 | *50.00* |

25th anniv. of the marriage of King George VI and Queen Elizabeth.

Type of 1938

Designs: 1p, Three Sisters. 1½p, Georgetown Pier. 2p, Green Mountain.

**Wmk. 4**

**1949, June 1 Engr. *Perf. 13***

| | | | | |
|---|---|---|---|---|
| *54* | A11 | 1p green & blk | 30 | 30 |

***Perf. 14***

| | | | | |
|---|---|---|---|---|
| *55* | A11 | 1½p lil rose & blk | 35 | 35 |
| *a* | | Perf. 13 ('53) | 1.80 | 1.80 |
| *56* | A11 | 2p red & blk | 50 | 50 |

Issue date: No. 55a, Feb. 25, 1953.

**UPU Issue**
Common Design Types

**Engr.; Name Typo. on Nos. 58, 59**

**1949, Oct. 10 *Perf. 13½, 11x11½***

| | | | | |
|---|---|---|---|---|
| *57* | CD306 | 3p rose carmine | 1.00 | 1.00 |
| *58* | CD307 | 4p indigo | 2.00 | 2.00 |
| *59* | CD308 | 6p olive | 2.50 | 2.50 |
| *60* | CD309 | 1sh slate | 5.00 | 5.00 |

UPU, 75th anniv.

**Coronation Issue**
Common Design Type

**1953, June 2 Engr. *Perf. 13½x13***

| | | | | |
|---|---|---|---|---|
| *61* | CD312 | 3p gray & black | 1.65 | 1.65 |

Reservoir A16

Designs: 1p, Map of Ascension. 1½p, Georgetown. 2p, Map showing Ascension between South America and Africa and cable lines. 2½p, Mountain road. 3p, Yellow-billed tropic bird. 4p, Longfinned tuna. 6p, Waves. 7p, Young green turtles. 1sh, Land crab. 2sh6p, Sooty tern (wideawake). 5sh, Perfect Crater. 10sh, View from Northwest.

**1956, Nov. 19 Wmk. 4 *Perf. 13***
**Center in Black**

| | | | | |
|---|---|---|---|---|
| *62* | A16 | ½p brown | 8 | 8 |
| *63* | A16 | 1p lilac rose | 12 | 12 |
| *64* | A16 | 1½p orange | 20 | 20 |
| *65* | A16 | 2p carmine | 28 | 28 |
| *66* | A16 | 2½p orange brn | 35 | 35 |
| *67* | A16 | 3p blue | 42 | 42 |
| *68* | A16 | 4p turq blue | 60 | 60 |
| *69* | A16 | 6p dark blue | 1.00 | 1.00 |
| *70* | A16 | 7p olive | 1.25 | 1.25 |
| *71* | A16 | 1sh scarlet | 1.65 | 1.40 |
| *72* | A16 | 2sh6p brn violet | 14.00 | 10.00 |
| *73* | A16 | 5sh bright grn | 17.50 | 11.50 |
| *74* | A16 | 10sh purple | 42.50 | 21.00 |
| | | *Nos. 62-74 (13)* | 79.95 | 48.20 |

Brown Booby — A17

Birds: 1½p, Black tern. 2p, Fairy tern. 3p, Red-billed tropic bird in flight. 4½p, Brown noddy. 6p, Sooty tern. 7p, Frigate bird. 10p, Blue-faced booby. 1sh, Yellow-billed tropic bird. 1sh6p, Red-billed tropic bird. 2sh6p, Madeiran storm petrel. 5sh, Red-footed booby (brown phase). 10sh, Frigate birds. £1, Red-footed booby (white phase).

***Perf. 14x14½***

**1963, May 23 Photo. Wmk. 314**

| | | | | |
|---|---|---|---|---|
| *75* | A17 | 1p brt bl, blk & yel | 6 | 5 |
| *a* | | Bklt. pane of 4 | 30 | |
| *76* | A17 | 1½p bis, blk & bl | 10 | 6 |
| *a* | | Bklt. pane of 4 | 50 | |
| *b* | | Blue omitted | 72.50 | |
| *77* | A17 | 2p brt ultra, blk & brn | 14 | 10 |
| *a* | | Bklt. pane of 4 | 1.10 | |
| *78* | A17 | 3p grnsh bl, ind & red | 16 | 14 |
| *a* | | Bklt. pane of 4 | 1.25 | |
| *79* | A17 | 4½p bl, dk brn & blk | 25 | 20 |
| *80* | A17 | 6p yel grn, blk & brn | 32 | 25 |
| *a* | | Bklt. pane of 4 | 3.25 | |
| *81* | A17 | 7p lil, blk & brn | 32 | 30 |
| *82* | A17 | 10p bluish grn, blk & yel | 50 | 40 |
| *83* | A17 | 1sh multicolored | 55 | 50 |
| *84* | A17 | 1sh6p multicolored | 1.10 | 1.00 |
| *a* | | Bklt. pane of 4 | 6.25 | |
| *85* | A17 | 2sh6p multicolored | 2.75 | 2.50 |
| *86* | A17 | 5sh multicolored | 5.00 | 5.00 |
| *87* | A17 | 10sh multicolored | 11.50 | 10.00 |
| *88* | A17 | £1 multicolored | 20.00 | 20.00 |
| | | *Nos. 75-88 (14)* | 42.75 | 40.50 |

**Freedom from Hunger Issue**
Common Design Type

**1963, June 4 Wmk. 314**

| | | | | |
|---|---|---|---|---|
| *89* | CD314 | 1sh6p car rose | 4.50 | 3.50 |

**Red Cross Centenary Issue**
Common Design Type
**Wmk. 314**

**1963, Sept. 2 Litho. *Perf. 13***

| | | | | |
|---|---|---|---|---|
| *90* | CD315 | 3p black & red | 1.10 | 1.10 |
| *91* | CD315 | 1sh6p ultra & red | 6.50 | 6.50 |

**ITU Issue**
Common Design Type
***Perf. 11x11½***

**1965, May 17 Litho. Wmk. 314**

| | | | | |
|---|---|---|---|---|
| *92* | CD317 | 3p mag & violet | 90 | 90 |
| *93* | CD317 | 6p grnsh bl & brn org | 1.90 | 1.90 |

**Intl. Cooperation Year Issue**
Common Design Type

**1965, Oct. 25 Wmk. 314 *Perf. 14½***

| | | | | |
|---|---|---|---|---|
| *94* | CD318 | 1p bl grn & cl | 45 | 28 |
| *95* | CD318 | 6p lt vio & grn | 1.75 | 1.65 |

**Churchill Memorial Issue**
Common Design Type

**1966, Jan. 24 Photo. *Perf. 14***
**Design in Black, Gold and Carmine Rose**

| | | | | |
|---|---|---|---|---|
| *96* | CD319 | 1p bright bl | 42 | 22 |
| *97* | CD319 | 3p green | 1.50 | 85 |
| *98* | CD319 | 6p brown | 2.00 | 1.65 |
| *99* | CD319 | 1sh6p violet | 6.25 | 4.75 |

**World Cup Soccer Issue**
Common Design Type

**1966, July 1 Litho. *Perf. 14***

| | | | | |
|---|---|---|---|---|
| *100* | CD321 | 3p multicolored | 70 | 55 |
| *101* | CD321 | 6p multicolored | 1.40 | 2.25 |

**WHO Headquarters Issue**
Common Design Type

**1966, Sept. 20 Litho. *Perf. 14***

| | | | | |
|---|---|---|---|---|
| *102* | CD322 | 3p multi | 1.25 | 1.00 |
| *103* | CD322 | 1sh6p multi | 3.25 | 3.00 |

Apollo Satellite Station, Ascension — A18

**Wmk. 314**

**1966, Nov. 7 Photo. *Perf. 14***

*104* A18 4p purple & blk 14 12
*105* A18 8p bl grn & blk 28 18
*106* A18 1sh3p brn ol & blk 55 35
*107* A18 2sh6p brt grnsh bl & blk 1.10 80

Opening of the Apollo communications satellite-earth station, part of the U.S. National Aeronautics and Space Administration's Apollo program.

**UNESCO Anniversary Issue**

Common Design Type

Designs: 3p, "Education." 6p, "Science." 1sh6p, "Culture."

**1967, Jan. 3 Litho. *Perf. 14***

*108* CD323 3p dp org, yel & dl vio 95 85
*109* CD323 6p vio, dk ol grn & yel 2.25 2.00
*110* CD323 1sh6p yel, mag & blk 6.25 6.25

BBC Emblem A19

**Photo.; Gold Impressed**

**1967, Dec. 1 Wmk. 314 *Perf. 14½***

*111* A19 1p ultra & gold 8 8
*112* A19 3p dk grn & gold 12 12
*113* A19 6p brt pur & gold 35 30
*114* A19 1sh6p brt red & gold 80 70

Opening of the British Broadcasting Company's South Atlantic Relay Station on Ascension Island.

Human Rights Flame and Chain — A20

***Perf. 14½x14***

**1968, July 8 Litho. Wmk. 314**

*115* A20 6p org, car & blk 28 20
*116* A20 1sh6p gray, mag & blk 60 55
*117* A20 2sh6p brt grn, plum & blk 1.10 90

International Human Rights Year.

Blackfish A21

Fish: No. 119, Sailfish. 6p, Oldwife. 8p, Leather jacks. 1sh6p, Yellowtails. 1sh9p, Tuna. 2sh3p, Mako sharks. 2sh11p, Rock hind (jack).

***Perf. 13x12½***

**1968-69 Wmk. 314 Litho.**

*118* A21 4p brt grnsh bl & blk 30 18
*119* A21 4p red & multi ('69) 35 24
*120* A21 6p yel olive & multi ('69) 45 35
*121* A21 8p brt rose lil & multi 60 38
*122* A21 1sh6p brown & multi ('69) 2.00 1.50
*123* A21 1sh9p emer & multi 1.10 95
*124* A21 2sh3p ocher & multi 1.75 1.25
*125* A21 2sh11p dp org & multi ('69) 3.50 2.25
*Nos. 118-125 (8)* 10.05 7.10

See Nos. 130-133.

Arms of R.N.S. Rattlesnake — A22

Coats of Arms of Royal Naval Ships: 9p, Weston. 1sh9p, Undaunted. 2sh3p, Eagle.

***Perf. 14x14½***

**1969, Oct. 1 Photo. Wmk. 314**

*126* A22 4p dk & lt bl, brn & gold 28 28
*127* A22 9p dk & lt bl, red & gold 55 55
*128* A22 1sh9p dk & lt bl & gold 1.40 1.40
*129* A22 2sh3p dk & lt bl, red, sil & gold 1.90 1.90
*a* Miniature sheet of 4 6.75 5.75

No. 129a contains one each of Nos. 126-129. Light blue ornamental margin. Size: 164x104mm.

See Nos. 134-137, 152-159, 166-169.

**Fish Type of 1968**

Deep-sea fish: 4p, Wahoo. 9p, Coalfish. 1sh9p, Dolphinfishes. 2sh3p, Soldierfish.

**1970, Apr. 6 Litho. *Perf. 14***

*130* A21 4p bluish grn & multi 55 35
*131* A21 9p org & multi 90 60
*132* A21 1sh9p ultra & multi 1.75 1.40
*133* A21 2sh3p gray & multi 3.25 2.00

**Naval Arms Type of 1969.**

Coats of Arms of Royal Naval Ships: 4p, Penelope. 9p, Carlisle. 1sh6p, Amphion. 2sh6p, Magpie.

***Perf. 12½x12***

**1970, Sept. 7 Photo. Wmk. 314**

*134* A22 4p ultra, gold & blk 25 25
*135* A22 9p lt bl, blk, gold & red 50 50
*136* A22 1sh6p grnsh bl, gold & blk 1.25 1.25
*137* A22 2sh6p lt grnsh bl, gold & blk 2.00 2.00
*a* Miniature sheet of 4 7.50 6.00

No. 137a contains one each of Nos. 134-137. Light blue ornamental margin. Size: 152x95mm.

**Decimal Currency Issue**

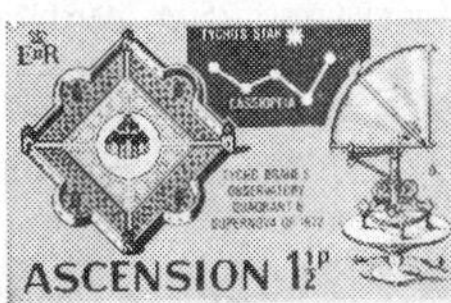


Tycho Brahe's Observatory, Quadrant and Supernova, 1572 — A23

Designs (Man into Space): ½p, Chinese rocket, 1232 (vert.). 1p, Medieval Arab astronomers (vert.). 2p, Galileo, his telescope and drawing of moon, 1609. 2½p, Isaac Newton, telescope and apple. 3½p, Harrison's chronometer and ship, 1735. 4½p, First American manned orbital flight (Project Mercury, 1962; vert.). 5p, Reflector of Palomar telescope and ring nebula in Lyra, Messier 57. 7½p, Jodrell Bank telescope. 10p, Mariner 7, 1969, and telescopic view of Mars. 12½p, Sputnik 2 and dog Laika, 1957. 25p, Astronaut walking in space, 1965 (Gemini 4; vert.). 50p, U.S. astronauts and moon landing module, 1969. £1, Future space research station.

**1971, Feb. 15 Litho. *Perf. 14½***

*138* A23 ½p multicolored 5 5
*a* Booklet pane of 4 35
*139* A23 1p multicolored 8 8
*a* Booklet pane of 4 50
*140* A23 1½p multicolored 12 12
*a* Booklet pane of 4 75
*141* A23 2p multicolored 18 18
*a* Booklet pane of 4 1.25
*142* A23 2½p multicolored 22 22
*a* Booklet pane of 4 1.65
*143* A23 3½p multicolored 30 30
*a* Booklet pane of 4 2.25
*144* A23 4½p multicolored 40 40
*145* A23 5p multicolored 45 45
*146* A23 7½p multicolored 50 50
*147* A23 10p multicolored 70 70
*148* A23 12½p multicolored 90 90
*149* A23 25p multicolored 1.90 1.90
*150* A23 50p multicolored 3.50 3.50
*151* A23 £1 multicolored 6.75 6.75
*Nos. 138-151 (14)* 16.05 16.05

Arms of H.M.S. Phoenix — A24

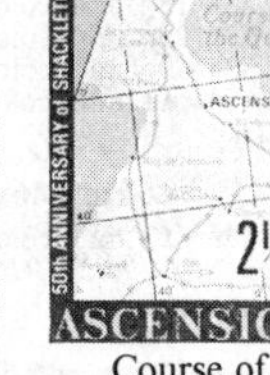


Course of Quest — A25

Coats of Arms of Royal Naval Ships: 4p, Milford. 9p, Pelican. 15p, Oberon.

**1971, Nov. 15 Photo. *Perf. 13½x13***

*152* A24 2p gold & multi 25 25
*153* A24 4p gold & multi 55 55
*154* A24 9p gold & multi 1.65 1.65
*155* A24 15p gold & multi 3.25 3.25
*a* Souvenir sheet of 4 9.75 12.50

No. 155a contains one each of Nos. 152-155. Blue ornamental margin. Size: 150x104mm.

**Naval Arms Type of 1969**

Coats of Arms of Royal Naval Ships: 1½p, Lowestoft. 3p, Auckland. 6p, Nigeria. 17½p, Bermuda.

**1972, May 22 Litho. *Perf. 14x14½***

*156* A22 1½p bl, gold & blk 24 24
*157* A22 3p grnsh bl, gold & blk 52 52
*158* A22 6p grn, gold, blk & bl 1.00 1.00
*159* A22 17½p lil, gold, blk & red 3.00 3.00
*a* Miniature sheet of 4 6.00 8.00

No. 159a contains one each of Nos. 156-159. Light blue ornamental margin. Size: 155x93mm.

**1972, Aug. 2 *Perf. 14***

Designs: 4p, Shackleton and "Quest" (horiz.). 7½p, Shackleton's cabin and Quest in pack ice (horiz.). 11p, Shackleton statue, London, and memorial cairn, South Georgia.

*160* A25 2½p multicolored 30 30
*161* A25 4p multicolored 50 50
*162* A25 7½p multicolored 1.00 1.00
*163* A25 11p multicolored 1.65 1.65
*a* Souvenir sheet of 4 4.75 4.75

50th anniv. of the death of Sir Ernest Henry Shackleton (1874-1922), explorer of Antarctica.

No. 163a contains one each of Nos. 160-163. Blue margin with commemorative inscription. Size: 140x104mm.

**Silver Wedding Issue, 1972**

Common Design Type

Design: Queen Elizabeth II, Prince Philip, land crab and shark.

**1972, Nov. 20 Photo. *Perf. 14x14½***

*164* CD324 2p violet & multi 14 14
*165* CD324 16p car rose & multi 1.00 1.00

**Naval Arms Type of 1969**

Coats of Arms of Royal Naval Ships: 2p, Birmingham. 4p, Cardiff. 9p, Penzance. 13p, Rochester.

**1973, May 28 Litho. Wmk. 314**

*166* A22 2p blue & multi 60 42
*167* A22 4p yel grn & multi 1.50 1.10
*168* A22 9p lt blue & multi 3.00 2.25
*169* A22 13p violet & multi 4.25 3.75
*a* Miniature sheet of 4 19.00 24.00

No. 169a contains one each of Nos. 166-169. Light blue decorative margin. Size: 107½x152mm.

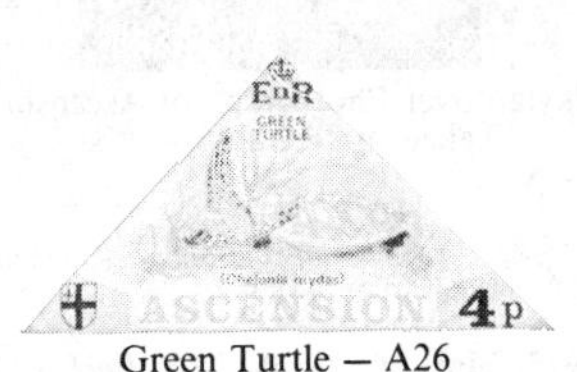


Green Turtle — A26

Turtles: 9p, Loggerhead. 12p, Hawksbill.

**1973, Aug. 28 *Perf. 13½***

*170* A26 4p pale lil & multi 1.40 1.10
*171* A26 9p gray grn & multi 2.75 2.25
*172* A26 12p yellow & multi 4.50 3.50

Light Infanty Marine Sergeant, 1900 — A27

Uniforms (Royal Marines): 6p, Private, 1816. 12p, Officer, Light Infantry, 1880. 20p, Color Sergeant, Artillery, 1910.

**1973, Oct. 31 *Perf. 14½***

*173* A27 2p multicolored 45 45
*174* A27 6p lt grn & multi 1.65 1.65
*175* A27 12p lt bl & multi 3.25 3.25
*176* A27 20p lt lil & multi 5.50 5.50

Departure of the Royal Marines from Ascension, 50th anniv.

**Princess Anne's Wedding Issue**

Common Design Type

**1973, Nov. 14 *Perf. 14***

*177* CD325 2p ocher & multi 25 25
*178* CD325 18p multicolored 1.25 1.25

Wedding of Princess Anne and Capt. Mark Phillips, Nov. 14, 1973.

Letter and UPU Emblem A29

Design: 9p, UPU emblem and Mercury.

**Wmk. 314**

**1974, Mar. 27 Litho. *Perf. 14½***

*179* A29 2p multicolored 22 22
*180* A29 9p vio bl & multi 90 90

Centenary of the Universal Postal Union.

Young Churchill and Blenheim Palace A30

Design: 25p, Churchill and United Nations Headquarters, New York.

**1974, Nov. 30 Litho. Unwmk.**

*181* A30 5p sl grn & multi 28 28
*182* A30 25p purple & multi 1.10 1.10
*a* Souvenir sheet of 2 2.25 2.00

Sir Winston Churchill (1874-1965), birth centenary. No. 182a contains one each of Nos. 181-182, dark red decorative margin. Size: 94x86mm.

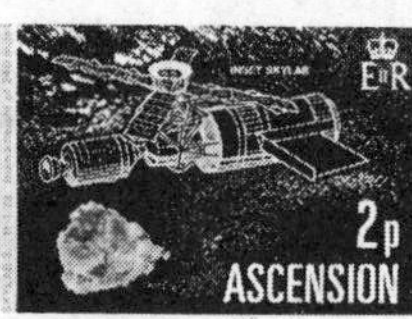


Skylab over Photograph of Ascension Taken by Skylab 3 — A31

Design: 18p, Command module and photo of Ascension from Skylab 4.

**1975, Mar. 20 Wmk. 314 *Perf. 14½***

| | | | | |
|---|---|---|---|---|
| *183* | A31 | 2p multicolored | 15 | 15 |
| *184* | A31 | 18p multicolored | 1.00 | 1.00 |

Skylab space station.

US Air Force C-141A Starlifter — A32

Aircraft: 5p, Royal Air Force C-130 Hercules. 9p, Vickers VC-10. 24p, U.S. Air Force C-5A Galaxy.

***Perf. 13½x14***

**1975, June 19 Litho. Wmk. 314**

| | | | | |
|---|---|---|---|---|
| *185* | A32 | 2p multicolored | 22 | 22 |
| *186* | A32 | 5p multicolored | 60 | 60 |
| *187* | A32 | 9p multicolored | 1.10 | 1.10 |
| *188* | A32 | 24p multicolored | 3.00 | 3.00 |
| *a* | | Souvenir sheet of 4 | 7.25 | 9.00 |

Wideawake Airfield, Ascension Island. No. 188a contains one each of Nos. 185-188; blue and violet blue margin. Size: 142½x98½mm.

Nos. 144, 148-149 Overprinted **APOLLO-SOYUZ LINK 1975**

**1975, Aug. Litho. *Perf. 14½***

| | | | | |
|---|---|---|---|---|
| *189* | A23 | 4½p multicolored | 30 | 30 |
| *190* | A23 | 12½p multicolored | 60 | 60 |
| *191* | A23 | 25p multicolored | 1.50 | 1.50 |

Apollo Soyuz space test project (Russo-American cooperation), launching July 15; link-up, July 17.

HMS Peruvian and Zenobia Arriving Oct. 22, 1815 A33

Designs: 5p, Water Supply, Dampiers Drip. 9p, First Landing, Oct. 1815. 15p, The Garden on Green Mountain. All designs after paintings by Isobel McManus.

**1975, Oct. 22 Wmk. 373 *Perf. 14½***

| | | | | |
|---|---|---|---|---|
| *192* | A33 | 2p lt bl & multi | 15 | 12 |
| *193* | A33 | 5p lt bl & multi | 32 | 25 |
| *194* | A33 | 9p red & multi | 52 | 50 |
| *195* | A33 | 15p red & multi | 1.00 | 85 |

British occupation, 160th anniv.

Canaries A34

Designs: 2p, Fairy tern (vert.). 3p, Waxbills. 4p, Black noddy (vert.). 5p, Brown noddy. 6p, Common mynah. 7p, Madeira storm petrels (vert.). 8p, Sooty terns. 9p, White booby (vert.). 10p, Red-footed booby. 15p, Red-throated francolin (vert.). 18p, Brown booby (vert.). 25p, Red-billed bo'sun bird. 50p, Yellow-billed bo'sun bird. £1, Ascension frigatebird (vert.). £2, Boatswain Island Bird Sanctuary and birds.

***Perf. 14x14½, 14½x14***

**1976, Apr. 26 Litho. Wmk. 373**

**Size: 35x27mm., 27x35mm.**

| | | | | |
|---|---|---|---|---|
| *196* | A34 | 1p multicolored | 7 | 5 |
| *197* | A34 | 2p multicolored | 10 | 6 |
| *198* | A34 | 3p multicolored | 12 | 8 |
| *199* | A34 | 4p multicolored | 15 | 10 |
| *200* | A34 | 5p multicolored | 20 | 12 |
| *201* | A34 | 6p multicolored | 22 | 16 |
| *202* | A34 | 7p multicolored | 25 | 18 |
| *203* | A34 | 8p multicolored | 30 | 22 |
| *204* | A34 | 9p multicolored | 40 | 24 |
| *205* | A34 | 10p multicolored | 45 | 25 |
| *206* | A34 | 15p multicolored | 65 | 40 |
| *207* | A34 | 18p multicolored | 85 | 48 |
| *208* | A34 | 25p multicolored | 1.25 | 65 |
| *209* | A34 | 50p multicolored | 2.25 | 1.25 |
| *210* | A34 | £1 multicolored | 3.25 | 2.75 |

***Perf. 13½***

**Size: 46x33mm.**

| | | | | |
|---|---|---|---|---|
| *211* | A34 | £2 multicolored | 6.50 | 5.25 |
| | | *Nos. 196-211 (16)* | 17.01 | 12.24 |

Great Britain Type A1 with Ascension Cancel — A35

Designs: 9p, Ascension No. 1 (vert.). 25p, Freighter Southampton Castle.

**1976, May 4 *Perf. 13½x14, 14x13½***

| | | | | |
|---|---|---|---|---|
| *212* | A35 | 5p lt brn, car & blk | 22 | 22 |
| *213* | A35 | 9p gray grn, grn & blk | 40 | 40 |
| *214* | A35 | 25p blue & multi | 1.25 | 1.25 |
| *a* | | Souvenir sheet of 3 | 3.00 | 3.00 |

Festival of Stamps 1976. No. 214a contains one each of Ascension No. 214, St. Helena No. 297 and Tristan da Cunha No. 208. Multicolored margin shows map with location of islands off Africa. Size: 133x121mm.

US Base A36

Designs: 9p, NASA Station, Devil's Ashpit. 25p, Viking satellite landing on Mars.

***Perf. 13½.***

**1976, July 4 Litho. Wmk. 373**

| | | | | |
|---|---|---|---|---|
| *215* | A36 | 8p blk & multi | 70 | 70 |
| *216* | A36 | 9p blk & multi | 85 | 85 |
| *217* | A36 | 25p blk & multi | 2.00 | 2.00 |

American Bicentennial. No. 215 also commemorates the 20th anniversary of Bahamas Long Range Proving Ground (extension) Agreement.

Queen in Coronation Coach — A37

Designs: 8p, Prince Philip on Ascension Island, 1957 (vert.). 12p, Queen leaving Buckingham Palace in coronation coach.

***Perf. 14x13½, 13½x14***

**1977, Feb. 7 Litho. Wmk. 373**

| | | | | |
|---|---|---|---|---|
| *218* | A37 | 8p multicolored | 30 | 30 |
| *219* | A37 | 12p multicolored | 42 | 42 |
| *220* | A37 | 25p multicolored | 90 | 90 |

25th anniversary of the reign of Queen Elizabeth II.

Water Pipe in Tunnel — A38

Designs: 5p, Breakneck Valley wells. 12p, Break tank in pipe line (horiz.). 25p, Dam and reservoir (horiz.).

**1977, June 27 Litho. *Perf. 14½***

| | | | | |
|---|---|---|---|---|
| *221* | A38 | 3p multicolored | 16 | 16 |
| *222* | A38 | 5p multicolored | 25 | 25 |
| *223* | A38 | 12p multicolored | 60 | 60 |
| *224* | A38 | 25p multicolored | 1.25 | 1.25 |

Water supplies constructed by Royal Marines, 1832 and 1881.

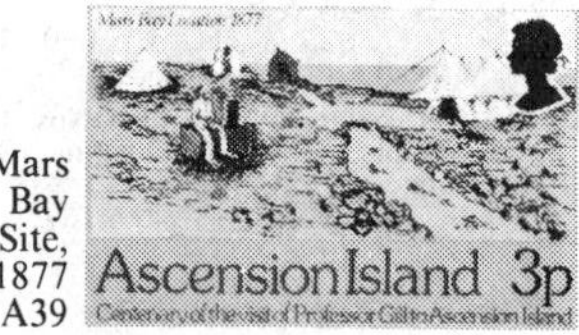


Mars Bay Site, 1877 A39

Designs: 8p, Mars Bay and instrument sites. 12p, Prof. and Mrs. Gill before their tent. 25p, Map of Ascension.

***Perf. 13½x14***

**1977, Oct. 3 Litho. Wmk. 373**

| | | | | |
|---|---|---|---|---|
| *225* | A39 | 3p multicolored | 18 | 16 |
| *226* | A39 | 8p multicolored | 45 | 38 |
| *227* | A39 | 12p multicolored | 75 | 65 |
| *228* | A39 | 25p multicolored | 1.50 | 1.25 |

Centenary of visit of Prof. David Gill (1843-1914), astronomer, to Ascension.

**Elizabeth II Coronation Anniversary Issue**

**Souvenir Sheet**

Common Design Types

**Unwmk.**

**1978, May 21 Litho. *Perf. 15***

| | | | | |
|---|---|---|---|---|
| *229* | | Sheet of 6, dk brn & multi | 4.00 | 4.00 |
| *a* | | CD326 25p Lion of England | 85 | 85 |
| *b* | | CD327 25p Elizabeth II | 85 | 85 |
| *c* | | CD328 25p Green turtle | 85 | 85 |

No. 229 contains 2 se-tenant strips of Nos. 229a-229c, separated by horizontal gutter with commemorative and descriptive inscriptions and showing central part of coronation procession with coach. Size: 100x135mm.

East Crater (Broken Tooth) — A40

Volcanoes: 5p, Hollands Crater (Hollow Tooth). 12p, Bears Back. 15p, Green Mountain. 25p, Two Boats village.

**1978, Sept. 4 Litho. *Perf. 14½***

| | | | | |
|---|---|---|---|---|
| *230* | A40 | 3p multicolored | 10 | 10 |
| *231* | A40 | 5p multicolored | 15 | 15 |
| *232* | A40 | 12p multicolored | 40 | 40 |
| *233* | A40 | 15p multicolored | 50 | 50 |
| *234* | A40 | 25p multicolored | 85 | 85 |
| *a* | | Souvenir sheet of 10 | 4.75 | 6.25 |
| | | *Nos. 230-234 (5)* | 2.00 | 2.00 |

Nos. 230-234 printed se-tenant showing panoramic view of volcanic terrain.

No. 234a contains 2 each of Nos. 230-234. Multicolored margin shows map of volcanic area. Size: 186x101mm.

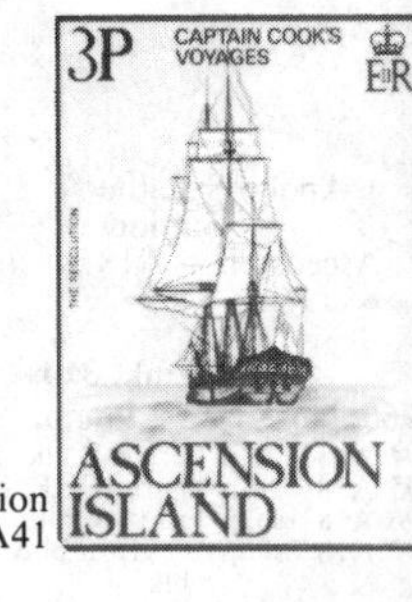


Resolution A41

Designs: 8p, Cook's chronometer. 12p, Green turtle. 25p, Capt. Cook after Flaxman/Wedgwood medallion.

**Litho.; Litho. & Engr. (25p)**

**1979, Jan. 8 *Perf. 11***

| | | | | |
|---|---|---|---|---|
| *235* | A41 | 3p multicolored | 15 | 12 |
| *236* | A41 | 8p multicolored | 35 | 28 |
| *237* | A41 | 12p multicolored | 60 | 45 |
| *238* | A41 | 25p multicolored | 1.25 | 90 |

Capt. Cook's voyages.

St. Mary's Church, Georgetown — A42

Designs: 12p, Old map of Ascension Island. 50p, Ascension, by Rembrandt.

**Wmk. 373**

**1979, May 24 Litho. *Perf. 14½***

| | | | | |
|---|---|---|---|---|
| *239* | A42 | 8p multicolored | 22 | 22 |
| *240* | A42 | 12p multicolored | 35 | 35 |
| *241* | A42 | 50p multicolored | 1.50 | 1.50 |

Ascension Day.

Landing Cable at Comfortless Cove — A43

Designs: 8p, Cable Ship Anglia. 12p, Map showing cables across the Atlantic (vert.). 15p, Cable-laying ship. 25p, Cable and earth station.

**Wmk. 373**

**1979, Sept. 15 Litho. *Perf. 14½***

| | | | | |
|---|---|---|---|---|
| *242* | A43 | 3p rose car & black | 8 | 8 |
| *243* | A43 | 8p dk yel grn & blk | 22 | 22 |
| *244* | A43 | 12p yel bister & blk | 35 | 35 |
| *245* | A43 | 15p violet & black | 45 | 45 |
| *246* | A43 | 25p deep org & black | 70 | 70 |
| | | *Nos. 242-246 (5)* | 1.80 | 1.80 |

Eastern Telegraph Company, 80th anniv.

Ascension No. 45 — A44

Ascension Stamps: 8p, No. 73. 12p, No. 14 (vert.). 50p, Hill portrait (vert.).

**1979, Dec. 17 Wmk. 373 *Perf. 14***

*247* A44 3p multicolored 8 8
*248* A44 8p multicolored 20 20
*249* A44 12p multicolored 28 28
*250* A44 50p multicolored 1.25 1.25

Sir Rowland Hill (1795-1879), originator of penny postage.

Anogramma Ascensionis A45

**1980, Feb. 18 Litho. *Perf. 14½***

*251* A45 3p shown 8 8
*252* A45 6p Xiphopteris ascensionense 15 15
*253* A45 8p Sporobolus caespitosus 20 20
*254* A45 12p Sporobolus durus, vert. 32 32
*255* A45 18p Dryopteris ascensionis, vert. 45 45
*256* A45 24p Marattia purpurascens, vert. 60 60
*Nos. 251-256 (6)* 1.80 1.80

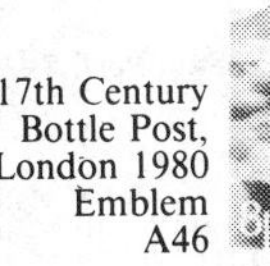

17th Century Bottle Post, London 1980 Emblem A46

**1980, May 1 Wmk. 373 *Perf. 14***

*257* A46 8p shown 20 20
*258* A46 12p 36-gun frigate, 19th century 32 32
*259* A46 15p "Garth Castle," 1863 40 40
*260* A46 50p "St. Helena," Lockheed C141 1.25 1.25
*a* Souvenir sheet of 4 2.50 3.50

London 1980 Intl. Stamp Exhib., May 6-14. No. 260a contains Nos. 257-260; light blue and black margin gives Ascension postal history. Sizes: 102x154mm.

**Queen Mother Elizabeth Birthday Issue**

Common Design Type

**1980, Aug. 11 Litho. *Perf. 14***

*261* CD330 15p multicolored 75 75

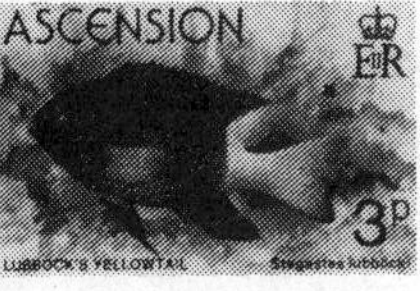

Lubbock's Yellowtail A47

**1980, Sept. 15 Litho. *Perf. 13½x14***

*262* A47 3p shown 8 8
*263* A47 10p Resplendent angelfish 30 30
*264* A47 25p Hedgehog butterflyfish 70 70
*265* A47 40p Marmalade razorfish 1.10 1.10

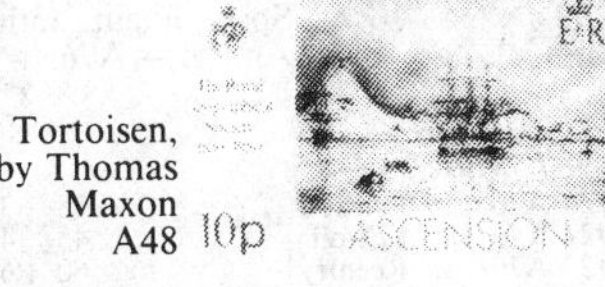

Tortoisen, by Thomas Maxon A48

Common Design Types are pictured in section before Great Britain.

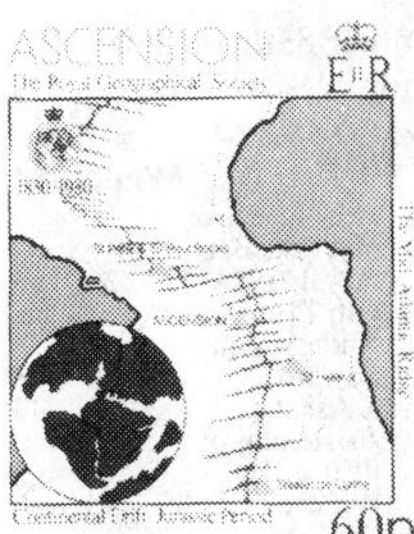

Map of South Atlantic Ridge and Contintental Drift — A49

Design: 15p, Wideawake Fair, by Linton Palmer, 1866.

**1980, Nov. 17 *Perf. 13½, 14 (60p)***

*266* A48 10p multicolored 25 25
*267* A48 15p multicolored 40 40
*268* A49 60p multicolored 1.50 1.50

Royal Geographical Soc., 50th anniv.

Green Mountain Farm, 1881 — A50

Designs: 15p, Two Boats, 1881. 20p, Green Mountain and Two Boats farms, 1981. 30p, Green Mountain Farm, 1981.

**1981, Feb. 15 Litho. *Perf. 14***

*269* A50 12p multicolored 30 30
*270* A50 15p multicolored 40 40
*271* A50 20p multicolored 50 50
*272* A50 30p multicolored 85 85

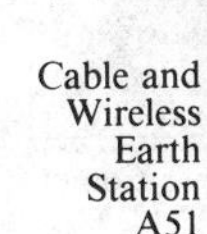

Cable and Wireless Earth Station A51

**1981, Apr. 27 Litho. *Perf. 14***

*273* Sheet of 10 4.00 4.00
*a* A51 15p multi 40 40

Flight of Columbia space shuttle. Gutter contains story of Ascension and space shuttle; margin shows craft and dish antenna. Size: 152x178mm.

Poinsettia — A52

**1981, May 11 Wmk. 373 *Perf. 13½***

*274* A52 1p shown 5 5
*275* A52 2p Clustererd wax flower 6 6
*276* A52 3p Kolanchoe, vert. 8 8
*277* A52 4p Yellow pops 10 10
*278* A52 5p Camel's foot creeper 12 12
*279* A52 8p White oleander 20 20
*280* A52 10p Ascension lily, vert. 25 25
*281* A52 12p Coral plant, vert. 32 32
*282* A52 15p Yellow allamanda 40 40
*283* A52 20p Ascention euphorbia 52 50
*284* A52 30p Flame of the forest, vert. 85 70
*285* A52 40p Bougainvillea 1.00 95

**Size: 42x53mm**

*286* A52 50p Solanum 1.25 1.10
*287* A52 £1 Ladies petticoat 2.75 2.25
*288* A52 £2 Red hibiscus 5.25 4.50
*Nos. 274-288 (15)* 13.20 11.58

Nos. 275-276, 280, 282-283 and 287 also issued inscribed 1982.

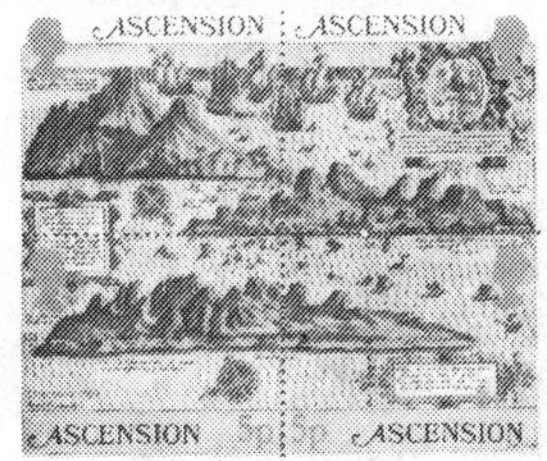

Linschoten's Map of Ascension, 1599 — A53

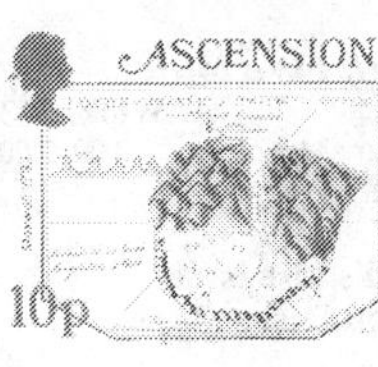

Maxwell's Map of Ascension, 1793 — A54

Designs: Old maps of Ascension.

**1981, May 22 *Perf. 14½***

*289* A53 Block of 4 60 60
*a.-d.* 5p, any single 15 15
*290* A54 10p shown 30 30
*291* A54 12p Maxwell, 1793, diff. 38 38
*292* A54 15p Eckberg & Chapman, 1811 45 45
*293* A54 40p Campbell, 1819 1.25 1.25
*Nos. 289-293 (5)* 2.98 2.98

**Royal Wedding Issue**

Common Design Type

**1981, July 22 Wmk. 373 *Perf. 14***

*294* CD331 10p Bouquet 25 25
*295* CD331 15p Charles 40 40
*296* CD331 50p Couple 1.25 1.25

Nos. 294-296 each se-tenant with label.

Man Shining Cannon — A55

**1981, Sept. 14 Litho. *Perf. 14***

*297* A55 5p shown 15 15
*298* A55 10p Mountain climbing 30 30
*299* A55 15p First aid treatment 45 45
*300* A55 40p Duke of Edinburgh 1.25 1.25

Duke of Edinburgh's Awards, 25th anniv.

Scouting Year A56

**1982, Feb. 22 Litho. *Perf. 14***

*301* A56 10p Parallel rope walking 28 28
*302* A56 15p 1st Ascension scout flag 45 45
*303* A56 25p Radio operators 70 70
*304* A56 40p Baden-Powell 1.10 1.10
*a* Souvenir sheet of 4 3.00 3.00

No. 304a contains stamps in designs of Nos. 301-304 (30x30mm., perf. 14½, diamond-shape); olive green and black margin shows emblems. Size: 121x121mm.

Sesquicentennial of Charles Darwin's Visit — A57

**1982, Apr. 19**

*305* A57 10p Portrait 25 25
*306* A57 12p Pistols 32 32
*307* A57 15p Rock crab 40 40
*308* A57 40p Beagle 1.10 1.10

40th Anniv. of Wideawake Airfield — A58

**1982, June 15 Litho. *Perf. 14***

*309* A58 5p Fairey Swordfish 14 14
*310* A58 10p North American B25C Mitchell 28 28
*311* A58 15p Boeing EC-135N Aria 45 45
*312* A58 50p Lockheed Hercules 1.40 1.40

**Princess Diana Issue**

Common Design Type

***Perf. 14½x14***

**1982, July 1 Wmk. 373**

*313* CD333 12p Arms 35 35
*314* CD333 15p Diana 45 45
*315* CD333 25p Wedding 70 70
*316* CD333 50p Portrait 1.40 1.40

Christmas and 50th Anniv. of BBC Overseas Broadcasting — A59

Anniv. Emblem and: 5p, Bush House (London headquarters). 10p, Atlantic relay station. 25p, Lord Reith, first director general. 40p, King George V delivering Christmas address, 1932.

**1982, Dec. 20 Litho. *Perf. 14***

*317* A59 5p multicolored 15 15
*318* A59 10p multicolored 28 28
*319* A59 25p multicolored 70 70
*320* A59 40p multicolored 1.10 1.10

Nos. 282-283 Overprinted: "1st PARTICIPATION / COMMONWEALTH GAMES 1982"

**1982 Litho. *Perf. 13½***

*321* A52 15p multicolored 45 45
*322* A52 20p multicolored 55 55

12th Commonwealth Games, Brisbane, Australia, Sept. 30-Oct. 9.

A60

**1983, Mar. 1 *Perf. 14***

*323* A60 7p Marasmius echinosphaerus 25 25
*324* A60 12p Chlorophyllum molybdites 42 42
*325* A60 15p Leucocoprinus cepaestipes 55 55
*326* A60 20p Lycoperdon marginatum 75 75
*327* A60 50p Marasmiellus distantifolius 1.75 1.75
*Nos. 323-327 (5)* 3.72 3.72

View of Georgetown A61

**1983, May 12 Litho. *Perf. 14***

*328* A61 12p shown 32 32
*329* A61 15p Farm, Green Mountain 40 40
*330* A61 20p Boatswain Bird Isld. 52 52
*331* A61 60p Telemetry Hill 1.65 1.65

See Nos. 359-362.

Manned Flight Bicentenary — A62

Military Aircraft.

**1983, Aug. 1 Wmk. 373 *Perf. 14***

*332* A62 12p Wessex Five helicopter 32 32
*333* A62 15p Vulcan B2 40 40
*334* A62 20p Nimrod MR2P 55 55
*335* A62 60p Victor K2 1.65 1.65

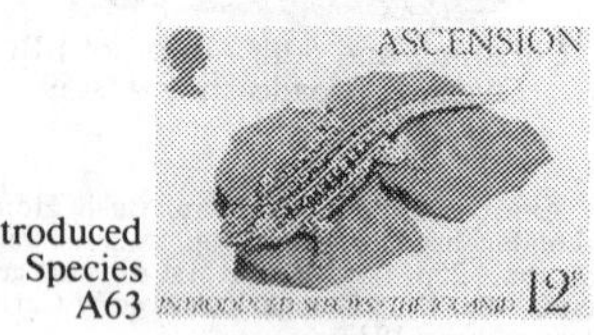


Introduced Species A63

**1983, Sept. Litho. Wmk. 373**

*336* A63 12p Iguanid 30 30
*337* A63 15p Rabbit 38 38
*338* A63 20p Cat 50 50
*339* A63 60p Donkey 1.50 1.50

Tellina Antonii Philippi A64

**Wmk. 373**

**1983, Nov. 28 Litho. *Perf. 14½***

*340* A64 7p shown 18 18
*341* A64 12p Nodipecten nodosus 30 30
*342* A64 15p Cypraea lurida oceanica 40 40
*343* A64 20p Nerita ascensionis gmelin 55 55
*344* A64 50p Micromelo undatus 1.40 1.40
*Nos. 340-344 (5)* 2.83 2.83

St. Helena Colony, 150th Anniv. — A65

Designs: First issue inscribed Ascension instead of overprinted.

**1984, Jan. 10 Litho. *Perf. 14***

*345* A65 12p No. 3 30 30
*346* A65 15p No. 4 38 38
*347* A65 20p No. 6 50 50
*348* A65 60p No. 9 1.50 1.50

**Souvenir Sheet**

Visit of Prince Andrew — A66

***Perf. 14½x14***

**1984, Apr. 10 Wmk. 373**

*349* Souvenir sheet of 2 2.00 2.00
*a* A66 12p Andrew 25 25
*b* A66 70p In naval uniform 1.75 1.75

**Lloyd's List Issue**

Common Design Type

**1984, May 28**

*351* CD335 12p Naval semaphore 25 25
*352* CD335 15p "Southampton Castle" 35 35
*353* CD335 20p Pier Head 45 45
*354* CD335 70p Dane 1.50 1.50

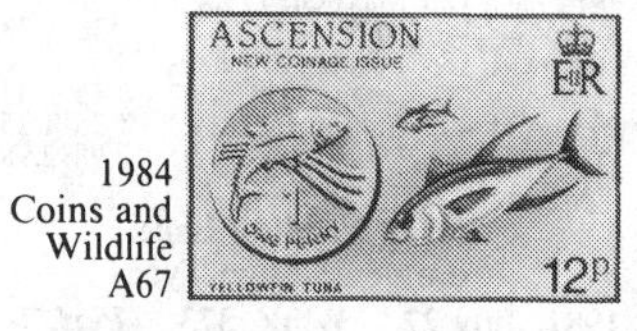


1984 Coins and Wildlife A67

**1984, June *Perf. 14***

*355* A67 12p One penny, yellowfin tuna 30 30
*356* A67 15p Two pence, donkeys 38 38
*357* A67 20p Fifty pence, green turtle 50 50
*358* A67 70p One pound, sooty terns 1.75 1.75

View Type of 1983

**1984, Oct. Litho. Wmk. 373**

*359* A61 12p Devil's Riding School 28 28
*360* A61 15p St. Mary's Church 35 35
*361* A61 20p Two Boats Village 48 48
*362* A61 70p Ascension Isld. 1.65 1.65

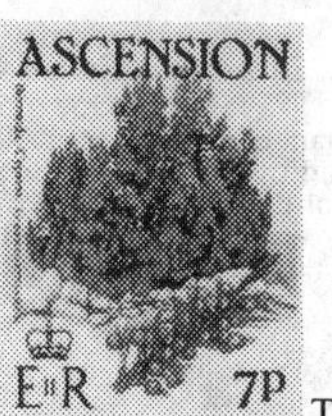


Trees — A68

**1985, Mar. 8 Litho. *Perf. 14½x14***

*363* A68 7p Bermuda cypress 14 14
*364* A68 12p Norfolk Island pine 25 25
*365* A68 15p Screwpine 28 28
*366* A68 20p Eucalyptus 40 40
*367* A68 65p Spore tree 1.40 1.40
*Nos. 363-367 (5)* 2.47 2.47

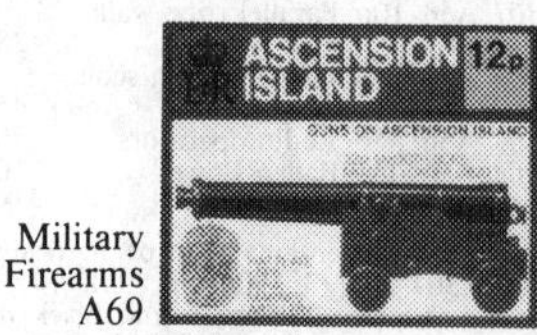


Military Firearms A69

Large guns and insignia: 12p, Thirty-two pounder small bore muzzle loader, c. 1820; Royal Marines hat plate, c. 1816. 15p, Seven-inch rifled muzzle loader, c. 1866; royal cipher. 20p, Seven-pounder rifled muzzle loader, c. 1877; Royal Artillery badge. 70p, HMS Hood 5.5-inch gun; ship crest.

**1985, July 21 Wmk. 373 *Perf. 14½***

*368* A69 12p multicolored 30 30
*369* A69 15p multicolored 38 38
*370* A69 20p multicolored 52 52
*371* A69 70p multicolored 1.75 1.75

**Queen Mother 85th Birthday**

Common Design Type

***Perf. 14½x14***

**1985, June 7 Wmk. 384**

*372* CD336 12p With the Duke of York, Balmoral, 1924 25 25
*373* CD336 15p With Princes Andrew and Edward 28 28
*374* CD336 20p At Ascot 40 40
*375* CD336 70p Christening of Prince Henry, Windsor Castle 1.40 1.40

**Souvenir Sheet**

*376* CD336 75p Leaving the QEII, 1968 1.55 1.50

No. 376 has multicolored margin continuing the design. Size: 92x74mm.

Intl. Youth Year, Girl Guides 75th Anniv. — A70

**1985, Oct. 4 Wmk. 373**

*377* A70 12p Guides' banner 30 30
*378* A70 15p First aid 38 38
*379* A70 20p Camping 52 52
*380* A70 70p Lady Baden-Powell 1.75 1.75

Wildflowers A71

Halley's Comet A72

**Wmk. 384**

**1985, Dec. 6 Litho. *Perf. 14***

*381* A71 12p Clerodendrum fragrans 30 30
*382* A71 15p Shell ginger 40 40
*383* A71 20p Cape daisy 52 52
*384* A71 70p Ginger lily 1.90 1.90

**1986, Mar. 7**

Designs: 12p, Newton's reflector telescope. 15p, Edmond Halley, Old Greenwich Observatory. 20p, Short's Gregorian telescope, comet, 1759. 70p, ICE space probe, Ascension satellite tracking station.

*385* A72 12p multicolored 30 30
*386* A72 15p multicolored 40 40
*387* A72 20p multicolored 52 52
*388* A72 70p multicolored 1.90 1.90

**Queen Elizabeth II 60th Birthday**

Common Design Type

Designs: 7p, Infant photograph, 1926. 15p, 1st worldwide Christmas broadcast, 1952. 20p, Garter Ceremony, Windsor Castle, 1983. 35p, Royal Tour, New Zealand, 1981. £1, Visiting Crown Agents' offices, 1983.

**1986, Apr. 21 *Perf. 14x14½***

*389* CD337 7p scar, blk & sil 20 20
*390* CD337 15p ultra, blk & sil 42 42
*391* CD337 20p green & multi 55 55
*392* CD337 35p violet & multi 1.00 1.00
*393* CD337 £1 rose vio & multi 2.75 2.75
*Nos. 389-393 (5)* 4.92 4.92

AMERIPEX '86 — A73

**1986, May 22 *Perf. 14½***

*394* A73 12p No. 183 35 35
*395* A73 15p No. 260 42 42
*396* A73 20p No. 215 55 55
*397* A73 70p No. 310 2.00 2.00

**Souvenir Sheet**

*398* A73 75p Statue of Liberty, New York Harbor 2.25 2.25

Statue of Liberty, cent. No. 398 has multicolored decorative margin picturing emblem, Ascension Island, latitude and longitude. Size: 60x75mm.

**Royal Wedding Issue, 1986**

Common Design Type

Designs: 15p, Couple kissing. 35p, Andrew in navy uniform, helicopter.

**Wmk. 384**

**1986, July 23 Litho. *Perf. 14***

*399* CD338 15p multicolored 42 42
*400* CD338 35p multicolored 1.00 1.00

Ships A74

**1986, Oct. 14 Wmk. 384 *Perf. 14½***

*401* A74 1p Ganymede, c. 1811 5 5
*402* A74 2p Kangaroo, c. 1811 6 6
*403* A74 4p Trinculo, c. 1811 10 10
*404* A74 5p Daring, c. 1811 12 12
*405* A74 9p Thais, c. 1811 22 22
*406* A74 10p Pheasant, 1819 24 24
*407* A74 15p Myrmidon, 1819 35 35
*408* A74 18p Atholl, 1825 44 44
*409* A74 20p Medina, 1830 48 48
*410* A74 25p Saracen, 1840 60 60
*411* A74 30p Hydra, c. 1845 70 70
*412* A74 50p Sealark, 1840 1.10 1.10
*413* A74 70p Rattlesnake, 1868 1.50 1.50
*414* A74 £1 Penelope, 1889 2.50 2.50
*415* A74 £2 Monarch, 1897 4.75 4.75
*Nos. 401-415 (15)* 13.21 13.21

Edible Bush Fruits A75

**1987, Jan. 29 *Perf. 14***

*416* A75 12p Cape gooseberry 38 38
*417* A75 15p Prickly pear 48 48
*418* A75 20p Guava 62 62
*419* A75 70p Loquat 2.15 2.15

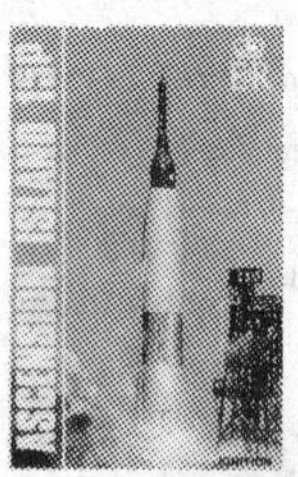


First Manned Space Flight, 25th Anniv. — A76

**1987, Mar. 30**

*420* A76 15p Ignition 38 38
*421* A76 18p Lift-off 45 45
*422* A76 25p Reentry 60 60
*423* A76 £1 Splashdown 2.50 2.50

**Souvenir Sheet**

*424* A76 70p Friendship 7 capsule 1.65 1.65

No. 424 has multicolored margin picturing the Earth, Moon, NASA emblem and flight data. Size: 94x78mm.

Military Uniforms, 1815-1820 — A77

Designs: a, Captains in full dress, 1st landing on Ascenion. b, Surgeon and sailors at campsite. c, Seaman returning from Dampier's Drip with water supply. d, Midshipman at lookout post. e, Commander and surveyor.

**1987, June 29**

| | | | | |
|---|---|---|---|---|
| *425* | | Strip of 5 | 4.00 | 4.00 |
| *a.-e.* | A77 | 25p multi | 80 | 80 |

See No. 454.

Butterflies A78

**1987, Aug. 10** ***Perf. 14½***

| | | | | |
|---|---|---|---|---|
| *426* | A78 | 15p Painted lady | 50 | 50 |
| *427* | A78 | 18p Monarch | 60 | 60 |
| *428* | A78 | 25p Diadem | 80 | 80 |
| *429* | A78 | £1 Long-tailed blue | 3.25 | 3.25 |

See Nos. 436-439, 455-458.

Birds — A79

Designs: a, Ascension frigatebirds (males). b, Brown booby, frigatebird, white boobies. c, Frigatebird, white booby. d, Ascension frigatebirds (females). e, Adult frigatebird feeding young.

**1987, Oct. 8 Wmk. 373** ***Perf. 14***

| | | | | |
|---|---|---|---|---|
| *430* | | Strip of 5 | 4.00 | 4.00 |
| *a.-e.* | A79 | 25p any single | 80 | 80 |

Printed se-tenant in continuous design.
See No. 449.

Nos. 389-393 Ovptd. "40TH WEDDING ANNIVERSARY" in Silver

***Perf. 14x14½***

**1987, Dec. 9 Litho. Wmk. 384**

| | | | | |
|---|---|---|---|---|
| *431* | CD337 | 7p scar, blk & sil | 24 | 24 |
| *432* | CD337 | 15p ultra, blk & sil | 50 | 50 |
| *433* | CD337 | 20p grn & multi | 68 | 68 |
| *434* | CD337 | 35p vio & multi | 1.20 | 1.20 |
| *435* | CD337 | £1 rose vio & multi | 3.40 | 3.40 |
| | | *Nos. 431-435 (5)* | 6.02 | 6.02 |

40th Wedding anniv. of Queen Elizabeth II and Prince Philip.

Insects Type of 1987

**1988, Jan. 18** ***Perf. 14½***

| | | | | |
|---|---|---|---|---|
| *436* | A78 | 15p Field cricket | 50 | 50 |
| *437* | A78 | 18p Bush cricket | 62 | 62 |
| *438* | A78 | 25p Ladybug | 85 | 85 |
| *439* | A78 | £1 Burnished brass moth | 3.40 | 3.40 |

Capt. William Bate (d. 1838), 1st Garrison Commander and Colonial Founder of Ascension
A80

Designs: 9p, Bate's Memorial, St. Mary's Church. 15p, Commodore's Cottage, Cross Hill. 18p, North East or Bate's Cottage, 1833. 25p, Landmarks on map. 70p, Bate and 3 soldiers.

**Wmk. 384**

**1988, Apr. 14 Litho.** ***Perf. 14***

| | | | | |
|---|---|---|---|---|
| *440* | A80 | 9p multi | 32 | 32 |
| *441* | A80 | 15p multi | 55 | 55 |
| *442* | A80 | 18p multi | 65 | 65 |
| *443* | A80 | 25p multi | 88 | 88 |
| *444* | A80 | 70p multi | 2.50 | 2.50 |
| | | *Nos. 440-444 (5)* | 4.90 | 4.90 |

Australia Bicentennial Emblem and Ships Named HMS *Resolution* — A81

**Wmk. 384**

**1988, June 23 Litho.** ***Perf. 14***

| | | | | |
|---|---|---|---|---|
| *445* | A81 | 9p 3-Masted square-rigger, 1667 | 35 | 35 |
| *446* | A81 | 18p 3-Masted square-rigger, 1772 | 68 | 68 |
| *447* | A81 | 25p Navy cruiser, 1892 | 95 | 95 |
| *448* | A81 | 65p Battleship, 1916 | 2.45 | 2.45 |

Australia bicentennial.

Bird Type of 1987

Behaviors of the wideawake tern, *Sterna fuscata:* a. Two adults, flock overhead. b. Nesting (two birds). c. Nesting (three birds). d. Adult and young. e. Tern flapping its wings. Printed se-tenant in a continuous design.

**1988, Aug. 15 Wmk.** ***Perf.***

| | | | | |
|---|---|---|---|---|
| *453* | | Strip of 5 | 4.25 | 4.25 |
| *a.-e.* | A79 | 25p any single | 85 | 85 |

**Lloyds of London, 300th Anniv.**

Common Design Type

Designs: 8p, Lloyd's Coffee House, Tower Street, 1688. 18p, Cable ship *Alert*, horiz. 25p, Satellite recovery in space, horiz. 65p, Ship *Good Hope Castle* on fire off Ascension, 1973.

**Wmk. 373**

**1988, Oct. 17 Litho.** ***Perf. 14***

| | | | | |
|---|---|---|---|---|
| *454* | CD341 | 8p multi | 28 | 28 |
| *455* | CD341 | 18p multi | 60 | 60 |
| *456* | CD341 | 25p multi | 85 | 85 |
| *457* | CD341 | 65p multi | 2.20 | 2.20 |

Military Uniforms Type of 1987

Uniforms of the Royal Marines: a, Marines arrive in Ascension (marines), 1821. b, Semaphore station (officer, marine), 1829. c, Octagonal tank (sergeant), 1831. d, Water pipe tunnel (officers), 1833. e, Constructing barracks (officer), 1834.

**1988, Nov. 21**

| | | | | |
|---|---|---|---|---|
| *458* | | Strip of 5 | 4.25 | 4.25 |
| *a.-e.* | A77 | 25p multi | 85 | 85 |

Insect Type of 1987

**Wmk. 384**

**1989, Jan. 16 Litho.** ***Perf.***

| | | | | |
|---|---|---|---|---|
| *459* | A78 | 15p Plume moth | 58 | 58 |
| *460* | A78 | 18p Green bottle | 68 | 68 |
| *461* | A78 | 25p Weevil | 95 | 95 |
| *462* | A78 | £1 Paper wasp | 3.75 | 3.75 |

## POSTAGE DUE STAMPS

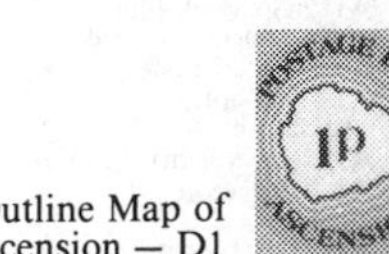
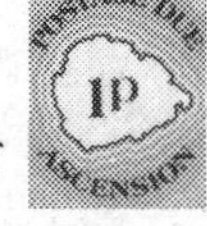

Outline Map of Ascension — D1

**1986 Litho.** ***Perf. 15x14***

| | | | | |
|---|---|---|---|---|
| *J1* | D1 | 1p beige & brown | 5 | 5 |
| *J2* | D1 | 2p orange & brown | 6 | 6 |
| *J3* | D1 | 5p org ver & brn | 12 | 12 |
| *J4* | D1 | 7p violet & black | 16 | 16 |
| *J5* | D1 | 10p ultra & black | 22 | 22 |
| *J6* | D1 | 25p pale grn & blk | 60 | 60 |
| | | *Nos. J1-J6 (6)* | 1.21 | 1.21 |

# AUSTRALIA

LOCATION — In Oceania, south of Indonesia, bounded on the west by the Indian Ocean.
GOVT. — A self-governing dominion of the British Commonwealth.
AREA — 2,967,909 sq. mi.
POP. — 15,276,100 (est. 1982)
CAPITAL — Canberra

Australia includes the former British colonies of New South Wales, Victoria, Queensland, South Australia, Western Australia and Tasmania.

12 Pence = 1 Shilling
20 Shillings = 1 Pound
100 Cents = 1 Dollar (1966)

**Catalogue values for unused stamps in this country are for Never Hinged items, beginning with Scott 197 in the regular postage section, Scott C6 in the air post section, Scott J71 in the postage due section, and all of the Australian Antarctic Territory.**

Kangaroo and Map — A1

Wmk. 8- Wide Crown and Wide A

**1913 Typo. Wmk. 8** ***Perf. 11½, 12***

| | | | | |
|---|---|---|---|---|
| *1* | A1 | ½p yel grn | 4.50 | 90 |
| *2* | A1 | 1p carmine | 4.00 | 18 |
| *d.* | | Wmkd. sideways | 800.00 | 210.00 |
| *3* | A1 | 2p gray | 16.00 | 3.25 |
| *4* | A1 | 2½p dark bl | 17.50 | 8.00 |
| *5* | A1 | 3p ol bis | 27.50 | 3.25 |
| *6* | A1 | 4p orange | 42.50 | 10.50 |
| *7* | A1 | 5p org brn | 35.00 | 16.00 |
| *8* | A1 | 6p ultra | 35.00 | 9.00 |
| *9* | A1 | 9p purple | 35.00 | 8.50 |
| *10* | A1 | 1sh bl grn | 42.50 | 7.75 |
| *11* | A1 | 2sh brown | 150.00 | 30.00 |
| *12* | A1 | 5sh yel & gray | 250.00 | 135.00 |
| *13* | A1 | 10sh pink & gray | 525.00 | 375.00 |
| *14* | A1 | £1 ultra & brn | 1,100. | 800.00 |
| *15* | A1 | £2 dp rose & blk | 1,800. | 1,050. |
| | | *Nos. 1-11 (11)* | 409.50 | 97.33 |

On No. 4 "2½d" is colorless in solid blue background.

See Nos. 38-59, 96-102, 121-129, 206.

King George V
A2

Kookaburra (Kingfisher)
A3

**1913-14 Unwmk. Engr.** ***Perf. 11***

| | | | | |
|---|---|---|---|---|
| *17* | A2 | 1p carmine | 3.75 | 4.00 |
| *a.* | | Vert. pair, imperf. between | *2,000.* | |
| *18* | A3 | 6p lake brn ('14) | 72.50 | 35.00 |

A4

Wmk. 9 - Wide Crown and Narrow A

ONE PENNY

Die I - Normal die, having outside the oval band with "AUSTRALIA" a white line and a heavy colored line.

Die Ia - As die I with a small white spur below the right serif at foot of the "1" in left tablet.

Die II - A heavy colored line between two white lines back of the emu's neck. A white scratch crossing the vertical shading lines at the lowest point of the bust.

TWO PENCE

Die I - The numeral "2" is thin. The upper curve is 1mm. across and a very thin line connects it with the foot of the figure.

Die II - The "2" is thicker than in die I. The top curve is 1½mm. across and a strong white line connects it with the foot of the figure. There are thin vertical lines across the ends of the groups of short horizontal lines at each side of "TWO PENCE".

THREE PENCE

Die I - The ends of the thin horizontal lines in the background run into the solid color of the various parts of the design. The numerals are thin and the letters of "THREE PENCE" are thin and irregular.

Die II - The oval about the portrait, the shields with the numerals, etc., are outlined by thin white lines which separate them from the horizontal background lines. The numerals are thick and the letters of "THREE PENCE" are heavy and regular.

FIVE PENCE

Die I - The top of the flag of the "5" is slightly curved.

Die II - The top of the flag of the "5" is flat. There are thin white vertical lines across the ends of the short horizontal lines at each side of "FIVE PENCE".

**1914-24 Typo. Wmk. 9** ***Perf. 14***

| | | | | |
|---|---|---|---|---|
| *19* | A4 | ½p emerald ('15) | 1.65 | 50 |
| *a.* | | Thin "½" at right | *1,400.* | *700.00* |
| *20* | A4 | ½p orange ('23) | 1.50 | 1.25 |
| *21* | A4 | 1p red (I) | 4.00 | 14 |
| *a.* | | 1p carmine rose (I) | 7.00 | 75 |
| *b.* | | 1p red (Ia) | 450.00 | 4.75 |
| *c.* | | 1p carmine (II) ('18) | 60.00 | 20.00 |
| *22* | A4 | 1p vio (I) ('22) | 2.50 | 45 |
| *a.* | | 1p red vio | 4.00 | 1.00 |
| *23* | A4 | 1p grn (I) ('24) | 1.25 | 16 |
| *24* | A4 | 1½p choc ('18) | 3.25 | 24 |
| *a.* | | 1½p red brown | 6.00 | 24 |
| *b.* | | 1½p black brown | 2.75 | 24 |
| *25* | A4 | 1½p emerald ('23) | 2.50 | 14 |
| *26* | A4 | 1½p scarlet ('24) | 90 | 14 |
| *27* | A4 | 2p brn org (I) ('20) | 3.25 | 16 |
| *a.* | | 2p orange (I) ('20) | 5.50 | 25 |
| *b.* | | Booklet pane of 6 | | |
| *28* | A4 | 2p red (I) ('22) | 3.50 | 14 |
| *29* | A4 | 2p red brn (I) ('24) | 11.50 | 2.25 |
| *30* | A4 | 3p ultra (I) ('24) | 11.50 | 52 |
| *31* | A4 | 4p orange ('15) | 12.50 | 2.00 |
| *a.* | | 4p yellow | 125.00 | 17.00 |
| *32* | A4 | 4p violet ('21) | 14.00 | 7.00 |
| *33* | A4 | 4p lt ultra ('22) | 32.50 | 4.25 |
| *34* | A4 | 4p ol bis ('24) | 13.00 | 1.75 |
| *35* | A4 | 4½p violet ('24) | 12.00 | 1.90 |
| *36* | A4 | 5p org brn (I) ('15) | 15.00 | 90 |
| *37* | A4 | 1sh4p lt blue ('20) | 50.00 | 14.00 |
| | | *Nos. 19-37 (19)* | 196.30 | 37.89 |

See Nos. 60-76, 113-120, 124.

**1915** *Perf. 11½, 12*

| | | | | |
|---|---|---|---|---|
| *38* | A1 | 2p gray | 35.00 | 7.00 |
| *39* | A1 | 2½p dark bl | 35.00 | 14.00 |
| *40* | A1 | 6p ultra | 105.00 | 14.00 |
| *41* | A1 | 9p violet | 100.00 | 15.00 |
| *42* | A1 | 1sh blue grn | 125.00 | 14.00 |
| *43* | A1 | 2sh brown | 325.00 | 42.50 |
| *44* | A1 | 5sh yel & gray | 700.00 | 150.00 |
| | | *Nos. 38-44 (7)* | 1,425. | 256.50 |

Wmk. 10 - Narrow Crown and Narrow A

**1915-24** **Wmk. 10**

| | | | | |
|---|---|---|---|---|
| *45* | A1 | 2p gray | 14.00 | 1.90 |
| *46* | A1 | 2½p dark blue | 12.50 | 3.50 |
| *a.* | | "1" of fraction omitted | *10,000.* | *3,500.* |
| *47* | A1 | 3p ol bister | 12.50 | 1.75 |
| *48* | A1 | 6p ultra | 32.50 | 3.75 |
| *a.* | | 6p chlky bl | 45.00 | 4.00 |
| *49* | A1 | 6p yel brn ('23) | 11.50 | 1.65 |
| *50* | A1 | 9p violet | 25.00 | 2.00 |
| *a.* | | 9p lil | 21.00 | 2.50 |
| *51* | A1 | 1sh bl grn ('16) | 20.00 | 1.75 |
| *a.* | | Wmkd. sideways ('20) | 57.50 | 57.50 |
| *52* | A1 | 2sh brown ('16) | 125.00 | 14.00 |
| *53* | A1 | 2sh vio brn ('24) | 32.50 | 8.50 |
| *54* | A1 | 5sh yel & gray ('18) | 145.00 | 47.50 |
| *a.* | | Wmkd. sideways | *2,500.* | *2,000.* |
| *55* | A1 | 10sh brt pink & gray ('17) | 285.00 | 100.00 |
| *a.* | | Wmkd. sideways | *3,500.* | *2,000.* |
| *56* | A1 | £1 ultra & brn ('16) | 1,100. | 550.00 |
| *a.* | | £1 ultra & brown orange ('16) | 1,100. | 550.00 |
| *b.* | | Wmkd. sideways | *5,000.* | *2,000.* |
| *57* | A1 | £1 gray ('24) | 450.00 | 175.00 |
| *58* | A1 | £2 dp rose & blk ('19) | 1,750. | 650.00 |
| *59* | A1 | £2 rose & vio brn ('24) | 1,500. | 650.00 |
| | | *Nos. 45-54 (10)* | 430.50 | 86.30 |

Wmk. 11 - Multiple Crown and A

*Perf. 14, 14½, 14½x14*

**1918-23** **Wmk. 11**

| | | | | |
|---|---|---|---|---|
| *60* | A4 | ½p emerald | 1.50 | 65 |
| *a.* | | Thin "½" at righ | 100.00 | 42.50 |
| *61* | A4 | 1p rose (I) | 17.00 | 6.00 |
| *62* | A4 | 1p dl grn (I) ('24) | 3.25 | 3.00 |
| *63* | A4 | 1½p choc ('19) | 4.75 | 65 |
| *a.* | | 1½p red brown ('19) | 6.25 | 80 |

**1924** **Unwmk.** *Perf. 14*

| | | | | |
|---|---|---|---|---|
| *64* | A4 | 1p green (I) | 3.00 | 2.25 |
| *65* | A4 | 1½p carmine | 3.50 | 2.50 |

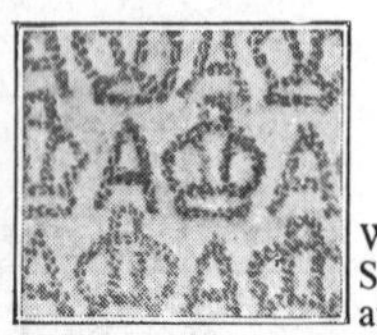

Wmk. 203 - Small Crown and A Multiple

*Perf. 14, 13½x12½*

**1926-30** **Wmk. 203**

| | | | | |
|---|---|---|---|---|
| *66* | A4 | ½p orange ('27) | 4.75 | 3.25 |
| *a.* | | Perf. 13½x12½ | 1.25 | 90 |
| *67* | A4 | 1p green (I) | 1.25 | 40 |
| *a.* | | 1p green (Ia) | 42.50 | 55.00 |
| *b.* | | Perf. 14 | 2.00 | 40 |
| *68* | A4 | 1½p rose red ('27) | 2.50 | 16 |
| *c.* | | Perf. 14 ('26) | 4.25 | 60 |
| *69* | A4 | 1½p red brn ('30) | 2.50 | 1.75 |
| *70* | A4 | 2p red brn (I) ('28) | 6.75 | 3.25 |
| *a.* | | Perf. 14 ('27) | 20.00 | 14.00 |
| *71* | A4 | 2p red (II) ('30) | 3.50 | 20 |
| *a.* | | 2p red (I) ('30) | 4.50 | 1.65 |
| *c.* | | Unwmkd. (II) ('31) | *1,900.* | *1,000.* |
| *72* | A4 | 3p ultra (I) | 18.00 | 1.25 |
| *a.* | | 3p ultra (II) ('29) | 12.50 | 1.50 |
| *b.* | | Perf. 14 | 15.00 | 3.50 |
| *73* | A4 | 4p ol bis ('29) | 15.00 | 60 |
| *a.* | | Perf. 14 ('28) | 40.00 | 15.00 |
| *74* | A4 | 4½p dk vio ('27) | 13.00 | 3.25 |
| *a.* | | Perf. 13½x12½ ('28) | 45.00 | 12.50 |
| *75* | A4 | 5p brn buff (II) ('30) | 16.00 | 80 |
| *76* | A4 | 1sh4p pale turq bl ('28) | 62.50 | 16.00 |
| *a.* | | Perf. 14 ('27) | 125.00 | 67.50 |
| | | *Nos. 66-76 (11)* | 145.75 | 30.91 |

Parliament House, Canberra — A5

**Unwmk.**

**1927, May 9** **Engr.** *Perf. 11*

| | | | | |
|---|---|---|---|---|
| *94* | A5 | 1½p brown red | 42 | 20 |
| *a.* | | Vert. pair, imperf. btwn. | *3,500.* | *2,500.* |

Opening of Parliament House at Canberra.

**Melbourne Exhibition Issue**

Kookaburra Type of 1914

**1928, Oct. 29**

| | | | | |
|---|---|---|---|---|
| *95* | A3 | 3p deep blue | 3.75 | 3.00 |
| *a.* | | Pane of 4 | 115.00 | *125.00* |

No. 95a was issued at the Melbourne Intl. Phil. Exhib. in October, 1928. No marginal inscription. Printed in sheets of 60 stamps (15 panes). No. 95 was also printed in sheets of 120 and issued Nov. 2 throughout Australia.

Kangaroo-Map Type of 1913

*Perf. 11½, 12*

**1929-30** **Wmk. 203** **Typo.**

| | | | | |
|---|---|---|---|---|
| *96* | A1 | 6p brown | 15.00 | 2.00 |
| *97* | A1 | 9p violet | 16.50 | 2.50 |
| *98* | A1 | 1sh bl green | 17.50 | 2.25 |
| *99* | A1 | 2sh red brown | 27.50 | 5.50 |
| *100* | A1 | 5sh yel & gray | 175.00 | 55.00 |
| *101* | A1 | 10sh pink & gray | 275.00 | 150.00 |
| *102* | A1 | £2 dl red & blk ('30) | 1,250. | 265.00 |
| | | *Nos. 96-102 (7)* | 1,776. | 482.25 |

Black Swan — A6

Capt. Charles Sturt — A7

**Unwmk.**

**1929, Sept. 28** **Engr.** *Perf. 11*

| | | | | |
|---|---|---|---|---|
| *103* | A6 | 1½p dull red | 65 | 32 |

Centenary of Western Australia.

**1930, June 2**

| | | | | |
|---|---|---|---|---|
| *104* | A7 | 1½p dark red | 40 | 12 |
| *105* | A7 | 3p dark blue | 3.50 | 3.00 |

Capt. Charles Sturt's exploration of the Murray River, cent.

Nos. 68 and 74a surcharged

**FIVE PENCE**

**1930** **Wmk. 203** *Perf. 13½x12½*

| | | | | |
|---|---|---|---|---|
| *106* | A4 | 2p on 1½p rose red | 60 | 20 |
| *107* | A4 | 5p on 4½p dk vio | 3.75 | 4.00 |

"Southern Cross" over Hemispheres A8

*Perf. 11, 11½*

**1931, Mar. 19** **Unwmk.**

| | | | | |
|---|---|---|---|---|
| *111* | A8 | 2p dull red | 60 | 14 |
| *112* | A8 | 3p blue | 3.50 | 3.25 |

Trans-oceanic flights (1928-1930) of Sir Charles Edward Kingsford-Smith (1897-1935). See No. C2.

Wmk. 228 - Small Crown and C of A Multiple

Types of 1913-23 Issues

*Perf. 13½x12½*

**1931-36** **Typo.** **Wmk. 228**

| | | | | |
|---|---|---|---|---|
| *113* | A4 | ½p orange ('32) | 1.25 | 1.40 |
| *114* | A4 | 1p green (I) | 80 | 32 |
| *115* | A4 | 1½p red brn ('36) | 3.50 | 3.25 |
| *116* | A4 | 2p red (II) | 1.00 | 18 |
| *117* | A4 | 3p ultra (II) ('32) | 13.00 | 38 |
| *118* | A4 | 4p ol bis ('33) | 14.00 | 42 |
| *120* | A4 | 5p brn buff (II) ('32) | 12.00 | 35 |

***Perf. 11½, 12; 13½x12½ (1sh4p)***

| | | | | |
|---|---|---|---|---|
| *121* | A1 | 6p yel brn ('36) | 11.50 | 7.75 |
| *122* | A1 | 9p violet ('32) | 11.50 | 1.75 |
| *124* | A4 | 1sh4p lt blue ('32) | 47.50 | 6.00 |
| *125* | A1 | 2sh red brn ('35) | 2.75 | 1.25 |
| *126* | A1 | 5sh yel & gray ('32) | 125.00 | 17.50 |
| *127* | A1 | 10sh pink & gray ('32) | 205.00 | 57.50 |
| *128* | A1 | £1 gray ('35) | 375.00 | 140.00 |
| *129* | A1 | £2 dl rose & blk ('34) | 1,350. | 250.00 |
| | | *Nos. 113-129 (15)* | 2,173. | 488.05 |

For redrawn 2sh, see No. 206.

Sydney Harbor Bridge — A9

**Unwmk.**

**1932, Mar. 14** **Engr.** *Perf. 11*

| | | | | |
|---|---|---|---|---|
| *130* | A9 | 2p red | 2.00 | 80 |
| *131* | A9 | 3p blue | 4.25 | 3.00 |
| *132* | A9 | 5sh gray green | 275.00 | 200.00 |

**Wmk. 228**

***Perf. 10½***

**Typo.**

| | | | | |
|---|---|---|---|---|
| *133* | A9 | 2p red | 1.75 | 80 |

Opening of the Sydney Harbor Bridge on March 19, 1932.

Kookaburra A14

Male Lyrebird A16

**1932, June 1** *Perf. 13½x12½*

| | | | | |
|---|---|---|---|---|
| *139* | A14 | 6p light brown | 11.50 | 65 |

**Unwmk.**

**1932, Feb. 15** **Engr.** *Perf. 11*

**Size: 21½x25mm.**

| | | | | |
|---|---|---|---|---|
| *141* | A16 | 1sh green | 30.00 | 75 |

See Nos. 175 and 300.

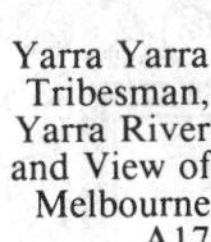

Yarra Yarra Tribesman, Yarra River and View of Melbourne
A17

*Perf. 10½, 11½*

| **1934, July 2** | **Engr.** | **Wmk. 228** | |
|---|---|---|---|
| *142* A17 | 2p vermilion | 1.10 | 48 |
| *143* A17 | 3p blue | 2.50 | 2.50 |
| *144* A17 | 1sh black | 35.00 | 15.00 |

Centenary of Victoria.

Merino Sheep — A18

| **1934, Nov. 1** | ***Perf. 11½*** | | |
|---|---|---|---|
| *147* A18 | 2p copper red | 2.50 | 20 |
| *148* A18 | 3p dark blue | 8.50 | 4.50 |
| *149* A18 | 9p dk violet | 30.00 | 27.50 |

Death centenary of Capt. John Macarthur (1767-1834), the "father of the New South Wales woolen industry."

Cenotaph in Whitehall, London
A19

King George V on His Charger "Anzac"
A20

| **1935, Mar. 18** | ***Perf. 13½x12½*** | | |
|---|---|---|---|
| *150* A19 | 2p red | 65 | 14 |
| | ***Perf. 11*** | | |
| *151* A19 | 1sh black | 37.50 | 27.50 |

20th anniv. of the Anzacs' landing at Gallipoli.

| **1935, May 2** | ***Perf. 11½*** | | |
|---|---|---|---|
| *152* A20 | 2p red | 20 | 15 |
| *153* A20 | 3p blue | 2.25 | 1.65 |
| *154* A20 | 2sh violet | 35.00 | 30.00 |

25th anniv. of the reign of King George V.

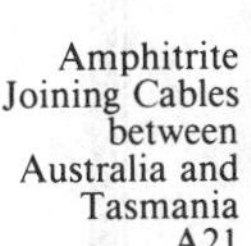

Amphitrite Joining Cables between Australia and Tasmania
A21

| **1936, Apr. 1** | | | |
|---|---|---|---|
| *157* A21 | 2p red | 32 | 9 |
| *158* A21 | 3p dark blue | 3.25 | 2.25 |

Linking of Australia and Tasmania by telephone.

Proclamation Tree and View of Adelaide, 1936 — A22

| **1936, Aug. 3** | | | |
|---|---|---|---|
| *159* A22 | 2p red | 45 | 9 |
| *160* A22 | 3p dark blue | 4.00 | 4.50 |
| *161* A22 | 1sh green | 12.50 | 5.00 |

Centenary of South Australia.

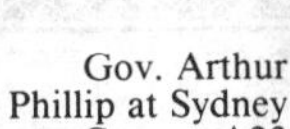

Gov. Arthur Phillip at Sydney Cove — A23

| **1937, Oct. 1** | ***Perf. 13x13½*** | | |
|---|---|---|---|
| *163* A23 | 2p red | 75 | 10 |
| *164* A23 | 3p ultra | 3.50 | 2.25 |
| *165* A23 | 9p violet | 15.00 | 10.50 |

150th anniversary of New South Wales.

Kangaroo
A24

Queen Elizabeth
A25

King George VI
A26 A27

Koala
A28

Merino Sheep
A29

Kookaburra (Kingfisher)
A30

Platypus
A31

Queen Elizabeth and King George VI in Coronation Robes
A32 A33

King George VI and Queen Elizabeth — A34

Two Types of A25 and A26.
Type I - Highlighted background. Lines around letters of Australia Postage and numerals of value.
Type II - Background of heavy diagonal lines without the highlighted effect. No lines around letters and numerals.

*Perf. 13½x14, 14x13½*

| **1937-46** | **Engr.** | **Wmk. 228** | |
|---|---|---|---|
| *166* A24 | ½p org, perf. 15x14 ('42) | 18 | 5 |
| *a.* | Perf. 13½x14 ('38) | 70 | 25 |
| *167* A25 | 1p emerald (I) | 20 | 8 |
| *168* A26 | 1½p dl red brn (II) | 3.50 | 2.00 |
| *a.* | Perf. 15x14 ('41) | 4.75 | 3.50 |
| *169* A26 | 2p scarlet (I) | 35 | 5 |
| *170* A27 | 3p dp ultra, thin paper ('38) | 10.50 | 35 |
| *a.* | 3p ultramarine | 13.00 | 1.00 |

171 A28 4p grn, perf. 15x14 ('42) 45 16
a. Perf. 13½x14 ('38) 3.00 90
172 A29 5p pale rose vio, perf. 14x15 ('46) 70 90
a. Perf. 14x13½ ('38) 2.50 55
173 A30 6p vio brn, perf. 15x14 ('42) 70 5
a. Perf. 13½x14 5.25 85
b. 6p choc, perf. 15x14 1.00 10
174 A31 9p sep, perf. 14x15 ('43) 1.00 10
a. Perf. 14x13½ ('38) 5.00 90
175 A16 1sh gray grn, perf. 15x14 ('41) 70 5
a. Perf. 13½x14 17.00 2.00
176 A27 1sh4p magenta ('38) 1.50 35

**Perf. 13½**

177 A32 5sh dl red brn ('38) 3.50 2.50
178 A33 10sh dl gray vio ('38) 25.00 12.00
179 A34 £1 bl gray ('38) 67.50 27.50
*Nos. 166-179 (14)* 115.78 46.14

No. 175 measures 17½x21½mm. See Nos. 223A, 293, 295, 298 and 300.

**1938-42** **Perf. 15x14**

180 A25 1p emerald (II) 52 25
181 A25 1p dl red brn (II) ('41) 52 5
181B A26 1½p bl grn (II) ('41) 60 5
182 A26 2p scarlet (II) 60 5
182B A26 2p red vio (II) ('41) 20 5
183 A27 3p dk ultra ('40) 13.00 70
183A A27 3p dk vio brn ('42) 20 5
*Nos. 180-183A (7)* 15.64 1.20

No. 183 differs from Nos. 170-170a in the shading lines on the king's left eyebrow which go downward, left to right, instead of the reverse. Also, more of the left epaulette shows.

Coil Perforation

A special perforation was applied to stamps intended for use in coils to make separation easier. It consists of small and large holes (2 small, 10 large, 2 small) on the stamps' narrow side. Some of the stamps so perforated were sold in sheets.

This coil perforation may be found on Nos. 166, 181, 182, 182B, 193, 215, 223A, 231, 257, 315-316, 319, 319a and others.

Nurse, Sailor, Soldier and Aviator — A35

**Perf. 13½x13**

**1940, July 15** **Engr.** **Wmk. 228**

184 A35 1p green 1.40 10
185 A35 2p red 1.40 10
186 A35 3p ultra 4.75 3.50
187 A35 6p chocolate 8.00 8.75

Australia's participation in WWII.

No. 182 Surcharged in Blue 2½d

**1941, Dec. 10** **Perf. 15x14**

188 A26 2½p on 2p red 32 10

No. 183 Surcharged in Blue and Yellow 3½d

189 A27 3½p on 3p dk ultra 65 52

No. 172a Surcharged in Purple 5½d

**Perf. 14 x 13½**

190 A29 5½p on 5p pale rose vio 3.25 3.50

Queen Elizabeth
A36 A37

King George VI
A38 A39

George VI and Blue Wrens
A40

Emu
A41

**1942-44** **Engr.** **Perf. 14½x14**

191 A36 1p brn vio ('43) 15 5
192 A37 1½p green 18 5
193 A38 2p lt rose vio ('44) 12 10
194 A39 2½p red 18 5
195 A40 3½p ultra 18 5
196 A41 5½p indigo 42 5
*Nos. 191-196 (6)* 1.23 35

See Nos. 224-225.

**Catalogue values for unused stamps in this section, from this point to the end of the section, are for Never Hinged items.**

Duke and Duchess of Gloucester — A42

**1945, Feb. 19** **Engr.** **Perf. 14½**

197 A42 2½p brown red 14 5
198 A42 3½p brt ultra 22 28
199 A42 5½p indigo 22 45

Inauguration of the Duke of Gloucester as Governor General.

Official Crest and Inscriptions
A43

Dove and Australian Flag
A44

Angel of Peace; "Motherhood" and "Industry"
A45

**1946, Feb. 18** **Wmk. 228** **Perf. 14½**

200 A43 2½p carmine 18 5
201 A44 3½p deep ultra 18 24
202 A45 5½p dp yel grn 38 38

End of WWII.

Sir Thomas Mitchell and Map of Queensland
A46

**1946, Oct. 14**

203 A46 2½p dark car 12 5
204 A46 3½p deep ultra 25 25
205 A46 1sh olive grn 85 38

Sir Thomas Mitchell's exploration of central Queensland, cent.

Kangaroo-Map Type of 1913 Redrawn

**1945, Dec.** **Typo.** **Perf. 11½**

206 A1 2sh dk red brn 4.50 1.65

The R and A of AUSTRALIA are separated at the base and there is a single line between the value tablet and "Two Shillings." On No. 125 the tail of the R touches the A, while two lines appear between value tablet and "Two Shillings." There are many other minor differences in the design.

John Shortland
A47

Pouring Steel
A48

Loading Coal — A49

**1947, Sept.** **Engr.** **Perf. 14½x14**

207 A47 2½p brown red 28 5

**Perf. 14½**

208 A48 3½p deep blue 22 30
209 A49 5½p deep green 38 30

150th anniv. of the discovery of the Hunter River estuary, site of Newcastle. The discoverer was Lieut. John Shortland, but by error the 2½p shows his father, Capt. John Shortland.

Princess Elizabeth — A50

**Perf. 14x14½**

**1947, Nov. 20** **Wmk. 228**

210 A50 1p brown violet 20 5

See No. 215.

Hereford Bull
A51

Crocodile
A52

**1948, Feb. 16** **Perf. 14½**

211 A51 1sh3p vio brown 1.90 70
212 A52 2sh chocolate 3.00 15

See No. 302.

William J. Farrer — A53

Design: No. 214, Ferdinand von Mueller.

**1948** **Perf. 14½x14**

213 A53 2½p red 18 5
214 A53 2½p dark red 24 5

William J. Farrer (1845-1906), wheat researcher, and Ferdinand von Mueller (1825-1896), German-born botanist.

Issue dates: #213, July 12. #214, Sept. 13.

Elizabeth Type of 1947

**1948, Aug.** **Unwmk.** **Perf. 14x14½**

215 A50 1p brown violet 10 5

Scout in Uniform
A55

Arms of Australia
A56

**1948, Nov. 15** **Engr.** **Wmk. 228**

216 A55 2½p brown red 20 5

Pan-Pacific Scout Jamboree, Victoria, December 29, 1948 to January 9, 1949. See No. 249.

**1949-50** **Wmk. 228** **Perf. 14x13½**

218 A56 5sh dark red 4.75 15
219 A56 10sh red violet 17.50 30
220 A56 £1 deep blue 30.00 3.00
221 A56 £2 green ('50) 115.00 15.00

Henry Lawson
A57

Outback Mail Carrier and Plane
A58

**Perf. 14½x14**

**1949, June 17** **Unwmk.**

222 A57 2½p rose brown 15 5

Henry Hertzberg Lawson (1867-1922), author and poet.

**1949, Oct. 10**

223 A58 3½p violet blue 25 16

UPU, 75th anniv.

Types of 1938, 1942-44 & A59

Aborigine
A59

John Forrest
A60

**1948-50** **Unwmk.** **Perf. 14½x14**

223A A24 ½p orange ('49) 12 5
224 A37 1½p green ('49) 28 5
225 A38 2p lt rose vio 32 5

**Wmk. 228**

226 A59 8½p dk brn ('50) 65 32

See No. 248.

**1949, Nov. 28** **Wmk. 228**

227 A60 2½p brown red 15 5

John Forrest (1847-1918), explorer and statesman.

*Australia stamps can be mounted in Scott's annually supplemented Australia and Dependencies Album.*

New South Wales A61

Victoria A62

First stamp designs.

*Perf. 14½x14*

| **1950, Sept. 27** | | | **Unwmk.** | |
|---|---|---|---|---|
| *228* | A61 | 2½p rose brown | 25 | 10 |
| *229* | A62 | 2½p rose brown | 25 | 10 |
| *a.* | | Se-tenant with No. 228 | 65 | 40 |

Cent. of Australian adhesive postage stamps. Issued in sheets of 160 stamps containing alternate copies of Nos. 228 and 229.

Queen Elizabeth A63

King George VI A64

| **1950-51** | | **Engr.** | **Unwmk.** | |
|---|---|---|---|---|
| *230* | A63 | 1½p deep green | 30 | 5 |
| *231* | A63 | 2p yel grn ('51) | 20 | 5 |
| *232* | A64 | 2½p vio brn ('51) | 20 | 5 |
| *233* | A64 | 3p dl grn ('51) | 30 | 5 |

King George VI
A65 A66

| **1950-52** | | | **Wmk. 228** | |
|---|---|---|---|---|
| *234* | A64 | 2½p red | 25 | 5 |
| *235* | A64 | 3p red ('51) | 30 | 5 |
| *236* | A65 | 3½p red brn ('51) | 30 | 5 |
| *237* | A65 | 4½p scarlet ('52) | 50 | 35 |
| *238* | A65 | 6½p choc ('52) | 50 | 35 |
| *238A* | A65 | 6½p bl grn ('52) | 35 | 5 |
| *239* | A66 | 7½p deep bl ('51) | 40 | 30 |

Sir Edmund Barton A67

Duke of York Opening First Federal Parliament A68

Designs: No. 241, Sir Henry Parkes. 1sh6p, Parliament House, Canberra.

*Perf. 14½x14*

| **1951, May 1** | | **Engr.** | **Unwmk.** | |
|---|---|---|---|---|
| *240* | A67 | 3p carmine | 60 | 5 |
| *241* | A67 | 3p carmine | 60 | 5 |
| *a.* | | Se-tenant with No. 240 | 1.25 | 65 |
| *242* | A68 | 5½p deep blue | 50 | *90* |
| *243* | A68 | 1sh6p red brown | 75 | 65 |

Founding of the Commonwealth of Australia, 50th anniv..

Edward Hammond Hargraves A69

King George VI A70

Design: No. 245, Charles Joseph Latrobe (1801-1875), first governor of Victoria.

| **1951, July 2** | | | | |
|---|---|---|---|---|
| *244* | A69 | 3p rose brown | 25 | 5 |
| *245* | A69 | 3p rose brown | 25 | 5 |
| *a.* | | Se-tenant with No. 244 | 65 | 65 |

Discovery of gold in Australia, cent. (No. 244); Establishment of representative government in Victoria, cent. (No. 245). Sheets contain alternate rows of Nos. 244 and 245.

| **1952, Mar. 19** | | **Wmk. 228** | ***Perf. 14½*** | |
|---|---|---|---|---|
| *247* | A70 | 1sh½p sl bl | 1.65 | 22 |

Aborigine Type of 1950 Redrawn

**Size: 20½x25mm**

| | | | | |
|---|---|---|---|---|
| *248* | A59 | 2sh6p dark brown | 3.50 | 25 |

Portrait as on A59; lettering altered and value repeated at lower left. See No. 303.

Scout Type of 1948
Dated "1952-53."

*Perf. 14x14½*

| **1952, Nov. 19** | | | **Wmk. 228** | |
|---|---|---|---|---|
| *249* | A55 | 3½p red brown | 18 | 5 |

Pan-Pacific Scout Jamboree, Greystanes, Dec. 30, 1952, to Jan. 9, 1953.

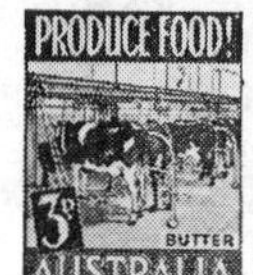


Modern Dairy, Butter Production — A71

*Perf. 14½*

| **1953, Feb. 11** | | **Unwmk.** | **Typo.** | |
|---|---|---|---|---|
| *250* | A71 | 3p green | 75 | 10 |
| *251* | A71 | 3p green *(Wheat)* | 75 | 10 |
| *252* | A71 | 3p green *(Beef)* | 75 | 10 |
| *a.* | | Strip of 3, Nos. 250-252 | 6.50 | 8.00 |
| *253* | A71 | 3½p red | 75 | 10 |
| *254* | A71 | 3½p red *(Wheat)* | 75 | 10 |
| *255* | A71 | 3½p red *(Beef)* | 75 | 10 |
| *a.* | | Strip of 3, Nos. 253-255 | 4.50 | *8.00* |
| | | *Nos. 250-255 (6)* | 4.50 | 60 |

Both the 3p and 3½p were printed in panes of 50 stamps: 17 Butter, 17 Wheat and 16 Beef. The stamps were issued to encourage food production.

Queen Elizabeth II — A72

*Perf. 14½x14*

| **1953-54** | | **Unwmk.** | **Engr.** | |
|---|---|---|---|---|
| *256* | A72 | 1p purple | 16 | 5 |
| *256A* | A72 | 2½p deep bl ('54) | 28 | 5 |
| *257* | A72 | 3p dark green | 28 | 5 |
| | | **Wmk. 228** | | |
| *258* | A72 | 3½p dark red | 28 | 5 |
| *258B* | A72 | 6½p orange ('54) | 90 | 10 |
| | | *Nos. 256-258B (5)* | 1.90 | 30 |

See Nos. 292 and 296.

**Coronation Issue**

Queen Elizabeth II A73

| **1953, May 25** | | | **Unwmk.** | |
|---|---|---|---|---|
| *259* | A73 | 3½p rose red | 28 | 5 |
| *260* | A73 | 7½p violet | 70 | 45 |
| *261* | A73 | 2sh dull grn | 2.25 | 1.10 |

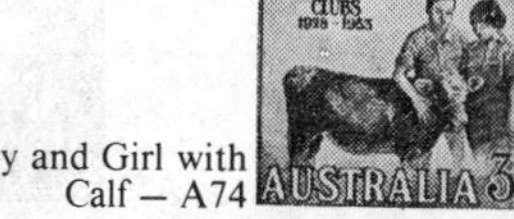


Boy and Girl with Calf — A74

| **1953, Sept. 3** | | | ***Perf. 14½*** | |
|---|---|---|---|---|
| *262* | A74 | 3½p dp grn & red brn | 25 | 5 |

Official establishment of Young Farmers' Clubs, 25th anniv..

Lieut. Gov. David Collins A75

Tasmania Stamp of 1853 A77

Sullivan Cove, Hobart A76

Design: No. 264, Lieut. Gov. William Paterson (facing left).

| **1953, Sept. 23** | | | ***Perf. 14½x14*** | |
|---|---|---|---|---|
| *263* | A75 | 3½p red brown | 35 | 5 |
| *264* | A75 | 3½p red brown | 35 | 5 |
| *a.* | | Se-tenant with No. 263 | 1.75 | 1.10 |
| *265* | A76 | 2sh green | 4.75 | 4.00 |

Settlement in Tasmania, 150th anniv. Sheets contain alternate rows of Nos. 263 and 264.

| **1953, Nov. 11** | | | ***Perf. 14½*** | |
|---|---|---|---|---|
| *266* | A77 | 3p red | 18 | 5 |

Tasmania's first postage stamps, cent.

Queen Elizabeth II and Duke of Edinburgh — A78

Queen Elizabeth II — A79

Telegraph Pole and Key — A80

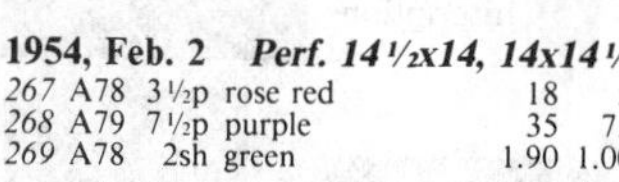

| **1954, Feb. 2** | | | ***Perf. 14½x14, 14x14½*** | |
|---|---|---|---|---|
| *267* | A78 | 3½p rose red | 18 | 5 |
| *268* | A79 | 7½p purple | 35 | 75 |
| *269* | A78 | 2sh green | 1.90 | 1.00 |

Visit of Queen Elizabeth II and the Duke of Edinburgh, 1954.

| **1954, Apr. 7** | | **Engr.** | ***Perf. 14*** | |
|---|---|---|---|---|
| *270* | A80 | 3½p dark red | 30 | 5 |

Inauguration of the telegraph in Australia, cent.

Red Cross and Globe — A81

Swan — A82

| **1954, June 9** | | | ***Perf. 14½x14*** | |
|---|---|---|---|---|
| *271* | A81 | 3½p deep bl & red | 18 | 5 |

Australian Red Cross Society.

| **1954, Aug. 2** | | **Unwmk.** | ***Perf. 14½*** | |
|---|---|---|---|---|
| *274* | A82 | 3½p black | 22 | 5 |

Western Australia's first postage stamp, cent.

Diesel and Early Steam Locomotives A83

| **1954, Sept. 13** | | | ***Perf. 14x14½*** | |
|---|---|---|---|---|
| *275* | A83 | 3½p red brown | 25 | 5 |

Centenary of Australian railroads.

Antarctic Flora and Fauna and Map A84

Olympic Circles and Arms of Melbourne A85

| **1954, Nov. 17** | | | ***Perf. 14*** | |
|---|---|---|---|---|
| *276* | A84 | 3½p black | 18 | 5 |

Australia's interest in the Antarctic continent.

| **1954, Dec. 1** | | | | |
|---|---|---|---|---|
| *277* | A85 | 2sh dark blue | 2.50 | 1.50 |

16th Olympic Games to be held in Melbourne Nov.-Dec. 1956. See No. 286.

Globe, Flags and Rotary Emblem — A86

| **1955, Feb. 23** | | | ***Perf. 14x14½*** | |
|---|---|---|---|---|
| *278* | A86 | 3½p carmine | 18 | 5 |

Rotary International, 50th anniv..

Queen Elizabeth II — A87

| **1955, Mar. 9** | | **Wmk. 228** | ***Perf. 14½*** | |
|---|---|---|---|---|
| *279* | A87 | 1sh½p dk gray bl | 4.00 | 25 |

Top of US Monument, Canberra — A88

| **1955, May 4** | | **Unwmk.** | ***Perf. 14x14½*** | |
|---|---|---|---|---|
| *280* | A88 | 3½p deep ultra | 18 | 5 |

Friendship between Australia and the United States.

Cobb and Company Mail Coach — A89

**1955, July 6** *Perf. 14½x14*
*281* A89 3½p dark brown 25 5
*282* A89 2sh brown 2.75 2.00

Pioneers of Australia's coaching era.

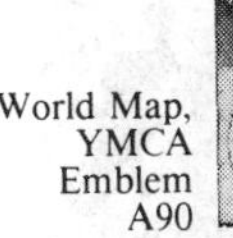

World Map, YMCA Emblem A90

**Engr. and Typo.**
**1955, Aug. 10** *Perf. 14*
*283* A90 3½p Prus grn & red 20 5

Centenary of YMCA.

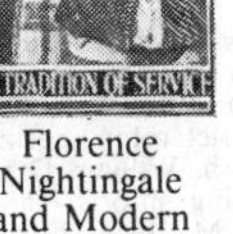
Florence Nightingale and Modern Nurse A91

Queen Victoria A92

**1955, Sept. 21 Engr.** *Perf. 14x14½*
*284* A91 3½p red violet 18 5

Centenary of Florence Nightingale's work in the Crimea and of the founding of modern nursing.

**1955, Oct. 17** *Perf. 14½*
*285* A92 3½p green 18 5

South Australia's first postage stamps, cent.

Olympic Type of 1954
**1955, Nov. 30 Unwmk.** *Perf. 14*
*286* A85 2sh deep green 2.25 1.65

16th Olympic Games at Melbourne, Nov. 22-Dec. 8, 1956.

Queen Victoria, Queen Elizabeth II and Badges of Victoria, New South Wales and Tasmania A93

**1956, Sept. 26** *Perf. 14½x14*
*287* A93 3½p brn carmine 25 5

Centenary of responsible government in Victoria, New South Wales and Tasmania.

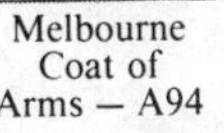
Melbourne Coat of Arms — A94

Southern Cross, Olympic Torch — A95

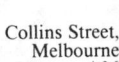

Collins Street, Melbourne A96

Design: 2sh, Melbourne across Yarra River.

**1956, Oct. 31 Engr.** *Perf. 14½, 14*
*288* A94 4p dark carmine 22 5
*289* A95 7½p ultramarine 55 42

**Photo.**
*Perf. 14x14½*
*290* A96 1sh multicolored 75 38

*Perf. 12x11½*
**Granite Paper**
*291* A96 2sh multicolored 1.40 60

16th Olympic Games, Melbourne, Nov. 22-Dec. 8.

A lithographed souvenir sheet incorporating reproductions of Nos. 288-291 in reduced size was of private origin and not postally valid.

Types of 1938-55 and

Queen Elizabeth II — A97

*Perf. 14½x14, 14x15, 15x14, 14½*
**1956-57 Engr. Unwmk.**
*292* A72 3½p dark red 60 5
*293* A28 4p green 1.65 16
*294* A97 4p claret ('57) 30 5
*a.* Bklt. pane of 6 ('57) 7.50
*295* A30 6p brown violet 2.75 16
*296* A72 6½p orange 1.75 8
*297* A97 7½p violet ('57) 3.00 35
*298* A31 9p sepia 9.00 52
*299* A97 10p gray blue ('57) 2.75 12
*300* A16 1sh gray green 6.00 35
*301* A87 1sh7p redsh brn ('57) 4.50 35
*302* A52 2sh chocolate 12.00 28
*303* A59 2sh6p brown ('57) 9.00 30
*Nos. 292-303 (12)* 53.30 2.77

No. 300 measures 17½x21½mm. No. 303 measures 20½x25mm. and is the redrawn type of 1952.

South Australia Coat of Arms — A99

**1957, Apr. 17 Unwmk.** *Perf. 14½*
*304* A99 4p brown red 18 5

Centenary of responsible government in South Australia.

Caduceus and Map of Australia A100

**1957, Aug. 21** *Perf. 14½x14*
*305* A100 7p violet blue 70 10

Royal Flying Doctor Service of Australia.

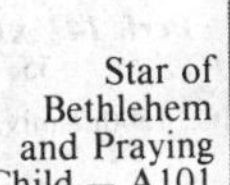

Star of Bethlehem and Praying Child — A101

**1957, Nov. 6 Engr.**
*306* A101 3½p dull rose 22 5
*307* A101 4p pale purple 22 5

Christmas.

Canberra War Memorial, Sailor and Airman A102

Design: No. 309, As No. 308 with soldier and service woman.

**1958, Feb. 10 Unwmk.**
*308* A102 5½p brn carmine 1.40 75
*309* A102 5½p brn carmine 1.40 75
*a.* Se-tenant with No. 308 4.50 3.50

Nos. 308-309 are printed in alternate rows in sheet.

Sir Charles Kingsford-Smith and "Southern Cross" — A103

**1958, Aug. 27** *Perf. 14x14½*
*310* A103 8p bright vio bl 1.25 1.00

First air crossing of the Tasman Sea, 30th anniv.

Broken Hill Mine A104

Nativity A105

**1958, Sept. 10** *Perf. 14½x14*
*311* A104 4p brown 25 5

Broken Hill mining field, 75th anniv.

**1958, Nov. 5** *Perf. 14½x15*
*312* A105 3½p dark red 15 5
*313* A105 4p dark purple 22 5

Christmas.

Queen Elizabeth II
A106 A107

A108

A109

A110

Platypus A111

Tasmanian Tiger A112

Flannel Flower A113

Aboriginal Stockman Cutting Out a Steer A114

Designs: 3p, Queen Elizabeth II facing right. 6p, Banded anteater. 8p, Spottedtailed cat. 9p, Kangaroos. 11p, Rabbit bandicoot. 1sh6p, Christmas bells (flower). 2sh3p, Wattle (flower). 2sh5p, Banksia (flower). 3sh, Waratah (flower).

FIVE PENCE

Die I - Four short lines inside "5" at right of ball; six short lines left of ball; full length line above ball is seventh from bottom. Odd numbered horizontal rows in each sheet are in Die I.

Die II - Five short lines inside "5" at right of ball; seven at left; full length line above ball is eighth from bottom. Even numbered horizontal rows in each sheet are in Die II.

*Perf. 14½x14, 14x14½, 14½*
**1959-64 Engr. Unwmk.**
*314* A106 1p dull violet 25 5
*315* A107 2p red brn ('62) 35 5
*316* A108 3p bluish green 25 5
*317* A108 3½p dark green 45 5
*318* A109 4p carmine 35 5
*a.* Bklt. pane of 6 25.00
*319* A110 5p dark bl (I) 65 5
*a.* 5p dark blue (II) 65 5
*b.* Bklt. pane of 6 ('60) 12.00
*320* A111 6p choc ('60) 65 5
*321* A111 8p red brn ('60) 60 5
*322* A111 9p brown black 2.50 20
*323* A111 11p dark bl ('61) 95 8
*324* A111 1sh slate green 3.75 10
*325* A112 1sh2p dk pur ('62) 1.50 20
*326* A113 1sh6p red, *yellow* ('60) 2.50 60
*327* A113 2sh dark blue 2.75 12
*328* A113 2sh3p green, *yel* 2.75 20
*328A* A113 2sh3p yel grn ('64) 6.75 1.00
*329* A113 2sh5p brown, *yellow* ('60) 9.00 40
*330* A113 3sh crimson 3.75 35

**Wmk. 228**
*331* A114 5sh red brn ('61) 25.00 1.00
*Nos. 314-331 (19)* 64.75 4.65

Luminescent Printings

Paper with an orange red phosphorescence (surface coating), was used for some printings of the Colombo Plan 1sh, No. 340, the Churchill 5p, No. 389, and several regular postage stamps. These include 2p, 3p, 6p, 8p, 9p, 11p, 1sh2p, 1sh6p and 2sh3p (Nos. 315, 316, 365, 367, 321, 368, 323, 325, 369, 328A).

Stamps printed only on phosphorescent paper include the Monash 5p, Hargrave 5p, ICY 2sh3p and Christmas 5p (Nos. 388, 390-393) and succeeding commemoratives; the 2sh, 2sh6p and 3sh regular birds (Nos. 370, 372, 373); and most of the regular series in decimal currency.

Ink with a phosphorescent content was used in printing most of the 5p red, No. 366, almost all of the 5p red booklets, No. 366a, most of the decimal 4c regular, No. 397, and its booklet pane, No. 397a, and all of No. 398.

Postmaster Isaac Nichols Boarding Vessel to Receive Mail — A115

**1959, Apr. 22** *Perf. 14½x14*
*332* A115 4p dark gray bl 25 5

First post office, Sydney, 150th anniv.

Parliament House, Brisbane, and Queensland Arms — A116

**1959, June 5** *Perf. 14x14½*
*333* A116 4p dk grn & vio 25 5

Centenary of self-government in Queensland.

Approach of the Magi — A117

**1959, Nov. 4** *Perf. 15x14½*
*334* A117 5p purple 25 5

Christmas.

Girl Guide and Lord Baden-Powell A118

**1960, Aug. 18** *Perf. 14½x14*
*335* A118 5p dark blue 32 5

50th anniversary of the Girl Guides.

The Overlanders by Sir Daryl Lindsay — A119

Melbourne Cup and Archer, 1861 Winner — A120

**1960, Sept. 21** *Perf. 14½*
*336* A119 5p lilac rose 35 8

Exploration of Australia's Northern Territory, cent.

**1960, Oct. 12** **Unwmk.**
*337* A120 5p sepia 35 8

Centenary of the Melbourne Cup.

Queen Victoria A121

Open Bible and Candle A122

**1960 Nov. 2** **Engr.** *Perf. 14½*
*338* A121 5p dark green 22 5

Centenary of the first Queensland stamps.

**1960, Nov. 9** **Unwmk.**
*339* A122 5p maroon 20 5

Christmas; beginning of 350th anniv. year of the publication of the King James translation of the Bible.

The Catalogue editors cannot undertake to appraise, identify or judge the genuineness or condition of stamps.

Colombo Plan Emblem — A123

**1961, June 30** *Perf. 14x14½*
*340* A123 1sh red brown 90 10

Colombo Plan for the peaceful development of South East Asia countries, 10th anniv.

Dame Nellie Melba, by Sir Bertram Mackennal — A124

**1961, Sept. 20** *Perf. 14½*
*341* A124 5p deep blue 35 8

Dame Nellie Melba, singer, birth cent.

Page from Book of Hours, 15th Century A125

John McDouall Stuart A126

**1961, Nov. 8** *Perf. 14½x14*
*342* A125 5p reddish brn 38 5

Christmas; end of the 350th anniv. year of the publication of the King James translation of the Bible.

**1962, July 25** **Unwmk.** *Perf. 14½*
*345* A126 5p carmine 35 8

First south-north crossing of Australia by John McDouall Stuart, cent.

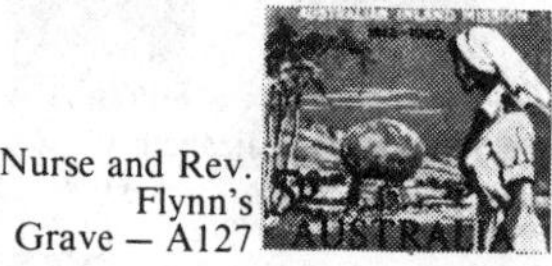
Nurse and Rev. Flynn's Grave — A127

**1962, Sept. 5** **Photo.** *Perf. 13½*
*346* A127 5p multicolored 35 8
*a.* Red omitted *275.00*

Australian Inland Mission founded by Rev. John Flynn, 50th anniv.

Woman and Globe A128

Madonna and Child A129

**1962, Sept. 26** **Engr.** *Perf. 14x14½*
*347* A128 5p dark green 35 8

World Conference of the Associated Country Women of the World, Melbourne, Oct. 2-12.

**1962, Oct. 17** *Perf. 14½*
*348* A129 5p deep violet 38 5

Christmas.

View of Perth and Kangaroo Paw — A130

Arms of Perth — A131

**1962, Nov. 1** **Photo.** *Perf. 14*
*349* A130 5p bl, dk grn, yel grn, blk & red 38 5
*a.* Red omitted *450.00*

*Perf. 14½x14*

*350* A131 2sh3p emer, blk, red & ultra 7.50 5.50

British Empire and Commonwealth Games, Perth, Nov. 22-Dec. 1.

Elizabeth II — A132

Elizabeth II and Prince Philip — A133

**1963, Feb. 18** **Engr.** *Perf. 14½*
*351* A132 5p dark green 30 5
*352* A133 2sh3 red brown 6.50 5.00

Visit of Elizabeth II and Prince Philip.

Walter Burley Griffin and Arms of Canberra A134

Red Cross Centenary Emblem A135

*Perf. 14½x14*

**1963, Mar. 8** **Unwmk.**
*353* A134 5p dark green 35 5

50th anniv. of Canberra; Walter Burley Griffin, American architect, who laid out plan for Canberra.

**1963, May 8** **Photo.** *Perf. 13½x13*
*354* A135 5p dk bl, red & gray 35 5

Centenary of the International Red Cross.

Explorers Blaxland, Lawson and Wentworth Looking West from Mt. York — A136

**1963, May 28** **Engr.** *Perf. 14½x14*
*355* A136 5p dark blue 35 5

1st crossing of the Blue Mts., 150th anniv.

Globe, Ship, Plane and Map of Australia A137

**1963, Aug. 28** **Unwmk.**
*356* A137 5p red 35 5

Importance of exports to Australian economy.

Elizabeth II — A138

Black-backed Magpie and Eucalyptus — A139

Abel Tasman and Ship A144

George Bass, Whaleboat A145

Designs: 6p, Yellow-tailed thornbill (horiz.). 1sh6p, Galah on tree stump. 2sh, Golden whistler. 2sh5p, Blue wren and bracken fern. 2sh6p, Scarlet robin (horiz.). 3sh, Straw-necked ibis. 5sh, William Dampier and "Roebuck" sailing ship. 7sh6p, Capt. James Cook. 10sh, Matthew Flinders and three-master "Investigator." £2, Admiral Philip Parker King.

**1963-65** **Unwmk.** **Engr.** *Perf. 15x14*
*365* A138 5p green 25 5
*a.* Bklt. pane of 6 ('64) 20.00
*b.* Pair, imperf. between 3.75 3.75
*366* A138 5p red ('65) 25 5
*a.* Bklt. pane of 6 ('65) 25.00

**Photo.**

*Perf. 13½*

*367* A139 6p lt grn, blk, brn & yellow ('64) 45 12
*a.* Vert. pair, imperf. between
*368* A139 9p lt grn, black & gray ('64) 2.50 1.90
*369* A139 1sh6p lil gray, blk, gray & rose ('64) 1.25 1.10
*370* A139 2sh pink, blk, yel & gray ('65) 2.50 38
*371* A139 2sh5p gray, blk, ultra & ocher ('64) 8.25 2.25
*372* A139 2sh6p gray, blk, green & red ('65) 3.75 1.50
*a.* Red omitted *1,000.*
*373* A139 3sh lt grn, buff, blk & red ('65) 2.50 1.25

**Engr.**

*Perf. 14½x14, 14½x15*

*374* A144 4sh vio blue 3.75 55

**Wmk. 228**

*375* A145 5sh red brown ('64) 5.25 1.25
*376* A144 7sh6p ol grn ('64) 24.00 15.00
*377* A144 10sh dp cl ('64) 30.00 7.25
*378* A145 £1 pur ('64) 45.00 22.50
*379* A145 £2 brown black ('64) 115.00 95.00
*Nos. 365-379 (15)* 244.70 150.15

No. 365a was printed in sheets of 288 which were sold intact by the Philatelic Bureau. These sheets have been broken to obtain pairs and blocks which are imperf. between (see No. 365b).

See Nos. 400-401, 406-417.

Star of Bethlehem — A146

**1963, Oct. 25 Unwmk. *Perf. 14½***

*380* A146 5p blue 25 5

Christmas.

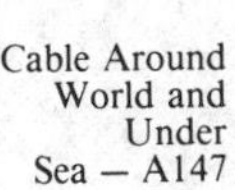

Cable Around World and Under Sea — A147

**1963, Dec. 3 Photo. *Perf. 13½***

*381* A147 2sh3p gray, ver, blk & bl 7.25 5.50

Opening of the Commonwealth Pacific (telephone) cable service (COMPAC).

Bleriot 60 Plane, 1914 — A148

**1964, July 1 Engr. *Perf. 14½x14***

*382* A148 5p olive green 20 10
*383* A148 2sh3p red 6.25 5.25

50th anniv. of the first air mail flight in Australia; Maurice Guillaux, aviator.

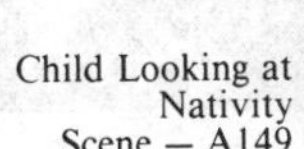

Child Looking at Nativity Scene — A149

**1964, Oct. 21 Photo. *Perf. 13½***

*384* A149 5p bl, blk, red & buff 28 5
*a.* Red omitted *375.00*
*b.* Black omitted *375.00*

Christmas.

"Simpson and His Donkey" by Wallace Anderson — A150

**1965, Apr. 14 Engr. *Perf. 14x14½***

*385* A150 5p ol bister 20 10
*386* A150 8p dark blue 1.40 90
*387* A150 2sh3p rose claret 6.50 4.75

50th anniv. of the landing of the Australian and New Zealand Army Corps (ANZAC) at Gallipoli, Turkey, Apr. 25, 1915. Private John Simpson Kirkpatrick saved the lives of many wounded soldiers. The statue erected in his honor stands in front of Melbourne's Shrine of Remembrance.

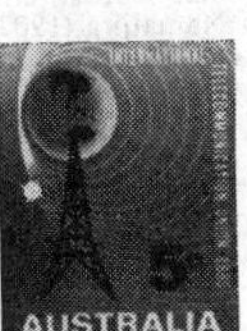


Radio Mast and Satellite Orbiting Earth A151

Winston Churchill A152

**1965, May 10 Photo. *Perf. 13½***

*388* A151 5p dk bl, ocher, brn & blk 25 8
*a.* Black ("5d" and pylon) omitted *650.00*

ITU, cent.

**1965, May 24**

*389* A152 5p lt bl, gray & blk 25 8

Sir Winston Spencer Churchill (1874-1965), statesman and WWII leader.

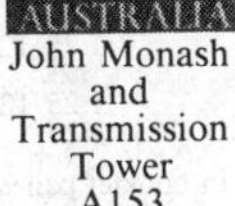


John Monash and Transmission Tower A153

Lawrence Hargrave and Sketch for 1902 Seaplane A154

**1965, June 23 Photo. *Perf. 13½***

*390* A153 5p red, yel, blk & lt brn 25 8

Birth cent. of General Sir John Monash (1865-1931), soldier, Vice-Chancellor of University of Melbourne and chairman of the Victoria state electricity commission.

**1965, Aug. 4 Unwmk. *Perf. 13½***

*391* A154 5p brn, ocher, blk & pur 30 8
*a.* Purple (5d) omitted *225.00*

50th anniv. of the death of Lawrence Hargrave (1850-1915), aviation pioneer.

ICY Emblem A155

Nativity A156

**1965, Sept. 1 Photo. *Perf. 13½***

*392* A155 2sh3p lt bl & grn 3.75 3.00

International Cooperation Year.

**1965, Oct. 20 Unwmk. *Perf. 13½***

*393* A156 5p gold, blk, ultra & redsh brn 30 5
*a.* Gold omitted *300.00*
*b.* Ultra. omitted 250.00

Christmas.

Types of 1963-65 and

Elizabeth II — A157

Humbug Fish — A158

Designs: No. 400, Yellow-tailed thornbill (horiz.). 6c, blue-faced honeyeater (horiz.). 8c, Coral fish. 9c, Hermit crab. 10c Anemone fish. 13c, Red-necked avocet. 15c, Galah on tree stump. 20c, Golden whistler. 24c Azure kingfisher (horiz.). 25c, Scarlet robin (horiz.). 30c Straw-necked ibis. 40c Abel Tasman and ship. 50c, William Dampier and "Roebuck" sailing ship. 75c, Capt. James Cook. $1, Matthew Flinders and three-master "Investigator." $2, George Bass and whaleboat. $4, Admiral Philip Parker King.

***Perf. 14½x14 (A157); 13½ (A158, A139)***

**Engr. (A157), Photo. (A158, A139)**

**1966-71**

*394* A157 1c red brown 35 5
*395* A157 2c olive green 65 5
*396* A157 3c Prus grn 90 5
*397* A157 4c red 9 5
*a.* Bklt. pane of 5 + label 30.00
*398* A157 5c on 4c red ('67) 1.00 8
*a.* Booklet pane of 5 + label ('67) 5.50
*399* A157 5c dk bl ('67) 1.25 5
*a.* Bklt. pane of 5 + label 11.00
*b.* Bklt. pane of 10 50.00
*400* A139 5c lt grn, blk, brn & yel 30 5
*a.* Bklt. pane of 10 45.00
*401* A139 6c gray, blk, lem & bl 75 15
*401A* A157 6c orange ('70) 24 10
*402* A158 7c brn, ver, blk & gray 1.40 5
*402A* A157 7c dp rose lilac ('71) 30 12
*403* A158 8c bl grn, grn, red & yel 1.50 12
*404* A158 9c ol grn, sep, blk & red brn 2.00 8
*405* A158 10c lt brn, blk, org & bl 1.50 25
*406* A139 13c lt bl grn, blk, gray & red 2.75 50
*a.* Red omitted 400.00
*407* A139 15c lt grn, blk, gray & rose 4.75 40
*a.* Gray omitted 1,500.
*408* A139 20c pink, blk, yel & gray 6.00 15
*a.* Yellow omitted 350.00
*409* A139 24c tan, blk, vio bl & org 1.50 40
*410* A139 25c gray, grn, blk & red 4.75 15
*a.* Red omitted 750.00
*411* A139 30c lt grn, buff, blk & red 25.00 50
*a.* Red omitted *575.00*

**Engr.**

***Perf. 14½x14, 14½x15***

*412* A144 40c vio blue 18.00 32
*413* A145 50c brown red 22.50 15
*414* A144 75c olive green 1.10 1.10
*415* A144 $1 deep claret 3.25 32
*416* A145 $2 purple 10.00 1.10
*417* A145 $4 sepia 7.25 4.50
*Nos. 394-417 (26)* 119.08 10.84

No. 398 issued in booklets only.

Booklet panes Nos. 399b and 400a were issued for the use of "Australian Defence Forces," as the covers read, in Viet Nam.

Coil Stamps

**1966-67 Photo. *Perf. 15 Horiz.***

*418* A157 3c emer, blk & buff 75 35
*419* A157 4c org red, blk & buff 60 12
*420* A157 5c bl, blk & buff ('67) 95 9

Rescue A159

**1966 July 6 Photo. *Perf. 13½***

*421* A159 4c bl, ultra & blk 35 10

Royal Life Saving Society, 75th anniv.

Adoration of the Shepherds A160

**1966, Oct. 19 Photo. *Perf. 13½***

*422* A160 4c olive & blk 24 10

Christmas.

Dutch Sailing Ship, 17th Century A161

Hands Reaching for Bible A162

**1966, Oct. 24 Photo. *Perf. 13½***

*423* A161 4c bl, blk, dp org & gold 24 10

350th anniv. of Dirk Hartog's discovery of the Australian west coast, and his landing on the island named after him.

**1967, Mar. 7 Photo. *Perf. 13½***

*424* A162 4c multicolored 24 8

British and Foreign Bible Soc., 150th anniv.

Combination Lock and Antique Keys — A163

**1967, Apr. 5 Photo. *Perf. 13½***

*425* A163 4c emer, blk & lt bl 38 8

150th anniv. of banking in Australia (Bank of New South Wales).

Lions Emblem — A164

**1967, June 7 Photo. *Perf. 13½***

*426* A164 4c ultra, blk & gold 24 10

Lions International, 50th anniversary.

YWCA Emblems and Flags — A165

**1967, Aug. 21 Photo. *Perf. 13½***

*427* A165 4c dk bl, lt bl & lil 32 8

World Council Meeting of the YWCA, Monash University, Victoria, Aug. 14-Sept. 1.

Seated Women Symbolizing Obstetrics and Gynecology, Female Symbol A166

**1967, Sept. 20 Photo. *Perf. 13½***

*428* A166 4c lil, dk bl & blk 24 10

5th World Congress of Gynecology and Obstetrics, Sydney, Sept. 23-30.

Gothic Arches and Christmas Bell Flower A167

Cross, Stars of David and Yin Yang Forming Mandala — A168

**1967 Photo. *Perf. 13½***

*429* A167 5c blk, ultra, org & yel 24 5
*430* A168 25c red & multi 3.00 2.75

Christmas.
Issue dates: 5c, Oct. 18; 25c, Nov. 27.

Satellite Orbiting Earth A169

Satellite and Antenna, Moree, N.S.W. A170

Design: 20c, World weather map connecting Washington, Moscow and Melbourne, and computer and teleprinter tape spools.

**1968, Mar. 20 Photo. *Perf. 13½***

*431* A169 5c dl yel, red, bl & dk blue 25 10
*432* A169 20c bl, blk & red 4.50 4.00
*433* A170 25c Prus bl, blk & lt green 4.50 4.50

Use of satellites for weather observations and communications.

Kangaroo Paw, Western Australia A171

Sturt's Desert Rose, Northern Territory A171a

State Flowers: 13c, Pink heath, Victoria. 15c, Tasmanian blue gum, Tasmania. 20c, Sturt's desert pea, South Australia. 25c, Cooktown orchid, Queensland. 30c, Waratah, New South Wales.

**1968, July 10 Photo. *Perf. 13½***
**Flowers in Natural Colors**

*434* A171 6c bis & dk brn 48 20
*435* A171 13c lt grnsh bl 60 12
*436* A171 15c dk brn & yel 2.50 25
*437* A171 20c lemon & blk 7.50 15
*438* A171 25c light ultra 6.00 15
*439* A171 30c chocolate 3.00 15
*Nos. 434-439 (6)* 20.08 1.02

Coil Stamps

**1970-75 *Perf. 14½ Horiz.***

Designs: 5c, Golden wattle, national flower. 7c, 10c, Sturt's desert pea.

*439A* A171a 2c dk grn & multi ('71) 20 5
*439B* A171a 4c gray & multi 50 40
*439C* A171a 5c gray & multi 20 12
*439D* A171a 6c gray & multi 1.10 50
*h.* Green omitted 300.00
*439E* A171a 7c blk, red & grn ('71) 35 15
*f.* Green omitted 150.00
*439G* A171a 10c blk, red & grn ('75) 30 15
*Nos. 439A-439G (6)* 2.65 1.37

Soil Testing Through Chemistry and by Computer A172

Hippocrates and Hands Holding Hypodermic A173

**1968, Aug. 6 Photo. *Perf. 13½***

*440* A172 5c multicolored 28 15
*441* A173 5c multicolored 28 15

9th Intl. Congress of Soil Science, University of Adelaide, Aug. 6-16 (No. 440); General Assembly of World Medical Associations, Sydney, Aug. 6-9 (No. 441). Nos. 440-441 printed in sheets of 100 in two separate panes of 50 connected by a gutter. Each sheet contains 10 gutter pairs.

Runner and Aztec Calendar Stone A174

Symbolic House and Money A175

Design: 25c, Aztec calendar stone and Mexican flag (horiz.).

**1968, Oct. 2**

*442* A174 5c multicolored 20 10
*443* A174 25c multicolored 2.75 2.50

19th Olympic Games, Mexico City, Oct. 12-27. Nos. 442-443 printed in sheets of 100 in two separate panes of 50 connected by a gutter. Each sheet contains 10 gutter pairs.

**1968, Oct. 16**

*444* A175 5c multicolored 25 18

11th Triennial Congress of the Intl. Union of Building Societies and Savings Associations, Sydney, Oct. 20-27.

View of Bethlehem and Church Window — A176

**1968, Oct. 23 Photo. *Perf. 13½***

*445* A176 5c lt bl, red, grn & gold 25 5
*a.* Red omitted 350.00

Christmas.

Edgeworth David (1858-1934), Geologist A177

Sir Edmund Barton (1849-1920) A178

Reginald C. and John R. Duigan, Aviators — A179

Famous Australians: No. 447, Caroline Chisholm (1808-1877), social worker and reformer. No. 448, Albert Namatjira (1902-1959), aborigine, artist. No. 449, Andrew Barton (Banjo) Paterson (1864-1941), poet and writer.

**1968, Nov. 6 Engr. *Perf. 15x14***

*446* A177 5c grn, *grnsh (David)* 1.25 12
*a.* Bklt pane of 5 + label 6.25
*447* A177 5c purple, *pink* 1.25 12
*a.* Bklt pane of 5 + label 6.25
*448* A177 5c dark brn, *buff* 1.25 12
*a.* Bklt pane of 5 + label 6.25
*449* A177 5c indigo, *lt blue* 1.25 12
*a.* Bklt pane of 5 + label 6.25

**1969, Oct. 22 Engr. *Perf. 15x14***

Prime Ministers: No. 451, Alfred Deakin (1856-1919). No. 452, John C. Watson (1867-1941). No. 453, Sir George H. Reid (1845-1918).

*450* A178 5c indigo, *grnish* 1.25 12
*a.* Bklt pane of 5 + label 6.25
*451* A178 5c indigo, *grnish* 1.25 12
*a.* Bklt pane of 5 + label 6.25
*452* A178 5c indigo, *grnish* 1.25 12
*a.* Bklt pane of 5 + label 6.25
*453* A178 5c indigo, *grnish* 1.25 12
*a.* Bklt pane of 5 + label 6.25

**1970, Nov. 16 Engr. *Perf. 15x14***

Famous Australians: No. 455, Lachlan Macquarie (1761-1824), Governor of New South Wales. No. 456, Adam Lindsay Gordon (1833-1870), poet. No. 457, Edward John Eyre (1815-1901), explorer.

*454* A179 6c dk bl *(Duigan brothers)* 1.25 12
*a.* Booklet pane of 5 + label 6.25
*455* A179 6c dk brn, *sal* 1.25 12
*a.* Booklet pane of 5 + label 6.25
*456* A179 6c mag, *brt pink* 1.25 12
*a.* Booklet pane of 5 + label 6.25
*457* A179 6c brn red, *sal* 1.25 12
*a.* Booklet pane of 5 + label 6.25

Nos. 446-457 were issued in booklet panes only; all stamps have 1 or 2 straight edges.

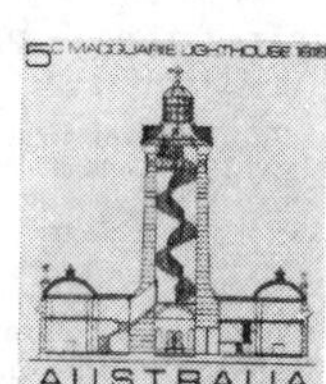


Macquarie Lighthouse A180

***Perf. 14½x13½***

**1968, Nov. 27 Engr.**

*458* A180 5c indigo, *buff* 35 15

Macquarie Lighthouse, Outer South Head, Sydney, 150th anniv.

Surveyor George W. Goyder and Assistants, 1869; Building in Darwin, 1969 — A181

**1969, Feb. 5 Photo. *Perf. 13½***

*459* A181 5c blk brn & dl yel 24 8

First permanent settlement of the Northern Territory of Australia, cent.

Melbourne Harbor Scene — A182

**1969, Feb. 26 Photo. *Perf. 13½***

*460* A182 5c dull bl & multi 24 8

6th Biennial Conference of the Intl. Assoc. of Ports and Harbors, Melbourne, March 3-8.

Overlapping Circles A183

**1969, June 5 Photo. *Perf. 13½***

*461* A183 5c gray, vio bl, bl & gold 24 8

ILO, 50th anniv.

Sugar Cane — A184

Designs (Primary industries): 15c, Eucalyptus (timber). 20c, Wheat. 25c, Ram, ewe and lamb (wool).

**1969, Sept. 17 *Perf. 13½x13***

*462* A184 7c blue & multi 1.25 1.10
*463* A184 15c emer & multi 7.25 5.25
*464* A184 20c org brn & multi 2.25 75
*465* A184 25c gray, blk & yel 2.75 70

Nativity — A185

Tree of Life — A186

***Perf. 13½x13, 13x13½***

**1969, Oct. 15 Photo.**

*466* A185 5c black & multi 20 5
*467* A186 25c mag, org, blk & gold 3.50 3.50

Christmas.

Vickers Vimy Flown by Ross Smith, England to Australia A187

Designs: No. 469, B.E. 2E plane, automobile and spectators. No. 470, Ford truck and surveyors Lieuts. Hudson Fysh and P.J. McGinness.

**1969, Nov. 12 *Perf. 13x13½***

*468* A187 5c bl, blk, cop red & ol 75 35
*469* A187 5c bl, blk, cop red & ol 75 35
*470* A187 5c cop red, blk & ol 75 35
Strip of 3, Nos. 468-470 4.75 5.00

50th anniv. of the first England to Australia flight by Capt. Ross Smith and Lieut. Keith Smith.

Nos. 468-470 are printed se-tenant with various combinations possible.

Diesel Locomotive and New Track Linking Melbourne, Sydney and Brisbane with Perth — A188

**1970, Feb. 11 Photo. *Perf. 13x13½***

*471* A188 5c multicolored 24 5

Completion of the standard gauge railroad between Sydney and Perth.

EXPO '70 Australian Pavilion A189

Design: 20c, Southern Cross and Japanese inscription: "From the country of the south with warm feeling."

**1970, Mar. 16 Photo. *Perf. 13x13½***
*472* A189 5c bl, blk, red & brnz 32 8
*473* A189 20c red & blk 1.25 45

EXPO '70 Intl. Exhib., Osaka, Japan, Mar. 15-Sept. 13.

Queen Elizabeth II and Prince Philip — A190

Australian Flag — A191

**1970, Mar. 31**
*474* A190 5c yel bis & black 25 8
*475* A191 30c vio bl & multi 3.00 2.75

Visit of Queen Elizabeth II, Prince Philip and Princess Anne to Australia.

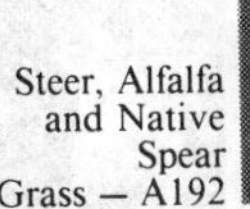

Steer, Alfalfa and Native Spear Grass — A192

**1970, Apr. 13 Photo. *Perf. 13x13½***
*476* A192 5c emerald & multi 28 22

11th Intl. Grasslands Congress, Surfers Paradise, Queensland, Apr. 13-23.

Capt. James Cook and "Endeavour" — A193

Designs: No. 478, Sextant and "Endeavour." No. 479, "Endeavour," landing party and kangaroo. No. 480, Daniel Charles Solander, Sir Joseph Banks, Capt. Cook, map and botanical drawing. No. 481, Capt. Cook taking possession with Union Jack; "Endeavour" and coral. 30c, Capt. Cook, "Endeavour," sextant, kangaroo and aborigines. Nos. 477-481 are printed se-tenant with continuous design.

**1970, Apr. 20 *Perf. 13½x13***
**Size: 24x35½mm.**
*477* A193 5c org brn & multi 60 10
*478* A193 5c org brn & multi 60 10
*479* A193 5c org brn & multi 60 10
*480* A193 5c org brn & multi 60 10
*481* A193 5c org brn & multi 60 10
Strip of 5, Nos. 477-481 3.50 4.75
**Size: 62x29mm.**
*482* A193 30c org brn & multi 3.75 4.00
a. Souvenir sheet of 6 15.00 15.00
*Nos. 477-482 (6)* 6.75 4.50

Captain Cook's discovery and exploration of the eastern coast of Australia, 200th anniv. No. 482a contains 6 imperf. stamps similar to Nos. 477-482 (Nos. 477-481 printed se-tenant). Black marginal inscriptions. Size: 155x127mm.

No. 482a with brown marginal overprint "Souvenir Sheet ANPEX 1970. . ." is of private origin.

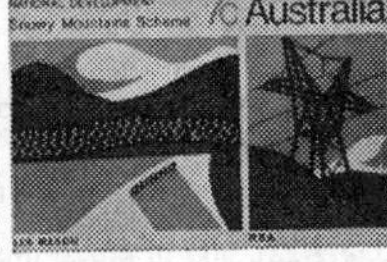

Snowy Mountains Hydroelectric Project A194

Designs: 8c, Ord River hydroelectric project (dam, cotton plant and boll). 9c, Bauxite and aluminum production (mine, conveyor belt and aluminum window frame). 10c, Oil and natural gas (off-shore drilling rig and pipelines).

**1970, Aug. 31 Photo. *Perf. 13x13½***
*483* A194 7c multicolored 1.90 32
*484* A194 8c multicolored 28 15
*485* A194 9c multicolored 28 15
*486* A194 10c multicolored 1.25 12

Australian economic development.

Flame Symbolizing Democracy and Freedom of Speech — A195

**1970, Oct. 2 Photo. *Perf. 13½x13***
*487* A195 6c green & multi 25 8

16th Commonwealth Parliamentary Assoc. Conference, Canberra, Oct. 2-9.

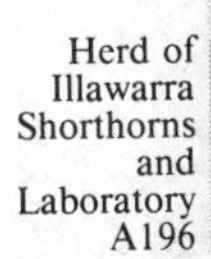

Herd of Illawarra Shorthorns and Laboratory A196

**1970, Oct. 7 *Perf. 13x13½***
*488* A196 6c multicolored 25 8

18th Intl. Dairy Cong., Sydney, Oct. 12-16.

Madonna and Child, by William Beasley A197

UN Emblem, Dove and Symbols A198

**1970, Oct. 14 *Perf. 13½x13***
*489* A197 6c multicolored 25 5

Christmas.

**1970, Oct. 19**
*490* A198 6c blue & multi 25 8

25th anniversary of the United Nations.

Qantas Boeing 707, and Avro 504 — A199

Design: 30c, Sunbeam Dyak powered Avro 504 on ground and Qantas Boeing 707 in the air.

**1970, Nov. 2 *Perf. 13x13½***
*491* A199 6c multicolored 24 8
*492* A199 30c multicolored 1.90 1.50

Qantas, Australian overseas airlines, 50th anniv.

Japanese Noh Actor, Australian Dancer and Chinese Opera Character — A200

Designs: 15c, Chinese pipe and trumpet, Australian aboriginal didgeridoo, Thai fiddle, Indian double oboe and Tibetan drums. 20c, Red Sea dhow, Chinese junk, Australian lifeguard's surfboat, Malaysian and South Indian river boats.

**1971, Jan. 6 Photo. *Perf. 13½x13***
*493* A200 7c multicolored 60 12
*494* A200 15c multicolored 1.90 1.00
*495* A200 20c multicolored 1.90 80

Link between Australia and Asia; 28th Intl. Congress of Orientalists, Canberra, Jan. 6-12.

Southern Cross — A201

**1971, Apr. 2 Photo. *Perf. 13x13½***
*496* A201 6c multicolored 28 8

Australian Natives Assoc., cent.

Symbolic Market Graphs — A202

**1971, May 5 *Perf. 13½x13***
*497* A202 6c silver & multi 28 8

Centenary of Sydney Stock Exchange.

Rotary Emblem A203

**1971, May 17 *Perf. 13x13½***
*498* A203 6c multicolored 25 8

First Intl. Rotary Convention held in Australia, Sydney, May 16-20.

DH-9A, Australian Mirage Jet Fighters A204

RSPCA Centenary A205

**1971, June 9 *Perf. 13½x13***
*499* A204 6c multicolored 35 8

Royal Australian Air Force, 50th anniv.

**1971, July 5 Photo. *Perf. 13½x13***

Designs: 12c, Man and lamb (animal science). 18c, Kangaroo (fauna conservation). 24c, Seeing eye dog (animals' aid to man).

*500* A205 6c blk, brown & org 28 6
*501* A205 12c blk, dk grn & yel 75 18
*502* A205 18c brown & multi 95 30
*503* A205 24c blue & multi 1.40 50

Royal Society for Prevention of Cruelty to Animals in Australia, cent.

Longnecked Tortoise, Painted on Bark — A206

Aboriginal Art: 25c, Mourners' body paintings, Warramunga tribe. 30c, Cave painting, Western Arnhem Land (vert.). 35c, Graveposts, Bathurst and Melville Islands (vert.).

***Perf. 13x13½, 13½x13***
**1971, Sept. 29**
*504* A206 20c multicolored 75 25
*505* A206 25c multicolored 75 90
*506* A206 30c multicolored 85 45
*507* A206 35c multicolored 75 65

Three Kings and Star — A207

**1971, Oct. 13 Photo. *Perf. 13½x13***
*508* A207 7c brt grn, dk bl & lil (Kings) 4.25 20
a. 7c brt grn, dk bl (Kings) & lil 12.00 50
b. 7c lil, red brn, grn & dk bl 7.75 20
c. 7c red brn & lil 2.75 20
d. 7c lil, red brn & brt grn 4.25 20
e. 7c red brn & dk bl 3.75 20
f. 7c lil, grn & dk bl 25.00 60
g. Block of 7, #508-508f 72.50

Christmas. Nos. 508-508f printed se-tenant in sheets of 50. Each sheet contains 2 green crosses formed by 4 No. 508 and three No. 508a.

Andrew Fisher (1862-1928) A208

Cameo Brooch A209

Prime Ministers: No. 515, Joseph Cook (1860-1947). No. 516, William Morris Hughes (1864-1952). No. 517, Stanley Melbourne Bruce (1883-1967).

**1972, Mar. 8 Engr. *Perf. 15x14***
*514* A208 7c dark blue 75 10
a. Booklet pane of 5 + label 4.25
*515* A208 7c dark red 75 10
a. Booklet pane of 5 + label 4.25
*516* A208 7c dark blue 75 10
a. Booklet pane of 5 + label 4.25
*517* A208 7c dark red 75 10
a. Booklet pane of 5 + label 4.25

Nos. 514-517 were issued in booklets only; all stamps have one or two straight edges.

**1972, Apr. 18 Photo. *Perf. 13½***
*518* A209 7c multicolored 25 10

Country Women's Assoc., 50th anniv.

Apple and Banana
A210

Designs (Primary Industries): 25c, Rice. 30c, Fish. 35c, Cattle.

**1972, June 14**
*519* A210 20c blue & multi 2.00 50
*520* A210 25c gray & multi 4.00 3.50
*521* A210 30c multicolored 4.00 75
*522* A210 35c bis & multi 13.00 10.00

Worker in Sheltered Workshop — A211

Designs: 18c, Amputee assembling electrical circuit (horiz.). 24c, Boy wearing Toronto splint, playing ball.

**1972, Aug. 2** ***Perf. 13½x13***
*523* A211 12c green & brn 32 15
*524* A211 18c orange & ol 1.50 22
*525* A211 24c brn & ultra 60 22

Rehabilitation of the handicapped.

Overland Telegraph Line — A212

**1972, Aug. 22 Photo.** ***Perf. 13x13½***
*526* A212 7c dk red, blk & lem 28 8

Centenary of overland telegraph line.

Athlete, Olympic Rings — A213

**1972, Aug. 28** ***Perf. 13½x13***
*527* A213 7c shown 24 12
*528* A213 7c Swimming 24 12
*529* A213 7c Rowing 24 12
*530* A213 35c Equestrian 5.75 5.75

20th Olympic Games, Munich, Aug. 26-Sept. 11.

Abacus, Numerals, Computer Circuits A214

**1972, Oct. 16 Photo.** ***Perf. 13x13½***
*531* A214 7c multicolored 22 10

10th Intl. Congress of Accountants.

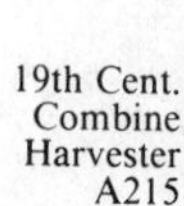

19th Cent. Combine Harvester A215

***Perf. 13½x13, 13x13½***

**1972, Nov. 15** **Photo.**
*532* A215 5c Pioneer family (vert.) 22 6
*533* A215 10c Water pump (vert.) 65 8
*534* A215 15c shown 50 14
*535* A215 40c Pioneer house 90 28
*536* A215 50c Cobb & Co. coach 1.75 32
*537* A215 60c Early Morse key (vert.) 1.40 55
*538* A215 80c Paddle-wheel steamer 1.75 45
*Nos. 532-538 (7)* 7.17 1.88

Australian pioneer life.

Jesus and Children — A216

Dove, Cross and "Darkness into Light" — A217

Metric Conversion, Mass — A218

***Perf. 14½x14, 13½x13***

**1972, Nov. 29**
*539* A216 7c tan & multi 45 6
*540* A217 35c blue & multi 13.00 13.00

Christmas.

**1973, Mar. 7 Photo.** ***Perf. 14x14½***

Metric conversion: No. 542, Temperature (horiz.). No. 543, Length. No. 544, Volume.

*541* A218 7c pale vio & multi 1.25 20
*542* A218 7c yellow & multi 1.25 20
*543* A218 7c yel grn & multi 1.25 20
*544* A218 7c brt rose & multi 1.25 20

Conversion to metric system.

Stylized Caduceus and Laurel A219

**1973, Apr. 4 Photo.** ***Perf. 14½x14***
*545* A219 7c dk bl, emer & lil rose 25 10

WHO, 25th anniv.

Dame Mary Gilmore, Writer A220

Shipping Industry A221

Famous Australians: No. 547, William Charles Wentworth, explorer. No. 548, Sir Isaac Isaacs, lawyer, first Australian-born Governor-General. No. 549, Marcus Clarke, writer.

**Engr. & Litho.**

**1973, May 16** ***Perf. 15x14***
*546* A220 7c bister & blk 2.25 12
*547* A220 7c bister & blk 2.25 12
*548* A220 7c blk & violet 2.25 12
*549* A220 7c blk & violet 2.25 12
Block of 4 (#546-549) 10.00

**1973, June 6 Photo.** ***Perf. 13½x13***

Designs: 25c, Iron ore and steel. 30c, Truck convoy (beef road). 35c, Aerial mapping.

*550* A221 20c ultra & multi 2.75 1.25
*551* A221 25c red & multi 2.25 1.65
*552* A221 30c ol brn & multi 8.00 2.75
*553* A221 35c olive & multi 4.00 *6.50*

Australian economic development.

Banded Coral Shrimp A222

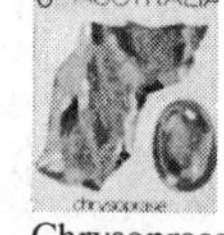

Chrysoprase A223

Helichrysum Thomsonii A223a

Wombat A224

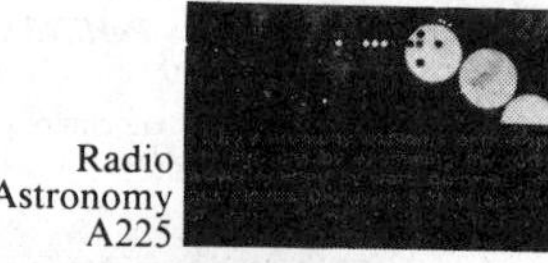
Radio Astronomy A225

Red Gums of the Far North, by Hans Heysen — A226

Coming South (Immigrants), by Tom Roberts — A226a

Paintings: $1, Sergeant of Light Horse, by George Lambert. $4, Shearing the Rams, by Tom Roberts. No. 575, Wallaby. No. 577, McMahon's Point, by Arthur Streeton. No. 578, Mentone.

***Perf. 14x15, 15x14 (A222, A223, A223a); Perf. 14x14½ (A224); Perf. 13x13½ (A225, A226, $1)***

**1973-84** **Photo.**
*554* A222 1c shown 8 5
*555* A222 2c Fiddler crab 8 5
*556* A222 3c Coral crab 10 5
*557* A222 4c Mauve stinger 12 5
*558* A223 6c shown 12 5
*559* A223 7c Agate 12 5
*560* A223 8c Opal 12 5
*561* A223 9c Rhodonite 15 5
*562* A223 10c Star sapphire ('74) 15 5
*563* A225 11c Atomic absorption spectrophotometry ('75) 55 28
*564* A223a 18c shown ('75) 50 12
*565* A224 20c shown ('74) 42 14
*566* A225 24c shown ('75) 1.00 52
*567* A224 25c Spiny anteater ('74) 1.25 35
*568* A224 30c Brushtail possum ('74) 70 30
*569* A225 33c Immunology ('75) 1.00 1.00
*570* A223a 45c Callistemon teretifolius (horiz.) ('75) 65 30
*571* A225 48c Oceanography ('75) 1.75 1.50
*572* A224 75c Feather-tailed glider ('74) 1.25 1.00
*573* A226a $1 multi ('74) 1.50 35
*574* A226 $2 shown ('74) 2.75 52
*575* A226 $2 multi ('81) 2.50 90
*576* A226 $4 multi ('74) 6.50 2.75

**Litho.**

***Perf. 14½***
*577* A226a $5 multi ('79) 6.50 2.00
*578* A226 $5 multi ('84) 6.00 1.50
*579* A226a $10 shown ('77) 12.00 3.25
*Nos. 554-579 (26)* 47.86 17.23

No. 560 Surcharged in Red =
9c

***Perf. 15x14***
*580* A223 9c on 8c multi ('74) 24 10

Hand Protecting Playing Children A227

**1973, Sept. 5 Photo.** ***Perf. 13x13½***
*581* A227 7c bis brn, grn & plum 25 12

50th anniv. of Legacy, an ex-servicemen's organization concerned with the welfare of widows and children of servicemen.

Baptism of Christ A228

The Good Shepherd A229

**1973, Oct. 3** ***Perf. 13x13½***
*582* A228 7c gold & multi 30 8
*583* A229 30c gold & multi 3.75 4.25

Christmas.

Buchanan's Hotel, Townsville A230

St. James' Church, Sydney A231

Designs: 7c, Opera House, Sydney. 40c, Como House, Melbourne.

**1973, Oct. 17 Photo.** ***Perf. 14½x14***
*584* A230 7c lt bl & ultra 65 6
*585* A230 10c bis & blk 90 32

***Perf. 13x13½, 13½x13***
*586* A230 40c dl pink, gray & blk 90 1.65
*587* A231 50c gray & multi 3.25 2.00

Australian architecture; opening of the Sydney Opera House, Oct. 14, 1973 (No. 584).

Radio and Gramophone Speaker A232

**1973, Nov. 21 Photo. *Perf. 13½x13***

| | | |
|---|---|---|
| *588* A232 7c dl bl, blk & brn | 25 | 12 |

Broadcasting in Australia, 50th anniv.

Supreme Court Judge on Bench A233

Australian Football A234

**1974, May 15 Photo. *Perf. 14x14½***

| | | |
|---|---|---|
| *589* A233 7c multicolored | 25 | 12 |

150th anniv. of the proclamation of the Charter of Justice in New South Wales and Van Diemen's Land (Australia's Third Charter).

**1974, July 24 Photo. *Perf. 14x14½***

| | | |
|---|---|---|
| *590* A234 7c shown | 38 | 16 |
| *591* A234 7c Cricket | 38 | 16 |
| *592* A234 7c Golf | 38 | 16 |
| *593* A234 7c Surfing | 38 | 16 |
| *594* A234 7c Tennis | 38 | 16 |
| *595* A234 7c Bowls (horiz.) | 38 | 16 |
| *596* A234 7c Rugby (horiz.) | 38 | 16 |
| *Nos. 590-596 (7)* | 2.66 | 1.12 |

Carrier Pigeon A235

Designs: 30c, Carrier pigeons (vert.).

***Perf. 14½x14, 14x14½***

**1974, Oct. 9 Photo.**

| | | |
|---|---|---|
| *597* A235 7c multicolored | 30 | 10 |
| *598* A235 30c multicolored | 1.25 | 1.25 |

UPU, cent. A booklet containing a strip of 5 each of Nos. 597-598 was produced and sold for $4 Australian by the National Stamp Week Promotion Council with government approval.

William Charles Wentworth A236

Adoration of the Kings, by Dürer A237

**Typo. and Litho.**

**1974, Oct. 9 *Perf. 14***

| | | |
|---|---|---|
| *599* A236 7c bister & blk | 35 | 15 |

Sesquicentennial of 1st Australian independent newspaper. W. C. Wentworth and Dr. Robert Wardell were the editors and the "A" is type from masthead of "The Australian."

**1974, Nov. 13 Engr. *Perf. 14x14½***

Design: 35c, Flight into Egypt, by Albrecht Dürer.

| | | |
|---|---|---|
| *600* A237 10c buff & black | 22 | 8 |
| *601* A237 35c buff & black | 1.10 | 1.10 |

Christmas.

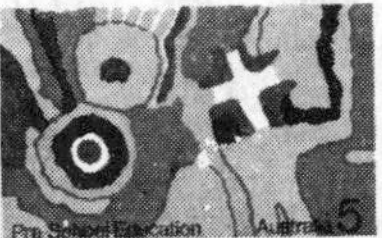


Pre-school Education A238

Correspondence Schools — A239

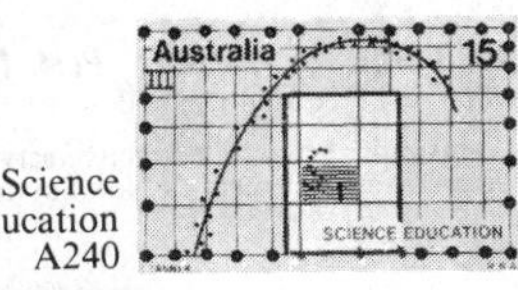


Science Education A240

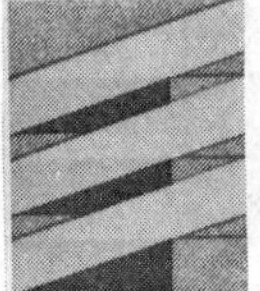


Advanced Education — A241

***Perf. 13x13½, 13½x13***

**1974, Nov. 20 Photo.**

| | | |
|---|---|---|
| *602* A238 5c multicolored | 25 | 12 |
| *603* A239 11c multicolored | 70 | 28 |
| *604* A240 15c multicolored | 75 | 30 |
| *605* A241 60c multicolored | 1.65 | 1.25 |

"Avoid Pollution" A242

"Road Safety" A243

Design: No. 607, "Avoid bush fires."

***Perf. 14½x14, 14x14½***

**1975, Jan. 29 Photo.**

| | | |
|---|---|---|
| *606* A242 10c multicolored | 40 | 12 |
| *607* A242 10c multicolored | 40 | 12 |
| *608* A243 10c multicolored | 40 | 12 |

Environmental dangers.

Symbols of Womanhood, Sun, Moon A244

Joseph B. Chifley (1885-1951) A245

**1975, Mar. 12 Photo. *Perf. 14x14½***

| | | |
|---|---|---|
| *609* A244 10c dk vio bl & grn | 28 | 8 |

International Women's Year.

**1975, Mar. 26**

| | | |
|---|---|---|
| *610* A245 10c shown | 30 | 10 |
| *611* A245 10c John Curtin, 1885-1945 | 30 | 10 |
| *612* A245 10c Arthur W. Fadden, 1895-1973 | 30 | 10 |
| *613* A245 10c Joseph A. Lyons, 1879-1939 | 30 | 10 |
| *614* A245 10c Earle Page, 1880-1963 | 30 | 10 |
| *615* A245 10c John H. Scullin, 1876-1953 | 30 | 10 |

Australian Prime Ministers.

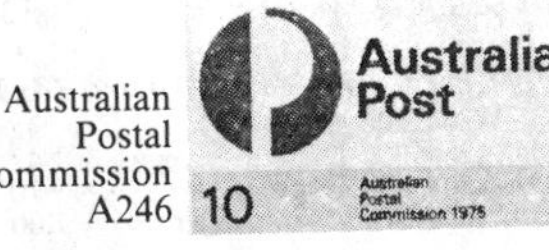


Australian Postal Commission A246

Design: No. 617, Australian Telecommunications Commission.

**1975, July 1 Photo. *Perf. 14½x14***

| | | |
|---|---|---|
| *616* A246 10c red, blk & gray | 50 | 20 |
| *617* A246 10c yel, blk & gray | 50 | 20 |

Formation of Australian Postal and Telecommunications Commissions. Nos. 616-617 printed checkerwise in sheets of 50.

Edith Cowan, Judge and Legislator A247

Truganini, Last Tasmanian Aborigine A248

Portraits: No. 619, Louisa Lawson (1848-1920), journalist. No. 620, Ethel Florence (Henry Handel) Richardson (1870-1946), novelist. No. 621, Catherine Spence (1825-1910), teacher, journalist, voting reformer. No. 622, Emma Constance Stone (1856-1902), first Australian woman physician.

**1975, Aug. 6 Photo. *Perf. 14x14½***

| | | |
|---|---|---|
| *618* A247 10c ol grn & multi | 45 | 38 |
| *619* A247 10c yel bis & multi | 45 | 38 |
| *620* A248 10c olive & multi | 45 | 38 |
| *621* A248 10c gray & multi | 45 | 38 |
| *622* A247 10c violet & multi | 45 | 38 |
| *623* A248 10c brown & multi | 45 | 38 |
| *Nos. 618-623 (6)* | 2.70 | 2.28 |

Famous Australian women.

Spirit House (PNG) and Sydney Opera House A249

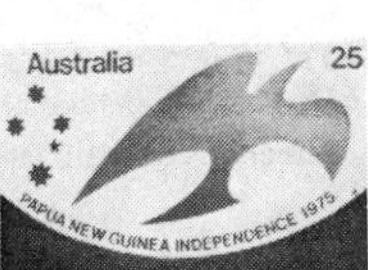


Bird in Flight and Southern Cross A250

**1975, Sept. 16 Photo. *Perf. 13½***

| | | |
|---|---|---|
| *624* A249 18c multicolored | 45 | 28 |
| *625* A250 25c multicolored | 80 | 50 |

Papua New Guinea independence, Sept. 16, 1975.

Adoration of the Kings — A251

"The Light Shineth in the Darkness" — A252

**1975, Oct. 29 Photo. *Perf. 14½x14***

| | | |
|---|---|---|
| *626* A251 15c multicolored | 28 | 8 |
| *627* A252 45c sil & multi | 2.75 | 2.75 |

Christmas.

Australian Coat of Arms — A253

**1976, Jan. 5 Photo. *Perf. 14½x14***

| | | |
|---|---|---|
| *628* A253 18c multicolored | 40 | 15 |

"Williams' Coffin" Telephone, 1878 — A254

**1976, Mar. 10 Photo. *Perf. 13½***

| | | |
|---|---|---|
| *629* A254 18c buff & multi | 35 | 18 |

Centenary of first telephone call by Alexander Graham Bell, Mar. 10, 1876.

John Oxley — A255

Designs: Australian explorers.

**1976, June 9 Photo. *Perf. 13½***

| | | |
|---|---|---|
| *630* A255 18c shown | 30 | 16 |
| *631* A255 18c Hamilton Hume and William Hovell | 30 | 16 |
| *632* A255 18c John Forrest | 30 | 16 |
| *633* A255 18c Ernest Giles | 30 | 16 |
| *634* A255 18c Peter Warburton | 30 | 16 |
| *635* A255 18c William Gosse | 30 | 16 |
| *Nos. 630-635 (6)* | 1.80 | 96 |

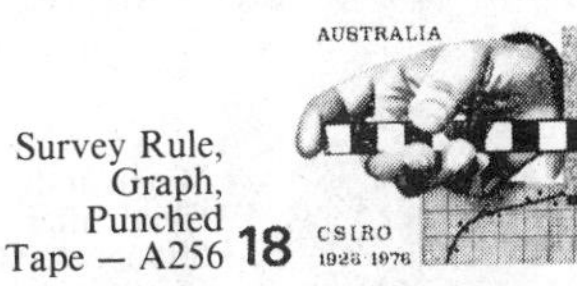


Survey Rule, Graph, Punched Tape — A256

**1976, June 15 *Perf. 15x14***

| | | |
|---|---|---|
| *636* A256 18c multicolored | 30 | 18 |

Commonwealth Scientific and Industrial Research Organization, 50th anniv.

Soccer Goalkeeper A257

Designs (Olympic Rings and): No. 638, Woman gymnast (vert.). 25c, Woman diver (vert.). 40c, Bicycling.

***Perf. 13x13½, 13½x13***

**1976, July 14 Photo.**

| | | |
|---|---|---|
| *637* A257 18c multicolored | 25 | 8 |
| *638* A257 18c multicolored | 25 | 8 |
| *639* A257 25c multicolored | 55 | 55 |
| *640* A257 40c multicolored | 65 | 65 |

21st Olympic Games, Montreal, Canada, July 17-Aug. 1.

An enhanced introduction to the Scott Catalogue begins on Page V. A thorough understanding of the material presented there will greatly aid your use of the catalogue itself.

Richmond Bridge, Tasmania A258

Mt. Buffalo, Victoria A259

Designs: 25c, Broken Bay, New South Wales. 35c, Wittenoom Gorge, Western Australia. 70c, Barrier Reef, Queensland. 85c, Ayers Rock, Northern Territory.

***Perf. 14½x14, 14x14½***

**1976, Aug. 25** **Photo.**

*641* A258 5c multicolored 25 6
*642* A258 25c multicolored 55 25
*643* A258 35c multicolored 42 42
*644* A259 50c multicolored 65 25
*645* A258 70c multicolored 90 42
*646* A258 85c multicolored 1.25 1.00
*Nos. 641-646 (6)* 4.02 2.40

Blamire Young and Australia No. 59 — A260

**1976, Sept. 27** **Photo.** ***Perf. 13½***

*647* A260 18c ap grn & multi 35 10

**Miniature Sheet**

*648* A260 Sheet of 4 2.50 1.50
a. yel & dk brn 80 35
b. rose, dk brn & yel 80 35
c. bl, dk brn, rose & yel 80 35

National Stamp Week, Sept. 27-Oct. 3. Blamire Young (1862-1935), designer of Australia's first issue. No. 648 shows different stages of 4-color printing. The 4th stamp in sheet is identical with No. 647. Dark brown marginal inscription. Size: 100x113mm.

Virgin and Child, after Simone Cantarini A261

Holly, Toy Koala, Christmas Tree and Decoration, Partridge A262

**1976, Nov. 1** **Photo.** ***Perf. 14½x14***

*649* A261 15c brt car & lt bl 35 20

***Perf. 13½***

*650* A262 45c multicolored 1.00 70

Christmas.

John Gould (1804-1881) Ornithologist A263

Violinists A264

Famous Australians: No. 652, Thomas Laby (1880-1946), nuclear scientist. No. 653, Sir Baldwin Spencer (1860-1929), anthropologist (aborigines). No. 654, Griffith Taylor (1880-1963), geographer and arctic explorer.

**1976, Nov. 10** ***Perf. 15x14***

*651* A263 18c shown 35 18
*652* A263 18c Laby 35 18
*653* A263 18c Spencer 35 18
*654* A263 18c Taylor 35 18

**1977, Jan. 19** **Photo.** ***Perf. 14x14½***

*655* A264 20c shown 35 20
*656* A264 30c Dramatic scene 42 30
*657* A264 40c Dancer 70 50
*658* A264 60c Opera singer 1.00 55

Performing arts in Australia.

Elizabeth II A265

Wicket Keeper and Slip Fieldsman A266

Design: 45c, Elizabeth II and Prince Philip.

**1977, Feb. 2**

*659* A265 18c multicolored 30 15
*660* A265 45c multicolored 85 80

Reign of Queen Elizabeth II, 25th anniv.

**1977, Mar. 9** **Photo.** ***Perf. 13½***

Cricket match, 19th century: No. 662, Umpire and batsman. No. 663, Two fieldsmen. No. 664, Batsman and umpire. No. 665, Bowler and fieldsman. 45c, Batsman facing bowler.

*661* A266 18c gray & multi 45 25
*662* A266 18c gray & multi 45 25
*663* A266 18c gray & multi 45 25
*664* A266 18c gray & multi 45 25
*665* A266 18c gray & multi 45 25
Strip of 5 (#661-665) 2.50 2.50
*666* A266 45c gray & multi 90 90
*Nos. 661-666 (6)* 3.15 2.15

Parliament House, Canberra A267

**1977, Apr. 13** ***Perf. 14½x14***

*667* A267 18c multicolored 40 8

Parliament House, Canberra, 50th anniv.

Trade Union Workers A268

**1977, May 9** **Photo.** ***Perf. 13***

*668* A268 18c multicolored 40 8

Australian Council of Trade Unions (ACTU), 50th anniv.

Surfing Santa A269

Virgin and Child A270

**1977, Oct. 31** **Photo.** ***Perf. 14x14½***

*669* A269 15c multicolored 35 8

***Perf. 13½x13***

*670* A270 45c multicolored 1.00 1.00

Christmas.

Australian Flag A271

**1978, Jan. 26** **Photo.** ***Perf. 13x13½***

*671* A271 18c multicolored 40 15

Australia Day, 190th anniversary of first permanent settlement in New South Wales.

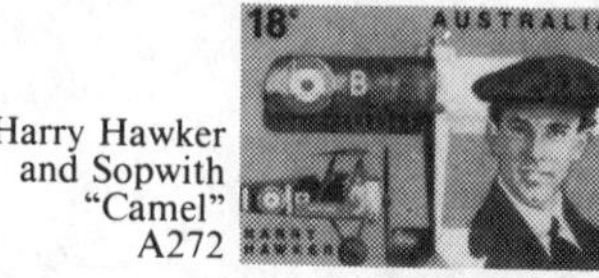


Harry Hawker and Sopwith "Camel" A272

Australian Aviators and their Planes: No. 673, Bert Hinkler and Avro Avian. No. 674, Charles Kingsford-Smith and Fokker "Southern Cross." No. 675, Charles Ulm and "Southern Cross."

**1978, Apr. 19** **Litho.** ***Perf. 15½***

*672* A272 18c ultra & multi 35 20
*673* A272 18c blue & multi 35 20
*674* A272 18c orange & multi 35 20
*675* A272 18c yellow & multi 35 20
a. Souvenir sheet of 4 2.00 2.50

50th anniv. of first Trans-Pacific flight from Oakland, Cal., to Brisbane (No. 675a). No. 675a contains 2 each of Nos. 674-675, imperf.; multicolored margin shows "Southern Cross" in flight from US to Australia. Size: 100x112mm.

Beechcraft Baron Landing A273

**1978, May 15** **Photo.** ***Perf. 13½***

*676* A273 18c multicolored 38 20

Royal Flying Doctor Service, 50th anniv.

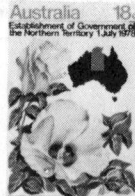

Illawarra Flame Tree A274

Sturt's Desert Rose, Map of Australia A275

Australian trees: 25c, Ghost gum. 40c, Grass tree. 45c, Cootamundra wattle.

**1978, June 1**

*677* A274 18c multicolored 30 15
*678* A274 25c multicolored 55 45
*679* A274 40c multicolored 70 90
*680* A274 45c multicolored 1.00 1.10

**1978, June 19** **Litho.** ***Perf. 15½***

*681* A275 18c multicolored 40 18

Establishment of Government of the Northern Territory.

Hooded Dotterel — A276

Australian birds: 20c, Little grebe. 25c, Spur-wing Plover. 30c, Pied oystercatcher. 55c, Lotus bird.

**1978** **Photo.** ***Perf. 13½***

*682* A276 5c multicolored 8 6
*683* A276 20c multicolored 38 5
*684* A276 25c multicolored 45 30
*685* A276 30c multicolored 50 35
*686* A276 55c multicolored 90 50
*Nos. 682-686 (5)* 2.31 1.26

Issue dates: Nos. 683, 686, July 3; others, July 17. See Nos. 713-718, 732-739, 768.

Australia No. 95 on Album Page — A277

Virgin and Child, by Simon Marmion — A278

**1978, Sept. 25** **Litho.** ***Perf. 15½***

*687* A277 20c multicolored 45 12
a. Miniature sheet of 4 1.90 1.90

National Stamp Week; 50th anniv. of Melbourne Intl. Phil. Exhib., Oct. 1928. Size of No. 687a: 78x112mm.

**1978** ***Perf. 15***

Paintings from National Gallery, Victoria: 15c, Virgin and Child, after Van Eyck. 55c, Holy Family, by Perino del Vaga.

*688* A278 15c multicolored 20 12
*689* A278 25c multicolored 50 52
*690* A278 55c multicolored 62 80

Christmas. Issue dates: 25c, Oct. 3, others, Nov. 1.

Tulloch A279

Race horses: 35c, Bernborough (vert.). 50c, Phar Lap (vert.). 55c, Peter Pan.

***Perf. 15x14, 14x15***

**1978, Oct. 18** **Photo.**

*691* A279 20c multicolored 28 12
*692* A279 35c multicolored 52 55
*693* A279 50c multicolored 75 80
*694* A279 55c multicolored 90 95

Australian horse racing.

Flag Raising at Sydney Cove — A280

**1979, Jan. 26** **Litho.** ***Perf. 15½***

*695* A280 20c multicolored 45 18

Australia Day, Jan. 26.

Passenger Steamer Canberra A281

Ferries and Murray River Steamers: 35c, M.V. Lady Denman. 50c, P.S. Murray River Queen. 55c, Hydrofoil Curl Curl.

**1979, Feb. 14 Photo. Perf. 13½**

*696* A281 20c multicolored 32 20
*697* A281 35c multicolored 52 40
*698* A281 50c multicolored 85 48
*699* A281 55c multicolored 85 90

Port Campbell A282

Designs: Australian National Parks.

**1979, Apr. 24 Litho. Perf. 15½**

*700* A282 20c shown 30 10
*701* A282 20c Uluru 30 10
*702* A282 20c Royal 30 10
*703* A282 20c Flinders Ranges 30 10
*704* A282 20c Namburg 30 10
*705* A282 20c Girraween (vert.) 30 10
*706* A282 20c Mount Field (vert.) 30 10
*Nos. 700-706 (7)* 2.10 70

Nos. 700-704 and 705-706 printed se-tenant.

Double Fairlie A283

Australian steam locomotives: 35c, Puffing Billy. 50c, Pichi Richi. 55c, Zig Zag.

**1979, May 16 Photo. Perf.**

*707* A283 20c multicolored 35 8
*708* A283 35c multicolored 65 55
*709* A283 50c multicolored 90 75
*710* A283 55c multicolored 95 75

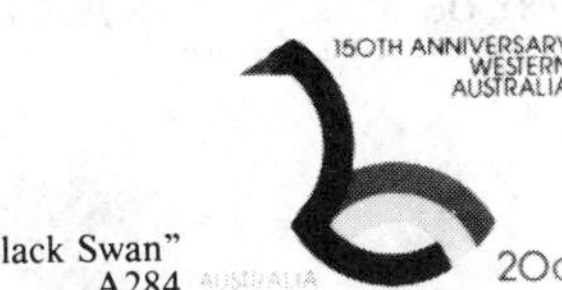

"Black Swan" A284

**1979, June 6 Photo.**

*711* A284 20c multicolored 38 20

150th anniversary of Western Australia.

Children Playing, IYC Emblem A285

**1979, Aug. 13 Litho. Perf. 13½x13**

*712* A285 20c multicolored 38 20

International Year of the Child.

Bird Type of 1978

Australian birds: 1c, Zebra finch. 2c, Crimson finch. 15c, Forest kingfisher (vert.). 20c, Eastern yellow robin. 40c, Lovely wren (vert.). 50c, Flame robin (vert.).

**1979, Sept. 17 Photo. Perf. 13½**

*713* A276 1c multicolored 5 5
*714* A276 2c multicolored 5 5
*715* A276 15c multicolored 30 6
*716* A276 20c multicolored 40 8
*717* A276 40c multicolored 70 40
*718* A276 50c multicolored 90 25
*Nos. 713-718 (6)* 2.40 89

Christmas Letters, Flag-wrapped Parcels A286

Trout Fishing A287

Christmas: 15c, Nativity, icon. 55c, Madonna and Child, by Buglioni.

**1979 Litho. Perf. 13**

*719* A286 15c multicolored 20 10
*720* A286 25c multicolored 40 35
*721* A286 55c multicolored 85 85

Issue dates: 25c, Sept. 24. Others, Nov. 1.

**1979, Oct. 24 Photo. Perf. 14x14½**

Sport fishing: 35c, Angler. 50c, Black marlin fishing. 55c, Surf fishing.

*722* A287 20c multicolored 28 9
*723* A287 35c multicolored 48 48
*724* A287 50c multicolored 85 48
*725* A287 55c multicolored 75 70

Matthew Flinders, Map of Australia A288

**1980, Jan. 23 Litho. Perf. 13½**

*726* A288 20c multicolored 38 10

Australia Day, Jan. 28.

Dingo — A289

**1980, Feb. 20 Litho. Perf. 13½x13**

*727* A289 20c shown 28 20
*728* A289 25c Border collie 32 35
*729* A289 35c Australian terrier 60 40
*730* A289 50c Australian cattle dog 85 70
*731* A289 55c Australian kelpie 85 80
*Nos. 727-731 (5)* 2.90 2.45

Bird Type of 1978

**Perf. 13½, 14x15 (22c), 13x12½(28c, 60c)**

**1980 Litho., Photo. (22c)**

*732* A276 10c Golden-shoulder parrot, vert. 15 6
*a.* Perf. 14½x14 1.25 40
*733* A276 22c White-tailed kingfisher, vert. 35 9
*734* A276 28c Rainbow bird, vert. 45 12
*735* A276 35c Regent bower bird, vert. 55 20
*736* A276 45c Masked woodswallow 3.00 1.00
*a.* Perf. 14x14½ 70 28
*737* A276 60c King parrot, vert. 1.00 30
*738* A276 80c Rainbow pitta 1.25 48
*739* A276 $1 Western magpie, vert. 1.50 60
*Nos. 732-739 (8)* 8.25 2.85

Issue dates: Nos. 733, 734, 737, Mar. 31; others, July 1.

Queen Elizabeth II, 54th Birthday — A290

**1980, Apr. 21 Litho. Perf. 13x13½**

*740* A290 22c multicolored 35 15

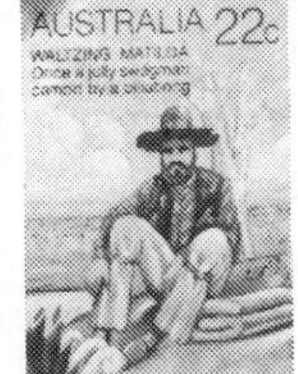

Wanderer A291

High Court Building, Canberra A292

**1980, May 7 Litho. Perf. 13x13½**

*741* Strip of 5 multi 1.75
*a.* A291 22c shown 32 10
*b.* A291 22c Stealing sheep 32 10
*c.* A291 22c Squatter on horseback 32 10
*d.* A291 22c Three troopers 32 10
*e.* A291 22c Wanderer's ghost 32 10

"Waltzing Matilda", poem by Andrew Barton Patterson (1864-1941). No. 741 in continuous design.

**1980, May 19**

*742* A292 22c multicolored 38 15

Opening of High Court of Australia Building, Canberra, May 26.

Salvation Army Officers A294

**Perf. 13x13½, 13½x13**

**1980, Aug. 11**

*747* A294 22c shown 32 12
*748* A294 22c St. Vincent de Paul Society, vert. 32 12
*749* A294 22c Meals on Wheels, vert. 32 12
*750* A294 22c "Life. Be in it." (Joggers, bicyclists) 32 12

Mailman c. 1900 A295

Holy Family, by Prospero Fontana A296

**1980, Sept. 29 Litho. Perf. 13x13½**

*751* A295 22c Mailbox 35 16
*752* A295 22c shown 35 16
*753* A295 22c Mail truck 35 16
*754* A295 22c Mailman, mailbox 35 16
*755* A295 22c Mailman, diff. 35 16
*a.* Souvenir sheet of 3 1.25
*Nos. 751-755 (5)* 1.75 80

National Stamp Week, Sept. 29-Oct. 5. Nos. 751-755 se-tenant. No. 755a contains stamps similar to Nos. 751, 753, 755; multicolored margin shows buildings in continuous design and commemorative cancel. Size: 95x130mm.

**1980 Perf. 13x13½**

Christmas: 15c, Virgin Enthroned, by Justin O'Brien. 60c, Virgin and Child, by Michael Zuern the Younger, 1680.

*756* A296 15c multicolored 22 9
*757* A296 28c multicolored 45 45
*758* A296 60c multicolored 90 65

CA-6 Wackett Trainer, 1941 — A297

Designs: Australian military training planes.

**1980, Nov. 19 Perf. 13½x14**

*759* A297 22c shown 32 32
*760* A297 40c Winjeel, 1955 60 60
*761* A297 45c Boomerang, 1944 65 52
*762* A297 60c Nomad, 1975 1.00 60

Bird Type of 1978

**1980, Nov. 17 Litho. Perf. 13½**

*768* A276 18c Spotted catbird, vert. 35 15

Flag on Map of Australia A298

**1981, Jan. 21**

*771* A298 22c multicolored 35 15

Australia Day, Jan. 21.

Jockey Darby Munro (1913-1966), by Tony Rafty — A299

Australian sportsmen (Cariactures by Tony Rafty): 35c, Victor Trumper (1877-1915), cricket batsman. 55c, Norman Brookes (1877-1968), tennis player. 60c, Walter Lindrum (1898-1960), billiards player.

**1981, Feb. 18 Perf. 14x13½**

*772* A299 22c multicolored 32 32
*773* A299 35c multicolored 52 42
*774* A299 55c multicolored 85 60
*775* A299 60c multicolored 90 60

Australia No. C2 and Cover A300

**Perf. 13x13½, 13½x13**

**1981, Mar. 25 Litho.**

*776* A300 22c Australia No. C2, vert. 32 32
*777* A300 60c shown 90 60

Australia-United Kingdom official airmail service, 50th anniv.

Map of Australia, APEX Emblem A301

**1981, Apr. 6 Photo. Perf. 13x13½**

*778* A301 22c multicolored 38 15

50th anniv. of APEX (young men's service club).

Prices of premium quality never hinged stamps will be in excess of catalogue price.

Queen Elizabeth's Personal Flag of Australia A302

**1981, Apr. 21** *Perf. 13*
779 A302 22c multicolored 38 15

Queen Elizabeth II, 55th birthday.

License Inspected, Forrest Creek, by S.T. Gill — A303

Gold Rush Era (Sketches by S.T. Gill): No. 781, Puddling. No. 782, Quality of Washing Stuff. No. 783, Diggers on Route to Deposit Gold.

**1981, May 20 Photo.** *Perf. 13x13½*
780 A303 22c multicolored 38 15
781 A303 22c multicolored 38 15
782 A303 22c multicolored 38 15
783 A303 22c multicolored 38 15

Lace Monitor — A303a

Tasmanian Tiger — A304

**1981 Litho.** *Perf. 13x13½*
784 A303a 1c shown 5 5
785 A303a 3c Corroboree frog 6 5
a. Perf. 14x14½ ('84) 6 5
786 A304 5c Queensland hairy-nosed wombat, vert. 8 5
a. Perf. 14½x14 ('84) 70 5
787 A303a 15c Eastern snake-necked tortoise 20 12
a. Perf. 14x14½ ('84) 70 14
788 A304 24c shown 35 18
789 A304 25c Greater bilby, vert. 35 18
a. Perf. 14½x14 80 24
790 A303a 27c Blue Mountains tree frog 40 20
a. Perf. 14x14½ 70 25
791 A304 30c Bridled nail-tailed wallaby, vert. 42 22
792 A303a 40c Smooth knob-tailed gecko 55 28
a. Perf. 14x14½ ('84) 2.00 35
793 A304 50c Leadbeater's opossum 85 40
a. Perf. 14x14½ ('84) 1.20 50
794 A304 55c Stick-nest rat, vert. 85 42
795 A303a 65c Yellow-faced whip snake 1.00 48
a. Perf. 14x14½ 1.25 48
796 A303a 70c Crucifix toad 1.10 55
797 A303a 75c Eastern water dragon 1.10 55
a. Perf. 14x14½ 1.40 55
798 A303a 85c Centralian blue-tongued lizard 1.25 65
799 A303a 90c Freshwater crocodile 1.40 70
800 A303a 95c Thorny devil 1.50 75
*Nos. 784-800 (17)* 11.51 5.83
*Nos. 785a-797a (9)* 8.81 2.61

Prince Charles and Lady Diana A305

**1981, July 29 Litho.** *Perf. 13*
804 A305 24c multicolored 42 32
805 A305 60c multicolored 1.15 75

Royal Wedding.

Cortinarius Cinnabarinus A306

Intl. Year of the Disabled A307

Designs: Fungi.

**1981, Aug. 19 Litho.** *Perf. 13*
806 A306 24c shown 35 32
807 A306 35c Coprinus comatus 52 42
808 A306 55c Armillaria luteobubalina 85 70
809 A306 60c Cortinarius austrovenetus 90 75

**1981, Sept. 16** *Perf. 14x13½*
810 A307 24c multicolored 38 15

Christmas Bush for His Adorning A308

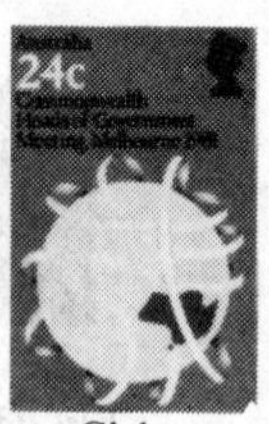

Globe A309

Christmas (Carols by William James and John Wheeler): 30c, The Silver Stars are in the Sky. 60c, Noeltime.

**1981 Litho.** *Perf. 13x13½*
811 A308 18c multicolored 50 18
812 A308 30c multicolored 80 35
813 A308 60c multicolored 1.75 70

Issue dates: 30c, Sept. 28; others, Nov. 2.

**1981, Sept. 30**
814 A309 24c multicolored 38 32
815 A309 60c multicolored 1.00 75

Commonwealth Heads of Government Meeting, Melbourne, Sept. 30-Oct. 7.

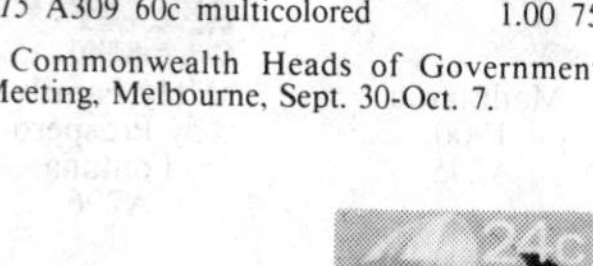

Yacht — A310

**1981, Oct. 14 Litho.** *Perf. 13x13½*
816 A310 24c Ocean racer 35 32
817 A310 35c Lightweight sharpie 52 45
818 A310 55c 12-Meter 85 70
819 A310 60c Sabot 90 75

Australia Day, Jan. 26 — A311

**1982, Jan. 20 Litho.** *Perf. 13x13½*
820 A311 24c multicolored 40 18

Sperm Whale A312

*Perf. 13x13½, 13½x13*
**1982, Feb. 17**
821 A312 24c shown 38 30
822 A312 35c Southern right whale, vert. 55 40
823 A312 55c Blue whale, vert. 90 65
824 A312 60c Humpback whale 1.00 75

Queen Elizabeth II, 56th Birthday A313

Roses A314

**1982, Apr. 21** *Perf. 13½*
825 A313 27c multicolored 42 18

**1982, May 19** *Perf. 13x13½*
826 A314 27c Marjorie Atherton 40 32
827 A314 40c Imp 65 60
828 A314 65c Minnie Watson 1.00 85
829 A314 75c Satellite 1.10 95

50th Anniv. of Australian Broadcasting Commission A315

**1982, June 16** *Perf. 13½x13*
830 A315 27c Announcer, microphone 45 25
831 A315 27c Emblem 45 25

Nos. 830-831 se-tenant in continuous design.

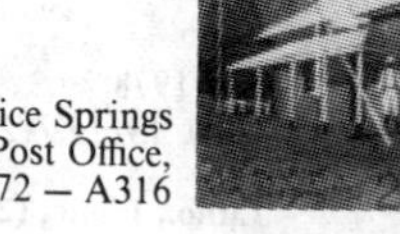

Alice Springs Post Office, 1872 — A316

**1982, Aug. 4** *Perf. 13½x14, 14x13½*
832 A316 27c shown 45 16
833 A316 27c Kingston, 1869 45 16
834 A316 27c York, 1893 45 16
835 A316 27c Flemington, 1890, vert. 45 16
836 A316 27c Forbes, 1881, vert. 45 16
837 A316 27c Launceston, 1889, vert. 45 16
838 A316 27c Rockhampton, 1892, vert. 45 16
*Nos. 832-838 (7)* 3.15 1.12

Christmas — A317

Designs: First Australian Christmas cards, 1881. 21c horiz.

**1982 Litho.** *Perf. 14½*
839 A317 21c multicolored 35 22
840 A317 35c multicolored 60 32
841 A317 75c multicolored 1.25 80

Issue dates: 35c, Sept. 15; others, Nov. 1.

12th Commonwealth Games, Brisbane, Sept. 30-Oct. 9 — A318

**1982, Sept. 22 Litho.** *Perf. 14x14½*
842 A318 27c Archery 45 22
843 A318 27c Boxing 45 22
844 A318 27c Weightlifting 45 22
a. Souvenir sheet of 3 1.50 1.40
845 A318 75c Pole vault 1.25 60

No. 844a contains Nos. 842-844. Size: 130x95mm.

Natl. Stamp Week A319

**1982, Sept. 27** *Perf. 13x13½*
846 A319 27c No. 132 45 15

Opening of Natl. Gallery, Canberra — A320

Design: Gurgurr (moon spirit), bark painting by Yirawala Gunwinggu tribe.

**1982, Oct. 12** *Perf. 14½*
847 A320 27c multicolored 45 15

Pink-flowered Marri — A321

Designs: Various eucalypts (gum trees).

*Perf. 12½x13½*
**1982, Nov. 17 Photo.**
848 A321 1c Pink-flowered marri 5 5
849 A321 2c Gungurru 6 5
850 A321 3c Red-flowering gum 8 5
851 A321 10c Tasmanian blue gum 32 10
852 A321 27c Forrest's marlock 80 25
a. Bklt. pane of 9 + label (2 #848-849, 850, 851, 3 #852) 3.00
b. Bklt. pane (2 each #848-849, 852) 1.75
*Nos. 848-852 (5)* 1.31 50

Nos. 848-852 issued in booklets only.

Mimi Spirits Singing and Dancing, by David Milaybuma A322

Aboriginal Bark Paintings: Music and dance of the Mimi Spirits, Gunwinggu Tribe.

**1982, Nov. 17 Litho.** *Perf. 13½x14*
853 A322 27c shown 40 28
854 A322 40c Lofty Nabardayal 65 45
855 A322 65c Jimmy Galareya 1.00 75

*856* A322 75c Dick Nguleingulei Murrumurru 1.10 85

Historic Fire Engines A323

**1983, Jan. 12** ***Perf. 13½x14***

*857* A323 27c Shand Mason Steam, 1891 40 28
*858* A323 40c Hotchkiss, 1914 65 45
*859* A323 65c Ahrens-Fox PS2, 1929 1.00 75
*860* A323 75c Merryweather Manual, 1851 1.10 85

Australia Day — A324

**1983, Jan. 26** **Litho.** ***Perf. 14½***

*861* A324 27c Sirius 45 25
*862* A324 27c Supply 45 25

Nos. 861-862 se-tenant.

Australia-New Zealand Closer Economic Relationship Agreement (ANZCER) — A325

**1983, Feb. 2** ***Perf. 14x13½***

*863* A325 27c multicolored 40 18

Commonwealth Day — A326

**1983, Mar. 9** **Litho.** ***Perf. 14½***

*864* A326 27c Equality, dignity 45 20
*865* A326 27c Social justice, co-operation 45 20
*866* A326 27c Liberty, freedom 45 20
*867* A326 75c Peace, harmony 1.25 60

Queen Elizabeth II, 57th Birthday A327

**1983, Apr. 20** ***Perf. 14½***

*868* A327 27c Britannia 40 18

World Communications Year — A328

**1983, May 18** **Litho.** ***Perf. 13½x14***

*869* A328 27c multicolored 42 18

50th Anniv. of Australian Jaycees Youth Organization A329

**1983, June 8**

*870* A329 27c multicolored 38 18

St. John Ambulance Centenary — A330

**1983, June 8** ***Perf. 13½x14***

*871* A330 27c multicolored 38 18

Regent Skipper — A331

**1983** ***Perf. 13½, 14½x14(30c)***

*872* A331 4c shown 8 5
*873* A331 10c Cairn's birdwing 15 6
*874* A331 20c Macleay's swal-lowtail 28 14
*875* A331 27c Ulysses 40 22
*875A* A331 30c Chlorinda hair-streak 45 22
*876* A331 35c Blue tiger 50 24
*877* A331 45c Big greasy 65 28
*878* A331 60c Wood white 85 35
*879* A331 80c Amaryllis azure 1.10 40
*880* A331 $1 Sword grass brown 1.40 65
*Nos. 872-880 (10)* 5.86 2.61

The Sentimental Bloke, by C.J. Dennis, 1909 — A332

Folktale scenes: a. The bloke. b. Doreen - the intro. c. The stror at coot. d. Hitched. e. The mooch of life.

**1983, Aug. 3** ***Perf. 14½***

*881* Strip of 5 2.00 1.00
*a.-e.* A332 27c multi, any single 40 20

Kookaburra Bird Wearing Santa Hat — A333

**1983, Sept. 14** **Litho.** ***Perf. 13½x14***

*882* A333 24c Nativity 35 35
*883* A333 35c multicolored 52 35
*884* A333 85c Holiday beach scene 1.25 60

Christmas. Nos. 882, 884 issued Nov. 2.

Inland Explorers — A334

Clay sculptures by Dianne Quinn: No. 885, Ludwig Leichhardt (1813-48). No. 886, William John Wills (1834-61), Robert O'Hara Burke (1821-61). No. 887, Paul Edmund de Strzelecki (1797-1873). No. 888, Alexander Forrest (1849-1901).

**1983, Sept. 26** ***Perf. 14½***

*885* A334 30c multicolored 40 16
*886* A334 30c multicolored 40 16
*887* A334 30c multicolored 40 16
*888* A334 30c multicolored 40 16

Australia Day — A335

**1984, Jan. 26** **Litho.** ***Perf. 13½x14***

*889* A335 30c Cooks' Cottage 40 18

50th Anniv. of Official Air Mail Service — A336

Designs:Pilot Charles Ulm (1898-1934); his plane, "Faith in Australia," and different flight covers.

**1984, Feb. 22** **Litho.** ***Perf. 13½***

*890* A336 45c Australia-New Zealand 1.00 60
*891* A336 45c Australia-Papua New Guinea 1.00 60

Thomson, 1898 — A337

Australian-made vintage cars: b. Tarrant, 1906. c. Australian Six, 1919. d. Summit, 1923. e. Chic, 1924.

**1984, Mar. 14** ***Perf. 14½***

*892* Strip of 5, multi 2.25 1.00
*a.-e.* A337 30c, any single 45 20

Queen Elizabeth II, 58th Birthday A338

**1984, Apr. 18** ***Perf. 14½***

*893* A338 30c multicolored 42 18

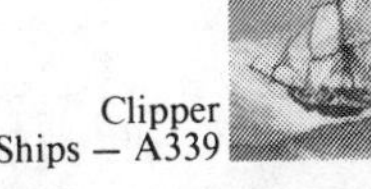

Clipper Ships — A339

***Perf. 14x13½, 13½x14***

**1984, May 23**

*894* A339 30c Cutty Sark, 1869, vert. 35 30
*895* A339 45c Orient, 1853 55 45
*896* A339 75c Sobraon, 1866 90 75
*897* A339 85c Thermopylae, 1868, vert. 1.10 85

Freestyle Skiing — A340

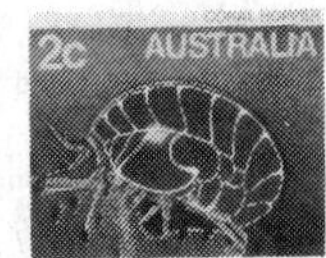


Coral Hopper — A341

**1984, June 6** **Litho.** ***Perf. 14½***

*898* A340 30c shown 56 20
*899* A340 30c Slalom, horiz. 56 20
*900* A340 30c Cross-country, horiz. 56 20
*901* A340 30c Downhill 56 20

***Perf. 13x13½, 14x14½ (Nos. 904, 906, 911, 911A, 916, 918)***

**1984-85** **Litho.**

*902* A341 2c shown 5 5
*903* A341 3c Jimble ('86) 5 5
*904* A341 5c Tasseled an-glerfish 8 5
*905* A341 10c Stonefish ('86) 12 5
*906* A341 20c Red handfish 22 12
*907* A341 25c Orange-tipped cowrie 35 22
*908* A341 30c Choat's wrasse 45 25
*909* A341 33c Leafy sea dragon 35 20
*910* A341 40c Red velvet fish 45 25
*911* A341 45c Texile cone shell ('86) 55 28
*912* A341 50c Blue-lined surge-onfish 75 48
*913* A341 55c Bennett's nudi-branch 85 50
*914* A341 60c Lionfish ('86) 70 38
*915* A341 65c Stingray ('86) 80 40
*916* A341 70c Blue-ringed octo-pus ('86) 85 42
*917* A341 80c Pineapple fish 95 52
*918* A341 85c Regal angelfish 1.25 70
*919* A341 90c Crab-eyed goby 1.00 55
*920* A341 $1 Crown of thorns starfish ('86) 1.25 60
*Nos. 902-920 (19)* 11.07 6.07

1984 Summer Olympics A342

Event stages.

***Perf. 13½x14, 14x13½***

**1984, July 25** **Litho.**

*922* A342 30c Start (facing down) 45 16
*923* A342 30c Competing (facing right) 45 16
*924* A342 30c Finish, vert. 45 16

Ausipex '84 — A343

Designs: No. 926a. Victoria No. 3. b. New South Wales No. 1. c. Tasmania No. 1. d. South Australia No. 1. e. Western Australia No. 1. f. Queensland No. 3.

**1984** **Litho.** ***Perf. 14½***

*925* A343 30c No. 2 45 16

**Souvenir Sheet**

*926* Sheet of 7 2.75 1.00
*a.-f.* A343 30c, any single 35 15

No. 926 contains Nos. 925, 926a-926f. Issue dates: No. 925, Aug. 22; No. 926, Sept. 21.

Christmas — A344

**1984 Litho. *Perf. 14x13½***

*927* A344 24c Angel and Child 30 22
*928* A344 30c Veiled Virgin and Child 35 25
*929* A344 40c Angel 50 35
*930* A344 50c Three Kings 65 45
*931* A344 85c Madonna and Child 1.10 70
*Nos. 927-931 (5)* 2.90 1.97

Stained-glass windows. Issue dates: 40c, Sept. 17; others, Oct. 30.

European Settlement Bicentenary A345

Settlement of Victoria Sesquicentenary A346

Design: No. 932, Bicentennial Emblem. Rock paintings: No. 933, Stick figures, Cobar Region, New South Wales. No. 934, Bunjil's Cave, Grampians, Western Victoria. No. 935, Quinkan Gallery, Cape York, Queensland. No. 936, Wandjina Spirit and Snake Babies, Gibb River, Western Australia. No. 937, Rock Python, Western Australia. No. 938, Silver Barramundi, Kakadu Natl. Park, Northern Territory. 85c, Rock Possum, Kakadu Natl. Park.

**1984, Nov. 7 Litho. *Perf. 14½***

*932* A345 30c multicolored 45 22
*933* A345 30c multicolored 45 22
*934* A345 30c multicolored 45 22
*935* A345 30c multicolored 45 22
*936* A345 30c multicolored 45 22
*937* A345 30c multicolored 45 22
*938* A345 30c multicolored 45 22
*939* A345 85c multicolored 1.25 60
*Nos. 932-939 (8)* 4.40 2.14

**1984, Nov. 19**

*940* A346 30c Helmeted honeyeater 45 20
*941* A346 30c Leadbeater's possum 45 20

Se-tenant.

Australia Day — A347

**1985, Jan. 25 Litho.**

*942* A347 30c Musgrave Ranges, by Sidney Nolan 45 20
*943* A347 30c The Walls of China, by Russell Drysdale 45 20

Se-tenant.

Intl. Youth Year — A348

**1985, Feb. 13 Litho. *Perf. 14x13½***

*944* A348 30c multicolored 40 15

Royal Victorian Volunteer Artillery — A349

Colonial military uniforms: b. Western Australian Pinjarrah Cavalry. c. New South Wales Lancers. d. New South Wales Contingent to the Sudan. e. Victorian Mounted Rifles.

**1985, Feb. 25 *Perf. 14½***

*945* Strip of 5 2.25 80
*a.-e.* A349 33c, any single 45 16

District Nursing Service Centenary — A350

**1985, Mar. 13**

*946* A350 33c multicolored 40 16

Australian Cockatoo — A351

***Perf. 14 Horiz. on 1 or 2 sides***

**1985, Mar. 13**

*947* A351 1c ap grn, yel & buff 5 5
*948* A351 33c ap grn, yel, & lt grnsh bl 90 16
*a.* Bklt. pane of 4 (1 #947, 3 #948) 2.75

Issued in booklets only.

Abel Tasman, Explorer A352

**1985, Apr. 10 *Perf. 13***

*949* A352 33c shown 55 32
*950* A352 33c The Eendracht 55 32
*951* A352 33c William Dampier 55 32
*952* A352 90c Globe and hand 1.50 90
*a.* Souvenir sheet of 4 3.50 2.00

No. 952a contains Nos. 949-952; multicolored margin shows Hessel Gerritsz' South Pacific map. Size: 150x115mm.

Queen Elizabeth II, 59th Birthday — A353

**1985, Apr. 22 *Perf. 14x13½***

*953* A353 33c Queen's Badge, Order of Australia 38 16

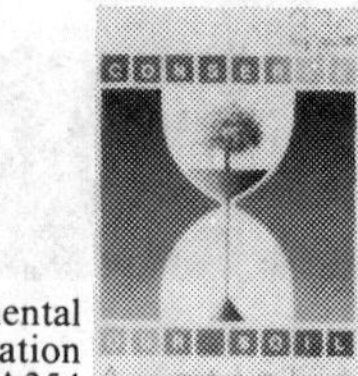


Environmental Conservation A354

**1985, May 15 Litho. *Perf. 14x13***

*954* A354 33c Soil 45 35
*955* A354 50c Air 65 52
*956* A354 80c Water 1.00 85
*957* A354 90c Energy 1.10 90

Elves & Fairies, by Annie Rentoul — A356

Illustrations from classic children's books: No. 960b, The Magic Pudding, text and illustrations by Norman Lindsay. No. 960c, Ginger Meggs, by James Charles Bancks. No. 960d, Blinky Bill, by Dorothy Wall. No. 960e, Snugglepot and Cuddlepie, by May Gibbs.

**1985, July 17 Litho. *Perf. 14½***

*960* Strip of 5 2.00 1.00
*a.-e.* A356 33c, any single 40 18

Electronic Mail — A357

**1985, Sept. 18 Litho.**

*961* A357 33c multicolored 38 16

Christmas A358

Angel in a ship, detail from a drawing by Albrecht Durer (1471-1528).

**1985, Sept. 18 Litho.**

*962* A358 45c multicolored 40 18

See Nos. 967-970.

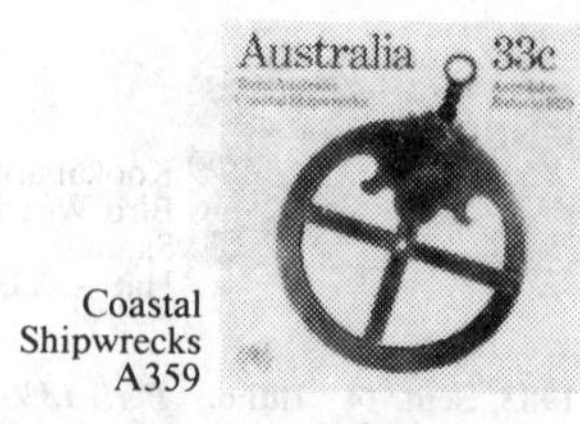


Coastal Shipwrecks A359

Salvaged antiquities: 33c, Astrolabe from Batavia, 1629. 50c, German beardman (Bellarmine) jug from Vergulde Draeck, 1656. 90c, Wooden bobbins from Batavia, and scissors from Zeewijk, 1727. $1, Silver buckle from Zeewijk.

**1985, Oct. 2 Litho. *Perf. 13***

*963* A359 33c multicolored 50 32
*964* A359 50c multicolored 75 55
*965* A359 90c multicolored 1.40 90
*966* A359 $1 multicolored 1.50 1.00

Christmas Type of 1985

Illustrations by Scott Hartshorne.

**1985, Nov. 1 Litho. *Perf. 14***

*967* A358 27c Angel with trumpet 28 18
*968* A358 33c Angel with bells 35 24
*969* A358 55c Angel with star 60 45
*970* A358 90c Angel with ornament 1.00 75

Australia Day A360

AUSSAT A361

**1986, Jan. 24 Litho. *Perf. 14½***

*971* A360 33c Aboriginal painting 42 16

**1986, Jan. 24**

Various communications satellites.

*972* A361 33c multicolored 35 16
*973* A361 80c multicolored 1.15 65

South Australia, Sesquicent. A362

**1986, Feb. 12 *Perf. 13½x14***

*974* A362 33c Sailing ship Buffalo 48 16
*975* A362 33c City Sign, sculpture by O.H. Hajek 48 16

Cook's New Holland Expedition A363

**1986, Mar. 12 *Perf. 13***

*976* A363 33c Hibiscus merankensis 45 30
*977* A363 33c Banksia serrata 45 30
*978* A363 50c Dillenia alata 68 45
*979* A363 80c Corria reflexa 1.10 85
*980* A363 90c Parkinson 1.25 85
*981* A363 90c Banks 1.25 85
*Nos. 976-981 (6)* 5.18 3.60

Australian bicentennial. Sydney Parkinson (d. 1775), artist. Sir Joseph Banks (1743-1820), naturalist.

Halley's Comet A364

Elizabeth II, 60th Birthday A365

**1986, Apr. 9 *Perf. 14x13½***

*982* A364 33c Radio telescope, trajectory diagram 42 18

**1986, Apr. 21 *Perf. 14½***

*983* A365 33c multicolored 42 18

Horses A366

**986, May 21**

84 A366 33c Brumbies 50 28
85 A366 80c Stock horse mustering 1.20 60
86 A366 90c Show-jumping 1.35 70
87 A366 $1 Australian pony 1.50 75

Click Go the Shears, Folk Song — A366a

Lines from the song: b, Old shearer stands. , Ringer looks around. d, Boss of the board. No. e, Tar-boy is there. f, Shearing is all over.

**986, July 21 Litho. *Perf. 14½***

987A Strip of 5 2.75 90
*b.-f.* A366a 33c, any single 55 18

Amalgamated Shearers' Union, predecessor of the Australian Workers' Union, cent.

Australia Bicentennial A367

Settling of Botany Bay penal colony: No. 988, King George III, c. 1767, by A. Ramsay. No. 989, Lord Sydney, secretary of state, 1783-1789, by Gilbert Stuart. No. 990, Capt. Arthur Phillip, 1st penal colony governor, by F. Wheatley, 1786. No. 991, Capt. John Hunter, governor, 1795-1800, by W. B. Bennett, 1815.

**1986, Aug. 6 Litho. *Perf. 13***

988 A367 33c multicolored 50 30
989 A367 33c multicolored 50 30
990 A367 33c multicolored 50 30
991 A367 $1 multicolored 1.50 1.00

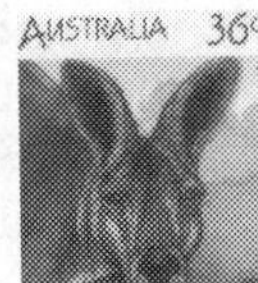


Wildlife — A368

Designs: a, Red kangaroo. b, Emu. c, Koala. d, Kookaburra. e, Platypus.

**1986, Aug. 13 *Perf. 14½x14***

992 Strip of 5 2.00 75
*a.-e.* A368 36c, any single 40 15

Alpine Wildflowers A369

***Rouletted 9½ Vert. on 1 or 2 sides***

**1986, Aug. 25**

993 A369 3c Royal bluebell 5 5
994 A369 5c Alpine marsh marigold 5 5
995 A369 25c Mount Buffalo sunray 50 10
996 A369 36c Silver snow daisy 75 15
*a.* Bklt. pane of 4, 1 #993, 1 #994, 2 #996 1.75
*b.* Bklt. pane of 4, 1 #993, 1 #995, 2 #996 2.00

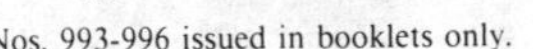

Nos. 993-996 issued in booklets only.

Orchids A370

America's Cup Triumph '83 A371

**1986, Sept. 18 *Perf. 14½***

997 A370 36c Elythranthera emarginata 50 30
998 A370 55c Dendrobium nindii 80 50
999 A370 90c Caleana major 1.25 80
1000 A370 $1 Thelymitra variegata 1.40 85

**1986, Sept. 26 *Perf. 14x13½***

1001 A371 36c Australia II crossing finish line 50 18
1002 A371 36c Trophy 50 18
1003 A371 36c Boxing kangaroo 50 18

Intl. Peace Year — A372

**1986, Oct. 22 Litho. *Perf. 14x13½***

1004 A372 36c multicolored 48 16

Christmas A373

Kindergarten nativity play: No. 1005, Holy Family, vert. No. 1006, Three Kings, vert. No. 1007, Angels. No. 1008a, Angels, peasants. No. 1008b, Holy Family, angels, vert. No. 1008c, Shepherd, angels, vert. No. 1008d, Three Kings. No. 1008e, Shepherds.

**1986, Nov. 3 Litho. *Perf. 14½***

1005 A373 30c multicolored 50 18
1006 A373 36c multicolored 60 24
1007 A373 60c multicolored 1.00 40

**Souvenir Sheet**

1008 Sheet of 5 2.50 80
*a.-e.* A373 30c, any single 50 15

No. 1008 has multicolored margin continuing the design. Size: 146x70mm.

Australia Day — A374

**1987, Jan. 23 Litho. *Perf. 13½x14***

1009 A374 36c Flag, circuit board 42 16
1010 A374 36c Made in Australia campaign emblem 42 16

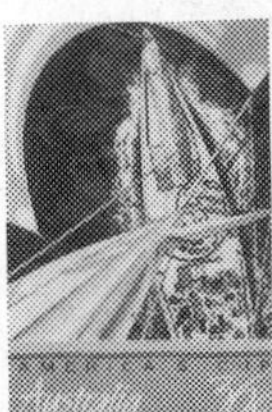


America's Cup — A375

Fruits — A376

Views of yachts racing.

**1987, Jan. 28 *Perf. 15x14½***

1011 A375 36c multicolored 42 28
1012 A375 55c multicolored 60 42
1013 A375 90c multicolored 1.10 70
1014 A375 $1 multicolored 1.25 75

**1987, Feb. 11 *Perf. 14x13½***

1015 A376 36c Melons, grapes 50 30
1016 A376 65c Tropical fruit 90 55
1017 A376 90c Pears, apples, oranges 1.25 80
1018 A376 $1 Berries, peaches 1.40 85

Agricultural Shows — A377

**1987, Apr. 10 Litho. *Perf. 14x13½***

1019 A377 36c Livestock 50 30
1020 A377 65c Produce 90 55
1021 A377 90c Carnival 1.25 80
1022 A377 $1 Farmers 1.40 85

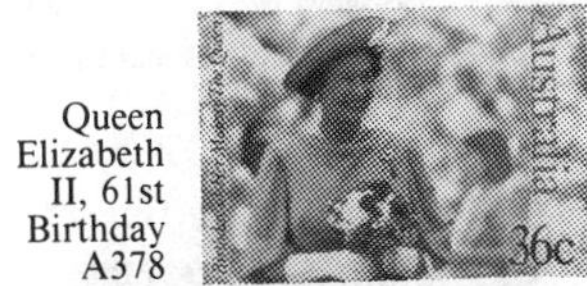


Queen Elizabeth II, 61st Birthday A378

**1987, Apr. 21 *Perf. 13½x14***

1023 A378 36c multicolored 45 18

First Fleet Leaving England A379

Continuous design: No. 1024a, Convicts awaiting transportation. No. 1024b, Capt. Arthur Phillip, Mrs. Phillip, longboat on shore. No. 1024c, Sailors relaxing and working. No. 1024d, Longboats heading from and to fleet. No. 1024e, Fleet in harbor. No. 1025a, Longboat approaching Tenerife, The Canary Isls. No. 1025b, Fishing in Tenerife Harbor. No. 1026, Fleet, dolphins.

**1987 *Perf. 13***

1024 Strip of 5 4.00 90
*a.-e.* A379 36c any single 80 18
1025 Pair 1.05 35
*a.-b.* A379 36c any single 52 18
1026 A379 $1 multicolored 1.50 50

Australia bicent.; departure of the First Fleet, May 13, 1787; arrival at Tenerife, June 1787. Issue dates: No. 1024, May 13; Nos. 1025-1026, June 3.

**1987, Aug. 6**

First Fleet arrives at Rio de Janeiro, Aug. 1787: a, Whale, storm in the Atlantic. b, Citrus grove. c, Market. d, Religious procession. e, Fireworks over harbor.

1027 Strip of 5 2.25 75
*a.-e.* A379 37c any single 45 15

Printed se-tenant in a continuous design.

**1987, Oct. 13**

First Fleet arrives at Cape of Good Hope, Oct. 1787: No. 1028a, British officer surveys livestock and supplies, Table Mountain. No. 1028b, Ships anchored in Table Bay. No. 1029, Fishermen pull in nets as the Fleet approaches the Cape.

1028 Pair 90 38
*a.-b.* A379 37c any single 45 18
1029 A379 $1 multi 1.25 50

Nos. 1028a-1028b are printed se-tenant in a continuous design.

**1988, Jan. 26 Litho. *Perf. 13***

Arrival of the First Fleet, Sydney Cove, Jan. 1788: a, Five aborigines on shore. b, Four aborigines on shore. c, Kangaroos. d, White cranes. e, Flag raising.

1030 Strip of 5 2.75 90
*a.-e.* A379 37c any single 55 18

Nos. 1030a-1030e printed se-tenant in a continuous design.

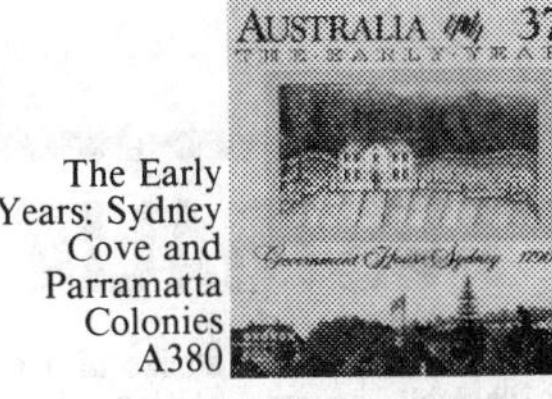


The Early Years: Sydney Cove and Parramatta Colonies A380

Details from panorama "View of Sydney from the East Side of the Cove," 1808, painted by convict artist John Eyre to illustrate *The Present Picture of New South Wales,* published in London in 1811, and paintings in British and Australian museums: a. *Government House, 1790, Sydney,* by midshipman George Raper. b. *Government Farm, Parramatta, 1791,* attributed to the Port Jackson Painter. c. *Parramatta Road, 1796,* attributed to convict artist Thomas Watling. d. *The Rocks and Sydney Cove, 1800,* an aquatint engraving by Edward Dayes. e. *Sydney Hospital, 1803,* by George William Evans, an explorer and surveyor-general of New South Wales. Printed se-tenant in a continuous design.

**1988, Apr. 13 Litho. *Perf. 13***

1031 Strip of 5 2.90 1.00
*a.-e.* A380 37c any single 58 20

Australia Bicentennial.

The Man from Snowy River, 1890, Ballad by A.B. Paterson — A381

Fauna — A382

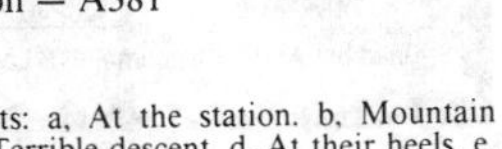

Excerpts: a, At the station. b, Mountain bred. c, Terrible descent. d, At their heels. e, Brought them back.

**1987, June 24 *Perf. 14x13½***

1034 Strip of 5 2.75 1.50
*a.-e.* A381 36c any single 55 30

Printed se-tenant in a continuous design.

**1987, July 1 *Perf. 14½x14***

Designs: a, Possum. b, Cockatoo. c, Wombat. d, Rosella. e, Echidna.

1035 Strip of 5 2.25 75
*a.-e.* A382 37c any single 45 15

Printed se-tenant in a continuous design.

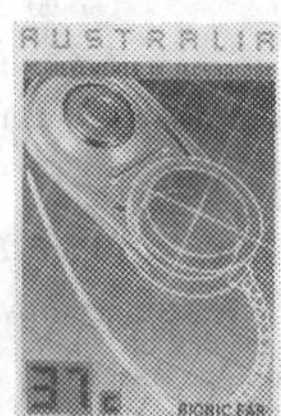
Technology A383

**1987, Aug. 19** *Perf. 14½*

| | | | | | |
|---|---|---|---|---|---|
| *1036* | A383 | 37c | Bionic ear | 38 | 18 |
| *1037* | A383 | 53c | Microchips | 55 | 28 |
| *1038* | A383 | 63c | Robotics | 70 | 32 |
| *1039* | A383 | 68c | Zirconia ceramics | 75 | 35 |

Children A384

**1987, Sept. 16**

| | | | | | |
|---|---|---|---|---|---|
| *1040* | A384 | 37c | Crayfishing | 45 | 18 |
| *1041* | A384 | 55c | Cat's cradle | 65 | 28 |
| *1042* | A384 | 90c | Eating meat pies | 1.00 | 45 |
| *1043* | A384 | $1 | Playing with a joey | 1.25 | 50 |

Christmas A385

Carolers: a. Woman, two girls. b. Man, two girls. c. Four children. d. Man, two women, boy. e. Six youths. 37c, three women, two men. Nos. 1044a-1044e are vert.

**1987, Nov. 2** **Litho.** *Perf. 14½*

| | | | | |
|---|---|---|---|---|
| *1044* | | Strip of 5 | 2.00 | 75 |
| *a.-e.* | A385 | 30c any single | 40 | 15 |

*Perf. 13½x14*

| | | | | | |
|---|---|---|---|---|---|
| *1045* | A385 | 37c | multicolored | 45 | 18 |
| *1046* | A385 | 63c | shown | 80 | 32 |

Carols by Candlelight, Christmas Eve, Sidney Myer Bowl, Melbourne.

Aboriginal Crafts — A386

Designs: 3c, Spearthrower, Western Australia. 15c, Shield, New South Wales. No. 1049, Basket, Queensland. No. 1050, Bowl, Central Australia. No. 1051, Belt, Northern Territory.

*Perf. 15½ Horiz.*

**1987, Oct. 13** **Photo.**

| | | | | | |
|---|---|---|---|---|---|
| *1047* | A386 | 3c | multicolored | 5 | 5 |
| *1048* | A386 | 15c | multicolored | 20 | 6 |
| *1049* | A386 | 37c | multicolored | 50 | 16 |
| *a.* | | | Bklt. pane of 4, 2 each #1047, #1049 | 1.10 | |
| *1050* | A386 | 37c | multicolored | 50 | 16 |
| *1051* | A386 | 37c | multicolored | 50 | 16 |
| *a.* | | | Bklt. pane of 6 (1 #1048, 3 #1050, 2 #1051) | 2.75 | |
| | | | *Nos. 1047-1051 (5)* | 1.75 | 59 |

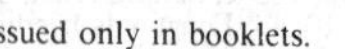

Issued only in booklets.

Caricature of Australian Koala and American Bald Eagle — A387

**1988, Jan. 26** *Perf. 13*

| | | | | | |
|---|---|---|---|---|---|
| *1052* | A387 | 37c | multi | 55 | 18 |

Australia bicentennial. See No. 1086 and US No. 2370.

Living Together — A388

Cartoons.

**1988** *Perf. 14*

| | | | | | |
|---|---|---|---|---|---|
| *1053* | A388 | 1c | Religion | 5 | 5 |
| *1054* | A388 | 2c | Industry | 5 | 5 |
| *1055* | A388 | 3c | Local government | 5 | 5 |
| *1056* | A388 | 4c | Trade unions | 6 | 5 |
| *1057* | A388 | 5c | Parliament | 8 | 5 |
| *1058* | A388 | 10c | Transportation | 18 | 6 |
| *1059* | A388 | 15c | Sports | 25 | 8 |
| *1060* | A388 | 20c | Commerce | 35 | 12 |
| *1061* | A388 | 25c | Housing | 42 | 14 |
| *1062* | A388 | 30c | Welfare | 52 | 16 |
| *1063* | A388 | 37c | Postal services | 62 | 20 |
| *a.* | | | Bklt. pane of 10 | 6.25 | |
| *1063B* | A388 | 39c | Tourism | 65 | 22 |
| *1064* | A388 | 40c | Recreation | 68 | 22 |
| *1065* | A388 | 45c | Health | 78 | 25 |
| *1066* | A388 | 50c | Mining | 85 | 28 |
| *1067* | A388 | 53c | Primary industry | 90 | 30 |
| *1068* | A388 | 55c | Education | 95 | 32 |
| *1069* | A388 | 60c | Armed Forces | 1.05 | 35 |
| *1070* | A388 | 63c | Police | 1.10 | 38 |
| *1071* | A388 | 65c | Telecommunications | 1.15 | 38 |
| *1072* | A388 | 68c | The media | 1.20 | 40 |
| *1073* | A388 | 70c | Science and technology | 1.20 | 40 |
| *1074* | A388 | 75c | Visual arts | 1.30 | 45 |
| *1075* | A388 | 80c | Performing arts | 1.40 | 48 |
| *1076* | A388 | 90c | Banking | 1.55 | 52 |
| *1077* | A388 | 95c | Law | 1.65 | 55 |
| *1078* | A388 | $1 | Rescue and emergency services | 1.70 | 58 |
| | | | *Nos. 1053-1078 (27)* | 20.74 | 7.09 |

Issue dates: 1c, 2c, 3c, 5c, 30c, 40c, 55c, 60c, 63c, 65c, 68c, 75c, 95c, Mar. 16. 39c, Sept. 28. Others, Feb. 17.

Queen Elizabeth II, 62nd Birthday A389

**1988, Apr. 21** *Perf. 14½*

| | | | | | |
|---|---|---|---|---|---|
| *1079* | A389 | 37c | multi | 58 | 20 |

EXPO '88, Brisbane, Apr. 30-Oct. 30 — A390

**1988, Apr. 29** *Perf. 13*

| | | | | | |
|---|---|---|---|---|---|
| *1080* | A390 | 37c | multi | 58 | 20 |

Opening of Parliament House, Canberra A391

**1988, May 9** *Perf. 14½*

| | | | | | |
|---|---|---|---|---|---|
| *1081* | A391 | 37c | multi | 58 | 2 |

Australia Bicentennial A392

Designs: No. 1082, Colonist, clipper ship. No. 1083, British and Australian parliaments, Queen Elizabeth II. No. 1084, Cricketer W.G. Grace. No. 1085, John Lennon (1940-1980), William Shakespeare (1564-1616) and Sydney Opera House. Stamps of the same denomination printed se-tenant in a continuous design picturing flag of Australia.

**1988, June 21** **Litho.** *Perf. 1.*

| | | | | | |
|---|---|---|---|---|---|
| *1082* | A392 | 37c | multi | 62 | 2 |
| *1083* | A392 | 37c | multi | 62 | 20 |
| *1084* | A392 | $1 | multi | 1.65 | 5 |
| *1085* | A392 | $1 | multi | 1.65 | 5 |

See Great Britain Nos. 1222-1225.

Caricature Type of 1988

Design: Caricature of an Australian koala and New Zealand kiwi.

**1988, June 21** **Litho.** *Perf. 13½*

| | | | | | |
|---|---|---|---|---|---|
| *1086* | A387 | 37c | multi | 62 | 20 |

Australia bicentennial. See New Zealand No. 907.

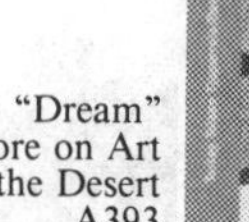
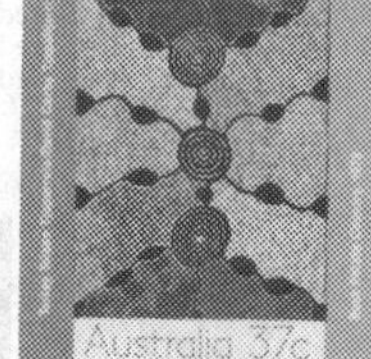
"Dream" Lore on Art of the Desert A393

Aboriginal paintings from Papunya Settlement in the Flinders University Art Museum: 37c, *Bush Potato Country*, by Turkey Tolson Tjupurrula with by David Corby Tjapaltjarri. 55c, *Courtship Rejected*, by Limpi Puntungka Tjapangati. 90c, *Medicine Story*, anonymous. $1, *Ancestor Dreaming*, by Tim Leura Tjapaltjarri.

**1988, Aug. 1** **Litho.** *Perf. 13*

| | | | | | |
|---|---|---|---|---|---|
| *1087* | A393 | 37c | multi | 62 | 20 |
| *1088* | A393 | 55c | multi | 90 | 30 |
| *1089* | A393 | 90c | multi | 1.50 | 50 |
| *1090* | A393 | $1 | multi | 1.65 | 55 |

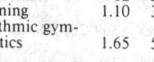

1988 Summer Olympics, Seoul — A394

**1988, Sept. 14** *Perf. 14½*

| | | | | | |
|---|---|---|---|---|---|
| *1091* | A394 | 37c | Basketball | 62 | 20 |
| *1092* | A394 | 65c | Running | 1.10 | 38 |
| *1093* | A394 | $1 | Rhythmic gymnastics | 1.65 | 55 |

34th Commonwealth Parliamentary Conference, Canberra — A395

**988, Sept. 19**

*094* A395 37c Scepter and mace 62 20

Works in the Contemporary Decorative Arts Collection at the Natl. Gallery — A396

**988, Sept. 28 Litho.** ***Perf. Horiz.***

*'095* A396 2c "Australian Fetish," by Peter Tully 5 5
*'096* A396 5c Vase by Colin Levy 8 5
*'097* A396 39c Teapot by Frank Bauer 65 22

Views A397

**1988, Oct. 17 Photo.** ***Perf. 13***

*1098* A397 39c The Desert 65 22
*1099* A397 55c The Top End 90 30
*1100* A397 65c The Coast 1.10 38
*1101* A397 70c The Bush 1.15 40

Christmas A398

Children's design contest winning drawings: 32c, Nativity scene, by Danielle Hush, age 7. 39c, Koala wearing a Santa hat, by Kylie Courtney, age 6. 63c, Cockatoo wearing a Santa hat, by Benjamin Stevenson, age 10.

**1988, Oct. 31** ***Perf. 13½x13***

*1102* A398 32c multi 55 18
*1103* A398 39c multi 65 22
*1104* A398 63c multi 1.05 35

## AIR POST STAMPS

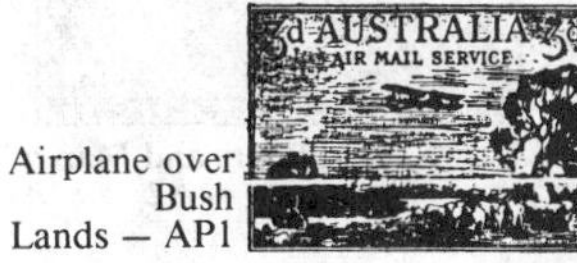

Airplane over Bush Lands — AP1

**Unwmk.**

**1929, May 20 Engr.** ***Perf. 11***

*C1* AP1 3p deep green 5.00 3.00
*a.* Bklt. pane of 4 ('30) 110.00

Airplane over Hemispheres AP2

**1931, Mar. 19**

*C2* AP2 6p gray violet 7.75 6.50

Trans-oceanic flights of Charles Kingsford-Smith.

AP3

**1931, Nov. 4**

*C3* AP3 6p olive brown 13.00 9.00

Mercury and Hemispheres — AP4

Mercury and Globe — AP5

**1934, Dec. 1** ***Perf. 11***

*C4* AP4 1sh6p violet brn 32.50 2.75

**1937, Oct. Wmk. 228** ***Perf. 13x13½***

*C5* AP4 1sh6p violet brn 3.50 25

**Catalogue values for unused stamps in this section, from this point to the end of the section, are for Never Hinged items.**

**1949, Sept. 1** ***Perf. 14½***

*C6* AP5 1sh6p sepia 1.90 10

**1956, Dec. 6 Unwmk.**

*C7* AP5 1sh6p sepia 14.00 85

Super-Constellation over Globe — AP6

**1958, Jan. 6** ***Perf. 14½x14***

*C8* AP6 2sh dark vio blue 2.50 1.75

Inauguration of Australian "Round the World" air service.

## AIR POST OFFICIAL STAMP

No. C3 Overprinted  

***Perf. 11, 11½***

**1931, Nov. 17 Unwmk.**

*CO1* AP3 6p olive brown 21.50 15.00

Issued primarily for official use, but to prevent speculation, a quantity was issued for public distribution.

## POSTAGE DUE STAMPS

D1

D2

Wmk. 55 - Large Crown and NSW

***Perf. 11½, 12***

**1902 Typo. Wmk. 55**

*J1* D1 ½p emerald 2.50 4.00
*J2* D1 1p emerald 7.50 4.50
*a.* Perf. 11 120.00 40.00
*J3* D1 2p emerald 9.00 4.50
*J4* D1 3p emerald 30.00 9.00
*J5* D1 4p emerald 21.00 6.00
*J6* D1 6p emerald 35.00 7.50
*J7* D1 8p emerald 100.00 75.00
*J8* D1 5sh emerald 180.00 35.00
*Nos. J1-J8 (8)* 385.00 145.50

The 1p, 2p and 4p, type D1, exist also in perforations compounding 11 with 11½ and 12.

***Perf. 11½, 12, 11 and 11 Compound with 11½, 12***

**1902-04**

*J9* D2 ½p emerald 6.50 6.75
*a.* Perf. 11 60.00 32.50
*J10* D2 1p emerald 5.00 2.00
*a.* Perf. 11 32.50 5.75
*J11* D2 2p emerald 11.50 1.25
*J12* D2 3p emerald 27.50 5.00
*J13* D2 4p emerald 20.00 5.25
*J14* D2 5p emerald 14.00 10.00
*a.* Perf. 11 65.00 10.00
*J15* D2 6p emerald 52.50 10.00
*J16* D2 8p emerald 65.00 22.50
*J17* D2 10p emerald 47.50 8.25
*J18* D2 1sh emerald 47.50 8.25
*a.* Perf. 11 65.00 20.00
*J19* D2 2sh emerald 60.00 13.00
*J20* D2 5sh emerald 115.00 10.00
*a.* Perf. 11 250.00 65.00
*J21* D2 10sh emerald *1,750. 950.00*
*J22* D2 20sh emerald *3,250. 1,750.*
*Nos. J9-J20 (12)* 472.00 102.25

Wmk. 12 - Crown and Single-lined A

Wmk. 13 - Large Crown and Double-lined A

***Perf. 11½, 12 Compound with 11***

**1906 Wmk. 12**

*J23* D2 ½p emerald 6.00 4.00
*J24* D2 1p emerald 9.50 1.75
*a.* Perf. 11 75.00 22.50
*J25* D2 2p emerald 32.50 5.00
*J26* D2 3p emerald 150.00 90.00
*J27* D2 4p emerald 40.00 12.00
*a.* Perf. 11 150.00 55.00
*J28* D2 6p emerald 50.00 18.00
*Nos. J23-J28 (6)* 288.00 130.75

**1907 Wmk. 13**

*J29* D2 ½p emerald 30.00 16.00
*J30* D2 1p emerald 45.00 30.00
*J31* D2 2p emerald 90.00 50.00
*J32* D2 4p emerald 185.00 65.00
*J33* D2 6p emerald 250.00 65.00
*Nos. J29-J33 (5)* 600.00 226.00

D3

D4

**1908-09 Wmk. 12**

*J34* D3 1sh emer ('09) 82.50 12.00
*J35* D3 2sh emerald *500.00 325.00*
*J36* D3 5sh emerald 165.00 45.00
*J37* D3 10sh emerald *1,750. 700.00*
*J38* D3 20sh emerald *4,500. 2,000.*

***Perf. 11, 12x12½, 12½, 14***

**1909 Wmk. 13**

*J39* D4 ½p green & car 7.75 3.00
*J40* D4 1p green & car 3.75 32
*J41* D4 2p green & car 9.50 50
*J42* D4 3p green & car 14.00 5.00
*J43* D4 4p green & car 11.00 2.75
*J44* D4 6p green & car 15.00 3.25
*J45* D4 1sh green & car 19.00 2.00
*J46* D4 2sh green & car 62.50 10.00
*J47* D4 5sh green & car 67.50 10.00
*J48* D4 10sh green & car 300.00 135.00
*J49* D4 £1 green & car 400.00 215.00
*Nos. J39-J49 (11)* 910.00 386.82

**1922-25 Wmk. 10** ***Perf. 14, 11***

*J50* D4 ½p grn & car ('23) 4.50 1.40
*J51* D4 1p green & car 2.75 40
*J52* D4 1½p yel green & rose ('25) 2.00 3.00
*J53* D4 2p green & car 7.00 2.75
*J54* D4 3p green & car 14.00 2.75
*J55* D4 4p green & car 17.50 3.25
*J56* D4 6p green & car 25.00 11.00
*Nos. J50-J56 (7)* 72.75 24.55

**1931-37 Wmk. 228** ***Perf. 11, 14***

*J57* D4 ½p yel green & rose ('34) 3.75 3.00
*J58* D4 1p yel grn & rose 2.50 32
*J59* D4 2p yel grn & rose 3.00 40
*J60* D4 3p yel green & rose ('37) 55.00 30.00
*J61* D4 4p yel green & rose ('34) 8.75 2.00
*J62* D4 6p yel green & rose ('36) 325.00 300.00
*J63* D4 1sh yel green & rose ('34) 32.50 20.00
*Nos. J57-J63 (7)* 430.50 355.72

D5

**Engraved; Value Typo.**

**1938** *Perf. 14½x14*

*J64* D5 ½p green & car 52 85
*J65* D5 1p green & car 1.40 30
*J66* D5 2p green & car 3.50 40
*J67* D5 3p green & car 12.00 3.25
*J68* D5 4p green & car 3.50 32
*J69* D5 6p green & car 27.50 13.00
*J70* D5 1sh green & car 27.50 4.00
*Nos. J64-J70 (7)* 75.92 22.12

**Catalogue values for unused stamps in this section, from this point to the end of the section, are for Never Hinged items.**

Type of 1938
Value Tablet Redrawn

Original

Redrawn

Pence denominations: "D" has melon-shaped center in redrawn tablet. The redrawn 3p differs slightly, having semi-melon-shaped "D" center, with vertical white stroke half filling it.
1sh. 1938: Numeral "1" narrow, with six background lines above.
1sh. 1947: Numeral broader, showing more white space around dotted central ornament. Three lines above.

**1946-57** **Wmk. 228**

*J71* D5 ½p grn & car ('56) 1.50 1.50
*J72* D5 1p grn & car ('47) 35 12
*J73* D5 2p green & car 1.00 20
*J74* D5 3p green & car 2.00 30
*J75* D5 4p grn & car ('52) 2.00 60
*J76* D5 5p grn & car ('48) 5.00 1.50
*J77* D5 6p grn & car ('47) 6.00 60
*J78* D5 7p grn & car ('53) 3.50 2.00
*J79* D5 8p grn & car ('57) 20.00 9.00
*J80* D5 1sh grn & car ('47) 17.50 90
*Nos. J71-J80 (10)* 58.85 16.72

**1953-54**

**White Tablet, Carmine Numeral**

*J81* D5 1sh grn & car ('54) 10.00 1.50
*J82* D5 2sh green & car 15.00 11.00
*J83* D5 5sh green & car 27.50 3.00

Redrawn Type of 1947-57

Two Types of Some Pence Values:
Type I - Background lines touch numeral, "D" and period.
Type II - Lines do not touch numeral, etc.
Second engraving of 1sh has sharper and thicker lines.

**Engr.; Denomination Typo.**

**1958-60** **Unwmk.** *Perf. 14½x14*

*J86* D5 ½p grn & car (II) 50 50
*J87* D5 1p grn & car (II) ('59) 2.50 40
*a.* Type I 3.75 95
*J88* D5 3p grn & car (II) ('60) 2.00 70
*J89* D5 4p grn & car (I) 5.00 3.50
*a.* Type II ('59) 12.00 3.50
*J90* D5 5p grn & car (I) 10.00 3.25
*a.* Type II ('59) 70.00 27.50
*J91* D5 6p grn & car (II) ('60) 5.00 2.00
*J92* D5 8p grn & car (II) 20.00 16.00
*J93* D5 10p grn & car (II) ('59) 8.50 3.25

**White Tablet, Carmine Numeral**

*J94* D5 1sh green & car 8.25 1.10
*a.* 2nd redrawing ('60) 5.00 70
*J95* D5 2sh grn & car ('60) 27.50 6.50
*Nos. J86-J95 (10)* 89.25 37.20

---

## MILITARY STAMPS

Nos. 166, 191, 183A, 173, 175, 206 and 177 Overprinted in Black:

B.C.O.F.
JAPAN
1946
a

B.C.O.F.
JAPAN
1946
b

B. C. O. F.
JAPAN
1946
c

*Perf. 14½x14, 15x14, 11½, 13½x13*

**1946-47** **Wmk. 228**

*M1* A24(a) ½p orange 4.75 2.00
*M2* A36(b) 1p brown vio 4.00 2.25
*a.* Blue overprint 165.00 67.50
*M3* A27(b) 3p dk vio brn 3.25 65
*M4* A30(a) 6p brn violet ('47) 4.75 2.50
*M5* A16(a) 1sh gray green ('47) 11.00 5.25
*M6* A1(c) 2sh dk red brown ('47) 26.00 21.00
*M7* A32(c) 5sh dl red brown ('47) 195.00 115.00
*Nos. M1-M7 (7)* 248.75 148.65

The letters in the overprints are the initials of "British Commonwealth Occupation Force."

---

## OFFICIAL STAMPS

Perforated Initials
In 1913-31, postage stamps were perforated "OS" for official use. This catalogue does not list varieties with perforated initials.

Overprinted 

On Regular Issue of 1931

**1931, May 4** **Unwmk.** *Perf. 11, 11½*

*O1* A8 2p dull red 60.00 20.00
*O2* A8 3p blue 175.00 37.50

These stamps were issued primarily for official use but to prevent speculation a quantity was issued for public distribution.

On Regular Issues of 1928-32

**1932** **Wmk. 203** *Perf. 13½x12½*

*O3* A4 2p red (II) 11.50 1.00
*O4* A4 4p olive bister 37.50 9.00

*Perf. 11½, 12*

*O5* A1 6p brown 67.50 32.50

**1932-33** **Wmk. 228** *Perf. 13½x12½*

*O6* A4 ½p orange 6.00 1.25
*a.* Inverted overprint 3,000. 1,500.
*O7* A4 1p green (I) 1.50 75
*O8* A4 2p red (II) 5.00 65
*a.* Inverted overprint 2,250.
*O9* A4 3p ultra (II) ('33) 14.00 8.50
*O10* A4 5p brown buff 50.00 21.00

*Perf. 11½, 12*

*O11* A1 6p yellow brown 35.00 18.00
*Nos. O6-O11 (6)* 111.50 50.15

**1932** **Unwmk.** *Perf. 11, 11½*

*O12* A9 2p red 6.00 4.50
*O13* A9 3p blue 18.00 18.00
*O14* A16 1sh gray green 57.50 32.50

---

## AUSTRALIAN ANTARCTIC TERRITORY

**Catalogue values for all unused stamps in this section are for Never Hinged items.**

All stamps are also valid for postage in Australia.

Edgeworth David, Douglas Mawson and A.F. McKay (1908-09 South Pole Expedition) — A1

Australian Explorers and Map of Antarctica — A2

Designs: 8p, Loading weasel (snow truck). 1sh, Dog team and iceberg (vert.). 2sh3p, Emperor penguins and map (vert.).

*Perf. 14½, 14½x14, 14x14½*

**1957-59** **Engr.** **Unwmk.**

*L1* A1 5p brown 55 6
*L2* A2 8p dark blue 2.50 1.10
*L3* A2 1sh dark green 4.50 1.90
*L4* A2 2sh ultra ('57) 3.75 28
*L5* A2 2sh3p green 12.50 5.50
*Nos. L1-L5 (5)* 23.80 8.84

Nos. L1 and L2 were printed as 4p and 7p stamps and surcharged typographically in black and dark blue before issuance.
Sizes of stamps: No. L2, 34x21mm; Nos. L3, L5, 21x34mm; No. L4, 43½x25½mm.

**1961, July 5** *Perf. 14½*

*L6* A1 5p dark blue 1.25 18

The denomination on No. L6 is not within a typographed circle, but is part of the engraved design.

Sir Douglas Mawson A3

Lookout and Iceberg A4

**1961, Oct. 18**

*L7* A3 5p dark green 75 18

50th anniv. of the 1911-14 Australian Antarctic Expedition.

*Perf. 13½x13, 13x13½*

**1966-68** **Photo.** **Unwmk.**

Designs: 1c, Aurora australis and camera dome. 2c, Banding penguins. 5c, Branding of elephant seals. 7c, Measuring snow strata. 10c, Wind gauges. 15c, Weather balloon. 20c, Helicopter. 25c, Radio operator. 50c, Ice compression tests. $1, "Mock sun" (parahelion) and dogs. (20c, 25c, 50c and $1 horizontal).

*L8* A4 1c multicolored 1.25 30
*L9* A4 2c multicolored 1.75 45
*L10* A4 4c multicolored 1.75 45
*L11* A4 5c multicolored 6.00 1.40
*L12* A4 7c multicolored 1.00 35
*L13* A4 10c multicolored 1.50 90
*L14* A4 15c multicolored 4.50 3.75
*L15* A4 20c multicolored 6.00 4.50
*L16* A4 25c multicolored 7.50 5.50
*L17* A4 50c multicolored 20.00 9.00
*L18* A4 $1 multicolored 50.00 20.00
*Nos. L8-L18 (11)* 101.25 46.60

Issue dates: 5c, Sept. 25, 1968. Others, Sept. 28, 1966.
Nos. L8-L18 are on phosphorescent helecon paper. Fluorescent orange is one of the colors used in printing the 10c, 15c, 20c and 50c.

*Australian Antarctic Territory stamps can be mounted in Scott's Australia and Dependencies Album.*

Sastrugi Snow Formation A5

Design: 30c, Pancake ice.

**1971, June 23** **Photo.** *Perf. 13x13½*

*L19* A5 6c blk, dp & brt bl 75 75
*L20* A5 30c multicolored 9.25 7.00

10th anniv. of the Antarctic Treaty pledging peaceful uses of and scientific cooperation in Antarctica.

Capt. Cook, Sextant, Azimuth Compass A6

Design: 35c, Chart of Cook's circumnavigation of Antarctica, and "Resolution."

**1972, Sept. 13** **Photo.** *Perf. 13x13½*

*L21* A6 7c bis & multi 2.00 95
*L22* A6 35c buff & multi 7.50 7.50

Bicentenary of Capt. James Cook's circumnavigation of Antarctica.

Plankton and Krill Shrimp — A7

Mawson's D.H. Gipsy Moth, 1931 — A8

Food Chain (Essential for Survival): 7c, Adelie penguin feeding on krill shrimp. 9c, Leopard seal pursuing fish (horiz.). 10c, Killer whale hunting seals (horiz.). 20c, Wandering albatross (horiz.). $1, Sperm whale attacking giant squid.
Explorers' Aircraft: 8c, Rymill's DH Fox Moth returning to Barry Island. 25c, Hubert Wilkins Lockheed Vega (horiz.). 30c, Lincoln Ellsworth's Northrop Gamma. 35c, Lars Christensen's Avro Avian and Framnes Mountains (horiz.). 50c, Richard Byrd's Ford Tri-Motor dropping US flag over South Pole.

*Perf. 13½x13, 13x13½*

**1973, Aug. 15**

*L23* A7 1c multicolored 8 8
*L24* A8 5c multicolored 8 16
*L25* A7 7c multicolored 1.65 60
*L26* A8 8c multicolored 35 35
*L27* A7 9c multicolored 30 30
*L28* A7 10c multicolored 4.00 1.25
*L29* A7 20c multicolored 42 42
*L30* A8 25c multicolored 42 42
*L31* A8 30c multicolored 42 42
*L32* A8 35c multicolored 40 55
*L33* A8 50c multicolored 1.50 85
*L34* A7 $1 multicolored 2.75 85
*Nos. L23-L34 (12)* 12.37 6.25

Adm. Byrd, Plane, Mountains A9

Design: 20c, Adm. Byrd, Floyd Bennett trimotored plane, map of Antarctica.

**1979, June 20** **Litho.** *Perf. 15½*

*L35* A9 20c multicolored 52 52
*L36* A9 55c multicolored 1.10 1.00

50th anniv. of first flight over South Pole by Richard Byrd (1888-1957).

S.Y. Nimrod
A10

*Perf. 13½x13, 13x13½*

**1974-81** **Litho.**

L37 A10 1c S.Y. Aurora 5 5
L38 A10 2c R.Y. Penola, vert. 5 5
L39 A10 5c M.V. Thala Dan, vert. 15 15
L40 A10 10c H.M.S. Challenger 15 15
L41 A10 15c shown 95 95
L42 A10 15c S.Y. Nimrod, stern view 25 22
L43 A10 20c R.R.S. Discovery II 32 30
L44 A10 22c R.Y.S. Terra Nova, vert. 28 28
L45 A10 25c S.S. Endurance, vert. 40 35
L46 A10 30c S.S. Fram 50 50
L47 A10 35c M.S. Nella Dan 45 45
L48 A10 40c M.S. Kista Dan, vert. 50 50
L49 A10 45c L'Astrolabe 55 55
L50 A10 50c S.S. Norvegia 70 70
L51 A10 55c S.Y. Discovery, vert. 80 80
L52 A10 $1 H.M.S. Resolution, vert. 1.25 65
*Nos. L37-L52 (16)* 7.35 6.65

Sir Douglas Mawson (1882-1958), Explorer — A11

**1982, May 5** **Litho.** *Perf. 14x13½*

L53 A11 27c Mawson, landscape 35 35
L54 A11 75c Mawson, map 1.25 1.25

Local Wildlife — A12

**1983, Apr. 6** **Litho.** *Perf. 14½*

L55 Strip of 5, multi 2.25 2.25
*a.* A12 27c Light-mantled sooty albatross 45 45
*b.* A12 27c Macquarie Isld. shags 45 45
*c.* A12 27c Elephant seals 45 45
*d.* A12 27c Royal penguins 45 45
*e.* A12 27c Antarctic prions 45 45

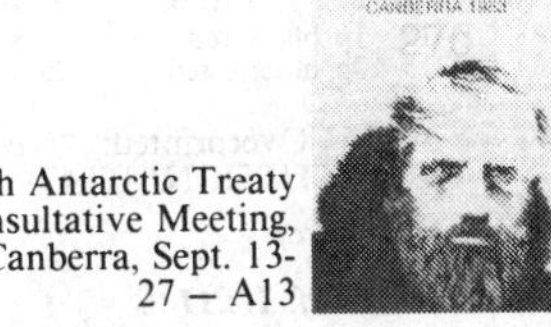
12th Antarctic Treaty Consultative Meeting, Canberra, Sept. 13-27 — A13

**1983, Sept. 7** **Litho.** *Perf. 14½*

L56 A13 27c multicolored 42 42

South Magnetic Pole Expedition, 75th Anniv. — A14

**1984, Jan. 16**

L57 A14 30c Prismatic compass 40 40
L58 A14 85c Aneroid barometer 1.25 1.25

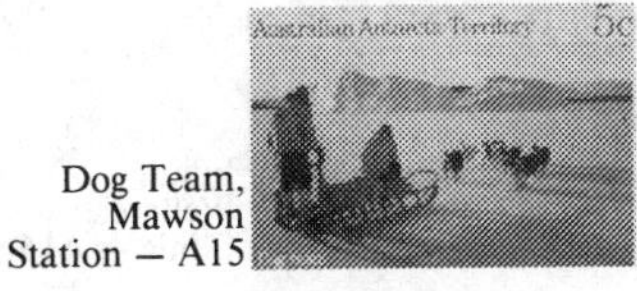
Dog Team, Mawson Station — A15

**1984-87** **Litho.** *Perf. 14½x15*

L60 A15 2c Summer afternoon 5 5
L61 A15 5c shown 8 8
L62 A15 10c Evening 14 14
L63 A15 15c Prince Charles Mts. 22 22
L64 A15 20c Morning 28 28
L65 A15 25c Sea ice, iceberg 40 40
L66 A15 30c Mt. Coates 48 48
L67 A15 33c Iceberg Alley, Mawson 48 48
L68 A15 36c Winter evening 50 50
L69 A15 45c Brash ice, vert. 65 65
L70 A15 60c Midwinter shadows 85 85
L71 A15 75c Coastline 1.20 1.20
L72 A15 85c Landing field 1.35 1.35
L73 A15 90c Pancake ice, vert. 1.30 1.30
L74 A15 $1 Emperor penguins, Auster Rookery 1.45 1.45
*Nos. L60-L74 (15)* 9.43 9.43

Antarctic Treaty, 25th Anniv. — A16

**1986, Sept. 17** **Litho.** *Perf. 14x13½*

L75 A16 36c multicolored 55 55

Environment, Conservation and Technology A17

Designs: a. Hour-glass dolphins and the *Nella Dan*. b. Emperor penguins and Davis Station. c. Crabeater seal and helicopters. d. Adelie penguins and snow-ice transport vehicle. e. Gray-headed albatross and photographer.

**1988, July 20** **Litho.** *Perf. 13*

L76 Strip of 5 3.10 1.20
*a.-e.* A17 37c any single 62 20

## BAHAMAS

LOCATION — A group of about 700 islands and 2,000 rocks in the West Indies, off the coast of Florida. Only 30 islands are inhabited.
GOVT. — Independent state in British Commonwealth.
AREA — 5,353 sq. mi.
POP. — 209,505 (1980).
CAPITAL — Nassau.

The principal island, on which the capital is located, is New Providence. The Bahamas obtained internal self-government on January 7, 1964, and independence on July 10, 1973.

12 Pence = 1 Shilling
20 Shillings = 1 Pound
100 Cents = 1 Dollar (1966)

**Catalogue values for unused stamps in this country are for Never Hinged items, beginning with Scott 130.**

Pen cancellations usually indicate revenue use. Such stamps sell for much less than postally canceled copies. Stamps with revenue or pen cancellations removed are often found with forged postal cancellations. Value, 50 cents to $2.50.

Queen Victoria
A1 A2

**1859-60** **Unwmk.** **Engr.** *Imperf.*

1 A1 1p dl lake ('60) 45.00 875.00
*a.* 1p redsh lake 6,000. 3,000.
*b.* 1p brnsh lake 3,000. 2,500.

Most unused copies of No. 1 are remainders, and false cancellations are plentiful. Nos. 1a and 1b are on thicker paper than No. 1.

**1861** *Rough Perf. 14 to 16*

2 A1 1p lake 725.00 200.00
*a.* Clean-cut perf. 1,400. 825.00
3 A2 4p dl rose 1,100. 500.00
*a.* Imperf. between, pair
4 A2 6p gray lil 3,750. 475.00

**1862** *Perf. 11½, 12*

5 A1 1p lake 475.00 140.00
*a.* Horiz. or vert. pair, imperf. between 8,000.
6 A2 4p dl rose 2,500. 250.00
7 A2 6p gray vio 2,750. 400.00

No. 5a was not issued in the Bahamas.
Nos. 5-7 exist with perf. 11½ or 12 compound with 11.

*Perf. 13*

8 A1 1p brn lake 300.00 125.00
*a.* 1p car lake 300.00 125.00
9 A2 4p rose 2,500. 250.00
10 A2 6p gray vio 3,000. 190.00
*a.* 6p dl vio 3,000. 375.00

Queen Victoria — A3

**1863-75** **Wmk. 1** *Perf. 12½*

11 A1 1p lake 45.00 40.00
*a.* 1p brn lake 45.00 40.00
*b.* 1p rose lake 45.00 40.00
12 A1 1p vermilion 42.50 42.50
13 A2 4p rose 225.00 50.00
*a.* 4p rose lake 250.00 67.50
*b.* 4p brt rose 140.00 50.00
14 A2 6p dk vio 110.00 40.00
*a.* 6p vio 250.00 65.00
*b.* 6p rose lil 4,750. 3,750.
*c.* 6p lil 300.00 65.00
15 A3 1sh grn ('64) 2,750. 275.00

**1863-81** *Perf. 14*

16 A1 1p vermilion 30.00 14.00
17 A1 1p car lake (anil) 2,250.
18 A2 4p rose 500.00 35.00
*a.* 4p dp rose 500.00 42.50
19 A3 1sh grn ('63) 5.00 5.00

**1882-98** **Wmk. Crown and C.A. (2)**

20 A1 1p vermilion 350.00 37.50
21 A2 4p rose 600.00 40.00
22 A3 1sh green 27.50 15.00
23 A3 1sh bl grn ('98) 25.00 15.00

*Perf. 12*

24 A1 1p vermilion 32.50 27.50
25 A2 4p rose 400.00 40.00

No. 14a Surcharged in Black **FOURPENCE**

**1883** **Wmk. 1** *Perf. 12½*

26 A2 4p on 6p vio 575.00 275.00

The surcharge, being handstamped, is found in various positions.

Queen Victoria
A5

Queen's Staircase
A6

**Wmk. Crown and C. A. (2)**

**1884-90** **Typo.** *Perf. 14*

27 A5 1p car rose 2.50 85
*a.* 1p pale rose 11.00 6.00
28 A5 2½p ultra 2.00 1.10
*a.* 2½p dl bl 11.00 7.50
29 A5 4p yellow 3.75 3.75
30 A5 6p violet 2.50 5.25
31 A5 5sh ol grn 40.00 50.00
32 A5 £1 brown 325.00 200.00
Revenue cancellation 45.00

Cleaned fiscally used copies of No. 32 are often found with postmarks of small post offices added.

**1901-03** **Engr.** **Wmk. 1**

33 A6 1p car & blk 2.25 3.25
34 A6 5p org & blk ('03) 8.25 14.00
35 A6 2sh ultra & blk ('03) 9.50 15.00
36 A6 3sh grn & blk ('03) 15.00 22.50

See Nos. 48, 58-62, 71, 78, 81-82.

Edward VII
A7

George V
A8

**1902** **Wmk. 2** **Typo.**

37 A7 1p car rose 1.90 80
38 A7 2½p ultra 6.00 2.25
39 A7 4p orange 5.00 8.75
40 A7 6p bis brn 6.00 7.75
41 A7 1sh gray blk & car 7.25 9.50
42 A7 5sh vio & ultra 32.50 40.00
43 A7 £1 grn & blk 225.00 375.00
*Nos. 37-43 (7)* 283.65 444.05

**1906-11** **Wmk. 3**

44 A7 ½p green 3.75 1.40
45 A7 1p car rose 5.00 90
46 A7 2½p ultra ('07) 14.00 17.50
47 A7 6p bis brn ('11) 42.50 55.00

**1910-16** **Engr.**

48 A6 1p red & gray blk ('16) 1.50 1.50
*a.* 1p car & blk 5.50 5.50

**1912-19** **Typo.**

49 A8 ½p green 85 1.25
50 A8 1p car rose 1.75 35
50A A8 2p gray ('19) 1.75 2.25
51 A8 2½p ultra 4.00 5.75
52 A8 4p orange 1.75 3.00
53 A8 6p bis brn 1.75 3.00

**Chalky Paper**

54 A8 1sh blk & red 2.50 3.00
55 A8 5sh vio & ultra 22.50 20.00
56 A8 £1 grn & blk 185.00 250.00
*Nos. 49-56 (9)* 221.85 288.60

**1917-19** **Engr.**

58 A6 3p pur, *yel* 8.50 9.50
59 A6 3p brn & blk ('19) 2.50 5.25
60 A6 5p vio & blk 2.50 7.50
61 A6 2sh ultra & blk 14.00 21.00
62 A6 3sh grn & blk 32.50 35.00
*Nos. 58-62 (5)* 60.00 78.25

**Peace Commemorative Issue**

King George V and Seal of Bahamas — A9

**1920, Mar. 1** **Engr.** *Perf. 14*

65 A9 ½p gray grn 42 2.25
66 A9 1p dp red 1.10 90
67 A9 2p gray 2.75 4.75

*68* A9 3p brown 2.75 *9.50*
*69* A9 1sh dk grn 22.50 *30.00*
*Nos. 65-69 (5)* 29.52 47.40

Types of 1901-12
**Typo., Engr. (A6)**

**1921-34** **Wmk. 4**
*70* A8 ½p grn ('24) 12 10
*71* A6 1p car & blk 85 85
*72* A8 1p car rose 16 12
*73* A8 1½p fawn ('34) 80 *1.25*
*74* A8 2p gray ('27) 65 *2.25*
*75* A8 2½p ultra ('22) 65 *2.25*
*76* A8 3p vio, *yel* ('31) 5.75 *11.00*
*77* A8 4p yel ('24) 1.50 *4.75*
*78* A6 5p red vio & gray blk ('29) 5.75 *9.00*
*79* A8 6p bis brn ('22) 90 *4.00*
*80* A8 1sh blk & red ('26) 3.00 *8.25*
*81* A6 2sh ultra & blk ('22) 30.00 *50.00*
*82* A8 3sh grn & blk ('24) 42.50 *55.00*
*83* A8 5sh vio & ultra ('24) 25.00 *32.50*
*84* A8 £1 grn & blk ('26) 140.00 *225.00*
*Nos. 70-84 (15)* 257.63 406.32

The 3p, 1sh, 5sh and £1 are on chalky paper.

Seal of Bahamas — A10

**1930, Jan. 2** **Engr.** ***Perf. 12***
*85* A10 1p red & blk 1.10 *2.75*
*86* A10 3p dp brn & blk 3.50 *7.75*
*87* A10 5p dk vio & blk 4.00 *7.75*
*88* A10 2sh ultra & blk 25.00 *40.00*
*89* A10 3sh dp grn & blk 32.50 *60.00*
*Nos. 85-89 (5)* 66.10 118.25

The dates on the stamps commemorate important events in the history of the colony. The first British occupation was in 1629. The Bahamas were ceded to Great Britain in 1729 and a treaty of peace was signed by that country, France and Spain. The third and second centenaries of those events are commemorated by the date 1929.

Type of 1930 Issue
Without Dates at Top

**1931-42**
*90* A10 2sh ultra & blk 80 80
*a.* 2sh ultra & sl pur ('42) 12.00 11.00
*91* A10 3sh dp grn & blk 90 90
*a.* 3sh dp grn & sl pur ('42) 11.00 11.00

**Silver Jubilee Issue**
Common Design Type

**1935, May 6** ***Perf. 13½x14***
*92* CD301 1½p car & bl 38 28
*93* CD301 2½p bl & brn 1.25 1.75
*94* CD301 6p ol grn & lt bl 3.00 *4.75*
*95* CD301 1sh brt vio & ind 4.75 *6.50*

Flamingos in Flight A11

**1935, May 22** ***Perf. 12½***
*96* A11 8p car & ultra 5.50 3.50

**Coronation Issue**
Common Design Type

**1937, May 12** ***Perf. 13½x14***
*97* CD302 ½p dp grn 12 12
*98* CD302 1½p brown 20 20
*99* CD302 2½p brt ultra 60 60

George VI — A12

Sea Gardens, Nassau — A13

Fort Charlotte A14

Flamingos in Flight A15

**1938-46** **Typo.** **Wmk. 4** ***Perf. 14***
*100* A12 ½p green 8 8
*101* A12 1p carmine 1.10 85
*101A* A12 1p gray ('41) 10 10
*102* A12 1½p red brn 14 14
*103* A12 2p gray 8.75 *14.00*
*103B* A12 2p car ('41) 18 18
*c.* "TWO PENCE" double *1,750.*
*104* A12 2½p ultra 1.40 85
*104A* A12 2½p lt vio ('43) 20 20
*105* A12 3p lt vio 5.50 *7.50*
*105A* A12 3p ultra ('43) 28 35

**Engr.**
***Perf. 12½***
*106* A13 4p red org & bl 52 45
*107* A14 6p bl & ol grn 35 28
*108* A15 8p car & ultra 70 60

**Typo.**
***Perf. 14***
*109* A12 10p yel org ('46) 48 48
*110* A12 1sh blk & car 85 70
*112* A12 5sh pur & ultra 7.50 6.00
*a.* 5sh lil & lt ultra 30.00 30.00
*113* A12 £1 grn & blk 27.50 *25.00*
*Nos. 100-113 (17)* 55.63 57.76

See Nos. 154-156.

No. 104 Surcharged in Black **3d.**

**1940, Nov. 28** ***Perf. 14***
*115* A12 3p on 2½p ultra 25 25

Stamps of 1931-42 Overprinted in Black **1492 LANDFALL OF COLUMBUS 1942**

**1942, Oct. 12** ***Perf. 14, 12½, 12***
*116* A12 ½p green 6 6
*117* A12 1p gray 6 6
*118* A12 1½p red brn 8 8
*119* A12 2p carmine 8 8
*120* A12 2½p ultra 12 12
*121* A12 3p ultra 12 12
*122* A13 4p red org & bl 15 15
*123* A14 6p bl & ol grn 26 26
*124* A15 8p car & ultra 30 30
*125* A12 1sh blk & car 40 40
*126* A10 2sh dk ultra & blk 3.75 *8.75*
*a.* 2sh ultra & sl pur 5.75 *13.00*
*127* A10 3sh dp grn & sl pur 2.25 *8.75*
*a.* 3sh dp grn & blk 7.00 *16.00*
*128* A12 5sh lil & ultra 3.00 *8.75*
*129* A12 £1 grn & blk 16.00 *27.50*
*Nos. 116-129 (14)* 26.63 55.38

Issued in commemoration of the 450th anniversary of the discovery of America by Columbus.

Two printings of the basic stamps were overprinted, the first with dark gum, the second with white gum.

**Catalogue values for unused stamps in this section, from this point to the end of the section, are for Never Hinged items.**

**Peace Issue**
Common Design Type
***Perf. 13½x14***

**1946, Nov. 11** **Engr.** **Wmk. 4**
*130* CD303 1½p brown 12 12
*131* CD303 3p dp bl 16 16

Infant Welfare Clinic — A16

Designs: 1p, Modern agriculture. 1½p, Sisal. 2p, Native straw work. 2½p, Modern dairying. 3p, Fishing fleet. 4p, Out island settlement. 6p, Tuna fishing. 8p, Paradise Beach. 10p, Modern hotel. 1sh, Yacht racing. 2sh, Water skiing. 3sh, Shipbuilding. 5sh, Modern transportation. 10sh, Modern salt production. £1, Parliament Building.

**1948, Oct. 11** **Unwmk.** ***Perf. 12***
*132* A16 ½p orange 12 12
*133* A16 1p ol grn 15 15
*134* A16 1½p ol bis 35 35
*135* A16 2p vermilion 24 24
*136* A16 2½p red brn 65 65
*137* A16 3p brt ultra 45 45
*138* A16 4p gray blk 48 1.65
*139* A16 6p emerald 65 1.65
*140* A16 8p violet 65 1.50
*141* A16 10p rose car 75 75
*142* A16 1sh ol brn 1.25 1.25
*143* A16 2sh claret 5.75 *10.50*
*144* A16 3sh brt bl 6.25 *10.50*
*145* A16 5sh purple 4.75 *9.25*
*146* A16 10sh dk gray 5.00 *12.50*
*147* A16 £1 red org 10.00 *19.00*
*Nos. 132-147 (16)* 37.49 70.51

Issued to commemorate the 300th anniversary, in 1947, of the settlement of the colony.

**Silver Wedding Issue**
Common Design Type
***Perf. 14x14½***

**1948, Dec. 1** **Wmk. 4** **Photo.**
*148* CD304 1½p red brn 16 7

**Engr.; Name Typo.**
***Perf. 11½x11***
*149* CD305 £1 gray grn 37.50 *42.50*

**UPU Issue**
Common Design Types
**Engr.; Name Typo. on #151 & 152.**

**1949, Oct. 10** ***Perf. 13½, 11x11½***
*150* CD306 2½p violet 25 25
*151* CD307 3p indigo 50 50
*152* CD308 6p bl gray 1.00 1.00
*153* CD309 1sh rose car 1.65 1.65

George VI Type of 1938
***Perf. 13½x14***

**1951-52** **Wmk. 4** **Typo.**
*154* A12 ½p cl ('52) 20 20
*a.* Wmk. 4a (error) *1,250.*
*155* A12 2p green 40 40
*156* A12 3p rose red ('52) 80 *3.00*

**Coronation Issue**
Common Design Type

**1953, June 3** **Engr.** ***Perf. 13½x13***
*157* CD312 6p bl & blk 60 60

Infant Welfare Clinic A17

Designs: 1p, Modern Agriculture. 1½p, Out island settlement. 2p, Native strawwork. 3p, Fishing fleet. 4p, Water skiing. 5p, Modern dairying. 6p, Modern transportation. 8p, Paradise Beach. 10p, Modern hotels. 1sh, Yacht racing. 2sh, Sisal. 2sh6p, Shipbuilding. 5sh, Tuna fishing. 10sh, Modern salt production. £1, Parliament Building.

**1954, Jan. 1** ***Perf. 11x11½***
*158* A17 ½p red org & blk 9 7
*159* A17 1p org brn & ol grn 10 7
*a.* Bklt pane of 4 52
*160* A17 1½p blk & bl 15 10
*a.* Bklt pane of 4 70
*161* A17 2p dk grn & brn org 15 9
*a.* Bklt pane of 4 70
*162* A17 3p dp car & blk 18 12
*163* A17 4p lil rose & bl grn 28 25
*a.* Bklt pane of 4 1.75
*164* A17 5p dp ultra & brn 65 *1.75*
*165* A17 6p blk & aqua 42 25
*a.* Bklt pane of 4 2.25
*166* A17 8p rose vio & blk 48 25
*a.* Bklt pane of 4 2.50
*167* A17 10p ultra & blk 55 35
*168* A17 1sh ol brn & ultra 65 52
*169* A17 2sh blk & brn org 1.10 75
*170* A17 2sh6p dp bl & blk 2.50 1.10
*171* A17 5sh dp org & emer 5.00 2.50
*172* A17 10sh grnsh blk & blk 7.00 5.00
*173* A17 £1 vio & grnsh blk 15.00 11.00
*Nos. 158-173 (16)* 34.30 24.17

See No. 203.

Queen Elizabeth II — A18

**Wmk. 314**

**1959, June 10** **Engr.** ***Perf. 13***
**Portrait in Black**
*174* A18 1p dk red 12 12
*175* A18 2p green 14 14
*176* A18 6p blue 28 28
*177* A18 10p brown 55 55

Cent. of the 1st postage stamp of Bahamas.

Christ Church Cathedral, Nassau — A19

Design: 10p, Public Library.

***Perf. 14x13***

**1962, Jan. 30** **Photo.** **Unwmk.**
*178* A19 8p emerald 60 60
*179* A19 10p violet 60 60

Centenary of the city of Nassau.

**Freedom from Hunger Issue**
Common Design Type
***Perf. 14x14½***

**1963, June 4** **Wmk. 314**
*180* CD314 8p sepia 1.25 1.10
*a.* "8d" and "BAHAMAS" omitted 1,000. 1,000.

Nos. 166-167 Overprinted: "BAHAMAS TALKS/ 1962"
***Perf. 11x11½***

**1963, July 15** **Engr.** **Wmk. 4**
*181* A17 8p rose vio & blk 1.00 85
*182* A17 10p ultra & blk 1.75 1.65

Meeting of Pres. Kennedy and Prime Minister Harold Macmillan, Dec. 1962.

**Red Cross Centenary Issue**
Common Design Type
**Wmk. 314**

**1963, Sept. 2** **Litho.** ***Perf. 13***
*183* CD315 1p blk & red 18 10
*184* CD315 10p ultra & red 2.00 1.40

Type of 1954 Overprinted: "NEW CONSTITUTION/ 1964"

Designs as Before

***Perf. 11x11½***

**1964, Jan. 7** **Engr.** **Wmk. 314**
*185* A17 ½p red org & blk 5 5
*186* A17 1p org brn & ol grn 5 5
*187* A17 1½p blk & bl 5 5
*188* A17 2p dk grn & brn org 7 7
*189* A17 3p dp car & blk 10 10
*190* A17 4p lil rose & bl grn 15 15
*191* A17 5p dp ultra & brn 18 18
*192* A17 6p blk & aqua 20 20
*193* A17 8p rose vio & blk 28 28
*194* A17 10p ultra & blk 38 32
*195* A17 1sh ol brn & ultra 52 45
*196* A17 2sh blk & brn org 1.10 95
*197* A17 2sh6p dp bl & blk 1.40 1.25
*198* A17 5sh dp org & emer 2.75 2.50
*199* A17 10sh grnsh blk & blk 5.00 4.75

*200* A17 £1 vio & grnsh blk 10.50 9.50
*Nos. 185-200 (16)* 22.78 20.85

**Shakespeare Issue**
Common Design Type
***Perf. 14x14½***

**1964, Apr. 23 Photo. Wmk. 314**
*201* CD316 6p grnsh bl 42 35

Type of 1954 Surcharged with Olympic Rings, New Value and Bars
***Perf. 11x11½***

**1964, Oct. 1 Engr. Wmk. 314**
*202* A17 8p on 1sh ol brn & ultra 45 45

18th Olympic Games, Tokyo, Oct. 10-25.

Queen Type of 1954

**1964, Oct. 6 Wmk. 314**
*203* A17 2p dk grn & brn org 50 50

Out Island Regatta A21

Designs: ½p, Colony badge. 1½p, Princess Margaret Hospital. 2p, High School. 3p, Flamingo. 4p, Liner "Queen Elizabeth." 6p, Island development. 8p, Yachting. 10p, Public Square, Nassau. 1sh, Sea Garden, Nassau. 2sh, Cannons at Fort Charlotte. 2sh6p, Sea plane and jetliner. 5sh, 1914 Williamson film project and 1939 underwater post office. 10sh, Conch shell. £1, Columbus' flagship.

**Engr. and Litho.**
***Perf. 13½x13***

**1965, Jan. 7 Wmk. 314**
*204* A21 ½p multi & bl, *bluish* 5 5
*205* A21 1p bl, dk grn & org 6 5
*a.* Bklt pane of 4 38
*206* A21 1½p grn, rose red & brn 9 7
*a.* Bklt pane of 4 45
*207* A21 2p grn, sl & bl 10 7
*a.* Bklt pane of 4 55
*208* A21 3p lt bl, red & pur 18 11
*209* A21 4p dl bl, brt grn & brn org 22 18
*a.* Bklt pane of 4 1.10
*210* A21 6p bl, dl grn & rose 30 18
*a.* Bklt pane of 4 1.25
*211* A21 8p grnsh bl, lil & ol grn 38 35
*a.* Bklt pane of 4 1.65
*212* A21 10p grn, lt brn & vio 35 18
*213* A21 1sh multi & grn, *grnsh* 55 30
*214* A21 2sh bl, brn & emer, *grnsh* 1.10 75
*215* A21 2sh6p bl, ol & ver rose 1.50 95
*216* A21 5sh brn org, dk bl & grn 3.00 1.90
*217* A21 10sh bl, pink & sep 6.00 4.25
*218* A21 £1 bl, brn & rose red 12.00 8.50
*Nos. 204-218 (15)* 25.88 17.89

Booklet panes were issued Mar. 23, 1965.
See Nos. 252-266.

**ITU Issue**
Common Design Type
***Perf. 11x11½***

**1965, May 17 Litho. Wmk. 314**
*219* CD317 1p emer & org 18 18
*220* CD317 2sh lil & ol 2.25 2.25

No. 211 Surcharged 9d

**Engr. & Litho.**

**1965, July 12 *Perf. 13½x13***
*221* A21 9p on 8p grnsh bl, lil & ol grn 60 60

**Intl. Cooperation Year Issue**
Common Design Type
**Wmk. 314**

**1965, Oct. 25 Litho. *Perf. 14½***
*222* CD318 ½p bl grn & cl 6 6
*223* CD318 1sh lt vio & grn 85 70

**Churchill Memorial Issue**
Common Design Type

**1966, Jan. 24 Photo. *Perf. 14***
*224* CD319 ½p multicolored 5 5
*225* CD319 2p multicolored 20 20
*226* CD319 10p multicolored 1.00 1.00
*227* CD319 1sh multicolored 1.50 1.50

**Royal Visit Issue**
Common Design Type Inscribed "Royal Visit / 1966"

**1966, Feb. 4 Litho. *Perf. 11x12***
*228* CD320 6p vio bl 65 65
*229* CD320 1sh dk car rose 1.65 1.65

Nos. 204-218 Surcharged 

**Engr. & Litho.**
***Perf. 13½x13***

**1966, May 25 Wmk. 314**
*230* A21 1c on ½p multi 5 5
*231* A21 2c on 1p multi 8 7
*232* A21 3c on 2p multi 10 8
*233* A21 4c on 3p multi 12 10
*234* A21 5c on 4p multi 14 12
*a.* Surch. omitted, vert. strip of 10 5,000.
*235* A21 8c on 6p multi 20 18
*236* A21 10c on 8p multi 24 20
*237* A21 11c on 1½p multi 35 20
*238* A21 12c on 10p multi 40 24
*239* A21 15c on 1sh multi 48 30
*240* A21 22c on 2sh multi 65 35
*241* A21 50c on 2sh6p multi 1.40 1.00
*242* A21 $1 on 5sh multi 2.75 2.00
*243* A21 $2 on 10sh multi 5.50 4.00
*244* A21 $3 on £1 multi 8.25 6.00
*Nos. 230-244 (15)* 20.71 14.89

The denominations are next to the bars instead of below on Nos. 232, 235-240; the length of the bars varies to cover old denomination.

No. 234a, if single, is identical with No. 209, but distinguishable if in vertical strip of 7 to 10. No. 234 was printed in sheets of 100 (10x10); No. 209 in sheets of 60 (10x6).

**World Cup Soccer Issue**
Common Design Type

**1966, July 1 Litho. *Perf. 14***
*245* CD321 8c multi 30 30
*246* CD321 15c multi 60 60

**WHO Headquarters Issue**
Common Design Type

**1966, Sept. 20 Litho. *Perf. 14***
*247* CD322 11c multi 52 52
*248* CD322 15c multi 70 70

**UNESCO Anniversary Issue**
Common Design Type

**1966, Dec. 1 Litho. *Perf. 14***
*249* CD323 3c "Education" 14 14
*250* CD323 15c "Science" 65 65
*251* CD323 $1 "Culture" 3.25 3.25

Type of 1965
Values in Cents and Dollars.
**Engr. and Litho.**
***Perf. 13½x13***

**1967, May 25 Wmk. 314**

Designs: 1c, Colony badge. 2c, Out Island Regatta. 3c, High School. 4c Flamingo. 5c, Liner "Oceanic." 8c, Island development. 10c, Yachting. 11c, Princess Margaret Hospital. 12c, Public Square, Nassau. 15c, Sea Garden, Nassau. 22c, Cannon at Fort Charlotte. 50c, Sea plane and jetliner. $1, 1914 Williamson film project and 1939 underwater post office. $2, Conch shell. $3, Columbus' flagship.

*252* A21 1c brn & multi 5 5
*253* A21 2c grn, sl & bl 8 7
*254* A21 3c grn, ind & vio 10 7
*255* A21 4c ultra, bl & red 15 8
*256* A21 5c pur, bl & ind 15 8
*257* A21 8c dk brn, bl & dl grn 22 16
*258* A21 10c car rose, bl & pur 25 16
*259* A21 11c bl, grn & rose red 35 24
*260* A21 12c ol grn, bl & lt brn 40 20
*261* A21 15c rose & multi 52 32
*262* A21 22c rose red, brn & bl 60 40
*263* A21 50c emer, ol & bl 1.40 90
*264* A21 $1 sep, brn org & dk bl 2.75 1.75
*265* A21 $2 grn & multi 5.50 4.25
*266* A21 $3 pur, bl & brn org 8.50 6.75
*Nos. 252-266 (15)* 21.02 15.48

Nos. 252-266 are on toned paper. Printings on very white, untinted paper appeared between late 1969 and May, 1971. Value, set $500.

Seal of Bahamas, Queen Elizabeth II and Lord Baden-Powell — A22

Designs: 15c, Scout emblem and portraits as on 3c.

***Perf. 14x13½***

**1967, Sept. 1 Photo. Wmk. 314**
*267* A22 3c multi 22 22
*268* A22 15c multi 85 85

60th anniversary of world Scouting.

Human Rights Flame and Globe A23

Designs: 12c, Human rights flame and scales of justice. $1, Human rights flame and Seal of Bahamas.

**1968, May 13 Litho. *Perf. 14***
*269* A23 3c multi 12 12
*270* A23 12c multi 50 50
*271* A23 $1 multi 2.25 2.25

International Human Rights Year 1968.

Golf — A24

Designs: 11c, Yachting. 15c, Horse racing. 50c, Water skiing.

**1968, Aug. Unwmk. *Perf. 13½***
*272* A24 5c multi 25 25
*273* A24 11c multi 52 52
*274* A24 15c multi 65 65
*275* A24 50c multi 2.25 2.25

Tourist publicity.

Olympic Monument and Sailboat — A25

Olympic Monument, San Salvador Island, Bahamas, and: 11c, Long jump. 50c, Running. $1, Sailing.

**1968, Sept. 30 Photo. *Perf. 14½x14***
*276* A25 5c multi 16 16
*277* A25 11c multi 40 40
*278* A25 50c multi 1.65 1.65
*279* A25 $1 multi 3.50 3.50

Issued to publicize the 19th Olympic Games, Mexico City, Oct. 12-27.

Legislative Building — A26

Designs: 10c, Bahamas mace and Big Ben, London (vert.). 12c, Local straw market (vert.). 15c, Horse-drawn surrey.

***Perf. 14½***

**1968, Nov. 1 Unwmk. Litho.**
*280* A26 3c brt bl & multi 14 14
*281* A26 10c yel, blk & bl 38 38
*282* A26 12c brt rose & multi 42 42
*283* A26 15c grn & multi 52 52

14th Commonwealth Parliamentary Conf., Nassau, Nov. 1-8.

$100 Coin with Queen Elizabeth II and Landing of Columbus — A27

Gold Coins with Elizabeth II on Obverse: 12c, $50 coin and Santa Maria flagship. 15c, $20 coin and Nassau Harbor Lighthouse. $1, $10 coin and Fort.

**Engr. on Gold Paper**

**1968, Dec. 2 Unwmk. *Perf. 13½***
*284* A27 3c dk red 18 18
*285* A27 12c dk grn 60 60
*286* A27 15c lilac 70 70
*287* A27 $1 black 4.25 2.25

First gold coinage in the Bahamas.

Bahamas Postal Card and Airplane Wing A28

Design: 15c, Seaplane, 1929.

***Perf. 14½x14***

**1969, Jan. 30 Litho. Unwmk.**
*288* A28 12c multi 90 90
*289* A28 15c multi 1.25 1.25

Issued to commemorate the 50th anniversary of the first flight from Nassau, Bahamas, to Miami, Fla., Jan. 30, 1919.

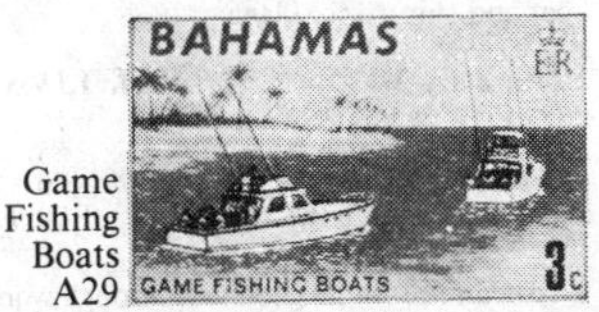

Game Fishing Boats A29

Designs: 11c, Paradise Beach. 12c, Sunfish sailboats. 15c, Parade on Rawson Square.

**1969, Aug. 26 Litho. Wmk. 314**
*290* A29 3c multi 16 16
*291* A29 11c multi 60 60
*292* A29 12c multi 65 65
*293* A29 15c multi 80 80
*a.* Souv. sheet of 4 4.25 4.25

Tourist publicity.

No. 293a contains one each of Nos. 290-293 with decorative margin and inscription. Size: 129x94mm.

Holy Family, by Nicolas Poussin — A30

Paintings: 3c, Adoration of the Shepherds, by Louis Le Nain. 12c, Adoration of the Kings, by Gerard David. 15c, Adoration of the Kings, by Vincenzo Foppa.

**1969, Oct. 15 Photo. *Perf. 12***

*294* A30 3c red & multi 15 15
*295* A30 11c emer & multi 60 60
*296* A30 12c ultra & multi 70 70
*297* A30 15c multi 90 90

Christmas 1969.

Girl Guides, Globe and Flags — A31

Designs: 12c, Yellow elder and Brownie emblem. 15c, Ranger emblem.

**1970, Feb. 23 Wmk. 314 *Perf. 14½***

*298* A31 3c vio bl, yel & red 18 18
*299* A31 12c dk brn, grn & yel 60 60
*300* A31 15c vio bl, bluish grn & yel 80 80

60th anniversary of the Girl Guides.

U.P.U. Headquarters, Bern — A32

**1970, May Litho. *Perf. 14½***

*301* A32 3c ver & multi 12 12
*302* A32 15c org & multi 75 75

Issued to commemorate the opening of the new U.P.U. Headquarters, Bern.

Bus and Globe A33

Designs (Globe and): 11c, Train. 12c, Sailboat and ship. 15c, Plane.

**1970, July 14 *Perf. 13½x13***

*303* A33 3c org & multi 16 16
*304* A33 11c emer & multi 65 65
*305* A33 12c multi 70 70
*306* A33 15c bl & multi 1.00 1.00
*a.* Souvenir sheet of 4 7.25 7.25

Issued to promote good will through world-wide travel and tourism. No. 306a contains one each of Nos. 303-306, blue decorative labels and emerald border. Size: 163x126mm.

People, Palms and Flamingo A34

Design: 15c, Red Cross Headquarters, Nassau, and marlin.

**1970, Aug. 18 *Perf. 14x14½***

*307* A34 3c multi 10 10
*308* A34 15c multi 80 80

Centenary of British Red Cross Society.

Nativity by G. B. Pittoni — A35

Designs: 11c, Holy Family, by Anton Raphael Mengs. 12c, Adoration of the Shepherds, by Giorgione. 15c, Adoration of the Shepherds, School of Seville.

***Perf. 12½x13***

**1970, Nov. 3 Litho. Wmk. 314**

*309* A35 3c multi 16 16
*310* A35 11c red org & multi 55 55
*311* A35 12c emer & multi 65 65
*312* A35 15c bl & multi 80 80
*a.* Souvenir sheet of 4 2.25 2.25

Christmas 1970.

No. 312a contains one each of Nos. 309-312, 3 labels and commemorative inscription. Size: 115x139mm.

International Airport A36

Designs: 2c, Breadfruit. 3c, Straw market. 4c, 6c, Hawksbill turtle. 5c, Grouper. 8c, Yellow elder. 10c, Bahamian sponge boat. 11c, Flamingos. 7c, 12c, Hibiscus. 15c, Bonefish. 18c, 22c, Royal poinciana. 50c, Post office, Nassau. $1, Pineapple (vert.). $2, Crayfish (vert.). $3, "Junkanoo" (costumed drummer) (vert.).

**Wmk. 314 Upright (Sideways on $1, $2, $3)**

**1971 Litho. *Perf. 14½x14, 14x14½***

*313* A36 1c bl & multi 7 7
*314* A36 2c red & multi 8 8
*315* A36 3c lil & multi 8 8
*316* A36 4c brn & multi 38 38
*317* A36 5c dp org & multi 28 26
*318* A36 6c brn & multi 14 14
*319* A36 7c grn & multi 28 26
*320* A36 8c yel & multi 60 38
*321* A36 10c red & multi 32 32
*322* A36 11c red & multi 35 35
*323* A36 12c grn & multi 1.00 1.00
*324* A36 15c gray & multi 28 28
*325* A36 18c multi 35 35
*326* A36 22c grn & multi 1.25 1.25
*327* A36 50c multi 1.40 1.25
*328* A36 $1 red & multi 3.00 2.50
*329* A36 $2 bl & multi 5.75 5.00
*330* A36 $3 vio bl & multi 9.00 8.00
*Nos. 313-330 (18)* 24.61 21.95

See Nos. 398-401, 426-443.

**Wmk. 314 Sideways (Upright on $1, $2, $3).**

**1973**

**Colors as Before**

*317a* A36 5c 15 15
*320a* A36 8c 25 25
*327a* A36 50c 1.50 1.50
*328a* A36 $1 3.00 3.00
*329a* A36 $2 5.75 5.75
*330a* A36 $3 8.75 8.75
*Nos. 317a-330a (6)* 19.40 19.40

**1976 Wmk. 373**

**Colors as Before**

*313a* A36 1c 5 5
*314a* A36 2c 5 5
*315a* A36 3c 7 7
*317b* A36 5c 14 14
*320b* A36 8c 15 15
*321a* A36 10c 18 18
*327b* A36 50c 1.25 1.25
*328b* A36 $1 2.50 2.50
*329b* A36 $2 4.75 4.75
*330b* A36 $3 7.50 7.50
*Nos. 313a-330b (10)* 16.64 16.64

Snowflake with Peace Signs A37

Designs: 11c, "Peace on Earth" with doves. 15c, Christmas wreath around old Bahamas coat of arms. 18c, Star of Bethlehem over palms.

***Perf. 14x14½***

**1971 Photo. Wmk. 314**

*331* A37 3c dp lil rose, gold & org 14 14
*332* A37 11c vio & gold 45 45
*333* A37 15c gold embossed & multi 65 65
*334* A37 18c brt bl, gold & vio bl 90 90
*a.* Souvenir sheet of 4 2.50 2.50

Christmas 1971. No. 334a contains one each of Nos. 331-334 perf. 15. Gold margin, violet inscription. Size: 126x95mm.

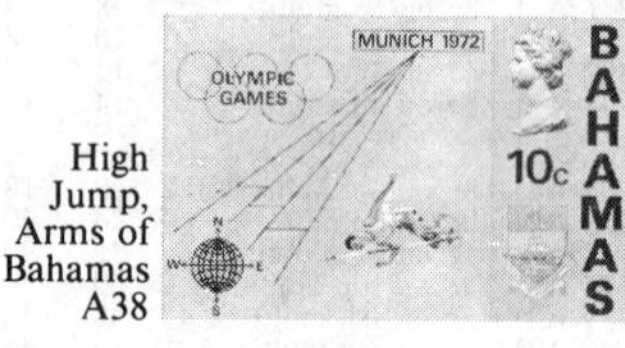

High Jump, Arms of Bahamas A38

Designs (Olympic Rings, Compass, Arms of Bahamas and): 11c, Bicycling. 15c, Running. 18c, Sailing.

**1972, June 27 Litho. *Perf. 13x13½***

*335* A38 10c lt vio & multi 40 40
*336* A38 11c ocher & multi 48 48
*337* A38 15c yel grn & multi 70 70
*338* A38 18c bl & multi 95 95
*a.* Souvenir sheet of 4 3.25 4.50

20th Olympic Games, Munich, Aug. 26-Sept. 10. No. 338a contains one each of Nos. 335-338. Yellow green margin. Size: 126x95mm.

Shepherd and Star of Bethlehem — A39

Designs: 6c, Bells. 15c, Holly and monstrance. 20c, Poinsettia.

**1972, Oct. 3 Wmk. 314 *Perf. 14***

*339* A39 3c gold & multi 14 14
*340* A39 6c blk & multi 28 28
*341* A39 15c blk & multi 70 70
*342* A39 20c gold & multi 95 95
*a.* Souvenir sheet of 4 2.75 3.25

Christmas 1972. Gold on 15c is embossed. No. 342a contains one each of Nos. 339-342. Violet margin, gold inscription. Size: 107½x139mm.

Souvenir Sheet

Map of Bahama Islands — A40

**1972, Nov. 1 Litho. *Perf. 15***

*343* A40 Souvenir sheet 3.75 4.75
*a.* 11c bl & multi 35 35
*b.* 15c bl & multi 45 45
*c.* 18c bl & multi 52 52
*d.* 50c bl & multi 1.50 1.50

Tourism Year of the Americas. No. 343 has yellow and multicolored margin. Size: 133x105mm.

**Silver Wedding Issue, 1972**

Common Design Type

Design: Queen Elizabeth II, Prince Philip, mace and galleon.

***Perf. 14x14½***

**1972, Nov. 13 Photo. Wmk. 314**

*344* CD324 11c car rose & multi 35 35
*345* CD324 18c vio & multi 55 55

Weather Satellite, WMO Emblem A41

Design: 18c, Weather radar.

**1973, Apr. 3 Litho. *Perf. 14***

*346* A41 15c dp bl & multi 65 65
*347* A41 18c bl grn & multi 90 90

Centenary of international meteorological cooperation.

Clarence A. Bain — A42

Virgin in Prayer, by Sassoferrato A43

Designs: 11c, New Bahamian coat of arms. 15c, New flag and Government House. $1, Milo B. Butler, Sr.

**1973 Wmk. 314 *Perf. 14½x14***

*348* A42 3c lil & multi 14 12
*349* A42 11c lt bl & multi 35 35
*350* A42 15c lt grn & multi 52 52
*351* A42 $1 yel & multi 2.50 2.50
*a.* Souvenir sheet of 4 4.00 4.75

Independence 1973. No. 351a contains one each of Nos. 348-351. Multicolored margin with black inscription. Size: 85½x120mm.

Issue dates: Nos. 348-350, July 10, Nos. 351, 351a, Aug. 1.

**1973, Oct. 16 Litho. *Perf. 14***

Paintings: 11c, Virgin and Child with St. John, by Filippino Lippi. 15c, Choir of Angels, by Marmion. 18c, The Two Trinities, by Murillo.

*352* A43 3c bl & multi 18 18
*353* A43 11c multi 60 60
*354* A43 15c gray grn & multi 80 80
*355* A43 18c lil rose & multi 1.10 1.10
*a.* Souvenir sheet of 4 2.75 3.75

Christmas 1973. No. 355a contains one each of Nos. 352-355. Blue, slate green and gold margin. Size: 124x99mm.

Agriculture, Science and Medicine — A44

Design: 18c, Symbols of engineering, art, and law.

**1974, Feb. 5 Litho. *Perf. 13½x14***
*356* A44 15c dl grn & multi 48 48
*357* A44 18 multi 65 65

25th anniversary of the University of the West Indies.

UPU Emblem A45

Designs: 13c, UPU emblem (vert.). 14c, UPU emblem. 18c, UPU monument, Bern (vert.).

**1974, Apr. 23 *Perf. 14***
*358* A45 3c multi 12 12
*359* A45 13c multi 45 45
*360* A45 14c ol bis & multi 52 52
*361* A45 18c multi 80 80
*a.* Souvenir sheet of 4 1.90 2.25

Centenary of Universal Postal Union. No. 361a contains one each of Nos. 358-361. Dark green margin with black ornaments and inscription. Size: 127x95mm.

Roseate Spoonbills, Trust Emblem — A46

Protected Birds (National Trust Emblem and): 14c, White-crowned pigeons. 21c, White-tailed tropic birds. 36c, Bahamian parrot.

**1974, Sept. 10 Litho. *Perf. 14***
*362* A46 13c multi 65 48
*363* A46 14c multi 65 48
*364* A46 21c multi 95 80
*365* A46 36c multi 1.65 1.25
*a.* Souvenir sheet of 4 5.25 6.00

15th anniversary of the Bahamas National Trust. No. 365a contains one each of Nos. 362-365, blue and multicolored margin. Size: 122x120mm.

Holy Family, by Jacques de Stella A47

Paintings: 10c, Virgin and Child, by Girolamo Romanino. 12c, Virgin and Child with St. John and St. Catherine, by Andrea Previtali. 21c, Virgin and Child with Angels, by Previtali.

**1974, Oct. Wmk. 314 *Perf. 13***
*366* A47 8c blk & multi 40 40
*367* A47 10c grn & multi 48 48
*368* A47 12c red & multi 60 60
*369* A47 21c ultra & multi 1.00 1.00
*a.* Souvenir sheet of 4 3.25 4.00

Christmas 1974. No. 369a contains one each of Nos. 366-369; gold and multicolored margin. Size: 125½x105mm.

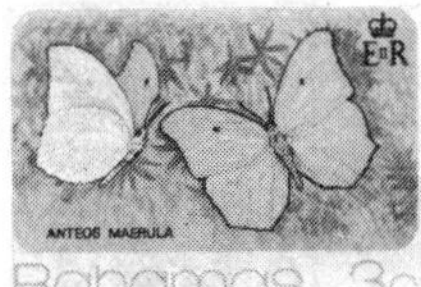

Anteos Maerula A48

**1975, Feb. 4 Litho. *Perf. 14x13½***
*370* A48 3c *shown* 26 22
*371* A48 14c *Eurema nicippe* 90 65
*372* A48 18c *Papilio andraemon* 1.15 90
*373* A48 21c *Euptoieta hegesia* 1.40 1.25
*a.* Souvenir sheet of 4 4.00 3.50

No. 373a contains one each of Nos. 370-373, light blue and multicolored margin. Size: 118x93mm.

Sheep Raising A49

Designs: 14c, Electric reel fishing (vert.). 18c, Growing food. 21c, Crude oil refinery (vert.).

**1975, May 27 Litho. *Perf. 14***
*374* A49 3c dl grn & multi 15 15
*375* A49 14c grn & multi 50 50
*376* A49 18c brn & multi 65 65
*377* A49 21c vio bl & multi 75 75
*a.* Souvenir sheet of 4 2.25 2.25

Economic diversification. No. 377a contains one each of Nos. 374-377; multicolored margin with red lilac inscription. Size: 126x94½mm.

Rowena Rand, Staff and Chrismon A50

Plant and IWY Emblem A51

**1975, July 22 Litho. *Perf. 14***
*378* A50 14c multi 60 60
*379* A51 18c multi 80 80

International Women's Year 1975.

Adoration of the Shepherds, by Perugino — A52

Paintings: 8c, 18c, Adoration of the Kings, by Ghirlandaio. 21c, like 3c.

**1975, Dec. 2 Litho. *Perf. 13½***
*380* A52 3c dk grn & multi 15 15
*381* A52 8c dk vio & multi 30 30
*382* A52 18c pur & multi 70 70
*383* A52 21c mar & multi 85 85
*a.* Souvenir sheet of 4 2.25 2.25

Christmas 1975. No. 383a contains one each of Nos. 380-383; multicolored decorative margin with black inscription. Size: 141x106mm.

Telephones, 1876 and 1976 — A53

Designs: 16c, Radio-telephone link, Deleporte, Nassau (radar). 21c, Alexander Graham Bell. 25c, Communications satellite.

**1976, March 23 Litho. *Perf. 14***
*384* A53 3c multi 9 9
*385* A53 16c multi 40 40
*386* A53 21c multi 52 52
*387* A53 25c multi 65 65

Centenary of first telephone call by Alexander Graham Bell, Mar. 10, 1876.

Bicycling and Olympic Rings — A54

Designs (Olympic Rings and): 16c, Long jump. 25c, Sailing. 40c, Boxing.

**1976, July 13 Litho. *Perf. 14***
*388* A54 8c mag & bl 24 24
*389* A54 16c org & brn 42 42
*390* A54 25c mag & bl 60 60
*391* A54 40c org & brn 1.10 1.10
*a.* Souvenir sheet of 4 2.75 2.75

21st Olympic Games, Montreal, Canada, July 17-Aug. 1.

No. 391a contains one each of Nos. 388-391; blue margin shows hurdling. Size: 102x127mm.

John Murray, Earl of Dunmore A55

Design: 16c, Map of US and Bahamas.

**1976, June 1 Wmk. 373 *Perf. 14***
*392* A55 16c multi 52 52
*393* A55 $1 multi 3.00 3.00
*a.* Souvenir sheet of 4 11.00 11.00

American Bicentennial. No. 393a contains 4 No. 393; yellow and black margin with Declaration of Independence. Size: 127x100mm.

Virgin and Child, Filippo Lippi — A56

Paintings: 21c, Adoration of the Shepherds, School of Seville. 25c, Adoration of the Kings, by Vincenzo Foppa. 40c, Virgin and Child, by Vivarini.

**1976, Oct. 19 Litho. *Perf. 14½x14***
*394* A56 3c brt bl & multi 12 12
*395* A56 21c dp org & multi 60 60
*396* A56 25c emer & multi 75 75
*397* A56 40c red lil & multi 1.10 1.10
*a.* Souvenir sheet of 4 2.75 2.75

Christmas 1976. No. 397a contains one each of Nos. 394-397; multicolored decorative margin. Size: 107x127mm.

Type of 1971

Designs: 16c, Hibiscus. 21c, Breadfruit. 25c, Hawksbill turtle. 40c, Bahamian sponge boat.

**1976, Nov. 2 Litho. Wmk. 373**
*398* A36 16c emer & multi 35 35
*399* A36 21c ver & multi 38 38
*400* A36 25c brn & multi 52 52
*401* A36 40c ver & multi 70 70

Elizabeth II Seated under Gold Canopy — A57

Designs: 16c, Coronation. 21c, Taking and signing of oath. 40c, Queen holding orb and scepter.

**1977, Feb. 7 *Perf. 12***
*402* A57 8c sil & multi 20 20
*403* A57 16c sil & multi 35 35
*404* A57 21c sil & multi 48 48
*405* A57 40c sil & multi 1.00 1.00
*a.* Souvenir sheet of 4 3.50 4.00

25th anniversary of the reign of Queen Elizabeth II. No. 405a contains one each of Nos. 402-405. Silver and black margin. Size: 123x90mm.

Featherduster — A58

Marine Life: 8c, Porkfish. 16c, Elkhorn coral. 21c, Soft coral and sponge.

**1977, May 24 Litho. *Perf. 13½***
*406* A58 3c multi 14 14
*407* A58 8c multi 28 28
*408* A58 16c multi 70 70
*409* A58 21c multi 85 85
*a.* Souvenir sheet of 4 2.50 3.00

No. 409a contains one each of Nos. 406-409, perf. 14½, multicolored margin shows underwater scene. Size: 118x92mm.

Campfire and Shower A59

Design: 21c, Boating.

**1977, Sept. 27 Litho. Wmk. 373**
*410* A59 16c multi 42 42
*411* A59 21c multi 52 52

6th Caribbean Jamboree, Kingston, Jamaica, Aug. 5-14.

Nos. 402-405a Overprinted: "Royal Visit / October 1977"

**1977, Oct. 19 Litho. *Perf. 12***
*412* A57 8c sil & multi 16 16
*413* A57 16c sil & multi 32 32
*414* A57 21c sil & multi 38 38
*415* A57 40c sil & multi 80 80
*a.* Souvenir sheet of 4 2.25 2.75

Caribbean visit of Queen Elizabeth II, Oct. 19-20.

*Bahamas stamps can be mounted in Scott's annually supplemented British North and West Caribbean Album.*

Virgin and Child — A60

Nassau Public Library — A61

Designs (Crèche Figurines): 16c, Three Kings. 21c, Adoration of the Kings. 25c, Three Kings.

**1977, Oct. 25 Litho. *Perf. 13½***

*416* A60 3c gold & multi 9 9
*417* A60 16c gold & multi 42 42
*418* A60 21c gold & multi 52 52
*419* A60 25c gold & multi 65 65
*a.* Souvenir sheet of 4 1.90 1.90

Christmas 1977. No. 419a contains one each of Nos. 416-419, perf. 14½; gold and black margin. Size: 137x74mm.

**1978, Mar. 28 Litho. *Perf. 14½x14***

Buildings: 8c, St. Matthew's Church. 16c, Government House. 18c, The Hermitage, Cat Island.

*420* A61 3c blk & yel grn 8 8
*421* A61 8c blk & lt bl 20 20
*422* A61 16c blk & lil rose 35 35
*423* A61 18c blk & sal 40 40
*a.* Souvenir sheet of 4 1.40 1.75

Architectural heritage. No. 423a contains one each of Nos. 420-423; lilac and black margin. Size: 91x91mm.

Scepter, St. Edward's Crown, Orb — A62

Design: $1, Elizabeth II.

***Perf. 14x13½***

**1978, June 27 Litho. Wmk. 373**

*424* A62 16c multi 28 28
*425* A62 $1 multi 1.65 1.65
*a.* Souvenir sheet of 2 2.25 2.25

25th anniversary of coronation of Queen Elizabeth II. No. 425a contains Nos. 424-425; multicolored margin shows Royal Guard on horseback. Size: 146x96mm.

### Type of 1971

Designs as before and: 16c, Hibiscus. 25c, Hawksbill turtle.

***Perf. 14½x14, 14x14½***

**1978, June Unwmk.**

*426* A36 1c bl & multi 5 5
*430* A36 5c dp org & multi 10 10
*436* A36 16c brt grn & multi 35 35
*439* A36 25c brn & multi 55 55
*440* A36 50c lem & multi 1.10 1.10
*441* A36 $1 lem & multi 2.25 2.25
*442* A36 $2 bl & multi 4.50 4.50
*443* A36 $3 vio bl & multi 6.75 6.75
*Nos. 426-443 (8)* 15.65 15.65

Angels and Palms A63

Design: 5c, Coat of arms within wreath, and sailing ships.

***Perf. 14x14½***

**1978, Nov. 14 Litho. Wmk. 373**

*444* A63 5c car, pink & gold 8 8
*445* A63 21c ultra, dk bl & gold 32 32
*a.* Souvenir sheet of 2 *2.75 2.75*

Christmas 1978. No. 445a contains Nos. 444-445; gold and black margin shows angel. Size: 95x95mm

Baby Walking, IYC Emblem — A64

Designs (IYC Emblem and): 16c, Children playing leapfrog. 21c, Girl skipping rope. 25c, Building blocks with "IYC" and emblem.

***Perf. 13½x13***

**1979, May 15 Litho. Wmk. 373**

*446* A64 5c multi 8 8
*447* A64 16c multi 25 25
*448* A64 21c multi 35 35
*449* A64 25c multi 40 40
*a.* Souvenir sheet of 4 1.10 1.10

International Year of the Child. No. 449a contains Nos. 446-449, perf. 14. Yellow and brown margin shows children dancing. Size: 112x126mm.

Rowland Hill and Penny Black — A65

Designs: 21c, Stamp printing press, 1840, and Bahamas No. 7. 25c, Great Britain No. 27 with 1850's Nassau cancellation, and Great Britain No. 29. 40c, Early mailboat and Bahamas No. 1.

**1979, Aug. 14 *Perf. 13½x14***

*450* A65 10c multi 16 16
*451* A65 21c multi 35 35
*452* A65 25c multi 40 40
*453* A65 40c multi 65 65
*a.* Souvenir sheet of 4 1.65 1.65

Sir Rowland Hill (1795-1879), originator of penny postage. No. 453a contains Nos. 450-453; multicolored margin. Size: 115x80mm.

Commonwealth Plaque over Map of Bahamas — A66

Designs: 21c, Parliament buildings. 25c, Legislative chamber. $1, Senate chamber.

**1979, Sept. 27 Litho. *Perf. 13½***

*454* A66 16c multi 25 25
*455* A66 21c multi 35 35
*456* A66 25c multi 40 40
*457* A66 $1 multi 1.65 1.65
*a.* Souvenir sheet of 4 2.75 2.75

Parliament of Bahamas, 250th anniv. No. 457a contains Nos. 454-457; light blue margin with black inscription. Size: 116x89mm.

> For unused stamps, more recent issues are valued as never hinged, with the beginning point determined on a country-by-country basis. Notes to show the beginning points are prominently placed in the text.

Headdress — A67

Designs: Goombay Carnival costumes.

**1979, Nov. 6 Litho. *Perf. 13***

*458* A67 5c multi 8 8
*459* A67 10c multi 16 16
*460* A67 16c multi 25 25
*461* A67 21c multi 35 35
*462* A67 25c multi 40 40
*463* A67 40c multi 65 65
*a.* Souvenir sheet of 6 2.00 2.00
*Nos. 458-463 (6)* 1.89 1.89

Christmas 1979. No. 463a contains Nos. 458-463, perf. 13½. Margin shows poinsettia. Size: 150x87½mm

Columbus' Landing, 1492 A68

**1980, July 9 Litho. *Perf. 15***

*464* A68 1c *shown* 6 6
*a.* Wmk. 384 6 6
*465* A68 3c *Blackbeard* 7 7
*a.* Wmk. 384 7 7
*466* A68 5c *Articles, 1647, Eleuthera map* 12 12
*467* A68 10c *Ceremonial mace* 24 24
*a.* Wmk. 384 24 24
*468* A68 12c *Col. Andrew Deveaux* 30 30
*469* A68 15c *Slave trading, Vendue House* 35 35
*470* A68 16c *Shipwreck salvage, 19th cent.* 38 38
*471* A68 18c *Blockade runner, 1860s* 42 42
*472* A68 21c *Bootlegging, 1919-1929* 50 50
*473* A68 25c *Pineapple cultivation* 30 30
*a.* Wmk. 384 60 60
*474* A68 40c *Sponge clipping* 95 95
*475* A68 50c *Victoria & Colonial Hotels* 1.25 1.25
*476* A68 $1 *Modern agriculture* 2.50 2.50
*477* A68 $2 *Ship, jet* 4.75 4.75
*478* A68 $3 *Central Bank, Arms* 7.25 7.25
*479* A68 $5 *Prince Charles, Prime Minister Pindling* 12.00 12.00
*Nos. 464-478 (15)* 19.44 19.44

Virgin and Child, Straw Figures — A69

**1980, Oct. 28 Litho. *Perf. 14½***

*480* A69 5c *shown* 8 8
*481* A69 21c *Three kings* 35 35
*482* A69 25c *Angel* 40 40
*483* A69 $1 *Christmas tree* 1.65 1.65
*a.* Souvenir sheet of 4 2.50 2.50

Christmas 1980. No. 483a contains Nos. 480-483; multicolored margin shows presents in straw bag. Size: 168x105mm.

Man with Crutch, Sun Rays A70

**1981, Feb. 10 Litho. *Perf. 14½***

*484* A70 5c shown 8 8
*485* A70 $1 Man in wheelchair 1.65 1.65
*a.* Souvenir sheet of 2 1.75 1.75

International Year of the Disabled. No. 485a contains Nos. 484-485; light blue and black margin shows globe, IYD emblem. Size: 120x60mm.

Grand Bahama Tracking Station A71

Satellite Views: 20c, Bahamas (vert.). 25c, Eleuthera. 50c, Andros and New Providence (vert.).

**Wmk. 373**

**1981, Apr. 21 Litho. *Perf. 13½***

*486* A71 10c multi 18 18
*487* A71 20c multi 35 35
*488* A71 25c multi 45 45
*489* A71 50c multi 90 90
*a.* Souvenir sheet of 4 2.00 2.75

No. 489a contains Nos. 486-489; multicolored margin shows rocket. Size: 115x100mm.

Prince Charles and Lady Diana A72

**Wmk. 373**

**1981, July 22 Litho. *Perf. 14½***

*490* A72 30c shown 52 52
*491* A72 $2 Charles, Prime Minister 3.50 3.50
*a.* Souvenir sheet of 2 4.25 4.75

Royal wedding. No. 491a contains Nos. 490-491; multicolored margin shows enlarged design of No. 491. Size: 142x120mm.

Bahama Ducks A73

**Wmk. 373**

**1981, Aug. 25 Litho. *Perf. 14***

*492* A73 5c shown 10 10
*493* A73 20c Reddish egrets 42 42
*494* A73 25c Brown boobies 52 52
*495* A73 $1 West Indian tree ducks 2.00 2.00
*a.* Souvenir sheet of 4 (#492-495) 4.00 4.00

See Nos. 514-517.

### Nos. 466-467, 473, 475 Overprinted: "COMMONWEALTH FINANCE MINISTERS' MEETING 21-23 SEPTEMBER 1981"

**1981, Sept. Litho. *Perf. 15***

*496* A68 5c multi 8 8
*497* A68 10c multi 16 16
*498* A68 25c multi 42 42
*499* A68 50c multi 85 85

World Food Day — A74

***Perf. 13x13½***

**1981, Oct. 16 Wmk. 373**

*500* A74 5c Chickens 8 8
*501* A74 20c Sheep 30 30
*502* A74 30c Lobster 45 45

*503* A74 50c Pigs 80 80
*a.* Souvenir sheet of 4 1.90 2.50

No. 503a contains Nos. 500-503; multicolored margin shows woman with produce. Size: 115x63mm.

Christmas 1981 — A75

**Wmk. 373**

**1981, Nov. 23 Litho. *Perf. 14***
*504* Sheet of 9 3.75 3.75
*a.* A75 5c Father Christmas 7 7
*b.* A75 5c shown 7 7
*c.* A75 5c St. Nicholas, Holland 7 7
*d.* A75 25c Lussibruden, Sweden 35 35
*e.* A75 25c Mother and child 35 35
*f.* A75 25c King Wenceslas, Czechoslovakia 35 35
*g.* A75 30c Mother and child 42 42
*h.* A75 30c Mother and child standing 42 42
*i.* A75 $1 Christkindl angel, Germany 1.50 1.50

No. 504 has silver margin. Size: 99x146mm.

TB Bacillus Centenary A76

**1982, Feb. 3 Litho. *Perf. 14***
*505* A76 5c Koch 9 9
*506* A76 16c X-ray 30 30
*507* A76 21c Microscopes 42 42
*508* A76 $1 Mantoux test 1.90 1.90
*a.* Souvenir sheet of 4 2.75 3.25

No. 508a contains Nos. 505-508, perf. 14½; multicolored margin shows bacillus. Size: 95x96mm.

Flamingoes A77

Designs: a. Females. b. Males. c. Nesting. d. Juvenile birds. e. Immature birds. No. 509 in continuous design.

**Wmk. 373**

**1982, Apr. 28 Litho. *Perf. 14***
*509* Strip of 5, multi 3.00 3.00
*a.-e.* A77 25c, any single 60 60

**Princess Diana Issue**
Common Design Type

**1982, July 1 Litho. *Perf. 14***
*510* CD333 16c Arms 25 25
*511* CD333 25c Diana 38 38
*512* CD333 40c Wedding 60 60
*513* CD333 $1 Portrait 1.50 1.50

Bird Type of 1981
**Wmk. 373**

**1982, Aug. 18 Litho. *Perf. 14***
*514* A73 10c Bat 18 18
*515* A73 16c Hutia 28 28
*516* A73 21c Racoon 35 35
*517* A73 $1 Dolphins 1.75 1.75
*a.* Souvenir sheet of 4 3.25 3.25

No. 517a contains Nos. 514-517; multicolored margin shows dolphins. Size: 115x77mm.

28th Commonwealth Parliamentary Conference A78

***Perf. 14x13½***
**1982, Oct. 16 Litho. Wmk. 373**
*518* A78 5c Plaque 9 9
*519* A78 25c Assoc. arms 45 45
*520* A78 40c Natl. arms 75 75
*521* A78 50c House of Assembly 90 90

Christmas 1982 — A79

Designs: 5c, Wesley Methodist Church, Baillou Hill Road. 12c, Centerville Seventh Day Adventist Church. 15c, Church of God of Prophecy, East Street. 21c, Bethel Baptist Church, Meeting Street. 25c, St. Francis Xavier Catholic Church, West Hill Street. $1, Holy Cross Anglican Church, Highbury Park.

**1982, Nov. 3 *Perf. 14***
*522* A79 5c multi 9 9
*523* A79 12c multi 24 24
*524* A79 15c multi 28 28
*525* A79 21c multi 40 40
*526* A79 25c multi 48 48
*527* A79 $1 multi 1.90 1.90
*Nos. 522-527 (6)* 3.39 3.39

**Commonwealth Day**
Common Design Type

**1983, Mar. 14 Litho.**
*528* CD334 5c Lynden O. Pindling 8 8
*529* CD334 25c Flags 40 40
*530* CD334 35c Map 55 55
*531* CD334 $1 Ocean liner 1.65 1.65

Nos. 469-472 Surcharged

**1983 Litho. *Perf. 15***
*532* A68 20c on 15c multi 35 35
*533* A68 31c on 21c multi 55 55
*534* A68 35c on 16c multi 65 65
*535* A68 80c on 18c multi 1.50 1.50

30th Anniv. of Customs Cooperation Council — A81

***Perf. 14x13½***
**1983, May 31 Wmk. 373**
*536* A81 31c Officers, ship 52 52
*537* A81 $1 Officers, jet 1.65 1.65

10th Anniv. of Independence A82

**Wmk. 373**

**1983, July 6 Litho. *Perf. 14***
*538* A82 $1 Flag raising 1.50 1.50
*a.* Souvenir sheet, perf. 12 1.50 1.50

Margin shows map. Size: 105x65mm.

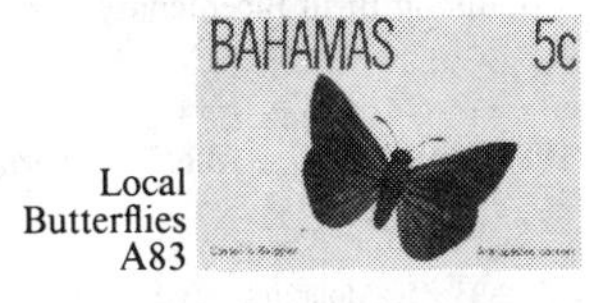

Local Butterflies A83

***Perf. 14½x14***
**1983, Aug. 24 Litho. Wmk. 373**
*539* A83 5c Carters skipper 10 10
*540* A83 25c Giant southern white 50 50
*541* A83 31c Large orange sulphur 62 62
*542* A83 50c Flambeau 1.00 1.00
*a.* Souvenir sheet of 4 2.25 2.50

No. 542a contains Nos. 539-542, perf. 14 and perf. 14½x14. Size: 121x81mm.

American Loyalists Arrival Bicentenary — A84

Paintings by Alton Lowe.

**Wmk. 373**

**1983, Sept. 28 Litho. *Perf. 14***
*543* A84 5c Loyalist Dreams 9 9
*544* A84 31c New Plymouth, Abaco 55 55
*545* A84 35c New Plymouth Hotel 60 60
*546* A84 50c Island Hope 90 90
*a.* Souvenir sheet of 4 2.25 2.25

No. 546a contains Nos. 543-546. Size: 111x76mm.

Christmas 1983 — A85

Children's designs: 5c, Christmas Bells, by Monica Pinder. 20c, The Flamingo by Cory Bullard 25c, The Yellow Hibiscus with Christmas Candle by Monique A. Bailey. 31c, Santa goes a Sailing by Sabrina Seiler (horiz.). 35c, Silhouette scene with palm trees by James Blake. 50c Silhouette scene with Pelicans, by Erik Russell (horiz.).

**1983, Nov. 1 *Perf. 14***
*547* A85 5c multi 8 8
*548* A85 20c multi 32 32
*549* A85 25c multi 42 42
*550* A85 31c multi 50 50
*551* A85 35c multi 60 60
*552* A85 50c multi 80 80
*Nos. 547-552 (6)* 2.72 2.72

125th Anniv. of Bahamas Stamps — A86

**Wmk. 373**

**1984, Feb. 22 Litho. *Perf. 14***
*553* A86 5c No. 3 8 8
*554* A86 $1 No. 1 1.65 1.65

**Lloyd's List Issue**
Common Design Type
**Wmk. 373**

**1984, Apr. 25 Litho. *Perf. 14½***
*555* CD335 5c Trent 9 9
*556* CD335 31c Orinoco 55 55
*557* CD335 35c Nassau Harbor 60 60
*558* CD335 50c Container ship Oropesa 85 85

1984 Summer Olympics A87

**1984, June 20 Litho. *Perf. 14x14½***
*559* A87 5c Running 8 8
*560* A87 25c Discus 42 42
*561* A87 31c Boxing 52 52
*562* A87 $1 Basketball 1.65 1.65
*a.* Souvenir sheet of 4 2.75 2.75

No. 562a contains Nos. 559-562. Size: 116x80mm.

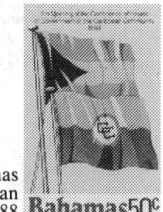

Flags of Bahamas and Caribbean Community — A88

**Wmk. 373**

**1984, July 4 Litho. *Perf. 14***
*563* A88 50c multi 90 90

Conference of Heads of Government of Caribbean Community, 5th Meeting.

Allen's Cay Iguana — A89

**1984, Aug. 15 *Perf. 14***
*564* A89 5c shown 8 8
*565* A89 25c Curly-tailed lizard 40 40
*566* A89 35c Greenhouse frog 55 55
*567* A89 50c Atlantic green turtle 80 80
*a.* Souvenir sheet of 4 2.00 2.00

No. 567a contains Nos. 564-567.

25th Anniv. of Natl. Trust — A90

Wildlife: a. Calliphlox evelynae. b. Megaceryle alcyon, Eleutherodactylus planirostris. c. Phoenicopterus ruber, Himantopus himantopus, Phoebus sennae. d. Urbanus proteus, Chelonia mydas. e. Pandion haliaetus. Continuous design.

**Wmk. 373**

**1984, Aug. 15 Litho. *Perf. 14***
*568* Strip of 5 2.50 2.50
*a.-e.* A90 31c, any single 50 50

Christmas 1984 — A91

Madonna and Child Paintings.

*Perf. 13½x13*

**1984, Nov. 7 Litho. Wmk. 373**

*569* A91 5c Titian 8 8
*570* A91 31c Anais Colin 50 50
*571* A91 35c Elena Caula 55 55
*a.* Souvenir sheet of 3 1.25 1.25

No. 571a contains Nos. 569-571; multicolored margin shows angels. Size:

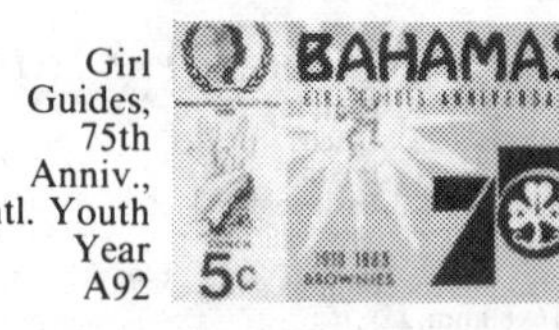
Girl Guides, 75th Anniv., Intl. Youth Year A92

**1985, Feb. 22 Litho. *Perf. 14***

*572* A92 5c Brownies 8 8
*573* A92 25c Camping 40 40
*574* A92 31c Girl Guides 50 50
*575* A92 35c Rangers 55 55
*a.* Souv. sheet of 4, #572-575 1.65 1.65

Audubon Birth Bicentenary — A93

**Wmk. 373**

**1985, Apr. 24 Litho. *Perf. 14***

*576* A93 5c Killdeer 7 7
*577* A93 31c Mourning dove, vert. 45 45
*578* A93 35c Mourning doves, diff., vert. 50 50
*579* A93 $1 Killdeers, diff. 1.50 1.50

**Queen Mother 85th Birthday**
Common Design Type

***Perf. 14½x14***

**1985, June 7 Litho. Wmk. 384**

*580* CD336 5c Portrait, 1927 8 8
*581* CD336 25c At christening of Peter Phillips 42 42
*582* CD336 35c Portrait, 1985 60 60
*583* CD336 50c Holding Prince Henry 85 85

**Souvenir Sheet**

*584* CD336 $1.25 In a pony and trap 2.00 2.00

No. 584 has multicolored margin continuing design. Size: 92x74mm.

UN and UN Food and Agriculture Org., 40th Annivs. A94

**Wmk. 373**

**1985, Aug. 26 Litho. *Perf. 14***

*585* A94 25c Wheat, emblems 42 42

Commonwealth Heads of Government Meeting, 1985 — A95

**1985, Oct. 16 Wmk. 373 *Perf. 14½***

*586* A95 31c Queen Elizabeth II 45 45
*587* A95 35c Flag, Commonwealth emblem 52 52

Christmas 1985 A96

Paintings by Alton Roland Lowe: 5c, Grandma's Christmas Bouquet. 25c, Junkanoo Romeo and Juliet, vert. 31c, Bunce Girl, vert. 35c, Home for Christmas.

**1985, Nov. 5 *Perf. 13***

*588* A96 5c multicolored 10 10
*589* A96 25c multicolored 48 48
*590* A96 31c multicolored 62 62
*591* A96 35c multicolored 65 65
*a.* Souvenir sheet of 4, #588-591, perf. 14 1.90 1.90

No. 591a has red and black decorative margin picturing mistletoe and bells. Size: 110x68mm.

**Queen Elizabeth II 60th Birthday**
Common Design Type

Designs: 10c, Age 1, 1927. 25c, Coronation, Westminster Abbey, 1953. 35c, Giving speech, royal visit, Bahamas. 40c, At Djakova, Jugoslavia, state visit, 1972. $1, Visiting Crown Agents, 1983.

**Wmk. 384**

**1986, Apr. 21 Litho. *Perf. 14½***

*592* CD337 10c scar, blk & sil 16 16
*593* CD337 25c ultra & multi 40 40
*594* CD337 35c grn & multi 55 55
*595* CD337 40c vio & multi 65 65
*596* CD337 $1 rose vio & multi 1.65 1.65
*Nos. 592-596 (5)* 3.41 3.41

AMERIPEX '86 — A97

**1986, May 19 *Perf. 14***

*597* A97 5c Nos. 464, 471 9 9
*598* A97 25c Nos. 288-289 45 45
*599* A97 31c No. 392 55 55
*600* A97 50c No. 489a 90 90
*601* A97 $1 Statue of Liberty, vert. 1.75 1.75
*a.* Souvenir sheet of one 1.75 1.75
*Nos. 597-601 (5)* 3.74 3.74

Statue of Liberty, cent. No. 601a has multicolored decorative margin picturing Chicago skyline, exhibition emblem.

**Royal Wedding Issue, 1986**
Common Design Type

Designs: 10c, Formal engagement. $1, Andrew in dress uniform.

**1986, July 23 *Perf. 14½x14***

*602* CD338 10c multi 16 16
*603* CD338 $1 multi 1.65 1.65

Fish A98

**1986-87 Litho. *Perf. 14***

*604* A98 5c Rock beauty 7 7
*605* A98 10c Stoplight parrotfish 14 14
*606* A98 15c Jacknife fish 22 22
*607* A98 20c Flamefish 28 28
*608* A98 25c Swissguard basslet 35 35
*609* A98 30c Spotfin butterflyfish 42 42
*610* A98 35c Queen triggerfish 50 50
*611* A98 40c Four-eyed butterflyfish 55 55
*612* A98 45c Fairy basslet 65 65
*613* A98 50c Queen angelfish 70 70
*614* A98 60c Blue chromis 85 85
*615* A98 $1 Spanish hogfish 1.40 1.40
*616* A98 $2 Harlequin bass 2.75 2.75
*617* A98 $3 Blackbar soldierfish 4.25 4.25
*618* A98 $5 Pygmy angelfish 7.00 7.00
*618A* A99 $10 Red hind ('87) 15.00 15.00
*Nos. 604-618A (16)* 35.13 35.13

**1987, June 25 Litho. *Perf. 14***

*604a* Wmk. 373 ('87) 7 7
*605a* Wmk. 373 ('87) 14 14
*606a* Wmk. 373 ('87) 22 22
*611a* Wmk. 373 ('87) 55 55
*612a* Wmk. 373 ('87) 65 65
*613a* Wmk. 373 ('87) 70 70
*614a* Wmk. 373 ('87) 85 85
*615a* Wmk. 373 ('87) 1.40 1.40
*616a* Wmk. 373 ('87) 2.75 2.75
*Nos. 604a-616a (9)* 7.33 7.33

Nos. 604a-616a dated 1987.

Christ Church Cathedral — A99

**Wmk. 373**

**1986, Sept. 16 Litho. *Perf. 14½***

*619* A99 10c View, 19th cent. 16 16
*620* A99 40c View, 1986 65 65
*a.* Souvenir sheet of 2, #619-620 85 85

City of Nassau, Diocese of Nassau and the Bahamas and Christ Church, 125th anniv. No. 620a has multicolored inscribed margin.

Christmas, Intl. Peace Year — A100

**Wmk. 384**

**1986, Nov. 4 Litho. *Perf. 14***

*621* A100 10c Nativity 16 16
*622* A100 40c Flight to Egypt 65 65
*623* A100 45c Children praying 75 75
*624* A100 50c Exchanging gifts 80 80
*a.* Souv. sheet of 4, #621-624 2.50 2.50

No. 624a has multicolored inscribed margin.

Pirates of the Caribbean A101

Map of the Bahamas — A102

**Wmk. 373**

**1987, June 2 Litho. *Perf. 14½***

*625* A101 10c Anne Bonney 16 16
*626* A101 40c Blackbeard (d. 1718) 65 65
*627* A101 45c Capt. Edward England 75 75
*628* A101 50c Capt. Woodes Rogers (c. 1679-1732) 85 85

**Souvenir Sheet**

*629* A102 $1.25 shown 2.00 2.00

No. 629 has multicolored margin picturing pirate ship attacking merchant vessel.

Lighthouses A103

Paintings by Alton Roland Lowe.

**1987, Mar. 31 Wmk. 384**

*630* A103 10c Great Isaac 16 16
*631* A103 40c Bird Rock 65 65
*632* A103 45c Castle Is. 75 75
*633* A103 $1 Hole in the Wall 1.65 1.65

Common Design Types are pictured in section before Great Britain.

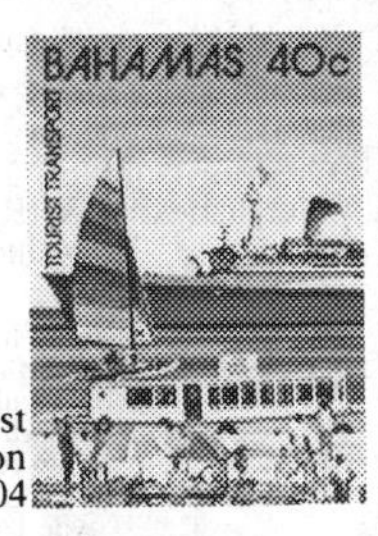


Tourist Transportation A104

Ships and aircraft: No. 634a, Cruise ship, ailboat. No. 634b, Cruise ships, tugboat, peedboat. No. 634c, Pleasure boat leaving arbor, sailboat. No. 634d, Pleasure boat docked, sailboats. No. 634e, Sailboats. No. 35a, Bahamasair plane. No. 635b, Bahamasair and Pan Am aircraft. No. 635c, Aircraft, radar tower. No. 635d, Control ower, aircraft. No. 635e, Helicopter, planes.

**1987, Aug. 26 Wmk. 373 *Perf. 14***

| | | | |
|---|---|---|---|
| 634 | Strip of 5 | 3.25 | 3.25 |
| *a.-e.* | A104 40c any single | 65 | 65 |
| 635 | Strip of 5 | 3.25 | 3.25 |
| *a.-e.* | A104 40c any single | 65 | 65 |

Orchids Painted by Alton Roland Lowe A105

**Wmk. 384**

**1987, Oct. 20 Litho. *Perf. 14½***

| | | | |
|---|---|---|---|
| 636 | A105 10c Cattleyopis lindenii | 16 | 16 |
| 637 | A105 40c Encyclia lucayana | 65 | 65 |
| 638 | A105 45c Encyclia hodgeana | 75 | 75 |
| 639 | A105 50c Encyclia lleidae | 80 | 80 |
| *a.* | Souv. sheet of 4, Nos. 636-639 | 2.50 | 2.50 |

Christmas 1987. No. 639a has multicolored decorative margin. Size: 120x92mm.

Discovery of America, 500th Anniv. (in 1992) — A106

Designs: 10c, Ferdinand and Isabella. 40c, Columbus before the Talavera Committee. 45c, Lucayan village. 50c, Lucayan potters. $1.50, Map, c. 1500.

***Perf. 14x14½***

**1988, Feb. 23 Litho. Wmk. 373**

| | | | |
|---|---|---|---|
| 640 | A106 10c multi | 16 | 16 |
| 641 | A106 40c multi | 65 | 65 |
| 642 | A106 45c multi | 75 | 75 |
| 643 | A106 50c multi | 80 | 80 |

**Souvenir Sheet**

| | | | |
|---|---|---|---|
| 644 | A106 $1.50 multi | 2.50 | 2.50 |

No. 644 has multicolored inscribed margin continuing the map. Size: 64x50mm.

World Wildlife Fund — A107

Whistling ducks, *Dendrocygna arborea.*

**1988, Apr. 29 *Perf. 14½***

| | | | |
|---|---|---|---|
| 645 | A107 5c Ducks in flight | 18 | 8 |
| 646 | A107 10c Among marine plants | 16 | 16 |
| 647 | A107 20c Adults, ducklings | 32 | 32 |
| 648 | A107 45c Wading | 75 | 75 |

Abolition of Slavery, 150th Anniv. A108

**1988, Aug. 9 Litho. Wmk. *Perf. 14***

| | | | |
|---|---|---|---|
| 649 | A108 10c African hut | 10 | 20 |
| 650 | A108 40c Basket weavers in hut, Grantstown | 80 | 80 |

1988 Summer Olympics, Seoul A109

Games emblem and details of painting by James Martin: 10c, Olympic flame, high jump, hammer throw, basketball and gymnastics. 40c, Swimming, boxing, weight lifting, fencing and running. 45c, Gymnastics, shot put and javelin. $1, Running, cycling and gymnastics.

**Wmk. 384**

**1988, Aug. 30 Litho. *Perf. 14***

| | | | |
|---|---|---|---|
| 651 | A109 10c multi | 20 | 20 |
| 652 | A109 40c multi | 80 | 80 |
| 653 | A109 45c multi | 90 | 90 |
| 654 | A109 $1 multi | 2.00 | 2.00 |
| *a.* | Souv. sheet of 4, Nos. 651-654 | 4.00 | 4.00 |

No. 654a has multicolored margin picturing athletes in silhouette. Size: 113x85mm.

**Lloyds of London, 300th Anniv.**

Common Design Type

Designs: 10c, Lloyds List No. 560, 1740. 40c, Freeport Harbor, horiz. 45c, Space shuttle over the Bahamas, horiz. $1, Supply ship *Yarmouth Castle* on fire.

**Wmk. 373**

**1988, Oct. 4 Litho. *Perf. 14***

| | | | |
|---|---|---|---|
| 655 | CD341 10c multi | 20 | 20 |
| 656 | CD341 40c multi | 80 | 80 |
| 657 | CD341 45c multi | 90 | 90 |
| 658 | CD341 $1 multi | 2.00 | 2.00 |

Christmas Carols — A110

Designs: 10c, *O' Little Town of Bethlehem.* 40c, *Little Donkey.* 45c, *Silent Night.* 50c, *Hark! The Herald Angels Sing.*

**Wmk. 384**

**1988, Nov. 21 Litho. *Perf. 14½***

| | | | |
|---|---|---|---|
| 659 | A110 10c multi | 20 | 20 |
| 660 | A110 40c multi | 80 | 80 |
| 661 | A110 45c multi | 90 | 90 |
| 662 | A110 50c multi | 1.00 | 1.00 |
| *a.* | Souv. sheet of 4, Nos. 659-662 | 2.90 | 2.90 |

No. 662a has multicolored margin picturing Star of Bethlehem, camels and the three wise men.

Discovery of America Type of 1988

Design: 10c, Columbus in cabin, map. 40c, Development of the caravel. 45c, Navigational tools. 50c, Arawak artifacts. $1.50, Caravel under construction, an illumination from the *Nuremburg Chronicles,* 15th cent.

**Wmk. 373**

**1989, Jan. 25 Litho. *Perf.***

| | | | |
|---|---|---|---|
| 663 | A106 10c multi | 20 | 20 |
| 664 | A106 40c multi | 80 | 80 |
| 665 | A106 45c multi | 90 | 90 |
| 666 | A106 50c multi | 1.00 | 1.00 |

**Souvenir Sheet**

| | | | |
|---|---|---|---|
| 667 | A106 $1.50 multi | 3.00 | 3.00 |

No. 667 has multicolored margin continuing the design.

## SEMI-POSTAL STAMPS

No. 48 Overprinted in Red

**1.1.17.**

**1917, May 18 Wmk. 3 *Perf. 14***

| | | | |
|---|---|---|---|
| B1 | A6 1p car & blk | 42 | 42 |

Type of 1911 Overprinted in Red

**WAR CHARITY 3.6.18.**

**1918, Jan.**

| | | | |
|---|---|---|---|
| B2 | A6 1p red & blk | 45 | 45 |
| *a.* | Double overprint | 2,000. | |

## AIR POST STAMPS

Manned Flight Bicentenary — AP1

Airplanes.

**Wmk. 373**

**1983, Oct. 13 Litho. *Perf. 14***

| | | | |
|---|---|---|---|
| C1 | AP1 10c Consolidated Catalina | 18 | 18 |
| *a.* | Without emblem ('85) | 18 | 18 |
| *b.* | Without emblem, wmk. 384 ('86) | 18 | 18 |
| C2 | AP1 25c Avro Tudor IV | 42 | 42 |
| *a.* | Without emblem ('85) | 45 | 45 |
| *b.* | Without emblem, wmk. 384 ('86) | 45 | 45 |
| C3 | AP1 31c Avro Lancastrian | 55 | 55 |
| *a.* | Without emblem ('85) | 55 | 55 |
| C4 | AP1 35c Consolidated Commodore | 60 | 60 |
| *a.* | Without emblem ('85) | 65 | 65 |

Aircraft AP2

**1987, July 7**

| | | | |
|---|---|---|---|
| C5 | AP2 15c Bahamasair Boeing 737 | 25 | 25 |
| C6 | AP2 40c Eastern Boeing 757 | 65 | 65 |
| C7 | AP2 45c Pan Am Airbus A300 B4 | 75 | 75 |
| C8 | AP2 50c British Airways Boeing 747 | 85 | 85 |

## SPECIAL DELIVERY STAMPS

No. 34 Overprinted **SPECIAL DELIVERY**

**1916 Wmk. 1 *Perf. 14***

| | | | |
|---|---|---|---|
| E1 | A6 5p org & blk | 9.25 | 9.25 |
| *a.* | Double overprint | 1,500. | 1,500. |
| *b.* | Inverted overprint | 1,500. | 1,500. |
| *c.* | Double overprint, one inverted | 1,900. | 1,900. |
| *d.* | Pair, one without overprint | 12,000. | 12,000. |

The No. E1 overprint exists in two types. Type I (illustrated) is much scarcer. Type II shows "SPECIAL" farther right, so that the letter "I" is slightly right of the vertical line of the "E" below it.

Type of Regular Issue of 1903 Overprinted **SPECIAL DELIVERY**

**1917, July 2 Wmk. 3**

| | | | |
|---|---|---|---|
| E2 | A6 5p org & blk | 1.25 | 1.65 |

No. 60 Overprinted in Red **SPECIAL DELIVERY**

**1918**

| | | | |
|---|---|---|---|
| E3 | A6 5p vio & blk | 85 | 1.65 |

## WAR TAX STAMPS

Stamps of 1912-18 Overprinted **WAR TAX**

**Wmk. Multiple Crown and C. A. (3)**

**1918, Feb. 21 *Perf. 14***

| | | | |
|---|---|---|---|
| MR1 | A8 ½p green | 3.00 | 4.00 |
| *a.* | Double overprint | 1,000. | 1,000. |
| *b.* | Inverted ovpt. | 1,000. | 1,000. |
| MR2 | A8 1p car rose | 80 | 1.10 |
| *a.* | Double overprint | 1,000. | 1,000. |
| *b.* | Inverted ovpt. | 1,000. | 1,000. |
| MR3 | A6 3p brn, *yel* | 3.75 | 4.75 |
| *a.* | Inverted ovpt. | 1,100. | 1,100. |
| *b.* | Double overprint | 1,000. | 1,000. |
| MR4 | A8 1sh blk & red | 100.00 | 125.00 |
| *a.* | Double ovpt. | 2,750. | 2,500. |

Same Overprint on No. 48a

**1918, July 10**

| | | | |
|---|---|---|---|
| MR5 | A6 1p car & blk | 3.50 | 6.00 |
| *a.* | Double overprint | 1,200. | |
| *b.* | Double overprint, one inverted | 1,000. | |
| *c.* | Inverted ovpt. | 1,100. | 1,100. |

Nos. 49-50, 54 Overprinted in Black or Red **WAR TAX**

| | | | |
|---|---|---|---|
| MR6 | A8 ½p green | 20 | 20 |
| MR7 | A8 1p car rose | 20 | 20 |
| *a.* | Watermarked sideways | 850.00 | |
| MR8 | A8 1sh blk & red (R) | 1.25 | 2.00 |

Nos. 58-59 Overprinted **WAR TAX**

**1918-19**

| | | | |
|---|---|---|---|
| MR9 | A6 3p brn, *yel* | 1.00 | *3.50* |
| MR10 | A6 3p brn & blk ('19) | 1.00 | *3.50* |

Nos. 49-50, 54 Overprinted in Red or Black **WAR TAX**

**1919, July 14**

| | | | |
|---|---|---|---|
| MR11 | A8 ½p grn (R) | 32 | 55 |
| MR12 | A8 1p car rose | 32 | 55 |
| MR13 | A8 1sh blk & red (R) | 3.00 | *10.50* |

No. 59 Overprinted **WAR TAX**

| | | | |
|---|---|---|---|
| MR14 | A6 3p brn & blk | 90 | 1.50 |

# BAHRAIN

LOCATION — An archipelago in the Persian Gulf, including the islands of Bahrain, Muharraq, Sitra, Nebi Saleh, Kasasifeh and Arad.

GOVT. — Independent sheikdom

AREA — 255 sq. mi.

POP. — 350,798 (1981)
CAPITAL — Manama

Bahrain was a British-protected territory until it became an independent state on August 15, 1971.

12 Pies = 1 Anna
16 Annas = 1 Rupee
100 Naye Paise = 1 Rupee (1957)
1000 Fils = 1 Dinar (1966)

**Catalogue values for unused stamps in this country are for Never Hinged items, beginning with Scott 52.**

### Indian Postal Administration

Stamps of India, 1926-32, Overprinted in Black

BAHRAIN
a

**Wmk. Multiple Stars. (196)**

**1933, Aug. 10** *Perf. 14*

*1* A46 3p gray 1.40 10
*2* A47 ½a green 3.50 70
*3* A68 9p dk grn 2.75 70
*4* A48 1a dk brn 4.25 1.65
*5* A69 1a3p violet 3.00 40
*6* A60 2a vermilion 3.00 3.25
*7* A51 3a blue 14.00 14.00
*8* A70 3a6p dp bl 1.50 60
*9* A61 4a ol grn 10.50 10.50
*10* A54 8a red vio 3.25 1.00
*11* A55 12a claret 4.25 1.65

Overprinted in Black

b BAHRAIN

*12* A56 1r grn & brn 8.00 6.75
*13* A56 2r brn org & car rose 27.50 24.00
*14* A56 5r dk vio & ultra 72.50 72.50
*Nos. 1-14 (14)* 159.40 137.80

Stamps of India, 1926-32, Overprinted Type "a" in Black

**1934**

*15* A72 1a dk brn 2.75 9
*16* A51 3a car rose 3.25 18
*17* A52 4a ol grn 4.50 28

India Nos. 138, 111, 111a Overprinted Type "a" in Black

**1935-37** *Perf. 13½x14, 14*

*18* A71 ½a green 2.50 9
*19* A49 2a vermilion 13.00 2.00
**a.** Small die ('37) 13.00 2.50

India Stamps of 1937 Overprinted Type "a" in Black

**1938-41 Wmk. 196** *Perf. 13½x14*

*20* A80 3p slate 1.50 90
*21* A80 ½a brown 10 10
*22* A80 9p green 22 18
*23* A80 1a carmine 22 10
*24* A81 2a scarlet 65 35
*26* A81 3a yel grn ('41) 8.75 2.50
*27* A81 3a6p ultra 1.00 *2.00*
*28* A81 4a dk brn ('41) 40.00 24.00
*30* A81 8a bl vio ('40) 50.50 32.50
*31* A81 12a car lake ('40) 45.00 42.50

**Overprinted Type "b" in Black**

*32* A82 1r brn & sl 1.90 70
*33* A82 2r dk brn & dk vio 8.75 2.50
*34* A82 5r dp ultra & dk grn 35.00 13.00
*35* A82 10r rose car & dk vio ('41) 50.00 18.00
*36* A82 15r dk grn & dk brn ('41) 24.00 24.00
*37* A82 25r dk vio & bl vio ('41) 65.00 57.50
*Nos. 20-37 (16)* 332.59 220.83

India Stamps of 1941-43 Overprinted Type "a" in Black

**1942-44 Wmk. 196** *Perf. 13½x14*

*38* A83 3p slate 5 5
*39* A83 ½a rose vio ('44) 9 9
*40* A83 9p lt grn ('43) 30 18
*41* A83 1a car rose ('44) 30 9
*42* A84 1a3p bis ('43) 60 *1.25*
*43* A84 1½a dk pur ('43) 90 18
*45* A84 2a scar ('43) 32 9
*46* A84 3a vio ('43) 1.25 1.25
*47* A84 3½a ultra 2.25 2.00
*48* A85 4a chocolate 35 24
*49* A85 6a pck bl 2.75 1.25
*50* A85 8a bl vio ('43) 30 20
*51* A85 12a car lake 60 50
*Nos. 38-51 (13)* 10.06 7.37

**Catalogue values for unused stamps in this section, from this point to the end of the section, are for Never Hinged items.**

### British Postal Administration

See Oman (Muscat) for similar stamps with surcharge of new value only.

Great Britain Nos. 258 to 263, 243 and 248 Surcharged in Black

BAHRAIN

ANNA c

**1948-49 Wmk. 251** *Perf. 14½x14*

*52* A101 ½a on ½p grn 25 25
*53* A101 1a on 1p ver 18 8
*54* A101 1½a on 1½p lt red brn 20 20
*55* A101 2a on 2p lt org 35 12
*56* A101 2½a on 2½p ultra 45 45
*57* A101 3a on 3p vio 30 15
*58* A102 6a on 6p rose lil 30 15
*59* A103 1r on 1sh brn 1.75 50

Great Britain Nos. 249A, 250 and 251A Surcharged in Black

BAHRAIN

2 RUPEES

**Wmk. 259** *Perf. 14*

*60* A104 2r on 2sh6p yel grn 3.75 3.00
*61* A104 5r on 5sh dl red 8.00 7.50
*61A* A105 10r on 10sh ultra ('49) 40.00 37.50
*Nos. 52-61A (11)* 55.53 49.90

Surcharge bars at bottom on No. 61A.
Issue dates: 10r, July 4, 1949. Others, Apr. 1, 1948.

### Silver Wedding Issue

Great Britain Nos. 267 and 268 Surcharged in Black

BAHRAIN
2½
ANNAS

*Perf. 14½x14, 14x14½*

**1948, Apr. 26 Wmk. 251**

*62* A109 2½a on 2½p brt ultra 18 18
*63* A110 15r on £1 dp chlky bl 37.50 60.00

Three bars obliterate the original denomination on No. 63.

### Olympic Issue

Great Britain Nos. 271 to 274 Surcharged "BAHRAIN" and New Value in Black

**1948, July 29** *Perf. 14½x14*

*64* A113 2½a on 2½p brt ultra 20 20
**a.** Double surcharge 425.00 *525.00*
*65* A114 3a on 3p dp vio 30 24
*66* A115 6a on 6p red vio 45 40
*67* A116 1r on 1sh dk brn 90 75

A square of dots obliterates the original denomination on No. 67.

### U. P. U. Issue

Great Britain Nos. 276 to 279 Surcharged "BAHRAIN," New Value and Square of Dots in Black

**1949, Oct. 10 Photo.** *Perf. 14½x14*

*68* A117 2½a on 2½p brt ultra 26 26
*69* A118 3a on 3p brt vio 45 32
*70* A119 6a on 6p red vio 75 65
*71* A120 1r on 1sh brn 1.90 1.40

Great Britain Nos. 280, 281, 283-285 Surcharged Type "c" in Black

**1950-51 Wmk. 251**

*72* A101 ½a on ½p lt org 7 7
*73* A101 1a on 1p ultra 18 18
*74* A101 1½a on 1½p grn 26 26
*75* A101 2a on 2p lt red brn 18 18
*76* A101 2½a on 2½p ver 26 26
*77* A102 4a on 4p ultra 42 35

Great Britain Nos. 286-288 Surcharged in Black

BAHRAIN

2 RUPEES

*Perf. 11x12*
**Wmk. 259**

*78* A121 2r on 2sh6p grn 5.00 3.75
*79* A121 5r on 5sh dl red 7.50 7.50
*80* A122 10r on 10sh ultra 16.00 16.00
*Nos. 72-80 (9)* 29.87 28.55

Longer bars, at lower right, on No. 80.
Issue dates: 4a, Nov. 2, 1950. Others, May 3, 1951.

Stamps of Great Britain, 1952-54, Surcharged "BAHRAIN" and New Value in Black or Dark Blue

**1952-54 Wmk. 298** *Perf. 14½x14*

*81* A126 ½a on ½p red org ('53) 9 5
**a.** "½" omitted 100.00 *125.00*
*82* A126 1a on 1p ultra ('53) 14 7
*83* A126 1½a on 1½p grn 14 12
*84* A126 2a on 2p red brn ('53) 14 12
*85* A127 2½a on 2½p scar 24 14
*86* A127 3a on 3p dk pur (Dk Bl) ('54) 30 14
*87* A128 4a on 4p ultra ('53) 70 35
*88* A129 6a on 6p lil rose 60 30
*89* A132 12a on 1sh3p dk grn ('53) 1.75 70
*90* A131 1r on 1sh6p dk bl ('53) 2.50 90
*Nos. 81-90 (10)* 6.60 2.89

Six stamps of this design picturing Sheik Sulman bin Hamad Al Kalifah were for local use in 1953-57.

Six stamps of similar design (same sheik, "Bahrain" vertical at left) were issued in 1961 for local use.

### Coronation Issue

Great Britain Nos. 313-316 Surcharged "BAHRAIN" and New Value in Black

*Perf. 14½x14*

**1953, June 3 Wmk. 298**

*92* A134 2½a on 2½p scar 40 40
*93* A135 4a on 4p brt ultra 65 65
*94* A136 12a on 1sh3p dk grn 1.50 1.50
*95* A137 1r on 1sh6p dk bl 2.00 2.00

Squares of dots obliterate the original denominations on Nos. 94 and 95.

Great Britain Nos. 309-311 Surcharged "BAHRAIN" and New Value in Black

**1955 Wmk. 308 Engr.** *Perf. 11x12*

*96* A133 2r on 2sh6p dk brn 3.00 1.25
*97* A133 5r on 5sh crim 9.50 4.00
*98* A133 10r on 10sh brt ultra 19.00 6.50

Three slightly different types of surcharge are found on the 2r; two on 5r and 10r.

Great Britain Nos. 317, 323, 325, 332-333 Surcharged "BAHRAIN" and New Value

*Perf. 14½x14*

**1956-57 Wmk. 308 Photo.**

*99* A126 ½a on ½p red org 25 20
*100* A128 4a on 4p ultra 5.00 6.25
*101* A129 6a on 6p lil rose 52 40
*102* A132 12a on 1sh3p dk grn 6.25 10.00
*103* A131 1r on 1sh6p dk bl ('57) 1.50 7
*Nos. 99-103 (5)* 13.52 17.6

Great Britain Nos. 317-325, 328, 33 Surcharged "BAHRAIN" and New Value

**1957, Apr. 1**

*104* A129 1np on 5p lt brn 9
*105* A126 3np on ½p red org 22
*106* A126 6np on 1p ultra 24
*107* A126 9np on 1½p grn 24
*108* A126 12np on 2p red brn 30 1
*109* A127 15np on 2½p scar, type I 35 1
**a.** Type II 38
*110* A127 20np on 3p dk pur 22 1
*111* A128 25np on 4p ultra 65 3
*112* A129 40np on 6p lil rose 65 3
*113* A130 50np on 9p dp ol grn 1.75 7
*114* A132 75np on 1sh3p dk grn 1.50 5
*Nos. 104-114 (11)* 6.21 2.5

The arrangement of the surcharge varies o different values: there are three bars throug value on No. 113.

### Jubilee Jamboree Issue

Great Britain Nos. 334-336 Surcharged "BAHRAIN," New Value and Square of Dots in Black

*Perf. 14½x14*

**1957, Aug. 1 Photo. Wmk. 30**

*115* A138 15np on 2½p scar 38 3
*116* A138 25np on 4p ultra 65 4
*117* A138 75np on 1sh3p dk grn 80 8

Great Britain No. 357 Surcharged "BAHRAIN/ NP 15 NP" in Black

**1960 Wmk. 322** *Perf. 14½x1*

*118* A127 15np on 2½p scar, type II 7.25 *11.0*

Sheik Sulman bin Hamad Al Khalifah
A1 A2

*Perf. 14½x14*

**1960, July 1 Photo. Unwmk**

*119* A1 5np lt ultra 10
*120* A1 15np orange 15
*121* A1 20np lt vio 22
*122* A1 30np ol bis 25
*123* A1 40np gray 30 12
*124* A1 50np emerald 35 12
*125* A1 75np red brn 60 22

**Engr.**
*Perf. 13x13½*

*126* A2 1r gray 95 25
*127* A2 2r carmine 1.90 42
*128* A2 5r ultra 5.50 2.25
*129* A2 10r ol grn 11.00 2.75
*Nos. 119-129 (11)* 21.32 6.41

Sheik Isa bin Sulman Al Khalifah — A3

Bahrain Airport — A4

Designs: 5r, 10r, Deep water jetty.

**1964, Feb. 22 Photo.** *Perf. 14½x14*

*130* A3 5np ultra 8 5
*131* A3 15np orange 12 6
*132* A3 20np brt pur 15 6
*133* A3 30np brn ol 18 9
*134* A3 40np slate 18 9
*135* A3 50np emerald 26 12
*136* A3 75np chestnut 45 38

Engr.

*Perf. 13½x13*

| | | | | |
|---|---|---|---|---|
| *137* | A4 | 1r black | 75 | 22 |
| *138* | A4 | 2r rose red | 2.25 | 85 |
| *139* | A4 | 5r vio bl | 5.75 | 2.25 |
| *140* | A4 | 10r dl grn | 11.00 | 3.75 |
| | | *Nos. 130-140 (11)* | 21.17 | 7.92 |

**Bahrain Postal Administration**

Sheik Isa bin Sulman Al Kalifah — A5

Sheik and Bahrain International Airport — A6

Pearl Divers — A7

Bab al Bahrain, Suq Al-Khamis Mosque, Sheik, Emblem, etc. — A8

Designs: 50f, 75f, Pier, Mina Sulman harbor. 200f, Falcon and horse race. 500f, "Hospitality," pouring coffee and Sheik's Palace.

*Perf. 14½x14*

**1966, Jan. 1 Photo. Unwmk.**

| | | | | |
|---|---|---|---|---|
| *141* | A5 | 5f green | 7 | 5 |
| *142* | A5 | 10f dk red | 9 | 5 |
| *143* | A5 | 15f ultra | 14 | 8 |
| *144* | A5 | 20f magenta | 20 | 12 |
| | | ***Perf. 13½x14*** | | |
| *145* | A6 | 30f grn & blk | 28 | 16 |
| *146* | A6 | 40f bl & blk | 32 | 20 |
| *147* | A6 | 50f dp car rose & blk | 42 | 25 |
| *148* | A6 | 75f vio & blk | 60 | 35 |
| | | ***Perf. 14½x14*** | | |
| *149* | A7 | 100f dk bl & yel | 1.00 | 50 |
| *150* | A7 | 200f dk grn & org | 3.00 | 1.00 |
| *151* | A7 | 500f red brn & yel | 6.25 | 2.50 |
| *152* | A8 | 1d multi | 12.50 | 5.00 |
| | | *Nos. 141-152 (12)* | 24.87 | 10.26 |

Produce, Date Palm, Ship, Truck and Plane A9

Map of Bahrain and WHO Emblem A10

**1966, Mar. 28 Litho.** ***Perf. 13x13½***

| | | | | |
|---|---|---|---|---|
| *153* | A9 | 10f red & bl grn | 25 | 25 |
| *154* | A9 | 20f grn & vio | 52 | 52 |
| *155* | A9 | 40f ol bis & lt bl | 1.00 | 1.00 |
| *156* | A9 | 200f vio bl & pink | 5.00 | 5.00 |

The 6th Bahrain Trade Fair and Agricultural Show.

**1968, June Unwmk.** ***Perf. 13½x14***

| | | | | |
|---|---|---|---|---|
| *157* | A10 | 20f gray & blk | 42 | 42 |
| *158* | A10 | 40f bl grn & blk | 1.10 | 1.10 |
| *159* | A10 | 150f dp rose & blk | 4.25 | 4.25 |

20th anniv. of the WHO.

Isa Town A11

Designs (Isa Town): 80f, Market. 120f, Stadium. 150f, Mosque.

**1968, Nov. 18 Litho.** ***Perf. 14½***

| | | | | |
|---|---|---|---|---|
| *160* | A11 | 50f brn & multi | 1.65 | 1.65 |
| *161* | A11 | 80f multi | 2.50 | 2.50 |
| *162* | A11 | 120f bl & multi | 4.25 | 4.25 |
| *163* | A11 | 150f red & multi | 6.75 | 6.75 |

Education Symbol — A12

**1969, Apr. Litho.** ***Perf. 13***

| | | | | |
|---|---|---|---|---|
| *164* | A12 | 40f multi | 85 | 85 |
| *165* | A12 | 60f multi | 1.40 | 1.40 |
| *166* | A12 | 150f multi | 2.75 | 2.75 |

50th anniversary of education in Bahrain.

Map of Arabian Gulf, Radar and Emblem A13

Designs: 40f, 150f, Radar installation and emblem of Cable & Wireless Ltd. (vert.).

***Perf. 14x13½, 13½x14***

**1969, July 14 Litho.**

| | | | | |
|---|---|---|---|---|
| *167* | A13 | 20f lt grn & multi | 90 | 90 |
| *168* | A13 | 40f vio bl & multi | 1.90 | 1.90 |
| *169* | A13 | 100f ocher & multi | 4.50 | 4.50 |
| *170* | A13 | 150f rose lil & multi | 7.75 | 7.75 |

Opening of the satellite earth station (connected through the Indian Ocean satellite Intelsat III) at Ras Abu Jarjur, July 14.

Municipal Building, Arms and Map of Bahrain A14

**1970, Feb. 23 Litho.** ***Perf. 12x12½***

| | | | | |
|---|---|---|---|---|
| *171* | A14 | 30f bl & multi | 1.40 | 1.40 |
| *172* | A14 | 150f multi | 5.00 | 5.00 |

Issued to publicize the 2nd Conference of the Arab Cities' Organization.

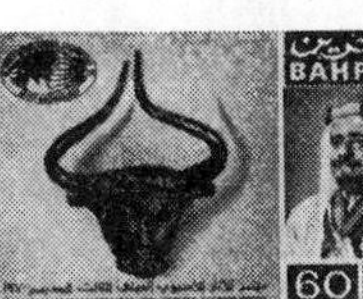

Copper Bull's Head A15

Designs (Conference Emblem and): 80f, Gateway to Qalat al Bahrain, 7th century B.C. 120f, Aerial view of grave mounds, Bahrain. 150f, Dilmun seal, 2000 B.C.

**1970, Mar. 1 Photo.** ***Perf. 14½***

| | | | | |
|---|---|---|---|---|
| *173* | A15 | 60f multi | 1.25 | 1.25 |
| *174* | A15 | 80f multi | 1.50 | 1.50 |
| *175* | A15 | 120f multi | 2.25 | 2.25 |
| *176* | A15 | 150f multi | 2.75 | 2.75 |

Issued to publicize the 3rd International Asian Archaeological Conference, Bahrain.

Vickers VC 10, Big Ben and Minaret A16

**1970, Apr. 5 Litho.** ***Perf. 14½x14***

| | | | | |
|---|---|---|---|---|
| *177* | A16 | 30f multi | 60 | 60 |
| *178* | A16 | 60f multi | 1.25 | 1.25 |
| *179* | A16 | 120f multi | 4.25 | 4.25 |

Issued to publicize the first flight to London from the Arabian Gulf Area by Gulf Aviation Company.

Education Year Emblem A17

Design: 120f, Education Year emblem and students.

**1970, Nov. 1 Litho.** ***Perf. 14½x14***

| | | | | |
|---|---|---|---|---|
| *180* | A17 | 60f blk, bl & org | 2.25 | 2.25 |
| *181* | A17 | 120f multi | 5.25 | 5.25 |

Issued for International Education Year.

**Independent State**

Government House, Manama — A18

U.N. Emblem and Sails — A19

Designs: 30f, "Freedom" with dove and torch, and globe. 120f, 150f, Bahrain coat of arms.

**1971, Oct. 2 Photo.** ***Perf. 14½x14***

| | | | | |
|---|---|---|---|---|
| *182* | A18 | 30f gold & multi | 1.25 | 1.25 |
| *183* | A18 | 60f gold & multi | 2.50 | 2.50 |
| *184* | A18 | 120f gold & multi | 5.00 | 5.00 |
| *185* | A18 | 150f gold & multi | 6.25 | 6.25 |

Declaration of Bahrain independence, Aug. 15, 1971.

***Perf. 14x14½, 14½x14***

**1972, Feb. 1 Litho.**

Designs: 30f, 60f, Dhow with sails showing U.N. and Arab League emblems (horiz.). 150f, as 120f.

| | | | | |
|---|---|---|---|---|
| *186* | A19 | 30f multi | 1.25 | 1.25 |
| *187* | A19 | 60f red, gray & multi | 3.00 | 3.00 |
| *188* | A19 | 120f dl bl & multi | 5.75 | 5.75 |
| *189* | A19 | 150f multi | 6.50 | 6.50 |

Bahrain's admission to the Arab League and the United Nations.

"Your Heart is your Health" — A20

**1972, Apr. 7 Litho.** ***Perf. 14½x14***

| | | | | |
|---|---|---|---|---|
| *190* | A20 | 30f blk & multi | 3.00 | 3.00 |
| *191* | A20 | 60f gray & multi | 6.00 | 6.00 |

World Health Day 1972.

UN and FAO Emblems A21

**1973, May 12 Litho.** ***Perf. 12½x13***

| | | | | |
|---|---|---|---|---|
| *192* | A21 | 30f org red, pur & grn | 2.75 | 2.75 |
| *193* | A21 | 60f ocher, brn & grn | 5.25 | 5.25 |

World Food Programs, 10th anniversary.

People of Various Races, Human Rights Flame A22

**1973, Nov. Litho.** ***Perf. 14x14½***

| | | | | |
|---|---|---|---|---|
| *194* | A22 | 30f bl, blk & brn | 2.75 | 2.75 |
| *195* | A22 | 60f lake, blk & brn | 5.25 | 5.25 |

25th anniversary of the Universal Declaration of Human Rights.

Flour Mill A23

Designs: 60f, International Airport. 120f, Sulmaniya Medical Center. 150f, ALBA aluminum smelting plant.

**1973, Dec. 16 Photo.** ***Perf. 14½***

| | | | | |
|---|---|---|---|---|
| *196* | A23 | 30f multi | 80 | 80 |
| *197* | A23 | 60f multi | 1.40 | 1.40 |
| *198* | A23 | 120f multi | 2.75 | 2.75 |
| *199* | A23 | 150f multi | 3.25 | 3.25 |

National Day.

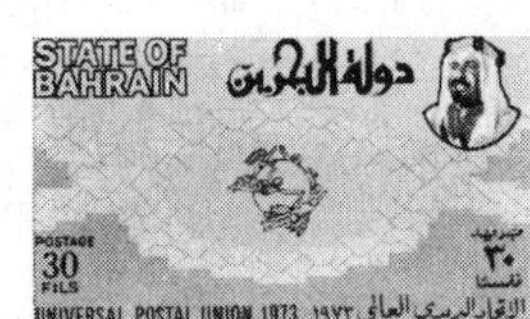

Letters and UPU Emblem — A24

Carrier Pigeon and UPU Emblem A25

Designs: 60f, UPU emblem and letters. 150f, Like 120f.

**1974, Feb. 4 Litho. *Perf. 13½***

*200* A24 30f bl & multi 60 60
*201* A24 60f emer & multi 1.00 1.00

***Perf. 12½x13½***

*202* A25 120f ultra & multi 2.00 2.00
*203* A25 150f yel & multi 2.50 2.50

Bahrain's admission to UPU.

Traffic Signals — A26

**1974, May 4 Litho. *Perf. 14½***

*204* A26 30f org brn & multi 1.10 1.10
*205* A26 60f brt bl & multi 2.50 2.50

International Traffic Day.

Jet, Globe, Mail Coach and UPU Emblem — A27

**1974, Sept. 1 Photo. *Perf. 14x14½***

*206* A27 30f multi 40 40
*207* A27 60f multi 80 80
*208* A27 120f multi 1.65 1.65
*209* A27 150f multi 2.00 2.00

Centenary of Universal Postal Union.

National Day Emblem, Sitra Power Station — A28

Woman's Silk Gown — A29

Designs (National Day Emblem and): 60f, like 30f. 120f, 150f, Bahrain dry dock.

**1974, Dec. 16 Litho. *Perf. 14½***

*210* A28 30f bl & multi 45 45
*211* A28 60f grn & multi 80 80
*212* A28 120f lil rose & multi 1.75 1.75
*213* A28 150f ver & multi 2.00 2.00

National Day.

**Photo.; Gold Embossed**

**1975, Feb. 1 *Perf. 14½x14***

Design: Various women's costumes.

*214* A29 30f bl grn & multi 42 42
*215* A29 60f vio bl & multi 80 80
*216* A29 120f rose red & multi 1.75 1.75
*217* A29 150f multi 2.00 2.00

A particular stamp may be scarce, but if few collectors want it, its market value may remain relatively low.

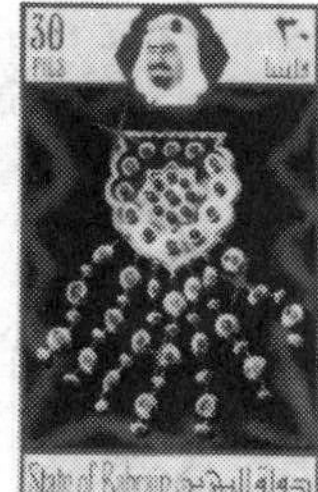


Pendant — A30

Woman Planting Flower, IWY Emblem — A31

Designs: Various jewelry.

**1975, Apr. 1 Photo. *Perf. 14½x14***

*218* A30 30f ol & multi 45 45
*219* A30 60f dp pur & multi 1.00 1.00
*220* A30 120f dp car & multi 2.00 2.00
*221* A30 150f dp bl & multi 2.50 2.50

**1975, July 28 Litho. *Perf. 14½***

Design: 60f, Educated woman holding IWY emblem.

*222* A31 30f multi 85 85
*223* A31 60f multi 1.75 1.75

International Women's Year 1975.

Miniature Sheet

Arabian Stallion — A32

Arabian horses: a. Brown head. b. White mare. c. Mare and foal. d. White head. e. White mare. f. Mare and stallion. g. Bedouins on horseback. Nos. 224a, 224b and 224d are vert.

***Perf. 14x14½, 14½x14***

**1975, Sept. 1 Photo.**

*224* Sheet of 8 37.50 26.00
*a.-h.* A32 60f any single 3.75 2.75

No. 224 has gold margin. Size: 127x152mm.

Flag of Bahrain A33

Map of Bahrain A34

Sheik Isa — A35

**1976-80 Litho. *Perf. 14½***

*225* A33 5f red & ultra 5 5
*226* A33 10f red & grn 5 5
*227* A33 15f red & blk 7 7
*228* A33 20f red & brn 10 10
*228A* A34 25f gray & blk ('79) 12 12
*229* A34 40f bl & blk 20 20
*229A* A34 50f yel grn & blk ('79) 25 25
*230* A34 60f dl grn & blk ('77) 30 30
*231* A34 80f rose lil & blk 40 40
*232* A34 100f lt red brn & blk ('77) 50 50
*233* A34 150f org & blk 75 75
*234* A34 200f yel & blk 1.00 1.00

**Engr.**

***Perf. 12x12½***

*235* A35 300f lt grn & grn 1.40 1.40
*236* A35 400f pink & red brn 2.00 2.00
*237* A35 500f lt bl & dk bl 2.50 2.50
*238* A35 1d gray & sep 5.00 4.50
*239* A35 2d rose & vio ('80) 10.00 8.25
*240* A35 3d buff & brn ('80) 15.00 12.50
*Nos. 225-240 (18)* 39.69 34.94

Concorde at London Airport — A36

Designs: No. 245, Concorde at Bahrain Airport. No. 246, Concorde over London to Bahrain map. No. 247, Concorde on runway at night.

**1976, Jan. 22 Photo. *Perf. 13x14***

*244* A36 80f gold & multi 1.90 1.90
*245* A36 80f gold & multi 1.90 1.90
*246* A36 80f gold & multi 1.90 1.90
*247* A36 80f gold & multi 1.90 1.90
*a.* Souvenir sheet of 4 6.75

First commercial flight of supersonic jet Concorde, London to Bahrain. Jan. 21. Nos. 244-247 printed se-tenant in sheets of 24. No. 247a contains 4 stamps similar to Nos. 244-247 with simulated perforations; blue margin with gold and white inscription and design. Size: 152x114mm.

Soldier, Flag and Arms of Bahrain — A37

**1976, Feb. 5 Litho. *Perf. 14½***

*248* A37 40f yel & multi 1.25 1.25
*249* A37 80f lt bl & multi 2.25 2.25

Defense Force Day.

Sheik Isa, King Khalid, Bahrain and Saudi Flags A38

**1976, Mar. 23 Litho. *Perf. 14½***

*250* A38 40f gold & multi 1.25 1.25
*251* A38 80f sil & multi 2.25 2.25

Visit of King Khalid of Saudi Arabia.

New Housing, Housing Ministry's Seal — A39

**1976, Dec. 16 Litho. *Perf. 14½***

*252* A39 40f rose & multi 1.10 1.10
*253* A39 80f bl & multi 2.25 2.25

National Day 1976.

APU Emblem A40

**1977, Apr. 12 Litho. *Perf. 14½***

*254* A40 40f sil & multi 85 85
*255* A40 80f rose & multi 1.75 1.75

Arab Postal Union, 25th anniversary.

Miniature Sheet

Dogs on Beach and Dhow A41

Designs: Saluki dogs.

**1977, July Photo. *Perf. 14x14½***

*256* 80f multi, sheet of 8 14.00 14.00
**a.** A41 *shown* 1.40 1.40
**b.** A41 *Dog and camels* 1.40 1.40
**c.** A41 *Dog and gazelles* 1.40 1.40
**d.** A41 *Dog and Ruler's Palace* 1.40 1.40
**e.** A41 *Dog's head* 1.40 1.40
**f.** A41 *Heads of two dogs* 1.40 1.40
**g.** A41 *Dog in dunes* 1.40 1.40
**h.** A41 *Playing dogs* 1.40 1.40

Students and Candle A42

**1977, Sept. 8 Litho. *Perf. 14½***

*257* A42 40f multi 1.10 1.10
*258* A42 80f multi 2.25 2.25

International Literacy Day.

Shipyard and Flags A43

**1977, Dec. 16 Litho. *Perf. 14½***

*259* A43 40f multi 90 90
*260* A43 80f multi 1.90 1.90

Inauguration of Arab Shipbuilding and Repair Yard Co.

Antenna, ITU Emblem A44

**1978, May 17 Litho. *Perf. 14½***

*261* A44 40f yel & multi 90 90
*262* A44 80f sil & multi 1.90 1.90

10th World Telecommunications Day.

Ghanja Dhow — A45

Designs: Dhows of the Arabian Gulf. Nos. 267-270 vertical.

***Perf. 14x14½, 14½x14***

**1979, June 16** **Photo.**

*263* A45 100f shown 1.90 1.90
*264* A45 100f Zarook 1.90 1.90
*265* A45 100f Shu'ai 1.90 1.90
*266* A45 100f Jaliboot 1.90 1.90
*267* A45 100f Baghla 1.90 1.90
*268* A45 100f Sambuk 1.90 1.90
*269* A45 100f Boom 1.90 1.90
*270* A45 100f Kotia 1.90 1.90
*Nos. 263-270 (8)* 15.20 15.20

Nos. 263-270 printed se-tenant in sheets of 40 (10x4).

Learning to Walk — A46

IYC Emblem and: 100f, Hands surrounding girl, U.N. emblem.

**1979** **Litho.** ***Perf. 14½***

*271* A46 50f multi 90 90
*272* A46 100f multi 1.90 1.90

International Year of the Child.

Hegira, 1,500th Anniv. — A47

**1980** **Photo.** ***Perf. 13x13½***

*273* A47 50f multi 55 55
*274* A47 100f multi 1.10 1.10
*a.* Miniature sheet 3.75 3.75
*275* A47 150f multi 1.65 1.65
*276* A47 200f multi 2.25 2.25

No. 274a contains No. 274. Blue and gold ornamental margin. Size: 83x90mm.

Falcon — A48

Designs: Falcons.

***Perf. 13½x14, 14x13½***

**1980, Nov. 1** **Photo.**

*277* Block of 8 12.50 12.50
*a.* A48 100f. any single 1.50 1.50

IYD Emblem, Sheik Isa — A49

**1981, Mar. 21** **Litho.** ***Perf. 14½***

*278* A49 50f multi 85 85
*279* A49 100f multi 1.75 1.75

International Year of the Disabled.

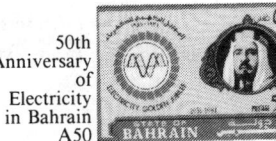

50th Anniversary of Electricity in Bahrain A50

**1981, Apr. 26** **Litho.** ***Perf. 14½***

*280* A50 50f multi 85 85
*281* A50 100f multi 1.75 1.75

Stone Cutting — A51

**1981, July 1** **Photo.** ***Perf. 14x13½***

*282* A51 50f shown 48 48
*283* A51 100f Pottery 95 95
*284* A51 150f Weaving 1.90 1.90
*285* A51 200f Basket making 1.90 1.90

Hegira (Pilgrimage Year) — A52

Designs: Various mosques.

**1981, Oct. 1** **Photo.** ***Perf. 14x13½***

*286* A52 50f multi 55 55
*287* A52 100f multi 1.10 1.10
*288* A52 150f multi 1.50 1.50
*289* A52 200f multi 2.25 2.25

Sheik Isa, 20th Anniv. of Coronation — A53

**1981, Dec. 16** **Photo.** ***Perf. 14x13½***

*290* A53 15f multi 18 18
*291* A53 50f multi 60 60
*292* A53 100f multi 1.25 1.25
*293* A53 150f multi 1.75 1.75
*294* A53 200f multi 2.50 2.50
*Nos. 290-294 (5)* 6.28 6.28

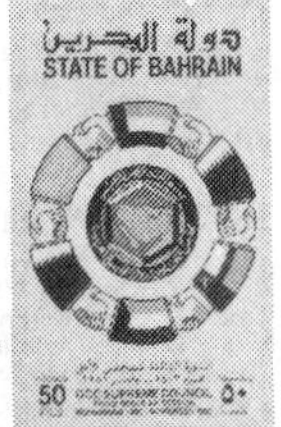

Wildlife in al Areen Park — A54

Designs: a. Gazelle. b. Oryx. c. Dhub lizard. d. Arabian hares. e. Oryxes. f. Reems.

**1982, Mar. 1** **Photo.** ***Perf. 13½x14***

*295* Sheet of 6 7.75 7.75
*a.-f.* A54 100f. any single 1.25 1.25

3rd Session of Gulf Supreme Council, Nov. — A55

**1982, Nov. 9** **Litho.** ***Perf. 14½***

*296* A55 50f bl & multi 60 60
*297* A55 100f grn & multi 1.25 1.25

Opening of Madinat Hamad Housing Development — A56

**1983, Dec. 1** **Litho.** ***Perf. 14½***

*298* A56 50f multi 60 60
*299* A56 100f multi 1.25 1.25

Al Khalifa Dynasty Bicentenary — A57

Sheiks or Emblems: a. 500fr, Isa bin Sulman. b. Emblem (tan & multi.). c. Isa bin Ali, 1869-1932. d. Hamad bin Isa, 1932-42. e. Sulman bin Hamad, 1942-61. f. Emblem (pale green & multi.). g. Emblem (lemon & multi.). h. Emblem (light blue & multi.). i. Emblem (gray & multi.).

**1983, Dec. 16** **Litho.** ***Perf. 14½***

*300* Sheet of 9 6.50 6.50
*a.-i.* A57 100f. any single 55 55

**Souvenir Sheet**

*301* A57 500f multi 4.25 4.25

No. 301 contains one stamp (60x38mm.); gold decorative margin. Size: 108x83mm.

Gulf Co-operation Council Traffic Week — A58

**1984, Apr. 30** **Litho.** ***Perf. 14½***

*302* A58 15f multi 12 12
*303* A58 50f multi 38 38
*304* A58 100f multi 75 75

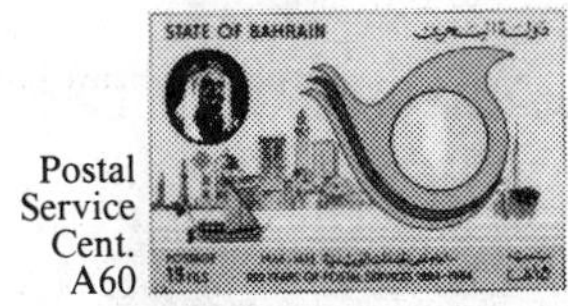

1984 Summer Olympics A59

**1984, Sept. 15** ***Perf. 14½***

*305* A59 15f Hurdles 14 14
*306* A59 50f Equestrian 42 42
*307* A59 100f Diving 85 85
*308* A59 150f Fencing 1.25 1.5
*309* A59 200f Shooting 1.75 1.75
*Nos. 305-309 (5)* 4.41 4.21

Postal Service Cent. A60

**1984, Dec. 8** **Photo.** ***Perf. 12x11½***

*310* A60 15f multi 8 8
*311* A60 50f multi 28 28
*312* A60 100f multi 52 52

**Miniature Sheet**

Coastal Fish A61

**1985, Feb. 10** **Photo.** ***Perf. 13½x14***

*313* Sheet of 10 5.25 5.25
*a.-j.* A61 100f. any single 52 52

1st Arab Gulf States Week for Social Work A62

**1985, Oct. 15** **Litho.** ***Perf. 14½***

*314* A62 15f multi 8 8
*315* A62 50f multi 25 25
*316* A62 100f multi 50 50

Intl. Youth Year A63

**1985, Nov. 16**

*317* A63 15f multi 8 8
*318* A63 50f multi 25 25
*319* A63 100f multi 50 50

Bahrain-Saudi Arabia Causeway Opening — A64

**1986, Nov.** **Litho.** ***Perf. 14½***

*320* A64 15f Causeway, aerial view 8 8
*321* A64 50f Island 25 25
*322* A64 100f Causeway 50 50

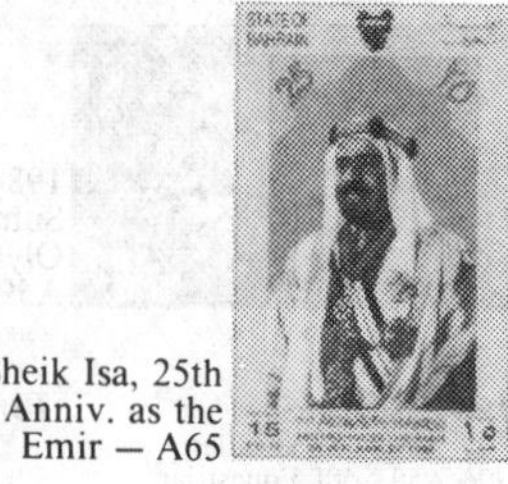

Sheik Isa, 25th Anniv. as the Emir — A65

**1986, Dec. 16**

| | | | | |
|---|---|---|---|---|
| *323* | A65 | 15f multi | 8 | 8 |
| *324* | A65 | 50f multi | 25 | 25 |
| *325* | A65 | 100f multi | 50 | 50 |
| *a.* | | Souv. sheet of 3, #323-325 | 85 | 85 |

No. 325a has inscribed decorative margin. Size: 148x110mm.

WHO, 40th Anniv. A66

**1988, Apr. 30 Litho.** ***Perf. 14½***

| | | | | |
|---|---|---|---|---|
| *326* | A66 | 50f multi | 28 | 28 |
| *327* | A66 | 150f multi | 80 | 80 |

Opening of Ahmed Al Fateh Islamic Center A67

**1988, June 2 Litho.** ***Perf. 14½***

| | | | | |
|---|---|---|---|---|
| *328* | A67 | 50f multi | 28 | 28 |
| *329* | A67 | 150f multi | 80 | 80 |

1988 Summer Olympics, Seoul A68

**1988, Sept. 17 Litho.** ***Perf. 14½***

| | | | | |
|---|---|---|---|---|
| *330* | A68 | 50f Running | 28 | 28 |
| *331* | A68 | 80f Equestrian | 45 | 45 |
| *332* | A68 | 150f Fencing | 80 | 80 |
| *333* | A68 | 200f Soccer | 1.10 | 1.10 |

### WAR TAX STAMP

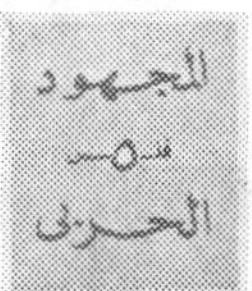

WT1

WT2

**1973, Nov. Litho.** ***Perf. 14½***

*MR1* WT1 5f sky blue

**1974 Litho.** ***Perf. 14½***

*MR2* WT2 5f lt blue 1.75 25

## BANGKOK

LOCATION — Capital of Siam (Thailand).

Stamps were issued by Great Britain under rights obtained in the treaty of 1855. These were in use until July 1, 1885, when the stamps of Siam were designated as the only official postage stamps to be used in the kingdom.

100 Cents = 1 Dollar

Excellent counterfeits of Nos. 1 to 22 are plentiful.

**B**

Stamps of Straits Settlements Overprinted in Black

**1882 Wmk. 1** ***Perf. 14***

| | | | | |
|---|---|---|---|---|
| *1* | A2 | 2c brown | 625.00 | 725.00 |
| *2* | A2 | 4c rose | 625.00 | 575.00 |
| *a.* | | Inverted overprint | | |
| *3* | A6 | 5c brn vio | 60.00 | 60.00 |
| *4* | A2 | 6c violet | 50.00 | 50.00 |
| *5* | A3 | 8c yel org | 900.00 | 55.00 |
| *6* | A7 | 10c slate | 72.50 | 50.00 |
| *7* | A3 | 12c blue | 400.00 | 165.00 |
| *8* | A3 | 24c green | 80.00 | 40.00 |
| *9* | A4 | 30c claret | 9,500. | 4,750. |
| *10* | A5 | 96c ol gray | 700.00 | 700.00 |

**1882-83 Wmk. Crown and C. A. (2)**

| | | | | |
|---|---|---|---|---|
| *11* | A2 | 2c brown | 50.00 | 50.00 |
| *12* | A2 | 2c rose ('83) | 15.00 | 15.00 |
| *a.* | | Inverted overprint | 11,500. | 3,000. |
| *b.* | | Double overprint | 1,750. | |
| *13* | A2 | 4c rose | 100.00 | 67.50 |
| *14* | A2 | 4c brn ('83) | 27.50 | 27.50 |
| *15* | A6 | 5c ultra ('83) | 72.50 | 50.00 |
| *16* | A2 | 6c vio ('83) | 50.00 | 40.00 |
| *a.* | | Double overprint | | |
| *17* | A3 | 8c yel org | 27.50 | 22.50 |
| *a.* | | Inverted overprint | | |
| *18* | A7 | 10c slate | 50.00 | 27.50 |
| *a.* | | Double overprint | | |
| *19* | A3 | 12c vio brn ('83) | 60.00 | 50.00 |
| *20* | A3 | 24c green | 1,100. | 1,000. |

**1883** **Wmk. 1**

*21* A5 2c on 32c pale red 675.00 775.00

On Straits Settlements No. 9

**1885 Wmk. Elephant's Head (38)**

*22* A7 32c on 2a yel (B+B) *8,250. 8,250.*

## BANGLADESH

LOCATION — In southern, central Asia, touching India, Burma, and the Bay of Bengal.
GOVT. — Republic in the British Commonwealth.
AREA — 55,598 sq. mi.
POP. — 87,052,024 (1981)
CAPITAL — Dacca

Bangladesh, formerly East Pakistan, broke away from Pakistan in April 1971, proclaiming its independence. It consists of 14 former eastern districts of Bengal and the former Assam district of Sylhet.

100 Paisas = 1 Rupee
100 Paisas (Poishas) = 1 Taka (1972)

**Catalogue values for all unused stamps in this country are for Never Hinged items.**

Various stamps of Pakistan were handstamped locally for use in Bangladesh during the first half of 1971.

Map of Bangladesh A1

Sheik Mujibur Rahman A2

Designs: 20p, "Dacca University Massacre." 50p, "A Nation of 75 Million People." 1r, Flag of Independence (showing map). 2r, Ballot box. 3r, Broken chain. 10r, "Support Bangladesh" and map.

***Perf. 14x14½***

**1971, July 29 Litho. Unwmk.**

| | | | | |
|---|---|---|---|---|
| *1* | A1 | 10p red, dk pur & lt bl | 5 | 5 |
| *2* | A1 | 20p bl, grn, red & yel | 6 | 6 |
| *3* | A1 | 50p dp org, gray & brn | 14 | 14 |
| *4* | A1 | 1r red, emer & yel | 25 | 25 |
| *5* | A1 | 2r lil rose, lt & dk bl | 50 | 50 |
| *6* | A1 | 3r bl, emer & grn | 70 | 70 |
| *7* | A2 | 5r dp org, tan & blk | 1.25 | 1.25 |
| *8* | A1 | 10r gold, dk bl & lil rose | 2.25 | 2.25 |
| | | *Nos. 1-8 (8)* | 5.20 | 5.20 |

A set of 15 stamps of types A1 and A2 in new paisa-taka values and colors was rejected by Bangladesh officials and not issued. Bangladesh representatives in England released these stamps, which were not valid, on Feb. 1, 1972.

Nos. 1-8 Overprinted in Black or Red: BANGLADESH LIBERATED বাংলাদেশের মুক্তি

**1971, Dec. 20**

| | | | | |
|---|---|---|---|---|
| *9* | A1 | 10p multi | 5 | 5 |
| *10* | A1 | 20p multi | 6 | |
| *11* | A1 | 50p multi | 12 | |
| *12* | A1 | 1r multi | 20 | |
| *13* | A1 | 2r multi | 40 | |
| *14* | A1 | 3r multi | 60 | |
| *15* | A2 | 5r multi (R) | 90 | 90 |
| *16* | A1 | 10r multi | 1.90 | 1.90 |
| | | *Nos. 9-16 (8)* | 4.23 | |

Liberation of Bangladesh.

The 10p, 5r and 10r were issued in Dacca, but Nos. 10-14 were not put on sale in Bangladesh.

Monument A3

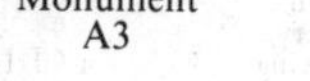

"Independence" A4

**1972, Feb. 21 Litho.** ***Perf. 13***

*32* A3 20p grn & rose 12 12

Martyrs of Bangladesh.

**1972, Mar. 26 Photo.** ***Perf. 13***

| | | | | |
|---|---|---|---|---|
| *33* | A4 | 20p mar & red | 6 | 6 |
| *34* | A4 | 60p dk bl & red | 18 | 18 |
| *35* | A4 | 75p pur & red | 20 | 20 |

First anniversary of independence.

Doves of Peace — A5

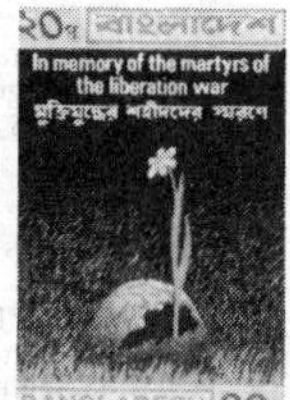

Flower Growing from Ruin — A6

**1972, Dec. 16 Litho.** ***Perf. 13***

| | | | | |
|---|---|---|---|---|
| *36* | A5 | 20p ocher & multi | 7 | 7 |
| *37* | A5 | 60p lil & multi | 18 | 18 |
| *38* | A5 | 75p yel grn & multi | 22 | 22 |

Victory Day, Dec. 16.

**1973, Mar. 25 Litho.** ***Perf. 13***

| | | | | |
|---|---|---|---|---|
| *39* | A6 | 20p ocher & multi | 6 | 6 |
| *40* | A6 | 60p brn & multi | 18 | 18 |
| *41* | A6 | 1.35t vio bl & multi | 40 | 40 |

Martyrs of the war of liberation.

Embroidered Quilt — A7

Hilsa — A8

Court of Justice — A9

Designs: 3p, Jute field. 5p, Jack fruit. 10p, Farmer plowing with ox team. 20p, Dahlia. 25p, Tiger. 60p, Bamboo and water lilies. 75p, Women picking tea. 90p, Handicraft. 2t, Coconut harvest (vert.). 5t, Net fishing. 10t, Sixty-dome Mosque.

**1973 Litho.** ***Perf. 14x14½, 14½x14***

**Size: 21x28mm, 28x21mm**

| | | | | |
|---|---|---|---|---|
| *42* | A7 | 2p black | 5 | 5 |
| *43* | A7 | 3p brt grn | 5 | 5 |
| *44* | A7 | 5p lt brn | 5 | 5 |
| *45* | A7 | 10p black | 5 | 5 |
| *46* | A7 | 20p olive | 6 | 6 |
| *47* | A7 | 25p red lil | 7 | 7 |
| *48* | A8 | 50p rose lil | 15 | 15 |
| *49* | A7 | 60p gray | 20 | 20 |
| *50* | A7 | 75p orange | 22 | 22 |
| *51* | A7 | 90p red brn | 28 | 28 |

**Taka Expressed as "TA"**

**Size: 35x22mm**

| | | | | |
|---|---|---|---|---|
| *52* | A9 | 1t violet | 30 | 30 |
| *53* | A9 | 2t grnsh gray | 60 | 60 |
| *54* | A9 | 5t grysh bl | 1.50 | 1.50 |
| *55* | A9 | 10t rose | 3.00 | 3.00 |
| | | *Nos. 42-55 (14)* | 6.58 | 6.58 |

See Nos. 82-85, 95-106, 165-176.

Human Rights Flame A10

Family, Chart, Map of Bangladesh A11

**1973, Dec. 10 Litho.** ***Perf. 13x13½***

| | | | | |
|---|---|---|---|---|
| *56* | A10 | 10p bl & multi | 5 | 5 |
| *57* | A10 | 1.25t vio & multi | 35 | 35 |

25th anniversary of the Universal Declaration of Human Rights.

**1974, Feb. 10 Litho.** ***Perf. 13½***

| | | | | |
|---|---|---|---|---|
| *58* | A11 | 20p bl grn & multi | 6 | 6 |
| *59* | A11 | 25p brt bl & multi | 7 | 7 |
| *60* | A11 | 75p red & multi | 20 | 20 |

First census in Bangladesh.

Copernicus, Heliocentric System A12

Flag and UN Headquarters A13

**1974, July 22 Litho. *Perf. 13½***

| | | | | |
|---|---|---|---|---|
| *61* | A12 | 25p vio, blk & org | 20 | 20 |
| *62* | A12 | 75p emer, blk & org | 60 | 60 |

500th anniversary of the birth of Nicolaus Copernicus (1473-1543), Polish astronomer.

**1974, Sept. 25 Litho. *Perf. 13½***

| | | | | |
|---|---|---|---|---|
| *63* | A13 | 25p lil & multi | 15 | 15 |
| *64* | A13 | 1t bl & multi | 60 | 60 |

Admission of Bangladesh to the UN.

Royal Bengal Tiger — A15

**1974, Nov. 4 Litho.**

| | | | | |
|---|---|---|---|---|
| *69* | A15 | 25p shown | 15 | 15 |
| *70* | A15 | 50p Tiger cub | 40 | 40 |
| *71* | A15 | 2t Swimming tiger | 1.50 | 1.50 |

"Save the Tiger," World Wildlife Fund.

Type of 1973
Taka Expressed in Bengali

**1974-75 *Perf. 14½x14, 14x14½***
**Size: 35x22mm**

| | | | | |
|---|---|---|---|---|
| *82* | A9 | 1t violet | 25 | 25 |
| *83* | A9 | 2t grysh grn | 50 | 50 |
| *84* | A9 | 5t grysh bl ('75) | 1.25 | 1.25 |
| *85* | A9 | 10t rose ('75) | 2.50 | 2.50 |

Family A16

Children A17

Family A18

**1974, Dec. 30 Litho. *Perf. 14***

| | | | | |
|---|---|---|---|---|
| *86* | A16 | 25p ocher & multi | 8 | 8 |
| *87* | A17 | 70p cl & multi | 22 | 22 |
| *88* | A18 | 1.25t multi | 35 | 35 |

Family planning. The numerals on No. 87 look like "90" but mean "70."

Betbunia Satellite Earth Station — A19

**1975, June 14 Litho. *Perf. 14***

| | | | | |
|---|---|---|---|---|
| *89* | A19 | 25p red, blk & sil | 8 | 8 |
| *90* | A19 | 1t vio bl, blk & sil | 25 | 25 |

Opening of Betbunia Satellite Earth Station.

Allegory, IWY Emblem A20

**1975, Dec. 31 Litho. *Perf. 15***

| | | | | |
|---|---|---|---|---|
| *91* | A20 | 50p rose & multi | 8 | 8 |
| *92* | A20 | 2t lt lil & multi | 45 | 45 |

International Women's Year 1975.

Types of 1973 Redrawn

**1976-77 Litho. *Perf. 15x14½***
**Size: 18x23mm, 23x18mm**

| | | | | |
|---|---|---|---|---|
| *95* | A7 | 5p green | 5 | 5 |
| *96* | A7 | 10p black | 5 | 5 |
| *97* | A7 | 20p ol grn | 5 | 5 |
| *98* | A7 | 25p rose lil | 5 | 5 |
| *99* | A7 | 50p rose lil | 8 | 8 |
| *100* | A7 | 60p gray | 10 | 10 |
| *101* | A7 | 75p olive | 12 | 12 |
| *102* | A7 | 90p red brn | 15 | 15 |

**Taka Expressed in Bengali**
**Size: 32x20mm, 20x32mm**

| | | | | |
|---|---|---|---|---|
| *103* | A9 | 1t violet | 16 | 16 |
| *104* | A9 | 2t grnsh gray | 30 | 30 |
| *105* | A9 | 5t grysh bl | 75 | 75 |
| *106* | A9 | 10t rose ('77) | 1.50 | 1.50 |
| | | *Nos. 95-106 (12)* | 3.36 | 3.36 |

Telephones, 1876 and 1976 — A21

Alexander Graham Bell — A22

**1976, Mar. 10 Litho. *Perf. 15***

| | | | | |
|---|---|---|---|---|
| *107* | A21 | 2.25t multi | 50 | 50 |
| *108* | A21 | 5t multi | 1.10 | 1.10 |

Centenary of first telephone call by Alexander Graham Bell, Mar. 10, 1876.

Eye and Healthful Food — A23

**1976, Apr. 7 Litho. *Perf. 15***

| | | | | |
|---|---|---|---|---|
| *109* | A23 | 30p yel & multi | 10 | 10 |
| *110* | A23 | 2.25t org & multi | 50 | 50 |

World Health Day: Foresight prevents blindness.

Liberty Bell — A24

Designs: 2.25t, Statue of Liberty, New York Skyline. 5t, Mayflower. 10t, Mt. Rushmore, presidents' heads.

**1976, May 29 Photo. *Perf. 13½x14***

| | | | | |
|---|---|---|---|---|
| *111* | A24 | 30p multi | 10 | 10 |
| *112* | A24 | 2.25t multi | 50 | 50 |
| *113* | A24 | 5t multi | 1.10 | 1.10 |
| *114* | A24 | 10t multi | 2.25 | 2.25 |
| | *a* | Souvenir sheet of 4 | 4.00 | 4.00 |

American Bicentennial. No. 114a contains one each of Nos. 111-114, perf. 13; multicolored margin showing center of "Declaration of Independence," by John Trumbull. Size: 166x95mm. Sheet exists imperf.

Weaver, Chemist, Farmer, Student and Emblem — A25

**1976, Aug. Litho. *Perf. 15***

| | | | | |
|---|---|---|---|---|
| *115* | A25 | 30p multi | 6 | 6 |
| *116* | A25 | 2.25t multi | 45 | 45 |

25th anniversary of Colombo Plan.

Hurdles — A26

Designs (Montreal Olympic Emblem and): 30p, Running (horiz.). 1t, High jump. 2.25t, Swimming (horiz.). 3.50t, Gymnastics. 5t, Soccer.

**1976, Nov. Litho. *Perf. 15***

| | | | | |
|---|---|---|---|---|
| *117* | A26 | 25p multi | 5 | 5 |
| *118* | A26 | 30p multi | 6 | 6 |
| *119* | A26 | 1t multi | 15 | 15 |
| *120* | A26 | 2.25t multi | 35 | 35 |
| *121* | A26 | 3.50t multi | 50 | 50 |
| *122* | A26 | 5t multi | 75 | 75 |
| | | *Nos. 117-122 (6)* | 1.86 | 1.86 |

21st Olympic Games, Montreal, Canada, July 17-Aug. 1.

Coronation Ceremony — A27

Designs: 2.25t, Queen Elizabeth II. 10t, Queen and Prince Philip.

**1977, Feb. 7 *Perf. 14x15***

| | | | | |
|---|---|---|---|---|
| *123* | A27 | 30p multi | 12 | 12 |
| *124* | A27 | 2.25t multi | 32 | 32 |
| *125* | A27 | 10t multi | 1.60 | 1.60 |
| | *a* | Souvenir sheet of 3 | 3.00 | 3.00 |

25th anniv. of the reign of Elizabeth II. No. 125a contains one each of Nos. 123-125, perf. 14½. Black and lilac rose decorative margin. Size: 127x114mm.

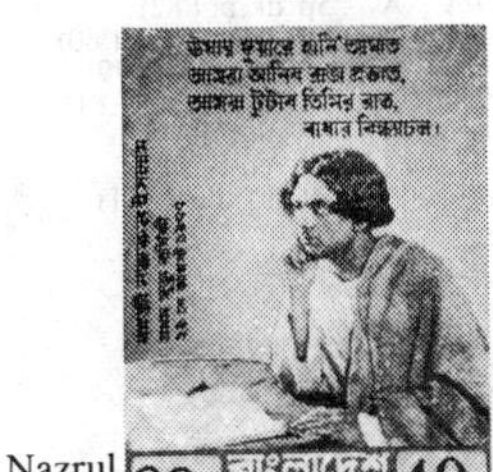


Qazi Nazrul Islam — A28

Demand, as well as supply, determines a stamp's market value. One is as important as the other.

Nazrul A29

**1977, Aug. 29 Litho. *Perf. 14***

| | | | | |
|---|---|---|---|---|
| *126* | A28 | 40p lt grn & blk | 6 | 6 |
| *127* | A29 | 2.25t multi | 30 | 30 |

Qazi Nazrul Islam (1899-1976), national poet.

Pigeon Carrying Letter A30

**1977, Sept. 29 Litho. *Perf. 14***

| | | | | |
|---|---|---|---|---|
| *128* | A30 | 30p multi | 5 | 5 |
| *129* | A30 | 2.25t multi | 30 | 30 |

Asian-Oceanic Postal Union (AOPU), 15th anniversary.

Leopard A31

40p and 1t are vert.

**1977, Nov. 9 Litho. *Perf. 13***

| | | | | |
|---|---|---|---|---|
| *130* | A31 | 40p Asiatic black bear | 8 | 8 |
| *131* | A31 | 1t Axis deer | 16 | 16 |
| *132* | A31 | 2.25t shown | 32 | 32 |
| *133* | A31 | 3.50t Gayal | 48 | 48 |
| *134* | A31 | 4t Elephant | 50 | 50 |
| *135* | A31 | 5t Bengal tiger | 65 | 65 |
| | | *Nos. 130-135 (6)* | 2.19 | 2.19 |

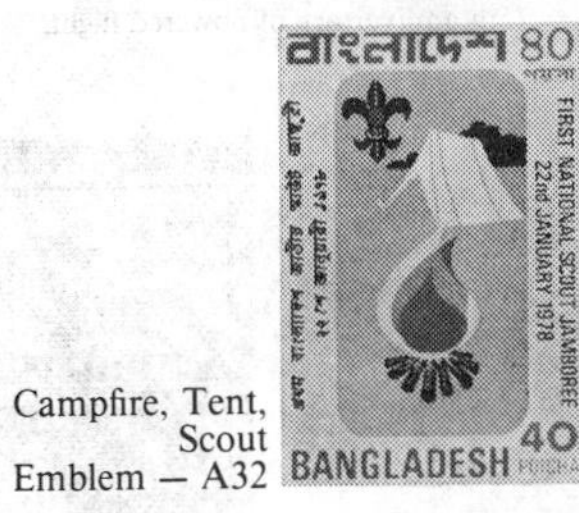


Campfire, Tent, Scout Emblem — A32

Designs: 3.50t, Emblem, first aid, signaling (horiz.). 5t, Scout emblem and oath.

**1978, Jan. 22 Litho. *Perf. 13***

| | | | | |
|---|---|---|---|---|
| *136* | A32 | 40p multi | 8 | 8 |
| *137* | A32 | 3.50t multi | 45 | 45 |
| *138* | A32 | 5t multi | 80 | 80 |

1st National Boy Scout Jamboree, Jan. 22.

Champac — A33

Flowers and Flowering Trees: 1t, Pudding pipe tree. 2.25t, Flamboyant tree. 3.50t, Water lilies. 4t, Butea. 5t, Anthocephalus indicus.

**1978, Mar. 31 Litho. Perf. 13**

| No. | Type | Value | Unused | Used |
|---|---|---|---|---|
| *139* | A33 | 40p multi | 6 | 6 |
| *140* | A33 | 1t multi | 15 | 15 |
| *141* | A33 | 2.25t multi | 30 | 30 |
| *142* | A33 | 3.50t multi | 50 | 50 |
| *143* | A33 | 4t multi | 55 | 55 |
| *144* | A33 | 5t multi | 65 | 65 |
| | | *Nos. 139-144 (6)* | 2.21 | 2.21 |

Crown, Scepter and Staff of State — A34

Designs: 3.50t, Royal family on balcony. 5t, Queen Elizabeth II and Prince Philip. 10t, Queen in coronation regalia, Westminster Abbey.

**1978, May Perf. 14**

| No. | Type | Value | Unused | Used |
|---|---|---|---|---|
| *145* | A34 | 40p multi | 8 | 8 |
| *146* | A34 | 3.50t multi | 55 | 55 |
| *147* | A34 | 5t multi | 80 | 80 |
| *148* | A34 | 10t multi | 1.50 | 1.50 |
| *a* | | Souvenir sheet of 4 | 3.00 | 3.00 |

Coronation of Queen Elizabeth II, 25th anniversary. No. 148a contains one each of Nos. 145-148, perf. 14½; tan margin with dark green inscription. Size: 89x121mm.

Alan Cobham's DH50, 1926 — A35

Planes: 2.25t, Capt. Hans Bertram's Junkers W33 Atlantis, 1932-33. 3.50t, Wright brothers' plane. 5t, Concorde.

**1978, June Litho. Perf. 13**

| No. | Type | Value | Unused | Used |
|---|---|---|---|---|
| *149* | A35 | 40p multi | 6 | 6 |
| *150* | A35 | 2.25t multi | 35 | 35 |
| *151* | A35 | 3.50t multi | 55 | 55 |
| *152* | A35 | 5t multi | 75 | 75 |

75th anniversary of powered flight.

Holy Kaaba, Mecca — A37

Design: 3.50t, Pilgrims at Mt. Arafat (horiz.).

**1978, Nov. 9 Litho. Perf. 13**

| No. | Type | Value | Unused | Used |
|---|---|---|---|---|
| *154* | A37 | 40p multi | 6 | 6 |
| *155* | A37 | 3.50t multi | 50 | 50 |

Pilgrimage to Mecca.

Jasim Uddin A38

**1979, Mar. 14 Litho. Perf. 14**

| No. | Type | Value | Unused | Used |
|---|---|---|---|---|
| *156* | A38 | 40p multi | 15 | 15 |

Jasim Uddin, poet.

Rowland Hill — A39

Moulana Bhashani — A40

Hill and Stamps of Bangladesh: 3.50t, No. 1 (horiz.). 10t, Unissued UPU stamp of 1974 (horiz.).

**1979, Aug. 27 Litho. Perf. 14**

| No. | Type | Value | Unused | Used |
|---|---|---|---|---|
| *157* | A39 | 40p multi | 8 | 8 |
| *158* | A39 | 3.50t multi | 45 | 45 |
| *159* | A39 | 10t multi | 1.40 | 1.40 |
| *a* | | Souvenir sheet of 3 | 1.75 | 1.75 |

Sir Rowland Hill (1795-1879), originator of penny postage. No. 159a contains Nos. 157-159. Multicolored margin shows Hill portrait. Size: 171½x96mm.

**1979, Nov. 17 Perf. 12½**

| No. | Type | Value | Unused | Used |
|---|---|---|---|---|
| *160* | A40 | 40p multi | 15 | 15 |

Moulana Abdul Hamid Khan Bhashani (1880-1976), philosopher and statesman.

Boys and Hoops, IYC Emblem — A41

IYC Emblem and: 3.50t, Children jumping. 5t, Boys flying kites.

**1979, Dec. 17 Litho. Perf. 14x14½**

| No. | Type | Value | Unused | Used |
|---|---|---|---|---|
| *161* | A41 | 40p multi | 6 | 6 |
| *162* | A41 | 3.50t multi | 55 | 55 |
| *163* | A41 | 5t multi | 80 | 80 |
| *a* | | Souvenir sheet of 3 | 1.75 | 1.75 |

International Year of the Child. No. 163a contains Nos. 161-163, perf. 14½; multicolored margin shows children playing games. Size: 170x121mm.

Type of 1973

Designs: 5p, Lalbag Fort. 10p, Fenchungan Fertilizer Factory (vert.). 15p, Pineapple. 20p, Gas well. 25p, Jute on boat. 30p, Banana tree. 40p, Baitul Mukarram Mosque. 50p, Baitul Mukarram Mosque. 80p, Garh excavations. 1ta, Dotara (musical instrument.) 2t, Karnaphuli Dam.

**1979-82 Photo. Perf. 14½**

**Size: 18x23mm, 23x18mm**

| No. | Type | Value | Unused | Used |
|---|---|---|---|---|
| *165* | A7 | 5p brn ('79) | 5 | 5 |
| *166* | A7 | 10p Prus bl | 5 | 5 |
| *167* | A7 | 15p yel org ('81) | 5 | 5 |
| *168* | A7 | 20p dk car ('79) | 5 | 5 |
| *169* | A7 | 25p dk bl ('82) | 5 | 5 |
| *169A* | A7 | 30p lt olive grn ('80) | 6 | 6 |
| *170* | A7 | 40p rose mag ('79) | 7 | 7 |
| *172* | A9 | 50p blk & gray ('81) | 8 | 8 |
| *173* | A7 | 80p dk brn ('80) | 12 | 12 |
| *175* | A7 | 1t red lil ('81) | 15 | 12 |
| *176* | A7 | 2t brt ultra ('81) | 28 | 28 |
| | | *Nos. 165-176 (11)* | 1.01 | 98 |

Rotary International, 75th Anniversary A42

Design: 40p, Rotary emblem (diff.).

**1980, Feb. 23 Litho. Perf. 14**

| No. | Type | Value | Unused | Used |
|---|---|---|---|---|
| *179* | A42 | 40p multi | 6 | 6 |
| *180* | A42 | 5t ultra & gold | 65 | 65 |

Canal Digging A43

**1980, Mar. Litho. Perf. 14**

| No. | Type | Value | Unused | Used |
|---|---|---|---|---|
| *181* | A43 | 40p multi | 12 | 12 |

A.K. Fazlul Huq — A44

**1980, Apr. 27 Litho. Perf. 14**

| No. | Type | Value | Unused | Used |
|---|---|---|---|---|
| *182* | A44 | 80p multi | 12 | 12 |

Sher-e-Bangla A.K. Fazlul Huq (1873-1962), national leader.

Early Mail Transport, London 1980 Emblem — A45

**1980, May 5**

| No. | Type | Value | Unused | Used |
|---|---|---|---|---|
| *183* | A45 | 1t *shown* | 12 | 12 |
| *184* | A45 | 10t *Modern mail transport* | 1.25 | 1.25 |
| *a* | | Souvenir sheet of 2 | 1.75 | 1.75 |

London 80 Intl. Stamp Exhib., May 6-14. No. 184a contains Nos. 183-184; multicolored margin shows London 80 emblem. Size: 140x96mm.

Dome of the Rock — A46

Adult Education — A47

**1980, Aug. 21 Litho. Perf. 14½**

| No. | Type | Value | Unused | Used |
|---|---|---|---|---|
| *185* | A46 | 50p vio rose | 15 | 15 |

For the families of Palestinians.

**1980, Aug. 23 Perf. 13½**

| No. | Type | Value | Unused | Used |
|---|---|---|---|---|
| *186* | A47 | 50p multi | 15 | 15 |

Beach Scene A48

**1980, Sept. Litho. Perf. 1**

| No. | Type | Value | Unused | Used |
|---|---|---|---|---|
| *187* | A48 | 50p *shown* | 12 | 1 |
| *188* | A48 | 5t *Beach scene,* diff. | 1.10 | 1.1 |
| *a* | | Souvenir sheet of 2 | 1.25 | 1.2 |

World Tourism Conference, Manila, Sept 27. Nos. 187-188 se-tenant in continuou design. No. 188a contains Nos. 187-188 green and black margin shows water sports Size: 140x88mm.

Hegira (Pilgrimage Year) — A49

**1980, Nov. 11 Photo. Perf. 14**

| No. | Type | Value | Unused | Used |
|---|---|---|---|---|
| *189* | A49 | 50p multi | 12 | 12 |

Deer and Boy Scout Emblem — A50

**1981, Jan. 1 Litho. Perf. 14**

| No. | Type | Value | Unused | Used |
|---|---|---|---|---|
| *190* | A50 | 50p multi | 8 | 8 |
| *191* | A50 | 5t multi | 75 | 75 |

5th Asia-Pacific and 2nd Bangladesh Scout Jamboree, 1980-1981.

Begum Roquiah (1880-1932), Educator — A51

**1980, Dec. Litho. Perf. 14**

| No. | Type | Value | Unused | Used |
|---|---|---|---|---|
| *192* | A51 | 50p multi | 12 | 12 |
| *193* | A51 | 2t multi | 45 | 45 |

Nos. 58-60 Overprinted: 2nd / CENSUS / 1981

**1981, Mar. 6 Perf. 13½**

| No. | Type | Value | Unused | Used |
|---|---|---|---|---|
| *194* | A11 | 20p multi | 5 | 5 |
| *195* | A11 | 25p multi | 5 | 5 |
| *196* | A11 | 75p multi | 15 | 15 |

Queen Mother Elizabeth, 80th Birthday (1980) — A52

**1981, Mar. 16 Litho. Perf. 14**

| No. | Type | Value | Unused | Used |
|---|---|---|---|---|
| *197* | A52 | 1t multi | 12 | 12 |
| *198* | A52 | 15t multi | 1.75 | 1.75 |
| *a* | | Souvenir sheet of 2 | 1.90 | 1.90 |

No. 198a contains Nos. 197-198; light blue and black margin. Size: 96x74mm.

Citizen Holding Rifle and Flag — A53

**1981, Mar. 26**
199 A53 50p shown 7 7
200 A53 2t People, map 25 25

10th anniversary of independence.

U.N. Conference on Least-developed Countries, Paris — A54

**1981, Sept. 1 Litho. *Perf. 14x13½***
201 A54 50p multi 15 15

Birth Centenary of Kemal Ataturk (First President of Turkey) — A55

**1981, Nov. 10 Litho. *Perf. 14***
202 A55 50p Portrait 8 8
203 A55 1t Portrait, diff. 12 12

Intl. Year of the Disabled A56

**1981, Dec. 26 Litho. *Perf. 14***
204 A56 50p Sign language, vert. 8 8
205 A56 2t Amputee 25 25

World Food Day, Oct. 16 — A57

**1981, Dec. 31 Litho. *Perf. 13½x14***
206 A57 50p multi 15 15

10th Anniv. of UN Conference on Human Environment A58

**1982, May 22 Litho. *Perf. 13½x14***
207 A58 50p Boat hauling rice straw 15 15

K. Hossain — A59

**1982, Oct. 9**
208 A59 50p multi 15 15

Scouting Year — A60

**1982, Oct. 21 Litho. *Perf. 14***
209 A60 50p Emblem, knots 8 8
210 A60 2t Baden-Powell, vert. 35 35

Capt. Mohiuddin Jahangir A61

Liberation Heroes (Tablet Color): b. Sepoy Hamidur Rahman (pale green). c. Sepoy Mohammed Mustafa Kamal (rose claret). d. Mohammad Ruhul Amin (yellow). e. M. Matiur Rahman (olive bister). f. Lance-Naik Munshi Abdur Rob (brown orange). g. Lance-Naik Nur Mouhammad (bright yellow green).

**1982, Dec. 16 Litho. *Perf. 14***
211 Strip of 7 60 60
*a.-g.* A61 50p multi 8 8

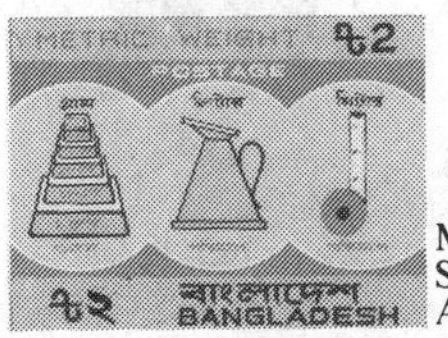

Metric System A62

**1983, Jan. 10 Litho. *Perf. 14***
212 A62 50p Mail scale, vert. 8 8
213 A62 2t Weights, measures 28 28

TB Bacillus Centenary — A63

**1983, Feb. 20 Litho. *Perf. 14***
214 A63 50p Koch 10 10
215 A63 1t Slides, microscope 20 20

**Commonwealth Day**
Common Design Type

**1983, Mar. 14 Litho. *Perf. 14***
216 CD334 1t Open stage theater 12 12
217 CD334 3t Boat race 35 35
218 CD334 10t Snake dance 1.10 1.10
219 CD334 15t Tea garden 1.75 1.75

Jnantapash Shahidullah (1885-1969), Patriot and Physician — A65

**1983, July 10 Litho. *Perf. 14***
220 A65 50p multi 15 15

Birds A66

**1983, Aug. 17 Litho. *Perf. 14***
221 A66 50p Copsychus saulari 7 7
222 A66 2t Halcyon smyrnensis, vert. 25 25
223 A66 3.75t Dinopium benghalense, vert. 40 40
224 A66 5t Carina scutulota 60 60
*a* Souvenir sheet of 4 1.75 1.75

Margin depicts various birds; black marginal inscription. Sold for 13t. Size: 165x111mm.

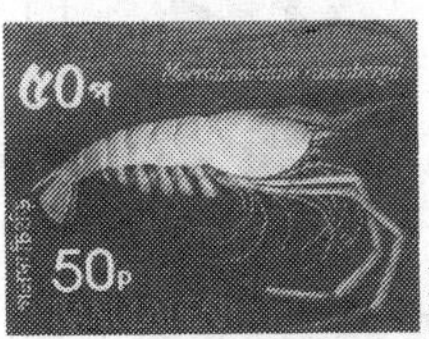

Local Fish — A67

**1983, Oct. 31 Litho. *Perf. 14***
225 A67 50p Macrobrachium rosengergii 7 7
226 A67 2t Stromateus cinereus 25 25
227 A67 3.75t Labeo rohita 40 40
228 A67 5t Anabas testudineus 60 60
*a* Souvenir sheet of 4 1.25 1.25

No. 228a contains Nos. 225-228 (imperf.); multicolored margin shows fish swimming. Size: 120x98mm. Sold for 13t.

**No. 148 Ovptd. "Nov. '83/Visit of Queen" in Red.**

**1983, Nov. 14 Litho. *Perf. 14***
228B A34 10t multi 1.75 1.75

World Communications Year — A68

**1983, Dec. 21 Litho. *Perf. 14***
229 A68 50p Messenger, vert. 7 7
230 A68 5t Jet, train, ship, vert. 60 60
231 A68 10t Dish antenna, messenger 1.10 1.10

Sangsad Bhaban Conference Hall A69

Mailboat A70

**1983, Dec. 5 Litho. *Perf. 14***
232 A69 50p shown 5 5
233 A69 5t Old Dhaka Fort 25 25

14th Islamic Foreign Ministers Conference.

***Perf. 11½x12½, 12½x11½***

**1983, Dec. 21**
234 A70 5p shown 5 5
235 A70 10p Dhaka P.O. interior 5 5
236 A70 15p IWTA Terminal 5 5
237 A70 20p Sorting mail 5 5
238 A70 25p Mail delivery 5 5
239 A70 30p Postman at mailbox 5 5
240 A70 50p Mobile post office 10 10

**Size: 30½x28½mm**

***Perf. 12x11½***
241 A70 1t Kamalapur Railway Station 10 10
242 A70 2t Zia Intl. Airport 20 20
242A A70 5t Khulna P.O. 50 50
*Nos. 234-242A (10)* 1.20 1.20

Nos. 235-237, 239-242A horiz.
See No. 270.

**Nos. 187-188 Overprinted "First Bangladesh National Philatelic Exhibition 1984" in English or Bengali in Red**

**1984, Feb. 1 Litho. *Perf. 14***
243 A48 50p Beach Scene 6 6
244 A48 5t Beach Scene, diff. 50 50

Se-tenant in continuous design.

Girl Examining Stamp Album — A71

**1984, May 17 *Perf. 14½***
245 A71 50p shown 6 6
246 A71 7.50t Boy updating collection 75 75
*a* Souv. sheet of 2, Nos. 245-246 1.20 1.20

Nos. 245-246 printed se-tenant in continuous design. No. 246a has multicolored inscribed margin. Sold for 10t. Size: 97x115mm.

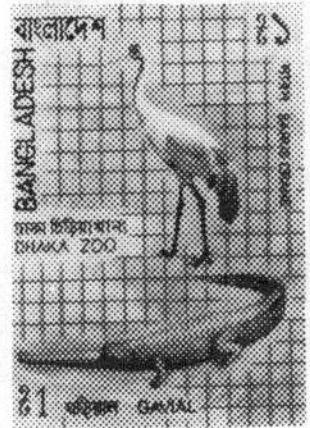

Dhaka Zoo — A72

Postal Life Insurance, Cent. — A73

**1984, July 17 Litho. *Perf. 14***
247 A72 1t Sarus crane, gavial 10 10
248 A72 2t Peafowl, royal Bengal tiger 20 20

**1984, Dec. 3**
249 A73 1t Chicken hawk, hen 10 10
250 A73 5t Beneficiaries 50 50

An enhanced introduction to the Scott Catalogue begins on Page V. A thorough understanding of the material presented there will greatly aid your use of the catalogue itself.

Abbasudin Ahmad, Bengali Singer — A74

**1984, Dec. 24**

*251* A74 3t multi 30 30

No. 116 Ovptd. for KHULNAPEX '84 Stamp Exhibition

৮৪—খুলনাপেক্স

**1984, Dec. 29 Litho. *Perf. 15***

*252* A25 2.25t multi 30 30

1984 Summer Olympics, Los Angeles A75

**1984, Dec. 31 *Perf. 14***

| | | | | |
|---|---|---|---|---|
| *253* | A75 | 1t Bicycling | 10 | 10 |
| *254* | A75 | 5t Field hockey | 50 | 50 |
| *255* | A75 | 10t Volleyball | 1.00 | 1.00 |

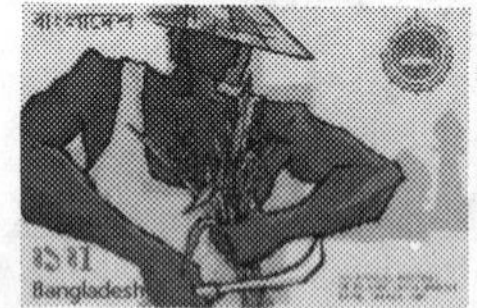

Islamic Development Bank, 9th Annual Congress, Dhaka — A76

**1985, Feb. 2**

| | | | | |
|---|---|---|---|---|
| *256* | A76 | 1t Farmer | 10 | 10 |
| *257* | A76 | 5t Four Bengalis | 50 | 50 |

UN Child Survival Campaign — A77

UN Decade for Women — A78

**1985, Mar. 14**

| | | | | |
|---|---|---|---|---|
| *258* | A77 | 1t Breastfeeding | 25 | 25 |
| *259* | A77 | 10t Growth monitoring | 1.25 | 1.25 |

Nos. 139-144 Ovptd. in Bengali for Local Elections.

উপজেলা নির্বাচন ১৯৮৫

**1985, May 16 Litho. *Perf. 13***

| | | | | |
|---|---|---|---|---|
| *259A* | A33 | 40p multi | 5 | 5 |
| *259B* | A33 | 1t multi | 7 | 7 |
| *259C* | A33 | 2.25t multi | 14 | 14 |
| *259D* | A33 | 3.50t multi | 22 | 22 |
| *259E* | A33 | 4t multi | 25 | 25 |
| *259F* | A33 | 5t multi | 30 | 30 |
| | | *Nos. 259A-259F (6)* | 1.03 | 1.03 |

**1985, July 18 *Perf. 14***

| | | | | |
|---|---|---|---|---|
| *260* | A78 | 1t shown | 10 | 10 |
| *261* | A78 | 10t Technology | 1.00 | 1.00 |

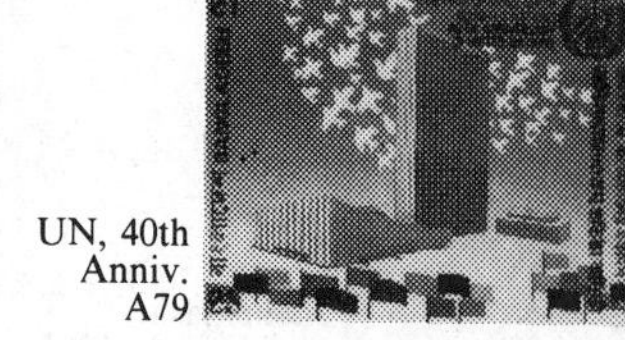
UN, 40th Anniv. A79

**1985, Sept. 15**

| | | | | |
|---|---|---|---|---|
| *262* | A79 | 1t UN building | 6 | 6 |
| *263* | A79 | 10t World map, natl. flag | 50 | 50 |

Admission of Bangladesh to UN, 11th anniv.

Intl. Youth Year — A80

**1985, Nov. 2 Litho. *Perf. 14***

| | | | | |
|---|---|---|---|---|
| *264* | A80 | 1t Scissors, pencil | 12 | 12 |
| *265* | A80 | 5t Hammer, wrenches | 50 | 50 |

Seven Doves, Council Emblem — A81

**1985, Dec. 8 Litho. *Perf. 14***

| | | | | |
|---|---|---|---|---|
| *266* | A81 | 1t shown | 10 | 10 |
| *267* | A81 | 5t Flags, lotus blossom | 50 | 50 |

1st South Asian Regional Council Summit, SARC, Dhaka.

Shilpacharya Zainul Abedin (1914-1976), Founder, Dhaka College of Art — A82

**1985, Dec. 28**

*268* A82 3t multi 30 30

No. 138 Ovptd. for the 3rd Natl. Scout Jamboree in Bengali.

**1985, Dec. 29 *Perf. 13***

*269* A32 5t multi 50 50

Postal Services Type of 1983-84

**1986, Jan. 11 Litho. *Perf. 12x11½***

**Size: 30½x19mm**

*270* A70 3t Sorting machine 30 30

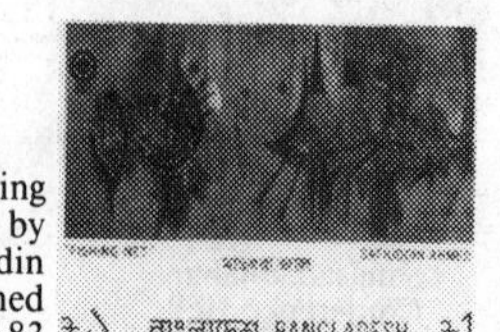

Fishing Net, by Safiuddin Ahmed A83

Paintings by Bengali artists: 5t, Happy Return, by Quamrul Hassan. 10t, Levelling the Plowed Field, by Zainul Abedin.

**1986, Apr. 6 Litho. *Perf. 14***

| | | | | |
|---|---|---|---|---|
| *275* | A83 | 1t multi | 10 | 10 |
| *276* | A83 | 5t multi | 50 | 50 |
| *277* | A83 | 10t multi | 1.00 | 1.00 |

1986 World Cup Soccer Championships, Mexico — A84

**1986, June 29 *Perf. 15x14***

| | | | | |
|---|---|---|---|---|
| *278* | A84 | 1t Stealing the ball | 10 | 10 |
| *279* | A84 | 10t Goal | 1.00 | 1.00 |

**Souvenir Sheet**

***Imperf***

*279A* A84 20t multi 3.25 3.25

No. 279A contains one stamp (size: 62x45mm) with simulated perfs.; multicolored inscribed margin continues the design. Size: 105x75mm.

Gen. M.A.G. Osmani (1918-1984), Liberation Forces Commander-in-Chief — A85

**1986, Sept. 10 Litho. *Perf. 14***

*280* A85 3t multi 55 55

A86

Intl. Peace Year — A87

**1986, Dec. 25 Litho. *Perf. 12x12½***

| | | | | |
|---|---|---|---|---|
| *282* | A86 | 1t shown | 10 | 10 |
| *283* | A86 | 10t City ruins, flower | 1.00 | 1.00 |

**Souvenir Sheet**

*284* A87 20t shown 2.00 2.00

No. 284 has multicolored margin continuing the war scene. Size: 110x79mm.

Nos. 179-180 Ovptd. or Surcharged "CONFERENCE FOR DEVELOPMENT '87"

**1987, Jan. 12 *Perf. 14***

| | | | | |
|---|---|---|---|---|
| *285* | A42 | 1t on 40p multi | 10 | 10 |
| *286* | A42 | 5t multi | 50 | 50 |

Language Movement, 35th Anniv. — A88

**1987, Feb. 21 *Perf. 12½x12***

| | | | | |
|---|---|---|---|---|
| *287* | A88 | 3t Protestors | 30 | 30 |
| *288* | A88 | 3t Memorial | 30 | 30 |

World Health Day — A89

**1987, Apr. 7 *Perf. 11½x12***

*289* A89 1t Child immunization 14 14

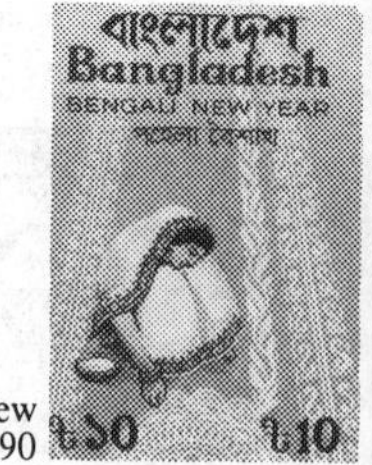

Bengali New Year — A90

**1987, Apr. 16 *Perf. 12x12½***

| | | | | |
|---|---|---|---|---|
| *290* | A90 | 1t Bengali script, embroidery | 10 | 10 |
| *291* | A90 | 10t shown | 1.00 | 1.00 |

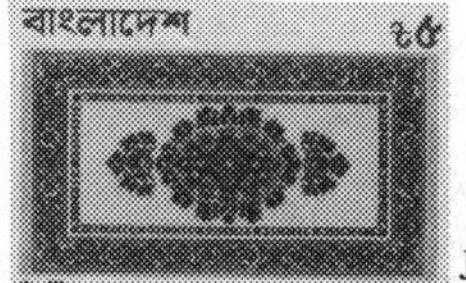

Jute Carpet A91

Exports: 1t, Jute shika (wall hanging, bowl-holder and mats), vert. 10t, Table lamp and shade, vert.

***Perf. 12x12½, 12½x12***

**1987, May 18 Litho.**

| | | | | |
|---|---|---|---|---|
| *292* | A91 | 1t multi | 12 | 12 |
| *293* | A91 | 5t shown | 55 | 55 |
| *294* | A91 | 10t multi | 1.10 | 1.10 |

Ustad Ayet Ali Khan (1884-1967), Composer, and Surbahar A92

**1987, Sept. 8 *Perf. 12x12½***

*295* A92 5t multi 55 55

Palanquin A93

Transportation.

**1987, Oct. 24 Litho. *Perf. 12½x12***

| | | | | |
|---|---|---|---|---|
| *296* | A93 | 2t shown | 24 | 24 |
| *297* | A93 | 3t Bicycle rickshaw | 35 | 35 |
| *298* | A93 | 5t Paddle steamer | 60 | 60 |
| *299* | A93 | 7t Train | 82 | 82 |
| *300* | A93 | 10t Ox cart | 1.20 | 1.20 |
| | | *Nos. 296-300 (5)* | 3.21 | 3.21 |

Hossain Shahid Suhrawardy (1893-1963), Politician — A94

**1987, Dec. 5** **Litho.** ***Perf. 12x12½***

| | | | | |
|---|---|---|---|---|
| *301* | A94 | 3t multi | 32 | 32 |

Intl. Year of Shelter for the Homeless A95

**1987, Dec. 15** ***Perf. 12½x12***

| | | | | |
|---|---|---|---|---|
| *302* | A95 | 5t shown | 55 | 55 |
| *303* | A95 | 5t Prosperous community | 55 | 55 |

Nos. 302-303 are printed se-tenant in a continuous design.

Natl. Democracy, 1st Anniv. — A96

Design: Pres. Hossain Mohammed Ershad addressing parliament.

**1987, Dec. 31**

| | | | | |
|---|---|---|---|---|
| *304* | A96 | 10t multi | 1.10 | 1.10 |

Woman Tending Crop A97

**1988, Jan. 26**

| | | | | |
|---|---|---|---|---|
| *305* | A97 | 3t shown | 22 | 22 |
| *306* | A97 | 5t Milking cow, village | 35 | 35 |

Intl. Fund for Agricultural Development (IFAD) Seminar on Loans for Women in Rural Areas.

## OFFICIAL STAMPS

Nos. 42-47, 49-50, 52, 82-84 and 54 Overprinted in Black or Red **SERVICE**

***Perf. 14x14½, 14½x14***

**1973-75** **Litho.**

| | | | | |
|---|---|---|---|---|
| *O1* | A7 | 2p blk (R) | 5 | 5 |
| *O2* | A7 | 3p brt grn | 5 | 5 |
| *O3* | A7 | 5p lt brn | 5 | 5 |
| *O4* | A7 | 10p blk (R) | 5 | 5 |
| *O5* | A7 | 20p olive | 6 | 6 |
| *O6* | A7 | 25p red lil | 8 | 8 |
| *O8* | A7 | 60p gray (R) | 20 | 20 |
| *O9* | A7 | 75p org ('74) | 25 | 25 |
| *O10* | A9 | 1t vio (#52) | 2.75 | 2.75 |
| *O11* | A9 | 1t vio (#82) | 32 | 32 |
| *O12* | A9 | 2t grysh grn ('74) | 64 | 64 |
| *O13* | A9 | 5t gray bl (#54) | 1.60 | 1.60 |
| *O14* | A9 | 5t grysh bl (#84) ('75) | 1.60 | 1.60 |
| | | *Nos. O1-O14 (13)* | 7.70 | 7.70 |

Nos. 95-101, 103-105 Overprinted "SERVICE" in Black or Red

**1976** **Litho.** ***Perf. 15x14½, 14½x15***

| | | | | |
|---|---|---|---|---|
| *O16* | A7 | 5p green | 5 | 5 |
| *O17* | A7 | 10p blk (R) | 5 | 5 |
| *O18* | A7 | 20p olive | 5 | 5 |
| *O19* | A7 | 25p rose | 5 | 5 |
| *O20* | A8 | 50p rose lil | 15 | 15 |
| *O21* | A7 | 60p gray (R) | 18 | 18 |
| *O22* | A7 | 75p olive | 22 | 22 |

***Perf. 15***

| | | | | |
|---|---|---|---|---|
| *O23* | A9 | 1t violet | 30 | 30 |
| *O24* | A9 | 2t grnsh gray | 60 | 60 |
| *O25* | A9 | 5t grysh bl | 1.50 | 1.50 |
| | | *Nos. O16-O25 (10)* | 3.15 | 3.15 |

Nos. 168, 169, 170, 172, 173, 175, 176 Overprinted "SERVICE"

**1979-82** **Photo.** ***Perf. 14½***

| | | | | |
|---|---|---|---|---|
| *O30* | A7 | 20p dk car | 5 | 5 |
| *O31* | A7 | 25p dk bl ('82) | 5 | 5 |
| *O32* | A9 | 40p rose mag | 8 | 8 |
| *O33* | A9 | 50p gray ('81) | 10 | 10 |
| *O34* | A7 | 80p dk brn | 15 | 15 |
| *O36* | A7 | 1t red lil ('81) | 20 | 20 |
| *O36A* | A7 | 2t brt ultra ('81) | 35 | 35 |
| | | *Nos. O30-O36A (7)* | 98 | 98 |

Nos. 234-242 ovptd. "SERVICE" in Red.

***Perf. 11½x12½, 12½x11½***

**1983, Dec. 21**

| | | | | |
|---|---|---|---|---|
| *O37* | A70 | 5p bluish grn | 5 | 5 |
| *O38* | A70 | 10p dp mag | 5 | 5 |
| *O39* | A70 | 15p blue | 5 | 5 |
| *O40* | A70 | 20p dk gray | 5 | 5 |
| *O41* | A70 | 25p slate | 5 | 5 |
| *O42* | A70 | 30p gray brn | 5 | 5 |
| *O43* | A70 | 50p yel brn | 5 | 5 |

**Size: 30½x28½mm**

***Perf. 12x11½***

| | | | | |
|---|---|---|---|---|
| *O44* | A70 | 1t ultra | 12 | 12 |
| *O45* | A70 | 2t Prus bl | 25 | 25 |
| | | *Nos. O37-O45 (9)* | 72 | 72 |

# BARBADOS

LOCATION — A West Indies island east of the Windwards.
GOVT. — Independent state in the British Commonwealth.
AREA — 166 sq. mi.
POP. — 270,500 (1981)
CAPITAL — Bridgetown

The British colony of Barbados became an independent state on November 30, 1966.

4 Farthings = 1 Penny
12 Pence = 1 Shilling
20 Shillings = 1 Pound
100 Cents = 1 Dollar (1950)

**Catalogue values for unused stamps in this country are for Never Hinged items, beginning with Scott 207 in the regular postage section, Scott B2 in the semi-postal section and Scott J1 in the postage due section.**

Britannia
A1 A2

**1852-55** **Unwmk.** **Engr.** ***Imperf.***

**Blued Paper**

| | | | | |
|---|---|---|---|---|
| *1* | A1 | (½p) dp grn | 90.00 | 175.00 |
| *a* | | (½p) yellow green | *7,500.* | 900.00 |
| *2* | A1 | (1p) blue | 16.00 | 125.00 |
| *a* | | (1p) dark blue | 16.00 | 45.00 |
| *3* | A1 | (2p) slate bl | 10.00 | |
| *a* | | (2p) grayish slate | 300.00 | |
| *b* | | Vert. half (#3a) used as 1p on cover | | 6,500. |
| *4* | A1 | (4p) brn red ('55) | 30.00 | 100.00 |

No. 3 was not placed in use. No. 3a was used only when bisected.

**1856-57**

**White Paper**

| | | | | |
|---|---|---|---|---|
| *5* | A1 | (½p) dp grn | 75.00 | 125.00 |
| *a* | | (½p) yellow green | 400.00 | 75.00 |
| *6* | A1 | (1p) blue | 17.50 | 30.00 |
| *a* | | (1p) pale blue | 30.00 | 30.00 |

It is believed that the (4p) brownish red on white paper exists only as No. 17b.

**1859**

| | | | | |
|---|---|---|---|---|
| *8* | A2 | 6p rose red | 400.00 | 110.00 |
| *9* | A2 | 1sh black | 125.00 | 50.00 |

***Pin-perf. 14***

| | | | | |
|---|---|---|---|---|
| *10* | A1 | (½p) pale yel grn | 2,250. | 250.00 |
| *11* | A1 | (1p) blue | 2,250. | 90.00 |

***Pin-perf. 12½***

| | | | | |
|---|---|---|---|---|
| *12* | A1 | (½p) pale yel grn | 5,500. | 400.00 |
| *12A* | A1 | (1p) blue | *15,000.* | 1,250. |

**1861** ***Clean-Cut Perf. 14 to 16***

| | | | | |
|---|---|---|---|---|
| *13* | A1 | (½p) dark bl grn | 40.00 | 9.00 |
| *14* | A1 | (1p) blue | 600.00 | 16.00 |
| *a* | | (1p) pale blue | 600.00 | 16.00 |
| *b* | | Half used as ½p on cover | | 3,250. |

***Rough Perf. 14 to 16***

| | | | | |
|---|---|---|---|---|
| *15* | A1 | (½p) blue green | 7.50 | 7.50 |
| *a* | | (½p) yellow green | 7.50 | 7.50 |
| *b* | | Imperf., pair | 500.00 | |
| *16* | A1 | (1p) blue | 11.00 | 3.25 |
| *a* | | Diagonal half used as ½p on cover | | *1,250.* |
| *b* | | Imperf., pair | 600.00 | |
| *17* | A1 | (4p) rose red | 35.00 | 15.00 |
| *a* | | (4p) brown red | 90.00 | 14.00 |
| *b* | | As "a," imperf., pair | 750.00 | |
| *c* | | (4p) rose red, imperf., pair | 800.00 | |
| *18* | A1 | (4p) vermilion | 150.00 | 50.00 |
| *a* | | Imperf., pair | 750.00 | |
| *19* | A2 | 6p rose red | 175.00 | 9.00 |
| *20* | A2 | 6p org ver | 27.50 | 7.50 |
| *a* | | 6p vermilion | 27.50 | 7.50 |
| *b* | | Imperf., pair | 400.00 | *1,000.* |
| *21* | A2 | 1sh black | 22.50 | 6.00 |
| *a* | | Horiz. pair, imperf. btwn. | *6,500.* | |
| *b* | | 1sh blue (error) | *22,500.* | |

No. 21b was never placed in use. All copies are pen-marked.

***Perf. 11 to 13***

| | | | | |
|---|---|---|---|---|
| *22* | A1 | (½p) deep green | *9,000.* | |
| *23* | A1 | (1p) blue | *4,250.* | |

Nos. 22 and 23 were never placed in use.

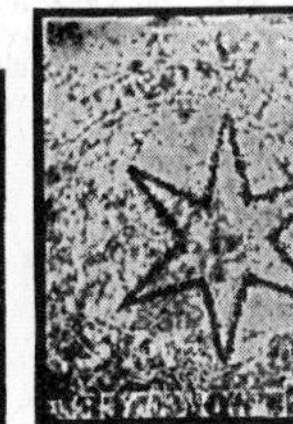

Wmk. 5- Small Star Wmk. 6- Large Star

**1871** **Wmk. 6** ***Rough Perf. 14 to 16***

| | | | | |
|---|---|---|---|---|
| *24* | A1 | (½p) yellow green | 70.00 | 10.00 |
| *a* | | Imperf., pair | 625.00 | |
| *25* | A1 | (1p) blue | 1,100. | 15.00 |
| *a* | | Imperf., pair | *1,300.* | |
| *26* | A1 | (4p) dull red | 750.00 | 37.50 |
| *27* | A2 | 6p vermilion | 750.00 | 45.00 |
| *28* | A2 | 1sh black | 200.00 | 15.00 |

**1871** **Wmk. 5**

| | | | | |
|---|---|---|---|---|
| *29* | A1 | (1p) blue | 60.00 | 3.00 |
| *30* | A1 | (4p) rose red | 500.00 | 15.00 |
| *31* | A2 | 6p vermilion | 325.00 | 17.50 |
| *32* | A2 | 1sh black | 110.00 | 10.00 |

***Clean-Cut Perf. 14½ to 16***

| | | | | |
|---|---|---|---|---|
| *33* | A1 | (1p) blue | 175.00 | 2.50 |
| *a* | | Diagonal half used as ½p on cover | | *1,000.* |
| *34* | A2 | 6p vermilion | 500.00 | 25.00 |
| *35* | A2 | 1sh black | 75.00 | 7.50 |

***Perf. 11 to 13 x 14½ to 16***

| | | | | |
|---|---|---|---|---|
| *36* | A1 | (½p) blue green | 250.00 | 15.00 |
| *37* | A1 | (4p) vermilion | 375.00 | 45.00 |

**1873** ***Perf. 14***

| | | | | |
|---|---|---|---|---|
| *38* | A2 | 3p claret | 350.00 | 60.00 |

**Wmk. 6**

***Clean-Cut Perf. 14½ to 16***

| | | | | |
|---|---|---|---|---|
| *39* | A1 | (½p) blue green | 175.00 | 15.00 |
| *40* | A1 | (4p) rose red | 750.00 | 110.00 |
| *41* | A2 | 6p vermilion | 600.00 | 65.00 |
| *a* | | Imperf., pair | 80.00 | *1,500.* |
| *b* | | Horiz. pair, imperf. btwn. | *4,000.* | |
| *42* | A2 | 1sh black | 75.00 | 11.00 |
| *a* | | Imperf. | | |

BARBADOS 5 SHILLINGS Britannia — A3

***Perf. 15½x15***

**Wmk. 5**

| | | | | |
|---|---|---|---|---|
| *43* | A3 | 5sh dull rose | 1,000. | 250.00 |

**1874** **Wmk. 6** ***Perf. 14***

| | | | | |
|---|---|---|---|---|
| *44* | A2 | ½p blue green | 10.00 | 7.50 |
| *45* | A2 | 1p blue | 75.00 | 2.50 |

***Clean-Cut Perf. 14½ to 16***

| | | | | |
|---|---|---|---|---|
| *45A* | A2 | 1p blue | | *6,000.* |

**1875** **Wmk. 1** ***Perf. 12½***

| | | | | |
|---|---|---|---|---|
| *46* | A2 | ½p yellow green | 10.00 | 2.50 |
| *47* | A2 | 4p scarlet | 110.00 | 10.00 |
| *48* | A2 | 6p orange | 650.00 | 50.00 |
| *49* | A2 | 1sh purple | 500.00 | 12.50 |

**1875-78** ***Perf. 14***

| | | | | |
|---|---|---|---|---|
| *50* | A2 | ½p yel grn ('76) | 4.00 | 1.50 |
| *51* | A2 | 1p ultramarine | 13.50 | 50 |
| *a* | | 1p gray blue | 16.00 | 50 |
| *b* | | Half used as ½p on cover | | 1,000. |
| *c* | | Watermarked sideways | | 1,750. |
| *52* | A2 | 3p violet ('78) | 55.00 | 10.00 |
| *53* | A2 | 4p rose red | 80.00 | 4.00 |
| *a* | | 4p scarlet | 100.00 | 5.00 |
| *b* | | As "a," perf. 14x12½ | *10,000.* | |
| *54* | A2 | 4p lake | 300.00 | 4.00 |
| *55* | A2 | 6p chrome yel | 75.00 | 3.25 |
| *a* | | 6p yellow | 350.00 | 11.00 |
| *56* | A2 | 1sh purple ('76) | 90.00 | 5.50 |
| *a* | | 1sh violet | 2,000. | 45.00 |
| *b* | | 1sh dull mauve | 350.00 | 6.00 |
| *c* | | Half used as 6p on cover | | *4,800.* |

Nos. 48, 49, 55 and 56 have the watermark sideways.
No. 53b was never placed in use.

A4

A5

Large Surcharge, ("1" 7mm High. "D" 2¾mm High).

**1878** **Wmk. 5** ***Perf. 15½x15***

**Slanting Serif**

| | | | | |
|---|---|---|---|---|
| *57* | A4 | 1p on half of 5sh dull rose | *4,800.* | 450.00 |
| *a* | | Unsevered pair | *15,000.* | *3,000.* |
| *b* | | Unsevered horiz. pairs, #57 + 58, imperf. between | | 4,750. |

**Straight Serif**

| | | | | |
|---|---|---|---|---|
| *58* | A4 | 1p on half of 5sh dull rose | *4,000.* | *1,400.* |
| *a* | | Unsevered pair | | *5,750.* |

**Small Surcharge, ("1" 6mm, "D" 2½mm High)**

| | | | | |
|---|---|---|---|---|
| *59* | A5 | 1p on half of 5sh dull rose | *5,000.* | *600.00* |
| *a* | | Unsevered pair | *12,500.* | *4,250.* |

On Nos. 57, 58 and 59 the surcharge is found reading upwards or downwards.
The perforation, which divides the stamp into halves, measures 11½ to 13.

Queen Victoria — A6

**1882-85** **Typo.** **Wmk. 2** ***Perf. 14***

| | | | | |
|---|---|---|---|---|
| *60* | A6 | ½p green | 1.50 | 45 |
| *61* | A6 | 1p carmine rose | 1.50 | 40 |
| *a* | | 1p rose | 4.50 | 55 |
| *b* | | Half used as ½p on cover | | 375.00 |
| *62* | A6 | 2½p dull blue | 11.00 | 50 |
| *a* | | 2½p ultramarine | 11.00 | 50 |
| *63* | A6 | 3p magenta | 1.75 | 1.75 |
| *a* | | 3p lilac | 22.50 | 18.75 |
| *64* | A6 | 4p slate | 175.00 | 1.40 |
| *65* | A6 | 4p brown ('85) | 1.25 | 50 |
| *66* | A6 | 6p olive gray | 7.50 | 7.50 |

67 A6 1sh org brown 6.00 5.00
68 A6 5sh bister 125.00 150.00
Nos. 60-68 (9) 330.50 167.50

No. 65 Surcharged in Black HALF-PENNY

**1892**
69 A6 ½p on 4p brown 90 1.00
a. Without hyphen 4.00 4.00
b. Double surcharge
c. Double surcharge, red and black 650.00 1,200.
d. As "c," without hyphen 2,000. 2,000.

Badge of Colony
A8 A9

**1892-1903** **Wmk. 2**
70 A8 1f sl & car ('96) 25 12
71 A8 ½p green 35 12
72 A8 1p carmine rose 35 10
73 A8 2p sl & org ('99) 3.25 1.50
74 A8 2½p ultramarine 2.50 30
75 A8 5p ol brn 4.00 2.50
76 A8 6p vio & car 4.00 2.50
77 A8 8p org & ultra 1.50 6.25
78 A8 10p bl grn & car 3.00 4.00
79 A8 2sh6p slate & org 12.50 14.00
80 A8 2sh6p pur & grn ('03) 45.00 55.00
Nos. 70-80 (11) 76.70 82.43

See Nos. 90-101.

### Victoria Jubilee Issue

**1897** **Wmk. 1**
81 A9 1f gray & car 20 20
a. Bluish paper 13.00 16.00
82 A9 ½p gray green 50 25
a. Bluish paper 13.00 16.00
83 A9 1p carmine rose 90 30
a. Bluish paper 22.50 25.00
84 A9 2½p ultra 3.75 60
a. Bluish paper 22.50 25.00
85 A9 5p dk olive brn 6.00 6.00
a. Bluish paper 140.00 150.00
86 A9 6p vio & car 7.00 7.00
a. Bluish paper 55.00 65.00
87 A9 8p org & ultra 6.00 7.00
a. Bluish paper 42.50 55.00
88 A9 10p bl grn & car 12.00 12.00
a. Bluish paper 75.00 85.00
89 A9 2sh6p slate & org 12.50 12.50
a. Bluish paper 55.00 65.00
Nos. 81-89 (9) 48.85 45.85
Nos. 81a-89a (9) 438.50

### Badge Type of 1892-1903

**1904-10** **Wmk. 3**
90 A8 1f gray & car 50 40
91 A8 1f brown ('09) 25 18
92 A8 ½p green 65 15
93 A8 1p carmine rose 1.50 20
94 A8 1p carmine ('09) 2.50 12
95 A8 2p gray ('09) 3.50 2.50
96 A8 2½p ultramarine 2.25 40
97 A8 6p vio & car 15.00 9.00
98 A8 6p dl vio & vio ('10) 4.25 4.25
99 A8 8p org & ultra 17.50 20.00
100 A8 1sh blk, grn ('10) 6.50 7.50
101 A8 2sh6p pur & grn 27.50 35.00
Nos. 90-101 (12) 81.90 79.70

### Nelson Centenary Issue

Lord Nelson Monument — A10

**1906** **Engr.** **Wmk. 1**
102 A10 1f gray & blk 85 60
103 A10 ½p green & blk 2.00 40
104 A10 1p car & blk 85 28
105 A10 2p org & blk 4.00 4.25
106 A10 2½p ultra & blk 5.00 4.00
107 A10 6p lilac & blk 14.00 14.00
108 A10 1sh rose & black 14.00 14.00
Nos. 102-108 (7) 40.70 37.53

See Nos. 110-112.

The "Olive Blossom" — A11

**1906, Aug. 15** **Wmk. 3**
109 A11 1p blk, green & blue 7.00 1.25

Tercentenary of the 1st British landing.

### Nelson Type of 1906

**1907, July 6** **Wmk. 3**
110 A10 1f gray & black 1.40 1.40
111 A10 2p org & blk 10.00 11.00
112 A10 2½p ultra & blk 10.00 11.00
a. 2½p indigo & black 1,100. 1,200.

A12 A13

King George V — A14

**1912** **Typo.**
116 A12 ¼p brown 22 12
117 A12 ½p green 50 16
a. Booklet pane of 6
118 A12 1p carmine 85 12
a. 1p scarlet 2.25 40
b. Booklet pane of 6
119 A12 2p gray 2.25 6.50
120 A12 2½p ultramarine 1.40 50
121 A13 3p vio, yel 1.50 3.50
122 A13 4p blk & scar, yel 1.40 4.25
123 A13 6p vio & red vio 2.25 2.50
124 A14 1sh blk, green 5.00 7.00
125 A14 2sh vio & ultra, bl 22.50 30.00
126 A14 3sh grn & violet 27.50 35.00
Nos. 116-126 (11) 65.37 89.65

Seal of the Colony — A15

**1916-18** **Engr.**
127 A15 ¼p brown 12 10
128 A15 ½p green 16 14
129 A15 1p red 50 10
130 A15 2p gray 3.50 5.50
131 A15 2½p ultramarine 85 65
132 A15 3p violet, yel 2.25 1.50
133 A15 4p red, yel 60 1.40
134 A15 4p red & black ('18) 85 1.00
135 A15 6p claret 85 85
136 A15 1sh blk, green 2.75 2.75
137 A15 2sh vio, blue 10.00 8.50
138 A15 3sh dark vio 27.50 42.50
139 A15 3sh dk vio & grn ('18) 14.00 16.00
a. 3sh bright vio & grn ('18) 140.00 150.00
Nos. 127-139 (13) 63.93 80.99

Nos. 134 and 139 are from a re-engraved die. The central medallion is not surrounded by a line and there are various other small alterations.

### Victory Issue

Victory
A16 A17

**1920, Sept. 9** **Wmk. 3**
140 A16 ¼p bister & blk 20 18
141 A16 ½p yel grn & blk 40 30
a. Booklet pane of 2
142 A16 1p org red & blk 65 22
a. Booklet pane of 2
143 A16 2p gray & blk 1.40 4.00
144 A16 2½p ultra & dk bl 1.40 2.00
145 A16 3p red lil & blk 85 1.50
146 A16 4p gray grn & blk 1.10 3.50
147 A16 6p orange & blk 1.50 3.50
148 A17 1sh yel grn & blk 4.25 8.00
149 A17 2sh brown & blk 8.25 12.00
150 A17 3sh orange & blk 13.50 16.00

**1921, Aug. 22** **Wmk. 4**
151 A16 1p orange red & blk 5.50 28
Nos. 140-151 (12) 39.00 51.48

A18 A19

**1921-24** **Wmk. 4**
152 A18 ¼p brown 15 10
153 A18 ½p green 35 18
154 A18 1p carmine 16 5
155 A18 2p gray 55 30
156 A18 2½p ultramarine 30 45
158 A18 6p claret 55 55
159 A18 1sh blk, emer ('24) 16.00 17.50
160 A18 2sh dk vio, blue 11.00 12.00
161 A18 3sh dark vio 11.00 12.00

**Wmk. 3**
162 A18 3p vio, yel 35 65
163 A18 4p red, yel 65 1.40
164 A18 1sh black, green 2.75 4.50
Nos. 152-164 (12) 43.81 49.68

**1925-35** **Wmk. 4** **Perf. 14**
165 A19 ¼p brown 6 6
166 A19 ½p green 6 5
a. Perf. 13½x12½ 16 6
b. Booklet pane of 10
167 A19 1p carmine 8 5
a. Perf. 13½x12½ 25 5
b. Booklet pane of 10
168 A19 1½p org, perf. 13½x12½ ('32) 65 14
a. Booklet pane of 6
b. Perf. 14 1.30 55
169 A19 2p gray 20 30
170 A19 2½p ultramarine 45 15
a. Perf. 13½x12½ 2.25 40
171 A19 3p vio brn, yel 35 25
172 A19 3p red brn, yel ('35) 6.00 6.00
173 A19 4p red, yel 45 40
174 A19 6p claret 80 80
175 A19 1sh blk, emerald 1.25 1.00
a. Perf. 13½x12½ 3.50 3.25
176 A19 1sh brn blk, yel grn ('32) 4.25 4.25
177 A19 2sh vio, bl 2.00 2.00
178 A19 2sh 6p car, bl ('32) 11.00 13.00
179 A19 3sh dark vio 3.75 3.75
Nos. 165-179 (15) 31.35 32.20

Stamps perf. 13½x12½ were issued in 1932.

Charles I and George V — A20

**1927, Feb. 17** **Perf. 12½**
180 A20 1p carmine lake 75 60

Tercentenary of the settlement of Barbados.

### Silver Jubilee Issue
Common Design Type

**1935, May 6** **Perf. 11x12**
186 CD301 1p car & dk bl 18 18
187 CD301 1½p blk & ultra 35 28
188 CD301 2½p ultra & brn 85 85
189 CD301 1sh brn vio & ind 4.00 4.00

### Coronation Issue
Common Design Type

**1937, May 14** **Perf. 13½x14**
190 CD302 1p carmine 7 7
191 CD302 1½p brown 20 20
192 CD302 2½p bright ultra 40 40

A21

**Perf. 13 to 14 and Compound**
**1938-47**
193 A21 ½p green 40 5
b. Perf. 14 22.50 1.40
c. Booklet pane of 10
193A A21 ½p bister ('42) 6 5
194 A21 1p carmine 1.75 14
b. Perf. 13½x13 50.00 1.40
c. Booklet pane of 10
194A A21 1p green ('42) 6 5
d. Perf. 13½x13 28 7
195 A21 1½p red orange 8 6
c. Perf. 14 60 10
d. Booklet pane of 6
195A A21 2p rose lake ('41) 1.10 22
195B A21 2p bright rose red ('43) 20 7
e. Perf. 14 12 10
196 A21 2½p ultramarine 20 14
197 A21 3p brown 20 16
b. Perf. 14 28 16
197A A21 3p deep bl ('47) 16 12
198 A21 4p black 16 10
a. Perf. 14 30 30
199 A21 6p violet 20 16
199A A21 8p red vio ('46) 65 65
200 A21 1sh brn ol 50 20
a. 1sh olive green 2.75 1.40
201 A21 2sh6p brn vio 1.75 65
201A A21 5sh indigo ('41) 2.75 1.40
Nos. 193-201A (16) 10.22 4.22

Kings Charles I, George VI Assembly Chamber and Mace A22

**Perf. 13½x14**
**1939, June 27** **Engr.** **Wmk. 4**
202 A22 ½p deep green 18 14
203 A22 1p scarlet 20 14
204 A22 1½p deep orange 35 25
205 A22 2½p ultramarine 60 60
206 A22 3p yellow brown 65 65
Nos. 202-206 (5) 1.98 1.78

Tercentenary of the General Assembly.

**Catalogue values for unused stamps in this section, from this point to the end of the section, are for Never Hinged items.**

### Peace Issue
Common Design Type

**1946, Sept. 18**
207 CD303 1½p deep orange 10 10
208 CD303 3p brown 15 15

Nos. 195e, 195B, Surcharged in Black ONE PENNY

**1947, Apr. 21** **Perf. 14**
209 A21 1p on 2p brt rose red 55 55
a. Double surcharge
b. Perf. 13½x13 65 65

### Silver Wedding Issue

Common Design Types

*Perf. 14x14½*

**1948, Nov. 24 Photo. Wmk. 4**

*210* CD304 1½p orange 15 15

**Engraved; Name Typographed**

*Perf. 11½x11*

*211* CD305 5sh dark blue 6.50 8.00

### UPU Issue

Common Design Types

**1949, Oct. 10** *Perf. 13½, 11x11½*

*212* CD306 1½p red orange 32 35
*213* CD307 3p indigo 55 55
*214* CD308 4p gray 1.00 1.00
*215* CD309 1sh olive 1.40 1.40

Dover Fort — A23

Admiral Nelson Statue — A24

Designs: 2c, Sugar cane breeding. 3c, Public buildings. 6c, Casting net. 8c, Intercolonial schooner. 12c, Flying Fish. 24c, Old Main Guard Garrison. 48c, Cathedral. 60c, Careenage. $1.20, Map. $2.40, Great Seal, 1660.

*Perf. 11x11½ (A23), 13x13½ (A24)*

**1950, May 1 Engr. Wmk. 4**

*216* A23 1c slate 12 12
*217* A23 2c emerald 12 12
*218* A23 3c slate & brn 15 12
*219* A24 4c carmine 20 20
*220* A23 6c blue 22 18
*221* A23 8c choc & blue 38 25
*222* A23 12c olive & aqua 75 45
*223* A23 24c gray & red 90 65
*224* A24 48c violet 2.50 1.75
*225* A23 60c brn car & bl grn 1.50 1.90
*226* A24 $1.20 olive & car 5.50 3.25
*227* A23 $2.40 gray 13.00 8.00
*Nos. 216-227 (12)* 25.34 16.99

### University Issue

Common Design Types

**1951, Feb. 16** *Perf. 14x14½*

*228* CD310 3c turq bl & choc 15 15
*229* CD311 12c ol brn & turq bl 75 75

Stamp of 1852 — A25

*Perf. 13½*

**1952, Apr. 15 Wmk. 4 Engr.**

*230* A25 3c sl bl & dp grn 15 15
*231* A25 4c rose pink & bl 25 25
*232* A25 12c emer & sl bl 40 40
*233* A25 24c gray blk & red brn 65 65

Centenary of Barbados postage stamps.

### Coronation Issue

Common Design Type

**1953, June 4** *Perf. 13½x13*

*234* CD312 4c red orange & blk 15 15

Harbor Police A26

Designs as in 1950 with portrait of Queen Elizabeth II. $2.40, Great Seal, 1660 ("E II R").

*Perf. 11x11½ (horiz.), 13x13½ (vert.)*

**1953-57 Engr.**

*235* A23 1c slate ('53) 10 8
*236* A23 2c greenish blue & deep orange 12 6
*237* A23 3c emerald & blk 14 6
*238* A24 4c orange & gray 14 6
*239* A26 5c dp car & dp bl 16 5
*240* A23 6c red brown 20 8
*241* A23 8c bright bl & blk 28 8
*242* A23 12c brn ol & aqua 38 10
*243* A23 24c gray & red ('56) 55 20
*244* A24 48c violet ('56) 1.75 1.10
*245* A23 60c brown carmine & blue green ('56) 3.00 1.75
*246* A24 $1.20 ol & car ('56) 5.25 3.25
*247* A23 $2.40 gray ('57) 11.00 6.25
*Nos. 235-247 (13)* 23.07 13.12

See Nos. 257-264.

### West Indies Federation

Common Design Type

*Perf. 11½x11*

**1958, Apr. 23 Wmk. 314**

*248* CD313 3c green 12 12
*249* CD313 6c blue 40 40
*250* CD313 12c carmine rose 50 50

Deep Water Harbor, Bridgetown A27

**1961, May 6 Engr.** *Perf. 11x11½*

*251* A27 4c orange & blk 14 14
*252* A27 8c ultra & black 28 28
*253* A27 24c black & pink 65 65

Opening of the Deep Water Harbor at Bridgetown.

Scout Emblem and Map of Barbados — A28

*Perf. 11½x11*

**1962, March 9 Wmk. 314**

*254* A28 4c orange & blk 14 14
*255* A28 12c gray & blue 30 30
*256* A28 $1.20 greenish gray & carmine rose 2.00 2.00

50th anniv. of the founding of the Boy Scouts of Barbados.

### Queen Types of 1953-57

*Perf. 11x11½, 13x13½*

**1964-65 Engr. Wmk. 314**

*257* A23 1c slate 35 35
*258* A24 4c orange & gray 45 45
*259* A23 8c brt bl & blk ('65) 60 50
*260* A23 12c brn ol & aqua ('65) 75
*261* A23 24c gray & red 75 60
*262* A24 48c violet 3.00 3.00
*263* A23 60c brn car & bl grn 4.25 4.25
*264* A23 $2.40 gray ('65) 6.75 6.75
*Nos. 257-264 (8)* 16.90

The 12c was never put on sale in Barbados.

### ITU Issue

Common Design Type

*Perf. 11x11½*

**1965, May 17 Litho. Wmk. 314**

*265* CD317 2c lilac & ver 10 10
*266* CD317 48c yellow & gray 1.50 1.50

Sea Horse A29

Designs: 1c, Deep sea coral. 2c, Lobster. 4c, Sea urchin. 5c, Staghorn coral. 6c, Butterflyfish. 8c, File shell. 12c, Balloonfish. 15c, Angelfish. 25c, Brain coral. 35c, Brittle star. 50c, Flyingfish. $1, Queen conch shell. $2.50, Fiddler crab.

**Wmk. 314 Upright**

**1965, July 15 Photo.** *Perf. 14x13½*

*267* A29 1c dark bl, pink & black 6 6
*268* A29 2c car rose, sepia & orange 8 8
*269* A29 3c org, brn & sep (*"Hippocampus"*) 10 10
*270* A29 4c ol grn & dk bl 10 8
*a.* Imperf., pair 450.00
*271* A29 5c lil, brn & pink 12 12
*272* A29 6c greenish bl, yel & blk 15 12
*273* A29 8c ultra, orange, red & black 25 18
*274* A29 12c rose lilac, yellow & blk 40 25
*275* A29 15c red, yel & blk 75 50
*276* A29 25c yel brn & ultra 1.10 80
*277* A29 35c green, rose brown & blk 1.75 1.00
*278* A29 50c yel grn & ultra 2.75 1.65
*279* A29 $1 gray & multi 5.50 4.00
*280* A29 $2.50 lt bl & multi 12.00 10.00
*Nos. 267-280 (14)* 25.11 18.94

**1966-69 Wmk. 314 Sideways**

Design: $5, "Dolphin" (coryphaena hippurus).

**Colors as Nos. 267-280**

*267a* A29 1c 5 5
*268a* A29 2c ('67) 8 5
*269A* A29 3c (*"Hippocampus"*) ('67) 18 10
*270b* A29 4c 10 5
*271a* A29 5c 15 10
*272a* A29 6c ('67) 20 12
*273a* A29 8c ('67) 25 20
*274a* A29 12c ('67) 35 20
*275a* A29 15c 50 35
*276a* A29 25c 60 55
*277a* A29 35c 85 60
*278a* A29 50c 1.25 1.10
*279a* A29 $1 2.50 1.90
*280a* A29 $2.50 6.25 6.00
*280B* A29 $5 dk ol & multi ('69) 12.50 12.50
*Nos. 267a-280B (15)* 25.81 23.87

### Churchill Memorial Issue

Common Design Type

**1966, Jan. 24 Wmk. 314** *Perf. 14*

**Design in Black, Gold and Carmine Rose**

*281* CD319 1c bright blue 7 7
*282* CD319 4c green 20 20
*283* CD319 25c brown 1.00 1.00
*284* CD319 35c violet 1.40 1.40

### Royal Visit Issue

Common Design Type

**1966, Feb. 4 Litho.** *Perf. 11x12*

*285* CD320 3c violet blue 20 20
*286* CD320 35c dark car rose 1.75 1.75

### UNESCO Anniversary Issue

Common Design Type

**1967, Jan. 6 Litho.** *Perf. 14*

*287* CD323 4c "Education" 16 16
*288* CD323 12c "Science" 60 60
*289* CD323 25c "Culture" 1.50 1.50

Arms of Barbados A30

Policeman and Anchor Monument A31

Designs: 25c, Hilton Hotel (horiz.). 35c, Garfield Sobers, captain of Barbados and West Indies Cricket Team. 50c, Pine Hill Dairy (horiz.).

**1966, Dec. 2 Unwmk. Photo.**

*290* A30 4c multicolored 10 10
*291* A30 25c multicolored 45 45
*292* A30 35c multicolored 65 65
*293* A30 50c multicolored 1.00 1.00

Barbados' independence, Nov. 30, 1966.

**1967, Oct. 9 Litho.** *Perf. 13½x14*

Designs: 25c, Policeman with telescope. 35c, Police motor launch (horiz.). 50c, Policemen at Harbor Gate.

*294* A31 4c multicolored 10 10
*295* A31 25c multicolored 35 35
*296* A31 35c multicolored 55 55
*297* A31 50c multicolored 90 90

Centenary of Bridgetown Harbor Police.

Independence Arch — A32

Designs: 4c, Sir Winston Scott, Governor-General (vert.). 35c, Treasury Building. 50c, Parliament Building.

*Perf. 14½x14, 14x14½*

**1967, Dec. 4 Photo. Unwmk.**

*298* A32 4c multicolored 10 10
*299* A32 25c multicolored 35 35
*300* A32 35c multicolored 50 50
*301* A32 50c multicolored 85 85

1st anniv. of independence.

UN Building, Santiago, Chile A33

**1968, Feb. 27** *Perf. 14½x14*

*302* A33 15c multicolored 25 25

20th anniv. of the UN Economic Commission for Latin America.

Radar Antenna on Top of Old Sugar Mill, Sugar Cane — A34

Designs: 25c, Caribbean Meteorological Institute, Barbados (horiz.). 50c, HARP gun used in High Altitude Research Program, at Paragon in Christ Church, Barbados.

*Perf. 14x14½, 14½x14*

**1968, June 4 Photo. Unwmk.**

*303* A34 3c violet & multi 8 8
*304* A34 25c ver & multi 35 35
*305* A34 50c orange & multi 80 80

World Meteorological Day.

Girl Scout at Campfire, Lady Baden-Powell and Queen Elizabeth II — A35

Designs (Lady Baden-Powell, Queen Elizabeth II and): 25c, Pax Hill Headquarters. 35c, Girl Scout badge.

*Perf. 14x14½*

**1968, Aug. 29 Photo. Unwmk.**

| | | | | |
|---|---|---|---|---|
| *306* | A35 | 3c dp ultra, blk & gold | 18 | 8 |
| *307* | A35 | 25c bluish green, black & gold | 45 | 45 |
| *308* | A35 | 35c org yel, blk & gold | 85 | 85 |

Barbados Girl Scouts' 50th anniv.

Human Rights Flame and Escape to Freedom A36

Designs: 4c, Human Rights flame, hands, and broken chain. 25c, Human Rights flame, family and broken chain.

*Perf. 11x11½*

**1968, Dec. 10 Litho. Unwmk.**

| | | | | |
|---|---|---|---|---|
| *309* | A36 | 4c violet, gray grn & red brown | 8 | 8 |
| *310* | A36 | 25c org, blk & blue | 45 | 45 |
| *311* | A36 | 35c greenish blue, blue, blk & org | 65 | 65 |

International Human Rights Year.

In the Paddock A37

Horse Racing: 25c, "They're off!" 35c, On the flat. 50c, The Finish.

**1969, Mar. 15 Litho.** *Perf. 14½*

| | | | | |
|---|---|---|---|---|
| *312* | A37 | 4c multicolored | 7 | 7 |
| *313* | A37 | 25c multicolored | 35 | 35 |
| *314* | A37 | 35c multicolored | 50 | 50 |
| *315* | A37 | 50c multicolored | 85 | 85 |
| *a.* | | Souvenir sheet of 4 | 2.50 | *3.00* |

No. 315a contains one each of Nos. 312-315 with brown marginal inscription. Size: 118½x84mm.

Map of Caribbean — A38

Design: 12c, 50c, "Strength in Unity" (horiz.).

*Perf. 14x14½, 14½x14*

**1969, May 6 Photo. Wmk. 314**

| | | | | |
|---|---|---|---|---|
| *316* | A38 | 5c brown & multi | 8 | 8 |
| *317* | A38 | 12c ultra & multi | 22 | 22 |
| *318* | A38 | 25c green & multi | 35 | 35 |
| *319* | A38 | 50c magenta & multi | 80 | 80 |

1st anniv. of CARIFTA (Caribbean Free Trade Area).

ILO Emblem A39

*Barbados stamps can be mounted in Scott's annually supplemented British East Caribbean Album.*

*Perf. 14x13*

**1969, Aug. 5 Litho. Unwmk.**

| | | | | |
|---|---|---|---|---|
| *320* | A39 | 4c bl grn, brt grn & blk | 10 | 10 |
| *321* | A39 | 25c red brn, brt mag & red | 50 | 50 |

50th anniv. of the ILO.

No. 294 Surcharged ONE CENT

**1969, Aug. 30** *Perf. 13½x14*

| | | | | |
|---|---|---|---|---|
| *322* | A31 | 1c on 4c multicolored | 40 | 40 |

Barbados Boy Scout Emblem — A40

Designs: 25c, Sea Scouts rowing in Bridgetown harbor. 35c, Campfire. 50c, Various Scouts in front of National Headquarters and Training Center, Hazelwood.

*Perf. 13½x13*

**1969, Dec. 16 Litho. Unwmk.**

| | | | | |
|---|---|---|---|---|
| *323* | A40 | 5c multicolored | 14 | 14 |
| *324* | A40 | 25c multicolored | 50 | 50 |
| *325* | A40 | 35c multicolored | 65 | 65 |
| *326* | A40 | 50c multicolored | 1.00 | 1.00 |
| *a.* | | Souvenir sheet of 4 | 8.50 | *10.00* |

Attainment of independence by the Barbados Boy Scout Association. No. 326a contains one each of Nos. 323-326. Boy Scout emblems and commemorative inscription in margin. Size: 154x115mm.

No. 271a Surcharged 4 X

**Wmk. 314 Sideways**

**1970, Mar. 11 Photo.** *Perf. 14x13½*

| | | | | |
|---|---|---|---|---|
| *327* | A29 | 4c on 5c multicolored | 18 | 18 |

This locally applied surcharge exists in several variations: double, triple, on back, in pair with one missing, etc.

Lion at Gun Hill — A41

Barbados Museum A42

Designs: 2c, Trafalgar Fountain. 3c, Montefiore Drinking Fountain. 4c, St. James' Monument. 5c, St. Ann's Fort. 6c, Old Sugar Mill, Morgan Lewis. 8c, Cenotaph. 10c, South Point Lighthouse. 15c, Sharon Moravian Church. 25c, George Washington House. 35c, St. Nicholas Abbey. 50c, Bowmanston Pumping Station. $1, Queen Elizabeth Hospital. $2.50, Modern sugar factory. $5, Seawell International Airport.

**Wmk. 314 Upright (A41), Sideways (A42)**

*Perf. 12½x13, 13x12½*

**1970, May 4 Photo.**

| | | | | |
|---|---|---|---|---|
| *328* | A41 | 1c bl grn & multi | 5 | 5 |
| *329* | A41 | 2c crim & multi | 5 | 5 |
| *330* | A41 | 3c blue & multi | 5 | 5 |
| *331* | A41 | 4c yellow & multi | 12 | 12 |
| *332* | A41 | 5c dp org & multi | 14 | 14 |
| *333* | A41 | 6c dl yel & multi | 18 | 18 |
| *334* | A41 | 8c dp bl & multi | 18 | 18 |
| *335* | A41 | 10c red & multi | 25 | 25 |
| *336* | A42 | 12c ultra & multi | 30 | 30 |
| *337* | A42 | 15c yel & multi | 35 | 30 |
| *338* | A42 | 25c org & multi | 60 | 60 |
| *339* | A42 | 35c pink & multi | 85 | 85 |
| *340* | A42 | 50c bl grn & multi | 1.00 | 1.00 |
| *341* | A42 | $1 emer & multi | 2.00 | 2.00 |
| *342* | A42 | $2.50 ver & multi | 5.00 | 5.00 |
| *343* | A42 | $5 yel & multi | 10.00 | 10.00 |
| | | *Nos. 328-343 (16)* | 21.12 | 21.07 |

Nos. 328-332, 334-343 were reissued in 1971 on glazed paper.

**Wmk. 314 Sideways (A41), Upright (A42)**

**1972-74**

**Colors as Before**

| | | | | |
|---|---|---|---|---|
| *331a* | A41 | 4c | 6 | 6 |
| *332a* | A41 | 5c | 7 | 7 |
| *333a* | A41 | 6c | 12 | 12 |
| *334a* | A41 | 8c | 15 | 15 |
| *335a* | A41 | 10c ('74) | 20 | 20 |
| *336a* | A42 | 12c | 20 | 20 |
| *337a* | A42 | 15c | 25 | 25 |
| *338a* | A42 | 25c | 45 | 45 |
| *339a* | A42 | 35c | 65 | 65 |
| *340a* | A42 | 50c | 1.00 | 1.00 |
| *341a* | A42 | $1 | 2.00 | 2.00 |
| *342a* | A42 | $2.50 ('73) | 5.00 | 5.00 |
| *343a* | A42 | $5 ('73) | 10.00 | 10.00 |
| | | *Nos. 331a-343a (13)* | 20.15 | 20.15 |

Primary Education, UN and Education Year Emblems A43

Designs (UN and Education Year Emblems and): 5c, Secondary education (student with microscope). 25c, Technical education (men working with power drill). 50c, University building.

**1970, June 26 Litho.** *Perf. 14*

| | | | | |
|---|---|---|---|---|
| *344* | A43 | 4c multicolored | 7 | 7 |
| *345* | A43 | 5c multicolored | 10 | 10 |
| *346* | A43 | 25c multicolored | 40 | 40 |
| *347* | A43 | 50c multicolored | 85 | 85 |

25th anniv. of the UN, and for Intl. Education Year, 1970.

Minnie Root A44

Flowers: 1c, Barbados Easter lily (vert.). 10c, Eyelash orchid. 25c, Pride of Barbados (vert.). 35c, Christmas hope.

**1970, Aug. 24 Litho. Wmk. 314**

**Flowers in Natural Colors**

| | | | | |
|---|---|---|---|---|
| *348* | A44 | 1c green | 5 | 5 |
| *349* | A44 | 5c deep magenta | 14 | 10 |
| *350* | A44 | 10c dark blue | 25 | 20 |
| *351* | A44 | 25c bright org brn | 65 | 50 |
| *352* | A44 | 35c blue | 1.00 | 80 |
| *a.* | | Souvenir sheet of 5 | 2.75 | 2.00 |
| | | *Nos. 348-352 (5)* | 2.09 | 1.65 |

No. 352a contains 5 imperf. stamps similar to Nos. 348-352 with simulated perforations. Green decorative margin inscribed "Flowers of Barbados." Size: 161x100mm.

Christ Carrying Cross — A45

Easter 1971: 10c, 50c, Resurrection, by Benjamin West, St. George's Anglican Church. 35c like 4c, Window from St. Margaret's Anglican Church, St. John.

**1971, Apr. 7 Wmk. 314** *Perf. 14*

| | | | | |
|---|---|---|---|---|
| *353* | A45 | 4c purple & multi | 8 | 8 |
| *354* | A45 | 10c silver & multi | 20 | 20 |
| *355* | A45 | 35c brt bl & multi | 65 | 65 |
| *356* | A45 | 50c gold & multi | 1.00 | 1.00 |

Sailfish Craft A46

Tourism: 5c, Tennis. 12c, Horseback riding. 25c, Water-skiing. 50c, Scuba diving.

**1971, Aug. 17** *Perf. 14x14½*

| | | | | |
|---|---|---|---|---|
| *357* | A46 | 1c multicolored | 5 | 5 |
| *358* | A46 | 5c multicolored | 10 | 10 |
| *359* | A46 | 12c multicolored | 20 | 20 |
| *360* | A46 | 25c multicolored | 50 | 50 |
| *361* | A46 | 50c multicolored | 1.00 | 1.00 |
| | | *Nos. 357-361 (5)* | 1.85 | 1.85 |



Samuel Jackman Prescod — A47

**1971, Sept. 26** *Perf. 14*

| | | | | |
|---|---|---|---|---|
| *362* | A47 | 3c orange & multi | 10 | 10 |
| *363* | A47 | 35c ultra & multi | 65 | 65 |

Samuel Jackman Prescod (1806-1871), 1st black member of Barbados Assembly.

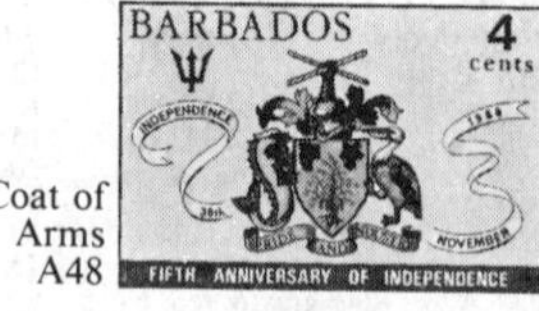


Coat of Arms A48

Designs: 15c, 50c, Flag and map of Barbados.

**1971, Nov. 23**

| | | | | |
|---|---|---|---|---|
| *364* | A48 | 4c light bl & multi | 10 | 10 |
| *365* | A48 | 15c multicolored | 30 | 30 |
| *366* | A48 | 25c yel grn & multi | 50 | 50 |
| *367* | A48 | 50c blue & multi | 1.00 | 1.00 |

5th anniv. of independence.

Telegraphy, 1872 and 1972 — A49

Designs: 10c, "Stanley Angwin" off St. Lawrence Coast. 35c, Earth station and Intelsat 4. 50c, Mt. Misery tropospheric scatter station.

**1972, Mar. 28 Litho.** *Perf. 14*

| | | | | |
|---|---|---|---|---|
| *368* | A49 | 4c purple & multi | 10 | 10 |
| *369* | A49 | 10c emer & multi | 30 | 30 |
| *370* | A49 | 35c red & multi | 65 | 65 |
| *371* | A49 | 50c orange & multi | 1.00 | 1.00 |

Centenary of telecommunications to and from Barbados.

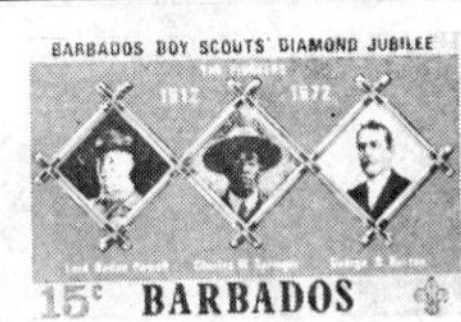


Lord Baden-Powell, Charles W. Springer, George B. Burton — A50

Designs: 5c, Map of Barbados and Combermere School (vert.). 25c, Photograph of 1922 troop. 50c, Flags of various Boy Scout troops.

**1972, Aug. 1**

*372* A50 5c ultra & multi 14 14
*373* A50 15c ultra & multi 40 40
*374* A50 25c ultra & multi 60 60
*375* A50 50c ultra & multi 1.10 1.10

60th anniv. of Barbados Boy Scouts and 4th Caribbean Jamboree.

Bookmobile, Open Book — A51

Designs: 15c, Visual aids truck. 25c, Central Library, Bridgetown. $1, Codrington College.

**1972, Oct. 31 Litho. Wmk. 314**

*376* A51 4c brt pink & multi 10 10
*377* A51 15c dull org & multi 30 30
*378* A51 25c buff & multi 50 50
*379* A51 $1 lt vio & multi 2.25 2.25

International Book Year 1972.

Pottery Wheels A52

Barbados pottery industry: 15c, Kiln. 25c, Finished pottery, Chalky Mount. $1, Pottery on sale at market.

**1973, Mar. 1 Wmk. 314 *Perf. 14***

*380* A52 5c dull red & multi 8 8
*381* A52 15c ol grn & multi 28 28
*382* A52 25c gray & multi 42 42
*383* A52 $1 yellow & multi 1.75 1.75

First Flight in Barbados, Wright Box Kite, 1911 A53

Aircraft: 15c, First flight to Barbados, De Havilland biplane, 1928. 25c, Passenger plane, 1939. 50c, Vickers VC-10 over control tower, 1973.

**1973, July 25 *Perf. 12½x12***

*384* A53 5c blue & multi 14 14
*385* A53 15c vio bl & multi 40 40
*386* A53 25c multicolored 65 65
*387* A53 50c blue & multi 1.40 1.40

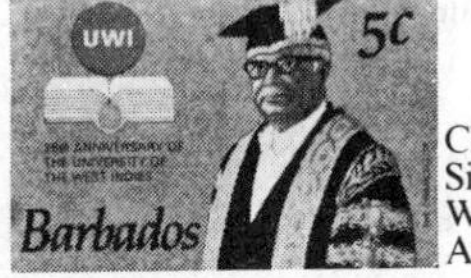


Chancellor Sir Hugh Wooding A54

Designs: 25c, Sherlock Hall, Cave Hill Campus. 35c, Cave Hill Campus.

**1973, Dec. 11 *Perf. 13x14***

*388* A54 5c deep org & multi 10 10
*389* A54 25c red brown & multi 40 40
*390* A54 35c multicolored 60 60

25th anniv. of the Univ. of the West Indies.

No. 338a Surcharged **4c.**

**1974, Apr. 30 Photo. *Perf. 13x12½***

*391* A42 4c on 25c multi 14 14
*a* "4c." omitted 20.00

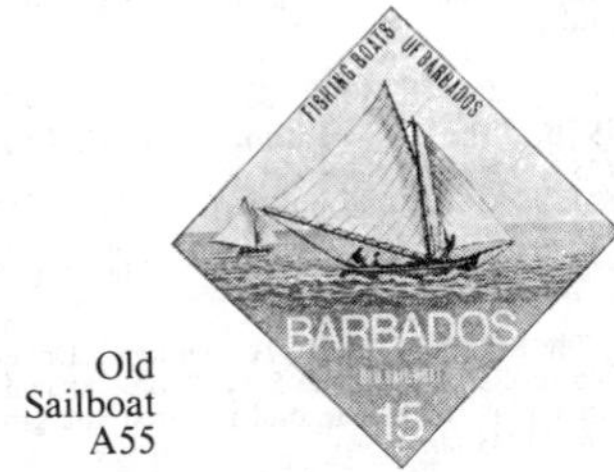


Old Sailboat A55

Designs: 25c, Rowboat. 50c, Motor-powered fishing boat. $1, Trawler "Calamar."

**1974, June 11 Wmk. 314 *Perf. 14***

*392* A55 15c blue & multi 25 25
*393* A55 35c multicolored 50 50
*394* A55 50c vio bl & multi 75 75
*395* A55 $1 blue & multi 1.50 1.50
*a* Souvenir sheet of 4 3.00 3.75

Fishing boats of Barbados. No. 395a contains one each of Nos. 392-395. Multicolored margin with fishing boats and red inscription. Size: 140x140mm.

Fire Orchid — A56

Designs: Orchids. 1c, 20c, 25c, $2.50, $5 horizontal.

**Wmk. 314 Sideways; Upright (1c, 20c, 25c, $1, $10)**

**1974-77 Photo. *Perf. 14***

*396* A56 1c *Cattleya gaskelliana alba* 5 5
*397* A56 2c *shown* 5 5
*398* A56 3c *Rose Marie* 8 5
*399* A56 4c *Fiery red orchid* 10 8
*400* A56 5c *Schomburgkia humboltii* 10 8
*401* A56 8c *Dancing dolls* 15 12
*402* A56 10c *Spider orchids* 18 15
*403* A56 12c *Dendrobium aggregatum* 20 18
*404* A56 15c *Lady slippers* 30 25
*404C* A56 20c *Spathoglottis* 35 30
*405* A56 25c *Eyelash* 50 40
*406* A56 35c *Bletia patula* 55 45
*406B* A56 45c *Sunset Glow* 75 60
*407* A56 50c *Sunset Glow* 75 60

***Perf. 14½x14, 14x14½***

*408* A56 $1 *Ascocenda red gem* 1.40 1.10
*409* A56 $2.50 *Brassolaeliocattleya nugget* 3.25 2.75
*410* A56 $5 *Caularthron bicornutum* 6.50 5.50
*411* A56 $10 *Moon orchid* 12.50 11.00
*Nos. 396-411 (18)* 27.76 23.71

Issue dates: 20c, 45c, May 3, 1977. Others, Sept. 16, 1974.

**Wmk. 314 Upright; Sideways (1c, 25c, $1)**

**1976 *Perf. 14***

*396a* A56 1c multicolored 12 6
*397a* A56 2c multicolored 15 6
*398a* A56 3c multicolored 20 15
*399a* A56 4c multicolored 25 20
*402a* A56 10c multicolored 45 40
*404a* A56 15c multicolored 80 70
*405a* A56 25c multicolored 1.00 90
*406a* A56 35c multicolored 1.50 1.25

***Perf. 14½x14***

*408a* A56 $1 multicolored 4.00 3.50
*Nos. 396a-408a (9)* 8.47 7.22

**1975 Wmk. 373 *Perf. 14***

*396b* A56 1c multicolored 6 6
*397b* A56 2c multicolored 12 9
*398b* A56 3c multicolored 15 12
*399b* A56 4c multicolored 25 22
*400b* A56 5c multicolored 15 12
*402b* A56 10c multicolored 20 18
*403b* A56 12c multicolored 25 22
*404b* A56 15c multicolored 50 45
*406c* A56 45c multicolored 1.10 90

***Perf. 14½x14, 14x14½***

*408b* A56 $1 multicolored 2.00 1.90
*409b* A56 $2.50 multicolored 5.00 4.50
*410b* A56 $5 multicolored 10.00 9.50
*411b* A56 $10 multicolored 18.00 18.00
*Nos. 396b-411b (13)* 37.78 36.26

UPU Emblem, Barbados No. 64 A57

Designs (UPU Emblem and): 35c, Letters encircling globe. 50c, Barbados coat of arms. $1, Map of Barbados, sailing ship and jet.

**1974, Oct. 9 Litho. *Perf. 14½***

*412* A57 8c brt rose, org & gray 14 14
*413* A57 35c red, blk, & ocher 50 50
*414* A57 50c vio bl, bl & sil 75 75
*415* A57 $1 ultra, blk & brn 1.50 1.50
*a* Souvenir sheet of 4 3.50 3.50

Centenary of the UPU. No. 415a contains one each of Nos. 412-415, gray margin with white inscription. Size: 126x100mm.

Yacht Britannia off Barbados A58

Royal Visit, Feb. 1975: 35c, $1, Palms and sunset.

**1975, Feb. 18**

*416* A58 8c brn & multi 12 12
*417* A58 25c blue & multi 40 40
*418* A58 35c pur & multi 65 65
*419* A58 $1 vio & multi 1.75 1.75

St. Michael's Cathedral — A59

Designs: 15c, Bishop Coleridge. 50c, All Saint's Church. $1, St. Michael, stained glass window, St. Michael's Cathedral.

**Wmk. 314**

**1975, July 29 Litho. *Perf. 14***

*420* A59 5c blue & multi 7 7
*421* A59 15c lilac & multi 20 20
*422* A59 50c green & multi 60 60
*423* A59 $1 multicolored 1.10 1.10
*a* Souvenir sheet of 4 2.25 2.75

Anglican Diocese in Barbados, sesquicentennial. No. 423a contains one each of Nos. 420-423, orange margin with red brown inscription. Size: 95x95mm.

Pony Float A60

Designs: 25c, Stiltsman (band and masqueraders). 35c, Maypole dancing. 50c, Cuban dancers.

**1975, Nov. 18 Litho. Wmk. 373**

*424* A60 8c yel & multi 14 14
*425* A60 25c buff & multi 40 40
*426* A60 35c ultra & multi 50 50
*427* A60 50c org & multi 80 80
*a* Souvenir sheet of 4 1.75 1.75

Crop-over (harvest) festival. No. 427a contains one each of Nos. 424-427; buff and multicolored margin. Size: 126x85mm.

Sailing Ship, 17th Cent. — A61

Coat of Arms — A62

Designs: 10c, Bearded fig tree and fruit. 25c, Ogilvy's 17th cent. map. $1, Capt. John Powell.

**1975, Dec. 17 Wmk. 373 *Perf. 13½***

*428* A61 4c lt bl & multi 150 8
*429* A61 10c lt bl & multi 20 16
*430* A61 25c yel & multi 50 45
*431* A61 $1 dk red & multi 1.75 1.50
*a* Souvenir sheet of 4 2.75 2.25

350th anniv. of 1st settlement. No. 431a contains one each of Nos. 428-431, multicolored margin with island scenes.

Coil Stamps

**1975, Dec. Unwmk. *Perf. 15x14***

*432* A62 5c light blue 6 6
*433* A62 25c violet 20 20

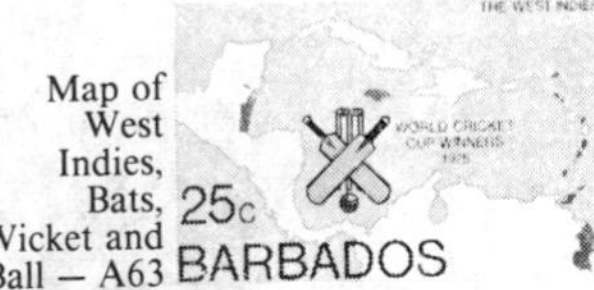


Map of West Indies, Bats, Wicket and Ball — A63

Prudential Cup — A64

**1976, July 7 Litho. *Perf. 14***

*438* A63 25c lt bl & multi 85 50
*439* A64 45c lil rose & blk 1.10 1.00

World Cricket Cup, won by West Indies Team, 1975.

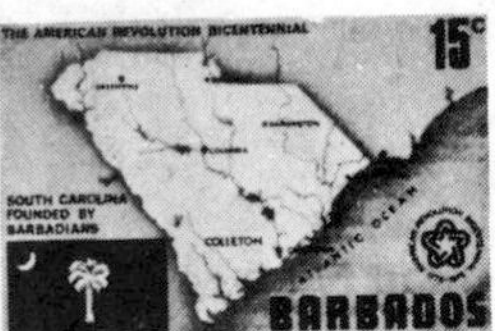


Map of South Carolina settled by Barbadians — A65

American Bicentennial: 25c, George Washington and map of Bridge Town area. 50c, Declaration of Independence. $1, Masonic emblem and Prince Hall, founder and Grand Master of African Grand Lodge, Boston, 1790-1807.

**1976, Aug. 17 Wmk. 373 *Perf. 13½***

| No. | Type | Value / Description | Unused | Used |
|---|---|---|---|---|
| *440* | A65 | 15c multicolored | 20 | 20 |
| *441* | A65 | 25c multicolored | 35 | 35 |
| *442* | A65 | 50c multicolored | 65 | 65 |
| *443* | A65 | $1 multicolored | 1.40 | 1.40 |

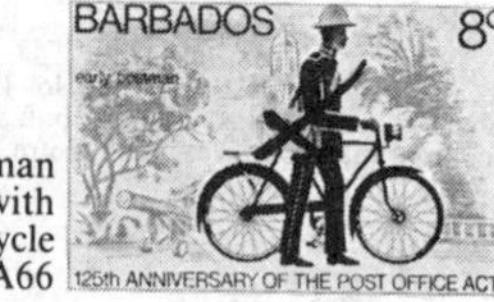


Mailman with Bicycle A66

PO Act, 125th anniv.: 35c, Mailman on motor scooter. 50c, Cover with Barbados No. 2. $1, Mail truck.

**1976, Oct. 19 Litho. *Perf. 14***

| No. | Type | Value / Description | Unused | Used |
|---|---|---|---|---|
| *444* | A66 | 8c rose red, blk & bis | 14 | 14 |
| *445* | A66 | 35c multicolored | 40 | 40 |
| *446* | A66 | 50c vio bl & multi | 60 | 60 |
| *447* | A66 | $1 red & multi | 1.10 | 1.10 |

Coast Guard Vessels A67

Designs: 15c, Bank note, reverse, showing Barbados Parliament. 25c, National anthem by Van Roland Edwards (music) and Irvine Burgie (lyrics). $1, Independence Day parade.

**1976, Nov. 30 *Perf. 13x13½***

| No. | Type | Value / Description | Unused | Used |
|---|---|---|---|---|
| *448* | A67 | 5c multicolored | 8 | 8 |
| *449* | A67 | 15c multicolored | 20 | 20 |
| *450* | A67 | 25c yel, brn & blk | 30 | 30 |
| *451* | A67 | $1 multicolored | 1.20 | 1.20 |
| *a* | | Souvenir sheet of 4 | 2.00 | 2.00 |

10th anniv. of independence. No. 451a contains one each of Nos. 448-451; multicolored margin with palms. Size: 125x90mm.

Queen Knighting Garfield Sobers, 1957 Visit – A68

Designs: 50c, Queen arriving at Westminster Abbey. $1, Queen leaving coach.

**1977, Feb. 7 *Perf. 14x13½***

| No. | Type | Value / Description | Unused | Used |
|---|---|---|---|---|
| *452* | A68 | 15c silver & multi | 20 | 20 |
| *453* | A68 | 50c silver & multi | 60 | 60 |
| *454* | A68 | $1 silver & multi | 1.25 | 1.25 |

25th anniv. of the reign of Queen Elizabeth II.

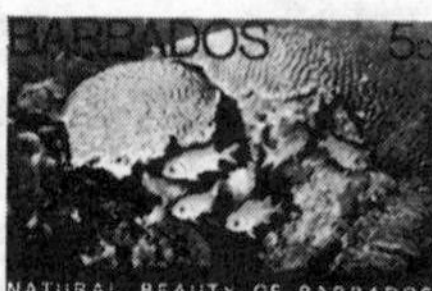


Underwater Park – A69

Beauty of Barbados: 35c, Royal palms (vert.). 50c, Underwater caves. $1, Stalagmite in Harrison's Cave (vert.).

**1977, May 3 Wmk. 373 *Perf. 14***

| No. | Type | Value / Description | Unused | Used |
|---|---|---|---|---|
| *455* | A69 | 5c multicolored | 7 | 7 |
| *456* | A69 | 35c multicolored | 50 | 50 |
| *457* | A69 | 50c multicolored | 65 | 65 |
| *458* | A69 | $1 multicolored | 1.40 | 1.40 |
| *a* | | Souvenir sheet of 4 | 2.75 | 2.75 |

No. 458a contains one each of Nos. 455-458; multicolored margin shows Barbados landscape. Size: 138½x92mm.

House of Commons Maces – A70

Charles I Handing Charter to Carlisle – A71

Designs: 25c, Speaker's chair. 50c, Senate Chamber. $1, Sam Lord's Castle (horiz.).

**1977, Aug. 2 Litho. *Perf. 13½***

| No. | Type | Value / Description | Unused | Used |
|---|---|---|---|---|
| *459* | A70 | 10c red brn & yel | 14 | 14 |
| *460* | A70 | 25c sl grn & org | 30 | 30 |
| *461* | A70 | 50c dk grn, grn & yel | 60 | 60 |
| *462* | A70 | $1 dk & lt bl & org | 1.10 | 1.10 |

13th Regional Conference of Commonwealth Parliamentary Association.

***Perf. 13½x13, 13x13½***

**1977, Oct. 11 Litho. Wmk. 373**

Designs: 12c, Charter scroll. 45c, Charles I and Earl of Carlisle (horiz.). $1, Map of Barbados, by Richard Ligon, 1657 (horiz.).

| No. | Type | Value / Description | Unused | Used |
|---|---|---|---|---|
| *463* | A71 | 12c buff & multi | 14 | 14 |
| *464* | A71 | 25c buff & multi | 30 | 30 |
| *465* | A71 | 45c buff & multi | 55 | 55 |
| *466* | A71 | $1 buff & multi | 1.10 | 1.10 |

350th anniv. of charter granting Barbados to the Earl of Carlisle.

Silver Jubilee Type, 1977, Inscribed: "ROYAL VISIT"

**1977, Oct. 31 Unwmk. *Roulette 5***

**Self-adhesive**

| No. | Type | Value / Description | Unused | Used |
|---|---|---|---|---|
| *467* | A68 | 15c sil & multi | 20 | 20 |
| *468* | A68 | 50c sil & multi | 60 | 60 |
| *469* | A68 | $1 sil & multi | 1.10 | 1.10 |

Caribbean visit of Queen Elizabeth II. Printed on peelable paper backing inscribed in ultramarine multiple rows: "SILVER JUBILEE ROYAL VISIT BARBADOS". Printed with die-cut label inscribed in black "BEND & PEEL" attached at left of stamp. Sheets of 50 stamps and 50 labels.

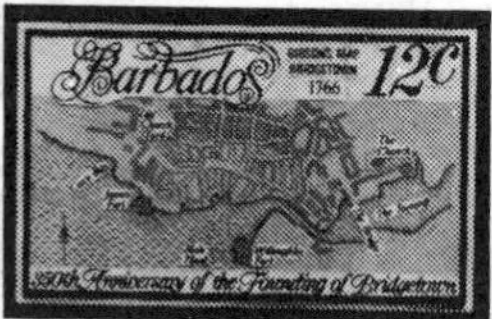


Gibson's Map of Bridgetown, 1766 – A72

Designs: 25c, Bridgetown, engraving by S. Copens, 1695. 45c, Trafalgar Square, Bridgetown, drawing by J. M. Carter, 1835. $1, The Bridges, 1978.

**Wmk. 373**

**1978, Mar. 1 Litho. *Perf. 14½***

| No. | Type | Value / Description | Unused | Used |
|---|---|---|---|---|
| *470* | A72 | 12c gold & multi | 14 | 14 |
| *471* | A72 | 25c gold & multi | 28 | 28 |
| *472* | A72 | 45c gold & multi | 50 | 50 |
| *473* | A72 | $1 gold & multi | 1.00 | 1.00 |

350th anniv. of founding of Bridgetown.

**Elizabeth II Coronation Anniv. Issue**

Souvenir Sheet

Common Design Types

**1978, Apr. 21 Unwmk. *Perf. 15***

| No. | Type | Value / Description | Unused | Used |
|---|---|---|---|---|
| *474* | | Sheet of 6 | 3.00 | 3.00 |
| *a* | | CD326 50c *Griffin of Edward III* | 50 | 50 |
| *b* | | CD327 50c *Elizabeth II* | 50 | 50 |
| *c* | | CD328 50c *Pelican* | 50 | 50 |

No. 474 contains 2 se-tenant strips of Nos. 474a-474c, separated by horizontal gutter with commemorative and descriptive inscriptions and showing central part of coronation with coach. Size: 100x135mm.

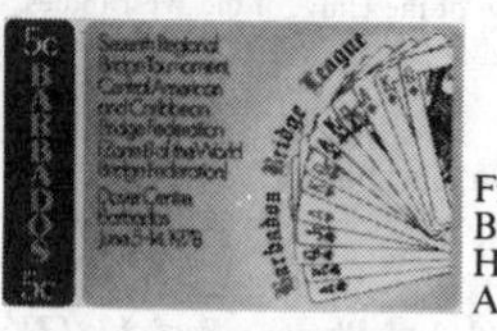


Freak Bridge Hand A73

Designs: 10c, World Bridge Fed. emblem. 45c, Central American and Caribbean Bridge Fed. emblem. $1, Map of Caribbean and cards.

**Wmk. 373**

**1978, June 6 Litho. *Perf. 14½***

| No. | Type | Value / Description | Unused | Used |
|---|---|---|---|---|
| *475* | A73 | 5c multi | 7 | 7 |
| *476* | A73 | 10c multi | 12 | 12 |
| *477* | A73 | 45c multi | 50 | 50 |
| *478* | A73 | $1 multi | 1.00 | 1.00 |
| *a* | | Souvenir sheet of 4 | 1.50 | 1.50 |

7th Regional Bridge Tournament, Dover Centre, Barbados, June 5-14. No. 478a contains Nos. 475-478, multicolored margin. Size: 134x84mm.

Girl Guides' Camp – A74

Designs: 28c, Girl Guides helping children and handicapped. 50c, Badge with "60" (vert.). $1, Badge with initials (vert.).

**1978, Aug. 1 Litho. *Perf. 13½***

| No. | Type | Value / Description | Unused | Used |
|---|---|---|---|---|
| *479* | A74 | 12c multi | 12 | 12 |
| *480* | A74 | 28c multi | 28 | 28 |
| *481* | A74 | 50c multi | 50 | 50 |
| *482* | A74 | $1 multi | 1.00 | 1.00 |

Girl Guides of Barbados, 60th anniv.

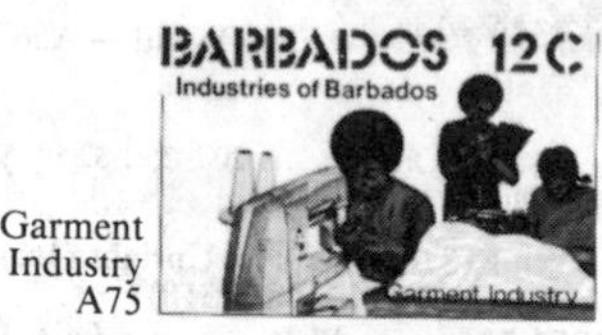


Garment Industry A75

Industries of Barbados: 28c, Cooper (vert.). 45c, Blacksmith (vert.). 50c, Wrought iron industry.

**1978, Nov. 14 Litho. *Perf. 14***

| No. | Type | Value / Description | Unused | Used |
|---|---|---|---|---|
| *483* | A75 | 12c multi | 10 | 10 |
| *484* | A75 | 28c multi | 28 | 28 |
| *485* | A75 | 45c multi | 42 | 42 |
| *486* | A75 | 50c multi | 50 | 50 |

Early Mail Steamer A76

Ships: 25c, Q.E.II in Deep Water Harbour. 50c, Ra II (raft) nearing Barbados. $1, Early mail steamer.

**1979, Feb. 8 Litho. *Perf. 13x13½***

| No. | Type | Value / Description | Unused | Used |
|---|---|---|---|---|
| *487* | A76 | 12c multi | 14 | 14 |
| *488* | A76 | 25c multi | 28 | 28 |
| *489* | A76 | 50c multi | 50 | 50 |
| *490* | A76 | $1 multi | 1.00 | 1.00 |

Barbados No. 235 A77

Designs: 28c, Barbados No. 430 (vert.). 45c, Penny Black and Maltese postmark (vert.). 50c, Barbados No. 21b.

**Wmk. 373**

**1979, May 8 Litho. *Perf. 14***

| No. | Type | Value / Description | Unused | Used |
|---|---|---|---|---|
| *491* | A77 | 12c multi | 8 | 8 |
| *492* | A77 | 28c multi | 20 | 20 |
| *493* | A77 | 45c multi | 30 | 30 |

**Souvenir Sheet**

| No. | Type | Value / Description | Unused | Used |
|---|---|---|---|---|
| *494* | A77 | 50c multi | 40 | 40 |

Sir Rowland Hill (1795-1879), originator of penny postage. Margin shows Mulready cover. Size: 137x91mm.

Birds – A78

Launcher Transported through Barbados – A79

**1979-81 Photo. Wmk. 373 *Perf. 14***

| No. | Type | Value / Description | Unused | Used |
|---|---|---|---|---|
| *495* | A78 | 1c Grass canaries | 6 | 5 |
| *496* | A78 | 2c Rain birds | 6 | 5 |
| *497* | A78 | 5c Sparrows | 6 | 5 |
| *498* | A78 | 8c Frigate birds | 7 | 6 |
| *499* | A78 | 10c Cattle egrets | 8 | 7 |
| *500* | A78 | 12c Green gaulins | 10 | 8 |
| *501* | A78 | 20c Humming-birds | 16 | 14 |
| *502* | A78 | 25c Ground doves | 20 | 16 |
| *503* | A78 | 28c Blackbirds | 22 | 20 |
| *504* | A78 | 35c Green-throated caribs | 28 | 24 |
| *505* | A78 | 45c Wood doves | 35 | 30 |
| *506* | A78 | 50c Ramiers | 40 | 35 |
| *506A* | A78 | 55c Black-breasted plover ('81) | 50 | 38 |
| *507* | A78 | 70c Yellow breasts | 50 | 45 |
| *508* | A78 | $1 Pee whistlers | 80 | 65 |
| *509* | A78 | $2.50 Christmas birds | 2.00 | 1.60 |
| *510* | A78 | $5 Kingfishers | 4.00 | 3.50 |
| *511* | A78 | $10 Red-seal coot | 8.50 | 6.50 |
| | | *Nos. 495-511 (18)* | 18.34 | 14.83 |

Issue dates: 55c, Sept. 1; others, Aug. 7.

See Nos. 570-572.

**1979, Oct. 9 Photo.**

Designs: 10c, Gun on landing craft, Foul Bay (horiz.). 20c, Firing of 16-inch launcher by day. 28c, Bath Earth Station and Intelsat IV-A (horiz.). 45c, Intelsat over Caribbean (horiz.). 50c, Intelsat IV-A over Atlantic, and globe. $1, Lunar landing module (horiz.).

| No. | Type | Value / Description | Unused | Used |
|---|---|---|---|---|
| *512* | A79 | 10c multi | 7 | 7 |
| *513* | A79 | 12c multi | 8 | 8 |
| *514* | A79 | 20c multi | 14 | 14 |
| *515* | A79 | 28c multi | 20 | 20 |
| *516* | A79 | 45c multi | 30 | 30 |
| *517* | A79 | 50c multi | 35 | 35 |
| | | *Nos. 512-517 (6)* | 1.14 | 1.14 |

**Souvenir Sheet**

| No. | Type | Value / Description | Unused | Used |
|---|---|---|---|---|
| *518* | A79 | $1 multi | 85 | 85 |

Space exploration. No. 518 commemorates 10th anniversary of first moon landing; multicolored margin shows moon surface, earth and spacecraft. Size: 119x90mm.

Family, IYC Emblem — A80

IYC Emblem and: 28c, Children holding hands and map of Barbados. 45c, Boy and teacher. 50c, Children playing. $1, Boy and girl flying kite.

**1979, Nov. 27 Litho. *Perf. 14***

| | | | | |
|---|---|---|---|---|
| *519* | A80 | 12c multi | 8 | 8 |
| *520* | A80 | 28c multi | 20 | 20 |
| *521* | A80 | 45c multi | 30 | 30 |
| *522* | A80 | 50c multi | 35 | 35 |
| *523* | A80 | $1 multi | 65 | 65 |
| | | *Nos. 519-523 (5)* | 1.58 | 1.58 |

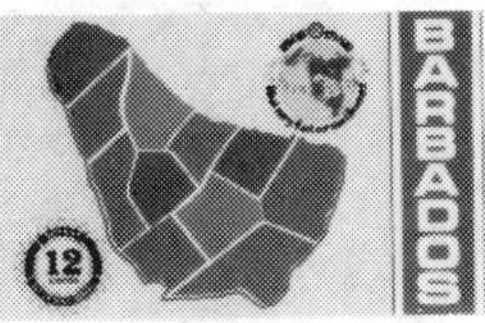

Map of Barbados, Anniversary Emblem — A81

Rotary Intl., 75th Anniv.: 28c, Map of district 404. 50c, 75th anniv. emblem. $1 Paul P. Harris, founder.

**1980, Feb. 19 Litho. *Perf. 13½***

| | | | | |
|---|---|---|---|---|
| *524* | A81 | 12c multi | 8 | 8 |
| *525* | A81 | 28c multi | 20 | 20 |
| *526* | A81 | 50c multi | 35 | 35 |
| *527* | A81 | $1 multi | 65 | 65 |

Regiment Volunteer, Artillery Company, 1909 — A82

**Wmk. 373**

**1980, Apr. 8 Litho. *Perf. 14½***

| | | | | |
|---|---|---|---|---|
| *528* | A82 | 12c *shown* | 8 | 8 |
| *529* | A82 | 35c *Drum major* | 22 | 22 |
| *530* | A82 | 50c *Sovereign's, regimental flags* | 35 | 35 |
| *531* | A82 | $1 *Women's corps* | 65 | 65 |

Barbados Regiment, 75th anniv.

Souvenir Sheets

Early Mailman, London 1980 Emblem — A83

**Wmk. 373**

**1980, May 6 Litho. *Perf. 14***

| | | | | |
|---|---|---|---|---|
| *532* | | Sheet of 6 | 1.10 | 1.10 |
| *a* | | A83 28c, any single | 20 | 20 |
| *533* | | Sheet of 6 | 2.25 | 2.25 |
| *a* | | A83 50c, any single | 35 | 35 |

London 80 Intl. Stamp Exhib., May 6-14. Slate blue and black margins show symbols of postal handling, emblem. Size: 123x125mm.

Underwater Scenes — A84

**1980, Sept. 30 Litho. *Perf. 13½***

| | | | | |
|---|---|---|---|---|
| *534* | A84 | 12c multi | 8 | 8 |
| *535* | A84 | 28c multi | 20 | 20 |
| *536* | A84 | 50c multi | 35 | 35 |
| *537* | A84 | $1 multi | 65 | 65 |
| *a* | | Souvenir sheet of 4 | 1.40 | 1.40 |

No. 537a contains Nos. 534-537. Multicolored margin shows underwater scene. Size: 137x110mm.

Bathsheba Railroad Station — A85

**1981, Jan. 13 Litho. *Perf. 14½***

| | | | | |
|---|---|---|---|---|
| *538* | A85 | 12c *shown* | 8 | 8 |
| *539* | A85 | 28c *Cab stand, The Green* | 20 | 20 |
| *540* | A85 | 45c *Mule-drawn tram* | 30 | 30 |
| *541* | A85 | 70c *Horse-drawn bus* | 50 | 50 |
| *542* | A85 | $1 *Fairchild St. railroad station* | 65 | 65 |
| | | *Nos. 538-542 (5)* | 1.73 | 1.73 |

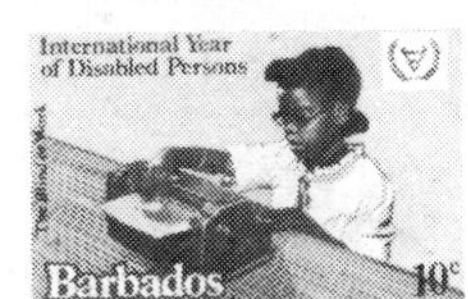

Visually Handicapped Girl at Typewriter — A86

**1981, May 19 Litho. *Perf. 14***

| | | | | |
|---|---|---|---|---|
| *543* | A86 | 10c shown | 7 | 7 |
| *544* | A86 | 25c Sign language alphabet, vert. | 16 | 16 |
| *545* | A86 | 45c Blind people crossing street, vert. | 30 | 30 |
| *546* | A86 | $2.50 Baseball game | 1.75 | 1.75 |

International Year of the Disabled.

**Royal Wedding Issue**

Common Design Type

**Wmk. 373**

**1981, July 22 Litho. *Perf. 13½***

| | | | | |
|---|---|---|---|---|
| *547* | CD331 | 28c Bouquet | 20 | 20 |
| *548* | CD331 | 50c Charles | 35 | 35 |
| *549* | CD331 | $2.50 Couple | 1.75 | 1.75 |

Tuk Band — A87

**1981, Aug. 11 Litho. *Perf. 14½***

| | | | | |
|---|---|---|---|---|
| *550* | A87 | 15c Landship maneuver | 15 | 15 |
| *551* | A87 | 20c Yoruba dancer | 20 | 20 |
| *552* | A87 | 40c shown | 40 | 40 |
| *553* | A87 | 55c Frank Collymore (sculpture) | 55 | 55 |
| *554* | A87 | $1 Barbados Harbor (painting) | 1.00 | 1.00 |
| | | *Nos. 550-554 (5)* | 2.30 | 2.30 |

4th Caribbean Arts Festival (CARIFESTA), July 19-Aug. 3.

Hurricane Gladys, View from Apollo A88

**1981, Sept. 29 Litho. *Perf. 14***

| | | | | |
|---|---|---|---|---|
| *555* | A88 | 35c Satellite view over Barbados | 35 | 35 |
| *556* | A88 | 50c shown | 50 | 50 |
| *557* | A88 | 60c Police watch | 60 | 60 |
| *558* | A88 | $1 Spotter plane | 1.00 | 1.00 |

Harrison's Cave — A89

***Perf. 14x14½***

**1981, Dec. 1 Litho. Wmk. 373**

| | | | | |
|---|---|---|---|---|
| *559* | A89 | 10c Twin Falls | 7 | 7 |
| *560* | A89 | 20c Rotunda Room Stream | 14 | 14 |
| *561* | A89 | 55c Rotunda Room formation | 35 | 35 |
| *562* | A89 | $2.50 Cascade Pool | 1.75 | 1.75 |

Nos. 503, 505, 507 Surcharged

**1982, Feb. 1 Photo. *Perf. 14***

| | | | | |
|---|---|---|---|---|
| *563* | A78 | 15c on 28c multi | 15 | 15 |
| *564* | A78 | 40c on 45c multi | 40 | 40 |
| *565* | A78 | 60c on 70c multi | 60 | 60 |

Black Belly Sheep A90

**1982, Feb. 9 Litho.**

| | | | | |
|---|---|---|---|---|
| *566* | A90 | 40c Ram | 40 | 40 |
| *567* | A90 | 50c Ewe | 50 | 50 |
| *568* | A90 | 60c Ewe, lambs | 60 | 60 |
| *569* | A90 | $1 Pair, map | 1.00 | 1.00 |

Bird Type of 1979

**Wmk. 373**

**1982, Mar. 1 Photo. *Perf. 14***

| | | | | |
|---|---|---|---|---|
| *570* | A78 | 15c like #503 | 15 | 15 |
| *571* | A78 | 40c like #506 | 40 | 40 |
| *572* | A78 | 60c like #507 | 60 | 60 |

Early Marine Transport A91

**1982, Apr. 6 Litho. *Perf. 14½***

| | | | | |
|---|---|---|---|---|
| *577* | A91 | 20c Lighter | 20 | 20 |
| *578* | A91 | 35c Rowboat | 35 | 35 |
| *579* | A91 | 55c Speightstown schooner | 55 | 55 |
| *580* | A91 | $2.50 Inter-colonial schooner | 2.50 | 2.50 |

Visit of Pres. Ronald Reagan A92

**1982, Apr. 8 Litho. *Perf. 14***

| | | | | |
|---|---|---|---|---|
| *581* | A92 | 20c Barbados Flag, arms | 25 | 20 |
| *582* | A92 | 20c US Flag, arms | 25 | 20 |
| *583* | A92 | 55c like #581 | 65 | 55 |
| *584* | A92 | 55c like #582 | 65 | 55 |

Stamps of same denomination printed in sheets of 8 with gutter showing Pres. Reagan and Prime Minister Tom Adams.

**Princess Diana Issue**

Common Design Type

**1982, July 1 Litho. *Perf. 14½***

| | | | | |
|---|---|---|---|---|
| *585* | CD333 | 20c Arms | 15 | 15 |
| *586* | CD333 | 60c Diana | 45 | 45 |
| *587* | CD333 | $1.20 Wedding | 90 | 90 |
| *588* | CD333 | $2.50 Portrait | 1.75 | 1.75 |

Scouting Year — A93

Washington's 250th Birth Anniv. — A94

**1982, Sept. 7 Wmk. 373 *Perf. 14***

| | | | | |
|---|---|---|---|---|
| *589* | A93 | 15c Helping woman | 10 | 10 |
| *590* | A93 | 40c Sign, emblem, flag, horiz. | 28 | 28 |
| *591* | A93 | 55c Religious service, horiz. | 35 | 35 |
| *592* | A93 | $1 Flags | 65 | 65 |

**Souvenir Sheet**

| | | | | |
|---|---|---|---|---|
| *593* | A93 | $1.50 Laws | 1.00 | 1.00 |

No. 593 has multicolored margin showing scouts holding law poster. Size: 120x94mm.

**1982, Nov. 2 *Perf. 13½x13***

| | | | | |
|---|---|---|---|---|
| *594* | A94 | 10c Arms | 10 | 10 |
| *595* | A94 | 55c Washington's house, Barbados | 55 | 55 |
| *596* | A94 | 60c Taking command | 60 | 60 |
| *597* | A94 | $2.50 Taking oath | 2.50 | 2.50 |

**Commonwealth Day Issue**

Common Design Type

**1983, Mar. 14 Litho. *Perf. 14***

| | | | | |
|---|---|---|---|---|
| *598* | CD334 | 15c Map, globe | 15 | 15 |
| *599* | CD334 | 40c Beach | 40 | 40 |
| *600* | CD334 | 60c Sugar cane harvest | 60 | 60 |
| *601* | CD334 | $1 Cricket game | 1.00 | 1.00 |

Gulf Fritillary A96

***Perf. 13½x13***

**1983, Feb. 8 Litho. Wmk. 373**

| | | | | |
|---|---|---|---|---|
| *602* | A96 | 20c shown | 20 | 20 |
| *603* | A96 | 40c Monarch | 40 | 40 |
| *604* | A96 | 55c Mimic | 55 | 55 |
| *605* | A96 | $2.50 Hanno Blue | 2.50 | 2.50 |

Manned Flight Bicentenary — A97

**1983, June 17 Litho. *Perf. 14***

| | | | | |
|---|---|---|---|---|
| *606* | A97 | 20c US Navy dirigible | 20 | 20 |
| *607* | A97 | 40c Douglas DC-3 | 40 | 40 |
| *608* | A97 | 55c Vickers Viscount | 55 | 55 |
| *609* | A97 | $1 Lockheed TriStar | 1.00 | 1.00 |

Common Design Types are pictured in section before Great Britain.

Nash 600, 1941
A98

**1983, Aug. 9 Litho. *Perf. 14***

| | | | | |
|---|---|---|---|---|
| *610* A98 | 25c shown | 25 | 25 |
| *611* A98 | 45c Dodge, 1938 | 45 | 45 |
| *612* A98 | 75c Ford Model AA, 1930 | 75 | 75 |
| *613* A98 | $2.50 Dodge Four, 1918 | 2.50 | 2.50 |

World Cup Table Tennis Championship
A99

**1983, Aug. 30 Litho. *Perf. 14***

| | | | |
|---|---|---|---|
| *614* A99 | 20c Players | 20 | 20 |
| *615* A99 | 65c Emblem, map | 65 | 65 |
| *616* A99 | $1 Cup | 1.00 | 1.00 |

Christmas 1983 — A100

Designs: 10c, 25c, Angel with lute, painting details. $2, The Virgin and Child, by Masaccio.

**1983, Nov. 1 *Perf. 14***

| | | | |
|---|---|---|---|
| *617* A100 | 10c multicolored | 10 | 10 |
| *618* A100 | 25c multicolored | 25 | 25 |

**Souvenir Sheet**

| | | | |
|---|---|---|---|
| *619* A100 | $2 multicolored | 2.00 | 2.00 |

No. 619 has multicolored margin continuing design. Size: 58x98mm.

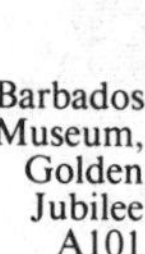

Barbados Museum, Golden Jubilee
A101

Museum Paintings: 45c, by Richard Day. 75c, St. Ann's Garrison in Barbados by W.S. Hedges. $2.50, Needham's Point, Carlisle Bay.

**1983, Nov. 1 *Perf. 14***

| | | | |
|---|---|---|---|
| *620* A101 | 45c multicolored | 45 | 45 |
| *621* A101 | 75c multicolored | 75 | 75 |
| *622* A101 | $2.50 multicolored | 2.50 | 2.50 |

1984 Olympics, Los Angeles
A102

**1984, Apr. 3 Litho. *Perf. 14***

| | | | |
|---|---|---|---|
| *623* A102 | 50c Track & field | 50 | 50 |
| *624* A102 | 65c Shooting | 65 | 65 |
| *625* A102 | 75c Sailing | 75 | 75 |
| *626* A102 | $1 Bicycling | 1.00 | 1.00 |
| *a* | Souvenir sheet of 4 | 3.00 | 3.00 |

No. 626a contains Nos. 623-626. Size: 115x88mm.

**Lloyd's List Issue**

Common Design Type

**1984, Apr. 25 Litho. *Perf. 14½***

| | | | |
|---|---|---|---|
| *627* CD335 | 45c World map | 45 | 45 |
| *628* CD335 | 50c Bridgetown Harbor | 50 | 50 |
| *629* CD335 | 75c Philosopher | 75 | 75 |
| *630* CD335 | $1 Sea Princess | 1.00 | 1.00 |

**Souvenir Sheet**

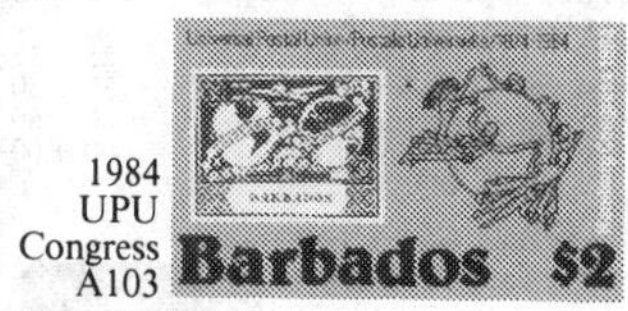


1984 UPU Congress
A103

**1984, June 6 Litho. *Perf. 13½***

| | | | |
|---|---|---|---|
| *631* A103 | $2 #213, UPU emblem | 2.00 | 2.00 |

No. 631 has yellow and black margin showing means of communication and mail transport. Size: 90x75mm.

World Chess Fed., 60th Anniv.
A104

**1984, Aug. 8 *Perf. 14x14½***

| | | | |
|---|---|---|---|
| *632* A104 | 25c Junior match | 25 | 25 |
| *633* A104 | 45c Knights | 45 | 45 |
| *634* A104 | 65c Queens | 65 | 65 |
| *635* A104 | $2 Rooks | 2.00 | 2.00 |

Christmas 1984 — A105

**1984, Oct. 24 Litho. *Perf. 14***

| | | | |
|---|---|---|---|
| *636* A105 | 50c Poinsettia | 50 | 50 |
| *637* A105 | 65c Snow-on-the-mountain | 65 | 65 |
| *638* A105 | 75c Christmas candle | 75 | 75 |
| *639* A105 | $1 Christmas hope | 1.00 | 1.00 |

Marine Life
A106

**1985 Litho. Wmk. 373 *Perf. 14***

| | | | |
|---|---|---|---|
| *640* A106 | 1c Bristle worm | 5 | 5 |
| *641* A106 | 2c Spotted trunk fish | 5 | 5 |
| *642* A106 | 5c Coney fish | 5 | 5 |
| *643* A106 | 10c Pink-tipped anemone | 10 | 10 |
| *645* A106 | 20c Christmas tree worm | 20 | 20 |
| *646* A106 | 25c Hermit crab | 25 | 25 |
| *648* A106 | 35c Animal flower | 35 | 35 |
| *649* A106 | 40c Vase sponge | 40 | 40 |
| *650* A106 | 45c Spotted moray | 45 | 45 |
| *651* A106 | 50c Ghost crab | 50 | 50 |
| *653* A106 | 65c Flaming tongue snail | 65 | 65 |
| *654* A106 | 75c Sergeant major fish | 75 | 75 |
| *656* A106 | $1 Caribbean warty anemone | 1.00 | 1.00 |
| *657* A106 | $2.50 Green turtle | 2.50 | 2.50 |
| *658* A106 | $5 Rock beauty | 5.00 | 5.00 |
| *659* A106 | $10 Elkhorn coral | 10.00 | 10.00 |
| | *Nos. 640-659 (16)* | 22.30 | 22.30 |

Issue dates: 10c, 20c, 25c, 50c, $2.50 and $5, Feb. 26; 5c, 35c, 40c, 65c and $10, Apr. 9; 1c, 2c, 45c, 75c and $1, May 7.

**1985, Dec. Wmk. 384**

| | | | |
|---|---|---|---|
| *642a* | Wmk. 384 | 5 | 5 |
| *643a* | Wmk. 384 | 7 | 7 |
| *645a* | Wmk. 384 | 14 | 14 |
| *646a* | Wmk. 384 | 16 | 16 |
| *648a* | Wmk. 384 | 25 | 25 |
| *651a* | Wmk. 384 | 35 | 35 |
| *657a* | Wmk. 384 | 1.75 | 1.75 |
| *658a* | Wmk. 384 | 3.50 | 3.50 |
| *659a* | Wmk. 384 | 6.50 | 6.50 |
| | *Nos. 642a-659a (9)* | 12.77 | 12.77 |

**1986 Wmk. 384 Sideways**

| | | | |
|---|---|---|---|
| *640a* | "1986" | 5 | 5 |
| *641a* | "1986" | 5 | 5 |
| *643b* | "1986" | 10 | 10 |
| *645b* | "1986" | 20 | 20 |
| *646b* | "1986" | 25 | 25 |
| *649a* | "1986" | 40 | 40 |
| *650a* | "1986" | 45 | 45 |
| *651b* | "1986" | 50 | 50 |
| *653a* | "1986" | 65 | 65 |
| *654a* | "1986" | 75 | 75 |
| *656a* | "1986" | 1.00 | 1.00 |
| *657b* | "1986" | 2.50 | 2.50 |
| *658b* | "1986" | 5.00 | 5.00 |
| *659b* | "1986" | 10.00 | 10.00 |
| | *Nos. 640a-659b (14)* | 21.90 | 21.90 |

No. 643b exists inscribed "1988."

**Queen Mother 85th Birthday**

Common Design Type

***Perf. 14½x14***

**1985, June 7 Litho. Wmk. 384**

| | | | |
|---|---|---|---|
| *660* CD336 | 25c At Buckingham Palace, 1930 | 25 | 25 |
| *661* CD336 | 65c With Lady Diana, 1981 | 65 | 65 |
| *662* CD336 | 75c At the docks | 75 | 75 |
| *663* CD336 | $1 Holding Prince Henry | 1.00 | 1.00 |

**Souvenir Sheet**

| | | | |
|---|---|---|---|
| *664* CD336 | $2 Opening the Garden Center, Syon House | 2.00 | 2.00 |

No. 664 has multicolored margin continuing design. Size: 92x74mm.

Audubon Birth Bicentenary — A107

Illustrations of North American bird species. Nos. 666-668 vert.

**Wmk. 373**

**1985, Aug. 6 Litho. *Perf. 14***

| | | | |
|---|---|---|---|
| *665* A107 | 45c Falco peregrinus | 45 | 45 |
| *666* A107 | 65c Dendroica discolor | 65 | 65 |
| *667* A107 | 75c Ardea herodias | 75 | 75 |
| *668* A107 | $1 Dendroica petechia | 1.00 | 1.00 |

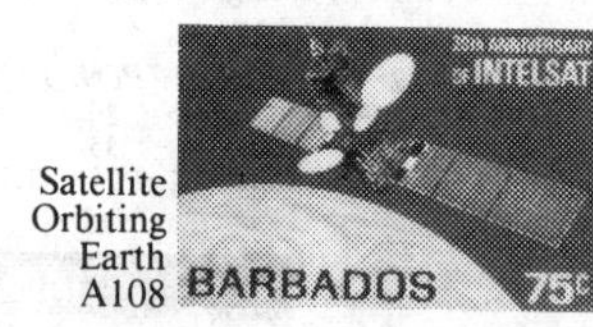


Satellite Orbiting Earth
A108

**1985, Sept. 10**

| | | | |
|---|---|---|---|
| *669* A108 | 75c multicolored | 75 | 75 |

INTELSAT, Intl. Telecommunications Satellite Consortium, 20th anniv.

Royal Barbados Police, 150th Anniv. — A109

**1985, Nov. 19**

| | | | |
|---|---|---|---|
| *670* A109 | 25c Traffic Dept. | 25 | 25 |
| *671* A109 | 50c Police Band | 50 | 50 |
| *672* A109 | 65c Dog Force | 65 | 65 |
| *673* A109 | $1 Mounted Police | 1.00 | 1.00 |

**Souvenir Sheet**

| | | | |
|---|---|---|---|
| *674* A109 | $2 Band on parade, horiz. | 2.00 | 2.00 |

No. 674 has multicolored inscribed margin continuing the design. Size: 86x60mm.

**Queen Elizabeth II 60th Birthday**

Common Design Type

Designs: 25c, Age 2. 50c, Senate House opening, University College of the West Indies, Jamaica, 1953. 65c, With Prince Philip, Caribbean Tour, 1985. 75c, Banquet, state visit to Sao Paulo, Brazil, 1968. $2, Visiting Crown Agents, 1983.

***Perf. 14x14½***

**1986, Apr. 21 Litho. Wmk. 384**

| | | | |
|---|---|---|---|
| *675* CD337 | 25c scar, blk & sil | 25 | 25 |
| *676* CD337 | 50c ultra & multi | 50 | 50 |
| *677* CD337 | 65c green & multi | 65 | 65 |
| *678* CD337 | 75c violet & multi | 75 | 75 |
| *679* CD337 | $2 rose vio & multi | 2.00 | 2.00 |
| | *Nos. 675-679 (5)* | 4.15 | 4.15 |

EXPO '86, Vancouver
A110

**1986, May 2 *Perf. 14***

| | | | |
|---|---|---|---|
| *680* A110 | 50c Trans-Canada North Star | 50 | 50 |
| *681* A110 | $2.50 Lady Nelson | 2.50 | 2.50 |

AMERIPEX '86 — A111

**1986, May 22 Wmk. 373**

| | | | |
|---|---|---|---|
| *682* A111 | 45c No. 441 | 45 | 45 |
| *683* A111 | 50c No. 442 | 50 | 50 |
| *684* A111 | 65c No. 558 | 65 | 65 |
| *685* A111 | $1 Nos. 583-584 | 1.00 | 1.00 |

**Souvenir Sheet**

| | | | |
|---|---|---|---|
| *686* A111 | $2 Statue of Liberty, NY Harbor | 2.00 | 2.00 |

Statue of Liberty, cent. No. 686 has multicolored decorative margin picturing natl. flag, exhibition emblem. Size: 90x80mm.

**Royal Wedding Issue, 1986**

Common Design Type

Designs: 45c, Informal portrait. $1, Andrew in navy uniform.

***Perf. 14½x14***

**1986, July 23 Litho. Wmk. 384**

| | | | |
|---|---|---|---|
| *687* CD338 | 45c multicolored | 45 | 45 |
| *688* CD338 | $1 multicolored | 1.00 | 1.00 |

Electrification of Barbados, 75th Anniv.
A112

Designs: 10c, Transporting utility poles, 1923. 25c, Heathfield ladder, 1935, vert. 65c, Transport fleet, 1941. $2, Bucket truck, 1986, vert.

**Wmk. 384**

**1986, Sept. 16 Litho. *Perf. 14***

| | | | |
|---|---|---|---|
| *689* A112 | 10c multicolored | 10 | 10 |
| *690* A112 | 25c multicolored | 25 | 25 |
| *691* A112 | 65c multicolored | 65 | 65 |
| *692* A112 | $2 multicolored | 2.00 | 2.00 |

Christmas — A113

Church windows and flowers.

**1986, Oct. 28** **Wmk. 373**
*693* A113 25c Alpinia purpurata 25 25
*694* A113 50c Anthurium andraeanum 50 50
*695* A113 75c Heliconia rostrata 75 75
*696* A113 $2 Heliconia psittacorum 2.00 2.00

Natl. Special Olympics, 10th Anniv. — A114

**1987, Mar. 10** **Wmk. 373** ***Perf. 14***
*697* A114 15c Shot put 15 15
*698* A114 45c Wheelchair race 45 45
*699* A114 65c Girl's long jump 65 65
*700* A114 $2 Emblem, creed 2.00 2.00

CAPEX '87 — A115

**1987, June 12**
*701* A115 25c Barn swallow 25 25
*702* A115 50c Yellow warbler 50 50
*703* A115 65c Audubon's shearwater 65 65
*704* A115 75c Black-whiskered vireo 75 75
*705* A115 $1 Scarlet tanager 1.00 1.00
*Nos. 701-705 (5)* 3.15 3.15

Natl. Scouting Movement, 75th Anniv. — A116

**1987, July 24** ***Perf. 14x14½***
*706* A116 10c Scout sign 10 10
*707* A116 25c Campfire 25 25
*708* A116 65c Merit badges, etc. 65 65
*709* A116 $2 Marching band 2.00 2.00

Bridgetown Synagogue Restoration A117

**1987, Oct. 6** **Wmk. 384** ***Perf. 14½***
*710* A117 50c Exterior 50 50
*711* A117 65c Interior 65 65
*712* A117 75c Ten Commandments, vert. 75 75
*713* A117 $1 Marble laver, vert. 1.00 1.00

Natl. Independence, 21st Anniv. — A118

E.W. Barrow (1920-87), Father of Independence A119

Designs: 25c, Coat of arms and seal of the colony. 45c, Natl. flag and the Union Jack. 65c, Silver dollar and penny. $2, Old and new regimental flags and Queen Elizabeth's colors.

**1987, Nov. 24** **Litho.** ***Perf. 14½***
*714* A118 25c multicolored 25 25
*715* A118 45c multicolored 45 45
*716* A118 65c multicolored 65 65
*717* A118 $2 multicolored 2.00 2.00

**Souvenir Sheet**

*718* A119 $1.50 multicolored 1.50 1.50

No. 718 has multicolored margin picturing map of Barbados, natl. flag and map of the Caribbean. Size: 94x56mm.

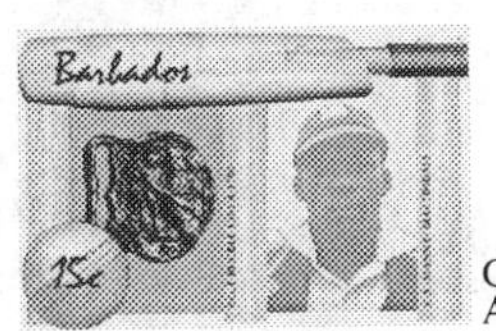

Cricket A120

Bat, wicket posts, ball, 18th cent. belt buckle and batters: 15c, E.A. "Manny" Martindale. 45c, George Challenor. 75c, Harold Austin. $2, Frank Worrell.

Bat, wicket posts, ball, 18th cent. belt buckle and batter: 50c, Herman C. Griffith.

**Wmk. 373**

**1988, June 6** **Litho.** ***Perf. 14***
*719* A120 15c multi 15 15
*720* A120 45c multi 45 45
*720A* A120 50c multi 50 50
*721* A120 75c multi 75 75
*722* A120 $2 multi 2.00 2.00

Issue date of No. 720A: July 11.

Lizards — A121

**1988, June 13**
*723* A121 10c Kentropyx borckianus 10 10
*724* A121 50c Hemidactylus mabouia 50 50
*725* A121 65c Anolis extremus 65 65
*726* A121 $2 Gymnophthalmus underwoodii 2.00 2.00

1988 Summer Olympics, Seoul — A122

**Wmk. 373**

**1988, Aug. 2** **Litho.** ***Perf. 14½***
*727* A122 25c Cycling 25 25
*728* A122 45c Running 45 45
*729* A122 75c Swimming 75 75
*730* A122 $2 Yachting 2.00 2.00
*a.* Souv. sheet of 4, Nos. 727-730 3.50 3.50

No. 730a has multicolored inscribed margin picturing grandstand and track. Size: 145x64mm.

**Lloyds of London, 300th Anniv.**

Common Design Type

Designs: 40c, Royal Exchange, 1774. 50c, Sugar mill (windmill), horiz. 65c, Container ship *Author*, horiz. $2, Sinking of the *Titanic*, 1912.

**Wmk. 373**

**1988, Oct. 18** **Litho.** ***Perf. 14***
*731* CD341 40c multi 40 40
*732* CD341 50c multi 50 50
*733* CD341 65c multi 65 65
*734* CD341 $2 multi 2.00 2.00

Harry Bayley Observatory, 25th Anniv. A123

Designs: 25c, Observatory, crescent Moon, Venus and Harry Bayley. 65c, Observatory and constellations. 75c, Andromeda Galaxy and telescope. $2, Orion Constellation.

**Wmk. 384**

**1988, Nov. 28** **Litho.** ***Perf. 14½***
*735* A123 25c multi 25 25
*736* A123 65c multi 65 65
*737* A123 75c multi 75 75
*738* A123 $2 multi 2.00 2.00

## SEMI-POSTAL STAMPS

No. 73 Surcharged in Red

Kingston Relief Fund. 1d.

**Wmk. 2**

**1907, Jan. 25** **Typo.** ***Perf. 14***
*B1* A8 1p on 2p sl & org 1.75 2.50
*a.* No period after 1d 15.00 17.50
*b.* Inverted surcharge 1.75 2.50
*c.* Inverted surcharge, no period after 1d 15.00 17.50
*d.* Double surcharge 1,100.
*e.* Dbl. surch., both invtd. 1,100.

**Catalogue values for unused stamps in this section, from this point to the end of the section, are for Never Hinged items.**

No. 406 Surcharged

28c + 4c

ST. VINCENT RELIEF FUND

**1979, May 29** **Photo.** **Wmk. 314**
*B2* A56 28c + 4c on 35c multi 30 30

The surtax was for victims of the eruption of Mt. Soufrière.

## POSTAGE DUE STAMPS

**Catalogue values for unused stamps in this section, from this point to the end of the section, are for Never Hinged items.**

D1

Flower and Numeral — D2

**1934-47** **Typo.** **Wmk. 4** ***Perf. 14***
*J1* D1 ½p green ('35) 60 70
*J2* D1 1p black 1.10 40
*J3* D1 3p dk car rose ('47) 17.50 22.50

A second die of the 1p was introduced in 1947.

**1950**
*J4* D1 1c green 18 18
*a.* Wmk. 4a (error) 57.50
*J5* D1 2c black 40 40
*a.* Wmk. 4a (error) 65.00
*J6* D1 6c carmine rose 1.50 1.75
*a.* Wmk. 4a (error) 75.00

Values are for 1953 chalky paper printing.

**1965-74** **Wmk. 314** ***Perf. 14***
*J7* D1 1c green 30 30
*J8* D1 2c black 35 35
*J9* D1 6c carmine rose 65 65
*a.* Watermarked sideways ('74) 2.25 2.25

***Perf. 13½x14***

**1976, May 12** **Litho.** **Wmk. 373**

Designs: Each stamp shows different stylized flower in background.

*J10* D2 1c brt pink & mag 5 5
*J11* D2 2c lt & dk vio bl 5 5
*J12* D2 5c yellow & brown 6 6
*J13* D2 10c lilac & purple 9 9
*J14* D2 25c yel grn & dk grn 22 22
*J15* D2 $1 rose & red 90 90
*Nos. J10-J15 (6)* 1.37 1.37

## WAR TAX STAMP

No. 118 Overprinted WAR TAX

**1917** **Wmk. 3** ***Perf. 14***
*MR1* A12 1p carmine 10 10
*a.* Imperf., pair 4,500.

# BARBUDA

LOCATION — Northernmost of the Leeward Islands, West Indies.
GOVT. — A dependency of Antigua.
AREA — 63 sq. mi.
POP. — 1,000 (estimated).
See Antigua.

12 Pence = 1 Shilling

Leeward Islands Stamps and Types of 1912-22 Overprinted in Black or Red

BARBUDA

Die II

For description of dies I and II see back of this section of the Catalogue.

**1922, July 13 Wmk. 4 Perf. 14**

| | | | | |
|---|---|---|---|---|
| 1 | A5 | ½p green | 1.10 | *1.65* |
| 2 | A5 | 1p rose red | 1.10 | *1.65* |
| 3 | A5 | 2p gray | 1.25 | *2.00* |
| 4 | A5 | 2½p ultra | 1.25 | *2.00* |
| 5 | A5 | 6p vio & red vio | 3.00 | *4.00* |
| 6 | A5 | 2sh vio & ultra, *bl* | 12.50 | *20.00* |
| 7 | A5 | 3sh grn & violet | 25.00 | *37.50* |
| 8 | A5 | 4sh blk & scar (R) | 25.00 | *37.50* |

**Wmk. 3**

| | | | | |
|---|---|---|---|---|
| 9 | A5 | 3p vio, *yel* | 1.10 | *2.00* |
| 10 | A5 | 1sh *emer* (R) | 2.50 | *4.00* |
| 11 | A5 | 5sh grn & red, *yel* | 75.00 | *125.00* |
| | | *Nos. 1-11 (11)* | 148.80 | *237.30* |

See For The Record. Recent issues are recorded in the Scott Chronicle of New Issues beginning with Vol. 1, No. 1.

## BASUTOLAND

LOCATION — An enclave in the state of South Africa.
GOVT. — Former British Crown Colony.
AREA — 11,716 sq. mi.
POP. — 733,000 (est. 1964).
CAPITAL — Maseru.

The Colony, a former independent native state, was annexed to the Cape Colony in 1871. In 1883 control was transferred directly to the British Crown. Stamps of the Cape of Good Hope were used from 1871 to 1910 and those of the Union of South Africa from 1910 to 1933. Basutoland became the independent state of Lesotho on Oct. 4, 1966.

12 Pence = 1 Shilling
100 Cents = 1 Rand (1961)

**Catalogue values for unused stamps in this country are for Never Hinged items, beginning with Scott 29 in the regular postage section and Scott J1 in the postage due section.**

King George V — A1

King George VI — A2

Crocodile and River Scene

*Perf. 12½*

**1933, Dec. 1 Engr. Wmk. 4**

| | | | | |
|---|---|---|---|---|
| 1 | A1 | ½p emerald | 20 | *60* |
| 2 | A1 | 1p carmine | 18 | 25 |
| 3 | A1 | 2p red vio | 40 | *1.25* |
| 4 | A1 | 3p ultra | 60 | *1.90* |
| 5 | A1 | 4p slate | 1.40 | *3.00* |
| 6 | A1 | 6p yellow | 2.00 | *3.00* |
| 7 | A1 | 1sh red org | 4.00 | *6.25* |
| 8 | A1 | 2sh6p dk brn | 18.00 | *25.00* |
| 9 | A1 | 5sh violet | 40.00 | *52.50* |
| 10 | A1 | 10sh ol grn | 110.00 | *140.00* |
| | | *Nos. 1-10 (10)* | 176.78 | 233.75 |

**Silver Jubilee Issue.**
Common Design Type

**1935, May 4 Perf. 13½x14**

| | | | | |
|---|---|---|---|---|
| 11 | CD301 | 1p car & bl | 20 | 20 |
| 12 | CD301 | 2p gray blk & ultra | 60 | *2.00* |
| 13 | CD301 | 3p bl & brn | 1.90 | *3.25* |
| 14 | CD301 | 6p brt vio & ind | 3.50 | *6.50* |

**Coronation Issue**
Common Design Type

**1937, May 12 Perf. 13½x14**

| | | | | |
|---|---|---|---|---|
| 15 | CD302 | 1p carmine | 10 | 10 |
| 16 | CD302 | 2p rose vio | 20 | 20 |
| 17 | CD302 | 3p brt ultra | 30 | 30 |

**1938, Apr. 1 Perf. 12½**

| | | | | |
|---|---|---|---|---|
| 18 | A2 | ½p emerald | 10 | 10 |
| 19 | A2 | 1p rose car | 12 | 10 |
| 20 | A2 | 1½p lt bl | 15 | 18 |
| 21 | A2 | 2p rose lil | 18 | 20 |
| 22 | A2 | 3p ultra | 20 | 22 |
| 23 | A2 | 4p gray | 25 | *85* |
| 24 | A2 | 6p yel ocher | 30 | 38 |
| 25 | A2 | 1sh red org | 50 | 60 |
| 26 | A2 | 2sh6p blk brn | 1.40 | 1.50 |
| 27 | A2 | 5sh violet | 6.50 | 7.00 |
| 28 | A2 | 10sh ol grn | 9.00 | 11.00 |
| | | *Nos. 18-28 (11)* | 18.70 | 22.13 |

**Catalogue values for unused stamps in this section, from this point to the end of the section, are for Never Hinged items.**

**Peace Issue**

South Africa Nos. 100-102 Overprinted **Basutoland**

Basic stamps inscribed alternately in English and Afrikaans.

**1945, Dec. 3 Wmk. 201 Perf. 14**

| | | | | |
|---|---|---|---|---|
| 29 | A42 | 1p rose pink & choc | 8 | 8 |
| *a.* | | Pair | 20 | 20 |
| 30 | A43 | 2p vio & sl bl | 8 | 8 |
| *a.* | | Pair | 22 | 22 |
| 31 | A43 | 3p ultra & dp ultra | 15 | 15 |
| *a.* | | Pair | 35 | 35 |

King George VI — A3

King George VI and Queen Elizabeth A4

Princess Margaret Rose and Princess Elizabeth A5

Royal British Family A6

*Perf. 12½*

**1947, Feb. 17 Wmk. 4 Engr.**

| | | | | |
|---|---|---|---|---|
| 35 | A3 | 1p red | 5 | 5 |
| 36 | A4 | 2p green | 6 | 6 |
| 37 | A5 | 3p ultra | 8 | 8 |
| 38 | A6 | 1sh dk vio | 20 | 20 |

Issued to commemorate the visit of the British Royal Family, March 11-12, 1947.

**Silver Wedding Issue**
Common Design Types

**1948, Dec. 1 Photo. Perf. 14x14½**

| | | | | |
|---|---|---|---|---|
| 39 | CD304 | 1½p brt ultra | 12 | 12 |

**Engr.; Name Typo.**
*Perf. 11½*

| | | | | |
|---|---|---|---|---|
| 40 | CD305 | 10sh dk brn ol | 16.00 | *32.00* |

**UPU Issue**
Common Design Types
**Engr.; Name Typo. on 3p, 6p**
*Perf. 13½, 11x11½*

**1949, Oct. 10 Wmk. 4**

| | | | | |
|---|---|---|---|---|
| 41 | CD306 | 1½p blue | 28 | 28 |
| 42 | CD307 | 3p indigo | 55 | 55 |
| 43 | CD308 | 6p org yel | 75 | 75 |
| 44 | CD309 | 1sh red brn | 1.10 | 1.10 |

**Coronation Issue.**
Common Design Type

**1953, June 3 Engr. Perf. 13½x13**

| | | | | |
|---|---|---|---|---|
| 45 | CD312 | 2p red vio & blk | 40 | 40 |

Qiloane Hill — A7

Shearing Angora Goats — A8

Designs: 1p, Orange River. 2p, Mosotho horseman. 3p, Basuto household. 4½p, Maletsunyane falls. 6p, Herdboy with lesiba. 1sh, Pastoral scene. 1sh 3p, Plane at Lancers Gap. 2sh6p, Old Fort Leribe. 5sh, Mission cave house.

**1954, Oct. 18 Wmk. 4 Perf. 13½**

| | | | | |
|---|---|---|---|---|
| 46 | A7 | ½p dk brn & gray | 8 | 6 |
| 47 | A7 | 1p dp grn & gray blk | 10 | 8 |
| 48 | A7 | 2p org & dp bl | 12 | 10 |
| 49 | A7 | 3p car & ol grn | 18 | 15 |
| 50 | A7 | 4½p dp bl & ind | 35 | 32 |
| 51 | A7 | 6p dk grn & org brn | 32 | 28 |
| 52 | A7 | 1sh rose vio & dk ol grn | 55 | 45 |
| 53 | A7 | 1sh3p aqua & brn | 70 | 55 |
| 54 | A7 | 2sh6p lil rose & dp ultra | 2.50 | 1.65 |
| 55 | A7 | 5sh dp car & blk | 3.75 | 3.00 |
| 56 | A8 | 10sh dp cl & blk | 7.50 | 5.50 |
| | | *Nos. 46-56 (11)* | 16.15 | 12.14 |

See Nos. 72-82, 87-91.

No. 48 Surcharged **½d.**

**1959, Aug. 1**

| | | | | |
|---|---|---|---|---|
| 57 | A7 | ½p on 2p org & dp bl | 20 | 20 |

Chief Moshoeshoe (Moshesh) — A9

Designs: 1sh, Council chamber. 1sh3p, Mosotho on horseback.

*Perf. 13x13½*

**1959, Dec. 15 Wmk. 314**

| | | | | |
|---|---|---|---|---|
| 58 | A9 | 3p lt yel, grn & blk | 15 | 15 |
| 59 | A9 | 1sh grn & pink | 45 | 45 |
| 60 | A9 | 1sh3p org & ultra | 75 | 75 |

Issued to commemorate the institution of the Basutoland National Council.

Nos. 46-56 Surcharged with New Value

**2½c** (I) **2½c** (II) **3½c** (I) **3½c** (II)
**5c** (I) **5c** (II) **10c** (I) **10c** (II)
**12½c** (I) **12½c** (II)
**25c** (I) **25c** (II) **25c** (III)
**50c** (I) **50c** (II) **R1** (I) **R1** (II) **R1** (III)

**1961, Feb. 14 Wmk. 4 Perf. 13½**

| | | | | |
|---|---|---|---|---|
| 61 | A7 | ½c on ½p dk brn & gray | 5 | 5 |
| *a.* | | Double surch. | *300.00* | |
| 62 | A7 | 1c on 1p dp grn & gray blk | 6 | 6 |
| 63 | A7 | 2c on 2p org & dp bl | 10 | 10 |
| *a.* | | Invert. surch. | *150.00* | |
| 64 | A7 | 2½c on 3p car & ol grn (II) | 10 | 10 |
| *a.* | | Type I | 12 | 12 |
| *b.* | | Inverted surch. (II) | *1,750.* | *1,000.* |
| 65 | A7 | 3½c on 4½p dp bl & ind (I) | 12 | 12 |
| *a.* | | Type II | 4.50 | 4.50 |
| 66 | A7 | 5c on 6p dk grn & org brn (II) | 12 | 12 |
| *a.* | | Type I | 15 | 15 |
| 67 | A7 | 10c on 1sh rose vio & dk ol grn (I) | 22 | 22 |
| *a.* | | Type II | 40.00 | 40.00 |
| 68 | A7 | 12½c on 1sh3p qua & brn (II) | 38 | 38 |
| *a.* | | Type I | 65 | 65 |
| 69 | A7 | 25c on 2sh6p lil rose & dp ultra (I) | 65 | 65 |
| *a.* | | Type II | 12.00 | 12.00 |
| *b.* | | Type III | 65 | 65 |
| 70 | A7 | 50c on 5sh dp car & blk (II) | 1.40 | 1.40 |
| *a.* | | Type I | 2.25 | 2.25 |
| 71 | A8 | 1r on 10sh dp cl & blk (III) | 2.75 | 2.75 |
| *a.* | | Type I | 12.00 | 12.00 |
| *b.* | | Type II | 12.00 | 12.00 |
| | | *Nos. 61-71 (11)* | 5.95 | 5.95 |

Surcharge types on Nos. 64-71 are numbered chronologically.

Types of 1954
Value in Cents and Rands.

Designs: ½c, Qiloane Hill. 1c, Orange River. 2c, Mosotho horseman. 2½c, Basuto household. 3½c, Maletsunyane Falls. 5c, Herdboy with lesiba. 10c, Pastoral scene. 12½c, Plane at Lancers Gap. 25c, Old Fort Leribe. 50c, Mission cave house. 1r, Shearing Angora goats.

**1961-63 Wmk. 4 Engr. Perf. 13½**

| | | | | |
|---|---|---|---|---|
| 72 | A7 | ½c dk brn & gray ('62) | 8 | 6 |
| 73 | A7 | 1c dp grn & gray blk ('62) | 10 | 8 |
| 74 | A7 | 2c org & dp bl ('62) | 12 | 10 |
| 75 | A7 | 2½c car & ol grn | 20 | 12 |
| 76 | A7 | 3½c dp bl & ind ('62) | 16 | 12 |
| 77 | A7 | 5c dk grn & org brn ('62) | 25 | 22 |
| 78 | A7 | 10c rose vio & dk ol ('62) | 38 | 32 |
| 79 | A7 | 12½c aqua & brn ('62) | 48 | 40 |
| 80 | A7 | 25c lil rose & dp ultra ('62) | 1.00 | 80 |
| 81 | A7 | 50c dp car & blk ('62) | 3.50 | 3.00 |

*Perf. 11½*

| | | | | |
|---|---|---|---|---|
| 82 | A8 | 1r dp cl & blk ('63) | 6.00 | 5.00 |
| | | *Nos. 72-82 (11)* | 12.27 | 10.22 |

See Nos. 87-91.

**Freedom from Hunger Issue**
Common Design Type
*Perf. 14x14½*

**1963, June 4 Photo. Wmk. 314**

| | | | | |
|---|---|---|---|---|
| 83 | CD314 | 12½c lilac | 50 | 40 |

**Red Cross Centenary Issue**
Common Design Type

**1963, Sept. 2 Litho. Perf. 13**

| | | | | |
|---|---|---|---|---|
| 84 | CD315 | 2½c blk & red | 20 | 20 |
| 85 | CD315 | 12½c ultra & red | 80 | 80 |

Queen Type of 1961-63

**1964 Engr. Perf. 13½**

| | | | | |
|---|---|---|---|---|
| 87 | A7 | 1c grn & gray blk | 9 | 7 |
| 88 | A7 | 2½c car & ol grn | 20 | 16 |
| 89 | A7 | 5c dk grn & org brn | 45 | 38 |
| 90 | A7 | 12½c aqua & brn | 1.10 | 95 |
| 91 | A7 | 50c dp car & blk | 4.00 | 3.25 |
| | | *Nos. 87-91 (5)* | 5.84 | 4.81 |

Mosotho Woman and Child — A10

Designs: 3½c, Maseru border post. 5c, Mountains. 12½c, Legislative Building.

*Perf. 14x13½*

**1965, May 10 Photo. Wmk. 314**

| | | | | |
|---|---|---|---|---|
| 97 | A10 | 2½c ultra & multi | 7 | 7 |
| 98 | A10 | 3½c bl & bis | 16 | 12 |
| 99 | A10 | 5c bl & ocher | 20 | 16 |
| 100 | A10 | 12½c lt bl, blk & buff | 40 | 40 |

Attainment of self-government.

Common Design Types pictured in section before Great Britain.

### ITU Issue
Common Design Type

**1965, May 17 Litho. *Perf. 11x11½***
*101* CD317 1c ver & red lil 10 8
*102* CD317 20c grnsh bl & org brn 85 65

### Intl. Cooperation Year Issue
Common Design Type

**1965, Oct. 25 Wmk. 314 *Perf. 14½***
*103* CD318 ½c bl grn & cl 8 6
*104* CD318 12½c lt vio & grn 1.00 75

### Churchill Memorial Issue
Common Design Type

**1966, Jan. 24 Photo. *Perf. 14***
**Design in Black, Gold and Carmine Rose**
*105* CD319 1c brt bl 8 8
*106* CD319 2½c green 12 12
*107* CD319 10c brown 50 50
*108* CD319 22½c violet 1.25 1.25

### POSTAGE DUE STAMPS

**Catalogue values for all unused stamps in this section are for Never Hinged items.**

D1

Coat of Arms — D2

**1933-38 Wmk. 4 Typo. *Perf. 14***
*J1* D1 1p dk red ('38) 20 20
a. 1p dk car 1.00 1.10
b. Wmk. 4a (error) 67.50
*J2* D1 2p lt vio 15 15
a. Wmk. 4a (error) 67.50

Nos. J1a and J2 also exist on chalky paper.

**1956, Dec. 1**
*J3* D2 1p carmine 22 22
*J4* D2 2p dk pur 25 25

Nos. J2-J4 Surcharged with New Value

**1961**
*J5* D2 1c on 1p car 8 8
*J6* D2 1c on 2p dk pur 8 8
*J7* D1 5c on 2p lt vio 3.00 3.00
a. Wmk. 4a (error) 400.00
*J8* D2 5c on 2p dark pur ("5" 7½mm high) 10 10
a. "5" 3½mm high 20.00 *27.50*

Value in Cents

**1964 Wmk. 314 *Perf. 14***
*J9* D2 1c carmine 10 10
*J10* D2 5c dk pur 20 20

### OFFICIAL STAMPS

Nos. 1-3 and 6 Overprinted "OFFICIAL."

**1934 Wmk. 4 Engr. *Perf. 12½***
*O1* A1 ½p emerald 3,000. 3,500.
*O2* A1 1p carmine 1,150. 1,500.
*O3* A1 2p red vio 850.00 750.00
*O4* A1 6p yellow 6,750.

Counterfeits exist.

## BATUM

LOCATION — A seaport on the Black Sea.

Batum is the capital of Adzhar, a territory which, in 1921, became an autonomous republic of the Georgian Soviet Socialist Republic.

Stamps of Batum were issued under the administration of British forces which occupied Batum and environs between December, 1918, and July, 1920, following the Treaty of Versailles.

100 Kopecks = 1 Ruble

Counterfeits exist of Nos. 1-65.

A1

**1919 Unwmk. Litho. *Imperf.***
*1* A1 5k green 22 28
*2* A1 10k ultra 22 28
*3* A1 50k yellow 22 24
*4* A1 1r red brown 35 35
*5* A1 3r violet 1.25 1.40
*6* A1 5r brown 1.50 1.75
*Nos. 1-6 (6)* 3.76 4.30

A14

Russian Stamps of 1909-17 Surcharged

БАТУМ. ОБ.
Руб 10 Руб.

**1919 On Stamps of 1917**
*7* A14 10r on 1k org 12.50 13.50
*8* A14 10r on 3k red 6.50 7.25

**On Stamp of 1909-12**
***Perf. 14x14½***
*9* A14 10r on 5k cl 80.00 80.00

**On Stamp of 1917**
*10* A14 10r on 10k on 7k lt bl 100.00 100.00

A15

Peter I — A19

Russian Stamps of 1909-13 Surcharged

БАТУМ. ОБ.
Коп 35 Коп.

**1919**
*11* A15 35k on 4k carmine *1,500.*
*12* A19 35k on 4k dl red *5,500.*

This surcharge was intended for postal cards. A few cards which bore adhesive stamps were also surcharged.

Type of 1919 Issue Overprinted

BRITISH
OCCUPATION

**1919 Unwmk. *Imperf.***
*13* A1 5k green 1.00 1.10
*14* A1 10k dark blue 1.00 1.10
*15* A1 25k orange 1.00 1.10
*16* A1 1r pale blue 75 85
*17* A1 2r sal pink 30 35
*18* A1 3r violet 30 35
*19* A1 5r brown 30 35
a. "CCUPATION" 50.00 60.00
*20* A1 7r dull red 1.00 1.10
*Nos. 13-20 (8)* 5.65 6.30

A11

A8

Russian Stamps of 1909-17 Surcharged in Various Colors:

БАТУМ ОБЛАС.
P 10 P.
BRITISH
OCCUPATION
a

БАТУМЪ
BRITISH
P. 15 P.
OCCUPATION
ОБЛ.
b

**On Stamps of 1917**

**1919-20 *Imperf.***
*21* A14(a) 10r on 3k red 12.00 12.00
*22* A14(b) 15r on 1k org (R) 27.50 30.00
*23* A14(b) 15r on 1k org (Bk) 30.00 30.00
*24* A14(b) 15r on 1k org (V) 30.00 30.00
*25* A14(a) 50r on 1k org 180.00 180.00
*26* A14(a) 50r on 2k grn 225.00 225.00

**Type "a" on Stamps of 1909-17**
***Perf. 14x14½***
*27* A14 50r on 2k green 300.00 300.00
*28* A14 50r on 3k red 450.00 450.00
*29* A15 50r on 4k car 275.00 275.00
*30* A14 50r on 5k cl 175.00 175.00
*31* A15 50r on 10k dk blue (R) 550.00 550.00
*32* A11 50r on 15k red brn & bl 225.00 225.00

Surcharged

БАТУМ.ОБЛ.
P.25P.
BRITISH
OCCUPATION

**On Stamps of 1909-17**
*33* A14 25r on 5k cl (Bk) 17.50 17.50
*34* A14 25r on 5k cl (Bl) 17.50 17.50
*35* A14 25r on 10k on 7k lt blue (Bk) 25.00 25.00
*36* A14 25r on 10k on 7k lt blue (Bl) 20.00 20.00
*37* A11 25r on 20k on 14k bl & rose (Bk) 25.00 25.00
*38* A11 25r on 20k on 14k bl & rose (Bl) 25.00 25.00
*39* A11 25r on 25k grn & gray vio (Bk) 30.00 30.00
*40* A11 25r on 25k grn & gray vio (Bl) 35.00 35.00
*41* A8 25r on 50k vio & grn (Bk) 12.50 12.50
*42* A8 25r on 50k vio & grn (Bl) 22.50 22.50
*43* A14 50r on 2k green 30.00 30.00
*44* A14 50r on 3k red 30.00 30.00
*45* A15 50r on 4k car 30.00 30.00
*46* A14 50r on 5k cl 35.00 35.00

**On Stamps of 1917**
***Imperf***
*47* A14 50r on 2k green 95.00 95.00
*48* A14 50r on 3k red 150.00 150.00
*49* A14 50r on 5k cl 350.00 350.00

**On Stamp of 1913**
***Perf. 13½***
*50* A19 50r on 4k dull red (Bl) 32.50 32.50

Nos. 3, 13 and 15 Surcharged in Black or Blue:

РУБ 25 ПЕН
BRITISH
OCCUPATION
25 РУБ. 25
e

R. 50 R.
BRITISH
OCCUPATION
РУБ.
f

**1920 *Imperf.***
*51* A1(e) 25r on 5k green 7.25 7.25
*52* A1(e) 25r on 5k grn (Bl) 8.50 8.50
*53* A1(e) 25r on 25k orange 7.25 7.25
*54* A1(e) 25r on 25k org (Bl) 17.50 17.50
*55* A1(f) 50r on 50k yellow 7.25 7.25
*56* A1(f) 50r on 50k yel (Bl) 17.50 17.50

The surcharges on Nos. 21-56 inclusive are handstamped and are known double, inverted, etc.

Tree Type of 1919 Overprinted

BRITISH
OCCUPATION

**1920**
*57* A1 1r orange brn 5 7
*58* A1 2r gray blue 5 7
*59* A1 3r rose 6 8
*60* A1 5r blk brown 6 8
*61* A1 7r yellow 8 10
*62* A1 10r dark green 10 12
*63* A1 15r violet 15 18
*64* A1 25r vermilion 30 35
*65* A1 50r dark blue 40 45
*Nos. 57-65 (9)* 1.25 1.50

The variety "BPITISH" occurs on #57-65.

## BECHUANALAND

### British Bechuanaland

LOCATION — Southern Africa.
GOVT. — A former British Crown Colony, annexed in 1895 to the Cape of Good Hope Colony which became a province in the Union of South Africa.
AREA — 51,424 sq. mi.
POP. — 84,210 (1904).
CAPITAL — Mafeking.

12 Pence = 1 Shilling
20 Shillings = 1 Pound

Cape of Good Hope Stamps of 1871-85 Overprinted

British
Bechuanaland

**Wmk. Crown and C. C. (1)**
**1886 *Perf. 14***
**Black Overprint.**
*1* A6 4p blue 45.00 42.50

**Wmk. Crown and C. A. (2)**
**Black Overprint.**
*3* A6 3p claret 20.00 22.50

**Red Overprint.**
*4* A6 ½p black 8.75 7.75
a. Double overprint in red & blk 900.00

**Wmk. Anchor. (16)**
**Black Overprint.**
*5* A6 ½p black 5.00 5.00
a. "ritish" 1,800. *1,800.*
*6* A6 1p rose 7.50 3.25
a. Double ovpt.
b. "ritish" 1,800. *1,600.*
*7* A6 2p bister 22.50 8.75
a. "ritish" 4,500. 4,500.
*8* A3 6p violet 32.50 22.50
*9* A3 1sh green 215.00 80.00
a. "ritish" *9,000.*

There is no period after Bechuanaland in the genuine stamps.

A2

Black Ovpt. on Great Britain #111

**1887 Wmk. Imperial Crown. (30)**
*10* A2 ½p vermilion 60 60
a. Double overprint 2,250.

The only foreign revenue stamps listed in this Catalogue are those authorized for prepayment of postage.

A3

A4

A5

Wmk.29

Wmk.14

**1887 Typo. Wmk. Orb. (29)**

**Country Name in Black**

*11* A3 1p lilac 12.00 4.75
*12* A3 2p lilac 18.00 3.00
*13* A3 3p lilac 3.25 4.75
*14* A3 4p lilac 27.50 5.50
*15* A3 6p lilac 32.50 19.00

**Wmk. V. R. in Italics. (14)**

*16* A4 1sh green 42.50 5.00
*17* A4 2sh green 47.50 20.00
*18* A4 2sh6p green 42.50 21.00
*19* A4 5sh green 90.00 82.50
*20* A4 10sh green 190.00 190.00

**Wmk. Orb. (29)**

*21* A5 £1 lilac 900.00 725.00
*22* A5 £5 lilac 2,000. 1,100.
Pen cancellation 165.00

A6

Surcharge of value in figures.

**1888**

**Country Name in Black**

**Black Surcharge.**

*23* A6 1p on 1p lil 5.25 5.00
**a.** Double surcharge
*24* A6 6p on 6p lil 90.00 22.50

**Red Surcharge.**

*25* A6 2p on 2p lil 6.00 3.00
**a.** "2" with curved tail 175.00 150.00
*26* A6 4p on 4p lil 110.00 80.00

**Green Surcharge.**

*27* A6 2p on 2p lil *2,750.*

**Blue Surcharge.**

*27A* A6 6p on 6p lil *2,500.*

**Wmk. V. R. in Italics. (14)**

**Black Surcharge.**

*28* A4 1sh on 1sh grn 85.00 47.50

A7

A8

Green Ovpt. on Cape of Good Hope

**1889 Wmk. Anchor. (16)**

*29* A7 ½p black 4.75 5.75
**a.** Double ovpt., one vert. 600.00
**b.** Double ovpt., one invtd. 600.00
**c.** Overprinted vertically
**d.** Double overprint 600.00
**e.** "British" omitted *2,500.*

**Wmk. Orb. (29)**

**Black Surcharge**

*30* A8 ½p on 3p lil & blk 125.00 135.00

Cape of Good Hope Nos. 43-44 Overprinted in Black

British
Bechuanaland.

**1891 Wmk. Anchor. (16)**

*31* A6 1p rose 10.00 9.25
**a.** No dots over the "i's" of "British" 150.00 150.00
**b.** "British" omitted 300.00
*32* A6 2p bister 3.00 3.00
**a.** Without period 200.00

See Nos. 38-39.

Stamps of Great Britain Overprinted in Black

BRITISH
BECHUANALAND

**Wmk. Imperial Crown. (30)**

**1891-94**

*33* A40 1p lilac 90 30
*34* A56 2p grn & car 2.50 75
*35* A59 4p brn & grn 2.50 75
**a.** Half used as 2p on cover *1,800.*
*36* A62 6p vio, *rose* 2.50 1.75
*37* A65 1sh grn ('94) 6.50 7.50
*Nos. 33-37 (5)* 14.90 11.05

Cape of Good Hope Nos. 43-44 Overprinted Like Nos. 31-32 but Reading Down.

**1893-95 Wmk. Anchor. (16)**

*38* A6 1p rose 2.50 2.75
**a.** No dots over the "i's" of "British" 75.00 75.00
**b.** "British" omitted 375.00
*39* A6 2p bis ('95) 4.75 2.75
**a.** Double overprint 900.00 900.00
**b.** No dots over the "i's" of "British" 125.00 125.00
**c.** "British" omitted 300.00 300.00

A16

Overprint Lines 13-13½mm Apart

**1897**

*40* A16 ½p light green 1.50 2.50

**Spaced 10 or 10½mm**

*41* A16 ½p light green 8.50 10.00

## BECHUANALAND PROTECTORATE

LOCATION — In central South Africa, north of the Republic of South Africa, east of South-West Africa and bounded on the north and east by Angola and Southern Rhodesia.

GOVT. — Former British Protectorate.

AREA — 222,000 sq. mi.

POP. — 540,400 (1964).

Bechuanaland Protectorate became the independent republic of Botswana Sept. 30, 1966.

12 Pence = 1 Shilling
20 Shillings = 1 Pound
100 Cents = 1 Rand (1961)

**Catalogue values for unused stamps in this country are for Never Hinged items, beginning with Scott 137 in the regular postage section and Scott J7 in the postage due section.**

Additional Overprint in Black on Bechuanaland No. 10.

Protectorate
a

Protectorate
b

Protectorate
c

**1888-90 Wmk. 30 *Perf. 14***

*51* A2 (a) ½p vermilion 80.00 80.00
**a.** Double overprint
*52* A2 (b) ½p vermilion ('89) 2.00 3.50
**a.** Double overprint ('90)
*53* A3 (c) ½p vermilion 80.00 80.00
**a.** Inverted overprint 40.00 40.00
**b.** Double overprint 40.00
**c.** As "a," dbl. 600.00 600.00

**Bechuanaland Nos. 16-20 Overprinted Type "b" in Black**

**Wmk. V. R. in Italics. (14)**

**Country Name in Black**

*54* A4 1sh green 55.00 30.00
**a.** First "o" omitted 2,600. 2,600.
*55* A4 2sh green 240.00 240.00
**a.** First "o" omitted 3,750. *4,250.*
*56* A4 2sh6p green 475.00 525.00
**a.** First "o" omitted 4,250. *4,500.*
*57* A4 5sh green 1,100. 1,400.
**a.** First "o" omitted 5,250. *6,000.*
*58* A4 10sh green 3,000. *3,500.*
**a.** First "o" omitted 12,000.

Bechuanaland Nos. 11-15 Overprinted Type "b" and Surcharged in Black

**1888 Wmk. Orb. (29)**

**Country Name in Black**

*60* A3 1p on 1p lil 2.75 3.00
**a.** Short "1" 225.00 275.00
*61* A3 2p on 2p lil 10.50 6.00
**a.** "2" with curved tail 300.00 300.00
*63* A3 3p on 3p lil 72.50 82.50
*64* A3 4p on 4p lil 100.00 125.00
*65* A3 6p on 6p lil 35.00 37.50

In No. 60 the "1" is 2½mm high; in No. 60a, 2mm.

**Value Surcharged in Red.**

*66* A3 4p on 4p lil 42.50 42.50

A7

Cape of Good Hope Type of 1886 Overprinted in Green

**1889 Wmk. Anchor. (16)**

*67* A7 ½p black 3.75 4.00
**a.** Double overprint 400.00 400.00
**b.** "Bechuanaland" omitted 675.00 675.00

**Black Surcharge on Bechuanaland Protectorate No. 52**

**Wmk. Imperial Crown. (30)**

*68* A2 4p on ½p ver 5.25 2.50
**a.** Inverted surch. *4,500.*

Stamps of Great Britain 1881-87, Overprinted in Black

BECHUANALAND
PROTECTORATE

**1897, Oct.**

*69* A54 ½p vermilion 26 26
*70* A40 1p lilac 65 40
*71* A56 2p grn & car 1.25 2.00
*72* A58 3p vio, *yel* 4.25 5.50
*73* A59 4p brn & grn 6.50 6.50
*74* A62 6p vio, *rose* 13.00 10.50
*Nos. 69-74 (6)* 25.91 25.16

Same on Great Britain No. 125

**1902, Feb. 25**

*75* A54 ½p blue green 1.00 1.25

Stamps of Great Britain, 1902, Overprinted in Black

BECHUANALAND
PROTECTORATE

**1904-12**

*76* A66 ½p gray grn ('06) 3.25 3.25
*77* A66 1p car ('05) 4.25 1.10
*78* A66 2½p ultra 5.75 5.25
*79* A74 1sh scar & grn ('12) 12.00 14.00

Same on Great Britain No. 143

**1908**

*80* A66 ½p pale yel grn 2.00 2.00

King Edward VII — A9

Transvaal No. 274 Overprinted

**1910 Wmk. 3**

*81* A9 6p brn org & blk 150.00 *210.00*

This stamp was issued for fiscal use, although it is known postally used.

King George V — A10

Great Britain No. 154 Overprinted

**1912, Sept. Wmk. 30 *Perf. 15x14***

*82* A10 1p scarlet 1.10 1.00

Great Britain Stamps of 1912-13 Overprinted

BECHUANALAND
PROTECTORATE

**1914-24 Wmk. 33**

*83* A82 ½p green 85 85
*84* A83 1p scarlet 1.90 60
*85* A84 1½p red brn ('20) 1.90 2.00
*86* A85 2p org (I) 1.90 1.00
**a.** 2p org (II)('24) 17.00 11.00
*87* A86 2½p ultra 1.50 1.65
*88* A87 3p bluish vio 3.75 3.75
*89* A88 4p sl grn 3.00 3.50
*90* A89 6p dl vio 4.25 3.75
*91* A90 1sh bister 5.75 5.75
*Nos. 83-91 (9)* 24.80 22.85

The dies of No. 86 are the same as in Great Britain 1912-13 issue.

Overprinted

BECHUANALAND
PROTECTORATE

**Wmk. Large Crown and G v R. (34)**

***Perf. 11x12***

*92* A91 2sh6p dk brn 95.00 125.00
**a.** 2sh6p lt brn ('16) 105.00 125.00
*93* A91 5sh rose car 150.00 190.00
**a.** 5sh car ('20) 190.00 225.00

Nos. 92, 93 were printed by Waterlow Bros. & Layton; Nos. 92a, 93a were printed by Thomas De La Rue & Co.

Same Overprint On Retouched Stamps of 1919

**1920-23**

*94* A91 2sh6p gray brn 115.00 125.00
*95* A91 5sh car rose 150.00 165.00

Great Britain Stamps of 1924 Overprinted like Nos. 83 to 91

**1925-26 Wmk. 35 *Perf. 15x14***

| No. | Type | Description | Unused | Used |
|---|---|---|---|---|
| *96* | A82 | ½p green | 90 | 1.50 |
| *97* | A83 | 1p scarlet | 1.10 | 1.50 |
| *99* | A85 | 2p dp org (II) | 2.25 | 2.00 |
| *101* | A87 | 3p violet | 3.00 | *6.00* |
| *102* | A88 | 4p sl grn | 3.75 | *11.00* |
| *103* | A89 | 6p dl vio | 4.75 | *15.00* |
| *104* | A90 | 1sh bister | 13.00 | *19.00* |
| | | *Nos. 96-104 (7)* | 28.75 | *56.00* |

George V
A11

George VI, Cattle and Baobab Tree
A12

***Perf. 12½***

**1932, Dec. 12 Engr. Wmk. 4**

| No. | Type | Description | Unused | Used |
|---|---|---|---|---|
| *105* | A11 | ½p green | 22 | 25 |
| *106* | A11 | 1p carmine | 32 | 35 |
| *107* | A11 | 2p red brn | 48 | 48 |
| *108* | A11 | 3p ultra | 95 | 1.10 |
| *109* | A11 | 4p orange | 95 | 1.10 |
| *110* | A11 | 6p red vio | 95 | 1.10 |
| *111* | A11 | 1sh blk & ol grn | 2.00 | 2.25 |
| *112* | A11 | 2sh blk & org | 11.00 | 12.00 |
| *113* | A11 | 2sh6p blk & car | 11.00 | 12.00 |
| *114* | A11 | 3sh blk & red vio | 16.00 | *21.00* |
| *115* | A11 | 5sh blk & ultra | 22.50 | *30.00* |
| *116* | A11 | 10sh blk & red brn | 75.00 | 82.50 |
| | | *Nos. 105-116 (12)* | 141.37 | 164.13 |

**Silver Jubilee Issue**
Common Design Type

**1935, May 4 *Perf. 11x12***

| No. | Type | Description | Unused | Used |
|---|---|---|---|---|
| *117* | CD301 | 1p car & bl | 25 | 28 |
| *118* | CD301 | 2p blk & ultra | 38 | 42 |
| *119* | CD301 | 3p ultra & blk | 55 | 60 |
| *120* | CD301 | 6p brn vio & ind | 1.10 | 1.25 |

**Coronation Issue**
Common Design Type

**1937, May 12 *Perf. 13½x14***

| No. | Type | Description | Unused | Used |
|---|---|---|---|---|
| *121* | CD302 | 1p carmine | 7 | 7 |
| *122* | CD302 | 2p brown | 14 | 14 |
| *123* | CD302 | 3p brt ultra | 25 | 25 |

**1938, Apr. 1 *Perf. 12½***

| No. | Type | Description | Unused | Used |
|---|---|---|---|---|
| *124* | A12 | ½p green | 7 | 8 |
| *125* | A12 | 1p rose car | 10 | 8 |
| *126* | A12 | 1½p lt bl | 18 | 8 |
| *127* | A12 | 2p brown | 22 | 8 |
| *128* | A12 | 3p ultra | 22 | 25 |
| *129* | A12 | 4p orange | 50 | 55 |
| *130* | A12 | 6p rose vio | 55 | *1.00* |
| *131* | A12 | 1sh blk & ol grn | 42 | 50 |
| *133* | A12 | 2sh6p blk & car | 2.25 | *4.75* |
| *135* | A12 | 5sh blk & ultra | 7.00 | 7.00 |
| *136* | A12 | 10sh blk & brn | 14.00 | 20.00 |
| | | *Nos. 124-136 (11)* | 25.51 | 34.37 |

**Catalogue values for unused stamps in this section, from this point to the end of the section, are for Never Hinged items.**

**Peace Issue**

South Africa Nos. 100-102 Overprinted **Bechuanaland**

Basic stamps inscribed alternately in English and Afrikaans.

**1945, Dec. 3 Wmk. 201 *Perf. 14***

| No. | Type | Description | Unused | Used |
|---|---|---|---|---|
| *137* | A42 | 1p rose pink & choc | 12 | 12 |
| *a.* | | Pair | 26 | 26 |
| *138* | A43 | 2p vio & sl bl | 16 | 16 |
| *a.* | | Pair | 32 | 32 |
| *139* | A43 | 3p ultra & dp ultra | 20 | 20 |
| *a.* | | Pair | 42 | 42 |

World War II victory of the Allies.

**Royal Visit Issue**
Types of Basutoland, 1947

***Perf. 12½***

**1947, Feb. 17 Wmk. 4 Engr.**

| No. | Type | Description | Unused | Used |
|---|---|---|---|---|
| *143* | A3 | 1p red | 6 | 6 |
| *144* | A4 | 2p green | 9 | 9 |
| *145* | A5 | 3p ultra | 12 | 12 |
| *146* | A6 | 1sh dk vio | 32 | 32 |

Visit of the British Royal Family, April 17, 1947.

**Silver Wedding Issue**
Common Design Types

**1948, Dec. 1 Photo. *Perf. 14x14½***

| No. | Type | Description | Unused | Used |
|---|---|---|---|---|
| *147* | CD304 | 1½p brt ultra | 12 | 12 |

**Engr.; Name Typo.**
***Perf. 11½x11***

| No. | Type | Description | Unused | Used |
|---|---|---|---|---|
| *148* | CD305 | 10sh gray blk | 17.50 | 27.50 |

**UPU Issue**
Common Design Types

**Engr.; Name Typo. on 3p and 6p**

**1949, Oct. 10 *Perf. 13½, 11x11½***

| No. | Type | Description | Unused | Used |
|---|---|---|---|---|
| *149* | CD306 | 1½p blue | 30 | 30 |
| *150* | CD307 | 3p indigo | 40 | 40 |
| *151* | CD308 | 6p red lil | 90 | 90 |
| *152* | CD309 | 1sh olive | 1.75 | 1.75 |

**Coronation Issue.**
Common Design Type

**1953, June 3 Engr. *Perf. 13½x13***

| No. | Type | Description | Unused | Used |
|---|---|---|---|---|
| *153* | CD312 | 2p brn & blk | 30 | 30 |

Elizabeth II
A13

Victoria, Elizabeth II and Water Hole
A14

**1955-58 *Perf. 13x13½***

| No. | Type | Description | Unused | Used |
|---|---|---|---|---|
| *154* | A13 | ½p green | 6 | 6 |
| *155* | A13 | 1p rose car | 8 | 8 |
| *156* | A13 | 2p brown | 15 | 12 |
| *157* | A13 | 3p ultra | 20 | 18 |
| *158* | A13 | 4p org ('58) | *2.25* | *2.50* |
| *159* | A13 | 4½p indigo | 65 | 65 |
| *160* | A13 | 6p rose vio | 45 | 45 |
| *161* | A13 | 1sh blk & ol grn | 80 | 80 |
| *162* | A13 | 1sh3p blk & rose vio | 1.10 | *3.50* |
| *163* | A13 | 2sh6p blk & car | 3.00 | 5.75 |
| *164* | A13 | 5sh blk & ultra | 5.75 | 8.75 |
| *165* | A13 | 10sh blk & brn | 12.50 | 16.00 |
| | | *Nos. 154-165 (12)* | 26.99 | 38.84 |

***Perf. 14½x14***

**1960, Jan. 21 Photo. Wmk. 314**

| No. | Type | Description | Unused | Used |
|---|---|---|---|---|
| *166* | A14 | 1p brn & blk | 10 | 10 |
| *167* | A14 | 3p car rose & blk | 16 | 16 |
| *168* | A14 | 6p ultra & blk | 32 | 32 |

Issued to commemorate the 75th anniversary of the Proclamation of the Protectorate.

Nos. 155-165 (A13) Surcharged with New Value

1c 1c 3½c 3½c 3½c
I II I II III

5c 5c R1 R1
I II I II

***Perf. 13x13½***

**1961, Feb. 14 Wmk. 4 Engr.**

| No. | Type | Description | Unused | Used |
|---|---|---|---|---|
| *169* | | 1c on 1p (I) | 9 | 9 |
| *a.* | | Type II | 10 | 10 |
| *170* | | 2c on 2p | 7 | 7 |
| *171* | | 2½c on 2p | 10 | 10 |
| *a.* | | Pair, one without surcharge | *700.00* | |
| *172* | | 2½c on 3p | 90 | 90 |
| *173* | | 3½c on 4p (III) | 18 | 18 |
| *a.* | | Type I | 52 | 52 |
| *b.* | | Type II | 1.65 | 1.65 |
| *174* | | 5c on 6p (II) | 22 | 22 |
| *a.* | | Type I | 75 | 75 |
| *175* | | 10c on 1sh | 32 | 32 |
| *a.* | | Pair, one without surch. | *700.00* | |
| *176* | | 12½c on 1sh3p ("12½c" 11¼mm wide) | 55 | 55 |
| *a.* | | "12½c" 12½mm wide | 75 | 75 |
| *177* | | 25c on 2sh6p | 90 | 90 |
| *178* | | 50c on 5sh | 1.90 | 1.90 |
| *179* | | 1r on 10sh (II, "R1" at lower center) | 4.50 | 4.50 |
| *a.* | | Type II, "R1" at lower left | 6.50 | 6.50 |
| *b.* | | Type I | 225.00 | 110.00 |
| | | *Nos. 169-179 (11)* | 9.73 | 9.73 |

Nos. 173a and 173b are found in the same sheet; each comes with "3½c" in both wide and narrow settings.

Surcharge types are numbered chronologically.

African Golden Oriole — A15

Baobab Tree — A16

Designs: 2c, African hoopoe. 2½c, Scarlet-chested sunbird. 3½c, Yellow bishop. 5c, Swallow-tailed bee-eater. 7½c, Gray hornbill. 10c, Red-headed weaver. 12½c, Brown-hooded kingfisher. 20c, Woman musician. 35c, Woman grinding corn. 50c, Bechuana ox. 1r, Lion. 2r, Police camel patrol.

***Perf. 14x14½, 14½x14***

**1961, Oct. 2 Photo. Wmk. 314**

| No. | Type | Description | Unused | Used |
|---|---|---|---|---|
| *180* | A15 | 1c lil, blk & yel | 14 | 5 |
| *181* | A15 | 2c pale ol, blk & org | 15 | 9 |
| *182* | A15 | 2½c bis, blk, grn & dp car | 18 | 10 |
| *183* | A15 | 3½c pink, blk & yel | 25 | 16 |
| *184* | A15 | 5c dl org, blk, grn & bl | 35 | 22 |
| *185* | A15 | 7½c yel grn, blk, red & brn | 48 | 30 |
| *186* | A15 | 10c aqua & multi | 60 | 38 |
| *187* | A15 | 12½c gray, yel, red & bl | 75 | 42 |
| *188* | A15 | 20c gray & brn | 1.00 | 75 |
| *189* | A16 | 25c yel & dk brn | 1.90 | 1.00 |
| *190* | A15 | 35c dp org & ultra | 2.00 | 1.25 |
| *191* | A16 | 50c lt ol grn & sep | 3.00 | 2.00 |
| *192* | A15 | 1r ocher & blk | 6.00 | 3.75 |
| *193* | A15 | 2r bl & brn | 12.00 | 7.75 |
| | | *Nos. 180-193 (14)* | 28.80 | 18.22 |

**Freedom from Hunger Issue**
Common Design Type

**1963, June 4 *Perf. 14x14½***

| No. | Type | Description | Unused | Used |
|---|---|---|---|---|
| *194* | CD314 | 12½c green | 48 | 48 |

**Red Cross Centenary Issue**
Common Design Type

**1963, Sept. 2 Litho. *Perf. 13***

| No. | Type | Description | Unused | Used |
|---|---|---|---|---|
| *195* | CD315 | 2½c blk & red | 20 | 20 |
| *196* | CD315 | 12½c ultra & red | 80 | 80 |

**Shakespeare Issue**
Common Design Type

**1964, Apr. 23 Photo. *Perf. 14x14½***

| No. | Type | Description | Unused | Used |
|---|---|---|---|---|
| *197* | CD316 | 12½c red brn | 28 | 28 |

Notwani River Dam, Gaberones Water Supply — A17

**Wmk. 314**

**1965, Mar. 1 Photo. *Perf. 14½***

| No. | Type | Description | Unused | Used |
|---|---|---|---|---|
| *198* | A17 | 2½c dk red & gold | 12 | 12 |
| *199* | A17 | 5c dp ultra & gold | 15 | 15 |
| *200* | A17 | 12½c brn & gold | 30 | 30 |
| *201* | A17 | 25c emer & gold | 55 | 55 |

Internal self-government, Mar. 1, 1965.

**ITU Issue**
Common Design Type

***Perf. 11x11½***

**1965, May 17 Litho. Wmk. 314**

| No. | Type | Description | Unused | Used |
|---|---|---|---|---|
| *202* | CD317 | 2½c ver & dl yel | 15 | 15 |
| *203* | CD317 | 12½c red lil & pale brn | 70 | 70 |

**Intl. Cooperation Year Issue**
Common Design Type

**1965, Oct. 25 *Perf. 14½***

| No. | Type | Description | Unused | Used |
|---|---|---|---|---|
| *204* | CD318 | 1c bl grn & cl | 22 | 22 |
| *205* | CD318 | 12½c lt vio & grn | 1.10 | 1.10 |

Common Design Types pictured in section before Great Britain.

**Churchill Memorial Issue**
Common Design Type

**1966, Jan. 24 Photo. *Perf. 14***
**Design in Black, Gold and Carmine Rose**

| No. | Type | Description | Unused | Used |
|---|---|---|---|---|
| *206* | CD319 | 1c brt bl | 7 | 7 |
| *207* | CD319 | 2½c green | 18 | 18 |
| *208* | CD319 | 12½c brown | 75 | 75 |
| *209* | CD319 | 20c violet | 1.25 | 1.25 |

Haslar Smoke Generator — A18

**Wmk. 314**

**1966, June 1 Photo. *Perf. 14½***

| No. | Type | Description | Unused | Used |
|---|---|---|---|---|
| *210* | A18 | 2½c shown | 12 | 12 |
| *211* | A18 | 5c Bugler | 18 | 18 |
| *212* | A18 | 15c Gun site | 48 | 48 |
| *213* | A18 | 35c Regimental cap badge | 1.10 | 1.10 |

25th anniv. of the Bechuanaland Pioneers and Gunners.

## POSTAGE DUE STAMPS

Postage Due Stamps of Great Britain Overprinted BECHUANALAND PROTECTORATE

On Stamp of 1914-22

**1926 Wmk. 33 *Perf. 14x14½***

| No. | Type | Description | Unused | Used |
|---|---|---|---|---|
| *J1* | D1 | 1p carmine | 3.75 | *40.00* |

**On Stamps of 1924-30**
**Wmk. 35**

| No. | Type | Description | Unused | Used |
|---|---|---|---|---|
| *J2* | D1 | ½pemerald | 3.75 | *40.00* |

Overprinted **BECHUANALAND PROTECTORATE**

| No. | Type | Description | Unused | Used |
|---|---|---|---|---|
| *J3* | D1 | 2p blk brn | 7.25 | *80.00* |

D2

**1932 Wmk. 4 Typo. *Perf. 14½***

| No. | Type | Description | Unused | Used |
|---|---|---|---|---|
| *J4* | D2 | ½p ol grn | 1.65 | *3.25* |
| *J5* | D2 | 1p car rose | 40 | 55 |
| *J6* | D2 | 2p dl vio | 65 | 65 |

**Catalogue values for unused stamps in this section, from this point to the end of the section, are for Never Hinged items.**

Nos. J4-J6 Surcharged

2c 2c
I. II

**1961, Feb. 14**

*J7* D2 1c on 1p car rose (II) 10 10
*a.* Type I 28 28
*b.* Double surcharge (II) 110.00
*J8* D2 2c on 2p dl vio (II) 25 25
*a.* Type I 35 35
*J9* D2 5c on ½p ol grn (I) 52 52

Nos. J7, J7a, J8 and J8a are on chalky paper. Nos. J7 and J8 printed on ordinary paper sell for much more.

Denominations in Cents

**1961 Wmk. 4 *Perf. 14***

*J10* D2 1c carmine rose 14 14
*J11* D2 2c dull violet 16 16
*J12* D2 5c olive green 40 *1.25*

## BELIZE

LOCATION — Central America bordering on Caribbean Sea to east, Mexico to north, Guatemala to west.
GOVT. — Independent state
AREA — 8,867 sq. mi.
POP. — 152,000 (1982 est.)
CAPITAL — Belmopan

Belize was known as British Honduras until 1973. The former British colony achieved independence in September 1981.

100 Cents = 1 Dollar

**Catalogue values for all unused stamps in this country are for Never Hinged items.**

Fish-Animal Type of British Honduras Regular Issue 1968-72 Overprinted in Black on Silver Panel

☼BELIZE☼

**Wmk. 314 (½c, 5c, $5), Unwmkd.**
**1973, June 1 Litho. *Perf. 13x12½***

*312* A37 ½c multi (#235) 5 5
*313* A37 1c multi (#214) 5 5
*314* A37 2c multi (#215) 6 6
*315* A37 3c multi (#216) 7 7
*316* A37 4c multi (#217) 7 7
*317* A37 5c multi (#238) 8 8
*318* A37 10c multi (#219) 16 16
*319* A37 15c multi (#220) 25 25
*320* A37 25c multi (#221) 40 40
*321* A37 50c multi (#222) 65 65
*322* A37 $1 multi (#223) 1.20 *1.60*
*323* A37 $2 multi (#224) 2.50 *3.25*
*324* A37 $5 multi (#240) 6.50 *8.75*
*Nos. 312-324 (13)* 12.04 15.44

**Princess Anne's Wedding Issue**
Common Design Type

**1973, Nov. 14 Wmk. 314 *Perf. 14***

*325* CD325 26c bl grn & multi 25 25
*326* CD325 50c ocher & multi 50 50

Crana — A50

**1974, Jan. 1 Litho. *Perf. 13½***

*327* A50 ½c *shown* 5 5
*328* A50 1c *Jewfish* 5 5
*329* A50 2c *White-lipped peccary* 5 5
*330* A50 3c *Grouper* 6 6
*331* A50 4c *Collared anteater* 7 7
*332* A50 5c *Bonefish* 8 8
*333* A50 10c *Paca* 18 18
*334* A50 15c *Dolphinfish* 25 25
*335* A50 25c *Kinkajou* 42 42
*336* A50 50c *Muttonfish* 85 85
*337* A50 $1 *Tayra* 1.65 1.65
*338* A50 $2 *Great barracudas* 3.25 3.25
*339* A50 $5 *Mountain lion* 8.50 8.50
*Nos. 327-339 (13)* 15.46 15.46

*Belize stamps can be mounted in Scott's annually supplemented British North and West Caribbean Album.*

Stag, Mayan Pottery A51

Designs: Mayan pottery decorations.

**1974, May 1 *Perf. 14½***

*340* A51 3c *shown* 7 7
*341* A51 6c *Fire snake* 12 12
*342* A51 16c *Mouse* 28 28
*343* A51 26c *Eagle* 48 48
*344* A51 50c *Parrot* 1.00 1.00
*Nos. 340-344 (5)* 1.95 1.95

Parides Arcas A52

Designs: Butterflies of Belize.

**Wmk. 314 Sideways**
**1974-77 *Perf. 14***

*345* A52 ½c *shown* 15 15
*346* A52 1c *Thecla regalis* 5 5
*347* A52 2c *Colobura dirce* 8 8
*348* A52 3c *Catonephele numilia* 10 10
*349* A52 4c *Battus belus* 15 15
*350* A52 5c *Callicore patelina* 20 20
*351* A52 10c *Callicore astala* 35 35

***Perf. 14x15; 14 (26, 35c)***

*352* A52 15c *Nessaea aglaura* 50 50
*a* Watermark upright ('75) 40 40
*353* A52 16c *Prepona pseudojoiceyi* 25 25
*354* A52 25c *Papilio thoas* 65 65
*a* Watermark upright ('77) 45 45
*355* A52 26c *Hamadryas arethusa* 4.00 *7.50*
*356* A52 50c *Thecla bathildis* 1.25 1.25
*a* Watermark upright ('77) 60 60
*357* A52 $1 *Caligo uranus* 1.20 1.20
*358* A52 $2 *Heliconius sapho* 2.40 2.40
*359* A52 $5 *Eurytides philolaus* 7.50 7.50
*a* Watermark upright ('75) 6.00 6.00
*360* A52 $10 *Philaethria dido* 12.00 12.00
*Nos. 345-360 (16)* 30.83 34.33

Issue dates: No. 355A, July 25, 1977; No. 360, Jan. 2, 1975; others Sept. 2, 1974.

Same Designs

**1975-78 Wmk. 373**

*345a* A52 ½c multi 5 5
*347a* A52 2c multi ('77) 5 5
*348a* A52 3c multi ('77) 5 5
*349a* A52 4c multi ('77) 5 5
*350a* A52 5c multi ('77) 15 15
*351a* A52 10c multi 30 30
*352b* A52 15c multi ('77) 40 40
*354b* A52 25c multi ('78) 60 60
*355A* A52 35c *Parides arcas* ('77) 90 90
*Nos. 345a-355A (9)* 2.55 2.55

Churchill and Coronation Coach of Queen Elizabeth II — A53

Design: $1, Churchill and Williamsburg (Va.) Liberty Bell.

**Wmk. 373**
**1974, Nov. 30 Litho. *Perf. 14***

*363* A53 50c multi 50 50
*364* A53 $1 multi 1.10 1.10

Sir Winston Churchill (1874-1965).

Mayan Urn — A54

Designs: Various Mayan vessels.

**1975, June 2 Wmk. 314 *Perf. 14***

*365* A54 3c lt grn & multi 6 6
*366* A54 6c lt bl & multi 15 15
*367* A54 16c dl yel & multi 22 22
*368* A54 26c lil & multi 35 35
*369* A54 50c lt brn & multi 75 75
*Nos. 365-369 (5)* 1.53 1.53

Musicians A55

Christmas: 26c, Nativity (Thatched hut and children). 50c, Drummers (vert.). $1, Map of Belize, star, fleeing family (vert.).

***Perf. 14x14½, 14½x14***
**1975, Nov. 17 Litho. Wmk. 314**

*370* A55 6c multi 12 12
*371* A55 26c multi 28 28
*372* A55 50c multi 50 50
*373* A55 $1 multi 1.10 1.10

William Wrigley, Jr., Sapodilla Tree A56

Designs (Bicentennial Emblem and): 35c, Charles Lindbergh and "Spirit of St. Louis." $1, John Lloyd Stephens and Mayan temple.

**Wmk. 373**
**1976, Mar. 29 Litho. *Perf. 14½***

*374* A56 10c multi 25 25
*375* A56 35c multi 55 55
*376* A56 $1 multi 1.50 1.50

American Bicentennial.

Bicycling A57

Designs (Olympic Rings and): 45c, Running. $1, Shooting.

**Wmk. 373**
**1976, July 17 Litho. *Perf. 14½***

*377* A57 35c org & multi 45 45
*378* A57 45c brn & multi 55 55
*379* A57 $1 grn & multi 1.25 1.25

21st Olympic Games, Montreal, Canada, July 17-Aug. 1.

No. 355 Surcharged with New Value and Bar

**Wmk. 314**
**1976, Aug. 30 Litho. *Perf. 14***

*380* A52 20c on 26c multi 50 50

**Cricket Cup Issue 1976**
Types of Barbados
**Unwmk.**
**1976, Oct. 18 Litho. *Perf. 14***

*381* A63 35c lt bl & multi 65 65
*382* A64 $1 lil rose & blk 1.90 1.90

World Cricket Cup, won by West Indies Team, 1975.

Royal Visit, 1975 A58

Designs: 35c, Rose window and Queen's head. $2, Queen surrounded by bishops.

**1977, Feb. 7 Litho. *Perf. 13½x14***

*383* A58 10c multi 14 14
*384* A58 35c multi 35 35
*385* A58 $2 multi 1.75 1.75

25th anniv. of the reign of Elizabeth II.

No. 352 Surcharged with New Value and Bar

**1977 Wmk. 314 *Perf. 14***

*386* A52 5c on 15c multi 30 30

Red-capped Manakin — A59

Designs: Birds of Belize.

**Wmk. 373**
**1977, Sept. 3 Litho. *Perf. 14½***

*387* A59 8c *shown* 25 15
*388* A59 10c *Hooded oriole* 30 18
*389* A59 25c *Blue-crowned motmot* 75 45
*390* A59 35c *Slaty-breasted tinamou* 85 60
*391* A59 45c *Ocellated turkey* 1.25 75
*392* A59 $1 *White hawk* 2.50 1.75
*a* Souvenir sheet of 6 7.50 4.25
*Nos. 387-392 (6)* 5.90 3.88

No. 392a contains Nos. 387-392; multicolored decorative margin. Size: 110x133mm.

See Nos. 398-403, 416-421, 424-425.

Medical Laboratory A60

Design: $1, Mobile medical unit and children receiving treatment.

**1977, Dec. 2 *Perf. 13½***

*393* A60 35c multi 38 38
*394* A60 $1 multi 1.00 1.00
*a* Souvenir sheet of 2 1.40 1.40

Pan American Health Organization, 75th anniversary. No. 394a contains one each of Nos. 393-394; multicolored margin shows mother and children and PAHO emblem. Size: 126x95mm.

Nos. 351 and 355A Overprinted in Gold: "BELIZE DEFENCE FORCE / 1ST JANUARY 1978"

**Wmk. 314, 373**
**1978, Feb. 15 Litho. *Perf. 14***

*395* A52 10c multi 10 10
*396* A52 35c multi 35 35

**Elizabeth II Coronation Anniversary Issue**
**Souvenir Sheet**
Common Design Types

**1978, Apr. 21 Unwmk. *Perf. 15***
*397* Sheet of 6 4.75 4.75
*a* CD326 75c *White lion of Mortimer* 75 75
*b* CD327 75c *Elizabeth II* 75 75
*c* CD328 75c *Jaguar (Maya god)* 75 75

No. 397 contains 2 se-tenant strips of Nos. 397a-397c, separated by horizontal gutter with commemorative and descriptive inscriptions and showing central part of coronation procession with coach. Size: 100x135mm.

Bird Type of 1977
**Wmk. 373**

**1978, July 31 Litho. *Perf. 14½***
*398* A59 10c *White-crowned parrot* 25 18
*399* A59 25c *Crimson-collared tanager* 55 42
*400* A59 35c *Citreoline trogon* 60 50
*401* A59 45c *Sungrebe* 75 60
*402* A59 50c *Muscovy duck* 80 65
*403* A59 $1 *King vulture* 1.50 1.25
*a* Souvenir sheet of 6 6.50 5.00
*Nos. 398-403 (6)* 4.45 3.60

No. 403a contains Nos. 398-403; multicolored decorative margin. Size: 110x133mm.

Russelia Sarmentosa A61

Wild Flowers and Ferns: 15c, Lygodium polymorphum. 35c, Heliconia aurantiaca. 45c, Adiantum tetraphyllum. 50c, Angelonia ciliaris. $1, Thelypteris obliterata.

**1978, Oct. 16 Litho. *Perf. 14x13½***
*404* A61 10c multi 15 15
*405* A61 15c multi 22 22
*406* A61 35c multi 40 40
*407* A61 45c multi 50 50
*408* A61 50c multi 55 55
*409* A61 $1 multi 1.10 1.10
*Nos. 404-409 (6)* 2.92 2.92

Christmas 1978.

Internal Airmail Service, 1937 A62

Mail Service: 10c, MV Heron, 1949. 35c, Dugout canoe on river, 1920. 45c, Stann Creek railroad, 1910. 50c, Mounted courier, 1882. $2, RMS Eagle, 1856, and "paid" cancel.

***Perf. 13½x14***
**1979, Jan. 15 Litho. Wmk. 373**
*410* A62 5c multi 6 6
*411* A62 10c multi 12 12
*412* A62 35c multi 42 42
*413* A62 45c multi 54 54
*414* A62 50c multi 60 60
*415* A62 $2 multi 1.65 1.65
*Nos. 410-415 (6)* 3.39 3.39

Centenary of membership in UPU.

Bird Type of 1977

**1979, Apr. 16 Litho. *Perf. 14½***
*416* A59 10c *Boat-billed heron* 30 25
*417* A59 25c *Gray-necked wood rail* 80 60
*418* A59 35c *Lineated woodpecker* 1.00 85
*419* A59 45c *Blue gray tanager* 1.25 1.10
*420* A59 50c *Laughing falcon* 1.50 1.20
*421* A59 $1 *Long-tailed hermit* 2.75 2.50
*a* Souvenir sheet of 6 8.50 7.00
*Nos. 416-421 (6)* 7.60 6.50

No. 421a contains Nos. 416-421; multicolored decorative margin. Size: 114x136mm.

Nos. 355A and 354b Surcharged with New Value and Bar

**1979 Litho. *Perf. 14***
*422* A52 15c on 35c multi 20 20

**1980, Mar. 31 Litho. *Perf. 14***
*423* A52 10c on 25c multi *80*

Bird Type of 1977
**Souvenir Sheets**

**1980, June 16 Litho. *Perf. 13½***
*424* A59 Sheet of 6 5.50 4.50
*a* 10c *Jabiru* 20 15
*b* 25c *Barred antshrike* 50 35
*c* 35c *Royal flycatcher* 65 50
*d* 45c *White-necked puffbird* 75 65
*e* 50c *Ornate hawk-eagle* 85 75
*f* $1 *Golden-masked tanager* 1.90 1.50
*g* Sheet of 12 11.00 9.00
*425* A59 Sheet of 2 8.00 8.00
*a* $2 *Jabiru* 3.00 3.00
*b* $3 *Golden-masked tanager* 4.50 4.50

Nos. 424-425 have multicolored margins with 1980 date and control number. No. 424g contains 2 each Nos. 424a-424f with gutter between, control number; inscribed "Protection of Environment" and "Wildlife Protection." Size of No. 424: 110x132mm; No. 425: 85x90mm.

No. 424 Overprinted or Surcharged with Exhibition Emblem

**1980, Oct. 3 Litho. *Perf. 13½***
*426* A59 Sheet of 6 4.00 4.00
*a* 10c multi 20 20
*b* 25c multi 50 50
*c* 35c multi 65 65
*d* 40c on 45c multi 85 85
*e* 40c on 50c multi 85 85
*f* 40c on $1 multi 85 85

ESPAMER '80 Stamp Exhibition, Madrid, Spain, Oct. 3-12.

Queen Mother Elizabeth, 80th Birthday — A63

**1980, Dec. 12**
*427* Sheet of 6 10.00 10.00
*a* A63 $1 multi 1.00 1.00

Gold margin shows royal emblem; black control number. Size: 117x113mm.

Cypraea Zebra A64

**1981, Jan. 7 Litho. *Perf. 14***
*428* A64 1c shown 5 5
*429* A64 2c Macrocallista maculata 5 5
*430* A64 3c Arca zebra, vert. 5 5
*431* A64 4c Chama macerophylla, vert. 5 5
*432* A64 5c Latirus cariniferus 6 6
*433* A64 10c Conus spurius, vert. 12 12
*434* A64 15c Murex cabritii, vert. 18 18
*435* A64 20c Atrina rigida 25 25
*436* A64 25c Chlamys imbricata, vert. 30 30
*437* A64 35c Conus granulatus 42 42
*438* A64 45c Tellina radiata, vert. 55 55
*439* A64 50c Leucozonia nassa 60 60
*440* A64 85c Tripterotyphis triangularis 1.05 1.05
*441* A64 $1 Strombus gigas, vert. 1.25 1.25
*442* A64 $2 Strombus gallus, vert. 2.50 2.50
*443* A64 $5 Fasciolaria tulipa 6.25 6.25
*a* Souvenir sheet of 2 (85c, $5) 7.50 7.50
*444* A64 $10 Arene cruentata 12.50 12.50
*a* Souvenir sheet of 2 ($2, $10) 15.00 17.50
*Nos. 428-444 (17)* 26.23 26.23

Nos. 443a-444a have black control numbers. Size: 127x93mm.

Mayan Monuments — A65

**1983, Nov. 14 Litho. *Perf. 13½x14***
*445* A65 10c Altun Ha 20 20
*446* A65 15c Xunantunich 30 30
*447* A65 75c Cerros 1.50 1.50
*448* A65 $2 Lamanai 4.00 4.00

**Souvenir Sheet**

*449* A65 $3 Xunantunich, diff. 7.50 7.50

Size of No. 449: 101x72mm.

World Communications Year — A66

**1983, Nov. 28 *Perf. 14***
*450* A66 10c Belmopan Earth Station 10 10
*451* A66 15c Telstar 2 15 15
*452* A66 75c UPU monument 75 75
*453* A66 $2 Mail boat 2.00 2.00

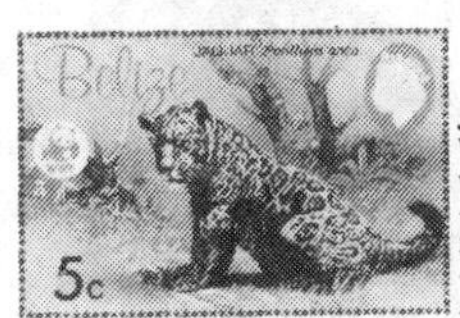

Jaguar, World Wildlife Fund Emblem A67

**1983, Dec. 9**
*454* A67 5c Sitting 7 7
*455* A67 10c Standing 14 14
*456* A67 85c Swimming 1.10 1.10
*457* A67 $1 Walking 1.40 1.40

**Souvenir Sheet**

*458* A67 $3 Sitting in tree 3.25 3.25

No. 458 contains one stamp (45x28mm.); multicolored margin shows jaguar walking. Size: 103x73mm.

Christmas 1983 — A68

Scenes from mass celebrated by Pope John Paul II during visit, Mar.

**1983, Dec. 22**
*459* A68 10c multi 10 10
*460* A68 15c multi 15 15
*461* A68 75c multi 75 75
*462* A68 $2 multi 2.00 2.00

**Souvenir Sheet**

*463* A68 $3 multi 2.75 2.75

Size of No. 463: 102x73mm.

Foureye Butterflyfish — A69

**1984, Feb. 27 *Perf. 15***
*464* A69 1c shown 5 5
*465* A69 2c Cushion star 5 5
*466* A69 3c Flower coral 5 5
*467* A69 4c Fairy basslets 5 5
*468* A69 5c Spanish hogfish 5 5
*469* A69 6c Star-eyed hermit crab 6 6
*470* A69 10c Sea fans, fire sponge 10 10
*a.* Perf. 13½ ('88) 10 10
*471* A69 15c Blueheads 15 15
*a.* Perf. 13½ ('88) 15 15
*472* A69 25c Blue-striped grunt 25 25
*a.* Perf. 13½ ('88) 25 25
*473* A69 50c Coral crab 50 50
*a.* Perf. 13½ ('88) 48 48
*474* A69 60c Tube sponge 60 60
*a.* Perf. 13½ ('88) 58 58
*475* A69 75c Brain coral 75 75
*476* A69 $1 Yellow-tail snapper 1.00 1.00
*a.* Perf. 13½ ('88) 95 95
*477* A69 $2 Common lettuce slug 2.00 2.00
*478* A69 $5 Yellow damselfish 5.00 5.00
*479* A69 $10 Rock beauty 10.00 10.00
*Nos. 464-479 (16)* 20.66 20.66

Nos. 470, 473 Overprinted: "VISIT OF THE LORD / ARCHBISHOP OF CANTERBURY / 8th-11th MARCH 1984"

**1984, Mar. 8**
*480* A69 10c multi 12 12
*481* A69 50c multi 60 60

1984 Summer Olympics — A70

**1984, Apr. 30 *Perf. 13½x14***
*482* A70 25c Shooting 18 18
*483* A70 75c Boxing 60 60
*484* A70 $1 Running 75 75
*485* A70 $2 Bicycling 1.50 1.50

**Souvenir Sheet**

*486* A70 $3 Discus 2.50 2.50

1984 Summer Olympics — A71

**1984, Apr. 30 Litho. *Perf. 14½***
**Booklet Stamps**
*487* A71 5c Running 7 7
*a* Bklt. pane of 4 30
*488* A71 20c Javelin 25 25
*a* Bklt. pane of 4 1.10
*489* A71 25c Shot put 35 35
*a* Bklt. pane of 4 1.50
*490* A71 $2 Torch 2.50 2.50
*a* Bklt. pane of 4 10.50

Ausipex '84 — A72

**1984, Sept. 26 Litho. *Perf. 15***

*491* A72 15c Br. Honduras #3 15 15
*492* A72 30c Bath-Bristol mail coach, 1784 34 34
*493* A72 65c Penny Black, Rowland Hill 65 65
*494* A72 75c Railroad Pier, Commerce Bight 75 75

***Perf. 14***

*495* A72 $2 Royal Exhibition Bldgs. 2.00 2.00
*Nos. 491-495 (5)* 3.89 3.89

**Souvenir Sheet**

*496* A72 $3 Australia #132, Br. Hond. #3 3.00 3.00

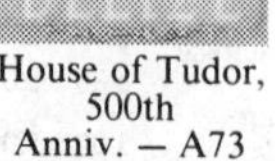


House of Tudor, 500th Anniv. — A73

White-fronted Parrot — A74

**1984, Oct. 15 *Perf. 14***

*497* A73 50c Queen Victoria 50 50
*498* A73 50c Prince Albert 50 50
*a* Sheet of 4, 2 each, #497-498 2.00
*499* A73 75c King George VI 75 75
*500* A73 75c Queen Elizabeth 75 75
*a* Sheet of 4, 2 each, #499-500 3.00
*501* A73 $1 Prince Charles 1.00 1.00
*502* A73 $1 Princess Diana 1.00 1.00
*a* Sheet of 4, 2 each, #501-502 4.00
*Nos. 497-502 (6)* 4.50 4.50

**Souvenir Sheet**

*503* Sheet of 2 3.00 3.00
*a* A73 $1.50 Prince Philip 1.50 1.50
*b* A73 $1.50 Queen Elizabeth II 1.50 1.50

**1984, Nov. 1 *Perf. 11***

Parrots: b. White-capped. c. Red-lored. d. Mealy. b, d, horiz.

*504* Block of 4 3.50 3.50
*a.-d.* A74 $1, any single 85 85

**Miniature Sheet**

***Perf. 14***

*505* A74 $3 Scarlet Macaw 2.50 2.50

No. 505 contains 1 stamp, size 48x32mm. Size of sheet: 103x73mm.

Mayan Artifacts — A75

**1984, Nov. 30 *Perf. 15***

*506* A75 25c Incense holder, 1450 25 25
*507* A75 75c Cylindrical vase, 675 75 75
*508* A75 $1 Tripod vase, 500 1.00 1.00
*509* A75 $2 Kinich Ahau (sun god) 2.00 2.00

Girl Guides 75th Anniv., Intl. Youth Year A76

**1985, Mar. 15 Litho. *Perf. 15***

*510* A76 25c Gov.-Gen. Gordon 25 25
*511* A76 50c Camping 50 50
*512* A76 90c Map reading 90 90
*513* A76 $1.25 Students in laboratory 1.25 1.25
*514* A76 $2 Lady Baden-Powell 2.00 2.00
*Nos. 510-514 (5)* 4.90 4.90

Each stamp shows the scouting and IYY emblems.

Audubon Bifth Bicentenary — A77

Illustrations by Audubon.

**1985, May 30 Litho. *Perf. 14***

*515* A77 10c White-tailed kite, vert. 10 10
*516* A77 15c Cuvier's kinglet 15 15
*517* A77 25c Painted bunting, vert. 25 25
*518* A77 75c Belted kingfisher, vert. 75 75
*519* A77 $1 Northern cardinal, vert. 1.00 1.00
*520* A77 $3 Long-billed curlew 3.00 3.00
*Nos. 515-520 (6)* 5.25 5.25

**Souvenir Sheet**

***Perf. 13½x14***

*521* A77 $5 Portrait of Audubon, 1826, by John Syme, vert. 5.00 5.00

No. 521 contains one stamp (38x51mm); multicolored decorative margin completes the portrait and pictures doves in flight at dusk. Size: 139x99mm.

Queen Mother, 85th Birthday — A78

Designs: 10c, The Queen Consort and Princess Elizabeth, 1928. 15c, Queen Mother, Elizabeth. 75c, Queen Mother waving a greeting. No. 525, Royal family photograph, christening of Prince Henry. $2, Holding the infant Prince Henry. No. 527, Queen Mother, diff.

**1985, June 20**

*522* A78 10c shown 10 10
*523* A78 15c multi 15 15
*524* A78 75c multi 75 75
*525* A78 $5 multi 5.00 5.00

**Souvenir Sheets**

*526* A78 $2 multi 2.00 2.00
*527* A78 $5 multi 5.00 5.00

Nos. 526-527 contain one stamp (size: 38x51mm); multicolored decorative margins complete each design and picture flowers or members of the royal family. Size: 139x99mm.

Miniature Sheet

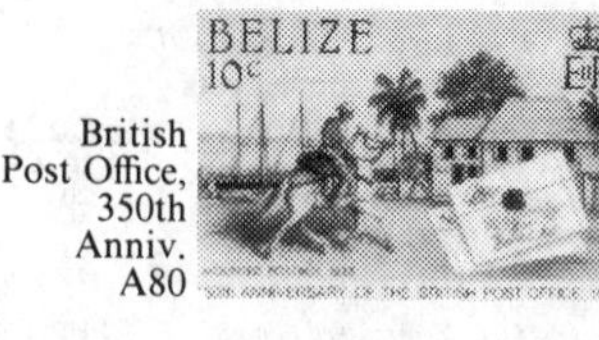

Commonwealth Stamp Omnibus, 50th Anniv. — A79

British Honduras Nos. 111-112, 127, 129, 143, 194, 307 and Belize Nos. 326, 385 and 397b on: a, George V and Queen Mary in an open carriage. b, George VI and Queen Consort Elizabeth crowned. c, Civilians celebrating the end of WW II. d, George VI and Queen Consort at mass service. e, Elizabeth II wearing robes of state and the imperial crown. f, Winston Churchill, WW II fighter planes. g, Bridal photograph of Elizabeth II and Prince Philip. h, Bridal photograph of Princess Anne and Capt. Mark Phillips. i, Elizabeth II. j, Imperial crown.

**1985, July 25 *Perf. 14½x14***

*528* Sheet of 10 5.00 5.00
*a.-j.* A79 50c, Any single 50 50

**Souvenir Sheet**

*529* A79 $5 Elizabeth II coronation photograph 5.00 5.00

No. 529 contains one stamp (size: 38x51mm, perf. 14); multicolored decorative margin continues the design and pictures No. 397b. Size: 139x98mm.

British Post Office, 350th Anniv. A80

**1985, Aug. 1 *Perf. 15***

*530* A80 10c Postboy, letters 10 10
*531* A80 15c Packet, privateer 15 15
*532* A80 25c Duke of Marlborough 25 25
*533* A80 75c Diana 75 75
*534* A80 $1 Falmouth P.O. packet 1.00 1.00
*535* A80 $3 S. S. Conway 3.00 3.00
*Nos. 530-535 (6)* 5.25 5.25

Nos. 522-527 Ovptd. in Silver "COMMONWEALTH SUMMIT / CONFERENCE, BAHAMAS / 16th-22nd OCTOBER 1985."

**1985, Sept. 5 Litho. *Perf. 15***

*536* A78 10c multi 10 10
*537* A78 15c multi 15 15
*538* A78 75c multi 75 75
*539* A78 $5 multi 5.00 5.00

**Souvenir Sheets**

*540* A78 $2 multi 2.00 2.00
*541* A78 $5 multi 5.00 5.00

Nos. 510-514 Ovptd. "80th ANNIVERSARY OF / ROTARY INTERNATIONAL."

**1985, Sept. 25 *Perf. 15***

*542* A76 25c multi 25 25
*543* A76 50c multi 50 50
*544* A76 90c multi 90 90
*545* A76 $1.25 multi 1.25 1.25
*546* A76 $2 multi 2.00 2.00
*Nos. 542-546 (5)* 4.90 4.90

Royal Visit — A81

**1985, Oct. 9 *Perf. 15x14½***

*547* A81 25c Royal and natl. flags 25 25
*548* A81 75c Elizabeth II 75 75

**Size 81x38mm**

*549* A81 $4 Britannia 4.00 4.00

**Souvenir Sheet**

*550* A81 $5 Elizabeth II, diff. 5.00 5.00

Nos. 547-549 printed se-tenant. No. 550 contains one stamp (size: 38x51mm, Perf. 13½x14), multicolored margin continues the portrait. Size: 139x99mm.

Disneyland, 30th Anniv. A82

Characters from "It's a Small World."

**1985, Nov. 1 *Perf. 11***

*551* A82 1c Royal Canadian Mounted Police 5 5
*552* A82 2c American Indian 5 5
*553* A82 3c Inca of the Andes 5 5
*554* A82 4c Africa 5 5
*555* A82 5c Far East 5 5
*556* A82 6c Belize 6 6
*557* A82 50c Balkans 50 50
*558* A82 $1.50 Saudi Arabia 1.50 1.50
*559* A82 $3 Japan 3.00 3.00
*Nos. 551-559 (9)* 5.31 5.31

**Souvenir Sheet**

***Perf. 14***

*560* A82 $4 Montage 4.00 4.00

Christmas 1985. No. 560 has multicolored margin continuing the design. Size: 127x101mm.

Nos. 528-529 Ovptd. "PRE 'WORLD CUP FOOTBALL' / MEXICO 1986."

**1985, Dec. 20 *Perf. 14½x14***

*561* Sheet of 10 5.00 5.00
*a.-j* A79 50c, any single 50 50

**Souvenir Sheet**

*562* A79 $5 multi 5.00 5.00

Women in Folk Costumes — A83

**1986, Jan. 15 *Perf. 15***

*563* A83 5c India 5 5
*564* A83 10c Maya 10 10
*565* A83 15c Garifuna 15 15
*566* A83 25c Creole 25 25
*567* A83 50c China 50 50
*568* A83 75c Lebanon 75 75
*569* A83 $1 Europe 1.00 1.00
*570* A83 $2 South America 2.00 2.00
*Nos. 563-570 (8)* 4.80 4.80

**Souvenir Sheet**

*571* A83 $5 Maya, So. America 5.00 5.00

No. 571 contains one stamp (size: 38x51mm, perf. 14), multicolored margin pictures six women in folk dress. Size: 139x98mm.

Miniature Sheet

A84

Easter — A85

Papal arms, crucifix and: No. 572a, Pius X. No. 572b, Benedict XV. No. 572c, Pius XI. No. 572d, Pius XII. No. 572e, John XXIII. No. 572f, Paul VI. No. 572g, John Paul I. No. 572h, John Paul II. No. 573, John Paul II saying mass in Belize.

**1986, Apr. 15 Litho. *Perf. 11***

*572* Sheet of 8 + label 4.00 4.00
*a.-h* A84 50c, any single 50 50

**Souvenir Sheet**

***Perf. 14***

*573* A85 $4 multi 4.00 4.00

No. 572 contains center label picturing the Vatican, and papal crest. Size: 180x142mm. No. 573 has multicolored margin continuing the design. Size: 148x93mm.

A86

Queen Elizabeth II, 60th Birthday A87

| **1986, Apr. 21** | | ***Perf. 14*** | |
|---|---|---|---|
| *574* | Strip of 3 | 1.50 | 1.50 |
| *a* | A86 25c Age 2 | 25 | 25 |
| *b* | A86 50c Coronation | 50 | 50 |
| *c* | A86 75c Riding horse | 75 | 75 |
| *575* | A86 $3 Wearing crown jewels | 3.00 | 3.00 |

**Souvenir Sheet**

*576* A87 $4 Portrait 4.00 4.00

No. 576 contains one stamp; multicolored margin continues the design and pictures Charles, Edward, Anne and Andrew. Size: 148x93mm.

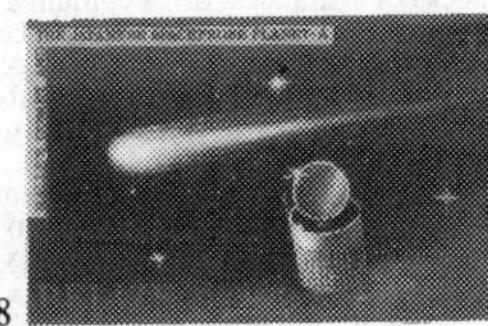

A88

$4 BELIZE

Halley's Comet A89

| **1986, Apr. 30** | | | |
|---|---|---|---|
| *577* | Strip of 3 | 75 | 75 |
| *a* | A88 10c Planet-A probe | 10 | 10 |
| *b* | A88 15c Sighting, 1910 | 15 | 15 |
| *c* | A88 50c Giotto probe | 50 | 50 |
| *578* | Strip of 3 | 3.75 | 3.75 |
| *a* | A88 75c Weather bureau | 75 | 75 |
| *b* | A88 $1 US space telescope, shuttle | 1.00 | 1.00 |
| *c* | A88 $2 Edmond Halley | 2.00 | 2.00 |

**Souvenir Sheet**

*579* A89 $4 Computer graphics 4.00 4.00

No. 579 contains one stamp; multicolored margin continues the design and pictures outer space and Halley. Size: 148x93mm.

Miniature Sheet

A90

US Presidents A91

| **1986, May 7** | | ***Perf. 11*** | |
|---|---|---|---|
| *580* | Sheet of 6 + 3 labels | 4.60 | 4.60 |
| *a* | A90 10c George Washington | 10 | 10 |
| *b* | A90 20c John Adams | 20 | 20 |
| *c* | A90 30c Thomas Jefferson | 30 | 30 |
| *d* | A90 50c James Madison | 50 | 50 |
| *e* | A90 $1.50 James Monroe | 1.50 | 1.50 |
| *f* | A90 $2 John Quincy Adams | 2.00 | 2.00 |

**Souvenir Sheet**

***Perf. 14***

*581* A91 $4 Washington 4.00 4.00

No. 580 contains 3 center labels picturing the great seal of the US. Size: 142x80mm. No. 581 has multicolored decorative margin continuing the design and picturing natl. emblem, flags and presidents. Size: 148x93mm.

A92

Statue of Liberty, Cent. — A93

Designs: 25c, Bartholdi, statue. 50c, Statue, US centennial celebration, Philadelphia, 1876. 75c, Statue close-up, flags, 1886 unveiling. $3, Flags, statue close-up. $4, Statue, New York City skyline.

| **1986, May 15** | | ***Perf. 14*** | |
|---|---|---|---|
| *582* | Strip of 3 | 4.00 | 4.00 |
| *a* | A92 25c multi | 25 | 25 |
| *b* | A92 75c multi | 75 | 75 |
| *c* | A92 $3 multi | 3.00 | 3.00 |
| *583* | A92 50c multi | 50 | 50 |

**Souvenir Sheet**

*584* A93 $4 multi 4.00 4.00

No. 584 contains one stamp; multicolored margin continues the design and pictures US, French flags. Size: 148x93mm.

A94

AMERIPEX '86, Chicago, May 22-June 1 — A95

| **1986, May 22** | | | |
|---|---|---|---|
| *585* | Strip of 3 | 75 | 75 |
| *a* | A94 10c British Honduras No. 3 | 10 | 10 |
| *b* | A94 15c Stamp of 1981 | 15 | 15 |
| *c* | A94 50c US No. C3a | 50 | 50 |
| *586* | Strip of 3 | 3.75 | 3.75 |
| *a* | A94 75c USS Constitution | 75 | 75 |
| *b* | A94 $1 Liberty Bell | 1.00 | 1.00 |
| *c* | A94 $2 White House | 2.00 | 2.00 |

**Souvenir Sheet**

*587* A95 $4 Capitol Building 4.00 4.00

No. 587 contains one stamp; multicolored margin continues the design. Size: 148x93mm.

1986 World Cup Soccer Championships, Mexico — A96

Designs: 25c, England vs. Brazil. 50c, Mexican player, Mayan statues. 75c, Belize players. $3, Aztec calendar stone, Mexico. $4, Flags composing soccer balls.

| **1986, June 16** | **Litho.** | ***Perf. 11*** | |
|---|---|---|---|
| *588* | A96 25c multi | 25 | 25 |
| *589* | A96 50c multi | 50 | 50 |
| *590* | A96 75c multi | 75 | 75 |
| *591* | A96 $3 multi | 3.00 | 3.00 |

**Souvenir Sheet**

***Perf. 14***

*592* A96 $4 multi 4.00 4.00

Nos. 588-591 printed in sheets of 8 plus label picturing Azteca Stadium, 2 each value. No. 592 has multicolored margin continuing the design, picturing crowded stadium. Size: 148x93mm.

Nos. 588-592 Overprinted "ARGENTINA - /WINNERS 1986."

| **1986, Aug. 15** | | | |
|---|---|---|---|
| *593* | A96 25c multi | 25 | 25 |
| *594* | A96 50c multi | 50 | 50 |
| *595* | A96 75c multi | 75 | 75 |
| *596* | A96 $3 multi | 3.00 | 3.00 |

**Souvenir Sheet**

*597* A96 $4 multi 4.00 4.00

The Scott Catalogue value is a retail price, what you could expect to pay for the stamp in a grade of Fine-Very Fine. The value listed is a reference which reflects recent actual dealer selling price.

A97

$1 BELIZE

Wedding of Prince Andrew and Sarah Ferguson — A98

| **1986, July 23** | | ***Perf. 14x14½*** | |
|---|---|---|---|
| *598* | Strip of 3 | 4.00 | 4.00 |
| *a* | A97 25c Sarah | 25 | 25 |
| *b* | A97 75c Andrew | 75 | 75 |
| *c* | A97 $3 Couple | 3.00 | 3.00 |

**Souvenir Sheet**

***Perf. 14½***

| | | | |
|---|---|---|---|
| *599* | Sheet of 2 | 4.00 | 4.00 |
| *a* | A98 $1 Sarah, diff. | 1.00 | 1.00 |
| *b* | A98 $3 Andrew, diff. | 3.00 | 3.00 |

Size of No. 598c: 92x41mm. No. 599 has multicolored decorative margin picturing Westminster Abbey. Size: 155x106mm.

Nos. 585-587 Ovptd. with STOCKHOLMIA '86 Emblems.

| **1986, Aug. 28** | **Litho.** | ***Perf. 14*** | |
|---|---|---|---|
| *600* | Strip of 3 | 75 | 75 |
| *a* | A94 10c multi | 10 | 10 |
| *b* | A94 15c multi | 15 | 15 |
| *c* | A94 50c multi | 50 | 50 |
| *601* | Strip of 3 | 3.75 | 3.75 |
| *a* | A94 75c multi | 75 | 75 |
| *b* | A94 $1 multi | 1.00 | 1.00 |
| *c* | A94 $2 multi | 2.00 | 2.00 |

**Souvenir Sheet**

*602* A95 $4 multi 4.00 4.00

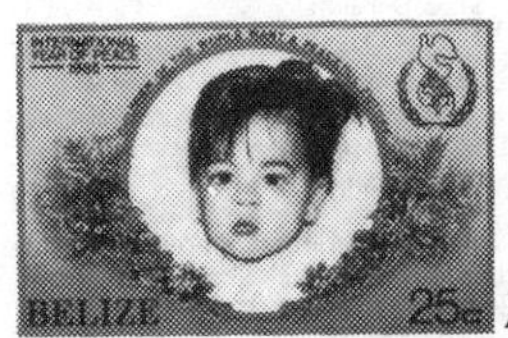


A99

Intl. Peace Year — A100

Children.

| **1986, Oct. 3** | **Litho.** | ***Perf. 14*** | |
|---|---|---|---|
| *603* | A99 25c Infant | 25 | 25 |
| *604* | A99 50c Caucasians | 50 | 50 |
| *605* | A99 75c Oriental | 75 | 75 |
| *606* | A99 $3 Indian, caucasian | 3.00 | 3.00 |

**Souvenir Sheet**

*607* A100 $4 shown 4.00 4.00

Nos. 603-606 printed se-tenant in sheets of 8 (2 each) plus center label. No. 607 has multicolored decorative margin picturing children. Size: 132x106mm.

Fungi — A101

Toucans — A102

**1986, Oct. 30** ***Perf. 14***

*608* A101 5c Amanita lilloi 5 5
*609* A102 10c Keel-billed toucan 10 10
*610* A101 20c Boletellus cubensis 20 20
*611* A102 25c Collared aracari 25 25
*612* A101 75c Psilocybe caerulescens 75 75
*613* A102 $1 Emerald toucanet 1.00 1.00
*614* A102 $1.25 Crimson-rumped toucan 1.25 1.25
*615* A101 $2 Russula puiggarii 2.00 2.00
*Nos. 608-615 (8)* 5.60 5.60

Stamps of the same design printed in sheets of 8 plus center label picturing Audubon Society emblem.

Christmas
A103

Disney characters.

**1986, Nov. 14** ***Perf. 11***

*616* Sheet of 9 4.75 4.75
*a.* A103 2c Jose Carioca 5 5
*b.* A103 3c Carioca, Panchito, Donald 5 5
*c.* A103 4c Daisy 5 5
*d.* A103 5c Mickey, Minnie 5 5
*e.* A103 6c Carioca playing music 5 5
*f.* A103 50c Panchito, Donald 50 50
*g.* A103 65c Donald, Carioca 65 65
*h.* A103 $1.35 Donald 1.35 1.35
*i.* A103 $2 Goofy 2.00 2.00

**Souvenir Sheet**

***Perf. 14***

*617* A103 $4 Donald 4.00 4.00

No. 617 has multicolored margin picturing Disney characters as the Three Caballeros. Size: 132x111mm.

A104

Marriage of Queen Elizabeth II and the Duke of Edinburgh, 40th Anniv. — A105

**1987, Oct. 7** **Litho.** ***Perf. 15***

*618* A104 25c Elizabeth, 1947 25 25
*619* A104 75c Couple, c. 1980 75 75
*620* A104 $1 Elizabeth, 1986 1.00 1.00
*621* A104 $4 Wearing robes of Order of the Garter 4.00 4.00

**Souvenir Sheet**

***Perf. 14***

*622* A105 $6 shown 6.00 6.00

No. 622 has multicolored inscribed margin picturing roses. Size: 172x113mm.

A106

America's Cup 1986-87 — A107

Yachts that competed in the 1987 finals.

**1987, Oct. 21** ***Perf. 15***

*623* A106 25c America II 25 25
*624* A106 75c Stars and Stripes 75 75
*625* A106 $1 Australia II 1.00 1.00
*626* A106 $4 White Crusader 4.00 4.00

**Souvenir Sheet**

***Perf. 14***

*627* A107 $6 Australia II sails 6.00 6.00

No. 627 has multicolored inscribed margin picturing flags of competing nations and race coat of arms. Size: 172x112mm.

A108

Woodcarvings by Sir George Gabb (b. 1928) — A109

**1987, Nov. 4** ***Perf. 15***

*628* A108 25c Mother and Child 25 25
*629* A108 75c Standing Form 75 75
*630* A108 $1 Love-Doves 1.00 1.00
*631* A108 $4 Depiction of Music 4.00 4.00

**Souvenir Sheet**

***Perf. 14***

*632* A109 $6 African Heritage 6.00 6.00

No. 632 has multicolored inscribed margin. Size: 173x114mm.

A110

Indigenous Primates — A111

**1987, Nov. 11** ***Perf. 15***

*633* A110 25c Black spider monkey 25 25
*634* A110 75c Male black howler 75 75
*635* A110 $1 Spider monkeys 1.00 1.00
*636* A110 $4 Howler monkeys 4.00 4.00

**Souvenir Sheet**

***Perf. 14***

*637* A111 $6 Black spider, diff. 6.00 6.00

No. 637 has multicolored inscribed margin continuing the design. Size: 172x112mm.

Natl. Girl Guides Movement, 50th Anniv. — A112

Lady Olave Baden-Powell, Founder — A113

**1987, Nov. 25** ***Perf. 15***

*638* A112 25c Flag-bearers 25 25
*639* A112 75c Camping 75 75
*640* A112 $1 On parade, camp 1.00 1.00
*641* A112 $4 Olave Baden-Powell 4.00 4.00

**Souvenir Sheet**

***Perf. 14***

*642* A113 $6 Lady Olave, diff. 6.00 6.00

No. 642 has multicolored inscribed margin continuing the design. Size: 173x114mm.

Intl. Year of Shelter for the Homeless
A114

**1987, Dec. 3** ***Perf. 15***

*643* A114 25c Tent dwellings 25 25
*644* A114 75c Urban slum 75 75
*645* A114 $1 Tents, diff. 1.00 1.00
*646* A114 $4 Construction 4.00 4.00

Orchids
A115

Designs: Illustrations from Reichenbachia, published by Henry F. Sander in 1886.

**1987, Dec. 16** **Litho.** ***Perf. 14***

*647* A115 1c Laelia euspatha 5 5
*648* A115 2c Cattleya citrina 5 5
*649* A115 3c Masdevallia bachousiana 5 5
*650* A115 4c Cypripedium tautzianum 5 5
*651* A115 5c Trichopilia suavis alba 5 5
*652* A115 6c Odontoglossum hebraicum 6 6
*653* A115 7c Cattleya trianaei schroederiana 6 6
*654* A115 10c Saccolabium giganteum 10 10
*655* A115 30c Cattleya warscewiczii 30 30
*656* A115 50c Chysis bractescens 50 50
*657* A115 70c Cattleya rochellensis 70 70
*658* A115 $1 Laelia elegans schilleriana 1.00 1.00
*659* A115 $1.50 Laelia anceps percivaliana 1.50 1.50
*660* A115 $3 Laelia gouldiana 3.00 3.00
*Nos. 647-660 (14)* 7.47 7.47

**Miniature Sheet**

*661* A115 $5 Cattleya dowiana aurea 5.00 5.00

Nos. 647-652 and 654-659 printed in blocks of six. Sheets of 14 contain 2 blocks of Nos. 647-652 plus 2 No. 653 and center label or 2 blocks of Nos. 654-659 plus center strip containing 2 No. 660 and center label. Center labels picture various illustrations from Reichenbachia.

No. 661 contains one stamp (size: 44x51mm); multicolored decorative margin pictures various orchids. Size: 172x113mm.

Miniature Sheet

Easter 1988 — A116

Stations of the Cross (in sequential order): a. Jesus condemned to death. b. Carries the cross. c. Falls the first time. d. Meets his mother, Mary. e. Cyrenean takes up the cross. f. Veronica wipes Jesus's face. g. Falls the second time. h. Consoles the women of Jerusalem. i. Falls the third time. j. Stripped of his robes. k. Nailed to the cross. l. Dies. m. Taken down from the cross. n. Laid in the sepulcher.

**1988, Mar. 21** ***Perf. 14***

*662* Sheet of 14+label 5.60 5.60
*a.-n.* A116 40c, any single 40 40

No. 662 contains center label picturing likeness of Jesus. Size: 140x279.

1988 Summer Olympics, Seoul — A117

**1988, Aug. 15 Litho. *Perf. 14***

*663* A117 10c Basketball 10 10
*664* A117 25c Volleyball 25 25
*665* A117 60c Table tennis 60 60
*666* A117 75c Diving 75 75
*667* A117 $1 Judo 1.00 1.00
*668* A117 $2 Field hockey 2.00 2.00
*Nos. 663-668 (6)* 4.70 4.70

**Souvenir Sheet**

*669* A117 $3 Women's gymnastics 3.00 3.00

No. 669 has multicolored inscribed margin continuing the design and picturing the natl. flag. Size: 76x106mm.

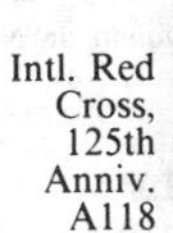

Intl. Red Cross, 125th Anniv. A118

**1988, Nov. 18 Litho. *Perf. 14***

*670* A118 60c Travelling nurse, 1912 60 60
*671* A118 75c Hospital ship, ambulance boat, 1937 75 75
*672* A118 $1 Ambulance, 1956 1.00 1.00
*673* A118 $2 Ambulance plane, 1940 2.00 2.00

Indigenous Small Animals A119

**1989, Jan. Litho. *Perf.***

*674* A119 25c Four-eyed opossum, vert. 25 25
*675* A119 50c Ant bear 50 50
*676* A119 60c Gibnut (agouti) 60 60
*677* A119 75c Antelope 75 75
*678* A119 $2 Peccary 2.00 2.00
*Nos. 674-678 (5)* 4.10 4.10

**POSTAGE DUE STAMPS**

Numeral — D2

Designs: Each denomination has different border.

**1976, July 1 Litho. Wmk. 373**

*J6* D2 1c grn & red 5 5
*J7* D2 2c vio & rose lil 5 5
*J8* D2 5c ocher & brt grn 7 7
*J9* D2 15c brn org & yel grn 25 25
*J10* D2 25c sl grn & org 40 40
*Nos. J6-J10 (5)* 82 82

## BERMUDA

LOCATION — A group of about 150 small islands of which only 20 are inhabited, lying in the Atlantic Ocean about 580 miles southeast of Cape Hatteras.
GOVT. — British Crown Colony
AREA — 20.5 sq. mi.
POP. — 54,893 (1980)
CAPITAL — Hamilton

Bermuda achieved internal self-government in 1968.

4 Farthings = 1 Penny
12 Pence = 1 Shilling
20 Shillings = 1 Pound
100 Cents = 1 Dollar (1970)

**Catalogue values for unused stamps in this country are for Never Hinged items, beginning with Scott 131.**

**POSTMASTER STAMPS.**

PM1

**1848-54 Unwmk. *Imperf.***

*X1* PM1 1p blk, *bluish* (1848, 1849) *125,000.*
*X2* PM1 1p red, *bluish* (1854, 1856) *125,000.*
*X3* PM1 1p red (1853) *160,000.*

PM2

**1860**

*X4* PM2 (1p) red, *yellowish* *100,000.*

Same inscribed "HAMILTON"

**1861**

*X5* PM2 (1p) red, *bluish* *125,000.*

Nos. X1-X3 were produced and used by Postmaster William B. Perot of Hamilton. No. X4 is attributed to Postmaster James H. Thies of St. George's.

**GENERAL ISSUES**

Queen Victoria
A1 A2

A3

A4

A5

**1865-74 Typo. Wmk. 1 *Perf. 14***

*1* A1 1p dl rose 30.00 2.00
*a.* 1p rose red 40.00 4.00
*b.* Imperf. *19,000.* *12,500.*
*2* A2 2p blue ('66) 55.00 10.00
*3* A3 3p buff ('73) 350.00 35.00
*4* A4 6p brn lilac 800. 100.00
*5* A4 6p lilac ('74) 12.00 12.00
*6* A5 1sh green 110.00 27.50

See Nos. 7-9, 19-21, 23, 25.

**1882-1903 *Perf. 14x12½***

*7* A3 3p buff 140.00 35.00
*8* A4 6p violet ('03) 14.50 16.00
*9* A5 1sh green ('94) 24.00 *50.00*
*a.* Vert. strip of 3, perf. all around & imperf. btwn. *12,500.*

Handstamped Diagonally **THREE PENCE**

**1874 *Perf. 14***

*10* A5 3p on 1sh green 1,300. 925.00

Handstamped Diagonally ***THREE PENCE***

*11* A1 3p on 1p rose *10,000.*
*12* A5 3p on 1sh green 2,000. 1,000.
*a.* "P" with top like "R" 2,400 1,000.

No. 11 is stated to be an essay, but a few copies are known used. Nos. 10-12 are found with double or partly double surcharges.

Surcharged in Black **One Penny.**

**1875**

*13* A2 1p on 2p blue 375.00 300.00
*a.* Without period *10,000.* *6,750.*
*14* A3 1p on 3p buff 375.00 225.00
*15* A5 1p on 1sh green 350.00 300.00
*a.* Inverted surcharge
*b.* Without period

A6

A7

**1880 Wmk. 1**

*16* A6 ½p brown 1.50 2.75
*17* A7 4p orange 5.50 2.50

See Nos. 18, 24.

A8

A9

**1883-1904 Wmk. 2**

*18* A6 ½p green ('92) 60 60
*19* A1 1p anil car ('89) 90 25
*a.* 1p dull rose 37.50 3.00
*b.* 1p rose red 24.00 1.75
*c.* 1p carmine rose ('86) 7.00 65
*20* A2 2p blue ('86)19 19.00 2.25
*21* A2 2p anil pur ('93) 7.00 3.50
*a.* 2p brown purple ('98) 2.25 2.50
*22* A8 2½p ultra ('84) 4.75 38
*23* A3 3p gray ('86) 9.25 3.50
*24* A7 4p brn org ('04) 19.00 22.50
*25* A5 1sh ol bis ('93) 14.00 12.00
*a.* 1sh yellow brown 14.00 13.00
*Nos. 18-25 (8)* 74.50 44.98

Black Surcharge

**1901**

*26* A9 1f on 1sh gray 15 15

Dry Dock — A10

**1902-03**

28 A10 ½p gray grn & blk ('03) 4.75 2.75
29 A10 1p car rose & brown 4.75 38
30 A10 3p ol grn & violet 2.00 4.00

**1906-10** **Wmk. 3**

31 A10 ¼p pur & brn ('08) 65 1.00
32 A10 ½p gray grn & blk 3.75 2.25
33 A10 ½p green ('09) 3.75 2.00
34 A10 1p car rose & brn 3.50 28
35 A10 1p carmine ('08) 2.50 32
36 A10 2p orange & gray 3.50 3.50
37 A10 2½p blue & brown 8.75 14.00
38 A10 2½p ultra ('10) 14.00 10.00
39 A10 4p vio brn & blue ('09) 3.50 8.25
*Nos. 31-39 (9)* 43.90 41.60

Caravel
A11

King George V
A12

**1910-20** **Engr.** ***Perf. 14***

40 A11 ¼p brown 45 *1.25*
41 A11 ½p yel green 90 25
 a. ½p dark green 3.00 1.40
42 A11 1p rose red (I) 40 12
 a. 1p carmine (I) 8.75 2.75
43 A11 2p gray 2.00 *3.75*
44 A11 2½p ultra (I) 2.25 60
45 A11 3p violet, *yel* 1.40 *3.25*
46 A11 4p red, *yellow* 2.75 *4.50*
47 A11 6p claret 8.00 *10.00*
48 A11 1sh blk, *green* 4.00 *5.75*
 a. 1sh black, *olive* 3.75 *5.75*

**Typographed**

**Chalky Paper**

49 A12 2sh ultra & dl vio, *bl* ('20) 7.25 *19.00*
50 A12 2sh6p red & blk, *bl* 18.00 *27.50*
51 A12 4sh car & black ('20) 47.50 *55.00*
52 A12 5sh red & grn, *yellow* 45.00 *62.50*
53 A12 10sh red & grn, *green* 130.00 *65.00*
54 A12 £1 black & vio, *red* 425.00 *550.00*
*Nos. 40-54 (15)* 694.90 *808.47*

Types I of 1p and 2½p are illustrated above Nos. 81-97.

The 1p was printed from two plates, the second of which, No. 42a, exists only in carmine on opaque paper with a bluish tinge. Compare Nos. MR1 (as No. 42) and MR2 (as No. 42a).

Revenue cancellations are found on Nos. 52-54.

See Nos. 81-97.

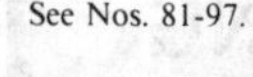

Seal of the Colony and King George V
A13

**1920-21** **Wmk. 3** **Ordinary Paper**

55 A13 ¼p brown 35 *1.25*
56 A13 ½p green 65 *2.25*
57 A13 2p gray 5.75 *8.50*

**Chalky Paper**

58 A13 3p vio & dl vio, *yellow* 4.50 *9.50*
59 A13 4p red & blk, *yellow* 5.75 *11.00*
60 A13 1sh blk, *gray grn* 11.00 *18.00*

**Ordinary Paper**

**Wmk. 4**

67 A13 1p rose red 65 60
68 A13 2½p ultra 4.50 *9.00*

**Chalky Paper**

69 A13 6p red vio & dl vio 9.50 *21.00*
*Nos. 55-60,67-69 (9)* 42.65 *81.10*

*Bermuda stamps can be mounted in Scott's annually supplemented British North and West Caribbean Album.*

King George V — A14

**1921** **Engr.**

71 A14 ¼p brown 45 *1.25*
72 A14 ½p green 3.50 *4.25*
73 A14 1p carmine 2.50 1.00

**Wmk. 3**

74 A14 2p gray 6.00 *8.00*
75 A14 2½p ultra 5.50 4.75
76 A14 3p vio, *orange* 4.25 *8.00*
77 A14 4p scarlet, *org* 6.00 *7.50*
78 A14 6p claret 7.50 *18.00*
79 A14 1sh blk, *green* 20.00 *27.50*
*Nos. 71-79 (9)* 55.70 *80.25*

Tercentenary of "Local Representative Institutions" (Nos. 55-79).

Types of 1910-20 Issue

Types of 1p: **1d** **1d** **1d**
I II III

Types of 2½p: **2½d** **2½d**
I II

**1922-34** **Wmk. 4**

81 A11 ¼p brown ('28) 12 *50*
82 A11 ½p green 10 9
83 A11 1p car, III ('28) 18 9
 a. 1p carmine, II ('26) 2.50 30
 b. 1p carmine, I 65 18
84 A11 1½p red brown ('34) 2.00 35
85 A11 2p gray ('23) 42 42
86 A11 2½p ap grn ('23) 1.00 1.00
87 A11 2½p ultra, II ('32) 90 32
 a. 2½p ultra, I ('26) 95 32
88 A11 3p ultra ('24) 12.00 *17.00*
89 A11 3p vio, *yellow* ('26) 45 45
90 A11 4p red, *yellow* ('24) 45 *85*
91 A11 6p cl ('24) 95 95
92 A11 1sh blk, *emer* ('27) 3.50 3.25
93 A11 1sh brn blk, *yel grn* ('34) 20.00 *30.00*

**Chalky Paper**

94 A12 2sh ultra & vio, *bl* ('27) 20.00 22.50
 a. 2sh bl & dp vio, *dp bl* ('31) 20.00 22.50
95 A12 2sh 6p red & blk, *bl* ('27) 35.00 35.00
 a. 2sh6p pale org ver & blk, *gray bl* ('30) 2,750. 2,750.
 b. 2sh6p dp ver & blk, *deep blue* ('31) 35.00 35.00
96 A12 10sh red & grn, *emer* ('24) 160.00 *190.00*
 a. 10sh dp red & pale grn, *dp emer* ('31) 160.00 *190.00*
97 A12 12sh 6p ocher & gray blk ('32) 375.00 400.00
*Nos. 81-97 (17)* 632.07 *702.77*

Revenue cancellations are found on Nos. 94-97.

**Silver Jubilee Issue**

Common Design Type

**1935, May 6** ***Perf. 11x12***

100 CD301 1p car & dk bl 12 12
101 CD301 1½p blk & ultra 48 48
102 CD301 2½p ultra & brn 1.50 1.50
103 CD301 1sh brn vio & ind 6.25 6.25

Hamilton Harbor — A15

South Shore — A16

Yacht "Lucie" — A17

Grape Bay
A18

Scene at Par-la-Ville
A20

Typical Cottage — A19

**1936-40** ***Perf. 12***

105 A15 ½p blue green 6 5
106 A16 1p car & black 22 14
107 A16 1½p choc & black 25 25
108 A17 2p lt bl & blk 1.90 1.90
109 A17 2p brn blk & turq bl ('38) 20.00 10.00
109A A17 2p red & ultra ('40) 22 18
110 A18 2½p dk bl & lt bl 45 45
111 A19 3p car & black 1.90 1.90
112 A20 6p vio & rose lake 22 18
113 A18 1sh deep green 4.50 5.00
114 A15 1sh6p brown 40 40
*Nos. 105-114 (11)* 30.12 20.45

No. 108, blue border and black center.
No. 109, black border, blue center.

**Coronation Issue**

Common Design Type

**1937, May 14** ***Perf. 13½x14***

115 CD302 1p carmine 10 10
116 CD302 1½p brown 16 16
117 CD302 2½p bright ultra 45 45

Hamilton Harbor — A21

Grape Bay — A22

St. David's Lighthouse
A23

King George VI
A25

Bermudian Water Scene and Yellow-billed Tropic Bird — A24

**1938-51** **Wmk. 4** ***Perf. 12***

118 A21 1p red & black ('40) 6 5
 a. 1p rose red & blk 8.50 85
119 A21 1½p vio brn & blue 6 5
 a. 1½p dl vio brn & bl ('43) 6 5
120 A22 2½p bl & lt bl 1.65 85
120A A22 2½p ol brn & lt bl ('41) 22 18
 b. 2½p dk ol blk & pale blue ('43) 22 18
121 A23 3p car & blk 3.25 2.25
121A A23 3p dp ultra & blk ('42) 22 15
 c. 3p brt ultra & blk ('41) 28 12
121D A24 7½p yel grn, bl & blk ('41) 85 85
122 A22 1sh green 65 42

**Typo.**

***Perf. 13***

123 A25 2sh ultra & red vio, *bl* ('50) 4.25 2.00
 a. 2sh ultra & vio, *bl*, perf. 14 4.00 3.00
 b. 2sh ultra & dl vio, *bl* (mottled paper), perf. 14 ('42) 3.75 3.50
124 A25 2sh 6p red & blk, *bl* 5.75 2.00
 a. Perf. 14 5.75 2.25
125 A25 5sh red & grn, *yel* 5.75 3.50
 a. Perf. 14 7.00 5.00
126 A25 10sh red & grn, *grn* ('51) 16.00 16.00
 a. 10sh brn lake & grn, *grn*, perf. 14 130.00 175.00
 b. 10sh red & grn, *grn*, perf. 14 ('39) 30.00 30.00
127 A25 12sh 6p org & gray blk 40.00 40.00
 a. 12sh6p orange & gray, perf. 14 32.50 32.50
 b. 12sh6p yellow & gray, perf. 14 ('47) 375.00 400.00

**Wmk. 3**

128 A25 £1 blk & vio, *red* ('51) 35.00 35.00
 a. £1 blk & pur, *red*, perf. 14 130.00 92.50
 b. £1 blk & dk vio, *salmon*, perf. 14 ('42) 30.00 30.00
*Nos. 118-128 (14)* 113.71 103.30

No. 127b is the so-called "lemon yellow" shade.

Revenue cancellations are found on Nos. 123-128.

**HALF PENNY**

**X** **X**

No. 118a Surcharged in Black

**1940, Dec. 20** **Wmk. 4** ***Perf. 12***

129 A21 ½p on 1p rose red & blk 20 20

**Catalogue values for unused stamps in this section, from this point to the end of the section, are for Never Hinged items.**

**Peace Issue**

Common Design Type

***Perf. 13½x14***

**1946, Nov. 6** **Engr.** **Wmk. 4**

131 CD303 1½p brown 18 18
132 CD303 3p deep blue 30 30

**Silver Wedding Issue**

Common Design Types

**1948, Dec. 1** **Photo.** ***Perf. 14x14½***

133 CD304 1½p red brown 12 6

**Engr.; Name Typo.**

***Perf. 11½x11***

134 CD305 £1 rose car 55.00 32.50

Postmaster Stamp of 1848
A26

**1949, Apr. 11** **Engr.** ***Perf. 13x13½***

135 A26 2½p dk brn & dp bl 18 18
136 A26 3p deep bl & blk 22 22
137 A26 6p grn & rose vio 45 45

No. 137 shows a different floral arrangement.

Bermuda's first postage stamp, cent.

**UPU Issue**

Common Design Types

***Perf. 13½, 11x11½***

**1949, Oct. 10** **Engr.; Name Typo.**

138 CD306 2½p slate 55 55
139 CD307 3p indigo 70 70
140 CD308 6p rose violet 1.10 1.10
141 CD309 1sh blue green 2.25 2.25

**Coronation Issue**
Common Design Type

**1953, June 4 Engr. *Perf. 13½x13***
*142* CD312 1½p dk bl & blk 38 22

A27

Easter Lilies — A28

Designs: 1p, 4p, Perot stamp. 2p, Racing dinghy. 2½p, Sir George Somers and "Sea Venture." 3p, 1sh3p, Map. 4½p, 9p, "Sea Venture," boat, hog coin and Perot stamp. 5p, 8p, Yellow-billed tropic bird. 1sh, Hog coins. 2sh, Arms of St. George. 2sh6p, Warwick Fort. 5sh, Hog coin. 10sh, Ealiest hog coin. £1, Arms of Bermuda.

**1953-58 *Perf. 13½x13, 13x13½***
*143* A27 ½p olive green 8 7
*144* A27 1p rose red & blk 7 5
*145* A28 1½p dull green 10 5
*146* A27 2p red & ultra 14 5
*147* A27 2½p carmine rose 18 14
*148* A27 3p vio *(Sandy's)* 48 26
*149* A27 3p violet *(Sandys)* ('57) 25 18
*150* A27 4p dp ultra & blk 18 18
*151* A27 4½p green 60 60
*152* A27 6p dk bluish grn & blk 35 22
*153* A27 8p red & blk ('55) 95 35
*154* A27 9p violet ('58) 2.00 95
*155* A27 1sh orange 40 22
*156* A27 1sh3p bl *(Sandy's)* 95 28
*157* A27 1sh3p blue *(Sandys)* ('57) 65 35
*158* A27 2sh yellow brn 2.00 65
*159* A28 2sh6p scarlet 2.00 1.25
*160* A27 5sh dp car rose 4.75 2.00
*161* A27 10sh deep ultra 8.50 4.50

**Engr. and Typo.**
*162* A27 £1 dp ol grn & multi 20.00 12.50
*Nos. 143-162 (20)* 44.63 24.85

Type of 1953 Inscribed "ROYAL VISIT 1953"

Design: 6p, Yellow-billed tropic bird.

**1953, Nov. 26 Engr.**
*163* A27 6p dk bluish grn & blk 42 38

Visit of Queen Elizabeth II and the Duke of Edinburgh, 1953.

Nos. 148 and 156 Overprinted in Violet Blue or Red

**Three Power Talks**
**December, 1953**

**1953, Dec. 8 *Perf. 13½x13***
*164* A27 3p violet 18 18
*165* A27 1sh3p blue (R) 48 42

Three Power Conference, Tucker's Town, December 1953.

Nos. 153 and 156 Overprinted in Black or Red

**50TH ANNIVERSARY**
**U S – BERMUDA**
**OCEAN RACE 1956**

**1956, June 22**
*166* A27 8p red & black 24 24
*167* A27 1sh3p blue (R) 38 38

Newport-Bermuda Yacht Race, 50th anniv.

Perot Post Office, Hamilton
A29

***Perf. 13½x13***
**1959, Jan. 1 Engr. Wmk. 4**
*168* A29 6p lilac & blk 42 32

Restoration and reopening of the post office operated at Hamilton by W. B. Perot in the mid-nineteenth century.

Arms of James I and Elizabeth II — A30

**Engr. and Litho.**
**1959, July 29 Wmk. 314 *Perf. 13***
**Coats of Arms in Blue, Yellow & Red**
*169* A30 1½p dark blue 15 15
*170* A30 3p gray 26 26
*171* A30 4p rose violet 35 35
*172* A30 8p violet gray 75 75
*173* A30 9p olive green 95 95
*174* A30 1sh3p orange brn 1.50 1.50
*Nos. 169-174 (6)* 3.96 3.96

350th anniv. of the shipwreck of the "Sea Venture" which resulted in the first permanent settlement of Bermuda.

The Old Rectory, St. George's, 1730 — A31

Designs: 2p, Church of St. Peter. 3p, Government House. 4p, Cathedral, Hamilton. 5p, No. 185A, H.M. Dockyard. 6p, Perot's Post Office, 1848. 8p, General Post Office, 1869. 9p, Library and Historical Society. 1sh, Christ Church, Warwick, 1719. 1sh3p, City Hall, Hamilton. 10p, No. 185, Bermuda Cottage, 1705. 2sh, Town of St. George. 2sh3p, Bermuda House, 1710. 2sh6p, Bermuda House, 18th century. 5sh, Colonial Secretariat, 1833. 10sh, Old Post Office, Somerset, 1890. £1, House of Assembly, 1815.

**Wmk. 314 Upright**
**1962-65 Photo. *Perf. 12½***
*175* A31 1p org, lil & blk 5 5
*176* A31 2p sl, lt vio, grn & yel 7 7
*a.* Light vio omitted 650.00
*b.* Green omitted
*d.* Imperf., pair 650.00
*177* A31 3p lt bl & yel brown 10 9
*a.* Yellow brn omitted 1,250.
*178* A31 4p car rose & red brn 15 14
*179* A31 5p dk bl & pink 32 32
*180* A31 6p emer, lt & dk blue 18 14
*181* A31 8p grn, dp org & ultra 35 30
*182* A31 9p org brn & grnsh bl 32 28
*182A* A31 10p brt vio & bister ('65) 65 55
*183* A31 1sh multicolored 42 26
*184* A31 1sh3p sl, lem & rose car 48 26
*185* A31 1sh6p brt vio & bis 2.75 2.25
*186* A31 2sh brown & org 1.25 85
*187* A31 2sh3p brn & brt yel green 2.50 2.00
*188* A31 2sh6p grn, yel & sep 1.50 1.10
*189* A31 5sh choc & brt green 2.50 1.65
*190* A31 10sh dl grn, buff & rose car 4.00 3.50
*191* A31 £1 cit, bis, blk & orange 9.50 7.75
*Nos. 175-191 (18)* 27.09 21.56

See No. 252a.

**1966-69 Wmk. 314 Sideways**
**Unnamed Colors as in 1962-65 Issue**
*176c* A31 2p ('69) 32 26
*181a* A31 8p ('67) 65 45
*182b* A31 10p 80 55
*183a* A31 1sh ('67) 80 60
*185A* A31 1sh6p ind & rose 1.65 1.50
*186a* A31 2sh ('67) 2.50 2.25
*Nos. 176c-186a (6)* 6.72 5.61

**Freedom from Hunger Issue**
Common Design Type

**1963, June 4 *Perf. 14x14½***
*192* CD314 1sh3p sepia 2.75 2.25

**Red Cross Centenary Issue**
Common Design Type
**Wmk. 314**
**1963, Sept. 2 Litho. *Perf. 13***
*193* CD315 3p blk & red 65 35
*194* CD315 1sh3p ultra & red 6.75 3.50

Finn Boat — A32

**Wmk. 314**
**1964, Sept. 28 Photo. *Perf. 13½***
*195* A32 3p bl, vio & red 28 28

18th Olympic Games, Tokyo, Oct. 10-25.

**ITU Issue**
Common Design Type
***Perf. 11x11½***
**1965, May 17 Litho. Wmk. 314**
*196* CD317 3p bl & emerald 42 30
*197* CD317 2sh yel & vio bl 3.50 3.50

Scout Badge and Royal Cipher
A33

**1965, July 24 Photo. *Perf. 12½***
*198* A33 2sh multi 85 85

50th anniversary of Scouting in Bermuda.

**Intl. Cooperation Year Issue**
Common Design Type
**1965, Oct. 25 Litho. *Perf. 14½***
*199* CD318 4p bl grn & cl 30 30
*200* CD318 2sh6p lt vio & grn 2.25 2.25

**Churchill Memorial Issue**
Common Design Type
**1966, Jan. 24 Photo. *Perf. 14***
**Design in Black, Gold and Carmine Rose**
*201* CD319 3p bright bl 30 20
*202* CD319 6p green 65 45
*203* CD319 10p brown 1.25 1.00
*204* CD319 1sh3p violet 2.50 2.00

**World Cup Soccer Issue**
Common Design Type
**1966, July 1 Litho. *Perf. 14***
*205* CD321 10p multicolored 65 65
*206* CD321 2sh6p multicolored 1.75 1.75

**UNESCO Anniversary Issue**
Common Design Type
**1966, Dec. 1 Litho. *Perf. 14***
*207* CD323 4p "Education" 40 40
*208* CD323 1sh3p "Science" 1.50 1.50
*209* CD323 2sh "Culture" 2.50 2.50

Post Office, Hamilton
A34
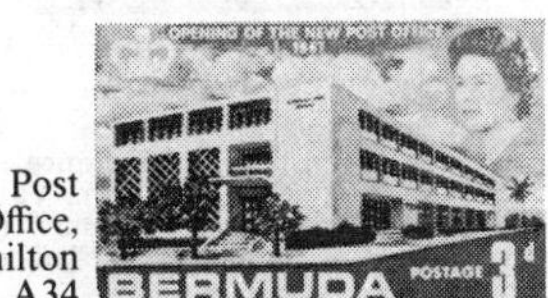


**Wmk. 314**
**1967, June 23 Photo. *Perf. 14½***
*210* A34 3p vio bl & multi 12 12
*211* A34 1sh orange & multi 40 40
*212* A34 1sh6p green & multi 70 70
*213* A34 2sh6p red & multi 1.10 1.10

Opening of the new GPO, Hamilton.

Cable Ship Mercury
A35

Designs: 1sh, Map of Bermuda and Virgin Islands, telephone and microphone. 1sh6p, Radio tower, television set, telephone and cable. 2sh6p, Cable at sea bottom and ship.

**1967, Sept. 14 Photo. Wmk. 314**
*214* A35 3p multicolored 12 12
*215* A35 1sh multicolored 40 40
*216* A35 1sh6p multicolored 70 70
*217* A35 2sh6p multicolored 1.10 1.10

Completion of the Bermuda-Tortola, Virgin Islands, telephone link.

Common Design Types pictured in section before Great Britain.

Human Rights Flame, Globe and Doves
A36

**1968, Feb. 1 Litho. *Perf. 14x14½***
*218* A36 3p ind, lt grn & bl 14 14
*219* A36 1sh brn, lt bl & bl 45 45
*220* A36 1sh6p blk, pink & blue 75 75
*221* A36 2sh6p grn, yellow & bl 95 95

International Human Rights Year.

Mace
A37

Design: 1sh6p, 2sh6p, House of Assembly, Bermuda; Parliament, London, and royal cipher.

**1968, July 1 Photo. *Perf. 14½***
*222* A37 3p rose red & multi 14 14
*223* A37 1sh ultra & multi 45 45
*224* A37 1sh6p yellow & multi 75 75
*225* A37 2sh6p multicolored 95 95

New constitution.

Olympic Sports and Rings
A38

**1968, Sept. 24 Wmk. 314 *Perf. 12½***
*226* A38 3p lilac & multi 14 14
*a.* Rose brown omitted ("3d BERMUDA") 2,000.
*227* A38 1sh multicolored 42 35
*228* A38 1sh6p multicolored 60 60
*229* A38 2sh6p multicolored 1.00 1.00

19th Olympic Games, Mexico City, Oct. 12-27.

Girl Guides A39

Designs: 1sh, Like 3p. 1sh6p, 2sh6p, Girl Guides and arms of Bermuda.

**1969, Feb. 17 Litho. *Perf. 14***

| | | | | |
|---|---|---|---|---|
| *230* | A39 | 3p lilac & multi | 14 | 14 |
| *231* | A39 | 1sh green & multi | 38 | 38 |
| *232* | A39 | 1sh6p gray & multi | 65 | 65 |
| *233* | A39 | 2sh6p red & multi | 1.10 | 1.10 |

Bermuda Girl Guides, 50th anniv.

Gold and Emerald Cross — A40

Design: 4p, 2sh, Different background.

**1969, Sept. 29 Photo. *Perf. 14½x14***
**Cross in Yellow, Brown and Emerald**

| | | | | |
|---|---|---|---|---|
| *234* | A40 | 4p violet | 24 | 24 |
| *235* | A40 | 1sh3p green | 75 | 75 |
| *236* | A40 | 2sh black | 1.10 | 1.10 |
| *237* | A40 | 2sh6p carmine rose | 1.40 | 1.25 |

Treasures salvaged off the coast of Bermuda. The cross shown is from the Tucker treasure from the 16th century Spanish galleon San Pedro.

Buildings Issue and Type of 1962-69 Surcharged with New Value and Bar in Black or Brown

**1970, Feb. 6 Wmk. 314 *Perf. 12½***

| | | | | |
|---|---|---|---|---|
| *238* | A31 | 1c on 1p multi | 5 | 5 |
| *239* | A31 | 2c on 2p multi | 8 | 8 |
| *a.* | | Watermark upright | 1.25 | 1.25 |
| *b.* | | Light violet omitted | *650.00* | |
| *c.* | | Pair, one without surch. | *2,000.* | |
| *240* | A31 | 3c on 3p multi | 10 | 10 |
| *241* | A31 | 4c on 4p multi (Br) | 12 | 12 |
| *242* | A31 | 5c on 8p multi | 14 | 14 |
| *243* | A31 | 6c on 6p multi | 14 | 14 |
| *244* | A31 | 9c on 9p multi (Br) | 22 | 22 |
| *245* | A31 | 10c on 10p multi | 28 | 28 |
| *246* | A31 | 12c on 1sh multi | 32 | 32 |
| *247* | A31 | 15c on 1sh3p multi | 70 | 60 |
| *248* | A31 | 18c on 1sh6p multi | 70 | 70 |
| *249* | A31 | 24c on 2sh multi | 85 | 85 |
| *250* | A31 | 30c on 2sh6p multi | 1.00 | 1.00 |
| *251* | A31 | 36c on 2sh3p multi | 1.25 | 1.25 |
| *252* | A31 | 60c on 5sh multi | 2.00 | 2.00 |
| *a.* | | Surcharge omitted | *450.00* | |
| *253* | A31 | $1.20 on 10sh multi | 4.00 | 4.00 |
| *254* | A31 | $2.40 on £1 multi | 8.00 | 8.00 |
| | | *Nos. 238-254 (17)* | 19.95 | 19.85 |

Watermark upright on 1c, 3c to 9c and 36c; sideways on others. Watermark is sideways on No. 252a, upright on No. 189.

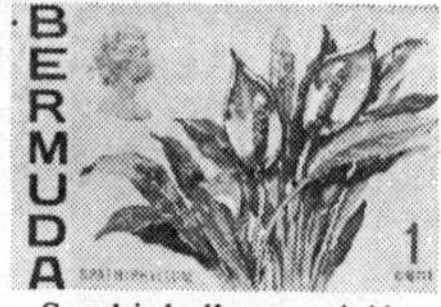


Spathiphyllum — A41

Flowers: 2c, Bottlebrush. 3c, Oleander (vert.). 4c, Bermudiana. 5c, Poinsettia. 6c, Hibiscus. 9c, Cereus. 10c, Bougainvillea (vert.). 12c, Jacaranda. 15c, Passion flower. 18c, Coralita. 24c, Morning glory. 30c, Tecoma. 36c, Angel's trumpet. 60c, Plumbago. $1.20, Bird of paradise. $2.40, Chalice cup.

**Wmk. 314, Sideways on Horiz. Stamps**

**1970, July 6 *Perf. 14***

| | | | | |
|---|---|---|---|---|
| *255* | A41 | 1c lt grn & multi | 5 | 5 |
| *256* | A41 | 2c pale bl & multi | 26 | 15 |
| *257* | A41 | 3c yellow & multi | 16 | 8 |
| *258* | A41 | 4c buff & multi | 18 | 9 |
| *259* | A41 | 5c pink & multi | 60 | 26 |
| *a.* | | Imperf., pair | 800.00 | |
| *260* | A41 | 6c orange & multi | 60 | 30 |
| *261* | A41 | 9c lt grn & multi | 35 | 16 |
| *262* | A41 | 10c pale salmon & multi | 35 | 16 |
| *263* | A41 | 12c pale yellow & multi | 1.65 | 85 |
| *264* | A41 | 15c buff & multi | 1.40 | 70 |
| *265* | A41 | 18c pale salmon & multi | 2.50 | 1.10 |
| *266* | A41 | 24c pink & multi | 1.65 | 75 |
| *267* | A41 | 30c plum & multi | 1.65 | 75 |
| *268* | A41 | 36c dark gray & multi | 2.50 | 1.10 |
| *269* | A41 | 60c gray & multi | 3.25 | 1.75 |
| *270* | A41 | $1.20 blue & multi | 7.50 | 3.50 |
| *271* | A41 | $2.40 multicolored | 15.00 | 8.25 |
| | | *Nos. 255-271 (17)* | 39.65 | 20.00 |

See Nos. 322-328.

**1974-76 Wmk. 314 Upright**

| | | | | |
|---|---|---|---|---|
| *259b* | A41 | 5c multicolored | 1.00 | 1.00 |
| *260a* | A41 | 6c multicolored | 2.25 | 2.25 |
| *263a* | A41 | 12c multicolored | 1.65 | 1.65 |
| *267a* | A41 | 30c multi ('76) | 3.00 | 3.00 |

**1975-76 Wmk. 373**

| | | | | |
|---|---|---|---|---|
| *256a* | A41 | 2c multicolored | 32 | 32 |
| *260b* | A41 | 6c multicolored | 1.00 | 1.00 |

State House, St. George's, 1622-1815 A42

Designs: 15c, The Sessions House, Hamilton, 1893. 18c, First Assembly House, St. Peter's Church, St. George's. 24c, Temporary Assembly House, Hamilton, 1815-26.

**1970, Oct. 12 Litho. *Perf. 14***

| | | | | |
|---|---|---|---|---|
| *272* | A42 | 4c multicolored | 15 | 15 |
| *273* | A42 | 15c multicolored | 45 | 45 |
| *274* | A42 | 18c multicolored | 65 | 65 |
| *275* | A42 | 24c multicolored | 1.10 | 1.10 |
| *a.* | | Souvenir sheet | 3.75 | 4.25 |

350th anniv. of Bermuda's Parliament. No. 275a contains one each of Nos. 272-275; light blue marginal inscription and decoration. Size: 129x95mm.

Street in St. George's A43

Designs: 15c, Horseshoe Bay. 18c, Gibb's Hill Lighthouse. 24c, View of Hamilton Harbor.

**1971, Feb. 8 Wmk. 314 *Perf. 14***

| | | | | |
|---|---|---|---|---|
| *276* | A43 | 4c multicolored | 24 | 24 |
| *277* | A43 | 15c multicolored | 70 | 70 |
| *278* | A43 | 18c multicolored | 90 | 90 |
| *279* | A43 | 24c multicolored | 1.50 | 1.50 |

"Keep Bermuda Beautiful."

Building of "Deliverance" — A44

Designs: 15c, "Deliverance" and "Patience" arriving in Jamestown, Va., 1610 (vert.). 18c, Wreck of "Sea Venture" (vert.). 24c, "Deliverance" and "Patience" under sail, 1610.

**1971, May 10 Litho. Wmk. 314**

| | | | | |
|---|---|---|---|---|
| *280* | A44 | 4c multicolored | 40 | 40 |
| *281* | A44 | 15c brn & multi | 1.40 | 1.40 |
| *282* | A44 | 18c pur & multi | 1.75 | 1.75 |
| *283* | A44 | 24c blue & multi | 2.50 | 2.50 |

Voyage of Sir George Somers to Jamestown, Va., from Bermuda, 1610.

Ocean View Golf Course A45

Golf Courses: 15c, Port Royal. 18c, Castle Harbour. 24c, Belmont.

**1971, Nov. 1 *Perf. 13***

| | | | | |
|---|---|---|---|---|
| *284* | A45 | 4c multicolored | 18 | 18 |
| *285* | A45 | 15c multicolored | 65 | 65 |
| *286* | A45 | 18c multicolored | 75 | 75 |
| *287* | A45 | 24c multicolored | 1.10 | 1.10 |

Golfing in Bermuda.

Nos. 258, 264-266 Overprinted: "HEATH-NIXON / DECEMBER 1971"

**1971, Dec. 20 Photo. *Perf. 14***

| | | | | |
|---|---|---|---|---|
| *288* | A41 | 4c buff & multi | 14 | 14 |
| *289* | A41 | 15c buff & multi | 42 | 42 |
| *290* | A41 | 18c pale sal & multi | 52 | 52 |
| *291* | A41 | 24c pink & multi | 70 | 70 |

Meeting of President Richard M. Nixon and Prime Minister Edward Heath of Great Britain, at Hamilton, Dec. 20-21, 1971.

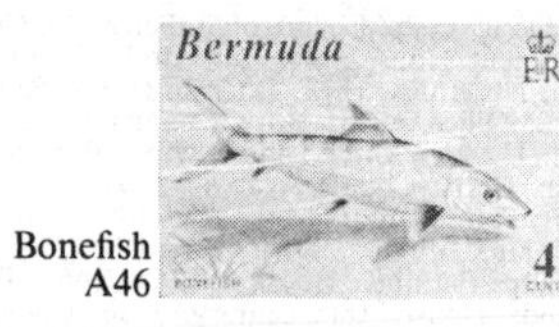


Bonefish A46

**1972, Aug. 7 Litho. *Perf. 13½x14***

| | | | | |
|---|---|---|---|---|
| *292* | A46 | 4c shown | 26 | 26 |
| *293* | A46 | 15c Wahoo | 75 | 75 |
| *294* | A46 | 18c Yellowfin tuna | 90 | 90 |
| *295* | A46 | 24c Greater amberjack | 1.40 | 1.40 |

World fishing records.

**Silver Wedding Issue, 1972**

Common Design Type

Design: Queen Elizabeth II, Prince Philip, Admiralty oar and mace.

**1972, Nov. 20 Photo. *Perf. 14x14½***

| | | | | |
|---|---|---|---|---|
| *296* | CD324 | 4c violet & multi | 14 | 14 |
| *297* | CD324 | 15c car rose & multi | 52 | 52 |

Palmettos — A47

**1973, Sept. 3 Wmk. 314 *Perf. 14***

| | | | | |
|---|---|---|---|---|
| *298* | A47 | 4c shown | 25 | 25 |
| *299* | A47 | 15c Olivewood | 75 | 75 |
| *300* | A47 | 18c Bermuda cedar | 1.00 | 1.20 |
| *301* | A47 | 24c Mahogany | 1.25 | 1.25 |

Bermuda National Trust, and "Plant a Tree" campaign.

**Princess Anne's Wedding Issue**

Common Design Type

**1973, Nov. 21 Litho.**

| | | | | |
|---|---|---|---|---|
| *302* | CD325 | 15c lilac & multi | 35 | 35 |
| *303* | CD325 | 18c slate & multi | 45 | 45 |

National Tennis Stadium, Pembroke, 1973 — A48

Designs: 15c, Bermuda's first tennis court Pembroke, 1873. 18c, Britain's first tennis court, Leamington Spa, 1872. 24c, First US tennis club, Staten Island, 1874.

**1973, Dec. 17 Wmk. 314**

| | | | | |
|---|---|---|---|---|
| *304* | A48 | 4c black & multi | 20 | 20 |
| *305* | A48 | 15c black & multi | 65 | 65 |
| *306* | A48 | 18c black & multi | 90 | 90 |
| *307* | A48 | 24c black & multi | 1.25 | 1.25 |

Centenary of tennis in Bermuda.

Rotary Emblem, Weather Vane, City Hall, Hamilton A49

Designs (Rotary Emblem and): 17c, St Peter's Church, St. George's. 20c, Somerset Drawbridge, Somerset. 25c, Map of Bermuda on globe, 1626.

**1974, June 24 *Perf. 14***

| | | | | |
|---|---|---|---|---|
| *308* | A49 | 5c emerald & multi | 22 | 22 |
| *309* | A49 | 17c blue & multi | 75 | 75 |
| *310* | A49 | 20c yel org & multi | 85 | 85 |
| *311* | A49 | 25c lt vio & multi | 1.10 | 1.10 |

50th anniv. of Rotary Intl. in Bermuda.

Jack of Clubs and a Good Bridge Hand — A50

Designs (Bermuda Bowl and): 17c, Queen of diamonds. 20c, King of hearts. 25c, Ace of spades.

**1975, Jan. 27 Litho. Wmk. 314**

| | | | | |
|---|---|---|---|---|
| *312* | A50 | 5c blue & multi | 24 | 24 |
| *313* | A50 | 17c dl yel & multi | 75 | 75 |
| *314* | A50 | 20c ver & multi | 80 | 80 |
| *315* | A50 | 25c lilac & multi | 1.10 | 1.10 |

World Bridge Championship, Bermuda, Jan. 1975.

Queen Elizabeth II and Prince Philip — A51

***Perf. 14x14½***

**1975, Feb. 17 Photo. Wmk. 373**

| | | | | |
|---|---|---|---|---|
| *316* | A51 | 17c multicolored | 60 | 60 |
| *317* | A51 | 20c dk bl & multi | 80 | 80 |

Royal Visit, Feb. 16-18, 1975.

British Cavalier Flying Boat, 1937 — A52

Designs: 17c, U.S. Navy airship "Los Angeles," 1925, flying from Lakehurst, N.J. to Hamilton, Bermuda. 20c, Constellation over Kindley Field, 1946. 25c, Boeing 747 on tarmac, 1970.

**1975, Apr. 28 Litho. Perf. 14**

| | | | | |
|---|---|---|---|---|
| *318* | A52 | 5c lt grn & multi | 42 | 42 |
| *319* | A52 | 17c lt ultra & multi | 1.25 | 1.25 |
| *320* | A52 | 20c multicolored | 1.75 | 1.75 |
| *321* | A52 | 25c rose lil & multi | 2.00 | 2.00 |
| *a.* | | Souvenir sheet of 4 | 6.00 | *7.50* |

Airmail service to Bermuda, 50th anniv. No. 321a contains one each of Nos. 318-321; bright blue border with black inscription. Size: 128x85mm.

Flower Type of 1970

**1975, June 2 Photo. Wmk. 314**

| | | | | |
|---|---|---|---|---|
| *322* | A41 | 17c Passion flower | 1.40 | 1.40 |
| *323* | A41 | 20c Coralita | 1.40 | 1.40 |
| *324* | A41 | 25c Morning glory | 1.40 | 1.40 |
| *325* | A41 | 40c Angel's trumpet | 1.40 | 1.40 |
| *326* | A41 | $1 Plumbago | 2.25 | 2.25 |
| *327* | A41 | $2 Bird-of-paradise flower | 3.75 | 3.75 |
| *328* | A41 | $3 Chalice cup | 6.50 | 6.50 |
| | | *Nos. 322-328 (7)* | 18.10 | 18.10 |

Royal Magazine Break-in A54

Designs: 17c, Sympathizers rowing towards magazine. 20c, Loading gun powder barrels onto ships. 25c, Gun powder barrels on beach.

***Perf. 13x13½***

**1975, Oct. 27 Litho. Wmk. 373**

| | | | | |
|---|---|---|---|---|
| *329* | A54 | 5c multicolored | 24 | 24 |
| *330* | A54 | 17c multicolored | 75 | 75 |
| *331* | A54 | 20c multicolored | 85 | 85 |
| *332* | A54 | 25c multicolored | 1.25 | 1.25 |
| *a.* | | Souvenir sheet of 4 | 4.00 | *5.00* |

Gunpowder Plot, 1775, American War of Independence. No. 332a contains one each of Nos. 329-332, perf. 14. Multicolored margin with map of Bermuda and descriptive inscription. Size: 164x137mm.

Bermuda Biological Station A55

Designs: 5c, Launching of bathysphere from "Ready" (vert.). 20c, Sailing ship Challenger, 1873. 25c, Descent of Beebe's bathysphere, 1934, and marine life (vert.).

**Wmk. 373**

**1976, Mar. 29 Litho. Perf. 14**

| | | | | |
|---|---|---|---|---|
| *333* | A55 | 5c multicolored | 28 | 28 |
| *334* | A55 | 17c multicolored | 70 | 70 |
| *335* | A55 | 20c multicolored | 85 | 85 |
| *336* | A55 | 25c multicolored | 1.00 | 1.00 |

Bermuda Biological Station, 50th anniversary.

Christian Radich, Norway A56

Tall Ships: 12c, Juan Sebastian de Elcano, Spain. 17c, Eagle, USA. 20c, Sir Winston Churchill, Great Britain. 40c, Kruzenshtern, USSR. $1, Cutty Sark (silver trophy).

**1976, June 15 Litho. Perf. 13**

| | | | | |
|---|---|---|---|---|
| *337* | A56 | 5c lt grn & multi | 30 | 30 |
| *338* | A56 | 12c violet & multi | 55 | 55 |
| *339* | A56 | 17c ultra & multi | 75 | 75 |
| *340* | A56 | 20c blue & multi | 1.00 | 1.00 |
| *341* | A56 | 40c yellow & multi | 1.50 | 1.50 |
| *342* | A56 | $1 sl grn & multi | 4.50 | 4.50 |
| | | *Nos. 337-342 (6)* | 8.60 | 8.60 |

Trans-Atlantic Cutty Sark International Tall Ships Race, Plymouth, England-New York City (Operation Sail '76).

Silver Cup Trophy and Crossed Club Flags A57

Designs: 17c, St. George's Cricket Club and emblem. 20c, Somerset Cricket Club and emblem. 25c, Cricket match.

**1976, Aug. 16 Wmk. 373 Perf. 14½**

| | | | | |
|---|---|---|---|---|
| *343* | A57 | 5c multicolored | 26 | 26 |
| *344* | A57 | 17c multicolored | 85 | 85 |
| *345* | A57 | 20c multicolored | 95 | 95 |
| *346* | A57 | 25c multicolored | 1.40 | 1.40 |

St. George's and Somerset Cricket Club matches, 75th anniversary.

Queen's Visit to Bermuda, 1975 — A58

Designs: 20c, St. Edward's Crown. $1, Queen seated in Chair of Estate.

**1977, Feb. 7 Litho. Perf. 14x13½**

| | | | | |
|---|---|---|---|---|
| *347* | A58 | 5c silver & multi | 12 | 12 |
| *348* | A58 | 20c silver & multi | 38 | 38 |
| *349* | A58 | $1 silver & multi | 1.65 | 1.65 |

25th anniv. of the reign of Queen Elizabeth II.

Stockdale House, St. George's A59

Designs (UPU Emblem and): 15c, Perot Post Office and Perot Stamp. 17c, St. George's Post Office, c. 1860. 20c, Old GPO, Hamilton, c. 1935. 40c, New GPO, Hamilton, 1967.

**1977, June 20 Litho. Perf. 13x13½**

| | | | | |
|---|---|---|---|---|
| *350* | A59 | 5c multicolored | 12 | 12 |
| *351* | A59 | 15c multicolored | 35 | 35 |
| *352* | A59 | 17c multicolored | 40 | 40 |
| *353* | A59 | 20c multicolored | 50 | 50 |
| *354* | A59 | 40c multicolored | 1.00 | 1.00 |
| | | *Nos. 350-354 (5)* | 2.37 | 2.37 |

Bermuda's UPU membership, cent..

Sailing Ship, 17th Century, Approaching Castle Island — A60

Designs: 15c, King's pilot leaving 18th century naval ship at Murray's Anchorage. 17c, Pilot gigs racing to meet steamship, early 19th century. 20c, Harvest Queen, late 19th century. 40c, Pilot cutter and Queen Elizabeth II off St. David's Lighthouse.

***Perf. 13½x14***

**1977, Sept. 26 Wmk. 373**

| | | | | |
|---|---|---|---|---|
| *355* | A60 | 5c multicolored | 15 | 15 |
| *356* | A60 | 15c multicolored | 42 | 42 |
| *357* | A60 | 17c multicolored | 48 | 48 |
| *358* | A60 | 20c multicolored | 60 | 60 |
| *359* | A60 | 40c multicolored | 1.25 | 1.25 |
| | | *Nos. 355-359 (5)* | 2.90 | 2.90 |

Piloting in Bermuda waters.

Elizabeth II — A61

Designs: 8c, Great Seal of Elizabeth I. 50c, Great Seal of Elizabeth II.

***Perf. 14x13½***

**1978, Aug. 28 Litho. Wmk. 373**

| | | | | |
|---|---|---|---|---|
| *360* | A61 | 8c gold & multi | 14 | 14 |
| *361* | A61 | 50c gold & multi | 85 | 85 |
| *362* | A61 | $1 gold & multi | 1.65 | 1.65 |

25th anniv. of coronation of Elizabeth II.

White-tailed Tropicbird — A62

***Perf. 14; 14x14½ (4c, 5c, $2, $3, $5)***

**1978-79 Photo. Wmk. 373**

| | | | | |
|---|---|---|---|---|
| *363* | A62 | 3c shown | 5 | 5 |
| *364* | A62 | 4c White-eyed vireo | 5 | 5 |
| *365* | A62 | 5c Eastern bluebird | 7 | 7 |
| *366* | A62 | 7c Whistling tree frog | 9 | 9 |
| *367* | A62 | 8c Cardinal | 10 | 10 |
| *368* | A62 | 10c Spiny lobster | 14 | 14 |
| *369* | A62 | 12c Land crab | 16 | 16 |
| *370* | A62 | 15c Skink | 20 | 20 |
| *371* | A62 | 20c Four-eyed butterflyfish | 26 | 26 |
| *372* | A62 | 25c Red hind | 35 | 35 |
| *373* | A62 | 30c Monarch butterfly | 40 | 40 |
| *374* | A62 | 40c Rock beauty | 55 | 55 |
| *375* | A62 | 50c Banded butterflyfish | 65 | 65 |
| *376* | A62 | $1 Blue angelfish | 1.40 | 1.40 |
| *377* | A62 | $2 Humpback whale | 2.75 | 2.75 |
| *378* | A62 | $3 Green turtle | 4.00 | 4.00 |
| *379* | A62 | $5 Bermuda Petrel | 6.75 | 6.75 |
| | | *Nos. 363-379 (17)* | 17.97 | 17.97 |

Issue dates: 3c, 4c, 5c, 8c, $5, 1978. Others, 1979.

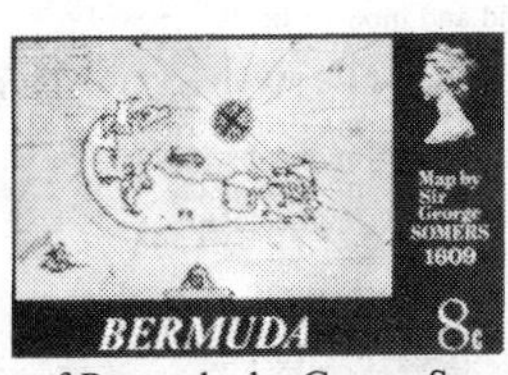

Map of Bermuda, by George Somers, 1609 — A63

Old Maps of Bermuda: 15c, by John Seller, 1685. 20c, by Herman Moll, 1729 (vert.). 25c, by Desbruslins, 1740. 50c, by John Speed, 1626.

**1979, May 14 Litho. Perf. 13½**

| | | | | |
|---|---|---|---|---|
| *380* | A63 | 8c multicolored | 16 | 16 |
| *381* | A63 | 15c multicolored | 30 | 30 |
| *382* | A63 | 20c multicolored | 40 | 40 |
| *383* | A63 | 25c multicolored | 45 | 45 |
| *384* | A63 | 50c multicolored | 95 | 95 |
| | | *Nos. 380-384 (5)* | 2.26 | 2.26 |

Bermuda Police Centenary — A64

Designs: 20c, Traffic direction (horiz.). 25c, Water patrol (horiz.). 50c, Motorbike and patrol car.

**1979, Nov. 26 Wmk. 373 Perf. 14**

| | | | | |
|---|---|---|---|---|
| *385* | A64 | 8c multicolored | 16 | 16 |
| *386* | A64 | 20c multicolored | 40 | 40 |
| *387* | A64 | 25c multicolored | 50 | 50 |
| *388* | A64 | 50c multicolored | 1.00 | 1.00 |

Bermuda No. X1, Penny Black — A65

Bermuda No. X1 and: 20c, Hill. 25c, "Paid 1" marking on cover. 50c, "Paid 1" marking.

**1980, Feb. 25 Litho. Perf. 13½x14**

| | | | | |
|---|---|---|---|---|
| *389* | A65 | 8c multicolored | 16 | 16 |
| *390* | A65 | 20c multicolored | 40 | 40 |
| *391* | A65 | 25c multicolored | 50 | 50 |
| *392* | A65 | 50c multicolored | 1.00 | 1.00 |

Sir Rowland Hill (1795-1879), originator of penny postage.

Tristar-500, London 1980 Emblem — A66

**1980, May 6 Litho. Perf. 13x14**

| | | | | |
|---|---|---|---|---|
| *393* | A66 | 25c shown | 42 | 42 |
| *394* | A66 | 50c "Orduna," 1926 | 85 | 85 |
| *395* | A66 | $1 "Delta," 1856 | 1.75 | 1.75 |
| *396* | A66 | $2 "Lord Sidmouth," 1818 | 3.50 | 3.50 |

London 1980 Intl. Stamp Exhib., May 6-14.

Gina Swainson, Miss World, 1979-80, Arms of Bermuda — A67

**1980, May 8 Perf. 14**

| | | | | |
|---|---|---|---|---|
| *397* | A67 | 8c shown | 14 | 14 |
| *398* | A67 | 20c After crowning ceremony | 35 | 35 |
| *399* | A67 | 50c Welcome home party | 90 | 90 |
| *400* | A67 | $1 In carriage | 1.75 | 1.75 |

**Queen Mother Elizabeth Birthday Issue**

Common Design Type

**1980, Aug. 4 Wmk. 373 *Perf. 14***

*401* CD330 25c multicolored 46 46

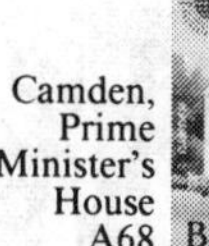

Camden, Prime Minister's House A68

**1980, Sept. 24 Litho. *Perf. 14***

*402* A68 8c View from satellite 16 16
*403* A68 20c shown 40 40
*404* A68 25c Princess Hotel, Hamilton 50 50
*405* A68 50c Government House 1.00 1.00

Commonwealth Finance Ministers Meeting, Bermuda, Sept.

18th Century Kitchen A69

**1981, May 21 Wmk. 373 *Perf. 14***

*406* A69 8c shown 14 14
*407* A69 25c Gathering Easter lilies 42 42
*408* A69 30c Fisherman 52 52
*409* A69 40c Stone cutting, 19th cent. 70 70
*410* A69 50c Onion shipping, 19th cent. 85 85
*411* A69 $1 Ships, 17th cent. 1.75 1.75
*Nos. 406-411 (6)* 4.38 4.38

**Royal Wedding Issue**

Common Design Type

**1981, July 22 Wmk. 373 *Perf. 14***

*412* CD331 30c Bouquet 52 52
*413* CD331 50c Charles 90 90
*414* CD331 $1 Couple 1.75 1.75

Girl Helping Blind Man Cross Street — A70

**1981, Sept. 28 Litho. *Perf. 14***

*415* A70 10c shown 18 18
*416* A70 25c Kayaking, Paget Island 48 48
*417* A70 30c Mountain climbing, St. David's Island 55 55
*418* A70 $1 Duke of Edinburgh 1.90 1.90

Duke of Edinburgh's Awards, 25th anniv.

Conus Species A71

**1982, May 13 Wmk. 373 *Perf. 14***

*419* A71 10c shown 20 20
*420* A71 25c Bursa finlayi 50 50
*421* A71 30c Sconsia striata 60 60
*422* A71 $1 Murex pterynotus lightbourni 1.90 1.90



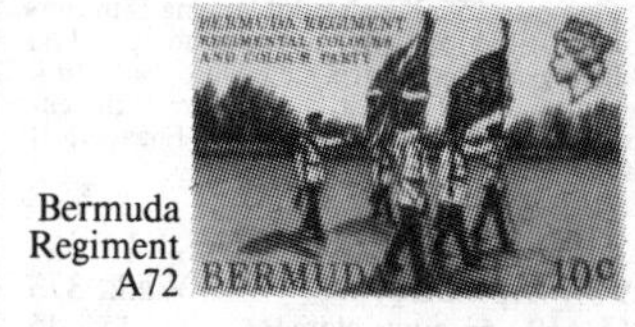

Bermuda Regiment A72

**1982, June 17 Litho. Wmk. 373**

*423* A72 10c Color guard 16 16
*424* A72 25c Queen's birthday parade 40 40
*425* A72 30c Governor inspecting honor guard 45 45
*426* A72 40c Beating the retreat 60 60
*427* A72 50c Ceremonial gunners 80 80
*428* A72 $1 Royal visit, 1975 1.65 1.65
*Nos. 423-428 (6)* 4.06 4.06

Southampton Fort — A73

**1982, Nov. 18 Litho. Wmk. 373**

*429* A73 10c Charles Fort, vert. 20 20
*430* A73 25c Pembroks Fort, vert. 50 50
*431* A73 30c shown 60 60
*432* A73 $1 Smiths and Pagets Forts 1.90 1.90

Arms of Sir Edwin Sandys (1561-1629) A74

Coats of Arms: 25c, Bermuda Company. 50c, William Herbert, 3rd Earl of Pembroke (1584-1630). $1 Sir George Somers (1554-1610).

**1983, Apr. 14 Litho. *Perf. 13½***

*433* A74 10c multicolored 18 18
*434* A74 25c multicolored 45 45
*435* A74 50c multicolored 90 90
*436* A74 $1 multicolored 1.75 1.75

See Nos. 457-460, 474-477.

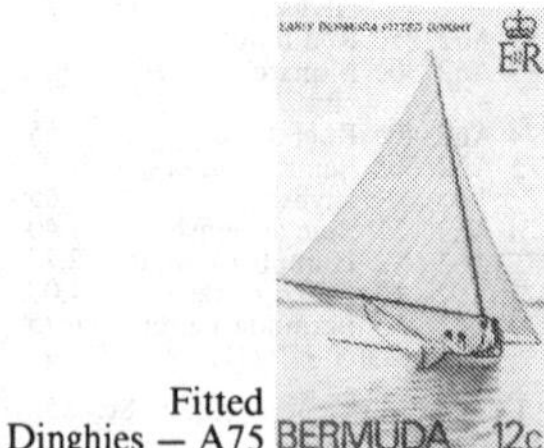

Fitted Dinghies — A75

Old and modern boats.

**1983, July 21 Wmk. 373 *Perf. 14***

*437* A75 12c multicolored 22 22
*438* A75 30c multicolored 55 55
*439* A75 40c multicolored 70 70
*440* A75 $1 multicolored 1.75 1.75

Manned Flight Bicentenary — A76

Designs: 12c, Curtiss Jenny, 1919 (first flight over Bermuda). 30c, Stinson Pilot Radio, 1930 (first completed US-Bermuda flight). 40c, Cavalier, 1937 (first scheduled passenger flight). $1, USS Los Angeles airship moored to USS Patoka, 1925.

**1983, Oct. 13 Litho. *Perf. 14***

*441* A76 12c multicolored 28 28
*442* A76 30c multicolored 65 65
*443* A76 40c multicolored 90 90
*444* A76 $1 multicolored 1.75 1.75

Newspaper and Postal Services, 200th Anniv. — A77

**1984, Jan. 26 Litho. *Perf. 14***

*445* A77 12c Joseph Stockdale 22 22
*446* A77 30c First Newspaper 55 55
*447* A77 40c Stockdale's Postal Service 70 70
*448* A77 $1 "Lady Hammond", horiz. 1.75 1.75

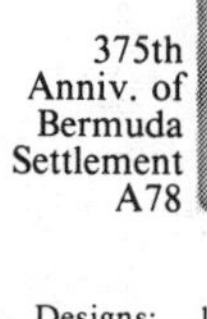

375th Anniv. of Bermuda Settlement A78

Designs: 12c, Thomas Gates, George Somers. 30c, Jamestown, Virginia, US. 40c, Sea Venture shipwreck. $1, Fleet leaving Plymouth, England.

**1984, May 3 Litho. Wmk. 373**

*449* A78 12c multicolored 22 22
*450* A78 30c multicolored 55 55
*451* A78 40c multicolored 70 70
*452* A78 $1 multicolored 1.75 1.75
*a.* Souvenir sheet of 2 2.75 2.75

No. 452a contains Nos. 450, 452; margin shows map.

1984 Summer Olympics A79

**1984, July 19 Litho. *Perf. 14***

*453* A79 12c Swimming, vert. 20 20
*454* A79 30c Track & field 48 48
*455* A79 40c Equestrian, vert. 65 65
*456* A79 $1 Sailing 1.65 1.65

Arms Type of 1983

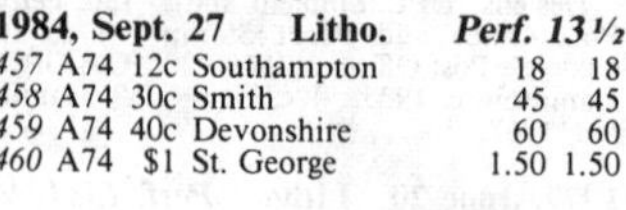

**1984, Sept. 27 Litho. *Perf. 13½***

*457* A74 12c Southampton 18 18
*458* A74 30c Smith 45 45
*459* A74 40c Devonshire 60 60
*460* A74 $1 St. George 1.50 1.50

Architecture, Butter — A80

**1985, Jan. 24 Litho. *Perf. 13½x13***

*461* A80 12c shown 25 25
*462* A80 30c Rooftops 60 60
*463* A80 40c Chimneys 85 85
*464* A80 $1.50 Archway 3.00 3.00

Audubon Birth Bicentenary — A81

**1985, Mar. 21 Wmk. 373 *Perf. 14***

*465* A81 12c Osprey, vert. 22 22
*466* A81 30c Yellow-crowned night heron, vert. 55 55
*467* A81 40c Great egret 75 75
*468* A81 $1.50 Bluebird, vert. 2.75 2.75

**Queen Mother 85th Birthday Issue**

Common Design Type

Designs: 12c, Queen Consort, 1937. 30c, With grandchildren, 80th birthday. 40c, At Clarence House, 83rd birthday. $1.50, Holding Prince Henry. No. 473, In coach with Prince Charles.

***Perf. 14½x14***

**1985, June 7 Wmk. 384**

*469* CD336 12c gray, bl & blk 25 25
*470* CD336 30c multicolored 60 60
*471* CD336 40c multicolored 85 85
*472* CD336 $1.50 multicolored 3.00 3.00

**Souvenir Sheet**

*473* CD336 $1 multicolored 2.00 2.00

No. 473 has multicolored margin continuing design. Size: 92x74mm.

Arms Type of 1983

Coats of Arms: 12c, James Hamilton, 2nd Marquess of Hamilton (1589-1625). 30c, William Paget, 4th Lord Paget (1572-1629). 40c, Robert Rich, 2nd Earl of Warwick (1587-1658). $1.50, Hamilton, 1957.

**1985, Sept. 19 Litho. *Perf. 13½***

*474* A74 12c multicolored 18 18
*475* A74 30c multicolored 45 45
*476* A74 40c multicolored 60 60
*477* A74 $1.50 multicolored 2.25 2.25

Halley's Comet A82

**1985, Nov. 21 Wmk. 384 *Perf. 14½***

*478* A82 15c Bermuda Archipelago 24 24
*479* A82 40c Nuremberg Chronicles, 1493 60 60
*480* A82 50c Peter Apian woodcut, 1532 80 80
*481* A82 $1.50 Painting by Samuel Scott (c. 1702-1772) 2.25 2.25

Shipwrecks — A83

**1986 Wmk. 373, 384 *Perf. 14***

*482* A83 3c Constellation, 1943 5 5
*483* A83 5c Early Riser, 1876 7 7
*484* A83 7c Madiana, 1903 10 10
*485* A83 10c Curlew, 1856 14 14
*486* A83 12c Warwick, 1619 16 16
*487* A83 15c HMS Vixen, 1890 20 20
*488* A83 20c San Pedro, 1594 26 26
*489* A83 25c Alert, 1877 35 35
*490* A83 40c North Carolina, 1880 52 52
*491* A83 50c Mark Antonie, 1777 70 70
*492* A83 60c Mary Celestia, 1864 80 80
*493* A83 $1 L'Herminie, 1839 1.40 1.40

*494* A83 $1.50 Caesar, 1818 2.00 2.00
*495* A83 $2 Lord Amherst, 1778 2.75 2.75
*496* A83 $3 Minerva, 1849 4.00 4.00
*497* A83 $5 Caraquet, 1923 6.75 6.75
*498* A83 $8 HMS Pallas, 1783 11.00 11.00
*Nos. 482-498 (17)* 31.25 31.25

**Queen Elizabeth II 60th Birthday**
Common Design Type

Designs: 15c, Age 3. 40c, With the Earl of Rosebury, Oaks May Meeting, Epsom, 1954. 50c, With Prince Philip, state visit, 1979. 60c, At the British embassy in Paris, state visit, 1972. $1.50, Visiting Crown Agents' offices, 1983.

**1986, Apr. 21 Wmk. 384 *Perf. 14½***
*499* CD337 15c scar, blk & sil 24 24
*500* CD337 40c ultra & multi 65 65
*501* CD337 50c green & multi 80 80
*502* CD337 60c violet & multi 95 95
*503* CD337 $1.50 rose vio & multi 2.50 2.50
*Nos. 499-503 (5)* 5.14 5.14

AMERIPEX '86 — A84

**1986, May 22 *Perf. 14***
*504* A84 15c No. 452a 24 24
*505* A84 40c No. 307 65 65
*506* A84 50c No. 441 80 80
*507* A84 $1 No. 339 1.65 1.65

**Souvenir Sheet**
*508* A84 1.50 Statue of Liberty, S.S. Queen of Bermuda 2.50 2.50

Statue of Liberty, cent.

No. 378 Surcharged
***Perf. 14x14½***
**1986, Dec. 4 Photo. Wmk. 373**
*509* A62 90c on $3 multi 1.50 1.50

Transport Railway, c. 1931-1947 — A85

**Wmk. 373**
**1987, Jan. 22 Litho. *Perf. 14***
*510* A85 15c Front Street, c. 1940 24 24
*511* A85 40c Springfield Trestle 65 65
*512* A85 50c No. 101, Bailey's Bay Sta. 80 80
*513* A85 $1.50 No. 31, ship Prince David 2.50 2.50

Paintings by Winslow Homer (1836-1910) A86

**1987, Apr. 30 *Perf. 14½***
*514* A86 15c Bermuda Settlers, 1901 24 24
*515* A86 30c Bermuda, 1900 48 48
*516* A86 40c Bermuda Landscape, 1901 65 65
*517* A86 50c Inland Water, 1901 80 80
*518* A86 $1.50 Salt Kettle, 1899 2.50 2.50
*Nos. 514-518 (5)* 4.67 4.67

**Booklet Stamps**
*519* A86 40c like 15c 65 65
*520* A86 40c like 30c 65 65
*521* A86 40c like No. 516 65 65
*522* A86 40c like 50c 65 65
*523* A86 40c like $1.50 65 65
*a.* Bklt. pane of 10 (2 each Nos. 519-523) 6.50

Nos. 519-523 printed in strips of 5 within pane. "ER" at lower left.

Intl. Flights Inauguration — A87

**1987, June 18 *Perf. 14***
*524* A87 15c Sikorsky S-42B, 1937 24 24
*525* A87 40c Shorts S-23 Cavalier 65 65
*526* A87 50c S-42B Bermuda Clipper 80 80
*527* A87 $1.50 Cavalier, Bermuda Clipper 2.50 2.50

Bermuda Telephone Company, Cent. — A88

**1987, Oct. 1 Litho. Wmk. 384**
*528* A88 15c Telephone poles on wagon 24 24
*529* A88 40c Operators 65 65
*530* A88 50c Telephones 80 80
*531* A88 $1.50 Satellite, fiber optics, world 2.50 2.50

Horse-drawn Commercial Vehicles, c. 1869-1930 — A89

**1988, Mar. 3 Litho. *Perf. 14***
*532* A89 15c Mail wagon, c. 1869 30 30
*533* A89 40c Open cart, c. 1823 80 80
*534* A89 50c Closed cart, c. 1823 1.00 1.00
*535* A89 $1.50 Two-wheel wagon, c. 1930 3.00 3.00

Old Garden Roses — A90

**1988, Apr. 21 Wmk. 373**
*536* A90 15c Old blush 30 30
*537* A90 30c Anna Olivier 60 60
*538* A90 40c Rosa chinensis semperflorens, vert. 80 80
*539* A90 50c Archduke Charles 1.00 1.00
*540* A90 $1.50 Rosa chinensis viridiflora, vert. 3.00 3.00
*Nos. 536-540 (5)* 5.70 5.70

**Lloyds of London, 300th Anniv.**
Common Design Type

Designs: 18c, Loss of the H.M.S. *Lutine*, 1799. 50c, Cable ship *Sentinel*, horiz. 60c, The *Bermuda*, Hamilton, 1931, horiz. $2, *Valerian*, lost during a hurricane, 1926.

**1988, Oct. 13 Litho. Wmk. 384**
*541* CD341 18c multi 35 35
*542* CD341 50c multi 1.00 1.00
*543* CD341 60c multi 1.20 1.20
*544* CD341 $2 multi 4.00 4.00

Shipwreck Type of 1986
**1988 Litho. Wmk. 384 *Perf. 14***
*545* A83 18c like 7c 35 35
*546* A83 70c like $1.50 1.40 1.40

Issue dates: 18c, Sept. 22; 70c, Oct. 27.

Military Uniforms — A91

Designs: 18c, Devonshire Parish Militia, 1812. 50c, 71st Regiment Highlander, 1831-34. 60c, Cameron Highlander, 1942. $2, Troop of Horse, 1774.

**1988, Nov. 10 Wmk. 373 *Perf.***
*547* A91 18c multi 35 35
*548* A91 50c multi 1.00 1.00
*549* A91 60c multi 1.20 1.20
*550* A91 $2 multi 4.00 4.00

Ferry Service A92



**1989 Litho. Wmk. *Perf.***
*551* A92 18c *Corona* 35 35
*552* A92 50c Rowboat ferry 1.00 1.00
*553* A92 60c *St. George's Ferry* 1.20 1.20
*554* A92 $2 *Laconia* 4.00 4.00

**WAR TAX STAMPS**

No. 42 Overprinted **WAR TAX**

**1918 Wmk. 3 *Perf. 14***
*MR1* A11 1p rose red 38 38

No. 42a Overprinted **WAR TAX**

**1920**
*MR2* A11 1p carmine 38 38

## BOTSWANA

LOCATION — In central South Africa, north of the Republic of South Africa, east of South-West Africa and bounded on the north and east by Angola and Zimbabwe.
GOVT. — Independent republic
AREA — 222,000 sq. mi.
POP. — 941,027 (1981)
CAPITAL — Gaborone

The former Bechuanaland Protectorate became an independent republic September 30, 1966, taking the name Botswana.

100 Cents = 1 Rand
100 Thebe = 1 Pula (1976)

**Catalogue values for all unused stamps in this country are for Never Hinged items.**

National Assembly Building A1

Designs: 5c, Abattoir, Lobatsi. 15c, Dakota plane. 35c, State House, Gaborone.

**Unwmk.**
**1966, Sept. 30 Photo. *Perf. 14***
*1* A1 2½c multi 8 8
*a.* Imperf., pair *200.00*
*2* A1 5c multi 15 15
*3* A1 15c multi 35 35
*4* A1 35c multi 75 75

Establishment of Republic of Botswana.

Bechuanaland Protectorate Nos. 180-193 Overprinted **REPUBLIC OF BOTSWANA**

***Perf. 14x14½, 14½x14***
**1966, Sept. 30 Wmk. 314**
*5* A15 1c multi 5 5
*6* A15 2c multi 6 6
*7* A15 2½c multi 8 8
*8* A15 3½c multi 10 10
*9* A15 5c multi 15 15
*10* A15 7½c multi 25 25
*11* A15 10c multi 30 30
*12* A15 12½c multi 1.50 35
*13* A15 20c gray & brn 1.50 50
*14* A15 25c yel & dk brn 70 70
*15* A15 35c dp org & ultra 90 90
*16* A15 50c lt ol grn & sep 2.25 1.65
*17* A15 1r ocher & blk 4.25 3.50
*18* A15 2r bl & brn 9.25 *11.25*
*Nos. 5-18 (14)* 21.34 *19.84*

European Golden Oriole — A2

Birds: 2c, African hoopoe. 3c, Ground-scraper thrush. 4c, Angolan cordon bleu. 5c, Secretary bird. 7c, Yellow-billed hornbill. 10c, Crimson-breasted shrike. 15c, Malachite kingfisher. 20c, Fish eagle. 25c, Gray lourie. 35c, Scimitar bill. 50c, Knob-billed duck. 1r, Crested barbet. 2r, Didrio cuckoo.

*Perf. 14x14½*

**1967, Jan. 3 Photo. Unwmk.**

| | | | | |
|---|---|---|---|---|
| *19* | A2 | 1c gray & multi | 6 | 5 |
| *20* | A2 | 2c lt bl & multi | 12 | 10 |
| *21* | A2 | 3c yel grn & multi | 20 | 15 |
| *22* | A2 | 4c sal & multi | 32 | 25 |
| *23* | A2 | 5c pink & multi | 35 | 28 |
| *24* | A2 | 7c sl & multi | 50 | 40 |
| *25* | A2 | 10c emer & multi | 65 | 50 |
| *26* | A2 | 15c lt grn & multi | 1.40 | 1.00 |
| *27* | A2 | 20c ultra & multi | 1.60 | 1.25 |
| *28* | A2 | 25c grn & multi | 2.00 | 1.60 |
| *29* | A2 | 35c multi | 2.50 | 2.00 |
| *30* | A2 | 50c dl yel & multi | 3.50 | 3.00 |
| *31* | A2 | 1r dl grn & multi | 7.50 | 6.00 |
| *32* | A2 | 2r org brn & multi | 14.50 | 10.00 |
| | | *Nos. 19-32 (14)* | 35.20 | 26.58 |

University Buildings and Graduates A3

**1967, Apr. 7** *Perf. 14x14½*

| | | | | |
|---|---|---|---|---|
| *33* | A3 | 3c yel, sep & dp bl | 6 | 6 |
| *34* | A3 | 7c bl, sep & dp bl | 15 | 15 |
| *35* | A3 | 15c dl rose, sep & dp bl | 25 | 25 |
| *36* | A3 | 35c lt vio, sep & dp bl | 60 | 60 |

Issued to commemorate the first conferment of degrees by the University of Botswana, Lesotho and Swaziland at Roma, Lesotho.

Chobe Bush Bucks A4

Designs: 7c, Sable antelopes. 35c, Fishing on the Chobe River.

**1967, Oct. 2 Photo.** *Perf. 14*

| | | | | |
|---|---|---|---|---|
| *37* | A4 | 3c multi | 10 | 10 |
| *38* | A4 | 7c multi | 22 | 22 |
| *39* | A4 | 35c multi | 1.10 | 1.10 |

Publicity for Chobe Game Reserve.

Human Rights Flame and Arms of Botswana A5

Design elements rearranged on 15c, 25c.

**1968, Apr. 8 Litho.** *Perf. 13½x13*

| | | | | |
|---|---|---|---|---|
| *40* | A5 | 3c brn red & multi | 8 | 6 |
| *41* | A5 | 15c emer & multi | 40 | 35 |
| *42* | A5 | 25c yel & multi | 65 | 50 |

International Human Rights Year.

A little time given to the study of the arrangement of the Scott Catalogue can make it easier to use effectively.

Rock Painting A6

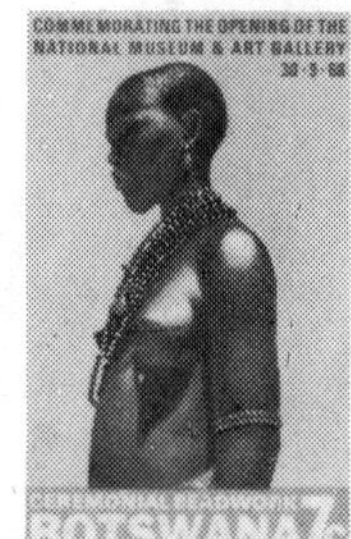


Girl Wearing Ceremonial Beads — A7

Designs: 10c, Baobab Trees, by Thomas Baines (34x25mm.). 15c, National Museum and Art Gallery (71½x19mm.).

*Perf. 13x13½ (3c, 10c); Perf. 12½ (7c); Perf. 12½x13 (15c)*

**1968, Sept. 30 Litho.**

| | | | | |
|---|---|---|---|---|
| *43* | A6 | 3c multi | 8 | 8 |
| *44* | A7 | 7c multi | 20 | 20 |
| *45* | A6 | 10c multi | 35 | 35 |
| *46* | A6 | 15c multi | 65 | 65 |
| *a.* | | Souv. sheet of 4 | 2.25 | 3.00 |

Issued to commemorate the opening of the National Museum and Art Gallery, Gaborone, Sept. 30, 1968. No. 46a contains Nos. 43-46 with perf. 13½. Black marginal inscription. Size: 133x82mm.

African Nativity Scene A8

**1968, Nov. 11 Unwmk.** *Perf. 13x14*

| | | | | |
|---|---|---|---|---|
| *47* | A8 | 1c car & multi | 5 | 5 |
| *48* | A8 | 2c brn & multi | 8 | 6 |
| *49* | A8 | 5c grn & multi | 20 | 15 |
| *50* | A8 | 25c dp vio & multi | 1.00 | 90 |

Christmas 1968.

Boy Scout, Botswana Scout Emblem and Lion — A9

Designs (Botswana Boy Scout Emblem, Lion and): 15c, Boy Scouts cooking (vert.). 25c, Boy Scouts around campfire.

**1969, Aug. 21 Litho.** *Perf. 13½*

| | | | | |
|---|---|---|---|---|
| *51* | A9 | 3c emer & multi | 15 | 15 |
| *52* | A9 | 15c lt brn & multi | 90 | 90 |
| *53* | A9 | 25c dk brn & multi | 1.65 | 1.65 |

Issued to publicize the 22nd World Scouting Conference, Helsinki, Finland, Aug. 21-27.

Mother, Child and Star of Bethlehem A10

Diamond Treatment Plant, Orapa A11

**1969, Nov. 6** *Perf. 14½x14*

| | | | | |
|---|---|---|---|---|
| *54* | A10 | 1c dk brn & lt bl | 5 | 5 |
| *55* | A10 | 2c dk brn & ap grn | 8 | 8 |
| *56* | A10 | 4c dk brn & dl yel | 18 | 18 |
| *57* | A10 | 35c dk brn & vio bl | 1.10 | 1.10 |
| *a.* | | Souvenir sheet of 4 | 2.00 | 1.40 |

Christmas 1969.

No. 57a contains one each of Nos. 54-57, perf. 14½. Multicolored marginal inscriptions. Size: 85x127mm.

*Perf. 14½x14, 14x14½*

**1970, Mar. 23 Litho.**

Designs: 7c, Copper and nickel mining, Selebi-Pikwe. 10c, Copper and nickel mining and metal bars, Selebi-Pikwe (horiz.). 35c, Orapa diamond mine and diamonds (horiz.).

| | | | | |
|---|---|---|---|---|
| *58* | A11 | 3c multi | 15 | 15 |
| *59* | A11 | 7c multi | 30 | 30 |
| *60* | A11 | 10c multi | 45 | 45 |
| *61* | A11 | 35c multi | 1.75 | 1.75 |

Botswana development program.

Mr. Micawber and Charles Dickens A12

Designs (Charles Dickens and): 7c, Scrooge. 15c, Fagin. 25c, Bill Sykes.

**1970, July 7 Litho.** *Perf. 11*

| | | | | |
|---|---|---|---|---|
| *62* | A12 | 3c gray grn & multi | 15 | 15 |
| *63* | A12 | 7c multi | 30 | 30 |
| *64* | A12 | 15c brn & multi | 60 | 60 |
| *65* | A12 | 25c dp vio & multi | 1.00 | 1.00 |
| *a.* | | Souvenir sheet of 4 | 3.50 | 3.50 |

Issued to commemorate the centenary of the death of Charles Dickens (1812-1870), English novelist. No. 65a contains one each of Nos. 62-65 with scenes from novels in margin. Size: 112x80mm.

U.N. Headquarters, Emblem — A13

**1970, Oct. 24 Litho.** *Perf. 11*

| | | | | |
|---|---|---|---|---|
| *66* | A13 | 15c ultra, red & sil | 60 | 60 |

United Nations' 25th anniversary.

Toy Crocodile A14

Toys: 2c, Giraffe. 7c, Elephant. 25c, Rhinoceros.

**1970, Nov. 3 Litho.** *Perf. 14*

| | | | | |
|---|---|---|---|---|
| *67* | A14 | 1c yel & multi | 5 | 5 |
| *68* | A14 | 2c yel grn & multi | 6 | 6 |
| *69* | A14 | 7c ultra & multi | 25 | 25 |
| *70* | A14 | 25c org & multi | 1.00 | 1.00 |
| *a.* | | Souvenir sheet of 4 | 2.75 | 2.75 |

Christmas 1970.

No. 70a contains one each of Nos. 67-70 with multicolored margin. Size: 127x89mm.

Sorghum A15

Important Crops: 7c, Millet. 10c, Corn. 35c, Peanuts.

**1971, Apr. 6 Litho.** *Perf. 14*

| | | | | |
|---|---|---|---|---|
| *71* | A15 | 3c multi | 8 | 8 |
| *72* | A15 | 7c multi | 20 | 20 |
| *73* | A15 | 10c multi | 25 | 25 |
| *74* | A15 | 35c multi | 1.00 | 1.00 |

Ox Head and Botswana Map — A16

King Bringing Gift — A17

Designs (Map of Botswana and): 4c, Cogwheels and waves. 7c, Zebra rampant. 10c, Tusk and corn. 20c, Coat of arms of Botswana.

**1971, Sept. 30** *Perf. 14½x14*

| | | | | |
|---|---|---|---|---|
| *75* | A16 | 3c yel grn, blk & brn | 10 | 10 |
| *76* | A16 | 4c lt bl, blk & bl | 15 | 15 |
| *77* | A16 | 7c org & blk | 20 | 20 |
| *78* | A16 | 10c yel & multi | 35 | 35 |
| *79* | A16 | 20c bl & multi | 75 | 75 |
| | | *Nos. 75-79 (5)* | 1.55 | 1.55 |

5th anniversary of independence.

**1971, Nov. 11** *Perf. 14*

Designs: 2c, King bringing gift. 7c, Kneeling King with gift. 20c, Three Kings and star.

| | | | | |
|---|---|---|---|---|
| *80* | A17 | 2c brt rose & multi | 8 | 8 |
| *81* | A17 | 3c lt bl & multi | 12 | 12 |
| *82* | A17 | 7c brt pink & multi | 25 | 25 |
| *83* | A17 | 20c vio bl & multi | 1.00 | 1.00 |
| *a.* | | Souvenir sheet of 4 | 2.25 | 2.25 |

Christmas 1971. No. 83a contains one each of Nos. 80-83. Light blue margin with commemorative inscriptions. Size: 85½x128mm.

Constellation Orion — A18

Night Sky over Botswana: 7c, Scorpio. 10c, Centaur. 20c, Southern Cross.

**1972, Apr. 24 Litho.** *Perf. 14*

| | | | | |
|---|---|---|---|---|
| *84* | A18 | 3c dp org, bl grn & blk | 25 | 25 |
| *85* | A18 | 7c org, bl & blk | 50 | 50 |
| *86* | A18 | 10c org, grn & blk | 75 | 75 |
| *87* | A18 | 20c emer, vio bl & blk | 1.50 | 1.50 |

Gubulawayo Cancel and Map of Trail — A19

Cross, Map of Botswana, Bells — A20

Sections of Mafeking-Gubulawayo Trail and: 4c, Bechuanaland Protectorate No. 65. 7c, Mail runners. 20c, Mafeking 638 killer cancellation.

**1972, Aug. 21** ***Perf. 13½x13***

| | | | | |
|---|---|---|---|---|
| *88* | A19 | 3c cr & multi | 15 | 15 |
| *89* | A19 | 4c cr & multi | 20 | 20 |
| *90* | A19 | 7c cr & multi | 50 | 50 |
| *91* | A19 | 20c cr & multi | 1.60 | 1.60 |
| *a.* | | Souv. sheet of 4 | 7.00 | 7.00 |

84th anniversary of Mafeking to Gubulawayo runner post. No. 91a contains one each of Nos. 88-91, arranged vertically to show map of trail. 638 oval killer cancellations of 1888 in margin. Size: 83x165mm.

**1972, Nov. 6** **Litho.** ***Perf. 14***

Designs (Cross, Map of Botswana and): 3c, Candle. 7c, Christmas tree. 20c, Star and holly.

| | | | | |
|---|---|---|---|---|
| *92* | A20 | 2c yel & multi | 8 | 8 |
| *93* | A20 | 3c pale lil & multi | 12 | 12 |
| *94* | A20 | 7c yel grn & multi | 30 | 30 |
| *95* | A20 | 20c pink & multi | 75 | 75 |
| *a.* | | Souvenir sheet of 4 | 2.25 | 2.25 |

Christmas 1972. No. 95a contains one each of Nos. 92-95. Pale lilac margin with black inscription and multicolored design. Size: 95x119mm.

Chariot of the Sun, Trundholm, Denmark — A21

Designs (WMO Emblem and): 3c, Thor, Norse thunder god (vert.). 7c, Ymir, Icelandic frost giant (vert.). 20c, Odin on 8-legged horse Sleipnir.

**1973, Mar. 23** **Litho.** ***Perf. 14***

| | | | | |
|---|---|---|---|---|
| *96* | A21 | 3c org & multi | 12 | 12 |
| *97* | A21 | 4c yel & multi | 18 | 18 |
| *98* | A21 | 7c ultra & multi | 35 | 35 |
| *99* | A21 | 20c gold & multi | 1.00 | 1.00 |

Centenary of international meteorological cooperation.

Livingstone and Boat on Lake Ngwami — A22

Design: 20c, Livingstone and his meeting with Henry Stanley.

**1973, Sept. 10** **Litho.** ***Perf. 13½x14***

| | | | | |
|---|---|---|---|---|
| *100* | A22 | 3c gray & multi | 12 | 12 |
| *101* | A22 | 20c yel grn & multi | 1.15 | 1.15 |

Centenary of the death of Dr. David Livingstone (1813-1873), medical missionary and explorer.

Shepherd and Flock A23

Designs: 3c, Ass and foal, African huts (vert.). 7c, African mother, child and star (vert.). 20c, Tribal meeting (kgotla), symbolic of Wise Men.

**1973, Nov. 12** **Litho.** ***Perf. 14½***

| | | | | |
|---|---|---|---|---|
| *102* | A23 | 3c multi | 10 | 10 |
| *103* | A23 | 4c multi | 15 | 15 |
| *104* | A23 | 7c multi | 30 | 30 |
| *105* | A23 | 20c multi | 90 | 90 |

Christmas 1973.

Gaborone Campus, Botswana A24

Designs: 7c, Kwaluseni Campus, Swaziland. 20c, Roma Campus, Lesotho. 35c, Map and flags of Botswana, Swaziland and Lesotho.

**1974, May 8** **Litho.** ***Perf. 14***

| | | | | |
|---|---|---|---|---|
| *106* | A24 | 3c lt bl & multi | 12 | 12 |
| *107* | A24 | 7c yel grn & multi | 30 | 30 |
| *108* | A24 | 20c yel grn & multi | 75 | 75 |
| *109* | A24 | 35c brt bl & multi | 1.10 | 1.10 |

10th anniversary of the University of Botswana, Lesotho and Swaziland.

UPU Emblem, Mail Vehicles — A25

Designs (UPU Emblem and): 3c, Post Office, Palapye, c. 1889. 7c, Bechuanaland police camel post, 1900. 20c, 1920 and 1974 planes.

**1974, May 22** **Litho.** ***Perf. 13½x14***

| | | | | |
|---|---|---|---|---|
| *110* | A25 | 2c car & multi | 15 | 12 |
| *111* | A25 | 3c grn & multi | 25 | 20 |
| *112* | A25 | 7c brn & multi | 65 | 50 |
| *113* | A25 | 20c bl & multi | 2.00 | 1.50 |

Centenary of the Universal Postal Union.

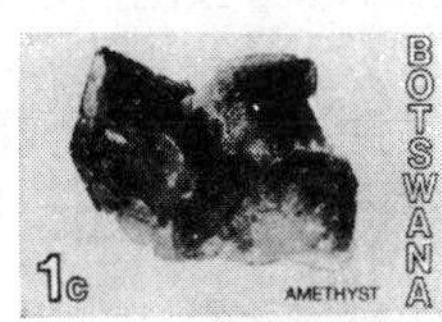


Amethyst A26

Designs: Minerals, precious and semiprecious stones.

**1974, July 1** **Photo.** ***Perf. 14x13***

| | | | | |
|---|---|---|---|---|
| *114* | A26 | 1c *shown* | 6 | 6 |
| *115* | A26 | 2c *Agate* | 12 | 12 |
| *116* | A26 | 3c *Quartz* | 15 | 15 |
| *117* | A26 | 4c *Niccolite* | 25 | 25 |
| *118* | A26 | 5c *Moss agate* | 30 | 30 |
| *119* | A26 | 7c *Agate* | 45 | 45 |
| *120* | A26 | 10c *Stilbite* | 60 | 60 |
| *121* | A26 | 15c *Moshaneng banded marble* | 90 | 90 |
| *122* | A26 | 20c *Gem diamonds* | 1.25 | 1.25 |
| *123* | A26 | 25c *Chrysotile* | 1.50 | 1.50 |
| *124* | A26 | 35c *Jasper* | 2.00 | 2.00 |
| *125* | A26 | 50c *Moss quartz* | 2.75 | 2.75 |
| *126* | A26 | 1r *Citrine* | 6.00 | 6.00 |
| *127* | A26 | 2r *Chalcopyrite* | 12.50 | 12.50 |
| | | *Nos. 114-127 (14)* | 28.83 | 28.83 |

Stapelia Variegata — A27

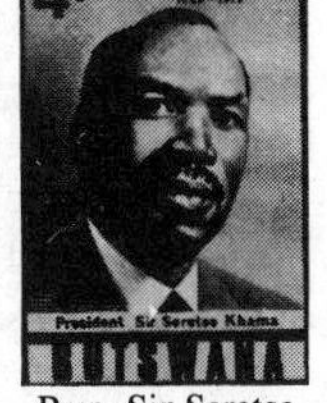


Pres. Sir Seretse Khama — A28

Flowers of Botswana: 7c, Hibiscus lunarifolius. 15c, Ceratotheca triloba. 20c, Nerine laticoma.

**1974, Nov. 4** **Litho.** ***Perf. 14***

| | | | | |
|---|---|---|---|---|
| *128* | A27 | 2c multi | 12 | 12 |
| *129* | A27 | 7c multi | 40 | 40 |
| *130* | A27 | 15c multi | 90 | 90 |
| *131* | A27 | 20c multi | 1.25 | 1.25 |
| *a.* | | Souvenir sheet of 4 | 2.50 | 2.50 |

No. 131a contains one each of Nos. 128-131; blue margin with black and white inscription. Size: 85x131mm.

**1975, Mar. 24** **Photo.** ***Perf. 13½x13***

| | | | | |
|---|---|---|---|---|
| *132* | A28 | 4c ol & multi | 12 | 12 |
| *133* | A28 | 10c yel & multi | 30 | 30 |
| *134* | A28 | 20c ultra & multi | 60 | 60 |
| *135* | A28 | 35c brn & multi | 1.00 | 1.00 |
| *a.* | | Souvenir sheet of 4 | 2.00 | 2.00 |

10th anniversary of self-government. No. 135a contains one each of Nos. 132-135; black and multicolored margin with ornaments and coat of arms. Size: 93x130mm.

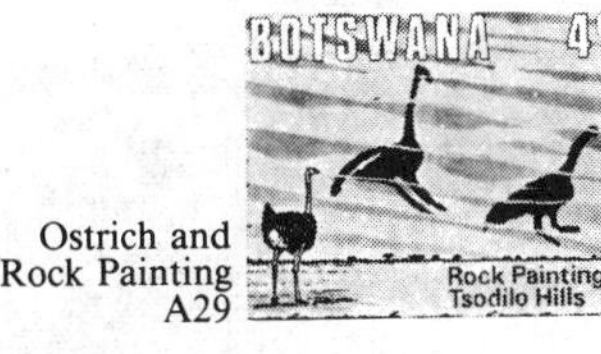


Ostrich and Rock Painting A29

Paintings and Animals: 10c, Rhinoceros. 25c, Hyena. 35c, Scorpion.

**1975, June 23** **Litho.** ***Perf. 14x14½***

| | | | | |
|---|---|---|---|---|
| *136* | A29 | 4c yel grn & multi | 25 | 25 |
| *137* | A29 | 10c buff & multi | 70 | 70 |
| *138* | A29 | 25c bl & multi | 1.60 | 1.60 |
| *139* | A29 | 35c lil & multi | 2.50 | 2.50 |
| *a.* | | Souvenir sheet of 4 | 6.50 | 6.50 |

Rock paintings from Tsodilo Hills. No. 139a contains one each of Nos. 136-139; black marginal drawings of Tsodilo Hills, maps and bushmen. Size: 148x150mm.

Map of British Bechuanaland A30

Chiefs Sebele, Bathoen and Khama A31

Design: 10c, Khama the Great and antelope.

***Perf. 14½x14, 14x14½***

**1975, Oct. 31** **Litho.**

| | | | | |
|---|---|---|---|---|
| *140* | A30 | 6c buff & multi | 35 | 35 |
| *141* | A30 | 10c rose & multi | 60 | 60 |
| *142* | A31 | 25c lt grn & multi | 1.60 | 1.60 |

Establishment of Protectorate, 90th anniversary (6c); Khama the Great (1828-1923), centenary of his accession as chief (10c); visit of the chiefs of the Bakwena, Bangwaketse and Bamangwato tribes to London, 80th anniversary (25c).

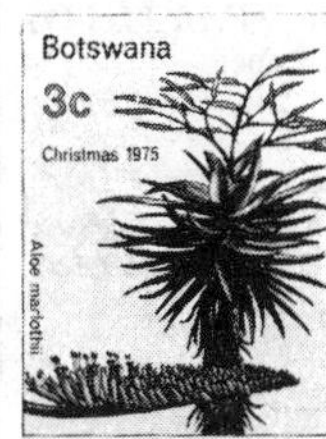


Aloe Marlothii — A32

Designs: 10c, Aloe lutescens. 15c, Aloe zebrina. 25c, Aloe littoralis.

**1975, Nov. 3** **Litho.** ***Perf. 14½x14***

| | | | | |
|---|---|---|---|---|
| *143* | A32 | 3c multi | 30 | 30 |
| *144* | A32 | 10c multi | 80 | 80 |
| *145* | A32 | 15c multi | 1.10 | 1.10 |
| *146* | A32 | 25c multi | 2.25 | 2.25 |

Christmas 1975.

Drum A33

Traditional Musical Instruments: 10c, Hand piano. 15c, Segankuru (violin). 25c, Kudu signal horn.

**1976, Mar. 1** **Litho.** ***Perf. 14***

| | | | | |
|---|---|---|---|---|
| *147* | A33 | 4c yel & multi | 15 | 15 |
| *148* | A33 | 10c lil & multi | 40 | 40 |
| *149* | A33 | 15c dl yel & multi | 65 | 65 |
| *150* | A33 | 25c lt bl & multi | 1.00 | 1.00 |

1-pula Bank Note with Seretse Khama A34

Designs (Reverse of Bank Notes): 10c, Farm workers. 15c, Antelopes. 25c, National Assembly building.

**1976, June 28** **Litho.** ***Perf. 14***

| | | | | |
|---|---|---|---|---|
| *151* | A34 | 4c rose & multi | 12 | 12 |
| *152* | A34 | 10c brt grn & multi | 35 | 35 |
| *153* | A34 | 15c yel grn & multi | 50 | 50 |
| *154* | A34 | 25c bl & multi | 90 | 1.10 |
| *a.* | | Souvenir sheet of 4 | 2.50 | 2.50 |

First national currency. No. 154a contains one each of Nos. 151-154; blue margin with black inscription. Size: 162x107mm.

Nos. 114-127 Surcharged in Black or Gold

**1976, Aug. 23** **Photo.** ***Perf. 14x13***

| | | | | |
|---|---|---|---|---|
| *155* | A26 | 1t on 1c multi | 5 | 5 |
| *156* | A26 | 2t on 2c multi | 8 | 7 |
| *157* | A26 | 3t on 3c multi (G) | 15 | 14 |
| *158* | A26 | 4t on 4c multi | 18 | 16 |
| *159* | A26 | 5t on 5c multi | 20 | 18 |
| *160* | A26 | 7t on 7c multi | 28 | 25 |
| *161* | A26 | 10t on 10c multi | 35 | 32 |
| *162* | A26 | 15t on 15c multi (G) | 60 | 55 |
| *163* | A26 | 20t on 20c multi | 80 | 75 |
| *164* | A26 | 25t on 25c multi | 1.10 | 90 |
| *165* | A26 | 35t on 35c multi | 1.25 | 1.10 |
| *166* | A26 | 50t on 50c multi | 1.75 | 1.50 |
| *167* | A26 | 1p on 1r multi | 3.50 | 3.25 |
| *168* | A26 | 2p on 2r multi (G) | 6.75 | 6.25 |
| | | *Nos. 155-168 (14)* | 17.04 | 15.47 |

Cattle Industry A35

Designs: 10t, Antelope, tourism (vert.). 15t, Schoolhouse and children, education. 25t, Rural weaving (vert.). 35t, Mining industry (vert.).

**1976, Sept. 30 Litho. *Perf. 14x14½***
**Textured Paper**

| | | | | |
|---|---|---|---|---|
| *169* | A35 | 4t multi | 10 | 10 |
| *170* | A35 | 10t multi | 25 | 25 |
| *171* | A35 | 15t multi | 30 | 30 |
| *172* | A35 | 25t multi | 50 | 50 |
| *173* | A35 | 35t multi | 75 | 75 |
| | | *Nos. 169-173 (5)* | 1.90 | 1.90 |

10th anniversary of independence.

Colophospermum Mopane — A36

Trees: 4t, Baikiaea plurijuga. 10t, Sterculia rogersii. 25t, Acacia nilotica. 40t, Kigelia africana.

**1976, Nov. 1 Litho. *Perf. 13***

| | | | | |
|---|---|---|---|---|
| *174* | A36 | 3t multi | 10 | 10 |
| *175* | A36 | 4t multi | 12 | 12 |
| *176* | A36 | 10t multi | 35 | 35 |
| *177* | A36 | 25t multi | 75 | 75 |
| *178* | A36 | 40t multi | 1.25 | 1.25 |
| | | *Nos. 174-178 (5)* | 2.57 | 2.57 |

Christmas 1976.

Pres. Seretse Khama and Elizabeth II — A37

Designs: 25t, Coronation coach in procession. 40t, Recognition scene.

**1977, Feb. 7 Litho. *Perf. 12***

| | | | | |
|---|---|---|---|---|
| *179* | A37 | 4t multi | 12 | 12 |
| *180* | A37 | 25t multi | 60 | 60 |
| *181* | A37 | 40t multi | 1.00 | 1.00 |

25th. anniversary of the reign of Queen Elizabeth II.

Clawless Otter A38

Designs (Wildlife Fund Emblem and): 4t, Serval. 10t, Bat-eared foxes. 25t, Pangolins. 40t, Brown hyena.

**1977, June 6 Litho. *Perf. 14***

| | | | | |
|---|---|---|---|---|
| *182* | A38 | 3t multi | 20 | 15 |
| *183* | A38 | 4t multi | 25 | 18 |
| *184* | A38 | 10t multi | 50 | 40 |
| *185* | A38 | 25t multi | 1.25 | 1.00 |
| *186* | A38 | 40t multi | 2.50 | 1.75 |
| | | *Nos. 182-186 (5)* | 4.70 | 3.48 |

Endangered wildlife.

Khama Memorial A39

Designs: 4t, Cwihaba Caves. 15t, Green's (expedition) tree. 20t, Mmajojo ruins. 25t, Ancient morabaraba board. 35t, Matsieng's footprints.

**1977, Aug. 22 Litho. *Perf. 14***

| | | | | |
|---|---|---|---|---|
| *187* | A39 | 4t multi | 12 | 12 |
| *188* | A39 | 5t multi | 20 | 20 |
| *189* | A39 | 15t multi | 50 | 50 |
| *190* | A39 | 20t multi | 65 | 65 |
| *191* | A39 | 25t multi | 90 | 90 |
| *192* | A39 | 35t multi | 1.25 | 1.25 |
| *a.* | | Souvenir sheet of 6 | 4.00 | *5.00* |
| | | *Nos. 187-192 (6)* | 3.62 | 3.62 |

Historical sites and national monuments. No. 192a contains one each of Nos. 187-192; multicolored margin shows landscape. Size: 154x105mm.

Hypoxis Nitida — A40

Lilies: 5t, Haemanthus magnificus. 10t, Boophane disticha. 25t, Vellozia retinervis. 40t, Ammocharis coranica.

**1977, Oct. 31 Litho. *Perf. 14***

| | | | | |
|---|---|---|---|---|
| *193* | A40 | 3t sep & multi | 12 | 12 |
| *194* | A40 | 5t gray & multi | 18 | 18 |
| *195* | A40 | 10t multi | 35 | 35 |
| *196* | A40 | 25t multi | 1.00 | 1.00 |
| *197* | A40 | 40t multi | 1.75 | 1.75 |
| | | *Nos. 193-197 (5)* | 3.40 | 3.40 |

Christmas 1977.

Black Korhaan — A41

Designs: Birds.

**1978, July 3 Photo. *Perf. 14***

| | | | | |
|---|---|---|---|---|
| *198* | A41 | 1t *shown* | 5 | 5 |
| *199* | A41 | 2t *Marabou storks* | 5 | 5 |
| *200* | A41 | 3t *Red-billed hoopoe* | 8 | 8 |
| *201* | A41 | 4t *Carmine bee-eaters* | 10 | 10 |
| *202* | A41 | 5t *African jacana* | 12 | 12 |
| *203* | A41 | 7t *Paradise flycatcher* | 16 | 16 |
| *204* | A41 | 10t *Bennett's woodpecker* | 25 | 25 |
| *205* | A41 | 15t *Red bishop* | 38 | 38 |
| *206* | A41 | 20t *Crowned plovers* | 50 | 50 |
| *207* | A41 | 25t *Giant kingfishers* | 62 | 62 |
| *208* | A41 | 30t *White-faced ducks* | 75 | 75 |
| *209* | A41 | 35t *Green-backed heron* | 88 | 88 |
| *210* | A41 | 45t *Black-headed herons* | 1.12 | 1.12 |
| *211* | A41 | 50t *Spotted eagle owl* | 1.25 | 1.25 |
| *212* | A41 | 1p *Gabar goshawk* | 2.50 | 2.50 |
| *213* | A41 | 2p *Martial eagle* | 5.00 | 5.00 |
| *214* | A41 | 5p *Saddlebill storks* | 10.00 | 10.00 |
| | | *Nos. 198-214 (17)* | 23.81 | 23.81 |

Tawana Making Kaross (garment) A42

Designs: 5t, Map of Okavango Delta. 15t, Bushman collecting roots. 20t, Herero woman milking cow. 25t, Yei pulling mokoro (boat). 35t, Mbukushu fishing.

**1978, Sept. 11 Litho. *Perf. 14***
**Textured Paper**

| | | | | |
|---|---|---|---|---|
| *215* | A42 | 4t multi | 10 | 10 |
| *216* | A42 | 5t multi | 12 | 12 |
| *217* | A42 | 15t multi | 25 | 25 |
| *218* | A42 | 20t multi | 40 | 40 |
| *219* | A42 | 25t multi | 50 | 50 |
| *220* | A42 | 35t multi | 65 | 65 |
| *a.* | | Souvenir sheet of 6 | 2.50 | *3.00* |
| | | *Nos. 215-220 (6)* | 2.02 | 2.02 |

People of the Okavango Delta. No. 220a contains Nos. 215-220; multicolored margin shows mokoro. Size: 150x98mm.

Caralluma Lutea — A43

Boy at Sip Well — A44

Flowers: 10t, Hoodia lugardii. 15t, Ipomoea transvaalensis. 25t, Ansellia gigantea.

**1978, Nov. 6**

| | | | | |
|---|---|---|---|---|
| *221* | A43 | 5t multi | 20 | 20 |
| *222* | A43 | 10t multi | 40 | 40 |
| *223* | A43 | 15t multi | 60 | 60 |
| *224* | A43 | 25t multi | 1.00 | 1.00 |

Christmas 1978.

**1979, Feb. 12 Litho. *Perf. 14***

Water Development: 5t, Watering pit. 10t, Hand-dug well and goats. 25t, Windmill, well and cattle. 40t, Modern drilling rig.

| | | | | |
|---|---|---|---|---|
| *225* | A44 | 3t multi | 6 | 6 |
| *226* | A44 | 5t multi | 8 | 8 |
| *227* | A44 | 10t multi | 15 | 15 |
| *228* | A44 | 25t multi | 40 | 40 |
| *229* | A44 | 40t multi | 65 | 65 |
| | | *Nos. 225-229 (5)* | 1.34 | 1.34 |

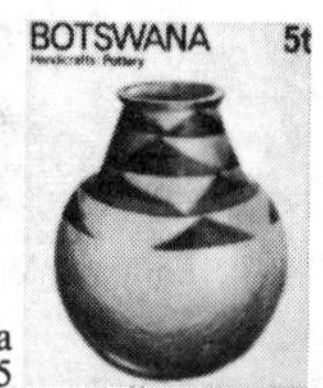


Botswana Pot — A45

Handicrafts: 10t, Clay buffalo. 25t, Woven covered basket. 40t, Beaded bag.

**1979, June 4 Litho. *Perf. 14***

| | | | | |
|---|---|---|---|---|
| *230* | A45 | 5t multi | 10 | 10 |
| *231* | A45 | 10t multi | 20 | 20 |
| *232* | A45 | 25t multi | 50 | 50 |
| *233* | A45 | 40t multi | 80 | 80 |
| *a.* | | Souvenir sheet of 4 | 1.75 | 1.75 |

No. 233a contains Nos. 230-233; multicolored margin repeats stamp designs. Size: 120x95mm.

Bechuanaland No 6, Rowland Hill — A46

Rowland Hill and: 25t, Bechuanaland Protectorate No. 107. 45t, Botswana No. 20.

**1979, Aug. 27 Litho. *Perf. 13½***

| | | | | |
|---|---|---|---|---|
| *234* | A46 | 5t rose & blk | 8 | 8 |
| *235* | A46 | 25t multi | 35 | 35 |
| *236* | A46 | 45t multi | 60 | 60 |

Sir Rowland Hill (1795-1879), originator of penny postage.

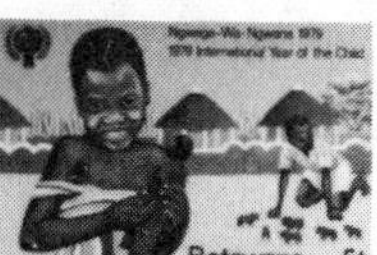


Children Playing A47

Design: 10t, Child playing with rag doll, and IYC emblem (vert.).

**1979, Sept. 24 *Perf. 14***

| | | | | |
|---|---|---|---|---|
| *237* | A47 | 5t multi | 12 | 12 |
| *238* | A47 | 10t multi | 25 | 25 |

International Year of the Child.

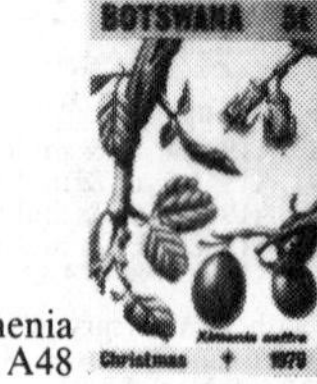


Ximenia Caffra — A48

Designs: 10t, Sclerocarya caffra. 15t, Hexalobus monopetalus. 25t, Ficus soldanella.

**1979, Nov. 12 Litho. *Perf. 14***

| | | | | |
|---|---|---|---|---|
| *239* | A48 | 5t multi | 10 | 10 |
| *240* | A48 | 10t multi | 20 | 20 |
| *241* | A48 | 15t multi | 30 | 30 |
| *242* | A48 | 25t multi | 50 | 50 |

Christmas 1979.

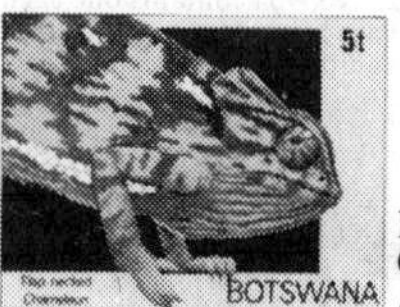


Flap-Necked Chameleon A49

**1980, Mar. 3 Litho. *Perf. 14***

| | | | | |
|---|---|---|---|---|
| *243* | A49 | 5t *shown* | 8 | 8 |
| *244* | A49 | 10t *Leopard tortoise* | 18 | 18 |
| *245* | A49 | 25t *Puff adder* | 45 | 45 |
| *246* | A49 | 40t *White-throated monitor* | 75 | 75 |

Rock Breaking (Early Mining) — A50

**1980, July 7 Litho. *Perf. 13½x14***

| | | | | |
|---|---|---|---|---|
| *247* | A50 | 5t *shown* | 8 | 8 |
| *248* | A50 | 10t *Ore hoisting* | 18 | 18 |
| *249* | A50 | 15t *Ore transport* | 25 | 25 |
| *250* | A50 | 20t *Ore crushing* | 35 | 35 |
| *251* | A50 | 25t *Smelting* | 40 | 40 |
| *252* | A50 | 35t *Tools, products* | 60 | 60 |
| | | *Nos. 247-252 (6)* | 1.86 | 1.86 |

Chiwele and the Giant — A51

Folktales: 10t, Kgori Is Not Deceived. 30t, Nyambi's Wife and Crocodile. 45t, Clever Hare (horiz.).

***Perf. 14, 14½ (10t, 30t)***

**1980, Sept. 8**

| | | | | |
|---|---|---|---|---|
| *253* | A51 | 5t multi | 10 | 10 |

**Size: 28x36mm.**

| | | | | |
|---|---|---|---|---|
| *254* | A51 | 10t multi | 20 | 20 |
| *255* | A51 | 30t multi | 60 | 60 |

**Size: 44x26mm.**

| | | | | |
|---|---|---|---|---|
| *256* | A51 | 45t multi | 90 | 90 |

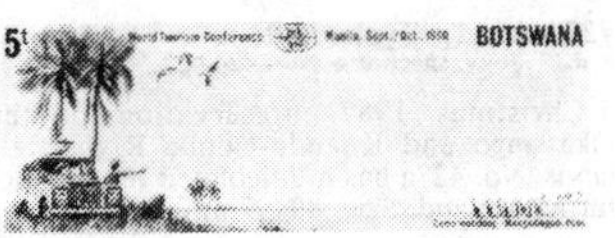

Game Watching — A52

**1980, Oct. 6 Litho. *Perf. 14***

| | | |
|---|---|---|
| *257* A52 5t multi | 20 | 20 |

World Tourism Conference, Manila, Sept. 27.

Acacia Gerrardii — A53

Christmas 1980: Flowering Trees.

**1980, Nov. 3 Litho. *Perf. 14***

| | | |
|---|---|---|
| *258* A53 5t *shown* | 8 | 8 |
| *259* A53 10t *Acacia nilotica* | 15 | 15 |
| *260* A53 25t *Acacia erubescens* | 35 | 35 |
| *261* A53 40t *Dichrostachys cinerea* | 50 | 50 |

Heinrich von Stephan, Bechuanaland Protectorate No. 150, Botswana No. 111 — A55

Design: 20t, Von Stephan, Bechuanaland Protectorate No. 151, Botswana No. 112.

**Wmk. 373**

**1981, Jan. 7 Litho. *Perf. 14***

| | | |
|---|---|---|
| *266* A55 6t multi | 8 | 8 |
| *267* A55 20t multi | 25 | 25 |

Von Stephan (1831-97), founder of UPU.

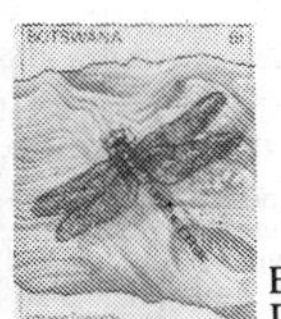
Emperor Dragonfly — A56

**1981, Feb. 23 Litho. *Perf. 14***

| | | |
|---|---|---|
| *268* A56 6t shown | 8 | 8 |
| *269* A56 7t Praying mantis | 10 | 10 |
| *270* A56 10t Elegant grasshopper | 15 | 15 |
| *271* A56 20t Dung beetle | 25 | 25 |
| *272* A56 30t Citrus swallowtail butterfly | 40 | 40 |
| *273* A56 45t Mopane worm | 60 | 60 |
| *a.* Souv. sheet of 6, Nos. 268-273 | 2.00 | 2.00 |
| *Nos. 268-273 (6)* | 1.58 | 1.58 |

No. 273a has brown and black margin continuing the design (log). Size: 181x89mm.

Blind Basket Weaver A57

**1981, Apr. 4 Litho. *Perf. 14***

| | | |
|---|---|---|
| *274* A57 6t Seamstress | 10 | 10 |
| *275* A57 20t shown | 30 | 30 |
| *276* A57 30t Carpenter | 40 | 40 |

International Year of the Disabled.

Woman Reading Letter (Literacy Campaign) — A58

**1981, June 8**

| | | |
|---|---|---|
| *277* A58 6t shown | 8 | 8 |
| *278* A58 7t Man sending telegram | 10 | 10 |
| *279* A58 20t Boy, newspaper | 25 | 25 |
| *280* A58 30t Father and daughter reading | 40 | 40 |

Pres. Seretse Khama and Flag — A59

First death anniv. of Pres. Khama: Portrait and local buildings.

**1981, July 13**

| | | |
|---|---|---|
| *281* A59 6t multi | 10 | 10 |
| *282* A59 10t multi | 15 | 15 |
| *283* A59 30t multi | 40 | 40 |
| *284* A59 45t multi | 60 | 60 |

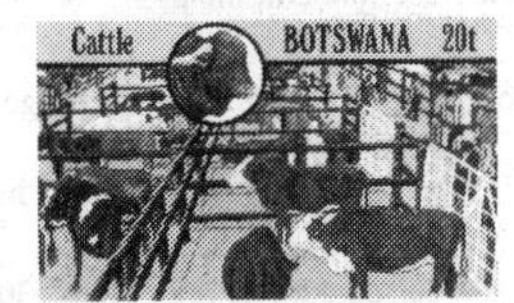

Cattle in Agricultural Show — A60

**1981, Sept. 21 Litho. *Perf. 14½***

| | | |
|---|---|---|
| *285* A60 6t Plowing | 8 | 8 |
| *286* A60 20t shown | 20 | 20 |
| *287* A60 30t Meat Commission | 35 | 35 |
| *288* A60 45t Vaccine Institute | 50 | 50 |

**Nos. 209, 204 Surcharged in Black**

**1981, Sept. Photo. *Perf. 14***

| | | |
|---|---|---|
| *289* A41 25t on 35t multi | 30 | 30 |
| *290* A41 30t on 10t multi | 40 | 40 |

Christmas 1981 — A61

Designs: Water lilies.

**1981, Nov. 2 Litho.**

| | | |
|---|---|---|
| *291* A61 6t Nymphaea caerulea | 10 | 10 |
| *292* A61 10t Nymphoides indica | 15 | 15 |
| *293* A61 25t Nymphaea lotus | 30 | 30 |
| *294* A61 40t Ottelia kunenensis | 50 | 50 |

Children's Drawings — A62

**1982, Feb. 15 Litho. *Perf. 14½x14***

| | | |
|---|---|---|
| *295* A62 6t Cattle | 10 | 10 |
| *296* A62 10t Kgotla meeting | 12 | 12 |
| *297* A62 30t Village | 40 | 40 |
| *298* A62 45t Huts | 60 | 60 |

Traditional Houses — A63

**1982, May 3 Litho. *Perf. 14***

| | | |
|---|---|---|
| *299* A63 6t Common type | 8 | 8 |
| *300* A63 10t Kgatleng | 12 | 12 |
| *301* A63 30t Northeastern | 40 | 40 |
| *302* A63 45t Sarwa | 60 | 60 |

Red-billed Teals — A64

***Perf. 14x14½, 14½x14***

**1982, July 1 Photo.**

| | | |
|---|---|---|
| *303* A64 1t Masked weaver | 5 | 5 |
| *304* A64 2t Lesser double-collared sunbirds | 5 | 5 |
| *305* A64 3t White-fronted bee-eaters | 8 | 8 |
| *306* A64 4t Ostriches | 10 | 10 |
| *307* A64 5t Grey-headed gulls | 12 | 12 |
| *308* A64 6t Pygmy geese | 15 | 15 |
| *309* A64 7t Cattle egrets | 16 | 16 |
| *310* A64 8t Lanner falcon | 18 | 18 |
| *311* A64 10t Yellow-billed storks | 22 | 22 |
| *312* A64 15t shown | 35 | 35 |
| *313* A64 20t Barn owls | 45 | 45 |
| *314* A64 25t Hamerkops | 60 | 60 |
| *315* A64 30t Stilts | 70 | 70 |
| *316* A64 35t Blacksmith plovers | 80 | 80 |
| *317* A64 45t Wattled plover | 1.00 | 1.00 |
| *318* A64 50t Crowned guinea-fowl | 1.10 | 1.20 |
| *319* A64 1p Cape vultures | 2.25 | 2.25 |
| *320* A64 2p Augur bustards | 4.50 | 4.50 |
| *Nos. 303-320 (18)* | 12.86 | 12.96 |

Nos. 303-310 vert.

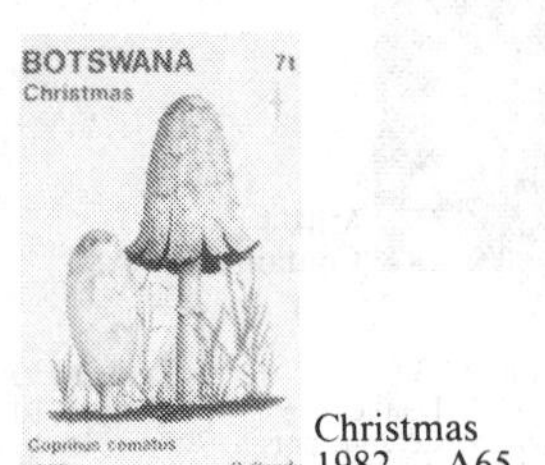

Christmas 1982 — A65

Designs: Mushrooms.

**1982, Nov. 2 Litho. *Perf. 14½***

| | | |
|---|---|---|
| *321* A65 7t Shaggy mane | 18 | 18 |
| *322* A65 15t Orange milk | 38 | 38 |
| *323* A65 35t Panther | 90 | 90 |
| *324* A65 50t King boletus | 1.25 | 1.25 |

**Commonwealth Day**

Common Design Type

**1983, Mar. 14 Litho. *Perf. 14***

| | | |
|---|---|---|
| *325* CD334 7t Pres. Quett Masire | 10 | 10 |
| *326* CD334 15t Dancers | 20 | 20 |
| *327* CD334 35t Melbourne Conference Center | 50 | 50 |
| *328* CD334 45t Heads of State meeting | 60 | 60 |

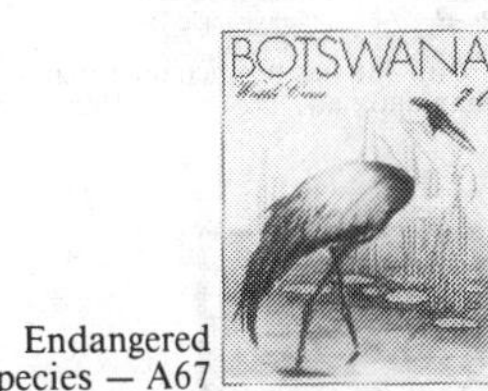

Endangered Species — A67

**1983, Apr. 19 Litho. *Perf. 14x14½***

| | | |
|---|---|---|
| *329* A67 7t Wattle crane | 12 | 12 |
| *330* A67 15t Aloe lutescens | 25 | 25 |
| *331* A67 35t Roan antelope | 60 | 60 |
| *332* A67 50t Hyphaene ventricosa | 80 | 80 |

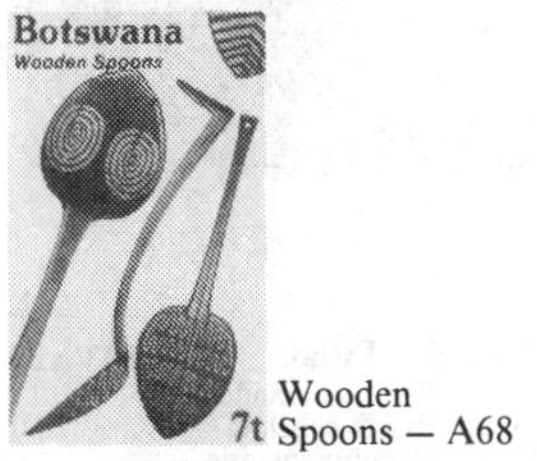

Wooden Spoons — A68

**1983, July 20 Litho. *Perf. 14***

| | | |
|---|---|---|
| *333* A68 7t shown | 15 | 15 |
| *334* A68 15t Jewelry | 30 | 30 |
| *335* A68 35t Ox-hide milk bag | 75 | 75 |
| *336* A68 50t Decorated knives | 1.00 | 1.00 |
| *a.* Souvenir sheet of 4 | 2.00 | 2.00 |

No. 336a contains Nos. 333-336. Size: 117x103mm.

Christmas 1983 — A69

Designs: Dragonflies.

**1983, Nov. 7 Litho. *Perf. 14½x14***

| | | |
|---|---|---|
| *337* A69 6t Pantala flavescens | 12 | 12 |
| *338* A69 15t Anax imperator | 30 | 30 |
| *339* A69 25t Trithemis arteriosa | 50 | 50 |
| *340* A69 45t Chlorolestes elegans | 90 | 90 |

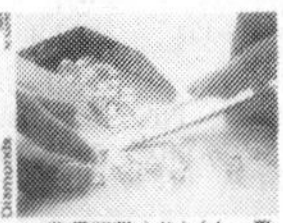

Mining Industry — A70

**1984, Mar. 19 Litho. *Perf. 14½***

| | | |
|---|---|---|
| *341* A70 7t Diamonds | 15 | 15 |
| *342* A70 15t Lime | 30 | 30 |
| *343* A70 35t Copper, nickel, vert. | 75 | 75 |
| *344* A70 50t Coal, vert. | 1.00 | 1.00 |

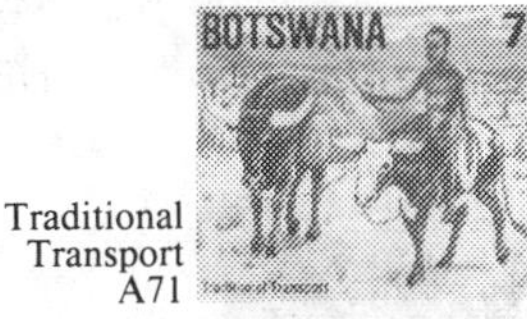

Traditional Transport A71

**1984, June 16 Litho. *Perf. 14½x14***

| | | |
|---|---|---|
| *345* A71 7t Man riding ox | 15 | 15 |
| *346* A71 25t Sled | 50 | 50 |
| *347* A71 35t Wagon | 75 | 75 |
| *348* A71 50t Cart | 1.00 | 1.00 |

Intl. Civil Aviation Org., 40th Anniv. — A72

**1984, Oct. 8 Litho. *Perf. 14x13½***

| | | |
|---|---|---|
| *349* A72 7t Avro 504 | 12 | 12 |
| *350* A72 10t Westland Wessex | 15 | 15 |
| *351* A72 15t Junkers 52-3M | 25 | 25 |
| *352* A72 25t Dragon Rapide | 40 | 40 |
| *353* A72 35t DC-3 | 60 | 60 |
| *354* A72 50t F27 Fokker Friendship | 80 | 80 |
| *Nos. 349-354 (6)* | 2.32 | 2.32 |

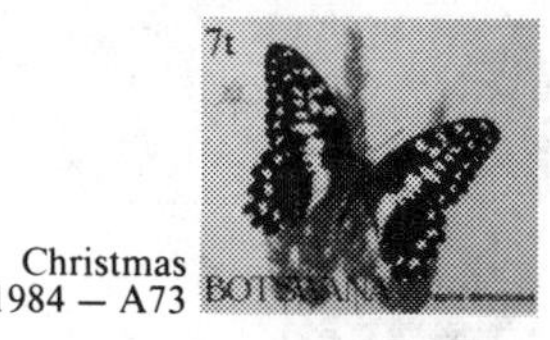

Christmas 1984 — A73

Butterflies.

**1984, Nov. 5 Litho. *Perf. 14½x14***
*355* A73 7t Papilio demodocus 15 15
*356* A73 25t Byblia acheloia 50 50
*357* A73 35t Hypolimnas missipus 75 75
*358* A73 50t Graphium taboranus 1.00 1.00

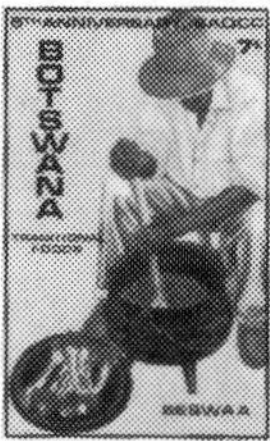

Traditional & Exotic Foods — A74

Bechuanaland No. 4 — A75

**1985, Mar. 18 Litho. *Perf. 14½***
*359* A74 7t Man preparing seswaa 8 8
*360* A74 15t Woman preparing bogobe 15 15
*361* A74 25t Girl eating madilla 25 25
*362* A74 50t Woman collecting caterpillars 50 50
*a.* Souvenir sheet of 4, #359-362 1.00 1.00

Southern African Development Coordination Conference, 5th anniv. No. 362a has multicolored decorative margin picturing woman cutting melon. Size: 118x104mm.

**1985, June 24**

Postage stamp cent.: 15t, Bechuanaland Protectorate No. 72. 25t, Bechuanaland Protectorate No. 106. 35t, Bechuanaland No. 199, 50t, Botswana No. 1, horiz.

*363* A75 7t multi 8 8
*364* A75 15t multi 18 18
*365* A75 25t multi 30 30
*366* A75 35t multi 42 42
*367* A75 50t multi 62 62
*Nos. 363-367 (5)* 1.60 1.60

Police Centenary A76

Designs: 7t, Bechuanaland Border Police, 1885-1895. 10t, Bechuanaland Mounted Police, 1894-1902. 25t, Bechuanaland Protectorate Police, 1903-1966. 50t, Botswana Motorcycle Police, 1966-1985.

**1985, Aug. 5 *Perf. 14½x14***
*368* A76 7t multi 8 8
*369* A76 10t multi 12 12
*370* A76 25t multi 30 30
*371* A76 50t multi 62 62

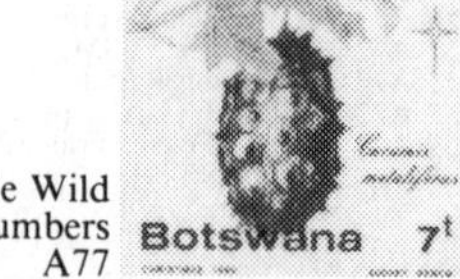

Edible Wild Cucumbers A77

**1985, Nov. 4**
*372* A77 7t Cucumis metuliferus 8 8
*373* A77 15t Acanthosicyos naudinianus 18 18
*374* A77 25t Coccinia sessifolia 30 30
*375* A77 50t Momordica balsamina 62 62

Christmas 1985.

Declaration of Protectorate, Cent. — A78

**1985, Dec. 30 Litho. *Perf. 14x14½***
*376* A78 7t Heads of state meet 8 8
*377* A78 15t Declaration reading, 1885 18 18
*378* A78 25t Mackenzie and Khama 30 30
*379* A78 50t Map 62 62
*a.* Souvenir sheet of 4, #376-379 1.20 1.20

No. 379a has multicolored margin picturing map of southern Africa. Size: 130x133mm.

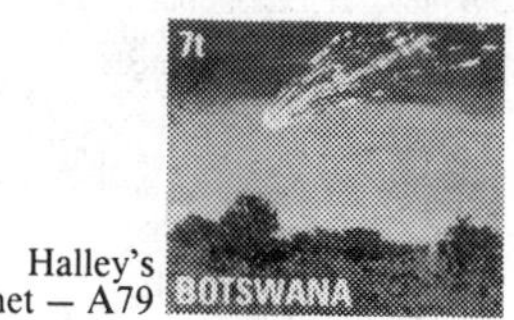

Halley's Comet — A79

**1986, Mar. 24 *Perf. 14½x14***
*380* A79 7t Comet over Serowe 8 8
*381* A79 15t Over Bobonong 18 18
*382* A79 35t Over Gomare swamps 42 42
*383* A79 50t Over Thamaga, Letlhakeng 62 62

Milk Containers — A80

**1986, June 23 *Perf. 14½***
*384* A80 8t Leather bag 10 10
*385* A80 15t Ceramic pots 18 18
*386* A80 35t Wood pot 42 42
*387* A80 50t Woman, pots 62 62

**Souvenir Sheet**

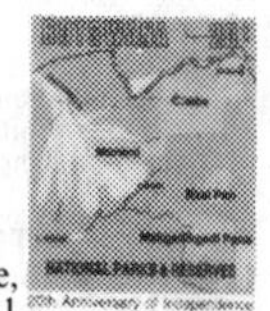
Natl. Independence, 20th Anniv. — A81

Designs: a, Map of natl. parks and reserves. b, Morupule Power Station. c, Cattle, Kgalagadi. d, Natl. Assembly.

**1986, Sept. 30 Litho. *Perf. 14½x14***
*388* Sheet of 4 90 90
*a.-d.* A81 20t, any single 22 22

No. 388 has multicolored margin picturing map and natl. flag. Size: 100x120mm.

Flowers of the Okavango Swamps — A82

**1986, Nov. 3 Litho. *Perf. 14x14½***
*389* A82 8t Ludwigia stogonifera 10 10
*390* A82 15t Sopubia mannii 16 16
*391* A82 35t Commelina diffusa 38 38
*392* A82 50t Hibiscus diversifolius 55 55

Christmas.

Traditional Medicine — A83

**1987, Mar. 2 Litho. *Perf. 14½x14***
*393* A83 8t Professional diviners 10 10
*394* A83 15t Lightning prevention 16 16
*395* A83 35t Rainmaker 38 38
*396* A83 50t Bloodletting 55 55

UN Child Survival Campaign — A84

**1987, June 1**
*397* A84 8t Oral rehydration therapy 10 10
*398* A84 15t Growth monitoring 16 16
*399* A84 35t Immunization 38 38
*400* A84 50t Breast-feeding 55 55

**Nos. 308, 311 and 318 Surcharged**

***Perf. 14x14½,14½x14***

**1987, Apr. 1 Photo.**
*401* A64 3t on 6t No. 308 5 5
*402* A64 5t on 10t No. 311 6 6
*403* A64 20t on 50t No. 318 30 30

Wildlife Conservation — A85

**1987, Aug. 3 *Perf. 14***
*404* A85 1t Cape fox 5 5
*405* A85 2t Lechwe 5 5
*406* A85 3t Zebra 5 5
*407* A85 4t Duiker 5 5
*408* A85 5t Banded mongoose 5 5
*409* A85 6t Rusty-spotted genet 5 5
*410* A85 8t Hedgehog 6 6
*411* A85 10t Scrub hare 8 8
*412* A85 12t Hippopotamus 10 10
*413* A85 15t Suricate 12 12
*414* A85 20t Caracal 16 16
*415* A85 25t Steenbok 20 20
*416* A85 30t Gemsbok 24 24
*417* A85 35t Square-lipped rhino 28 28
*418* A85 40t Mountain reedbuck 32 32
*419* A85 50t Rock dassie 40 40
*420* A85 1p Giraffe 80 80
*421* A85 2p Tsessebe 1.60 1.60
*422* A85 3p Side-striped jackal 2.40 2.40
*423* A85 5p Hartebeest 4.00 4.00
*Nos. 404-423 (20)* 11.06 11.06

Wetland Grasses — A86

**1987, Oct. 26 *Perf. 14x14½***
*424* A86 8t Cyperus articulatus 6 6
*425* A86 15t Miscanthus junceus 12 12
*426* A86 30t Cyperus alopecuroides 24 24
*427* A86 1p Typha latifolia 80 80
*a.* Souv. sheet of 4, Nos. 424-427 1.25 1.25

Christmas 1987, preservation of the Okavango and Kuando-Chobe River wetlands. No. 427a has multicolored margin picturing wetland. Size: 89x99mm.

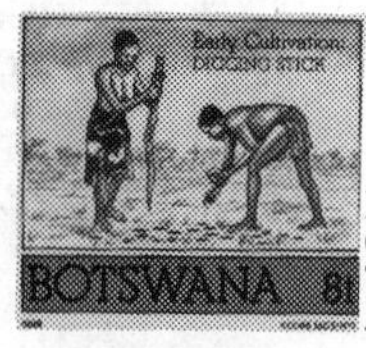

Early Cultivation Techniques A87

**1988, Mar. 14 Litho. *Perf. 14½x14***
*428* A87 8t Digging stick 10 10
*429* A87 15t Iron hoe 18 18
*430* A87 35t Wooden plow 42 42
*431* A87 50t Communal planting, Lesotla 60 60

World Wildlife Fund — A88

Designs: WWF emblem and various red lechwe, *Kobus leche*.

**1988, June 6 Litho. *Perf. 14½x14***
*432* A88 10t Adult wading 12 12
*433* A88 15t Adult, sun 18 18
*434* A88 35t Cow, calf 40 40
*435* A88 75t Herd 85 85

Runner Post, Cent. — A89

Routes and: 10t, Gubulawayo, Bechuanaland, cancellation dated Aug. 21 '88. 15t, Bechuanaland Protectorate No. 65. 30t, Pack traders. 60t, Mafeking killer cancel No. 638.

**1988, Aug. 22 Litho. *Perf. 14½***
*436* A89 10t multi 12 12
*437* A89 15t multi 18 18
*438* A89 30t multi 35 35
*439* A89 60t multi 65 65
*a.* Souv. sheet of 4, Nos. 436-439 1.30 1.30

Printed in a continuous design picturing the Mafeking-Gubulawayo route and part of the Shoshong runner post route. No. 439a has multicolored inscribed margin. Size: 81x152mm.

State Visit of Pope John Paul II, Sept. 13 — A90

Natl. Museum and Art Gallery, Gaborone, 20th Anniv. — A91

**1988, Sept. 13 Litho. *Perf. 14x14½***
*440* A90 10t Map, portrait 10 10
*441* A90 15t Portrait 15 15
*442* A90 30t Map, portrait, diff. 32 32
*443* A90 80t Portrait, diff. 82 82

**1988, Sept. 30 *Perf. 14½***
*444* A91 8t Museum 10 10
*445* A91 15t Pottery, c. 400-1300 18 18
*446* A91 30t Buffalo bellows 35 35
*447* A91 60t Children, mobile museum 68 68

Flowering Plants of Southeastern Botswana — A92

**1988, Oct. 11 Litho. *Perf. 14x14½***

| No. | Type | Denom. | Description | Unused | Used |
|---|---|---|---|---|---|
| *448* | A92 | 8t | Grewia flava | 8 | 8 |
| *449* | A92 | 15t | Cienfuegosia digitata | 15 | 15 |
| *450* | A92 | 40t | Solanum seaforthianum | 42 | 42 |
| *451* | A92 | 75t | Carissa bispinosa | 78 | 78 |

Christmas 1988.

## POSTAGE DUE STAMPS

Bechuanaland Protectorate Nos. J10-J12 Overprinted: "REPUBLIC OF / BOTSWANA"

**Wmk. 4**

**1967, Mar. 1 Typo. *Perf. 14***

| No. | Type | Denom. | Description | Unused | Used |
|---|---|---|---|---|---|
| *J1* | D2 | 1c | carmine rose | 15 | *1.00* |
| *J2* | D2 | 2c | dull violet | 25 | *1.50* |
| *J3* | D2 | 5c | olive green | 60 | *2.00* |

Elephant D1

Zebra D2

***Perf. 13½***

**1971, June 9 Litho. Unwmk.**

| No. | Type | Denom. | Description | Unused | Used |
|---|---|---|---|---|---|
| *J4* | D1 | 1c | carmine rose | 20 | *75* |
| *J5* | D1 | 2c | violet blue | 25 | *90* |
| *J6* | D1 | 6c | sepia | 45 | *1.50* |
| *J7* | D1 | 14c | green | 80 | *2.25* |

**1978 *Perf. 12½***

| No. | Type | Denom. | Description | Unused | Used |
|---|---|---|---|---|---|
| *J8* | D2 | 1t | red orange & blk | 5 | 5 |
| a. | | | Perf. 14½x14 ('84) | 5 | 5 |
| *J9* | D2 | 2t | emerald & blk | 5 | 5 |
| a. | | | Perf. 14½x14 ('84) | 5 | 5 |
| *J10* | D2 | 4t | red & black | 10 | 10 |
| a. | | | Perf. 14½x14 ('84) | 10 | 10 |
| *J11* | D2 | 10t | dark blue & blk | 25 | 25 |
| a. | | | Perf. 14½x14 ('84) | 25 | 25 |
| *J12* | D2 | 16t | brown & blk | 40 | 40 |
| a. | | | Perf. 14½x14 ('84) | 40 | 40 |
| | | | *Nos. J8-J12 (5)* | 85 | 85 |

# BRITISH ANTARCTIC TERRITORY

LOCATION — South Atlantic Ocean between 20-80 degrees longitude and south of 60 degrees latitude.

GOVT. — British territory

POP. — About 100 scientific staff at research stations.

This territory includes Graham Land (Palmer Peninsula), South Shetland Islands and South Orkney Islands. Formerly part of Falkland Islands Dependency.

12 Pence = 1 Shilling

20 Shillings = 1 Pound

100 Pence = 1 Pound (1971)

**Catalogue values for all unused stamps in this country are for Never Hinged items.**

M. V. Kista Dan — A1

Designs: 1p, Skiers hauling load. 1½p, Muskeg (tractor). 2p, Skiers. 2½p, Beaver seaplane. 3p, R.R.S. John Biscoe. 4p, Camp scene. 6p, H.M.S. Protector. 9p, Dog sled. 1sh, Otter ski-plane. 2sh, Huskies and aurora australis. 2sh6p, Helicopter. 5sh, Snocat (truck). 10sh, R.R.S. Shackleton. £1, Map of Antarctica.

***Perf. 11x11½***

**1963, Feb. 1 Engr. Wmk. 314**

| No. | Type | Denom. | Description | Unused | Used |
|---|---|---|---|---|---|
| *1* | A1 | ½p | dk bl | 25 | 18 |
| *2* | A1 | 1p | brown | 18 | 15 |
| *3* | A1 | 1½p | plum & red | 22 | 18 |
| *4* | A1 | 2p | rose vio | 30 | 22 |
| *5* | A1 | 2½p | dl grn | 35 | 25 |
| *6* | A1 | 3p | Prus bl | 48 | 40 |
| *7* | A1 | 4p | sepia | 52 | 45 |
| *8* | A1 | 6p | dk bl & ol | 95 | 75 |
| *9* | A1 | 9p | olive | 1.10 | 95 |
| *10* | A1 | 1sh | stl bl | 1.50 | 1.25 |
| *11* | A1 | 2sh | dl vio & bis | 7.50 | 6.00 |
| *12* | A1 | 2sh6p | blue | 8.25 | 7.50 |
| *13* | A1 | 5sh | rose red & org | 16.00 | 16.00 |
| *14* | A1 | 10sh | grn & vio bl | 40.00 | 40.00 |
| *15* | A1 | £1 | blk & bl | 95.00 | 75.00 |
| | | | *Nos. 1-15 (15)* | 172.60 | 149.28 |

See No. 24.

**Churchill Memorial Issue**

Common Design Type

**1966, Jan. 24 Photo. *Perf. 14***

| No. | Type | Denom. | Description | Unused | Used |
|---|---|---|---|---|---|
| *16* | CD319 | ½p | brt bl | 38 | 30 |
| *17* | CD319 | 1p | green | 1.50 | 75 |
| *18* | CD319 | 1sh | brown | 18.00 | 15.00 |
| *19* | CD319 | 2sh | violet | 25.00 | 16.00 |

Lemaire Channel, Iceberg and Adelie Penguins A2

Designs: 6p, Weather sonde and operator. 1sh, Muskeg (tractor) pulling tent equipment. 2sh, Surveyors with theodolite.

**1969, Feb. 6 Litho.**

| No. | Type | Denom. | Description | Unused | Used |
|---|---|---|---|---|---|
| *20* | A2 | 3½p | bl, vio bl & blk | 1.25 | 1.10 |
| *21* | A2 | 6p | emer, blk & dp org | 2.00 | 1.90 |
| *22* | A2 | 1sh | ultra, blk & ver | 3.50 | 3.50 |
| *23* | A2 | 2sh | grnsh bl, blk & ocher | 6.75 | 6.75 |

Issued to commemorate 25 years of continuous scientific work in the Antarctic.

Type of 1963

Design: £1, H.M.S. Endurance and helicopter.

**1969, Dec. 1 Engr. *Perf. 11x11½***

| No. | Type | Denom. | Description | Unused | Used |
|---|---|---|---|---|---|
| *24* | A1 | £1 | blk & rose red | 165.00 | 165.00 |

Common Design Types pictured in section before Great Britain.

Nos. 1-14 Surcharged in Decimal Currency; Three Bars Overprinted

**1971, Feb. 15 Wmk. 314**

| No. | Type | Denom. | Description | Unused | Used |
|---|---|---|---|---|---|
| *25* | A1 | ½p | on ½p dk bl | 12 | 12 |
| *26* | A1 | 1p | on 1p brn | 20 | 18 |
| *27* | A1 | 1½p | on 1½p plum & red | 28 | 25 |
| *28* | A1 | 2p | on 2p rose vio | 30 | 30 |
| *29* | A1 | 2½p | on 2½p dl grn | 35 | 40 |
| *30* | A1 | 3p | on 3p Prus bl | 70 | 60 |
| *31* | A1 | 4p | on 4p sep | 1.00 | 95 |
| *32* | A1 | 5p | on 6p dk bl & ol | 1.40 | 1.25 |
| *33* | A1 | 6p | on 9p ol | 1.75 | 1.50 |
| *34* | A1 | 7½p | on 1sh stl bl | 2.00 | 2.00 |
| *35* | A1 | 10p | on 2sh dl vio & bis | 4.50 | 4.25 |
| *36* | A1 | 15p | on 2sh6p bl | 14.00 | 13.00 |
| *37* | A1 | 25p | on 5sh rose red & org | 27.50 | 25.00 |
| *38* | A1 | 50p | on 10sh grn & vio bl | 62.50 | 62.50 |
| | | | *Nos. 25-38 (14)* | 116.60 | 112.30 |

*British Antarctic Territory stamps can be mounted in Scott's British South Atlantic Album.*

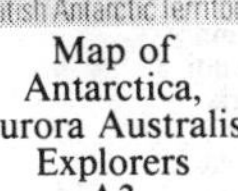


Map of Antarctica, Aurora Australis, Explorers A3

Capt. Cook and "Resolution" A4

Map of Antarctica, Aurora Australis and: 4p, Sea gulls. 5p, Seals. 10p, Penguins.

**Litho. and Engr.**

**1971, June 23 *Perf. 14x13***

| No. | Type | Denom. | Description | Unused | Used |
|---|---|---|---|---|---|
| *39* | A3 | 1½p | multi | 3.25 | 1.25 |
| *40* | A3 | 4p | multi | 6.00 | 4.00 |
| *41* | A3 | 5p | multi | 8.00 | 6.00 |
| *42* | A3 | 10p | multi | 13.00 | 10.00 |

Tenth anniversary of the Antarctic Treaty pledging peaceful uses of and scientific cooperation in Antarctica.

**Silver Wedding Issue, 1972**

Common Design Type

Design: Queen Elizabeth II, Prince Philip, seals and emperor penguins.

**1972, Dec. 13 Photo. *Perf. 14x14½***

| No. | Type | Denom. | Description | Unused | Used |
|---|---|---|---|---|---|
| *43* | CD324 | 5p | rose brn & multi | 2.00 | 2.00 |
| *44* | CD324 | 10p | ol & multi | 4.00 | 4.00 |

**Wmk. 314**

**1973, Feb. 14 Litho. *Perf. 14½***

Polar Explorers and their Crafts: 1p, Thaddeus von Bellingshausen and "Vostok." 1½p, James Weddell and "Jane." 2p, John Biscoe and "Tula." 2½p, J. S. C. Dumont d'Urville and "Astrolabe." 3p, James Clark Ross and "Erebus." 4p, C. A. Larsen and "Jason." 5p, Adrien de Gerlache and "Belgica." 6p, Otto Nordenskjöld and "Antarctic." 7½p, W. S. Bruce and "Scotia." 10p, Jean-Baptiste Charcot and "Pourquoi Pas?" 15p, Ernest Shackleton and "Endurance." 25p, Hubert Wilkins and airplane "San Francisco." 50p, Lincoln Ellsworth and airplane "Polar Star." £1, John Rymill and "Penola."

| No. | Type | Denom. | Description | Unused | Used |
|---|---|---|---|---|---|
| *45* | A4 | ½p | multi | *2.00* | *2.00* |
| *46* | A4 | 1p | multi | *2.50* | *2.75* |
| *47* | A4 | 1½p | multi | *4.00* | *4.00* |
| *48* | A4 | 2p | multi | 28 | 14 |
| *49* | A4 | 2½p | multi | 35 | 18 |
| *50* | A4 | 3p | multi | 35 | 20 |
| *51* | A4 | 4p | multi | 35 | 20 |
| *52* | A4 | 5p | multi | 48 | 32 |
| *53* | A4 | 6p | multi | 45 | 32 |
| *54* | A4 | 7½p | multi | 65 | 52 |
| *55* | A4 | 10p | multi | 1.25 | 60 |
| *56* | A4 | 15p | multi | 2.00 | 1.00 |
| *57* | A4 | 25p | multi | 2.50 | 1.75 |
| *58* | A4 | 50p | multi | 4.75 | 3.25 |
| *59* | A4 | £1 | multi | 14.00 | 13.00 |
| | | | *Nos. 45-59 (15)* | 35.91 | 30.23 |

**1975-80 Wmk. 373**

| No. | Type | Denom. | Description | Unused | Used |
|---|---|---|---|---|---|
| *45a* | A4 | ½p | multi | 5 | 5 |
| *46a* | A4 | 1p | multi ('78) | 5 | 5 |
| *47a* | A4 | 1½p | multi ('78) | 7 | 7 |
| *48a* | A4 | 2p | multi ('79) | 10 | 10 |
| *49a* | A4 | 2½p | multi ('79) | 13 | 13 |
| *50a* | A4 | 3p | multi ('79) | 15 | 15 |
| *51a* | A4 | 4p | multi, perf. 12 ('80) | 20 | 20 |
| *52a* | A4 | 5p | multi ('79) | 24 | 24 |
| *53a* | A4 | 6p | multi, perf. 12 ('80) | 30 | 30 |
| *54a* | A4 | 7½p | multi, perf. 12 ('80) | 38 | 38 |
| *55a* | A4 | 10p | multi ('79) | 48 | 48 |
| *56a* | A4 | 15p | multi ('79) | 72 | 72 |
| *57a* | A4 | 25p | multi ('79) | 1.20 | 1.20 |
| *58a* | A4 | 50p | multi ('79) | 2.40 | 2.40 |
| *59a* | A4 | £1 | multi ('78) | 4.00 | 4.00 |
| | | | *Nos. 45a-59a (15)* | 10.47 | 10.47 |

Nos. 55a-59a exist perf. 12. Same values.

**Princess Anne's Wedding Issue**

Common Design Type

**1973, Nov. 14 Wmk. 314 *Perf. 14***

| No. | Type | Denom. | Description | Unused | Used |
|---|---|---|---|---|---|
| *60* | CD325 | 5p | ocher & multi | 55 | 55 |
| *61* | CD325 | 15p | bl grn & multi | 1.40 | 1.40 |

Wedding of Princess Anne and Capt. Mark Phillips, Nov. 14, 1973.

Churchill and Map of Churchill Peninsula A5

Design: 15p, Churchill and "Trepassey" of Operation Tabarin, 1943.

**1974, Nov. 30 Litho. *Perf. 14***

| No. | Type | Denom. | Description | Unused | Used |
|---|---|---|---|---|---|
| *62* | A5 | 5p | multi | 1.25 | 80 |
| *63* | A5 | 15p | multi | 2.50 | 2.50 |
| a. | | | Souvenir sheet of 2 | 6.75 | 4.50 |

Sir Winston Churchill (1874-1965), birth centenary. No. 63a contains one each of Nos. 62-63, light blue and multicolored margin with British Antarctic Territory coat of arms. Size: 114x88mm.

Humpback Whale — A6

**Wmk. 373**

**1977, Jan. 4 Litho. *Perf. 14***

| No. | Type | Denom. | Description | Unused | Used |
|---|---|---|---|---|---|
| *64* | A6 | 2p | Sperm whale | 2.00 | 1.00 |
| *65* | A6 | 8p | Fin whale | 2.50 | 1.50 |
| *66* | A6 | 11p | shown | 5.00 | 3.00 |
| *67* | A6 | 25p | Blue whale | 6.00 | 4.50 |

Conservation of whales.

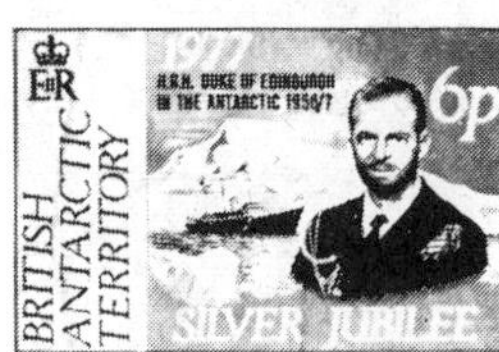


Prince Philip in Antarctica, 1956-57 — A7

Designs: 11p, Coronation oath. 33p, Queen before taking oath.

**1977, Feb. 7 *Perf. 13½x14***

| No. | Type | Denom. | Description | Unused | Used |
|---|---|---|---|---|---|
| *68* | A7 | 6p | multi | 40 | 40 |
| *69* | A7 | 11p | multi | 65 | 65 |
| *70* | A7 | 33p | multi | 2.25 | 2.25 |

25th anniv. of the reign of Elizabeth II.

**Elizabeth II Coronation Anniversary Issue**

Common Design Types

Souvenir Sheet

**Unwmk.**

**1978, June 2 Litho. *Perf. 15***

| No. | Type | Denom. | Description | Unused | Used |
|---|---|---|---|---|---|
| *71* | | | Sheet of 6 | 7.00 | 7.00 |
| a. | CD326 | 25p | *Black bull of Clarence* | 1.00 | 1.00 |
| b. | CD327 | 25p | *Elizabeth II* | 1.00 | 1.00 |
| c. | CD328 | 25p | *Emperor penguin* | 1.00 | 1.00 |

No. 71 contains 2 se-tenant strips of Nos. 71a-71c, separated by horizontal gutter with commemorative and descriptive inscriptions and showing central part of coronation procession with coach. Size: 100x135mm.

Macaroni Penguins — A8

***Perf. 13½x14***

**1979, Jan. 14 Litho. Wmk. 373**

| No. | Type | Denom. | Description | Unused | Used |
|---|---|---|---|---|---|
| *72* | A8 | 3p | shown | *7.25* | *2.50* |
| *73* | A8 | 8p | Gentoo | *2.00* | *1.25* |
| *74* | A8 | 11p | Adelie | *1.65* | *1.65* |
| *75* | A8 | 25p | Emperor | *4.25* | *2.00* |

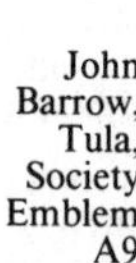

John Barrow, Tula, Society Emblem A9

Royal Geographical Society Sesquicentennial (Past Presidents and Expedition Scenes): 7p, Clement Markham 11p, Lord Curzon. 15p, William Goodenough. 22p, James Wordie. 30p, Raymond Priestley.

**Wmk. 373**

**1980, Dec. 1 Litho. *Perf. 13½***

| | | | | |
|---|---|---|---|---|
| *76* | A9 | 3p multi | 10 | 10 |
| *77* | A9 | 7p multi | 22 | 22 |
| *78* | A9 | 11p multi | 35 | 35 |
| *79* | A9 | 15p multi | 60 | 60 |
| *80* | A9 | 22p multi | 90 | 90 |
| *81* | A9 | 30p multi | 1.10 | 1.10 |
| | | *Nos. 76-81 (6)* | 3.27 | 3.27 |

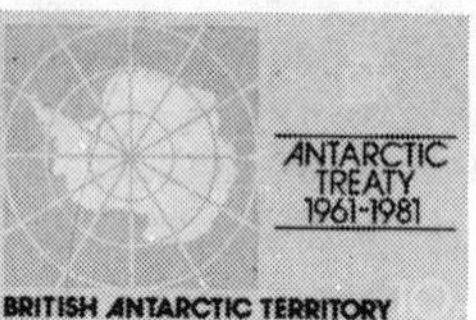


20th Anniv. of Antarctic Treaty — A10

***Perf. 13½x14***

**1981, Dec. 1 Litho. Wmk. 373**

| | | | | |
|---|---|---|---|---|
| *82* | A10 | 10p Map | 32 | 32 |
| *83* | A10 | 13p Conservation research | 42 | 42 |
| *84* | A10 | 25p Satellite image mapping | 80 | 80 |
| *85* | A10 | 26p Global geophysics | 85 | 85 |

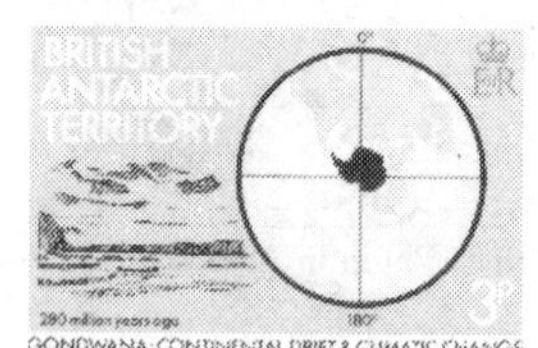

Continental Drift and Climatic Change — A11

**1982, Mar. 8 Litho. *Perf. 13½x14***

| | | | | |
|---|---|---|---|---|
| *86* | A11 | 3p Land, water | 15 | 15 |
| *87* | A11 | 6p Shrubs | 30 | 30 |
| *88* | A11 | 10p Dinosaur | 50 | 50 |
| *89* | A11 | 13p Volcano | 65 | 65 |
| *90* | A11 | 25p Trees | 1.25 | 1.25 |
| *91* | A11 | 26p Penguins | 1.30 | 1.30 |
| | | *Nos. 86-91 (6)* | 4.15 | 4.15 |

**Princess Diana Issue**

Common Design Type

**1982, July 1 Litho. *Perf. 14½x14***

| | | | | |
|---|---|---|---|---|
| *92* | CD333 | 5p Arms | 16 | 16 |
| *93* | CD333 | 17p Diana, by Bryan Organ | 55 | 55 |
| *94* | CD333 | 37p Wedding | 1.25 | 1.25 |
| *95* | CD333 | 50p Portrait | 1.65 | 1.65 |

10th Anniv. of Convention for Conservation of Antarctic Seals — A12

**1982, Nov. Litho.**

| | | | | |
|---|---|---|---|---|
| *96* | A12 | 5p shown | 16 | 16 |
| *97* | A12 | 10p Weddell seals | 32 | 32 |
| *98* | A12 | 13p Elephant seals | 42 | 42 |
| *99* | A12 | 17p Fur seals | 55 | 55 |
| *100* | A12 | 25p Ross seal | 55 | 55 |
| *101* | A12 | 34p Crabeater seals | 1.10 | 1.10 |
| | | *Nos. 96-101 (6)* | 3.10 | 3.10 |

Corethron Criophilum — A13

**1984, Mar. 15 Litho. *Perf. 14***

| | | | | |
|---|---|---|---|---|
| *102* | A13 | 1p shown | 5 | 5 |
| *103* | A13 | 2p Desmonema gaudichaudi | 6 | 6 |
| *104* | A13 | 3p Tomopteris carpenteri | 10 | 10 |
| *105* | A13 | 4p Pareuchaeta antarctica | 14 | 14 |
| *106* | A13 | 5p Antarctomysis maxima | 16 | 16 |
| *107* | A13 | 6p Antarcturus signiensis | 20 | 20 |
| *108* | A13 | 7p Serolis comuta | 22 | 22 |
| *109* | A13 | 8p Parathemisto gaudichaudii | 25 | 25 |
| *110* | A13 | 9p Bovallia gigantea | 30 | 30 |
| *110A* | A13 | 10p Euphausia superba | 32 | 32 |
| *111* | A13 | 15p Colossendeis australis | 50 | 50 |
| *112* | A13 | 20p Todarodes sagittatus | 65 | 65 |
| *113* | A13 | 25p Notothenia neglecta | 85 | 85 |
| *114* | A13 | 50p Chaenocephalus aceratus | 1.65 | 1.65 |
| *115* | A13 | £1 Lobodon carcinophagus | 3.25 | 3.25 |
| *116* | A13 | £3 Antarctic marine food chain | 8.25 | *11.50* |
| | | *Nos. 102-116 (16)* | 16.95 | 20.20 |

Manned Flight Bicentenary — A14

**Wmk. 373**

**1983, Dec. 17 Litho. *Perf. 14***

| | | | | |
|---|---|---|---|---|
| *117* | A14 | 5p De Havilland Twin Otter | 12 | 12 |
| *118* | A14 | 13p De Havilland Single Otter | 30 | 30 |
| *119* | A14 | 17p Consolidated Canso | 40 | 40 |
| *120* | A14 | 50p Lockheed Vega | 1.25 | 1.25 |

British-Graham Land Expedition, 1934-1937 — A15

Designs: 7p, M. Y. Penola in Stella Creek. 22p, Northern base, Winter Island. 27p, D. H. Fox Moth at southern base, Barry Island. 54p, Dog team near Ablation Point, George VI Sound.

**1985, Mar. 23 Litho. *Perf. 14½***

| | | | | |
|---|---|---|---|---|
| *121* | A15 | 7p multi | 18 | 18 |
| *122* | A15 | 22p multi | 55 | 55 |
| *123* | A15 | 27p multi | 65 | 65 |
| *124* | A15 | 54p multi | 1.30 | 1.30 |

Robert McCormick (1800-1890), Catharacta Skua Maccormicki A16

Naturalists, fauna and flora: 22p, Sir Joseph Dalton Hooker (1817-1911), Deschampsea antarctica. 27p, Jean Rene C. Quoy (1790-1869), Lagenorhynchus cruciger. 54p, James Weddell (1787-1834), Leptonychotes weddelli.

**1985, Nov. 4 Litho. *Perf. 14½***

| | | | | |
|---|---|---|---|---|
| *125* | A16 | 7p multi | 18 | 18 |
| *126* | A16 | 22p multi | 62 | 62 |
| *127* | A16 | 27p multi | 75 | 75 |
| *128* | A16 | 54p multi | 1.50 | 1.50 |

Halley's Comet — A17

**Wmk. 373**

**1986, Jan. 6 Litho. *Perf. 14***

| | | | | |
|---|---|---|---|---|
| *129* | A17 | 7p Edmond Halley | 20 | 20 |
| *130* | A17 | 22p Halley Station | 65 | 65 |
| *131* | A17 | 27p Trajectory, 1531 | 78 | 78 |
| *132* | A17 | 54p Giotto space probe | 1.50 | 1.50 |

Intl. Glaciological Society, 50th Anniv. — A18

Different snowflakes.

**Wmk. 384**

**1986, Dec. 6 Litho. *Perf. 14½***

| | | | | |
|---|---|---|---|---|
| *133* | A18 | 10p dp bl & lt bl | 30 | 30 |
| *134* | A18 | 24p bl grn & lt bl grn | 70 | 70 |
| *135* | A18 | 29p dp rose lil & lt lil | 85 | 85 |
| *136* | A18 | 58p dp vio & pale vio bl | 1.70 | 1.70 |

Capt. Robert Falcon Scott, CVO RN (1868-1912) A19

Designs: 24p, The Discovery at Hut Point, 1902-1904. 29p, Cape Evans Hut, 1911-1913. 58p, South Pole, 1912.

**Wmk. 373**

**1987, Mar. 19 Litho. *Perf. 14½***

| | | | | |
|---|---|---|---|---|
| *137* | A19 | 10p multi | 30 | 30 |
| *138* | A19 | 24p multi | 70 | 70 |
| *139* | A19 | 29p multi | 85 | 85 |
| *140* | A19 | 58p multi | 1.70 | 1.70 |

Intl. Geophysical Year, 30th Anniv. A20

Commonwealth Trans-Antarctic Expedition A21

**Wmk. 384**

**1987, Dec. 25 Litho. *Perf. 14½***

| | | | | |
|---|---|---|---|---|
| *141* | A20 | 10p Emblem | 35 | 35 |
| *142* | A20 | 24p Port Lockroy | 82 | 82 |
| *143* | A20 | 29p Argentine Islands | 1.00 | 1.00 |
| *144* | A20 | 58p Halley Bay | 2.00 | 2.00 |

**1988, Mar. 19 *Perf. 14***

| | | | | |
|---|---|---|---|---|
| *145* | A21 | 10p Aurora over South Ice | 38 | 38 |
| *146* | A21 | 24p Otter aircraft | 88 | 88 |
| *147* | A21 | 29p Seismic ice-depth sounding | 1.10 | 1.10 |
| *148* | A21 | 58p Sno-cat over crevasse | 2.15 | 2.15 |

Lichens A22

**1988, Dec. Litho. Wmk. 373 *Perf.***

| | | | | |
|---|---|---|---|---|
| *149* | A22 | 10p Xanthoria elegans | 35 | 35 |
| *150* | A22 | 24p Usnea aurantiaco-atra | 82 | 82 |
| *151* | A22 | 29p Cladonia chlorophaea | 1.00 | 1.00 |
| *152* | A22 | 58p Umbilicaria antarctica | 2.00 | 2.00 |

# BRITISH CENTRAL AFRICA

LOCATION — In Central Africa, on the west shore of Lake Nyassa.
GOVT. — A former British territory, under charter to the British South Africa Company.
AREA — 37,800 sq. mi.
POP. — 1,639,329.
CAPITAL — Zomba.

In 1907 the name was changed to Nyasaland Protectorate, and stamps so inscribed replaced those of British Central Africa.

12 Pence = 1 Shilling
20 Shillings = 1 Pound

Rhodesia Nos. 2, 4-19 Overprinted in Black **B.C.A.**

**1891-95 Unwmk. *Perf. 14***

| | | | | |
|---|---|---|---|---|
| *1* | A1 | 1p black | 2.00 | 2.00 |
| *2* | A2 | 2p gray green & ver | 75 | 90 |
| *3* | A2 | 4p red brn & blk | 1.00 | 1.25 |
| *4* | A1 | 6p ultra | 45.00 | 24.00 |
| *5* | A1 | 6p dark blue | 4.50 | 6.00 |
| *6* | A2 | 8p rose & blue | 6.00 | *10.50* |
| *7* | A1 | 1sh bis brown | 4.75 | 4.75 |
| *8* | A1 | 2sh vermilion | 14.00 | 17.00 |
| *9* | A1 | 2sh6p gray lilac | 27.50 | 30.00 |
| *10* | A2 | 3sh brown & green ('95) | 32.50 | 32.50 |
| *11* | A2 | 4sh gray & vermilion ('93) | 32.50 | 32.50 |
| *12* | A1 | 5sh yellow | 37.50 | 37.50 |
| *13* | A1 | 10sh green | 60.00 | 67.50 |
| *14* | A3 | £1 blue | 325.000 | 350.00 |
| *15* | A3 | £2 rose red | 525.00 | *525.00* |
| *16* | A3 | £5 yel green | 1,500. | *1,650.* |
| *17* | A3 | £10 red brown | *3,000.* | *3,000.* |
| | | *Nos. 1-13 (13)* | 268.00 | *266.40* |

High values with fiscal cancellation are fairly common and can be purchased at a small fraction of the above values. This applies to subsequent issues also.

Rhodesia Nos. 13-14 Surcharged in Black **B.C.A. THREE SHILLINGS.**

**1892-93**

| | | | | |
|---|---|---|---|---|
| *18* | A2 | 3sh on 4sh gray & ver ('93) | 175.00 | 175.00 |
| *19* | A1 | 4sh on 5sh yellow | 47.50 | 47.50 |

No. 2 Surcharged in Black, with Bar **ONE PENNY.**

**1895**

| | | | | |
|---|---|---|---|---|
| *20* | A2 | 1p on 2p gray grn & ver | 7.50 | 10.00 |
| *a.* | | Double surch. | *3,250.* | *2,250.* |

A double surcharge, without period after "Penny," and measuring 16 mm instead of 18 mm, is from a trial printing.

Coat of Arms of the Protectorate
A4 A5

**1895 Unwmk. Typo. *Perf. 14***

*21* A4 1p black 3.75 3.75
*22* A4 2p grn & blk 10.00 10.00
*23* A4 4p org & blk 17.50 20.00
*24* A4 6p ultra & blk 20.00 7.50
*25* A4 1sh rose & blk 25.00 17.50
*26* A5 2sh6p vio & blk 75.00 55.00
*27* A5 3sh yel & blk 55.00 27.50
*28* A5 5sh ol & blk 70.00 45.00
*29* A5 £1 org & blk 750.00 350.00
*30* A5 £10 ver & blk *3,250. 3,000.*
*31* A5 £25 bl grn & blk *6,000. 4,500.*
*Nos. 21-28 (8)* 276.25 186.25

**1896 Wmk. 2**

*32* A4 1p black 4.50 4.50
*33* A4 2p grn & blk 9.00 5.75
*34* A4 4p org brown & blk 13.00 16.00
*35* A4 6p ultra & blk 9.00 6.75
*36* A4 1sh rose & blk 13.00 9.00

**Wmk. 1 Sideways**

*37* A5 2sh6p vio rose & blk 45.00 42.50
*38* A5 3sh yel & blk 30.00 16.00
*39* A5 5sh ol & blk 57.50 62.50
*40* A5 £1 bl & blk 600.00 475.00
*41* A5 £10 ver & blk *3,500. 2,250.*
*42* A5 £25 bl grn & blk *7,500. 7,500.*
*Nos. 32-39 (8)* 181.00 163.00

A6 A7

**1897-1901 Wmk. 2**

*43* A6 1p ultra & blk 75 40
*44* A6 1p rose & violet ('01) 90 90
*45* A6 2p yel & black 65 70
*46* A6 4p car rose & blk 3.75 2.50
*47* A6 4p ol. green & violet ('01) 3.00 3.00
*48* A6 6p grn & black 9.00 3.00
*49* A6 6p red brown & violet ('01) 4.00 3.75
*50* A6 1sh gray lil & blk 5.00 6.25

**Wmk. 1**

*51* A7 2sh6p ultra & blk 27.50 30.00
*52* A7 3sh gray grn & black 100.00 100.00
*53* A7 4sh car rose & blk 25.00 25.00
*54* A7 10sh ol & black 55.00 65.00
*55* A7 £1 dp vio & blk 225.00 150.00
*56* A7 £10 org & black *3,000. 1,250.*
*Nos. 43-54 (12)* 234.55 240.50

No. 52 Surcharged in Red

ONE

PENNY

**1897**

*57* A7 1p on 3s gray grn & blk 4.50 4.50
*a.* "PNNEY" 1,000.
*b.* "PENN" 525.00
*c.* Double surcharge 750.00 600.00

A8

**1898, Mar. 11 Unwmk. *Imperf.***

*58* A8 1p ver & ultra 1,250. 11.00
*a.* Center inverted *10,000.*
*b.* Double oval
*c.* Pair, one without oval *6,000.*
*d.* Pair with three ovals
*e.* Initials of P.M. Gen'l on back *250.00*

***Perf. 12***

*59* A8 1p ver & blue 900.00 5.00

There are two settings of Nos. 58-59, with 30 types of each.

King Edward VII
A9 A10

**1903-04 Wmk. 2**

*60* A9 1p car & black 2.25 75
*61* A9 2p vio & dl vio 4.75 2.50
*62* A9 4p blk & gray green 4.50 5.75
*63* A9 6p org brn & black 4.50 4.50
*64* A9 1sh pale bl & black ('04) 5.50 4.00

**Wmk. 1**

*65* A10 2sh6p gray green 25.00 30.00
*66* A10 4sh vio & dl vio 25.00 47.50
*67* A10 10sh blk & gray green 60.00 67.50
*68* A10 £1 scar & blk 175.00 135.00
*69* A10 £10 ultra & blk *4,500. 3,500.*
*Nos. 60-68 (9)* 306.50 297.50

**1907 Wmk. 3**

*70* A9 1p carmine & blk 75 65
*71* A9 2p vio & dl vio *10,000.*
*72* A9 4p blk & gray grn *10,000.*
*73* A9 6p org brn & blk 22.50 27.50

British Central Africa stamps were replaced by those of Nyasaland Protectorate in 1908.

## BRITISH COLUMBIA AND VANCOUVER ISLAND

LOCATION — On the northwest coast of North America.
GOVT. — A former British Colony.
AREA — 355,900 sq. mi.
POP. — 694,300.

In 1871 the colony became a part of the Canadian Confederation and the postage stamps of Canada have since been used.

12 Pence = 1 Shilling
20 Shillings = 1 Pound
100 Cents = 1 Dollar (1865)

Queen Victoria — A1

**1860 Unwmk. Typo. *Imperf.***

*1* A1 2½p dull rose 2,750.

No. 1 was not placed in use.

***Perf. 14***

*2* A1 2½p dull rose 175.00 110.00

*British Columbia and Vancouver Island stamps can be mounted in Scott's Canada Specialty Album.*

### VANCOUVER ISLAND.

A2 A3

**1865 Wmk. 1 *Imperf.***

*3* A2 5c rose *25,000 6,750.*
*4* A3 10c blue 1,000 800.00

***Perf. 14***

*5* A2 5c rose 175.00 110.00
*6* A3 10c blue 175.00 110.00

### BRITISH COLUMBIA.

Seal — A4

**1865, Nov. 1**

*7* A4 3p blue 42.50 38.00

Type of 1865 Surcharged in Various Colors

**TWO CENTS** **5.CENTS.5**
a b

**1867-69 *Perf. 14***

*8* A4(a) 2c on 3p brown (Blk) 42.50 42.50
*9* A4(b) 5c on 3p brt red (Blk) ('69) 65.00 65.00
*10* A4(b) 10c on 3p lilac rose (Bl) 550.00
*11* A4(b) 25c on 3p orange (V) ('69) 75.00 75.00
*12* A4(b) 50c on 3p violet (R) 300.00
*13* A4(b) $1 on 3p green (G) 500.00

Nos. 10 and 13 were not placed in use.

**1869 *Perf. 12½***

*14* A4(b) 5c on 3p bright red (Blk) 400.00 400.00
*15* A4(b) 10c on 3p lilac rose (Bl) 275.00 265.00
*16* A4(b) 25c on 3p org (V) 275.00 225.00
*17* A4(b) 50c on 3p vio (R) 350.00 250.00
*18* A4(b) $1 on 3p grn (G) 550.00 600.00

## BRITISH EAST AFRICA

LOCATION — Formerly included all of the territory in East Africa under British control.

Postage stamps were issued by the British East Africa Company in 1896. Later the territory administered by this company was incorporated in the East Africa and Uganda Protectorate which, together with Kenya, became officially designated Kenya Colony.

16 Annas = 1 Rupee

Queen Victoria — A1

A2 A3

**1890 Wmk. 30 *Perf. 14***

*1* A1 ½a on 1p lil 325.00 200.00
*2* A2 1a on 2p grn & car rose 350.00 190.00
*3* A3 4a on 5p lil & bl 375.00 275.00

Sun and Crown Symbolical of "Light and Liberty"
A4 A5

**1890-94 Unwmk. Litho. *Perf. 14***

*14* A4 ½a bis brn 70 90
*b.* Pair, imperf. btwn. 700.00 575.00
*15* A4 1a green 70 70
*16* A4 2a vermilion 90 1.10
*17* A4 2½a *yel* ('91) 1.40 1.40
*b.* Pair, imperf. btwn. 525.00 450.00
*18* A4 3a *red* ('91) 70 1.40
*b.* Pair, imperf. btwn. 500.00 400.00
*19* A4 4a yel brn 1.40 1.65
*20* A4 4½a brn vio ('91) 1.10 1.40
*b.* 4½a gray vio ('91) 11.00 7.25
*c.* Pair, imperf. btwn. 700.00 525.00
*21* A4 5a *bl* ('94) 70 1.75
*22* A4 7½a blk ('94) 70 1.75
*23* A4 8a blue 1.40 3.25
*24* A4 8a gray 275.00 325.00
*25* A4 1r rose 1.40 3.50
*26* A4 1r gray 200.00 225.00
*27* A5 2r brick red 5.75 6.50
*28* A5 3r gray vio 5.75 7.25
*29* A5 4r ultra 11.00 12.50
*30* A5 5r gray grn 32.50 25.00
*Nos. 14-30 (17)* 541.10 620.05

Some of the paper used for this issue had a papermaker's watermark and parts of it often can be seen on the stamps.

***Imperf***

**Unwmk.**

**1890-94 Litho.1890-91 *Perf. 14***

Values for Pairs except No. 19b.

*14a* A4 ½a bis brn 400.00 275.00
*15a* A4 1a green 600.00 400.00
*16a* A4 2a vermilion 1,200. 525.00
*17a* A4 2½a *yellow* 550.00 375.00
*18a* A4 3a *red* 725.00 600.00
*19a* A4 4a yel brn 1,200. 600.00
*19b* A4 4a gray 1,750. 1,900.
*20a* A4 4½a dl vio 1,100. 525.00
*23a* A4 8a blue 1,100. 600.00
*25a* A4 1r rose 2,400. 625.00

A6 A7

Handstamped Surcharges

**1891 *Perf. 14***

*31* A6 ½a on 2a ver ("A.D.") 1,800. 800.00
*32* A6 1a on 4a yel brn ("A.B.") 4,000. 1,200.

Nos. 31-32 are initialed in manuscript "A.D." or "A.B." See note below No. 35.

Manuscript Surcharges

**1891-95**

*33* A6 ½a on 2a ver ("A.B.") 3,000. 675.00
*a.* "½ Annas" ("A.B.") 1,200.
*b.* Initialed "A.D." 675.00
*c.* "½ Annas" ("A.D.") 1,600.
*34* A6 ½a on 3a *red* ("T.E.C.R.") 200.00 50.00
*b.* Initialed "A.B." 2,400. 1,100
*34A* A6 1a on 3a *red* ("V.H.M.") 2,400. 1,200.
*c.* Initialed "T.E.C.R." 2,400. 1,500.
*35* A6 1a on 4a yel brn ("A.B.") 1,600. 950.00

The manuscript initials on Nos. 31-35, given in parentheses, stand for Andrew Dick, Archibald Brown, Victor H. Mackenzie (1891) and T. E. C. Remington (1895).

Printed Surcharges

**1894**

*36* A7 5a on 8a bl 52.50 70.00
*37* A7 7½a on 1r rose 52.50 70.00

Stamps of 1890-94 Handstamped in Black

BRITISH
EAST
AFRICA

**1895**

| | | | | |
|---|---|---|---|---|
| *38* | A4 | ½a bis brn | 40.00 | 24.00 |
| *39* | A4 | 1a green | 60.00 | 65.00 |
| *40* | A4 | 2a vermilion | 125.00 | 125.00 |
| *41* | A4 | 2½a *yellow* | 100.00 | 40.00 |
| *42* | A4 | 3a *red* | 37.50 | 37.50 |
| *43* | A4 | 4a yel brn | 37.50 | 37.50 |
| *44* | A4 | 4½a gray vio | 100.00 | 95.00 |
| **a.** | | 4½a brn vio | 475.00 | 375.00 |
| *45* | A4 | 5a *blue* | 125.00 | 87.50 |
| *46* | A4 | 7½a black | 87.50 | 80.00 |
| *47* | A4 | 8a blue | 100.00 | 100.00 |
| *48* | A4 | 1r rose | 45.00 | 47.50 |
| *49* | A5 | 2r brick red | 125.00 | 125.00 |
| *50* | A5 | 3r gray vio | 110.00 | 125.00 |
| *51* | A5 | 4r ultra | 125.00 | 125.00 |
| *52* | A5 | 5r gray grn | 300.00 | 350.00 |
| | | *Nos. 38-52 (15)* | 1,517. | 1,464. |

This overprint exists double on most denominations and inverted on the 8a.

Surcharged in Red 2½

**1895**

| | | | | |
|---|---|---|---|---|
| *53* | A4 | 2½a on 4½a gray vio | 100.00 | 90.00 |

Stamps of India 1874-95 Overprinted or Surcharged

British
East
Africa

2½ a  2½ b  2½ c

**1895** **Wmk. Star. (39)**

| | | | | |
|---|---|---|---|---|
| *54* | A17 | ½a green | 1.65 | 2.00 |
| *55* | A19 | 1a maroon | 2.00 | 2.00 |
| *56* | A20 | 1a6p bis brn | 3.50 | 3.00 |
| *57* | A21 | 2a ultra | 2.00 | 2.25 |
| *58* | A28 | 2a6p green | 2.75 | 2.75 |
| *59* | A20(a) | 2½a on 1a6p bis brn | 32.50 | 27.50 |
| **a.** | | "½" without fraction line | 70.00 | |
| **b.** | | Surcharge "b" | 175.00 | |
| **c.** | | Surcharge "c" | 175.00 | |
| **d.** | | As "a." "1" of "½" inverted | 300.00 | 350.00 |
| *62* | A22 | 3a orange | 5.50 | 5.50 |
| *63* | A23 | 4a ol grn | 7.50 | 7.50 |
| *64* | A25 | 8a red vio | 16.00 | 16.00 |
| **a.** | | 8a red lil | 27.50 | 35.00 |
| *65* | A26 | 12a vio, *red* | 8.50 | 9.00 |
| *66* | A27 | 1r gray | 42.50 | 42.50 |
| *67* | A29 | 1r car & grn | 17.00 | 18.00 |
| **a.** | | Double ovpt., one sideways | 125.00 | 175.00 |
| *68* | A30 | 2r bis & rose | 27.50 | 30.00 |
| *69* | A30 | 3r grn & brn | 50.00 | 55.00 |
| *70* | A30 | 5r vio & ultra | 50.00 | 55.00 |
| **a.** | | Double overprint | 1,200. | |

**Wmk. Elephant's Head. (38)**

| | | | | |
|---|---|---|---|---|
| *71* | A14 | 6a bister | 7.25 | 7.25 |
| | | *Nos. 54-59,62-71 (16)* | 276.15 | 285.25 |

Varieties of the overprint include: "Britlsh," "Brltish," "Bpitish" and "Biitish" for "British", "Afrlca" for "Africa"; "Eas" and "Easa" for "East."

No. 59 is surcharged in bright red; Nos. 59b and 59c in brown red. Nos. 59b and 59c were prepared for use but not issued.

Queen Victoria and British Lions — A8

**Wmk. Crown and C. A. (2)**

**1896-1903** **Engr.** ***Perf. 14***

| | | | | |
|---|---|---|---|---|
| *72* | A8 | ½a yel grn | 15 | 15 |
| *73* | A8 | 1a carmine | 2.25 | 8 |
| **a.** | | 1a red | 2.25 | 10 |
| *74* | A8 | 1a dp rose ('03) | 26.00 | 2.75 |
| *75* | A8 | 2a chocolate | 3.25 | 2.50 |
| *76* | A8 | 2½a dk bl | 1.25 | 80 |
| *77* | A8 | 3a gray | 1.25 | 1.25 |
| *78* | A8 | 4a dp grn | 1.90 | 1.00 |
| *79* | A8 | 4½a orange | 1.25 | 1.25 |
| *80* | A8 | 5a dk ocher | 1.25 | 1.25 |
| *81* | A8 | 7½a lilac | 2.50 | 2.50 |
| *82* | A8 | 8a ol gray | 1.40 | 1.40 |
| *83* | A8 | 1r ultra | 10.50 | 7.25 |
| *84* | A8 | 2r red org | 35.00 | 13.00 |
| *85* | A8 | 3r dp vio | 32.50 | 10.50 |
| *86* | A8 | 4r lake | 32.50 | 16.00 |
| *87* | A8 | 5r dk brn | 32.50 | 26.00 |
| | | *Nos. 72-87 (16)* | 185.45 | 87.68 |

Zanzibar Nos. 38-40, 44-46 Overprinted in Black

British
East
Africa

**1897** **Wmk. Rosette (71)**

| | | | | |
|---|---|---|---|---|
| *88* | A2 | ½a yel grn & red | 26.00 | 17.00 |
| *89* | A2 | 1a ind & red | 65.00 | 65.00 |
| *90* | A2 | 2a red brn & red | 26.00 | 13.00 |
| *91* | A2 | 4½a org & red | 26.00 | 17.00 |
| *92* | A2 | 5a bis & red | 30.00 | 13.00 |
| *93* | A2 | 7½a lil & red | 42.50 | 30.00 |
| **a.** | | Overprinted on front and back | | |
| | | *Nos. 88-93 (6)* | 215.50 | 155.00 |

The 1a with red overprint, which includes a period after "Africa", was sent to the UPU, but never placed in use. Nos. 88, 90-93 and 95-100 also exist with period (in black) in sets sent to the UPU. Some experts consider these essays.

Black Ovpt. on Zanzibar #39, 42 New Value Surcharged in Red

**1897**

| | | | | |
|---|---|---|---|---|
| *95* | A2 (a) | 2½a on 1a ind & red | 52.50 | 45.00 |
| **a.** | | Black ovpt. double | 6,500. | |
| **b.** | | "2" over "1" for "½" | 1,200. | |
| *96* | A2 (b) | 2½a on 1a ind & red | 75.00 | 67.50 |
| *97* | A2 (c) | 2½a on 1a ind & red | 52.50 | 37.50 |
| *98* | A2 (a) | 2½a on 3a sl & red | 45.00 | 30.00 |
| **a.** | | "2" over "1" for "½" | 1,200. | |
| *99* | A2 (b) | 2½a on 3a sl & red | 67.50 | 60.00 |
| *100* | A2 (c) | 2½a on 3a sl & red | 45.00 | 32.50 |
| | | *Nos. 95-100 (6)* | 337.50 | 272.50 |

A10

**1898** **Wmk. 1** **Engr.**

| | | | | |
|---|---|---|---|---|
| *102* | A10 | 1r ultra | 7.50 | 6.00 |
| *103* | A10 | 2r orange | 27.50 | 24.00 |
| *104* | A10 | 3r dk vio | 32.50 | 32.50 |
| *105* | A10 | 4r carmine | 77.50 | *87.50* |
| *106* | A10 | 5r blk brn | 110.00 | 125.00 |
| *107* | A10 | 10r bister | 160.00 | 175.00 |
| *108* | A10 | 20r yel grn | 575.00 | 500.00 |
| *109* | A10 | 50r lilac | 2,500. | 2,750. |
| | | *Nos. 102-107 (6)* | 415.00 | 450.00 |

The stamps of this country were superseded in 1904 by the stamps of East Africa and Uganda Protectorate.

## BRITISH GUIANA

LOCATION — On the northeast coast of South America.
GOVT. — Former British Crown Colony.
AREA — 83,000 sq. mi.
POP. — 628,000 (estimated 1964).
CAPITAL — Georgetown.

*British Guiana stamps can be mounted in Scott's British East Caribbean Album.*

British Guiana became the independent state of Guyana May 26, 1966.

100 Cents = 1 Dollar

**Catalogue values for unused stamps in this country are for Never Hinged items, beginning with Scott 242 in the regular postage section and Scott J1 in the postage due section.**

Values of early British Guiana stamps vary according to condition. Quotations for Nos. 1-16 are for fine copies. Very fine to superb specimens sell at higher prices, and inferior or poor copies sell at much reduced prices, depending on the condition of the individual specimen.

A1

**1850-51** **Typeset** **Unwmk.** ***Imperf.***

| | | | | |
|---|---|---|---|---|
| *1* | A1 | 2c *pale rose*, cut to shape ('51) | | *65,000.* |
| *2* | A1 | 4c *orange* | | *18,000.* |
| **a.** | | 4c *yellow* | | *25,000.* |
| | | Cut to shape | | *4,000.* |
| *3* | A1 | 4c *yellow* (pelure) | | *35,000.* |
| | | Cut to shape | | *4,000.* |
| *4* | A1 | 8c *green* | | *12,500.* |
| | | Cut to shape | | *2,500.* |
| *5* | A1 | 12c *blue* | | *5,250.* |
| | | Cut to shape | | *1,900.* |
| **a.** | | 12c *pale blue* | | *10,500.* |
| **b.** | | 12c *indigo* | | *12,500.* |
| **c.** | | "1" of "12" omitted | | |

These stamps were initialed before use by the Deputy Postmaster General or by one of the clerks of the Colonial Postoffice at Georgetown. The following initials are found:—E. T. E. D(alton); E. D. W(ight); G. B. S(mith); H. A. K(illikelley); W. H. L(ortimer). As these stamps are type-set there are several types of each value.

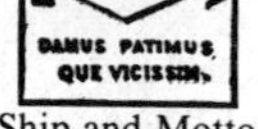


Ship and Motto of Colony — A2

Seal of the Colony — A3

**1852** **Litho.**

| | | | | |
|---|---|---|---|---|
| *6* | A2 | 1c *magenta* | *9,000.* | *5,000.* |
| *7* | A2 | 4c *blue* | *14,000.* | *5,000.* |

Both 1c and 4c are found in two types. Copies with paper cracked or rubbed sell for much less.

*The reprints are on thicker paper and the colors are brighter. They are perforated 12½ and imperforate. Value $15 each.*

**1853-59** ***Imperf.***

**Without Line above Value.**

| | | | | |
|---|---|---|---|---|
| *8* | A3 | 1c vermilion | 4,000. | 1,000. |

**Full or Partial White Line Above Value.**

| | | | | |
|---|---|---|---|---|
| *9* | A3 | 1c red | 2,250. | 550.00 |
| *10* | A3 | 4c blue | 825.00 | 375.00 |

On No. 9, "ONE CENT" varies from 11 to 13mm. in width.

**No. 10 Retouched; White Line above Value Removed.**

| | | | | |
|---|---|---|---|---|
| *11* | A3 | 4c blue | 1,250. | 400.00 |
| **a.** | | 4c dk bl | 1,600. | 425.00 |

*Reprints of Nos. 8 and 10 are on thin paper, perf. 12½ or imperf. The 1c is orange red, the 4c sky blue.*

**1860**

**Numerals in Corners Framed.**

| | | | | |
|---|---|---|---|---|
| *12* | A3 | 4c blue | 3,000. | 375.00 |

A4

**1856** **Typeset** ***Imperf.***

| | | | | |
|---|---|---|---|---|
| *13* | A4 | 1c *magenta* | | |
| *14* | A4 | 4c *magenta* | | *7,500.* |
| **a.** | | 4c *rose car* | | *10,500.* |
| *15* | A4 | 4c *blue* | | *45,000.* |
| *16* | A4 | 4c *bl, paper colored through* | | *60,000.* |

These stamps were initialed before being issued and the following initials are found:—E. T. E. D.; E. D. W.; W. H. L.; C. A. W. No. 13 is unique.

A5

Wide space between value and "Cents."

**1860-61** **Litho.** ***Perf. 12.***

**Thick Paper.**

| | | | | |
|---|---|---|---|---|
| *17* | A5 | 1c brn red ('61) | 225.00 | 65.00 |
| *18* | A5 | 1c pink | 1,000. | 165.00 |
| *19* | A5 | 2c orange | 80.00 | 25.00 |
| *20* | A5 | 8c rose | 225.00 | 35.00 |
| *21* | A5 | 12c gray | 250.00 | 25.00 |
| **a.** | | 12c lil | 300.00 | 25.00 |
| *22* | A5 | 24c green | 750.00 | 55.00 |

All denominations of type A5 above four cents are expressed in Roman numerals.

*The reprints of the 1c pink are perforated 12½; the other values have not been reprinted.*

Thin Paper

**1862**

| | | | | |
|---|---|---|---|---|
| *23* | A5 | 1c brown | 250.00 | 125.00 |
| *24* | A5 | 1c black | 50.00 | 20.00 |
| **a.** | | Imperf. | | |
| *25* | A5 | 2c orange | 40.00 | 15.00 |
| *26* | A5 | 8c rose | 52.50 | 25.00 |
| **a.** | | Imperf. | | |
| *27* | A5 | 12c lilac | 52.50 | 16.00 |
| *28* | A5 | 24c green | 500.00 | 47.50 |
| **a.** | | Imperf. | | |

***Perf. 12½ and 13***

| | | | | |
|---|---|---|---|---|
| *29* | A5 | 1c black | 18.00 | 9.00 |
| *30* | A5 | 2c orange | 40.00 | 10.00 |
| *31* | A5 | 8c rose | 110.00 | 32.50 |
| *32* | A5 | 12c lilac | 325.00 | 47.50 |
| *33* | A5 | 24c green | 100.00 | 40.00 |

***Perf. 10***

| | | | | |
|---|---|---|---|---|
| *34* | A5 | 12c gray lil | 225.00 | 22.50 |

See Nos. 44-62.

A6 A7

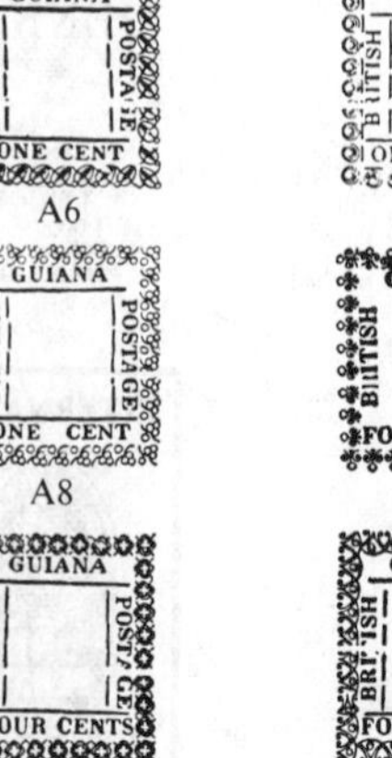


A8 A9

A10

A11

**1862 Typeset *Rouletted***

35 A6 1c *rose* 1,100. 175.00
Unsigned 140.00
36 A7 1c *rose* 1,200. 200.00
Unsigned 150.00
37 A8 1c *rose* 2,250. 300.00
Unsigned 275.00
38 A6 2c *yellow* 1,100. 200.00
Unsigned 125.00
39 A7 2c *yellow* 1,500. 225.00
Unsigned 150.00
40 A8 2c *yellow* 2,500. 375.00
Unsigned 300.00
41 A9 4c *blue* 1,200. 250.00
Unsigned 225.00
42 A10 4c *blue* 2,500. 1,250.
Unsigned 425.00
a. Without inner lines 1,200. 300.00
As "a" Unsigned 200.00
43 A11 4c *blue* 1,000. 125.00
Unsigned 225.00

Nos. 35-43 were typeset, there being 24 types of each value. They were initialed before use "R. M. Ac. R. G"., being the initials of Robert Mather, Acting Receiver General.

Black ink was used on the rose stamps, red ink on the yellow and an alkali was used on the blue stamps, which, destroying the color of the paper, caused the initials to appear to be written in white.

Uninitialed stamps are remainders, few sheets having been found.

Specimens with roulette on all sides are valued higher.

Narrow space between value and "Cents"

**1860 Thick Paper. Litho. *Perf. 12.***

44 A5 4c blue 175.00 32.50

**Thin Paper.**

44A A5 4c blue 32.50 17.50

Medium Paper.

**1863 *Perf. 12½ and 13***

45 A5 1c black 25.00 12.00
46 A5 2c orange 27.50 5.00
a. Imperf., pair 82.50
47 A5 4c blue 50.00 9.00
a. Imperf., pair 150.00
48 A5 8c rose 90.00 16.00
49 A5 12c lilac 225.00 22.50

**1866 *Perf. 10.***

50 A5 1c black 5.00 4.00
51 A5 2c orange 7.00 2.00
52 A5 4c blue 32.50 5.75
a. Half used as 2c on cover 3,500.
53 A5 8c rose 55.00 6.00
a. Diagonal half used as 4c on cover
54 A5 12c lilac 65.00 10.00
a. Third used as 4c on cover

**1875 *Perf. 15***

58 A5 1c black 18.00 5.00
59 A5 2c orange 85.00 8.00
60 A5 4c blue 150.00 55.00
61 A5 8c rose 100.00 40.00
62 A5 12c lilac 275.00 32.50

Seal of Colony
A12 A13

**1863 *Perf. 12***

63 A12 24c green 75.00 6.00

***Perf. 12½ to 13.***

64 A12 6c blue 60.00 27.50
65 A12 24c green 70.00 6.50
a. Imperf. 125.00
66 A12 48c deep red 80.00 22.50
a. 48c rose 150.00 22.50

**1866 *Perf. 10***

67 A12 6c blue 65.00 10.00
a. 6c ultra 65.00 16.00
68 A12 24c green 95.00 5.00
69 A12 48c rose red 175.00 17.50

**1875 *Perf. 15***

70 A12 6c ultra 200.00 40.00
71 A12 24c green 300.00 17.50

**Wmk. Crown and C. C. (1)**

**1876 Typo. *Perf. 14.***

72 A13 1c slate 2.50 35
a. Perf. 14x12½ 150.00
73 A13 2c orange 10.00 1.10
74 A13 4c ultra 50.00 4.75
a. Perf. 12½ 1,100. 125.00
75 A13 6c chocolate 30.00 6.50
76 A13 8c rose 50.00 1.90
77 A13 12c lilac 35.00 3.50
78 A13 24c green 35.00 5.00
79 A13 48c red brn 65.00 9.25
80 A13 96c bister 325.00 190.00
*Nos. 72-80 (9)* 602.50 222.35

See Nos. 107-111.

Stamps Surcharged by Brush-like Pen Lines

Surcharge Types:
Type a- Two horiz. lines.
Type b- Two lines, one horiz., one vert.
Type c- Three lines, two horiz., one vert.
Type d- One horiz. line.

On Nos. 75 and 67

**1878 *Perf. 10, 14***

82 A13(a) (1c) on 6c choc 32.50 32.50
83 A12(b) (1c) on 6c bl 125.00 45.00
84 A13(b) (1c) on 6c choc 125.00 35.00

**On Nos. O3, O8-O10**

85 A13(c) (1c) on 4c ultra 70.00 45.00
a. Type b 3,000.
86 A13(c) (1c) on 6c choc 110.00 45.00
87 A5 (c) (2c) on 8c rose 95.00 45.00
88A A13(b) (2c) on 8c rose 125.00 45.00

**On Nos. O1, O3, O6-O7**

89 A5 (d) (1c) on 1c blk 110.00 45.00
89A A5 (d) (2c) on 8c rose
90 A13(d) (1c) on 1c sl 125.00 20.00
91 A13(d) (2c) on 2c org 125.00 30.00

The provisional values of Nos. 82 to 91 were established by various official decrees. The horizontal lines crossed out the old value, "OFFICIAL," or both.

A19 A19a

A20 A21

Issues of 1866-76 Surcharged with New Values in Black.

**1881**

92 A19 1c on 48c red 17.50 4.25
93 A19a 1c on 96c bis 3.75 4.00
94 A20 2c on 96c bis 4.00 6.00
95 A21 2c on 96c bis 25.00 25.00

A22 A23

A24 A25

A26

Official Stamps Surcharged with New Values

**1881**

96 A22 1c on 12c lil 50.00 25.00
97 A23 1c on 48c red brn 52.50 45.00
98 A24 2c on 12c lil 110.00 110.00
99 A25 2c on 12c lil 30.00 15.00
a. "2" inverted
b. "2" double 450.00 425.00
100 A24 2c on 24c grn 600.00 600.00
101 A25 2c on 24c grn 42.50 32.50
a. "2" inverted
d. Double surcharge 650.00
102 A26 2c on 24c grn 110.00 110.00

A27

Typeset

ONE AND TWO CENTS.
Type I. Ship with three masts.
Type II. Brig with two masts.

"SPECIMEN"

Perforated Diagonally across Stamp

**1882 Unwmk. *Perf. 12***

103 A27 1c *lilac rose*, I 30.00 17.50
a. Without "Specimen" 50.00 50.00
104 A27 1c *lilac rose*, II 30.00 22.50
a. Without "Specimen" 50.00 50.00
105 A27 2c *yellow*, I 35.00 40.00
a. Without "Specimen" 50.00 50.00
b. Diagonal half used as 1c on cover
106 A27 2c *yellow*, II 32.50 32.50
a. Without "Specimen" 50.00 50.00

Nos. 103-106 were typeset, 12 to a sheet, and, to prevent fraud on the government, the word *"Specimen"* was perforated across them before they were issued. There were 2 settings of the 1c and 3 settings of the 2c, thus there are 24 types of the former and 36 of the latter.

Type of 1876

**Wmk. Crown and C. A. (2)**

**1882 Typo. *Perf. 14***

107 A13 1c slate 2.25 35
108 A13 2c orange 7.75 45
a. "2 CENTS" double
109 A13 4c ultra 27.50 7.00
110 A13 6c brown 3.75 7.75
111 A13 8c rose 40.00 1.40
*Nos. 107-111 (5)* 81.25 16.95

A28 A29

4 CENTS and $4
Type I. Figure "4" is 3mm high.
Type II. Figure "4" is 3½mm high.
6 CENTS.
Type I. Top of "6" is flat.
Type II. Top of "6" turns downward.

"INLAND REVENUE" Overprint and Surcharged in Black.

**1889**

112 A28 1c lilac 1.65 70
113 A28 2c lilac 1.00 45
114 A28 3c lilac 1.00 45
115 A28 4c lilac, I 1.00 45
116 A28 4c lilac, II 20.00 14.00
117 A28 6c lilac, I 4.00 4.00
118 A28 6c lilac, II 3.00 3.00
119 A28 8c lilac 1.10 80
120 A28 10c lilac 2.00 2.00
121 A28 20c lilac 4.25 3.75
122 A28 40c lilac 7.25 5.50
123 A28 72c lilac 9.00 8.75
124 A28 $1 green 325.00 250.00
125 A28 $2 green 110.00 110.00
126 A28 $3 green 52.50 52.50
127 A28 $4 green, I 225.00 175.00
127A A28 $4 green, II 600.00 600.00
128 A28 $5 green 125.00 125.00
*Nos. 112-128 (18)* 1,492. 1,356.

No. 113 Surcharged "2" in Red.

**1889**

129 A29 2c on 2c lilac 80 40

Inverted and double surcharges of "2" were privately made.

A30 A31

**1889-1903 Typo.**

130 A30 1c lil & gray 75 22
131 A30 1c grn ('90) 30 16
131A A30 1c gray grn ('00) 1.00 14
132 A30 2c lil & org 70 14
133 A30 2c lil & rose ('00) 2.50 14
134 A30 2c vio & blk, *red* ('01) 1.00 14
135 A30 4c lil & ultra 2.00 1.00
a. 4c lil & bl 7.50 1.25
136 A30 5c ultra ('91) 2.25 25
137 A30 6c lil & mar 4.25 1.50
a. 6c lil & brn 11.00 5.50
138 A30 6c gray blk & ultra ('02) 4.25 3.00
139 A30 8c lil & rose 5.00 75
140 A30 8c lil & blk ('90) 2.25 1.40
141 A30 12c lil & vio 3.25 1.00
142 A30 24c lil & grn 2.75 1.40
143 A30 48c lil & ver 12.50 4.25
144 A30 48c dk gray & lil brn ('01) 8.25 7.00
145 A30 60c gray grn & car ('03) 50.00 60.00
146 A30 72c lil & org brn 15.00 14.00
147 A30 96c lil & rose 37.50 37.50
*Nos. 130-147 (19)* 155.50 133.99

Stamps of the 1889-1903 issue with pen or revenue cancellation sell for a small fraction of the above quotations.

See Nos. 160-177.

Red Surcharge

**1890**

148 A31 1c on $1 grn & blk 55 40
a. Double surcharge 40.00 40.00
149 A31 1c on $2 grn & blk 32 32
a. Double surcharge 82.50 82.50
150 A31 1c on $3 grn & blk 65 65
a. Double surcharge 55.00 55.00
151 A31 1c on $4 grn & blk, type I 1.40 1.40
a. Double surcharge 67.50
151B A31 1c on $4 grn & blk, type II 8.75 8.75
c. Double surcharge
*Nos. 148-151B (5)* 11.67 11.52

Mt. Roraima
A32

Kaieteur (Old Man's) Falls — A33

**1898 Wmk. 1 Engr.**

152 A32 1c car & gray blk 2.50 90
153 A33 2c bl & brn 2.50 90
a. Horiz. pair, imperf. between 4,500.
154 A32 5c brn & grn 10.50 4.75
155 A33 10c red & bl blk 12.00 12.00
156 A32 15c bl & red brn 10.50 12.00
*Nos. 152-156 (5)* 38.00 30.55

60th anniv. of Queen Victoria's accession to the throne.

Nos. 154-156 Surcharged in Black. **TWO CENTS.**

**1899**

157 A32 2c on 5c brn & grn 1.40 1.65
a. Without period 22.50 22.50
158 A33 2c on 10c red & bl blk 85 1.10
a. "GENTS" 45.00 45.00
b. Inverted surch 200.00 225.00
c. Without period 22.50 22.50
159 A32 2c on 15c bl & red brn 1.40 1.40
a. Without period 40.00 40.00
b. Double surcharge 60.00
c. Inverted surch. 300.00 300.00

There are many slight errors in the setting of this surcharge, such as: small "E" in

"CENTS;" no period and narrow "C"; comma between "T" and "S"; dash between "TWO" and "CENTS;" comma between "N" and "T."

Ship Type of 1889-1903.

**1905-10** **Wmk. 3**

**Chalky Paper**

*160* A30 1c gray grn 40 12
*a.* 1c bl grn, ordinary paper ('10) 40 12
*b.* Booklet pane of 6
*161* A30 2c vio & blk, *red* 1.75 22
*162* A30 4c lil & ultra 12.00 6.75
*163* A30 5c lil & bl, *bl* 7.75 1.75
*164* A30 6c gray blk & ultra 14.00 12.50
*165* A30 12c lil & vio 14.00 12.50
*166* A30 24c lil & grn ('06) 3.50 3.50
*167* A30 48c gray & vio brn 9.25 12.50
*168* A30 60c gray grn & car rose 11.00 12.50
*169* A30 72c lil & org brn ('07) 27.50 25.00
*170* A30 96c blk & red, *yel* ('06) 22.50 *27.50*
*Nos. 160-170 (11)* 123.65 *114.84*

The 2c-60c exist on ordinary paper.

A34

George V — A35

**Black Overprint.**

*171* A34 $2.40 grn & vio 140.00 *140.00*

Ship Type of 1889-1903.
Ordinary Paper.

TWO CENTS.
Type I. Only the upper right corner of the flag touches the mast.
Type II. The entire right side of the flag touches the mast.

**1907**

*172* A30 2c red, type I 2.25 18
*a.* Booklet pane of 6, type I
*b.* 2c red, type II 60 12
*174* A30 4c brn & vio 1.95 1.00
*175* A30 5c blue 3.00 42
*176* A30 6c gray & blk 7.50 3.00
*177* A30 12c org & vio 3.25 3.00
*Nos. 172-177 (5)* 17.95 7.60

**1913-16** ***Perf. 14***

*178* A35 1c green 1.00 12
*179* A35 2c scarlet 52 8
*a.* 2c car 38 8
*180* A35 4c brn & red vio 65 20
*181* A35 5c ultra 65 25
*182* A35 6c gray & blk 65 55
*183* A35 12c org & vio 90 90

**Chalky Paper**

*184* A35 24c dl vio & grn 1.40 1.40
*185* A35 48c blk & vio brn 3.50 3.50
*186* A35 60c grn & car 7.75 11.00
*187* A35 72c dl vio & org brn 14.00 17.00

**Surface Colored Paper**

*188* A35 96c blk & red, *yel* 14.00 18.00

**Paper Colored Through**

*189* A35 96c blk & red, *yel* ('16) 10.00 12.50
*Nos. 178-189 (12)* 55.02 65.50

The 72c and late printings of the 2c and 5c are from redrawn dies. The ruled lines behind the value are thin and faint, making the tablet appear lighter than before. The shading lines in other parts of the stamps are also lighter.

**1921-27** **Wmk. 4**

*191* A35 1c green 32 18
*a.* Booklet pane of 6
*192* A35 2c rose red 65 8
*193* A35 2c dp vio ('23) 55 6
*a.* Booklet pane of 6
*194* A35 4c brn & vio 1.00 14
*a.* Booklet pane of 6
*195* A35 6c ultra 1.10 22
*196* A35 12c org & vio 1.65 80

**Chalky Paper**

*197* A35 24c dl vio & grn 2.75 1.90
*198* A35 48c blk & vio brn ('26) 6.75 2.00
*199* A35 60c grn & car ('26) 7.50 *11.00*
*200* A35 72c dl vio & brn org 8.00 9.00
*201* A35 96c blk & red, *yel* ('27) 9.50 *12.00*
*Nos. 191-201 (11)* 39.77 37.38

Plowing a Rice Field — A36

Indian Shooting Fish — A37

Kaieteur Falls — A38

Georgetown, Public Buildings — A39

**1931, July 21** **Engr.** ***Perf. 12½***

*205* A36 1c bl grn 38 38
*206* A37 2c dk brn 1.00 45
*207* A38 4c car rose 2.75 1.75
*208* A39 6c ultra 2.25 1.90
*209* A38 $1 violet 24.00 26.00
*Nos. 205-209 (5)* 30.38 30.48

Issued in commemoration of the centenary of the union of Berbice, Demerara and Essequibo to form the Colony of British Guiana.

Plowing a Rice Field — A40

Indian Shooting Fish — A41

Gold Mining — A42

Kaieteur Falls — A43

Shooting Logs over Falls — A44

Stabroek Market — A45

Sugar Cane in Punts — A46

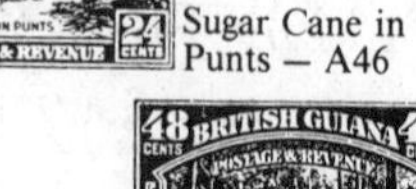

Forest Road — A47

The first price column gives the catalogue value of an unused stamp, the second that of a used stamp.

Victoria Regia Lilies — A48

Mt. Roraima — A49

Sir Walter Raleigh and Son — A50

Botanical Gardens — A51

**1934-51** ***Perf. 12½***

*210* A40 1c green 10 5
*211* A41 2c brown 20 5
*212* A42 3c carmine 5 5
*a.* Bklt pane of 4 ('38) 9.00
*b.* Perf. 12½x13½ ('43) 28 5
*c.* Perf. 13x13½ ('49) 6 7
*213* A43 4c vio blk 90 9
*a.* Imperf. horiz., pair *8,000.*
*214* A44 6c dp ultra 1.50 1.40
*215* A45 12c orange 10 5
*a.* Perf. 13½x13 ('51) 10 5
*216* A46 24c rose vio 3.00 1.25
*217* A47 48c black 10.50 9.25
*218* A43 50c green 12.00 15.00
*219* A48 60c brown 21.00 24.00
*220* A49 72c rose vio 1.25 1.00
*221* A50 96c black 20.00 21.00
*222* A51 $1 violet 19.00 17.00
*Nos. 210-222 (13)* 89.60 90.19

See Nos. 236, 238, 240.

**Silver Jubilee Issue.**
Common Design Type

**1935, May 6** ***Perf. 13½x14***

*223* CD301 2c gray blk & ultra 18 18
*224* CD301 6c bl & brn 85 42
*225* CD301 12c ind & grn 1.40 1.00
*226* CD301 24c brt vio & ind 3.25 3.25

**Coronation Issue.**
Common Design Type

**1937, May 12** ***Perf. 13½x14***

*227* CD302 2c brown 8 8
*228* CD302 4c gray blk 14 14
*229* CD302 6c brt ultra 20 20

Plowing a Rice Field — A52

Kaieteur Falls — A53

Map of South America A54

Indian Shooting Fish A55

Sugar Cane in Punts — A56

Shooting Logs over Falls — A57

Botanical Gardens — A58

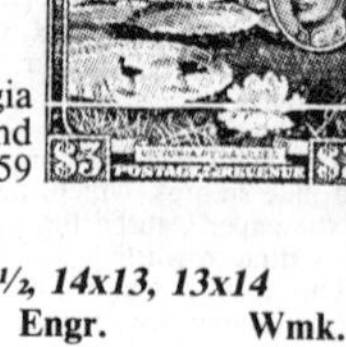
Victoria Regia Lilies and Jacanas — A59

***Perf. 12½, 14x13, 13x14***

**1938-52** **Engr.** **Wmk. 4**

*230* A52 1c green 5 5
*a.* Booklet pane of 4 3.75
*b.* Perf. 14x13 ('49) 5 5
*231* A53 2c vio blk 5 5
*a.* Booklet pane of 4 5.75
*b.* Perf. 13x14 ('49) 5 5
*232* A54 4c blk & rose, perf. 13x14 ('52) 15 9
*a.* Perf. 12½ 8 5
*b.* Booklet pane of 4
*c.* Vert. pair, imperf. between *5,500.* *3,000.*
*233* A55 6c dp ultra 8 5
*a.* Perf. 13x14 ('49) 9 5
*234* A56 24c dp grn 95 18
*a.* Wmk. upright 4.75 3.00
*235* A53 36c pur, perf. 13x14 ('51) 95 95
*a.* Perf. 12½ 35 16
*236* A47 48c org yel 55 32
*a.* Perf. 14x13 ('51) 1.10 1.10
*237* A57 60c brown 65 35
*238* A50 96c brn vio, perf. 12½ 2.05 1.00
*a.* Perf. 12½x13½ ('44) 2.00 1.00
*239* A58 $1 dp vio 1.25 55
*a.* Perf. 14x13 ('51) 200.00 375.00
*240* A49 $2 rose vio, perf. 14x13 ('50) 3.25 3.00
*a.* Perf. 12½ ('45) 3.25 3.00
*241* A59 $3 org brn, perf. 12½ ('45) 3.75 3.00
*a.* Perf. 14x13 ('52) 7.50 6.25
*Nos. 230-241 (12)* 13.73 9.59

The watermark on No. 234 is sideways.

**Catalogue values for unused stamps in this section, from this point to the end of the section, are for Never Hinged items.**

**Peace Issue.**
Common Design Type

**1946, Oct. 21** ***Perf. 13½x14***

*242* CD303 3c carmine 8 8
*243* CD303 6c dp bl 16 16

**Silver Wedding Issue.**
Common Design Types

**1948, Dec. 20** **Photo.** ***Perf. 14x14½***

*244* CD304 3c scarlet 9 9

**Engr.**
***Perf. 11½x11***

*245* CD305 $3 org brn 10.00 *16.00*

**UPU Issue**
Common Design Types
**Engr.; Name Typo. on 6c and 12c**
***Perf. 13½, 11x11½***

**1949, Oct. 10** **Wmk. 4**

*246* CD306 4c rose car 35 12
*247* CD307 6c indigo 55 55
*248* CD308 12c orange 70 70
*249* CD309 24c bl grn 1.40 1.40

**University Issue**
Common Design Types

**1951, Feb. 16** **Engr.** ***Perf. 14x14½***

*250* CD310 3c car & blk 32 22
*251* CD311 6c dp ultra & blk 42 42

**Coronation Issue.**
Common Design Type

**1953, June 2** *Perf. 13½x13*
*252* CD312 4c car & blk 20 10

---

Common Design Types pictured in section before Great Britain.

---

General Post Office, Georgetown — A60

Indian Shooting Fish — A61

Designs: 2c, Botanical gardens. 3c, Victoria regia lilies and jacanas. 5c, Map. 6c, Rice combine. 8c, Sugar cane entering factory. 12c, Felling greenheart tree. 24c, Bauxite mining. 36c, Mt. Roraima. 48c, Kaieteur Falls. 72c, Arapaima (fish). $1, Toucan. $2, Dredging gold. $5, Coat of Arms.

**Engraved, Center Litho on $1.**
*Perf. 12½x13, 13*

**1954, Dec. 1** **Wmk. 4**
*253* A60 1c black 7 5
*254* A60 2c dk grn 7 5
*255* A60 3c red brn & ol 10 6
*256* A61 4c violet 14 6
*257* A60 5c blk & red 16 7
*258* A60 6c yel grn 16 7
*259* A60 8c ultra 16 9
*260* A61 12c brn & blk 35 10
*261* A60 24c org & blk 75 18
*262* A60 36c blk & rose 1.10 42
*263* A61 48c red brn & ultra 1.40 70
*264* A61 72c emer & rose 2.00 1.60
*265* A60 $1 blk, yel, grn & sal 3.25 90
*266* A60 $2 magenta 4.25 2.25
*267* A61 $5 blk & ultra 9.25 7.75
*Nos. 253-267 (15)* 23.21 14.35

See Nos. 279-287.

Clasped Hands — A62

*Perf. 14½x14*

**1961, Oct. 23** **Photo.** **Wmk. 314**
*268* A62 5c sal pink & brn 14 14
*269* A62 6c lt bl grn & brn 16 16
*270* A62 30c lt org & brn 42 42

Fourth annual History and Culture Week.

**Freedom from Hunger Issue**
Common Design Type

**1963, June 4** *Perf. 14x14½*
*271* CD314 20c lilac 48 40

**Red Cross Centenary Issue**
Common Design Type
**Wmk. 314**

**1963, Sept. 2** **Litho.** *Perf. 13*
*272* CD315 5c blk & red 12 12
*273* CD315 20c ultra & red 65 65

Queen Types of 1954

**Engraved; Center Litho. on $1.**
*Perf. 12½x13, 13*

**1963-65** **Wmk. 314**
*279* A60 3c red brn & ol ('65) 85 65
*280* A60 5c blk & red ('64) 15 5
*281* A61 12c brn & blk ('64) 30 5
*282* A60 24c org & blk 52 7
*283* A60 36c blk & rose 85 7
*284* A61 48c red brn & ultra 1.50 1.10
*285* A61 72c emer & rose 4.25 3.00
*286* A60 $1 blk, yel, grn & sal 5.25 2.50
*287* A60 $2 magenta 7.50 4.75
*Nos. 279-287 (9)* 21.17 12.24

Weight Lifter A63

**1964, Oct. 1** **Photo.** *Perf. 13x13½*
*290* A63 5c orange 8 8
*291* A63 8c blue 14 14
*292* A63 25c car rose 42 42

18th Olympic Games, Tokyo, Oct. 10-25.

**ITU Issue**
Common Design Type
*Perf. 11x11½*

**1965, May 17** **Litho.** **Wmk. 314**
*293* CD317 5c emer & ol 12 8
*294* CD317 25c lt bl & brt pink 45 45

**Intl. Cooperation Year Issue**
Common Design Type

**1965, Oct. 25** **Wmk. 314** *Perf. 14½*
*295* CD318 5c bl grn & cl 12 12
*296* CD318 25c lt vio & grn 50 50

Winston Churchill and St. George's Cathedral, Georgetown — A64

**1966, Jan. 24** **Photo.** *Perf. 14x14½*
*297* A64 5c multi 14 8
*298* A64 25c dp bl, blk & gold 60 48

Sir Winston Leonard Spencer Churchill (1874-1965), statesman and WW II leader.

**Royal Visit Issue**
Common Design Type

**1966, Feb. 4** **Litho.** *Perf. 11x12*
*299* CD320 3c vio blue 25 18
*300* CD320 25c dk car rose 1.40 1.10

---

## POSTAGE DUE STAMPS

**Catalogue values for unused stamps in this section, from this point to the end of the section, are for Never Hinged items.**

D1

*Perf. 13½x14*

**1940-52** **Typo.** **Wmk. 4**
*J1* D1 1c green 26 26
*a.* Wmk. 4a (error) 40.00
*J2* D1 2c black 32 32
*a.* Wmk. 4a (error) 35.00
*J3* D1 4c ultra ('52) 80 80
*a.* Wmk. 4a (error) 35.00
*J4* D1 12c carmine 1.65 *4.00*

The 2c and 12c are on chalky paper as well as ordinary paper.

---

## WAR TAX STAMP

Regular Issue No. 179 Overprinted **War Tax**

**1918, Jan. 4** **Wmk. 3** *Perf. 14*
*MR1* A35 2c scarlet 12 12

---

## OFFICIAL STAMPS

No. 50 Overprinted in Red **OFFICIAL**

**1875** **Unwmk.** *Perf. 10*
*O1* A5 1c black 35.00 10.00

Nos. 51, 53-54, 68 Overprinted in Black **OFFICIAL**

*O2* A5 2c orange 125.00 11.00
*O3* A5 8c rose 300.00 100.00
*O4* A5 12c lilac 1,000. 500.00
*O5* A12 24c green 600.00 225.00

Same Overprint on Nos. 72-76

**1877** **Wmk. 1** *Perf. 14*
*O6* A13 1c slate 225.00 85.00
*O7* A13 2c orange 75.00 7.50
*O8* A13 4c ultramarine 100.00 35.00
*O9* A13 6c chocolate 2,750. 675.00
*O10* A13 8c rose 2,500. 525.00

The type A13 12c lilac, 24c green and 48c red brown overprinted "OFFICIAL" were never placed in use. A few copies of the 12c and 24c have been seen but the 48c is only known surcharged with new value for provisional use in 1881.

---

# BRITISH HONDURAS

LOCATION — Central America bordering on Caribbean on east, Mexico on north and Guatemala on west.
GOVT. — British Crown Colony.
AREA — 8,867 sq. mi.
POP. — 130,000 (est. 1972).
CAPITAL — Belmopan.

Before British Honduras became a colony (subordinate to Jamaica) in 1862, it was a settlement under British influence. In 1884 it became an independent colony. In 1973 the colony changed its name to Belize. Issues of Belize are listed under that name in this volume.

12 Pence = 1 Shilling
100 Cents = 1 Dollar (1888)

**Catalogue values for unused stamps in this country are for Never Hinged items, beginning with Scott 127 in the regular postage section, Scott J1 in the postage due section.**

Queen Victoria — A1

**1866** **Unwmk.** **Typo.** *Perf. 14*
*1* A1 1p blue 30.00 30.00
*a.* Horiz. pair, imperf. betwn.
*2* A1 6p rose 125.00 82.50
*3* A1 1sh green 150.00 72.50

**1872-73** **Wmk. 1** *Perf. 12½*
*4* A1 1p blue 30.00 12.00
*5* A1 3p brown 70.00 45.00
*6* A1 6p rose 140.00 27.50
*a.* Imperf.
*7* A1 1sh green 175.00 18.00
*a.* Horiz. pair, imperf. betwn. *18,000.*

**1872-79** *Perf. 14.*
*8* A1 1p blue 26.00 12.00
*a.* Horiz. strip of 3, imperf. betwn. *4,500.*
*9* A1 3p brown 60.00 16.00
*10* A1 4p vio ('79) 110.00 10.00
*11* A1 6p rose 225.00 165.00
*12* A1 1sh green 150.00 6.50

**1882-87** **Wmk. Crown and C.A. (2)**
*13* A1 1p bl ('84) 22.50 18.00
*14* A1 1p rose ('84) 9.50 6.50
*a.* Diagonal half used as ½p on cover
*15* A1 4p violet 45.00 4.00
*16* A1 6p yel ('85) 240.00 150.00
*17* A1 1sh gray ('87) 175.00 110.00

Stamps of 1872-87 Surcharged in Black — a **2 CENTS**

**1888** **Wmk. 1** *Perf. 12½*
*18* A1 2c on 6p rose 95.00 95.00
*19* A1 3c on 3p brn *8,000.* *3,000.*

*Perf. 14.*
*20* A1 2c on 6p rose 62.50 62.50
*a.* Diagonal half used as 1c on cover *225.00*
*b.* Double surcharge 1,300. 1,300.
*c.* "2" with curved tail 725.00 725.00
*21* A1 3c on 3p brn 47.50 47.50

**Wmk. Crown and C. A. (2)**
*22* A1 2c on 1p rose 6.00 *15.00*
*a.* Diagonal half used as 1c on cover 250.00
*b.* Double surcharge 1,100. 1,000.
*c.* Inverted surcharge 1,300. 1,250.
*23* A1 10c on 4p vio 20.00 9.00
*a.* Inverted surch.
*24* A1 20c on 6p yel 18.00 15.00
*25* A1 50c on 1sh gray 325.00 425.00

No. 25 with Additional Surcharge in Red or Black — b **TWO**

*26* A1 2c (R) on 50c on 1sh gray 21.00 *37.50*
*a.* "TWO" in blk *10,000.* *9,000.*
*b.* "TWO" double (Blk + R) *10,000.* *8,500.*
*c.* Diagonal half used as 1c on cover 325.00

Stamps of 1872-87 Surcharged in Black — c **2 CENTS**

**1888-89**
*28* A1 2c on 1p rose 45 *85*
*a.* Diagonal half used as 1c on cover 110.00
*29* A1 3c on 3p brn 50 *1.00*
*30* A1 10c on 4p vio 1.75 *1.75*
*31* A1 20c on 6p yel 4.50 *11.00*
*32* A1 50c on 1sh gray 12.00 *22.50*

No. 30 with Additional Surcharge in Black or Red — d **6**

**1891**
*33* A1 6c (Blk) on 10c on 4p 1.00 *3.75*
*a.* "6" and bar inverted *3,000.* *900.00*
*b.* "6" only inverted *3,000.*
*34* A1 6c (R) on 10c on 4p 65 *2.50*
*a.* "6" and bar inverted *500.00* *500.00*
*b.* "6" only inverted *3,000.*

Stamps similar to No. 33 but with "SIX" instead of "6," both with and without bar, were prepared but not regularly issued.

No. 29 with Additional Surcharge in Black **FIVE**

*35* A1 5c on 3c on 3p brn (Bk) 1.50 *3.25*
*a.* Double surcharge of "Five" and bar 225.00 *250.00*

**Black Surcharge, Type "c".**
*36* A1 6c on 3p bl 75 1.40

No. 36 with Additional Surcharge in Red

**1891**
*37* A1 (c+d) 15c (R) on 6c on 3p bl 5.00 *8.75*
*a.* Double surcharge

*British Honduras stamps can be mounted in Scott's British North and West Caribbean Album.*

A8

A9

**1891-98 Wmk. 2 *Perf. 14***

*38* A8 1c green 90 1.00
*39* A8 2c car rose 75 24
*40* A8 3c brown 95 1.25
*41* A8 5c ultra ('95) 10.00 90
*42* A8 6c ultra 1.75 50
*43* A8 10c vio & grn ('95) 5.25 4.75
*44* A8 12c vio & grn 3.50 2.50
*45* A8 24c yel & bl 3.00 3.50
*46* A8 25c red brn & grn ('98) 10.00 *15.00*
*Nos. 38-46 (9)* 36.10 29.64

Numeral tablet on Nos. 43-46 has lined background with colorless value and "c".

Type of 1866 Surcharged Type "c"

**1892**

*47* A1 1c on 1p grn 22 22

Regular Issue Overprinted in Black REVENUE

**1899**

*48* A8 5c ultra 1.75 2.25
*a.* "BEVENUE" 50.00 *57.50*
*49* A8 10c lil & grn 3.50 *6.50*
*a.* "BEVENUE" 175.00 *250.00*
*50* A8 25c red brn & grn 2.50 4.25
*a.* "BEVENUE" 72.50 *87.50*
*51* A1 50c on 1sh gray (No. 32) 100.00 *140.00*
*a.* "BEVENUE" 2,750. 2,750.

The overprint is found in two lengths: 12mm. (43 to the pane) and 11mm. (17 to the pane). The "U" is found in both a tall, narrow type and the more common small type.

**1899-1901**

*52* A9 5c gray blk & ultra, *bl* ('00) 1.90 60
*53* A9 10c vio & grn ('01) 2.50 *3.75*
*54* A9 50c grn & car rose 7.50 *12.50*
*55* A9 $1 grn & car rose 11.00 *13.00*
*56* A9 $2 grn & ultra 26.00 *32.50*
*57* A9 $5 grn & blk 210.00 *250.00*
*Nos. 52-57 (6)* 258.90 312.35

Numeral tablet on Nos. 53-54 has lined background with colorless value and "c".

King Edward VII — A10

**1902-04 Typo. Wmk. 2**

*58* A10 1c gray grn & grn ('04) 6.00 *7.25*
*59* A10 2c vio & blk, *red* 2.00 38
*60* A10 5c gray blk & ultra, *bl* 3.00 1.00
*61* A10 20c dl vio & vio ('04) 7.25 *12.00*

**1904-06 Chalky Paper Wmk. 3**

*62* A10 1c green 30 22
*63* A10 2c vio & blk, *red* 1.25 10
*64* A10 5c blk & ultra, *bl* ('05) 1.25 28
*65* A10 10c vio & grn ('06) 2.50 1.25
*67* A10 25c vio & org ('06) 4.00 6.00
*68* A10 50c grn & car rose ('06) 6.00 *13.00*
*69* A10 $1 grn & car rose ('06) 12.00 *20.00*
*70* A10 $2 grn & ultra ('06) 45.00 57.50
*71* A10 $5 grn & blk ('06) 200.00 225.00
*Nos. 62-71 (9)* 272.30 323.35

The 1c and 2c exist also on ordinary paper.

**1909**

**Ordinary Paper.**

*72* A10 2c carmine 2.00 28
*73* A10 5c ultra 2.25 48

**1911**

*74* A10 25c *green* 8.25 *11.00*

Numeral tablet on #61, 65-68, 74 has lined background with colorless value and "c".

King George V
A11 A12

**1913-17 Wmk. 3 *Perf. 14***

*75* A11 1c green 35 35
*76* A11 2c scarlet 65 18
*a.* 2c car 85 85
*77* A11 3c org ('17) 45 18
*78* A11 5c ultra 2.25 1.10

**Chalky Paper.**

*79* A12 10c dl vio & ol grn 2.50 *3.75*
*80* A12 25c *gray grn* 3.75 3.75
*a.* 25c *emer* 2.50 2.50
*b.* 25c *bl grn, ol back* 3.25 3.75
*81* A12 50c vio & ultra, *bl* 4.50 *6.00*
*82* A11 $1 blk & scar 6.00 7.75
*83* A11 $2 grn & dl vio 22.50 *30.00*
*84* A11 $5 vio & blk, *red* 210.00 *225.00*
*Nos. 75-84 (10)* 252.95 278.06

See No. 91.

With Moire Overprint in Violet.

**1915**

*85* A11 1c green 95 *4.00*
*86* A11 2c carmine 1.10 *3.25*
*87* A11 5c ultramarine 1.25 *3.25*

**Peace Commemorative Issue**

Seal of Colony and George V — A13

**1921 Engr.**

*89* A13 2c carmine 2.50 1.00

Similar to A13 but without "Peace Peace"

**1922 Wmk. 4**

*90* A13 4c dk gray 2.50 95

Type of 1913-17.

**1921 Typo. Wmk. 4**

*91* A11 1c green 2.00 1.65

A14

**1922-33 Typo. Wmk. 4**

*92* A14 1c grn ('29) 48 38
*93* A14 2c dk brn 35 20
*94* A14 2c rose red ('27) 85 70
*95* A14 3c org ('33) 95 75
*96* A14 4c gray ('29) 85 20
*97* A14 5c ultra 75 20

**Chalky Paper.**

*98* A14 10c ol grn & lil 1.25 35
*99* A14 25c *emerald* 1.50 1.90
*100* A14 50c ultra & vio, *bl* 3.25 *5.50*
*101* A14 $1 scar & blk 6.50 *9.00*
*102* A14 $2 red vio & grn 17.50 *26.00*

**Wmk. Multiple Crown and C. A. (3)**

*103* A14 25c *emerald* 4.25 *13.00*
*104* A14 $5 blk & vio, *red* 140.00 *175.00*
*Nos. 92-104 (13)* 178.48 233.18

**Silver Jubilee Issue**
Common Design Type
***Perf. 11x12***

**1935, May 6 Engr. Wmk. 4**

*108* CD301 3c blk & ultra 65 65
*109* CD301 4c ind & grn 1.10 1.40
*110* CD301 5c ultra & brn 2.00 2.00
*111* CD301 25c brn vio & ind 4.00 *6.00*

**Coronation Issue.**
Common Design Type

**1937, May 12 *Perf. 13½x14***

*112* CD302 3c dp org 12 12
*113* CD302 4c gray blk 15 15
*114* CD302 5c brt ultra 18 18

Mayan Figures A15

Chicle Tapping A16

Cohune Palm A17

Local Products A18

Grapefruit Industry A19

Mahogany Logs in River — A20

Sergeant's Cay — A21

Dory — A22

Chicle Industry A23

Court House, Belize — A24

Mahogany Cutting — A25

Seal of Colony — A26

**1938-47 *Perf. 11x11½, 11½x11.***

*115* A15 1c grn & vio 7 7
*116* A16 2c car & blk 9 9
*a.* Perf. 12 ('47) 2.25 2.00
*117* A17 3c brn & dk vio 10 10
*118* A18 4c grn & blk 14 14
*119* A19 5c sl bl & red vio 14 14
*120* A20 10c brn & yel grn 22 22
*121* A21 15c bl & brn 40 32
*122* A22 25c grn & ultra 70 45
*123* A23 50c dk vio & blk 1.40 1.40
*124* A24 $1 ol grn & car 2.25 2.25
*125* A25 $2 rose lake & ind 4.50 4.50
*126* A26 $5 brn & car 18.00 16.00
*Nos. 115-126 (12)* 28.01 25.68

**Catalogue values for unused stamps in this section, from this point to the end of the section, are for Never Hinged items.**

**Peace Issue.**
Common Design Type
***Perf. 13½x14***

**1946, Sept. 9 Engr. Wmk. 4**

*127* CD303 3c brown 9 9
*128* CD303 5c dp bl 14 14

**Silver Wedding Issue.**
Common Design Types

**1948, Oct. 1 Photo. *Perf. 14x14½***

*129* CD304 4c dk grn 18 18

**Engraved; Name Typographed**
***Perf. 11½x11***

*130* CD305 $5 lt brn 22.50 *25.00*

St. George's Cay — A27

H.M.S. Merlin — A28

**1949, Jan. 10 Engr. *Perf. 12½***

*131* A27 1c grn & ultra 14 14
*132* A27 3c yel brn & dp bl 18 18
*133* A27 4c pur & brn ol 28 28
*134* A28 5c dk bl & brn 28 28
*135* A28 10c vio brn & bl grn 50 50
*136* A28 15c ultra & emer 90 90
*Nos. 131-136 (6)* 2.28 2.28

Issued to commemorate the 150th anniversary of the Battle of St. George's Cay.

**UPU Issue.**
Common Design Types
***Perf. 13½, 11x11½***

**1949, Oct. 10 Engr. Wmk. 4**

*137* CD306 4c bl grn 35 35
*138* CD307 5c indigo 55 55
*139* CD308 10c chocolate 90 90
*140* CD309 25c blue 1.50 1.50

**University Issue.**
Common Design Types

**1951, Feb. 16 Engr. *Perf. 14x14½***

*141* CD310 3c choc & pur 32 32
*142* CD311 10c choc & grn 65 65

**Coronation Issue.**
Common Design Type

**1953, June 2 *Perf. 13½x13***

*143* CD312 4c dk grn & blk 43 43

Arms — A29

Maya — A30

Designs: 2c, Tapir. 3c, Legislative Council Chamber and mace. 4c, Pine industry. 5c, Spiny lobster. 10c, Stanley Field Airport. 15c, Mayan frieze. 25c, Blue butterfly. $1, Armadillo. $2, Hawkesworth Bridge. $5, Pine Ridge orchid.

**1953-57 Engr. Perf. 13, 14**

| | | | | |
|---|---|---|---|---|
| *144* | A29 | 1c gray blk & grn | 7 | 5 |
| *145* | A29 | 2c gray blk & brn, perf. 14 ('57) | 12 | 10 |
| *a.* | | Perf. 13 | 28 | 24 |
| *146* | A29 | 3c mag & rose lil, perf. 14 ('57) | 12 | 10 |
| *a.* | | Perf. 13 | 12 | 10 |
| *147* | A29 | 4c grn & dk brn | 10 | 9 |
| *148* | A29 | 5c car & ol brn, perf. 14 ('57) | 22 | 18 |
| *a.* | | Perf. 13 | 42 | 42 |
| *149* | A29 | 10c ultra & bl gray | 22 | 20 |
| *150* | A29 | 15c vio & yel grn | 35 | 35 |
| *151* | A29 | 25c brn & ultra | 80 | 60 |
| *152* | A30 | 50c pur & brn | 2.00 | 1.10 |
| *153* | A29 | $1 red brn & sl bl | 2.75 | 2.50 |
| *154* | A29 | $2 gray & car | 7.00 | 6.50 |
| *155* | A30 | $5 bl gray & pur | 14.00 | 11.00 |
| | | *Nos. 144-155 (12)* | 27.75 | 22.77 |

View of Belize, 1842 — A31

Designs: 10c, Public seals, 1860 and 1960. 15c, Tamarind Tree, Newtown Barracks.

***Perf. 11½x11***

**1960, July 1 Wmk. 314**

| | | | | |
|---|---|---|---|---|
| *156* | A31 | 2c green | 8 | 8 |
| *157* | A31 | 10c carmine | 28 | 28 |
| *158* | A31 | 15c blue | 48 | 48 |

Cent. of the establishment of a local PO.

Nos. 145-146 and 149-150 Overprinted: "NEW CONSTITUTION/1960"

**1961, Mar. 1 Wmk. 4 Perf. 14, 13**

| | | | | |
|---|---|---|---|---|
| *159* | A29 | 2c gray blk & brn | 8 | 8 |
| *160* | A29 | 3c mag & rose lil | 16 | 16 |
| *161* | A29 | 10c ultra & bl gray | 35 | 35 |
| *162* | A29 | 15c vio & yel grn | 60 | 60 |

Nos: 144, 149, 151 and 152 Overprinted: "HURRICANE/HATTIE"

**1962, Jan. 15 Perf. 13**

| | | | | |
|---|---|---|---|---|
| *163* | A29 | 1c gray blk & grn | 7 | 7 |
| *164* | A29 | 10c ultra & bl gray | 14 | 14 |
| *165* | A29 | 25c brn & ultra | 32 | 32 |
| *166* | A30 | 50c pur & brn | 70 | 70 |

Hurricane Hattie struck Belize, Oct. 31, 1961.

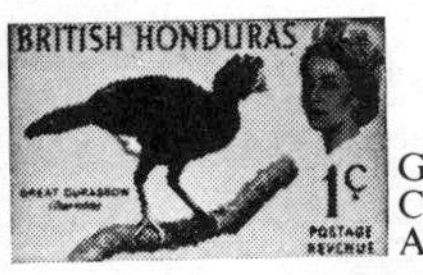


Great Curassow A32

Birds: 2c, Red-legged honeycreeper. 3c, American jacana. 4c, Great kiskadee. 5c, Scarlet-rumped tanager. 10c, Scarlet macaw. 15c, Massena trogon. 25c, Redfooted booby. 50c, Keel-billed toucan. $1, Magnificent frigate bird. $2, Rufoustailed jacamar. $5, Montezuma oropendola.

***Perf. 14x14½***

**1962, Apr. 2 Photo. Wmk. 314**

**Birds in Natural Colors; Black Inscriptions**

| | | | | |
|---|---|---|---|---|
| *167* | A32 | 1c yellow | 8 | 5 |
| *168* | A32 | 2c gray | 8 | 5 |
| *a.* | | Green omitted | *100.00* | |
| *169* | A32 | 3c lt yel grn | 10 | 6 |
| *a.* | | Dark grn (legs) omitted | *175.00* | |
| *170* | A32 | 4c lt gray | 12 | 10 |
| *171* | A32 | 5c buff | 15 | 10 |
| *172* | A32 | 10c beige | 28 | 16 |
| *a.* | | Blue omitted | *150.00* | |
| *173* | A32 | 15c pale lem | 40 | 25 |
| *174* | A32 | 25c bluish gray & pink | 75 | 45 |
| *175* | A32 | 50c pale bl | 2.50 | 1.65 |
| *b.* | | Blue (beak & claw) omitted | | |
| *176* | A32 | $1 blue | 5.75 | 3.75 |
| *177* | A32 | $2 pale gray | 8.00 | 6.50 |
| *178* | A32 | $5 lt bl | 25.00 | 20.00 |
| | | *Nos. 167-178 (12)* | 43.21 | 33.12 |

**1967 Wmk. 314 Sideways**

**Colors as in 1962 Issue.**

| | | | | |
|---|---|---|---|---|
| *167a* | A32 | 1c | 9 | 5 |
| *168b* | A32 | 2c | 14 | 12 |
| *170a* | A32 | 4c | 28 | 24 |
| *171a* | A32 | 5c | 55 | 32 |
| *172b* | A32 | 10c | 80 | 65 |
| *173a* | A32 | 15c | 1.10 | 95 |
| *175a* | A32 | 50c | 4.25 | 3.50 |
| | | *Nos. 167a-175a (7)* | 7.21 | 5.83 |

**Freedom from Hunger Issue**

Common Design Type

**1963, June 4 Perf. 14x14½**

| | | | | |
|---|---|---|---|---|
| *179* | CD314 | 22c green | 85 | 85 |

**Red Cross Centenary Issue**

Common Design Type

**Wmk. 314**

**1963, Sept. 2 Litho. Perf. 13**

| | | | | |
|---|---|---|---|---|
| *180* | CD315 | 4c blk & red | 8 | 8 |
| *181* | CD315 | 22c ultra & red | 1.40 | 1.40 |

Nos. 167, 169, 170, 172 and 174 Overprinted: "SELF GOVERNMENT / 1964"

**1964 Photo. Perf. 14x14½**

| | | | | |
|---|---|---|---|---|
| *182* | A32 | 1c multi | 5 | 5 |
| *a.* | | Yellow omitted | *125.00* | |
| *183* | A32 | 3c multi | 7 | 7 |
| *184* | A32 | 4c multi | 12 | 12 |
| *185* | A32 | 10c multi | 30 | 30 |
| *186* | A32 | 25c multi | 55 | 55 |
| | | *Nos. 182-186 (5)* | 1.09 | 1.09 |

Attainment of self-government.

**ITU Issue**

Common Design Type

***Perf. 11x11½***

**1965, May 17 Litho. Wmk. 314**

| | | | | |
|---|---|---|---|---|
| *187* | CD317 | 2c ver & grn | 6 | 6 |
| *188* | CD317 | 50c yel & red lil | 1.00 | 1.00 |

**Intl. Cooperation Year Issue**

Common Design Type

**1965, Oct. 25 Perf. 14½**

| | | | | |
|---|---|---|---|---|
| *189* | CD318 | 1c bl grn & cl | 7 | 7 |
| *190* | CD318 | 22c lt vio & grn | 75 | 75 |

**Churchill Memorial Issue**

Common Design Type

**1966, Jan. 24 Photo. Perf. 14**

**Design in Black, Gold and Carmine Rose**

| | | | | |
|---|---|---|---|---|
| *191* | CD319 | 1c brt bl | 5 | 5 |
| *192* | CD319 | 4c green | 8 | 8 |
| *193* | CD319 | 22c brown | 65 | 65 |
| *194* | CD319 | 25c violet | 90 | 90 |

Bird Type of 1962 Overprinted: "DEDICATION OF SITE / NEW CAPITAL / 9th OCTOBER 1965"

**Wmk. 314 Sideways**

**1966, July 1 Perf. 14x14½**

| | | | | |
|---|---|---|---|---|
| *195* | A32 | 1c multi | 5 | 5 |
| *196* | A32 | 3c multi | 6 | 6 |
| *197* | A32 | 4c multi | 7 | 7 |
| *198* | A32 | 10c multi | 25 | 25 |
| *199* | A32 | 25c multi | 52 | 52 |
| | | *Nos. 195-199 (5)* | 95 | 95 |

Citrus Grove — A33

Designs: 10c, Half Moon Cay and Lighthouse Reef. 22c, Hidden Valley Falls and Mountain Pine Ridge. 25c, Xunantunich Mayan ruins in Cayo district.

***Perf. 14x14½***

**1966, Oct. 1 Photo. Wmk. 314**

| | | | | |
|---|---|---|---|---|
| *200* | A33 | 5c multi | 10 | 10 |
| *201* | A33 | 10c multi | 22 | 22 |
| *202* | A33 | 22c multi | 48 | 48 |
| *203* | A33 | 25c multi | 65 | 65 |

Issued to commemorate the centenary of the first British Honduras stamp issue.

International Tourist Year — A34

**1967, Dec. 4 Perf. 12½**

| | | | | |
|---|---|---|---|---|
| *204* | A34 | 5c Sailfish | 8 | 8 |
| *205* | A34 | 10c Deer | 20 | 20 |
| *206* | A34 | 22c Jaguar | 42 | 42 |
| *207* | A34 | 25c Tarpon | 52 | 52 |

Schomburgkia Tibicinis — A35

Belizean Patriots' Memorial, Belize City, and Human Rights Flame — A36

Orchids: 10c, Maxillaria tenuifolia. 22c, Bletia purpurea. 25c, Sobralia macrantha.

Inscribed: "20th Anniversary of E.C.L.A."

***Perf. 14½x14***

**1968, Apr. 16 Photo. Wmk. 314**

| | | | | |
|---|---|---|---|---|
| *208* | A35 | 5c vio & multi | 12 | 12 |
| *209* | A35 | 10c grn & multi | 22 | 22 |
| *210* | A35 | 22c multi | 55 | 55 |
| *211* | A35 | 25c ol & multi | 70 | 70 |

20th anniv. of the Economic Commission for Latin America. See Nos. 226-229, 255-258.

***Perf. 13x13½***

**1968, July 15 Litho. Wmk. 314**

Design: 50c, Mayan motif stele, monument at new capital site and Human Rights flame.

| | | | | |
|---|---|---|---|---|
| *212* | A36 | 22c multi | 30 | 30 |
| *213* | A36 | 50c multi | 70 | 70 |

International Human Rights Year.

Jewfish A37

Designs: 2c, White-lipped peccary. 3c, Grouper (sea bass). 4c, Collared anteater. 5c, Bonefish. 10c, Paca. 15c, Dolphinfish. 25c, Kinkajou. 50c, Yellow-and-green-banded muttonfish. $1, Tayra. $2, Great barracudas. $5, Mountain lion.

***Perf. 13x12½***

**1968, Oct. 15 Litho. Unwmk.**

| | | | | |
|---|---|---|---|---|
| *214* | A37 | 1c yel & multi | 5 | 5 |
| *215* | A37 | 2c brt yel & multi | 6 | 5 |
| *216* | A37 | 3c pink & multi | 6 | 5 |
| *217* | A37 | 4c brt grn & multi | 7 | 5 |
| *218* | A37 | 5c brick red & multi | 9 | 7 |
| *219* | A37 | 10c lil & multi | 18 | 15 |
| *220* | A37 | 15c org yel & multi | 26 | 22 |
| *221* | A37 | 25c multi | 45 | 42 |
| *222* | A37 | 50c bl grn & multi | 95 | 85 |
| *223* | A37 | $1 ocher & multi | 1.90 | 1.75 |
| *224* | A37 | $2 vio & multi | 3.75 | 3.50 |
| *225* | A37 | $5 ultra & multi | 8.25 | 7.50 |
| | | *Nos. 214-225 (12)* | 16.07 | 14.66 |

See Nos. 234-240, 327-339.

Orchid Type of 1968

Inscribed "Orchids of Belize"

Designs: 5c, Rhyncholaetia digbyana. 10c, Cattleya bowringiana. 22c, Lycaste cochleatum. 25c, Coryanthes speciosum.

***Perf. 14½x14***

**1969, Apr. 9 Photo. Wmk. 314**

| | | | | |
|---|---|---|---|---|
| *226* | A35 | 5c Prus bl & multi | 15 | 15 |
| *227* | A35 | 10c ol bis & multi | 30 | 30 |
| *228* | A35 | 22c yel grn & multi | 70 | 70 |
| *229* | A35 | 25c vio bl & multi | 85 | 85 |

Hardwood Trees — A38

Virgin and Child, by Giovanni Bellini — A39

**1969, Sept. 1 Litho. Perf. 14**

| | | | | |
|---|---|---|---|---|
| *230* | A38 | 5c Ziricote | 10 | 10 |
| *231* | A38 | 10c Rosewood | 20 | 20 |
| *232* | A38 | 22c Mayflower | 42 | 42 |
| *233* | A38 | 25c Mahogany | 50 | 50 |

Issued to publicize the timber industry of British Honduras. Issued in sheets of 9 (3x3) on simulated wood background.

Fish-Animal Type of 1968

Designs: ½c, Crana (fish). Others as before.

**Wmk. 314 Sideways**

**1969-72 Litho. Perf. 13x12½**

| | | | | |
|---|---|---|---|---|
| *234* | A37 | ½c vio bl, yel & blk | 14 | 14 |
| *235* | A37 | ½c cit, blk & bl ('71) | 6 | 6 |
| *236* | A37 | 2c brt yel, blk & grn ('72) | 8 | 8 |
| *237* | A37 | 3c pink & multi ('72) | 16 | 16 |
| *a.* | | Wmk. upright ('72) | 16 | 16 |
| *238* | A37 | 5c brick red & multi, wmk. upright ('72) | 22 | 22 |
| *239* | A37 | 10c lil & multi ('72) | 40 | 40 |
| *a.* | | Wmk. upright ('72) | 40 | 40 |
| *240* | A37 | $5 ultra & multi ('70) | 6.00 | 6.00 |
| | | *Nos. 234-240 (7)* | 7.06 | 7.06 |

**Christmas Issue**

Design: 22c, 25c, Adoration of the Kings, by Veronese.

**1969, Oct. 1 Litho. Perf. 14**

| | | | | |
|---|---|---|---|---|
| *247* | A39 | 5c multi | 9 | 9 |
| *248* | A39 | 15c dp org & multi | 26 | 26 |
| *249* | A39 | 22c lil rose & multi | 45 | 45 |
| *250* | A39 | 25c emer & multi | 60 | 60 |

Nos. 238-239 and Type of 1968 Overprinted "POPULATION/CENSUS 1970"

**Wmk. 314 Sideways**

**1970, Feb. 2 Photo. Perf. 13x12½**

| | | | | |
|---|---|---|---|---|
| *251* | A37 | 5c brick red & multi | 7 | 7 |
| *252* | A37 | 10c lil & multi | 20 | 20 |
| *253* | A37 | 15c org yel & multi | 28 | 28 |
| *254* | A37 | 25c multi | 48 | 48 |

Orchid Type of 1968

Inscribed: "Orchids of Belize"

Orchids: 5c, Black orchid. 15c, White butterfly orchid. 22c, Swan orchid. 25c, Butterfly orchid.

**Wmk. 314**

**1970, Apr. 2 Litho. Perf. 14**

| | | | | |
|---|---|---|---|---|
| *255* | A35 | 5c gray & multi | 12 | 12 |
| *256* | A35 | 15c brt grnsh bl & multi | 38 | 38 |
| *257* | A35 | 22c ol & multi | 60 | 60 |
| *258* | A35 | 25c brn org & multi | 70 | 70 |

For unused stamps, more recent issues are valued as never hinged, with the beginning point determined on a country-by-country basis. Notes to show the beginning points are prominently placed in the text.

Santa Maria Tree and Wood (Calophyllum Brasiliense) A40

Nativity, by Arthur Hughes A41

Hardwood Trees and Woods: 15c, Nargusta (terminalia amazonia). 22c, Cedar (cedrela mexicana). 25c, Sapodilla (achras sapota).

**1970, Sept. 7** *Perf. 14*

*259* A40 5c multi 9 9
*260* A40 15c multi 30 30
*261* A40 22c multi 45 45
*262* A40 25c multi 55 55

**Christmas Issue**

Designs: 5c, 15c, 50c, Mystic Nativity, by Botticelli.

**1970, Nov. 2** *Perf. 14*

*263* A41 ½c blk & multi 5 5
*264* A41 5c brn & multi 9 9
*265* A41 10c multi 18 18
*266* A41 15c sl bl & multi 28 28
*267* A41 22c dk grn & multi 45 45
*268* A41 50c blk & multi 95 95
*Nos. 263-268 (6)* 2.00 2.00

Legislative Assembly House A42

Designs: 5c, View of South Side of Belize. 10c, Government Plaza, Belmopan. 22c, Magistrates' Court. 25c, Police Headquarters. 50c, New General Post Office.

**1971, Jan. 31 Litho.** *Perf. 13½x14*

**Size: 59x22mm.**

*269* A42 5c multi 6 6
*270* A42 10c multi 12 12

**Size: 37x21½mm.**

*271* A42 15c multi 25 25
*272* A42 22c multi 38 38
*273* A42 25c multi 45 45
*274* A42 50c multi 85 85
*Nos. 269-274 (6)* 2.11 2.11

New capital at Belmopan.

Tabebuia Chrysantha — A43

Flowers: 5c, 22c, Hymenocallis littoralis. 10c, 25c, Hippeastrum equestre. 15c, like ½c.

**1971, Mar. 27 Litho.** *Perf. 14*

*275* A43 ½c vio bl & multi 5 5
*276* A43 5c ol & multi 10 10
*277* A43 10c vio & multi 22 22
*278* A43 15c multi 32 32
*279* A43 22c multi 48 48
*280* A43 25c lt brn & multi 60 60
*Nos. 275-280 (6)* 1.77 1.77

Easter, 1971.

Type of 1968 Overprinted: "RACIAL EQUALITY / YEAR—1971"

*Perf. 13x12½*

**1971, June 14 Litho. Wmk. 314**

*281* A37 10c lil & multi 14 14
*282* A37 50c bl grn & multi 70 70

International year against racial discrimination.

Tubroos (Enterolobium Cyclocarpum) A44

Hardwood Trees of Belize: 15c, Yemeri (Vochysia hondurensis). 26c, Billyweb (Sweetia panamensis). 50c, Logwood (Haematoxylum campechiaum).

**1971, Aug. 16** *Perf. 14*

**Queen's Head in Silver**

*283* A44 5c grn, brn & blk 15 15
*284* A44 15c multi 50 50
*285* A44 26c multi 85 85
*286* A44 50c multi 1.50 1.50
*a.* Souvenir sheet of 4 5.25 5.25

No. 286a contains one each of Nos. 283-286. Wood grain design in margin and black inscription. Size: 97x170mm.

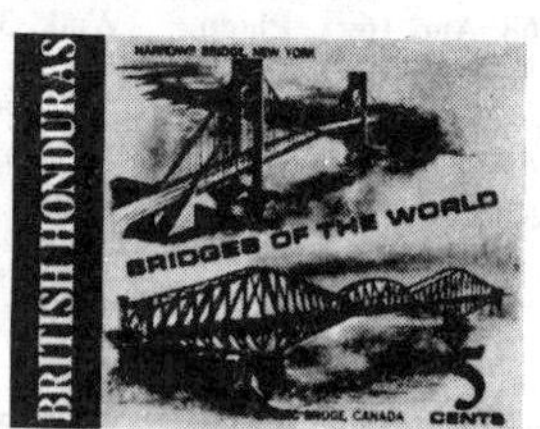

Verrazano-Narrows Bridge, New York, and Quebec Bridge, Canada — A45

Bridges of the World: ½c, Hawksworth Bridge connecting San Ignacio and Santa Helena and Belcan Bridge, Belize, Br. Honduras. 26c, London Bridge in 1871, and at Lake Havasu City, Ariz., in 1971. 50c, Belize-Mexico Bridge and Belize Swing Bridge.

**1971, Sept. 23** **Litho.**

*287* A45 ½c bl, pink & blk 5 5
*288* A45 5c dp rose lil, org & blk 9 9
*289* A45 26c multi 55 55
*290* A45 50c multi 1.10 1.10

Petrae Volubis — A46

Seated Jade Figure — A47

Wild Flowers: 15c, Vochysia hondurensis. 26c, Tabebuia pentaphylla. 50c, Erythrina americana.

**1972, Feb. 28**

**Flowers in Natural Colors; Black Inscriptions**

*292* A46 6c lil & yel 12 12
*293* A46 15c lt bl & pale grn 32 32
*294* A46 26c pink & lt bl 60 60
*295* A46 50c org & lt grn 1.10 1.10

Easter 1972.

*Perf. 14x13½, 13½x14*

**1972, May 22 Unwmk.**

Mayan Carved Jade, 4th-8th centuries: 6c, Dancing priest. 16c, Sun god's head (horiz.). 26c, Priest on throne and sun god's head. 50c, Figure and mask.

*296* A47 3c rose red & multi 5 5
*297* A47 6c vio bl & multi 12 12
*298* A47 16c brn & multi 32 32
*299* A47 26c ol grn & multi 52 52
*300* A47 50c pur & multi 95 95
*Nos. 296-300 (5)* 1.96 1.96

Black inscription with details of designs on back of stamps.

Banak (Virola Koschnyi) — A48

Hardwood Trees of Belize: 5c, Quamwood (Schizolobium parahybum). 16c, Waika chewstick (Symphonia globulifera). 26c, Mammee-apple (Mammea americana). 50c, My lady (Aspidosperma megalocarpon).

**1972, Aug. 21 Wmk. 314** *Perf. 14*

**Queen's Head in Gold**

*301* A48 3c brt pink & multi 5 5
*302* A48 5c gray & multi 10 10
*303* A48 16c grn & multi 32 32
*304* A48 26c lem & multi 52 52
*305* A48 50c lt vio & multi 1.00 1.00
*Nos. 301-305 (5)* 1.99 1.99

**Silver Wedding Issue, 1972**

Common Design Type

Design: Queen Elizabeth II, Prince Philip and Belize orchids.

**1972, Nov. 20 Photo.** *Perf. 14x14½*

*306* CD324 26c slate grn & multi 42 42
*307* CD324 50c vio & multi 80 80

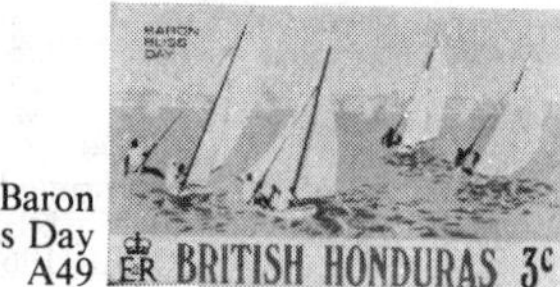

Baron Bliss Day A49

Festivals of Belize: 10c, Labor Day boat race. 26c, Carib Settlement Day dance. 50c, Pan American Day parade.

**1973, Mar. 9 Litho.** *Perf. 14½*

*308* A49 3c dl bl & blk 5 5
*309* A49 10c red & multi 20 20
*310* A49 26c ver & multi 45 45
*311* A49 50c blk & multi 85 85

See Belize for later issues inscribed "Belize."

---

### SEMI-POSTAL STAMPS

Regular Issue of 1921-29 Surcharged in Black or Red

BELIZE
RELIEF FUND
PLUS
3 CENTS

**1932 Wmk. 4** *Perf. 14*

*B1* A14 1c + 1c grn 1.50 4.75
*B2* A14 2c + 2c rose red 1.50 4.75
*B3* A14 3c + 3c org 2.50 6.25
*B4* A14 4c + 4c gray (R) 3.25 9.50
*B5* A14 5c + 5c ultra 5.00 16.00
*Nos. B1-B5 (5)* 13.75 41.25

The surtax was for a fund to aid sufferers from the destruction of the city of Belize by a hurricane in September, 1931.

---

### POSTAGE DUE STAMPS

**Catalogue values for unused stamps in this section, from this point to the end of the section, are for Never Hinged items.**

D1

**1923 Typo. Wmk. 4** *Perf. 14*

*J1* D1 1c black 90 2.50
*J2* D1 2c black 1.10 2.50
*J3* D1 4c black 3.00 10.00

Nos. J1-J3 were re-issued on chalky paper in 1956.

*Perf. 13½x13, 13½x14*

**1965-72 Wmk. 314**

*J4* D1 2c black ('72) 50 2.00
*J5* D1 4c black 1.25 3.00

---

### WAR TAX STAMPS

Nos. 85, 75 and 77 Overprinted **WAR**

**1916-17 Wmk. 3** *Perf. 14*

**With Moire Overprint**

*MR1* A11 1c green 18 18
*a.* Inverted overprint 250.00 250.00

**Without Moire Overprint**

*MR2* A11 1c green ('17) 18 18
*MR3* A11 3c orange ('17) 75 75
*a.* Double overprint 450.00 450.00

Nos. 75 and 77 Overprinted **WAR**

**1918**

*MR4* A11 1c green 18 18
*MR5* A11 3c orange 22 22

---

## BRITISH INDIAN OCEAN TERRITORY

LOCATION — Indian Ocean.
GOVT. — British Dependency.
POP. — 558 (1972).

B.I.O.T. was established Nov. 8, 1965. This island group lies 1,180 miles north of Mauritius. It consisted of Chagos Archipelago (chief island: Diego Garcia), Aldabra, Farquhar and Des Roches Islands until June 23, 1976, when the last three islands were returned to Seychelles.

100 Cents = 1 Rupee

**Catalogue values for all unused stamps in this country are for Never Hinged items.**

Seychelles Nos. 198-202, 204-212 Overprinted **B.I.O.T.**

***Perf. 14½x14, 14x14½***

**968, Jan. 17 Photo. Wmk. 314**

**Size: 24x31, 31x24mm.**

| | | | | | |
|---|---|---|---|---|---|
| | A17 | 5c | multi | 5 | 6 |
| | A17 | 10c | multi | 6 | 7 |
| | A17 | 15c | multi | 12 | 12 |
| | A17 | 20c | multi | 12 | 14 |
| | A17 | 25c | multi | 14 | 15 |
| | A18 | 40c | multi | 35 | 38 |
| | A18 | 45c | multi | 45 | 48 |
| | A17 | 50c | multi | 48 | 55 |
| | A17 | 75c | multi | 60 | 65 |
| | A18 | 1r | multi | 1.50 | 1.60 |
| | A18 | 1.50r | multi | 2.75 | 3.00 |
| | A18 | 2.25r | multi | 4.75 | 5.00 |
| | A18 | 3.50r | multi | 7.50 | 8.00 |
| | A18 | 5r | multi | 16.25 | 17.50 |

***Perf. 13x14***

**Size: 22½x39mm.**

| | | | | | |
|---|---|---|---|---|---|
| | A17 | 10r | multi | 32.00 | 34.00 |
| | | | *Nos. 1-15 (15)* | 67.12 | 71.70 |

Lascar A1

Marine Fauna: 10c, Hammerhead shark (vert.). 15c, Tiger shark. 20c, Sooty eagle ray. 25c, Butterflyfish (vert.). 30c, Robber crab. 40c, Green carangue. 45c, Needlefish (vert.). 50c, Barracuda. 60c, Spotted pebble crab. 75c, Parrotfish. 85c, Rainbow runner (fish). 1r, Giant hermit crab. 1.50r, Humphead. 2.25r, Rock cod. 3.50r, Black marlin. 5r, Whale shark (vert.). 10r, Lionfish.

***Perf. 14x13½, 13½x14; 14 (30c, 60c, 85c)***

**1968-73 Litho. Wmk. 314**

| | | | | | |
|---|---|---|---|---|---|
| *16* | A1 | 5c | multi | 55 | 40 |
| *a.* | | | Wmk. upright ('73) | 65 | 50 |
| *17* | A1 | 10c | multi | 12 | 10 |
| *18* | A1 | 15c | multi | 16 | 12 |
| *19* | A1 | 20c | multi | 18 | 14 |
| *20* | A1 | 25c | multi | 45 | 35 |
| *21* | A1 | 30c | multi ('70) | 55 | 40 |
| *22* | A1 | 40c | multi | 45 | 35 |
| *23* | A1 | 45c | multi | 3.50 | 3.25 |
| *24* | A1 | 50c | multi | 45 | 45 |
| *25* | A1 | 60c | multi ('70) | 1.10 | 1.10 |
| *26* | A1 | 75c | multi | 5.25 | 3.75 |
| *27* | A1 | 85c | multi ('70) | 2.25 | 1.75 |
| *28* | A1 | 1r | multi | 1.75 | 1.40 |
| *29* | A1 | 1.50r | multi | 2.25 | 1.75 |
| *30* | A1 | 2.25r | multi | 18.00 | 17.00 |
| *31* | A1 | 3.50r | multi | 5.00 | 4.25 |
| *32* | A1 | 5r | multi | 7.75 | 6.50 |
| *33* | A1 | 10r | multi | 22.50 | 17.50 |
| | | | *Nos. 16-33 (18)* | 72.26 | 60.56 |

No. 16 has watermark sideways.

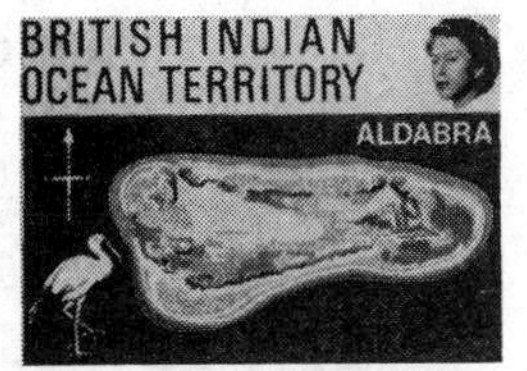

Aldabra Atoll and Sacred Ibis — A2

**1969, July 10 Litho. *Perf. 13½x13***

| | | | | | |
|---|---|---|---|---|---|
| *34* | A2 | 2.25r | vio bl & multi | 3.75 | 2.75 |

Outrigger Canoe — A3

Designs: 75c, Beaching canoe. 1r, Merchant ship Nordvaer. 1.50r, Yacht, Isle of Farquhar.

***Perf. 13½x14***

**1969, Dec. 15 Litho. Wmk. 314**

| | | | | | |
|---|---|---|---|---|---|
| *35* | A3 | 45c | multi | 65 | *65* |
| *36* | A3 | 75c | multi | 1.25 | *1.10* |
| *37* | A3 | 1r | multi | 2.00 | *1.75* |
| *38* | A3 | 1.50r | multi | 3.00 | *2.50* |

Common Design Types pictured in section before Great Britain.

Giant Land Tortoise — A4

Designs: 75c, Aldabra lily. 1r, Aldabra tree snail. 1.50r, Dimorphic egrets.

**1971, Feb. 1 Litho. Wmk. 314**

| | | | | | |
|---|---|---|---|---|---|
| *39* | A4 | 45c | multi | 1.75 | 1.25 |
| *40* | A4 | 75c | multi | 2.50 | 1.75 |
| *41* | A4 | 1r | multi | 5.00 | 3.50 |
| *42* | A4 | 1.50r | multi | 6.50 | 4.50 |

Aldabra Nature Reserve.

Society Coat of Arms and Flightless Rail — A5

**1971, June 30 Litho. *Perf. 13½***

| | | | | | |
|---|---|---|---|---|---|
| *43* | A5 | 3.50r | multi | 12.00 | 8.00 |

Opening of Royal Society Research Station at Aldabra.

Acropora Formosa A6

Corals: 60c, Goniastrea pectinata. 1r, Fungia fungites. 1.75r, Tubipora musica.

**1972, March 1**

| | | | | | |
|---|---|---|---|---|---|
| *44* | A6 | 40c | bl & multi | 1.00 | 1.00 |
| *45* | A6 | 60c | brt pink & multi | 1.75 | 1.75 |
| *46* | A6 | 1r | bl & multi | 3.50 | 3.50 |
| *47* | A6 | 1.75r | brt pink & multi | 7.75 | 7.75 |

**Silver Wedding Issue, 1972**

Common Design Type

Design: Queen Elizabeth II, Prince Philip, flightless rail and sacred ibis.

**1972, Nov. 20 Photo. *Perf. 14x14½***

| | | | | | |
|---|---|---|---|---|---|
| *48* | CD324 | 95c | multi | 1.10 | 50 |
| *49* | CD324 | 1.50r | vio & multi | 1.50 | 75 |

Crucifixion, 17th Century — A7

Upsidedown Jellyfish — A8

Paintings, Ethiopian Manuscripts, 17th Century: 75c, 1.50r, Joseph and Nicodemus burying Jesus. 1r, Like 45c.

**1973, Apr. 9 Litho. *Perf. 14***

| | | | | | |
|---|---|---|---|---|---|
| *50* | A7 | 45c | buff & multi | 50 | 35 |
| *51* | A7 | 75c | buff & multi | 75 | 60 |
| *52* | A7 | 1r | buff & multi | 1.00 | 75 |
| *53* | A7 | 1.50r | buff & multi | 1.75 | 1.25 |
| *a.* | | | Souvenir sheet of 4 | 7.75 | 5.00 |

Easter 1973.

No. 53a contains one each of Nos. 50-53. Buff and multicolored margin with inscription. Size: 133x104½mm.

**1973, Nov. 12 Litho. Wmk. 314**

| | | | | | |
|---|---|---|---|---|---|
| *54* | A8 | 50c | *shown* | 1.40 | 1.00 |
| *55* | A8 | 1r | *Butterflies* | 2.25 | 1.50 |
| *56* | A8 | 1.50r | *Spider* | 3.75 | 2.50 |

Nordvaer and July 14, 1969 Cancel — A9

Design: 2.50r, Nordvaer offshore and cancel.

**1974, July 14**

| | | | | | |
|---|---|---|---|---|---|
| *57* | A9 | 85c | multi | 85 | 65 |
| *58* | A9 | 2.50r | multi | 2.25 | 1.50 |

5th anniversary of Nordvaer traveling post office.

Terebra Maculata and Terebra Subulata — A10

Sea Shells: 75c, Turbo marmoratus. 1r, Drupa rubusidaeus. 1.50r, Cassis rufa.

**1974, Nov. 12 Litho. *Perf. 13½x14***

| | | | | | |
|---|---|---|---|---|---|
| *59* | A10 | 45c | multi | 40 | 30 |
| *60* | A10 | 75c | multi | 65 | 50 |
| *61* | A10 | 1r | multi | 1.10 | 90 |
| *62* | A10 | 1.50r | multi | 1.90 | 1.40 |

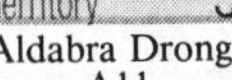
Aldabra Drongo A11

Grewia Salicifolia A12

Birds: 10c, Malagasy coucal. 20c, Red-headed forest fody. 25c, Fairy tern. 30c, Crested tern. 40c, Brown booby. 50c, Noddy tern. 60c, Gray heron. 65c, Blue-faced booby. 95c, Malagasy white-eye. 1r, Green-backed heron. 1.75r, Lesser frigate bird. 3.50r, White-tailed tropic bird. 5r, Souimanga sunbird. 10r, Malagasy turtledove. Nos. 69, 71-77 horizontal.

**Wmk. 314**

**1975, Feb. 28 Litho. *Perf. 14***

| | | | | | |
|---|---|---|---|---|---|
| *63* | A11 | 5c | buff & multi | 7 | *5* |
| *64* | A11 | 10c | lt ultra & multi | 10 | *15* |
| *65* | A11 | 20c | dp yel & multi | 20 | *15* |
| *66* | A11 | 25c | ultra & multi | 22 | *16* |
| *67* | A11 | 30c | dl yel & multi | 32 | *22* |
| *68* | A11 | 40c | bis & multi | 40 | *28* |
| *69* | A11 | 50c | lt bl & multi | 48 | *40* |
| *70* | A11 | 60c | yel & multi | 55 | *45* |
| *71* | A11 | 65c | yel grn & multi | 65 | *45* |
| *72* | A11 | 95c | cit & multi | 80 | *75* |
| *73* | A11 | 1r | bis & multi | 1.00 | *1.00* |
| *74* | A11 | 1.75r | yel & multi | 2.00 | *1.50* |
| *75* | A11 | 3.50r | bl & multi | 4.00 | *3.75* |
| *76* | A11 | 5r | pale sal & multi | 6.50 | *4.75* |
| *77* | A11 | 10r | brt yel & multi | 10.00 | *7.25* |
| | | | *Nos. 63-77 (15)* | 27.29 | 21.31 |

**1975, July 10 Litho. Wmk. 314**

Native Plants: 65c, Cassia aldabrensis. 1r, Hypoestes aldabrensis. 1.60r, Euphorbia pyrifolia.

| | | | | | |
|---|---|---|---|---|---|
| *78* | A12 | 50c | multi | 40 | 35 |
| *79* | A12 | 65c | multi | 55 | 50 |
| *80* | A12 | 1r | multi | 90 | 75 |
| *81* | A12 | 1.60r | multi | 1.50 | 1.25 |

Nature protection.

Aldabra and Compass Rose — A13

Maps of Islands: 1r, Desroches. 1.50r, Farquhar. 2r, Diego Garcia.

**1975, Nov. 8 Litho. *Perf. 13½x14***

| | | | | | |
|---|---|---|---|---|---|
| *82* | A13 | 50c | blk, bl & grn | 40 | 30 |
| *83* | A13 | 1r | grn & multi | 80 | 60 |
| *84* | A13 | 1.50r | blk, ultra & grn | 1.25 | 85 |
| *85* | A13 | 2r | blk, lil & grn | 1.75 | 1.25 |
| *a.* | | | Souvenir sheet of 4 | 5.00 | 4.00 |

British Indian Ocean Territory, 10th anniversary. No. 85a contains one each of Nos. 82-85 and descriptions of islands. Lemon margin with black inscription. Size: 147x146mm.

Crimson Speckled Moth — A14

Insects: 1.20r, Dysdercus fasciatus. 1.50r, Sphex torridus. 2r, Oryctes rhinoceros.

***Perf. 13½x14***

**1976, Mar. 22 Litho. Wmk. 373**

| | | | | | |
|---|---|---|---|---|---|
| *86* | A14 | 65c | multi | 50 | 50 |
| *87* | A14 | 1.20r | multi | 80 | 80 |
| *88* | A14 | 1.50r | multi | 1.10 | 1.10 |
| *89* | A14 | 2r | multi | 1.75 | 1.75 |

## BRUNEI

LOCATION — On the northwest coast of Borneo.
GOVT. — Independent state
AREA — 2,226 sq. mi.
POP. — 191,770 (1981)
CAPITAL — Bandar Seri Begawan

Brunei became a British protectorate in 1888. A treaty between the sultan and the British Government in 1979 provided for independence in 1983.

100 Cents (Sen) = 1 Dollar

**Catalogue values for unused stamps in this country are for Never Hinged items, beginning with Scott 62.**

Labuan Stamps of 1902-03 Overprinted or Surcharged in Red:

**BRUNEI.**

**BRUNEI.** **TWO CENTS.**

**1906 Unwmk. Perf. 12 to 16**

*1* A38 1c vio & blk 12.50 *17.50*
*a.* Black overprint *2,500. 2,750.*
*2* A38 2c on 3c brn & blk 1.50 *3.00*
*a.* "BRUNEI." double *4,250. 3,000.*
*3* A38 2c on 8c org & blk 15.00 *25.00*
*a.* "TWO CENTS." double *5,000.*
*b.* "TWO CENTS." omitted, in pair with normal *6,500.*
*4* A38 3c brn & blk 15.00 *30.00*
*5* A38 4c on 12c yel & blk 1.75 *3.25*
*6* A38 5c on 16c org brn & grn 20.00 *25.00*
*7* A38 8c org & blk 5.00 *10.00*
*8* A38 10c on 16c org brn & grn 6.00 *7.00*
*9* A38 25c on 16c org brn & grn 70.00 *100.00*
*10* A38 30c on 16c org brn & grn 65.00 *95.00*
*11* A38 50c on 16c org brn & grn 65.00 *95.00*
*12* A38 $1 on 8c org & blk 70.00 *100.00*
*Nos. 1-12 (12)* 346.75 *510.75*

The 25c surcharge reads: "25 CENTS."

Scene on Brunei River — A1

Two Types of 1908 1c, 3c:
I. Dots form bottom line of water shading (Double plate.)
II. Dots removed. (Single plate.)

**Wmk. Multiple Crown and C. A. (3)**

**1907-21 Engr. Perf. 14.**

*13* A1 1c yel grn & blk 1.50 *2.75*
*14* A1 1c grn, (II) ('08) 40 40
*a.* Type I ('19) 60 *1.50*
*15* A1 2c red & blk 1.50 *3.00*
*16* A1 2c brn & blk ('11) 60 *1.40*
*17* A1 3c red brn & blk 12.50 *15.00*
*18* A1 3c car, (I) ('08) 85 *1.50*
*a.* Type II ('17) 12.50 *17.50*
*19* A1 4c lil & blk 5.00 *9.00*
*20* A1 4c cl ('12) 4.00 50
*21* A1 5c ultra & blk 35.00 *50.00*
*22* A1 5c org & blk ('08) 3.50 4.00
*23* A1 5c org ('16) 1.75 2.25
*24* A1 8c org & blk 5.50 *20.00*
*25* A1 8c bl ('08) 4.25 6.25
*26* A1 8c ultra ('16) 2.00 2.25
*27* A1 10c dk grn & blk 9.00 *15.00*
*28* A1 10c vio, *yel* ('12) 1.00 1.25
*29* A1 25c yel brn & bl 19.00 *30.00*
*30* A1 25c vio ('12) 1.90 *4.00*
*31* A1 30c blk & pur 19.00 *30.00*
*32* A1 30c org & red vio ('12) 6.50 *12.50*
*33* A1 50c brn & grn 19.00 *30.00*
*34* A1 50c *grn* ('12) 19.00 30.00
*35* A1 50c *grnsh bl* ('21) 5.50 *13.50*
*36* A1 $1 sl & red 60.00 *65.00*
*37* A1 $1 red & blk, *bl* ('12) 24.00 *50.00*
*38* A1 $5 lake, *grn* ('08) 55.00 *100.00*
*39* A1 $25 *red* ('08) 375.00 *500.00*
*Nos. 13-38 (26)* 317.25 *499.55*

Stamps of 1908-21 Overprinted in Black: "MALAYA-BORNEO EXHIBITION, 1922" in Four Lines.

**1922**

*14b* A1 1c green 3.50 *9.00*
*16a* A1 2c brn & blk 4.00 *11.00*
*18b* A1 3c carmine 4.00 *17.50*
*20a* A1 4c claret 4.00 *25.00*
*23a* A1 5c orange 6.00 *40.00*
*28a* A1 10c vio, *yel* 9.00 *50.00*
*30a* A1 25c violet 27.50 *70.00*
*35a* A1 50c grnsh bl 62.50 *140.00*
*37a* A1 $1 red & blk, *bl* 87.50 *225.00*
*Nos. 14b-37a (9)* 208.00 587.50

Industrial fair, Singapore, Mar. 31-Apr. 15.

Type of 1907 Issue.

**1924-37 Wmk. 4**

*43* A1 1c blk ('26) 20 25
*44* A1 2c dp brn 70 *1.75*
*45* A1 2c grn ('33) 25 30
*46* A1 3c green 70 *2.50*
*47* A1 4c cl brn 1.90 1.75
*48* A1 4c org ('29) 50 65
*49* A1 5c orange 65 70
*50* A1 5c lt gray ('31) 3.50 4.00
*51* A1 5c brn ('33) 1.75 40
*52* A1 8c ultra ('27) 2.50 3.00
*53* A1 8c gray ('33) 2.75 50
*54* A1 10c vio, *yel* ('37) 6.25 9.00
*55* A1 25c dk vio ('31) 4.00 5.00
*56* A1 30c org & red vio ('31) 4.75 5.00
*57* A1 50c *grn* ('31) 6.00 10.00
*58* A1 $1 red & blk, *bl* ('31) 25.00 42.50
*Nos. 43-58 (16)* 61.40 87.30

Dwellings in Town of Brunei — A2

**1924-31**

*59* A2 6c black 3.50 3.50
*60* A2 6c red ('31) 2.75 3.50
*61* A2 12c blue 5.00 5.50

See note after Nos. N1-N19.

**Catalogue values for unused stamps in this section, from this point to the end of the section, are for Never Hinged items.**

Types of 1907-24

**1947-51 Engr. Perf. 14, 14x13½**

*62* A1 1c brown 6 6
*63* A1 2c gray 8 8
*a.* Perf. 14½x13½ ('50) *1.50 2.00*
*64* A2 3c dk grn 30 30
*65* A1 5c dp org 10 10
*a.* Perf. 14½x13½ ('50) *6.00 7.50*
*66* A2 6c gray blk 1.50 1.50
*67* A1 8c scarlet 15 15
*a.* Perf. 13 ('51) 18 18
*68* A1 10c violet 15 15
*a.* Perf. 14½x13½ ('50) *1.50 2.50*
*69* A1 15c brt ultra 3.00 3.00
*70* A1 25c red vio 30 30
*a.* Perf. 14½x13½ ('51) 50 *1.00*
*71* A1 30c dp org & gray blk 35 35
*a.* Perf. 14½x13½ ('51) 45 *1.00*
*72* A1 50c black 35 35
*a.* Perf. 13 ('50) 3.00 *10.00*
*73* A1 $1 scar & gray blk 1.00 1.00
*74* A1 $5 red org & grn ('48) 12.50 *12.50*
*75* A1 $10 dp cl & gray blk ('48) 25.00 *35.00*
*Nos. 62-75 (14)* 44.84 54.84

Sultan Ahmed and Pile Dwellings — A3

**1949, Sept. 22 Wmk. 4 Perf. 13**

*76* A3 8c car & blk 1.60 1.60
*77* A3 25c red org & pur 1.60 1.60
*78* A3 50c bl & blk 2.00 2.00

25th anniv. of the reign of Sultan Ahmed Tajudin Akhazul Khair Wad-din.

**UPU Issue**

Common Design Types

**Engr.; Name Typo. on 15c and 25c**

**1949, Oct. 10 Perf. 13½, 11x11½**

*79* CD306 8c rose car 50 50
*80* CD307 15c indigo 75 75
*81* CD308 25c red lil 1.25 1.25
*82* CD309 50c slate 2.50 2.50

Sultan Omar Ali Saifuddin — A4

River Kampong — A5

Canceled-to-order stamps are often from remainders. Most collectors of canceled stamps prefer postally used specimens.

*Perf. 13½x13*

**1952, Mar. 1 Engr. Wmk. 4**

**Center in Black.**

*83* A4 1c black 5 5
*84* A4 2c red org 9 5
*85* A4 3c red brn 12 9
*86* A4 4c green 12 9
*87* A4 6c gray 18 15
*88* A4 8c carmine 24 18
*89* A4 10c ol brn 25 15
*90* A4 15c violet 30 22
*91* A4 15c blue 40 20
*92* A4 25c purple 60 50
*93* A4 50c ultra 90 60

*Perf. 13*

*94* A5 $1 dl grn 2.50 1.00
*95* A5 $2 red 3.75 3.00
*96* A5 $5 dp plum 12.00 9.00
*Nos. 83-96 (14)* 21.50 15.28

See Nos. 101-114.

Mosque and Sultan Omar — A6

**1958, Sept. 24 Wmk. 314 Perf. 13**

**Center in Black**

*97* A6 8c dl grn 30 30
*98* A6 15c car rose 35 35
*99* A6 35c rose vio 75 75

Opening of the Brunei Mosque.

**Freedom from Hunger Issue**

Common Design Type with Portrait of Sultan Omar.

**1963, June 4 Photo. Perf. 14x14½**

*100* CD314 12c sepia 1.50 1.50

Types of 1952

**Wmk. 314 Upright**

**1964-70 Engr. Perf. 13½x13**

**Center in Black**

*101* A4 1c black 5 5
*102* A4 2c red org 6 6
*103* A4 3c red brn 12 6
*104* A4 4c green 15 10
*105* A4 6c black 20 12
*106* A4 8c dk car 22 15
*107* A4 10c ol brn 25 20
*108* A4 12c violet 35 20
*109* A4 15c blue 40 25
*110* A4 25c purple 75 28
*111* A4 50c ultra 1.60 1.00

*Perf. 13*

*112* A5 $1 dl grn ('68) 3.00 2.00
*113* A5 $2 red ('70) 10.00 6.50
*114* A5 $5 dp plum ('70) 20.00 16.50
*Nos. 101-114 (14)* 37.15 27.47

Nos. 101-112 were reissued in 1968-70 on whiter, glazed paper; the $2 and $5 are only on this paper.

**Wmk. 314 Sideways**

**1972-73 Perf. 13½x13**

**Center in Black**

*102a* A4 2c red org 18 18
*103a* A4 3c red brn 25 25
*104a* A4 4c green 30 30
*105a* A4 6c black 45 45
*106a* A4 8c dk car 60 60
*107a* A4 10c ol brn 75 75
*108a* A4 12c violet 90 90
*109a* A4 15c blue 1.25 1.25
*Nos. 102a-109a (8)* 4.68 4.68

The stamps with watermark sideways are on the whiter, glazed paper.

**ITU Issue**

Common Design Type with Portrait of Sultan Omar

*Perf. 11x11½*

**1965, May 17 Litho. Wmk. 314**

*116* CD317 4c red lil & org brn 8 7
*117* CD317 75c org & emer 1.40 1.40

**Intl. Cooperation Year Issue**

Common Design Type with Portrait of Sultan Omar

**1965, Oct. 25 Perf. 14½**

*118* CD318 4c bl grn & cl 8 8
*119* CD318 15c lt vio & grn 70 70

**Churchill Memorial Issue**

Common Design Type with Portrait of Sultan Omar

**1966, Jan. 24 Photo. Perf. 14**

**Design in Black, Gold and Carmine Rose**

*120* CD319 3c brt bl 25 15
*121* CD319 10c green 65 35
*122* CD319 15c brown 1.00 60
*123* CD319 75c violet 3.50 2.50

**World Cup Soccer Issue**

Common Design Type with Portrait of Sultan Omar

**1966, July 4 Litho. Perf. 14**

*124* CD321 4c multi 8 8
*125* CD321 75c multi 1.25 1.25

**WHO Headquarters Issue**

Common Design Type with Portrait of Sultan Omar

**1966, Sept. 20 Litho. Perf. 14**

*126* CD322 12c multi 22 18
*127* CD322 25c multi 75 75

**UNESCO Anniversary Issue**

Common Design Type with Portrait of Sultan Omar

**1966, Dec. 1 Litho. Wmk. 314**

*128* CD323 4c "Education" 12 8
*129* CD323 15c "Science" 45 45
*130* CD323 75c "Culture" 2.25 2.25

State Religious Building and Sultan Hassanal Bolkiah — A7

**1967, Dec. 19 Photo. Perf. 12½**

*131* A7 4c vio & multi 6 6
*132* A7 10c red & multi 14 14
*133* A7 25c org & multi 35 35
*134* A7 50c lt vio & multi 65 65

A three-stamp set (12c, 25c, 50c) showing views of the new Language and Communications Headquarters was prepared and announced for release in April, 1968. The Crown Agents distributed sample sets, but the stamps were not issued. Later, Nos. 144-146 were issued instead.

Sultan Hassanal Bolkiah, Brunei Mosque and Flags — A8

Design: 12c, Sultan, Mosque and flags (horiz.).

*Perf. 13x14, 14x13*

**1968, July 9 Photo. Unwmk.**

*135* A8 4c grn & multi 15 15
*136* A8 12c dp bis & multi 30 30
*137* A8 25c vio & multi 75 75

Installation of Sultan Hassanal Bolkiah.

Sultan Hassanal Bolkiah A9

**Wmk. 314**

**1968, July 15 Litho. *Perf. 12***

| | | |
|---|---|---|
| *138* A9 4c multi | 8 | 8 |
| *139* A9 12c multi | 22 | 22 |
| *140* A9 25c multi | 45 | 45 |

Sultan Hassanal Bolkiah's birthday.

Sultan Hassanal Bolkiah — A10

**1968, Aug. 1 Photo. *Perf. 14½x14***

| | | |
|---|---|---|
| *141* A10 4c Prus bl & multi | 8 | 8 |
| *142* A10 12c rose lil & multi | 22 | 22 |
| *143* A10 25c multi | 45 | 45 |

Coronation of Sultan Hassanal Bolkiah, Aug. 1, 1968.

A11

Hall of Language and Culture — A12

***Perf. 13½, 12½x13½ (A12)***

**1968, Sept. 29 Photo. Wmk. 314**

| | | |
|---|---|---|
| *144* A11 10c bl grn & multi | 15 | 15 |
| *145* A12 15c ocher & multi | 22 | 22 |
| *146* A12 30c ultra & multi | 45 | 45 |

Issued to commemorate the opening of the Hall of Language and Culture and of the Broadcasting and Information Department Building. Nos. 144-146 are overprinted "1968" and 4 bars over the 1967 date. They were not issued without this overprint.

Human Rights Flame and Struggling Man — A13

**Unwmk.**

**1968, Dec. 16 Litho. *Perf. 14***

| | | |
|---|---|---|
| *147* A13 12c grn, yel & blk | 15 | 15 |
| *148* A13 25c ultra, yel & blk | 35 | 35 |
| *149* A13 75c dk plum, yel & blk | 90 | 90 |

International Human Rights Year.

Sultan and WHO Emblem A14

**1968, Dec. 19 Litho. *Perf. 14***

| | | |
|---|---|---|
| *150* A14 4c lt bl, org & blk | 6 | 6 |
| *151* A14 15c brt pur, org & blk | 22 | 22 |
| *152* A14 25c ol, org & blk | 38 | 38 |

20th anniv. of the WHO.

Sultan Hassanal Bolkiah, Pengiran Shahbandar and Oil Rig — A15

***Perf. 14x13***

**1969, July 10 Photo. Wmk. 314**

| | | |
|---|---|---|
| *153* A15 12c grn & multi | 20 | 20 |
| *154* A15 40c dk rose brn & multi | 60 | 60 |
| *155* A15 50c vio & multi | 75 | 75 |

Installation of Pengiran Shahbandar as Second Minister (Di-Galong Sahibol Mal).

Royal Assembly Hall and Council Chamber — A16

Design: 50c, Front view of buildings.

**Unwmk.**

**1969, Sept. 23 Litho. *Perf. 15***

| | | |
|---|---|---|
| *156* A16 12c multi | 15 | 15 |
| *157* A16 25c multi | 35 | 35 |
| *158* A16 50c vio & pink | 65 | 65 |

Issued to commemorate the opening of the Royal Assembly Hall and Council Chamber.

Youth Center — A17

**1969, Dec. 20 Litho. Wmk. 314**

| | | |
|---|---|---|
| *159* A17 6c lt org, blk & di vio | 8 | 8 |
| *160* A17 10c cit, blk & dl Prus grn | 15 | 15 |
| *161* A17 30c yel grn, blk & brn | 45 | 45 |

Opening of Youth Center, Mar. 15, 1969.

Helicopter and Emblem — A18

Designs: 10c, Soldier and emblem (vert.). 75c, Patrol boat and emblem.

**1971, May 31 Litho. *Perf. 14***

| | | |
|---|---|---|
| *162* A18 10c grn & multi | 38 | 15 |
| *163* A18 15c Prus bl & multi | 45 | 25 |
| *164* A18 75c lt ultra & multi | 2.75 | 1.75 |

10th anniv. of Royal Brunei Malay Reg.

50th Anniv. of the Royal Brunei Police Force — A19

**1971, Aug. 14 *Perf. 14½***

| | | |
|---|---|---|
| *165* A19 10c Superintendent | 40 | 25 |
| *166* A19 15c Constable | 50 | 32 |
| *167* A19 50c Traffic policeman | 2.25 | 1.60 |

Sultan, Heir Apparent and View of Brunei — A20

Designs (Portraits and): 25c, View of Brunei with Mosque. 50c, Mosque and banner.

**1971, Aug. 27 Litho. Wmk. 314**

| | | |
|---|---|---|
| *168* A20 15c multi | 38 | 22 |
| *169* A20 25c multi | 75 | 55 |
| *170* A20 50c multi | 1.40 | 1.10 |

Installation of Sultan Hassanal Bolkiah's brother Muda Omar Ali Saifuddin as heir apparent (Perdana Wazir).

Brass and Copper Goods A21

Designs: 12c, Basketware. 15c, Leather goods. 25c, Silverware. 50c, Brunei Museum.

**1972, Feb. 29 *Perf. 13½x14***

**Size: 37x21mm.**

**Portrait in Black**

| | | |
|---|---|---|
| *171* A21 10c brn, sal & yel grn | 15 | 12 |
| *172* A21 12c org, yel & grn | 18 | 15 |
| *173* A21 15c dk grn, emer & org | 25 | 22 |
| *174* A21 25c brn, org & sl | 70 | 60 |

**Size: 58x21mm.**

| | | |
|---|---|---|
| *175* A21 50c dl bl & multi | 1.50 | 1.10 |
| *Nos. 171-175 (5)* | 2.78 | 2.19 |

Opening of Brunei Museum.

Queen Elizabeth II, Sultan and View — A22

Designs (Queen Elizabeth II, Sultan Hassanal Bolkiah and): 15c, View of Brunei. 25c, Mosque and barge. 50c, Royal Assembly Hall.

**1972, Feb. 29 Photo. *Perf. 13x13½***

| | | |
|---|---|---|
| *176* A22 10c lt brn & multi | 24 | 20 |
| *177* A22 15c lt bl & multi | 35 | 30 |
| *178* A22 25c lt grn & multi | 70 | 60 |
| *179* A22 50c dl pur & multi | 2.00 | 2.00 |

Visit of Queen Elizabeth II, Feb. 29.

Bangunan Secretariat (Government Buildings) — A23

Designs (Sultans Omar Ali Saifuddin and Hassanal Bolkiah): 15c, Istana Darul Hana (Sultan's residence). 25c, View of capital. 50c, View of new Mosque.

**1972, Oct. 4 Litho. *Perf. 13½***

| | | |
|---|---|---|
| *180* A23 10c org, blk & grn | 15 | 15 |
| *181* A23 15c grn & multi | 22 | 22 |
| *182* A23 25c ultra & multi | 45 | 45 |
| *183* A23 50c rose red & multi | 90 | 90 |

Change of capital's name from Brunei to Bandar Seri Begawan, Oct. 4, 1970.

Beverley Plane Landing — A24

Design: 25c, Blackburn Beverley plane dropping supplies by parachute (vert.).

***Perf. 14x13½, 13½x14*** **Litho.**

**1972, Nov. 15**

| | | |
|---|---|---|
| *184* A24 25c bl & multi | 1.25 | 1.25 |
| *185* A24 75c ultra & multi | 3.00 | 3.00 |

Opening of Royal Air Force Museum, Hendon, London.

**Silver Wedding Issue, 1972**

Common Design Type

Design: Queen Elizabeth II, Prince Philip; girl and boy with traditional gifts.

**1972, Nov. 20 Photo. *Perf. 14x14½***

| | | |
|---|---|---|
| *186* CD324 12c multi | 40 | 12 |
| *187* CD324 75c multi | 1.25 | 1.25 |

INTERPOL Emblem and Headquarters, Paris — A25

Design: 50c, similar to 25c.

**1973, Sept. 7 Litho. *Perf. 14x14½***

| | | |
|---|---|---|
| *188* A25 25c emer & multi | 75 | 75 |
| *189* A25 50c multi | 1.50 | 1.50 |

50th anniversary of International Criminal Police Organization (INTERPOL).

Princess Anne and Mark Phillips — A26

**1973, Nov. 14 Litho. *Perf. 13½***

| | | |
|---|---|---|
| *190* A26 25c vio bl & multi | 20 | 20 |
| *191* A26 50c red lil & multi | 40 | 40 |

Wedding of Princess Anne and Capt. Mark Phillips, Nov. 14, 1973.

Churchill Painting Outdoors
A27

Sultan Hassanal Bolkiah
A28

Design: 50c, Churchill making "V" sign.

***Perf. 14x13½***

**1973, Dec. 31 Litho. Wmk. 314**

*192* A27 12c car rose & multi 14 14
*193* A27 50c dk grn & multi 55 55

Winston Churchill Memorial Exhibition.

**Wmk. 314 Sideways**

**1974-76 Photo. *Perf. 13x15***

*194* A28 4c bl grn & multi 5 5
*195* A28 5c dl bl & multi 5 5
*196* A28 6c ol grn & multi 6 5
*197* A28 10c lt vio & multi 7 6
**b.** Watermark upright ('76) 12 12
*198* A28 15c brn & multi 12 9
*199* A28 20c buff & multi 15 12
**b.** Watermark upright ('76) 15 15
*200* A28 25c ol & multi 16 15
**b.** Watermark upright ('76) 18 16
*201* A28 30c multi 20 18
*202* A28 35c gray & multi 24 20
*203* A28 40c multi 30 25
*204* A28 50c yel brn & multi 35 30
*205* A28 75c multi 55 45
*206* A28 $1 dl org & multi 70 60
*207* A28 $2 multi 1.50 1.20
*208* A28 $5 sil & multi 3.25 3.00
*209* A28 $10 gold & multi 7.50 7.50
*Nos. 194-209 (16)* 15.25 14.25

Nos. 194-209 issued July 15, 1974.

**1975-76 Wmk. 373**

**Same Colors**

*194a* A28 4c 5 5
*195a* A28 5c 5 5
**b.** Booklet pane of 4 ('76) 20 20
*196a* A28 6c 5 5
*197a* A28 10c 8 8
**c.** Booklet pane of 4 ('76) 35 35
*198a* A28 15c 12 12
*199a* A28 20c 16 16
*200a* A28 25c 20 20
*201a* A28 30c 24 24
*202a* A28 35c 28 28
*203a* A28 40c 32 32
*204a* A28 50c 40 40
*205a* A28 75c 60 60
*206a* A28 $1 80 80
*207a* A28 $2 1.60 1.60
*208a* A28 $5 4.00 4.00
*209a* A28 $10 8.00 8.00
*Nos. 194a-209a (16)* 16.95 16.95

Brunei Airport
A29

Design: 75c, Sultan Hassanal Bolkiah in uniform and jet over airport.

***Perf. 14x14½***

**1974, July 18 Litho. Wmk. 314**

**Size: 44x28mm**

*215* A29 50c multi 1.00 1.00

**Size: 47x36mm**

***Perf. 12½x13***

*216* A29 75c multi 1.35 1.35

Opening of Brunei Airport.

UPU Emblem
A30

**1974, Oct. 28 *Perf. 14½***

*217* A30 12c org & multi 15 15
*218* A30 50c bl & multi 50 50
*219* A30 75c emer & multi 75 75

Centenary of Universal Postal Union.

Winston Churchill
A31

Design: 75c, Churchill smoking cigar.

**1974, Nov. 30 Wmk. 373 *Perf. 14***

*220* A31 12c vio bl, bl & gold 15 15
*221* A31 75c dk grn, blk & gold 90 90

Sir Winston Churchill (1874-1965).

Boeing 737 Planes at Airport
A32

Designs: 35c, Boeing 737 over Bandar Seri Begawan Mosque. 75c, Boeing 737 in flight. All planes with crest of Royal Brunei Airlines.

***Perf. 12½x12***

**1975, May 14 Unwmk.**

*222* A32 12c multi 30 25
*223* A32 35c multi 1.00 75
*224* A32 75c multi 2.00 2.00

Inauguration of Royal Brunei Airlines.

**10**
**sen**

No. 196a Surcharged in Silver

***Perf. 13x15***

**1976, Aug. 16 Photo. Wmk. 373**

*225* A28 10c on 6c multi 25 25

British Royal Coat of Arms – A33

Designs: 20c, Imperial State Crown. 75c, Elizabeth II.

**Wmk. 373**

**1977, June 7 Litho. *Perf. 14***

*226* A33 10c dk bl & multi 8 8
*227* A33 20c pur & multi 20 20
*228* A33 75c yel & multi 65 65

25th anniv. of the reign of Elizabeth II.

Values quoted in this catalogue are for stamps graded at Fine-Very Fine and with no faults. An illustrated guide to grade is provided in introductory material, beginning on Page V.

Coronation of Elizabeth II – A34

Designs: 20c, Elizabeth II with coronation regalia. 75c, Departure from Westminster Abbey (coach).

**1978, June 2 Litho. *Perf. 13½x13***

*229* A34 10c multi 8 8
*230* A34 20c multi 20 20
*231* A34 75c multi 65 65

25th anniv. of coronation of Elizabeth II.

Sultan's Coat of Arms – A35

Struggling Man, Human Rights Flame – A36

Designs: 20c, Coronation ceremony. 75c, Royal crown.

**Wmk. 373**

**1978, Aug. 1 Litho. *Perf. 12***

*232* A35 10c multi 12 10
*233* A35 20c multi 22 18
*234* A35 75c multi 90 75
**a.** Souvenir sheet of 3 4.50 3.50

10th anniversary of coronation of Sultan Hassanal Bolkiah. No. 234a contains Nos. 232-234; multicolored margin shows Brunei views. Size: 182x188mm.

**1978, Dec. 10 Litho. *Perf. 14***

*235* A36 10c red, blk & yel 9 9
*236* A36 20c vio, blk & yel 18 18
*237* A36 75c ol, blk & yel 65 65

Universal Declaration of Human Rights, 30th anniversary.

Children and IYC Emblem
A37

Design: $1, IYC emblem.

**Wmk. 373**

**1979, June 30 Litho. *Perf. 14***

*238* A37 10c multi 10 10
*239* A37 $1 dl grn & blk 90 90

Telisai Earth Satellite Station
A38

Designs: 20c, Radar screen and satellite. 75c, Cameraman, telex operator, telephone.

***Perf. 14½x14***

**1979, Sept. 23 Litho. Wmk. 37**

*240* A38 10c multi 12 1
*241* A38 20c multi 18 1
*242* A38 75c multi 75 7

Hajeer Emblem – A39

**1979, Nov. 21**

*243* A39 10c multi 10 10
*244* A39 20c multi 20 20
*245* A39 75c multi 75 75
**a.** Souvenir sheet of 3 2.50 2.50

Hegira, 1400th anniversary. No. 245a contains Nos. 243-245. Light blue and ultramarine margin shows mosque. Size: 179x200mm.

Installation Ceremony – A40

**1980 Litho. *Perf. 14***

*246* A40 10c *shown* 8 8
*247* A40 10c *Ceremony, diff.* 8 8
*248* A40 75c *Jefri Bolkiah* 60 60
*249* A40 75c *Sufri Bolkiah* 60 60

Installation of Jefri Bolkiah and Sufri Bolkiah as Wizars (Ministers of State for Royalty) 1st anniv. Issue dates: Nos. 246, 248, Nov. 8; others, Dec. 6.

Umbrella – A41

**1981, Jan. 19 Litho. *Perf. 12x11½***

*255* A41 10c *shown* 12 12
*256* A41 15c *Dagger, shield* 18 18
*257* A41 20c *Spears* 25 25
*258* A41 30c *Gold pouch* 35 35

**Size: 22½x40mm.**

***Perf. 14x13½***

*259* A41 50c *Headdress* 60 60
**a.** Souvenir sheet of 5 2.25 2.25
*Nos. 255-259 (5)* 1.50 1.50

No. 259a contains Nos. 255-259; multicolored margin shows street scene. Size: 98x142mm.

13th World Telecommunications Day – A42

**981, May 17 Litho. *Perf. 13x13½***
*60* A42 10c car rose & blk 10 10
*61* A42 75c dp vio & blk 75 75

Dagger and Case — A43

***Perf. 12½x12, 12 (75c)***
**1981, July 15 Litho.**
*262* A43 10c shown 10 10
*263* A43 15c Rifle, powder pouch 15 15
*264* A43 20c Spears 18 18
*265* A43 30c Sword, tunic, shield 30 30
*266* A43 50c Horns 50 50

**Size: 28½x45mm.**
*267* A43 75c Gold bowl and table 75 75
*Nos. 262-267 (6)* 1.98 1.98

**Royal Wedding Issue**
Common Design Type
**1981, July 29 *Perf. 14***
*268* CD331 10c Bouquet 8 8
*269* CD331 $1 Charles 80 80
*270* CD331 $2 Couple 1.60 1.60

World Food Day — A44

**1981, Oct. 16 Litho. *Perf. 12***
*271* A44 10c Fishermen 8 8
*272* A44 $1 Produce 80 80

Intl. Year of the Disabled — A45

**Wmk. 373**
**1981, Dec. 16 Litho. *Perf. 12***
*273* A45 10c Blind man 8 8
*274* A45 20c Sign language 16 16
*275* A45 75c Man in wheelchair 60 60

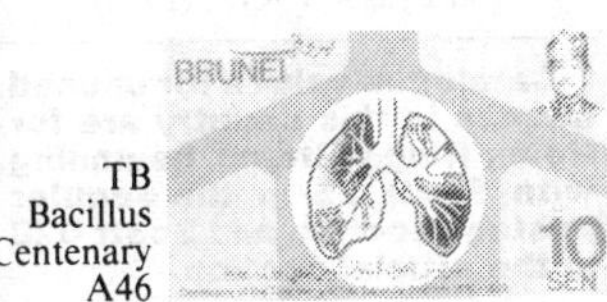


TB Bacillus Centenary A46

***Perf. 12, 13½ (75c)***
**1982, Mar. 24 Litho.**
*276* A46 10c Lungs 8 8
*277* A46 75c Bacillus, microscope 60 60

Silver Urn — A47

**1982, May 31 Litho. *Perf. 12½x12***
*278* A47 10c shown 10 10
*279* A47 15c Pedestal urn 15 15
*280* A47 20c Silver bowl 20 20
*281* A47 30c Candle 30 30
*282* A47 50c Gold pipe 50 50

**Size: 28x44mm.**
***Perf. 13½***
*283* A47 75c Silver pointer 75 75
*Nos. 278-283 (6)* 2.00 2.00

**1982, July 15 Litho. *Perf. 12½x12***
*284* A47 10c Urn 10 10
*285* A47 15c Crossed banners 15 15
*286* A47 20c Golden fan 20 20
*287* A47 30c Lid 30 30
*288* A47 50c Sword, sheath 50 50

**Size: 28x44mm.**
***Perf. 12***
*289* A47 75c Golden chalice pole 75 75
*Nos. 284-289 (6)* 2.00 2.00

**Commonwealth Day**
Common Design Type
**1983, Mar. 14 Litho. *Perf. 13½***
*290* CD334 10c Flag 12 12
*291* CD334 20c Natl. palace 20 20
*292* CD334 75c Oil drilling 75 75
*293* CD334 $2 Sultan Bolkiah 2.00 2.00

Nos. 290-293 se-tenant.

World Communications Year — A48

**1983, July 15 Litho. *Perf. 13½***
*294* A48 10c Mail delivery 10 10
*295* A48 75c Typewriter, phone 80 80
*296* A48 $2 Dish antenna, satellite, TV 2.00 2.00

Opening of Hassanal Bolkiah National Stadium — A49

**1983, Sept. 23 Litho. *Perf. 12***
*297* A49 10c Soccer, vert. 15 15
*298* A49 75c Runners, vert. 1.00 1.00
*299* A49 $1 shown 1.25 1.25

Size, Nos. 297-298: 26x33mm.

Fishing Industry — A50

**1983, Sept. 23 Litho. *Perf. 13½***
*300* A50 10c Shrimp, lobster 12 12
*301* A50 50c Pacific jacks 60 60
*302* A50 75c Parrotfish, flatfish 90 90
*303* A50 $1 Tuna 1.25 1.25

State Assembly Building A51

Map of Southeast Asia, Flag — A52

Sultan Hassanal Bolkiah — A53

**1984, Jan. 1 Litho. *Perf. 13***
*304* A51 10c shown 12 12
*305* A51 20c State Secretariat building 25 25
*306* A51 35c New Law Court 40 40
*307* A51 50c Liquid natural gas well 60 60
*308* A51 75c Omar Ali Saifuddin Mosque 90 90
*309* A51 $1 Sultan's Palace 1.20 1.20
*310* A52 $3 shown 3.60 3.60
**a.** Souvenir sheet of 7 7.00 7.00
*Nos. 304-310 (7)* 7.07 7.07

**Souvenir Sheets**
*311* Sheet of 4, Constitution signing, 1959 1.25 1.25
**a.-d.** A53 25c, any single 25 25
*312* Sheet of 4, Brunei U.K. Friendship Agreement, 1979 1.25 1.25
**a.-d.** A53 25c, any single 25 25

No. 310a contains Nos. 304-310; red and orange decorative margin. Size: 150x106mm. Nos. 311-312 have gold decorative margins. Size: 150x122mm.

Forestry Resources — A54

**1984, Apr. 21 Litho. *Perf. 13½***
*313* A54 10c Forests, enrichment planting 12 12
*314* A54 50c Irrigation canal 60 60
*315* A54 75c Recreation forest 90 90
*316* A54 $1 Wildlife 1.20 1.20

Philakorea 1984 — A55

**Litho. & Engr.**
**1984, Oct. 22 *Perf. 13***
*317* A55 10c No. 93 12 12
**a.** Souvenir sheet of 1 12 12
*318* A55 75c No. 27 90 90
**a.** Souvenir sheet of 1 90 90
*319* A55 $2 1985 regional issue 2.50 2.50
**a.** Souvenir sheet of 1 2.50 2.50

Multicolored margin on souvenir sheets show view of Bandar Seri Begawan, capital city. Souvenir sheet sizes: 117 x 99 mm.

Brunei Admission to Intl. Organizations A56

**1985, Sept. 23 Litho. *Perf. 13***
*320* A56 50c UN 45 45
*321* A56 50c Commonwealth 45 45
*322* A56 50c ASEAN 45 45
*323* A56 50c OIC 45 45
**a.** Souvenir Sheet of 4 #320-323 2.00 2.00

No. 323a has center label picturing Sultan Bolkiah; multicolored margin pictures national crest and colors. Size: 110x152mm.

Intl. Youth Year — A57

**1985, Oct. 17 *Perf. 12***
*324* A57 10c shown 8 8
*325* A57 75c Industry, education 55 55
*326* A57 $1 Public Service 70 70

Intl. Day of Solidarity with the Palestinian People — A58

**1985, Nov. 29 *Perf. 12x12½***
*327* A58 10c lt bl & multi 12 12
*328* A58 50c pink & multi 55 55
*329* A58 $1 lt grn & multi 1.10 1.10

Natl. Scout Jamboree, Dec. 14-20 — A59

Sultan Hassanal Bolkiah — A60

**1985, Dec. 14 *Perf. 13½***
*330* A59 10c Scout handshake 10 10
*331* A59 20c Semaphore 18 18
*332* A59 $2 Jamboree emblem 1.75 1.75

**1985-86 *Perf. 13½x14½***
*333* A60 10c multi 10 10
*334* A60 15c multi 14 14
*335* A60 20c multi 18 18
*336* A60 25c multi 22 22
*337* A60 35c multi ('86) 32 32
*338* A60 40c multi ('86) 36 36
*339* A60 50c multi ('86) 45 45
*340* A60 75c multi ('86) 68 68

**Size: 35x42mm.**
***Perf. 14***
*341* A60 $1 multi ('86) 90 90
*342* A60 $2 multi ('86) 1.75 1.75
*343* A60 $5 multi ('86) 4.50 4.50
*344* A60 $10 multi ('86) 9.00 9.00
*Nos. 333-344 (12)* 18.60 18.60

Issue dates: Nos. 333-336, Dec. 23. Nos. 337-340, Jan. 15. Nos. 341-343, Feb. 23. No. 344, Mar. 29.

Admission to Intl. Organizations A61

**Wmk. 382 Cartor**

**1986, Apr. 30 Litho.** ***Perf. 13***

| | | | | |
|---|---|---|---|---|
| *345* | A61 | 50c WMO | 45 | 45 |
| *346* | A61 | 50c ITU | 45 | 45 |
| *347* | A61 | 50c UPU | 45 | 45 |
| *348* | A61 | 50c ICAO | 45 | 45 |
| *a.* | | Souvenir sheet of 4, Nos. 345-348 | 1.80 | 1.80 |

No. 348a has gold and bright brown orange decorative margin; center label pictures natl. flag. Size: 105x155mm.

Royal Brunei Armed Forces, 25th Anniv. A62

**1986, May 31** ***Perf. 13½***

| | | | |
|---|---|---|---|
| *349* | Strip of 4 | 1.40 | 1.40 |
| *a.* | A62 10c In combat | 10 | 10 |
| *b.* | A62 20c Communications | 18 | 18 |
| *c.* | A62 50c Air and sea defense | 45 | 45 |
| *d.* | A62 75c On parade, Royal Palace | 68 | 68 |

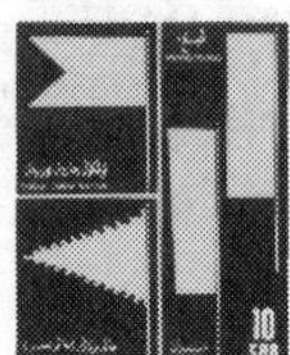

Royal Ensigns — A63

Designs: No. 350, Tunggul charok buritan, Pisang-pisang, Alam bernaga, Sandaran. No. 351, Dadap, Tunggul kawan, Ambal, Payong ubor-ubor, Sapu-sapu ayeng and Rawai lidah. No. 352, Ula-ula besar, Payong haram, Sumbu layang. No. 353, Payong ubor-ubor tiga ringkat and Payong tinggi. No. 354, Panji-panji, Chogan istiadat, Chogan ugama. No. 355, Lambang duli yang maha mulia and Mahligai.

**1986 Litho.** ***Perf. 12½***

| | | | | |
|---|---|---|---|---|
| *350* | A63 | 10c multi | 10 | 10 |
| *351* | A63 | 10c multi | 10 | 10 |
| *352* | A63 | 75c multi | 68 | 68 |
| *353* | A63 | 75c multi | 68 | 68 |
| *354* | A63 | $2 multi | 1.75 | 1.75 |
| *355* | A63 | $2 multi | 1.75 | 1.75 |
| | | *Nos. 350-355 (6)* | 5.06 | 5.06 |

Intl. Peace Year — A64

**1986, Oct. 24 Litho.** ***Perf. 12***

| | | | | |
|---|---|---|---|---|
| *356* | A64 | 50c Peace doves | 48 | 48 |
| *357* | A64 | 75c Hands | 68 | 68 |
| *358* | A64 | $1 Peace symbols | 88 | 88 |

Natl. Anti-Drug Campaign Posters — A65

**1987, Mar. 15 Litho.** ***Perf. 12***

| | | | | |
|---|---|---|---|---|
| *359* | A65 | 10c Jail | 8 | 8 |
| *360* | A65 | 75c Noose | 65 | 65 |
| *361* | A65 | $1 Execution | 88 | 88 |

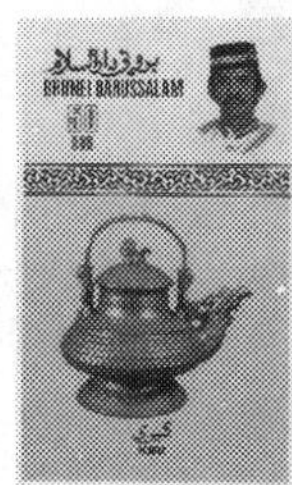

Brass Artifacts — A66

**1987, July 15**

| | | | | |
|---|---|---|---|---|
| *362* | A66 | 50c Kiri (kettle) | 45 | 45 |
| *363* | A66 | 50c Langguai (bowl) | 45 | 45 |
| *364* | A66 | 50c Badil (cannon) | 45 | 45 |
| *365* | A66 | 50c Pelita (lamp) | 45 | 45 |

See Nos. 388-391.

Dewan Bahasa Dan Pustaka, 25th Anniv. — A67

Illustration reduced.

**1987, Sept. 29** ***Perf. 13½x13***

| | | | |
|---|---|---|---|
| *366* | A67 Strip of 3 | 2.30 | 2.30 |
| *a.* | 10c multi | 8 | 8 |
| *b.* | 50c multi | 45 | 45 |
| *c.* | $2 multi | 1.75 | 1.75 |

Language and Literature Bureau. Printed se-tenant in a continuous design.

ASEAN, 20th Anniv. — A68

**1987, Aug. 8 Litho.** ***Perf. 14x13½***

| | | | | |
|---|---|---|---|---|
| *367* | A68 | 20c Map | 18 | 18 |
| *368* | A68 | 50c Year dates | 45 | 45 |
| *369* | A68 | $1 Flags, emblem | 90 | 90 |

World Food Day A70

Fruit: a. Artocarpus odoratissima. b. Canarium odontophyllum mig. c. Litsea garciae. d. Mangifera foetida lour.

**1987, Oct. 31** ***Perf. 12½***

| | | | |
|---|---|---|---|
| *370* | Strip of 4 | 1.80 | 1.80 |
| *a.-d.* | A70 50c any single | 45 | 45 |

See No. 374.

Intl. Year of Shelter for the Homeless A71

Various houses.

**1987, Nov. 28 Litho.** ***Perf. 13***

| | | | | |
|---|---|---|---|---|
| *371* | A71 | 50c multi | 45 | 45 |
| *372* | A71 | 75c multi, diff. | 68 | 68 |
| *373* | A71 | $1 multi, diff. | 90 | 90 |

Fruit Type of 1987
Without FAO Emblem, Dated 1988.

Fruit: a, Durio. b, Durio oxleyanus. c, Durio graveolens (cross section at L). d, Durio graveolens (cross section at R).

**1988, Jan. 30 Litho.** ***Perf. 12***

| | | | |
|---|---|---|---|
| *374* | Strip of 4 | 2.00 | 2.00 |
| *a.-d.* | A70 50c, any single | 50 | 50 |

Opening of Malay Technology Museum — A72

**1988, Feb. 29** ***Perf. 12½x12***

| | | | | |
|---|---|---|---|---|
| *375* | A72 | 10c Wooden lathe | 10 | 10 |
| *376* | A72 | 75c Water wheel, buffalo | 75 | 75 |
| *377* | A72 | $1 Bird caller in blind | 1.00 | 1.00 |

Handwoven Cloth — A73

Designs: 10c, Kain Beragi Bunga Sakah-Sakah Dan Bunga Cengkih. 20c, Kain Jong Sarat. 25c, Kain Si Pugut. 40c, Kain Si Pugut Bunga Berlapis. 75c, Kain Si Lobang Bangsi Bunga Belitang Kipas.

**1988, Apr. 30 Litho.** ***Perf. 12***

| | | | | |
|---|---|---|---|---|
| *378* | A73 | 10c multi | 10 | 10 |
| *379* | A73 | 20c org brn & blk | 20 | 20 |
| *380* | A73 | 25c multi | 25 | 25 |
| *381* | A73 | 40c multi | 40 | 40 |
| *382* | A73 | 75c multi | 75 | 75 |
| *a.* | | Souv. sheet of 5 (Nos. 378-382) + label | 1.70 | 1.70 |
| | | *Nos. 378-382 (5)* | 1.70 | 1.70 |

No. 382a contains label picturing youth wearing exotic cloth vestments; multicolored inscribed margin pictures cloth pattern. Size: 150x204mm.

Brass Artifacts Type of 1987

**1988, June 30 Litho.** ***Perf. 12***

| | | | | |
|---|---|---|---|---|
| *388* | A66 | 50c Celapa (repousse box) | 50 | 50 |
| *389* | A66 | 50c Gangsa (footed plate) | 50 | 50 |
| *390* | A66 | 50c Periok (lidded pot) | 50 | 50 |
| *391* | A66 | 50c Lampong (candle-stick) | 50 | 50 |

Coronation of Sultan Hassanal Bolkiah, 20th Anniv. — A74

**1988, Aug. 1 Litho.** ***Perf. 14***

| | | | | |
|---|---|---|---|---|
| *392* | A74 | 20c shown | 20 | 20 |
| *393* | A74 | 75c Reading from the Koran | 75 | 75 |

**Size: 26x62mm**

***Perf. 12½x13***

| | | | | |
|---|---|---|---|---|
| *394* | A74 | $2 In full regalia | 2.00 | 2.00 |
| *a.* | | Souv. sheet of 3, Nos. 392-394 | 3.00 | 3.00 |

No. 394a has multicolored margin picturing an aerial view of Bandar Seri Begawan, the nation's capital. Size: 164x125mm.

## OCCUPATION STAMPS

**Issued under Japanese Occupation.**
Stamps and Types of 1908-37 Handstamped in Violet, Red Violet, Blue or Red

府政国帝本日大

***Perf. 14, 14x11½ (#N7)***

**1942-44** **Wmk. 4**

| | | | | | |
|---|---|---|---|---|---|
| *N1* | A1 | 1c | black | 6.50 | 12.00 |
| *N2* | A1 | 2c | green | 65.00 | *100.00* |
| *N3* | A1 | 2c | dl org | 3.50 | *6.00* |
| *N4* | A1 | 3c | green | 27.50 | *65.00* |
| *N5* | A1 | 4c | orange | 5.00 | *14.00* |
| *N6* | A1 | 5c | brown | 5.00 | *14.00* |
| *N7* | A2 | 6c | sl gray | 70.00 | *140.00* |
| *N8* | A2 | 6c | red | 525.00 | 600.00 |
| *N9* | A1 | 8c | gray (RV) | 525.00 | 825.00 |
| *N10* | A2 | 8c | carmine | 5.00 | *10.00* |
| *N11* | A1 | 10c | vio, *yel* | 10.00 | *17.50* |
| *N12* | A2 | 12c | blue | 10.00 | *17.50* |
| *N13* | A2 | 15c | ultra | 10.00 | *17.50* |
| *N14* | A1 | 25c | dk vio | 22.50 | *65.00* |
| *N15* | A1 | 30c | org & red vio | 110.00 | *375.00* |
| *N16* | A1 | 50c | blk, *green* | 27.50 | 80.00 |
| *N17* | A1 | $1 | red & blk, *bl* | 50.00 | 100.00 |

**Wmk. 3**

| | | | | | |
|---|---|---|---|---|---|
| *N18* | A1 | $5 | lake, *grn* | 1,125. | 750.00 |
| *N19* | A1 | $25 | blk, *red* | 1,200. | 1,500. |

Overprints vary in shade. Nos. N3, N7, N10 and N13 without overprint are not believed to have been regularly issued.

本日大

No. 43 Surcharged in Red

便郵国帝

**1944 Wmk. 4** ***Perf. 14***

| | | | |
|---|---|---|---|
| *N20* | A1 $3 on 1c blk | *2,250.* | *1,875.* |
| *a.* | On No. N1 | *2,250.* | *1,875.* |

## BURMA

LOCATION — Bounded on the north by China; east by China, Laos and Thailand; south and west by the Bay of Bengal, Bangladesh and India.
GOVT. — Republic
AREA — 261,789 sq. mi.
POP. — 35,313,905 (1983)
CAPITAL — Rangoon

Burma was part of India from 1826 until April 1, 1937, when it became a self-governing unit of the British Commonwealth and received a constitution. On January 4, 1948, Burma became an independent nation.

12 Pies = 1 Anna
16 Annas = 1 Rupee
100 Pyas = 1 Kyat (1953)

**Catalogue values for unused stamps in this country are for Never Hinged items, beginning with Scott 35 in the regular postage section and Scott O28 in the official section.**

Stamps of India 1926-36 Overprinted **BURMA**

**1937, Apr. 1 Wmk. 196** ***Perf. 14***

| | | | | | |
|---|---|---|---|---|---|
| *1* | A46 | 3p | slate | 5 | 5 |
| *2* | A71 | ½a | green | 5 | 5 |
| *3* | A68 | 9p | dk grn | 7 | 5 |
| *4* | A72 | 1a | dk brn | 10 | 5 |
| *5* | A49 | 2a | ver (small die) | 10 | 5 |
| *6* | A57 | 2a6p | buff | 12 | 5 |
| *7* | A51 | 3a | car rose | 30 | 12 |
| *8* | A70 | 3a6p | dp bl | 30 | 12 |
| *9* | A52 | 4a | ol grn | 30 | 5 |
| *10* | A53 | 6a | bister | 30 | 12 |
| *11* | A54 | 8a | red vio | 32 | 10 |
| *12* | A55 | 12a | claret | 35 | 35 |

Overprinted **BURMA**

| | | | | |
|---|---|---|---|---|
| 3 | A56 | 1r grn & brn | 50 | 20 |
| 4 | A56 | 2r brn org & car rose | 1.40 | 32 |
| 5 | A56 | 5r dk vio & ultra | 2.75 | 2.00 |
| 6 | A56 | 10r car & grn | 17.50 | 5.00 |
| 7 | A56 | 15r ol grn & ultra | 75.00 | 50.00 |
| 8 | A56 | 25r bl & ocher | 150.00 | 125.00 |
| | | *Nos. 1-18 (18)* | 249.51 | 183.68 |

King George VI
A1 A2

Royal Barge — A3

Elephant Moving Teak Log — A4

Farmer Plowing Rice Field — A5

Sailboat on Irrawaddy River — A6

Peacock — A7

King George VI — A8

Wmk. 254- Elephant Heads

***Perf. 13½x14***

**1938-40 Litho. Wmk. 254**

| | | | | |
|---|---|---|---|---|
| *18A* | A1 | 1p red org ('40) | 5 | 5 |
| *19* | A1 | 3p violet | 5 | 5 |
| *20* | A1 | 6p ultra | 5 | 5 |
| *21* | A1 | 9p yel grn | 16 | 16 |
| *22* | A2 | 1a brn vio | 5 | 5 |
| *23* | A2 | 1½a turq grn | 5 | 5 |
| *24* | A2 | 2a carmine | 5 | 5 |

***Perf. 13***

| | | | | |
|---|---|---|---|---|
| *25* | A3 | 2a6p rose lake | 20 | 20 |
| *26* | A4 | 3a dk vio | 65 | 30 |
| *27* | A5 | 3a6p dp bl & brt bl | 1.65 | *3.25* |
| *28* | A2 | 4a sl bl, perf. 13½x14 | 14 | 14 |
| *29* | A6 | 8a sl grn | 16 | 16 |

***Perf. 13½***

| | | | | |
|---|---|---|---|---|
| *30* | A7 | 1r brt ultra & dk vio | 55 | 32 |
| *31* | A7 | 2r dk vio & red brn | 1.75 | 80 |
| *32* | A8 | 5r car & dl vio | 20.00 | 6.75 |
| *33* | A8 | 10r gray grn & brn | 40.00 | 32.50 |
| | | *Nos. 18A-33 (16)* | 65.56 | 44.88 |

See Nos. 51-65.

No. 25 Surcharged in Black

COMMEMORATION
POSTAGE STAMP
6th MAY 1840

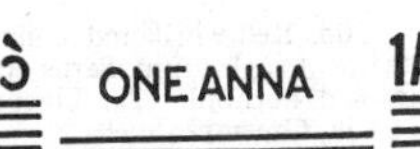


**1940, May 6** ***Perf. 13***

| | | | | |
|---|---|---|---|---|
| *34* | A3 | 1a on 2a6p rose lake | 1.00 | 80 |

Centenary of first postage stamp.

**Catalogue values for unused stamps in this section, from this point to the end of the section, are for Never Hinged items.**

Nos. 18A to 33 Overprinted in Black:

MILY ADMN — a

MILY ADMN — b

**1945**

| | | | | |
|---|---|---|---|---|
| *35* | A1(a) | 1p red org | 5 | 5 |
| *36* | A1(a) | 3p violet | 5 | 5 |
| *37* | A1(a) | 6p ultra | 7 | 7 |
| *38* | A1(a) | 9p yel grn | 7 | 7 |
| *39* | A2(a) | 1a brn vio | 8 | 8 |
| *40* | A2(a) | 1½a turq grn | 10 | 8 |
| *41* | A2(a) | 2a carmine | 10 | 8 |
| *42* | A3(b) | 2a6p rose lake | 10 | 10 |
| *43* | A4(b) | 3a dk vio | 10 | 10 |
| *44* | A5(b) | 3a6p dp bl & brt bl | 10 | 10 |
| *45* | A2(a) | 4a sl bl | 12 | 12 |
| *46* | A6(b) | 8a sl grn | 18 | 18 |
| *47* | A7(b) | 1r brt ultra & dk vio | 26 | 26 |
| *48* | A7(b) | 2r dk vio & red brn | 42 | 42 |
| *49* | A8(b) | 5r car & dl vio | 80 | 80 |
| *50* | A8(b) | 10r gray grn & brn | 1.50 | 1.50 |
| | | *Nos. 35-50 (16)* | 4.10 | 4.06 |

Types of 1938.

***Perf. 13½x14***

**1946, Jan. 1 Litho. Wmk. 254**

| | | | | |
|---|---|---|---|---|
| *51* | A1 | 3p brown | 5 | 5 |
| *52* | A1 | 6p violet | 5 | 5 |
| *53* | A1 | 9p dl grn | 5 | 5 |
| *54* | A2 | 1a dp bl | 5 | 5 |
| *55* | A2 | 1½a salmon | 5 | 5 |
| *56* | A2 | 2a rose lake | 6 | 6 |

***Perf. 13***

| | | | | |
|---|---|---|---|---|
| *57* | A3 | 2a6p grnsh bl | 8 | 8 |
| *58* | A4 | 3a bl vio | 10 | 10 |
| *59* | A5 | 3a6p ultra & gray blk | 12 | 12 |
| *60* | A2 | 4a rose lil, perf. 13½x14 | 12 | 12 |
| *61* | A6 | 8a dp mag | 20 | 20 |

***Perf. 13½***

| | | | | |
|---|---|---|---|---|
| *62* | A7 | 1r dp mag & dk vio | 28 | 24 |
| *63* | A7 | 2r sal & red brn | 70 | 60 |
| *64* | A8 | 5r red brn & dk grn | 1.40 | 1.20 |
| *65* | A8 | 10r dk vio & car | 2.25 | 2.25 |
| | | *Nos. 51-65 (15)* | 5.56 | 5.22 |

Burmese Man — A9

Burmese Woman — A10

Common Design Types are pictured in section before Great Britain.

Mythological Chinze — A11

Elephant Hauling Teak — A12

**1946, May 2** ***Perf. 13***

| | | | | |
|---|---|---|---|---|
| *66* | A9 | 9p pck grn | 8 | 8 |
| *67* | A10 | 1½a brt vio | 8 | 8 |
| *68* | A11 | 2a carmine | 10 | 10 |
| *69* | A12 | 3a6p ultra | 12 | 12 |

Victory of the Allied Nations in WW II.

Nos. 51 to 65 Overprinted in Black

ကြားဖြတ်
အစိုးရ။

**1947, Oct. 1** ***Perf. 13½x14, 13, 13½***

| | | | | |
|---|---|---|---|---|
| *70* | A1 | 3p brown | 6 | 6 |
| *71* | A1 | 6p violet | 6 | 6 |
| *72* | A1 | 9p dl grn | 6 | 6 |
| *a.* | | Inverted overprint | 8.00 | 8.00 |
| *73* | A2 | 1a dp bl | 6 | 6 |
| *74* | A2 | 1½a salmon | 6 | 6 |
| *75* | A2 | 2a rose lake | 6 | 6 |
| *76* | A3 | 2a6p grnsh bl | 8 | 6 |
| *77* | A4 | 3a bl vio | 8 | 8 |
| *78* | A5 | 3a6p ultra & gray blk | 10 | 10 |
| *79* | A2 | 4a rose lil | 10 | 10 |
| *80* | A6 | 8a dp mag | 20 | 20 |
| *81* | A7 | 1r dp mag & dk vio | 40 | 30 |
| *82* | A7 | 2r sal & red brn | 80 | 55 |
| *83* | A8 | 5r red brn & dk grn | 1.00 | 75 |
| *84* | A8 | 10r dk vio & car | 1.75 | 1.50 |
| | | *Nos. 70-84 (15)* | 4.87 | 4.00 |

The overprint is slightly larger on Nos. 76 to 78 and 80 to 84. The Burmese characters read "Interim Government."

Other denominations are known with the overprint inverted or double.

**Issues of the Republic.**

U Aung San Map and Chinze — A13

Martyrs' Memorial — A14

***Perf. 12½x12***

**1948, Jan. 6 Litho. Unwmk.**

| | | | | |
|---|---|---|---|---|
| *85* | A13 | ½a emerald | 6 | 5 |
| *86* | A13 | 1a dp rose | 7 | 6 |
| *87* | A13 | 2a carmine | 10 | 8 |
| *88* | A13 | 3½a blue | 15 | 12 |
| *89* | A13 | 8a lt choc | 20 | 18 |
| | | *Nos. 85-89 (5)* | 58 | 49 |

Attainment of independence, Jan. 4, 1948.

**1948, July 19 Engr.** ***Perf. 14x13½***

| | | | | |
|---|---|---|---|---|
| *90* | A14 | 3p ultra | 5 | 5 |
| *91* | A14 | 6p green | 5 | 5 |
| *92* | A14 | 9p dp car | 5 | 5 |
| *93* | A14 | 1a purple | 5 | 5 |
| *94* | A14 | 2a lil rose | 5 | 5 |
| *95* | A14 | 3½a dk sl grn | 6 | 6 |
| *96* | A14 | 4a yel brn | 7 | 7 |
| *97* | A14 | 8a org red | 12 | 12 |
| *98* | A14 | 12a claret | 16 | 14 |
| *99* | A14 | 1r bl grn | 20 | 16 |
| *100* | A14 | 2r dp bl | 48 | 35 |
| *101* | A14 | 5r chocolate | 1.25 | 80 |
| | | *Nos. 90-101 (12)* | 2.59 | 1.95 |

1st anniv. of the assassination of Burma's leaders in the fight for independence.

Ball Game (Chinlon) A15

Bell A16

Mythical Bird — A17

Rice Planting — A18

Throne — A19

Designs: 6p, Dancer. 9p, Musician. 3a, Spinning. 3a6p, Royal Palace. 4a, Cutting teak. 8a, Plowing rice field.

***Perf. 12½ (A15-A17), 12x12½ (A18), 13 (A19)***

**1949, Jan. 4**

| | | | | |
|---|---|---|---|---|
| *102* | A15 | 3p ultra | 8 | 8 |
| *103* | A15 | 6p green | 5 | 5 |
| *104* | A15 | 9p carmine | 5 | 5 |
| *105* | A16 | 1a red org | 5 | 5 |
| *106* | A17 | 2a orange | 6 | 5 |
| *107* | A18 | 2a6p lil rose | 8 | 8 |
| *108* | A18 | 3a purple | 8 | 6 |
| *109* | A18 | 3a6p dk sl grn | 6 | 6 |
| *110* | A16 | 4a chocolate | 8 | 6 |
| *111* | A18 | 8a carmine | 16 | 12 |
| *112* | A19 | 1r bl grn | 35 | 20 |
| *a.* | | Perf. 14 | | 2.50 |
| *113* | A19 | 2r dp bl | 80 | 32 |
| *114* | A19 | 5r chocolate | 1.65 | 70 |
| *115* | A19 | 10r org red | 3.25 | 1.00 |
| | | *Nos. 102-115 (14)* | 6.80 | 2.88 |

UPU Monument, Bern — A20

**Unwmk.**

**1949, Oct. 9 Engr.** ***Perf. 13***

| | | | | |
|---|---|---|---|---|
| *116* | A20 | 2a orange | 7 | 7 |
| *117* | A20 | 3½a ol grn | 10 | 8 |
| *118* | A20 | 6a lilac | 16 | 14 |
| *119* | A20 | 8a crimson | 24 | 16 |
| *120* | A20 | 12½a ultra | 32 | 16 |
| *121* | A20 | 1r bl grn | 52 | 50 |
| | | *Nos. 116-121 (6)* | 1.41 | 1.11 |

75th anniv. of the UPU.

Types of 1949.
Designs as Before.

***Perf. 13½x14, 14x13½, 13***

**1952-53 Litho. Wmk. 254**

| | | | | |
|---|---|---|---|---|
| *122* | A15 | 3p brn org | 10 | 5 |
| *123* | A15 | 6p dp plum | 5 | 5 |
| *124* | A15 | 9p blue | 5 | 5 |
| *125* | A16 | 1a vio bl | 5 | 5 |
| *126* | A17 | 2a grn ('52) | 5 | 5 |
| *127* | A18 | 2a6p green | 14 | 14 |
| *128* | A18 | 3a sal pink ('52) | 7 | 5 |
| *129* | A18 | 3a6p brn org | 14 | 14 |
| *130* | A16 | 4a vermilion | 10 | 5 |
| *131* | A18 | 8a lt bl ('52) | 14 | 8 |
| *132* | A19 | 1r rose vio | 24 | 14 |
| *133* | A19 | 2r yel grn | 52 | 26 |
| *134* | A19 | 5r ultra | 1.65 | 85 |
| *135* | A19 | 10r aqua | 3.25 | 1.65 |
| | | *Nos. 122-135 (14)* | 6.55 | 3.61 |

See Nos. 139-152.

Map of Burma and Monument — A21

**1953, Jan. 4** ***Perf. 14***

**Size: 21½x18mm.**

*136* A21 14p green 5 5

***Perf. 13***

**Size: 36½x26mm.**

*137* A21 20p sal pink 8 5
*138* A21 25p ultra 10 8

Fifth anniversary of independence.

Types of 1949.

Designs: 2p, Dancer. 3p, Musician. 20p, Spinning. 25p, Royal Palace. 30p, Cutting teak. 50p, Plowing rice field.

**1954, Jan. 4** ***Perf. 14x13½, 13, 14***

*139* A15 1p brn org 5 5
*140* A15 2p plum 5 5
*141* A15 3p blue 5 5
*142* A16 5p ultra 5 5
*143* A18 10p yel grn 5 5
*144* A17 15p green 5 5
*145* A18 20p vermilion 5 5
*146* A18 25p lt red org 7 5
*147* A16 30p vermilion 10 8
*148* A18 50p blue 24 5
*149* A19 1k rose vio 50 8
*150* A19 2k green 1.00 10
*151* A19 5k ultra 2.75 14
*152* A19 10k lt bl 5.00 26
*Nos. 139-152 (14)* 10.01 1.11

Peace Pagoda, Monks' Hostels and Meeting-cave — A22

Designs: 10p, Sangha (community) of Cambodia. 15p, Council meeting. 50p, Sangha of Thailand. 1k, Sangha of Ceylon. 2k, Sangha of Laos.

**1954** **Typo.** ***Perf. 13***

*153* A22 10p dp bl 5 5
*154* A22 15p dp cl 5 5
*155* A22 35p dk brn 14 7
*156* A22 50p green 16 8
*157* A22 1k carmine 32 16
*158* A22 2k violet 60 40
*Nos. 153-158 (6)* 1.32 81

6th Buddhist Council, Rangoon, 1954-56.

Marble Markers of 5th Buddhist Council A23

Designs: 40p, Thatbyinnyu Pagoda. 60p, Shwedagon Pagoda, Rangoon. 1.25k, Aerial View of 6th Buddhist Council, Yegu.

***Perf. 11x11½***

**1956, May 24** **Litho.** **Unwmk.**

*159* A23 20p bl & gray ol 7 5
*160* A23 40p bl & brt yel grn 14 8
*161* A23 60p grn & lem 16 12
*162* A23 1.25k gray bl & yel 32 20

Issued in honor of the 2500th anniversary of the Buddhist Era.

Nos. 146, 149-150 Surcharged or Overprinted

မြို့မန္တလာ-နှစ်တရာ

၁၂၂၁-၁၃၂၁

**15 P** ၁၅ါး

**1959, Nov. 9** **Wmk. 254** ***Perf. 13, 14***

*163* A18 15p on 25p lt red org 7 5
*164* A19 1k rose vio 30 16
*165* A19 2k green 55 45

Centenary of Mandalay, former capital.

The two lines of overprint are 4mm. apart on No. 163; 7mm. on Nos. 164-165.

No. 136 Surcharged: ၁၅ါး

**1961, June** ***Perf. 14***

*166* A21 15p on 14p grn 32 16

Children A24

**Unwmk.**

**1961, Dec. 11** **Litho.** ***Perf. 13***

*167* A24 15p cl & rose cl 7 5

15th anniversary of UNICEF.

Runner with Torch — A25

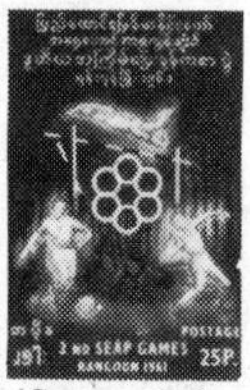

Soccer, Pole Vault and Shot Put — A26

Designs: 50p, Women runners. 1k, Hurdling, weight lifting, boxing, bicycling and swimming.

**1961, Dec. 11** **Photo.** ***Perf. 14x13***

*168* A25 15p red & ultra 7 5
*169* A26 25p dk grn & ocher 10 7
*170* A26 50p vio bl & pink 20 10
*171* A25 1k brt grn & yel 35 26

Issued to commemorate the 2nd South East Asia Peninsular Games, Rangoon.

Map and Flag of Burma — A27

**Wmk. 254**

**1963, Mar. 2** **Engr.** ***Perf. 13***

*172* A27 15p red 16 7

First anniversary of new government.

Nos. 143 and 148 Overprinted in Violet or Red: "FREEDOM FROM HUNGER"

**1963, Mar. 21** **Litho.**

*173* A18 10p yel grn (V) 7 5
*174* A18 50p bl (R) 20 14

"Freedom from Hunger" campaign of the UNFAO.

No. 145 Overprinted

အလုပ်သမားနေ့

၁၉၆၃

**1963, May 1**

*175* A18 20p vermilion 10 8

Issued for May Day 1963.

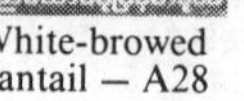

White-browed Fantail — A28

Indian Roller — A29

Birds: 20p, Red-whiskered bulbul. 25p, Crested serpent eagle. 50p, Sarus crane. 1k, Malabar pied hornbill. 2k, Lineated kalij pheasant. 5k, Green peafowl.

**Unwmk.**

**1964, Apr. 16** **Photo.** ***Perf. 13***

**Size: 25x21mm.**

*176* A28 1p gray 5 5
*177* A28 2p car rose 5 5
*178* A28 3p bl grn 5 5

**Size: 22x26½mm.**

*179* A29 5p vio bl 5 5
*180* A29 10p org brn 8 5
*181* A29 15p olive 14 5

**Size: 35x25mm.**

*182* A28 20p rose & brn 16 5

**Size: 27x36½mm., 36½x27mm.**

*183* A29 25p yel & brn 20 5
*184* A29 50p red, blk & gray 50 7
*185* A29 1k gray, ind & yel 1.00 10
*186* A28 2k pale ol, ind & red 2.00 32
*187* A29 5k cit, dk bl & red 4.75 65
*Nos. 176-187 (12)* 9.03 1.54

See also Nos. 197-208.

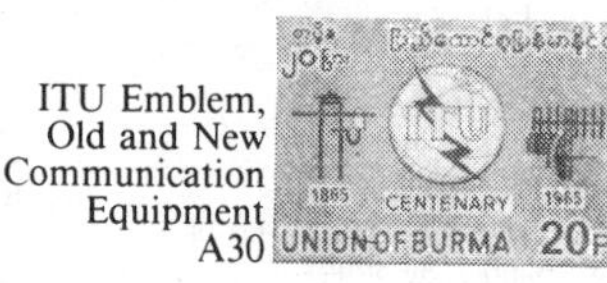

ITU Emblem, Old and New Communication Equipment A30

**1965, May 17** **Litho.** ***Perf. 15***

**Size: 32x22mm.**

*188* A30 20p brt pink 9 5

***Perf. 13***

**Size: 34x24½mm.**

*189* A30 50p dl grn 24 26

Centenary of the ITU.

ICY Emblem A31

**1965, July 1** **Unwmk.** ***Perf. 13***

*190* A31 5p vio bl 5 5
*191* A31 10p brn org 5 5
*192* A31 15p olive 9 5

International Cooperation Year, 1965.

Rice Farmer — A32

**1966, Mar. 2**

*193* A32 15p multi 9 5

Issued for Farmers' Day.

Cogwheel and Hammer — A33

**1967, May 1** **Litho.** **Unwmk.**

*194* A33 15p lt bl, yel & blk 9 5

Issued for Labor Day, May 1, 1967.

Aung San, Tractor and Farmers A34

**1968, Jan. 4** **Unwmk.** ***Perf. 13***

*195* A34 15p sky bl, blk & ocher 9 7

20th anniversary of independence.

Largest Burmese Pearl — A35

**1968, Mar. 4** **Litho.** ***Perf. 13½x13***

*196* A35 15p bl, ultra, gray & yel 9 5

Burmese pearl industry.

Bird Types of 1964 in Changed Sizes; Designs as Before.

**Unwmk.**

**1968, July 1** **Photo.** ***Perf. 14***

**Size: 21x17mm.**

*197* A28 1p gray 5 5
*198* A28 2p car rose 5 5
*199* A28 3p bl grn 5 5

**Size: 23½x28mm.**

*200* A29 5p vio bl 5 5
*201* A29 10p org brn 7 5
*202* A29 15p olive 10 5

**Size: 38½x21, 21x38½mm.**

*203* A28 20p rose & brn 14 5
*204* A29 25p yel & brn 16 5
*205* A29 50p ver, blk, & gray 32 5
*206* A29 1k gray, ind & yel 65 8
*207* A28 2k dl cit, ind & red 1.40 24
*208* A29 5k yel, dk bl & red 3.25 55
*Nos. 197-208 (12)* 6.29 1.32

Wheat — A36

**Unwmk.**

**1969, Mar. 2** **Litho.** ***Perf. 13***

*209* A36 15p bl, emer & yel 5 5

Issued for Peasant's Day.

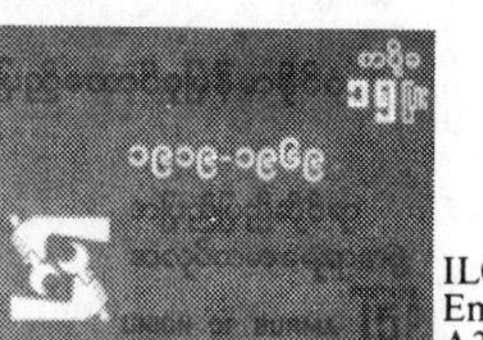

ILO Emblem A37

**1969, Oct. 29** **Photo.** **Wmk. 254**

*210* A37 15p dk bl grn & gold 5 5
*211* A37 50p dp car & gold 15 12

50th anniv. of the ILO.

Soccer — A38

Designs: 25p, Runner (horiz.). 50p, Weight lifter. 1k, Women's volleyball.

*Perf. 12½x13, 13x12½*

**1969, Dec. 1 Litho. Wmk. 254**

| | | | | |
|---|---|---|---|---|
| *212* | A38 | 15p brt ol & multi | 6 | 5 |
| *213* | A38 | 25p brn & multi | 12 | 9 |
| *214* | A38 | 50p brt grn & multi | 24 | 15 |
| *215* | A38 | 1k bl, yel grn & blk | 45 | 30 |

5th South East Asia Peninsular Games, Rangoon.

Burmese Flags and Marching Soldiers — A39

**1970, Mar. 27** *Perf. 13*

| | | | | |
|---|---|---|---|---|
| *216* | A39 | 15p multi | 5 | 5 |

Issued for Armed Forces Day.

Solar System and U.N. Emblem A40

**1970, June 26 Photo. Unwmk.**

| | | | | |
|---|---|---|---|---|
| *217* | A40 | 15p lt ultra & multi | 5 | 5 |

25th anniversary of the United Nations.

Scroll, Marchers, Peacock Emblem A41

Designs: 25p, Students' boycott demonstration. 50p, Banner and marchers at Shwedagon Camp.

**1970, Nov. 23 Litho.** *Perf. 13x13½*

| | | | | |
|---|---|---|---|---|
| *218* | A41 | 15p ultra & multi | 8 | 5 |
| *219* | A41 | 25p multi | 12 | 5 |
| *220* | A41 | 50p lt bl & multi | 24 | 12 |

For the 50th National Day (Students' 1920 uprising).

Workers, Farmers, Technicians — A42

Designs: 15p, Burmese of various races, and flags. 25p, Hands holding document. 50p, Red party flag.

**1971, June 28 Litho.** *Perf. 13½*

| | | | | |
|---|---|---|---|---|
| *221* | A42 | 5p bl & multi | 5 | 5 |
| *222* | A42 | 15p bl & multi | 7 | 5 |
| *223* | A42 | 25p bl & multi | 10 | 5 |
| *224* | A42 | 50p bl & multi | 22 | 10 |
| *a.* | | Souvenir sheet of 4 | 45 | 45 |

First Congress of Burmese Socialist Program Party. No. 224a contains one each of Nos. 221-224. Gold ornament and blue inscription in margin. Size: 177x126mm.

Child Drinking Milk — A43

Design: 50p, Marionettes.

**1971, Dec. 11** *Perf. 14½*

| | | | | |
|---|---|---|---|---|
| *225* | A43 | 15p lt ultra & multi | 14 | 7 |
| *226* | A43 | 50p emer & multi | 32 | 16 |

25th anniv. of UNICEF.

Aung San, Independence Monument, Pinlon — A44

Designs: 50p, Bogyoke Aung San and people in front of Independence Monument. 1k, Map of Burma with flag pointing to Pinlon (vert.).

**1972, Feb. 12** *Perf. 14*

| | | | | |
|---|---|---|---|---|
| *227* | A44 | 15p ocher & multi | 6 | 5 |
| *228* | A44 | 50p bl & multi | 24 | 10 |
| *229* | A44 | 1k grn, ultra & red | 40 | 22 |

Union Day, 25th anniversary.

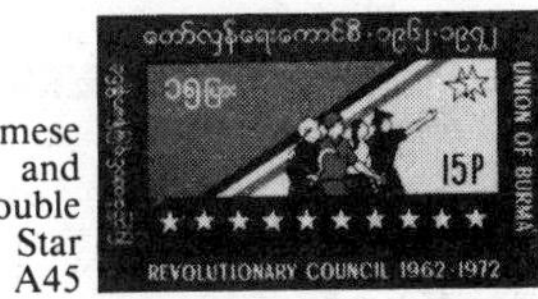
Burmese and Double Star A45

**1972 Litho.** *Perf. 14*

| | | | | |
|---|---|---|---|---|
| *230* | A45 | 15p bis & multi | 5 | 5 |

Revolutionary Council, 10th anniversary.

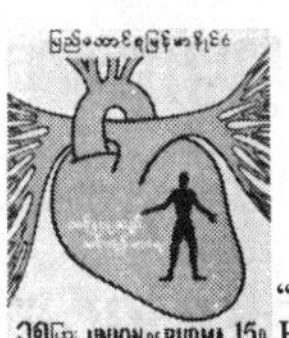
"Your Heart is your Health" — A46

**1972, Apr. 7** *Perf. 14x14½*

| | | | | |
|---|---|---|---|---|
| *231* | A46 | 15p yel, red & blk | 5 | 5 |

World Health Day.

Burmese of Various Ethnic Groups A47

**1973, Feb. 12 Litho.** *Perf. 14*

| | | | | |
|---|---|---|---|---|
| *232* | A47 | 15p multi | 5 | 5 |

1973 census.

Casting Vote — A48

Designs: 10p, Voters holding map of Burma. 15p, Farmer and soldier holding ballots (vert.).

*Perf. 14x14½, 14½x14*

**1973, Dec. 15 Litho.**

| | | | | |
|---|---|---|---|---|
| *233* | A48 | 5p dp org & blk | 5 | 5 |
| *234* | A48 | 10p bl & multi | 5 | 5 |
| *235* | A48 | 15p bl & multi | 5 | 5 |

National Referendum.

Open-air Meeting A49

Designs: 15p, Regional flags. 1k, Scales of justice and Burmese emblem.

**1974, Mar. 2 Photo.** *Perf. 13*

**Size: 80x26mm.**

| | | | | |
|---|---|---|---|---|
| *236* | A49 | 15p bl & multi | 5 | 5 |

**Size: 37x25mm.**

| | | | | |
|---|---|---|---|---|
| *237* | A49 | 50p bl & multi | 20 | 14 |
| *238* | A49 | 1k lt bl, bis & blk | 40 | 26 |

First meeting of People's Parliament.

Messenger Bird and UPU Emblem A50

Designs (UPU emblem and): 20p, Mother reading letter to child (vert.). 50p, Simulated block of stamps (vert.). 1k, Burmese doll (vert.). 2k, Mailman delivering letter to family.

**1974, May 22**

| | | | | |
|---|---|---|---|---|
| *239* | A50 | 15p grn, lt grn & org | 6 | 5 |
| *240* | A50 | 20p multi | 10 | 5 |
| *241* | A50 | 50p grn & multi | 22 | 12 |
| *242* | A50 | 1k ultra & multi | 48 | 25 |
| *243* | A50 | 2k bl & multi | 95 | 50 |
| | | *Nos. 239-243 (5)* | 1.81 | 97 |

Centenary of Universal Postal Union.

Children A51

Man and Woman A52

Designs: 3p, Girl. 5p, 15p, Man and woman. 10p, Children (like 1p). 50p, Woman with fan. 1k, Seated woman. 5k, Drummer.

*Perf. 13, 13x13½ (#248-251)*

**1974-78 Photo.**

| | | | | |
|---|---|---|---|---|
| *244* | A51 | 1p rose & lil rose | 5 | 5 |
| *245* | A51 | 3p dk brn & pink | 5 | 5 |
| *246* | A51 | 5p pink & vio | 5 | 5 |
| *246A* | A51 | 10p Prus bl ('78) | 5 | 5 |
| *247* | A51 | 15p lt grn & ol | 5 | 5 |
| *248* | A52 | 20p lt bl & multi | 7 | 5 |
| *249* | A52 | 50p ocher & multi | 24 | 14 |
| *250* | A52 | 1k brt rose & multi | 48 | 28 |
| *251* | A52 | 5k ol grn & multi | 2.00 | 1.40 |
| | | *Nos. 244-251 (9)* | 3.04 | 2.12 |

IWY Emblem, Woman and Globe A53

Design: 2k, Symbolic flower, globe and IWY emblem (vert.).

**1975, Dec. 15 Photo.** *Perf. 13½*

| | | | | |
|---|---|---|---|---|
| *252* | A53 | 50p grn & blk | 18 | 12 |
| *253* | A53 | 2k blk & bl | 70 | 48 |

International Women's Year 1975.

Burmese with Raised Fists — A54

Designs: 50p, Demonstrators with banners and emblem. 1k, People and map of Burma, emblem.

**1976, Jan. 3** *Perf. 14*

**Size: 36x21mm.**

| | | | | |
|---|---|---|---|---|
| *254* | A54 | 20p bl & blk | 8 | 5 |
| *255* | A54 | 50p bl, blk & brn | 22 | 12 |

**Size: 56x20mm.**

| | | | | |
|---|---|---|---|---|
| *256* | A54 | 1k bl & multi | 45 | 22 |

Constitution Day.

Students, Campaign Emblem — A55

Abacus A56

Designs: 50p, Campaign emblem. 1k, Emblem, book and globe.

**1976, Sept. 8 Photo.** *Perf. 14*

| | | | | |
|---|---|---|---|---|
| *257* | A55 | 10p sal & blk | 5 | 5 |
| *258* | A56 | 15p bl grn & multi | 6 | 5 |
| *259* | A56 | 50p ultra, org & blk | 24 | 15 |
| *260* | A55 | 1k multi | 60 | 30 |

International Literacy Year.

Steam Locomotive A57

Diesel Train Emerging from Tunnel A58

Designs: 20p, Early train and oxcart. 25p, Old and new trains approaching station. 50p, Railroad bridge.

**1977, May 1** *Perf. 13½*

**Size: 26x17mm.**

| | | | | |
|---|---|---|---|---|
| *261* | A57 | 15p multi | 5 | 5 |

**Size: 38x26, 26x38mm.**

| | | | | | |
|---|---|---|---|---|---|
| *262* | A57 | 20p multi | | 6 | 5 |
| *263* | A57 | 25p multi | | 10 | 8 |
| *264* | A57 | 50p multi | | 26 | 14 |
| *265* | A58 | 1k multi | | 52 | 26 |
| | | *Nos. 261-265 (5)* | | 99 | 58 |

Centenary of Burma's railroad.

Karaweik Pagoda A59

Design: 1k, Karaweik Pagoda, front view.

**1977**

**Size: 37x25mm.**

*266* A59 50p lt brn 18 12

**Size: 78x25mm.**

*267* A59 1k multi 35 24

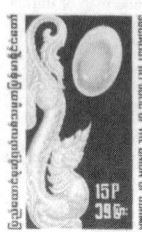

Jade Dragon — A60

Precious Jewelry: 20p, Gold bird with large pearl. 50p, Hand holding pearl necklace with pendant. 1k, Gold dragon (horiz.).

**1978 Photo. *Perf. 13, 14 (1k)***

**Sizes: 15p, 20p, 50p, 25x37mm. 1k, 55x20mm.**

| | | | | |
|---|---|---|---|---|
| *268* | A60 | 15p grn & yel grn | 6 | 5 |
| *269* | A60 | 20p multi | 8 | 5 |
| *270* | A60 | 50p multi | 32 | 16 |
| *271* | A60 | 1k multi | 48 | 32 |

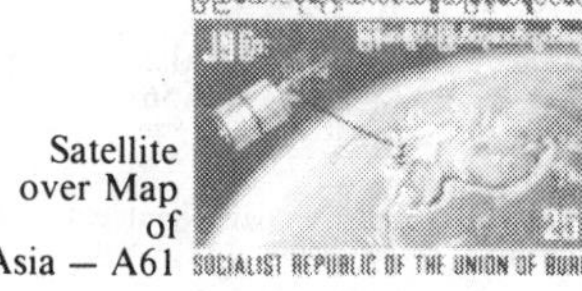

Satellite over Map of Asia — A61

**1979, Feb., 12 Photo. *Perf. 13***

*272* A61 25p multi 10 7

IYC Emblem in Map of Burma — A62

**1979, Dec. Photo. *Perf. 13½***

| | | | | |
|---|---|---|---|---|
| *273* | A62 | 25p multi | 16 | 10 |
| *274* | A62 | 50p multi | 32 | 16 |

International Year of the Child.

Weather Balloon, WMO Emblem — A63

**1980, Mar. 23 Photo. *Perf. 13½***

| | | | | |
|---|---|---|---|---|
| *275* | A63 | 25p shown | 16 | 10 |
| *276* | A63 | 50p Weather satellite, cloud | 32 | 16 |

World Meteorological Day.

Weight Lifting, Olympic Rings A64

**1980, Dec. Litho. *Perf. 14***

| | | | | |
|---|---|---|---|---|
| *277* | A64 | 20p shown | 8 | 5 |
| *278* | A64 | 50p Boxing | 20 | 14 |
| *279* | A64 | 1k Soccer | 40 | 25 |

22nd Summer Olympic Games, Moscow, July 19-Aug. 3.

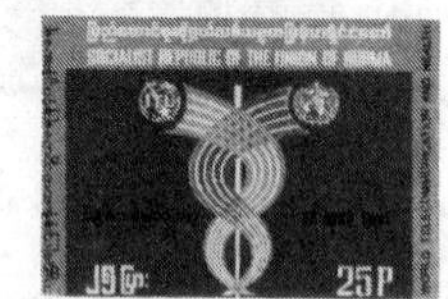

13th World Telecommunications Day — A65

**1981, May 17 Photo. *Perf. 13½***

*280* A65 25p org & blk 10 7

World Food Day — A66

**1981, Oct. 16 Photo. *Perf. 13½***

| | | | | |
|---|---|---|---|---|
| *281* | A66 | 25p Livestock, produce | 10 | 7 |
| *282* | A66 | 50p Farmer, rice, produce | 20 | 14 |
| *283* | A66 | 1k Emblems | 40 | 25 |

Intl. Year of the Disabled A67

**1981, Dec. 12**

*284* A67 25p multi 10 7

World Communications Year — A68

**1983, Sept. 15 Litho. *Perf. 14½x14***

| | | | | |
|---|---|---|---|---|
| *285* | A68 | 15p pale blue & blk | 9 | 7 |
| *286* | A68 | 25p dull lake & blk | 15 | 10 |
| *287* | A68 | 50p pale brn, blk & lake | 30 | 20 |
| *288* | A68 | 1k buff, blk, beige & yel grn | 60 | 40 |

World Food Day — A69

Design: Fish, ship, globe, FAO emblem.

**1983, Oct. 16 Photo. *Perf. 14x14½***

| | | | | |
|---|---|---|---|---|
| *289* | A69 | 15p brt blue, bister & blk | 9 | 7 |
| *290* | A69 | 25p yel grn, pale org & blk | 15 | 10 |
| *291* | A69 | 50p org, pale grn & blk | 30 | 20 |
| *292* | A69 | 1k yel, ultra & blk | 60 | 40 |

World Food Day A70

Designs: Stylized trees, hemispheres and log.

**1984, Oct. 16 *Perf. 14½x14***

| | | | | |
|---|---|---|---|---|
| *293* | A70 | 15p org, blk & blue | 9 | 7 |
| *294* | A70 | 25p pale yel, blk & lt vio | 15 | 10 |
| *295* | A70 | 50p pale pink, blk & lt grn | 30 | 20 |
| *296* | A70 | 1k yel, blk & lt rose vio | 60 | 40 |

Intl. Youth Year — A71

**1985, Oct. 15 *Perf. 14x14½***

*297* A71 15p multi 10 7

## OFFICIAL STAMPS

Stamps of India, 1926-34, Overprinted in Black **BURMA** **SERVICE**

**1937 Wmk. 196 *Perf. 14***

| | | | | |
|---|---|---|---|---|
| *O1* | A46 | 3p gray | 5 | 5 |
| *O2* | A71 | ½a green | 5 | 5 |
| *O3* | A68 | 9p dk grn | 8 | 5 |
| *O4* | A72 | 1a dk brn | 8 | 5 |
| *O5* | A49 | 2a vermilion | 10 | 5 |
| *O6* | A57 | 2a6p buff | 10 | 8 |
| *O7* | A52 | 4a ol grn | 15 | 9 |
| *O8* | A53 | 6a bister | 50 | 75 |
| *O9* | A54 | 8a red vio | 28 | 10 |
| *O10* | A55 | 12a claret | 25 | 22 |

Overprinted **BURMA** **SERVICE**

| | | | | |
|---|---|---|---|---|
| *O11* | A56 | 1r grn & brn | 1.00 | 25 |
| *O12* | A56 | 2r buff & car rose | 2.50 | 3.00 |
| *O13* | A56 | 5r dk vio & ultra | 7.50 | 10.00 |
| *O14* | A56 | 10r car & grn | 30.00 | *35.00* |
| | | *Nos. O1-O14 (14)* | 42.64 | 49.74 |

Regular Issue of 1938 Overprinted in Black **SERVICE**

**Wmk. Elephant Heads. (254)**

**1939 *Perf. 13½x14, 13, 13½.***

| | | | | |
|---|---|---|---|---|
| *O15* | A1 | 3p violet | 5 | 5 |
| *O16* | A1 | 6p ultra | 5 | 5 |
| *O17* | A1 | 9p yel grn | 7 | 5 |
| *O18* | A2 | 1a brn vio | 10 | 5 |
| *O19* | A2 | 1½a turq grn | 8 | 5 |
| *O20* | A2 | 2a carmine | 10 | 5 |
| *O21* | A2 | 4a sl bl | 32 | 10 |

Overprinted **SERVICE**

| | | | | |
|---|---|---|---|---|
| *O22* | A3 | 2a6p rose lake | 32 | 20 |
| *O23* | A6 | 8a sl grn | 75 | 26 |
| *O24* | A7 | 1r brt ultra & dk vio | 1.00 | 40 |
| *O25* | A7 | 2r dk vio & red brn | 6.75 | 2.00 |
| *O26* | A8 | 5r car & dl vio | 24.00 | 5.00 |
| *O27* | A8 | 10r gray grn & brn | 40.00 | 17.00 |
| | | *Nos. O15-O27 (13)* | 73.59 | 25.26 |

**Catalogue values for unused stamps in this section, from this point to the end of the section, are for Never Hinged items.**

Nos. 51-56, 60 Ovptd. Like Nos. O15-O21

**1946 *Perf. 13½x14***

| | | | | |
|---|---|---|---|---|
| *O28* | A1 | 3p brown | 5 | 5 |
| *O29* | A1 | 6p violet | 5 | 5 |
| *O30* | A1 | 9p dl grn | 5 | 5 |
| *O31* | A2 | 1a dp bl | 5 | 5 |
| *O32* | A2 | 1½a salmon | 6 | 5 |
| *O33* | A2 | 2a rose lake | 6 | 5 |
| *O34* | A2 | 4a rose lil | 12 | 6 |

**Nos. 57, 61-65 Ovptd. Like Nos. O22-O27**

***Perf. 13, 13½***

| | | | | |
|---|---|---|---|---|
| *O35* | A3 | 2a6p grnsh bl | 12 | 8 |
| *O38* | A6 | 8a dp mag | 16 | 14 |
| *O39* | A7 | 1r dp mag & dk vio | 28 | 20 |
| *O40* | A7 | 2r sal & red brn | 2.50 | 1.65 |
| *O41* | A8 | 5r red brn & dk grn | 4.00 | 4.00 |
| *O42* | A8 | 10r dk vio & car | 8.00 | *12.00* |
| | | *Nos. O28-O42 (13)* | 15.50 | 18.43 |

Nos. O28 to O42 Overprinted in Black ကြားဖြတ် အစိုးရ။

**1947**

| | | | | |
|---|---|---|---|---|
| *O43* | A1 | 3p brown | 5 | 5 |
| *O44* | A1 | 6p violet | 5 | 5 |
| *O45* | A1 | 9p dl grn | 7 | 7 |
| *O46* | A2 | 1a dp bl | 5 | 5 |
| *O47* | A2 | 1½a salmon | 10 | 6 |
| *O48* | A2 | 2a rose lake | 15 | 7 |
| *O49* | A3 | 2a6p grnsh bl | 15 | 10 |
| *O50* | A2 | 4a rose lil | 18 | 10 |
| *O51* | A6 | 8a dp mag | 30 | 15 |
| *O52* | A7 | 1r dp mag & dk vio | 45 | 30 |
| *O53* | A7 | 2r sal & red brn | *2.50* | *2.50* |
| *O54* | A8 | 5r red brn & dk grn | *7.50* | *7.50* |
| *O55* | A8 | 10r dk vio & car | *10.00* | *10.00* |
| | | *Nos. O43-O55 (13)* | 21.55 | 21.00 |

The overprint is slightly larger on Nos. O49 and O51 to O55. The Burmese characters read "Interim Government."

**Issues of the Republic**

Nos. 102 to 106 and 109 to 115 Overprinted in Carmine or Black အစိုးရကိစ္စ

a. Overprint 13mm Long.
b. Overprint 15mm Long.

**1949 Unwmk. *Perf. 12½, 13***

| | | | | |
|---|---|---|---|---|
| *O56* | A15(a) | 3p ultra (C) | 5 | 5 |
| *O57* | A15(a) | 6p grn (C) | 5 | 5 |
| *O58* | A15(a) | 9p carmine | 5 | 5 |
| *O59* | A16(a) | 1a red org | 5 | 5 |
| *O60* | A17(a) | 2a orange | 5 | 5 |
| *O61* | A18(b) | 3a6p dk sl grn (C) | 6 | 5 |
| *O62* | A16(a) | 4a chocolate | 8 | 6 |
| *O63* | A18(b) | 8a carmine | 16 | 12 |
| *O64* | A19(b) | 1r bl grn (C) | 32 | 24 |
| *O65* | A19(b) | 2r dp bl (C) | 65 | 40 |
| *O66* | A19(b) | 5r chocolate | 1.65 | 1.25 |
| *O67* | A19(b) | 10r org red | 3.25 | 2.50 |
| | | *Nos. O56-O67 (12)* | 6.42 | 4.87 |

Same Overprint in Black on Nos. 139-142, 144-152

***Perf. 14x13½, 13, 14***

**1954-57 Wmk. 254**

| | | | | |
|---|---|---|---|---|
| *O68* | A15(a) | 1p brn org | 5 | 5 |
| *O69* | A15(a) | 2p plum | 5 | 5 |
| *O70* | A15(a) | 3p blue | 5 | 5 |
| *O71* | A16(a) | 5p ultra | 5 | 5 |
| *O72* | A17(a) | 15p green | 7 | 5 |
| *O72A* | A18(b) | 20p ver ('57) | 8 | 5 |
| *O73* | A18(b) | 25p lt red org | 10 | 5 |
| *O74* | A16(a) | 30p vermilion | 12 | 5 |
| *O75* | A18(b) | 50p blue | 20 | 8 |
| *O76* | A19(b) | 1k rose vio | 40 | 12 |
| *O77* | A19(b) | 2k green | 85 | 20 |

*O78* A19(b) 5k ultra 1.65 32
*O79* A19(b) 10k lt bl 3.25 45
*Nos. O68-O79 (13)* 6.92 1.57

Nos. 176-179, 181-187 Overprinted in Black or Red အစိုးရကိစ္စ

**1967 Unwmk. Photo. *Perf. 13***

**Overprint: 15mm**

**Size: 25x21mm**

*O80* A28 1p gray 5 5
*O81* A28 2p car rose 5 5
*O82* A28 3p bl grn 5 5

**Size: 22x26½mm**

*O83* A29 5p vio bl 5 5
*O85* A29 15p olive 7 5

**Size: 35x25mm**

*O86* A28 20p rose & brn 10 5

**Size: 27x36½mm, 36½x27mm**

*O87* A29 25p yel & brn (R) 14 5
*O88* A29 50p red, blk & gray 26 10
*O89* A29 1k gray, ind & yel (R) 52 14
*O90* A28 2k pale ol, ind & red (R) 1.10 30
*O91* A29 5k cit, dk bl & red (R) 2.75 65
*Nos. O80-O91 (11)* 5.14 1.54

Similar Overprint on Nos. 197-200, 202-208 in Black or Red

**1968 Unwmk. *Perf. 14***

**Size: 21x17mm**

**Overprint: 13mm**

*O92* A28 1p gray 5 5
*O93* A28 2p car rose 5 5
*O94* A28 3p bl grn 5 5

**Size: 23½x28mm**

**Overprint: 15mm**

*O95* A29 5p vio bl 5 5
*O96* A29 15p olive 7 5

**Size: 38½x21mm, 21x38½mm**

**Overprint: 14mm**

*O97* A28 20p rose & brn 10 6
*O98* A29 25p yel & brn (R) 14 5
*O99* A29 50p ver, blk & gray 26 5
*O100* A29 1k gray, ind & yel (R) 52 8
*O101* A28 2k dl cit, ind & red (R) 1.10 24
*O102* A29 5k yel, dk bl & red (R) 2.75 55
*Nos. O92-O102 (11)* 5.14 1.28

## OCCUPATION STAMPS

**Issued by Burma Independence Army (in conjunction with Japanese occupation officials)**

Stamps of Burma, 1937-40, Overprinted in Blue, Black Blue, Black or Red

**Henzada Issue**

Nos. 1, 3 and 5 Overprinted in Blue or Black

Henzada Type I

**1942, May Wmk. 196 *Perf. 14***

*1N1* A46 3p slate 5.00 *7.50*
*1N2* A68 9p dk grn 17.50 *25.00*
*1N3* A49 2a vermilion 50.00 *75.00*

**On 1938-40 George VI Issue**

***Perf. 13½x14***

**Wmk. 254**

*1N4* A1 1p red org 75.00 *87.50*
*1N5* A1 3p violet 17.50 *35.00*
*1N6* A1 6p ultra 15.00 *30.00*
*1N7* A1 9p yel grn 200.00
*1N8* A2 1a brn vio 5.00 *7.50*
*1N9* A2 1½a turq grn 12.50 *17.50*
*1N10* A2 2a carmine 15.00 *17.50*
*1N11* A2 4a sl bl 30.00 *37.50*

**On Official Stamps of 1939**

*1N12* A1 3p violet 50.00 *62.50*
*1N13* A1 6p ultra 45.00 *62.50*
*1N14* A2 1½a turq grn 65.00 *87.50*
*1N15* A2 2a carmine 150.00 150.00
*1N16* A2 4a slate bl 200.00 250.00

Authorities believe this overprint was officially applied only to postal stationery and that the adhesive stamps existing with it were not regularly issued. It has been called "Henzada Type II."

**Myaungmya Issue**

1937 George V Issue Overprinted in Black

Myaungmya Type I

**1942, May Wmk. 196 *Perf. 14***

*1N25* A68 9p dk grn 50.00 62.50
*1N26* A70 3a6p dp bl 25.00 32.50

**On Official Stamp of 1937, No. O8**

*1N27* A53 6a bister 50.00 62.50

**On 1938-40 George VI Issue**

***Perf. 13½x14***

**Wmk. 254**

*1N28* A1 9p yel grn 100.00 125.00
*1N29* A2 1a brn vio 175.00 225.00
*1N30* A2 4a sl bl (blk ovpt. over red) 100.00 125.00

**On Official Stamps of 1939**

*1N31* A1 3p violet 15.00 15.00
*1N32* A1 6p ultra 7.50 10.00
*1N33* A2 1a brn vio 7.50 10.00
*1N34* A2 1½a turq grn 300.00
*1N35* A2 2a carmine 15.00 20.00
*1N36* A2 4a slate bl 12.50 17.50

1938-40 George VI Issue Overprinted

Myaungmya Type II

**1942, May**

*1N37* A1 3p violet 12.50 *20.00*
*1N38* A1 6p ultra 25.00 *30.00*
*1N39* A1 9p yel grn 10.00 *15.00*
*1N40* A2 1a brn vio 10.00 12.50
*1N41* A2 2a carmine 15.00 20.00
*1N42* A2 4a sl bl 15.00 *25.00*

Nos. 30-31 Overprinted

Myaungmya Type III

*1N43* A7 1r brt ultra & dk vio 200.00
*1N44* A7 2r dk vio & red brn 110.00

**Pyapon Issue**

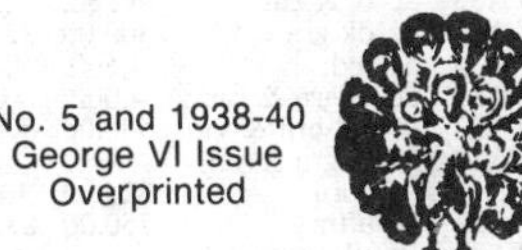

No. 5 and 1938-40 George VI Issue Overprinted

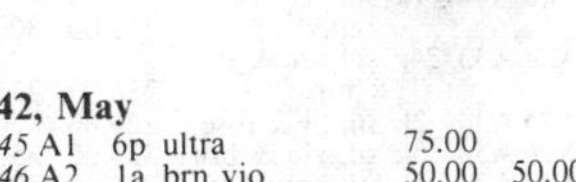

**1942, May**

*1N45* A1 6p ultra 75.00
*1N46* A2 1a brn vio 50.00 50.00
*1N47* A49 2a vermilion 75.00
*1N48* A2 2a carmine 45.00 62.50
*1N49* A2 4a sl bl 150.00 *200.00*

Counterfeits of the peacock overprints exist.

## OCCUPATION OFFICIAL STAMP

**Myaungmya Issue**

Burma No. O23 Overprinted in Black

**1942, May Wmk. 254 *Perf. 13***

*1NO1* A6 8a sl grn 50.00 62.50

Overprint characters translate: "Office use." Two types of overprint differ mainly in base of peacock which is either 5mm or 8mm.

## ISSUED UNDER JAPANESE OCCUPATION

Yano Seal — OS1

**Wmk. ABSORBO DUPLICATOR and Outline of Elephant in Center of Sheet.**

**Handstamped**

**1942, June 1 *Perf. 12x11***

**Without Gum**

*2N1* OS1I(a) vermilion 30.00 37.50

This stamp is the handstamped impression of the personal chop or seal of Shizuo Yano, chairman of the committee appointed to re-establish the Burmese postal system. It was prepared in Rangoon on paper captured from the Burma Government Offices. Not every stamp shows a portion of the watermark.

Farmer Plowing — OS2

Vertically Laid Paper

Without Gum

**Wmk. ELEPHANT BRAND and Outline of Trumpeting Elephant Covering Several Stamps.**

**1942, June 15 Litho. *Perf. 11x12***

*2N2* OS2 1a scarlet 20.00 25.00

See illustration OS4.

Same, Surcharged with New Value.

**1942, Oct. 15**

*2N3* OS2 5c on 1a scar 12.50 10.50

Rice Harvest — A83

General Nogi — A84

Power Plant — A85

Admiral Togo — A86

Diamond Mountains, Korea — A89

Meiji Shrine, Tokyo — A90

Yomei Gate, Nikko — A91

Mount Fuji and Cherry Blossoms — A94

Torii of Miyajima Shrine — A96

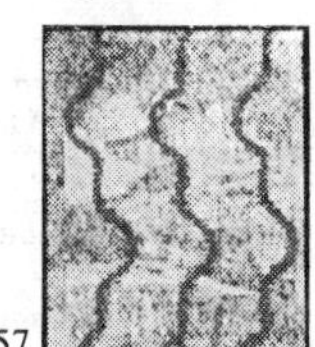

Wmk.257

Stamps of Japan, 1937-42, Surcharged with New Value in Black or Red

**Wmk. Curved Wavy Lines. (257)**

**1942, Sept. *Perf. 13***

*2N4* A83 ¼a on 1s fawn 12.50 15.00
*2N5* A84 ½a on 2s crim 12.50 15.00
*2N6* A85 ¾a on 3s grn 20.00 20.00
**a.** Inverted surcharge
*2N7* A86 1a on 5s brn lake 17.50 20.00
*2N8* A89 3a on 7s dp grn 30.00 32.50
*2N9* A86 4a on 4s dk grn 22.50 25.00
**a.** 4a on 4s + 2s dk grn (#B5) 75.00 87.50
*2N10* A90 8a on 8s dk pur & pale vio (B) 100.00 100.00
**a.** Red surcharge 140.00 150.00
*2N11* A91 1r on 10s lake 12.50 12.50
*2N12* A94 2r on 20s ultra (B) 30.00 35.00
**a.** Red surcharge 37.50 37.50
*2N13* A96 5r on 30s pck bl (B) 10.00 10.00
**a.** Red surcharge 15.00 15.00

Re-surcharged in Black or Red

**1942, Oct. 15**

*2N14* A83 1c on ¼a on 1s fawn 25.00 25.00
*2N15* A84 2c on ½a on 2s crim 25.00 25.00
*2N16* A85 3c on ¾a on 3s grn 30.00 30.00
**a.** "3C." in blue 75.00 *100.00*
*2N17* A86 5c on 1a on 5s brn lake 37.50 37.50
*2N18* A89 10c on 3a on 7s dp grn 37.50 37.50
*2N19* A86 15c on 4a on 4s dk grn 10.50 10.50
*2N20* A90 20c on 8a on 8s dk pur & pale vio (# 2N10) 87.50 60.00
**a.** On No. 2N10a 100.00 62.50

No. 2N16a was issued in the Shan States.

Stamps of Japan, 1937-42, Surcharged with New Value in Black or Red

**1942, Oct. 15**

*2N21* A83 1c on 1s fawn 10.00 12.50
*2N22* A84 2c on 2s crim 17.50 20.00
*2N23* A85 3c on 3s grn 20.00 25.00
**a.** "3C." in bl 75.00 87.50
*2N24* A86 5c on 5s brn lake 20.00 25.00
**a.** "5C." in vio 87.50 100.00

| | | | | |
|---|---|---|---|---|
| *2N25* A89 | 10c on 7s dp grn | | 25.00 | 30.00 |
| *2N26* A86 | 15c on 4s dk grn | | 10.00 | 12.50 |
| *2N27* A90 | 20c on 8s dk pur & pale vio | | 62.50 | 50.00 |

Nos. 2N23a and 2N24a were issued in the Shan States.

Burma State Government Crest — OS3

**Unwmk.**

**1943, Feb. 15 Litho. *Perf. 12***

**Without Gum.**

| | | | |
|---|---|---|---|
| *2N29* OS3 5c carmine | | 10.00 | 12.50 |
| *a.* Imperf. | | 12.50 | 15.00 |

This stamp was intended to be used to cover the embossed George VI envelope stamp and generally was sold affixed to such envelopes. It is also known used on private envelopes.

Farmer Plowing — OS4

**Denomination Typographed**

**1943, Mar.**

**Without Gum**

| | | | |
|---|---|---|---|
| *2N30* OS4 | 1c dp org | 1.00 | 1.00 |
| *2N31* OS4 | 2c yel grn | 1.00 | 1.50 |
| *2N32* OS4 | 3c blue | 1.00 | 1.00 |
| *a.* | Laid paper | 10.00 | 10.00 |
| *2N33* OS4 | 5c carmine | 50 | 65 |
| *a.* | Small "5c" | 3.00 | 4.00 |
| *b.* | Imperf. | | |
| *2N34* OS4 | 10c vio brn | 75 | 90 |
| *2N35* OS4 | 15c red vio | 25 | 25 |
| *a.* | Laid paper | 10.00 | |
| *2N36* OS4 | 20c dl pur | 25 | 75 |
| *2N37* OS4 | 30c bl grn | 25 | 75 |
| | *Nos. 2N30-2N37 (8)* | 5.00 | 6.80 |

Small "c" in Nos. 2N34 to 2N37.

Burmese Soldier Carving "Independence" OS5

Farmer Rejoicing OS6

Boy with Burmese Flag — OS7

***Hyphen-hole Perf., Pin-Perf. x Hyphen-hole Perf.***

**1943, Aug. 1 Typo.**

| | | | |
|---|---|---|---|
| *2N38* OS5 | 1c orange | 1.00 | *2.00* |
| *a.* | Perf. 11 | 3.50 | 4.00 |
| *2N39* OS6 | 3c blue | 1.00 | *2.00* |
| *a.* | Perf. 11 | 3.50 | 4.00 |
| *2N40* OS7 | 5c rose | 1.00 | *2.00* |
| *a.* | Perf. 11 | 3.50 | 4.00 |

Declaration of the independence of Burma by the Ba Maw government, Aug. 1, 1943.

Burmese Girl Carrying Water Jar — OS8

Elephant Carrying Teak Log — OS9

Watch Tower of Mandalay Palace — OS10

**1943, Oct. 1 Litho. *Perf. 12½***

| | | | |
|---|---|---|---|
| *2N41* OS8 | 1c dp sal | 3.00 | *4.50* |
| *2N42* OS8 | 2c yel grn | 15 | *50* |
| *2N43* OS8 | 3c violet | 15 | *38* |
| *2N44* OS9 | 5c rose | 20 | *38* |
| *2N45* OS9 | 10c blue | 25 | 25 |
| *2N46* OS9 | 15c vermilion | 15 | *38* |
| *2N47* OS9 | 20c yel grn | 20 | *50* |
| *2N48* OS9 | 30c brown | 25 | *50* |
| *2N49* OS10 | 1r vermilion | 25 | *1.25* |
| *2N50* OS10 | 2r violet | 30 | *2.00* |
| | *Nos. 2N41-2N50 (10)* | 4.90 | 10.64 |

No. 2N49 exists imperforate. Canceled to order copies of Nos. 2N42-2N50 same values as unused.

Bullock Cart — OS11

Shan Woman — OS12

**1943, Oct. 1 *Perf. 12½***

| | | | |
|---|---|---|---|
| *2N51* OS11 | 1c brown | 20.00 | *30.00* |
| *2N52* OS11 | 2c yel grn | 20.00 | *30.00* |
| *2N53* OS11 | 3c violet | 17.50 | *25.00* |
| *2N54* OS11 | 5c ultra | 3.75 | *10.00* |
| *2N55* OS12 | 10c blue | 17.50 | *30.00* |
| *2N56* OS12 | 20c rose | 20.00 | *30.00* |
| *2N57* OS12 | 30c brown | 20.00 | *30.00* |
| | *Nos. 2N51-2N57 (7)* | 118.75 | 185.00 |

For use only in the Shan States. Perak No. N34 also used in Shan States. CTO's ½ used value.

ဗမာနိုင်ငံတော်

Surcharged in Black

၁ ဆင့်။

**1944, Nov. 1**

| | | | |
|---|---|---|---|
| *2N58* OS11 | 1c brown | 1.75 | 2.00 |
| *2N59* OS11 | 2c yel grn | 15 | *50* |
| *a.* | Inverted surcharge | 150.00 | *200.00* |
| *2N60* OS11 | 3c violet | 1.00 | *1.75* |
| *2N61* OS11 | 5c ultra | 50 | 65 |
| *2N62* OS12 | 10c blue | 1.00 | *1.50* |
| *2N63* OS12 | 20c rose | 25 | *65* |
| *2N64* OS12 | 30c brown | 30 | *65* |
| | *Nos. 2N58-2N64 (7)* | 4.95 | 7.70 |

Top line of surcharge reads: "Bama naing ngan daw" (Burma State). Bottom line repeats denomination in Burmese. Surcharge applied when the Shan States came under Burmese government administration, Dec. 24, 1943. CTO's same value as unused.

## BUSHIRE

LOCATION — On Persian Gulf.

Bushire is a Persian port which British troops occupied Aug. 8, 1915.

20 Chahis (or Shahis) = 1 Kran
10 Krans = 1 Toman

### ISSUED UNDER BRITISH OCCUPATION

Iranian Stamps of 1911-13 Overprinted in Black

BUSHIRE
Under British
Occupation.

Shah Ahmed — A32

**Typographed and Engraved**

***Perf. 11½, 11½x11***

**1915, Aug. 15 Unwmk.**

| | | | | |
|---|---|---|---|---|
| *N1* | A32 | 1c grn & org | 10.00 | 10.00 |
| *N2* | A32 | 2c red & sep | 10.00 | 10.00 |
| *N3* | A32 | 3c gray brn & grn | 10.00 | 10.00 |
| *N4* | A32 | 5c brn & car | 125.00 | 125.00 |
| *N5* | A32 | 6c grn & red brn | 12.50 | 12.50 |
| *N6* | A32 | 9c yel brn & vio | 12.50 | 12.50 |
| *a.* | | Double ovrerprint | | |
| *N7* | A32 | 10c red & org brn | 12.50 | 12.50 |
| *N8* | A32 | 12c grn & ultra | 17.50 | 17.50 |
| *N9* | A32 | 1k ultra & car | 17.50 | 17.50 |
| *a.* | | Double overprint | 5,250. | |
| *N10* | A32 | 24c vio & grn | 17.50 | 17.50 |
| *N11* | A32 | 2k grn & red vio | 55.00 | 50.00 |
| *N12* | A32 | 3k vio & blk | 100.00 | 112.50 |
| *N13* | A32 | 5k red & ultra | 42.50 | 40.00 |
| *N14* | A32 | 10k ol bis & cl | 37.50 | 35.00 |
| | | *Nos. N1-N14 (14)* | 480.00 | 482.50 |

Nos. N1-N14, except No. N4, exist without period after "Occupation." This variety sells for more.

Forged overprints exist of Nos. N1-N30.

The Bushire overprint exists on Iran No. 537 but is considered a forgery.

Same Ovpt. on Iranian Stamps of 1915

Imperial Crown A33

King Darius, Ahura-Mazda Overhead A34

Ruins of Persepolis — A35

Wmk. 161- Lion

***Perf. 11, 11½***

**1915, Sept. Wmk. 161**

| | | | |
|---|---|---|---|
| *N15* A33 | 1c car & ind | 250.00 | 250.00 |
| *N16* A33 | 2c bl & car | 6,250. | *7,500.* |
| *N17* A33 | 3c dk grn | 300.00 | 325.00 |
| *N18* A33 | 5c red | 4,500. | *4,750.* |
| *N19* A33 | 6c ol grn & car | 4,000. | *4,500.* |
| *N20* A33 | 9c yel brn & vio | 550.00 | *600.00* |
| *N21* A33 | 10c bl grn & yel brn | 925.00 | 1,000. |
| *N22* A33 | 12c ultra | 750.00 | 825.00 |
| *N23* A34 | 1k sil, yel brn & gray | 275.00 | 300.00 |
| *N24* A33 | 24c yel brn & dk brn | 250.00 | 275.00 |
| *N25* A34 | 2k sil, bl & rose | 225.00 | 250.00 |
| *N26* A34 | 3k sil, vio & brn | 325.00 | 350.00 |
| *N27* A34 | 5k sil, brn & grn | 275.00 | 325.00 |
| *a.* | Inverted overprint | | |
| *N28* A35 | 1t gold, pur & blk | 300.00 | *325.00* |
| *N29* A35 | 3t gold, cl & red brn | 2,000. | *2,250.* |

Persia resumed administration of Bushire post office Oct. 16, 1915.

## CAMEROONS

LOCATION — West coast of Africa, north of equator.
GOVT. — Former British Mandate.
AREA — 34,081 sq. mi.
POP. — 868,637 (estimated).
CAPITAL — Buea.

Prior to World War I, Cameroons (Kamerun) was a German Protectorate. It was occupied during the War by Great Britain and France and in 1922 was mandated to these countries by the League of Nations. Stamps of Nigeria were used in the British part until 1960. The northern section of the British Cameroons became part of the independent state of Nigeria in 1960, and the southern section became a United Kingdom Trust Territory. After a referendum, this U.K.T.T. joined the independent State of Cameroun to form the Federal Republic of Cameroun, Oct. 1, 1961.

Stamps of the German Protectorate, the French Mandate, the independent state and the Cameroun Federal Republic are listed in Volume II of the Standard Postage Stamp Catalogue.

**Catalogue values for unused stamps in this country are for Never Hinged items, beginning with Scott 66.**

**Issued under British Occupation**

Kaiser's Yacht "Hohenzollern"
A3

A4

Wmk. 125- Lozenges

Stamps of German Cameroun Surcharged

C. E. F.
½ d.

**Wmk. 125 (5, 10, 20pf and 5m); Unwmk. (Other Values)**

**1915 *Perf. 14, 14½***

**Blue Surcharge**

| | | | |
|---|---|---|---|
| *53* A3 | ½p on 3pf brn | 7.50 | 11.00 |
| *54* A3 | ½p on 5pf grn | 3.00 | 5.00 |
| *a.* | Double surcharge | 400.00 | 200.00 |
| *b.* | Black surcharge | 8.00 | 10.00 |
| *55* A3 | 1p on 10pf car | 3.00 | 5.00 |
| *a.* | "1" with thin serifs | 10.50 | 13.00 |
| *b.* | Double surcharge | 175.00 | 175.00 |
| *c.* | Black surcharge | 22.50 | 30.00 |

**Black Surcharge**

| | | | |
|---|---|---|---|
| *56* A3 | 2p on 20pf ultra | 3.25 | *10.00* |
| *57* A3 | 2½pon 25pf org & blk, *yel* | 15.00 | 21.00 |
| *a.* | Double surcharge | *3,500.* | |

| | | | | |
|---|---|---|---|---|
| 58 | A3 | 3p on 30pf org & blk, *sal* | 11.00 | 21.00 |
| 59 | A3 | 4p on 40pf lake & blk | 11.00 | 21.00 |
| 60 | A3 | 6p on 50pf pur & blk, *sal* | 11.00 | 21.00 |
| 61 | A3 | 8p on 80pf lake & blk, *rose* | 11.00 | 21.00 |

Surcharged **C. E. F. 1s.**

| | | | | |
|---|---|---|---|---|
| 62 | A4 | 1sh on 1m car | 175.00 | *225.00* |
| a. | | "S" inverted | 650.00 | *1,000.* |
| 63 | A4 | 2sh on 2m bl | 175.00 | *225.00* |
| a. | | "S" inverted | 650.00 | *1,000.* |
| 64 | A4 | 3sh on 3m blk vio | 175.00 | *225.00* |
| a. | | "S" inverted | 650.00 | *1,000.* |
| b. | | Double surcharge | *4,000.* | |
| 65 | A4 | 5sh on 5m sl & car | 175.00 | *225.00* |
| a. | | "S" inverted | 650.00 | *1,000.* |
| | | *Nos. 53-65 (13)* | 775.75 | 1,036. |

The letters "C. E. F." are the initials of "Cameroons Expeditionary Force."

**Catalogue values for unused stamps in this section, from this point to the end of the section, are for Never Hinged items.**

### Southern Cameroons

Stamps and Type of Nigeria, 1953, Overprinted in Red **CAMEROONS U.K.T.T.**

***Perf. 13½, 14***

**1960, Oct. 1 Wmk. 4 Engr.**

**Size: 35½x22½mm**

| | | | | |
|---|---|---|---|---|
| 66 | A17 | ½p red org & blk | 5 | 5 |
| 67 | A17 | 1p ol gray & blk | 6 | 6 |
| 68 | A17 | 1½p bl grn | 8 | 8 |
| 69 | A17 | 2p gray (II) | 9 | 9 |
| 70 | A17 | 3p pur & blk | 12 | 12 |
| 71 | A17 | 4p ultra & blk | 15 | 15 |
| 72 | A18 | 6p blk & org brn, perf. 14 | 18 | 18 |
| a. | | Perf. 13x13½ ('61) | 18 | 18 |
| 73 | A17 | 1sh brn vio & blk | 30 | 30 |

**Size: 40½x24½mm**

| | | | | |
|---|---|---|---|---|
| 74 | A17 | 2sh6p grn & blk | 75 | 75 |
| 75 | A17 | 5sh ver & blk | 1.50 | 1.50 |
| 76 | A17 | 10sh red brn & blk | 3.00 | 3.00 |

**Size: 42x31½mm**

| | | | | |
|---|---|---|---|---|
| 77 | A17 | £1 vio & blk | 5.75 | 5.75 |
| | | *Nos. 66-77 (12)* | 12.03 | 12.03 |

Nos. 66-77 were withdrawn Sept. 30, 1961, when this territory joined the Cameroun Federal Republic.

## CANADA

LOCATION — Northern part of North American continent, except for Alaska.
GOVT. — Self-governing dominion in the British Commonwealth of Nations.
AREA — 3,851,809 sq. mi.
POP. — 24,907,100 (est. 1983)

Included in the dominion are British Columbia, Vancouver Island, Prince Edward Island, Nova Scotia, New Brunswick and Newfoundland, all of which formerly issued stamps.

12 Pence = 1 Shilling
100 Cents = 1 Dollar (1859)

**Catalogue values for unused stamps in this country are for Never Hinged items, beginning with Scott 268 in the regular postage section, Scott C9 in the air post section, Scott CE3 in the air post special delivery section, Scott CO1 in the air post official section, Scott E11 in the special delivery section, Scott EO1 in the special delivery official section, Scott J15 in the postage due section, and Scott O1 in the official section.**

The Scott Catalogue value is a retail price, what you could expect to pay for the stamp in a grade of Fine-Very Fine. The value listed is a reference which reflects recent actual dealer selling price.

Values of early Canada stamps vary according to condition. Quotations for Nos. 1-13 are for fine copies. Very fine to superb specimens sell at much higher prices, and inferior or poor copies sell at reduced prices, depending on the condition of the individual specimen.

### Province of Canada.

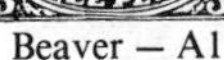
Beaver — A1

Prince Albert — A2

Queen Victoria — A3

**1851 Unwmk. Engr. *Imperf.***

**Laid Paper.**

| | | | | |
|---|---|---|---|---|
| 1 | A1 | 3p red | 10,000. | 350.00 |
| 2 | A2 | 6p grysh pur | 10,000. | 525.00 |
| a | | Diagonal half used as 3p on cover | | |
| 3 | A3 | 12p black | 65,000. | 50,000. |

On some stamps the laid lines of Nos. 1-3 are practically invisible.

**1852-55**

**Wove Paper**

| | | | | |
|---|---|---|---|---|
| 4 | A1 | 3p red | 1,000. | 110.00 |
| a | | 3p brn red ('53) | 1,050. | 125.00 |
| b | | Diagonal half used as 1½p on cover | | *30,000.* |
| c | | Ribbed paper | 2,000. | 275.00 |
| d | | Thin paper | 1,000. | 175.00 |
| 5 | A2 | 6p sl gray ('55) | 7,500. | 450.00 |
| a | | 6p brnsh gray | 9,000. | 700.00 |
| b | | 6p grnsh gray | 7,500. | 650.00 |
| c | | Diagonal half used as 3p on cover | | *15,500.* |
| d | | Thick hard paper (gray vio) | 9,000. | 800.00 |

Re-entries of the 3p are numerous. The main re-entry is distinguishable most easily by the line through "EE" and "PEN."

Most authorities believe the 12p black does not exist on wove paper.

Jacques Cartier — A4

**1855**

| | | | | |
|---|---|---|---|---|
| 7 | A4 | 10p blue | 5,000. | 700.00 |
| a | | Thick paper | 6,000. | 1,000. |

Queen Victoria
A5 A6

**1857**

| No. | Type | Description | Unused | Used |
|---|---|---|---|---|
| 8 | A5 | ½p rose | 450.00 | 265.00 |
| a | | Horizontally ribbed paper | 3,000. | 1,350. |
| b | | Vertically ribbed paper | 3,750. | 1,750. |
| 9 | A6 | 7½p green | 5,000. | 1,100. |

**Very Thick Soft Wove Paper.**

| No. | Type | Description | Unused | Used |
|---|---|---|---|---|
| 10 | A2 | 6p redsh pur | 11,000. | 2,250. |
| a | | Half used as 3p on cover | | *25,000.* |

**1858-59 Wove Paper. *Perf. 12.***

| No. | Type | Description | Unused | Used |
|---|---|---|---|---|
| 11 | A5 | ½p rose | 1,400. | 425.00 |
| 12 | A1 | 3p red | 2,500. | 275.00 |
| 13 | A2 | 6p brn vio ('59) | 5,500. | 2,250. |
| a | | 6p gray vio | 5,500. | 2,250. |
| b | | Diagonal half used as 3p on cover | | |

A7 A8

A9 A10

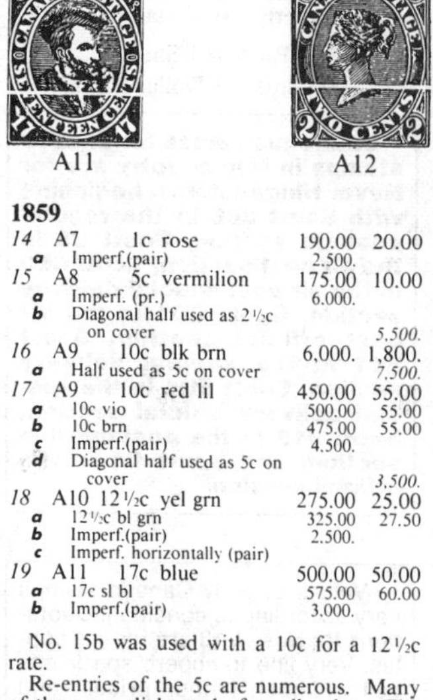

A11 A12

**1859**

| No. | Type | Description | Unused | Used |
|---|---|---|---|---|
| 14 | A7 | 1c rose | 190.00 | 20.00 |
| a | | Imperf.(pair) | 2,500. | |
| 15 | A8 | 5c vermilion | 175.00 | 10.00 |
| a | | Imperf. (pr.) | 6,000. | |
| b | | Diagonal half used as 2½c on cover | | *5,500.* |
| 16 | A9 | 10c blk brn | 6,000. | 1,800. |
| a | | Half used as 5c on cover | | *7,500.* |
| 17 | A9 | 10c red lil | 450.00 | 55.00 |
| a | | 10c vio | 500.00 | 55.00 |
| b | | 10c brn | 475.00 | 55.00 |
| c | | Imperf.(pair) | 4,500. | |
| d | | Diagonal half used as 5c on cover | | *3,500.* |
| 18 | A10 | 12½c yel grn | 275.00 | 25.00 |
| a | | 12½c bl grn | 325.00 | 27.50 |
| b | | Imperf.(pair) | 2,500. | |
| c | | Imperf. horizontally (pair) | | |
| 19 | A11 | 17c blue | 500.00 | 50.00 |
| a | | 17c sl bl | 575.00 | 60.00 |
| b | | Imperf.(pair) | 3,000. | |

No. 15b was used with a 10c for a 12½c rate.

Re-entries of the 5c are numerous. Many of them are slight and of small value. The major re-entry has many lines of the design double, especially the outlines of the ovals and frame at left. Value, used, about $300.

**1864**

| No. | Type | Description | Unused | Used |
|---|---|---|---|---|
| 20 | A12 | 2c rose | 325.00 | 125.00 |
| a | | 2c dp cl rose | 400.00 | 150.00 |
| b | | Imperf.(pair) | 1,750. | |

**Dominion of Canada.**

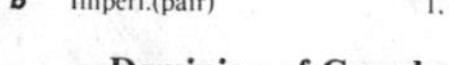

Queen Victoria
A13 A14

A15 A16

A17 A18

A19 A20

**1868-76 *Perf. 12***

| No. | Type | Description | Unused | Used |
|---|---|---|---|---|
| 21 | A13 | ½c black | 25.00 | 21.00 |
| a | | Perf. 11½ x 12 ('73) | 25.00 | 21.00 |
| b | | Wmkd. | *16,500.* | *7,000.* |
| c | | Thin paper | 30.00 | 27.50 |
| 22 | A14 | 1c brn red | 225.00 | 32.50 |
| a | | Wmkd. | 1,750. | 150.00 |
| b | | Thin paper | 350.00 | 32.50 |
| 23 | A14 | 1c yel org | 425.00 | 50.00 |
| a | | 1c dp org | 450.00 | 55.00 |
| 24 | A15 | 2c green | 225.00 | 22.50 |
| a | | Wmkd. | 1,750. | 150.00 |
| b | | Thin paper | 250.00 | 30.00 |
| c | | Diagonal half used as 1c on cover | | *3,000.* |
| 25 | A16 | 3c red | 400.00 | 8.00 |
| a | | Wmkd. | 2,000. | 125.00 |
| b | | Thin paper | 450.00 | 12.00 |
| 26 | A17 | 5c ol grn, perf. 11½x12 ('75) | 500.00 | 42.50 |
| 27 | A18 | 6c dk brn | 400.00 | 30.00 |
| a | | 6c yel brn | 375.00 | 27.50 |
| b | | Wmkd. | 2,500. | 850.00 |
| c | | Thin paper | 550.00 | 45.00 |
| d | | Diagonal half used as 3c on cover | | *2,500.* |
| e | | Vertical half used as 3c on cover | | |
| 28 | A19 | 12½c blue | 250.00 | 30.00 |
| a | | Wmkd. | 1,500. | 125.00 |
| b | | Thin paper | 275.00 | 50.00 |
| c | | Imperf. vert., pair | | |
| d | | Imperf. horiz., pair | | |
| 29 | A20 | 15c gray vio | 30.00 | 14.00 |
| a | | Perf. 11½x12 ('74) | 525.00 | 80.00 |
| b | | 15c red lil | 600.00 | 42.50 |
| c | | Wmkd. (Clutha Mills) | 3,000. | 500.00 |
| d | | Imperf. (pair) | 700.00 | |
| e | | Thin paper | 450.00 | 55.00 |
| 30 | A20 | 15c gray | 25.00 | 14.00 |
| a | | Perf. 11½x12 ('73) | 600.00 | 80.00 |
| b | | 15c bl gray ('75) | 27.50 | 17.00 |
| c | | Very thick paper (dp vio) | 3,000. | 800.00 |
| d | | Script wmk., Perf. 11½x12. ('76) | 6,500. | 2,250. |

The watermark on Nos. 21b, 22a, 24a, 25a, 27b, 28a and 29c consists of double-lined letters reading: "E. & G. BOTHWELL CLUTHA MILLS". The script watermark on No. 30d reads in full: "Alexr. Pirie & Sons".

**1868 Laid Paper**

| No. | Type | Description | Unused | Used |
|---|---|---|---|---|
| 31 | A14 | 1c brn red | 10,000. | 2,000. |
| 32 | A15 | 2c green | | *60,000* |
| 33 | A16 | 3c brt red | 9,500. | 400.00 |

**Montreal and Ottawa Printings.**

A21 A22 A23

A24 A25

A26

A27

**370-89 Wove Paper. *Perf. 12.***

A21 ½c blk ('82) 4.25 4.25
- *a* Imperf. (pair) 300.00
- *b* Pair, imperf. between 650.00

A22 1c yellow 15.00 50
- *a* 1c org ('70) 70.00 4.50
- *b* Imperf. (pair) 200.00
- *c* Diagonal half used as ½c on cover 3,500.

A23 2c grn ('72) 15.00 90
- *a* Imperf. (pair) 250.00
- *b* Diagonal half used as 1c on cover 575.00
- *c* Vertical half used as 1c on cover
- *d* 2c bl grn ('89) 30.00 2.50
- *f* Dbl impression

A24 3c dl red ('72) 35.00 1.25
- *a* 3c rose ('71) 200.00 5.00
- *b* 3c cop red ('70) 600.00 17.50
- *c* 3c org red ('73) 32.50 90

A25 5c sl grn ('76) 185.00 8.25

A26 6c yel brn ('72) 165.00 8.25
- *a* Diagonal half used as 3c on cover 500.00

A27 10c dl rose lil ('77) 200.00 21.00
- *a* 10c mag ('80) 200.00 22.50
- *b* 10c dp lil rose 200.00 22.50

Copies of Nos. 36b and 36c postmarked Halifax" are a private speculation.

**370 *Perf. 12½***

*d* A24 3c cop red (Ottawa) 4,500. 500.00

**873-79 *Perf. 11½x12.***

*d* A22 1c orange 90.00 6.50
*e* A23 2c green 105.00 10.00
*e* A24 3c red 110.00 5.00
*a* A25 5c sl grn 250.00 17.00
*b* A26 6c yel brn 250.00 17.00
*c* A27 10c pale mlky rose lil ('74) 450.00 135.00

The gum on Nos. 35d-40c is always dull nd usually blotchy or streaky. It is distinct om the earlier clear, smooth gum and from e bright shiny gums of the later periods.

Nos. 38 and 40 were printed at Montreal. Printings of Nos. 34 to 37, and 39 were made at Ottawa or Montreal and can be separated only by differences in paper and gum.

**Ottawa Printing.**

A28

A29

**1888-93 *Perf. 12***

*41* A24 3c brt ver 10.50 30
- *a* 3c rose car 200.00 2.75
- *b* Imperf. (pair) 200.00

*42* A25 5c gray 22.50 2.00
- *a* Imperf. (pair) 300.00

*43* A26 6c red brn 25.00 4.75
- *a* 6c choc ('90) 32.50 7.25
- *b* Imperf. (pair) 350.00

*44* A28 8c gray ('93) 25.00 1.75
- *a* 8c bl gray 25.00 1.75
- *b* 8c sl 25.00 1.75
- *c* 8c vio blk 25.00 1.75
- *d* Imperf. (pair) 300.00

*45* A27 10c brn red 75.00 18.00
- *a* 10c dl rose 75.00 18.00
- *b* 10c pink 75.00 22.50
- *c* Imperf. (pair) 250.00

*46* A29 20c ver ('93) 115.00 30.00
- *a* Imperf. (pair) 675.00

*47* A29 50c dp bl ('93) 165.00 20.00
- *a* Imperf. (pair) 675.00

Stamps of the 1870-93 issues are found on paper varying from very thin to thick, also occasionally on paper showing a distinctly ribbed surface.

The gum on Nos. 41-47 appears bright and shiny, often with a yellowish tint.

**Jubilee Issue.**

Queen Victoria, "1837" and "1897" — A30

**1897, June 19 Unwmk. *Perf. 12***

*50* A30 ½c black 45.00 55.00
*51* A30 1c orange 4.00 3.00
*52* A30 2c green 4.50 4.50
*53* A30 3c brt rose 3.75 85
*54* A30 5c dp bl 14.00 12.50
*55* A30 6c yel brn 60.00 85.00
*56* A30 8c dk vio 11.00 9.50
*57* A30 10c brn vio 37.50 37.50
*58* A30 15c stl bl 85.00 85.00
*59* A30 20c vermilion 87.50 87.50
*60* A30 50c ultra 100.00 92.50
*61* A30 $1 lake 400.00 475.00
*62* A30 $2 dk pur 625.00 350.00
*63* A30 $3 yel bis 750.00 600.00
*64* A30 $4 purple 750.00 600.00
*65* A30 $5 ol grn 800.00 600.00
*Nos. 50-60 (11)* 452.25 472.85

60th year of Queen Victoria's reign.

Roller and smudged cancels on Nos. 61-65 sell for less.

A31

A32

**1897-98**

*66* A31 ½c black 3.00 2.75
- *a* Imperf., pair 300.00

*67* A31 1c bl grn 6.50 45
- *a* Imperf., pair 300.00

*68* A31 2c purple 7.50 65
- *a* Imperf., pair 300.00

*69* A31 3c car ('98) 7.50 12
- *a* Imperf., pair 600.00

*70* A31 5c dk bl, *bluish* 32.50 2.75
- *a* Imperf., pair 300.00

*71* A31 6c brown 30.00 10.50
- *a* Imperf., pair 600.00

*72* A31 8c orange 45.00 4.25
- *a* Imperf., pair 300.00

*73* A31 10c brn vio ('98) 82.50 30.00
- *a* Imperf., pair 350.00

*Nos. 66-73 (8)* 214.50 51.47

**1898-1902**

TWO CENTS:

Type I. Frame of four very thin lines.
Type II. Frame of a thick line between two thin ones.

*74* A32 ½c black 90 70
- *a* Imperf., pair 225.00

*75* A32 1c gray grn 5.50 8
- *a* Imperf., pair 600.00

*76* A32 2c pur (I) 6.25 8
- *a* Thick paper 65.00 6.00

*77* A32 2c car (I) ('99) 7.75 6
- *a* 2c car (II) 8.50 18
- *b* Booklet pane of 6 (II) 650.00 *650.00*
- *c* Imperf., pair 180.00

*78* A32 3c carmine 10.50 25

*79* A32 5c bl, *bluish* 37.50 52
- *a* Imperf., pair 600.00

*80* A32 6c brown 55.00 20.00
- *a* Imperf., pair 600.00

*81* A32 7c ol yel ('02) 32.50 9.00
- *a* Imperf., pair 225.00

*82* A32 8c orange 75.00 11.00
- *a* Imperf., pair 600.00

*83* A32 10c brn vio 87.50 9.00
- *a* Imperf., pair 600.00

*84* A32 20c ol grn ('00) 160.00 42.50
- *a* Imperf., pair 1,500.

*Nos. 74-84 (11)* 478.40 93.19

**Imperial Penny Postage Issue.**

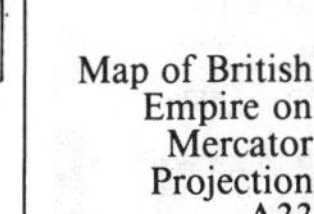

Map of British Empire on Mercator Projection A33

**1898, Dec. 7 Engr. & Typo.**

*85* A33 2c blk, lav & car 11.00 3.00
- *a* Imperf., pair 300.00

*86* A33 2c blk, bl & car 11.00 3.00
- *a* Imperf., pair 300.00

Nos. 69 and 78 Surcharged in Black **2 CENTS**

**1899, July**

*87* A31 2c on 3c car 4.00 2.25
*88* A32 2c on 3c car 4.50 2.00

No. 78 Surcharged in Blue or Violet

A32a

A32b

**1899, Jan. 5**

| | | | | |
|---|---|---|---|---|
| *88B* | A32a | 1(c) on one-third of 3c car (Bl) | | |
| *88C* | A32b | 2(c) on two-thirds of 3c car (V) | | |

Nos. 88B-88C were prepared and used at Port Hood, Nova Scotia, without official authorization.

King Edward VII — A34

**1903-08** **Engr.**

| | | | | |
|---|---|---|---|---|
| *89* | A34 | 1c green | 5.75 | 10 |
| *a* | | Imperf. (pair) | 400.00 | |
| *90* | A34 | 2c carmine | 5.75 | 5 |
| *a* | | Imperf. (pair) | 22.50 | 22.50 |
| *b* | | Booklet pane of 6 | 725.00 | *725.00* |
| *91* | A34 | 5c blue, *blue* | 27.50 | 1.50 |
| *a* | | Imperf. (pair) | 625.00 | |
| *92* | A34 | 7c ol bis | 18.00 | 1.75 |
| *a* | | Imperf. (pair) | 400.00 | |
| *93* | A34 | 10c brn lil | 57.50 | 3.50 |
| *a* | | Imperf. (pair) | 700.00 | |
| *94* | A34 | 20c ol grn | 150.00 | 14.00 |
| *95* | A34 | 50c pur ('08) | 225.00 | 35.00 |
| | | *Nos. 89-95 (7)* | 489.50 | 55.90 |

**Quebec Tercentenary Issue**

Prince and Princess of Wales, 1908 — A35

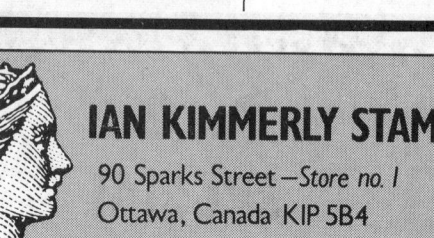

Jacques Cartier and Samuel de Champlain A36

Queen Alexandra and King Edward A37

Champlain's Home in Quebec A38

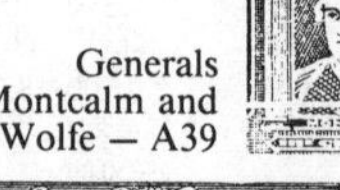

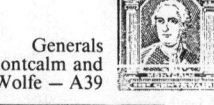

Generals Montcalm and Wolfe — A39

View of Quebec in 1700 — A40

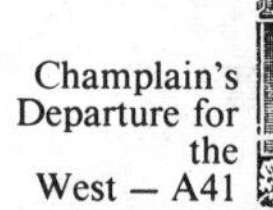

Champlain's Departure for the West — A41

Arrival of Cartier at Quebec A42

**1908, July 16**

| | | | | |
|---|---|---|---|---|
| *96* | A35 | ½c blk brn | 2.00 | 2.00 |
| *a* | | Imperf., pair | 400.00 | |
| *97* | A36 | 1c bl grn | 4.00 | 2.00 |
| *a* | | Imperf., pair | 400.00 | |
| *98* | A37 | 2c carmine | 6.25 | 60 |
| *a* | | Imperf., pair | 400.00 | |
| *99* | A38 | 5c dk bl | 24.00 | 14.00 |
| *a* | | Imperf., pair | 400.00 | |
| *100* | A39 | 7c ol grn | 30.00 | 18.00 |
| *a* | | Imperf., pair | 400.00 | |
| *101* | A40 | 10c dk vio | 45.00 | 30.00 |
| *a* | | Imperf., pair | 400.00 | |
| *102* | A41 | 15c red org | 55.00 | 45.00 |
| *a* | | Imperf., pair | 400.00 | |
| *103* | A42 | 20c yel brn | 75.00 | 50.00 |
| *a* | | Imperf., pair | 400.00 | |
| | | *Nos. 96-103 (8)* | 241.25 | 161.60 |

King George V — A43

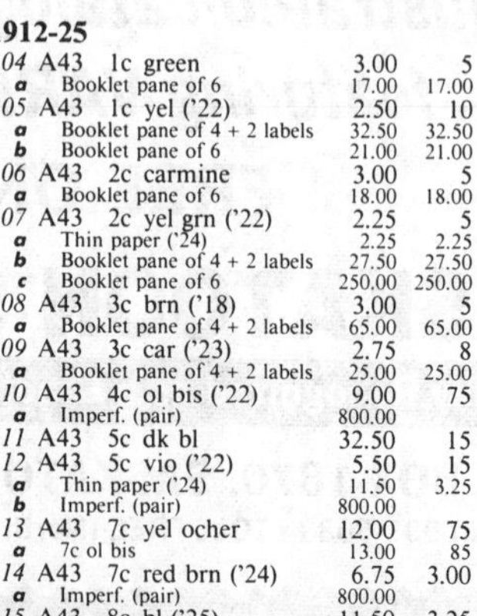

**1912-25**

| | | | | |
|---|---|---|---|---|
| *104* | A43 | 1c green | 3.00 | 5 |
| *a* | | Booklet pane of 6 | 17.00 | 17.00 |
| *105* | A43 | 1c yel ('22) | 2.50 | 10 |
| *a* | | Booklet pane of 4 + 2 labels | 32.50 | 32.50 |
| *b* | | Booklet pane of 6 | 21.00 | 21.00 |
| *106* | A43 | 2c carmine | 3.00 | 5 |
| *a* | | Booklet pane of 6 | 18.00 | 18.00 |
| *107* | A43 | 2c yel grn ('22) | 2.25 | 5 |
| *a* | | Thin paper ('24) | 2.25 | 2.25 |
| *b* | | Booklet pane of 4 + 2 labels | 27.50 | 27.50 |
| *c* | | Booklet pane of 6 | 250.00 | 250.00 |
| *108* | A43 | 3c brn ('18) | 3.00 | 5 |
| *a* | | Booklet pane of 4 + 2 labels | 65.00 | 65.00 |
| *109* | A43 | 3c car ('23) | 2.75 | 8 |
| *a* | | Booklet pane of 4 + 2 labels | 25.00 | 25.00 |
| *110* | A43 | 4c ol bis ('22) | 9.00 | 75 |
| *a* | | Imperf. (pair) | 800.00 | |
| *111* | A43 | 5c dk bl | 32.50 | 15 |
| *112* | A43 | 5c vio ('22) | 5.50 | 15 |
| *a* | | Thin paper ('24) | 11.50 | 3.25 |
| *b* | | Imperf. (pair) | 800.00 | |
| *113* | A43 | 7c yel ocher | 12.00 | 75 |
| *a* | | 7c ol bis | 13.00 | 85 |
| *114* | A43 | 7c red brn ('24) | 6.75 | 3.00 |
| *a* | | Imperf. (pair) | 800.00 | |
| *115* | A43 | 8c bl ('25) | 11.50 | 3.25 |
| *a* | | Imperf. (pair) | 800.00 | |
| *116* | A43 | 10c plum | 50.00 | |
| *117* | A43 | 10c bl ('22) | 15.00 | |
| *118* | A43 | 10c bis brn ('25) | 12.00 | |
| *a* | | Imperf. (pair) | 800.00 | |
| *119* | A43 | 20c ol grn | 22.50 | |
| *a* | | Imperf. (pair) | 900.00 | |
| *120* | A43 | 50c blk brn ('25) | 24.00 | |
| *a* | | 50c blk | 40.00 | |
| *b* | | Imperf. (pair) | 1,100. | |
| *122* | A43 | $1 org ('23) | 45.00 | 3 |
| *a* | | Imperf. (pair) | 1,100. | |
| | | *Nos. 104-122 (18)* | 262.25 | 14 |

For type A43 perforated 12 x 8 see No. 18

Coil Stamps.

**1912** ***Perf. 8 Horizonta***

| | | | | |
|---|---|---|---|---|
| *123* | A43 | 1c dk grn | 27.50 | 26 |
| *124* | A43 | 2c carmine | 27.50 | 26 |

**1912-24** ***Perf. 8 Vertica***

| | | | | |
|---|---|---|---|---|
| *125* | A43 | 1c green | 5.25 | |
| *126* | A43 | 1c yel ('23) | 4.00 | 3 |
| *a* | | Block of 4 | 25.00 | 2 |
| *127* | A43 | 2c carmine | 10.50 | |
| *128* | A43 | 2c grn ('22) | 4.00 | |
| *a* | | Block of 4 | 25.00 | 2 |
| *129* | A43 | 3c brn ('18) | 3.75 | |
| *130* | A43 | 3c car ('24) | 27.50 | 3 |
| *a* | | Block of 4 | 450.00 | 45 |
| | | *Nos. 125-130 (6)* | 55.00 | 7 |

Nos. 126a, 128a and 130a were supplied the Postal Agency in sheets. Nos. 126a a 128a exist on thick and thin paper. No. 1 exists on thick paper only.

**1915-24** ***Perf. 12 Horizonta***

| | | | | |
|---|---|---|---|---|
| *131* | A43 | 1c dk grn | 3.25 | 4 |
| *132* | A43 | 2c carmine | 8.50 | 6 |
| *133* | A43 | 2c yel grn ('24) | 40.00 | 42 |
| *134* | A43 | 3c brn ('21) | 3.25 | 3 |

"The Fathers of Confederation" — A44

**1917, Sept. 15** ***Perf.***

| | | | | |
|---|---|---|---|---|
| *135* | A44 | 3c brown | 11.50 | |
| *a* | | Imperf. (pair) | 300.00 | |

50th anniv. of the Canadian Confederatio

**1924** ***Impe***

| | | | | |
|---|---|---|---|---|
| *136* | A43 | 1c yellow | 27.50 | 27. |
| *137* | A43 | 2c green | 27.50 | 27. |
| *138* | A43 | 3c carmine | 12.00 | 14. |

No. 109 Surcharged:

**2 CENTS**
a

**2**
**CENTS**
b

**1926** ***Perf.***

| | | | | |
|---|---|---|---|---|
| *139* | A43(a) | 2c on 3c car | 32.50 | 35. |
| *a* | | Pair, one without surcharge | 250.00 | |
| *b* | | Double surcharge | 175.00 | |
| *140* | A43(b) | 2c on 3c car | 12.50 | 14. |
| *a* | | Double surcharge | 175.00 | |
| *b* | | Triple surcharge | 175.00 | |

Sir John A. Macdonald A45

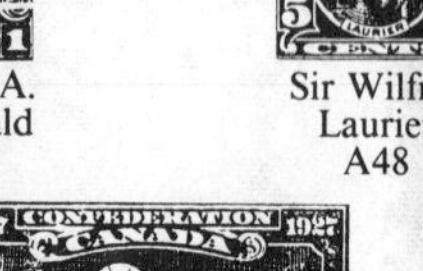

Sir Wilfri Laurier A48

"The Fathers of Confederation" — A46

*Canada stamps can be mounted in Scott's annually supplemented Canada Specialty Album.*

# CANADA

## CANADA ANNUAL SOUVENIR COLLECTION FROM THE POST OFFICE

| | | | | | |
|---|---|---|---|---|---|
| 1974....... | $90.00 | 1979....... | $22.50 | 1983....... | $34.20 |
| 1975....... | $67.50 | 1980....... | $15.30 | 1984....... | $25.20 |
| 1976....... | $67.50 | 1981....... | $16.20 | 1985....... | $29.70 |
| 1977....... | $45.00 | 1982....... | $31.50 | 1986....... | $27.00 |
| 1978....... | $22.50 | | | | |

## MINT CANADA F-VF NH

**COILS INCLUDED** (TAGGED and TAX stamps excluded.)

1942 to 1949 #248-288 NET $175.50
1950 to 1960 inclusive #289-390 NET $123.30
1961 to 1970 inclusive #391-531 NET $59.40
1971 to 1980 inclusive #532-877 B1-12 NET $118.80
1981 to 1986 inclusive #878-1121 NET $108.90

## CANADIAN DUCK STAMPS BOOKLET

1985 $10.80 | 1987 $10.80
1986 $14.40 | 1988 $9.00

## 1988 QUEBEC DUCK STAMPS

BOOKLET $6.75
SOUVENIR SHEET OF 4 $27.00

## CANADIAN PLATE BLOCKS

Scott #274 to 700
50% OFF Scott Canada Specialized.
#701 AND UP - 30% OFF!

## CANADA YEAR SETS F-VF NH
### WITH TAX TAGGED AND BOOKLETS STAMPS

| YEAR | SCOTT # | PRICE | YEAR | SCOTT# | PRICE |
|---|---|---|---|---|---|
| 1950 | 289-301.................. | 24.30 | 1968 | 478-489.................. | 3.70 |
| 1951 | 302-315.................. | 61.20 | 1969 | 490-504.................. | 8.30 |
| 1951 | 303-315.................. | 7.55 | 1970 | 505-531.................. | 15.05 |
| 1952 | 316-320.................. | 1.70 | 1971 | 532-558.................. | 5.60 |
| 1953 | 321-334.................. | 19.10 | 1972 | 559-610.................. | 20.60 |
| 1954 | 335-350.................. | 5.15 | 1973 | 611-628.................. | 4.60 |
| 1955 | 351-358.................. | 2.20 | 1974 | 629-55 B1-3.............. | 9.00 |
| 1956 | 359-364.................. | 3.80 | 1975 | 656-80 B4-9.............. | 15.60 |
| 1957 | 365-374.................. | 4.35 | 1976 | 681-703 B10-12........ | 16.95 |
| 1958 | 375-382.................. | 1.95 | 1977 | 704-51.................. | 14.00 |
| 1959 | 383-388.................. | 1.50 | 1978* | 752-79.................. | 9.90 |
| 1960 | 389-390.................. | .55 | 1979 | 780-846.................. | 12.50 |
| 1961 | 391-395.................. | 1.20 | 1980 | 847-77.................. | 8.85 |
| 1962 | 396-400.................. | 1.20 | 1981 | 878-908.................. | 8.30 |
| 1963 | 401-413.................. | 27.65 | 1982* | 909-75.................. | 37.35 |
| 1964 | 414-436.................. | 6.90 | 1983 | 976-1008.................. | 25.20 |
| 1965 | 437-444.................. | 1.45 | 1984* | 1009-44.................. | 16.95 |
| 1966 | 445-452.................. | 1.40 | 1985* | 1045-76.................. | 16.40 |
| 1967 | 453-477.................. | 20.45 | 1986* | 1077-1121............... | 24.30 |

*SOUVENIR SHEET INCLUDED.

**WE PAY HIGH PRICES FOR EXCLUSIVE STAMPS AND COVERS**
Let Us Know What You Have.
**ALSO BUYING COLLECTIONS!**

**WE SPECIALIZE IN ERRORS AND VARIETIES**
Ask For Our FREE Catalogue.

**MAIL AUCTIONS CATALOGUE FREE ON REQUEST!**

**WE WELCOME YOUR WANT LISTS**

## ALL PRICES IN U.S. DOLLARS

Call or write for all your needs.
Veruska, Marc, Luc,
Alfredo and Jean
will be pleased to serve you.

**"SPECIALIZING IN CANADA & FRANCE"**

## TERMS:

- Allow ten days after receipt of order.
- Full payment required with order
- Visa, MasterCard, Diners Club, Amex
- Ten days money back guarantee
- Quebec Res. 9% Sales Tax

**Minimum order $50.00.**
All Stamps sent Registered Mail.

# LA TIMBRAGIE - JEAN LAPOINTE

1329 STE-CATHERINE EAST, MONTREAL, QUEBEC H2L 2H4 CANADA
FAX: #514-598-5498 PHONE: (514) 598-1571

CSDA

Parliament Building at Ottawa
A47

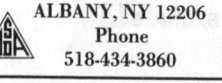

Map of Canada
A49

**1927, June 29**

| No. | Type | Description | Unused | Used |
|---|---|---|---|---|
| *141* | A45 | 1c orange | 1.50 | 30 |
| a | | Imperf., pair | 75.00 | |
| *142* | A46 | 2c green | 1.10 | 6 |
| a | | Imperf., pair | 75.00 | |
| *143* | A47 | 3c brn car | 4.75 | 1.90 |
| a | | Imperf., pair | 75.00 | |
| *144* | A48 | 5c violet | 3.25 | 95 |
| a | | Imperf., pair | 75.00 | |
| *145* | A49 | 12c dk bl | 9.75 | 1.90 |
| a | | Imperf., pair | 75.00 | |
| | | *Nos. 141-145 (5)* | 20.35 | 5.11 |

60th year of the Canadian Confederation. Nos. 141-145 exist partly perforated.

Thomas d'Arcy McGee
A50

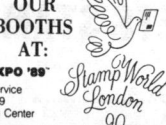

Laurier and Macdonald
A51

Robert Baldwin and Sir Louis Hippolyte Lafontaine
A52

**1927, June 29**

| No. | Type | Description | Unused | Used |
|---|---|---|---|---|
| *146* | A50 | 5c violet | 1.75 | 1.00 |
| a | | Imperf., pair | 80.00 | |
| *147* | A51 | 12c green | 4.75 | 2.00 |
| a | | Imperf., pair | 80.00 | |
| *148* | A52 | 20c brn car | 11.00 | 2.50 |
| a | | Imperf., pair | 80.00 | |

Nos. 146-148 were to have been issued in July, 1926, as a commemorative series, but were withheld and issued June 29, 1927. They exist partly perforated.

King George V — A53

Mt. Hurd from Bell-Smith's Painting "The Ice-crowned Monarch of the Rockies" — A54

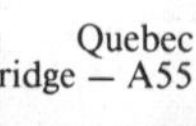

Quebec Bridge — A55

Harvesting Wheat — A56

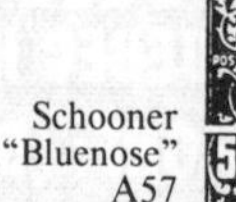

Schooner "Bluenose" A57

Parliament Building
A58

**1928-29**

| No. | Type | Description | Unused | Used |
|---|---|---|---|---|
| *149* | A53 | 1c orange | 90 | 16 |
| a | | Booklet pane of 6 | 9.00 | 9.00 |
| b | | Imperf. pair | 45.00 | |
| *150* | A53 | 2c green | 40 | 5 |
| a | | Booklet pane of 6 | 18.00 | 18.00 |
| b | | Imperf. pair | 45.00 | |
| *151* | A53 | 3c dk car | 5.25 | 5.50 |
| a | | Imperf. pair | 52.50 | |
| *152* | A53 | 4c bis ('29) | 5.25 | 3.00 |
| a | | Imperf. pair | 52.50 | |
| *153* | A53 | 5c dp vio | 2.00 | 1.40 |
| a | | Booklet pane of 6 | 50.00 | 50.00 |
| b | | Imperf. pair | 52.50 | |
| *154* | A53 | 8c blue | 4.00 | 2.75 |
| a | | Imperf. pair | 52.50 | |
| *155* | A54 | 10c green | 3.25 | 45 |
| a | | Imperf. pair | 85.00 | |
| *156* | A55 | 12c gray ('29) | 5.25 | 2.75 |
| a | | Imperf. pair | 85.00 | |
| *157* | A56 | 20c dk car ('29) | 10.50 | 4.25 |
| a | | Imperf. pair | 85.00 | |
| *158* | A57 | 50c dk bl ('29) | 110.00 | 25.00 |
| a | | Imperf. pair | 450.00 | |
| *159* | A58 | $1 ol grn ('29) | 125.00 | 30.00 |
| a | | Imperf. pair | 450.00 | |
| | | *Nos. 149-159 (11)* | 271.80 | 75.31 |

Nos. 149 to 159 exist partly perforated.

## Coil Stamps.

**1929** ***Perf. 8 Vertically***

| No. | Type | Description | Unused | Used |
|---|---|---|---|---|
| *160* | A53 | 1c orange | 14.00 | 14.00 |
| *161* | A53 | 2c green | 9.25 | 1.75 |

King George V
A59

Library of Parliament
A60

The Citadel at Quebec
A61

Harvesting Wheat — A62

Museum at Grand Pre and Monument to Evangeline
A63

Mt. Edith Cavell — A64

Two dies of 2c.

Die I. The top of the letter "P" encloses a tiny dot of color.

Die II. The top of the "P" encloses a larger spot of color than in die I. The "P" appears almost like a "D."

There are two dies of the 1c also, but differences are trivial.

**1930-31** ***Perf. 11***

| No. | Type | Description | Unused | Used |
|---|---|---|---|---|
| *162* | A59 | 1c orange | 65 | 35 |
| *163* | A59 | 1c dp grn | 1.25 | 8 |
| a | | Booklet pane of 4 + 2 labels | 80.00 | 80.00 |
| c | | Booklet pane of 6 | 9.00 | 9.00 |
| d | | Imperf. (pair) | 1.100. | |
| *164* | A59 | 2c dl grn (I) | 80 | 5 |
| a | | Booklet pane of 6 | 15.00 | 15.00 |
| *165* | A59 | 2c dp red (II) | 1.40 | 8 |
| a | | Die I | 1.00 | 10 |
| b | | Booklet pane of 6 (I) | 13.00 | 13.00 |
| *166* | A59 | 2c dk brn (II) ('31) | 90 | |
| a | | Booklet pane of 4 + 2 labels (II) | 75.00 | 75. |
| b | | Die I | 2.50 | 2. |
| c | | Booklet pane of 6 (I) | 17.50 | 17. |
| *167* | A59 | 3c dp red ('31) | 1.25 | |
| a | | Booklet pane of 4 + 2 labels | 17.50 | 17. |
| *168* | A59 | 4c yel bis | 4.00 | 2. |
| *169* | A59 | 5c dl vio | 2.50 | 1. |
| *170* | A59 | 5c dl bl | 2.25 | |
| *171* | A59 | 8c dk bl | 8.00 | 3. |
| *172* | A59 | 8c red org | 2.75 | 1. |
| *173* | A60 | 10c ol grn | 4.00 | |
| a | | Imperf. pair | 1.100. | |
| *174* | A61 | 12c gray blk | 6.25 | 3.( |
| a | | Imperf., pair | 500.00 | |
| *175* | A62 | 20c brn red | 12.00 | |
| a | | Imperf., pair | 500.00 | |
| *176* | A63 | 50c dl bl | 85.00 | 10.( |
| a | | Imperf., pair | 750.00 | |
| *177* | A64 | $1 dk ol grn | 85.00 | 16.( |
| a | | Imperf., pair | 750.00 | |
| | | *Nos. 162-177 (16)* | 218.00 | 40. |

No. 169 was printed from both flat an[d] rotary press plates.

See also No. 201.

## Coil Stamps.

**1930-31** ***Perf. 8 ½ Verticall[y]***

| No. | Type | Description | Unused | Used |
|---|---|---|---|---|
| *178* | A59 | 1c orange | 6.00 | 4.7 |
| *179* | A59 | 1c dp grn | 3.50 | 3.5 |
| *180* | A59 | 2c dl grn | 3.00 | 2.0 |
| *181* | A59 | 2c dp red | 7.50 | 1.5 |
| *182* | A59 | 2c dk brn ('31) | 5.25 | 4 |
| *183* | A59 | 3c dp red ('31) | 7.50 | 3 |
| | | *Nos. 178-183 (6)* | 32.75 | 12.5 |

## George V Type of 1912-25

**1931, June 24** ***Perf. 12x***

| No. | Type | Description | Unused | Used |
|---|---|---|---|---|
| *184* | A43 | 3c carmine | 1.75 | 1.7 |

Sir Georges Etienne Cartier — A65

**1931, Sept. 30** ***Perf. 1***

| No. | Type | Description | Unused | Used |
|---|---|---|---|---|
| *190* | A65 | 10c dk grn | 4.75 | |
| a | | Imperf., pair | 250.00 | |

Nos. 165, 165a Surcharged

**1932, June 21**

| No. | Type | Description | Unused | Used |
|---|---|---|---|---|
| *191* | A59 | 3c on 2c dp red (II) | 70 | |
| a. | | Die I | 1.50 | 1.0 |

King George V
A66

Edward, Prince of Wales
A67

Allegory of British Empire
A68

**1932, July 12**

| No. | Type | Description | Unused | Used |
|---|---|---|---|---|
| *192* | A66 | 3c dp red | 45 | ( |
| *193* | A67 | 5c dl bl | 4.00 | 1.4( |
| *194* | A68 | 13c dp grn | 5.00 | 3.2 |

Imperial Economic Conference, Ottawa.

Type of 1930 and

King George V — A69

**932, Dec. 1**

*95* A69 1c dk grn 45 5
*a* Booklet pane of 4 + 2 labels 75.00 75.00
*b* Booklet pane of 6 22.50 22.50
*c* Imperf., pair 150.00
*96* A69 2c blk brn 55 5
*a* Booklet pane of 4 + 2 labels 75.00 75.00
*b* Booklet pane of 6 15.00 15.00
*c* Imperf., pair 150.00
*97* A69 3c dp red 75 5
*a* Booklet pane of 4 + 2 labels 20.00 20.00
*b* Imperf., pair 150.00
*98* A69 4c ocher 18.00 2.75
*a* Imperf., pair 150.00
*99* A69 5c dk bl 3.50 5
*a* Imperf. vert., pair 500.00
*b* Imperf., pair 150.00
*00* A69 8c red org 11.00 1.75
*a* Imperf., pair 150.00
*01* A61 13c dl vio 21.00 1.50
*a* Imperf., pair 500.00
*Nos. 195-201 (7)* 55.25 6.20

Type A66 has at the foot of the stamp OTTAWA-CONFERENCE 1932". This ıscription does not appear on the stamps of ype A69.

Government Buildings, Ottawa — A70

**933, May 18**

*02* A70 5c dk bl 5.00 2.50
*a* Imperf., pair 500.00

Issued in commemoration of the meeting of the Executive Committee of the Universal Postal Union at Ottawa, May and June, 1933.

No. 175 Overprinted in Blue

WORLD'S GRAIN EXHIBITION & CONFERENCE
REGINA 1933

**1933, July 24**

*203* A62 20c brn red 21.00 10.50
*a* Imperf., pair 500.00

Issued to commemorate the World's Grain Exhibition and Conference at Regina.

Steamship Royal William A71

**1933, Aug. 17**

*204* A71 5c dk bl 5.75 2.50
*a* Imperf., pair 500.00

Issued in commemoration of the centenary of the linking by steam of the Dominion, then a colony, with Great Britain, the mother country. The Royal William's 1833 voyage was the first Trans-Atlantic passage under steam all the way.

George V Type of 1932.
Coil Stamps.

**1933** ***Perf. 8 1/2 Vertically***

*205* A69 1c dk grn 10.50 1.50
*206* A69 2c blk brn 11.50 60
*207* A69 3c dp red 8.25 24

Cartier's Arrival at Quebec — A72

**1934, July 1** ***Perf. 11***

*208* A72 3c blue 1.90 80
*a* Imperf., pair 500.00

Issued in commemoration of the 400th anniversary of the landing of Jacques Cartier.

Group from Loyalists Monument, Hamilton, Ontario A73

**1934, July 1**

*209* A73 10c ol grn 12.50 6.00
*a* Imperf., pair 850.00

150th anniv. of the emigration of the United Empire Loyalists from the USA to Canada.

Seal of New Brunswick — A74

**1934, Aug. 16**

*210* A74 2c red brn 1.10 1.10
*a* Imperf., pair 500.00

150th anniv. of the founding of the Province of New Brunswick.

Princess Elizabeth A75

Duke of York A76

King George V and Queen Mary A77

Prince of Wales A78

Windsor Castle — A79

Royal Yacht Britannia A80

**1935, May 4** ***Perf. 12***

*211* A75 1c green 28 18
*a* Imperf., pair 100.00
*212* A76 2c brown 55 12
*a* Imperf., pair 100.00
*213* A77 3c carmine 1.40 6
*a* Imperf., pair 100.00
*214* A78 5c blue 3.00 1.90
*a* Imperf., pair 100.00
*215* A79 10c green 3.50 1.65
*a* Imperf., pair 100.00
*216* A80 13c dk bl 4.75 3.50
*a* Imperf., pair 100.00
*Nos. 211-216 (6)* 13.48 7.41

25th anniv. of the accession to the throne of George V.

King George V — A81

Royal Canadian Mounted Police — A82

Confederation Conference at Charlottetown, 1864 — A83

Niagara Falls — A84

Parliament Buildings, Victoria, B.C. — A85

Champlain Monument, Quebec A86

**1935, June 1**

*217* A81 1c green 18 7
*a* Booklet pane of 4 + 2 labels 40.00 40.00
*b* Booklet pane of 6 13.00 13.00
*c* Imperf., pair 85.00
*218* A81 2c brown 20 5
*a* Booklet pane of 4 + 2 labels 40.00 40.00
*b* Booklet pane of 6 7.50 7.50
*c* Imperf., pair 85.00
*219* A81 3c dk car 30 5
*a* Booklet pane of 4 + 2 labels 9.00 9.00
*b* Imperf., pair 85.00
*220* A81 4c yellow 1.75 30
*a* Imperf., pair 85.00
*221* A81 5c blue 1.75 7
*a* Imperf. vertically (pair) 95.00
*b* Imperf., pair 85.00
*222* A81 8c dp org 1.75 1.25
*a* Imperf., pair 85.00
*223* A82 10c car rose 4.75 10
*a* Imperf., pair 140.00
*224* A83 13c violet 4.75 52
*a* Imperf., pair 140.00
*225* A84 20c ol grn 13.00 32
*a* Imperf., pair 140.00
*226* A85 50c dl vio 18.00 3.25
*a* Imperf., pair 140.00
*227* A86 $1 dp bl 35.00 6.50
*a* Imperf., pair 160.00
*Nos. 217-227 (11)* 81.43 12.48

Coil Stamps

**1935** ***Perf. 8 Vertically***

*228* A81 1c green 6.50 1.65
*229* A81 2c brown 5.50 50
*230* A81 3c dk car 5.50 25

King George VI — A87

King George VI and Queen Elizabeth — A88

**1937** ***Perf. 12***

*231* A87 1c green 25 5
*a* Booklet pane of 4 + 2 labels 8.50 8.50
*b* Booklet pane of 6 1.00 1.00
*c* Imperf., pair 85.00
*232* A87 2c brown 35 5
*a* Booklet pane of 4 + 2 labels 5.00 5.00
*b* Booklet pane of 6 2.50 2.50
*c* Imperf., pair 85.00
*233* A87 3c carmine 40 5
*a* Booklet pane of 4 + 2 labels 1.50 1.50
*b* Imperf., pair 85.00
*234* A87 4c yellow 1.90 15
*a* Imperf., pair 85.00
*235* A87 5c blue 1.65 5
*a* Imperf., pair 85.00

*236* A87 8c orange 2.00 45
*a* Imperf., pair 85.00
*Nos. 231-236 (6)* 6.55 80

**1937, May 10**
*237* A88 3c carmine 15 8
*a* Imperf., pair 300.00

Issued in commemoration of the coronation of King George VI and Queen Elizabeth.

George VI Types of 1937.
Coil Stamps.

**1937** ***Perf. 8 Vertically.***
*238* A87 1c green 70 50
*239* A87 2c brown 1.10 12
*240* A87 3c carmine 1.75 6

Memorial Chamber, Parliament Building, Ottawa
A89

Entrance to Halifax Harbor
A90

Fort Garry Gate, Winnipeg
A91

Vancouver Harbor — A92

Chateau de Ramezay, Montreal
A93

**1938** ***Perf. 12***
*241* A89 10c dk car 2.50 7
*a* 10c car rose 4.00 8
*b* Imperf., pair 125.00
*242* A90 13c dp bl 4.50 25
*a* Imperf., pair 125.00
*243* A91 20c red brn 9.00 18
*a* Imperf., pair 125.00
*244* A92 50c green 11.50 3.00
*a* Imperf., pair 125.00
*245* A93 $1 dl vio 35.00 3.50
*a* Imperf. horiz. (pair) 1,750.
*b* Imperf., pair 250.00
*Nos. 241-245 (5)* 62.50 7.00

Princess Elizabeth and Princess Margaret Rose
A94

War Memorial, Ottawa
A95

King George VI and Queen Elizabeth
A96

Unwmk.
**1939, May 15** **Engr.** ***Perf. 12***
*246* A94 1c grn & blk 15 12
*a* Imperf., pair 140.00
*247* A95 2c brn & blk 15 8
*a* Imperf., pair 140.00
*248* A96 3c dk car & blk 15 5
*a* Imperf., pair 140.00

Visit of George VI and Queen Elizabeth to Canada and the US.

King George VI
A97 A98 A99

Grain Elevators
A100

Farm Scene
A101

Parliament Buildings
A102

"Ram" Tank
A103

Corvette
A104

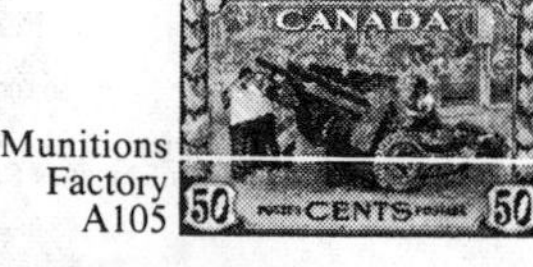

Munitions Factory
A105

Destroyer
A106

**1942-43** **Unwmk.** **Engr.** ***Perf. 12.***
*249* A97 1c green 10 5
*a* Booklet pane of 4 + 2 labels 2.50 2.50
*b* Booklet pane of 6 1.00 1.00
*c* Booklet pane of 3 1.00 1.00
*d* Imperf., pair 90.00
*250* A98 2c brown 22 5
*a* Booklet pane of 4 + 2 labels 2.50 2.50
*b* Booklet pane of 6 2.50 2.50
*c* Imperf., pair 90.00
*251* A99 3c dk car 22 5
*a* Booklet pane of 4 + 2 labels 1.10 1.10
*b* Imperf., pair 90.00
*252* A99 3c rose vio ('43) 20 5
*a* Booklet pane of 4 + 2 labels 1.00 1.00
*b* Booklet pane of 3 1.40 1.40
*c* Booklet pane of 6 2.50 2.50
*d* Imperf., pair 90.00
*253* A100 4c grnsh blk 80 60
*a* Imperf., pair 90.00
*254* A98 4c dk car ('43) 20 5
*a* Booklet pane of 6 1.10 1.10
*b* Booklet pane of 3 1.25 1.25
*c* Imperf., pair 90.00
*255* A97 5c dp bl 55 5
*a* Imperf., pair 90.00
*256* A101 8c red brn 1.10 25
*a* Imperf., pair 90.00
*257* A102 10c brown 2.25 10
*a* Imperf., pair 250.00
*258* A103 13c dl grn 3.00 2.00
*a* Imperf., pair 250.00
*259* A103 14c dl grn ('43) 4.50 15
*a* Imperf., pair 250.00
*260* A104 20c chocolate 3.75 12
*a* Imperf., pair 250.00
*261* A105 50c violet 15.00 1.10
*a* Imperf., pair 250.00
*262* A106 $1 dp bl 40.00 4.00
*a* Imperf., pair 400.00
*Nos. 249-262 (14)* 71.89 8.62

Issued to publicize Canada's contribution to the war effort of the Allied Nations.

Types of 1942.
Coil Stamps.

**1942-43** ***Perf. 8 Vertically***
*263* A97 1c green 50 20
*264* A98 2c brown 75 45
*265* A99 3c dk car 75 45
*266* A99 3c rose vio ('43) 1.25 10
*267* A98 4c dk car ('43) 1.75 9
*Nos. 263-267 (5)* 5.00 1.29

See Nos. 278-281.

**Catalogue values for unused stamps in this section, from this point to the end of the section, are for Never Hinged items.**

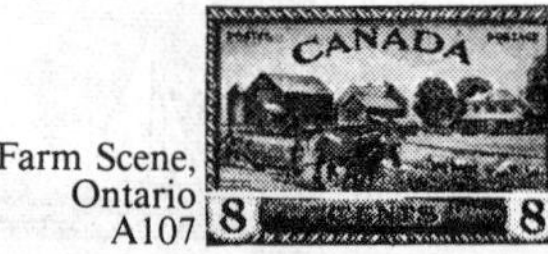

Farm Scene, Ontario
A107

Great Bear Lake, Mackenzie
A108

Hydroelectric Station, Saint Maurice River — A109

Combine
A110

Logging, British Columbia
A111

Train Ferry, Prince Edward Island — A112

**1946, Sept. 16** **Engr.** ***Perf. 12***
*268* A107 8c red brn 90 30
*269* A108 10c olive 90 6
*270* A109 14c blk brn 2.00 12
*271* A110 20c sl blk 2.00 9
*272* A111 50c dk bl grn 12.00 1.25
*273* A112 $1 red vio 27.50 1.65
*Nos. 268-273 (6)* 45.30 3.47

Alexander Graham Bell
A113

Citizen of Canada
A114

**1947, Mar. 3**
*274* A113 4c dp bl 16 8

Birth centenary of Alexander Graham Bell.

**1947, July 1**
*275* A114 4c dp bl 16 8

Issued on July 1, 1947, the 80th anniversary of the Canadian Confederation, to mark the advent of Canadian Citizenship.

Princess Elizabeth
A115

Parliament Buildings Ottawa
A116

**1948, Feb. 16**
*276* A115 4c dp bl 16 8

Marriage of Princess Elizabeth to Lieut. Philip Mountbatten, R. N., on Nov. 20, 1947.

**1948, Oct. 1**
*277* A116 4c gray 16 5

Centenary of Responsible Government.

George VI Types of 1942.
Coil Stamps.

**1948** ***Perf. 9½ Vertically***
*278* A97 1c green 3.25 1.50
*279* A98 2c brown 11.00 6.75
*280* A99 3c rose vio 6.50 2.25
*281* A98 4c dk car 10.00 2.75

John Cabot's Ship "Matthew"
A117

**1949, Apr. 1** **Engr.** ***Perf. 12***
*282* A117 4c dp grn 16 5

Issued to commemorate the entry of Newfoundland into confederation with Canada.

"Founding of Halifax, 1749" — A118

**949, June 21** **Unwmk.**
83 A118 4c purple 16 8

Issued to commemorate the 200th anniver-ary of the founding of Halifax, Nova Scotia.

A119 A120 A121

A122 A123

**1949, Nov. 19**
284 A119 1c green 6 5
a Bklt. pane of 3 ('50) 70 70
285 A120 2c sepia 15 5
286 A121 3c rose vio 18 5
a Bklt. pane of 3 ('50) 85 85
b Booklet pane of 4 + 2 labels 1.10 1.10
287 A122 4c dk car 30 5
a Bklt. pane of 3 ('50) 6.50 6.50
b Bklt. pane of 6 ('51) 9.75 9.75
288 A123 5c dp bl 70 12
*Nos. 284-288 (5)* 1.39 32

Stamps from booklet panes of 3 are imperf. on 2 or 3 sides.

"POSTES POSTAGE" Omitted

**1950, Jan. 19**
289 A119 1c green 6 5
290 A120 2c sepia 18 8
291 A121 3c rose vio 14 5
292 A122 4c dk car 16 5
293 A123 5c dp bl 80 70
*Nos. 289-293 (5)* 1.34 93

See Nos. 295-300.

Oil Wells, Alberta A124

**1950, Mar. 1** **Engr.** ***Perf. 12***
294 A124 50c dl grn 12.00 90

Development of oil wells in Canada.

Coil Stamps
Types of 1949
"POSTES POSTAGE" Omitted

**1950** ***Perf. 9½ Vertically***
295 A119 1c green 25 22
296 A121 3c rose vio 50 40

With "POSTES POSTAGE"
***Perf. 9½ Vertically.***
297 A119 1c green 25 18
298 A120 2c sepia 1.50 95
299 A121 3c rose vio 85 14
300 A122 4c dk car 10.00 55

See note after No. 288.

Indians Drying Skins on Stretchers A125

**1950, Oct. 2** ***Perf. 12***
301 A125 10c blk brn 65 8

Issued to publicize Canada's fur resources.

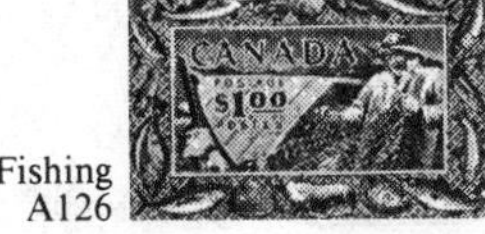
Fishing A126

**1951, Feb. 1** **Unwmk.**
302 A126 $1 brt ultra 55.00 11.50

Issued to publicize Canada's fish resources.

Sir Robert Laird Borden — A127

William L. Mackenzie King — A128

**1951, June 25** ***Perf. 12***
303 A127 3c turq grn 20 10
304 A128 4c rose pink 22 10

George VI Types of 1949.

**1951** ***Perf. 12***
305 A120 2c ol grn 12 5
306 A122 4c org ver 20 5
a Booklet pane of 3 1.50 1.50
b Booklet pane of 6 1.75 1.75

Coil Stamps.
***Perf. 9½ Vertically***
309 A120 2c ol grn 1.00 50
310 A122 4c org ver 1.65 60

Trains of 1851 and 1951 — A129

"Threepenny Beaver" of 1851 — A130

Designs: 5s, Steamships City of Toronto and Prince George. 7c, Stagecoach and Plane.

**1951, Sept. 24** **Unwmk.** ***Perf. 12***
311 A129 4c dk gray 48 8
312 A129 5c purple 1.50 1.10
313 A129 7c dp bl 90 25
314 A130 15c brt red 90 22

Issued to commemorate the centenary of British North American postal administration.

Princess Elizabeth and Duke of Edinburgh A131

**1951, Oct. 26** **Engr.**
315 A131 4c violet 16 6

Issued to commemorate the visit of Princess Elizabeth, Duchess of Edinburgh and the Duke of Edinburgh to Canada and the United States.

Symbols of Newsprint Paper Production A132

**1952, Apr. 1** **Unwmk.** ***Perf. 12***
316 A132 20c gray 1.25 5

Canada's paper production.

Red Cross on Sun — A133

**1952, July 26** **Engr. and Litho.**
317 A133 4c bl & red 16 5

Issued to publicize the 18th International Red Cross Conference, Toronto, July 1952.

Sir John J. C. Abbott A134

Alexander Mackenzie A135

**1952, Nov. 3** **Engr.**
318 A134 3c rose lil 15 6
319 A135 4c org ver 18 6

Canada Goose A136

**1952, Nov. 3**
320 A136 7c blue 35 5

Pacific Coast Indian House and Totem Pole — A137

**1953, Feb. 2**
321 A137 $1 gray 14.00 60

Polar Bear A138

Elizabeth II A139

Designs: 3c, Moose. 4c, Bighorn Sheep.

**1953, Apr. 1**
322 A138 2c dp bl 12 8
323 A138 3c blk brn 15 5
324 A138 4c slate 20 5

National Wildlife Week, 1953.

**1953, May 1**
325 A139 1c vio brn 8 5
a Booklet pane of 3 80 60
326 A139 2c green 12 5
327 A139 3c car rose 15 5
a Booklet pane of 3 1.25 80
b Booklet pane of 4 + 2 labels 1.40 1.40
328 A139 4c violet 22 5
a Booklet pane of 3 1.50 1.40
b Booklet pane of 6 1.50 1.40
329 A139 5c ultra 30 5
*Nos. 325-329 (5)* 87 25

Stamps from booklet panes of 3 are imperf. on 2 or 3 sides.

The indexes in each volume of the Scott Catalogue contain many listings which help to identify stamps.

**Coronation Issue.**

Queen Elizabeth II — A140

**1953, June 1**
330 A140 4c violet 16 5

Coil Stamps.

**1953** ***Perf. 9½ Vertically***
331 A139 2c green 1.25 75
332 A139 3c car rose 1.25 75
333 A139 4c violet 3.00 1.25

See note after No. 329.

Bobbin, Cloth and Spinning Wheel — A141

**1953, Nov. 2** ***Perf. 12***
334 A141 50c lt grn 4.00 18

Walrus A142

Beaver A143

**1954, Apr. 1**
335 A142 4c gray 22 5
336 A143 5c ultra 25 5
a Bklt. pane of 5 + label 2.00 2.00

National Wildlife Week, 1954.

Elizabeth II A144

Gannet A145

**1954-61**
337 A144 1c vio brn 5 5
a Bklt. pane of 5 + label 80 75
338 A144 2c green 7 5
a Pane of 25 ('61) 5.00 5.00
339 A144 3c car rose 9 5
a Imperf. vert., pair 900.00
340 A144 4c violet 11 5
a Bklt pane of 5 + label 1.40 1.25
b Booklet pane of 6 4.50 4.50
341 A144 5c brt bl 16 5
a Bklt pane of 5 + label 1.50 1.25
b Pane of 20 (5 x 4) ('61) 9.00 9.00
342 A144 6c orange 25 10
343 A145 15c gray 80 10
*Nos. 337-343 (7)* 1.53 45

Panes of 20 and 25 are imperf. on 4 sides.

Luminescence

The overprinting of regular stamps with vertical luminescent bands began experimentally in 1962 when Nos. 337p-341p were released at Winnipeg. The bands are of varying number, position and chemical content.

Tagged varieties of stamps which were issued both untagged and with luminescent overprint are listed with suffix letter "p".

Tagged

**1962, Jan. 13**
337p A144 1c vio brn 90 1.10
338p A144 2c green 90 90
339p A144 3c car rose 90 90

*340p* A144 4c violet 2.50 3.00
*341p* A144 5c brt bl 2.75 2.25
*Nos. 337p-341p (5)* 7.95 8.15

Coil Stamps.

**1954** ***Perf. 9½ Vertically***
*345* A144 2c green 32 12
*347* A144 4c violet 1.10 15
*348* A144 5c brt bl 1.75 12

Sir John Sparrow David Thompson A146

Sir Mackenzie Bowell A147

**1954, Nov. 1** ***Perf. 12***
*349* A146 4c violet 20 8
*350* A147 5c brt bl 20 8

Eskimo and Kayak — A148

**1955, Feb. 21**
*351* A148 10c vio brn 24 5

Musk Ox A149

Whooping Cranes A150

**1955, Apr. 4**
*352* A149 4c purple 24 5
*353* A150 5c blue 28 5

National Wildlife Week, April 10-16.

Torch, Dove and Maple Leaves — A151

**1955, June 1** **Unwmk.**
*354* A151 5c lt bl 24 12

Issued to commemorate the 10th anniversary of the founding of the International Civil Aviation Organization.

Pioneer Settlers A152

**1955, June 30** ***Perf. 12***
*355* A152 5c ultra 24 15

Issued to commemorate the 50th anniversary of the founding of the provinces of Alberta and Saskatchewan.

Globe and Scout Emblem A153

**1955, Aug. 20** **Engr.**
*356* A153 5c grn & org brn 24 12

Issued to commemorate the 8th Boy Scout World Jamboree, Niagara-on-the-Lake, Ont.

Richard Bedford Bennett A154

Sir Charles Tupper A155

**1955, Nov. 8**
*357* A154 4c violet 22 8
*358* A155 5c ultra 22 8

Ice Hockey Players A156

**1956, Jan. 23**
*359* A156 5c ultra 22 10

Issued to publicize Canada's most popular winter sport.

Caribou A157

Mountain Goat A158

**1956, Apr. 12**
*360* A157 4c dp vio 22 5
*361* A158 5c ultra 22 5

National Wildlife Week, 1956.

"Paper Industry" A159

"Chemical Industry" A160

**1956, June 7** **Engr.**
*362* A159 20c green 1.10 8
*363* A160 25c red 1.40 10

House on Fire A161

Canada's Outdoor Recreation Facilities A162

**1956, Oct. 9** **Unwmk.** ***Perf. 12***
*364* A161 5c gray & red 22 5

Issued to emphasize the needless waste caused by preventable fires.

**1957, Mar. 7**
*365* A162 5c Fishing 30 20
*366* A162 5c Swimming 30 20
*367* A162 5c Hunter and dog 30 20
*368* A162 5c Skiing 30 20

All four designs are printed alternating in sheets of 50, with various combinations possible.

Loon A163

David Thompson and Map of Western Canada A164

**1957, Apr. 10** ***Perf. 12***
*369* A163 5c black 30 5

**1957, June 5** **Unwmk.**
*370* A164 5c ultra 22 10

Issued to honor David Thompson (1770-1857), explorer and geographer.

Parliament Building Ottawa A165

Post Horn and Globe A166

**1957, Aug. 14** ***Perf. 12***
*371* A165 5c dk bl 22 5
*372* A166 15c dk bl 1.90 1.50

Universal Postal Union, 14th Congress, Ottawa, Aug. 1957.

Miner With Pneumatic Drill A167

Queen Elizabeth II and Prince Philip A168

**1957, Sept. 5**
*373* A167 5c black 22 10

Issued to honor Canada's mining industry and the Sixth Commonwealth Mining and Metallurgical Congress, Vancouver, Sept. 8-Oct. 8.

**1957, Oct. 10** **Unwmk.**
*374* A168 5c black 22 10

Issued to commemorate the visit of Queen Elizabeth II and Prince Philip to Canada, Oct. 12-16.

Newspapers and Symbols of Industry A169

Microscope and Globe A170

**1958, Jan. 22** **Engr.**
*375* A169 5c black 28 15

Issued to honor the Canadian press and emphasize the importance of a free press.

**1958, Mar. 5** ***Perf. 12***
*376* A170 5c blue 25 10

Issued to publicize the International Geophysical Year, 1957-1958.

Miner Panning Gold — A171

**1958, May 8** **Unwmk.**
*377* A171 5c bluish grn 22 10

Issued to commemorate the centenary of the province of British Columbia.

La Verendrye A172

**1958, June 4** ***Perf. 12***
*378* A172 5c brt ultra 22 10

Issued in honor of Pierre Gaultier de Varenne, Sieur de la Verendrye, 18th century French explorer of Western Canada.

Champlain and View of Quebec A173

**1958, June 26**
*379* A173 5c dk grn & bis brn 22 10

Issued to commemorate the 350th anniversary of the founding of Quebec.

Nurse — A174

Kerosene Lamp and Refinery — A175

**1958, July 30** **Engr.**
*380* A174 5c rose lil 22 8

Issued to emphasize the importance of health, both to the individual and to the nation.

**1958, Sept. 10** ***Perf. 12***
*381* A175 5c ol & red 22 8

Centennial of Canada's oil industry.

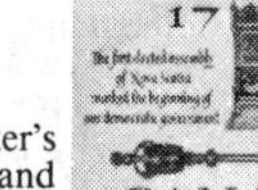

Speaker's Chair and Mace — A176

**1958, Oct. 2**
*382* A176 5c sl bl 22 10

Issued to commemorate the bicentennial of the meeting of the first House of Representatives in Canada, Halifax, Oct. 2, 1758.

"Silver Dart" and Delta Wing Planes A177

**1959, Feb. 23** ***Perf. 12***
*383* A177 5c bl & blk 22 8

50th anniv. of the 1st airplane flight in Canada near Baddeck, N. S., with J. A. D. McCurdy as pilot.

Globe and Dove — A178

**1959, Apr. 2**
384 A178 5c vio bl 22 8

Issued to commemorate the 10th anniversary of the North Atlantic Treaty Organization.

Woman Tending Tree — A179

Elizabeth II — A180

**1959, May 13**
385 A179 5c ap grn & blk 22 8

Associated Country Women of the World.

**1959, June 18**
386 A180 5c dk car 22 5

Issued to commemorate the visit of Queen Elizabeth and Prince Philip to Canada, June 18-Aug. 1.

Great Lakes, Maple Leaf and Eagle Emblems A181

**1959, June 26** **Engr.**
387 A181 5c red & bl 22 8
a Center invtd. 8,000. 6,500.

Issued to commemorate the opening of the St. Lawrence Seaway, June 26, 1959.
See United States No. 1131.

British Lion, Fleur-de-Lis and Maple Leaves A182

**1959, Sept. 10** ***Perf. 12***
388 A182 5c crim rose & dk grn 22 8

Issued to commemorate the bicentenary of the Battle of the Plains of Abraham.

Girl Guide Emblem A183

Dollard des Ormeaux and Battle Scene A184

**1960, Apr. 20** **Unwmk.**
389 A183 5c brn org & ultra 22 8

Issued to commemorate the 50th anniversary of the Canadian Girl Guides Association.

**1960, May 19**
390 A184 5c ultra & bis brn 22 8

Issued to commemorate the 300th anniversary of the Battle of the Long Sault.

Compass Rose, Earth Mover and Surveyor A185

Emily Pauline Johnson A186

**1961, Feb. 8** **Engr.** ***Perf. 12***
391 A185 5c grn & ver 22 8

Development of Canada's Northland.

**1961, March 10**
392 A186 5c grn & red 22 8

Issued to commemorate the centenary of the birth of Emily Pauline Johnson (1861-1913), Mohawk princess and poet.

Arthur Meighen A187

Power Plant and Men Holding Blueprint A188

**1961, Apr. 19**
393 A187 5c ultra 22 8

Issued to honor Arthur Meighen, Prime Minister of Canada, (1920-21, 1926).

**1961, June 28** **Unwmk.** ***Perf. 12***
394 A188 5c lt red brn & bl 22 8

Issued to commemorate the tenth anniversary of the Colombo Plan, initiated to assist underdeveloped countries by providing trained manpower and resources.

Natural Resources and Hands Holding Cogwheel — A189

**1961, Oct. 12** **Engr.** ***Perf. 12***
395 A189 5c brn & bl grn 22 8

Issued to publicize Canada's "Resources for Tomorrow Program" and to publicize the close link between industry and the country's renewable natural resources.

Young Adults and Education Symbols — A190

**1962, Feb. 28** **Unwmk.** ***Perf. 12***
396 A190 5c blk & lt red brn 22 8
a Lt. red brn (symbols) omitted

Issued to stimulate public awareness of the importance of education.

Scottish Settler and Lord Selkirk A191

**1962, May 3** ***Perf. 12***
397 A191 5c lt grn & vio brn 22 8

Issued to commemorate the 150th anniversary of the Red River Settlement in Western Canada (Prairie Provinces).

Jean Talon Presenting Gifts to Young Farm Couple — A192

**1962, June 13** **Unwmk.** ***Perf. 12***
398 A192 5c dk bl 22 8

Issued to honor Jean Talon, administrator of New France (Canada), 1665-1668.

British Columbia Legislative Building and Stamp of 1860 — A193

**1962, Aug. 22** **Engr.** ***Perf. 12***
399 A193 5c blk & rose 22 8

Centenary of Victoria as incorporated city.

Arms of the Provinces A194

**1962, Aug. 31**
400 A194 5c brn org & blk 22 10

Issued to commemorate the official opening of the Trans-Canada Highway, Rogers Pass, Glacier National Park, Sept. 4.

Queen Elizabeth II and Wheat — A195

Designs (Symbol in upper left corner): 1c, Mineral crystals. 2c, Tree. 3c, Fish. 4c, Electric high tension tower.

**1962-63** **Engr.** ***Perf. 12***

| | | |
|---|---|---|
| 401 A195 1c dp brn ('63) | 6 | 5 |
| a Bklt pane 5 + label ('63) | 2.75 | 2.75 |
| 402 A195 2c grn ('63) | 9 | 5 |
| a Pane of 25 ('63) | 3.75 | 3.75 |
| 403 A195 3c pur ('63) | 12 | 5 |
| 404 A195 4c car ('63) | 15 | 5 |
| a Bklt pane 5 + label ('63) | 3.50 | 3.50 |
| b Pane of 25 ('63) | 5.25 | 5.25 |
| 405 A195 5c vio bl | 18 | 5 |
| a Bklt pane of 5 + label ('63) | 4.25 | 3.75 |
| b Pane of 20 ('63) | 5.75 | 5.50 |
| *Nos. 401-405 (5)* | 60 | 25 |

Nos. 402a, 404b, and 405b are imperf. on four sides.

Tagged

**1963**

| | | |
|---|---|---|
| 401p A195 1c dp brn | 12 | 9 |
| 402p A195 2c green | 16 | 12 |
| 403p A195 3c purple | 25 | 9 |
| 404p A195 4c carmine | 85 | 50 |
| 405p A195 5c vio bl | 50 | 25 |
| q Pane of 20 | 35.00 | |
| *Nos. 401p-405p (5)* | 1.88 | 1.05 |

See note after No. 343.

Coil Stamps

**1963-64** ***Perf. 9½ Horiz.***

| | | |
|---|---|---|
| 406 A195 2c green | 3.00 | 1.40 |
| 407 A195 3c pur ('64) | 2.00 | 1.00 |
| 408 A195 4c carmine | 3.00 | 1.40 |
| 409 A195 5c vio bl | 3.00 | 52 |

Casimir Stanislaus Gzowski — A196

**1963, Mar. 5** **Unwmk.** ***Perf. 12***
410 A196 5c rose lil 22 7

Issued to commemorate the 150th anniversary of the birth of Sir Casimir Stanislaus Gzowski (1813-1898), engineer, soldier and educator.

Export Crate and Mercator Map — A197

**1963, June 14** **Unwmk.** ***Perf. 12***
411 A197 $1 rose car 16.00 1.65

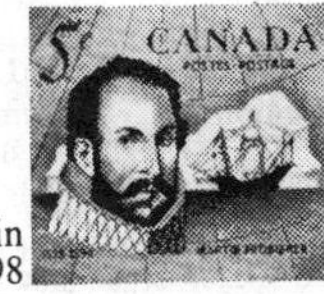
Martin Frobisher — A198

**1963, Aug. 21** **Engr.**
412 A198 5c ultra 22 8

Issued to honor Sir Martin Frobisher, 1535-1594, explorer and discoverer of Frobisher Bay.

Postrider and First Land Mail Routes A199

**1963, Sept. 25**
413 A199 5c grn & red brn 22 8

Issued to commemorate the bicentennial of the first regular postal service between Quebec, Three Rivers and Montreal.

Jet at Ottawa Airport — A200

Canada Geese — A201

**1963-64**
414 A200 7c bl ('64) 60 60
415 A201 15c dp ultra 3.75 25

See No. 436.

"Peace on Earth" — A202

**Engr. and Litho.**

**1964, Apr. 8** ***Perf. 12***
416 A202 5c grnsh bl, Prus bl & ocher 22 8

Issued to promote world peace.

Three-Maple-Leaf Emblem (Canadian Unity) — A203

White Trillium and Arms of Ontario A204

Design: No. 419, White garden lily and arms of Quebec. No. 420, Mayflower (trailing arbutus) and arms of Nova Scotia. No. 421, Purple violet and arms of New Brunswick. No. 422, Prairie crocus and arms of Manitoba. No. 423, Dogwood and arms of British Columbia. No. 424, Lady's slipper and arms of Prince Edward Island. No. 425, Prairie lily and arms of Saskatchewan. No. 426, Wild rose and arms of Alberta. No. 427, Pitcher plant and arms of Newfoundland. No. 428, Fireweed and arms of Yukon. No. 429, Mountain avens and arms of Northwest Territories. No. 429A, Maple leaf and arms of Canada.

**Engraved and Lithographed**

**1964-66 Unwmk. *Perf. 12***

*417* A203 5c lt bl & dk car 20 5
*418* A204 5c red brn, buff & grn 20 10
*419* A204 5c grn, yel & org 20 8
*420* A204 5c bl, pink & grn ('65) 20 8
*421* A204 5c car, grn & vio ('65) 20 8
*422* A204 5c red brn, lil & dl grn ('65) 20 8
*423* A204 5c lil, grn & bis ('65) 20 8
*424* A204 5c vio, grn & dp rose ('65) 20 8
*425* A204 5c sep, org & grn ('66) 20 10
*426* A204 5c dl grn, yel & car ('66) 20 8
*427* A204 5c blk, grn & car ('66) 20 8
*428* A204 5c dk bl, rose & grn ('66) 20 10
*429* A204 5c ol, yel & grn ('66) 20 8
*429A* A204 5c dk bl & dp red ('66) 20 8
*Nos. 417-429A (14)* 2.80 1.15

No. 414 Surcharged 8

**1964, July 15 Engr.**
*430* A200 8c on 7c bl 28 28
*a* Pair, one without surch. *2,000.*

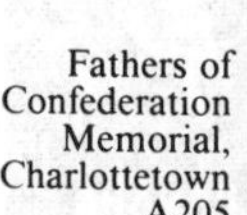

Fathers of Confederation Memorial, Charlottetown A205

**1964, July 29 Engr.**
*431* A205 5c black 22 8

Issued to commemorate the centenary of the Charlottetown, P.E.I., Conference, Sept. 1-9, 1864, which led to the creation of the Canadian nation in 1867.

Maple Leaf and Hand Holding Quill Pen — A206

**1964, Sept. 9 Unwmk. *Perf. 12***
*432* A206 5c dk brn & rose 20 5

Issued to commemorate the centenary of the Quebec Conference, Oct. 10-27, 1864, which led to the creation of the Canadian nation.

Queen Elizabeth II A207

Family and Star of Bethlehem A208

**1964, Oct. 5 Engr.**
*433* A207 5c claret 20 8

Issued to commemorate Queen Elizabeth's visit to Canada, Oct. 6-13.

**1964, Oct. 14 *Perf. 12***
*434* A208 3c red 12 5
*a* Pane of 25 6.25 6.25
*p* Tagged 1.00 25
*q* As "a," tagged 10.00 10.00
*435* A208 5c blue 18 5
*p* Tagged 1.00 25

Panes of 25 are imperf. on four sides.

Jet Type of 1964

**1964, Nov. 18 Unwmk. *Perf. 12***
*436* A200 8c blue 40 18

Maple Leaf and I.C.Y. Emblem A209

**1965, Mar. 3 Engr. *Perf. 12***
*437* A209 5c sl grn 18 10

International Cooperation Year.

Sir Wilfred Grenfell at Wheel of Hospital Ship Strathcona II — A210

**1965, June 9 Engr. *Perf. 12***
*438* A210 5c Prus bl 18 10

Issued to commemorate the centenary of the birth of Sir Wilfred Grenfell, author, medical missionary and founder of the Grenfell Mission.

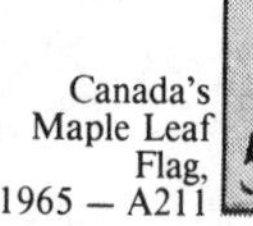
Canada's Maple Leaf Flag, 1965 — A211

**1965, June 30 Unwmk.**
*439* A211 5c bl & red 18 10

Winston Churchill A212

Peace Tower, Ottawa A213

**1965, Aug. 12 Litho. *Perf. 12***
*440* A212 5c brown 25 10

Issued in memory of Sir Winston Spencer Churchill (1874-1965).

**1965, Sept. 8 Engr. *Perf. 12***
*441* A213 5c sl grn 18 10

Issued to commemorate the meeting of the Inter-Parliamentary Union, Ottawa, Sept. 8-17.

Parliament and Ottawa River — A214

**1965, Sept. 8**
*442* A214 5c brown 18 10

Issued to commemorate the centenary of the selection of Ottawa as national capital.

Gifts of the Wise Men — A215

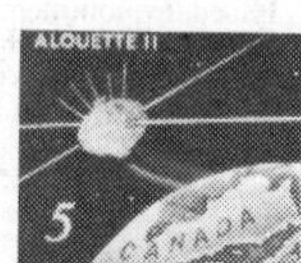
Alouette II Orbiting Globe — A216

**1965, Oct. 13 Engr.**
*443* A215 3c olive 12 5
*a* Pane of 25 5.75 5.75
*p* Tagged 20 15
*q* As "a" tagged 6.75 6.75
*444* A215 5c vio bl 15 5
*p* Tagged 28 20

Christmas 1965.
Panes of 25 are imperf. on four sides.

**1966, Jan. 5 Unwmk. *Perf. 12***
*445* A216 5c dk vio bl 18 10

Issued to commemorate the launching (in California) of the Canadian satellite Alouette II, Nov. 28, 1965, as part of the Canadian-American program of space research.

La Salle, Map of 17th Century Canada, Ship, Canoe, Spyglass and Compass — A217

**1966, Apr. 13 Engr. *Perf. 12***
*446* A217 5c bl grn 18 8

Issued to commemorate the tercentenary of the arrival in Canada of Rene Robert Cavelier, Sieur de La Salle (1643-1687).

Traffic Signs — A218

**1966, May 2**
*447* A218 5c blk, bl & yel 18 10

Issued to publicize traffic safety.

House of Commons, Thames River and Canadian Delegates A219

**1966, May 26**
*448* A219 5c brown 18 8

Centenary of the London Conference, Dec 4, 1866, which resulted in the British North America Act.

Atomic Reactor, Heavy Water Atom Symbol and Microscope A220

**1966, July 27 Engr. *Perf. 12***
*449* A220 5c dp ultra 18 8

Issued to publicize peaceful uses of atomic power. The design shows a stylized view of the Douglas Point Nuclear Power Station, Lake Huron, Ontario.

Parliamentary Library, Ottawa A221

Praying Hands, by Albrecht Dürer A222

**1966, Sept. 8 Engr. *Perf. 12***
*450* A221 5c plum 18 6

Issued to commemorate the 12th General Conference of the Commonwealth Parliamentary Association, Ottawa, Sept. 8-Oct. 5.

**1966, Oct. 12 Engr. *Perf. 12***
*451* A222 3c car rose 9 5
*a* Pane of 25 3.25 3.25
*p* Tagged 15 10
*q* As "a" tagged 4.00 4.00
*452* A222 5c orange 15 5
*p* Tagged 40 25

Christmas 1966.
Panes of 25 are imperf. on four sides.

Canadian Flag over Globe and Centennial Emblem — A223

**1967, Jan. 11 Engr. *Perf. 12***
*453* A223 5c bl & red 22 5
*p* Tagged 40 28

Canada's centenary as a nation.

Northern Lights and Dog Team A224

"Alaska Highway" by A. Y. Jackson A225

Two types of 6c black:

Type I

Type II

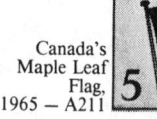

Designs: 2c, Totem pole (Pacific Area). 3c, Combine and oil rig (Prairie Region). 4c, Ship in lock (Central Canada). 5c, Lobster ıps and boat (Atlantic Provinces). 6c, ansportation means. 10c, "The Jack Pine" Tom Thomson. 15c, "Bylot Island" by ıwren Harris. 20c, "The Ferry, Quebec" by mes Wilson Morrice. 25c, "The Solemn ınd" by J. E. H. MacDonald. 50c, "Summer's Stores" by John Ensor (grain elevators). ı. Oilfield near Edmonton, by H. G. Glyde.

**967-72 Engr. *Perf. 12***

54 A224 1c brown 5 5
a Booklet pane of 5 + label 65 65
b Bklt pane (1 #454d, 4 #459 + label), perf. 10 ('68) 2.10 2.10
c Bklt pane (5 #454d + 5 #457d) perf. 10 ('68) 3.75 3.75
d Perf. 10 25 15
e Perf. 12½x12 50 18
55 A224 2c green 5 5
a Bklt pane (4 #455, 4 #456 with gutter btwn.) 2.50 2.50
56 A224 3c dl pur 8 5
a Perf. 12½x12 80 40
57 A224 4c car rose 12 5
a Booklet pane of 5 + label 1.75 1.75
b Pane of 25 (5x5) 14.00
c Booklet pane of 25 + 2 labels, perf. 10 ('68) 8.00
d Perf. 10 75 25
58 A224 5c blue 8 5
a Booklet pane of 5 + label 5.50 5.25
b Pane of 20 20.00
c Bklt pane of 20, perf. 10 ('68) 8.00
d Perf. 10 75 25
59 A224 6c org, perf. 10 ('68) 40 5
a Booklet pane of 25 + 2 labels, perf. 10 ('69) 6.75
b Perf. 12½x12 ('69) 35 5
60 A224 6c blk (I), perf. 12½x12 ('70) 20 5
a Blkt pane of 25 + 2 labels (I), perf. 10 ('70) 19.00 19.00
b As "a", perf. 12½x12 17.50
c Type II, perf. 12½x12 24 5
d As "c", booklet pane of 4 4.25 4.25
e As "d", perf. 10 ('70) 8.75 5.50
f Type II, perf. 12 ('72) 42 15
g Type I, perf. 10 1.75 35
h Type II, perf. 10 2.25 1.00
61 A225 8c vio brn 40 10
62 A225 10c ol grn 40 5
63 A225 15c dl pur 80 5
64 A225 20c dk bl 80 8
65 A225 25c sl grn 1.50 5
65A A225 50c brn org 4.75 8
65B A225 $1 car rose 10.00 50
*Nos. 454-465B (14)* 19.63 1.26

Nos. 454d, 457d, 458d, 460g and 460h are rom booklet panes.
See Nos. 543-544, 549-550.

**Tagged**

54p A224 1c brown 20 20
ep Perf. 12½x12 ('71) 10 5
455p A224 2c green 16 15
456p A224 3c dl pur 16 15
457p A224 4c car rose 52 25
458p A224 5c blue 52 25
bp Pane of 20 37.50 37.50
459p A224 6c org, perf. 10 ('68) 52 25
pb Perf. 12½x12 ('69) 70 40
460 A224 6c blk. (I), perf. 12½x12 ('70) 24 15
cp blk (II), perf. 12½x12 ('70) 50 50
fp As "cp", perf. 12 ('72) 35 12
462p A225 10c ol grn ('70) 90 50
463p A225 15c dl pur ('70) 90 50
464p A225 20c dk bl ('70) 1.40 75
465p A225 25c sl grn ('70) 2.75 1.50
*Nos. 454p-465p (11)* 8.27 4.65

See note after No. 343.

## Coil Stamps

**1967-70 *Perf. 9½ Horiz.***

466 A224 3c dl pur 1.75 1.25
467 A224 4c car rose 90 75
468 A224 5c blue 1.75 1.00

***Perf. 10 Horiz.***

468A A224 6c org ('69) 35 8
c Imperf., pair 200.00
468B A224 6c blk, die II ('70) 35 8
d Imperf., pair 550.00
*Nos. 466-468B (5)* 5.10 3.16

Horizontal pairs or blocks of Nos. 468A and 468B may be found with a fine vertical score line between the stamps. These sell for little more than vertical pairs or strips.

EXPO '67 Emblem and Canadian Pavilion A226

**1967, Apr. 28 Engr. *Perf. 12***
*469* A226 5c bl & red 18 10

EXPO '67, Intl. Exhib., Montreal, Apr. 28-Oct. 27.

Symbolic Woman and Ballot A227

Queen Elizabeth II A228

**1967, May Litho. *Perf. 12***
*470* A227 5c blk & rose lil 18 8

50th anniversary of woman suffrage.

**1967, June 30 Engr. *Perf. 12***
*471* A228 5c dp org & pur 18 8

Issued to commemorate the Centennial Year visit of Queen Elizabeth II and the Duke of Edinburgh.

Runner A229

**1967, July 19 Engr. *Perf. 12***
*472* A229 5c red 18 8

Pan-American Games, Winnipeg, Manitoba, July 22-Aug. 7.

Globe and Flash — A230

**1967, Aug. 31**
*473* A230 5c dp ultra 18 8

Issued to commemorate the 50th anniversary of the Canadian Press, news gathering and distributing service.

Georges Philia Vanier A231

**Engraved and Lithographed**

**1967, Sept. 15 Unwmk. *Perf. 12***
*474* A231 5c black 18 8

Issued in memory of Georges Philias Vanier (1888-1967), Governor General of Canada, 1959-1967.

Toronto in 1967 and Citizens of 1867 — A232

**1967, Sept. 28 Engr.**
*475* A232 5c sl grn & sal pink 18 8

Centenary of Toronto as capital of Ontario.

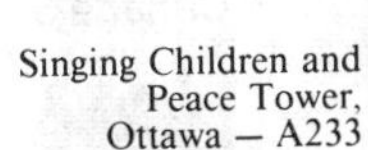

Singing Children and Peace Tower, Ottawa — A233

**1967, Oct. 11 Engr. *Perf. 12***
*476* A233 3c carmine 9 5
a Pane of 25 2.50 2.50
p Tagged 15 12
q As "a" tagged 3.50 3.50
*477* A233 5c green 15 5
p Tagged 25 20

Christmas 1967.

Panes of 25 are imperf. on four sides.

Gray Jays — A234

Weather Map and Composite of Instruments — A235

**1968, Feb. 15 Litho.**
*478* A234 5c grn, blk & red 35 10

**1968, Mar. 13 *Perf. 11***
*479* A235 5c dk & lt bl, yel & red 18 8

Issued to commemorate the 200th anniversary of Canada's first long-term fixed point weather observations at Fort Prince of Wales, Churchill, by William Wales and Joseph Dymond.

Male Narwhal A236

**1968, Apr. 10 Litho. *Perf. 11***
*480* A236 5c multi 18 8

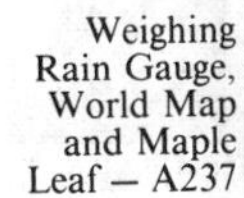

Weighing Rain Gauge, World Map and Maple Leaf — A237

**1968, May 8 Litho. *Perf. 11***
*481* A237 5c multi 18 8

Issued to publicize the International Hydrological Decade, 1967-74.

The Nonsuch A238

**Photogravure and Engraved**

**1968, June 5 *Perf. 10***
*482* A238 5c dk bl & multi 18 8

Issued to commemorate the 300th anniversary of the voyage of the Nonsuch which opened the way to Canada's West through the fur trade.

Contemporary and Indian Lacrosse Players — A239

**1968, July 3 Photo. & Engr.**
*483* A239 5c yel, blk & red 18 8

George Brown, "Globe" Front Page and Legislature, Prince Edward Island A240

**1968, Aug. 21 *Perf. 10***
*484* A240 5c multi 18 8

Issued to commemorate the sesquicentennial of the birth of George Brown (1818-80), founder of Toronto "Globe" and political leader.

Henri Bourassa and Newspaper Page A241

Canadian Memorial, Vimy Near France A242

**Lithographed and Engraved**

**1968, Sept. 4 *Perf. 12***
*485* A241 5c ver, buff & blk 18 8

Issued to commemorate the centenry of the birth of Henri Bourassa (1868-1952), jounalist and statesman.

**1968, Oct. 15 Engr. *Perf. 12***
*486* A242 15c slate 1.40 1.00

50th anniv. of the Armistice which ended WW I. The stamp shows "The Defenders and the Breaking of the Sword," a detail from the memorial designed by W. S. Allward.

John McCrae and "Flanders Fields" A243

Eskimo Family, Carving A244

**1968, Oct. 15 Litho. & Engr.**
*487* A243 5c multi 18 8

Issued to commemorate the 50th anniversary of the death of Lt. Col. John McCrae (1872-1918), author of "In Flanders Fields."

**1968, Nov. Photo. *Perf. 12***

Design (Eskimo soapstone carving): 6c, Mother and infant, by Munamee of Cape Dorset.

*488* A244 5c brt bl & blk 12 5
a Bklt pane of 10 2.75
p Tagged 20 16
q As "a" tagged 4.00
*489* A244 6c dp bis & blk 15 5
p Tagged 25 16

Christmas 1968.
Issue dates: 5c, Nov. 1; 6c, Nov. 15.

Curling A245

Vincent Massey A246

**Photogravure and Engraved**

**1969, Jan. 15**
*490* A245 6c blk, brt bl & car 18 8

**Lithographed and Engraved**

**1969, Feb. 20 *Perf. 12***
*491* A246 6c yel ol & dk brn 18 5

Vincent Massey (1887-1967), 1st Canadian-born Governor General of Canada, 1952-59.

Return from the Harvest Field, by Aurele de Foy Suzor-Cote
A247

**1969, Mar. 14** **Photo.**
*492* A247 50c multi 3.00 1.65

Aurele de Foy Suzor-Cote (1869-1937), painter.

Globe and Tools of Various Trades — A248

**1969, May 21** **Engr.** ***Perf. 12x12½***
*493* A248 6c dk ol grn 18 8

50th anniv. of the ILO.

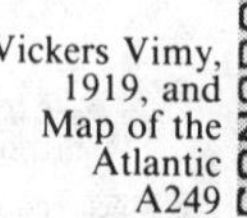

Vickers Vimy, 1919, and Map of the Atlantic
A249

**1969, June 13** **Photo. and Engr.**
*494* A249 15c red brn, yel grn & lt ultra 1.40 1.75

Issued to commemorate the 50th anniversary of the first non-stop Atlantic flight from Newfoundland to Ireland of Capt. John Alcock and Lt. Arthur Whitten Brown.

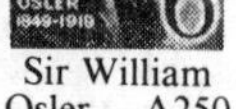

Sir William Osler — A250

Ipswich Sparrow — A251

**1969, June 23** ***Perf. 12½x12***
*495* A250 6c dk bl & lt red brn 18 10

Issued in memory of Sir William Osler (1849-1919), physician, professor of physiology and pathology in Canada, United States and England.

**1969, July 23** **Litho.** ***Perf. 12***

Birds: 6c, White-throated sparrows (vert.). 25c, Hermet thrush.

*496* A251 6c multi 50 8
*497* A251 10c ultra & multi 1.00 60
*498* A251 25c blk & multi 2.50 2.25

Map of Prince Edward Island
A252

**Photo. and Engr.**
**1969, Aug. 15** ***Perf. 12x12½***
*499* A252 6c ultra, org brn & blk 18 15

Bicentenary of Charlottetown as capital of Prince Edward Island.

Prices of premium quality never hinged stamps will be in excess of catalogue price.

Flags of Summer and Winter Canada Games — A253

**Litho. and Engr.**
**1969, Aug. 15** ***Perf. 14***
*500* A253 6c ultra, brt grn & red 18 10

Issued to publicize the Firt Canada Summer Games, Halifax and Dartmouth, N.S., Aug. 16-24.

Sir Isaac Brock and Memorial Queenston Heights — A254

**1969, Sept. 12** **Litho. and Engr.**
*501* A254 6c yel brn, brn & pale sal 18 5

Issued to commemorate the 200th anniversary of the birth of Major General Sir Isaac Brock (1769-1812), administrator of Upper Canada and leader in the war of 1812.

Children of Various Races — A255

**1969, Oct. 8** **Litho.** ***Perf. 12***
*502* A255 5c bl & multi 12 5
 *a* Bklt pane of 10 3.75
 *p* Tagged 20 12
 *q* As "a" tagged 4.50
*503* A255 6c red & multi 12 5
 *a* Black (inscriptions & frame line) omitted 1.250. 1.250.
 *p* Tagged 25 16

Christmas 1969.

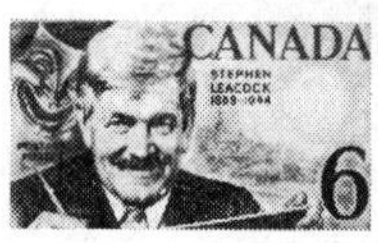

Stephen Leacock, Comedy Mask and Mariposa View — A256

**Photo. and Engr.**
**1969, Nov. 12** ***Perf. 12x12½***
*504* A256 6c multi 18 10

Issued to commemorate the centenary of the birth of Stephen Butler Leacock (1869-1944), humorist, historian and economist.

Manitoba, Crossroads of Canada
A257

**1970, Jan. 27** **Litho.** ***Perf. 12***
*505* A257 6c vio bl & multi 18 5
 *p* Tagged 30 20

Centenary of the province of Manitoba.

Enchanted Owl, by Kenojuak — A258

**1970, Jan. 27** **Engr.** ***Perf. 12***
*506* A258 6c dk red & blk 18 7

Centenary of Nortwest Territories.

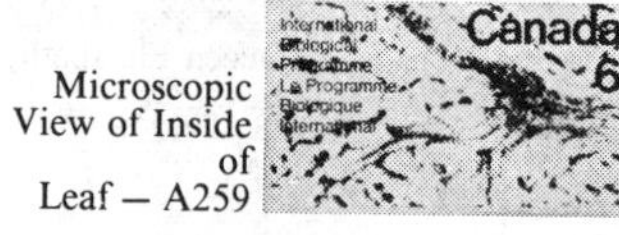

Microscopic View of Inside of Leaf — A259

**1970, Feb. 18** **Photo. and Engr.**
*507* A259 6c grn, lt org & bl 18 10

Issued to publicize Canada's participation in the International Biological Program, 1967-1972.

Emblems of EXPO '67 and '70 — A260

EXPO '70 Emblem and Dogwood, British Columbia
A261

Designs: No. 510, EXPO '70 emblem and white garden lily, Quebec. No. 511, EXPO '70 emblem and white trillium, Ontario.

**1970, Mar. 18** **Litho.** ***Perf. 12***
*508* A260 25c red emblem 1.75 1.75
 *p* Tagged 2.50 2.50
*509* A261 25c vio emblem 1.75 1.75
 *p* Tagged 2.50 2.50
*510* A261 25c grn emblem 1.75 1.75
 *p* Tagged 2.50 2.50
*511* A261 25c bl emblem 1.75 1.75
 *p* Tagged 2.50 2.50

EXPO '70 International Exhibition, Osaka, Japan, Mar. 15-Sept. 13. Nos. 508-511 printed se-tenant in sheets of 50 (5x10), with various combinations possible.

Henry Kelsey
A262

**Photo. and Engr.**
**1970, Apr. 15** ***Perf. 12x12½***
*512* A262 6c multi 18 10

Issued to commemorate the 300th anniversary of the birth of Henry Kelsey, explorer of Canada's western plains.

"A Divided World, with Energy Focused on Unification..."
A263

**1970, May 13** **Litho.** ***Perf. 11***
*513* A263 10c blue 60 45
 *p* Tagged 1.00 1.00
*514* A263 15c lil & dk red 90 60
 *p* Tagged 1.50 1.50

25th anniversary of the United Nations.

Louis Riel
A264

Mackenzie Rock, Dean Channel
A265

**1970, June 19** **Photo.** ***Perf. 12½x1***
*515* A264 6c red & brt bl 18

Issued to memory of Louis Riel (184 1885), Metis leader who became president the Council of Assiniboin in 1870.

**1970, June 25** **Engr.** ***Perf.***
*516* A265 6c brown 18

Issued in memory of Sir Alexander Ma kenzie (1764-1820), Scottish explorer who 1793 completed the first crossing of the Nor American continent north of Mexico.

Sir Oliver Mowat and Parliament, Ottawa
A266

**Photo. and Engr.**
**1970, Aug. 12** ***Perf. 12x12***
*517* A266 6c red & blk 18 1

Issued to commemorate the 150th annive sary of the birth of Sir Oliver Mowat (182 1903), government leader and a Father Confederation.

Isle of Spruce, by Arthur Lismer
A267

**1970, Sept. 18** **Litho.** ***Perf. 1***
*518* A267 6c multi 18

Issued to commemorate the 50th annive sary of "The Group of Seven," Canadia landscape artists.

Santa Claus — A268

Christ Child — A269

Child in the Manger and Star-studded Sky — A270

Designs by Canadian School Children.

**1970, Oct. 7** **Litho.** ***Perf. 12***
*519* A268 5c *Santa Claus* 28 8
*520* A268 5c *Horse-drawn Sleigh* 28 8
*521* A268 5c *Nativity* 28 8
*522* A268 5c *Children Skiing* 28 8
*523* A268 5c *Snowmen and Christmas Tree* 28 8
*524* A269 6c *Christ Child* 35 8
*525* A269 6c *Christmas Tree and Children* 35 8
*526* A269 6c *Toy Store* 35 8
*527* A269 6c *Santa Claus* 35 8
*528* A269 6c *Church* 35 8
*529* A270 10c *Christ Child* 45 35
*530* A270 15c *Snowmobile and Trees* 90 90
 *Nos. 519-530 (12)* 4.50 2.05

**Tagged**

*519p* A268 5c multi 50 18
*520p* A268 5c multi 50 18
*521p* A268 5c multi 50 18
*522p* A268 5c multi 50 18
*523p* A268 5c multi 50 18
*524p* A269 6c multi 60 18
*525p* A269 6c multi 60 18
*526p* A269 6c multi 60 18
*527p* A269 6c multi 60 18
*528p* A269 6c multi 60 18
*529p* A270 10c multi 80 65
*530p* A270 15c multi 1.65 1.65
 *Nos. 519p-530p (12)* 7.95 4.10

Christmas 1970.

The Sheets of 100 of both 5c and 6c contain all 5 designs, generally alternating, and arranged to permit vertical and horizontal pairs of each design in the two center vertical and horizontal rows. The center block of 4 is entirely of No. 522 (5c) and 525 (6c). The sheet may also be broken to provide 20 strips of 5, each stamp of different design.

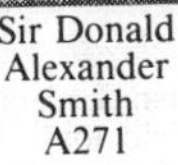

Sir Donald Alexander Smith A271

Big Raven, by Emily Carr A272

**1970, Nov. 4 Litho. *Perf. 12***
*531* A271 6c dk grn, yel & blk 18 5

Issued to commemorate the 150th anniversary of the birth of Sir Donald Alexander Smith (1820-1914), railroad builder and Canadian High Commissioner, 1896-1914.

**1971, Feb. 12 Litho. *Perf. 12***
*532* A272 6c multi 18 5

Centenary of the birth of Emily Carr (1871-1945), painter and writer.

Laboratory Equipment Used for Insulin Discovery — A273

**1971, Mar. 3 Litho. *Perf. 11***
*533* A273 6c multi 18 5

Discovery of insulin by Dr. Frederick G. Banting and Dr. Charles H. Best, 50th anniversary.

A274

**1971, Mar. 24 Litho. *Perf. 11***
*534* A274 6c red, org & blk 18 5

Centenary of the birth of Sir Ernest Rutherford (1871-1937), physicist, developer of theory of spontaneous disintegration of the atom.

Spring, Winged Maple Seed A275

Louis Joseph Papineau A276

**1971 Litho. *Perf. 11***
*535* A275 6c shown 22 5
*a* Imperf., pair *775.00*
*536* A275 6c Summer 22 5
*537* A275 7c Autumn 22 5
*538* A275 7c Winter 22 5

Issue dates: No. 535, Apr. 14; No. 536, June 16; No. 537, Sept. 3; No. 538, Nov. 19.

**Litho. & Engr.**

**1971, May 7 *Perf. 12***
*539* A276 6c multi 18 8

Centenary of the death of Louis Joseph Papineau (1786-1871), member of Legislative Assembly and leader of French Canadian Patriote party.

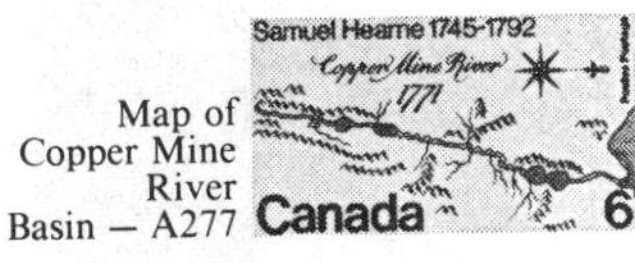


Map of Copper Mine River Basin — A277

**1971, May 7**
*540* A277 6c buff, red & brn 18 8

Bicentenary of Samuel Hearne's expedition to the Copper Mine River.

Maple Leaves A278

**1971, June 1**
*541* A278 15c blk, red org & yel 1.50 1.10
*p* Tagged 2.50 2.25

Inauguration of new transmitters for Radio Canada International.

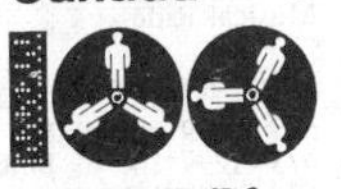


Computer Tape and Reels — A279

**1971, June 1**
*542* A279 6c blk, ultra & red 18 10

Centenary of measured progress through census.

---

Migrating Phosphor

Canada's "Ottawa/General" tagging of engraved stamps printed March-October, 1972, used a phosphor which migrates onto or through other stamps, booklet covers and album pages. It fluoresces yellow under ultraviolet light.

This bleeding, contaminating "OP4" phosphor can be somewhat contained in mounts or envelopes of acetate, glassine or polyethylene, but it may leak or penetrate.

The migrating phosphor is found on all copies of Nos. 560p-561p, and on some of Nos. 544p, 544q, 544r, 544s, 562p-565p and 594-598.

---

Transportation Means — A280

Design: 8c, Library of Parliament.

**1971-72 Engr. *Perf. 12½x12***
*543* A280 7c sl grn 24 8
*a* Booklet pane of 5 + label (#454e, #456a + 3#543) 2.75
*b* Bklt. pane of 20 (4 #454e, 4 #456a, 12 #543) 9.25
*p* Tagged 60 22
*544* A280 8c slate 15 5
*a* Bklt. pane of 6 (3 #454e, 1 #460c, 2 #544) 2.25
*b* Bklt. pane of 18 (6 #454e, 1 #460c, 11 #544) 7.50
*c* Bklt. pane of 10 (4 #454e, 1 #460c, 5 #544 ('72) 1.90
*p* Tagged 30 16
*q* As "a," tagged 2.00
*r* As "b," tagged 6.50
*s* As "c," tagged 2.75

Coil Stamps

**1971 *Perf. 10 Horiz.***
*549* A280 7c sl grn 40 10
*a* Imperf., pair 750.00
*550* A280 8c slate 32 8
*a* Imperf., pair 200.00
*p* Tagged 30 8

See note below No. 468B.

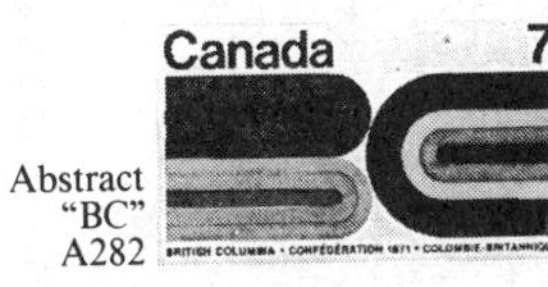


Abstract "BC" A282

**1971, July 20 Litho. *Perf. 12***
*552* A282 7c multi 18 5

Centenary of British Columbia's entry into Canadian Confederation.

Indian Encampment on Lake Huron, by Kane A283

**1971, Aug. 11 *Perf. 12½***
*553* A283 7c multi 28 10

Centenary of the death of Paul Kane (1810-1871), painter.

Snowflake A284

Pierre Laporte A285

**1971, Oct. 6 Engr. *Perf. 12***
**Size: 24x30mm.**
*554* A284 6c dk bl 14 5
*p* Tagged 18 6
*555* A284 7c brt grn 18 5
*p* Tagged 24 6

**Litho. and Engr.**
**Size: 30x30mm.**
*556* A284 10c dp car & sil 28 30
*p* Tagged 35 30
*557* A284 15c lt ultra, dp car & sil 55 65
*p* Tagged 75 75

Christmas 1971.

**1971, Oct. 20 Engr. *Perf. 12***
*558* A285 7c black 18 10

Pierre Laporte (1921-1970), Minister of Labor, kidnapped and killed.

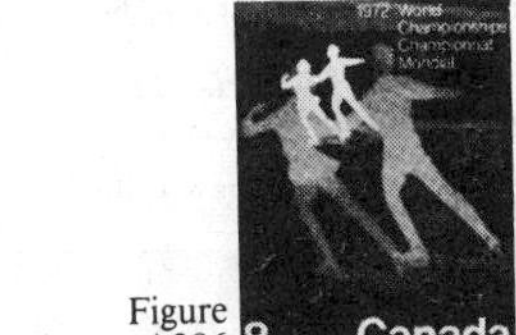


Figure Skating — A286

**1972, Mar. 1 Litho. *Perf. 12***
*559* A286 8c dp red lil 18 8

World Figure Skating Championships, Calgary, Alberta, Mar. 6-12.

"Your Heart is your Health" A287

**1972, Apr. 7 Engr. *Perf. 12x12½***
*560* A287 8c red 28 12
*p* Tagged 60 35

World Health Day, Apr. 7.

Frontenac, by Philippe Hébert and Fort Saint Louis, Quebec A288

**Photo. and Engr.**

**1972, May 17 *Perf. 12x12½***
*561* A288 8c red brn & multi 18 6
*p* Tagged 52 52

Tercentenary of the appointment of Louis de Buade, Count of Frontenac and Palluau (1622-1698), as Governor of New France.

**Indians of Canada**

Buffalo Chase, by George Catlin A289

Thunderbird, Assiniboin Pattern A290

In Nos. 562-581, the first two and last two stamps of each annual set are printed checkerwise in same sheet of 50.

**1972 Litho. *Perf. 12x12½***
*562* A289 8c *shown* 40 10
*p* Tagged 38 20
*563* A289 8c *Plains Indian artifacts* 40 10
*p* Tagged 38 20

**Photogravure and Engraved**
***Perf. 12½x12***
*564* A290 8c *shown* 40 10
*p* Tagged 38 20
*565* A290 8c *Ceremonial sun dance costume* 40 10
*p* Tagged 38 20

Honoring the Plains Indians of Canada.
Issue dates: Nos. 562-563, July 6. Nos. 564-565, Oct. 4.

Tagged (Nos. 566-581)

**1973 Litho. *Perf. 12x12½***
*566* A289 8c *Algonkian artifacts* 40 10
*567* A289 8c *"Micmac Indians"* 40 10

**Photogravure and Engraved**
***Perf. 12½x12***
*568* A290 8c *Thunderbird and belt* 32 10
*569* A290 8c *Algonkian man and woman* 32 10

Honoring the Algonkian-speaking Indians of Canada (Malecite, Micmac, Montagnais, Algonquin and Ojibwa).
Issue dates: Nos. 566-567, Feb. 21. Nos. 568-569, Nov. 28.

**1974 Litho. *Perf. 12x12½***
*570* A289 8c *Nootka Sound, house, inside* 32 10
*571* A289 8c *Artifacts* 32 10

**Photogravure and Engraved**
***Perf. 12½x12***
*572* A290 8c *Chief wearing Chilkat blanket* 32 10
*573* A290 8c *Thunderbird from Kwakiutl house* 32 10

Honoring the Pacific Coast Indians of Canada (Haida, Salish, Tsimshian, Chilkat and Kwakiutl).

Issue dates: Nos. 570-571, Jan. 16. Nos. 572-573, Feb. 22.

**1975, Apr. 4 Litho. *Perf. 13½***

574 A289 8c *Montagnais-Naskapi artifacts* 24 8
575 A289 8c *Dance of the Kutcha-Kutchin* 24 8

***Perf. 12½***

576 A290 8c *Kutchin ceremonial costume* 24 8

**Litho. and Embossed**

577 A290 8c *Ojibwa thunderbird and Naskapi pattern* 24 8

Honoring Subarctic Indians.

**1976, Sept. 17 Litho. *Perf. 13½***

578 A289 10c *Cornhusk mask, artifacts* 24 8
579 A289 10c *Iroquoian Encampment, by George Heriot* 24 8

***Perf. 12½***

**Lithographed and Engraved**

580 A290 10c *Iroquoian thunderbird* 24 8

**Litho.**

581 A290 10c *Iroquoian man, woman* 24 8
*Nos. 562-581 (20)* 6.24 1.84

Honoring the Iroquois (Mohawk, Cayuga, Seneca, Oneida, Onondaga and Tuscarora).

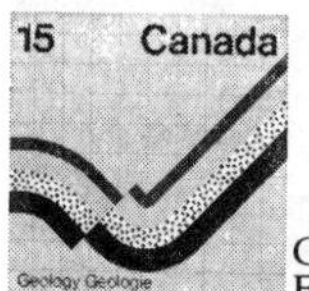

Geological Fault — A291

**1972, Aug. 2 *Perf. 12***

582 A291 15c *shown* 1.50 1.25
p Tagged 2.50 2.50
583 A291 15c *Bird's eye view of town* 1.50 1.25
p Tagged 2.50 2.50
584 A291 15c *Aerial map photography* 1.50 1.25
p Tagged 2.50 2.50
585 A291 15c *Contour lines* 1.50 1.25
p Tagged 2.50 2.50

Earth sciences: 24th International Geological Congress (No. 582); 22nd International Geographical Congress (No. 583); 12th Congress of International Society of Photogrammetry (No. 584); 6th Congress of International Cartographic Association (No. 585). Se-tenant in sheets of 16.

Sir John A. Macdonald — A292

Elizabeth II — A292a

Forest, Central Canada — A293

Vancouver, B.C. — A294

Designs: 2c, Sir Wilfrid Laurier. 3c, Sir Robert L. Borden. 4c, William Lyon Mackenzie King. 5c Richard Bedford Bennett. 6c, Lester B. Pearson. 7c, Louis St. Laurent. 15c, Mountain sheep, Western Canada. 20c, Grain fields, Prairie. 25c, Polar bears, North. 50c, Seashore. $2, Quebec.

**1972-76 Engr. *Perf. 12x12½***

**Tagged**

586 A292 1c org ('73) 5 5
a Booklet pane of 6 (3 #586, 1 #591, 2 #593) ('74) 55
b Booklet pane of 18 (6 #586, 1 #591, 11 #593) ('75) 2.10
c Booklet pane of 10 (2 #586, 4 #587, 4 #593c) ('76) 1.60
587 A292 2c grn ('73) 6 5
588 A292 3c brn ('73) 6 5
589 A292 4c blk ('73) 8 5
590 A292 5c lil ('73) 12 5
591 A292 6c dk red ('73) 14 5
592 A292 7c dk brn ('74) 14 5
593 A292a 8c ultra ('73) 14 5
b Perf. 13 x 13½ ('76) 50 12

***Perf. 13x13½***

593A A292a 10c dk car ('76) 18 5
c Perf. 12 x 12½ 22 6

***Perf. 12½x12***

**Photogravure and Engraved**

**1972-76 Engr *Perf. 12x12½***

594 A293 10c multi 18 6
595 A293 15c multi 25 8
596 A293 20c multi 35 6
597 A293 25c multi 40 6
598 A293 50c multi 80 8
599 A294 $1 multi ('73) 1.90 40

***Perf. 11***

**Lithographed and Engraved**

600 A294 $1 multi 3.75 1.40
601 A294 $2 multi 3.25 1.90
*Nos. 586-601 (17)* 11.85 4.49

No. 599 has engraved shading added in some areas.

Plates 1 and 2 of the scenic 10c differ in impression and colors. Plate 1 has distinct crosshatching of "Canada" background. On plate 2, released in 1974, this area appears solidly inked. A 1974 printing of the 50c has darker shading and a deeper tone for the dark blue areas of the photogravure impression.

Nos. 600 and 601 are untagged.

**Photogravure and Engraved**

**1976-77 *Perf. 13½***

594a A293 10c multi 22 5
595a A293 15c multi 32 5
596a A293 20c multi 50 5
597a A293 25c multi 60 5
598a A293 50c multi 1.65 10
599a A294 $1 multi ('77) 2.25 25
*Nos. 594a-599a (6)* 5.54 55

Coil Stamps

**1974-76 *Perf. 10 Vert.***

604 A292a 8c ultra 20 5
605 A292a 10c dk car ('76) 28 8

See note below No. 468B. No. 604 also exists in horizontal multiples without score line.

Candles A295

Candles and Fruit A296

Christmas: 8c, Like 6c. 15c, Candles, 15th century prayer book, boxes and brass vase.

**1972, Nov. 1 Litho. *Perf. 12½x12***

606 A295 6c red & multi 16 5
p Tagged 25 25
607 A295 8c vio bl & multi 20 5
p Tagged 30 25

***Perf. 11***

608 A296 10c grn & multi 45 38
p Tagged 60 60
609 A296 15c yel bis & multi 70 65
p Tagged 1.10 1.25

"The Blacksmith's Shop," by Krieghoff A297

**1972, Nov. 29 Litho. *Perf. 12½***

610 A297 8c multi 22 10
p Tagged 24 15

Centenary of the death of Cornelius Krieghoff (1815-1872), painter.

---

Tagged
From No. 611 onward, all stamps are tagged unless otherwise noted.

---

Monsignor de Laval — A298

**1973, Jan. 31 Litho. *Perf. 11***

611 A298 8c sil, ultra & gold 18 8

350th anniversary of the birth of François-Xavier de Montmorency-Laval de Montigny (1623-1708), first Bishop of Quebec and founder of many educational institutions; one of the builders of New France.

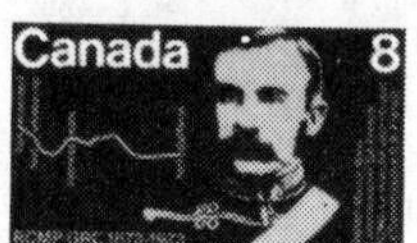

Commissioner G. A. French and Map of 1874 Trek — A299

Designs: 10c, Spectrograph. 15c, R.C.M.P. Musical Ride.

**1973, Mar. 9 Litho. *Perf. 11***

612 A299 8c dk brn, org & red 22 8
613 A299 10c dk bl & multi 38 20
614 A299 15c yel grn & multi 75 38
a Imperf., pair 500.00

Centenary of the Royal Canadian Mounted Police.

Jeanne Mance A300

Joseph Howe A301

**1973, Apr. 18**

615 A300 8c multi 18 8

300th anniversary of death of Jeanne Mance (1606-1673), first secular nurse in North America and founder of first hospital, the Hotel-Dieu in Montreal settlement.

**1973, May 16 Litho. *Perf. 11***

616 A301 8c gold & blk 18 8

Centenary of the death of Joseph Howe (1804-1873), journalist, poet and Lieutenant-Governor of Nova Scotia.

Mist Fantasy, by James MacDonald — A302

**1973, June 8 Litho. *Perf. 12½***

617 A302 15c multi 45 45

Centenary of the birth of James E. H. MacDonald (1873-1932), painter.

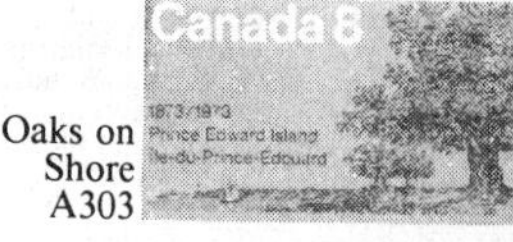

Oaks on Shore A303

**Photo. and Engr.**

**1973, June 22 *Perf. 12x12½***

618 A303 8c org & red brn 18 8

Centenary of Prince Edward Island's entry into Confederation.

Scottish Settlers and "Hector" A304

**1973, July 20 Litho. *Perf. 12x12½***

619 A304 8c multi 18 8

Bicentenary of arrival of Scottish settlers at Pictou, N.S.

Queen Elizabeth II — A305

**1973, Aug. 2 Photo. and Engr.**

620 A305 8c sil & multi 27 8
621 A305 15c gold & multi 80 48

Visit to Ottawa of Queen Elizabeth II and the Duke of Edinburgh, July 31-Aug. 4, and meeting of Commonwealth Heads of Government, Ottawa, Aug. 2-10.

Nellie McClung A306

Montreal Olympic Games A307

**1973, Aug. 29 Litho. *Perf. 10½x11***

622 A306 8c multi 18 8

Centenary of the birth of Nellie McClung (1873-1951), leader of women's suffrage movement, social reformer and writer.

**1973, Sept. 20 Litho. *Perf. 12x12½***

**Size: 26x44mm.**

623 A307 8c sil & multi 16 8
624 A307 15c gold & multi 60 30

21st Olympic Games, Montreal, 1976.
See Nos. B1-B3.

Ice Skate
A308

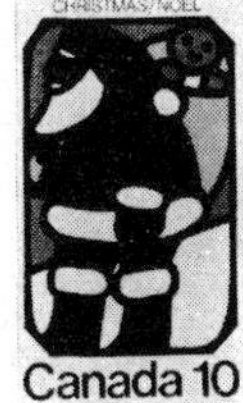

Santa Claus
A309

**1973, Nov. 7 Litho. *Perf. 12½x12***

*625* A308 6c *shown* 12 5
*626* A308 8c *Dove* 15 5

***Perf. 10½***

*627* A309 10c *shown* 24 24
*628* A309 15c *Shepherd and star* 50 50

Christmas 1973.

Children Diving from Dock — A310

**1974, Mar. 22 Engr. *Perf. 12***

*629* A310 8c *shown* 22 10
*630* A310 8c *Joggers* 22 10
*631* A310 8c *Bicycling family* 22 10
*632* A310 8c *Hikers* 22 10

"Keep Fit." 21st Summer Olympic Games, Montreal, 1976. When stamps are observed at an angle the Montreal Olympic Games' emblem can be seen. Se-tenant in sheets of 50 (10x5).

Main St. and Portage Ave., Winnipeg, 1872 — A311

**Litho. and Engr.**

**1974, May 3 *Perf. 12x12½***

*633* A311 8c multi 18 8

Centenary of Winnipeg's incorporation as a city.

Postmaster A312

**1974, June 11 Litho. *Perf. 13½x13***

*634* A312 8c *shown* 35 20
*635* A312 8c *Mail collector and truck* 35 20
*636* A312 8c *Mail handler* 35 20
*637* A312 8c *Mail sorters* 35 20
*638* A312 8c *Mailman* 35 20
*639* A312 8c *Rural mail delivery* 35 20
*a* Block of 6, #634-639 2.50 2.50
*Nos. 634-639 (6)* 2.10 1.20

Centenary of letter carrier delivery service. Nos. 634-639 printed se-tenant in sheets of 50 (5x10).

Agricultural Education — A313

**1974, July 12 Litho. *Perf. 12½x12***

*640* A313 8c multi 24 8

Ontario Agricultural College centenary.

Pedestal, Gallows Frame and Contempra Telephones A314

**1974, July 26 *Perf. 12½***

*641* A314 8c multi 24 8

Centenary of the idea for the telephone by Alexander Graham Bell while visiting Brantford, Canada.

Bicycle Wheel and Cycling Emblem A315

**Photo. and Engr.**

**1974, Aug. 7 *Perf. 12x12½***

*642* A315 8c blk, red & sil 24 8

World Cycling Championships, Montreal, Aug. 14-25.

Mennonite Settlers A316

**1974, Aug. 28 Litho. *Perf. 12x12½***

*643* A316 8c multi 24 8

Centenary of arrival of Mennonite settlers in Manitoba.

Snowshoeing A317

**1974, Sept. 23 Engr. *Perf. 13½***

*644* A317 8c *shown* 25 15
*645* A317 8c *Skiing* 25 15
*646* A317 8c *Skating* 25 15
*647* A317 8c *Curling* 25 15

"Keep Fit." 1976 Winter Olympic Games. When the stamps are observed at an angle the Montreal Olympic Games' emblem can be seen. Se-tenant in sheets of 50.

Mercury with Winged Horses, UPU Emblem A318

**Photo. and Engr**

**1974, Oct. 9 *Perf. 12x12½***

*648* A318 8c vio, red & bl 18 8
*649* A318 15c vio, red & bl 70 50

Centenary of Universal Postal Union.

Nativity, by Jean Paul Lemieux A319

Skaters at Hull, by Henri Masson — A320

Paintings: 10c, The Ice Cone, Montmorency Falls, by Robert C. Todd. 15c, Village in the Laurentian Mountains, by Clarence A. Gagnon.

**1974, Nov. 1 Litho. *Perf. 13½***

*650* A319 6c multi 12 5
*651* A320 8c multi 15 5
*652* A319 10c multi 30 18
*653* A319 15c multi 50 35

Christmas 1974.

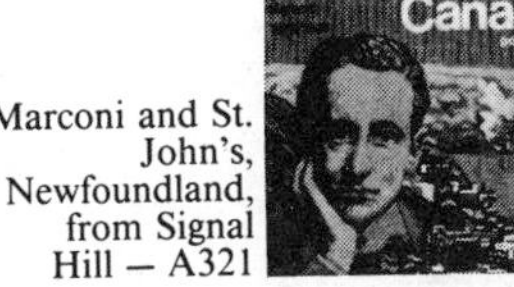

Marconi and St. John's, Newfoundland, from Signal Hill — A321

**1974, Nov. 15 Litho. *Perf. 13***

*654* A321 8c multi 18 8

Centenary of the birth of Guglielmo Marconi (1874-1937), Italian electrical engineer and inventor.

Merritt and Welland Canal A322

**Litho. and Engr.**

**1974, Nov. 29 *Perf. 13x13½***

*655* A322 8c multi 18 8

Sesquicentennial of the start of construction of the Welland Canal between Lakes Ontario and Erie, a project conceived and supervised by William Hamilton Merritt (1793-1862). Portrait by Robert Whale.

The Sprinter A323

The Plunger A324

Designs: Sculptures by Robert Tait McKenzie, M.D. (1867-1938), and Montreal Olympic Games' emblem.

***Perf. 12½x12, 12x12½***

**1975, Mar. 14 Litho.; Embossed**

*656* A323 $1 multi 2.75 2.00
*657* A324 $2 multi 5.25 4.25

21st Olympic Games, Montreal, July 17-Aug. 1, 1976.

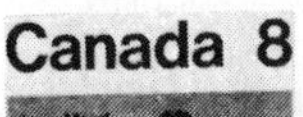

Anne of Green Gables A325

Maria Chapdelaine A326

**1975, May 15 Litho. *Perf. 13***

*658* A325 8c bl & multi 18 8
*659* A326 8c brn & multi 18 8

Birth centenary of Lucy Maud Montgomery (1874-1942), writer and author of "Anne of Green Gables"; Louis Hemon (1880-1913), writer and author of "Maria Chapdelaine." Nos. 658-659 printed checkerwise in sheets of 50 (10x5).

Illustration of Anne by Peter Swan, of Maria by Clarence Gagnon.

Marguerite Bourgeoys A327

Alphonse Desjardins A328

**1975, May 30 Litho. *Perf. 12½x12***

*660* A327 8c red & multi 18 8
*661* A328 8c red & multi 18 8

Marguerite Bourgeoys (1620-1700), founder of the Congregation de Notre-Dame, Montreal, first girls' school in New France; Alphonse Desjardins (1854-1920), journalist, founder of first credit union in North America.

Samuel Dwight Chown — A329

John Cook — A330

**Photo. and Engr.**

**1975, May 30 *Perf. 12x12½***

*662* A329 8c dk brn, yel & buff 18 8
*663* A330 8c dk brn, yel & buff 18 8

Samuel Dwight Chown (1853-1933), Methodist minister, leader of temperance movement, founder of United Church. Dr. John Cook (1805-1892), First Moderator of the United Presbyterian Church in Canada.

Nos. 662-663 printed checkerwise in sheets of 50 (10x5).

Pole Vaulting — A331

Hurdling — A332

Design: 25c, Marathon running and Montreal Olympic Games' emblem.

**1975, June 11 Litho. *Perf. 12x12½***

*664* A331 20c dk bl & multi 55 50
*665* A331 25c mar & multi 65 55
*666* A331 50c multi 1.25 1.00

21st Olympic Games, Montreal, July 17-Aug. 1, 1976.

"Untamed" (Wild Horse Race) A333

**1975, July 3** *Perf. 12x12½*

*667* A333 8c gray & multi 18 8

Centenary of the founding of Calgary.

Female Symbol A334

"Justice," by Walter S. Allward A335

**Photogravure and Engraved**

**1975, July 14** *Perf. 13*

*668* A334 8c dp yel, gray & blk 18 8

International Women's Year.

**1975, Sept. 2 Litho.** *Perf. 12½*

*669* A335 8c multi 18 8

Supreme Court of Canada, centenary.

"Wm. D. Lawrence" A336

**Photogravure and Engraved**

**1975, Sept. 24** *Perf. 13*

| | | | |
|---|---|---|---|
| *670* A336 8c *shown* | 45 | 35 |
| *671* A336 8c *"Beaver"* | 45 | 35 |
| *672* A336 8c *"Neptune"* | 45 | 35 |
| *673* A336 8c *"Quadra"* | 45 | 35 |

Coastal ships. Nos. 670-673 printed se-tenant in sheets of 50 (5x10).

Santa Claus — A337

Child — A338

Trees — A339

Designs by Canadian School Children: "What Christmas Means to Me."

**1975, Oct. 22 Litho.** *Perf. 13½*

| | | |
|---|---|---|
| *674* A337 6c *shown* | 12 | 7 |
| *675* A337 6c *Skater* | 12 | 7 |
| *676* A338 8c *shown* | 15 | 7 |
| *677* A338 8c *Family and Christmas tree* | 15 | 7 |
| *678* A338 10c *Gift box* | 20 | 20 |
| *679* A339 15c *shown* | 40 | 40 |
| *Nos. 674-679 (6)* | 1.14 | 88 |

Christmas 1975.

Stamps of same denomination printed checkerwise in sheets of 50.

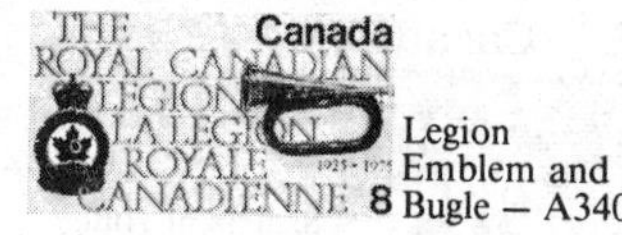

Legion Emblem and Bugle — A340

**Photogravure and Engraved**

**1975, Nov. 10** *Perf. 13*

*680* A340 8c gray & multi 18 8

Royal Canadian Legion, 50th anniversary.

Olympic Torch Ignited by Satellite in Canada A341

Communication Arts — A342

High-rise Tower, Notre Dame Church, Montreal, and Games' Emblem — A343

Snowflake, Winter Olympics' Emblem — A344

Designs (Montreal Olympic Games' Emblem and): 20c, Canadian athletes carrying Olympic flag. 25c, Women athletes receiving Olympic medals.

**1976, June 18 Litho.** *Perf. 13*

| | | |
|---|---|---|
| *681* A341 8c blk & multi | 10 | 7 |
| *682* A341 20c blk & multi | 45 | 35 |
| *683* A341 25c blk & multi | 55 | 55 |

1976 Olympic Games ceremonies.

**1976, Feb. 6 Photo.** *Perf. 12x12½*

Designs: 25c, Handicraft tools. 50c, Performing arts.

| | | |
|---|---|---|
| *684* A342 20c gray & multi | 80 | 38 |
| *685* A342 25c ocher & multi | 90 | 45 |
| *686* A342 50c bl & multi | 1.50 | 80 |

Olympic Fine Arts and Cultural Program.

**Photogravure and Engraved**

**1976, Mar. 12** *Perf. 13*

Design: $2, Olympic Stadium, Velodrome, flags and emblem.

| | | |
|---|---|---|
| *687* A343 $1 sil & multi | 2.75 | 2.00 |
| *688* A343 $2 gold & multi | 5.25 | 4.25 |

Nos. 681-688 were issued in commemoration of, or in connection with the 21st Olympic Games, Montreal, July 17-Aug. 1. Nos. 687-688 were issued in panes of 8.

**Photo. and Embossed**

**1976, Feb. 6** *Perf. 12½*

*689* A344 20c multi 90 45

12th Winter Olympic Games, Innsbruck, Austria, Feb. 4-15.

Flower Growing from City — A345

**1976, May 12 Litho.** *Perf. 12x12½*

*690* A345 20c multi 42 40

Habitat, U.N. Conference on Human Settlements, Vancouver, May 31-June 11.

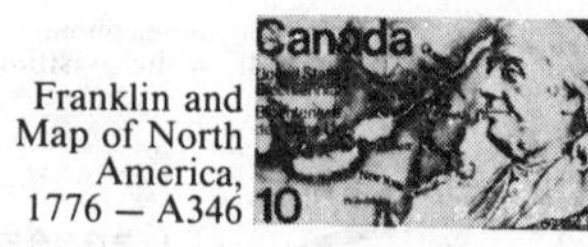

Franklin and Map of North America, 1776 — A346

**Lithographed and Engraved**

**1976, June 1** *Perf. 13*

*691* A346 10c multi 22 14

American Bicentennial; Benjamin Franklin (1706-1790), deputy postmaster general for the colonies (1753-1774).

See U.S. No. 1690.

Color Parade, Memorial Arch — A347

Wing Parade, Mackenzie Building — A348

**1976, June 1 Litho.** *Perf. 12*

| | | |
|---|---|---|
| *692* A347 8c red & multi | 15 | 8 |
| *693* A348 8c red & multi | 15 | 8 |

Royal Military College, Kingston, Ont., centenary.

Archer in Wheelchair A349

**1976, Aug. 3 Litho.** *Perf. 12x12½*

*694* A349 20c grn & multi 45 42

Olympiad for the Physically Disabled (25th Stoke Mandeville Games), Toronto, Aug. 3-11.

The Cremation of Sam McGee A350

The Outlander A351

**1976, Aug. 17** *Perf. 13½*

| | | |
|---|---|---|
| *695* A350 8c multi | 15 | 8 |
| *696* A351 8c multi | 15 | 8 |

Robert W. Service (1874-1958), author of poem "The Cremation of Sam McGee"; Germaine Guevremont, author of "Le Survenant" (The Outlander). Nos. 695-696 printed se-tenant in sheets of 50 (10x5).

Illustration of the Cremation by David Bierk, of The Outlander by Antoine Dumas.

Nativity, St. Michael's, Toronto — A352

Nativity, Stained-glass windows: 10c, St. Jude, London, Ontario. 20c, Designed and owned by Yvonne Williams.

**1976, Nov. 3 Litho.** *Perf. 13½*

| | | |
|---|---|---|
| *697* A352 8c multi | 12 | 5 |
| *698* A352 10c multi | 15 | 5 |
| *699* A352 20c multi | 40 | 60 |

Christmas 1976.

Northcote A353

Inland Vessels: No. 701, Chicora. No. 702, Passport. No. 703, Athabasca.

**Lithographed and Engraved**

**1976, Nov. 19** *Perf. 12*

| | | |
|---|---|---|
| *700* A353 10c shown | 32 | 25 |
| *701* A353 10c Chicora | 32 | 25 |
| *702* A353 10c Passport | 32 | 25 |
| *703* A353 10c Athabasca | 32 | 25 |

Nos. 700-703 printed se-tenant in sheets of 50 with various combination possible. Nos. 700 and 702 alternate in first row, Nos. 701 and 703 in next.

Queen Elizabeth II — A354

**Litho. and Typo.**

**1977, Feb. 4** *Perf. 12½x12*

*704* A354 25c sil & multi 70 40

25th anniv. of the reign of Elizabeth II.

Bottle Gentian — A355

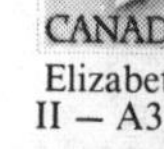

Elizabeth II — A356

Parliament, Ottawa A357

Trembling Aspen A358

Main Street, Prairie Town — A359

*Canada stamps can be mounted in Scott's annually supplemented Master Canada Album.*

Fundy National Park — A359a

Designs: 2c, Western columbine. 3c, Canada lily. 4c, Hepatica. 5c, Shooting star. 10c, Franklin's lady's-slipper. No. 712, Jewelweed. No. 715, Parliament, Ottawa. No. 716, Queen Elizabeth II. 20c, Douglas fir. 25c, Maple. 30c, Red oak.

75c, Old houses, eastern City Street. 80c, Street leading to the sea, Eastern Maritime Provinces.

**Lithographed and Engraved**

**1977-79** ***Perf. 12x12½***

| No. | Type | Description | Unused | Used |
|---|---|---|---|---|
| *705* | A355 | 1c multi | 5 | 5 |
| *707* | A355 | 2c multi | 6 | 5 |
| *708* | A355 | 3c multi | 6 | 5 |
| *709* | A355 | 4c multi | 6 | 5 |
| *710* | A355 | 5c multi | 6 | 5 |
| *711* | A355 | 10c multi | 12 | 6 |
| a | | Perf. 13 ('78) | 12 | 6 |

**Photo. & Engr.**

***Perf. 13x13½***

| No. | Type | Description | Unused | Used |
|---|---|---|---|---|
| *712* | A355 | 12c multi ('78) | 35 | 6 |
| *713* | A356 | 12c bl & multi | 20 | 5 |
| a | | Perf. 12 x 12½ | 35 | 6 |

**Engraved**

***Perf. 13***

| No. | Type | Description | Unused | Used |
|---|---|---|---|---|
| *714* | A357 | 12c blue | 18 | 5 |
| *715* | A357 | 14c red ('78) | 18 | 5 |

**Photo. & Engr.**

***Perf. 13x13½***

| No. | Type | Description | Unused | Used |
|---|---|---|---|---|
| *716* | A356 | 14c red & blk ('78) | 18 | 5 |
| a | | Perf. 12x12½ | 20 | 6 |
| b | | As "a," bklt. pane of 25 + 2 labels ('78) | 7.50 | |
| c | | Red omitted | *1,000.* | |

***Perf. 13½***

| No. | Type | Description | Unused | Used |
|---|---|---|---|---|
| *717* | A358 | 15c multi | 35 | 10 |
| *718* | A358 | 20c multi | 24 | 6 |
| *719* | A358 | 25c multi | 40 | 8 |
| *720* | A358 | 30c multi ('78) | 45 | 12 |
| *721* | A358 | 35c multi ('79) | 45 | 20 |
| *723* | A359 | 50c multi ('78) | 90 | 15 |
| *723A* | A359 | 50c multi, litho. & engr. ('78) | 75 | 15 |
| *724* | A359 | 75c multi ('78) | 1.10 | 22 |
| *725* | A359 | 80c multi ('78) | 1.10 | 24 |

**Lithographed and Engraved**

***Perf. 13***

| No. | Type | Description | Unused | Used |
|---|---|---|---|---|
| *726* | A359a | $1 multi ('79) | 1.25 | 45 |
| a | | Untagged | 1.40 | 60 |
| *727* | A359a | $2 Kluane Natl. Park ('79) | 2.50 | 1.10 |
| | | *Nos. 705-727 (22)* | 10.99 | 3.44 |

On No. 723A license plate on yellow car reads "1978." See Nos. 781-806, 1084.

Coil Stamps

**1977-78** **Engr.** ***Perf. 10 Vert.***

| No. | Type | Description | Unused | Used |
|---|---|---|---|---|
| *729* | A357 | 12c blue | 20 | 8 |
| a | | Imperf., pair | 100.00 | |
| *730* | A357 | 14c red ('78) | 22 | 8 |
| a | | Imperf., pair | 100.00 | |

See note below No. 468B.

Eastern Cougar A360

**1977, Mar. 30** **Litho.** ***Perf. 12½***

| No. | Type | Description | Unused | Used |
|---|---|---|---|---|
| *732* | A360 | 12c multi | 20 | 8 |

Wildlife protection.

April in Algonquin Park, by Thomson — A361

Design: No. 734, Autumn Birches, by Tom Thomson.

**1977, May 26** **Litho.** ***Perf. 12***

| No. | Type | Description | Unused | Used |
|---|---|---|---|---|
| *733* | A361 | 12c blk & multi | 20 | 10 |
| *734* | A361 | 12c ocher & multi | 20 | 10 |

Tom Thomson (1877-1917), landscape painter, birth centenary. Nos. 733-734 printed checkerwise in sheets of 50 (10x5).

Names of Governors General and Standard A362

**1977, June 30** ***Perf. 12½***

| No. | Type | Description | Unused | Used |
|---|---|---|---|---|
| *735* | A362 | 12c vio bl & multi | 20 | 8 |

Honoring Canadian-born Governors General: Vincent Massey, Georges Philias Vanier, Daniel Roland Michener and Jules Léger.

Order of Canada A363

**1977, June 30** **Litho. & Embossed**

| No. | Type | Description | Unused | Used |
|---|---|---|---|---|
| *736* | A363 | 12c multi | 20 | 8 |

Order of Canada, 10th anniversary.

Peace Bridge, Canadian, U.S. and U.N. Flags A364

**1977, Aug. 4** **Litho.** ***Perf. 12½***

| No. | Type | Description | Unused | Used |
|---|---|---|---|---|
| *737* | A364 | 12c bl & multi | 20 | 8 |

50th anniversary of the Peace Bridge, connecting Fort Erie, Ontario, with Buffalo, N.Y.

Joseph E. Bernier, CGS Arctic A365

Sandford Fleming, Railroad Bridge A366

**1977, Sept. 16** **Engr.** ***Perf. 13***

| No. | Type | Description | Unused | Used |
|---|---|---|---|---|
| *738* | A365 | 12c dk bl | 20 | 10 |
| *739* | A366 | 12c brown | 20 | 10 |

Joseph-Elzéar Bernier (1852-1934), explorer; Sandford Fleming (1827-1915), mapped route for Intercolonial Railway and designed Canada's first stamp.

Nos. 738-739 printed checkerwise in sheets of 50 (5x10).

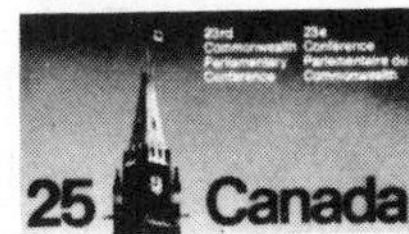

Peace Tower, Parliament, Ottawa A367

**1977, Sept. 19** **Litho.** ***Perf. 12½***

| No. | Type | Description | Unused | Used |
|---|---|---|---|---|
| *740* | A367 | 25c multi | 52 | 60 |

23rd Commonwealth Parliamentary Conference, Ottawa, Sept. 19-25.

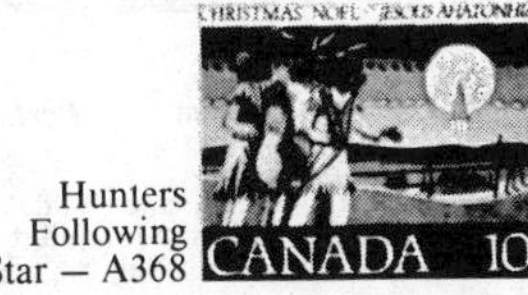

Hunters Following Star — A368

Designs: 12c, Angelic choir in northern light. 25c, Christ Child in Ring of Glory blessing chiefs from afar. Illustrations for Canada's first Christmas carol, written by Father Brebeuf, 1649.

**1977, Oct. 26** **Litho.** ***Perf. 13½***

| No. | Type | Description | Unused | Used |
|---|---|---|---|---|
| *741* | A368 | 10c multi | 15 | 8 |
| *742* | A368 | 12c multi | 18 | 8 |
| *743* | A368 | 25c multi | 35 | 35 |

Christmas 1977.

Pinky A369

Designs: Canadian sailing ships.

**Litho. and Engr.**

**1977, Nov. 18** ***Perf. 12x12½***

**Light Brown & Multicolored**

| No. | Type | Description | Unused | Used |
|---|---|---|---|---|
| *744* | A369 | 12c *shown* | 20 | 15 |
| *745* | A369 | 12c *Tern schooner* | 20 | 15 |
| *746* | A369 | 12c *5-masted schooner* | 20 | 15 |
| *747* | A369 | 12c *Mackinaw boat* | 20 | 15 |

Nos. 744-747 printed se-tenant vertically in sheets of 50 (5x10); Nos. 744, 746 alternate in one horizontal row, Nos. 745, 747 in next.

Seal Hunter, Soapstone Sculpture A370

Disguised Caribou Hunter, Print — A371

Designs (Inuit Art): No. 749, Spear fishing. No. 751, Walrus hunt. Nos. 749-751 are after stonecut prints.

**1977, Nov. 18** **Litho.** ***Perf. 12x12½***

| No. | Type | Description | Unused | Used |
|---|---|---|---|---|
| *748* | A370 | 12c multi | 20 | 15 |
| *749* | A371 | 12c multi | 20 | 15 |
| *750* | A371 | 12c multi | 20 | 15 |
| *751* | A371 | 12c multi | 20 | 15 |

Inuit hunting. Nos. 748-749 and Nos. 750-751 printed se-tenant checkerwise in sheets of 50 (5x10).

Peregrine Falcon A372

**1978, Jan. 18** **Litho.** ***Perf. 12½***

| No. | Type | Description | Unused | Used |
|---|---|---|---|---|
| *752* | A372 | 12c multi | 20 | 8 |

Endangered wildlife.

Canada No. 3, 1851 — A373

**1978** **Photo. & Engr.** ***Perf. 13½***

| No. | Type | Description | Unused | Used |
|---|---|---|---|---|
| *753* | A373 | 12c shown | 14 | 5 |
| *754* | A373 | 14c No. 7 | 18 | 6 |
| *755* | A373 | 30c No. 8 | 42 | 22 |
| *756* | A373 | $1.25 No. 2 | 1.65 | 65 |
| a | | Souvenir sheet of 3 | 2.00 | |

CAPEX '78, Canadian Intl. Phil. Exhib., Toronto, June 9-18 (cent. of Canada's admission to UPU).

No. 756a contains one each of Nos. 754-756 ($1.25 untagged); silver margin with black inscription. Size: 99x76mm.

Issue dates: 12c, Jan. 18. Others, June 10.

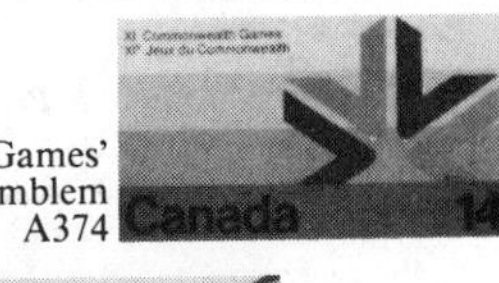

Games' Emblem A374

Stadium A375

Design: 30c, Badminton.

**1978, Mar. 31** **Litho.** ***Perf. 12½***

| No. | Type | Description | Unused | Used |
|---|---|---|---|---|
| *757* | A374 | 14c sil & multi | 24 | 10 |
| *758* | A374 | 30c sil & multi | 52 | 35 |

**1978, Aug. 3**

Designs: No. 760, Running. No. 761, Alberta Legislature building, Edmonton. No. 762, Bowls.

| No. | Type | Description | Unused | Used |
|---|---|---|---|---|
| *759* | A375 | 14c sil & multi | 20 | 8 |
| *760* | A375 | 14c sil & multi | 20 | 8 |
| *761* | A375 | 30c sil & multi | 50 | 35 |
| *762* | A375 | 30c sil & multi | 50 | 35 |

Nos. 757-762 commemorate 11th Commonwealth Games, Edmonton, Aug. 3-12.

Stamps of same denomination printed checkerwise in sheets of 50.

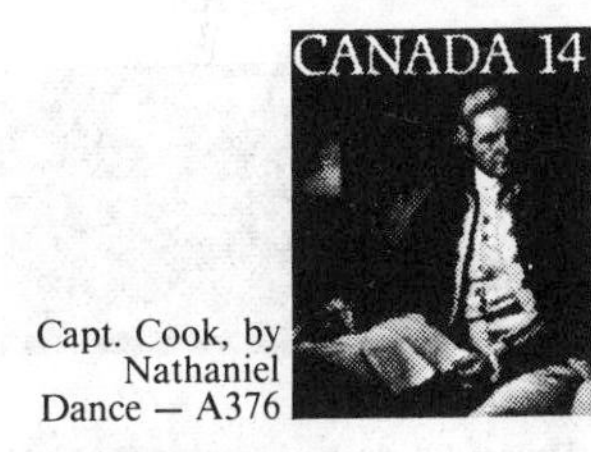

Capt. Cook, by Nathaniel Dance — A376

Nootka Sound, by John Webber — A377

**1978, Apr. 26** **Litho.** ***Perf. 13***

| No. | Type | Description | Unused | Used |
|---|---|---|---|---|
| *763* | A376 | 14c multi | 20 | 10 |
| *764* | A377 | 14c multi | 20 | 10 |

Capt. James Cook (1728-1779), explorer of Canada's East and West Coasts and bicentenary of his anchorage near Anchorage, June 1, 1778. Nos. 763-764 printed checkerwise in sheets of 50.

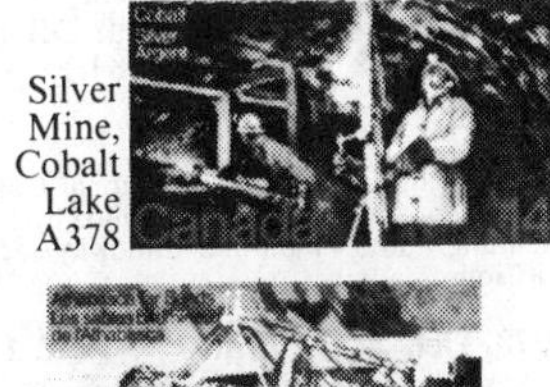

Silver Mine, Cobalt Lake A378

Stripmining, Athabasca Tar Sands — A379

**1978, May 19** **Litho.** ***Perf. 12½***

| No. | Type | Description | Unused | Used |
|---|---|---|---|---|
| *765* | A378 | 14c multi | 20 | 10 |
| *766* | A379 | 14c multi | 20 | 10 |

Development of national resources. Nos. 765-766 printed checkerwise in sheets of 50.

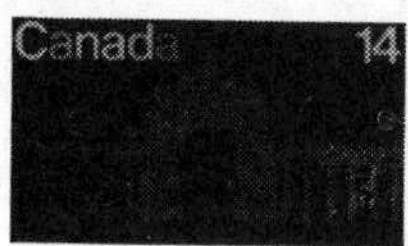

Prince's Gate A380

**1978, Aug. 16 Litho. *Perf. 12½***

| | | |
|---|---|---|
| *767* A380 14c multi | 20 | 10 |

Canadian National Exhibition, centenary.

Mère d'Youville and Miracle of Food — A381

**1978, Sept. 21 Litho. *Perf. 13x13½***

| | | |
|---|---|---|
| *768* A381 14c multi | 20 | 10 |

Marguerite d'Youville (1701-1771), founder of the Gray Nuns, beatified 1959.

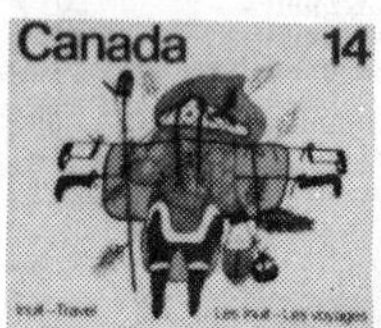

Woman Walking, by Pitseolak A382

Migration, Soapstone by Joe Talurinili A383

Designs (Works by Eskimo Artists): No. 771, Plane over village, stonecut and stencil print by Pudlo. No. 772, Dogteam and sled, ivory sculpture by Abraham Kingmeatook.

**1978, Sept. 27 *Perf. 13½***

| | | |
|---|---|---|
| *769* A382 14c multi | 22 | 14 |
| *770* A383 14c multi | 22 | 14 |
| *771* A382 14c multi | 22 | 14 |
| *772* A383 14c multi | 22 | 14 |

Travels of the Inuit. Nos. 769-770 and 771-772 printed se-tenant checkerwise in sheets of 50.

Madonna of the Flowering Pea, Cologne School — A384

Renaissance Paintings in National Gallery of Canada: 14c, Virgin and Child, by Hans Memling. 30c, Virgin and Child, by Jacopo Di Cione.

**1978, Oct. 20 Litho. *Perf. 12½***

| | | |
|---|---|---|
| *773* A384 12c multi | 15 | 8 |
| *774* A384 14c multi | 20 | 8 |
| *775* A384 30c multi | 45 | 28 |

Christmas 1978.

"Chief Justice Robinson," 1842 A385

**Lithographed and Engraved**

**1978, Nov. 15 *Perf. 13***

| | | |
|---|---|---|
| *776* A385 14c *shown* | 22 | 15 |
| *777* A385 14c *"St. Roch,"* 1928 | 22 | 15 |
| *778* A385 14c *"Northern Light," 1928* | 22 | 15 |
| *779* A385 14c *"Labrador," 1954* | 22 | 15 |

Ice vessels. Nos. 776-779 printed setenant in sheets of 50 (5x10).

Quebec Carnival — A386

**1979, Feb. 1 Litho. *Perf. 13***

| | | |
|---|---|---|
| *780* A386 14c multi | 22 | 10 |

Flower, Queen & Parliament Types of 1977

Designs: 1c, Bottle gentian. 2c, Western columbine. 3c, Canada lily. 4c, Hepatica. 5c, Shooting star. 10c, Franklin's lady's-slipper. 15c, Canada violet. No. 789, Elizabeth II. No. 790, Parliament, Ottawa.

**Photo. & Engr., (#790)**

**1977-83 *Perf. 13x13½***

| | | |
|---|---|---|
| *781* A355 1c multi ('79) | 5 | 5 |
| *a* Perf. 12x12½ ('77) | 5 | 5 |
| *b* Bklt. pane of 6 (2 #781a, 4 #713a) | 1.50 | |
| *782* A355 2c multi (79) | 5 | 5 |
| *a* Bklt. pane of 7 (4 #782, 3 #716a, label) | 1.00 | |
| *b* Perf. 12x12½ ('78) | 5 | 5 |
| *783* A355 3c multi ('79) | 6 | 5 |
| *784* A355 4c multi ('79) | 8 | 5 |
| *785* A355 5c multi ('79) | 10 | 5 |
| *786* A355 10c multi ('79) | 14 | 10 |
| *787* A355 15c multi ('79) | 24 | 15 |
| *789* A356 17c grn & blk ('79) | 24 | 5 |
| *a* Perf. 12x12½ | 28 | 8 |
| *b* Bklt. pane of 25 + 2 labels | 7.50 | |
| *790* A357 17c sl grn ('79) | 24 | 5 |
| *791* A356 30c multi ('82) | 45 | 5 |
| *792* A356 32c multi ('83) | 45 | 5 |

Nos. 781a, 782b, 789a are from booklet panes. No. 782b has one straight edge, others one or two.

Booklet Stamps

Parliament Type of 1977

**1979, Mar. 28 Engr. *Perf. 12x12½***

| | | |
|---|---|---|
| *797* A357 1c sl bl | 5 | 5 |
| *a* Bklt. pane of 6 (1 #797, 3 #800, 2 #789a) | 1.00 | |
| *800* A357 5c vio brn | 15 | 8 |

Nos. 797, 800 are from booklet panes. No. 797 has one straight edge, No. 800 has one or two.

Coil Stamp

**1979, Mar. 8 Engr. *Perf. 10 Vert.***

| | | |
|---|---|---|
| *806* A357 17c sl grn | 28 | 5 |
| *a* Imperf., pair | 200.00 | |

Endangered Wildlife — A392

**1979, Apr. 10 Litho. *Perf. 12½***

| | | |
|---|---|---|
| *813* A392 17c Turtle | 22 | 9 |
| *814* A392 35c Whale | 60 | 35 |

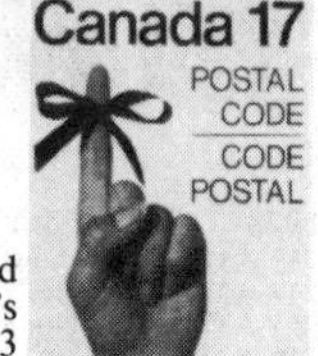

Ribbon Around Woman's Finger — A393

Design: No. 816, String around man's finger.

**1979, Apr. 10**

| | | |
|---|---|---|
| *815* A393 17c multi | 28 | 8 |
| *816* A393 17c multi | 28 | 8 |

Use postal code. Nos. 815-816 printed checkerwise in sheets of 50 (10x5).

Fruits of the Earth, by F. P. Grove — A394

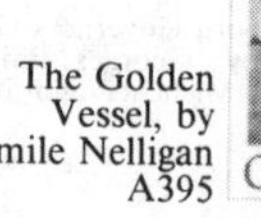

The Golden Vessel, by Emile Nelligan A395

**1979, May 3 Litho. *Perf. 13x13½***

| | | |
|---|---|---|
| *817* A394 17c multi | 28 | 10 |
| *818* A395 17c multi | 28 | 10 |

Frederick Philip Grove (1879-1948), teacher and writer; Emile Nelligan (1879-1941), French-Canadian poet. Nos. 817-818 printed se-tenant checkerwise in sheets of 50.

De Salaberry A396

John By A397

**1979, May 11 *Perf. 13½***

| | | |
|---|---|---|
| *819* A396 17c multi | 28 | 10 |
| *820* A397 17c multi | 28 | 10 |

Charles-Michel d'Irumberry de Salaberry (1778-1829), and John By (1779-1836), Canadian colonels. Nos. 819-820 printed se-tenant checkerwise in sheets of 50.

Flag of Ontario — A398

Designs: Provincial and Territorial flags.

**1979, June 15 Litho. *Perf. 13***

| | | |
|---|---|---|
| *821* A398 17c *shown* | 32 | 20 |
| *822* A398 17c *Quebec* | 32 | 20 |
| *823* A398 17c *Nova Scotia* | 32 | 20 |
| *824* A398 17c *New Brunswick* | 32 | 20 |
| *825* A398 17c *Manitoba* | 32 | 20 |
| *826* A398 17c *British Columbia* | 32 | 20 |
| *827* A398 17c *Prince Edward Island* | 32 | 20 |
| *828* A398 17c *Saskatchewan* | 32 | 20 |
| *829* A398 17c *Alberta* | 32 | 20 |
| *830* A398 17c *Newfoundland* | 32 | 20 |
| *831* A398 17c *Northwest Territories* | 32 | 20 |
| *832* A398 17c *Yukon Territory* | 32 | 20 |
| *a* Sheet of 12 | 4.00 | |
| *Nos. 821-832 (12)* | 3.84 | 2.40 |

Printed se-tenant in sheets of 12 (3x4).

White Water Kayak Race A399

**1979, July 3 Litho. *Perf. 12½***

| | | |
|---|---|---|
| *833* A399 17c multi | 28 | 10 |

Canoe-Kayak (Slalom and Wild Water) World Championships, Jonquière and Desbiens, Quebec, June 30-July 8.

Women's Field Hockey A400

**1979, Aug. 16**

| | | |
|---|---|---|
| *834* A400 17c multi | 28 | 10 |

Women's Field Hockey Championship, Vancouver, B.C., Aug. 16-30.

Summer Tent, Print by Kiakshuk A401

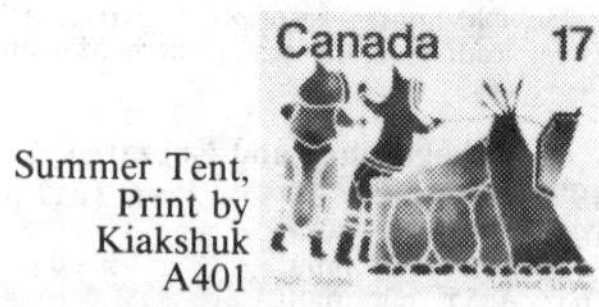

Eskimos Building Igloo, by Abraham of Povungnituk A402

Designs (Works by Eskimo Artists): No. 837, The Dance, print by Kalvak of Holman Island. No. 838, Two soapstone figures from Repulse Bay, by Madeleine Isserkut and Jean Mapsalak.

**1979, Sept. 13 Litho. *Perf. 13½***

| | | |
|---|---|---|
| *835* A401 17c multi | 24 | 10 |
| *836* A402 17c multi | 24 | 10 |
| *837* A401 17c multi | 24 | 10 |
| *838* A402 17c multi | 24 | 10 |

Inuit shelters and community. Nos. 835-836 and 837-838 printed se-tenant checkerwise in sheets of 50.

Painted Wooden Train A403

Antique Toys: 17c, Horse, pull toy. 35c, Knitted doll (vert.).

**1979, Oct. 17 Litho. *Perf. 13***

| | | |
|---|---|---|
| *839* A403 15c multi | 24 | 6 |
| *840* A403 17c multi | 25 | 8 |
| *841* A403 35c multi | 52 | 28 |

Christmas 1979.

Girl Watering Tree of Life — A404

**1979, Oct. 24**

| | | |
|---|---|---|
| *842* A404 17c multi | 24 | 10 |

International Year of the Child.

Curtiss HS-2L A405

**1979, Nov. 15 Litho. *Perf. 12½***

| | | |
|---|---|---|
| *843* A405 17c *shown* | 28 | 10 |
| *844* A405 17c *Canadair CL-215* | 28 | 10 |
| *845* A405 35c *Vichers Vedette* | 55 | 50 |
| *846* A405 35c *Consolidated Canso* | 55 | 50 |

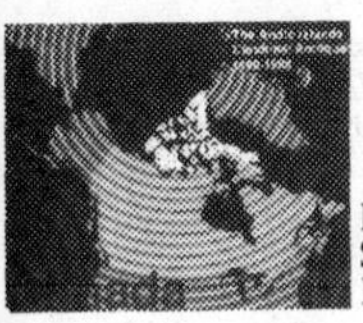

Map of Canada Showing Arctic Islands — A406

**1980, Jan. 23** **Litho.** ***Perf. 13½***
*847* A406 17c multi 24 10

Acquisition of the Arctic Islands, centenary.

Downhill Skiing — A407

**1980, Jan. 23**
*848* A407 35c multi 45 30

13th Winter Olympic Games, Lake Placid, N.Y., Feb. 12-24.

Meeting of the School Trustees, by Robert Harris A408

Royal Canadian Academy of Arts Centenary: No. 850, Inspiration, bronze sculpture, by Louis-Philippe Hebert (1850-1917). No. 851, Parliament Buildings, by Thomas Fuller (1822-1919). No. 852, Sunrise on the Saguenay, by Lucius O'Brien (1832-99).

**1980, Mar. 6** **Litho.**
*849* A408 17c multi 25 10
*850* A408 17c multi 25 10
*851* A408 35c multi 52 40
*852* A408 35c multi 52 40

Nos. 849-850 and 851-852 printed se-tenant checkerwise in sheets of 50.

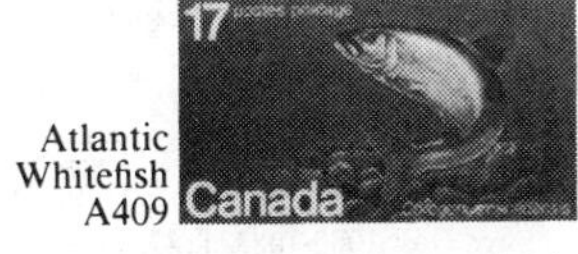


Atlantic Whitefish A409

Endangered wildlife. No. 854, Greater prairie chicken.

**1980, May 6** **Litho.** ***Perf. 12½***
*853* A409 17c multi 28 10
*854* A409 17c multi 28 10

Garden A410

Helping Hands A411

**1980, May 29** **Litho.** ***Perf. 13½***
*855* A410 17c multi 24 10

International Flower Show, Montreal, May 17-Sept. 1.

**Litho. & Embossed**

**1980, May 29** ***Perf. 12½***
*856* A411 17c ultra & gold 24 10

14th World Congress of Rehabilitation International, Winnipeg, June 22-27.

"O Canada" Opening Bars A412

Composers Lavallee, Routhier, Weir A413

**1980, June 6** **Litho.** ***Perf. 12½***
*857* A412 17c multi 24 10
*858* A413 17c multi 24 10

"O Canada" centenary. Printed checkerwise in sheets of 16.

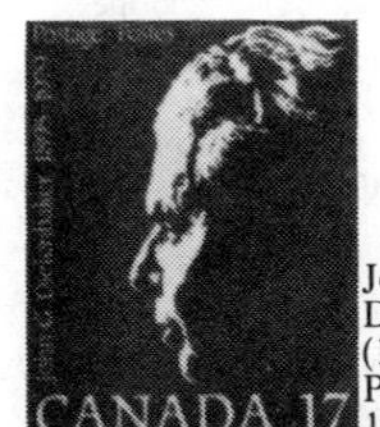


John George Diefenbaker (1895-1979), Prime Minister, 1956-63 — A414

**1980, June 20** **Engr.** ***Perf. 13½***
*859* A414 17c dark blue 24 10

Emma Albani (1847-1930), Soprano — A415

Design: No. 861, Healey Willan (1880-1968), organist and composer. Nos. 860-861 se-tenant, checkerwise.

**1980, July 4** **Litho.** ***Perf. 13½***
*860* A415 17c multi 24 10
*861* A415 17c multi 24 10

Ned Hanlan (1855-1908), Oarsman A416

**1980, July 4** **Litho.**
*862* A416 17c multi 24 10

Wheat Fields, Saskatchewan A417

Design: No. 864, Strip mining and town, Alberta.

**1980, Aug. 27** **Litho.** ***Perf. 13½***
*863* A417 17c multi 24 10
*864* A417 17c multi 24 10

75th anniversary of Saskatchewan's and Alberta's entry into Confederation.

Uraninite Molecular Structure — A418

**1980, Sept. 3**
*865* A418 35c multi 48 28

Discovery of uranium in Canada, 80th anniversary.

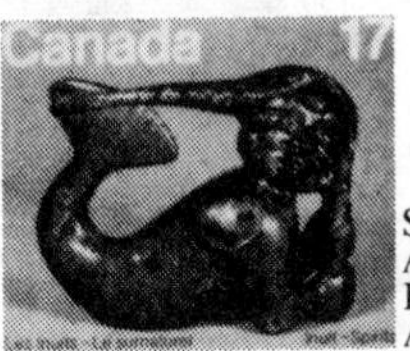


Sedna, by Ashoona Kiawak A419

Return of the Sun, Print by Kenojouak A420

Designs (Works by Eskimo Artists): No. 868, Bird Spirit, by Doris Hagiolok. No. 869, Shaman, print by Simon Tookoome.

**1980, Sept. 25** **Litho.** ***Perf. 13½***
*866* A419 17c multi 25 15
*867* A420 17c multi 25 15
*868* A419 35c multi 52 50
*869* A420 35c multi 52 50

Inuit spirits. Nos. 866-867 and 868-869 printed se-tenant checkerwise in sheets of 50.

Christmas Morning, by Frank Charles Hennessey — A421

Christmas 1980 (Greeting Cards, 1931): 17c, Sleigh Ride, by Joseph Sydney Hallam. 35c, McGill Cab Stand, by Kathleen Morris.

**1980, Oct. 22** **Litho.** ***Perf. 12½x12***
*870* A421 15c multi 22 8
*871* A421 17c multi 25 8
*872* A421 35c multi 52 25

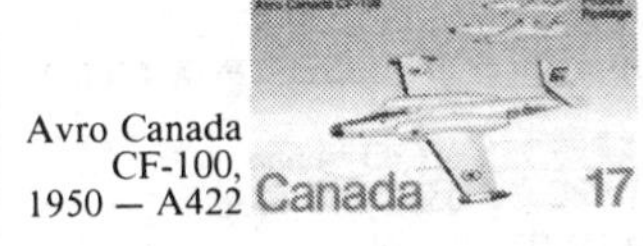


Avro Canada CF-100, 1950 — A422

Military Aircraft: No. 874, Avro Lancaster, 1941. No. 875, Curtiss JN-4 Canuck. No. 876, Hawker Hurricane, 1935.

**1980, Nov. 10** ***Perf. 13x13½***
*873* A422 17c multi 25 8
*874* A422 17c multi 25 8
*875* A422 35c multi 55 35
*876* A422 35c multi 55 35

Nos. 873-874 and 875-876 printed checkerwise in sheets of 50.

Emmanuel-Persillier Lachapelle, Caduceus — A423

**1980, Dec. 5** ***Perf. 13½***
*877* A423 17c multi 25 10

Emmanuel-Persillier Lachapelle (1845-1918), physician, founded Notre Dame Hospital, Montreal, 1880.

Mandora, 18th Century A424

**1981, Jan. 19** **Litho.** ***Perf. 12½***
*878* A424 17c multi 25 10

"The Look of Music" rare musical instrument exhibition, Vancouver, Nov. 2, 1980-Apr. 5, 1981.

Emily Stowe (1831-1903) and Toronto General Hospital — A425

Designs: No. 880, Louise McKinney, (1868-1931) Alberta legislative building. No. 881, Idola Saint-Jean, (1875-1945) Quebec legislative building. No. 882, Henrietta Edwards, (1849-1931) clubwomen.

**1981, Mar. 4** **Litho.** ***Perf. 13x13½***
*879* A425 17c multi 28 8
*880* A425 17c multi 28 8
*881* A425 17c multi 28 8
*882* A425 17c multi 28 8

Vancouver Island Marmot, by Michael Dumas A426

Endangered Wildlife: 35c, Wood bison, by Robert Bateman.

**1981, Apr. 6** **Litho.**
*883* A426 17c multi 24 10
*884* A426 35c multi 60 50

Kateri Tekakwitha ("Lily of the Mohawks"), by Emile Brunet — A427

Brunet Sculpture: No. 886, Marie de L'Incarnation.

**1981, Apr. 24** ***Perf. 12½***
*885* A427 17c brn & pale grn 25 10
*886* A427 17c lt bl & ultra 25 10

Beatification of Kateri Tekakwitha (1656-1680), first North American Indian saint, and

Marie De L'Incarnation (1599-1672), founder of Ursuline Order. Nos. 885-886 se-tenant.

At Baie Saint-Paul, by Marc-Aurele Fortin (1888-1970) — A428

Paintings: No. 888, Self-portrait, by Frederick H. Varley (1881-1969) (vert.). 35c, Untitled No. 6, by Paul-Emile Borduas (1905-1960) (vert.).

**1981, May 22 Litho. *Perf. 12½***
*887* A428 17c multi 25 10
*888* A428 17c multi 25 10

**Photo. *Perf. 13***
*889* A428 35c multi 40 30

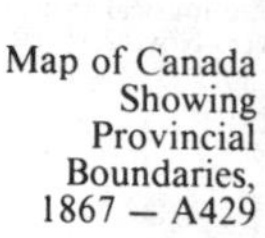

Map of Canada Showing Provincial Boundaries, 1867 — A429

**1981, June 30 Litho. *Perf. 13½***
*890* A429 17c shown 30 15
*891* A429 17c 1873 30 15
*892* A429 17c 1905 30 15
*893* A429 17c 1949 30 15

Canada Day. Nos. 890-893 se-tenant in sheets of 16 (4x4).

Frere Marie-Victorin (1885-1944) Botanist — A430

Montreal Rose — A431

Botanists: No. 895, John Macoun (1831-1920). Nos. 894-895 se-tenant.

**1981, July 22 Litho. *Perf. 12½***
*894* A430 17c multi 25 10
*895* A430 17c multi 25 10

**1981, July 22 *Perf. 13½***
*896* A431 17c multi 25 10

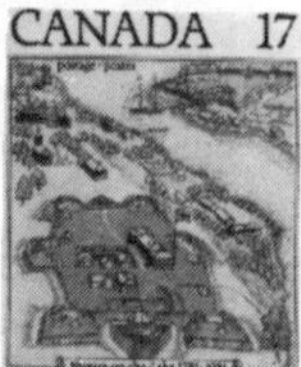


Niagara-on-the-Lake (First Capital of Upper Canada) — A432

Acadian Congress Centenary A433

**Photo. & Engr.**
**1981, July 31 *Perf. 13½***
*897* A432 17c multi 25 10

**1981, Aug. 14 Litho.**
*898* A433 17c multi 25 10

Aaron Mosher (1881-1959) Labor Congress Founder — A434

**1981, Sept. 8**
*899* A434 17c multi 25 10

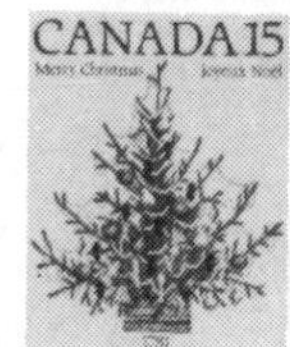


Christmas Tree, 1781 — A435

**1981, Nov. 16 Litho. *Perf. 13½***
*900* A435 15c shown 24 8
*901* A435 15c 1881 24 8
*902* A435 15c 1981 24 8

Christmas 1981; bicentenary of 1st illuminated Christmas tree in Canada.

Canadair CL-41 Tutor A436

**1981, Nov. 24 Litho. *Perf. 12½***
*903* A436 17c shown 25 15
*904* A436 17c de Havilland Tiger Moth 25 15
*905* A436 35c Avro Canada C-102 52 40
*906* A436 35c de Havilland Canada Dash-7 52 40

Stamps of same denomination se-tenant.

A437

**1981, Dec. 29 Engr. *Perf. 13x13½***
*907* A437 (30c) red 55 10

**Coil Stamp**
***Perf. 10 Vert.***
*908* A437 (30c) red 85 20

See Nos. 923-924, 941-951.

CANADA '82 Intl. Philatelic Youth Exhibition, Toronto, May 20-24 — A438

**1982 Litho. *Perf. 13½***
*909* A438 30c No. 1 45 16
*910* A438 30c No. 102 45 16
*911* A438 35c No. 223 52 30
*912* A438 35c No. 155 52 30
*913* A438 60c No. 158 1.00 55
**a** Souvenir sheet (#909-913) 3.25 2.00
*Nos. 909-913 (5)* 2.94 1.47

Issue dates: Nos. 909, 911, Mar. 11; others, May 20.

Jules Leger (1913-1980), 26th Governor General A439

Terry Fox (1958-1981), Marathon of Hope A440

**1982, Apr. 2 Litho. *Perf. 13½***
*914* A439 30c multi 42 10

**1982, Apr. 13 *Perf. 12½***
*915* A440 30c multi 42 10

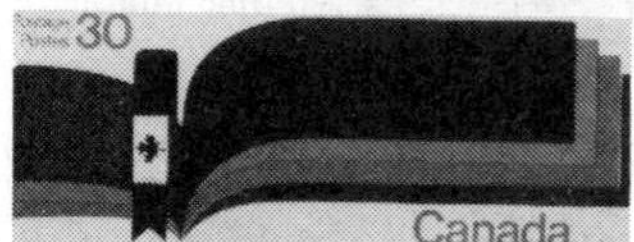


1982 Constitution — A441

**1982, Apr. 16 Litho. *Perf. 12x12½***
*916* A441 30c multi 42 10

Types of 1981-82 and

Decoy A442

Parliament (Library) A443

Parliament (West Block) A444

Parliament (East Block) A445

Elizabeth II — A446

Designs: Artifacts, 18th and 19th cent.

**1982-87 Litho. *Perf. 14x13½***
*917* A442 1c shown 5 5
**a.** Perf. 13x13½ ('85) 5 5
*918* A442 2c Fishing spear 5 5
**a.** Perf. 13x13½ ('84) 5 5
*919* A442 3c Stable lantern 6 5
**a.** Perf. 13x13½ ('85) 6 5
*920* A442 5c Bucket 8 5
**a.** Perf. 13x13½ ('84) 10 5
*921* A442 10c Weathercock 18 8
**a.** Perf. 13x13½ ('85) 20 8
*922* A442 20c Ice skates 35 15

**Photo. & Engr.**
***Perf. 13x13½***
*923* A437 30c lt bl, bl, & red 48 5
**a.** Bklt. pane of 20 (perf. 12x12½) 10.00
**b.** Perf. 12x12½ 60 15
*924* A437 32c beige, red & brn ('83) 52 5
**a.** Bklt. pane of 25 (perf. 12x12½) 14.00
**b.** Perf. 12x12½ 60 15

**Litho. *Perf. 13½x13***
*925* A443 34c multi ('85) 50 5
**a.** Bklt. pane of 25 12.50
**b.** Bluer sky, perf. 13½x14 50 5
**c.** Bklt. pane of 25, perf. 13½x14 12.50

**Photo. & Engr.**
***Perf. 13x13½***
*926* A446 34c lt bl & int bl ('85) 55 5

***Perf. 13½x14***
*926A* A446 36c plum ('87) 55 12

***Perf. 13½x13***
*926B* A443 36c multi ('87) 55 12
**c.** Bklt. pane of 10 5.50
**d.** Bklt. pane of 25 13.75

***Perf. 12x12½, 12½x12***
**Litho.**
**Size: 26x20mm**
*927* A442 37c Wooden plow ('83) 75 30
*928* A442 39c Settle-bed ('85) 60 20
*929* A442 48c Cradle 1.00 40
*930* A442 50c Sleigh ('85) 75 25
*931* A359 60c Street scene, Ontario City, Perf. 13½ 1.20 30
*932* A442 64c Wood stove ('83) 1.30 50
*933* A442 68c Spinning wheel ('85) 1.00 35

***Perf. 13½***
*934* A359a $1 Glacier Natl. Park, 1.50 60
*935* A359a $1.50 Waterton Lakes Natl. Park 3.00 75
*936* A359a $2 Moraine Lake, Banff Park 3.00 1.50
*937* A359a $5 Point Pelee Natl. Park ('83) 10.00 2.75
*Nos. 917-938 (24)* 28.07 8.82

**Booklet Stamps**
***Perf. 12x12½ (A437), 12½x12***
**Engr.**
*938* A445 1c sage grn ('87) 5 5
*939* A444 2c myr ('85) 5 5
*940* A437 5c dp cl 12 5
*941* A445 5c dp brn ('85) 8 5
*942* A444 6c henna brn ('87) 10 5
*943* A437 8c dk bl ('83) 16 5
*944* A437 10c dk grn 25 5
*945* A437 30c red 65 15
**a.** Bklt. pane of 4 (2 #940, 944, 945) 1.25
*946* A437 32c brn ('83) 65 5
**b.** Bklt. pane of 4 (2 #941, 943, 946) 1.00
*947* A443 34c dp sl bl ('85) 50 5
**a.** Bklt. pane of 6 (3 2c, 2 #941, 34c) 1.30
*948* A443 36c dark lil rose ('87) 55 12
**a.** Bklt. pane of 5 (2 No. 938, 2 No. 942, No. 948) 85

**Coil Stamps**
***Perf. 10 Vert. or Horiz.***
**Engr.**
*950* A437 30c red 1.00 20
*951* A437 32c brn ('83) 65 5
*952* A443 34c dl red brn ('85) 50 5
*953* A443 36c dark red ('87) 55 12

See Nos. 1080-1083, 1187, 1191.

Centenary of Salvation Army in Canada A457

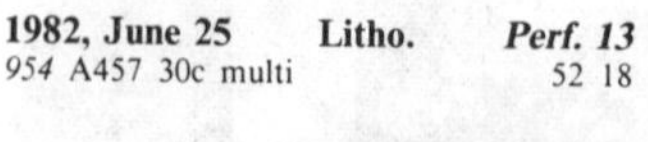

**1982, June 25 Litho. *Perf. 13***
*954* A457 30c multi 52 18

Canada Day — A458

Paintings: No. 955, The Highway near Kluana Lake, by A.Y. Jackson. No. 956, Montreal Street Scene, by Adrien Hebert. No. 957, Breakwater, by Christopher Pratt. No. 958, Along Great Slave Lake, by Rene Richard. No. 959, Tea Hill, by Molly Lamb. No. 960, Family and Rainstorm, by Alex Colville. No. 961, Brown Shadows, by Dorothy Knowles. No. 962, The Red Brick House, by David Milne. No. 963, Campus Gates, by

Bruno Bobak. No. 964, Prairie Town—Early Morning, by Illingworth Kerr. No. 965, Totems at Ninstints, by Joe Plaskett. No. 966, Doc Snider's House, by Lionel LeMoine FitzGerald.

**1982, June 30** ***Perf. 12½x12***

| | | |
|---|---|---|
| *955* A458 30c multi | 60 | 38 |
| *956* A458 30c multi | 60 | 38 |
| *957* A458 30c multi | 60 | 38 |
| *958* A458 30c multi | 60 | 38 |
| *959* A458 30c multi | 60 | 38 |
| *960* A458 30c multi | 60 | 38 |
| *961* A458 30c multi | 60 | 38 |
| *962* A458 30c multi | 60 | 38 |
| *963* A458 30c multi | 60 | 38 |
| *964* A458 30c multi | 60 | 38 |
| *965* A458 30c multi | 60 | 38 |
| *966* A458 30c multi | 60 | 38 |
| *a* Miniature sheet of 12 | 8.50 | |
| *Nos. 955-966 (12)* | 7.20 | 4.56 |

No. 966a contains Nos. 955-966; black marginal inscription.

Regina Centenary A459

**1982, Aug. 3** ***Perf. 13½x13***

*967* A459 30c multi 52 18

Centenary of Royal Canadian Henley Regatta, St. Catharines, Aug. 4-8 A460

**1982, Aug. 4**

*968* A460 30c multi 52 18

Fairchild FC-2W1 A461

**1982, Oct. 5** **Litho.** ***Perf. 12½***

| | | |
|---|---|---|
| *969* A461 30c shown | 48 | 18 |
| *970* A461 30c De Havilland Canada Beaver | 48 | 18 |
| *971* A461 60c Noorduyn Norseman | 1.00 | 45 |
| *972* A461 60c Fokker Super Universal | 1.00 | 45 |

Stamps of same denomination se-tenant.

Christmas 1982 — A462

Designs: Creche figures.

**1982, Nov. 3** ***Perf. 13½***

| | | |
|---|---|---|
| *973* A462 30c Holy Family | 48 | 18 |
| *974* A462 35c Shepherds | 60 | 20 |
| *975* A462 60c Three Kings | 1.00 | 35 |

World Communications Year — A463

**1983, Mar. 10** **Litho.** ***Perf. 12x12½***

*976* A463 32c multi 55 20

Commonwealth Day — A464

**1983, Mar. 14**

*977* A464 $2 multi 3.00 1.65

Scene from Angeline de Montbrun, by Laure Conan (1845-1924), Painted by Rene Milot — A465

Design: No. 979, Sea Gulls, by Edwin John Pratt (1882-1966), woodcut by Claire Pratt. Nos. 978-979 se-tenant.

**1983, Apr. 22** **Litho.** ***Perf. 13½***

| | | |
|---|---|---|
| *978* A465 32c multi | 52 | 20 |
| *979* A465 32c multi | 52 | 20 |

St. John Ambulance Centenary A466

**1983, June 3** ***Perf. 13½***

*980* A466 32c Emblem 52 20

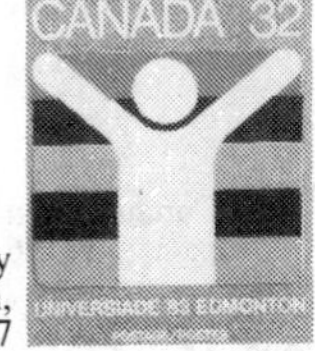

World University Games, Edmonton, July 1-11 — A467

**1983, June 28** ***Perf. 13½***

| | | |
|---|---|---|
| *981* A467 32c multi | 42 | 20 |
| *982* A467 64c multi | 1.25 | 60 |

Canada Day A468

Forts: No. 983, Fort Henry, Ontario. No. 984, Fort William, Ontario. No. 985, Fort Rodd Hill, British Columbia. No. 986, Fort Wellington, Ontario. No. 987, Fort Prince of Wales, Manitoba. No. 988, Halifax Citadel, Nova Scotia. No. 989, Fort Chambly, Quebec. No. 990, Fort No. 1, Point Levis, Quebec. No. 991, Fort at Coteau-du-Lac, Quebec. No. 992, Fort Beausejour, New Brunswick. Sizes: Nos. 983, 988: 44x22mm.; Nos. 984-985, 989-990, 36x22mm.; Nos. 986-987, 991-992, 28x22mm. Nos. 983-992 issued in booklet only.

**1983, June 30** ***Perf. 12½x13***

| | | |
|---|---|---|
| *983* A468 32c multi | 65 | 28 |
| *984* A468 32c multi | 65 | 28 |
| *985* A468 32c multi | 65 | 28 |
| *986* A468 32c multi | 65 | 28 |
| *987* A468 32c multi | 65 | 28 |
| *988* A468 32c multi | 65 | 28 |
| *989* A468 32c multi | 65 | 28 |
| *990* A468 32c multi | 65 | 28 |
| *991* A468 32c multi | 65 | 28 |
| *992* A468 32c multi | 65 | 28 |
| *a* Bklt. pane of 10 | 7.00 | |
| *Nos. 983-992 (10)* | 6.50 | 2.80 |

Scouting Year — A469

**1983, July 6** ***Perf. 13½***

*993* A469 32c multi 52 20

Church Council Emblem — A470

Humphrey Gilbert — A471

**1983, July 22** **Litho.**

*994* A470 32c tan & grn 52 20

6th World Council of Churches Assembly, Vancouver, July 24-Aug. 10.

**1983, Aug. 3** **Litho.**

*995* A471 32c multi 52 20

400th anniv. of discovery of Newfoundland by Sir Humphrey Gilbert (1537-1583).

Centenary of Discovery of Nickel, Sudbury, Ontario A472

**Photo. & Embossed**

**1983, Aug. 12** ***Perf. 13***

*996* A472 32c multi 52 20

Josiah Henson (1789-1883), Preacher A473

**1983, Sept. 16** ***Perf. 13x13½***

*997* A473 32c multi 52 20

Antoine Labelle (1833-1891), Deputy Minister for Settlement A474

**1983, Sept. 16** ***Perf. 13½***

*998* A474 32c multi 52 20

Locomotives A475

**1983, Oct. 3** ***Perf. 12½x13***

| | | |
|---|---|---|
| *999* A475 32c Toronto 4-4-0, 1853 | 52 | 30 |
| *1000* A475 32c Dorchester 0-4-0, 1836 | 52 | 30 |
| *1001* A475 37c Samson 0-6-0, 1838 | 60 | 52 |
| *1002* A475 64c Adam Brown 4-4-0, 1860 | 1.05 | 90 |

Nos. 999-1000 se-tenant.

Dalhousie Law School Centenary A476

**1983, Oct. 28** **Litho.** ***Perf. 13***

*1003* A476 32c Arms 52 20

Christmas 1983 — A477

**1983, Nov. 3** **Litho.** ***Perf. 13½***

| | | |
|---|---|---|
| *1004* A477 32c Urban church | 52 | 20 |
| *1005* A477 37c Family going to church | 60 | 38 |
| *1006* A477 64c Rural church | 1.05 | 75 |

Army Regiment Centenaries A478

19th Cent. Uniforms: No. 1007, Royal Canadian Regiment, British Columbia Regiment. No. 1008, Royal Winnipeg Rifles, Royal Canadian Dragoons. Se-tenant.

**1983, Nov. 10** ***Perf. 13½x13***

| | | |
|---|---|---|
| *1007* A478 32c multi | 52 | 20 |
| *1008* A478 32c multi, shown | 52 | 20 |

50th Anniv. of Yellowknife A479

**1984, Mar. 15** **Litho.** ***Perf. 13½***

*1009* A479 32c Gold mine 52 20

50th Anniv. of Montreal Symphony Orchestra A480

**1984, Mar. 24** **Litho.** ***Perf. 12½***

*1010* A480 32c multi 52 20

450th Anniv. of Cartier's Landing in Quebec A481

**1984, Apr. 20** **Photo. & Engr.**

*1011* A481 32c multi 60 20

See France No. 1923.

Values quoted in this catalogue are for stamps graded at Fine-Very Fine and with no faults. An illustrated guide to grade is provided in introductory material, beginning on Page V.

Voyage of Tall Ships, Saint-Malo, France, to Quebec City — A482

**1984, May 18 Litho.** ***Perf. 12x12½***
*1012* A482 32c multi 65 20

450th anniv. of Cartier's landing in Quebec.

Canadian Red Cross Society, 75th Anniv. — A483

**1984, May 28 Litho.** ***Perf. 13***
*1013* A483 32c Meritorious Service Medal 65 20

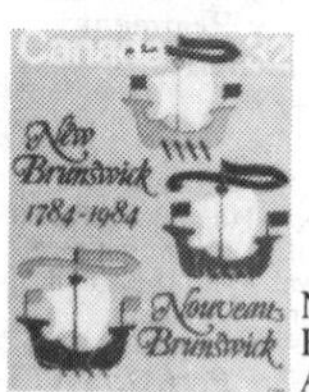

New Brunswick Bicentenary A484

**Photo. & Engr.**
**1984, June 18** ***Perf. 13***
*1014* A484 32c Galleys 65 20

St. Lawrence Seaway, 25th Anniv. — A485

**1984, June 26 Litho.** ***Perf. 13***
*1015* A485 32c Seaway, Lake Superior 65 20

Canada Day A486

Provincial Landscapes by Jean Paul Lemieux (b. 1904).

**1984, June 29** ***Perf. 13***
*1016* A486 32c New Brunswick 65 20
*1017* A486 32c British Columbia 65 20
*1018* A486 32c Yukon Territory 65 20
*1019* A486 32c Quebec 65 20
*1020* A486 32c Manitoba 65 20
*1021* A486 32c Alberta 65 20
*1022* A486 32c Prince Edward Island 65 20
*1023* A486 32c Saskatchewan 65 20
*1024* A486 32c Nova Scotia, vert. 65 20
*1025* A486 32c Northwest Territories 65 20
*1026* A486 32c Newfoundland 65 20
*1027* A486 32c Ontario, vert. 65 20
*a* Miniature sheet of 12 6.50
*Nos. 1016-1027 (12)* 7.80 2.40

Nos. 1018 and 1025 incorrectly inscribed. No. 1018 shows Northwest Territories landscape; No. 1025, Yukon Territory church. No. 1027a contains Nos. 1016-1027; black marginal inscription. Size: 138x123mm.

Loyalists, British Flag (1606-1801) A487

**1984, July 3**
*1028* A487 32c multi 52 20

United Empire Loyalists, American colonists who remained loyal to British throne and therefore emigrated to Canada during American Revolution.

Roman Catholic Church in Newfoundland A488

**1984, Aug. 17 Litho.** ***Perf. 13½***
*1029* A488 32c St. John's Basilica 52 25

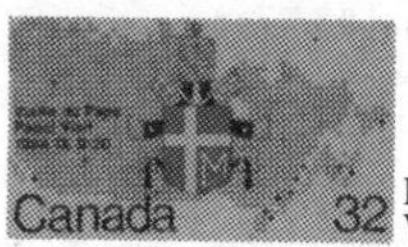

Papal Visit — A489

**1984, Aug. 31 Litho.** ***Perf. 12½***
*1030* A489 32c multi 52 25
*1031* A489 64c multi 1.05 50

Lighthouses A490

**1984, Sept. 21 Litho.** ***Perf. 12½***
*1032* A490 32c Louisbourg, 1734 60 15
*1033* A490 32c Fisgard, 1860 60 15
*1034* A490 32c Ile Verte, 1809 60 15
*1035* A490 32c Gibraltar Point, 1808 60 15

Printed se-tenant.

Steam Locomotives — A491

**1984, Oct. 25 Litho.** ***Perf. 12½x13***
*1036* A491 32c Scotia 60 25
*1037* A491 32c Countess of Dufferin 60 25
*1038* A491 37c Grand Trunk Class E3 70 28
*1039* A491 64c Canadian Pacific D10a 1.25 50
*a* Souvenir sheet 3.50 1.50

Nos. 1036-1037 se-tenant. No. 1039a contains Nos. 1036-1039 in changed colors. Size: 152x104mm.

Christmas 1984 — A492

Paintings: 32c, The Annunciation, by Jean Dallaire. 37c, The Three Kings, by Simone Mary Bouchard. 64c, Snow in Bethlehem, by David Milne.

**1984, Nov. 2 Litho.** ***Perf. 13***
*1040* A492 32c multi 52 25
*1041* A492 37c multi 60 28
*1042* A492 64c multi 1.05 50

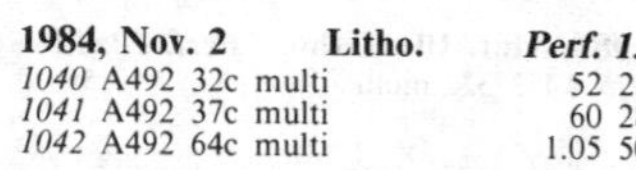

Royal Canadian Air Force — A493

**1984, Nov. 9 Litho.** ***Perf. 12x12½***
*1043* A493 32c Pilots 52 25

Centenary of La Presse — A494

**1984, Nov. 16 Litho.** ***Perf. 13x13½***
*1044* A494 32c Treffle Berthiaume 52 25

International Youth Year — A495

**1985, Feb. 8 Litho.** ***Perf. 12½***
*1045* A495 32c Heart, arrow, jeans 50 25

Canadians in Space — A496

**1985, Mar. 15 Litho.** ***Perf. 13½***
*1046* A496 32c Astronaut 50 25

Therese Casgrain A497

Emily Murphy A498

**1985, April 17 Litho.**
*1047* A497 32c multi 55 24
*1048* A498 32c multi 55 24

Issued se-tenant.

Gabriel Dumont (1837-1906) A499

**1985, May 6 Litho.** ***Perf. 13***
*1049* A499 32c multi 55 24

Centenary of the Northwest Rebellion.

Canada Day 1985 A500

Forts: No. 1050, Lower Ft. Garry, Manitoba. No. 1051, Ft. Anne, Nova Scotia. No. 1052, Ft. York, Ontario. No. 1053, Castle Hill, Newfoundland. No. 1054, Ft. Whoop Up, Alberta. No. 1055, Ft. Erie, Ontario. No. 1056, Ft. Walsh, Saskatchewan. No. 1057, Ft. Lennox, Quebec. No. 1058, York Redoubt, Nova Scotia. No. 1059, Ft. Frederick, Ontario. Sizes: Nos. 1050, 1055: 48x26mm. Nos. 1051-1052, 1056-1057: 40x26mm. Nos. 1053-1054, 1058-1059, 32x26mm. Nos. 1050-1059 issued in booklets only.

**1985, June 28 Litho.** ***Perf. 12½x13***
*1050* A500 34c multi 70 20
*1051* A500 34c multi 70 20
*1052* A500 34c multi 70 20
*1053* A500 34c multi 70 20
*1054* A500 34c multi 70 20
*1055* A500 34c multi 70 20
*1056* A500 34c multi 70 20
*1057* A500 34c multi 70 20
*1058* A500 34c multi 70 20
*1059* A500 34c multi 70 20
*a* Bklt. pane of 10 7.25
*Nos. 1050-1059 (10)* 7.00 2.00

Louis Hebert (1575-1627), 1st French Apothecary in North America — A501

Interparliamentary Union '85, Ottawa — A502

**1985, Aug. 30 Litho.** ***Perf. 12½***
*1060* A501 34c multi 50 25

Intl. Pharmaceutical Federation Congress.

**1985, Sept. 3** ***Perf. 13½***
*1061* A502 34c multi 50 25

Natl. Girl Guides Movement, Cent. — A503

**1985, Sept. 12 Photo.** ***Perf. 13½x13***
*1062* A503 34c Guide, brownie saluting 50 25

Lighthouses A504

**1985, Oct. 3 Litho. *Perf. 13½***

*1063* A504 34c Sisters Islets 50 25
*1064* A504 34c Pelee Passage 50 25
*1065* A504 34c Haut-fond Prince 50 25
*1066* A504 34c Rose Blanche 50 25
*a* Block of 4, #1063-1066 2.00 1.00
*b* Souvenir sheet of 4 2.00 1.00

No. 1066b contains Nos. 1063-1066; multicolored margin continues the design. Size: 108x90mm.

Santa Claus Parade — A505

Paintings by Barbara Carroll.

**1985, Oct. 23 Litho. *Perf. 13½***

*1067* A505 34c Santa Claus 50 25
*1068* A505 39c Horse-drawn coach 60 30
*1069* A505 68c Christmas tree 1.00 50

***Perf. 13½ on 3 Sides***

*1070* A505 32c Polar float 48 24
*a* Bklt. pane of 10 4.80

No. 1070 printed in booklets only.

Locomotives, 1905-1925 — A506

**1985, Nov. 7 *Perf. 12½x13***

*1071* A506 34c Grand Trunk K2 50 25
*1072* A506 34c Canadian Pacific P2a 50 25
*a* Pair, #1071-1072 1.00 50
*1073* A506 39c Canadian Northern O10a 60 30
*1074* A506 68c Canadian Govt. Railways H4D 1.00 50

See Nos. 1118-1121.

1910 Gunner's Mate, World War II Officer, 1985 Woman Recruit — A507

**1985, Nov. 8 *Perf. 13½x13***

*1075* A507 34c multi 50 25

Royal Canadian Navy, 75th anniv.

Old Holton House, Sherbrooke Street, Montreal, by James Wilson Morrice (1865-1924) A508

**1985, Nov. 15 *Perf. 13½***

*1076* A508 34c multi 50 25

Montreal Museum of Fine Arts, 120th anniv.

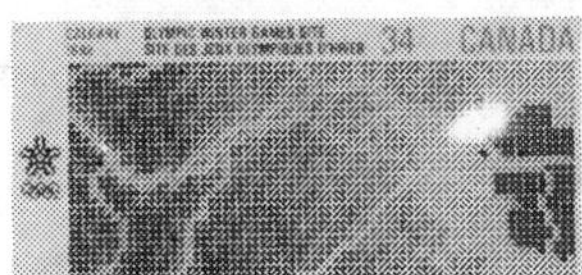


Southwestern Alberta, Computer Design Map — A509

**1986, Feb. 13 Litho. *Perf. 12½x13***

*1077* A509 34c multi 50 25

1988 Winter Olympics, Calgary, Alberta, Feb. 13-28.

EXPO '86, Vancouver, May 2-Oct. 13 — A510

**1986, Mar. 7 Photo. & Engr.**

*1078* A510 34c Canada Pavilion 50 25
*1079* A510 39c Communications 58 28

Heritage Artifacts Type of 1982

**1987, May 6 Litho. *Perf. 14x13½***

*1080* A442 25c Butter stamp 38 10

**Size: 20x26mm**

***Perf. 12x12½***

*1081* A442 42c Linen chest 65 15
*1082* A442 55c Iron kettle 85 20
*1083* A442 72c Hand-drawn cart 1.10 25

Park Type of 1982

**Litho. & Engr.**

**1986, Mar. 14 *Perf. 13½***

*1084* A359a $5 La Mauricie Natl. Park 7.00 3.50

Philippe Aubert de Gaspe (1786-1871), Novelist A511

Molly Brant (1736-1796), Iroquois Leader and Loyalist A512

***Perf. 12½, 13½ (No. 1091)***

**1986, Apr. 14 Litho.**

*1090* A511 34c multi 50 25
*1091* A512 34c multi 50 25

EXPO '86 — A513

**Photo. & Engr.**

**1986, Apr. 28 *Perf. 13x13½***

*1092* A513 34c Expo Center, Vancouver 50 25
*1093* A513 68c Transportation 1.00 50

Canadian Forces Postal Service, 75th Anniv. — A514

**1986, May 9 Litho. *Perf. 13½***

*1094* A514 34c multi 50 25

Indigenous Birds — A515

**1986, May 22**

*1095* A515 34c Great blue heron 50 25
*1096* A515 34c Snow goose 50 25
*1097* A515 34c Great horned owl 50 25
*1098* A515 34c Spruce grouse 50 25
*a* Block of 4, #1095-1098 2.00 1.00

Canada Day — A516

Invention blueprints.

**1986, June 27 Litho.**

*1099* A516 34c Rotary snowplow, 1869 50 25
*1100* A516 34c Canadarm, 1986 50 25
*1101* A516 34c Anti-gravity flight suit, 1938 50 25
*1102* A516 34c Variable pitch propeller, 1923 50 25
*a* Block of 4, #1099-1102 2.00 1.00

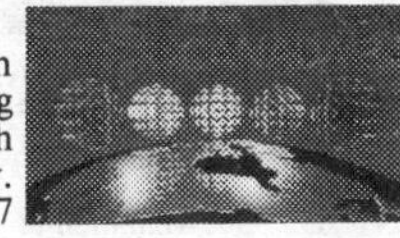

Canadian Broadcasting Corp., 50th Anniv. A517

**1986, July 23 Litho. *Perf. 12½***

*1103* A517 34c Emblem, map 50 25

Exploration of Canada A518

Designs: No. 1104, Siberian Indians discover and inhabit No. America, 10,000 B.C. No. 1105, Viking settlement, A.D. 1000. No. 1106, John Cabot lands, 1498. No. 1107, Henry Hudson pioneers Hudson Strait and Bay, 1610.

**1986, Aug. 29 Litho. *Perf. 12½x13***

*1104* A518 34c multi 50 25
*1105* A518 34c multi 50 25
*1106* A518 34c multi 50 25
*1107* A518 34c multi 50 25
*a* Block of 4, #1104-1107 2.00 1.00
*b* Souvenir sheet of 4, #1104-1107 2.00 1.00

No. 1107b issued Oct. 1 for CAPEX '87; multicolored decorative margin pictures exhibition emblem and map-like design.

See Nos. 1126-1129.

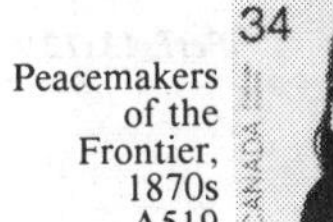

Peacemakers of the Frontier, 1870s A519

Designs: No. 1108, Crowfoot (1830-1890), Blackfoot Indian chief. No. 1109, James F. Macleod (1836-1894), asst. commissioner of Northwest Mounted Police.

**1986, Sept. 5 *Perf. 13x13½***

*1108* A519 34c scar, gray & ind 50 25
*1109* A519 34c ind, gray & scar 50 25

Printed se-tenant.

Intl. Peace Year — A520

**Litho. & Embossed**

**1986, Sept. 16 *Perf. 13½***

*1110* A520 34c multi 50 25

1988 Calgary Winter Olympics — A521

**1986, Oct. 15 Litho. *Perf. 13½x13***

*1111* A521 34c Ice hockey 50 25
*1112* A521 34c Biathlon 50 25
*a* Pair, #1111-1112 1.00 50

See Nos. 1130-1131, 1152-1153, 1195-1198.

Christmas — A522

Angels.

**1986, Oct. 29 Litho. *Perf. 12½***

*1113* A522 34c multi 50 25
*1114* A522 39c multi 58 30
*1115* A522 68c multi 1.00 50

**Size: 72x26mm**

*1116* A522 29c multi 45 22
*a* Bklt. pane of 10 4.50

No. 1116 has bar code in at left, for use on covers with printed postal code matrix. Issued in booklets only.

John Molson (1763-1836), Entrepreneur — A523

**1986, Nov. 4**

*1117* A523 34c multi 50 25

Locomotives Type of 1985

**1986, Nov. 21 *Perf. 12½x13***

*1118* A506 34c CN V1a 50 25
*1119* A506 34c CP T1a 50 25
*a* Pair, #1118-1119 1.00 50
*1120* A506 39c CN U2a 55 28
*1121* A506 68c CP H1c 1.00 50

CAPEX '87 A524

**1987 Litho. & Engr. *Perf. 13x13½***

*1122* A524 34c 1st Toronto P.O. 50 25
*1123* A524 36c Nelson-Miramichi P.O. 55 28
*1124* A524 42c Saint Ours P.O. 65 32
*1125* A524 72c Battleford P.O. 1.10 55

**Souvenir Sheet**

*1125A* Sheet of 4 3.00 1.50
*b* A524 36c like No. 1122, yel grn inscription 55 28

*c* A524 36c like No. 1123, yel grn inscription 55 28
*d* A524 42c like No. 1124, yel grn inscription 65 32
*e* A524 72c like No. 1125, yel grn inscription 1.10 55

No. 1125A has inscribed multicolored margin picturing lithographic and engraved impressions of No. 1122. Size: 155x92mm.

Issue dates: 34c, Feb. 16. Others, June 12.

### Exploration Type of 1986

Pioneers of New France: No. 1126, Etienne Brule (c. 1592-1633), first European to see the Great Lakes. No. 1127, Pierre Esprit Radisson (c. 1636-1710) and Medard Chouart des Groseilliers (1625-1698), British expedition to Hudson Bay, 1668. No. 1128, Louis Jolliet (1645-1700) and Fr. Jacques Marquette (1637-1675) discovering the Mississippi River, 1673. No. 1129, Recollet wilderness mission, 1615.

**1987, Mar. 13 Litho.** ***Perf. 12½x13***

*1126* A518 34c multi 50 25
*1127* A518 34c multi 50 25
*1128* A518 34c multi 50 25
*1129* A518 34c multi 50 25
*a* Block of 4, #1126-1129 2.00 1.00

### Olympics Type of 1986

**1987, Apr. 3** ***Perf. 13½x13***

*1130* A521 36c Speed skating 55 28
*1131* A521 42c Bobsledding 65 32

Volunteers Week — A525

**1987, Apr. 13** ***Perf. 12½x13***

*1132* A525 36c multi 55 28

Law Day — A526

**1987, Apr. 15** ***Perf. 14x13½***

*1133* A526 36c Coat of arms 55 28

Canadian Charter of Rights and Freedoms, 5th anniv.

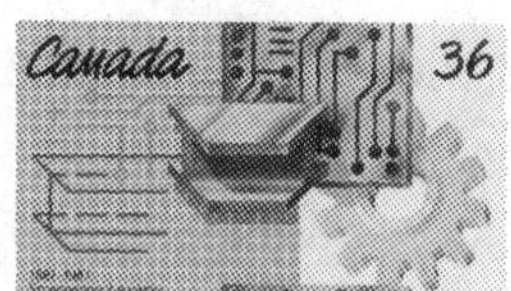


Engineering Institute of Canada, Cent. — A527

**1987, May 19** ***Perf. 12½x13***

*1134* A527 36c multi 55 28

Canada Day — A528

Inventors and communications innovations: No. 1135, Reginald Aubrey Fessenden (1866-1932), AM radio, 1900. No. 1136, Charles Fenerty, newsprint, 1838. No. 1137, Georges-Edouard Desbarats and William Leggo, half-tone engraving, 1869. No. 1138, Frederick Newton Gisborne, No. America's first undersea cable, 1852, New Brunswick to Prince Edward Is.

**1987, June 25 Litho.** ***Perf. 13½***

*1135* A528 36c multi 55 28
*1136* A528 36c multi 55 28
*1137* A528 36c multi 55 28
*1138* A528 36c multi 55 28
*a* Block of 4, Nos. 1135-1138 2.25 1.15

Steamships — A529

**1987, July 20** ***Perf. 13½x13***

*1139* A529 36c Segwun, 1887 55 28
*1140* A529 36c Princess Marguerite, 1948 55 28

Nos. 1139-1140 are printed se-tenant.

Shipwrecks — A530

**1987, Aug. 7**

*1141* A530 36c Hamilton & Scourge, 1813 55 28
*1142* A530 36c San Juan, 1565 55 28
*1143* A530 36c Breadalbane, 1853 55 28
*1144* A530 36c Ericsson, 1892 55 28
*a* Block of 4, Nos. 1141-1144 2.25 1.15

Air Canada, 50th Anniv. — A531

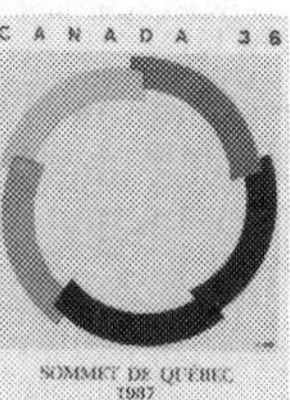


2nd Intl. Francophone Summit, Quebec, Sept. 2-4 — A532

**1987, Sept. 1** ***Perf. 13½***

*1145* A531 36c multi 58 30

**1987, Sept. 2** ***Perf. 13x12½***

*1146* A532 36c multi 58 30

9th Commonwealth Meeting, Vancouver, Oct. 13-17 — A533

**1987, Oct. 13**

*1147* A533 36c multi 58 30

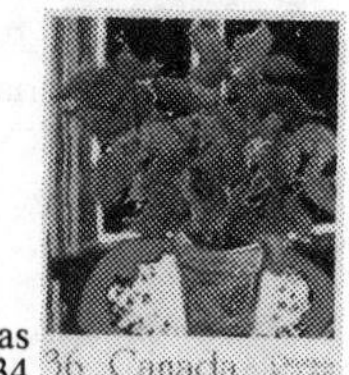


Christmas A534

**1987, Nov. 2 Litho.** ***Perf. 13½***

*1148* A534 36c Poinsettia 58 30
*1149* A534 42c Holly wreath 65 32
*1150* A534 72c Mistletoe, Christmas tree 1.15 58

**Size: 39x25mm**

*1151* A534 31c multi 48 25
*a* Bklt. pane of 10 4.80

No. 1151 has bar code at left, for use on covers with printed postal code matrix. Issued in booklets only.

### 1988 Olympics Type of 1986

**1987, Nov. 13** ***Perf. 13½x13***

*1152* A521 36c Cross-country skiing 58 30
*1153* A521 36c Ski jumping 58 30
*a* Pair, #1152-1153 1.16 60

75th Grey Cup, Vancouver, Nov. 29 — A535

**1987, Nov. 20** ***Perf. 12½***

*1154* A535 36c multi 58 30

### Types of 1985 and

Elizabeth II — A536

Parliament (Center Block) — A537

Mammals A538

Parliament (Close-up of Clock Tower) A539

**1987-88 Litho.** ***Perf. 13x13½***

**Size: 22x18mm**

*1155* A538 1c Flying squirrel 5 5
*1156* A538 2c Prickly porcupine 5 5
*1157* A538 3c Muskrat 5 5
*1158* A538 5c Varying hare 10 5
*1159* A538 6c Red fox 10 5
*1160* A538 10c Skunk 18 5
*1162* A538 25c Beaver 42 5

***Perf. 13½x13***

*1165* A536 37c multi 58 5
*1166* A537 37c multi 58 5
*a.* Bklt. pane of 10, perf. 13½x14 ('88) 5.80
*b.* Bklt. pane of 25 ('88) 14.50
*c.* Perf. 13½x14 58 5
*1167* A536 38c multi ('88) 65 5
*1168* A539 38c multi ('88) 65 5

***Perf. 12x12½***

**Size: 26x20mm**

*1170* A538 43c Lynx 68 22
*1171* A538 44c Walrus ('89) 75 25
*1173* A538 57c Killer whale 90 30
*1174* A538 59c Musk-ox (89) 1.00 35
*1177* A538 74c Wapiti 1.15 38
*1178* A538 76c Grizzly bear ('89) 1.30 45
*Nos. 1155-1178 (12)* 4.84 1.35

**Booklet Stamps**

***Perf. 12½x12 on 2 or 3 sides***

**Engr.**

*1187* A443 37c dark blue 58 5
*a.* Bklt. pane of 4 + 2 labels (No. 938, 2 No. 942, No. 1187) 85

**Booklet Stamps**

**Engr.**

***Perf. on 2 or 3 Sides***

*1188* A537 38c ('89) 65 5
*a.* Bklt. pane of 5 (3No. 939, No. 943 and No. 1188) ('89) 90

**Coil Stamp**

***Perf. Perf. 10 Horiz.***

**Engr.**

*1191* A443 37c dark blue 58 5

**Coil Stamp**

***Perf. Horiz.***

*1192* A443 38c ('89) 65 5

Issue dates: 1c, 2c, 3c, 5c, 6c, 10c, 25c, Oct. 3, 1988. Nos. 1165-1166, Dec. 30, 1987. Nos. 1170, 1173, 1177, Jan. 18, 1988. No. 1187, Feb. 3, 1988. No. 1191, Feb. 22, 1988.

This is an expanding set. Numbers will change if necessary.

Issue dates: Nos. 1167-1168, Dec. 29. Nos. 1171, 1174, 1178 and 1188, Jan. 18. No. 1192, Feb. 1.

### Olympics Type of 1986

**1988, Feb. 12 Litho.** ***Perf. 12x12½***

*1195* A521 37c Alpine skiing 58 30
*1196* A521 37c Curling 58 30
*a.* Pair, Nos. 1195-1196 1.20 60
*1197* A521 43c Figure skating 68 35
*1198* A521 74c Luge 1.15 58

### Exploration Type of 1986

18th Cent. explorers of the western territories: No. 1199, Anthony Henday traveled the Prairies in 1754 from the Hayes River to Red Deer, Alberta. No. 1200, George Vancouver (1757-1798), circumnavigated Vancouver Is. and explored the Pacific Coast, 1792-94. No. 1201, Simon Fraser (1776-1862), fur trader who discovered and navigated the Fraser River. No. 1202, John Palliser (1807-1887), geographer who determined the topographical boundary between Canada and the US from Lake Superior to the Pacific Coast.

**1988, Mar. 17 Litho.** ***Perf. 12½x13***

*1199* A518 37c multi 60 30
*1200* A518 37c multi 60 30
*1201* A518 37c multi 60 30
*1202* A518 37c multi 60 30
*a* Block of 4, Nos. 1199-1202 2.40 1.20

The Young Reader, by Ozias Leduc A546

**Photo. & Engr.**

**1988, May 20** ***Perf. 13x13½***

*1203* A546 50c multi 82 40

Masterpieces of Canadian art. Printed in sheets of 16 with extra wide margin containing information.

Wildlife and Habitat Conservation A547

**1988, June 1 Litho.** *Perf. 13x13½*

*1204* A547 37c Duck 60 30
*1205* A547 37c Moose at water hole 60 30
*a.* Pair, Nos. 1204-1205 1.20 60

Grey Owl, ne Archibald Belaney, (b. 1888), conservationist; Ducks Unlimited Canada, 50th anniv.

Science and Technology — A548

Inventions: No. 1206, Kerosene, invented by Abraham Gesner (1797-1864), patented in 1854. No. 1207, Marquis wheat, developed in 1908 by Charles Saunders. No. 1208, Electron microscope, developed in 1938 at the University of Toronto by James Hillier and Albert Prebus under the supervision of Eli Burton. No. 1209, Cobalt cancer therapy, introduced by Dr. Harold Johns and Atomic Energy of Canada, Ltd., in 1951.

**1988, June 17** *Perf. 12½x13*

*1206* A548 37c multi 60 30
*1207* A548 37c multi 60 30
*1208* A548 37c multi 60 30
*1209* A548 37c multi 60 30
*a* Block of 4, Nos. 1206-1209 2.40 1.20

Intl. Entomology Congress, Vancouver A549

**1988, July 4 Litho.** *Perf. 12*

*1210* A549 37c Short-tailed swallowtail 62 30
*1211* A549 37c Northern blue 62 30
*1212* A549 37c Macoun's Arctic 62 30
*1213* A549 37c Canadian tiger swallowtail 62 30
*a.* Block of 4, Nos. 1210-1213 2.50 1.20

St. John's City, Newfoundland, Cent. of Incorporation — A550

**1988, July 22** *Perf. 13½x13*

*1214* A550 37c Harbor entrance, skyline 62 30

Canadian 4-H Council, 75th Anniv. A551

**1988, Aug. 5**

*1215* A551 37c Motto, farm, young scientists 62 30

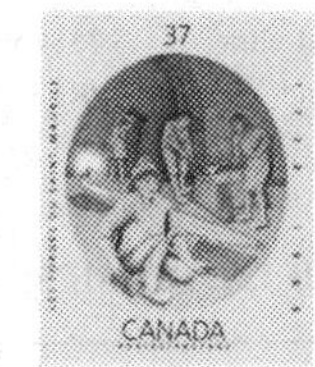
Les Forges Du St. Maurice (1738-1883), Canada's 1st Industrial Complex — A552

**Litho. & Engr.**

**1988, Aug. 19** *Perf. 13½*

*1216* A552 37c multi 62 30

Canadian Kennel Club, Cent. A553

**1988, Aug. 26** *Perf. 12½x12*

*1217* A553 37c Tahltan bear dog 62 30
*1218* A553 37c Nova Scotia duck-tolling retriever 62 30
*1219* A553 37c Canadian Eskimo dog 62 30
*1220* A553 37c Newfoundland 62 30
*a.* Block of 4, Nos. 1217-1220 2.50 1.20

*Canada stamps can be mounted in Scott's annually supplemented Canada Specialty and Master Canada Albums.*

Sesquicentennial of the 1st Baseball Game, Beachville, Canada, June 4, 1838 — A554

**1988, Sept. 9 Litho.** *Perf. 13½x13*

*1221* A554 37c multi 62 30

Christmas 1988 — A555

Icons of the Eastern Church: 32c, Nativity. 37c, Conception. 43c, Virgin and Child. 74c, Virgin and Child, diff.

**1988, Oct. 27 Litho.** *Perf. 13½*

*1222* A555 37c multi 62 30
*1223* A555 43c multi 72 35
*1224* A555 74c multi 1.25 62

**Booklet Stamp**

**Size:**

***Perf.***

*1225* A555 32c multi 55 28
*a.* Bklt. pane of 10 5.50

Millennium of Christianity in the Ukraine. No. 1225 has bar code at left; used on covers with printed postal code matrix. Issued in booklets only.

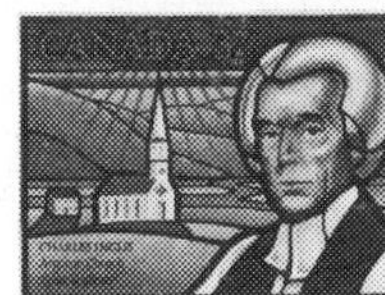
Inglis and Anglican Church A556

**1988, Nov. 1** *Perf. 12½x12*

*1226* A556 37c multi 62 30

Charles Inglis (1734-1816), Canada's 1st Anglican bishop and founder of the Kings-Edgehill School, Nova Scotia, and the University of King's College at Halifax, bicent.

Hopkins and *Canoe Manned by Voyageurs* A557

**1988, Nov. 18** ***Perf.***

*1227* A557 37c multi 62 30

Frances Ann Hopkins (1838-1918), painter.

The *Bluenose* and Capt. Walters — A558

**1988, Nov. 18** *Perf.*
*1228* A558 37c multi 62 30

Angus Walters (1882-1968), mariner.

## SEMI-POSTAL STAMPS

Olympic Type of 1973 and

SP1

SP2

**1974, Apr. 17** **Litho.** ***Perf. 12½***
**Size: 20x36mm**

| | | | | |
|---|---|---|---|---|
| *B1* | A307 | 8c + 2c brnz & multi | 22 | 22 |
| *B2* | A307 | 10c + 5c sil & multi | 35 | 35 |
| *B3* | A307 | 15c + 5c gold & multi | 45 | 45 |

**1975, Feb. 5** **Litho.** ***Perf. 13***

| | | | | |
|---|---|---|---|---|
| *B4* | SP1 | 8c + 2c Swimming | 22 | 22 |
| *B5* | SP1 | 10c + 5c Rowing | 35 | 35 |
| *B6* | SP1 | 15c + 5c Sailing | 45 | 45 |

**1975, Aug. 6** **Litho.** ***Perf. 13***

| | | | | |
|---|---|---|---|---|
| *B7* | SP2 | 8c + 2c Woman fencer | 22 | 22 |
| *B8* | SP2 | 10c + 5c Boxing | 35 | 35 |
| *B9* | SP2 | 15c + 5c Judo | 45 | 45 |

**1976, Jan. 7**

| | | | | |
|---|---|---|---|---|
| *B10* | SP2 | 8c + 2c Basketball | 22 | 22 |
| *B11* | SP2 | 10c + 5c Vaulting | 35 | 35 |
| *B12* | SP2 | 20c + 5c Soccer | 45 | 45 |

Nos. B1-B12 commemorate the 21st Olympic Games, Montreal, July 17-Aug. 1, 1976. The surtax was for the Canadian Olympic Committee.

## AIR POST STAMPS

Allegory of Flight — AP1

**Unwmk.**

**1928, Sept. 21** **Engr.** ***Perf. 12***
*C1* AP1 5c brown olive 5.25 1.65
*a.* Imperf., pair 175.00

C1 is known imperforate horizontally and imperforate vertically.

Allegory-Air Mail Circles Globe AP2

**1930, Dec. 4** ***Perf. 11***
*C2* AP2 5c olive brown 20.00 13.00

No. C1 Surcharged

6

**1932, Feb. 22** ***Perf. 12***
*C3* AP1 6c on 5c brn ol 3.25 1.50
*a.* Inverted surcharge 150.00
*b.* Double surcharge 500.00
*c.* Triple surcharge 150.00
*d.* Pair, one without surcharge 600.00

Counterfeit surcharges exist.

No. C2 Surcharged in Dark Blue

6 6
**OTTAWA CONFERENCE**
**1932**

**1932, July 12** ***Perf. 11***
*C4* AP2 6c on 5c ol brn 8.00 6.00

Daedalus AP3

**1935, June 1** **Engr.** ***Perf. 12***
*C5* AP3 6c red brown 1.50 80
*a.* Horiz. pair, imperf. vert. 1,750.
*b.* Imperf., pair 400.00

Mackenzie River Steamer and Seaplane AP4

**1938, June 15**
*C6* AP4 6c blue 1.65 14
*a.* Imperf., pair 425.00

Planes and Student Flyers — AP5

**1942-43**
*C7* AP5 6c deep blue 2.50 50
*a.* Imperf., pair 425.00
*C8* AP5 7c deep blue ('43) 45 5
*a.* Imperf., pair 425.00

Canada's contribution to the war effort of the Allied Nations.

**Catalogue values for unused stamps in this section, from this point to the end of the section, are for Never Hinged items.**

Canada Geese in Flight — AP6

**1946, Sept. 16**
*C9* AP6 7c deep blue 48 10
*a.* Booklet pane of 4 2.25 1.75

Foreign postal stationery (stamped envelopes, postal cards and air letter sheets) lies beyond the scope of this Catalogue, which is limited to adhesive postage stamps.

## AIR POST SPECIAL DELIVERY STAMPS

Trans-Canada Airplane and Aerial View of a City — APSD1

**1942-43** **Unwmk.** **Engr.** ***Perf. 12***
*CE1* APSD1 16c bright ultra 1.50 1.40
*a.* Imperf., pair 350.00
*CE2* APSD1 17c brt ultra ('43) 2.25 2.00
*a.* Imperf., pair 350.00

Canada's contribution to the war effort of the Allied Nations.

**Catalogue values for unused stamps in this section, from this point to the end of the section, are for Never Hinged items.**

DC-4 Transatlantic Mail Plane Over Quebec — APSD2

**1946, Sept. 16**
*CE3* APSD2 17c bright ultra 3.75 4.50

Circumflex accent on second "E" of "EXPRES".

Corrected Die

**1947**
*CE4* APSD2 17c bright ultra 3.75 4.50

Grave accent on the 2nd "E" of "EXPRES".

## AIR POST OFFICIAL STAMPS

**Catalogue values for unused stamps in this section, from this point to the end of the section, are for Never Hinged items.**

No. C9 Overprinted in Black **O.H.M.S.**

**1949** **Unwmk.** ***Perf. 12.***
*CO1* AP6 7c deep blue 5.00 3.00
*a.* No period after "S" 60.00 45.00

Same Overprinted **G**

**1950**
*CO2* AP6 7c deep blue 15.00 15.00

## SPECIAL DELIVERY STAMPS

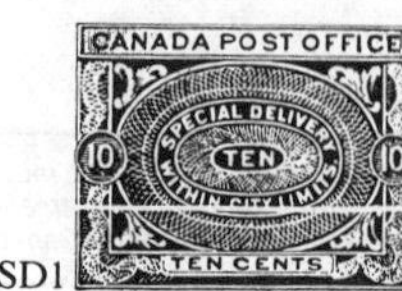


SD1

**Unwmk.**

**1898, June 28** **Engr.** ***Perf. 12***
*E1* SD1 10c blue green 27.50 3.75

SD2

**1922, Sept.**
*E2* SD2 20c carmine 32.50 4.25

Five Stages of Mail Transportation SD3

**1927, June**
*E3* SD3 20c orange 4.50 4.25
*a.* Imperf., pair 125.00

No. E3 forms part of the Confederation Commemorative issue. It is known imperforate vertically and imperforate horizontally.

SD4

**1930, Sept. 2** ***Perf. 11***
*E4* SD4 20c henna brown 26.00 7.50

SD5

**1933**
*E5* SD5 20c henna brown 22.50 8.75
*a.* Imperf., pair 300.00

Symbolical of Progress — SD6

**1935, June 1** ***Perf. 12***
*E6* SD6 20c dark carmine 4.50 3.50
*a.* Imperf., pair 250.00

Arms of Canada SD7

**1938-39**
*E7* SD7 10c dk green ('39) 3.00 1.40
*a.* Imperf., pair 400.00
*E8* SD7 20c dark carmine 20.00 20.00
*a.* Imperf., pair 400.00

No. E8 Surcharged in Black

**10** **10**

**1939, Mar. 1**
*E9* SD7 10c on 20c dk car 3.50 3.00

Coat of Arms and Flags SD8

**1942, July 1** **Engr.**
*E10* SD8 10c green 1.50 85
*a.* Imperf., pair 400.00

Canada's contribution to the war effort of the Allied Nations.

**Catalogue values for unused stamps in this section, from this point to the end of the section, are for Never Hinged items.**

Arms of Canada SD9

**1946, Sept. 16**
*E11* SD9 10c green 1.10 45

The laurel and olive branches symbolize Victory and Peace.

## SPECIAL DELIVERY OFFICIAL STAMPS

**Catalogue values for unused stamps in this section, from this point to the end of the section, are for Never Hinged items.**

No. E11 Overprinted in Black **O.H.M.S.**

**1950** **Unwmk.** ***Perf. 12***
*EO1* SD9 10c green 14.00 12.50

Same Overprinted **G**

*EO2* SD9 10c green 25.00 22.50

## REGISTRATION STAMPS

R1

**1875-88** **Unwmk.** **Engr.** ***Perf. 12.***
*F1* R1 2c orange 32.50 1.25
*a.* 2c vermilion 47.50 4.50
*b.* 2c rose carmine 115.00 47.50
*c.* Imperf., pair *1,000.*
*d.* Perf. 12x11½ 185.00 47.50
*F2* R1 5c dark green 47.50 1.50
*a.* 5c blue green ('88) 57.50 1.50
*b.* 5c yellow green 47.50 1.50
*c.* Imperf., pair *850.00*
*d.* Perf. 12x11½ 325.00 100.00
*F3* R1 8c blue 200.00 150.00

## POSTAGE DUE STAMPS

D1

D2

**1906-28** **Unwmk.** **Engr.** ***Perf. 12***
*J1* D1 1c violet 4.00 1.40
*a.* Thin paper 4.50 2.75
*b.* Imperf., pair 175.00
*J2* D1 2c violet 4.00 32
*a.* Thin paper 4.50 3.25
*b.* Imperf., pair 175.00
*J3* D1 4c violet ('28) 18.00 5.50
*J4* D1 5c violet 4.00 55
*a.* Thin paper 3.25 2.75
*b.* Imperf., pair 175.00
*J5* D1 10c violet ('28) 12.50 4.00
*Nos. J1-J5 (5)* 42.50 11.77

In 1924 there was a printing of Nos. J1, J2 and J4 on thin semi-transparent paper.

**1930-32** ***Perf. 11.***
*J6* D2 1c dark violet 3.50 1.65
*J7* D2 2c dark violet 2.50 42
*J8* D2 4c dark violet 5.25 1.25
*J9* D2 5c dark violet 5.25 2.25
*J10* D2 10c dark vio ('32) 30.00 4.00
*a.* Vert. pair, imperf. horiz. 225.00
*Nos. J6-J10 (5)* 46.50 9.57

D3

D4

**1933-34**
*J11* D3 1c dark vio ('34) 4.25 2.25
*a.* Imperf., pair 200.00
*J12* D3 2c dark violet 1.75 40
*J13* D3 4c dark violet 4.50 2.50
*J14* D3 10c dark violet 7.75 1.90

**Catalogue values for unused stamps in this section, from this point to the end of the section, are for Never Hinged items.**

**1935-65** ***Perf. 12***
*J15* D4 1c dark violet 15 7
*a.* Imperf., pair 85.00
*J16* D4 2c dark violet 15 7
*a.* Imperf., pair 85.00
*J16B* D4 3c dark vio ('65) 1.75 85
*J17* D4 4c dark vio 25 7
*a.* Imperf., pair 85.00
*J18* D4 5c dark vio ('48) 35 20
*J19* D4 6c dark vio ('57) 1.75 1.00
*J20* D4 10c dark violet 25 5
*a.* Imperf., pair 85.00
*Nos. J15-J20 (7)* 4.65 2.31

D5

**1967, Feb. 8** **Litho.** ***Perf. 12***
**Size: 20x17mm**
*J21* D5 1c carmine rose 15 15
*J22* D5 2c carmine rose 20 20
*J23* D5 3c carmine rose 22 20
*J24* D5 4c carmine rose 25 25
*J25* D5 5c carmine rose 1.25 1.25
*J26* D5 6c carmine rose 25 25
*J27* D5 10c carmine rose 25 25
*Nos. J21-J27 (7)* 2.57 2.55

**1969-78** ***Perf. 12***
**Size: 20x15¾mm**
*J28* D5 1c car rose ('70) 45 28
*a.* Perf. 12½x12 ('77) 8 6
*J29* D5 2c car rose ('72) 12 8
*J30* D5 3c car rose ('74) 12 8
*J31* D5 4c carmine rose 12 8
*a.* Perf. 12½x12 ('77) 8 6
*J32* D5 5c car rose, perf. 12½x12 ('77) 10 6
*a.* Perf. 12 18.00 18.00
*J33* D5 6c car rose ('72) 12 8
*J34* D5 8c carmine rose 18 14
*a.* Perf. 12½x12 ('78) 30 12
*J35* D5 10c carmine rose 12 8
*a.* Perf. 12½x12 ('77) 15 8
*J36* D5 12c carmine rose 2.50 80
*a.* Perf. 12½x12 ('77) 30 12
*J37* D5 16c carmine rose ('74) 25 20

***Perf. 12½x12***
*J38* D5 20c carmine rose ('77) 25 20
*J39* D5 24c carmine rose ('77) 38 22
*J40* D5 50c carmine rose ('77) 80 60
*Nos. J28-J40 (13)* 5.51 2.90

## WAR TAX STAMPS

WT1

WT2

**Unwmk.**
**1915, Mar. 25** **Engr.** ***Perf. 12***
*MR1* WT1 1c green 4.00 10
*MR2* WT1 2c carmine 4.00 15

In 1915 postage stamps of 5, 20 and 50 cents were overprinted "WAR TAX" in two lines. These stamps were intended for fiscal use, the war tax on postal matter being 1 cent. A few of these stamps were used to pay postage.

**1916**

TWO DIES:
Die I. There is a colored line between two white lines below the large letter "T."
Die II. The right half of the colored line is replaced by two short diagonal lines and five small dots.

*MR3* WT2 2c + 1c car (I) 4.00 10
*a.* 2c + 1c carmine (II) 35.00 1.65
*MR4* WT2 2c + 1c brn (II) 2.75 5
*a.* 2c + 1c brown (I) 12.00 4.00
*b.* Imperf., pair (I) 90.00
*c.* Imperf., pair (II) 600.00

***Perf. 12x8***
*MR5* WT2 2c + 1c car (I) 14.00 12.00

**Coil Stamps.**
***Perf. 8 Vertically***
*MR6* WT2 2c + 1c car (I) 37.50 2.50
*MR7* WT2 2c + 1c brn (II) 5.50 40
*a.* 2c + 1c brown (I) 45.00 2.50

## OFFICIAL STAMPS

With Perforated Initials O H M S
On March 28, 1939 the Treasury Board ruled that on and after June 30, 1939 all stamps used by government departments throughout the country should be perforated O H M S (On His Majesty's Service) and that "the Post Office Department is to make arrangements required to provide that all stamps sold to Government Departments are perforated with the letters O H M S." The sale of such perforated stamps was discontinued in 1948.
We do not list varieties with perforated initials.

**Catalogue values for unused stamps in this section, from this point to the end of the section, are for Never Hinged items.**

Nos. 249, 250, 252 and 254 Overprinted in Black **O.H.M.S.**

**1949-50** **Unwmk.** ***Perf. 12***
*O1* A97 1c green 3.00 2.00
*a.* No period after "S" 40.00 40.00
*O2* A98 2c brown 11.50 7.50
*a.* No period after "S" 55.00 55.00
*O3* A99 3c rose violet 3.00 1.25
*O4* A98 4c dark carmine 3.25 60

Nos. 269 to 273 Overprinted in Black **O.H.M.S.**

*O6* A108 10c olive 4.50 60
*a.* No period after "S" 45.00 42.50
*O7* A109 14c black brown 4.75 2.25
*a.* No period after "S" 57.50 52.50
*O8* A110 20c slate black 15.00 3.00
*a.* No period after "S" 70.00 65.00
*O9* A111 50c dk bl grn 190.00 100.00
*a.* No period after "S" 400.00 375.00
*O10* A112 $1 red violet 45.00 30.00
*a.* No period after "S" 1,000. 750.00
*Nos. O1-O4,O6-O10 (9)* 280.00 147.20

Same Overprint on No. 294

**1950**
*O11* A124 50c dull green 27.50 15.00

Nos. 284 to 288 Overprinted in Black **O.H.M.S.**

**1950**
*O12* A119 1c green 24 20
*O13* A120 2c sepia 70 60
*O14* A121 3c rose violet 90 30
*O15* A122 4c dark carmine 90 9
*b.* No period after "S" 45.00 35.00
*O15A* A123 5c deep blue 1.50 1.10
*c.* No period after "S" 42.50 40.00
*Nos. O12-O15A (5)* 4.24 2.29

Stamps of 1946-50 Overprinted in Black **G** *a* **G** *b* **G** *c*

**1950**
*O16* A119(a) 1c green (#284) 28 12
*O17* A120(a) 2c sepia (#285) 1.40 80
*O18* A121(a) 3c rose vio (#286) 1.40 15
*O19* A122(a) 4c dk car (#287) 1.40 10
*O20* A123(a) 5c dp bl (#288) 1.65 85
*O21* A108(b) 10c olive 2.75 45
*O22* A109(b) 14c blk brn 5.50 2.00
*O23* A110(b) 20c slate blk 14.00 1.00
*O24* A124(b) 50c dull grn 7.75 5.50
*O25* A112(b) $1 red violet 72.50 60.00
*Nos. O16-O25 (10)* 108.63 70.97

Nos. 301-302 Overprinted Type "b"

**1950-51**
*O26* A125 10c black brown 85 12
*a.* Pair, one without "G" 400.00 400.00
*O27* A126 $1 brt ultra ('51) 60.00 60.00

Nos. 305-306 Overprinted Type "a"

**1951-52** **Unwmk.** ***Perf. 12***
*O28* A120 2c olive green 35 10
*O29* A122 4c org ver ('52) 52 10

No. 316 Overprinted Type "b"

**1952**
*O30* A132 20c gray 1.65 15

Nos. 320-321 Overprinted Type "b"

**1952-53**
*O31* A136 7c blue 2.75 65
*O32* A137 $1 gray ('53) 11.50 6.50

Same Overprints on Nos. 325-329, 334.

**1953-61**
*O33* A139(a) 1c violet brown 18 6
*O34* A139(a) 2c green 20 6
*O35* A139(a) 3c carmine rose 20 5
*O36* A139(a) 4c violet 30 5
*O37* A139(a) 5c ultramarine 30 6
*O38* A141(b) 50c light green 4.00 75
*a.* Overprinted type "c" ('61) 3.25 1.10
*Nos. O33-O38 (6)* 5.18 1.03

No. 351 Overprinted Type "b"

**1955-62**
*O39* A148 10c violet brown 85 10
*a.* Overprinted type "c" ('62) 1.40 65

Nos. 337-338, 340-341 Overprinted Type "a"

**1955-56**
*O40* A144 1c vio brn ('56) 18 14
*O41* A144 2c green ('56) 24 5
*O43* A144 4c violet ('56) 75 5
*O44* A144 5c bright blue 28 5

No. 362 Overprinted Type "b"

**1956-62**
*O45* A159 20c green 1.25 9
*a.* Overprinted type "c" ('62) 3.75 30

Nos. 401-402, 404-405 Overprinted Type "a"

**1963, May 15 Engr. *Perf. 12***

*O46* A195 1c deep brown 50 50
*O47* A195 2c green 50 50
**a.** Pair, one without "G" 750.00
*O48* A195 4c carmine 55 55
*O49* A195 5c violet blue 32 32

## CAPE OF GOOD HOPE

LOCATION — In the extreme southern part of South Africa.
GOVT. — Former British Colony.
AREA — 276,995 sq mi. (1911).
POP. — 2,564,965 (1911).
CAPITAL — Cape Town.

Cape of Good Hope joined with Natal, the Transvaal and the Orange River Colony in 1910, forming the Union of South Africa.

12 Pence = 1 Shilling

> Values of early Cape of Good Hope stamps vary according to condition. Quotations for Nos. 1-15 are for copies with two ample margins, the third close or touching the design but with no faults. Very fine to superb specimens sell at much higher prices, and inferior to poor copies sell at reduced prices, depending on the condition of the individual specimen.

"Hope" Seated A1

Wmk. 15- Anchor

**Printed by Perkins, Bacon & Co.**

**Wmk. 15**

**1853, Sept. 1 Engr. *Imperf.***

**Bluish Paper**

*1* A1 1p red 2,750. 165.00
**a.** Deeply blued paper 3,250. 175.00
*2* A1 4p blue 1,700. 100.00
**a.** Deeply blued paper 1,700. 125.00

**1855-58**

**White Paper**

*3* A1 1p rose ('57) 275.00 100.00
**a.** 1p dl red 325.00 150.00
*4* A1 4p blue 165.00 45.00
*5* A1 6p lil ('58) 575.00 125.00
**a.** 6p gray *3,750.* 200.00
**b.** bluish paper *3,000.* 200.00
**c.** Half used as 3p on cover
*6* A1 1sh yel grn ('58) *1,500.* 110.00
**a.** 1sh dk grn 225.00 250.00
**b.** Half used as 6p on cover

Nos. 3 to 6 are known rouletted unofficially.

No. 4 was reproduced by the collotype process in a souvenir sheet distributed at the London International Stamp Exhibition 1950. The paper is unwatermarked.

A2

**Printed by Saul Solomon & Co.**

**1861 Laid Paper Unwmk. Typo.**

*7* A2 1p red *18,000.* 1,600.
**a.** 1p car *17,000.* 1,600.
**b.** 1p bl (error) *32,500.*
*9* A2 4p blue *7,250.* 2,000.
**a.** 4p dk bl *14,000.* 4,250.
**b.** 4p red (error) *90,000.* *35,000.*
**c.** 4p bl, right corner retouched 4,250.

Nos. 7 and 9 are usually called Wood Blocks. The plates were made locally and composed of cliches mounted on wood. The errors were caused by a cliché of each value being mounted in the plate of the other value.

In 1883 plate proofs of both values on white paper, usually called "reprints," were made. The 1p is in dull orange red; the 4p in dark blue. These are known canceled, as a few were misused as stamps. The proofs do not include the errors.

**Printed by De La Rue & Co.**

**1863-64 Wmk. Anchor. (15) Engr.**

*12* A1 1p brn red 125.00 125.00
**a.** 1p dk car 87.50 *125.00*
*13* A1 4p dk bl 110.00 35.00
**a.** 4p sl bl 1,700. 275.00
*14* A1 6p purple 150.00 *300.00*
*15* A1 1sh emerald 225.00 325.00
**a.** 1sh pale emer 750.00

Nos. 12-15 can be distinguished from Nos. 3-6 not only by colors but because Nos. 12-15 often appear in a granular ink or with the background lightly printed in whole or part.

No. 12a, wmk 1, is believed to be a proof.

"Hope" and Symbols of Colony

A3 A6

Frame Line Around Stamp

**Wmk. Crown and C. C. (1)**

**1864-65 Typo. *Perf. 14***

*16* A3 1p rose ('65) 35.00 5.50
*17* A3 4p bl ('65) 50.00 1.75
**a.** 4p pale bl 50.00 1.90
**b.** 4p dl ultra 150.00 45.00
*18* A3 6p brt vio 45.00 1.75
**a.** 6p dl vio 50.00 8.00
*19* A3 1sh yel grn 35.00 1.75
**a.** 1sh bl grn 42.50 2.50

Imperf. stamps are believed to be proofs.

Stamps of 1864 Surcharged in Red or Black:

**Four Pence.** **ONE PENNY**

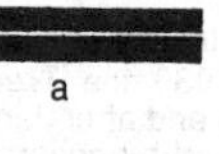

a b

**1868-74 Red Surcharge**

*20* A3 (a) 4p on 6p vio 80.00 10.00
**a.** "Peuce" for "Pence" *1,900.*
**b.** "Fonr" for "Four" 750.00
*21* A3 (b) 1p on 6p vio ('74) 200.00 20.00
**a.** "E" of PENNY omitted 525.00

Space between words and bars varies from 12½ to 16mm. on No. 20, and 16½ to 18mm. on No. 21.

**1876 Black Surcharge**

*22* A3 (b) 1p on 1sh grn 14.00 14.00

Without Frame Line Around Stamp

**1871-81 *Perf. 14***

*23* A6 ½p gray blk ('75) 4.00 4.00
*24* A6 1p rose ('72) 8.00 48
*25* A6 3p lil rose ('80) 100.00 8.00
*26* A6 3p cl ('81) 25.00 2.25
*27* A6 4p bl ('76) 35.00 65
**a.** 4p ultra 125.00 37.50
*28* A6 5sh orange 100.00 8.25

**THREE PENCE**

No. 27 Surcharged in Red

**1879**

*29* A6 3p on 4p bl 47.50 2.50
**a.** "THE.EE" 1,800. 425.00
**b.** "PENCB" 1,700. 325.00
**c.** Double surcharge *9,000.* *1,800.*
**d.** As "a," double surcharge

Type of 1871 Surcharged in Black **THREEPENCE**

**1880**

*30* A6 3p on 4p lil rose 21.00 1.65

No. 25 Surcharged in Black

**3** **3**

e f

*31* A6 (e) 3p on 3p lil rose 55.00 3.25
**a.** Inverted surcharge *9,500.* 1,300.
*32* A6 (f) 3p on 3p lil rose 16.00 1.10
**a.** Inverted surcharge 375.00 35.00

**1882-83 Wmk. Crown and C. A. (2)**

*33* A6 ½p gray blk 2.00 50
*34* A6 1p rose 8.00 25
*35* A6 2p bister 24.00 25
*36* A6 3p claret 2.00 40
*37* A3 6p brt vio 24.00 90
*38* A6 5sh org ('83) 950.00 175.00

Nos. 26 and 36 Surcharged in Black **One Half-penny.**

**1882 Wmk. Crown and C. C. (1)**

*39* A6 ½p on 3p cl *2,500.* 110.00
**a.** Hyphen omitted

**Wmk. Crown and C. A. (2)**

*40* A6 ½p on 3p cl 2.75 2.50
**a.** "ENNY" 1,800. 900.00
**b.** "PENN" 875.00 350.00
**c.** Hyphen omitted 375.00 350.00

Wmk.16

**1884-98 Wmk. Anchor. (16)**

*41* A6 ½p gray blk ('86) 20 6
*42* A6 ½p grn ('96) 12 8
*43* A6 1p rose ('85) 20 5
*44* A6 2p bister 30 8
*45* A6 2p choc brn ('97) 1.50 1.50
*46* A6 3p red vio ('98) 55 38
*47* A6 4p bl ('90) 50 14
*48* A6 4p pale ol grn ('97) 65 25
*49* A3 6p violet 65 20
*50* A3 1sh grn ('85) 24.00 1.65
*51* A6 1sh bl grn ('94) 11.00 52
*52* A6 1sh yel buff ('96) 1.10 25
*53* A6 5sh org ('87) 27.50 2.25
*54* A6 5sh brn org ('96) 11.00 2.25
*Nos. 41-54 (14)* 79.27 9.66

Type of 1871 Surcharged in Black **2½d**

**1891, Mar.**

*55* A6 2½p on 3p vio rose 80 80
**a.** "1" of "½" has straight serif 50.00 27.50

Hope Seated — A13

**1892-96**

*56* A13 2½p ol grn 95 15
*57* A13 2½p ultra ('96) 32 10

**ONE PENNY.**

No. 44 Surcharged in Black

**1893, Mar.**

*58* A6 1p on 2p bis 45 22
**a.** Double surcharge 475.00
**b.** No period after "PENNY" 20.00 14.00

Hope Standing A15

Table Mountain and Bay; Coat of Arms A16

**1893-1902**

*59* A15 ½p grn ('98) 12 9
*60* A15 1p rose 7 5
*61* A15 3p red vio ('02) 1.10 70

**1900, Jan.**

*62* A16 1p car rose 10 6

King Edward VII — A17

A18

A19

A20

A21

A22

A23

A24

A25

**1902-04 Wmk. 16**

*63* A17 ½p emerald 24 10
*64* A18 1p car rose 14 6
*65* A19 2p brn ('04) 60 24
*66* A20 2½p ultra ('04) 95 *1.40*
*67* A21 3p red vio ('03) 1.40 20
*68* A22 4p ol grn ('03) 60 20
*69* A23 6p vio ('03) 1.65 48
*70* A24 1sh bister 1.65 24
*71* A25 5sh brn org ('03) 12.00 2.75
*Nos. 63-71 (9)* 19.23 5.67

Imperf. stamps are proofs.

Cape of Good Hope stamps were replaced by those of Union of South Africa.

**Issued in Mafeking**

Excellent forgeries of Nos. 162-177 are known.

Stamps of Cape of Good Hope Surcharged **MAFEKING, 1d. BESIEGED.**

**1900, Mar. 24**
162 A6 1p on ½p grn 140.00 47.50
163 A15 1p on ½p grn 165.00 52.50
164 A15 3p on 1p rose 140.00 37.50
165 A6 6p on 3p red vio 3,250. 275.00
166 A6 1sh on 4p pale ol grn 3,000. 275.00

MAFEKING
3d.
Stamps of Bechuanaland Protectorate Surcharged
BESIEGED.

**1900 Wmk. Imperial Crown (30)**
167 A54 1p on ½p ver 125.00 47.50
a. Inverted surcharge 4,000.
168 A40 3p on 1p lil 950.00 60.00
a. Double surcharge 7,000.
169 A56 6p on 2p grn & car 1,000. 85.00
170 A58 6p on 3p vio, *yel* 3,250. 190.00
a. Inverted surcharge 5,000.
b. Double surcharge

The lettering of "Mafeking Besieged" shows varying breaks in various letters, and may have either a period or no punctuation after "Mafeking."

On Stamps of Bechuanaland
**Wmk. Orb. (29)**
171 A3 6p on 3p vio 400.00 62.50

**Wmk. Imperial Crown. (30)**
172 A59 1sh on 4p brn & grn 1,200. 52.50
a. Double surcharge, one inverted 7,000.
b. Triple surcharge 7,000.
c. Inverted surcharge 5,750.
d. Double surcharge 5,750.

MAFEKING
3d.
Stamps of Bechuanaland Protectorate Surcharged
BESIEGED.

173 A40 3p on 1p lil 1,100. 65.00
a. Double surcharge 7,250.
174 A56 6p on 2p grn & car 1,200. 65.00
175 A62 1sh on 6p vio, *rose* 2,400. 85.00

**On Stamps of Bechuanaland**
176 A62 1sh on 6p vio, *rose* 4,500. 725.00
177 A65 2sh on 1sh grn 4,000. 350.00

Sgt. Major Goodyear M1

Gen. Robert S. S. Baden-Powell M2

**Photographic Print**
**1900, Apr. 9 Unwmk. Perf. 12**
**Laid Paper**
178 M1 1p blue, *blue* 700.00 225.00
a. Imperf., pair
179 M2 3p blue, *blue*, 18½mm wide 1,275. 375.00
a. Horiz. pair, imperf. between
b. Double impression
c. Reversed design
180 M2 3p blue, *blue*, 21mm wide 6,500. 925.00

The color of the paper varies from pale to deep blue.

**ISSUED IN VRYBURG**

**Under Boer Occupation**

½ PENCE
Cape of Good Hope Stamps of 1884-96 Surcharged
Z.A.R.

Two Types of Surcharge.
I. Surcharge 10mm. high. Space between lines 5½mm.
II. Surcharge 12mm. high. Space between lines 7½mm.

**1899, Nov. Wmk. 16 Perf. 14**
N1 A6 ½p on ½p emer (I) 225.00 85.00
a. Type II 625.00
N2 A15 1p on 1p rose (I) 275.00 95.00
a. Double surcharge
b. Type II 750.00
N3 A3 2p on 6p vio (II) 3,500. 450.00
N4 A13 2½p on 2½p ultra (I) 2,500. 450.00
a. Type II

"Z.A.R." stands for Zuid Afrikaansche Republiek (South African Republic).

**Under British Occupation**

Transvaal Stamps of 1895-96 Handstamped
V. R.
SPECIAL
POST

**1900 Unwmk. Perf. 12½**
N5 A13 ½p green 2,250.
N6 A13 1p rose & grn 9,000. 2,750.
N7 A13 2p brn & grn
N8 A13 2½p ultra & grn

# CAYMAN ISLANDS

LOCATION — Three islands in the Caribbean Sea, about 200 miles northwest of Jamaica.
GOVT. — British Crown Colony, formerly a dependency of Jamaica.
AREA — 100 sq. mi.
POP. — 18,285 (1982)
CAPITAL — George Town, located on Grand Cayman.

12 Pence = 1 Shilling
20 Shilling = 1 Pound
100 Cents = 1 Dollar (1969)

**Catalogue values for unused stamps in this country are for Never Hinged items, beginning with Scott 112.**

Queen Victoria — A1

**Wmk. Crown and C. A. (2)**
**1900 Typo. Perf. 14**
1 A1 ½p green 1.10 1.40
2 A1 1p car rose 2.25 65

King Edward VII — A2

**1901-03**
3 A2 ½p grn ('02) 2.25 3.75
4 A2 1p car rose ('03) 3.75 3.75
5 A2 2½p ultra 4.25 5.00
6 A2 6p chocolate 12.00 15.00
7 A2 1sh brn org 40.00 45.00
*Nos. 3-7 (5)* 62.25 72.50

**Wmk. Multiple Crown and C. A. (3)**
**1905**
8 A2 ½p green 1.10 2.00
9 A2 1p car rose 6.75 7.50
10 A2 2½p ultra 2.50 3.00
11 A2 6p chocolate 16.00 18.50
12 A2 1sh brn org 32.50 40.00
*Nos. 8-12 (5)* 58.85 71.00

**1907**
13 A2 4p brn & bl 17.50 21.00
14 A2 6p ol grn & rose 17.50 21.00
15 A2 1sh vio & grn 30.00 40.00
16 A2 5sh ver & grn 150.00 165.00

Numerals of 4p, 1sh and 5sh of type A2 are in color on colorless tablet.

Stamps of 1905-07 Handstamped

One Halfpenny.
a

½D
b

1D
c

2½D
d

**1907-08**
17 A2 (a) ½p on 1p car rose 30.00 42.50
18 A2 (b) ½p on 5sh ver & grn 210.00 250.00
a Inverted surch. 15,000.
b Double surcharge 9,000. 10,000.
c Double surcharge, one inverted
d Pair, one without surcharge 22,500.
19 A2 (c) 1p on 5sh ver & grn 200.00 225.00
a Double surch. 15,000.
20 A2 (d) 2½p on 4p brn & bl ('08) 2,250. 3,000.
a Double surcharge 27,500.

The 1p on 4p is a revenue stamp not authorized for postal use. Price about $150.

A3

A4

**1907-09 Perf. 14**
21 A3 ½p green 95 1.40
22 A3 1p car rose 60 90
23 A3 2½p ultra 3.00 5.25

**Chalky Paper**
24 A3 3p vio, *yel* 3.00 5.25
25 A3 4p blk & red, *yel* 40.00 42.50
26 A3 6p violet 5.25 7.75
27 A3 1sh *grn* ('09) 3.75 6.50
28 A3 5sh grn & red, *yel* 35.00 42.50
*Nos. 21-28 (8)* 91.55 112.05

**1908 Wmk. Crown and C. A. (2)**
29 A3 1sh *green* 35.00 42.50
30 A3 10sh grn & red, *grn* 200.00 300.00

Numerals of 3p, 4p, 1sh and 5sh of type A3 are in color on plain tablet.

**1908 Wmk. 3**
**Ordinary Paper**
31 A4 ¼p brown 10 18

King George V
A5 A6

**1912-20**
32 A5 ¼p brown 10 12
33 A5 ½p green 42 1.25
34 A5 1p car ('13) 70 85
35 A5 2p gray 40 1.50
36 A5 2½p ultra ('14) 3.50 4.50

**Chalky Paper**
37 A5 3p vio, *yel* ('15) 1.10 2.50
38 A5 4p blk & red, *yel* ('13) 85 1.50
39 A5 6p vio & red vio ('13) 1.50 3.25
40 A5 1sh *grn* ('16) 4.00 5.50
41 A5 2sh vio & ultra, *bl* 7.50 12.50
42 A5 3sh grn & vio 8.75 12.50
43 A5 5sh grn & red, *yel* ('14) 25.00 35.00
44 A5 10sh grn & red, *bl grn, olive back* ('20) 62.50 87.50
a 10sh grn & red, *grn* ('15) 70.00 100.00
*Nos. 32-44 (13)* 116.32 168.47

**1913, Nov. 19**
**Surface-colored Paper**
45 A5 3p vio, *yel* 1.90 3.25
46 A5 1sh *green* 3.25 5.50
47 A5 10sh grn & red, *grn* 70.00 82.50

Numeral of ¼p, 2p, 3p, 4p, 1sh, 2sh, 3sh and 5sh of type A5 are in color on plain tablet.

**1921-26 Wmk. 4 Perf. 14**
50 A6 ¼p yel brn 12 16
51 A6 ½p gray grn 35 35
52 A6 1p rose red 55 85
53 A6 1½p org brn 42 85
54 A6 2p gray 1.10 2.25
55 A6 2½p ultra 85 1.40
56 A6 3p vio, *yel* ('23) 70 1.10
57 A6 4½p ol grn ('23) 1.40 3.75
58 A6 6p claret 4.25 6.75
59 A6 1sh *grn* ('25) 3.25 6.75
60 A6 2sh vio, *bl* 5.50 8.25
61 A6 3sh violet 14.00 19.00
62 A6 5sh grn, *yel* ('25) 17.00 22.50
63 A6 10sh car, *grn* ('26) 45.00 55.00
*Nos. 50-63 (14)* 94.49 128.96

**1921, Apr. Wmk. 3**
64 A6 3p vio, *org* 1.25 1.65
65 A6 4p red, *yel* 85 1.25
66 A6 1sh *green* 2.50 3.25
67 A6 5sh grn, *yel* 13.00 21.00
68 A6 10sh car, *grn* 52.50 65.00
*Nos. 64-68 (5)* 70.10 92.15

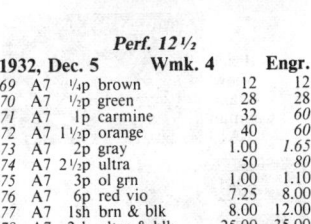

King William IV, King George V
A7

**Perf. 12½**
**1932, Dec. 5 Wmk. 4 Engr.**
69 A7 ¼p brown 12 12
70 A7 ½p green 28 28
71 A7 1p carmine 32 60
72 A7 1½p orange 40 60
73 A7 2p gray 1.00 1.65
74 A7 2½p ultra 50 80
75 A7 3p ol grn 1.00 1.10
76 A7 6p red vio 7.25 8.00
77 A7 1sh brn & blk 8.00 12.00
78 A7 2sh ultra & blk 25.00 35.00
79 A7 5sh grn & blk 100.00 125.00
80 A7 10sh car & blk 275.00 350.00
*Nos. 69-80 (12)* 418.87 535.15

Centenary of the formation of the Cayman Islands Assembly.

**Silver Jubilee Issue**
Common Design Type
**1935, May 6 Perf. 13½x14**
81 CD301 ½p grn & blk 18 22
82 CD301 2½p bl & brn 2.00 2.25
83 CD301 6p ol grn & lt bl 2.75 2.25
84 CD301 1sh brt vio & ind 3.50 3.25

King George V
A8

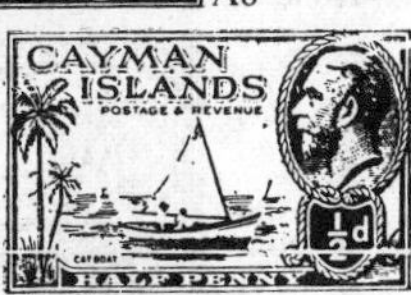

Catboat
A9

Red-footed Boobies
A10

Conches and Coconut Palms — A11

Hawksbill Turtles A12

**1935-36** *Perf. 12½*

*85* A8 ¼p brn & blk 8 8
*86* A9 ½p yel grn & ultra ('36) 12 10
*87* A10 1p car & ultra 80 48
*88* A11 1½p org & blk 42 40
*89* A9 2p brn vio & ultra 1.10 60
*90* A12 2½p dp bl & blk ('36) 4.25 1.90
*91* A8 3p ol grn & blk 2.25 1.10
*92* A12 6p red vio & blk ('36) 8.50 8.00
*93* A9 1sh org & ultra ('36) 4.50 5.25
*94* A10 2sh blk & ultra 22.50 24.00
*95* A12 5sh grn & blk 30.00 *37.50*
*96* A11 10sh car & blk 67.50 80.00
*Nos. 85-96 (12)* 142.02 159.41

**Coronation Issue**

Common Design Type

**1937, May 13** *Perf. 11x11½*

*97* CD302 ½p dp grn 18 18
*98* CD302 1p dk car 22 22
*99* CD302 2½p dp ultra 55 55

Beach View, Grand Cayman A13

Dolphin — A14

Map of the Islands A15

Hawksbill Turtles — A16

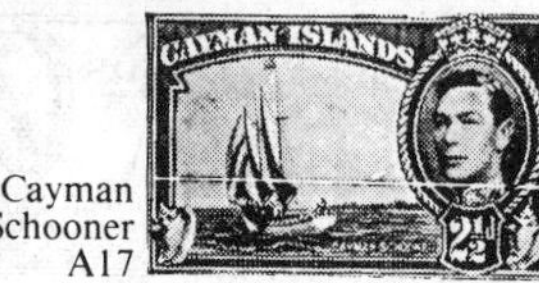

Cayman Schooner A17

***Perf. 12½; 11½x13 or 13x11½ (A14, #111); 14 (#104, 107)***

**1938-43** **Engr.**

*100* A13 ¼p red org 5 5
*a* Perf. 13½x12½ ('43) 5 5
*101* A14 ½p yel grn 5 5
*a* Perf. 14 ('43) 5 5
*102* A15 1p carmine 7 7
*103* A13 1½p black 7 7
*104* A16 2p dp vio ('43) 15 15
*a* Perf. 11½x13 24 24
*105* A17 2½p ultra 9 9
*106* A15 3p orange 15 15
*107* A16 6p dk ol grn ('43) 65 45
*a* Perf. 11½x13 1.00 1.00
*108* A14 1sh redsh brn 1.25 1.25
*a* Perf. 14 ('43) 1.25 1.25
*109* A13 2sh green 6.00 6.00
*110* A17 5sh dp rose 4.75 4.75
*111* A16 10sh dk brn 9.50 8.50
*a* Perf. 14 ('43) 7.25 7.25
*Nos. 100-111 (12)* 22.78 21.58

See Nos. 114-115.

**Catalogue values for unused stamps in this section, from this point to the end of the section, are for Never Hinged items.**

**Peace Issue**

Common Design Type

**1946, Aug. 26** **Wmk. 4** *Perf. 13½*

*112* CD303 1½p black 12 12
*113* CD303 3p orange 20 20

Types of 1938

**1947** *Perf. 12½*

*114* A17 2½p orange 2.00 30
*115* A15 3p ultra 42 42

**Silver Wedding Issue**

Common Design Types

**1948, Nov. 29** **Photo.** *Perf. 14x14½*

*116* CD304 ½p dk grn 12 12

**Engr.; Name Typo.**

***Perf. 11½x11***

*117* CD305 10sh bl vio 16.00 16.00

**UPU Issue**

Common Design Types

**Engr.; Name Typo. on #119, 120**

**1949, Oct. 10** *Perf. 13½, 11x11½*

*118* CD306 2½p orange 42 42
*119* CD307 3p indigo 70 70
*120* CD308 6p olive 1.25 1.25
*121* CD309 1sh red brn 2.50 2.50

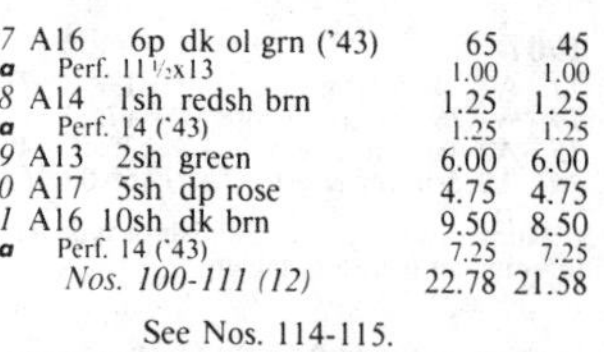

Catboat A18

Designs: ½p, Coconut grove. 1p, Green turtle. 1½p, Thatch rope industry. 2p, Caymanian seamen. 2½p, Map. 3p, Parrot fish. 6p, Bluff, Cayman Brac. 9p, Georgetown harbor. 1sh, Turtle "crawl". 2sh, Cayman schooner. 5sh, Boat-building. 10sh, Government offices.

***Perf. 11½x11***

**1950, Oct. 2** **Wmk. 4** **Engr.**

*122* A18 ¼p rose red & bl 20 20
*123* A18 ½p bl grn & red vio 28 28
*124* A18 1p dp bl & ol 55 55
*125* A18 1½p choc & bl grn 45 45
*126* A18 2p rose car & vio 45 45
*127* A18 2½p sep & aqua 80 80
*128* A18 3p bl & bl grn 2.25 2.25
*129* A18 6p dp bl & org brn 1.90 1.90
*130* A18 9p dk grn & rose red 3.25 3.25
*131* A18 1sh red org & brn 3.25 3.25
*132* A18 2sh red vio & vio 6.50 6.50
*133* A18 5sh vio & ol 13.00 13.00
*134* A18 10sh rose red & blk 19.00 19.00
*Nos. 122-134 (13)* 51.88 51.88

Types of 1950 with Portrait of Queen Elizabeth II and

Lighthouse, South Sound — A20

Elizabeth II and Turtles — A21

***Perf. 11½x11, 11x11½***

**1953-59** **Engr.**

*135* A18 ¼p rose red & bl ('55) 5 5
*136* A18 ½p bl grn & red vio ('54) 6 5
*137* A18 1p dp bl & ol ('54) 8 5
*138* A18 1½p choc & bl grn ('54) 10 8
*139* A18 2p rose car & vio ('54) 15 15
*140* A18 2½p blk & aqua ('54) 15 15
*141* A18 3p bl & bl grn ('55) 18 18
*142* A20 4p dp bl & blk 25 24
*143* A18 6p dp bl & red brn ('54) 22 22
*144* A18 9p dk grn & rose red ('54) 40 38
*145* A18 1sh red org & brn ('55) 85 75
*146* A18 2sh red vio & vio ('55) 2.50 2.50
*147* A18 5sh vio & ol ('55) 6.00 5.50
*148* A18 10sh rose red & blk ('55) 9.00 10.50
*149* A21 £1 brt bl ('59) 30.00 27.50
*Nos. 135-149 (15)* 49.99 48.30

**Coronation Issue**

Common Design Type

**1953, June 2** *Perf. 13½x13*

*150* CD312 1p brt grn & blk 25 25

Arms of Cayman Islands A22

**Wmk. 4**

**1959, July 4** **Photo.** *Perf. 12*

*151* A22 2½p dl bl & blk 60 60
*152* A22 1sh red org & blk 60 60

Granting of a new constitution.

Cayman Parrot — A23

Catboat A24

Designs: 1½p, Orchid. 2p, May of Islands. 2½p, Fisherman casting net. 3p, West Bay Beach. 4p, Green turtle. 6p, Cayman schooner. 9p, Angler with kingfish. 1sh, Iguana. 1sh3p, Swimming pool, Cayman Brac. 1sh9p, Girl and sailboat. 5sh, Fort George. 10sh, Coat of Arms. £1, Queen Elizabeth II.

***Perf. 11x11½, 11½x11***

**1962, Nov. 28** **Wmk. 314** **Engr.**

*153* A23 ¼p rose red & emer 8 8
*154* A24 1p ol & blk 8 8
*155* A24 1½p pur & yel 8 8
*156* A24 2p sep & bl 8 8
*157* A24 2½p grn & vio 10 10
*158* A24 3p car & bl 14 14
*159* A24 4p pur & grn 16 16
*160* A24 6p sep & grn 25 25
*161* A23 9p pur & vio bl 40 40
*162* A24 1sh rose & sep 60 60
*163* A24 1sh3p brn org & lt grn 1.50 1.50
*164* A24 1sh9p vio & bl grn 2.00 2.00
*165* A24 5sh grn & dl pur 5.00 5.00
*166* A23 10sh bl & ol 7.25 7.25
*167* A23 £1 blk & car rose 14.00 14.00
Revenue cancel 75
*Nos. 153-167 (15)* 31.72 31.72

**Freedom from Hunger Issue**

Common Design Type

**1963, June 4** **Photo.** *Perf. 14x14½*

*168* CD314 1sh9p car rose 1.90 1.90

**Red Cross Centenary Issue**

Common Design Type

**Wmk. 314**

**1963, Sept. 2** **Litho.** *Perf. 13*

*169* CD315 1p blk & red 15 15
*170* CD315 1sh 9p ultra & red 2.50 2.50

**Shakespeare Issue**

Common Design Type

**1964, Apr. 23** **Photo.** *Perf. 14x14½*

*171* CD316 6p dp lil rose 28 28

**ITU Issue**

Common Design Type

**1965, May 17** **Litho.** **Wmk. 314**

*172* CD317 1p ultra & red lil 8 8
*173* CD317 1sh 3p rose lil & grn 1.40 1.40

**Intl. Cooperation Year Issue**

Common Design Type

**1965, Oct. 25** **Wmk. 314** *Perf. 14½*

*174* CD318 1p bl grn & cl 8 8
*175* CD318 1sh lt vio & grn 85 85

**Churchill Memorial Issue**

Common Design Type

**1966, Jan. 24** **Photo.** *Perf. 14*

**Design in Black, Gold and Carmine Rose**

*176* CD319 ¼p brt bl 6 6
*177* CD319 1p green 10 10
*178* CD319 1sh brown 80 80
*179* CD319 1sh 9p vio 1.40 1.40

**Royal Visit Issue**

Common Design Type

**1966, Feb. 4** **Litho.** *Perf. 11x12*

*180* CD320 1p vio bl 6 6
*181* CD320 1sh 9p dk car rose 1.10 1.10

**World Cup Soccer Issue**

Common Design Type

**1966, July 1** **Litho.** *Perf. 14*

*182* CD321 1½p multi 8 8
*183* CD321 1sh 9p multi 85 85

Common Design Types pictured in section before Great Britain.

**WHO Headquarters Issue**

Common Design Type

**1966, Sept. 20** **Litho.** *Perf. 14*

*184* CD322 2p multi 20 20
*185* CD322 1sh3p multi 90 90

**UNESCO Anniversary Issue**

Common Design Type

**1966, Dec. 1** **Litho.** *Perf. 14*

*186* CD323 1p "Education" 6 6
*187* CD323 1sh9p "Science" 90 90
*188* CD323 5sh "Culture" 2.75 2.75

Telephone and Map of Caymans — A25

***Perf. 14½x14***

**1966, Dec. 5** **Litho.** **Wmk. 314**

*189* A25 4p multi 25 25
*190* A25 9p multi 60 60

Issued to commemorate the linking of the Cayman telephone system with the international system.

BAC 1-11 Jet Liner over Schooner A26

**1966, Dec. 17**

191 A26 1sh bl. ol & blk 30 30
192 A26 1sh9p ultra. grn & sep 60 60

Issued to publicize the opening of the Grand Cayman Airport jet service.

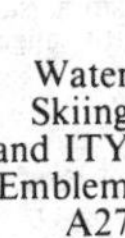
Water Skiing and ITY Emblem A27

Designs (ITY Emblem and): 6p, Skin diving. 1sh, Sport fishing. 1sh9p, Sailing.

*Perf. 14½x14*

**1967, Dec. 1 Photo. Wmk. 314**

193 A27 4p multi & gold 10 10
a. gold omitted 100.00
194 A27 6p multi & gold 15 15
195 A27 1sh multi & gold 32 32
196 A27 1sh9p multi & gold 55 55

Issued for International Tourist Year, 1967.

Human Rights Flame and Freed Slaves A28

**1968, June 3 Photo. Wmk. 314**

197 A28 3p sl bl, grn & gold 6 6
198 A28 9p lt brn, grn & gold 28 28
199 A28 5sh ultra, grn & gold 1.40 1.40

International Human Rights Year 1968.

Long Jump A29

Designs: 1sh3p, High jump. 2sh, Pole vault (vert.).

**1968, Oct. 1 Litho. *Perf. 13½***

200 A29 1sh multi 30 30
201 A29 1sh3p multi 40 40
a. Imperf., pair 225.00
202 A29 2sh yel & multi 75 75

Issued to publicize the 19th Olympic Games, Mexico City, Oct. 12-27.

Adoration of Shepherds, by Carel Fabritius A30

Design: 1p, 8p, 2sh, Adoration of the Shepherds, by Rembrandt.

*Perf. 14x14½*

**1968, Nov. 18 Photo. Wmk. 314**

203 A30 ¼p brn & multi 5 5
a. gold omitted 190.00
204 A30 1p vio & multi 5 5
205 A30 6p multi 18 18
206 A30 8p car & multi 28 28
207 A30 1sh3p multi 45 45
208 A30 2sh gray & multi 75 75
*Nos. 203-208 (6)* 1.76 1.76

Christmas 1968.

**1969, Jan. 8 Unwmk.**

209 A30 ¼p red lil & multi 5 5

Grand Cayman Thrush A31

Designs: 1p, Brahman cattle. 2p, Blowholes on coast. 2½p, Map of Grand Cayman. 3p, Town scene in Georgetown. 4p, Royal poinciana. 6p, Map of Cayman Brac and Little Cayman. 8p, Ships in harbor. 1sh, Basket making. 1sh3p, Beach scene. 1sh6p, Rope making. 2sh, Barracudas. 4sh, Government House. 10sh, Coat of arms (vert.). £1, Queen Elizabeth II (vert.).

**Unwmk.**

**1969, June 5 Litho. *Perf. 14***

210 A31 ¼p multi 8 5
211 A31 1p multi 8 5
212 A31 2p multi 8 6
213 A31 2½p multi 8 8
214 A31 3p multi 8 8
215 A31 4p multi 10 10
216 A31 6p multi 15 15
217 A31 8p multi 22 22
218 A31 1sh multi 35 35
219 A31 1sh3p multi 52 52
220 A31 1sh6p multi 60 60
221 A31 2sh multi 80 80
222 A31 4sh multi 1.65 1.65
223 A31 10sh multi 3.50 3.50
224 A31 £1 multi 7.00 7.00
*Nos. 210-224 (15)* 15.29 15.21

See Nos. 262-276.

**1969, Aug. 11 Wmk. 314 Sideways**

225 A31 ¼p multi 15 15

Type of 1969 Surcharged

C-DAY
8th September 1969
¼c

**1969, Sept. 8 Wmk. 314 *Perf. 14***

227 A31 ¼c on ¼p multi 5 5
228 A31 1c on 1p multi 5 5
229 A31 2c on 2p multi 8 8
230 A31 3c on 4p multi 10 10
231 A31 4c on 2½p multi 8 8
232 A31 5c on 6p multi 12 12
233 A31 7c on 8p multi 20 20
234 A31 8c on 3p multi 20 20
235 A31 10c on 1s multi 28 28
236 A31 12c on 1sh3p multi 38 38
237 A31 15c on 1sh6p multi 48 48
238 A31 20c on 2sh multi 65 65
239 A31 40c on 4sh multi 1.40 1.40
240 A31 $1 on 10sh multi 3.75 3.75
241 A31 $2 on £1 multi 7.50 7.50
*Nos. 227-241 (15)* 15.32 15.32

The surcharge is arranged differently on various denominations.

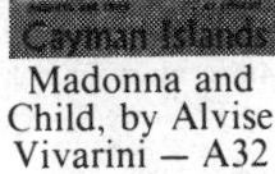
Madonna and Child, by Alvise Vivarini — A32

"Noli me Tangere," by Titian — A33

Designs: 1c, 7c, 20c, The Adoration of the Kings, by Jan Gossaert.

**1969, Nov. 4 Photo. *Perf. 14***

242 A32 ¼c bl & multi 5 5
243 A32 ¼c emer & multi 5 5
244 A32 ¼c red org & multi 5 5
245 A32 ¼c brt pink & multi 5 5
246 A32 1c vio bl & multi 5 5
247 A32 5c red org & multi 12 12
248 A32 7c dk grn & multi 18 18
249 A32 12c emer & multi 38 38
250 A32 20c multi 60 60
*Nos. 242-250 (9)* 1.53 1.53

Christmas 1969.

**1970, Mar. 23 Litho. Unwmk.**

251 A33 ¼c dl grn & multi 5 5
252 A33 ¼c dk car & multi 5 5
253 A33 ¼c vio & multi 5 5
254 A33 ¼c bis & multi 5 5
255 A33 10c vio bl & multi 30 30
256 A33 12c red brn & multi 35 35
257 A33 40c brn vio & multi 1.25 1.25
*Nos. 251-257 (7)* 2.10 2.10

Easter 1970.

Barnaby from "Barnaby Rudge" by Dickens (1812-70), English Novelist — A34

Characters from Charles Dickens: 12c, Sairey Gamp, from "Martin Chuzzlewit." 20c, Mr. Micawber and David, from "David Copperfield." 40c, The Marchioness from "The Old Curiosity Shop."

**1970, June 17 Photo. *Perf. 14½x14***

258 A34 1c ol grn, yel & blk 5 5
259 A34 12c red brn, brick red & blk 45 45
260 A34 20c dk ol bis, gold & blk 75 75
261 A34 40c dp ultra, lt bl & blk 1.50 1.50

Type of Regular Issue 1969 Values in Cents and Dollars

Designs: ¼c, Grand Cayman thrush. 1c, Brahman cattle. 2c, Blowholes on coast. 3c, Royal poinciana. 4c, Map of Grand Cayman. 5c, Map of Cayman Brac and Little Cayman. 7c, Ships in harbor. 8c, Town scene in Georgetown. 10c, Basket making. 12c, Beach scene. 15c, Rope making. 20c, Barracudas. 40c, Government House. $1, Coat of arms (vert.). $2, Queen Elizabeth II (vert.).

**Wmk. 314**

**1970, Sept. 8 Litho. *Perf. 14***

262 A31 ¼c multi 5 5
263 A31 1c multi 5 5
264 A31 2c multi 6 6
265 A31 3c multi 10 10
266 A31 4c multi 14 14
267 A31 5c multi 16 16
268 A31 7c multi 25 25
269 A31 8c multi 30 30
270 A31 10c multi 40 40
271 A31 12c multi 45 45
272 A31 15c multi 60 60
273 A31 20c multi 80 80
274 A31 40c multi 1.65 1.65
275 A31 $1 multi 5.00 5.00
276 A31 $2 multi 8.25 8.25
*Nos. 262-276 (15)* 18.26 18.26

The Three Wise Men A35

Design: 1c, 10c, 20c, Nativity and globe.

**1970, Oct. 8 Litho. *Perf. 14***

277 A35 ¼c brt grn & yel grn 5 5
278 A35 1c bl grn, yel grn & blk 5 5
279 A35 5c dp cl & org 16 16
280 A35 10c red org, yel & blk 35 35
281 A35 12c ultra & lt grnsh bl 42 42
282 A35 20c grn, yel grn & blk 70 70
*Nos. 277-282 (6)* 1.73 1.73

Christmas 1970.

Grand Cayman Terrapin A36

Cayman Islands Turtles: 7c, Green turtle. 12c, Hawksbill turtle. 20c, Turtle farm.

**1971, Jan. 28 *Perf. 14x14½***

283 A36 5c multi 42 42
284 A36 7c multi 60 60
285 A36 12c multi 1.10 1.10
286 A36 20c multi 1.90 1.90

Dendrophylax Fawcetii — A37

Adoration of the Kings, 15th Century — A38

Wild Orchids of West Indies: 2c, Schomburgkia thomsoniana. 10c, Vanilla claviculata. 40c, Oncidium variegatum.

**Wmk. 314**

**1971, Apr. 7 Litho. *Perf. 14***

287 A37 ¼c brn & multi 5 5
288 A37 2c ol grn & multi 22 22
289 A37 10c gray bl & multi 90 90
290 A37 40c lt vio & multi 3.00 3.00

**1971, Sept. 27 *Perf. 14***

Christmas: 1c, 15c, Nativity (detail), Paris, 14th cent. 5c, 20c, Adoration of the Kings (detail), Burgundian, 15th cent.

291 A38 ¼c gold & multi 5 5
292 A38 1c gold & multi 6 6
293 A38 5c gold & multi 18 18
294 A38 12c gold & multi 45 45
295 A38 15c gold & multi 60 60
296 A38 20c gold & multi 1.00 1.00
a. Souvenir sheet of 6 4.00 4.00
*Nos. 291-296 (6)* 2.34 2.34

No. 296a contains one each of Nos. 291-296. Decorative margin in gold, ultramarine and red. Size: 113x150mm.

Underwater Cable, Turtle and Telephone — A39

**1972, Jan. 10**

297 A39 2c multi 8 8
298 A39 10c multi 45 45
299 A39 40c multi 2.00 2.00

Coaxial cable for world communications.

Courthouse — A40

Designs: 15c, 40c, Legislative Assembly Building, Georgetown.

**1972, Aug. 15 *Perf. 13½x14***

300 A40 5c dp car & multi 14 14
301 A40 15c lil rose & multi 42 42
302 A40 25c dl grn & multi 70 70
303 A40 40c dk bl & multi 1.25 1.25
a. Souv. sheet of 4 3.00 3.00

New Cayman Islands government buildings. No. 303a contains one each of Nos. 300-303. Gold and blue margin. Size: 121x107½mm.

### Silver Wedding Issue, 1972

Common Design Type

Design: Queen Elizabeth II, Prince Philip, hawksbill turtle and conch.

**1972, Nov. 20 Photo. *Perf. 14x14½***

*304* CD324 12c vio blk & multi 32 32
*305* CD324 30c ol & multi 75 75

$1 Note and 1c Coin A41

Designs: 6c, $5 note and 5c coin. 15c, $10 note and 10c coin. 25c, $25 note and 25c coin.

**1973, Jan. 15**

*306* A41 3c emer & multi 10 10
*307* A41 6c yel & multi 10 10
*308* A41 15c lil & multi 55 55
*309* A41 25c org & multi 90 90
*a* Souvenir sheet of 4 3.00 3.00

First Cayman Islands coinage and bank notes, May 1, 1972. No. 309a contains one each of Nos. 306-309. Silver marginal inscription. Size: 126x106mm.

Last Supper A42

Stained Glass Windows: 10c, Christ Carrying Cross (vert.). 12c, Resurrection (vert.). 30c, Crucifixion.

***Perf. 14½x14, 14x14½***

**1973, Apr. 11 Litho.**

*310* A42 10c pink & multi 28 28
*311* A42 12c yel grn & multi 38 38
*312* A42 20c lt bl & multi 75 75
*313* A42 30c yel & multi 1.10 1.10
*a* Souvenir sheet of 4 3.25 3.25

Easter 1973. No. 313a contains 4 stamps similar to Nos. 310-313 with simulated perforations. Multicolored border. Size: 120x104mm.

Nativity — A43

White-winged Dove — A44

Christmas: 5c, 12c, 25c, Adoration of the Magi, from Breviary of Queen Isabella. 9c, 15c, Like 3c, Nativity from Sforza Book of Hours.

**1973, Oct. 2 *Perf. 14½***

*314* A43 3c dl grn & multi 10 10
*315* A43 5c dl pur & multi 16 16
*316* A43 9c sep & multi 28 28
*317* A43 12c dk bl & multi 38 38
*318* A43 15c dp rose & multi 48 48
*319* A43 25c blk & multi 75 75
*Nos. 314-319 (6)* 2.15 2.15

### Princess Anne's Wedding Issue

Common Design Type

**1973, Nov. 14 Wmk. 314 *Perf. 14***

*320* CD325 10c brt grn & multi 25 25
*321* CD325 30c lil & multi 70 70

**1974, Jan. 2 Litho. *Perf. 14x14½***

*322* A44 3c *shown* 30 25
*323* A44 10c *Vitelline warblers* 85 75
*324* A44 12c *Greater Antillean grackles* 1.25 1.00
*325* A44 20c *West Indian red-bellied woodpecker* 2.00 1.75
*326* A44 30c *Stripe-headed tanagers* 3.00 2.50
*327* A44 50c *Yucatan vireos* 5.00 4.50
*Nos. 322-327 (6)* 12.40 10.75

See Nos. 354-359.

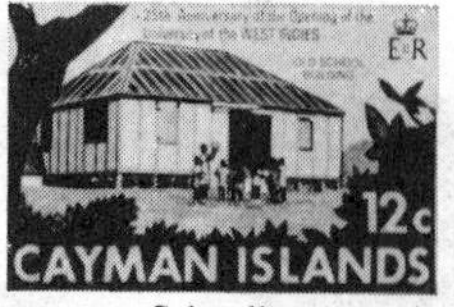


One-room Schoolhouse — A45

Designs: 20c, New comprehensive school. 30c, Creative Arts Center, Mona, Jamaica.

**1974, May 1 *Perf. 14***

*328* A45 12c multi 32 32
*329* A45 20c multi 65 65
*330* A45 30c multi 95 95

25th anniversary of the University College of the West Indies.

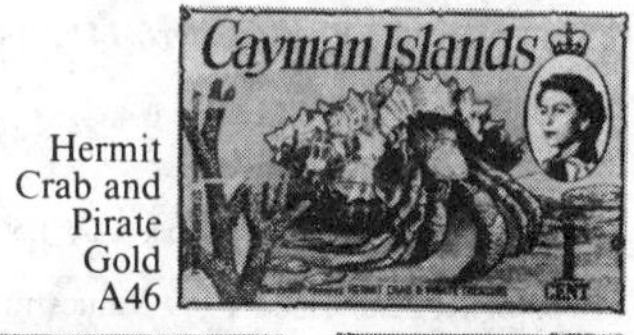


Hermit Crab and Pirate Gold A46

Coat of Arms — A47

Elizabeth II — A48

Designs: 3c, Pirate, treasure chest and lion's paw. 4c, Spotted scorpionfish and crown. 5c, Flint-lock pistol and brain coral. 6c, Blackbeard on Grand Cayman and green turtle. 8c, 9c, Jeweled pomander and porkfish. 10c, Spiny lobster and gold coins. 12c, Jeweled sword, dagger and sea fan. 15c, Cabrit's murex and jeweled necklace. 20c, Queen conch, pistol and gold cup. 25c, Hogfish and pirate chest. 40c, Gold chalice and sea whip.

**Wmk. 314 Upright, Sideways (#336, 344-345)**

**1974-75 Litho. *Perf. 14***

*331* A46 1c multi 20 20
*a* Wmk. sideways ('75) 16 16
*332* A46 3c multi 42 42
*a* Wmk. sideways 30 30
*333* A46 4c multi 26 26
*334* A46 5c multi 26 26
*335* A46 6c multi 12 12
*336* A46 8c multi 45 45
*337* A46 9c multi 2.75 2.75
*338* A46 10c multi 65 65
*339* A46 12c multi 24 24
*340* A46 15c multi 32 32
*341* A46 20c multi 1.10 1.10
*342* A46 25c multi 52 52
*343* A46 40c multi 85 85
*344* A47 $1 multi 5.25 5.25
*345* A48 $2 multi 10.50 10.50
*Nos. 331-345 (15)* 23.89 23.89

**1976 Wmk. 373**

*331b* A46 1c multi ('78) 10 8
*332b* A46 3c multi 10 8
*333a* A46 4c multi ('77) 12 10
*334a* A46 5c multi ('77) 15 12
*336b* A46 8c multi 20 15
*338b* A46 10c multi 15 12
*341b* A46 20c multi 50 38
*344a* A47 $1 multi ('77) 3.00 2.50
*345b* A48 $2 multi 5.00 5.00
*Nos. 331b-345b (9)* 9.32 8.53

Sea Captain and Ship A49

**1974, Oct. 7 Wmk. 314 *Perf. 14***

*349* A49 8c *shown* 22 22
*350* A49 12c *Thatch weaver* 28 28
*351* A49 20c *Farmer* 48 48
*a* Miniature sheet of 3 1.75 1.75

No. 351a contains one each of Nos. 349-351; multicolored margin. Size: 86x123mm.

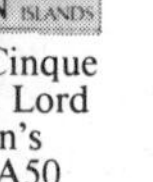

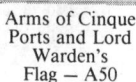

Arms of Cinque Ports and Lord Warden's Flag — A50

Churchill Coat of Arms — A51

**1974, Nov. 30**

*352* A50 12c multi 30 30
*353* A51 50c multi 1.25 1.25
*a* Souvenir sheet of 2 2.25 2.25

Sir Winston Churchill (1874-1965), birth centenary. No. 353a contains one each of Nos. 352-353, lemon and black margin showing Churchill statue. Size: 98x85mm.

Bird Type of 1974

**Wmk. 314**

**1975, Jan. 1 Litho. *Perf. 14***

*354* A44 3c *Yellow-shafted flicker* 15 15
*355* A44 10c *West Indian tree duck* 55 55
*356* A44 12c *Yellow warblers* 70 70
*357* A44 20c *White-bellied dove* 1.20 1.20
*358* A44 30c *Magnificent frigate bird* 1.80 1.80
*359* A44 50c *Cayman amazon* 3.00 3.00
*Nos. 354-359 (6)* 7.40 7.40

Ivory Crosier with Crucifixion — A52

Design: 35c, Crucifixion, ivory and gilt. Designs show heads of 14th century French pastoral staffs.

**Wmk. 314**

**1975, Mar. 24 Litho. *Perf. 14***

*360* A52 15c plum & multi 35 35
*361* A52 35c gray & multi 90 90
*a* Souvenir sheet of 2 1.50 1.50

Easter 1975. No. 361a contains one each of Nos. 360-361, purple margin with black inscription. Size: 128x97mm. No. 361a exists imperf.

See Nos. 366-367.

Israel Hands A53

Designs: Pirates and various scenes.

**1975, July 25 Wmk. 314**

*362* A53 10c *shown* 38 38
*363* A53 12c *John Fenn* 50 50
*364* A53 20c *Thomas Anstis* 85 85
*365* A53 30c *Edward Low* 1.25 1.25

Easter Type of 1975

Designs after ivory carved pastoral staffs showing Virgin and Child with angels. French, 14th century.

**Wmk. 373**

**1975, Oct. 31 Litho. *Perf. 14***

*366* A52 12c dk grn & multi 32 32
*367* A52 50c multi 1.25 1.25
*a* Souvenir sheet of 2 2.00 2.00

Christmas 1975. No. 367a contains one each of Nos. 366-367; brown margin with black and white inscription. Size: 112x85mm.

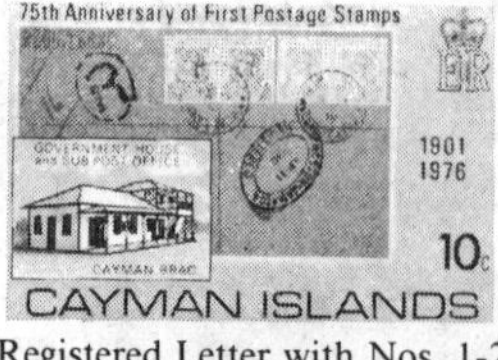


Registered Letter with Nos. 1-2; Cayman Brac Government House and Sub Post Office — A54

Designs: 20c, Cayman Islands No. 1 and cancelation used 1890-94. 30c, Nos. 2 and 20. 50c, Nos. 1-2.

**1976, Mar. 12 Litho. *Perf. 13½x14***

*368* A54 10c lt bl & multi 30 30
*369* A54 20c pink & multi 60 60
*370* A54 30c multi 90 90
*371* A54 50c yel & multi 1.50 1.50
*a* Souvenir sheet of 4 3.50 3.50

75th anniversary of Cayman Islands first postage stamps. No. 371a contains one each of Nos. 368-371; yellow and multicolored margin showing historic postal markings. Size: 116½x144mm.

Seals of Georgia, Delaware and New Hampshire — A55

Designs: 15c, Seals of South Carolina, New Jersey and Maryland. 20c, Seals of Virginia, Rhode Island and Massachusetts. 25c, Seals of New York, Connecticut and North Carolina. 30c, Seal of Pennsylvania, Liberty Bell and Great Seal of the U.S.

**Wmk. 373**

**1976, May 29 Litho. *Perf. 14***

*372* A55 10c ol & multi 40 40
*373* A55 15c bl & multi 60 60
*374* A55 20c multi 80 80
*375* A55 25c bl grn & multi 1.00 1.00
*376* A55 30c red brn & multi 1.25 1.25
*a* Souvenir sheet of 5 + label 5.00 5.00
*Nos. 372-376 (5)* 4.05 4.05

American Bicentennial. Nos. 372-376 printed in sheets of 5 with same border and size as No. 376a. No. 376a contains one each of Nos. 372-376 and corner label inscribed "USA 200." Multicolored margin with border showing stars, Cayman turtle and Great Seal of the U.S. Size: 160x122mm.

French Class 470 Racing
Dinghies — A56

Queen Elizabeth II — A57

Design: 50c, One racing dinghy.

**976, Aug. 16 Litho. *Perf. 14***

*77* A56 20c multi 65 65
*78* A56 50c multi 1.65 1.65

21st Olympic Games, Montreal, Canada, uly 17-Aug. 1.

***Perf. 14x13½, 13½x14***

**977, Feb. 7 Litho. Wmk. 373**

Designs: 8c, Prince Charles, 1973 visit. 0c, Preparation for anointing ceremony oriz.).

*79* A57 8c multi 18 18
*80* A57 30c multi 70 70
*81* A57 50c multi 1.25 1.25

25th anniv. of the reign of Elizabeth II.

Scuba Diving
A58

Designs: 10c, Divers examining underwa-r wreck. 20c, Fairy basslets (fish). 25c, Ser-eant majors (fish).

**977, July 25 *Perf. 13½***

*82* A58 5c multi 20 20
*83* A58 10c multi 38 38
*84* A58 20c multi 75 75
*85* A58 25c multi 95 95
*a* Souvenir sheet of 4 2.25 2.25

Tourist publicity. No. 385a contains one ach of Nos. 382-385, perf. 14½; ultramarine nd dark blue margin shows scuba divers. ize: 146x90mm.

Composia Fidelissima
A59

Butterflies: 8c, Heliconius charitonius. 0c, Danaus gilippus. 15c, Agraulis vanillae. 0c, Junonia evarete. 30c, Anartia jatrophae.

***Perf. 14x13***

**977, Dec. 2 Litho. Wmk. 373**

*86* A59 5c multi 22 22
*87* A59 8c multi 38 38
*88* A59 10c multi 45 45
*89* A59 15c multi 70 70
*90* A59 20c multi 90 90
*91* A59 30c multi 1.40 1.40
*Nos. 386-391 (6)* 4.05 4.05

Cruise Ship "Southward"
A60

Designs: 5c, "Renaissance." 30c, New har-bor (vert.). 50c, "Daphne" (vert.).

**1978, Jan. 23 Litho. *Perf. 14***

*392* A60 3c multi 9 9
*393* A60 5c multi 15 15
*394* A60 30c multi 65 65
*395* A60 50c multi 1.10 1.10

New harbor and cruise ships.

Crucifixion, by Dürer — A61

Explorers, Singing Game — A62

Etchings by Dürer: 15c, Christ at Emmaus. 20c, Entry into Jerusalem. 30c, Christ washing Peter's feet.

**1978, Mar. 20 Litho. *Perf. 12***

*396* A61 10c multi 22 22
*397* A61 15c multi 30 30
*398* A61 20c multi 42 42
*399* A61 30c multi 60 60
*a* Souvenir sheet of 4 1.65 1.65

Easter 1978 and 450th death anniversary of Albrecht Dürer (1471-1528). Nos. 396-399 issued in sheets of 6. No. 399a contains one each of Nos. 396-399; gray black margin shows hands of Apostle, 1508. Size: 131x119mm.

**1978, Apr. 28 Litho. *Perf. 14***

Designs: 10c, Girls' Brigade presenting flag. 20c, Guides studying Bible, playing guitar, tennis and volleyball. 50c, Guides setting table.

*400* A62 3c multi 10 10
*401* A62 10c multi 30 30
*402* A62 20c multi 55 55
*403* A62 50c multi 1.25 1.25

Third International Council Meeting of Girls' Brigade.

**Elizabeth II Coronation Anniversary Issue**

Common Design Types

**Souvenir Sheet**

**1978, June 2 Unwmk. *Perf. 15***

*404* Sheet of 6 3.75 *3.75*
*a* CD326 30c *Yale of Beaufort* 60 60
*b* CD327 30c *Elizabeth II* 60 60
*c* CD328 30c *Screech owl* 60 60

No. 404 contains 2 se-tenant strips of Nos. 404a-404c, separated by horizontal gutter with commemorative and descriptive inscriptions and showing central part of coronation procession with coach. Size: 100x135mm.

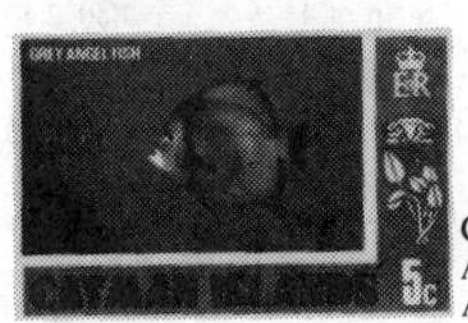


Gray Angelfish
A63

Fish: 1c, Trumpetfish. No. 406, Four-eyed butterflyfish. No. 407, Nassau grouper. No. 409, French angelfish. No. 412, Squirrelfish. No. 413, Schoolmaster snappers. 15c, Parrotfish. No. 415, Spanish hogfish. No. 416, Banded butterflyfish. 30c, Queen angelfish. 50c, Black-bar soldierfish.

**1978-79 Wmk. 373 Litho. *Perf. 14***

*405* A63 1c multi ('79) 5 5
*406* A63 3c multi 9 9
*407* A63 3c multi ('79) 6 6
*408* A63 5c multi 15 15
*409* A63 5c multi 8 8
*412* A63 10c multi 28 28
*413* A63 10c multi 28 28
*414* A63 15c multi 38 38
*415* A63 20c multi 45 45
*416* A63 20c multi 45 45
*417* A63 30c multi 75 75
*418* A63 50c multi 1.10 1.10
*Nos. 405-418 (12)* 4.12 4.12

Lockheed Lodestar
A64

Aircraft: 5c, Consolidated PBY. 10c, Vickers Viking. 15c, BAC1-11. 20c, Piper Cheyenne, HS 125 and Bell 47. 30c, BAC1-11.

**1979, Feb. 5 *Perf. 14½***

*420* A64 3c multi 8 8
*421* A64 5c multi 12 12
*422* A64 10c multi 24 24
*423* A64 15c multi 32 32
*424* A64 20c multi 48 48
*425* A64 30c multi 65 65
*Nos. 420-425 (6)* 1.89 1.89

25th anniversary of opening of Owen Roberts Airport.

Rowland Hill and No. 2 — A65

Rowland Hill and: 10c, Great Britain No. 132. 20c, Cayman Islands No. 149. 50c, Cayman Islands No. 20.

***Perf. 13½x14½***

**1979, Aug. 15 Litho.**

*426* A65 5c multi 12 12
*427* A65 10c multi 22 22
*428* A65 20c multi 45 45

**Souvenir Sheet**

*429* A65 50c multi 1.10 1.10

Sir Rowland Hill (1795-1879), originator of penny postage. No. 429 has multicolored margin showing Mulready envelope. Size: 138x90mm.

Flight into Egypt
A66

Christmas 1979: 20c, Shepherds, Star of Bethlehem. 30c, Nativity. 40c, Three Kings, Star of Bethlehem.

**1979, Nov. 20 Litho. *Perf. 13½***

*430* A66 10c multi 20 20
*431* A66 20c multi 42 42
*432* A66 30c multi 60 60
*433* A66 40c multi 85 85

Bonaventure House, Rotary Emblem — A67

***Perf. 14x13½, 13½x14***

**1980, Feb. 14 Litho. Wmk. 373**

*434* A67 20c *shown* 45 45
*435* A67 30c *Paul P. Harris,* vert. 65 65
*436* A67 50c *Anniversary emblem,* vert. 1.10 1.10

Rotary International, 75th anniversary.

Mailman, London 1980 Emblem
A68

**1980, May 6 Litho. *Perf. 14***

*437* A68 5c *shown* 9 9
*438* A68 10c *Cat boat* 20 20
*439* A68 15c *Mounted mailman* 28 28
*440* A68 30c *Mail wagon* 60 60
*441* A68 40c *Mailman on bicycle* 75 75
*442* A68 $1 *Mail truck* 1.90 *1.90*
*Nos. 437-442 (6)* 3.82 3.82

London '80 Intl. Stamp Exhib., May 6-14.

**Queen Mother Elizabeth Birthday Issue**

Common Design Type

**1980, Aug. 4 Litho. *Perf. 14***

*443* CD330 20c multi 45 45

Spondylus Americanus
A69

**1980, Aug. 12 *Perf. 14½x14***

*444* A69 5c *shown* 10 10
*445* A69 10c *Murex brevifrons* 22 22
*446* A69 30c *Cymatium femorale* 65 65
*447* A69 50c *Vasum muricatum* 1.10 1.10

See Nos. 502-505.

Lantana — A70

**1980, Oct. 21 Litho. *Perf. 14***

*448* A70 5c *shown* 12 12
*449* A70 15c *Bauhinia* 35 35
*450* A70 30c *Hibiscus* 70 70
*451* A70 $1 *Milk and wine lily* 2.25 2.25

See Nos. 478-481.

Juvenile Tarpon and Fire Sponges — A71

**1980, Dec. 9 Litho. *Perf. 13½x13***

*452* A71 3c *shown* 6 6
*453* A71 5c *Mangrove root oysters* 9 9
*454* A71 10c *Mangrove crab* 20 20
*455* A71 15c *Lizard, crescent spot butterfly* 30 30
*456* A71 20c *Tricolored heron* 38 38
*457* A71 30c *Red mangrove flower* 60 60
*458* A71 40c *Red mangrove seeds* 80 80
*459* A71 50c *Waterhouse's leaf-nosed bat* 95 95
*460* A71 $1 *Black-crowned night heron* 1.90 1.90
*461* A71 $2 *Cayman Islds. arms* 3.75 3.75
*462* A71 $4 *Queen Elizabeth II* 7.75 7.75
*Nos. 452-462 (11)* 16.78 16.78

Also issued inscribed 1982.

Bread and Wine — A72

**1981, Mar. 17 Wmk. 373 *Perf. 14***
*463* A72 3c shown 5 5
*464* A72 10c Crown of thorns 18 18
*465* A72 20c Crucifix 35 35
*466* A72 $1 Christ 1.75 1.75

Easter 1981.

Wood Slave A73

**1981, June 16 Litho. *Perf. 13½***
*467* A73 20c shown 45 45
*468* A73 30c Cayman iguana 70 70
*469* A73 40c Lion lizard 90 90
*470* A73 50c Freshwater turtle 1.10 1.10

**Royal Wedding Issue**
Common Design Type

**1981, July 22 Litho. *Perf. 14***
*471* CD331 20c Bouquet 38 38
*472* CD331 30c Charles 60 60
*473* CD331 $1 Couple 1.90 1.90

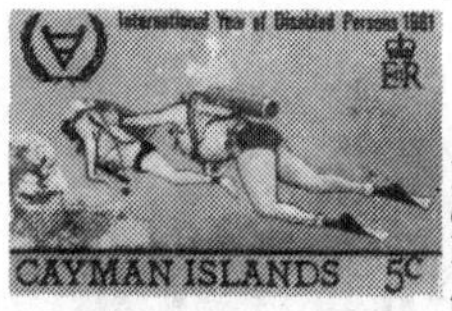

Intl. Year of the Disabled A74

**1981, Sept. 29 Litho. *Perf. 14***
*474* A74 5c Scuba divers 9 9
*475* A74 15c Old School for Handicapped 28 28
*476* A74 20c New School for Handicapped 38 38
*477* A74 $1 Beach scene 1.90 1.90

Flower Type of 1980

**1981, Oct. 20 Litho. *Perf. 14***
*478* A70 3c Bougainvillea 7 7
*479* A70 10c Morning glory 22 22
*480* A70 20c Wild amaryllis 45 45
*481* A70 $1 Cordia 2.25 2.25

TB Bacillus Centenary A75

**1982, Mar. 24 Litho. *Perf. 14½***
*482* A75 15c Koch, horizontal microscope 38 38
*483* A75 30c Koch, vert. 75 75
*484* A75 40c Microscope, vert. 1.00 1.00
*485* A75 50c Koch, diff., vert. 1.25 1.25

**Princess Diana Issue**
Common Design Type

**1982, July 1 Litho. *Perf. 13***
*486* CD333 20c Arms 40 40
*487* CD333 30c Diana 60 60
*488* CD333 40c Wedding 80 80
*489* CD333 50c Portrait 1.00 1.00

Scouting Year A76

**1982, Aug. 24 Wmk. 373 *Perf. 14***
*490* A76 3c Pitching tent 7 7
*491* A76 20c Cooking 45 45
*492* A76 30c Troop 70 70
*493* A76 50c Boating skills 1.10 1.10

Christmas 1982 — A77

Virgin and Child Paintings by Raphael.

**1982, Oct. 26 *Perf. 14½***
*494* A77 3c multi 7 7
*495* A77 10c multi 22 22
*496* A77 20c multi 45 45
*497* A77 30c multi 65 65

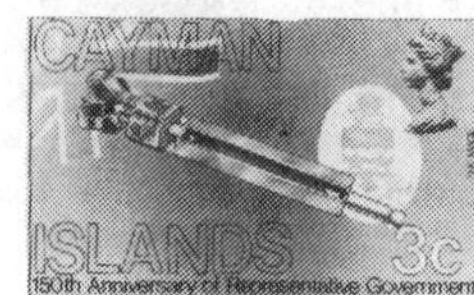

Representative Govt. Sesquicentennial — A78

**1982, Nov. 9 Litho. Wmk. 373**
*498* A78 3c Mace 7 7
*499* A78 10c Old Courthouse 22 22
*500* A78 20c Commonwealth Parliamentary Assoc. arms 42 42
*501* A78 30c Legislative Assembley building 65 65

Shell Type of 1980

**1983, Jan. 11 Litho. *Perf. 13½***
*502* A69 5c Natica canrena 12 12
*503* A69 10c Cassis tuberosa 25 25
*504* A69 20c Strombus gallus 50 50
*505* A69 $1 Cypraecassis testiculus 2.50 2.50

Visit of Queen Elizabeth II and Prince Philip A79

**1983, Feb. 15 Litho. *Perf. 14***
*506* A79 20c Legislative Building, Cayman Brac 45 45
*507* A79 30c Leg. Bldg., Grand Cayman 70 70
*508* A79 50c Prince Philip 1.10 1.10
*509* A79 $1 Queen Elizabeth II 2.25 2.25
*a* Souvenir sheet of 4 4.50 *4.50*

No. 509a contains Nos. 506-509.

**Commonwealth Day**
Common Design Type

**1983, Mar. 14**
*510* CD334 3c Globe 9 9
*511* CD334 15c Flags 42 42
*512* CD334 20c Fisherman 55 55
*513* CD334 40c Elizabeth II 1.10 1.10

Manned Flight Bicentenary and Mosquito Research and Control Unit — A81

Airplanes.

**1983, Oct. 10 Litho. *Perf. 14½***
*514* A81 3c MRCU Cessna 8 8
*515* A81 10c Consolidated Catalina PBY 25 25
*516* A81 20c Boeing 727 50 50
*517* A81 40c Hawker Siddeley HS-748 1.00 1.00

Shell Type of 1980

**1984, Jan. 18 *Perf. 14x14½***
*518* A69 3c Natica Floridana 9 9
*519* A69 10c Conus Austini 28 28
*520* A69 30c Colubrania Obscura 80 80
*521* A69 50c Turbo Cailletii 1.40 1.40

**Lloyd's List Issue**
Common Design Type

**1984, May 16 Litho. *Perf. 14***
*522* CD335 5c Cruise ship 12 12
*523* CD335 10c The Old Harbor 22 22
*524* CD335 25c Ridgefield 60 60
*525* CD335 50c Goldfield 1.25 1.25

**Souvenir Sheet**

*526* CD335 $1 Goldfield, diff. 2.50 2.50

No. 526 has multicolored margin showing map. Size: 105x75mm.

No. 525 Overprinted: "U.P.U. CONGRESS / HAMBURG 1984"

**1984, June 18**
*527* CD335 50c multi 1.40 1.40

Local Birds — A82

***Perf. 14x14½***
**1984, Aug. 15 Litho. Wmk. 373**
*528* A82 5c Snowy egret 12 12
*529* A82 10c Bananaquit 24 24
*530* A82 35c Kingfisher 85 85
*531* A82 $1 Brown booby 2.50 2.50

Christmas 1984 — A83

Designs: Nos. 532a-532d, evening beach scenes. Nos. 533a-533d, daytime boating and beach scenes.

**1984, Oct. 17 Litho. *Perf. 14***
*532* Strip of 4 50 50
*a.-d.* A83 5c Any single 12 12
*533* Strip of 4 2.50 2.50
*a.-d.* A83 25c Any single 62 62

**Souvenir Sheet**

*534* A83 $1 Bonfire, diff. 2.50 2.50

No. 534 contains one stamp, size: 29x48mm. Margin continues design. Size: 59x77mm.

Orchids — A84

**1985, Mar. 13 Litho. *Perf. 14x13½***
*535* A84 5c Schomburgkia thomsoniana var. 10 10
*536* A84 10c Schomburgkia thomsoniana 20 20
*537* A84 25c Encyclia plicata 50 50
*538* A84 50c Dendrophylax fawcetti 1.00 1.00

Shipwrecks A85

Unspecified shipwrecks found in Cayma waters.

**1985, May 22 *Perf. 1***
*539* A85 5c multi 10
*540* A85 25c multi 50
*541* A85 35c multi 70
*542* A85 40c multi 80

Intl. Youth Year — A86

Designs: 5c, Natl. Athletic Assoc. trac competition. 15c, High school students stu ying in Grand Cayman Campus Library. 25 Amateur League Competition Football. 50 Natl. Netball Assoc. competition.

**1985, Aug. 14 *Perf. 14***
*543* A86 5c multi 10
*544* A86 15c multi 30
*545* A86 25c multi 50
*546* A86 50c multi 1.00 1.0

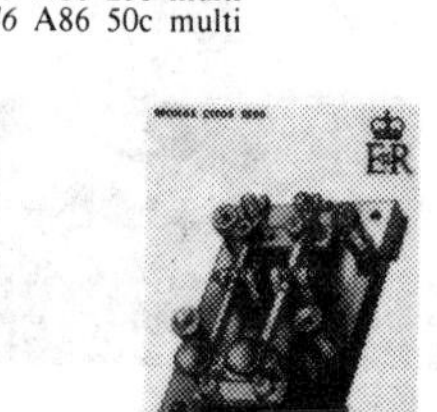

Telecommunications, 50th Anniv. — A87

Designs: 5c, Morse Code transmitter, 193 10c, Hand-cranked telephone, 1935. 25 Tropospheric scatter dish, 1966. 50c, Eart dish receiver, 1979.

**1985, Oct. 25 *Perf. 1***
*547* A87 5c multi 10 1
*548* A87 10c multi 20 2
*549* A87 25c multi 50 5
*550* A87 50c multi 1.00 1.0

Birds A88

**Wmk. 384**
**1986, Mar. 20 Litho. *Perf. 1***
*551* A88 10c Magnificent frigatebird 12 1
*552* A88 25c West Indian whistling duck 35 3
*553* A88 35c La Sagra's flycatcher 60 6
*554* A88 40c Yellow-faced grassquit 95 9

Nos. 552-553 vert.

**Queen Elizabeth II 60th Birthday**
Common Design Type

Designs: 5c, As bridesmaid at wedding o Lady Mary Cambridge, 1931. 10c, Roya visit to Norway, 1955. 25c, Inspecting Wes Indian troop, royal tour, 1985. 50c, Gu tour, 1979. $1, Visiting Crown Agents offices, 1983.

**1986, Apr. 21 *Perf. 14x14½***
*555* CD337 5c scar, blk & sil 12 1
*556* CD337 10c ultra, blk & sil 24 2
*557* CD337 25c grn & multi 60 6
*558* CD337 50c vio & multi 1.20 1.2
*559* CD337 $1 rose vio & multi 2.40 2.4
*Nos. 555-559 (5)* 4.56 4.5

**Royal Wedding Issue, 1986**

Common Design Type

Designs: 5c, Informal portrait. 50c, Andrew in uniform, helicopter.

***Perf. 14½x14***

**1986, July 23 Litho. Wmk. 384**

| | | | | |
|---|---|---|---|---|
| *560* | CD338 | 5c multi | 12 | 12 |
| *561* | CD338 | 50c multi | 1.20 | 1.20 |

Marine Life — A89

***Perf. 13½x13***

**1986, Sept. 15 Litho. Wmk. 373**

| | | | | |
|---|---|---|---|---|
| *562* | A89 | 5c Rhynchocinetes rigeus | 10 | 10 |
| *563* | A89 | 10c Nemaster rubiginosa | 18 | 18 |
| *564* | A89 | 15c Calcinus tibicen | 28 | 28 |
| *565* | A89 | 20c Rhodactis sanctithomae | 38 | 38 |
| *566* | A89 | 25c Spirobranchus gigantea | 48 | 48 |
| *567* | A89 | 35c Diodon holacanthus | 65 | 65 |
| *568* | A89 | 50c Pseudocorynactis aribbeorum | 95 | 95 |
| *569* | A89 | 60c Astrophyton muricatum | 1.10 | 1.10 |
| *570* | A89 | 75c Cyphoma gibbosum | 1.40 | 1.40 |
| *571* | A89 | $1 Conolylactis gigantea | 1.90 | 1.90 |
| *572* | A89 | $2 Malacoctenus boehlkei | 3.75 | 3.75 |
| *573* | A89 | $4 Lima scabra | 7.50 | 7.50 |
| | | *Nos. 562-573 (12)* | 18.67 | 18.67 |

Nos. 562-565, 571-573 exist inscribed "1979.".

Tourism A90

***Perf. 13x13½***

**1987, Jan. 26 Litho. Wmk. 384**

| | | | | |
|---|---|---|---|---|
| *574* | A90 | 10c Golfing | 24 | 24 |
| *575* | A90 | 15c Sailing | 35 | 35 |
| *576* | A90 | 25c Snorkeling | 60 | 60 |
| *577* | A90 | 35c Parasailing | 85 | 85 |
| *578* | A90 | $1 Fishing | 2.40 | 2.40 |
| | | *Nos. 574-578 (5)* | 4.44 | 4.44 |

Fruit — A91

**1987, May 20** ***Perf. 14½***

| | | | | |
|---|---|---|---|---|
| *579* | A91 | 5c Akee | 12 | 12 |
| *580* | A91 | 25c Breadfruit | 60 | 60 |
| *581* | A91 | 35c Pawpaw | 85 | 85 |
| *582* | A91 | $1 Soursop | 2.40 | 2.40 |

Lizards — A92

**1987, Aug. 26 Litho.** ***Perf. 14***

| | | | | |
|---|---|---|---|---|
| *583* | A92 | 10c Lion lizard | 24 | 24 |
| *584* | A92 | 50c Iguana | 1.20 | 1.20 |
| *585* | A92 | $1 Anole | 2.40 | 2.40 |

Flowers — A93

**1987, Nov. 18** ***Perf. 14½x14***

| | | | | |
|---|---|---|---|---|
| *586* | A93 | 5c Poinsettia | 12 | 12 |
| *587* | A93 | 25c Periwinkle | 60 | 60 |
| *588* | A93 | 35c Yellow allamanda | 85 | 85 |
| *589* | A93 | 75c Blood lily | 1.75 | 1.75 |

Butterflies A94

Designs: 5c, *Hemiargus ammon erembisand Strymon martialis.* 25c, *Phocides pigmalion batabano.* 50c, *Anaea troglodyta cubana.*$1, *Papilio andraemon andraemon.*

**Wmk. 384**

**1988, Mar. 29 Litho.** ***Perf. 14***

| | | | | |
|---|---|---|---|---|
| *590* | A94 | 5c multi | 12 | 12 |
| *591* | A94 | 25c multi | 60 | 60 |
| *592* | A94 | 50c multi | 1.20 | 1.20 |
| *593* | A94 | $1 multi | 2.40 | 2.40 |

Herons — A95

**1988, Jan. 26 Litho.** ***Perf. 14***

| | | | | |
|---|---|---|---|---|
| *594* | A95 | 5c Butorides striatus | 12 | 12 |
| *595* | A95 | 25c Egretta tricolor | 60 | 60 |
| *596* | A95 | 50c Nycticorax violaceus | 1.20 | 1.20 |
| *597* | A95 | $1 Egretta caerulea | 2.40 | 2.40 |

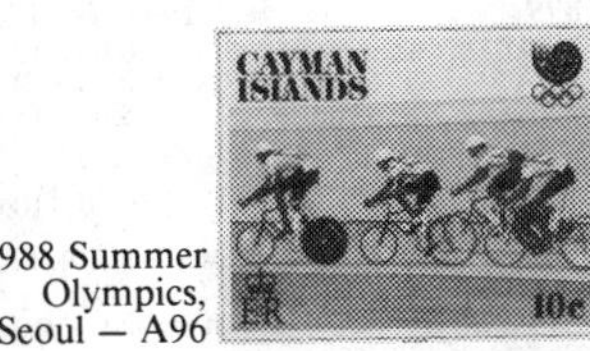


1988 Summer Olympics, Seoul — A96

**1988, Sept. 21** ***Perf. 14½***

| | | | | |
|---|---|---|---|---|
| *598* | A96 | 10c Cycling | 24 | 24 |
| *599* | A96 | 50c Natl. team, passenger jet | 1.20 | 1.20 |
| *600* | A96 | $1 Yachting | 2.40 | 2.40 |

**Souvenir Sheet**

**Wmk. 373**

| | | | | |
|---|---|---|---|---|
| *601* | A96 | $1 Tennis | 2.40 | 2.40 |

No. 601 has inscribed multicolored margin inscribed to commemorate the 75th anniv. of the Intl. Tennis Federation. Size: 53x60mm.

Common Design Types are pictured in section before Great Britain.

Visit of Princess Alexandra A97

**Wmk. 373**

**1988, Nov. 1 Litho.** ***Perf. 15***

| | | | | |
|---|---|---|---|---|
| *602* | A97 | 5c Portrait | 12 | 12 |
| *603* | A97 | $1 Seated in garden | 2.40 | 2.40 |

---

### WAR TAX STAMPS

No. 36 Surcharged:

| WAR STAMP. 1½d | WAR STAMP. 1½d |
|---|---|
| a | b |

**1917 Wmk. 3** ***Perf. 14***

| | | | | |
|---|---|---|---|---|
| *MR1* | A5(a) 1½p on 2½p | | 2.25 | *3.50* |
| | **a.** Fraction bar omitted | | 70.00 | *110.00* |
| *MR2* | A5(b) 1½p on 2½p | | 65 | *2.50* |
| | **a.** Fraction bar omitted | | 52.50 | *70.00* |

Surcharged WAR STAMP 1½d

| | | | | |
|---|---|---|---|---|
| *MR3* | A5 | 1½p on 2½p ultra | 950.00 | *1,500.* |

Surcharged WAR STAMP 1½d

| | | | | |
|---|---|---|---|---|
| *MR4* | A5 | 1½p on 2½p ultra | 20 | 22 |

No. 33 Overprinted WAR STAMP

**1919**

| | | | | |
|---|---|---|---|---|
| *MR5* | A5 | ½p green | 12 | 20 |

Type of 1912-16 Surcharged WAR STAMP 1½d

| | | | | |
|---|---|---|---|---|
| *MR6* | A5 | 1½p on 2½p orange | 1.40 | *2.00* |

No. 35 Surcharged WAR STAMP 1½d.

**1920**

| | | | | |
|---|---|---|---|---|
| *MR7* | A5 | 1½p on 2p gray | 1.50 | *3.90* |

---

## CEYLON

LOCATION — An island in the Indian Ocean separated from India by the Gulf of Manaar.

GOVT. — Independent republic within the British Commonwealth.

AREA — 25,332 sq. mi.

POP. — 12,670,000 (est. 1971).

CAPITAL — Colombo.

Ceylon changed its name to Republic of Sri Lanka on May 22, 1972. Issues of Sri Lanka are listed under that name in this volume.

12 Pence = 1 Shilling

100 Cents = 1 Rupee (1872)

Values of early Ceylon stamps vary according to condition.

The quotations for Nos. 1-13 are for cut-square copies with small margins and design intact. Copies with larger margins all around sell at higher prices. Inferior specimens with designs partly cut away sell at greatly reduced prices. Cut to shape copies of Nos. 5, 8, 9, 12, 12a or 13 sell for very little.

Perforated issues of 1861 to 1868 are seldom found well centered. Values shown are for stamps with perforations cutting into the design.

**Catalogue values for unused stamps in this country are for Never Hinged items, beginning with Scott 290 in the regular postage section and Scott B1 in the semi-postal section.**

Queen Victoria

A1 A2

Wmk. 6- Large Star

**1857 Engr. Wmk. 6** ***Imperf.***

**Blued Paper**

| | | | | |
|---|---|---|---|---|
| *1* | A1 | 1p blue | *2,000.* | 65.00 |
| *2* | A1 | 6p plum | *10,000.* | 200.00 |

**1857-59**

**White Paper**

| | | | | |
|---|---|---|---|---|
| *3* | A1 | 1p blue | 250.00 | 12.00 |
| *4* | A1 | 2p yel grn | 400.00 | 110.00 |
| | **a.** | 2p dp grn | 175.00 | 40.00 |
| *5* | A2 | 4p dl rose ('59) | *75,000.* | 4,000. |
| *6* | A1 | 5p org brn | 2,000. | 200.00 |
| *6A* | A1 | 6p plum | 1,500. | 80.00 |
| *7* | A1 | 6p brown | 4,500. | 225.00 |
| *8* | A2 | 8p brn ('59) | *15,000.* | 1,500. |
| *9* | A2 | 9p lil brn ('59) | 30,000. | 1,500. |
| *10* | A1 | 10p vermilion | 850.00 | 125.00 |
| *11* | A1 | 1sh violet | 3,500. | 115.00 |
| *12* | A2 | 1sh9p grn ('59) | 900.00 | 300.00 |
| | **a.** | 1sh9p yel grn | 2,250. | 750.00 |
| *13* | A2 | 2sh bl ('59) | 5,500. | 700.00 |

Stamps of type A2 frequently have repaired corners.

Nos. 3-4 exist unofficially rouletted.

No. 5 was reproduced by the collotype process in a souvenir sheet distributed at the London International Stamp Exhibition 1950. The paper is unwatermarked.

A3

**1857-58 Typo. Unwmk.**

| | | | | |
|---|---|---|---|---|
| *14* | A3 | ½p lilac ('58) | 100.00 | 47.50 |
| *15* | A3 | ½p lil, *bluish* | 4,000. | 300.00 |

No. 14 exists unofficially rouletted.

### Clean-Cut Perf. 14 to 15½

**1861 Wmk. 6 Engr.**

17 A1 1p blue 32.50 11.00
18 A1 2p yel grn 32.50 20.00
19 A2 4p dl rose 675.00 110.00
20 A1 5p org brn 40.00 8.50
20A A1 6p brown 775.00 47.50
b. 6p bis brn 60.00
21 A2 8p brown 850.00 210.00
22 A2 9p lil brn 2,500. 135.00
23 A1 1sh violet 40.00 14.00
24 A2 2sh blue 850.00 200.00

### Rough Perf. 14 to 15½

25 A1 1p blue 27.50 5.50
b. Blued paper 200.00 15.00
26 A1 2p yel grn 35.00 24.00
27 A2 4p rose red 90.00 27.50
28 A1 6p bis brn 175.00 22.50
a. 6p dp brn 180.00 22.50
29 A2 8p brown 925.00 165.00
30 A2 8p yel brn 775.00 165.00
31 A2 9p ol brn 175.00 20.00
32 A2 9p dp brn 40.00 20.00
33 A1 10p vermilion 77.50 15.00
a. Imperf. vert., pair
34 A1 1sh violet 175.00 11.50
35 A2 1sh9p green 275.00
36 A2 2sh blue 500.00 82.50

The 1sh9p green was never placed in use.

**1863 Perf. 12½**

37 A1 10p vermilion 150.00 13.00

**1862 Typo. Unwmk.**

38 A3 ½p lilac 90.00 67.50

**1863 Engr. Perf. 13**

39 A1 1p blue 35.00 8.00
40 A1 5p car brn 600.00 82.50
41 A1 6p brown 40.00 19.00
42 A2 9p brown 360.00 32.50
43 A1 1sh grysh vio 1,500. 60.00

Parts of the papermaker's sheet watermark, "T. H. SAUNDERS 1862," may be found on some copies of Nos. 39-43.

**Perf. 12**

44 A1 1p blue 385.00 67.50

Two Types of Watermark Crown and C. C. (1)

Wmk.1a

Wmk.1b

Wmk. 1a—22½mm. high, oval letters.
Wmk. 1b—21mm. high, round letters.

**1863-67 Typo. Wmk. 1a Perf. 12½**

45 A3 ½p lilac 9.00 4.50

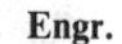

**Engr.**

46 A1 1p blue 13.00 3.50
a. 1p dk bl 13.00 3.75
c. Perf. 11½ 200.00 37.50
47 A1 2p gray grn 26.00 6.00
48 A1 2p emerald 55.00 45.00
48A A1 2p yel grn 3,000. 150.00
49 A1 2p olive 140.00 100.00
50 A2 4p rose 52.50 8.00
51 A1 5p car brn 80.00 27.50
52 A1 5p ol grn 37.50 13.00
e. 5p dp sage grn 1,050. 140.00
53 A1 6p choc brn 19.00 7.00
a. 6p brn 19.00 8.00
c. Perf. 13 360.00 32.50
54 A2 8p red brn 19.00 11.00
55 A2 9p brown 150.00 15.00
c. Perf. 13 2,000. 250.00
56 A1 10p orange 200.00 22.50
a. 10p ver 550.00 15.00
58 A2 2sh blue 100.00 10.00

The ½p, 1p blue, 2p olive, 4p and 5p green exist imperf.

**Wmk. 1b**

46d A1 1p blue 14.00 3.75
e. 1p dk bl 11.00 3.75
49d A1 2p org yel 12.50 4.00
e. 2p ol yel 12.50 4.25
f. 2p ol grn 125.00 30.00
50b A2 4p rose 12.50 4.75
52b A1 5p myr grn 15.00 5.00
c. 5p ol grn 17.50 6.75
d. 5p brnz grn 15.00 6.75
53d A1 6p choc brn 12.50 4.75
e. 6p brn 14.00 4.75
54a A2 8p red brn 14.00 8.75
55a A2 9p dk brn 14.00 3.75
b. 9p bis brn 110.00 25.00
56b A1 10p orange 17.50 5.50
c. 10p org red 17.50 5.50
d. 10p ver 260.00 125.00
57 A1 1sh purple 50.00 6.25
58a A2 2sh dp bl 35.00 7.00
b. 2sh ind 42.50 7.00

The 1p blue and 6p brown exist imperf.

A4

A5

**Wmk. Crown and C. C. (1)**

**1866 Typo. Perf. 12½**

59 A5 3p rose 90.00 20.00
a. Imperf., pair 160.00

**1868 Perf. 14**

61 A4 1p blue 7.25 4.25
62 A5 3p rose 20.00 9.50

A6

A7

A8

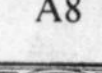
A9

A10

A11

A12

A13

A14

A15

A16

**1872-80 Perf. 14**

63 A6 2c brown 1.65 65
64 A7 4c gray 5.00 18
65 A7 4c lil rose ('80) 8.75 50
66 A8 8c orange 5.50 1.25
a. 8c org yel 5.50 1.25
67 A9 16c violet 8.75 1.65
68 A10 24c green 12.50 1.65
69 A11 32c sl bl ('77) 22.50 3.00
70 A12 36c blue 25.00 4.25
71 A13 48c rose 27.50 5.00
72 A14 64c red brn ('77) 65.00 22.50
73 A15 96c ol gray 32.50 5.00
Nos. 63-73 (11) 214.65 45.63

**1872 Perf. 12½**

74 A6 2c brown 500.00 25.00
75 A7 4c gray 240.00 55.00

**1879 Perf. 14x12½**

77 A6 2c brown 90.00 12.50
78 A7 4c gray 90.00 4.25
79 A8 8c orange 65.00 15.00

**Perf. 12½x14**

82 A16 2r50c claret 250.00 110.00

The 32c and 64c are known perf. 14x12½, but were not regularly issued.
No. 82, perf. 12½, was not regularly issued.
See Nos. 142, 158.

SIXTEEN

16

CENTS

Nos. 68, 72 Surcharged

**1882 Perf. 14**

83 A10 16c on 24c grn 11.00 4.25
84 A14 20c on 64c red brn 6.50 2.25
a. Double surcharge 425.00

**Wmk. Crown and C. A. (2)**

85 A6 2c pale brn 12.50 75
86 A6 2c grn ('84) 45 8
a. Perf. 12 800.00
87 A6 2c org brn ('99) 22 15
88 A7 4c lil rose 40 8
89 A7 4c rose ('84) 1.25 1.25
a. Perf. 12 1,000.
90 A7 4c brt rose ('98) 85 1.40
91 A7 4c yel ('99) 25 50
92 A8 8c orange 1.75 2.00
93 A9 16c violet 350.00 100.00
94 A10 24c pur brn 350.00
b. Perf. 12 1,250.

Nos. 86a, 89a, 94 and 94b were never placed in use. A 48c brown, perf. 12, was prepared but not issued.

Issues of 1872-82 Surcharged:

Postage &

FIVE CENTS

Revenue

a

TEN CENTS

b

Twenty Cents

c

One Rupee Twelve Cents

d

**1885 Wmk. 1 Perf. 14**

94A A9 (a) 5c on 16c
95 A10 (a) 5c on 24c 375.00 30.00
96 A11 (a) 5c on 32c 12.50 3.00
a. Inverted surcharge 225.00
97 A12 (a) 5c on 36c 17.50 1.75
a. Inverted surcharge 250.00
98 A13 (a) 5c on 48c 87.50 12.50
99 A14 (a) 5c on 64c 15.00 2.25
a. Double surcharge 175.00
100 A15 (a) 5c on 96c 67.50 15.00
101 A9 (b) 10c on 16c 300.00
102 A10 (b) 10c on 24c 225.00 37.50
103 A12 (b) 10c on 36c 75.00 37.50
104 A14 (b) 10c on 64c 35.00 20.00
105 A10 (b) 20c on 24c 17.50 6.75
106 A11 (c) 20c on 32c 9.75 6.75
107 A11 (c) 25c on 32c 9.75 4.00
108 A13 (c) 28c on 48c 7.50 2.75
a. Double surcharge 300.00
109 A12 (b) 30c on 36c 4.75 4.50
a. Inverted surcharge 75.00 37.50
110 A15 (b) 56c on 96c 9.75 6.00

**Perf. 12½**

111 A16 (d) 1r12c on 2r50c 75.00 25.00

**Perf. 14x12½**

112 A11 (a) 5c on 32c 32.50 6.75
113 A14 (a) 5c on 64c 35.00 10.00
114 A14 (b) 10c on 64c 15.00 16.00
a. Vert. pair, imperf. btwn. 750.00

**Perf. 12½x14**

115 A16 (d) 1r12c on 2r50c 20.00 15.00

**Wmk. Crown and C. A. (2)**

**Perf. 14**

116 A7 (a) 5c on 4c lil rose 65.00 50.00
a. Inverted surcharge
117 A7 (a) 5c on 4c rose 3.75 25
a. Inverted surcharge 100.00 50.00
118 A8 (a) 5c on 8c org 5.00 1.50
a. Inverted surcharge 225.00 175.00
b. Double surcharge 180.00 150.00
119 A9 (a) 5c on 16c vio 12.50 4.00
a. Inverted surcharge 195.00 100.00
120 A10 (a) 5c on 24c pur brn 160.00 85.00
121 A9 (b) 10c on 16c vio 575.00 175.00
122 A10 (b) 10c on 24c pur brn 6.50 4.00
123 A9 (b) 15c on 16c vio 6.50 4.25

Types of 1872-80 Surcharged

REVENUE AND POSTAGE

5 CENTS

e

10 CENTS

f

1 R. 12 C.

g

**1885-87**

124 A8 (e) 5c on 8c lil 2.50 18
125 A10 (f) 10c on 24c pur brn 6.25 2.50
126 A9 (f) 15c on 16c org 12.50 4.25
127 A11 (f) 28c on 32c sl bl 8.00 1.75
128 A12 (f) 30c on 36c ol grn 12.50 10.00
129 A15 (f) 56c on 96c ol gray 9.25 3.75

**Wmk. 1 Sideways**

130 A16 (g) 1r12c on 2r50c cl 16.00 16.00

A23

A24

FIVE CENTS
Type I. Thin lines in background. Hair and curl clear.
Type II. Thicker lines in background. Heavier shading under chin.

**1886 Wmk. Crown and C. A. (2)**
131 A23 5c lil, type I 18 6
a. 5c lil, type II 2.00 8

**1886-1900**
132 A24 3c org brn & grn ('93) 65 15
133 A24 3c grn ('00) 75 15
134 A24 6c rose & blk ('99) 75 15
135 A24 12c ol grn & car ('00) 1.10 1.25
136 A24 15c ol grn 90 15
137 A24 15c ultra ('00) 1.25 75
138 A24 25c brown 65 45
a. 25c brn, value in ol yel 40.00 35.00
139 A24 28c slate 1.10 75
140 A24 30c vio & org brn ('93) 1.25 65
141 A24 75c blk & org brn ('00) 2.50 2.00
*Nos. 132-141 (10)* 10.90 6.45

Numeral tablet of 3c, 12c and 75c has lined background with colorless value and "c".

**1887 Wmk. Crown and C. C. (1)**
142 A16 1r12c claret 7.50 6.25

Issue of 1883-84 Surcharged **TWO CENTS**

**1888-90 Wmk. 2**
143 A7 2c on 4c lil rose 22 18
a. Inverted surcharge 3.50 3.50
b. Double surcharge, one inverted 16.00
144 A7 2c on 4c rose 22 18
a. Inverted surcharge 3.50 3.50
b. Double surcharge 12.50

Surcharged **TWO**

145 A7 2c on 4c lil rose 45 25
a. Inverted surcharge 8.75 8.75
b. Double surcharge 14.00 11.00
c. Double surcharge, one inverted 6.00 6.00
146 A7 2c on 4c rose 50 14
a. Double surcharge, one inverted 11.00 11.00
b. Double surcharge 11.00 11.00
c. Inverted surcharge 22.50 22.50

Surcharged **2 Cents**

147 A7 2c on 4c lil rose 27.50 27.50
a. Inverted surcharge 32.50
b. Double surcharge, one inverted 40.00
148 A7 2c on 4c rose 70 70
a. Inverted surcharge 6.00 6.00
b. Double surcharge, one inverted 4.00 4.00
c. Double surcharge

Surcharged **Two Cents**

149 A7 2c on 4c lil rose 27.50 27.50
a. Inverted surcharge 40.00 27.50
150 A7 2c on 4c rose 55 25
a. Inverted surcharge 3.50 3.50
b. Double surcharge 8.75 8.75
c. Double surcharge, one inverted 4.00 4.00

Surcharged **2 Cents**

151 A7 2c on 4c rose 1.25 38
a. Inverted surcharge 3.25 3.25
b. Double surcharge 17.50 17.50
c. Double surcharge, one inverted 6.75 6.75
i. "S" of "Cents" inverted 20.00
151D A7 2c on 4c lil rose 15.00 15.00
e. Inverted surcharge 24.00 24.00
f. Double surcharge 16.00
g. Double surcharge, one inverted 20.00 20.00
h. "S" of "Cents" inverted

Counterfeit errors of surcharges of Nos. 143 to 151D are prevalent.

No. 136 Surcharged **POSTAGE Five Cents REVENUE**

**1890**
152 A24 5c on 15c ol grn 50 50
a. "Flve" instead of "Five" 35.00 30.00
b. "REVENUE" omitted 40.00 32.50
c. Inverted surcharge 6.00 6.00
d. Double surcharge 55.00 50.00

Nos. 138-139 Surcharged **FIFTEEN CENTS**

**1891**
153 A24 15c on 25c brn 4.00 3.50
154 A24 15c on 28c sl 3.50 3.50

Nos. 88, 89 and 139 Surcharged **3 Cents**

**1892**
155 A7 3c on 4c lil rose 28 30
156 A7 3c on 4c rose 70 75
a. Double surcharge, one inverted 
157 A24 3c on 28c slate 28 32
a. Double surcharge 27.50 17.50

Type of 1879

**1898**
158 A16 2r50c vio, *red* 13.00 13.00

No. 136 Surcharged in Black **Six Cents**

**1899**
159 A24 6c on 15c ol grn 20 20

A34

A35

Black Surcharge

**1899 Wmk. Crown and C. C. (1)**
160 A34 1r50c on 2r50c gray 16.00 16.00
161 A34 2r25c on 2r50c yel 22.50 22.50

**1900 Wmk. Crown and C. C. (1)**
162 A35 1r50c car rose 10.00 9.00
163 A35 2r25c dl bl 15.00 15.00

King Edward VII
A36 A37

A38

A39

A40

**1903-05 Wmk. Crown and C. A. (2)**
166 A36 2c org brn 85 16
167 A37 3c green 1.40 25
168 A37 4c yel & bl 1.50 1.25
169 A38 5c dl lil 1.10 12
170 A39 6c car rose 1.25 50
171 A37 12c ol grn & car 3.00 3.00
172 A40 15c ultra 4.25 1.65
173 A40 25c bister 3.50 5.50
174 A40 30c vio & grn 1.75 1.10
175 A37 75c bl & org ('05) 4.25 6.25
176 A40 1r50c gray ('04) 37.50 37.50
177 A40 2r25c brn & grn ('04) 35.00 32.50
*Nos. 166-177 (12)* 95.35 89.78

**1904-10 Wmk. 3**
178 A36 2c org brn 12 7
a. 2c org 12 7
179 A37 3c green 25 8
180 A37 4c yel & bl 22 22
181 A38 5c dl lil 2.75 8
a. Booklet pane of 12
182 A39 6c car rose 40 10
183 A40 10c ol grn & vio ('10) 85 32
184 A37 12c ol grn & car 1.00 65
185 A40 15c ultra 85 20
186 A40 25c bis ('05) 2.25 1.65
187 A40 25c sl ('10) 2.50 2.50
188 A40 30c vio & grn ('05) 1.00 32
189 A40 50c brn ('10) 3.00 2.75
190 A37 75c bl & org ('05) 3.00 3.00
191 A40 1r vio, *yel* ('10) 8.50 6.50
192 A40 1r50c gray ('05) 5.75 6.50
193 A40 2r scar, *yel* ('10) 13.00 20.00
194 A40 2r25c brn & grn 13.00 16.00
195 A40 5r *grn* ('10) 32.50 50.00
196 A40 10r *red* ('10) 52.50 82.50
*Nos. 178-196 (19)* 143.44 193.44

No. 181 exists on ordinary and chalky paper.

A41

A42

**1908**
197 A41 5c dp red vio 22 8
a. Booklet pane of 12
198 A42 6c car rose 30 10

**1911**
199 A40 3c green 2.00 8

King George V
A44 A45

3 AND 6 CENTS
Type I. Small "c" after value, 2¼mm wide and 2mm high.
Type II. Large "c" after value, 2½mm wide and 2¼mm high.

**Die I**

For description of the dies see back of this section of the Catalogue.

**1912-25 Wmk. 3**
200 A44 1c dp brn (Die Ib) ('20) 6 6
201 A44 2c brn org 10 6
202 A44 3c dp grn (Die Ia, type II) 12 5
a. 3c dp grn (Die I, type I) 35 10
203 A44 5c red vio 12 5
204 A44 6c car (Die Ib, type II) 1.25 6
a. 6c car (Die I, type I) 1.75 8
b. Bklt. pane of 6 (Die I, type I)
205 A44 10c ol grn 50 18
206 A44 15c ultra 60 20

**Chalky Paper**
207 A44 25c yel & ultra 60 20
208 A44 30c grn & vio 75 28
209 A44 50c blk & scar 75 28
210 A44 1r vio, *yel* 1.10 60
211 A44 2r blk & red, *yel* 1.50 1.25
212 A44 5r *green* 12.00 10.50
a. 5r *bl grn*, olive back 13.00 15.00
b. 5r *emer* (Die II) ('20) 45.00 45.00
213 A44 10r vio & blk, *red* 27.50 25.00
a. 10r vio & blk, *red* (Die II) ('20) 42.50 40.00
214 A44 20r blk & red, *bl* 55.00 35.00
215 A45 50r dl vio 275.00
216 A45 100r gray blk 1,250.
217 A45 500r gray grn *3,750.*
218 A45 1000r vio, *red* ('25) *20,000.*
*Nos. 200-214 (15)* 101.95 73.77

Although Nos. 217 and 218 were theoretically available for postage it is not probable that they were ever used for other than fiscal purposes.
The 1r through 100r with revenue cancellations sell for minimal prices.

**Die I**
**Surface-colored Paper**

**1913-14**
220 A44 1r vio, *yel* 1.50 1.65
221 A44 2r blk & red, *yel* 1.65 2.00
222 A44 5r blk, *green* 7.50 7.50

No. 203 Surcharged **ONE CENT**

**1918**
223 A44 1c on 5c red vio 8 8

**Die I**

**1921-33 Wmk. 4**

**Ordinary Paper**
225 A44 1c dp brn (Die Ib, type II) ('27) 10 6
226 A44 2c brn org (Die II) 10 6
227 A44 3c grn (Die Ia, type II) 45 6
228 A44 3c sl (Die Ia, type II) ('22) 8 6
229 A44 5c red vio (Die I, type II) 8 5
230 A44 6c car (Die Ib, type II) 22 6
231 A44 6c vio (Die Ib, type II) ('22) 10 5
232 A44 9c red, *yel* (Die II, type II) ('26) 20 10
233 A44 10c ol grn 52 10
a. Die II 30 7
234 A44 12c scar ('25) 2.00 1.65
a. Die II 95 70
235 A44 15c ultra 1.25 1.00
236 A44 15c grn, *yel* ('22) 2.00 1.00
a. Die II 95 32
237 A44 20c ultra ('22) 1.10 42
a. Die II 32 20
238 A44 25c yel & bl 1.00 30
a. Die II 70 38

**Chalky Paper**
239 A44 30c grn & vio 1.10 45
a. Die II 90 22
240 A44 50c blk & scar (Die II) 1.65 35
a. Die I 32.50 40.00
241 A44 1r vio, *yel* 10.00 5.25
a. Die II 6.00 6.50
242 A44 2r blk & red, *yel* (Die II) 4.00 3.25
243 A44 5r *emer*, (Die II) 16.00 22.50
244 A44 20r blk & red, *bl*, (Die II) 65.00 65.00
245 A45 50r dl vio 450.00
246 A45 100r gray blk 2,250.
247 A45 100r ultra & dl vio ('27) 1,750.
*Nos. 225-244 (20)* 106.95 101.77

Nos. 228, 231 Surcharged **2 Cents.**

**1926**
248 A44 2c on 3c slate 30 20
a. Double surcharge 40.00 40.00
b. Bar omitted 27.50
249 A44 5c on 6c violet 22 20
a. Double surcharge

A46

**1927-28 Chalky Paper Wmk. 4**
254 A46 1r red vio & dl vio 2.50 85
255 A46 2r car & grn 3.50 1.25
256 A46 5r brn vio & grn 12.00 10.00
257 A46 10r org & grn 24.00 30.00
258 A46 20r ultra & dl vio 55.00 65.00
*Nos. 254-258 (5)* 97.00 107.10

### Silver Jubilee Issue
Common Design Type

**1935, May 6 Engr. *Perf. 13½x14***

| | | | | |
|---|---|---|---|---|
| 260 | CD301 6c gray blk & ultra | | 6 | 5 |
| 261 | CD301 9c ind & grn | | 30 | 20 |
| 262 | CD301 20c bl & grn | | 65 | 45 |
| 263 | CD301 50c brt vio & ind | | 1.50 | 1.00 |

Tapping Rubber Tree — A47

Colombo Harbor — A49

Picking Tea — A50

Coconut Palms — A53

Adam's Peak — A48

Rice Terraces A51

River Scene — A52

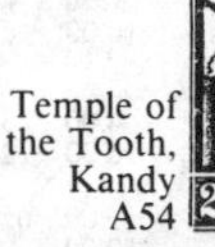

Temple of the Tooth, Kandy A54

Ancient Reservoir A55

Wild Elephants A56

View of Trincomalee A57

***Perf. 11x11½, 11½x11; 11½x13, 13x11½ (A47, A48, A53); 14 (A56)***

**1935 Wmk. 4**

| | | | |
|---|---|---|---|
| 264 A47 2c car rose & blk | 8 | 8 |
| a. Perf. 14 | 1.50 | 45 |
| 265 A48 3c ol & blk | 20 | 8 |
| a. Perf. 14 | 1.50 | 45 |
| 266 A49 6c bl & blk | 8 | 7 |
| 267 A50 9c org red & ol grn | 32 | 12 |
| 268 A51 10c dk vio & blk | 40 | 10 |
| 269 A52 15c grn & org brn | 60 | 10 |
| 270 A53 20c ultra & blk | 1.10 | 18 |
| 271 A54 25c choc & dk ultra | 80 | 15 |
| 272 A55 30c grn & lake | 1.50 | 45 |
| 273 A56 50c dk vio & blk | 4.75 | 48 |
| 274 A57 1r brn & vio | 4.50 | 2.25 |
| *Nos. 264-274 (11)* | 14.33 | 4.06 |

### Coronation Issue
Common Design Type

**1937, May 12 *Perf. 11x11½***

| | | |
|---|---|---|
| 275 CD302 6c dk car | 6 | 6 |
| a. Bklt pane of 10 | | |
| 276 CD302 9c dp grn | 10 | 10 |
| a. Bklt pane of 10 | 150.00 | |
| 277 CD302 20c dp ultra | 20 | 20 |

Tapping Rubber Tree — A58

Colombo Harbor — A60

Picking Tea — A63

Ancient Guard Stone — A68

Adam's Peak, 7360 Ft. — A59

Sigiriya (Lion Rock) — A61

River Scene — A62

Temple of the Tooth — A64

Ancient Reservior A65

Wild Elephants A66

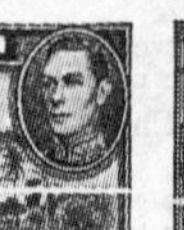

View of Trincomalee — A67

King George VI — A69

***Perf. 11x11½, 11½x11; 12 (#278-279, 286)***

**1938-52 Engr. Wmk. 4**

| | | |
|---|---|---|
| 278 A58 2c car rose & blk ('49) | 8 | 5 |
| a. Perf. 13½x13 ('38) | 6.00 | 10 |
| b. Perf. 13½ ('38) | 8 | 5 |
| c. Perf. 11x11½ ('44) | 5 | 5 |
| d. Perf. 11½x13 ('38) | 1.75 | 6 |
| 279 A59 3c dk grn & blk ('46) | 8 | 5 |
| a. Perf. 13x13½ ('38) | 100.00 | 2.50 |
| b. Perf. 14 ('41) | 25.00 | 40 |
| c. Perf. 13½ ('38) | 15 | 5 |
| d. Perf. 11½x11 ('42) | 8 | 5 |
| e. Perf. 13x11½ | 1.75 | 15 |
| 280 A60 6c bl & blk | 6 | 5 |
| 281 A61 10c bl & blk | 12 | 6 |
| 282 A62 15c red brn & grn | 12 | 6 |
| 283 A63 20c dl bl & blk | 10 | 6 |
| 284 A64 25c choc & dk ultra | 15 | 6 |
| 285 A65 30c dk grn & rose car | 55 | 12 |
| 286 A66 50c dk vio & blk ('46) | 50 | 12 |
| a. Perf. 14 ('42) | 4.25 | 1.25 |
| b. Perf. 13x11½ ('38) | 62.50 | 25.00 |
| c. Perf. 13x13½ ('38) | 75.00 | 1.75 |
| d. Perf. 13½ ('38) | 75 | 20 |
| e. Perf. 11½x11 ('42) | 45 | 12 |
| 287 A67 1r dk brn & bl vio | 1.20 | 35 |
| 288 A68 2r dk car & blk | 1.75 | 90 |

**Typo. *Perf. 14***

| | | |
|---|---|---|
| 289 A69 5r brn vio & grn | 5.00 | 1.25 |
| 289A A69 10r yel org & dl grn ('52) | 40.00 | 25.00 |
| *Nos. 278-289 (12)* | 9.71 | 3.13 |

No. 289A differs from type A69 in having "REVENUE" inscribed vertically at either side of the frame. This revenue 10r was valid for postage Dec. 1, 1952-Mar. 14, 1954.

See Nos. 292, 295.

**Catalogue values for unused stamps in this section, from this point to the end of the section, are for Never Hinged items.**

No. 283 Surcharged in Black

**1940, Nov. 5 *Perf. 11x11½***

| | | |
|---|---|---|
| 290 A63 3c on 20c dl bl & blk | 25 | 25 |

No. 280 Surcharged with New Value and Bars

**1941, May 10**

| | | |
|---|---|---|
| 291 A60 3c on 6c bl & blk | 10 | 10 |

Coconut Palms — A70

**1943-47 Wmk. 4 Engr. *Perf. 12***

| | | |
|---|---|---|
| 292 A70 5c red org & ol grn ('47) | 6 | 5 |
| a. Perf. 13½ ('43) | 8 | 6 |

### Peace Issue
Common Design Type

**1946, Dec. 10 *Perf. 13½x14***

| | | |
|---|---|---|
| 293 CD303 6c dp bl | 8 | 8 |
| 294 CD303 15c brown | 15 | 15 |

Guard Stone Type of 1938

**1947, Mar. 15 *Perf. 11x11½***

| | | |
|---|---|---|
| 295 A68 2r vio & blk | 1.50 | 55 |

Parliament Building, Colombo — A71

Adam's Peak A72

Dagoba at Anuradhapura A74

Temple of the Tooth, Kandy A73

**1947, Nov. 25 *Perf. 11x12, 12x11***

| | | |
|---|---|---|
| 296 A71 6c dp ultra & blk | 8 | 6 |
| 297 A72 10c car, org & blk | 12 | 10 |
| 298 A73 15c red vio & grnsh blk | 16 | 14 |
| 299 A74 25c brt grn & bis | 20 | 20 |

New constitution of 1947.

National Flag A75

D. S. Senanayake A76

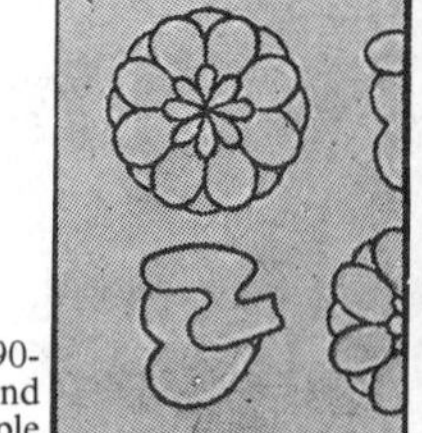

Wmk. 290- Lotus and "Sri" Multiple

**Engr., Flag Typo. (A75); Engr. (A76)**
***Perf. 12½x12, 12x12½, 13x12½***

**1949 Wmk. 4**

| | | |
|---|---|---|
| 300 A75 4c org brn, car & yel | 10 | 7 |
| 301 A76 5c dk grn & brn | 10 | 6 |

**Wmk. 290**

| | | |
|---|---|---|
| 302 A75 15c red org, car & yel | 16 | 15 |
| 303 A76 25c dp bl & brn | 28 | 14 |

Size of No. 302: 28x22¼mm.

1st anniv. of Ceylon's independence.

Dates of issue: Nos. 300-301, Feb. 4, Nos. 302-303, Apr. 5.

A77

A78

Design: 15c, Lion Rock and UPU symbols.

**Wmk. 290**

**1949, Oct. 10 Engr. *Perf. 12***

*304* A77 5c dk grn & brn 22 6
*305* A77 15c dk car & blk 65 25
*306* A78 25c ultra & blk 90 25

75th anniv. of the UPU.

Kandyan Dancer A79

Kiri Vehera, Polonnaruwa A80

Vesak Orchid A81

Sigiriya A82

Ratmalana, Plane — A83

Vatadage Ruins at Madirigiriya A84

**1950, Feb. 4 *Perf. 12x12½***

*307* A79 4c brt red & choc 5 5
*308* A80 5c green 6 5
*a.* Booklet pane of 10 60
*309* A81 15c pur & bl grn 18 6
*310* A82 30c car & yel 18 6

***Perf. 11x11½, 11½x11***

*311* A83 75c red org & bl 40 15
*a.* Booklet pane of 4 2.00
*312* A84 1r red brn & dp bl 50 20
*Nos. 307-312 (6)* 1.37 57

See Nos. 340-345.

Coconut Palms A85

Star Orchid A86

**1951-52 Unwmk. Photo. *Perf. 11½***

*313* A85 10c gray & dk grn 20 5
*314* A86 35c dk grn & rose brn ('52) 50 8
*a.* Corrected inscription 30 6

On No. 314a a dot has been added above the third character in the second line of the Tamil inscription.
See No. 351.

Mace and Symbols of Industry A87

***Perf. 12½x14***

**1952, Feb. 23 Wmk. 290**

*315* A87 5c green 12 5
*316* A87 15c brt ultra 30 25

Colombo Plan Exhibition, February 1952.

**Coronation Issue**

Queen Elizabeth II — A88

**1953, June 2 Engr. *Perf. 12x12½***

*317* A88 5c green 12 5

Royal Procession A89

**1954, Apr. 10 *Perf. 13x12½***

*318* A89 10c dp bl 12 5

Visit of Queen Elizabeth II and the Duke of Edinburgh, 1954.

Sambar in Ruhuna National Park — A90

Rubber Trees — A91

Designs: 3c, Ancient guard stone. 6c and 10r, Harvesting rice. 25c, Sigiriya fresco. 50c, Outrigger fishing canoe. 85c, Tea Picker. 2r, Gal Oya dam. 5r, Bas-relief, "The Lovers."

**1954 Unwmk. Photo. *Perf. 11½***

**Size: 21x25½mm**

*319* A90 2c grn & brn 6 5
*320* A90 3c vio & blk 8 5
*321* A90 6c yel grn & blk brn 8 5
*322* A90 25c vio bl, bl & brn org 16 5

**Size: 25½x21mm**

*323* A91 40c blk brn 25 8
*324* A91 50c indigo 25 8

**Size: 23x32½mm, 32½x23mm**

*325* A90 85c dk grn & gray 45 18
*326* A91 2r bl & blk brn 1.75 32
*327* A90 5r dp org & blk brn 4.50 80
*328* A90 10r brown 10.00 2.25
*Nos. 319-328 (10)* 17.58 3.91

See Nos. 346-356.
Nos. 327-328 with revenue cancellations sell for minimal prices.

King Coconuts A92

Symbols of Agriculture A93

**1954, Dec. 1**

*329* A92 10c brn & org 10 5

See No. 349.

***Perf. 14x14½***

**1955, Dec. 10 Wmk. 290**

*330* A93 10c org & brn 8 5

Issued to publicize the Royal Agricultural and Food Exhibition.

House of Representatives — A94

**1956, Mar. 26 Unwmk. *Perf. 11½***

**Granite Paper.**

*331* A94 10c dp grn 8 5

Issued to commemorate the 25th anniversary of Prime Minister Sir John Kotelawala's entry into the Ceylon Legislature.

Arrival of Vijaya in Ceylon — A95

Dharmachakra Encircling Globe — A96

**1956, May 23 Granite Paper**

*332* A95 3c dl vio gray & saph 6 5
*333* A96 15c ultra 25 10

Issued to commemorate the 2500th anniversary of the birth of Buddha. See also Nos. B1-B2.

Methods of Transportation — A97

Designs: 35c, 85c, Ceylon's first stamp and coat of arms.

**1957, Apr. 1 Photo. *Perf. 12½x13***

*334* A97 4c bl grn & ver 18 6
*335* A97 10c bl & ver 22 6

***Perf. 11½***

**Granite Paper**

*336* A97 35c bl, yel & brn 35 12
*337* A97 85c dl grn, yel & brn 65 55

Nos. 334-337 were issued to commemorate the centenary of the first postage stamps of Ceylon.

Nos. B1-B2 Overprinted with Black Bars and Squares

**1958, Jan. 15 Unwmk.**

**Granite Paper**

*338* SP1 4c dp bl & lt yel 5 5
*a.* Inverted ovpt. 12.50
*b.* Double ovpt. 12.50
*339* SP1 10c dk gray, yel & brt pink 8 5
*a.* Inverted ovpt. 20.00

The overprint obliterates the surtax and inscription at right.

Types of 1950-1954 Redrawn

***Perf. 12x12½***

**1958-59 Engr. Wmk. 290**

*340* A79 4c brt red & choc 5 5
*341* A80 5c green 6 5
*342* A81 15c pur & bl grn 8 5
*343* A82 30c car & yel ('59) 12 5

***Perf. 11½x11***

*344* A83 75c red org & bl ('59) 28 10

***Perf. 11x11½***

*345* A84 1r red brn & dp bl 38 10
*Nos. 340-345 (6)* 97 40

**1958-59 Unwmk. Photo. *Perf. 11½***

**Granite Paper**

*346* A90 2c grn & brn 5 5
*347* A90 3c vio & blk 5 5
*348* A90 6c yel grn & blk brn 5 5
*349* A92 10c brn & org 10 5
*350* A90 25c vio bl, bl & brn org 12 5
*351* A86 35c dk grn & rose brn 22 5
*352* A91 50c indigo 25 6
*353* A90 85c dk grn & gray ('59) 1.90 12
*354* A91 2r bl & blk brn 75 25
*355* A90 5r dp org & blk brn 1.90 60
*356* A90 10r brown 3.75 1.25
*Nos. 346-356 (11)* 9.14 2.58

Designs and sizes of Nos. 340-356 remain as before, but wording has been changed to be predominantly Singhalese. "Ceylon" appears in small letters only in English and Tamil.
Nos. 355-356 with revenue cancellations sell for minimal prices.

Hands Reaching for UN Symbol A98

***Perf. 13x12½***

**1958, Dec. 10 Photo. Unwmk.**

*357* A98 10c red brn & red 10 6
*358* A98 85c Prus grn & red 50 45

10th anniv. of the signing of the Universal Declaration of Human Rights.

Pirivena Universities and Founders A99

**1959, Dec. 31**

*359* A99 10c brt ultra & dp org 8 5

Issued to commemorate the institution of Pirivena Universities and to honor their founders Hikkaduwe Sri Sumangala Nayaka Thero and Ratmalane Sri Dharmaloka Nayake Thero.

Uprooted Oak Emblem A100

Prime Minister Bandaranaike A101

**1960, Apr. 7 Photo. *Perf. 11½***

**Granite Paper**

*360* A100 4c choc & gold 8 5
*361* A100 25c vio bl & gold 18 12

Issued to publicize World Refugee Year, July 1, 1959-June 30, 1960.

**1961, Jan. 8 Granite Paper**

Two types: I. Gray hair at temple.
II. Dark hair at temple (redrawn).

*362* A101 10c vio bl & gray bl (I) 8 5
*a.* Type II 40 25

Issued to honor Solomon West Ridgeway Dias Bandaranaike, assassinated Sept. 26, 1959.

The lack of a price for a listed item does not necessarily indicate rarity.

Badge of Singhalese Scouts
A102

Malaria Eradication Emblem
A103

**1962, Feb. 26 Unwmk. *Perf. 11½***
**Granite Paper**

*363* A102 35c dk bl & ocher 30 15

Issued to commemorate the 50th anniversary of the Boy Scouts of Ceylon.

***Perf. 14½x14***

**1962, Apr. 7 Photo. Wmk. 290**

*364* A103 25c lt sep, red org & brn 15 8

Issued for the World Health Organization drive to eradicate malaria.

Monoplane 1938, and De Havilland Comet IV — A104

**1963, Feb. 28 Unwmk. *Perf. 11½***
**Granite Paper**

*365* A104 50c lt grnsh bl & blk 30 18

Issued to commemorate the 25th anniversary of Ceylonese airmail service.

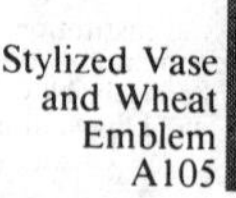

Stylized Vase and Wheat Emblem
A105

**1963, Mar. 21**
**Granite Paper**

*366* A105 5c bl & org ver 20 5
*367* A105 25c ol & brn 50 10

Issued for the "Freedom from Hunger" campaign of the U.N. Food and Agriculture Organization.

No. 340 Surcharged

ශත
2
சதம்

***Perf. 12x12½***

**1963, June 1 Engr. Wmk. 290**

*368* A79 2c on 4c brt red & choc 8 5
- *a.* Inverted surch. 25.00
- *b.* Double surch. 17.50

Rural Life — A106

**1963, July 5 Photo. *Perf. 14x14½***

*369* A106 60c dl red & blk 30 18

Issued to commemorate the 50th anniversary of the Cooperative Movement.

Landscape and Elephant
A107

**1963, Dec. 2 Wmk. 290**

*370* A107 5c bl & blk 8 5

National Conservation Week.

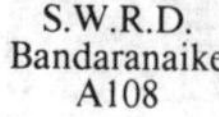

S.W.R.D. Bandaranaike
A108

Anagarika Dharmapala
A109

***Perf. 11½***

**1963, Sept. 26 Unwmk. Engr.**
**Granite Paper**

*371* A108 10c blue 10 6

Redrawn

**1964, July 1 Photo.**
**Granite Paper**

*372* A108 10c grnsh gray & bl vio 8 5

Frame redrawn on No. 372; inscription in bottom panel replaced by ornament.

**1964, Sept. 16 Unwmk. *Perf. 11½***
**Granite Paper**

*373* A109 25c gray brn & dl yel 12 8

Issued to commemorate the centenary of the birth of Anagarika Dharmapala, Buddhist missionary.

Ceylon Jungle Fowl — A110

Vatadage Ruins at Madirigiriya
A111

Tea Picker
A112

Designs: 5c, Hill myna. 15c, Blue peafowl. 75c, Asiatic black-headed oriole. 5r, Girls, working in rice field. 10r, Map of Ceylon on scroll, showing agricultural development stations.

**Wmk. 290; Unwmkd. (20c)**

**1964-69 Photo. *Perf. 14; 11½ (20c)***

*374* A110 5c brt bl, blk, yel & grn ('66) 10 5
*375* A110 15c yel, grn, blk, brt bl & rose ('66) 8 5
*376* A111 20c dk red brn, *buff* 12 5
*377* A110 60c yel & multi ('66) 40 10
- *a.* Blue omitted 50.00
- *b.* Red omitted 50.00

*378* A110 75c ol, blk, org & brn ('66) 48 10
- *a.* Souvenir sheet of 4 2.00
- *b.* As "a," overprinted ('67) 1.00

*379* A112 1r brn & grn 32 8
- *c.* Brown omitted 125.00

*379A* A111 5r multi ('69) 1.50 35
*379B* A112 10r brn & multi ('69) 3.25 80
*Nos. 374-379B (8)* 6.25 1.58

No. 378a contains four imperf. stamps with simulated perforations similar to Nos. 374-375 and 377-378. Gray and light olive margin with trilingual black inscription and bird design. Size: 149x175mm.

No. 378b is overprinted "First National Stamp Exhibition 1967" in two lines of black capitals.

No. 376 is on granite paper. See No. 325.

Exhibition Buildings, Cogwheels
A113

**1964, Dec. 1 Unwmk. *Perf. 11***
**"Industrial Exhibition" in Singhalese and English**

*380* A113 5c multi 8 5

**"Industrial Exhibition" in Singhalese and Tamil**

*381* A113 5c multi 8 5

Issued to publicize the 1965 Industrial Exhibition; Nos. 380 and 381 are printed in alternating vertical rows in sheets of 100.

Railroad Trains, 1864-1964
A114

**Wmk. 290**

**1964, Dec. 21 Photo. *Perf. 14***
**"Railway Centenary" in Singhalese and English**

*382* A114 60c lil rose, bl & yel grn 60 20

**"Railway Centenary" in Singhalese and Tamil**

*383* A114 60c lil rose, bl & yel grn 60 20

Issued to commemorate the centenary of Ceylonese railroads. Nos. 382-383 are printed in alternating horizontal rows of sheets of 100.

ITU Emblem, Old and New Communication Equipment — A115

**1965, May 17 *Perf. 14***

*384* A115 2c ultra & red 12 12
*385* A115 30c brn & red 50 30

Issued to commemorate the centenary of the International Telecommunication Union.

ICY Emblem
A116

**1965, June 26 Unwmk. *Perf. 11½***
**Granite Paper**

*386* A116 3c rose car & dk bl 10 10
*387* A116 50c gold, rose car & blk 50 40

International Cooperation Year, 1965.

Municipal Council Building
A117

**1965, Oct. 29 Photo. *Perf. 11½***
**Granite Paper**

*388* A117 25c gray & grn 15 8

Centenary of Colombo Municipal Council.

No. 372 Surcharged **5**

**1965, Dec. 18 Photo. *Perf. 11½***

*389* A108 5c on 10c grnsh gray & bl vio 5 5

D. S. Senanayake
A118

View and Arms of Kandy
A119

**1966, Mar. 22 Unwmk. *Perf. 11½***
**Granite Paper**

*390* A118 10c brt grn 10 5

Issued in memory of D. S. Senanayake, first prime minister of Ceylon, on the 14th anniversary of his death. See No. 418.

***Perf. 14x13½***

**1966, June 15 Photo. Wmk. 290**

*391* A119 25c multi 15 8

Centenary of Kandy Municipal Council.

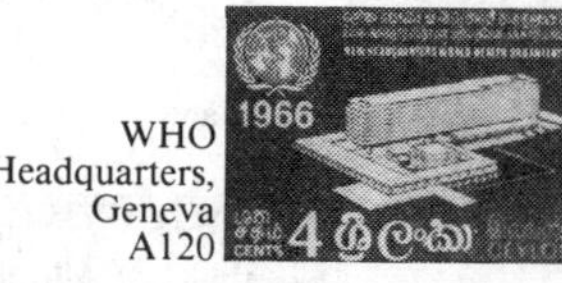

WHO Headquarters, Geneva
A120

**Unwmk.**

**1966, Oct. 8 Litho. *Perf. 14***

*392* A120 4c multi 8 8
*393* A120 1r multi 50 50

Issued to commemorate the opening of World Health Organization Headquarters, Geneva.

Rice, Map of Ceylon, FAO Emblem
A121

UNESCO Emblem
A122

Design: 30c, Rice and globe.

**1966, Oct. 25 Photo. *Perf. 11½***
**Granite Paper**

*394* A121 6c dk grn, org & brn 5 5
*395* A121 30c brt bl, org & brn 22 15

Issued to publicize the International Rice Year under sponsorship of the U.N. Food and Agricultural Organization.

**1966, Nov. 3 Litho. *Perf. 12***

*396* A122 3c tan & multi 5 5
*397* A122 50c brt grn & multi 25 20

20th anniv. of UNESCO.

Values quoted in this catalogue are for stamps graded at Fine-Very Fine and with no faults. An illustrated guide to grade is provided in introductory material, beginning on Page V.

Map of Ceylon and UNESCO Emblem A123

Worshippers at Buddhist Shrine A124

**1966, Dec. 1 Unwmk. Perf. 14**

*398* A123 2c yel brn. yel & bl 5 5
*399* A123 2r multi 60 45

Issued to publicize the International Hydrological Decade (UNESCO). 1965-74.

**1967, Jan. 2 Photo. Perf. 12**

Designs: 20c. Muhintale Rock. 35c. Sacred Bo Tree. 60c. Adam's Peak.

*400* A124 5c multi 5 5
*401* A124 20c multi 8 6
*402* A124 35c multi 14 8
*403* A124 60c multi 24 14

Issued to commemorate the first anniversary of the Poya Holiday System. Buddhist holiday replacing Sunday.

Dutch Ramparts, Clock Tower and Arms of Galle A125

***Perf. 14x13½***

**1967, Jan. 5 Litho. Unwmk.**

*404* A125 25c dk grn & multi 12 8

Centenary of Galle Municipal Council.

Tea Research A126

Designs: 40c. Tea tasting (cup and loose tea). 50c. Tea picking. 1r. Tea export (crate and freighter).

**1967, Aug. 1 Unwmk. Perf. 13½**

*405* A126 4c multi 5 5
*406* A126 40c multi 16 12
*407* A126 50c multi 20 14
*408* A126 1r multi 40 24

Centenary of the Ceylonese tea industry.

Elephant and ITY Emblem A127

**1967, Aug. 15 Litho.**

*409* A127 45c multi 40 15

Issued for International Tourist Year 1967.

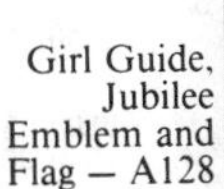

Girl Guide, Jubilee Emblem and Flag — A128

**1967, Sept. 19 Perf. 12x12½**

*410* A128 3c grn & multi 10 5
*411* A128 25c org yel & multi 20 20

Issued to commemorate the 50th anniversary of the Ceylon Girl Guide Association.

Henry S. Olcott and Buddhist Flag — A129

***Perf. 13½***

**1967, Dec. 12 Unwmk. Litho.**

*412* A129 15c multi 10 6

Issued in memory of Colonel Henry S. Olcott (1832-1907), an American who reorganized the Buddhist hierarchy and school system in Ceylon and was the first president of the Theosophical Society.

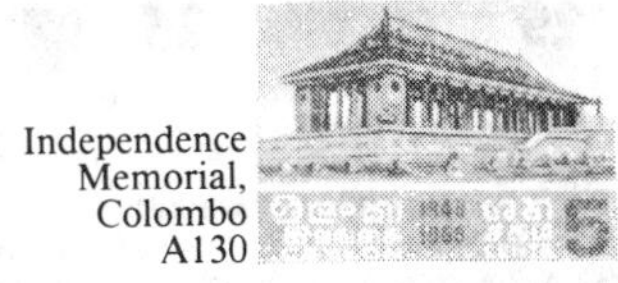


Independence Memorial, Colombo A130

Design: 1r. Flag of Ceylon and mace.

**1968, Feb. 4 Wmk. 290 Perf. 14**

*413* A130 5c multi 5 5
*414* A130 1r multi 40 30

20th anniversary of independence.

D. B. Jayatilaka — A131

**1968, Feb. 14 Photo.**

*415* A131 25c brown 12 6

Issued to commemorate the centenary of the birth of Sir Don Baron Jayatilaka (1868-1944), Buddhist leader and scholar.

Hygiene Institute, Kalutara A132

***Perf. 11½x12***

**1968, Apr. 4 Litho. Wmk. 290**

*416* A132 50c multi 15 12

Issued for the 20th anniversary of the World Health Organization.

Jet over Colombo Terminal A133

**1968, Aug. 5 Perf. 13½**

*417* A133 60c org brn, dk bl & org 22 12

Opening of Colombo Airport.

D. S. Senanayake — A134

**1968, Sept. 23 Photo. Perf. 14**

*418* A134 10c dp grn 5 5

See No. 390.

Open Koran — A135

**1968, Oct. 14 Photo. Perf. 14**

*419* A135 25c org brn, blk, bl & emer 12 8

1,400th anniversary of the Koran.

Human Rights Flame — A136

***Perf. 12½x13½***

**1968, Dec. 10 Unwmk.**

**Vignette in Greenish Blue, Orange & Red.**

*420* A136 2c pale rose 5 5
*421* A136 20c sal pink 8 6
*422* A136 40c lilac 14 8
*423* A136 2r lemon 55 48

International Human Rights Year.

Ceylon Buddhist Headquarters, Colombo — A137

**1968, Dec. 19 Litho. Perf. 13½**

*424* A137 5c multi 8 5

Issued to commemorate the 50th anniversary of the All-Ceylon Buddhist Congress.

A multicolored 50c showing the Sri Padmaya (Sacred Footprint) on Adam's Peak was prepared but the issuance order was countermanded on Dec. 18. Some were sold in ignorance of the withdrawal order.

E. W. Perera A138

"Strength in Saving" A139

**Wmk. 290**

**1969, Feb. 17 Photo. Perf. 14**

*425* A138 60c brown 30 20

Issued to honor E. W. Perera, member of Legislative Council.

**1969, Mar. 20**

*426* A139 3c bl, yel & blk 5 5

Issued to publicize the 25th anniversary of the National Savings Movement in Ceylon.

Seat of Enlightenment under Bodhi Tree — A140

Design: 6c, Buduresmala (disk symbolic of six-fold Buddha rays).

**Wmk. 290**

**1969, Apr. 10 Litho. Perf. 15**

*427* A140 4c org & multi 5 5
*428* A140 6c gold & multi 5 5
*429* A140 35c scar & multi 18 12

Issued for Vesak Day which commemorates the birth, enlightenment and death of Buddha.

Alexander Ekanayake Goonesingha — A141

**1969, Apr. 29 Photo. Perf. 14x14½**

*430* A141 15c org yel & multi 10 5

Issued to honor Alexander Ekanayake Goonesingha (1891-1967), trade unionist, political leader and diplomat.

ILO Emblem A142

**1969, May 4 Perf. 14½x14**

*431* A142 5c grnsh bl & blk 5 5
*432* A142 25c car rose & blk 20 8

Issued to commemorate the 50th anniversary of the International Labor Organization.

Convocation Hall, University of Ceylon — A143

Elephant Lamp (Ath Pana) — A144

Designs: 35c, "Lamp of Education," globe and flags. 50c, Uranium atom diagram. 60c, Symbols of science education. 1r, Aerial view of Sigiriya rock fortress.

**Unwmk.**

**1969, Aug. 1 Litho. Perf. 14**

**Inscribed: "SIYAWASA"**

*433* A143 4c yel & multi 5 5
*434* A144 6c multi 5 5
*435* A143 35c multi 12 6
*436* A144 50c red & multi 16 8
*437* A143 60c bl & multi 18 10
*438* A144 1r yel & multi 32 20
*Nos. 433-438 (6)* 88 54

Issued to commemorate the centenary of public education and archaeological research.

Wild Water Buffalo — A145

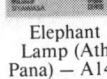

Designs: 15c, Slender loris. 50c, Axis deer. 1r, Leopard.

*Perf. 14x13½*

**1970, May 11 Litho. Unwmk.**

| | | | | |
|---|---|---|---|---|
| *439* A145 | 5c lt bl & multi | 8 | 5 |
| *440* A145 | 15c buff & multi | 16 | 5 |
| *441* A145 | 50c sal & multi | 48 | 16 |
| *442* A145 | 1r gray & multi | 1.00 | 42 |

Symbols of Agriculture and Industry A146

**1970, June 17**

*443* A146 60c multi 15 12

Asian Productivity Year, 1970.

U.P.U. Headquarters, Bern — A147

**1970, Aug. 14 Litho. Unwmk.**

| | | | |
|---|---|---|---|
| *444* A147 | 50c org, blk & bl | 20 | 10 |
| *445* A147 | 1.10r red, blk & bl | 44 | 22 |

Issued to commemorate the inauguration of the new Universal Postal Union Headquarters in Bern.

Caduceus and Oil Lamp — A148

**1970, Sept. 1** *Perf. 13½x14*

| | | | |
|---|---|---|---|
| *446* A148 | 5c multi | 5 | 5 |
| *447* A148 | 45c gray & multi | 30 | 15 |

Centenary of the Ceylon Medical School.

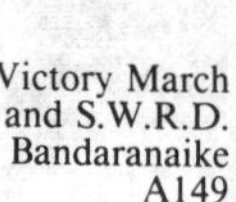

Victory March and S.W.R.D. Bandaranaike A149

**1970, Sept. 25** *Perf. 14*

*448* A149 10c red & multi 5 5

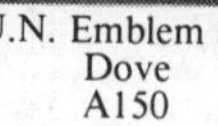

U.N. Emblem and Dove A150

Keppetipola Dissawe A151

**1970, Oct. 24 Photo.** *Perf. 12½x14*

*449* A150 2r dp org & multi 60 38

25th anniversary of the United Nations.

**1970, Nov. 26 Litho.** *Perf. 14x14½*

*450* A151 25c multi 10 6

The 152nd anniversary of the execution of Keppetipola Dissawe, leader of the Great Rebellion of 1817-18.

Ola Leaf Manuscript and Education Year Emblem — A152

**1970, Dec. 21 Photo.** *Perf. 13*

*451* A152 15c brn & multi 8 6

International Education Year.

Charles Henry de Soysa A153

Edward Henry Pedris A154

**1971, March 3 Litho.** *Perf. 14x13½*

*452* A153 20c org & multi 8 5

135th anniversary of the birth of Charles Henry de Soysa (1836-1890), philanthropist who founded hospitals and schools.

**1971, July 8 Litho.** *Perf. 14x14½*

*453* A154 25c bl & multi 10 6

Edward Henry Pedris (1888-1925), patriot.

Globe and Buddhist Flag — A155

**1971 Litho.** *Perf. 14½x13½*

*454* A155 5c org brn & multi 5 5

10th Conference of World Fellowship of Buddhists, Ceylon, May 9-13. See No. 471.

Lenin A156

Cumaratunga Munidasa A157

**1971, Aug. 31** *Perf. 14½*

*455* A156 40c dp car & multi 16 10

In memory of Lenin (1870-1924), Russian communist leader.

**1971, Oct. 29** *Perf. 14*

Poets and Philosophers: No. 457, Ananda Coomaraswamy (1887-1947). No. 458, Rev. S. Mahinda Thero (1905-1951). No. 459, Anada Rajakaruna (1885-1957). No. 460, Arumuga Navalar (1822-1878).

| | | | |
|---|---|---|---|
| *456* A157 | 5c brown | 5 | 5 |
| *457* A157 | 5c slate | 5 | 5 |
| *458* A157 | 5c dp org | 5 | 5 |
| *459* A157 | 5c dp vio bl | 5 | 5 |
| *460* A157 | 5c brn red | 5 | 5 |
| | *Nos. 456-460 (5)* | 25 | 25 |

CARE Package A158

**1971, Dec. 28** *Perf. 14x13*

*461* A158 50c pur, bl & pink 20 12

25th anniversary of CARE, a U.S.-Canadian Co-operative for American Relief Everywhere.

Map of Ceylon, Colombo Plan Emblem A159

**1971, Dec. 28 Litho.** *Perf. 14x14½*

*462* A159 20c multi 9 6

20th anniversary of the Colombo Plan.

Issues of 1969-70 Surcharged

5 X 5 a ■ b 15 ● c

25 ▮ d 25 ■ e

**Wmk. 290, Unwmkd.**

**1971, Dec. 5** *Perf. 15, 14*

| | | | | |
|---|---|---|---|---|
| *463* A140(a) | 5c on 4c (#427) | 20 | 20 |
| *464* A143(b) | 5c on 4c (#433) | 12 | 12 |
| *465* A149(c) | 15c on 10c (#448) | 8 | 8 |
| *466* A140(d) | 25c on 6c (#428) | 20 | 20 |
| *467* A144(e) | 25c on 6c (#434) | 20 | 20 |
| | *Nos. 463-467 (5)* | 80 | 80 |

Nos. 463-466 exist with surcharge inverted.

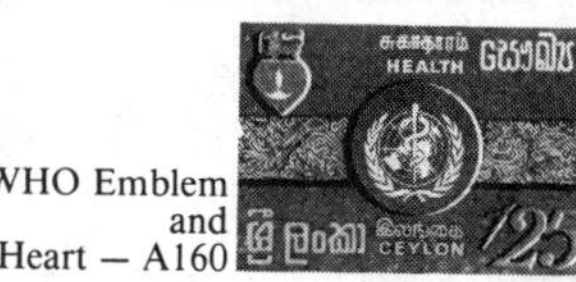

WHO Emblem and Heart — A160

**1972, May 2 Unwmk.** *Perf. 13x13½*

*468* A160 25c multi 12 8

"Your heart is your health," World Health Day.

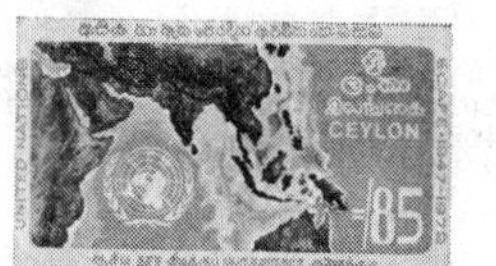

UN Emblem, Map Showing Asian Highway A161

**1972, May 2** *Perf. 13x12½*

*469* A161 85c lt bl & multi 40 27

Economic Commission for Asia and the Far East (ECAFE), 25th anniversary.

Sri Lanka

Succeeding issues, inscribed "Sri Lanka," are listed under that name in this volume.

## SEMI-POSTAL STAMPS

**Catalogue values for unused stamps in this section, from this point to the end of the section, are for Never Hinged items.**

Lamp and Dharmachakra — SP1

Design: 10c+5c, Hand of Peace.

*Perf. 11½*

**1956, May 10 Unwmk. Photo.**

**Granite Paper**

| | | | |
|---|---|---|---|
| *B1* SP1 | 4c + 2c dp bl & lt yel | 28 | 28 |
| *B2* SP1 | 10c + 5c dk gray, yel & brt pink | 45 | 38 |

Issued to commemorate the 2500th anniversary of the birth of Buddha. The surtax went to the Buddha Jayanti Fund. See also Nos. 338-339.

## WAR TAX STAMPS

Nos. 201, 202, 202a and 203 Overprinted **WAR STAMP**

**Die I**

**1918 Wmk. 3** *Perf. 14.*

| | | | |
|---|---|---|---|
| *MR1* A44 | 2c brn org | 8 | 8 |
| *a.* | Double ovpt. | 40.00 | 35.00 |
| *b.* | Inverted ovpt. | 40.00 | 35.00 |
| *MR2* A44 | 3c dp grn (Die Ia, type II) | 10 | 10 |
| *a.* | 3c dp grn (Die I, type I) | 15 | 8 |
| *b.* | Double ovpt. (Die I) | 80.00 | 80.00 |
| *MR3* A44 | 5c red vio | 12 | 12 |
| *a.* | Double overprint | 30.00 | 30.00 |
| *b.* | Inverted ovpt. | 40.00 | 40.00 |

Same Overprint on No. 223

| | | | |
|---|---|---|---|
| *MR4* A44 | 1c on 5c red vio | 7 | 7 |
| *a.* | Double overprint | | |

## OFFICIAL STAMPS

Regular Issues Overprinted **SERVICE**

**1869 Wmk. 1** *Perf. 12½, 14*

**Black Overprint**

| | | | |
|---|---|---|---|
| *O1* A4 | 1p blue | 55.00 | |
| *O2* A1 | 2p yellow | 55.00 | |
| *O3* A5 | 3p rose | 72.50 | |
| *O4* A2 | 8p red brn | 72.50 | |
| *O5* A1 | 1sh gray lil | 92.50 | |

**Red Overprint**

| | | | |
|---|---|---|---|
| *O6* A1 | 6p brown | 72.50 | |
| *O7* A2 | 2sh blue | 92.50 | |
| *a.* | Imperf. | *800.00* | |

Nos. O1 to O7 were never placed in use.

The overprint measures 15 mm. on Nos. O1 and O3.

Regular Issues Overprinted in Black or Red **On Service**

**1895-1900 Wmk. 2** *Perf. 14*

| | | | |
|---|---|---|---|
| *O8* A6 | 2c green | 3.00 | 12 |
| *O9* A6 | 2c org brn ('00) | 35 | 9 |
| *O10* A24 | 3c org brn & grn | 3.50 | 60 |
| *O11* A24 | 3c grn ('00) | 60 | 30 |
| *O12* A23 | 5c lilac | 45 | 7 |
| *O13* A24 | 15c ol grn | 3.50 | 20 |
| *O14* A24 | 15c ultra ('00) | 3.50 | 30 |
| *O15* A24 | 25c brown | 3.50 | 30 |
| *O16* A24 | 30c vio & org brn | 4.50 | 15 |
| *O17* A24 | 75c blk & org brn (R) ('99) | 4.50 | 75 |

**Wmk. 1**

| | | | |
|---|---|---|---|
| *O18* A16 | 1r12c claret | 30.00 | 18.00 |
| | *Nos. O8-O18 (11)* | 57.40 | 20.88 |

**1903-04 Wmk. 2**

| | | | |
|---|---|---|---|
| *O19* A36 | 2c org brn | 1.00 | 80 |
| *O20* A37 | 3c green | 80 | 80 |
| *O21* A38 | 5c dl lil | 1.00 | 38 |
| *O22* A40 | 15c ultra | 4.75 | 1.40 |

23 A40 25c bister 15.00 15.00
24 A40 30c vio & grn 5.50 95
*Nos. O19-O24 (6)* 28.05 19.33

## CHRISTMAS ISLAND

OCATION — In the Indian Ocean, 230 miles south of Java.
OVT. — A territory of Australia.
REA — 135 sq. mi.
OP. — 3,000 (est. 1983)

Australia took over Christmas Island rom Singapore in 1958.

**Catalogue values for all unused stamps in this country are for Never Hinged items.**

Queen Elizabeth II — A1

**Engr.; Name and Value Typo. in Black**

**958, Oct. 15 Unwmk. *Perf. 14½***
A1 2c yel org 15 10
A1 4c brown 28 18
A1 5c lilac 40 30
A1 6c dl bl 50 35
A1 8c gray brn 80 45
A1 10c violet 1.00 60
A1 12c car rose 1.10 75
A1 20c ultra 3.50 2.50
A1 50c yel grn 20.00 8.00
0 A1 $1 grnsh bl 27.50 12.00
*Nos. 1-10 (10)* 55.23 25.23

Map of Island — A2

Island Scene — A3

Designs: 4c. Moonflower. 5c. Robber crab. 8c. Phosphate train. 10c. Crane loading phosphate. 12c. Flying fish cove. 20c. Loading ship. 50c. Frigate bird. $1. Yellow-billed ropic bird.

***Perf. 14x14½, 14½x14***

**1963, Aug. 28 Engr.**

**Size: 20x26mm, 26x20mm**

11 A2 2c orange 12 9
12 A2 4c red brn 25 18
13 A2 5c rose lil 32 25
14 A3 6c slate 40 30
15 A2 8c black 80 35
16 A2 10c violet 60 38
17 A3 12c dl red 80 55
18 A3 20c dk bl 2.00 1.50
19 A3 50c green 4.00 1.75

**Size: 35x21mm**

20 A3 $1 org yel 10.00 4.50
*Nos. 11-20 (10)* 19.29 9.85

**ANZAC Issue**

Type of Australia, 1965

**1965, Apr. 14 Photo. *Perf. 13½x13***
21 A150 10c brt grn, sep & blk 1.10 1.10

See note after Australia No. 387.

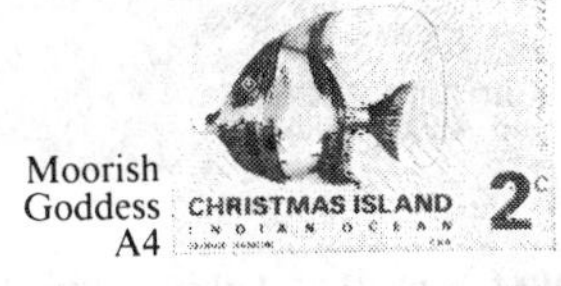

Moorish Goddess A4

Fish: 1c. Golden striped grouper. 3c. Forceps fish. 4c. Queen triggerfish. 5c. Regal angelfish. 9c. Surgeonfish. 10c. Turkeyfish. 15c. Saddleback butterflyfish. 20c. Clown butterflyfish. 30c. Ghost pipefish. 50c. Lined surgeonfish. $1. Meyer's butterflyfish.

**1968-70 Photo. *Perf. 13½***
22 A4 1c multi 16 16
23 A4 2c multi 32 32
24 A4 3c multi 40 40
25 A4 4c multi 48 48
26 A4 5c multi 55 55
27 A4 9c multi 1.25 1.25
28 A4 10c multi 1.40 1.40
29 A4 15c multi ('70) 11.50 11.50
30 A4 20c multi 4.00 4.00
31 A4 30c multi ('70) 11.50 11.50
32 A4 50c multi 14.00 14.00
33 A4 $1 multi 25.00 25.00
*Nos. 22-33 (12)* 70.56 70.56

**Christmas Issues**

"Hark the Herald Angels Sing" A5

Virgin and Child, by Morando A6

Adoration of the Shepherds, Seville School — A7

**1969, Nov. 10 Photo. *Perf. 13½***
34 A5 5c dk bl, gold, buff & red 60 60

**1970, Oct. 26 Photo. *Perf. 14x14½***

Design: 3c. The Ansidei Madonna, by Raphael.

35 A6 3c gold & multi 35 35
36 A6 5c sil & multi 50 50

**1971, Oct. 4**

Design: 20c. Adoration of the Shepherds, by Guido Reni.

37 A7 6c blk & multi 85 85
38 A7 20c dk bl & multi 2.50 2.50

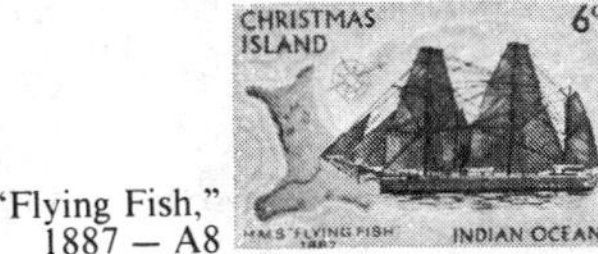

"Flying Fish," 1887 — A8

Ships and Map of Christmas Island: 1c, "Eagle," 1714. 2c, "Redpole," 1890. 3c, "Hoi Houw," 1959. 4c, "Pigot," 1771. 5c, "Valetta," 1968. 7c, "Asia," 1805. 8c, "Islander," 1929-60. 9c, "Imperieuse," 1888. 10c, "Egeria," 1887. 20c, "Thomas," 1615. 25c, "Gordon," 1864. 30c, "Cygnet," 1688. 35c, "Triadic," 1958. 50c, "Amethyst," 1857. $1, "Royal Mary," 1643. (The 9c is incorrectly inscribed "Imperious.")

**1972-73 Photo. *Perf. 14½x13½***
39 A8 1c yel grn & multi 6 5
40 A8 2c lt red brn & multi 10 8
41 A8 3c dp rose & multi 15 12
42 A8 4c multi ('73) 22 20
43 A8 5c multi ('73) 28 25
44 A8 6c lil & multi 30 28
45 A8 7c lt grn & multi 30 28
46 A8 8c bl & multi 40 35
47 A8 9c org & multi ('73) 45 40
48 A8 10c lem & multi ('73) 45 40
49 A8 20c tan & multi 1.00 90
50 A8 25c multi ('73) 1.10 1.00
51 A8 30c multi ('73) 1.25 1.10
52 A8 35c tan & multi ('73) 1.25 1.10
53 A8 50c ultra & multi ('73) 1.40 1.25
54 A8 $1 yel & multi 3.50 3.25
*Nos. 39-54 (16)* 12.21 11.01

Issue dates: 6c, 7c, 8c, 20c, Feb. 5; 1c, 2c, 3c, $1, June 5; 4c, 5c, 9c, 50c, Feb. 6, 1973; 10c, 25c, 30c, 35c, June 4, 1973.

"Joy" — A9

Designs: Nos. 55, 57, "Peace," angel facing right. No. 58, Like No. 56.

**1972, Oct. 2 Litho. *Perf. 14½***
55 A9 3c blk & multi 1.00 90
56 A9 3c blk & multi 1.00 90
57 A9 7c blk & multi 1.40 1.25
58 A9 7c blk & multi 1.40 1.25

Christmas 1972. Stamps of same denomination printed se-tenant.

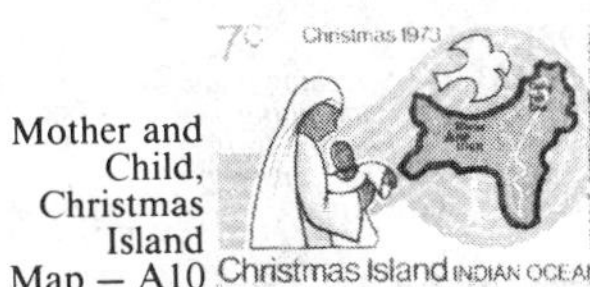

Mother and Child, Christmas Island Map — A10

**1973, Oct. 2 Photo. *Perf. 14½x13½***
59 A10 7c bl & multi 1.40 1.40
60 A10 25c brt grn & multi 6.50 6.50

Christmas 1973.

Mother and Child with Star and Cross — A11

**1974, Oct. 2 Photo. *Perf. 13½x14½***
61 A11 7c blk & lil rose 75 75
62 A11 30c blk & yel 4.50 4.50

Christmas 1974.

Flight into Egypt — A12

**1975, Oct. 2 Photo. *Perf. 14½x13½***
63 A12 10c gold, blk & yel 65 65
64 A12 35c gold, vio blk & rose 2.25 2.25

Christmas 1975.

Star of Bethlehem and Dove A13 A14

**1976, Oct. 2 Photo. *Perf. 13½***
65 A13 10c red & multi 40 40
66 A14 10c red & multi 40 40
67 A13 35c bl & multi 1.60 1.60
68 A14 35c bl & multi 1.60 1.60

Christmas 1976. Stamps of same denomination printed se-tenant in sheets of 50.

Andrew Clunies-Ross (first settler) — A15

Famous Visitors: 1c, William Dampier, explorer, buccaneer. 2c, Capt. Willem de Vlamingh, Dutch explorer. 3c, Vice Adm. John F. L. P. Maclear, Royal Navy. 4c, John Murray, oceanographer, scientist. 5c, Adm. Pelham Aldrich and crew collecting specimen. 7c, Joseph Jackson Lister, naturalist, and arenga listeri plant. 8c, Adm. William Henry May. 9c, Henry Nicholas Ridley, botanist. 10c, George Clunies-Ross, pioneer phosphate miner. 20c, Capt. Joshua Slocum. 45c, Charles William Andrews, zoologist, and frigate birds. 50c, Karl Richard Hanitsch, zoologist, and fruit pigeon. 75c, Victor W. W. Saunders Purcell, Sinologist. $1, Fam Choo Beng, educator. $2, Harold Spencer-Jones, astronomer.

**1977-78 Photo. *Perf. 14x13½***
69 A15 1c multi 5 5
70 A15 2c multi 5 5
71 A15 3c multi 6 6
72 A15 4c multi 7 7
73 A15 5c multi 8 8
74 A15 6c multi 10 10
75 A15 7c multi 10 10
76 A15 8c multi 14 14
77 A15 9c multi 14 14
78 A15 10c multi 18 18
79 A15 20c multi 35 35
80 A15 45c multi 50 50
81 A15 50c multi 65 65
82 A15 75c multi 1.00 1.00
83 A15 $1 multi 1.40 1.40
84 A15 $2 multi 2.00 2.00
*Nos. 69-84 (16)* 6.87 6.87

Issue dates: Nos. 69, 74, 77 and 83, Apr. 30, 1977. Others, 1978.

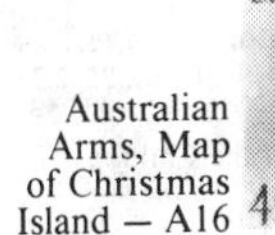
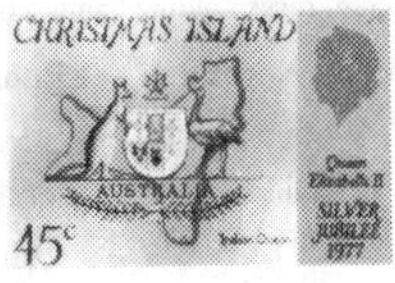

Australian Arms, Map of Christmas Island — A16

**1977, June 2 Litho. *Perf. 14½x13½***
85 A16 45c multi 1.25 1.25

25th anniv. of reign of Elizabeth II.

**Souvenir Sheet**

Partridge in a Pear Tree — A17

Designs (Twelve Days of Christmas): a. Partridge in a pear tree. b. 2 turtle doves. c. 3 French hens. d. 4 calling birds. e. 5 gold rings. f. 6 geese. g. 7 swans. h. 8 maids a-milking. i. 9 ladies dancing. j. 10 lords a-leaping. k. 11 pipers piping. l. 12 drummers drumming.

**Unwmk.**

**1977, Oct. 20 Litho. *Perf. 14***
86 A17 Sheet of 12 2.75 2.75
*a.-l.* 10c. single stamp 20 20
*m.* Wmk. 373 ('78) 2.25 2.25

Christmas 1977. No. 86 has red and black marginal inscription and bars of carol. Size: 142x170mm.

**Elizabeth II Coronation Anniversary Issue**

Common Design Types

**Souvenir Sheet**

**1978, Apr. 21 Litho. *Perf. 15***

| | | | |
|---|---|---|---|
| *87* | Sheet of 6 | 5.50 | 5.50 |
| *a* | CD326 45c *white swan of Bohun* | 90 | 90 |
| *b* | CD327 45c *Elizabeth II* | 90 | 90 |
| *c* | CD328 45c *Abbott's booby* | 90 | 90 |

No. 87 contains 2 se-tenant strips of Nos. 87a-87c, separated by horizontal gutter with commemorative and descriptive inscriptions and showing central part of coronation procession with coach. Size: 100x135mm.

**Souvenir Sheet**

Christ Child — A18

Designs (Song of Christmas): a. Christ Child. b. Herald angels. c. Redeemer. d. Israel. e. Star. f. Three Wise Men. g. Manger. h. "All He stands for." i. "Shepherds came."

**1978, Oct. 2 Litho. *Perf. 14***

| | | | |
|---|---|---|---|
| *88* | A18 Sheet of 9 | 1.75 | 1.75 |
| *a.-i.* | 10c. single stamp | 18 | 18 |

Christmas 1978. Each stamp design incorporates one letter of "Christmas;" multicolored margin with bars of carol. Size: 143x160mm.

IYC Emblem, Oriental Children — A19

Design: IYC emblem and children of different races holding hands, continuous design.

**1979, Apr. 20 Litho. *Perf. 14***

| | | | |
|---|---|---|---|
| *89* | Strip of 5 | 2.25 | 2.25 |
| *a* | A19 20c single stamp | 40 | 40 |

International Year of the Child.

Rowland Hill and No. 25 — A20

Designs: Rowland Hill and Christmas Island stamps.

**1979, Aug. 27 Litho. *Perf. 13x13½***

| | | | |
|---|---|---|---|
| *90* | Strip of 5 | 1.75 | 1.75 |
| *a* | A20 20c No. 1 | 30 | 30 |
| *b* | A20 20c No. 11 | 30 | 30 |
| *c* | A20 20c No. 21 | 30 | 30 |
| *d* | A20 20c *shown* | 30 | 30 |
| *e* | A20 20c No. 34 | 30 | 30 |

Sir Rowland Hill (1795-1879), originator of penny postage.

Three Kings Bearing Gifts — A21

Christmas: 55c, Virgin and Child, globe.

**1979, Oct. 22 Litho. *Perf. 14x14½***

| | | | |
|---|---|---|---|
| *91* | A21 20c multi | 35 | 35 |
| *92* | A21 55c multi | 90 | 90 |

25 Years of Golf — A22

**1980, Feb. 12 Litho. *Perf. 14½x14***

| | | | |
|---|---|---|---|
| *93* | A22 20c *shown* | 30 | 30 |
| *94* | A22 55c *Clubhouse* | 80 | 80 |

Surveyor, Phosphate Industry A23

**1980, May 5 Litho. *Perf. 14x14½***

| | | | |
|---|---|---|---|
| *95* | A23 15c *shown* | 25 | 25 |
| *96* | A23 22c *Drilling for samples* | 38 | 38 |
| *97* | A23 40c *Sample analysis* | 70 | 70 |
| *98* | A23 55c *Mine planning* | 90 | 90 |

**1980, July 14**

| | | | |
|---|---|---|---|
| *99* | A23 15c *Jungle clearing* | 25 | 25 |
| *100* | A23 22c *Overburden removal* | 38 | 39 |
| *101* | A23 40c *Open cut mining* | 70 | 70 |
| *102* | A23 55c *Restoration* | 90 | 90 |

**1981, Feb. 9**

| | | | |
|---|---|---|---|
| *103* | A23 22c *Screening and stockpiling* | 38 | 38 |
| *104* | A23 28c *Loading train* | 50 | 50 |
| *105* | A23 40c *Rail transport* | 70 | 70 |
| *106* | A23 60c *Drying* | 1.00 | 1.00 |

**1981, May 4**

| | | | |
|---|---|---|---|
| *107* | A23 22c *Crushing* | 38 | 38 |
| *108* | A23 28c *Pipeline* | 50 | 50 |
| *109* | A23 40c *Bulk storage* | 70 | 70 |
| *110* | A23 60c *Loading ship* | 1.00 | 1.00 |
| | *Nos. 95-110 (16)* | 9.62 | 9.63 |

**Souvenir Sheet**

Virgin and Child — A24

**1980, Oct. 6 Litho. *Perf. 13½x13***

| | | | |
|---|---|---|---|
| *111* | Sheet of 6 | 3.00 | 3.00 |
| *a* | A24 15c *Angel* | 25 | 25 |
| *b* | A24 22c *shown* | 35 | 35 |
| *c* | A24 60c *Angel* | 85 | 85 |
| *d* | A24 15c *Angel holding soldier* | 25 | 25 |
| *e* | A24 22c *Kneeling woman and man* | 35 | 35 |
| *f* | A24 60c *Chinese, Indian, European children* | 85 | 85 |

Christmas 1980. No. 111 contains 2 strips of 3 (Nos. 111a-111c and 111d-111f) with gutter between. Multicolored margin shows angels and verse from carol "It Came upon a Midnight Clear." Size: 115x150mm.

Cryptoblepharus Egeriae — A25

Designs: Reptiles.

**1981, Aug. 10 Litho. *Perf. 13x13½***

| | | | |
|---|---|---|---|
| *112* | A25 24c shown | 35 | 35 |
| *113* | A25 30c Emoia nativitata | 50 | 50 |
| *114* | A25 40c Lepidodactylus listeri | 60 | 60 |
| *115* | A25 60c Cyrtodactylus nov. | 85 | 85 |

*Christmas Island stamps can be mounted in Scott's Australia and Dependencies Album.*

**Souvenir Sheet**

Nativity A26

**1981, Oct. 19 Litho. *Perf. 14½x14***

| | | | |
|---|---|---|---|
| *116* | Sheet of 4 | 2.50 | 2.50 |
| *a* | A26 18c Angels, star | 30 | 30 |
| *b* | A26 24c shown | 40 | 40 |
| *c* | A26 40c Children praying to Jesus | 70 | 70 |
| *d* | A26 60c Children praying | 90 | 90 |

Christmas 1981. No. 116 has multicolored margin showing children praying. Size: 112x112mm.

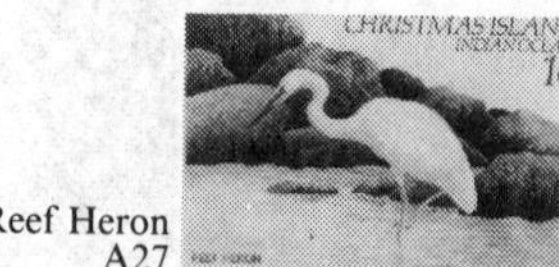


Reef Heron A27

**1982 Litho. *Perf. 14***

| | | | |
|---|---|---|---|
| *117* | A27 1c shown | 5 | 5 |
| *118* | A27 2c Noddies | 5 | 5 |
| *119* | A27 3c Glossy swiftlet | 6 | 6 |
| *120* | A27 4c Imperial pigeon | 8 | 8 |
| *121* | A27 5c Christmas Isld. silvereyes | 9 | 9 |
| *122* | A27 10c Thrush | 16 | 16 |
| *123* | A27 25c Silver bosunbird | 45 | 45 |
| *124* | A27 30c Christmas Isld. emerald doves | 50 | 50 |
| *125* | A27 40c Brown boobies | 70 | 70 |
| *126* | A27 50c Red-footed boobies | 90 | 90 |
| *127* | A27 65c Christmas Isld. frigatebird | 1.25 | 1.25 |
| *128* | A27 75c Golden bosunbirds | 1.40 | 1.40 |
| *129* | A27 80c Nankeen kestrel, vert. | 1.50 | 1.50 |
| *130* | A27 $1 Christmas Isld. hawk owl, vert. | 1.75 | 1.75 |
| *131* | A27 $2 Goshawk, vert. | 3.25 | 3.25 |
| *132* | A27 $4 Abbott's boobies, vert. | 7.25 | 7.25 |
| | *Nos. 117-132 (16)* | 19.44 | 19.44 |

Christmas 1982 — A28

25th Anniv. of Boat Club — A29

Designs: Paper sculptures. Nos. 135-137 se-tenant.

**Lithographed & Embossed**

**1982, Oct. 18**

| | | | |
|---|---|---|---|
| *135* | A28 27c Joseph | 40 | 40 |
| *136* | A28 50c Angel | 65 | 65 |
| *137* | A28 75c Wise Man | 1.00 | 1.00 |

***Perf. 14x14½, 14½x14***

**1983, May 2 Litho.**

Designs: Various boating activities.

| | | | |
|---|---|---|---|
| *138* | A29 27c multi | 40 | 40 |
| *139* | A29 35c multi | 55 | 55 |
| *140* | A29 50c multi, horiz. | 85 | 85 |
| *141* | A29 75c multi, horiz. | 1.10 | 1.10 |

25th Anniv. of Australian Territory A30

**1983, Oct. 1 Litho. *Perf. 1***

| | | | |
|---|---|---|---|
| *142* | A30 24c Maps. golden bosun bird, kangaroo | 35 | 3 |
| *143* | A30 30c Map, flag | 40 | 4 |
| *144* | A30 85c Boeing 727, maps | 1.25 | 1.2 |

Christmas 1983 — A31

Designs: Christmas candles.

**1983, Oct. 31 Litho. *Perf. 13½x1***

| | | | |
|---|---|---|---|
| *145* | A31 24c multi | 35 | 3 |
| *146* | A31 30c multi | 40 | 4 |
| *147* | A31 85c multi | 1.25 | 1.2 |

Red Land Crab — A32

**1984, Feb. 20 Litho. *Perf. 14x14½***

| | | | |
|---|---|---|---|
| *148* | A32 30c Feeding | 55 | 5 |
| *149* | A32 40c Migration | 75 | 7 |
| *150* | A32 55c Developmental stages | 1.00 | 1.0 |
| *151* | A32 85c Adult female, young | 1.50 | 1.5 |

Local Fungi — A33

**1984, Apr. 30 *Perf. 13½x14½***

| | | | |
|---|---|---|---|
| *152* | A33 30c Leucocoprinus fragilissimus | 65 | 65 |
| *153* | A33 40c Microporus xanthopus | 90 | 90 |
| *154* | A33 45c Trogia anthidepas | 1.00 | 1.00 |
| *155* | A33 55c Haddowia longipes | 1.20 | 1.20 |
| *156* | A33 85c Phillipsia domingensis | 1.85 | 1.85 |
| | *Nos. 152-156 (5)* | 5.60 | 5.60 |

Cricket on Christmas Isld., 25th Anniv. A34

**1984, July 23 Litho. *Perf. 14***

| | | | |
|---|---|---|---|
| *157* | A34 30c Runout | 60 | 60 |
| *158* | A34 40c Catch at point | 80 | 80 |
| *159* | A34 55c Batsman | 1.10 | 1.10 |
| *160* | A34 85c Batsman hitting | 1.65 | 1.65 |

**Souvenir Sheet**

Christmas 1984 and Ausipex '84 A35

**1984, Sept. 21 Litho. *Perf. 13½***

| | | | |
|---|---|---|---|
| *161* | Sheet of 3 | 3.75 | 3.75 |
| *a* | A35 30c Father Christmas arriving | 65 | 65 |
| *b* | A35 55c Distributing gifts | 1.20 | 1.20 |
| *c* | A35 85c Waving good-bye | 1.85 | 1.85 |

Size: 100x100mm.

Crabs — A36

**1985 Litho. Perf. 13x13½**

*162* A36 30c Birgus latro 48 48
*163* A36 33c Cardiosoma hirtipes 55 55
*164* A36 33c Gecarcoidea natalis 55 55
*165* A36 40c Ocypode ceratophthalma 65 65
*166* A36 45c Ceonobita rugosa 70 70
*167* A36 45c Metasesarma rousseauxi 70 70
*168* A36 55c Coenobita brevimana 90 90
*169* A36 60c Geograpsus stormi 1.00 1.00
*170* A36 60c Grapsus tenuicrustatus 1.00 1.00
*171* A36 85c Geograpsus grayi 1.40 1.40
*172* A36 90c Ocypode cordimana 1.50 1.50
*173* A36 90c Geograpsus crinipes 1.50 1.50
*Nos. 162-173 (12)* 10.93 10.93

Issue dates: 30c, 40c, 55c, 85c, Jan. 30. Nos. 163, 166, 169 and 172, Apr. 29. Nos. 164, 167, 170 and 173, July 22.

Once in Royal David's City — A37

Songs: 33c, While Shepherds Watched Their Flocks by Night. 45c, Away in a Manger. 60c, We Three Kings of Orient Are. 90c, Hark! The Herald Angels Sing.

**1985, Oct. 28 Litho. Perf. 14x14½**

*174* A37 27c multi 50 50
*175* A37 33c multi 65 65
*176* A37 45c multi 85 85
*177* A37 60c multi 1.10 1.10
*178* A37 90c multi 1.65 1.65
*a* Strip of 5, #174-178 5.00 5.00

Christmas 1985.

Halley's Comet — A38

**1985, Apr. 30 Litho. Perf. 14**

*179* A38 33c Over island 58 58
*180* A38 45c Edmond Halley 75 75
*181* A38 60c Over phosphate shipping 1.10 1.10
*182* A38 90c Over Flying Fish Cove 1.60 1.60

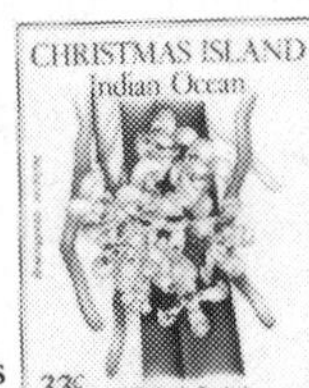

Indigenous Flowers — A39

**1986, June 30 Litho. Perf. 14**

*183* A39 33c Ridley's orchid 58 30
*184* A39 45c Hanging flower 75 40
*185* A39 60c Hoya 1.10 60
*186* A39 90c Sea hibiscus 1.60 85

**Royal Wedding Issue, 1986**

Common Design Type

Designs: 33c, Couple in Buckingham Palace garden. 90c, Andrew operating helicopter.

**1986, July 23 Litho. Perf. 14½x14**

*187* CD338 33c multi 65 65
*188* CD338 90c multi 1.75 1.75

Christmas A40

Santa Claus at Christmas Island.

**1986, Sept. 30 Litho. Perf. 13x13½**

*189* A40 30c Speedboating 50 50
*190* A40 36c At the beach 60 60
*191* A40 55c Fishing 85 85
*192* A40 70c Golfing 1.10 1.10
*193* A40 $1 Sleeping in hammock 1.60 1.60
*Nos. 189-193 (5)* 4.65 4.65

Visiting Ships, Cent. A41

**1987, Jan. 21 Perf. 14½**

*194* A41 36c Flying Fish 48 48
*195* A41 90c Egeria 1.20 1.20

Wildlife A42

**1987-88 Litho. Perf. 14**

*196* A42 1c Blind snake 5 5
*197* A42 2c Blue-tailed skink 5 5
*198* A42 3c Insectivorous bat 5 5
*199* A42 5c Green cricket 8 8
*200* A42 10c Christmas Is. fruit bat 15 15
*201* A42 25c Gecko 38 38
*202* A42 30c Praying mantis 42 42
*203* A42 36c Hawk owl 52 52
*204* A42 40c Bull-mouth helmet shell 58 58
*205* A42 50c Textile cone shell 75 75
*206* A42 65c Brittle-stars 95 95
*207* A42 75c Royal angelfish 1.10 1.10
*208* A42 90c Christmas Is. white butterfly 1.30 1.30
*209* A42 $1 Mimic butterfly 1.45 1.45
*210* A42 $2 Shrew 3.00 3.00
*211* A42 $5 Green turtle 7.25 7.25
*a.* Sheet of 16, Nos. 196-211 18.08 18.08
*Nos. 196-211 (16)* 18.08 18.08

Issue dates: 1c, 2c, 25c, $5, Mar. 25; 3c, 10c, 36c, $2, June 24; 40c, 50c, 65c, 75c, Aug. 26. 5c, 30c, 90c, $1, Mar. 1, 1988.

Stamps contained in No. 211a inscribed "1988" at bottom. Size of No. 211a: 176x125mm.

**Souvenir Sheet**

Santa Claus Delivering Presents — A43

Illustration reduced.

**1987, Oct. 7 Litho. Perf. 13½**

*212* A43 Sheet of 4 3.85 3.85
*a* 30c multi 45 45
*b* 37c multi 55 55
*c* 90c multi 1.35 1.35
*d* $1 multi 1.50 1.50

Christmas. No. 212 has multicolored decorative margin; stamps printed in a continuous design. Size: 165x65mm.

Australia Bicentennial A44

Designs: a. First Fleet sighted by 5 Aborginals on land. b. Four Aboriginals on land, one in canoe. c. Ships entering bay, kangaroos. d. Europeans land. e. Flag raising.

**1988, Jan. 26 Litho. Perf. 13**

*213* Strip of 5 2.60 2.60
*a.-e.* A44 37c, any single 52 52

No. 213a-213e printed in a continuous design. See Cocos Islands No. 172.

Annexation of the Island, Cent. — A45

**Perf. 14½**

**1988, June 8 Litho. Unwmk.**

*214* A45 37c Capt William Henry May 55 55
*215* A45 53c Annexation ceremony 78 78
*216* A45 95c HMS *Imperieuse* 1.40 1.40
*217* A45 $1.50 Building cairn of stones 2.20 2.20

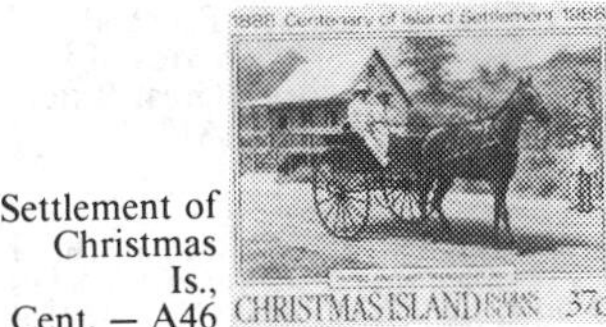

Settlement of Christmas Is., Cent. — A46

Transportation: 37c, Horse and cart, 1910. 55c, Phosphate mining, 1910. 70c, Steam locomotive, 1914. $1, Arrival of first aircraft, 1957.

**Perf. 14½**

**1988, Aug. 24 Litho. Unwmk.**

*218* A46 37c multi 60 60
*219* A46 55c multi 90 90
*220* A46 70c multi 1.15 1.15
*221* A46 $1 multi 1.65 1.65

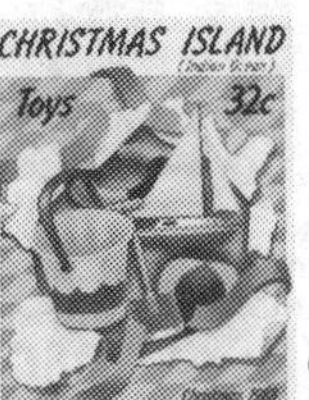

Christmas Presents — A47

**1988, Nov. 15 Perf. 14x14½**

*222* A47 32c Bucket, shovel, boat 50 50
*223* A47 39c Snorkeling equipment 60 60
*224* A47 90c Toy soldier, doll, stuffed animals 1.40 1.40
*225* A47 $1 Race car, truck, plane 1.55 1.55

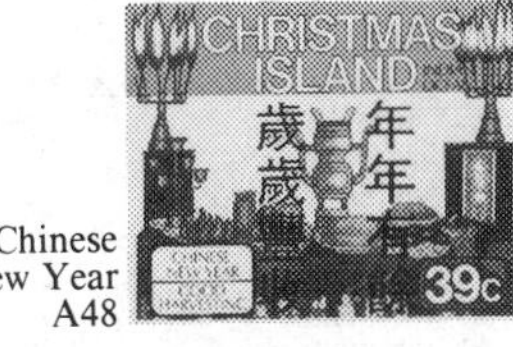

Chinese New Year A48

**1989, Jan. 31 Litho. Unwmk. Perf.**

*226* A48 39c Good harvest 60 60
*227* A48 55c Prosperity 90 90
*228* A48 90c Good fortune 1.40 1.40
*229* A48 $1 Progress 1.55 1.55

## COCOS ISLANDS

### (Keeling Islands)

LOCATION — Indian Ocean, 1,330 miles northwest of Australia, 580 miles southwest of Java.

GOVT. — A territory of Australia.

AREA — 6 sq. mi.

POP. — 579 (1983)

Of 27 small coral islands making up two atolls, two islands are inhabited. Cocos Islands stamps are also valid within Australia.

12 Pence = 1 Shilling
100 Cents = 1 Dollar (1969)

**Catalogue values for all unused stamps in this country are for Never Hinged items.**

Copra Industry — A1

Super Constellation — A2

Map of Islands — A3

Designs: 1sh, Coco palms. 2sh, Sailboat (dukong). 2sh3p, Fairy tern.

**Perf. 14½**

**1963, June 11 Unwmk. Engr.**

*1* A1 3p dk red brn 5.00 4.00
*2* A2 5p vio bl 2.00 2.00
*3* A3 8p red 10.00 5.50
*4* A1 1sh green 6.50 2.75
*5* A3 2sh dl pur 17.50 11.00
*6* A2 2sh3p green 35.00 30.00
*Nos. 1-6 (6)* 76.00 55.25

**ANZAC Issue**

Type of Australia

**1965, Apr. 14 Photo. Perf. 13½x13**

*7* A150 5p brt grn, sep & blk 1.40 1.25

See note after Australia No. 387.

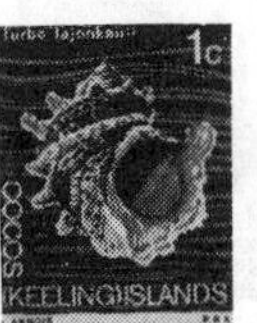

Turbo Lajonkairii A4

Blenny A5

Designs: 2c, Tridacna crocea (shell). 3c, Tridacna derasa (shell). 5c, Porites cocosensis (coral). 6c, Flyingfish. 10c, Banded rail (bird). 15c, Java sparrow. 20c, Red-tailed tropic bird. 30c, Sooty tern. 50c, Eastern reef heron. $1, Great frigate bird.

**Perf. 13½**

**1969, July 9 Unwmk. Photo.**

**Size: 21½x27mm, 26½x22mm**

| No. | Type | Description | Unused | Used |
|---|---|---|---|---|
| 8 | A4 | 1c multi | 8 | 7 |
| 9 | A4 | 2c multi | 90 | 75 |
| 10 | A5 | 3c multi | 20 | 15 |
| 11 | A5 | 4c multi | 30 | 25 |
| 12 | A5 | 5c multi | 35 | 30 |
| 13 | A5 | 6c multi | 55 | 45 |
| 14 | A5 | 10c multi | 1.40 | 1.25 |
| 15 | A5 | 15c multi | 1.10 | 90 |
| 16 | A5 | 20c multi | 1.10 | 90 |
| 17 | A5 | 30c multi | 1.90 | 1.50 |
| 18 | A5 | 50c multi | 3.25 | 2.00 |

**Size: 21½x34mm**

| No. | Type | Description | Unused | Used |
|---|---|---|---|---|
| 19 | A4 | $1 multi | 5.50 | 5.50 |
| | | *Nos. 8-19 (12)* | 16.63 | 14.02 |

"Dragon" — A6

"Juno" — A7

**Perf. 13½x13, 13x13½**

**1976, Mar. 29 Photo.**

| No. | Type | Description | Unused | Used |
|---|---|---|---|---|
| 20 | A6 | 1c *shown* | 5 | 5 |
| 21 | A7 | 2c *shown* | 12 | 12 |
| 22 | A7 | 5c *"Beagle"* | 25 | 25 |
| 23 | A7 | 10c *"Sydney"* | 40 | 40 |
| 24 | A7 | 15c *"Emden"* | 75 | 75 |
| 25 | A7 | 20c *"Ayesha"* | 90 | 90 |
| 26 | A6 | 25c *"Islander"* | 1.40 | 1.40 |
| 27 | A6 | 30c *"Cheshire"* | 1.50 | 1.50 |
| 28 | A7 | 35c *"Jukung"* | 1.75 | 1.75 |
| 29 | A7 | 40c *"Scotia"* | 1.40 | 1.40 |
| 30 | A6 | 50c *"Orontes"* | 1.75 | 1.75 |
| 31 | A6 | $1 *Royal Yacht "Gothic"* | 3.25 | 3.25 |
| | | *Nos. 20-31 (12)* | 13.52 | 13.52 |

Historic ships.

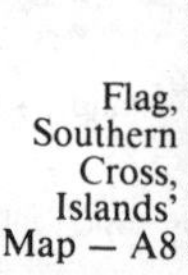

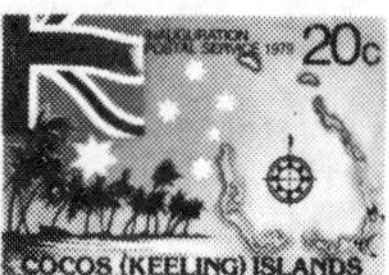


Flag, Southern Cross, Islands' Map — A8

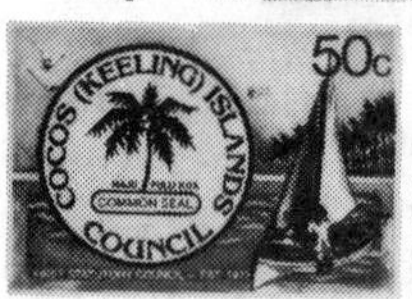


Council Emblem, Sailboat A9

**1979, Sept. 3 Litho. Perf. 15½**

| No. | Type | Description | Unused | Used |
|---|---|---|---|---|
| 32 | A8 | 20c multi | 32 | 32 |
| 33 | A9 | 50c multi | 90 | 90 |

Inauguration of Cocos Islands' postal service (20c), and establishment of Cocos Islands Council (50c).

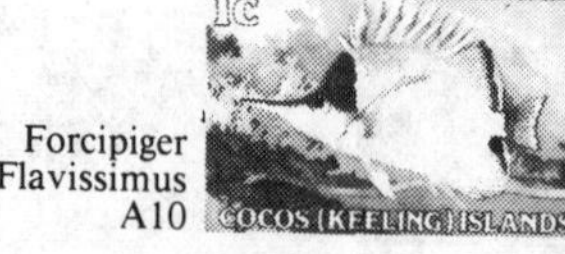


Forcipiger Flavissimus A10

Fish: 2c, Chaetodon ornatissimus. 5c, Anthias. 10c, Meyer's coralfish. 15c, Halichoeres. 20c, Amphiprion clarkii. 22c, Balistapus undulatus. 25c, Maori wrasse. 28c, Macropharyngodon meleagris. 30c, Chaetodon madagascariensis. 35c, Centropyge colini. 40c, Bodianus axillaris. 50c, Corisgaimardi. 55c, Spotted wrasse. 60c, Epinepnelus tauvina. $1, Paracanthurus hepatus. $2, Striped butterflyfish.

**1979-80 Litho. Perf. 15½**

| No. | Type | Description | Unused | Used |
|---|---|---|---|---|
| 34 | A10 | 1c multi | 5 | 5 |
| 35 | A10 | 2c multi | 6 | 6 |
| 36 | A10 | 5c multi | 14 | 14 |
| 37 | A10 | 10c multi ('80) | 28 | 28 |
| 38 | A10 | 15c multi | 40 | 40 |
| 39 | A10 | 20c multi | 48 | 48 |
| 40 | A10 | 22c multi ('80) | 45 | 45 |
| 41 | A10 | 25c multi ('80) | 60 | 60 |
| 42 | A10 | 28c multi ('80) | 55 | 55 |
| 43 | A10 | 30c multi | 75 | 75 |
| 44 | A10 | 35c multi | 80 | 80 |
| 45 | A10 | 40c multi | 90 | 90 |
| 46 | A10 | 50c multi | 1.25 | 1.25 |
| 47 | A10 | 55c multi ('80) | 1.40 | 1.40 |
| 48 | A10 | 60c multi ('80) | 60 | 60 |
| 49 | A10 | $1 multi | 1.25 | 1.25 |
| 50 | A10 | $2 multi ('80) | 2.50 | 2.50 |
| | | *Nos. 34-50 (17)* | 12.46 | 12.46 |

Sailboats in Lagoon A11

Christmas: 25c, Yachts and seagulls (vert.).

**1979, Oct. 22 Litho. Perf. 15½**

| No. | Type | Description | Unused | Used |
|---|---|---|---|---|
| 51 | A11 | 25c multi | 40 | 40 |
| 52 | A11 | 55c multi | 90 | 90 |

Star of Bethlehem, Map of Cocos Islands — A12

Christmas (Map of Cocos Islands and): 28c, Three kings. 60c, Nativity.

**1980, Oct. 22 Litho. Perf. 13½x13**

| No. | Type | Description | Unused | Used |
|---|---|---|---|---|
| 53 | A12 | 15c multi | 25 | 25 |
| 54 | A12 | 28c multi | 40 | 40 |
| 55 | A12 | 60c multi | 80 | 80 |

Flag and Arms of Great Britain A13

Australian Territory Status, 25th Anniversary (British Flag and Arms of Past Administrators): No. 57, Ceylon, 1878, 1942-1946. No. 58, Straits Settlements, 1886. No. 59, Singapore, 1946. No. 60, Australia (flag), 1955. Nos. 56-60 se-tenant.

**1980, Nov. 24 Litho. Perf. 13½x13**

| No. | Type | Description | Unused | Used |
|---|---|---|---|---|
| 56 | A13 | 22c multi | 25 | 25 |
| 57 | A13 | 22c multi | 25 | 25 |
| 58 | A13 | 22c multi | 25 | 25 |
| 59 | A13 | 22c multi | 25 | 25 |
| 60 | A13 | 22c multi | 25 | 25 |
| | | *Nos. 56-60 (5)* | 1.25 | 1.25 |

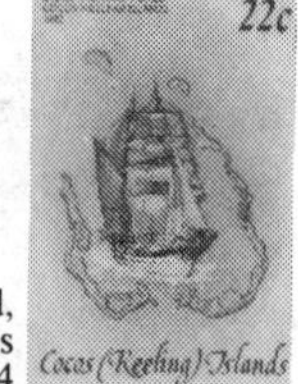


Eye of the Wind, Map of Cocos Islands — A14

**Perf. 13x13½, 13½x13**

**1980, Dec. 18**

| No. | Type | Description | Unused | Used |
|---|---|---|---|---|
| 61 | A14 | 22c *shown* | 40 | 40 |
| 62 | A14 | 28c *Expedition routes, horiz.* | 50 | 50 |
| 63 | A14 | 35c *Francis Drake, Golden Hinde* | 80 | 80 |
| 64 | A14 | 60c *Prince Charles, Eye of the Wind* | 75 | 75 |

Operation Drake circumnavigation.

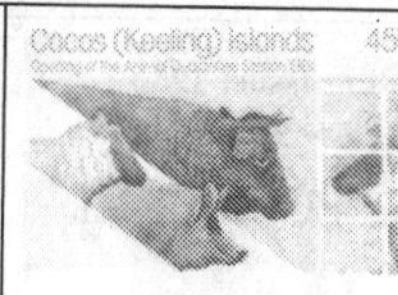


Livestock in Quarantine A15

**1981, May 12 Litho. Perf. 13½x13**

| No. | Type | Description | Unused | Used |
|---|---|---|---|---|
| 65 | A15 | 22c Aerial view of station | 35 | 35 |
| 66 | A15 | 45c shown | 70 | 70 |
| 67 | A15 | 60c Livestock, diff. | 90 | 90 |

West Island Quarantine Station opening.

Catalina Guba II — A16

Inauguration of Air Service to Indian Ocean: No. 69, Avro Lancastrian. No. 70, Douglas DC4 Skymaster, Lockheed Constellation. No. 71, Lockheed Electra. No. 72, Boeing 727. Nos. 68-72 se-tenant

**1981, June 23 Litho. Perf. 13½x13**

| No. | Type | Description | Unused | Used |
|---|---|---|---|---|
| 68 | A16 | 22c multi | 38 | 38 |
| 69 | A16 | 22c multi | 38 | 38 |
| 70 | A16 | 22c multi | 38 | 38 |
| 71 | A16 | 22c multi | 38 | 38 |
| 72 | A16 | 22c multi | 38 | 38 |
| | | *Nos. 68-72 (5)* | 1.90 | 1.90 |

Prince Charles and Lady Diana — A17

**1981, July 29 Litho. Perf. 13½x13**

| No. | Type | Description | Unused | Used |
|---|---|---|---|---|
| 73 | A17 | 24c multi | 50 | 50 |
| 74 | A17 | 60c multi | 1.10 | 1.10 |

Royal Wedding.

Angels We Have Heard on High — A18

Christmas: Carols.

**1981, Oct. 22 Photo. Perf. 13½x13**

| No. | Type | Description | Unused | Used |
|---|---|---|---|---|
| 75 | A18 | 18c shown | 35 | 35 |
| 76 | A18 | 30c Shepherds Why this Jubilee | 55 | 55 |
| 77 | A18 | 60c Come to Bethlehem and See Him | 1.10 | 1.10 |

Sesquicentennial of Charles Darwin's Visit — A19

**1981, Dec. 28 Litho. Perf. 13½x13**

| No. | Type | Description | Unused | Used |
|---|---|---|---|---|
| 78 | A19 | 24c Coral | 38 | 38 |
| 79 | A19 | 45c Darwin, coral | 65 | 65 |
| 80 | A19 | 60c Beagle, coral | 90 | 90 |

**Souvenir Sheet**

| No. | Type | Description | Unused | Used |
|---|---|---|---|---|
| 81 | | Sheet of 2 | 1.25 | 1.25 |
| *a.* | A19 | 24c Atoll | 60 | 60 |
| *b.* | A19 | 24c Atoll, diff. | 60 | 60 |

No. 81 has multicolored margin showing portrait, text and diagram. Size: 131x95mm.

*Cocos Islands stamps can be mounted in Scott's Australia and Dependencies Album.*

125th Anniv. of Annexation to the British Dominions A20

**1982, Mar. 31 Litho. Perf. 13½x14**

| No. | Type | Description | Unused | Used |
|---|---|---|---|---|
| 82 | A20 | 24c Queen Victoria | 40 | 40 |
| 83 | A20 | 45c British flag | 70 | 70 |
| 84 | A20 | 60c Capt. Fremantle | 1.00 | 1.00 |

Scouting Year — A21

**Perf. 13½x14, 14x13½**

**1982, July 21 Litho.**

| No. | Type | Description | Unused | Used |
|---|---|---|---|---|
| 85 | A21 | 27c Baden-Powell | 50 | 50 |
| 86 | A21 | 75c Emblem, map, vert. | 1.40 | 1.40 |

Macroglossum Corythus — A22

**1982, Sept. 6**

| No. | Type | Description | Unused | Used |
|---|---|---|---|---|
| 87 | A22 | 1c Presic villida, vert. | 5 | 5 |
| 88 | A22 | 2c Cephonodes picus | 5 | 5 |
| 89 | A22 | 5c shown | 7 | 7 |
| 90 | A22 | 10c Chasmina candida, vert. | 12 | 12 |
| 91 | A22 | 20c Nagia linteola | 25 | 25 |
| 92 | A22 | 25c Eublemma rivula, vert. | 35 | 35 |
| 93 | A22 | 30c Eurrhyparodes tricoloralis, vert. | 40 | 40 |
| 94 | A22 | 35c Hippotion boerhaviae | 52 | 52 |
| 95 | A22 | 40c Euploea core corinna, vert. | 52 | 52 |
| 96 | A22 | 45c Psara hipponalis | 60 | 60 |
| 97 | A22 | 50c Danaus chrysippus | 65 | 65 |
| 98 | A22 | 55c Hypolimas misippus, vert. | 80 | 80 |
| 99 | A22 | 60c Spodoptera litura, vert. | 75 | 75 |
| 100 | A22 | $1 Achaea janata, vert. | 1.00 | 1.00 |
| 101 | A22 | $2 Hippotion velox | 2.25 | 2.25 |
| 102 | A22 | $3 Utetheisa pulchelloides | 3.25 | 3.25 |
| | | *Nos. 87-102 (16)* | 11.63 | 11.63 |

Christmas 1982 — A23

**1982, Oct. 25 Perf. 13x13½**

| No. | Type | Description | Unused | Used |
|---|---|---|---|---|
| 104 | A23 | 21c Holy Family | 40 | 40 |
| 105 | A23 | 35c Angel | 52 | 52 |
| 106 | A23 | 75c Flight into Egypt | 1.10 | 1.10 |

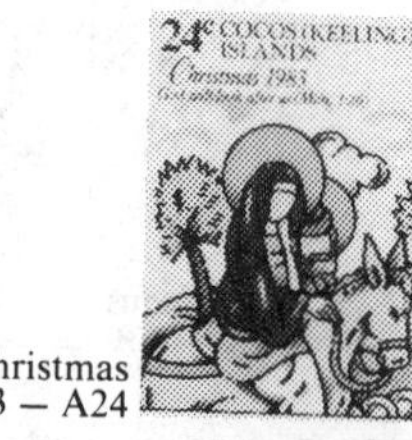


Christmas 1983 — A24

The Birth of Christ: a. God Will Look After Us; b. Our Baby King Jesus; c. Your Saviour is Born; d. Wise Men Followed the Star; e. And Worship the Lord.

**1983, Oct. 31 Litho. Perf. 14x13½**

| No. | Type | Description | Unused | Used |
|---|---|---|---|---|
| 107 | | Strip of 5 | 2.00 | 2.00 |
| *a.-e.* | A24 | 24c Any single | 40 | 40 |

Cocos-Malay Culture — A25

Festive Occasions.

**1984, Jan. 27 Litho. *Perf. 14x13½***

| | | | |
|---|---|---|---|
| *108* A25 45c Hari Raya | 1.00 | 1.00 |
| *109* A25 75c Melenggok dance | 1.75 | 1.75 |
| *110* A25 85c Wedding | 1.90 | 1.90 |

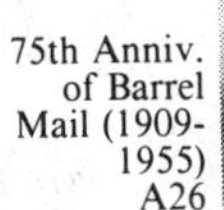

75th Anniv. of Barrel Mail (1909-1955) A26

Designs: 35c, Mail distribution, Direction Isld. 55c, Jukongs retrieving barrels from ocean liner. 70c, Morea receiving outgoing barrel mail, 1909. $1, Barrel mail recovery.

**1984, Apr. 20 Litho. *Perf. 13½x14***

| | | |
|---|---|---|
| *111* A26 35c multi | 85 | 85 |
| *112* A26 55c multi | 1.40 | 1.40 |
| *113* A26 70c multi | 1.75 | 1.75 |

**Souvenir Sheet**

| | | |
|---|---|---|
| *114* A26 $1 multi | 2.50 | 2.50 |

No. 114 has multicolored margin showing ships that carried barrel mail. Size: 125x95mm.

375th Anniv. of Islands' Discovery — A27

**1984, July 10 Litho. *Perf. 14x13½***

| | | |
|---|---|---|
| *115* A27 30c Capt. William Keeling | 65 | 65 |
| *116* A27 65c The Hector | 1.40 | 1.40 |
| *117* A27 95c Astrolabe | 2.00 | 2.00 |
| *118* A27 $1.10 Map, 1666 | 2.25 | 2.25 |

AUSIPEX '84 — A28

**1984, Sept. 21 Litho. *Perf. 13½***

| | | |
|---|---|---|
| *119* A28 45c Malay Settlement, Home Island | 1.60 | 1.60 |
| *120* A28 55c West Island Air Strip, settlement | 2.00 | 2.00 |

**Souvenir Sheet**

| | | |
|---|---|---|
| *121* A28 $2 Jukong ships racing, Melbourne Exhibition Center | 4.25 | 4.25 |

No. 121 has multicolored margin continuing design.

Christmas A29

**1984, Oct. 31 Litho. *Perf. 13½***

| | | |
|---|---|---|
| *122* A29 24c Fish | 60 | 60 |
| *123* A29 35c Butterfly | 90 | 90 |
| *124* A29 55c Bird | 1.40 | 1.40 |

**Souvenir Sheet**

Act of Self-Determination — A30

Integration with Australia: No. 125a, Australians welcoming Cocos islanders. No. 125b, Australian flag over the islands.

**1984, Nov. 30 Litho. *Perf. 13½x14***

| | | |
|---|---|---|
| *125* Sheet of 2 | 2.40 | 2.40 |
| ***a.-b*** A30 30c, any single | 1.10 | 1.10 |

No. 125 has multicolored inscribed margin. Size: 90x52mm.

Crafts — A31

**1985, Jan. 30 *Perf. 14x13½***

| | | |
|---|---|---|
| *126* A31 30c Boat building | 70 | 70 |
| *127* A31 45c Blacksmith | 1.00 | 1.00 |
| *128* A31 55c Woodcarving | 1.40 | 1.40 |

Cable-laying Ships — A32

**1985, Apr. 24 *Perf. 13½x14***

| | | |
|---|---|---|
| *129* A32 33c Scotia | 65 | 65 |
| *130* A32 65c Anglia | 1.10 | 1.10 |
| *131* A32 80c Patrol | 1.75 | 1.75 |

Birds A33

**1985, July 17 *Perf. 13½***

| | | |
|---|---|---|
| *132* A33 33c Redfooted booby, vert. | 70 | 70 |
| *133* A33 60c Nankeen night heron | 1.10 | 1.10 |
| *134* A33 $1 Buff-banded rail | 2.25 | 2.25 |
| ***a*** "Block" of 3 | 3.00 | 3.00 |

Nos. 132-134 printed in a continuous design.

Seashells A34

**1985-86 Litho. *Perf. 13½x14***

| | | |
|---|---|---|
| *135* A34 1c Trochus maculatus | 5 | 5 |
| *136* A34 2c Smaragdia rangiana | 5 | 5 |
| *137* A34 3c Chama | 5 | 5 |
| *138* A34 4c Cypraea moneta | 6 | 6 |
| *139* A34 5c Drupa morum | 7 | 7 |
| *140* A34 10c Conus miles | 12 | 12 |
| *141* A34 15c Terebra maculata | 16 | 16 |
| *142* A34 20c Fragum fragum | 22 | 22 |
| *143* A34 30c Turbo lajonkairii | 35 | 35 |
| *144* A34 33c Mitra fissurata | 40 | 40 |
| *145* A34 40c Lambis lambis | 45 | 45 |
| *146* A34 50c Tridacna squamosa | 55 | 55 |
| *147* A34 60c Cypraea histrio | 80 | 80 |
| *148* A34 $1 Phillidia varicosa | 1.40 | 1.40 |
| *149* A34 $2 Halgerda tessellata | 3.25 | 3.25 |
| *150* A34 $3 Harminoea cymbalum | 4.00 | 4.00 |
| *Nos. 135-150 (16)* | 11.98 | 11.98 |

Issue dates: 1c, 5c, 33c, $1, Sept. 18. 2c, 3c, 10c, $3, Jan. 29, 1986. 15c-30c, 40c, Apr. 30, 1986. 4c, 50c, 60c, $2, July 30, 1986.

**Souvenir Sheet**

Christmas A35

Designs: a, Star LR. b, Star LL. c, Star UR. d, Star UL.

**1985, Oct. 30 *Perf. 13½x14***

| | | |
|---|---|---|
| *151* Sheet of 4 | 2.75 | 2.75 |
| ***a.-d*** A35 27c, any single | 65 | 65 |

No. 151 has multicolored decorative margin. Size: 121x88mm.

Darwin's Visit to the Islands — A36

**1986, Apr. 1 Litho. *Perf. 14x13½***

| | | |
|---|---|---|
| *152* A36 33c Charles Darwin | 75 | 75 |
| *153* A36 60c Map of voyage | 1.40 | 1.40 |
| *154* A36 $1 HMS Beagle | 2.25 | 2.25 |

Christmas 1986 — A37

**1986, Oct. 20 Litho. *Perf. 13½x14***

| | | |
|---|---|---|
| *155* A37 30c Coconut palm, holly | 60 | 60 |
| *156* A37 90c Shell, ornament | 1.75 | 1.75 |
| *157* A37 $1 Tropical fish, bell | 2.00 | 2.00 |

Sailboats A38

Se-tenant in a continuous design: a, Jukong. b, Ocean racers. c, Sarimanok. d, Ayesha.

**1987, Jan. 28**

| | | |
|---|---|---|
| *158* Strip of 4 | 2.00 | 2.00 |
| ***a.-d.*** A38 36c any single | 50 | 50 |

Island Views — A39

**1987, Apr. 8**

| | | |
|---|---|---|
| *159* A39 70c Direction Is. | 85 | 85 |
| *160* A39 90c West Is. | 1.10 | 1.10 |
| *161* A39 $1 Golf course, Cocos | 1.25 | 1.25 |

Communications — A40

**1987, July 29 Litho. *Perf. 13½x14***

| | | |
|---|---|---|
| *162* A40 70c Radio | 1.05 | 1.05 |
| *163* A40 75c Air service | 1.10 | 1.10 |
| *164* A40 90c Satellite | 1.35 | 1.35 |
| *165* A40 $1 Airmail | 1.50 | 1.50 |

Industries A41

**1987, Sept. 16**

| | | |
|---|---|---|
| *166* A41 45c Batik printing | 68 | 68 |
| *167* A41 65c Boat building | 95 | 95 |
| *168* A41 75c Copra production | 1.10 | 1.10 |

Industrial activities of the Cocos Malay people.

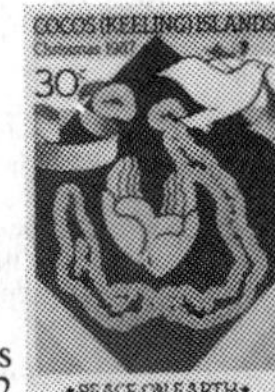

Christmas 1987 — A42

**1987, Oct. 28 *Perf. 14x13½***

| | | |
|---|---|---|
| *169* A42 30c Peace on Earth | 40 | 40 |
| *170* A42 90c Unity | 1.25 | 1.25 |
| *171* A42 $1 Goodwill Towards All | 1.40 | 1.40 |

Australia Bicentennial A43

Arrival of the First Fleet, Sydney Cove, Jan. 1788: a. Five aboriginals on shore. b. Four aboriginals on shore, one in canoe. c. Ships entering bay, kangaroos. d. Europeans land, white cranes. e. Flag raising.

**1988, Jan. 26 Litho. *Perf. 13***

| | | |
|---|---|---|
| *172* Strip of 5 | 2.60 | 2.60 |
| ***a.-e.*** A43 37c any single | 52 | 52 |

Nos. 172a-172e are printed se-tenant in a continuous design. See Christmas Is. No. 213.

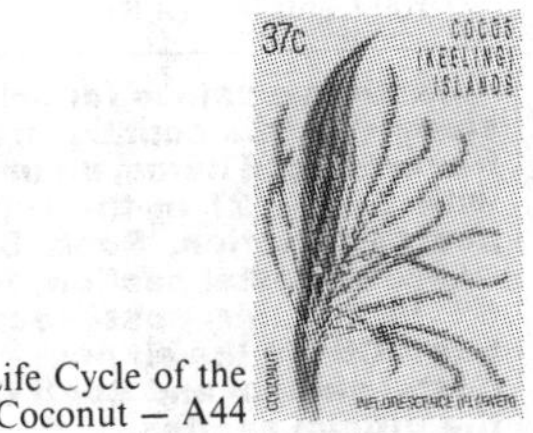

Life Cycle of the Coconut — A44

**1988, Apr. 13 Litho. *Perf. 14x13½***

| | | |
|---|---|---|
| *173* A44 37c Flower | 58 | 58 |
| *174* A44 65c Small nut stage | 1.00 | 1.00 |
| *175* A44 90c Mature nuts | 1.40 | 1.40 |
| *176* A44 $1 Seedlings | 1.55 | 1.55 |
| ***a*** Souv. sheet of 4, Nos. 173-176 | 4.55 | 4.55 |

No. 176a has multicolored margin picturing lifecycle. Size: 102x91mm.

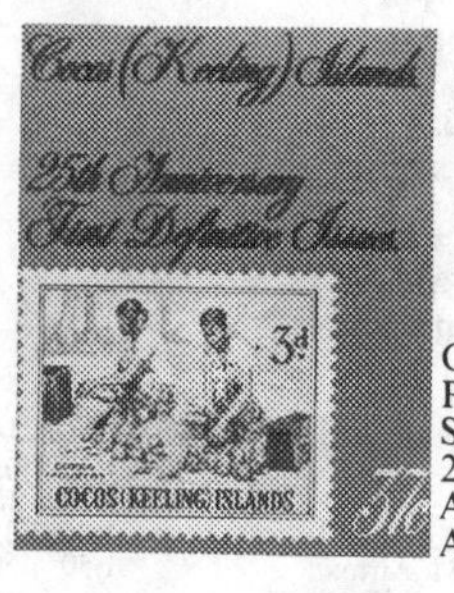

Cocos Postage Stamps, 25th Anniv. A45

**Litho. & Engr.**

**1988, June 15** *Perf. 15x14*

*177* A45 37c No. 1 60 60
*178* A45 55c No. 4 90 90
*179* A45 65c No. 2 1.05 1.05
*180* A45 70c No. 3 1.15 1.15
*181* A45 90c No. 5 1.45 1.45
*182* A45 $1 No. 6 1.60 1.60
*Nos. 177-182 (6)* 6.75 6.75

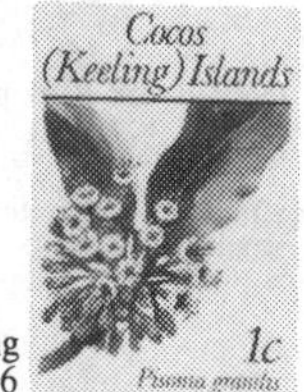

Flowering Plants — A46

**1988, July 29 Litho.** *Perf. 14x13½*

*183* A46 1c Pisonia grandis 5 5
*185* A46 5c Morinda citrifolia 8 8
*190* A46 37c Calophyllum inophyllum 60 60
*198* A46 $3 Hibiscus tiliaceus 4.75 4.75

Souvenir Sheet

**1988, July 30**

*199* A46 $3 like No. 198 *4.75 4.75*

SYDPEX '88. No. 199 has multicolored margin continuing the design and picturing the Sydney Opera House and Sydney Harbor Bridge. Size: 70x85mm.

## COOK ISLANDS

## (Rarotonga)

LOCATION — South Pacific Ocean, northeast of New Zealand.
GOVT. — Internal self-government, linked to New Zealand.
AREA — 117 sq. mi.
POP. — 17,754 (1981)
CAPITAL — Rarotonga

Fifteen islands in Northern and Southern groups extend over 850,000 square miles of ocean.

Separate stamp issues used by Aitutaki (1903-32 and 1972 onward) and Penrhyn Islands (1902-32 and 1973 onward). Niue is included geographically, but administered separately. It continues to issue separate stamps.

12 Pence = 1 Shilling
20 Shillings = 1 Pound
100 Cents = 1 Dollar (1967)

**Catalogue values for unused stamps in this country are for Never Hinged items, beginning with Scott 127 in the regular postage section, Scott B1 in the semi-postal section, Scott C1 in the air post section, Scott CB1 in the air post semi-postal section and Scott O1 in the official section.**

A1

**1892 Unwmk. Typo.** *Perf. 12½*

**Toned Paper**

*1* A1 1p black 15.00 15.00
*a* Vertical pair, imperf. between *7,500.*
*2* A1 1½p violet 20.00 20.00
*3* A1 2½p blue 25.00 25.00
*4* A1 10p carmine 150.00 87.50

**White Paper**

*5* A1 1p black 19.00 22.50
*6* A1 1½p violet 24.00 27.50
*7* A1 2½p blue 40.00 37.50
*8* A1 10p carmine 125.00 100.00

Queen Makea Takau A2

Wrybill (Torea) A3

Wmk. 62- Single-lined N Z and Star Wide Apart

**1893-94 Wmk. 62** *Perf. 12x11½*

*9* A2 1p brown 40.00 *48.00*
*10* A2 1p bl ('94) 4.00 2.50
*11* A2 1½p brt vio 5.00 3.50
*12* A2 2½p rose 17.50 *20.00*
*13* A2 5p ol gray 7.50 10.00
*14* A2 10p green 35.00 *50.00*
*Nos. 9-14 (6)* 109.00 134.00

Perf. 11½ examples of Nos. 9-14 are from a part of the normal perf. 12x11½ sheets. They were caused by a partial deviation of the original perforating.

**1898-1900** *Perf. 11*

*15* A3 ½p bl ('00) 3.50 5.00
*16* A2 1p brown 3.50 5.00
*17* A2 1p blue 2.50 2.50
*18* A2 1½p violet 2.50 2.50
*19* A3 2p chocolate 4.00 5.00
*20* A2 2½p car rose 4.00 5.00
*21* A2 5p ol gray 17.50 21.00
*22* A3 6p red vio 12.50 17.50
*23* A2 10p green 22.50 25.00
*24* A3 1sh car rose 40.00 50.00
*Nos. 15-24 (10)* 112.50 138.50

No. 17 Surcharged in Black

**ONE HALF PENNY**

**1899**

*25* A2 ½p on 1p bl 40.00 45.00
*a* Double surcharge 1,000. 1,000.
*b* Inverted surch. 1,000. 1,000.

No. 16 Overprinted in Black

**1901**

*26* A2 1p brown 125.00 110.00
*a* Inverted overprint 1,750. 1,750.
*b* Overprint sideways *2,250. 2,250.*
*c* Double overprint 1,750. 2,000.
*d* Triple overprint *2,500.*

**1902** **Unwmk.**

*27* A3 ½p green 4.00 5.00
*a* imperf. horiz., pair 1,000.
*28* A2 1p rose 5.00 5.00
*29* A2 2½p dl bl 14.00 *17.50*

Wmk. 61- Single-lined N Z and Star Close Together

**1902 Wmk. 61** *Perf. 11*

*30* A3 ½p green 90 80
*31* A2 1p rose 90 *1.25*
*32* A2 1½p brt vio 1.90 1.50
*33* A3 2p chocolate 2.75 *3.75*
*a* Value omitted 1,500. 1,250.
*b* Perf. 11x14 *500.00*
*34* A2 2½p dl bl 2.25 *4.00*
*35* A2 5p ol gray 7.00 *9.00*
*36* A3 6p purple 8.00 *13.00*
*37* A2 10p bl grn 24.00 *32.50*
*38* A3 1sh car rose 32.50 *25.00*
*a* Perf. 11x14 *325.00*
*Nos. 30-38 (9)* 80.20 90.80

**1909-19** *Perf. 14, 14x14½, 14½x14*

*39* A3 ½p grn ('11) 1.00 *1.75*
*40* A2 1p red 90 *1.40*
*41* A2 1½p pur ('15) 2.25 1.50
*42* A3 2p dp brn ('19) 6.50 11.00
*43* A2 10p dp grn ('18) 11.00 18.00
*44* A3 1sh car rose ('19) 9.00 18.00
*Nos. 39-44 (6)* 30.65 51.65

Nos. 39-40 are on both ordinary and chalky paper; Nos. 41-44 on chalky paper.

**RAROTONGA**

New Zealand Stamps of 1909-19 Surcharged in Dark Blue or Red

**APA PENE**

**1919 Typo.** *Perf. 14x13½, 14x14½*

*48* A43 ½p yel grn (R) 12 18
*a* Pair, one without surcharge
*49* A42 1p carmine 15 18
*50* A47 1½p brn org (R) 20 30
*51* A43 2p yel (R) 90 1.75
*52* A43 3p chocolate 2.25 2.50

**Engr.**

*53* A44 2½p dl bl (R) 1.00 1.50
*54* A45 3p vio brn 1.50 1.75
*55* A45 4p purple 1.50 1.75
*56* A44 4½p dk grn 90 *3.00*
*57* A45 6p car rose 1.50 *3.00*
*58* A44 7½p red brn 1.50 *3.00*
*59* A45 9p ol grn (R) 1.75 3.50
*60* A45 1sh vermilion 2.50 4.50
*Nos. 48-60 (13)* 15.77 26.91

The Polynesian surcharge restates the denomination of the basic stamp.

Landing of Capt. Cook A4

Avarua Waterfront A5

Capt. James Cook — A6

Palm — A7

Houses at Arorangi — A8

Avarua Harbor — A9

**1920 Unwmk. Engr.** *Perf. 14*

*61* A4 ½p grn & blk 1.50 *3.25*
*62* A5 1p car & blk 1.40 *2.50*
*a* Center inverted *550.00*
*63* A6 1½p bl & blk 2.00 2.25
*64* A7 3p red brn & blk 3.25 3.50
*65* A8 6p org & red brn 3.25 3.50
*66* A9 1sh vio & blk 3.25 3.50
*Nos. 61-66 (6)* 14.65 18.50

The stamps overprinted or inscribed "Rarotonga" were used throughout the Cook Islands.

New Zealand Postal-Fiscal Stamps of 1906-13 Overprinted in Red or Dark Blue

a **RAROTONGA**

*Perf. 14, 14½, 14x14½*

**1921 Typo. Wmk. 61**

*67* PF1 2sh bl (R) 21.00 25.00
*68* PF1 2sh6p brown 20.00 25.00
*69* PF1 5sh grn (R) 20.00 25.00
*70* PF1 10sh claret 45.00 *70.00*
*71* PF2 £1 rose 75.00 90.00

Types of 1920 Issue

**1925-26 Engr.** *Perf. 14*

*72* A4 ½p yel grn & blk 65 70
*73* A5 1p car & blk 1.75 1.75

New Zealand Stamps of 1926 Overprinted Type "a" in Red

**1926-28 Typo.** *Perf. 14, 14½x14*

*74* A56 2sh blue 12.00 *20.00*
*a* 2sh dark blue 14.00 *19.00*
*75* A56 3sh violet 18.00 *30.00*

Rarotongan Chief (Te Po) — A10

Avarua Harbor — A11

**1927 Engr.** *Perf. 14*

*76* A10 2½p dk bl & red brn 1.75 2.25
*77* A11 4p dl vio & bl grn 4.25 4.50

No. 63 Surcharged in Red **TWO PENCE**

**1931** **Unwmk.**

*78* A6 2p on 1½p bl & blk 85 1.00

Same Surcharge on Type of 1920

**Wmk. 61**

*79* A6 2p on 1½p bl & blk 1.40 1.50

No. 79 was not issued without surcharge.

New Zealand Postal-Fiscal Stamps of 1931-32 Overprinted Type "a" in Blue or Red

**1931-32** **Typo.**

*80* PF5 2sh6p dp brn (Bl) 9.00 10.00
*81* PF5 5sh grn (R) 15.00 18.00
*82* PF5 10sh dk car (Bl) 32.50 35.00
*83* PF5 £1 pink (Bl) ('32) 50.00 60.00

See Nos. 103-108, 124A-126C.

Landing of Capt. Cook — A12

Capt. James Cook — A13

Double Canoe — A14

Islanders Unloading Ship — A15

View of Avarua Harbor A16

R.M.S. Monowai A17

King George V — A18

**Unwmk.**

**1932, Mar. 16 Engr. *Perf. 13***
**Center in Black**

84 A12 ½p dp grn 40 55
a Perf. 14 20.00 25.00
85 A13 1p brn lake 45 55
a Center invtd. 1,500. 1,750.
b Perf. 14 9.00 12.50
86 A14 2p brown 3.00 3.00
a Center inverted
b Perf. 14 3.75 3.75
87 A15 2½p dk ultra 5.75 6.25
a Center invtd. 650.00
b Perf. 14 5.75 5.75

***Perf. 14***

88 A16 4p ultra 5.75 6.25
a Perf. 13 5.75 6.25
b Perf. 14x13 32.50 47.50
89 A17 6p orange 3.00 3.25
a Perf. 13 8.00 8.50
90 A18 1sh dp vio 3.00 5.00
*Nos. 84-90 (7)* 21.35 24.85

Nos. 84 to 90 were available for postage in Aitutaki, Penrhyn and Rarotonga and replaced the special issues for those islands.

**1933-36 Wmk. 61 *Perf. 14***

91 A12 ½p dp grn & blk 12 16
92 A13 1p dk car & blk ('35) 20 28
93 A14 2p brn & blk ('36) 28 35
94 A15 2½p dk ultra & blk 32 40
95 A16 4p bl & blk 60 80
96 A17 6p org & blk ('36) 80 1.00
97 A18 1sh dp vio & blk ('36) 10.00 11.00
*Nos. 91-97 (7)* 12.32 13.99

See Nos. 116-121.

**Silver Jubilee Issue**

Types of 1932 Overprinted in Black or Red

SILVER JUBILEE OF KING GEORGE V. 1910-1935.

**1935, May 7**

98 A13 1p dk car & brn red 25 30
99 A15 2½p dk ultra & bl (R) 80 90
100 A17 6p dl org & grn 3.75 4.00

The vertical spacing of the overprint is wider on No. 100.

New Zealand Stamps of 1926 Overprinted in Black

COOK ISLANDS
b

**1936 Typo. *Perf. 14***

101 A56 2sh blue 12.50 14.00
102 A56 3sh violet 15.00 17.50

New Zealand Postal-Fiscal Stamps of 1931-35 Overprinted Type "b" in Black or Red

**1932-36**

103 PF5 2sh6p brn ('36) 8.50 *12.50*
104 PF5 5sh grn (R) ('36) 10.00 *12.50*
105 PF5 10sh dk car ('36) 16.00 *27.50*
106 PF5 £1 pink ('36) 27.50 *35.00*
107 PF5 £3 lt grn (R) 100.00 *200.00*
108 PF5 £5 dk bl (R) 125.00 *175.00*
*Nos. 103-108 (6)* 287.00 462.50

New Zealand Stamps of 1937 Overprinted in Black

COOK IS'DS.

***Perf. 14x13½***

**1937, June 1 Engr. Wmk. 253**

109 A78 1p rose car 10 10
110 A78 2½p dk bl 20 20
111 A78 6p vermilion 30 30

King George VI A19

Village and Palms A20

Coastal Scene with Canoe — A21

**1938, May 2 Wmk. 61 *Perf. 14***

112 A19 1sh dp vio & blk 1.40 1.40
113 A20 2sh dk red brn & blk 2.00 2.00
114 A21 3sh yel grn & bl 4.00 4.00

See Nos. 122-124

Mt. Ikurangi behind Avarua — A22

Wmk. 253- Multiple N Z and Star

***Perf. 13½x14***

**1940, Sept. 2 Engr. Wmk. 253**

115 A22 3p on 1½p vio & blk 14 14

Types of 1932-38

**1944-46 Engr. *Perf. 14***

116 A12 ½p dk ol grn & blk ('45) 25 25
117 A13 1p dk car & blk ('45) 16 16
118 A14 2p brn & blk ('46) 75 75
119 A15 2½p dk bl & blk ('45) 25 25
120 A16 4p bl & blk 38 38
121 A17 6p org & blk 55 55
122 A19 1sh dp vio & blk 75 75
123 A20 2sh dk red brn & blk 1.90 1.90
124 A21 3sh yel grn & bl ('45) 2.75 2.75
*Nos. 116-124 (9)* 7.74 7.74

New Zealand Nos. AR76, AR78, AR85 and Type of 1931 Postal-Fiscal Stamps Overprinted Type "b" in Black or Red

**1943-50 Wmk. 253 Typo. *Perf. 14***

124A PF5 2sh6p brn ('46) 3.25 4.00
125 PF5 5sh grn (R) 4.75 *8.00*
126 PF5 10sh dp pink ('48) 14.00 *20.00*
126A PF5 £1 pink ('47) 17.50 *24.00*
126B PF5 £3 lt grn (R) ('46) 90.00 *140.00*
126C PF5 £5 dk bl (R) ('50) 150.00 *225.00*
*Nos. 124A-126C (6)* 279.50 421.00

Catalogue values for unused stamps in this section, from this point to the end of the section, are for Never Hinged items.

**Peace Issue**

New Zealand Nos. 248, 250, 254 and 255 Overprinted in Black or Blue:

COOK ISLANDS
c

COOK ISLANDS
d

***Perf. 13x13½, 13½x13***

**1946, June 1 Engr.**

127 A94 (c) 1p emerald 15 15
128 A96 (d) 2p rose vio (Bl) 22 22
129 A100(c) 6p org red & red brn 30 30
130 A101(c) 8p brn lake & blk (Bl) 35 35

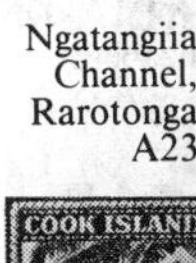

Ngatangiia Channel, Rarotonga A23

Capt. James Cook Statue and Map of Cook Islands — A24

Designs: 1p, . Cook and map of Hervey Isls. 2p, Rev. John Williams, his ship Messenger of Peace, and map of Rarotonga. 3p, Aitutaki map and palms. 5p, Mail plane landing at Rarotonga airport. 6p, Tongareva (Penrhyn) scene. 8p, Islander's house, Rarotonga. 2sh, Thatched house, mat weaver. 3sh, Steamer Matua offshore.

***Perf. 13½x13, 13x13½***

**1949, Aug.1 Engr. Wmk. 253**

131 A23 ½p brn & vio 12 12
132 A23 1p grn & org 55 55
133 A23 2p car & brn 35 35
134 A23 3p ultra & grn 30 30
135 A23 5p pur & grn 1.75 1.75
136 A23 6p car rose & blk 90 90
137 A23 8p org & ol 1.25 1.25
138 A24 1sh choc & bl 2.00 2.00
139 A24 2sh rose car & brn 4.75 4.75
140 A24 3sh bl grn & lt ultra 5.50 5.50
*Nos. 131-140 (10)* 17.47 17.47

**Coronation Issue**

Type of New Zealand

**1953, May 25 Photo. *Perf. 14x14½***

145 A113 3p brown 45 45
146 A114 6p sl blk 90 90

No. 135 Surcharged with New Value and Two Dots

**1960, Apr. 1 Engr. *Perf. 13½x13***

147 A23 1sh6p on 5p pur & grn 50 75

Tiare Maori — A25

Fishing God — A26

Queen Elizabeth II — A27

Island Scene A28

Designs: 3sh, Administration building, Mangaia. 5sh, Ship in Rarotonga harbor. (3p, 5p, 6p, 1sh horizontal.)

***Perf. 13½x13, 13x13½***

**1963, June 4 Litho.; Engr.; (1sh6p)**

148 A25 1p shown 8 12
149 A26 2p shown 12 16
150 A25 3p Frangipani 20 25
151 A26 5p Fairy tern 32 35
152 A25 6p Hibiscus 35 40
153 A26 8p Bonito 52 60
154 A25 1sh Oranges 80 1.00
155 A27 1sh6p shown 1.60 2.50
156 A28 2sh gray & brn 2.50 3.25
157 A28 3sh emer & blk 3.50 4.50
158 A28 5sh ultra & brn 5.00 6.00
*Nos. 148-158 (11)* 14.99 19.13

Solar Eclipse and Palm Tree — A29

**1965, May 31 Litho. *Perf. 13x13½***

159 A29 6p blk, lt bl & yel 30 30

Observation of the solar eclipse on Manuae Island, May 30, 1965.

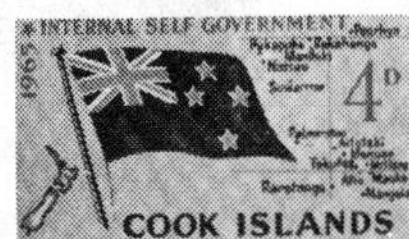
Flag of New Zealand and Map of Cook Islands A30

Designs: 10p, London Missionary Society Chruch and graveyard. 1sh, Reading of Proclamation of Cession, Oct. 8, 1900, and Queen Elizabeth II. 1sh9p, Nikao School and flag of New Zealand.

***Perf. 13½x13***

**1965, Sept. 16 Litho. Wmk. 253**

160 A30 4p bl and red 15 15
161 A30 10p multi 40 40
162 A30 1sh multi 45 45
163 A30 1sh9p multi 75 75

Establishment of internal self-government.

Nos. 160-162 and 156-158 Overprinted in Red: "In Memoriam / Sir Winston Churchill / 1874-1965"

**1966, Jan. 24 Litho. Wmk. 253**

164 A30 4p bl & red 35 25
165 A30 10p multi 75 65
a. Inverted overprint 375.00
166 A30 1sh multi 85 75
167 A28 2sh gray & brn 2.00 1.75
168 A28 3sh emer & blk 3.00 2.75
169 A28 5sh ultra & brn 5.00 4.50
*Nos. 164-169 (6)* 11.95 10.65

Statesman and WW II leader.

Adoration of the Wise Men, by Fra Angelico — A31

Paintings: 2p, Nativity, by Hans Memling (vert.). 4p, Adoration of the Wise Men, by Velazquez. 10p, Adoration of the Wise Men, by Hieronymus Bosch. 1sh6p, Adoration of the Shepherds, by Jose Ribera (vert.).

***Perf. 13x14½, 14½x13***

**1966, Nov. 28 Photo. Unwmk.**

170 A31 1p multi 7 5
a. Perf. 13x12 22 14
171 A31 2p multi 12 7
a. Perf. 12x13 7.00 3.50
172 A31 4p multi 22 12
a. Perf. 13x12 45 35
173 A31 10p multi 50 40
a. Perf. 13x12 1.10 1.10
174 A31 1sh6p multi 90 70
a. Perf. 12x13 2.25 1.75
*Nos. 170-174 (5)* 1.81 1.34

Christmas 1966. Issued in sheets of 6 with ornamental gold border.

Tennis and Queen Elizabeth A32

Sport: 1p, Women's basketball and Games' emblem. 4p, Boxing and team emblem. 7p, Soccer and Queen Elizabeth II.

**1967, Jan. 12** *Perf. 13½*

| No. | Type | Description | Unused | Used |
|---|---|---|---|---|
| *175* | A32 | ½p brt ol & multi | 5 | 5 |
| *176* | A32 | 1p brt bl & multi | 6 | 6 |
| *177* | A32 | 4p pur & multi | 12 | 12 |
| *178* | A32 | 7p red & multi | 20 | 20 |
| | | *Nos. 175-178,C10-C11 (6)* | 1.43 | 1.43 |

Second South Pacific Games, Noumea, New Caledonia, Dec. 8-18, 1966.

### Nos. 148-155, 157-158, 161 Surcharged with New Value or Black or Red

2½c 2½c
I II

**1967**

| No. | Type | Description | Unused | Used |
|---|---|---|---|---|
| *179* | A25 | 1c on 1p pale yel & grn | 1.75 | 1.75 |
| *180* | A26 | 2c on 2p yel & red brn | 7 | 7 |
| *181* | A25 | 2½c on 3p multi (I) | 8 | 8 |
| *a.* | | Type II | 8 | 8 |
| *182* | A30 | 3c on 4p bl & red | 10 | 10 |
| *183* | A26 | 4c on 5p ultra & blk | 35 | 35 |
| *184* | A25 | 5c on 6p multi (152) | 14 | 14 |
| *185* | A29 | 5c on 6p multi (159) | 1.00 | 65 |
| *186* | A26 | 7c on 8p bl & blk | 20 | 20 |
| *187* | A25 | 10c on 1sh lt grn & yel | 28 | 28 |
| *188* | A27 | 15c on 1sh6p vio (R) | 2.00 | 1.00 |
| *189* | A28 | 30c on 3sh emer & blk (R) | 6.50 | 5.00 |
| *190* | A28 | 50c on 5sh ultra & brn (R) | 4.25 | 2.75 |
| *191* | A30 | $1 on 10p multi (R) | 14.00 | 10.00 |
| | | *Nos. 179-191 (13)* | 30.72 | 22.37 |

Issue Dates: Apr. 3, 2c, 2½c, 3c, 5c, 7c, 10c; others May 4.

No. 191 is surcharged "10/ $1.00" and 3 bars over old value.

Numerous varieties of surcharge include wrong-font "c", thin numerals, etc.

### Nos. 126A, 126B and 126C Surcharged in Red

**Wmk. 253**

**1967, June 6** **Typo.** *Perf. 14*

| No. | Type | Description | Unused | Used |
|---|---|---|---|---|
| *192* | PF5 | $2 on £1 pink | 110.00 | 110.00 |
| *193* | PF5 | $6 on £3 lt grn | 125.00 | 125.00 |
| *194* | PF5 | $10 on £5 dk bl | 190.00 | 190.00 |

Stamp of 1892, Village and Queen Victoria A33

Designs: 3c (4p), PO, Rarotonga, and Elizabeth II. 8c (10p), View of Avarua, Rarotonga, and 10p stamp of 1892. 18c (1sh9p), Map of Cook Islands, DC-3, S.S. Moana Roa and Capt. Cook.

*Perf. 13½*

**1967, July 3** **Photo.** **Unwmk.**

| No. | Type | Description | Unused | Used |
|---|---|---|---|---|
| *195* | A33 | 1c (1p) multi | 7 | 7 |
| *196* | A33 | 3c (4p) multi | 20 | 20 |
| *197* | A33 | 8c (10p) multi | 40 | 40 |
| *198* | A33 | 10c (1sh9p) multi | 80 | 80 |
| *a.* | | Souvenir sheet of 4 | 1.50 | 1.50 |

75th anniv. of the 1st Cook Islands stamps. Issued in sheets of 8 stamps and 1 label with inscription in yellow margin. No. 198a contains one each f Nos. 195-195; black inscription and gold border in blue margin. Size: 134x109mm.

Hibiscus — A34

Elizabeth II — A35

Elizabeth II and Flowers — A36

Flowers: 1c, Rose of Sharon. 2c, 15c, Frangipani. 2½c, Butterfly pea. 3c, Suva queen and Queen Elizabeth II. 4c, Water lily. 5c, Bauhania. 6c, Yellow hibiscus. 8c, Alamanda and Queen Elizabeth II. 9c, Stephanotis. 10c, Flaymboyant poinciana. 20c, Thunbergia. 25c, Canna lily and Queen Elizabeth II. 30c, Poinsettia. 50c, Gardenia.

**1967-69** **Photo.** *Perf. 14x13½*

| No. | Type | Description | Unused | Used |
|---|---|---|---|---|
| *199* | A34 | ½c gold & multi | 5 | 5 |
| *200* | A34 | 1c gold & multi | 5 | 5 |
| *201* | A34 | 2c gold & multi | 6 | 6 |
| *202* | A34 | 2½c gold & multi | 7 | 7 |
| *203* | A34 | 3c gold & multi | 8 | 8 |
| *204* | A34 | 4c *Walter Lily* | 1.75 | 1.75 |
| *205* | A34 | 4c *Water Lily* | 10 | 10 |
| *206* | A34 | 5c gold & multi | 12 | 12 |
| *207* | A34 | 6c gold & multi | 14 | 14 |
| *208* | A34 | 8c gold & multi | 16 | 16 |
| *209* | A34 | 9c gold & multi | 20 | 20 |
| *210* | A34 | 10c gold & multi | 22 | 22 |
| *211* | A34 | 15c gold & multi | 35 | 35 |
| *212* | A34 | 20c gold & multi | 50 | 50 |
| *213* | A34 | 25c gold & multi | 60 | 60 |
| *214* | A34 | 30c gold & multi | 75 | 75 |
| *215* | A34 | 50c gold & multi | 1.10 | 1.10 |
| *216* | A35 | $1 gold & multi | 2.25 | 2.25 |
| *217* | A35 | $2 gold & multi | 3.50 | 3.50 |
| *218* | A36 | $4 multi ('68) | 6.50 | 6.50 |
| *219* | A36 | $6 multi ('68) | 10.00 | 10.00 |
| *219A* | A36 | $8 multi ('69) | 11.00 | 11.00 |
| *220* | A36 | $10 multi ('68) | 15.00 | 15.00 |
| | | *Nos. 199-220 (23)* | 54.55 | 54.55 |

The $4 exists with "FOUR DOLLARS" in two widths: 32½mm and 33½mm.

Nos. 214-215 were surcharged "Plus 20c United Kingdom Special Mail Service" in 5 lines of capitals for use during the 1971 British mail strike. The strike ended Mar. 8, the day the 50c+20c, was released.

---

**Fluorescence**

Since 1968 a number of stamps have been issued with a "fluorescent security underprinting" in a multiple coat of arms pattern. Some issues have this underprint, some do not.

Stamps issued both with and without the underprint are Nos. 199-203, 205-220, 283, 290-291.

From Nos. 292-296 onward, all stamps have this underprint unless otherwise noted.

---

Ia Orana Maria, by Gauguin A37

Gauguin Paintings: 3c, Riders on the Beach. 5c, Still Life with Flowers. 8c, Whispered Words. 15c, Maternity. 22c, Why Are You Angry?

**1967, Oct. 23** **Photo.** *Perf. 13½*

| No. | Type | Description | Unused | Used |
|---|---|---|---|---|
| *221* | A36 | 1c gold & multi | 5 | 5 |
| *222* | A37 | 3c gold & multi | 6 | 6 |
| *223* | A37 | 5c gold & multi | 9 | 9 |
| *224* | A37 | 8c gold & multi | 14 | 14 |
| *225* | A37 | 15c gold & multi | 30 | 30 |
| *226* | A37 | 22c gold & multi | 45 | 45 |
| *a.* | | Souvenir sheet of 6 | 1.50 | 1.40 |
| | | *Nos. 221-226 (6)* | 1.09 | 1.09 |

Nos. 221-226 are printed in sheets of 6 (3x2). No. 226a contains one each of Nos. 221-226. Sheets of each denomination and No. 226a have gold ornamental border and black inscription. Size: 155x131mm.

Holy Family by Rubens — A38

Paintings: 3c, Adoration of the Magi, by Albrecht Durer. 4c, The Lucca Madonna, by Jan Van Eyck. 8c, Adoration of the Shepherds, by Jacopo da Bassano. 15c, Nativity, by El Greco. 25c, Madonna and Child, by Antonio Allegri da Correggio.

**1967, Dec. 4** *Perf. 12x13*

| No. | Type | Description | Unused | Used |
|---|---|---|---|---|
| *227* | A38 | 1c gold & multi | 6 | 6 |
| *228* | A38 | 3c gold & multi | 7 | 7 |
| *229* | A38 | 4c gold & multi | 9 | 9 |
| *230* | A38 | 8c gold & multi | 18 | 18 |
| *231* | A38 | 15c gold & multi | 35 | 35 |
| *232* | A38 | 25c gold & multi | 65 | 65 |
| | | *Nos. 227-232 (6)* | 1.40 | 1.40 |

Christmas. Issued in sheets of 6 (2x4) with gold ornamental margin reproducing a 15th cent. illuminated manuscript of the Flemish School.

Capt. Cook and Matavai Bay, Tahiti, by Sydney Parkinson — A39

Designs; 1c, Ships off Huahine Island, Tahiti, by John and James Clevely. 2c, town and harbor of Kamchatka, by John Webber, and Queen Elizabeth II. 4c, "The Ice Islands" (Antarctica), by William Hodges.

**1968, Sept. 12** **Photo.** *Perf. 13*

| No. | Type | Description | Unused | Used |
|---|---|---|---|---|
| *233* | A39 | ½c gold & multi | 5 | 5 |
| *234* | A39 | 1c gold & multi | 6 | 6 |
| *235* | A39 | 2c gold & multi | 8 | 8 |
| *236* | A39 | 4c gold & multi | 20 | 20 |

Bicent. of Capt. Cook's 1st voyage of discovery. Printed in sheets of 10 stamps and 2 labels (3x4). Labels show portraits of Elizabeth II and Cook.

Gymnast A40

**1968, Oct. 21**

| No. | Type | Description | Unused | Used |
|---|---|---|---|---|
| *237* | A40 | 1c Sailing | 5 | 5 |
| *238* | A40 | 5c shown | 7 | 7 |
| *239* | A40 | 15c High jump | 22 | 22 |
| *240* | A40 | 20c Woman diver | 30 | 30 |
| *241* | A40 | 30c Bicyclist | 45 | 45 |
| *242* | A40 | 50c Woman hurdler | 75 | 75 |
| | | *Nos. 237-242 (6)* | 1.84 | 1.84 |

19th Olympic Games, Mexico City, Oct. 12-27. Printed in sheets of 10 stamps and 2 labels (3x4).

Virgin and Child, by Titian — A41

Paintings: 4c, Holy Family, by Raphael. 10c, Madonna of the Rosary, by Murillo. 20c, Adoration of the Magi, by Memling. 30c, Adoration of the Magi, by Ghirlandajo.

**1968, Dec. 2** **Photo.** *Perf. 13*

| No. | Type | Description | Unused | Used |
|---|---|---|---|---|
| *243* | A41 | 1c gold & multi | 5 | 5 |
| *244* | A41 | 4c gold & multi | 6 | 6 |
| *245* | A41 | 10c gold & multi | 15 | 15 |
| *246* | A41 | 20c gold & multi | 30 | 30 |
| *247* | A41 | 30c gold & multi | 45 | 45 |
| *a.* | | Souvenir sheet of 5 | 1.75 | 1.75 |
| | | *Nos. 243-247 (5)* | 1.01 | 1.01 |

Issued in sheets of 6 (2x3) with decorative borders. No. 247a contains one each of Nos. 243-247 plus label showing portrait of Queen Elizabeth II; decorative borders inscribed "Christmas 1968," Size: 123x177mm.

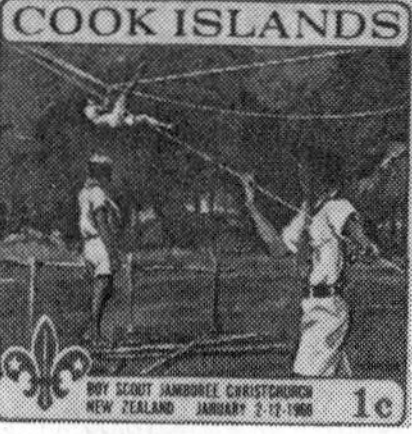


Training on Ropeway A42

Designs: ½c, Boy Scouts cooking over campfire. 5c, Training with signal flags, and Queen Elizabeth II. 10c, Planting a tree. 20c, Erecting a hut. 30c, Lord Baden-Powell, lake and mountains (visit to Rarotonga in 1935).

**1969, Feb. 6** **Photo.** *Perf. 13½*

| No. | Type | Description | Unused | Used |
|---|---|---|---|---|
| *248* | A42 | ½c multi | 5 | 5 |
| *249* | A42 | 1c multi | 5 | 5 |
| *250* | A42 | 5c multi | 12 | 12 |
| *251* | A42 | 20c multi | 25 | 25 |
| *252* | A42 | 20c multi | 50 | 50 |
| *253* | A42 | 30c multi | 75 | 75 |
| | | *Nos. 248-253 (6)* | 1.72 | 1.72 |

5th Natl. Boy Scout Jamboree, Christchurch, New Zealand, Jan. 2-12.

Issued in sheets of 10 stamps and 2 labels (4x3); gold decorative border.

Soccer — A43

Sports: No. 255, Pole vault. No. 256, Weight lifting. No. 257, Basketball, Elizabeth II. No. 258, Long jump. No. 259, Tennis. No. 260, Running. No. 261, Javelin, Elizabeth II. No. 262, Boxing. No. 263, Golf.

*Perf. 13½x13*

**1969, July 7 Photo. Unwmk.**

*254* A43 ½c gold & multi 5 5
*255* A43 ½c gold & multi 5 5
*256* A43 1c gold & multi 5 5
*257* A43 1c gold & multi 5 5
*258* A43 4c gold & multi 6 6
*259* A43 4c gold & multi 6 6
*260* A43 10c gold & multi 20 20
*261* A43 10c gold & multi 20 20
*262* A43 15c gold & multi 35 35
*263* A43 15c gold & multi 35 35
**a.** Souvenir sheet of 10 2.00 2.00
*Nos. 254-263 (10)* 1.42 1.42

3rd South Pacifc Games, Port Moresby, Papua and New Guinea, Aug. 13-23.

Stamps of the same denomination are printed se-tenant in sheets of 10. No.263a contains one each of Nos. 254-263 and 2 labels with Cook Islands coat of arms and emblem of 3rd South Pacific Games. Gold border with black inscription. Size: 175x129mm.

Map of Cook Islands and Capt. Cook — A44

Designs (Map of Cook Islands and): 5c, Premier Albert Henry of New Zealand. 25c, Coat of arms of New Zealand. 30c, Queen Elizabeth II.

**1969, Oct. 8 Photo. *Perf. 13***

*264* A44 5c red & multi 15 15
*265* A44 10c lem & multi 35 35
*266* A44 25c grn & multi 85 85
*267* A44 30c bl & multi 1.00 1.00

South Pacific Conf., Noumea, Oct. 1969.

Madonna and Child, by Filippino Lippi A45

Paintings: 4c, Holy Family, by Baccio della Porta. 10c, Madonna and Child, by Anton Raphael Mengs. 20c, Madonna and Child, by Le Maitre de Flemalle. 30c, Madonna and Child by Correggio.

**1969, Nov. 21 Photo. *Perf. 13½***

*268* A45 1c buff & multi 5 5
*269* A45 4c buff & multi 8 8
*270* A45 10c buff & multi 22 22
*271* A45 20c buff & multi 45 45
*272* A45 30c buff & multi 65 65
**a.** Souvenir sheet of 5 1.75 1.75
*Nos. 268-272 (5)* 1.45 1.45

Issued in Sheets of 8 stamps, one label with portrait of Queen Elizabeth II and ornamental border.

No. 272a contains one each of Nos. 268-272 and label with Queen's portrait. Ornamental border. Size: 129x95mm.

Resurrection of Christ, by Raphael — A46

The Resurrection of Christ by: 8c, Dirk Bouts. 20c, Albert Altdorfer. 25c, Murillo.

**1970, Mar. 12 Photo. *Perf. 13½***

**Size: 25½x56mm**

*273* A46 4c gold & multi 10 10
*274* A46 8c gold & multi 20 20
*275* A46 20c gold & multi 50 50
*276* A46 25c gold & multi 60 60
**a.** Souvenir sheet of 4 1.50 1.50

Easter 1970.

Printed in sheets of 8 stamps and a label (3x3) showing portrait of Queen Elizabeth II and name of painting and painter. No. 276a contains one each of Nos. 273-276 and 2 labels; decorative border. Size: 131x160mm.

See Nos. 316-318.

Nos. 205, 208, 211-212, 214, 217 Overprinted: "KIA ORANA / APOLLO 13 /ASTRONAUTS / Te Atua to / Tatou Irinakianga"

**1970, Apr. *Perf. 14x13½***

*277* A34 4c gold & multi 7 7
*278* A34 8c gold & multi 10 10
*279* A34 15c gold & multi 16 16
*280* A34 20c gold & multi 22 22
*281* A34 30c gold & multi 35 35
*282* A35 $2 gold & multi 2.00 2.00

**No. 218 Overprinted: "KIA ORANA / APOLLO 13 /ASTRONAUTS"**

*283* A36 $4 gold & multi 5.00 5.00
*Nos. 277-283 (7)* 7.90 7.90

Splashdown of Apollo 13 west of Rarotonga, Apr. 17, 1970. Nos. 277-282 were issued Apr. 17; No. 283, Apr. 30.

Values for Nos. 283, 290-291 are for stamps with fluorescence. Stamps without fluorescene sell for more.

Queen Elizabeth II, Prince Philip, Princess Anne and Prince Charles — A47

Design: 30c, Wedgwood bust of Capt. Cook and "Endeavour." $1, Royal visit commemorative coin, obverse and reverse.

**1970, June 12 Photo. *Perf. 13½***

*284* A47 5c gold & multi 20 20
*285* A47 30c gold & multi 1.40 1.25
*286* A47 $1 gold & multi 4.50 4.00
**a.** Souvenir sheet of 3 7.50 7.00

Vist of the British royal family.

No. 286a contains one each of Nos. 284-286 and decorative label; New Zealand coat of arms in margin. Size: 144x95.

Nos. 284-286 Overprinted in Silver or Black: "Fifth Anniversary Self-Government August 1970"

**1970, Aug. 27 Photo. *Perf. 13½***

*287* A47 5c gold & multi (S) 18 14
*288* A47 30c gold & multi 1.00 90
*289* A47 $1 gold & multi 3.50 3.00

5th anniv. of self-government. The overprint on No. 287 is arranged in one line around 3 sides of the design; the overprint on Nos. 288-289 is in 3 horizontal lines.

Nos. 219A-220 Surcharged

**FOUR DOLLARS**

**$4.00**

**1970, Nov. 11 Photo. *Perf. 14x13½***

*290* A36 $4 on $8 multi 16.00 16.00
*291* A36 $4 on $10 multi 12.00 12.00

In each sheet of 15, 3 stamps have 2 surcharged bars instead of one. See second note after No. 283.

Nativity A48

Designs (Illuminations from 14th Century Robert de Lisle Psalter): 4c, Angel and shepherds. 10c, The Circumcision. 20c, The Adoration of the Kings. 30c, The Presentation at the Temple.

**1970, Nov. 30 Photo. *Perf. 13½***

*292* A48 1c gold & multi 5 5
*293* A48 4c gold & multi 10 10
*294* A48 10c gold & multi 25 25
*295* A48 20c gold & multi 50 50
*296* A48 30c gold & multi 75 75
**a** Souvenir sheet of 5 + label 2.00 2.00
*Nos. 292-296 (5)* 1.65 1.65

Christmas 1970.

Issued in sheets of 5 stamps and a label (3x2) showing portrait of Queen Elizabeth II and source of design. No. 296a contains one each of Nos. 292-296 and a label. Decorative multicolored border. Size: 100x138mm.

Queen Elizabeth II and Prince Philip — A49

Designs: 4c, Royal family at Balmoral. 10c, Prince Philip sailing. 15c, Prince Philip as polo player. 25c, Prince Philip and royal yacht.

**1971, Mar. 11 Litho. *Perf. 13½***

*297* A49 1c brt bl & multi 5 5
*298* A49 4c brt bl & multi 25 25
*299* A49 10c brt bl & multi 65 65
*300* A49 15c brt bl & multi 1.00 1.00
*301* A49 25c brt bl & multi 1.75 1.75
**a** Souvenir sheet of 5 5.00 5.00
*Nos. 297-301 (5)* 3.70 3.70

Visit of Prince Philip, Duke of Edinburgh to Rarotonga, Feb. 27, 1971. Printed in sheets of 10 stamps and 2 labels showing Queen Elizabeth II commemorative coin and a portrait of Prince Philip. No. 301a contains one each of Nos. 297-301 plus 2 labels; silver and pink ornamental margin and black inscription. Size: 169x122mm.

Nos. 210, 213-214 Overprinted

**1971, Sept. 8 Photo. *Perf. 14x13½***

*302* A34 10c gold & multi 15 15
*303* A34 25c gold & multi 30 30
*304* A34 30c gold & multi 40 40
*Nos. 302-304 (3)* 85 85

4th South Pacific Games, Papeete, French Polynesia, Sept. 8-19.

Nos. 202, 205, 208-209 and 211 Surcharged with New Value and Three Bars

**1971, Oct. 20**

*305* A34 10c on 2½c multi 28 28
*306* A34 10c on 4c multi 28 28
*307* A34 10c on 8c multi 28 28
*308* A34 10c on 9c multi 28 28
*309* A34 10c on 15c multi 28 28
*Nos. 305-309 (5)* 1.40 1.40

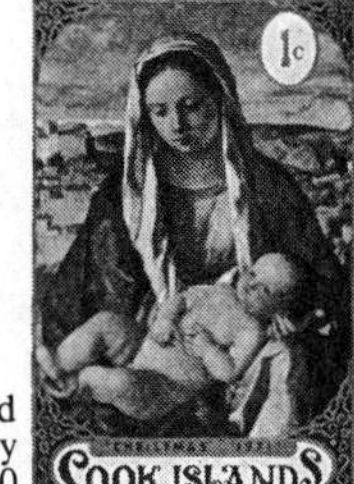


Madonna and Child, by Bellini — A50

Christmas: Paintings of the Madonna and Child, by Giovanni Bellini.

**1971, Nov. 30 *Perf. 13½***

*310* A50 1c gold & multi 5 5
*311* A50 4c gold & multi 10 10
*312* A50 10c gold & multi 25 25
*313* A50 20c gold & multi 50 50
*314* A50 30c gold & multi 75 75
**a** Souvenir sheet of 5 2.50 2.25
*Nos. 310-314 (5)* 1.65 1.65

No. 314a contains Nos. 310-314 and ornamental label. Multicolored border in floral design. Size: 136x147mm. See No. B14.

No. 216 Overprinted: "SOUTH PACIFIC / COMMISSION / FEB. 1947-1972"

**1972, Feb. 17 Photo. *Perf. 14x13½***

*315* A35 $1 gold & multi 2.00 1.75

South Pacific Commission, 25th anniv.

Easter Type of 1970

Designs (Illuminations from 14th century Robert de Lisle Psalter): 5c, St. John. 10c, Christ crucified. 20c, Virgin Mary.

**1972, Mar. 6 Photo. *Perf. 13½***

**Size: 21x68mm**

*316* A46 5c gold & multi 12 12
*317* A46 10c gold & multi 25 25
*318* A46 30c gold & multi 90 90
**a** Souvenir sheet of 3 2.25 2.00

Printed in sheets of 12. No. 318a contains one each of Nos. 316-318. The sheet reproduces original page of psalter from which stamp designs were taken. Size: 79x112mm.

Rocket over Moon — A51

**1972, Apr. 17**

*319* A51 5c *shown* 10 10
*320* A51 5c *Earth over moon* 10 10
*321* A51 10c *Landing module and astronaut* 20 20
*322* A51 10c *Astronaut collecting moon rocks* 20 20
*323* A51 25c *Earth and rocket over moon* 50 50
*324* A51 25c *Lunar rover and astronaut* 50 50
*325* A51 30c *Helicopter over raft in Pacific* 65 65
*326* A51 30c *Capsule and parachutes* 65 65
**a** Souvenir sheet of 8 4.50 4.25
*Nos. 319-326 (8)* 2.90 2.90

Apollo moon explorations. Stamps of the same denomination are printed setenant in sheets of 12.

No. 326a contains one each of Nos. 319-326 arranged in 2 blocks of 4 divided by a map showing splashdown area of Apollo X, XII and XIII in blue, gold and black. Size: 82x204mm.

*Cook Islands stamps can be mounted in Scott's annual New Zealand Dependencies Supplement.*

High Jump, Olympic Rings A52

Rest on Flight to Egypt, by Caravaggio A53

**1972, June 26**

| | | | | |
|---|---|---|---|---|
| *327* | A52 | 10c *shown* | 35 | 35 |
| *328* | A52 | 25c *Running* | 90 | 90 |
| *329* | A52 | 30c *Boxing* | 1.00 | 1.00 |
| *a* | | Souvenir sheet of 3 | 3.00 | 3.00 |

20th Olympic Games, Munich, Aug. 26-Sept. 10. Sheets of 8 stamps and label. No. 329a contains one each of Nos. 327-329 and label. Multicolored border. Size: 84x126mm. See No. B29.

**1972, Oct. 11 Photo. *Perf. 13½***

Paintings: 5c, Virgin of the Swallows, by Guercino. 10c, Virgin with Green Cushion, by Andrea Solario. 20c, Virgin and Child, by Lorenzo di Credi. 30c, Virgin and Child, by Giovanni Bellini.

| | | | | |
|---|---|---|---|---|
| *330* | A53 | 1c gold & multi | 5 | 5 |
| *331* | A53 | 5c gold & multi | 12 | 12 |
| *332* | A53 | 10c gold & multi | 28 | 28 |
| *333* | A53 | 20c gold & multi | 55 | 55 |
| *334* | A53 | 30c gold & multi | 90 | 90 |
| *a* | | Souv. sheet of 5 | 2.50 | 2.50 |
| | | *Nos. 330-334 (5)* | 1.90 | 1.90 |

Christmas 1972. No. 334a contains one each of Nos. 330-334 and label. Multicolored border with cherubs and flowers. Size: 140x152mm. See No. B30.

Princess Elizabeth and Prince Philip — A54

Designs: 5c, Wedding ceremony, Westminster Abbey. 15c, Bridal portrait. 30c, Official wedding picture of royal family.

**1972, Nov. 20**

**Size: 29x40mm**

| | | | | |
|---|---|---|---|---|
| *335* | A54 | 5c sil & multi | 12 | 12 |
| *336* | A54 | 10c sil & multi | 30 | 30 |

**Size: 40x40mm**

| | | | | |
|---|---|---|---|---|
| *337* | A54 | 15c sil & multi | 50 | 50 |

**Size: 66x40mm**

| | | | | |
|---|---|---|---|---|
| *338* | A54 | 30c sil & multi | 1.00 | 1.00 |

25th anniversary of the marriage of Queen Elizabeth II and Prince Philip.

Nos. 335-337 printed in sheets of 8 stamps and one label; No. 338 in sheets of 6.

1c Coin with Queen Elizabeth II and Taro Leaf — A55

Queen Elizabeth II Coins: 2c, Pineapples. 5c, Hibiscus. 10c, Oranges. 20c, Fairy terns. 50c, Bonito. $1, Tangaroa, Polynesian god of creation (vert.).

**1973, Mar. 15 Photo. *Perf. 13x13½***

**Size: 37x24mm**

| | | | | |
|---|---|---|---|---|
| *339* | A55 | 1c dp car, blk & gold | 5 | 5 |
| *340* | A55 | 2c bl, blk & gold | 5 | 5 |

| | | | | |
|---|---|---|---|---|
| *341* | A55 | 5c grn, blk & gold | 12 | 12 |

**Size: 46x30mm**

| | | | | |
|---|---|---|---|---|
| *342* | A55 | 10c vio, bl, blk & sil | 22 | 22 |
| *343* | A55 | 20c dk grn, blk & sil | 45 | 45 |
| *344* | A55 | 50c dp car, blk & sil | 1.10 | 1.10 |

**Size: 32x54½mm**

| | | | | |
|---|---|---|---|---|
| *345* | A55 | $1 bl, blk & sil | 2.25 | 2.25 |
| | | *Nos. 339-345 (7)* | 4.24 | 4.24 |

Coinage commemorating silver wedding anniversary of Queen Elizabeth II.

Printed in sheets of 20 stamps and label showing Westminster Abbey.

"Noli me Tangere," by Titian — A56

Paintings: 10c, Descent from the Cross, by Rubens. 30c, The Lamentation of Christ, by Dürer.

**1973, Apr. 9**

| | | | | |
|---|---|---|---|---|
| *346* | A56 | 5c gold & multi | 12 | 12 |
| *347* | A56 | 10c gold & multi | 25 | 25 |
| *348* | A56 | 30c gold & multi | 75 | 75 |
| *a* | | Souvenir sheet of 3 | 1.75 | 1.75 |

Easter 1973. Printed in sheets of 15 stamps and one label. No. 348a contains one each of Nos. 346-348. Gold, violet and black margins. Size: 131x67mm. See Nos. 378-380, B31-B33, B39-B41.

Queen Elizabeth II in Coronation Regalia — A57

**1973, June 1 Photo. *Perf. 14x13½***

| | | | | |
|---|---|---|---|---|
| *349* | A57 | 10c gold & multi | 3.00 | 2.00 |

**Souvenir Sheet**

| | | | | |
|---|---|---|---|---|
| *350* | A57 | 50c gold & multi | 7.50 | 5.00 |

20th anniversary of the coronation of Queen Elizabeth II. No. 349 printed in sheets of 5 stamps and one label.

No. 350 contains one stamp, perf. 13½x14½. Sheet shows official coronation portrait of 1953. Size: 64x88mm.

Nos. 206, 208, 210, 212-214 Overprinted: "TENTH ANNIVERSARY / CESSATION OF / NUCLEAR TESTING / TREATY"

**1973, July 25 Photo. *Perf. 14x13½***

| | | | | |
|---|---|---|---|---|
| *351* | A34 | 5c gold & multi | 12 | 12 |
| *352* | A34 | 8c gold & multi | 20 | 20 |
| *353* | A34 | 10c gold & multi | 25 | 25 |
| *354* | A34 | 20c gold & multi | 50 | 50 |
| *355* | A34 | 25c gold & multi | 65 | 65 |
| *356* | A34 | 30c gold & multi | 75 | 75 |
| | | *Nos. 351-356 (6)* | 2.47 | 2.47 |

Nuclear Test Ban Treaty, 10th anniversary and as protest against French nuclear testing on Mururoa atoll.

Tipairua A58

Designs: Historic South Pacific sailing vessels.

**1973, Sept. 17 Photo. *Perf. 13½x13***

| | | | | |
|---|---|---|---|---|
| *357* | A58 | ½c *shown* | 5 | 5 |
| *358* | A58 | 1c *Wa'a Kaulua* | 5 | 5 |
| *359* | A58 | 1½c *Tainui* | 6 | 6 |
| *360* | A58 | 5c *War canoe* | 12 | 12 |
| *361* | A58 | 10c *Pahi* | 25 | 25 |
| *362* | A58 | 15c *Amatasi* | 40 | 40 |
| *363* | A58 | 25c *Vaka* | 65 | 65 |
| | | *Nos. 357-363 (7)* | 1.58 | 1.58 |

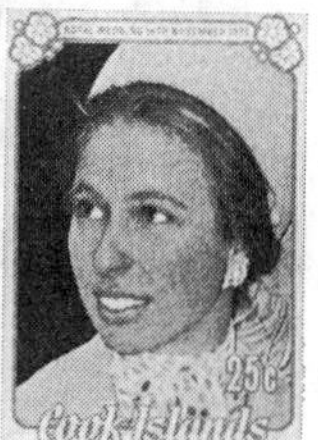


Annunciation A59

Princess Anne A60

Designs from 15th Century Prayer Book: 5c, The Visitation. 10c, Adoration of the Shepherds. 20c, Adoration of the Kings. 30c, Slaughter of the Innocents.

**1973, Oct. 30 Photo. *Perf. 13x13½***

| | | | | |
|---|---|---|---|---|
| *364* | A59 | 1c multi | 5 | 5 |
| *365* | A59 | 5c multi | 10 | 10 |
| *366* | A59 | 10c multi | 18 | 18 |
| *367* | A59 | 20c multi | 40 | 40 |
| *368* | A59 | 30c multi | 65 | 65 |
| *a* | | Souvenir sheet of 5 + label | 1.75 | 1.50 |
| | | *Nos. 364-368 (5)* | 1.38 | 1.38 |

Christmas 1973. No. 368a contains one each of Nos. 364-368 and gold label with portrait of Queen Elizabeth II and black inscription. Size: 121x128mm.

See Nos. B34-B38.

**1973, Nov. 14 Photo. *Perf. 14***

| | | | | |
|---|---|---|---|---|
| *369* | A60 | 25c *shown* | 40 | 40 |
| *370* | A60 | 30c *Mark Phillips* | 60 | 60 |
| *371* | A60 | 50c *Princess and Mark Phillips* | 1.00 | 1.00 |
| *a* | | Souvenir sheet of 3 + label | 2.50 | 2.50 |

Wedding of Princess Anne and Capt. Mark Phillips.

No. 371a contains one each of Nos. 369-371 and label showing interior of Westminster Abbey. View of Westminster Abbey in multicolored margin. Size: 118½x98½mm.

Running and Games Emblem A61

Designs (Games Emblem and): 1c, Diving (vert.). 3c, Boxing (vert.). 10c, Weight lifting. 30c, Bicycling. 50c, Discobolus (vert.).

**1974, Jan. 24 Photo. *Perf. 14***

| | | | | |
|---|---|---|---|---|
| *372* | A61 | 1c multi | 5 | 5 |
| *373* | A61 | 3c multi | 8 | 8 |
| *374* | A61 | 5c multi | 12 | 12 |
| *375* | A61 | 10c multi | 25 | 25 |
| *376* | A61 | 30c multi | 75 | 75 |
| | | *Nos. 372-376 (5)* | 1.25 | 1.25 |

**Souvenir Sheet**

| | | | | |
|---|---|---|---|---|
| *377* | A61 | 50c multi | 1.25 | 1.25 |

10th British Commonwealth Games, Christchurch, New Zealand, Jan. 24-Feb. 2. No. 377 contains one stamp (35x45mm.). Multicolored margin with flags of Cook Islands and New Zealand and gold inscription. Size: 114x89mm.

Easter Type of 1973 Dated "1974"

Paintings: 5c, Jesus Carrying Cross, by Raphael. 10c, Jesus in the Arms of God, by El Greco. 30c, Descent from the Cross, by Caravaggio.

**1974, Mar. 25 *Perf. 13½x13***

| | | | | |
|---|---|---|---|---|
| *378* | A56 | 5c gold & multi | 12 | 12 |
| *379* | A56 | 10c gold & multi | 25 | 25 |
| *380* | A56 | 30c gold & multi | 65 | 65 |
| *a* | | Souvenir sheet of 3 | 1.40 | 1.40 |

Easter 1974. No. 380a contains one each of Nos. 378-380, gold and multicolored margin. Size: 130x70mm.

See Nos. B39-B41.

Phallicium Glaucum A62

Queen Elizabeth II — A63

Queen and Shells — A64

Designs: Cook Islands sea shells. The designs of the 2c, 5c, 10c and 30c include portrait of Queen Elizabeth II.

**1974-75 Photo. *Perf. 13½***

| | | | | |
|---|---|---|---|---|
| *381* | A62 | ½c *shown* | 6 | 5 |
| *382* | A62 | 1c *Vasum turbinellus* | 6 | 5 |
| *383* | A62 | 1½c *Corculum cardissa* | 6 | 5 |
| *384* | A62 | 2c *Terebellum terebellum* | 7 | 5 |
| *385* | A62 | 3c *Aulica vespertilio* | 8 | 7 |
| *386* | A62 | 4c *Strombus gibberulus* | 10 | 8 |
| *387* | A62 | 5c *Cymatium pileare* | 12 | 10 |
| *388* | A62 | 6c *Cyprae caputserpentis* | 14 | 12 |
| *389* | A62 | 8c *Bursa granularis* | 16 | 15 |
| *390* | A62 | 10c *Tenebra muscaria* | 20 | 18 |
| *391* | A62 | 15c *Mitra mitra* | 30 | 28 |
| *392* | A62 | 20c *Natica alapillonis roding* | 40 | 35 |
| *393* | A62 | 25c *Gloripallium pallium* | 50 | 42 |
| *394* | A62 | 30c *Conus miles* | 60 | 50 |
| *395* | A62 | 50c *Conus textile* | 1.00 | 90 |
| *396* | A62 | 60c *Oliva sericea roding* | 1.10 | 1.00 |
| *397* | A63 | $1 multi | 1.75 | 1.75 |
| *398* | A63 | $2 multi ('75) | 3.50 | 3.50 |

***Perf. 14x13½***

| | | | | |
|---|---|---|---|---|
| *399* | A64 | $4 multi ('75) | 5.00 | 5.00 |
| *400* | A64 | $6 multi ('75) | 8.00 | 8.00 |
| *401* | A64 | $8 multi ('75) | 10.00 | 10.00 |
| *402* | A64 | $10 multi ('75) | 14.00 | 14.00 |
| | | *Nos. 381-402 (22)* | 47.20 | 46.60 |

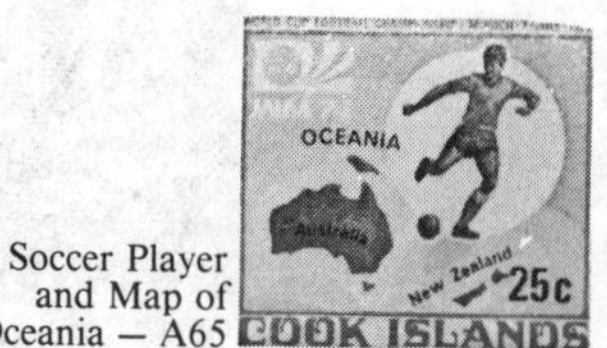


Soccer Player and Map of Oceania — A65

Designs: 50c, Munich stadium and map of Oceania. $1, Soccer player, Munich stadium and World Cup.

**1974, July 5 Photo. *Perf. 13½***

**Size: 31x29mm**

| | | | | |
|---|---|---|---|---|
| *403* | A65 | 25c multi | 45 | 45 |
| *404* | A65 | 50c multi | 90 | 90 |

**Size: 68x28½mm**

*405* A65 $1 multi 1.75 1.75
*a* Souvenir sheet of 3 3.75 3.75

World Cup Soccer Championship, Munich, June 13-July 7. Nos. 403-405 printed in sheets of 8 and commemorative label. No. 405a contains one each of Nos. 403-405. Gold margin and inscription. Size: 89x100mm.

$2.50 Capt. Cook Silver Coin — A66

Designs (Commemorative Silver Coins): $7.50, $7.50 coin with Queen Elizabeth II on obverse; Capt. Cook, map of Islands and "Resolution" on reverse. $2.50 coin shows "Resolution," "Adventure" and globe on reverse.

**1974, July 22 Photo. *Perf. 14***

*406* A6 $2.50 sil, vio & blk 6.25 5.00
*407* A6 $7.50 grn, sil & blk 17.50 15.00
*a* Souvenir sheet of 2 30.00 27.50

Bicentenary of Capt. Cook's 2nd voyage of discovery. Nos. 406-407 printed in sheets of 5 and commemorative label. No. 407a contains one each of Nos. 406-407; silver, green and violet border. Size: 73x73mm.

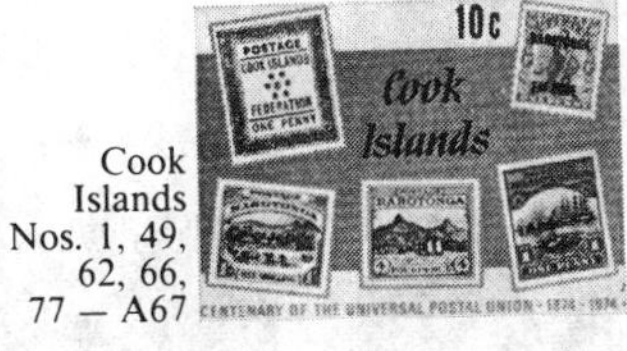


Cook Islands Nos. 1, 49, 62, 66, 77 — A67

Designs (Stamps of Cook Islands): 25c, DC-3 over old Rarotonga landing strip, and No. 19. 30c, Rarotonga Post Office, UPU emblem and No. 65. 50c, UPU emblem and Nos. 1, 19, 49, 62, 65-66 and 77.

**1974, Sept. 16 Photo. *Perf. 13½x14***

*408* A67 10c gold & multi 22 22
*409* A67 25c gold & multi 55 55
*410* A67 30c gold & multi 65 65
*411* A67 50c gold & multi 1.20 1.20
*a* Souvenir sheet of 4 2.75 2.75

Cent. of UPU. Nos. 408-411 printed in sheets of 8 and commemorative label.
No. 411a contains one each of Nos. 408-411, perf. 13½. Multicolored margin showing UPU Monument, Bern, and gold inscription. Size: 117x78mm.

Virgin and Child, with St. John, by Raphael — A68

Paintings: 5c, Holy Family, by Andrea del Sarto. 10c, Nativity, by Correggio. 20c, Holy Family, by Rembrandt. 30c, Nativity, by Van der Weyden.

**1974, Oct. 15 Photo. *Perf. 13½***

*412* A68 1c multi 5 5
*413* A68 5c multi 10 10
*414* A68 10c multi 20 20
*415* A68 20c multi 45 45
*416* A68 30c multi 65 65
*a* Souvenir sheet of 5 + label 1.65 1.65
*Nos. 412-416 (5)* 1.45 1.45

Christmas 1974. Nos. 412-416 printed in sheets of 15 and one label showing Queen Elizabeth II. No. 416a contains one each of Nos. 412-416 and label with Queen's portrait. Gold and multicolored margin. Size: 111x130mm.
See Nos. B42-B46.

Churchill and Blenheim Palace A69

Designs (Churchill and): 10c, Parliament. 25c, Chartwell. 30c, Buckingham Palace. 50c, St. Paul's Cathedral.

**1974, Nov. 20 Photo. *Perf. 14***

*417* A69 3c vio & multi 12 12
*418* A69 10c mar & multi 25 25
*419* A69 25c dk bl & multi 65 65
*420* A69 30c brn & multi 85 85
*421* A69 50c multi 1.65 1.65
*a* Souvenir sheet of 5 + label 3.75 3.75
*Nos. 417-421 (5)* 3.52 3.52

Sir Winston Churchill (1874-1965), birth centenary. Nos. 417-421 printed in sheets of 5 stamps and one label showing $100 commemorative gold coin. No. 421a contains one each of Nos. 417-421, perf. 13, and label showing $50 commemorative silver coin. Silver and claret margin. Size: 108x114mm.

Vasco Nunez de Balboa — A70

Designs: 5c, Ferdinand Magellan and route around South America. 10c, Juan Sebastian del Cano and ship. 25c, Andres de Urdaneta and ship. 25c, Miguel Lopez de Legaspi and ship.

**1975, Feb. 3 *Perf. 13½***

*422* A70 1c multi 6 5
*423* A70 5c multi 15 10
*424* A70 10c multi 30 20
*425* A70 25c multi 85 65
*426* A70 30c multi 1.00 75
*Nos. 422-426 (5)* 2.36 1.75

16th century explorers of the Pacific Ocean.

Apollo and Apollo-Soyuz Emblem — A71

Designs (Apollo-Soyuz Emblem and): No. 428, Soyuz. No. 429, Aleksei A. Leonov and Valery N. Kubasov. No. 430, Donald K. Slayton, Vance D. Brand and Thomas P. Stafford. No. 431, Cosmonaut inside Soyuz capsule. No. 432, American astronauts inside Apollo capsule.

**1975, July 15 Photo. *Perf. 13½***

*427* A71 25c multi 50 50
*428* A71 25c multi 50 50
*429* A71 30c multi 60 60
*430* A71 30c multi 60 60
*431* A71 50c multi 1.00 1.00
*432* A71 50c multi 1.00 1.00
*a* Souvenir sheet of 6 3.75 3.75
*Nos. 427-432 (6)* 4.20 4.20

Apollo Soyuz space test project (Russo-American space cooperation), launching July 15; link-up, July 17. Stamps of same denomination printed se-tenant in sheets of 18 stamps and 2 labels showing flags. No. 432a contains one each of Nos. 427-432; blue and multicolored margin with gold inscription. Size: 117x119mm.

$100 Gold Commemorative Coin — A72

**1975, Aug. 8 Photo. *Perf. 13½x13***

*433* A72 $2 gold & dp vio 4.00 3.75

Bicentenary of the completion of Capt. Cook's second voyage of discovery.

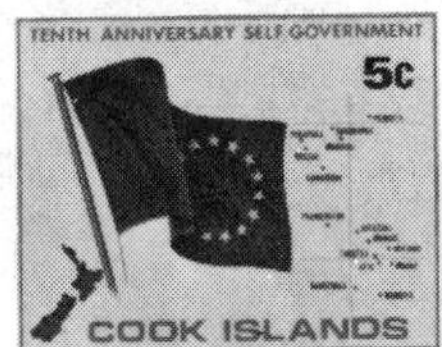


Cook Islands' Flag, Map of Islands and New Zealand A73

Prime Minister Sir Albert Henry — A74

Design: 25c, View of Rarotonga and flag.

**1975, Aug. 8 *Perf. 13½x13, 13x13½***

*434* A73 5c gold & multi 12 9
*435* A74 10c gold & multi 25 20
*436* A73 25c gold & multi 65 50

Tenth anniversary of self-government.

Virgin and Child, 15th Century, Flemish — A75

Paintings: 10c, Madonna in the Field, by Raphael. 15c, Holy Family, by Raphael. 20c, Adoration of the Shepherds, by J. B. Mayno. 35c, Annunciation, by Murillo.

**1975, Dec. 1 Photo. *Perf. 13½***

*437* A75 6c gold & multi 12 12
*438* A75 10c gold & multi 20 20
*439* A75 15c gold & multi 30 30
*440* A75 20c gold & multi 40 40
*441* A75 35c gold & multi 65 65
*a* Souvenir sheet of 5 1.75 1.75
*Nos. 437-441 (5)* 1.67 1.67

Christmas 1975. No. 441a contains one each of Nos. 437-441 and label; multicolored margin. Size: 110x125mm. See Nos. B47-B51.

Descent from the Cross, by Raphael A76

Paintings: 15c, Pieta, by Veronese. 35c, Pieta, by El Greco.

**1976, Mar. 29 Photo. *Perf. 13½***

*442* A76 7c gold & multi 12 12
*443* A76 15c gold & multi 28 28
*444* A76 35c gold & multi 70 70
*a* Souvenir sheet of 3 1.10 1.10

Easter 1976. No. 444a contains one each of Nos. 442-444; purple and gold margin. Size: 145x57mm. Nos. 442-444 printed in sheets of 20 with label showing Queen Elizabeth II.
See Nos. B52-B54.

Benjamin Franklin and "Resolution" — A77

Designs: $2, Capt. James Cook and "Resolution." $3, Cook, "Resolution" and Franklin.

**1976, May 29 Photo. *Perf. 13½***

*445* A77 $1 gold & multi 3.75 2.00
*446* A77 $2 gold & multi 7.50 4.00

**Souvenir Sheet**

***Perf. 13***

*447* A77 $3 gold & multi 8.75 5.00

American Bicentennial. No. 447 contains one stamp (73x31mm.); gold and multicolored margin showing Bicentennial emblem. Size: 118x59mm. Nos. 445-446 printed in sheets of 5 and corner label with Franklin's request to assist Capt. Cook.

Nos. 445-447 Overprinted "Royal Visit July 1976"

**1976, July 6 Photo. *Perf. 13½***

*448* A77 $1 gold & multi 1.50 1.25
*449* A77 $2 gold & multi 3.75 3.50

**Souvenir Sheet**

***Perf. 13***

*450* A77 $3 gold & multi 8.75 6.00

Visit of Queen Elizabeth II and Prince Philip to the United States.

High Hurdles
A78 A79

**1976, July 22 *Perf. 13½***

*451* A78 7c *shown* 12 12
*452* A79 7c *shown* 12 12
*453* A78 15c *Field hockey* 25 25
*454* A79 15c *Field hockey* 25 25
*455* A78 30c *Fencing* 50 50
*456* A79 30c *Fencing* 50 50
*457* A78 35c *Soccer* 60 60
*458* A79 35c *Soccer* 60 60
*a* Souvenir sheet of 8 3.25 3.25
*Nos. 451-458 (8)* 2.94 2.94

21st Olympic Games, Montreal, Canada, July 17-Aug. 1. Stamps of same denomination printed se-tenant in sheets of 10 stamps and 2 labels (4x3), showing flags of New Zealand and Cook Islands and Montreal Olympic Games emblem. No. 458a contains one each of Nos. 451-458; gold, violet and light blue margin. Size: 104x146mm.

The Visitation — A80

Designs: 10c, Virgin and Child. 15c, Adoration of the Shepherds. 20c, Adoration of the Kings. 35c, Holy Family. After painted Renaissance altar sculptures.

**1976, Oct. 12 Photo. *Perf. 14x13½***

| | | | |
|---|---|---|---|
| *459* A80 | 6c gold & multi | 12 | 12 |
| *460* A80 | 10c gold & multi | 18 | 18 |
| *461* A80 | 15c gold & multi | 25 | 25 |
| *462* A80 | 20c gold & multi | 35 | 35 |
| *463* A80 | 35c gold & multi | 60 | 60 |
| *a* | Souvenir sheet of 5 | 1.75 | 1.75 |
| | *Nos. 459-463 (5)* | 1.50 | 1.50 |

Christmas 1976. Nos. 459-463 printed in sheets of 20 with label showing Queen Elizabeth II. No. 463a contains one each of Nos. 459-463 and label; multicolored margin. Size: 116x109mm.

$5 Silver Coin, 1976 — A81

**1976, Nov. 15 Photo. *Perf. 13½***

| | | | |
|---|---|---|---|
| *464* A81 | $1 multi | 2.00 | 1.75 |

National Wildlife and Conservation Day. Issued in sheets of 5 stamps and commemorative label. See No. 502.

Elizabeth II in Coronation Vestments — A82

Designs: No. 465, Crown. No. 467, Westminster Abbey. No. 468, Coach in procession. No. 469, Queen and Prince Philip after coronation. No. 470, Investiture of Sir Albert Henry, Premier of Cook Islands, 1974.

**1977, Feb. 7 Photo. *Perf. 13½x13***

| | | | |
|---|---|---|---|
| *465* A82 | 25c sil & multi | 50 | 40 |
| *466* A82 | 25c sil & multi | 50 | 40 |
| *467* A82 | 50c sil & multi | 1.25 | 1.00 |
| *468* A82 | 50c sil & multi | 1.25 | 1.00 |
| *469* A82 | $1 sil & multi | 2.50 | 2.00 |
| *470* A82 | $1 sil & multi | 2.50 | 2.00 |
| *a* | Souvenir sheet of 6 | 8.75 | 7.50 |
| | *Nos. 465-470 (6)* | 8.50 | 6.80 |

25th anniversary of the reign of Queen Elizabeth II. Stamps of same denomination printed se-tenant in sheets of 8 (4x2) with decorative silver margin. No. 470a contains one each of Nos. 465-470, perf. 13, with violet blue and multicolored margin showing coat of arms. Size: 130x136mm.

The Catalogue editors cannot undertake to appraise, identify or judge the genuineness or condition of stamps.

Crucifixion, by Rubens — A83

Virgin and Child, by Memling — A84

Paintings by Rubens: 15c, Christ Between the Thieves. 35c, Descent from the Cross.

**1977, Mar. 28 Photo. *Perf. 14x13½***

| | | | |
|---|---|---|---|
| *471* A83 | 7c gold & multi | 10 | 10 |
| *472* A83 | 15c gold & multi | 20 | 20 |
| *473* A83 | 35c gold & multi | 50 | 50 |
| *a* | Souvenir sheet of 3 | 90 | 90 |

Easter 1977, and 400th birth anniversary of Peter Paul Rubens (1577-1640), Flemish painter. Nos. 471-473 printed in sheets of 24 stamps and corner label with portrait of Queen Elizabeth II and description. No. 473a contains one each of Nos. 471-473, perf. 13; gold and dark blue decorative margin. Size: 118x64mm.

**1977, Oct. 3 Photo. *Perf. 13½***

Virgin and Child by: 10c, Hans Memling. 15c, Geertgen Tot Sin Jans. 20c, Carlo Crivelli. 35c, School of Henry Blex.

| | | | |
|---|---|---|---|
| *474* A84 | 6c gold & multi | 8 | 8 |
| *475* A84 | 10c gold & multi | 14 | 14 |
| *476* A84 | 15c gold & multi | 20 | 20 |
| *477* A84 | 20c gold & multi | 28 | 28 |
| *478* A84 | 35c gold & multi | 50 | 50 |
| *a* | Souvenir sheet of 5 | 1.25 | 1.25 |
| | *Nos. 474-478 (5)* | 1.20 | 1.20 |

Christmas 1977. Nos. 474-478 printed in sheets of 24 and label. No. 478a contains one each of Nos. 474-478 and label; multicolored margin. Size: 117x111mm.

$5-silver Coin, 1977 — A85

**1977, Nov. 15 Photo. *Perf. 13½***

| | | | |
|---|---|---|---|
| *479* A85 | $1 sil & multi | 3.50 | 1.65 |

National Wildlife Conservation Day. No. 479 issued in sheets of 5 stamps and one label with commemorative inscription.

Capt. Cook, by Nathaniel Dance and "Resolution" — A86

Designs: $1, "Capt. Cook Landing at Owyhee" and Capt. Cook. $2, Cook Islands $200 commemorative coin, 1978, and Cook Monument, Hawaii, 1825.

**1978, Jan. 20 Litho. *Perf. 13½***

| | | | |
|---|---|---|---|
| *480* A86 | 50c gold & multi | 75 | 75 |
| *481* A86 | $1 gold & multi | 1.50 | 1.50 |
| *482* A86 | $2 gold multi | 3.00 | 3.00 |
| *a* | Souvenir sheet of 3 | 5.00 | 5.00 |

Bicentennial of Capt. Cook's arrival in Hawaii. No. 482a contains one each of Nos. 480-482; gold, black and blue decorative margin. Size: 118x95mm.

Nos. 480-482 issued in sheets of 5 with corner label showing ship off Hawaiian coast.

Pieta, by Rogier van der Weyden A87

Paintings, National Gallery, London: 35c, Burial of Jesus, by Michelangelo. 75c, Jesus at Emmaus, by Caravaggio.

**1978, Mar. 20 Photo. *Perf. 13½x13***

| | | | |
|---|---|---|---|
| *483* A87 | 15c gold & multi | 22 | 22 |
| *484* A87 | 35c gold & multi | 50 | 50 |
| *485* A87 | 75c gold & multi | 1.10 | 1.10 |
| *a* | Souvenir sheet of 3 | 1.40 | 1.40 |

Easter 1978. No. 485a contains one each of Nos. 483-485 and label showing National Gallery, London; multicolored margin. Size: 114x96mm. Nos. 483-485 printed in sheets of 5 and corner label showing National Gallery.

**Souvenir Sheets**

Elizabeth II — A88

**1978, June 6 Photo. *Perf. 13***

| | | | |
|---|---|---|---|
| *486* | Sheet of 4 + 2 labels | 2.00 | 2.00 |
| *a* | A88 50c *shown* | 75 | 75 |
| *b* | A88 50c *Lion of England* | 75 | 75 |
| *c* | A88 50c *Imperial State Crown* | 75 | 75 |
| *d* | A88 50c *Tangaroa figure* | 75 | 75 |
| *487* | Sheet of 4 + label | 3.00 | 3.00 |
| *a* | A88 70c *like 486a* | 1.00 | 1.00 |
| *b* | A88 70c *Scepter with Cross* | 1.00 | 1.00 |
| *c* | A88 70c *St. Edward's Crown* | 1.00 | 1.00 |
| *d* | A88 70c *Rarotongan staff god* | 1.00 | 1.00 |
| *e* | Souvenir sheet of 8 | 6.25 | 6.25 |

25th anniversary of coronation of Queen Elizabeth II. Labels of Nos. 486-487 give design descriptions. Size: 102x100mm. No. 487e contains one each of Nos. 486a-487d and label with date and commemorative inscription. Size: 103x141mm.

Nos. 381, 383, 388-389, 393-396 Surcharged with New Value and Three Bars in Silver, Black or Gold

**1978, Nov. 10 Photo. *Perf. 13½***

| | | | |
|---|---|---|---|
| *488* A62 | 5c on 1½c multi (S) | 14 | 14 |
| *489* A62 | 7c on ½c multi | 20 | 20 |
| *490* A62 | 10c on 6c multi (G) | 28 | 28 |
| *491* A62 | 10c on 8c multi (G) | 28 | 28 |
| *492* A62 | 15c on ½c multi | 42 | 42 |
| *493* A62 | 15c on 25c multi (S) | 42 | 42 |
| *494* A62 | 15c on 30c multi | 42 | 42 |
| *495* A62 | 15c on 50c multi (S) | 42 | 42 |
| *496* A62 | 15c on 60c multi (G) | 42 | 42 |
| *497* A62 | 17c on ½c multi | 48 | 48 |
| *498* A62 | 17c on 50c multi (S) | 48 | 48 |
| | *Nos. 488-498 (11)* | 3.96 | 3.96 |

Nos. 480-482a Overprinted in Black on Silver Panel: "1728--250th ANNIVERSARY OF COOK'S BIRTH--1978"

**1978, Nov. 13 Litho. *Perf. 13½***

| | | | |
|---|---|---|---|
| *499* A86 | 50c gold & multi | 75 | 75 |
| *500* A86 | $1 gold & multi | 1.50 | 1.50 |
| *501* A86 | $2 gold & multi | 3.00 | 3.00 |
| *a* | Souvenir sheet of 3 | 6.00 | 6.00 |

250th anniversary of Capt. Cook's birth. Similar overprint in 4 lines was applied to labels. Label of No. 501a overprinted only with dates 1728, 1978.

Coin Type of 1976

Design: $1, $5 Silver coin, 1978 (Polynesian warbler).

**1978, Nov. 15 Photo. *Perf. 13½***

| | | | |
|---|---|---|---|
| *502* A81 | $1 multi | 2.25 | 2.00 |

National Wildlife and Conservation Day. Sheets of 24 containing 4 panes of 6

Virgin and Child, by Rogier van der Weyden — A89

Pieta, by Gaspar de Crayer — A90

Virgin and Child by: 17c, Carlo Crivelli. 35c, Murillo.

**1978, Dec. 8 Photo. *Perf. 13***

| | | | |
|---|---|---|---|
| *503* A89 | 15c multi | 20 | 20 |
| *504* A89 | 17c multi | 25 | 25 |
| *505* A89 | 35c multi | 50 | 50 |
| *a* | Souvenir sheet of 3 | 1.25 | 1.25 |

Christmas 1978. No. 505a contains Nos. 503-505. Multicolored decorative margin. Size: 107x71mm.

**1979, Apr. 5 Photo. *Perf. 13***

Descent from the Cross, by Gaspar de Crayer (Details): 12c, St. John. 15c, Mary Magdalene. 20c, Cherubs.

| | | | |
|---|---|---|---|
| *506* A90 | 10c multi | 14 | 14 |
| *507* A90 | 12c multi | 18 | 18 |
| *508* A90 | 15c multi | 24 | 24 |
| *509* A90 | 20c multi | 50 | 50 |

Easter 1979.

Capt. Cook, by John Weber — A91

Rowland Hill, Postrider — A92

Designs: 30c, Resolution, by Henry Roberts. 35c, Endeavour. 50c, Death of Capt. Cook, by George Carter.

**1979, July 23 Photo. *Perf. 14x13½***

| | | | |
|---|---|---|---|
| *510* A91 | 20c multi | 35 | 35 |
| *511* A91 | 30c multi | 50 | 50 |
| *512* A91 | 35c multi | 60 | 60 |
| *513* A91 | 50c multi | 80 | 80 |
| *a* | Souvenir sheet of 4 | 2.00 | 2.00 |

Capt. Cook (1728-79), explorer. No. 513a contains 4 stamps similar to Nos. 510-513 with black frames; gray blue and gold margin. Size: 78x113mm.

**1979, Sept. 10 *Perf. 14½***

Rowland Hill and: No. 515, Stagecoach. No. 516, Automobile. No. 517, Streamlined train. No. 518, Cap-Horniers, sailing ship. No. 519, River steamer. No. 520, Liner Deutschland. No. 521, Liner United States. No. 522, Balloon Neptune. No. 523, Junkers F13. No. 524, Graf Zeppelin. No. 525, Concorde.

| | | | |
|---|---|---|---|
| *514* A92 | 30c multi | 30 | 30 |
| *515* A92 | 30c multi | 30 | 30 |
| *516* A92 | 30c multi | 30 | 30 |
| *517* A92 | 30c multi | 30 | 30 |
| *518* A92 | 35c multi | 35 | 35 |
| *519* A92 | 35c multi | 35 | 35 |
| *520* A92 | 35c multi | 35 | 35 |
| *521* A92 | 35c multi | 35 | 35 |
| *522* A92 | 50c multi | 50 | 50 |
| *523* A93 | 50c multi | 50 | 50 |
| *524* A93 | 50c multi | 50 | 50 |
| *525* A93 | 50c multi | 50 | 50 |
| *a* | Souvenir sheet of 12 | 5.00 | 5.00 |
| | *Nos. 514-525 (12)* | 4.60 | 4.60 |

Sir Rowland Hill (1795-1879), originator of penny postage. Stamps of same denomination printed se-tenant in sheets of 40. No. 525a contains Nos. 514-525 in 3 horizontal rows: gold and purple margin. Size: 132x104mm.

Nos. 381, 383, 396 Surcharged

**1979, Sept. 12 Photo. *Perf. 13½***

| | | | |
|---|---|---|---|
| *526* A62 | 6c on ½c gold & multi | 18 | 18 |
| *527* A62 | 10c on 1½c gold & multi | 28 | 28 |
| *528* A62 | 15c on 60c gold & multi | 42 | 42 |

Nos. 526-528 have 3 thick bars of equal length over old value.

Girl and Baby, IYC Emblem — A93

IYC Emblem and: 50c, Boy playing tree drum. 65c, Children dancing.

**1979, Oct. 10 *Perf. 13***

| | | | |
|---|---|---|---|
| *529* A93 | 30c multi | 42 | 42 |
| *530* A93 | 50c multi | 70 | 70 |
| *531* A93 | 65c multi | 90 | 90 |

IYC. See No. B75.

Apollo 11 Emblem — A94

Designs: 50c, Apollo 11 crew, lunar map. 60c, Astronaut walking on moon. 65c, Splashdown.

**1979, Nov. 7 *Perf. 14***

| | | | |
|---|---|---|---|
| *532* A94 | 30c multi | 40 | 40 |
| *533* A94 | 50c multi | 60 | 60 |
| *534* A94 | 60c multi | 75 | 75 |
| *535* A94 | 65c multi | 85 | 85 |
| *a* | Souvenir sheet of 4 | 3.00 | 3.00 |

Apollo 11 moon landing, 10th anniv. No. 535a contains Nos. 532-535, perf. 13. Multi margin shows lunar landscape and earth; gold inscription. Size: 119x115mm.

Coin Type of 1976

Design: $1, $5 Silver coin, 1979 (Raratonga fruit dove).

***Perf. 13½x14½***

**1979, Nov. 15 Photo.**

| | | | |
|---|---|---|---|
| *536* A81 | $1 multi | 2.00 | 2.00 |

National Wildlife and Conservation Day.

Christmas Tree Ornaments — A95

Christmas (Flowers and): 10c, Star. 12c, Bells and candle. 15c, Ancestral statue.

**1979, Dec. 14 *Perf. 14***

| | | | |
|---|---|---|---|
| *537* A95 | 6c multi | 10 | 10 |
| *538* A95 | 10c multi | 14 | 14 |
| *539* A95 | 12c multi | 15 | 15 |
| *540* A95 | 15c multi | 20 | 20 |
| | *Nos. 537-540,B76-B79 (8)* | 1.47 | 1.47 |

Flagellation, by DorE — A96

**1980, Mar. 31 Photo. *Perf. 13***

| | | | |
|---|---|---|---|
| *541* A96 | 20c *shown* | 28 | 28 |
| *542* A96 | 20c *Jesus Wearing Crown of Thorns* | 28 | 28 |
| *543* A96 | 30c *Jesus Mocked* | 45 | 45 |
| *544* A96 | 30c *Jesus Falls* | 45 | 45 |
| *545* A96 | 35c *The Crucifixion* | 50 | 50 |
| *546* A96 | 35c *Descent from the Cross* | 50 | 50 |
| | *Nos. 541-546 (6)* | 2.46 | 2.46 |

Easter 1980 (Bible illustrations by Gustave DorE, 1833-83). Stamps of same denomination se-tenant. See Nos. B80-B86.

Doves with Olive Branch, Rotary Emblem A97

**1980, May 27 Photo. *Perf. 14***

| | | | |
|---|---|---|---|
| *547* A97 | 30c *shown* | 45 | 45 |
| *548* A97 | 35c *Flowers* | 50 | 50 |
| *549* A97 | 50c *Flags, globe* | 70 | 70 |

Rotary International, 75th anniversary.

New Zealand No. 1 and Postrider — A98

Designs (Four different designs for each denomination, stamp of New Zealand): 30c, No. 1; coach, automobile and train. 35c, No. 2; sailing ship, river steamer, early transatlantic liner and ocean liner. 50c, No. 3; 1870-71 mail balloon, 1919 plane, Graf Zeppelin and Concorde.

**1980, Aug. 22 Photo. *Perf. 14***

| | | | |
|---|---|---|---|
| *550* | 30c Block of 4 | 1.50 | 1.25 |
| *a* | A98 single stamp | 35 | 30 |
| *551* | 35c Block of 4 | 2.00 | 1.75 |
| *a* | A98 single stamp | 50 | 42 |
| *552* | 50c Block of 4 | 3.00 | 2.50 |
| *a* | A98 single stamp | 75 | 60 |
| *b* | Souvenir sheet of 12 | 7.50 | 6.50 |

Easter Type of 1980

**Souvenir Sheet**

***Perf. 13***

| | | | |
|---|---|---|---|
| *553* A96 | Sheet of 6 (#541-546) | 5.00 | 3.50 |

ZEAPEX '80, New Zealand Intl. Stamp Exhib., Auckland, Aug. 23-31. Stamps of same denomination se-tenant in blocks of 4, sheets of 40. No. 552b contains stamps of Nos. 550-552 arranged se-tenant horizontally (4x3); multicolored margin. Size: 133x105mm. No. 553 has multicolored margin with black on gold overprint: "ZEAPEX / '80 / Auckland / +10c". Size: 120½x110mm.

Queen Mother Elizabeth, 80th Birthday — A99

**1980, Sept. 22 Photo. *Perf. 13***

| | | | |
|---|---|---|---|
| *554* A99 | 50c multi | 1.50 | 1.00 |

**Souvenir Sheet**

| | | | |
|---|---|---|---|
| *555* A99 | $2 multi | 2.75 | 2.75 |

No. 554 issued in sheets of 9 (3x3). No. 555 has multicolored margin with continuous design. Size: 64x78mm.

Johannes Kepler, Spacecraft — A100

Designs: Nos. 557, 562, Kepler, spacecraft (diff.). No. 563, Kepler, lunar rover, astronaut on moon. Nos. 558-561, Jules Verne, various scenes from From Earth to Moon (vert.). Stamps of same denomination se-tenant.

**1980, Nov. 7 Photo. *Perf. 13***

| | | | |
|---|---|---|---|
| *556* A100 | 12c multi | 25 | 25 |
| *557* A100 | 12c multi | 25 | 25 |
| *558* A100 | 20c multi | 25 | 25 |
| *559* A100 | 20c multi | 25 | 25 |
| *560* A100 | 30c multi | 65 | 65 |
| *561* A100 | 30c multi | 65 | 65 |
| *a* | Souvenir sheet of 4 | 2.25 | 2.25 |
| *562* A100 | 50c multi | 1.10 | 1.10 |
| *563* A100 | 50c multi | 1.10 | 1.10 |
| *a* | Souvenir sheet of 4 | 2.75 | 2.75 |
| | *Nos. 556-563 (8)* | 4.50 | 4.50 |

Death anniversaries of Johannes Kepler, German astronomer and Jules Verne, French science fiction writer. Nos. 561a and 563a contain Nos. 558-561 and Nos. 556-557, 562-563 respectively. Multicolored margins show lunar map (No. 561a) and Old World map (No. 563a). Size: 122x122mm.

Burning Bush Coral — A101

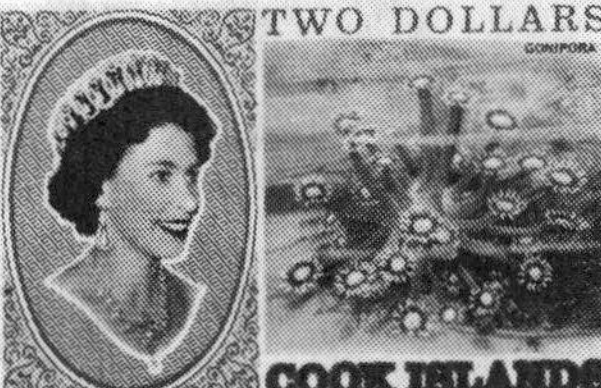


Daisy Coral — A101a

**1980-82 *Perf. 13½x13***

| | | | |
|---|---|---|---|
| *564* A101 | 1c Siphonogorgia | 5 | 5 |
| *565* A101 | 1c Pavona practorta | 5 | 5 |
| *566* A101 | 1c Stylaster echinatus | 5 | 5 |
| *567* A101 | 1c Tubastraea | 5 | 5 |
| *568* A101 | 3c Millepora alcicornis | 7 | 7 |
| *569* A101 | 3c Junceella gemmaea | 7 | 7 |
| *570* A101 | 3c Fungia fungites | 7 | 7 |
| *571* A101 | 3c Heliofungia actiniformis | 7 | 7 |
| *572* A101 | 4c Distichopora violacea | 8 | 8 |
| *573* A101 | 4c Stylaster | 8 | 8 |
| *574* A101 | 4c Gonipora | 8 | 8 |
| *575* A101 | 4c Caulastraea echinulata | 8 | 8 |
| *576* A101 | 5c Ptilosarcus gurneyi | 10 | 10 |
| *577* A101 | 5c Stylophora pistillata | 10 | 10 |
| *578* A101 | 5c Melithaea squamata | 10 | 10 |
| *579* A101 | 5c Porites andrewsi | 10 | 10 |
| *580* A101 | 6c Lobophyllia bemprichii | 12 | 12 |
| *581* A101 | 6c Palauastrea ramosa | 12 | 12 |
| *582* A101 | 6c Bellonella indica | 12 | 12 |
| *583* A101 | 6c Pectinia alcicornis | 12 | 12 |
| *584* A101 | 8c Sarcophyton digitatum | 16 | 16 |
| *585* A101 | 8c Melithaea albitincta | 16 | 16 |
| *586* A101 | 8c Plerogyra sinuosa | 16 | 16 |
| *587* A101 | 8c Dendrophyllia gracilis | 16 | 16 |
| *588* A101 | 10c like #564 | 20 | 20 |
| *589* A101 | 10c like #565 | 20 | 20 |
| *590* A101 | 10c like #566 | 20 | 20 |
| *591* A101 | 10c like #567 | 20 | 20 |
| *592* A101 | 12c like #568 | 24 | 24 |
| *593* A101 | 12c like #569 | 24 | 24 |
| *594* A101 | 12c like #570 | 24 | 24 |
| *595* A101 | 12c like #571 | 24 | 24 |
| *596* A101 | 15c like #572 | 28 | 28 |
| *597* A101 | 15c like #573 | 28 | 28 |
| *598* A101 | 15c like #574 | 28 | 28 |
| *599* A101 | 15c like #575 | 28 | 28 |
| *600* A101 | 20c like #576 | 35 | 35 |
| *601* A101 | 20c like #577 | 35 | 35 |
| *602* A101 | 20c like #578 | 35 | 35 |
| *603* A101 | 20c like #579 | 35 | 35 |
| *604* A101 | 25c like #580 | 50 | 50 |
| *605* A101 | 25c like #581 | 50 | 50 |
| *606* A101 | 25c like #582 | 50 | 50 |
| *607* A101 | 25c like #583 | 50 | 50 |
| *608* A101 | 30c like #584 | 60 | 60 |
| *609* A101 | 30c like #585 | 60 | 60 |
| *610* A101 | 30c like #586 | 60 | 60 |
| *611* A101 | 30c like #587 | 60 | 60 |
| *612* A101 | 35c like #564 | 65 | 65 |
| *613* A101 | 35c like #565 | 65 | 65 |
| *614* A101 | 35c like #566 | 65 | 65 |
| *615* A101 | 35c like #567 | 65 | 65 |
| *616* A101 | 50c like #568 | 90 | 90 |
| *617* A101 | 50c like #569 | 90 | 90 |
| *618* A101 | 50c like #570 | 90 | 90 |
| *619* A101 | 50c like #571 | 90 | 90 |
| *620* A101 | 60c like #572 | 1.10 | 1.10 |
| *621* A101 | 60c like #573 | 1.10 | 1.10 |
| *622* A101 | 60c like #574 | 1.10 | 1.10 |
| *623* A101 | 60c like #575 | 1.10 | 1.10 |
| *624* A101 | 70c like #576 | 1.25 | 1.25 |
| *625* A101 | 70c like #577 | 1.25 | 1.25 |
| *626* A101 | 70c like #578 | 1.25 | 1.25 |
| *627* A101 | 70c like #579 | 1.25 | 1.25 |
| *628* A101 | 80c like #580 | 1.40 | 1.40 |
| *629* A101 | 80c like #581 | 1.40 | 1.40 |
| *630* A101 | 80c like #582 | 1.40 | 1.40 |
| *631* A101 | 80c like #583 | 1.40 | 1.40 |
| *632* A101 | $1 like #584 | 1.50 | 1.50 |
| *633* A101 | $1 like #585 | 1.50 | 1.50 |
| *634* A101 | $1 like #586 | 1.50 | 1.50 |
| *635* A101 | $1 like #587 | 1.50 | 1.50 |

***Perf. 14x13½***

| | | | |
|---|---|---|---|
| *636* A101a | $2 like #574 | 3.50 | 3.50 |
| *637* A101a | $3 like #571 | 5.00 | 5.00 |
| *638* A101a | $4 like #577 | 6.50 | 6.50 |
| *639* A101a | $6 like #566 | 10.00 | 10.00 |
| *640* A101a | $10 like #585 | 15.00 | 15.00 |
| | *Nos. 564-640 (77)* | 78.20 | 78.20 |

Stamps of same denomination se-tenant in continuous design.

Annunciation, 13th Century Prayerbook Illustration A102

**1980, Dec. 1 Photo. *Perf. 14***

| | | | |
|---|---|---|---|
| *652* A102 | 15c *shown* | 20 | 20 |
| *653* A102 | 30c *Visitation* | 42 | 42 |
| *654* A102 | 40c *Nativity* | 50 | 50 |
| *655* A102 | 50c *Epiphany* | 70 | 70 |
| *a* | Souvenir sheet of 4 | 2.00 | 2.00 |

Christmas 1980. No. 655a contains Nos. 652-655, multicolored decorative margin. Size: 89x114mm.

Crucifixion, 12th Cent. Prayerbook Illustration — A103

**1981, Apr. 10** *Perf. 14*

*656* A103 15c shown 22 22
*657* A103 25c Placing in Tomb 38 38
*658* A103 40c Marys at the Tomb 60 60

Easter 1981.

Prince Charles and Lady Diana — A104

**1981, July 29** **Photo.** *Perf. 14*

*659* A104 $1 Charles 1.75 1.75
*660* A104 $2 shown 3.50 3.50
*a* Souv. sheet of 2, #659-660 5.00 5.00

Royal Wedding. Issued in sheets of 4. No. 660a has multicolored margin showing arms of Prince of Wales. Size: 107x60mm.

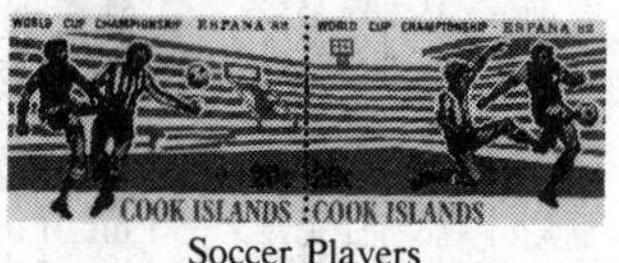


Soccer Players
A105 A106

Designs: Various soccer players.

**1981, Oct 20** **Photo.** *Perf. 14*

*661* A105 20c multi 25 25
*662* A106 20c multi 25 25
*663* A105 30c multi 40 40
*664* A106 30c multi 40 40
*665* A105 35c multi 50 50
*666* A106 35c multi 50 50
*667* A105 50c multi 65 65
*668* A106 50c multi 65 65
*Nos. 661-668 (8)* 3.60 3.60

ESPANA '82 World Cup Soccer Championships. Stamps of same denomination se-tenant in continuous design.

Virgin and Child, by Rubens — A107

Christmas 1981: Rubens Paintings.

**1981, Dec. 14** **Photo.** *Perf. 14x13½*

*669* A107 8c shown 10 10
*670* A107 15c Coronation of St. Catherine 20 20
*671* A107 40c Adoration of the Shepherds 50 50
*672* A107 50c Adoration of the Kings 60 60

**Souvenir Sheets**

**1982, Jan. 18**

*673* A107 75 +5c like #669 1.10 1.10
*674* A107 75 +5c like #670 1.10 1.10
*675* A107 75 +5c like #671 1.10 1.10
*676* A107 75 +5c like #672 1.10 1.10

Nos. 673-676 have multicolored margins showing entire painting. Size: 62x78mm. Surtax was for school children.

21st Birthday of Princess Diana A108

**1982, June 21** **Photo.** *Perf. 14*

*677* A108 $1.25 Portrait 2.50 2.50
*677A* A108 $1.25 1 July 1982 2.50 2.50
*678* A108 $2.50 Wedding portrait 5.00 5.00
*b* Souvenir sheet of 2 6.50 6.50
*678A* A108 $2.50 1 July 1982 5.00 5.00

No. 678b contains $1.25 and $2.50 stamps inscribed in two lines: 21st Birthday 1 July 1982. Perf. 13½; multicolored margin shows arms of Prince of Wales, gold inscription. Size 92x72mm.

Nos. 659-660a Overprinted: "ROYAL BIRTH 21 JUNE 1982" or "PRINCE WILLIAM OF WALES"

**1982, July 12**

*679* A104 $1 Royal Birth 1.75 1.75
*679A* A104 $1 Prince William 1.75 1.75
*680* A104 $2 Royal Birth 3.25 3.25
*b* Souvenir sheet of 2 6.75 6.75
*680A* A104 $2 Prince William 3.25 3.25

Type A108 Inscribed: "Royal Birth" and/or "21 June 1982"

**1982, Aug. 3**

*681* A108 $1.25 Royal Birth 1.75 1.75
*681A* A108 $1.25 21 June 1982 1.75 1.75
*682* A108 $2.50 Royal Birth 3.50 3.50
*b* Souvenir sheet of 2 5.00 5.00
*682A* A108 $2.50 21 June 1982 3.50 3.50

Serenade, by Norman Rockwell (1894-1978) A109

**1982, Sept. 10** **Photo.** *Perf. 14*

*683* A109 5c shown 8 8
*684* A109 10c The Hikers 15 15
*685* A109 20c The Doctor and the Doll 30 30
*686* A109 30c Home From Camp 45 45

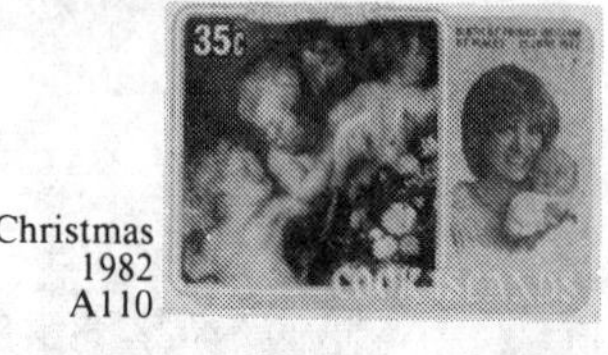


Christmas 1982 A110

Princess Diana Holding Prince William, Various Details from Virgin with Garlands, by Rubens.

**1982, Nov. 30** **Photo.** *Perf. 14*

*687* A110 35c multi 50 50
*688* A110 48c multi 65 65
*689* A110 60c multi 75 75
*690* A110 $1.70 multi 2.25 2.25

**Souvenir Sheets**

*Perf. 13½*

*691* Sheet of 4 3.50 3.50
*a* A110 60c like 35c 85 85
*b* A110 60c like 48c 85 85
*c* A110 60c like #689 85 85
*d* A110 60c like $1.70 85 85
*692* A110 75 + 5c like 35c 1.25 1.25
*693* A110 75 + 5c like 48c 1.25 1.25
*694* A110 75 + 5c like 60c 1.25 1.25
*695* A110 75 + 5c like $1.70 1.25 1.25

No. 691 contains 4 stamps (27x32mm., showing only painting details) plus 2 labels showing Diana and William. Size: 105x83mm. Nos. 692-695 show Diana and William (27x39mm.), multicolored margins show painting details. Size: 73x59mm. Surtax was for child welfare.

An enhanced introduction to the Scott Catalogue begins on Page V. A thorough understanding of the material presented there will greatly aid your use of the catalogue itself.

Commonwealth Day — A111

**1983, Mar. 14** **Photo.** *Perf. 14*

*696* A111 60c Tangaroa statue 65 65
*697* A111 60c Rarotonga oranges 65 65
*698* A111 60c Rarotonga Airport 65 65
*699* A111 60c Prime Minister Thomas Davis 65 65

Nos. 696-699 se-tenant.

Scouting Year
A112 A113

**1983, Apr. 5** **Photo.** *Perf. 13x13½*

*700* Pair, shown 35 35
*a* A112 12c multi 16 16
*b* A113 12c multi 16 16
*701* Pair, Camping 1.10 1.10
*a* A112 36c multi 50 50
*b* A113 36c multi 50 50
*702* Pair, Rope swing 1.40 1.40
*a* A112 48c multi 70 70
*b* A113 48c multi 70 70
*703* Pair, Tree planting 1.75 1.75
*a* A112 60c multi 85 85
*b* A113 60c multi 85 85

**Souvenir Sheet**

*704* Sheet of 8 4.50 4.50
*a* 12 + 2c like #700 40 40
*b* 36 + 2c like #701 1.00 1.00
*c* 48 + 2c like #702 1.40 1.40
*d* 60 + 2c like #703 1.65 1.65

No. 704 contains Nos. 704a-704d. Size: 162x133mm.

Nos. 700-704 Overprinted: "XV WORLD JAMBOREE ALBERTA CANADA 1983"

**1983, July 4** **Photo.** *Perf. 13x13½*

*705* Pair 35 35
*a* A112 12c multi 16 16
*b* A113 12c multi 16 16
*706* Pair 1.10 1.10
*a* A112 36c multi 50 50
*b* A113 36c multi 50 50
*707* Pair 1.40 1.40
*a* A112 48c multi 65 65
*b* A113 48c multi 65 65
*708* Pair 1.75 1.75
*a* A112 60c multi 85 85
*b* A113 60c multi 85 85

**Souvenir Sheet**

*709* Sheet of 8 5.00 5.00
*a* 12c + 2c like #705 42 42
*b* 36c + 2c like #706 1.10 1.10
*c* 48c + 2c like #707 1.50 1.50
*d* 60c + 2c like #708 1.90 1.90

Size: 162x132mm.

Nos. 584-587, 596-599, 608-611, 604-607, 624-627, 660, 639 Surcharged in Black or Gold.

*Perf. 13½x13, 14x13½, 14*

**1983, Aug. 12** **Photo.**

*710* A101 18c on 8c #584 40 40
*711* A101 18c on 8c #585 40 40
*712* A101 18c on 8c #586 40 40
*713* A101 18c on 8c #587 40 40
*714* A101 36c on 15c #596 65 65
*715* A101 36c on 15c #597 65 65
*716* A101 36c on 15c #598 65 65
*717* A101 36c on 15c #599 65 65
*718* A101 36c on 30c #608 65 65
*719* A101 36c on 30c #609 65 65
*720* A101 36c on 30c #610 65 65
*721* A101 36c on 30c #611 65 65
*722* A101 48c on 25c #604 1.00 1.00
*723* A101 48c on 25c #605 1.00 1.00
*724* A101 48c on 25c #606 1.00 1.00
*725* A101 48c on 25c #607 1.00 1.00
*726* A101 72c on 70c #624 1.50 1.50
*727* A101 72c on 70c #625 1.50 1.50
*728* A101 72c on 70c #626 1.50 1.50
*729* A101 72c on 70c #627 1.50 1.50
*730* A104 96c on $2 #660 (G) 2.00 2.00
*731* A101a $5.60 on $6 #639 (G) 11.00 11.00
*Nos. 710-731 (22)* 29.80 29.80

A114

A115

**1983, Sept. 9** *Perf. 14*

*732* Pair 15 15
*a* A114 6c Gt. Britain 7 7
*b* A115 6c Cook Islds. Group Federal flag 7 7
*733* Pair 25 25
*a* A114 12c Raratonga ensign 12 12
*b* A115 12c New Zealand 12 12
*734* Pair 30 30
*a* A114 15c Cook Islds. 1973-79 15 15
*b* A115 15c Cook Islds. 1983 15 15
*c* Souvenir sheet of 6 (#732-734) 75 75
*735* Pair 45 45
*a* A114 20c like #732a 20 20
*b* A115 20c like #732b 20 20
*736* Pair 60 60
*a* A114 30c like #733a 30 30
*b* A115 30c like #733b 30 30
*737* Pair 70 70
*a* A114 35c like #734a 35 35
*b* A115 35c like #734b 35 35
*c* Souvenir sheet of 6 (#735-737) 1.75 1.75
*Nos. 732-737 (6)* 2.45 2.45

Nos. 732-737 have different background landscapes; Nos. 735-737 airmail with silver background. Nos. 734c, 737c perf. 13½; multicolored margins show map of Cook Isld. group. Size: 132x120mm.

Nos. 612-615, 640, 678 Surcharged in Black or Gold.

*Perf. 13½x13, 14x13½, 14*

**1983, Aug. 30** **Photo.**

*738* A101 36c on 35c #612 65 65
*739* A101 36c on 35c #613 65 65
*740* A101 36c on 35c #614 65 65
*741* A101 36c on 35c #615 65 65
*742* A108 96c on $2.50 #678 (G) 2.00 2.00
*742A* A108 96c on $2.50 #678A 2.00 2.00
*743* A101a $5.60 on $10 #640 (G) 10.00 10.00
*Nos. 738-743 (7)* 16.60 16.60

Satellite Earth Station — A116

Designs: Various satellites in orbit.

**1983, Oct. 10** **Litho.** *Perf. 13½*

*744* A116 36c multi 50 50
*745* A116 48c multi 65 65
*746* A116 60c multi 75 75
*747* A116 96c multi 1.25 1.25

**Souvenir Sheet**

*748* A116 $2 multi 3.50 3.50

World Communications Year. Multicolored margin shows emblem; black and blue inscription. Size: 89x65mm.

Christmas 1983 — A117

Raphael Paintings: 12c, La Belle Jardiniere. 18c, Madonna and Child with Five Saints. 36c, Madonna and Child with Saint John. 48c, Madonna of the Fish. 60c, Madonna of the Baldacchino.

**1983 Photo. *Perf. 14***

| | | | | |
|---|---|---|---|---|
| *749* | A117 | 12c multi | 15 | 15 |
| *750* | A117 | 18c multi | 22 | 22 |
| *751* | A117 | 36c multi | 45 | 45 |
| *752* | A117 | 48c multi | 55 | 55 |
| *753* | A117 | 60c multi | 75 | 75 |
| | | *Nos. 749-753 (5)* | 2.12 | 2.12 |

**Souvenir Sheets**

***Perf. 13½***

| | | | | |
|---|---|---|---|---|
| *754* | | Sheet of 5 | 3.25 | 3.25 |
| *a* | A117 | 12c + 3c like #749 | 24 | 24 |
| *b* | A117 | 18c + 3c like #750 | 32 | 32 |
| *c* | A117 | 36c + 3c like #751 | 60 | 60 |
| *d* | A117 | 48c + 3c like #752 | 78 | 78 |
| *e* | A117 | 60c + 3c like #753 | 95 | 95 |
| *755* | A117 | 85c + 5c like #749 | 1.35 | 1.35 |
| *756* | A117 | 85c + 5c like #750 | 1.35 | 1.35 |
| *757* | A117 | 85c + 5c like #751 | 1.35 | 1.35 |
| *758* | A117 | 85c + 5c like #752 | 1.35 | 1.35 |
| *759* | A117 | 85c + 5c like #753 | 1.35 | 1.35 |

Nos. 749-753 sheets of 5 + label. No. 754 has multicolored margin showing Raphael self-portrait. Size: 140x103 mm. Nos. 755-759 have multicolored margins showing entire paintings. Size: 66x82 mm. Surtax was for children's charities. Issue dates: Nos. 749-754 Nov. 14; others Dec. 9.

Manned Flight Bicentenary — A118

Various balloons.

**1984, Jan. 16 Photo. *Perf. 13***

| | | | | |
|---|---|---|---|---|
| *760* | A118 | 36c 1st manned flight, 1783 | 50 | 50 |
| *761* | A118 | 48c Ascent of Adorne, Strasbourg, 1784 | 65 | 65 |
| *762* | A118 | 60c 1785 | 75 | 75 |
| *763* | A118 | 72c Man on horse, 1785 | 1.10 | 1.10 |
| *764* | A118 | 96c Godard's aerial acrobatics, 1850 | 1.25 | 1.25 |
| | | *Nos. 760-764 (5)* | 4.25 | 4.25 |

**Souvenir Sheets**

| | | | | |
|---|---|---|---|---|
| *765* | A118 | $2.50 Blanchard & Jefferies, 1785 | 4.00 | 4.00 |
| *766* | | Sheet of 5 | 10.25 | 10.25 |
| *a* | A118 | 36c + 5c like 36c | 1.25 | 1.25 |
| *b* | A118 | 48c + 5c like 48c | 1.55 | 1.55 |
| *c* | A118 | 60c + 5c like 60c | 2.00 | 2.00 |
| *d* | A118 | 72c + 5c like 72c | 2.25 | 2.25 |
| *e* | A118 | 96c + 5c like 96c | 3.00 | 3.00 |

No. 765 contains one stamp (30x48mm, perf. 13½): multicolored margin continues design. Size: 105x85mm. Size of No. 766: 122x132mm.

Save the Whales Campaign A119

**1984, Feb. 10 Photo. *Perf. 13***

| | | | | |
|---|---|---|---|---|
| *767* | A119 | 10c Cuvier's beaked whale | 18 | 18 |
| *768* | A119 | 18c Risso's dolphin | 30 | 30 |
| *769* | A119 | 20c True's beaked whale | 32 | 32 |
| *770* | A119 | 24c Long-finned pilot whale | 40 | 40 |
| *771* | A119 | 30c Narwhal | 50 | 50 |
| *772* | A119 | 36c Beluga whale | 60 | 60 |
| *773* | A119 | 42c Common dolphin | 70 | 70 |
| *774* | A119 | 48c Commerson's dolphin | 75 | 75 |
| *775* | A119 | 60c Bottle-nosed dolphin | 1.00 | 1.00 |
| *776* | A119 | 72c Sowerby's whale | 1.25 | 1.25 |
| *777* | A119 | 96c Common porpoise | 1.50 | 1.50 |
| *778* | A119 | $2 Boutu | 3.25 | 3.25 |
| | | *Nos. 767-778 (12)* | 10.75 | 10.75 |

1984 Summer Olympics A120

Posters of Various Summer Olympics. 72c, 96c, $1.20 airmail.

**1984, Mar. 8 Photo. *Perf. 13½***

| | | | | |
|---|---|---|---|---|
| *779* | A120 | 18c Athens, 1896 | 28 | 28 |
| *780* | A120 | 24c Paris, 1900 | 36 | 36 |
| *781* | A120 | 36c St. Louis, 1904 | 55 | 55 |
| *782* | A120 | 48c London, 1948 | 72 | 72 |
| *783* | A120 | 60c Tokyo, 1964 | 90 | 90 |
| *784* | A120 | 72c Berlin, 1936 | 1.10 | 1.10 |
| *785* | A120 | 96c Rome, 1960 | 1.50 | 1.50 |
| *786* | A120 | $1.20 Los Angeles, 1932 | 1.80 | 1.80 |
| | | *Nos. 779-786 (8)* | 7.21 | 7.21 |

Coral — A121

**1984 *Perf. 13½x13***

| | | | | |
|---|---|---|---|---|
| *787* | A121 | 1c Siphonogorgia | 5 | 5 |
| *788* | A121 | 2c Millepora alcicornis | 5 | 5 |
| *789* | A121 | 3c Distichopora violacea | 5 | 5 |
| *790* | A121 | 5c Ptilosarcus gurneyi | 8 | 8 |
| *791* | A121 | 10c Lobophyllia bemprichii | 15 | 15 |
| *792* | A121 | 12c Sarcophyton digitatum | 18 | 18 |
| *793* | A121 | 14c Pavona praetorta | 22 | 22 |
| *794* | A121 | 18c Junceela gemmacea | 28 | 28 |
| *795* | A121 | 20c Stylaster | 30 | 30 |
| *796* | A121 | 24c Stylophora pistillata | 36 | 36 |
| *797* | A121 | 30c Palauastrea ramosa | 45 | 45 |
| *798* | A121 | 36c Melithaea albitincta | 55 | 55 |
| *799* | A121 | 40c Stylaster echinatus | 60 | 60 |
| *800* | A121 | 42c Fungia fungites | 65 | 65 |
| *801* | A121 | 48c Gonipora | 72 | 72 |
| *802* | A121 | 50c Melithaea squamata | 75 | 75 |
| *803* | A121 | 52c Bellonella indica | 78 | 78 |
| *804* | A121 | 55c Plerogyra sinuosa | 82 | 82 |
| *805* | A121 | 60c Tubastraea | 90 | 90 |
| *806* | A121 | 70c Heliofungia actinformis | 1.05 | 1.05 |
| *807* | A121 | 85c Caulastraea echinulata | 1.30 | 1.30 |
| *808* | A121 | 96c Porites andrewsi | 1.45 | 1.45 |
| *809* | A121 | $1.10 Pectinia alcicornis | 1.65 | 1.65 |
| *810* | A121 | $1.20 Dendrophyllia gracilis | 1.80 | 1.80 |

***Perf. 14x13½***

**Size: 59½x38½mm.**

| | | | | |
|---|---|---|---|---|
| *811* | A121 | $3.60 Gonipora | 4.50 | 4.50 |
| *812* | A121 | $4.20 Heliofungia actiniformis | 5.00 | 5.00 |
| *813* | A121 | $5 Stylophora pistillata | 6.00 | 6.00 |
| *814* | A121 | $7.20 Stylaster echinatus | 8.00 | 8.00 |
| *815* | A121 | $9.60 Melithaea albitincta | 10.00 | 10.00 |
| | | *Nos. 787-815 (29)* | 48.69 | 48.69 |

Issue dates: Nos. 787-801, Mar. 23. Nos. 802-810, May 15. Nos. 811-813, June 28. No. 814, July 20. No. 815, Aug. 10.

### Nos. 784-786 Overprinted With Winners

**1984, Aug. 24 Photo. *Perf. 13½***

| | | | | |
|---|---|---|---|---|
| *826* | A120 | 72c Team Dressage, Germany | 75 | 75 |
| *827* | A120 | 96c Daley Thompson, Great Britain | 1.00 | 1.00 |
| *828* | A120 | $1.20 Carl Lewis, USA | 1.25 | 1.25 |

1984 Summer Olympics. Nos. 826-828 airmail.

AUSIPEX '84 — A123

**1984, Sept. 20**

| | | | | |
|---|---|---|---|---|
| *829* | A123 | 36c Captain Cook's cottage | 40 | 40 |
| *830* | A123 | 48c The Endeavour | 50 | 50 |
| *831* | A123 | 60c Cook's landing | 60 | 60 |
| *832* | A123 | $2 Portrait, by John Webber | 2.00 | 2.00 |
| *a* | | Souvenir sheet of 4, Nos. 829-832, 90c each | 3.75 | 3.75 |
| *b* | | Sheet of 4, STAMPEX '86 emblem | 2.75 | 2.75 |

No. 832a has multicolored margin showing ships, gold emblem; black marginal inscription. Size: 140x100mm.

No. 832b issued Aug. 4, 1986, for STAMPEX '86, Adelaide, Aug. 4-10; margin ovptd. with exhibition emblem, stamp picturing James Cook ovptd. with gold circle and black "Stampex 86 / Adelaide."

### No. 659 Ovptd. "Royal Birth/Prince Henry/15 Sept. 1984" and Surcharged in Silver.

### Nos. 677-677A, 678-678A Ovptd.: "Commemorating -/15 Sept. 1984" or "Birth H.R.H./Prince Henry" and Surcharged in Gold.

**1984, Oct. 15 Photo. *Perf. 14***

| | | | | |
|---|---|---|---|---|
| *833* | A108 | $1.25 No. 677 | 1.00 | 1.00 |
| *834* | A108 | $1.25 No. 677A | 1.00 | 1.00 |
| *835* | A108 | $2.50 No. 678 | 2.25 | 2.25 |
| *836* | A108 | $2.50 No. 678A | 2.25 | 2.25 |
| *837* | A104 | $3 on $1 No. 659 | 2.75 | 2.75 |
| | | *Nos. 833-837 (5)* | 9.25 | 9.25 |

Nos. 833-836 printed in sheets of 4, two each of same denomination. No. 837 printed in sheets of 4.

Christmas 1984 — A124

Paintings: 36c, Virgin on Throne with Child, by Giovanni Bellini (c. 1430-1516). 48c, Virgin and Child, 15th century, artist unknown. 60c, Virgin and Child with Saints, by Alvise Vivarini (c. 1446-1505). 96c, Virgin and Child with Angels, by Hans Memling (c. 1435-1494). $1.20, Adoration of the Magi, by Giovanni Tiepolo (1696-1770).

**1984, Nov. 21**

| | | | | |
|---|---|---|---|---|
| *838* | A124 | 36c multi | 48 | 48 |
| *839* | A124 | 48c multi | 65 | 65 |
| *840* | A124 | 60c multi | 80 | 80 |
| *841* | A124 | 96c multi | 1.25 | 1.25 |
| *842* | A124 | $1.20 multi | 1.50 | 1.50 |
| | | *Nos. 838-842 (5)* | 4.68 | 4.68 |

**Souvenir Sheets**

***Perf. 13½***

| | | | | |
|---|---|---|---|---|
| *843* | | Sheet of 5 | 4.00 | 4.00 |
| *a* | A124 | 36c +5c like #838 | 45 | 45 |
| *b* | A124 | 48c +5c like #839 | 55 | 55 |
| *c* | A124 | 60c +5c like #840 | 65 | 65 |
| *d* | A124 | 96c +5c like #841 | 1.10 | 1.10 |
| *e* | A124 | $1.20 +5c like #842 | 1.25 | 1.25 |

**1984, Dec. 10**

| | | | | |
|---|---|---|---|---|
| *844* | A124 | 95c + 5c like #838 | 1.25 | 1.25 |
| *845* | A124 | 95c + 5c like #839 | 1.25 | 1.25 |
| *846* | A124 | 95c + 5c like #840 | 1.25 | 1.25 |
| *847* | A124 | 95c + 5c like #841 | 1.25 | 1.25 |
| *848* | A124 | 95c + 5c like #842 | 1.25 | 1.25 |

No. 843 has multicolored decorative margin. Size: 120x115mm. Surtax for children's organizations.

Nos. 844-848 have multicolored margins continuing each portrait. Sizes: 63x77mm. Surtax for youth education.

Audubon Birth Bicentenary A125

Illustrations of North American bird species by artist, naturalist John J. Audubon.

**1985, Apr. 23 *Perf. 13x13½***

| | | | | |
|---|---|---|---|---|
| *849* | A125 | 30c Downy woodpecker | 28 | 28 |
| *850* | A125 | 55c Black-throated blue warbler | 52 | 52 |
| *851* | A125 | 65c Yellow-throated warbler | 60 | 60 |
| *852* | A125 | 75c Chestnut-sided warbler | 70 | 70 |
| *853* | A125 | 95c Dickcissel | 90 | 90 |
| *854* | A125 | $1.15 White-crowned sparrow | 1.00 | 1.00 |
| | | *Nos. 849-854 (6)* | 4.00 | 4.00 |

**Souvenir Sheets**

| | | | | |
|---|---|---|---|---|
| *855* | A125 | $1.30 Red-cockaded woodpecker | 1.25 | 1.25 |
| *856* | A125 | $2.80 Seaside sparrow | 2.50 | 2.50 |
| *857* | A125 | $5.30 Zenaida dove | 5.00 | 5.00 |

Nos. 855-857 have multicolored margins continuing the illustrations and picturing a portrait of Audubon. Size: 77x75mm.

Locomotives — A126

**1985, May 14 Litho. *Perf. 14x13½***

| | | | | |
|---|---|---|---|---|
| *858* | A126 | 20c Kingston Flyer, New Zealand | 20 | 20 |
| *859* | A126 | 55c Class 640, Italy | 52 | 52 |
| *860* | A126 | 65c Gotthard, Switzerland | 60 | 60 |
| *861* | A126 | 75c Union Pacific 6900, USA | 70 | 70 |
| *862* | A126 | 95c Super Continental, Canada | 90 | 90 |
| *863* | A126 | $1.15 TGV, France | 1.00 | 1.00 |
| *864* | A126 | $2.20 Flying Scotsman, U.K. | 2.00 | 2.00 |
| *865* | A126 | $3.40 Orient Express, Europe | 3.00 | 3.00 |
| | | *Nos. 858-865 (8)* | 8.92 | 8.92 |

Intl. Youth Year — A127

Paintings: 55c, Helena Fourment, by Rubens. 65c, Vigee-Lebrun and Daughter, by Elizabeth Vigee-Lebrun (1755-1842). 75c, On the Terrace, by Renoir. $1.30, Young Mother Sewing, by Mary Cassatt (1845-1926).

**1985, June 6 Photo. *Perf. 13x13½***

| | | | | |
|---|---|---|---|---|
| *866* | A127 | 55c multi | 50 | 50 |
| *867* | A127 | 65c multi | 60 | 60 |
| *868* | A127 | 75c multi | 70 | 70 |
| *869* | A127 | $1.30 multi | 1.15 | 1.15 |

**Souvenir Sheet**

| | | | |
|---|---|---|---|
| *870* | Sheet of 4 | 3.50 | 3.50 |
| *a* | A127 55c + 10c like #866 | 60 | 60 |
| *b* | A127 65c + 10c like #867 | 70 | 70 |
| *c* | A127 75c + 10c like #868 | 80 | 80 |
| *d* | A127 $1.30 + 10c like #869 | 1.25 | 1.25 |

No. 870 has multicolored decorative margin picturing the IYY emblem. Size: 105x107mm. Surtax for youth organizations.

Queen Mother, 85th Birthday — A128

Portraits: 65c, Lady Elizabeth, 1908, by Mable Hankey. 75c, Duchess of York, 1923, by Savely Sorine. $1.15, Duchess of York, 1925, by Philip De Laslo. $2.80, $5.30, Queen Elizabeth, 1938, by Sir Gerald Kelly.

**1985, June 28**

| | | | | |
|---|---|---|---|---|
| *871* | A128 | 65c multi | 45 | 45 |
| *872* | A128 | 75c multi | 50 | 50 |
| *873* | A128 | $1.15 multi | 80 | 80 |
| *874* | A128 | $2.80 multi | 1.75 | 1.75 |
| *874A* | | Sheet of 4 | 2.25 | 2.25 |
| *b.-e* | A128 | 55c, like #871-874 | 55 | 55 |

**Souvenir Sheet**

| | | | | |
|---|---|---|---|---|
| *875* | A128 | $5.30 multi | 4.75 | 4.75 |

Nos. 871-874 printed in sheets of four. No. 875 has multicolored inscribed margin continuing the portrait. Size: 69x82mm.

No. 874A issued Aug. 4, 1986, for 86th birthday; has multicolored decorative margin. Size: 91x116mm.

Self-government, 20th Anniv. — A129

Portraits of prime ministers.

**1985, July 29**

| | | | | |
|---|---|---|---|---|
| *876* | A129 | 30c Albert Henry, 1965-78 | 32 | 32 |
| *877* | A129 | 50c Sir Thomas Davis, 1978-83 | 55 | 55 |
| *878* | A129 | 65c Geoffrey Henry, 1983 | 70 | 70 |

**Souvenir Sheet**

| | | | |
|---|---|---|---|
| *879* | Sheet of 3 | 1.75 | 1.75 |
| *a* | A129 55c like #876 | 58 | 58 |
| *b* | A129 55c like #877 | 58 | 58 |
| *c* | A129 55c like #878 | 58 | 58 |

No. 879 has multicolored margin inscribed with historical data and picturing the flags of the U.K., New Zealand and Cook Islands. Size: 135x70mm.

South Pacific Mini Games, Rarotonga, July 31-Aug. 10 A130

**1985, July 29 *Perf. 14***

| | | | | |
|---|---|---|---|---|
| *880* | A130 | 55c Golf | 65 | 65 |
| *881* | A130 | 65c Rugby | 70 | 70 |
| *882* | A130 | 75c Tennis | 80 | 80 |

**Souvenir Sheet**

| | | | |
|---|---|---|---|
| *883* | Sheet of 3 | 2.50 | 2.50 |
| *a* | A130 55c + 10c like #880 | 70 | 70 |
| *b* | A130 65c + 10c like #881 | 80 | 80 |
| *c* | A130 75c + 10c like #882 | 90 | 90 |

No. 883 has multicolored decorative margin picturing the national flag and Games emblem. Size: 127x70mm. Surtax for the benefit of the Mini Games.

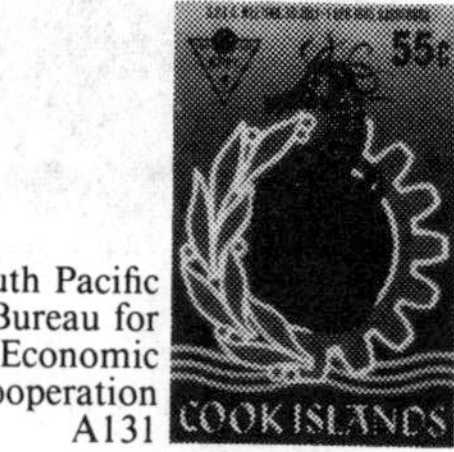

South Pacific Bureau for Economic Cooperation A131

Seahorse & conf. emblems: 65c, South Pacific Forum. 75c, Pacific Islands Conf.

**1985, July 29 *Perf. 14***

| | | | | |
|---|---|---|---|---|
| *884* | A131 | 55c blk, scar & gold | 60 | 60 |
| *885* | A131 | 65c blk, vio & gold | 70 | 70 |
| *886* | A131 | 75c blk, brt grn & gold | 80 | 80 |

**Souvenir Sheet**

| | | | |
|---|---|---|---|
| *887* | Sheet of 3 | 1.75 | 1.75 |
| *a* | A131 50c like #884 | 55 | 55 |
| *b* | A131 50c like #885 | 55 | 55 |
| *c* | A131 50c like #886 | 55 | 55 |

Pacific islands conferences, Rarotonga, July 30-Aug. 10. No. 887 has gold, blue and black margin picturing an aerial view of Rarotonga. Size: 127x81mm.

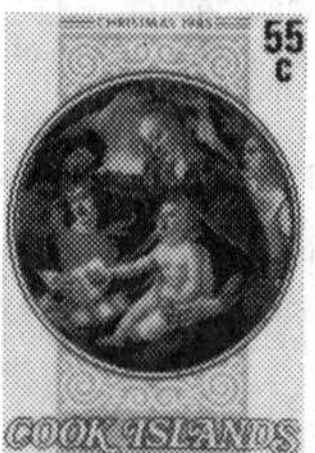

Virgin and Child Paintings by Botticelli — A132

**1985, Nov. 18**

| | | | | |
|---|---|---|---|---|
| *888* | A132 | 55c Madonna of the Magnificent | 65 | 65 |
| *889* | A132 | 65c Madonna with Pomegranate | 78 | 78 |
| *890* | A132 | 75c Madonna with Child & Six Angels | 90 | 90 |
| *891* | A132 | 95c Madonna & Child with St. John | 1.15 | 1.15 |

**Souvenir Sheets**

***Perf. 13½***

| | | | |
|---|---|---|---|
| *892* | Sheet of 4 | 2.50 | 2.50 |
| *a* | A132 50c like #888 | 60 | 60 |
| *b* | A132 50c like #888 | 60 | 60 |
| *c* | A132 50c like #890 | 60 | 60 |
| *d* | A132 50c like #891 | 60 | 60 |

**1985, Dec. 9 *Imperf.***

| | | | | |
|---|---|---|---|---|
| *893* | A132 | $1.20 like #888 | 1.50 | 1.50 |
| *894* | A132 | $1.45 like #889 | 1.75 | 1.75 |
| *895* | A132 | $2.20 like #890 | 2.75 | 2.75 |
| *896* | A132 | $2.75 like #891 | 3.25 | 3.25 |

Christmas 1985. No. 892 has multicolored decorative margin. Size: 90x104mm. Nos. 893-896 have multicolored margins framing details of each painting. Sizes: 50x51mm.

Halley's Comet A133

Elizabeth II, 60th Birthday A134

Paintings: 55c, No. 902a, The Eve of the Deluge, by John Martin (1789-1854). 65c, No. 902b, Lot and His Daughters, by Lucas van Leyden (1494-1533). 75c, No. 902c, Auspicious Comet, 1587, anonymous. $1.25, No. 902d, Events Following Charles I, by Herman Saftleven (1609-1658). $2, No. 902e, Ossian Receiving Napoleonic Officers, by Anne Louis Girodet-Trioson (1764-1824). $4, Halley's Comet over the Thames, 1759, by Samuel Scott (1702-1772).

**1986, Mar. 13 Photo. *Perf. 14***

| | | | | |
|---|---|---|---|---|
| *897* | A133 | 55c multi | 52 | 52 |
| *898* | A133 | 65c multi | 62 | 62 |
| *899* | A133 | 75c multi | 72 | 72 |
| *900* | A133 | $1.25 multi | 1.25 | 1.25 |
| *901* | A133 | $2 multi | 2.00 | 2.00 |
| | | *Nos. 897-901 (5)* | 5.11 | 5.11 |

**Souvenir Sheets**

***Perf. 13½***

| | | | |
|---|---|---|---|
| *902* | Sheet of 5 + label | 3.50 | 3.50 |
| *a.-e* | A133 70c, each single | 68 | 68 |
| *903* | A133 $4 multi | 3.75 | 3.75 |

No. 902 has multicolored decorative margin, label picturing Halley. Size: 130x101mm. No. 903 has multicolored margin continuing the design. Size: 84x64mm.

**1986, Apr. 21 *Perf. 13x13½***

Various portraits.

| | | | | |
|---|---|---|---|---|
| *904* | A134 | 95c multi | 1.15 | 1.15 |
| *905* | A134 | $1.25 multi | 1.50 | 1.50 |
| *906* | A134 | $1.50 multi | 1.75 | 1.75 |

**Souvenir Sheets**

| | | | | |
|---|---|---|---|---|
| *907* | A134 | $1.10 like #904 | 1.25 | 1.25 |
| *908* | A134 | $1.95 like #905 | 2.25 | 2.25 |
| *909* | A134 | $2.45 like #906 | 3.00 | 3.00 |

Nos. 907-909 have multicolored margins continuing the designs. Sizes: 44x75mm.

AMERIPEX '86 — A135

Designs: $1, US No. 1, The Resolution, Rarotonga. $1.50, Downtown Chicago. $2, No. 398, Benjamin Franklin, The Resolution.

**1986, May 21 Photo. *Perf. 14***

| | | | | |
|---|---|---|---|---|
| *910* | A135 | $1 multi | 1.20 | 1.20 |
| *911* | A135 | $1.50 multi | 1.75 | 1.75 |
| *912* | A135 | $2 multi | 2.25 | 2.25 |

Statue of Liberty, Cent. — A136

Wedding of Prince Andrew and Sarah Ferguson — A137

**1986, July 4**

| | | | | |
|---|---|---|---|---|
| *913* | A136 | $1 Head | 1.10 | 1.10 |
| *914* | A136 | $1.25 Torch | 1.40 | 1.40 |
| *915* | A136 | $2.75 Liberty Is. | 3.00 | 3.00 |

**1986, July 23**

| | | | | |
|---|---|---|---|---|
| *916* | A137 | $1 Sarah Ferguson | 1.10 | 1.10 |
| *917* | A137 | $2 Prince Andrew | 2.20 | 2.20 |

**Size: 60x33½mm.**

***Perf. 13½x13***

| | | | | |
|---|---|---|---|---|
| *918* | A137 | $3 Couple | 3.30 | 3.30 |

Nos. 916-918 each printed in sheets of 4.

Christmas A138

Paintings by Rubens: 55c, No. 922a, The Holy Family. $1.30, $6.40, No. 922b, Virgin with Garland. $2.75, No. 922c, Adoration of Magi.

**1986, Nov. 17 Litho. *Perf. 13½***

| | | | | |
|---|---|---|---|---|
| *919* | A138 | 55c multi | 60 | 60 |
| *920* | A138 | $1.30 multi | 1.40 | 1.40 |
| *921* | A138 | $2.75 multi | 2.90 | 2.90 |

**Souvenir Sheets**

| | | | |
|---|---|---|---|
| *922* | Sheet of 3 | 7.50 | 7.50 |
| *a.-c* | A138 $2.40, any single | 2.50 | 2.50 |
| *923* | A138 $6.40 multi | 6.75 | 6.75 |

No. 922 contains 3 stamps (size: 38½x49mm) picturing expanded designs; bright pink, gold and sage green margin inscribed with names of paintings. No. 923 has multicolored inscribed margin continuing the painting. Size: 81x71mm.

## Stamps of 1980-86 Surcharged in Black, Black and Gold or Gold

***Perfs. as before***

**1987, Feb. 10-12 Litho.**

| | | | | |
|---|---|---|---|---|
| *924* | A121 | 5c on 1c #787 | 6 | 6 |
| *925* | A121 | 5c on 2c #788 | 6 | 6 |
| *926* | A121 | 5c on 3c #789 | 6 | 6 |
| *927* | A121 | 5c on 12c #792 | 6 | 6 |
| *928* | A121 | 5c on 14c #793 | 6 | 6 |
| *929* | A101 | 10c on 15c #596 | 12 | 12 |
| *930* | A101 | 10c on 15c #597 | 12 | 12 |
| *931* | A101 | 10c on 15c #598 | 12 | 12 |
| *932* | A101 | 10c on 15c #599 | 12 | 12 |
| *933* | A101 | 10c on 15c #604 | 12 | 12 |
| *934* | A101 | 10c on 25c #605 | 12 | 12 |
| *935* | A101 | 10c on 25c #606 | 12 | 12 |
| *936* | A101 | 10c on 25c #607 | 12 | 12 |
| *937* | A121 | 18c on 24c #796 | 20 | 20 |
| *938* | A101 | 18c on 12c #592 | 20 | 20 |
| *939* | A101 | 18c on 12c #593 | 20 | 20 |
| *940* | A101 | 18c on 12c #594 | 20 | 20 |
| *941* | A101 | 18c on 12c #595 | 20 | 20 |
| *942* | A101 | 18c on 20c #600 | 20 | 20 |
| *943* | A101 | 18c on 20c #601 | 20 | 20 |
| *944* | A101 | 18c on 20c #602 | 20 | 20 |
| *945* | A101 | 18c on 20c #603 | 20 | 20 |
| *946* | A121 | 55c on 52c #803 | 65 | 65 |
| *947* | A101 | 55c on 35c #612 | 65 | 65 |
| *948* | A101 | 55c on 35c #613 | 65 | 65 |
| *949* | A101 | 55c on 35c #614 | 65 | 65 |
| *950* | A101 | 55c on 35c #615 | 65 | 65 |
| *951* | A121 | 65c on 42c #800 | 75 | 75 |
| *952* | A101 | 65c on 50c #616 | 75 | 75 |
| *953* | A101 | 65c on 50c #617 | 75 | 75 |
| *954* | A101 | 65c on 50c #618 | 75 | 75 |
| *955* | A101 | 65c on 50c #619 | 75 | 75 |
| *956* | A101 | 65c on 60c #620 | 75 | 75 |
| *957* | A101 | 65c on 60c #621 | 75 | 75 |
| *958* | A101 | 65c on 60c #622 | 75 | 75 |
| *959* | A101 | 65c on 60c #623 | 75 | 75 |
| *960* | A121 | 75c on 48c #801 | 90 | 90 |
| *961* | A101 | 75c on 70c #624 | 90 | 90 |
| *962* | A101 | 75c on 70c #625 | 90 | 90 |
| *963* | A101 | 75c on 70c #626 | 90 | 90 |
| *964* | A101 | 75c on 70c #627 | 90 | 90 |
| *965* | A121 | 95c on 96c #808 | 1.10 | 1.10 |
| *966* | A121 | 95c on $1.10 #809 | 1.10 | 1.10 |
| *967* | A121 | 95c on $1.20 #810 | 1.10 | 1.10 |
| *968* | A123 | $1.30 on 36c #829 (B&G) | 1.50 | 1.50 |
| *969* | A123 | $1.30 on 48c #830 (B&G) | 1.50 | 1.50 |

*970* A123 $1.30 on 60c #831 (B&G) 1.50 1.50
*971* A123 $1.30 on $2 #832 (G) 1.50 1.50
*972* A134 $2.80 on 95c #904 (G) 3.25 3.25
*973* A134 $2.80 on $1.25 #905 (G) 3.25 3.25
*974* A134 $2.80 on $1.50 #906 (G) 3.25 3.25
*975* A137 $2.80 on $1 #916 (B&G) 3.25 3.25
*976* A137 $2.80 on $2 #917 (B&G) 3.25 3.25
*977* A137 $2.80 on $3 #918 (B&G) 3.25 3.25
*978* A101a $6.40 on $4 #638 7.00 7.00
*979* A101a $7.20 on $6 #639 8.00 8.00
*980* A104 $9.40 on $1 #659 (G) 11.00 11.00
*981* A104 $9.40 on $2 #660 (G) 11.00 11.00
*982* A108 $9.40 on $2.50 #678 (G) 11.00 11.00
*983* A108 $9.40 on $2.50 #678A (G) 11.00 11.00
*Nos. 924-983 (60)* 105.36 105.36

Stamps of 1980-82 Surcharged in Black or Gold

***Perfs. as before***

**1987, June 17** **Photo.**
*984* A101a $2.80 on $2 #636 3.50 3.50
*985* A101a $5 on $3 #637 6.15 6.15
*986* A101a $9.40 on $10 #640 11.50 11.50
*987* A104 $9.40 on $1 #679 (G) 11.50 11.50
*988* A104 $9.40 on $1 #679A (G) 11.50 11.50
*989* A104 $9.40 on $2 #680 (G) 11.50 11.50
*a* Souv. sheet of 2 (on #680b) 22.50 22.50
*990* A104 $9.40 on $2 #680A (G) 11.50 11.50
*Nos. 984-990 (7)* 67.15 67.15

No. 989a contains 2 stamps (Nos. 679-680), each surcharged $9.20.

Nos. 399 and 638 Ovptd. "ROYAL / WEDDING / FORTIETH / ANNIVERSARY" in Black on Gold Bar

**1987, Nov. 20** **Photo.** ***Perf. 14x13½***
*991* A64 $4 on #399 4.90 4.90
*992* A101a $4 on #638 4.90 4.90

Christmas — A139

The Holy Family, religious paintings by Rembrandt in European museums: $1.25, No. 996a, The Louvre, Paris. $1.50, No. 996b, $6, The Holy Family with Angels, The Hermitage, Leningrad. $1.95, No. 996c, The Alte Pinakothek, Munich.

**1987, Dec. 7** **Photo.** ***Perf. 13½***
*993* A139 $1.25 multi 1.55 1.55
*994* A139 $1.50 multi 1.85 1.85
*995* A139 $1.95 multi 2.40 2.40

**Souvenir Sheets**

*996* Sheet of 3 4.40 4.40
*a.-c.* A139 $1.15 any single 1.45 1.45

***Perf. 13x13½***

*997* A139 $6 multi 7.75 7.75

No. 996 has multicolored decorative margin; size of Nos. 996a-996c: 49½x38½mm. No. 997 contains 1 stamp (size: 39½x31½mm); multicolored inscribed margin continues the painting. Size: 100x140mm (No. 996), 70x80mm (No. 997).

1988 Summer Olympics, Seoul A140

Designs: a. Cook Islands commemorative silver coin (obverse and reverse) issued on Aug. 20, 1987, for the '88 Summer Games. b. Seoul Olympic Park, torch and emblem. c. Steffi Graf, women's tennis champion, and '88 gold medal.

**1988, Apr. 26** **Photo.** ***Perf. 13½x14***
*998* Strip of 3 5.85 5.85
*a.-c.* A140 $1.50 multi 1.95 1.95

**Souvenir Sheet**

***Perf. 13½***

*999* A140 $10 multi 13.00 13.00

Participation of national athletes in the Olympics for the first time, introduction of tennis as an Olympic gold-medal event.

No. 999 has inscribed silver margin; contains one stamp (size: 114x47mm) combining the designs of Nos. 998a-998c. Size: 132x82mm.

Nos. 998-999 Ovptd. for Olympic Winners

*a.* "MILOSLAV MECIR / CZECHOSLOVAKIA / GOLD MEDAL WINNER / MEN'S TENNIS"

*b.* "TIM MAYOTTE / UNITED STATES / GABRIELA SABATINI / ARGENTINA / SILVER MEDAL WINNERS"

*c.* "GOLD MEDAL WINNER / STEFFI GRAF / WEST GERMANY"

*d.* "GOLD MEDAL WINNER / SEOUL OLYMPIC GAMES / STEFFI GRAF - WEST GERMANY"

**1988, Oct. 12** **Photo.** ***Perf. 13½x14***
*1000* Strip of 3 5.85 5.85
*a.* A140(a) $1.50 on #998a 1.95 1.95
*b.* A140(b) $1.50 on #998b 1.95 1.95
*c.* A140(c) $1.50 on #998c 1.95 1.95

**Souvenir Sheet**

***Perf. 13½***

*1001* A140(d) $10 on No. 999 13.00 13.00

Margin of No. 1001 ovptd.: "STEFFI GRAF, WINNER OF AUSTRALIAN OPEN 24 JULY 1988, FRENCH OPEN / 4 JUNE 1988, WIMBLEDON 2 JULY 1988, U.S. OPEN 10 SEPTEMBER 1988. / FIRST GRAND SLAM WINNER IN 18 YEARS. GOLD MEDAL WINNER SEOUL / OLYMPICS 1 OCTOBER 1988."

Christmas A141

Paintings by Albrecht Durer: 70c, *Virgin and Child.* 85c, *Virgin and Child,* diff. 95c, *Virgin and Child,* diff. $1.25, *Virgin and Child,* diff. $6.40, *The Nativity.*

**1988, Nov. 11** ***Perf. 13½***
*1002* A141 70c multi 90 90
*1003* A141 85c multi 1.10 1.10
*1004* A141 95c multi 1.20 1.20
*1005* A141 $1.25 multi 1.60 1.60

**Souvenir Sheet**

*1006* A141 $6.40 multi 8.25 8.25

No. 1006 contains one stamp (size: 45x60mm); multicolored inscribed margin continues the painting. Size: 80x100mm.

## SEMI-POSTAL STAMPS

**Catalogue values for unused stamps in this section, from this point to the end of the section, are for Never Hinged items.**

Nos. 203-204, 223, 210, 213, 215-216 Surcharged

HURRICANE
RELIEF
PLUS 2c

***Perf. 14x13½, 13½***

**1968, Feb. 12** **Photo.**
*B1* A34 3c + 1c multi 7 7
*B2* A34 4c + 1c multi 8 8
*B3* A37 5c + 2c multi 10 10
*B4* A34 10c + 2c multi 22 22
*B5* A34 25c + 5c multi 40 40
*B6* A34 50c + 10c multi 90 90
*B7* A35 $1 + 10c multi 1.75 1.75
*Nos. B1-B7 (7)* 3.52 3.52

Surtax for the victims of hurricane of Dec. 15-18, 1967. The surch. on No. B3 is printed on a silver rectangle. The surch. on No. B7 is in smaller type with serifs, measuring 7½mm in depth.

Nos. 210, 213-214 Surcharged in Ultramarine

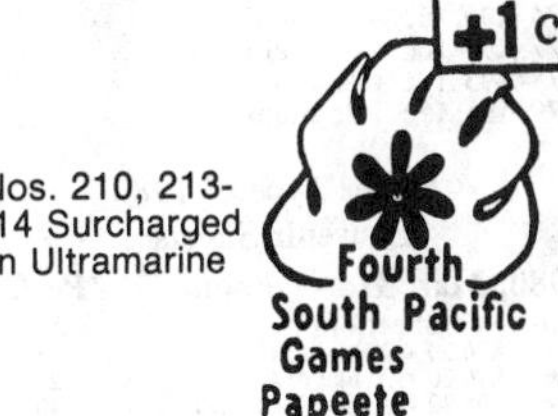


**1971, Sept. 8** **Photo.** ***Perf. 14x13½***
*B8* A34 10c + 1c multi 25 25
*B9* A34 10c + 3c multi 25 25
*B10* A34 25c + 1c multi 65 65
*B11* A34 25c + 3c multi 65 65
*B12* A34 30c + 1c multi 75 75
*B13* A34 30c + 3c multi 75 75
*Nos. B8-B13 (6)* 3.30 3.30

4th South Pacific Games, Papeete, French Polynesia, Sept. 8-19.

Christmas Type of Regular Issue

Design: 50c+5c, Holy Family in a Garland of Flowers, by Jan Brueghel and Pieter van Avont.

**Souvenir Sheet**

**1971, Nov. 30** **Photo.** ***Perf. 13½***
*B14* A50 50c + 5c gold & multi 1.75 1.75

Christmas. No. B14 contains one stamp (size 45x40mm). Flower design of painting extends into sheet margin, which also contains head of Elizabeth II and gold inscription. Size: 91x98mm.

Nos. 316-318, 211, 213 and 215 Surcharged in Red or Black

HURRICANE RELIEF PLUS 2c — a
Hurricane Relief Plus 5c — b

**1972, Mar. 30** **Photo.** ***Perf. 13½***
*B15* A46(a) 5c + 2c multi (R) 10 10
*B16* A46(a) 10c + 2c multi (R) 20 20
*B17* A34(b) 15c + 5c multi 35 35
*B18* A34(b) 25c + 5c multi 65 65
*B19* A46(a) 30c + 5c multi (R) 75 75
*B20* A34(b) 50c + 10c multi 1.40 1.40
*Nos. B15-B20 (6)* 3.45 3.45

Surtax was for victims of hurricane of March 22-26.

Nos. 319-326a with Surcharge Similar to Type "a"

**1972, May 24** **Photo.** ***Perf. 13½***
*B21* A51 5c + 2c multi 10 10
*B22* A51 5c + 2c multi 10 10
*B23* A51 10c + 2c multi 20 20
*B24* A51 10c + 2c multi 20 20
*B25* A51 25c + 2c multi 50 50
*B26* A51 25c + 2c multi 50 50
*B27* A51 30c + 2c multi 75 75
*B28* A51 30c + 2c multi 75 75
*a.* Souvenir sheet of 8 3.50 3.50
*Nos. B21-B28 (8)* 3.10 3.10

Surtax for victims of hurricane of Mar. 22-26. Stamps of No. B28a each surcharged 3c.

Olympic Type of Regular Issue

Design: 50c+5c, Pierre de Coubertin and Olympic rings.

**Souvenir Sheet**

**1972, June 26**
*B29* A52 50c + 5c multi 3.25 3.25

20th Olympic Games, Munich, Aug. 26-Sept. 10. No. B29 contains one stamp. Multicolored margin with Discobolus, New Zealand flag and list of previous Olympic Games. Size: 87x78mm.

Christmas Type of Regular Issue

Design: 50c+5c, Nativity, by Correggio.

**Souvenir Sheet**

**1972, Oct. 11** **Photo.** ***Perf. 13½***
*B30* A53 50c + 5c multi 2.25 2.00

Christmas 1972. No. B30 contains one stamp (30x40mm.). Design of painting continued into margin. Multicolored border with cherubs and flowers. Size: 100x82mm.

Easter Type of Regular Issue

Designs: No. B31, Like No. 346. No. B32, Like No. 347. No. B33, Like No. 348.

**Souvenir Sheets**

**1973, Apr. 30** **Photo.** ***Perf. 13½x14***
*B31* A56 50c + 5c multi 1.10 1.10
*B32* A56 50c + 5c multi 1.10 1.10
*B33* A56 50c + 5c multi 1.10 1.10

The sheets show paintings from which designs of stamps were taken. Surtax was for school children. Size: 67x87 mm.

Christmas Type of Regular Issue

Designs from 15th Century Prayer Book: No. B34, Like No. 364. No. B35, Like No. 365. No. B36, Like No. 366. No. B37, Like No. 367. No. B38, Like No. 368.

**Souvenir Sheets**

**1973, Dec. 3** **Photo.** ***Perf. 13x13½***
*B34* A59 50c + 5c multi 75 75
*B35* A59 50c + 5c multi 75 75
*B36* A59 50c + 5c multi 75 75
*B37* A59 50c + 5c multi 75 75
*B38* A59 50c + 5c multi 75 75
*Nos. B34-B38 (5)* 3.75 3.75

Each sheet shows the illuminated page from which the designs were taken. Surtax was for school children. Size: 50x70mm.

Easter Type of 1973 Dated "1974"

Paintings: No. B39, Like No. 378. No. B40, Like No. 379. No. B41, Like No. 380.

**Souvenir Sheets**

**1974, Apr. 22** ***Perf. 13½x14***
*B39* A56 50c + 5c multi 1.00 1.00
*B40* A56 50c + 5c multi 1.00 1.00
*B41* A56 50c + 5c multi 1.00 1.00

The sheets show paintings from which designs of stamps were chosen. Size: 59x87mm.

Christmas Type of 1974

Paintings: No. B42, Like No. 412. No. B43, Like No. 413. No. B44, Like No. 414. No. B45, Like No. 415. No. B46, Like No. 416.

**Souvenir Sheets**

**1974 Photo. *Perf. 13½x13***
*B42* A68 50c + 5c multi 75 75
*B43* A68 50c + 5c multi 75 75
*B44* A68 50c + 5c multi 75 75
*B45* A68 50c + 5c multi 75 75
*B46* A68 50c + 5c multi 75 75
*Nos. B42-B46 (5)* 3.75 3.75

The sheets show paintings from which designs of stamps were chosen. Size: 53x68mm.

### Christmas Type of 1975

Designs: No. B47, Like No. 437. No. B48, Like No. 438. No. B49, Like No. 439. No. B50, Like No. 440. No. B51, Like No. 441.

**Souvenir Sheets**

**1975, Dec. 1 *Perf. 13½***
*B47* A75 75c + 5c multi 1.10 1.10
*B48* A75 75c + 5c multi 1.10 1.10
*B49* A75 75c + 5c multi 1.10 1.10
*B50* A75 75c + 5c multi 1.10 1.10
*B51* A75 75c + 5c multi 1.10 1.10
*Nos. B47-B51 (5)* 5.50 5.50

The sheets show paintings from which designs of stamps were taken. Size of stamps: 23x40mm., size of sheets: 52x72mm.

### Easter Type of 1976

Paintings: No. B52, Like No. 442. No. B53, Like No. 443. No. B54, Like No. 444.

**Souvenir Sheets**

**1976, May 3 Photo. *Perf. 13½***
*B52* A76 60c + 5c multi 1.00 1.00
*B53* A76 60c + 5c multi 1.00 1.00
*B54* A76 60c + 5c multi 1.00 1.00

The sheets show paintings from which designs of stamps were taken. Size of stamps: 36x36mm., size of sheets: 69x69mm.

### Christmas Type of 1976

Designs: No. B55, like No. 459. No. B56, like No. 460. No. B57, like No. 461. No. B58, like No. 462. No. B59, like No. 463.

**Souvenir Sheets**

**1976, Nov. 2 Photo. *Perf. 14x13½***
*B55* A80 75c + 5c multi 1.10 1.10
*B56* A80 75c + 5c multi 1.10 1.10
*B57* A80 75c + 5c multi 1.10 1.10
*B58* A80 75c + 5c multi 1.10 1.10
*B59* A80 75c + 5c multi 1.10 1.10
*Nos. B55-B59 (5)* 5.50 5.50

The sheets show altarpieces from which designs were taken; gold border and marginal inscription. Size: 66x80mm.

### Easter Type of 1977

Designs: No. B60, Like No. 471. No. B61, Like No. 472. No. B62, Like No. 473.

**Souvenir Sheets**

**1977, Apr. 18 Photo. *Perf. 13½x14***
*B60* A83 60c + 5c multi 1.00 1.00
*B61* A83 60c + 5c multi 1.00 1.00
*B62* A83 60c + 5c multi 1.00 1.00

Easter 1977, and 400th birth anniversary of Peter Paul Rubens (1577-1640).

Sheets show paintings from which designs of stamps were taken. Size of stamps: 30x42mm., size of sheets: 60x78mm.

### Christmas Type of 1977

Designs: No. B63, like No. 474. No. B64, like No. 475. No. B65, like No. 476. No. B66, like No. 477. No. B67, like No. 478.

**Souvenir Sheets**

**1977, Oct. 31 Photo. *Perf. 14x13½***
*B63* A84 75c + 5c multi 1.10 1.10
*B64* A84 75c + 5c multi 1.10 1.10
*B65* A84 75c + 5c multi 1.10 1.10
*B66* A84 75c + 5c multi 1.10 1.10
*B67* A84 75c + 5c multi 1.10 1.10
*Nos. B63-B67 (5)* 5.50 5.50

Christmas 1977. The sheets show paintings from which designs were taken; gold border and marginal inscription. Size: 69x69mm.

### Easter Type of 1978

Designs: No. B68, like No. 483. No. B69, like No. 484. No. B70, like No. 485.

**Souvenir Sheets**

**1978, Apr. 10 Photo. *Perf. 14x13½***
*B68* A87 60c + 5c multi 85 75
*B69* A87 60c + 5c multi 85 75
*B70* A87 60c + 5c multi 85 75

The sheets show paintings from which designs were taken; gold marginal inscriptions and multicolored border. Size: 85x72mm.

### Christmas Type of 1978

**Souvenir Sheets**

**1979, Jan. 12 Photo. *Perf. 13***
*B71* A89 75c + 5c multi 90 90
*B72* A89 75c + 5c multi 90 90
*B73* A89 75c + 5c multi 90 90

Sheets show paintings from which designs were taken. Size: 57x87mm.

### Easter Type of 1979.

**Souvenir Sheet**

**1979, Apr. 5 Photo. *Perf. 13***
*B74* Sheet of 4 1.00 1.00
*a.* A90 10c + 2c like #506 16 16
*b.* A90 12c + 2c like #507 20 20
*c.* A90 15c + 2c like #508 25 25
*d.* A90 20c + 2c like #509 35 35

Sheet shows painting from which stamp designs were taken. Green and gold border. Size: 83x110mm.

### IYC Type of 1979

**Souvenir Sheet**

**1979, Oct. 10**
*B75* Sheet of 3 2.25 2.25
*a.* A93 30c + 5c multi 45 45
*b.* A93 60c + 5c multi 75 75
*c.* A93 65c + 5c multi 90 90

Decorative margin shows IYC emblem. Size 102x76mm.

### Christmas Type of 1979

**1980, Jan. 15 Photo. *Perf. 14***
*B76* A95 6c + 2c multi 15 15
*B77* A95 10c + 2c multi 20 20
*B78* A95 12c + 2c multi 25 25
*B79* A95 15c + 2c multi 28 28

### Easter Type of 1980

**Souvenir Sheets**

**1980, Mar. 31 Photo. *Perf. 13***
*B80* Sheet of 6 2.25 2.25
*a.* A96 20 + 2c like #542 25 25
*b.* A96 20 + 2c like #541 25 25
*c.* A96 30 + 2c like #543 40 40
*d.* A96 30 + 2c like #544 40 40
*e.* A96 35 + 2c like #545 45 45
*f.* A96 35 + 2c like #546 45 45

**1980, Apr. 23**
*B81* A96 75c + 5c like #541 1.00 1.00
*B82* A96 75c + 5c like #542 1.00 1.00
*B83* A96 75c + 5c like #543 1.00 1.00
*B84* A96 75c + 5c like #544 1.00 1.00
*B85* A96 75c + 5c like #545 1.00 1.00
*B86* A96 75c + 5c like #546 1.00 1.00
*Nos. B81-B86 (6)* 6.00 6.00

Easter 1980. Surtax was for school children. No. B80 has multicolored decorative margin. Size: 120½x110mm. Nos. B81-B86 have multicolored margins showing entire illustrations. Size: 60x72mm.

### Rotary Type of 1980

**Souvenir Sheet**

**1980, May 27 Photo. *Perf. 14***
*B87* Sheet of 3 1.75 1.75
*a.* A97 30c + 3c like #547 45 45
*b.* A97 35c + 3c like #548 55 55
*c.* A97 50c + 3c like #549 75 75

No. B87 has dark blue and gold decorative margin. Size: 72x113½mm.

### Christmas Type of 1980

**Souvenir Sheets**

**1981, Jan. 9 Photo. *Imperf.***
*B88* A102 75c + 5c like #652 1.00 1.00
*B89* A102 75c + 5c like #653 1.00 1.00
*B90* A102 75c + 5c like #654 1.00 1.00
*B91* A102 75c + 5c like #655 1.00 1.00

Nos. B88-B91 have multicolored decorative margins. Size: 56x68½mm.

### Easter Type of 1981

**Souvenir Sheets**

**1981, Apr. 10 Photo. *Perf. 13½***
*B92* Sheet of 3 1.50 1.50
*a.* A103 15c + 2c like #656 25 25
*b.* A103 25c + 2c like #657 50 50
*c.* A103 40c + 2c like #658 75 75

**1981, Apr. 28 *Imperf.***
*B93* A103 75c + 5c like #656 1.50 1.50
*B94* A103 75c + 5c like #657 1.50 1.50
*B95* A103 75c + 5c like #658 1.50 1.50

Surtax was for school children. Nos. B92-B95 have multicolored decorative margins. Size of No. B92: 72x116mm; Nos. B93-B95, 64x54mm.

### Espana '82 Type of 1981

**Souvenir Sheet**

**1981 Photo. *Perf. 13½***
*B96* Sheet of 8 3.75 3.75
*a.* A105 20c + 3c multi 25 25
*b.* A106 20c + 3c multi 25 25
*c.* A105 30c + 3c multi 40 40
*d.* A106 30c + 3c multi 40 40
*e.* A105 35c + 3c multi 50 50
*f.* A106 35c + 3c multi 50 50
*g.* A105 50c + 3c multi 70 70
*h.* A106 50c + 3c multi 70 70

No. B96 has multicolored margin showing Espana '82 emblem. Size: 180x95mm.

### Royal Wedding Type of 1981 Nos. 659-660a Surcharged in Black

**1981, Nov. 10 Photo. *Perf. 14***
*B97* A104 $1 + 5c multi 2.25 2.25
*B98* A104 $2 + 5c multi 4.50 4.50
*a.* Souvenir sheet of 2 7.50 7.50

Intl. Year of the Disabled. No. B98a contains Nos. B97-B98 each with 10¢ surtax, which was for benefit of the disabled; black overprint in margin.

### Christmas Type of 1981

**Souvenir Sheet**

**1981, Dec. 14 Photo. *Perf. 13½***
*B99* Sheet of 4 3.50 3.50
*a.* A107 8 + 3c like #669 25 25
*b.* A107 15 + 3c like #670 40 40
*c.* A107 40 + 3c like #671 1.10 1.10
*d.* A107 50 + 3c like #672 1.40 1.40

Surtax was for school children. No. B99 has multicolored decorative margin. Size: 86x111mm.

### Nos. 919-923 Surcharged "FIRST PAPAL VISIT TO SOUTH PACIFIC / POPE JOHN PAUL II / *NOV 21-24 1986* " and Value in Silver

**1986, Nov. 21 Litho. *Perf. 13½***
*B100* A138 55c + 10c multi 70 70
*B101* A138 $1.30 + 10c multi 1.50 1.50
*B102* A138 $2.75 + 10c multi 3.00 3.00

**Souvenir Sheets**

*B103* Sheet of 3 8.00 8.00
*a.-c.* A138 $2.40 + 10c on No. 922a-922c 2.65 2.65
*B104* A138 $6.40 + 50c multi 7.25 7.25

No. B103 ovptd. in margin "VISIT TO SOUTH PACIFIC / OF POPE JOHN PAUL II" and "FIRST PAPAL VISIT / NOVEMBER 21-24 1986." No. B104 ovptd. around margin only, "*FIRST PAPAL VISIT TO SOUTH PACIFIC NOVEMBER 21-24 1986" and "PRE-CHRISTMAS VISIT OF HIS HOLINESS POPE JOHN PAUL II."

### Stamps of 1982 and 1987 Surcharged "HURRICANE RELIEF" in Sans-serif Capitals Plus New Value

***Perfs. as before***

**1987, June 30 Photo.**
*B105* A121 55c +25c on #946 1.00 1.00
*B106* A121 65c +25c on #951 1.10 1.10
*B107* A121 75c +25c on #960 1.25 1.25
*B108* A121 95c +25c on #965 1.50 1.50
*B109* A101 $2.80 +50c on #636 4.10 4.10
*B110* A101 $5 +50c on #637 6.75 6.75
*B111* A101a $6.40 +50c on #978 8.50 8.50
*Nos. B105-B111 (7)* 24.20 24.20

### Stamps of 1985-86 Surcharged "HURRICANE RELIEF / +50c" in Silver or Black

**1987 *Perfs. as before***
*B112* A138 55c +50c on #B100 1.30 1.30
*B113* A133 55c +50c on #897 (B) 1.30 1.30
*B114* A128 65c +50c on #871 1.40 1.40
*B115* A133 65c +50c on #898 1.40 1.40
*B116* A128 75c +50c on #872 1.50 1.50
*B117* A133 75c +50c on #899 1.50 1.50
*B118* A134 95c +50c on #908 (B) 1.80 1.80
*B119* A135 $1 +50c on #910 1.85 1.85
*B120* A136 $1 +50c on #913 1.85 1.85
*B121* A137 $1 +50c on #916 1.85 1.85
*B122* A128 $1.15 +50c on #873 2.00 2.00
*B123* A133 $1.25 +50c on #900 2.15 2.15
*B124* A134 $1.25 +50c on #905 2.15 2.15
*B125* A136 $1.25 +50c on #914 (B) 2.15 2.15
*B126* A138 $1.30 +50c on #920 2.20 2.20
*B127* A134 $1.50 +50c on #906 (B) 2.50 2.50
*B128* A135 $1.50 +50c on #911 (B) 2.50 2.50
*B129* A133 $2 +50c on #901 (B) 3.10 3.10
*B130* A135 $2 +50c on #912 (B) 3.10 3.10
*B131* A137 $2 +50c on #917 3.10 3.10
*B132* A136 $2.75 +50c on #915 4.00 4.00
*B133* A138 $2.75 +50c on #921 4.00 4.00
*B134* A128 $2.80 +50c on #874 4.10 4.10
*B135* A137 $3 +50c on #918 4.30 4.30
*Nos. B112-B135 (23)* 55.10 55.10

**Souvenir Sheets**

*B136* A134 $1.10 +50c on #907 (B) 2.00 2.00
*B137* A134 $1.95 +50c on #908 3.00 3.00
*B138* on #922 (sheet of 3) 10.80 10.80
*a.-c.* A138 $2.40 +50c, any single 3.60 3.60
*B139* A134 $2.45 +50c on #909 (B) 3.65 3.65
*B140* A128 $5.30 +50c on #875 7.15 7.15
*B141* A138 $6.40 +50c on #923 8.50 8.50

Issue dates: Nos. B112-B117, B119-B120, B122-B123, B125-B126, B128, B130, B132-B134, B138, B141-B142, June 30. Others July 31.

---

## AIR POST STAMPS

**Catalogue values for unused stamps in this section, from this point to the end of the section, are for Never Hinged items.**

Stamps of 1936-63 Overprinted and Surcharged

**Airmail**

***Perf. 13x13½, 13½x13***

**Litho., Engr.**

**1966, Apr. 22 Wmk. 253**
*C1* A25 6p multi (#152) 25 20
*C2* A26 7p on 8p bl & blk (#153) 30 25
*C3* A25 10p on 3p multi (#150) 40 35
*C4* A25 1sh lt grn & yel (#154) 50 45
*C5* A27 1sh6p vio (#155) 75 65
*C6* A28 2sh3p on 3sh emer & blk (#157) 1.25 1.00
*C7* A28 5sh ultra & brn (#158) 2.00 1.75
*C8* A28 10sh on 2sh gray & brn (#156) 4.00 4.00

**Typo. *Perf. 14***
*C9* PF5 £1 pink (#106) 15.00 14.00
*Nos. C1-C9 (9)* 24.45 22.65

The position of the airplane in relationship to "Airmail" varies. The surcharges are printed on silver ovals.

### Games' Type of Regular Issue

Sport: 10p, Women runners and Games' emblem. 2sh3p, Runner and team emblem.

***Perf. 13½***

**1967, Jan. 12 Unwmk. Photo.**
*C10* A32 10p org & multi 25 25
*C11* A32 2sh3p multi 75 75

See note after No. 178.

### Capt. Cook Type of Regular Issue

Designs: 6c, The "Resolution" and "Discovery" Beating Through the Ice, by Webber. 10c, The Island of Otaheite, by Hodges, and Queen Elizabeth II. 15c, View of Karakakooa (Kealakekua), Hawaii, by Webber. 25c, The Landing at Middleburg, Tonga, by Hodges, and Captain Cook. (All horizontal.)

**1968, Sept. 12 Photo. *Perf. 13***

| No. | Type | Description | Unused | Used |
|---|---|---|---|---|
| *C12* | A39 | 6c gold & multi | 25 | 25 |
| *C13* | A39 | 10c gold & multi | 40 | 40 |
| *C14* | A39 | 15c gold & multi | 50 | 50 |
| *C15* | A39 | 25c gold & multi | 1.00 | 1.00 |

See note after No. 236.

Christmas Type of 1979

Designs: 20c, like No. 537. 25c, like No. 538. 30c, like No. 539. 35c, like No. 540.

**1979, Dec. 14 Photo. *Perf. 14***

| No. | Type | Description | Unused | Used |
|---|---|---|---|---|
| *C16* | A95 | 20c multi | 25 | 25 |
| *C17* | A95 | 25c multi | 35 | 35 |
| *C18* | A95 | 30c multi | 40 | 40 |
| *C19* | A95 | 35c multi | 50 | 50 |

Franklin D. Roosevelt (1882-1945) AP1

Portraits: 80c, Benjamin Franklin (1706-1790). $1.40, George Washington (1732-1799), by Gilbert Stuart.

**1982, Sept. 30 Photo. *Perf. 14***

| No. | Type | Description | Unused | Used |
|---|---|---|---|---|
| *C20* | AP1 | 60c multi | 90 | 90 |
| *C21* | AP1 | 80c multi | 1.10 | 1.10 |
| *C22* | AP1 | $1.40 multi | 2.00 | 2.00 |
| *a.* | | Souvenir sheet of 3 | 4.25 | 4.25 |

No. C22a contains Nos. C20-C22, perf. 13½ with portraits in square frames. Size: 117x60mm.

No. C22 Overprinted in Gold and Black

**1983, Aug. 12 Photo. *Perf. 14***

| No. | Type | Description | Unused | Used |
|---|---|---|---|---|
| *C23* | AP1 | 96c on $1.40 multi | 2.00 | 2.00 |

## AIR POST SEMI-POSTAL STAMPS

**Catalogue values for unused stamps in this section, from this point to the end of the section, are for Never Hinged items.**

Christmas Type of 1979

Designs: 20c+4c, like No. C16. 25c+4c, like No. C17. 30c+4c, like No. C18. 35c+4c, like No. C19.

**1980, Jan. 15 Photo. *Perf. 14***

| No. | Type | Description | Unused | Used |
|---|---|---|---|---|
| *CB1* | A95 | 20c + 4c multi | 40 | 40 |
| *CB2* | A95 | 25c + 4c multi | 45 | 45 |
| *CB3* | A95 | 30c + 4c multi | 50 | 50 |
| *CB4* | A95 | 35c + 4c multi | 60 | 60 |

## OFFICIAL STAMPS

**Catalogue values for unused stamps in this section, from this point to the end of the section, are for Never Hinged items.**

Flower Issue of 1967-69 Overprinted or Surcharged in Black on Silver

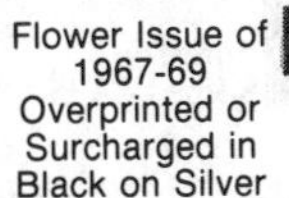

**1975 Photo. Unwmk. *Perf. 14x13½***

| No. | Type | Description | Value |
|---|---|---|---|
| *O1* | A34 | 1c multi (#200) | 5 |
| *O2* | A34 | 2c multi (#201) | 7 |
| *O3* | A34 | 3c multi (#203) | 9 |
| *O4* | A34 | 4c multi (#205) | 12 |
| *O5* | A34 | 5c on 2½c multi (#202) | 16 |
| *O6* | A34 | 8c multi (#208) | 25 |
| *O7* | A34 | 10c on 6c multi (#207) | 28 |
| *O8* | A34 | 18c on 20c multi (#212) | 40 |
| *O9* | A34 | 25c on 9c multi (#209) | 60 |
| *O10* | A34 | 30c on 15c multi (#211) | 80 |
| *O11* | A34 | 50c multi (#215) | 1.25 |
| *O12* | A35 | $1 multi (#216) | 2.75 |
| *O13* | A35 | $2 multi (#217) | 4.75 |
| *O14* | A36 | $4 multi (#218) | 8.00 |
| *O15* | A36 | $6 multi (#219) | 10.00 |
| | | *Nos. O1-O15 (15)* | 29.57 |

No. O1-O15 were not sold to the public unused. Arrangement of surcharge varies on different denominations.

Silver panel on Nos. O14-O15 measures 26½x6mm. and is rounded at both ends.

Issue dates: 1c-$2, Mar. 17, $4-$6, May 19.

Nos. 381-382, 389, 393-396, 469-470, 446 Overprinted or Surcharged in Silver or Black **O.H.M.S.**

**Photo., Litho.**

**1978, Oct. 19 *Perf. 13½***

| No. | Type | Description | Unused | Used |
|---|---|---|---|---|
| *O16* | A62 | 1c multi (S) | 5 | 5 |
| *O17* | A62 | 2c on ½c multi | 5 | 5 |
| *O18* | A62 | 5c on ½c multi | 8 | 6 |
| *O19* | A62 | 10c on 8c multi (S) | 15 | 10 |
| *O20* | A62 | 15c on 50c multi (S) | 20 | 15 |
| *O21* | A62 | 18c on 60c multi (S) | 25 | 20 |
| *O22* | A62 | 25c multi | 35 | 25 |
| *O23* | A62 | 30c multi (S) | 40 | 30 |
| *O24* | A62 | 35c on 60c multi (S) | 50 | 35 |
| *O25* | A62 | 50c multi (S) | 65 | 50 |
| *O26* | A62 | 60c multi (S) | 75 | 60 |
| *O27* | A82 | $1 multi (S) | 1.30 | 1.00 |
| *O28* | A82 | $1 multi (S) | 1.30 | 1.00 |
| *O29* | A77 | $2 multi | 2.50 | 2.00 |
| *O30* | A64 | $4 multi ('79) | 5.00 | 4.00 |
| *O31* | A64 | $6 multi ('79) | 7.00 | 6.50 |
| | | *Nos. O16-O31 (16)* | 20.53 | 17.11 |

Diagonal overprint on Nos. O27-O28. Overprint on No. O29: 19x4mm.

Nos. 790-791, 795, 797, 799, 805, 807, 809-810 Ovptd. or Surcharged "O.H.M.S." in Silver

**1985, July 10 Photo. *Perf. 13½x13***

| No. | Type | Description | Unused | Used |
|---|---|---|---|---|
| *O32* | A121 | 5c multi | 5 | 5 |
| *O33* | A121 | 10c multi | 10 | 10 |
| *O34* | A121 | 20c multi | 20 | 20 |
| *O35* | A121 | 30c multi | 30 | 30 |
| *O36* | A121 | 40c multi | 40 | 40 |
| *O37* | A121 | 55c on 85c multi | 55 | 55 |
| *O38* | A121 | 60c multi | 60 | 60 |
| *O39* | A121 | $1.10 multi | 1.10 | 1.10 |
| *O40* | A121 | $2 on $1.20 multi | 2.00 | 2.00 |
| | | *Nos. O32-O40 (9)* | 5.30 | 5.30 |

Nos. 792-794, 802, 806, 696-699 and 637 Ovptd. or Surcharged "O.H.M.S." in Silver, Gold or Black and Silver

**1986, May 5 Photo. *Perfs. as before***

| No. | Type | Description | Unused | Used |
|---|---|---|---|---|
| *O41* | A121 | 12c multi | 15 | 15 |
| *O42* | A121 | 14c multi | 16 | 16 |
| *O43* | A121 | 18c multi | 22 | 22 |
| *O44* | A121 | 50c multi | 60 | 60 |
| *O45* | A121 | 70c multi | 85 | 85 |
| *O46* | A111 | 75c on 60c #696 (G) | 90 | 90 |
| *O47* | A111 | 75c on 60c #697 (G) | 90 | 90 |
| *O48* | A111 | 75c on 60c #698 (G) | 90 | 90 |
| *O49* | A111 | 75c on 60c #699 (G) | 90 | 90 |
| *O50* | A101a | $5 on $3 (BK & S) | 6.00 | 6.00 |
| | | *Nos. O41-O50 (10)* | 11.58 | 11.58 |

# CRETE

LOCATION — An island in the Mediterranean Sea south of Greece.
GOVT. — Joint administration of France, Great Britain, Italy and Russia.
AREA — 3,235 sq. mi.
POP. — 301,273 (1900).
CAPITAL — Canea.

Formerly Crete was a province of Turkey. After an extended period of civil wars, France, Great Britain, Italy and Russia intervened and declaring Crete an autonomy, placed it under the administration of Prince George of Greece as High Commissioner.

Stamps issued for use in the Russian Sphere of Administration and those issued by the Cretan government are listed in Vol. II.

40 Paras = 1 Piaster

**British Sphere of Administration District of Heraklion (Candia)**

A1

A2

**Handstamped**

**1898 Unwmk. *Imperf.***

| No. | Type | Description | Unused | Used |
|---|---|---|---|---|
| *1* | A1 | 20pa violet | 500.00 | 300.00 |

**1898 Litho. *Perf. 11½***

| No. | Type | Description | Unused | Used |
|---|---|---|---|---|
| *2* | A2 | 10pa blue | 5.50 | 5.00 |
| *a.* | | Horiz. pair, imperf. btwn. | | |
| *b.* | | Imperf., pair | 400.00 | |
| *3* | A2 | 20pa green | 5.50 | 5.00 |
| *a.* | | Imperf., pair | 400.00 | |

**1899**

| No. | Type | Description | Unused | Used |
|---|---|---|---|---|
| *4* | A2 | 10pa brown | 5.50 | 5.00 |
| *a.* | | Horiz. pair, imperf. btwn. | | |
| *b.* | | Imperf., pair | 400.00 | |
| *5* | A2 | 20pa rose | 5.50 | 5.00 |
| *a.* | | Imperf., pair | 400.00 | |

Used values for Nos. 2-5 are for CTO's (single-line Heraklion cancel.)

Counterfeits exist of Nos. 1-5.

*Reprints exist of Nos. 2-5.*

# CYPRUS

LOCATION — An island in the Mediterranean Sea off the coast of Turkey.
GOVT. — Republic
AREA — 3,572 sq. mi.
POP. — 645,500 (1982)
CAPITAL — Nicosia

The British Crown Colony of Cyprus became a republic in 1960.

12 Pence = 1 Shilling
40 Paras = 1 Piastre
9 Piastres = 1 Shilling
20 Shillings = 1 Pound
1000 Milliemes = 1 Pound (1955)
100 Cents = 1 Cyprus Pound (1983)

**Catalogue values for unused stamps in this country are for Never Hinged items, beginning with Scott 156 in the regular postage section and Scott RA1 in the postal tax section.**

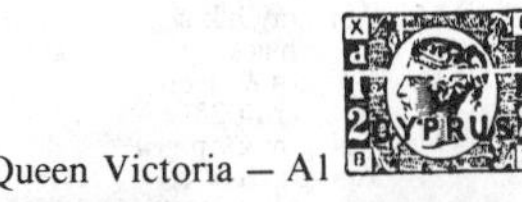

Queen Victoria — A1

A2

A3

A4

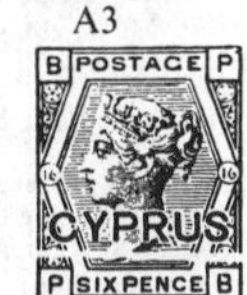

A5

A6

A7

**Various Watermarks as in Great Britain (20, 23, 25, 27 & 29)**

**1880 *Perf. 14***

| No. | Type | Description | Unused | Used |
|---|---|---|---|---|
| *1* | A1 | ½p rose (Plate 15) | 50.00 | 60.00 |
| *b* | | Dbl. ovpt. (Plate 15) | | *5,000.* |
| | | Plate 12 | 82.50 | 125.00 |
| | | Plate 19 | 2,500. | 750.00 |
| *2* | A2 | 1p red (P 201, 215-217) | 6.50 | 8.00 |
| *a* | | Dbl. ovpt. (Plate 208) | *8,500.* | |
| *b* | | As "a" (Plate 218) | 4,250. | |
| *c* | | Pair, one without overprint (P 208) | *8,500.* | |
| | | Plate 174 | 800.00 | 775.00 |
| | | Plate 181 | 60.00 | 67.50 |
| | | Plate 184 | 7,500. | 3,000. |
| | | Plates 193, 196 | 650.00 | |
| | | Plate 205 | 16.00 | 19.00 |
| | | Plate 208 | 55.00 | 17.50 |
| | | Plate 218 | 9.50 | 14.00 |
| | | Plate 220 | 750.00 | 400.00 |
| *3* | A3 | 2½p cl(P 14) | 1.65 | 2.75 |
| | | Plate 15 | 1.90 | 4.50 |
| *4* | A4 | 4p lt ol grn (P 16) | 110.00 | 125.00 |
| *5* | A5 | 6p ol gray (P 16) | 265.00 | 325.00 |
| *6* | A6 | 1sh green (P 13) | 450.00 | 350.00 |

**Black Surcharge**

| No. | Type | Description | Unused | Used |
|---|---|---|---|---|
| *7* | A7 | 30 paras on 1p red (P 216) | 42.50 | 55.00 |
| *a* | | Double surcharge, one inverted (P 216) | 2,250. | |
| *b* | | Same as "a" (Plate 220) | 1,250. | 1,500. |
| | | Plates 201, 217 | 72.50 | 77.50 |
| | | Plate 220 | 90.00 | 90.00 |

One Penny Stamps of Preceding Issue Surcharged

**HALF-PENNY**
18mm Long

**1881**

| No. | Type | Description | Unused | Used |
|---|---|---|---|---|
| *8* | A2 | ½p on #2 (201, 216) | 20.00 | 22.50 |
| | | Plate 174 | 45.00 | 90.00 |
| | | Plate 181 | 45.00 | 55.00 |
| | | Plate 205 | 25.00 | 27.50 |
| | | Plate 208 | 55.00 | 80.00 |
| | | Plate 215 | 135.00 | 225.00 |
| | | Plate 217 | 225.00 | 210.00 |
| | | Plate 218 | 150.00 | 180.00 |
| | | Plate 220 | 75.00 | 90.00 |

**HALF-PENNY**
16mm Long

| No. | Type | Description | Unused | Used |
|---|---|---|---|---|
| *9* | A2 | ½p on £2 (P 201) | 60.00 | 67.50 |
| *a* | | Double surch. (P 201) | 2,500. | |
| | | Plate 216 | 110.00 | 165.00 |

**HALF-PENNY**
13mm Long

| No. | Type | Description | Unused | Used |
|---|---|---|---|---|
| *10* | A2 | ½p on 1p red (P 215, 218) | 22.50 | 25.00 |
| *b* | | Dbl. surch. (P 205) | 675.00 | |
| *c* | | As "b" (P 215) | 600.00 | 600.00 |
| *d* | | Triple surch. (P 205) | *2,500.* | |
| *e* | | As "d" (P 215) | 675.00 | |
| *f* | | As "d" (P 217) | | |
| *g* | | As "d" (P 218) | *1,250.* | |
| *h* | | Quadruple surch. (P 205) | *2,500.* | |
| *i* | | As "h" (P 215) | *2,500.* | |
| *j* | | "CYPRUS" dbl. (P 218) | *5,000.* | |
| | | Plate 205 | 82.50 | *165.00* |
| | | Plate 217 | 30.00 | 32.50 |

A8

**1881, July Typo. Wmk. 1**

| No. | Type | Description | Unused | Used |
|---|---|---|---|---|
| *11* | A8 | ½pi emerald grn | 110.00 | 22.50 |
| *12* | A8 | 1pi rose | 150.00 | 32.50 |
| *13* | A8 | 2pi ultramarine | 350.00 | 21.50 |
| *14* | A8 | 4pi olive green | 750.00 | 175.00 |
| *15* | A8 | 6pi olive gray | 1,100. | 225.00 |

Postage and revenue stamps of Cyprus with "J.A.B." (the initials of Postmaster J.A. Bulmer) in manuscript, or with "POSTAL SURCHARGE" (with or without "J. A. B."), were not Postage Due stamps but were employed for accounting purposes between the chief PO at Larnaca and the sub-offices.

A9

A10

Black Surcharge

**1882** **Wmk. 1**

| No. | Type | Description | Unused | Used |
|---|---|---|---|---|
| 16 | A9 | ½pi on ½pi grn | 140.00 | 50.00 |
| 17 | A10 | 30pa on 1pi rose | 1,500. | 75.00 |

**1884** **Wmk. 2**

| No. | Type | Description | Unused | Used |
|---|---|---|---|---|
| 18 | A9 | ½pi on ½pi grn | 47.50 | 10.00 |
| a | | Double surch. | | 2,250. |

See Nos. 26, 27.

**1882-84** **Die B**

For explanation of Dies A and B, see back of this section of the Catalogue.

| No. | Type | Description | Unused | Used |
|---|---|---|---|---|
| 19 | A8 | ½pi green | 3.25 | 32 |
| a | | Die A | 3.50 | 22 |
| b | | ½pi emerald, Die A | 5,000. | 300.00 |
| 20 | A8 | 30pa violet | 1.50 | 1.10 |
| a | | 30pa lilac, die A | 27.50 | 11.00 |
| 21 | A8 | 1pi rose | 9.00 | 2.50 |
| a | | Die A | 30.00 | 1.65 |
| 22 | A8 | 2pi blue | 6.25 | 85 |
| a | | Die A | 55.00 | 1.65 |
| 23 | A8 | 4pi olive green | 15.00 | 10.00 |
| a | | Die A | 165.00 | 22.50 |

**Die A**

| No. | Type | Description | Unused | Used |
|---|---|---|---|---|
| 24 | A8 | 6pi olive gray | 30.00 | 10.00 |
| a | | Die B | 110.00 | 140.00 |
| 25 | A8 | 12pi brown org | 110.00 | 25.00 |
| a | | Die B | 90.00 | *100.00* |
| | | *Nos. 19-25 (7)* | 175.00 | 49.77 |

A11

Type I - Figures "½" 8 mm. apart.
Type II - Figures "½" 6 mm. apart.
The space between the fraction bars varies from 5½ to 8½mm. but is usually 6 or 8mm.

Black Surcharge

**1886** **Wmk. 2**

| No. | Type | Description | Unused | Used |
|---|---|---|---|---|
| 26 | A11 | ½pi on ½pi grn type I | 100.00 | 6.50 |
| a | | Type II | 100.00 | 32.50 |
| b | | Double surcharge, type II | | |

**Wmk. 1**

| No. | Type | Description | Unused | Used |
|---|---|---|---|---|
| 27 | A11 | ½pi on ½pi grn, type I | 5,000. | 350.00 |
| a | | Type II | 5,000. | |

**1894-96** **Wmk. 2**

| No. | Type | Description | Unused | Used |
|---|---|---|---|---|
| 28 | A8 | ½pi grn & car rose | 1.25 | 18 |
| 29 | A8 | 30pa violet & green | 1.75 | 30 |
| 30 | A8 | 1pi rose & ultra | 2.00 | 24 |
| 31 | A8 | 2pi ultra & maroon | 2.00 | 30 |
| 32 | A8 | 4pi ol green & vio | 3.75 | 2.00 |
| 33 | A8 | 6pi ol gray & grn | 5.25 | 3.75 |
| 34 | A8 | 9pi brown & rose | 6.50 | 3.00 |
| 35 | A8 | 12pi brn org & blk | 11.50 | 13.00 |
| 36 | A8 | 18pi slate & brown | 30.00 | 27.50 |
| 37 | A8 | 45pi dk vio & ultra | 72.50 | 72.50 |
| | | *Nos. 28-37 (10)* | 136.50 | 122.77 |

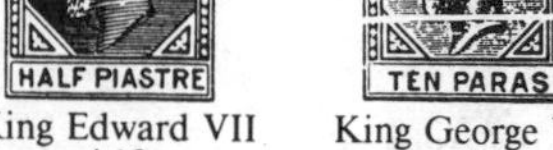

King Edward VII A12 King George V A13

**1903** **Typo.**

| No. | Type | Description | Unused | Used |
|---|---|---|---|---|
| 38 | A12 | ½pi grn & car rose | 75 | 22 |
| 39 | A12 | 30pa violet & green | 35 | 35 |
| 40 | A12 | 1pi car rose & ultra | 4.25 | 50 |
| 41 | A12 | 2pi ultra & maroon | 8.00 | 1.50 |
| 42 | A12 | 4pi ol green & vio | 10.50 | 5.50 |
| 43 | A12 | 6pi ol brown & grn | 22.50 | 27.50 |
| 44 | A12 | 9pi brn & car rose | 45.00 | 62.50 |
| 45 | A12 | 12pi org brn & blk | 3.75 | 7.25 |
| 46 | A12 | 18pi black & brown | 40.00 | 50.00 |
| 47 | A12 | 45pi dk vio & ultra | 150.00 | 240.00 |
| | | *Nos. 38-47 (10)* | 285.10 | 395.32 |

**1904-07** **Wmk. 3**

| No. | Type | Description | Unused | Used |
|---|---|---|---|---|
| 48 | A12 | 5pa bis & blk ('07) | 22 | 12 |
| 49 | A12 | 10pa org & grn ('07) | 28 | 12 |
| 50 | A12 | ½pi grn & car rose | 3.75 | 8 |
| 51 | A12 | 30pa violet & green | 1.65 | 60 |
| 52 | A12 | 1pi car rose & ultra | 95 | 28 |
| 53 | A12 | 2pi ultra & maroon | 4.75 | 28 |
| 54 | A12 | 4pi ol grn & red vio | 6.75 | 2.50 |
| 55 | A12 | 6pi ol brn & green | 11.00 | 4.50 |
| 56 | A12 | 9pi brn & car rose | 3.00 | 3.00 |
| 57 | A12 | 12pi org brn & blk | 16.00 | 11.00 |
| 58 | A12 | 18pi black & brown | 22.50 | 8.25 |
| 59 | A12 | 45pi dk vio & ultra | 45.00 | 45.00 |
| | | *Nos. 48-59 (12)* | 115.85 | 75.73 |

**1912**

| No. | Type | Description | Unused | Used |
|---|---|---|---|---|
| 61 | A13 | 10pa orange & green | 22 | 10 |
| 62 | A13 | ½pi grn & car rose | 22 | 6 |
| 63 | A13 | 30pa violet & green | 45 | 8 |
| 64 | A13 | 1pi car & ultra | 80 | 32 |
| 65 | A13 | 2pi ultra & maroon | 80 | 32 |
| 66 | A13 | 4pi ol grn & red vio | 1.65 | 70 |
| 67 | A13 | 6pi ol brn & green | 1.50 | 1.25 |
| 68 | A13 | 9pi brn & car rose | 9.75 | 9.75 |
| 69 | A13 | 12pi org brn & blk | 9.00 | 9.75 |
| 70 | A13 | 18pi black & brown | 9.75 | 6.50 |
| 71 | A13 | 45pi dl vio & ultra | 35.00 | 32.50 |
| | | *Nos. 61-71 (11)* | 69.14 | 61.33 |

**1921-23** **Wmk. 4**

| No. | Type | Description | Unused | Used |
|---|---|---|---|---|
| 72 | A13 | 10pa orange & grn | 50 | 22 |
| 73 | A13 | 10pa gray & yellow ('23) | 2.75 | 7.50 |
| 74 | A13 | 30pa violet & grn | 1.75 | 22 |
| 75 | A13 | 30pa green ('23) | 1.25 | 22 |
| 76 | A13 | 1pi rose & ultra | 5.00 | 6.75 |
| 77 | A13 | 1pi violet & car ('23) | 3.25 | 1.60 |
| 78 | A13 | 1½pi orange & blk ('23) | 3.25 | 3.25 |
| 79 | A13 | 2pi ultra & red violet | 4.50 | 4.00 |
| 80 | A13 | 2pi rose & ultra ('23) | 4.50 | 6.00 |
| 81 | A13 | 2¾pi ultra & red violet ('23) | 5.75 | *7.75* |
| 82 | A13 | 4pi ol grn & red violet | 2.75 | 1.90 |
| 83 | A13 | 6pi ol brn & green | 6.75 | 10.50 |
| 84 | A13 | 9pi brn & carmine | 11.50 | *11.50* |
| 85 | A13 | 18pi black & brown | 45.00 | 55.00 |
| 86 | A13 | 45pi dl vio & ultra | 100.00 | 110.00 |
| | | *Nos. 72-86 (15)* | 198.50 | 226.41 |

**Wmk. 3**

| No. | Type | Description | Unused | Used |
|---|---|---|---|---|
| 87 | A13 | 10sh grn & red, *yellow* ('23) | 275.00 | *500.00* |
| 88 | A13 | £1 vio & black, *red* ('23) | 950.00 | *1,500.* |

A14

**1924-28** **Chalky Paper** **Wmk. 4**

| No. | Type | Description | Unused | Used |
|---|---|---|---|---|
| 89 | A14 | ¼pi gray & brn orange | 14 | 9 |
| 90 | A14 | ½pi gray blk & black | 1.00 | 1.60 |
| 91 | A14 | ½pi grn & deep grn ('25) | 1.00 | 8 |
| 92 | A14 | ¾pi grn & dp grn | 40 | 10 |
| 93 | A14 | ¾pi gray blk & blk ('25) | 1.10 | 6 |
| 94 | A14 | 1pi brn vio & org brown | 32 | 10 |
| 95 | A14 | 1½pi org & black | 1.00 | 55 |
| 96 | A14 | 1½pi car ('25) | 1.00 | 28 |
| 97 | A14 | 2pi car & green | 1.00 | 1.75 |
| 98 | A14 | 2pi org & black ('25) | 2.50 | 2.50 |
| 99 | A14 | 2½pi ultra ('25) | 2.00 | 20 |
| 100 | A14 | 2¾pi ultra & dl violet | 75 | 1.00 |
| 101 | A14 | 4pi ap grn & vio | 60 | 1.25 |
| 102 | A14 | 4½pi blk & yel, *emer* | 1.75 | 2.00 |
| 103 | A14 | 6pi grn ol & grn | 1.75 | 2.25 |
| 104 | A14 | 9pi brn & dk vio | 1.65 | 1.75 |
| 105 | A14 | 12pi org brn & black | 5.75 | *16.00* |
| 106 | A14 | 18pi blk & orange | 9.00 | 6.75 |
| | | Revenue cancel | | 15 |
| 107 | A14 | 45pi gray vio & ultra | 13.00 | 15.00 |
| | | Revenue cancel | | 40 |
| 108 | A14 | 90pi grn & red, *yel* | 40.00 | 50.00 |
| | | Revenue cancel | | 1.00 |
| 109 | A14 | £5 *yellow* ('28) | 3,750. | *5,500.* |
| | | Revenue cancel | | 125.00 |

**Wmk. 3**

| No. | Type | Description | Unused | Used |
|---|---|---|---|---|
| 110 | A14 | £1 vio & black, *red* | 300.00 | 350.00 |
| | | Revenue cancel | | 2.75 |
| | | *Nos. 89-108 (20)* | 85.71 | 103.31 |

Nos. 96 and 99 are on ordinary paper.

Silver Coin of Amathus — A15
Philosopher Zeno — A16

Map of Cyprus — A17

Discovery of Body of St. Barnabas — A18

Cloisters of Bella Paise Monastery — A19

Badge of the Colony — A20

Hospice of Umm Haram at Larnaca — A21

Statue of Richard Coeur de Lion, London A22

St. Nicholas Cathedral, Famagusta A23

King George V — A24

**Wmk. 4**

**1928, Feb. 1** **Engr.** ***Perf. 12***

| No. | Type | Description | Unused | Used |
|---|---|---|---|---|
| 114 | A15 | ¾pi dark violet | 52 | 30 |
| 115 | A16 | 1pi Prus bl & blk | 1.00 | 1.00 |
| 116 | A17 | 1½pi red | 4.00 | 2.50 |
| 117 | A18 | 2½pi ultramarine | 1.00 | 1.00 |
| 118 | A19 | 4pi deep red brn | 3.00 | 3.75 |
| 119 | A20 | 6pi dark blue | 4.50 | 8.25 |
| 120 | A21 | 9pi violet brn | 5.75 | 8.00 |
| 121 | A22 | 18pi dk brn & blk | 14.00 | 20.00 |
| 122 | A23 | 45pi deep bl & vio | 27.50 | 30.00 |
| 123 | A24 | £1 ol brn & deep blue | 210.00 | 275.00 |
| | | *Nos. 114-123 (10)* | 271.27 | 349.80 |

50th year of Cyprus as a British colony.

Ruins of Vouni Palace — A25

Columns at Salamis — A26

Peristerona Church — A27

Soli Theater — A28

Kyrenia Castle and Harbor — A29

Kolossi Castle — A30

St. Sophia Cathedral — A31

Bairakdar Mosque — A32

Queen's Window, St. Hilarion Castle — A33

Buyuk Khan, Nicosia — A34

Forest Scene — A35

**1934, Dec. 1** **Engr.** ***Perf. 12½***

| No. | Type | Description | Unused | Used |
|---|---|---|---|---|
| 125 | A25 | ¼pi yel brn & ultra | 9 | 9 |
| a | | Vert. pair, imperf. between | 9,000. | |
| 126 | A26 | ½pi green | 12 | 12 |
| a | | Vert. pair, imperf. between | 7,500. | 8,000. |
| 127 | A27 | ¾pi violet & blk | 10 | 7 |
| 128 | A28 | 1pi brown & blk | 18 | 15 |
| a | | Vert. pair, imperf. between | 7,500. | 8,000. |
| b | | Horiz. pair, imperf. between | 6,000. | |
| 129 | A29 | 1½pi rose red | 24 | 20 |
| 130 | A30 | 2½pi dark ultra | 30 | 28 |

*131* A31 4½pi dk car & blk 4.25 65
*132* A32 6pi blue & black 4.00 4.25
*133* A33 9pi dl vio & blk brown 4.00 4.25
*134* A34 18pi ol grn & black 22.50 20.00
*135* A35 45pi blk & emer 42.50 40.00
*Nos. 125-135 (11)* 78.28 70.06

**Silver Jubilee Issue**
Common Design Type

**1935, May 6** ***Perf. 11x12***
*136* CD301 ¾pi gray blk & ultra 60 25
*137* CD301 1½pi car & dk bl 5.00 3.00
*138* CD301 2½pi ultra & brn 4.25 4.25
*139* CD301 9pi brn vio & indigo 17.00 19.00

**Coronation Issue**
Common Design Type

**1937, May 12** ***Perf. 11x11½***
*140* CD302 ¾pi dark gray 18 15
*141* CD302 1½pi dark carmine 35 30
*142* CD302 2½pi deep ultra 65 55

Ruins of Vouni Palace — A36

Columns at Salamis — A37

Peristerona Church — A38

Soli Theater — A39

Kyrenia Castle and Harbor — A40

Kolossi Castle — A41

Map of Cyprus — A42 Bairakdar Mosque — A43

The indexes in each volume of the Scott Catalogue contain many listings which help to identify stamps.

Citadel, Famagusta A44

Buyuk Khan A45

Forest Scene A46

King George VI A47

**1938-44** **Wmk. 4** ***Perf. 12½***
*143* A36 ¼pi yel brn & ultra 14 5
*144* A37 ½pi green 10 6
*145* A38 ¾pi violet & blk 3.75 10
*146* A39 1pi orange 18 6
***a*** Perf. 13½x12½ ('44) 250.00 22.50
*147* A40 1½pi rose carmine 50 35
*147A* A40 1½pi lt vio ('43) 18 8
*147B* A38 2pi carmine & blk ('42) 18 10
***c*** Perf. 12½x13½ ('44) 1.40 *3.00*
*148* A41 2½pi ultramarine 4.00 3.50
*148A* A41 3pi dp ultra ('42) 28 14
*149* A42 4½pi gray 28 14
*150* A43 6pi blue & black 55 25
*151* A44 9pi dk vio & blk 45 22
*152* A45 18pi ol grn & blk 1.50 65
*153* A46 45pi blk & emerald 3.75 1.50
*154* A47 90pi blk & brt vio 18.00 13.00
*155* A47 £1 ind & dl red 35.00 18.00
*Nos. 143-155 (16)* 68.84 38.20

See Nos. 164-166.

**Catalogue values for unused stamps in this section, from this point to the end of the section, are for Never Hinged items.**

**Peace Issue**
Common Design Type

**1946, Oct. 21** **Engr.** ***Perf. 13½x14***
*156* CD303 1½pi purple 10 10
*157* CD303 3pi deep blue 15 15

**Silver Wedding Issue**
Common Design Types

**1948, Dec. 20** **Photo.** ***Perf. 14x14½***
*158* CD304 1½pi purple 12 12

**Engr.; Name Typo.**
***Perf. 11½x11***
*159* CD305 £1 dark blue 47.50 47.50

**UPU Issue**
Common Design Types

***Perf. 13½, 11x11½***
**1949, Oct. 10** **Engr.** **Wmk. 4**
*160* CD306 1½pi violet 45 45
*161* CD307 2pi deep car 75 75
*162* CD308 3pi indigo 1.50 1.50
*163* CD309 9pi rose violet 3.50 3.25

Types of 1938-43

**1951, July 2** **Engr.** ***Perf. 12½***
*164* A37 ½pi purple 20 6
*165* A40 1½pi deep green 30 8
*166* A41 4pi deep ultra 50 12

**Coronation Issue**
Common Design Type

**1953, June 2** ***Perf. 13½x13***
*167* CD312 1½pi brt grn & blk 50 35

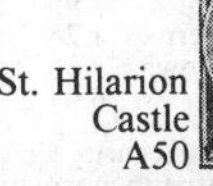
Carobs A48

Copper Pyrites Mine A49

St. Hilarion Castle A50

Queen Elizabeth II and Cyprian Coin Devices — A51

Designs: 3m, Grapes. 5m, Oranges. 15m, Troodos forest. 20m, Aphrodite beach. 25m, Coin of Paphos. 30m, Kyrenia. 35m, Harvest in Mesaoria. 40m, Famagusta harbor. 100m, Hala Sultan Tekke. 250m, Kanakaria church. £1, Queen Elizabeth II and devices of Byzantium, Lusignan, Ottoman Empire and Venice.

***Perf. 11½***
**1955, Aug. 1** **Engr.** **Wmk. 4**
*168* A48 2m chocolate 8 8
*169* A48 3m violet blue 8 8
*170* A48 5m orange 8 6
*171* A49 10m gray grn & chocolate 9 6
*172* A49 15m indigo & olive 25 10
*173* A49 20m ultra & brown 25 10
*174* A49 25m aquamarine 40 24
*175* A49 30m carmine & blk 25 12
*176* A49 35m aqua & orange 35 28
*177* A49 40m choc & dk grn 55 35

***Perf. 13½***
*178* A50 50m red brn & aqua 1.00 30
*179* A50 100m bl green & mag 2.75 65
*180* A50 250m vio brn & dk blue gray 6.50 4.00

***Perf. 11x11½***
*181* A51 500m lilac rose & grnsh gray 20.00 10.00
*182* A51 £1 grnsh gray & brn red 32.50 22.50
Revenue cancel 1.00
*Nos. 168-182 (15)* 65.13 38.92

**Republic**

Nos. 168-182 Overprinted in Dark Blue

ΚΥΠΡΙΑΚΗ
ΔΗΜΟΚΡΑΤΙΑ

KIBRIS
CUMHURIYETİ

**1960, Aug. 16** **Ovpt. 10x6½mm**
*183* A48 2m chocolate 15 12
*184* A48 3m violet blue 15 12
*185* A48 5m orange 18 12

**Overprint 12½x11mm**
*186* A49 10m gray grn & chocolate 25 8
*187* A49 15m indigo & ol 40 20
*188* A49 20m ultra & brn 40 20
***a*** Double overprint *6,000.*
*189* A49 25m aquamarine 60 35
*190* A49 30m car & black 75 30
***a*** Double overprint *6,000.*
*191* A49 35m aqua & org 85 45
*192* A49 40m choc & dk green 1.10 65

**2-line overprint 2½mm apart**
*193* A50 50m red brown & aqua 1.25 75
*194* A50 100m bl grn & mag 3.50 2.00
*195* A50 250m vio brn & dk blue gray 12.00 6.00

**2-line overprint 22mm apart**
*196* A51 500m lil rose & grnsh gray 42.50 18.00
*197* A51 £1 grnsh gray & brn red 105.00 45.00
*Nos. 183-197 (15)* 169.08 74.34

The overprint, in Greek and Turkish, reads "Republic of Cyprus."

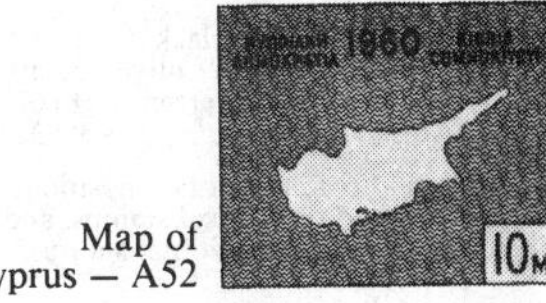
Map of Cyprus — A52

**Wmk. 314**
**1960, Aug. 16** **Engr.** ***Perf. 11½***
*198* A52 10m brown & grn 35 32
*199* A52 30m blue & brown 1.50 95
*200* A52 100m purple & blk 3.50 3.25

Independence of Republic of Cyprus.

**Europa Issue, 1961**

Nineteen Doves Flying as One — CD4

***Perf. 14x13½***
**1962, Mar. 19** **Litho.** **Unwmk.**
*201* CD4 10m lilac 12 9
*202* CD4 40m deep ultra 55 45
*203* CD4 100m emerald 1.10 1.10

Admission of Cyprus to Council of Europe.

Malaria Eradication Emblem A54

**1962, May 14** ***Perf. 14x13½***
*204* A54 10m gray grn & bl 25 18
*205* A54 30m red brn & blk 95 80

WHO drive to eradicate malaria.

Iron Age Jug — A55

Wmk. 344- Map of Cyprus and KC/K Delta

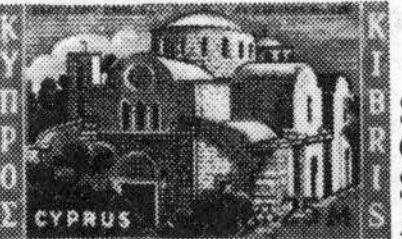
St. Barnabas Church, Salamis A56

Designs: 5m, Grapes. 10m, Head of Apollo. 15m, St. Sophia Church, Nicosia. 30m, Temple of Apollo. 35m, Head of Aphrodite. 40m, Skiing on Mt. Troodos. 50m, Ruins of Gymnasium, Salamis. 100m, Hala Sultan Tekke (sheep, Salt Lake Larnaca and tomb). 250m, Bella Paise Monastery. 500m, Cyprus mouflon. £1, St. Hilarion Castle.

***Perf. 13½x14, 14x13½***
**1962, Sept. 17** **Wmk. 344**
*206* A55 3m dark brn & sal 7 6
*207* A55 5m dl grn & red lilac 10 6
*208* A55 10m dk sl grn & yel green 15 7
*209* A55 15m dk brn & rose violet 22 12
*210* A56 25m salmon & brown 40 20
*211* A56 30m lt bl & dk bl 60 25
*212* A55 35m dk bl & pale green 85 42
*213* A56 40m vio bl & dk bl 1.10 55
*214* A56 50m ol bister & dk grn 1.65 50
*215* A55 100m brn & yel brn 3.25 1.25

*216* A56 250m tan & black 11.50 4.00
*217* A55 500m brown & olive 32.50 13.00
*218* A56 £1 gray & green 40.00 27.50
*Nos. 206-218 (13)* 92.39 47.98

Wmk. 344 is found in two positions: normal or inverted on vertical stamps, and reading up or down on horizontal stamps.

**Europa Issue, 1962**
Common Design Type
***Perf. 14x13½***
**1963, Jan. 28** **Wmk. 344**
**Size: 36x20mm**

*219* CD5 10m ultra & black 35 22
*220* CD5 40m red & black 2.50 1.65
*221* CD5 150m green & black 10.00 4.50

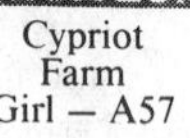

Cypriot Farm Girl — A57

Cub Scout and Tents — A58

Design: 75m, Statue of Demeter, goddess of agriculture.

**1963, Mar. 21** ***Perf. 13½x14***
*222* A57 25m blk, ultra & ocher 85 85
*223* A57 75m dk car, gray & blk 3.50 3.50

"Freedom from Hunger" campaign of the FAO.

**1963, Aug. 21** **Wmk. 344**

Designs: 20m, Sea Scout. 150m, Boy Scout and mouflon.

*224* A58 3m multicolored 12 10
*225* A58 20m multicolored 1.10 70
*226* A58 150m multicolored 4.25 3.25
*a* Souvenir sheet of 3 165.00 *125.00*

50th anniv. of the Boy Scout movement in Cyprus. No. 226a contains 3 imperf. stamps similar to Nos. 224-226 with simulated perforations. Gray marginal inscription. Size: 110x90mm. Sold for 250m.

Red Cross Nurse — A59

Children's Home, Kyrenia A60

***Perf. 13½x14, 14x13½***
**1963, Sept. 9** **Litho.**
*227* A59 10m multicolored 28 16
*228* A60 100m multicolored 3.25 1.75

Intl. Red Cross, cent.

**Europa Issue, 1963**

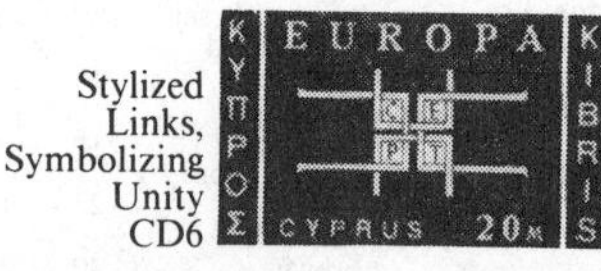

Stylized Links, Symbolizing Unity CD6

***Perf. 14x13½***
**1963, Nov. 4** **Wmk. 344**
*229* CD6 20m multi 70 55
*230* CD6 30m multi 80 60
*231* CD6 150m multi 9.00 5.25

Nos. 208, 211, 213-215 Overprinted in Ultramarine

**1964, May 5** ***Perf. 13½x14, 14x13½***
*232* A55 10m dk sl grn & yel green 24 22
*233* A55 30m lt bl & dk blue 60 45
*234* A55 40m vio bl & dl bl 95 80
*235* A55 50m ol bis & dk grn 1.25 95
*236* A55 100m brn & yel brown 3.00 2.75
*Nos. 232-236 (5)* 6.04 5.17

Decision by the UN and its Security Council to help restore the country to normality and to seek a solution of its problems.

Clay Mask and Soli Theater A62

Designs: 35m, Curium theater. 50m, Salamis theater. 100m, Performance of "Othello" in front of Othello Tower.

***Perf. 13½x14***
**1964, June 15** **Litho.** **Wmk. 344**
*237* A62 15m multicolored 16 10
*238* A62 35m multicolored 42 32
*239* A62 50m multicolored 60 45
*240* A62 100m multicolored 1.50 1.10

400th anniversary of Shakespeare's birth.

Boxers A63

Designs (14th century B.C. art): 10m, Runners (vert.). 75m, Chariot.

**1964, July 6** ***Perf. 13½x14, 14x13½***
*241* A63 10m brn, bis & blk 12 10
*242* A63 25m gray bl, bl & brn 40 32
*243* A63 75m brick red, blk & brown 1.25 1.00
*a* Souv. sheet of 3 9.75 7.50

18th Olympic Games, Tokyo, Oct. 10-25, 1964. No. 243a contains three imperf. stamps similar to Nos. 241-243 with gray marginal inscription. Size: 110x90mm. Sheet sold for 250m; the difference between face value and selling price went for the promotion of classical athletics in Cyprus.

Symbolic Daisy — CD7

Satyr Drinking Wine, 5th Century B.C. Statuette — A65

Modern Winery A66

**Europa Issue, 1964**
***Perf. 13½x14***
**1964, Sept. 14** **Litho.** **Wmk. 344**
*244* CD7 20m bis brn & red brn 40 35
*245* CD7 30m lt bl & dark blue 60 55
*246* CD7 150m green & ol green 7.25 4.50

CEPT, 5th anniv. The 22 petals of the flower symbolize the 22 members of the organization.

***Perf. 14x13½, 13½x14***
**1964, Oct. 26** **Wmk. 344**

Designs: 10m, Dionysus and Acme drinking wine, 3rd century mosaic. 50m, Commandaria wine, Knight Templar and Kolossi Castle.

*247* A66 10m multicolored 14 8
*248* A65 40m multicolored 75 45
*249* A65 50m multicolored 1.25 65
*250* A66 100m multicolored 4.00 2.00

Cypriot wine industry.

Pres. John F. Kennedy A67

***Perf. 14x13½***
**1965, Feb. 15** **Litho.** **Wmk. 344**
*251* A67 10m violet blue 15 12
*252* A67 40m green 70 48
*253* A67 100m rose claret 2.00 1.25
*a* Souv. sheet of 3 5.50 4.50

In memory of Pres. John F. Kennedy (1917-63). No. 253a contains 3 imperf. stamps similar to Nos. 251-253 with simulated perforations. Gray marginal inscription. Size: 110x90mm. Sold for 250m, 100m going to charitable organizations in Cyprus.

Old Couple A68

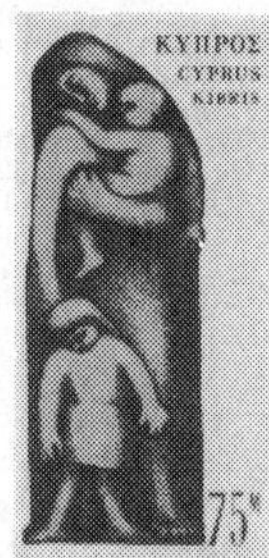

Mother and Children by A. Diamantis A69

Design: 45m, Man with broken leg (accident insurance).

**1965, Apr. 12** ***Perf. 13½x14***
*254* A68 30m dl grn & tan 70 40
*255* A68 45m dk vio bl, bl & gray 1.25 90
***Perf. 13½x12½***
*256* A69 75m buff & red brn 3.50 2.00

Introduction of Social Insurance Law.

ITU Emblem, Old and New Communication Equipment — A70

**1965, May 17** **Litho.** ***Perf. 14x13½***
*257* A70 15m brn, yel & black 40 18
*258* A70 60m grn, lt grn & blk 2.50 1.25
*259* A70 75m dk & lt bl & blk 3.50 1.65

ITU, cent.

ICY Emblem A71

**1965, May 17** **Wmk. 344**
*260* A71 50m lt brn, brn & sl grn 1.65 95
*261* A71 100m pale lil, pur & sl grn 3.00 1.90

International Cooperation Year.

**Europa Issue, 1965**

Leaves and Fruit CD8

***Perf. 14x13½***
**1965, Sept. 27** **Litho.** **Wmk. 344**
*262* CD8 5m org, org brn & black 16 10
*263* CD8 45m lt grn, org brn & black 1.65 1.25
*264* CD8 150m gray, org brn & black 5.00 4.00

Nos. 206, 208, 211 and 216 Overprinted in Dark Blue

**U. N.**
**Resolution on Cyprus**
**18 Dec. 1965**

***Perf. 13½x14, 14x13½***
**1966, Jan. 31**
*265* A55 3m dk brn & salmon 14 12
*266* A55 10m dk sl grn & yel grn 28 20
*267* A56 30m lt bl & dk blue 65 50
*268* A56 250m tan & black 5.00 4.75

UN General Assembly's resolution to mediate the dispute between Greeks and Turks on Cyprus, Dec. 18, 1965.

St. Barnabas, Ancient Icon — A73

Chapel over Tomb of St. Barnabas A74

Bishop Anthemios of Constantine Dreaming of St. Barnabas, Discovering Tomb, etc. — A75

Design: 15m, Discovery of body of St. Barnabas (scene as in type A18).

***Perf. 13x14, 14x13***
**1966, Apr. 25** **Litho.** **Wmk. 344**
*269* A73 15m multicolored 15 12
*270* A74 25m multicolored 38 35
*271* A73 100m multicolored 1.90 1.50

**Miniature Sheet**
***Imperf***
*272* A75 250m multicolored 11.00 9.50

1900th anniv. of the death of St. Barnabas. No. 272 has gray simulated perforations and narginal inscription. Size: 110x91mm. The vo lower fresco scenes show Emperor Zenon eceiving Gospel of St. Matthew from nthemios, and granting privileges to Church f Cyprus.

**No. 206 Surcharged with New Value and Three Bars**

***Perf. 13½x14***

**1966, May 30 Litho. Wmk. 344**
73 A55 5m on 3m dk brn & sal 15 15

Gen. K. S. Thimayya A76

**1966, June 6** ***Perf. 14x13½***
274 A76 50m tan & black 50 40

In memory of Gen. Kodendera Subayya Thimayya (1906-1965), commander of the UN Peace-keeping Force on Cyprus.

**Europa Issue, 1966**

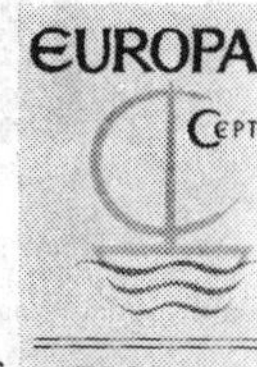


Symbolic Sailboat — CD9

***Perf. 13½x14***

**1966, Sept. 26 Litho. Wmk. 344**
275 CD9 20m multicolored 18 14
276 CD9 30m multicolored 32 28
277 CD9 150m multicolored 2.75 2.75

Stavrovouni Monastery A78

St. Nicholas Cathedral, Famagusta A79

Ingot Bearer, Bronze Age — A80

Designs: 5m, St. James' Church, Tricomo (vert.). 10m, Zeno of Citium, marble bust (vert.). 15m, Ship from 7th century B.C. vase (horiz.). 20m, Silver coin, 4th century B.C. (head of Hercules with lion skin). 25m, Sleeping Eros (first century marble statue; horiz.). 35m, Hawks on 11th century gold and enamel scepter from Curium. 40m, Marriage of David (7th century silver disc). 50m, Silver coin of Alexander the Great showing Hercules and Zeus (horiz.). 100m, Bird catching fish on 7th century B.C. jug. 250m, The Rape of Ganymede (3rd century mosaic). £1, Aphrodite (first century marble statue).

***Perf. 12x12½, 12½x12***

**1966, Nov. 21 Litho. Wmk. 344**
278 A78 3m bl, dl yel, grn & black 6 6
279 A78 5m dk bl, ol & blk 6 6
280 A78 10m olive & black 7 5

***Perf. 14x13½, 13½x14***
281 A79 15m org brn, blk & red brown 9 8
282 A79 20m red brown & blk 14 9
283 A79 25m red brn, gray & black 15 8
284 A79 30m aqua, tan & blk 20 8
285 A79 35m dk car, yel & black 28 20
286 A79 40m brt bl, gray & black 35 15
287 A79 50m org brn, gray & black 55 22
288 A79 100m gray, buff, blk & red 1.40 60

***Perf. 13x14***
289 A80 250m dl yellow, grn & blk 3.50 1.75
290 A80 500m multicolored 9.00 4.75
291 A80 £1 gray, lt gray & black 21.00 12.00
*Nos. 278-291 (14)* 36.85 20.17

Electric Power Station, Limassol — A81

Arghaka-Maghounda Dam — A82

Designs: 35m, Troodos Highway. 50m, Cyprus Hilton Hotel. 100m, Ships in Famagusta Harbor.

***Perf. 14x13½, 13½x14***

**1967, Apr. 10 Litho. Wmk. 344**
292 A81 10m lt brn, dark brn & yel 7 5
293 A82 15m lt blue, blue & grn 10 6
294 A82 35m dark gray, indigo & dark grn 30 24
295 A82 50m gray, olive & blue 50 32
296 A82 100m gray, indigo & blue 1.40 1.00
*Nos. 292-296 (5)* 2.37 1.67

Completion of the first development program, 1962-66.

**Europa Issue, 1967**
**Common Design Type**

**1967, May 2** ***Perf. 13x14***
**Size: 21x37mm**
297 CD10 20m yel grn & olive 28 22
298 CD10 30m rose vio & pur 40 32
299 CD10 150m pale brn & brn 2.00 1.65

Javelin Thrower, Map of Eastern Mediterranean and "Victory" — A83

Designs (Map of Eastern Mediterranean, Victory Statue and): 35m, Runner. 100m, High jumper. 250m, Amphora, map of Eastern Mediterranean and Victory statue.

***Perf. 13½x13***

**1967, Sept. 4 Litho. Wmk. 344**
300 A83 15m multi 12 8
301 A83 35m multi 55 48
302 A83 100m multi 1.25 1.10

**Miniature Sheet**

***Imperf***
303 A83 250m multi 4.50 4.00

Cyprus-Crete-Salonika Athletic Games. No. 303 contains one stamp (97x77mm) with simulated perforations. Size of sheet: 110x90mm.

Marble Forum at Salamis, Church of St. Barnabas and Bellapais Abbey A84

Designs (ITY Emblem and): 40m, Famagusta Beach. 50m, Plane and Nicosia International Airport. 100m, Youth Hostel and skiing on Mt. Troodos.

***Perf. 13½x13***

**1967, Oct. 16 Litho. Wmk. 344**
304 A84 10m multicolored 8 6
305 A84 40m multicolored 30 22
306 A84 50m multicolored 48 32
307 A84 100m multicolored 1.00 90

Intl. Tourist Year, 1967.

St. Andrew, 6th Century Mosaic — A85

Crucifixion, 15th Century — A86

The Three Kings, 15th Century Fresco — A87

**1967, Nov. 8** ***Perf. 13x13½***
308 A85 25m multicolored 18 18
309 A86 50m multicolored 28 28
310 A87 75m multicolored 50 50

St. Andrew's Monastery, cent. (25m); Exhibition of Art of Cyprus, Paris, Nov. 7, 1967-Jan. 3, 1968 (50m); 20th anniv. of UNESCO (75m).

Human Rights Flame and Stars — A88

Designs: 90m, Human Rights flame and UN emblem. 250m, Scroll showing Article One of the Declaration of Human Rights.

***Perf. 13½x14***

**1968, Mar. 18 Litho. Wmk. 344**
311 A88 50m multicolored 24 24
312 A88 90m multicolored 65 65

**Miniature Sheet**

***Imperf***
313 A88 250m multicolored 2.25 2.25

Issued for Intl. Human Rights Year. Size of No. 313: 110x90mm.

**Europa Issue, 1968**
**Common Design Type**

**1968, Apr. 29** ***Perf. 14x13½***
314 CD11 20m multicolored 20 10
315 CD11 30m dk car rose, gray brn & blk 35 22
316 CD11 150m multicolored 1.75 1.40

Boy Holding Milk, UNICEF Emblem A89

Aesculapius and WHO Emblem — A90

***Perf. 14x13½, 13½x14***

**1968, Sept. 2 Wmk. 344**
317 A89 35m dk red, lt brn & blk 18 18
318 A90 50m gray ol, blk & grn 28 28

21st anniv. of UNICEF (No. 317), 20th anniv. of the WHO (No. 318).

Discus Thrower A91

ILO Emblem A92

Designs: 25m, Runners. 100m, Stadium, Mexico City (horiz.).

***Perf. 13½x14, 14x13½***

**1968, Oct. 24 Litho.**
319 A91 10m multicolored 8 8
320 A91 25m vio bl & multi 15 15
321 A91 100m bl & multi 70 70

19th Olympic Games, Mexico City, Oct. 12-27.

***Perf. 12x13½***

**1969, Mar. 3 Wmk. 344**
322 A92 50m bl, vio bl & org brn 20 20
323 A92 90m gray, blk & org brn 55 55

ILO, 50th anniv.

Ancient Map of Cyprus A93

Design: 50m, Medieval map of Cyprus.

***Perf. 13½x13***

**1969, Apr. 7 Wmk. 344**
324 A93 35m multicolored 35 28
325 A93 50m ol & multi 35 28

1st Intl. Congress of Cypriot Studies.

*Cyprus stamps can be mounted in Scott's annually supplemented British Europe Album.*

**Europa Issue, 1969**

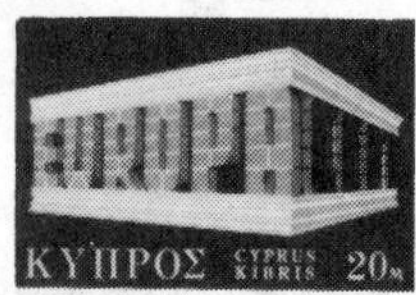


"EUROPA" and "CEPT" CD12

**1969, Apr. 28 Litho. *Perf. 14x13½***

| | | | | |
|---|---|---|---|---|
| *326* CD12 | 20m | bl, blk & gray | 16 | 8 |
| *327* CD12 | 30m | cop red, blk & ocher | 32 | 16 |
| *328* CD12 | 150m | grn, blk & yel | 1.40 | 1.00 |

CEPT, 10th anniv.

European Roller — A95

Birds: 15m, Audouin's gull. 20m, Cyprus warbler. 30m, Eurasian jay (vert.). 40m, Hoopoe (vert.). 90m, Eleonora's falcon (vert.).

***Perf. 13½x12, 12x13½***

**1969, July 7 Wmk. 344**

| | | | | |
|---|---|---|---|---|
| *329* A95 | 5m | multicolored | 8 | 8 |
| *330* A95 | 15m | multicolored | 22 | 12 |
| *331* A95 | 20m | multicolored | 25 | 16 |
| *332* A95 | 30m | multicolored | 38 | 24 |
| *333* A95 | 40m | multicolored | 55 | 35 |
| *334* A95 | 90m | multicolored | 1.75 | 1.40 |
| | | *Nos. 329-334 (6)* | 3.23 | 2.35 |

Nativity, Mural, 1192 A96

Christmas: 45m, Nativity, mural in Church of Ayios Nicolaos tis Steghis, 14th century. 250m, Virgin and Child between Archangels Michael and Gabriel, mosaic in Church of Panayia Angeloktistos, 6th-7th centuries. Design of 20m is a mural in Church of Panayia tou Arakos, Lagoudhera.

**1969, Nov. 24 Litho. *Perf. 13½x13***

| | | | | |
|---|---|---|---|---|
| *335* A96 | 20m | multicolored | 16 | 14 |
| *336* A96 | 45m | multicolored | 40 | 35 |

**Miniature Sheet**

***Imperf***

| | | | | |
|---|---|---|---|---|
| *337* A96 | 250m | dk bl & multi | 4.50 | 3.50 |

Size of No. 337: 109x89mm.

Mahatma Gandhi A97

***Perf. 14x13½***

**1970, Jan. 26 Wmk. 344**

| | | | | |
|---|---|---|---|---|
| *338* A97 | 25m | brn, vio bl, blk & gray | 16 | 12 |
| *339* A97 | 75m | brn, lt brn, blk & gray | 55 | 50 |

Birth cent. of Mohandas K. Gandhi (1869-1948), leader in India's struggle for independence.

**Europa Issue, 1970**

Interwoven Threads CD13

**1970, May 4 Litho. Wmk. 344**

| | | | | |
|---|---|---|---|---|
| *340* CD13 | 20m | brn, yel & org | 18 | 12 |
| *341* CD13 | 30m | brt bl, yel & org | 30 | 24 |
| *342* CD13 | 150m | brt rose lil, yel & orange | 1.75 | 1.50 |

Landscape with Flowers — A99

Designs: Various landscapes with flowers.

***Perf. 13x14***

**1970, Aug. 3 Litho. Wmk. 344**

| | | | | |
|---|---|---|---|---|
| *343* A99 | 10m | multicolored | 8 | 8 |
| *344* A99 | 50m | multicolored | 38 | 35 |
| *345* A99 | 90m | multicolored | 1.10 | 1.10 |

European Nature Conservation Year.

Education Year Emblem — A100

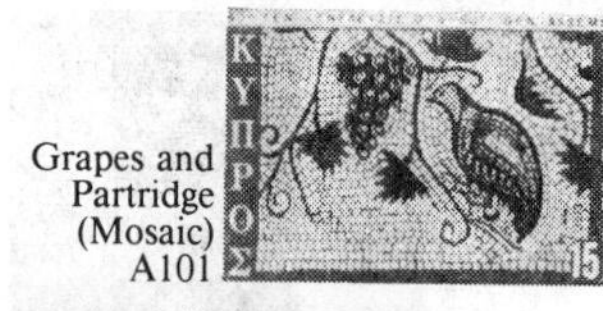


Grapes and Partridge (Mosaic) A101

UN Emblem, Dove, Globe and Wheat A102

***Perf. 13x14, 14x13***

**1970, Sept. 7 Litho. Wmk. 344**

| | | | | |
|---|---|---|---|---|
| *346* A100 | 5m | tan, blk & brn | 6 | 5 |
| *347* A101 | 15m | multicolored | 10 | 8 |
| *348* A102 | 75m | multicolored | 48 | 42 |

Intl. Education Year (No. 346); 50th General Assembly of the Intl. Vine and Wine Office (No. 347); 25th anniv. of the UN (No. 348).

Virgin and Child, Mural from Podhithou Church, 16th Century — A103

***Perf. 14x14½***

**1970, Nov. 23 Photo. Unwmk.**

| | | | | |
|---|---|---|---|---|
| *349* A103 | | Strip of three | 45 | 45 |
| *a* | 25m | *Left angel* | 15 | 15 |
| *b* | 25m | *Virgin and Child* | 15 | 15 |
| *c* | 25m | *Right angel* | 15 | 15 |
| *350* A103 | 75m | multicolored | 45 | 45 |

Christmas.

Design of No. 349 is same as No. 350, but divided by perforation into 3 stamps with 25m denomination each. Size of No. 349: 71x46mm.; size of No. 350: 42x31mm.

Cotton Napkin A104

Festive Costume A105

Drinking Cup, 7th Cent. B.C. A106

Mouflon from Mosaic Pavement, 3rd Century — A107

Cypriot Art: 5m, St. George, bas-relief on pine board, 19th cent. 20m, kneeling donors, painting, Church of St. Mamas, 1465. 25m, Mosaic head, 5th cent. A.D. 30m, Athena mounting horse-drawn chariot, terracotta figurine, 5th cent. B.C. 40m, Shepherd playing pipe, 14th cent. fresco. 50m, Woman's head, limestone, 3rd cent. B.C. 75m, Angel, mosaic, 6th cent. 90m, Mycenaean silver bowl, 14th cent. B.C. 500m, Woman and tree, decoration from amphora, 7th-6th cent. B.C. £1, God statue (horned helmet), from Enkomi, 12th cent. B.C. (vert.).

***Perf. 12½x13½ (A104), 13x14 (A105), 14x13 (A106), 13 ½x13, 13x13½ (A107)***

**1971, Feb. 22 Litho. Wmk. 344**

| | | | | |
|---|---|---|---|---|
| *351* A104 | 3m | blk, red & brn | 5 | 5 |
| *352* A104 | 5m | cit, red brn & black | 5 | 5 |
| *353* A105 | 10m | multicolored | 6 | 5 |
| *354* A106 | 15m | bis brn, blk & slate | 10 | 6 |
| *355* A105 | 20m | sl, red brn & black | 12 | 8 |
| *356* A105 | 25m | multicolored | 15 | 8 |
| *357* A106 | 30m | multicolored | 18 | 12 |
| *358* A105 | 40m | gray & multi | 30 | 18 |
| *359* A105 | 50m | bl, bis & blk | 35 | 24 |
| *360* A105 | 75m | cit & multi | 55 | 38 |
| *361* A106 | 90m | multicolored | 80 | 60 |
| *362* A107 | 250m | lt red brn, brn & black | 4.25 | 2.25 |
| *363* A107 | 500m | tan & multi | 6.75 | 5.00 |
| *364* A107 | £1 | multicolored | 12.50 | 8.50 |
| | | *Nos. 351-364 (14)* | 26.21 | 17.64 |

**Europa Issue, 1971**

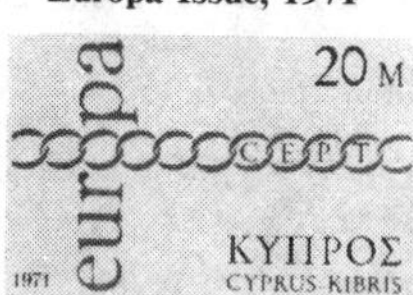


"Fraternity, Co-operation, Common Effort" — CD14

**1971, May 3 Litho. *Perf. 14x13½***
**Size: 36½x23½mm**

| | | | | |
|---|---|---|---|---|
| *365* CD14 | 20m | lt bl, vio bl & blk | 16 | 12 |
| *366* CD14 | 30m | brt yel grn, grn & blk | 28 | 22 |
| *367* CD14 | 150m | yel, grn & blk | 1.65 | 1.50 |

Archbishop Kyprianos, 1821 — A109

Paintings: 30m, Young Greek Taking Oath (horiz.). 100m, Bishop Germanos of Patras Declaring Greek Independence.

***Perf. 13x13½, 13½x13***

**1971, July 9 Wmk. 344**

| | | | | |
|---|---|---|---|---|
| *368* A109 | 15m | multicolored | 8 | 6 |
| *369* A109 | 30m | multicolored | 15 | 10 |
| *370* A109 | 100m | multicolored | 70 | 55 |

150th anniversary of Greek independence.

Arch and Castle A110

Designs: 25m, Decorated gourd and sun over shore (vert.). 60m, Mountain road (vert.). 100m, Village church.

***Perf. 13½x13, 13x13½***

**1971, Sept. 20**

| | | | | |
|---|---|---|---|---|
| *371* A110 | 15m | vio bl & multi | 9 | 9 |
| *372* A110 | 25m | ocher & multi | 12 | 12 |
| *373* A110 | 60m | green & multi | 35 | 35 |
| *374* A110 | 100m | blue & multi | 70 | 70 |

Tourist publicity.

Virgin and Child A111

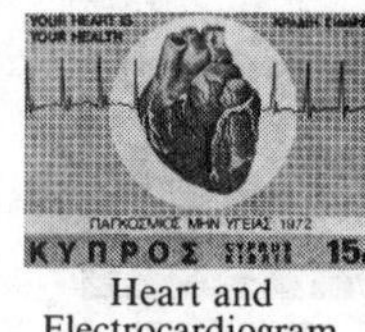


Heart and Electrocardiogram A112

**1971, Nov. 22 *Perf. 13½x14***

| | | | | |
|---|---|---|---|---|
| *375* A111 | 10m | shown | 8 | 8 |
| *376* A111 | 50m | The Three Kings | 45 | 35 |
| *377* A111 | 100m | Shepherds | 90 | 70 |

Christmas. Nos. 375-377 printed se-tenant in sheets of 36.

**1972, Apr. 11 *Perf. 13½x12½***

| | | | | |
|---|---|---|---|---|
| *378* A112 | 15m | bis & multi | 10 | 8 |
| *379* A112 | 50m | brn & multi | 40 | 38 |

"Your heart is your health," World Health Day.

**Europa Issue 1972**

Sparkles, Symbolic of Communications CD15

**1972, May 22 *Perf. 12½x13½***

| | | | | |
|---|---|---|---|---|
| *380* CD15 | 20m | brn, org & fawn | 22 | 15 |
| *381* CD15 | 30m | pur, org & lil | 38 | 32 |
| *382* CD15 | 150m | dk ol, org & brt green | 2.00 | 1.90 |

Archery, Olympic and Motion Emblems A114

Designs (Olympic and Motion Emblems): 40m, Wrestling. 100m, Soccer.

**1972, July 24** *Perf. 14x13½*

*383* A114 10m bl & multi 8 8
*384* A114 40m org & multi 38 35
*385* A114 100m multicolored 1.10 1.00

20th Olympic Games, Munich, Aug. 26-Sept. 11.

Apollo, Silver Stater, Marion, 5th Century B.C. A115

Silver Staters of Cyprus: 30m, Eagle's head, Paphos, c. 460 B.C. 40m, Pallas Athena, Lapithos, 388-387 B.C. 100m, Sphinx (obverse) and lotus flower (reverse), Idalion, c. 460 B.C.

**1972, Sept. 25 Litho. Wmk. 344**

**Coins in Silver**

*386* A115 20m lt grnsh bl & blk 12 10
*387* A115 30m pale bl & silver 20 18
*388* A115 40m ol bister & black 32 30
*389* A115 100m pale brown & blk 1.25 1.10

Bathing the Christ Child — A116

Christmas: 20m, The Three Kings. 100m, Nativity. 250m, The Nativity, 1466, mural in Church of the Holy Cross, Platanistasa. The designs of the 10m, 20m, 100m, show details from mural shown entirely on 250m.

**1972, Nov. 20 Litho.** *Perf. 13½x14*

*390* A116 10m multicolored 8 8
*391* A116 20m multicolored 22 22
*392* A116 100m multicolored 1.40 1.25

**Miniature Sheet**

***Imperf***

*393* A116 250m multicolored 4.50 4.25

Size of No. 393: 110x90mm.

Landscape, Troodos Mountains A117

Design: 100m, FIS Congress emblem and map of Cyprus.

*Perf. 14x13½*

**1973, Mar. 13 Wmk. 344**

*394* A117 20m bl & multi 18 18
*395* A117 100m bl & multi 80 80

29th Meeting of the Intl. Ski Fed. (FIS), Nicosia, June 1973.

**Europa Issue 1973**

Post Horn of Arrows CD16

**1973, May 7 Size: 37x21mm**

*396* CD16 20m dl bl & multi 22 18
*397* CD16 30m multicolored 45 35
*398* CD16 150m multicolored 2.25 2.00

Archbishop's Palace, Nicosia — A119

Traditional Architecture: 30m, Konak, Nicosia, 18th century (vert.). 50m, House, Gourri, 1850 (vert.). 100m, House, Rizokarpaso, 1772.

**1973, July 23** *Perf. 14x13, 13x14*

*399* A119 20m multicolored 16 15
*400* A119 30m multicolored 32 30
*401* A119 50m multicolored 50 42
*402* A119 100m multicolored 95 85

No. 354 Surcharged **20M**

**1973, Sept. 24** *Perf. 14x13*

*403* A106 20m on 15m multi 22 22

Cyprus Scout Emblem A120

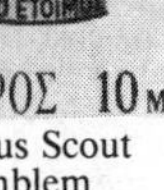
Cyprus Airways Emblem A122

EEC Emblem A121

Designs: 35m, FAO emblem. 100m, INTERPOL emblem.

**1973, Sept. 24** *Perf. 13x14, 14x13*

*404* A120 10m brn ol, ol & buff 14 7
*405* A121 25m purple, bl & plum 20 18
*406* A121 35m grn, gray grn & citron 30 28
*407* A122 50m black & blue 45 42
*408* A120 100m brown & fawn 90 85
*Nos. 404-408 (5)* 1.99 1.80

60th anniv.of Cyprus Boy Scout Organ.; association of Cyprus with EEC; 10th anniv. of FAO; 25th anniv. of Cyprus Airways; 50th anniv. of Intl. Criminal Police Organization.

Archangel Gabriel — A123

Virgin and Child — A124

Christmas: 100m, Panaya tou Araka Church (horiz.). Designs of 10m, 20m are from wall paintings in Arakas Church.

**1973, Nov. 26 Wmk. 344**

*409* A123 10m multicolored 8 7
*410* A124 20m multicolored 15 14
*411* A124 100m multicolored 1.00 90

Grapes A125

Rape of Europa A126

**1974, Mar. 18 Litho.** *Perf. 13x14*

*412* A125 25m shown 14 12
*413* A125 50m Grapefruit 38 35
*414* A125 50m Oranges 38 35
*415* A125 50m Lemons 38 35

No. 412 printed in sheets of 100; Nos. 413-415 se-tenant in sheets of 36.

**Europa Issue 1974**

**1974, Apr. 29**

Design shows a silver stater of Marion, second half of 5th century B.C.

*416* A126 10m org brn & multi 9 9
*417* A126 40m multicolored 38 38
*418* A126 150m dk car & multi 1.40 1.40

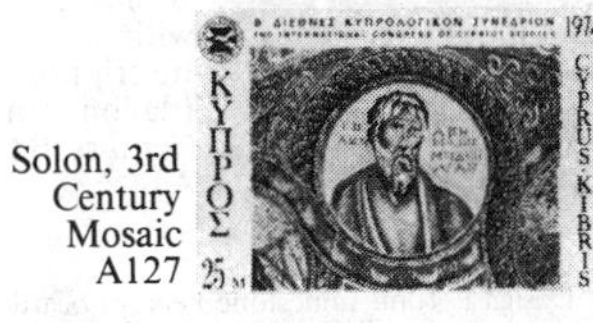
Solon, 3rd Century Mosaic A127

Designs: 10m, Front page of "History of Cyprus," by Archimandrite Kyprianos, 1788 (vert.). 100m, St. Neophytos, mural (vert.). 250m, Maps of Cyprus and Greek Islands, by Abraham Ortelius, 1584.

*Perf. 13x14, 14x13*

**1974, July 22 Litho. Wmk. 344**

*419* A127 10m multicolored 10 8
*420* A127 25m multicolored 16 14
*421* A127 100m multicolored 70 70

**Miniature Sheet**

***Imperf***

*422* A127 250m multicolored 2.00 1.90

2nd Intl. Congress of Cypriot Studies, Nicosia, Sept. 15-21. No. 422 has simulated perforations. Size: 110x90mm.

Nos. 353, 358-359, 362 Overprinted

SECURITY
COUNCIL
RESOLUTION
353
20 JULY 1974

*Perf. 13x14, 13½x13*

**1974, Oct. 14 Litho.**

*424* A105 10m multicolored 10 8
*425* A105 40m multicolored 50 45
*426* A105 50m multicolored 65 60
*427* A107 250m multicolored 3.25 3.00

UN Security Council Resolution No. 353 to end hostilities on Cyprus. Overprint is in 3 lines on No. 427.

Virgin and Child, 1466 A129

Adoration of the Kings, c. 1500 — A130

Christmas: 100m, Flight into Egypt, mural, Monastery Church of Ayios Meophytos, c. 1500. (50m is from same church). Mural on 10m is in Church of Stavros tou Ahiasmati.

*Perf. 14x13, 13x14*

**1974, Dec. 2 Wmk. 344**

*429* A129 10m multicolored 8 5
*430* A130 50m multicolored 25 22
*431* A129 100m multicolored 65 55

Disabled Persons, Emblem A131

Council of Europe Flag A132

**1975, Feb. 17 Unwmk.** *Perf. 14½*

*432* A131 30m ocher & ultra 25 22
*433* A132 100m multicolored 85 75

8th European Meeting of the Intl. Society for the Rehabilitation of Disabled Persons (30m; design shows society's emblem); 25th anniv. of Council of Europe (100m).

First Mail Coach in Cyprus A133

**1975, Feb. 17**

*434* A133 20m multicolored 14 14
*435* A133 50m ultra & multi 1.50 50

Centenary (in 1974) of UPU.

**Europa Issue 1975**

The Distaff, by Michael Kashalos — A134

Paintings: 30m, Still Life, by Christoforos Savva. 150m, Virgin and Child of Liopetri, by Georghios P. Georghiou.

*Perf. 13½x14½*

**1975, Apr. 28 Photo.**

*436* A134 20m multicolored 12 10
*437* A134 30m multicolored 20 15
*438* A134 150m multicolored 1.00 85

Nos. 436-438 printed se-tenant in sheets of 30 (6x5).

A particular stamp may be scarce, but if few collectors want it, its market value may remain relatively low.

Red Cross Flag over Cyprus A135

Nurse and Nurses Emblem A136

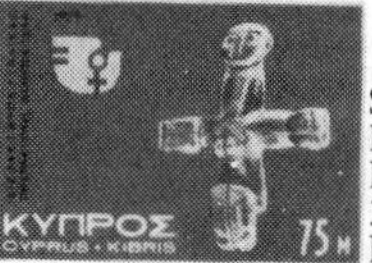

Steatite Female Figure, c. 3000 B.C. — A137

*Perf. 12½x13½, 13½x12½*

**1975, Aug. 4 Litho. Wmk. 344**

| | | | | |
|---|---|---|---|---|
| *439* | A135 | 25m bl green & red | 16 | 15 |
| *440* | A136 | 30m dp bl & lt grn | 22 | 20 |
| *441* | A137 | 75m multicolored | 55 | 48 |

Cyprus Red Cross, 25th anniv.; Intl. Nurses' Day 1975; IWY.

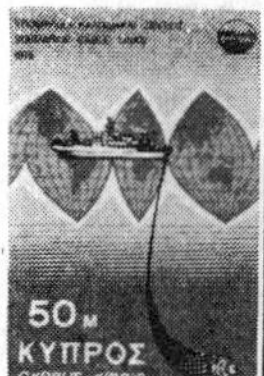

Submarine Cable — A138

International Telephone — A139

*Perf. 12½x13½, 13½x12½*

**1975, Oct. 13 Litho.**

| | | | | |
|---|---|---|---|---|
| *442* | A138 | 50m multicolored | 25 | 22 |
| *443* | A139 | 100m purple & org | 50 | 42 |

Telecommunications achievements.

No. 351 Surcharged 10M

**1976, Jan. 5** *Perf. 12½x13½*

| | | | | |
|---|---|---|---|---|
| *444* | A104 | 10m on 3m multi | 12 | 12 |

**Europa Issue 1976**

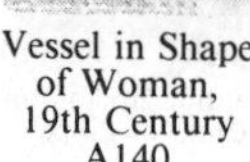

Vessel in Shape of Woman, 19th Century A140

Composite Vessel, 2100-2000 B.C. A141

Design: 100m, Byzantine goblet, 15th cent.

*Perf. 13x14*

**1976, May 3 Litho. Wmk. 344**

| | | | | |
|---|---|---|---|---|
| *445* | A140 | 20m violet & multi | 15 | 15 |
| *446* | A141 | 60m gray & multi | 40 | 40 |
| *447* | A140 | 100m brown & multi | 65 | 65 |

Self-help Housing A142

Cyprus Airways Jet — A143

Designs: 25m, Women sewing in front of tents. 30m, Aforestation.

**1976, May 3** *Perf. 14x13*

| | | | | |
|---|---|---|---|---|
| *448* | A142 | 10m multicolored | 7 | 7 |
| *449* | A142 | 25m multicolored | 14 | 14 |
| *450* | A142 | 30m multicolored | 15 | 15 |
| *451* | A143 | 60m multicolored | 35 | 35 |

Re-activation of the economy.

Terracotta Statue, 7th-6th Centuries B.C. — A144

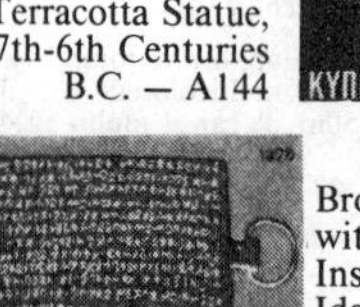

Bronze Plate with Inscription, Idalion, 5th Century B.C. A145

Designs: 10m, Limestone head of bearded man, 5th cent. B.C. 20m, Gold necklace, Lamboussa, 6th cent. A.D. 25m, Terracotta warrior on horseback, 7th cent. B.C. 30m, Limestone figure, priest of Aphrodite, 5th cent. B.C. 50m, Mycenaean crater, 13th cent. B.C. 60m, Limestone sarcophagus, Amathus, 550-500 B.C. 100m, Gold bracelet, Lamboussa, 6th cent. A.D. 250m, Silver dish, Lamboussa, 6th cent. A.D. 500m, Bronze stand, 12th cent. B.C. £1, Marble statue of Artemis, Larnaca, 4th cent. B.C.

*Perf. 12x13½*

**1976, June 7 Wmk. 344**

**Size: 22x33mm**

| | | | | |
|---|---|---|---|---|
| *452* | A144 | 5m brown & multi | 5 | 5 |
| *453* | A144 | 10m gray & multi | 6 | 6 |

**Size: 24x37mm, 37x24mm**

*Perf. 13x14, 14x13*

| | | | | |
|---|---|---|---|---|
| *454* | A144 | 20m red & multi | 9 | 9 |
| *455* | A144 | 25m lt brn & blk | 12 | 10 |
| *456* | A144 | 30m green & multi | 14 | 12 |
| *457* | A145 | 40m bis gray & blk | 20 | 18 |
| *458* | A145 | 50m brown & multi | 22 | 20 |
| *459* | A145 | 60m dk brown & multi | 28 | 25 |
| *460* | A145 | 100m crim & multi | 48 | 45 |

**Size: 28x40mm**

*Perf. 13x12½*

| | | | | |
|---|---|---|---|---|
| *461* | A144 | 250m dk bl & multi | 1.10 | 1.00 |
| *462* | A144 | 500m yel & multi | 2.25 | 2.25 |
| *463* | A144 | £1 slate & multi | 4.75 | 4.50 |
| | | *Nos. 452-463 (12)* | 9.74 | 9.25 |

George Washington A146

**1976, July 5** *Perf. 13x13½*

| | | | | |
|---|---|---|---|---|
| *464* | A146 | 100m multicolored | 70 | 60 |

American Bicentennial.

Montreal Olympic Games Emblem — A147

Various Sports A148

Design: 100m, like 60m, with different sports.

**1976, July 5 Unwmk.** *Perf. 14*

| | | | | |
|---|---|---|---|---|
| *465* | A147 | 20m yel, blk & dk car | 12 | 12 |
| *466* | A148 | 60m ultra & multi | 38 | 38 |
| *467* | A148 | 100m lilac & multi | 60 | 60 |

21st Olympic Games, Montreal, Canada, July 17-Aug. 1.

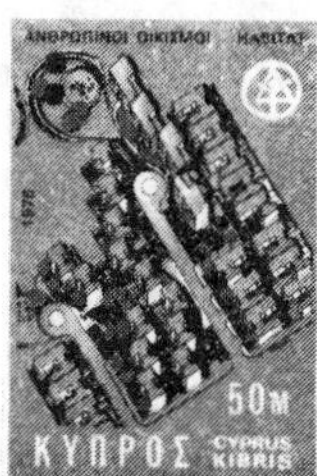

Children in Library A149

Low-cost Housing Development A150

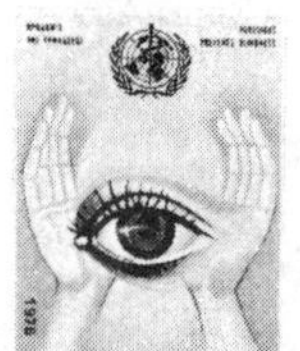

Hands Shielding Eye — A151

*Perf. 13½x14, 13x13½*

**1976, Sept. 27 Litho. Wmk. 344**

| | | | | |
|---|---|---|---|---|
| *468* | A149 | 40m black & multi | 28 | 28 |
| *469* | A150 | 50m multicolored | 24 | 20 |
| *470* | A151 | 80m ultra & multi | 40 | 35 |

Books for Children (40m); Habitat, UN Conference on Human Settlements, Vancouver, Canada, May 31-June 11 (50m); World Health Day: Foresight prevents blindness (80m).

Archangel Michael — A152

Christmas: 15m, Archangel Gabriel. 150m, Nativity. Icons in Ayios Neophytis Monastery, 16th century.

**1976, Nov. 15 Unwmk.** *Perf. 12½*

| | | | | |
|---|---|---|---|---|
| *471* | A152 | 10m multicolored | 6 | 6 |
| *472* | A152 | 15m multicolored | 8 | 8 |
| *473* | A152 | 150m multicolored | 95 | 85 |

**Europa Issue 1977**

Landscape, by A. Diamantis — A154

Paintings: 60m, Trees and Meadow, by T. Kanthos. 120m, Harbor, by V. Ioannides.

*Perf. 13½x13*

**1977, May 2 Litho. Unwmk.**

| | | | | |
|---|---|---|---|---|
| *475* | A154 | 20m multicolored | 14 | 12 |
| *476* | A154 | 60m multicolored | 48 | 45 |
| *477* | A154 | 120m multicolored | 90 | 80 |

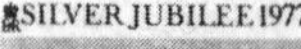

SILVER JUBILEE 1977

Cyprus No. 196 — A155

*Perf. 13x13½*

**1977, June 13 Litho. Wmk. 344**

| | | | | |
|---|---|---|---|---|
| *478* | A155 | 120m multicolored | 65 | 48 |

25th anniv. of reign of Queen Elizabeth II.

Silver Tetradrachm of Demetrios Poliorcetes — A156

Ancient Coins of Cyprus: 10m, Bronze coin of Emperor Trajan. 60m, Silver Tetradrachm of Ptolemy VIII. 100m, Gold octadrachm of Arsinoe II.

**1977, June 13 Unwmk.** *Perf. 14*

| | | | | |
|---|---|---|---|---|
| *479* | A156 | 10m multicolored | 8 | 8 |
| *480* | A156 | 40m multicolored | 22 | 20 |
| *481* | A156 | 60m multicolored | 35 | 32 |
| *482* | A156 | 100m multicolored | 52 | 52 |

Archbishop Makarios — A157

Designs: 20m, Archbishop in full vestments. 250m, Head.

*Perf. 13x14*

**1977, Sept. 10 Litho. Unwmk.**

| | | | | |
|---|---|---|---|---|
| *483* | A157 | 20m multicolored | 10 | 8 |
| *484* | A157 | 60m multicolored | 30 | 8 |
| *485* | A157 | 250m multicolored | 1.10 | 1.00 |

Archbishop Makarios (1913-77), Pres. of Cyprus.

Handicrafts A158

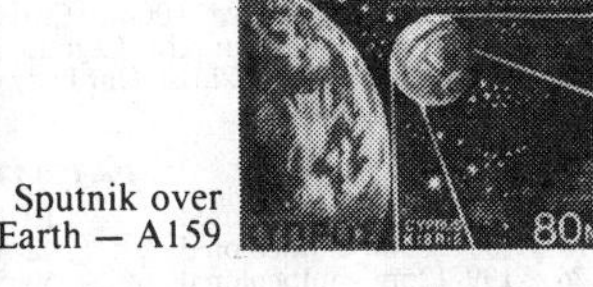
Sputnik over Earth — A159

Designs: 40m, Map of Cyprus. 60m, Gold medals and sports emblems.

*Perf. 13½x12*

**1977, Oct. 17** **Wmk. 344**

| | | | | |
|---|---|---|---|---|
| *486* | A158 | 20m multicolored | 12 | 10 |
| *487* | A158 | 40m multicolored | 20 | 18 |
| *488* | A158 | 60m multicolored | 30 | 28 |
| *489* | A159 | 80m multicolored | 45 | 38 |

Revitalization of handicrafts (20m); Man and the biosphere (40m); Gold medals won by secondary school students in France for long jump and 200 meter race (60m); 60th anniv. of Bolshevik Revolution (80m).

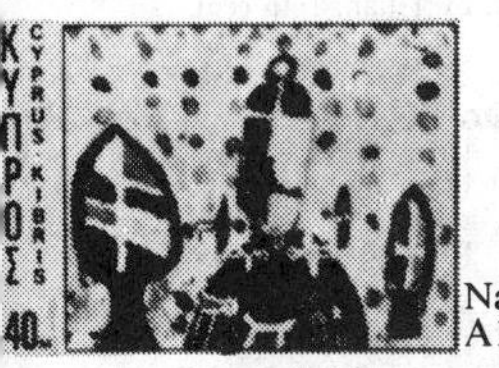
Nativity A160

Christmas (Children's Drawings): 10m, Three Kings following the star. 150m, Flight into Egypt.

*Perf. 14x13½*

**1977, Nov. 21** **Litho.** **Unwmk.**

| | | | | |
|---|---|---|---|---|
| *490* | A160 | 10m multicolored | 8 | 8 |
| *491* | A160 | 40m multicolored | 20 | 18 |
| *492* | A160 | 150m multicolored | 75 | 70 |

Demetrios Libertis (1866-1937) — A161

Design: 150m, Vasilis Michaelides (1849-1917).

**1978, Mar. 6** **Wmk. 344** ***Perf. 14x13***

| | | | | |
|---|---|---|---|---|
| *493* | A161 | 40m bister & olive | 22 | 20 |
| *494* | A161 | 150m gray, ver & blk | 70 | 65 |

Cypriot poets.

**Europa Issue 1978**

Chrysorrhogiatissa Monastery — A162

Designs: 75m, Kolossi Castle. 125m, Municipal Library, Paphos.

*Perf. 14½x13*

**1978, Apr. 24** **Litho.** **Unwmk.**

| | | | | |
|---|---|---|---|---|
| *495* | A162 | 25m multicolored | 12 | 10 |
| *496* | A162 | 75m multicolored | 35 | 35 |
| *497* | A162 | 125m multicolored | 60 | 60 |

Makarios as Archbishop 1950-1977 — A163

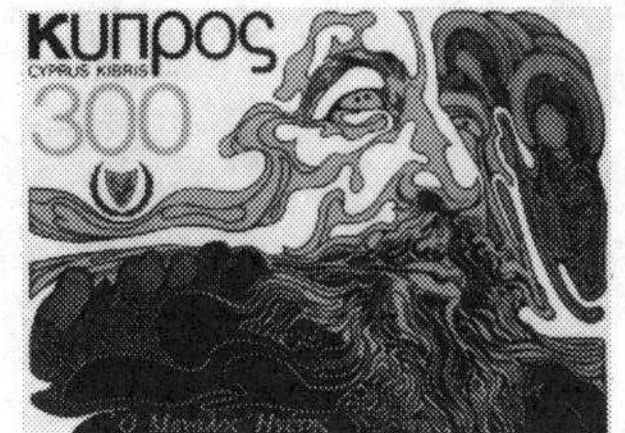
"The Great Leader" — A164

Designs (Archbishop Makarios): 25m, Exiled, Seychelles, 1956-1957. 50m, President of Cyprus, 1960-1977. 75m, Soldier of Christ. 100m, Freedom fighter.

*Perf. 14x14½*

**1978, Aug. 3** **Litho.** **Unwmk.**

| | | | | |
|---|---|---|---|---|
| *498* | A163 | 15m multicolored | 8 | 8 |
| *499* | A163 | 25m multicolored | 12 | 12 |
| *500* | A163 | 50m multicolored | 30 | 30 |
| *501* | A163 | 75m multicolored | 42 | 42 |
| *502* | A163 | 100m multicolored | 60 | 60 |
| | | *Nos. 498-502 (5)* | 1.52 | 1.52 |

**Miniature Sheet**

***Imperf***

| | | | | |
|---|---|---|---|---|
| *503* | A164 | 300m multicolored | 8.25 | 7.25 |

Archbishop Makarios, President of Cyprus. Size of No. 503: 110x80mm.

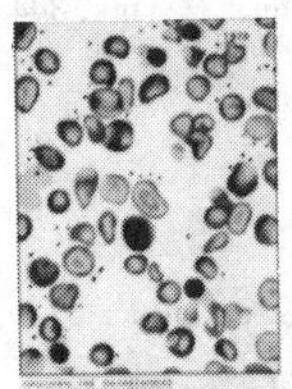
Blood Cells with Low Hemoglobin A165

Bust of Aristotle A166

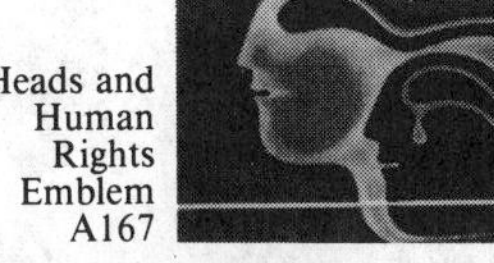
Heads and Human Rights Emblem A167

Wilbur and Orville Wright, Flyer I — A168

*Perf. 13x14, 14x13*

**1978, Oct. 23** **Unwmk.** **Litho.**

| | | | | |
|---|---|---|---|---|
| *504* | A165 | 15m multicolored | 7 | 7 |
| *505* | A166 | 35m multicolored | 20 | 20 |
| *506* | A167 | 75m black | 40 | 40 |
| *507* | A168 | 125m multicolored | 55 | 55 |

Anemia prevention (15m); 2300th birth anniv. of Aristotle (35m); 30th anniv. of Universal Declaration of Human Rights (75m); 75th anniv. of first powered flight (125m).

Kiti Icon Stand — A169

Christmas: 35m, Athienou icon stand. 150m, Omodhos icon stand.

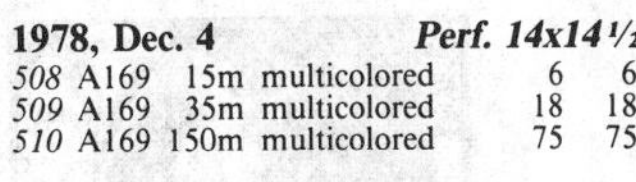

**1978, Dec. 4** ***Perf. 14x14½***

| | | | | |
|---|---|---|---|---|
| *508* | A169 | 15m multicolored | 6 | 6 |
| *509* | A169 | 35m multicolored | 18 | 18 |
| *510* | A169 | 150m multicolored | 75 | 75 |

Venus Statue from Soli A170

Design: 125m, Birth of Venus, by Botticelli (detail).

**1979, Mar. 12** **Litho.** ***Perf. 14x13½***

| | | | | |
|---|---|---|---|---|
| *511* | A170 | 75m multicolored | 35 | 35 |
| *512* | A170 | 125m multicolored | 55 | 55 |

**Europa Issue 1979**

Mail Coach, Envelope and Truck A171

Designs: 75m, Old telephone, dish antenna and satellite. 125m, Steamship, jet and envelopes.

**1979, Apr. 30** **Litho.** ***Perf. 14x13½***

| | | | | |
|---|---|---|---|---|
| *513* | A171 | 25m multicolored | 12 | 12 |
| *514* | A171 | 75m multicolored | 35 | 35 |
| *515* | A171 | 125m multicolored | 55 | 55 |

Peacock Wrasse A172

Designs: 50m, Black partridge (vert.). 75m, Cyprus cedar (vert.). 125m, Mule.

*Perf. 13½x12½, 12½x13½*

**1979, June 25** **Litho.**

| | | | | |
|---|---|---|---|---|
| *516* | A172 | 25m multi | 12 | 10 |
| *517* | A172 | 50m multi | 24 | 22 |
| *518* | A172 | 75m multi | 35 | 32 |
| *519* | A172 | 125m multi | 55 | 50 |

Children Holding Globe, UNESCO Emblem — A173

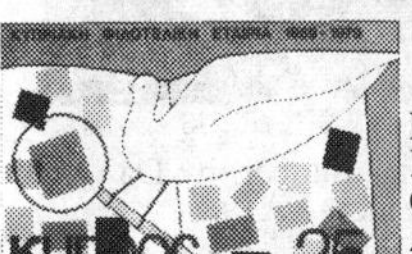

Dove, Magnifying Glass, Album A174

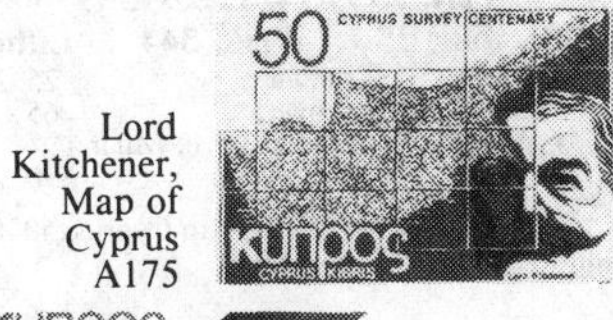
Lord Kitchener, Map of Cyprus A175

Smiling Child, IYC Emblem A176

Soccer A177

Rotary Emblem — A178

**1979, Oct. 1** **Litho.** ***Perf. 12½***

| | | | | |
|---|---|---|---|---|
| *520* | A173 | 15m multicolored | 8 | 8 |
| *521* | A174 | 25m multicolored | 12 | 12 |
| *522* | A175 | 50m multicolored | 24 | 24 |
| *523* | A176 | 75m multicolored | 32 | 28 |
| *524* | A177 | 100m multicolored | 48 | 45 |
| *525* | A178 | 125m multicolored | 55 | 48 |
| | | *Nos. 520-525 (6)* | 1.79 | 1.65 |

Intl. Bureau of Education, Geneva, 50th anniv.; Cyprus Philatelic Society, 20th anniv.; Horatio Herbert Kitchener's survey of Cyprus, cent.; IYC; European Soccer Assoc., 25th anniv.; Rotary Club of Cyprus, 75th anniv..

Jesus, Icon, 12th Century — A179

Christmas (Icons): 35m, Nativity, 16th cent. 150m, Virgin and Child, 12th cent.

*Perf. 13½x14, 13x14*

**1979, Nov. 5** **Litho.**

**Sizes: 24x37mm; 27x40mm (35m)**

| | | | | |
|---|---|---|---|---|
| *526* | A179 | 15m multicolored | 9 | 9 |
| *527* | A179 | 35m multicolored | 20 | 18 |
| *528* | A179 | 150m multicolored | 70 | 60 |

Cyprus No. 1, Nicosia Cancel A180

Cyprus Stamp Centenary: 125m, No. 3, Kyrenia cancel. 175m, No. 6, Larnaca cancel. 500m, Nos. 1-6.

**1980, Mar. 17** **Litho.** ***Perf. 14x13***

| | | | | |
|---|---|---|---|---|
| *529* | A180 | 40m multicolored | 22 | 22 |
| *530* | A180 | 125m multicolored | 65 | 65 |
| *531* | A180 | 175m multicolored | 95 | 95 |

**Size: 105x85mm.**

| | | | | |
|---|---|---|---|---|
| *532* | A180 | 500m multicolored | 3.00 | 3.00 |

**Europa Issue 1980**

Holy Cross, St. Barnabas Church, Ayiasmati — A181

Design: 125m, Zenon of Citium, Ny Carsberg Glyptothek, Copenhagen.

**1980, Apr. 28** *Perf. 12½*

533 A181 40m multicolored 20 20
534 A181 125m multicolored 62 62

Sailing, Moscow '80 Emblem
A182

**1980, June 23** **Litho.** *Perf. 14x13*

535 A182 40m shown 20 20
536 A182 125m Swimming 62 62
537 A182 200m Gymnast 1.00 1.00

22nd Summer Olympic Games, Moscow, July 19-Aug. 3.

Gold Necklace
A183

Clay Amphora
A184

Designs: Archaeological finds on Cyprus, 12th century B.C. to 3rd century A.D. 15m, 40m, 150m, 500m, horiz.

*Perf. 13½x14, 14x13½*

**1980, Sept. 15** **Litho.** **Wmk. 344**

538 A183 10m shown 5 5
539 A183 15m Bronze cow 8 8
540 A183 25m shown 10 10
541 A183 40m Lion, gold ring 18 18
542 A183 50m Bronze cauldron 22 22
543 A183 75m Stele 35 35
544 A183 100m Clay jug 45 45
545 A183 125m Warrior, terracotta bust 55 55
546 A183 150m Lions attacking bull 65 65
547 A183 175m Faience and enamel vase 80 80
548 A183 200m Warrior god, bronze 90 90
549 A183 500m Stone bowl 2.25 2.25
550 A183 £1 Ivory plaque 4.50 4.50
551 A183 £2 Leda and the swan, mosaic 9.00 9.00
*Nos. 538-551 (14)* 20.08 20.08

Cyprus Flag
A185

Archbishop Makarios
A187

Treaty Signing Establishing Republic, 20th Anniversary — A186

**1980, Oct. 1** *Perf. 13½x14, 14x13*

552 A185 40m multicolored 20 20
553 A186 125m multicolored 62 62
554 A187 175m multicolored 90 90

Dove and Woman
A188

*Perf. 14x13*

**1980, Nov. 29** **Litho.** **Wmk. 344**

555 A188 40m shown 20 20
556 A188 125m Dove and man 62 62

Intl. Palestinian Solidarity Day. Nos. 555-556 se-tenant.

Pulpit, Tripiotis Church, Nicosia — A189

Christmas: 100m. Iconostatis (Holy Door), Panayia Church, Paralimni. 125m, Pulpit, Ayios Lazaros Church, Larnaca.

**1980, Nov. 29** *Perf. 13½x14*

557 A189 25m multicolored 12 12

**Size: 24x37mm**

558 A189 100m multicolored 50 50

**Size: 21x37mm**

559 A189 125m multicolored 62 62

**Europa Issue 1981**

Folk Dance — A190

**1981, May 4** **Photo.** *Perf. 14*

560 A190 40m shown 20 20
561 A190 175m Dance, diff. 90 90

Self-portrait, by Da Vinci — A191

The Last Supper, by Da Vinci — A192

*Perf. 13½x14, 12½x13½*

**1981, June 15** **Wmk. 344** **Litho.**

562 A191 50m shown 25 25
563 A192 125m shown 65 65
564 A191 175m Lace pattern, Milan Cathedral 90 90

Leonardo Da Vinci's visit to Cyprus, 500th anniv.

Ophrys Kotschyi — A193

Designs: Orchids. Nos. 565-568 se-tenant.

**1981, July 6** *Perf. 13½x14*

565 A193 25m shown 14 14
566 A193 50m Orchis puntulata 28 28
567 A193 75m Ophrys argolica elegantis 42 42
568 A193 150m Epipactis veratrifolia 85 85

Prince Charles and Lady Diana, St. Paul's Cathedral
A194

*Perf. 14x13*

**1981, Sept. 28** **Litho.** **Wmk. 344**

569 A194 200m multicolored 1.00 1.00

Royal wedding.

Heinrich von Stephan (1831-1897), UPU Founder — A195

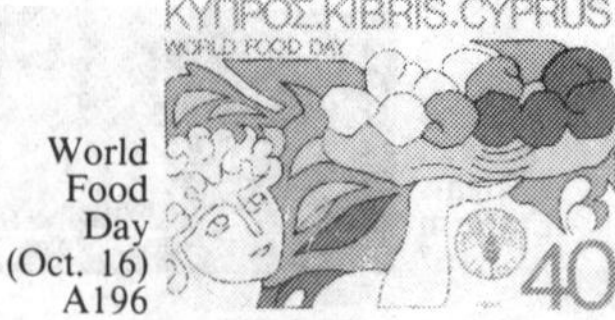


World Food Day (Oct. 16)
A196

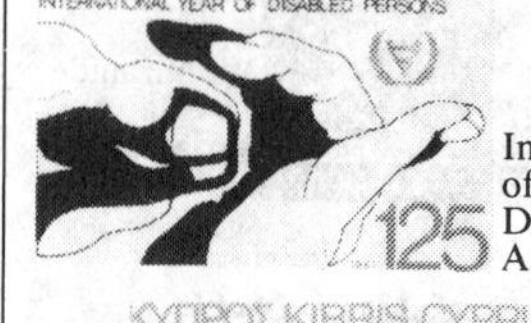


Intl. Year of the Disabled
A197

European Campaign for Urban Renaissance — A198

**1981, Sept. 28**

570 A195 25m multicolored 10 10
571 A196 40m multicolored 18 18
572 A197 125m multicolored 55 55
573 A198 150m multicolored 65 65

Our Lady of the Angels, Transfiguration Church, Palekhori — A199

Christmas (Frescoes): 100m, Christ, Madonna of Arakas Church, Lagoudera (vert.). 125m, Baptism of Christ, Our Lady of Assinou Church, Nikitari.

**1981, Nov. 16** *Perf. 12½*

574 A199 25m multicolored 10 10
575 A199 100m multicolored 42 42
576 A199 125m multicolored 50 50

Bathing Aphrodite, Sculpture, Soloi, 250 B.C. — A200

Design: 175m, Aphrodite Emerging from the Water, by Titian, 16th cent.

*Perf. 13½x14*

**1982, Apr. 12** **Litho.** **Wmk. 344**

577 A200 125m multicolored 50 50
578 A200 175m multicolored 75 75

**Europa Issue 1982**

Liberation by Emperor Nicephorus II Phocas, 965 A.D.
A201

*Perf. 12½*

**1982, May 3** **Photo.** **Unwmk.**

579 A201 40m shown 15 15
580 A201 175m Conversion of Sergius Paulus, 45 A.D. 65 65

Mosaic Chrismon
A202

Cultural Heritage: 125m, King of Palaepaphos (High Priest of Aphrodite), sculpture (vert.). 225m, Theseus Struggling with the Minotaur, mosaic.

**Wmk. 344**

**1982, July 5** **Litho.** *Perf. 12½*

581 A202 50m multicolored 20 20
582 A202 125m multicolored 50 50
583 A202 225m multicolored 95 95

No. 543 Surcharged

**1982, Sept. 6** **Litho.** *Perf. 13½x14*

584 A184 100m on 75m multi 38 38

Scouting Year
A203

Christmas
A204

*Perf. 13½x12½, 12½x13½*

**1982, Nov. 8** **Wmk. 344**

585 A203 100m Emblem, horiz. 40 40
586 A203 125m Baden-Powell 50 50
587 A203 175m Camp site, horiz. 70 70

*Perf. 12½, 13½x14 (100m)*

**1982, Dec. 6**

Designs: 25m, 250m, Christ Giving Holy Communion (bread, 25m: wine, 250m) to the Apostles, St. Neophytos Monastery Church,

Paphos (horiz.). 100m, Chalice, Church of St. Savvas, Nicosia.

588 A204 25m multicolored 10 10
589 A204 100m multicolored 45 45
590 A204 250m multicolored 1.10 1.10

**Commonwealth Day**
Common Design Type

**1983, Mar. 14** ***Perf. 14x13½***

591 CD334 50m Cyprus Forest Industries, Ltd. 18 18
592 CD334 125m Mosaic, 3rd cent. 45 45
593 CD334 150m Dancers 55 55
594 CD334 175m Royal Exhibition Building, Melbourne 65 65

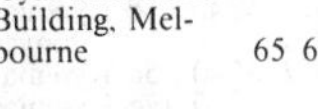

Europa A205

Designs: 50m, Cyprosyllabic script funerary stele, 6th cent., BC. 200m, Copper ore, Enkomi ingot, 1400-1250 BC, bronze jug, 2nd cent.

**1983, May 3 Photo.** ***Perf. 14½x14***

595 A205 50m multicolored 18 18
596 A205 200m multicolored 75 75

Local Butterflies A206

**Wmk. 344**

**1983, June 28 Litho.** ***Perf. 12½***

597 A206 60m Pararge aegeria 24 24
598 A206 130m Aricia medon 52 52
599 A206 250m Glaucopsyche paphos 1.00 1.00

Nos. 538-549 Surcharged

***Perf. 13½x14, 14x13½***

**1983, Oct. 3 Litho. Wmk. 344**

600 A183 1c on 10m multi 5 5
601 A184 2c on 15m multi 8 8
602 A184 3c on 25m multi 12 12
603 A183 4c on 40m multi 16 16
604 A183 5c on 50m multi 20 20
605 A184 6c on 75m multi 24 24
606 A183 10c on 100m multi 40 40
607 A183 13c on 125m multi 52 52
608 A183 15c on 150m multi 60 60
609 A183 20c on 200m multi 80 80
610 A183 25c on 175m multi 1.00 1.00
611 A183 50c on 500m multi 2.00 2.00
*Nos. 600-611 (12)* 6.17 6.17

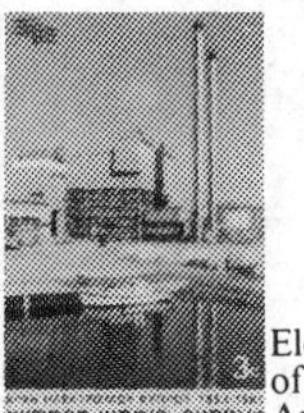

Electricity Authority of Cyprus, 30th Anniv. — A207

World Communications Year — A208

Intl. Maritime Org., 25th Anniv. — A209

Universal Declaration of Human Rights, 35th Anniv. — A210

Nicos Kazantzakis, 100th Birth Anniv. — A211

Archbishop Makarios III, 70th Birth Anniv. — A212

**1983, Oct. 31 Litho.** ***Perf. 13½x14***

612 A207 3c multicolored 12 12
613 A208 6c multicolored 24 24
614 A209 13c multicolored 52 52
615 A210 15c multicolored 60 60
616 A211 20c multicolored 80 80
617 A212 25c multicolored 1.00 1.00
*Nos. 612-617 (6)* 3.28 3.28

Christmas — A213

Designs: 4c, Belfry, St. Lazaros Church, Larnaca. 13c, Belfry, St. Varvara Church, Kaimakli, Nicosia. 20c, Belfry, St. Ioannis Church, Larnaca.

**1983, Dec. 12** ***Perf. 12½x14***

618 A213 4c multicolored 14 14
619 A213 13c multicolored 48 48
620 A213 20c multicolored 70 70

Waterside Cafe at the Marina, Larnaca — A214

19th Century engravings. Size of 6c: 41x27mm; 75c, 110x85mm.

***Perf. 14½x14 (6c), 14, Imperf. (75c)***

**1984, Mar. 6**

621 A214 6c shown 22 22
622 A214 20c Bazaar, Larnaca 70 70
623 A214 30c East Gate, Nicosia 1.00 1.00
624 A214 75c St. Lazarus Church Interior, Larnaca 2.75 2.75

Europa (1959-1984) A215

**1984, Apr. 30 Wmk. 344** ***Perf. 12½***

625 A215 6c multicolored 28 28
626 A215 15c multicolored 65 65

1984 Summer Olympics A216

**1984, June 18 Litho.** ***Perf. 14***

627 A216 3c Running 12 12
628 A216 4c Olympic column 16 16
629 A216 13c Swimming 52 52
630 A216 20c Gymnastics 80 80

Turkish Invasion, 10th Anniv. A217

**1984, July 20 Litho.** ***Perf. 14x13½***

631 A217 15c Prisoners, barbed wire 60 60
632 A217 20c Map 85 85

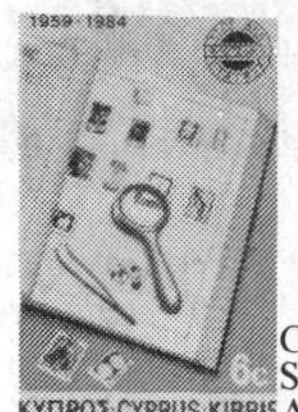

Cyprus Philatelic Society, 25th Anniv. — A218

Cyprus Soccer Assoc., 50th Anniv. A219

George Papanicolaou (1883-1962), Cancer Researcher — A220

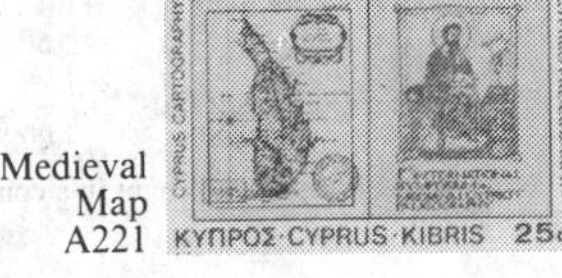

Medieval Map A221

**1984, Oct. 15 Wmk. 344** ***Perf. 12½***

633 A218 6c multicolored 18 18
634 A219 10c multicolored 30 30
635 A220 15c multicolored 50 50
636 A221 25c multicolored 95 95

Intl. Symposium of Cyprus Cartography and First Intl. Symposium on Medieval Paleography (25c).

Christmas — A222

**1984, Nov. 26 Litho.** ***Perf. 12½***

637 A222 4c St. Mark 10 10
638 A222 13c Gospel page (St. Mark) 48 48
639 A222 20c St. Luke 75 75

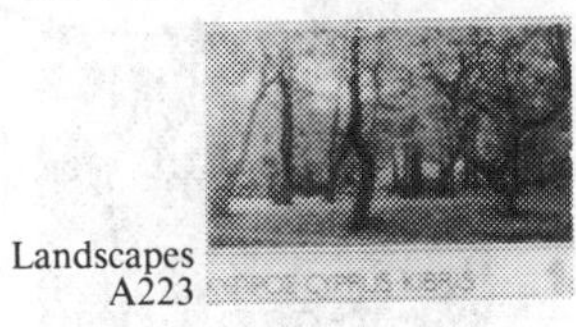

Landscapes A223

***Perf. 15x14, 14x15***

**1985, Mar. 18 Litho.**

640 A223 1c Autumn at Platania 5 5
641 A223 2c Ayia Napa Monastery 5 5
642 A223 3c Phine Village 8 8
643 A223 4c Kykko Monastery 12 12
644 A223 5c Beach at Makronissos 16 16
645 A223 6c Village Street, Omodhos, vert. 18 18
646 A223 10c Sea view 30 30
647 A223 13c Water sports 40 40
648 A223 15c Beach at Protaras 48 48
649 A223 20c Forestry, vert. 60 60
650 A223 25c Sunrise at Protaras, vert. 90 75
651 A223 30c Village houses, Pera Orinis 1.25 90
652 A223 50c Apollo Hylates Sanctuary 2.50 1.50
653 A223 £1 Troodos Mountain, vert. 5.00 5.00
654 A223 £5 Personification of Autumn, Dionyssos House, vert. 19.00 15.00
*Nos. 640-654 (15)* 31.07 25.57

Europa A224

Designs: 6c, Ceramic figures playing the double flute, lyre and tambourine, 7th-6th century B.C. 15c, Cypriot violin, lute, flute, the Fourth Women's Dance from the Cyprus Suite.

**1985, May 6 Litho.** ***Perf. 12½***

655 A224 6c multicolored 22 22
656 A224 15c multicolored 55 55

Republic of Cyprus, 25th Anniv. — A225

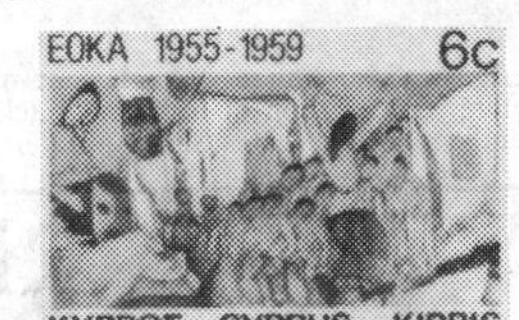

Natl. Liberation Movement, 30th Anniv. — A226

Intl. Youth Year A227

Demand, as well as supply, determines a stamp's market value. One is as important as the other.

Solon Michaelides (1905-1979), Conductor, European Music Year — A228

UN 40th Anniv. — A229

***Perf. 14½ (#657), 14½x14, 15 (#661)***

**1985, Sept. 23** **Litho.**

*657* A225 4c multicolored 10 10
*658* A226 6c multicolored 22 22
*659* A227 13c multicolored 48 48
*660* A228 15c multicolored 55 55
*661* A229 20c multicolored 75 75
*Nos. 657-661 (5)* 2.10 2.10

Christmas — A230

Murals of the St. Ioannis Lampadistis Monastery, Kalopanyiotis: 4c, Virgin Mary's Visit to Elizabeth. 13c, The Nativity. 20c, The Candlemas, Church of Our Lady of Assinous, Nikitari.

**1985, Nov. 18** **Litho.** ***Perf. 12½***

*662* A230 4c multicolored 15 15
*663* A230 13c multicolored 52 52
*664* A230 20c multicolored 80 80

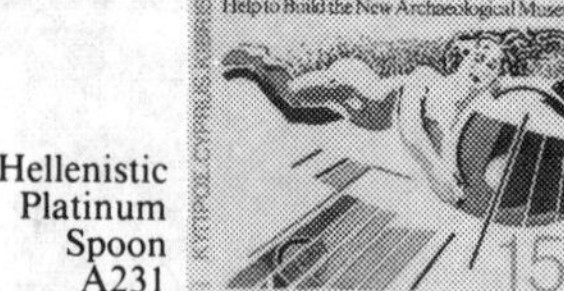


Hellenistic Platinum Spoon A231

Designs: 20c, Ionian helmet, foot of a sculpture. 25c, Union of Eros and Intellect personified, abstract. 30c, Statue profile.

**1986, Feb. 17** ***Perf. 15x14***

*665* A231 15c multicolored 60 60
*666* A231 20c multicolored 80 80
*667* A231 25c multicolored 1.00 1.00
*668* A231 30c multicolored 1.25 1.25
*a.* Souvenir sheet of 4, #665-668 9.00 9.00

Construction of the New Archaeological Museum, Nicosia. Department of Antiquities, 50th anniv. No. 668a sold for £1.

Europa A232

**1986, Apr. 28** **Litho.** ***Perf. 14x13***

*669* A232 7c Mouflon, cedar trees 30 30
*670* A232 17c Flamingos, Larnaca Salt Lake 80 80

Seashells A233

**1986, July 1** ***Perf. 14x13½***

*671* A233 5c Chlamys pesfelis 24 24
*672* A233 7c Charonia variegata 60 60
*673* A233 18c Murex brandaris 60 60
*674* A233 25c Cypraea spurca 85 85

Overseas Cypriots Year A234

Halley's Comet A235

Anniversaries and events.

***Perf. 13½x13***

**1986, Oct. 13** **Litho.** **Wmk. 344**

*675* A234 15c multi 80 80
*676* A235 18c shown 1.00 1.00
*677* A235 18c Comet tail, Edmond Halley 1.00 1.00

Nos. 676-677 printed se-tenant in a continuous design.

Road Safety A236

**1986, Nov. 10** ***Perf. 14x13***

*678* A236 5c Pedestrian crossing 20 20
*679* A236 7c Helmet, motorcycle controls 28 28
*680* A236 18c Seatbelt, rearview mirror 70 70

Intl. Peace Year, Christmas — A237

Nativity frescoes (details): 5c, Church of Panayia tou Araka. 15c, Church of Panayia tou Moutoulla. 17c, Church of St. Nicholaos tis Steyis.

**1986, Nov. 24** ***Perf. 13½x14***

*681* A237 5c multicolored 25 25
*682* A237 15c multicolored 75 75
*683* A237 17c multicolored 85 85

Nos. 645 and 647 Surcharged

***Perf. 14x15, 15x14***

**1986, Oct. 13** **Litho.** **Wmk. 344**

*684* A223 7c on 6c multi 30 30
*685* A223 18c on 13c multi 75 75

**Miniature Sheet**

Troodos Churches on UNESCO World Heritage List — A238

Churches and frescoes: a, Assinou, Nikitari. b, Moutoulla, Moutoullas. c, Podithou, Galata. d, Ayios Ioannis Lampadistis, Kalopanayiotis. e, Timios Stavros, Pelentri. f, Stavros Ayiasmati, Platanistasa. g, Archangelos Pedoula, Pedoulas. h, Ayios Nicolaos tis Steyis, Kakopetria. i, Araka, Lagoudera.

***Perf. 12½***

**1987, Apr. 22** **Photo.** **Unwmk.**

*686* Sheet of 9 6.00 6.00
*a.-i.* 15c, any single 65 65

No. 686 has inscribed margin with black control number. Size: 152x121mm.

Europa A239

Modern architecture.

***Perf. 14x13½***

**1987, May 11** **Litho.** **Wmk. 344**

*687* A239 7c Central Bank of Cyprus 28 28
*688* A239 18c Cyprus Communications Authority 75 75

Ships Named Kyrenia A240

**1987, Oct. 3**

*689* A240 2c The Kyrenia, Kyrenia Castle 10 10
*690* A240 3c Kyrenia II, Perama Shipyard 14 14
*691* A240 5c Kyrenia II, Paphos 22 22
*692* A240 17c Kyrenia II, New York Harbor 75 75

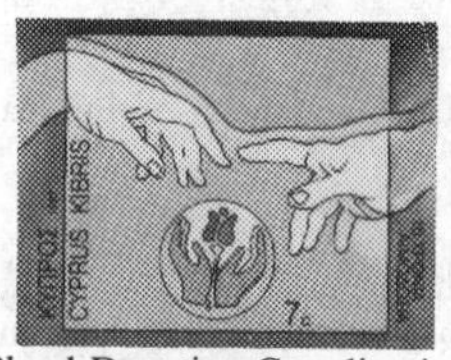


Blood Donation Coordinating Committee, 10th Anniv. — A241

European Campaign for Countryside — A242

TROODOS '87 — A243

***Perf. 14x13½***

**1987, Nov. 2** **Litho.** **Wmk. 344**

*693* A241 7c multicolored 30 30
*694* A242 15c multicolored 65 65
*695* A243 20c multicolored 85 85

Christmas A244

**1987, Nov. 30** ***Perf. 14***

*696* A244 5c Babe in a manger 22 22
*697* A244 15c Ornament 65 65
*698* A244 17c Fruit bowl 72 72

Cyprus Customs Union in Cooperation with the EEC — A245

***Perf. 13x13½***

**1988, Jan. 11** **Wmk. 344**

*699* A245 15c Natl. and EEC flags 65 65
*700* A245 18c Maps 80 80

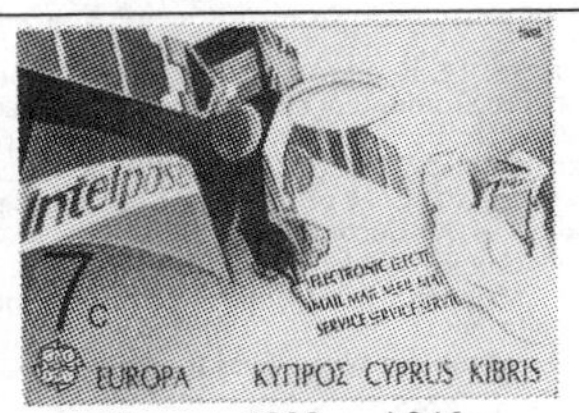

Europa 1988 — A246

Communication and transportation: No. 701, Electronic mail (Intelpost). No. 702, Cellular telephone system. No. 703, Cyprus Airways, technology vs. ecology (jet, 3 flamingos). No. 704, Cyprus Airways (jet, 4 flamingos).

**1988, May 9** *Perf. 14x14½*

| No. | Type | Description | Unused | Used |
|---|---|---|---|---|
| *701* | A246 | 7c multi | 32 | 32 |
| *702* | A246 | 7c multi | 32 | 32 |
| *703* | A246 | 18c multi | 82 | 82 |
| *704* | A246 | 18c multi | 82 | 82 |

Stamps of the same denomination printed se-tenant.

1988 Summer Olympics, Seoul — A247

**Unwmk.**

**1988, June 27 Photo.** *Perf. 12*

**Granite Paper**

| No. | Type | Description | Unused | Used |
|---|---|---|---|---|
| *705* | A247 | 5c Sailing | 22 | 22 |
| *706* | A247 | 7c Track | 32 | 32 |
| *707* | A247 | 10c Marksmanship | 45 | 45 |
| *708* | A247 | 20c Judo | 90 | 90 |

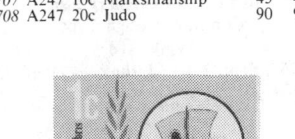

Non-Aligned Foreign Minister's Conference — A248

Designs: 10c, Natl. coat of arms. 50c, Jawaharlal Nehru, Tito, Gamal Abdel Nasser and Makarios III (1913-77).

*Perf. 14x13½*

**1988, Sept. 5 Litho. Wmk. 344**

| No. | Type | Description | Unused | Used |
|---|---|---|---|---|
| *709* | A248 | 1c shown | 5 | 5 |
| *710* | A248 | 10c multi | 45 | 45 |
| *711* | A248 | 50c multi | 2.15 | 2.15 |

No. 643 Surcharged 15c ═

**1988, Oct. 3 Litho.** *Perf. 15x14*

| No. | Type | Description | Unused | Used |
|---|---|---|---|---|
| *712* | A223 | 15c on 4c multi | 85 | 85 |

Christmas A249

*Perf. 13½x14*

**1988, Nov. 28 Litho. Wmk. 344**

| No. | Type | Description | Unused | Used |
|---|---|---|---|---|
| *713* | A249 | 5c Candlemas | 22 | 22 |
| *714* | A249 | 15c Madonna and child | 65 | 65 |
| *715* | A249 | 17c Adoration of the Magi | 75 | 75 |

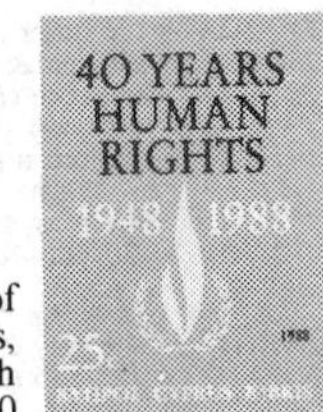

UN Declaration of Human Rights, 40th Anniv. — A250

**1988, Dec. 10**

| No. | Type | Description | Unused | Used |
|---|---|---|---|---|
| *716* | A250 | 25c lt ultra & intense bl | 1.10 | 1.10 |

## POSTAL TAX STAMPS

**Catalogue values for unused stamps in this section, from this point to the end of the section, are for Never Hinged items.**

No. 352 Surcharged

REFUGEE FUND
ΤΑΜΕΙΟΝ
ΠΡΟΣΦΥΓΩΝ
GOCMENLER FONU
10M

*Perf. 12x12½*

**1974, Dec. 2 Wmk. 344**

| No. | Type | Description | Unused | Used |
|---|---|---|---|---|
| *RA1* | A104 | 10m on 5m multi | 15 | 15 |

Refugee Fund.

Old Woman and Child — PT1

**1974, Oct. 1** *Perf. 12½x13½*

| No. | Type | Description | Unused | Used |
|---|---|---|---|---|
| *RA2* | PT1 | 10m gray & black | 12 | 12 |

Refugee Fund.

Child and Barbed Wire — PT2

**1977, Jan. 10 Litho. Wmk. 344**

| No. | Type | Description | Unused | Used |
|---|---|---|---|---|
| *RA3* | PT2 | 10m black | 10 | 8 |

Plight of the refugees. Refugee Fund.

Inscribed 1984

**1984, June 18** *Perf. 13*

| No. | Type | Description | Unused | Used |
|---|---|---|---|---|
| *RA4* | PT2 | 1c black | 10 | 5 |

Inscribed 1988

**1988, Sept. 12** *Perf. 13x12½*

| No. | Type | Description | Unused | Used |
|---|---|---|---|---|
| *RA5* | PT2 | 1c blk & pale gray | 6 | 5 |

# DOMINICA

LOCATION — The largest island of the Windward group in the West Indies. Southeast of Puerto Rico.
GOVT. — Republic in British Commonwealth.
AREA — 290 sq. mi.
POP. — 74,859 (1981).
CAPITAL — Roseau.

Formerly a Presidency of the Leeward Islands, Dominica became a separate colony under the governor of the Windward Islands on January 1, 1940. Dominica joined the West Indies federation April 22, 1958. In 1968, Dominica became an associate state of Britain; in 1978, an independent nation.

12 Pence = 1 Shilling
20 Shillings = 1 Pound
100 Cents = 1 Dollar (1949)

**Catalogue values for unused stamps in this country are for Never Hinged items, beginning with Scott 112.**

Queen Victoria — A1

**Wmk. Crown and C. C. (1)**

**1874 Typo.** *Perf. 12½*

| No. | Type | Description | Unused | Used |
|---|---|---|---|---|
| *1* | A1 | 1p violet | 85.00 | 30.00 |
| *2* | A1 | 6p green | 325.00 | 60.00 |
| *3* | A1 | 1sh dp lil rose | 250.00 | 45.00 |

**1877-79** *Perf. 14*

| No. | Type | Description | Unused | Used |
|---|---|---|---|---|
| *4* | A1 | ½p bis ('79) | 8.50 | *9.50* |
| *5* | A1 | 1p violet | 4.00 | 1.75 |
| *a* | | Diagonal or vertical half used as ½p on cover | | 1,500. |
| *6* | A1 | 2½p red brn ('79) | 95.00 | 20.00 |
| *7* | A1 | 4p bl ('79) | 65.00 | 7.00 |
| *8* | A1 | 6p green | 100.00 | 25.00 |
| *9* | A1 | 1sh dp lil rose | 90.00 | 40.00 |

No. 5 Bisected and Surcharged in Black or Red:

½ (a) HALF PENNY (b) 1/2 (c)

**1882**

| No. | Type | Description | Unused | Used |
|---|---|---|---|---|
| *10* | A1(a) | ½p on half of 1p vio | 100.00 | 50.00 |
| *a* | | Inverted surcharge | 1,000. | 800.00 |
| *b* | | Surcharge tete beche pair | 1,400. | 1,400. |
| *11* | A1(b) | ½p on half of 1p vio | 27.50 | 30.00 |
| *a* | | Surcharge reading downward | 27.50 | 30.00 |
| *b* | | Double surcharge | 750.00 | |
| *12* | A1(c) | ½p on half of 1p vio (R) | 14.00 | 10.00 |
| *a* | | Inverted surcharge | 900.00 | 775.00 |
| *b* | | Double surcharge | 1,750. | |

Nos. 8 and 9 Surcharged in Black

Half Penny

**1886**

| No. | Type | Description | Unused | Used |
|---|---|---|---|---|
| *13* | A1 | ½p on 6p grn | 7.50 | 7.25 |
| *14* | A1 | 1p on 6p grn | *1,750.* | *14,000.* |
| *15* | A1 | 1p on 1sh | 9.90 | *12.50* |
| *a* | | Double surcharge | 7,500. | 3,750. |

**1883-88 Wmk. Crown and C. A. (2)**

| No. | Type | Description | Unused | Used |
|---|---|---|---|---|
| *16* | A1 | ½p bis ('83) | 2.50 | *3.50* |
| *17* | A1 | ½p grn ('86) | 50 | 1.50 |
| *18* | A1 | 1p vio ('86) | 9.00 | 12.50 |
| *a* | | Half used as ½p on cover | | 1,400. |
| *19* | A1 | 1p car rose ('87) | 50 | 50 |
| *a* | | 1p rose | 6.50 | 6.50 |
| *b* | | Vert. half used as ½p on cover | | 1,500. |
| *20* | A1 | 2½p red brn ('84) | 75.00 | 7.00 |
| *21* | A1 | 2½p ultra ('88) | 3.00 | 2.00 |
| *22* | A1 | 4p gray ('86) | 2.50 | 1.50 |
| *23* | A1 | 6p org ('88) | 11.00 | *35.00* |
| *24* | A1 | 1sh dp lil rose ('88) | 130.00 | *250.00* |
| | | *Nos. 16-24 (9)* | 234.00 | 313.50 |

Roseau, Capital of Dominica — A6

King Edward VII — A7

**1903 Wmk. 1** *Perf. 14*

| No. | Type | Description | Unused | Used |
|---|---|---|---|---|
| *25* | A6 | ½p gray grn | 1.75 | *2.25* |
| *26* | A6 | 1p car & blk | 1.75 | 40 |
| *27* | A6 | 2p brn & gray grn | 5.00 | *7.50* |
| *28* | A6 | 2½p ultra & blk | 7.50 | 9.00 |
| *29* | A6 | 3p blk & vio | 7.50 | 10.00 |
| *30* | A6 | 6p org brn & blk | 11.00 | 15.00 |
| *31* | A6 | 1sh gray grn & red vio | 12.00 | *16.00* |
| *32* | A6 | 2sh red vio & blk | 15.50 | 20.00 |
| *33* | A6 | 2sh6p ocher & gray grn | 16.00 | *30.00* |
| *34* | A7 | 5sh brn & blk | 95.00 | *150.00* |
| | | *Nos. 25-34 (10)* | 173.00 | 260.15 |

Nos. 25 to 29 and 31 are on both ordinary and chalky paper.

**1907-20 Wmk. 3**

**Chalky Paper**

| No. | Type | Description | Unused | Used |
|---|---|---|---|---|
| *35* | A6 | ½p gray grn | 70 | 1.00 |
| *36* | A6 | 1p car & blk | 1.40 | 40 |
| *37* | A6 | 2p brn & gray grn | 4.50 | 6.00 |
| *38* | A6 | 2½p ultra & blk | 6.00 | 8.00 |
| *39* | A6 | 3p blk & vio | 5.50 | 7.00 |
| *40* | A6 | 3p vio, *yel* ('09) | 1.50 | 1.50 |
| *41* | A6 | 6p org brn & blk ('08) | 50.00 | 50.00 |
| *42* | A6 | 6p vio & dl vio ('09) | 2.00 | 2.50 |
| *43* | A6 | 1sh gray grn & red vio | 12.50 | 13.75 |
| *44* | A6 | 1sh *green*('10) | 3.25 | 3.50 |
| *45* | A6 | 2sh red vio & blk ('08) | 18.75 | *21.25* |
| *46* | A6 | 2sh ultra & vio, *bl* ('19) | 12.50 | *23.75* |
| *47* | A6 | 2sh6p ocher & gray grn ('08) | 20.00 | *26.25* |
| *48* | A6 | 2sh6p red & blk, *bl* ('20) | 9.00 | *15.00* |
| *49* | A7 | 5sh brn & blk ('08) | 55.00 | 50.00 |
| | | *Nos. 35-49 (15)* | 202.60 | 229.90 |

Nos. 40 and 42 are on both ordinary and chalky paper.

**1908-09 Ordinary Paper**

| No. | Type | Description | Unused | Used |
|---|---|---|---|---|
| *50* | A6 | ½p green | 45 | 42 |
| *51* | A6 | 1p scarlet | 42 | 15 |
| *a* | | 1p carmine | 42 | 15 |
| *52* | A6 | 2p gray ('09) | 2.25 | 2.50 |
| *53* | A6 | 2½p ultra | 1.75 | 1.50 |

King George V — A8

**1914 Chalky Paper** *Perf. 14*

| No. | Type | Description | Unused | Used |
|---|---|---|---|---|
| *54* | A8 | 5sh grn & scar, *yel* | 42.50 | *62.50* |

Type of 1903 Surcharged ═1½D.═

**1920**

| No. | Type | Description | Unused | Used |
|---|---|---|---|---|
| *55* | A6 | 1½p on 2½p org | 1.00 | 75 |

**1921-22 Wmk. 4**

**Ordinary Paper**

| No. | Type | Description | Unused | Used |
|---|---|---|---|---|
| *56* | A6 | ½p green | 2.25 | 3.50 |
| *57* | A6 | 1p rose red | 1.50 | 2.25 |
| *58* | A6 | 1½p orange | 5.00 | 8.50 |
| *59* | A6 | 2p gray | 6.00 | 9.00 |
| *60* | A6 | 2½p ultra | 3.50 | *8.50* |
| *61* | A6 | 6p vio & dl vio | 5.00 | *15.00* |
| *62* | A6 | 2sh ultra & vio, *bl* | 22.50 | *50.00* |
| *63* | A6 | 2sh6p red & blk, *bl* | 27.50 | *55.00* |
| | | *Nos. 56-63 (8)* | 73.25 | 151.75 |

No. 61 is on chalky paper.

Seal of Colony and George V — A9

**1923-33 Chalky Paper Wmk. 4**

65 A9 ½p grn & blk 20 15
66 A9 1p vio & blk 1.25 50
67 A9 1p scar & blk ('33) 2.50 2.00
68 A9 1½p car & blk 75 35
69 A9 1½p dp brn & blk ('33) 2.50 35
70 A9 2p gray & blk 60 45
71 A9 2½p org & blk 65 2.50
72 A9 2½p ultra & blk ('28) 1.40 1.50
73 A9 3p ultra & blk 65 3.75
74 A9 3p red & blk, *yel* ('28) 1.00 1.25
75 A9 4p brn & blk 1.25 4.25
76 A9 6p red vio & blk 1.40 3.25
77 A9 1sh *emerald* 2.25 3.00
78 A9 2sh ultra & blk, *bl* 4.00 7.50
79 A9 2sh 6p red & blk, *bl* 7.50 10.00
80 A9 3sh vio & blk, *yel* ('27) 6.25 10.00
81 A9 4sh red & blk, *emer* 7.50 14.00
82 A9 5sh grn & blk, *yel* ('27) 11.50 16.00
*Nos. 65-82 (18)* 53.15 80.80

**1923 Wmk. 3**

83 A9 3sh vio & blk, *yel* 7.50 12.50
84 A9 5sh grn & blk, *yel* 8.75 17.50
85 A9 £1 vio & blk, *red* 225.00 325.00

**Silver Jubilee Issue**
Common Design Type
***Perf. 13½x14***

**1935, May 6 Wmk. 4 Engr.**

90 CD301 1p car & bl 25 25
91 CD301 1½p gray blk & ultra 75 75
92 CD301 2½p bl & brn 2.50 2.75
93 CD301 1sh brt vio & ind 4.50 5.00

**Coronation Issue.**
Common Design Type

**1937, May 12 *Perf. 11x11½***

94 CD302 1p dk car 8 8
95 CD302 1½p brown 10 10
96 CD302 2½p dp ultra 20 20

Fresh-Water Lake — A10

Layou River — A11

Picking Limes — A12

Boiling Lake — A13

**1938-47 Wmk. 4 *Perf. 12½***

97 A10 ½p grn & red brn 5 5
98 A11 1p car & gray 6 6
99 A12 1½p rose vio & grn 8 6
100 A13 2p brn blk & dp rose 9 9
101 A12 2½p ultra & rose vio 8 8
102 A11 3p red brn & ol 9 9
103 A12 3½p red vio & brt ultra ('47) 15 15
104 A10 6p vio & yel grn 18 18
105 A10 7p org brn & grn ('47) 28 28
106 A13 1sh ol & vio 32 32
107 A11 2sh red vio & blk ('47) 2.00 2.00
108 A10 2sh 6p scar ver & blk 1.10 1.10
109 A11 5sh dk brn & bl 1.75 1.75
110 A13 10sh dl org & blk ('47) 6.25 7.50
*Nos. 97-110 (14)* 12.48 13.71

King George VI — A14

**1940, Apr. 15 Photo. *Perf. 14½x14***

111 A14 ¼p brn vio 5 5

**Catalogue values for unused stamps in this section, from this point to the end of the section, are for Never Hinged items.**

**Peace Issue**
Common Design Type

**1946, Oct. 14 Engr. *Perf. 13½x14***

112 CD303 1p carmine 6 6
113 CD303 3½p dp bl 12 12

**Silver Wedding Issue.**
Common Design Types

**1948, Dec. 1 Photo. *Perf. 14x14½***

114 CD304 1p scarlet 12 12

**Engraved; Name Typographed**
***Perf. 11½x11***

115 CD305 10sh org brn 13.00 15.00

**UPU Issue**
Common Design Types
**Engr.: Name Typo. on 6c and 12c**

**1949, Oct. 10 *Perf. 13½, 11x11½***

116 CD306 5c blue 18 18
117 CD307 6c chocolate 45 45
118 CD308 12c rose vio 75 75
119 CD309 24c olive 1.25 1.25

**University Issue**
Common Design Types

**1951, Feb. 16 Engr. *Perf. 14x14½***

120 CD310 3c pur & grn 32 32
121 CD311 12c dp car & dk bl grn 70 70

George VI — A15

Drying Cocoa — A16

Picking Oranges — A17

Designs: 2c and 60c, Carib Baskets. 3c and 48c, Lime Plantation. 4c, Picking Oranges. 5c, Bananas. 6c, Botanical Gardens. 8c, Drying Vanilla Beans. 12c and $1.20, Fresh Water Lake. 14c, Layou River. 24c, Boiling Lake.

***Perf. 14½x14***

**1951, July 1 Photo. Wmk. 4**

122 A15 ½c brown 7 5

**Engr. *Perf. 13x13½***

123 A16 1c red org & blk 16 15
124 A16 2c dp grn & red brn 18 16
125 A16 3c red vio & bl grn 18 16
126 A16 4c dk brn & brn org 25 20
127 A16 5c rose red & blk 25 22
128 A16 6c org brn & ol grn 25 22
129 A16 8c dp bl & dp grn 42 35
130 A16 12c emer & gray 45 40
131 A16 14c pur & bl 1.00 90
132 A16 24c rose car & red vio 85 70
133 A16 48c red org & bl grn 2.25 4.25
134 A16 60c gray & car 4.75 6.50
135 A16 $1.20 gray & emer 7.25 9.00

***Perf. 13½x13***

136 A17 $2.40 gray & org 15.00 17.50
*Nos. 122-136 (15)* 33.31 40.76

Nos. 125, 127, 129 and 131 Overprinted in Black or Carmine: **NEW CONSTITUTION 1951**

**1951, Oct. 15 *Perf. 13x13½***

137 A16 3c red vio & bl grn 20 20
138 A16 5c rose red & blk 25 25
139 A16 8c dp bl & dp grn (C) 35 35
140 A16 14c pur & bl (C) 50 50

Adoption of a new constitution for the Windward Islands, 1951.

**Coronation Issue.**
Common Design Type

**1953, June 2 Engr. *Perf. 13½x13***

141 CD312 2c dk grn & blk 20 20

Types of 1951 with Portrait of Queen Elizabeth II

**1954, Oct. 1 Photo. *Perf. 14½x14***

142 A15 ½c brown 5 5

**Engr. *Perf. 13x13½***

143 A16 1c red org & blk 5 5
144 A16 2c dp grn & red brn 7 6
145 A16 3c red vio & bl grn 30 28
146 A16 4c dk brn & brn org 7 6
147 A16 5c rose red & blk 38 35
148 A16 6c org brn & ol grn 12 10
149 A16 8c dp bl & dp grn 15 12
150 A16 12c emer & gray 20 18
151 A16 14c pur & bl 22 20
152 A16 24c rose car & red vio 38 28
153 A16 48c red org & bl grn 6.50 6.00
154 A16 60c gray & car 1.10 1.00
155 A16 $1.20 gray & emer 2.75 2.50

***Perf. 13½x13***

156 A17 $2.40 gray & org 6.50 5.50
*Nos. 142-156 (15)* 18.84 16.73

Mat Making — A18

Designs: 5c, Canoe making. 10c, Bananas.

***Perf. 13x13½***

**1957, Oct. 15 Wmk. 4**

157 A18 3c car rose & blk 12 10
158 A18 5c brn & bl 14 11
159 A18 10c redsh brn & brt grn 25 20
160 A18 48c vio & brn 4.50 4.00

**West Indies Federation**
Common Design Type
***Perf. 11½x11***

**1958, Apr. 22 Wmk. 314**

161 CD313 3c green 6 6
162 CD313 6c blue 15 15
163 CD313 12c car rose 25 25

Sailing Canoe A19 — Traditional Costume A20

Designs: 1c, Seashore, Rosalie. 2c, 5c, Queen Elizabeth II by Annigoni. 4c, Sulphur Springs. 6c, Road making. 8c, Dugout canoe. 10c, Frog (mountain chicken). 12c, Boats and Scotts Head. 15c, Bananas. 24c, Imperial parrot. 48c, View of Goodwill. 60c, Cacao tree. $1.20, Coat of Arms. $2.40, Trafalgar Falls. $4.80, Coconut palm.

Two types of 14c:
I. Mountain light violet. Girl's eyes look straight out.
II. Mountain blue. Eyes look sideways.

***Perf. 14½x14, 14x14½***

**1963, May 16 Photo. Wmk. 314**

164 A19 1c bl, brn & grn 5 5
165 A20 2c ultra 5 5
166 A19 3c lt ultra & blk 5 5
167 A19 4c sl, grn & brn 6 6
168 A20 5c magenta 6 6
169 A19 6c lt grn, vio & buff 7 7
170 A19 8c tan, blk & lt grn 10 10
171 A19 10c pink & brn 10 10
172 A19 12c bl, blk, grn & brn 12 12
173 A20 14c multi (I) 40 40
*a* Type II 16 16
174 A19 15c grn, yel & brn 16 16
175 A20 24c multi 50 35
176 A19 48c bl, blk & grn 85 65
177 A19 60c blk, grn, org & brn 1.10 1.00
178 A19 $1.20 multi 2.25 2.25
179 A20 $2.40 grn, bl, brn & blk 4.00 4.00
180 A20 $4.80 bl, brn & grn 8.00 8.00
*Nos. 164-180 (17)* 17.92 17.47

**1966-67 Wmk. 314 Sideways**
**Colors as in 1963 Issue**

167a A19 4c ('67) 12 12
169a A19 6c 25 25
170a A19 8c 40 40
171a A19 10c ('67) 45 45
174a A19 15c ('67) 75 75
*Nos. 167a-174a (5)* 1.97 1.97

**Freedom from Hunger Issue**
Common Design Type

**1963, June 4 *Perf. 14x14½***

181 CD314 15c lilac 35 35

**Red Cross Centenary Issue**
Common Design Type
**Wmk. 314**

**1963, Sept. 2 Litho. *Perf. 13***

182 CD315 5c blk & red 20 20
183 CD315 15c ultra & red 90 90

**Shakespeare Issue**
Common Design Type

**1964, Apr. 23 Photo. *Perf. 14x14½***

184 CD316 15c lil rose 30 30

**ITU Issue**
Common Design Type

**1965, May 17 Litho. *Perf. 11x11½***

185 CD317 2c emer & bl 6 6
186 CD317 48c grnsh bl & sl 90 90

**Intl. Cooperation Year Issue**
Common Design Type

**1965, Oct. 25 *Perf. 14½***

187 CD318 1c bl grn & cl 5 5
188 CD318 15c lt vio & grn 35 35

**Churchill Memorial Issue**
Common Design Type

**1966, Jan. 24 Photo. *Perf. 14***
**Design in Black, Gold and Carmine Rose**

189 CD319 1c brt bl 5 5
*a* Gold omitted 750.00
190 CD319 5c green 10 10
191 CD319 15c brown 30 30
192 CD319 24c violet 65 65

**Royal Visit Issue**
Common Design Type

**1966, Feb. 4 Litho. *Perf. 11x12***

193 CD320 5c vio bl 15 12
194 CD320 15c dk car rose 40 40

**World Cup Soccer Issue**
Common Design Type

**1966, July 1 Litho. *Perf. 14***

195 CD321 5c multi 10 10
196 CD321 24c multi 45 45

**WHO Headquarters Issue**
Common Design Type

**1966, Sept. 20 Litho. *Perf. 14***

197 CD322 5c multi 10 10
198 CD322 24c multi 45 45

**UNESCO Anniversary Issue**
Common Design Type

**1966, Dec. 1 Litho. *Perf. 14***
*199* CD323 5c "Education" 10 10
*200* CD323 15c "Science" 30 30
*201* CD323 24c "Culture" 50 50

Carib, Negro and Caucasian Children — A21

Designs: 10c, Columbus' ship Santa Maria and banderol. 15c, Hands with banderol. 24c, Belaire dancers.

***Perf. 14½x14***
**1967, Nov. 3 Photo. Wmk. 314**
*202* A21 5c multi 5 5
*203* A21 10c multi 10 10
*204* A21 15c multi 15 15
*205* A21 24c multi 25 25

Issued for National Day, Nov. 3.

---

Common Design Types pictured in section before Great Britain.

---

John F. Kennedy and Human Rights Flame — A22

Designs (Human Rights Flame and): 10c, Cecil E. A. Rawle (1891-1938), Dominican crusader for human rights. 12c, Pope John XXIII. 48c, Florence Nightingale. 60c, Dr. Albert Schweitzer.

**Wmk. 314 Sideways**
**1968, Apr. Litho. *Perf. 14***
*206* A22 1c multi 5 5
*207* A22 10c multi 8 8
*208* A22 12c multi 10 10
*209* A22 48c multi 40 40
*210* A22 60c multi 60 60
*Nos. 206-210 (5)* 1.23 1.23

International Human Rights Year.

Stamps and Types of 1963-67 Overprinted in Silver or Black: "ASSOCIATED / STATEHOOD"
***Perf. 14½x14, 14x14½***
**1968, July 8 Photo. Wmk. 314**
*211* A19 1c multi (S) 5 5
*212* A20 2c ultra (S) 5 5
*213* A19 3c lt ultra & blk (S) 5 5
*214* A19 4c multi (S) 5 5
*215* A20 5c mag (S) 5 5
*216* A19 6c multi (B) 5 5
*217* A19 8c multi (B) 6 6
*218* A19 10c pink & brn (S) 8 8
*219* A19 12c multi (S) 8 8
*a* Watermark upright 8 8
*220* A20 14c multi (II) (S) 10 10
*221* A19 15c multi (S) 12 12
*222* A20 24c multi (S) 20 20
*223* A19 48c multi (S) 50 50
*a* Watermark upright 3.50 3.50
*224* A19 60c multi (B) 50 50
*225* A19 $1.20 multi (B) 1.00 1.00
*226* A20 $2.40 multi (S) 2.00 2.00
*227* A20 $4.80 multi (S) 4.00 4.00
*Nos. 211-227 (17)* 8.94 8.94

In this set, overprint was applied to 2c, 3c, 12c, 14c, 24c, 48c, 60c, $1.20, $2.40 and $4.80 with watermark upright. A reprinting of the 1c, 4c, 6c, 8c, 10c, 12c No. 219, 15c and 48c No. 223 on paper with watermark sideways was made.

Nos. 164-166, 173 and 178 Overprinted: "NATIONAL DAY / 3 NOVEMBER 1968"
***Perf. 14½x14, 14x14½***
**1968, Nov. 3 Photo. Wmk. 314**
*228* A19 1c bl, brn & grn 5 5
*229* A20 2c ultra 5 5
*230* A19 3c lt ultra & blk 5 5
*231* A20 14c multi (I) 15 15
*232* A19 $1.20 multi 1.00 1.00
*Nos. 228-232 (5)* 1.30 1.30

Basketball A23

Designs: No. 233, Three soccer players. No. 234, Soccer player and goalie. No. 235, Swimmers at start. No. 236, Divers. No. 237, Javelin thrower and hurdlers. No. 238, Hurdlers. No. 240, Three basketball players.

***Perf. 11½***
**1968, Nov. 23 Unwmk. Litho.**
*233* A23 1c brt lil & multi 5 5
*234* A23 1c brt lil & multi 5 5
*235* A23 5c brt grnsh bl & multi 5 5
*236* A23 5c brt grnsh bl & multi 5 5
*237* A23 48c lt ol & multi 40 40
*238* A23 48c lt ol & multi 40 40
*239* A23 60c dp org & multi 50 50
*240* A23 60c dp org & multi 50 50
*Nos. 233-240 (8)* 2.00 2.00

Issued to commemorate the 19th Olympic Games, Mexico City, Oct. 12-27. The stamps of the same denomination are printed se-tenant in sheets of 40 with continuous design across each se-tenant pair (10 rows of 2 horizontal pairs separated by vertical gutter).

The Small Cowper Madonna, by Raphael A24

***Perf. 12½x12***
**1968, Dec. 16 Photo. Unwmk.**
*241* A24 5c multi 8 8

Christmas 1968.
No. 241 printed in sheets of 20. Sheets of 6 (3x2) exist containing two each of 12c, 24c, and $1.20 stamps, each picturing a different madonna painting. Value $2.50.

Venus and Adonis, by Rubens — A25

Citrus Fruit Picker — A26

Paintings: 15c, The Death of Socrates, by Louis Jacques David. 24c, Christ at Emmaus, by Velazquez. 50c, Pilate Washing his Hands, by Rembrandt.

***Perf. 14½x15***
**1969, Jan. 30 Litho. Wmk. 314**
*242* A25 5c lil & multi 5 5
*243* A25 15c emer & multi 12 12
*244* A25 24c lt bl & multi 20 20
*245* A25 50c crim & multi 40 40

20th anniv. (in 1968) of the WHO.

**1969, Mar. 10 *Perf. 14½***

Designs: No. 247, Woman and child. No. 248, Hotel. No. 249, Red-necked parrots. No. 250, Calypso band. No. 251, Women dancers. No. 252, Tropical fish and coelenterates. No. 253, Diver and turtle.

*246* A26 10c multi 8 8
*247* A26 10c multi 8 8
*248* A26 12c multi 10 10
*249* A26 12c multi 10 10
*250* A26 24c multi 25 25
*251* A26 24c multi 25 25
*252* A26 48c multi 50 50
*253* A26 48c multi 50 50
*Nos. 246-253 (8)* 1.86 1.86

Tourist publicity. Stamps of same denomination are printed se-tenant.

Spinning, by Millet, Flags and ILO Emblem — A27

Designs (Etchings by Jean F. Millet, Flags and ILO Emblem): 30c, Threshing. 30c, Flax pulling.

**1969, July Unwmk. *Perf. 13½***
*254* A27 15c multi 12 12
*255* A27 30c multi 30 30
*256* A27 38c multi 40 40

50th anniv. of the ILO.

"Strength in Unity," Bananas and Cacao A28

Designs ("Strength in Unity" Emblem and): 8c, Map of Dominica and Hawker Siddeley 748. 12c, Map of Caribbean. 24c, Ships in harbor.

**1969, July Litho.**
*257* A28 5c org & multi 7 7
*258* A28 8c gray & multi 10 10
*259* A28 12c lil & multi 16 16
*260* A28 24c lt bl & multi 40 40

Issued to publicize the Caribbean Free Trade Area (CARIFTA).

Gandhi at Spinning Wheel and Big Ben, London A29

Designs: 38c, Gandhi, Nehru and Fatehpur Sikri Mausoleum. $1.20, Gandhi and Taj Mahal.

**1969, Oct. Litho. *Perf. 14½***
*261* A29 6c multi 8 8
*262* A29 38c multi 50 50
*263* A29 $1.20 multi 1.75 1.75

Mohandas K. Gandhi (1869-1948), leader in India's fight for independence. "Gandhi" is misspelled "Ghandi" on Nos. 261-263.

> The only foreign revenue stamps listed in this Catalogue are those authorized for prepayment of postage.

St. Joseph — A30

Stained Glass Windows, from 17th Century French Churches: 8c, St. John. 12c, St. Peter. 60c, St. Paul.

**1969, Nov. 10 Litho. *Perf. 14***
*264* A30 6c blk & multi 6 6
*265* A30 8c blk & multi 9 9
*266* A30 12c blk & multi 15 15
*267* A30 60c blk & multi 75 75

Issued to commemorate National Day, Nov. 3. Issued in sheets of 16 (4x4) with control numbers and 4 tabs with a patriotic poem by W. O. M. Pond.

Queen Elizabeth II — A31

Purplethroated Carib (Hummingbird) — A32

Designs: 2c, Poinsettia. 3c, Red-necked pigeon. 4c, Imperial parrot. 5c, Swallowtail butterfly. 6c, Brown Julia butterfly. 8c, Banana shipment. 10c, Portsmouth Harbor. 12c, Copra processing plant. 15c, Women with straw work. 25c, Timber plant. 30c, Mining pumice. 38c, Cricket, Grammar School. 50c, Roman Catholic Cathedral. 60c, Government headquarters. $1.20, Melville Hall Airport. $2.40, Coat of Arms. $4.80, Queen Elizabeth II.

***Perf. 13½***
**1969, Nov. 26 Unwmk. Photo.**
*268* A31 ½c sil & multi 5 5
*269* A32 1c yel & multi 5 5
*270* A32 2c yel & multi 5 5
*271* A32 3c yel & multi 5 5
*272* A32 4c yel & multi 7 5
*273* A32 5c yel & multi 8 7
*274* A32 6c brn & multi 10 8
*275* A32 8c brn & multi 12 9
*276* A32 10c yel & multi 14 12
*277* A32 12c cit & multi 18 16
*278* A32 15c bl & multi 22 20
*279* A32 25c pink & multi 35 32
*280* A32 30c ol & multi 45 40
*281* A32 38c multi 60 55
*282* A32 50c brn & multi 70 65

**Wmk. Rectangles (334)**
***Perf. 14***
**Size: 38x26mm., 26x38mm.**
*283* A32 60c yel & multi 90 80
*284* A32 $1.20 yel & multi 1.75 1.60
*285* A32 $2.40 gold & multi 4.00 3.50
*286* A31 $4.80 gold & multi 8.00 7.25
*Nos. 268-286 (19)* 17.86 16.04

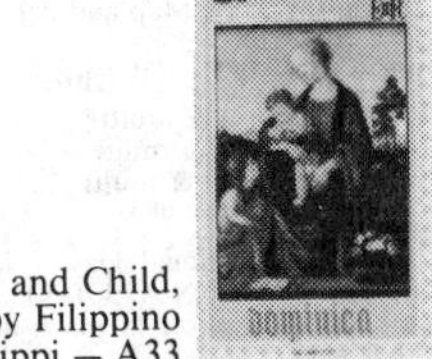


Madonna and Child, by Filippino Lippi — A33

Paintings: 10c, Holy Family with Lamb, by Raphael. 15c, Virgin and Child, by Perugino. $1.20, Madonna of the Rose Hedge, by Botticelli.

*Perf. 14½*

**1969, Dec. Unwmk. Litho.**

*287* A33 6c lt bl & multi 8 8
*288* A33 10c multi 12 12
*289* A33 15c lil & multi 20 20
*290* A33 $1.20 lt grn & multi 1.25 1.25
a Souv. sheet of 2 1.75 1.75

Christmas 1969.

No. 290a contains 2 imperf. stamps with simulated perforations similar to Nos. 289-290. Multicolored Christmas border and inscription. Size: 88x76mm.

Neil A. Armstrong, First Man on the Moon — A34

Designs: 5c, American flag and astronauts on moon. 8c, Astronauts collecting moon rocks. 30c, Landing module, moon and earth. 50c, Memorial tablet left on moon. 60c, Astronauts Armstrong, Aldrin and Collins.

**1970, Feb. 2 Litho. *Perf. 12½***

*291* A34 ½c lil & multi 5 5
*292* A34 5c lt bl & multi 5 5
*293* A34 8c org & multi 8 8
*294* A34 30c bl & multi 25 25
*295* A34 50c red brn & multi 50 50
*296* A34 60c rose & multi 60 60
a Souvenir sheet of 4 2.00 2.00
*Nos. 291-296 (6)* 1.53 1.53

See note after U.S. No. C76. No. 296a contains 4 stamps similar to Nos. 293-296, but imperf. with simulated perforations. Blue margin with black commemorative inscription. Size: 115x110mm.

Giant Green Turtle — A35

Designs: 24c, Flying fish. 38c, Anthurium lily. 60c, Imperial and red-necked parrots.

**1970, Sept. 6 Litho. *Perf. 13½x13***

*297* A35 6c lt grn & multi 10 10
*298* A35 24c multi 30 30
*299* A35 38c grn & multi 50 50
*300* A35 60c yel & multi 85 85
a Souvenir sheet of 4 3.25 3.25

No. 300a contains one each, Nos. 297-300. Greenish blue marginal decorations. Size: 160x108mm.

Women in 18th Century Dress A36

Designs: 8c, Carib mace and wife leader, 18th century. $1, Map and flag of Dominica.

**1970, Nov. 3 Litho. *Perf. 14***

*301* A36 5c yel & multi 5 5
*302* A36 8c grn & multi 8 8
*303* A36 $1 lt bl & multi 1.50 1.50
a Souvenir sheet of 3 1.50 1.50

Issued for National Day. No. 303a contains one each of Nos. 301-303 and 3 labels. Marginal inscription in black and red. Size: 150x85mm.

Marley's Ghost — A37

Designs (from A Christmas Carol, by Dickens): 15c, Fezziwig's Ball. 24c, Scrooge and his Nephew's Christmas Party. $1.20, The Ghost of Christmas Present.

**1970, Nov. 23 Litho. *Perf. 14x14½***

*304* A37 2c bl & multi 5 5
*305* A37 15c multi 20 20
*306* A37 24c red & multi 30 30
*307* A37 $1.20 multi 1.40 1.40
a Souvenir sheet of 4 3.00 3.00

Issued for Christmas and to commemorate the centenary of the death of Charles Dickens (1812-1870). No. 307a contains one each of Nos. 304-307; red decorative margin with black inscription. Size: 140x87mm.

Hands and Red Cross A38

Designs: 8c, The Doctor, by Sir Luke Fildes. 15c, Dominica flag and Red Cross. 50c, The Sick Child, by Edvard Munch.

**1970, Dec. 28 *Perf. 14½x14***

*308* A38 8c multi 8 8
*309* A38 10c multi 10 10
*310* A38 15c multi 20 20
*311* A38 50c multi 75 75
a Souvenir sheet of 4 1.50 1.50

Issued to commemorate the centenary of the British Red Cross Society. No. 311a contains one each of Nos. 308-311. Decorative multicolored margin with commemorative inscription. Size: 107x75mm.

Marigot Primary School — A39

Designs (Education Year Emblem and): 8c, Goodwill Junior High School. 14c, University of the West Indies. $1, Trinity College, Cambridge, England.

**1971, March 1 Litho. *Perf. 13½***

*312* A39 5c multi 6 6
*313* A39 8c multi 9 9
*314* A39 14c multi 20 20
*315* A39 $1 multi 90 90
a Souvenir sheet of 2 1.25 1.25

International Education Year. No. 315a contains one each of Nos. 314-315. Multicolored decorative margin. Size: 90x90mm.

Waterfall and Bird-of-Paradise Flower — A40

Designs: 10c, Boat building. 30c, Sailboat along North Coast. 50c, Speed boat and steamer.

**1971, March 22 *Perf. 13½x14***

*316* A40 5c multi 5 5
*317* A40 10c multi 10 10
*318* A40 30c multi 30 30
*319* A40 50c multi 65 65
a Souvenir sheet of 4 1.25 1.25

Tourist publicity. No. 319a contains one each of Nos. 316-319. Multicolored margin with black inscription. Size: 129½x87mm.

UNICEF Emblem, Letter "D" A41

**1971, June 14 Litho. *Perf. 14***

*320* A41 5c dk grn, gold & vio 6 6
*321* A41 10c yel, gold & dk grn 9 9
*322* A41 38c emer, gold & dk grn 30 30
*323* A41 $1.20 org, gold & dk grn 90 90
a Souv. sheet of 2 1.25 1.25

25th anniv. of UNICEF. No. 323a contains one each of Nos. 321 and 323. Orange margin with dark green inscription and emblem. Size: 82x77½mm.

Boy Scout, Jamboree Emblem, Torii, Camp and Mt. Fuji — A42

Designs: 24c, British Scout and flag. 30c, Japanese Scout and flag. $1, Dominican Scout and flag.

**1971, Oct. 18 Unwmk. *Perf. 11***

*324* A42 20c bis & multi 20 20
*325* A42 24c grn & multi 25 25
*326* A42 30c red lil & multi 30 30
*327* A42 $1 bl & multi 1.25 1.25
a Souvenir sheet of 2 2.00 2.00

13th Boy Scout World Jamboree, Asagiri Plain, Japan, Aug. 2-10.

No. 327a contains one each of Nos. 326-327, multicolored margin. Size: 114x101mm.

Boats at Portsmouth — A43

Designs: 15c, Carnival street scene. 20c, $1.20, Anthea Mondesire, Carifta Queen (vert.). 50c, Rock of Atkinson (vert.).

***Perf. 13½x14, 14x13½***

**1971, Nov. 15 Litho.**

*328* A43 8c multi 10 10
*329* A43 15c multi 15 15
*330* A43 20c multi 20 20
*331* A43 50c multi 50 50

**Souvenir Sheet**

***Perf. 15***

*332* A43 $1.20 multi 1.25 1.25

National Day. No. 332 contains one stamp with gray and multicolored margin, black inscription. Size: 63x83½mm.

First Dominica Coin, 8 Reals, 1761 — A44

Early Dominica Coins: 30c, Eleven and 3-bit pieces, 1798. 35c, Two-real coin, 1770 (vert.). 50c, Three "mocos" and piece of 8, 1798.

**1972, Feb. 7 Litho. *Perf. 14***

*333* A44 10c vio, sil & blk 10 10
*334* A44 30c grn, sil & blk 30 30
*335* A44 35c ultra, sil & blk 60 60
*336* A44 50c red, sil & blk 60 60
a Souvenir sheet of 2 1.50 1.50

No. 336a contains one each of Nos. 335-336. Multicolored margin inscribed "Christmas 1971." Size: 85x90mm.

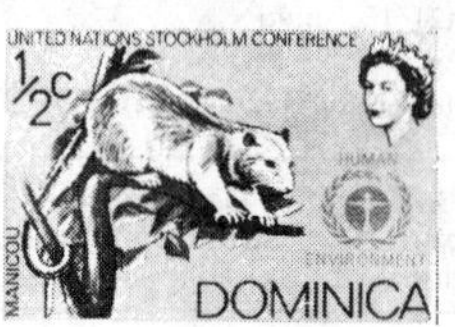

Common Opossum, Environment Emblem — A45

Designs (Environment Emblem and): 35c, Agouti. 60c, Oncidium papillo (orchid). $1.20, Hibiscus.

**1972, June 5**

*337* A45 ½c yel grn & multi 5 5
*338* A45 35c org brn & multi 35 35
*339* A45 60c lt bl & multi 65 65
*340* A45 $1.20 yel & multi 1.25 1.25
a Souv. sheet of 4, #337-340 5.00 5.00

UN Conf. on Human Environment, Stockholm, June 5-16. No. 340a has yellow decorative margin with green inscription. Size: 138x92mm.

100-meter Sprint, Olympic Rings A46

Designs (Olympic Rings and): 35m, 400-meter hurdles. 58c, Hammer throw (vert.). 72c, Broad jump (vert.).

**1972, Oct. 9 Litho. *Perf. 14***

*341* A46 30c dp org & multi 30 30
*342* A46 35c bl & multi 35 35
*343* A46 58c lil rose & multi 60 60
*344* A46 72c yel grn & multi 75 75
a Souv. sheet of 2 2.75 2.75

20th Olympic Games, Munich, Aug. 26-Sept. 11. No. 344a contains one each of Nos. 343-344, perf. 15. Yellow green margin with brown inscription and sports scenes. Size: 98x96mm.

General Post Office A47

**1972, Nov. 1 *Perf. 13½***

*345* A47 10c *shown* 8 8
*346* A47 20c *Morne Diablotin Mountain* 15 15
*347* A47 30c *Rodney's Rock* 30 30
a Souvenir sheet of 2 85 85

National Day. No. 347a contains one each of Nos. 346-347, perf. 15; multicolored margin. Size: 82x95mm.

Adoration of the Shepherds, by Caravaggio — A48

Paintings: 14c, Madonna and Child, by Rubens. 30c, Madonna and Child, with St. Anne by Orazio Gentileschi. $1, Adoration of the Kings, by Jan Mostaert. (On 8c, painting is mistakenly attributed to Boccaccino, according to Fine Arts Philatelists.)

**1972, Dec. 4.**

*348* A48 8c gold & multi 9 9
*349* A48 14c gold & multi 15 15
*350* A48 30c gold & multi 30 30
*351* A48 $1 gold & multi 1.00 1.00
*a* Souvenir sheet of 2 2.50 2.50

Christmas 1972. No. 351a contains one each of Nos. 350-351 with simulated perforations. Multicolored margin. Size: 100x79mm.

**Silver Wedding Issue, 1972**
Common Design Type

Design: Queen Elizabeth II, Prince Philip, bananas, sisseron parrot.

***Perf. 14x14½***
**1972, Nov. 13 Photo. Wmk. 314**

*352* CD324 5c ol & multi 6 6
*353* CD324 $1 multi 60 60

See note after Antigua No. 296.

Launching of Tiros Weather Satellite — A49

Designs: 1c, Nimbus satellite. 2c, Radiosonde balloon and equipment. 30c, Radarscope. 35c, General circulation of atmosphere. 50c, Picture of hurricane transmitted by satellite. $1, Computer weather map. (30c, 35c, 50c, $1, horizontal).

***Perf. 14½***
**1973, July 16 Unwmk. Litho.**

*354* A49 ½c blk & multi 5 5
*355* A49 1c blk & multi 5 5
*356* A49 2c blk & multi 5 5
*357* A49 30c blk & multi 25 25
*358* A49 35c blk & multi 30 30
*359* A49 50c blk & multi 45 45
*360* A49 $1 blk & multi 90 90
*a* Souvenir sheet of 2 2.00 2.00
*Nos. 354-360 (7)* 2.05 2.05

Centenary of international meteorological cooperation. No. 360a contains one each of Nos. 359-360. Green, blue and black margin with Greek allegorical figures of winds. Size: 90x105mm.

Going to the Hospital A50

Designs (WHO Emblem and): 1c, Maternity and infant care. 2c, Inoculation against smallpox. 30c, Emergency service. 35c, Waiting patients. 50c, Examination. $1, Traveling physician.

**1973, Aug. 20 Unwmk. *Perf. 14½***

*361* A50 ½c lt bl & multi 5 5
*362* A50 1c gray grn & multi 5 5
*363* A50 2c yel & multi 5 5
*364* A50 30c lt vio & multi 25 25
*365* A50 35c yel grn & multi 30 30
*366* A50 50c multi 45 45
*367* A50 $1 bis & multi 90 90
*a* Souvenir sheet of 2 2.25 2.25
*Nos. 361-367 (7)* 2.05 2.05

WHO, 25th anniv.. No. 367a contains one each of Nos. 366-367. Gray and multicolored margin with commemorative inscription. Size: 112x110mm.

Cyrique Crab — A51

**1973, Oct.**

*368* A51 ½c *shown* 5 5
*369* A51 22c *Blue land crab* 30 30
*370* A51 25c *Breadfruit* 35 35
*371* A51 $1.20 *Sunflower* 1.40 1.40
*a* Souvenir sheet of 4 3.50 3.50

No. 371a contains one each of Nos. 368-371. Prussian blue margin with black inscription. Size: 91x127mm.

Princess Anne and Mark Phillips — A52

**1973, Nov. 14 *Perf. 13½***

*372* A52 25c sal & multi 15 15
*373* A52 $2 bl & multi 1.20 1.20
*a* Souv. sheet of 2 (75c, $1.20) 1.75 1.75

Wedding of Princess Anne and Capt. Mark Phillips.

Nos. 372-373 were issued in sheets of 5 plus label, with multicolored, inscribed margins.

No. 373a contains 2 stamps of type A52: 75c in colors of the 25c, and $1.20 in colors of the $2. Multicolored margins with commemorative inscriptions. Size: 78x99mm.

Nativity, by Brueghel A53

Paintings of the Nativity by: 1c, Botticelli. 2c, Dürer. 12c, Botticelli. 22c, Rubens. 35c, Dürer. $1, Giorgione (inscribed "Giorgeone").

**1973 Unwmk. *Perf. 14½x15***

*374* A53 ½c gray & multi 5 5
*375* A53 1c gray & multi 5 5
*376* A53 2c gray & multi 5 5
*377* A53 12c gray & multi 10 10
*378* A53 22c gray & multi 20 20
*379* A53 35c gray & multi 25 25
*380* A53 $1 gray & multi 75 75
*a* Souvenir sheet of 2 2.25 2.25
*Nos. 374-380 (7)* 1.45 1.45

Christmas 1973. No. 380a contains one each of Nos. 379-380 in changed colors. Multicolored margin with angel and gold inscription. Size: 121x97mm.

Carib Basket Weaving — A54

Designs: 10c, Staircase of the Snake. 50c, Miss Caribbean Queen, Kathleen Telemacque (vert.). 60c, Miss Carifta Queen, Esther Fadelle (vert.). $1, La Jeune Etoille Dancers.

***Perf. 13½x14, 14x13½***
**1973, Dec. 17**

*381* A54 5c buff & multi 5 5
*382* A54 10c multi 6 6
*383* A54 50c multi 30 30
*384* A54 60c multi 40 40
*385* A54 $1 multi 65 65
*a* Souvenir sheet of 3 1.10 1.10
*Nos. 381-385 (5)* 1.46 1.46

National Day 1973. No. 385a contains one each of Nos. 381-382, 385. Blue and multicolored margin. Size: 94x126mm.

U.W.I. Center, Dominica — A55

Designs: 30c, Graduation. $1, University coat of arms.

**1974, Jan. 21 Litho. *Perf. 13½x14***

*386* A55 12c dp org & multi 10 10
*387* A55 30c vio & multi 25 25
*388* A55 $1 multi 85 85
*a* Souvenir sheet of 3 1.25 1.25

25th anniversary of the University of the West Indies. No. 388a contains one each of Nos. 386-388. Bright blue margin with black inscription. Size: 97x130mm.

Dominica No. 1 and Map of Island A56

Designs: 1c, 50c, No. 8 and post horn. 2c, $1.20, No. 9 and coat of arms. 10c, Like ½c.

**1974, May 4 Litho. *Perf. 14½***

*389* A56 ½c brt pur & multi 5 5
*390* A56 1c sal & multi 5 5
*391* A56 2c ultra & multi 5 5
*392* A56 10c vio & multi 16 16
*393* A56 50c yel grn & multi 50 50
*394* A56 $1.20 rose & multi 1.10 1.10
*a* Souvenir sheet of 3 2.25 2.25
*Nos. 389-394 (6)* 1.91 1.91

Centenary of Dominican postage stamps. No. 394a contains one each of Nos. 392-394, perf. 15. Green margin with commemorative inscription. Size: 105x120mm.

Soccer Player and Cup, Brazilian Flag — A57

Designs: Soccer cup, various players and flags.

**1974, July Litho. *Perf. 14½***

*395* A57 ½c *shown* 5 5
*396* A57 1c *Germany, Fed. Rep.* 5 5
*397* A57 2c *Italy* 5 5
*398* A57 30c *Scotland* 25 25
*399* A57 40c *Sweden* 35 35
*400* A57 50c *Netherlands* 40 40
*401* A57 $1 *Jugoslavia* 85 85
*a* Souvenir sheet of 2 1.50 1.50
*Nos. 395-401 (7)* 2.00 2.00

World Cup Soccer Championship, Munich, June 13-July 7. No. 401a contains one each of Nos. 400-401, perf. 13½; multicolored margin. Size: 88x86mm.

Indian Hole A58

Designs: 40c, Teachers' Training College. $1, Petite Savane Co-operative Bay Oil Distillery.

**1974, Nov. 1 Litho. *Perf. 13½x14***

*402* A58 10c multi 8 8
*403* A58 40c multi 35 35
*404* A58 $1 multi 85 85
*a* Souvenir sheet of 3 1.50 1.50

No. 404a contains one each of Nos. 402-404, multicolored decorative margin. Size: 96x142mm.

Churchill at Race Track A59

Designs (Churchill): 1c, with Gen. Eisenhower. 2c, with Franklin D. Roosevelt. 20c, as First Lord of the Admiralty. 45c, painting outdoors. $2, giving "V" sign.

**1974, Nov. 25 Litho. *Perf. 14½***

*405* A59 ½c multi 5 5
*406* A59 1c multi 5 5
*407* A59 2c multi 5 5
*408* A59 20c multi 20 20
*409* A59 45c multi 40 40
*410* A59 $2 multi 1.75 1.75
*a* Souvenir sheet of 2 2.50 2.50
*Nos. 405-410 (6)* 2.50 2.50

Sir Winston Churchill (1874-1965), birth centenary. No. 410a contains one each of Nos. 409-410, perf. 13½, multicolored margin showing St. Paul's Cathedral under attack. Size: 125x100mm.

Virgin and Child, by Oronzo Tiso — A60

Paintings (Virgin and Child): 1c, by Lorenzo Costa. 2c, by unknown Master. 10c, by G. F. Romanelli. 25c, Holy Family, by G. S. da Sermoneta. 45c, Adoration of the Shepherds, by Guido Reni. $1, Adoration of the Kings, by Cristoforo Caselli.

**1974, Dec. 16 Litho. *Perf. 14***

*411* A60 ½c multi 5 5
*412* A60 1c multi 5 5
*413* A60 2c multi 5 5
*414* A60 10c multi 18 18
*415* A60 25c multi 40 40
*416* A60 45c multi 65 65
*417* A60 $1 multi 1.50 1.50
*a* Souvenir sheet of 2 3.25 3.25
*Nos. 411-417 (7)* 2.88 2.88

Christmas 1974. No. 417a contains one each of Nos. 416-417; greenish gray and multicolored margin. Size: 113x78mm.

Seamail, "Orinoco," 1851, and "Geest-haven," 1966 — A61

Cent. of UPU: $2, Airmail, De Havilland 4, 1918, and Boeing 747, 1974.

**1974, Dec. 4 Litho. *Perf. 13½***

*418* A61 10c multi 20 20
*419* A61 $2 multi 2.75 2.75
*a* Souv. sheet of 2 ($1.20, $2.40) 3.75 3.75

No. 419a contains a $1.20 stamp of 10c design and a $2.40 of $2 design, both multicolored. Margin multicolored with UPU emblem and black inscription. Size: 105½x92mm.

Oldwife A62

**1975, June 2 Litho. *Perf. 14½***

*421* A62 ½c *shown* 5 5
*422* A62 1c *Ocyurus chrysurus* 5 5
*423* A62 2c *Blue marlin* 5 5
*424* A62 3c *Swordfish* 7 5
*425* A62 20c *Great barracuda* 45 30
*426* A62 $2 *Grouper* 3.50 2.75
*a* Souvenir sheet 4.00 3.25
*Nos. 421-426 (6)* 4.17 3.25

No. 426a contains one stamp, perf. 13½. Multicolored margin shows underwater plants. Size: 104x79mm.

Myscelia Antholia A63

Designs: Butterflies.

**1975, July 28 Litho. *Perf. 14½***

*427* A63 ½c *shown* 5 5
*428* A63 1c *Lycorea ceres* 5 5
*429* A63 2c *Siderone nemesis* 10 5
*430* A63 6c *Battus polydamas* 15 12
*431* A63 30c *Anartia lytrea* 65 60
*432* A63 40c *Morpho peleides* 80 65
*433* A63 $2 *Dryas julia* 4.75 3.50
*a* Souvenir sheet 4.25 4.25
*Nos. 427-433 (7)* 6.55 5.02

No. 433a contains one stamp, perf. 13½. Multicolored margin showing shore and palms. Size: 107x80mm.

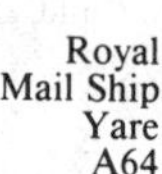
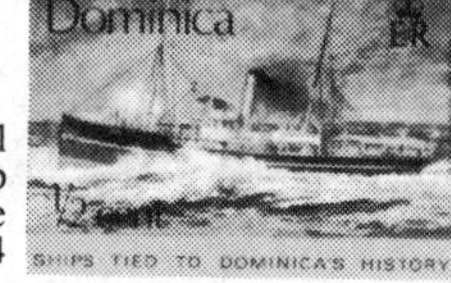


Royal Mail Ship Yare A64

Designs: 1c, Royal mail ship Thames. 2c, Canadian National S.S. Lady Nelson. 20c, C.N. S.S. Lady Rodney. 45c, Harrison Line M.V. Statesman. 50c, Geest Line M.V. Geestcape. $2, Geest Line M.V. Geeststar.

**1975, Sept. 1 *Perf. 14***

*434* A64 ½c blk & multi 5 5
*435* A64 1c blk & multi 5 5
*436* A64 2c blk & multi 5 5
*437* A64 20c blk & multi 40 30
*438* A64 45c blk & multi 75 65
*439* A64 50c blk & multi 90 75
*440* A64 $2 blk & multi 4.50 3.00
*a* Souvenir sheet of 2 4.50 4.00
*Nos. 434-440 (7)* 6.70 4.85

Ships tied in with Dominican history. No. 440a contains one each of Nos. 439-440. Multicolored margin showing ships. Size: 77x102mm.

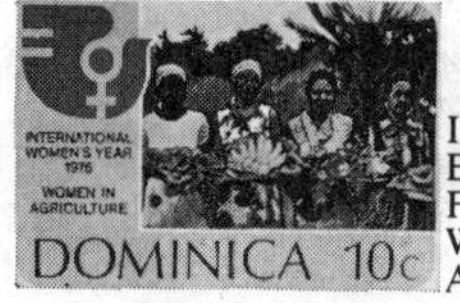


IWY Emblem, Farm Women A65

Design: $2, IWY emblem, dressmaker and saleswoman.

**1975, Oct. 30 Litho. *Perf. 14***

*441* A65 10c pink & multi 12 12
*442* A65 $2 yel & multi 2.50 2.50

International Women's Year 1975.

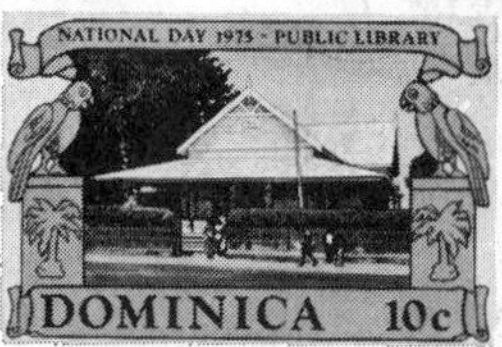


Public Library — A66

Designs: 5c, Miss Caribbean Queen 1975 (vert.). 30c, Citrus factory. $1, National Day Cup (vert.).

**1975, Nov. 6**

*443* A66 5c multi 5 5
*444* A66 10c multi 12 12
*445* A66 30c multi 40 40
*446* A66 $1 multi 1.50 1.50
*a* Souvenir sheet of 3 2.10 2.10

National Day 1975. No. 446a contains 3 stamps similar to Nos. 444-446 with simulated perforations; multicolored margin. Size: 128x97mm.

Virgin and Child, by Mantegna — A67

Designs: Paintings of the Virgin and Child.

**1975, Nov. 24**

*447* A67 ½c *shown* 5 5
*448* A67 1c *Fra Filippo Lippi* 5 5
*449* A67 2c *Bellini* 5 5
*450* A67 10c *Botticelli* 12 12
*451* A67 25c *Bellini* 30 30
*452* A67 45c *Correggio* 65 65
*453* A67 $1 *Durer* 1.50 1.50
*a* Souvenir sheet of 2 3.00 3.00
*Nos. 447-453 (7)* 2.72 2.72

Christmas. No. 453a contains one each of Nos. 452-453; buff and multicolored margin with Nativity scene. Size: 137x84mm.

Hibiscus A68

Queen Elizabeth II — A69

Designs: 1c, African tulip. 2c, Castor oil tree. 3c, White cedar flower. 4c, Eggplant. 5c, Garfish. 6c, Okra. 8c, Zenaida doves. 10c, Screw pine. 20c, Mangoes. 25c, Crayfish. 30c, Manicou. 40c, Bay leaf groves. 50c, Tomatoes. $1, Lime factory. $2, Rum distillery. $5, Bay oil distillery.

**1975, Dec. Litho. *Perf. 14½***

*454* A68 ½c ultra & multi 5 5
*455* A68 1c lil & multi 5 5
*456* A68 2c org & multi 5 5
*457* A68 3c multi 8 5
*458* A68 4c pink & multi 10 5
*459* A68 5c multi 12 7
*460* A68 6c gray & multi 15 10
*461* A68 8c multi 15 12
*462* A68 10c vio & multi 18 15
*463* A68 20c yel & multi 40 32
*464* A68 25c lem & multi 45 40
*465* A68 30c sal & multi 52 45
*466* A68 40c multi 80 65
*467* A68 50c red & multi 1.00 80
*468* A68 $1 cit & multi 2.00 1.50
*469* A68 $2 multi 4.00 3.25
*470* A68 $5 multi 10.00 8.00

***Perf. 14***

*471* A69 $10 bl & multi 20.00 16.00
*Nos. 454-471 (18)* 40.10 32.06

American Infantry — A70

Rowing — A71

Designs: 1c, English three-decker, 1782. 2c, George Washington. 45c, English sailors. 75c, English ensign with regimental flag. $2, Admiral Hood. All designs have old maps in background.

**1976, Apr. 12 Litho. *Perf. 14½***

*472* A70 ½c grn & multi 5 5
*473* A70 1c pur & multi 5 5
*474* A70 2c org & multi 5 5
*475* A70 45c brn & multi 75 60
*476* A70 75c ultra & multi 1.25 1.00
*477* A70 $2 red & multi 3.50 3.00
*a* Souvenir sheet of 2 6.00 4.50
*Nos. 472-477 (6)* 5.65 4.75

American Bicentennial. No. 477a contains 2 stamps similar to Nos. 476-477, perf. 13; black margin shows naval battle. Size: 105x92mm.

**1976, May 24 Litho. *Perf. 14½***

Designs (Olympic Rings and): 1c, Shot put. 2c, Swimming. 40c, Relay race. 45c, Gymnastics. 60c, Sailing. $2, Archery.

*478* A71 ½c ocher & multi 5 5
*479* A71 1c ocher & multi 5 5
*480* A71 2c ocher & multi 5 5
*481* A71 40c ocher & multi 38 38
*482* A71 45c ocher & multi 40 40
*483* A71 60c ocher & multi 60 60
*484* A71 $2 ocher & multi 1.75 1.75
*a* Souvenir sheet of 2 3.50 3.50
*Nos. 478-484 (7)* 3.28 3.28

21st Olympic Games, Montreal, Canada, July 17-Aug. 1. No. 484a contains one each of Nos. 483-484, perf. 13; multicolored margin with Olympic rings. Size: 90x104mm.

Ringed Kingfisher A72

Birds: 1c, Mourning dove. 2c, Green heron. 15c, Broad-winged hawk. 30c, Blue-headed hummingbird. 45c, Banana-quit. $2, Imperial parrot. 15c, 30c, 45c, $2, vert.

**1976, June 28**

*485* A72 ½c multi 12 5
*486* A72 1c multi 12 5
*487* A72 2c multi 12 5
*488* A72 15c multi 60 30
*489* A72 30c multi 1.10 60
*490* A72 45c multi 2.25 1.00
*491* A72 $2 multi 10.00 5.00
*a* Souvenir sheet of 3 15.00 7.50
*Nos. 485-491 (7)* 14.31 7.05

No. 491a contains one each of Nos. 489-491, perf. 13; multicolored margin showing various birds. Size: 134x101mm.

**Cricket Cup Issue**

Types of Barbados 1976

**1976, July 26 Litho. *Perf. 14***

*492* A63 15c lt bl & multi 50 25
*493* A64 25c lil rose & blk 1.00 50

World Cricket Cup, won by West Indies Team, 1975.

Viking Spacecraft A73

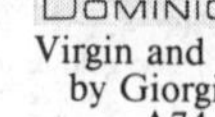


Virgin and Child, by Giorgione A74

Designs: 1c, Titan launch center (horiz.). 2c, Titan 3-D and Centaur D-IT. 3c, Orbiter and landing capsule. 45c, Capsule with closed parachute. 75c, Capsule with open parachute. $1, Landing capsule descending on Mars (horiz.). $2, Viking on Mars (horiz.).

**1976, Sept. 20 Litho. *Perf. 15***

*494* A73 ½c multi 5 5
*495* A73 1c multi 5 5
*496* A73 2c multi 5 5
*497* A73 3c multi 5 5
*498* A73 45c multi 35 35
*499* A73 75c multi 60 60
*500* A73 $1 multi 75 75
*501* A73 $2 multi 1.50 1.50
*a* Souvenir sheet of 2 2.50 2.50
*Nos. 494-501 (8)* 3.40 3.40

Viking mission to Mars. No. 501a contains one each of Nos. 500-501, perf. 13½; multicolored margin showing rocket. Size: 103x78mm.

**1976, Nov. 1 Litho. *Perf. 14***

Virgin and Child by: 1c, Bellini. 2c, Mantegna. 6c, Mantegna. 25c, Memling. 45c, 50c, Correggio. $1, $3, Raphael.

*502* A74 ½c multi 5 5
*503* A74 1c multi 5 5
*504* A74 2c multi 5 5
*505* A74 6c multi 6 6
*506* A74 25c multi 22 22
*507* A74 45c multi 38 38
*508* A74 $3 multi 2.75 2.75
*Nos. 502-508 (7)* 3.56 3.56

**Souvenir Sheet**

*509* A74 Sheet of 2 2.00 2.00
*a.* 50c multi 50
*b.* $1 multi 1.00

Christmas 1976. No. 509 has bister and multicolored margin showing angel playing harp. Size: 140x85mm.

Island Craft Co-operative — A75

Designs: 50c, Banana harvest, Castle Bruce Co-operative. $1, Banana shipping plant, Bourne Farmers' Co-operative.

**1976, Nov. 22 Litho. *Perf. 13½x14***

*510* A75 10c multi 12 12
*511* A75 50c multi 60 60
*512* A75 $1 multi 1.20 1.20
*a* Souvenir sheet of 3 2.00 2.00

National Day. No. 512a contains one each of Nos. 510-512; multicolored margin with banana tree. Size: 96x123mm.

Common Sundial — A76

Sea Shells: 1c, Flame helmet. 2c, Mouse cone. 20c, Caribbean vase. 40c, West Indian fighting conch. 50c, Short coral shell. $2, Long-spined star shell. $3, Apple murex.

**1976, Dec. 20 Litho. *Perf. 14***

*513* A76 ½c blk & multi 5 5
*514* A76 1c blk & multi 5 5
*515* A76 2c blk & multi 5 5
*516* A76 20c blk & multi 22 18
*517* A76 40c blk & multi 45 35
*518* A76 50c blk & multi 50 45
*519* A76 $3 blk & multi 3.50 2.50
*Nos. 513-519 (7)* 4.82 3.63

**Souvenir Sheet**

*520* A76 $2 blk & multi 2.75 1.75

No. 520 has multicolored margin showing sea shells. Size: 102x76mm.

Queen Enthroned — A77

Designs: 1c, Imperial crown. 45c, Elizabeth II and Princess Anne. $2, Coronation ring. $2.50, Ampulla and spoon. $5, Royal visit to Dominica.

**1977, Feb. 7 *Perf. 14***

*521* A77 ½c multi 5 5
*522* A77 1c multi 5 5
*523* A77 45c multi 42 42
*524* A77 $2 multi 1.75 1.75
*525* A77 $2.50 multi 2.25 2.25
*Nos. 521-525 (5)* 4.52 4.52

**Souvenir Sheet**

*526* A77 $5 multi 4.50 4.50

25th anniv. of the reign of Elizabeth II. No. 526 has green and tan margin. Size: 104x79mm.

Nos. 521-525 were printed in sheets of 40 (4x10), perf. 14, and sheets of 5 plus label, perf. 12, in changed colors.

Joseph Haydn — A78

Designs: 1c, Fidelio, act I, scene IV. 2c, Dancer Maria Casentini. 15c, Beethoven working on Pastoral Symphony. 30c, "Wellington's Victory." 40c, Soprano Henriette Sontag. $2, Young Beethoven.

**1977, Apr. 25 Litho. *Perf. 14***

*527* A78 ½c multi 5 5
*528* A78 1c multi 5 5
*529* A78 2c multi 5 5
*530* A78 15c multi 15 15
*531* A78 30c multi 30 30
*532* A78 40c multi 38 38
*533* A78 $2 multi 1.75 1.75
*a* Souvenir sheet of 3 3.00 3.00
*Nos. 527-533 (7)* 2.73 2.73

Ludwig van Beethoven (1770-1827), composer. 150th death anniversary. No. 533a contains one each of Nos. 531-533; black margin showing Beethoven bust. Size: 138x93mm.

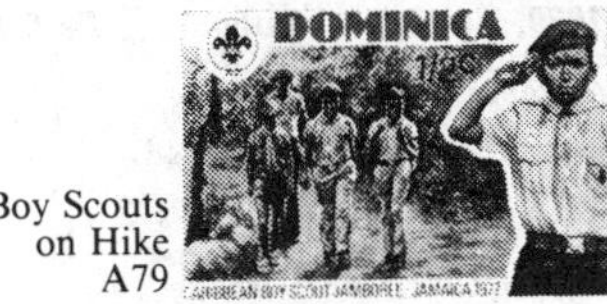

Boy Scouts on Hike A79

Designs (Saluting Boy Scout and): 1c, First aid. 2c, Scouts setting up camp. 45c, Rock climbing. 50c, Kayaking. 75c, Map reading. $2, Campfire. $3, Sailing.

**1977, Aug. 8 Litho. *Perf. 14***

*534* A79 ½c multi 5 5
*535* A79 1c multi 5 5
*536* A79 2c multi 5 5
*537* A79 45c multi 40 40
*538* A79 50c multi 42 42
*539* A79 $3 multi 2.50 2.50
*Nos. 534-539 (6)* 3.47 3.47

**Souvenir Sheet**

*540* A79 Sheet of 2 3.50 3.50
*a* 75c multi 90
*b* $2 multi 2.50

6th Caribbean Jamboree, Kingston, Jamaica, Aug. 5-14. No. 540 has brown, yellow and black margin with hand raised for Scout oath. Size: 111x115mm.

Nativity A80

Designs: 1c, Annunciation to the Shepherds. 2c, 45c, Presentation at the Temple (different). 6c, $2, $3, Flight into Egypt (different). 15c, Adoration of the Kings. 50c, Virgin and Child with Angels. ½c to 45c are illustrations from De Lisle Psalter, 14th century. 50c, $2, $3 are from other Psalters.

**1977, Nov. 14 Litho. *Perf. 14***

*541* A80 ½c multi 5 5
*542* A80 1c multi 5 5
*543* A80 2c multi 5 5
*544* A80 6c multi 6 6
*545* A80 15c multi 10 10
*546* A80 45c multi 30 30
*547* A80 $3 multi 1.90 1.90
*Nos. 541-547 (7)* 2.51 2.51

**Souvenir Sheet**

*548* A80 Souvenir sheet of 2 2.75 2.75
*a* 50c multi 35
*b* $2 multi 1.25

Christmas 1977. No. 548 has multicolored margin showing 3 Kings. Size: 112x85mm.

### Nos. 521-526 Overprinted "ROYAL VISIT / W.I. 1977"

**1977, Nov. 24 Litho. *Perf. 12, 14***

*549* A77 ½c multi 5 5
*550* A77 1c multi 5 5
*551* A77 45c multi 30 30
*552* A77 $2 multi 1.40 1.40
*553* A77 $2.50 multi 1.75 1.75
*Nos. 549-553 (5)* 3.55 3.55

**Souvenir Sheet**

***Perf. 14***

*554* A77 $5 multi 3.50 3.50

Caribbean visit of Queen Elizabeth II. Nos. 549-550 are perf. 12, others perf. 12 and 14.

Two types of No. 554: I. Overprinted only on stamp. II. Overprinted "W.I. 1977" on stamp and "Royal Visit W.I. 1977" on margin.

Masqueraders — A81

Designs: 1c, Sensay costume. 2c, Street musicians. 45c, Douiette band. 50c, Pappy Show wedding. $2, $2.50, Masquerade band.

**1978, Jan. 9 *Perf. 14***

*555* A81 ½c multi 5 5
*556* A81 1c multi 5 5
*557* A81 2c multi 5 5
*558* A81 45c multi 30 30
*559* A81 50c multi 35 35
*560* A81 $2 multi 1.40 1.40
*Nos. 555-560 (6)* 2.20 2.20

**Souvenir Sheet**

*561* A81 $2.50 multi 1.75 1.75

History of Carnival. No. 561 has multicolored margin. Size: 115x88mm.

Lindbergh and Spirit of St. Louis A82

Designs: 10c, Spirit of St. Louis take-off, Long Island, May 20, 1927. 15c, Lindbergh and map of route New York to Paris. 20c, Lindbergh and plane in Paris. 40c, 1st Zeppelin, trial over Lake Constance. 50c, Spirit of St. Louis. 60c, Count Zeppelin and Zeppelin LZ-2, 1906. $2, Graf Zeppelin, 1928. $3, LZ-127, 1928.

**1978, Mar. 13 Litho. *Perf. 14½***

*562* A82 6c multi 6 6
*563* A82 10c multi 8 8
*564* A82 15c multi 12 12
*565* A82 20c multi 15 15
*566* A82 40c multi 30 30
*567* A82 60c multi 45 45
*568* A82 $3 multi 2.25 2.25
*Nos. 562-568 (7)* 3.41 3.41

**Souvenir Sheet**

*569* A82 Sheet of 2 2.75 2.75
*a* 50c multi 50
*b* $2 multi 2.00

Charles A. Lindbergh's solo transatlantic flight from New York to Paris, 50th anniversary, and flights of Graf Zeppelin. No. 569 has multicolored margin with map showing flight routes. Size: 140x107mm.

Royal Family on Balcony — A83

Designs: 45c, Coronation. $2.50, Elizabeth II and Prince Philip. $5, Elizabeth II.

**1978, June 2 Litho. *Perf. 14***

*570* A83 45c multi 30 30
*571* A83 $2 multi 1.40 1.40
*572* A83 $2.50 multi 1.75 1.75

**Souvenir Sheet**

*573* A83 $5 multi 3.50 3.50

25th anniversary of coronation of Queen Elizabeth II. No. 573 has multicolored margin showing royal beasts. Size: 76x107mm. Nos. 570-572 were issued in sheets of 50, and in sheets of 3 stamps and label, in changed colors, perf. 12. Multicolored sheet margins have inscriptions and show royal beasts.

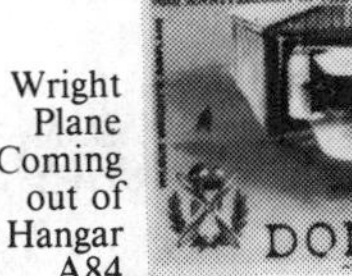

Wright Plane Coming out of Hangar A84

Designs: 40c, 1908 plane. 60c, Flyer I gliding. $2, Flyer I taking off. $3, Wilbur and Orville Wright and Flyer I.

**1978, July 10 Litho. *Perf. 14½***

*574* A84 30c multi 20 20
*575* A84 40c multi 28 28
*576* A84 60c multi 40 40
*577* A84 $2 multi 1.50 1.50

**Souvenir Sheet**

*578* A84 $3 multi 2.75 2.75

75th anniversary of first powered flight. No. 578 has multicolored margin showing various flying machines. Size: 115x88mm.

Two Apostles, by Rubens — A85

Rubens Paintings: 45c, Descent from the Cross. 50c, St. Ildefonso Receiving Chasuble. $2, Holy Family. $3, Assumption of the Virgin.

**1978, Oct. 16 Litho. *Perf. 14***

*579* A85 20c multi 20 20
*580* A85 45c multi 45 45
*581* A85 50c multi 50 50
*582* A85 $3 multi 3.00 3.00

**Souvenir Sheet**

*583* A85 $2 multi 2.25 2.25

Christmas 1978. No. 583 has light blue and black margin showing Rubens portrait. Size: 114x83mm.

### Nos. 454-471 Overprinted: "INDEPENDENCE / 3rd NOVEMBER 1978"

**1978 Nov. 1 Litho. *Perf. 14½***

*584* A68 ½c ultra & multi 5 5
*585* A68 1c lil & multi 5 5
*586* A68 2c org & multi 5 5
*587* A68 3c multi 5 5
*588* A68 4c pink & multi 5 5
*589* A68 5c multi 5 5
*590* A68 6c gray & multi 6 6
*591* A68 8c multi 8 8
*592* A68 10c vio & multi 10 10
*a* Perf. 13½ ('79) 10 10
*593* A68 20c yel & multi 20 20
*594* A68 25c lem & multi 25 25
*595* A68 30c sal & multi 30 30
*596* A68 40c multi 40 40
*597* A68 50c red & multi 50 50
*598* A68 $1 cit & multi 1.00 1.00
*599* A68 $2 multi 2.00 2.00
*600* A68 $5 multi 4.50 4.50

***Perf. 14***

*601* A69 $10 bl & multi 9.00 9.00
*Nos. 584-601 (18)* 18.69 18.69

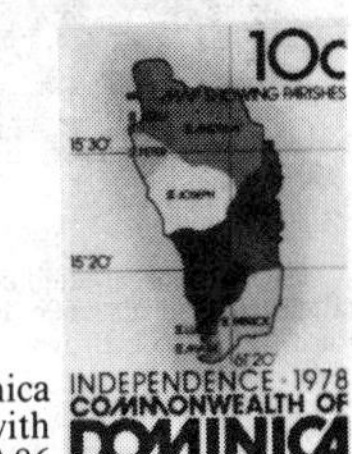

Map of Dominica with Parishes — A86

Designs: 25c, Sabinea carinalis, national flower, and map. 45c, New flag and map. 50c, Coat of arms and map. $2, Prime Minister Patrick John.

**1978, Nov. 1 *Perf. 14***

*602* A86 10c multi 8 8
*603* A86 25c multi 20 20
*604* A86 45c multi 35 35
*605* A86 50c multi 40 40
*606* A86 $2 multi 1.60 1.60
*Nos. 602-606 (5)* 2.63 2.63

**Souvenir Sheet**

*607* A86 $2.50 multi *15.00 10.00*

Dominican independence.
No. 607 has multicolored margin showing map of Caribbean. Size: 115x91mm.

Rowland Hill — A87

Designs: 45c, Great Britain No. 2. 50c, Dominica No. 1. $2, Maltese Cross handstamps. $5, Penny Black.

**1979, Mar. 19**

*608* A87 25c multi 16 16
*609* A87 45c multi 30 30
*610* A87 50c multi 35 35
*611* A87 $2 multi 1.40 1.40

**Souvenir Sheet**

*612* A87 $5 multi 7.50 7.50

Sir Rowland Hill (1795-1879), originator of penny postage. No. 612 has multicolored margin with portrait of Rowland Hill. Size: 186x95mm.

Nos. 608-611 printed in sheets of 5 plus label, perf. 12x12½, in changed colors.

Boys and Dugout Canoe A88

Designs (IYC Emblem and): 40c, Children carrying bananas. 50c, Boys playing cricket. $3, Child feeding rabbits. $5, Boy showing catch of fish.

**1979, Apr. 23 Litho. *Perf. 14***

*613* A88 30c multi 25 25
*614* A88 40c multi 35 35
*615* A88 50c multi 40 40
*616* A88 $3 multi 2.50 2.50

**Souvenir Sheet**

*617* A88 $5 multi 4.50 4.50

IYC. No. 617 has multicolored margin showing beach and boat. Size: 117x85mm.

Grouper A89

Designs: 30c, Spotted dolphin. 50c, White-tailed tropic birds. 60c, Brown pelicans. $1, Pilot whale. $2, Brown booby. $3, Elkhorn coral.

**1979, May 21 Litho. *Perf. 14***

*618* A89 10c multi 10 10
*619* A89 30c multi 30 30
*620* A89 50c multi 50 50
*621* A89 60c multi 60 60
*622* A89 $1 multi 1.00 1.00
*623* A89 $2 multi 2.00 2.00
*Nos. 618-623 (6)* 4.50 4.50

**Souvenir Sheet**

*624* A89 $3 multi 3.25 3.25

Wildlife protection. No. 624 has multicolored margin showing underwater scene. Size: 120x95mm.

Capt. Cook, Bark Endeavour — A90

Designs (Capt. Cook and): 50c, Resolution, map of 2nd voyage. 60c, Discovery, map of 3rd voyage. $2, Cook's map of New Zealand, 1770. $5, Portrait.

**1979, July 16 Litho. *Perf. 14***

*625* A90 10c multi 8 8
*626* A90 50c multi 40 40
*627* A90 60c multi 50 50
*628* A90 $2 multi 1.60 1.60

**Souvenir Sheet**

*629* A90 $5 multi 3.75 3.75

200th death anniversary of Capt. James Cook (1728-1779). No. 629 has ocher and brown margin showing bark Endeavour on Endeavour River. Size: 97x91mm.

Girl Guides Cooking A91

Girl Guides: 20c, Setting up emergency rain tent. 50c, Raising flag of independent Dominica. $2.50, Playing accordion and singing. $3, Leader and Guides of different ages.

**1979, July 30**

*630* A91 10c multi 10 10
*631* A91 20c multi 16 16
*632* A91 50c multi 40 40
*633* A91 $2.50 multi 2.00 2.00

**Souvenir Sheet**

*634* A91 $3 multi 3.00 3.00

50th anniversary of Dominican Girl Guides. No. 634 has multicolored margin showing pier and boats. Size: 110x87mm.

Colvillea — A92

Flowering Trees: 40c, Lignum vitae. 60c, Dwarf poinciana. $2, Fern tree. $3, Perfume tree.

**1979, Sept. 3 Litho. *Perf. 14***

*635* A92 20c multi 20 20
*636* A92 40c multi 40 40
*637* A92 60c multi 60 60
*638* A92 $2 multi 2.00 2.00

**Souvenir Sheet**

*639* A92 $3 multi 3.50 3.50

No. 639 has multicolored margin showing flowers and beach scene. Size: 114x90mm.

Nos. 459, 466, 470-471 Overprinted: "HURRICANE / RELIEF"

***Perf. 14½, 13½, 13½x14, 14***

**1979, Oct. 29 Litho.**

*640* A68 5c multi 5 5
*641* A68 40c multi 40 40
*642* A68 $5 multi 5.00 5.00
*643* A68 $10 multi 10.00 10.00

Hurricane devastation, Aug. 29. Vertical overprint on No. 643, others horizontal.

Music Scenes A92a

**1979, Nov. 2 Litho. *Perf. 11***

*644* A92a ½c *Mickey Mouse* 5 5
*645* A92a 1c *Goofy playing guitar* 5 5
*646* A92a 2c *Mickey Mouse and Goofy* 5 5
*647* A92a 3c *Donald Duck* 5 5
*648* A92a 4c *Minnie Mouse* 5 5
*649* A92a 5c *Goofy playing accordion* 5 5
*650* A92a 10c *Horace Horsecollar and Dale* 8 8
*651* A92a $2 *Huey, Dewey, Louie* 1.60 1.60
*652* A92a $2.50 *Donald and Huey* 2.00 2.00
*Nos. 644-652 (9)* 3.98 3.98

**Souvenir Sheet**

***Perf. 13***

*653* A92a $3 *Mickey Mouse playing piano* 2.50 2.50

No. 653 has multicolored margin showing notes and piano. Size: 127½x102mm.

Cathedral of the Assumption — A93

Cathedrals: 40c, St. Patrick's, New York. 45c, St. Paul's, London (vert.). 60c, St. Peter's; Rome. $2, Cologne Cathedral. $3, Notre Dame, Paris (vert.).

**1979, Nov. 26 Litho. *Perf. 14***

*654* A93 6c multi 5 5
*655* A93 45c multi 30 30
*656* A93 60c multi 40 40
*657* A93 $3 multi 2.00 2.00

**Souvenir Sheet**

*658* Sheet of 2 1.75 1.75
*a.* A93 40c multi 28 28
*b.* A93 $2 multi 1.40 1.40

Christmas 1979. No. 658 has multicolored decorative margin. Size: 114x85mm.

Nurse and Patients, Rotary Emblem A94

**1980, Mar. 31 Litho. *Perf. 14***

*659* A94 10c *shown* 7 7
*660* A94 20c *Electrocardiogram machine* 14 14
*661* A94 40c *Mental hospital* 28 28
*662* A94 $2.50 *Paul Harris, founder* 1.75 1.75

**Souvenir Sheet**

*663* A94 $3 *Map of Africa and Europe* 2.25 2.25

Rotary International, 75th anniversary. Nos. 659-662 each contain quadrant of Rotary emblem. No. 663 has multicolored margin showing Rotary emblem and world map. Size: 128x114mm.

Nos. 608-611 Overprinted "LONDON 1980"

**1980, May 6 Litho. *Perf. 12***

*663A* A87 25c multi 50 50
*663B* A87 45c multi 90 90
*663C* A87 50c multi 1.00 1.00
*663D* A87 $2 multi 4.00 4.00

London 80 Intl. Stamp Exhib., May 6-14.

Shot Put, Moscow '80 Emblem A95

**1980, May 27 Litho. *Perf. 14***

*664* A95 30c *shown* 20 20
*665* A95 40c *Basketball* 28 28
*666* A95 60c *Swimming* 40 40
*667* A95 $2 *Gymnast* 1.40 1.40

**Souvenir Sheet**

*668* A95 $3 *Running* 2.00 2.00

22nd Summer Olympic Games, Moscow, July 19-Aug. 3. No. 668 has multicolored margin showing runners and Moscow '80 emblem. Size: 114x86½mm.

Embarkation for Cythera, by Watteau — A96

Paintings: 20c, Supper at Emmaus, by Caravaggio. 25c, Charles I Hunting, by Van Dyck (vert.). 30c, The Maids of Honor, by Velazquez (vert.). 45c, Rape of the Sabine Women, by Poussin. $1, Embarkation for Cythera, by Watteau. $3, Holy Family, by Rembrandt. $5, Girl before a Mirror, by Picasso (vert.).

***Perf. 14x13½, 13½x14***

**1980, June Litho.**

*669* A96 20c multi 16 16
*670* A96 25c multi 20 20
*671* A96 30c multi 22 22
*672* A96 45c multi 35 35
*673* A96 $1 multi 80 80
*674* A96 $5 multi 4.00 4.00
*Nos. 669-674 (6)* 5.73 5.73

**Souvenir Sheet**

*675* A96 $3 multi 2.50 2.50

No. 675 has multicolored margin showing entire painting. Size: 114½x112mm.

Queen Mother Elizabeth, 80th Birthday — A97

**1980, Aug. 4 *Perf. 14***

*676* A97 40c multi 40 40
*677* A97 $2.50 multi 2.50 2.50

**Souvenir Sheet**

*678* A97 $3 multi 3.50 3.50

No. 678 has multicolored margin showing flowers. Size: 85½x66½mm.

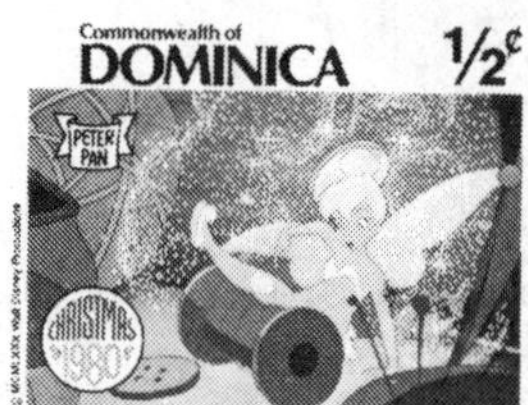

Tinkerbell — A98

Designs: Scenes from Disney's Peter Pan.

**1980, Oct. 1 Litho. *Perf. 11***

*679* A98 ½c multi 5 5
*680* A98 1c multi 5 5
*681* A98 2c multi 5 5
*682* A98 3c multi 5 5
*683* A98 4c multi 5 5
*684* A98 5c multi 5 5
*685* A98 10c multi 8 8
*686* A98 $2 multi 1.60 1.60
*687* A98 $2.50 multi 2.00 2.00
*Nos. 679-687 (9)* 3.98 3.98

**Souvenir Sheet**

688 A98 $4 multi 3.56 3.50

Christmas 1980. No. 688 contains a vertical stamp; multicolored margin shows Wendy, John and Michael. Size: 124x99mm.

Douglas Bay A99

| 1981, Feb. 12 | Litho. | Perf. 14 | |
|---|---|---|---|
| 689 A99 | 20c shown | 15 | 15 |
| 690 A99 | 30c Valley of Desolation | 22 | 22 |
| 691 A99 | 40c Emerald Pool, vert. | 30 | 30 |
| 692 A99 | $3 Indian River, vert. | 2.25 | 2.25 |

**Souvenir Sheet**

693 A99 $4 Trafalgar Falls 3.00 3.00

No. 693 has multicolored margin showing forest. Size: 86x105mm.

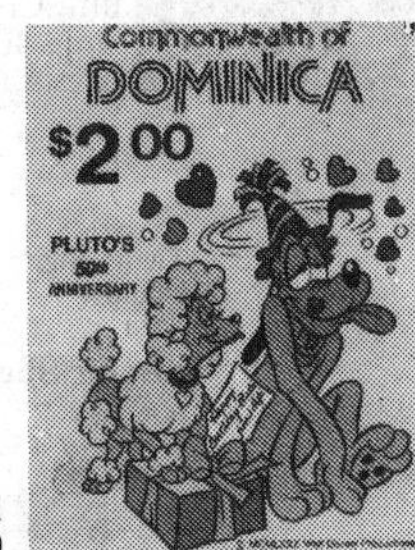

Pluto and Fifi — A100

Design: $4, Pluto in Blue Note (1947 cartoon).

**1981, Apr. 30 Litho. Perf. 13½x14**

694 A100 $2 multi 2.00 2.00

**Souvenir Sheet**

695 A100 $4 multi 4.00 4.00

50th anniversary of Walt Disney's Pluto. No. 695 has multicolored margin showing entire scene. Size: 127x102mm.

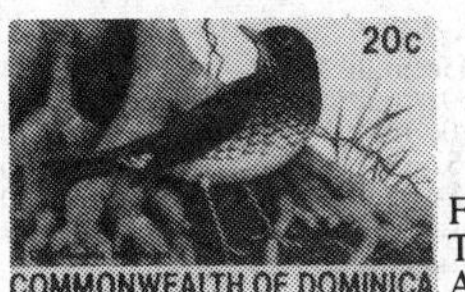

Forest Thrush A101

| 1981, Apr. 30 | | Perf. 14 | |
|---|---|---|---|
| 696 A101 | 20c shown | 16 | 16 |
| 697 A101 | 30c Stolid flycatcher | 24 | 24 |
| 698 A101 | 40c Blue-hooded euphonia | 32 | 32 |
| 699 A101 | $5 Lesser antillean peewee | 4.00 | 4.00 |

**Souvenir Sheet**

700 A101 $3 Sisserou parrot 2.25 2.25

No. 700 has multicolored margin showing sisserou parrots in tree. Size: 121½x95½mm.

**Royal Wedding Issue**

Common Design Type

| 1981, June 16 | Litho. | Perf. 14 | |
|---|---|---|---|
| 701 CD331 | 45c Couple | 35 | 35 |
| 702 CD331 | 60c Windsor Castle | 45 | 45 |
| 703 CD331 | $4 Charles | 3.00 | 3.00 |

**Souvenir Sheet**

704 CD331 $5 Helicopter 3.00 3.00

**Booklet**

705 CD331 11.75
- a Pane of 6 (3x25c, Lady Diana, 3x$2, Charles) 6.75
- b Pane of 1, $5, Couple 5.00

No. 704 has light green and black margin showing heraldic designs. Size: 96x83mm. No. 705 contains imperf., self-adhesive stamps.

Nos. 701-703 also printed in sheets of 5 plus label, perf. 12, in changed colors.

Elves Repairing Santa's Sleigh — A102

Christmas 1981: Scenes from Walt Disney's Santa's Workshop.

| 1981, Nov. 2 | Litho. | Perf. 14 | |
|---|---|---|---|
| 706 A102 | ½c multi | 5 | 5 |
| 707 A102 | 1c multi | 5 | 5 |
| 708 A102 | 2c multi | 5 | 5 |
| 709 A102 | 3c multi | 5 | 5 |
| 710 A102 | 4c multi | 5 | 5 |
| 711 A102 | 5c multi | 5 | 5 |
| 712 A102 | 10c multi | 8 | 8 |
| 713 A102 | 45c multi | 35 | 35 |
| 714 A102 | $5 multi | 3.75 | 3.75 |
| | Nos. 706-714 (9) | 4.48 | 4.48 |

**Souvenir Sheet**

715 A102 $4 multi 3.00 3.00

No. 715 has multicolored margin continuing design. Size: 129x103mm.

Ixora A103

| 1981, Dec. 1 | Litho. | Perf. 14 | |
|---|---|---|---|
| 716 A103 | 1c shown | 5 | 5 |
| 717 A103 | 2c Flamboyant | 5 | 5 |
| 718 A103 | 4c Poinsettia | 5 | 5 |
| 719 A103 | 5c Sabinea carinalis | 5 | 5 |
| 720 A103 | 8c Annatto roucou | 7 | 7 |
| 721 A103 | 10c Passion fruit | 8 | 8 |
| 722 A103 | 15c Breadfruit | 12 | 12 |
| 723 A103 | 20c Allamanda buttercup | 16 | 16 |
| 724 A103 | 25c Cashew | 20 | 20 |
| 725 A103 | 35c Soursop | 28 | 28 |
| 726 A103 | 40c Bougainvillea | 32 | 32 |
| 727 A103 | 45c Anthurium | 35 | 35 |
| 728 A103 | 60c Cacao | 48 | 48 |
| 729 A103 | 90c Pawpaw tree | 70 | 70 |
| 730 A103 | $1 Coconut palm | 80 | 80 |
| 731 A103 | $2 Coffee tree | 1.60 | 1.60 |
| 732 A103 | $5 Lobster claw | 4.00 | 4.00 |
| a | Perf. 12½x12 ('85) | 2.50 | 2.50 |
| 733 A103 | $10 Banana fig | 8.00 | 8.00 |
| | Nos. 716-733 (18) | 17.36 | 17.36 |

Intl. Year of the Disabled A104

Bathers, by Picasso A105

| 1981, Dec. 22 | Litho. | Perf. 14 | |
|---|---|---|---|
| 734 A104 | 45c Ramp curb | 30 | 30 |
| 735 A104 | 60c Bus steps | 40 | 40 |
| 736 A104 | 75c Hand-operated car | 50 | 50 |
| 737 A104 | $4 Bus lift | 2.75 | 2.75 |

**Souvenir Sheet**

738 A104 $5 Elevator buttons 3.50 3.50

No. 738 has multicolored margin showing emblem. Size: 82x96mm.

| 1981, Dec. 30 | | Perf. 14½ | |
|---|---|---|---|
| 739 A105 | 45c Olga in Armchair | 35 | 35 |
| 740 A105 | 60c shown | 45 | 45 |
| 741 A105 | 75c Woman in Spanish Costume | 55 | 55 |
| 742 A105 | $4 Dog and Cock | 3.00 | 3.00 |

**Souvenir Sheet**

743 A105 $5 Sleeping Peasants 3.75 3.75

No. 743 has multicolored margin showing entire painting. Size: 140x115mm.

1982 World Cup Soccer — A106

Designs: Various Disney characters playing soccer.

| 1982, Jan. 29 | | Perf. 14 | |
|---|---|---|---|
| 744 A106 | ½c multi | 5 | 5 |
| 745 A106 | 1c multi | 5 | 5 |
| 746 A106 | 2c multi | 5 | 5 |
| 747 A106 | 3c multi | 5 | 5 |
| 748 A106 | 4c multi | 5 | 5 |
| 749 A106 | 5c multi | 5 | 5 |
| 750 A106 | 10c multi | 8 | 8 |
| 751 A106 | 60c multi | 45 | 45 |
| 752 A106 | $5 multi | 3.75 | 3.75 |
| | Nos. 744-752 (9) | 4.58 | 4.58 |

**Souvenir Sheet**

753 A106 $4 multi 3.00 3.00

Golden Days, by Norman Rockwell A107

| 1982, Mar. 10 | Litho. | Perf. 14x13½ | |
|---|---|---|---|
| 754 A107 | 10c shown | 8 | 8 |
| 755 A107 | 25c The Morning News | 18 | 18 |
| 756 A107 | 45c The Marbles Champ | 35 | 35 |
| 757 A107 | $1 Speeding Along | 75 | 75 |

Intl. Decade for Women (1975-85) A108

Famous Women: 10c, Elma Napier (1890-1973), first woman elected to Legislative Council in British West Indies, 1940. 45c, Margaret Mead (1901-1978), anthropologist. $1, Mabel Caudiron (1909-1968), musician and folk historian. $3, Florence Nightingale, founder of modern nursing. $4, Eleanor Roosevelt.

| 1982, Apr. 15 | Litho. | Perf. 14 | |
|---|---|---|---|
| 758 A108 | 10c multi | 8 | 8 |
| 759 A108 | 45c multi | 35 | 35 |
| 760 A108 | $1 multi | 75 | 75 |
| 761 A108 | $4 multi | 3.00 | 3.00 |

**Souvenir Sheet**

762 A108 $3 multi 2.25 2.25

No. 762 has multicolored margin showing women in 19th dresses. Size: 92x63mm.

George Washington and Independence Hall, Philadelphia — A109

Washington or Roosevelt and: 60c, Capitol Building. 90c, The Surrender of Cornwallis, by John Trumbull. $2, Dam construction during New Deal (mural by William Gropper). $5, Washington, Roosevelt.

| 1982, May 1 | | Perf. 14½ | |
|---|---|---|---|
| 763 A109 | 45c multi | 35 | 35 |
| 764 A109 | 60c multi | 45 | 45 |
| 765 A109 | 90c multi | 70 | 70 |
| 766 A109 | $2 multi | 1.50 | 1.50 |

**Souvenir Sheet**

767 A109 $5 multi 4.00 4.00

George Washington's 250th birth anniv. and Franklin D. Roosevelt's birth cent. No. 767 has multicolored margin showing Liberty Bell, US flag, eagle. Size: 116x91mm.

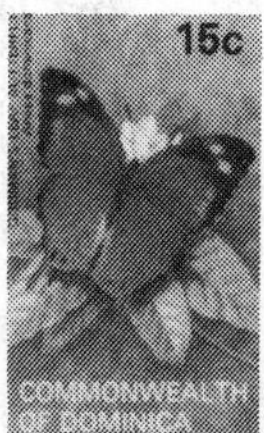



Godman's Leaf Butterfly — A110

| 1982, June 1 | Litho. | Perf. 14 | |
|---|---|---|---|
| 768 A110 | 15c shown | 12 | 12 |
| 769 A110 | 45c Zebra | 35 | 35 |
| 770 A110 | 60c Mimic | 45 | 45 |
| 771 A110 | $3 Red rim | 1.50 | 1.50 |

**Souvenir Sheet**

772 A110 $5 Southern dagger tail 3.75 3.75

No. 772 has multicolored margin continuing design. Size: 77x105mm.

**Princess Diana Issue**

Common Design Type

| 1982, July 1 | Litho. | Perf. 14½x14 | |
|---|---|---|---|
| 773 CD332 | 45c Buckingham Palace | 35 | 35 |
| 774 CD332 | $2 Engagement portrait | 1.50 | 1.50 |
| 775 CD332 | $4 Wedding | 3.00 | 3.00 |

**Souvenir Sheet**

776 CD332 $5 Diana, diff. 3.75 3.75

No. 776 has multicolored margin showing family tree, John Adams. Size: 103x76mm.
Also issued in sheet of 5 plus label.

Scouting Year A111

| 1982, July 1 | Litho. | Perf. 14 | |
|---|---|---|---|
| 777 A111 | 45c Cooking | 35 | 35 |
| 778 A111 | 60c Meteorological study | 45 | 45 |
| 779 A111 | 75c Sisserou parrot, cub scouts | 55 | 55 |
| 780 A111 | $3 Canoeing, Indian River | 2.25 | 2.25 |

**Souvenir Sheet**

781 A111 $5 Flagbearer 3.75 3.75

No. 781 has multicolored margin continuing design. Size: 100x70mm.

**Nos. 773-776 Overprinted: "ROYAL BABY / 21.6.82"**

| 1982, Sept. 1 | Litho. | Perf. 14½x14 | |
|---|---|---|---|
| 782 CD332 | 45c multi | 35 | 35 |
| 783 CD332 | $2 multi | 1.50 | 1.50 |
| 784 CD332 | $4 multi | 3.00 | 3.00 |

**Souvenir Sheet**

785 CD332 $5 multi 3.75 3.75

Birth of Prince William of Wales, June 21.
Also issued in sheet of 5 plus label.

Christmas 1982 — A112

Holy Family Paintings by Raphael.

**1982, Oct. 18 Litho. *Perf. 14***

*786* A112 25c multi 18 18
*787* A112 30c multi 22 22
*788* A112 90c multi 70 70
*789* A112 $4 multi 3.00 3.00

**Souvenir Sheet**

*790* A112 $5 multi 3.75 3.75

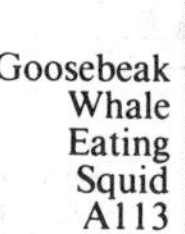
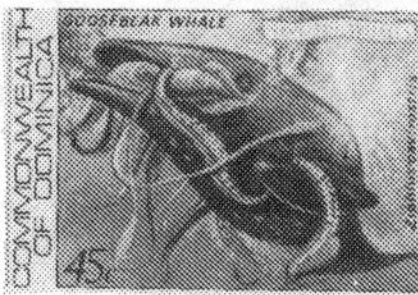
Goosebeak Whale Eating Squid A113

**1983, Feb. 15 Litho. *Perf. 14***

*791* A113 45c shown 35 35
*792* A113 60c Humpback whale 45 45
*793* A113 75c Great right whale 55 55
*794* A113 $3 Melonhead whale 2.25 2.25

**Souvenir Sheet**

*795* A113 $5 Pygmy sperm whale 3.75 3.75

**Commonwealth Day**
Common Design Type

**1983, Mar. 14**

*796* CD334 25c Banana industry 18 18
*797* CD334 30c Road construction 22 22
*798* CD334 90c Community nursing 70 70
*799* CD334 $3 Basket weavers 2.25 2.25

World Communications Year — A114

**1983, Apr. 18 Litho. *Perf. 14***

*800* A114 45c Hurricane pattern, map 35 35
*801* A114 60c Air-to-ship communication 45 45
*802* A114 90c Columbia shuttle, dish antenna 70 70
*803* A114 $2 Walkie-talkie 1.50 1.50

**Souvenir Sheet**

*804* A114 $5 Satellite 3.75 3.75

No. 804 has multicolored margin continuing design. Size: 111x85mm.

Manned Flight Bicentenary A115

**1983, July 19 Litho. *Perf. 15***

*805* A115 45c Mayo Composite 35 35
*806* A115 60c Macchi M-39 45 45
*807* A115 90c Fairey Swordfish 70 70
*808* A115 $4 Zeppelin LZ-3 3.00 3.00

**Souvenir Sheet**

*809* A115 $5 Double Eagle II, vert. 3.75 3.75

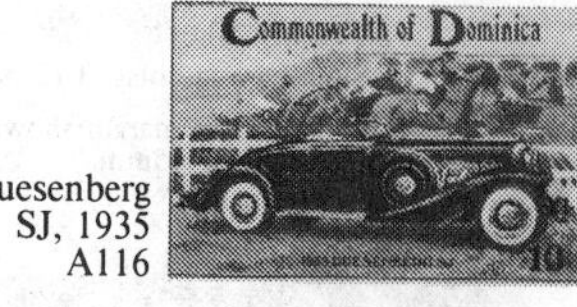
Duesenberg SJ, 1935 A116

**1983, Sept. 1 Litho. *Perf. 14***

*810* A116 10c shown 8 8
*811* A116 45c Studebaker Avanti, 1962 35 35
*812* A116 60c Cord 812, 1936 45 45
*813* A116 75c MG-TC, 1945 55 55
*814* A116 90c Camaro 350-SS, 1967 70 70
*815* A116 $3 Porsche 356, 1948 2.25 2.25
*Nos. 810-815 (6)* 4.38 4.38

**Souvenir Sheet**

*816* A116 $5 Ferrari 312-T, 1975 3.75 3.75

No. 816 has multicolored margin continuing design. Size: 105x75mm.

Christmas 1983 — A117

Raphael Paintings.

**1983, Oct. 4 Litho. *Perf. 13½***

*817* A117 45c multi 25 25
*818* A117 60c multi 35 35
*819* A117 90c multi 52 52
*820* A117 $4 multi 2.25 2.25

**Souvenir Sheet**

*821* A117 $5 multi 2.75 2.75

23rd Olympic Games, Los Angeles, July 28-Aug. 12 — A118

**1984, Mar. Litho. *Perf. 14***

*822* A118 30c Gymnastics 22 22
*823* A118 45c Javelin 35 35
*824* A118 60c Diving 45 45
*825* A118 $4 Fencing 2.75 2.75

**Souvenir Sheet**

*826* A118 $5 Equestrian 3.75 3.75

No. 826 has multicolored margin continuing design.

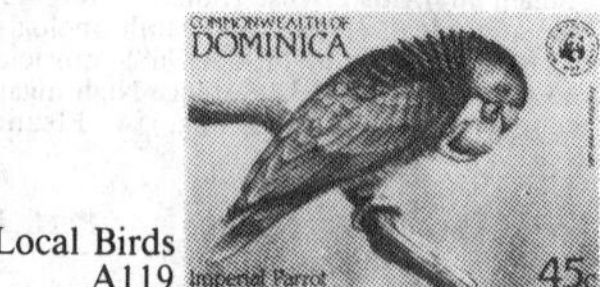
Local Birds A119

**1984, May Litho.**

*827* A119 5c Plumbeous warbler 5 5
*828* A119 45c Imperial parrot 35 35
*829* A119 60c Blue-headed hummingbird 45 45
*830* A119 90c Red-necked parrot 70 70

**Souvenir Sheet**

*831* A119 $5 Roseate flamingoes 3.75 3.75

Easter 1984 — A120

Various Disney characters and Easter bunnies.

**1984, Apr. 15 Litho. *Perf. 11***

*832* A120 ½c multi 5 5
*833* A120 1c multi 5 5
*834* A120 2c multi 5 5
*835* A120 3c multi 5 5
*836* A120 4c multi 5 5
*837* A120 5c multi 5 5
*838* A120 10c multi 8 8
*839* A120 $2 multi 1.60 1.60
*840* A120 $4 multi 3.25 3.25
*Nos. 832-840 (9)* 5.23 5.23

**Souvenir Sheet**
***Perf. 14***

*841* A120 $5 multi 4.00 4.00

No. 841 has multicolored margin continuing design. Size: 127x102mm.

Ships A121

**1984, June 14 Litho. *Perf. 14***

*842* A121 45c Atlantic Star 34 34
*843* A121 60c Atlantic 45 45
*844* A121 90c Carib fishing pirogue 68 68
*845* A121 $4 Norway 3.00 3.00

**Souvenir Sheet**

*846* A121 $5 Santa Maria 3.75 3.75

No. 846 has multicolored margin continuing design. Size: 107x81mm.

Local Plants — A122

Correggio & Degas — A122a

**1983, July**

*847* A122 45c Guzmania lingulata 34 34
*848* A122 60c Pitcairnia angustifolia 45 45
*849* A122 75c Tillandsia fasciculata 56 56
*850* A122 $3 Aechmea smithiorum 2.25 2.25

**Souvenir Sheet**

*851* A122 $5 Tillandsia utriculata 3.75 3.75

Ausipex Intl. Stamp Exhibition. No. 851 has multicolored margin continuing design. Size: 76x105mm.

Nos. 721, 732 Overprinted: "19th UPU / CONGRESS HAMBURG"

**1984 Litho. *Perf. 14***

*852* A103 10c multi 8 8
*853* A103 $5 multi 3.75 3.75

**1984, Nov. Litho. *Perf. 15***

Correggio: 25c, Virgin and Child with Young St. John. 60c, Christ Bids Farewell to the Virgin Mary. 90c, Do Not Touch Me. $4, The Mystical Marriage of St. Catherine. No. 862, Adoration of the Magi. Degas (horiz.): 30c, Before the Start. 45c, On the Racecourse. $1, Jockeys at the Flagpole. $3, Racehorses at Longchamp. No. 863, Self-portrait.

*854* A122a 25c multi 18 18
*855* A122a 30c multi 22 22
*856* A122a 45c multi 34 34
*857* A122a 60c multi 45 45
*858* A122a 90c multi 68 68
*859* A122a $1 multi 75 75
*860* A122a $3 multi 2.25 2.25
*861* A122a $4 multi 3.00 3.00
*Nos. 854-861 (8)* 7.87 7.87

**Souvenir Sheets**

*862* A122a $5 multi 3.75 3.75
*863* A122a $5 multi 3.75 3.75

No. 862 has multicolored margin continuing design. Size: 89x60mm.

Intl. Civil Aviation Org., 40th Anniv. — A123

**1984, Dec. *Perf. 14***

*864* A123 30c Avro 748 22 22
*865* A123 60c Twin Otter 45 45
*866* A123 $1 Islander 75 75
*867* A123 $3 Casa 2.25 2.25

**Souvenir Sheet**

*868* A123 $5 Boeing 747 3.75 3.75

Christmas 1984 and 50th Anniv. of Donald Duck — A124

Scenes from various Donald Duck movies.

**1984, Nov. Litho.**

*869* A124 45c multi 34 34
*870* A124 60c multi 45 45
*871* A124 90c multi 70 70
*872* A124 $2 perf. 12x12½ 1.50 1.50
*873* A124 $4 multi 3.00 3.00
*Nos. 869-873 (5)* 5.99 5.99

**Souvenir Sheet**
***Perf. 13½x14***

*874* A124 $5 multi 3.75 3.75

No. 874 has multicolored margin continuing design.

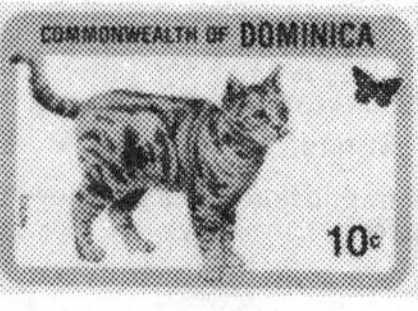
Cats A125

**1984, Nov. 12 Litho. *Perf. 15***

*875* A125 10c Tabby 8 8
*876* A125 15c Calico shorthair 12 12
*877* A125 20c Siamese 15 15
*878* A125 25c Manx 18 18
*879* A125 45c Abyssinian 32 32
*880* A125 60c Tortoise shell longhair 42 42
*881* A125 $1 Rex 72 72
*882* A125 $2 Persian 1.50 1.50
*883* A125 $3 Himalayan 2.25 2.25
*884* A125 $5 Burmese 3.50 3.50
*Nos. 875-884 (10)* 9.24 9.24

**Souvenir Sheet**

885 A125 $5 Gray Burmese, Persian, American shorthair 3.50 3.50

No. 885 has multicolored margin picturing Siamese cat. Size: 105x77mm.

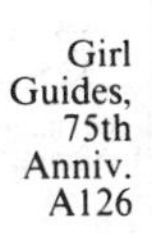
Girl Guides, 75th Anniv. A126

**1985, Feb. 18** *Perf. 14*

886 A126 35c Lady Baden-Powell 25 25
887 A126 45c Inspecting Dominican troop 35 35
888 A126 60c With Dominican troop leaders 45 45
889 A126 $3 Lord and Lady Baden-Powell, vert. 2.25 2.25

**Souvenir Sheet**

890 A126 $5 Flag ceremony 3.75 3.75

No. 890 has a multicolored margin continuing design. Size: 77x106mm.

John James Audubon A127

**1985, Apr. 4**

891 A127 45c King rails 35 35
892 A127 $1 Black-winged hawks, vert. 75 75
893 A127 $2 Broad-winged hawks, vert. 1.50 1.50
894 A127 $3 Ring-necked ducks 2.25 2.25

**Souvenir Sheet**

895 A127 $5 Reddish egrets, vert. 3.75 3.75

Nos. 891-894 exist vertically se-tenant with labels showing additional bird species. No. 895 has multicolored margin continuing design. Size: 103x73mm.
See Nos. 965-969.

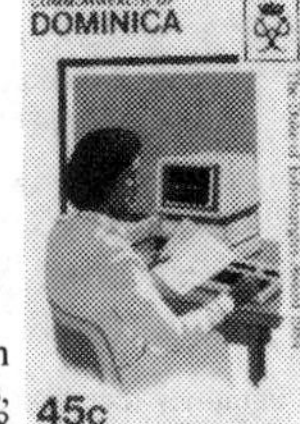


Duke of Edinburgh Awards, 1984 — A128

**1985, Apr. 30**

896 A128 45c Woman at computer terminal 35 35
897 A128 60c Medical staff, patient 45 45
898 A128 90c Runners 68 68
899 A128 $4 Family jogging 3.00 3.00

**Souvenir Sheet**

900 A128 $5 Duke of Edinburgh 3.75 3.75

No. 900 has multicolored margin continuing design and showing an award recipient. Size: 101x98mm.

Intl. Youth Year A129

**1985, July 8** **Litho.** *Perf. 14*

901 A129 45c Cricket match 30 30
902 A129 60c Environmental study, parrot 40 40
903 A129 $1 Stamp collecting 65 65
904 A129 $3 Boating, leisure 2.00 2.00

**Souvenir Sheet**

905 A129 $5 Youths join hands 3.25 3.25

No. 905 has multicolored margin continuing design and picturing a world map. Size: 97x66mm.

Queen Mother, 85th Birthday A130

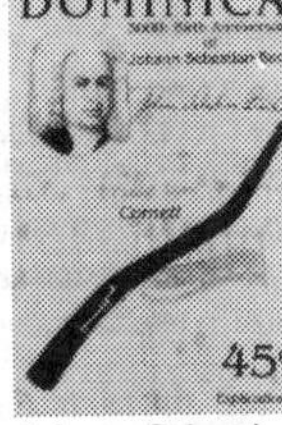


Johann Sebastian Bach A131

**1985, July 15**

906 A130 60c Visiting Sadlers Wells 40 40
907 A130 $1 Fishing 65 65
908 A130 $3 At Clarence House, 1984 2.00 2.00

**Souvenir Sheet**

909 A130 $5 Attending Windsor Castle Garter Ceremony 3.25 3.25

No. 909 has multicolored margin continuing the portrait. Size: 52x85mm.

**1985, Sept. 2**

Portrait, signature, music from Explication and: 45c, Cornett 60c, Coiled trumpet. $1, Piccolo. $3, Violoncello piccolo.

910 A131 45c multi 30 30
911 A131 60c multi 40 40
912 A131 $1 multi 65 65
913 A131 $3 multi 2.00 2.00

**Souvenir Sheet**

914 A131 $5 Portrait 3.25 3.25

No. 913 has black margin picturing a line drawing of Eisenach, Bach s birthplace. Size: 110x76mm.

State Visit of Elizabeth II, Oct. 25 — A132

**1985, Oct. 25** *Perf. 14½*

915 A132 60c Flags of U.K., Dominica 40 40
916 A132 $1 Elizabeth II, vert. 65 65
917 A132 $4 HMS Britannia 2.75 2.75

**Souvenir Sheet**

918 A132 $5 Map 3.25 3.25

No. 918 has multicolored margin continuing the map of the Caribbean Sea and picturing the Britannia. Size: 112x83mm.

Mark Twain — A133

Disney characters in Tom Sawyer.

**1985, Nov. 11** **Litho.** *Perf. 14*

919 A133 20c multi 15 15
920 A133 60c multi 45 45
921 A133 $1 multi 75 75
922 A133 $1.50 multi 1.10 1.10
923 A133 $2 multi 1.50 1.50
*Nos. 919-923 (5)* 3.95 3.95

**Souvenir Sheet**

924 A133 $5 multi 3.75 3.75

Christmas 1985. No. 924 has multicolored margin continuing the design. Size: 126x101mm.

The Brothers Grimm — A134

Disney characters in Little Red Cap (Little Red Riding Hood).

**1985, Nov. 11**

925 A134 10c multi 8 8
926 A134 45c multi 32 32
927 A134 90c multi 65 65
928 A134 $1 multi 75 75
929 A134 $3 multi 2.25 2.25
*Nos. 925-929 (5)* 4.05 4.05

**Souvenir Sheet**

930 A134 $5 multi 3.75 3.75

Christmas 1985. No. 930 has multicolored margin continuing the design. Size: 127x101mm.

UN, 40th Anniv. A135

Stamps of UN, famous men and events: 45c, No. 442 and Lord Baden-Powell. $2, No. 157 and Maimonides (1135-1204) Judaic scholar. $3, No. 278 and Sir Rowland Hill. $5, Apollo-Soyuz Mission, 10th anniv.

**1985, Nov. 22** *Perf. 14½*

931 A135 45c multi 32 32
932 A135 $2 multi 1.50 1.50
933 A135 $3 multi 2.25 2.25

**Souvenir Sheet**

934 A135 $5 multi 3.75 3.75

No. 934 has multicolored margin picturing anniv. emblem, UN Geneva No. 110, flag of Dominica and space probe. Size: 110x85mm.

1986 World Cup Soccer Championships, Mexico — A136

Various soccer plays.

**1986, Mar. 26** *Perf. 14*

935 A136 45c multi 32 32
936 A136 60c multi 45 45
937 A136 $1 multi 75 75
938 A136 $3 multi 2.25 2.25

**Souvenir Sheet**

939 A136 $5 multi 3.75 3.75

No. 939 has multicolored margin continuing the design. Size: 113x84mm.

Statue of Liberty, Cent. A137

Statue and: 15c, New York police pursuing river pirates, c. 1890. 25c, Police patrol boat. 45c, Hoboken Ferry Terminal, c. 1890. $4, Holland Tunnel.

**1986, Mar. 26**

940 A137 15c multi 12 12
941 A137 25c multi 18 18
942 A137 45c multi 32 32
943 A137 $4 multi 3.00 3.00

**Souvenir Sheet**

944 A137 $5 Statue, vert. 3.75 3.75

No. 944 has multicolored margin picturing emigrants, Fritz Lang (1890-1976), film director, John Muir, naturalist, Igor Stravinsky, composer, and Dr. Werner von Braun (1912-77), rocket scientist. Size: 105x76mm.

Halley's Comet A138

Designs: 5c, Jantal Mantar Observatory, Delhi, India, Nasir al Din al Tusi (1201-1274), astronomer. 10c, US Bell X-1 rocket plane breaking sound barrier. 45c, Astronomicum Caesareum, 1540, manuscript diagram of comet's trajectory, 1531. $4, Mark Twain, comet appeared at birth and death. $5, Comet.

**1986, Apr. 17**

945 A138 5c multi 5 5
946 A138 10c multi 8 8
947 A138 45c multi 32 32
948 A138 $4 multi 3.00 3.00

**Souvenir Sheet**

949 A138 $5 multi 3.75 3.75

No. 949 has multicolored margin continuing the design. Size: 104x71mm.
See Nos. 984-988.

**Queen Elizabeth II, 60th Birthday**
Common Design Type

**1986, Apr. 21** **Litho.** *Perf. 14*

950 CD339 2c Wedding, 1947 5 5
951 CD339 $1 With Pope John Paul II, 1982 75 75
952 CD339 $4 Royal visit, 1971 3.00 3.00

**Souvenir Sheet**

953 CD339 $5 Age 10 3.75 3.75

No. 953 has beige and gray inscribed margin. Size: 120x85mm.

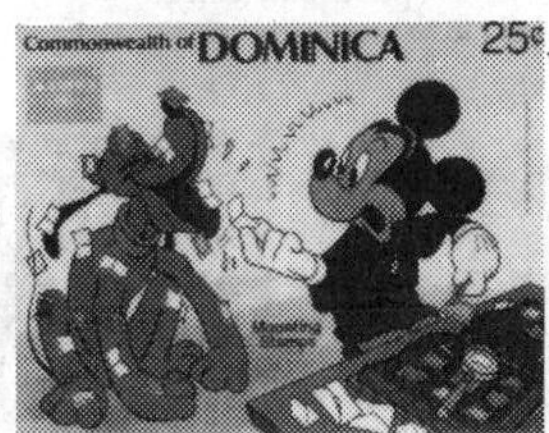


AMERIPEX '86 — A139

Walt Disney characters involved in stamp collecting.

**1986, May 22** *Perf. 11*

954 A139 25c Mickey Mouse and Pluto 18 18
955 A139 45c Donald Duck 32 32
956 A139 60c Chip-n-Dale 45 45
957 A139 $4 Donald, nephews 3.00 3.00

**Souvenir Sheet**
*Perf. 14*

958 A139 $5 Uncle Scrooge 3.75 3.75

No. 958 has multicolored margin continuing the design and picturing Disney characters at stamp auction. Size: 127x102mm.

A little time given to the study of the arrangement of the Scott Catalogue can make it easier to use effectively.

British Monarchs — A140

**1986, June 9** *Perf. 14*

*959* A140 10c William I 8 8
*960* A140 40c Richard II 30 30
*961* A140 50c Henry VIII 38 38
*962* A140 $1 Charles II 75 75
*963* A140 $2 Queen Anne 1.50 1.50
*964* A140 $4 Queen Victoria 3.00 3.00
*Nos. 959-964 (6)* 6.01 6.01

Audubon Type of 1985

*Perf. 12½x12, 12x12½*

**1986, June 18**

*965* A127 25c Black-throated diver 20 20
*966* A127 60c Great blue heron 45 45
*967* A127 90c Yellow-crowned night heron 65 65
*968* A127 $4 Shoveler duck 3.00 3.00

**Souvenir Sheet**

*Perf. 14*

*969* A127 $5 Goose 3.75 3.75

Nos. 966-967 vert. No. 969 has multicolored margin continuing the design. Size: 73x103mm.

**Royal Wedding Issue, 1986**

Common Design Type

**1986, July 23** *Perf. 14*

*970* CD340 45c Couple 32 32
*971* CD340 60c Prince Andrew 45 45
*972* CD340 $4 Prince, aircraft 3.00 3.00

**Souvenir Sheet**

*973* CD340 $5 Couple, diff. 3.75 3.75

No. 973 has multicolored margin picturing Prince Andrew at the helm of a royal navy ship. Size: 88x88mm.

Nos. 935-939 Ovptd. "WINNERS / Argentina 3 / W. Germany 2" in Gold.

**1986, Sept. 15** **Litho.** *Perf. 14*

*974* A136 45c multi 32 32
*975* A136 60c multi 45 45
*976* A136 $1 multi 75 75
*977* A136 $3 multi 2.25 2.25

**Souvenir Sheet**

*978* A136 $5 multi 3.75 3.75

Paintings by Albrecht Durer
A141 A142

**1986, Dec. 2** **Litho.** *Perf. 14*

*979* A141 45c Virgin in Prayer 35 35
*980* A141 60c Madonna and Child 48 48
*981* A141 $1 Madonna and Child, diff. 80 80
*982* A141 $3 Madonna and Child with St. Anne 2.40 2.40

**Souvenir Sheet**

*983* A142 $5 Nativity 4.00 4.00

No. 983 has multicolored margin continuing the painting. Size: 76x102mm.

Nos. 945-949 Printed with Halley's Comet Logo in Black or Silver.

**1986, Dec. 16**

*984* A138 5c multi 5 5
*985* A138 10c multi 8 8
*986* A138 45c multi 35 35
*987* A138 $4 multi 3.60 3.60

**Souvenir Sheet**

*988* A138 $5 multi (S) 4.00 4.00

Birds — A143

**1987, Jan. 20** **Litho.** *Perf. 15*

*989* A143 1c Broad-winged hawk 5 5
*990* A143 2c Ruddy quail dove 5 5
*991* A143 5c Red-necked pigeon 5 5
*992* A143 10c Green heron 8 8
*993* A143 15c Common gallinule 12 12
*994* A143 20c Ringed kingfisher 16 16
*995* A143 25c Brown pelican 20 20
*996* A143 35c White-tailed tropicbird 28 28
*997* A143 45c Red-legged thrush 35 35
*998* A143 60c Purple throated carib 48 48
*999* A143 90c Magnificent frigatebird 72 72
*1000* A143 $1 Trembler 80 80
*1001* A143 $2 Black-capped petrel 1.60 1.60
*1002* A143 $5 Barn owl 4.00 4.00
*1003* A143 $10 Imperial parrot 8.00 8.00
*Nos. 989-1003 (15)* 16.94 16.94

Paintings by Marc Chagall (1887-1985) A144

Designs: 25c, Artist and His Model. 35c, Midsummer Night's Dream. 45c, Joseph the Shepherd. 60c, the Cellist. 90c, Woman with Pigs. $1, the Blue Circus. $3, For Vava. $4, the Rider. No. 1012, Purim. No. 1013, Firebird design for the curtain of the Stravinsky Ballet production.

**1987, Mar. 2** *Perf. 14*

*1004* A144 25c multi 20 20
*1005* A144 35c multi 28 28
*1006* A144 45c multi 35 35
*1007* A144 60c multi 48 48
*1008* A144 90c multi 72 72
*1009* A144 $1 multi 80 80
*1010* A144 $3 multi 2.40 2.40
*1011* A144 $4 multi 3.20 3.20

**Size: 110x95mm**

***Imperf***

*1012* A144 $5 multi 4.00 4.00
*1013* A144 $5 multi 4.00 4.00
*Nos. 1004-1013 (10)* 16.43 16.43

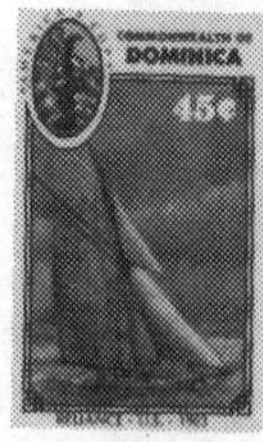


A145

Conch Shells — A147

America's Cup — A146

**1987, Feb. 5** *Perf. 15*

*1014* A145 45c Reliance, 1903 35 35
*1015* A145 60c Freedom, 1980 48 48
*1016* A145 $1 Mischief, 1881 80 80
*1017* A145 $3 Australia, 1977 2.40 2.40

**Souvenir Sheet**

*1018* A146 $5 Courageous, Australia, 1977 4.00 4.00

No. 1018 has multicolored margin continuing the design and picturing flag of the US and America's cup. Size: 113x84mm.

**1987, Apr. 13** **Litho.**

Designs: 35c, Morch Poulsen's triton. 45c, Swainson globe purple sea snail. 60c, Banded tulip. No. 1022, Lamarck deltoid rock shell. No. 1023, Junoia volute.

*1019* A147 35c multi 28 28
*1020* A147 45c multi 35 35
*1021* A147 60c multi 48 48
*1022* A147 $5 multi 4.00 4.00

**Souvenir Sheet**

*1023* A147 $5 multi 4.00 4.00

No. 1023 has multicolored decorative margin picturing coral.

CAPEX '87 A148

Mushrooms.

**1987, June 15** **Litho.** *Perf. 14*

*1024* A148 45c Cantharellus cinnabarinus 35 35
*1025* A148 60c Boletellus cubensis 45 45
*1026* A148 $2 Eccilia cystiophorus 1.50 1.50
*1027* A148 $3 Xerocomus guadelupae 2.25 2.25

**Souvenir Sheet**

*1028* A148 $5 Gymnopilus chrysopellus 3.75 3.75

No. 1028 has multicolored decorative margin picturing flora and coastline. Size: 85x86mm.

A149

Discovery of America, 500th Anniv. (in 1992) — A150

Explorations of Christopher Columbus: 10c, Discovery of Dominica. 15c, Ships greeted by Carib Indians. 45c, Claiming New World for Spain. 60c, Wrecking of the Santa Maria. 90c, Fleet setting sail. $1, Sighting land. $3, Trading with the Indians. No. 1036, First settlement. No. 1037, Arrival of Second Fleet at Dominica, Nov. 3, 1493. No. 1038, Map of exploration of the Leeward Islands.

**1987, July 27** *Perf. 15*

*1029* A149 10c multi 8 8
*1030* A149 15c multi 12 12
*1031* A149 45c multi 35 35
*1032* A149 60c multi 45 45
*1033* A149 90c multi 68 68
*1034* A149 $1 multi 75 75
*1035* A149 $3 multi 2.25 2.25
*1036* A149 $5 multi 3.75 3.75
*Nos. 1029-1036 (8)* 8.43 8.43

**Souvenir Sheets**

*1037* A150 $5 multi 3.75 3.75
*1038* A150 $5 multi 3.75 3.75

Nos. 1037-1038 have multicolored margins continuing the designs. Sizes: 110x80mm.

Transportation — A151

Designs: 10c, Warrior, first iron-clad warship. 15c, Maglev-MLU 001, fastest passenger train. 25c, Clipper Flying Cloud, fastest New York to San Francisco voyage, 1852. 35c, First elevated railway, New York City. 45c, Tom Thumb, first U.S. passenger train locomotive. 60c, Joshua Slocum, first solo circumnavigation of the world in a sloop. 90c, Se-Land Commerce, fastest Pacific crossing. $1, First cable car, San Francisco. $3, Orient Express. $4, The North River Steamboat of Clermont, invented by Robert Fulton, first successful commercial steamboat.

**1987** **Litho.** *Perf. 14*

*1039* A151 10c multi 8 8
*1040* A151 15c multi 10 10
*1041* A151 25c multi, vert. 18 18
*1042* A151 35c multi, vert. 25 25
*1043* A151 45c multi 32 32
*1044* A151 60c multi, vert. 45 45
*1045* A151 90c multi, vert. 65 65
*1046* A151 $1 multi 72 72
*1047* A151 $3 multi 2.15 2.15
*1048* A151 $4 multi 2.90 2.90
*Nos. 1039-1048 (10)* 7.80 7.80

Issue dates: 10c, 5c, 45c, 60c, $4, Sept. 28; others Aug. 1.

Christmas — A152

Paintings (details): 20c, Virgin and Child with St. Anne, by Durer. 25c, The Virgin and Child, by Murillo. $2, Madonna and Child, by Vincenzo Foppa (c. 1427-1516). $4, Madonna and Child, by Paolo Veronese (1528-1588). $5, Angel of the Annunciation, anonymous.

**1987, Nov. 16**

*1049* A152 20c multi 15 15
*1050* A152 25c multi 18 18
*1051* A152 $2 multi 1.45 1.45
*1052* A152 $4 multi 2.90 2.90

**Souvenir Sheet**

*1053* A152 $5 multi 3.60 3.60

No. 1053 has multicolored decorative margin continuing the painting. Size: 100x76mm.

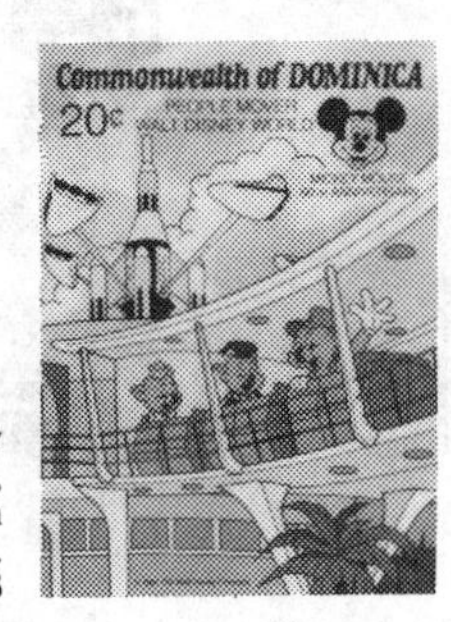


Mickey Mouse, 60th Anniv. A153

Disney theme parks and trains: 20c, People Mover, Disney World. 25c, Horse-drawn Trolley, Disneyland. 45c, Roger E. Broggie, Disney World. 60c, Big Thunder Mountain, Disneyland. 90c, Walter E. Disney, Disneyland. $1, Monorail, Disney World. $3, Casey Jr. from Dumbo. $4, Lilly Belle, Disney World. No. 1062, Rainbow Caverns Mine Train, Disneyland, horiz. No. 1063, Toy train from movie Out of Scale, horiz.

**1987, Dec. 7 Litho. *Perf. 14***

*1054* A153 20c multi 15 15
*1055* A153 25c multi 20 20
*1056* A153 45c multi 35 35
*1057* A153 60c multi 48 48
*1058* A153 90c multi 65 65
*1059* A153 $1 multi 75 75
*1060* A153 $3 multi 2.25 2.25
*1061* A153 $4 multi 3.00 3.00
*Nos. 1054-1061 (8)* 7.83 7.83

**Souvenir Sheets**

*1062* A153 $5 multi 3.80 3.80
*1063* A153 $5 multi 3.80 3.80

Nos. 1062-1063 have multicolored margins continuing the designs. Sizes: 127x102mm.

40th Wedding Anniv. of Queen Elizabeth II and Prince Philip — A154

1988 Summer Olympics, Seoul — A155

**1988, Feb. 15 Litho. *Perf. 14***

*1064* A154 45c Couple, wedding party, 1947 35 35
*1065* A154 60c Elizabeth, Charles, c. 1952 45 45
*1066* A154 $1 Royal Family, c. 1952 78 78
*1067* A154 $3 Queen with tiara, c. 1960 2.30 2.30

**Souvenir Sheet**

*1068* A154 $5 Elizabeth, 1947 3.80 3.80

No. 1068 has multicolored margin picturing Irish State coach on wedding day. Size: 101x76mm.

**1988, Mar. 15**

*1069* A155 45c Kayaking 35 35
*1070* A155 60c TaeKwon-Do 45 45
*1071* A155 $1 Diving 78 78
*1072* A155 $3 Parallel bars 2.30 2.30

**Souvenir Sheet**

*1073* A155 $5 Soccer 3.80 3.80

No. 1073 has multicolored margin picturing aerial view of stadium, birds and natl. flag. Size: 81x110mm.

Reunion '88 Tourism Campaign A156

**1988, Apr. 13 Litho. *Perf. 15***

*1074* A156 10c Carib Indian, vert. 8 8
*1075* A156 25c Mountainous interior 20 20
*1076* A156 35c Indian River, vert. 28 28
*1077* A156 60c Belaire dancer, vert. 45 45
*1078* A156 90c The Boiling Lake, vert. 68 68
*1079* A156 $3 Coral reef 2.25 2.25
*Nos. 1074-1079 (6)* 3.94 3.94

**Souvenir Sheet**

*1080* A156 $5 Belaire dancer, diff., vert. 3.80 3.80

Independence, 10th anniv. No. 1080 has multicolored decorative margin continuing the design and picturing beach, light aircraft. Size: 113x83mm.

Nos. 1046-1047, 1037-1038 Ovptd. for Philatelic Exhibitions in Black

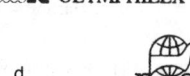

a 

b 

c 

d 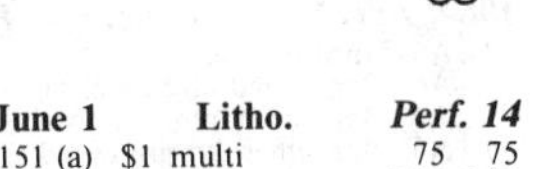


**1988, June 1 Litho. *Perf. 14***

*1081* A151 (a) $1 multi 75 75
*1082* A151 (b) $3 multi 2.25 2.25

**Souvenir Sheets**

***Perf. 15***

*1083* A150 (c) $5 multi 3.75 3.75
*1084* A150 (d) $5 multi 3.75 3.75

FINLANDIA '88 ($1), INDEPENDENCE 40 ($3), OLYMPHILEX '88 (No. 1083), PRAGA '88 (No. 1084).

Miniature Sheet

Rain Forest Flora and Fauna — A157

Designs: a. White-tailed tropicbirds. b. Blue-throated euphonia. c. Smooth-billed ani. d. Scaly-breasted thrasher. e. Purple-throated carib. f. Southern daggertail and Clench's hairstreak. g. Trembler. h. Imperial parrot. i. Mangrove cuckoo. j. Hercules beetle. k. Orion. l. Red-necked parrot. m. Tillandsia. n. *Polystacha luteola* and bananaquit. o. False chameleon. p. Iguana. q. Hypolimnas. r. Green-throated carib. s. Heliconia. t. Agouti.

**1988, July 25 *Perf. 14½***

*1085* Sheet of 20 7.00 7.00
*a.-t.* A157 45c any single 35 35

Size: 178x178mm.

Intl. Fund for Agricultural Development (IFAD), 10th Anniv. — A158

**1988, Sept. 5 Litho. *Perf. 14***

*1086* A158 45c Hen house 35 35
*1087* A158 60c Pig farm 45 45
*1088* A158 90c Cattle 70 70
*1089* A158 $3 Black-belly sheep 2.25 2.25

**Souvenir Sheet**

*1090* A158 $5 Mixed crops, vert. 3.75 3.75

No. 1090 has multicolored inscribed margin continuing the design. Size: 96x68mm.

Entertainers A159

**1988, Sept. 8**

*1091* A159 10c Gary Cooper 8 8
*1092* A159 35c Josephine Baker 28 28
*1093* A159 45c Maurice Chevalier 35 35
*1094* A159 60c James Cagney 45 45
*1095* A159 $1 Clark Gable 75 75
*1096* A159 $2 Louis Armstrong 1.50 1.50
*1097* A159 $3 Liberace 2.25 2.25
*1098* A159 $4 Spencer Tracy 3.00 3.00
*Nos. 1091-1098 (8)* 8.66 8.66

**Souvenir Sheets**

*1099* A159 $5 Elvis Presley 3.75 3.75
*1100* A159 $5 Humphrey Bogart 3.75 3.75

Nos. 1099-1100 have multicolored decorative margins continuing the designs and picturing Graceland, Presley's estate in Memphis, Tennessee, or John Houston directing Bogart in a scene from *The African Queen.* Sizes: 105x75mm.

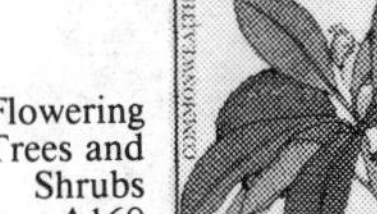

Flowering Trees and Shrubs A160

**1988, Sept. 29 Litho. *Perf. 14***

*1101* A160 15c Sapodilla 12 12
*1102* A160 20c Tangerine 15 15
*1103* A160 25c Avocado pear 18 18
*1104* A160 45c Amherstia 35 35
*1105* A160 90c Lipstick tree 68 68
*1106* A160 $1 Cannonball tree 75 75
*1107* A160 $3 Saman 2.25 2.25
*1108* A160 $4 Pineapple 3.00 3.00
*Nos. 1101-1108 (8)* 7.48 7.48

**Souvenir Sheets**

*1109* A160 $5 Lignum vitae 3.75 3.75
*1110* A160 $5 Sea grape 3.75 3.75

Nos. 1109-1110 have multicolored margins continuing the designs. Sizes: 95x66mm.

Paintings by Titian A161

Designs: 25c, *Jacopo Strada,* c. 1567. 35c, *Titian's Daughter Lavinia,* c. 1565. 45c, *Andrea Navagero,* c. 1515. 60c, *Judith with Head of Holoferenes,* c. 1570. $1, *Emilia di Spilimbergo,* c. 1560. $2, *Martyrdom of St. Lawrence,* c. 1548. $3, *Salome With the Head of St. John the Baptist,* 1560. $4, *St. John the Baptist,* c. 1540. No. 1119, *Self-portrait,* c. 1555. No. 1120, *Sisyphus,* 1549.

**1988, Oct. 10 Litho. *Perf. 13½x14***

*1111* A161 25c multi 18 18
*1112* A161 35c multi 28 28
*1113* A161 45c multi 35 35
*1114* A161 60c multi 45 45
*1115* A161 $1 multi 75 75
*1116* A161 $2 multi 1.50 1.50
*1117* A161 $3 multi 2.25 2.25
*1118* A161 $4 multi 3.00 3.00
*Nos. 1111-1118 (8)* 8.76 8.76

**Souvenir Sheets**

*1119* A161 $5 multi 3.75 3.75
*1120* A161 $5 multi 3.75 3.75

Nos. 1119-1120 have multicolored margins continuing the paintings. Sizes: 110x95mm.

Independence, 10th Anniv. A162

John F. Kennedy A163

**1988, Oct. 31 Litho. *Perf. 14***

*1121* A162 20c Imperial parrot 15 15
*1122* A162 45c No. 1, landscape 35 35
*1123* A162 $2 No. 602, waterfall 1.50 1.50
*1124* A162 $3 Carib wood 2.25 2.25

**Souvenir Sheet**

*1125* A162 $5 Natl. band performing 3.75 3.75

Nos. 1122-1123 horiz. No. 1125 has multicolored margin continuing the design. Size: 116x94mm.

**1988, Nov. 22**

*1126* A163 20c With Jackie 15 15
*1127* A163 25c Sailing *Vicuna* 20 20
*1128* A163 $2 Walking in Hyannis Port 1.50 1.50
*1129* A163 $4 Berlin Wall speech 3.00 3.00

**Souvenir Sheet**

*1130* A163 $5 Portrait 3.75 3.75

Nos. 1126-1128 horiz. No. 1130 has multicolored inscribed margin picturing eternal flame from grave site in Arlington Cemetery. Size: 100x70mm.

Miniature Sheet

Christmas, Mickey Mouse 60th Anniv. — A164

Designs: No. 1131a, Huey, Dewey and Louie. No. 1131b, Daisy Duck. No. 1131c, Winnie-the-Pooh. No. 1131d, Goofy. No. 1131e, Donald Duck. No. 1131f, Mickey Mouse. No. 1131g, Minnie Mouse. No. 1131h, Chip-n-Dale. No. 1132, Mickey, Morty and Ferdy. No. 1133, Characters visiting shopping mall Santa.

**1988, Dec. 1 *Perf. 13½x14***

*1131* A164 Sheet of 8 3.60 3.60
*a.-h.* 60c any single 45 45

**Souvenir Sheets**

*1132* A164 $6 multi 4.50 4.50
*1133* A164 $6 multi, horiz. 4.50 4.50

Nos. 1132-1133 have multicolored decorative margins continuing the designs. Sizes: 179x140mm (No. 1131); 127x102mm (Nos. 1132-1133).

UN Declaration of Human Rights, 40th Anniv. — A165

Designs: $3, Flag of Sweden and Raoul Wallenberg, who helped save 100,000 Jews in Budapest from deportation to Nazi concentration camps. $5, Human Rights Flame.

**1988, Dec. 12** ***Perf.***

| | | | | |
|---|---|---|---|---|
| *1134* | A165 | $3 multi | 2.25 | 2.25 |

**Souvenir Sheet**

| | | | | |
|---|---|---|---|---|
| *1135* | A165 | $5 multi, vert. | 3.75 | 3.75 |

No. 1135 has multicolored margin picturing US Capitol Building, Martin Luther King, Jr., Gandhi, the Taj Mahal, the Glockenspiel in Market Square, Munich, Albert Einstein, Eleanor Roosevelt and the White House.

## WAR TAX STAMPS

No. 50 Surcharged in Red — WAR TAX ONE HALFPENNY

**1916** **Wmk. 3** ***Perf. 14.***

| | | | | |
|---|---|---|---|---|
| *MR1* | A6 | ½p on ½p green | 8 | 8 |

No. 50 Overprinted in Black — WAR TAX

**1918**

| | | | | |
|---|---|---|---|---|
| *MR2* | A6 | ½p green | 20 | 20 |

Nos. 50, 40 in Black or Red — WAR TAX

**1918**

| | | | | |
|---|---|---|---|---|
| *MR3* | A6 | ½p green | 6 | *10* |
| *MR4* | A6 | 3p vio, *yel* (R) | 10 | *40* |

Type of 1908-09 Surcharged in Red — WAR TAX 1½D.

**1919**

| | | | | |
|---|---|---|---|---|
| *MR5* | A6 | 1½p on 2½p orange | 8 | *35* |

# DUBAI

LOCATION — Oman Peninsula, Arabia, on Persian Gulf.
GOVT. — Sheikdom under British protection.
AREA — 1,500 sq. mi.
POP. — 60,000.
CAPITAL — Dubai.

Dubai is one of six Persian Gulf sheikdoms to join the United Arab Emirates which proclaimed its independence Dec. 2, 1971. See United Arab Emirates.

100 Naye Paise = 1 Rupee
100 Dirhams = 1 Riyal (1966)

Imperforate
Many issues were accompanied by smaller quantities of imperforate stamps.

**Catalogue values for all unused stamps in this country are for Never Hinged items.**

Hermit Crab — A1

Sheik Rashid bin Said al Maktum — A2

Designs: 2np, 20np, Cuttlefish. 3np, 25np, Snail. 4np, 30np, Crab. 5np, 35np, Sea urchin. 10np, 50np, Sea shell. 1r, Fortress wall. 2r, View of Dubai. 3r, Fortress wall. 5r, View of Dubai.

***Perf. 12x11½***

**1963, June 15** **Litho.** **Unwmk.**

| | | | | | |
|---|---|---|---|---|---|
| *1* | A1 | 1np | dl bl & car rose | 12 | 5 |
| *2* | A1 | 2np | lt bl & bis brn | 12 | 5 |
| *3* | A1 | 3np | grn & sep | 12 | 5 |
| *4* | A1 | 4np | pink & org | 12 | 5 |
| *5* | A1 | 5np | vio & blk | 12 | 5 |
| *6* | A1 | 10np | brn org & blk | 12 | 5 |
| *7* | A1 | 15np | gray ol & dp car | 20 | 6 |
| *8* | A1 | 20np | rose red & org brn | 22 | 7 |
| *9* | A1 | 25np | ap grn & red brn | 25 | 8 |
| *10* | A1 | 30np | gray & red | 30 | 10 |
| *11* | A1 | 35np | dl lil & dl vio | 35 | 10 |
| *12* | A1 | 50np | org & sep | 55 | 15 |
| *13* | A1 | 1r | brt bl & red org | 1.10 | 30 |
| *14* | A1 | 2r | dl yel & brn | 2.25 | 60 |
| *15* | A1 | 3r | rose car & blk | 3.50 | 90 |
| *16* | A1 | 5r | grn & dl red brn | 5.50 | 1.50 |

***Perf. 12***

| | | | | | |
|---|---|---|---|---|---|
| *17* | A2 | 10r | rose lake, grnsh bl & blk | 11.25 | 3.00 |
| | | | *Nos. 1-17 (17)* | 26.19 | 7.16 |

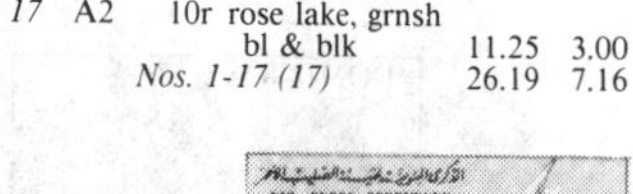

Dhows — A3

Designs: 2np, First-aid tent. 3np, Camel caravan. 4np, Butterfly.

**1963, Sept. 1** **Unwmk.** ***Perf. 12***

| | | | | | |
|---|---|---|---|---|---|
| *18* | A3 | 1np | ultra, yel & red | 10 | 10 |
| *19* | A3 | 2np | brn, yel & red | 10 | 10 |
| *20* | A3 | 3np | red brn, org & red | 10 | 10 |
| *21* | A3 | 4np | brn, brt grn & red | 10 | 10 |
| | | | *Nos. 18-21,C9-C12 (8)* | 2.10 | 2.10 |

Centenary of International Red Cross. Exist perf. 10½.

Four imperf. souvenir sheets exist in the denominations and designs of Nos. C9-C12, with "Air-Mail" omitted and colors changed. Size: 119x99mm.

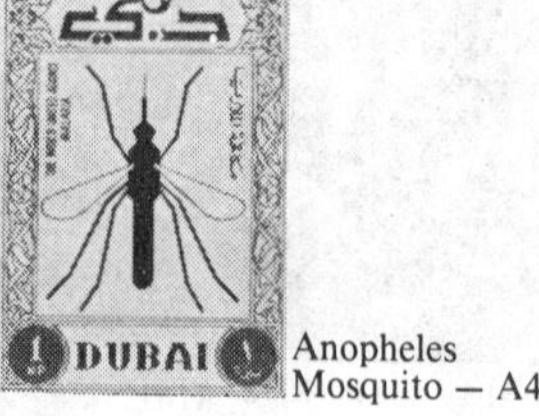

Anopheles Mosquito — A4

Designs: 2np, Mosquito and entwined snakes. 3np, Mosquitoes over swamp.

**1963, Dec. 20** **Unwmk.** ***Perf. 12***

| | | | | | |
|---|---|---|---|---|---|
| *22* | A4 | 1np | emer & red brn | 12 | 12 |
| *23* | A4 | 1np | red & dk brn | 12 | 12 |
| *24* | A4 | 1np | bl & car | 12 | 12 |
| *25* | A4 | 2np | brn & org | 12 | 12 |
| *26* | A4 | 2np | car & bl | 12 | 12 |
| *27* | A4 | 3np | org brn & bl | 12 | 12 |
| | | | *Nos. 22-27,C13-C15 (9)* | 2.05 | 2.05 |

Issued for the World Health Organization drive to eradicate malaria.

Scouts Forming Pyramid — A5

Designs: 2np, Bugler. 3np, Cub Scouts. 4np, Scouts and bugler. 5np, Scouts presenting flag.

**1964** **Unwmk.**

| | | | | | |
|---|---|---|---|---|---|
| *28* | A5 | 1np | dk brn & ocher | 8 | 8 |
| *29* | A5 | 2np | car rose & sep | 8 | 8 |
| *30* | A5 | 3np | bl & red org | 8 | 8 |
| *31* | A5 | 4np | car & bl | 8 | 8 |
| *32* | A5 | 5np | ind & bluish grn | 8 | 8 |
| | | | *Nos. 28-32,C20-C24 (10)* | 1.97 | 1.97 |

Issued to commemorate the 11th Boy Scout Jamboree, Marathon, Greece, August, 1963.

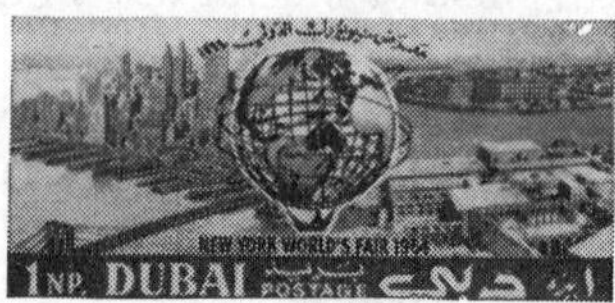

Unisphere, New York Skyline and Dubai Harbor — A6

Design: 2np, 4np, 10np, Views of New York and Dubai.

**1964, Apr. 22** **Litho.** ***Perf. 12***

| | | | | | |
|---|---|---|---|---|---|
| *33* | A6 | 1np | dk bl & rose red | 10 | 10 |
| *34* | A6 | 2np | dl red, lil rose & bl | 10 | 10 |
| *35* | A6 | 3np | brn & grn | 10 | 10 |
| *36* | A6 | 4np | emer, brt grn & red | 10 | 10 |
| *37* | A6 | 5np | ol, sl grn & lil | 10 | 10 |
| *38* | A6 | 10np | brn org, red org & blk | 35 | 35 |
| | | | *Nos. 33-38,C36-C38 (9)* | 3.30 | 3.30 |

New York World's Fair, 1964-65.

Gymnast — A8

Designs: 2np, 5np, 20np, 40np, Various exercises on bar. 3np, 30np, Various exercises on vaulting horse. 4np, 10np, 1r, Various exercises on rings.

**1964** **Photo.** ***Perf. 14***

| | | | | | |
|---|---|---|---|---|---|
| *43* | A8 | 1np | org brn & yel grn | 5 | 5 |
| *44* | A8 | 2np | dk brn & grnsh bl | 5 | 5 |
| *45* | A8 | 3np | ultra & org brn | 7 | 7 |
| *46* | A8 | 4np | dk pur & yel | 10 | 10 |
| *47* | A8 | 5np | ocher & dk bl | 14 | 14 |
| *48* | A8 | 10np | brt bl & ocher | 25 | 25 |
| *49* | A8 | 20np | ol & lil rose | 55 | 55 |
| *50* | A8 | 30np | dk bl & yel | 65 | 65 |
| *51* | A8 | 40np | Prus grn & dl org | 1.10 | 1.10 |
| *52* | A8 | 1r | rose vio & grnsh bl | 2.50 | 2.50 |
| | | | *Nos. 43-52 (10)* | 5.46 | 5.46 |

Issued to commemorate the 18th Olympic Games, Tokyo, Oct. 10-25, 1964. An imperf. miniature sheet contains a stamp similar to No. 52. Size of stamp: 67x67mm. Size of sheet: 102x102mm. Value $4.

Palace — A9

Sheik Rashid bin Said — A10

Designs: 20np, 25np, View of new Dubai. 35np, 40np, Bridge and dhow. 60np, 1r, Bridge. 1.25r, Minaret. 1.50r, 3r, Old Dubai.

***Perf. 14x14½***

**1966, May 30** **Photo.** **Unwmk.**

**Size: 23x18mm**

| | | | | | |
|---|---|---|---|---|---|
| *53* | A9 | 5np | brn & ind | 20 | 20 |
| *54* | A9 | 10np | blk & org | 20 | 20 |
| *55* | A9 | 15np | ultra & brn | 22 | 22 |

***Perf. 13***

**Size: 27½x20½mm**

| | | | | | |
|---|---|---|---|---|---|
| *56* | A9 | 20np | bl & red brn | 30 | 30 |
| *57* | A9 | 25np | org ver & ultra | 38 | 38 |
| *58* | A9 | 35np | vio & emer | 52 | 52 |
| *59* | A9 | 40np | grnsh bl & bl | 55 | 55 |

***Perf. 14½***

**Size: 31½x24mm**

| | | | | | |
|---|---|---|---|---|---|
| *60* | A9 | 60np | yel grn & org ver | 90 | 90 |
| *61* | A9 | 1r | ultra & bl | 1.50 | 1.50 |
| *62* | A9 | 1.25r | brn org & blk | 1.90 | 1.90 |
| *63* | A9 | 1.50r | rose lil & yel grn | 2.25 | 2.25 |
| *64* | A9 | 3r | dk ol bis & vio | 4.50 | 4.50 |

**Engr.**

***Perf. 14***

| | | | | | |
|---|---|---|---|---|---|
| *65* | A10 | 5r | rose car | 7.50 | 7.50 |
| *66* | A10 | 10r | dk bl | 15.00 | 15.00 |
| | | | *Nos. 53-66 (14)* | 35.92 | 35.92 |

Nos. 53-62, 64-66 Overprinted with New Currency Names and Bars

**1967**

| | | | | |
|---|---|---|---|---|
| *67* | A9 | 5d on 5np | 12 | 12 |
| *68* | A9 | 10d on 10np | 12 | 12 |
| *69* | A9 | 15d on 15np | 15 | 15 |
| *70* | A9 | 20d on 20np | 18 | 18 |
| *71* | A9 | 25d on 25np | 25 | 25 |
| *72* | A9 | 35d on 35np | 30 | 30 |
| *73* | A9 | 40d on 40np | 38 | 38 |
| *74* | A9 | 60d on 60np | 65 | 65 |
| *75* | A9 | 1r on 1r | 90 | 90 |
| *76* | A9 | 1.25r on 1.25r | 1.25 | 1.25 |
| *77* | A9 | 3r on 3r | 3.25 | 3.25 |
| *78* | A10 | 5r on 5r | 5.00 | 5.00 |
| *79* | A10 | 10r on 10r | 10.00 | 10.00 |
| | | *Nos. 67-79 (13)* | 22.55 | 22.55 |

Sheik and Falcon — A11

Dhow — A12

**Litho. and Engr.**

**1967, Aug. 21** ***Perf. 13½***

| | | | | | |
|---|---|---|---|---|---|
| *80* | A11 | 5d | dp car & org | 12 | 12 |
| *81* | A11 | 10d | sep & grn | 12 | 12 |
| *82* | A11 | 20d | dp cl & bl gray | 12 | 12 |
| *83* | A11 | 35d | sl & car | 32 | 32 |
| *84* | A11 | 60d | vio bl & emer | 65 | 65 |
| *85* | A11 | 1r | grn & lil | 90 | 90 |
| *86* | A12 | 1.25r | lt bl & cl | 1.25 | 1.25 |
| *87* | A12 | 3r | dl vio & cl | 3.00 | 3.00 |
| *88* | A12 | 5r | brt grn & vio | 5.00 | 5.00 |
| *89* | A12 | 10r | lil rose & grn | 5.75 | 5.75 |
| | | | *Nos. 80-89 (10)* | 17.23 | 17.23 |

S. S. Bamora, 1914 — A13

Designs: 35d, De Havilland 66 plane, 1930. 60d, S. S. Sirdhana, 1947. 1r, Armstrong Whitworth 15 "Atlanta," 1938. 1.25r, S. S. Chandpara, 1949. 3r, BOAC Sunderland amphibian plane, 1943. No. 96, Freighter Bombala, 1961, and BOAC Super VC10, 1967.

**1969, Feb. 12 Litho. *Perf. 14x13½***

*90* A13 25d lt grn, bl & blk 12 5
*91* A13 35d multi 16 5
*92* A13 60d multi 32 5
*93* A13 1r lil, blk & dl yel 52 *10*
*94* A13 1.25r gray, blk & dp org 65 *12*
*95* A13 3r pink, blk & bl grn 1.60 *32*
*Nos. 90-95 (6)* 3.37 69

**Miniature Sheet**

***Imperf***

*96* A13 1.25r pink, blk & bl grn 3.25 3.25

Issued to commemorate 60 years of postal service. Size of No. 96: 117x79mm.

Mother and Children, by Rubens A14

Designs: 60d, Madonna and Child, by Murillo. 1r, Mother and Child, by Francesco Mazzuoli. 3r, Madonna and Child, by Correggio.

**1969, Mar. 21 Litho. *Perf. 13½***

*97* A14 60d sil & multi 50 5
*98* A14 1r sil & multi 90 *12*
*99* A14 1.25r sil & multi 1.10 *15*
*100* A14 3r sil & multi 2.50 *38*

Issued for Arab Mother's Day.

Porkfish — A15

**1969, May 26 Litho. *Perf. 11***

*101* A15 60d shown 65 *32*
*102* A15 60d Spotted grouper 65 *32*
*103* A15 60d Moonfish 65 *32*
*104* A15 60d Sweetlips 65 *32*
*105* A15 60d Blue angel 65 *32*
*106* A15 60d Texas skate 65 *32*
*107* A15 60d Striped butterflyfish 65 *32*
*108* A15 60d Imperial angelfish 65 *32*
*Nos. 101-108 (8)* 5.20 2.56

Nos. 101-108 printed in same sheet of 16 (4x4).

Explorers and Map of Arabia A16

**1969, July 21 Litho. *Perf. 13½x13***

*109* A16 35d brn & grn 50 5
*110* A16 60d vio & sep 90 5
*111* A16 1r grn & dl bl 1.50 *12*
*112* A16 1.25r gray & rose car 2.00 *15*

Issued to honor European explorers of Arabia: Sir Richard Francis Burton (1821-1890), Charles Montagu Doughty (1843-1926), Johann Ludwig Burckhardt (1784-1817) and Wilfred Patrick Thesiger (1910- ).

Construction of World's First Underwater Oil Storage Tank — A17

Designs: 20d, Launching of oil storage tank. 35d, Oil storage tank in place on ocean ground. 60d, Sheik Rashid bin Said, offshore drilling platform and monument commemorating first oil export. 1r, Offshore production platform and helicopter port.

**1969, Oct. 13 Litho. *Perf. 11***

*113* A17 5d bl & multi 20 5
*114* A17 20d bl & multi 32 5
*115* A17 35d bl & multi 60 5
*116* A17 60d bl & multi 1.00 5
*117* A17 1r bl & multi 1.25 *10*
*Nos. 113-117 (5)* 3.37 30

Astronauts Collecting Moon Rocks — A18

Designs: 1r, Astronaut at foot of ladder. 1.25r, Astronauts planting American flag.

**1969, Dec. 15 Litho. *Perf. 14½***

*118* A18 Strip of 3 2.25 *30*
**a.** 60d multi 30 *6*
**b.** 1r multi 60 *10*
**c.** 1.25r multi (airmail) 1.25 *12*

Nos. 118a-118c were printed se-tenant. The 1.25r is inscribed "AIRMAIL."
Sizes: 60d and 1r, 28½x41mm.; 1.25r, 60½x41mm.
See note after U.S. No. C76.

Ocean Weather Ship Launching Radio Sonde, and Hastings Plane — A19

Designs (WMO Emblem and): 1r, Kew-type radio sonde, weather balloon and radar antenna. 1.25r, Tiros satellite and weather sounding rocket. 3r, Ariel satellite and rocket launching.

**1970, Mar. 23 Litho. *Perf. 11***

*121* A19 60d dl grn, brn & blk 32 5
*122* A19 1r brn & multi 60 9
*123* A19 1.25r dk bl & multi 70 *12*
*124* A19 3r multi 1.65 *28*

9th World Meteorological Day.

UPU Headquarters and Monument, Bern — A20

Design: 60d, UPU monument, Bern, telecommunications satellite and London PO tower.

**1970, May 20 Litho. *Perf. 13½x14***

*125* A20 5d lt grn & multi 35 5
*126* A20 60d dp bl & multi 1.00 5

Opening of the new UPU Headquarters, Bern, May 20, 1970.

Charles Dickens, London Skyline — A21

Designs: 60d, Dickens' portrait (vert.). 1.25r, Dickens and "Old Curiosity Shop." 3r, Bound volumes.

**1970, July 23 Litho. *Perf. 13½***

*127* A21 60d ol & multi 50 5
*128* A21 1r multi 75 *15*
*129* A21 1.25r buff & multi 1.00 *20*
*130* A21 3r multi 2.50 *50*

Charles Dickens (1812-70), English novelist.

The Graham Children, by William Hogarth — A22

Paintings: 60d, Caroline Murat and her Children, by François Pascal Gerard (vert.). 1r, Napoleon with the Children on the Terrace in St. Cloud, by Louis Ducis.

**1970, Oct. 1 Litho. *Perf. 13½***

*131* A22 35d multi 40 *5*
*132* A22 60d multi 70 *5*
*133* A22 1r multi 1.10 *8*

Issued for Children's Day.

National Bank of Dubai — A24

Sheik Rashid bin Said — A23

Television Station — A25

Designs: 10d, Boat building. 20d, Al Maktum Bascule Bridge. 35d, Great Mosque, Dubai (vert.). 1r, Dubai International Airport (horiz.). 1.25r, Port Rashid harbor project (horiz.). 3r, Rashid Hospital (horiz.). 5r, Dubai Trade School (horiz.).

***Perf. 14x14½, 14½x14***

**1970-71 Litho.**

*134* A23 5d multi ('71) 18 5
*135* A24 10d multi ('71) 20 5
*136* A24 20d multi ('71) 30 5
*137* A24 35d multi ('71) 40 5
*138* A24 60d multi 65 5

***Perf. 14***

*139* A25 1r multi 90 *6*
*140* A25 1.25r multi 1.00 *10*
*141* A25 3r multi 2.00 *25*
*142* A25 5r multi 3.25 *40*
*143* A25 10r multi ('71) 5.75 *85*
*Nos. 134-143 (10)* 14.63 *1.91*

Dubai Airport A26

Designs: 1.25r, Airport entrance.

**1971, May 15 Litho. *Perf. 13½x14***

*144* A26 1r multi 1.00 *15*
*145* A26 1.25r multi 1.25 *20*

Opening of Dubai International Airport.

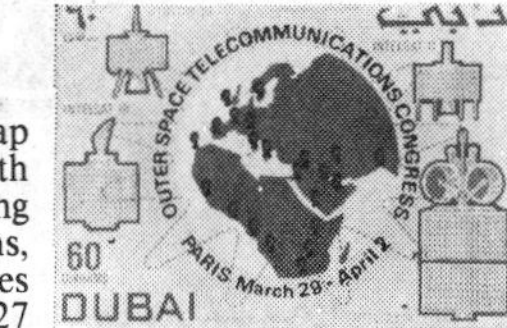

Map With Tracking Stations, Satellites A27

**1971, June 21 Litho. *Perf. 14½***

*146* A27 60d multi 45 *28*

Outer Space Telecommunications Cong., Paris, Mar. 29-Apr. 2. See Nos. C55-C56.

Fan, Scout Emblem, Map of Japan — A28

Designs: 1r, Boy Scouts in kayaks. 1.25r, Mountaineering. 3r, Campfire (horiz.).

***Perf. 14x13½, 13½x14***

**1971, Aug. 30 Litho.**

*147* A28 60d multi 42 *5*
*148* A28 1r multi 75 *10*
*149* A28 1.25r multi 90 *12*
*150* A28 3r multi 2.00 *30*

13th Boy Scout World Jamboree, Asagiri Plain, Japan, Aug. 2-10.

Albrecht Dürer, Self-portrait A29

**1971, Oct. 18** ***Perf. 14x13½***
*151* A29 60d gold & multi 50 5

See Nos. C57-C59.

Boy in Meadow A30

Design: 5r, Boys playing and UNICEF emblem (horiz.).

**1971, Dec. 11** ***Perf. 13½***
*152* A30 60d gold & multi 42 5
*153* A30 5r gold & multi 2.00 *25*

25th anniv. of UNICEF. See No. C60.

Ludwig van Beethoven — A31

Portrait: 10d, Leonardo da Vinci.

**1972, Feb. 7**
*154* A31 10d lt tan & multi 10 5
*155* A31 35d lt tan & multi 25 5

See Nos. C61-C62.

Olympic Emblems, Gymnast on Rings — A32

**1972, July 31** **Litho.** ***Perf. 13½***
*156* A32 35d *shown* 30 5
*157* A32 40d *Fencing* 38 5
*158* A32 65d *Hockey* 45 5
*Nos. 156-158,C65-C67 (6)* 3.03 48

20th Olympic Games, Munich, Aug. 26-Sept. 11.

Stamps of Dubai were replaced in 1972 by those of United Arab Emirates.

## AIR POST STAMPS

Type of Regular Issue and

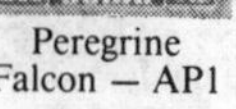
Peregrine Falcon — AP1

Wheat — AP2

Design: A1, Falcon over bridge.

***Perf. 12x11½, 11½x12***

**1963, June 15** **Litho.** **Unwmk.**
*C1* A1 20np dk red brn & lt bl 45 12
*C2* AP1 25np ol & blk brn 50 15
*C3* A1 30np red org & blk 60 18
*C4* AP1 40np grysh brn & dk vio 80 25
*C5* A1 50np emer & rose cl 1.10 30
*C6* AP1 60np brn org & blk 1.25 35
*C7* A1 75np vio & dp grn 1.50 45
*C8* AP1 1r org & red brn 2.25 60
*Nos. C1-C8 (8)* 8.45 2.40

Red Cross Type of Regular Issue

Designs: 20np, Dhows. 30np, First-aid tent. 30np, Camel caravan. 4np, Butterfly.

**1963, Sept. 1** **Unwmk.** ***Perf. 12***
*C9* A3 20np brn, yel & red 25 25
*C10* A3 30np dk bl, buff & red 35 35
*C11* A3 40np blk, yel & red 50 50
*C12* A3 50np vio, lt bl & red 60 60

Malaria Type of Regular Issue

Designs: 30np, Anopheles mosquito. 40np, Mosquito and coiled arrows. 70np, Mosquitoes over swamp.

**1963, Dec. 20** **Unwmk.** ***Perf. 12***
*C13* A4 30np pur & emer 30 30
*C14* A4 40np red & dl grn 38 38
*C15* A4 70np sl & cit 65 65

Three imperf. souv. sheets exist containing 4 stamps each in changed colors similar to Nos. C13-C15. Size: 100x120mm.

**1963, Dec. 30** **Litho.**

Designs: 40np, Wheat and palm tree. 70np, Hands holding wheat. 1r, Woman carrying basket.

*C16* AP2 20np vio bl & ocher 30 30
*C17* AP2 40np red & ol 45 45
*C18* AP2 70np grn & org 65 65
*C19* AP2 1r org brn & Prus bl 1.00 1.00

Boy Scout Type of Regular Issue

Designs: 20np, Human pyramid. 30np, Bugler. 40np, Cub Scouts. 70np, Scouts and bugler. 1r, Scouts presenting flag.

**1964, Jan. 20**
*C20* A5 20np grn & dk brn 12 12
*C21* A5 30np lil & ocher 20 20
*C22* A5 40np vio bl & yel grn 25 25
*C23* A5 70np dk grn & gray 40 40
*C24* A5 1r vio bl & red org 60 60
*Nos. C20-C24 (5)* 1.57 1.57

Five imperf. souv. sheets exist containing 4 stamps each in changed colors similar to Nos. C20-C24. Size: 100x120mm.

John F. Kennedy and US Seal — AP3

**1964, Jan. 15** **Litho.**
*C25* AP3 75np grn & blk, *lt grn* 52 52
*C26* AP3 1r ocher & blk, *tan* 65 65
*C27* AP3 1.25r mag & blk, *gray* 85 85

Issued in memory of Pres. John F. Kennedy (1917-63). A souvenir sheet contains one imperf. 1.25r in buff and black with simulated perforations and red brown margin with white inscription. Size: 99x60mm.

Spacecraft — AP4

Designs: 1np, 5np, Ascending rocket (vert.). 2np, 1r, Mercury capsule (vert.). 4np, 2r, Twin spacecraft.

**1964, Jan. 25** **Unwmk.** ***Perf. 12***
*C28* AP4 1np emer & org 12 12
*C29* AP4 2np multi 12 12
*C30* AP4 3np multi 12 12
*C31* AP4 4np multi 12 12
*C32* AP4 5np bl & org 12 12
*C33* AP4 1r vio bl, dp car & buff 60 60
*C34* AP4 1.50r vio bl, dp car & buff 90 90
*C35* AP4 2r bl, yel & red 1.25 1.25
*Nos. C28-C35 (8)* 3.35 3.35

Issued to honor the astronauts. An imperf. souvenir sheet contains one stamp similar to No. C35. Ocher margin with green inscription. Size: 90x64mm.

New York World's Fair Type of Regular Issue

Design: Statue of Liberty and ships in Dubai harbor.

**1964, Apr. 22** **Litho.**
*C36* A6 75np gray bl, ultra & blk 50 50
*C37* A6 2r gray grn, dk brn & bis 85 85
*C38* A6 3r dl grn, gray ol & dp org 1.10 1.10

An imperf. souvenir sheet contains 2 stamps in Statue of Liberty design: 2r dark brown and rose carmine, and 3r ultramarine and gold. Light blue margin. Size: 110x90mm.

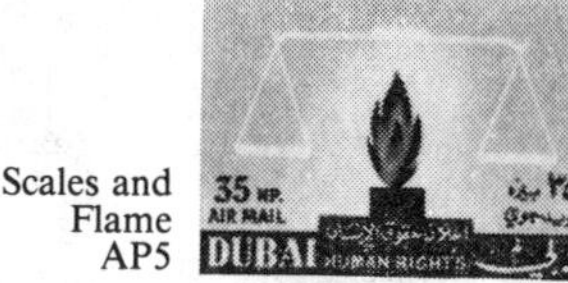

Scales and Flame AP5

**1964, Apr. 30** **Litho.** ***Perf. 12***
*C39* AP5 35np bl, brn & scar 28 28
*C40* AP5 50np lt bl, dk grn & scar 35 35
*C41* AP5 1r grnsh bl, blk & scar 60 60
*C42* AP5 3r lt ultra, ultra, & scar 2.00 2.00

Issued to commemorate the 15th anniversary of the Universal Declaration of Human Rights. An imperf. souvenir sheet contains one 3r light green, ultramarine and scarlet stamp. Pale gray olive margin with ultramarine and white inscription. Size: 100x60mm.

Nos. C20-C24 Overprinted in Red and Black (Shield in Red)

**1964, June 20**
*C47* A5 20np grn & dk brn 75 38
*C48* A5 30np lil & ocher 1.00 50
*C49* A5 40np vio bl & yel grn 1.50 75
*C50* A5 70np dk grn & gray 2.50 1.25
*C51* A5 1r vio bl & red org 3.75 1.75
*Nos. C47-C51 (5)* 9.50 4.63

Issued to commemorate the 9th Winter Olympic Games, Innsbruck, Austria, Jan. 29-Feb. 9, 1964.

A similar but unauthorized overprint, with shield in black, exists on Nos. 28-32, C20-C24, and the five souvenir sheets mentioned below No. C24. The Dubai G.P.O. calls this black-shield overprint "bogus."

Nos. C25-C27 Overprinted in Brown or Green

MAY
29

**1964, Sept. 15**
*C52* AP3 75np (BR) 1.50 1.50
*C53* AP3 1r (G) 1.75 1.75
*C54* AP3 1.25r (G) 2.25 2.25

Pres. John F. Kennedy 48th birth anniv. The same overprint in black was applied to the souv. sheet noted after No. C27.

No. 118c is inscribed "AIRMAIL."

Communications Type of Regular Issue

Designs: 1r, Intelsat 4, tracking station on globe and rocket. 5r, Eiffel Tower, Syncom 3 and Goonhilly radar station.

**1971, June 21** **Litho.** ***Perf. 14½***
*C55* A27 1r lt brn & multi 45 *10*
*C56* A27 5r multi 2.25 *45*

Portrait Type of Regular Issue

Portraits: 1r, Sir Isaac Newton. 1.25r, Avicenna. 3r, Voltaire.

**1971, Oct. 18** **Litho.** ***Perf. 14x13½***
*C57* A29 1r gold & multi 60 *12*
*C58* A29 1.25r gold & multi 75 *15*
*C59* A29 3r gold & multi 2.25 *45*

UNICEF Type of Regular Issue

Design: 1r, Mother, children and UNICEF emblem.

**1971, Dec. 11** ***Perf. 13½***
*C60* A30 1r gold & multi 50 *10*

Portrait Type of Regular Issue

Portraits: 75d, Khalil Gibran. 5r, Charles de Gaulle.

**1972, Feb. 7** **Litho.** ***Perf. 13½***
*C61* A31 75d lt tan & multi 25 *5*
*C62* A31 5r lt tan & multi 1.75 *32*

Infant Health Care AP6

Design: 75d, Nurse supervising children at meal, and WHO emblem (vert.).

**1972, Apr. 7** **Litho.** ***Perf. 14x13½***
*C63* AP6 75d multi 1.00 *15*
*C64* AP6 1.25r multi 1.50 *25*

World Health Day 1972.

Olympic Type of Regular Issue

**1972, July 31** **Litho.** ***Perf. 13½***
*C65* A32 75d *Water polo* 50 *6*
*C66* A32 1r *Steeplechase* 65 *12*
*C67* A32 1.25r *Running* 75 *15*

## POSTAGE DUE STAMPS

Type of Regular Issue, 1963.

Designs: 1np, 4np, 15np, Clam. 2np, 5np, 25np, Mussel. 3np, 10np, 35np, Oyster.

***Perf. 12x11½***

**1963, June 15** **Litho.** **Unwmk.**
*J1* A1 1np gray grn & ver 25 15
*J2* A1 2np lem & brt bl 30 20
*J3* A1 3np dl rose & grn 50 35
*J4* A1 4np lt grn & mag 75 50
*J5* A1 5np ver & blk 85 60
*J6* A1 10np cit & vio 1.10 80
*J7* A1 15np brt ultra & ver 1.50 1.00
*J8* A1 25np buff & ol grn 1.75 1.10
*J9* A1 35np turq bl & dp org 2.00 1.25
*Nos. J1-J9 (9)* 9.00 5.95

Sheik Rashid bin Said — D1

**1972, May 22** **Litho.** ***Perf. 14x14½***
*J10* D1 5d blk & gray grn 40 40
*J11* D1 10d vio bl, blk & bis 40 40
*J12* D1 20d sl grn, blk & brick red 60 60

| | | | | |
|---|---|---|---|---|
| J13 | D1 | 30d grnsh gray, blk & lil | 90 | 90 |
| J14 | D1 | 50d lil, brn & bis | 1.50 | 1.50 |
| | | *Nos. J10-J14 (5)* | 3.80 | 3.80 |

# EAST AFRICA AND UGANDA PROTECTORATES

LOCATION — In central East Africa, bordering on the Indian Ocean.
GOVT. — Former British Protectorate.
AREA — 350,000 sq. mi. (approx.).
POP. — 6,503,507 (approx.).
CAPITAL — Mombasa.

This territory, formerly administered by the British East Africa Colony, was divided between Kenya Colony and the Uganda Protectorate. See Kenya, Uganda and Tanzania.

16 Annas = 1 Rupee
100 Cents = 1 Rupee (1907)

King Edward VII
A1 A2

**Wmk. Crown and C. A. (2)**

**1903 Typo. *Perf. 14***

| | | | | |
|---|---|---|---|---|
| 1 | A1 | ½a gray grn | 2.00 | 1.65 |
| 2 | A1 | 1a car & blk | 1.90 | 28 |
| 3 | A1 | 2a vio & dl vio | 4.00 | 4.00 |
| 4 | A1 | 2½a ultra | 8.25 | *8.25* |
| 5 | A1 | 3a gray grn & brn | 6.50 | 7.25 |
| 6 | A1 | 4a blk & gray grn | 6.50 | 6.50 |
| 7 | A1 | 5a org brn & blk | 12.50 | *19.00* |
| 8 | A1 | 8a pale bl & blk | 12.50 | 15.00 |

**Wmk. Crown and C. C. (1)**

| | | | | |
|---|---|---|---|---|
| 9 | A2 | 1r gray grn | 8.25 | 6.75 |
| 10 | A2 | 2r vio & dl vio | 15.00 | 19.00 |
| 11 | A2 | 3r blk & gray grn | 22.50 | *27.50* |
| 12 | A2 | 4r lt grn & blk | 30.00 | *35.00* |
| 13 | A2 | 5r car & blk | 32.50 | *37.50* |
| 14 | A2 | 10r ultra & blk | 75.00 | 95.00 |
| 15 | A2 | 20r ol gray & blk | 500.00 | *575.00* |
| 16 | A2 | 50r org brn & blk | 1,050. | *1,150.* |
| | | *Nos. 1-13 (13)* | 162.40 | 187.68 |

Nos. 9 and 14 are on both ordinary and chalky paper.

**1904-07 Wmk. 3 Chalky Paper**

| | | | | |
|---|---|---|---|---|
| 17 | A1 | ½a gray grn | 55 | 20 |
| 18 | A1 | 1a car & blk | 1.10 | 18 |
| 19 | A1 | 2a vio & dl vio | 1.50 | 1.10 |
| 20 | A1 | 2½a ultra | 4.75 | 4.50 |
| a. | | 2½a bl | 6.00 | 4.00 |
| 21 | A1 | 3a gray grn & brn | 3.50 | 6.00 |
| 22 | A1 | 4a blk & gray grn | 9.00 | 7.50 |
| 23 | A1 | 5a org brn & blk | 5.00 | *9.00* |
| 24 | A1 | 8a pale bl & blk | 6.00 | 7.50 |
| 25 | A2 | 1r gray grn | 12.00 | 12.00 |
| 26 | A2 | 2r vio & dl vio | 18.00 | 12.00 |
| 27 | A2 | 3r blk & gray grn | 24.00 | 35.00 |
| 28 | A2 | 4r lt grn & blk | 30.00 | *42.50* |
| 29 | A2 | 5r car & blk | 35.00 | 45.00 |
| 29A | A2 | 10r ultra & blk | 150.00 | 150.00 |
| 30 | A2 | 20r ol gray & blk | 300.00 | 300.00 |
| 30A | A2 | 50r org brn & blk | 1,150. | *1,150.* |
| | | *Nos. 17-29 (13)* | 150.40 | 182.48 |

Nos. 17-19, 21-24 are on both ordinary and chalky paper. No. 20 is on ordinary paper.

**1907-08**

| | | | | |
|---|---|---|---|---|
| 31 | A1 | 1c brn ('08) | 14 | 10 |
| 32 | A1 | 3c gray grn | 1.90 | 16 |
| 33 | A1 | 6c carmine | 1.00 | 20 |
| 34 | A1 | 10c cit & vio | *7.00* | *5.50* |
| 35 | A1 | 12c red vio & dl vio | 3.75 | 1.75 |
| 36 | A1 | 15c ultra | 5.25 | 5.25 |
| 37 | A1 | 25c blk & bl grn | 5.50 | 2.75 |
| 38 | A1 | 50c org brn & grn | 6.25 | 7.00 |
| 39 | A1 | 75c pale bl & gray blk ('08) | 7.00 | *10.50* |
| | | *Nos. 31-39 (9)* | 37.79 | 33.21 |

Nos. 31, 32, 33 and 36 are on ordinary paper.
There are two dies of the 6c differing very slightly in many details.

King George V
A3 A4

**1912-18 Ordinary Paper Wmk. 3**

| | | | | |
|---|---|---|---|---|
| 40 | A3 | 1c black | 90 | 10 |
| 41 | A3 | 3c green | 1.50 | 10 |
| a. | | Booklet pane of 6 | | |
| 42 | A3 | 6c carmine | 1.50 | 8 |
| a. | | Booklet pane of 6 | | |
| 43 | A3 | 10c orange | 2.00 | 15 |
| 44 | A3 | 12c gray | 1.90 | 40 |
| 45 | A3 | 15c ultra | 1.90 | 30 |

**Chalky Paper**

| | | | | |
|---|---|---|---|---|
| 46 | A3 | 25c scar & blk, *yel* | 1.40 | 45 |
| 47 | A3 | 50c vio & blk | 1.40 | 75 |
| 48 | A3 | 75c *green* | 3.50 | 3.50 |
| a. | | 75c *emer* | 4.50 | 3.00 |
| b. | | 75c *blue grn*, olive back | 7.50 | 4.50 |
| c. | | 75c *emer*, olive back | 45.00 | *60.00* |
| 49 | A4 | 1r *green* | 5.00 | 4.75 |
| a. | | 1r *emerald* | 4.75 | 4.50 |
| 50 | A4 | 2r blk & red, *bl* | 15.00 | 16.00 |
| 51 | A4 | 3r gray grn & vio | 16.00 | 16.00 |
| 52 | A4 | 4r grn & red, *yel* | 32.50 | 35.00 |
| 53 | A4 | 5r dl vio & ultra | 35.00 | *42.50* |
| 54 | A4 | 10r grn & red, *grn* | 47.50 | *65.00* |
| 55 | A4 | 20r vio & blk, *red* | 200.00 | 150.00 |
| 56 | A4 | 20r bl & vio, *bl* ('18) | 265.00 | 150.00 |
| 57 | A4 | 50r gray grn & rose red | 500.00 | 500.00 |
| 58 | A4 | 100r blk & vio, *red* | *3,250.* | *2,000.* |
| 59 | A4 | 500r red & grn, *grn* | | |
| | | *Nos. 40-54 (15)* | 167.00 | 185.08 |

The 1r through 50r with revenue cancellations sell for minimal prices. The 100r and 500r were available for postage but were nearly always used fiscally.

**1914 Surface-colored Paper**

| | | | | |
|---|---|---|---|---|
| 60 | A3 | 25c scar & blk, *yel* | 1.25 | 1.75 |
| 61 | A3 | 75c *green* | 1.90 | *4.75* |

Stamps of types A3 and A4 with watermark 4 are listed under Kenya, Uganda and Tanzania.

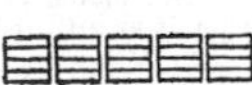

No. 42 Surcharged **4 cents**

**1919**

| | | | | |
|---|---|---|---|---|
| 62 | A3 | 4c on 6c carmine | 15 | 15 |
| a. | | Double surcharge | 125.00 | 150.00 |
| b. | | Without squares over old value | 14.00 | 14.00 |
| c. | | Pair, one without surcharge | 400.00 | *450.00* |
| d. | | Inverted surcharge | 150.00 | 175.00 |

For later issues see Kenya, Uganda and Tanzania.
For stamps of East Africa and Uganda overprinted "G. E. A." see German East Africa in this volume.

# FALKLAND ISLANDS

LOCATION — A group of islands about 300 miles east of the Straits of Magellan at the southern limit of South America.
GOVT. — British Crown Colony.
AREA — 4,700 sq. mi.
POP. — 1,813 (1980).
CAPITAL — Stanley.

Dependencies of the Falklands are South Georgia and South Sandwich. In March 1962, three other dependencies —South Shetland Islands, South Orkneys and Graham Land—became the new separate colony of British Antarctic Territory.

12 Pence = 1 Shilling
20 Shillings = 1 Pound
100 Pence = 1 Pound (1971)

**Catalogue values for unused stamps in this country are for Never Hinged items, beginning with Scott 97 in the regular postage section, Scott B1 in the semi-postal section, Scott 1L1 in Falkland Island Dependencies regular issues, and Scott 1LB1 in Falkland Island Dependencies semi-postals.**

*Falkland Islands stamps can be mounted in Scott's annually supplemented British South Atlantic Album.*

Queen Victoria — A1

**1878-79 Unwmk. Engr. *Perf. 14***

| | | | | |
|---|---|---|---|---|
| 1 | A1 | 1p claret | 450.00 | *550.00* |
| 2 | A1 | 4p dk gray ('79) | 1,200. | 200.00 |
| 3 | A1 | 6p green | 27.50 | 45.00 |
| 4 | A1 | 1sh bis brn | 27.50 | 45.00 |

**1883-95 Wmk. 2**

| | | | | |
|---|---|---|---|---|
| 5 | A1 | 1p brt claret ('94) | 24.00 | 24.00 |
| a. | | 1p claret | 350.00 | 100.00 |
| b. | | Imperf. vertically, horiz. pair | *42,500.* | |
| c. | | Diagonal half used as ½p on cover | | *3,250.* |
| 6 | A1 | 4p olive gray ('95) | 12.50 | 25.00 |
| a. | | 4p gray black | 22.50 | 32.50 |

**1886 Wmk. 2 Sideways**

| | | | | |
|---|---|---|---|---|
| 7 | A1 | 1p claret | 37.50 | 27.50 |
| a. | | Diagonal half used as ½p on cover | | *3,250.* |
| 8 | A1 | 4p olive gray | 175.00 | 32.50 |

**1891-96 Wmk. 2**

| | | | | |
|---|---|---|---|---|
| 9 | A1 | ½p blue green | 12.50 | 14.00 |
| 10 | A1 | ½p yel grn ('92) | 60 | 1.00 |
| 11 | A1 | 1p orange brown | 21.00 | 21.00 |
| a. | | Diagonal half used as ½p on cover | | *3,250.* |
| 12 | A1 | 1p org red ('95) | 2.50 | 2.50 |
| a. | | 1p red brn | 3.50 | 2.50 |
| 13 | A1 | 2p magenta ('96) | 3.50 | 5.50 |
| 14 | A1 | 2½p deep blue | 200.00 | 180.00 |
| 15 | A1 | 2½p deep ultra | 3.75 | 3.75 |
| a. | | 2½p pale ultra | 55.00 | 30.00 |
| 16 | A1 | 6p orange ('92) | 10.00 | 14.00 |
| a. | | 6p yellow ('96) | 11.00 | 12.50 |
| 17 | A1 | 9p ver ('96) | 19.00 | 40.00 |
| 18 | A1 | 1sh bis brn ('96) | 16.00 | *24.00* |
| | | *Nos. 9-18 (10)* | 288.85 | 305.75 |

Nos. 7, 5a and 11 Surcharged **½d.** in Black

**1891 Wmk. 2 Sideways**

| | | | | |
|---|---|---|---|---|
| 19 | A1 | ½p on half of 1p cl (No. 7) | 550.00 | 285.00 |
| d. | | Unsevered pair | 1,650. | 1,000. |

**Wmk. 2**

| | | | | |
|---|---|---|---|---|
| 19E | A1 | ½p on half of 1p cl (No. 5a) | 350.00 | 150.00 |
| f. | | Unsevered pair | | 425.00 |
| 19G | A1 | ½p on half of 1p org brn (No. 11) | 475.00 | 175.00 |
| i. | | Unsevered pair | 1,450. | 500.00 |

Genuine used bisects should be canceled with a segmented circular cork cancel. Any other cancel must be linked by date to known mail ship departures. This surcharge exists on "souvenir" bisects and can be found inverted, double and sideways.

A3 A4

**1898 Wmk. 1**

| | | | | |
|---|---|---|---|---|
| 20 | A3 | 2sh6p dark blue | 200.00 | 225.00 |
| 21 | A4 | 5sh brown red | 175.00 | 225.00 |

King Edward VII
A5 A6

**1904-07 Wmk. 3 *Perf. 14***

| | | | | |
|---|---|---|---|---|
| 22 | A5 | ½p yellow grn | 1.05 | 1.05 |
| 23 | A5 | 1p red | 2.50 | 42 |
| a. | | Wmk. sideways ('07) | 70 | *1.05* |
| 24 | A5 | 2p dl vio ('05) | 5.25 | *12.00* |
| 25 | A5 | 2½p ultra | 11.50 | 10.00 |
| a. | | 2½p deep blue | 350.00 | 300.00 |
| 26 | A5 | 6p orange ('05) | 20.00 | *27.50* |
| 27 | A5 | 1sh bis brn ('05) | 20.00 | *26.00* |
| 28 | A6 | 3sh gray green | 80.00 | 87.50 |
| 29 | A6 | 5sh dl red ('05) | 105.00 | 115.00 |
| | | *Nos. 22-29 (8)* | 245.30 | *279.47* |

King George V
A7 A8

**1912-14**

| | | | | |
|---|---|---|---|---|
| 30 | A7 | ½p yellow grn | 1.50 | 1.50 |
| 31 | A7 | 1p red | 1.75 | 85 |
| 32 | A7 | 2p brn violet | 2.50 | 4.25 |
| 33 | A7 | 2½p deep ultra | 8.00 | *9.00* |
| 34 | A7 | 6p orange | 8.75 | *10.50* |
| 35 | A7 | 1sh bister brn | 16.00 | *18.00* |
| 36 | A8 | 3sh dark green | 45.00 | *47.50* |
| 37 | A8 | 5sh brown red | 50.00 | *57.50* |
| 38 | A8 | 5sh plum ('14) | 50.00 | *57.50* |

| | | | | | |
|---|---|---|---|---|---|
| *39* | A8 | 10sh | red, *grn* | 165.00 | *175.00* |
| *40* | A8 | £1 | *red* | 300.00 | *365.00* |
| | | | *Nos. 30-40 (11)* | 648.50 | *746.60* |

**1921-29** **Wmk. 4**

| | | | | | |
|---|---|---|---|---|---|
| *41* | A7 | ½p | yellow green | 90 | 1.00 |
| *42* | A7 | 1p | red ('24) | 90 | 90 |
| *43* | A7 | 2p | brn vio ('23) | 2.25 | 2.75 |
| *44* | A7 | 2½p | dark blue | 2.50 | 3.00 |
| **a.** | | | Prussian blue ('29) | 325.00 | *425.00* |
| *45* | A7 | 2½p | vio, *yel* ('23) | 5.00 | *8.75* |
| *46* | A7 | 6p | orange ('25) | 5.50 | *10.00* |
| *47* | A7 | 1sh | bister brown | 16.00 | *25.00* |
| *48* | A8 | 3sh | dk grn ('23) | 75.00 | *100.00* |
| | | | *Nos. 41-48 (8)* | 108.05 | *151.40* |

No. 43 Surcharged 2½D

**1928**

| | | | | | |
|---|---|---|---|---|---|
| *52* | A7 | 2½p on 2p | brn vio | 1,050. | 1,200. |

King George V — A9

**1929-32** ***Perf. 14***

| | | | | | |
|---|---|---|---|---|---|
| *54* | A9 | ½p | green | 12 | 18 |
| *55* | A9 | 1p | scarlet | 16 | 16 |
| *56* | A9 | 2p | gray | 35 | 45 |
| *57* | A9 | 2½p | blue | 80 | *1.25* |
| *58* | A9 | 4p | dp org ('32) | 3.00 | *6.00* |
| *59* | A9 | 6p | brn violet | 3.75 | *4.50* |
| *60* | A9 | 1sh | *green* | 5.00 | *6.00* |
| **a.** | | | 1sh *emerald* | *20.00* | *35.00* |
| *61* | A9 | 2sh6p | red, *blue* | 12.00 | 20.00 |
| *62* | A9 | 5sh | green, *yel* | 26.00 | 30.00 |
| *63* | A9 | 10sh | red, *green* | 40.00 | 60.00 |

**Wmk. 3**

| | | | | | |
|---|---|---|---|---|---|
| *64* | A9 | £1 | *red* | 300.00 | 360.00 |
| | | | *Nos. 54-64 (11)* | 391.18 | *488.54* |

Romney Marsh Ram — A10

Iceberg A11

Whaling Ship — A12

Port Louis — A13

Map of the Islands A14

South Georgia A15

Blue Whale A16

Government House A17

Battle Memorial A18

King Penguin A19

Coat of Arms — A20

King George V — A21

**1933, Jan. 2** **Wmk. 4** ***Perf. 12***

| | | | | | |
|---|---|---|---|---|---|
| *65* | A10 | ½p | green & blk | 80 | 1.00 |
| *66* | A11 | 1p | dl red & blk | 1.00 | 1.00 |
| *67* | A12 | 1½p | lt bl & blk | 2.25 | *3.00* |
| *68* | A13 | 2p | ol brn & blk | 3.25 | *4.50* |
| *69* | A14 | 3p | dl vio & blk | 5.75 | *8.00* |
| *70* | A15 | 4p | orange & blk | 7.75 | *11.00* |
| *71* | A16 | 6p | gray & black | 40.00 | *52.50* |
| *72* | A17 | 1sh | ol grn & blk | 30.00 | *50.00* |
| *73* | A18 | 2sh6p | dp vio & blk | 85.00 | *100.00* |
| *74* | A19 | 5sh | yellow & blk | 425.00 | *575.00* |
| **a.** | | | 5sh yel org & blk | 1,350. | *1,525.* |
| *75* | A20 | 10sh | lt brn & blk | 550.00 | *650.* |
| *76* | A21 | £1 | rose & black | 1,150. | *1,600.* |
| | | | *Nos. 65-76 (12)* | 2,300. | *3,056.* |

Cent. of the permanent occupation of the islands as a British colony.

**Silver Jubilee Issue**

Common Design Type

**1935, May 7** ***Perf. 11x12***

| | | | | | |
|---|---|---|---|---|---|
| *77* | CD301 | 1p | carmine & bl | 35 | 35 |
| *78* | CD301 | 2½p | ultra & brown | 70 | 70 |
| *79* | CD301 | 4p | indigo & grn | 1.25 | 1.50 |
| *80* | CD301 | 1sh | brn vio & ind | 3.00 | 3.50 |

**Coronation Issue**

Common Design Type

**1937, May 12** ***Perf. 11x11½***

| | | | | | |
|---|---|---|---|---|---|
| *81* | CD302 | ½p | deep green | 12 | 12 |
| *82* | CD302 | 1p | dk carmine | 25 | 25 |
| *83* | CD302 | 2½p | deep ultra | 38 | 38 |

Whale Jawbones (Centennial Monument) A22

Designs: Nos. 85, 86A, Black-necked swan. Nos. 85B, 86, Battle memorial. 2½p, 3p, Flock of sheep. 4p, Upland goose. 6p, R.R.S. "Discovery II." 9p, R.R.S. "William Scoresby." 1sh, Mt. Sugar Top. 1sh3p, Turkey vultures. 2sh6p, Gentoo penguins. 5sh, Sea lions. 10sh, Deception Island. £1, Arms of Colony.

**1938-46** ***Perf. 12***

| | | | | | |
|---|---|---|---|---|---|
| *84* | A22 | ½p | green & blk | 10 | 10 |
| *85* | A22 | 1p | red & black | 1.10 | 85 |
| **a.** | | | 1p rose car & black | 6.00 | 6.00 |
| *85B* | A22 | 1p | dk vio & black ('41) | 12 | 12 |
| *86* | A22 | 2p | dk vio & blk | 75 | 55 |
| *86A* | A22 | 2p | rose car & black ('41) | 20 | 20 |
| *87* | A22 | 2½p | ultra & blk | 65 | 55 |
| *87A* | A22 | 3p | dp bl & black ('41) | 35 | 35 |
| *88* | A22 | 4p | rose vio & black | 75 | 75 |
| *89* | A22 | 6p | brown & blk | 2.00 | 2.00 |
| *90* | A22 | 9p | sl bl & blk | 75 | 65 |
| *91* | A22 | 1sh | dull blue | 2.50 | 1.50 |
| *92* | A22 | 1sh3p | carmine & blk ('46) | 75 | *1.25* |
| *93* | A22 | 2sh6p | gray black | 15.00 | 10.00 |
| *94* | A22 | 5sh | org brown & ultra | 22.50 | 20.00 |
| **a.** | | | 5sh yel brn & indigo | 300.00 | 150.00 |
| *95* | A22 | 10sh | orange & blk | 25.00 | 20.00 |
| *96* | A22 | £1 | dk vio & blk | 50.00 | 40.00 |
| | | | *Nos. 84-96 (16)* | 122.52 | 98.87 |

See Nos. 101-102.

**Catalogue values for unused stamps in this section, from this point to the end of the section, are for Never Hinged items.**

**Peace Issue**

Common Design Type

***Perf. 13½x14***

**1946, Oct. 7** **Engr.** **Wmk. 4**

| | | | | |
|---|---|---|---|---|
| *97* | CD303 | 1p purple | 30 | 30 |
| *98* | CD303 | 3p deep blue | 45 | 45 |

**Silver Wedding Issue**

Common Design Types

**1948, Nov. 1** **Photo.** ***Perf. 14x14½***

| | | | | |
|---|---|---|---|---|
| *99* | CD304 | 2½p bright ultra | 25 | 25 |

**Engr.; Name Typo.**

***Perf. 11½x11***

| | | | | |
|---|---|---|---|---|
| *100* | CD305 | £1 purple | 80.00 | 67.50 |

Types of 1938-46

Designs: 2½p, Upland geese. 6p, R.R.S. "Discovery II"

**Wmk. 4**

**1949, June 15** **Engr.** ***Perf. 12***

| | | | | | |
|---|---|---|---|---|---|
| *101* | A22 | 2½p | dp bl & blk | 2.00 | *5.00* |
| *102* | A22 | 6p | gray black | 2.00 | 2.00 |

**UPU Issue**

Common Design Types

**Engr.; Name Typo. on 3p, 1sh3p**

**1949, Oct. 10** ***Perf. 13½, 11x11½***

| | | | | |
|---|---|---|---|---|
| *103* | CD306 | 1p violet | 50 | 50 |
| *104* | CD307 | 3p indigo | 90 | 90 |
| *105* | CD308 | 1sh3p green | 3.00 | 3.00 |
| *106* | CD309 | 2sh blue | 6.00 | 6.00 |

Sheep — A35

Arms of the Colony — A36

Designs: 1p, R.M.S. Fitzroy. 2p Upland goose. 2½p, Map. 4p, Auster plane. 6p, M.S.S. John Biscoe. 9p, "Two Sisters" peaks. 1sh, Gentoo penguins. 1sh 3p, Kelp goose and gander. 2sh 6p, Sheet shearing. 5sh, Battle memorial. 10sh, Sea lion and clapmatch. £1, Hulk of "Great Britain."

***Perf. 13½x13, 13x13½***

**1952, Jan. 2** **Engr.** **Wmk. 4**

| | | | | | |
|---|---|---|---|---|---|
| *107* | A35 | ½p | green | 50 | 42 |
| *108* | A35 | 1p | red | 60 | 50 |
| *109* | A35 | 2p | violet | 1.50 | 1.25 |
| *110* | A35 | 2½p | ultra & blk | 1.00 | 85 |
| *111* | A36 | 3p | deep ultra | 1.00 | 85 |
| *112* | A35 | 4p | claret | 1.25 | 1.10 |
| *113* | A35 | 6p | yellow brn | 3.00 | 95 |
| *114* | A35 | 9p | orange yel | 2.50 | 2.00 |
| *115* | A36 | 1sh | black | 5.00 | 4.00 |
| *116* | A35 | 1sh3p | red orange | 3.00 | *8.50* |
| *117* | A36 | 2sh6p | olive | 7.50 | *8.50* |
| *118* | A36 | 5sh | red violet | 8.00 | *6.75* |
| *119* | A35 | 10sh | gray | 15.00 | *27.50* |
| *120* | A35 | £1 | black | 32.50 | *37.50* |
| | | | *Nos. 107-120 (14)* | 82.35 | *100.67* |

**Coronation Issue**
Common Design Type

**1953, June 4** ***Perf. 13½x13***
121 CD312 1p car & black 95 95

Types of 1952 with Portrait of Queen Elizabeth II

**1955-57** ***Perf. 13½x13, 13x13½***
122 A35 ½p green ('57) 35 35
123 A35 1p red ('57) 80 40
124 A35 2p violet ('56) 2.00 1.65
125 A35 6p light brown 3.50 2.00
126 A35 9p ocher ('57) 16.00 16.00
127 A36 1sh black 10.00 8.25
*Nos. 122-127 (6)* 32.65 28.65

Falkland Islands Thrush A37

Birds: 1p, Dominican gull. 2p, Gentoo penguins. 2½p, Marsh starling. 3p, Upland geese. 4p, Steamer ducks. 5½p, Rock-hopper penguin. 6p, black-browed albatross. 9p, Silver grebe. 1sh, Pied oystercatchers. 1sh3p, Yellow-billed teal. 2sh, Kelp geese. 5sh, King shag. 10sh, Guadelupe caracara. £1, Black-necked swan.

***Perf. 13½x13***
**1960, Feb. 10** **Engr.** **Wmk. 314**
**Center in Black**
128 A37 ½p green 22 18
*a.* Wmk. sideways ('66) 35 30
129 A37 1p rose red 25 22
130 A37 2p blue 35 30
131 A37 2½p bis brown 1.10 40
132 A37 3p olive 50 28
133 A37 4p rose car 75 28
134 A37 5½p violet 85 40
135 A37 6p sepia 1.10 75
136 A37 9p orange 1.25 80
137 A37 1sh dull pur 1.10 80
138 A37 1sh3p ultra 3.00 2.25
139 A37 2sh brown car 6.25 2.50
140 A37 5sh grnsh bl 12.50 9.25
141 A37 10sh rose lil 30.00 15.00
142 A37 £1 yel org 55.00 37.50
*Nos. 128-142 (15)* 114.22 70.91

Morse Key — A38

**1962, Oct. 5** **Photo.** ***Perf. 11½x11***
143 A38 6p dp orange & dk red 1.25 70
144 A38 1sh brt ol grn & dp grn 1.50 1.40
145 A38 2sh brt ultra & violet 2.50 2.50

50th anniv. of the Falkland Islands radio station.

**Freedom from Hunger Issue**
Common Design Type

**1963, June 4** ***Perf. 14x14½***
146 CD314 1sh ultramarine 10.50 8.50

**Red Cross Centenary Issue**
Common Design Type
**Wmk. 314**

**1963, Sept.2** **Litho.** ***Perf. 13***
147 CD315 1p black & red 1.65 1.10
148 CD315 1sh ultra & red 12.50 10.50

**Shakespeare Issue**
Common Design Type

**1964, Apr. 23** **Photo.** ***Perf. 14x14½***
149 CD316 6p black 1.10 1.10

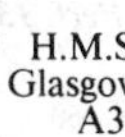
H.M.S. Glasgow A39

Designs: 6p, H.M.S. Kent. 1sh, H.M.S. Invincible. 2sh, Falkland Islands Battle Memorial (vert.).

**1964, Dec. 8** **Engr.** ***Perf. 13***
150 A39 2½p ver & black 2.25 1.40
151 A39 6p blue & black 90 90
*a.* "Glasgow" vignette 20,000.
152 A39 1sh carmine & blk 2.00 1.75

***Perf. 13x14***
153 A39 2sh dark blue & blk 4.00 3.25

50th anniv. of the Battle of the Falkland Islands between the British and German navies.

**ITU Issue**
Common Design Type
***Perf. 11x11½***

**1965, May 26** **Litho.** **Wmk. 314**
154 CD317 1p bl & dl dk bl 40 40
155 CD317 2sh lilac & dl yel 6.75 3.25

**Intl. Cooperation Year Issue**
Common Design Type

**1965, Oct. 25** ***Perf. 14½***
156 CD318 1p bl grn & cl 40 28
157 CD318 1sh lt vio & grn 3.25 2.50

**Churchill Memorial Issue**
Common Design Type

**1966, Jan. 24** **Photo.** ***Perf. 14***
**Design in Black, Gold and Carmine Rose**
158 CD319 ½p bright bl 18 15
159 CD319 1p green 95 30
160 CD319 1sh brown 3.00 2.25
161 CD319 2sh violet 6.50 4.75

Human Rights Flame and Globe A40

***Perf. 14x14½***
**1968, July 4** **Photo.** **Wmk. 314**
162 A40 2p brt rose & multi 20 15
163 A40 6p brt grn & multi 42 42
164 A40 1sh orange & multi 65 65
165 A40 2sh ultra & multi 1.25 1.25

International Human Rights Year.

Dusty Miller — A41

Falkland Islands flora: 1½p, Pig vine (horiz.). 2p, Pale maiden. 3p, Dog orchard. 3½p, Sea cabbage (horiz.). 4½p, Vanilla daisy. 5½p, Arrowleaf marigold (horiz.). 6p, Diddle-dee (horiz.). 1sh, Scurvy grass (horiz.). 1sh 6p, Prickly burr. 2sh, Fachine. 3sh, Lavender. 5sh, Felton's flower (horiz.). £1, Yellow orchid.

**1968, Oct. 9** **Photo.** ***Perf. 14***
166 A41 ½p multicolored 10 10
167 A41 1½p multicolored 14 14
168 A41 2p multicolored 18 18
169 A41 3p multicolored 30 30
170 A41 3½p multicolored 45 45
171 A41 4½p multicolored 60 60
172 A41 5½p multicolored 75 75
173 A41 6p multicolored 95 95
174 A41 1sh multicolored 1.90 1.90
175 A41 1sh6p multicolored 4.75 2.75
176 A41 2sh multicolored 6.00 4.00
177 A41 3sh multicolored 7.50 5.75
178 A41 5sh multicolored 22.50 11.00
179 A41 £1 multicolored 13.00 13.00
*Nos. 166-179 (14)* 59.12 41.87

See Nos. 210-222.

Common Design Types pictured in section before Great Britain.

Beaver DHC 2 Seaplane A42

Designs: 6p, Norseman seaplane. 1sh, Auster plane. 2sh, Falkland Islands arms.

**1969, Apr. 8** **Litho.** ***Perf. 14***
180 A52 2p multicolored 22 18
181 A52 6p multicolored 55 50
182 A52 1sh multicolored 1.00 1.00
183 A42 2sh multicolored 2.75 2.00

21st anniv. of Government Air Service.

Bishop Stirling A43

Designs: 2p, Holy Trinity Church, 1869. 6p, Christ Church Cathedral, 1969. 2sh, Bishop's miter.

**1969, Oct. 30** ***Perf. 14***
184 A43 2p emerald & blk 18 18
185 A43 6p red org & blk 45 45
186 A43 1sh lilac & black 90 90
187 A43 2sh yellow & multi 1.75 1.75

Consecration of Waite Hocking Stirling (1829-1923), as first Bishop of the Bishopric of the Falkland Islands, cent.

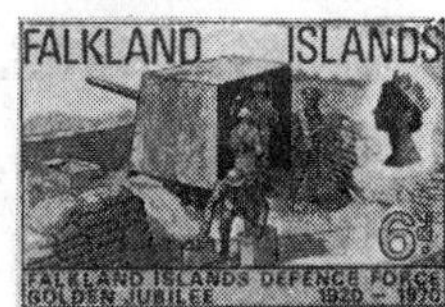

Gun Emplacement — A44

Designs: 2p, Volunteer on horseback (vert.). 1sh, Volunteer in dress uniform (vert.). 2sh, Defense Force badge.

***Perf. 13½x13, 13x13½***
**1970, Apr. 30** **Litho.** **Wmk. 314**
188 A44 2p ultra & multi 50 30
189 A44 6p multicolored 1.00 75
190 A44 1sh buff & multi 2.00 1.25
191 A44 2sh yel & multi 4.25 2.50

50th anniv. of the Falkland Islands Defense Force.

The Great Britain, 1843 A45

Designs (The Great Britain in ): 4p, 1845. 9p, 1876. 1sh, 1886. 2sh, 1970.

**1970, Oct. 30** **Litho.** ***Perf. 14½***
192 A45 2p lemon & multi 40 24
193 A45 4p lilac & multi 80 55
194 A45 9p bister & multi 1.50 1.25
195 A45 1sh org brn & multi 2.75 2.00
196 A45 2sh multicolored 5.25 4.25
*Nos. 192-196 (5)* 10.70 8.29

Nos. 166-178 Surcharged with New Value (Decimal Currency) and Bar

**1971, Feb. 15** **Photo.** ***Perf. 14***
197 A41 ½p on ½p multi 80 80
198 A41 1p on 1½p multi 20 20
199 A41 1½p on 2p multi 28 28
200 A41 2p on 3p multi 35 35
201 A41 2½p on 3½p multi 48 48
202 A41 3p on 4½p multi 55 55
203 A41 4p on 5½p multi 70 70
204 A41 5p on 6p multi 90 90
205 A41 6p on 1sh multi 1.40 1.10
206 A41 7½p on 1sh6p multi 1.75 1.40
207 A41 10p on 2sh multi 2.75 2.00
208 A41 15p on 3sh multi 5.00 3.50
209 A41 25p on 5sh multi 10.00 7.25
*Nos. 197-209 (13)* 25.16 19.51

Flower Type of 1968
"p" instead of "d"

Designs as before. 1p, 2½p, 4p, 5p, 6p, 25p, horizontal.

**Wmk. 314, Sideways on Vert. Stamps**
**1972, June 1** ***Perf. 14***
210 A41 ½p Dusty miller 75 75
*a.* Wmk. upright ('74) 4.25 6.25
*b.* Wmk. 373 ('75) 80 80
211 A41 1p Pig vine 25 14
212 A41 1½p Pale maiden 30 22
213 A41 2p Dog orchid 2.00 2.00
*a.* Wmk. upright ('74) 2.50 2.50
214 A41 2½p Sea cabbage 60 50
215 A41 3p Vanilla daisy 60 55
216 A41 4p Arrowleaf marigold 70 70
217 A41 5p Diddle-dee 85 85
218 A41 6p Scurvy grass 9.50 8.50
*a.* Wmk. sideways ('74) 2.00 2.00
219 A41 7½p Prickly burr 2.00 2.00
220 A41 10p Fachine 4.25 4.25
221 A41 15p Lavender 3.75 3.75
222 A41 25p Felton's flower 7.25 7.25
*Nos. 210-222 (13)* 32.80 31.46

No. 213 has watermark sideways

**Silver Wedding Issue, 1972**
Common Design Type

Design: Queen Elizabeth II, Prince Philip, Romney Marsh sheep and giant sea lions.

**1972, Nov 20** **Photo.** ***Perf. 14x14½***
223 CD324 1p sl grn & multi 28 28
224 CD324 10p ultra & multi 1.40 1.40

**Princess Anne's Wedding Issue**
Common Design Type

**1973, Nov. 14** **Litho.** ***Perf. 14***
225 CD325 5p lilac & multi 30 30
226 CD325 15p citron & multi 1.00 1.00

Fur Seals A46

Designs: 4p, Trout fishing. 5p, Rockhopper penguins. 15p, Military starling.

**1974, Mar. 6** **Litho.** **Wmk. 314**
227 A46 2p lt ultra & multi 1.65 1.10
228 A46 4p brt blue & multi 2.25 1.65
229 A46 5p yellow & multi 2.75 1.65
230 A46 15p lt ultra & multi 4.50 3.50

Tourist publicity.

Early 19th Century Mail Coach, UPU Emblem — A47

UPU cent. (UPU Emblem and): 5p, Packet, 1841. 8p, First British mail planes, 1911. 16p, Catapult mail, 1920's.

**1974, July 31** ***Perf. 14***
231 A47 2p multicolored 16 16
232 A47 5p multicolored 42 42
233 A47 8p multicolored 75 75
234 A47 16p multicolored 1.50 1.50

UPU, cent.

Churchill, Parliament and Big Ben — A48

Design: 20p, Churchill and warships.

**1974, Nov. 30** *Perf. 13x13½*

| | | | | |
|---|---|---|---|---|
| 235 | A48 | 16p multicolored | 1.00 | 1.00 |
| 236 | A48 | 20p multicolored | 1.25 | 1.25 |
| a. | | Souvenir sheet 2 | 6.00 | 6.00 |

Sir Winston Churchill (1874-1965), birth centenary. No. 236a contains one each of Nos. 235-236, multicolored margin with Churchill's coat of arms. Size: 107x83mm.

HMS Exeter A49

Battleships: 6p, HMNZS Achilles. 8p, Admiral Graf Spee. 16p, HMS Ajax.

**1974, Dec. 13** *Perf. 14*

| | | | | |
|---|---|---|---|---|
| 237 | A49 | 2p multicolored | 1.50 | 85 |
| 238 | A49 | 6p multicolored | 2.50 | 2.00 |
| 239 | A49 | 8p multicolored | 3.00 | 3.00 |
| 240 | A49 | 16p multicolored | 7.50 | 7.50 |

35th anniv. of the Battle of the River Plate between British ships and the German battleship Graf Spee.

Seal and Flag Badge — A50

Designs: 7½p, Coat of arms, 1925. 10p, Arms, 1948. 16p, Arms (Falkland Islands Dependencies), 1952.

**Wmk. 373**

**1975, Oct. 28** **Litho.** *Perf. 14*

| | | | | |
|---|---|---|---|---|
| 241 | A50 | 2p multicolored | 30 | 30 |
| 242 | A50 | 7½p multicolored | 1.00 | 1.00 |
| 243 | A50 | 10p multicolored | 1.25 | 1.25 |
| 244 | A50 | 16p multicolored | 2.00 | 2.00 |

Falkland Islands heraldic arms, 50th anniv.

½p-Coin and Trout A51

Designs: 5½p, 1p-coin and gentoo penguins. 8p, 2p-coin and upland geese. 10p, 5p-coin and black-browed albatross. 16p, 10p-coin and sea lions.

**1975, Dec. 31** **Litho.** **Wmk. 373**

| | | | | |
|---|---|---|---|---|
| 245 | A51 | 2p copper & multi | 42 | 42 |
| 246 | A51 | 5½p copper & multi | 85 | 85 |
| 247 | A51 | 8p copper & multi | 1.65 | 1.65 |
| 248 | A51 | 10p silver & multi | 2.50 | 2.50 |
| 249 | A51 | 16p silver & multi | 7.50 | 7.50 |
| | | *Nos. 245-249 (5)* | 12.92 | 12.92 |

New coinage.

Gathering Sheep — A52

Sheep Farming: 7½p, Shearing. 10p, Dipping sheep. 20p, Motor Vessel Monsunen collecting wool.

**Wmk. 373**

**1976, Apr. 28** **Litho.** *Perf. 13½*

| | | | | |
|---|---|---|---|---|
| 250 | A52 | 2p multicolored | 25 | 18 |
| 251 | A52 | 7½p multicolored | 1.75 | 55 |
| 252 | A52 | 10p multicolored | 95 | 75 |
| 253 | A52 | 20p multicolored | 1.90 | 1.90 |

Prince Philip, 1957 Visit A53

Designs: 11p, Queen, ampulla and spoon. 33p, Queen awaiting anointment, and Knights of the Garter.

**1977, Feb. 7** *Perf. 13½x14*

| | | | | |
|---|---|---|---|---|
| 254 | A53 | 6p multicolored | 35 | 35 |
| a. | | Booklet pane of 4 | 2.50 | |
| 255 | A53 | 11p multicolored | 60 | 60 |
| a. | | Booklet pane of 4 | 2.75 | |
| 256 | A53 | 33p multicolored | 1.50 | 1.50 |
| a. | | Booklet pane of 4 | 6.25 | |

25th anniv. of the reign of Elizabeth II. No. 254a has watermark 314.

Map of West and East Falkland with Communications Centers — A54

Telecommunications: 11p, Ship to shore communications at Fox Bay. 40p, Globe with Telex tape and telephone.

**1977, Oct. 24** **Litho.** *Perf. 14½x14*

| | | | | |
|---|---|---|---|---|
| 257 | A54 | 3p yel brn & multi | 30 | 25 |
| 258 | A54 | 11p lt ultra & multi | 70 | 60 |
| 259 | A54 | 40p rose & multi | 3.00 | 3.00 |

A.E.S., 1957-1974 A55

Designs: Mail ships.

**Wmk. 373**

**1978, Jan. 25** **Litho.** *Perf. 14*

| | | | | |
|---|---|---|---|---|
| 260 | A55 | 1p shown | 6 | 6 |
| 261 | A55 | 20 Darwin, 1957-75 | 12 | 12 |
| 262 | A55 | 3p Merak-N 1951-53 | 18 | 18 |
| 263 | A55 | 4p Fitzroy, 1936-57 | 22 | 22 |
| 264 | A55 | 5p Lafonia 1936-41 | 28 | 28 |
| 265 | A55 | 6p Fleurus, 1924-33 | 35 | 35 |
| 266 | A55 | 7p S.S. Falkland, 1914-34 | 40 | 40 |
| 267 | A55 | 8p Oravia, 1900-12 | 45 | 45 |
| 268 | A55 | 9p Memphis, 1890-97 | 50 | 50 |
| 269 | A55 | 10p Black Hawk, 1873-80 | 60 | 60 |
| 270 | A55 | 20p Foam, 1963-72 | 1.10 | 1.10 |
| 271 | A55 | 25p Fairy, 1857-61 | 1.40 | 1.40 |
| 272 | A55 | 50p Amelia, 1852-54 | 2.75 | 2.75 |
| 273 | A55 | £1 Nautilus, 1846-48 | 5.50 | 5.50 |
| 274 | A55 | £3 Hebe, 1842-46 | 15.00 | 15.00 |
| | | *Nos. 260-274 (15)* | 28.91 | 28.91 |

The 1p, 3p, 5p, 6p and 10p were also issued in booklet panes of 4.

Nos. 260-274 also issued inscribed 1982.

**Elizabeth II Coronation Anniversary Issue**

**Souvenir Sheet**

Common Design Type

**1978, June 2** **Unwmk.** *Perf. 15*

| | | | | |
|---|---|---|---|---|
| 275 | | Sheet of 6 | 6.00 | 6.00 |
| a. | | CD326 25p Red Dragon of Wales | 95 | 95 |
| b. | | CD327 25p Elizabeth II | 95 | 95 |
| c. | | CD328 25p Hornless ram | 95 | 95 |

No. 275 contains 2 se-tenant strips of Nos. 275a-275c, separated by horizontal gutter with commemorative and descriptive inscriptions and showing central part of coronation procession with coasch. Size: 100x135mm.

Short Sunderland Mark III — A56

Design: 33p, Pane in flight and route Southampton to Stanley.

**Wmk. 373**

**1978, Apr. 28** **Litho.** *Perf. 14*

| | | | | |
|---|---|---|---|---|
| 276 | A56 | 11p multi | 1.50 | 1.50 |
| 277 | A56 | 33p multi | 2.50 | 2.50 |

First direct flight Southampton, England to Stanley, Falkland Islands, 26th anniv.

First Fox Bay PO and No. 1 — A57

Macrocystis Pyrifera — A58

Designs: 11p, Second Stanley Post Office and No. 2. 15p, New Island Post Office and No. 3. 22p, First Stanley Post Office and No. 4.

**1978, Aug. 8** **Litho.** *Perf. 13½x13*

| | | | | |
|---|---|---|---|---|
| 278 | A57 | 3p multicolored | 25 | 16 |
| 279 | A57 | 11p multicolored | 60 | 60 |
| 280 | A57 | 15p multicolored | 80 | 80 |
| 281 | A57 | 22p multicolored | 1.25 | 1.25 |

Falkland Islands postage stamps, cent.

**1979, Feb. 19** **Litho.** *Perf. 14*

Kelp: 7p, Durvillea. 11p, Lessoniae (horiz.). 15p, Callophyllis (horiz.). 25p, Iridea.

| | | | | |
|---|---|---|---|---|
| 282 | A58 | 3p multicolored | 20 | 20 |
| 283 | A58 | 7p multicolored | 45 | 45 |
| 284 | A58 | 11p multicolored | 70 | 70 |
| 285 | A58 | 15p multicolored | 90 | 90 |
| 286 | A58 | 25p multicolored | 1.50 | 1.50 |
| | | *Nos. 282-286 (5)* | 3.75 | 3.75 |

Britten-Norman Islander over Map — A59

Designs: 11p, Fokker F27 over map. 15p, Fokker F28 over Stanley. 25p, Cessna 172 Skyhawk, Islander and Fokkers F27, F28 aver runway.

**1979, May 1** **Litho.** *Perf. 13½*

| | | | | |
|---|---|---|---|---|
| 287 | A59 | 3p multicolored | 22 | 18 |
| 288 | A59 | 11p multicolored | 70 | 70 |
| 289 | A59 | 15p multicolored | 90 | 90 |
| 290 | A59 | 25p multicolored | 1.65 | 1.65 |

Opening of Stanley Airport.

Rowland Hill and No. 121 A60

Rowland Hill and: 11p, Falkland Islands No. 1 (vert.). 25p, Penny Black. 33p, Falkland Islands No. 37 (vert.).

**1979, Aug. 27** *Perf. 14*

| | | | | |
|---|---|---|---|---|
| 291 | A60 | 3p multicolored | 12 | 12 |
| 292 | A60 | 11p multicolored | 42 | 42 |
| 293 | A60 | 25p multicolored | 90 | 90 |

**Souvenir Sheet**

| | | | | |
|---|---|---|---|---|
| 294 | A60 | 33p multicolored | 1.40 | 1.40 |

Sir Rowland Hill (1795-1879), originator of penny postage. No. 294 has multicolored margin showing packet. Size: 137x98mm.

Mail Delivery by Air, UPU Emblem A61

UPU Emblem and Modes of Mail Delivery: 11p, Horseback. 25p, Schooner Gwendolin.

**1979, Nov. 26**

| | | | | |
|---|---|---|---|---|
| 295 | A61 | 3p multicolored | 16 | 16 |
| 296 | A61 | 11p multicolored | 60 | 60 |
| 297 | A61 | 25p multicolored | 1.25 | 1.25 |

UPU, membership centenary.

Commerson's Dolphin — A62

**1980, Feb. 25** **Wmk. 373** *Perf. 14*

| | | | | |
|---|---|---|---|---|
| 298 | A62 | 3p Peale's porpoise, vert. | 16 | 12 |
| 299 | A62 | 6p shown | 28 | 24 |
| 300 | A62 | 7p Hour-glass dolphin | 32 | 32 |
| 301 | A62 | 11p Spectacled porpose, vert. | 48 | 48 |
| 302 | A62 | 15p Dusky dolphin | 65 | 65 |
| 303 | A62 | 25p Killer whale | 1.25 | 1.25 |
| | | *Nos. 298-303 (6)* | 3.14 | 3.06 |

**Miniature Sheet**

Falkland Islands Cancel, 1878 A63

**1980, May 6** **Litho.** *Perf. 14*

| | | | | |
|---|---|---|---|---|
| 304 | | Sheet of 6 | 2.50 | 2.50 |
| a. | | A63 11p shown | 40 | 40 |
| b. | | A63 11p New Islds., 1915 | 40 | 40 |
| c. | | A63 11p Falklands Islds., 1901 | 40 | 40 |
| d. | | A63 11p Port Stanley, 1935 | 40 | 40 |
| e. | | A63 11p Port Stanley airmail, 1952 | 40 | 40 |
| f. | | A63 11p Fox Bay, 1934 | 40 | 40 |

London 1980 Intl. Stamp Exhibition, May 6-14. Size: 147x77mm.

**Queen Mother Elizabeth Birthday Issue**

Common Design Type

**1980, Aug. 4** **Litho.** *Perf. 14*

| | | | | |
|---|---|---|---|---|
| 305 | CD330 | 11p multicolored | 50 | 50 |

Striated Caracara A64

**1980, Aug. 11** **Wmk. 373** *Perf. 13½*

| | | | | |
|---|---|---|---|---|
| 306 | A64 | 3p shown | 16 | 12 |
| 307 | A64 | 11p Red-backed buzzard | 60 | 60 |

308 A64 15p Crested caracara 70 70
309 A64 25p Cassin's falcon 1.40 1.40

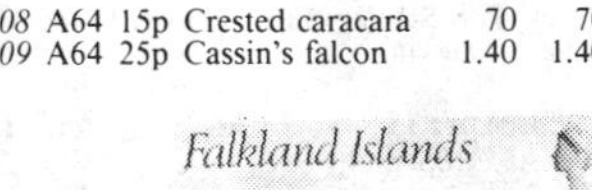

Port Egmont, Early Settlement
A65

**1980, Dec. 22 Litho. *Perf. 14***
310 A65 3p Stanley 16 12
311 A65 11p shown 60 60
312 A65 25p Port Louis 1.25 70
313 A65 33p Mission House, Keppel Island 1.50 1.25

Polwarth Sheep
A66

**1981, Jan. 19 Litho. *Perf. 14***
314 A66 3p shown 15 15
315 A66 11p Frisian cow and calf 50 50
316 A66 25p Horse 1.10 1.10
317 A66 33p Welsh collies 1.50 1.50

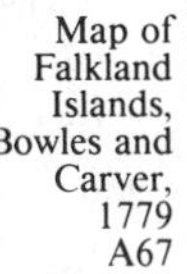

Map of Falkland Islands, Bowles and Carver, 1779
A67

**1981, May 22 Litho. *Perf. 14***
318 A67 3p shown 12 8
319 A67 10p Hawkin's Mainland, 1773 32 28
320 A67 13p New Isles, 1747 42 35
321 A67 15p French & British Islands 50 42
322 A67 25p Falklands, 1771 80 65
323 A67 26p Falklands, 1764 80 70
*Nos. 318-323 (6)* 2.96 2.48

**Royal Wedding Issue**
Common Design Type

**1981, July 22 Litho. *Perf. 13½x13***
324 CD331 10p Bouquet 40 40
325 CD331 13p Charles 52 52
326 CD331 52p Couple 2.00 2.00

Duke of Edinburgh's Awards, 25th Anniv. — A68

**1981, Sept. 28 Litho. *Perf. 14***
327 A68 10p Spinning 30 30
328 A68 13p Camping 40 40
329 A68 15p Kayaking 45 45
330 A68 26p Duke of Edinburgh 80 80

The Holy Virgin, by Guido Reni (1575-1642)
A69

Rock Cod
A70

Christmas: 3p, Adoration of the Holy Child, 16th cent. Dutch. 13p, Holy Family in an Italian Landscape, 17th cent. Italian.

**1981, Nov. 2 Litho. *Perf. 14***
331 A69 3p multicolored 12 12
332 A69 13p multicolored 52 52
333 A69 26p multicolored 1.00 1.00

**1981, Dec. 7**

Designs: Shelf fish. 5p, 15p, 25p horiz.

334 A70 5p Falkland herring 15 15
335 A70 13p shown 42 42
336 A70 15p Patagonian hake 50 50
337 A70 25p Southern blue whiting 85 85
338 A70 26p Gray-tailed skate 85 85
*Nos. 334-338 (5)* 2.77 2.77

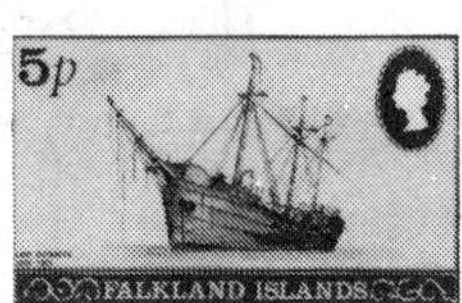

Shipwrecks — A71

**Wmk. 373**

**1982, Feb. 15 Litho. *Perf. 14½***
339 A71 5p Lady Elizabeth, 1913 18 18
340 A71 13p Capricorn, 1882 48 48
341 A71 15p Jhelum, 1870 55 55
342 A71 25p Snowsquall, 1864 95 95
343 A71 26p St. Mary, 1890 95 95
*Nos. 339-343 (5)* 3.11 3.11

Sesquicentennial of Charles Darwin's Visit — A72

**1982, Apr. 19 *Perf. 14***
344 A72 5p Darwin 15 15
345 A72 17p Microscope 55 55
346 A72 25p Warrah 85 85
347 A72 34p Beagle 1.10 1.10

**Princess Diana Issue**
Common Design Type
**Wmk. 373**

**1982, July 5 Litho. *Perf. 13***
348 CD333 5p Arms 14 14
349 CD333 17p Diana 48 48
350 CD333 37p Wedding 1.00 1.00
351 CD333 50p Portrait 1.40 1.40

Nos. 264, 271 Overprinted: "1st PARTICIPATION / COMMONWEALTH GAMES 1982"
**Wmk. 373**

**1982, Oct. 7 Litho. *Perf. 14***
352 A55 5p multicolored 18 18
353 A55 25p multicolored 90 90

12th Commonwealth Games, Brisbane, Australia, Sept. 30-Oct. 9.

Tussock Bird — A73

**1982, Dec. 6 *Perf. 15x14½***
354 A73 5p shown 15 15
355 A73 10p Black-chinned siskin 32 32
356 A73 13p Grass wren 42 42
357 A73 17p Black-throated finch 55 55
358 A73 25p Falkland-correndera pipit 85 85
359 A73 34p Dark-faced ground-tyrant 1.10 1.10
*Nos. 354-359 (6)* 3.39 3.39

British Occupation Sesquicentennial — A74

Designs: 1p, Raising the Standard, Port Louis, 1833 (vert.). 2p, Chelsea pensioners and barracks, 1849. 5p, Wool trade, 1874 (vert.). 10p, Ship repairing trade, 1850-90. 15p, Government House, early 20th cent. 20p, Battle of the Falkland Islds, 1914 (vert.). 25p, Whalebone Arch centenary, 1933. 40p, Contribution to World War II effort, 1939-45 (vert.). 50p, Visit of Duke of Edinburgh, 1957. £1, Royal Marines, 1933, 1983 (vert.). £2, Queen Elizabeth II (vert.).

**1983, Jan. 1 Litho. *Perf. 14***
360 A74 1p multicolored 5 5
361 A74 2p multicolored 8 8
362 A74 5p multicolored 14 14
363 A74 10p multicolored 25 25
364 A74 15p multicolored 40 40
365 A74 20p multicolored 52 52
366 A74 25p multicolored 65 65
367 A74 40p multicolored 1.10 1.10
368 A74 50p multicolored 1.40 1.40
369 A74 £1 multicolored 2.75 2.75
370 A74 £2 multicolored 6.00 6.00
*Nos. 360-370 (11)* 13.34 13.34

**Commonwealth Day**
Common Design Type

**1983, Mar. 14**
371 CD334 5p No. 69 12 12
372 CD334 17p No. 65 55 55
373 CD334 34p No. 75, vert. 1.25 1.25
374 CD334 50p No. 370, vert. 1.25 1.25

First Anniv. of Liberation
A76

**Wmk. 373**

**1983, June 14 Litho. *Perf. 14***
375 A76 5p Army 12 12
376 A76 13p Merchant Navy 30 30
377 A76 17p Royal Air Force 45 45
378 A76 50p Royal Navy 1.25 1.25
*a.* Souvenir sheet of 4 2.50 2.50

No. 378a contains Nos. 375-378; multicolored margin shows badges of participating British units. Size: 168x130mm.

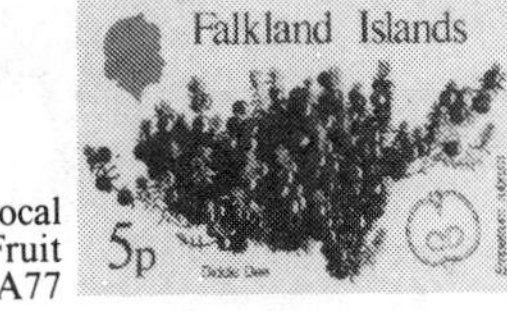

Local Fruit
A77

**Wmk. 373**

**1983, Oct. 10 Litho. *Perf. 14***
379 A77 5p Diddle dee 10 10
380 A77 17p Tea berries 34 34
381 A77 25p Mountain berries 50 50
382 A77 34p Native strawberries 70 70

Britten-Norman Islander — A78

**1983, Nov. 14 Litho. *Perf. 14***
383 A78 5p shown 8 8
384 A78 13p DHC-2 Beaver 22 22
385 A78 17p Noorduyn Norseman 30 30
386 A78 50p Auster 85 85

Green Spider — A79

Insects and Spiders.

**1984, Jan. 1 Litho. *Perf. 14***
387 A79 1p shown 5 5
388 A79 2p Ichneumon-Fly 5 5
389 A79 3p Brocade Moth 6 6
390 A79 4p Black Beetle 8 8
391 A79 5p Fritillary 10 10
392 A79 6p Green Spider, diff. 14 14
393 A79 7p Ichneumon-Fly, diff. 16 16
394 A79 8p Ochre Shoulder 18 18
395 A79 9p Clocker Weevil 20 20
396 A79 10p Hover Fly 22 22
397 A79 20p Weevil 45 45
398 A79 25p Metallic Beetle 55 55
399 A79 50p Camel Cricket 1.10 1.10
400 A79 £1 Beauchene Spider 2.25 2.25
401 A79 £3 Southern Painted Lady 6.85 6.85
*Nos. 387-401 (15)* 12.44 12.44

No. 388 exists inscribed "1986."

Nos. 364, 366 Surcharged

**1984, Jan. 3 Litho. *Perf. 14***
402 A74 17p on 15p multi 30 30
403 A74 22p on 25p multi 38 38

**Lloyd's List Issue**
Common Design Type
**Wmk. 373**

**1984, May 7 Litho. *Perf. 14½***
404 CD335 6p Wavertree 10 10
405 CD335 17p Port Stanley, 1910 30 30
406 CD335 22p Oravia 40 40
407 CD335 52p Cunard Countess 95 95

Great Grebe — A80

**1984, Aug. 6 *Perf. 14½x14***
408 A80 17p shown 42 42
409 A80 22p Silver grebe 55 55
410 A80 52p Rolland's grebe 1.40 1.40

1984 UPU Congress
A81

**1984, June 22 Litho. *Perf. 14***
411 A81 22p Emblem, jet, ship 60 60

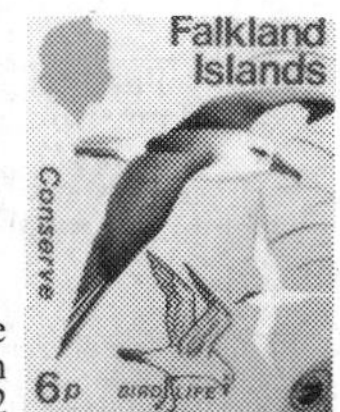

Wildlife Conservation
A82

**1984, Nov. 5 Litho. *Perf. 14½***
412 A82 6p Birds 12 12
413 A82 17p Plants 34 34
414 A82 22p Mammals 45 45
415 A82 52p Marine Life 1.05 1.05
*a.* Souv. sheet of 4, #412-415 2.00 2.00

Camber Railway, 1915-1927
A83

**1985, Feb. 18 Litho. *Perf. 14***

*416* A83 7p multicolored 14 14
*417* A83 22p multicolored 45 45
*418* A83 27p multicolored 55 55

**Size: 77x26mm.**

*419* A83 54p multicolored 1.10 1.10

**Queen Mother 85th Birthday**

Common Design Type

***Perf. 14½x14***

**1985, June 7 Litho. Wmk. 384**

*420* CD336 7p Commonwealth Visitor's Reception 20 20
*421* CD336 22p With Prince Charles, Mark Phillips, Princess Anne 60 60
*422* CD336 27p 80th birthday celebration 75 75
*423* CD336 54p Holding Prince Henry 1.50 1.50

**Souvenir Sheet**

*424* CD336 £1 In coach with Princess Diana 2.75 2.75

No. 424 has multicolored margin continuing design. Size: 92x74mm.

Mount Pleasant Airport Opening
A84

**1985, May 12 Litho. *Perf. 14½***

*425* A84 7p Pioneer camp, docked ship 18 18
*426* A84 22p Construction site 55 55
*427* A84 27p Runway layout 65 65
*428* A84 54p Aircraft landing 1.25 1.25

Captain J. McBride, HMS Jason, 1765 — A85

18th-19th century naval explorers: 22p, Commodore J. Byron, HMS Dolphin and Tamar, 1765. 27p, Vice-Adm. R. Fitzroy, HMS Beagle, 1831. 54p, Adm. Sir B.J. Sulivan, HMS Philomel, 1842.

**1985, Sept. 23**

*429* A85 7p multicolored 18 18
*430* A85 22p multicolored 55 55
*431* A85 27p multicolored 65 65
*432* A85 54p multicolored 1.40 1.40

Philibert Commerson (1727-1773), Commerson's Dolphin — A86

Naturalists, endangered species: 22p, Rene Primevere Lesson (1794-1849), kelp. 27p, Joseph Paul Gaimard (1796-1858), diving petrel. 54p, Charles Darwin (1803-1882), Calceolaria darwinii.

**1985, Nov. 4 *Perf. 14½***

*433* A86 7p multicolored 16 16
*434* A86 22p multicolored 50 50
*435* A86 27p multicolored 60 60
*436* A86 54p multicolored 1.25 1.25

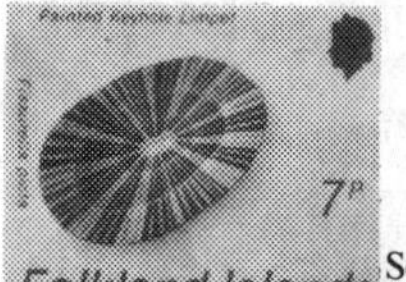


Seashells
A87

**Wmk. 384**

**1986, Feb. 10 Litho. *Perf. 14½***

*437* A87 7p Painted keyhole limpet 16 16
*438* A87 22p Magellanic volute 52 52
*439* A87 27p Falkland scallop 65 65
*440* A87 54p Rough thorn drupe 1.25 1.25

**Queen Elizabeth II 60th Birthday**

Common Design Type

Designs: 10p, With Princess Margaret at St. Paul's, Waldenbury, 1932. 24p, Christmas broadcast from Sandringham, 1958. 29p, Order of the Thistle, St. Giles Cathedral, Edinburgh, 1962. 45p, Royal reception on the Britannia, US visit, 1976. 58p, Visiting Crown Agents' offices, 1983.

**1986, Apr. 21 Litho. *Perf. 14x14½***

*441* CD337 10p scar, blk & sil 30 30
*442* CD337 24p ultra, blk & sil 72 72
*443* CD337 29p green & multi 88 88
*444* CD337 45p violet & multi 1.35 1.35
*445* CD337 58p rose vio & multi 1.75 1.75
*Nos. 441-445 (5)* 5.00 5.00

AMERIPEX '86 — A88

SS Great Britain's arrival in the Falkland Isls., Cent.: 10p, Maiden voyage, crossing the Atlantic, 1845. 24p, Wreck in Sparrow Cove, 1937. 29p, Refloating wreck, 1970. 58p, Restored vessel, Bristol, 1986.

**1986, May 22**

*446* A88 10p multicolored 25 25
*447* A88 24p multicolored 60 60
*448* A88 29p multicolored 75 75
*449* A88 58p multicolored 1.50 1.50
*a.* Souvenir sheet of 4, #446-449 3.25 3.25

No. 449a has multicolored margin picturing the steamship in New York after her maiden voyage. Size: 109x110mm.

Rockhopper Penguins — A89

**Wmk. 373**

**1986, Aug. 25 Litho. *Perf. 14½***

*450* A89 10p Adult 28 28
*451* A89 24p Adults swimming 65 65
*452* A89 29p Adults, diff. 80 80
*453* A89 58p Adult and young 1.65 1.65

Wedding of Prince Andrew and Sarah Ferguson — A90

Various photographs: 17p, Presenting Queen's Polo Cup, Windsor, 1986. 22p, Open carriage, wedding. 29p, Andrew wearing military fatigues.

**Wmk. 384**

**1986, Nov. 10 Litho. *Perf. 14½***

*454* A90 17p multicolored 50 50
*455* A90 22p multicolored 65 65
*456* A90 29p multicolored 85 85

Royal Engineers, 200th Anniv.
A91

**1987, Feb. 9 Litho. *Perf. 14½***

*457* A91 10p Surveying Sapper Hill 25 25
*458* A91 24p Explosives disposal 60 60
*459* A91 29p Boxer Bridge, Pt. Stanley 70 70
*460* A91 58p Postal services, Stanley Airport 1.50 1.50

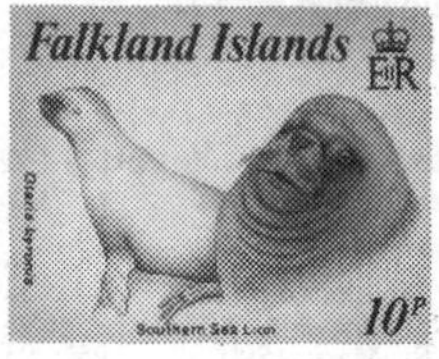


Seals
A92

**1987, Apr. 27**

*461* A92 10p Southern sea lion 30 30
*462* A92 24p Falkland fur seal 70 70
*463* A92 29p Southern elephant seal 85 85
*464* A92 58p Leopard seal 1.65 1.65

Hospitals — A93

Designs: 10p, Victorian Cottage Home, c. 1912. 24p, King Edward VII Memorial Hospital, c. 1914. 29p, Churchill Wing, 1953. 58p, Prince Andrew Wing, 1987.

**1987, Dec. 8 *Perf. 14***

*465* A93 10p multicolored 30 30
*466* A93 24p multicolored 70 70
*467* A93 29p multicolored 85 85
*468* A93 58p multicolored 1.65 1.65

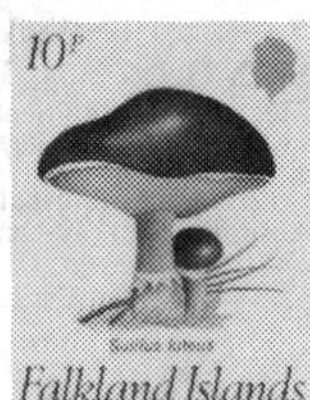


Fungi — A94

**1987, Sept. 14 Litho. *Perf. 14½***

*469* A94 10p Suillus luteus 35 35
*470* A94 24p Mycena 80 80
*471* A94 29p Camarophyllus adonis 1.00 1.00
*472* A94 58p Gerronema schusteri 2.00 2.00

1940 Morris Truck, Fitzroy
A95

Classic automobiles: 24p, 1929 Citroen Kegresse, San Carlos. 29p, 1933 Ford 1-Ton Truck, Port Stanley. 58p, 1935 Ford Model T Saloon, Darwin.

**1988, Apr. 11 Litho. *Perf. 14***

*473* A95 10p multi 35 35
*474* A95 24p multi 85 85
*475* A95 29p multi 1.05 1.05
*476* A95 58p multi 2.05 2.05

Geese
A96

**1988, July 25**

*477* A96 10p Kelp 38 38
*478* A96 24p Upland 90 90
*479* A96 29p Ruddy-headed 1.10 1.10
*480* A96 58p Ashy-headed 2.15 2.15

**Lloyds of London, 300th Anniv.**

Common Design Type

Designs: 10p, Lloyd's Nelson Collection silver service. 24p, Hydroponic Gardens, horiz. 29p, Supply ship *A.E.S.*, horiz. 58p, Wreck of the *Charles Cooper* near the Falklands, 1866.

**1988, Nov. 14 Litho. Wmk. 373**

*481* CD341 10p multi 35 35
*482* CD341 24p multi 80 80
*483* CD341 29p multi 98 98
*484* CD341 58p multi 1.95 1.95

Ships of Cape Horn
A97

**1989 Litho. Wmk. 384 *Perf.***

*485* A97 1p *Padua* 5 5
*486* A97 2p *Priwall*, vert. 8 8
*487* A97 3p *Passat* 10 10
*488* A97 4p *Archibald Russell*, vert. 15 15
*489* A97 5p *Pamir*, vert. 18 18
*490* A97 6p *Mozart* 22 22
*491* A97 7p *Pommern* 25 25
*492* A97 8p *Preussen* 30 30
*493* A97 9p *Fennia* 32 32
*494* A97 10p *Cassard* 38 38
*495* A97 20p *Lawhill* 75 75
*496* A97 25p *Garthpool* 92 92
*497* A97 50p *Grace Harwar* 1.85 1.85
*498* A97 £1 *Criccieth Castle* 3.65 3.65
*499* A97 £3 *Cutty Sark*, vert. 11.00 11.00
*500* A97 £5 *Flying Cloud* 18.25 18.25
*Nos. 485-500 (16)* 38.45 38.45

**SEMI-POSTAL STAMP**

**Catalogue values for unused stamps in this section, from this point to the end of the section, are for Never Hinged items.**

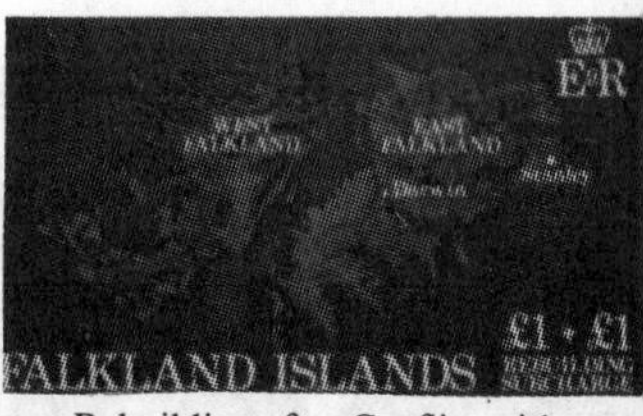


Rebuilding after Conflict with Argentina — SP1

**Wmk. 373**

**1982, Sept. 13 Litho. *Perf. 11***

*B1* SP1 £1 + £1 Battle sites 5.00 5.00

## WAR TAX STAMPS

Regular Issue of 1912-14 Overprinted **WAR STAMP**

**1918 Wmk. 3 *Perf. 14***

| No. | Type | Value | Color | Unused | Used |
|---|---|---|---|---|---|
| *MR1* | A7 | ½p | yellow grn | 50 | *3.00* |
| *MR2* | A7 | 1p | red | 32 | *2.00* |
| a. | | | Double overprint | *2,500.* | |
| *MR3* | A7 | 1sh | bister brn | 7.50 | *35.00* |
| a. | | | Pair, one without overprint | 6,000. | |

## FALKLAND ISLANDS DEPENDENCIES

**Catalogue values for unused stamps in this section, from this point to the end of the section, are for Never Hinged items.**

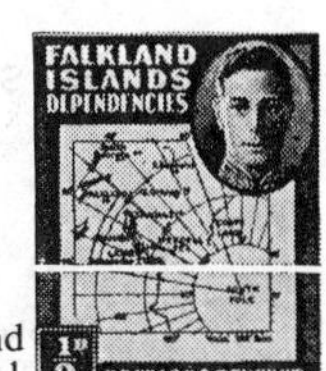


Map of Falkland Islands — A1

**Engr., Center Litho. in Black**

**1946, Feb. 1 Wmk. 4 *Perf. 12***

| No. | Type | Value | Color | Unused | Used |
|---|---|---|---|---|---|
| *1L1* | A1 | ½p | yel green | 55 | 1.00 |
| *1L2* | A1 | 1p | bl violet | 55 | 1.25 |
| *1L3* | A1 | 2p | deep car | 55 | 1.25 |
| *1L4* | A1 | 3p | ultra | 1.00 | 1.25 |
| *1L5* | A1 | 4p | deep plum | 1.00 | 2.00 |
| *1L6* | A1 | 6p | orange yel | 1.65 | 2.50 |
| *1L7* | A1 | 9p | brown | 1.65 | 2.50 |
| *1L8* | A1 | 1sh | rose violet | 3.25 | 5.00 |
| | | | *Nos. 1L1-1L8 (8)* | 10.20 | 16.75 |

Nos. 1L1-1L8 were reissued in 1948, printed on more opaque paper with the lines of the map finer and clearer. See No. 1L13.

**Peace Issue**

Common Design Type

**1946, Oct. 4 *Perf. 13½x14***

| No. | Type | Value | Color | Unused | Used |
|---|---|---|---|---|---|
| *1L9* | CD303 | 1p | purple | 40 | 40 |
| *1L10* | CD303 | 3p | deep blue | 75 | 75 |

**Silver Wedding Issue**

Common Design Types

**1948, Dec. 6 Photo. *Perf. 14x14½***

| No. | Type | Value | Color | Unused | Used |
|---|---|---|---|---|---|
| *1L11* | CD304 | 2½p | brt ultra | 50 | 50 |

***Perf. 11½x11***

**Engr.**

| No. | Type | Value | Color | Unused | Used |
|---|---|---|---|---|---|
| *1L12* | CD305 | 1sh | blue vio | 8.50 | 8.50 |

Type of 1946

**1949, Mar. 6 *Perf. 12***

**Center Litho. in Black**

| No. | Type | Value | Color | Unused | Used |
|---|---|---|---|---|---|
| *1L13* | A1 | 2½p | deep blue | 9.00 | 9.00 |

**UPU Issue**

Common Design Types

**Engr.; Name Typo. on 2p, 3p**

**1949, Oct. 10 *Perf. 13½, 11x11½***

| No. | Type | Value | Color | Unused | Used |
|---|---|---|---|---|---|
| *1L14* | CD306 | 1p | violet | 2.50 | 1.65 |
| *1L15* | CD307 | 2p | deep car | 5.00 | 2.00 |
| *1L16* | CD308 | 3p | indigo | 7.50 | 4.25 |
| *1L17* | CD309 | 6p | red org | 12.50 | 8.50 |

**Coronation Issue**

Common Design Type

**1953, June 4 *Perf. 13½x13***

| No. | Type | Value | Color | Unused | Used |
|---|---|---|---|---|---|
| *1L18* | CD312 | 1p | pur & black | 1.65 | 1.65 |

John Biscoe — A2

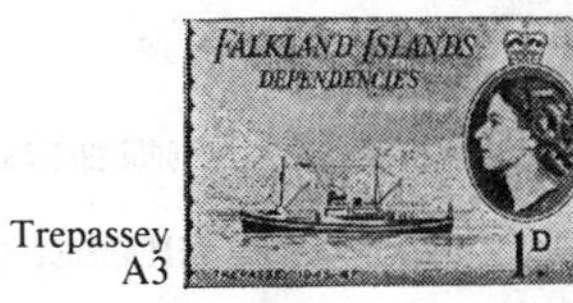


Trepassey — A3

Ships: 1½p, Wyatt Earp. 2p, Eagle. 2½p, Penola. 3p, Discovery II. 4p, William Scoresby. 6p, Discovery. 9p, Endurance. 1sh, Deutschland. 2sh, Pourquoi-pas? 2sh 6p, Français. 5sh, Scotia. 10sh, Antarctic. £1, Belgica.

**1954, Feb. 1 Engr. *Perf. 12½***

**Center in Black**

| No. | Type | Value | Color | Unused | Used |
|---|---|---|---|---|---|
| *1L19* | A2 | ½p | bl green | 22 | 22 |
| *1L20* | A3 | 1p | sepia | 22 | 22 |
| *1L21* | A3 | 1½p | olive | 30 | 30 |
| *1L22* | A3 | 2p | rose red | 45 | 45 |
| *1L23* | A3 | 2½p | yellow | 45 | 45 |
| *1L24* | A3 | 3p | ultra | 55 | 55 |
| *1L25* | A3 | 4p | red vio | 65 | 65 |
| *1L26* | A2 | 6p | rose vio | 1.10 | 1.10 |
| *1L27* | A2 | 9p | black | 2.00 | 1.75 |
| *1L28* | A3 | 1sh | org brn | 2.50 | 2.50 |
| *1L29* | A3 | 2sh | lil rose | 4.50 | 4.00 |
| *1L30* | A2 | 2sh6p | bl gray | 6.75 | 6.75 |
| *1L31* | A2 | 5sh | violet | 22.50 | 18.00 |
| *1L32* | A3 | 10sh | brt blue | 45.00 | 35.00 |
| *1L33* | A2 | £1 | black | 110.00 | 100.00 |
| | | | *Nos. 1L19-1L33 (15)* | 197.19 | 171.94 |

Stamps of 1954 Overprinted in Black **TRANS-ANTARCTIC EXPEDITION 1955-1958**

**1956, Jan 30 Center in Black**

| No. | Type | Value | Color | Unused | Used |
|---|---|---|---|---|---|
| *1L34* | A3 | 1p | sepia | 16 | 16 |
| *1L35* | A3 | 2½p | yellow | 85 | 85 |
| *1L36* | A3 | 3p | ultra | 95 | 95 |
| *1L37* | A2 | 6p | rose vio | 1.10 | 1.10 |

Trans-Antarctic Expedition, 1955-1958.

Map of Falkland Islands Dependencies — A4

**Wmk. 373**

**1980, May 5 Litho. *Perf. 13½***

| No. | Type | Value | Design | Unused | Used |
|---|---|---|---|---|---|
| *1L38* | A4 | 1p | shown | 5 | 5 |
| *1L39* | A4 | 2p | Shag Rocks | 6 | 6 |
| *1L40* | A4 | 3p | Bird and Willis Islds. | 8 | 8 |
| *1L41* | A4 | 4p | Gulbrandsen Lake | 10 | 10 |
| *1L42* | A4 | 5p | King Edward Point | 12 | 12 |
| *1L43* | A4 | 6p | Shackleton's Memorial Cross | 15 | 15 |
| *1L44* | A4 | 7p | Shackleton's grave | 18 | 18 |
| *1L45* | A4 | 8p | Grytviken Church | 20 | 20 |
| *1L46* | A4 | 9p | Coaling Hulk "Louise" | 28 | 28 |
| *1L47* | A4 | 10p | Clerke Rocks | 25 | 25 |
| *1L48* | A4 | 20p | Candlemas Island | 50 | 50 |
| a. | | | Wmk. 384 | 50 | 50 |
| *1L49* | A4 | 25p | Twitcher Rock, Cook Island | 65 | 65 |
| a. | | | Wmk. 384 | 60 | 60 |
| *1L50* | A4 | 50p | "John Biscoe" | 1.25 | 1.25 |
| a. | | | Wmk. 384 | 1.65 | 1.65 |
| *1L51* | A4 | £1 | "Bransfield" | 2.50 | 2.50 |
| a. | | | Wmk. 384 | 2.25 | 2.25 |
| *1L52* | A4 | £3 | "Endurance" | 8.00 | 8.00 |
| a. | | | Wmk. 384 | 7.25 | 7.25 |
| | | | *Nos. 1L38-1L52 (15)* | 14.37 | 14.37 |
| | | | *Nos. 1L48a-1L52a (5)* | 12.25 | 12.25 |

Magellanic Clubmoss — A5

**1981, Feb. 5 Litho. *Perf. 14***

| No. | Type | Value | Design | Unused | Used |
|---|---|---|---|---|---|
| *1L53* | A5 | 3p | shown | 10 | 10 |
| *1L54* | A5 | 6p | Alpine cat's-tail | 25 | 25 |
| *1L55* | A5 | 7p | Greater burnet | 30 | 30 |
| *1L56* | A5 | 11p | Antarctic bedstraw | 45 | 45 |
| *1L57* | A5 | 15p | Brown rush | 60 | 60 |
| *1L58* | A5 | 25p | Antarctic hair grass | 85 | 85 |
| | | | *Nos. 1L53-1L58 (6)* | 2.55 | 2.55 |

**Royal Wedding Issue**

Common Design Type

**1981, July 22 Litho. *Perf. 14***

| No. | Type | Value | Design | Unused | Used |
|---|---|---|---|---|---|
| *1L59* | CD331 | 10p | Bouquet | 40 | 40 |
| *1L60* | CD331 | 13p | Charles | 52 | 52 |
| *1L61* | CD331 | 52p | Couple | 1.25 | 1.25 |

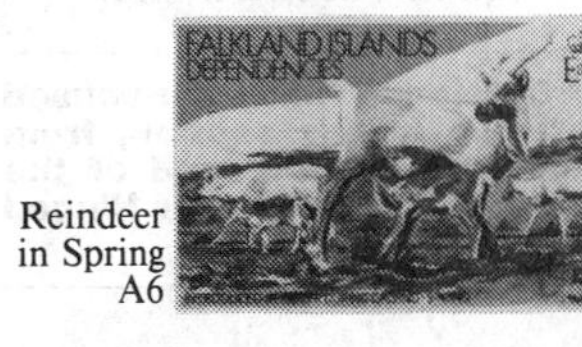


Reindeer in Spring — A6

**1982, Jan. 29 Litho. *Perf. 14***

| No. | Type | Value | Design | Unused | Used |
|---|---|---|---|---|---|
| *1L62* | A6 | 5p | shown | 20 | 20 |
| *1L63* | A6 | 13p | Autumn | 52 | 52 |
| *1L64* | A6 | 25p | Winter | 1.00 | 1.00 |
| *1L65* | A6 | 26p | Late winter | 1.00 | 1.00 |

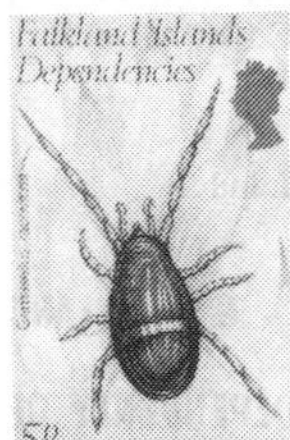


Gamasellus Racovitzai — A7

**1982, Mar. 16 Litho. *Perf. 14***

| No. | Type | Value | Design | Unused | Used |
|---|---|---|---|---|---|
| *1L66* | A7 | 5p | shown | 12 | 12 |
| *1L67* | A7 | 10p | Alaskozetes antarcticus | 25 | 25 |
| *1L68* | A7 | 13p | Cryptopygus antarcticus | 32 | 32 |
| *1L69* | A7 | 15p | Notiomaso australis | 38 | 38 |
| *1L70* | A7 | 25p | Hydromedion sparsutum | 60 | 60 |
| *1L71* | A7 | 26p | Parochlus steinenii | 65 | 65 |
| | | | *Nos. 1L66-1L71 (6)* | 2.32 | 2.32 |

**Princess Diana Issue**

Common Design Type

**1982, July 1 Litho. *Perf. 14x14½***

| No. | Type | Value | Design | Unused | Used |
|---|---|---|---|---|---|
| *1L72* | CD333 | 5p | Arms | 15 | 15 |
| *1L73* | CD333 | 17p | Diana | 55 | 55 |
| a. | | | Perf. 14 | 15.00 | 15.00 |
| *1L74* | CD333 | 37p | Wedding | 1.25 | 1.25 |
| *1L75* | CD333 | 50p | Portrait | 1.65 | 1.65 |

Crustacea — A8

***Perf. 14½x14***

**1984, Mar. 23 Litho. Wmk. 373**

| No. | Type | Value | Design | Unused | Used |
|---|---|---|---|---|---|
| *1L76* | A8 | 5p | Euphausia superba | 15 | 15 |
| *1L77* | A8 | 17p | Glyptonotus antarcticus | 55 | 55 |
| *1L78* | A8 | 25p | Epimeria monodon | 85 | 85 |
| *1L79* | A8 | 34p | Serolis pagenstecheri | 1.10 | 1.10 |

Manned Flight Bicentenary — A9

**1983, Dec. 23 Litho. *Perf. 14***

| No. | Type | Value | Design | Unused | Used |
|---|---|---|---|---|---|
| *1L80* | A9 | 5p | Westland Whirlwind | 12 | 12 |
| *1L81* | A9 | 13p | Westland Wasp | 30 | 30 |
| *1L82* | A9 | 17p | Saunders-Roe Walrus | 40 | 40 |
| *1L83* | A9 | 50p | Auster | 1.25 | 1.25 |

South Sandwich Islds. Volcanoes — A10

**Wmk. 373**

**1984, Nov. 8 Litho. *Perf. 14½***

| No. | Type | Value | Design | Unused | Used |
|---|---|---|---|---|---|
| *1L84* | A10 | 6p | Zavodovski Isld. | 15 | 15 |
| *1L85* | A10 | 17p | Mt. Michael, Saunders Isld. | 40 | 40 |
| *1L86* | A10 | 22p | Bellingshausen Isld. | 52 | 52 |
| *1L87* | A10 | 52p | Bristol Isld. | 1.25 | 1.25 |

Albatrosses — A11

**Wmk. 384**

**1985, May 5 Litho. *Perf. 14½***

| No. | Type | Value | Design | Unused | Used |
|---|---|---|---|---|---|
| *1L88* | A11 | 7p | Diomedea chrysostoma | 18 | 18 |
| *1L89* | A11 | 22p | Diomedea melanophris | 55 | 55 |
| *1L90* | A11 | 27p | Diomedea exulans | 65 | 65 |
| *1L91* | A11 | 54p | Phoebetria palpebrata | 1.25 | 1.25 |

**Queen Mother 85th Birthday**

Common Design Type

Designs: 7p, 14th birthday celebration. 22p, With Princess Anne, Lady Sarah Armstrong-Jones, Prince Edward. 27p, Queen Mother. 54p, Holding Prince Henry. £1, On the Britannia.

**1985, June 23 *Perf. 14½x14***

| No. | Type | Value | Color | Unused | Used |
|---|---|---|---|---|---|
| *1L92* | CD336 | 7p | multi | 20 | 20 |
| *1L93* | CD336 | 22p | multi | 60 | 60 |
| *1L94* | CD336 | 27p | multi | 75 | 75 |
| *1L95* | CD336 | 54p | multi | 1.50 | 1.50 |

**Souvenir Sheet**

| No. | Type | Value | Color | Unused | Used |
|---|---|---|---|---|---|
| *1L96* | CD336 | £1 | multi | 2.75 | 2.75 |

No. 1L96 has multicolored margin continuing design. Size: 92x74mm.

Falkland Islands Naturalists Type of 1985

Naturalists, endangered species: 7p, Dumont d'Urville (1790-1842), kelp. 22p, Johann Reinhold Forster (1729-98), king penguin. 27p, Johann Georg Adam Forster (1754-94), tussock grass. 54p, Sir Joseph Banks (1743-1820), dove prion.

**1985, Nov. 4 *Perf. 13½x14***

| No. | Type | Value | Color | Unused | Used |
|---|---|---|---|---|---|
| *1L97* | A86 | 7p | multi | 20 | 20 |
| *1L98* | A86 | 22p | multi | 60 | 60 |
| *1L99* | A86 | 27p | multi | 75 | 75 |
| *1L100* | A86 | 54p | multi | 1.50 | 1.50 |

## South Georgia and South Sandwich Islands

**Queen Elizabeth II 60th Birthday**

Common Design Type

Designs: 10p, With King George and Queen Mary at christening of Prince Charles, 1948. 24p, Engagement of Prince Charles and Lady Diana, Buckingham Palace Music Room, 1981. 29p, Order of the British Empire, service at St. Paul's Cathedral, London, 1974. 45p, Banquet for Canadian Prime Minister Trudeau during the 1976 Olympics. 58p, Visiting Crown Agents' offices, 1983.

**Wmk. 384**

**1986, Apr. 21 Litho. *Perf. 14½***

| No. | Type | Value | Color | Unused | Used |
|---|---|---|---|---|---|
| *1L101* | CD337 | 10p | multi | 25 | 25 |
| *1L102* | CD337 | 24p | multi | 60 | 60 |
| *1L103* | CD337 | 29p | multi | 75 | 75 |
| *1L104* | CD337 | 45p | multi | 1.10 | 1.10 |
| *1L105* | CD337 | 58p | multi | 1.50 | 1.50 |
| | | | *Nos. 1L101-1L105 (5)* | 4.20 | 4.20 |

Wedding of Prince Andrew and Sarah Ferguson — A12

**1986, Nov. 10 Litho. *Perf. 14½***

*1L106* A12 17p Couple at Ascot 50 50
*1L107* A12 22p Wedding 65 65
*1L108* A12 29p Andrew, helicopter 85 85

Birds A13

**1987, Apr. 24 Litho. Wmk. 384**

*1L109* A13 1p Dominican gull 5 5
*1L110* A13 2p Blue-eyed cormorant 6 6
*1L111* A13 3p Wattled sheathbill 10 10
*1L112* A13 4p Brown skua 14 14
*1L113* A13 5p Cape pigeon 18 18
*1L114* A13 6p South Georgia diving petrel 20 20
*1L115* A13 7p South Georgia pipit 24 24
*1L116* A13 8p South Georgia pintail 28 28
*1L117* A13 9p Fairy prion 30 30
*1L118* A13 10p Chinstrap penguin 35 35
*1L119* A13 20p Macaroni penguin 68 68
*1L120* A13 25p Light-mantled sooty albatross 85 85
*1L121* A13 50p Southern giant petrel 1.75 1.75
*1L122* A13 £1 Wandering albatross 3.50 3.50
*1L123* A13 £3 King penguin 10.25 10.25
*Nos. 1L109-1L123 (15)* 18.93 18.93

1, 2, 7, 8, 20, 25, 50p and £3 vert.

Intl. Geophysical Year, 30th Anniv. — A14

**1987, Dec. 5 Litho. *Perf. 14½***

*1L124* A14 24p shown 82 82
*1L125* A14 29p Grytviken Whaling Station 98 98
*1L126* A14 58p Glaciologist 1.95 1.95

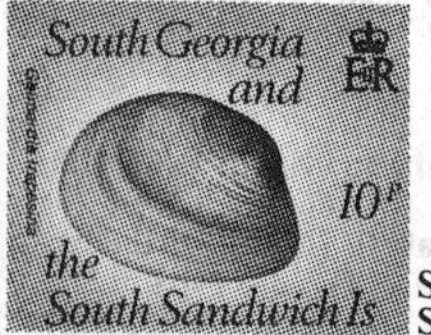

Sea Shells — A15

**Wmk. 384**

**1988, Feb. 26 Litho. *Perf. 14½***

*1L127* A15 10p Gaimardia trapesina 38 38
*1L128* A15 24p Margarella tropidophoroides 88 88
*1L129* A15 29p Trophon scotianus 1.05 1.05
*1L130* A15 58p Chlanidota densesculpta 2.10 2.10

**Lloyds of London, 300th Anniv.**
Common Design Type

Designs: 10p, Queen Mother at the official opening of the Lloyds Building, Lime Street, 1957. 24p, *Lindblad Explorer*, horiz. 29p, Leith Harbor whaling station, horiz. 58p, Whale oil tanker *Horatio* on fire.

**1988, Sept. 17 *Perf. 14***

*1L131* CD341 10p multi 35 35
*1L132* CD341 24p multi 80 80
*1L133* CD341 29p multi 98 98
*1L134* CD341 58p multi 1.95 1.95

## SEMI-POSTAL STAMP

**Catalogue values for unused stamps in this section, from this point to the end of the section, are for Never Hinged items.**

Rebuilding Type of Falkland Islands

**1982, Sept. 13 Litho. *Perf. 11***

*1LB1* SP1 £1 Map of South Georgia 5.00 5.00

## ISSUES FOR THE SEPARATE ISLANDS

### Graham Land

Falkland Islands Stamps of 1938-41, Overprinted in Red — GRAHAM LAND DEPENDENCY OF

**1944, Feb. 12 Wmk. 4 *Perf. 12***

*2L1* A22 ½p green & black 45 40
*2L2* A22 1p dk vio & black 50 50
*2L3* A22 2p rose car & blk 75 70
*2L4* A22 3p deep bl & blk 1.00 90
*2L5* A22 4p rose vio & blk 1.25 1.20
*2L6* A22 6p brown & black 3.25 3.00
*2L7* A22 9p slate bl & blk 2.50 2.50
*2L8* A22 1sh dull blue 2.50 2.25
*Nos. 2L1-2L8 (8)* 12.20 11.45

### South Georgia

Stamps of 1938-41, Overprinted in Red — SOUTH GEORGIA DEPENDENCY OF

**1944, Apr. 3 Wmk. 4 *Perf. 12***

*3L1* A22 ½p green & black 50 40
*3L2* A22 1p dark vio & blk 55 50
*3L3* A22 2p rose car & blk 85 70
*3L4* A22 3p deep bl & blk 1.10 90
*3L5* A22 4p rose vio & blk 1.40 1.25
*3L6* A22 6p brown & black 3.50 3.00
*3L7* A22 9p slate bl & blk 2.75 2.50
*3L8* A22 1sh dull blue 2.75 2.25
*Nos. 3L1-3L8 (8)* 13.40 11.50

### South Orkneys

Stamps of 1938-41 Overprinted in Red — SOUTH ORKNEYS DEPENDENCY OF

**1944, Feb. 21 Wmk. 4 *Perf. 12***

*4L1* A22 ½p green & black 45 40
*4L2* A22 1p dark vio & blk 50 50
*4L3* A22 2p rose car & blk 75 70
*4L4* A22 3p deep bl & blk 1.00 90
*4L5* A22 4p rose vio & blk 1.25 1.25
*4L6* A22 6p brown & black 3.25 3.00
*4L7* A22 9p slate bl & blk 2.50 2.50
*4L8* A22 1sh dull blue 2.50 2.25
*Nos. 4L1-4L8 (8)* 12.20 11.50

### South Shetlands

Stamps of 1938-41, Overprinted in Red — SOUTH SHETLANDS DEPENDENCY OF

**1944 Wmk. 4 *Perf. 12***

*5L1* A22 ½p green & black 45 40
*5L2* A22 1p dark vio & blk 50 50
*5L3* A22 2p rose car & blk 75 70
*5L4* A22 3p deep bl & blk 1.00 90
*5L5* A22 4p rose vio & blk 1.25 1.25
*5L6* A22 6p brown & black 3.25 3.00
*5L7* A22 9p slate bl & blk 2.50 2.50
*5L8* A22 1sh dull blue 2.50 2.25
*Nos. 5L1-5L8 (8)* 12.20 11.50

# FIJI

LOCATION — A group of about 844 islands (106 inhabited) in the South Pacific Ocean east of Vanuatu.
GOVT. — Independent nation in British Commonwealth.
AREA — 7,078 sq. mi.
POP. — 646,561 (1981).
CAPITAL — Suva.

A British colony since 1874, Fiji became fully independent in 1970.

12 Pence = 1 Shilling
20 Shillings = 1 Pound
100 Cents = 1 Dollar (1872-74, 1969)

**Catalogue values for unused stamps in this country are for Never Hinged items, beginning with Scott 137 in the regular postage section and Scott B1 in the semi-postal section.**

**Values for Nos. 1-10 are for stamps with roulettes on two sides and small faults thatr do not detract from the stamps appearance. Values for unused stamps are for copies without gum.**

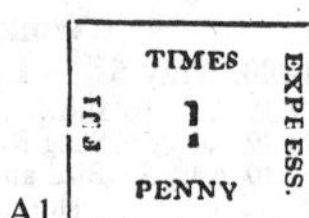

A1

**1870 Unwmk. Typeset *Rouletted***
**Quadrille Paper**

*1* A1 1p *pink* 2,500. 2,750.
*2* A1 3p *pink* 1,700. 1,900.
*3* A1 6p *pink* 2,250. 2,750.
*5* A1 1sh *pink* 1,700. 2,250.

**1871 Laid Batonne Paper**

*6* A1 1p *pink* 1,250. 1,250.
*7* A1 3p *pink* 1,500. 1,400.
*8* A1 6p *pink* 1,300. 1,200.
*9* A1 9p *pink* 1,500. 1,700.
*10* A1 1sh *pink* 1,500. 1,400.

*Official imitations exist on pink laid paper, pin-perforated, measuring 22½x16mm. Originals measure 22½x18½mm. A later printing was made on pink wove paper.*

Crown and "CR" (Cakobau Rex)
A2 A3

A4

Wmk. 17- FIJI POSTAGE Across Center Row of Sheet

**1871 Typo. Wmk. 17 *Perf. 12½***
**Wove Paper**

*15* A2 1p blue 72.50 90.0
*16* A3 3p green 110.00 150.0
*17* A4 6p rose 150.00 250.0

Sheets of 50 (10x5).

Stamps of 1871 Surcharged in Black — Tw… Cent…

**1872, Jan. 13**

*18* A2 2c on 1p blue 16.00 17.5
*19* A3 6c on 3p green 18.00 22.5
*20* A4 12c on 6p rose 37.50 37.5

Nos. 18-20 with Additional Overprin… in Black:

V.R. — b    ¥.R — c

**1874, Oct. 10**

*21* A2(b) 2c on 1p bl 425.00 125.0
*22* A2(c) 2c on 1p bl 500.00 180.0
*a* Inverted "A" instead of "V" 1,500
*b* Period after "R" is a Maltese Cross 1,500
*23* A3(b) 6c on 3p grn 1,250. 850.0
*24* A3(c) 6c on 3p grn 900.00 550.0
*a* Inverted "A" 3,000.
*b* Period after "R" is a Maltese Cross
*25* A4(b) 12c on 6p rose 550.00 250.0
*a* "V.R." inverted 3,750.
*26* A4(c) 12c on 6p rose 400.00 140.0
*a* Inverted "A" 1,350
*b* Period after "R" is a Maltese Cross 1,350
*c* "V.R." inverted 3,750

Nos. 23-26 with Additional Surcharge in Black or Red — 2d

**1875**

*27* A3(b) 2p on 6c on 3p grn 1,250. 550.00
*a* Period between "2" and "d"
*b* "V.R." double 2,750
*28* A3(b) 2p on 6c on 3p grn (R) 500.00 165.00
*a* Period between "2" and "d"
*29* A3(c) 2p on 6c on 3p grn 850.00 325.00
*a* Inverted "A" 2,500. 1,250
*b* Period after "R" is a Maltese Cross 2,500. 1,250
*c* No period after "2d" 2,500. 1,250
*30* A3(c) 2p on 6c on 3p grn (R) 375.00 225.00
*a* Inverted "A" 1,750. 675.00
*b* Period after "R" is a Maltese Cross 1,750. 725.00
*c* No period after "2d" 1,850. 725.00
*31* A4(b) 2p on 12c on 6p rose 1,000. 650.00
*a* Period between "2" and "d"
*b* No period after "2d"
*c* "2d, VR" double 1,750
*32* A4(c) 2p on 12c on 6p rose 775.00 400.00
*a* Inverted "A" 1,000. 600.00
*b* No period after "2d"
*c* "2d, VR" double 2,000

Types of 1871 Overprinted or Surcharged in Black:

e

Two Pence
f

**1876, Jan. 31** **Unwmk.**

**Wove Paper**

| | | | | |
|---|---|---|---|---|
| *33* | A2(e) | 1p ultra | 30.00 | 30.00 |
| a | | Inverted surcharge | | |
| b | | Dbl. impression of stamp | 2,000. | |
| *34* | A3(e+f) | 2p on 3p dk grn | 37.50 | 37.50 |
| a | | Double surcharge "Two Pence" | | |
| *35* | A4(e) | 6p rose | 65.00 | 60.00 |
| a | | Imperf. vertically | | |
| b | | Surcharge inverted | | |
| c | | Dbl. impression of stamp | | |

**1877** **Laid Paper**

| | | | | |
|---|---|---|---|---|
| *36* | A2(e) | 1p ultra | 9.50 | 9.00 |
| a | | Imperf. vert., pair | 1,100. | |
| *37* | A3(e+f) | 2p on 3p dk grn | 62.50 | 62.50 |
| *38* | A3(e+f) | 4p on 3p lil | 40.00 | 25.00 |
| *39* | A4(e) | 6p rose | 13.00 | 5.75 |

Many of the preceding stamps are known imperforate. They are printer's waste and were never issued.

A12

A13

Queen Victoria
A14 A15

***Perf. 10-13½ & Compound***

**1878-91** **Wove Paper** **Typo.**

| | | | | |
|---|---|---|---|---|
| *40* | A12 | 1p ultra | 2.50 | 85 |
| a | | 1p blue | 17.00 | 6.50 |
| *41* | A12 | 2p green | 5.75 | 2.50 |
| a | | Imperf. horiz., pair | | |
| b | | 2p ultra (error) | | |
| *42* | A12 | 4p brt vio ('91) | 4.50 | 4.50 |
| a | | 4p mauve | 7.50 | 9.00 |
| *43* | A13 | 6p bright rose | 5.75 | 4.75 |
| a | | Printed on both sides | 525.00 | 425.00 |
| *44* | A14 | 1sh yel brn ('81) | 13.00 | 5.40 |
| a | | 1sh deep brown | 17.50 | 7.00 |

**Litho.**

| | | | | |
|---|---|---|---|---|
| *45* | A15 | 5sh blk & red brn ('81) | 42.50 | 42.50 |
| | | *Nos. 40-45 (6)* | 74.00 | 60.50 |

Facsimiles of the 5sh were officially made in 1900, differing in shades and detail of design from No. 45. They exist imperf., perf. 10 and 12; are all canceled "SUVA" and usually dated "15 Dec., 00."

Surcharged type "f" in Black

**1878-90** **Typo.**

| | | | | |
|---|---|---|---|---|
| *46* | A12 | 2p on 3p green | 4.75 | 7500 |
| *47* | A12 | 4p on 1p vio ('90) | 8.00 | 8.00 |
| *48* | A12 | 4p on 2p lil ('83) | 17.00 | 7.25 |

Nos. 40-43 Surcharged in Black:

½d.
g

2½d.
h

5d
j

FIVE
PENCE
k

**1891-92** ***Perf. 10***

| | | | | |
|---|---|---|---|---|
| *49* | A12(g) | ½p on 1p ultra ('92) | 37.50 | 37.50 |
| *50* | A12(h) | 2½p on 2p grn | 32.50 | 32.50 |
| a | | Wider space (2mm.) between "2" and "½" | 150.00 | 150.00 |
| *51* | A12(j) | 5p on 4p redsh vio ('92) | 50.00 | 50.00 |
| *52* | A13(k) | 5p on 6p rose ('92) | 37.50 | 37.50 |
| a | | "FIVE" and "PENCE" 3mm. apart. | 37.50 | 37.50 |

A18

Fijian Canoe — A19

A20

**1891-96** ***Perf. 10-12 & Compound***

| | | | | |
|---|---|---|---|---|
| *53* | A18 | ½p grnsh blk ('92) | 1.75 | 1.75 |
| a | | ½p gray | 1.75 | 1.75 |
| *54* | A19 | 1p black ('93) | 2.75 | 2.50 |
| *55* | A19 | 1p lilac rose ('96) | 3.00 | 1.00 |
| *56* | A19 | 2p green ('93) | 4.25 | 85 |
| a | | Perf. 10x12 | | 325.00 |
| *57* | A20 | 2½ red brown | 3.50 | 2.25 |
| *58* | A19 | 5p ultra ('93) | 6.25 | 6.25 |
| | | *Nos. 53-58 (6)* | 21.50 | 14.60 |

Stamps of the issues of 1878 to 1896 occasionally show letters of paper makers' watermarks, "T.H. Saunders", "Sanderson", "Cowan", and "New South Wales Government".

Edward VII
A22

George V
A23

**1903** **Wmk. 2** ***Perf. 14***

| | | | | |
|---|---|---|---|---|
| *59* | A22 | ½p gray grn & pale grn | 60 | 42 |
| *60* | A22 | 1p vio & blk, *red* | 7.00 | 32 |
| *61* | A22 | 2p vio & orange | 48 | 48 |
| *62* | A22 | 2½p vio & ultra, *bl* | 9.50 | *12.00* |
| *63* | A22 | 3p vio & red vio | 1.40 | *3.50* |
| *64* | A22 | 4p violet & blk | 1.65 | *3.00* |
| *65* | A22 | 5p vio & green | 1.65 | *4.00* |
| *66* | A22 | 6p vio & car rose | 3.00 | *4.75* |
| *67* | A22 | 1sh grn & car rose | 12.00 | *17.00* |
| *68* | A22 | 5sh green & blk | 30.00 | *47.50* |
| *69* | A22 | £1 gray & ultra | 375.00 | *475.00* |
| | | *Nos. 59-68 (10)* | 67.28 | *92.97* |

Numerals of 2p, 4p, 6p and 5sh of type A22 are in color on plain tablet.

**1904-12** **Wmk. 3**

**Ordinary Paper**

| | | | | |
|---|---|---|---|---|
| *70* | A22 | ½p green ('04) | 48 | 30 |
| *71* | A22 | 1p vio & black, *red* ('04) | 4.00 | 25 |
| *72* | A22 | 1p carmine ('06) | 1.10 | 30 |
| *73* | A22 | 2½p ultra ('10) | 1.25 | *2.00* |

**Chalky Paper**

| | | | | |
|---|---|---|---|---|
| *74* | A22 | 6p violet ('10) | 3.75 | *4.00* |
| *75* | A22 | 1sh grn & carmine rose ('09) | 20.00 | *25.00* |
| *76* | A22 | 1sh *green* ('11) | 4.00 | *8.25* |
| *77* | A22 | 5sh grn & scarlet, *yel* ('11) | 25.00 | *35.00* |
| *78* | A22 | £1 vio & black, *red* ('12) | 260.00 | 275.00 |
| | | *Nos. 70-77 (8)* | 59.58 | *75.10* |

Die I

For description of Dies I and II see back of this section of the Catalogue.

**1912-23**

**Ordinary Paper**

| | | | | |
|---|---|---|---|---|
| *79* | A23 | ¼p brown ('16) | 20 | 22 |
| *80* | A23 | ½p green | 45 | 45 |
| *81* | A23 | 1p scarlet | 70 | 14 |
| a | | 1p carmine ('16) | 1.10 | 52 |
| *82* | A23 | 2p gray ('14) | 1.40 | 55 |
| *83* | A23 | 2½p ultra ('14) | 4.75 | 5.00 |
| *84* | A23 | 3p violet, *yel* | 1.50 | 1.50 |
| a | | Die II ('21) | 1.50 | 1.75 |
| *85* | A23 | 4p black & red, *yel* ('14) | 2.25 | 2.25 |
| a | | Die II ('23) | 6.25 | *15.00* |

**Chalky Paper**

| | | | | |
|---|---|---|---|---|
| *86* | A23 | 5p dl vio & ol grn ('14) | 3.50 | 4.00 |
| *87* | A23 | 6p dl vio & red vio ('14) | 2.75 | 2.75 |
| *88* | A23 | 1sh *green* | 3.50 | 3.50 |
| a | | 1sh *blue green*, ol back | 2.75 | 3.00 |
| b | | 1sh *emerald* ('21) | 2.75 | 2.75 |
| c | | Die II ('22) | 4.25 | *8.25* |
| *89* | A23 | 2sh 6p black & red, *blue* | 16.00 | *21.00* |
| *90* | A23 | 5sh grn & scar, *yellow* | 22.50 | *30.00* |
| *91* | A23 | £1 vio & black, *red* | 260.00 | 300.00 |
| a | | Die II ('21) | 260.00 | 300.00 |

**Surface-colored Paper**

| | | | | |
|---|---|---|---|---|
| *92* | A23 | 1sh *green* | 2.00 | 2.00 |
| | | *Nos. 79-90,92 (13)* | 61.50 | *73.36* |

Numerals of ¼p, 1½p, 2p, 4p, 6p, 2sh, 2sh6p and 5sh of type A23 are in color on plain tablet.

Die II

**1922-27** **Wmk. 4**

**Ordinary Paper**

| | | | | |
|---|---|---|---|---|
| *93* | A23 | ¼p dark brown | 1.00 | *8.50* |
| *94* | A23 | ½p green | 65 | 65 |
| *95* | A23 | 1p rose red | 1.25 | 1.65 |
| *96* | A23 | 1p violet ('27) | 40 | 25 |
| *97* | A23 | 1½p rose red ('27) | 2.75 | 2.75 |
| *98* | A23 | 2p gray | 1.25 | 25 |
| *99* | A23 | 3p ultra ('23) | 65 | 65 |
| *100* | A23 | 4p blk & red, *yel* | 2.75 | 3.50 |
| *101* | A23 | 5p dl vio & ol green | 2.00 | 1.10 |
| *102* | A23 | 6p dl vio & red violet | 2.00 | 2.50 |

**Chalky Paper**

| | | | | |
|---|---|---|---|---|
| *103* | A23 | 1sh *emerald* | 2.00 | 2.50 |
| *104* | A23 | 2sh vio & ultra, *bl* ('27) | 16.00 | *27.50* |
| *105* | A23 | 2sh6p blk & red, *bl* | 12.00 | *22.50* |
| *106* | A23 | 5sh grn & scar, *yellow* | 35.00 | *52.50* |
| | | *Nos. 93-106 (14)* | 79.70 | *126.80* |

**Silver Jubilee Issue**

Common Design Type

**1935, May 6** ***Perf. 13½x14***

| | | | | |
|---|---|---|---|---|
| *110* | CD301 | 1½p carmine & blue | 42 | 42 |
| *111* | CD301 | 2p gray blk & ultra | 70 | 70 |
| *112* | CD301 | 3p blue & brown | 1.40 | 2.00 |
| *113* | CD301 | 1sh brt vio & indigo | 2.25 | 2.50 |

**Coronation Issue**

Common Design Type

**1937, May 12** ***Perf. 11x11½***

| | | | | |
|---|---|---|---|---|
| *114* | CD302 | 1p dark violet | 10 | 10 |
| *115* | CD302 | 2p gray black | 22 | 22 |
| *116* | CD302 | 3p indigo | 25 | 25 |

Outrigger Canoe — A24

Fijian Village — A25

Outrigger Canoe A26

Map of Fiji Islands A27

Canoe and Arms of Fiji — A28

The first price column gives the catalogue value of an unused stamp, the second that of a used stamp.

Sugar Cane — A29

Spear Fishing at Night — A30

Arms of Fiji — A31

Suva Harbor — A32

River Scene — A33

Fijian House — A34

Papaya Tree — A35

Bugler — A36

Designs: No. 121, Government buildings. 8p, 1sh5p, 1sh6p, Arms of Fiji.

***Perf. 12, 12½, 13½, 13x11½, 13½x14, 14, 14½x14***

**1938-55** **Engr.** **Wmk. 4**

| | | | | |
|---|---|---|---|---|
| *117* | A24 | ½p green, perf. 13½ | 7 | 7 |
| c | | Perf. 14 ('41) | 3.00 | 3.00 |
| d | | Perf. 12 ('48) | 12 | 12 |
| *118* | A25 | 1p bl & brn, perf. 12½ | 7 | 7 |
| *119* | A26 | 1½p rose car (empty canoe) perf. 13½ | 3.25 | 2.00 |
| *120* | A27 | 2p grn & org brn (no "180 degree"), perf. 13½ | 3.75 | 50 |
| *121* | A27 | 2p mag & grn, perf. 13½ ('41) | 15 | 12 |
| a | | Perf. 12 ('46) | 22 | 22 |
| *122* | A28 | 3p dp ultra, perf. 12½ | 15 | 15 |
| *123* | A29 | 5p rose red & bl, perf. 12½ | 12.50 | 8.50 |
| *124* | A29 | 5p rose red & yel grn, perf. 12½ ('40) | 25 | 25 |
| *125* | A27 | 6p blk (no "180 degree"), perf. 13x12 | 21.00 | 12.50 |
| *126* | A31 | 8p rose car, perf. 13 ('48) | 65 | 65 |
| a | | Perf. 14 ('48) | 42 | 42 |
| *127* | A30 | 1sh blk & yel, perf. 12½ | 45 | 45 |
| *128* | A31 | 1sh5p car & blk, perf. 14 ('40) | 50 | 50 |

*128A* A31 1sh6p ultra, perf. 14 ('50) 1.10 70
*b* Perf. 13 ('55) 2.00 1.50

***Perf. 12½***

*129* A32 2sh vio & org 75 75
*130* A33 2sh6p brn & grn 1.10 1.10
*131* A34 5sh dk vio & green 1.65 1.65
*131A* A35 10sh emer & brn org ('50) 15.00 17.00
*131B* A36 £1 carmine & ultra ('50) 24.00 24.00
*Nos. 117-131B (18)* 86.39 70.96

Types of 1938-40 Redrawn

**1940-49 Wmk. 4 *Perf. 12, 13½, 14***

*132* A26 1½p rose car (man in canoe) perf. 12 ('49) 25 25
*a* perf. 13½ ('40) 25 25
*b* perf. 14 ('42) 6.75 8.50
*133* A27 2p grn & org brn ("180 degree"), perf. 13½ 1.50 1.25
*134* A27 2½p grn & org brn, perf. 12 ('48) 25 22
*a* Perf. 14 ('42) 22 22
*b* Perf. 13½ ('42) 25 22
*135* A27 6p blk ("180 degree"), perf. 12 ('47) 60 60
*a* Perf. 13½ ('40) 48 48

No. 132, type A26, has a man sitting in the canoe.

Nos. 133-135, type A27, have 180 degree added to the lower right hand corner of the design.

No. 133 Surcharged in Black

**2½d.**

**1941, Feb. 10 *Perf. 13½***

*136* A27 2½p on 2p grn & org brn 18 18

**Catalogue values for unused stamps in this section, from this point to the end of the section, are for Never Hinged items.**

**Peace Issue**

Common Design Type

**1946, Aug. 17 *Perf. 13½***

*137* CD303 2½p bright green 14 14
*138* CD303 3p deep blue 18 18

**Silver Wedding Issue**

Common Design Types

**1948, Dec. 17 Photo. *Perf. 14x14½***

*139* CD304 2½p dark green 26 26

**Engr.; Name Typo.**

***Perf. 11½x11***

*140* CD305 5sh blue vio 19.00 16.00

**UPU Issue**

Common Design Types

**Engr.; Name Typo. on 3p, 8p**

***Perf. 13½, 11x11½***

**1949, Oct. 10 Wmk. 4**

*141* CD306 2p red violet 48 48
*142* CD307 3p indigo 85 85
*143* CD308 8p dp carmine 1.50 1.50
*144* CD309 1sh6p blue 3.00 3.00

**Coronation Issue**

Common Design Type

**1953, June 2 *Perf. 13½x13***

*145* CD312 2½p dk grn & blk 90 90

Type of 1938-40 with Portrait of Queen Elizabeth II Inscribed: "Royal Visit 1953"

**1953, Dec. 16 *Perf. 13***

*146* A31 8p carmine lake 25 25

Visit of Queen Elizabeth II and the Duke of Edinburgh, 1953.

Types of 1938-50 with Portrait of Queen Elizabeth II, and:

A39

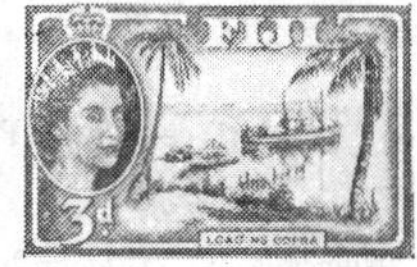



Loading Copra — A40

Designs: 1sh6p, Sugar cane train. 2sh, Bananas for export. 5sh, Gold industry.

***Perf. 11½, 11½x11, 12, 12½, 13***

**1954-56 Engr.**

*147* A24 ½p green 6 5
*148* A39 1p grnsh bl ('56) 12 8
*149* A39 1½p brown ('56) 15 10
*150* A27 2p mag & green 25 10
*151* A39 2½p bl vio ('56) 1.00 50
*152* A40 3p purple & brown ('56) 42 8
*154* A27 6p black 45 30
*155* A31 8p car lake 60 38
*156* A30 1sh black & yel 1.25 65
*157* A40 1sh6p grn & dp ultra ('56) 3.00 1.50
*158* A40 2sh brt car & black ('56) 3.25 1.50
*159* A33 2sh6p brn & bl grn 1.40 80
*160* A40 5sh dp ultra & yel ('56) 12.50 2.75
*161* A35 10sh emer & brown org 25.00 17.50
*162* A36 £1 car & ultra 35.00 14.00
*Nos. 147-162 (15)* 84.45 40.29

No. 154 has "180 degree" added in lower right corner of design.

Types of 1954-56 and:

Nautilus Shells A41

Hibiscus A42

Kandavu Parrot — A43

Designs: ½p, 2p, 2½p, Queen Elizabeth II (A39). 1p, Queen, turtles in bottom panels. 6p, Fijian beating drum (lali). 10p, Yaqona ceremony. 1sh, South Pacific map. 2sh6p, Nadi Airport. 10sh, Cutting sugar cane. £1, Arms of Fiji.

***Perf. 11½ (A39, A41); 11½x11 (A40); 14½x14 (A42); 14x14½ (A43)***

**Engr. (A39, A40, A41); others Photo.**

**1959-63 Wmk. 4**

*163* A39 ½p green ('61) 5 5
*164* A41 1p dark bl ('62) 15 14
*165* A41 1½p dark brn ('62) 20 18
*166* A39 2p crim rose ('61) 35 32
*167* A39 2½p brown org ('62) 65 60
*168* A40 6p blk & carmine rose ('61) 80 75
*169* A42 8p gray, red, yel & grn ('61) 1.00 90
*170* A40 10p car & brn ('63) 1.90 1.40
*171* A40 1sh dk bl & bl ('61) 60 50
*172* A40 2sh6p pur & blk ('61) 2.50 2.50
*173* A43 4sh dk grn, red, bl & emer 3.00 2.25
*174* A40 10sh sep & emerald ('61) 11.00 10.50
*175* A40 £1 org & blk ('61) 32.50 22.50
*Nos. 163-175 (13)* 54.70 42.59

Types of 1954-63 and:

Queen Elizabeth II — A44

Designs: 1sh6p, 180th meridian and International Date Line. 2sh, White orchids. 5sh, Orange dove.

***Perf. 11½ (A41); 12½ (A44); 11½x11 (A40); 14x14½ (A43)***

**Engr. (A40, A41); others Photo.**

**1962-67 Wmk. 314**

*176* A41 1p dark blue ('64) 65 55
*177* A39 2p crim rose ('65) 75 65
*178* A44 3p rose cl & multi 18 8
*179* A40 6p blk & carmine rose ('64) 95 52
*180* A42 9p ultra, red, yel & grn ('63) 95 42
*181* A40 10p car & brn ('64) 95 65
*182* A40 1sh dk bl & bl ('66) 1.65 1.10
*183* A43 1sh6p dk bl & multi 1.95 95
*184* A42 2sh gold, yel grn & grn 2.75 1.10
*185* A40 2sh6p pur & blk. ('65) 1.95 1.25
*186* A43 4sh dark green & multi ('66) 4.00 3.25
*a* 4sh green & multi ('64) 3.50 3.25
*b* As "a", wmk. sideways ('67) 2.50 2.25
*187* A43 5sh dk gray, yel & red 7.25 3.50
*188* A40 10sh sep & emerald ('64) 11.00 10.50
*189* A40 £1 org & blk ('64) 20.00 13.00
*Nos. 176-189 (14)* 54.98 37.52

Nos. 178 and 171 Overprinted: "ROYAL VISIT 1963"

**1963, Feb. 1**

*196* A44 3p multicolored 20 20
*197* A40 1sh dark bl & bl 65 65

Visit of Elizabeth II & Prince Philip, Feb. 3.

**Freedom from Hunger Issue**

Common Design Type

**1963, June 4 Photo. *Perf. 14x14½***

*198* CD314 2sh ultramarine 6.50 4.00

Running A45

Designs: 9p, Throwing the discus (vert.). 1sh, Field hockey (vert.). 2sh6p, Women's high jump.

***Perf. 14½x14, 14x14½***

**1963, Aug. 6 Wmk. 314**

*199* A45 3p yel, blk & brn 22 22
*200* A45 9p vio, blk & brn 40 40
*201* A45 1sh grn, blk & brn 52 52
*202* A45 2sh6p blue, blk & brn 1.65 1.65

First South Pacific Games, Suva, Aug. 29-Sept. 7.

**Red Cross Centenary Issue**

Common Design Type

**1963, Sept. 2 Litho. *Perf. 13***

*203* CD315 2p black & red 38 32
*204* CD315 2sh ultra & red 4.50 3.75

Type of 1959-63 Overprinted

COMPAC CABLE
IN SERVICE
DECEMBER 1963

**1963, Dec. 2 Engr. *Perf. 11½x11***

*205* A40 1sh dark bl & bl 95 95

Opening of the Commonwealth Pacific (telephone) Cable service, COMPAC.

Fiji Scout Badge — A46

Scouts of India, Fiji and Europe Tying Knot — A47

**1964, Aug. 3 Photo. *Perf. 12½***

*206* A46 3p grn, ultra, red & gold 18 18
*207* A47 1sh ocher & purple 95 95

50th anniv. of the founding of the Fiji Boy Scouts.

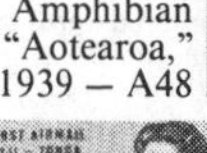

Amphibian "Aotearoa," 1939 — A48

Map of Fiji and Tonga Islands and Plane A49

Design: 6p, Heron plane.

**1964, Oct. 24 *Perf. 12½, 14½***

*208* A48 3p brt red & blk 16 16
*209* A48 6p ultra & red 38 38
*210* A49 1sh grnsh bl & blk 75 75

Fiji-Tonga airmail service, 25th anniv.

**ITU Issue**

Common Design Type

***Perf. 11x11½***

**1965, May 17 Litho. Wmk. 314**

*211* CD317 3p bl & rose red 35 35
*212* CD317 2sh yel & bister 3.00 3.00

**Intl. Cooperation Year Issue**

Common Design Type

**1965, Oct. 25 *Perf. 14½***

*213* CD318 2p bl grn & cl 32 32
*214* CD318 2sh6p lt vio & grn 2.00 1.75

**Churchill Memorial Issue**

Common Design Type

**1966, Jan. 24 Photo. *Perf. 14***

**Design in Black, Gold and Carmine Rose**

*215* CD319 3p bright bl 28 28
*216* CD319 9p green 90 90
*217* CD319 1sh brown 1.10 1.10
*218* CD319 2sh6p violet 3.00 3.00

**World Cup Soccer Issue**

Common Design Type

**1966, July 1 Litho. *Perf. 14***

*219* CD321 2p multicolored 28 28
*220* CD321 2sh multicolored 2.00 1.40

H.M.S. Pandora and Split Island, Rotuma A50

Designs: 10p, Rotuma chiefs, Pandora, and Rotuma's position in Pacific. 1sh6p, Rotuma islanders welcoming Pandora.

***Perf. 14x13***

**1966, Aug. 29 Photo. Wmk. 314**

*221* A50 3p multicolored 14 14
*222* A50 10p multicolored 35 35
*223* A50 1sh6p multicolored 70 70

175th anniv. of the discovery of Rotuma, a group of eight islands forming part of the colony of Fiji.

**WHO Headquarters Issue**

Common Design Type

**1966, Sept. 20 Litho. *Perf. 14***

*224* CD322 6p multicolored 52 45
*225* CD322 2sh6p multicolored 3.75 2.50

Woman Runner A51

Designs: 9p, Shot put (vert.). 1sh, Diver.

**1966, Dec. 8 Photo. *Perf. 14x14½***

| | | | | |
|---|---|---|---|---|
| *226* | A51 | 3p ol, blk & lt brn | 9 | 9 |
| *227* | A51 | 9p brt bl, blk & brn | 30 | 30 |
| *228* | A51 | 1sh bl grn & multi | 48 | 48 |

2nd South Pacific Games, Noumea, New Caledonia, Dec. 8-18.

Common Design Types pictured in section before Great Britain.

Military Band A52

Designs (ITY Emblem and): 9p, Reef diving. 1sh, Beqa fire walkers. 2sh, Liner Oriana and Mt. Rama volcano.

**1967, Oct. 20 *Perf. 14x13***

| | | | | |
|---|---|---|---|---|
| *229* | A52 | 3p multi & gold | 15 | 12 |
| *230* | A52 | 9p multi & silver | 28 | 28 |
| *231* | A52 | 1sh multi & gold | 32 | 32 |
| *232* | A52 | 2sh multi & silver | 75 | 60 |

International Tourist Year.

Admiral Bligh, H.M.S. Providence and Old Map of "Feejee" A53

Designs: 1sh, Bligh's longboat being chased by double canoe and map of Fiji Islands. 2sh6p, Bligh's tomb, St. Mary's Cemetery, Lambeth, London.

***Perf. 15x14, 12½x13 (1sh)***

**1967, Dec. 7 Photo. Wmk. 314**

**Size: 35x21mm**

| | | | | |
|---|---|---|---|---|
| *233* | A53 | 4p emer, blk & yel | 9 | 9 |

**Size: 54x20mm**

| | | | | |
|---|---|---|---|---|
| *234* | A53 | 1sh brt bl, brn org & blk | 28 | 28 |

**Size: 35x21mm**

| | | | | |
|---|---|---|---|---|
| *235* | A53 | 2sh6p sep & multi | 70 | 70 |

150th anniv. of the death of Adm. William Bligh (1754-1817), captain of the Bounty and principal discoverer of the Fiji Islands.

Simmonds "Spartan" Seaplane A54

Designs: 6p, Fiji Airways Hawker-Siddeley H748 and emblems of various airlines. 1sh, Fokker "Southern Cross," Capt. Charles Kingsford-Smith, his crew and Southern Cross constellation. 2sh, Lockheed Altair "Lady Southern Cross."

***Perf. 14x14½***

**1968, June 5 Photo. Wmk. 314**

| | | | | |
|---|---|---|---|---|
| *236* | A54 | 2p green & black | 7 | 7 |
| *237* | A54 | 6p brt bl, car & blk | 18 | 18 |
| *238* | A54 | 1sh deep vio & green | 35 | 35 |
| *239* | A54 | 2sh org brn & dark bl | 70 | 70 |

40th anniv. of the first Trans-Pacific Flight through Fiji under Capt. Charles Kingsford-Smith.

Fijian Bures — A55

Eastern Reef Heron — A56

Designs: 1p, Passion fruit flowers. 2p, Nautilus pompilius shell. 4p, Hawk moth. 6p, Reef butterflyfish. 9p, Bamboo raft (bilibili). 10p, Tiger moth. 1sh, Black marlin. 1sh6p, Orange-breasted honey eaters. 2sh, Ringed sea snake (horiz.). 2sh6p, Outrigger canoes (takia) (horiz.). 3sh, Golden cowrie shell. 4sh, Emperor gold mine and gold ore. 5sh, Bamboo orchids (horiz.). 10sh, Tabua (ceremonial whale's tooth). £1, Coat of Arms and Queen Elizabeth II (horiz.).

***Perf. 13½ (A55), 14 (A56)***

**1968, July 15 Photo. Wmk. 314**

| | | | | |
|---|---|---|---|---|
| *240* | A55 | ½p multicolored | 5 | 5 |
| *241* | A55 | 1p multicolored | 7 | 7 |
| *242* | A55 | 2p multicolored | 12 | 12 |
| *243* | A56 | 3p multicolored | 16 | 16 |
| *244* | A55 | 4p multicolored | 20 | 20 |
| *245* | A55 | 6p multicolored | 32 | 32 |
| *246* | A55 | 9p multicolored | 50 | 50 |
| *247* | A55 | 10p multicolored | 65 | 65 |
| *248* | A56 | 1sh multicolored | 70 | 70 |
| *249* | A56 | 1sh6p multicolored | 80 | 80 |
| *250* | A56 | 2sh multicolored | 1.00 | 1.00 |
| *251* | A56 | 2sh6p multicolored | 1.40 | 1.40 |
| *252* | A55 | 3sh multicolored | 1.65 | 1.65 |
| *253* | A56 | 4sh multicolored | 2.00 | 2.00 |
| *254* | A56 | 5sh multicolored | 3.00 | 3.00 |
| *255* | A56 | 10sh multicolored | 5.75 | 5.75 |
| *256* | A56 | £1 red & multi | 11.00 | 11.00 |
| | | *Nos. 240-256 (17)* | 29.37 | 29.37 |

WHO Emblem, Map of Fiji and Nurses — A57

Designs (WHO Emblem and): 9p, Medical team loading patient on stretcher on dinghy and medical ship "Vuniwai." 3sh, People playing on beach.

**1968, Dec. 9 Litho. *Perf. 14***

| | | | | |
|---|---|---|---|---|
| *257* | A57 | 3p bl grn & multi | 9 | 9 |
| *258* | A57 | 9p brt bl & multi | 30 | 30 |
| *259* | A57 | 3sh dk bl & multi | 90 | 90 |

WHO, 20th anniv.

Types of 1968
Values in Cents and Dollars

Designs: 1c, Passion fruit flowers. 2c, Nautilus pompilius shell. 3c, Reef heron. 4c, Hawk moth. 5c, Reef butterflyfish. 6c, Fijian bures. 8c, Bamboo raft. 9c, Tiger moth. 10c, Black marlin. 15c, Orange-breasted honey-eater. 20c, Ringed sea snake (horz.). 25c, Outrigger canoes (takia) (horz.). 30c, Golden cowrie shell. 40c Emperor gold mine and gold ore. 50c, Bamboo orchids (horiz.). $1, Tabua (ceremonial whale's tooth). $2, Coat of Arms and Queen Elizabeth II (horiz.).

***Perf. 13½ (A55), 14 (A56)***

**1969, Jan. 13 Photo. Wmk. 314**

| | | | | |
|---|---|---|---|---|
| *260* | A55 | 1c multicolored | 5 | 5 |
| *a* | | Bklt. pane of 2 ('70) | 25 | |
| *261* | A55 | 2c multicolored | 6 | 5 |
| *a* | | Bklt. pane of 2 | 25 | |
| *b* | | Bklt. pane of 4 | 50 | |
| *262* | A56 | 3c multicolored | 9 | 7 |
| *263* | A55 | 4c multicolored | 12 | 9 |
| *264* | A55 | 5c multicolored | 16 | 12 |
| *265* | A55 | 6c multicolored | 18 | 12 |
| *266* | A55 | 8c multicolored | 25 | 18 |
| *267* | A55 | 9c multicolored | 32 | 25 |
| *268* | A56 | 10c multicolored | 38 | 28 |
| *269* | A56 | 15c multicolored | 1.90 | 1.25 |
| *270* | A56 | 20c multicolored | 95 | 55 |
| *271* | A56 | 25c multicolored | 1.10 | 75 |
| *272* | A55 | 30c multicolored | 3.25 | 1.10 |
| *273* | A56 | 40c multicolored | 2.25 | 1.50 |
| *274* | A56 | 50c multicolored | 3.75 | 1.90 |
| *275* | A56 | $1 multicolored | 5.75 | 3.75 |
| *276* | A56 | $2 red & multi | 9.50 | 7.75 |
| | | *Nos. 260-276 (17)* | 30.06 | 19.76 |

Fiji Soldiers and Map of Solomon Islands A58

Designs: 10c, Flags of Fiji Military Force, soldiers in full and battle dress. 25c, Cpl. Sefanaia Sukanaivalu and Victoria Cross.

**1969, June 23 Wmk. 314 *Perf. 14***

| | | | | |
|---|---|---|---|---|
| *277* | A58 | 3c emer & multi | 7 | 7 |
| *278* | A58 | 10c red & multi | 25 | 25 |
| *279* | A58 | 25c blk & multi | 65 | 65 |

25th anniv. of the Fiji Military Forces campaign in the Solomon Islands and of the posthumous award of the Victoria Cross to Cpl. Sefanaia Sukanaivalu.

Yachting — A59

Designs: 4c, Javelin. 20c, Winners and South Pacific Games medal.

***Perf. 14½x14***

**1969, Aug. 18 Photo. Wmk. 314**

| | | | | |
|---|---|---|---|---|
| *280* | A59 | 4c red, brn & blk | 10 | 10 |
| *281* | A59 | 8c blue & black | 22 | 22 |
| *282* | A59 | 20c olive grn, blk & ocher | 55 | 55 |

3rd South Pacific Games, Port Moresby, Papua New Guinea, Aug. 13-23.

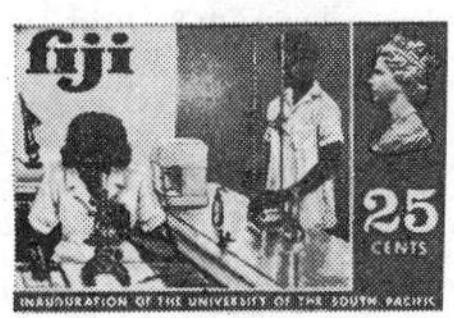

Students in Laboratory — A60

Designs: 2c, Map of South Pacific and mortarboard. 8c, Site of University at Royal New Zealand Air Force Seaplane Station, Laucala Bay, RNZAF badge and Sunderland flying boat.

**1969, Nov. 10 *Perf. 14x14½***

| | | | | |
|---|---|---|---|---|
| *283* | A60 | 2c multicolored | 7 | 7 |
| *284* | A60 | 8c red & multi | 22 | 22 |
| *285* | A60 | 25c dark grn & multi | 70 | 70 |

Inauguration of the University of the South Pacific, Laucala Bay, Suva.

Nos. 261, 268 and 271 Overprinted: "ROYAL VISIT / 1970."

**1970, Mar. 4 *Perf. 13½, 14***

| | | | | |
|---|---|---|---|---|
| *286* | A55 | 2c multicolored | 9 | 9 |
| *287* | A56 | 10c multicolored | 35 | 35 |
| *288* | A55 | 25c multicolored | 90 | 90 |

Visit of Queen Elizabeth II, Prince Philip and Princess Anne, Mar. 4-5.

Nuns Sitting under Chaulmoogra Tree, and Chaulmoogra Fruit — A61

Designs: 10c, Paintings by Semisi Maya (former patient). No. 290, Cascade, vert. No. 291, Sea urchins, vert. 30c, Aerial view of Makogai Hospital.

***Perf. 14x14½, 14½x14***

**1970, May 25 Photo. Wmk. 314**

| | | | | |
|---|---|---|---|---|
| *289* | A61 | 2c brt pink & multi | 6 | 6 |
| *290* | A61 | 10c gray grn & blk | 28 | 28 |
| *291* | A61 | 10c blue, car & blk | 28 | 28 |
| *292* | A61 | 30c orange & multi | 75 | 75 |

Closing of the Leprosy Hospital on Makogai Island in 1969. Nos. 290-291 printed se-tenant.

Abel Tasman and Ship's Log, 1643 — A62

Designs: 3c, Capt. James Cook and "Endeavorur." 8c, Capt. William Bligh and longboat, 1789. 25c, Man of Fiji and Fijian ocean-going canoe.

***Perf. 13x12½***

**1970, Aug. 18 Litho. Wmk. 314**

| | | | | |
|---|---|---|---|---|
| *293* | A62 | 2c blue grn & multi | 28 | 14 |
| *294* | A62 | 3c gray grn & multi | 55 | 20 |
| *295* | A62 | 8c multicolored | 1.10 | 70 |
| *296* | A62 | 25c dull lil & multi | 3.25 | 2.25 |

Discoverers and explorers of Fiji Islands.

King Cakobau and Cession Stone at Lavuka A63

Designs: 3c, Chinese, Fijian, Indian and European children. 10c, Prime Minister Ratu Sir Kamisese Mara and flag of Fiji. 25c, Fijian male dancer and Indian female dancer.

**1970, Oct. 10 Wmk. 314 *Perf. 14***

| | | | | |
|---|---|---|---|---|
| *297* | A63 | 2c multicolored | 6 | 5 |
| *298* | A63 | 3c multicolored | 9 | 8 |
| *299* | A63 | 10c multicolored | 32 | 26 |
| *300* | A63 | 25c multicolored | 90 | 65 |

Fijian independence.

Fiji Nos. 1 and 3 — A64

Designs: 15c, Fiji Nos. 15, 44, 59, 81, 127 and 166. 20c, Fiji Times Office, Levuka, and Gerneral Post Office, Suva.

**1970, Nov. 2 Photo. *Perf. 14½x14***

**Size: 35x21mm**

| | | | | |
|---|---|---|---|---|
| *301* | A64 | 4c multicolored | 10 | 10 |

**Size: 60x21½mm**

| | | | | |
|---|---|---|---|---|
| *302* | A64 | 15c multicolored | 45 | 45 |

**Size: 35x21mm**

| | | | | |
|---|---|---|---|---|
| *303* | A64 | 20c multicolored | 70 | 70 |

Centenary of first postage stamps of Fiji.

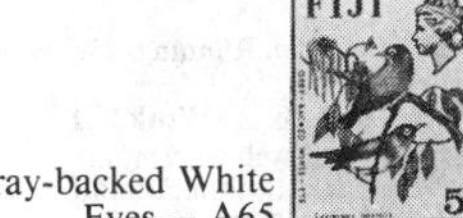

Gray-backed White Eyes — A65

For unused stamps, more recent issues are valued as never hinged, with the beginning point determined on a country-by-country basis. Notes to show the beginning points are prominently placed in the text.

Yellow-breasted Musk Parrots — A66

Designs: 1c, Cirrhopetalum umbellatum. 2c, Cardinal honey eaters. 3c, Calanthe furcata. 4c, Bulbophyllum. 6c, Phaius tancarvilliae. 8c, Blue-crested broadbills. 10c, Acanthephippium vitiense. 15c, Dendrobium tokai. 20c, Slaty flycatchers. 25c, Kandavu honey eaters. 30c, Dendrobium gordonii. 50c, White-throated pigeon. $1, Collared lories (kula). $2, Dendrobium platygastrium. (Orchids shown on 1c, 3c, 4c, 6c, 10c, 15c, 30c, $2.)

**Wmk. 314 Upright**

**1971-73 Litho. *Perf. 13½x14***

*305* A65 1c blk & multi ('72) 6 5
*306* A65 2c carmine & multi 12 9
*307* A65 3c multi ('72) 20 14
*308* A65 4c blk & multi ('72) 26 20
*309* A65 5c brown & multi 42 26
*310* A65 6c lt bl & multi ('72) 45 30
*311* A65 8c black & multi 52 35
*312* A65 10c multi ('72) 55 38
*313* A56 15c multi ('72) 75 55
*314* A65 20c gray & multi 95 60

***Perf. 14***

*315* A66 25c sepia & multi 1.50 95
*316* A66 30c grn & multi ('72) 1.90 95
*317* A66 40c blue & multi 2.50 1.50
*318* A66 50c gray & multi 3.00 1.90
*319* A66 $1 red & multi 6.25 3.75
*320* A66 $2 multi ('72) 12.50 7.25
*Nos. 305-320 (16)* 31.93 19.22

**1972-74 Wmk. 314 Sideways**

*306c* A65 2c car & multi ('73) 16 12
*307a* A65 3c dk brn & multi ('73) 24 16
*308a* A65 4c black & multi ('73) 28 18
*309a* A65 5c brown & multi ('73) 32 24
*310a* A65 6c lt bl & multi ('73) 38 28
*311a* A65 8c black & multi ('73) 52 38
*313a* A65 15c emer & multi ('73) 95 70
*314a* A65 20c gray & multi 1.40 95
*315a* A66 25c sepia & multi ('73) 1.65 1.10
*317a* A66 40c blue & multi ('74) 2.75 1.90
*318a* A66 50c gray & multi ('74) 3.75 2.25
*319a* A66 $1 red & multi 7.00 4.75
*320a* A66 $2 car rose & multi 14.00 9.25
*Nos. 306c-320a (13)* 33.40 22.26

**1975-77 Wmk. 373 Same Colors**

*305b* A65 1c 15 10
*306d* A65 2c 18 14
*307b* A65 3c 25 20
*308b* A65 4c ('76) 25 20
*309b* A65 5c 30 24
*310b* A65 6c ('76) 35 28
*311b* A65 8c ('76) 50 35
*312b* A65 10c 80 60
*313b* A65 15c ('76) 1.25 90
*314b* A65 20c ('77) 1.50 1.00
*316b* A66 30c ('76) 2.50 1.75
*317b* A66 40c ('76) 2.25 1.50
*318b* A66 50c ('76) 2.75 2.00
*319b* A66 $1 ('76) 6.00 4.50
*320b* A66 $2 ('76) 12.00 9.00
*Nos. 305b-320b (15)* 31.03 22.76

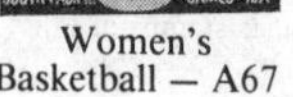

Women's Basketball — A67

Community Education — A68

Designs: 10c, Running. 25c, Weight lifting.

**1971, Sept. 6 Wmk. 314 *Perf. 14***

*321* A67 8c yellow & multi 30 30
*322* A67 10c lt ultra & multi 35 35
*323* A67 25c lt grn & multi 90 90

4th South Pacific Games, Papeete, French Polynesia, Sept. 8-19.

**1972, Feb. 7**

Designs: 4c, Public health. 50c, Economic growth (farm scenes).

*324* A68 2c brt rose & multi 6 6
*325* A68 4c gray & multi 12 12
*326* A68 50c brt blue & multi 1.50 1.50

South Pacific Commission, 25th anniv.

Arts Festival Emblem — A69

Rugby — A70

**1972, Apr. 10**

*327* A69 10c blue, org & black 32 32

South Pacific Festival of Arts, May 6-20.

**Silver Wedding Issue, 1972**

Common Design Type

Design: Queen Elizabeth II, Prince Philip, flowers and shells.

***Perf. 14x14½***

**1972, Nov. 20 Photo. Wmk. 314**

*328* CD324 10c sl grn & multi 28 28
*329* CD324 25c red lil & multi 60 60

**1973, Mar. 9 Photo. *Perf. 14***

*330* A70 2c shown 9 9
*331* A70 8c Tackle 38 38
*332* A70 25c Kicking ball 1.10 1.10

60th anniversary of Fiji Rugby Union.

Forestry Development — A71

Development projects: 8c, Irrigation of rice field. 10c, Low income housing. 25c, Highway construction.

**1973, July 23 *Perf. 14***

*333* A71 5c multicolored 16 16
*334* A71 8c multicolored 22 22
*335* A71 10c multicolored 30 30
*336* A71 25c multicolored 80 80

Holy Family — A72

Runners — A73

Festivals: 10c, Diwali (Candles; Indian New Year). 20c, Id-Ul-Fitar (Friendly greeting and mosque; Moslem, Ramadan). 25c, Chinese New Year (dragon dance).

**1973, Oct. 26 *Perf. 14x14½***

*337* A72 3c blue & multi 14 14
*338* A72 10c purple & multi 32 32
*339* A72 20c emer & multi 65 65
*340* A72 25c red & multi 95 95

Festivals celebrated by various groups in Fiji.

**1974, Jan. 7**

*341* A73 3c shown 8 8
*342* A73 8c Boxing 18 18
*343* A73 50c Lawn bowling 2.25 1.25

10th British Commonwealth Games, Christchurch, N.Z., Jan. 24-Feb. 2.

Centenary of Cricket in Fiji — A74

Designs: 3c, Bowler. 25c, Batsman and wicketkeeper. 40c, Fielder (horiz.).

***Perf. 14x14½, 14½x14***

**1974, Feb. 21 Litho.**

*344* A74 3c multicolored 18 8
*345* A74 25c multicolored 1.25 65
*346* A74 40c multicolored 2.00 1.10

Mailman and UPU Emblem A75

Designs (UPU Emblem and): 8c, Loading mail on ship. 30c, Post office and truck. 50c, Jet.

**1974, May 22 Wmk. 314 *Perf. 14***

*347* A75 3c org & multi 16 12
*348* A75 8c multicolored 38 30
*349* A75 30c lt bl & multi 90 70
*350* A75 50c multicolored 1.50 1.25

Centenary of the Universal Postal Union.

Cub Scouts A76

Designs: 10c, Boy Scouts reading map. 40c, Scouts and Fiji flag (vert.).

**1974, Aug. 30**

*351* A76 3c multicolored 12 12
*352* A76 10c multicolored 45 45
*353* A76 40c multicolored 1.65 1.65

First National Boy Scout Jamboree, Lautoka, Viti Levu Island.

Cakobau Club and Flag — A77

King Cakobau, Queen Victoria A78

Design: 50c, Signing ceremony at Levuka.

**1974, Oct. 9 Litho. *Perf. 13½x13***

*354* A77 3c multicolored 10 10
*355* A78 8c multicolored 25 25
*356* A78 50c multicolored 1.65 1.65

Deed of Cession, cent. and 4th anniv. of independence.

Diwali, Hindu Festival of Lights — A79

Designs: 15c, Id-Ul-Fitar (women exchanging greetings under moon). 25c, Chinese New Year (girl twirling streamer, and fireworks). 30c, Christmas (man and woman singing hymns, and star).

**1975, Oct. 31 Wmk. 373 *Perf. 14***

*357* A79 3c black & multi 9 9
*358* A79 15c black & multi 45 45
*359* A79 25c black & multi 75 75
*360* A79 30c black & multi 90 90
*a* Souvenir sheet of 4 5.50 4.25

Festivals celebrated by various groups in Fiji. No. 360a contains one each of Nos. 357-360; multicolored candles in black margin with symbols of each group and inscription. Size: 120x100mm.

Steam Locomotive No. 21 — A80

Sugar mill trains: 15c, Diesel locomotive No. 8. 20c, Diesel locomotive No. 1. 30c, Free passenger train.

**1976, Jan. 26 Litho. *Perf. 14½***

*361* A80 4c yel & multi 24 16
*362* A80 15c sal & multi 65 50
*363* A80 20c multicolored 85 65
*364* A80 30c blue & multi 1.25 1.10

Fiji Blind Society and Rotary Emblems A81

Design: 25c, Ambulance and Rotary emblems.

***Perf. 13x13½***

**1976, Mar. 26 Wmk. 373**

*365* A81 10c lt grn, brn ultra 32 32
*366* A81 25c multicolored 80 80

Rotary Intl. of Fiji, 40th anniv.

De Havilland Drover — A82

Planes: 15c, BAC One-Eleven. 25c, Hawker-Siddeley 748. 30c, Britten Norman Trislander.

**1976, Sept. 1 Litho. *Perf. 14***

*367* A82 4c multicolored 22 22
*368* A82 15c multicolored 60 42
*369* A82 25c multicolored 1.40 70
*370* A82 30c multicolored 1.65 90

Fiji air service, 25th anniversary.

Queen's Visit, 1970 — A83

Designs: 25c, King Edward's Chair. 30c, Queen wearing cloth-of-gold supertunica.

**1977, Feb. 7 Litho. *Perf. 14x13½***

| | | | | |
|---|---|---|---|---|
| *371* | A83 | 10c silver & multi | 16 | 16 |
| *372* | A83 | 25c silver & multi | 42 | 42 |
| *373* | A83 | 30c silver & multi | 60 | 60 |

25th anniv. of reign of Elizabeth II.

World Map, Sinusoidal Projection — A84

Design: 30c, Map showing Fiji Islands.

**Wmk. 373**

**1977, Apr. 12 Litho. *Perf. 14½***

| | | | | |
|---|---|---|---|---|
| *374* | A84 | 4c multicolored | 14 | 12 |
| *375* | A84 | 30c multicolored | 1.00 | 70 |

First Joint Council of Ministers Conference of the European Economic Community (EEC) and of African, Caribbean and Pacific States (ACP).

Red Hibiscus A85

Designs: 15c, Orange hibiscus. 30c, Pink hibiscus. 35c, Yellow hibiscus.

**1977, Aug. 27 Wmk. 373 *Perf. 14***

| | | | | |
|---|---|---|---|---|
| *376* | A85 | 4c lilac & multi | 14 | 12 |
| *377* | A85 | 15c lilac & multi | 42 | 35 |
| *378* | A85 | 30c lilac & multi | 90 | 70 |
| *379* | A85 | 35c lilac & multi | 1.10 | 90 |

Fiji Hibiscus Festival, 21st anniversary.

Drua, Double Canoe A86

Canoes: 15c, Tabilai. 25c, Takia, dugout outrigger canoe. 40c, Camakau.

**1977, Nov. 7 Litho. *Perf. 14½***

| | | | | |
|---|---|---|---|---|
| *380* | A86 | 4c multicolored | 14 | 12 |
| *381* | A86 | 15c multicolored | 42 | 35 |
| *382* | A86 | 25c multicolored | 70 | 60 |
| *383* | A86 | 40c multicolored | 1.10 | 1.00 |

**Elizabeth II Coronation Anniversary Issue**

**Souvenir Sheet**

Common Design Types

**Unwmk.**

**1978, Apr. 21 Litho. *Perf. 15***

| | | | |
|---|---|---|---|
| *384* | Sheet of 6 | 3.25 | 3.25 |
| *a.* | CD326 25c White hart of Richard II | 52 | 52 |
| *b.* | CD327 25c Elizabeth II | 52 | 52 |
| *c.* | CD328 25c Banded iguana | 52 | 52 |

No. 384 contains 2 se-tenant strips of Nos. 348a-348c, separated by horizontal gutter with commemorative and descriptive inscriptions and showing central part of coronation procession with coach. Size: 100x135mm.

Southern Cross on Naselai Beach A87

Designs: 4c, Fiji Defence Force surrounding Southern Cross. 25c, Wright Flyer. 30c, Bristol F2B.

**1978, June 26 Wmk. 373 *Perf. 14½***

| | | | | |
|---|---|---|---|---|
| *385* | A87 | 4c multicolored | 15 | 12 |
| *386* | A87 | 15c multicolored | 42 | 32 |
| *387* | A87 | 25c multicolored | 75 | 60 |
| *388* | A87 | 30c multicolored | 1.10 | 75 |

50th anniv. of Kingsford-Smith's Trans-Pacific flight, May 31-June 10, 1928 (4c, 15c); 75th anniv. of Wright brothers' first powered flight, Dec. 17, 1903 (25c); 60th anniv. of Royal Air Force, Apr. 1, 1918 (30c).

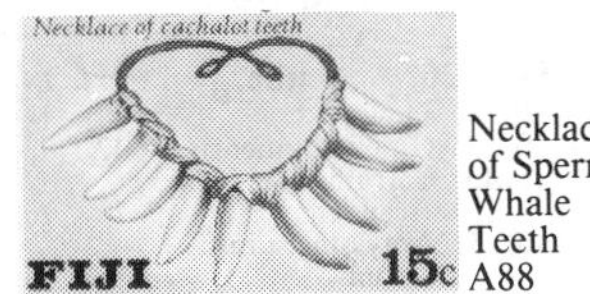

Necklace of Sperm Whale Teeth A88

Fiji artifacts: 4c, Wooden oil dish in shape of man (vert.). 25c, Twin water bottles. 30c, Carved throwing club (Ula; vert.).

**1978, Aug. 14 Litho. *Perf. 14***

| | | | | |
|---|---|---|---|---|
| *389* | A88 | 4c multicolored | 8 | 8 |
| *390* | A88 | 15c multicolored | 25 | 25 |
| *391* | A88 | 25c multicolored | 45 | 45 |
| *392* | A88 | 30c multicolored | 55 | 55 |

Christmas Wreath and Candles A89

Festivals: 15c, Diwali (oil lamps). 25c, Id-Ul-Fitr (fruit, coffeepot and cups). 40c, Chinese New Year (paper dragon).

**1978, Oct. 30 *Perf. 14***

| | | | | |
|---|---|---|---|---|
| *393* | A89 | 4c multicolored | 8 | 8 |
| *394* | A89 | 15c multicolored | 30 | 30 |
| *395* | A89 | 25c multicolored | 48 | 48 |
| *396* | A89 | 40c multicolored | 80 | 80 |

Banded Iguana — A90

Endangered species and Wildlife Fund emblem: 15c, Tree frog. 25c, Long-legged warbler. 30c, Pink-billed parrot finch.

**1979, Mar. 19 Litho. Wmk. 373**

| | | | | |
|---|---|---|---|---|
| *397* | A90 | 4c multicolored | 12 | 12 |
| *398* | A90 | 15c multicolored | 45 | 45 |
| *399* | A90 | 25c multicolored | 70 | 70 |
| *400* | A90 | 30c multicolored | 85 | 85 |

Indian Women Making Music A91

Designs: 15c, Indian men sitting around kava bowl. 30c, Indian sugar cane and houses. 40c, Sailing ship Leonidas and map of South Pacific.

**1979, May 11 Wmk. 373 *Perf. 14***

| | | | | |
|---|---|---|---|---|
| *401* | A91 | 4c multicolored | 8 | 8 |
| *402* | A91 | 15c multicolored | 24 | 24 |
| *403* | A91 | 30c multicolored | 48 | 48 |
| *404* | A91 | 40c multicolored | 65 | 65 |

Arrival of Indians as indentured laborers, cent.

Soccer A92

Designs (Games Emblem and): 15c, Rugby. 30c, Tennis. 40c, Weight lifting.

**1979, July 2 Litho. *Perf. 14***

| | | | | |
|---|---|---|---|---|
| *405* | A92 | 4c multicolored | 8 | 8 |
| *406* | A92 | 15c multicolored | 30 | 30 |
| *407* | A92 | 30c multicolored | 60 | 60 |
| *408* | A92 | 40c multicolored | 80 | 80 |

6th South Pacific Games.

Old Town Hall, Suva A93

Designs: 2c, Dudley Church, Suva. 3c, Telecommunications building, Suva. 4c, 5c, Lautoka Mosque. 6c, GPO, Suva. 8c, 12c, Levuka Public School. 10c, Visitors' Bureau, Suva. 15c, Colonial War Memorial Hospital Suva. 18c, Labasa Sugar Mill. 20c, Rewa Bridge, Nausori. 30c Sacred Heart Cathedral, Suva (vert.). 35c Grand Pacific Hotel, Suva. 45c, Shiva Temple, Suva. 50c Serua Island Village. $1, Solo Lighthouse (vert.). $2, Baker memorial Hall, Nausori. $5, Government House.

***Perf. 14, 14x13½ ($1), 13½x14 ($2, $5)***

**1979-88 Wmk. 373, 384 (8c)**

| | | | | |
|---|---|---|---|---|
| *409* | A93 | 1c multicolored | 5 | 5 |
| *410* | A93 | 2c multicolored | 5 | 5 |
| *a.* | | Wmk. 384 ('86) | 5 | 5 |
| *411* | A93 | 3c multicolored | 5 | 5 |
| *411A* | A93 | 4c multi ('88) | 7 | 7 |
| *412* | A93 | 5c multi ('80) | 8 | 8 |
| *413* | A93 | 6c multi ('80) | 10 | 10 |
| *413A* | A93 | 8c multi ('86) | 14 | 14 |
| *414* | A93 | 10c multicolored | 18 | 18 |
| *415* | A93 | 12c multicolored | 20 | 20 |
| *416* | A93 | 15c multicolored | 26 | 26 |
| *417* | A93 | 18c multi ('80) | 30 | 30 |
| *418* | A93 | 20c multicolored | 35 | 35 |
| *419* | A93 | 30c multicolored | 40 | 40 |
| *420* | A93 | 35c multi ('80) | 48 | 48 |
| *421* | A93 | 45c multi ('80) | 60 | 60 |
| *422* | A93 | 50c multi ('80) | 70 | 70 |

**Size: 29x45mm, 45x29mm**

| | | | | |
|---|---|---|---|---|
| *423* | A93 | $1 multi ('80) | 1.40 | 1.40 |
| *424* | A93 | $2 multi ('80) | 2.75 | 2.75 |

**Size: 48x31mm**

| | | | | |
|---|---|---|---|---|
| *425* | A93 | $5 multicolored | 6.75 | 6.75 |
| | | *Nos. 409-425 (19)* | 14.91 | 14.91 |

Nos. 410, 412 and 413 reissued inscribed 1983.

Southern Cross, 1873, London 1980 Emblem A94

**Wmk. 373**

**1980, Apr. 28 Litho. *Perf. 13½***

| | | | | |
|---|---|---|---|---|
| *426* | A94 | 6c shown | 9 | 9 |
| *427* | A94 | 20c Levuka, 1910 | 32 | 32 |
| *428* | A94 | 45c Matua, 1936 | 70 | 70 |
| *429* | A94 | 50c Oronsay, 1951 | 80 | 80 |

London 80 Intl. Stamp Exhib., May 6-14.

Sovi Bay A95

**1980, Aug. 18 *Perf. 13½x14***

| | | | | |
|---|---|---|---|---|
| *430* | A95 | 6c shown | 9 | 9 |
| *431* | A95 | 20c Yanuca Island, evening scene | 30 | 30 |
| *432* | A95 | 45c Dravuni Beach | 65 | 65 |
| *433* | A95 | 50c Wakaya Island | 75 | 75 |

Opening of Parliament, 1979 — A96

**1980, Oct. 6 Litho. *Perf. 13***

| | | | | |
|---|---|---|---|---|
| *434* | A96 | 6c shown | 8 | 8 |
| *435* | A96 | 20c Coat of arms, vert. | 28 | 28 |
| *436* | A96 | 45c Fiji flag | 60 | 60 |
| *437* | A96 | 50c Queen Elizabeth II, vert. | 70 | 70 |

Independence, 10th anniversary.

Coastal Scene, by Semisi Maya A97
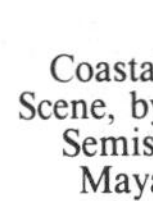

International Year of the Disabled: Paintings and portrait of disabled artist Semisi Maya.

**1981, Apr. 21 Wmk. 373 *Perf. 14***

| | | | | |
|---|---|---|---|---|
| *438* | A97 | 6c shown | 8 | 8 |
| *439* | A97 | 35c Underwater Scene | 50 | 50 |
| *440* | A97 | 50c Maya Painting, vert. | 70 | 70 |
| *441* | A97 | 60c Peacock, vert. | 85 | 85 |

**Royal Wedding Issue**

Common Design Type

**1981, July 22 Wmk. 373 *Perf. 14***

| | | | | |
|---|---|---|---|---|
| *442* | CD331 | 6c Bouquet | 8 | 8 |
| *443* | CD331 | 45c Charles | 60 | 60 |
| *444* | CD331 | $1 Couple | 1.25 | 1.25 |

Operator Assistance Center A98

**1981, Aug. 7 Litho. *Perf. 14***

| | | | | |
|---|---|---|---|---|
| *445* | A98 | 6c shown | 10 | 10 |
| *446* | A98 | 35c Microwave station, map | 65 | 65 |
| *447* | A98 | 50c Satellite earth station | 90 | 90 |
| *448* | A98 | 60c Cableship Retriever | 1.10 | 1.10 |

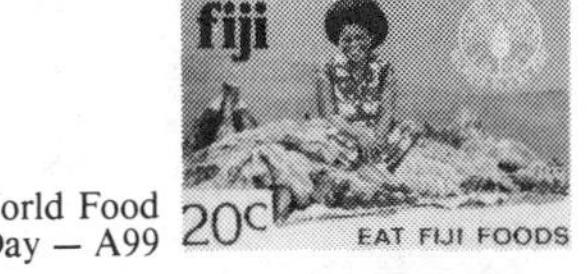

World Food Day — A99

**1981, Sept. 21 Litho. *Perf. 14½x14***

| | | | | |
|---|---|---|---|---|
| *449* | A99 | 20c multicolored | 40 | 40 |

Ratu Sir Lala Sukuna, First Legislative Council Speaker
A100

**1981, Oct. 19 Litho. *Perf. 14***

| | | | |
|---|---|---|---|
| *450* A100 6c | shown | 9 | 9 |
| *451* A100 35c | Mace, flag | 55 | 55 |
| *452* A100 50c | Suva Civic Center | 75 | 75 |

**Souvenir Sheet**

| | | | |
|---|---|---|---|
| *453* A100 60c | Emblem, participants' flags | 90 | 90 |

27th Commonwealth Parliamentary Assoc. Conf., Suva. No. 453 has multicolored margin showing participants' flags. Size: 73x53mm.

World War II Aircraft
A101

**1981, Dec. 7 Litho. *Perf. 14***

| | | | |
|---|---|---|---|
| *454* A101 6c | Bell P-39 Aircobra | 10 | 10 |
| *455* A101 18c | Consolidated PBY-5 Catalina | 32 | 32 |
| *456* A101 35c | Curtiss P-40 Warhawk | 65 | 65 |
| *457* A101 60c | Short Singapore | 1.00 | 1.00 |

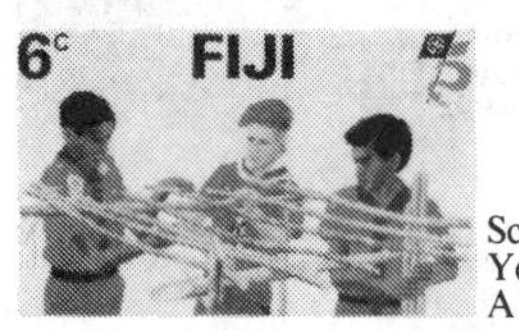

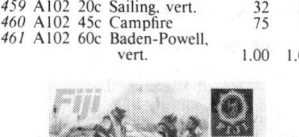

Scouting Year
A102

**1982, Feb. 22 Litho. *Perf. 14½***

| | | | |
|---|---|---|---|
| *458* A102 6c | Building | 10 | 10 |
| *459* A102 20c | Sailing, vert. | 32 | 32 |
| *460* A102 45c | Campfire | 75 | 75 |
| *461* A102 60c | Baden-Powell, vert. | 1.00 | 1.00 |

Disciplined Forces — A103

**1982, May 10 Wmk. 373 *Perf. 14***

| | | | |
|---|---|---|---|
| *462* A103 12c | U.N. checkpoint | 20 | 20 |
| *463* A103 30c | Construction project | 50 | 50 |
| *464* A103 40c | Police, car | 65 | 65 |
| *465* A103 70c | Navy ship | 1.25 | 1.25 |

1982 World Cup
A104

**1982, June 15 Litho. *Perf. 14***

| | | | |
|---|---|---|---|
| *466* A104 6c | Fiji Soccer Assoc. emblem | 10 | 10 |
| *467* A104 18c | Flag, ball | 30 | 30 |
| *468* A104 50c | Stadium | 80 | 80 |
| *469* A104 90c | Emblem | 1.50 | 1.50 |

**Princess Diana Issue**
Common Design Type

**1982, July 1 *Perf. 14½x14***

| | | | |
|---|---|---|---|
| *470* CD333 20c | Arms | 32 | 32 |
| *471* CD333 35c | Diana | 55 | 55 |
| *472* CD333 45c | Wedding | 70 | 70 |
| *473* CD333 $1 | Portrait | 1.50 | 1.50 |

October Royal Visit — A105

**1982, Nov. 1 Litho. *Perf. 14***

| | | | |
|---|---|---|---|
| *474* A105 6c | Duke of Edinburgh | 10 | 10 |
| *475* A105 45c | Elizabeth II | 80 | 80 |

**Souvenir Sheet**

| | | | |
|---|---|---|---|
| *476* | Sheet of 3 | 2.75 | 2.75 |
| *c* A105 $1 | Britannia | 1.65 | 1.65 |

No. 476 contains Nos. 474-475 and 476c, Size of No. 476: 128x89mm.

Christmas
A106

**1982, Nov. 22 *Perf. 14x14½***

| | | | |
|---|---|---|---|
| *477* A106 6c | Holy Family | 12 | 12 |
| *478* A106 20c | Adoration of the Kings | 40 | 40 |
| *479* A106 35c | Carolers | 75 | 75 |

**Souvenir Sheet**

| | | | |
|---|---|---|---|
| *480* A106 $1 | Faith, from The Three Virtues, by Raphael | 2.00 | 2.00 |

Red-throated Lory — A107

Parrots.

**1983, Feb. 14 Litho. *Perf. 14***

| | | | |
|---|---|---|---|
| *481* A107 20c | shown | 45 | 45 |
| *482* A107 40c | Blue-crowned lory | 95 | 95 |
| *483* A107 55c | Sulphur-breasted musk parrot | 1.25 | 1.25 |
| *484* A107 70c | Red-breasted musk parrot | 1.65 | 1.65 |

**Commonwealth Day Issue**
Common Design Type

**1983, Mar. 14**

| | | | |
|---|---|---|---|
| *485* CD334 8c | Traditional house | 14 | 14 |
| *486* CD334 25c | Barefoot firewalkers | 42 | 42 |
| *487* CD334 50c | Sugar cane crop | 85 | 85 |
| *488* CD334 80c | Kava Yagona ceremony | 1.40 | 1.40 |

Manned Flight Bicentenary — A109

**1983, July 18 Wmk. 373 *Perf. 14***

| | | | |
|---|---|---|---|
| *489* A109 8c | Montgolfiere, 1783 | 14 | 14 |
| *490* A109 20c | Wright Flyer | 35 | 35 |
| *491* A109 25c | DC-3 | 42 | 42 |
| *492* A109 40c | DeHavilland Comet | 70 | 70 |
| *493* A109 50c | Boeing 747 | 85 | 85 |
| *494* A109 58c | Columbia space shuttle | 1.00 | 1.00 |
| | *Nos. 489-494 (6)* | 3.46 | 3.46 |

Cordia Subcordata
A110

Earth Satellite Station, Fijian Playing Lali
A111

Flowers.

**1983, Sept. 26 Litho. *Perf. 14***

| | | | |
|---|---|---|---|
| *495* A110 8c | shown | 14 | 14 |
| *496* A110 25c | Gmelina vitiensis | 42 | 42 |
| *497* A110 40c | Carruthersia scandens | 70 | 70 |
| *498* A110 $1 | Amylotheca insularum | 1.75 | 1.75 |

See Nos. 505-508.

***Perf. 14x13½***

**1983, Nov. 7 Litho. Wmk. 373**

| | | | |
|---|---|---|---|
| *499* A111 50c | multicolored | 85 | 85 |

Dacryopinax S spathularia
A112

Various fungi.

***Perf. 14x13½, 13½x14***

**1984, Jan. 9 Wmk. 373**

| | | | |
|---|---|---|---|
| *500* A112 8c | shown | 18 | 18 |
| *501* A112 15c | Podoscypha involuta | 32 | 32 |
| *502* A112 40c | Lentinus squarrosulus | 85 | 85 |
| *503* A112 50c | Scleroderma flavidum | 1.10 | 1.10 |
| *504* A112 $1 | Phillipsia domingensis | 2.00 | 2.00 |
| | *Nos. 500-504 (5)* | 4.45 | 4.45 |

Flower Type of 1983

**1984 Litho. *Perf. 14x14½***

| | | | |
|---|---|---|---|
| *505* A110 15c | Pseuderanthemum laxiflorum | 28 | 28 |
| *506* A110 20c | Storkiella vitiensis | 38 | 38 |
| *507* A110 50c | Paphia vitiensis | 95 | 95 |
| *508* A110 70c | Elaeocarpus storkii | 1.25 | 1.25 |

**Lloyd's List Issue**
Common Design Type
***Perf. 14½x14***

**1984, May 7 Wmk. 373**

| | | | |
|---|---|---|---|
| *509* CD335 8c | Tui Lau on reef | 14 | 14 |
| *510* CD335 40c | Tofua | 70 | 70 |
| *511* CD335 55c | Canberra | 1.00 | 1.00 |
| *512* CD335 60c | Suva Wharf | 1.10 | 1.10 |

**Souvenir Sheet**

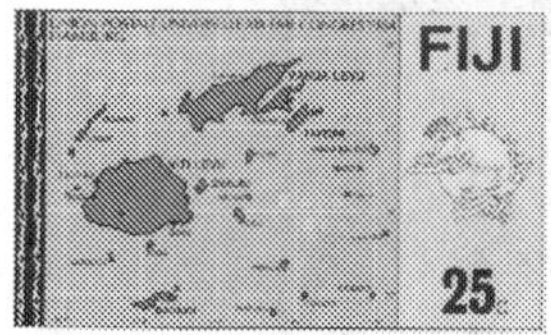


1984 UPU Congress — A113

**1984, June 14 Litho. *Perf. 14½***

| | | | |
|---|---|---|---|
| *513* A113 25c | Map | 52 | 52 |

Size: 78x64mm.

Ausipex '84 — A114

**1984, Sept. 17 Wmk. 373 *Perf. 14***

| | | | |
|---|---|---|---|
| *514* A114 8c | Yalavou cattle | 15 | 15 |
| *515* A114 25c | Wailoa Power Station, vert. | 48 | 48 |
| *516* A114 40c | Boeing 737 | 75 | 75 |
| *517* A114 $1 | Cargo ship Fua Kavenga | 1.90 | 1.90 |

Christmas
A115

**1984, Nov. 5 Litho. *Perf. 14***

| | | | |
|---|---|---|---|
| *518* A115 8c | Church on hill | 15 | 15 |
| *519* A115 20c | Sailing | 38 | 38 |
| *520* A115 25c | Santa, children, tree | 45 | 45 |
| *521* A115 40c | Going to church | 75 | 75 |
| *522* A115 $1 | Family, tree, vert. | 1.90 | 1.90 |
| | *Nos. 518-522 (5)* | 3.63 | 3.63 |

Butterflies
A116

**1985, Feb. 4 *Perf. 14***

| | | | |
|---|---|---|---|
| *523* A116 8c | Monarch | 24 | 24 |
| *524* A116 25c | Common eggfly | 75 | 75 |
| *525* A116 40c | Long-tailed blue, vert. | 1.20 | 1.20 |
| *526* A116 $1 | Meadow argus, vert. | 3.00 | 3.00 |

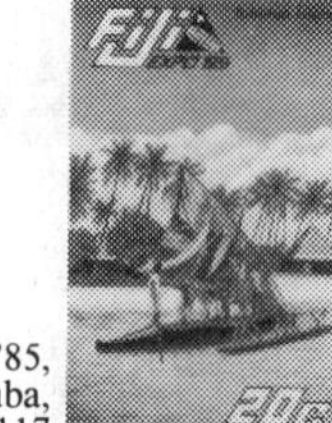


EXPO '85, Tsukuba, Japan — A117

**1985, Mar. 18 Litho. *Perf. 14***

| | | | |
|---|---|---|---|
| *527* A117 20c | Outrigger canoe, Toberua Isl. | 35 | 35 |
| *528* A117 25c | Wainivula Falls | 42 | 42 |
| *529* A117 50c | Mana Island | 85 | 85 |
| *530* A117 $1 | Sawa-I-Lau Caves | 1.75 | 1.75 |

**Queen Mother 85th Birthday Issue**

Common Design type

*Perf. 14½x14*

**1985, June 7** **Wmk. 384**

*531* CD336 8c Holding Prince Andrew 16 16
*532* CD336 25c With Prince Charles 50 50
*533* CD336 40c On Oaks Day, Epsom Races 80 80
*534* CD336 50c Holding Prince Henry 1.00 1.00

**Souvenir Sheet**

*535* CD336 $1 In Royal Wedding Cavalcade, 1981 2.00 2.00

No. 535 has multicolored margin continuing design. Size: 92x74mm.

Shallow Water Fish A118

**1985, Sept. 23** ***Perf. 14½***

*536* A118 40c Horned squirrel fish 70 70
*537* A118 50c Yellow-banded goatfish 85 85
*538* A118 55c Fairy cod 95 95
*539* A118 $1 Peacock rock cod 1.75 1.75

Sea Birds — A119

**1985, Nov. 4** ***Perf. 14***

*540* A119 15c Collared petrel 25 25
*541* A119 20c Lesser frigate bird 35 35
*542* A119 50c Brown booby 85 85
*543* A119 $1 Crested tern 1.75 1.75

**Queen Elizabeth II 60th Birthday Issue**

Common Design Type

Designs: 20c, With the Duke of York at the Royal Tournament, 1936. 25c, On Buckingham Palace balcony, wedding of Princess Margaret and Anthony Armstrong-Jones, 1960. 40c, Inspecting the Guard of Honor, Suva, 1982. 50c, State visit to Luxembourg, 1976. $1, Visiting Crown Agents' offices, 1983.

*Perf. 14x14½*

**1986, Apr. 21** **Litho.** **Wmk. 384**

*544* CD337 20c scar, blk & sil 38 38
*545* CD337 25c ultra & multi 48 48
*546* CD337 40c green & multi 75 75
*547* CD337 50c violet & multi 95 95
*548* CD337 $1 rose vio & multi 1.85 1.85
*Nos. 544-548 (5)* 4.41 4.41

Intl. Peace Year — A120

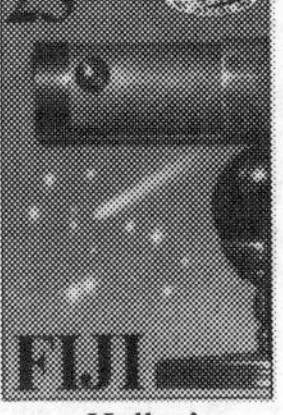


Halley's Comet — A121

**1986, June 23** **Wmk. 373** ***Perf. 14½***

*549* A120 8c shown 15 15
*550* A120 40c Dove 75 75

**1986, July 7** ***Perf. 13½***

*551* A121 25c Newton's reflector telescope 48 48
*552* A121 40c Comet over Lomaiviti 75 75
*553* A121 $1 Comet nucleus, Giotto probe 1.85 1.85

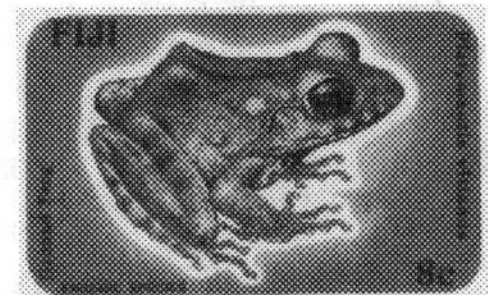


Reptiles and Amphibians — A122

**1986, Aug. 1** ***Perf. 14½***

*554* A122 8c Ground frog 15 15
*555* A122 20c Burrowing snake 38 38
*556* A112 25c Spotted gecko 48 48
*557* A122 40c Crested iguana 75 75
*558* A122 50c Blotched skink 92 92
*559* A122 $1 Speckled skink 1.85 1.85
*Nos. 554-559 (6)* 4.53 4.53

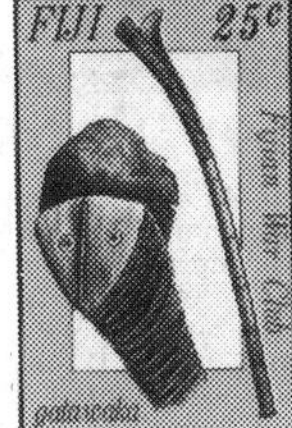


Ancient War Clubs — A123

**1986, Nov. 10** **Wmk. 384** ***Perf. 14***

*560* A123 25c Gatawaka 48 48
*561* A123 40c Siriti 75 75
*562* A123 50c Bulibuli 95 95
*563* A123 $1 Culacula 1.85 1.85

Cone Shells — A124

**1987, Feb. 26** **Litho.** ***Perf. 14x14½***

*564* A124 15c Weasel 28 28
*565* A124 20c Pertusus 38 38
*566* A124 25c Admiral 48 48
*567* A124 40c Leaden 75 75
*568* A124 50c Imperial 92 92
*569* A124 $1 Geography 1.85 1.85
*Nos. 564-569 (6)* 4.66 4.66

**Souvenir Sheet**

Tagimoucia Flower — A125

**1987, Apr. 23** **Wmk. 373** ***Perf. 14½***

*570* A125 $1 multicolored 1.85 1.85

No. 570 has multicolored margin picturing tagimoucia garland.

No. 570 Overprinted with CAPEX '87 Emblem

**1987, June 13**

*571* A125 $1 multicolored 1.85 1.85

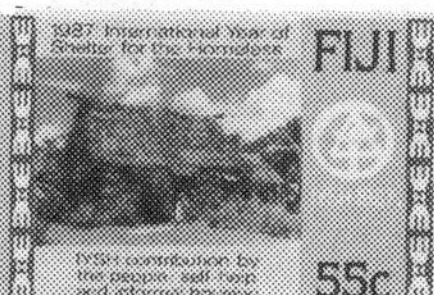


Intl. Year of Shelter for the Homeless A126

**1987, July 20** ***Perf. 14***

*572* A126 55c Hut 1.00 1.00
*573* A126 70c Government housing 1.30 1.30

Beetles A127

**1987, Sept. 7** **Wmk. 384**

*574* A127 20c Bulbogaster ctenostomoides 38 38
*575* A127 25c Paracupta flaviventris 48 48
*576* A127 40c Cerambyrhynchus schoenherri 75 75
*577* A127 50c Rhinoscapha lagopyga 92 92
*578* A127 $1 Xixuthrus heros 1.85 1.85
*Nos. 574-578 (5)* 4.38 4.38

Christmas — A128

**1987, Nov. 19**

*579* A128 8c Holy Family, vert. 12 12
*580* A128 40c Shepherds see star 65 65
*581* A128 50c Three Kings follow star 80 80
*582* A128 $1 Adoration of the Magi 1.60 1.60

World Expo '88, Apr. 30-Oct. 30, Brisbane, Australia A129

**Wmk. 384**

**1988, Apr. 27** **Litho.** ***Perf. 14***

*583* A129 30c Windsurfing 42 42

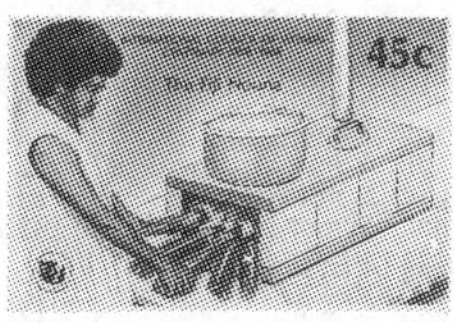


Intl. Council of Women, Cent. A130

**1988, June 14**

*584* A130 45c Fiji Nouna 62 62

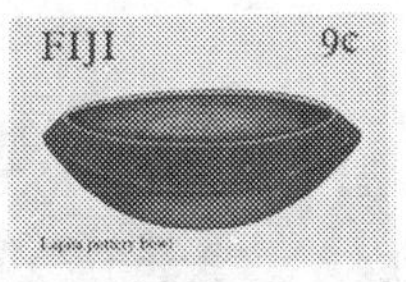


Pottery A131

**Wmk. 384, 373 (69c)**

**1988, Aug. 29** **Litho.** ***Perf. 13½***

*585* A131 9c Lapita (bowl) 14 14
*586* A131 23c Kuro (cooking pot) 35 35
*587* A131 58c Saqa (ritual drinking vessel) 85 85
*588* A131 63c Saqa, diff. 90 90
*589* A131 69c Ramarama (oil lamp) 1.00 1.00
*590* A131 75c Kuro, diff., vert. 1.10 1.10
*Nos. 585-590 (6)* 4.34 4.34

World Wildlife Fund — A132

Tree frogs, *Platymantis vitiensis*, diff.

**1988, Oct. 3** **Wmk. 384** ***Perf. 14***

*591* A132 18c multi 25 25
*592* A132 23c multi, diff. 35 35
*593* A132 30c multi, diff. 42 42
*594* A132 45c multi, diff. 65 65

Indigenous Flowering Plants — A133

**1988, Nov. 21** **Wmk. 373**

*595* A133 9c Dendrobium mohlianum 14 14
*596* A133 30c Dendrobium cattilare 42 42
*597* A133 45c Degeneria vitiensis 62 62
*598* A133 $1 Degeneria roseiflora 1.40 1.40

---

## SEMI-POSTAL STAMPS

**Catalogue values for unused stamps in this section, from this point to the end of the section, are for Never Hinged items.**

Children at Play — SP1

Rugby Player — SP2

*Perf. 13x13½*

**1951, Sept. 17** **Engr.** **Wmk. 4**

*B1* SP1 1p + 1p brown 25 25
*B2* SP2 2p + 1p deep grn 32 32

Bamboo River Raft — SP3

Design: 2½p+½p, Cross of Lorraine.

**1954, Apr. 1** *Perf. 11x11½*

| | | | | |
|---|---|---|---|---|
| *B3* | SP3 | 1½p + ½p green & brn | 25 | 25 |
| *B4* | SP3 | 2½p + ½p black & org | 32 | 32 |

Nos. 269 and 272 Surcharged — HURRICANE RELIEF +5c

**1972, Dec. 4** **Photo.** *Perf. 14, 13½*

| | | | | |
|---|---|---|---|---|
| *B5* | A56 | 15c + 5c multi | 52 | 52 |
| *B6* | A55 | 30c + 10c multi | 1.10 | 1.10 |

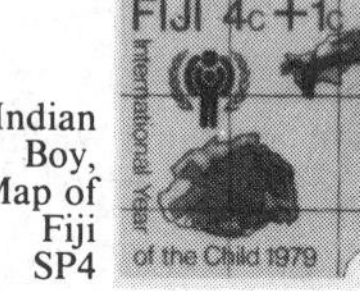


Indian Boy, Map of Fiji SP4

Map of Fiji and: 15c+2c, European girl. 30c+3c, Chinese girl. 40c+4c, Fijian boy.

**Wmk. 373**

**1979, Sept. 17** **Litho.** *Perf. 14½*

| | | | | |
|---|---|---|---|---|
| *B7* | SP4 | 4c + 1c multi | 7 | 7 |
| *B8* | SP4 | 15c + 2c multi | 26 | 26 |
| *B9* | SP4 | 30c + 3c multi | 50 | 50 |
| *B10* | SP4 | 40c + 4c multi | 70 | 70 |

The surtax was for IYC fund.

## POSTAGE DUE STAMPS

D1

D2

D3

**1917** **Unwmk.** **Typeset** *Perf. 11*
**Laid Papers; Without Gum**

| | | | | |
|---|---|---|---|---|
| *J1* | D1 | ½p black | 450.00 | 425.00 |
| *J2* | D2 | ½p black | 500.00 | 300.00 |
| *J3* | D3 | 1p black | 250.00 | 85.00 |
| *J4* | D3 | 2p black | 275.00 | 72.50 |
| *J5* | D3 | 3p black | 400.00 | 100.00 |
| *J6* | D3 | 4p black | 675.00 | 425.00 |
| | | *Nos. J1-J6 (6)* | 2,550. | 1,407. |

There were two printings of the 1 penny stamps. In the first printing the stamps were 25mm. wide including the margins. In the second printing the cliches were set a little closer, and the stamps were 23mm. wide.

D4

D5

**Wmk. 3**

**1918, June 1** **Typo.** *Perf. 14*

| | | | | |
|---|---|---|---|---|
| *J7* | D4 | ½p black | 3.75 | *6.00* |
| *J8* | D4 | 1p black | 3.75 | *4.75* |
| *J9* | D4 | 2p black | 4.75 | *7.25* |
| *J10* | D4 | 3p black | 6.00 | *8.50* |
| *J11* | D4 | 4p black | 7.25 | *12.00* |
| | | *Nos. J7-J11 (5)* | 25.50 | *38.50* |

**1940** **Wmk. 4** *Perf. 12½*

| | | | | |
|---|---|---|---|---|
| *J12* | D5 | 1p bright grn | 1.25 | *4.50* |
| *J13* | D5 | 2p bright grn | 1.40 | *6.25* |
| *J14* | D5 | 3p bright grn | 1.40 | *6.25* |
| *J15* | D5 | 4p bright grn | 2.50 | *10.00* |
| *J16* | D5 | 5p bright grn | 3.25 | *12.00* |
| *J17* | D5 | 6p bright grn | 8.50 | *32.50* |
| *J18* | D5 | 1sh dk carmine | 10.00 | *40.00* |
| *J19* | D5 | 1sh 6p dk carmine | 20.00 | *70.00* |
| | | *Nos. J12-J19 (8)* | 48.30 | *181.50* |

## WAR TAX STAMPS

Regular Issue of 1912-16 Overprinted — WAR STAMP

Die I

**1916** **Wmk. 3** *Perf. 14*

| | | | | |
|---|---|---|---|---|
| *MR1* | A23 | ½p green | 15 | 35 |
| *a.* | | Inverted ovpt. | 400.00 | |
| *b.* | | Double ovpt. | | |
| *MR2* | A23 | 1p scarlet | 35 | 40 |
| *a.* | | 1p carmine | 7.00 | 7.00 |
| *b.* | | Pair, one without overprint | *10,000.* | |
| *c.* | | Inverted ovpt. | 400.00 | |

# FUJEIRA

LOCATION — Oman Peninsula, Arabia, on Persian Gulf.
GOVT. — Sheikdom under British protection.

Fujeira is one of six Persian Gulf sheikdoms to join the United Arab Emirates which proclaimed independence Dec. 2, 1971. See United Arab Emirates.

100 Naye Paise = 1 Rupee

**Catalogue values for all unused stamps in this country are for Never Hinged items.**

Sheik Hamad bin Mohammed al Sharqi and Grebe A1

Designs (Sheik and): 2np, 50np, Arabian oryx. 3np, 70np, Hoopoe. 4np, 1r, Wild ass. 5np, 1.50r, Herons in flight. 10np, 2r, Arabian horses. 15np, 3r, Leopard. 20np, 5r, Camels. 30np, 10r, Hawks.

**Photogravure and Lithographed**
**1964** **Unwmk.** *Perf. 14*
**Size: 36x24mm**

| | | | | |
|---|---|---|---|---|
| *1* | A1 | 1np gold & multi | 5 | 5 |
| *2* | A1 | 2np gold & multi | 5 | 5 |
| *3* | A1 | 3np gold & multi | 6 | 5 |
| *4* | A1 | 4np gold & multi | 5 | 5 |
| *5* | A1 | 5np gold & multi | 8 | 5 |
| *6* | A1 | 10np gold & multi | 5 | 5 |
| *7* | A1 | 15np gold & multi | 5 | 5 |
| *8* | A1 | 20np gold & multi | 5 | 5 |
| *9* | A1 | 30np gold & multi | 15 | 5 |

**Size: 43x28mm**

| | | | | |
|---|---|---|---|---|
| *10* | A1 | 40np gold & multi | 9 | 5 |
| *11* | A1 | 50np gold & multi | 12 | 6 |
| *12* | A1 | 70np gold & multi | 28 | 8 |
| *13* | A1 | 1r gold & multi | 22 | 12 |
| *14* | A1 | 1.50r gold & multi | 65 | 18 |
| *15* | A1 | 2r gold & multi | 45 | 22 |

**Size: 53½x35mm**

| | | | | |
|---|---|---|---|---|
| *16* | A1 | 3r gold & multi | 65 | 32 |
| *17* | A1 | 5r gold & multi | 1.10 | 55 |
| *18* | A1 | 10r gold & multi | 3.50 | 1.10 |
| | | *Nos. 1-18 (18)* | 7.65 | 3.13 |

Dates of issue: Sept. 22, for 1np, 2np, 3np, 4np, 5np, 10np, 15np, 40np, 50np, 1r, 2r and 5r; Nov. 14, for 20np, 30np, 70np, 1.50r, 3r and 10r.

Sheik Hamad and Shot Put A2

Designs (Sheik and): 50np, Discus. 75np, Fencing. 1r, Boxing. 1.50r, Relay race. 2r, Soccer. 3r, Pole vaulting. 5r, Hurdling. 7.50r, Equestrian.

**1964, Dec. 6** *Perf. 14*
**Size: 43x28mm**

| | | | | |
|---|---|---|---|---|
| *19* | A2 | 25np gold & multi | 5 | 5 |
| *20* | A2 | 50np gold & multi | 10 | 5 |
| *21* | A2 | 75np gold & multi | 15 | 6 |
| *22* | A2 | 1r gold & multi | 20 | 9 |
| *23* | A2 | 1.50r gold & multi | 30 | 15 |
| *24* | A2 | 2r gold & multi | 40 | 20 |

**Size: 53½x35mm**

| | | | | |
|---|---|---|---|---|
| *25* | A2 | 3r gold & multi | 60 | 30 |
| *26* | A2 | 5r gold & multi | 1.00 | 50 |
| *27* | A2 | 7.50r gold & multi | 1.50 | 75 |
| | | *Nos. 19-27 (9)* | 4.30 | 2.15 |

Issued to commemorate the 18th Olympic Games, Tokyo, Oct. 10-25, 1964.

John F. Kennedy — A3

John F. Kennedy: 10np, As sailor in the Pacific. 15np, As naval lieutenant. 20np, On speaker's rostrum. 25np, Sailing with family. 50np, With crowd of people. 1r, with Mrs. Kennedy and Lyndon B. Johnson. 2r, With Dwight D. Eisenhower on White House porch. 3r, With Mrs. Kennedy and Caroline. 5r, Portrait.

**1965, Feb. 23** **Photo.** *Perf. 13½*
**Size: 29x44mm**
**Black Design with Gold Inscriptions**

| | | | | |
|---|---|---|---|---|
| *28* | A3 | 5np pale gray | 5 | 5 |
| *29* | A3 | 10np pale yel | 5 | 5 |
| *30* | A3 | 15np pink | 5 | 5 |
| *31* | A3 | 20np pale grnsh gray | 5 | 5 |
| *32* | A3 | 25np pale bl | 6 | 5 |
| *33* | A3 | 50np pale rose | 12 | 5 |

**Size: 33x51mm**

| | | | | |
|---|---|---|---|---|
| *34* | A3 | 1r pale gray | 22 | 10 |
| *35* | A3 | 2r pale grn | 45 | 22 |
| *36* | A3 | 3r pale gray | 55 | 32 |
| *37* | A3 | 5r pale yel | 80 | 55 |
| | | *Nos. 28-37 (10)* | 2.40 | 1.49 |

Issued in memory of Pres. John F. Kennedy (1917-63). A souvenir sheet contains 2 stamps similar to Nos. 36-37 with pale blue (3r) and pale rose (5r) backgrounds, size: 29x44mm. Marginal gold design and green inscription. Size: 89"1/2x80mm. Nos. 28-37 exist imperf.

Stamps of Fujeira were replaced in 1972 by those of United Arab Emirates.

## AIR POST STAMPS

Arabian Oryx AP1

Designs (Sheik and): 15np, Grebe. 35np, Hoopoe. 50np, Wild ass. 75np, Herons in flight. 1r, Arabian horses. 2r, Leopard. 3r, Camels. 5r, Hawks.

**Photogravure and Lithographed**
**1965, Aug. 16** **Unwmk.** *Perf. 13½*
**Size: 43x28mm.**

| | | | | |
|---|---|---|---|---|
| *C1* | AP1 | 15np gold & multi | 12 | 5 |
| *C2* | AP1 | 25np gold & multi | 6 | 5 |
| *C3* | AP1 | 35np gold & multi | 18 | 5 |
| *C4* | AP1 | 50np gold & multi | 12 | 5 |
| *C5* | AP1 | 75np gold & multi | 35 | 7 |
| *C6* | AP1 | 1r gold & multi | 22 | 10 |

**Size: 53½x35mm.**

| | | | | |
|---|---|---|---|---|
| *C7* | AP1 | 2r gold & multi | 45 | 16 |
| *C8* | AP1 | 3r gold & multi | 60 | 28 |
| *C9* | AP1 | 5r gold & multi | 1.50 | 50 |
| | | *Nos. C1-C9 (9)* | 3.60 | 1.31 |

## AIR POST OFFICIAL STAMPS

Type of Air Post Issue, 1965

Designs: 75np, Arabian horses. 2r, Leopard. 3r, Camels. 5r, Hawks.

**Photogravure and Lithographed**
**1965, Nov. 10** **Unwmk.** *Perf. 13½*
**Size: 43x28mm.**

| | | | | |
|---|---|---|---|---|
| *CO1* | AP1 | 75np sil & multi | 20 | 10 |

*Perf. 13*
**Size: 53½x35mm.**

| | | | | |
|---|---|---|---|---|
| *CO2* | AP1 | 2r sil & multi | 50 | 28 |
| *CO3* | AP1 | 3r sil & multi | 65 | 40 |
| *CO4* | AP1 | 5r sil & multi | 1.75 | 65 |

## OFFICIAL STAMPS

Type of Air Post Issue, 1965

Designs: 25np, Grebe. 40np, Arabian oryx. 50np, Hoopoe. 75np, Wild ass. 1r, Herons in flight.

**Photogravure and Lithographed**
**1965, Oct. 14** **Unwmk.** *Perf. 13½*
**Size: 43x28mm.**

| | | | | |
|---|---|---|---|---|
| *O1* | AP1 | 25np sil & multi | 7 | 5 |
| *O2* | AP1 | 40np sil & multi | 12 | 6 |
| *O3* | AP1 | 50np sil & multi | 14 | 8 |
| *O4* | AP1 | 75np sil & multi | 20 | 12 |
| *O5* | AP1 | 1r sil & multi | 28 | 16 |
| | | *Nos. O1-O5 (5)* | 81 | 47 |

# GAMBIA

LOCATION — Extending inland from the mouth of the Gambia River on the west coast of Africa.
GOVT. — Republic in British Commonwealth.
AREA — 4,068 sq. mi.
POP. — 695,886 (1983).
CAPITAL — Banjul.

The British Crown Colony and Protectorate of Gambia became independent in 1965 and a republic in 1970.

12 Pence = 1 Shilling
100 Bututs = 1 Dalasy (1971)

**Catalogue values for unused stamps in this country are for Never Hinged items, beginning with Scott 144.**

Queen Victoria — A1

**Typographed and Embossed**
**1869, Jan.** **Unwmk.** *Imperf.*

| | | | | |
|---|---|---|---|---|
| *1* | A1 | 4p pale brn | 175.00 | 90.00 |
| *a.* | | 4p brown | 250.00 | 90.00 |
| *2* | A1 | 6p blue | 175.00 | 125.00 |
| *a.* | | 6p pale blue | *3,000.* | *2,000.* |

**1874, Aug.** **Wmk. 1**

| | | | | |
|---|---|---|---|---|
| *3* | A1 | 4p brown | 250.00 | 150.00 |
| *4* | A1 | 6p blue | 225.00 | 150.00 |

**1880, June** *Perf. 14*

| | | | | |
|---|---|---|---|---|
| *5* | A1 | ½p orange | 2.50 | 3.25 |
| *6* | A1 | 1p maroon | 3.25 | 3.75 |
| *7* | A1 | 2p rose | 14.00 | 5.00 |
| *8* | A1 | 3p ultra | 30.00 | 12.50 |
| *9* | A1 | 4p brown | 140.00 | 10.00 |
| *10* | A1 | 6p blue | 65.00 | 40.00 |
| *11* | A1 | 1sh green | 225.00 | 110.00 |

The watermark on Nos. 5-11 exists both upright and sideways.

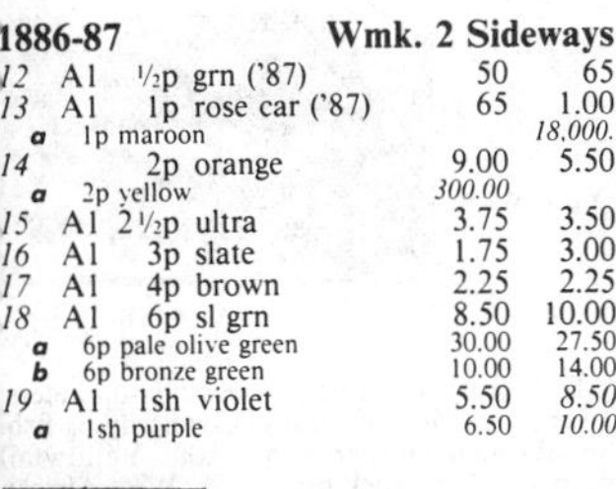

**1886-87 Wmk. 2 Sideways**

12 A1 ½p grn ('87) 50 65
13 A1 1p rose car ('87) 65 1.00
a 1p maroon 18,000.
14 2p orange 9.00 5.50
a 2p yellow 300.00
15 A1 2½p ultra 3.75 3.50
16 A1 3p slate 1.75 3.00
17 A1 4p brown 2.25 2.25
18 A1 6p sl grn 8.50 10.00
a 6p pale olive green 30.00 27.50
b 6p bronze green 10.00 14.00
19 A1 1sh violet 5.50 *8.50*
a 1sh purple 6.50 *10.00*

Queen Victoria — A2

**1898, Jan. Typo. Wmk. 2**

20 A2 ½p gray grn 1.00 1.25
21 A2 1p car rose 1.50 1.50
22 A2 2p brn org & pur 2.50 4.00
23 A2 2½p ultra 1.75 3.00
24 A2 3p red vio & ultra 4.50 7.00
25 A2 4p brn & ultra 6.00 9.00
26 A2 6p ol grn & car rose 9.00 12.00
27 A2 1sh vio & grn 12.00 *21.00*
*Nos. 20-27 (8)* 38.25 58.75

King Edward VII — A3

**1902-05 Perf. 14**

28 A3 ½p green 65 75
29 A3 1p car rose 1.10 40
30 A3 2p org & pur 1.75 *2.50*
31 A3 2½p ultra 6.50 7.00
32 A3 3p red vio & ultra 6.50 4.00
33 A3 4p brn & ultra 3.00 5.00
34 A3 6p ol grn & rose 4.00 5.00
35 A3 1sh bluish vio & grn 27.50 35.00
36 A3 1sh6p grn & red, *yel* ('05) 14.00 15.00
37 A3 2sh blk & org 16.00 20.00
38 A3 2sh6p pur & brn, *yel* ('05) 17.50 20.00
39 A3 3sh red & grn, *yel* ('05) 22.50 25.00
*Nos. 28-39 (12)* 121.00 139.65

Numerals of 5p, 7½p, 10p, 1sh6p, 2sh, 2sh6p and 3sh of type A3 are in color on plain tablet.

**1904-09 Wmk. 3**

41 A3 ½p green 32 32
42 A3 1p car rose 45 32
a 1p carmine ('09) 45 32
43 A3 2p org & pur ('06) 6.25 5.00
44 A3 2p gray ('09) 1.10 1.10
45 A3 2½p ultra 1.45 1.50
46 A3 3p red vio & ultra 3.75 4.00
47 A3 3p vio, *yel* ('09) 3.25 2.50
48 A3 4p brn & ultra ('06) 12.00 15.00
49 A3 4p blk & red, *yel* ('09) 1.25 1.90
50 A3 5p gray & blk 6.25 7.50
51 A3 5p org & vio ('09) 1.90 2.25
52 A3 6p ol grn & rose ('06) 12.00 12.75
53 A3 6p dl vio ('09) 1.50 1.90
54 A3 7½p bl grn & red 5.25 7.50
55 A3 7½p brn & ultra ('09) 1.90 3.00
56 A3 10p ol bis & red 15.00 16.50
57 A3 10p ol grn & car rose ('09) 2.00 2.75
58 A3 1sh vio & grn 19.00 25.00
59 A3 1sh *grn* ('09) 2.50 3.75
60 A3 1sh 6p vio & grn ('09) 6.25 7.50
61 A3 2sh blk & org 50.00 62.50
62 A3 2sh vio & bl, *bl* ('09) 9.50 12.00
63 A3 2sh 6pblk & red, *bl* ('09) 16.00 19.00
64 A3 3sh yel & grn ('09) 28.00 30.00
*Nos. 41-64 (24)* 206.87 245.54

Surcharged in Black:

HALF PENNY

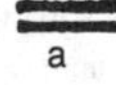

a

ONE PENNY

b

Type a (I). The word "PENNY" is 5mm from the horizontal bars.
Type a (II). "PENNY" is 4mm from the bars.

**1906, Apr. Wmk. 2**

65 A3 ½p on 2sh6p pur & brn, *yel*, type I 50.00 55.00
a Type II 50.00 55.00
66 A3 1p on 3sh red & grn, *yel* 62.50 67.50
a Double surcharge *2,500. 4,500.*

King George V — A4

**1912-22 Wmk. 3**

70 A4 ½p green 20 20
71 A4 1p scarlet 20 12
a 1p car 20 12
72 A4 1½p ol brn & grn 42 50
73 A4 2p gray 35 50
74 A4 2½p ultra 70 70
75 A4 3p vio, *yel* 35 50
76 A4 4p blk & red, *yel* 50 75
77 A4 5p org & vio 1.10 1.25
78 A4 6p dl vio & red vio 70 90
79 A4 7½p brn & ultra 70 90
80 A4 10p ol grn & car rose 1.40 *3.00*
81 A4 1sh *green* 55 70
a 1sh *emerald* 90 1.00
82 A4 1sh6p vio & grn 5.00 6.25
83 A4 2sh vio & bl, *bl* 5.00 6.25
84 A4 2sh6p blk & red, *bl* 6.25 10.00
85 A4 3sh yel & grn 7.50 12.50
86 A4 5sh grn & red, *yel* ('22) *27.50 37.50*
*Nos. 70-86 (17)* 58.42 82.52

Numerals of 1½p, 5p, 7½p, 10p, 1sh6p, 2sh, 2sh6p, 3sh, 4sh and 5sh of type A3 are in color on colorless tablet. No. 86 is on chalky paper.

**1921-22 Wmk. 4**

87 A4 ½p green 25 *1.50*
88 A4 1p carmine 65 *75*
89 A4 1½p ol grn & bl grn 2.50 *5.00*
90 A4 2p gray 1.40 *2.50*
91 A4 2½p ultra 70 *1.75*
92 A4 5p org & vio 2.25 *5.00*
93 A4 6p dl vio & red vio *3.00 5.00*
94 A4 7½p brn & ultra *3.75 7.50*
95 A4 10p yel grn & car rose *4.25 10.00*
96 A4 4sh blk & red ('22) *30.00 55.00*
*Nos. 87-96 (10)* 48.75 94.00

No. 96 is on chalky paper.

George V and Elephant — A5

King George V — A6

**1922-27 Engr. Wmk. 4**
**Head and Shield in Black**

102 A5 ½p green 12 12
103 A5 1p brown 12 12
104 A5 1½p carmine 15 15
105 A5 2p gray 50 65
106 A5 2½p orange 65 *2.50*
107 A5 3p ultra 65 50
108 A5 4p car, *org* ('27) 2.25 3.00
109 A5 5p yel grn 1.75 *4.50*
110 A5 6p claret 90 1.00
111 A5 7½p vio, *yel* ('27) 2.25 *6.50*
112 A5 10p blue 3.00 *7.50*
113 A6 1sh vio, *org* ('24) 2.50 1.50
114 A6 1sh6p blue 4.00 *7.50*
115 A6 2sh vio, *bl* 3.75 3.75
116 A6 2sh6p dk grn 5.50 *9.00*
117 A6 3sh anil vio 7.50 *15.00*
a 3sh blk pur 175.00 *400.00*
118 A6 4sh brown 5.75 *10.00*
119 A6 5sh dk grn, *yel* ('26) 10.00 *17.50*
120 A6 10sh yel grn 27.50 42.50
*Nos. 102-120 (19)* 78.84 133.29

**1922 Wmk. 3**

121 A5 4p car, *yel* 65 *1.50*
122 A5 7½p vio, *yel* 1.40 *3.75*
123 A6 1sh vio, *org* 5.00 *10.00*
124 A6 5sh dk grn, *yel* 22.50 32.50

**Silver Jubilee Issue**
Common Design Type

**1935, May 6 Wmk. 4 *Perf. 11x12***

125 CD301 1½p car & bl 35 35
126 CD301 3p ultra & brn 85 85
127 CD301 6p ol grn & lt bl 1.75 1.75
128 CD301 1sh brn vio & ind 1.75 1.75

**Coronation Issue**
Common Design Type

**1937, May 12 *Perf. 11x11½***

129 CD302 1p brown 8 8
130 CD302 1½p dk car 10 10
131 CD302 3p dp ultra 20 20

King George VI and Elephant Badge of Gambia — A7

**1938-46 *Perf. 12***

132 A7 ½p bl grn & blk 5 5
133 A7 1p brn & red vio 6 8
134 A7 1½p rose red & brn lake 15 15
134A A7 1½p gray blk & ultra ('44) 12 12
135 A7 2p gray blk & ultra 65 65
135A A7 2p rose red & brn lake ('43) 12 12
136 A7 3p bl & brt bl 15 15
136A A7 5p dk vio brn & ol ('41) 18 18
137 A7 6p plum & ol grn 50 50
138 A7 1sh vio & sl blk 75 75
138A A7 1sh3p bl & choc ('46) 40 40
139 A7 2sh bl & dp rose 1.10 1.10
140 A7 2sh6p sl grn & sep 1.25 1.25
141 A7 4sh dk vio & red org 3.75 3.25
142 A7 5sh org red & dk bl 4.00 4.00
143 A7 10sh blk & yel org 8.75 8.75
*Nos. 132-143 (16)* 21.98 21.50

**Catalogue values for unused stamps in this section, from this point to the end of the section, are for Never Hinged items.**

**Peace Issue.**
Common Design Type

**1946, Aug. 6 Engr. *Perf. 13½***

144 CD303 1½p black 12 12
145 CD303 3p dp bl 20 20

**Silver Wedding Issue.**
Common Design Types

**1948, Dec. 24 Photo. *Perf. 14x14½***

146 CD304 1½p black 15 15

**Engraved; Name Typographed**
***Perf. 11½x11.***

147 CD305 £1 purple 12.50 *17.50*

**UPU Issue**
Common Design Types
**Engr.; Name Typo. on 3p, 6p**
***Perf. 13½, 11x11½***

**1949, Oct. 10 Wmk. 4**

148 CD306 1½p slate 30 30
149 CD307 3p indigo 55 55
150 CD308 6p red lilac 1.10 1.10
151 CD309 1sh violet 2.00 2.00

**Coronation Issue**
Common Design Type

**1953, June 2 Engr. *Perf. 13½x13***

152 CD312 1½p dk bl & blk 20 20

Palm Wine Tapping — A8

Palm Leaf and Elizabeth II, by Annigoni — A9

Designs: 1p, 1sh 3p, Cutter. 1½p, 5sh, Wollof woman. 2½p, 2sh, Barra canoe. 3p, 10sh, "Lady Wright." 4p, 4sh, James Island. 1sh, 2sh 6p, Woman farming. £1, Elephant badge of Gambia.

**1953, Nov. 2 *Perf. 13½***

153 A8 ½p dk grn & car 8 8
154 A8 1p dk brn & ultra 10 10
155 A8 1½p gray & dk brn 15 15
156 A8 2½p car & blk 30 30
157 A8 3p pur & ind 32 32
158 A8 4p dp bl & blk 25 25
159 A8 6p dp plum & brn 25 25
160 A8 1sh grn & yel brn 50 50
161 A8 1sh3p bl & vio bl 65 65
162 A8 2sh car & ind 1.60 1.60
163 A8 2sh6p brn & bl grn 1.75 1.75
164 A8 4sh brn org & dp bl 2.75 2.75
165 A8 5sh ultra & red brn 3.25 3.25
166 A8 10sh dk yel grn & ultra 5.75 5.75
167 A8 £1 blk & bl grn 12.50 12.50
*Nos. 153-167 (15)* 30.20 30.20

**Wmk. 314**
**1961, Dec. 2 Engr. *Perf. 11½***

Design: 3p, 6p, Map of West Africa.

168 A9 2p lil & grn 6 6
169 A9 3p brn & Prus grn 9 9
170 A9 6p car rose & dk bl 15 15
171 A9 1sh3p grn & vio 35 35

Visit of Elizabeth II to Gambia, Dec., 1961.

**Freedom from Hunger Issue**
Common Design Type

**1963, June 4 Photo. *Perf. 14x14½***

172 CD314 1sh 3p car rose 50 50

**Red Cross Centenary Issue**
Common Design Type

**1963, Sept. 2 Litho. *Perf. 13***

173 CD315 2p blk & red 8 8
174 CD315 1sh 3p ultra & red 75 75

Beautiful Long-tailed Sunbird — A10

Birds: 1p, Yellow-mantled whydah. 1½p, Cattle egret. 2p, Yellow-bellied parrot. 3p, Ring-necked parakeet. 4p, Amethyst starling. 6p, Village weaver. 1sh, Rufous-crowned roller. 1sh3p, Red-eyed turtle dove. 2sh6p, Double-spurred francolin. 5sh, Palm-nut vulture. 10sh, Orange-cheeked waxbill. £1, Emerald cuckoo.

***Perf. 12½x13***
**1963, Nov. 4 Photo. Wmk. 314**
**Multicolored Design & Inscription**

175 A10 ½p rose buff 6 5
176 A10 1p gray grn 12 10
177 A10 1½p pale vio 18 15
178 A10 2p buff 15 12
179 A10 3p lt gray 30 25
180 A10 4p lt yel grn 50 45
181 A10 6p lt bl 60 50
182 A10 1sh pale grysh grn 1.00 90
183 A10 1sh3p lt bl 2.50 1.50
184 A10 2sh6p pale grn 3.50 2.75
185 A10 5sh blue 6.50 5.00
186 A10 10sh tan 12.50 10.00
187 A10 £1 pale rose 30.00 20.00
*Nos. 175-187 (13)* 57.91 41.77

Nos. 176, 179, 182 and 183 Overprinted: "SELF GOVERNMENT/1963"

**1963, Nov. 7**

188 A10 1p multi 6 6
189 A10 3p multi 9 9
190 A10 1sh multi 30 30
191 A10 1sh3p multi 40 40

**Shakespeare Issue**
Common Design Type

**1964, Apr. 23 Photo.** ***Perf. 14x14½***

| | | | | |
|---|---|---|---|---|
| *192* | CD316 | 6p ultra | 22 | 22 |

Nos. 175-187 Overprinted: "INDEPENDENCE / 1965"

***Perf. 12½x13***

**1965, Feb. 18 Photo. Wmk. 314**
**Multicolored Design & Inscription**

| | | | | |
|---|---|---|---|---|
| *193* | A10 | ½p rose buff | 5 | 5 |
| *194* | A10 | 1p gray grn | 8 | 8 |
| *195* | A10 | 1½ pale vio | 12 | 12 |
| *196* | A10 | 2p buff | 12 | 12 |
| *197* | A10 | 3p lt gray | 15 | 15 |
| *198* | A10 | 4p lt yel grn | 20 | 20 |
| *199* | A10 | 6p lt bl | 25 | 25 |
| *200* | A10 | 1sh pale grysh grn | 45 | 45 |
| *201* | A10 | 1sh3p lt bl | 60 | 60 |
| *202* | A10 | 2sh6p pale grn | 1.25 | 1.25 |
| *203* | A10 | 5sh blue | 2.50 | 2.50 |
| *204* | A10 | 10sh tan | 4.00 | 4.00 |
| *205* | A10 | £1 pale rose | 7.50 | 7.50 |
| | | *Nos. 193-205 (13)* | 17.27 | 17.27 |

In the overprint, "1965" is flush at left side under "Independence" on the ½p, 1½p, 6p, 1sh3p and 2sh6p; it is centered on the others.

Flag of Gambia over Gambia River — A11

Design: 2p, 1sh6p, Coat of arms.

**1965, Feb. 18 Unwmk.** ***Perf. 14***

| | | | | |
|---|---|---|---|---|
| *206* | A11 | ½p sl & multi | 5 | 5 |
| *207* | A11 | 2p lt brn & multi | 6 | 6 |
| *208* | A11 | 7½p dk brn & multi | 15 | 15 |
| *209* | A11 | 1sh6p lt grn & multi | 30 | 30 |

Gambia's Independence.

ITU Emblem, Old and New Communication Equipment — A12

**1965, May 17 Photo.** ***Perf. 14½x14***

| | | | | |
|---|---|---|---|---|
| *210* | A12 | 1p dl bl & sil | 8 | 8 |
| *211* | A12 | 1sh6p vio & gold | 65 | 65 |

Cent. of the ITU.

Winston Churchill and Parliament A13

**1966, Jan. 24** ***Perf. 14x14½***

| | | | | |
|---|---|---|---|---|
| *212* | A13 | 1p multi | 7 | 7 |
| *213* | A13 | 6p multi | 30 | 30 |
| *214* | A13 | 1sh6p multi | 85 | 85 |

Sir Winston Leonard Spencer Churchill, statesman and WW II leader.

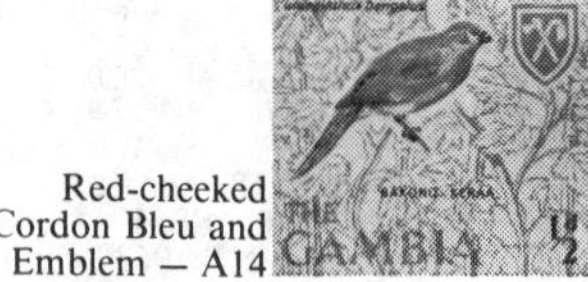

Red-cheeked Cordon Bleu and Emblem — A14

Birds: 1p, White-faced tree duck. 1½p, Red-throated bee eater. 2p, Pied kingfisher. 3p, Yellow-crowned bishop. 4p, Fish eagle. 6p, Bruce's green pigeon. 1sh, Blue-bellied roller. 1sh6p, African pigmy kingfisher. 2sh6p, Spur-winged goose. 5sh, Little woodpecker. 10sh, Violet plantain eater. £1, Pintailed whydah (vert.).

***Perf. 12½x13***

**1966, Feb. 18 Photo. Unwmk.**
**Size: 29x25mm.**
**Multicolored Design & Inscription**

| | | | | |
|---|---|---|---|---|
| *215* | A14 | ½p gray | 5 | 5 |
| *216* | A14 | 1p bluish grn | 6 | 6 |
| *217* | A14 | 1½p yel grn | 8 | 8 |
| *218* | A14 | 2p rose lil | 75 | 38 |
| *219* | A14 | 3p lilac | 12 | 12 |
| *220* | A14 | 4p blue | 15 | 15 |
| *221* | A14 | 6p gray | 22 | 22 |
| *222* | A14 | 1sh lt grn | 38 | 38 |
| *223* | A14 | 1sh6p brt bl | 55 | 55 |
| *224* | A14 | 2sh6p tan | 90 | 90 |
| *225* | A14 | 5sh gray grn | 1.75 | 1.75 |
| *226* | A14 | 10sh ocher | 3.75 | 3.75 |

***Perf. 14x14½***
**Size: 25x39mm.**

| | | | | |
|---|---|---|---|---|
| *227* | A14 | £1 pink | 6.00 | 6.00 |
| | | *Nos. 215-227 (13)* | 14.76 | 14.39 |

Coat of Arms, Old and New Views of Bathurst — A15

**Photo.; Silver Impressed (Arms)**
**1966, June 24** ***Perf. 14½x14***

| | | | | |
|---|---|---|---|---|
| *228* | A15 | 1p org & dk brn | 5 | 5 |
| *229* | A15 | 2p lt ultra & dk brn | 6 | 6 |
| *230* | A15 | 6p emer & dk brn | 16 | 16 |
| *231* | A15 | 1sh6p brt pink & dk brn | 40 | 40 |

150th anniv. of the founding of Bathurst.

Adonis and Atlantic Hotels and ITY Emblem — A16

**Photo.; Silver Impressed (Emblem)**
**1967, Dec. 20** ***Perf. 14½x14***

| | | | | |
|---|---|---|---|---|
| *232* | A16 | 2p lt yel grn & brn | 6 | 6 |
| *233* | A16 | 1sh org & brn | 20 | 20 |
| *234* | A16 | 1sh6p lil rose & brn | 30 | 30 |

International Tourist Year, 1967.

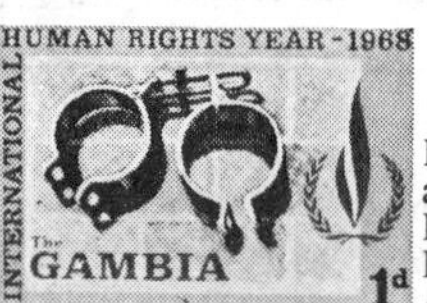

Handcuffs and Human Rights Flame A17

Designs: 1sh, Fort Bullen. 5sh, Methodist Church.

***Perf. 14x13***

**1968, July 15 Unwmk. Photo.**

| | | | | |
|---|---|---|---|---|
| *235* | A17 | 1p gold & multi | 5 | 5 |
| *236* | A17 | 1sh gold & multi | 15 | 15 |
| *237* | A17 | 5sh gold & multi | 90 | 90 |

International Human Rights Year, 1968

Gambia No. 1, Victoria and Elizabeth II — A18

Designs: 6p, Gambia No. 2, Queens Victoria and Elizabeth II. 2sh6p, Gambia Nos. 1-2 and Queen Elizabeth II.

**Photo. and Embossed**
***Perf. 14x13½***

**1969, Jan. 20 Wmk. 314**

| | | | | |
|---|---|---|---|---|
| *238* | A18 | 4p dl yel & dk brn | 12 | 12 |
| *239* | A18 | 6p dp yel grn & bl | 18 | 18 |
| *240* | A18 | 2sh6p dk bl gray, brn & bl | 90 | 90 |

Centenary of Gambian postage stamps.

Dornier Wal, Route Gambia to Brazil and Lufthansa Emblem — A19

Designs: 2p, Plane and ship Westfalen, route Gambia to Brazil and Lufthansa emblem. 1sh6p, Zeppelin, route Gambia to Brazil and Lufthansa emblem.

***Perf. 13½x14***

**1969, Dec. 15 Litho. Unwmk.**

| | | | | |
|---|---|---|---|---|
| *241* | A19 | 2p pink, org red & blk | 6 | 6 |
| *242* | A19 | 1sh buff, dl yel & blk | 30 | 30 |
| *243* | A19 | 1sh6p lt bl, ultra & blk | 75 | 75 |

35th anniversary of pioneer air services.

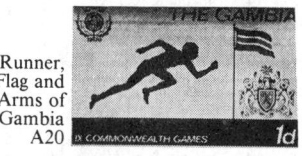

Runner, Flag and Arms of Gambia A20

**1970, July 16** ***Perf. 14½x14***
**Flag in Red, Blue & Green**

| | | | | |
|---|---|---|---|---|
| *244* | A20 | 1p pink & brn | 5 | 5 |
| *245* | A20 | 1sh ultra & brn | 20 | 20 |
| *246* | A20 | 5sh grn & brn | 1.00 | 1.00 |

Issued to publicize the 9th Commonwealth Games, Edinburgh, Scotland, July 16-25.

Pres. Jawara and State House A21

Designs: 1sh, Pres. Sir Dauda Kairaba Jawara (vert.). 1sh6p, Pres. Jawara and Gambia flag (vert.).

**1970, Nov. 2 Litho.** ***Perf. 14***

| | | | | |
|---|---|---|---|---|
| *247* | A21 | 2p gray & multi | 5 | 5 |
| *248* | A21 | 1sh multi | 20 | 20 |
| *249* | A21 | 1sh6p pink & multi | 30 | 30 |

Republic Day, Apr. 24, 1970.

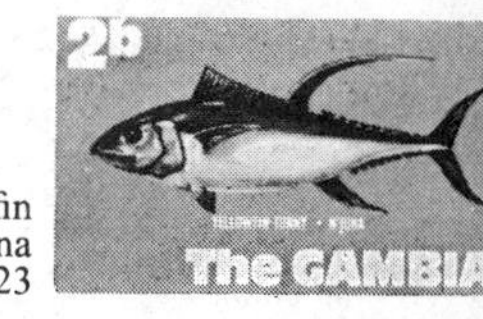

Methodist Church, Georgetown — A22

Designs: 1sh, Map of Africa and cross (vert.). 1sh6p, John Wesley.

**1971, Apr. 16 Unwmk.** ***Perf. 14***

| | | | | |
|---|---|---|---|---|
| *250* | A22 | 2p multi | 5 | 5 |
| *251* | A22 | 1sh vio bl & multi | 20 | 20 |
| *252* | A22 | 1sh6p grn & multi | 40 | 40 |

150th anniversary of establishment of Methodist Mission.

Yellowfin Tuna A23

Fish from Gambian Waters: 4b, Peters mormyrid. 6b, Tropical two-wing flying fish 8b, African sleeper goby. 10b, Yellowtail snapper. 13b, Rock hind. 25b, West African eel cat. 38b, Tiger shark. 50b, Electric catfish. 63b, Swamp eel. 1.25d, Smalltooth sawfish. 2.50d, Barracuda. 5d, Brown bullhead.

**1971, July 1 Litho.** ***Perf. 14***
**Fish in Natural Colors**

| | | | | |
|---|---|---|---|---|
| *253* | A23 | 2b blue | 5 | 5 |
| *254* | A23 | 4b lemon | 7 | 7 |
| *255* | A23 | 6b lt bl grn | 8 | 8 |
| *256* | A23 | 8b org brn | 12 | 10 |
| *257* | A23 | 10b lt Prus bl | 14 | 12 |
| *258* | A23 | 13b org yel | 18 | 16 |
| *259* | A23 | 25b green | 40 | 38 |
| *260* | A23 | 38b brick red | 50 | 50 |
| *261* | A23 | 50b Prus bl | 85 | 65 |
| *262* | A23 | 63b bister | 1.00 | 1.00 |
| *263* | A23 | 1.25d yel grn | 2.00 | 2.00 |
| *264* | A23 | 2.50d dp rose | 4.00 | 4.00 |
| *265* | A23 | 5d ultra | 8.50 | 8.50 |
| | | *Nos. 253-265 (13)* | 17.89 | 17.61 |

Mungo Park, Scottish Landscape, Map of Gambia Basin — A24

Designs (Map of Gambia River Basin and): 25b, Park traveling in dugout canoe. 37b, Park's death under attack at Busa Rapids.

***Perf. 13½x14***

**1971, Sept. 10 Litho. Unwmk.**

| | | | | |
|---|---|---|---|---|
| *270* | A24 | 4b ultra & multi | 6 | 6 |
| *271* | A24 | 25b yel grn & multi | 35 | 35 |
| *272* | A24 | 37b brick red & multi | 55 | 55 |

Bicentenary of the birth of Mungo Park (1771-1806), Scottish explorer of the Gambia and Niger Rivers.

Radio Gambia and Pres. Jawara A25

Designs: 25b, Map showing area reached by Radio Gambia. 37b, Like 4b.

**1972, July 1** ***Perf. 14***

| | | | | |
|---|---|---|---|---|
| *273* | A25 | 4b blk & dl yel | 7 | 7 |
| *274* | A25 | 25b blk, bl & red | 40 | 40 |
| *275* | A25 | 37b blk & yel grn | 60 | 60 |

Radio Gambia, 10th anniversary, May 1, 1972.

High Jump A26

**1972, Aug. 31** ***Perf. 13½***

| | | | | |
|---|---|---|---|---|
| *276* | A26 | 4b emer & multi | 5 | 5 |
| *277* | A26 | 25b lt ultra & multi | 25 | 25 |
| *278* | A26 | 37b red & multi | 40 | 40 |

20th Olympic Games, Munich, Aug. 26-Sept. 11.

Mandingo Woman — A27

Designs: 25b, Musician playing Mandingo 21-stringed lute (kora). 37b, Map of Mali empire and area of Mandingo language.

**1972, Oct. 18 Litho. *Perf. 14x14½***

| | | | | |
|---|---|---|---|---|
| *279* | A27 | 2b rose red & multi | 5 | 5 |
| *280* | A27 | 25b lt ultra & multi | 35 | 35 |
| *281* | A27 | 37b emer & multi | 50 | 50 |

International Conference on Mandingo Studies, London, June 30-July 3.

Ship Model with Lanterns A28

Design: 2b, Lighted ship (lantern) carried by boys.

**1972, Dec. 1 Litho. *Perf. 13x13½***

| | | | | |
|---|---|---|---|---|
| *282* | A28 | 2b vio & multi | 5 | 5 |
| *283* | A28 | 1.25d bl & multi | 1.50 | 1.50 |

Christmas 1972.

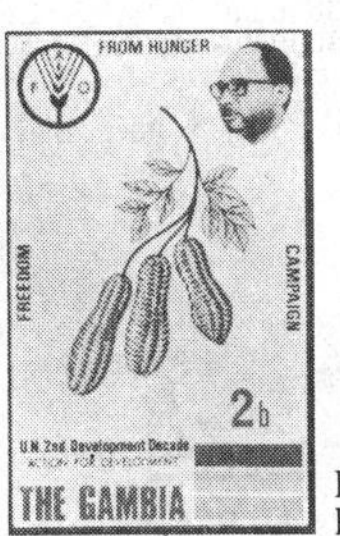


Peanuts, FAO Emblem — A29

**1973, Mar. 31 Litho. *Perf. 14½x14***

| | | | | |
|---|---|---|---|---|
| *284* | A29 | 2b red & multi | 8 | 8 |
| *285* | A29 | 25b lt bl & multi | 40 | 40 |
| *286* | A29 | 37b emer & multi | 65 | 65 |

Freedom from Hunger, 2nd U.N. development campaign.

Planting and Drying Rice — A30

Oil Palms — A31

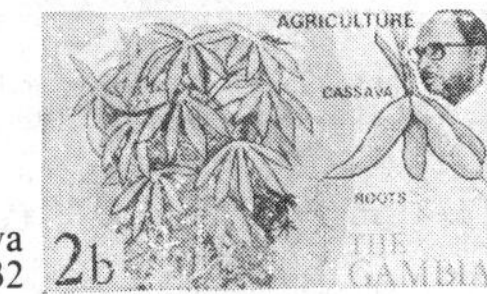


Cassava A32

**1973, Apr. 30 *Perf. 14½x14***

| | | | | |
|---|---|---|---|---|
| *287* | A30 | 2b *shown* | 5 | 5 |
| *288* | A30 | 25b *Sorghum (Guinea corn)* | 35 | 35 |
| *289* | A30 | 37b *Rice crop* | 50 | 50 |

**1973, July 16**

| | | | | |
|---|---|---|---|---|
| *290* | A31 | 2b *shown* | 6 | 6 |
| *291* | A31 | 25b *Limes* | 35 | 35 |
| *292* | A31 | 37b *Oil palm fruits* | 60 | 60 |

**1973, Oct. 15**

| | | | | |
|---|---|---|---|---|
| *293* | A32 | 2b *shown* | 7 | 7 |
| *294* | A32 | 50b *Cotton* | 75 | 75 |
| | | *Nos. 287-294 (8)* | 2.73 | 2.73 |

Gambian agriculture.

OAU Emblem — A33

**1973, Nov. 1 Unwmk. *Perf. 13½x13***

| | | | | |
|---|---|---|---|---|
| *295* | A33 | 4b grn, yel & blk | 6 | 6 |
| *296* | A33 | 25b dp mag, yel & blk | 40 | 40 |
| *297* | A33 | 37b bl, yel & blk | 60 | 60 |

10th anniv. of the OAU.

Red Cross — A34

***Perf. 14½x14***

**1973, Nov. 30 Wmk. 314**

| | | | | |
|---|---|---|---|---|
| *298* | A34 | 4b red & blk | 6 | 6 |
| *299* | A34 | 25b ultra, red & blk | 40 | 40 |
| *300* | A34 | 37b emer, red & blk | 60 | 60 |

25th anniv. of Gambia Red Cross Soc.

Flag of Gambia and Arms of Banjul — A35

***Perf. 13½x13***

**1973, Dec. 17 Litho. Unwmk.**

| | | | | |
|---|---|---|---|---|
| *301* | A35 | 4b yel grn & multi | 6 | 6 |
| *302* | A35 | 25b ver & multi | 35 | 35 |
| *303* | A35 | 37b lt ultra & multi | 50 | 50 |

Change of name of Bathurst to Banjul and of St. Mary's Island to Banjul Island.

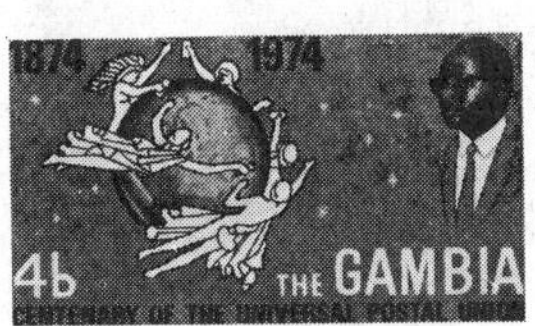


UPU Emblem — A36

**1974, Aug. 24 Litho. *Perf. 13½x13***

| | | | | |
|---|---|---|---|---|
| *304* | A36 | 4b lil & multi | 6 | 6 |
| *305* | A36 | 37b bl & multi | 65 | 65 |

Centenary of Universal Postal Union.

Canceled-to-order stamps are often from remainders. Most collectors of canceled stamps prefer postally used specimens.

Churchill at Harrow — A37

Churchill in Uniform of 4th Hussars — A38

Designs: 50b, Churchill as Prime Minister.

**1974, Nov. 30 Litho. *Perf. 13½***

| | | | | |
|---|---|---|---|---|
| *306* | A37 | 4b multi | 6 | 6 |
| *307* | A37 | 37b multi | 40 | 40 |
| *308* | A37 | 50b multi | 65 | 65 |

Sir Winston Churchill (1874-1965).

WPY Emblem, Races of Man A39

Symbolic Designs and WPY Emblem: 37b, Races multiplying and dividing like atom. 50b, World population.

**1974, Dec. 16 Litho. *Perf. 14***

| | | | | |
|---|---|---|---|---|
| *309* | A39 | 4b multi | 5 | 5 |
| *310* | A39 | 37b multi | 35 | 35 |
| *311* | A39 | 50b multi | 50 | 50 |

World Population Year.

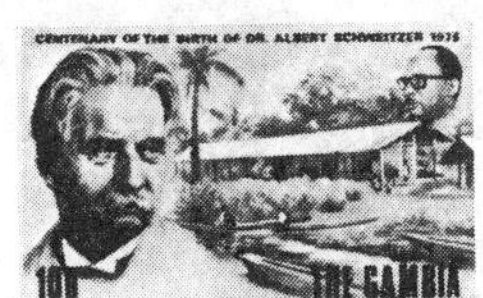


Dr. Schweitzer and Hospital, Lambarene — A40

Designs (Portrait and): 50b, Dr. Schweitzer examining patient. 1.25d, Dr. Schweitzer in boat on Ogowe River.

**1975, Jan. 14 Litho. *Perf. 14***

| | | | | |
|---|---|---|---|---|
| *312* | A40 | 10b multi | 9 | 9 |
| *313* | A40 | 50b multi | 42 | 42 |
| *314* | A40 | 1.25d multi | 1.10 | 1.10 |

Dr. Albert Schweitzer (1875-1965), medical missionary, birth centenary.

Peace Dove A41

Designs: 10b, Gambia flag. 50b, Gambia coat of arms. 1.25d, Map of Gambia and Gambia River.

**1975, Feb. 18 *Perf. 13***

| | | | | |
|---|---|---|---|---|
| *315* | A41 | 4b multi | 5 | 5 |
| *316* | A41 | 10b multi | 8 | 8 |
| *317* | A41 | 50b multi | 40 | 40 |
| *318* | A41 | 1.25d multi | 1.00 | 1.00 |

10th anniversary of independence.

Public Services Graph, A.D.B. Emblem A42

David, by Michelangelo A43

Designs (African Development Bank Emblem and): 50b, Plant symbolizing growth of Africa, fed by Development Bank. 1.25d, A.D.B. emblem surrounded by symbols of water, education, roads and hospitals.

**1975, Mar. 31 Litho. *Perf. 14***

| | | | | |
|---|---|---|---|---|
| *319* | A42 | 10b multi | 8 | 8 |
| *320* | A42 | 50b multi | 40 | 40 |
| *321* | A42 | 1.25d multi | 1.00 | 1.00 |

African Development Bank, 10th anniversary.

**1975, Nov. 14 *Perf. 14½***

Bas-reliefs by Michelangelo: 50b, Madonna of the Steps. 1.25d, Battle of the Centaurs (horiz.).

| | | | | |
|---|---|---|---|---|
| *322* | A43 | 10b dl bl & multi | 8 | 8 |
| *323* | A43 | 50b sep & multi | 40 | 40 |
| *324* | A43 | 1.25d grn & multi | 1.00 | 1.00 |

500th birth anniversary of Michelangelo Buonarroti (1475-1564), Italian painter, sculptor and architect.

Gambia High School A44

Designs: 50b, Pupil in laboratory and school emblem. 1.50d, School emblem.

**1975, Nov. 17**

| | | | | |
|---|---|---|---|---|
| *325* | A44 | 10b multi | 8 | 8 |
| *326* | A44 | 50b multi | 40 | 40 |
| *327* | A44 | 1.50d multi | 1.00 | 1.00 |

Gambia High School, centenary.

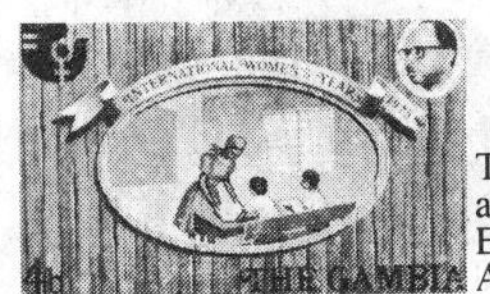


Teacher and IWY Emblem A45

Designs: 10b, Women planting rice. 50b, Nurse holding baby. 1.50d, Woman traffic officer.

**1975, Dec. 15 Litho. *Perf. 14½***

| | | | | |
|---|---|---|---|---|
| *328* | A45 | 4b yel & multi | 5 | 5 |
| *329* | A45 | 10b multi | 10 | 10 |
| *330* | A45 | 50b multi | 60 | 60 |
| *331* | A45 | 1.50d bl & multi | 1.50 | 1.50 |

International Women's Year 1975.

Woman Golfer A46

Designs: 50b, Golfer addressing ball. 1.50d, Golfer finishing iron shot.

**1976, Feb. 18 Litho. Perf. 14½**

*332* A46 10b multi 14 10
*333* A46 50b multi 65 55
*334* A46 1.50d multi 1.75 1.50

11th anniversary of independence.

American Militiaman A47

Designs: 50b, Continental Army soldier. 1.25d, Declaration of Independence.

**1976, May 15 Litho. Perf. 14x13½**

*335* A47 25b multi 25 22
*336* A47 50b multi 55 45
*337* A47 1.25d multi 1.40 1.40
*a* Souvenir sheet of 3 3.25 3.25

American Bicentennial. No. 337a contains one each of Nos. 335-337; light blue margin with indigo inscription and Bicentennial emblem. Size: 98x90mm.

Mother and Child, Christmas Decoration — A48

**1976, Oct. 28 Litho. Perf. 14**

*338* A48 10b lt ultra & multi 10 10
*339* A48 50b rose & multi 50 50
*340* A48 1.25d yel grn & multi 1.40 1.40

Christmas 1976.

Serval Cat and Wildlife Fund Emblem — A49

Designs: 25b, Harnessed antelope. 50b, Sitatunga. 1.25d, Leopard.

**1976, Nov. 29 Perf. 13½x14**

*341* A49 10b multi 22 12
*342* A49 25b multi 70 38
*343* A49 50b multi 1.10 70
*344* A49 1.25d multi 2.75 1.75
*a* Souvenir sheet of 4 7.50 4.00

Abuko Nature Reserve. No. 344a contains one each of Nos. 341-344; multicolored margin shows forest. Size: 135x110mm.

Queen's Visit, 1961 — A50

Designs: 50b, The spurs and jeweled sword. 1.25d, The oblation of the sword.

**1977, Feb. 7 Litho. Perf. 13½x14**

*345* A50 25b multi 1.75 1.25
*346* A50 50b multi 2.50 1.25
*347* A50 1.25d multi 7.50 2.25

25th anniv. of the reign of Elizabeth II.

Festival Emblem and Weaver A51

**1977, Jan. 12 Litho. Perf. 14**

*348* A51 25b multi 25 25
*349* A51 50b multi 45 45
*350* A51 1.25d multi 1.10 1.10
*a* Souvenir sheet of 3 2.50 2.50

2nd World Black and African Festival, Lagos, Nigeria, Jan. 15-Feb. 12. No. 350a contains one each of Nos. 348-350; multicolored margin showing Festival (Benin head) emblem. Size: 127x114mm.

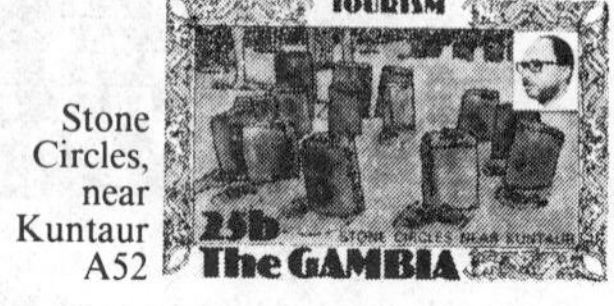


Stone Circles, near Kuntaur A52

Tourism: 50b, Ruins of Fort on James Island. 1.25d, Mungo Park Monument.

**1977, Feb. 18 Litho. Perf. 14½**

*351* A52 25b multi 25 25
*352* A52 50b multi 50 50
*353* A52 1.25d multi 1.10 1.10

Clerodendrum Splendens — A53

Flowers and Shrubs: 4b, White water lily. 6b, Fireball lily. 8b, Mussaenda elegans. 10b, Broad-leaved ground orchid. 13b, Fiber plant. 25b, False kapok. 38b, Baobab. 50b, Coral tree. 63b, Gloriosa lily. 1.25d, Bell-flowered mimosa. 2.50d, Kindin dolo. 5d, African tulip tree. 6b, 8b, 10b, 13b, 25b, 38b, 1.25d, 2.50d, vertical.

**1977, July 1 Litho. Perf. 14½**

*354* A53 2b multi 5 5
*355* A53 4b multi 5 5
*356* A53 6b multi 6 6
*357* A53 8b multi 9 9
*358* A53 10b multi 12 12
*359* A53 13b multi 15 15
*a* Pale olive background 18 18
*360* A53 25b multi 30 30
*361* A53 38b multi 45 45
*362* A53 50b multi 60 60
*363* A53 63b multi 75 75
*364* A53 1.25d multi 1.50 1.50
*365* A53 2.50d multi 3.00 3.00
*366* A53 5d multi 6.25 6.25
*Nos. 354-366 (13)* 13.37 13.37

Crowned Crane, Nile Crocodile, Bush Buck — A54

Madonna, Flight into Egypt, by Rubens — A55

Designs: 25b, Banjul Declaration, excerpt, flag colors. 50b, Banjul Declaration. 1.25d, Climbing lily, butterfly and moth.

**1977, Oct. 15 Litho. Perf. 14**

*367* A54 10b lt bl & blk 14 10
*368* A54 25b multi 30 25
*369* A54 50b multi 55 50
*370* A54 1.25d red & blk 1.40 1.10

Banjul Declaration, for the conservation of flora and fauna, Feb. 18, 1977.

**1977, Dec. 15 Litho. Perf. 14x13½**

Rubens Paintings: 25b, Education of Mary by St. Ann. 50b, Child's head. 1d, Madonna surrounded by saints.

*371* A55 10b multi 10 10
*372* A55 25b multi 25 25
*373* A55 50b multi 60 60
*374* A55 1d multi 1.40 1.40

Peter Paul Rubens (1577-1640), 400th birth anniversary. Nos. 371-374 printed in sheets of 5 stamps and decorative label; bister margin with Rubens drawings.

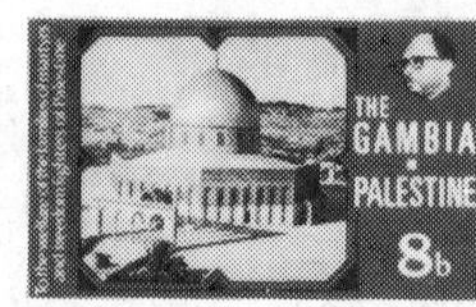


Dome of the Rock, Jerusalem — A56

**1978, Jan. 3 Litho. Perf. 14½**

*375* A56 8b ol grn & multi 50 50
*376* A56 25b red & multi 2.00 2.00

Palestinian fighters and their families.

Walking on Greased Pole — A57

Designs: 50b, Pillow fight on greased pole. 1.25d, Rowers in long boat.

**1978, Feb. 18 Perf. 14**

*377* A57 10b multi 8 8
*378* A57 50b multi 50 50
*379* A57 1.25d multi 1.40 1.40

Independence Regatta celebrating 13th anniversary of independence.

**Elizabeth II Coronation Anniversary Issue**

Souvenir Sheet

Common Design Types

**1978, Apr. 15 Litho. Perf. 15**

*380* Sheet of 6 5.00 5.00
*a* CD326 1d *White grayhound of Richmond* 80 80
*b* CD327 1d *Elizabeth II* 80 80
*c* CD328 1d *Lion* 80 80

No. 380 contains 2 se-tenant strips of Nos. 380a-380c, separated by horizontal gutter with commemorative and descriptive inscriptions and showing central part of coronation procession with coach. Size: 100x135mm.

Verreaux's Eagle Owl — A58

Birds of Prey and Wildlife Fund Emblem: 25b, Lizard buzzard. 50b, West African harrier hawk. 1.25d, Long-crested hawk eagle.

**1978, Oct. 28 Litho. Perf. 14x13½**

*381* A58 20b multi 60 45
*382* A58 25b multi 70 50
*383* A58 50b multi 1.25 1.00
*384* A58 1.25d multi 3.00 2.50

Abuko Nature Reserve.

MV Lady Wright A59

New river vessels: 25b, River vessel Lady Chilel Jawara. 1d, Cross section of Lady Chilel Jawara.

**1978, Dec. 1 Litho. Perf. 14½**

*385* A59 8b multi 15 12
*386* A59 25b multi 45 35
*387* A59 1d multi 1.75 1.50

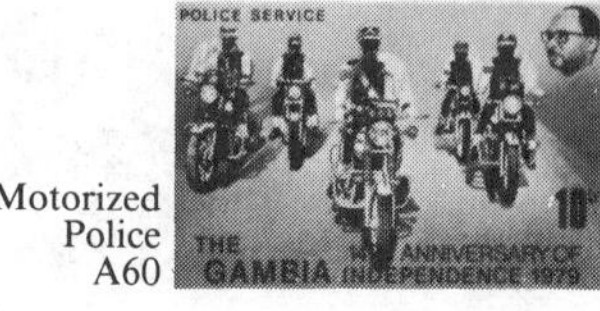


Motorized Police A60

**1979, Feb. 18 Litho. Perf. 14**

*388* A60 10b shown 12 12
*389* A60 50b Fire engine 65 65
*390* A60 1.25d Ambulance 1.60 1.60

14th anniversary of independence.

Nos. 359, 363-364 Surcharged.

**1979 Litho. Perf. 14½**

*390A* A53 25b on 13b multi 22 22
*390B* A53 25b on 63b multi 22 22
*390C* A53 25b on 1.25d multi 22 22

Issue dates: No. 390A, Mar. 5; others, Mar. 26.

Ramsgate Sands, by William P. Frith — A61

Designs: 10b, 25b, IYC emblem and details from painting shown on 1d. 25b vert.

**1979, May 25 Litho. Perf. 14**

**Size: 38x21mm, 21x38mm**

*391* A61 10b multi 9 9
*392* A61 25b multi 22 22

**Size: 56x21mm**

*393* A61 1d multi 90 90

International Year of the Child.

Gambia No. 15, Maltese Cross Postmark — A62

Designs (Gambian Stamps and Maltese Cross Postmark): 25b, No. 1. 50b, No. 208. 1.25d, No. 125.

**1979, Aug. 16 Litho. Perf. 14½**

*394* A62 10b multi 8 8
*395* A62 25b multi 14 14
*396* A62 50b multi 40 40
*397* A62 1.25d multi 1.00 1.00
*a* Souvenir sheet 1.25 1.25

Sir Rowland Hill (1795-1879), originator of penny postage. No. 397a contains No. 397; multicolored margin with portrait of Rowland Hill. Size: 119x85.

Abuko Earth Station, Construction — A63

Telecommunications: 50b, Newly opened station. 1d, Intelsat satellites orbiting earth.

**1979, Sept. 20 Litho. Perf. 14**

*398* A63 25b multi 25 25
*399* A63 50b multi 50 50
*400* A63 1d multi 1.00 1.00

Apollo 11 Lift-off — A64

**1979, Oct. 17 Litho. Perf. 14**

*401* A64 25b *shown* 25 25
*402* A64 38b *Orbiting moon* 38 38
*403* A64 50b *Splashdown* 50 50
*a* Souvenir booklet 4.00
*b* Pane of 6 (2 each of 25b,38b,50b) 1.90
*c* Pane of 1 (2d *Lunar module*) 1.75

Apollo 11 moon landing, 10th anniversary. No. 403a contains Nos. 403b-403c printed on peelable, self-adhesive paper backing with Apollo 11 emblems on back. Stamps and panes are die-cut and have 1 to 3 sides rouletted 9½. Size of panes: 149x89mm.

Large Spotted Acraea, Wildlife Fund Emblem — A65

Wildlife Fund Emblem and Butterflies: 50b, Yellow pansy. 1d, Veined swallowtail. 1.25d, Foxy charaxes.

**1980, Jan. 3 Litho. Perf. 13½x14**

*404* A65 25b multi 32 32
*405* A65 50b multi 65 65
*406* A65 1d multi 1.40 1.40
*407* A65 1.25d multi 1.65 1.65
*a* Souvenir sheet of 4 4.00 4.00

Abuko Nature Reserve. No. 407a contains Nos. 404-407; multicolored margin shown butterflies. Size: 145x122mm.

Steam Launch "Vampire" — A66

**1980, May 6 Litho. Perf. 14½**

*408* A66 10b *shown* 10 10
*409* A66 25b *"Lady Denham"* 25 25

**Perf. 13½x14½**
**Size: 49x21mm**

*410* A66 50b *"Mansa Kila Ba"* 50 50
*411* A66 1.25d *"Prince of Wales"* 1.25 1.25

London 80 Intl. Stamp Exhib., May 6-14.

**Queen Mother Elizabeth Birthday Issue**
Common Design Type

**1980, Aug. 4 Litho. Perf. 14**

*412* CD330 67b multi 60 60

Phoenician Trading Vessel — A67

**1980, Oct. 2 Litho. Perf. 14½**

*413* A67 8b *shown* 7 7
*414* A67 67b *Egyptian seagoing ship* 52 52
*415* A67 75b *Portuguese caravel* 60 60
*416* A67 1d *Spanish galleon* 80 80

Virgin and Child, by Francesco de Mura — A68

Christmas 1980: 67b, Praying Virgin with Crown of Stars, by Correggio. 75b, Rest on the Flight, after Correggio.

**1980, Dec. 18 Litho. Perf. 14**

*417* A68 8b multi 7 7
*418* A68 67b multi 52 52
*419* A68 75b multi 60 60

New Atlantic Hotel, Conference Emblem A69

**1981, Feb. 18 Litho. Perf. 14**

*420* A69 25b *shown* 25 25
*421* A69 75b Ancient stone circle 75 75
*422* A69 85b Conference emblem 85 85

World Tourism Conference, Manila, Sept. 27 and 16th anniversary of independence.

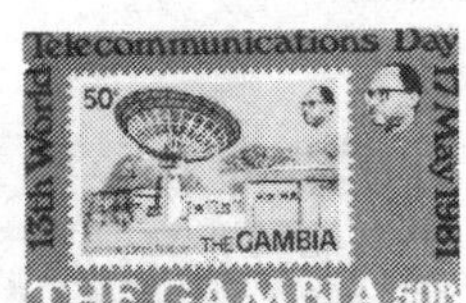


13th World Telecomunications Day — A70

**1981, May 17 Litho. Perf. 14**

*423* A70 50b No. 399 35 35
*424* A70 50b No. 313 35 35
*425* A70 85b ITU, WHO emblems 60 60

**Royal Wedding Issue**
Common Design Type

**1981, July 22 Litho. Perf. 13½x13**

*426* CD331 75b Bouquet 55 55
*427* CD331 1d Charles 75 75
*428* CD331 1.25d Couple 90 90

Planting Rice Seedlings A71

**1981, Sept. 4 Litho. Perf. 14**

*429* A71 10b shown 8 8
*430* A71 50b Spraying 40 40
*431* A71 85b Winnowing and drying 65 65

West African Rice Development Assoc., 10th anniv.

Abuko Nature Reserve A72

Designs: Wildlife Fund emblem and reptiles.

**1981, Nov. 17 Litho. Perf. 14**

*432* A72 40b Bosc's monitor 40 40
*433* A72 60b Dwarf crocodile 60 60
*434* A72 80b Royal python 80 80
*435* A72 85b Chameleon 85 85

30th Anniv. of West African Examinations Council — A73

**1982, Mar. 16 Litho. Perf. 14**

*436* A73 60b Test room 40 40
*437* A73 85b 1st high school 55 55
*438* A73 1.10d Council office 75 75

No. 426 Surcharged.

**1982, Apr. 19 Litho. Perf. 13½x13**

*439* CD331 60b on 75b multi

Scouting Year A74

**1982, May Perf. 14**

*440* A74 85b Tree planting 55 55
*441* A74 1.25d Woodworking 80 80
*442* A74 1.27d Baden-Powell 90 90

1982 World Cup A75

**1982, June 13 Litho. Perf. 14**

*443* A75 10b Team 7 7
*444* A75 1.10d Players 75 75
*445* A75 1.25d Stadium 80 80
*446* A75 1.55d Cup 1.00 1.00
*a* Souvenir sheet of 4 2.75 2.75

No. 446a contains Nos. 443-446; black marginal inscription. Size: 115x85mm.

**Princess Diana Issue**
Common Design Type

**1982, July 1 Perf. 14½x14**

*447* CD333 10b Arms 8 8
*448* CD333 85b Diana 65 65
*449* CD333 1.10d Wedding 85 85
*450* CD333 2.50d Portrait 1.75 1.75

Economic Community of West African States Development A76

**1982, Nov. 5 Litho. Perf. 14x14½**

*451* A76 10b Yundum Experimental Farm 8 8
*452* A76 60b Banjul/Kaolack Microwave Tower 45 45
*453* A76 90b Soap Factory, Denton Bridge Banjul 70 70
*454* A76 1.25d Control Tower, Yundum 90 90

Kassina Cassinoides — A77

**1982, Dec. Litho. Perf. 14**

*455* A77 10b shown 7 7
*456* A77 20b Hylarana galamensis 14 14
*457* A77 85b Euphlyctis occipitalis 60 60
*458* A77 2d Kassina senegalensis 1.40 1.40

**Commonwealth Day**
Common Design Type
**Wmk. 373**

**1983, Mar. 14 Litho. Perf. 12**

*459* CD334 10b Globe showing Gambia 6 6
*460* CD334 60b Batik cloth 35 35
*461* CD334 1.10d Bagging peanuts 60 60
*462* CD334 2.10d Flag 1.10 1.10

Sisters of St. Joseph of Cluny Centenary — A79

**1983, Apr. 8 Litho. Perf. 14**

*463* A79 10b Founder Anne Marie Javouhey, vert. 7 7
*464* A79 85b Javouhey with children, house 60 60

River Boats A80

**1983, July 11 Litho. Perf. 14**

*465* A80 1b Canoes 5 5
*466* A80 2b Upstream ferry 5 5
*467* A80 3b Dredging vessel 5 5
*468* A80 4b Harbor launch 5 5
*469* A80 5b Freighter 5 5
*470* A80 10b 60-foot launch 7 7
*471* A80 20b Multi-purpose vessel 14 14
*472* A80 30b Large sailing canoe 20 20
*473* A80 40b Passenger-cargo ferry 28 28
*474* A80 50b Cargo liner, diff. 35 35
*475* A80 75b Fishing boats 50 50
*476* A80 1d Peanut river train 65 65
*477* A80 1.25d Groundnutter 80 80
*478* A80 2.50d Banjul-Barra ferry 1.75 1.75
*479* A80 5d Binlang Bolong 3.50 3.50
*480* A80 10d Passenger-cargo ferry, diff. 6.50 6.50
*Nos. 465-480 (16)* 14.99 14.99

The Scott Catalogue value is a retail price, what you could expect to pay for the stamp in a grade of Fine-Very Fine. The value listed is a reference which reflects recent actual dealer selling price.

World Communications Year — A81

**1983, Oct. 10**
*481* A81 10b Local ferry 8 8
*482* A81 85b GPO telex, Banjul 65 65
*483* A81 90b Radio Gambia 70 70
*484* A81 1.10d Loading mail, Yundum Airport 85 85

Osprey, Breeding Range A82

Designs: Birds, Maps of Europe and Africa.

**1983, Sept. 12 Litho. *Perf. 14***
*485* A82 10b multi 8 8
*486* A82 60b multi 48 48
*487* A82 85b multi 70 70
*488* A82 1.10d multi 90 90

Raphael, 500th Birth Anniv. A83

Details from St. Paul Preaching at Athens.

**1983, Nov. 1 Litho. *Perf. 14***
*489* A83 60b multi 30 30
*490* A83 85b multi 40 40
*491* A83 1d multi 50 50

**Souvenir Sheet**

*492* A83 2d multi (vert.) 1.00 1.00

No. 492 has multicolored margin showing entire painting. Size: 105x84mm.

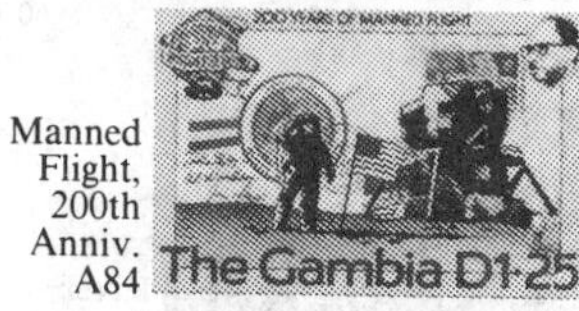

Manned Flight, 200th Anniv. A84

flown covers and: 60b, Montgolfier Balloon. 85b, British Caledonian Aircraft. 96b, Junkers Airplane. 1.25d, Lunar module. 4d, Zeppelin.

**1983, Dec. 12 Litho. *Perf. 14***
*493* A84 60b multi 55 55
*494* A84 85b multi 75 75
*a* Bklt pane, 2 each #493, 494 2.75
*495* A84 90b multi 80 80
*496* A84 1.25d multi 1.10 1.10
*a* Bklt pane, 2 each #495, 496 4.00

**Souvenir Sheet**

*497* A84 4d multi 6.00 6.00

No. 497 issued in booklet containing 497, 494a, 496a. Cover shows Gambia Nos. 102, 105 and 128.

### Nos. 411, 445, 428 and 449 Surcharged with Black Bars and New Value.

**1983, Dec. 14 Litho. *Perfs. as before***
*497A* A66 1.50d on 1.25d, #411
*497B* A75 1.50d on 1.25d, #445
*497C* CD331 2d on 1.25d, #428
*497D* CD333 2d on 1.10d, #449

Easter 1984 — A85

Various Disney characters painting Easter eggs.

**1984, Apr. 15 Litho. *Perf. 11***
*498* A85 1b multi 5 5
*499* A85 2b multi 5 5
*500* A85 3b multi 5 5
*501* A85 4b multi 5 5
*502* A85 5b multi 5 5
*503* A85 10b multi 7 7
*504* A85 60b multi 40 40
*505* A85 90b multi 60 60
*506* A85 5d multi 3.50 3.50
*Nos. 498-506 (9)* 4.82 4.82

**Souvenir Sheet**
***Perf. 14***

*507* A85 5d multi 3.50 3.50

No. 507 has multicolored margin continuing design. Size: 127x102mm.

1984 Summer Olympics A86

**1984, Mar. 30 Litho. *Perf. 14***
*508* A86 60b Shot put, vert. 35 35
*509* A86 85b High jump 48 48
*510* A86 90b Wrestling, vert. 50 50
*511* A86 1d Gymnastics, vert. 55 55
*512* A86 1.25d Swimming 70 70
*513* A86 2d Diving 1.10 1.10
*Nos. 508-513 (6)* 3.68 3.68

**Souvenir Sheet**

*514* A86 5d Yachting, vert. 2.75 2.75

No. 514 has multicolored margin continuing design. Size: 100x80mm.

Nile Crododile A87

**1984, May 23**
*515* A87 4b Young hatching 5 5
*516* A87 6b Adult carrying young 5 5
*517* A87 90b Adult 52 52
*518* A87 1.50d Adult, diff. 90 90
*a* Souvenir sheet of 4 1.50 1.50

No. 518a contains Nos. 515-518. Size: 127x94mm.

### Lloyd's List Issue
Common Design Type

**1984, June 1 Litho. *Perf. 14***
*519* CD335 60b Banjul Port 35 35
*520* CD335 85b Bulk cargo carrier 50 50
*521* CD335 90b Sinking of the Dagomba 52 52
*522* CD335 1.25d 19th-cent. frigate 70 70

### Nos. 478-479 Overprinted: "19th UPU / CONGRESS HAMBURG"

**1984, June 19 Litho. *Perf. 14***
*523* A80 2.50d multi 2.00 2.00
*524* A80 5d multi 4.00 4.00

1984 Summer Olympics A88

**1984, July 28 Litho. *Perf. 14***
*525* A88 60b Running 36 36
*526* A88 85b Long jump 52 52
*527* A88 90b Running, diff. 55 55
*528* A88 1.25d Long jump, diff. 75 75

Gambia-South America Transatlantic Flight, 50th Anniv. — A89

**1984, Nov. 1 Litho. *Perf. 14***
*529* A89 60b Graf Zeppelin D-LZ127 30 30
*530* A89 85b Dornier Wal on S.S. Westfalen 50 50
*531* A89 90b Dornier DO-18 D-ABYM 52 52
*532* A89 1.25d Dornier Wal D-2069 70 70

Butterflies and Marine Life A90

**1984, Nov. 27**
*533* A90 10b Antanartia hippomene 5 5
*534* A90 55b Penaeus duorarum 30 30
*535* A90 75b Caretta caretta 45 45
*536* A90 85b Pseudacraea eurytus 48 48
*537* A90 90b Charaxes lactitinctus 50 50
*538* A90 1.50d Physalia 85 85
*539* A90 2.35d Uca pugilator 1.25 1.25
*540* A90 3d Graphium pylades 1.50 1.50
*Nos. 533-540 (8)* 5.38 5.38

**Souvenir Sheets**

*541* A90 5d Eurema hapale 2.75 2.75
*542* A90 5d Cowrie snail 2.75 2.75

Nos. 541-542 have multicolored margins continuing each design. Sizes: 106x76mm; 106x70mm (#542).

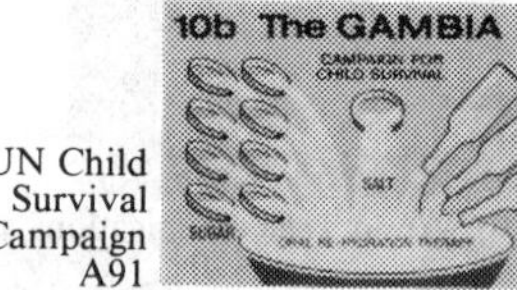

UN Child Survival Campaign A91

**1985, Feb. 27**
*543* A91 10b Oral rehydration therapy 5 5
*544* A91 85b Growth monitoring 50 50
*545* A91 1.10d Breast-feeding 65 65
*546* A91 1.50d Universal immunization 90 90

UN Decade for Women A92

Design: 1d, 1.25d, Woman working in office.

**1985, Mar. 11**
*547* A92 60b multi 30 30
*548* A92 85b multi 45 45
*549* A92 1d multi 55 55
*550* A92 1.25d multi 65 65

Audubon Birth Bicent. — A93

Queen Mother, 85th Birthday — A94

Illustrations of North American bird species by John J. Audubon (1785-1851).

**1985, July 15**
*551* A93 60b Cathartes aura 32 32
*552* A93 85b Anhinga anhinga 50 50
*553* A93 1.50d Butoroides striatus 90 90
*554* A93 5d Aix sponsa 3.00 3.00

**Souvenir Sheet**

*555* A93 10d Gavia immer 5.50 5.50

No. 555 has multicolored decorative margin continuing the design. Size: 100x99mm.

**1985, July 24**
*556* A94 85b Inspecting troops 50 50
*557* A94 3d Portrait 1.65 1.65
*558* A94 5d Portrait, diff. 3.00 3.00

**Souvenir Sheet**

*559* A94 10d On parade with Prince Charles 5.50 5.50

No. 559 has multicolored margin picturing fiber plants and coral tree blooms. Size: 57x85mm.

Life on the Mississippi, by Mark Twain (1835-1910) — A95

Walt Disney characters.

**1985, Oct. 30**
*560* A95 60b Portrait 30 30
*561* A95 85b Treasure 40 40
*562* A95 1.50d Helm of Calamity Jane 90 90
*563* A95 2d Antebellum Mansion, Missouri Shore 1.20 1.20
*564* A95 2.35d Music 1.20 1.20
*565* A95 2.50d Measuring Channel Depth, Natchez 1.40 1.40
*566* A95 3d Card Game aboard the Gold Dust 1.65 1.65
*567* A95 5d Statue 2.50 2.50
*Nos. 560-567 (8)* 9.55 9.55

**Souvenir Sheet**

*568* A95 10d Landing, St. Louis 6.00 6.00
*569* A95 10d Goofy 5.00 5.00

No. 568 has multicolored margin continuing the design, picturing Goofy and Donald Duck. Size: 127x101mm.

No. 569 has multicolored margin continuing the design, picturing characters celebrating Faithful John's recovery. Size: 127x102mm.

### Nos. 508-514 Ovptd. "GOLD MEDALIST" or "GOLD MEDAL," Name of Winner and Country.

Designs: 60b, Claudia Losch, West Germany, women's shot put. 85b, Ulrike Meyfarth, West Germany, women's high jump. 90b, Pasquale Passarelli, West Germany, 126-pound Greco-Roman wrestling.

1d, Li Ning, China, men's gymnastic floor exercises. 1.25d, Michael Gross, West Germany, men's 100-meter butterfly and 200-meter freestyle swimming. 2d, Sylvie Bernier, Canada, women's springboard diving. 5d, US, Star Class yachting.

**1985, Nov. 11** *Perf. 14*

*570* A86 60b multi 28 28
*571* A86 85b multi 40 40
*572* A86 90b multi 48 48
*573* A86 1d multi 50 50
*574* A86 1.25d multi 65 65
*575* A86 2d multi 1.00 1.00
*Nos. 570-575 (6)* 3.31 3.31

**Souvenir Sheet**

*576* A86 5d multi 2.50 2.50

UN 40th Anniv. A97

Views of Banjul.

**1985, Nov. 15**

*577* A97 85b Independence Stadium 45 45
*578* A97 2d Central Bank 1.10 1.10
*579* A97 4d Port 2.25 2.25
*580* A97 6d Oyster Creek Bridge 3.50 3.50

Natl. independence, 20th anniv.

UN FAO, 40th Anniv. A98

**1985, Nov. 15**

*581* A98 60b Corn 30 30
*582* A98 1.10d Paddy 60 60
*583* A98 3d Cow, calf 1.75 1.75
*584* A98 5d Fruit 2.75 2.75

Diocese of Gambia and Guinea, 50th Anniv. A99

Designs: 60b, Fishermen, Fotoba, Guinea. 85b, St. Mary's Primary School, Banjul. 1.10d, St. Mary's Cathedral, Banjul. 1.50d, Mobile Dispensary at Christy, Kunda, 1935-45.

**1985, Dec. 24**

*585* A99 60b multi 30 30
*586* A99 85b multi 45 45
*587* A99 1.10d multi 60 60
*588* A99 1.50d multi 90 90

Girl Guides, 75th Anniv. A100

Christmas A101

**1985, Dec. 27**

*589* A100 60b Application, horiz. 30 30
*590* A100 85b 2nd Bathurst, horiz. 45 45
*591* A100 1.50d Lady Baden-Powell 90 90
*592* A100 5d Rosamond Fowlis, leader 2.75 2.75

**Souvenir Sheet**

*593* A100 10d Guides 5.50 5.50

No. 593 has multicolored margin continuing the design, picturing Gambian troop and anniv. emblem. Size: 98x67mm.

**1985, Dec. 27** *Perf. 15*

Painting details: 60b, Virgin and Child, by Dirck Bouts (c. 1400-1475). 85b, The Annunciation, by Robert Campin (c. 1378-1444). 1.50d, Adoration of the Shepherds, by Gerard David (c. 1460-1523). 5d, The Nativity, by Gerard David. 10d, Adoration of the Magi, by Hieronymus Bosch (1450-1516).

*594* A101 60b multi 30 30
*595* A101 85b multi 45 45
*596* A101 1.50d multi 90 90
*597* A101 5d multi 2.75 2.75

**Souvenir Sheet**

*598* A101 10d multi 5.50 5.50

No. 598 has multicolored decorative margin continuing the painting. Size: 106x84mm.

Intl. Youth Year A102

**1985, Dec. 31** *Perf. 14*

*599* A102 60b Mother's helper 30 30
*600* A102 85b Wrestling 45 45
*601* A102 1.10d Griot storyteller 60 60
*602* A102 1.50d Crocodile pool 90 90

**Souvenir Sheet**

*603* A102 5d Cow herder 2.75 2.75

No. 603 has multicolored margin continuing the design and picturing river bank. Size: 106x77mm.

A103

Halley's Comet A104

Designs: 10b, Maria Mitchell (1818-1889), American astronomer, Kitt Peak Natl. Observatory, Papago Indian Reservation, Arizona. 20b, Apollo 11, Neil Armstrong steps on moon, 1969. 75b, Skylab 4, Kohoutek Comet, 1973. 1d, NASA Infrared Astronomical Satellite, 1983. 2d, Comet sighting, 1577, Turkish art. No. 609, NASA Intl. Cometary Explorer satellite. No. 610, Comet.

**1986, Mar.**

*604* A103 10b multi 5 5
*605* A103 20b multi 12 12
*606* A103 75b multi 40 40
*607* A103 1d multi 60 60
*608* A103 2d multi 1.10 1.10
*609* A103 10d multi 5.50 5.50
*Nos. 604-609 (6)* 7.77 7.77

**Souvenir Sheet**

*610* A104 10d multi 5.75 5.75

No. 610 pictures the comet over Gambia River. Size: 102x70mm.

**Queen Elizabeth II, 60th Birthday**
Common Design Type

Designs: 1d, Royal family at Royal Tournament, 1936. 2.50d, Christening, 1983. No. 613, State visit to West Germany, 1978. No. 614, At Balmoral, 1935.

**1986, Apr. 21**

*611* CD339 1d lt yel bis & blk 60 60
*612* CD339 2.50d pale grn & multi 1.40 1.40
*613* CD339 10d dl lil & multi 5.50 5.50

**Souvenir Sheet**

*614* CD339 10d tan & blk 5.50 5.50

No. 614 has tan, gray and black inscribed margin. Size: 120x85mm.

1986 World Cup Soccer Championships, Mexico — A105

**1986, May 2**

*615* A105 75b Block 45 45
*616* A105 1d Kneeing the ball 60 60
*617* A105 2.50d Kick 1.40 1.40
*618* A105 10d Heading the ball 5.50 5.50

**Souvenir Sheet**

*619* A105 10d Goalie catching ball 5.50 5.50

No. 619 has multicolored margin picturing gloves, Rimet Cup, ball and cleated shoes. Size: 100x70mm.

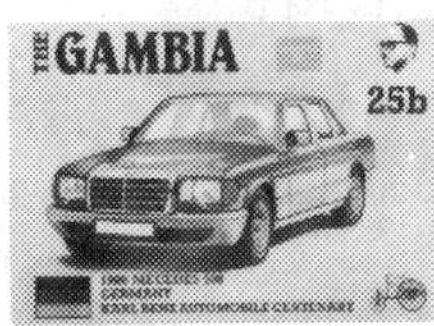


AMERIPEX '86 — A106

Exhibition emblem, automobiles and flags: 25b, 1986 Mercedes 500, Germany. 75b, 1935 Cord 810, US. 1d, 1957 Borgward Isabella Coupe, Germany. 1.25d, 1985-6 Lamborghini Countach, Italy. 2d, 1955 Ford Thunderbird, US. 2.25d, 1956 Citroen DS19, France. 5d, 1936 Bugatti Atlante, France. 10d, 1936 Horch 853, Germany. No. 628, 1913 Benz 8/20, Germany. No. 629, 1924 Steiger 10/50, Germany.

**1986, May 22** *Perf. 15*

*620* A106 25b multi 15 15
*621* A106 75b multi 40 40
*622* A106 1d multi 60 60
*623* A106 1.25d multi 70 70
*624* A106 2d multi 1.10 1.10
*625* A106 2.25d multi 1.25 1.25
*626* A106 5d multi 2.75 2.75
*627* A106 10d multi 5.50 5.50
*Nos. 620-627 (8)* 12.45 12.45

**Souvenir Sheets**

*628* A106 12d multi 6.75 6.75
*629* A106 12d multi 6.75 6.75

Karl Benz automobile cent. Nos. 628-629 have light blue or light yellow bister inscribed margins picturing Benz automobile. Sizes: 100x70mm.

Statue of Liberty, Cent. A107

Statue and famous emigrants: 20b, John Jacob Astor (1763-1848), financier. 1d, Jacob Riis (1849-1914), journalist. 1.25d, Igor Sikorsky (1889-1972), aeronautics engineer. 5d, Charles Boyer (1899-1978), actor. 10d, Statue, vert.

**1986, June 10** *Perf. 14*

*630* A107 20b multi 12 12
*631* A107 1d multi 60 60
*632* A107 1.25d multi 70 70
*633* A107 5d multi 2.75 2.75

**Souvenir Sheet**

*634* A107 10d multi 5.50 5.50

No. 634 has multicolored margin picturing aerial view of New York City and: Ludwig Mies van der Rohe (1886-1969), architect; Ottmar Mergenthaler (1854-1899), inventor; Walter Damrosch (1862-1950), conductor, composer; and Arnold Schoenberg (1874-1951), composer. Size: 114x81mm.

**Royal Wedding Issue, 1986**
Common Design Type

Designs: 1d, Engagement of Prince Andrew and Sarah Ferguson. 2.50d, Andrew. 4d, Andrew in flight uniform, other helicopter pilot. 7d, Couple, diff.

**1986, July 23**

*635* CD340 1d multi 60 60
*636* CD340 2.50d multi 1.40 1.40
*637* CD340 4d multi 2.25 2.25

**Souvenir Sheet**

*638* CD340 7d multi 4.00 4.00

No. 638 has multicolored margin picturing couple touring ship. Size: 88x88mm.

Nos. 615-619 Overprinted "WINNERS / Argentina 3 / W. Germany 2" in Gold.

**1986, Sept. 16** **Litho.** *Perf. 14*

*639* A105 75b multi 40 40
*640* A105 1d multi 60 60
*641* A105 2.50d multi 1.50 1.50
*642* A105 10d multi 5.50 5.50

**Souvenir Sheet**

*643* A105 10d multi 5.50 5.50

Christmas, STOCKHOLMIA '86 — A108

Disney characters mailing letters in various countries.

**1986, Nov. 4** *Perf. 11*

*644* A108 1d Great Britain 30 30
*645* A108 1.25d United States 40 40
*646* A108 2d France 60 60
*647* A108 2.35d Australia 70 70
*648* A108 5d Germany 1.60 1.60
*Nos. 644-648 (5)* 3.60 3.60

**Souvenir Sheet**

*649* A108 10d Sweden 3.00 3.00

No. 649 has multicolored margin continuing the design.

Nos. 604-610 Ovptd. with Halley's Comet Logo in Silver.

**1986, Oct. 21** **Litho.** *Perf. 14*

*650* A103 10b multi 5 5
*651* A103 20b multi 6 6
*652* A103 75b multi 22 22
*653* A103 1d multi 30 30
*654* A103 2d multi 55 55
*655* A103 10d multi 3.00 3.00
*Nos. 650-655 (6)* 4.18 4.18

**Souvenir Sheet**

*656* A104 10d multi 3.00 3.00

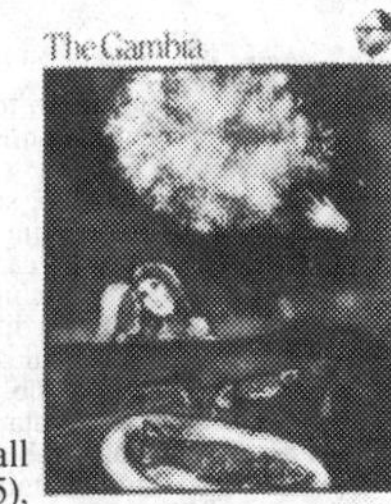


Marc Chagall (1887-1985), Artist — A109

Paintings, ceramicware, sculpture: 75b, Snowing. 85b, The Boat, 1957. 1d, Maternity, 1913. 1.25d, The Flute Player. 2.35d, Lovers and the Beast, 1957. 4d, Fishes at Saint Jean. 5d, Entering the Ring, 1968. 10d, Three Acrobats, 1956. No. 665, The Sabbath. No. 666, The Cattle Driver.

**1987, Feb. 6** **Litho.**

657 A109 75b multi 20 20
658 A109 85b multi 22 22
659 A109 1d multi 25 25
660 A109 1.25d multi 32 32
661 A109 2.35d multi 60 60
662 A109 4d multi 1.00 1.00
663 A109 5d multi 1.25 1.25
664 A109 10d multi 2.50 2.50

**Sizes: 110x95mm, 110x68mm**

***Imperf***

665 A109 12d multi 3.00 3.00
666 A109 12d multi 3.00 3.00
*Nos. 657-666 (10)* 12.34 12.34

Musical Instruments — A110

Various instruments from the Manding Empire.

**1987, Jan. 21** **Litho.** ***Perf. 15***

667 A110 75b Bugarab, tabala 22 22
668 A110 1d Balaphong, fiddle 30 30
669 A110 1.25d Bolongbato, konting 35 35
670 A110 10d Koras 2.75 2.75

**Souvenir Sheet**

671 A110 12d Sabarrs 3.25 3.25

Nos. 669-670 vert. No. 671 has inscribed muticolored margin picturing hunting and defense weapons. Size: 100x70mm.

America's Cup A111

**1987, Apr. 3** ***Perf. 14***

672 A111 20b America, 1851 8 8
673 A111 1d Courageous, 1974 38 38
674 A111 2.50d Volunteer, 1887 95 95
675 A111 10d Intrepid, 1967 3.75 3.75

**Souvenir Sheet**

676 A111 12d Australia II, 1983 4.50 4.50

No. 676 has multicolored margin picturing builder's draft of boat. Size: 114x89mm.

Statue of Liberty, Cent. A112

Photographs of restoration and unveiling in 1986.

**1987, Apr. 9** **Litho.**

677 A112 1b Shoulder, torch 5 5
678 A112 2b Operation Sail flotilla 5 5
679 A112 3b Tall ship, ships 5 5
680 A112 5b Luxury liner, aircraft carrier 5 5
681 A112 50b Statue's coiffure 18 18
682 A112 75b Coiffure, diff. 28 28
683 A112 1d Workmen scaling statue 38 38
684 A112 1.25d Back of statue 48 48
685 A112 10d Front of Statue 3.75 3.75
686 A112 12d Side of statue 4.50 4.50
*Nos. 677-686 (10)* 9.77 9.77

Nos. 677, 681-686 vert.

Prices of premium quality never hinged stamps will be in excess of catalogue price.

Flowers from Abuko Nature Reserve A113

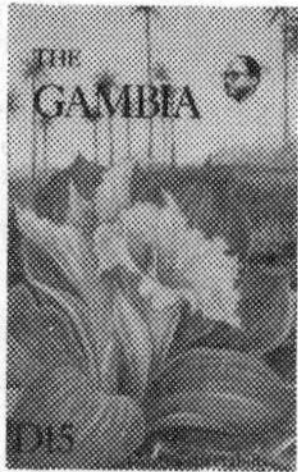


Costus Spectabilis A114

**1987, May 25**

687 A113 75b Lantana camara 28 28
687A A113 1d Clerodendrum thomsoniae 38 38
688 A113 1.50d Haemanthus multiflorus 58 58
688A A113 1.70d Gloriosa simplex 65 65
689 A113 1.75d Combretum microphyllum 65 65
689A A113 2.25d Eulophia guineensis 85 85
689B A113 5d Erythrina senegalensis 1.90 1.90
690 A113 15d Dichrostachys glomerata 5.50 5.50
*Nos. 687-690 (8)* 10.79 10.79

**Souvenir Sheets**

691 A114 15d multi 5.50 5.50
691A A114 15d Strophanthus preussii 5.50 5.50

Nos. 691-691A have multicolored margins continuing the designs, picturing Gambian woman in nature reserve and Abuko Reserve lodge, respectively. Sizes: 101x70mm.

CAPEX '87 A115

Various buses.

**1987, June 15**

692 A115 20b multi, vert. 8 8
693 A115 75b multi 28 28
694 A115 1d multi 38 38
695 A115 10d multi, vert. 3.75 3.75

**Souvenir Sheet**

696 A115 12d multi 4.50 4.50

No. 696 has multicolored margin picturing African wildlife. Size: 77x70mm.

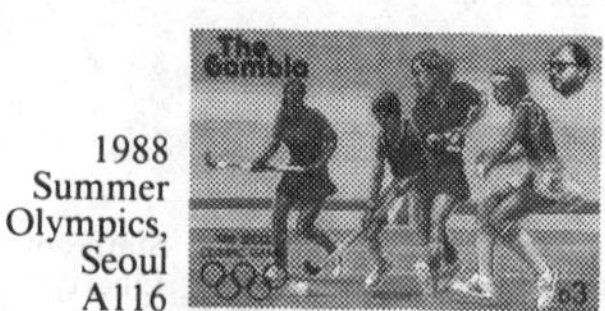


1988 Summer Olympics, Seoul A116

**1987, July 3**

697 A116 50b Women's basketball 20 20
698 A116 1d Volleyball 38 38
699 A116 3d Field hockey 1.15 1.15
700 A116 10d Handball 3.75 3.75

**Souvenir Sheet**

701 A116 15d Soccer 5.50 5.50

Nos. 697-698 vert. No. 701 has inscribed decorative margin picturing five-ring emblem and athletes. Size: 102x85mm.

A117

The Twelve Days of Christmas, Medieval Counting Song — A118

Designs: 20b, Partridge in a pear tree. 40b, 2 turtle doves. 60b, 3 French hens. 75b, 4 calling birds. 1d, 5 golden rings. 1.25d, 6 geese a-laying. 1.50d, 7 swans a-swimming. 2d, 8 maids a-milking. 3d, 9 ladies dancing. 5d, 10 lords a-leaping. 10d, 11 pipers piping. 12d, 12 drummers drumming.

**Miniature Sheet**

**1987, Nov. 2** **Litho.** ***Perf. 14***

702 Sheet of 12 14.00 14.00
a A117 20b multi 8 8
b A117 40b multi 15 15
c A117 60b multi 22 22
d A117 75b multi 28 28
e A117 1d multi 38 38
f A117 1.25d multi 48 48
g A117 1.50d multi 58 58
h A117 2d multi 75 75
i A117 3d multi 1.15 1.15
j A117 5d multi 1.90 1.90
k A117 10d multi 3.75 3.75
l A117 12d multi 4.50 4.50

**Souvenir Sheet**

703 A118 15d multi 5.50 5.50

Size of No. 702: 111x193mm. No. 703 has multicolored margin continuing the design. Size: 100x70mm.

16th Boy Scout Jamboree, Australia, 1987-88 A119

**1987, Nov. 9**

704 A119 75b Singing around campfire 28 28
705 A119 1d Nature study, African katydid 38 38
706 A119 1.25d Bird watching, red-tailed tropicbird 48 48
707 A119 12d Boarding bus 4.50 4.50

**Souvenir Sheet**

708 A119 15d Nature study 5.50 5.50

No. 708 has multicolored inscribed margin continuing the design and picturing flora and fauna. Size: 72xx98mm.

Mickey Mouse, 60th Anniv. — A120

Disney animated characters and historic locomotives: 60b, Richard Trevithick's locomotive, 1804. 75b, Empire State Express 999, 1893. 1d, George Stephenson's Rocket, 1829. 1.25d, Santa Fe Mountain 2-10-2, 1920. 2d, Class GG-1 Pennsylvania, 1933. 5d, Stourbridge Lion, 1829. 10d, Best Friend of Charleston, 1830. 12d, M10001 Union Pacific, 1934. No. 717, Tres Grande Vitesse-SNCF, 1981, France. No. 718, The General, Western & Atlantic, 1855.

**1987, Dec. 9** **Litho.** ***Perf. 14x13½***

709 A120 60b multi 18 18
710 A120 75b multi 22 22
711 A120 1d multi 30 30
712 A120 1.25d multi 38 38
713 A120 2d multi 60 60
714 A120 5d multi 1.50 1.50
715 A120 10d multi 3.00 3.00
716 A120 12d multi 3.60 3.60
*Nos. 709-716 (8)* 9.78 9.78

**Souvenir Sheets**

717 A120 15d multi 4.50 4.50
718 A120 15d multi 4.50 4.50

Nos. 717-718 have multicolored margins continuing the designs. Size: 127x102mm.

Fauna and Flora A121

**1988, Feb. 9** **Litho.** ***Perf. 15***

719 A121 50b Duiker, acacia 15 15
720 A121 75b Red-billed hornbill, casuarina 22 22
721 A121 90b West African dwarf crocodile, rice 28 28
722 A121 1d Leopard, papyrus 30 30
723 A121 1.25d Crested cranes, millet 38 38
724 A121 2d Waterbuck, baobab tree 60 60
725 A121 3d Oribi, Senegal palm 90 90
726 A121 5d Hippopotamus, papaya 1.50 1.50
*Nos. 719-726 (8)* 4.33 4.33

**Souvenir Sheets**

727 A121 12d Great white pelican 3.60 3.60
728 A121 12d Red-throated bee-eater 3.60 3.60

Nos. 720, 722, 724, 726 and 728 vert. Nos. 727-728 have multicolored decorative margins continuing the designs and picturing mangrove (No. 727) or acacia trees (No. 728). Sizes: 98x69mm.

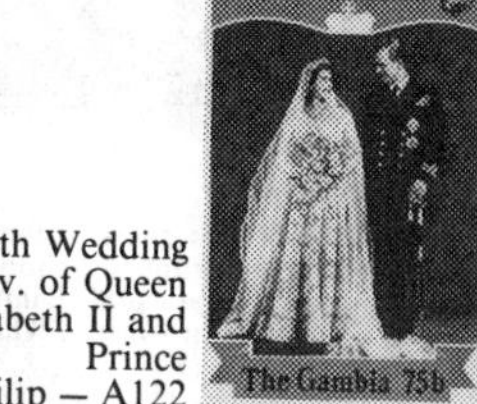


40th Wedding Anniv. of Queen Elizabeth II and Prince Philip — A122

**1988, Mar. 15** ***Perf. 14***

729 A122 75b Wedding portrait, 1947 22 22
730 A122 1d Couple at leisure 30 30
731 A122 3d Wedding portrait, diff. 90 90
732 A122 10d Couple, c. 1987 3.00 3.00

**Souvenir Sheet**

733 A122 15d Wedding party 4.50 4.50

No. 733 has multicolored margin continuing the photograph. Size: 100x75mm.

1988 Summer Olympics, Seoul A123

**1988, May 3** **Litho.** ***Perf. 14***

734 A123 1d Archery, vert. 30 30
735 A123 1.25d Boxing, vert. 38 38
736 A123 5d Gymnastics, vert. 1.50 1.50
737 A123 10d 100-Meter sprint 3.00 3.00

**Souvenir Sheet**

| | | | | |
|---|---|---|---|---|
| *738* | A123 | 15d Award ceremony, Olympic stadium | 4.50 | 4.50 |

No. 738 has multicolored inscribed margin continuing the design. Size: 75x103mm.

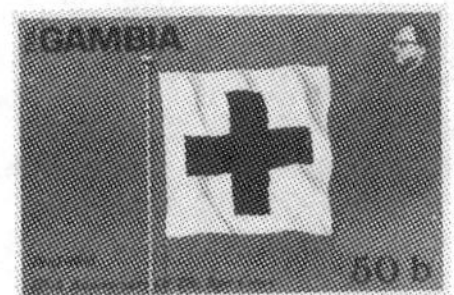


Anniversaries & Events — A124

Designs: 50b, Red Cross flag. 75b, Friendship 7, piloted by John Glenn, 1963. 1d, British Airways Concorde jet. 1.25d, *Spirit of St. Louis*, piloted by Charles Lindbergh, 1927. 2d, X-15, piloted by Major William Knight, 1967. 3d, Bell X-1, piloted by Capt. Charles Yeager, 1947. 10d, Spanish galleon, British warship, 1588. 12d, The *Titanic*. No. 747, Kangaroo and joey. No. 748, Cathedral, modern church, vert.

**1988, May 15**

| | | | | |
|---|---|---|---|---|
| *739* | A124 | 50b multi | 16 | 16 |
| *740* | A124 | 75b multi | 24 | 24 |
| *741* | A124 | 1d multi | 32 | 32 |
| *742* | A124 | 1.25d multi | 38 | 38 |
| *743* | A124 | 2d multi | 62 | 62 |
| *744* | A124 | 3d multi | 95 | 95 |
| *745* | A124 | 10d multi | 3.10 | 3.10 |
| *746* | A124 | 12d multi | 3.75 | 3.75 |
| | | *Nos. 739-746 (8)* | 9.52 | 9.52 |

**Souvenir Sheets**

| | | | | |
|---|---|---|---|---|
| *747* | A124 | 15d multi | 4.50 | 4.50 |
| *748* | A124 | 15d multi | 4.50 | 4.50 |

Intl. Red Cross, 125th anniv. (50b); first American in space, 25th anniv. in 1987 (75b); 1st London-New York scheduled Concorde flight, 10th anniv. in 1987 (1d); first solo transatlantic flight, 60th anniv. in 1987 (1.25d); fastest speed flown, 6.72 Mach, 20th anniv. in 1987 (2d); 1st supersonic flight, 40th anniv. in 1987 (3d); defeat of the Spanish Armada, 400th anniv. (10d); maiden voyage of the *Titanic*,75th anniv. in 1987 (12d); founding of Australia, bicentennial (No. 747); and founding of Berlin, 750th anniv. in 1987 (No. 748).

Nos. 747-748 have multicolored inscribed margins picturing map of Australia, or view of Berlin and Berlin Lion, respectively. Sizes: 121x90mm (No. 747), 114x85mm (No. 748).

Nos. 694, 670, 675 and 690 Ovptd. for Philatelic Exhibitions

a

b

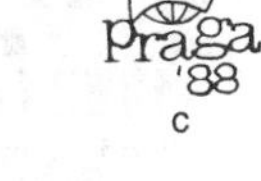


c

d

OLYMPHILEX '88

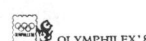

**1988, Apr. 19 Litho. *Perf. 14, 15***

| | | | | |
|---|---|---|---|---|
| *749* | A115 (a) | 1d multi | 32 | 32 |
| *750* | A110 (b) | 10d multi | 3.10 | 3.10 |
| *751* | A111 (c) | 10d multi | 3.25 | 3.25 |
| *752* | A113 (d) | 15d multi | 4.75 | 4.75 |

INDEPENDENCE 40, FINLANDIA 88, PRAGA 88, OLYMPHILEX '88.

Paintings by Titian — A125

Designs: 25b, *Emperor Charles V*, 1549. 50b, *St. Margaret and the Dragon*, 1565. 60b, *Ranuccio Farnese*, 1542. 75b, *Tarquin and Lucretia*, 1570. 1d, *The Knight of Malta*, c. 1550. 5d, *Spain Succouring Faith*, 1571. 10d, *Doge Francesco Venier*, 1555. 12d, *Doge Grimani Before the Faith*, c. 1555-1576. No. 761, *Jealous Husband*, 1511. No. 762, *Venus Blindfolding Cupid*, 1560.

**1988, July 7 Litho. *Perf. 13½x14***

| | | | | |
|---|---|---|---|---|
| *753* | A125 | 25b multi | 8 | 8 |
| *754* | A125 | 50b multi | 16 | 16 |
| *755* | A125 | 60b multi | 20 | 20 |
| *756* | A125 | 75b multi | 25 | 25 |
| *757* | A125 | 1d multi | 32 | 32 |
| *758* | A125 | 5d multi | 1.60 | 1.60 |
| *759* | A125 | 10d multi | 3.10 | 3.10 |
| *760* | A125 | 12d multi | 3.75 | 3.75 |
| | | *Nos. 753-760 (8)* | 9.46 | 9.46 |

**Souvenir Sheets**

| | | | | |
|---|---|---|---|---|
| *761* | A125 | 15d multi | 4.50 | 4.50 |
| *762* | A125 | 15d multi | 4.50 | 4.50 |

Nos. 761-762 have multicolored inscribed margins continuing the paintings. Sizes: 110x95mm.

*See Addenda for Nos. 763-767*

Entertainers — A127

Designs: 20b, Emmett Lee Kelly (1898-1979), clown. 1d, Gambia Natl. Ensemble. 1.25d, Jackie Gleason (1916-87), comedian, and *The Honeymooners* cast. 1.50d, Stan Laurel (1890-1965) and Oliver Hardy (1892-1957), film comedy team. 2.50d, Yul Brynner (c. 1920-85), actor. 3d, Cary Grant (1904-86), actor. 10d, Danny Kaye (1918-87), comedian, actor. 20d, Charlie Chaplin (1889-1977), comedian, actor. No. 776, Harpo (1893-1964), Chico (1891-1961), Zeppo (1901-79) and Groucho (1890-1977) Marx, comedy team. No. 777, Fred Astaire (1899-1987) and Rita Hayworth (1918-87), dancers and film stars. Nos. 768-775 vert.

**1988, Nov. 9 Litho.**

| | | | | |
|---|---|---|---|---|
| *768* | A127 | 20b multi | 6 | 6 |
| *769* | A127 | 1d multi | 30 | 30 |
| *770* | A127 | 1.25d multi | 38 | 38 |
| *771* | A127 | 1.50d multi | 45 | 45 |
| *772* | A127 | 2.50d multi | 75 | 75 |
| *773* | A127 | 3d multi | 90 | 90 |
| *774* | A127 | 10d multi | 3.00 | 3.00 |
| *775* | A127 | 20d multi | 6.00 | 6.00 |
| | | *Nos. 768-775 (8)* | 11.84 | 11.84 |

**Souvenir Sheets**

| | | | | |
|---|---|---|---|---|
| *776* | A127 | 15d multi | 4.50 | 4.50 |
| *777* | A127 | 15d multi | 4.50 | 4.50 |

Kelly's name is spelled incorrectly; Brynner's and Grant's dates are incorrect.

Nos. 776-777 have multicolored margins picturing the Marx Brothers, or Astaire and Hayworth dancing. Sizes: 110x78.

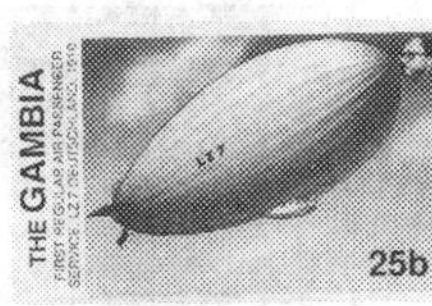


Zeppelin LZ7 *Deutschland*, 1910 — A128

Transportation innovations: 50b, Stephenson's *Locomotion*, 1825. 75b, General Motors *Sun Racer*, 1987. 1d, Sprague's *Premiere*, 1888. 1.25d, *Gold Rush* bicycle, 1986. 2.50d, 1st Liquid-fuel rocket, invented by Robert Goddard, 1925. 10d, *Orukter Amphibolos*, 1805. 12d, *Sovereign of the Seas*, 1988. No. 786, USS *Nautilus*, 1954, vert. No. 787, *Fulton's Nautilus*, early 19th cent.

**1988, Nov. 21 Litho. *Perf. 14***

| | | | | |
|---|---|---|---|---|
| *778* | A128 | 25b multi | 8 | 8 |
| *779* | A128 | 50b multi | 15 | 15 |
| *780* | A128 | 75b multi | 22 | 22 |
| *781* | A128 | 1d multi | 30 | 30 |
| *782* | A128 | 1.25d multi | 38 | 38 |
| *783* | A128 | 2.50d multi | 75 | 75 |
| *784* | A128 | 10d multi | 3.00 | 3.00 |
| *785* | A128 | 12d multi | 3.60 | 3.60 |
| | | *Nos. 778-785 (8)* | 8.48 | 8.48 |

**Souvenir Sheets**

| | | | | |
|---|---|---|---|---|
| *786* | A128 | 15d multi | 4.50 | 4.50 |
| *787* | A128 | 15d multi | 4.50 | 4.50 |

Nos. 786-787 have multicolored margins continuing the designs. Size: 71x93mm.

Discovery of America, 500th Anniv. (in 1992) A129

Designs: 50b, Caravel, Henry the Navigator (1394-1460), Prince of Portugal, and coat of arms, vert. 75b, Jesse Ramsden's sextant, map of Africa, arms, vert. 1d, Hour glass, 15th cent., and map, vert. 1.25d, Henry and Vasco da Gama, vert. 2.50d, Da Gama and 15th cent. caravel, vert. 5d, Mungo Park (1771-1806), Scottish explorer, arms and map of Gambia River. 10d, Map of west African coast, 1563. 12d, Portuguese caravel, arms. No. 796, Caravel off the Gambian coast, 15th cent., vert. No. 797, European ship off Gambian coast, 15th cent., vert.

**1988, Dec. 1 Litho. *Perf. 14***

| | | | | |
|---|---|---|---|---|
| *788* | A129 | 50b multi | 15 | 15 |
| *789* | A129 | 75b multi | 22 | 22 |
| *790* | A129 | 1d multi | 30 | 30 |
| *791* | A129 | 1.25d multi | 38 | 38 |
| *792* | A129 | 2.50d multi | 75 | 75 |
| *793* | A129 | 5d shown | 1.50 | 1.50 |
| *794* | A129 | 10d multi | 3.00 | 3.00 |
| *795* | A129 | 12d multi | 3.60 | 3.60 |
| | | *Nos. 788-795 (8)* | 9.90 | 9.90 |

**Souvenir Sheets**

| | | | | |
|---|---|---|---|---|
| *796* | A129 | 15d multi | 4.50 | 4.50 |
| *797* | A129 | 15d multi | 4.50 | 4.50 |

Nos. 796-797 have multicolored margins continuing the designs. Sizes: 65x101mm.

Space Achievements — A130

Galileo and: 50b, Futuristic aerospace plane and Ernst Mach (1838-1916), Austrian physicist who studied projectiles and after whom the mach was named, vert. 75b, OAO III astronomical satellite and Niels Bohr (1885-1962), Danish physicist and Nobel lauerate in 1922, vert. 1d, NASA space shuttle, future space station and Robert Goddard (1882-1945), American rocket scientist. 1.25d, Flyby of JPL probe past Jupiter, 1979, and Edward Barnard (1857-1923), American astronomer who discovered Jupiter's 5th satellite in 1892. 2d, *Voyager*, 1st circumnavigation of the world without refueling, 1987, and the Wright Brothers. 3d, Precision measurement of the distance between the Earth and the Moon by laser and Albert A. Michelson (1852-1931), Nobel laureate in 1907 for research on the speed of light. 10d, HEAO-2 Einstein orbital satellite and Albert Einstein, vert. 20d, Hubble Space Telescope and George Hale (1868-1938), American astronomer, vert. No. 806, Galilean moon Ganymede passing the Great Red Spot on Jupiter. No. 807, *Apollo* and Neil Armstrong, 1st man on the Moon, July 20, 1969, vert.

**1988, Dec. 12 *Perf.***

| | | | | |
|---|---|---|---|---|
| *798* | A130 | 50b multi | 15 | 15 |
| *799* | A130 | 75b multi | 22 | 22 |
| *800* | A130 | 1d multi | 30 | 30 |
| *801* | A130 | 1.25d multi | 38 | 38 |
| *802* | A130 | 2d multi | 60 | 60 |
| *803* | A130 | 3d multi | 90 | 90 |
| *804* | A130 | 10d multi | 3.00 | 3.00 |
| *805* | A130 | 20d multi | 6.00 | 6.00 |
| | | *Nos. 798-805 (8)* | 11.55 | 11.55 |

**Souvenir Sheets**

| | | | | |
|---|---|---|---|---|
| *806* | A130 | 15d multi | 4.50 | 4.50 |
| *807* | A130 | 15d multi | 4.50 | 4.50 |

350th anniv. of the publication of *Discourses*, by Galileo. Nos. 806-807 have multicolored inscribed margins continuing the designs.

## GERMAN EAST AFRICA

LOCATION — In East Africa, bordering on the Indian Ocean.
GOVT. — Former German Colony.
AREA — 384,180 sq. mi.
POP. — 7,651,106.
CAPITAL — Dar-es-Salaam.

Following World War I, the greater part of this German Colonial possession was mandated to Great Britain. The British ceded to the Belgians the provinces of Ruanda and Urundi (Belgian East Africa.) The Kionga triangle was awarded to the Portuguese and became part of the Mozambique Colony. The remaining area became the British Mandated Territory of Tanganyika.

12 Pence = 1 Shilling
100 Cents = 1 Rupee (1917)

**Issued Under British Occupation**

Stamps of Nyasaland Protectorate, 1913-15 Overprinted **N. F.**

**1916 Wmk. 3 *Perf. 14***

| | | | | |
|---|---|---|---|---|
| *N101* | A3 | ½p green | 1.40 | *4.25* |
| *a.* | | Double overprint (R & Bk) | | |
| *N102* | A3 | 1p carmine | 70 | *2.00* |
| *N103* | A3 | 3p vio, *yel* | 8.75 | *17.50* |
| *a.* | | Double overprint | | *8,500.* |
| *N104* | A3 | 4p scar & blk, *yel* | 30.00 | *52.50* |
| *N105* | A3 | 1sh *green* | 30.00 | *52.50* |
| | | *Nos. N101-N105 (5)* | 70.85 | *128.75* |

The letters "N.F." are the initials of "Nyasaland Force."

Stamps of East Africa and Uganda, 1912-14, Overprinted in Black or Red **G.E.A.**

**1917**

| | | | | |
|---|---|---|---|---|
| *N106* | A3 | 1c blk (R) | 10 | 10 |
| *N107* | A3 | 3c bl grn | 10 | 10 |
| *N108* | A3 | 6c carmine | 12 | 12 |
| *N109* | A3 | 10c brn org | 15 | 15 |
| *a.* | | Inverted overprint | | |
| *N110* | A3 | 12c gray | 30 | *90* |
| *N111* | A3 | 15c ultra | 25 | *1.50* |
| *N112* | A3 | 25c scar & blk, *yel* | 25 | *2.00* |
| *N113* | A3 | 50c vio & blk | 2.50 | *3.00* |
| *N114* | A3 | 75c *bl grn*, olive back (R) | 90 | *3.50* |
| *a.* | | 75c *emerald* (R) | 1.10 | *3.00* |

Overprinted **G.E.A.**

| | | | | |
|---|---|---|---|---|
| *N115* | A4 | 1r *green* (R) | 1.10 | *3.50* |
| *a.* | | 1r *emerald* (R) | 1.40 | *4.50* |
| *N116* | A4 | 2r blk & red, *bl* | 3.50 | *6.00* |
| *N117* | A4 | 3r gray grn & vio | 5.50 | *9.00* |
| *N118* | A4 | 4r grn & red, *yel* | 9.00 | *15.00* |
| *N119* | A4 | 5r dl vio & ultra | 10.50 | *18.00* |
| *N120* | A4 | 10r grn & red, *grn* | 42.50 | *60.00* |
| *a.* | | 10r grn & red, *emer* | 47.50 | *75.00* |
| *N121* | A3 | 20r vio & blk, *red* | 85.00 | *125.00* |
| *N122* | A3 | 50r gray grn & red | 575.00 | 625.00 |
| | | *Nos. N106-N120 (15)* | 76.77 | *122.87* |

See Tanganyika for "G.E.A." overprints on stamps inscribed "East Africa and Uganda Protectorates" and watermarked multiple crown and script CA.

## GHANA

LOCATION — West Africa between Benin and Ivory Coast.
GOVT. — Republic.
AREA — 92,010 sq. mi.
POP. — 12,827,000 (est. 1983).
CAPITAL — Accra.

Ghana is the former British colony of Gold Coast, which achieved independence on March 6, 1957. It

Common Design Types are pictured in section before Great Britain.

includes the former trusteeship territory of British Togoland.

12 Pence = 1 Shilling
20 Shillings = 1 Pound
100 Pesewas = 1 Cedi (1965, 1972)
100 New Pesewas = 1 New Cedi (1967)

Used Values in Italics
In 1961 the government canceled all remainder stocks, using cancellations which closely resemble genuine postmarks. Catalogue values in italics (in Ghana) are for canceled-to-order stamps. Postally used copies are worth more.

**Catalogue values for all unused stamps in this country are for Never Hinged items.**

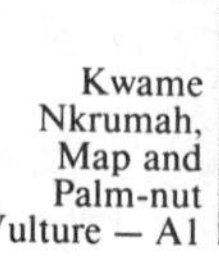

Kwame Nkrumah, Map and Palm-nut Vulture — A1

*Perf. 14x14½*

**1957, Mar. 6 Wmk. 4 Photo.**

| | | | | |
|---|---|---|---|---|
| 1 | A1 | 2p rose red | 5 | *5* |
| 2 | A1 | 2½p green | 5 | *5* |
| 3 | A1 | 4p brown | 7 | *5* |
| 4 | A1 | 1sh3p dk bl | 20 | *8* |

Independence, Mar. 6, 1957.

Stamps of Gold Coast, 1952-54, Overprinted in Black or Red

GHANA
INDEPENDENCE
6TH MARCH.
1957.

*Perf. 11½x12, 12x11½*

**1957, Mar. 6 Engr.**

| | | | | |
|---|---|---|---|---|
| 5 | A14 | ½p yel brn & car | 5 | *5* |
| 6 | A14 | 1p dp bl (R) | 5 | *5* |
| 7 | A14 | 1½p green | 5 | *5* |
| 8 | A14 | 3p rose | 5 | *5* |
| 9 | A15 | 6p org & blk (R) | 7 | *6* |
| 10 | A14 | 1sh red org & blk | 12 | *7* |
| 11 | A14 | 2sh rose car & ol brn | 32 | *10* |
| 12 | A14 | 5sh gray & red vio | 75 | *32* |
| 13 | A15 | 10sh ol grn & blk | 1.50 | *45* |
| | | *Nos. 5-13 (9)* | 2.96 | *1.20* |

Nos. 5-6 exist in vertical coils.
See Nos. 25-27.

Viking Ship and Angelfish A2

Designs: 1sh3p, Medieval galleon and swordfish. 5sh, Modern cargo ship and flyingfish.

*Perf. 12x11½*

**1957, Dec. 27 Engr. Unwmk.**

| | | | | |
|---|---|---|---|---|
| 14 | A2 | 2½p emerald | 12 | *8* |
| 15 | A2 | 1sh3p dk bl | 45 | *45* |
| 16 | A2 | 5sh red lil | 1.75 | *1.75* |

Black Star Line inauguration.

Ambassador Hotel — A3

Coat of Arms — A4

Design: 2½p, Opening of Parliament. 1sh 3p, National monument.

*Perf. 14x14½, 14½x14*

**1958, Mar. 6 Photo. Wmk. 4**

**Flags in Original Colors.**

| | | | | |
|---|---|---|---|---|
| 17 | A3 | ½p car rose & blk | 5 | *5* |
| 18 | A3 | 2½p org yel, red & blk | 5 | *5* |
| 19 | A3 | 1sh3p bl & blk | 18 | *18* |
| 20 | A4 | 2sh multi | 30 | *25* |

First anniversary of Independence.

Map of Africa — A5

Map and Torch — A6

**1958, Apr. 15** *Perf. 13½x14½*

| | | | | |
|---|---|---|---|---|
| 21 | A5 | 2½p multi | 5 | *5* |
| 22 | A5 | 3p multi | 6 | *5* |
| 23 | A6 | 1sh multi | 15 | *12* |
| 24 | A6 | 2sh6p multi | 30 | *25* |

1st conf. of Independent African States, Accra, Apr. 15-22.

Gold Coast Nos. 151-152 and 154 Overprinted Like Nos. 5-13

*Perf. 11½x12, 12x11½*

**1958, May 26 Engr. Wmk. 4**

| | | | | |
|---|---|---|---|---|
| 25 | A15 | 2p chocolate | 6 | *5* |
| 26 | A15 | 2½p red | 8 | *6* |
| 27 | A14 | 4p deep blue | 18 | *15* |

Nos. 25-27 were prepared in 1957 and some were sold without authorization. The set was officially released in 1958.

Ghana Nos. 1-4 Overprinted: "Prime Minister's Visit U. S. A. and Canada."

**1958, July 18 Photo.** *Perf. 14x14½*

| | | | | |
|---|---|---|---|---|
| 28 | A1 | 2p rose red | 5 | *5* |
| 29 | A1 | 2½p green | 6 | *5* |
| 30 | A1 | 4p brown | 8 | *8* |
| 31 | A1 | 1sh3p dk bl | 18 | *18* |

Prime Minister Kwame Nkrumah's visit to the US and Canada, July, 1958.

Palm-nut Vulture over Globe — A7

"Britannia" Plane — A8

Designs: 2sh, Stratocruiser and albatross. 2sh6p, Palm-nut vulture and jet plane (horiz.).

*Perf. 14x14½, 14½x14*

**1958, July 15**

| | | | | |
|---|---|---|---|---|
| 32 | A7 | 2½p multi | 5 | *5* |
| 33 | A8 | 1sh3p multi | 20 | *18* |
| 34 | A8 | 2sh multi | 25 | *20* |
| 35 | A7 | 2sh6p ol bis & blk | 35 | *30* |

Inauguration of Ghana Airways.

Black Hand Shaking White Below UN Emblem — A9

*Perf. 14x14½*

**1958, Oct. 24 Wmk. 4 Litho.**

| | | | | |
|---|---|---|---|---|
| 36 | A9 | 2½p multi | 6 | *5* |
| 37 | A9 | 1sh3p multi | 20 | *18* |
| 38 | A9 | 2sh6p multi | 25 | *20* |

United Nations Day, Oct. 24.

Lincoln Memorial and Kwame Nkrumah — A10

Wmk. 325- Stars and G Multiple

*Perf. 14x14½*

**1959, Feb. 12 Photo. Wmk. 325**

| | | | | |
|---|---|---|---|---|
| 39 | A10 | 2½p dp plum & brt pink | 6 | *5* |
| 40 | A10 | 1sh3p dp bl & lt bl | 20 | *18* |
| 41 | A10 | 2sh6p ol gray & org yel | 28 | *25* |
| a. | | Souv. sheet of 3 | 2.25 | *2.25* |

Lincoln's birth sesquicentennial.
No. 41a contains one each of Nos. 39-41, imperforate.

Kente Cloth with Traditional Symbols A11

Symbol of Greeting — A12

Designs: 2½p, Talking drums and elephant horn-blower. 2sh, Map of Africa, flag and palm tree.

*Perf. 14½x14, 14x14½*

**1959, Mar. 6 Photo. Wmk. 325**

| | | | | |
|---|---|---|---|---|
| 42 | A11 | ½p multi | 5 | *5* |
| 43 | A11 | 2½p multi | 7 | *6* |
| 44 | A12 | 1sh3p multi | 22 | *18* |
| 45 | A11 | 2sh multi | 30 | *25* |

Independence, 2nd anniversary.

Flags of Independent States of Africa and Globe — A13

**1959, Apr. 15** *Perf. 14½x14*

| | | | | |
|---|---|---|---|---|
| 46 | A13 | 2½p multi | 6 | *5* |
| 47 | A13 | 8½p multi | 18 | *18* |

Africa Freedom Day, Apr. 15.

Kente Cloth and "God's Omnipotence" Symbol — A13a

Nkrumah Statue, Accra — A14

Shell Ginger — A15

Cacao A16

"God's Omnipotence" Symbol — A16a

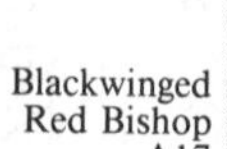

Blackwinged Red Bishop A17

Designs: 1½p, Ghana timber. 2p, Volta river. 4p, Diamond and mine. 11p, Golden spider lily. 2sh6p, Great blue turaco. 5sh, Tiger orchid. 10sh, Jewelfish (tropical African cichlid).

*Perf. 11½x12, 12x11½, 14x14½, 14½x14*

**1959, Oct. 5 Photo. Wmk. 325**

**Size: 30½x21mm, 21x30½mm**

| | | | | |
|---|---|---|---|---|
| 48 | A13a | ½p multi *(God's Omnipotence)* | 5 | *5* |
| 49 | A14 | 1p multi | 5 | *5* |

**Size: 26½x37mm, 37x26½mm**

| | | | | |
|---|---|---|---|---|
| 50 | A15 | 1½p multi | 5 | *5* |
| 51 | A16 | 2p multi | 6 | *5* |
| 52 | A16 | 2½p multi | 8 | *8* |

53 A16a 3p multi *(God's Omnipotence)* 10 5
54 A16 4p multi 12 5
55 A17 6p multi 25 5
a Booklet pane of 4 75
56 A15 11p multi 33 12
57 A15 1sh multi 27 8
58 A17 2sh6p multi 70 30
59 A15 5sh multi 1.35 65

**Size: 45x26mm**

60 A16 10sh multi 2.70 1.65
*Nos. 48-60 (13)* 6.11 3.23

Nos. 48 and 53 inscribed "God's Omnipotence." Nos. 95-96 inscribed "Gye Nyame." See Nos. C1-C2.

Map and Gold Cup — A18

Designs: 1p, Soccer players (vert.). 3p, Flags and goalkeeper in stadium. 8p, Soccer player at goal. 2sh6p, Kwame Nkrumah Gold Cup (vert.).

***Perf. 14½x14, 14x14½.***

**1959, Oct. 15**

61 A18 ½p multi 5 5
62 A18 1p multi 5 5
63 A18 3p multi 8 5
64 A18 8p multi 20 8
65 A18 2sh6p multi 65 28
*Nos. 61-65 (5)* 1.03 51

West African Soccer Competitions.

Prince Philip A19

***Perf. 14½x14***

**1959, Nov. 24 Photo. Wmk. 325**

66 A19 3p brt pink & blk 14 8

Visit of Prince Philip.

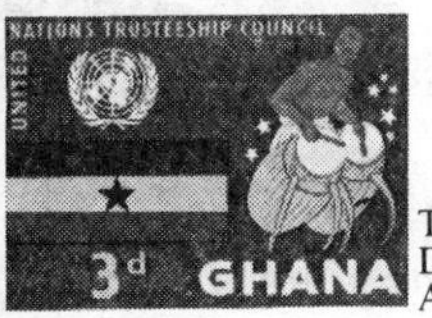

Talking Drums A20

Designs: 6p, 1sh3p, Ghana flag and U. N. emblem (vert.). 2sh6p, Pile of Ceremonial Stools and "UNTC" (vert.).

***Perf. 14½x14, 14x14½***

**1959, Dec. 10**

**Flag in Original Colors**

67 A20 3p vio & org yel 6 5
68 A20 6p Prus grn & blk 12 6
69 A20 1sh3p grnsh bl, blk & vio 22 12
70 A20 2sh6p dk bl & blk 45 30

United Nations Trusteeship Council.

Three Flying Eagles — A21

Designs: 3p, Three clusters of fireworks. 1sh3p, Ghana flag forming "3" and dove. 2sh, Ghana flag forming triple sail of symbolic ship.

***Perf. 13½x14½***

**1960, Mar. 6 Wmk. 325**

71 A21 ½p multi 8 5
72 A21 3p multi 8 5
73 A21 1sh3p multi 25 10
74 A21 2sh multi 40 20

Independence, 3rd anniversary.

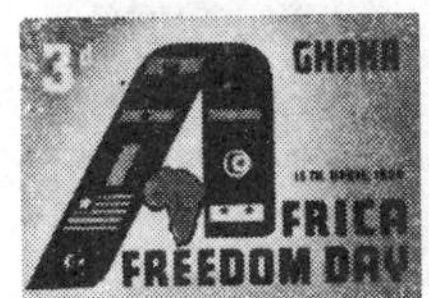

Flags Forming "A" and Map — A22

Designs: 6p, Letter "F". 1sh, "D".

**1960, Apr. 15 Photo. Wmk. 325**

**Flags in Original Colors.**

75 A22 3p grn, red & blk 8 5
76 A22 6p rose & blk 12 6
77 A22 1sh bl, blk & red 20 8

Africa Freedom Day, Apr. 15.

President Kwame Nkrumah — A23

Olympic Rings and Hand Holding Torch — A24

Designs: 1sh3p, Flag and star. 2sh, Hand holding torch. 10sh, Coat of Arms and flag of Ghana (horiz.).

***Perf. 14x14½, 14½x14***

**1960, July 1 Litho.**

78 A23 3p multi 8 5
79 A23 1sh3p multi 28 22
80 A23 2sh multi 45 35
81 A23 10sh multi 1.75 1.50
a Souvenir sheet of 4, imperf. 2.75 2.75

Declaration of the Republic, July 1, 1960.
No. 81a contains one each of Nos. 78-81 with black marginal inscription. Size: 101x72mm.

**1960, Aug. 15 Photo. Wmk. 325**

Design: 1sh3p, 2sh6p, Runner, Map of Africa and Olympic Rings (horiz.).

82 A24 3p multi 6 5
83 A24 6p multi 15 12
84 A24 1sh3p multi 18 15
85 A24 2sh6p multi 40 30

Issued to commemorate the 17th Olympic Games, Rome, Aug. 25-Sept. 11.

Map and Arch — A25

U.N. Emblem and Ghana Flag — A26

Designs: 3p, Flag and Kwame Nkrumah (horiz.). 6p, Star and Nkrumah.

**1960, Sept. 21 Photo.**

86 A25 3p multi 7 5
87 A25 6p multi 14 12
88 A25 1sh3p multi 28 20

Issued to commemorate Founder's Day, Sept. 21, birthday of Dr. Kwame Nkrumah.

**1960, Dec. 10** ***Perf. 14x14½***

Designs: 6p, Flame and emblem. 1sh3p, U.N. Emblem.

89 A26 3p multi 6 5
90 A26 6p multi 10 7
91 A26 1sh3p multi 20 12

Human Rights Day, Dec. 10, 1960.

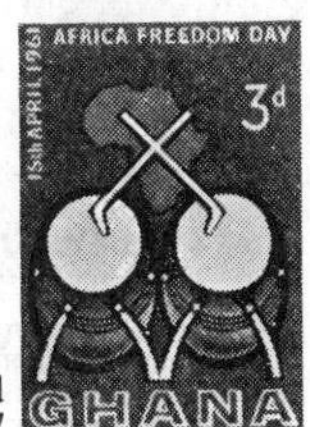

Talking Drums and Map — A27

Designs: 6p, Map of Africa showing 25 independent states. 2sh, Map of Africa and flags of independent nations in 1958 (horiz.).

***Perf. 14x14½, 14½x14***

**1961, Apr. 15 Wmk. 325**

92 A27 3p multi 8 5
93 A27 6p multi 15 12
94 A27 2sh multi 40 28

Africa Freedom Day, Apr. 15, 1961.

Types of 1959 Redrawn and

Red-fronted Gazelle — A28

***Perf. 11½x12, 14½x14***

**1961, Apr. 29 Photo. Wmk. 325**

95 A13a ½p multi *(Gye Nyame)* 5 5
96 A16a 3p multi *(Gye Nyame)* 8 6
a Bklt pane of 4 35

***Perf. 14x14½***

97 A28 £1 multi 5.00 3.00

Nos. 95-96 are the same sizes as Nos. 48 and 53 which are inscribed "God's Omnipotence."

Column, Eagle and Star — A29

Dove with Olive Branch — A30

World Map, Chain and Olive Branch A31

Designs: 1sh3p, Symbolic flower and star. 2sh, Star and 3 Ghana flags.

**1961, July 1** ***Perf. 14x14½***

98 A29 3p multi 6 5
99 A29 1sh3p multi 30 22
100 A29 2sh multi 50 30

First anniversary of the Republic.

***Perf. 14x14½, 14½x14***

**1961, Sept. 1 Photo. Wmk. 325**

Design: 5sh, Rostrum and olive branch.

101 A30 3p green 8 6
102 A31 1sh3p dk bl 25 18
103 A31 5sh rose car 1.00 80

Issued to commemorate the Conference of Non-aligned Nations, Belgrade, September, 1961.

Kwame Nkrumah and Globe A32

Designs: 1sh3p, Kente cloth and Nkrumah (vert.). 5sh, Kwame Nkrumah (vert.).

***Perf. 14½x14, 14x14½***

**1961, Sept. 21 Wmk. 325**

104 A32 3p multi 8 7
a Souvenir sheet of 4, imperf. 60 60
105 A32 1sh3p multi 35 25
a Souvenir sheet of 4, imperf. 1.75 1.75
106 A32 5sh multi 1.65 1.40
a Souvenir sheet of 4, imperf. 10.00 10.00

Issued to commemorate Founder's Day.
The souvenir sheets contain four imperf. stamps each with simulated perforations. No. 104a has pale brown margin and inscription; No. 105a has ultramarine margin and inscription and No. 106a, has gray margin and inscription. Sizes: 106x84½mm. (No. 104a); 84½x106mm. (Nos. 105a and 106a).

Elizabeth II and Map of Africa A33

**1961, Nov. 10** ***Perf. 14½x14***

**Gold Inscriptions: Design in Black, Red, Yellow & Green**

107 A33 3p claret 8 5
108 A33 1sh3p Prus bl 28 18
109 A33 5sh vio bl 1.10 90
a Souvenir sheet of 4 6.00 6.00

Issued to commemorate the visit of Queen Elizabeth II to Ghana, Nov. 10-22.
No. 109a contains four imperf. copies of No. 109 with simulated perforations, light violet blue margin and black inscription. Size: 106x85mm.

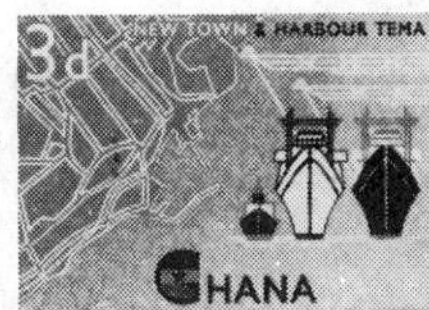

Map of Tema Harbor and Ships A34

***Perf. 14x13***

**1962, Feb. 10 Litho. Unwmk.**

110 A34 3p multi 10 6

Opening of Tema Harbor, as part of Volta River Project.

Dove Flying over Map of Africa — A35

**1962, March 6** ***Perf. 13x14***

111 A35 3p multi 10 6

Issued to commemorate the first anniversary of the conference of African heads of state at Casablanca. See Nos. C5-C6.

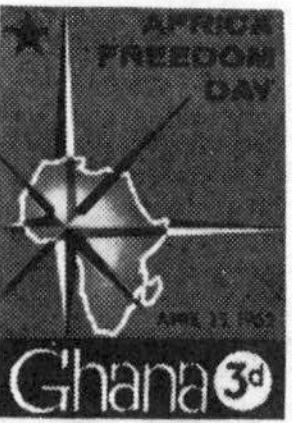


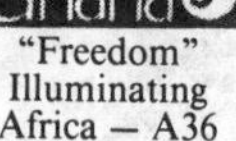


"Freedom" Illuminating Africa — A36

"Five Continents at Peace" — A37

*Perf. 14x14½*

**1962, Apr. 15 Photo. Wmk. 325**

| | | | | |
|---|---|---|---|---|
| *112* | A36 | 3p multi | 8 | 6 |
| *113* | A36 | 6p multi | 15 | 12 |
| *114* | A36 | 1sh3p multi | 28 | 20 |

Africa Freedom Day, Apr. 15.

**1962, June 21 Wmk. 325**

Designs: 6p, Atom bomb blast in shape of skull. 1sh3p, Peace dove and globe.

| | | | | |
|---|---|---|---|---|
| *115* | A37 | 3p dp rose & blk | 8 | 5 |
| *116* | A37 | 6p blk & dk red | 20 | 14 |
| *117* | A37 | 1sh3p grnsh bl | 50 | 35 |

Issued to commemorate the Accra Assembly of Africans for a "World Without Bomb," Accra, June 21-28.

Patrice Lumumba A38

**1962, June 30** *Perf. 14½x14*

| | | | | |
|---|---|---|---|---|
| *118* | A38 | 3p blk & org | 8 | 5 |
| *119* | A38 | 6p mar, grn & blk | 15 | 12 |
| *120* | A38 | 1sh3p dk grn, pink & blk | 40 | 22 |

Issued to commemorate the first anniversary (on Feb. 12) of the death of Patrice Lumumba, premier of Congo.

Arch and Star — A39

Kwame Nkrumah — A40

Designs: 6p, Torch in flag colors and globe. 1sh3p, Palm-nut vulture trailing flag (horiz.).

*Perf. 13x13½, 13½x13*

**1962, July 1 Unwmk.**

| | | | | |
|---|---|---|---|---|
| *121* | A39 | 3p multi | 10 | 6 |
| *122* | A39 | 6p multi | 25 | 20 |
| *123* | A39 | 1sh3p multi | 65 | 50 |

Second anniversary of the republic.

**1962, Sept. 21 Litho.** *Perf. 13x14*

Designs: 3p, Nkrumah medal. 1sh3p, Nkrumah's head and stars. 2sh, Hands with trowel and building block.

| | | | | |
|---|---|---|---|---|
| *124* | A40 | 1p multi | 5 | 5 |
| *125* | A40 | 3p multi | 9 | 6 |
| *126* | A40 | 1sh3p ultra & blk | 35 | 25 |
| *127* | A40 | 2sh multi | 55 | 30 |

Founder's Day, Nkrumah's 53rd birthday.

Malaria Eradication Emblem — A41

Wheat Emblem and Globe — A42

*Perf. 14x14½*

**1962, Dec. 1 Photo. Wmk. 325**

| | | | | |
|---|---|---|---|---|
| *128* | A41 | 1p car rose | 5 | 5 |
| *129* | A41 | 4p yel grn | 12 | 8 |
| *130* | A41 | 6p ol bis | 18 | 14 |
| *131* | A41 | 1sh3p violet | 35 | 25 |
| *a* | | Souv. sheet of 4, imperf. | 90 | 90 |

Issued for the World Health Organization drive to eradicate malaria.

No. 131a contains one each of Nos. 128-131, with simulated perforation. Pale violet margin, violet inscription. Size: 89½x114mm.

*Perf. 14x14½, 14½x14*

**1963, Mar. 21 Wmk. 325**

Designs: 4p, Hands holding Wheat Emblem (horiz.). 1sh3p, Globe (horiz.).

| | | | | |
|---|---|---|---|---|
| *132* | A42 | 1p multi | 5 | 5 |
| *133* | A42 | 4p multi | 8 | 6 |
| *134* | A42 | 1sh3p multi | 25 | 18 |

Issued for the "Freedom from Hunger" campaign of the U.N. Food and Agriculture Organization.

Map of Africa in Sun — A43

Cross, Flag and Centenary Emblem — A44

Designs: 4p, Symbolic wood carving (horiz.). 1sh3p, Map of Africa and ceremonial fire. 2sh6p, Gazelle and flag.

**1963, Apr. 15 Photo.**

| | | | | |
|---|---|---|---|---|
| *135* | A43 | 1p crim & gold | 5 | 5 |
| *136* | A43 | 4p org, blk & red | 9 | 6 |
| *137* | A43 | 1sh3p multi | 28 | 20 |
| *138* | A43 | 2sh6p multi | 55 | 40 |

Africa Freedom Day, Apr. 15.

*Perf. 14x14½, 14½x14*

**1963, May 28 Wmk. 325**

Designs: 1½p, Centenary emblem (horiz.). 4p, Family and emblem (horiz.). 1sh3p, Emblem and globe.

| | | | | |
|---|---|---|---|---|
| *139* | A44 | 1p multi | 5 | 5 |
| *140* | A44 | 1½p multi | 5 | 5 |
| *141* | A44 | 4p multi | 8 | 5 |
| *142* | A44 | 1sh3p multi | 25 | 18 |
| *a* | | Souv. sheet of 4, imperf. | 50 | 50 |

Issued to commemorate the centenary of the founding of the International Red Cross.

No. 142a contains one each of Nos. 139-142, with simulated perforation. Light blue margin, black inscription. Size: 96x120mm.

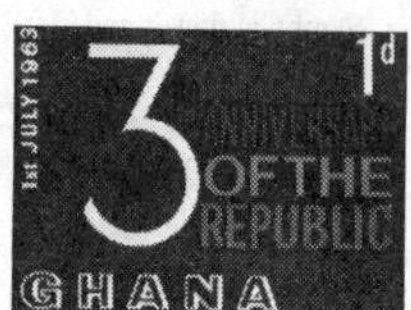


A45

Designs: 4p, Three flags. 1sh3p, Map of Africa with Ghana (vert.). 2sh6p, Torch (vert.).

*Perf. 14½x14, 14x14½*

**1963, July 1 Photo.**

| | | | | |
|---|---|---|---|---|
| *143* | A45 | 1p multi | 5 | 5 |
| *144* | A45 | 4p multi | 8 | 5 |
| *145* | A45 | 1sh3p multi | 25 | 18 |
| *146* | A45 | 2sh6p multi | 50 | 35 |

The 3rd anniversary of the republic.

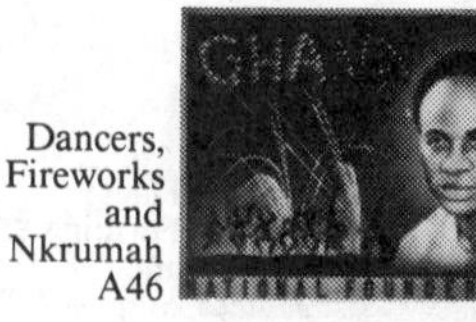


Dancers, Fireworks and Nkrumah A46

Designs: 1p, Nkrumah and streamer (vert.). 4p, Nkrumah and flag (vert.). 5sh, Wisdom symbol.

*Perf. 14x14½, 14½x14*

**1963, Sept. 21 Wmk. 325**

| | | | | |
|---|---|---|---|---|
| *147* | A46 | 1p multi | 5 | 5 |
| *148* | A46 | 4p multi | 9 | 5 |
| *149* | A46 | 1sh3p multi | 28 | 18 |
| *150* | A46 | 5sh multi | 1.10 | 75 |

Founder's Day, Nkrumah's 54th birthday.

Ramses II at Abu Simbel — A47

Designs: 1½p, Rock painting, bird and fish (horiz.). 2p, Queen Nefertari (horiz.). 4p, Sphinx of Wadi es-Sebua. 1sh3p, Statues of Ramses II at Abu Simbel (horiz.).

*Perf. 11½x11*

**1963, Nov. 1 Photo. Unwmk.**

| | | | | |
|---|---|---|---|---|
| *151* | A47 | 1p multi | 5 | 5 |
| *152* | A47 | 1½p multi | 6 | 5 |
| *153* | A47 | 2p multi | 8 | 6 |
| *154* | A47 | 4p multi | 15 | 10 |
| *155* | A47 | 1sh3p multi | 55 | 40 |
| | | *Nos. 151-155 (5)* | 89 | 66 |

Issued to publicize the UNESCO world campaign to save historic monuments in Nubia.

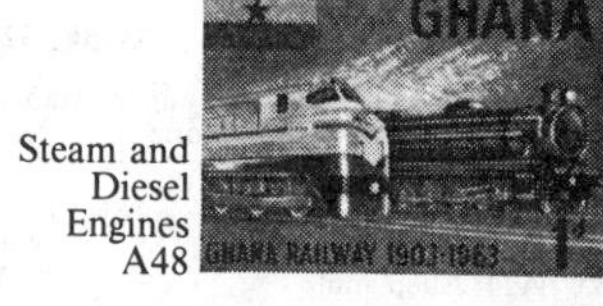


Steam and Diesel Engines A48

*Perf. 14½x14*

**1963, Nov. 1 Wmk. 325**

| | | | | |
|---|---|---|---|---|
| *156* | A48 | 1p multi | 5 | 5 |
| *157* | A48 | 6p multi | 25 | 15 |
| *158* | A48 | 1sh3p multi | 60 | 50 |
| *159* | A48 | 2sh6p multi | 1.50 | 1.25 |

The 60th anniversary of Ghana's railroads.

Eleanor Roosevelt and Flame — A49

IQSY Emblem and Satellites — A50

Designs: 6p, Mrs. Roosevelt and flag. 1sh3p, Mrs. Roosevelt, flag, flame and Ghanaian symbols (horiz.).

*Perf. 11½x11, 11x11½*

**1963, Dec. 10 Unwmk.**

| | | | | |
|---|---|---|---|---|
| *160* | A49 | 1p multi | 5 | 5 |
| *161* | A49 | 4p multi | 12 | 8 |
| *162* | A49 | 6p multi | 18 | 10 |
| *163* | A49 | 1sh3p multi | 35 | 25 |

Issued to honor Eleanor Roosevelt on the 15th anniversary of the Universal Declaration of Human Rights.

Imperforates

Starting in 1964, certain sets of Ghana exist imperf.

**1964, June 1 Photo.** *Perf. 14*

| | | | | |
|---|---|---|---|---|
| *164* | A50 | 3p multi | 9 | 6 |
| *165* | A50 | 6p multi | 18 | 8 |
| *166* | A50 | 1sh3p multi | 35 | 25 |
| *a* | | Souv. sheet of four | 1.50 | 1.50 |

Issued to publicize the International Quiet Sun Year, 1964-65. No. 166a contains 4 imperf. stamps similar to No. 166 with simulated perforations. Dark blue margin; size: 89x89mm. See also Nos. 186-188.

Harvest on State Farm — A51

Designs: 6p, Oil refinery, Tema. 1sh3p, Communal labor. 5sh, Ghana flag and people.

**1964, July 1** *Perf. 13x14*

| | | | | |
|---|---|---|---|---|
| *167* | A51 | 3p multi | 9 | 6 |
| *168* | A51 | 6p multi | 18 | 8 |
| *169* | A51 | 1sh3p multi | 35 | 25 |
| *170* | A51 | 5sh multi | 1.10 | 1.00 |
| *a* | | Souv. sheet of 4 | 2.00 | 2.00 |

Issued to commemorate the fourth anniversary of the Republic. No. 170a contains four stamps similar to Nos. 167-170 with simulated perforations. Bright yellow margin with white and brown inscription and Nkrumah medal. Size: 126x100mm.

Dove, Globe, Olive Branch and Flag — A52

Designs: 6p, Map of Africa and quill pen (vert.). 1sh3p, Knotted rope and map of Africa. 5sh, Hands planting symbolic tree (vert.).

**1964, July 6** *Perf. 14*

| | | | | |
|---|---|---|---|---|
| *171* | A52 | 3p multi | 8 | 6 |
| *172* | A52 | 6p blk & red | 15 | 6 |
| *173* | A52 | 1sh3p bl & multi | 28 | 20 |
| *174* | A52 | 5sh yel & multi | 1.10 | 75 |

First anniversary of the signing of the African Unity Charter.

Nkrumah and Hibiscus — A53

Boxing — A54

*Perf. 14x14½*

**1964, Sept. 21 Photo. Wmk. 325**

**Design in Brown, Green and Rose Red**

| | | | | |
|---|---|---|---|---|
| *175* | A53 | 3p lt bl | 9 | 6 |
| *176* | A53 | 6p yellow | 18 | 8 |
| *177* | A53 | 1sh3p gray | 35 | 30 |

*178* A53 2sh6p emerald 70 50
*a* Souv. sheet of 4 3.00 2.50

Founder's Day, Nkrumah's 55th birthday.
No. 178a contains four of No. 178 with simulated perforation. The blue green margin shows music of national anthem. Size: 90x122mm.

**1964, Oct. 25** ***Perf. 14½x14***

Sport: 1p, Hurdling (horiz.). 2½p, Running (horiz.). 4p, Broad jump. 6p, Soccer. 1sh3p, Athlete with Olympic torch. 5sh, Banners and Tokyo Olympic emblem (horiz.).

*179* A54 1p yel & multi 5 5
*180* A54 2½p multi 7 5
*181* A54 3p red & multi 8 6
*182* A54 4p bl & multi 10 7
*183* A54 6p multi 14 7
*184* A54 1sh3p bl & multi 28 20
*185* A54 5sh gray & multi 1.10 80
*a* Souvenir sheet of 3 3.00 3.00
*Nos. 179-185 (7)* 1.82 1.30

18th Olympic Games, Tokyo, Oct. 10-25.
No. 185a contains stamps similar to Nos. 183-185 with simulated perforation. Size: 128x102mm.

Quiet Sun Year Type of 1964

**1964, Oct. Unwmk. Photo.** ***Perf. 14***

*186* A50 3p gray, bl, grn, yel & red 1.25 1.25
*187* A50 6p pink, bl, grn, yel & red 2.50 2.50
*188* A50 1sh3p tan, bl, grn, yel, & red 4.00 4.00

Each issued in sheets of 12, with star-strewn blue border inscribed "Ghana International Quiet Sun Year." Stamps arranged in square surrounding vignette of New York World's Fair Unisphere in blue. Size: 149x149mm.

G. W. Carver and Sweet Potato A55

Design: 1sh3p, Albert Einstein, theory of relativity formula and atom symbol.

**1964, Dec. 7** ***Perf. 14½ Wmk. 325***

*189* A55 6p grn & dk bl 18 14
*190* A55 1sh3p Prus bl & cl 35 25
*191* A55 5sh org ver & brn blk 1.50 1.25
*a* Souv. sheet of 3 2.25 2.00

Issued for Human Rights Day, and to honor Albert Einstein (1878-1955) and George Washington Carver (1864-1943), scientists.
No. 191a commemorates UNESCO Week and contains one each of Nos. 189-191 with simulated perforations. Sheet background in salmon with dark blue UNESCO emblem. Size: 127x76½mm.

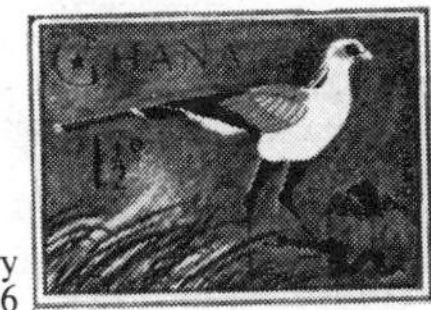
Secretary Bird — A56

Designs: 1p, Elephant (vert.). 2½p, Purple wreath (vert.). 3p, Gray parrot (vert.). 4p, Blue-naped mousebird. 6p, African tulip tree flowers. 1sh3p, Amethyst starling. 2sh6p, Hippopotamuses.

***Perf. 11½x11, 11x11½***

**1964, Dec. 14 Photo. Unwmk.**

*192* A56 1p bl & multi 7 5
*193* A56 1½p org & multi 10 5
*194* A56 2½p lt grn & multi 20 14
*a* Souv. sheet of 3 1.00 1.00
*195* A56 3p lt grn & multi 20 18
*196* A56 4p multi 28 20
*197* A56 6p multi 28 7
*198* A56 1sh3p multi 50 35
*199* A56 2sh6p multi 1.00 60
*a* Souv. sheet of 5 3.00 3.00
*Nos. 192-199 (8)* 2.63 1.64

No. 194a contains one each of Nos. 192-194, imperf.; size 150x86mm. No. 199a contains one each of Nos. 195-199, imperf.; size 150x110mm. Both sheets inscribed "Pictorial Issue," with green frameline and flaglike decorations.

ICY Emblem — A57

**1965, Feb. 15 Litho.** ***Perf. 14x13***
**Design in Black, Red and Green**

*200* A57 1p gray 5 5
*201* A57 4p bister 12 8
*202* A57 6p tan 18 14
*203* A57 1sh3p lt grn 45 30
*a* Souv. sheet of 4 1.75 1.75

Issued to publicize the United Nations International Cooperation Year. No. 203a contains 4 imperf. stamps similar to No. 203. Rose red margin with green inscription. Size: 100x100mm.

ITU Emblem, Old and New Communication Equipment — A58

**1965, Apr. 12** ***Perf. 13½***

*204* A58 1p multi 5 5
*205* A58 6p multi 15 12
*206* A58 1sh3p multi 28 18
*207* A58 5sh multi 1.10 90
*a* Souv. sheet of 4 1.75 1.75

Cent. of the ITU. No. 207a contains 4 imperf. stamps similar to Nos. 204-207 with simulated perforations. Light blue border with red inscription. Size: 133x115mm.

Lincoln's Home, Springfield, Ill. — A59

Designs: 1sh3p, Inaugural Address and Lincoln. 2sh, Lincoln and his signature. 5sh, Adaptation of 1869 U.S. Lincoln stamp (No. 122).

**Wmk. 325**
**1965, Apr. Photo.** ***Perf. 12½***

*208* A59 6p multi 15 10
*209* A59 1sh3p multi 28 18
*210* A59 2sh multi 42 35
*211* A59 5sh red & blk 1.10 75
*a* Souv. sheet of 4 2.00 1.50

Centenary of death of Abraham Lincoln.
No. 211a contains one each of Nos. 208-211 with simulated perforation. Blue margin. Size: 114x114mm.

5-Pesewa Coin, Nkrumah's Head — A60

Coins: 10pa, 10 pesewas. 25pa, 25 pesewas. 50pa, 50 pesewas.

***Perf. 11x13***
**1965, July 19 Unwmk. Litho.**
**Coin in Silver and Black**
**Size: 45x32mm**

*212* A60 5pa red, grn & lt grn 12 10
*213* A60 10pa red, grn, & pink 25 20

**Size: 62x39mm**

*214* A60 25pa red, grn, & pink 70 55

**Size: 71x43½mm**

*215* A60 50pa red, grn & lt grn 1.40 1.10

Introduction of decimal currency.

Regular Issue of 1959-61 Surcharged in Red, Blue, Brown, Black or White with New Value and: "Ghana New Currency / 19th July, 1965"

***Perf. 12x11½, 14½x14, 14x14½***
**1965, July 19 Photo. Wmk. 325**

*216* A14 1pa on 1p (R) 5 5
*217* A16 2pa on 2p (Bl) 6 5
*218* A16a 3pa on 3p (#96, Br) 14 5
*219* A16 4pa on 4p (Bl) 14 5
*220* A17 6pa on 6p (Bk) 22 5
*221* A15 11pa on 11p (W) 30 10
*222* A15 12pa on 1sh (Bl) 35 9
*223* A17 30pa on 2sh6p (Bl) 1.25 55
*224* A15 60pa on 5sh (Bl) 2.25 1.10
*225* A16 1.20c on 10s (Bl) 4.00 2.75
*226* A28 2.40c on £1 (Bl) 9.00 7.25
*Nos. 216-226 (11)* 17.76 12.09

The two lines of the overprint are diagonal on the 1pa, 11pa, 12pa, 60pa, 1.20c and 2.40c.
The surcharge exists double or inverted on six or more denominations.

Summit Conference, Accra — A61

Map of Africa and Flags — A62

Designs: 2pa, "OAU" and three heads (triangle pointing up). 5pa, Symbol of African Unity. 15pa, Sunburst and map of Africa. 24pa, Map of Africa.

***Perf. 14, 14½x14***
**1965, Oct. 21 Photo.**
**Ghana Flag in Red, Black & Green**

*227* A61 1pa multi 5 5
*228* A61 2pa multi 6 5
*229* A61 5pa multi 15 8
*230* A62 6pa org & blk 18 8
*231* A62 15pa lt bl & blk 50 30
*232* A62 24pa lt ultra & grn 75 65
*Nos. 227-232 (6)* 1.69 1.21

Summit Conference of the Organization for African Unity, Accra, Oct. 1965.

Soccer Goalkeeper — A63

Designs: 15pa, Soccer player and cup. (vert.). 24pa, Two soccer players and cup.

***Perf. 14x13, 13x14***
**1965, Nov. 15 Photo. Unwmk.**

*233* A63 6pa ocher & multi 10 5
*234* A63 15pa multi 25 12
*235* A63 24pa lt bl & multi 50 30

African Soccer Cup competition.

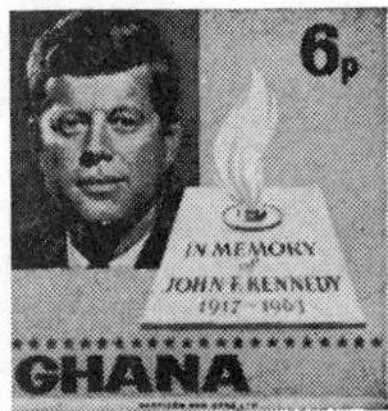

John F. Kennedy and Eternal Flame — A64

Various Kennedy Portraits

**1965, Dec. 15 Wmk. 325** ***Perf. 12½***

*236* A64 6pa blk, yel, gold & grn 18 14
*237* A64 15pa vio, crim & brt grn 55 35
*238* A64 24pa dp pur & blk 90 90
*239* A64 30pa vio brn & blk 1.25 1.25
*a* Souv. sheet of 4 ('66) 3.75 3.00

Issued in memory of President John F. Kennedy (1917-63).
No. 239a contains four imperf. stamps similar to Nos. 236-239. Green margin with white inscription. Size: 114x114mm.

Generators, Volta River Project A65

Designs: 15pa, Dam and Lake Volta. 24pa, "Ghana" forming dam. 30pa, Grain.

***Perf. 11x11½***
**1966, Jan. 22 Photo. Unwmk.**

*240* A65 6pa sep & multi 15 12
*241* A65 15pa multi 40 30
*242* A65 24pa multi 60 38
*243* A65 30pa brt bl & blk 85 60

Issued to commemorate the opening of the Volta River dam and electric power station at Akosombo.

Nos. 233-235 Overprinted Diagonally: "Black Stars Retain Africa Cup / 21st Nov. 1965"

**1966, Feb. 7** ***Perf. 14x13, 13x14***

*244* A63 6pa ocher & multi 20 15
*245* A63 15pa multi 45 35
*246* A63 24pa lt bl & multi 70 45

Ghana's soccer victory, Nov. 21, 1965.

WHO Headquarters, Geneva — A66

Designs: 24pa, 30pa, WHO Headquarters from the west and WHO emblem.

***Perf. 14x14½***
**1966, July 1 Photo. Wmk. 325**

*247* A66 6pa multi 15 12
*248* A66 15pa multi 35 25
*249* A66 24pa multi 55 32
*250* A66 30pa multi 70 50
*a* Souv. sheet of 4 2.00 1.75

Issued to commemorate the inauguration of World Health Organization Headquarters, Geneva.
No. 250a contains 4 imperf. stamps similar to Nos. 247-250 with simulated perforations. Gray margin with commemorative inscription. Size: 120x101mm.

6p GHANA
Herring, Fishermen and Flag A67

Designs: 15pa, Flatfish and canoes. 24pa, Spadefish and schooner. 30pa, Red snapper and fishing trawler "Shama." 60pa, Mackerel and steamer.

*Perf. 14x13*

**1966, Aug. 10 Photo. Unwmk.**

| | | | | |
|---|---|---|---|---|
| *251* | A67 | 6pa ocher & multi | 18 | 10 |
| *252* | A67 | 15pa yel grn & multi | 40 | 25 |
| *253* | A67 | 24pa ver & multi | 65 | 28 |
| *254* | A67 | 30pa bl & multi | 1.00 | 40 |
| *a* | | Souv. sheet of 4 | 3.50 | 2.00 |
| *255* | A67 | 60pa grn & multi | 1.40 | 85 |
| | | *Nos. 251-255 (5)* | 3.63 | 1.88 |

Issued to publicize the 1966 Freedom from Hunger campaign "Young World Against Hunger."

No. 254a contains 4 imperf. stamps similar to No. 254. Blue margin with commemorative inscription and ship designs. Size: 125x109mm.

Flags of African Unity Charter Signers, Map and Diamond A68

Designs: 6p, Ghana flag and links enclosing map of Africa (vert.). 24p, Ship's wheel enclosing map of Africa, and cacao pod.

**1966, Sept. Unwmk. *Perf. 13x13½***

| | | | | |
|---|---|---|---|---|
| *256* | A68 | 6pa brt bl & multi | 18 | 14 |
| *257* | A68 | 15pa bl & multi | 55 | 40 |
| *258* | A68 | 24pa dp grn & multi | 90 | 55 |

Issued to commemorate the third anniversary of the signing of the African Unity Charter.

Soccer Player and Rimet Cup — A69

Various Soccer Scenes

*Perf. 14½x14*

**1966, Nov. 14 Photo. Wmk. 325**

| | | | | |
|---|---|---|---|---|
| *259* | A69 | 5pa brn & multi | 12 | 10 |
| *260* | A69 | 15pa bl & multi | 35 | 25 |
| *261* | A69 | 24pa grn & multi | 55 | 32 |
| *262* | A69 | 30pa brt rose & multi | 75 | 50 |
| *263* | A69 | 60pa lil & multi | 1.50 | 1.00 |
| *a* | | Souv. sheet of 4 | 5.00 | 5.00 |
| | | *Nos. 259-263 (5)* | 3.27 | 2.17 |

Issued to commemorate the World Cup Soccer Championship, Wembley, England, July 11-30.

No. 263a contains 4 imperf. stamps similar to No. 263 with simulated perforations. Lilac margin with commemorative inscription. Size: 121x102mm.

UNESCO Emblem A70

**1966, Dec. 23 Wmk. 325 *Perf. 14½***

| | | | | |
|---|---|---|---|---|
| *264* | A70 | 5pa multi | 12 | 8 |
| *265* | A70 | 15pa multi | 35 | 20 |
| *266* | A70 | 24pa multi | 52 | 45 |
| *267* | A70 | 30pa multi | 70 | 50 |
| *268* | A70 | 60pa multi | 1.40 | 1.00 |
| *a* | | Souv. sheet of 5 | 3.25 | 2.25 |
| | | *Nos. 264-268 (5)* | 3.09 | 2.23 |

Issued to commemorate the 20th anniversary of UNESCO (United Nations Educational, Scientific and Cultural Organization). No. 268a contains 5 imperf. stamps similar to Nos. 264-268 with simulated perforations. Green margin with white inscription. Size: 140x144 mm.

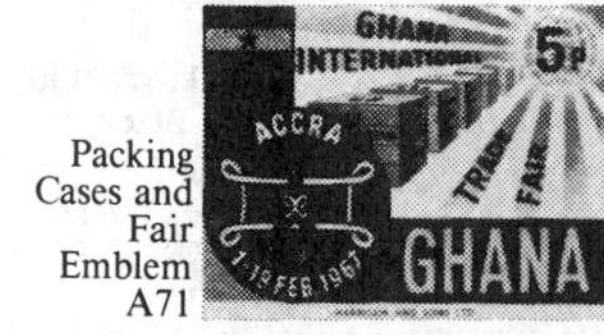


Packing Cases and Fair Emblem A71

Designs (Fair Emblem and): 15pa, World map and trade routes to Accra. 24pa, Freighters and loading crane (vert.). 36pa, Hand holding cargo net.

**1967, Feb. 1 *Perf. 14½x14, 14x14½***

| | | | | |
|---|---|---|---|---|
| *269* | A71 | 5pa multi | 12 | 8 |
| *270* | A71 | 15pa multi | 45 | 25 |
| *271* | A71 | 24pa multi | 60 | 50 |
| *272* | A71 | 36pa multi | 1.10 | 75 |

International Trade Fair, Accra, Feb. 1-19.

Eagle and Flag — A72

*Perf. 14x14½*

**1967, Feb. 24 Photo. Wmk. 325**

**Flag in Red, Yellow, Black and Green**

| | | | | |
|---|---|---|---|---|
| *273* | A72 | 1np gray bl & dk brn | 5 | 5 |
| *274* | A72 | 4np ocher & dk brn | 20 | 20 |
| *275* | A72 | 12½np ol grn & dk brn | 65 | 65 |
| *276* | A72 | 25np dl cl & dk brn | 1.50 | 1.50 |
| *a* | | Souv. sheet of 4 | 3.25 | 2.50 |

1st anniv. of the revolution which overthrew the regime of Kwame Nkrumah.

No. 276a contains one each of Nos. 273-276 with dull claret marginal inscriptions. Size: 89x107mm. A similar imperf. sheet has solid margins of dull claret, colorless inscriptions. Value $2.

Nos. 51, 54-58, 60 and 97 Surcharged in Black, Red or White

*Perf. 14½x14, 14x14½*

**1967, Feb. 27 Photo. Wmk. 325**

**Size: 30½x21mm, 21x30½mm**

| | | | | |
|---|---|---|---|---|
| *277* | A16 | 1½np on 2p (B) | 9.00 | 3.00 |
| *278* | A16 | 3½np on 4p (R) | 18 | 6 |
| *279* | A17 | 5np on 6p (R) | 20 | 9 |
| *280* | A15 | 9np on 11p (W) | 32 | 16 |
| *281* | A15 | 10np on 1sh (W) | 35 | 22 |
| *282* | A17 | 25np on 2sh6p (R) | 2.50 | 1.50 |

**Size: 45x26mm**

| | | | | |
|---|---|---|---|---|
| *283* | A16 | 1nc on 10sh (R) | 9.00 | 7.25 |
| *284* | A28 | 2nc on £1 (R) | 15.75 | 14.00 |
| | | *Nos. 277-284 (8)* | 37.30 | 26.28 |

Corn A73

Forest Kingfisher A74

African Lungfish A75

Designs: 2np, Ghana Mace (golden staff). 2½np, Commelina flower. 4np, Rufous-crowned roller (vert.). 6np, Akosombo Dam, Volta River. 8np, Adomi Bridge, Volta River. 9np, Chemeleon. 10np, Quay No. 2, Tema Harbor. 20np, Cape hare. 50np, Black-winged stilt. 1nc, Chief's ceremonial stool. 2nc, Frangipani. 2.50nc, State Chair.

*Perf. 11½x12, 12x11½ (A73), 14x14½, 14½x14 (A74-A75)*

**1967 Photo. Wmk. 325**

| | | | | |
|---|---|---|---|---|
| *286* | A73 | 1np multi | 5 | 5 |
| *287* | A74 | 1½np multi | 5 | 5 |
| *288* | A74 | 2np multi | 5 | 5 |
| *289* | A74 | 2½np multi | 5 | 5 |
| *290* | A75 | 3np multi | 6 | 6 |
| *291* | A73 | 4np multi | 7 | 5 |
| *292* | A75 | 6np multi | 9 | 6 |
| *293* | A73 | 8np multi | 12 | 7 |
| *294* | A75 | 9np multi | 14 | 7 |
| *295* | A75 | 10np multi | 15 | 8 |
| *296* | A74 | 20np blue | 30 | 22 |
| *297* | A74 | 50np multi | 90 | 75 |
| *298* | A74 | 1nc multi | 1.90 | 1.25 |
| *299* | A74 | 2nc multi | 3.75 | 2.75 |
| *300* | A74 | 2.50nc multi | 4.75 | 3.25 |
| | | *Nos. 286-300 (15)* | 12.43 | 8.81 |

Kumasi Fort, 1896 A76

Castles on Ghana Coast: 12½np, Christiansborg Castle, 1659, and British galleon. 20np, Elmina Castle, 1482, and Portuguese galleon. 25np, Cape Coast Castle, 1664, and Spanish galleon.

**1967, June 12 *Perf. 14½***

| | | | | |
|---|---|---|---|---|
| *301* | A76 | 4np grnsh bl & multi | 15 | 10 |
| *302* | A76 | 12½np red org & multi | 55 | 38 |
| *303* | A76 | 20np brt grn & multi | 1.10 | 60 |
| *304* | A76 | 25np lt red brn & multi | 1.50 | 75 |

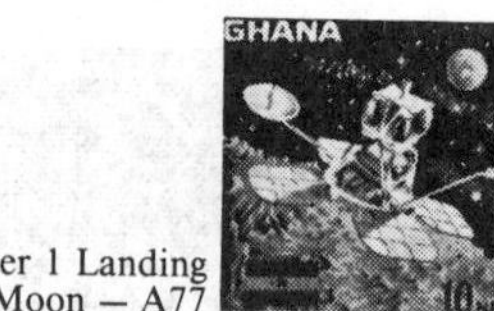


Orbiter 1 Landing on Moon — A77

Designs: 4np, Luna 10 on the moon, and globe. 12½np, Astronaut walking in space.

*Perf. 13½*

**1967, Aug. 16 Unwmk. Photo.**

| | | | | |
|---|---|---|---|---|
| *305* | A77 | 4np multi | 12 | 9 |
| *306* | A77 | 10np multi | 30 | 22 |
| *307* | A77 | 12½np multi | 38 | 30 |
| *a* | | Souv. sheet of 3 | 1.50 | 1.50 |

Issued to publicize achievements in space. Issued in Ghana in sheets of 30. Sheets of 12 with ornamented, inscribed border also exist; these were sold in Ghana in 1968.

No. 307a contains 3 imperf. stamps similar to Nos. 305-307. Blue margin with commemorative inscription. Size: 140x90mm.

Boy Scouts at Campfire A78

Designs: 10np, Hiking Boy Scout. 12½np, Lord Baden-Powell.

**1967, Sept. 18 Photo. *Perf. 14x13½***

| | | | | |
|---|---|---|---|---|
| *308* | A78 | 4np multi | 15 | 12 |
| *309* | A78 | 10np multi | 40 | 30 |
| *310* | A78 | 12½np multi | 50 | 40 |
| *a* | | Souv. sheet of 3 | 1.10 | 90 |

Issued to commemorate the 50th anniversary of the Ghana (Gold Coast) Boy Scouts. Issued in Ghana in sheets of 30. Sheets of 12 with ornamented, inscribed border also exist; these were sold in Ghana in 1968.

No. 310a contains 3 imperf. stamps similar to Nos. 308-310 with simulated perforations. Pink margin with gold inscription and blue design. Size: 168x95mm.

U.N. Secretariat Building — A79

Design: 50np, 2.50nc, U.N. Headquarters.

**1967, Oct. 24 Litho. *Perf. 13½x13***

| | | | | |
|---|---|---|---|---|
| *311* | A79 | 4np multi | 12 | 8 |
| *312* | A79 | 10np multi | 25 | 14 |
| *313* | A79 | 50np multi | 65 | 50 |
| *314* | A79 | 2.50nc multi | 5.50 | 5.50 |
| *a* | | Souv. sheet | 6.75 | 6.75 |

Issued for United Nations Day. No. 314a contains one imperf. stamp similar to No. 314 with simulated perforations. U.N. emblem and black inscription in margin. Size: 75x75mm.

Leopard — A80

Designs: 12½np, Christmas butterfly. 20np, Nubian carmine bee-eaters. 50np, Waterbuck.

**Wmk. 325**

**1967, Dec. 28 Photo. *Perf. 12½***

| | | | | |
|---|---|---|---|---|
| *315* | A80 | 4np multi | 12 | 5 |
| *316* | A80 | 12½np multi | 35 | 20 |
| *317* | A80 | 20np multi | 75 | 40 |
| *318* | A80 | 50np multi | 1.75 | 1.10 |
| *a* | | Souv. sheet of 3 | 3.00 | 2.00 |

Issued for International Tourist Year 1967. No. 318a contains 3 imperf. stamps similar to Nos. 316-318 with simulated perforations. Blue and white margin with ITY emblem and black inscription. Size: 126x126mm.

Convoy Entering Accra A81

Designs: 12½np, Victory parade. 20np, Waving crowd. 40np, Singing and dancing crowd.

**Unwmk.**

**1968, Feb. 24 Litho. *Perf. 14***

| | | | | |
|---|---|---|---|---|
| *319* | A81 | 4np sal & multi | 8 | 6 |
| *320* | A81 | 12½np multi | 40 | 30 |
| *321* | A81 | 20np multi | 65 | 50 |
| *322* | A81 | 40np yel & multi | 1.40 | 1.10 |

2nd anniversary of Feb. 24th Revolution.

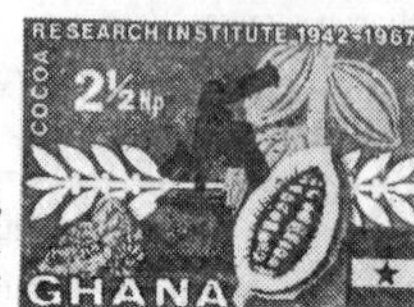


Cacao Beans and Microscope A82

Designs: 4np, 25np, Cacao tree and beans, microscope.

*Perf. 14½x14*

**1968, Mar. 18 Photo. Wmk. 325**

| No. | Type | Description | Unused | Used |
|---|---|---|---|---|
| 323 | A82 | 2½np grn & multi | 6 | 5 |
| 324 | A82 | 4np gray & multi | 7 | 6 |
| 325 | A82 | 10np scar & multi | 20 | 20 |
| 326 | A82 | 25np multi | 50 | 50 |
| a |  | Souv. sheet of 4 | 1.10 | 1.10 |

Issued to publicize Ghana's cocoa production. Sheets of 30.

No. 326a contains four imperf. stamps similar to Nos. 323-326 with simulated perforations. Deep rose margin with black inscription. Size: 103x101mm.

Nos. 323-326 also exist in sheets of 12 with ornamental border, inscription and reproduction of a still life by Jan Paul Gillemans; these are believed not to have been on sale in Ghana.

Lt. Gen. E. K. Kotoka A83

Designs: Various portraits of Lt. Gen. Kotoka. 40np vertical.

**1968, Apr. 17 Unwmk. *Perf. 14***

| No. | Type | Description | Unused | Used |
|---|---|---|---|---|
| 327 | A83 | 4np pur & multi | 12 | 12 |
| 328 | A83 | 12½np grn & multi | 45 | 45 |
| 329 | A83 | 20np multi | 90 | 90 |
| 330 | A83 | 40np gray & multi | 1.75 | 1.75 |

Issued to commemorate the first anniversary of the death of Lt. Gen. Emmanuel Kwasi Kotoka (1926-1967), leader of the Revolution of 1966 against Nkrumah.

Tobacco — A84

Designs: 5np, Crested porcupine. 12½np, Tapped rubber tree. 20np, Cymothoe sangaris butterfly. 40np, Charaxes ameliae butterfly.

**1968, Aug. Photo. *Perf. 14x14½***

| No. | Type | Description | Unused | Used |
|---|---|---|---|---|
| 331 | A84 | 4np multi | 8 | 6 |
| 332 | A84 | 5np multi | 12 | 8 |
| 333 | A84 | 12½np multi | 45 | 45 |
| 334 | A84 | 20np multi | 75 | 75 |
| 335 | A84 | 40np multi | 1.50 | 1.50 |
| a |  | Souvenir sheet of 4 | 3.00 | 3.00 |
|  |  | *Nos. 331-335 (5)* | 2.90 | 2.84 |

No. 335a contains 4 stamps similar to Nos. 331, 332-335 with simulated perforations. Light blue margin with white design and inscription. Size: 89x114mm.

Surgical Team A85

**1968, Nov. 11 *Perf. 14x13***

| No. | Type | Description | Unused | Used |
|---|---|---|---|---|
| 336 | A85 | 4np grn & multi | 12 | 10 |
| 337 | A85 | 12½np multi | 45 | 30 |
| 338 | A85 | 20np pur & multi | 70 | 65 |
| 339 | A85 | 40np bl & multi | 1.65 | 1.50 |
| a |  | Souv. sheet of 4 | 3.25 | 3.25 |

Issued to commemorate the 20th anniversary of the World Health Organization. No. 339a contains 4 imperf. stamps similar to Nos. 336-339. Yellow margin with brown commemorative inscription. Size: 132x110mm.

Hurdling — A86

Designs: 12½np, Boxing. 20np, Torch bearer, flags and Olympic rings. 40np, Soccer.

*Perf. 14x14½*

**1968, Dec. Unwmk. Photo.**

| No. | Type | Description | Unused | Used |
|---|---|---|---|---|
| 340 | A86 | 4np gray & multi | 9 | 8 |
| 341 | A86 | 12½np gray & multi | 35 | 25 |
| 342 | A86 | 20np ultra & multi | 70 | 60 |
| 343 | A86 | 40np gray & multi | 1.40 | 1.25 |
| a |  | Souv. sheet of 4 | 3.50 | 3.50 |

Issued to commemorate the 19th Olympic Games, Mexico City, Oct. 12-27, 1968. No. 343a contains 4 imperf. stamps with simulated perforations similar to Nos. 340-343. Light green margin with commemorative inscription. Size: 89x114mm.

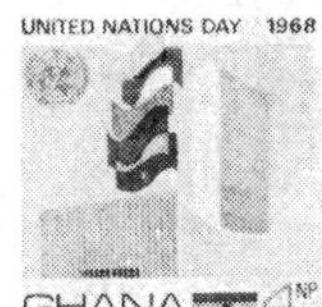

U.N. Headquarters and Flags — A87

Designs: 12np, U.N. emblem and Ghanaian staff and stool. 20np, U.N. Headquarters, New York, U.N. emblem and Ghana flag. 40np, U.N. emblem surrounded by flags.

**1969, Feb. 1 Litho. *Perf. 13x13½***

| No. | Type | Description | Unused | Used |
|---|---|---|---|---|
| 344 | A87 | 4np multi | 9 | 8 |
| 345 | A87 | 12½np pink & multi | 35 | 22 |
| 346 | A87 | 20np blk & multi | 75 | 50 |
| 347 | A87 | 40np lt bl & multi | 1.40 | 1.20 |
| a |  | Souv. sheet of 4 | 3.50 | 3.00 |

Issued for United Nations Day 1968. No. 347a contains 4 imperf. stamps with simulated perforations similar to Nos. 344-347. Black marginal inscription. Size: 127x117mm.

Joseph Boakye Danquah A88

Design: 12½np, 20np, Dr. Martin Luther King, Jr., Human Rights flame and flag of Ghana.

**1969, Mar. 7 Photo. *Perf. 14½x14***

| No. | Type | Description | Unused | Used |
|---|---|---|---|---|
| 348 | A88 | 4np gray & multi | 12 | 10 |
| 349 | A88 | 12½np multi | 45 | 30 |
| 350 | A88 | 20np bl & multi | 85 | 80 |
| 351 | A88 | 40np grn & multi | 1.50 | 1.50 |
| a |  | Souv. sheet of 4 | 3.25 | 3.25 |

Issued for International Human Rights Year, and to honor the Rev. Martin Luther King, Jr. (1929-1968), American civil rights leader, and Joseph Boakye Danquah (1895-1965), lawyer, writer and Ghanaian political leader.

No. 351a contains 4 imperf. stamps with simulated perforations similar to Nos. 348-351. Bister brown margin with white inscription. Size: 115x90mm.

Parliament A89

Design: 12½np, 40np, Coat of Arms.

*Perf. 14½x14*

**1969, Sept. Photo. Wmk. 325**

| No. | Type | Description | Unused | Used |
|---|---|---|---|---|
| 352 | A89 | 4np multi | 12 | 10 |
| 353 | A89 | 12½p multi | 45 | 30 |
| 354 | A89 | 20np multi | 75 | 70 |
| 355 | A89 | 40np multi | 1.50 | 1.40 |
| a |  | Souv. sheet of 4 | 3.00 | 3.00 |

Issued to commemorate the 3rd anniversary of the revolution. No. 355a contains 4 imperf. stamps with simulated perforations similar to Nos. 352-355. Light greenish blue margin with commemorative inscription. Size: 114x88mm.

Nos. 286-300 Overprinted in Black, Yellow or Red: NEW CONSTITUTION 1969

*Perf. 11½x12, 12x11½ (A73), 14x14½, 14½x14 (A74-A75)*

**1969, Oct. 1 Photo. Wmk. 325**

| No. | Type | Description | Unused | Used |
|---|---|---|---|---|
| 356 | A73 | 1np multi | 5 | 5 |
| 357 | A74 | 1½np multi | 5 | 5 |
| 358 | A73 | 2np multi | 6 | 5 |
| 359 | A73 | 2½np multi | 7 | 6 |
| 360 | A75 | 3np multi | 8 | 6 |
| 361 | A73 | 4np multi (Y) | 10 | 9 |
| 362 | A75 | 6np multi | 14 | 10 |
| 363 | A73 | 8np multi | 16 | 14 |
| 364 | A75 | 9np multi | 16 | 15 |
| 365 | A75 | 10np multi | 20 | 16 |
| 366 | A74 | 20np blue | 50 | 45 |
| 367 | A74 | 50np multi | 1.75 | 1.25 |
| 368 | A74 | 1nc multi | 2.25 | 1.90 |
| 369 | A74 | 2nc multi (R) | 5.25 | 4.50 |
| 370 | A74 | 2.50nc multi | 6.75 | 5.25 |
|  |  | *Nos. 356-370 (15)* | 17.57 | 14.26 |

Overprint vertical on vertical stamps.

The 4np also exists with overprint in black and in red.

Map of Africa, Two Ghana Flags Rising from Ghana — A90

Designs: 12½np, "2" with laurel and star. 20np, Three hands and egg (symbol of rebirth) and Kente cloth. 40np, like 4np.

**Unwmk.**

**1969, Dec. 4 Litho. *Perf. 14***

| No. | Type | Description | Unused | Used |
|---|---|---|---|---|
| 371 | A90 | 4np multi | 12 | 10 |
| 372 | A90 | 12½np bl & multi | 40 | 30 |
| 373 | A90 | 20np multi | 75 | 70 |
| 374 | A90 | 40np bl & multi | 1.50 | 1.40 |

Issued to commemorate the inauguration of the Second Republic, Oct. 1969.

Cogwheels and ILO Emblem A91

*Perf. 14½x14*

**1970, Jan. 5 Photo. Wmk. 325**

| No. | Type | Description | Unused | Used |
|---|---|---|---|---|
| 375 | A91 | 4np rose red & multi | 12 | 10 |
| 376 | A91 | 12½np multi | 45 | 30 |
| 377 | A91 | 20np multi | 75 | 65 |
| a |  | Souvenir sheet of 3 | 1.75 | 1.10 |

Issued to commemorate the 50th anniversary of the International Labor Organization. No. 377a contains 3 imperf. stamps similar to Nos. 375-377 with simulated perforations. Dark gray and black margin with white commemorative inscription. Size: 115x88½ mm.

Nos. 375-377 printed in sheets of 12 arranged around reproduction of a painting and with commemorative inscription in margin.

Foreign postal stationery (stamped envelopes, postal cards and air letter sheets) lies beyond the scope of this Catalogue, which is limited to adhesive postage stamps.

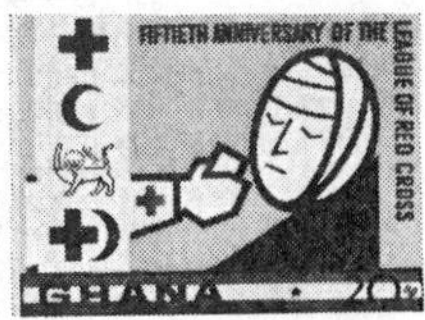

Red Cross Helping Wounded A92

Designs: 4np, Red Cross and globe (vert.). 12½np, Henri Dunant, Red Cross, Red Crescent, Lion and Sun emblems. 40np, Red Cross and first aid.

**1970, Feb. 2 *Perf. 14x14½, 14½x14***

| No. | Type | Description | Unused | Used |
|---|---|---|---|---|
| 378 | A92 | 4np gold & multi | 10 | 6 |
| 379 | A92 | 12½np gold & multi | 30 | 10 |
| 380 | A92 | 20np bl & multi | 60 | 25 |
| 381 | A92 | 40np multi | 1.25 | 50 |
| a |  | Souvenir sheet of 4 | 2.25 | 2.00 |

Issued to commemorate the 50th anniversary of the League of Red Cross Societies. No. 381a contains 4 imperf. stamps similar to Nos. 378-381 with simulated perforations. Bright pink margin with white commemorative inscription. Size: 114x88mm.

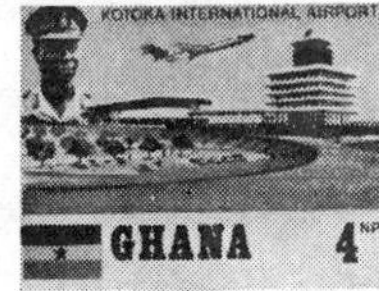

Kotoka Airport, Gen. Kotoka and VC10 — A93

Designs: 12½np, Control tower and tail section of VC10. 20np, Bird's eye view of airport and runway. 40np, Flags in front of Kotoka Airport.

*Perf. 13x14*

**1970, Apr. Unwmk. Litho.**

| No. | Type | Description | Unused | Used |
|---|---|---|---|---|
| 382 | A93 | 4np multi | 10 | 8 |
| 383 | A93 | 12½np multi | 35 | 20 |
| 384 | A93 | 20np multi | 65 | 50 |
| 385 | A93 | 40np multi | 1.25 | 1.00 |

Inauguration of Kotoka Airport.

Lunar Landing Module and Spacecraft — A94

Designs: 12½np, Neil A. Armstrong stepping onto the moon. 20np, Scientific experiments on the moon (horiz.). 40np, Neil A. Armstrong, Michael Collins and Edwin E. Aldrin, Jr., after return to earth (horiz.).

**1970, June 15 Litho. *Perf. 12½***

| No. | Type | Description | Unused | Used |
|---|---|---|---|---|
| 386 | A94 | 4np multi | 30 | 25 |
| 387 | A94 | 12½np multi | 1.50 | 1.25 |
| 388 | A94 | 20np multi | 1.75 | 1.50 |
| 389 | A94 | 40np multi | 6.00 | 5.00 |
| a |  | Souvenir sheet of 4 | 9.00 | 8.00 |

See note after U.S. No. C76. No. 389a contains 4 imperf. stamps similar to Nos. 386-389. Exists with and without simulated perfs. Sheet has black commemorative inscription, frame in Ghanaian colors and picture of lunar landing module. Size: 140x140mm.

Nos. 386-389 and 389a were overprinted "PHILYMPIA/LONDON 1970" in black or silver in Sept. 1970. They are believed not to have been regularly issued.

Adult Education A95

Designs (Education Year Emblem and): 12½np, Children of various races studying together. 20np, "Ntesie" symbol of wisdom and knowledge. 40np, Nursery school children.

**1970, Aug. 10 Litho. *Perf. 13x12½***

| | | | | |
|---|---|---|---|---|
| *390* | A95 | 4np bl & multi | 8 | 6 |
| *391* | A95 | 12½np bl & multi | 32 | 25 |
| *392* | A95 | 20np bl & multi | 52 | 40 |
| *393* | A95 | 40np bl & multi | 1.00 | 80 |

Issued for International Education Year.

Inauguration of Second Republic A96

Designs: 12½np, Mace and words of proclamation by K. A. Busia. 20np, Mace and globe with doves. 40np, Opening of Parliament of Second Republic.

**1970, Oct. 1 Litho. *Perf. 13***

| | | | | |
|---|---|---|---|---|
| *398* | A96 | 4np multi | 10 | 8 |
| *399* | A96 | 12½np multi | 40 | 30 |
| *400* | A96 | 20np multi | 65 | 50 |
| *401* | A96 | 40np lt bl & multi | 1.25 | 1.10 |

First anniversary of the Second Republic.

Amaryllis A97

Designs: 12½np, Lioness. 20np, African orchid. 40np, Elephant.

***Perf. 14½x14***

**1970 Photo. Wmk. 325**

| | | | | |
|---|---|---|---|---|
| *402* | A97 | 4np multi | 10 | 6 |
| *403* | A97 | 12½np multi | 30 | 15 |
| *404* | A97 | 20np pink & multi | 75 | 30 |
| *405* | A97 | 40np multi | 1.50 | 75 |

Kuduo Brass Casket A98

Designs: 12½np, Akan traditional house, Danmum. 20np, Larabanga Mosque. 40np, Akan funerary clay head.

**1970, Dec. 7 Litho. *Perf. 14½x14***

| | | | | |
|---|---|---|---|---|
| *406* | A98 | 4np gray & multi | 8 | 7 |
| *407* | A98 | 12½np bl & multi | 32 | 25 |
| *408* | A98 | 20np multi | 52 | 40 |
| *a* | | Souvenir sheet of 4 | 2.25 | 2.25 |
| *409* | A98 | 40np bl & multi | 1.00 | 90 |

No. 408a contains stamps similar to Nos. 406 and 408, a 12½np (Pompeii Basilica) and a 40np (Pompeii scene). Simulated perforation. Gray margin with violet inscription. Size: 89x76½mm.

Fair Building and Emblem A99

Designs (Fair Emblem and): 12½np, Drugstore merchandise. 20np, Automotives and tools. 40np, Cranes and trucks. 50np, Cargo, ship and plane (vert.).

***Perf. 14½x14, 14x14½***

**1971, Feb. 5 Photo. Wmk. 325**

| | | | | |
|---|---|---|---|---|
| *410* | A99 | 4np multi | 9 | 9 |
| *411* | A99 | 12½np lil & multi | 28 | 28 |
| *412* | A99 | 20np bl & multi | 45 | 45 |
| *413* | A99 | 40np multi | 90 | 90 |
| *414* | A99 | 50np multi | 1.10 | 1.10 |
| | | *Nos. 410-414 (5)* | 2.82 | 2.82 |

2nd Ghana International Trade Fair, Accra, Feb. 1-14, 1971.

Crucifixion A100

Design: 12½np, Jesus and disciples. 20np, Resurrection.

***Perf. 13½***

**1971, May 19 Litho. Unwmk.**

| | | | | |
|---|---|---|---|---|
| *415* | A100 | 4np multi | 12 | 10 |
| *416* | A100 | 12½np multi | 40 | 35 |
| *417* | A100 | 20np multi | 75 | 70 |

Easter, 1971.

Corn and FAO Emblem — A101

***Perf. 14x14½***

**1971, June Wmk. 325 Photo.**

| | | | | |
|---|---|---|---|---|
| *418* | A101 | 4np lil & multi | 28 | 20 |
| *419* | A101 | 12½np lt bl & multi | 1.10 | 65 |
| *420* | A101 | 20np multi | 2.00 | 1.25 |

Freedom from Hunger, second development decade, 1970-1980.

The overprint "In Memoriam / Lord Boyd ORR / 1880-1971" was applied to Nos. 418-420 in October, 1971. The 4np was also surcharged "60NP".

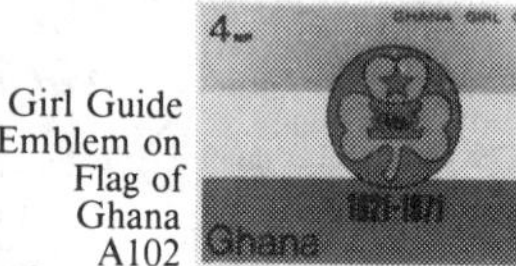


Girl Guide Emblem on Flag of Ghana A102

Designs (Emblem and): 12½np, Mrs. Elsie Ofuatey-Kodjoe, national founder. 20np, Girl Guides at play. 40np, Campfire and tent. 50np, Girl Guides signalling.

**Unwmk.**

**1971, July 22 Litho. *Perf. 14***

| | | | | |
|---|---|---|---|---|
| *421* | A102 | 4np multi | 10 | 10 |
| *422* | A102 | 12½np yel & multi | 28 | 28 |
| *423* | A102 | 20np sal & multi | 50 | 50 |
| *424* | A102 | 40np multi | 1.00 | 1.00 |
| *425* | A102 | 50np lil & multi | 1.25 | 1.10 |
| *a* | | Souvenir sheet of 5 | 3.00 | 2.75 |
| | | *Nos. 421-425 (5)* | 3.13 | 2.98 |

50th anniversary of the Girl Guides of Ghana. No. 425a contains 5 imperf. stamps similar to Nos. 421-425. Gray margin with multicolored border. Size: 132x106mm.

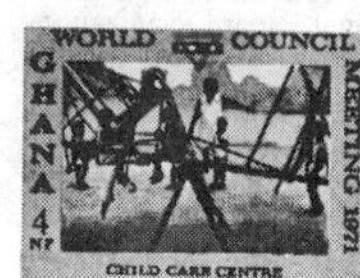


Child Care Center — A103

Designs (Y.W.C.A. Emblem and): 12½np, World Council Meeting and map of Ghana. 20np, Typing class. 40np, Building fund day.

**1971, Aug. 5 *Perf. 13***

| | | | | |
|---|---|---|---|---|
| *426* | A103 | 4np multi | 8 | 7 |
| *427* | A103 | 12½np ultra & multi | 30 | 30 |
| *428* | A103 | 20np bl & multi | 50 | 50 |
| *429* | A103 | 40np yel & multi | 90 | 90 |
| *a* | | Souvenir sheet of 4 | 2.50 | 2.50 |

World Council Meeting of Young Women's Christian Association, Accra, Aug. 5. No. 429a contains 4 stamps similar to Nos. 426-429 with simulated perforations. Black marginal inscription. Size: 82x82mm.

African Nativity Scene A104

Designs: 1np, Fireworks (vert.). 6np, Flight into Egypt.

***Perf. 14x14½, 14½x14***

**1971, Nov. Photo. Wmk. 325**

| | | | | |
|---|---|---|---|---|
| *433* | A104 | 1np multi | 5 | 5 |
| *434* | A104 | 3np org & multi | 8 | 7 |
| *435* | A104 | 6np bl & multi | 18 | 15 |

Christmas 1971.

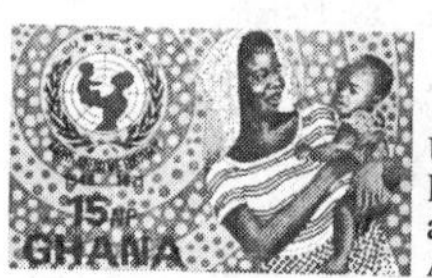


UNICEF Emblem, and Child A105

UNICEF Emblem and: 5np, Infant weighed in net scale (vert.). 30np, Student midwife (vert.). 50np, Boy in day care center.

***Perf. 13½x13, 13x13½***

**1971, Dec. 20 Litho. Unwmk.**

| | | | | |
|---|---|---|---|---|
| *436* | A105 | 5np grn & multi | 12 | 10 |
| *437* | A105 | 15np yel & multi | 45 | 40 |
| *438* | A105 | 30np pink & multi | 85 | 70 |
| *439* | A105 | 50np bl & multi | 1.65 | 1.50 |
| *a* | | Souvenir sheet of 4 | 3.50 | 3.50 |

25th anniv. of UNICEF. No. 439a contains 4 stamps with simulated perforations similar to Nos. 436-439. Black inscription and UNICEF emblem. Size: 111x119mm.

Fair Emblem, Map of Africa, Symbol of Unity A106

Designs (Fair Emblem and): 15np, Horn of Plenty. 30np, Fireworks over Africa. 60np, 1nc, Names of participating nations over map of Africa.

**1972, Feb. 23 Litho. *Perf. 14***

| | | | | |
|---|---|---|---|---|
| *440* | A106 | 5np lt brn & multi | 18 | 15 |
| *441* | A106 | 15np lt bl & multi | 65 | 50 |
| *442* | A106 | 30np grn & multi | 1.40 | 1.25 |
| *443* | A106 | 60np yel & multi | 2.00 | 1.90 |
| *444* | A106 | 1nc lt bl & multi | 3.50 | 3.25 |
| | | *Nos. 440-444 (5)* | 7.73 | 7.05 |

First All-Africa Trade Fair, Nairobi, Kenya, Feb. 23-Mar. 5.

Nos. 440-444 were overprinted "BELGICA 72" in red for release June 24, 1972. The regularity of this issue has been questioned.

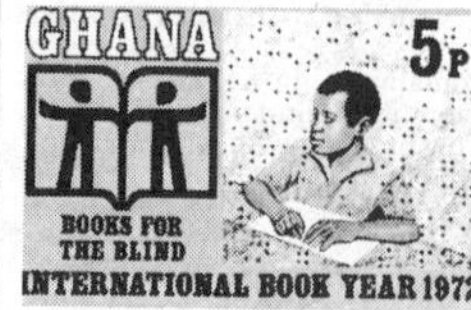


Books for the Blind A107

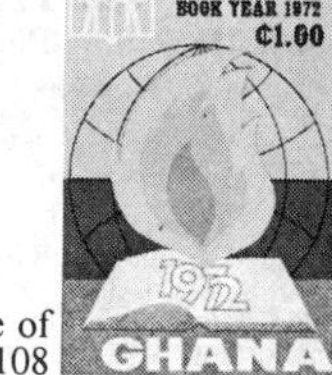


Book and Flame of Knowledge — A108

Book Year Emblem and: 15p, Books for Children ("Anansi and Snake the Postman"). 30p, Books for Recreation (Accra Central Library). 50p, Books for Students (2 students).

**1972, Apr. 21 *Perf. 13½***

| | | | | |
|---|---|---|---|---|
| *445* | A107 | 5p bl & multi | 12 | 12 |
| *446* | A107 | 15p yel & multi | 35 | 35 |
| *447* | A107 | 30p lil & multi | 75 | 75 |
| *448* | A107 | 50p grn & multi | 1.10 | 1.10 |
| *449* | A108 | 1ce bl & multi | 1.75 | 1.75 |
| *a* | | Souvenir sheet of 5 | 4.50 | 4.25 |
| | | *Nos. 445-449 (5)* | 4.07 | 4.07 |

International Book Year 1972. No. 449a contains one each of Nos. 445-449 with simulated perforations. Yellow margin with black inscription and Book Year emblem. Size: 100x100mm.

Star Grass A109

**1972, July 3 Litho. *Perf. 13½***

| | | | | |
|---|---|---|---|---|
| *450* | A109 | 5p *shown* | 10 | 8 |
| *451* | A109 | 15p *Mona monkey* | 35 | 25 |
| *452* | A109 | 30p *Amaryllis* | 1.00 | 50 |
| *453* | A109 | 1ce *Side-striped squirrel* | 3.50 | 1.75 |

Olympic Emblems, Soccer — A110

**1972, Sept. 5 Litho. *Perf. 13½x13***

| | | | | |
|---|---|---|---|---|
| *454* | A110 | 5p *shown* | 12 | 8 |
| *455* | A110 | 15p *Running* | 38 | 25 |
| *456* | A110 | 30p *Boxing* | 75 | 55 |
| *457* | A110 | 50p *Long jump* | 1.25 | 1.00 |
| *458* | A110 | 1ce *High jump* | 2.75 | 2.25 |
| | | *Nos. 454-458 (5)* | 5.25 | 4.13 |

**Souvenir Sheet**

| | | | | |
|---|---|---|---|---|
| *459* | A110 | Sheet of 2 | 4.50 | 2.50 |
| *a* | | 40p *like 30p* | 75 | 50 |
| *b* | | 60p *like 5p* | 1.10 | 75 |

20th Olympic Games, Munich, Aug. 26-Sept. 11. No. 459 has black marginal inscription and Olympic emblems. Size: 85x43mm.

Senior and Cub Scouts, Badge A111

Designs: 15p, Scout in front of tent. 30p, 40p, Sea Scouts in canoe. 50p, Cub Scouts with den mother. 60p, 1ce, Scouts studying.

**1972, Oct. Litho. *Perf. 14***

| | | | | |
|---|---|---|---|---|
| *460* | A111 | 5p bl grn & multi | 12 | 10 |
| *461* | A111 | 15p ocher & multi | 40 | 30 |
| *462* | A111 | 30p lil & multi | 80 | 65 |
| *463* | A111 | 50p multi | 1.25 | 1.10 |
| *464* | A111 | 1ce bl & multi | 2.50 | 2.25 |
| | | *Nos. 460-464 (5)* | 5.07 | 4.40 |

Souvenir Sheet

**Perf. 13½**

*465* A111 Souv. sheet of 2 3.75 3.75
*a* 40p brn & multi 60 38
*b* 60p grn & multi 90 55

Boy Scout Movement, 65th anniversary. No. 465 has light blue margin with fleur-de-lis design and black inscription. Size: 110x110mm.

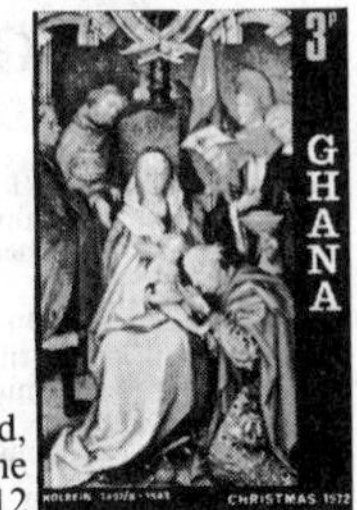


Virgin and Child, by Holbein the Younger — A112

Paintings: 1p, Holy Night, by Correggio. 15p, Virgin and Child, by Andrea Rico. 30p, Melchior. 60p, Virgin and Child with Caspar. 1ce, Balthasar. 30p, 60p, 1ce, are from early 16th century stained glass windows.

**1972, Dec. 2** ***Perf. 14x13½***

*466* A112 1p blk & multi 5 5
*467* A112 3p blk & multi 6 5
*468* A112 15p blk & multi 28 20
*469* A112 30p blk & multi 55 45
*470* A112 60p blk & multi 1.25 90
*471* A112 1ce blk & multi 2.25 1.50
*a* Souvenir sheet of 3 4.00 3.00
*Nos. 466-471 (6)* 4.44 3.15

Christmas 1972. No. 471a contains one each of Nos. 469-471 with simulated perforations. Multicolored margin with bright blue margin. Size: 138x89mm.

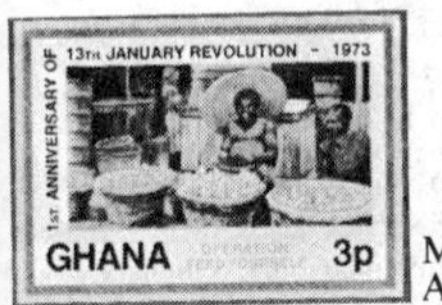


Market A113

Designs: 1p, Unity Declaration at Kumasi Durbar. 5p, Woman with child selling bananas (vert.). 15p, Farmer at rest and produce (vert.). 30p, Market. 40p, 1ce, Farmer cutting palm nuts with cutlass. 60p, Miners.

***Perf. 14x13½, 13½x14***

**1973, Apr.** **Litho.**

*472* A113 1p multi 5 5
*473* A113 3p multi 8 8
*474* A113 5p multi 12 12
*475* A113 15p multi 40 35
*476* A113 30p multi 75 70
*477* A113 1ce multi 2.50 2.40
*Nos. 472-477 (6)* 3.90 3.70

Souvenir Sheet

*478* A113 Sheet of 2 3.00 2.75
*a* 40p multi 80 50
*b* 60p multi 1.20 75

Operation "Feed Yourself" and for first anniversary of the October 13 Revolution. No. 478 has black marginal inscription. Size: 89x55mm.

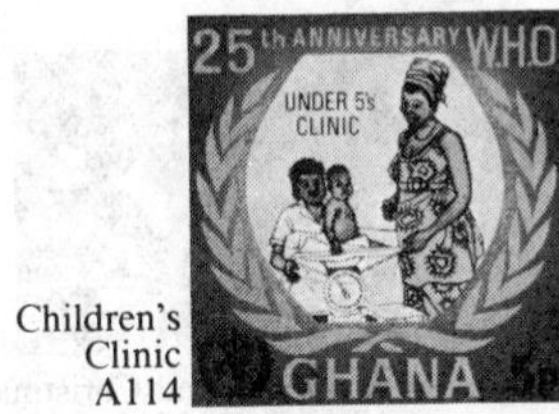


Children's Clinic A114

Designs (WHO Emblem and): 15p, Radiology. 30p, Immunization. 50p, Fight against malnutrition (starving child). 1ce, WHO Headquarters, Geneva.

**1973, July** ***Perf. 14x13½***

*479* A114 5p rose red & multi 10 10
*480* A114 15p bl & multi 28 28
*481* A114 30p bis & multi 60 55
*482* A114 50p grn & multi 1.00 90
*483* A114 1ce multi 2.00 1.75
*Nos. 479-483 (5)* 3.98 3.58

World Health Organization, 25th anniversary.

Nos. 460-465 Overprinted: "1st WORLD SCOUTING CONFERENCE IN AFRICA"

**1973, July** **Litho.** ***Perf. 14***

*484* A111 5p grn & multi 12 12
*485* A111 15p ocher & multi 35 35
*486* A111 30p lil & multi 75 70
*487* A111 50p multi 1.25 1.10
*488* A111 1ce bl & multi 2.50 2.25
*Nos. 484-488 (5)* 4.97 4.52

**Souvenir Sheet**

***Perf. 13½***

*489* A111 Souv. sheet of 2 3.25 3.00
*a* 40p brn & multi 90 60
*b* 60p grn & multi 1.25 90

24th Boy Scout World Conference (1st in Africa), Nairobi, Kenya, July 16-21.

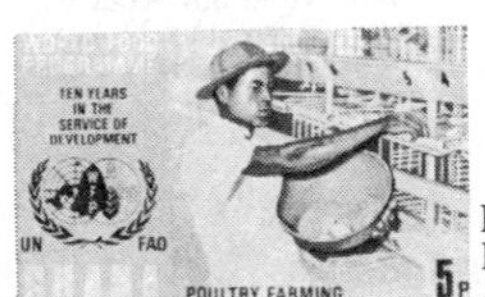


Poultry Farming A115

Designs (FAO/UN Emblem and): 15p, 40p, Tractor. 50p, Cacao harvest. 60p, 1ce, FAO Headquarters, Rome.

**1973** **Litho.** ***Perf. 14½x14***

*490* A115 5p bl & multi 14 14
*491* A115 15p bl & multi 50 45
*492* A115 50p bl & multi 1.50 1.35
*493* A115 1ce bl & multi 3.00 2.75

**Souvenir Sheet**

*494* A115 Souv. sheet of 2 3.00 2.75
*a* 40p bl & multi 80 50
*b* 60p bl & multi 1.20 75

World Food Program, 10th anniversary. No. 494 has lemon margin with grain design and black inscription. Size: 92½x104mm.

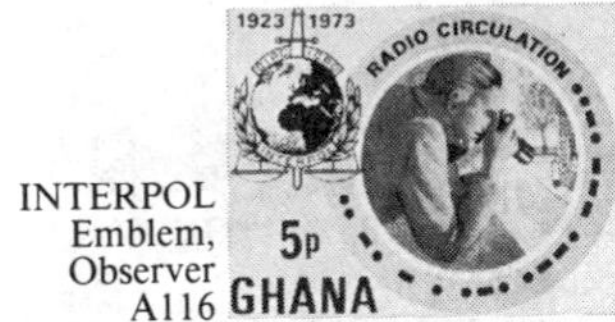


INTERPOL Emblem, Observer A116

Designs (INTERPOL Emblem and): 30p, Dentures, poison bottle, handcuffs. 50p, photograph and fingerprint. 1ce, Corpse and question mark.

**1973** ***Perf. 13x13½***

*495* A116 5p emer & multi 12 12
*496* A116 30p rose red & multi 65 60
*497* A116 50p ultra & multi 1.00 90
*498* A116 1ce gray & multi 2.25 2.00

50th anniversary of the International Criminal Police Organization (INTERPOL).

Handclasp and "OAU" A117

Designs ("OAU" and): 30p, Africa Hall, Addis Ababa. 50p, OAU emblem (map of Africa). 1ce, "X" in Ghana flag colors.

**1973, Oct. 22** **Litho.** ***Perf. 14x14½***

*499* A117 5p lt bl, blk & brn 10 10
*500* A117 30p bluish grn, blk & brn 65 60
*501* A117 50p pink, blk & ol 1.00 90
*502* A117 1ce multi 2.25 2.00

10th anniversary of the Organization for African Unity.

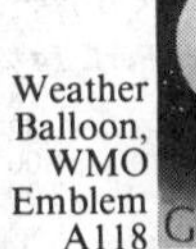

Weather Balloon, WMO Emblem A118

**1973, Nov. 16**

Designs (WMO Emblem and): 15p, 40p, Tiros weather satellite. 30p, 60p, Computer weather map. 1ce, Radar cloud scanner.

*503* A118 5p multi 9 9
*504* A118 15p multi 30 25
*505* A118 30p multi 60 50
*506* A118 1ce multi 1.75 1.50

**Souvenir Sheet**

*507* A118 Sheet of 2 2.50 2.25
*a* 40p multi 75 40
*b* 60p multi 1.10 60

Centenary of international meteorological cooperation. No. 507 has pale green and multicolored margin showing cloud formation over Ghana map. Size: 120x95mm.

Adoration of the Kings — A119

Christmas: 3p, 40p, Madonna and Child (contemporary). Nos. 510, 511d, Madonna and Child, by Murillo. No. 511, 60p, Adoration of the Kings, by Tiepolo. No. 511b as 1p.

**1973, Dec. 10** ***Perf. 14***

*508* A119 1p blk & multi 5 5
*509* A119 3p gray & multi 8 8
*510* A119 30p multi 90 90
*511* A119 50p multi 1.75 1.75

**Souvenir Sheet**

***Imperf***

*511A* A119 Sheet of 4 2.75 2.75
*b* 30p blk & multi 45 45
*c* 40p gray & multi 60 60
*d* 50p multi 75 75
*e* 60p multi 90 90

No. 511A has simulated perforations, yellow margin with black inscription. Size: 76x103mm.

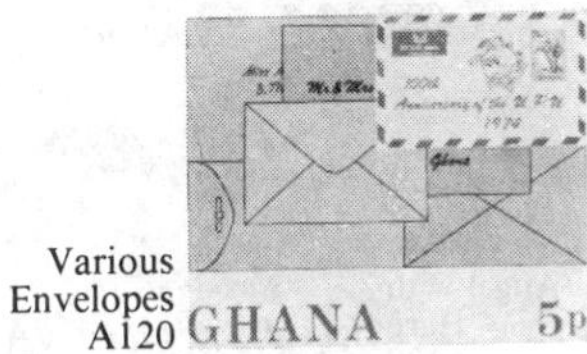


Various Envelopes A120

Designs (UPU Emblem and): 9p, 30p, UPU Headquarters, Bern. 40p, 50p, Airmail envelope with Ghana No. 296. 60p, 1ce, Ghana No. 296.

**1974, May** **Litho.** ***Perf. 14½***

*512* A120 5p bl, blk & org 8 6
*513* A120 9p bl, blk & org 15 12
*514* A120 50p bl, blk & org 90 80
*515* A120 1ce bl, blk & org 1.90 1.75

**Souvenir Sheet**

*515A* A120 Sheet of 4 3.00 2.75
*b* 20p bl, blk & org 25 25
*c* 30p bl, blk & org 50 50
*d* 40p bl, blk & org 75 75
*e* 50p bl, blk & org 90 90

Centenary of Universal Postal Union. No. 515A has salmon pink margin with black inscriptions. Size: 108x90mm.

The Betrayal — A121

Designs: 5p, 15p, Jesus Carrying Cross, painting by Thomas de Coloswar, 1427. 20p, 30p, The Betrayal. 25p, 50p, The Deposition. 40p, 1ce, Risen Christ and Mary Magdalene. The designs (except 5p, 15p) are from 15th century English ivory carvings.

**1974, Apr.** **Litho.** ***Perf. 14***

*516* A121 5p blk & multi 8 8
*517* A121 30p sil, ultra & brn 48 48
*518* A121 50p sil, red & brn 80 80
*519* A121 1ce sil, ol & brn 1.60 1.60

**Souvenir Sheet**

***Imperf***

*520* A121 Sheet of 4 1.65 1.65
*a* 15p blk & multi 22
*b* 20p sil, ultra & brn 30
*c* 25p sil, red & brn 38
*d* 40p sil, ol & brn 60

Easter 1974. No. 520 contains 4 stamps with simulated perforations, yellow margin and black inscription. Size: 110x105mm.

Nos. 512-515A Overprinted "INTERNABA 1974"

**1974, June 7** ***Perf. 14½***

*521* A120 5p bl, blk & org 12 8
*522* A120 9p bl, blk & org 20 12
*523* A120 50p bl, blk & org 1.35 1.00
*524* A120 1ce bl, blk & org 2.75 2.00

**Souvenir Sheet**

*524A* A120 Sheet of 4 3.75 3.00
*b* 20p bl, blk & org 28 28
*c* 30p bl, blk & org 52 52
*d* 40p bl, blk & org 75 75
*e* 60p bl, blk & org 1.00 1.00

INTERNABA 1974 International Philatelic Exhibition, Basel, June 7-16.

Overprint is applied to individual stamps of No. 524A.

Soccer and World Cup Emblem A122

Designs: Various soccer scenes and world cup emblem.

**1974, June 17** **Litho.** ***Perf. 14½, 13***

*525* A122 5p multi 9 6
*526* A122 30p multi 55 45
*527* A122 50p multi 90 80
*528* A122 1ce multi 1.75 1.60

**Souvenir Sheet**

***Perf. 14½***

*529* A122 Sheet of 4 3.75 3.25
*a* 25p multi 40
*b* 40p multi 65
*c* 55p multi 90
*d* 60p multi 1.00

World Cup Soccer Championship, June 13-July 7. No. 529 has multicolored margin and black inscription. Size: 146x93mm.

Nos. 525-528 were issued in sheets of 30, perf. 14½, and in sheets of 5 plus label, perf. 13.

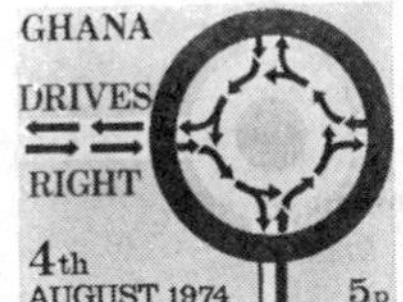


Traffic Diagram at Traffic Circle A123

Designs: 15p, Traffic sign "Two-way traffic." 30p, "Change to right hand drive!" (vert.). 50p, Warning hands sign (vert.). 1ce, 2 hands and car symbolizing traffic change (vert.).

**1974, July 16** *Perf. 13½*

**Size: 35x28½mm.**

*530* A123 5p yel grn, red & blk 8 6
*531* A123 15p lil, red & blk 25 18

**Size: 28½x41mm.**

*Perf. 14½*

*532* A123 30p multi 50 40
*533* A123 50p multi 80 65
*534* A123 1ce red, grn & blk 1.75 1.50
*Nos. 530-534 (5)* 3.38 2.79

Publicity for change to right-hand driving, Aug. 4, 1974.

Nos. 525-529 Overprinted: "WEST GERMANY WINNERS"

**1974, Aug. 30 Litho.** *Perf. 14½, 13*

*535* A122 5p multi 12 12
*536* A122 30p multi 65 65
*537* A122 50p multi 1.10 1.10
*538* A122 1ce multi 2.00 2.00

**Souvenir Sheet**

*539* A122 Sheet of 4 3.75 3.25
*a* 25p multi 40
*b* 40p multi 65
*c* 55p multi 90
*d* 60p multi 1.00

World Cup Soccer Championship, 1974, victory of German Federal Republic. Overprint is applied to individual stamps of No. 539.

Family and WPY Emblem A124

**1974, Sept. 27** *Perf. 12½*

*540* A124 5p *shown* 8 7
*541* A124 30p *Clinic* 50 40
*542* A124 50p *Immunization of children* 80 75
*543* A124 1ce *Census* 1.75 1.75

World Population Year, 1974.

Angel — A125

Nativity — A127

Three Kings, Candles — A126

Design: 60p, 1ce, Annunciation.

*Perf. 13½, 14 (7p)*

**1974, Dec. 19** **Litho.**

*544* A125 5p red & multi 10 6
*545* A126 7p bl & multi 14 8
*546* A127 9p org & multi 20 15
*547* A127 1ce org & multi 2.50 2.50

**Souvenir Sheet**

*Imperf*

*548* Sheet of 4 2.75 2.75
*a* A125 15p red & multi 22
*b* A126 30p bl & multi 45
*c* A127 45p org & multi 70
*d* A127 60p org & multi 90

Christmas 1974. No. 548 contains 4 stamps with simulated perforations; yellow margin with black inscription and border. Size: 127x127mm.

Nos. 525-529 Overprinted "APOLLO / SOYUZ / JULY 15, 1975"

**1975, Aug. 15 Litho.** *Perf. 14½, 13*

*549* A122 5p multi 8 6
*550* A122 30p multi 52 40
*551* A122 50p multi 1.00 80
*552* A122 1ce multi 2.00 1.60

**Souvenir Sheet**

*Perf. 14½*

*553* A122 Sheet of 4 3.75 3.75
*a* 25p multi 40
*b* 40p multi 65
*c* 55p multi 90
*d* 60p multi 1.00

Apollo Soyuz space test project (Russo-American cooperation), launching July 15, link-up, July 17.

Overprint is applied to individual stamps of No. 553.

Nos. 549-552 with perf. 13 are from the sheets of 5 plus label.

IWY Emblem, Woman Tractor Driver — A128

Designs (International Women's Year Emblem and): 15p, like 7p. 30p, 40p, Automobile mechanic. 60p, 65p, Factory workers. 80p, 1ce, Cocoa research.

**1975, Sept. 3 Litho.** *Perf. 14*

*554* A128 7p multi 15 15
*555* A128 30p lt vio & multi 55 55
*556* A128 60p multi 1.10 1.10
*557* A128 1ce lil & multi 1.75 1.75

**Souvenir Sheet**

*Imperf*

*558* A128 Sheet of 4 3.75 3.75
*a* 15p Prus grn & multi 22
*b* 40p lt vio & multi 60
*c* 65p dl grn & multi 1.00
*d* 80p lil & multi 1.20

International Women's Year 1975. No. 558 contains 4 stamps with simulated perforations; light blue margin with black inscription and IWY emblems. Size: 135x109mm.

Angel over Child in Crib A129

Angel with Harp A130

Designs: 7p, 40p, Angels with lute and bell. 30p, 65p, Angel with viol. 1ce, 80p, Angels with trumpets. 15p, like 5p.

**1975, Dec. 31 Litho.** *Perf. 14x13½*

*559* A129 2p org & multi 5 5
*560* A130 5p yel, brn & grn 8 6
*561* A130 7p yel, brn & grn 12 7
*562* A130 30p yel, brn & grn 48 25
*563* A130 1ce yel, brn & grn 1.60 1.00
*Nos. 559-563 (5)* 2.33 1.43

**Souvenir Sheet**

*Imperf*

*564* A130 Sheet of 4 3.50 3.50
*a* 15p yel, grn & brn 25
*b* 40p yel, grn & brn 25
*c* 65p yel, grn & brn 1.10
*d* 80p yel, grn & brn 1.25

Christmas 1975. No. 564 has simulated perforations, light green and brown margin. Size: 98x87mm.

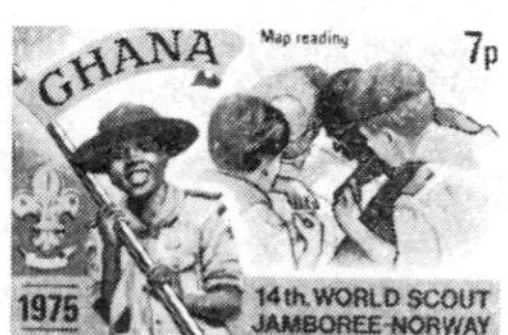


Boy Scouts Reading Map — A131

Designs: 30p, 40p, Sailing. 60p, 65p, Hiking. 80p, 1ce, Life saving (swimmers). 15p, like 7p.

**1976, Jan. 5** *Perf. 13½x14*

*565* A131 7p ocher & multi 12 6
*566* A131 30p bl & multi 45 22
*567* A131 60p grn & multi 90 45
*568* A131 1ce multi 1.50 90

**Souvenir Sheet**

*569* A131 Sheet of 4 3.50 3.50
*a* 15p ocher & multi 25
*b* 40p bl & multi 65
*c* 65p grn & multi 1.10
*d* 80p rose cl & multi 1.25

Nordjamb 75, 14th World Boy Scout Jamboree, Lillehammer, Norway, July 29-Aug. 7. No. 569 has yellow margin with black inscription. Size: 133x99mm.

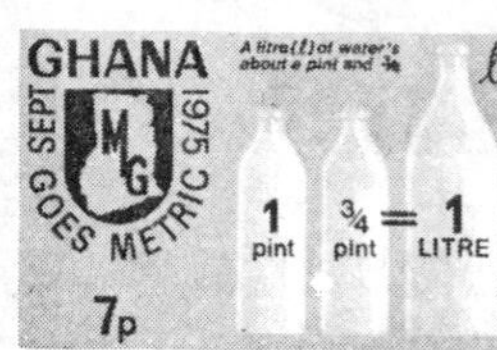


1¾ Pints Equal 1 Liter A132

Designs (Map of Ghana and): 30p, "2¼ lbs of jam a little more than a kilogram." 60p, "A meter of cloth will be a little more than 3 foot 3." 1ce, Thermometer, ice and boiling tea kettle.

**1976, Jan. 5 Litho.** *Perf. 14x13½*

*570* A132 7p bluish gray & blk 12 6
*571* A132 30p vio bl & multi 45 22
*572* A132 60p ocher & multi 90 45
*573* A132 1ce multi 1.50 90

Introduction of metric system, Sept. 1975.

Fair Grounds — A133

Designs: Various exhibition halls.

**1976, Apr. 6 Litho.** *Perf. 14*

*574* A133 7p multi 12 6
*575* A133 30p yel & multi 45 22
*576* A133 60p multi 90 45
*577* A133 1ce sal & multi 1.50 90

International Trade Fair, Accra, Feb. 1-15.

Nos. 565-569 Overprinted in Violet Blue

'INTERPHIL' 76 BICENTENNIAL EXHIBITION

**1976, May 29 Litho.** *Perf. 13½x14*

*578* A131 7p ocher & multi 15 6
*579* A131 30p bl & multi 55 22
*580* A131 60p grn & multi 1.10 45
*581* A131 1ce multi 1.50 90

**Souvenir Sheet**

*582* A131 Sheet of 4 3.50 2.25
*a* 15p ocher & multi 25
*b* 40p bl & multi 65
*c* 65p grn & multi 1.10
*d* 80p rose cl & multi 1.25

Interphil 76 International Philatelic Exhibition, Philadelphia, Pa., May 29-June 6. Overprint applied to individual stamps of No. 582.

Shot Put — A134

Designs (Olympic Rings, Map of Ghana and): 15p, like 7p. 30p, 40p, Soccer. 60p, 65p, Women's 1500 meters. 80p, 1ce, Boxing.

**1976, Aug. 9 Litho.** *Perf. 14x13½*

*583* A134 7p lt bl & multi 12 7
*584* A134 30p yel & multi 48 25
*585* A134 60p multi 1.00 48
*586* A134 1ce yel & multi 1.60 1.00

**Souvenir Sheet**

*587* A134 Sheet of 4 3.50 3.50
*a* 15p lt bl & multi 25
*b* 40p yel & multi 65
*c* 65p emer & multi 1.00
*d* 80p yel & multi 1.25

21st Olympic Games, Montreal, Canada, July 17-Aug. 1. No. 587 has multicolored margin showing flags of Ghana and Canada and various sports. Size: 103x135mm.

Supreme Court, Accra A135

Designs: Various views of Supreme Court Building, Scales of Justice, law book.

**1976, Sept. 7 Litho.** *Perf. 14*

*588* A135 8p lil & multi 12 12
*589* A135 30p bl & multi 50 50
*590* A135 60p ver & multi 1.00 1.00
*591* A135 1ce multi 1.75 1.75

Ghana Supreme Court, centenary.

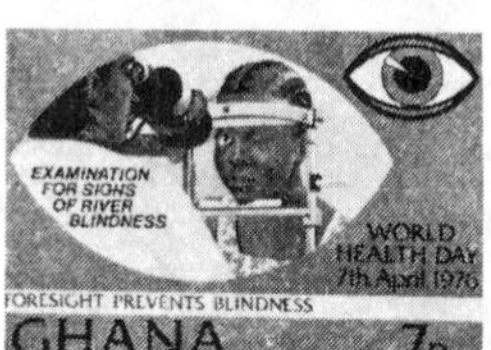


Examination for River Blindness — A136

Designs: 30p, Ghanaian entomologist with microscope. 60p, Flowers. 1ce, Boatmen checking effectiveness of black fly larvae insecticide.

**1976, Oct. 28 Litho.** *Perf. 14½x14*

*592* A136 7p multi 12 12
*593* A136 30p multi 50 50
*594* A136 60p multi 1.00 1.00
*595* A136 1ce multi 1.75 1.75

World Health Day. Prevention of blindness.

Children with Gifts and Christmas Tree — A137

Designs: 6p, 15p, Children with firecrackers. 30p, 65p, Family at Christmas dinner. 40p, 80p, 1ce, like 8p.

**1976, Dec. 15 Litho. Perf. 13½**

596 A137 6p multi 12 12
597 A137 8p multi 15 15
598 A137 30p multi 55 55
599 A137 1ce multi 1.75 1.75

**Souvenir Sheet**
***Imperf***

600 A137 Sheet of 4 3.50 3.50
a. 15p multi 22
b. 40p multi 60
c. 65p multi 1.00
d. 80p multi 1.25

Christmas 1976. No. 600 has simulated perforations, blue margin with black inscription and design. Size: 123x98mm.

1876 Gallows Frame Telephone and A. G. Bell — A138

Designs (A. G. Bell and): 15p, like 8p. 30p, 40p, 1895 telephone. 60p, 65p, 1929 telephone. 80p, 1ce, 1976 telephone.

**1976, Dec. 17 Perf. 14½**

601 A138 8p multi 12 6
602 A138 30p multi 50 25
603 A138 60p multi 1.10 50
604 A138 1ce multi 1.75 90

**Souvenir Sheet**
***Perf. 13***

605 A138 Sheet of 4 3.50 3.50
a. 15p multi 22
b. 40p multi 60
c. 65p multi 1.00
d. 80p multi 1.20

Centenary of first telephone call by Alexander Graham Bell, Mar. 10, 1876. No. 605 has light blue and black margin. Size: 126x92mm.

Nos. 583-587 Overprinted:
a. EAST GERMANY / WINNERS
b. U.S.S.R. WINNERS
c. U.S.A. WINNERS

**1977, Feb. 22 Litho. Perf. 14x13½**

606 A134 (a) 7p multi 10 6
607 A134 (a) 30p multi 40 20
608 A134 (b) 60p multi 80 40
609 A134 (c) 1ce multi 1.75 65

**Souvenir Sheet**

610 A134 Sheet of 4 3.50 2.50
a. (a) 15p multi 35
b. (a) 40p multi 75
c. (b) 65p multi 1.10
d. (c) 80p multi 1.25

1976 Montreal Olympic Games' winners.

Klama Dance, Dipo Tribe — A139

Designs (Festival Emblem and): 15p, like 8p. 30p, 40p, African artifacts. 60p, 65p, Acon dance. 80p, 1ce, Mud, straw and wooden huts.

**1977, Mar. 24 Litho. Perf. 14x13½**

611 A139 8p multi 12 6
612 A139 30p multi 45 22
613 A139 60p multi 90 45
614 A139 1ce multi 1.50 75

**Souvenir Sheet**

615 A139 Sheet of 4 3.50 2.50
a. 15p multi 35
b. 40p multi 75
c. 65p multi 1.10
d. 80p multi 1.25

2nd World Black and African Festival of Arts and Culture, Lagos, Nigeria, Jan. 15-Feb. 12. No. 615 has light blue and black margin. Size: 163x119mm.

Nos. 601-605 Overprinted: "PRINCE CHARLES / VISITS GHANA / 17th TO 25th / MARCH, 1977"

**1977, June 2 Litho. Perf. 14½**

616 A138 8p multi 12 5
617 A138 30p multi 40 18
618 A138 60p multi 90 35
619 A138 1ce multi 1.40 60

**Souvenir Sheet**
***Perf. 13***

620 A138 Sheet of 4 3.50 2.50
a. 15p multi 35
b. 40p multi 75
c. 65p multi 1.10
d. 80p multi 1.25

Visit of Prince Charles, March 17-25. Overprint applied to individual stamps of No. 620.

Olive Colobus A140

Designs (Wildlife Fund Emblem and): 15p, like 8p. 20p, 40p, Ebien palm squirrel. 30p, 65p, African wild dog. 60p, 80p, West African manatee.

**1977, June 22 Litho. Perf. 13½x14**

621 A140 8p multi 14 6
622 A140 20p multi 35 14
623 A140 30p multi 30 20
624 A140 60p multi 1.00 40

**Souvenir Sheet**

625 A140 Sheet of 4 3.50 2.50
a. 15p multi 35
b. 40p multi 75
c. 65p multi 1.10
d. 80p multi 1.25

Wildlife protection. No. 625 has multicolored margin. Size: 139x100mm.

Suzanne Fourment in Velvet Hat, by Rubens — A141

Paintings: 15p, like 8p. 30p, 40p, Isabella of Portugal, by Titian. 60p, 65p, Duke and Duchess of Cumberland, by Gainsborough. 80p, 1ce, Rubens and his wife Isabella, by Rubens.

**1977, Sept. Litho. Perf. 14x13½**

626 A141 8p lt bl & multi 16 16
627 A141 30p lt bl & multi 60 60
628 A141 60p lt bl & multi 1.20 1.20
629 A141 1ce lt bl & multi 2.00 2.00

**Souvenir Sheet**

630 A141 Sheet of 4 4.25 4.25
a. 15p lt bl & multi 30
b. 40p lt bl & multi 80
c. 65p lt bl & multi 1.30
d. 80p lt bl & multi 1.60

Painters, Birth Anniversaries: Peter Paul Rubens (1577-1640); Titian (1477-1576); Thomas Gainsborough (1727-1788). No. 630 has ocher and black margin. Size: 99x150mm.

Adoration of the Kings — A142

Guild of the Good Shepherd, Abossey Okai — A143

Designs: 6p, 40p, Methodist Church, Wesley, Accra. 8p, Virgin and Child, and Star. 15p, like 2p. 30p, 65p, Holy Spirit Cathedral, Accra. 80p, 1ce, Ebenezer Presbyterian Church, Osu, Accra. Type A143 designs include score of "Hark the Herald Angels Sing."

***Perf. 14x14½, 14***

**1977, Dec. 30 Litho.**

631 A142 1p multi 5 5
632 A143 2p multi 5 5
633 A143 6p multi 10 6
634 A142 8p multi 12 7
635 A143 30p multi 48 25
636 A143 1ce multi 1.60 80
*Nos. 631-636 (6)* 2.40 1.28

**Souvenir Sheet**
***Imperf***

637 A143 Sheet of 4 3.75 3.75
a. 15p multi 25
b. 40p multi 65
c. 65p multi 1.00
d. 80p multi 1.40

Christmas 1977. No. 637 has light blue and black margin with bar of music; simulated perforations. Size: 122x97mm.

No. 631-637 Overprinted: "REFERENDUM 1978 VOTE EARLY"

***Perf. 14x14½, 14***

**1978, Mar. 28 Litho.**

638 A142 1p multi 5 5
639 A143 2p multi 5 5
640 A143 6p multi 10 6
641 A142 8p multi 12 7
642 A143 30p multi 48 25
643 A143 1ce multi 1.60 80
*Nos. 638-643 (6)* 2.40 1.28

**Souvenir Sheet**
***Imperf***

644 A143 Sheet of 4 *35.50*
a. 15p multi *1.50*
b. 40p multi *3.75*
c. 60p multi *6.00*
d. 80p multi *7.50*

Banana Harvest — A144

Designs: 8p, Vegetable garden. 30p, Produce market. 60p, Fishing. 1ce, Tractor.

**1978, May 15 Perf. 14**

645 A144 2p multi 5 5
646 A144 8p multi 12 6
647 A144 30p multi 45 22
648 A144 60p multi 90 45
649 A144 1ce multi 1.50 75
*Nos. 645-649 (5)* 3.02 1.53

Operation feed yourself.

Wright Biplane and Crowd — A145

Planes and Crowd: 15p, like 8p. 30p, 40p, Heracles, 1st practical airliner. 60p, 65p, D. H. Comet, 1st jet airliner. 80p, 1ce, Concorde, 1st supersonic airliner.

**1978, June 6 Litho. Perf. 14x13½**

650 A145 8p multi 12 6
651 A145 30p multi 45 22
652 A145 60p multi 90 45
653 A145 1ce multi 1.50 75

**Souvenir Sheet**

654 A145 Sheet of 4 3.00 3.00
a. 15p multi 22
b. 40p multi 60
c. 65p multi 1.00
d. 80p multi 1.10

75th anniversary of first powered flight. No. 654 has dark brown margin with picture of Wright brothers. Size: 168x100mm. The "cheering crowd" forms a continuing design on Nos. 650-654.

Nos. 650-653, 654a-654d Overprinted: "CAPEX 78 / JUNE 9-18 1978"

**1978, June 9**

655 A145 8p multi 12 7
656 A145 30p multi 48 25
657 A145 60p multi 1.00 48
658 A145 1ce multi 1.60 80

**Souvenir Sheet**

659 A145 Sheet of 4 3.00 3.00
a. 15p multi 22
b. 40p multi 60
c. 65p multi 90
d. 80p multi 1.10

CAPEX, Canadian International Philatelic Exhibition, Toronto, Ont., June 9-18.

Soccer, Africa Cup Emblem and Ghana Flag — A146

Designs: 15p, like 8p. 30p, 40p, Three soccer players, Africa Cup emblem, Ghana flag. 60p, 65p, Two soccer players, Argentina '78 emblem, Argentine flag. 80p, 1ce, Goalkeeper, Argentina '78 emblem and Argentine flag.

**1978, July 1 Litho. Perf. 13½x14**

660 A146 8p multi 12 7
661 A146 30p multi 45 22
662 A146 60p multi 90 45
663 A146 1ce multi 1.50 75

**Souvenir Sheet**

664 Sheet of 4 3.00 3.00
a. A146 15p multi 22
b. A146 40p multi 60
c. A146 65p multi 90
d. A146 80p multi 1.10

11th African Cup of Nations, Ghana, Mar. 5-19, and 11th World Cup Soccer Championship, Argentina, June 1-25. No. 664 has margin showing flag colors of Argentina and Ghana. Size: 111x105mm.

Nos. 660-661, 664a-664b Overprinted: "GHANA WINNERS"
Nos. 662-663, 664c-664d Overprinted: "ARGENTINA WINS"

**1978, Aug. 21 Litho. Perf. 13½x14**

665 A146 8p multi 12 7
666 A146 30p multi 45 22
667 A146 60p multi 90 45
668 A146 1ce multi 1.50 75

**Souvenir Sheet**

669 Sheet of 4 3.00 3.00
a. A146 15p multi 22
b. A146 40p multi 60
c. A146 65p multi 90
d. A146 80p multi 1.10

Winners, 11th African Cup and 11th World Cup Soccer Championships.
Overprint on 60p and 65p is in two lines.

Values quoted in this catalogue are for stamps graded at Fine-Very Fine and with no faults. An illustrated guide to grade is provided in introductory material, beginning on Page V.

The Betrayal, by Dürer — A147

Etchings by Albrecht Dürer: 39p, The Crucifixion. 60p, The Deposition. 1ce, The Resurrection.

**1978, Sept. 1 Litho. *Perf. 14x13½***

| | | | | | |
|---|---|---|---|---|---|
| *670* | A147 | 11p | lil & blk | 7 | 7 |
| *671* | A147 | 39p | sal & blk | 28 | 28 |
| *672* | A147 | 60p | org & blk | 40 | 40 |
| *673* | A147 | 1ce | yel grn & blk | 65 | 65 |

Easter 1978.

Bauhinia Purpurea A148

Flowers: 39p, Cassia fistula. 60p, Frangipani. 1ce, Jacaranda mimosifolia.

**1978, Nov. 20 Litho. *Perf. 14x13½***

| | | | | | |
|---|---|---|---|---|---|
| *674* | A148 | 11p | multi | 8 | 6 |
| *675* | A148 | 39p | multi | 25 | 20 |
| *676* | A148 | 60p | multi | 50 | 30 |
| *677* | A148 | 1ce | multi | 75 | 50 |

Mail Railroad Car — A149

Designs: 39p, Pay and bank car. 60p, Locomotive, 1922. 1ce, Diesel locomotive, 1960.

**1978, Dec. 4 Litho. *Perf. 13½***

| | | | | | |
|---|---|---|---|---|---|
| *678* | A149 | 11p | multi | 15 | 10 |
| *679* | A149 | 39p | multi | 50 | 40 |
| *680* | A149 | 60p | multi | 1.00 | 60 |
| *681* | A149 | 1ce | multi | 1.50 | 1.00 |

Ghana railroad, 75th anniversary.

Orbiter Spacecraft — A150

Designs: 15p, like 11p. 39p, 40p, Multiprobe spacecraft. 60p, 65p, Orbiter and Multiprobe circling Venus. 2ce, 3ce, Radar chart of Venus.

**1979, July 5 Litho. *Perf. 14x13½***

| | | | | | |
|---|---|---|---|---|---|
| *682* | A150 | 11p | multi | 8 | 8 |
| *683* | A150 | 39p | multi | 35 | 35 |
| *684* | A150 | 60p | multi | 50 | 50 |
| *685* | A150 | 3ce | multi | 2.50 | 2.50 |

**Souvenir Sheet**

***Imperf***

| | | | |
|---|---|---|---|
| *686* | Sheet of 4 | 3.25 | 3.25 |
| *a* | A150 15p multi | 15 | |
| *b* | A150 40p multi | 40 | |
| *c* | A150 65p multi | 65 | |
| *d* | A150 2ce multi | 2.00 | |

Pioneer Venus Space Project. No. 686 has multicolored margin showing split-up of Multiprobe. Size: 135x94mm.

O Come All Ye Faithful A152

Christmas Carols: 10p, O Little Town of Bethlehem. 15p, 65p, We Three Kings of Orient Are. 20p, I Saw Three Ships Come Sailing By. 25p, like 8p. No. 696, 1ce, Away in a Manger. 4ce, No. 698d, Ding Dong Merrily on High.

**1979, Dec. 20 *Perf. 14½***

| | | | | | |
|---|---|---|---|---|---|
| *692* | A152 | 8p | multi | 14 | 7 |
| *693* | A152 | 10p | multi | 16 | 8 |
| *694* | A152 | 15p | multi | 25 | 12 |
| *695* | A152 | 20p | multi | 32 | 15 |
| *696* | A152 | 2ce | multi | 3.25 | 1.60 |
| *697* | A152 | 4ce | multi | 5.75 | 3.25 |
| | | | *Nos. 692-697 (6)* | 9.87 | 5.27 |

**Souvenir Sheet**

| | | | |
|---|---|---|---|
| *698* | Sheet of 4 | 6.25 | 3.00 |
| *a* | A152 25p multi | 40 | 18 |
| *b* | A152 65p multi | 90 | 50 |
| *c* | A152 1ce multi | 1.50 | 75 |
| *d* | A152 2ce multi | 3.00 | 1.50 |

Christmas 1979. No. 698 has multicolored margin showing ships and Bethlehem. Size: 110x95½mm.

J.B. Danquah (1895-1965) A153

National Leaders: 65p, John Mensah Sarbah (1864-1910). 80p, J.E.K. Aggrey (1875-1925). 2ce, Kwame Nkrumah (1909-1972). 4ce, G.E. Grant (1878-1956).

**1980, Jan. 21 Litho. *Perf. 13½x14***

| | | | | | |
|---|---|---|---|---|---|
| *699* | A153 | 20p | multi | 32 | 16 |
| *700* | A153 | 65p | multi | 1.10 | 50 |
| *701* | A153 | 80p | multi | 1.25 | 65 |
| *702* | A153 | 2ce | multi | 3.25 | 1.60 |
| *703* | A153 | 4ce | multi | 6.50 | 3.25 |
| | | | *Nos. 699-703 (5)* | 12.42 | 6.16 |

Man with Clack Bells, Hill A154

Hill and: 25p, Man with clack bells. 50p, 65p, Chief, elephant staff. 1ce, 2ce, Drummer. 4ce, 5ce, Chief, ivory staff.

**1980, Mar. 12 Litho. *Perf. 14½***

| | | | | | |
|---|---|---|---|---|---|
| *704* | A154 | 20p | multi | 20 | 10 |
| *705* | A154 | 65p | multi | 65 | 35 |
| *706* | A154 | 2ce | multi | 2.00 | 1.00 |
| *707* | A154 | 4ce | multi | 4.00 | 2.00 |

**Souvenir Sheet**

| | | | |
|---|---|---|---|
| *708* | Sheet of 4 | 7.00 | 4.00 |
| *a* | A154 25p multi | 25 | 15 |
| *b* | A154 50p multi | 50 | 35 |
| *c* | A154 1ce multi | 1.00 | 65 |
| *d* | A154 5ce multi | 5.00 | 3.50 |

Sir Rowland Hill (1795-1879), originator of penny postage. No. 708 has multicolored decorative margin. Size: 115x89mm.

Students, IYC Emblem — A155

IYC Emblem and: 25p like 20p. 50p, 65p, Boys playing soccer. 1ce, 2ce, Boys in canoe. 3ce, 4ce, Mother and child.

**1980, Apr. 2 Litho. *Perf. 15***

| | | | | | |
|---|---|---|---|---|---|
| *709* | A155 | 20p | multi | 20 | 10 |
| *710* | A155 | 65p | multi | 65 | 35 |
| *711* | A155 | 2ce | multi | 2.00 | 1.00 |
| *712* | A155 | 4ce | multi | 4.00 | 2.00 |

**Souvenir Sheet**

| | | | |
|---|---|---|---|
| *713* | Sheet of 4 | 8.75 | 4.00 |
| *a* | A155 25p multi | 50 | 25 |
| *b* | A155 50p multi | 1.00 | 50 |
| *c* | A155 1ce multi | 1.75 | 75 |
| *d* | A155 3ce multi | 5.50 | 2.50 |

International Year of the Child (1979). No. 713 has multicolored margin showing IYC Emblem. Size: 155x94mm.

Nos. 704-708 Overprinted: "LONDON 1980" 6th-14th May 1980

**1980, May 6 Litho. *Perf. 14½***

| | | | | | |
|---|---|---|---|---|---|
| *714* | A154 | 20p | multi | 20 | 10 |
| *715* | A154 | 65p | multi | 65 | 35 |
| *716* | A154 | 2ce | multi | 2.00 | 1.00 |
| *717* | A154 | 4ce | multi | 4.00 | 2.00 |

**Souvenir Sheet**

| | | | |
|---|---|---|---|
| *718* | Sheet of 4 | 7.50 | 4.00 |
| *a* | A154 25p multi | 30 | 20 |
| *b* | A154 50p multi | 60 | 30 |
| *c* | A154 1ce multi | 1.10 | 60 |
| *d* | A154 5ce multi | 5.50 | 2.75 |

London 1980 International Stamp Exhibition, May 6-14. Sheet margin overprinted: Earl's Court 6th-14th May "London 1980."

Nos. 709-713 Overprinted: "PAPAL VISIT" 8th-9th May 1980

**1980, May 8 *Perf. 15***

| | | | | | |
|---|---|---|---|---|---|
| *719* | A155 | 20p | multi | 20 | 10 |
| *720* | A155 | 65p | multi | 65 | 35 |
| *721* | A155 | 2ce | multi | 2.00 | 1.00 |
| *722* | A155 | 4ce | multi | 4.00 | 2.00 |

**Souvenir Sheet**

| | | | |
|---|---|---|---|
| *723* | Sheet of 4 | 8.00 | 4.00 |
| *a* | A155 25p multi | 40 | 20 |
| *b* | A155 50p multi | 80 | 40 |
| *c* | A155 1ce multi | 1.75 | 75 |
| *d* | A155 3ce multi | 5.00 | 2.25 |

Visit of Pope John Paul II to Ghana, May 8-9.

Parliament House A156

**1980, Aug. 4 Litho. *Perf. 14***

| | | | | | |
|---|---|---|---|---|---|
| *724* | A156 | 20p | *shown* | 20 | 10 |
| *725* | A156 | 65p | *Supreme Court* | 75 | 32 |
| *726* | A156 | 2ce | *The Castle* | 2.00 | 1.00 |

**Souvenir Sheet**

| | | | |
|---|---|---|---|
| *727* | Sheet of 3 | 4.25 | 2.25 |
| *a* | A156 25p *like #724* | 25 | 15 |
| *b* | A156 1ce *like #725* | 1.00 | 50 |
| *c* | A156 3ce *like #726* | 3.00 | 1.50 |

Third Republic. No. 727 has multicolored decorative margin. Size: 72x104mm.

Map of West African Member Countries, Flag of Ghana, Jet — A157

**1980, Nov. 5 Litho. *Perf. 14½***

| | | | | | |
|---|---|---|---|---|---|
| *728* | A157 | 20p | *shown* | 20 | 10 |
| *729* | A157 | 65p | *Dish antenna* | 65 | 35 |
| *730* | A157 | 80p | *Cogwheels* | 80 | 40 |
| *731* | A157 | 2ce | *Corn* | 2.00 | 1.00 |

5th Anniversary of ECOWAS (Economic Community of West African States).

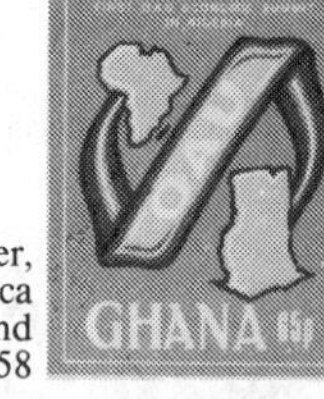

OAU Banner, Maps of Africa and Ghana — A158

**1980, Nov. 26**

| | | | | | |
|---|---|---|---|---|---|
| *732* | A158 | 20p | *"OAU"* | 20 | 20 |
| *733* | A158 | 65p | *shown* | 70 | 35 |
| *734* | A158 | 80p | *Waves on map of Africa* | 80 | 40 |
| *735* | A158 | 2ce | *Flag, banner, map* | 2.00 | 1.00 |

Organization for African Unity summit conference, Lagos, Nigeria, Apr. 28-29.

Adoration of the Magi, by Fra Angelico — A159

Christmas 1980 (Fra Angelico Paintings): 20p, 50p, Virgin and Child Enthroned with Four Angels. 1ce, 2ce, Virgin and Child Enthroned with Eight Angels. 3ce, 4ce, Annunciation.

**1980, Dec. 10 *Perf. 14***

| | | | | | |
|---|---|---|---|---|---|
| *736* | A159 | 15p | multi | 15 | 10 |
| *737* | A159 | 20p | multi | 20 | 12 |
| *738* | A159 | 2ce | multi | 2.00 | 1.00 |
| *739* | A159 | 4ce | multi | 4.00 | 2.00 |

**Souvenir Sheet**

| | | | |
|---|---|---|---|
| *740* | Sheet of 4 | 4.50 | 2.50 |
| *a* | A159 25p multi | 25 | 15 |
| *b* | A159 50p multi | 50 | 25 |
| *c* | A159 1ce multi | 75 | 50 |
| *d* | A159 3ce multi | 2.75 | 1.50 |

No. 740 has silver and black decorative margin. Size: 77x112½mm.

Nurse Weighing Newborn, Rotary Emblem A160

**1980, Dec. 18**

| | | | | | |
|---|---|---|---|---|---|
| *741* | A160 | 20p | *shown* | 25 | 15 |
| *742* | A160 | 65p | *Map of Ghana and world* | 90 | 45 |
| *743* | A160 | 2ce | *Helping hands, world map* | 2.50 | 1.40 |
| *744* | A160 | 4ce | *Food distribution* | 5.50 | 2.50 |

**Souvenir Sheet**

| | | | |
|---|---|---|---|
| *745* | Sheet of 4 | 6.00 | 3.25 |
| *a* | A160 25p *like #741* | 35 | 15 |
| *b* | A160 50p *like #742* | 65 | 35 |
| *c* | A160 1ce *like #743* | 1.25 | 65 |
| *d* | A160 3ce *like #744* | 3.75 | 2.00 |

Rotary International, 75th anniversary. No. 745 has multicolored margin showing cogwheels. Size: 122x93½mm.

The lack of a price for a listed item does not necessarily indicate rarity.

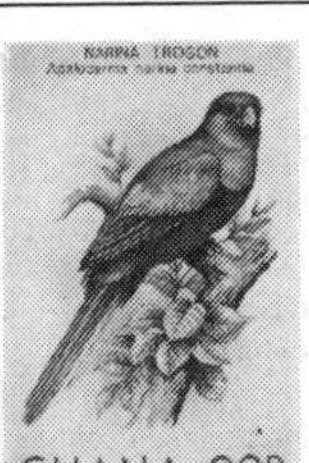


Narina Trogon — A161

**1981, Jan. 12 Litho. *Perf. 14***

746 A161 20p *shown* 20 10
747 A161 65p *White-crowned robin-chat* 65 35
748 A161 2ce *Swallow-tailed bee-eater* 2.00 1.00
749 A161 4ce *Long-tailed parakeet* 4.00 2.00

**Souvenir Sheet**

750 Sheet of 4 5.25 2.75
*a* A161 25p *like #746* 30 15
*b* A161 50p *like #747* 60 30
*c* A161 1ce *like #748* 1.10 55
*d* A161 3ce *like #749* 3.25 1.60

No. 750 has multicolored margin showing flowers. Size: 89½x121mm.

Pope John Paul II, Pres. Limann, Archbishop of Canterbury — A162

**1981, Mar. 3 Litho. *Perf. 14***

751 A162 20p multi 30 15
752 A162 65p multi 1.00 50
753 A162 80p multi 1.20 60
754 A162 2ce multi 3.00 1.50

Visit of Pope John Paul II, May 8-10, 1980.

Earth Satellite Station — A163

**1981, Sept. 28 Litho. *Perf. 14***

755 A163 20p shown 18 18
756 A163 65p Satellites orbiting earth 60 60
757 A163 80p Satellite 75 75
758 A163 4ce Satellite, earth 3.50 3.50

**Souvenir Sheet**

758A Sheet of 4 4.25 4.25
*b.* A163 25p like #755 22 22
*c.* A163 50p like #756 45 45
*d.* A163 1ce like #757 90 90
*e.* A163 3ce like #758 2.50 2.50

Earth Satellite Station commission. No. 758A has multicolored margin showing waves beaming to earth. Size: 112x100mm.

**Royal Wedding Issue**

Common Design Type

**1981 Litho. *Perf. 14***

759 CD331 20p Couple 15 15
759A CD331 65p like 20p 48 48
760 CD331 80p Charles 60 60
760A CD331 1ce like 80p 75 75
760B CD331 3ce like 4ce 2.25 2.25
761 CD331 4ce Royal yacht Britannia 3.00 3.00
*Nos. 759-761 (6)* 8.40 8.40

**Souvenir Sheet**

762 CD331 7ce St. Paul's Cathedral 4.75 4.75

Nos. 759-761 each printed se-tenant with label showing heraldic design. No. 762 has orange and black decorative margin. Size: 96x85½mm.

Issue dates: 20p, 80p, 4ce, 7ce, July 8. 65p, 1ce, 3ce, Sept. 16.

**1981, Sept. 16 Litho. *Perf. 14***

763 CD331 2ce like 4ce 2.00 2.00
764 CD331 5ce like 20p 5.00 5.00
*a* Bklt. pane of 4 (2 each #763-764) 14.00

Nos. 763-764 issued only in booklets.

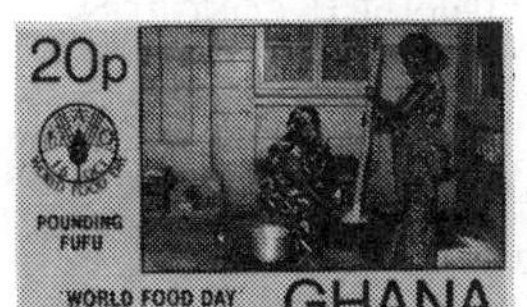


World Food Day A164

**1981, Oct. 16 Litho. *Perf. 14***

765 A164 20p Women pounding fufu 15 15
766 A164 65p Plucking cocoa 50 50
767 A164 80p Preparing banku 65 65
768 A164 2ce Processing garri 1.50 1.50

**Souvenir Sheet**

769 Sheet of 4 3.50 3.50
*a* A164 25p like #765 15 15
*b* A164 50p like #766 35 35
*c* A164 1ce like #767 75 75
*d* A164 3ce like #768 2.25 2.25

No. 769 has multicolored margin showing cocoa trees and flowers. Size: 131x99mm.

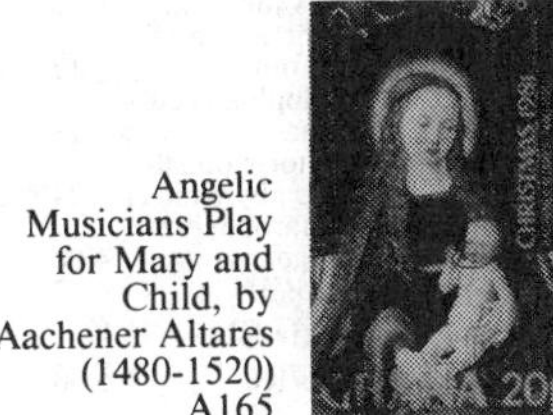


Angelic Musicians Play for Mary and Child, by Aachener Altares (1480-1520) A165

Christmas 1981 (Paintings): 15p, The Betrothal of St. Catherine of Alexandria, by Lucas Cranach (1472-1553). 65p, Child Jesus Embracing His Mother, by Gabriel Metsu (1629-1667). 80p, Virgin and Child, by Fra Filippo Lippi (1406-1469). $2, The Virgin with Infant Jesus, by Barnaba da Modena (1361-1383). $4, The Immaculate Conception, by Bartolome Murillo (1618-1682). $6, Virgin and Child, by Hans Memling (1430-1494).

**1981, Nov. 26 *Perf. 14***

770 A165 15p multi 10 10
771 A165 20p multi 14 14
772 A165 65p multi 45 45
773 A165 80p multi 50 50
774 A165 $2 multi 1.40 1.40
775 A165 $4 multi 2.50 2.50
*Nos. 770-775 (6)* 5.09 5.09

**Souvenir Sheet**

776 A165 $6 multi 4.00 4.00

No. 776 has multicolored margin showing entire painting. Size: 83x103mm.

Intl. Year of the Disabled A166

**1982, Feb. 8 Litho. *Perf. 14***

777 A166 20p Blind man 15 15
778 A166 65p Woman, crutch 50 50
779 A166 80p Girl reading Braille 60 60
780 A166 4ce Couple 3.00 3.00

**Souvenir Sheet**

781 A166 6ce Group 4.75 4.75

No. 781 has multicolored margin showing emblem, Braille. Size: 109x85mm.

Clawless Otter — A167

**1982, Feb. 22**

782 A167 20p shown 15 15
783 A167 65p Bushbuck 50 50
784 A167 80p Aardvark 60 60
785 A167 1ce Scarlet bell tree 75 75
786 A167 2ce Glory lilies 1.50 1.50
787 A167 4ce Blue peas 3.00 3.00
*Nos. 782-787 (6)* 6.50 6.50

**Souvenir Sheet**

788 A167 5ce Chimpanzees 3.75 3.75

No. 788 has multicolored design showing chimpanzees in trees. Size: 75x101mm.

Blue-spot Commodore A168

**1982, Apr. 27 Litho. *Perf. 14***

789 A168 20p shown 15 15
790 A168 65p Emperor swallowtail 50 50
791 A168 2ce Orange admiral 1.50 1.50
792 A168 4ce Giant charaxes 3.00 3.00

**Souvenir Sheet**

***Perf. 14½***

793 Sheet of 4 3.75 3.75
*a* A168 25p like #789 18 18
*b* A168 50p like #790 35 35
*c* A168 1ce like #791 75 75
*d* A168 3ce like #792 2.25 2.25

No. 793 has multicolored margin showing butterflies. Size: 99x123mm.

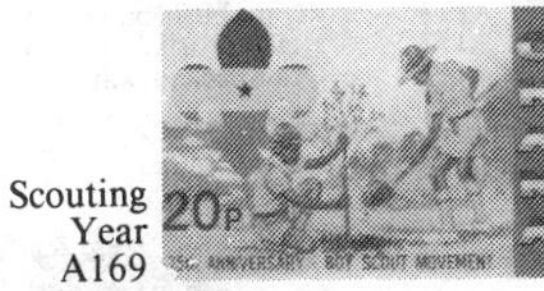


Scouting Year A169

**1982, June 1 Litho. *Perf. 15***

794 A169 20p Tree planting 15 15
795 A169 65p Camping 50 50
796 A169 80p Sailing 60 60
797 A169 3ce Watching elephant 2.25 2.25

**Souvenir Sheet**

798 A169 5ce Baden-Powell, vert. 3.75 3.75

No. 798 has multicolored margin continuing design. Size: 101x71mm.

Kpong Hydroelectric Dam Opening — A170

**1982, June 28 Litho. *Perf. 14***

799 A170 20p Cranes, lifts 15 15
800 A170 65p Construction 50 50
801 A170 80p Turbines 60 60
802 A170 2ce Aerial view 1.50 1.50

1982 World Cup A171

***Perf. 15, 14½x15 (30p, No. 807, 1ce, 3ce)***

**1982, July 19 Litho.**

803 A171 20p multi 15 15
804 A171 30p multi, like 20p 22 22
805 A171 65p multi 50 50
806 A171 80p multi, like 65p 60 60
807 A171 80p multi, diff. 60 60
808 A171 1ce multi, like #807 75 75
809 A171 3ce multi 2.25 2.25
810 A171 4ce multi, like 3ce 3.00 3.00
*Nos. 803-810 (8)* 8.07 8.07

**Souvenir Sheet**

811 A171 6ce multi 4.50 4.50

Nos. 804, 807-809 in sheets of 5 plus label. No. 811 has multicolored margin showing plays, cup. Size: 110x91mm.

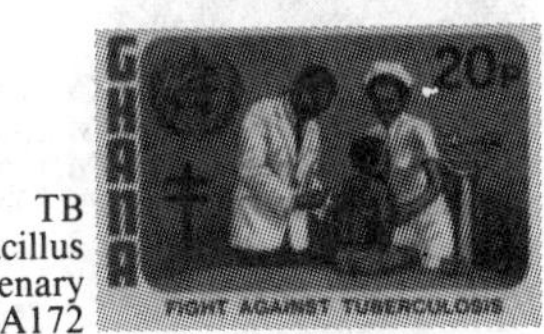


TB Bacillus Centenary A172

**1982, Aug. 9 *Perf. 14***

812 A172 20p Child immunization 15 15
813 A172 65p Koch, Berlin 50 50
814 A172 80p Koch, Africa 60 60
815 A172 1ce Looking through microscope 75 75
816 A172 2ce Koch, 1905 Nobel medal 1.50 1.50
*Nos. 812-816 (5)* 3.50 3.50

Christmas 1982 — A173

**1982, Dec. Litho. *Perf. 15***

817 A173 15p Angel with banner 12 12
818 A173 20p Holy Family 15 15
819 A173 65p Three Kings 50 50
820 A173 4ce Nativity 3.00 3.00

**Souvenir Sheet**

821 A173 6ce Nativity, diff. 4.50 4.50

Size of No. 821, 91x110mm.

**Commonwealth Day**

Common Design Type

**1983, Mar. 10 Litho. *Perf. 15***

822 CD334 20p Flags 15 15
823 CD334 55p Aerial view 40 40
824 CD334 80p Minerals 60 60
825 CD334 3ce Eagle 2.25 2.25

Nos. 803-811 Overprinted in Gold: "WINNER ITALY / 3-1"

**1983, June Litho.**

826 A171 20p multi 15 15
827 A171 30p multi 22 22
828 A171 65p multi 50 50
829 A171 80p multi, on #806 60 60
830 A171 80p multi, on #807 60 60
831 A171 1ce multi 75 75
832 A171 3ce multi 2.25 2.25
833 A171 4ce multi 3.00 3.00
*Nos. 826-833 (8)* 8.07 8.07

**Souvenir Sheet**

834 A171 6ce multi 4.50 4.50

Italy's victory in 1982 World Cup.

World Communications Year — A173a

**1983, Nov. Litho. *Perf. 14***

*835* A173a 1ce shown 75 75
*836* A173a 1.40ce Dish antenna 1.00 1.00
*837* A173a 2.30ce Cable ship 1.75 1.75
*838* A173a 3ce Switchboard 2.25 2.25
*839* A173a 5ce Control tower 3.75 3.75
*Nos. 835-839 (5)* 9.50 9.50

**Souvenir Sheet**

*840* A173a 6ce Satellite 4.50 4.50

Coastal Marine Mammals A173b

**1983, Nov. 15 Litho. *Perf. 15***

*841* A173b 1ce Short fin pilot whale 55 55
*842* A173b 1.40ce Gray dolphin 75 75
*843* A173b 2.30ce False killer whale 1.25 1.25
*844* A173b 3ce Spinner dolphin 1.75 1.75
*845* A173b 5ce Atlantic humpback dolphin 2.75 2.75
*Nos. 841-845 (5)* 7.05 7.05

**Souvenir Sheet**

*846* A173b 6ce White Alantic humpback dolphin 3.25 3.25

Margin shows various marine mammals. Size: 102x76mm.

A174

Christmas 1983 — A175

***Perf. 14x13½, 14½x14***

**1983, Dec. 28**

*852* A174 70p Children receiving gifts 5 5
*853* A175 1ce Nativity 6 6
*854* A175 1.40ce Children playing 9 9
*855* A175 2.30ce Family praying 15 15
*856* A174 3ce Bongo drums, festivities 18 18
*Nos. 852-856 (5)* 53 53

**Souvenir Sheet**

*857* A175 6ce like #855 38 38

Previous Issues Surcharged

**1983, Dec.**

*858* A74 1ce on 20np #296 8 8
*859* CD331 1ce on 20p #759 8 8
*860* CD334 1ce on 20p #822 8 8
*861* A171 1ce on 20p #803 8 8
*862* A171 1ce on 20p #826 8 8
*863* CD334 9ce on 55p #823 65 65
*864* A171 9ce on 65p #805 65 65
*865* A171 9ce on 65p #828 65 65
*866* CD331 9ce on 80p #760 65 65
*867* A169 10ce on 20p #794 70 70
*868* A171 10ce on 80p #806 70 70
*869* A171 10ce on 80p #830 70 70
*870* A169 19ce on 65p #795 1.40 1.40
*871* CD331 20ce on 4ce #761 1.45 1.45
*872* A171 20ce on 4ce #810 1.45 1.45
*873* A171 20ce on 4ce #833 1.45 1.45
*874* CD334 30ce on 80p #824 2.00 2.00
*875* A169 30ce on 3ce #797 2.00 2.00
*876* CD334 50ce on 3ce #825 3.50 3.50
*Nos. 858-876 (19)* 18.35 18.35

**Souvenir Sheets**

*877* A169 60ce on 5ce #798 4.25 4.25
*878* A171 60ce on 6ce #811 4.25 4.25
*879* A171 60ce on 6ce #834 4.25 4.25
*880* CD331 60ce on 7ce #762 4.25 4.25

Namibia Day — A176

**1984, Jan. 26 *Perf. 14***

*881* A176 50p Soldiers raising rifles 5 5
*882* A176 1ce Soldiers, tank 8 8
*883* A176 1.40ce Machete cutting chains 12 12
*884* A176 2.30ce Namibian woman 20 20
*885* A176 3ce Soldiers in combat 24 24
*Nos. 881-885 (5)* 69 69

Scorpion Weight — A177

**1983, Dec. 12 Litho. *Perf. 14***

*886* A177 5p Banded Jewelfish, horiz. 5 5
*887* A177 10p Jewelfish, map, horiz. 5 5
*888* A177 20p Blood lily 5 5
*889* A177 50p Mounted warrior (gold statuette) 5 5
*890* A177 1ce shown 8 8
*891* A177 2ce Jet, horiz. 16 16
*892* A177 3ce White-collared mangabey 24 24
*893* A177 4ce Pigmy bush baby 32 32
*894* A177 5ce Nigerian iris 40 40
*895* A177 10ce Gray-backed warbler 80 80
*Nos. 886-895 (10)* 2.20 2.20

Easter 1984 — A178

**1984, Apr. Litho. *Perf. 14½***

*906* A178 1ce Cross, crown of thorns 8 8
*907* A178 1.40ce Jesus praying 12 12
*908* A178 2.30ce Jesus going to Jerusalem 18 18
*909* A178 3ce Jesus entering Jerusalem 24 24
*910* A178 50ce Jesus with Disciples 4.00 4.00
*Nos. 906-910 (5)* 4.62 4.62

**Souvenir Sheet**

*911* A178 60ce Cross, crown of thorns 4.50 4.50

No. 911 has multicolored margin showing crosses. Size: 102x77mm.

Nos. 804, 807, 809, 827, 830, 832 Surcharged.

**1984 Litho.**

*912* A171 9ce on 3ce #809 72 72
*913* A171 9ce on 3ce #832 72 72
*914* A171 10ce on 30p #804 80 80
*915* A171 10ce on 30p #827 80 80
*916* A171 20ce on 80p #807 1.60 1.60
*917* A171 20ce on 80p #830 1.60 1.60
*Nos. 912-917 (6)* 6.24 6.24

Nos. 844-846 Surcharged and Overprinted in Red with UPU Emblem and: "19th U.P.U. CONGRESS-HAMBURG"

**1984 Litho. *Perf. 14½***

*918* A173 10ce on 3ce multi 70 70
*919* A173 50ce on 5ce multi 3.50 3.50

**Souvenir Sheet**

*920* A173 60ce on 6ce multi 4.25 4.25

Local Flowers — A179

**1984, July Litho. *Perf. 14***

*921* A179 1ce Amorphophallus johnsonii 8 8
*922* A179 1.40ce Pancratium trianthum 12 12
*923* A179 2.30ce Eulophia cucullata 18 18
*924* A179 3ce Amorphophallus abyssinicus 24 24
*925* A179 50ce Chlorophytum togoense 4.00 4.00
*Nos. 921-925 (5)* 4.62 4.62

**Souvenir Sheet**

*926* A179 60ce like 1ce 5.00 5.00

Size of No. 926: 70x96mm.

Endangered Species A180

**1984, Aug. *Perf. 14***

*927* A180 1ce Bongo 8 8
*928* A180 2.30ce Males locking horns 18 18
*929* A180 3ce Family 24 24
*930* A180 20ce Herd 1.60 1.60

**Souvenir Sheets**

*931* A180 70ce Kob 6.00 6.00
*932* A180 70ce Bushbuck 6.00 6.00

Nos. 932-933 have multicolored margins continuing design. Size: 101x72mm.

1984 Summer Olympics A181

Native Dancers A182

**1984, Aug. *Perf. 15***

*933* A181 1ce Running 8 8
*934* A181 1.40ce Boxing 12 12
*935* A181 2.30ce Field hockey 18 18
*936* A181 3ce Hurdles 24 24
*937* A181 50ce Rhythmic gymnastics 4.00 4.00
*Nos. 933-937 (5)* 4.62 4.62

**Souvenir Sheet**

*938* A181 70ce Soccer 6.00 6.00

No. 938 has multicolored margin showing flags. Size: 104x79mm.

**1984, Sept. *Perf. 14***

*939* A182 1ce Dipo 8 8
*940* A182 1.40ce Adowa 12 12
*941* A182 2.30ce Agbadza 18 18
*942* A182 3ce Damba 24 24
*943* A182 50ce Dipo, diff. 4.00 4.00
*Nos. 939-943 (5)* 4.62 4.62

**Souvenir Sheet**

*944* A182 70ce Mandolin player 6.00 6.00

No. 944 has multicolored margin continuing design. Size: 70x84mm.

Nos. 933-938 Ovptd. in Gold with Winner and Country.

**1984, Oct. Litho. *Perf. 15***

*945* A181 1ce Valerie Brisco-Hooks, USA 5 5
*946* A181 1.40ce US winners 6 6
*947* A181 2.30ce Pakistan, (field hockey) 10 10
*948* A181 3ce Edwin Moses, USA 12 12
*949* A181 50ce Lauri Fung, Canada 2.00 2.00
*Nos. 945-949 (5)* 2.33 2.33

**Souvenir Sheet**

*950* A181 70ce France 2.75 2.75

Christmas 1984 A183

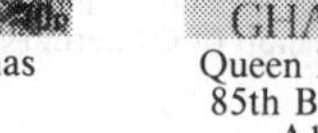

Queen Mother, 85th Birthday A184

**1984, Nov. 19 *Perf. 12x12½***

*951* A183 70p Adoration of the Magi 5 5
*952* A183 1ce Chorus of angels 5 5
*953* A183 1.40ce Adoration of the shepherds 6 6
*954* A183 2.30ce Flight into Egypt 10 10
*955* A183 3ce King holding Christ 12 12
*956* A183 50ce Adoration of the angels 2.00 2.00
*Nos. 951-956 (6)* 2.38 2.38

**Souvenir Sheet**

*957* A183 70ce like 70p 2.75 2.75

No. 957 has multicolored margin picturing woodgrain and ornament. Size: 70x90mm.

**1985 *Perf. 14***

Portraits.

*958* A184 5ce multi 20 20
*959* A184 8ce like 5ce 32 32
*960* A184 12ce multi 48 48
*961* A184 20ce like 12ce 80 80
*962* A184 70ce multi 2.75 2.75
*963* A184 100ce like 70ce 4.00 4.00
*Nos. 958-963 (6)* 8.55 8.55

**Souvenir Sheet**

*964* A184 110ce multi 4.50 4.50

Issue dates: 5ce, 12ce, 100ce, 110ce, July 29. 8ce, 20ce, 70ce, Dec. Nos. 959, 961-962 issued in sheets of 5 + label. No. 964 has multicolored decorative margin picturing exotic flowers. Size: 56x84mm.

Id-El-Fitr Islamic Festival A185

Intl. Youth Year A186

**1985, Aug. 1**

965 A185 5ce Entering mosque 20 20
966 A185 8ce Prayer rug 32 32
967 A185 12ce Mosque 48 48
968 A185 18ce Public Koran reading 72 72
969 A185 50ce Map, Banda Nkwanta Mosque 2.00 2.00
*Nos. 965-969 (5)* 3.72 3.72

**1985, Aug. 9**

970 A186 5ce Street clean-up 20 20
971 A186 8ce Tree planting 32 32
972 A186 12ce Food production 48 48
973 A186 100ce Education 4.00 4.00

**Souvenir Sheet**

974 A186 110ce like 8ce 4.50 4.50

No. 974 has multicolored margin picturing IYY emblem and natl. flag. Size: 103x77mm.

Motorcycle Centenary A187

**1985, Sept. 9**

975 A187 5ce 1984 Honda Interceptor 20 20
976 A187 8ce 1938 DKW 32 32
977 A187 12ce 1923 BMW R 32 48 48
978 A187 100ce 1900 NSU 4.00 4.00

**Souvenir Sheet**

979 A187 110ce 1973 Zundapp 4.50 4.50

No. 979 has multicolored margin continuing design, picturing motorcycle rally. Size: 79x109mm.

Audubon Birth Bicent. — A188

**1985, Oct. 16**

980 A188 5ce York-tailed fly-catcher 20 20
981 A188 8ce Barred owl 32 32
982 A188 12ce Black-throated mango 48 48
983 A188 100ce White-crowned pigeon 4.00 4.00

**Souvenir Sheet**

984 A188 110ce Downy woodpecker 4.50 4.50

No. 984 has multicolored margin continuing design. Size: 85x115mm.

UN, 40th Anniv. A189

**1985, Oct. 24** *Perf. 14½x14*

985 A189 5ce UN building 20 20
986 A189 8ce UN building, diff. 32 32
987 A189 12ce Dove 48 48
988 A189 18ce General Assembly 72 72
989 A189 100ce Flags 4.00 4.00
*Nos. 985-989 (5)* 5.72 5.72

**Souvenir Sheet**

990 A189 110ce UN No. 36 4.50 4.50

No. 990 has multicolored margin picturing flags and emblem. Size: 90x70mm.

UNCTAD, 20th Anniv. — A190

**1985, Nov. 4** *Perf. 14*

991 A190 5ce Coffee 20 20
992 A190 8ce Cocoa 32 32
993 A190 12ce Lumber 48 48
994 A190 18ce Bauxite mining 72 72
995 A190 100ce Gold mining 4.00 4.00
*Nos. 991-995 (5)* 5.72 5.72

**Souvenir Sheet**
***Perf. 15x14***

996 A190 110ce Produce 4.50 4.50

UN Conference on Trade and Development. No. 996 has multicolored Size: 104x74mm.

UN Child Survival Campaign A191

**1985, Dec. 16** *Perf. 14*

997 A191 5ce Weighing 20 20
998 A191 8ce Oral rehydration therapy 32 32
999 A191 12ce Breast-feeding 48 48
1000 A191 100ce Immunization 4.00 4.00

**Souvenir Sheet**
***Perf. 15x14***

1001 A191 110ce Emblem, pinwheel 4.50 4.50

No. 1001 has multicolored margin picturing oral rehydration therapy and breast-feeding. Size: 99x70mm.

AMERIPEX '86 — A192

***Perf. 14½x14, 14x14½***
**1986, Oct. 27** **Litho.**

1002 A192 5ce Young collectors 15 15
1003 A192 25ce Earth, jet 75 75
1004 A192 100ce Stewardess, vert. 3.00 3.00

**Souvenir Sheet**

1005 A192 150ce Young collectors, diff. 4.50 4.50

No. 1005 has blue and gray inscribed margin. Size: 90x70mm.

INTER-TOURISM '86, Nov. 8-17 — A193

Designs: 5ce, Kejetia Roundabout, Jumasi. 15ce, Fort St. Jago, Elmina. 25ce, Warriors. 100ce, Chief, retinue. 150ce, Elephants.

**1986, Nov. 10** *Perf. 14*

1006 A193 5ce multi 15 15
1007 A193 15ce multi 45 45
1008 A193 25ce multi 75 75
1009 A193 100ce multi 3.00 3.00

**Souvenir Sheet**
***Perf. 15x14***

1010 A193 150ce multi 4.50 4.50

No. 1010 has dull green decorative margin. Size: 110x71mm.

1986 World Cup Soccer Championships, Mexico — A194

Fertility Dolls — A195

Various soccer plays.

**1987, Jan. 16** **Litho.** *Perf. 14x14½*

1011 A194 5ce multi 15 15
1012 A194 15ce multi 45 45
1013 A194 25ce multi 75 75
1014 A194 100ce multi 3.00 3.00

**Souvenir Sheet**

1015 A194 150ce multi 4.50 4.50

No. 1015 has multicolored margin continuing the design. Size: 90x70mm.

**1987, Jan. 22**

Various dolls.

1016 A195 5ce multi 15 15
1017 A195 15ce multi 45 45
1018 A195 25ce multi 75 75
1019 A195 100ce multi 3.00 3.00

**Souvenir Sheet**

1020 A195 150ce like #1016 4.50 4.50

No. 1020 has multicolored margin picturing fertility dolls. Size: 90x71mm.

Intl. Peace Year A196

***Perf. 14½x14, 14x14½***
**1987, Mar. 2** **Litho.**

1021 A196 5ce Children playing 15 15
1022 A196 25ce Plow 75 75
1023 A196 100ce Earth, doves, vert. 3.00 3.00

**Souvenir Sheet**

1024 A196 150ce Dove, plow, vert. 4.50 4.50

No. 1024 has multicolored margin reproducing design pictured on 100ce stamp. Size: 90x70mm.

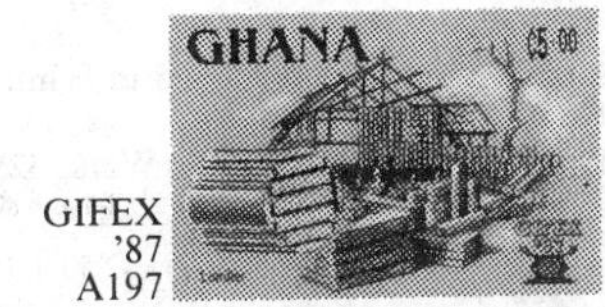


GIFEX '87 A197

**1987, Mar. 10** *Perf. 14*

1025 A197 5ce Lumber, house construction 10 10
1026 A197 15ce Furniture 30 30
1027 A197 25ce Tree stumps 50 50
1028 A197 200ce Logs, art objects 4.00 4.00

Ghana Intl. Forestry Expostiion, Accra.

A198

Halley's Comet A199

Designs: 5ce, Mikhail Vasilyevich Lomonosov (1711-1765), Russian scientist, and the Chamber of Curiosities. 25ce, Landing of the US probe Surveyor on the Moon's surface, 1966. 200ce, Wedgewood memorial to Sir Isaac Newton, the appearance of Halley's Comet in 1790 and US astronauts Armstrong and Aldrin landing Eagle on the Moon in 1969. 250ce, Comet over Fishermen near Christianborg Castle.

**1987, Apr. 8** *Perf. 14½x14*

1029 A198 5ce multi 10 10
1030 A198 25ce multi 50 50
1031 A198 200ce multi 4.00 4.00

**Souvenir Sheet**

1032 A199 250ce multi 5.00 5.00

No. 1032 has inscribed multicolored margin continuing the design. Size: 100x70mm.

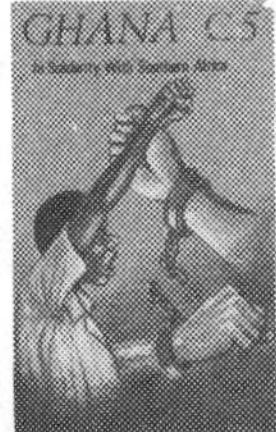


Solidarity with South Africans for Abolition of Apartheid — A200

**1987, May 18** *Perf. 14x14½*

1033 A200 5ce Liberated prisoner 10 10
1034 A200 15ce Miner, gold ingots 30 30
1035 A200 25ce Zulu warrior 50 50
1036 A200 100ce Nelson Mandela, shackles 2.00 2.00

**Souvenir Sheet**

1037 A200 150ce Mandela, map, star 3.00 3.00

No. 1037 has multicolored decorative margin. Size: 70x90mm.

Traditional Musical Instruments — A201

**1987, July 13** *Perf. 14½x14*

1038 A201 5ce Horns 10 10
1039 A201 15ce Xylophone 30 30
1040 A201 25ce String instruments 50 50
1041 A201 100ce Drums 2.00 2.00

**Souvenir Sheet**

1042 A201 200ce Percussion instruments 3.00 3.00

No. 1042 has inscribed decorative margin. Size: 90x70mm.

The Catalogue editors cannot undertake to appraise, identify or judge the genuineness or condition of stamps.

Intl. Year of Shelter for the Homeless A202

**1987, Sept. 21 Litho. *Perf. 14***

*1043* A202 5ce Public well 10 10
*1044* A202 15ce Home construction 30 30
*1045* A202 25ce Village, bridge, car 50 50
*1046* A202 100ce Village, electric power lines 2.00 2.00

Festivals A203

UN Universal Immunization Campaign A204

Designs: Preparation of Kpokpoi, Homowo Festival. 15ce, Hunters with catch, Aboakyir Festival. 25ce, Chief dancing, Odwira Festival. 100ce, Chief held aloft in a palanquin, Yam Festival.

**1988, Jan. 6 Litho. *Perf. 15***

*1047* A203 5ce multi 10 10
*1048* A203 15ce multi 30 30
*1049* A203 25ce multi 50 50
*1050* A203 100ce multi 2.00 2.00

**1988, Feb. 1**

Child Survival Campaign emblem and: 5ce, Nurse immunizing woman. 15ce, Child receiving intramuscular vaccine. 25ce, Youth crippled by polio. 100ce, Nurse handing infant to mother.

*1051* A204 5ce multi 10 10
*1052* A204 15ce multi 30 30
*1053* A204 25ce multi 50 50
*1054* A204 100ce multi 2.00 2.00

Tribal Costumes — A205

**1988, May 9 Litho. *Perf. 14***

*1055* A205 5ce Akwadjan 5 5
*1056* A205 25ce Banaa 22 22
*1057* A205 250ce Agwasen 2.25 2.25

1988 Summer Olympics, Seoul — A206

**1988, Oct. 10**

*1058* A206 20ce Boxing 20 20
*1059* A206 60ce Running 60 60
*1060* A206 80ce Discus 80 80
*1061* A206 100ce Javelin 1.00 1.00
*1062* A206 350ce Weight lifting 3.50 3.50
*Nos. 1058-1062 (5)* 6.10 6.10

**Souvenir Sheet**

*1063* A206 500ce like 80ce 5.00 5.00

No. 1063 has multicolored margin continuing the design and picturing discus thrower and natl. flag. Size: 75x105mm.

Intl. Red Cross, 125th Anniv. — A207

**1988, Dec. 14 Litho. *Perf.***

*1064* A207 20ce Nutrition 20 20
*1065* A207 50ce Voluntary service 50 50
*1066* A207 60ce Disaster relief (flood) 60 60
*1067* A207 200ce Medical assistance 2.00 2.00

## AIR POST STAMPS

Type of Regular Issue

Designs: 1sh3p, Pennant-winged nightjar. 2sh, Crowned cranes (vert.).

***Perf. 14½x14, 14x14½.***

**1959, Oct. 5 Photo. Wmk. 325**

*C1* A17 1sh3p multi 40 15
*a.* Booklet pane of 4 1.75
*C2* A17 2sh multi 55 45

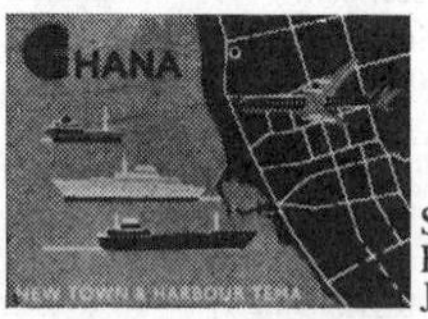

Ships, Tema Harbor and Jet — AP1

***Perf. 14x13***

**1962, Feb. 10 Litho. Unwmk.**

*C3* AP1 1sh3p multi 65 65
*C4* AP1 2sh6p multi 1.25 1.25

Opening of Tema Harbor, as part of the Volta River Project.

Type of Regular Issue, 1962

**1962, Mar. 6 *Perf. 13x14***

*C5* A35 1sh3p multi 50 35
*C6* A35 2sh6p multi 1.00 70

Nos. C1-C2 Surcharged in White or Green with New Value and: "Ghana New Currency / 19th July, 1965"

***Perf. 14½x14, 14x14½***

**1965, July 19 Photo. Wmk. 325**

*C7* A17 15pa on 1sh3p multi (W) 35 22
*C8* A17 24pa on 2sh multi (G) 70 35

The two lines of the overprint are diagonal on No. C8.

Nos. C1 and C8 Surcharged in White or Red

**1967, Feb. 27 Photo. Wmk. 325**

*C9* A17 12½np on 1sh3p (W) 1.10 80
*C10* A17 20np on 24pa on 2sh (R) 2.50 1.75

## POSTAGE DUE STAMPS

Gold Coast Nos. J2-J6 Overprinted "GHANA" and Bar in Red.

**Wmk. 4**

**1958, June 25 Typo. *Perf. 14***

*J1* D1 1p black 5 5
*J2* D1 2p black 6 6
*J3* D1 3p black 8 8
*J4* D1 6p black 15 15
*J5* D1 1sh black 25 25
*Nos. J1-J5 (5)* 59 59

Type of Gold Coast Inscribed "Ghana."

**1958, Dec. 1 *Perf. 14***

*J6* D1 1p car rose 5 5
*J7* D1 2p green 5 5
*J8* D1 3p orange 6 6
*J9* D1 6p ultra 12 12
*J10* D1 1sh purple 20 20
*Nos. J6-J10 (5)* 48 48

Nos. J6-J10 Surcharged in Black, Blue or Red with New Value and "Ghana New Currency / 19th July, 1965."

**1965**

*J11* D1 1pa on 1p car rose 5 5
*J12* D1 2pa on 2p grn (Bl) 8 8
*J13* D1 3pa on 3p org (Bl) 18 18
*J14* D1 6pa on 6p ultra (R) 35 35
*J15* D1 12pa on 1sh pur (Bl) 65 65
*Nos. J11-J15 (5)* 1.31 1.31

The overprint is diagonal on Nos. J11 and J15.

No. J12 with additional surcharge, "1½Np" in red, was reported to have been used at one branch post office (Burma Camp) despite official intention. Four similar added surcharges were prepared: 1np on 1pa, 2½np on 3pa, 5np on 6pa, and 10np on 12pa.

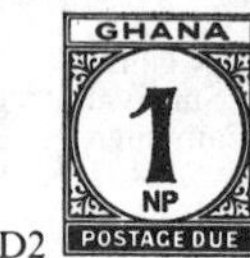

D2

**1970 Unwmk. Litho. *Perf. 14½x14***

*J16* D2 1np car rose 5 5
*J17* D2 1½np green 5 5
*J18* D2 2½np orange 5 5
*J19* D2 5np ultra 10 10
*J20* D2 10np dl pur 20 20
*Nos. J16-J20 (5)* 45 45

**1981 Litho. *Perf. 14½x14***

*J21* D2 2p red org 5 5
*J22* D2 3p brown 6 5

# GIBRALTAR

LOCATION — A fortified promontory, including the Rock, extending from Spain's southeast coast at the entrance to the Mediterranean Sea.
GOVT. — British Crown Colony.
AREA — 2.5 sq. mi.
POP. — 31,183 (1982).
CAPITAL — Gibraltar.

12 Pence = 1 Shilling
20 Shillings = 1 Pound
100 Centimos = 1 Peseta (1889-95)
100 Pence = 1 Pound (1971)

**Catalogue values for unused stamps in this country are for Never Hinged items, beginning with Scott 119 in the regular postage section and Scott J1 in the in the postage due section.**

Types of Bermuda Overprinted in Black **GIBRALTAR**

**1886, Jan. 1 Wmk. 2 *Perf. 14***

*1* A6 ½p green 3.75 3.75
*2* A1 1p rose 11.50 4.50
*3* A2 2p vio brn 50.00 27.50
*4* A8 2½p ultra 60.00 3.25
*5* A7 4p org brn 60.00 50.00
*6* A3 6p violet 135.00 90.00
*7* A4 1sh bis brn 300.00 225.00
*Nos. 1-7 (7)* 620.25 404.00

Forged overprints of No. 7 are plentiful.

Victoria — A6

A7

A8

A9

**1886-98 Typo.**

*8* A6 ½p dl grn 1.10 1.10
*9* A6 ½p gray grn ('98) 45 45
*10* A7 1p rose 5.50 1.40
*11* A7 1p car rose ('98) 80 35
*12* A8 2p brn vio 15.00 14.00
*13* A8 2p brn vio & ultra ('98) 3.50 3.50
*14* A9 2½p brt ultra ('98) 1.90 80
*a* 2½p ultra 22.50 4.00
*16* A8 4p org brn 40.00 37.50
*17* A8 4p org brn & grn ('98) 9.00 9.50
*18* A8 6p violet 57.50 57.50
*19* A8 6p vio & car rose ('98) 14.00 11.50
*20* A8 1sh bister 125.00 100.00
*21* A8 1sh bis & car rose ('98) 14.00 11.50
*Nos. 8-14,16-21 (13)* 287.75 249.10

Stamps of 1886 Issue Surcharged in Black **10 CENTIMOS**

**1889, July**

*22* A6 5c on ½p grn 4.00 4.00
*23* A7 10c on 1p rose 3.75 3.75
*24* A8 25c on 2p brn vio 1.10 1.10
*a* Small "I" in "CENTIMOS" 200.00 200.00
*b* Broken "N" 200.00 200.00
*25* A9 25c on 2½p ultra 7.25 2.75
*a* Small "I" in "CENTIMOS" 150.00 150.00
*b* Broken "N" 150.00 150.00
*26* A8 40c on 4p org brn 25.00 25.00
*27* A8 50c on 6p vio 25.00 25.00
*28* A8 75c on 1sh bis 30.00 30.00
*Nos. 22-28 (7)* 96.10 91.60

There are two varieties of the figure "5" in the 5c, 25c, 50c and 75c.

A11

**1889-95**

*29* A11 5c green 65 28
*30* A11 10c rose 65 18
*a* Value omitted 6,500.
*31* A11 20c ol grn ('95) 3.50 5.75
*31A* A11 20c ol grn & brn ('95) 4.75 4.75
*32* A11 25c ultra 1.50 24
*33* A11 40c org brn 80 1.40
*34* A11 50c violet 2.25 2.25
*35* A11 75c ol grn 19.00 24.00
*36* A11 1p bister 24.00 21.00
*36A* A11 1p bis & bl ('95) 2.25 2.25
*37* A11 2p blk & car rose ('95) 4.75 *8.25*
*38* A11 5p stl bl 24.00 30.00
*Nos. 29-38 (12)* 88.10 100.35

King Edward VII
A12 A13

**1903**

*39* A12 ½p grn & bl grn 1.65 2.75
*40* A12 1p vio, *red* 6.75 55
*41* A12 2p grn & car rose 8.25 7.50
*42* A12 2½p vio & blk, *bl* 1.40 1.40
*43* A12 6p vio & pur 5.50 5.50
*44* A12 1sh blk & car rose 8.25 6.75

| | | | | |
|---|---|---|---|---|
| 45 | A13 | 2sh grn & ultra | 30.00 | 35.00 |
| 46 | A13 | 4sh vio & grn | 32.50 | 42.50 |
| 47 | A13 | 8sh vio & blk, *bl* | 60.00 | 77.50 |
| 48 | A13 | £1 vio & blk, *red* | 425.00 | 500.00 |
| | | *Nos. 39-48 (10)* | 579.30 | 679.45 |

**1904-11** **Wmk. 3**

**Ordinary or Chalky Paper.**

| | | | | |
|---|---|---|---|---|
| 49 | A12 | ½p gray grn | 70 | 70 |
| a | | ½p bl grn ('07) | 28 | 14 |
| 50 | A12 | 1p vio, *red* | 90 | 14 |
| 51 | A12 | 1p car ('07) | 50 | 14 |
| 52 | A12 | 2p grn & car rose | 60 | 60 |
| 53 | A12 | 2p gray ('10) | 3.75 | 4.50 |
| 54 | A12 | 2½p vio & blk, *bl* | 12.50 | 14.00 |
| 55 | A12 | 2½p ultra ('07) | 90 | 80 |
| 56 | A12 | 6p vio & pur ('06) | 1.50 | 2.75 |
| a | | 6p vio & red vio ('07) | 80.00 | *185.00* |
| 57 | A12 | 1sh blk & car rose | 5.75 | 5.75 |
| 58 | A12 | 1sh *grn* ('10) | 6.25 | 6.75 |
| 59 | A13 | 2sh grn & ultra ('05) | 16.00 | 20.00 |
| 60 | A13 | 2sh vio & bl, *bl* ('10) | 18.00 | 22.50 |
| 61 | A13 | 4sh vio & grn | 45.00 | 52.50 |
| 62 | A13 | 4sh blk & red ('10) | 25.00 | 26.00 |
| 63 | A13 | 8sh vio & grn ('11) | 145.00 | 170.00 |
| 64 | A12 | £1 vio & blk, *red* | 375.00 | 425.00 |
| | | *Nos. 49-64 (16)* | 657.35 | 752.13 |

Nos. 49a, 51, 53, 55 are on ordinary paper. Nos. 54, 58, 60-64 are on chalky paper. Others come on both papers.

King George V
A14 A15

**1912** **Ordinary Paper**

| | | | | |
|---|---|---|---|---|
| 66 | A14 | ½p green | 38 | 10 |
| 67 | A14 | 1p scarlet | 95 | 10 |
| a | | 1p car | 95 | 16 |
| 68 | A14 | 2p gray | 2.50 | 1.75 |
| 69 | A14 | 2½p ultra | 1.90 | 55 |

**Chalky Paper**

| | | | | |
|---|---|---|---|---|
| 70 | A14 | 6p dl vio & red vio | 5.00 | 4.50 |
| 71 | A14 | 1sh *green* | 2.75 | 2.75 |
| a | | 1sh *emer* | 8.25 | 8.25 |
| b | | 1sh *bl grn*, olive back | 5.50 | 5.50 |
| c | | 1sh *emer*, ol back | 3.50 | 3.50 |
| 72 | A15 | 2sh vio & ultra, *bl* | 9.50 | 6.75 |
| 73 | A15 | 4sh blk & scar | 15.00 | 17.00 |
| 74 | A15 | 8sh vio & grn | 32.50 | 45.00 |
| 75 | A15 | £1 vio & blk, *red* | 135.00 | 165.00 |
| | | *Nos. 66-75 (10)* | 205.48 | 243.50 |

**1921-32** **Ordinary Paper** **Wmk. 4**

| | | | | |
|---|---|---|---|---|
| 76 | A14 | ½p grn ('27) | 18 | 14 |
| 77 | A14 | 1p rose red | 18 | 12 |
| 78 | A14 | 1½p red brn ('22) | 40 | 14 |
| 79 | A14 | 2p gray | 45 | 50 |
| 80 | A14 | 2½p ultra | 5.75 | 5.75 |
| 81 | A14 | 3p ultra | 55 | 35 |

**Chalky Paper**

| | | | | |
|---|---|---|---|---|
| 82 | A14 | 6p dl vio & red vio ('23) | 80 | 80 |
| a | | 6p gray lil & red vio ('26) | 80 | 80 |
| 83 | A14 | 1sh *emer* ('24) | 6.75 | 7.25 |
| 84 | A14 | 1sh ol grn & blk ('29) | 4.25 | 4.50 |
| a | | 1sh brn ol & blk ('32) | 4.25 | 4.50 |
| 85 | A15 | 2sh vio & ultra, *bl* ('24) | 3.00 | *6.75* |
| 86 | A15 | 2sh red brn & blk ('29) | 11.50 | 12.50 |
| 87 | A15 | 2sh6p grn & blk ('25) | 4.50 | 5.00 |
| 88 | A15 | 4sh blk & scar ('24) | 37.50 | *45.00* |
| 89 | A15 | 5sh car & blk ('25) | 11.50 | 14.00 |
| 90 | A15 | 8sh vio & grn ('24) | 110.00 | 135.00 |
| 91 | A15 | 10sh ultra & blk ('25) | 17.00 | 19.00 |
| 92 | A15 | £1 org & blk ('27) | 100.00 | 150.00 |
| 93 | A15 | £5 dl vio & blk ('25) | 1,300. | *2,000.* |
| | | *Nos. 76-92 (17)* | 314.31 | 406.80 |

Type of 1912 Issue
Inscribed: "THREE PENCE"

**1930** **Ordinary Paper**

| | | | | |
|---|---|---|---|---|
| 94 | A14 | 3p ultra | 9.50 | 2.25 |

Rock of Gibraltar
A16

**1931-33** **Engr.** ***Perf. 14***

| | | | | |
|---|---|---|---|---|
| 96 | A16 | 1p red | 50 | 50 |
| a | | Perf. 13½x14 | 8.50 | 2.00 |
| 97 | A16 | 1½p red brn | 90 | 50 |
| a | | Perf. 13½x14 | 3.75 | 1.25 |
| 98 | A16 | 2p gray ('32) | 1.75 | 80 |
| a | | Perf. 13½x14 | 6.00 | 1.10 |
| 99 | A16 | 3p dk bl ('33) | 1.75 | 1.75 |
| a | | Perf. 13½x14 | 9.00 | 12.00 |

**Silver Jubilee Issue**

Common Design Type

**1935, May 6** ***Perf. 11x12***

| | | | | |
|---|---|---|---|---|
| 100 | CD301 | 2p blk & ultra | 1.10 | 70 |
| 101 | CD301 | 3p ultra & brn | 2.25 | 1.90 |
| 102 | CD301 | 6p ind & grn | 3.75 | 3.75 |
| 103 | CD301 | 1sh brn vio & ind | 7.50 | 7.50 |

**Coronation Issue.**

Common Design Type

**1937, May 12** ***Perf. 11x11½***

| | | | | |
|---|---|---|---|---|
| 104 | CD302 | ½p dp grn | 20 | 12 |
| 105 | CD302 | 2p gray blk | 45 | 35 |
| 106 | CD302 | 3p dp ultra | 1.10 | 65 |

King George VI — A17

Rock of Gibraltar
A18

Designs: 2p, Rock from north side. 3p, 5p, Europa Point. 6p, Moorish Castle. 1sh, Southport Gate. 2sh, Eliott Memorial. 5sh, Government House. 10sh, Catalan Bay.

***Perf. 13½x14, 14, 13½, 13.***

**1938-49** **Engr.** **Wmk. 4**

| | | | | |
|---|---|---|---|---|
| 107 | A17 | ½p gray grn, perf. 13½x14 | 8 | 8 |
| 108 | A18 | 1p red brn, perf. 13 ('42) | 16 | 16 |
| a | | 1p chnt, perf. 14 | 20 | 16 |
| b | | 1p chnt, perf. 13½ | 65 | 50 |
| c | | Perf. 13½, wmkd. sideways ('41) | 20 | 20 |
| 109 | A18 | 1½p car rose, perf. 14 | 1.65 | 55 |
| b | | Perf. 13½ | 77.50 | 32.50 |
| 109A | A18 | 1½p gray vio, perf. 13 ('43) | 10 | 8 |
| 110 | A18 | 2p dk gray, perf. 13 ('42) | 50 | 50 |
| a | | Perf. 14 | 1.40 | 32 |
| c | | Perf. 13½ | 50 | 32 |
| d | | Perf. 13½, wmkd. sideways ('41) | 225.00 | 27.50 |
| 110B | A18 | 2p car rose, perf. 13 ('44) | 20 | 14 |
| 111 | A18 | 3p bl, perf. 13 ('42) | 25 | 14 |
| a | | Perf. 14 | 25.00 | 7.25 |
| b | | Perf. 13½ | 1.25 | 25 |
| 112 | A18 | 5p red org, perf. 13 ('47) | 80 | 80 |
| 113 | A18 | 6p dl vio & car rose, perf. 13 | 75 | 40 |
| a | | Perf. 14 | 70.00 | 1.10 |
| b | | Perf. 13½ | 2.25 | 1.10 |
| 114 | A18 | 1sh grn & blk, perf. 13 ('42) | 1.65 | 80 |
| a | | Perf. 14 | 4.00 | 3.25 |
| b | | Perf. 13½ | 14.00 | 5.25 |
| 115 | A18 | 2sh org brn & blk, perf. 13 ('42) | 2.75 | 2.25 |
| a | | Perf. 14 | 17.50 | 16.00 |
| b | | Perf. 13½ | 20.00 | 18.00 |
| 116 | A18 | 5sh dk car & blk, perf. 13 ('44) | 5.50 | 4.00 |
| a | | Perf 14 | 32.50 | *40.00* |
| b | | Perf. 13½ | 6.75 | 5.50 |
| 117 | A18 | 10sh bl & blk, perf. 13 ('43) | 19.00 | 14.00 |
| a | | Perf. 14 | 25.00 | 20.50 |
| 118 | A17 | £1 org, perf. 13½x14 | 27.50 | 27.50 |
| | | *Nos. 107-118 (14)* | 60.89 | 51.40 |

Nos. 108c and 110d were issued in coils.

No. 108 (1p, perf. 13) exists with watermark both normal and sideways. Nos. 110 and 110B (both 2p, perf. 13) have watermark sideways.

**Catalogue values for unused stamps in this section, from this point to the end of the section, are for Never Hinged items.**

**Peace Issue**

Common Design Type

**1946, Oct. 12** ***Perf. 13½x14***

| | | | | |
|---|---|---|---|---|
| 119 | CD303 | ½p brt grn | 12 | 12 |
| 120 | CD303 | 3p brt ultra | 20 | 20 |

**Silver Wedding Issue**

Common Design Types

**1948, Dec. 1** **Photo.** ***Perf. 14x14½***

| | | | | |
|---|---|---|---|---|
| 121 | CD304 | ½p dk grn | 12 | 12 |

**Engr.; Name Typo.**

***Perf. 11½x11.***

| | | | | |
|---|---|---|---|---|
| 122 | CD305 | £1 brn org | 80.00 | 55.00 |

**UPU Issue**

Common Design Types

**Engr.; Name Typo. on 3p, 6p**

***Perf. 13½, 11x11½***

**1949, Oct. 10** **Wmk. 4**

| | | | | |
|---|---|---|---|---|
| 123 | CD306 | 2p rose car | 1.75 | 1.40 |
| 124 | CD307 | 3p indigo | 2.00 | 1.60 |
| 125 | CD308 | 6p rose vio | 3.00 | 3.00 |
| 126 | CD309 | 1sh bl grn | 7.50 | 7.50 |

Nos. 110B, 111, 113-114 overprinted in Black or Carmine

**NEW CONSTITUTION 1950**

**1950, Aug. 1** ***Perf. 13x12½***

| | | | | |
|---|---|---|---|---|
| 127 | A18 | 2p car rose | 50 | 50 |
| 128 | A18 | 3p blue | 55 | 55 |
| 129 | A18 | 6p dl vio & car rose | 1.25 | 1.25 |
| a | | Dbl. overprint | 500.00 | *600.00* |
| 130 | A18 | 1sh grn & blk (C) | 2.00 | 2.00 |

Adoption of Constitution of 1950.

**Coronation Issue.**

Common Design Type

**1953, June 2** **Engr.** ***Perf. 13½x13***

| | | | | |
|---|---|---|---|---|
| 131 | CD312 | ½p ol grn & blk | 25 | 18 |

Wharves
A26

Moorish Castle — A27

Designs: 1p, South view. 1½p, Tunny fishing industry. 2p, Southport Gate. 2½p, Sailing in the bay. 3p, Ocean liner. 4p, Coaling wharf. 5p, Airport. 6p, Europa Point. 1sh, Strait from Buena Vista. 2sh, Rosia Bay. 5sh, Government House. £1, Arms of Gibraltar.

**1953, Oct. 19** ***Perf. 12½***

| | | | | |
|---|---|---|---|---|
| 132 | A26 | ½p dk grn & ind | 10 | 8 |
| 133 | A26 | 1p bl grn | 12 | 10 |
| 134 | A26 | 1½p dk gray | 15 | 14 |
| 135 | A26 | 2p sepia | 25 | 16 |
| 136 | A26 | 2½p car lake | 35 | 28 |
| 137 | A26 | 3p grnsh bl | 32 | 16 |
| 138 | A26 | 4p ultra | 42 | 32 |
| 139 | A26 | 5p dp plum | 45 | 42 |
| 140 | A26 | 6p bl & blk | 70 | 50 |
| 141 | A26 | 1sh red brn & bl | 1.25 | 95 |
| 142 | A26 | 2sh vio & org | 8.50 | 3.50 |
| 143 | A26 | 5sh dk brn | 15.00 | 6.50 |
| 144 | A27 | 10sh ultra & brn | 60.00 | 30.00 |
| 145 | A27 | £1 yel & red | 105.00 | 37.50 |
| | | *Nos. 132-145 (14)* | 192.61 | 80.61 |

Inscribed: "ROYAL VISIT 1954"

**1954, May 10**

| | | | | |
|---|---|---|---|---|
| 146 | A26 | 3p grnsh bl | 42 | 35 |

Candytuft
A28

Rock and Badge of Gibraltar Regiment
A30

Moorish Castle
A29

Designs: 2p, St. George's Hall and cannons. 2½p, The keys. 3p, Rock by moonlight. 4p, Catalan Bay. 6p, Map. 7p, Air terminal. 9p, American war memorial. 1sh, Barbary ape. 2sh, Barbary partridge. 5sh, Blue rock thrush. 10sh, Narcissus.

**Wmk. 314**

**1960, Oct. 29** **Photo.** ***Perf. 12½***

| | | | | |
|---|---|---|---|---|
| 147 | A28 | ½p brt grn & lil | 10 | 8 |
| 148 | A29 | 1p blk & yel grn | 10 | 8 |
| 149 | A29 | 2p org brn & sl | 12 | 10 |
| 150 | A28 | 2½p bl & blk | 14 | 12 |
| 151 | A29 | 3p dk bl & ver | 16 | 15 |
| 152 | A29 | 4p choc & grnsh bl | 45 | 38 |
| a | | Wmkd. sideways ('66) | 25 | 18 |
| 153 | A28 | 6p brn & emer | 35 | 30 |
| 154 | A28 | 7p gray & car | 48 | 40 |
| 155 | A28 | 9p grnsh bl & bluish gray | 75 | 65 |
| 156 | A29 | 1sh brn & grn | 75 | 65 |
| 157 | A29 | 2sh dk red brn & ultra | 3.00 | 1.90 |
| 158 | A29 | 5sh ol & Prus grn | 9.25 | 5.25 |
| 159 | A28 | 10sh bl, yel & grn | 15.00 | 18.00 |

**Engr.** ***Perf. 14***

| | | | | |
|---|---|---|---|---|
| 160 | A30 | £1 org red & sl | 30.00 | 10.50 |
| | | *Nos. 147-160 (14)* | 60.65 | 38.56 |

**Freedom from Hunger Issue**

Common Design Type

**1963, June 4** ***Perf. 14x14½***

| | | | | |
|---|---|---|---|---|
| 161 | CD314 | 9p sepia | 16.00 | 10.50 |

**Red Cross Centenary Issue**

Common Design Type

**1963, Sept. 2** **Litho.** ***Perf. 13***

| | | | | |
|---|---|---|---|---|
| 162 | CD315 | 1p blk & red | 38 | 22 |
| 163 | CD315 | 9p ultra & red | 20.00 | 15.00 |

**Shakespeare Issue**

Common Design Type

**1964, Apr. 23** **Photo.** ***Perf. 14x14½***

| | | | | |
|---|---|---|---|---|
| 164 | CD316 | 7p brown | 1.10 | 1.00 |

Nos. 151 and 153 Overprinted: "NEW / CONSTITUTION / 1964."

**1964, Oct. 16** ***Perf. 12½***

| | | | | |
|---|---|---|---|---|
| 165 | A29 | 3p dk bl & ver | 25 | 25 |
| 166 | A28 | 6p brn & emer | 42 | 42 |
| a | | No period in overprint | 15.00 | 12.50 |

**ITU Issue**

Common Design Type

***Perf. 11x11½***

**1965, May 17** **Litho.** **Wmk. 314**

| | | | | |
|---|---|---|---|---|
| 167 | CD317 | 4p emer & yel | 90 | 50 |
| 168 | CD317 | 2sh ap grn & dk bl | 27.50 | 17.50 |

**Intl. Cooperation Year Issue**

Common Design Type

**1965, Oct. 25** ***Perf. 14½***

| | | | | |
|---|---|---|---|---|
| 169 | CD318 | ½p lt vio & grn | 12 | 12 |
| 170 | CD318 | 4p bl grn & cl | 1.75 | 1.40 |

**Churchill Memorial Issue**
Common Design Type

**1966, Jan. 24 Photo. *Perf. 14***
**Design in Black, Gold and Carmine Rose**

171 CD319 ½p brt bl 8 8
172 CD319 1p green 12 12
173 CD319 4p brown 80 80
174 CD319 9p violet 1.90 1.90

**World Cup Soccer Issue**
Common Design Type

**1966, July 1 Litho. *Perf. 14***

175 CD321 2½p multi 70 28
176 CD321 6p multi 1.50 1.10

Sea Bream A30a

Fish: 7p, Orange scorpionfish. 1sh, Stone bass (vert.).

***Perf. 14x13½, 13½x14***
**1966, Aug. 27 Photo. Wmk. 314**

177 A30a 4p ultra, rose red & blk 8 8
178 A30a 7p ol, rose red & blk 22 22
*a* Value omitted 625.00
179 A30a 1sh brt grn, brn & blk 35 35

Issued to publicize the European Sea Angling Championships, Gibraltar, Aug. 28–Sept. 3.

**WHO Headquarters Issue**
Common Design Type

**1966, Sept. 20 Litho. *Perf. 14***

180 CD322 6p multi 1.40 1.00
181 CD322 9p multi 2.75 2.00

"Our Lady of Europa" A31

***Perf. 14x14½***
**1966, Nov. 15 Photo. Wmk. 314**

182 A31 2sh ultra & blk 1.50 1.50

Centenary of the enthronement of the recovered statue of the Madonna in its new shrine.

**UNESCO Anniversary Issue**
Common Design Type

**1966, Dec. 1 Litho. *Perf. 14***

183 CD323 2p "Education" 22 10
184 CD323 7p "Science" 65 35
185 CD323 5sh "Culture" 4.00 3.00

Victory, Nelson's Flagship A32

Ships and Arms of Gibraltar: 1p, S.S. Arab. 2p, H.M.S. Carmania. 2½p, M.V. Mons Calpe. 3p, S.S. Canberra. 4p, H.M.S. Hood. 5p, Cable Ship Mirror. 6p, Xebec, Moorish vessel. 7p, Amerigo Vespucci, Italian training ship (sails). 9p, Raffaello, Italian liner. 1sh, H.M.S. Royal Katherine, 17th century British warship. 2sh, H.M.S. Ark Royal, aircraft carrier. 5sh, H.M.S. Dreadnought, atomic submarine. 10sh, S.S. Neuralia, troopship. £1, Mary Celeste, 19th century mystery ship (sails).

***Perf. 14x14½***
**1967-69 Photo. Wmk. 314**
**Design in Black, Red and Gold; Background as Indicated**

186 A32 ½p dp rose 6 6
187 A32 1p yellow 10 8
188 A32 2p ultra 12 10
189 A32 2½p orange 15 10
190 A32 3p violet 20 10
191 A32 4p rose 22 15
191A A32 5p brn & multi ('69) 80 60
192 A32 6p gray 32 22
193 A32 7p yel grn 40 25
194 A32 9p green 60 35
195 A32 1sh rose brn 80 45
196 A32 2sh brt yel 2.75 1.65
197 A32 5sh brick red 5.00 4.00
198 A32 10sh emerald 11.50 10.00
199 A32 £1 lt ultra 27.50 22.50
*Nos. 186-199 (15)* 50.52 40.61

Common Design Types pictured in section before Great Britain.

Cable Car and ITY Emblem — A33

Designs (ITY emblem and): 9p, Bull shark (horiz.). 1sh, Skin diver (horiz.).

***Perf. 14½x14, 14x14½***
**1967, June 15 Photo. Wmk. 314**

200 A33 7p red brn, red & blk 22 18
201 A33 9p brt bl, blk & sl 35 25
202 A33 1sh emer, blk & org brn 45 38

International Tourist Year, 1967.

Holy Family — A34

Christmas: 6p, Church window (vert.).

**1967, Nov. 1 *Perf. 14½***

203 A34 2p dk red & multi 10 10
204 A34 6p dk grn & multi 20 20

General Eliott and Map of Europe and Great Britain A35

Designs: 9p, Eliott Memorial and tower. 1sh, Gen. Eliott and map of Gibraltar (vert.). 2sh, Gen. Eliott directing rescue operations for enemy sailors during Great Siege 1779-83.

***Perf. 14½x14, 14x14½***
**1967, Dec. 11 Photo. Wmk. 314**
**Size: 37x21mm, 21x37mm**

205 A35 4p multi 12 12
206 A35 9p multi 20 20
207 A35 1sh multi 30 30

**Size: 58x21½mm**

208 A35 2sh multi 60 60

250th anniv. of the birth of General George Augustus Eliott (1717-90), Governor of Gibraltar during Great Siege.

Lord Baden-Powell — A36

Designs: 7p, Scout flag, Rock of Gibraltar and globe with map of Europe. 9p, Symbolic tents, heads and Scout salute. 1sh, Three Scout badges.

***Perf. 14x14½***
**1968, Mar. 27 Photo. Wmk. 314**

209 A36 4p dl yel & pur 8 8
210 A36 7p brn org, brn & grn 16 16
211 A36 9p ultra, blk & org 25 25
212 A36 1sh yel & emer 32 32

60th anniv. of the Gibraltar Scout Assoc.

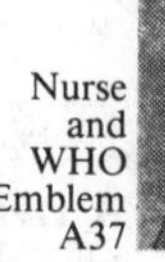

Nurse and WHO Emblem A37

Design: 4p, Physician with microscope and WHO emblem.

**1968, July 1 Photo. Wmk. 314**

213 A37 2p yel, ultra & blk 14 14
214 A37 4p pink, blk & sl 30 30

20th anniv. of WHO.

King John Signing Magna Carta A38

Shepherd, Lamb and Star A39

Design: 2sh, Rock of Gibraltar, "Freedom" and Human Rights flame.

***Perf. 13½x14½***
**1968, Aug. 26 Photo. Wmk. 314**

215 A38 1sh org, gold & dk brn 30 30
216 A38 2sh brt grn & gold 55 55

International Human Rights Year

***Perf. 14x13½***
**1968, Nov. 1 Photo. Wmk. 314**

Design: 9p, Mary, Jesus and lamb.

217 A39 4p lt brn & multi 18 18
218 A39 9p rose & multi 35 35

Christmas 1968.

Government House, Gilbraltar — A40

Designs: 9p, Rock of Gibraltar and Commonwealth Parliamentary Association emblem. 2sh, Big Ben, London, and arms of Gibraltar.

***Perf. 14½x14, 14x14½***
**1969, May 26 Photo. Wmk. 314**

219 A40 4p grn & gold 8 8
220 A40 9p brt vio & gold 22 22
221 A40 2sh lt ultra, gold & red 55 55

Issued to publicize the meeting of the Executive Committee of the General Council of the Commonwealth Parliamentary Association, Gibraltar, May, 1969.

Rock of Gibraltar A41

***Perf. 14½x13½***
**1969, July 30 Photo. Wmk. 314**

222 A41 ½p org & gold 5 5
223 A41 5p emer & sil 12 10
224 A41 7p brt rose lil & sil 20 18
225 A41 5sh ultra & gold 1.40 1.30

Gibraltar's new constitution.

Royal Artillery Officer, 1758 — A42

Madonna della Seggiola, by Raphael — A43

Uniforms: 6p, Contemporary soldier of the Royal Anglian Regiment. 9p, Soldier, Royal Engineers, 1786. 2sh, Private of Fox's Marines, 1704.

**Wmk. 314**
**1969, Nov. 6 Photo. *Perf. 14***

226 A42 1p gold & multi 12 12
227 A42 6p sil, gold & multi 70 70
228 A42 9p sil, gold & multi 95 95
229 A42 2sh gold & multi 4.00 3.25

Design descriptions are printed on back on top of gum.

See Nos. 234-237, 276-279, 286-289, 299-302, 310-313, 318-321, 330-333.

***Perf. 13½x Roulette 9***
**1969, Dec. 1 Photo.**

Paintings: 7p, Madonna and Child, by Luis Morales. 1sh, Virgin of the Rocks, by Leonardo da Vinci.

230 A43 5p gold & multi 30 30
231 A43 7p gold & multi 50 50
232 A43 1sh gold & multi 85 85
Triptych, Nos. 230-232 1.65 1.65

Christmas 1969.

Nos. 230-232 are printed se-tenant (sequence: 5p-1sh-7p) in sheets of 30.

**Europa Issue**

Europa Point — A44

**1970, June 8 *Perf. 13½***

233 A44 2sh multi 85 75

Uniform Type of 1969.

Uniforms: 2p, Royal Scots officer, 1839. 5p, Private of South Wales Borderers. 7p, Private of Queen's Royal Regiment, 1742. 2sh, Piper of Royal Irish Rangers, 1969.

**1970, Aug. 28 Photo. *Perf. 14***

234 A42 2p gold & multi 25 25
235 A42 5p gold & multi 75 75
236 A42 7p gold & multi 1.10 1.10
237 A42 2sh gold & multi 3.75 3.50

Design descriptions are printed on back on top of gum.

No. 178a and Rock of Gibraltar A45

Design: 2sh, No. 30a and Moorish Castle.

**1970, Sept. 18** *Perf. 13*
*238* A45 1sh red & ol 30 28
*239* A45 2sh ultra & rose 60 55

Issued to publicize Philympia, London Philatelic Exhibition, Sept. 18-26.

Virgin Mary by Gabriel Loire A46

**1970, Dec. 1 Photo.** *Perf. 13x14*
*240* A46 2sh multi 1.10 85

Christmas 1970. The design is after a stained glass window in the Church of Our Lady of Perpetual Succour, Glasgow.

**Decimal Currency Issue**

Battery, Rosia; 20th Century A47

Designs show for each denomination a 19th century print and a contemporary photograph of the same view: 1p, Prince George of Cambridge Quarters, and Trinity Church. 1½p, Wellington Monument, Alameda Gardens. 2p, View from North Bastion. 2½p, Catalan Bay. 3p, Convent, seen from garden. 4p, The Exchange and Spanish Chapel. 5p, Commercial Square, Library and Main Guard. 7p, South Barracks and Rosia Magazine. 8p, Moorish Mosque and Castle. 9p, Europa Pass. 10p, South Barracks, from Rosia Bay. 12½p, Southport Gates. 25p, Guards on Alameda. 50p, Europa Pass Gorge (vert.). £1 Prince Edward Gate (vert.).
In the listing the 1st number is for the 19th cent. design, the 2nd for the 20th cent. design.

**Wmk. 314 Sideways**

**1971, Feb. 15 Litho.** *Perf. 14*
*241* A47 ½p brn red & multi 5 5
*242* A47 ½p brn red & multi 5 5
*243* A47 1p lt bl & multi 18 14
*244* A47 1p lt bl & multi 18 14
*245* A47 1½p emer & multi 10 10
*246* A47 1½p emer & multi 10 10
*247* A47 2p dk brn & multi 45 45
*248* A47 2p dk brn & multi 45 45
*249* A47 2½p ver & multi 15 15
*250* A47 2½p ver & multi 15 15
*251* A47 3p pale grn & multi 18 18
*252* A47 3p pale grn & multi 18 18
*253* A47 4p gray & multi 1.10 1.10
*254* A47 4p gray & multi 1.10 1.10
*255* A47 5p dk grn & multi 25 25
*256* A47 5p dk grn & multi 25 25
*257* A47 7p org & multi 38 38
*258* A47 7p org & multi 38 38
*259* A47 8p dk bl & multi 45 45
*260* A47 8p dk bl & multi 45 45
*261* A47 9p brick red & multi 48 48
*262* A47 9p brick red & multi 48 48
*263* A47 10p blk & multi 55 55
*264* A47 10p blk & multi 55 55
*265* A47 12½p bis & multi 65 65
*266* A47 12½p bis & multi 65 65
*267* A47 25p dp pur & multi 1.40 1.40
*268* A47 25p dp pur & multi 1.40 1.40
*269* A47 50p bl & multi 2.25 2.25
*270* A47 50p bl & multi 2.25 2.25
*271* A47 £1 sep & multi 4.75 4.75
*272* A47 £1 sep & multi 4.75 4.75
*Nos. 241-272 (32)* 26.74 26.66

The stamps of the same denomination are printed se-tenant both horizontally and vertically in sheets of 100.

**1973, Sept. 12 Wmk. 314 Upright**
*247a* A47 2p dk brn & multi 15 15
*248a* A47 2p dk brn & multi 15 15
*253a* A47 4p gray & multi 30 30
*254a* A47 4p gray & multi 30 30

**1975, July 9 Wmk. 373**
*243a* A47 1p bl & multi 14 14
*244a* A47 1p bl & multi 14 14

Queen Elizabeth II — A48

Regimental Coat of Arms — A49

Coil Stamps
*Perf. 14½x14*

**1971, Feb. 15 Photo. Wmk. 314**
*273* A48 ½p red org 10 10
*274* A48 1p brt bl 20 20
*275* A48 2p lt yel grn 50 50
*a* Strip of 5 (½p, ½p, 1p, 1p, 2p) 1.40 1.40

Uniform Type of 1969

Uniforms: 1p, Soldier, Black Watch, 1845. 2p, Drum Major with antelope mascot, Royal Fusiliers, 1971. 4p, Soldier, Kings Own Royal Border Regiment, 1704. 10p, Soldier, Devonshire and Dorset Regiment, 1801.

**1971, Sept. 6 Litho.** *Perf. 14*
*276* A42 1p sil & multi 25 25
*277* A42 2p gold & multi 60 60
*278* A42 4p gold & multi 1.50 1.50
*279* A42 10p sil, gold & multi 4.50 3.75

Design descriptions are printed on back on top of gum.

**1971, Sept. 25** *Perf. 13x12*
*280* A49 3p red, bis & blk 55 50

Presentation of colors to Gibraltar Regiment, Sept. 25, 1971.

Nativity — A50

Christmas: 5p, Journey to Bethlehem.

**1971, Dec. 1 Photo.** *Perf. 13x13½*
*281* A50 3p sil & multi 75 65
*282* A50 5p gold & multi 1.25 1.10

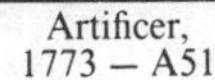

Artificer, 1773 — A51

"Our Lady of Europa" — A52

Designs: 3p, Tunneler with drill, 1969. 5p, Royal Engineers, 1772 and 1972, and regimental crest (horiz.).

**1972, Mar. 6** *Perf. 14x13½, 13½x14*
*283* A51 1p dk bl & multi 30 25
*284* A51 3p red & multi 1.00 80
*285* A51 5p grn & multi 1.75 1.35

Bicent. of the Royal Engineers in Gibraltar.

Uniform Type of 1969

Uniforms: 1p, Soldier, Duke of Cornwall's Light Infantry, 1704. 3p, Officer, King's Royal Rifle Corps, 1830. 7p, Officer, 37th North Hampshire Regiment, 1825. 10p, Sailor, Royal Navy, 1972.

**1972, July 19 Litho.** *Perf. 14*
*286* A42 1p sil & multi 25 22
*287* A42 3p sl & multi 85 70
*288* A42 7p sil & multi 2.00 1.75
*289* A42 10p gold & multi 3.75 3.25

Design descriptions printed on back on top of gum.

**1972, Oct. 1** *Perf. 14½x14*
*290* A52 3p brn & multi 22 22
*291* A52 5p grn & multi 50 50

Christmas. Design description printed on back.

**Silver Wedding Issue, 1972**
Common Design Type

Design: Queen Elizabeth II, Prince Philip, keys of Gibraltar and white narcissus.

**1972, Nov. 20 Photo.** *Perf. 14x14½*
*292* CD324 5p car rose & multi 35 35
*293* CD324 7p sl grn & multi 45 45

Flags of EEC Members and EEC Emblem — A53

*Perf. 14½x14*

**1973, Feb. 22 Litho. Unwmk.**
*294* A53 5p red & multi 52 45
*295* A53 10p ultra & multi 1.00 95

Entry into European Economic Community.

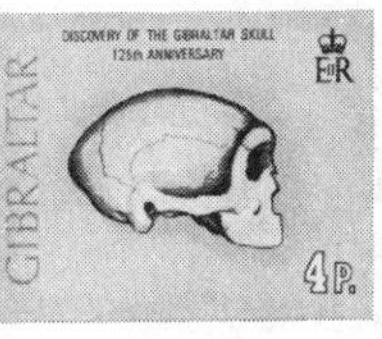

Gibraltar Skull — A54

Designs: 6p, Head of Neanderthal man. 10p, Neanderthal family.

**1973, May 22 Wmk. 314** *Perf. 13½*
*296* A54 4p lil rose & multi 65 55
*297* A54 6p lt ultra & multi 1.00 80
*298* A54 10p yel grn & multi 1.60 1.30

125th anniv. of the discovery of the Gibraltar skull.

Uniform Type of 1969

Uniforms: 1p, Fifer, King's Own Scottish Borderers, 1770. 4p, Officer, Royal Welsh Fusiliers, 1800. 6p, Soldier, Royal Northumberland Fusiliers, 1736. 10p, Private, Grenadier Guards, 1898.

**1973, Aug. 22 Litho.** *Perf. 14*
*299* A42 1p multicolored 35 22
*300* A42 4p multicolored 1.65 1.10
*301* A42 6p multicolored 2.50 1.50
*302* A42 10p multicolored 4.25 2.50

Design descriptions printed on back on top of gum.

*Gibraltar stamps can be mounted in Scott's annually supplemented British Europe Album.*

Nativity, by Justus Danckerts A55

**1973, Oct. 17 Litho.** *Perf. 12½x12*
*303* A55 4p brn org & blue 60 40
*304* A55 6p green & claret 85 60

Christmas.

**Princess Anne's Wedding Issue**
Common Design Type

**1973, Nov. 14** *Perf. 14*
*305* CD325 6p bl grn & multi 55 45
*306* CD325 14p brt grn & multi 1.20 1.00

Wedding of Princess Anne and Capt. Mark Phillips, Nov. 14, 1973.

V.R. (Queen Victoria) Pillar Box — A56

Virgin with Green Cushion, Andrea Solario — A57

Pillar Boxes: 6p, G.R. (King George). 14p, E.R. (Queen Elizabeth).

**1974, May 2 Litho.** *Perf. 14*
*307* A56 2p yel grn & multi 18 18
*308* A56 6p gray & multi 55 55
*309* A56 14p dull yel & multi 1.25 1.25
*a* Souvenir booklet 14.00

UPU, cent.
No. 309a contains 2 self-adhesive panes printed on peelable paper backing with multicolored advertising on back. One pane of 6 contains 3 each similar to Nos. 307-308; the other pane of 3 contains one each similar to Nos. 307-309. Stamps are imperf. x roulette.

Uniform Type of 1969

Uniforms: 4p, Officer, East Lancashire Regiment, 1742. 6p, Sergeant, Somerset Light Infantry, 1833. 10p, Company man, Royal Sussex Regiment, 1790. 16p, Officer, Royal Air Force, 1974.

**1974, Aug. 21** *Perf. 14*
*310* A42 4p silver & multi 55 45
*311* A42 6p silver & multi 95 75
*312* A42 10p silver & multi 1.65 1.25
*313* A42 16p silver & multi 2.50 2.75

Design descriptions are printed on back on top of gum.

**1974, Nov. 5 Litho.**

Painting: 6p, Madonna of the Meadow, by Giovanni Bellini.

*314* A57 4p gold & multi 60 42
*315* A57 6p gold & multi 1.10 70

Christmas.

Churchill, Parliament and Big Ben — A58

Design: 20p, Churchill and King George V-class battleship.

**1974, Nov. 30** *Perf. 14x14½*

| | | | | |
|---|---|---|---|---|
| *316* | A58 | 6p violet & multi | 35 | 35 |
| *317* | A58 | 20p multicolored | 90 | 90 |
| *a* | | Souvenir sheet of 2 | 3.00 | 3.00 |

Sir Winston Churchill, (1874-1965), birth centenary. No. 317a contains one each of Nos. 316-317, black marginal inscription and Churchill portrait in light violet. Size: 113x92mm.

### Uniform Type of 1969

Uniforms: 4p, Officer, East Surrey Regiment, 1846. 6p, Private, Highland Light Infantry, 1777. 10p, Officer, Coldstream Guards, 1704. 20p, Sergeant, Gibraltar Regiment, 1974.

**1975, Mar. 14 Wmk. 373** *Perf. 14*

| | | | | |
|---|---|---|---|---|
| *318* | A42 | 4p multicolored | 32 | 25 |
| *319* | A42 | 6p multicolored | 50 | 42 |
| *320* | A42 | 10p multicolored | 1.00 | 70 |
| *321* | A42 | 20p multicolored | 2.00 | 1.50 |

Design descriptions are printed on back on top of gum.

Girl Guides Emblem A59

*Perf. 13½x13*

**1975, Oct. 10 Litho. Wmk. 373**

| | | | | |
|---|---|---|---|---|
| *322* | A59 | 5p violet, gold & blue | 35 | 35 |
| *323* | A59 | 7p red brn, gold & blk | 52 | 52 |
| *324* | A59 | 15p ocher, silver & blk | 1.10 | 1.10 |

Girl Guides, 50th anniversary.

Child and Bird A60

Bruges Madonna, by Michelangelo A61

*Perf. 14x14½*

**1975, Nov. 25 Litho. Wmk. 373**

| | | | | |
|---|---|---|---|---|
| *325* | | Block of 6 | 3.00 | 3.00 |
| *a* | | A60 6p shown | 48 | 48 |
| *b* | | A60 6p Angel playing lute | 48 | 48 |
| *c* | | A60 6p Singing boy | 48 | 48 |
| *d* | | A60 6p Mother and children | 48 | 48 |
| *e* | | A60 6p Praying child | 48 | 48 |
| *f* | | A60 6p Child and lamb | 48 | 48 |

Christmas. No. 325 printed in sheets of 60 containing 10 blocks of 6 (3x2) stamps with horizontal and vertical gutters between blocks.

**1975, Dec. 17 Litho.** *Perf. 14x13½*

Sculptures by Michelangelo: 9p, Traddei Madonna. 15p, Pieta.

| | | | | |
|---|---|---|---|---|
| *326* | A61 | 6p vio blk & multi | 28 | 28 |
| *327* | A61 | 9p blk brn & multi | 45 | 45 |
| *328* | A61 | 15p dk pur & multi | 75 | 75 |
| *a* | | Souvenir booklet | 5.50 | |

500th birth anniversary of Michelangelo Buonarroti (1475-1564), Italian sculptor, painter and architect.

No. 328a contains 2 self-adhesive panes printed on peelable paper backing with stamp dealer's advertisements on back. One pane of 6 contains 2 each similar to Nos. 326-328; the other pane of 3 contains one each similar to Nos. 326-328. Stamps are imperf. x roulette.

Common Design Types are pictured in section before Great Britain.

American Bicentennial Emblem, Arms of Gibraltar — A62

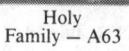

Holy Family — A63

*Perf. 14x14½*

**1976, May 28 Litho. Wmk. 373**

| | | | | |
|---|---|---|---|---|
| *329* | A62 | 25p multicolored | 1.50 | 1.10 |
| *a* | | Souvenir sheet of 4 | 4.50 | 4.50 |

American Bicentennial. No. 329a contains 4 No. 329; Spirit of 76 design in margin. Size: 84x133mm. Sheet is rouletted all around.

### Uniform Type of 1969

Uniforms: 1p, Suffolk Regiment, 1795. 6p, Northamptonshire Regiment, 1779. 12p, Lancashire Fusiliers, 1793. 25p, Royal Army Ordinance Corps, 1896.

**Wmk. 373**

**1976, July 21 Litho.** *Perf. 14*

| | | | | |
|---|---|---|---|---|
| *330* | A42 | 1p multicolored | 9 | 8 |
| *331* | A42 | 6p multicolored | 30 | 20 |
| *332* | A42 | 12p multicolored | 75 | 45 |
| *333* | A42 | 25p multicolored | 1.50 | 1.10 |

Design descriptions printed on back on top of gum.

**1976, Nov. 3 Litho. Wmk. 373**

Stained Glass Windows: 9p, St. Bernard of Clairvaux. 12p, St. John the Evangelist. 20p, Archangel Michael.

| | | | | |
|---|---|---|---|---|
| *334* | A63 | 6p ultra & multi | 40 | 30 |
| *335* | A63 | 9p brt grn & multi | 50 | 40 |
| *336* | A63 | 12p orange & multi | 65 | 52 |
| *337* | A63 | 20p dk car & multi | 1.50 | 90 |

Christmas.

Elizabeth II and Royal Crest — A64

**1977, Feb. 7 Litho.** *Perf. 14x13½*

| | | | | |
|---|---|---|---|---|
| *338* | A64 | 6p multicolored | 30 | 30 |
| *339* | A64 | £1 multicolored | 3.25 | 3.25 |
| *a* | | Souvenir sheet of 2 | 6.75 | 5.25 |

25th anniversary of the reign of Queen Elizabeth II. Nos. 338-339 issued in sheets of 9. No. 339a contains one each of Nos. 338-339, perf. 13; multicolored margin showing ampulla and imperial state crown. Size: 127x115mm.

Red Mullet A65

Designs: ½p, 3p, 9p, 25p, Flowers. 1p, 4p, 10p, 50p, Fish. 2p, 5p, 12p, £1, Butterflies. 2½p, 6p, 20p, £2, Birds. ½p, 2½p, 3p, 6p, 9p, 20p, 25p, £2, vertical.

**1977-80** *Perf. 14½x14, 14x14½*

| | | | | |
|---|---|---|---|---|
| *340* | A65 | ½p Toothed orchid | 5 | 5 |
| *341* | A65 | 1p shown | 5 | 5 |
| *342* | A65 | 2p Large blue | 6 | 6 |
| *343* | A65 | 2½p Sardinian warbler | 8 | 8 |
| *344* | A65 | 3p Giant squill | 10 | 10 |
| *345* | A65 | 4p Gray wrasse | 12 | 12 |
| *346* | A65 | 5p Red admiral | 14 | 14 |
| *347* | A65 | 6p Black kite | 15 | 15 |
| *348* | A65 | 9p Scorpion vetch | 24 | 24 |
| *349* | A65 | 10p John Dory | 28 | 28 |
| *350* | A65 | 12p Clouded yellow | 35 | 35 |
| *350A* | A65 | 15p Winged asparagus pea ('80) | 35 | 35 |
| *351* | A65 | 20p Andouin's gull | 55 | 55 |
| *352* | A65 | 25p Barbary nut | 70 | 70 |
| *353* | A65 | 50p Swordfish | 1.40 | 1.40 |
| *354* | A65 | £1 Swallowtail | 2.75 | 2.75 |
| *355* | A65 | £2 Hoopoe | 5.50 | 5.50 |
| *355A* | A65 | £5 Coat of Arms ('79) | 12.00 | 12.00 |
| | | *Nos. 340-355A (18)* | 24.87 | 24.87 |

½p also comes inscribed 1982, the 4p, 10p, 12p, 25p & 50p inscribed 1981, 9p inscribed 1978.

Gibraltar No. 182 — A66

Designs: 12p, Gibraltar No. 233 (vert.). 25p, Gibraltar No. 294 (vert.).

**1977, May 27 Litho.** *Perf. 14*

| | | | | |
|---|---|---|---|---|
| *356* | A66 | 6p multicolored | 20 | 20 |
| *357* | A66 | 12p multicolored | 42 | 42 |
| *358* | A66 | 25p multicolored | 90 | 90 |

Amphilex 77 Intl. Phil. Exhib., Amsterdam, May 26-June 5. Issued in sheets of 6.

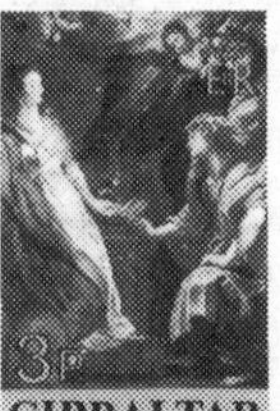


Annunciation, by Rubens — A67

Rubens Paintings: 9p, Nativity. 12p, Adoration of the Kings (horiz.). 15p, Holy Family under Apple Tree.

*Perf. 14x13½, 13½x14*

**1977, Nov. 2 Litho.**

| | | | | |
|---|---|---|---|---|
| *359* | A67 | 3p multicolored | 10 | 10 |
| *360* | A67 | 9p multicolored | 32 | 32 |
| *361* | A67 | 12p multicolored | 42 | 42 |
| *362* | A67 | 15p multicolored | 52 | 52 |
| *a* | | Souvenir sheet of 4 | 2.25 | 2.25 |

Christmas and 400th birth anniv. of Peter Paul Rubens. No. 362a contains one each of Nos. 359-362; orange and black margin with Rubens drawings. Size: 118x210mm.

Gibraltar from Space A68

Design: 25p, Strait of Gibraltar, aerial view.

**1978, May 3 Litho.** *Perf. 13½*

| | | | | |
|---|---|---|---|---|
| *363* | A68 | 12p multicolored | 52 | 45 |

**Souvenir Sheet**

| | | | | |
|---|---|---|---|---|
| *364* | A68 | 25p multicolored | 1.10 | 95 |

No. 363 issued in sheets of 10.

No. 364 contains one stamp; multicolored margin shows Skylab 3, map of Europe and North Africa. Size: 149x108½mm.

Holyroodhouse — A69

Royal Houses: 9p, St. James Palace. 12p, Sandringham House. 18p, Balmoral.

**1978, June 12 Litho.** *Perf. 13½*

| | | | | |
|---|---|---|---|---|
| *365* | A69 | 6p multicolored | 18 | 18 |
| *366* | A69 | 9p multicolored | 28 | 28 |
| *367* | A69 | 12p multicolored | 35 | 35 |
| *368* | A69 | 18p multicolored | 55 | 55 |
| *a* | | Souvenir booklet | 4.50 | |

25th anniversary of coronation of Queen Elizabeth II. No. 368a contains 2 panes printed on peelable paper backing with pictures of castles. One pane contains 6 rouletted stamps, 3 each similar to Nos. 367-368; the other pane contains one 25p (Windsor Castle) rouletted stamp.

Sunderland Seaplane Landing — A70

Designs (Gibraltar and): 9p, Two-tiered Caudron taking off, 1918. 12p, Shackleton, 1953-1966. 16p, Hunter warplane, 1954-1966. 18p, Nimrod, 1969-1978.

**1978, Sept. 6 Litho.** *Perf. 14*

| | | | | |
|---|---|---|---|---|
| *369* | A70 | 3p multicolored | 12 | 9 |
| *370* | A70 | 9p multicolored | 35 | 24 |
| *371* | A70 | 12p multicolored | 45 | 32 |
| *372* | A70 | 16p multicolored | 60 | 48 |
| *373* | A70 | 18p multicolored | 75 | 60 |
| | | *Nos. 369-373 (5)* | 2.27 | 1.73 |

Royal Air Force, 60th anniversary.

Madonna with Goldfinch, by Dürer — A71

Paintings by Albrecht Dürer: 5p, Madonna with Animals. 9p, Nativity. 15p, Adoration of the Kings.

**1978, Nov. 1 Litho.** *Perf. 14*

| | | | | |
|---|---|---|---|---|
| *374* | A71 | 5p multicolored | 20 | 15 |
| *375* | A71 | 9p multicolored | 32 | 25 |
| *376* | A71 | 12p multicolored | 50 | 42 |
| *377* | A71 | 15p multicolored | 55 | 50 |

Christmas.

Rowland Hill and Gibraltar No. 10 — A72

Designs (Rowland Hill and): 9p, Gibraltar No. 274. 12p, Parchment scroll with early postal regulations. 25p, "Barred G" cancellation used on British stamps in Gibraltar.

**1979, Feb. 7 Litho. *Perf. 13½***
*378* A72 3p multicolored 10 8
*379* A72 9p multicolored 30 28
*380* A72 12p yel grn & blk 45 38
*381* A72 25p yellow & blk 90 75

Sir Rowland Hill (1795-1879), originator of penny postage.

Satellite Earth Station, Post Horn, Telephone — A73

**1979, May 16 *Perf. 13½x14***
*382* A73 3p lt grn & green 22 8
*383* A73 9p lt brn & brown 70 25
*384* A73 12p gray & ultra 80 35

European telecommunications system.

Children, IYC Emblem, Nativity — A74

**Litho.; Silver Embossed**

**1979, Nov. 14 *Perf. 14***
*385* Block of 6 3.50 3.25
*a* A74 12p African girl 50 40
*b* A74 12p Chinese girl 50 40
*c* A74 12p Pacific islands girl 50 40
*d* A74 12p American Indian girl 50 40
*e* A74 12p shown 50 40
*f* A74 12p Scandinavian boy 50 40

Christmas; IYC. No. 385 printed in sheets of 12 containing 2 No. 385 with vertical rouletted gutter between.

Officers, Exchange and Commercial Library, 1830 — A75

Gibraltar Police Force, 150th anniv.: 6p, Early and modern uniforms, Rock of Gibraltar. 12p, Traffic Officer, ambulance. 37p, Policeman and woman, Police Station, Irish Town.

***Perf. 14x14½***

**1980, Feb. 5 Litho. Wmk. 373**
*386* A75 3p multicolored 12 10
*387* A75 6p multicolored 25 20
*388* A75 12p multicolored 50 45
*389* A75 37p multicolored 1.50 1.35

**Europa Issue 1980**

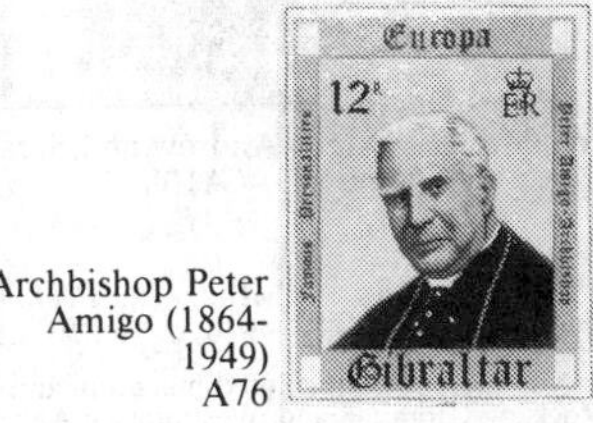

Archbishop Peter Amigo (1864-1949) A76

Designs: No. 391, Gustavo Charles Bacarisas (1872-1971), artist. No. 392, John Mackintosh (1865-1940), philanthropist.

**1980, May 6 Wmk. 373 *Perf. 14½***
*390* A76 12p multicolored 50 40
*391* A76 12p multicolored 50 40
*392* A76 12p multicolored 50 40

**Queen Mother Elizabeth Birthday Issue**

Common Design Type

**1980, Aug. 4 Litho. *Perf. 14***
*393* CD330 15p multicolored 38 38

"Victory" and Rock of Gibraltar, by Monamy Swaine A77

Paintings: 3p, Lord Nelson, by John Francis Rigaud, 1781 (vert.). 15p, Lord Nelson, by William Beechey (vert.). 40p, Victory Towed into Gibraltar by Clarkson Stanfield.

**1980, Aug. 20 Litho. *Perf. 14***
*394* A77 3p multicolored 25 25
*395* A77 9p multicolored 38 38
*396* A77 15p multicolored 65 65
*a* Souvenir sheet 1.40 1.40
*397* A77 40p multicolored 1.65 1.65

Horatio Nelson (1758-1805), 175th death anniv. No. 396a contains No. 396; multicolored margin shows Victory Towed into Gibraltar. Size: 160x99½mm.

Holy Family A78

**1980, Nov. 12**
*398* A78 15p shown 50 50
*399* A78 15p Three kings 50 50

Christmas. Nos. 398-399 se-tenant in continuous design.

**Europa Issue 1981**

Hercules Separating Africa and Europe — A79

Design: 15p, Hercules standing on Rock of Gibraltar and Morocco.

***Perf. 14x13½***

**1981, Feb. 24 Wmk. 373**
*400* A79 9p multicolored 38 38
*401* A79 15p multicolored 65 65

Dining Room, The Convent — A80

**1981, May 22 Litho. *Perf. 14½x14***
*402* A80 4p shown 14 14
*403* A80 14p King's Chapel 45 45
*404* A80 15p Aerial view 50 50
*405* A80 55p Cloister 1.85 1.85

450th anniv. of The Convent (Governor's residence, originally Franciscan monastery).

Prince Charles and Lady Diana A81

**1981, July 27 Litho. *Perf. 14½***
*406* A81 £1 multicolored 3.25 3.25

Royal wedding. Se-tenant with decorative label.

Queen Elizabeth II — A82

**1981, Sept. 29 *Perf. 14½***
*407* A82 1p black 5 5
*a* Bklt. pane of 10 + 2 labels (2 #407, 2 #408, 6 #409) 3.00
*b* Bklt. pane of 5 + label (#407, #408, 3 #409) 1.50
*408* A82 4p dark blue 12 12
*409* A82 15p green 40 40

Nos. 407-409 issued in booklets only.

Airmail Service, 50th Anniv. A83

**1981, Sept. 29 *Perf. 14½***
*410* A83 14p Paper plane 45 45
*411* A83 15p Envelopes, aerogram 50 50
*412* A83 55p Airplane circling globe 1.85 1.85

Intl. Year of the Disabled A84

**1981, Nov. 19 Litho. Wmk. 373**
*413* A84 14p multicolored 45 45

Christmas A85

**1981, Nov. 19 *Perf. 14***
*414* A85 15p Children singing carols 50 50
*415* A85 55p Decorated mailbox, vert. 1.85 1.85

Douglas DC-3 — A86

**1982, Feb. 10 Litho. *Perf. 14***
*416* A86 1p shown 5 5
*417* A86 2p Vickers Viking 8 8
*a* Wmk. 384, dated 1986 ('87) 8 8
*418* A86 3p Airspeed Ambassador 10 10
*419* A86 4p Vickers Viscount 14 14
*420* A86 5p Boeing 727 18 18
*a* Wmk. 384, dated 1986 ('87) 18 18
*421* A86 10p Vickers Vanguard 35 35
*422* A86 14p Short Solent 45 45
*423* A86 15p Fokker F-27 Friendship 50 50
*424* A86 17p Boeing 737 60 60
*425* A86 20p BAC One-eleven 70 70
*426* A86 25p Lockheed Constellation 85 85
*427* A86 50p De Havilland Comet 4B 1.75 1.75
*428* A86 £1 Saro Windhover 2.50 2.50
*429* A86 £2 Hawker Siddeley Trident 2 5.50 5.50
*430* A86 £5 DH-89A Dragon Rapide 15.00 15.00
*Nos. 416-430 (15)* 28.75 28.75

No. 425 exists with 1985 imprint.

Royal Navy Ship Crests — A87

**1982, Apr. 14 Litho. *Perf. 14***
*431* A87 ½p Opossum 5 5
*432* A87 15½p Norfolk 45 45
*433* A87 17p Fearless 55 55
*434* A87 60p Rooke 1.90 1.90

See Nos. 449-452, 465-468, 474-477, 492-495, 501-504, 528-531.

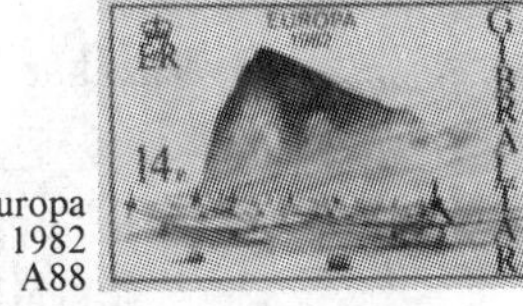

Europa 1982 A88

Designs: Operation Torch, 1943.

**1982, June 11 Litho. *Perf. 14***
*435* A88 14p Planes preparing for takeoff 45 45
*436* A88 17p Generals Eisenhower and Giraud 60 60

Chamber of Commerce Centenary — A89

Anniversaries: 15½p, British Forces Postal Service centenary. 60p, Scouting year.

**1982, Sept. 22**
*437* A89 ½p multicolored 5 5
*438* A89 15½p multicolored 42 42
*439* A89 60p multicolored 1.75 1.75

Intl. Direct Telephone Dialing System Inauguration — A90

**1982, Oct. 1 *Perf. 14½***
*440* A90 17p Map 60 60

Gibraltar
14p CHRISTMAS 1982

Christmas A91

***Perf. 14x14½***

**1982, Nov. 18 Litho. Wmk. 373**
*441* A91 14p Holly 45 45
*442* A91 17p Mistletoe 60 60

**Commonwealth Day Issue**
Common Design Type

**1983, Mar. 14 Litho. *Perf. 14***

*443* CD334 4p Local street 12 12
*444* CD334 14p Scouts on parade 38 38
*445* CD334 17p Flag, vert. 50 50
*446* CD334 60p Queen Elizabeth II, vert. 1.75 1.75

Europa 1983 — A92

**1983, May 21 *Perf. 14x13½***

*447* A92 16p St. George's Hall 48 48
*448* A92 19p Water catchments 65 65

Royal Navy Crest Type of 1982

**1983, July 1 Litho. *Perf. 14***

*449* A87 4p Faulkner 12 12
*450* A87 14p Renown 38 38
*451* A87 17p Sheffield 50 50
*452* A87 60p Ark Royal 1.75 1.75

Fortresses — A94

**1983, Sept. 13 *Perf. 13½x14***

*453* A94 4p Landport Gate, 1729 10 10
*454* A94 17p Koehler gun, 1782 45 45
*455* A94 77p King's Bastion, 1799 2.00 2.00
*a* Souvenir sheet, #453-455 3.00 3.00

Christmas A95

Raphael Paintings.

**1983, Nov. 17 Litho. *Perf. 14***

*456* A95 4p Adoration of the Magi 12 12
*457* A95 17p Madonna of Foligno, vert. 55 55
*458* A95 60p Sistine Madonna, vert. 1.90 1.90

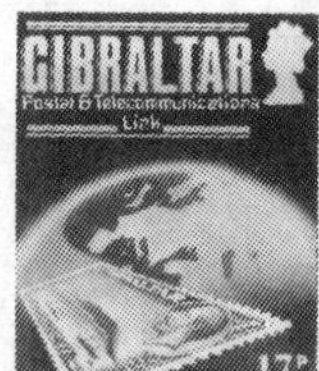

Europa (1959-1984) — A96

Intl. Postal and Telecommunication Links.

**1984, Mar. 6 Litho. *Perf. 14½***

*459* A96 17p No. 98 60 60
*460* A96 23p Communications circuit 75 75

Field Hockey A97

**1984, May 25 Litho. *Perf. 14***

*461* A97 20p shown 60 60
*462* A97 21p Basketball 65 65
*463* A97 26p Rowing 75 75
*464* A97 29p Soccer 85 85

Royal Navy Crest Type of 1982

**1984, Sept. 21 Litho. *Perf. 13½x13***

*465* A87 20p Active 65 65
*466* A87 21p Foxhound 65 65
*467* A87 26p Valiant 80 80
*468* A87 29p Hood 90 90

Christmas A98

***Perf. 14x14½***

**1984, Nov. 7 Litho. Wmk. 373**

*469* A98 20p Parade float 55 55
*470* A98 80p Float, diff. 2.25 2.25

Europa 1985 — A99

Musical symbols.

**1985, Feb. 26 Photo. *Perf. 12½***
**Granite Paper**

*471* A99 20p multicolored 42 42
*472* A99 29p multicolored 60 60

Save the Children Fund — A100

Designs: Globe and legend in various positions.

**1985, May 3 Litho. *Perf. 13x13½***

*473* Strip of 4 2.50 2.50
*a.-d* A100 26p, Any single 60 60

Royal Navy Crests Type of 1982

**1985, July 3 Litho. *Perf. 14***

*474* A87 4p Duncan 10 10
*475* A87 9p Fury 20 20
*476* A87 21p Firedrake 52 52
*477* A87 80p Malaya 1.90 1.90

Intl. Youth Year — A101

**1985, Sept. 6 *Perf. 14½***

*478* A101 4p Emblem 10 10
*479* A101 20p Hands, diamond 52 52
*480* A101 80p Girl Guides anniv. emblem 2.00 2.00

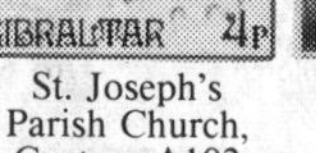

St. Joseph's Parish Church, Cent. — A102

Creche, Detail — A103

***Perf. 13½ x Roulette 7 Between, 13½***

**1985, Oct. 25 Wmk. 373 Litho.**

*481* A102 Pair 24 24
*a* 4p Centenary seal 12 12
*b* 4p Church 12 12
*c* No. 481a, perf. 13½ on 4 sides 12 12
*482* A103 80p multicolored 2.25 2.25

Christmas. Nos. 481a-481b rouletted between. Printed in sheets of 10 pairs with the bottom row containing 5 No. 481c. Strips of 3, Nos. 481a-481c exist.

Europa 1986 A104

**1986, Feb. 10 Litho. *Perf. 13x13½***

*483* A104 22p Butterfly, house 65 65
*484* A104 29p Seagull, hotel 85 85

Postage Stamp Cent. — A105

**1986, Mar. 25 *Perf. 13½x13***

*485* A105 4p No. 18 12 12
*486* A105 22p No. 42 68 68
*487* A105 32p No. 67 95 95
*488* A105 36p No. 118 1.10 1.10

**Size: 32x48mm**
***Perf. 14***

*489* A105 44p No. 131 1.40 1.40
*Nos. 485-489 (5)* 4.25 4.25

**Souvenir Sheet**

*490* A105 29p No. 2 85 85

No. 490 has multicolored decorative margin picturing map of surrounding region and postmark used on British stamps, 1859-1885. Size: 102x73mm.

Queen Elizabeth II, 60th Birthday — A106

**1986, May 22 Litho. *Perf. 14***

*491* A106 £1 multicolored 3.00 3.00

Royal Naval Crests Type of 1982

**1986, Aug. 28 Litho. *Perf. 14***

*492* A87 22p Lightning 62 62
*493* A87 29p Hermione 82 82
*494* A87 32p Laforey 90 90
*495* A87 44p Nelson 1.25 1.25

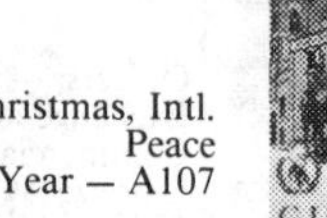

Christmas, Intl. Peace Year — A107

**1986, Oct. 14 Litho. *Perf. 14½x14***

*496* A107 18p St. Mary the Crowned Cathedral 55 55
*497* A107 32p St. Andrew's Church 95 95

**Souvenir Sheet**

Wedding of Prince Andrew and Sarah Ferguson — A108

**1986, Aug. 28 Litho. *Perf. 15***

*498* A108 44p multicolored 1.50 1.50

No. 498 has multicolored margin picturing Rock of Gibraltar and Westminster Abbey. Size: 115x85mm.

The indexes in each volume of the Scott Catalogue contain many listings which help to identify stamps.

Europa 1987 — A109

**1987, Feb. 17 Wmk. 384 *Perf. 15***

| | | |
|---|---|---|
| *499* A109 22p Neptune House | 70 | 70 |
| *500* A109 29p Ocean Heights | 90 | 90 |

Royal Navy Crests Type of 1982

**1987, Apr. 2 *Perf. 13½x13***

| | | |
|---|---|---|
| *501* A87 18p Wishart | 60 | 60 |
| *502* A87 22p Charybdis | 72 | 72 |
| *503* A87 32p Antelope | 1.05 | 1.05 |
| *504* A87 44p Eagle | 1.50 | 1.50 |

Warrant Granted to the Royal Engineers, 200th Anniv. — A110

**Wmk. 373**

**1987, Apr. 25 Litho. *Perf. 14½***

| | | |
|---|---|---|
| *505* A110 18p Victoria Stadium | 55 | 55 |
| *506* A110 32p Casket, Freedom Scroll | 1.00 | 1.00 |
| *507* A110 44p Monogram | 1.35 | 1.35 |

Guns and Artillery A111

Designs: 1p. 13-inch mortar, 1783. 2p. 6-inch Coast, 1909. 3p. 8-inch Howitzer, 1783. 4p. Bofors L40/70, 1951. 5p. 100-ton RML, 1882. 10p. 5.25 HAA, 1953. 18p. 25-pounder Gun-howitzer, 1943. 19p. 64-pounder RML, 1873. 22p. 12-pounder, 1758. 50p.

**1987, June 1 Wmk. 373 *Perf. 12½***

| | | |
|---|---|---|
| *508* A111 1p multicolored | 5 | 5 |
| *509* A111 2p multicolored | 6 | 6 |
| *510* A111 3p multicolored | 8 | 8 |
| *511* A111 4p multicolored | 12 | 12 |
| *512* A111 5p multicolored | 15 | 15 |
| *513* A111 10p multicolored | 30 | 30 |
| *514* A111 18p multicolored | 50 | 50 |
| *515* A111 19p multicolored | 55 | 55 |
| *516* A111 22p multicolored | 60 | 60 |
| *517* A111 50p multicolored | 1.50 | 1.50 |
| *518* A111 £1 multicolored | 3.00 | 3.00 |
| *519* A111 £3 multicolored | 8.50 | 8.50 |
| *520* A111 £5 multicolored | 15.00 | 15.00 |
| *Nos. 508-520 (13)* | 30.41 | 30.41 |

Christmas — A112

**1987, Nov. 12 Wmk. 384 *Perf. 14½***

| | | |
|---|---|---|
| *521* A112 4p Three Wise Men | 12 | 12 |
| *522* A112 22p Holy Family | 60 | 60 |
| *523* A112 44p Shepherds | 1.25 | 1.25 |

Europa 1988 A113

Transport and communication: No. 524, Rock of Gibraltar, cruise ship. No. 525, Passenger jet, yacht, dish aerial. No. 526, Bus, buggy. No. 527, Rock of Gibraltar, automobile, telephone.

***Perf. 14½x14 on 3 Sides; Rouletted Between***

**1988, Feb. 16 Litho. Wmk. 373**

| | | |
|---|---|---|
| *524* A113 22p multicolored | 85 | 85 |
| *525* A113 22p multicolored | 85 | 85 |
| *526* A113 32p multicolored | 1.20 | 1.20 |
| *527* A113 32p multicolored | 1.20 | 1.20 |

Stamps of the same denomination printed se-tenant in continuous designs.

Royal Navy Crests Type of 1982

***Perf. 13½x13***

**1988, Apr. 7 Litho. Wmk. 384**

| | | |
|---|---|---|
| *528* A87 18p Clyde | 58 | 58 |
| *529* A87 22p Foresight | 72 | 72 |
| *530* A87 32p Severn | 1.05 | 1.05 |
| *531* A87 44p Rodney | 1.45 | 1.45 |

Birds — A114

**Wmk. 373**

**1988, June 15 Litho. *Perf. 14***

| | | |
|---|---|---|
| *532* A114 4p Bee eater | 8 | 8 |
| *533* A114 22p Common puffin | 85 | 85 |
| *534* A114 32p Honey buzzard | 1.20 | 1.20 |
| *535* A114 44p Blue rock thrush | 1.70 | 1.70 |

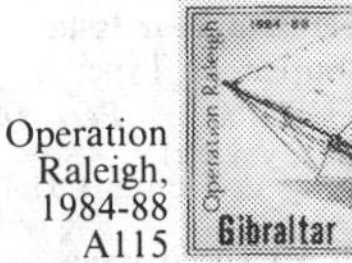

Operation Raleigh, 1984-88 A115

Designs: 19p. Square-rigger. 22p. Sir Walter Raleigh and expedition emblem. 32p. Maps and modern transport ship *Sir Walter Raleigh*. 44p. *Sir Walter Raleigh*.

***Perf. 13x13½***

**1988, Sept. 14 Litho. Wmk. 373**

| | | |
|---|---|---|
| *536* A115 19p multi | 65 | 65 |
| *537* A115 22p multi | 75 | 75 |
| *538* A115 32p multi | 1.10 | 1.10 |

**Souvenir Sheet**

| | | |
|---|---|---|
| *539* Sheet of 2, #537, 539a | 2.25 | 2.25 |
| ***a.*** A115 44p multi | 1.50 | 1.50 |

400th anniv. of Sir Walter Raleigh's voyage to the New World to establish the 1st English-speaking colony, in what is now North Carolina.

No. 539 has multicolored margin picturing map with Operation Raleigh expedition routes highlighted. Size: 135x87mm.

Christmas A116

Children's drawings: 4p. Snowman, by Rebecca Falero. 22p. Nativity, by Dennis Penalver. 44p. Santa Claus, by Gavin Key.

**Wmk. 384**

**1988, Nov. 2 Litho. *Perf. 14***

| | | |
|---|---|---|
| *540* A116 4p multi | 15 | 15 |
| *541* A116 22p multi | 80 | 80 |

**Size: 25x33mm**

| | | |
|---|---|---|
| *542* A116 44p multi | 1.60 | 1.60 |

## POSTAGE DUE STAMPS

**Catalogue values for unused stamps in this section, from this point to the end of the section, are for Never Hinged items.**

Type of Barbados 1934-47

**Wmk. 4**

**1956, Dec. 1 Typo. *Perf. 14***

**Chalky Paper**

| | | |
|---|---|---|
| *J1* D1 1p green | 3.50 | 4.00 |
| *J2* D1 2p brown | 6.50 | 6.00 |
| *J3* D1 4p ultra | 8.25 | 9.25 |

"p" instead of "d"

***Perf. 17½x18***

**1971, Feb. 15 Typo. Wmk. 314**

**Chalky Paper**

| | | |
|---|---|---|
| *J4* D1 ½p green | 62 | 62 |
| *J5* D1 1p dark brown | 62 | 62 |
| *J6* D1 2p dark blue | 1.00 | 1.00 |

Gibraltar Arms — D2

***Perf. 14x13½***

**1976, Oct. 13 Litho. Wmk. 373**

| | | |
|---|---|---|
| *J7* D2 1p orange | 5 | 5 |
| *J8* D2 3p bright ultra | 12 | 12 |
| *J9* D2 5p vermilion | 15 | 18 |
| *J10* D2 7p brt red lilac | 25 | 25 |
| *J11* D2 10p gray | 38 | 38 |
| *J12* D2 20p green | 75 | 75 |
| *Nos. J7-J12 (6)* | 1.70 | 1.73 |

D3

**1984, July 2 *Perf. 14½x14***

| | | |
|---|---|---|
| *J13* D3 1p black | 5 | 5 |
| *J14* D3 3p red | 8 | 8 |
| *J15* D3 5p blue | 14 | 14 |
| *J16* D3 10p sky blue | 25 | 25 |
| *J17* D3 25p lilac | 65 | 65 |
| *J18* D3 50p orange | 1.25 | 1.25 |
| *J19* D3 £1 green | 2.50 | 2.50 |
| *Nos. J13-J19 (7)* | 4.92 | 4.92 |

## WAR TAX STAMP

No. 66 Overprinted **WAR TAX**

**1918, Apr. Wmk. 3 *Perf. 14***

| | | |
|---|---|---|
| *MR1* A14 ½p green | 25 | 25 |
| ***a.*** Double overprint | 750.00 | |

# GILBERT AND ELLICE ISLANDS

LOCATION — Groups of islands in the Pacific Ocean northeast of Australia.
GOVT. — British Crown Colony.
AREA — 375 sq. mi.
POP. — 57,816 (est. 1973).
CAPITAL — Tarawa.

The Gilbert group of which Butaritari, Tarawa and Tamana are the more important, is on the Equator. Ellice Islands, Phoenix Islands, Line Islands (Fanning, Washington and Christmas), and Ocean Island are included in the Colony. The islands were annexed by Great Britain in 1892 and formed into the Gilbert and Ellice Islands Colony in 1915 on request of the native governments.

The colony divided into the Gilbert Islands and Tuvalu, Jan. 1, 1976.

12 Pence = 1 Shilling
20 Shillings = 1 Pound
100 Cents = 1 Dollar (1966)

**Catalogue values for unused stamps in this country are for Never Hinged items, beginning with Scott 52.**

Edward VII A1

Pandanus A2

Stamps and Type of Fiji Overprinted in Black or Red

**1911, Jan. 1 Wmk. 3 *Perf. 14***

**Ordinary Paper**

| | | |
|---|---|---|
| *1* A1 ½p green | 9.25 | 9.25 |
| *2* A1 1p carmine | 30.00 | 30.00 |
| ***a.*** Pair, one without ovpt. | | |
| *3* A1 2p gray | 6.50 | 5.50 |
| *4* A1 2½p ultra | 12.50 | 11.00 |

**Chalky Paper**

| | | |
|---|---|---|
| *5* A1 5p vio & ol grn | 19.00 | *27.50* |
| *6* A1 6p violet | 22.50 | 27.50 |
| *7* A1 1sh *green* | 19.00 | 22.50 |
| *Nos. 1-7 (7)* | 118.75 | 133.25 |

**1911, Mar. Engr.**

**Ordinary Paper**

| | | |
|---|---|---|
| *8* A2 ½p green | 2.00 | *5.25* |
| *9* A2 1p carmine | 1.40 | *2.00* |
| *10* A2 2p gray | 1.40 | 1.50 |
| *11* A2 2½p ultra | 1.40 | *4.00* |

King George V — A3

For description of Dies I and II, see back of this section of the Catalogue.

Die I

**1912-24 Typo.**

| | | |
|---|---|---|
| *14* A3 ½p dp grn | 55 | *1.40* |
| *15* A3 1p carmine | 80 | *1.65* |
| ***a.*** 1p scar | 2.75 | *5.50* |
| *16* A3 2p gray ('16) | 8.00 | *13.00* |
| *17* A3 2½p ultra ('16) | 2.50 | *4.25* |

**Chalky Paper**

| | | |
|---|---|---|
| *18* A3 3p vio, *yel* ('19) | 2.25 | *4.00* |
| *19* A3 4p blk & red, *yel* | 80 | *3.50* |
| *20* A3 5p vio & ol grn | 3.00 | *11.00* |
| *21* A3 6p vio & red vio | 1.90 | *5.50* |
| *22* A3 1sh *green* | 3.75 | *6.75* |
| *23* A3 2sh vio & ultra, *bl* | 9.50 | *15.00* |
| *24* A3 2sh6p blk & red, *bl* | 11.00 | *16.00* |
| *25* A3 5sh grn & red, *yel* | 24.00 | *45.00* |

**Die II**

| | | |
|---|---|---|
| *26* A3 £1 vio & blk, *red* ('24) | 875.00 | *1,750.* |
| *Nos. 14-25 (12)* | 68.05 | 127.05 |

Die II

**1921-27 Ordinary Paper Wmk. 4**

| | | |
|---|---|---|
| *27* A3 ½p green | 28 | *1.40* |
| *28* A3 1p dp vio ('27) | 52 | *1.75* |
| *29* A3 1½p scar ('24) | 1.90 | *4.25* |
| *30* A3 2p gray | 3.75 | *8.50* |

**Chalky Paper**

| | | |
|---|---|---|
| *31* A3 10sh green & red, *emer* ('24) | 190.00 | *325.00* |
| *Nos. 27-31 (5)* | 196.45 | 340.90 |

**Silver Jubilee Issue**
Common Design Type

**1935, May 6 Engr.** ***Perf. 11x12***

*33* CD301 1p blk & ultra 1.50 1.75
*34* CD301 1½ car & bl 1.10 1.25
*35* CD301 3p ultra & brn 3.75 *5.00*
*36* CD301 1sh brn vio & ind 10.00 *17.00*

**Coronation Issue**
Common Design Type

**1937, May 12** ***Perf. 13½x14***

*37* CD302 1p dk pur 15 15
*38* CD302 1½p carmine 26 26
*39* CD302 3p brt ultra 45 45

Great Frigate Bird — A4

Pandanus — A5

Designs: 1½p, Canoe crossing reef. 2p, Canoe and boat house. 2½p, Islander's house. 3p, Seascape. 5p, Ellice Islands canoe. 6p, Coconut trees. 1sh, Phosphate loading jetty, Ocean Island. 2sh, Cutter "Nimanoa." 2sh6p, Gilbert Islands canoe. 5sh, Coat of arms of colony.

***Perf. 11½x11 (Nos. 40, 43, 50), 12½ (Type A5), 13½ (Nos. 42, 44, 45, 48)***

**1939, Jan. 14 Engr. Wmk. 4**

*40* A4 ½p dk grn & sl bl 14 14
*41* A5 1p dk vio & brt bl grn 20 20
*42* A4 1½p car & blk 20 20
*43* A5 2p blk & brn 26 26
*44* A4 2½p ol grn & blk 35 35
*45* A4 3p ultra & blk 26 26
*a.* Perf. 12 ('55) 50 50
*46* A5 5p dk brn & ultra 75 75
*47* A5 6p dl vio & ol 75 75
*48* A4 1sh gray bl & blk 52 52
*a.* Perf. 12 ('51) 3.00 3.00
*49* A5 2sh red org & ultra 4.75 4.75
*50* A4 2sh6p brt bl grn & bl 4.75 4.75
*51* A5 5sh dp bl & red 6.50 6.50
*Nos. 40-51 (12)* 19.43 19.43

**Catalogue values for unused stamps in this section, from this point to the end of the section, are for Never Hinged items.**

**Peace Issue**
Common Design Type

**1946, Dec. 16** ***Perf. 13½x14***

*52* CD303 1p dp mag 15 15
*53* CD303 3p dp bl 25 25

Common Design Types pictured in section before Great Britain.

**Silver Wedding Issue**
Common Design Types

**1949, Aug. 29 Photo.** ***Perf. 14x14½***

*54* CD304 1p violet 16 16

**Engraved; Name Typographed**
***Perf. 11½x11***

*55* CD305 £1 red 26.00 *47.50*

**UPU Issue.**
Common Design Types

**Engr.; Name Typo. on 2p, 3p.**

**1949, Oct. 1** ***Perf. 13½, 11x11½***

*56* CD306 1p rose vio 60 60
*57* CD307 2p gray blk 1.25 1.25
*58* CD308 3p indigo 1.90 1.90
*59* CD309 1sh blue 4.50 4.50

**Coronation Issue**
Common Design Type

**1953, June 2 Engr.** ***Perf. 13½x13***

*60* CD312 2p gray & blk 85 85

Types of 1939-42 with Portrait of Queen Elizabeth II, and

Canoe Crossing Reef — A6

***Perf. 11½x11 (Nos. 61, 63, 70), 12½ (Type A5), 12 (Nos. 64-65, 68, 72)***

**1956, Aug. 1**

*61* A4 ½p brt ultra & blk 8 6
*62* A5 1p vio & ol 16 10
*63* A4 2p dl pur & brt grn 20 14
*64* A4 2½p grn & blk 25 16
*65* A4 3p dk car & blk 32 25
*66* A5 5p red org & brt ultra 75 50
*67* A5 6p dk gray & red brn 90 55
*68* A4 1sh ol grn & blk 1.40 1.00
*69* A5 2sh dk brn & brt ultra 5.50 3.75
*70* A4 2sh6p dp ultra & rose red 6.50 4.25
*71* A5 5sh grn & bl 12.50 10.00
*72* A6 10sh turq bl & blk 26.00 25.00
*Nos. 61-72 (12)* 54.56 45.76

See Nos. 84-85.

Loading Phosphate on Freighter A7

Designs: 2½p, Original lump of phosphate. 1sh, Loading phosphate on truck, Ocean Island.

**Wmk. 314**

**1960, May 1 Photo.** ***Perf. 12***

*73* A7 2p rose lil & grn 55 38
*74* A7 2½p ol & blk 70 45
*75* A7 1sh grnsh bl & blk 1.65 1.50

60th anniversary of the discovery of phosphate deposits at Ocean Island.

**Freedom from Hunger Issue**
Common Design Type

**1963, June 4** ***Perf. 14x14½***

*76* CD314 10p ultra 5.00 4.50

**Red Cross Centenary Issue**
Common Design Type
**Wmk. 314**

**1963, Sept. 2 Litho.** ***Perf. 13***

*77* CD315 2p blk & red 1.10 45
*78* CD315 10p ultra & red 6.00 5.50

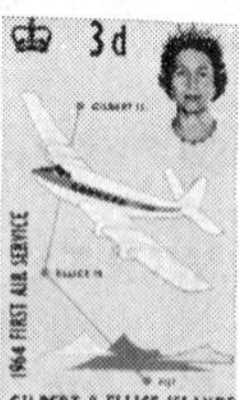

Plane and Fiji-Ellice-Gilbert Route — A8

Designs: 1sh, Eastern reef heron in flight (horiz.). 3sh7p, Plane and Tarawa sailboat.

***Perf. 11½x11, 11x11½***

**1964, July 20 Litho. Wmk. 314**

*79* A8 3p lt bl, bl & blk 24 18
*80* A8 1sh dk bl, bl & blk 60 45
*81* A8 3sh7p lt grn, grn & blk 2.00 1.75

Inauguration of air service between Fiji and Gilbert and Ellice Islands.

Queen Types of 1956
***Perf. 11½x11, 12½***

**1964-65 Engr. Wmk. 314**

*84* A4 2p dl pur & brt grn 95 95
*85* A5 6p dk gray & red brn ('65) 2.00 2.00

**ITU Issue**
Common Design Type

**1965, June 4 Litho.** ***Perf. 11x11½***

*87* CD317 3p dp org & turq bl 24 24
*88* CD317 2sh6p grnsh bl & red lil 2.25 2.25

Village Elder Blowing Conch and Meeting House (Maneaba) — A9

Designs: 1p, Ellice Islanders torch fishing. 2p, Gilbertese girl weaving frangipani garland. 3p, Gilbertese woman dancing The Ruoia. 4p, Gilbertese man dancing. 5p, Gilbertese woman drawing water. 6p, Ellice kosu dance. 7p, Fatele taua dance, Ellice men. 1sh, Gilbertese woman harvesting taro roots (babai). 1sh6p, Ellice man and woman dancing fatele toka. 2sh, Ellice Islanders pounding taro roots. 3sh7p, Gilbertese sitting dance, ruoia (horiz.). 5sh, Gilbertese boys playing stick game (horiz.). 10sh, Ellice men beating box-drum (horiz.). £1, Coat of arms (horiz.).

***Perf. 12x11, 11x12***

**1965, Aug. 16 Litho. Wmk. 314**

*89* A9 ½p bl grn & multi 5 5
*90* A9 1p vio bl & multi 5 5
*91* A9 2p lt ol & multi 6 6
*92* A9 3p red & multi 9 9
*93* A9 4p pur & multi 12 12
*94* A9 5p car rose & multi 15 15
*95* A9 6p multi 18 18
*96* A9 7p brn & multi 32 32
*97* A9 1sh bl vio & multi 48 48
*98* A9 1sh6p yel & multi 95 95
*99* A9 2sh multi 1.40 1.40
*100* A9 3sh7p ultra & multi 3.00 3.00
*101* A9 5sh multi 4.00 4.00
*102* A9 10sh grn & multi 7.00 7.00
*103* A9 £1 bl & multi 11.00 11.00
*Nos. 89-103 (15)* 28.85 28.85

See Nos. 135-149.

**Intl. Cooperation Year Issue**
Common Design Type

**1965, Oct. 25 Litho.** ***Perf. 14½***

*104* CD318 ½p bl grn & cl 7 7
*105* CD318 3sh7p lt vio & grn 1.65 1.65

**Churchill Memorial Issue**
Common Design Type

**1966, Jan. 24 Photo.** ***Perf. 14***

**Design in Black, Gold and Carmine Rose**

*106* CD319 ½p brt bl 5 5
*107* CD319 3p green 18 18
*108* CD319 3sh brown 1.65 1.65
*109* CD319 3sh7p violet 1.90 1.90

Nos. 89-103 Surcharged with New Value and Three Bars
***Perf. 12x11, 11x12***

**1966, Feb. 14 Litho.**

*110* A9 1c on 1p multi 8 8
*111* A9 2c on 2p multi 12 12
*112* A9 3c on 3p multi 16 16
*113* A9 4c on ½p multi 24 24
*114* A9 5c on 6p multi 28 28
*115* A9 6c on 4p multi 35 35
*116* A9 8c on 5p multi 48 48
*117* A9 10c on 1sh multi 60 60
*118* A9 15c on 7p multi 95 95
*119* A9 20c on 1sh6p multi 1.25 1.25
*120* A9 25c on 2sh multi 1.50 1.50
*121* A9 35c on 3sh7p multi 2.25 2.25
*122* A9 50c on 5sh multi 3.50 3.50
*123* A9 $1 on 10sh multi 4.75 4.75
*124* A9 $2 on £1 multi 10.00 10.00
*Nos. 110-124 (15)* 26.51 26.51

**World Cup Soccer Issue**
Common Design Type

**1966, July 1 Litho.** ***Perf. 14***

*125* CD321 3c multi 14 14
*126* CD321 35c multi 1.40 1.40

**WHO Headquarters Issue**
Common Design Type

**1966, Sept. 20 Litho.** ***Perf. 14***

*127* CD322 3c multi 12 12
*128* CD322 12c multi 95 95

**UNESCO Anniversary Issue**
Common Design Type

**1966, Dec. 1 Litho.** ***Perf. 14***

*129* CD323 5c "Education" 55 55
*130* CD323 10c "Science" 1.40 1.40
*131* CD323 20c "Culture" 3.25 3.25

H.M.S. Royalist, 1892, and Union Jack A10

Designs: 10c, Cutter and canoe at trading post. 35c, Family.

***Perf. 14½x14***

**1967, Sept. 1 Photo. Wmk. 314**

*132* A10 3c grn, bl & red 8 8
*133* A10 10c multi 28 28
*134* A10 35c multi 90 90

75th anniversary of the Gilbert and Ellice Islands as a British Protectorate.

Type of 1965

Designs: 1c, Ellice Islanders torch fishing. 2c, Gilbertese girl weaving frangipani garland. 3c, Gilbertese woman dancing the ruoia. 4c, Village elder blowing conch, and Meeting House. 5c, Ellice kosu dance. 6c, Gilbertese man dancing. 8c, Gilbertese woman drawing water. 10c, Gilbertese woman harvesting taro roots. 15c, Fatele taua dance, Ellice men. 20c, Ellice man and woman dancing fatele toka. 25c, Ellice Islanders pounding taro roots. 35c, Gilbertese sitting dance, ruoia (horiz.). 50c, Gilbertese boys playing stick game (horiz.). $1, Ellice men beating box-drum (horiz.). $2, Coat of Arms (horiz.).

***Perf. 12x11, 11x12***

**1968, Jan. 1 Litho. Wmk. 314**

*135* A9 1c vio bl & multi 5 5
*136* A9 2c lt ol & multi 10 8
*137* A9 3c red & multi 14 12
*138* A9 4c bl grn & multi 18 16
*139* A9 5c multi 22 20
*140* A9 6c pur & multi 26 22
*141* A9 8c car rose & multi 32 30
*142* A9 10c bl vio & multi 52 45
*143* A9 15c brn & multi 80 75
*144* A9 20c yel & multi 1.10 1.00
*145* A9 25c multi 1.65 1.40
*146* A9 35c ultra & multi 1.90 1.75
*147* A9 50c multi 2.50 2.00
*148* A9 $1 grn & multi 5.00 4.25
*149* A9 $2 bl & multi 9.50 8.00
*Nos. 135-149 (15)* 24.24 20.73

Map of Tarawa Atoll — A11

Designs: 10c, U.S. Marines wading ashore at Betio. 15c, Battle scene on Betio. 35c, Raising U.S. and British flags on Betio.

**1968, Nov. 21 Photo.** ***Perf. 14***

*150* A11 3c multi 8 8
*151* A11 10c multi 26 26
*152* A11 15c multi 40 40
*153* A11 35c multi 1.00 1.00

Issued to commemorate the 25th anniversary of the Battle of Tarawa against Japan.

School Boy and Map of Abemama Atoll A12

Designs: 10c, Secondary school boy and girl on map of Tarawa, with rest of Gilbert and Ellice Islands. 35c, Student in cap and grown on main Fiji island (Viti Levu) and map of South Pacific Islands.

**1969, June 2 Litho. *Perf. 12½***

*154* A12 3c dl org & multi 10 10
*155* A12 10c blk & multi 32 32
*156* A12 35c dl grn & multi 1.10 1.10

Issued to commemorate the first anniversary of the University of the South Pacific in Fiji, and to show the progress of education in the area it serves.

Polynesian Madonna A13

**1969, Oct. 20 *Perf. 11½***

*157* A13 2c multi 20 20
*158* A13 10c multi 1.00 1.00

Christmas 1969.

Canceled to Order
The Philatelic Bureau of Gilbert and Ellice Islands began in 1970 to sell canceled sets of new issues. Values in the second ("used") column are for these canceled-to-order stamps.

Melanesian Resuscitating White Man — A14

Designs: 10c, White man resuscitating Melanesian: Red Cross at right. 35c, Melanesian resuscitating Melanesian man.

**1970, Mar. 9 Litho. *Perf. 14½***

*159* A14 10c yel & multi 30 30
*160* A14 15c pale vio & multi 48 48
*161* A14 35c dk bl & multi 1.25 1.25

Centenary of the British Red Cross.

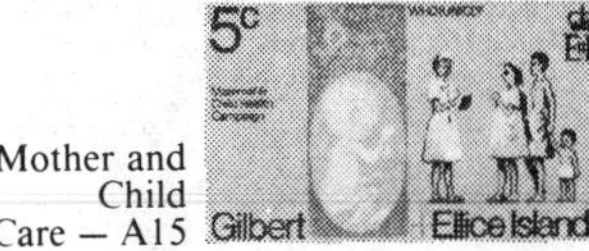

Mother and Child Care — A15

Designs: 10c, Woman physician and laboratory equipment. 15c, Chest X-ray and technician. 35c, Map of Gilbert and Ellice Islands and U.N. emblem.

***Perf. 12½x13***

**1970, June 26 Litho. Wmk. 314**

*162* A15 5c lil & multi 14 14
*163* A15 10c blk, gray & red 28 28
*164* A15 15c yel & multi 50 50
*165* A15 35c bl grn, bl & blk 1.10 1.10

25th Anniversary of the United Nations.

Map of Onotoa, Beru, Tamana and Arorae Islands A16

Designs: 10c, Sailing ship "John Williams III" (vert.). 25c, Rev. Samuel James Whitmee (vert.). 35c, Map of Islands and steamship "John Williams VII."

***Perf. 14x14½, 14½x14***

**1970, Sept. 1 Litho. Wmk. 314**

*166* A16 2c bl & multi 7 7
*167* A16 10c brt grn & blk 32 32
*168* A16 25c lt ultra & red brn 80 80
*169* A16 35c ver, blk & lt gray 1.10 1.10

Issued to commemorate the centenary of the landing in the Southern Gilbert Islands by the first missionaries of the London Missionary Society.

Island Child with Halo on Pandanus Mat — A17

Designs: 10c, Sanctuary of New Tarawa Cathedral. 35c, Three Gilbertese sailing canoes within Star of Bethlehem.

**1970, Oct. 3 *Perf. 14½***

*170* A17 2c ocher & multi 6 6
*171* A17 10c ocher & multi 35 35
*172* A17 35c pink & multi 1.25 1.25

Christmas 1970.

Harvesting Copra — A18

Lagoon Fishing A19

Designs: 3c, Women cleaning pandanus leaves. 4c, Fishermen casting nets. 5c, Gilbertese canoes. 6c, Dehusking coconuts. 8c, Woman weaving pandanus fronds. 10c, Basket weaving. 15c, Tiger shark. 20c, Beating rolled pandanus leaf. 25c, Loading copra. 35c, Night fishing. 50c, Local handicraft. $1, Woman weaving coconut screen. $2, Coat of arms.

**Wmk. 314 Upright (A18), Sideways (A19)**

**1971, May 31 Litho. *Perf. 14***

*173* A18 1c multi 8 5
*174* A19 2c multi 20 16
*175* A19 3c multi 16 12
*176* A19 4c multi 20 15
*177* A19 5c multi 35 32
*178* A18 6c multi 40 35
*179* A18 8c multi 40 35
*180* A18 10c multi 50 45
*181* A18 15c multi 2.00 95
*182* A19 20c multi 2.50 1.90
*183* A19 25c multi 2.00 1.50
*184* A19 35c multi 2.75 2.00
*185* A18 50c multi 3.25 2.50
*186* A18 $1 multi 8.25 5.00
*187* A18 $2 multi 14.00 10.00
*Nos. 173-187 (15)* 37.04 25.80

**Wmk. 314 Upright (A19), Sideways (A18)**

**1972-73**

*174a* A19 2c multi ('73) 20 16
*177a* A19 25c multi 50 40
*178a* A18 6c multi ('73) 65 52
*181a* A18 15c multi 1.90 1.50
*182a* A19 20c multi 2.50 2.00
*Nos. 174a-182a (5)* 5.75 4.58

Legislative Council, 1971 (former House of Representatives) — A20

Design: 10c, Meeting House.

**1971, Aug. 1 Wmk. 314 *Perf. 14***

*188* A20 3c org & multi 18 18
*189* A20 10c grn & multi 70 70

New Constitution, 1971.

Nativity Scene — A21

Christmas: 10c, Star of Bethlehem and palm fronds. 35c, Fishermen in outrigger canoe looking at Star.

**1971, Oct. 1**

*190* A21 3c vio bl, blk & yel 12 12
*191* A21 10c grnsh bl, blk & gold 38 38
*192* A21 35c car rose, blk & rose 1.10 1.10

Children and UNICEF Emblem A22

Designs (UNICEF Emblem and): 10c, Seated child. 35c, Child's head.

**1971, Dec. 11**

*193* A22 3c brt pink & multi 16 16
*194* A22 10c blk & multi 55 55
*195* A22 35c bl & multi 1.65 1.65

25th anniv. UNICEF.

Commission Flag, Map of South Pacific — A23

South Pacific Commission Flag and: 10c, Island boats. 35c, Flags of 8 member nations plus Tonga, a non-member.

**1972, Feb. 21 *Perf. 13½x14***

*196* A23 3c gray & multi 10 10
*197* A23 10c tan, ultra & brn 32 32
*198* A23 35c ultra & multi 1.10 1.10

South Pacific Commission, 25th anniv.

Alveopora A24

Corals: 10c, Euphyllia. 15c, Melithea. 35c, Spongodes.

***Perf. 14x14½***

**1972, May 26 Litho. Wmk. 314**

*199* A24 3c yel bis & multi 9 9
*200* A24 10c grn & multi 45 45
*201* A24 15c gray & multi 60 60
*202* A24 35c ultra & multi 2.25 1.75

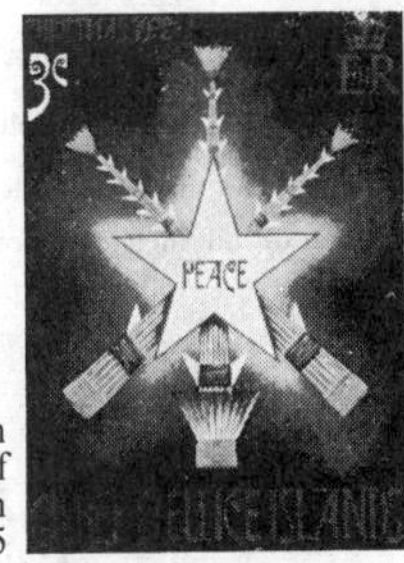

"Peace" on Star of Bethlehem A25

Christmas: 10c, Holy Family, made of shells. 35c, Christ child sleeping in giant clam and covered with dawn cowrie (horiz.).

**1972, Sept. 15 *Perf. 13½***

*203* A25 3c gold & multi 28 8
*204* A25 10c gold & multi 35 35
*205* A25 35c gold & multi 1.10 1.10

**Silver Wedding Issue, 1972**
Common Design Type

Design: Queen Elizabeth II, Prince Philip and kaue floral headdress.

**1972, Nov. 20 Photo. *Perf. 14x14½***

*206* CD324 3c ol & multi 7 7
*207* CD324 35c rose brn & multi 80 80

Funafuti, Land of Bananas A26

Designs: 10c, Butaritari, the smell of the sea. 25c, Tarawa, the center of the world. 35c, Abemama, the land of the moon.

**1973, Mar. 5 Litho. *Perf. 14½x14***

*208* A26 3c yel & multi 12 12
*209* A26 10c brt grn & multi 35 35
*210* A26 25c dl bl & multi 1.10 1.10
*211* A26 35c org & multi 1.50 1.50

Legends of island names.

Ellice Dancer — A27

Christmas: (Within Outline of Nautilus Shell). 10c, Outrigger canoe in lagoon. 35c, Evening on the lagoon. 50c, Map of Christmas Island, Pacific Ocean.

**1973, Sept. 24 *Perf. 14***

*212* A27 3c vio bl & multi 12 12
*213* A27 10c multi 38 38
*214* A27 35c multi 1.10 1.10
*215* A27 50c vio bl & multi 1.65 1.65

**Princess Anne's Wedding Issue**
Common Design Type

**1973, Nov. 14** ***Perf. 14***

| No. | Type | Description | Unused | Used |
|---|---|---|---|---|
| *216* | CD325 | 3c brt grn & multi | 8 | 8 |
| *217* | CD325 | 35c sl & multi | 75 | 75 |

Meteorological Observation — A28

Designs (WMO Emblem and): 10c, Island observation station. 35c, Wind finding radar. 50c, Map of Gilbert and Ellice Islands world weather watch stations.

**1973, Nov. 26** **Litho.** ***Perf. 14½***

| No. | Type | Description | Unused | Used |
|---|---|---|---|---|
| *218* | A28 | 3c org & multi | 25 | 25 |
| *219* | A28 | 10c dp bis & multi | 90 | 90 |
| *220* | A28 | 35c gray & multi | 2.75 | 2.75 |
| *221* | A28 | 50c dk bl & multi | 3.75 | 3.75 |

Cent. of intl. meteorological cooperation.

Te-Mataaua Crest and Canoe — A29

Designs: Various family crests and canoes.

**1974, Mar. 4** **Litho.** ***Perf. 13½***

| No. | Type | Description | Unused | Used |
|---|---|---|---|---|
| *222* | A29 | 3c tan & multi | 12 | 12 |
| *223* | A29 | 10c lt bl & multi | 40 | 40 |
| *224* | A29 | 35c yel & multi | 1.25 | 1.25 |
| *225* | A29 | 50c pink & multi | 1.65 | 1.65 |
| *a.* | | Souvenir sheet of 4 | 5.75 | 5.75 |

No. 225a contains one each of Nos. 222-225. Multicolored margin. Size: 154x130mm.

UPU Emblem, "Te Koroba" and No. 26 — A30

UPU cent.: 10c, Sailing ship "Kiakia" and No. 51. 25c, BAC 111 jet and No. 187. 35c, UPU emblem.

**1974, June 10** ***Perf. 14***

| No. | Type | Description | Unused | Used |
|---|---|---|---|---|
| *226* | A30 | 4c bl grn & multi | 12 | 12 |
| *227* | A30 | 10c org & multi | 32 | 32 |
| *228* | A30 | 25c dp bl & multi | 80 | 80 |
| *229* | A30 | 35c red org & blk | 1.10 | 1.10 |

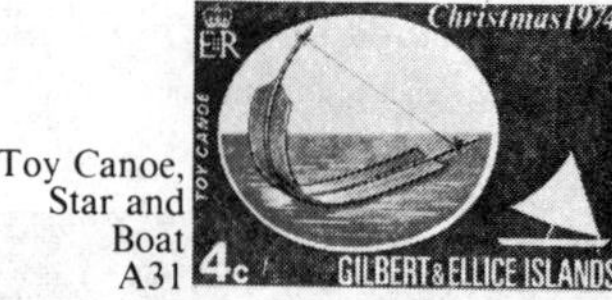

Toy Canoe, Star and Boat A31

Designs (Star of Bethlehem and): 10c, Pinwheel and boat. 25c, Coconut ball (crate) and boat. 35c, Three boats (Wise Men) and stars.

**1974, Sept. 23**

| No. | Type | Description | Unused | Used |
|---|---|---|---|---|
| *230* | A31 | 4c yel grn & multi | 12 | 12 |
| *231* | A31 | 10c red brn & multi | 30 | 30 |
| *232* | A31 | 25c multi | 75 | 75 |
| *233* | A31 | 35c red brn & multi | 1.10 | 1.10 |

Christmas 1974.

A particular stamp may be scarce, but if few collectors want it, its market value may remain relatively low.

Blenheim Palace, Entrance — A32

Churchill Painting — A33

Design: 35c, Churchill Statue, London.

**1974, Nov. 30** **Litho.** ***Perf. 14***

| No. | Type | Description | Unused | Used |
|---|---|---|---|---|
| *234* | A32 | 4c multi | 16 | 16 |
| *235* | A33 | 10c ultra & blk | 35 | 35 |
| *236* | A33 | 35c bl, ocher & blk | 1.10 | 1.10 |

Sir Winston Churchill (1874-1965).

Carpilius Maculatus A34

Crabs: 10c, Ranina ranina. 25c, Portunus pelagicus. 35c, Ocypode ceratophthalma.

**1975, Jan. 27** **Litho.** ***Perf. 14***

| No. | Type | Description | Unused | Used |
|---|---|---|---|---|
| *237* | A34 | 4c vio & multi | 18 | 18 |
| *238* | A34 | 10c grn & multi | 55 | 55 |
| *239* | A34 | 25c buff & multi | 1.50 | 1.50 |
| *240* | A34 | 35c lt bl & multi | 2.25 | 2.25 |

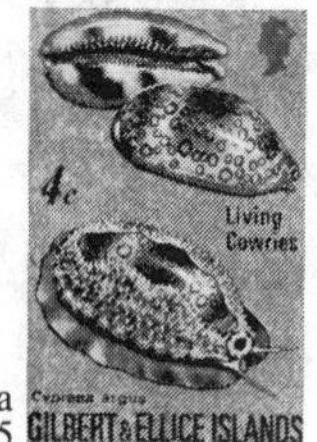

Cypraea Argus — A35

Designs: Living cowries and empty shells.

**Wmk. 314**

**1975, May 26** **Litho.** ***Perf. 14***

| No. | Type | Description | Unused | Used |
|---|---|---|---|---|
| *241* | A35 | 4c *shown* | 25 | 25 |
| *242* | A35 | 10c *Cypraea cribraria* | 60 | 60 |
| *243* | A35 | 25c *Cypraea talpa* | 1.50 | 1.50 |
| *244* | A35 | 35c *Cypraea mappa* | 2.25 | 2.25 |
| *a.* | | Souvenir sheet of 4 | 8.50 | 8.50 |

No. 244a contains one each of Nos. 241-244, multicolored margin showing lagoon. Size: 146x135mm.

Map of Beru (The Bud) A36

Designs: 10c, Map of Onotoa (Six Giants). 25c, Map of Abaiang (Land to the North). 35c, Map of Marakei (Floating fish trap).

**Wmk. 314**

**1975, Aug. 1** **Litho.** ***Perf. 14***

| No. | Type | Description | Unused | Used |
|---|---|---|---|---|
| *245* | A36 | 4c brt grn & multi | 14 | 14 |
| *246* | A36 | 10c brn & multi | 35 | 35 |
| *247* | A36 | 25c vio bl & multi | 85 | 85 |
| *248* | A36 | 35c org red & multi | 1.25 | 1.25 |

Legends of island names.

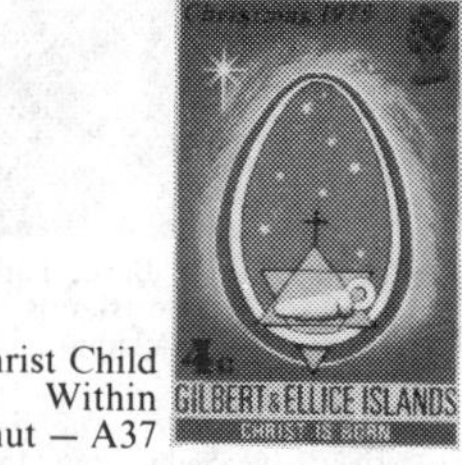

Christ Child Within Coconut — A37

Christmas: 10c, Sadd Memorial Chapel (Protestant), Tarawa. 25c, R.C. Church, Ocean Island. 35c, Fishermen in outrigger canoes seeing star.

**1975, Sept. 22** ***Perf. 14***

| No. | Type | Description | Unused | Used |
|---|---|---|---|---|
| *249* | A37 | 4c brn & multi | 12 | 12 |
| *250* | A37 | 10c brt bl & multi | 28 | 28 |
| *251* | A37 | 25c vio & multi | 85 | 75 |
| *252* | A37 | 35c grn & multi | 1.25 | 1.10 |

## POSTAGE DUE STAMPS

D1

**1940, Aug.** **Typo.** **Wmk. 4** ***Perf. 12***

| No. | Type | Description | Unused | Used |
|---|---|---|---|---|
| *J1* | D1 | 1p emerald | 1.25 | *1.90* |
| *J2* | D1 | 2p dk red | 2.25 | *3.25* |
| *J3* | D1 | 3p chocolate | 3.25 | *4.75* |
| *J4* | D1 | 4p dp bl | 4.25 | *6.50* |
| *J5* | D1 | 5p dp grn | 5.25 | *8.25* |
| *J6* | D1 | 6p brt red vio | 6.50 | *10.00* |
| *J7* | D1 | 1sh dl vio | 10.50 | *16.00* |
| *J8* | D1 | 1sh6p turq grn | 26.00 | *37.50* |
| | | *Nos. J1-J8 (8)* | 59.25 | 88.15 |

## WAR TAX STAMP

No. 15a Overprinted **WAR TAX**

**1918** **Wmk. 3** ***Perf. 14.***

| No. | Type | Description | Unused | Used |
|---|---|---|---|---|
| *MR1* | A3 | 1p scarlet | 60 | 50 |

# GILBERT ISLANDS

LOCATION — A group of islands in the Pacific Ocean northeast of Australia.
GOVT. — British Crown Colony.
AREA — 270 sq. mi.
POP. — 52,000 (1973).
CAPITAL — Tarawa.

The Gilbert Islands Colony consists of the Gilbert Islands, Phoenix, Ocean and Line Islands. They were part of the Gilbert and Ellice Islands colony until 1976. See Tuvalu.

**Catalogue values for all unused stamps in this country are for Never Hinged items.**

Stamps and Types of Gilbert and Ellice Islands 1971 Overprinted in Red, Black or Gold

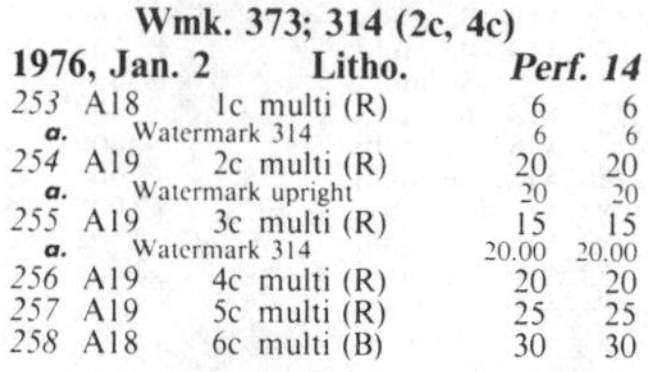


**Wmk. 373; 314 (2c, 4c)**

**1976, Jan. 2** **Litho.** ***Perf. 14***

| No. | Type | Description | Unused | Used |
|---|---|---|---|---|
| *253* | A18 | 1c multi (R) | 6 | 6 |
| *a.* | | Watermark 314 | 6 | 6 |
| *254* | A19 | 2c multi (R) | 20 | 20 |
| *a.* | | Watermark upright | 20 | 20 |
| *255* | A19 | 3c multi (R) | 15 | 15 |
| *a.* | | Watermark 314 | 20.00 | 20.00 |
| *256* | A19 | 4c multi (R) | 20 | 20 |
| *257* | A19 | 5c multi (R) | 25 | 25 |
| *258* | A18 | 6c multi (B) | 30 | 30 |
| *259* | A18 | 8c multi (R) | 35 | 35 |
| *260* | A18 | 10c multi (B) | 45 | 45 |
| *261* | A18 | 15c multi (B) | 90 | 80 |
| *262* | A19 | 20c multi (R) | 1.40 | 1.40 |
| *a.* | | Wmk. 314 sideways | 2.00 | 1.75 |
| *b.* | | Wmk. 314 upright | 70.00 | 70.00 |
| *263* | A19 | 25c multi (B) | 1.90 | 1.65 |
| *a.* | | Watermark 314 | 45.00 | 45.00 |
| *264* | A19 | 35c multi (G) | 2.75 | 2.00 |
| *265* | A18 | 50c multi (B) | 5.00 | 4.00 |
| *266* | A18 | $1 multi (R) | 30.00 | 25.00 |
| | | *Nos. 253-266 (14)* | 43.91 | 36.81 |

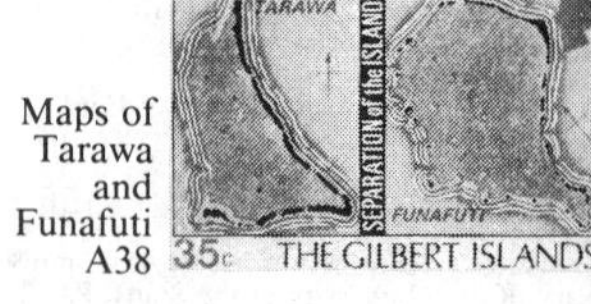

Maps of Tarawa and Funafuti A38

Design: 4c, Charts of Gilbert and Tuvalu Islands.

**1976, Jan. 2** **Wmk. 373**

| No. | Type | Description | Unused | Used |
|---|---|---|---|---|
| *267* | A38 | 4c multi | 32 | 25 |
| *268* | A38 | 35c multi | 4.00 | 3.00 |

Separation of the Gilbert and Ellice Islands.

M.V. Teraaka A39

Designs: 3c, M.V. Tautunu. 4c, Moorish idol. 5c, Hibiscus. 6c, Reef egret. 7c, Roman Catholic Cathedral, Tarawa. 8c, Frangipani. 10c, Maneaba meeting house. 12c, Betio Harbor. 15c, Sunset. 20c, Marakei Atoll. 35c, Chapel, Tangintebu. 40c, Flamboyant tree. 50c, Hypolimnas bolina elliciana (butterfly). $1, Landing craft, Tabakea. $2, Gilbert Islands flag.

**1976, July 1** **Litho.** ***Perf. 14***

| No. | Type | Description | Unused | Used |
|---|---|---|---|---|
| *269* | A39 | 1c multi | 5 | 5 |
| *270* | A39 | 3c multi | 8 | 8 |
| *271* | A39 | 4c multi | 12 | 12 |
| *272* | A39 | 5c multi | 15 | 15 |
| *273* | A39 | 6c multi | 16 | 16 |
| *274* | A39 | 7c multi | 18 | 18 |
| *275* | A39 | 8c multi | 22 | 22 |
| *276* | A39 | 10c multi | 25 | 25 |
| *277* | A39 | 12c multi | 30 | 30 |
| *278* | A39 | 15c multi | 40 | 40 |
| *279* | A39 | 20c multi | 45 | 45 |
| *280* | A39 | 35c multi | 65 | 65 |
| *281* | A39 | 40c multi | 90 | 90 |
| *282* | A39 | 50c multi | 1.00 | 1.00 |
| *283* | A39 | $1 multi | 1.75 | 1.75 |
| *284* | A39 | $2 multi | 3.75 | 3.75 |
| | | *Nos. 269-284 (16)* | 10.41 | 10.41 |

Church A40

Children's Drawings: 15c, Feasting (vegetables, fish, pig, chicken; vert.). 20c, Communal meeting house (vert.). 35c, Children watching dancer.

**1976, Sept. 15** **Litho.** ***Perf. 14***

| No. | Type | Description | Unused | Used |
|---|---|---|---|---|
| *285* | A40 | 5c bl & multi | 35 | 30 |
| *286* | A40 | 15c grn & multi | 65 | 60 |
| *287* | A40 | 20c rose & multi | 1.10 | 90 |
| *288* | A40 | 35c sal & multi | 2.75 | 2.50 |

Christmas 1976.

Porcupine Fish Helmet — A41

Prince Charles, 1970 Visit — A42

Scout Emblem, Beach Scene A45

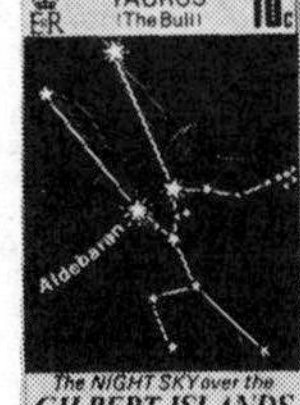

Taurus with Aldebaran A46

Artifacts: 15c, Shark's teeth dagger. 20c, Fighting gauntlet. 35c, Coconut body armor.

**1976, Dec. 6 Litho. *Perf. 13½x13***

| | | | |
|---|---|---|---|
| *289* A41 | 5c multi | 40 | 35 |
| *290* A41 | 15c multi | 65 | 60 |
| *291* A41 | 20c multi | 1.10 | 90 |
| *292* A41 | 35c multi | 2.75 | 2.50 |
| *a.* | Souvenir sheet of 4 | 12.50 | 10.00 |

No. 292a contains one each of Nos. 289-292; multicolored margin shows warrior in full armor. Size: 140x128mm.

**1977, Feb. 7 *Perf. 14***

Designs: 20c, Prince Philip, 1959 visit. 40c, Queen in coronation robes.

| | | | |
|---|---|---|---|
| *293* A42 | 8c multi | 25 | 20 |
| *294* A42 | 20c multi | 50 | 40 |
| *295* A42 | 40c multi | 1.25 | 90 |

25th anniversary of the reign of Queen Elizabeth II.

John Byron and Dolphin, 1765 A43

Explorers: 15c, Edmund Fanning, 1798, and "Betsey." 20c, Fabian Gottlieb von Bellingshausen, 1820, and "Vostok." 35c, Charles Wilkes, 1838-42, and "Vincennes."

**1977, June 1 Wmk. 373 *Perf. 14***

| | | | |
|---|---|---|---|
| *296* A43 | 5c multi | 75 | 60 |
| *297* A43 | 15c multi | 1.50 | 1.10 |
| *298* A43 | 20c multi | 2.50 | 2.00 |
| *299* A43 | 35c multi | 4.50 | 3.75 |

Resolution and Discovery off Christmas Island — A44

Designs: 15c, Capt. Cook's logbook entry, 1777 (horiz.). 20c, Capt. Cook on board ship. 40c, Capt. Cook landing on Christmas Island (horiz.).

**1977, Sept. 12 Litho. *Perf. 14***

| | | | |
|---|---|---|---|
| *300* A44 | 8c multi | 75 | 60 |
| *301* A44 | 15c multi | 90 | 80 |
| *302* A44 | 20c multi | 1.50 | 1.25 |
| *303* A44 | 40c multi | 3.00 | 2.50 |
| *a.* | Souvenir sheet of 4 | 11.00 | 11.00 |

Christmas 1977 and bicentenary of Capt. Cook's discovery of Christmas Island. No. 303a contains one each of Nos. 300-303; blue and multicolored margin shows map and route of "Resolution." Size: 143x142mm.

Designs: 15c, Patrol meeting (horiz.). 20c, Scout weaving mat (horiz.). 40c, Canoeing.

**1977, Dec. 5 Litho. *Perf. 13***

| | | | |
|---|---|---|---|
| *304* A45 | 8c gold & multi | 60 | 50 |
| *305* A45 | 15c gold & multi | 80 | 75 |
| *306* A45 | 20c gold & multi | 1.25 | 1.00 |
| *307* A45 | 40c gold & multi | 2.50 | 1.75 |

50th anniversary of Gilbert Islands Scouting.

**1978, Feb. 20 Litho. *Perf. 14***

Night Sky over Gilbert Islands: 20c, Canis Major with Sirius. 25c, Scorpio with Antares. 45c, Orion with Betelgeuse and Rigel.

| | | | |
|---|---|---|---|
| *308* A46 | 10c bl & blk | 35 | 28 |
| *309* A46 | 20c dp rose & blk | 90 | 70 |
| *310* A46 | 25c ol grn & blk | 1.10 | 90 |
| *311* A46 | 45c org & blk | 2.25 | 1.75 |

**Elizabeth II Coronation Anniversary Issue**

Souvenir Sheet

Common Design Types

**1978, Apr. 21 Unwmk.**

| | | | |
|---|---|---|---|
| *312* | Sheet of 6 | 4.50 | 4.50 |
| *a.* | CD326 45c *Unicorn of Scotland* | 75 | 75 |
| *b.* | CD327 45c *Elizabeth II* | 75 | 75 |
| *c.* | CD328 45c *Great frigate bird* | 75 | 75 |

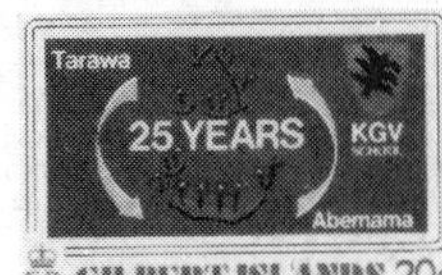

Arrows, Tarawa and Abemama Islands, School Insignia A47

Designs: 10c, Birds inscribed Bikenibeu, Abemama, Bairiki (school locations). 25c, Children greeting each other from maps of Islands. 45c, Abemama and Tarawa school buildings.

***Perf. 14x13½***

**1978, June 5 Litho. Wmk. 373**

| | | | |
|---|---|---|---|
| *313* A47 | 10c multi | 38 | 25 |
| *314* A47 | 20c multi | 75 | 50 |
| *315* A47 | 25c multi | 1.00 | 75 |
| *316* A47 | 45c multi | 1.90 | 1.50 |

King George V School, 25th anniversary of return from Abemama to Tarawa.

Garland A48

Designs: Various garlands.

**1978, Sept. 4 Litho. *Perf. 14***

| | | | |
|---|---|---|---|
| *317* A48 | 10c multi | 40 | 35 |
| *318* A48 | 20c multi | 50 | 45 |
| *319* A48 | 25c multi | 85 | 80 |
| *320* A48 | 45c multi | 1.75 | 1.50 |
| *a.* | Souvenir sheet of 4 | 7.50 | 7.50 |

Christmas 1978. No. 320a contains Nos. 317-320, perf. 13x13½; multicolored margin shows Gilbert Islanders. Size: 148x98mm.

Endeavour A49

Designs: 20c, Green turtle. 25c, Quadrant. 45c, Capt. Cook after Flaxman/Wedgwood medallion.

**1979, Jan. 15 Litho. *Perf. 11***

| | | | |
|---|---|---|---|
| *321* A49 | 10c multi | 40 | 30 |
| *322* A49 | 20c multi | 55 | 50 |
| *323* A49 | 25c multi | 75 | 70 |

**Litho.; Embossed**

| | | | |
|---|---|---|---|
| *324* A49 | 45c multi | 1.10 | 90 |

Capt. Cook's voyages.

Gilbert Islands stamps were replaced in 1979 by those of Kiribati.

## GOLD COAST

LOCATION — West Africa between Dahomey and Ivory Coast.
GOVT. — Former British Crown Colony.
AREA — 91,843 sq. mi.
POP. — 3,089,000 (1952).
CAPITAL — Accra.

Attached to the colony were Ashanti and Northern Territories (protectorate). Togoland, under British mandate, was also included for administrative porposes.

Gold Coast became the independent state of Ghana in 1957. (See Ghana.)

12 Pence = 1 Shilling
20 Shillings = 1 Pound

**Catalogue values for unused stamps in this country are for Never Hinged items, beginning with Scott 128.**

Queen Victoria
A1 A3

***Perf. 12½***

**1875, July Typo. Wmk. 1**

| | | | |
|---|---|---|---|
| *1* A1 | 1p blue | 350.00 | 70.00 |
| *2* A1 | 4p red violet | 375.00 | 125.00 |
| *3* A1 | 6p orange | 525.00 | 100.00 |

**1876-79 *Perf. 14.***

| | | | |
|---|---|---|---|
| *4* A1 | ½p bis ('79) | 16.00 | 17.50 |
| *5* A1 | 1p blue | 10.50 | 4.25 |
| *a.* | Half used as ½p on cover | | 1,600. |
| *6* A1 | 2p grn ('79) | 25.00 | 10.50 |
| *a.* | Half used as 1p on cover | | 1,800. |
| *7* A1 | 4p red vio | 125.00 | 6.75 |
| *a.* | Quarter used as 1p on cover | | 4,000. |
| *8* A1 | 6p orange | 67.50 | 13.00 |
| *a.* | One sixth used as 1p on cover | | |

Handstamp Surcharged "1D" in Black

**1883, May**

*9* A1 1p on 4p red vio

Some experts question the status of No. 9.

**1883-91 Wmk. Crown and C. A. (2)**

| | | | |
|---|---|---|---|
| *10* A1 | ½p bis ('83) | 100.00 | 32.50 |
| *11* A1 | ½p grn ('84) | 40 | 35 |
| *12* A1 | 1p bl ('83) | 625.00 | 50.00 |
| *13* A1 | 1p rose ('84) | 65 | 32 |
| *a.* | Half used as ½p on cover | | 2,500. |
| *14* A1 | 2p gray ('84) | 1.60 | 52 |
| *a.* | Value omitted | | |
| *b.* | Half used as 1p on cover | | |
| *15* A1 | 2½p bl & org ('91) | 80 | 52 |
| *16* A1 | 3p ol grn ('89) | 1.50 | 1.50 |
| *a.* | 3p ol bis | 2.00 | 2.00 |
| *17* A1 | 4p dl vio ('84) | 1.25 | 1.00 |
| *a.* | 4p cl | 3.25 | 3.50 |
| *b.* | Half used as 2p on cover | | |
| *18* A1 | 6p org ('89) | 2.00 | 1.10 |
| *a.* | One sixth used as 1p on cover | | |
| *19* A1 | 1sh pur ('88) | 3.25 | 1.25 |
| *20* A1 | 2sh brn ('84) | 13.00 | 11.00 |
| *a.* | 2sh yel brn | 57.50 | 52.50 |

ONE PENNY

No. 18 Surcharged in Black

**1889, Mar.**

| | | | |
|---|---|---|---|
| *21* A1 | 1p on 6p org | 100.00 | 40.00 |

The surcharge exists in two spacings between "PENNY" and bar: 7mm and 8mm.

**1889**

| | | | |
|---|---|---|---|
| *22* A3 | 5sh lil & ultra | 26.00 | 8.75 |
| *23* A3 | 10sh lil & red | 52.50 | 15.00 |
| *24* A3 | 20sh grn & red | 3,750. | |

**1894**

| | | | |
|---|---|---|---|
| *25* A3 | 20sh vio & blk, *red* | 140.00 | 22.50 |

**1898-1902**

| | | | |
|---|---|---|---|
| *26* A3 | ½p lil & grn | 55 | 18 |
| *27* A3 | 1p lil & car rose | 24 | 12 |
| *28* A3 | 2p lil & red ('02) | 12.50 | *52.50* |
| *29* A3 | 2½p lil & ultra | 3.00 | 2.50 |
| *30* A3 | 3p lil & yel | 3.00 | 1.40 |
| *31* A3 | 6p lil & pur | 3.00 | 85 |
| *32* A3 | 1sh gray grn & blk | 5.00 | 2.75 |
| *33* A3 | 2sh gray grn & car rose | 15.00 | 12.00 |
| *34* A3 | 5sh grn & lil ('00) | 37.50 | 17.00 |
| *35* A3 | 10sh grn & brn ('00) | 77.50 | 30.00 |
| | *Nos. 26-35 (10)* | 157.29 | 119.30 |

Numerals of 2p, 3p and 6p of type A3 are in color on colorless tablet.

ONE PENNY

Nos. 29 and 31 Surcharged in Black

**1901, Oct. 6**

| | | | |
|---|---|---|---|
| *36* A3 | 1p on 2½p lilac & ultra | 90 | 90 |
| *37* A3 | 1p on 6p lil & pur | 45 | 1.50 |
| *a.* | "ONE" omitted | 500.00 | *575.00* |

King Edward VII
A5 A6

**1902 Wmk. Crown and C. A. (2)**

| | | | |
|---|---|---|---|
| *38* A5 | ½p vio & grn | 24 | 15 |
| *39* A5 | 1p vio & car rose | 18 | 12 |
| *40* A5 | 2p vio & red org | 3.00 | 2.50 |
| *41* A5 | 2½p vio & ultra | 3.00 | 1.65 |
| *42* A5 | 3p vio & org | 1.75 | 75 |
| *43* A5 | 6p vio & pur | 3.25 | 1.00 |
| *44* A5 | 1sh grn & blk | 3.00 | 1.25 |
| *45* A5 | 2sh grn & car rose | 12.00 | 7.50 |
| *46* A5 | 5sh grn & vio | 15.00 | 18.00 |
| *47* A5 | 10sh grn & brn | 32.50 | *45.00* |
| *48* A5 | 20sh vio & blk, *red* | 110.00 | 100.00 |
| | *Nos. 38-48 (11)* | 183.92 | 177.92 |

Numerals of 2p, 3p, 6p and 2sh6p of type A5 are in color on colorless tablet.

**1904-07 Wmk. 3**

| | | | |
|---|---|---|---|
| *49* A5 | ½p vio & grn ('07) | 3.25 | 45 |
| *50* A5 | 1p vio & car rose | 2.25 | 28 |
| *51* A5 | 2p vio & red org | 1.65 | 40 |
| *52* A5 | 2½p vio & ultra ('06) | 24.00 | 13.00 |
| *53* A5 | 3p vio & org ('05) | 5.25 | 80 |
| *54* A5 | 6p vio & pur ('06) | 7.75 | 1.50 |
| *55* A5 | 2sh 6p grn & yel ('06) | 26.00 | *55.00* |
| | *Nos. 49-55 (7)* | 70.15 | *71.43* |

Nos. 49 and 52 are on ordinary paper. Nos. 50, 51, 53 and 54 are on both ordinary and chalky paper. No. 55 is on chalky paper.

**1907-13** **Ordinary Paper.**

*56* A5 ½p green 20 12
*57* A5 1p carmine 2.00 8
*58* A5 2p gray ('09) 1.25 50
*59* A5 2½p ultra 1.25 65

**Chalky Paper**

*60* A5 3p vio, *yel* ('09) 1.65 40
*61* A5 6p dl vio ('08) 4.00 1.40
**a.** 6p dl vio & red vio 1.25 1.25
*62* A5 1sh *grn* ('09) 3.75 1.00
*63* A5 2sh vio & bl, *bl* ('10) 6.25 6.25
*64* A5 2sh 6p blk & red, *bl* ('11) 10.00 *25.00*
*65* A5 5sh grn & red, *yel* ('13) 25.00 *55.00*
*Nos. 56-65 (10)* 55.35 *90.40*

No. 63 is on both ordinary and chalky paper.

**1908** **Ordinary Paper**

*66* A6 1p carmine 15 5

King George V
A7 A8

For description of Dies I and II, see back of this section of the Catalogue.

Die I

**1913-21** **Ordinary Paper**

*69* A7 ½p green 24 9
*70* A8 1p carmine 12 5
**a.** 1p scar 30 5
*71* A7 2p gray 1.75 60
*72* A7 2½p ultra 70 454

**Chalky Paper.**

*73* A7 3p vio, *yel* ('15) 70 14
**a.** Die II ('19) 5.75 4.75
*74* A7 6p dl vio & red vio 1.00 90
*75* A7 1sh *green* 1.00 70
**a.** 1sh *emer* 1.90 80
**b.** 1sh *bl grn*, ol back 1.00 70
**c.** Die II ('21) 1.90 80
*76* A7 2sh vio & bl, *bl* 5.75 1.75
**a.** Die II ('21) 225.00 60.00
*77* A7 2sh6pblk & red, *bl* 5.75 4.25
**a.** Die II ('21) 22.50 22.50
*78* A7 5sh grn & red, *yel* 9.00 11.00
**a.** Die II ('21) 16.00 *35.00*
*79* A7 10sh grn & red, *grn* ('16) 14.00 18.00
**a.** 10sh grn & red, *emer* 18.00 18.00
**b.** 10sh grn & red, *bl grn*, ol back 16.00 18.00
*80* A7 20sh vio & blk, *red* ('16) 80.00 45.00
*Nos. 69-80 (12)* 120.01 87.02

**Surface-colored Paper**

*81* A7 3p vio, *yel* 45 45
*82* A7 5sh grn & red, *yel* 7.00 *17.50*

Numerals of 2p, 3p, 6p and 2sh6p of type A7 are in color on plain tablet.

Die II

**1921-25** **Ordinary Paper** **Wmk. 4**

*83* A7 ½p grn ('22) 12 6
*84* A8 1p brn ('22) 14 5
*85* A7 1½p car ('22) 45 5
*86* A7 2p gray 55 18
*87* A7 2½p org ('23) 40 *3.25*
*88* A7 3p ultra ('22) 55 22

**Chalky Paper**

*89* A7 6p dl vio & red vio ('22) 65 90
*90* A7 1sh blk, *emer* ('25) 2.25 3.25
*91* A7 2sh vio & bl, *bl*('24) 2.25 *4.25*
*92* A7 2sh6pblk & red, *bl*('25) 3.75 *8.75*
*93* A7 5sh grn & red, *yel*('25) 8.75 *16.00*

**Die I**

*94* A7 15sh dl vio & grn ('21) 130.00 *250.00*
**a.** Die II ('25) 120.00 *250.00*
*95* A7 £2 grn & org 250.00 *625.00*
*Nos. 83-94 (12)* 149.86 *286.96*

Christiansborg Castle — A9

**1928** **Photo.** ***Perf. 13½x14½***

*98* A9 ½p green 5 5
*99* A9 1p red brn 6 5
*100* A9 1½p scarlet 26 18
*101* A9 2p slate 14 9
*102* A9 2½p yellow 65 *2.25*
*103* A9 3p ultra 30 18
*104* A9 6p dl vio & blk 45 22
*105* A9 1sh red org & blk 1.10 90
*106* A9 2sh pur & blk 4.50 4.00
*107* A9 5sh ol grn & car 17.50 17.50
*Nos. 98-107 (10)* 25.01 25.42

**Silver Jubilee Issue.**
Common Design Type

**1935, May 6** **Engr.** ***Perf. 11x12***

*108* CD301 1p blk & ultra 25 18
*109* CD301 3p ultra & brn 90 65
*110* CD301 6p ind & grn 3.00 2.75
*111* CD301 1sh brn vio & ind 3.25 3.50

**Coronation Issue.**
Common Design Type

**1937, May 12** ***Perf. 11x11½***

*112* CD302 1p brown 8 8
*113* CD302 2p dk gray 15 15
*114* CD302 3p dp ultra 25 25

George VI and Christiansborg Castle
A10 A11

**1938-41** **Wmk. 4** ***Perf. 12***

*115* A10 ½p green 5 5
*116* A10 1p red brn 6 5
*117* A10 1½p rose red 7 5
*118* A10 2p gray blk 24 5
*119* A10 3p ultra 8 7
*120* A10 4p rose lil 9 8
*121* A10 6p rose vio 14 12
*122* A10 9p red org 30 30
*123* A11 1sh gray grn & blk 30 18
*124* A11 1sh3p turq grn & red brn ('41) 28 25
*125* A11 2sh dk vio & dp bl 1.50 35
*126* A11 5sh rose car & ol grn 1.50 1.25
*127* A11 10sh pur & blk ('40) 3.00 2.75
*Nos. 115-127 (13)* 7.61 5.55

**Catalogue values for unused stamps in this section, from this point to the end of the section, are for Never Hinged items.**

**Peace Issue**
Common Design Type

**1946, Oct. 14** ***Perf. 13½***

*128* CD303 2p purple 15 15
**a.** Perf. 13½x14 2.25 75
*129* CD303 4p dp red vio 22 22
**a.** Perf. 13½x14 4.25 1.50

Mounted Constable — A12

Christiansborg Castle — A13

Designs: 1½p, Emblem of Joint Provincial Council. 2p, Talking Drums. 2½p, Map. 3p, Manganese mine. 4p, Lake Bosumtwi. 6p, Cacao farmer. 1sh, Breaking cacao pods. 2sh, Trooping the colors. 5sh, Surfboats. 10sh, Forest.

**Wmk. 4**

**1948, July 1** **Engr.** ***Perf. 12***

*130* A12 ½p emerald 7 7
*131* A13 1p dp bl 15 7
*132* A13 1½p red 18 15
*133* A12 2p chocolate 22 7
*134* A13 2½p lt brn & red 50 26
*135* A13 3p blue 30 18
*136* A13 4p dk car rose 65 50
*137* A12 6p org & blk 42 26
*138* A13 1sh red org & blk 75 26
*139* A13 2sh rose car & ol brn 2.50 60
*140* A13 5sh gray & red vio 7.75 2.50
*141* A12 10sh ol grn & blk 10.00 5.00
*Nos. 130-141 (12)* 23.49 9.92

**Silver Wedding Issue**
Common Design Types

**1948, Dec. 20** **Photo.** ***Perf. 14x14½***

*142* CD304 1½p scarlet 14 14

**Engraved; Name Typographed**
***Perf. 11½x11***

*143* CD305 10sh dk brn ol 10.00 10.00

**UPU Issue**
Common Design Types

**Engr.; Name Typo. on 2½p and 3p**

**1949, Oct. 10** ***Perf. 13½, 11x11½***

*144* CD306 2p red brn 22 22
*145* CD307 2½p dp org 35 35
*146* CD308 3p indigo 85 85
*147* CD309 1sh bl grn 2.25 2.25

Common Design Types pictured in section before Great Britain.

Map of West Africa A14 — Mounted Constable A15

Designs: 1p, Christiansborg Castle. 1½p, Emblem of Joint Provincial Council. 2p, Talking drums. 3p, Manganese mine. 4p, Lake Bosumtwi. 6p, Cacao farmer. 1sh, Breaking cacao pods. 2sh, Trooping the colors. 5sh, Surfboats. 10sh, Forest.

***Perf. 11½x12, 12x11½***

**1952-54** **Engr.**

*148* A14 ½p yel brn & car ('53) 12 7
*149* A14 1p dp bl 9 5
*150* A14 1½p grn ('53) 9 7
*151* A15 2p chocolate 12 5
*152* A15 2½p red ('52) 16 12
*153* A14 3p rose ('53) 20 8
*154* A14 4p dp bl ('53) 22 12
*155* A15 6p org & blk 28 9
*156* A14 1sh red org & blk 55 14
*157* A14 2sh rose car & ol brn 1.10 40
*158* A14 5sh gray & red vio 5.50 90
*159* A15 10sh ol grn & blk 9.00 2.00
*Nos. 148-159 (12)* 17.43 4.09

Nos. 148-149 exist in vertical coils.

**Coronation Issue**
Common Design Type

**1953, June 2** ***Perf. 13½x13***

*160* CD312 2p dk brn & blk 18 7

Gold Coast stamps were replaced in 1957 by those of Ghana.

**POSTAGE DUE STAMPS**

D1

**1923-52** **Typo.** **Wmk. 4** ***Perf. 14***

*J1* D1 ½p black 19.00 *80.00*
*J2* D1 1p black 55 55
*J3* D1 2p black 55 *1.90*
**a.** Wmk. 4a (error) 85.00
*J4* D1 3p black 70 *2.75*
**a.** Wmk. 4a (error) 85.00
*J5* D1 6p black ('52) 1.40 *5.50*
**a.** Wmk. 4a (error) 125.00
*J6* D1 1sh black ('52) 2.75 *8.00*
**a.** Wmk. 4a (error) 175.00
*Nos. J1-J6 (6)* 24.95 98.70

**WAR TAX STAMP**

WAR TAX
ONE PENNY

Regular Issue of 1913 Surcharged

**1918, June** **Wmk. 3** ***Perf. 14***

*MR1* A8 1p on 1p scar 12 9

## GRENADA

LOCATION — in Windward Islands, West Indies.
GOVT. — Independent nation in the British Commonwealth.
AREA — 133 sq. mi.
POP. — 115,000 (est. 1981)
CAPITAL — St. George's

Grenada consists of Grenada Island and the southern Grenadines, including Carriacou. This colony was granted associated statehood with Great Britain in 1967 and became an independent state Feb. 7, 1974.

12 Pence = 1 Shilling
100 Cents = 1 Dollar (1949)

**Catalogue values for unused stamps in this country are for Never Hinged items, beginning with Scott 143 in the regular postage section, Scott B1 in the semi-postal section, Scott C1 in the air post section, Scott J15 in the postage due section, and Scott O1 in the official section.**

Queen Victoria — A1

***Rough Perf. 14 to 16***

**1861** **Engr.** **Unwmk.**

*1* A1 1p green 65.00 55.00
**a** 1p bl grn 3,500. 300.00
**b** Horiz. pair, imperf. btwn.
*2* A1 6p rose 625.00 100.00
**b** 6p lake red, perf. 11-12 1,000.

No. 2b was not issued. No. 2 imperf. is a proof.

Wmk. 5- Small Star

Wmk. 6- Large Star

**1863-71** **Wmk. 5**

*3* A1 1p grn ('64) 65.00 15.00
*4* A1 6p rose 400.00 25.00
*5* A1 6p ver ('71) 500.00 25.00
**a** 6p dl red 2,250. 175.00
**g** Double impression 2,000.

**1873-78** ***Clean-Cut Perf. about 15***

*5B* A1 1p dp grn 45.00 35.00
**c** 1p bl grn ('78) 300.00 40.00
**h** Half used as ½p on cover 7,500.
*5D* A1 6p ver ('75) 625.00 40.00
**e** 6p dl red 625.00 40.00
**f** Double impression 1,750.

**1873** **Wmk. 6**

6 A1 1p bl grn 42.50 20.00
 a Diagonal half used as ½p on cover 7,500.
7 A1 6p vermilion 500.00 35.00

**1875** ***Perf. 14***

7A A1 1p yel grn 35.00 15.00
 b Half used as ½p on cover 7,500.

A2

A2a

Revenue Stamps Surcharged in Black.

**1875-81** ***Perf. 14, 14½***

8 A2 ½p pur ('81) 6.00 6.00
 a "OSTAGE" 150.00 125.00
 b Imperf., pair 300.00
 c "ALF" 2,000.
 d "PEN"
 e No hyphen between "HALF" and "PENNY" 150.00 100.00
 f Double surcharge 250.00 250.00
9 A2a 2½p lake ('81) 35.00 12.50
 a Imperf., pair 400.00
 b Imperf. vertically, pair 2,000.
 c "PENCF" 300.00 250.00
 d No period after "PENNY" 100.00 75.00
 e "PENOE" 150.00
10 A2 4p bl ('81) 80.00 25.00

**Revenue Stamps Surcharged in Dark Blue**

11 A2 1sh purple 400.00 22.50
 a "SHLLIING" 4,000. 850.00
 b "NE SHILLING" 2,500.
 c "OSTAGE" 1,400.
 d Inverted "S" in "POSTAGE" 3,500. 1,000.

Large Star with Broad Points

**1881** **Wmk. 7**

12 A2 2½p lake 225.00 35.00
 a 2½p cl 500.00 110.00
 b "PENCF" 550.00 190.00
 c No period after "PENNY" 500.00 175.00
13 A2 4p blue 190.00 160.00

A3

A4

A5

A6

Revenue Stamp Overprinted "POSTAGE" in Black

**1883** **Wmk. 5**

**Denomination & Crown in 2nd Color**

14 A3 ½p org & grn 700.00 200.00
 a Unsevered pair 4,000. 1,500.
15 A4 ½p org & grn 125.00 90.00
 a Unsevered pair 1,250. 500.00
16 A5 1p org & grn 100.00 35.00
 a Invtd. overprint 1,250. 600.00
 b Double overprint 900.00 575.00
 c Inverted "S" in "Postage" 500.00 475.00

**"Postage" in Manuscript, Red or Black**

18 A6 1p org & grn (R) 2,500.
19 A6 1p org & grn 1,250.

On Nos. 14 to 19 the words "ONE PENNY" measure from 10 to 11¼mm. in length.

On No. 15, the lower "POSTAGE" is always inverted.

It has been claimed that although Nos. 18 and 19 were used, they were not officially issued.

A8

A10

**1883** **Wmk. 2** ***Perf. 14***

20 A8 ½p green 1.10 1.10
 a Tete beche pair 2.75 4.50
21 A8 1p rose 22.50 3.50
 a Tete beche pair 150.00 175.00
22 A8 2½p ultra 5.50 .75
 a Tete beche pair 20.00 25.00
23 A8 4p slate 3.50 3.50
 a Tete beche pair 14.00 17.50
24 A8 6p red lil 5.00 6.50
 a Tete beche pair 20.00 30.00
25 A8 8p bister 10.00 12.00
 a Tete beche pair 30.00 37.50
26 A8 1sh violet 65.00 42.50
 a Tete beche pair 900.00 900.00
 *Nos. 20-26 (7)* 112.60 69.85

Stamps of types A8, A10 and D2 were printed with alternate horizontal rows inverted.

Revenue Stamps Surcharged

d.
1
POSTAGE.

**1886** **Wmk. Large Star. (6)**

27 A2 1p on 1½ org 25.00 20.00
 a Invtd. surch. 250.00 250.00
 b Diagonal half used as ½ on cover 1,500.
 c Dbl. surch. 250.00 250.00
 d "HALH" instead of "HALF" 250.00 250.00
28 A2 1p on 1sh org 22.50 22.50
 a "SHILLING" instead of "SHILLING" 450.00 400.00
 b No period after "POSTAGE"
 c Half used as ½p on cover 1,750.

**Wmk. Small Star. (5)**

29 A2 1p on 4p org 150.00 100.00

**1887** **Wmk. Crown and C. A. (2)**

30 A10 1p rose 25 25
 a Tete beche pair 2.25 4.50

Revenue Stamps Surcharged:

HALF
PENNY
POSTAGE
h

4d.
POSTAGE
i

POSTAGE
d.
AND 1
REVENUE
k

POSTAGE
AND
REVENUE
1d.
l

**1888-91** **Wmk. 5** ***Perf. 14½***

31 A2 (h) ½p on 2sh org ('89) 17.50 19.00
 a Double surch. 400.00 400.00
 b First "S" in "SHILLINGS" inverted 350.00 350.00
32 A2 (i) 4p on 2sh org 22.50 22.50
 a "4d" and "POSTAGE" 5mm apart 25.00 30.00
 b "S" inverted, as in #31b 550.00 550.00
 c As "a," invert. "S," as in #31b 500.00 500.00

**"d" vertical instead of slanting.**

33 A2 (i) 4p on 2sh org 600.00 600.00
34 A2 (k) 1p on 2sh org ('90) 55.00 55.00
 a Inverted surcharge 350.00 350.00
35 A2 (l) 1p on 2sh org ('91) 40.00 40.00
 a Inverted surcharge 350.00 350.00
 b No period after "d" 275.00 275.00

No. 25 Surcharged in Black:

POSTAGE
AND
REVENUE
1d. 2½d.

**Wmk. Crown and C.A. (2)**

36 A8 1p on 8p bis 12.50 12.50
 a Tete beche pair 90.00 125.00
 b Inverted surcharge 325.00 325.00
 c No period after "d" 300.00 300.00

**"2" of "½" Upright**

37 A8 2½p on 8p bis 22.50 22.50
 a Tete Beche pair 110.00 150.00
 b Inverted surcharge
 c Double surch. 600.00 750.00
 d Triple surcharge 1,100.
 e Double surcharge, one inverted 450.00 450.00

**"2" of "½" Italic**

38 A8 2½p on 8p bis 22.50 22.50
 a Tete beche pair 125.00 175.00
 b Tete beche pair, #37, 38 110.00
 c Inverted surcharge
 d Double surch. 650.00 750.00
 e Triple surcharge 1,100.
 f Triple surch., two inverted 1,000.

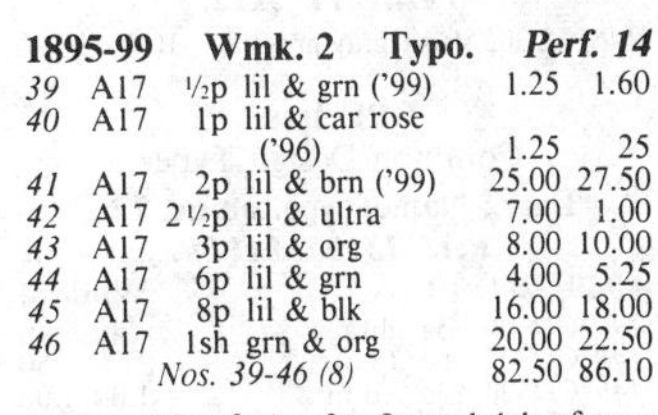
Queen Victoria — A17

**1895-99** **Wmk. 2** **Typo.** ***Perf. 14***

39 A17 ½p lil & grn ('99) 1.25 1.60
40 A17 1p lil & car rose ('96) 1.25 25
41 A17 2p lil & brn ('99) 25.00 27.50
42 A17 2½p lil & ultra 7.00 1.00
43 A17 3p lil & org 8.00 10.00
44 A17 6p lil & grn 4.00 5.25
45 A17 8p lil & blk 16.00 18.00
46 A17 1sh grn & org 20.00 22.50
 *Nos. 39-46 (8)* 82.50 86.10

Numerals of ½p, 3p, 8p and 1sh of type A17 are in color on colorless tablet.

Columbus' Flagship, La Concepcion
A18

King Edward VII
A19

**1898, Aug. 15** **Engr.** **Wmk. 1**

47 A18 2½p ultra 10.00 10.00
 a Bluish paper 50.00 60.00

Discovery of the island by Columbus, Aug. 15th, 1498.

**1902** **Wmk. 2** **Typo.**

48 A19 ½p vio & grn 30 35
49 A19 1p vio & car rose 40 15
50 A19 2p vio & brn 1.90 3.50
51 A19 2½p vio & ultra 2.25 2.50
52 A19 3p vio & org 2.25 2.75
53 A19 6p vio & grn 2.25 3.50
54 A19 1sh grn & org 5.00 7.50
55 A19 2sh grn & ultra 11.25 21.00
56 A19 5sh grn & car rose 20.00 30.00
57 A19 10sh grn & vio 82.50 100.00
 *Nos. 48-57 (10)* 128.10 171.25

Numerals of ½p, 3p, 1sh, 2sh and 10sh of type A19 are in color on colorless tablet.

**1904-06** **Wmk. 3** ***Perf. 14***

58 A19 ½p vio & grn 6.25 10.00
59 A19 1p vio & car rose 4.50 2.00
60 A19 2p vio & brn 17.50 20.00
61 A19 2½p vio & ultra 17.50 20.00
62 A19 3p vio & org 3.00 3.50
63 A19 6p vio & grn 4.50 5.00
64 A19 1sh grn & org 5.00 7.50
65 A19 2sh grn & ultra 7.50 15.00
66 A19 5sh grn & car rose 20.00 37.50
67 A19 10sh grn & vio 87.50 125.00
 *Nos. 58-67 (10)* 173.25 245.50

Nos. 62, 63 and 65 are on both ordinary and chalky paper.

Issue years: Nos. 58, 60-62, 64, 1905. Nos. 63, 65-67, 1906.

Seal of Colony
A20

King George V
A21

**1906-11** **Engr.**

68 A20 ½p green 70 15
69 A20 1p carmine 1.00 8
70 A20 2p yellow 1.75 3.25
71 A20 2½p blue 2.75 3.00
 a 2½p ultra 4.00 2.25

**Typo.**

**Chalky Paper**

**Numerals white on dark ground**

72 A20 3p vio, *yel* ('08) 1.75 2.50
73 A20 6p vio ('08) 6.25 7.50
74 A20 1sh *grn* ('11) 1.75 2.50
75 A20 2sh vio & bl, *bl* ('08) 6.25 7.50
76 A20 5sh red & grn, *yel* ('08) 20.00 27.50
 *Nos. 68-76 (9)* 42.20 53.98

**1908** **Wmk. Crown and C. A. (2)**

77 A20 1sh *green* 8.75 12.50
78 A20 10sh red & grn, *grn* 82.50 95.00

**1913** **Ordinary Paper.** **Wmk. 3**

79 A21 ½p green 12 12
80 A21 1p scarlet 75 40
 a 1p car 50 40
81 A21 2p orange 20 22
82 A21 2½p ultra 1.00 1.50

**Chalky Paper.**

83 A21 3p vio, *yel* 30 40
84 A21 6p dl vio & red vio 1.50 3.00
85 A21 1sh *green* 2.50 2.75
 a 1sh *emer* 1.75 2.00
 b 1sh *bl grn*, olive back 30.00 45.00
 c As "a," olive back 1.75 2.00
86 A21 2sh vio & ultra, *bl* 3.25 6.25
87 A21 5sh grn & red, *yel* 7.50 11.25
88 A21 10sh grn & red, *grn* 30.00 37.50
 a 10sh grn & red, *emer* 30.00 37.50
 *Nos. 79-88 (10)* 47.12 63.39

**1914** **Surface-colored Paper.**

89 A21 3p vio, *yel* 50 1.50
90 A21 1sh *green* 1.40 3.75

**1921-29** **Ordinary Paper** **Wmk. 4**

91 A21 1½p green 15 10
92 A21 1p rose red 20 10
93 A21 1p brn ('22) 20 10
94 A21 1½p rose red ('22) 40 25
95 A21 2p orange 25 25
96 A21 2p gray ('26) 2.00 1.90
97 A21 2½p ultra 75 1.00
98 A21 2½p gray ('22) 50 2.50
99 A21 3p ultra ('22) 1.75 3.25

**Chalky Paper.**

100 A21 3p vio, *yel* ('26) 1.25 2.50
101 A21 4p blk & red, *yel* ('26) 1.00 3.00
102 A21 5p gray vio & ol grn 65 2.50
103 A21 6p dl vio & red vio 1.90 4.00
104 A21 6p blk & red ('26) 2.00 3.25
105 A21 9p gray vio & blk 1.75 3.50
106 A21 1sh *emerald* 2.50 5.00
107 A21 1sh org brn ('26) 5.00 6.50
108 A21 2sh vio & ultra, *bl* 5.00 6.25
109 A21 2sh6p blk & red, *bl* ('29) 7.50 11.25
110 A21 3sh grn & vio 7.50 15.00
111 A21 5sh grn & red, *yel* 10.00 20.00
112 A21 10sh grn & red, *emer* 32.50 50.00
 *Nos. 91-112 (22)* 84.75 142.20

Demand, as well as supply, determines a stamp's market value. One is as important as the other.

Grand Anse Beach — A22

Seal of the Colony — A23

View of Grand Etang A24

View of St. George's A25

**1934, Oct. 23 Engr. *Perf. 12½***

| | | | | |
|---|---|---|---|---|
| *114* | A22 | ½p green | 14 | 14 |
| ***a*** | | Perf. 12½x13 ('36) | 4.50 | 6.50 |
| *115* | A23 | 1p blk brn & blk | 30 | 30 |
| ***a*** | | Perf. 13x12½ | 1.75 | 2.25 |
| *116* | A24 | 1½p car & blk | 90 | 75 |
| ***a*** | | Perf. 12½x13 ('36) | 2.75 | 3.00 |
| *117* | A23 | 2p org & blk | 40 | 45 |
| *118* | A25 | 2½p dp bl | 40 | 38 |
| *119* | A23 | 3p ol grn & blk | 1.75 | 2.00 |
| *120* | A23 | 6p cl & blk | 2.50 | 2.75 |
| *121* | A23 | 1sh brn & blk | 2.75 | 3.00 |
| *122* | A23 | 2sh6p ultra & blk | 15.00 | *17.50* |
| *123* | A23 | 5sh vio & blk | 22.50 | *30.00* |
| | | *Nos. 114-123 (10)* | 46.64 | 57.27 |

**Silver Jubilee Issue.**
Common Design Type

**1935, May 6 *Perf. 11x12***

| | | | | |
|---|---|---|---|---|
| *124* | CD301 | ½p grn & blk | 22 | 22 |
| *125* | CD301 | 1p blk & ultra | 340 | 340 |
| *126* | CD301 | 1½p car & bl | 80 | 80 |
| *127* | CD301 | 1sh brn vio & ind | 3.50 | 3.75 |

**Coronation Issue.**
Common Design Type
***Perf. 11x11½***

**1937, May 12 Wmk. 4**

| | | | | |
|---|---|---|---|---|
| *128* | CD302 | 1p dk pur | 18 | 18 |
| *129* | CD302 | 1½p dk car | 30 | 30 |
| *130* | CD302 | 2½p dp ultra | 38 | 38 |

King George VI — A26

Seal of the Colony — A28

Grand Anse Beach — A27

View of Grand Etang — A29

View of St. George's A30

Seal of the Colony A31

**1937, July 12 Photo. *Perf. 14½x14***

| | | | | |
|---|---|---|---|---|
| *131* | A26 | ¼p chestnut | 5 | 5 |

**1938-43 Engr. *Perf. 12½***

| | | | | |
|---|---|---|---|---|
| *132* | A27 | ½p green | 8 | 8 |
| ***a*** | | Perf. 12½x13½ | 75 | 75 |
| *133* | A28 | 1p blk brn & blk | 12 | 9 |
| ***a*** | | Perf. 13½x12½ | 14 | 12 |
| *134* | A29 | 1½p scar & blk | 12 | 9 |
| ***a*** | | 1½p car & blk, perf. 12½x13½ | 1.75 | 38 |
| *135* | A28 | 2p org & blk | 14 | 12 |
| ***a*** | | Perf. 13½x12½ | 18 | 14 |
| *136* | A30 | 2½p ultra | 14 | 14 |
| ***a*** | | Perf. 12½x13½ | *3,750.* | 275.00 |
| *137* | A28 | 3p ol grn & blk | 18 | 18 |
| ***a*** | | Perf. 13½x12½ | 38 | 38 |
| *138* | A28 | 6p red vio & blk | 22 | 22 |
| ***a*** | | Perf. 13½x12½ ('42) | 38 | 35 |
| *139* | A28 | 1sh org brn & blk | 50 | 50 |
| ***a*** | | Perf. 13½x12½ ('42) | 50 | 50 |
| *140* | A28 | 2sh ultra & blk | 1.25 | 1.25 |
| ***a*** | | Perf. 13½x12½ | 3.00 | 3.00 |
| *141* | A28 | 5sh pur & blk | 2.25 | 2.25 |
| ***a*** | | Perf. 13½x12½ | 4.50 | 4.75 |

***Perf. 14***

| | | | | |
|---|---|---|---|---|
| *142* | A31 | 10sh rose car & gray bl | 6.50 | 6.50 |
| ***a*** | | 10sh dp car & gray bl, perf. 12 ('43) | 200.00 | 200.00 |
| ***b*** | | Perf. 12x13 | 6.50 | 6.75 |
| | | *Nos. 131-142 (12)* | 11.55 | 11.47 |

**Catalogue values for unused stamps in this section, from this point to the end of the section, are for Never Hinged items.**

**Peace Issue.**
Common Design Type

**1946, Sept. 25 *Perf. 13½x14***

| | | | | |
|---|---|---|---|---|
| *143* | CD303 | 1½p carmine | 10 | 10 |
| *144* | CD303 | 3½p dp bl | 15 | 15 |

**Silver Wedding Issue.**
Common Design Types

**1948, Oct. 27 Photo. *Perf. 14x14½***

| | | | | |
|---|---|---|---|---|
| *145* | CD304 | 1½p scarlet | 12 | 12 |

**Engr.; Name Typo.**
***Perf. 11½x11.***

| | | | | |
|---|---|---|---|---|
| *146* | CD305 | 10sh gray grn | 10.00 | 10.00 |

**UPU Issue**
Common Design Types
**Engr.; Name Typo. on 6c, 12c.**
***Perf. 13½, 11x11½***

**1949, Oct. 10 Wmk. 4**

| | | | | |
|---|---|---|---|---|
| *147* | CD306 | 5c ultra | 40 | 40 |
| *148* | CD307 | 6c dp ol | 50 | 50 |
| *149* | CD308 | 12c red lil | 1.00 | 1.00 |
| *150* | CD309 | 24c red brn | 1.50 | 1.50 |

A32

A33

A34

**1951, Jan. 8 Engr. *Perf. 11½***
**Center in Black**

| | | | | |
|---|---|---|---|---|
| *151* | A32 | ½c chestnut | 18 | 18 |
| *152* | A32 | 1c bl grn | 18 | 18 |
| *153* | A32 | 2c dk brn | 20 | 18 |
| *154* | A32 | 3c carmine | 25 | 18 |
| *155* | A32 | 4c dp org | 30 | 25 |
| *156* | A32 | 5c purple | 50 | 50 |
| *157* | A32 | 6c olive | 50 | 45 |
| *158* | A32 | 7c blue | 50 | 40 |
| *159* | A32 | 12c red vio | 1.90 | 1.40 |

***Perf. 11½x12½***

| | | | | |
|---|---|---|---|---|
| *160* | A33 | 25c dk brn | 1.75 | 85 |
| *161* | A33 | 50c ultra | 1.60 | 1.00 |
| *162* | A33 | $1.50 orange | 7.50 | 6.00 |

***Perf. 11½x13.***
**Center in Gray Blue**

| | | | | |
|---|---|---|---|---|
| *163* | A34 | $2.50 dp car | 9.50 | 7.50 |
| | | *Nos. 151-163 (13)* | 24.86 | 19.07 |

See Nos. 180-183, 202.

**University Issue.**
Common Design Types

**1951, Feb. 16 *Perf. 14x14½***

| | | | | |
|---|---|---|---|---|
| *164* | CD310 | 3c dp car & gray blk | 30 | 30 |
| *165* | CD311 | 6c olive & blk | 50 | 50 |

**NEW CONSTITUTION**

Nos. 154-156 and 159 Overprinted in Black or Carmine

**1951**

**1951, Sept. 21 *Perf. 11½***

| | | | | |
|---|---|---|---|---|
| *166* | A32 | 3c car & blk | 22 | 22 |
| *167* | A32 | 4c dp org & blk | 32 | 32 |
| *168* | A32 | 5c pur & blk (C) | 35 | 35 |
| *169* | A32 | 12c red vio & blk | 55 | 55 |

Adoption of a new constitution for the Windward Islands.

**Coronation Issue.**
Common Design Type

**1953, June 3 *Perf. 13½x13***

| | | | | |
|---|---|---|---|---|
| *170* | CD312 | 3c car & blk | 20 | 20 |

Types of 1951 Inscribed "E II R" and

Queen Elizabeth II — A35

**1953-59 Engr. *Perf. 11½***
**Center in Black.**

| | | | | |
|---|---|---|---|---|
| *171* | A35 | ½c chnt ('54) | 5 | 5 |
| *172* | A35 | 1c bl grn | 6 | 5 |
| *173* | A35 | 2c dk brn | 8 | 6 |
| *174* | A35 | 3c car ('54) | 8 | 7 |
| *175* | A35 | 4c dp org ('54) | 12 | 10 |
| *176* | A35 | 5c pur ('54) | 14 | 12 |
| *177* | A35 | 6c olive | 24 | 20 |
| *178* | A35 | 7c bl ('55) | 28 | 25 |
| *179* | A35 | 12c red vio | 28 | 25 |

***Perf. 11½x12½***

| | | | | |
|---|---|---|---|---|
| *180* | A33 | 25c dk brn ('55) | 48 | 40 |
| *181* | A33 | 50c ultra ('55) | 2.25 | 1.50 |
| *182* | A33 | $1.50 org ('55) | 8.00 | 7.00 |

***Perf. 11½x13***
**Center in Gray Blue.**

| | | | | |
|---|---|---|---|---|
| *183* | A34 | $2.50 dp car ('59) | 8.00 | 7.00 |
| | | *Nos. 171-183 (13)* | 20.06 | 17.05 |

See Nos. 195-202.

No. 182 was locally surcharged "2" and two black horizontal lines and issued Dec. 23, 1965, for revenue use. It was used postally, though not authorized for postal use. The "2" is found in two type faces.

**West Indies Federation**
Common Design Type
***Perf. 11½x11***

**1958, Apr. 22 Wmk. 314**

| | | | | |
|---|---|---|---|---|
| *184* | CD313 | 3c green | 10 | 10 |
| *185* | CD313 | 6c blue | 20 | 20 |
| *186* | CD313 | 12c car rose | 40 | 40 |

Victoria and Elizabeth II and Mail Truck A36

Designs (Queens and): 8c, "La Concepcion" and Dakota plane. 25c, Steam Packet "Solent" and B.O.A.C. plane.

***Perf. 14½x14***

**1961, June 1 Photo. Wmk. 314**

| | | | | |
|---|---|---|---|---|
| *187* | A36 | 3c gray & dp car | 20 | 20 |
| *188* | A36 | 8c org & ultra | 48 | 48 |
| *189* | A36 | 25c bl & mar | 1.00 | 1.00 |

Centenary of first Grenada postage stamps.

**Freedom from Hunger Issue**
Common Design Type

**1963, June 4 *Perf. 14x14½***

| | | | | |
|---|---|---|---|---|
| *190* | CD314 | 8c green | 35 | 35 |

**Red Cross Centenary Issue**
Common Design Type

**1963, Sept. 2 Litho. *Perf. 13***

| | | | | |
|---|---|---|---|---|
| *191* | CD315 | 3c blk & red | 12 | 12 |
| *192* | CD315 | 25c ultra & red | 65 | 65 |

Types of 1953-55
**Wmk. 314**

**1963-64 Engr. *Perf. 11½***
**Center in Black**

| | | | | |
|---|---|---|---|---|
| *195* | A35 | 2c dk brn | 8 | 8 |
| *196* | A35 | 3c carmine | 9 | 9 |
| *197* | A35 | 4c dp org | 9 | 9 |
| *198* | A35 | 5c purple | 16 | 16 |
| *199* | A35 | 6c olive | 250.00 | 90.00 |
| *201* | A35 | 12c red vio | 35 | 35 |

***Perf. 11½x12½***

| | | | | |
|---|---|---|---|---|
| *202* | A33 | 25c dk brn | 80 | 80 |
| | | *Nos. 195-198,201-202 (6)* | 1.57 | 1.57 |

Issue dates: 6c in 1963; others, May 12, 1964.

**ITU Issue**
Common Design Type
***Perf. 11x11½***

**1965, May 17 Litho. Wmk. 314**

| | | | | |
|---|---|---|---|---|
| *205* | CD317 | 2c ver & ol | 6 | 6 |
| *206* | CD317 | 50c yel & ver | 70 | 70 |

**Intl. Cooperation Year Issue**
Common Design Type

**1965, Oct. 25 Litho. *Perf. 14½***

| | | | | |
|---|---|---|---|---|
| *207* | CD318 | 1c bl grn & cl | 6 | 6 |
| *208* | CD318 | 25c lt vio & grn | 50 | 50 |

**Churchill Memorial Issue**
Common Design Type

**1966, Jan. 24 Photo. *Perf. 14***
**Design in Black, Gold and Carmine Rose**

| | | | | |
|---|---|---|---|---|
| *209* | CD319 | 1c brt bl | 6 | 6 |
| *210* | CD319 | 3c green | 8 | 8 |
| *211* | CD319 | 25c brown | 45 | 45 |
| *212* | CD319 | 35c violet | 80 | 80 |

**Royal Visit Issue**
Common Design Type

**1966, Feb. 4 Litho. *Perf. 11x12***

| | | | | |
|---|---|---|---|---|
| *213* | CD320 | 3c vio bl | 12 | 12 |
| *214* | CD320 | 35c dk car rose | 75 | 75 |

Careenage, St. George's A37

Queen Elizabeth II — A38

Designs: 1c, Hillsborough, Carriacou. 2c, Bougainvillea. 3c, Flamboyant plant. 5c, Levera Beach. 8c, Annandale Falls. 10c, Cacao pods. 12c, Inner Harbor. 15c, Nutmeg. 25c, St. George's. 35c, Grand Anse Beach. 50c, Bananas. $1, Seal of Colony. $3, Map of Grenada.

***Perf. 14½x13½, 14½ (A38)***

**1966, Apr. 1 Photo. Wmk. 314**

| | | | | |
|---|---|---|---|---|
| *215* | A37 | 1c bl, grn & yel | 5 | 5 |
| *216* | A37 | 2c dk grn & dp car rose | 5 | 5 |
| *217* | A37 | 3c multi | 6 | 6 |
| *218* | A37 | 5c multi | 7 | 7 |
| *219* | A37 | 6c ultra, grn & car rose | 7 | 7 |
| *220* | A37 | 8c dp grn, ind & yel | 10 | 10 |
| *221* | A37 | 10c yel grn, brn & dk car | 12 | 12 |
| *222* | A37 | 12c multi | 15 | 15 |
| *223* | A37 | 15c multi | 20 | 20 |
| *224* | A37 | 25c dk bl, grn & car rose | 40 | 40 |
| *225* | A37 | 35c multi | 60 | 60 |
| *226* | A37 | 50c vio & grn | 80 | 80 |
| *227* | A38 | $1 brn, ultra & dl grn | 1.60 | 1.60 |
| *228* | A38 | $2 multi | 3.25 | 3.25 |
| *229* | A38 | $3 brt grnsh bl, dk bl & dl yel | 4.75 | 4.75 |
| | | *Nos. 215-229 (15)* | 12.27 | 12.27 |

The overprint "Children Need Milk" and surcharges were applied in 1968 in Grenada to Nos. 227-229. The surcharges respectively are 1c+3c, 2c+3c and 3c+3c. The surcharge exists in two sizes on the $2 stamp.

**World Cup Soccer Issue**
Common Design Type

**1966, July 1 Litho. *Perf. 14***
*230* CD321 5c multi 8 8
*231* CD321 50c multi 75 75

**WHO Headquarters Issue**
Common Design Type

**1966, Sept. 20 Litho. *Perf. 14***
*232* CD322 8c multi 12 12
*233* CD322 25c multi 40 40

**UNESCO Anniversary Issue**
Common Design Type

**1966, Dec. 1 Litho. *Perf. 14***
*234* CD323 2c "Educatin" 5 5
*235* CD323 15c "Science" 25 25
*236* CD323 50c "Culture" 90 90

Nos. 216-217, 220 and 224 Overprinted "ASSOCIATED STATEHOOD 1967" in Silver

***Perf. 14½x13½***
**1967, Mar. 3 Photo. Wmk. 314**
*237* A37 2c dk grn & dp car rose 5 5
*238* A37 3c multi 8 8
*239* A37 8c dp grn, ind & yel 20 20
*240* A37 25c dk bl, grn & car rose 60 60

Nos. 216, 221, 223 and 227-228 Surcharged

1c

***Perf. 14½x13½, 14½ (A38)***
**1967, July 1 Photo. Wmk. 314**
*241* A37 1c on 15c multi 5 5
*242* A37 2c dk grn & dp car rose 6 6
*243* A37 3c on 10c multi 6 6
*244* A38 $1 multi 1.10 1.10
*245* A38 $2 multi 2.20 2.20
*Nos. 241-245 (5)* 3.47 3.47

EXPO '67 International Exhibition, Montreal, Apr. 28-Oct. 27.

Nos. 215-229 Overprinted in Black: "ASSOCIATED STATEHOOD"

**1967-68 Photo. Wmk. 314**
*246* A37 1c multi 5 5
*247* A37 2c multi 5 5
*248* A37 3c multi 5 5
*249* A37 5c multi 6 6
*250* A37 6c multi 7 7
*251* A37 8c multi 9 9
*252* A37 10c multi 12 12
*253* A37 12c multi 14 14
*254* A37 15c multi 18 18
*255* A37 25c multi 35 35
*256* A37 35c multi 45 45
*257* A37 50c multi 75 75
*258* A38 $1 multi 1.75 1.75
*259* A38 $2 multi 3.50 3.50
*260* A38 $3 multi 5.50 5.50

**Overprinted and Surcharged**
*261* A38 $5 on $2 multi ('68) 7.50 7.50
*Nos. 246-261 (16)* 20.61 20.61

Issue dates: $5, May 18, 1968. Others, Oct. 19, 1967.

Pres. John F. Kennedy — A39

Designs (Pres. Kennedy and): 25c, 50c, Bird-of-paradise flower. 35c, $1, Roses.

***Perf. 14½x14***
**1968, Jan. 13 Photo. Unwmk.**
*262* A39 1c lt bl & multi 5 5
*263* A39 15c org & multi 25 25
*264* A39 25c vio & multi 35 35
*265* A39 35c multi 45 45
*266* A39 50c bl & multi 60 60
*267* A39 $1 multi 1.25 1.25
*Nos. 262-267 (6)* 2.95 2.95

Issued to commemorate the 50th anniversary of the birth of Pres. John F. Kennedy.

Bugler and Jamboree Emblem — A40

Designs (Jamboree Emblem and): 2c, 50c, Boy Scouts sitting in tent. 3c, $1, Lord Baden-Powell.

**1968, Feb. 1 Photo. *Perf. 13x14***
*268* A40 1c org & multi 5 5
*269* A40 2c emer & multi 6 6
*270* A40 3c yel & multi 7 7
*271* A40 35c multi 40 40
*272* A40 50c bl & multi 50 50
*273* A40 $1 multi 1.00 1.00
*Nos. 268-273 (6)* 2.08 2.08

12th Boy Scout Jamboree, Farragut State Park, Idaho, Aug. 1-9, 1967.

Seascape, by Winston Churchill — A41

Paintings: 12c, Pine at the shore. 15c, 35c, Houses at the shore. 50c, Churchill painting a seascape.

***Perf. 14x14½***
**1968, Mar. 23 Photo. Unwmk.**
*274* A41 10c multi 15 15
*275* A41 12c multi 20 20
*276* A41 15c multi 25 25
*277* A41 25c multi 40 40
*278* A41 35c multi 55 55
*279* A41 50c multi 90 90
*Nos. 274-279 (6)* 2.45 2.45

Issued to honor Winston Churchill as a painter.

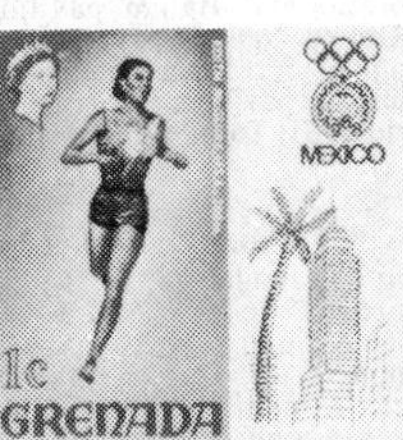


Edith McGuire, U.S.A., 200m. Dash, 1964 — A42

Gold Medal Winners: 2c, 50c, Arthur Wint, Jamaica, 400m. run, 1948. 3c, 60c, Adhemar Ferreira da Silva, Brazil, hop, step and jump, 1952 & 1956. 10c, Like 1c.

**1968, Sept. 24 Photo. *Perf. 12½***
*280* A42 1c ultra & multi 5 5
*281* A42 2c lil & multi 5 5
*282* A42 3c grn & multi 8 8
*283* A42 10c red org & multi 20 20
*284* A42 50c Prus bl & multi 75 75
*285* A42 60c org & multi 1.00 1.00
*Nos. 280-285 (6)* 2.13 2.13

19th Olympic Games, Mexico City, Oct. 12-27. Nos. 280-282 and 283-285 are printed in sheets of 9 (3 of each denomination).

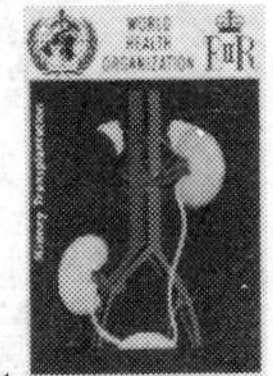


Transplant Operations — A43

***Perf. 13x13½***
**1968, Nov. 25 Photo. Unwmk.**
*286* A43 5c Kidney 5 5
*287* A43 25c Heart 28 28
*288* A43 35c Lung 40 40
*289* A43 50c Cornea 55 55

20th anniv. of WHO.

Adoration of the Magi, by Veronese A44

Paintings: 15c, Madonna and Child with St. John and St. Catherine, by Titian. 35c, Adoration of the Magi, by Botticelli. $1, "A Knight Adoring the Infant Christ" by Vincenzo di Biagio Catena.

**1968, Dec. 3 *Perf. 12½***
*290* A44 5c vio bl & multi 8 8
*291* A44 15c crim & multi 25 25
*292* A44 35c dk grn & multi 55 55
*293* A44 $1 dk bl & multi 1.40 1.40

Christmas 1968.

Hibiscus and "La Concepcion" — A45

Yacht in St. George's Harbour — A45a

Designs: 2c, Bird-of-paradise flower. 3c, Bougainvillea. 5c, Rock hind (fish; horiz.). 6c, Sailfish. 8c, Red snapper (horiz.). 10c, Giant toad (horiz.). 12c, Yellowfoot tortoise. No. 302, Tree boa (horiz.). No. 302A, Thunbergia. 25c, Mouse opossum. 35c Armadillo (horiz.). 50c, Mona monkey. $1, Bananaquit (bird). $2, Brown pelican. $3, Magnificent frigate bird. $5, Bare-eyed thrush.

***Perf. 14x14½, 14½x14; 14x13½ (#302A); 13½x14 (#305A)***
**Photo.; Litho. (#302A, 305A)**
**1968-71 Unwmk.**
*294* A45 1c dl yel & multi 5 5
*295* A45 2c brt pink & multi 6 5
*296* A45 3c bl & multi ('69) 8 6
*297* A45 5c vio & multi ('69) 10 8
*298* A45 6c emer & multi 12 10
*299* A45 8c multi ('69) 25 15
*300* A45 10c multi ('69) 18 15
*301* A45 12c ver & multi 24 20
*302* A45 15c emer & multi 85 75
*302A* A45 15c gray & multi ('70) 4.25 3.00
*303* A45 25c multi ('69) 60 50
*304* A45 35c multi ('69) 80 70
*305* A45 50c ultra & multi 1.25 1.00
*305A* A45a 75c bl & multi ('71) 3.00 2.50
*306* A45 $1 multi 2.25 2.00
*307* A45 $2 multi ('69) 3.50 3.00
*308* A45 $3 yel & multi 5.00 4.50
*309* A45 $5 multi ('69) 8.00 7.50
*Nos. 294-309 (18)* 30.58 26.29

Nos. 294-309 vary in size from 25x44mm to 29x46mm.

The overprint "VOTE/FEB. 28 1972" was applied to the 2c, 3c, 6c and 25c in Feb., 1972.

Nos. 280-285 Surcharged in Carmine

VISIT CARIFTA EXPO 69
April 5-30

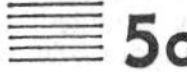


**1969, Feb. *Perf. 12½***
*310* A42 5c on 1c multi 6 6
*311* A42 8c on 2c multi 10 10
*312* A42 25c on 3c multi 35 35
*313* A42 35c on 10c multi 50 50
*314* A42 $1 on 50c multi 1.25 1.25
*315* A42 $2 on 60c multi 2.50 2.50
*Nos. 310-315 (6)* 4.76 4.76

Issued to publicize the CARIFTA (Caribbean Free Trade Area) Exposition, St. George's, Apr. 5-30.

Gov. Hilda Bynoe and View of St. George's A46

Designs: 15c, Premier Eric M. Gairy, fruits and St. George's. 60c, Emblems of Brussels, New York and Montreal World's Fairs.

**1969, May 1 Litho. *Perf. 13x13½***
*316* A46 5c multi 6 6
*317* A46 15c multi 18 18
*318* A46 50c multi 50 50
*319* A46 60c multi 55 55

Issued to commemorate the CARIFTA Exposition, St. George's, Apr. 5-30.

Gov. Hilda Bynoe — A47

Designs: 25c, Dr. Martin Luther King, Jr. $1, Belshazzar's Feast, by Rembrandt (horiz.).

***Perf. 13x12½, 12½x13***
**1969, June 8 Photo. Unwmk.**
*320* A47 5c multi 6 6
*321* A47 25c multi 25 25
*322* A47 35c multi 40 40
*323* A47 $1 multi 1.00 1.00

International Human Rights Year, 1968.

**Cricket Issue**

Batsman Playing Off-drive — A48

Designs: 10c, Batsman playing defensive stroke. 25c, Batsman sweeping ball. 35c, Batsman playing on-drive.

**1969, Aug. 1** *Perf. 14x14½*

| No. | Type | Description | Unused | Used |
|---|---|---|---|---|
| *324* | A48 | 3c dk bl & multi | 15 | 12 |
| *325* | A48 | 10c fawn & multi | 60 | 50 |
| *326* | A48 | 25c dp grn & multi | 1.50 | 1.00 |
| *327* | A48 | 35c brt pur & multi | 2.00 | 1.50 |

Astronaut Collecting Moon Rocks, Landing Module and Earth — A49

Designs: ½c, like $1. 1c, Apollo 11, moon and earth. 2c, Landing module "Eagle." 3c, Memorial tablet left on moon. 8c, Separation of rocket and spaceship. 25c, Take off from Cape Kennedy (vert.). 35c, Apollo 11 circling the moon (vert.). 50c, Splashdown (vert.). ½c, 2c, 25c, 50c, $1 inscribed: "We came in peace for all mankind." 1c, 3c, 8c, 35c inscribed: "Like the moon it shall be established forever" Psalms 89:37.

*Perf. 13x13½ (½c), 12½*

**1969, Sept.** **Litho.** **Unwmk.**

**Size: 56x35mm**

| No. | Type | Description | Unused | Used |
|---|---|---|---|---|
| *328* | A49 | ½c multi | 5 | 5 |

**Size: 44½x28mm, 28x44½mm**

| No. | Type | Description | Unused | Used |
|---|---|---|---|---|
| *329* | A49 | 1c multi | 5 | 5 |
| *330* | A49 | 2c multi | 5 | 5 |
| *331* | A49 | 3c multi | 5 | 5 |
| *332* | A49 | 8c multi | 18 | 18 |
| *333* | A49 | 25c multi | 42 | 42 |
| *334* | A49 | 35c multi | 75 | 75 |
| *335* | A49 | 50c multi | 1.00 | 1.00 |
| *336* | A49 | $1 multi | 2.00 | 2.00 |
| *a* | | Souv. sheet of 2 | 1.40 | 1.40 |
| | | *Nos. 328-336 (9)* | 4.55 | 4.55 |

Man's first moonlanding (Apollo 11), July 20, 1969.

No. 336a contains stamps similar to Nos. 331 and 336 with simulated perforations. Portraits of Michael Collins, Neil A. Armstrong and Edwin E. Aldrin, Jr., in blue margin, inscribed, "One small step for man, one giant leap for mankind." Size: 115x90mm.

Mahatma Gandhi — A50

Designs: Gandhi in various positions. 15c, 25c are vertical.

**1969, Oct. 8** *Perf. 11½x12, 12x11½*

**Queen's Head in Gold**

| No. | Type | Description | Unused | Used |
|---|---|---|---|---|
| *337* | A50 | 6c multi | 15 | 15 |
| *338* | A50 | 15c multi | 35 | 35 |
| *339* | A50 | 25c multi | 65 | 65 |
| *340* | A50 | $1 multi | 1.75 | 1.75 |
| *a* | | Souvenir sheet of 4 | 3.00 | 3.00 |

Issued to commemorate the centenary of the birth of Mohandas K. Gandhi (1869-1948), leader in India's fight for independence.

No. 340a contains stamps similar to Nos. 337-340 with simulated perforation. Size: 155x122mm.

**Christmas Issue**

Nos. 290-293 Overprinted in Black or Silver with Bars and "1969"

**1969, Dec.** **Photo.** *Perf. 12½*

| No. | Type | Description | Unused | Used |
|---|---|---|---|---|
| *341* | A44 | 2c on 15c multi | 5 | 5 |
| *342* | A44 | 5c multi (S) | 6 | 6 |
| *343* | A44 | 35c multi (S) | 35 | 35 |
| *344* | A44 | $1 multi (S) | 90 | 90 |

An enhanced introduction to the Scott Catalogue begins on Page V. A thorough understanding of the material presented there will greatly aid your use of the catalogue itself.

Edward Teach (Blackbeard) A51

Pirates: 25c, Anne Bonney and sailboats. 50c, Jean Lafitte and sailboats. $1, Mary Read, ships and fighting pirates.

**1970, Feb. 1** **Engr.** *Perf. 13x13½*

| No. | Type | Description | Unused | Used |
|---|---|---|---|---|
| *345* | A51 | 15c black | 60 | 35 |
| *346* | A51 | 25c emerald | 1.00 | 70 |
| *347* | A51 | 50c purple | 2.25 | 1.50 |
| *348* | A51 | $1 carmine | 5.00 | 3.25 |

No. 328 Surcharged

Type I Type II

**1970, Mar. 18** **Litho.** *Perf. 13x13½*

| No. | Type | Description | Unused | Used |
|---|---|---|---|---|
| *349* | A49 | 5c on ½c multi (I) | 15 | 15 |
| *a* | | Type II | 1.50 | 1.50 |

Christ, from "The Last Supper," by Andrea del Sarto — A52

Paintings: No. 351 (5c), St. John, from Last Supper by Andrea del Sarto. Nos. 352-353 (15c), Christ Crowned with Thorns, by Anthony Van Dyck. Nos. 354-355 (25c), Passion of Christ, by Hans Memling. Nos. 356-357 (60c), Christ in the Tomb, by Peter Paul Rubens. Nos. 350, 352, 354 and 356 have denomination in lower right corner; others in lower left corner. The stamps of the same denomination are printed se-tenant without separating margin, reproducing continuous picture.

*Perf. 11½x11*

**1970, Apr. 13** **Litho.** **Unwmk.**

| No. | Type | Description | Unused | Used |
|---|---|---|---|---|
| *350* | A52 | 5c rose car & multi | 8 | 8 |
| *351* | A52 | 5c rose car & multi | 8 | 8 |
| *352* | A52 | 15c ultra & multi | 20 | 20 |
| *353* | A52 | 15c ultra & multi | 20 | 20 |
| *354* | A52 | 25c brt vio & multi | 32 | 32 |
| *355* | A52 | 25c brt vio & multi | 32 | 32 |
| *356* | A52 | 60c dl org & multi7 | 70 | 70 |
| *357* | A52 | 60c dl org & multi | 70 | 70 |
| *a* | | Souvenir sheet of 4 | 2.50 | 2.50 |
| | | *Nos. 350-357 (8)* | 2.60 | 2.60 |

Easter 1970.

No. 357a contains one each of Nos. 354-357. Light blue margin with figures of saints and lilac inscription. Size: 119x140mm.

Girl Pushing Carriage with Kittens — A53

Designs: 15c, Girl playing with puppy and kitten. 30c, Boy fishing and cat. 60c, Children with pets.

**1970, May 27** **Litho.** *Perf. 11*

| No. | Type | Description | Unused | Used |
|---|---|---|---|---|
| *358* | A53 | 5c multi | 10 | 10 |
| *359* | A53 | 15c multi | 25 | 25 |
| *360* | A53 | 30c multi | 45 | 45 |
| *a* | | Souvenir sheet of 2 | 75 | 75 |
| *361* | A53 | 60c multi | 90 | 90 |
| *a* | | Souvenir sheet of 2 | 2.00 | 2.00 |

Issued to commemorate the bicentenary of the birth of William Wordsworth (1770-1850), English poet. No. 360a contains stamps similar to Nos. 358 and 360; No. 361a contains stamps similar to Nos. 359 and 361. Sheets have simulated perforations, gray margins with pictures of cats and dogs and quotations from Wordsworth. Size: 113x124mm.

Indian Parliament — A54

Designs (Commonwealth Parliamentary Association Emblem and): 25c, British Parliament. 50c, Canadian Parliament. 60c, Grenadian Parliament.

**1970, June 15** *Perf. 14½x14*

| No. | Type | Description | Unused | Used |
|---|---|---|---|---|
| *362* | A54 | 5c multi | 8 | 8 |
| *363* | A54 | 25c multi | 35 | 35 |
| *364* | A54 | 50c multi | 70 | 70 |
| *365* | A54 | 60c multi | 85 | 85 |
| *a* | | Souvenir sheet of 4 | 2.25 | 2.25 |

Issued to publicize the 7th Caribbean Regional Conference of the Commonwealth Parliamentary Association, St. George's, Grenada. June 13-20. No. 365a contains one each of Nos. 362-365; decorative margin and commemorative inscription. Size: 126x90mm.

Sun Tower and EXPO Emblem A55

Designs (EXPO Emblem and): 2c, Livelihood Industry pavilion (horiz.). 3c, Ikenobo, Japanese floral art (vert.). 10c, Adam and Eve, by Tintoretto and Italian pavilion (horiz.). 25c, United Nations pavilion and flags reflected in pool. 50c, Peace statue of St. Francis, San Francisco pavilion, cable car and Golden Gate Bridge. $1, Toshiba-Ihi pavilion (horiz.).

**1970, Aug. 8** **Litho.** *Perf. 13½*

| No. | Type | Description | Unused | Used |
|---|---|---|---|---|
| *366* | A55 | 1c brt bl & multi | 5 | 5 |
| *367* | A55 | 2c multi | 5 | 5 |
| *368* | A55 | 3c buff & multi | 5 | 5 |
| *369* | A55 | 10c multi | 20 | 20 |
| *370* | A55 | 25c gray & multi | 40 | 40 |
| *371* | A55 | 50c gray & multi | 80 | 80 |
| | | *Nos. 366-371 (6)* | 1.55 | 1.55 |

**Souvenir Sheet**

| No. | Type | Description | Unused | Used |
|---|---|---|---|---|
| *372* | A55 | $1 gold & multi | 1.50 | 1.50 |

EXPO '70 International Exhibition, Osaka, Japan, Mar. 15-Sept. 13. No. 372 has Prussian blue margin with view of EXPO '70, dancers and noh mask. Size: 121x90½mm.

Pres. Roosevelt and Flag-Raising on Iwo Jima — A56

Designs: 5c, Marshal Georgi K. Zhukov and fall of Berlin. 15c, Winston Churchill and evacuation of Dunkirk. 25c, Charles de Gaulle and liberation of Paris. 50c, General Dwight D. Eisenhower and D-Day landing. 60c, Field Marshal Bernard Montgomery and Battle of Alamein.

**1970, Sept. 3** *Perf. 11*

| No. | Type | Description | Unused | Used |
|---|---|---|---|---|
| *373* | A56 | ½c multi | 8 | 5 |
| *374* | A56 | 5c multi | 20 | 10 |
| *375* | A56 | 15c multi | 50 | 25 |
| *376* | A56 | 25c multi | 1.40 | 80 |
| *377* | A56 | 50c multi | 2.75 | 1.50 |
| *378* | A56 | 60c multi | 3.00 | 2.00 |
| *a* | | Souvenir sheet of 4 | 6.50 | 4.50 |
| | | *Nos. 373-378 (6)* | 7.93 | 4.70 |

End of World War II, 25th anniversary.

No. 378a contains one each of Nos. 373, 375, 377-378. Light blue margin with commemorative inscription and flags of Great Britain, United States, Russia and France. Size: 162x112mm.

Nos. 333-336 Overprinted in Black or Silver: "PHILYMPIA / LONDON 1970"

**1970, Sept. 18** *Perf. 12½*

| No. | Type | Description | Unused | Used |
|---|---|---|---|---|
| *379* | A49 | 25c multi | 30 | 30 |
| *380* | A49 | 35c multi | 40 | 40 |
| *381* | A49 | 50c multi | 65 | 65 |
| *382* | A49 | $1 multi (S) | 1.25 | 1.25 |

Issued to commemorate Philympia 1970, London philatelic exhibition, Sept. 18-26. The overprint on No. 382 is vertical, reading up.

This overprint was applied in silver to No. 336a.

U.P.U. Headquarters, Emblem and Old Transportation — A57

Designs (U.P.U. Headquarters, emblem and): 25c, Jet plane, ship and diesel train. 50c, Rowland Hill (vert.). $1, Abraham Lincoln (vert.).

**1970, Oct. 17** **Litho.** *Perf. 14½*

| No. | Type | Description | Unused | Used |
|---|---|---|---|---|
| *383* | A57 | 15c org & multi | 25 | 25 |
| *384* | A57 | 25c bl & multi | 35 | 35 |
| *385* | A57 | 50c multi | 65 | 65 |
| *386* | A57 | $1 rose & multi | 1.25 | 1.25 |
| *a* | | Souvenir sheet of 2 | 2.50 | 2.50 |

Issued to commemorate the opening of the new Universal Postal Union Headquarters in Bern. No. 386a contains stamps similar to Nos. 385-386. Light blue margin with deep rose inscription. Size: 78x84mm.

Madonna of the Goldfinch, by Tiepolo — A58

Paintings: No. 388, 35c, Virgin and Child with Sts. Peter and Paul, by Dirk Bouts. No. 389, $1, Virgin and Child, by Bellini. 3c, Like No. 387. 2c, 50c, Madonna of the Basket, by Correggio.

**1970, Dec. 5** *Perf. 14x13½*

| No. | Type | Description | Unused | Used |
|---|---|---|---|---|
| *387* | A58 | ½c yel grn & multi | 5 | 5 |
| *388* | A58 | ½c pink & multi | 5 | 5 |
| *389* | A58 | ½c yel & multi | 5 | 5 |
| *390* | A58 | 2c lt bl & multi | 5 | 5 |
| *391* | A58 | 3c dp rose & multi | 5 | 5 |
| *392* | A58 | 35c dk grn & multi | 65 | 55 |
| *393* | A58 | 50c brn & multi | 1.00 | 85 |
| *394* | A58 | $1 pur & multi | 2.00 | 1.75 |
| *a* | | Souvenir sheet of 2 | 3.50 | 2.75 |
| | | *Nos. 387-394 (8)* | 3.90 | 3.40 |

Christmas 1970.

No. 394a contains Nos. 393-394. Decorative multicolored border with inscription. Size: 102x87½mm.

Nursing in 19th Century A59

Designs: 15c, Horse-drawn ambulance, Northern France, 1918. 25c, First aid station, 1941. 60c, Red Cross truck loaded on plane, 1970 emergency aid.

**1970, Dec. 12 Litho. *Perf. 14½x14***

| | | | | |
|---|---|---|---|---|
| *395* | A59 | 5c red & multi | 10 | 10 |
| *396* | A59 | 15c red & multi | 25 | 25 |
| *397* | A59 | 25c red & multi | 45 | 45 |
| *398* | A59 | 60c red & multi | 1.25 | 1.25 |
| *a* | | Souvenir sheet of 4 | 2.25 | 2.25 |

Issued to commemorate the centenary of the British Red Cross Society. No. 398a contains one each of Nos. 395-398. Decorative margin with commemorative inscription. Size: 114x81½mm.

John Dewey, Children Learning to Paint — A60

Designs: 10c, Jean-Jacques Rousseau and students. 50c, Moses Maimonides and biology student. $1, Bertrand Russell and boys.

**1971, May 8 Litho. *Perf. 13½***

| | | | | |
|---|---|---|---|---|
| *399* | A60 | 5c multi | 10 | 10 |
| *400* | A60 | 10c multi | 20 | 20 |
| *401* | A60 | 50c multi | 1.25 | 1.25 |
| *402* | A60 | $1 multi | 2.50 | 2.50 |
| *a* | | Souvenir sheet of 2 | 3.75 | 3.75 |

International Education Year. No. 402a contains Nos. 401-402. Light blue and multicolored margin with black inscription. Size: 90x108mm.

Jennifer Hosten and Map of Grenada A61

**1971, June 1 Litho. *Perf. 13½***

| | | | | |
|---|---|---|---|---|
| *403* | A61 | 5c vio bl & multi | 15 | 12 |
| *404* | A61 | 10c red lil & multi | 35 | 20 |
| *405* | A61 | 15c brt rose & multi | 75 | 35 |
| *406* | A61 | 25c vio & multi | 1.25 | 60 |
| *407* | A61 | 35c bl & multi | 1.75 | 1.20 |
| *408* | A61 | 50c red & multi | 3.50 | 2.00 |
| *a* | | Souvenir sheet of 1 | 2.75 | 2.75 |
| | | *Nos. 403-408 (6)* | 7.75 | 4.47 |

Honoring Miss Jennifer Hosten of Grenada, Miss World, 1971. No. 408a, printed on silk, contains imperf. stamp similar to No. 408. Dull blue margin with full length photograph of Miss Hosten and black inscription. Size: 92x80mm.

Nos. 403-408 and 408a were overprinted "INTERPEX/1972" in March, 1972.

Canadian and French Boy Scouts — A62

Boy Scouts from: 35c, West Germany and U.S.A. 50c, Australia and Japan. 75c, Grenada and Great Britain.

**1971, Aug. Litho. *Perf. 11***

| | | | | |
|---|---|---|---|---|
| *409* | A62 | 5c multi | 10 | 10 |
| *410* | A62 | 35c multi | 70 | 60 |
| *411* | A62 | 50c multi | 1.00 | 90 |
| *412* | A62 | 75c multi | 1.50 | 1.50 |
| *a* | | Souvenir sheet of 2 | 3.50 | 3.25 |

13th Boy Scout World Jamboree, Asagiri Plain, Japan, Aug. 2-10. No. 412a contains Nos. 411-412. Multicolored margin with merit badges. Sizes: 101x114mm.

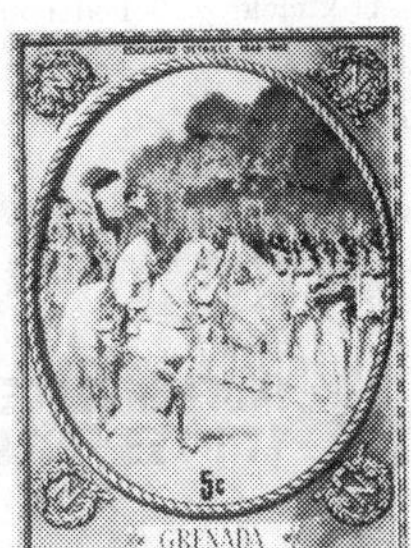


Napoleon, by Edouard Detaille A63

Paintings of Napoleon: 15c, Outside Madrid, by Carle Vernet. 35c, Crossing the Alps, by Jacques Louis David. $2, Portrait, by David.

**1971, Sept. *Perf. 13x13½***

| | | | | |
|---|---|---|---|---|
| *413* | A63 | 5c multi | 10 | 10 |
| *414* | A63 | 15c multi | 25 | 25 |
| *415* | A63 | 35c multi | 65 | 65 |
| *a* | | Souvenir sheet of 1 | 1.25 | 1.25 |
| *416* | A63 | $2 multi | 3.00 | 3.00 |

Sesquicentennial of the death of Napoleon Bonaparte (1769-1821).

No. 415a contains stamp similar to No. 415 with simulated perforations. Imperial cipher in margin. Size: 101x76mm.

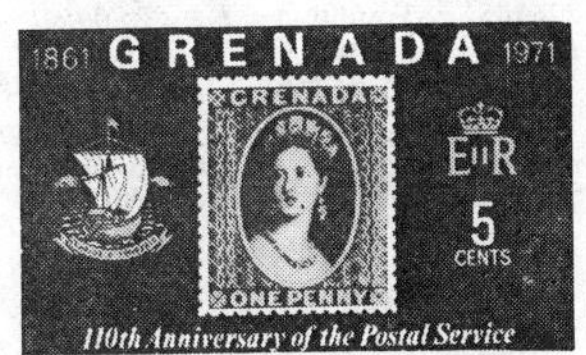


Grenada No. 1 — A64

Designs: 15c, Grenada No. 2 and Queen Elizabeth II. 35c, Grenada Nos. 1 and 2. 50c, Grenada No. 1 and scroll.

**1971, Nov. 6 Litho. *Perf. 11***

| | | | | |
|---|---|---|---|---|
| *417* | A64 | 5c dk red & multi | 10 | 10 |
| *418* | A64 | 15c multi | 25 | 25 |
| *419* | A64 | 35c dl org & multi | 75 | 75 |
| *420* | A64 | 50c dk grn & multi | 1.25 | 1.25 |
| *a* | | Souvenir sheet of 2 | 2.10 | 2.10 |

110th anniversary of postal service. No. 420a contains Nos. 419-420. Dark red decorative margin. Size: 96x113½mm.

Splashdown, Apollo 13 — A65

Designs: 2c, Capsule and rafts in ocean, Apollo 13. 3c, Separation of landing module from rocket, Apollo 14. 10c, Astronauts collecting moon rocks, Apollo 14. 25c, Astronauts in moon rover, Apollo 15. 50c, $1, Rocket blast-off, Apollo 15 (vert.).

**1971, Nov.**

| | | | | |
|---|---|---|---|---|
| *421* | A65 | 1c multi | 5 | 5 |
| *422* | A65 | 2c multi | 5 | 5 |
| *423* | A65 | 3c blk & multi | 6 | 6 |
| *424* | A65 | 10c blk & multi | 22 | 22 |
| *425* | A65 | 25c multi | 55 | 55 |
| *426* | A65 | $1 multi | 2.25 | 2.25 |
| | | *Nos. 421-426 (6)* | 3.18 | 3.18 |

**Souvenir Sheet**

| | | | | |
|---|---|---|---|---|
| *427* | A65 | 50c multi | 2.25 | 2.25 |

U.S. moon missions of Apollo 13, 14 and 15. No. 427 has blue border with insignia of missions and names of astronauts. Size: 77x109mm.

67th Regiment of Foot, 1787 — A66

Designs: 1c, 45th Regiment of Foot, 1792. 2c, 29th Regiment of Foot, 1794. 10c, 9th Regiment of Foot, 1801. 25c, 2nd Regiment of Foot, 1815. $1, 70th Regiment of Foot, 1764.

**1971, Dec. *Perf. 13½x14***

| | | | | |
|---|---|---|---|---|
| *428* | A66 | ½c red & multi | 5 | 5 |
| *429* | A66 | 1c red & multi | 5 | 5 |
| *430* | A66 | 2c red & multi | 5 | 5 |
| *431* | A66 | 10c red & multi | 30 | 30 |
| *432* | A66 | 25c red & multi | 90 | 90 |
| *433* | A66 | $1 red & multi | 3.50 | 3.50 |
| *a* | | Souvenir sheet of 2 | 5.00 | 5.00 |
| | | *Nos. 428-433 (6)* | 4.85 | 4.85 |

Uniforms of British units stationed in Grenada. No. 433a contains Nos. 432-433, perf. 15. Light blue and multicolored margin. Size: 108x99mm.

Adoration of the Kings, by Memling — A67

Designs: 25c, Madonna and Child, sculpture by Michelangelo. 35c, Madonna and Child, by Murillo. 50c, Madonna with the Apple, by Memling. $1, Adoration of the Kings, by Jan Mostaert.

**1971, Dec. *Perf. 14x13½***

| | | | | |
|---|---|---|---|---|
| *434* | A67 | 15c gold & multi | 25 | 25 |
| *435* | A67 | 25c gold & multi | 45 | 45 |
| *436* | A67 | 35c gold & multi | 65 | 65 |
| *437* | A67 | 50c gold & multi | 1.00 | 1.00 |

**Souvenir Sheet**

| | | | | |
|---|---|---|---|---|
| *438* | A67 | $1 gold & multi | 2.00 | 2.00 |

Christmas 1971.

No. 438 has decorative multicolored margin. Size: 106x81mm.

### No. 430 Surcharged with New Value, Olympic Rings and: "WINTER OLYMPICS / FEB. 3-13, 1972 / SAPPORO, JAPAN"

**1972, Feb. 3 *Perf. 13½x14***

| | | | | |
|---|---|---|---|---|
| *439* | A66 | $2 on 2c red & multi | 3.50 | 3.50 |
| *a* | | Souvenir sheet of 2 | 5.00 | 5.00 |

11th Winter Olympic Games, Sapporo, Japan, Feb. 3-13. See Nos. C1-C2.

No. 439a is overprinted in red on No. 433a (no surcharge); margin inscribed in red: "SAPPORO 1972."

King Arthur, UNICEF Emblem A68

Designs (UNICEF Emblem and): 1c, 50c, Robin Hood. 2c, 75c, Robinson Crusoe (vert.). 25c, like ½c. $1, Mary and her Little Lamb (vert.).

**1972, Mar. 4 *Perf. 14½x14, 14x14½***

| | | | | |
|---|---|---|---|---|
| *450* | A68 | ½c dp bl & multi | 5 | 5 |
| *451* | A68 | 1c yel & multi | 5 | 5 |
| *452* | A68 | 2c dp yel & multi | 5 | 5 |
| *453* | A68 | 25c sal & multi | 30 | 30 |
| *454* | A68 | 50c multi | 60 | 60 |
| *455* | A68 | 75c bl & multi | 90 | 90 |
| *456* | A68 | $1 multi | 1.20 | 1.20 |
| *a* | | Souvenir sheet of 1 | 2.00 | 2.00 |
| | | *Nos. 450-456 (7)* | 3.15 | 3.15 |

25th anniversary (in 1971) of the United Nations International Children's Fund (UNICEF). No. 456a has No. 456. Buff decorative margin with black UNICEF emblem. Size: 64x88mm.

Yachting A69

Designs (Olympic rings and): 1c, 50c, Equestrian. 2c, 35c, Running (vert.).

**1972, Sept. 8 Litho. *Perf. 14***

| | | | | |
|---|---|---|---|---|
| *457* | A69 | ½c multi | 5 | 5 |
| *458* | A69 | 1c lt bl & multi | 5 | 5 |
| *459* | A69 | 2c org & multi | 5 | 5 |
| *460* | A69 | 35c yel & multi | 70 | 70 |
| *461* | A69 | 50c yel grn & multi | 1.00 | 1.00 |
| | | *Nos. 457-461,C20-C21 (7)* | 2.90 | 2.90 |

20th Olympic Games, Munich, Aug. 26-Sept. 11. See No. C22.

### Nos. 294-296, 403 Surcharged with New Value and Two Bars

***Perf. 14x14½, 13½***

**1972, Oct. Photo.**

| | | | | |
|---|---|---|---|---|
| *462* | A45 | 12c on 1c multi | 45 | 45 |
| *463* | A45 | 12c on 2c multi | 45 | 45 |
| *464* | A45 | 12c on 3c multi | 45 | 45 |
| *465* | A61 | 12c on 5c multi | 45 | 45 |

### Silver Wedding Issue, 1972

Common Design Type

Design: Queen Elizabeth II, Prince Philip, seal of Grenada and myristica fragrans.

***Perf. 14x14½***

**1972, Nov. 20 Photo. Wmk. 314**

| | | | | |
|---|---|---|---|---|
| *466* | CD324 | 8c ol & multi | 18 | 18 |
| *467* | CD324 | $1 multi | 1.40 | 1.40 |

Boy Scout Saluting A70

Designs: 1c, Two Scouts knotting ropes. 2c, 70c, 75c, Scouts from different nations. 3c, 60c, $1, Lord Baden-Powell.

**Unwmk.**

**1972, Dec. 2 Litho. *Perf. 14***

| | | | | |
|---|---|---|---|---|
| *468* | A70 | ½c yel & multi | 5 | 5 |
| *469* | A70 | 1c red & multi | 5 | 5 |
| *470* | A70 | 2c yel & multi | 5 | 5 |
| *471* | A70 | 3c brt lil & multi | 5 | 5 |
| *472* | A70 | 75c lt bl & multi | 1.40 | 1.40 |
| *473* | A70 | $1 multi | 2.00 | 2.00 |
| | | *Nos. 468-473,C27-C28 (8)* | 4.70 | 4.70 |

**Souvenir Sheet**

| | | | | |
|---|---|---|---|---|
| *474* | A70 | Sheet of 2 | 3.50 | 3.50 |
| *a* | | 60c ocher & multi | 1.50 | 1.50 |
| *b* | | 70c pale lil & multi | 1.90 | 1.90 |

Boy Scouts, 65th anniversary. No. 474 has buff and brown margin with Scout design. Size: 86x88mm.

Virgin and Child, Crosier — A71

Designs: 3c, 35c, 70c, The Three Kings. 5c, $1, Holy Family. 25c, 60c, Like 1c.

**1972, Dec. 9 Litho. *Perf. 14x13½***

*475* A71 1c bl & multi 5 5
*476* A71 3c gray & multi 5 5
*477* A71 5c multi 5 5
*478* A71 25c multi 40 40
*479* A71 35c lt bl & multi 70 70
*480* A71 $1 ocher & multi 2.25 2.25
*Nos. 475-480 (6)* 3.50 3.50

**Souvenir Sheet**

***Perf. 15***

*481* A71 Sheet of 2 3.00 2.75
*a* 60c bl & multi 1.10 1.10
*b* 70c brt pink & multi 1.25 1.25

Christmas 1972.

No. 481 has multicolored margin. Size: 101x76mm.

Flamingos A72

**1973, Jan. 5 Litho. *Perf. 14***

*482* A72 25c *shown* 40 40
*483* A72 35c *Tapir* 60 60
*484* A72 60c *Macaws* 1.20 1.20
*485* A72 70c *Ocelot* 1.40 1.40

National Zoo of Grenada.

Class II Ocean Racing Yacht A73

**1973, Jan. 26 Litho. *Perf. 13½x14***

*486* A73 25c *shown* 40 40
*487* A73 35c *Boats in St. George's Harbour* 55 55
*488* A73 60c *Yacht "Bloodhound"* 95 95
*489* A73 70c *St. George's Harbour* 1.10 1.10

Yachting off Grenada.

Sun God Helios, Equinoxes and Solstices — A74

Designs (WMO Emblem and): 1c, Poseidon and Nomad automatic storm detector. 2c, Zeus and radarscope. 3c, Goddess Iris, rainbow, weather balloon. 35c, Hermes, ATS 3 satellite. 50c, Zephyr and circulation of atmosphere. 75c, Demeter, space photograph of storm. $1, Selene, globe showing world rainfall. $2, Computer weather map (42x31mm.).

**1973, July 6 Litho. *Perf. 13½***

*490* A74 ½c multi 5 5
*491* A74 1c multi 5 5
*492* A74 2c multi 5 5
*493* A74 3c multi 6 6
*494* A74 35c multi 50 50
*495* A74 50c multi 75 75
*496* A74 75c multi 1.15 1.15
*497* A74 $1 multi 1.50 1.50
*Nos. 490-497 (8)* 4.11 4.11

**Souvenir Sheet**

*498* A74 $2 multi 3.00 2.75

Centenary of international meteorological cooperation.

No. 498 shows Chinese weather gods in multicolored margin. Size: 123x92mm.

Racing Class Yachts A75

**1973, Aug. 3 Litho. *Perf. 13½***

*499* A75 ½c *shown* 5 5
*500* A75 1c *Cruising class* 5 5
*501* A75 2c *Open-decked sloops* 5 5
*502* A75 35c *Sloop Mermaid* 50 50
*503* A75 50c *St. George's Harbour* 75 75
*504* A75 75c *Map of Carriacou* 1.15 1.15
*505* A75 $1 *Boat building* 1.50 1.50
*Nos. 499-505 (7)* 4.05 4.05

**Souvenir Sheet**

*506* A75 $2 *End of race* 3.00 2.75

Carriacou Regatta, August 1973.

No. 506 has multicolored margin. Size: 108x88mm.

Ignaz Philipp Semmelweiss — A76

Designs: Physicians and scientists.

**1973, Sept. 17 Litho. *Perf. 14½***

*507* A76 ½c *shown* 5 5
*508* A76 1c *Louis Pasteur* 5 5
*509* A76 2c *Edward Jenner* 5 5
*510* A76 3c *Sigmund Freud* 5 5
*511* A76 25c *Emil von Behring* 35 35
*512* A76 35c *Carl Jung* 50 50
*513* A76 50c *Charles Calmette* 75 75
*514* A76 $1 *William Harvey* 1.50 1.50
*Nos. 507-514 (8)* 3.30 3.30

**Souvenir Sheet**

*515* A76 $2 *Marie Curie* 3.00 2.75

World Health Organization, 25th anniversary. No. 515 has multicolored margin with flower design and emblems. Size: 105x80mm.

Princess Anne and Mark Phillips — A77

**1973, Nov. 14 Wmk. 34 *Perf. 13½***

*516* A77 25c dp org & multi 30 30
*517* A77 $2 grn & multi 2.25 2.25
*a* Souv. sheet of 2 (75c, $1) 2.25 2.25

Wedding of Princess Anne and Capt. Mark Phillips.

Nos. 516-517 were issued only in sheets of 5 plus label, with multicolored, inscribed margins.

No. 517a has multicolored margins with commemorative inscriptions. Size: 78x99mm. Colors of 75c and $1 are as those of 25c and $2.

Virgin and Child, by Carlo Maratti — A78

Paintings: 1c, Virgin and Child, by Carlo Crivelli. 2c, Virgin and Child, by Verrocchio. 3c, Adoration of the Shepherds, by Roberti. 25c, Holy Family, by Federigo Baroccio. 35c, Holy Family, by Bronzino. 75c, Mystic Nativity, by Botticelli. $1, Adoration of the Kings, by Geertgen tot Sint Jans. $2, Adoration of the Kings, by Jan Mostaert (30x45mm.).

***Perf. 14½***

**1973, Nov. Unwmk. Litho.**

*519* A78 ½c lt brn & multi 5 5
*520* A78 1c cit & multi 5 5
*521* A78 2c bl & multi 5 5
*522* A78 3c grn & multi 8 8
*523* A78 25c multi 50 50
*524* A78 35c multi 70 70
*525* A78 75c vio bl & multi 1.50 1.50
*526* A78 $1 multi 2.00 2.00
*Nos. 519-526 (8)* 4.93 4.93

**Souvenir Sheet**

***Perf. 13½x14***

*527* A78 $2 red & multi 3.50 3.50

Christmas 1973. No. 527 has multicolored margin. Size: 89x89mm.

Nos. 294-297, 299-301, 303-304, 305A-309 Overprinted **INDEPENDENCE 7TH FEB 1974**

***Perf. 14x14½, 14½x14***

**1974, Feb. 7 Photo.**

*528* A45 1c multi 5 5
*529* A45 2c multi 5 5
*530* A45 3c multi 15 12
*531* A45 5c multi 22 15
*532* A45 8c multi 30 22
*533* A45 10c multi 35 30
*534* A45 12c multi 50 45
*535* A45 25c multi 1.10 90
*536* A45 35c multi 1.75 1.40

**Litho.**

***Perf. 13½x14***

*537* A45a 75c multi *5.25 3.50*

**Photo.**

***Perf. 14x14½***

*538* A45 $1 multi *7.50 4.50*
*539* A45 $2 multi *16.00 10.00*
*540* A45 $3 multi *25.00 15.00*
*541* A45 $5 multi *67.50 22.50*
*Nos. 528-541 (14)* 125.72 59.14

Grenada's independence, Feb. 7, 1974. Size of overprint on vertical stamps 16x5mm.; on horizontal stamps 20x6mm.

Creative Arts Theater, Jamaica Campus — A79

Designs: 25c, Marryshow House, University Center. 50c, Chapel (vert.). $1, $2, University coat of arms (vert.).

**1974, Apr. 10 Litho. *Perf. 13½***

*542* A79 10c multi 22 22
*543* A79 25c multi 60 60
*544* A79 50c multi 1.10 1.10
*545* A79 $1 multi 2.25 2.25

**Souvenir Sheet**

*546* A79 $2 multi 3.00 3.00

25th anniversary of the University of the West Indies. No. 546 has yellow and multicolored border. Size: 68½x85mm.

Prime Minister Eric M. Gairy — A80

Soccer, Flags of West Germany and Chile — A81

**1974, Aug. 19 Litho. *Perf. 13½***

*547* A80 3c *Nutmeg and mace* 5 5
*548* A80 8c *Map of Grenada* 22 22
*549* A80 25c *shown* 50 50
*550* A80 35c *Anse Beach and Flag* 75 75
*551* A80 $1 *Coat of arms* 2.50 2.50
*Nos. 547-551 (5)* 4.02 4.02

**Souvenir Sheet**

*552* A80 $2 *Coat of arms* 3.00 3.00

Grenada's independence. No. 552 has multicolored margin showing new Grenada flag and map of islands. Size: 91x124mm.

**1974, Sept. 3 Litho. *Perf. 14½***

Designs (Soccer Games and Flags): 1c, East Germany and Australia. 2c, Jugoslavia and Brazil. 10c, Scotland and Zaire. 25c, Netherlands and Uruguay. 50c, Sweden and Bulgaria. 75c, Italy and Haiti. $1, Poland and Argentina. $2, Flags of participating nations (horiz.).

*553* A81 ½c multi 5 5
*554* A81 1c multi 5 5
*555* A81 2c multi 5 5
*556* A81 10c multi 10 10
*557* A81 25c multi 25 25
*558* A81 50c multi 50 50
*559* A81 75c multi 85 85
*560* A81 $1 multi 1.00 1.00
*Nos. 553-560 (8)* 2.85 2.85

**Souvenir Sheet**

***Perf. 13***

*561* A81 $2 multi 2.75 2.50

World Cup Soccer Championship, Munich, June 13-July 7. No. 561 has multicolored margin showing soccer cup. Size: 113x76mm.

19th Century US Mail Train, Concorde and UPU Emblem — A82

Designs (UPU Emblem and): 1c, Sailing ship "Caesar," 1839, and helicopter. 2c, Zeppelin, jet and early planes. 8c, Pigeon post, 1480, telephone dial. 15c, Bellman, 18th century and radar. 25c, German Imperial messenger, 1450, satellite. 35c, French pillar box and ocean liner. $1, German mailman, 18th century, and futuristic mail train. $2, St. Gotthard mail coach, 1735 (vert.).

**1974, Oct. 8 Litho. *Perf. 14½***

*562* A82 ½c rose & multi 5 5
*563* A82 1c gray & multi 5 5
*564* A82 2c dl pink & multi 5 5
*565* A82 8c yel & multi 8 8
*566* A82 15c yel grn & multi 20 20
*567* A82 25c dl yel & multi 35 35
*568* A82 35c lil & multi 45 45
*569* A82 $1 lt bl & multi 1.25 1.25
*Nos. 562-569 (8)* 2.48 2.48

**Souvenir Sheet**

***Perf. 13***

*570* A82 $2 multi 2.50 2.50

Centenary of Universal Postal Union. Margin design of No. 570 simulates airmail envelope with 2 airmail labels, UPU emblem and black inscription. Size: 104x66mm.

Sir Winston Churchill — A83

Design: $2, Churchill, different portrait.

**1974, Oct. 28 Litho. Perf. 13½**

*571* A83 35c multi 45 45
*572* A83 $2 multi 2.50 2.50

**Souvenir Sheet**

*573* A83 Sheet of 2 2.50 2.50
*a* 75c like 35c 1.00 1.00
*b* $1 like $2 1.25 1.25

Winston Churchill (1874-1965), birth centenary. No. 573 has multicolored border showing World War II battle scene. Size: 129x96mm.

Virgin and Child, by Botticelli — A84

Designs: Paintings of the Virgin and Child.

**1974, Nov. 18 Perf. 14½**

*574* A84 ½c *shown* 5 5
*575* A84 1c *Niccolo di Pietro* 5 5
*576* A84 2c *Van der Weyden* 5 5
*577* A84 3c *Bastiani* 6 6
*578* A84 10c *Giovanni* 12 12
*579* A84 25c *Van der Weyden* 30 30
*580* A84 50c *Botticelli* 60 60
*581* A84 $1 *Mantegna* 1.20 1.20
*Nos. 574-581 (8)* 2.43 2.43

**Souvenir Sheet**

**Perf. 13½**

*582* A84 $2 *Niccolo di Pietro* 2.00 2.00

Christmas 1974. No. 582 has multicolored margin showing 3 Kings. Size: 117x96mm.

Yachts and Point Saline A85

Designs: 1c, Grenada Yacht Club race, St. George's. 2c, Careenage taxi (boat). 3c, Large working boats. 5c, Deep Water Dock, St. George's. 6c, Cacao beans in drying trays. 8c, Nutmeg branch. 10c, River Antoine Estate rum distillery, c. 1785. 12c, Cacao branch. 15c, Fishermen landing catch at Fontenoy. 20c, Parliament Building, St. George's. 25c, Fort George cannons. 35c, Pearls Airport. 50c, General Post Office. 75c, Carib Leap, Sauteurs Bay. $1, Careenage, St. George's. $2, St. George's harbor at night. $3, Grand Anse Beach. $5, Canoe Bay and Black Bay from Point Saline Lighthouse. $10, Sugarloaf Island from Levera Beach.

**1975 Litho. Perf. 14½**

**Size: 38x25mm**

*583* A85 ½c multi 5 5
*584* A85 1c multi 5 5
*585* A85 2c multi 5 5
*586* A85 3c multi 5 5
*587* A85 5c multi 5 5
*588* A85 6c multi 6 6
*589* A85 8c multi 8 8
*590* A85 10c multi 10 10
*591* A85 12c multi 12 12
*592* A85 15c multi 15 15
*593* A85 20c multi 20 20
*594* A85 25c multi 25 25
*595* A85 35c multi 35 35
*596* A85 50c multi 50 50

**Perf. 13½x14**

**Size: 45x28mm**

*597* A85 75c multi 75 75
*598* A85 $1 multi 1.00 1.00
*599* A85 $2 multi 2.00 2.00
*600* A85 $3 multi 3.00 3.00
*601* A85 $5 multi 5.00 5.00
*602* A85 $10 multi 10.00 10.00
*Nos. 583-602 (20)* 23.81 23.81

Issue dates: Nos. 583-596, Jan. 13; Nos. 597-601, Jan. 22; No. 602, Mar. 26.

In 1978, 10 denominations were issued perf. 13 (Nos. 584-588, 590, 592-594, 596). Values similar.

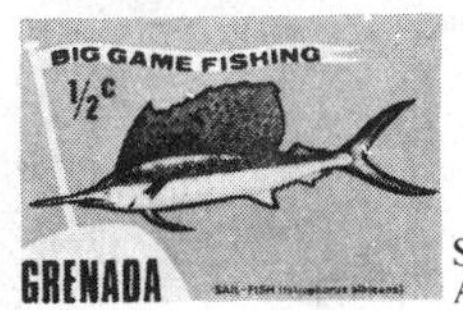


Sailfish A86

Designs: Big game fish.

**1975, Feb. 3 Perf. 14½**

*603* A86 ½c *shown* 5 5
*604* A86 1c *Blue marlin* 5 5
*605* A86 2c *White marlin* 5 5
*606* A86 10c *Yellowfin tuna* 10 10
*607* A86 25c *Wahoo* 25 25
*608* A86 50c *Dolphin* 48 48
*609* A86 70c *Grouper* 70 70
*610* A86 $1 *Great barracuda* 1.00 1.00
*Nos. 603-610 (8)* 2.68 2.68

**Souvenir Sheet**

**Perf. 13**

*611* A86 $2 *Mako shark* 2.75 2.75

No. 611 has multicolored margin. Size: 105x79mm.

Passiflora Quadrangularis — A87

Designs: Flowers of Grenada.

**1975, Feb. 26 Litho. Perf. 14½**

*612* A87 ½c *shown* 5 5
*613* A87 1c *Bleeding heart* 5 5
*614* A87 2c *Poinsettia* 5 5
*615* A87 3c *Obroma cacao* 5 5
*616* A87 10c *Gladioli* 20 20
*617* A87 25c *Red head-yellow head* 45 45
*618* A87 50c *Plumbago* 85 85
*619* A87 $1 *Orange blossoms* 1.60 1.60
*Nos. 612-619 (8)* 3.30 3.30

**Souvenir Sheet**

**Perf. 13½**

*620* A87 $2 *Barbados gooseberry* 2.75 2.75

No. 620 has multicolored margin showing flower garden. Size: 102x82mm.

Grenada Flag and UN Emblem — A88

Designs: 1c, UN and Grenada flags. 2c, $1, UN emblem and Grenada coat of arms. 35c, UN emblem over map of Grenada. 50c, Grenada flag in front of UN Headquarters. 75c, like ½c. $2, UN emblem and scroll.

**1975, Mar. 19 Perf. 14½**

*621* A88 ½c multi 5 5
*622* A88 1c multi 5 5
*623* A88 2c multi 5 5
*624* A88 35c multi 40 40
*625* A88 50c multi 55 55
*626* A88 $2 multi 2.25 2.25
*Nos. 621-626 (6)* 3.35 3.35

**Souvenir Sheet**

**Perf. 13½**

*627* A88 Sheet of 2 2.25 2.25
*a* 75c multi 85 85
*b* $1 multi 1.10 1.10

Grenada's admission to the United Nations, Sept. 17, 1974. No. 627 has blue and multicolored margin. Size: 122x91mm.

Midnight Ride of Paul Revere — A89

Designs: 1c, Crispus Attucks at Boston Massacre. 2c, Patrick Henry. 3c, Franklin visiting Washington at the front. 5c, Lexington-Concord. 10c, John Paul Jones. No. 634, Arms of Grenada and United States. No. 635, Flags of Grenada and United States.

**1975, May 6 Litho. Perf. 14½, 13**

*628* A89 ½c Prus bl & multi 5 5
*629* A89 1c buff & multi 5 5
*630* A89 2c dp org & multi 5 5
*631* A89 3c org & multi 5 5
*632* A89 5c Prus bl & multi 8 5
*633* A89 10c ultra & multi 12 6
*Nos. 628-633,C29-C32 (10)* 4.10 1.21

**Souvenir Sheets**

**Perf. 13½**

*634* A89 $2 tan & multi 2.75 *50*
*635* A89 $2 gray & multi 2.75 *50*

American Revolution Bicentennial.

Nos. 634-635 have multicolored margins showing battle scene and historic American flags. Size: stamps, 47x34mm.; sheets 130x102mm.

Nos. 628-633 issued in sheets of 40. Each denomination was also printed in sheets of 5 plus label, perf. 13.

Angel Collecting Jesus' Blood in Grail, by Bellini — A90

Paintings: 1c, Pieta, by Bellini. 2c, The Deposition, by Rogier van der Weyden. 3c, Pieta, by Bellini. 35c, Descent from the Cross, by Bellini. 75c, Jesus Rising from the Tomb, by Bellini. $1, Descent from the Cross, by Procaccini. $2, Pieta, by Botticelli.

**1975, May 21**

*636* A90 ½c multi 5 *5*
*637* A90 1c multi 5 *5*
*638* A90 2c multi 5 *5*
*639* A90 3c multi 5 *5*
*640* A90 35c multi 60 *15*
*641* A90 75c multi 1.35 *25*
*642* A90 $1 multi 1.80 *50*
*Nos. 636-642 (7)* 3.95 *1.10*

**Souvenir Sheet**

**Perf. 13½**

*643* A90 $2 multi 3.75 *70*

Easter 1975. No. 643 has orange and multicolored margin. Size: 116½x100mm.

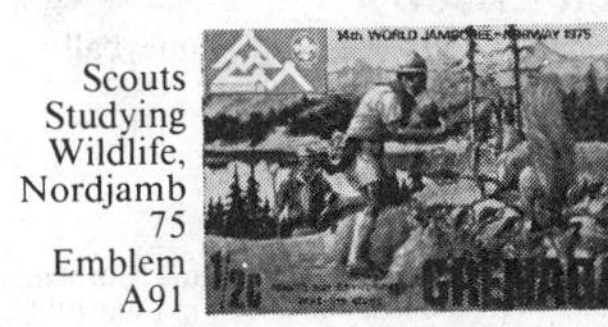


Scouts Studying Wildlife, Nordjamb 75 Emblem A91

Designs (Nordjamb 75 Emblem and): 1c, Seamanship; Scouts in sailboat. 2c, Survival; Scouts reading map. 35c, First aid. 40c, Physical fitness; gymnastics. 75c, Mountaineering. $1, Emergency boat building. $2, Scouts singing.

**1975, July 2 Litho. Perf. 14**

*644* A91 ½c bl & multi 5 *5*
*645* A91 1c bl & multi 5 *5*
*646* A91 2c bl & multi 5 *5*
*647* A91 35c bl & multi 50 *20*
*648* A91 40c bl & multi 60 *20*
*649* A91 75c bl & multi 1.00 *30*
*650* A91 $2 bl & multi 2.75 *65*
*Nos. 644-650 (7)* 5.00 *1.50*

**Souvenir Sheet**

*651* A91 $1 bl & multi 3.00 *50*

Nordjamb 75, 14th Boy Scout World Jamboree, Lillehammer, Norway, July 29-Aug. 7.

No. 651 has multicolored margin showing landscape with lake. Size: 106x80mm.

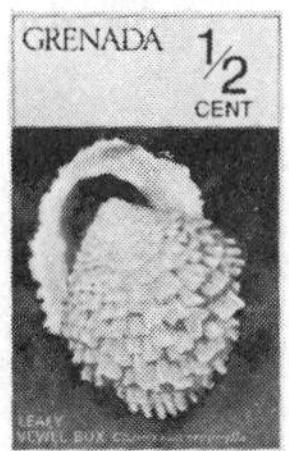


Leafy Jewel Box — A92

Butterflies — A93

Designs: Sea shells.

**1975, Aug. 1 Litho. Perf. 14**

*652* A92 ½c *shown* 5 *5*
*653* A92 1c *Emerald nerite* 5 *5*
*654* A92 2c *Yellow cockle* 5 *5*
*655* A92 25c *Purple sea snail* 50 *20*
*656* A92 50c *Turkey wing* 1.00 *40*
*657* A92 75c *West Indian fighting conch* 1.50 *1.50*
*658* A92 $1 *Noble wentletrap* 2.00 *60*
*Nos. 652-658 (7)* 5.15 2.85

**Souvenir Sheet**

*659* A92 $2 *Music volute* 4.50 *1.00*

No. 659 has multicolored margin. Size: 100x75mm.

**1975, Sept. 22 Litho. Perf. 14**

*660* A93 ½c *Large tiger* 5 *5*
*661* A93 1c *Five continents* 5 *5*
*662* A93 2c *Large striped bl* 5 *5*
*663* A93 35c *Gonatryx* 50 *22*
*664* A93 45c *Spear-winged cattle heart* 65 *30*
*665* A93 75c *Risty nymula* 1.10 *40*
*666* A93 $2 *Blue night* 3.00 *75*
*Nos. 660-666 (7)* 5.40 *1.82*

**Souvenir Sheet**

*667* A93 $1 *Lycrophon* 2.50 *60*

No. 667 has multicolored margin in floral design. Size: 107x83mm.

Crew Race A94

Young Man, by Michelangelo A95

**1975, Oct. 13 Litho. Perf. 14**

*668* A94 ½c *shown* 5 *5*
*669* A94 1c *Women's swimming* 5 *5*
*670* A94 2c *Steeplechase* 5 *5*
*671* A94 35c *Gymnastics* 35 *15*
*672* A94 45c *Soccer* 45 *18*
*673* A94 75c *Boxing* 75 *25*
*674* A94 $2 *Bicycling* 2.00 *50*
*Nos. 668-674 (7)* 3.70 *1.23*

**Souvenir Sheet**

*675* A94 $1 *Sailing* 1.50 *35*

7th Pan-American Games, Mexico City, Oct. 13-26.

No. 675 has multicolored margin showing beach and palms. Size: 106x81mm.

**1975, Nov. 3**

Works by Michelangelo (except 50c): ½c, David. 2c, Moses. 40c, Zachariah. 50c, St.

John the Baptist (sculpture). 75c, Judith and Holofernes (detail). $1, Madonna (head from Pieta). $2, Doni Madonna (detail from Holy Family).

| | | | | |
|---|---|---|---|---|
| *676* | A95 | ½c blk & multi | 5 | *5* |
| *677* | A95 | 1c blk & multi | 5 | *5* |
| *678* | A95 | 2c blk & multi | 5 | *5* |
| *679* | A95 | 40c blk & multi | 45 | *15* |
| *680* | A95 | 50c blk & multi | 55 | *20* |
| *681* | A95 | 75c blk & multi | 85 | *25* |
| *682* | A95 | $2 blk & multi | 2.25 | *50* |
| | | *Nos. 676-682 (7)* | 4.25 | *1.25* |

**Souvenir Sheet**

| | | | | |
|---|---|---|---|---|
| *683* | A95 | $1 blk & multi | 1.25 | *30* |

500th birth anniversary of Michelangelo Buonarroti (1475-1564), Italian painter, sculptor and architect. No. 683 has marble-colored margin with blue inscription. Size: 103x88mm.

Virgin and Child Paintings A96

Bananaquit A97

**1975, Dec. 8**

| | | | | |
|---|---|---|---|---|
| *684* | A96 | ½c *Filippino Lippi* | 5 | *5* |
| *685* | A96 | 1c *Mantegna* | 5 | *5* |
| *686* | A96 | 2c *Luis de Morales* | 5 | *5* |
| *687* | A96 | 35c *G. M. Morandi* | 35 | *15* |
| 688 | A96 | 50c *Antonello da Messina* | 50 | *20* |
| *689* | A96 | 75c *Durer* | 75 | *25* |
| *690* | A96 | $1 *Velazquez* | 1.00 | *30* |
| | | *Nos. 684-690 (7)* | 2.75 | 1.05 |

**Souvenir Sheet**

| | | | | |
|---|---|---|---|---|
| *691* | A96 | $2 *Bellini* | 3.75 | *60* |

Christmas 1975. No. 691 has multicolored margin showing angels. Size: 125x97mm.

**1976, Jan. 20 Litho. *Perf. 14***

Designs: 1c, Orange-rumped agouti. 2c, Hawksbill turtle (horiz.). 5c, Dwarf poinciana. 35c, Albacores (horiz.). 40c, Cardinal's guard flower. $1, Belted kingfisher. $2, Antillean armadillo (horiz.).

| | | | | |
|---|---|---|---|---|
| *692* | A97 | ½c multi | 5 | 5 |
| *693* | A97 | 1c multi | 5 | 5 |
| *694* | A97 | 2c multi | 5 | 5 |
| *695* | A97 | 5c multi | 5 | 5 |
| *696* | A97 | 35c multi | 75 | 75 |
| *697* | A97 | 40c multi | 85 | 85 |
| *698* | A97 | $2 multi | 4.25 | 4.25 |
| | | *Nos. 692-698 (7)* | 6.05 | 6.05 |

**Souvenir Sheet**

| | | | | |
|---|---|---|---|---|
| 699 | A97 | $1 multi | 3.00 | 3.00 |

No. 699 contains one stamp, multicolored decorative margin. Size: 82x88½mm.

Carnival Dancers A98

Designs: 1c, Scuba diving. 2c, Cruise ship in St. George's Harbor. 35c, Game fishing. 50c, St. George's Golf Course. 75c, Tennis. $1, Mount Rich rock carvings. $2, Sailboats.

**1976, Feb. 25 Litho. *Perf. 14***

| | | | | |
|---|---|---|---|---|
| *700* | A98 | ½c multi | 5 | 5 |
| *701* | A98 | 1c multi | 5 | 5 |
| *702* | A98 | 2c multi | 5 | 5 |
| *703* | A98 | 35c multi | 40 | 40 |
| *704* | A98 | 50c multi | 55 | 55 |
| *705* | A98 | 75c multi | 80 | 80 |
| *706* | A98 | $1 multi | 1.10 | 1.10 |
| | | *Nos. 700-706 (7)* | 3.00 | 3.00 |

**Souvenir Sheet**

| | | | | |
|---|---|---|---|---|
| *707* | A98 | $2 multi | 2.20 | 2.20 |

Tourist publicity. No. 707 has multicolored margin showing sports, fish, musicians. Size: 100x74mm.

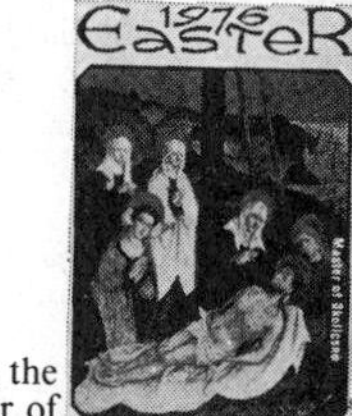


Descent from the Cross, by Master of Okolicsno — A99

Paintings: 1c, Pieta, by Correggio. 2c, Crucifixion, by van der Weyden. 3c, Burial of Christ, by Dürer. 35c, God the Father Holding Crucified Christ, by unknown master (Florence). 75c, Ascension, by Raphael. $1, Burial of Christ, by Raphael. $2, Pieta, by Crespi.

**1976, Mar. 29**

| | | | | |
|---|---|---|---|---|
| *708* | A99 | ½c multi | 5 | 5 |
| *709* | A99 | 1c multi | 5 | 5 |
| *710* | A99 | 2c multi | 5 | 5 |
| *711* | A99 | 3c multi | 5 | 5 |
| *712* | A99 | 35c multi | 35 | 35 |
| *713* | A99 | 75c multi | 75 | 75 |
| *714* | A99 | $1 multi | 1.00 | 1.00 |
| | | *Nos. 708-714 (7)* | 2.30 | 2.30 |

**Souvenir Sheet**

| | | | | |
|---|---|---|---|---|
| *715* | A99 | $2 multi | 1.75 | 1.75 |

Easter 1976. No. 715 has yellow and multicolored margin with picture of Risen Christ. Size: 108x86mm.

Sharpshooters, 1780 — A100

Designs (First Stars and Stripes and): 1c, Defense of Liberty Pole. 2c, Men loading muskets. 35c, 75c, Fight for Liberty. 50c, $2, Peace Treaty, 1783. $1, Drumming march on Breed's Hill. $3, Gunboat, c. 1776.

**1976, Apr. 15 Litho. *Perf. 14***

| | | | | |
|---|---|---|---|---|
| *716* | A100 | ½c multi | 5 | 5 |
| *717* | A100 | 1c multi | 5 | 5 |
| *718* | A100 | 2c multi | 5 | 5 |
| *719* | A100 | 35c multi | 35 | 35 |
| *720* | A100 | 50c multi | 50 | 50 |
| *721* | A100 | $1 multi | 1.00 | 1.00 |
| *722* | A100 | $3 multi | 3.00 | 3.00 |
| | | *Nos. 716-722 (7)* | 5.00 | 5.00 |

**Souvenir Sheet**

| | | | | |
|---|---|---|---|---|
| *723* | A100 | Sheet of 2 | 3.00 | 3.00 |
| *a.* | | 75c multi | 75 | 75 |
| *b.* | | $2 multi | 2.00 | 2.00 |

American Bicentennial. No. 723 has blue margin with black and white inscription and shows Boston Massacre. Size: 93x80mm.

Girl Guide Emblems, Nature Study A101

Volleyball A102

Designs (Various Girl Guide Emblems and): 1c, Cooking. 2c, $2, First aid (diff.). 50c, Tenting. 75c, Home economics. $1, Drawing.

**1976, June 1 Litho. *Perf. 14***

| | | | | |
|---|---|---|---|---|
| *724* | A101 | ½c multi | 5 | 5 |
| *725* | A101 | 1c multi | 5 | 5 |
| *726* | A101 | 2c multi | 5 | 5 |
| *727* | A101 | 50c multi | 50 | 50 |
| *728* | A101 | 75c multi | 75 | 75 |
| *729* | A101 | $2 multi | 2.25 | 2.25 |
| | | *Nos. 724-729 (6)* | 3.65 | 3.65 |

**Souvenir Sheet**

| | | | | |
|---|---|---|---|---|
| *730* | A101 | $1 multi | 2.25 | 2.25 |

Girl Guides of Grenada, 50th anniv.

No. 730 has multicolored margin showing Girl Guide emblems and flags. Size: 110x85mm.

**1976, June 21 Litho. *Perf. 14***

Designs (Olympic Rings and): 1c, Bicycling. 2c, Rowing. 35c, Judo. 45c, Hockey. 75c, Women's gymnastics. $1, High jump. $3, Equestrian.

| | | | | |
|---|---|---|---|---|
| *731* | A102 | ½c multi | 5 | 5 |
| *732* | A102 | 1c multi | 5 | 5 |
| *733* | A102 | 2c multi | 5 | 5 |
| *734* | A102 | 35c multi | 28 | 28 |
| *735* | A102 | 45c multi | 35 | 35 |
| *736* | A102 | 75c multi | 60 | 60 |
| *737* | A102 | $1 multi | 80 | 80 |
| | | *Nos. 731-737 (7)* | 2.18 | 2.18 |

**Souvenir Sheet**

| | | | | |
|---|---|---|---|---|
| *738* | A102 | $3 multi | 2.50 | 2.50 |

21st Olympic Games, Montreal, Canada, July 17-Aug. 1. No. 738 has multicolored margin showing various sports. Size: 105x80mm.

Moulin Rouge, by Toulouse-Lautrec A103

Paintings by Toulouse-Lautrec: 1c, Start of the Quadrille. 2c, Woman's Head. 3c, Hall at the Moulin Rouge. 40c, Man Delivering Laundry. 50c, Dancing the Bolero. $1, Lady with Boa. $2, Signor Boileau at the Cafe.

**1976, July 20 Litho. *Perf. 14***

| | | | | |
|---|---|---|---|---|
| *739* | A103 | ½c multi | 5 | 5 |
| *740* | A103 | 1c multi | 5 | 5 |
| *741* | A103 | 2c multi | 5 | 5 |
| *742* | A103 | 3c multi | 5 | 5 |
| *743* | A103 | 40c multi | 40 | 40 |
| *744* | A103 | 50c multi | 50 | 50 |
| *745* | A103 | $2 multi | 2.00 | 2.00 |
| | | *Nos. 739-745 (7)* | 3.10 | 3.10 |

**Souvenir Sheet**

| | | | | |
|---|---|---|---|---|
| *746* | A103 | $1 multi | 1.20 | 1.20 |

Henri de Toulouse-Lautrec (1864-1901), painter, 75th death anniversary. No. 746 has yellow green and black margin showing easel and paint brushes. Size: 163x125mm.

**Cricket Cup Issue**

Types of Barbados 1976

**1976, July 26**

| | | | | |
|---|---|---|---|---|
| *747* | A63 | 35c lt bl & multi | 70 | 70 |
| *748* | A64 | $1 lil rose & blk | 2.00 | 2.00 |

World Cricket Cup, won by West Indies Team, 1975.

Piper Apache A104

Airplanes: 1c, Beech Twin Bonanza. 2c, D. H. Twin Otter. 40c, Britten Norman Islander. 50c, D. H. Heron. $2, Hawker Siddeley Avro 748. $3, B.A.C. One-Eleven.

**1976, Aug. 18**

| | | | | |
|---|---|---|---|---|
| *749* | A104 | ½c multi | 5 | 5 |
| *750* | A104 | 1c multi | 5 | 5 |
| *751* | A104 | 2c multi | 5 | 5 |
| *752* | A104 | 40c multi | 40 | 40 |
| *753* | A104 | 50c multi | 50 | 50 |
| *754* | A104 | $2 multi | 2.00 | 2.00 |
| | | *Nos. 749-754 (6)* | 3.05 | 3.05 |

**Souvenir Sheet**

| | | | | |
|---|---|---|---|---|
| *755* | A104 | $3 multi | 3.30 | 3.30 |

No. 755 has dark brown margin showing aircraft. Size: 75x83mm.

Helios Mission, Assembly — A105

Designs: 1c, Helios spacecraft in space 2c, Helios assembled. 15c, Helios, system test and checkout. 45c, Viking nearing Mars (horiz.). 75c, Viking on Mars. $2, Viking spacecraft assembled. $3, Helios orbiter and Viking lander.

**1976, Sept. 1 Litho. *Perf. 14***

| | | | | |
|---|---|---|---|---|
| *756* | A105 | ½c multi | 5 | 5 |
| *757* | A105 | 1c multi | 5 | 5 |
| *758* | A105 | 2c multi | 5 | 5 |
| *759* | A105 | 15c multi | 12 | 12 |
| *760* | A105 | 45c multi | 35 | 35 |
| *761* | A105 | 75c multi | 60 | 60 |
| *762* | A105 | $2 multi | 1.60 | 1.60 |
| | | *Nos. 756-762 (7)* | 2.82 | 2.82 |

**Souvenir Sheet**

| | | | | |
|---|---|---|---|---|
| *763* | A105 | $3 multi | 2.75 | 2.75 |

Helios (solar probe) mission and Viking Mars missions. No. 763 has multicolored margin showing rocket. Size: 109x85mm.

S.S. Geestland, Geest Line Flag — A106

Ships: 1c, M.V. Federal Palm, West Indies Shipping Service. 2c, H.M.S. Blake and ship's crest. 25c, M.V. Vistafjord and Norwegian-American Line flag. 75c, S.S. Canberra and P. & O. Line flag. $1, S.S. Regina and Chandris Line flag. $2, Santa Maria and Spanish flag, 1492. $5, S.S. Arandora and Blue Star Line flag.

**1976, Nov. 3 Litho. *Perf. 14½***

| | | | | |
|---|---|---|---|---|
| *764* | A106 | ½c bl & multi | 5 | 5 |
| *765* | A106 | 1c bl & multi | 5 | 5 |
| *766* | A106 | 2c bl & multi | 5 | 5 |
| *767* | A106 | 25c bl & multi | 25 | 25 |
| *768* | A106 | 75c bl & multi | 75 | 75 |
| *769* | A106 | $1 bl & multi | 1.00 | 1.00 |
| *770* | A106 | $5 bl & multi | 5.00 | 5.00 |
| | | *Nos. 764-770 (7)* | 7.15 | 7.15 |

**Souvenir Sheet**

| | | | | |
|---|---|---|---|---|
| *771* | A106 | $2 multi | 2.75 | 2.75 |

Ships connected with Grenada's development. No. 771 has green and dark brown margin showing ships. Size: 91½x79mm.

Altarpiece of San Barnaba, by Botticelli A107

Paintings: 1c, Annunciation, by Botticelli. 2c, Madonna with Chancellor Rolin, by Jan van Eyck. 35c, Annunciation, by Fra Filippo Lippi. 50c, Madonna of the Magnificat, by Botticelli. 75c, Madonna of the Pomegranate, by Botticelli. $2, Gipsy Madonna, by Titian. $3, Madonna with St. Cosmas and Saints, by Botticelli.

**1976, Dec. 8 Litho. *Perf. 14***

| | | | | |
|---|---|---|---|---|
| *772* | A107 | ½c multi | 5 | 5 |
| *773* | A107 | 1c multi | 5 | 5 |
| *774* | A107 | 2c multi | 5 | 5 |
| *775* | A107 | 35c multi | 45 | 45 |
| *776* | A107 | 50c multi | 65 | 65 |

| | | |
|---|---|---|
| *777* A107 75c multi | 1.00 | 1.00 |
| *778* A107 $3 multi | 4.00 | 4.00 |
| *Nos. 772-778 (7)* | 6.25 | 6.25 |

**Souvenir Sheet**

| | | |
|---|---|---|
| *779* A107 $2 multi | 2.20 | 2.20 |

Christmas 1976. No. 779 has light violet margin with stars. Size: 72x57mm.

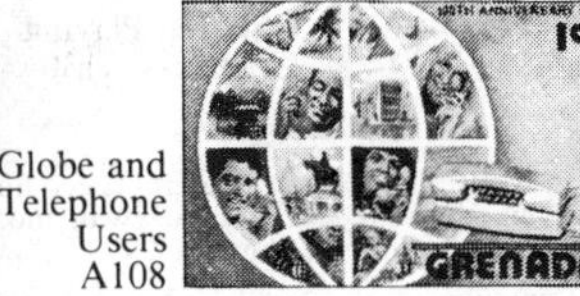

Globe and Telephone Users A108

Designs: ½c, A. G. Bell, 1876 and modern telephones. 2c, Satellites around globe, world map. 18c, Videophone. 40c, Satellite and ground stations. $1, Satellite and telephone communication with ships. $2, British "Trimphone" and radar station. $5, Flags of the world surrounding globe, and telephone.

**1976, Dec. 17 Litho. *Perf. 14***

| | | |
|---|---|---|
| *780* A108 ½c multi | 5 | 5 |
| *781* A108 1c multi | 5 | 5 |
| *782* A108 2c multi | 5 | 5 |
| *783* A108 18c multi | 18 | 18 |
| *784* A108 40c multi | 40 | 40 |
| *785* A108 $1 multi | 1.00 | 1.00 |
| *786* A108 $2 multi | 2.00 | 2.00 |
| *Nos. 780-786 (7)* | 3.73 | 3.73 |

**Souvenir Sheet**

| | | |
|---|---|---|
| *787* A108 $5 multi | 4.00 | 4.00 |

Centenary of first telephone conversation by Alexander Graham Bell, Mar. 10, 1876. No. 787 has gray margin with black inscription and multicolored abstract telephone design. Size: 107x80mm.

Coronation of Elizabeth II — A109

Designs: 1c, $1, Orb and scepter. 35c, $3, Trooping of the Guards. 50c, $2, Spoon and ampulla. 35c (bklt.), $2.50, Elizabeth II and Prince Philip. $5, Royal visit to Grenada.

**1977, Feb. 8 Litho. *Perf. 14, 12***

| | | |
|---|---|---|
| *788* A109 ½c multi | 5 | 5 |
| *789* A109 1c multi | 5 | 5 |
| *790* A109 35c multi | 25 | 25 |
| *791* A109 $2 multi | 1.40 | 1.40 |
| *792* A109 $2.50 multi | 1.75 | 1.75 |
| *a* Bklt. pane of 6 (35c) | 2.00 | |
| *b* Bklt. pane of 3 (50c, $1, $3) | 6.00 | |
| *Nos. 788-792 (5)* | 3.50 | 3.50 |

**Souvenir Sheet**

| | | |
|---|---|---|
| *793* A109 $5 multi | 3.25 | 3.25 |

25th anniversary of the reign of Queen Elizabeth II.

Nos. 792a-792b are self-adhesive, roulette x imperf. Marginal inscriptions.

No. 793 has blue and multicolored margin showing royal coat of arms. Size: 104x78mm.

Nos. 788-792 were printed in sheets of 40 (10x4), perf. 14, and sheets of 5 plus label, perf. 12, in changed colors.

Water Skiing, One-ski Slalom A110

Designs: 1c, Speedboat racing around Grand Anse. 2c, Crew racing, St. George's. 22c, Swimming, Grand Anse. 35c, Local work boat races. 75c, Water polo, careenage, St. George's. $2, Game fishing. $3, South Coast yacht race.

**1977, Apr. 13 Litho. *Perf. 14***

| | | |
|---|---|---|
| *794* A110 ½c multi | 5 | 5 |
| *795* A110 1c multi | 5 | 5 |
| *796* A110 2c multi | 5 | 5 |
| *797* A110 22c multi | 22 | 22 |
| *798* A110 35c multi | 35 | 35 |
| *799* A110 75c multi | 75 | 75 |
| *800* A110 $2 multi | 2.00 | 2.00 |
| *Nos. 794-800 (7)* | 3.47 | 3.47 |

**Souvenir Sheet**

| | | |
|---|---|---|
| *801* A110 $3 multi | 3.00 | 3.00 |

1977 Easter Water Parade. No. 801 has blue and multicolored margin showing various water sports. Size: 115x85mm.

Tent, OAS Emblem A111

**1977, June 14 Litho. *Perf. 14***

| | | |
|---|---|---|
| *802* A111 35c multi | 35 | 35 |
| *803* A111 $1 multi | 1.00 | 1.00 |
| *804* A111 $2 multi | 2.00 | 2.00 |

7th Regular Session, General Assembly of Organization of American States.

Scouts on Raft A112

Designs: 1c, Tug-of-war. 2c, Boy Scout regatta. 18c, Scouts around camp fire. 40c, Field kitchen. $1, Boy Scouts and Sea Scouts. $2, Hiking and map reading. $3, Semaphore.

**1977, Sept. 6 Litho. *Perf. 14***

| | | |
|---|---|---|
| *805* A112 ½c multi | 5 | 5 |
| *806* A112 1c multi | 5 | 5 |
| *807* A112 2c multi | 5 | 5 |
| *808* A112 18c multi | 18 | 18 |
| *809* A112 40c multi | 40 | 40 |
| *810* A112 $1 multi | 1.00 | 1.00 |
| *811* A112 $2 multi | 2.00 | 2.00 |
| *Nos. 805-811 (7)* | 3.73 | 3.73 |

**Souvenir Sheet**

| | | |
|---|---|---|
| *812* A112 $3 multi | 3.30 | 3.30 |

6th Caribbean Jamboree, Kingston, Jamaica, Aug. 5-14. No. 812 has multicolored margin showing Boy Scout emblem, map of Caribbean and Scouts signaling "Welcome." Size: 108x85mm.

Annunciation to the Shepherds — A113

Ceiling Paintings, St. Martin's Church, Zillis, Switzerland, 12th Century: 1c, Joseph on his way. 2c, Virgin and Child, Flight into Egypt. 22c, Angel leading the way. 35c, King on way to Herod. 75c, Three horses. $2, Virgin and Child. $3, Adoration of the Kings.

**1977, Nov. 3 Litho. *Perf. 14***

| | | |
|---|---|---|
| *813* A113 ½c multi | 5 | 5 |
| *814* A113 1c multi | 5 | 5 |
| *815* A113 2c multi | 5 | 5 |
| *816* A113 22c multi | 15 | 15 |
| *817* A113 35c multi | 25 | 25 |
| *818* A113 75c multi | 50 | 50 |
| *819* A113 $2 multi | 1.40 | 1.40 |
| *Nos. 813-819 (7)* | 2.45 | 2.45 |

**Souvenir Sheet**

| | | |
|---|---|---|
| *820* A113 $3 multi | 2.25 | 2.25 |

Christmas 1977. No. 820 has multicolored margin showing angel and candle. Size: 85x113mm.

Nos. 788-793 Overprinted "Royal Visit W.I. 1977"

**1977, Nov. 10 *Perf. 12, 14***

| | | |
|---|---|---|
| *821* A109 ½c multi | 5 | 5 |
| *822* A109 1c multi | 5 | 5 |
| *823* A109 35c multi | 25 | 25 |
| *824* A109 $2 multi | 1.40 | 1.40 |
| *825* A109 $2.50 multi | 1.75 | 1.75 |
| *Nos. 821-825 (5)* | 3.50 | 3.50 |

**Souvenir Sheet**

***Perf. 14***

| | | |
|---|---|---|
| *826* A109 $5 multi | 3.25 | 3.25 |

Caribbean visit of Queen Elizabeth II. Nos. 821-822 are perf. 12, others perf. 12 and 14.

Christjaan Eijkman — A114

Portraits: 1c, Winston Churchill, Literature, 1953. 2c, Woodrow Wilson, Peace, 1919. 35c, Frederic Passy, Peace 1901. $1, Albert Einstein, Physics, 1921. $2, Alfred Nobel, founder. $3, Carl Bosch, Chemistry, 1931.

**1978, Jan. 25 Litho. *Perf. 14***

| | | |
|---|---|---|
| *827* A114 ½c multi | 5 | 5 |
| *828* A114 1c multi | 5 | 5 |
| *829* A114 2c multi | 5 | 5 |
| *830* A114 35c multi | 28 | 28 |
| *831* A114 $1 multi | 75 | 75 |
| *832* A114 $3 multi | 2.25 | 2.25 |
| *Nos. 827-832 (6)* | 3.43 | 3.43 |

**Souvenir Sheet**

| | | |
|---|---|---|
| *833* A114 $2 multi | 1.50 | 1.50 |

Nobel Prize winners. No. 833 contains one stamp. Multicolored margin shows medals? of Nobel Peace awards. Size: 113x88mm.

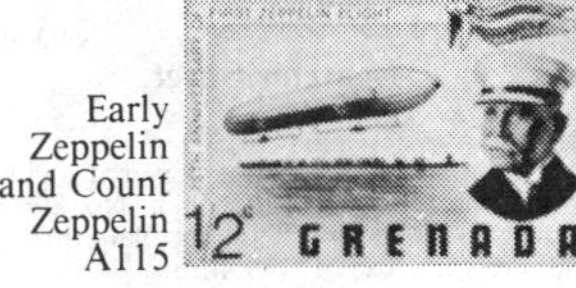

Early Zeppelin and Count Zeppelin A115

Designs: 1c, Lindbergh and Spirit of St. Louis. 2c, "Deutschland" airship. 22c, Lindbergh landing in Paris. 35c, Lindbergh in cockpit. 75c, Lindbergh and Spirit of St. Louis in flight. $1, Zeppelin over Alps. $2, Count Zeppelin and early airship. $3, Zeppelin over White House.

**1978, Feb. 13 Litho. *Perf. 14***

| | | |
|---|---|---|
| *834* A115 ½c multi | 5 | 5 |
| *835* A115 1c multi | 5 | 5 |
| *836* A115 2c multi | 5 | 5 |
| *837* A115 22c multi | 18 | 18 |
| *838* A115 75c multi | 60 | 60 |
| *839* A115 $1 multi | 80 | 80 |
| *840* A115 $3 multi | 2.50 | 2.50 |
| *Nos. 834-840 (7)* | 4.23 | 4.23 |

**Souvenir Sheet**

| | | |
|---|---|---|
| *841* A115 Sheet of 2 | 2.50 | 2.50 |
| *a* 35c multi | 35 | |
| *b* $2 multi | 2.00 | |

Aviation history. No. 841 has multicolored border showing early airships, balloon and double-decker plane. Size: 113x85mm.

Launching of Space Shuttle — A116

Space Shuttle: 1c, Booster separation. 2c, External tank separation. 18c, In orbit. 75c, Satellite placement. $2, Landing approach. $3, On landing pad.

**1978, Feb. 28**

| | | |
|---|---|---|
| *842* A116 ½c multi | 5 | 5 |
| *843* A116 1c multi | 5 | 5 |
| *844* A116 2c multi | 5 | 5 |
| *845* A116 18c multi | 18 | 18 |
| *846* A116 75c multi | 75 | 75 |
| *847* A116 $2 multi | 2.00 | 2.00 |
| *Nos. 842-847 (6)* | 3.08 | 3.08 |

**Souvenir Sheet**

| | | |
|---|---|---|
| *848* A116 $3 multi | 3.30 | 3.30 |

U.S. space shuttle. No. 848 has black and blue margin showing space shuttle over earth. Size: 114x85mm.

Black-headed Gulls — A117

Wild Birds of Grenada and Wildlife Fund Emblem: 1c, Wilson's petrels. 2c, Killdeers. 50c, White-necked jacobin and hibiscus. 75c, Blue-faced booby. $1, Broad-winged hawk. $2, Scaley-necked pigeon. $3, Scarlet ibis.

**1978, Mar. 8 Litho. *Perf. 14***

| | | |
|---|---|---|
| *849* A117 ½c multi | 5 | 5 |
| *850* A117 1c multi | 5 | 5 |
| *851* A117 2c multi | 5 | 5 |
| *852* A117 50c multi | 40 | 40 |
| *853* A117 75c multi | 60 | 60 |
| *854* A117 $1 multi | 80 | 80 |
| *855* A117 $2 multi | 1.60 | 1.60 |
| *Nos. 849-855 (7)* | 3.55 | 3.55 |

**Souvenir Sheet**

| | | |
|---|---|---|
| *856* A117 $3 multi | 3.30 | 3.30 |

No. 856 has multicolored margin showing ibis and large Wildlife Fund emblem. Size: 102x94mm.

Marquise de Spinola, by Rubens A118

Ludwig van Beethoven A119

Rubens Paintings: 5c, Reception of Marie de Medicis. 15c, Rubens and Helena Fourment. 25c, Ludovicus Nonnius. 45c, Helena Fourment with her Children. 75c, Child's head. $3, Suzanne Fourment in Velvet Hat.

**1978, Mar. 30 Litho. *Perf. 13½x14***

| | | |
|---|---|---|
| *857* A118 5c lt bl & multi | 5 | 5 |
| *858* A118 15c lt bl & multi | 12 | 12 |
| *859* A118 18c lt bl & multi | 15 | 15 |
| *860* A118 25c lt bl & multi | 20 | 20 |
| *861* A118 45c lt bl & multi | 35 | 35 |
| *862* A118 75c lt bl & multi | 60 | 60 |
| *863* A118 $3 lt bl & multi | 2.50 | 2.50 |
| *Nos. 857-863 (7)* | 3.97 | 3.97 |

**Souvenir Sheet**

| | | |
|---|---|---|
| *864* A118 $5 lt bl & multi | 4.00 | 4.00 |

Peter Paul Rubens (1577-1640), 400th birth anniversary. No. 864 contains one stamp; blue and purple margin. Size: 64x100mm.

**1978, Apr. 24 *Perf. 14***

Designs: 15c, Woman violinist playing concerto. 18c, Various musical instruments. 22c, Piano. 50c, Two violins. 75c, Beethoven's piano and score. $2, Beethoven and score. $3, Beethoven and his house. (15c, 18c, 22c, 75c, $2, $3 horiz.).

| No. | Type | Denomination | Unused | Used |
|---|---|---|---|---|
| *865* | A119 | 5c multi | 5 | 5 |
| *866* | A119 | 15c multi | 12 | 12 |
| *867* | A119 | 18c multi | 14 | 14 |
| *868* | A119 | 22c multi | 18 | 18 |
| *869* | A119 | 50c multi | 38 | 38 |
| *870* | A119 | 75c multi | 55 | 55 |
| *871* | A119 | $3 multi | 2.25 | 2.25 |
| | | *Nos. 865-871 (7)* | 3.67 | 3.67 |

**Souvenir Sheet**

| No. | Type | Denomination | Unused | Used |
|---|---|---|---|---|
| *872* | A119 | $2 multi | 2.25 | 2.25 |

Ludwig van Beethoven (1770-1827), composer, death sesquicentennial.

No. 872 has buff and black margin. Size: 83x62mm.

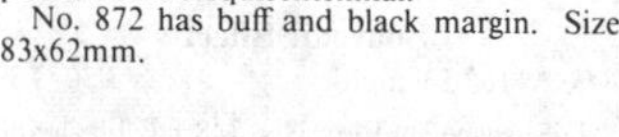

Elizabeth II with Crown, Scepter and Orb — A120

Trooping of the Colors — A121

Designs: 35c, Coronation. $2.50, St. Edward's crown. $5, Elizabeth II and Prince Philip.

**1978, June 2 Litho. *Perf. 14***

| No. | Type | Denomination | Unused | Used |
|---|---|---|---|---|
| *873* | A120 | 35c multi | 25 | 25 |
| *874* | A120 | $2 multi | 1.50 | 1.50 |
| *875* | A120 | $2.50 multi | 1.75 | 1.75 |

**Souvenir Sheet**

| No. | Type | Denomination | Unused | Used |
|---|---|---|---|---|
| *876* | A120 | $5 multi | 3.25 | 3.25 |

**Litho.**

***Imperf***

**Self-adhesive**

Designs: 35c, Elizabeth II at Maundy Money distribution ceremony. $5, Elizabeth II and Prince Philip.

| No. | Description | Unused | Used |
|---|---|---|---|
| *877* | Souvenir booklet | 5.75 | 5.75 |
| *a* | A121 Bklt. pane of 6 (3 each 25c and 35c) | 1.50 | |
| *b* | A121 Bklt. pane of 1 ($5) | 4.00 | |

Coronation of Queen Elizabeth II, 25th anniv. No. 876 has multicolored margin with flowers and Royal crowns. Size: 102x76mm.

Nos. 873-875 were printed in sheets of 40 (10x4), perf. 14, and sheets of 3 plus label, perf. 12, in changed colors. Labels show royal insignia; multicolored margin with coats of arms.

No. 877 contains 2 booklet panes printed on peelable paper backing showing coins. Size of panes: 155x92mm.

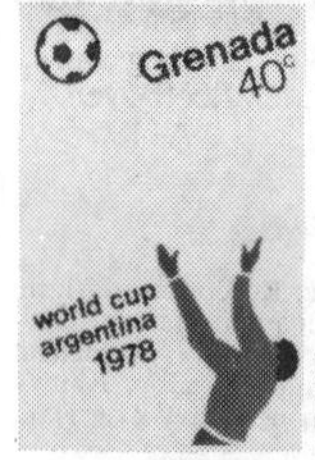


Goalkeeper Reaching for Ball — A122

Designs: Goalkeeper reaching for ball, various stages of motion.

**1978, Aug. 1 Litho. *Perf. 15***

| No. | Type | Denomination | Unused | Used |
|---|---|---|---|---|
| *878* | A122 | 40c multi | 28 | 28 |
| *879* | A122 | 60c multi | 40 | 40 |
| *880* | A122 | 90c multi | 60 | 60 |
| *881* | A122 | $2 multi | 1.40 | 1.40 |

**Souvenir Sheet**

| No. | Type | Denomination | Unused | Used |
|---|---|---|---|---|
| *882* | A122 | $2.50 multi | 2.00 | 2.00 |

11th World Cup Soccer Championship, Argentina, June 1-25. No. 882 contains one stamp; multicolored margin shows ball flying over stands. Size: 130x97mm.

*Grenada stamps can be mounted in Scott's annually supplemented British Windward Islands Album.*

Flying Objects, 16th Century Drawing and Flying Saucer, 1962
A123

Designs: 35c, Radar probing skies, and Mars surface. $2, Prime Minister Eric Gairy and U.N. General Assembly Building. $3, Flying saucer with downwards beam, and UFO photograph.

**1978, Aug. 17**

| No. | Type | Denomination | Unused | Used |
|---|---|---|---|---|
| *883* | A123 | 5c multi | 5 | 5 |
| *884* | A123 | 35c multi | 28 | 28 |
| *885* | A123 | $3 multi | 2.25 | 2.25 |

**Souvenir Sheet**

| No. | Type | Denomination | Unused | Used |
|---|---|---|---|---|
| *886* | A123 | $2 multi | 1.75 | 1.75 |

Proposal by Prime Minister Eric Gairy of Grenada to the U.N. General Assembly to study unidentified flying objects, Oct. 7, 1977. No. 886 has multicolored margin showing United Nations, N.Y., and flying saucer. Size: 112x89mm.

Wright Glider and Allegory of Flight
A124

Designs: 15c, Flyer I, 1903, and eagle. 18c, Flyer III and allegory of flight. 22c, Flyer III and eagle. 50c, Orville Wright, Flyer and allegory of flight. 75c, Flyer, 1908, and eagle. $2, Flyer and allegory of flight. $3, Wilbur Wright, Flyer and allegory of flight.

**1978, Aug. 24 *Perf. 14***

| No. | Type | Denomination | Unused | Used |
|---|---|---|---|---|
| *887* | A124 | 5c multi | 5 | 5 |
| *888* | A124 | 15c multi | 12 | 12 |
| *889* | A124 | 18c multi | 15 | 15 |
| *890* | A124 | 22c multi | 18 | 18 |
| *891* | A124 | 50c multi | 38 | 38 |
| *892* | A124 | 75c multi | 55 | 55 |
| *893* | A124 | $3 multi | 2.25 | 2.25 |
| | | *Nos. 887-893 (7)* | 3.68 | 3.68 |

**Souvenir Sheet**

| No. | Type | Denomination | Unused | Used |
|---|---|---|---|---|
| *894* | A124 | $2 multi | 1.50 | 1.50 |

75th anniversary of first powered flight by Wright brothers, Dec. 17, 1903. No. 894 has multicolored margin showing plane in flight and crowd. Size: 114x85mm.

Hawaiian Feast in Capt. Cook's Honor
A125

Designs (Capt. Cook and): 35c, Hawaiian warriors' dance. 75c, Honolulu harbor. $3, "Resolution." $4, Death scene.

**1978, Dec. 5 Litho. *Perf. 14***

| No. | Type | Denomination | Unused | Used |
|---|---|---|---|---|
| *895* | A125 | 18c multi | 15 | 15 |
| *896* | A125 | 35c multi | 28 | 28 |
| *897* | A125 | 75c multi | 60 | 60 |
| *898* | A125 | $3 multi | 2.50 | 2.50 |

**Souvenir Sheet**

| No. | Type | Denomination | Unused | Used |
|---|---|---|---|---|
| *899* | A125 | $4 multi | 2.75 | 2.75 |

Bicentenary of Capt. Cook's arrival in Hawaii and 250th anniversary of his birth. No. 899 has multicolored margin showing map of Capt. Cook's voyages. Size: 116x89mm.

Detail from Paumgartner Altar, by Dürer — A126

Convention and Cultural Center — A127

Dürer Paintings: 60c, The Three Kings. 90c, Virgin and Child. $2, Head of the Virgin. $4, Virgin and Child.

**1978, Dec. 20 Litho. *Perf. 14***

| No. | Type | Denomination | Unused | Used |
|---|---|---|---|---|
| *900* | A126 | 40c multi | 30 | 30 |
| *901* | A126 | 60c multi | 45 | 45 |
| *902* | A126 | 90c multi | 70 | 70 |
| *903* | A126 | $2 multi | 1.50 | 1.50 |

**Souvenir Sheet**

| No. | Type | Denomination | Unused | Used |
|---|---|---|---|---|
| *904* | A126 | $4 multi | 2.75 | 2.75 |

Christmas 1978 and 450th death anniversary of Albrecht Dürer (1471-1528), German painter. No. 904 has multicolored margin showing entire painting. Size: 113x84mm.

**1979, Feb. 8 Litho. *Perf. 14***

Designs: 18c, Geodesic Dome. 22c, Rowboat race, Easter parade, St. George's. 35c, Prime Minister Eric M. Gairy. $3, Cross at Fort Frederick at night.

| No. | Type | Denomination | Unused | Used |
|---|---|---|---|---|
| *905* | A127 | 5c multi | 5 | 5 |
| *906* | A127 | 18c multi | 12 | 12 |
| *907* | A127 | 22c multi | 15 | 15 |
| *908* | A127 | 35c multi | 25 | 25 |
| *909* | A127 | $3 multi | 2.00 | 2.00 |
| | | *Nos. 905-909 (5)* | 2.57 | 2.57 |

5th anniversary of independence.

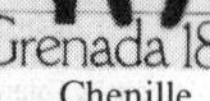

Chenille Plant — A128

Birds in Flight — A129

Native Flowers: 50c, Red hibiscus. $1, Skyflower. $2, Pink pride of India. $3, Rosebay.

**1979, Feb. 26**

| No. | Type | Denomination | Unused | Used |
|---|---|---|---|---|
| *910* | A128 | 18c multi | 15 | 15 |
| *911* | A128 | 50c multi | 40 | 40 |
| *912* | A128 | $1 multi | 80 | 80 |
| *913* | A128 | $3 multi | 2.50 | 2.50 |

**Souvenir Sheet**

| No. | Type | Denomination | Unused | Used |
|---|---|---|---|---|
| *914* | A128 | $2 multi | 2.00 | 2.00 |

No. 914 has multicolored margin showing flowers of African tulip tree. Size: 115x90mm.

**1979, Mar. 15**

Design: $2, Bird in flight and Human Rights emblem.

| No. | Type | Denomination | Unused | Used |
|---|---|---|---|---|
| *915* | A129 | 15c multi | 12 | 12 |
| *916* | A129 | $2 multi | 1.50 | 1.50 |

Universal Declaration of Human Rights, 30th anniversary.

Children Playing Cricket — A130

Designs (IYC Emblem and): 22c, Boys playing baseball. $4, Children with model spaceship. $5, Three children.

**1979, Apr. 23 Litho. *Perf. 14***

| No. | Type | Denomination | Unused | Used |
|---|---|---|---|---|
| *917* | A130 | 18c multi | 18 | 18 |
| *918* | A130 | 22c multi | 22 | 22 |
| *919* | A130 | $5 multi | 5.00 | 5.00 |

**Souvenir Sheet**

| No. | Type | Denomination | Unused | Used |
|---|---|---|---|---|
| *920* | A130 | $4 multi | 4.25 | 4.25 |

International Year of the Child. No. 920 has multicolored margin showing children's heads. Size: 114x92mm.

Balloon and Space Shuttle
A131

Designs: 35c, Octopus holding sailors, nuclear submarine. 75c, Rocket and moon. $3, Imaginary plane and space ship. $4, Multi-propellered ship and U.S. space shuttle.

**1979, May 4**

| No. | Type | Denomination | Unused | Used |
|---|---|---|---|---|
| *921* | A131 | 18c multi | 15 | 15 |
| *922* | A131 | 35c multi | 25 | 25 |
| *923* | A131 | 75c multi | 55 | 55 |
| *924* | A131 | $3 multi | 2.25 | 2.25 |

**Souvenir Sheet**

| No. | Type | Denomination | Unused | Used |
|---|---|---|---|---|
| *925* | A131 | $4 multi | 2.75 | 2.75 |

Jules Verne (1828-1905), science fiction writer. No. 925 has multicolored margin with portrait of Jules Verne. Size: 111x85mm.

African Mail Runner
A132

Rowland Hill and: 40c, American Pony Express. $1, Oriental pigeon post. $3, European mail coach. $5, Tete-beche stamps with revenue surcharge, 1883.

**1979, June Litho. *Perf. 14***

| No. | Type | Denomination | Unused | Used |
|---|---|---|---|---|
| *926* | A132 | 20c multi | 14 | 14 |
| *927* | A132 | 40c multi | 28 | 28 |
| *928* | A132 | $1 multi | 65 | 65 |
| *929* | A132 | $3 multi | 2.00 | 2.00 |

**Souvenir Sheet**

| No. | Type | Denomination | Unused | Used |
|---|---|---|---|---|
| *930* | A132 | $5 multi | 3.25 | 3.25 |

Sir Rowland Hill (1795-1879), originator of penny postage. No. 930 has lilac and black margin showing Penny Black and mail coach. Size: 128x100mm.

Nos. 926-929 were printed in sheets of 40, perf. 14, and in sheets of 5 plus label, perf. 12, in changed colors.

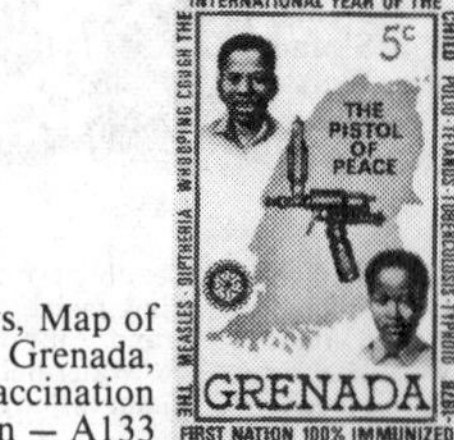


Boys, Map of Grenada, Vaccination Gun — A133

**1979, Aug. 2 Litho. *Perf. 14***

*931* A133 5c multi 5 5
*932* A133 $1 multi 1.50 1.50

International Year of the Child, immunization of children.

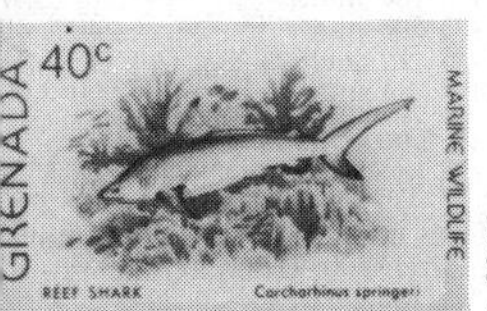

Reef Shark A134

Designs: 45c, Spotted eagle ray. 50c, Manytooth conger. 60c, Golden olive shells. 70c, West Indian murex. 75c, Giant tuns. 90c, Brown boobies. $1, Magnificent frigate bird. $2.50, Sooty tern.

**1979, Aug. 22 Litho. *Perf. 14***

*933* A134 40c multi 28 28
*934* A134 45c multi 30 30
*935* A134 50c multi 35 35
*936* A134 60c multi 40 40
*937* A134 70c multi 50 50
*938* A134 75c multi 55 55
*939* A134 90c multi 60 60
*940* A134 $1 multi 65 65
*Nos. 933-940 (8)* 3.63 3.63

**Souvenir Sheet**

*941* A134 $2.50 multi 2.75 2.75

Flight into Egypt, Tapestry A135

Tapestries: 25c, Virgin and Child. 30c, Angel (vert.). 40c, Infant Jesus, by Doge Marino Grimani (vert.). 90c, Shepherds (vert.). $1, Flight into Egypt (vert.). $2, Virgin in Glory (vert.). $4, Virgin and Child, by Grimani (vert.).

**1979, Oct. 16 Litho. *Perf. 14***

*942* A135 6c multi 6 6
*943* A135 25c multi 18 18
*944* A135 30c multi 20 20
*945* A135 40c multi 28 28
*946* A135 90c multi 60 60
*947* A135 $1 multi 65 65
*948* A135 $2 multi 1.40 1.40
*Nos. 942-948 (7)* 3.37 3.37

**Souvenir Sheet**

*949* A135 $4 multi 2.75 2.75

Christmas 1979. No. 949 has light blue and black decorative margin. Size: 112x149mm.

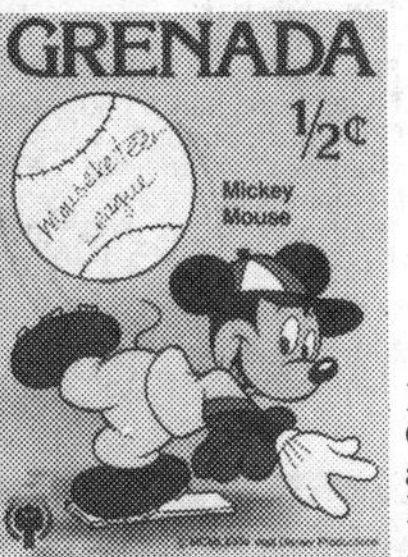

Disney Characters and IYC Emblem A135a

Designs: Sport scenes.

**1979, Nov. 2 Litho. *Perf. 11***

*950* A135a ½c *Mickey Mouse, baseball* 5 5
*951* A135a 1c *Donald, high jump* 5 5
*952* A135a 2c *Goofy, basketball* 5 5
*953* A135a 3c *Goofy, hurdles* 5 5
*954* A135a 4c *Donald Duck, golf* 5 5
*955* A135a 5c *Mickey, cricket* 5 5
*956* A135a 10c *Mickey, soccer* 10 10
*957* A135a $2 *Mickey, tennis* 2.00 2.00
*958* A135a $2.50 *Minnie, equestrian* 2.50 2.50
*Nos. 950-958 (9)* 4.90 4.90

**Souvenir Sheet**

***Perf. 13½***

*959* CD329 $3 *Goofy in riding habit* 3.00 3.00

No. 959 has multicolored margin showing Goofy on horseback. Size: 126x100mm.

See Nos. 1031-1032.

Hands, Paul P. Harris, Rotary Emblem — A136

Rotary Emblem and Hands Holding: 30c, Caduceus. 90c, Wheat. $2, Family. $4, Emblem.

**1980, Feb. 25 Litho. *Perf. 14***

*960* A136 6c multi 6 6
*961* A136 30c multi 20 20
*962* A136 90c multi 60 60
*963* A136 $2 multi 1.40 1.40

**Souvenir Sheet**

*964* A136 $4 multi 2.75 2.75

Rotary International, 75th anniversary. No. 964 has multicolored margin showing Rotary president's medal. Size: 114x89mm.

Nos. 585-586, 588-591, 593-594, 596-602 Overprinted in Black:
PEOPLE'S REVOLUTION
13 MARCH 1979

**1980 *Perf. 15, 13½***

*965* A85 2c multi 5 5
*966* A85 3c multi 5 5
*967* A85 6c multi 6 6
*968* A85 8c multi 6 6
*969* A85 10c multi 7 7
*970* A85 12c multi 8 8
*971* A85 20c multi 14 14
*972* A85 25c multi 16 16
*973* A85 50c multi 35 35
*974* A85 75c multi 50 50
*975* A85 $1 multi 65 65
*976* A85 $2 multi 1.40 1.40
*977* A85 $3 multi 2.00 2.00
*978* A85 $5 multi 3.50 3.50
*979* A85 $10 multi 6.50 6.50
*Nos. 965-979 (15)* 15.57 15.57

Issue dates: 25c, Apr. 7; others, Feb. 28.

Boxing, Kremlin, Olympic Rings A137

**1980, Mar. 24 *Perf. 14***

*980* A137 25c *shown* 16 16
*981* A137 40c *Bicycling* 28 28
*982* A137 90c *Equestrian* 60 60
*983* A137 $2 *Running* 1.40 1.40

**Souvenir Sheet**

*984* A137 $4 *Yachting* 2.75 2.75

22nd Summer Olympic Games, Moscow, July 19-Aug. 3. No. 984 has multicolored margin showing yacht and Kremlin. Size: 127½x95mm.

Tropical Kingbirds — A138

**1980, Apr. 8**

*985* A138 20c *shown* 20 20
*986* A138 40c *Rufous-breasted hermits* 40 40
*987* A138 $1 *Troupials* 1.00 1.00
*988* A138 $2 *Ruddy quail doves* 2.00 2.00

**Souvenir Sheet**

*989* A138 $3 *Prairie warblers* 2.75 2.75

No. 989 has multicolored margin showing birds in tree. Size: 85x113½mm.

Nos. 926-929 Overprinted: "LONDON 1980"

**1980, May 6 Litho. *Perf. 12***

*989A* A132 20c multi 14 14
*989B* A132 40c multi 28 28
*989C* A132 $1 multi 65 65
*989D* A132 $3 multi 2.00 2.00

London '80 Intl. Stamp Exhibition, May 6-14.

Free School Hot Lunches A139

**1980, May 19 Litho. *Perf. 14***

*990* A139 10c *shown* 7 7
*991* A139 40c *Food canning* 28 28
*992* A139 $1 *Health care* 65 65
*993* A139 $2 *Housing projects* 1.40 1.40

**Souvenir Sheet**

*994* A139 $5 *Prime Minister Bishop*, vert. 3.50 3.50

People's Revolution, 1st anniversary. No. 994 has multicolored margin showing crowd. Size: 110x85mm.

Jamb Statues, West Portal, Chartres Cathedral — A140

Masterpieces: 10c, Les Desmoiselles d'Avignon, by Picasso. 40c, Winged Victory of Samothrace. 50c, The Night Watch, by Rembrandt. $1, Edward VI as a Child, by Holbein, the Younger. $3, Queen Nefertiti. $4, Weier Haws, by Durer (vert.).

**1980, June Litho. *Perf. 14***

*995* A140 8c multi 6 6
*996* A140 10c multi 7 7
*997* A140 40c multi 28 28
*998* A140 50c multi 35 35
*999* A140 $1 multi 65 65
*1000* A140 $3 multi 2.00 2.00
*Nos. 995-1000 (6)* 3.41 3.41

**Souvenir Sheet**

*1001* A140 $4 multi 2.75 2.75

No. 1001 has multicolored margin showing entire painting. Size: 101½x102mm.

Carib Canoes A141

**1980, July Litho. *Perf. 14***

*1002* A141 ½c *shown* 5 5
*1003* A141 1c *Boat building* 5 5
*1004* A141 2c *Small workboat* 5 5
*1005* A141 4c *"Santa Maria"* 5 5
*1006* A141 5c *West India man barque, 1840* 5 5
*1007* A141 6c *"Orinoco," 1851* 6 6
*1008* A141 10c *Schooner* 8 8
*1009* A141 12c *Trimaran* 9 9
*1010* A141 15c *"Petite Amie," Spice Island cruising yacht* 12 12
*1011* A141 20c *Fishing pirogue* 15 15
*1012* A141 25c *Harbor police launch* 18 18
*1013* A141 30c *Grand Anse speedboat* 22 22
*1014* A141 40c *"Seimstrand"* 30 30
*1015* A141 50c *"Ariadne," 3-masted schooner* 38 38
*1016* A141 90c *"Geestide," banana boat* 70 70
*1017* A141 $1 *"Cunard Countess," cruise ship* 75 75
*1018* A141 $3 *Rumrunner* 2.25 2.25
*1019* A141 $5 *"Statendam"* 3.75 3.75
*1020* A141 $10 *Coast Guard patrol boat* 7.50 7.50
*Nos. 1002-1020 (19)* 16.78 16.78

Nos. 1002, 1006, 1008, 1011-1014, 1018-1019 reprinted inscribed 1982.

Snow White at Well — A142

Christmas 1980: Various scenes from Walt Disney's Snow White and the Seven Dwarfs.

**1980, Sept. 25 Litho. *Perf. 11***

*1021* A142 ½c multi 5 5
*1022* A142 1c multi 5 5
*1023* A142 2c multi 5 5
*1024* A142 3c multi 5 5
*1025* A142 4c multi 5 5
*1026* A142 5c multi 5 5
*1027* A142 10c multi 9 8
*1028* A142 $2.50 multi 2.00 2.00
*1029* A142 $3 multi 2.50 2.50
*Nos. 1021-1029 (9)* 4.89 4.88

**Souvenir Sheet**

*1030* A142 $4 multi 3.25 3.25

No. 1030 contains a vertical stamp. Multicolored margin shows dwarfs around Snow White's bier. Size: 127x102mm.

Disney Type of 1980

50th Anniversary of Pluto Character: $2, Pluto and birthday cake. $4, Pluto.

**1981, Jan. 19 Litho. *Perf. 14***

*1031* A135a $2 multi 2.00 2.00

**Souvenir Sheet**

*1032* A135a $4 multi 3.50 3.50

No. 1032 has multicolored margin showing scene from Pueblo Pluto, 1949. Size: 127x101mm. No. 1031 issued in sheets of 8.

Adult Education — A143

**1981, Mar. 13 Litho. *Perf. 12½***

*1033* A143 5c Flags of the Revolution and Grenada 5 5
*1034* A143 10c shown 8 8
*1035* A143 15c Food processing plant 12 12
*1036* A143 25c Agriculture 18 18
*1037* A143 40c Fishing boat, crawfish 30 30
*1038* A143 90c Ships 70 70
*1039* A143 $1 Palm trees 75 75
*1040* A143 $3 Map 2.25 2.25
*Nos. 1033-1040 (8)* 4.43 4.43

2nd Festival of the Revolution.

Mickey Mouse and Goofy with Easter Basket A144

Designs: Various Disney characters with Easter baskets.

**1981, Apr. 7** — *Perf. 11*

*1041* A144 35c multi 35 35
*1042* A144 40c multi 40 40
*1043* A144 $2 multi 2.00 2.00
*1044* A144 $2.50 multi 2.50 2.50

**Souvenir Sheet**

*1045* A144 $4 multi 4.00 4.00

Easter 1981. No. 1045 has multicolored margin showing Goofy dropping Easter basket. Size: 127x101½mm.

Large Heads, by Picasso — A145

Picasso Paintings: 25c, Woman-Flower. 30c, Portrait of Madame. 90c, Cavalier with Pipe. $5, Woman on the Bank of the Seine.

**1981, Apr. 28** — *Perf. 14*

*1046* A145 25c multi 20 20
*1047* A145 30c multi 25 25
*1048* A145 90c multi 70 70
*1049* A145 $4 multi 3.25 3.25

**Souvenir Sheet**

*1050* A145 $5 multi 3.50 3.50

Pablo Picasso (1881-1973). Size of No. 1050: 128½x103½mm.

**Royal Wedding Issue**
Common Design Type

**1981, June 16** — **Litho.** — *Perf. 15*

*1051* CD331 50c Couple 38 38
*1052* CD331 $2 Holyrood House 1.50 1.50
*1053* CD331 $4 Charles 3.00 3.00

**Souvenir Sheet**

*1054* CD331 $5 Glass coach 3.75 3.75

**Souvenir Booklet**

*1055* CD331 14.00
 *a* Pane of 6 (3x$1, Lady Diana, 3x$2, Charles) 9.00
 *b* Pane of 1, $5, Couple 5.00

No. 1054 has light brown and black margin showing heraldic designs. Size: 97x84mm. No. 1055 contains imperf., self-adhesive stamps.

Sheets of 5 plus label contain 30c, 40c or $4 in changed colors, perf. 14x14½.

The Bath, by Mary Cassatt (1845-1926) — A146

Decade for Women (Paintings by Women): 40c, Mademoiselle Charlotte du Val d'Ognes, by Constance Marie Charpentier. 60c, Self-portrait, by Mary Beale. $3, Woman in White Stockings, by Suzanne Valadon. $5, The Artist Hesitating between the Arts of Music and Painting (horiz.).

**1981, Oct. 13** — **Litho.** — *Perf. 14*

*1058* A146 15c multi 12 12
*1059* A146 40c multi 30 30
*1060* A146 60c multi 45 45
*1061* A146 $3 multi 2.25 2.25

**Souvenir Sheet**

*1062* A146 $5 multi 3.50 3.50

No. 1062 has multicolored margin showing women at easels. Size: 101x76mm.

Cinderella and Prince Charming Dancing at the Ball — A147

Christmas 1981: Scenes from Walt Disney's Cinderella.

**1981, Nov. 2** — **Litho.** — *Perf. 14x13½*

*1063* A147 ½c multi 5 5
*1064* A147 1c multi 5 5
*1065* A147 2c multi 5 5
*1066* A147 3c multi 5 5
*1067* A147 4c multi 5 5
*1068* A147 5c multi 5 5
*1069* A147 10c multi 9 9
*1070* A147 $2.50 multi 2.25 2.25
*1071* A147 $3 multi 2.75 2.75
 *Nos. 1063-1071 (9)* 5.39 5.39

**Souvenir Sheet**

*1072* A147 $5 multi 4.25 4.25

No. 1072 has multicolored margin continuing design. Size: 127x104mm.

Columbia Space Shuttle — A148

Designs: Views of the Columbia space shuttle.

**1981, Nov. 12**

*1073* A148 30c multi 20 20
*1074* A148 60c multi 40 40
*1075* A148 70c multi 50 50
*1076* A148 $3 multi 2.00 2.00

**Souvenir Sheet**

*1077* A148 $5 multi 3.75 3.75

No. 1077 has multicolored margin continuing design. Size: 118x90mm.

UPU Membership Centenary — A149

**1981, Dec. 10** — **Litho.** — *Perf. 15*

*1078* A149 25c St. George's P.O. 16 16
*1079* A149 30c No. 1 20 20
*1080* A149 90c No. 384 60 60
*1081* A149 $4 No. 189 2.75 2.75

**Souvenir Sheet**

*1082* A149 $5 No. 562 3.75 3.75

No. 1082 has multicolored margin showing flag emblem, headquarters. Size: 113x87mm.

Intl. Year of the Disabled (1981) — A150

**1982, Feb. 4** — *Perf. 14*

*1083* A150 30c Artist 20 20
*1084* A150 40c Computer operator 28 28
*1085* A150 70c Teaching Braille 50 50
*1086* A150 $3 Drummer 2.00 2.00

**Souvenir Sheet**

*1087* A150 $4 Auto mechanic 3.00 3.00

Scouting Year A151

**1982, Feb. 19** — *Perf. 15*

*1088* A151 70c Gardening 50 50
*1089* A151 90c Map reading 60 60
*1090* A151 $1 Bee keeping 65 65
*1091* A151 $4 Hospital reading 2.00 2.00

**Souvenir Sheet**

*1092* A151 $5 Trophy presentation 3.00 3.00

Flambeaux A152

Norman Rockwell A153

**1982, Mar. 24** — **Litho.** — *Perf. 14*

*1093* A152 10c shown 7 7
*1094* A152 60c Large orange sulphurs 40 40
*1095* A152 $1 Red anartias 65 65
*1096* A152 $3 Polydamas swallowtails 2.00 2.00

**Souvenir Sheet**

*1097* A152 $5 Caribbean buckeyes 3.00 3.00

**1982, Apr. 12** — **Litho.** — *Perf. 14x13½*

*1098* A153 15c shown 10 10
*1099* A153 30c Card Tricks 20 20
*1100* A153 60c Pharmacist 40 40
*1101* A153 70c Pals 50 50

**Princess Diana Issue**
Common Design Type

**1982, July 1** — **Litho.** — *Perf. 14½x14*

*1101A* CD332 50c Kensington Palace 35 35
*1102* CD332 60c Kensington Palace 40 40
*1102A* CD332 $1 Couple in field 65 65
*1103* CD332 $2 Honeymoon 1.40 1.40
*1103A* CD332 $3 Diana in green dress 2.00 2.00
*1104* CD332 $4 Diana 2.75 2.75

**Souvenir Sheet**

*1105* CD332 $5 Diana, diff. 3.50 3.50

No. 1105 has multicolored margin showing family tree, Humphrey Bogart. Size: 103x76mm.

Franklin Roosevelt Birth Centenary A154

Designs: 10c, Mary McLeod Bethune, director of Negro Affairs, 1942. 60c, Leadbelly (Huddie Ledbetter, Works Progress Administration). $1.10, Signing Fair Employment Act, 1941. $3, Farm Security Administration.

**1982, July 27** — **Litho.** — *Perf. 14*

*1106* A154 10c multi 7 7
*1107* A154 60c multi 40 40
*1108* A154 $1.10 multi 75 75
*1109* A154 $3 multi 2.00 2.00

**Souvenir Sheet**

*1110* A154 $5 multi 3.50 3.50

No. 1110 has multicolored margin continuing design. Size: 100x71mm.

Easter 1982 A155

Details from Raphael's On the Way to Calvary. 70c, $1.10, $4, $5, vert.

**1982, Sept. 2** — *Perf. 14½*

*1111* A155 40c multi 28 28
*1112* A155 70c multi 40 40
*1113* A155 $1.10 multi 65 65
*1114* A155 $4 multi 2.75 2.75

**Souvenir Sheet**

*1115* A155 $5 multi 3.50 3.50

No. 1115 has multicolored margin showing entire painting. Size: 103x127mm.

**Nos. 1102-1105 Overprinted: "ROYAL BABY / 21.6.82"**

**1982, Sept. 27** — **Litho.** — *Perf. 14½x14*

*1115A* CD332 50c multi 35 35
*1116* CD332 60c multi 40 40
*1116A* CD332 $1 multi 65 65
*1117* CD332 $2 multi 1.40 1.40
*1117A* CD332 $3 multi 2.00 2.00
*1118* CD332 $3 multi 2.75 2.75

**Souvenir Sheet**

*1119* CD332 $5 multi 3.50 3.50

Birth of Prince William of Wales, June 21.

Orient Express A156

**1982, Oct. 4**

*1120* A156 30c shown 20 20
*1121* A156 60c Trans-Siberian Express 40 40
*1122* A156 70c Fleche D'or 50 50
*1123* A156 90c Flying Scotsman 60 60
*1124* A156 $1 German Federal Railways 65 65
*1125* A156 $3 German Natl. Railways 2.00 2.00
 *Nos. 1120-1125 (6)* 4.35 4.35

**Souvenir Sheet**

*1126* A156 $5 20th Century Limited, US 3.50 3.50

Christmas 1982 — A157

Designs: Scenes from Walt Disney's Robin Hood.

**1982, Dec. 7 Litho. Perf. 14**

1127 A157 ½c multi 5 5
1128 A157 1c multi 5 5
1129 A157 2c multi 5 5
1130 A157 3c multi 5 5
1131 A157 4c multi 5 5
1132 A157 5c multi 5 5
1133 A157 10c multi 8 8
1134 A157 $2.50 multi 1.75 1.75
1135 A157 $3 multi 2.25 2.25
*Nos. 1127-1135 (9)* 4.38 4.38

**Souvenir Sheet**

1136 A157 $5 multi 3.75 3.75

No. 1136 has multicolored margin continuing design. Size: 127x102mm.

Italy's Victory in 1982 World Cup A158

**1982, Dec. 2 Perf. 14x13½**

1137 A158 60c Stolen ball 45 45
1138 A158 $4 Captain holding trophy 3.00 3.00

**Souvenir Sheet**

1139 A158 $5 Flags 3.75 3.75

Killer Whale — A159

**1982, Dec. 15 Perf. 14**

1140 A159 15c shown 12 12
1141 A159 40c Sperm whale 30 30
1142 A159 70c Blue whale 50 50
1143 A159 $3 Common dolphins 2.25 2.25

**Souvenir Sheet**

1144 A159 $5 Humpback whale 3.75 3.75

500th Birth Anniv. of Raphael — A160

**1983, Feb. 15 Litho. Perf. 14**

1145 A160 25c Construction of the Ark 18 18
1146 A160 30c Jacob's Vision 22 22
1147 A160 90c Joseph Interprets the Dreams 70 70
1148 A160 $4 Joseph Interprets Pharaoh's Dream 3.00 3.00

**Souvenir Sheet**

1149 A160 $5 Creation of the Animals 3.75 3.75

Size of No. 1149: 129x101mm.

**Commonwealth Day**
Common Design Type

**1983, Mar. 14**

1150 CD334 10c Dental care 8 8
1151 CD334 70c Airport runway construction 55 55
1152 CD334 $1.10 Beach 85 85
1153 CD334 $3 Boat building 2.25 2.25

World Communication Year — A162

**1983, Apr. 18**

1154 A162 30c Ship-satellite communication 22 22
1155 A162 40c Rural telephone installation 30 30
1156 A162 $2.50 Weather map 1.75 1.75
1157 A162 $3 Airport control tower 2.25 2.25

**Souvenir Sheet**

1158 A162 $5 Satellite 3.75 3.75

Franklin Sport Sedan, 1928 A163

**1983, May 4 Litho. Perf. 15**

1159 A163 6c shown 6 6
1160 A163 10c Delage D8, 1933 8 8
1161 A163 40c Alvis, 1938 30 30
1162 A163 60c Invicta S-type Tourer, 1931 45 45
1163 A163 70c Alfa-Romeo 1750 Gran Sport, 1930 50 50
1164 A163 90c Isotta Fraschini, 1930 70 70
1165 A163 $1 Bugatti Royal Type 41, 1941 75 75
1166 A163 $2 BMW 328, 1938 1.50 1.50
1167 A163 $3 Marmon V-16, 1931 2.25 2.25
1168 A163 $4 Lincoln KB Saloon, 1932 3.00 3.00
*Nos. 1159-1168 (10)* 9.59 9.59

**Souvenir Sheet**

1169 A163 $5 Cougar XR-7, 1972 3.75 3.75

No. 1169 has multicolored margin showing emblems. Size: 115x90mm.

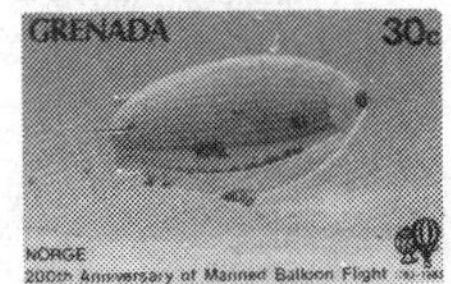

Manned Flight Bicentenary — A164

**1983, July 18 Litho. Perf. 14**

1170 A164 30c Norge blimp 22 22
1171 A164 60c Gloster-VI sea plane 45 45
1172 A164 $1.10 Curtiss NC-4 80 80
1173 A164 $4 Dornier Do-18 3.00 3.00

**Souvenir Sheet**

1174 A164 $5 Hot air ballooning, vert. 3.75 3.75

No. 1174 has multicolored margin showing balloons. Size. 114x86mm.

Christmas 1983 — A165

Designs: Walt Disney's Its Beginning to look a lot like Christmas.

**1983, Nov. Perf. 11**

1175 A165 ½c Morty and Patches 5 5
1176 A165 1c Ludwig von Drake 5 5
1177 A165 2c Gyro Gearloose 5 5
1178 A165 3c Pluto and Figaro 5 5
1179 A165 4c Morty and Ferdy 5 5
1180 A165 5c Mickey Mouse and Goofy 5 5
1181 A165 10c Chip'n'Dale 6 6
1182 A165 $2.50 Mickey and Minnie 1.40 1.40
1183 A165 $3 Donald and Grandma Duck 1.75 1.75
*Nos. 1175-1183 (9)* 3.51 3.51

**Souvenir Sheet**

1184 A165 $5 Goofy 2.75 2.75

Multicolored margin shows Disney characters. Size: 127x102mm.

1984 Olympics — A166

Designs: Various Disney characters.

**1983, Dec. 19 Litho. Perf. 13½**

1185 A166 ½c Pommel Horse 5 5
1186 A166 1c Boxing 5 5
1187 A166 2c Archery 5 5
1188 A166 3c Uneven bars 5 5
1189 A166 4c Hurdles 5 5
1190 A166 5c Weightlifting 5 5
1191 A166 $1 Kayak 75 75
1192 A166 $2 Marathon 1.50 1.50
1193 A166 $3 Pole Vault 2.25 2.25
*Nos. 1185-1193 (9)* 4.80 4.80

**Souvenir Sheet**

1194 A166 $5 Medley Relay, vert. 3.75 3.75

No. 1194 has multicolored margin continuing design.

1984 Los Angeles Olympics Type of 1983 Inscribed with Olympic Rings Emblem

**1984 Litho.**

1185a Perf. 12½x12 5 5
1186a Perf. 12½x12 5 5
1187a Perf. 12½x12 5 5
1188a Perf. 12½x12 5 5
1189a Perf. 12½x12 5 5
1190a Perf. 12½x12 5 5
1191a Perf. 12½x12 75 75
1192a Perf. 12½x12 1.50 1.50
1193a Perf. 12½x12 2.25 2.25
*Nos. 1185a-1193a (9)* 4.80 4.80

**Souvenir Sheet**

1194a Olympic rings emblem inscribed 3.75 3.75

Nos. 1185a-1193a inscribed with Olympic rings emblem. Printed in sheets of 5.

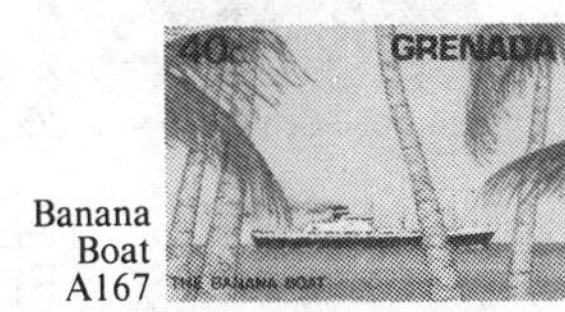

Banana Boat A167

**1984, July 16 Litho. Perf. 15**

1195 A167 40c shown 30 30
1196 A167 70c Queen Elizabeth 2 50 50
1197 A167 90c Working sailboats 70 70
1198 A167 $4 Amerikanis 3.00 3.00

**Souvenir Sheet**

1199 A167 $5 Spanish galleon, flotilla 3.75 3.75

No. 1199 has multicolored margin continuing design. Size: 108x81mm.

King William I, 1066-87 — A168

British Kings or Queens and Years of their reigns: No. 1200b, William II, 1087-1100. c. Henry I, 1100-35. d. Stephen, 1135-54. e. Henry II, 1154-89. f. Richard I, 1189-99. g. John, 1199-1216.

No. 1201a, Henry III, 1216-72. b. Edward I, 1272-1307. c. Edward II, 1307-27. d. Edward III, 1327-77. e. Richard II, 1377-99. f. Henry IV, 1399-1413. g. Henry V, 1413-22.

No. 1202a, Henry VI, 1422-61. b. Edward IV, 1461-83. c. Edward V, 1483. d. Richard III, 1483-85. e. Henry VII, 1485-1509. f. Henry VIII, 1509-47. g. Edward VI, 1547-53.

No. 1203a, Jane Grey, 1553. b. Mary I, 1553-58. c. Elizabeth I, 1558-1603. d. James I, 1603-25. e. Charles I, 1625-49. f. Charles II, 1660-85. g. James II, 1685-88.

No. 1204a, William III, 1688-1702. b. Mary II, 1688-94. c. Anne, 1702-14. d. George I, 1714-27. e. George II, 1727-60. f. George III, 1760-1820. g. George IV, 1820-30.

No. 1205a, William IV, 1830-37. b. Victoria, 1837-1901. c. Edward VII, 1901-10. d. George V, 1910-36. e. Edward VIII, 1936. f. George VI, 1936-52. g. Elizabeth II, since 1952. Size: 141x128mm.

**1984, Jan. 25 Litho. Perf. 14**

1200-1205 Sheets of 7 + label, any sheet 21.00 21.00
*a.-g.* A168, $4, any single 3.00 3.00

Local Flowers A169

**1984, May Perf. 15**

1206 A169 25c Lantana 18 18
1207 A169 30c Plumbago 22 22
1208 A169 90c Spider lily 70 70
1209 A169 $4 Giant alocasia 3.00 3.00

**Souvenir Sheet**

1210 A169 $5 Orange trumpet vine 3.75 3.75

Coral Reef Fish, World Wildlife Fund Emblem A170

**1984, May Litho. Perf. 14**

1211 A170 10c Blue parrot fish 8 8
1212 A170 30c Flame-back cherub fish 22 22
1213 A170 70c Painted wrasse 52 52
1214 A170 90c Straight-tailed razorfish 68 68

**Souvenir Sheet**

1215 A170 $5 Spanish hogfish 3.75 3.75

No. 1215 has multicolored margin showing diver. Size: 82x85mm.

Nos. 1208-1210 Overprinted: "19th U.P.U. CONGRESS—HAMBURG"

**1984 Litho. Perf. 15**

1216 A169 90c multi 68 68
1217 A169 $4 multi 3.00 3.00

**Souvenir Sheet**

1218 A169 $5 multi 3.75 3.75

The only foreign revenue stamps listed in this Catalogue are those authorized for prepayment of postage.

AUSIPEX '84 — A171

**1984, Sept. 21** *Perf. 14*
*1219* A171 $1.10 Puffing Billy 82 82
*1220* A171 $4 Australia II 3.00 3.00

**Souvenir Sheet**

*1221* A171 $5 Melbourne tram 3.75 3.75

No. 1221 has multicolored margin continuing design. Size: 107x76mm.

Correggio & Degas — A171a

Correggio: 10c, The Night (detail). 30c, Virgin Adoring the Child. 90c, Mystical Marriage of St. Catherine with St. Sebastian. $4, Madonna and the Fruit Basket. No. 1230, Madonna at the Spring. Degas: 25c, L'Absinthe. 70c, Pouting (horiz.). $1.10, The Millinery Shop. $3, The Bellelli Family. No. 1231, The Cotton Market.

**1984, Aug. Litho.** *Perf. 14*
*1222* A171a 10c multi 8 8
*1223* A171a 25c multi 20 20
*1224* A171a 30c multi 22 22
*1225* A171a 70c multi 52 52
*1226* A171a 90c multi 68 68
*1227* A171a $1.10 multi 82 82
*1228* A171a $3 multi 2.25 2.25
*1229* A171a $4 multi 3.00 3.00
*Nos. 1222-1229 (8)* 7.77 7.77

**Souvenir Sheets**

*1230* A171a $5 multi 3.75 3.75
*1231* A171a $5 multi 3.75 3.75

Nos. 1230 and 1231 have multicolored margins showing entire paintings. Size: 53x83mm; 74x54mm.

19th Cent. Locomotives — A172

**1984, Oct.** *Perf. 14½*
*1232* A172 30c Locomotion, '25 22 22
*1233* A172 40c Novelty, '29 30 30
*1234* A172 60c Washington Farmer, '36 45 45
*1235* A172 70c French Crampton, '59 52 52
*1236* A172 90c Dutch State, '73 68 68
*1237* A172 $1.10 Champion, '82 82 82
*1238* A172 $2 Webb Compound, '93 1.50 1.50
*1239* A172 $4 Berlin 74, 1900 3.00 3.00
*Nos. 1232-1239 (8)* 7.49 7.49

**Souvenir Sheets**

*1240* A172 $5 Crampton Phoenix, '63 3.75 3.75
*1241* A172 $5 2-82 Mikado, '97 3.75 3.75

Size of No. 1240: 100x70mm.

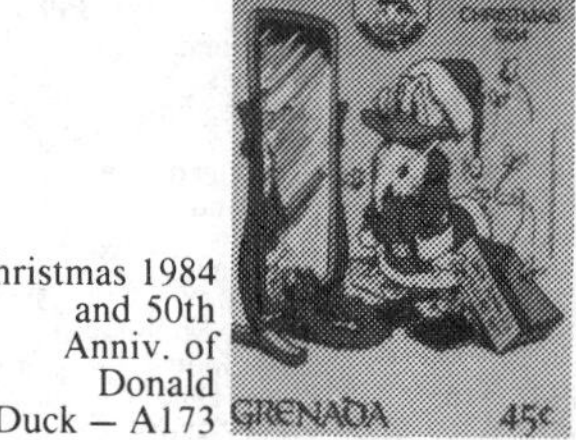

Christmas 1984 and 50th Anniv. of Donald Duck — A173

Scenes from various Donald Duck movies.

**1984, Nov. Litho.** *Perf. 13½x14*
*1242* A173 45c multi 35 35
*1243* A173 60c multi 50 50
*1244* A173 90c multi 75 75
*1245* A173 $2 multi 1.65 1.65
*1246* A173 $4 multi 3.25 3.25
*Nos. 1242-1246 (5)* 6.50 6.50

**Souvenir Sheet**

*1247* A173 $5 multi 4.25 4.25

No. 1247 has multicolored margin continuing design. Size:

Overprinted: "OPENING OF/POINT SALINE/INT'L AIRPORT"

**1984, Oct. 28 Litho.** *Perf. 14½x14*
*1248* A162 40c on #1155 30 30
*1249* A162 $3 on #1157 2.25 2.25

**Souvenir Sheet**

**No. 1158 Overprinted in Margin**

*1250* A162 $5 multi 3.75 3.75

Audubon Birth Bicentenary A174

**1985, Feb. Litho.** *Perf. 14*
*1251* A174 50c Clapper Rail 37 37
*1252* A174 70c Hooded Warbler 52 52
*1253* A174 90c Flicker 66 66
*1254* A174 $4 Bohemian Waxwing 3.00 3.00

**Souvenir Sheet**

*1255* A174 $5 Pigeon Hawk, horiz. 3.75 3.75

No. 1255 has design continuing into margin. Size: 82x112mm.

Motorcycle Centenary — A175

**1985, Mar. 11 Litho.** *Perf. 14*
*1256* A175 25c Honda XL500R 12 12
*1257* A175 50c Suzuki GS1100ES 28 28
*1258* A175 90c Kawasaki KZ700 45 45
*1259* A175 $4 BMW K100 1.75 1.75

**Souvenir Sheet**

*1260* A175 $5 Yamaha 500CC 3.75 3.75

No. 1260 has multicolored margin continuing the design picturing a race. Size: 110x82mm.

Girl Guides, 75th Anniv. A176

**1985, Apr. 15**
*1261* A176 25c Nature hike 16 16
*1262* A176 60c Cookout 45 45
*1263* A176 90c Singing around campfire 65 65
*1264* A176 $3 Public service 2.25 2.25

**Souvenir Sheet**

*1265* A176 $5 Flags 3.75 3.75

No. 1265 has multicolored margin picturing merit badges. Size: 98x71mm.

Opening of Point Saline Intl. Airport, Oct. 28, 1984 A177

Inaugural flights.

**1985, Apr. 30**
*1266* A177 70c From Barbados 60 60
*1267* A177 $1 From New York 85 85
*1268* A177 $4 To Miami 3.25 3.25

**Souvenir Sheet**

*1269* A177 $5 Point Saline Intl. Airport 3.75 3.75

No. 1269 has multicolored margin continuing the design. Size: 102x72mm.

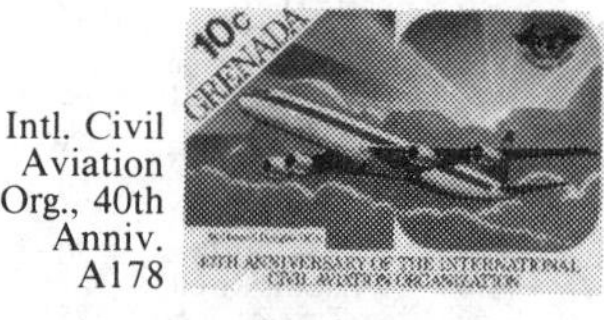

Intl. Civil Aviation Org., 40th Anniv. A178

**1985, May 15**
*1270* A178 10c McDonnell Douglas DC-8 5 5
*1271* A178 50c Super Constellation 42 42
*1272* A178 60c Vickers Vanguard 48 48
*1273* A178 $4 DeHavilland Twin Otter 3.00 3.00

**Souvenir Sheet**

*1274* A178 $5 Avro 748 Turboprop 3.75 3.75

No. 1274 has multicolored margin picturing the ICAO emblem and inscribed: 40. Size: 102x64mm.

Water Sports A179

**1985, June 15** *Perf. 15*
*1275* A179 10c Model boat racing 5 5
*1276* A179 50c Snorkeling, Sandy Island carriacou 42 42
*1277* A179 $1.10 Sailing, Grand Anse Beach 90 90
*1278* A179 $4 Windsurfing 3.00 3.00

**Miniature Sheet**

*1279* A179 $5 Snorkelers, surfers, sailboats 3.75 3.75

No. 1279 has multicolored margin continuing the design. Size: 107x78mm.

Island Flowers — A180

**1985, July 1** *Perf. 14*
*1280* A180 ½c Strelitzia reginae 5 5
*1281* A180 1c Passiflora coccinea 5 5
*1282* A180 2c Nerium oleander 5 5
*1283* A180 4c Ananas comosus 5 5
*1284* A180 5c Anthurium andraeanum 5 5
*1285* A180 6c Bougainvillea glabra 5 5
*1286* A180 10c Hibiscus rose-sinensis 5 5
*1287* A180 15c Alpinia purpurata 8 8
*1288* A180 25c Euphorbia pulcherrima 15 15
*1289* A180 30c Antigonon leptopus 20 20
*1290* A180 40c Datura candida 30 30
*1291* A180 50c Hippeastrum puniceum 35 35
*1292* A180 60c Opuntia megacantha 40 40
*1293* A180 70c Acalypha hispida 45 45
***1293B*** A180 75c *Cordia sebestina* ('88) 60 60
*1294* A180 $1 Catharanthus roseus 68 68
*1295* A180 $1.10 Ixora macrothyrsa 75 75
*1296* A180 $3 Justicia brandegeeana 2.00 2.00
*1297* A180 $5 Plumbago capensis 3.25 3.25
*1297A* A180 $10 Lantana camara 6.50 6.50
*1297B* A180 $20 Jatropha integerrima 13.00 13.00
*Nos. 1280-1297B (20)* 28.46 28.46

**1986** **Litho.**

| | | | |
|---|---|---|---|
| *1280a* | Perf. 12x12½ | 5 | 5 |
| *1281a* | Perf. 12x12½ | 5 | 5 |
| *1282a* | Perf. 12x12½ | 5 | 5 |
| *1283a* | Perf. 12x12½ | 5 | 5 |
| *1284a* | Perf. 12x12½ | 5 | 5 |
| *1285a* | Perf. 12x12½ | 5 | 5 |
| *1286a* | Perf. 12x12½ | 5 | 5 |
| *1287a* | Perf. 12x12½ | 8 | 8 |
| *1288a* | Perf. 12x12½ | 15 | 15 |
| *1289a* | Perf. 12x12½ | 20 | 20 |
| *1290a* | Perf. 12x12½ | 30 | 30 |
| *1291a* | Perf. 12x12½ | 35 | 35 |
| *1292a* | Perf. 12x12½ | 40 | 40 |
| *1293a* | Perf. 12x12½ | 45 | 45 |
| *1294a* | Perf. 12x12½ | 68 | 68 |
| *1295a* | Perf. 12x12½ | 75 | 75 |
| *1296a* | Perf. 12x12½ | 2.00 | 2.00 |
| *1297c* | $5 Perf. 12x12½ | 3.25 | 3.25 |
| *1297d* | $10 Perf. 12x12½ | 6.50 | 6.50 |
| | *Nos. 1280a-1297d (19)* | 15.46 | 15.46 |

Nos. 1289, 1291a, 1292 and 1294a reprinted with "1987" imprint, No. 1286 with "1988" imprint.

Queen Mother, 85th Birthday A181

Photographs: $1, At the Royal Opera, vert. $1.50, Playing pool, London Press Club. $2.50, At Epsom for the Oaks Day races, vert. $5, In open carriage with Prince Charles, Thanksgiving Day, 1980, vert.

**1985, July 5**
*1298* A181 $1 multi 68 68
*1299* A181 $1.50 multi 1.05 1.05
*1300* A181 $2.50 multi 1.75 1.75

**Souvenir Sheet**

*1301* A181 $5 multi 3.25 3.25

No. 1301 has multicolored margin picturing bleanders and chenille plants. Size: 57x85mm.

**1986, Jan. 20 Litho.** *Perf. 12x12½*
*1301A* A181 90c like #1298 65 65
*1301B* A181 $1 like #1299 75 75
*1301C* A181 $3 like #1300 2.25 2.25

Nos. 1301A-1301C issued in sheets of 5 plus label. Size: 130x126mm.

Intl. Youth Year — A182

**1985, Aug. 21** *Perf. 15*

*1302* A182 25c Gardening 15 15
*1303* A182 50c At the beach 35 35
*1304* A182 $1.10 Education 75 75
*1305* A182 $3 Health care 2.00 2.00

**Souvenir Sheet**

*1306* A182 $5 Harmonizing 3.25 3.25

No. 1306 has multicolored margin continuing the design and picturing flags of Great Britain, Italy, Singapore, Venezuela, Canada, U.S., Kenya, Sweden, France and Grenada. Size: 112x81mm.

4th Caribbean Cuboree, Aug. 17-23 A183

**1985, Sept. 5** *Perf. 14*

*1307* A183 10c Pitching tents 5 5
*1308* A183 50c Swimming 42 42
*1309* A183 $1 Stamp collecting 85 85
*1310* A183 $4 Bird watching 3.25 3.25

**Souvenir Sheet**

*1311* A183 $5 Grand Circle ritual 4.00 4.00

No. 1311 has multicolored margin continuing the design and inscribed: Growing to Participate and Serve. Size: 103x75mm.

Johann Sebastian Bach — A184

Portrait, signature, music from Ciaccona and: 25c, Crumhorn. 70c, Oboe d'amore. $1, Violin. $3, Harpsichord. $5, Portrait.

**1985, Sept. 19**

*1312* A184 25c multi 15 15
*1313* A184 70c multi 45 45
*1314* A184 $1 multi 68 68
*1315* A184 $3 multi 2.00 2.00

**Souvenir Sheet**

*1316* A184 $5 multi 3.50 3.50

No. 1316 has violet black and black margin picturing Bach playing the violin, his signature and music from Ciaccona. Size: 105x75mm.

The Prince & the Pauper — A185

Walt Disney characters.

**1985, Oct. 30**

*1317* A185 25c Prince & Pauper meet 18 18
*1318* A185 50c Exchange clothes 45 45
*1319* A185 $1.10 Prince as the Pauper 95 95
*1320* A185 $1.50 Prince rescued 1.40 1.40
*1321* A185 $2 Pauper as the Prince 1.75 1.75
*Nos. 1317-1321 (5)* 4.73 4.73

**Souvenir Sheet**

*1322* A185 $5 Prince & Pauper celebrate 4.25 4.25

Intl. Youth Year. Mark Twain (1835-1910), children's book author. No. 1322 has multicolored margin continuing the design and picturing the Intl. Youth Year emblem and a cameo portrait of Twain. Size: 127x101mm.

Elizabeth II, Royal Visit to Spice Island — A186

**1985, Oct. 31** *Perf. 14½*

*1323* A186 50c Flags of Grenada, U.K. 42 42
*1324* A186 $1 Elizabeth II, vert. 80 80
*1325* A186 $4 HMS Britannia 3.00 3.00

**Souvenir Sheet**

*1326* A186 $5 Map 3.75 3.75

No. 1326 has multicolored margin continuing map of the Caribbean Sea and picturing the HMS Britannia. Size: 111x83mm.

The Brothers Grimm — A187

Disney characters in The Fisherman and His Wife.

**1985, Nov. 4** **Litho.** *Perf. 14*

*1327* A187 30c multi 25 25
*1328* A187 60c multi 55 55
*1329* A187 70c multi 60 60
*1330* A187 $1 multi 90 90
*1331* A187 $3 multi 2.75 2.75
*Nos. 1327-1331 (5)* 5.05 5.05

**Souvenir Sheet**

*1332* A187 $5 multi 4.50 4.50

No. 1332 has multicolored margin continuing the design. Size: 126x100mm.

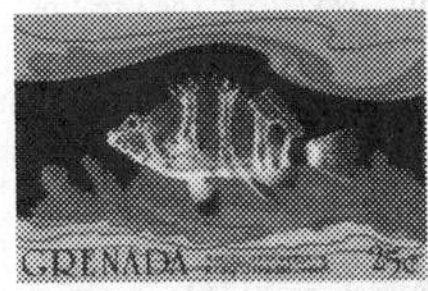


Indigenous Fish and Coral A188

**1985, Nov. 15**

*1333* A188 25c Red-spotted hawkfish 18 18
*1334* A188 50c Spotfin butterflyfish 38 38
*1335* A188 $1.10 Fire coral, orange sponge 80 80
*1336* A188 $3 Pillar coral 2.25 2.25

**Souvenir Sheet**

*1337* A188 $5 Bigeye 3.75 3.75

No. 1337 has multicolored margin continuing the design. Size: 128x101mm.

UN, 40th Anniv. A189

UN stamps and famous people: 50c, No. 258, Mary McLeod Bethune (1875-1955), American educator. $2, No. 156, Maimonides (1135-1204), Judaic scholar. $2.50, No. 41, Alexander Graham Bell (1847-1922), inventor of the telephone. $5, Dag Hammarskjold (1905-1961), 2nd UN secretary general.

**1985, Nov. 22** *Perf. 14½*

*1338* A189 50c multi 38 38
*1339* A189 $2 multi 1.50 1.50
*1340* A189 $2.50 multi 1.75 1.75

**Souvenir Sheet**

*1341* A189 $5 multi 3.75 3.75

No. 1341 has gray margin picturing UN No. 38 and anniv. emblem. Size: 111x86mm.

Christmas A190

Religious paintings: 25c, Adoration of the Shepherds, by Andre Mantegna (1431-1506). 60c, Journey of the Magi, by Sassetta (d. 1450). 90c, Madonna and Child Enthroned with Saints, by Raphael (1483-1520). $4, Nativity, by Monaco. $5, Madonna and Child Enthroned with Saints, by Agnolo Gaddi (c. 1350-1396).

**1985, Dec. 23** *Perf. 15*

*1342* A190 25c multi 18 18
*1343* A190 60c multi 45 45
*1344* A190 90c multi 65 65
*1345* A190 $4 multi 3.00 3.00

**Souvenir Sheet**

*1346* A190 $5 multi 3.75 3.75

No. 1346 has multicolored margin continuing the design. Size: 107x80mm.

Statue of Liberty, Cent. A191

Views of New York City.

**1986, Jan. 6**

*1347* A191 5c Columbus Circle, 1893 5 5
*1348* A191 25c Circle, 1986 18 18
*1349* A191 40c Central Park Mounted Police, 1895 30 30
*1350* A191 $4 Mounted Police, 1986 3.00 3.00

**Souvenir Sheet**

*1351* A191 $5 Statue of Liberty 3.75 3.75

Nos. 1347-1348, 1351 vert. No. 1351 has multicolored margin picturing prominent emigrants, Gustave Mahler (1860-1911), composer, conductor; Bertrand Russell (1872-1970), mathematician and Nobel laureate in literature; Carl Schurz (1829-1906), politician; and Dr. Stephen S. Wise (1874-1949), clergyman. Size: 104x76mm.

### Audubon Type of 1985

**1986, Jan. 20** *Perf. 12x12½*

*1352* A174 50c Snowy egret 38 38
*1353* A174 90c Red flamingo 65 65
*1354* A174 $1.10 Barnacle goose 80 80
*1355* A174 $3 Smew 2.25 2.25

**Souvenir Sheet**

*Perf. 14*

*1356* A174 $5 Brant Goose, horiz. 3.75 3.75

No. 1356 has multicolored margin continuing the design. Size: 103x73mm.

### Nos. 1291 and 1297 Ovptd. "VISIT OF / PRES. REAGAN / 20 FEB. 1986."

**1986, Feb. 20** *Perf. 14*

*1357* A180 50c multi 38 38
*1358* A180 $5 multi 3.75 3.75

St. George Methodist Church, Bicent. A192

**1986, Feb. 24** *Perf. 15*

*1359* A192 60c multi 45 45

**Souvenir Sheet**

*1360* A192 $5 multi 3.75 3.75

Heritage Year. No. 1360 has multicolored margin continuing the design, picturing St. George's Harbor. Size: 102x73mm.

1986 World Cup Soccer Championships, Mexico — A193

Various soccer plays.

**1986, Mar. 6** *Perf. 14*

*1361* A193 50c multi 38 38
*1362* A193 70c multi 52 52
*1363* A193 90c multi 65 65
*1364* A193 $4 multi 3.00 3.00

**Souvenir Sheet**

*1365* A193 $5 multi 3.75 3.75

No. 1365 has multicolored margin continuing the design. Size: 101x71mm.

Halley's Comet A194

Designs: 5c, Clyde Tombaugh, discovered Pluto, 1930, and Dudley Observatory. 20c, US X-24B space shuttle prototype, 1973. 40c, Medallic art, Catholic Church, 1618. $4, Lot and his daughters fleeing Sodom and Gomorrah, 1949 B.C. $5, Comet over Grand Anse Beach.

**1986, Mar. 20**

*1366* A194 5c multi 5 5
*1367* A194 20c multi 15 15
*1368* A194 40c multi 30 30
*1369* A194 $4 multi 3.00 3.00

**Souvenir Sheet**

*1370* A194 $5 multi 3.75 3.75

No. 1370 has multicolored margin continuing the design. Size: 102x70mm.

### Queen Elizabeth II, 60th Birthday
Common Design Type

Designs: 2c, Signing the log, 1951. $1.50, Presenting polo trophy, Windsor, 1965. $4, Derby Day, 1977. $5, Royal family portrait, 1939.

**1986, Apr. 21** *Perf. 14*

*1371* CD339 2c yel & blk 5 5
*1372* CD339 $1.50 pale grn & multi 1.15 1.15
*1373* CD339 $4 dl lil & multi 3.00 3.00

**Souvenir Sheet**

*1374* CD339 $5 tan & blk 3.75 3.75

No. 1374 has tan, black and gray inscribed margin. Size: 120x85mm.

Common Design Types are pictured in section before Great Britain.

AMERIPEX '86 — A195

Walt Disney characters playing baseball.

**1986, May 22 Litho. *Perf. 11***

| | | | | | |
|---|---|---|---|---|---|
| *1375* | A195 | 1c | Pitcher | 5 | 5 |
| *1376* | A195 | 2c | Catcher | 5 | 5 |
| *1377* | A195 | 3c | Strike | 5 | 5 |
| *1378* | A195 | 4c | Force out | 5 | 5 |
| *1379* | A195 | 5c | Fly ball | 5 | 5 |
| *1380* | A195 | 6c | Third base | 5 | 5 |
| *1381* | A195 | $2 | Manager | 1.50 | 1.50 |
| *1382* | A195 | $3 | Error | 2.25 | 2.25 |
| | | | *Nos. 1375-1382 (8)* | 4.05 | 4.05 |

**Souvenir Sheets**

***Perf. 14***

| | | | | | |
|---|---|---|---|---|---|
| *1383* | A195 | $5 | Batter | 3.75 | 3.75 |
| *1384* | A195 | $5 | Grand slam | 3.75 | 3.75 |

Nos. 1383-1384 have multicolored margins continuing the designs. Sizes: 127x101mm.

**Royal Wedding Issue, 1986**
Common Design Type

Designs: 2c, Prince Andrew and Sarah Ferguson. $1.10, Andrew. $4, Andrew in flight suit, helicopter. $5, Couple, diff.

**1986, July 23 *Perf. 14***

| | | | | | |
|---|---|---|---|---|---|
| *1385* | CD340 | 2c | multi | 5 | 5 |
| *1386* | CD340 | $1.10 | multi | 82 | 82 |
| *1387* | CD340 | $4 | multi | 3.00 | 3.00 |

**Souvenir Sheet**

| | | | | | |
|---|---|---|---|---|---|
| *1388* | CD340 | $5 | multi | 3.75 | 3.75 |

No. 1388 has multicolored margin picturing Andrew through helicopter portal. Size: 88x88mm.

Seashells
A196

Designs: 25c, Gmelin brown-lined latirus. 60c, Lamarck lamellose wentletrap. 70c, Swainson turkey wing. $4, Linne rooster-tail conch. $5, Linne angular triton.

**1986, July 15 Litho. *Perf. 15***

| | | | | | |
|---|---|---|---|---|---|
| *1389* | A196 | 25c | multi | 18 | 18 |
| *1390* | A196 | 60c | multi | 45 | 45 |
| *1391* | A196 | 70c | multi | 52 | 52 |
| *1392* | A196 | $4 | multi | 3.00 | 3.00 |

**Souvenir Sheet**

| | | | | | |
|---|---|---|---|---|---|
| *1393* | A196 | $5 | multi | 3.75 | 3.75 |

No. 1393 has multicolored margin picturing marine life. Size: 110x75mm.

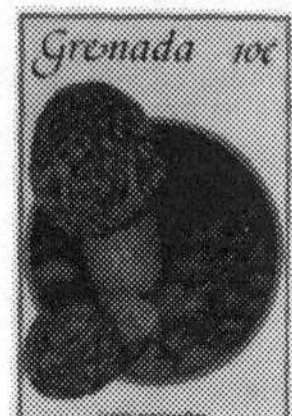


Mushrooms
A197

**1986, Aug. 1 *Perf. 15***

| | | | | | |
|---|---|---|---|---|---|
| *1394* | A197 | 10c | Lepiota roselamellata | 8 | 8 |
| *1395* | A197 | 60c | Lentinus bertieri | 45 | 45 |
| *1396* | A197 | $1 | Lentinus retinervis | 75 | 75 |
| *1397* | A197 | $4 | Eccilia cystiophorus | 3.00 | 3.00 |

**Souvenir Sheet**

| | | | | | |
|---|---|---|---|---|---|
| *1398* | A197 | $5 | Cystolepiota eriophora | 3.75 | 3.75 |

No. 1398 has multicolored margin continuing the design and picturing island flora. Size: 127x100mm.

**Nos. 1361-1365 Ovptd. "WINNERS Argentina 3 / W. Germany 2" in Gold.**

**1986, Sept. 15 Litho. *Perf. 14***

| | | | | | |
|---|---|---|---|---|---|
| *1399* | A193 | 50c | multi | 38 | 38 |
| *1400* | A193 | 70c | multi | 52 | 52 |
| *1401* | A193 | 90c | multi | 65 | 65 |
| *1402* | A193 | $4 | multi | 3.00 | 3.00 |

**Souvenir Sheet**

| | | | | | |
|---|---|---|---|---|---|
| *1403* | A193 | $5 | multi | 3.75 | 3.75 |

Disarmament Week and Intl. Peace Year — A198

Designs: 60c, Mahatma Gandhi, rifles, dove, vert. $4, Martin Luther King, Jr., hands, olive branch.

**1986, Sept. 15 *Perf. 11***

| | | | | | |
|---|---|---|---|---|---|
| *1404* | A198 | 60c | multi | 45 | 45 |
| *1405* | A198 | $4 | multi | 3.00 | 3.00 |

Christmas — A199

Disney characters. Nos. 1406-1407, 1411-1412 vert.

**1986, Nov. 3**

| | | | | | |
|---|---|---|---|---|---|
| *1406* | A199 | 30c | Mickey, hearth | 22 | 22 |
| *1407* | A199 | 45c | Mickey, Santa | 32 | 32 |
| *1408* | A199 | 60c | Donald, Mickey Mouse phone | 45 | 45 |
| *1409* | A199 | 70c | Goofy, toy band | 52 | 52 |
| *1410* | A199 | $1.10 | Daisy, dolls | 82 | 82 |
| *1411* | A199 | $2 | Goofy as Santa | 1.50 | 1.50 |
| *1412* | A199 | $2.50 | Goofy playing piano | 1.85 | 1.85 |
| *1413* | A199 | $3 | Train ride | 2.25 | 2.25 |
| | | | *Nos. 1406-1413 (8)* | 7.93 | 7.93 |

**Souvenir Sheets**

| | | | | | |
|---|---|---|---|---|---|
| *1414* | A199 | $5 | Donald, Goofy, Mickey | 3.75 | 3.75 |
| *1415* | A199 | $5 | Dewey | 3.75 | 3.75 |

Nos. 1414-1415 have multicolored margins continuing the designs.

**Nos. 1366-1370 Ovptd. with Halley's Comet Logo.**

**1986, Oct. 15 Litho. *Perf. 14***

| | | | | | |
|---|---|---|---|---|---|
| *1416* | A194 | 5c | multi | 5 | 5 |
| *1417* | A194 | 20c | multi | 15 | 15 |
| *1418* | A194 | 40c | multi | 30 | 30 |
| *1419* | A194 | $4 | multi | 3.00 | 3.00 |

**Souvenir Sheet**

| | | | | | |
|---|---|---|---|---|---|
| *1420* | A194 | $5 | multi | 3.75 | 3.75 |

Fauna and Flora
A200

**1986, Nov. 17 *Perf. 14***

| | | | | | |
|---|---|---|---|---|---|
| *1421* | A200 | 10c | Chicken, rooster | 8 | 8 |
| *1422* | A200 | 30c | Fish-eating bat | 24 | 24 |
| *1423* | A200 | 60c | Goat | 48 | 48 |
| *1424* | A200 | 70c | Cow | 58 | 58 |
| *1425* | A200 | $1 | Anthurium | 80 | 80 |
| *1426* | A200 | $1.10 | Royal poinciana | 90 | 90 |
| *1427* | A200 | $2 | Frangipani | 1.60 | 1.60 |
| *1428* | A200 | $4 | Orchid | 3.25 | 3.25 |
| | | | *Nos. 1421-1428 (8)* | 7.93 | 7.93 |

**Souvenir Sheets**

| | | | | | |
|---|---|---|---|---|---|
| *1429* | A200 | $5 | Horse | 4.00 | 4.00 |
| *1430* | A200 | $5 | Trees | 4.00 | 4.00 |

Nos. 1429-1430 have multicolored margin continuing the designs. Sizes: 104x72mm, 104x73mm (#1430).

Automobile, Cent. — A202

1886 Daimler and modern automobiles.

**1986, Nov. 20 *Perf. 15***

| | | | | | |
|---|---|---|---|---|---|
| *1431* | A202 | 10c | 1984 Maserati Biturbo | 8 | 8 |
| *1432* | A202 | 30c | 1960 AC Cobra | 24 | 24 |
| *1433* | A202 | 60c | 1963 Corvette | 48 | 48 |
| *1434* | A202 | 70c | 1932 Duesenberg SJ7 | 55 | 55 |
| *1435* | A202 | 90c | 1957 Porsche | 72 | 72 |
| *1436* | A202 | $1.10 | 1930 Stoewer | 88 | 88 |
| *1437* | A202 | $2 | 1957 VW Beetle | 1.60 | 1.60 |
| *1438* | A202 | $3 | 1963 Mercedes 600 Limo | 2.40 | 2.40 |
| | | | *Nos. 1431-1438 (8)* | 6.95 | 6.95 |

**Souvenir Sheets**

| | | | | | |
|---|---|---|---|---|---|
| *1439* | A202 | $5 | 1914 Stutz | 4.00 | 4.00 |
| *1440* | A202 | $5 | 1941 Packard | 4.00 | 4.00 |

Nos. 1439-1440 have multicolored margins picturing manufacturer's symbols. Size: 106x77mm.

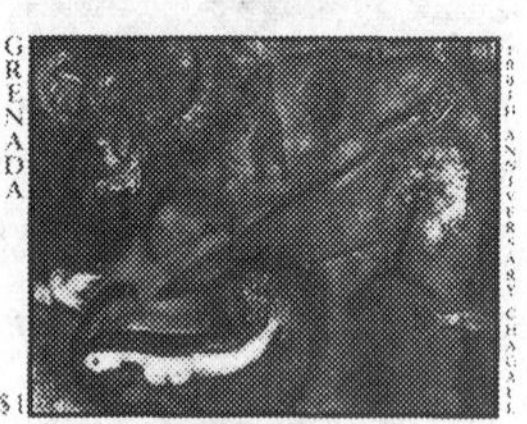


Song of Songs, by Marc Chagall (1887-1984) — A203

Paintings: No. 1441, The Rooster. No. 1442, Lovers in the Moonlight. No. 1443, Woman and Haystack. No. 1444, Snow-Covered Church. No. 1445, Peasant Life. No. 1446, Moses Receiving the Tablets. No. 1447, Vitebsk: From Mt. Zadunuv. No. 1449, Song of Songs, diff. No. 1450, The Creation of Man. No. 1451, Spring. No. 1452, Jacob's Struggle with the Angel. No. 1453, Song of Songs (wedding detail). No. 1454, The Painter to the Moon, 1917. No. 1455, Moses Striking the Rock. No. 1456, To My Betrothed, 1911. No. 1457, Sacrifice of Isaac. No. 1458, Monkey Acting as Judge Over Dispute Between Wolf and Fox, 1925. No. 1459, Song of Songs (bride riding Pegasus). No. 1460, Lovers in the Lilac, 1930. No. 1461, Song of Songs (sun, spirits). No. 1462, Jacob's Dream. No. 1463, Purim, 1916. No. 1464, Fantastic Horsecart. No. 1465, Listening to the Cock, 1944. No. 1466, Self-portrait, 1914. No. 1467, The Juggler, 1943. No. 1468, Noah and the Rainbow. No. 1469, Moses Before the Burning Bush. No. 1470, Around Her, 1945. No. 1471, The Trough, 1925. No. 1472, The Poet of Half-Past-Three. No. 1473, The Tree of Life, 1948. No. 1474, Woman with the Blue Face, 1932. No. 1475, Chrysanthemums, 1926. No. 1476, Spoonful of Milk, 1912. No. 1477, The Soldier Drinks, 1911. No. 1478, Noah's Ark. No. 1479, Flowers and Fruit. No. 1480, Adam and Eve Expelled fron Paradise. No. 1481, Return from Synagogue. No. 1482, Aleko: A Fantasy of St. Petersburg. No. 1483, The Orchard. No. 1484, Solitude. No. 1485, Paris Through the Window, 1913. No. 1486, The Wedding, 1910. No. 1487, Paradise. No. 1488, The Dream, 1939. No. 1489, Abraham and the Three Angels. No. 1490, Water Carrier Under the Moon, 1914.

**1986, Dec. 19**

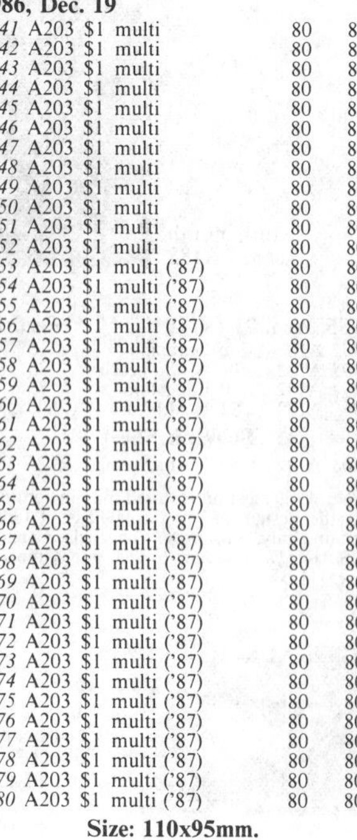

| | | | | | |
|---|---|---|---|---|---|
| *1441* | A203 | $1 | multi | 80 | 80 |
| *1442* | A203 | $1 | multi | 80 | 80 |
| *1443* | A203 | $1 | multi | 80 | 80 |
| *1444* | A203 | $1 | multi | 80 | 80 |
| *1445* | A203 | $1 | multi | 80 | 80 |
| *1446* | A203 | $1 | multi | 80 | 80 |
| *1447* | A203 | $1 | multi | 80 | 80 |
| *1448* | A203 | $1 | multi | 80 | 80 |
| *1449* | A203 | $1 | multi | 80 | 80 |
| *1450* | A203 | $1 | multi | 80 | 80 |
| *1451* | A203 | $1 | multi | 80 | 80 |
| *1452* | A203 | $1 | multi | 80 | 80 |
| *1453* | A203 | $1 | multi ('87) | 80 | 80 |
| *1454* | A203 | $1 | multi ('87) | 80 | 80 |
| *1455* | A203 | $1 | multi ('87) | 80 | 80 |
| *1456* | A203 | $1 | multi ('87) | 80 | 80 |
| *1457* | A203 | $1 | multi ('87) | 80 | 80 |
| *1458* | A203 | $1 | multi ('87) | 80 | 80 |
| *1459* | A203 | $1 | multi ('87) | 80 | 80 |
| *1460* | A203 | $1 | multi ('87) | 80 | 80 |
| *1461* | A203 | $1 | multi ('87) | 80 | 80 |
| *1462* | A203 | $1 | multi ('87) | 80 | 80 |
| *1463* | A203 | $1 | multi ('87) | 80 | 80 |
| *1464* | A203 | $1 | multi ('87) | 80 | 80 |
| *1465* | A203 | $1 | multi ('87) | 80 | 80 |
| *1466* | A203 | $1 | multi ('87) | 80 | 80 |
| *1467* | A203 | $1 | multi ('87) | 80 | 80 |
| *1468* | A203 | $1 | multi ('87) | 80 | 80 |
| *1469* | A203 | $1 | multi ('87) | 80 | 80 |
| *1470* | A203 | $1 | multi ('87) | 80 | 80 |
| *1471* | A203 | $1 | multi ('87) | 80 | 80 |
| *1472* | A203 | $1 | multi ('87) | 80 | 80 |
| *1473* | A203 | $1 | multi ('87) | 80 | 80 |
| *1474* | A203 | $1 | multi ('87) | 80 | 80 |
| *1475* | A203 | $1 | multi ('87) | 80 | 80 |
| *1476* | A203 | $1 | multi ('87) | 80 | 80 |
| *1477* | A203 | $1 | multi ('87) | 80 | 80 |
| *1478* | A203 | $1 | multi ('87) | 80 | 80 |
| *1479* | A203 | $1 | multi ('87) | 80 | 80 |
| *1480* | A203 | $1 | multi ('87) | 80 | 80 |

**Size: 110x95mm.**

***Imperf***

| | | | | | |
|---|---|---|---|---|---|
| *1481* | A203 | $5 | multi | 4.00 | 4.00 |
| *1482* | A203 | $5 | multi | 4.00 | 4.00 |
| *1483* | A203 | $5 | multi | 4.00 | 4.00 |
| *1484* | A203 | $5 | multi ('87) | 4.00 | 4.00 |
| *1485* | A203 | $5 | multi ('87) | 4.00 | 4.00 |
| *1486* | A203 | $5 | multi ('87) | 4.00 | 4.00 |
| *1487* | A203 | $5 | multi ('87) | 4.00 | 4.00 |
| *1488* | A203 | $5 | multi ('87) | 4.00 | 4.00 |
| *1489* | A203 | $5 | multi ('87) | 4.00 | 4.00 |
| *1490* | A203 | $5 | multi ('87) | 4.00 | 4.00 |
| | | | *Nos. 1441-1490 (50)* | 72.00 | 72.00 |

Nos. 1441-1446, 1450-1452 1455-1458, 1464-1467 and 1470-1479 vert.

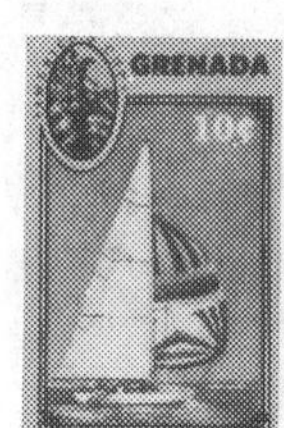


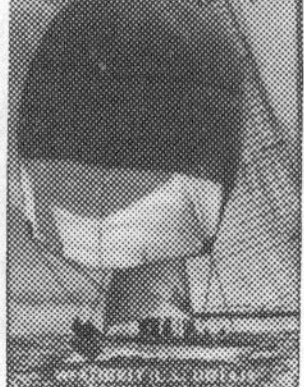


America's Cup
A204 A205

**1987, Feb. 5 Litho. *Perf. 15***

| | | | | | |
|---|---|---|---|---|---|
| *1491* | A204 | 10c | Columbia, 1958 | 8 | 8 |
| *1492* | A204 | 60c | Resolute, 1920 | 48 | 48 |
| *1493* | A204 | $1.10 | Endeavor, 1934 | 88 | 88 |
| *1494* | A204 | $4 | Rainbow, 1934 | 3.25 | 3.25 |

**Souvenir Sheet**

| | | | | | |
|---|---|---|---|---|---|
| *1495* | A205 | $5 | Weatherly, Gretel, 1962 | 4.00 | 4.00 |

No. 1495 has multicolored margin picturing the crew of the Weatherly, US flag and America's cup. Size: 114x84mm.

Virgin Mary
A206

Map of Voyage, Columbus' Signature
A207

**987, Apr. 27** *Perf. 15*

*496* A206 10c shown 8 8
*497* A206 30c Nina, Pinta, Santa Maria 22 22
*498* A206 50c Columbus, map 38 38
*499* A206 60c Columbus 45 45
*500* A206 90c Isabella, Ferdinand 68 68
*501* A206 $1.10 Discovering the Antilles 82 82
*502* A206 $2 Carib Indians 1.50 1.50
*a.* Souv. sheet of 3 (#1497, 1500, 1502 2.40 2.40
*503* A206 $3 American Indians, 1493 2.25 2.25
*a.* Souv. sheet of 5 + label (#1496, 1498-1499, 1501, 1503) 4.00 4.00
*Nos. 1496-1503 (8)* 6.38 6.38

**Souvenir Sheets**

*504* A207 $5 shown 3.75 3.75
*505* A207 $5 Columbus, Christ child 3.75 3.75

Discovery of America 500th anniv. (in 992). Nos. 1497, 1500 and 1502 horiz. Nos. 504-1505 have multicolored margins continuing the designs. Size: 104x73mm.

CAPEX '87 — A208

Fish. Nos. 1506, 1508 vert.

**1987, June 15**

*506* A208 10c Black grouper 8 8
*507* A208 30c Blue marlin 22 22
*508* A208 60c White marlin 45 45
*509* A208 70c Big-eye thresher shark 52 52
*1510* A208 $1 Bonefish 75 75
*1511* A208 $1.10 Wahoo 82 82
*1512* A208 $2 Sailfish 1.50 1.50
*1513* A208 $4 Albacore 3.00 3.00
*Nos. 1506-1513 (8)* 7.34 7.34

**Souvenir Sheets**

*1514* A208 $5 Barracuda 4.50 4.50
*1515* A208 $5 Yellowfin tuna, vert. 4.50 4.50

Nos. 1514-1515 have multicolored margins continuing the designs. Sizes: 100x70mm.

Transportation Innovations — A209

**1987, May 18** *Perf. 14*

*1516* A209 10c Cornu's Helicopter, 1907 8 8
*1517* A209 15c The Monitor and Merrimack, 1862 12 12
*1518* A209 30c LZ1 Zeppelin, c. 1900 22 22
*1519* A209 50c S.S. Sirius, 1838 38 38
*1520* A209 60c Trans-Siberian Railway 45 45
*1521* A209 70c USS Enterprise, 1960 52 52
*1522* A209 90c Blanchard's Balloon, 1785 68 68
*1523* A209 $1.50 USS Holland 1, 1900 1.15 1.15
*1524* A209 $2 S.S. Oceanic, 1871 1.50 1.50
*1525* A209 $3 1984 Lamborghini Countach 2.25 2.25
*Nos. 1516-1525 (10)* 7.35 7.35

Statue of Liberty, Cent. A210

**1987, Aug. 5**

*1526* A210 10c Computer structural diagrams 8 8
*1527* A210 25c Fireworks around statue 20 20
*1528* A210 50c Fireworks in front of statue 38 38
*1529* A210 60c Statue, boats 45 45
*1530* A210 70c Structural diagram, close-up 52 52
*1531* A210 $1 Rear of statue, close-up 75 75
*1532* A210 $1.10 Liberty and Manhattan Isls. 82 82
*1533* A210 $2 Statue, boats, diff. 1.50 1.50
*1534* A210 $4 Ocean liner, New York Harbor 3.00 3.00
*Nos. 1526-1534 (9)* 7.70 7.70

Nos. 1529, 1531-1534 vert.

Inventors and Innovators A211

Designs: 50c, Sir Isaac Newton (1642-1727), law of gravity. $1.10, Jons Jakob Berzelius (1779-1848), symbols of chemical elements. $2, Robert Boyle (1627-1691), and Boyle's Law of pressure and volume. $3, James Watt (1736-1819), and diagram of steam engine. $5, Wright Flyer, Voyager.

**1987, Sept. 9**

*1535* A211 50c multi 38 38
*1536* A211 $1.10 multi 82 82
*1537* A211 $2 multi 1.50 1.50
*1538* A211 $3 multi 2.25 2.25

**Souvenir Sheet**

*1539* A211 $5 multi 3.75 3.75

No. 1536 inscribed with incorrect spelling of inventors name, "John Jacob Berzelius." No. 1538 inscribed with incorrect caption; James Watt and Watt engine are pictured, not Rudolf Diesel and the diesel engine. No. 1539 has multicolored margin continuing the design and picturing Dick Rutan, Jeana Yeager, Wilbur and Orville Wright.

**Miniature Sheets**

Fairy Tales A212

Snow White: No. 1540a, Snow White scrubs stairs. b, Wicked Queen, looking glass. c, Snow White fleeing. d, Dwarfs, mine. e, Snow White at cottage. f, Snow White, dwarfs. g, Snow White dancing with dwarfs. h, Eating poison apple. i, Prince kissing Snow White.

Sleeping Beauty: No. 1541a, Royal family. b, Maleficent cursing infant (Aurora). c, Merryweather altering curse. d, Three good fairies. e, Briar Rose (Aurora), forest animals. f, Aurora, spinning wheel. g, Sleeping Beauty (Aurora). h, Prince Phillip battling dragon (Maleficent). i, Sleeping Beauty awakes.

Cinderella: No. 1542a, Ella (Cinderella) and father. b, Cinderella sweeping. c, Cinderella, animals in barn. d, Cinderella, stepmother, stepsisters. e, Mice. f, Fairy Godmother. g, Cinderella transformed, coach. h, i, Duke puts glass slipper on Cinderella's foot.

Pinocchio: No. 1543a, Geppetto and puppet. b, Jiminy Cricket. c, Pinocchio, J. Worthington Foulfellow and Gideon. d, Pinocchio, Master Stromboli. e, Blue Fairy rescues Pinocchio. f, Pinocchio, donkeys. g, Pinocchio riding fish. h, Pinocchio and Geppetto at sea. i, Pinocchio transformed into a boy.

Alice in Wonderland: No. 1544a, Alice, rabbit hole. b, Alice in bottle. c, Walrus and Carpenter. d, White Rabbit in pink house. e, Alice, pink butterfly. f, March Hare, Mad Hatter. g, Alice in garden. h, Queen of Hearts. i, Alice on trial.

Peter Pan: No. 1545a, Nana. b, Peter Pan. c, Peter Pan, Tinker Bell, Wendy, John and Michael Darling flying. d, In NeverNever Land. e, Peter Pan and Tiger Lily. f, Captain Hook and First Mate Smee. g, Pater Pan dueling with Captain Hook. h, Tinker Bell, pirate ship. i, Captain Hook, crocodile.

No. 1546, Snow White and Prince riding off into sunset. No. 1547, Aurora and Prince Phillip dancing. No. 1548, Cinderella and Prince Charming marry. No. 1549, Pinocchio, Jiminy Cricket and Gepetto. No. 1550, Alice, cat, mother. No. 1551, Darling children waving goodbye to Peter Pan.

**1987, Sept. 9** *Perf. 14x13½*

*1540* Sheet of 9 2.00
*a.-i* A212 30c any single 22 22
*1541* Sheet of 9 2.00
*a.-i* A212 30c any single 22 22
*1542* Sheet of 9 2.00
*a.-i* A212 30c any single 22 22
*1543* Sheet of 9 2.00
*a.-i* A212 30c any single 22 22
*1544* Sheet of 9 2.00
*a.-i* A212 30c any single 22 22
*1545* Sheet of 9 2.00
*a.-i* A212 30c any single 22 22
*Nos. 1540-1545 (6)* 12.00

**Souvenir Sheets**

*1546* A212 $5 multi 3.75 3.75
*1547* A212 $5 multi 3.75 3.75
*1548* A212 $5 multi 3.75 3.75
*1549* A212 $5 multi 3.75 3.75
*1550* A212 $5 multi 3.75 3.75
*1551* A212 $5 multi 3.75 3.75

Snow White and the Seven Dwarfs, 50th anniv.; Sleeping Beauty; Cinderella; Pinocchio; Alice in Wonderland; Peter Pan. Size of Nos. 1540-1545: 176x144mm. Nos. 1546-1551 have multicolored margins continuing the designs. Sizes: 128x103mm (No. 1546), 128x102mm (Nos. 1547-1548), 127x102mm (Nos. 1549-1551).

**Souvenir Sheet**

Baseball All-Star Game, Oakland, July 14 — A213

Athletes and team emblems: No. 1552a, Wade Boggs, Boston Red Sox. No. 1552b, Eric Davis, Cincinnati Reds.

**1987, Nov. 2** **Litho.** *Perf. 14*

*1552* A213 Sheet of 2 1.45 1.45
*a.-b* $1 any single 72 72

No. 1552 has multicolored margin picturing American and Natl. League all-star lineups. Size: 115x82mm.

Massachusetts State Crest — A214

Designs: 15c, Independence Hall, Philadelphia. 50c, Benjamin Franklin. $4, Robert Morris (1734-1806), financier of American Revolution. $5, Pres. James Madison.

**1987, Nov. 2**

*1553* A214 15c multi, vert. 10 10
*1554* A214 50c multi, vert. 35 35
*1555* A214 60c shown 45 45
*1556* A214 $4 multi, vert. 2.90 2.90

**Souvenir Sheet**

*1557* A214 $5 multi, vert. 3.60 3.60

US Constitution bicent. No. 1557 has multicolored inscribed margin continuing the design and picturing Independence Hall and score of President Madison's March. Size: 105x75mm.

Nos. 1286, 1291 and 1296 Overprinted

International Social Security Association

**1987, Nov. 2**

*1558* A180 10c multi 5 5
*1559* A180 50c multi 35 35
*1560* A180 $3 multi 2.00 2.00

HAFNIA '87 — A215

Disney animated characters in adaptation of fairy tales by Hans Christian Andersen.

**1987, Nov. 16** **Litho.** *Perf. 14*

*1561* A215 25c The Shadow 20 20
*1562* A215 30c The Storks 22 22
*1563* A215 50c The Emperor's New Clothes 38 38
*1564* A215 60c The Tinderbox 45 45
*1565* A215 70c The Shepherdess and the Chimney Sweep 55 55
*1566* A215 $1.50 The Little Mermaid 1.15 1.15
*1567* A215 $3 The Princess and the Pea 2.25 2.25
*1568* A215 $4 The Marsh King's Daughter 3.00 3.00
*Nos. 1561-1568 (8)* 8.20 8.20

**Souvenir Sheets**

*1569* A215 $5 The Flying Trunk, horiz. 3.75 3.75
*1570* A215 $5 The Sandman, horiz. 3.75 3.75

Nos. 1569-1570 have multicolored margins continuing the designs. Sizes: 127x102mm.

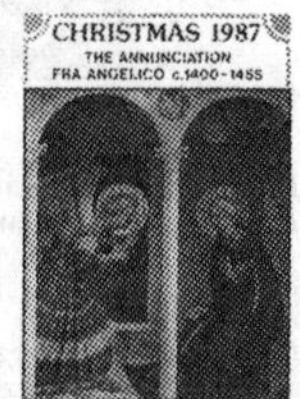

Christmas — A216

Religious paintings: 15c, The Annunciation, by Fra Angelico. 30c, The Annunciation, attributed to Hubert van Eyck (c. 1370-1426). 60c, Adoration of the Magi, by Januarius Zick (1730-1797). $4, The Flight Into Egypt, by David. $5, The Circumcision, produced by artists of the Giovanni Bellini Studio, 14th cent.

**1987, Dec. 15**

*1571* A216 15c multi 12 12
*1572* A216 30c multi 22 22
*1573* A216 60c multi 45 45
*1574* A216 $4 multi 3.00 3.00

**Souvenir Sheet**

*1575* A216 $5 multi 3.75 3.75

No. 1575 has multicolored margin continuing the painting. Size: 100x76mm.

For unused stamps, more recent issues are valued as never hinged, with the beginning point determined on a country-by-country basis. Notes to show the beginning points are prominently placed in the text.

T. Albert Marryshow (b. 1887) — A217

**1988, Jan. 22 Litho. *Perf. 14***

*1576* A217 25c scar, red brn & brn blk 20 20

40th Wedding Anniv. of Queen Elizabeth II and Prince Philip — A218

**1988, Feb. 15**

*1577* A218 15c Wedding portrait, 1947 12 12
*1578* A218 50c Elizabeth, Charles, Anne 38 38
*1579* A218 $1 Elizabeth, Anne 75 75
*1580* A218 $4 Elizabeth, c. 1980 3.00 3.00

**Souvenir Sheet**

*1581* A218 $5 Elizabeth, 1947 3.75 3.75

No. 1581 has multicolored margin continuing the photograph. Size: 76x100mm.

Disney Animated Characters and 1988 Summer Olympics, Seoul A219

**1988, Apr. 13 Litho. *Perf. 13½x14***

*1582* A219 1c Lighting torch, Olympia 5 5
*1583* A219 2c Torch bearers 5 5
*1584* A219 3c Flag bearers 5 5
*1585* A219 4c Releasing doves 5 5
*1586* A219 5c Opening ceremony 5 5
*1587* A219 10c Olympic motto 8 8
*1588* A219 $6 Tiger character trademark 4.50 4.50
*1589* A219 $7 Oldest Korean p.o. 5.25 5.25
*Nos. 1582-1589 (8)* 10.08 10.08

**Souvenir Sheets**

*1590* A219 $5 Sportsmanship oath 3.80 3.80
*1591* A219 $5 Closing ceremony 3.80 3.80

Nos. 1590-1591 have multicolored decorative margins continuing the designs. Size: 127x102mm.

Boy Scouts A220

**1988, May 3 Litho. *Perf. 14***

*1592* A220 20c Fishing, vert. 15 15
*1593* A220 70c Hiking 55 55
*1594* A220 90c First-aid 70 70
*1595* A220 $3 Canoeing, vert. 2.25 2.25

**Souvenir Sheet**

*1596* A220 $5 Scout holding koala, vert. 3.75 3.75

No. 1596 has multicolored inscribed margin announcing the 16th World Jamboree, Australia, and picturing Cataract Scout Park entrance. Size: 110x73mm.

Rotary Conference, District 405, St. George, May 5-7 — A221

Rotary Intl emblem and: $2, Map of District 405 island nations (Grenada, Guyana, Surinam and French Guiana), 15th cent. Spanish galleon *Santa Maria*, vert. $10, Motto "Service Above Self."

**1988, May 5 *Perf. 13½x14***

*1597* A221 $2 multi 1.50 1.50

**Souvenir Sheet**

***Perf. 14x13½***

*1598* A221 $10 shown 7.50 7.50

No. 1598 has multicolored margin picturing Concorde jet over St. George. Size: 134x91mm.

Nos. 1522-1525 Overprinted for Philatelic Exhibitions

a  OLYMPHILEX '88

b  INDEPENDENCE 40

c  FINLANDIA 88

d 

**1988, Apr. 19 Litho. *Perf. 14***

*1599* A209 (a) 90c multi 68 68
*1600* A209 (b) $1.50 multi 1.15 1.15
*1601* A209 (c) $2 multi 1.50 1.50
*1602* A209 (d) $3 multi 2.25 2.25

OLYMPHILEX '88; INDEPENDENCE 40; FINLANDIA '88; PRAGA '88.

Birds — A222

**1988, May 31**

*1603* A222 10c Roseate tern 8 8
*1604* A222 25c Laughing gull 18 18
*1605* A222 50c Osprey 38 38
*1606* A222 60c Rose-breasted grosbeak 45 45
*1607* A222 90c Purple gallinule 68 68
*1608* A222 $1.10 White-tailed tropicbird 82 82
*1609* A222 $3 Blue-faced booby 2.25 2.25
*1610* A222 $4 Northern shoveler 3.00 3.00
*Nos. 1603-1610 (8)* 7.84 7.84

**Souvenir Sheet**

*1611* A222 $5 Belted kingfisher 3.75 3.75
*1612* A222 $5 Rusty-tailed flycatcher 3.75 3.75

Nos. 1611-1612 have multicolored margins continuing the designs. Sizes: 100x70mm.

Miniature Sheets

Classic Automobiles A223

Cars (US or): No. 1613a, 1934 Tatra Type 77, Czechoslovakia. b, 1938 Rolls-Royce Phantom III, Britain. c, 1947 Studebaker Champion Starlight. d, 1948 Porsche Gmund, Germany. e, 1948 Tucker. f, 1931 Peerless V-16. g, 1931 Minerva AL, Belgium. h, 1933 REO Royale. i, 1933 Pierce-Arrow Silver Arrow. j, 1934 Hupmobile Aerodynamic.

No. 1614a, 1925 Vauxhall Type OE30/98, Britain. b, 1926 Wills Sainte Claire. c, 1928 Bucciali, France. d, 1929 Irving Napier Golden Arrow, Britain. e, 1930 Studebaker President. f, 1907 Thomas Flyer. g, 1908 Isotta-Fraschini Tipo J, Italy. h, 1910 Fiat 10/14HP, Italy. i, 1911 Mercer Type 35 Raceabout. j, 1917 Marmon Model 34 Cloverleaf.

No. 1615a, 1965 Peugeot 404, France. b, 1969 Ford Capri, Britain. c, 1975 Ferrari 312T, Italy. d, 1978 Lotus T-79, Britain. e, 1979 Williams-Cosworth FW07, Britain. f, 1948 H.R.G. 1500 Sports, Britain. g, 1949 Crosley Hotshot. h, 1955 Volvo PV444, Sweden. i, 1960 Maserati Tipo 61, Italy. j, 1963 Saab 96, Sweden.

**1988, June 1 *Perf. 13x13½***

*1613* Sheet of 10 14.50 14.50
*a.-j.* A223 $2 any single 1.45 1.45
*1614* Sheet of 10 14.50 14.50
*a.-j.* A223 $2 any single 1.45 1.45
*1615* Sheet of 10 14.50 14.50
*a.-j.* A223 $2 any single 1.45 1.45

Size of Nos. 1613-1615: 216x130mm.

Paintings by Titian (c. 1488-1576) A224

Paintings by Titian: 10c, *Lavinia Vecellio*, c. 1546. 20c, *Portrait of a Man*, c. 1510. 25c, *Andrea De Franceschi*, 1532. 90c, *Head of a Soldier*, 1511. $1, *Man With a Flute*.$2, *Lucrezia and Tarquinius*, c. 1515. $3, *Duke of Mantua with Dog*, 1525. $4, *La Bella Di Tiziano*, 1536. No. 1624, *Allegory of Alfonso D'Avalos*. No. 1625, *Fall of Man*, 1570, horiz.

**1988, June 15 *Perf. 13½x14***

*1616* A224 10c multi 8 8
*1617* A224 20c multi 15 15
*1618* A224 25c multi 18 18
*1619* A224 90c multi 68 68
*1620* A224 $1 multi 75 75
*1621* A224 $2 multi 1.50 1.50
*1622* A224 $3 multi 2.25 2.25
*1623* A224 $4 multi 3.00 3.00
*Nos. 1616-1623 (8)* 8.59 8.59

**Souvenir Sheets**

*1624* A224 $5 multi 3.75 3.75

***Perf. 14x13½***

*1625* A224 $5 multi 3.75 3.75

Nos. 1624-1625 have multicolored margins continuing the paintings. Size: 110x95mm.

Zeppelins — A225

Designs: 10c, *Graf Zeppelin* over the Federal Building, Chicago, 1933 World's Fair, vert. 15c, *LZ-1* over Lake Konstance, 1900. 25c, *Washington* aerial balloon lifting off the aircraft carrier USS *George Washington Curtis* off Port Royal, South Carolina, 1862, vert. 45c, *Hindenburg* over a Maybach Zeppelin automobile, Friedrichshaven, 1936. 50c, Goodyear Blimp over the Statue of Liberty, 1986, vert. 60c, *Hindenburg* passing over the Statue of Liberty during its final flight, 1937. 90c, Experimental docking of aircraft (piloted by Ernst Udet) with the *Hindenburg*, 1936. $2, *Hindenburg* over the Olympic stadium, Berlin, 1936, vert. $3, *Hindenburg* over Christ of the Andes statue, Rio de Janeiro, 1937, vert. $4, *Hindenburg* over mail plane catapult ship *Bremen*, 1936. No. 1636, Zepplin over DLH base, Bathurst, Gambia, 1935. No. 1637, *Graf Zeppelin* over mosque, Moscow, 1930.

**1988, July 1 *Perf. 14***

*1626* A225 10c multi 8 8
*1627* A225 15c multi 12 12
*1628* A225 25c multi 18 18
*1629* A225 45c multi 35 35
*1630* A225 50c multi 38 38
*1631* A225 60c multi 45 45
*1632* A225 90c multi 68 68
*1633* A225 $2 multi 1.50 1.50
*1634* A225 $3 multi 2.25 2.25
*1635* A225 $4 multi 3.00 3.00
*Nos. 1626-1635 (10)* 8.99 8.99

**Souvenir Sheets**

*1636* A225 $5 multi 3.75 3.75
*1637* A225 $5 multi 3.75 3.75

Nos. 1636-1637 have multicolored inscribed margins continuing the designs. Size: 76x95mm.

SYDPEX '88, Sydney, Australia — A226

Walt Disney characters in Australian settings: 1c, Camping in the Outback, a howling Tasmanian wolf. 2c, Offering peanuts to wallabies. 3c, With a kangaroo and joey against Ayers Rock. 4c, Riding emus, emu-wrens. 5c, Camp and wombat. 10c, Duck-billed platypuses. No. 1664, Photographing a kookaburra. $6, Koala and Mickey waving flags of Grenada, Australia and the United States, map. No. 1646, Flags and candles atop Cake in the shape of Australia. No. 1647, Mickey, Minnie Pluto and Goofy taking a break during a walkabout.

**1988, Aug. 1 Litho. *Perf. 14x13½***

*1638* A226 1c multi 5 5
*1639* A226 2c multi 5 5
*1640* A226 3c multi 5 5
*1641* A226 4c multi 5 5
*1642* A226 5c multi 5 5
*1643* A226 10c multi 8 8
*1644* A226 $5 multi 3.75 3.75
*1645* A226 $6 multi 4.50 4.50
*Nos. 1638-1645 (8)* 8.58 8.58

**Souvenir Sheet**

*1646* A226 $5 multi 3.75 3.75
*1647* A226 $5 multi 3.75 3.75

Mickey Mouse, 60th anniversary. Nos. 1646-1647 have multicolored inscribed margins continuing the designs and picturing the exhibition emblem plus an Australian cattle dog and dingo (No. 1646) or Australian parrots, cockatoos and rosellas (No. 1647). Sizes: 127x101mm (No. 1646).

Intl. Fund for Agricultural Development, 10th Anniv. — A227

**1988, Aug. 11** **Litho.** ***Perf. 14***

*1648* A227 25c Pineapple, vert. 20 20
*1649* A227 75c Banana, vert. 58 58
*1650* A227 $3 Mace, nutmeg 2.25 2.25

Flowering Trees and Shrubs of the Caribbean A228

**1988, Sept. 30** **Litho.**

*1651* A228 15c Lignum vitae 10 10
*1652* A228 25c Saman 18 18
*1653* A228 35c Red frangipani 25 25
*1654* A228 45c Flowering maple 32 32
*1655* A228 60c Yellow poui 42 42
*1656* A228 $1 Wild chestnut 70 70
*1657* A228 $3 Mountain immortelle 2.10 2.10
*1658* A228 $4 Queen of flowers 2.75 2.75
*Nos. 1651-1658 (8)* 6.82 6.82

**Souvenir Sheets**

*1659* A228 $5 Flamboyant 3.50 3.50
*1660* A228 $5 Orchid tree 3.50 3.50

Nos. 1659-1660 have multicolored margins continuing the designs. Size: 117x88mm.

Miniature Sheet

Christmas, Mickey Mouse 60th Anniv. — A229

Designs: No. 1661a, Huey draping garland. No. 1661b, Goofy stringing popcorn. No. 1661c, Chip'n'Dale decorating tree. No. 1661d, Santa Claus in his sleigh. No. 1661e, Dewey hanging stockings. No. 1661f, Louie unpacking decorations. No. 1661g, Donald Duck. No. 1661h, Mickey Mouse. No. 1662, Morty and Ferdie leaving milk and cookies for Santa, horiz. No. 1663, Morty and Ferdie dreaming of presents, horiz.

***Perf. 13½x14, 14x13½***

**1988, Dec. 1** **Litho.**

*1661* A229 Sheet of 8 6.00 6.00
*a.-h.* $1 any single 75 75

**Souvenir Sheets**

*1662* A229 $5 multi 3.75 3.75
*1663* A229 $5 multi 3.75 3.75

Nos. 1662-1663 have multicolored decorative margins continuing the designs. Size: 127x103mm.

Miniature Sheets

Major League Baseball Players — A230

No. 1664: a. Mickey Mantle. b. Roger Clemens. c. Rod Carew. d. Ryne Sandberg. e. Mike Scott. f. Tim Raines. g. Willie Mays. h. Bret Saberhagen. i. Honus Wagner.

No. 1665: a. Roberto Clemente. b. Cal Ripken, Jr. c. Bob Feller. d. George Bell. e. Mark McGwire. f. Alvin Davis. g. Pete Rose. h. Dan Quisenberry. i. Babe Ruth.

No. 1666: a. Jackie Robinson. b. Dwight Gooden. c. Brooks Robinson. Jr. d. Nolan Ryan. e. Mike Schmidt. f. Gary Gaetti. g. Nellie Fox. h. Tony Gwynn. i. Dizzy Dean.

No. 1667: a. Ernie Banks. b. National League emblem. c. Julio Franco. d. Jack Morris. e. Fernando Valenzuela. f. Lefty Grove. g. Ted Williams. h. Darryl Strawberry. i. Dale Murphy.

No. 1668: a. Johnny Bench. b. Dave Stieb. c. Reggie Jackson. d. Harold Baines. e. Wade Boggs. f. Pete O'Brien. g. Stan Musial. h. Wally Joyner. i. Grover Cleveland Alexander.

No. 1669: a. Jose Cruz. b. American League emblem. c. Al Kaline. d. Chuck Klein. e. Don Mattingly. f. Mike Witt. g. Mark Langston. h. Hubie Brooks. i. Harmon Killebrew.

No. 1670: a. George Brett. b. Joe Carter. c. Frank Robinson. d. Mel Ott. e. Benito Santiago. f. Teddy Higuera. g. Lloyd Moseby. h. Bobby Bonilla. i. Warren Spahn.

No. 1671: a. Gary Carter. b. Hank Aaron. c. Gaylord Perry. d. Ty Cobb. e. Andre Dawson. f. Charlie Hough. g. Kirby Puckett. h. Robin Yount. i. Don Drysdale.

No. 1672: a. Luis Aparicio. b. Paul Molitor. c. Lou Gehrig. d. Jeffrey Leonard. e. Eric Davis. f. Pete Incaviglia. g. Steve Rogers. h. Ozzie Smith. i. Randy Jones.

**1988, Nov. 28** **Litho.** ***Perf. 14***

*1664* Sheet of 9 2.00
*a.-i.* A230 30c any single 22 22
*1665* Sheet of 9 2.00
*a.-i.* A230 30c any single 22 22
*1666* Sheet of 9 2.00
*a.-i.* A230 30c any single 22 22
*1667* Sheet of 9 2.00
*a.-i.* A230 30c any single 22 22
*1668* Sheet of 9 2.00
*a.-i.* A230 30c any single 22 22
*1669* Sheet of 9 2.00
*a.-i.* A230 30c any single 22 22
*1670* Sheet of 9 2.00
*a.-i.* A230 30c any single 22 22
*1671* Sheet of 9 2.00
*a.-i.* A230 30c any single 22 22
*1672* Sheet of 9 2.00
*a.-i.* A230 30c any single 22 22
*Nos. 1664-1672 (9)* 18.00

Nos. 1664-1672 have multicolored decorative margins picturing emblems. Sizes: 186x152mm.

Singers — A231

**1988, Dec. 5** **Litho.** ***Perf. 14***

*1673* A231 10c Tina Turner 8 8
*1674* A231 25c Lionel Ritchie 18 18
*1675* A231 45c Whitney Houston 35 35
*1676* A231 60c Joan Armatrading 45 45
*1677* A231 75c Madonna 58 58
*1678* A231 $1 Elton John 75 75
*1679* A231 $3 Bruce Springsteen 2.25 2.25
*1680* A231 $4 Bob Marley 3.00 3.00
*Nos. 1673-1680 (8)* 7.64 7.64

**Souvenir Sheet**

*1681* Sheet of 4 (2 55c + 2 $1) 2.35 2.35
*a.* A231 55c Yoko Minamino 42 42
*b.* A231 $1 Yoko Minamino, diff. 75 75

Armatrading is misspelled "Ammertrading" on No. 1676.

No. 1681 has multicolored decorative margin.

## SEMI-POSTAL STAMPS

**Catalogue values for unused stamps in this section, from this point to the end of the section, are for Never Hinged items.**

ESPANA '82 World Cup Soccer SP1

Designs: Players and Flags of Winning Countries.

**1981, Nov. 30** **Litho.** ***Perf. 14***

*B1* SP1 25c + 10c West Germany, 1974 35 35
*B2* SP1 40c + 20c Argentina, 1978 60 60
*B3* SP1 50c + 25c Brazil, 1970 75 75
*B4* SP1 $1 + 50c Gt. Britain, 1966 1.50 1.50

**Souvenir Sheet**

*B5* SP1 $5 + 50c World Cup, ESPANA '82 3.75 3.75

Nos. B1-B4 each issued in sheets of 12 with sheet background showing soccer ball. No. B5 has multicolored margin showing players and flags, soccer ball. Size: 142x128mm.

1988 Seoul Olympics — SP2

**1986, Dec. 1** **Litho.** ***Perf. 15***

*B6* SP2 10c + 5c Pole vault 7 7
*B7* SP2 50c + 20c Balance beam 30 30
*B8* SP2 70c + 30c Shot put 40 40
*B9* SP2 $2 + $1 High jump 1.20 1.20

**Souvenir Sheet**

*B10* SP2 $3 + $1 Swimming 1.75 1.75

Surtax for natl. Olympic team. No. B10 has multicolored inscribed margin picturing yachting. Size: 80x100mm.

## AIR POST STAMPS

**Catalogue values for unused stamps in this section, from this point to the end of the section, are for Never Hinged items.**

Nos. 428-429, Surcharged with New Value, Olympic Rings, "Air Mail" and: "WINTER OLYMPICS / FEB. 3-13, 1972 / SAPPORO, JAPAN"

***Perf. 13½x14***

**1972, Feb. 3** **Litho.** **Unwmk.**

*C1* A66 35c on ½c multi 50 50
*C2* A66 50c on 1c multi 75 75

11th Winter Olympic Games, Sapporo, Japan, Feb. 3-13.

Nos. 294-300, 302A, 303-309 Overprinted Type "a" or Surcharged Type "b"

AIR MAIL
a

AIR MAIL
30c
b

***Perfs. as Before***

**1972, May 2** **Photo.; Litho.**

*C3* A45 5c vio & multi 7 7
*C4* A45 8c multi 10 10
*C5* A45 10c org & multi 12 12
*C6* A45 15c gray & multi 16 16
*C7* A45 25c multi 32 32
*C8* A45 30c on 1c multi 35 35
*C9* A45 35c multi 40 40
*C10* A45 40c on 2c multi 45 45
*C11* A45 45c on 3c multi 48 48
*C12* A45 50c multi 55 55
*C13* A45 60c on 5c multi 70 70
*C14* A45 70c on 6c multi 80 80
*C15* A45 $1 multi 1.10 1.10
*C16* A45 $1.35 on 8c multi 1.60 1.60
*C17* A45 $2 multi 2.25 2.25
*C18* A45 $3 multi 3.25 3.25
*C19* A45 $5 multi 5.50 5.50
*Nos. C3-C19 (17)* 18.20 18.20

"AIR MAIL" reading down on 5c, 15c, 25c, 35c, 60c and $5.

Olympic Type of Regular Issue

Designs (Olympic Rings and): 25c, 60c, $1, Boxing. 70c, Equestrian (not inscribed air mail).

**1972, Sept. 8** **Litho.** ***Perf. 14***

*C20* A69 25c bl & multi 40 40
*C21* A69 $1 grn & multi 65 65

**Souvenir Sheet**

*C22* A69 Sheet of 2 2.25 2.25
*a.* 60c bl & multi 85 85
*b.* 70c dp yel & multi 1.00 1.00

No. C22 has blue margin with black inscription and white sports design. Size: 81x84mm.

Nos. 409-412 Overprinted Vertically, Reading Up "AIR MAIL"

**1972, Oct.** **Litho.** ***Perf. 11***

*C23* A62 5c multi 12 12
*C24* A62 35c multi 50 50
*C25* A62 50c multi 85 85
*C26* A62 75c multi 1.50 1.50

Boy Scout Type of Regular Issue

Designs: 25c, Scout saluting. 35c, Two Scouts knotting ropes.

**1972, Nov.** ***Perf. 14***

*C27* A70 25c dp bl & multi 45 45
*C28* A70 35c brn org & multi 65 65

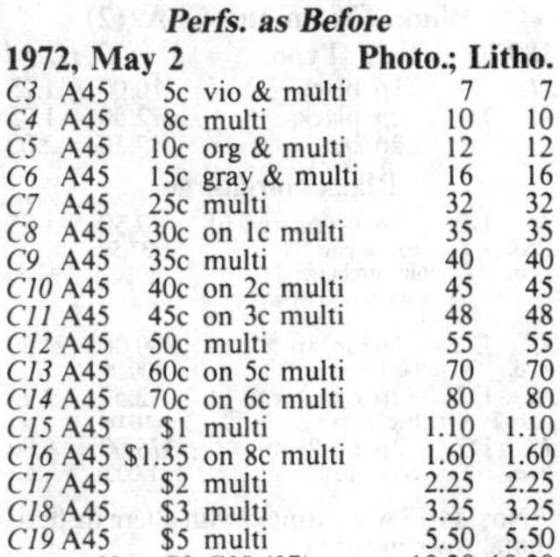

John Hancock — AP1

Designs: 50c, Benjamin Franklin. 75c, John Adams. $1, Marquis de Lafayette.

**1975, May 6** **Litho.** ***Perf. 14½, 13***

*C29* AP1 40c multi 55 *15*
*C30* AP1 50c multi 65 *20*
*C31* AP1 75c multi 1.00 *25*
*C32* AP1 $1 multi 1.50 *30*

American Revolution Bicentennial.

Nos. C29-C32 issued in sheets of 40. Each denomination was also printed in sheets of 5 plus label, perf. 13.

## POSTAGE DUE STAMPS

D1

D2

**Wmk. Crown and C. A. (2)**

**1892 Typo. *Perf. 14***

*J1* D1 1p black 10.00 1.25
*J2* D1 2p black 12.50 1.75
*J3* D1 3p black 17.50 2.00

**Black Surcharge**

*J4* D2 1p on 6p red lil 27.50 1.75
**a.** Tete beche pair 37.50
**b.** Double surcharge 42.50
**c.** Same as "b." tete beche pair
*J5* D2 1p on 8p bis 200.00 4.50
**a.** Tete beche pair 500.00
*J6* D2 2p on 6p red lil 42.50 3.25
**a.** Tete beche pair 110.00
*J7* D2 2p on 8p bis 375.00 8.00
**a.** Tete beche pair 1.000.

Nos. J4-J7 were printed with alternate horizontal rows inverted.

**1906-11 Wmk. 3**

*J8* D1 1p black 1.00 1.00
*J9* D1 2p black 2.00 1.60
*J10* D1 3p black 4.00 2.75

D3

**1921-22 Wmk. 4**

*J11* D3 1p black 45 45
*J12* D3 1½p black 2.00 2.00
*J13* D3 2p black 1.40 90
*J14* D3 3p black 1.50 1.50

**Catalogue values for unused stamps in this section, from this point to the end of the section, are for Never Hinged items.**

**1952**

*J15* D3 2c black 15 15
**a.** Wmk. 4a (error) 25.00
*J16* D3 4c black 15 15
**a.** Wmk. 4a (error) 25.00
*J17* D3 6c black 20 20
**a.** Wmk. 4a (error) 50.00
*J18* D3 8c black 30 30
**a.** Wmk. 4a (error) 50.00

### WAR TAX STAMPS

Nos. 80a, 80 Overprinted **WAR TAX**

**1916 Wmk. 3 *Perf. 14***

*MR1* A21 1p carmine 1.25 1.50
**a.** 1p scarlet 3.00 3.00
**b.** Double overprint 225.00
**c.** Inverted overprint 225.00

No. 80 Overprinted **WAR TAX**

*MR2* A21 1p scarlet 15 15

### OFFICIAL STAMPS

**Catalogue values for unused stamps in this section, from this point to the end of the section, are for Never Hinged items.**

Nos. 1006-1018, 1020, 1051-1053 Overprinted: "P.R.G."

**1982, July 15 Litho. *Perf. 14, 15***

*O1* A141 5c multi 5 5
*O2* A141 6c multi 6 6
*O3* A141 10c multi 8 8
*O4* A141 12c multi 10 10
*O5* A141 15c multi 12 12
*O6* A141 20c multi 16 16
*O7* A141 25c multi 20 20
*O8* A141 30c multi 25 25
*O9* A141 40c multi 32 32
*O10* A141 50c multi 40 40
*O11* CD331 50c multi 40 40
*O12* A141 90c multi 75 75
*O13* A141 $1 multi 80 80
*O14* CD331 $2 multi 1.60 1.60
*O15* A141 $3 multi 2.50 2.50
*O16* CD331 $4 multi 3.25 3.25
*O17* A141 $10 multi 8.00 8.00
*Nos. O1-O17 (17)* 19.04 19.04

PRG stands for People's Revolutionary Government.

## GRIQUALAND WEST

LOCATION — In South Africa west of the Orange Free State and north of the Orange River.
GOVT. — Former British Crown Colony.
AREA — 15,197 sq. mi.
POP. — 83,375 (1891).
CAPITAL — Kimberley.

Originally a territorial division of the Cape of Good Hope Colony, Griqualand West was declared a British Crown Colony in 1873 and together with Griqualand East was annexed to the Cape Colony in 1880.

12 Pence = 1 Shilling

Stamps of Cape of Good Hope 1864-65 (Type I, 4p, 6p, 1sh) and 1871-76 (Type II, ½p, 1p, 4p, 5sh) Surcharged or Overprinted

Type I. With frame line around stamp.
Type II. Without frame line.

"Hope" — A1

Manuscript Surcharge in Dark Red.

**1874 Wmk. 1 *Perf. 14***

*1* A1 1p on 4p bl (type I) 500.00 *750.00*

Overprinted **G. W.**

**1877 Black Overprint**

*2* 1p rose 325.00 50.00

**Red Overprint**

*3* 4p bl (type II) 200.00 50.00

G G G G
a b c d
G G G
e f g

In Black on the One Penny, in Red on the Other Values

*4* (a) ½p gray blk 7.00 6.75
*5* (a) 1p rose 6.25 5.00
*6* (a) 4p bl (type I) 100.00 10.00
*7* (a) 4p bl (type II) 80.00 6.25
*8* (a) 6p dl vio 65.50 15.00
*9* (a) 1sh green 50.00 12.50
**a.** Inverted overprint 225.00
*10* (a) 5sh orange 250.00 7.25
*11* (b) ½p gray blk 15.00 11.00
*12* (b) 1p rose 22.50 19.00
*13* (b) 4p bl (type I) 275.00 37.50
*15* (b) 4p bl (type II)
*15* (b) 6p dl vio 75.00 19.00
*16* (b) 1sh green 75.00 20.00
**a.** Inverted overprint
*17* (b) 5sh orange 275.00 25.00
*18* (c) ½p gray blk 15.00 15.00
*19* (c) 1p rose 25.00 19.00
*20* (c) 4p bl (type I) 200.00 30.00
*21* (c) 4p bl (type II) *275.00* 25.00
*22* (c) 6p dl vio 62.50 22.50
*23* (c) 1sh green 90.00 19.00
*24* (c) 5sh orange 22.50
*25* (d) ½p gray blk 6.75 6.25
*26* (d) 1p rose 10.00 7.50
*27* (d) 4p bl (type I) 225.00 22.50
*28* (d) 4p bl (type II) 75.00 12.50
*29* (d) 6p dl vio 50.00 10.00
*30* (d) 1sh green 22.50 8.00
*31* (d) 5sh orange 275.00 8.00
*32* (e) ½p gray blk 15.00 15.00
*33* (e) 1p rose 15.00 10.00
*34* (e) 4p bl (type I) 250.00 80.00
*35* (e) 4p bl (type II) 100.00 14.00
*36* (e) 6p dl vio 100.00 40.00
*37* (e) 1sh green 80.00 14.00
**a.** Inverted ovpt.
*38* (e) 5sh orange 17.50
*39* (f) ½p gray blk 16.00 15.00
*40* (f) 1p rose 25.00 19.00
*41* (f) 4p bl (type I) 300.00 150.00
*42* (f) 4p bl (type II) 175.00 37.50
*43* (f) 6p dl vio 100.00 37.50
*44* (f) 1sh green 100.00 16.00
*45* (f) 5sh orange 375.00 22.50
*46* (g) ½p gray blk 6.75 6.25
*47* (g) 1p rose 6.75 5.00
*48* (g) 4p bl (type I) 200.00 25.00
*49* (g) 4p bl (type II) 75.00 15.00
*50* (g) 6p dl vio 37.50 15.00
*51* (g) 1sh green 37.50 6.50
**a.** Inverted overprint
*52* (g) 5sh orange 275.00 6.50

There are minor varieties of types *"e"* and *"f"*.

Overprinted in Black

G G G G G
i k l m n
G G G G
o p q r

**1878**

*54* (g) 4p bl (type II) 175.00 27.50
*55* (g) 6p dl vio 275.00 62.50
*56* (i) 1p rose 6.00 5.50
*57* (i) 4p bl (type II) 37.50 7.00
*58* (i) 6p dl vio 150.00 22.50
*59* (k) 1p rose 6.75 6.00
*60* (k) 4p bl (type II) 150.00 27.50
*61* (k) 6p dl vio 275.00 55.00
*62* (l) 1p rose 15.00 15.00
*63* (l) 4p bl (type II) 55.00 15.00
*64* (l) 6p dl vio 150.00 35.00
*65* (m) 1p rose
*66* (m) 4p bl (type II)
*67* (m) 6p dl vio
*68* (n) 1p rose 75.00
*69* (n) 4p bl (type II) 300.00 125.00
*70* (n) 6p dl vio 300.00
*71* (o) 1p rose 15.00 15.00
*72* (o) 4p bl (type II) 175.00 27.50
*73* (o) 6p dl vio 400.00 175.00
*74* (p) 1p rose 27.50 20.00
*75* (p) 4p bl (type II) 225.00 35.00
*76* (p) 6p dl vio 325.00 110.00
*77* (q) 1p rose 55.00 50.00
*78* (q) 4p bl (type II) 275.00 80.00
*79* (q) 6p dl vio 375.00 225.00
*80* (r) 1p rose 225.00 165.00
*81* (r) 4p bl (type II) *350.00* 90.00
*82* (r) 6p dl vio *625.00* 350.00

There are two minor varieties of type *"i"* and one of type *"p"*.

Overprinted

G G
s t

**1878**

*83* (s) ½p gray blk 3.00 3.00
**a.** Double overprint 25.00
**b.** Inverted overprint 3.50 3.50
**c.** Double overprint, inverted 42.50
*84* (s) 4p bl (type II) 275.00 100.00
**a.** Invtd. overprint 275.00 100.00
*85* (t) ½p gray blk 3.25 3.25
**a.** Double overprint 40.00
**b.** Inverted overprint 4.00 4.00
*86* (t) 4p bl (type II) 350.00 50.00
**a.** Invtd. overprint 350.00 50.00

**Black Overprint**

*87* (s) ½p gray blk 225.00 125.00
**a.** Invtd. overprint 225.00 350.00
**b.** With second overprint *(s)* in red, inverted 250.00
**c.** With second overprint *(t)* in red, inverted 110.00
*88* (s) 1p rose 3.75 2.25
**a.** Double overprint 75.00 25.00
**b.** Inverted overprint 4.00 4.00
**c.** Double overprint, inverted 75.00 30.00
**d.** With second overprint *(s)* in red, inverted 17.50 17.50
*89* (s) 4p bl (type I) 175.00
*90* (s) 4p bl (type II) 62.50 14.00
**a.** Double overprint 90.00
**b.** Inverted overprint 110.00 50.00
**c.** Double overprint, inverted
*91* (s) 6p dl vio 40.00 22.50
*92* (s) ½p gray blk 30.00 30.00
**a.** Inverted overprint 35.00 35.00
**b.** With second overprint inverted 125.00
*93* (t) 1p rose 3.25 2.75
**a.** Double overprint 40.00
**b.** Inverted overprint 35.00 12.50
**c.** Double overprint, inverted 55.00
**d.** With second overprint *(t)* in red, inverted 35.00 35.00
*94* (t) 4p bl (type I) 150.00
*95* (t) 4p bl (type II) 175.00 5.50
**a.** Double overprint 125.00
**b.** Inverted overprint 200.00 20.00
**c.** Double overprint, inverted
*96* (t) 6p dl vio 27.50

Overprinted in Black

G
u

*97* (u) ½p gray blk 3.25 2.75
**a.** Double overprint 150.00 150.00
*98* (u) 1p rose 2.75 1.65
**a.** Double overprint 75.00
**b.** Triple overprint
**c.** Inverted overprint 55.00
*99* (u) 4p bl (type II) 3.75 1.65
**a.** Double overprint 75.00
*100* (u) 6p brt vio 50.00 4.00
**a.** Double overprint 250.00 110.00
**b.** Inverted overprint 32.50
*101* (u) 1sh green 35.00 2.75
**a.** Double overprint 150.00 100.00
*102* (u) 5sh orange 190.00 4.00
**a.** Double overprint 200.00 45.00
**b.** Triple overprint 175.00

These stamps were declared obsolete in 1880 and the remainders were used in Cape of Good Hope offices as ordinary stamps.

## GUYANA

LOCATION — Northeast coast of South America.
GOVT. — Republic.
AREA — 83,000 sq. mi.
POP. — 900,000 (est. 1983).
CAPITAL — Georgetown.

The former Crown Colony of British Guiana became an independent member of the British Commonwealth May 26, 1966, taking the name Guyana. On February 23, 1970, Guyana became a republic, remaining a Commonwealth nation.

100 Cents = 1 Dollar

**Catalogue values for all unused stamps in this country are for Never Hinged items.**

British Guiana Stamps of 1954 Overprinted **GUYANA INDEPENDENCE 1966**

***Perf. 12½x13, 13***

**1966, May 26 Wmk. 4 Engr.**

*1* A60 2c dk grn (#254) 5 5
*1A* A60 3c red brn & ol (#255) 2.50 2.50
*2* A61 4c vio (#256) 15 12
*3* A60 6c yel grn (#258) 7 7
*4* A60 8c ultra (#259) 15 12
*5* A61 12c brn & blk (#260) 25 25
*6* A61 $5 blk & ultra (#267) 47.50 47.50
*Nos. 1-6 (7)* 50.67 50.61

Same Overprint on British Guiana Stamps and Types of 1954

**Engr.; Center Litho. on $1**

**1966-67 Wmk. 314 Upright**

*7* A60 1c black ('67) 6 6
*8* A60 3c red brn & ol (#279) 6 5
*9* A61 4c violet ('67) 8 8
*10* A60 5c blk & red (#280) 6 5
*10A* A60 6c yel grn ('67) 9 7
*11* A60 8c ultra ('67) 9 7
*12* A61 12c brn & blk (#281) 8 6
*13* A60 24c org & blk (#282) 40 20
*14* A60 36c blk & rose (#283) 25 20
*15* A61 48c red brn & ultra (#284) 3.25 3.25
*16* A61 72c emer & rose (#285) 40 35
*17* A60 $1 blk & multi (#286) 55 45
*18* A60 $2 mag (#287) 1.10 75
*19* A61 $5 blk & ultra 3.75 3.25
*Nos. 7-19 (14)* 10.22 8.89

**1966-67 Wmk. 314 Sideways**

*7a* A60 1c black 5 5
*9a* A61 4c violet 6 5
*11a* A60 8c ultra 6 6
*12a* A61 12c brn & blk ('67) 10 8
*13a* A60 24c org & blk 20 12
*14a* A60 36c blk & rose ('67) 28 20
*15a* A61 48c red brn & ultra 40 28
*16a* A61 72c emer & rose ('67) 50 45
*17a* A60 $1 blk & multi ('67) 1.00 80
*18a* A60 $2 mag ('67) 2.00 1.75
*19a* A61 $5 blk & ultra ('67) 6.00 5.50
*Nos. 7a-19a (11)* 10.65 9.34

See Nos. 32-32T and note.

Flag and Map of Guyana — A1

Designs: 25c, $1, Arms of Guyana.

Unwmk.

**1966, May 26 Photo. *Perf. 14***

| | | | | |
|---|---|---|---|---|
| *20* | A1 | 5c vio & multi | 6 | 6 |
| *21* | A1 | 15c dk red brn & multi | 15 | 15 |
| *22* | A1 | 25c brt bl & multi | 22 | 22 |
| *23* | A1 | $1 sep & multi | 80 | 80 |

Guyana's independence, May 26, 1966.

Bank of Guyana A2

**1966, Oct. 11 *Perf. 13½x14***

| | | | | |
|---|---|---|---|---|
| *24* | A2 | 5c yel grn, bl, blk & gold | 6 | 6 |
| *25* | A2 | 25c bl, blk & gold | 22 | 22 |

Establishment of the Bank of Guyana.

British Guiana No. 13 — A3

**1967, Feb. 23 Litho. *Perf. 12½***

| | | | | |
|---|---|---|---|---|
| *26* | A3 | 5c multi | 8 | 5 |
| | *a* | Imperf., pair | | |
| *27* | A3 | 25c multi | 22 | 8 |

Issued to honor the unique British Guiana 1c black on magenta stamp of 1856.

---

Canceled to Order

Remainders of Nos. 26-30, 33-38 and 54-67 were canceled and sold by the Post Office in 1969. Values are for these canceled to order stamps. Postally used copies do not command a significant premium.

---

Chateau Margot — A4

Designs: 15c, Independence Arch. 25c, Guyana Fort, Fort Island (horiz.). $1, Parliament, National Assembly Hall (horiz.).

***Perf. 14, 14½x14, 14x14½***

**1967, May 26 Photo. Unwmk.**

| | | | | |
|---|---|---|---|---|
| *28* | A4 | 6c multi | 6 | 5 |
| *29* | A4 | 15c multi | 15 | 5 |
| *30* | A4 | 25c multi | 20 | 8 |
| *31* | A4 | $1 multi | 80 | 80 |

First anniversary of independence.

British Guiana Stamps and Types of 1954 Locally Overprinted

**GUYANA INDEPENDENCE 1966**

**1967 Wmk. 4**

| | | | | |
|---|---|---|---|---|
| *32* | A60 | 1c black | 5 | 5 |
| *32A* | A60 | 2c dk grn | 5 | 5 |
| *32B* | A60 | 3c red brn & ol | 7 | 6 |
| *32C* | A61 | 4c violet | 8 | 6 |
| *32D* | A60 | 6c yel grn | 10 | 7 |
| *32E* | A60 | 8c ultra | 12 | 8 |
| *32F* | A61 | 12c brn & blk | 14 | 12 |
| *32G* | A60 | $2 magenta | 2.50 | 2.50 |
| *32H* | A61 | $5 blk & ultra | 4.50 | 4.50 |
| | | *Nos. 32-32H (9)* | 7.61 | 7.49 |

The 24c with Wmk. 4 also exists with this overprint. Value $100.

**1967-68 Wmk. 314 Upright**

| | | | | |
|---|---|---|---|---|
| *32I* | A60 | 1c blk ('68) | 5 | 5 |
| *32J* | A60 | 2c dk grn ('68) | 6 | 5 |
| *32K* | A60 | 3c red brn & ol | 7 | 6 |
| *32L* | A61 | 4c vio ('68) | 8 | 7 |
| *32M* | A60 | 5c blk & red | 35 | 35 |
| *32N* | A60 | 6c yel grn ('68) | 20 | 12 |
| *32O* | A60 | 24c org & blk | 30 | 25 |
| *32P* | A60 | 36c blk & rose | 40 | 30 |
| *32Q* | A61 | 48c red brn & ultra | 60 | 50 |
| *32R* | A61 | 72c emer & rose | 75 | 75 |
| *32S* | A60 | $1 blk & multi | 1.00 | 1.00 |
| *32T* | A60 | $2 magenta | 2.25 | 2.00 |
| | | *Nos. 32I-32T (12)* | 6.11 | 5.50 |

The 1c, 4c, 6c, 8c and $5 with Wmk. 314 were not issued without overprint.

"Millie," the Bilingual Macaw — A5

Wicketkeeper, Emblem of West Indies Cricket Team — A6

**Christmas Issues**

**1967, Nov. 6 *Perf. 14½x14***

| | | | | |
|---|---|---|---|---|
| *33* | A5 | 5c ol grn & multi | 6 | 5 |
| *33A* | A5 | 25c pur & multi | 28 | 8 |

**1968, Jan. 22**

| | | | | |
|---|---|---|---|---|
| *34* | A5 | 5c red & multi | 6 | 5 |
| *35* | A5 | 25c yel grn & multi | 28 | 8 |

**1968, Jan. 8 Photo. *Perf. 14***

Designs: 6c, Batsman and emblem of Marylebone Cricket Club. 25c, Bowler and emblem of West Indies Cricket Team.

| | | | | |
|---|---|---|---|---|
| *36* | A6 | 5c multi | 8 | 5 |
| *37* | A6 | 6c multi | 10 | 5 |
| *38* | A6 | 25c multi | 35 | 12 |

Issued to publicize the visit of the Marylebone Cricket Club to the West Indies, Jan.-Feb. 1968. Nos. 36-38 are printed in sheets of 6 (3x3) in se-tenant strips of 3. Sheets have decorative borders.

Pike Cichlid — A7

Marail Guan — A8

Christ of St. John of the Cross, by Salvador Dali — A9

Designs: 2c, Piranha. 3c, Cichla ocellaris (fish). 5c, Armored catfish. 6c, Two-spotted cichlid. 15c, Harpy eagle. 20c, Hoatzin. 25c, Andean cock-of-the-rock. 40c, Great kiskadee. 50c, Agouti. 60c, Peccary. $1, Paca. $2, Armadillo. $5, Ocelot.

***Perf. 14x14½, 14½x14***

**1968, Mar. 4 Photo. Unwmk.**

| | | | | |
|---|---|---|---|---|
| *39* | A7 | 1c chlky bl & multi | 5 | 5 |
| *40* | A7 | 2c gray & multi | 5 | 5 |
| *41* | A7 | 3c grnsh bl & multi | 5 | 5 |
| *42* | A7 | 5c ultra & multi | 5 | 5 |
| *43* | A7 | 6c brt ol & multi | 6 | 5 |
| *44* | A8 | 10c yel grn & multi | 7 | 6 |
| *45* | A8 | 15c grn & multi | 12 | 8 |
| *46* | A8 | 20c ap grn & multi | 15 | 10 |
| *47* | A8 | 25c brt grn & multi | 20 | 12 |
| *48* | A8 | 40c pale brn & multi | 32 | 20 |
| *49* | A7 | 50c rose brn & multi | 40 | 28 |
| *50* | A7 | 60c lil rose & multi | 50 | 30 |
| *51* | A7 | $1 dp org & multi | 80 | 65 |
| *52* | A7 | $2 ocher & multi | 2.00 | 1.50 |
| *53* | A7 | $5 red & multi | 5.75 | 4.50 |
| | | *Nos. 39-53 (15)* | 10.57 | 8.04 |

See Nos. 68-82.

**1968, Mar. 25 *Perf. 14x14½***

| | | | | |
|---|---|---|---|---|
| *54* | A9 | 5c car rose & multi | 6 | 5 |
| *55* | A9 | 25c brt vio & multi | 28 | 6 |

Easter 1968.

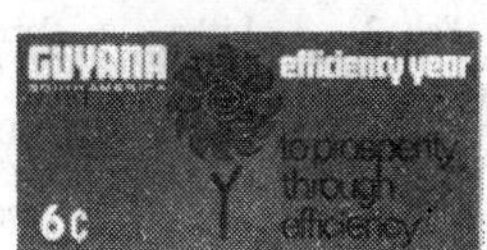

"Efficiency Year" — A10

Designs: 30c, 40c, "Savings bonds."

**1968, July 22 Litho. *Perf. 14***

| | | | | |
|---|---|---|---|---|
| *56* | A10 | 6c grn & multi | 6 | 5 |
| *57* | A10 | 25c fawn & multi | 22 | 7 |
| *58* | A10 | 30c multi | 25 | 7 |
| *59* | A10 | 40c multi | 35 | 7 |

Issued to promote the sale of savings bonds and to publicize Efficiency Year.

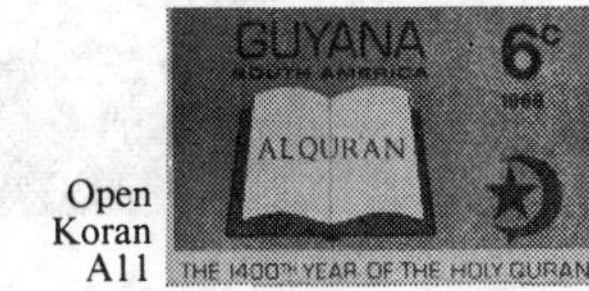

Open Koran A11

***Perf. 14x13½***

**1968, Oct. 9 Photo. Unwmk.**

| | | | | |
|---|---|---|---|---|
| *60* | A11 | 6c sal pink, gold & blk | 6 | 5 |
| *61* | A11 | 25c pale vio, gold & blk | 22 | 6 |
| *62* | A11 | 30c pale yel grn, gold & blk | 25 | 8 |
| *63* | A11 | 40c pale bl, gold & blk | 35 | 8 |

Koran's 1400th anniversary.

Dish Aerials, Thomas Lands, Guyana — A12

Wmk.364

Designs: 30c, 40c, Map showing connection between Guyana and Trinidad. All stamps are inscribed: "Guyana Sends Christmas Greetings to the World."

**Wmk. Lotus Bud Multiple (364)**

**1968, Nov. 11 Litho. *Perf. 14***

| | | | | |
|---|---|---|---|---|
| *64* | A12 | 6c bl, gray, ocher & emer | 6 | 5 |
| *65* | A12 | 25c brt rose lil, brn & emer | 18 | 6 |
| *66* | A12 | 30c bl grn & dk bl grn | 25 | 6 |
| *67* | A12 | 40c bl grn & red | 32 | 8 |

Issued for Christmas and to publicize the communications link with Trinidad by the tropospheric scatter system.

Types of 1968

Designs as before

***Perf. 14x14½, 14½x14***

**1968 Photo. Wmk. 364**

| | | | | |
|---|---|---|---|---|
| *68* | A7 | 1c chlky bl & multi | 5 | 5 |
| *69* | A7 | 2c gray & multi | 5 | 5 |
| *70* | A7 | 3c grnsh bl & multi | 5 | 5 |
| *71* | A7 | 5c ultra & multi | 5 | 5 |
| *72* | A7 | 6c brt ol & multi | 7 | 5 |
| *73* | A8 | 10c yel grn & multi | 12 | 10 |
| *74* | A8 | 15c grn & multi | 18 | 12 |
| *75* | A8 | 20c ap grn & multi | 25 | 15 |
| *76* | A8 | 25c brt grn & multi | 32 | 20 |
| *77* | A8 | 40c pale brn & multi | 55 | 32 |
| *78* | A7 | 50c rose brn & multi | 75 | 45 |
| *79* | A7 | 60c lil rose & multi | 90 | 65 |
| *80* | A7 | $1 dp org & multi | 1.25 | 1.10 |
| *81* | A7 | $2 ocher & multi | 2.50 | 2.00 |
| *82* | A7 | $5 red & multi | 6.50 | 6.00 |
| | | *Nos. 68-82 (15)* | 13.59 | 11.34 |

Celebrants Spraying Perfumed Powder — A13

Designs: 25c, 40c, Two celebrants spraying colored water.

**1969, Feb. 26 Litho. *Perf. 13½***

| | | | | |
|---|---|---|---|---|
| *83* | A13 | 6c multi | 6 | 6 |
| *84* | A13 | 25c multi | 18 | 18 |
| *85* | A13 | 30c multi | 22 | 22 |
| *86* | A13 | 40c multi | 30 | 30 |

Phagwah (Holi) Hindu festival.

The Last Supper, by Salvador Dali A14

**1969, Mar. 10 Photo. *Perf. 13***
*87* A14 6c dp car & multi 6 6
*88* A14 25c grn & multi 18 18
*89* A14 30c org brn & multi 25 22
*90* A14 40c dp vio & multi 35 30

Easter 1969.

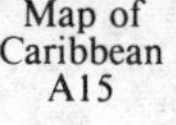

Map of Caribbean A15

Prow of Aluminum Ship A16

Design: 25c, "Strength in Unity" (horiz.).

**Wmk. 364**

**1969, Apr. 30 Litho. *Perf. 13½***
*91* A15 6c vio bl & multi 7 6
*92* A15 25c brt rose, yel & brn 20 18

Issued to commemorate the 1st anniversary of CARIFTA (Caribbean Free Trade Area).

**1969, Apr. 30 *Perf. 12x11, 11x12***

Design: 40c, Bauxite processing plant (horiz.).

*93* A16 30c blk, bl & sil 20 20
*94* A16 40c multi 25 25

50th anniv. of the ILO.

Flag Raising A17

Designs: 8c, 30c, Campfire.

***Perf. 13½x13***

**1969, Aug. 13 Litho. Wmk. 364**
*95* A17 6c pale grn & multi 5 5
*96* A17 8c org & multi 6 6
*97* A17 25c pale brn & multi 18 18
*98* A17 30c multi 25 25
*99* A17 50c rose & multi 50 50
*Nos. 95-99 (5)* 1.04 1.04

Issued to commemorate the 60th anniversary of Scouting in Guyana and to publicize the 3rd Caribbean Scout Jamboree, Georgetown, Aug. 13-22.

Gandhi and Spinning Wheel A18

***Perf. 14½x14***

**1969, Oct. 1 Litho. Wmk. 364**
*100* A18 6c ol, blk & lt brn 18 12
*101* A18 15c rose lil, blk & lt brn 60 45

Issued to commemorate the centenary of the birth of Mohandas K. Gandhi (1868-1948), leader in India's fight for independence.

Mother Sally Troupe A19

City Hall, Georgetown A20

**1969, Nov. 17 *Perf. 14x13½***
*102* A19 5c multi 6 6
*103* A20 6c bl & multi 7 7
*104* A19 25c multi 20 20
*105* A20 60c org & multi 45 45

Christmas 1969.

The 5c, 6c, and 25c exist without the "Christmas 1969" overprint.

Prime Minister Forbes Burnham and Map — A21

Descent from the Cross, by Rubens — A22

Designs: 6c, "Rural Self Help Project" (man and woman building house). 15c, University of Guyana (horiz.). 25c, President's Residence (horiz.).

**1970, Feb. 23 Litho. *Perf. 14***
*106* A21 5c bl, brn & ocher 6 5
*107* A21 6c bl, blk ocher & brn 7 6
*108* A21 15c ap grn & multi 15 10
*109* A21 25c multi 20 18

Issued for Republic Day, Feb. 23, 1970.

**1970, Mar. 24 *Perf. 14x14½***

Design: 6c, 25c, Christ on the Cross, by Rubens.

*110* A22 5c bl & multi 6 5
*111* A22 6c rose lil & multi 7 6
*112* A22 15c dk red & multi 20 18
*113* A22 25c yel & multi 35 30

Easter 1970.

"Peace" and U.N. Emblem A23

Design: 6c, 25c, U.N. emblem, panning for gold and drilling for minerals.

**1970, Oct. 26 *Perf. 14½x14***
*114* A23 5c red & multi 5 5
*115* A23 6c bl & multi 6 6
*116* A23 15c multi 18 18
*117* A23 25c brn & multi 28 28

25th anniversary of the United Nations.

Mother and Child, by Philip Moore — A24

**1970, Dec. 8 Litho. *Perf. 13½***
*118* A24 5c vio & multi 5 5
*119* A24 6c brn & multi 6 6
*120* A24 15c dk grn & multi 18 18
*121* A24 25c mar & multi 28 28

Christmas 1970.

National Cooperative Bank — A25

**1971, Feb. 23 Wmk. 364 *Perf. 14***
*122* A25 6c red & multi 6 6
*123* A25 15c yel & multi 12 12
*124* A25 25c ultra & multi 20 20

Republic Day, 1971.

"Togetherness, Vision, Understanding" A26

Volunteer Felling Tree, by John Criswick A27

**1971, Mar. 22 *Perf. 14½x14***
*125* A26 5c yel grn & multi 5 5
*126* A26 6c lil rose & multi 6 6
*127* A26 15c multi 12 12
*128* A26 25c yel & multi 20 20

Intl. year against racial discrimination.

**1971, July 19 *Perf. 14***
*129* A27 5c bl & multi 5 5
*130* A27 20c grn & multi 12 12
*131* A27 25c yel & multi 20 20
*132* A27 50c brn & multi 45 45

First anniversary of the National Self-help Road Project.

Yellow Allamanda — A28

Flora: 1c, Pitcher plant of Mt. Roraima. 3c, Hanging heliconia. 5c, Annatto tree. 6c, Cannonball tree. 10c, Cattleya violacea. 15c, Christmas orchid. 20c, Paphinia cristata. 25c, Gongora quinquinervis. 40c, Tiger beard. 50c, Guzmania lingulata. 60c, Soldier's cap. $1, Chelonanthus uliginoides. $2, Norantea guianensis. $5, Odontadenia grandiflora.

**1971-76 Litho. *Perf. 13x13½***
*133* A28 1c multi ('72) 5 5
*134* A28 2c lil & multi 5 5
*135* A28 3c multi 5 5
*136* A28 5c lt bl & multi 5 5
*137* A28 6c dl rose & multi 6 6

***Perf. 13½***
*138* A28 10c multi ('72) 10 10
*139* A28 15c multi ('72) 15 15
*a* Perf. 13 ('76) 15 15
*140* A28 20c multi ('72) 20 20
*141* A28 25c multi, flowers downward ('72) 50 50
*141A* A28 25c multi, flowers upward ('73) 25 25
*b* Perf. 13 ('76) 25 25
*142* A28 40c multi ('72) 40 40
*143* A28 50c multi ('73) 50 50
*144* A28 60c multi ('73) 60 60
*145* A28 $1 multi ('73) 1.00 1.00
*146* A28 $2 multi ('73) 2.00 2.00
*147* A28 $5 multi ('73) 5.00 5.00
*Nos. 133-147 (16)* 10.96 10.96

No. 141 has 2 blossoms at left, 3 at right; this is reversed on No. 141A.

The overprint "REVENUE / ONLY" between rules was applied to Nos. 134-136, 141A, 142-147 in 1975. Postal use was permitted in November-December, 1975.

The Lord's Prayer, by School Girl Veronica Bassoo — A29

Guyana Masker, by School Boy Michael Austin — A30

***Perf. 13½x14, 14x13½***

**1971, Nov. 15 Litho. Wmk. 364**
*148* A29 5c brt grn & multi 6 6
*149* A29 20c brt grn & multi 18 18
*150* A30 25c multi 20 20
*151* A30 50c multi 45 45

Christmas 1971.

Guyana Dollar — A31

Handclasp and Mosque — A32

**1972, Feb. 23 Litho. *Perf. 14½x14***
*152* A31 5c blk, dp org & sil 5 5
*153* A31 20c blk, dp lil rose & sil 20 20
*154* A31 25c blk, ultra & sil 22 22
*155* A31 50c blk, emer & sil 45 45

Republic Day 1972.

**1972, Apr. 3 *Perf. 14***
*156* A32 5c brn & multi 5 5
*157* A32 25c bl & multi 20 20
*158* A32 30c grn & multi 25 25
*159* A32 60c yel brn & multi 50 50

Youman Nabi (Peaceful Prophet), Mohammedan festival.

Map of South America, Emblem of Non-aligned Countries — A33

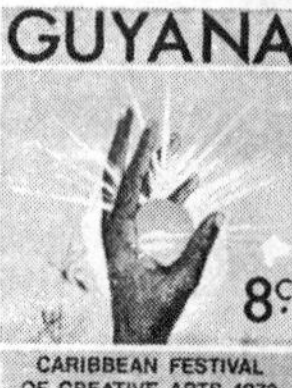

CARIFESTA '72 Emblem — A34

**1972, July 20**

*160* A33 8c vio & multi 10 10
*161* A33 25c yel grn & multi 20 20
*162* A33 40c org & multi 25 25
*163* A33 50c red brn & multi 40 40

Conf. of Foreign Ministers of Nonaligned Countries, Georgetown, Aug. 7-12.

**1972, Aug. 25**

*164* A34 8c org & multi 10 10
*165* A34 25c org & multi 20 20
*166* A34 40c org & multi 25 25
*167* A34 50c org & multi 40 40

Caribbean Festival of Arts (CARIFESTA), Georgetown, Aug. 25-Sept. 15.

Holy Family — A35

Umana Yana (Meeting Place of Wai Wai Chiefs) — A36

**1972, Oct. 18 Litho. *Perf. 13x13½***

*168* A35 8c bl & multi 6 6
*169* A35 25c bl & multi 15 15
*170* A35 40c bl & multi 20 20
*171* A35 50c bl & multi 30 30

Christmas 1972.

**1973, Feb. 23 Litho. *Perf. 14x14½***

Designs: 25c, 40c, Bethel Chapel. 50c, Like 8c.

*172* A36 8c brt bl & multi 6 6
*173* A36 25c rose red & multi 20 20
*174* A36 40c emer & multi 25 25
*175* A36 50c blk & multi 40 40

Republic Day 1973.

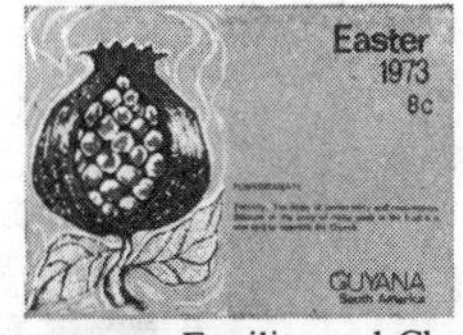


Pomegranate, Fertility and Church Symbol — A37

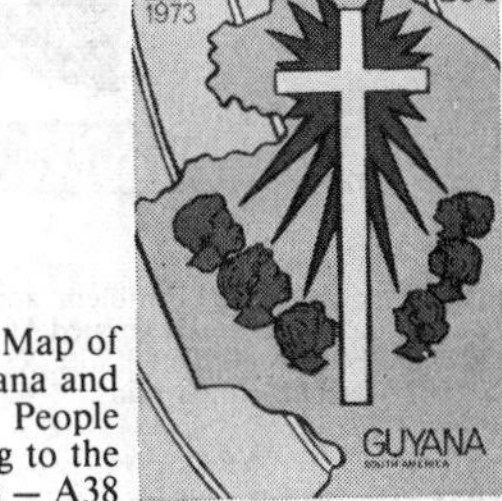


Map of Guyana and People Looking to the Cross — A38

**1973, Apr. 19 *Perf. 14x14½, 13½***

*176* A37 8c pink & multi 6 6
*177* A38 25c yel & multi 18 18
*178* A38 40c ultra & multi 25 25
*179* A37 50c yel & multi 35 35

Easter 1973.

Symbolic of Blood Donation — A39

***Perf. 14x14½***

**1973, Oct. 1 Wmk. 364**

*180* A39 8c red & blk 7 7
*181* A39 25c red & lil 20 20
*182* A39 40c red & vio bl 32 32
*183* A39 50c red & brn 40 40

Guyana Red Cross, 25th anniversary.

Steel Band, Star, Pegasus Hotel — A40

Madonna and Child, St. Philip's Anglican Church, Georgetown — A41

**1973, Nov. 20 Litho. *Perf. 14x14½***

*184* A40 8c lil & multi 6 6
*185* A40 25c lil & multi 18 18

***Perf. 13½x14***

*186* A41 40c vio bl & multi 25 25
*187* A41 50c vio bl & multi 38 38

Christmas 1973.

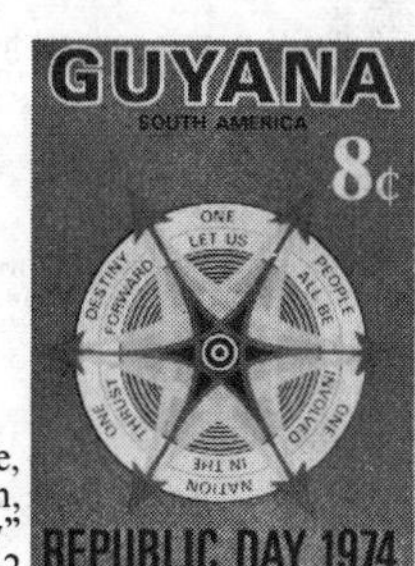


"One People, One Nation, One Destiny" — A42

Designs: 25c, 50c, Wai Wai Indian. 40c, Like 8c.

**1974, Feb. 23 Litho. *Perf. 13½***

*188* A42 8c multi 6 6
*189* A42 25c multi 18 18
*190* A42 40c multi 30 30
*191* A42 50c multi 40 40

Republic Day, 1974.

No. 137 Surcharged with New Value and 2 Bars

***Perf. 13x13½***

**1974, Mar. 18 Wmk. 364**

*192* A28 8c on 6c multi 12 10

Crucifix Super-imposed on Eddy Bow Kite — A43

Crucifix in Pre-Columbian Timehri Style — A44

**1974, Apr. 8 *Perf. 13½x14***

*193* A43 8c grn & multi 6 6
*194* A44 25c blk, grn & gray 18 18
*195* A44 40c blk, gray & car 25 25
*196* A43 50c gold & multi 35 35

Easter 1974.

UPU Emblem and British Guiana Type of 1863 — A45

Mailman and UPU Emblem — A46

**1974, June 18 Litho. *Perf. 14, 14½***

*197* A45 8c rose & multi 6 6
*198* A46 25c yel grn & multi 18 18
*199* A45 40c bl & multi 25 25
*200* A46 50c yel grn & multi 35 35

Centenary of Universal Postal Union.

Girl Guides Holding Banner — A47

Designs: 25c, 40c, Guides in camp cooking and carrying water. 50c, Like 8c.

**1974, Aug. 1 *Perf. 14½***

*201* A47 8c multi 6 6
*202* A47 25c multi 18 18
*203* A47 40c multi 30 30
*204* A47 50c multi 40 40
*a* Souvenir sheet of 4 1.50 1.50

50th anniversary of the Girl Guides of Guyana. No. 204a contains one each of Nos. 201-204. Multicolored margin. Size: 160x132mm.

Buck Toyeau — A48

Golden Arrow of Courage — A49

Fruit: 35c, Five-fingers and awaras. 50c, Pawpaw and tangerine. $1, Pineapple and sapodillas.

**1974, Nov. 18 Litho. *Perf. 14x13½***

*205* A48 8c multi 6 6
*206* A48 35c multi 28 28
*207* A48 50c multi 40 40
*208* A48 $1 multi 75 75
*a* Souvenir sheet of 4 1.75 1.75

Christmas 1974. No. 208a contains one each of Nos. 205-208, multicolored decorative margin. Size: 93x126mm.

No. 135 Surcharged with New Value and Two Bars

**1975, Jan. 20 Litho. *Perf. 13x13½***

*209* A28 8c on 3c multi 12 10

**1975, Feb. 23 *Perf. 13x13½***

Designs: 35c, Cacique's Crown of Honour. 50c, Cacique's Crown of Valour. $1, Order of Excellence.

*210* A49 10c brn & multi 8 8
*211* A49 35c brn red & multi 25 25
*212* A49 50c grn & multi 35 35
*213* A49 $1 vio bl & multi 65 65

Republic Day 1975.

Old Sluice Gate — A50

Modern Sluice Gate A51

**1975, May 2 *Perf. 14***

*214* A50 10c bis & multi 6 6
*215* A51 35c brn & multi 20 20
*216* A50 50c bis & multi 30 30
*217* A51 $1 grn & multi 60 60
*a* Souvenir sheet of 4 1.75 1.75

International Commission on Irrigation and Drainage, 25th anniversary. No. 217a contains one each of Nos. 214-217; pink and green margin showing dam and inscription. Size: 160x120mm.

IWY Emblem, Symbolic Man and Woman A52

Designs: IWY emblem and petroglyph designs of men and women.

**1975, July 1 Litho. Wmk. 364**

*218* A52 10c yel & dl grn 8 8
*219* A52 35c Prus bl & pur 25 25
*220* A52 50c org & dk bl 35 35
*221* A52 $1 ultra & brn 65 65
*a* Souvenir sheet of 4 1.75 1.75

International Women's Year 1975. No. 221a contains one each of Nos. 218-221, perf. 14½. Blue and purple ornament, brown inscription in margin. Size: 173x89mm.

The Scott Catalogue value is a retail price, what you could expect to pay for the stamp in a grade of Fine-Very Fine. The value listed is a reference which reflects recent actual dealer selling price.

Freedom Monument, Georgetown A53

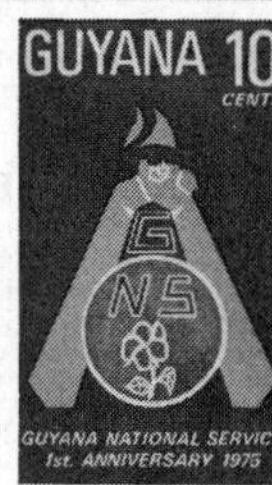

"GNS," Flower and Clasped Hands A54

Designs: Various views of Freedom Monument, Georgetown.

**1975, Aug. 26 Litho. *Perf. 14***

*222* A53 10c gray & multi 8 8
*223* A53 35c yel & multi 25 25
*224* A53 50c lil & multi 35 35
*225* A53 $1 ol & multi 65 65

Namibia Day (independence for South-West Africa).

**1975, Oct. 2 Wmk. 364 *Perf. 14***

Designs ("GNS" and Clasped hands): 35c, Wheel. 50c, Soccer ball. $1, Uniform cap.

*226* A54 10c vio, yel & grn 8 8
*227* A54 35c brt bl, org & grn 25 25
*228* A54 5c lt brn, brt bl & grn 35 35
*229* A54 $1 grn, vio & brt grn 65 65
*a* Souvenir sheet of 4 1.50 1.50

Guyana National Service, first anniversary. No. 229a contains one each of Nos. 226-229. Emerald GNS emblem and inscription in margin. Size: 194x133mm.

Foresters' Building and Badge A55

Designs: 35c, Rock painting of hunter. 50c, Crossed axes and hunting horn. $1, Bow and arrow.

**1975, Nov. 14 Litho. Wmk. 364**

*230* A55 10c red, blk & gold 8 8
*231* A55 35c red, blk & gold 25 25
*232* A55 50c gold & multi 35 35
*233* A55 $1 gold & multi 65 65
*a* Souvenir sheet of 4 1.50 1.50

Ancient Order of Foresters, centenary. No. 233a contains one each of Nos. 230-233; black and red marginal ornaments and inscription. Size: 128x96mm.

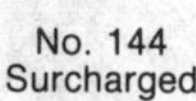
No. 144 Surcharged

35c

**1976, Feb. 10 *Perf. 13½***

*234* A28 35c on 60c multi 25 25

St. John Ambulance Emblem — A56

Independence Arch, 1966 — A57

**1976, Mar. 29 Litho. *Perf. 14***

*235* A56 8c blk, lil rose & sil 6 6
*236* A56 15c blk, org & sil 10 10
*237* A56 35c blk, emer & sil 25 25
*238* A56 40c blk, bl & sil 30 30

Guyana St. John Ambulance, 50th anniversary.

**1976, May 25 *Perf. 13½***

Stylized Designs: 15c, Victoria regia. 35c, Letter "S" for socialism. 40c, Worker with pitchfork.

*239* A57 8c sil & multi 6 6
*240* A57 15c sil & multi 10 10
*241* A57 35c sil & multi 25 25
*242* A57 40c sil & multi 30 30
*a* Souvenir sheet of 4 75 75

10th anniversary of independence. No. 242a contains one each of Nos. 239-242, perf. 14; multicolored margin shows stylized Victoria regia. Size: 120x103mm.

## Cricket Cup Issue

Types of Barbados 1976

**Unwmk.**

**1976, Aug. 3 Litho. *Perf. 14***

*243* A63 15c lt bl & multi 25 25
*244* A64 15c lil rose & blk 25 25

World Cricket Cup, won by West Indies Team, 1975.

Lamp — A58

Guitar-Sitar, Benin Head — A59

Designs: 15c, Hand and flame. 35c, Flame. 40c, Lakshmi, Hindu goddess of wealth.

**1976, Oct. 21 *Perf. 14***

*245* A58 8c multi 8 8
*246* A58 15c org & multi 15 15
*247* A58 35c pur & multi 35 35
*248* A58 40c ultra & multi 40 40
*a* Souvenir sheet of 4 1.25 1.25

Deepavali, Hindu Festival of Lights.
No. 248a contains one each of Nos. 245-248, light green and multicolored margin. Size: 93x107½mm.

**1977, Feb. 1 Litho. *Perf. 14½***

*249* A59 10c gold & multi 8 8
*250* A59 35c gold & multi 25 25
*251* A59 50c gold & multi 40 40
*252* A59 $1 gold & multi 75 75
*a* Souvenir sheet of 4 2.00 2.00

2nd World Black and African Festival, Lagos, Nigeria, Jan. 15-Feb. 12. No. 252a contains one each of Nos. 249-252; multicolored margin. Size: 84x157mm. Nos. 249-252a were not issued without black bar.

1c and 5c Coins A60

Coins (Obverse): 15c, 10c and 25c. 35c, 50c and $1. 40c, $5 and $10. $1, $50 and $100. $2, Reverse, Coat of arms.

**1977, May 26 *Perf. 14***

*253* A60 8c multi 6 6
*254* A60 15c multi 10 10
*255* A60 35c multi 25 25
*256* A60 40c multi 30 30
*257* A60 $1 multi 65 65
*258* A60 $2 multi 1.40 1.40
*Nos. 253-258 (6)* 2.76 2.76

New coinage.

Hand Pump, c. 1850 A61

Fire Engines: 15c, Steam engine, c. 1860. 35c, Fire engine, c. 1930. 40c, Fire engine, 1977.

***Perf. 14x14½***

**1977, Nov. 15 Litho. Wmk. 364**

*259* A61 8c multi 6 6
*260* A61 15c multi 12 12
*261* A61 35c multi 28 28
*262* A61 40c multi 30 30

National Fire Prevention Week.

Cuffy Monument A62

Harpy Eagle A63

Designs: 8c, 35c, Cuffy statue from monument. 40c, like 15c.

**1977, Dec. 7 Litho. *Perf. 14***

*263* A62 8c multi 6 6
*264* A62 15c multi 12 12
*265* A62 35c multi 28 28
*266* A62 40c multi 30 30

Cuffy, Guyana's national hero, led a slave revolution in 1763. The monument was unveiled in 1976.

**1978, Feb. 15 *Perf. 14***

Designs: 8c, Manatee (horiz.). 15c, Giant sea turtle (horiz.). 40c, Iguana.

*267* A63 8c multi 8 8
*268* A63 15c multi 15 15
*269* A63 35c multi 35 35
*270* A63 40c multi 40 40

Wildlife protection.

Parliament and Prime Minister Burnham — A64

Designs (Prime Minister and): 15c, Student and school children. 35c, Bauxite mine. 40c, Cooperative village.

**1978, Apr. 27 Litho. *Perf. 13½x14***

*271* A64 8c vio & blk 6 6
*272* A64 15c gray, blk & bl 10 10
*273* A64 35c multi 25 25
*274* A64 40c gray, blk & org 30 30
*a* Souvenir sheet of 4 75 75

Prime Minister Linden Forbes Burnham, 25th anniversary of his entry into parliament. No. 274a contains one each of Nos. 271-274; gray and black margin shows Parliament. Size: 177x120mm.

Dr. George Giglioli, Anopheles Mosquito — A65

Agrias Claudina — A66

Designs: 30c, Institute of Applied Science and Technology, proposed for University of Guyana (horiz.). 50c, Map of Guyana and National Science Research Council emblem. 60c, Commonwealth Science Council emblem (horiz.).

***Perf. 13½x14, 14x13½***

**1978, Sept. 4 Litho. Wmk. 364**

*275* A65 10c multi 6 6
*276* A65 30c multi 15 15
*277* A65 50c multi 25 25
*278* A65 60c multi 30 30

**1978, Oct. 1 *Perf. 14x13½***

*279* A66 5c Prepona pheridamas 5 5
*280* A66 10c Archonias bellona 8 8
*281* A66 15c Eryphania palyzena 12 12
*282* A66 20c Helicopis cupido 15 15
*283* A66 25c Nessaea batesli 18 18
*283A* A66 30c Nymphidium mantus ('80) 22 22
*284* A66 35c Siderone galanthis 28 28
*285* A66 40c Morpho rhetenor, male 30 30
*286* A66 50c Hamadryas amphinone 40 40
*286A* A66 60c Papilio androgens ('80) 45 45

**Size: 25x39mm**

***Perf. 13½x13***

*287* A66 $1 Agrias claudina 75 75
*288* A66 $2 Morpho rhetenor, female 1.50 1.50
*289* A66 $5 Morpho deidamia 3.75 3.75
*289A* A66 $10 Elbella patrobas, perf. 14 ('80) 7.50 7.50
*Nos. 279-289A (14)* 15.73 15.73

Indian Making Stone Chip Grater — A67

Designs (UNESCO Emblem and): 30c, Arawak Cassiri jar and decorated Amerindian jar. 50c, Gate to old Dutch fort, Kykover-al. 60c, Fort Island, Dutch ruins.

**Wmk. 364**

**1978, Dec. 27 Litho. *Perf. 14***

*290* A67 10c grn & multi 8 8
*291* A67 30c grn & multi 20 20
*292* A67 50c grn & multi 35 35
*293* A67 60c grn & multi 40 40

National and International Heritage Year.

Earth Station at Dawn, Georgetown A68

Designs: 30c, Earth Station in daylight, Georgetown. 50c, Intelsat V. $3, Intelsat IVa.

**1979, Feb. 7 Litho. *Perf. 14x14½***

*294* A68 10c multi 8 8
*295* A68 30c multi 20 20
*296* A68 50c multi 35 35
*297* A68 $3 multi 2.00 2.00

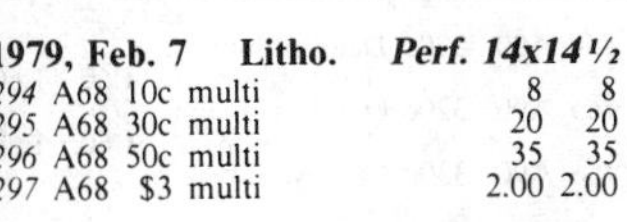

British Guyana No. 5 — A69

Designs: 30c, British Guiana No. 13 (vert.). 50c, British Guiana No. 152. $3, Printing press used for 1c Magenta (vert.).

**Wmk. 364**

**1979, May 30 Litho. *Perf. 14***

*298* A69 10c multi 8 8
*299* A69 30c multi 20 20
*300* A69 50c multi 35 35
*301* A69 $3 multi 2.00 2.00

Sir Rowland Hill (1795-1879), originator of penny postage.

"Fun with the Fowls" and IYC Emblem — A70

Children's Drawings and IYC Emblem: 10c, "Me and my sister" (vert.). 50c, "Two boys catching ducks." $3, "Mango season."

**1979, Aug. 20 Litho. *Perf. 13½***

*302* A70 10c multi 8 8
*303* A70 30c multi 20 20
*304* A70 50c multi 35 35
*305* A70 $3 multi 2.00 2.00

International Year of the Child.

H. N. Critchlow, Worker Hauling Sack — A71

Critchlow and: 30c, Baker (horiz.). 50c, Flag and crowd. $3, Portrait only.

**1979, Sept. 27 Litho. *Perf. 14***

*306* A71 10c multi 8 8
*307* A71 30c multi 20 20
*308* A71 50c multi 35 35
*309* A71 $3 multi 2.00 2.00

Guyana Labor Union, 60th anniversary.

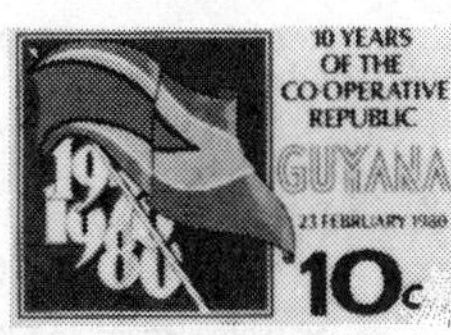


Cooperative Republic Centenary — A72

**Wmk. 364**

**1980, Feb. 23 Litho. *Perf. 14***

*313* A72 10c *shown* 8 8
*314* A72 35c *Demerara River Bridge* 25 25
*315* A72 60c *Kaieteur Falls* 40 40
*316* A72 $3 *Makanaima, American Indian* 2.00 2.00

Miniature Sheet

Snoek, London 1980 Emblem A73

London 80 Emblem and Fish: a, Snoek. b, Haimara. c, Electric eel. d, Golden rivulus. e, Pencil fish. f, Four-eyed fish. g, Pirai. h, Smoking hassar. i, Devil ray. j, Flying patwa. k, Arapaima. l, Lukanani.

**Wmk. 373**

**1980, May 6 Litho. *Perf. 14***

*317* Sheet of 12 3.00 3.00
*a.-l.* A73 35c multi, any stamp 25 25

London 1980 International Stamp Exhibition, May 6-14. No. 317 has black decorative margin. Size: 162x140mm.

Children's Convalescent Home, Rotary Emblem A74

Rotary International, 75th Anniversary (Emblem and): 30c, Georgetown club emblem. 50c, District 404 emblem (hibiscus; vert.). $3, Anniversary emblem (vert.).

***Perf. 14x14½, 14½x14***

**1980, June 23 Litho. Wmk. 364**

*318* A74 10c multi 10 10
*319* A74 30c multi 30 30
*320* A74 50c multi 50 50
*321* A74 $3 multi 3.00 3.00

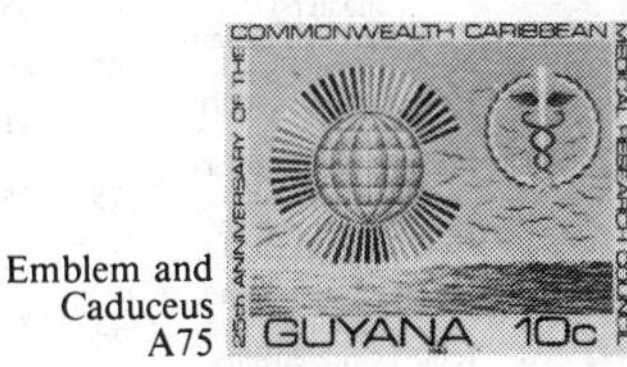


Emblem and Caduceus A75

**Wmk. 364**

**1980, Sept. 23 Litho. *Perf. 13½***

*322* A75 10c *shown* 8 8
*323* A75 60c *Scientist, beach scene* 40 40
*324* A75 $3 *Emblems over island* 2.00 2.00

Commonwealth Caribbean Medical Research Council, 25th anniversary.

Virola Surinamensis (Christmas 1980) — A76

**1980, Nov. 1 Wmk. 373 *Perf. 14***

*325* A76 10c *shown* 8 8
*326* A76 30c *Hymenaea courbaril* 20 20
*327* A76 50c *Mora excelsa* 35 35
*328* A76 $3 *Peltogyne venosa* 2.00 2.00

A77

Designs: a, Tree porcupine. b, Howler monkeys. c, Squirrel monkeys. d, Two-toed sloth. e, Tapir. f, Collared peccary. g, Six-banded armadillo. h, Anteater. i, Great anteaters. j, Mouse opossums. k, Four-eyed opossum. l, Orange-rumped agouti.

**Wmk. 364**

**1981, Mar. 2 Litho. *Perf. 14***

*329* Sheet of 12 2.75 2.75
*a.-l.* A77 30c, any single 20 20
*m* As #329g, perf. 12 20 20

16th Anniv. of the Guyana Defense Force — A78

**Wmk. 364**

**1981, Oct. 1 Litho. *Perf. 13½***

*330* A78 15c on 10c Armed Ranger, 1772 12 12
*331* A78 50c Private, Foot Regiment, 1825 40 40
*332* A78 $1 on 30c Marine Private, 1775 75 75
*333* A78 $1.10 on $3 Defense Force officers, 1966 80 80

Nos. 330, 332-333 not issued without surcharge.

Louis Braille and Boy Reading Braille — A79

Intl. Year of the Disabled: 50c, Helen Keller and Rajkumari Singh. $1, Beethoven and Sonny Thomas. $1.10, Renoir and painting.

**1981, Nov. 2 *Perf. 13½x14***

*334* A79 15c on 10c multi 12 12
*335* A79 50c multi 40 40
*336* A79 $1 on 60c multi 75 75
*337* A79 $1.10 on $3 multi 80 80

Nos. 334, 336-337 not issued without surcharge.

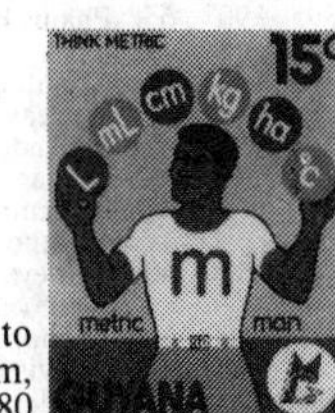


Conversion to Metric System, Jan. 2. — A80

Designs: a. Tape measure. b. Juggler. c. Man, envelope. d. Baby on scale. e. Canje Bridge. f. Liter bucket.

***Perf. 14½x14***

**1982, Jan. 18 Wmk. 364 Litho.**

*338* Sheet of 6 75 75
*a-f* A80 15c, any single 12 12

Flag A81

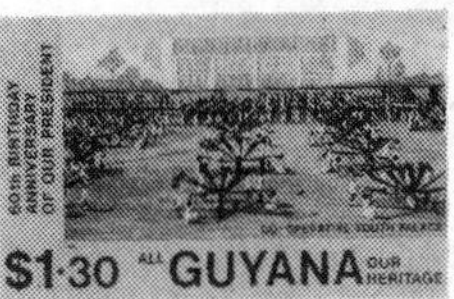


Cooperative Youth Palace — A82

**1983, Feb. 19 Litho.**

*339* A81 Pair 40 40
*a* 25c Flag flying right 20 20
*b* 25c Flag flying left 20 20
*340* A82 $1.30 shown 1.00 1.00

**Size: 43x25mm**

*341* A82 $6 Map 4.50 4.50

60th birthday of Pres. Linden Forbes Burnham. No. 339a inscribed for birthday; No. 339b for Burnham's 30th anniv. of election to parliament. No. 339, perf. 14½x14; No. 340, perf. 13½; No. 341, perf. 14½.

See Nos. 359-360.

River Steamers A83

**1983, July 11 Litho. *Perf. 14***

*342* A83 30c Kurupukari 18 18
*343* A83 60c Makouria 36 36
*344* A83 120c Powis 72 72
*345* A83 130c Pomeroon 78 78
*346* A83 150c Lukanani 90 90
*Nos. 342-346 (5)* 2.94 2.94

Great Britain, Postal Use In British Guiana, 150th Anniv. — A84

**1983, Oct. 1 Litho. *Perf. 14***

**Inscribed in Black**

*347* A84 25c #20 15 15
*348* A84 30c #26 18 18
*349* A84 60c #27 36 36
*350* A84 120c #28 72 72

**Inscribed in Blue**

*351* Block of 4 60 60
*a* A84 25c #20 15 15
*b* A84 25c #26 15 15
*c* A84 25c #27 15 15
*d* A84 25c #28 15 15
*352* Block of 4 72 72
*a* A84 30c #20 18 18
*b* A84 30c #26 18 18
*c* A84 30c #27 18 18
*d* A84 30c #28 18 18
*353* Block of 4 1.12 1.12
*a* A84 45c #20 28 28
*b* A84 45c #26 28 28
*c* A84 45c #27 28 28
*d* A84 45c #28 28 28
*354* Block of 4 3.60 3.60
*a* A84 120c #20 72 72
*b* A84 130c #26, Demerara 78 78
*c* A84 150c #27, Berbice 90 90
*d* A84 200c #28, Essequibo 1.20 1.20
*Nos. 347-354 (8)* 7.45 7.45

Nos. 347-350 printed in sheets with bottom two rows inverted. Nos. 351-353 printed in sheets of 60. No. 354 printed in sheets with blue marginal text.

Teachers' Assoc. Centenary — A85

**Wmk. 364**

**1984, July 16 Litho. *Perf. 14***

*355* A85 25c Children dancing 15 15
*356* A85 25c Torch, graduate 15 15
*357* A85 25c Torch concentric circles 15 15
*358* A85 25c Teachers, school 15 15

Nos. 355-358 se-tenant.

Type A81 Without Inscription.

**1983, July 1 Litho. *Perf. 14½x14***

*359* A81 Pair 30 30
*a* 25c. Flag flying right 15 15
*b* 25c. Flag flying left 15 15

Type A82 Inscribed "OLYMPIC GAMES 1984 / LOS ANGELES."

**1984, Nov. 16 *Perf. 13½***

*360* A82 $1.20 multi 60 60

Elanoides Forficatus A86

Designs: No. 361a, Pair in tree. No. 361b, Landing on branch. No. 361c, In flight, wings up. No. 361d, In flight, wings down. No. 361e, In flight, wings outstretched.

**1984, Dec. 3 *Perf. 14½***

*361* Strip of 5 1.50 1.50
*a.-e* A86 60c. any single 30 30

High Street Architecture A87

Designs: 25c, St. George's Cathedral, 1892, Colonial Life Insurance Co. 60c, No. 364a, Demerara Mutual Life Assurance Soc., Ltd. No. 364b, 200c, Town Hall, 1888, City Engineers Office. No. 364c, 300c, Victoria Law Courts, 1887.

**1985, Feb. 8 *Perf. 14***

*362* A87 25c multi 14 14
*363* A87 60c multi 30 30
*364* Triptych 1.80 1.80
*a.-c* A87 120c. any single 60 60
*365* A87 200c multi 1.00 1.00
*366* A87 300c multi 1.50 1.50
*Nos. 362-366 (5)* 4.74 4.74

Ocelot Cub Xica — A88

Macaw Nena — A89

***Perf. 12½x13***

**1985, Mar. 11 Wmk. 364**

*367* A88 25c multi 14 14
*368* A88 60c multi 30 30
*369* Triptych 1.80 1.80
*a.-c* A88 120c. like #367-368, 370 60 60
*d* Triptych, perf. 14 ('87) 75 75
*370* A88 130c multi 65 65

***Perf. 14½***

*371* A89 320c shown 1.60 1.60
*372* A89 330c Cub on hind legs 1.65 1.65
*Nos. 367-372 (6)* 6.14 6.14

Stamps in No. 369d inscribed "1986."

Orchids from Reichenbachia, by Sanders A90

Natl. Arms A91

**1985-86 Unwmk. *Perf. 14***

*373* A90 25c Cattleya lawrenceana 14 14
*374* A90 25c Laelia elegans schilleriana 14 14
*375* A90 25c Cattleya warscewiczii 14 14
*376* A90 25c Cypripedium io 14 14
*377* A90 25c Laelia euspatha 14 14
*378* A90 25c Cypripedium rothschildianum 14 14
*379* A90 25c Phalaenopsis speciosa 14 14
*380* A90 25c Oncidium ampliatum majus 14 14
*381* A90 25c Dendrobium aureum 14 14
*382* A90 25c Laelia gouldiana 14 14
*a* Dark red flowers ('86) 14 14
*383* A90 25c Renanthera lowii 14 14
*384* A90 30c Zygopetalum wendlandi 15 15
*a.* Wmk. 364 ('86) 15 15
*385* A90 30c Odontoglossum triumphans 15 15
*386* A90 40c Cattleya guttata leopoldi 20 20
*387* A90 40c Odontoglossum schroderianum 20 20
*388* A90 45c Cypripedium selligerum majus 22 22
*389* A90 45c Cattleya trianae alba 22 22
*390* A90 50c Dendrobium brymerianum 25 25
*391* A90 55c Saccolabium giganteum 28 28
*a* Wmk. 364 ('86) 28 28
*392* A90 55c Dendrobium wardianum 28 28
*a* Wmk. 364 ('86) 28 28
*393* A90 55c Odontoglossum harryanum 28 28
*a* Wmk. 364 ('86) 28 28
*394* A90 55c Oncidium macranthum 28 28
*a* Wmk. 364 ('86) 28 28
*395* A90 55c Phaius humblotii 28 28
*396* A90 60c Odontoglossum insleayi splendens 30 30
*397* A90 60c Laelia autumnalis xanthotropis 30 30
*398* A90 60c Cattleya percivaliana 30 30
*399* A90 60c Trichopilia suavis alba 30 30
*400* A90 60c Masdevallia backhousiana 30 30
*401* A90 60c Sobralia xantholeuca 30 30
*402* A90 60c Epidendrum vitellinum 30 30
*403* A90 60c Angraecum articulatum 30 30
*404* A90 60c Vanda coerulea 30 30
*405* A90 60c Oncidium lanceanum 30 30
*406* A90 60c Cattleya labiata gaskelliana 30 30
*407* A90 60c Cattleya labiata warneri 30 30
*408* A90 60c Cattleya eldorado crocata 30 30
*409* A90 75c Angraecum articulatum 38 38
*a* Wmk. 364 38 38
*410* A90 75c Cattleya dowiana aurea 38 38
*411* A90 90c Odontoglossum luteo-purpureum prionopetalum 45 45
*412* A90 90c Cypropedium lemoinierianum 45 45
*413* A90 100c Cypripedium tautzianum 50 50
*a* Wmk. 364 50 50
*414* A90 100c Laelia albida 50 50
*415* A90 100c Oncidium tigrinum 50 50
*416* A90 120c Vanda teres 60 60
*417* A90 120c Laelia anceps percivaliana 60 60
*418* A90 120c Odontoglossum hallii xanthoglossum 60 60
*419* A90 120c Phalaenopsis grandiflora aurea 60 60
*420* A90 120c Odontoglossum crispum 60 60
*421* A90 120c Cattleya trianaei schroederiana 60 60
*422* A90 120c Odontoglossum hebraicum 60 60
*423* A90 120c Angraecum caudatum 60 60
*424* A90 120c Laelia anceps sanderiana 60 60
*425* A90 120c Dendrobium nobile sanderianum 60 60
*426* A90 120c Odontoglossum roezlii 60 60
*427* A90 130c Cypripedium sanerianum 65 65
*428* A90 130c Chysis bractescens 65 65
*429* A90 130c Oncidium concolor 65 65
*430* A90 130c Odontoglossum crispum hrubyanum 65 65
*431* A90 130c Coelogyne cristata maxima 65 65
*a* Wmk. 364 ('86) 65 65
*432* A90 130c Maxillaria sanderiana 65 65
*a* Wmk. 364 ('86) 65 65
*433* A90 130c Masdevallia shuttleworthii and xanthocorys 65 65
*a* Wmk. 364 ('86) 65 65
*434* A90 130c Cattleya citrina 65 65
*a* Wmk. 364 ('86) 65 65
*435* A90 130c Zygopetalum intermedium 65 65
*436* A90 130c Cypripedium oenanthum superbum 65 65
*437* A90 130c Cymbidium mastersi 65 65
*438* A90 130c Cattleya ballantiniana 65 65
*439* A90 150c Vanda sanderiana 75 75
*440* A90 150c Cattleya superba splendens 75 75
*441* A90 150c Stanhopea shuttleworthii 75 75
*442* A90 150c Cypripedium niveum 75 75
*443* A90 150c Laelia anceps stella and barkeriana 75 75
*444* A90 150c Lycaste skinneri and alba 75 75
*445* A90 150c Odontoglossum crispum kinlesideanum 75 75
*a* Wmk. 364 ('86) 75 75
*446* A90 150c Phalaenopsis stuartiana 75 75
*a* Wmk. 364 ('86) 75 75
*447* A90 150c Laelia harpophylla 75 75
*a* Wmk. 364 ('86) 75 75
*448* A90 150c Odontoglossum edwardii 75 75
*449* A90 150c Oncidium splendidum 75 75
*450* A90 150c Phalaenopsis casta 75 75
*451* A90 150c Epidendrum prismatocarpum 75 75
*452* A90 180c Cattleya mendelii 90 90
*453* A90 200c Odontoglossum rossii 1.00 1.00
*454* A90 200c Aeranthus sesquipedalis 1.00 1.00
*455* A90 200c Cattleya trianaei ernesti 1.00 1.00
*a* Wmk. 364 ('86) 1.00 1.00
*456* A90 200c Oncidium jonesianum and phaeanthum 1.00 1.00
*457* A90 200c Odontoglossum luteo-purpureum 1.00 1.00
*458* A90 200c Odontoglossum hebraicum aspersum 1.00 1.00
*459* A90 225c Odontoglossum blandum 1.15 1.15
*a.* Wmk. 364 ('86) 1.15 1.15
*460* A90 225c Odontoglossum grande 1.15 1.15
*461* A90 250c Vanda hookeriana 1.25 1.25
*462* A90 260c Dendrobium superbiens 1.30 1.30
*463* A90 300c Cypripedium argus 1.50 1.50
*464* A90 320c Dendrobium leechianum 1.60 1.60
*465* A90 320c Odontoglossum humeanum 1.60 1.60
*466* A90 330c Cattleya dowiana chrysotoxa 1.65 1.65
*467* A90 350c Odontoglossum sanderianum 1.75 1.75
*468* A90 360c Cattleya rochellensis 1.80 1.80
*469* A90 375c Catasetum bungerothii 1.90 1.90
*Nos. 373-469 (97)* 59.09 59.09

See note below No. 567. Issue dates: Nos. 373, 396-400, 416, 427-434, 453, July 9. Nos. 374, 391-394, 401-402, 417, 435-436, 439-444, Aug. 12. Nos. 375-381, 418-420, 445-447, 454-456, Sept. 16. No. 403, Oct. 7. Nos. 382, 384, 404-406, 409, 413, 421-425, 437, 448, 457, 459, Nos. 385, 395, 408, 414, 438, 461-462, 469, July 10. Nos. 387, 389, 412, 415, 451-452, 465-466, July 24. Nov. 4. Nos. 386, 388, 390, 407, 410-411, 449, 458, 463-464, 468, Feb. 26, 1986. Nos. 383, 426, 450, 460, 467, Apr. 4, 1986.

Some stamps printed in sheets of 25, blocks of 4 each of different stamps separated by gutter containing 2 No. 566 and strip of 5 No. 567. Margin contains separation marks for Nos. 566-567. Nos. 383, 404-406, 418-420, 426, 445-447, 450, 455-457, 467 horiz.

**1986 Litho. *Perf. 14***

*470* A90 30c Saccolabium coeleste 15 15
*471* A90 40c Cattleya ballantiniana 20 20
*472* A90 45c Odontoglossum coradinei 22 22
*473* A90 45c Cattleya schroederae alba 22 22
*474* A90 50c Laelia grandis 25 25
*475* A90 60c Selenipedium hybridum nitidissimum 30 30
*476* A90 75c Cypripedium boxalli atratum 38 38
*477* A90 75c Coelogyne sanderae 38 38
*478* A90 80c Dendrobium phalaenopsis 40 40
*479* A90 85c Cypripedium castleanum 42 42
*480* A90 90c Phaius tuberculosus 45 45
*481* A90 90c Laelia anceps schroderiana 45 45
*482* A90 130c Cypripedium laucheanum and eyermanianum 65 65
*483* A90 160c Odontoglossum crispum mundyanum 80 80
*484* A90 200c Odontoglossum wattianum 1.00 1.00
*485* A90 200c Odontoglossum naevium 1.00 1.00
*486* A90 300c Dendrobium venus and cassiope 1.50 1.50
*487* A90 320c Dendrobium melanodiscus 1.60 1.60
*488* A90 320c Cypripedium lathamianum inversum 1.60 1.60
*489* A90 350c Odontoglossum vexillarium 1.75 1.75
*490* A90 360c Cattleya labiata lueddemanniana 1.80 1.80
*491* A90 390c Laelia praestans 1.95 1.95
*Nos. 470-491 (22)* 17.47 17.47

Issue dates: Nos. 470, 472, 476, 478, 480, 482-484, 487, 489-490, Sept. 23. No. 471, Sept. 26. Others, Oct. 31. Nos. 472, 478, 483 and 489 horiz.

**1986 Litho. *Perf. 14***

*492* A90 25c Laelio cattleya elegans blenheimensis 12 12
*493* A90 40c Laelia albida 20 20
*494* A90 40c Dendrobium phalaenopsis statterianum 20 20
*495* A90 50c Laelia anceps schroederiana 25 25
*496* A90 80c Phaius humblotii 40 40
*497* A90 85c Disa grandiflora 42 42
*498* A90 90c Dendrobium formosum 45 45
*499* A90 120c Phaius hybridus cooksonii 60 60
*500* A90 130c Miltonia bleuana 65 65

*501* A90 150c Odontoglossum wilckeanum rothschildianum 75 75
*502* A90 320c Lycaste skinnerii armeniaca 1.60 1.60
*503* A90 330c Cattleya mendelii measuresiana 1.65 1.65
*Nos. 492-503 (12)* 7.29 7.29

Issue dates: Nos. 492, 494, 497-501, 502-503, Dec. 27, 1986. Nos. 493, 496, Nov. 25, 1986. No. 495, Dec. 3, 1986.

**1986, Aug. 21 Litho. *Perf. 14***

*504* A90 40c Catasetum bungerothii 20 20
*505* A90 45c Cattleya guttata leopoldi 22 22
*506* A90 45c Oncidium splendidum 22 22
*507* A90 45c Odontoglossum luteo-purpureum prionopetalum 22 22
*508* A90 45c Cattleya rochellensis 22 22
*509* A90 50c Dendrobium wardianum 25 25
*510* A90 50c Saccolabium giganteum 25 25
*511* A90 50c Odontoglossum blandum 25 25
*512* A90 50c Zygopetalum wendlandi 25 25
*513* A90 50c Cypripedium tautzianum 25 25
*514* A90 55c Cattleya mendelii 28 28
*515* A90 55c Cattleya trianae alba 28 28
*516* A90 55c Odontoglossum humeanum 28 28
*517* A90 55c Cypripedium lemoinierianum 28 28
*518* A90 60c Cattleya dowiana aurea 30 30
*519* A90 60c Dendrobium leechianum 30 30
*520* A90 60c Cypripedium selligerum majus 30 30
*521* A90 60c Odontoglossum roezlii 30 30
*522* A90 60c Renanthera lowii 30 30
*523* A90 60c Odontoglossum hebraicum aspersum 30 30
*524* A90 60c Philaenopsis casta 30 30
*525* A90 60c Odontoglossum sanderianum 30 30
*526* A90 65c Epidendrum prismatocarpum 32 32
*527* A90 65c Cattleya dowiana chrysotoxa 32 32
*528* A90 65c Oncidium tigrinum 32 32
*529* A90 65c Odontoglossum schroderianum 32 32
*530* A90 75c Odontoglossum grande 38 38
*531* A90 75c Cypripedium argus 38 38
*532* A90 75c Dendrobium brymerianum 38 38
*533* A90 75c Cattleya labiata warneri 38 38
*534* A90 80c Dendrobium superbiens 40 40
*535* A90 80c Vanda hookeriana 40 40
*536* A90 80c Cattleya eldorado crocata 40 40
*537* A90 100c Coelogyne cristata maxima 50 50
*538* A90 100c Masdevallia shuttleworthii and xanthocorys 50 50
*539* A90 100c Cattleya citrina 50 50
*540* A90 100c Maxillaria sanderiana 50 50
*541* A90 100c Laelia harpophylla 50 50
*542* A90 100c Phalaenopsis stuartiana 50 50
*543* A90 100c Cattleya trianaei ernesti 50 50
*544* A90 100c Odontoglossum crispum kinlesideanum 50 50
*Nos. 504-544 (41)* 13.85 13.85

Nos. 521-522, 524-525, 541-544 horiz. Nos. 504-544 sold in booklets only. Two booklets of 48 stamps each contain Nos. 504-544 and previous values issued in the series.

**1986-87**

*545* A90 35c Cypripedium castleanum ('87) 18 18
*546* A90 40c Odontoglossum triumphans 20 20
*547* A90 50c Oncidium macranthum 25 25
*548* A90 50c Odontoglossum harryanum 25 25
*549* A90 50c Disa grandiflora ('87) 25 25
*550* A90 50c Angraecum articulatum ('87) 25 25
*551* A90 85c Cattleya intermedia punctatissima 42 42
*552* A90 85c Lycaste skinnerii armeniaca ('87) 42 42
*553* A90 90c Cypripedium lathamianum inversum 45 45
*554* A90 90c Selenipedium hybridium nitidissimum 45 45
*555* A90 90c Cattleya bowringiana ('87) 45 45
*556* A90 180c Odontoglossum ramosissimum ('87) 45 45
*557* A90 200c like No. 555 1.00 1.00
*558* A90 225c like No. 551 1.15 1.15
*559* A90 230c Laelia purpurata ('87) 58 58
*560* A90 300c Cattleya victoria regina ('87) 75 75
*561* A90 330c Thunia brymeriana ('87) 85 85
*562* A90 425c Laelia autumnalis alba ('87) 1.05 1.05
*563* A90 440c Spathoglottis kimballiana ('87) 1.10 1.10
*564* A90 590c Cattleya mossiae reineckiana ('87) 1.50 1.50
*565* A90 650c Arachnanthe clarkei ('87) 1.65 1.65
*Nos. 545-565 (21)* 13.65 13.65

See note after No. 567A. Issue dates: Nos. 546 and 553, Oct. 23, 1986. Nos. 547, 551 and 554, Dec. 15. No. 548, Dec. 22. Nos. 545, 549, 552 and 555, Jan. 5, 1987. No. 550, Jan. 16. Nos. 556, 559-565, Feb. 14. Nos. 557-558, Nov. 25, 1986.

See Nos. 583-624D, 631-675, O1-O17.

**1985, July 9 *Perf. 14 Vert.***

*566* A91 25c multi 14 14
*566A* A91 25c multi ('87) 5 5

***Perf. 14 Horiz.***

*567* A91 25c multi 14 14
*567A* A91 25c multi ('87) 5 5

Nos. 566-567 were cut from orchid sheet gutters. Stamps vary considerably in size.

Nos. 566A and 567A are Nos. 566 and 567 redrawn to include black border. Issued June 2.

Abolition of Slavery, Sesquicent. A92

**1985, July 29 *Perf. 14***

*568* A92 25c Revolution leaders, 1763 12 12
*569* A92 60c Damon's execution, 1834 28 28
*570* A92 130c Demerara Uprising, 1823 60 60
*571* A92 150c Den Arendt slave ship 70 70

Clive Lloyd, Cricketeer A93

Lloyd Holding Intl. Cup A94

Designs: No. 572a, $2.25, Lloyd playing cricket. No. 572b, $1.30, Lloyd, bat and wicket. No. 572c, 60c, Gloves, wicket, bat, natl. flag.

**1985, Nov. 7 *Perf. 14½x14***

*572* Triptych 38 38
*a.-c.* A93 25c, any single 12 12

**Size: 30x38mm.**

***Perf. 14x14½***

*573* A93 60c multi 28 28
*574* A93 $1.30 multi 60 60
*575* A93 $2.25 multi 1.10 1.10
*576* A94 $3.50 multi 1.75 1.75
*Nos. 572-576 (5)* 4.11 4.11

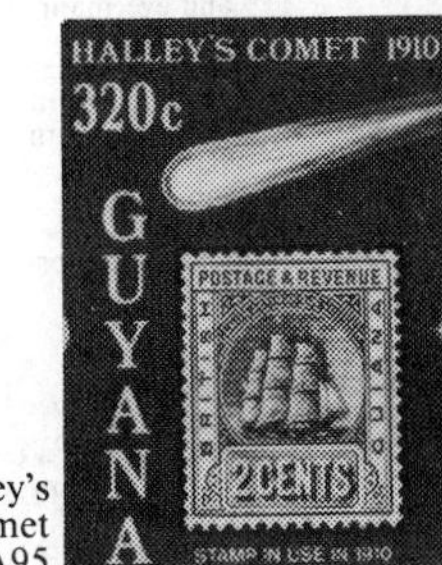


Halley's Comet A95

**1986, July 19 *Perf. 14***

*577* A95 320c Br. Guiana No. 172 1.60 1.60
*578* A95 320c No. 371 1.60 1.60

Printed se-tenant, in a continuous design. Exists imperf and imperf between.

L.F.S. Burnham, President 1980-85 A96

**1986, Dec. 13 Litho. *Perf. 12½x13***

*579* A96 25c Tomb 12 12
*580* A96 120c Flags, map 60 60
*581* A96 130c Government building 65 65
*582* A96 $6 Portrait, necklace, vert. 3.00 3.00

### Orchids Type of 1985

**1987, Apr. 24 *Perf. 14***

*583* A90 240c Cattleya amethystoglossa 55 55
*584* A90 260c Cychnoches chlorochilon 58 58
*585* A90 275c Coelogyne pandurata 62 62
*586* A90 390c Odontoglossum leroyanum 88 88
*587* A90 450c Odontoglossum excellens 1.00 1.00
*588* A90 460c Oncidium loxense 1.05 1.05
*589* A90 500c Selenipedium weidlichianum 1.15 1.15
*590* A90 560c Cypripedium morganiae burfordiense 1.25 1.25
*Nos. 583-590 (8)* 7.08 7.08

See note after No. 567A.

**1987, June 2**

*591* A90 500c Zygopetalum klabochorum 1.00 1.00
*592* A90 520c Laelio-cattleya 1.05 1.05
*593* A90 $20 Miltonia moreliana 4.00 4.00

**1987**

*594* A90 200c Coelogyne swaniana 40 40
*595* A90 200c Cattleya arnoldiana 40 40
*596* A90 200c Cypripedium pollettianum and maynardii 40 40
*597* A90 325c Phalaenopsis sanderiana and intermedia portei 65 65
*598* A90 400c Lissochilus giganteus 80 80
*599* A90 420c Dendrobium imperatrix 85 85
*600* A90 480c Cypripedium calypso 95 95
*601* A90 575c Oncidium superbiens 1.15 1.15
*602* A90 600c Epidendrum atro-purpureum randianum 1.20 1.20
*603* A90 $25 Cattleya rex 5.00 5.00
*Nos. 594-603 (10)* 11.80 11.80

Issue dates: 200c, Sept. 29. 325c, 420c, 575c, Oct. 26. 400c, 480c, 600c, $25, July 22. Nos. 597, 599 horiz. A 900c stamp printed in sheets of four and picturing *Cattleya luedemanniana alba* issued on September 29, 1987. Two stamps from each sheet of four surcharged 600c; issued only in pairs of one 900c stamp plus one 600c surcharge.

**1987, Nov. 23**

*604* A90 255c Dendrobium johnsoniae 45 45
*605* A90 290c Cymbidium lowianum 52 52
*606* A90 375c Vanda parishii marriottiana 68 68
*607* A90 680c Cattleya mendelii quorndon house 1.25 1.25
*608* A90 720c Cattleya labiata 1.30 1.30
*609* A90 750c Zygopetalum burtii 1.35 1.35
*610* A90 800c Miltonia phalaenopsis 1.45 1.45
*611* A90 850c Masdevallias courtauldiana, geleniana and measuresiana 1.55 1.55
*Nos. 604-611 (8)* 8.55 8.55

### Miniature Sheets

Designs: Nos. 612a, 613b, 614c, 615d, Cattleya hardyana. Nos. 612b, 613a, 614d, 615c, Odontoglossum cervantesii decorum. Nos. 612c, 613d, 614a, 615b, Aerides savageanum. Nos. 612d, 613c, 614b, 615a, Cypripedium leeanum giganteum.

**1988 Litho. *Perf. 14***

*612* Sheet of 4 3.00 3.00
*a* A90 320c multi 65 65
*b* A90 330c multi 65 65
*c* A90 350c multi 70 70
*d* A90 500c multi 1.00 1.00
*613* Sheet of 4 3.00 3.00
*a* A90 320c multi 65 65
*b* A90 330c multi 65 65
*c* A90 350c multi 70 70
*d* A90 500c multi 1.00 1.00
*614* Sheet of 4 3.00 3.00
*a* A90 320c multi 65 65
*b* A90 330c multi 65 65
*c* A90 350c multi 70 70
*d* A90 500c multi 1.00 1.00
*615* Sheet of 4 3.00 3.00
*a* A90 320c multi 65 65
*b* A90 330c multi 65 65
*c* A90 350c multi 70 70
*d* A90 500c multi 1.00 1.00

Inscribed "REICHENBACHIA" and "1886-1986." Sizes: 102x128mm.

**1988 Litho. *Perf. 14***

*616* A90 320c Selenipedium hybridum grande 95 95
*617* A90 350c Cattleya luedemanniana alba 70 70
*618* A90 475c Zygopetalum crinitum 1.40 1.40
*619* A90 525c Cattleya granulosa schofieldiana 1.55 1.55
*620* A90 530c Phaius blumei assamicus 1.60 1.60
*621* A90 700c Laelia hybrida behrensiana 1.40 1.40
*622* A90 775c Schomburgkia sanderiana 1.55 1.55
*623* A90 875c Cypripedium hybridum youngianum 1.75 1.75

*624* A90 950c Masdevallia chimaera mooreana 1.90 1.90
*624A* A90 $10 Cattleya o'brieniana 2.00 2.00
*624B* A90 $12 Zygopetalum rostratum 2.40 2.40
*624C* A90 $15 Cattleya parthenia 4.45 4.45
*Nos. 616-624C (12)* 21.65 21.65

Issue dates: Nos. 616, 618-620 and 624C, June 1. No. 617, June 22. Nos. 621-624, June 15. Nos. 624A-624B, Mar. 24.
See note after No. 567A.

A97

A98

Locomotives — A99

Designs: Nos. 625a, 626a, Alexandra 4. Nos. 625b, 626b, Diesel locomotive facing right. Nos. 625c, 626c, Steam locomotive facing right. Nos. 625d, 626d, Diesel locomotive No. 21 facing left.
Nos. 628a, 629b, Alexandra 4. Nos. 628b, 629a, Diesel locomotive. Nos. 628c, 629d, Steam locomotive facing right. Nos. 628d, 629c, Diesel locomotive No. 21. No. 629e, Photograph of trains in Georgetown Station. No. 630, Steam locomotive pulling cattle cars, map of routes from Parika to Vreedenhoop and from Georgetown to Rosignol.

**1987, Aug. 3** ***Perf. 15***
*625* Block of 4 1.00 1.00
*a.-d.* A97 $1.20 any single 24 24
*626* Block of 5 3.25 3.25
*a.-d.* A97 $3.20 any single 65 65
*e.* A98 $3.20 shown 65 65
*627* A99 $12 shown 2.40 2.40
*Nos. 625-627 (3)* 6.65 6.65

Sizes: Nos. 626e, 84x57mm; No. 627, 90x40mm.

**1987, Dec. 4** ***Perf. 15***
*628* Block of 4 1.15 1.15
*a.-d.* A97 $1.20 rose lake, any single 28 28
*629* Block of 5 3.75 3.75
*a.-d.* A98 $3.30 blk, any single 75 75
*e.* A98 $3.30 blk 75 75
*630* A99 $10 multi 2.25 2.25
*Nos. 628-630 (3)* 7.15 7.15

Sizes: No. 629e, 84x57mm. No. 630, 90x40mm.

Orchids Type of 1985

**Unwmk.**

**1988, Aug. 15 Litho.** ***Perf. 14***
*631* A90 270c Phaius hybridus marthiae and amabilis 55 55
*632* A90 360c Oncidium kramerianum 72 72
*633* A90 550c Angraecum humblotii 1.10 1.10
*634* A90 670c Odontoglossum pescatorei 1.35 1.35

Nos. 633-634 horiz.

**1988, Aug. 23 Litho.** ***Perf. 14***
*635* A90 30c Cattleya mendelii measuresiana 12 12
*636* A90 30c Dendrobium phalaenopsis statterianum 12 12
*637* A90 30c Odontoglossum wilckeanum rothschildianum 12 12
*638* A90 30c Phaius hybridus cooksonii 12 12
*639* A90 50c Dendrobium formosum 18 18
*640* A90 50c Laelia praestans 18 18
*641* A90 50c Laelio-cattleya elegans blenheimensis 18 18
*642* A90 50c Miltonia bleuana 18 18
*643* A90 70c Cattleya schroederae alba 25 25
*644* A90 70c Cypripedium boxalli atratum 25 25
*645* A90 70c Dendrobium melanodiscus 25 25
*646* A90 70c Odontoglossum wattianum 25 25
*647* A90 100c Laelia grandis 72 72
*648* A90 100c Odontoglossum naevium 72 72
*649* A90 130c Dendrobium phalaenopsis 48 48
*650* A90 130c Odontoglossum vexillarium 48 48
*651* A90 130c Odontoglossum crispum mundyanum 48 48
*652* A90 140c Cattleya labiata lueddemanniana 50 50
*653* A90 140c Cypripedium laucheanum and eyermanianum 50 50
*654* A90 140c Laelia purpurata 50 50
*655* A90 140c Odontoglossum ramosissimum 50 50
*656* A90 140c Phaius tuberculosus 50 50
*657* A90 175c Cattleya amethystoglossa 62 62
*658* A90 175c Cychnoches chlorochilon 62 62
*659* A90 175c Cypripedium morganiae burfordiense 62 62
*660* A90 175c Odontoglossum excellens 62 62
*661* A90 175c Odontoglossum leroyanum 62 62
*662* A90 200c Cypripedium lawrenceanum hyeanum 72 72
*663* A90 200c Masdevallia harryana splendens 72 72
*664* A90 200c Paphinia rugosa and zygopetalum xanthinum 72 72
*665* A90 225c Odontoglossum cervantesii decorum 80 80
*666* A90 250c Cattleya o'brieniana 90 90
*667* A90 380c Odontoglossum coronarium 1.35 1.35
*Nos. 635-667 (33)* 15.89 15.89

Nos. 649-651 and 660-661 horiz. See note after No. 567A.

**1988, Nov. 3 Litho.** ***Perf. 14***
*668* A90 160c like No. 486 32 32
*669* A90 175c like No. 589 35 35
*670* A90 250c like No. 610 50 50
*671* A90 280c like No. 621 55 55
*672* A90 285c like No. E2 58 58
*Nos. 668-672 (5)* 2.30 2.30

**1988, Nov. 3 Litho.** ***Perf. 14***
*673* A90 200c Cymbidium winnianum 40 40
*674* A90 200c Laelio-cattleya phoebe 40 40

**Special Delivery Stamps**

Orchid Type of 1985 Inscribed "Express"

**1987 Litho.** ***Perf. 14***
*E1* A90 $15 Paphinia rugosa, Zygopetalum xanthinum 3.00 3.00
*E2* A90 $25 Calanthes victoria regina, bella and burfordiense 5.00 5.00
*E3* A90 $45 Odontoglossum coronarium 9.00 9.00

Issue dates: $15, Sept. 29. $25, Oct. 26. $45, Sept. 1.

**1988, May 17**
*E4* A90 $20 Laelio-cattleya phoebe 5.65 5.65

## POSTAGE DUE STAMPS

Type of British Guiana Inscribed "Guyana"

***Perf. 13½x14***

**1967-68 Wmk. 314 Typo.**
*J2* D1 2c black ('68) 60 60
*J3* D1 4c ultramarine 18 18
*J4* D1 12c carmine 40 40

**1973 Wmk. 364**
*J5* D1 1c green 10 10
*J6* D1 2c black 10 10
*J7* D1 4c ultramarine 10 10
*J8* D1 12c carmine 25 25

## OFFICIAL STAMPS

Orchid Type of 1985

**1987, Oct. 5 Litho.** ***Perf. 14***
*O1* A90 225c Masdevallia harryana splendens 45 45
*O2* A90 275c Phaius hybridus amabilis and marthiae 55 55
*O3* A90 320c Cymbidium winnianum 62 62
*O4* A90 330c Cypripedium lawrenceanum hyeanum 65 65
*O5* A90 600c Angraecum humblotii 1.20 1.20
*O6* A90 $12 Odontoglossum pescatorei 2.40 2.40
*O7* A90 $15 Oncidium kramerianum 3.00 3.00

Nos. O5-O6 horiz.

**1987, Oct. 5**
*O8* A90 120c Cattleya arnoldiana 24 24
*O9* A90 130c Coelogyne swaniana 25 25
*O10* A90 150c Cypripedium pollettianum and maynardii 30 30
*O11* A90 200c Dendrobium johnsoniae 40 40
*O12* A90 230c Phalaenopsis sanderiana and intermedia portei 45 45
*O13* A90 350c Dendrobium imperatrix 70 70

**1988, Oct. 5 Litho.** ***Perf. 14***
*O14* A90 140c like No. 619 28 28
*O15* A90 175c like No. 623 38 38
*O16* A90 250c like No. 622 52 52
*O17* A90 260c like No. 620 55 55
*Nos. O1-O17 (17)* 12.94 12.94

# HELIGOLAND

LOCATION — An island in the North Sea near the northern coast of Germany.
GOVT. — Former British Possession.
AREA — ¼ sq. mi.
POP. — 2,307 (1900).

Great Britain ceded Heligoland to Germany in 1890. It became part of Schleswig-Holstein province. Stamps of Heligoland were superseded by those of the German Empire.

16 Schillings = 1 Mark
100 Pfennig = 1 Mark = 1 Schilling (1875)

Queen Victoria
A1 A2

A3 A4

HALF SCHILLING.
Type A1: Curl below chignon is rounded.
Type A2: Curl resembles hook or comma.
Color of frame comes first, center second.

**Typo., Head Embossed**

**1867-68 Unwmk.** ***Rouletted***
*1* A1 ½sch bl grn & rose, type I 300.00 *625.00*
*1A* A2 ½sch bl grn & rose, type II 825.00 *1,200.*
*2* A1 1sch rose & dp grn 165.00 *175.00*
*3* A3 2sch rose & pale grn 8.25 *55.00*
*4* A3 6sch gray grn & rose 10.00 *275.00*

*Reprints of No. 2 have not the large curl, those of 1A are not in blue green, and those of 3 and 4 are on slightly porous paper and the colors are either too deep or too bright. The 2sch and 6sch perforated exist only as reprints.*

**1869-71** ***Perf. 13½x14½.***

**Thick Soft Paper.**
*5* A2 ½sch yel grn & rose 140.00 *165.00*
*a.* ½sch blue green & rose 165.00 *200.00*
*6* A2 1sch rose & yel grn 140.00 *165.00*

*Reprints are on thinner paper and in too dark colors.*

**1873 Thick Quadrille Paper.**
*7* A4 ¼sch pale rose & pale grn 19.00 *1,500.*
*a.* ¼sch dp rose & pale grn 19.00 *1,500.*
*8* A4 ¼sch yel grn & rose 110.00 *1,900.*
*9* A2 ½sch brt grn & rose 62.50 *190.00*
*10* A4 ¾sch gray grn & pale rose 20.00 *1,100.*
*a.* ¾sch gray grn & dp rose 24.00 *1,100.*
*11* A2 1sch rose & pale grn 125.00 *200.00*
*12* A4 1½sch yel grn & rose 62.50 *250.00*

*Reprints are never on quadrille paper.*

**1874 Thin Wove Paper**
*13* A4 ¼sch rose & yel grn 12.50

*Originals have the large curl. The early reprints have the small curl. The later reprints are on thin hard paper with smooth white gum and the colors are too bright.*

A5

A6

A7

Coat of Arms — A8

**1875 Wove Paper.**
*14* A5 1pf dk rose & dk grn 9.00 *500.00*
*15* A5 2pf yel grn & dk rose 9.00 *750.00*
*16* A6 5pf dk rose & dk grn 9.00 *21.00*

*17* A6 10pf bl grn & red 9.00 *21.00*
*a.* 10pf yel grn & dk rose 15.00 *24.00*
*b.* 10pf lt grn & pale red 110.00 25.00
*18* A7 25pf rose & dk grn 12.50 *30.00*
*a.* 25pf dk rose & dk grn 12.50 *30.00*
*19* A7 50pf dl grn & dk rose 22.50 *30.00*

*The 1pf and 2pf have been reprinted on very white paper with white gum. The colors are too bright and too light.*

**1876-90 Typo.**

*20* A8 3pf dp grn & dl red 225.00 *950.00*
*a.* 3pf grn & brt red 140.00 *950.00*
*21* A8 20pf ver & brt grn 8.25 *25.00*
*a.* 20pf brn org & grn 8.25 *25.00*
*b.* 20pf vio car & yel grn 200.00 150.00
*c.* 20pf anil rose & dk grn 225.00 62.50
*d.* 20pf lil rose & dk grn 225.00 150.00
*e.* 20pf rose red & dk grn 225.00 150.00

The coat-of-arms on Nos. 20, 21 and sub-varieties is printed in three colors: varying shades of yellow, red and green.

*The 3pf has been reprinted. The colors are usually too pale, especially the red, which is either orange or orange red.*

A9

A10

**1879 Typo.**

*22* A9 1m dp grn & car 150.00 *190.00*
*a.* 1m bl grn & sal 150.00 *190.00*
*b.* 1m dk grn & ver 60.00
*23* A10 5m bl grn & sal 150.00 *825.00*

**Perf. 11½**

*24* A9 1m dp grn & car 625.00
*25* A10 5m bl grn & rose red 625.00
*a.* Imperf. vert., pair 2,750.

Nos. 13, 20a, 22b, 24 and 25 were never placed in use. Forged cancellations of Nos. 1-23 are plentiful.

Heligoland stamps were replaced by those of the German Empire in 1890.

## HONG KONG

LOCATION — A peninsula and island in southeast China at the mouth of the Canton River.
GOVT. — British Crown Colony.
AREA — 426 sq. mi.
POP. — 5,313,000 (est. 1983).
CAPITAL — Victoria.

100 Cents = 1 Dollar

**Catalogue values for unused stamps in this country are for Never Hinged items, beginning with Scott 174 in the regular postage section and Scott J13 in the postage due section.**

Queen Victoria — A1

**Unwmk.**

**1862, Dec. 8 Typo. Perf. 14**

*1* A1 2c pale brn 150.00 25.00
*2* A1 8c buff 225.00 30.00
*3* A1 12c blue 165.00 21.00
*4* A1 18c lilac 187.50 18.00
*5* A1 24c green 375.00 35.00
*6* A1 48c rose 2,000. 140.00
*7* A1 96c gray 2,750. 165.00

**1863-80 Wmk. Crown and C. C. (1)**

*8* A1 2c brn ('65) 32.50 2.50
*a* Imperf.
*9* A1 2c dl rose ('80) 19.00 4.00
*10* A1 4c slate 19.00 1.50
*11* A1 5c ultra ('80) 90.00 10.00
*12* A1 6c lilac 125.00 3.75
*a* 6c vio 125.00 4.50
*13* A1 8c org buff ('65) 100.00 4.50
*a* 8c brt org 125.00 4.50
*14* A1 10c vio ('80) 90.00 3.75
*15* A1 12c lt bl 3.75 4.00
*a* 12c lt grnsh bl 200.00 20.00
*16* A1 16c yel ('77) 275.00 30.00
*17* A1 18c lil ('66) 2,000. 150.00
*a* Imperf.
*18* A1 24c grn ('65) 85.00 5.00
*19* A1 30c vermilion 200.00 10.50
*20* A1 30c vio ('71) 65.00 4.00
*a* Imperf.
*21* A1 48c rose ('65) 325.00 16.00
*a* Imperf.
*22* A1 48c brn ('80) 275.00 35.00
*23* A1 96c bis ('65) *15,000.* 375.00
*24* A1 96c gray ('66) 300.00 16.00

**1874 Perf. 12½**

*25* A1 4c slate 4,500. 200.00

See Nos. 36-49.

A2

A3

A4

**Wmk. Crown and C. C. (1)**

**1874 Engr. Perf. 15½x15**

*26* A2 $2 sage grn 150.00 17.50
*27* A3 $3 violet 100.00 12.50
*28* A4 $10 rose 4,500. 500.00

Nos. 26-28 are revenues which were used postally. Used values are for postally canceled copies. See Nos. 57-59.

Nos. 17 and 20 Surcharged in Black:

**16 cents.** 28 cents.

**1876 Perf. 14.**

*29* A1 16c on 18c lil 1,150. 75.00
*30* A1 28c on 30c vio 575.00 32.50

Stamps of 1863-80 Surcharged in Black — 5 cents.

**1879-80**

*31* A1 5c on 8c org ('80) 175.00 32.50
*a* Inverted surcharge 7,500.
*b* Double surch.
*32* A1 5c on 18c lil 150.00 22.50
*33* A1 10c on 12c bl 175.00 35.00
*34* A1 10c on 16c yel 650.00 80.00
*a* Inverted surch. 17,000.
*35* A1 10c on 24c grn 300.00 30.00

Nos. 16-17, 35B Surcharged in Black

A5

A6

**1879**

*35A* A5 3c on 16c yel 150.00 300.00
*35B* A5 3c on 18c lil 150.00 300.00
*35C* A6 3c on 5c on 18c lil 4,000. *6,000.*

Nos. 35A-35C were sold affixed to postal cards. Values are for copies on card.

**1882-1902 Wmk. 2 Perf. 14**

*36* A1 2c rose 1.75 25
*a* 2c dl rose 30.00 9.50
*37* A1 2c grn ('00) 50 25
*38* A1 4c sl ('96) 2.75 60
*39* A1 4c car rose ('00) 50 42
*40* A1 5c ultra 2.00 20
*41* A1 5c yel ('00) 2.25 1.75
*42* A1 10c lilac 225.00 7.50
*43* A1 10c green 25.00 1.00
*a* 10c bl grn 1,350. 25.00
*44* A1 10c vio, *red* ('90) 2.00 22
*45* A1 10c ultra ('00) 4.25 22
*46* A1 12c bl ('02) 10.00 *15.00*
*47* A1 30c gray grn ('90) 12.50 4.50
*a* 30c dl grn 45.00 19.00
*48* A1 30c brn ('01) 3.50 3.50

**1882 Perf. 12**

*49* A1 2c rose *15,000.*

No. 28 Surcharged in Black — 12 CENTS.

**1882 Wmk. 1 Perf. 15½x15**

*50* A4 12c on $10 rose 250.00 100.00

Surcharged in Black — 20 CENTS

**1885-91 Wmk. 2 Perf. 14**

*51* A1 20c on 30c ver 24.00 4.00
*a* Double surch.
*52* A1 20c on 30c gray grn ('91) 40.00 16.00
*53* A1 50c on 48c brn 120.00 9.00
*54* A1 50c on 48c lil ('91) 130.00 100.00
*55* A1 $1 on 96c ol gray 150.00 16.00
*56* A1 $1 on 96c vio, *red* ('91) 325.00 175.00

**1890-1902 Wmk. 1 Perf. 14**

*57* A2 $2 gray grn 175.00 125.00
*58* A3 $3 lil ('02) 175.00 125.00
*59* A4 $10 gray grn ('92) *2,300.* *2,000.*

Type of 1874 Surcharged in Black — 5 DOLLARS

**1891 Wmk. Crown and C. A. (2)**

*60* A4 $5 on $10 vio, *red* 150.00 55.00

Nos. 52, 54 and 56 Handstamped with Chinese characters

弍 *g* 五十 *h* 壹員 *i*

*61* A1 (g) 20c on 30c gray grn 3.50 1.10
*a* 20c on 30c dl grn 20.00 3.75
*b* "20 CENTS" double
*62* A1 (h) 50c on 48c lil 20.00 2.25
*63* A1 (i) $1 on 96c vio, *red* 95.00 6.00

No. 61 may be found with Chinese character 2, 2½ or 3 mm. high.

The handstamped Chinese surcharges on Nos. 61-63 exist in several varieties including inverted, double, triple, misplaced and omitted.

Nos. 43 and 20 Surcharged — 7 cents.

**1891**

*64* A1 7c on 10c grn 19.00 25.00
*a* Double surcharge 3,500. 1,500.

**Wmk. Crown and C. C. (1)**

*65* A1 14c on 30c vio 47.50 42.50

No. 36 Overprinted in Black — 1841 Hong Kong JUBILEE 1891

**1891, Jan. 22 Wmk. 2**

*66* A1 2c rose 95.00 32.50
*a* Double overprint *10,000.* *8,500.*
*b* "U" of "JUBILEE" shorter 250.00 150.00
*c* "J" of "JUBILEE" shorter 250.00 150.00
*d* Tall "K" in "KONG" 750.00 450.00

50th anniversary of the colony.

Common Design Types pictured in section before Great Britain.

No. 26 Surcharged

ONE DOLLAR

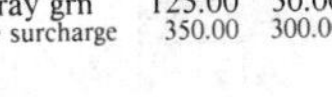

**1897 Wmk. 1 Perf. 15½x15.**

*67* A2 $1 on $2 sage grn 80.00 30.00
*a* Without Chinese surcharge 1,000. 800.00

**On No. 57.**

**Perf. 14.**

*68* A2 $1 on $2 gray grn 125.00 50.00
*a* Without Chinese surcharge 350.00 300.00

Handstamp Surcharged in Black — 拾 10 CENTS

**1898 Wmk. Crown and C.A. (2)**

*69* A1 10c on 30c gray grn 6.00 10.00
*a* Large Chinese surcharge 350.00 275.00
*70* A1 $1 on 96 blk 30.00 11.00

See notes below Nos. 61-63.

King Edward VII — A10

**1903 Wmk. Crown and C. A. (2)**

*71* A10 1c brn & lil 8 8
*72* A10 2c gray grn 1.65 12
*73* A10 4c vio, *red* 1.40 8
*74* A10 5c org & gray grn 1.10 55
*75* A10 8c vio & blk 70 28
*76* A10 10c ultra & lil, *bl* 3.25 20
*77* A10 12c red vio & gray grn, *yel* 1.10 70
*78* A10 20c org brn & blk 1.40 95
*79* A10 30c blk & gray grn 2.25 80
*80* A10 50c red vio & gray grn 10.00 2.75
*81* A10 $1 ol grn & lil 16.00 3.25
*82* A10 $2 scar & blk 45.00 19.00
*83* A10 $3 dp bl & blk 50.00 37.50
*84* A10 $5 bl grn & lil 125.00 110.00
*85* A10 $10 org & blk, *bl* 375.00 325.00
*Nos. 71-85 (15)* 633.93 501.26

**1904-11 Wmk. 3**

**Ordinary or Chalky Paper.**

*86* A10 1c brn ('10) 35 10
*a* Booklet pane of 4
*87* A10 2c gray grn 65 10
*88* A10 2c dp grn 65 5
*a* Booklet pane of 4
*b* Booklet pane of 12
*89* A10 4c vio, *red* 1.10 6
*90* A10 4c carmine 80 5
*a* Booklet pane of 4
*b* Booklet pane of 12
*91* A10 5c org & gray grn 45 16
*92* A10 6c red vio & org ('07) 2.25 65
*93* A10 8c vio & blk ('07) 1.40 90
*94* A10 10c ultra & lil, *bl* 3.50 22
*95* A10 10c ultra 2.25 16

96 A10 12c red vio & gray grn, *yel* ('07) 2.25 1.60
97 A10 20c org brn & blk 2.25 65
98 A10 20c ol grn & vio ('11) 13.00 5.75
99 A10 30c blk & gray grn 5.75 2.75
100 A10 30c org & vio ('11) 8.00 2.75
101 A10 50c red vio & gray grn 7.75 1.60
102 A10 50c *grn* ('11) 6.75 2.75
103 A10 $1 ol grn & lil 9.00 4.50
104 A10 $2 scar & blk 32.50 18.00
105 A10 $2 blk & car ('10) 40.00 32.50
106 A10 $3 dp bl & blk 35.00 27.50
107 A10 $5 bl grn & lil 90.00 57.50
108 A10 $10 org & blk, *bl* 300.00 250.00
*Nos. 86-108 (23)* 565.65 410.30

Nos. 86, 88, 90, 94 and 95 are on ordinary paper only. Nos. 92, 93, 96, 98, 100, 102, 105, 106 and 107 are on chalky paper and the others of the issue are on both papers.
The 4c, 5c, 8c, 12c 20c, 50c, $2 and $5 denominations of type A10 are expressed in colored letters or numerals and letters on a colorless background.

King George V
A11 A12

A13

A14

A15

**1912-14 Ordinary Paper**
109 A11 1c brown 60 14
a Booklet pane of 12
110 A11 2c dp grn 40 5
a Booklet pane of 12
111 A12 4c carmine 50 6
a Booklet pane of 12
b Booklet pane of 4
112 A13 6c orange 35 20
113 A12 8c gray 3.25 1.00
114 A11 10c ultra 3.00 5

**Chalky Paper**
115 A14 12c vio, *yel* 2.50 2.50
116 A14 20c ol grn & vio 1.25 35
117 A15 25c red vio & dl vio 6.00 3.75
118 A13 30c org & vio 3.25 60
119 A14 50c *green* 2.75 30
a 50c *emer* 3.75 2.75
b 50c *bl grn,* ol back 80.00 3.75
c 50c *emer,* ol back 6.00 3.00
120 A11 $1 bl & vio, *bl* 4.00 2.25
121 A14 $2 blk & red 12.00 6.00
122 A13 $3 vio & grn 24.00 12.00
123 A14 $5 red & grn, *grn* 80.00 50.00
a $5 red & grn, *bl grn,* ol back 225.00 32.50
124 A13 $10 blk & vio, *red* 100.00 20.00
*Nos. 109-124 (16)* 243.85 99.25

**1914 Surface-colored Paper**
125 A14 12c vio, *yel* 1.65 1.00
126 A14 50c *green* 1.75 40
127 A14 $5 red & grn, *grn* 90.00 80.00

Stamp of 1912-14 Redrawn

弍 instead of 貳 at upper left.

**1919 Chalky Paper**
128 A15 25c red vio & dl vio 22.50 16.00

Types of 1912-14 Issue

**1921-37 Wmk. (4)**

**Ordinary Paper**
129 A11 1c brown 10 8
130 A11 2c dp grn 16 8
131 A11 2c gray ('37) 3.25 3.25
132 A12 3c gray ('31) 2.75 2.00
133 A12 4c rose red 16 10
134 A12 5c vio ('31) 1.40 16
135 A12 8c gray 2.00 *4.00*
136 A12 8c orange 40 12
137 A11 10c ultra 40 12

**Chalky Paper**
138 A14 12c vio, *yel* ('33) 2.75 80
139 A14 20c ol grn & dl vio 1.00 16
140 A15 25c red vio & dl vio, type of No. 128 40 14
141 A13 30c yel & vio 1.10 14
142 A14 50c *emerald* 1.10 14
143 A11 $1 ultra & vio, *bl* 3.00 30
144 A14 $2 blk & red 22.50 2.50
145 A13 $3 dl vio & grn ('26) 57.50 13.00
146 A14 $5 red & grn, *emer* ('25) 80.00 20.00
*Nos. 129-146 (18)* 179.97 47.09

**Silver Jubilee Issue.**
Common Design Type

**1935, May 6 Engr. *Perf. 11x12***
147 CD301 3c blk & ultra 1.00 1.00
148 CD301 5c ind & grn 3.75 1.00
149 CD301 10c ultra & brn 8.75 2.75
150 CD301 20c brn vio & ind 11.00 6.00

**Coronation Issue.**
Common Design Type

**1937, May 12 *Perf. 11x11½***
151 CD302 4c dp grn 22 10
152 CD302 15c dk car 50 22
153 CD302 25c dp ultra 90 50

King George VI — A16

**1938-48 Typo. *Perf. 14.***

**Ordinary Paper.**
154 A16 1c brown 5 5
155 A16 2c gray 6 5
156 A16 4c orange 6 5
157 A16 5c green 6 5
157B A16 8c brn red ('41) 6 6
c Imperf., pair 2,400.
158 A16 10c violet 9 5
159 A16 15c carmine 6 7
159A A16 20c gray ('46) 18 9
159B A16 20c rose red ('48) 6 6
160 A16 25c ultra 1.75 9
160A A16 25c gray ol ('46) 18 12
161 A16 30c ol bis 32.50 2.50
161B A16 30c lt ultra ('46) 18 7
162 A16 50c red vio 28 9

**Chalky Paper.**
162B A16 80c lil rose ('48) 30 15
163 A16 $1 lil & ultra 35 20
163B A16 $1 dp org & grn ('46) 35 9
164 A16 $2 dp org & grn 30.00 3.50
164A A16 $2 vio & red ('46) 1.10 60
165 A16 $5 lil & red 7.50 1.25
165A A16 $5 grn & vio ('46) 9.00 90
166 A16 $10 grn & vio 95.00 30.00
166A A16 $10 vio & ultra ('46) 20.00 2.50
*Nos. 154-166A (23)* 199.17 42.59

Coarse Impressions.
Ordinary Paper.

**1941-46 *Perf. 14½x14.***
155a A16 2c gray 32 32
156a A16 4c org ('46) 1.75 1.75
157a A16 5c green 20 20
158a A16 10c violet 42 24
161a A16 30c dl ol bis 60 60
162a A16 50c red lil 60 60
*Nos. 155a-162a (6)* 3.89 3.71

A17

**1938, Jan. 11 Wmk. 4**
167 A17 5c green 8.00 8.00

No. 167 is a revenue stamp officially authorized to be sold and used for postal purposes. Used Jan. 11-21, 1938. The used price is for the stamp on cover.
CTO covers exist.

Street Scene — A18

Hong Kong Bank — A22

Liner and Junk — A19

University of Hong Kong — A20

Harbor — A21

China Clipper and Seaplane A23

***Perf. 13½x13, 13x13½***

**1941, Feb. 26 Engr. Wmk. 4**
168 A18 2c sep & org 20 20
169 A19 4c rose car & vio 50 50
170 A20 5c yel grn & blk 25 12
171 A21 15c red & blk 85 50
172 A22 25c dp bl & dk brn 1.75 1.00
173 A23 $1 brn org & brt bl 5.00 3.00
*Nos. 168-173 (6)* 8.55 5.32

Centenary of British rule.

**Catalogue values for unused stamps in this section, from this point to the end of the section, are for Never Hinged items.**

**Peace Issue.**

Phoenix Rising from Flames A24

**1946, Aug. 29 *Perf. 13x12½***
174 A24 30c car & dp bl 1.00 1.00
175 A24 $1 car & brn 2.00 2.50

Issued to commemorate the return to peace at the close of World War II.

**Silver Wedding Issue.**
Common Design Types

***Perf. 14x14½***

**1948, Dec. 22 Photo. Wmk. 4**
178 CD304 10c purple 40 20

**Engr.; Name Typo.**

***Perf. 11½x11.***
179 CD305 $10 rose car 65.00 40.00

**UPU Issue**
Common Design Types

**Engr.; Name Typo. on 20c & 30c**

**1949, Oct. 10 *Perf. 13½, 11x11½***
180 CD306 10c violet 2.25 1.10
181 CD307 20c dp car 3.75 2.25
182 CD308 30c indigo 5.00 2.25
183 CD309 80c red vio 11.00 7.75

**Coronation Issue.**
Common Design Type

**1953, June 2 Engr. *Perf. 13½x13***
184 CD312 10c pur & blk 50 15

Queen Elizabeth II A25

Arms of University A26

**1954-60 Typo. *Perf. 13½x14***
185 A25 5c orange 10 5
a Imperf., pair 1,250.
186 A25 10c violet 15 10
187 A25 15c green 15 6
188 A25 20c brown 18 6
189 A25 25c rose red 22 8
190 A25 30c gray 38 6
191 A25 40c blue 52 10
192 A25 50c red vio 52 6
193 A25 65c lt gray ('60) 10.50 2.25
194 A25 $1 org & grn 95 12
195 A25 $1.30 bl & ver ('60) 10.50 1.50
196 A25 $2 vio & red 5.25 25
197 A25 $5 grn & vio 22.50 55
198 A25 $10 vio & ultra 37.50 1.50
*Nos. 185-198 (14)* 89.42 6.74

Nos. 185-187 are on ordinary paper; Nos. 188-198 on chalky paper.

***Perf. 11½x12***

**1961, Sept. 11 Photo. Wmk. 314**
199 A26 $1 bl, blk, red, grn & gold 3.50 1.50
a Gold omitted 1,000.

Issued to commemorate the 50th anniversary of the University of Hong Kong.

Queen Victoria Statue, Victoria Park, Hong Kong — A27

Queen Elizabeth II — A28

**1962, May 4 *Perf. 14***
200 A27 10c car rose & blk 18 8
201 A27 20c bl & blk 75 35
202 A27 50c bis & blk 1.50 75

Issued to commemorate the centenary of the first postage stamps of Hong Kong.

**Wmk. 314 Upright**

**1962, Oct. 4 Photo. *Perf. 14½x14***

**Size: 17x21mm.**
203 A28 5c red org 8 5
a Bklt. pane of 4 65
204 A28 10c purple 15 5
a Bklt. pane of 4 1.25
205 A28 15c green 35 5
206 A28 20c red brn 40 7
a Bklt. pane of 4 2.50
207 A28 25c lil rose 50 7
208 A28 30c dk bl 55 8
209 A28 40c Prus grn 65 8
210 A28 50c crimson 65 5
a Bklt. pane of 4 6.00
211 A28 65c ultra 3.25 1.50
212 A28 $1 dk brn 3.25 8

***Perf. 14x14½***

**Size: 25½x30½mm.**

**Portrait in Natural Colors**
213 A28 $1.30 sky bl 2.25 10
a Ocher (sash) omitted 27.50
b Yel. omitted 27.50
214 A28 $2 fawn 3.25 15
a Yel. and ocher (sash) omitted 37.50
b Yel. omitted
215 A28 $5 orange 7.00 75
a Ocher (sash) omitted 30.00

*216* A28 $10 green 15.00 1.00
*217* A28 $20 vio bl 32.50 6.00
*Nos. 203-217 (15)* 69.83 10.08

**Wmk. 314 Sideways**

**1966-72** ***Perf. 14½x14***

**Size: 17x21mm.**

*203b* A28 5c red org ('67) 10 5
*204b* A28 10c pur ('67) 15 5
*205a* A28 15c grn ('67) 25 5
*206b* A28 20c red brn 32 6
*207a* A28 25c lil rose ('67) 42 5
*208a* A28 30c dk bl ('70) 50 8
*209a* A28 40c Prus grn ('67) 55 12
*210b* A28 50c crim ('67) 90 10
*211a* A28 65c ultra ('67) 3.75 2.00
*212a* A28 $1 dk brn ('67) 3.75 18

***Perf. 14x14½***

**Size: 25½x30½mm.**

*213c* A28 $1.30 multi ('72) 2.50 75
*214c* A28 $2 multi ('71) 7.50 1.75
*215b* A28 $5 multi ('71) 30.00 4.00
*217a* A28 $20 vio bl ('72) 85.00 40.00
*Nos. 203b-217a (14)* 135.69 49.24

**Freedom from Hunger Issue**
Common Design Type

***Perf. 14x14½***

**1963, June 4** **Photo.** **Wmk. 314**
*218* CD314 $1.30 green 25.00 7.50

**Red Cross Centenary Issue**
Common Design Type

**1963, Sept. 2** **Litho.** ***Perf. 13***
*219* CD315 10c blk & red 42 12
*220* CD315 $1.30 ultra & red 12.50 3.50

**ITU Issue**
Common Design Type

**1965, May 17** ***Perf. 11x11½***
*221* CD317 10c red lil & yel 35 8
*222* CD317 $1.30 ap grn & turq bl 10.50 2.75

**Intl. Cooperation Year Issue**
Common Design Type

**1965, Oct. 25** ***Perf. 14½***
*223* CD318 10c bl grn & cl 16 8
*224* CD318 $1.30 lt vio & grn 7.75 2.75

**Churchill Memorial Issue**
Common Design Type

**1966, Jan. 24** **Photo.** ***Perf. 14***
**Design in Black, Gold and Carmine Rose**
*225* CD319 10c brt bl 28 10
*226* CD319 50c green 1.50 45
*227* CD319 $1.30 brown 4.50 2.75
*228* CD319 $2 violet 8.75 3.50

**WHO Headquarters Issue**
Common Design Type

**1966, Sept. 20** **Litho.** ***Perf. 14***
*229* CD322 10c multi 15 10
*230* CD322 50c multi 2.50 1.00

**UNESCO Anniversary Issue**
Common Design Type

**1966, Dec. 1.** **Litho.** ***Perf. 14***
*231* CD323 10c "Education" 32 10
*232* CD323 50c (Science" 1.75 85
*233* CD323 $2 "Culture" 14.00 6.50

Three Rams' Heads A29

Lunar New Year: $1.30, Three rams.

**1967, Jan. 17** **Photo.** ***Perf. 14***
*234* A29 10c red, cit & grn 50 12
*235* A29 $1.30 red, cit & brt grn 11.00 4.00

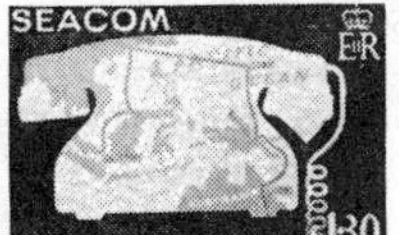

Outline of Telephone with Map of South East Asia and Australia A30

**1967, Mar. 30** **Photo.** ***Perf. 12½***
*236* A30 $1.30 dk red & bl 6.75 1.90

Issued to commemorate the completion of the Hong Kong-Malaysia link of the South East Asia Commonwealth Cable, SEACOM.

Monkeys A31

Lunar New Year: $1.30, Two monkey families.

**1968, Jan. 23** **Wmk. 314** ***Perf. 14***
*237* A31 10c crim, blk & gold 50 10
*238* A31 $1.30 crim, blk & gold 10.00 4.00

Liner and New Sea Terminal A32

Seacraft: 20c, Pleasure launch and sailing cruiser. 40c, Vehicle ferry. 50c, Passenger ferry. $1, Sampan. $1.30, Junk.

***Perf. 13x12½***

**1968, Apr. 24** **Litho.** **Unwmk.**
*239* A32 10c multi 28 8
*240* A32 20c sky bl, bis & blk 70 24
*241* A32 40c org, rose lil & blk 1.75 90
*242* A32 50c brt red, emer & blk 2.00 35
*243* A32 $1 yel, cop red & blk 5.25 1.40
*244* A32 $1.30 dk bl, brt pink & blk 8.75 2.75
*Nos. 239-244 (6)* 18.73 5.72

Bauhinia Blakeana — A33

Design: $1, Coat of Arms.

***Perf. 14x14½***

**1968, Sept. 25** **Photo.** **Wmk. 314**
*245* A33 65c bl & multi 90 30
*a* Wmkd. sideways ('72) 2.25 75
*246* A33 $1 brn & multi 1.10 30
*a* Wmkd. sideways ('71) 2.00 60

Human Rights Flame and "Lamp of Life" A34

**1968, Nov. 20** **Litho.** ***Perf. 13½***
*247* A34 10c grn, org & blk 25 10
*248* A34 50c mag, yel & blk 2.25 1.25

International Human Rights Year.

Cock A35

Design: $1.30, Cock (vert.).

***Perf. 13x13½, 13½x13***

**1969, Feb. 11** **Photo.** **Unwmk.**
*249* A35 10c brn, blk, org & red 50 10
*a* Red omitted
*250* A35 $1.30 ocher, blk, org & red 14.00 5.00

Lunar New Year, Feb. 17, 1969.

Chinese University Seal — A36

**1969, Aug. 26** **Unwmk.** ***Perf. 13***
*251* A36 40c multi 2.00 75

Issued to publicize the Chinese University of Hong Kong, founded 1963.

Radar, Globe and Satellite A37

***Perf. 14x14½***

**1969, Sept. 24** **Photo.** **Wmk. 314**
*252* A37 $1 scar, blk, sil & bl 4.00 1.75

Issued to publicize the opening of the satellite earth station (connected through the Indian Ocean satellite Intelsat III) on Stanley Peninsula, Hong Kong.

Chow A38

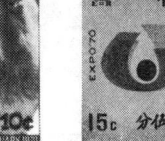

Emblem A39

Lunar New Year: $1.30, Chow (horiz.).

**1970, Jan. 28** ***Perf. 14***
*253* A38 10c blk & multi 75 10
*254* A38 $1.30 grn & multi 14.00 6.00

***Perf. 13½x13, 13x13½***

**1970, Mar. 14** **Litho.** **Wmk. 314**

Design: 25c, Emblem and Chinese junks (horiz.).

*255* A39 15c multi 42 20
*256* A39 25c multi 70 35

Issued to publicize EXPO '70 International Exposition, Osaka, Japan, Mar. 15-Sept. 13.

"A Compassionate Ship on the Bitter Sea" — A40

**1970, Apr. 9** **Photo.** ***Perf. 14***
*257* A40 10c yel grn & multi 25 8
*258* A40 50c scar & multi 1.40 1.00

Issued to commemorate the centenary of the Tung Wah Group of Hospitals (including schools and various charitable organizations).

A.P.Y. Emblem — A41

**1970, Aug. 5** **Litho.** **Wmk. 314**
*259* A41 10c yel & multi 35 18

Issued for Asian Productivity Year.

Boar A42

***Perf. 13x13½***

**1971, Jan. 20** **Photo.** **Unwmk.**
*260* A42 10c yel grn, gold & blk 60 10
*261* A42 $1.30 vio, gold & blk 8.00 2.75

Lunar New Year 1971.

Scout Emblem and "60" — A43

***Perf. 14x14½***

**1971, July 23** **Litho.** **Wmk. 314**
*262* A43 10c red, yel & blk 16 10
*263* A43 50c bl, emer & blk 90 35
*264* A43 $2 vio, lil rose & blk 3.50 2.00

60th anniversary of Hong Kong Boy Scouts.

Festival Emblem A44

Symbolic Flower A45

Design: 50c, Dancers (horiz.).

**1971, Nov. 2** ***Perf. 14***
*265* A44 10c lil & org 25 15

***Perf. 14½***

*266* A45 50c lil & multi 1.25 75
*267* A45 $1 lil & multi 2.50 1.50

Festival of Hong Kong 1971.

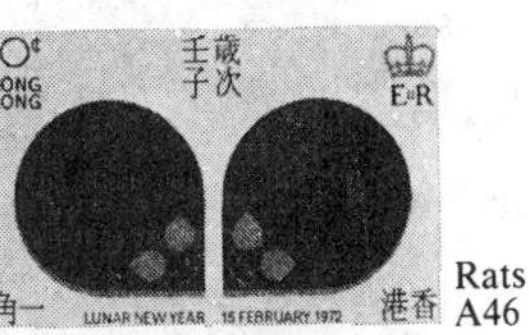

Rats A46

***Perf. 13½x13***

**1972, Feb. 8** **Photo.** **Unwmk.**
*268* A46 10c blk, red & gold 25 10
*269* A46 $1.30 blk, gold & red 4.00 2.00

Lunar New Year 1972.

Cross Harbor Tunnel Entrance — A47

**Perf. 14x14½**

**1972, Oct. 20 Litho. Wmk. 314**

*270* A47 $1 multi 1.25 62

Inauguration of Cross Harbor Tunnel linking Victoria and Kowloon.

**Silver Wedding Issue, 1972**

Common Design Type

Design: Queen Elizabeth II, Prince Philip, phoenix and dragon.

**1972, Nov. 20 Photo. *Perf. 14x14½***

*271* CD324 10c cit & multi 12 6
*272* CD324 50c gray & multi 85 38

Ox A48

Lunar New Year: 10c, Ox (vert.).

**1973, Feb. 3 *Perf. 14***

*273* A48 10c dk brn & red 50 10
*274* A48 $1.30 dk brn, yel & org 3.25 1.00

Queen Elizabeth II — A49

**Wmk. 314 Upright; Sideways (15c, 30c, 40c)**

**1973, June 12 Photo. *Perf. 14½x14***

**Size: 20x24mm.**

*275* A49 10c orange 12 5
*b* Booklet pane of 4 ('75) 48
*d* Watermark sideways (coil) 20 5
*276* A49 15c ol grn 20 5
*b* Booklet pane of 4 ('75) 1.00
*277* A49 20c brt pur 28 5
*b* Booklet pane of 4 ('75) 1.25
*278* A49 25c dp brn 35 12
*279* A49 30c ultra 45 12
*280* A49 40c bl grn 45 16
*281* A49 50c red 52 12
*b* Booklet pane of 4 ('75) 2.50
*282* A49 65c dp bis 1.25 40
*283* A49 $1 dk sl grn 1.40 20

**Perf. 14x14½**

**Wmk. 314 Sideways**

**Size: 28x32mm.**

*284* A49 $1.30 dk pur & yel 1.50 40
*285* A49 $2 dp brn & lt grn 1.50 60
*286* A49 $5 dk vio bl & rose 4.00 1.75
*287* A49 $10 dk sl grn & pink 8.75 4.00
*288* A49 $20 blk & rose 17.50 6.50
*Nos. 275-288 (14)* 38.27 14.52

**1975-78 Wmk. 373 *Perf. 14½x14***

**Size: 20x24mm.**

*275a* A49 10c orange 5 5
*c* Booklet pane of 4 ('76) 20
*276a* A49 15c ol grn 8 5
*c* Booklet pane of 4 32
*277a* A49 20c brt pur 10 5
*c* Booklet pane of 4 ('76) 40
*278a* A49 25c dp brn 12 8
*279a* A49 30c ultra 15 8
*280a* A49 40c bl grn 20 10
*281a* A49 50c red 23 10
*c* Booklet pane of 4 92
*282a* A49 65c dp bis 35 30
*283a* A49 $1 dk sl grn 55 35

**Perf. 14x14½**

**Size: 28x32mm.**

*284a* A49 $1.30 dk pur & yel 70 50
*285a* A49 $2 dp brn & lt grn 1.10 85
*286a* A49 $5 dk vio bl & rose ('78) 2.50 2.00
*287a* A49 $10 dk sl grn & pink ('78) 5.00 4.00
*288a* A49 $20 blk & rose ('78) 10.00 8.00
*Nos. 275a-288a (14)* 21.13 16.51

See Nos. 316-327.

**Princess Anne's Wedding Issue**

Common Design Type

**Wmk. 314**

**1973, Nov. 14 Litho. *Perf. 14***

*289* CD325 50c ocher & multi 40 20
*290* CD325 $2 lil & multi 2.00 1.00

Chinese Character "Hong" A50

Designs: 50c, "Kong." $1, "Festival."

**1973, Nov. 23 Litho. *Perf. 14½x14***

*291* A50 10c red & grn 15 8
*292* A50 50c plum & red 60 35
*293* A50 $1 emer & plum 1.50 1.00

Festival of Hong Kong 1973.

Tiger A51

Lunar New Year: $1.30, Tiger (vert.).

***Perf. 14½x14, 14x14½***

**1974, Jan. 8 Wmk. 314**

*294* A51 10c grn & multi 30 6
*295* A51 $1.30 lil & multi 3.00 80

Chinese Opera Mask — A52

Designs: Chinese opera masks.

**1974, Feb. 1 Photo. *Perf. 12x12½***

*296* A52 10c blk, red & org 10 6
*297* A52 $1 multi 1.25 62
*298* A52 $2 blk, org & gold 3.00 1.50
*a* Souvenir sheet of 3 16.00 16.00

Hong Kong Arts Festival. No. 298a contains one each of Nos. 296-298, perf. 14x13; English and Chinese black marginal inscriptions. Size: 158x91mm.

Carrier Pigeons A53

Cent. of UPU: 50c, Symbolic globe in envelope. $2, Hands holding letters.

**1974, Oct. 9 Litho. *Perf. 14***

*299* A53 10c bl, grn & blk 10 8
*a* Unwmk. 50.00
*300* A53 50c mag & multi 45 25
*301* A53 $2 vio & multi 1.90 95

Prices of premium quality never hinged stamps will be in excess of catalogue price.

Rabbit A54

Lunar New Year: $1.30, Two rabbits.

**1975, Feb. 5 Wmk. 314 *Perf. 14***

*302* A54 10c sil & red 22 6
*a* Unwmk. 16 8
*303* A54 $1.30 gold & grn 2.50 90
*a* Unwmk. 2.25 1.10

Queen Elizabeth II, Prince Philip, Hong Kong Arms — A55

**Wmk. 373**

**1975, Apr. 30 Litho. *Perf. 13½***

*304* A55 $1.30 bl & multi 1.40 40
*305* A55 $2 yel & multi 2.25 70

Royal Visit 1975.

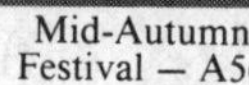


Mid-Autumn Festival — A56

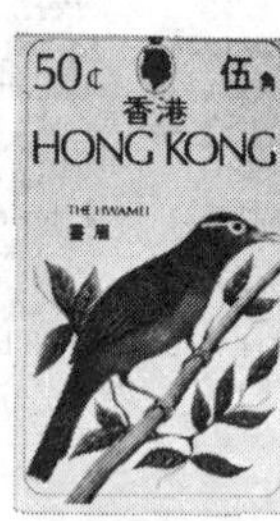


Brown Laughing Thrush — A57

Abstract Designs: $1, Dragon Boat Festival (boats). $2, Tin Hau Festival (ships with flags).

**1975, July 31 Unwmk. *Perf. 14***

*306* A56 50c rose lil & multi 55 28
*307* A56 $1 brt grn & multi 1.10 1.10
*308* A56 $2 org & multi 2.25 2.25
*a* Souvenir sheet of 3 6.50 6.50

Hong Kong Festivals, 1975. No. 308a contains one each of Nos. 306-308; black marginal inscription. Size: 102x82mm.

**1975, Oct. 29 Litho. Wmk. 373**

Birds: $1.30, Chinese bulbul. $2, Black-capped kingfisher.

*309* A57 50c lt bl & multi 1.00 50
*310* A57 $1.30 pink & multi 3.75 1.00
*311* A57 $2 yel & multi 4.00 1.50

Dragon A58

Lunar New Year: $1.30, like 20c, pattern reversed.

**1976, Jan. 21 Litho. *Perf. 14½***

*312* A58 20c gold, pur & lil 25 12
*313* A58 $1.30 gold, red & grn 3.00 1.00

**Queen Elizabeth Type of 1973**

**Wmk. 373 (#320-322), Unwmkd.**

**1976-81 Photo. *Perf. 14½x14***

**Size: 20x24mm**

*316* A49 20c brt pur 42 8
*318* A49 30c ultra 75 12
*320* A49 60c lt vio ('77) 75 16
*321* A49 70c yel ('77) 85 16
*322* A49 80c brt mag ('77) 1.10 22
*323* A49 90c sep ('81) 38 30

**Size: 28x32mm**

**Perf. 14x14½**

*324* A49 $2 dp brn & lt grn 5.00 85
*325* A49 $5 dk vio bl & rose 12.50 3.50
*326* A49 $10 dk sl grn & pink 32.50 10.50
*327* A49 $20 blk & rose 85.00 35.00
*Nos. 316-327 (10)* 139.25 50.89

"60" and Girl Guides Emblem A59

Design: $1.30, "60," tents and Girl Guides emblem.

**Wmk. 314**

**1976, Apr. 23 Photo. *Perf. 14½***

*328* A59 20c sil & multi 25 12
*329* A59 $1.30 sil & multi 2.00 1.00

60th anniversary of Hong Kong Girl Guides.

"Postal Services" (in Chinese) — A60

Designs: $1.30, General Post Office, 1911-1976. $2, New G.P.O., 1976.

**1976, Aug. 11 Litho. Wmk. 373**

*330* A60 20c gray, grn & blk 20 8
*331* A60 $1.30 gray, red & blk 90 60
*332* A60 $2 gray, yel & blk 1.50 75

Opening of new General Post Office building.

Snake A61

Lunar New Year: $1.30, Snake and branch face left.

**1977, Jan. 6 *Perf. 13½***

*333* A61 20c multi 22 8
*334* A61 $1.30 multi 1.65 55

Queen Dotting Eye of Dragon, 1975 Visit — A62

Designs: 20c, Presentation of the orb. $2, Orb (vert.).

**1977, Feb. 7 Litho.**

*335* A62 20c multi 12 8
*336* A62 $1.30 multi 75 45
*337* A62 $2 multi 1.25 60

25th anniv. of the reign of Elizabeth II.

Streetcars A63

Buttercup Orchid A64

Designs: 60c, Star ferryboat. $1.30, Funicular railway. $2, Junk and sampan.

**Wmk. 373**

**1977, June 30 Litho.** ***Perf. 13½***

*338* A63 20c multi 10 6
*339* A63 60c multi 45 25
*340* A63 $1.30 multi 75 50
*341* A63 $2 multi 1.50 62

Tourist publicity.

**Wmk. 373**

**1977, Oct. 12 Litho.** ***Perf. 14***

Designs: $1.30, Lady's-slipper. $2, Susan orchid.

*342* A64 20c bl & multi 15 10
*343* A64 $1.30 yel & multi 1.10 65
*344* A64 $2 grn & multi 2.00 65

Horse and Chinese Character "Ma" — A65

**1978, Jan. 26 Litho.** ***Perf. 14½***

*345* A65 20c multi 14 8
*346* A65 $1.30 multi 1.10 55

Lunar New Year 1978.

Elizabeth II — A66

***Perf. 14x14½***

**1978, June 2 Litho. Wmk. 373**

*347* A66 20c car & dk bl 9 9
*348* A66 $1.30 dk bl & car 60 30

25th anniv. of coronation of Elizabeth II.

Boy and Girl A67

Design: $1.30, Ring-around-a-rosy.

**Wmk. 373**

**1978, Nov. 8 Litho.** ***Perf. 14½***

*349* A67 20c multi 7 7
*350* A67 $1.30 multi 70 40

Centenary of Po Leung Kuk, society for help and education of orphans and poor children.

Electronics — A68

Industries: $1.30, Toy (bear and drum). $2, Garment (mannequins).

**1979, Jan. 9 Litho.** ***Perf. 14½***

*351* A68 20c multi 7 7
*352* A68 $1.30 multi 40 28
*353* A68 $2 multi 70 55

Precis Orithya — A69

Butterflies: $1, Graphium sarpedon. $1.30, Heliophorus epicles phoenicoparyphus. $2, Danaus genutia.

**1979, June 20 Photo. Unwmk.**

*354* A69 20c multi 7 7
*355* A69 $1 multi 32 32
*356* A69 $1.30 multi 45 28
*357* A69 $2 multi 55 55

Cross Section of Station A70

Mass Transit Railroad: $1.30, Front, rear and side views of train. $2, Map of routes.

**1979, Oct. 1 Litho.** ***Perf. 13½***

*358* A70 20c multi 6 6
*359* A70 $1.30 multi 20 20
*360* A70 $2 multi 65 50

Ching Chung Koon Temple, Tuen Mun — A71

Rural Architecture: 20c, Tsui Shing Lau Pagoda, Sheung Cheung Wai (vert.). $1.30, Village house, Sai O.

***Perf. 13x13½, 13½x13***

**1980, May 14 Litho. Wmk. 373**

*361* A71 20c multi 6 6
*362* A71 $1.30 multi 42 32
*363* A71 $2 multi 65 50

**Queen Mother Elizabeth Birthday Issue**

Common Design Type

**1980, Aug. 4 Litho.** ***Perf. 14***

*364* CD330 $1.30 multi 40 30

The first price column gives the catalogue value of an unused stamp, the second that of a used stamp.

Botanical Gardens — A72

**1980, Nov. 12 Litho.** ***Perf. 13½***

*365* A72 20c *shown* 6 6
*366* A72 $1 *Ocean Park* 25 25
*367* A72 $1.30 *Kowloon Park* 32 32
*368* A72 $2 *Country Park* 50 50

Epinephelus Akaara — A73

**1981, Jan. 28 Litho.** ***Perf. 13½***

*369* A73 20c *shown* 6 6
*370* A73 $1 *Nemipterus virgatus* 28 28
*371* A73 $1.30 *Choerodon azurio* 35 35
*372* A73 $2 *Scarus ghobban* 55 40

**Royal Wedding Issue**

Common Design Type

**1981, July 29 Photo.** ***Perf. 14***

*373* CD331 20c Bouquet 6 6
*374* CD331 $1.30 Charles 35 28
*375* CD331 $5 Couple 1.10 1.10

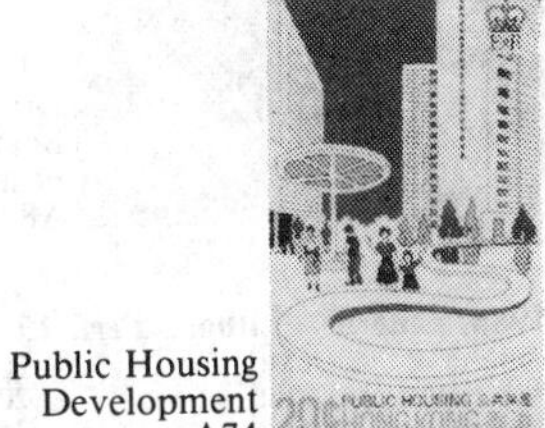

Public Housing Development A74

Designs: Various public housing developments.

**1981, Nov. Litho.** ***Perf. 13½***

*376* A74 20c multi 6 6
*377* A74 $1 multi 30 30
*378* A74 $1.30 multi 40 30
*379* A74 $2 multi 45 45
*a* Souvenir sheet of 4 1.25 1.25

No. 379a contains Nos. 376-379; multicolored margin. Size: 148x105mm.

Port of Hong Kong A75

Designs: Various views of Port of Hong Kong.

**1982, Jan. 12 Litho.** ***Perf. 14½***

*380* A75 20c multi 9 9
*381* A75 $1 multi 45 45
*382* A75 $1.30 multi 55 55
*383* A75 $2 multi 65 65

Five-banded Civet — A76

**1982, May 4 Litho.** ***Perf. 14½***

*384* A76 20c shown 8 8
*385* A76 $1 Pangolin 30 30
*386* A76 $1.30 Chinese porcupine 55 55
*387* A76 $5 Barking deer 1.65 1.65

Queen Elizabeth II
A77 A78

**Wmk. 373, Unwmkd. ($1.70)**

**1982, Aug. 30 Photo.** ***Perf. 14½x14***

*388* A77 10c yel & dk red 5 5
*a* Unwmk. 5 5
*389* A77 20c bl vio & vio 8 8
*a.* Unwmkd. 30 30
*390* A77 30c org & pur 12 12
*391* A77 40c lt bl & red 16 16
*a* Unwmk. ('87) 16 16
*392* A77 50c pale grn & brn 20 20
*a* Unwmk. 20 20
*393* A77 60c gray & brt mag 25 25
*a* Unwmk. 25 25
*394* A77 70c brt org & dk grn 30 30
*a* Unwmk. 30 30
*395* A77 80c gray ol & brn ol 32 32
*a* Unwmk. 32 32
*396* A77 90c grnsh bl & grn 35 35
*a* Unwmk. 35 35
*397* A77 $1 brt pink & brn org 35 35
*a* Unwmk. 35 35
*398* A77 $1.30 rose vio & dk bl 40 40
*b.* Unwmkd. 40 40
*398A* A77 $1.70 brt yel grn & dp bl ('85) 20 20
*399* A77 $2 buff & bl 60 60
*a* Unwmk. 60 60

***Perf. 14x14½***

**Photogravure & Embossed**

*400* A78 $5 lem & lake 1.50 1.50
*a* Unwmk. 1.50 1.50
*401* A78 $10 brn & blk brn 2.75 2.75
*a* Unwmk. 2.75 2.75
*402* A78 $20 lt bl & lake 5.50 5.50
*a* Unwmk. 5.50 5.50
*403* A78 $50 gray & lake 12.00 12.00
*a* Unwmk. 12.00 12.00
*Nos. 388-403 (17)* 25.13 25.13
*Nos. 388a-403a (13)* 24.33 24.33

Unwmkd. stamps issued in 1985, except for 20c. Nos. 388 and 397 also issued in coils.

3rd Far East and South Pacific Games for the Disabled — A79

**1982, Oct. 31 Litho.** ***Perf. 14x14½***

*404* A79 30c Table tennis 12 12
*405* A79 $1 Racing 42 42
*406* A79 $1.30 Basketball 55 55
*407* A79 $5 Archery 1.65 1.65

Performing Arts — A80

***Perf. 14½x14***

**1983, Jan. 26 Litho. Wmk. 373**

*408* A80 30c Dancing 12 12
*409* A80 $1.30 Theater 55 55
*410* A80 $5 Music 1.65 1.65

### Commonwealth Day
Common Design Type

**1983, Mar. 14** *Perf. 14½x13½*

| | | | | |
|---|---|---|---|---|
| *411* CD334 | 30c | Aerial view | 12 | 12 |
| *412* CD334 | $1 | Liverpool Bay | 42 | 42 |
| *413* CD334 | $1.30 | Flag | 55 | 55 |
| *414* CD334 | $5 | Queen Elizabeth II | 1.65 | 1.65 |

Views by Night A82

**1983, Aug. 17** **Litho.** *Perf. 14½*

| | | | | |
|---|---|---|---|---|
| *415* A82 | 30c | Victoria Harbor | 10 | 10 |
| *416* A82 | $1 | Space Museum | 30 | 30 |
| *417* A82 | $1.30 | Chinese New Year Fireworks | 40 | 40 |
| *418* A82 | $5 | Jumbo Restaurant | 1.00 | 1.00 |

Royal Observatory Centenary — A83

**1983, Nov. 23** **Litho.** *Perf. 14½*

| | | | | |
|---|---|---|---|---|
| *419* A83 | 40c | Technical facilities | 12 | 12 |
| *420* A83 | $1 | Wind measurement | 30 | 30 |
| *421* A83 | $1.30 | Temperature measurement | 40 | 40 |
| *422* A83 | $5 | Earthquake measurement | 1.00 | 1.00 |

Training Plane, Dorado — A84

**Wmk. 373**

**1984, Mar. 7** **Litho.** *Perf. 13½*

| | | | | |
|---|---|---|---|---|
| *423* A84 | 40c | shown | 12 | 12 |
| *424* A84 | $1 | Hong Kong Clipper seaplane | 30 | 30 |
| *425* A84 | $1.30 | Jumbo jet, Kai Tak Airport | 40 | 40 |
| *426* A84 | $5 | Baldwin Brothers balloon, vert. | 1.00 | 1.00 |

Map of Hong Kong, 19th Cent. A85

Various maps.

**1984, June 21** **Litho.** *Perf. 14*

| | | | | |
|---|---|---|---|---|
| *427* A85 | 40c | multi | 12 | 12 |
| *428* A85 | $1 | multi | 30 | 30 |
| *429* A85 | $1.30 | multi | 30 | 30 |
| *430* A85 | $5 | multi | 1.00 | 1.00 |

Chinese Lanterns A86

**1984, Sept. 6** **Litho.** *Perf. 13½x13*

| | | | | |
|---|---|---|---|---|
| *431* A86 | 40c | Rooster | 12 | 12 |
| *432* A86 | $1 | Bull | 30 | 30 |
| *433* A86 | $1.30 | Butterfly | 40 | 40 |
| *434* A86 | $5 | Fish | 1.00 | 1.00 |

Jockey Club Centenary — A87

**1984, Nov. 21** **Litho.** *Perf. 14½*

| | | | | |
|---|---|---|---|---|
| *435* A87 | 40c | Supporting health care | 12 | 12 |
| *436* A87 | $1 | Supporting disabled | 28 | 28 |
| *437* A87 | $1.30 | Supporting the arts | 25 | 25 |
| *438* A87 | $5 | Supporting Ocean Park | 1.00 | 1.00 |
| *a* | | Souvenir sheet of 4 | 2.10 | 2.10 |

No. 438a contains Nos. 435-438 with horse racing in margin. Size: 178x98mm.

Historic Buildings A88

**1985, Mar. 14** **Litho.** *Perf. 13½*

| | | | | |
|---|---|---|---|---|
| *439* A88 | 40c | Hung Sing Temple | 10 | 10 |
| *440* A88 | $1 | St. John's Cathedral | 28 | 28 |
| *441* A88 | $1.30 | Old Supreme Court Building | 35 | 35 |
| *442* A88 | $5 | Wan Chai Post Office | 1.00 | 1.00 |

Intl. Dragon Boat Festival A89

**1985, June 19** **Litho.** *Perf. 13½x13*

| | | | | |
|---|---|---|---|---|
| *443* A89 | 40 | multi | 10 | 10 |
| *444* A89 | $1 | multi | 20 | 20 |
| *445* A89 | $1.30 | multi | 25 | 25 |
| *446* A89 | $5 | multi | 1.00 | 1.00 |
| *a* | | Strip of four (Nos. 443-446) | 2.00 | 2.00 |
| *b* | | Souvenir sheet of 4 | 2.00 | 2.00 |

Nos. 443-446 were printed se-tenant in continuous design picturing a dragon boat. No. 446b contains No. 446a (perf. 13x12½); multicolored margin pictures Chinese dragon and historical data. Size: 190x100mm.

### Queen Mother 85th Birthday Issue
Common Design Type

**1985, Aug. 7** **Litho.** *Perf. 14½x14*

| | | | | |
|---|---|---|---|---|
| *447* CD336 | 40c | At Glamis Castle, age 9 | 10 | 10 |
| *448* CD336 | $1 | On balcony with Princes William and Charles | 20 | 20 |
| *449* CD336 | $1.30 | Photograph by Cecil Beaton, 1980 | 25 | 25 |
| *450* CD336 | $5 | Holding Prince Henry | 1.00 | 1.00 |

Indigenous Flowers — A90

**1985, Sept. 25** **Litho.** *Perf. 13½*

| | | | | |
|---|---|---|---|---|
| *451* A90 | 40c | Melastoma | 10 | 10 |
| *452* A90 | 50c | Chinese lily | 14 | 14 |
| *453* A90 | 60c | Grantham's camellia | 16 | 16 |
| *454* A90 | $1.30 | Narcissus | 25 | 25 |
| *455* A90 | $1.70 | Bauhinia | 30 | 30 |
| *456* A90 | $5 | Chinese New Year flower | 1.00 | 1.00 |
| | | *Nos. 451-456 (6)* | 1.95 | 1.95 |

Modern Architecture — A91

**1985, Nov. 27** *Perf. 15*

| | | | | |
|---|---|---|---|---|
| *457* A91 | 50c | Hong Kong Academy for Performing Arts | 14 | 14 |
| *458* A91 | $1.30 | Exchange Square, vert. | 25 | 25 |
| *459* A91 | $1.70 | Hong Kong Bank Hdqtrs., vert. | 35 | 35 |
| *460* A91 | $5 | Hong Kong Coliseum | 1.00 | 1.00 |

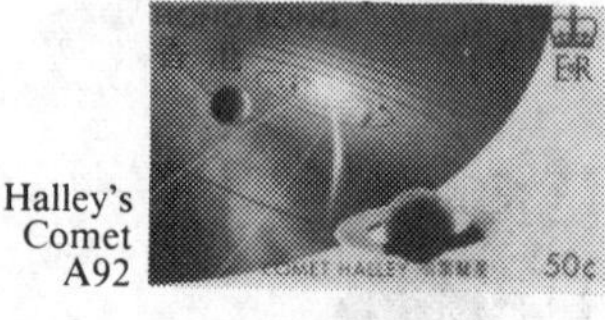


Halley's Comet A92

**1986, Feb. 26** **Litho.** *Perf. 13½x13*

| | | | | |
|---|---|---|---|---|
| *461* A92 | 50c | Comet, solar system | 14 | 14 |
| *462* A92 | $1.30 | Edmond Halley | 25 | 25 |
| *463* A92 | $1.70 | Hong Kong, trajectory | 35 | 35 |
| *464* A92 | $5 | Comet, Earth | 1.00 | 1.00 |
| *a* | | Souvenir sheet of 4, #461-464 | 2.30 | 2.30 |

No. 464a has multicolored decorative margin picturing satellite view of Earth. Size: 135x80mm.

### Queen Elizabeth II 60th Birthday
Common Design Type

Designs: 50c, At the wedding of Cecillia Bowes-Lyon, Brompton Parish Church, 1939. $1, Most Noble Order of the Garter, service at St. George's Chapel, Windsor Castle, 1977. $1.30, State visit, 1975. $1.70, Queen Mother's 80th birthday celebration, Royal Lodge, Windsor, 1980. $5, Visiting Crown Agents' offices, 1983.

**1986, Apr. 21** *Perf. 14½*

| | | | | |
|---|---|---|---|---|
| *465* CD337 | 50c | scar, blk & sil | 14 | 14 |
| *466* CD337 | $1 | ultra & multi | 20 | 20 |
| *467* CD337 | $1.30 | grn & multi | 25 | 25 |
| *468* CD337 | $1.70 | vio & multi | 35 | 35 |
| *469* CD337 | $5 | rose vio & multi | 1.10 | 1.10 |
| | | *Nos. 465-469 (5)* | 2.04 | 2.04 |

EXPO '86, Vancouver — A93

**1986, July 18** **Litho.** *Perf. 13½*

| | | | | |
|---|---|---|---|---|
| *470* A93 | 50c | Transportation | 14 | 14 |
| *471* A93 | $1.30 | Finance | 25 | 25 |
| *472* A93 | $1.70 | Trade | 35 | 35 |
| *473* A93 | $5 | Communications | 1.10 | 1.10 |

Fishing Vessels A94

**1986, Sept. 24** **Litho.**

| | | | | |
|---|---|---|---|---|
| *474* A94 | 50c | Hand-liner sampan | 14 | 14 |
| *475* A94 | $1.30 | Stern trawler | 25 | 25 |
| *476* A94 | $1.70 | Long liner junk | 45 | 45 |
| *477* A94 | $5 | Junk trawler | 1.10 | 1.10 |

19th Cent. Paintings — A95

Designs: 50c, Possibly, Second puan khequa, by Spoilum. $1.30, Chinese woman, artist unknown. $1.70, Self-portrait at age 52, by Kwan Kiu Chin. $5, Possibly, Wife of a merchant, by George Chinnery.

**1986, Dec. 9** **Litho.** *Perf. 14*

| | | | | |
|---|---|---|---|---|
| *478* A95 | 50c | multi | 14 | 14 |
| *479* A95 | $1.30 | multi | 35 | 35 |
| *480* A95 | $1.70 | multi | 35 | 35 |
| *481* A95 | $5 | multi | 1.10 | 1.10 |

New Year 1987 (Year of the Hare) A96

Embroideries of various rabbits.

**1987, Jan. 21** **Litho.** *Perf. 13½x14*

| | | | | |
|---|---|---|---|---|
| *482* A96 | 50c | multi | 14 | 14 |
| *483* A96 | $1.30 | multi | 38 | 38 |
| *484* A96 | $1.70 | multi | 48 | 48 |
| *485* A96 | $5 | multi | 1.40 | 1.40 |
| *a* | | Souv. sheet of 4, #482-485 | 2.50 | 2.50 |

No. 485a has silver and red inscribed margin. Size: 133x83mm.

19th Century Paintings in the Hong Kong Museum of Art and Shanghai Banking Corp. — A97

Scenes: 50c, A Village Square, Hong Kong Island, 1838, by Auguste Borget (1809-1877). $1.30, Boat Dwellers in Kowloon Bay, 1838, by Borget. $1.70, Flagstaff House, Lt. Governor D'Aguilar's Residence, 1846, by Murdoch Bruce. $5, A View of Wellington Street, late 19th century, by C. Andrasi.

**1987, Apr. 23** **Litho.** *Perf. 14*

| | | | | |
|---|---|---|---|---|
| *486* A97 | 50c | multi | 12 | 12 |
| *487* A97 | $1.30 | multi | 35 | 35 |
| *488* A97 | $1.70 | multi | 45 | 45 |
| *489* A97 | $5 | multi | 1.25 | 1.25 |

Elizabeth II, Hong Kong Waterfront A98

Queen, Natl. Landmarks A99

**1987, July 13** **Litho.** *Perf. 14½x14*

| | | | | |
|---|---|---|---|---|
| *490* A98 | 10c | yel grn, gray & blk | 5 | 5 |
| *491* A98 | 40c | bluish grn, lt yel & blk | 10 | 10 |
| *492* A98 | 50c | brn org, buff & blk | 12 | 12 |
| *493* A98 | 60c | lt blue, pale rose & blk | 15 | 15 |
| *494* A98 | 70c | vio, pale rose & blk | 16 | 16 |

*495* A98 80c brt rose lil, lt blue & blk 18 18
*496* A98 90c pink, pale beige & blk 22 22
*497* A98 $1 brt lem & blk 24 24
*498* A98 $1.30 rose claret, brt yel grn & blk 32 32
*499* A98 $1.70 lt blue & blk 40 40
*500* A98 $2 yel grn, cream & blk 45 45
*501* A99 $5 Tsim Shah Tsui, Kowloon 1.25 1.25
*502* A99 $10 Victoria Harbor 2.25 2.25
*503* A99 $20 Legislative Council Building 4.75 4.75
*504* A99 $50 Government House 12.00 12.00
*Nos. 490-504 (15)* 22.64 22.64

See Nos. 532-533.

Nethersole Hospital, Cent. — A100

**1987, Sept. 8** ***Perf. 14½***
*505* A100 50c Hospital, 1887 14 14
*506* A100 $1.30 Patients, staff 38 38
*507* A100 $1.70 Technology, 1987 48 48
*508* A100 $5 Treatment 1.40 1.40

Natl. Flag — A101

Coil Stamps

**1987, July 13** ***Perf. 15x14***
*509* A101 10c shown 5 5
*510* A101 50c Map 14 14

Folk Costumes — A102

**1987, Nov. 18** ***Perf. 13½***
*511* A102 50c multi 10 10
*512* A102 $1.30 multi, diff. 28 28
*513* A102 $1.70 multi, diff. 35 35
*514* A102 $5 multi, diff. 1.10 1.10

New Year 1988 (Year of the Dragon) A103

**1988, Jan. 27** **Litho.** ***Perf. 13½***
*515* A103 50c multi 12 12
*516* A103 $1.30 multi, diff. 35 35
*517* A103 $1.70 multi, diff. 45 45
*518* A103 $5 multi, diff. 1.30 1.30
***a*** Souv. sheet of 4, Nos. 515-518 2.25 2.25

No. 518a has dark red and silver decorative margin. Size: 134x88mm.

Indigenous Birds — A104

**1988, Apr. 20** ***Perf. 13½x14***
*519* A104 50c White-breasted kingfisher 12 12
*520* A104 $1.30 Fukien niltava 35 35
*521* A104 $1.70 Black kite 45 45
*522* A104 $5 Pied kingfisher 1.30 1.30

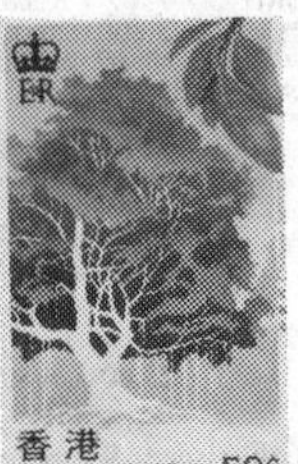

Indigenous Trees — A105

**1988, June 16** **Litho.** ***Perf. 13½***
*523* A105 50c Chinese banyan 14 14
*524* A105 $1.30 *Bauhinia blakeana* 35 35
*525* A105 $1.70 Cotton tree 45 45
*526* A105 $5 Schima 1.25 1.25
***a.*** Souv. sheet of 4, Nos. 523-526 2.25 2.25

Peak Tramway, Victoria, Cent. — A106

Various views of Hong Kong and the tram line.

**1988, Aug. 4** **Litho.** ***Perf. 15***
*527* A106 50c multi 14 14
*528* A106 $1.30 multi, diff. 35 35
*529* A106 $1.70 multi, diff. 45 45
*530* A106 $5 multi, diff. 1.30 1.30
***a.*** Souv. sheet of 4, Nos. 527-530 2.25 2.25

No. 530a has multicolored inscribed margin picturing an illustration by Kathryn Blomfield. Size: 161x90mm.

Catholic Cathedral, Caine Road, Cent. — A107

**1988, Sept. 30** **Litho.** ***Perf. 14***
*531* A107 60c multi 15 15

Queen and Waterfront Type of 1987

**1988, Sept. 1** **Litho.** ***Perf. 13½x14***
*532* A98 $1.40 multi 35 35
*533* A98 $1.80 multi 48 48

## SEMI-POSTAL STAMPS

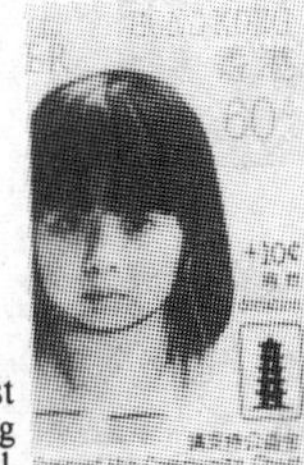

Community Chest of Hong Kong — SP1

**1988, Nov. 30** **Litho.** ***Perf. 14½***
*B1* SP1 60c +10c Girl 18 18
*B2* SP1 $1.40 +20c Elderly woman 40 40
*B3* SP1 $1.80 +30c Blind youth 55 55
*B4* SP1 $5 +$1 Mother and child 1.55 1.55

Surtax for the social welfare organization.

## POSTAGE DUE STAMPS

Scales Showing Letter Overweight — D1

**1924-56** **Typo.** **Wmk. 4** ***Perf. 14***
*J1* D1 1c brown 75 60
***a.*** Wmkd. sideways ('56) 35 35
*J2* D1 2c green 2.25 1.25
*J3* D1 4c red 3.25 1.65
*J4* D1 6c orange 9.00 6.00
*J5* D1 10c ultra 13.00 2.75
*Nos. J1-J5 (5)* 28.25 12.25

**1938-47** ***Perf. 14***
*J6* D1 2c gray 35 35
*J7* D1 4c org yel 1.10 45
*J8* D1 6c carmine 2.75 1.40
*J9* D1 8c fawn ('46) 2.75 1.40
*J10* D1 10c violet 1.40 65
*J11* D1 20c blk ('46) 2.75 2.00
*J12* D1 50c bl ('47) 16.00 11.50
*Nos. J6-J12 (7)* 27.10 17.75

Nos. J1, J6-J7 and J10 exist on both ordinary and chalky paper.

**Catalogue values for unused stamps in this section, from this point to the end of the section, are for Never Hinged items.**

**Wmk. 314 Sideways**

**1965-69** ***Perf. 14***
*J13* D1 4c org yel 1.75 1.75
*J14* D1 5c org ver ('69) 75 40
***a.*** 5c car, wmk. upright ('67) 75 40
*J15* D1 10c pur ('67) 2.00 90
*J16* D1 20c black 4.00 2.00
*J17* D1 50c dk bl 7.00 3.00
***a.*** Wmk. upright ('70) 8.00 5.00
*Nos. J13-J17 (5)* 15.50 8.05

Size of 5c, 21x18mm.; others, 22x18mm.

**Wmk. 314 Upright**

**1972-74** ***Perf. 13½x14***
*J18* D1 5c red brn ('74) 15 15

***Perf. 14x14½***
*J19* D1 10c lilac 60 60
*J20* D1 20c black 1.25 1.25
*J21* D1 50c dl bl 3.50 3.50

Nos. J18-J22 are on glazed paper.

**1976** **Wmk. 373**
*J19a* D1 10c lilac 8 8
*J20a* D1 20c black 12 12
*J21a* D1 50c dull blue 30 30
***b.*** Unwmk. 30 30
*J22* D1 $1 yellow 60 60
***a.*** Unwmk. 60 60

Size of $1, 20½x17mm.; others, 22x18mm.

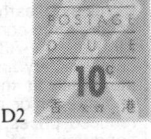

D2

**1986** **Litho.** ***Perf. 14x15***
*J23* D2 10c lt grn 5 5
*J24* D2 20c dk red brn 6 6
*J25* D2 50c lilac 12 12
*J26* D2 $1 lt org 22 22
*J27* D2 $5 grysh bl 1.10 1.10
*J28* D2 $10 rose red 2.25 2.25
*Nos. J23-J28 (6)* 3.80 3.80

## OCCUPATION STAMPS

**Issued under Japanese Occupation**

War Factory Girl — A144

Gen. Maresuke Nogi — A84

Admiral Heihachiro Togo — A86

Stamps of Japan, 1942-43 Surcharged in Black

**1945** **Wmk. 257** **Typo.** ***Perf. 13***
*N1* A144 1½y on 1s org brn 8.25 8.25
*N2* A84 3y on 2s ver 5.50 8.25
*N3* A86 5y on 5s brn lake 325.00 42.50

# INDIA

LOCATION — In southern, central Asia.
GOVT. — Republic.
AREA — 1,266,732 sq. mi.
POP. — 683,810,051 (1981).
CAPITAL — New Delhi.

On August 15, 1947, India was divided into two self-governing dominions: Pakistan and India. India became a republic in 1950.

The stamps of pre-partition India fall into three groups: 1) Issues inscribed simply "India," for use mainly in British India proper, but available and valid throughout the country; 2) Issues as above and overprinted with one of the names of the six states (Chamba, Faridkot, Gwalior, Jind, Nabha and Patiala) which had a postal convention with British India, for use in these states. 3) Issues of the feudatory states, over which the British India government exercised little internal control, valid only within the states issuing them.

12 Pies = 1 Anna
16 Annas = 1 Rupee
100 Naye Paise = 1 Rupee (1957)
100 Paise = 1 Rupee (1964)

Values of early India stamps vary according to condition. Quotations for Nos. A1-A3, 1-7 are for fine copies. Very fine to superb specimens sell at much higher prices, and inferior or poor copies sell at reduced prices, depending on the condition of the individual specimen.

**Catalogue values for unused stamps in this country are for Never Hinged items, beginning with Scott 168 in the regular postage section, Scott C7 in the air post section, Scott M44 in the military section, Scott O113 in the official section, Scott RA1 in the postal tax section, Scott 51 in Hyderabad regular issues, Scott O54 in Hyderabad officials, Scott 49 in Jaipur regular issues, Scott O30 in Jaipur officials, Scott 39 in Soruth regular issues and Scott O19 in Soruth official; all of the values are for Never Hinged for all of the items in the sections for the International Commission in Indo-China, Jasdan, Rajasthan, and Travancore-Cochin.**

## SCINDE DISTRICT POST

A1

**1852, July 1 — Embossed — *Imperf.***

| No. | Type | Description | Unused | Used |
|---|---|---|---|---|
| *A1* | A1 | ½a *white* | 4,000. | 600.00 |
| *A2* | A1 | ½a blue | 12,000. | 1,650. |
| *A3* | A1 | ½a *red* | | 5,250. |

Obsolete October, 1854.

No. A3 is embossed on red sealing wax.

## GENERAL ISSUES

### East India Company

Queen Victoria
A1 A2

A3

A4

A5

**Lithographed; Typographed (#5)**

**1854 — Wmk. 37 — *Imperf.***

| No. | Type | Description | Unused | Used |
|---|---|---|---|---|
| *1* | A1 | ½a red | 550.00 | |
| *2* | A2 | ½a blue | 30.00 | 7.25 |
| a | | ½a deep blue | 37.50 | 9.25 |
| b | | Printed on both sides | | *5,000.* |
| *4* | A3 | 1a red | 35.00 | 22.50 |
| a | | 1a scarlet | 35.00 | 27.50 |
| *5* | A4 | 2a green | 52.50 | 14.00 |
| *6* | A5 | 4a red & bl | 2,800. | 200.00 |
| a | | 4a deep red & blue | 2,000. | 325.00 |
| | | Cut to shape | | 14.00 |
| c | | Head inverted | | *65,000.* |
| | | As "c," cut to shape | | *35,000.* |
| e | | Double impression of head | | |

No. 1 was not placed in use.

Nos. 2, 4, 5 and 6 are known with unofficial perforation.

There are 3 dies of No. 2, and 2 dies of No. 4, showing slight differences.

There are 4 dies of the head and 2 dies of the frame of No. 6.

Wmk. 37- Coat of Arms in Sheet. (Reduced illustration. Watermark covers a large section of the sheet.)

A6

**1855**

| No. | Type | Description | Unused | Used |
|---|---|---|---|---|
| *7* | A6 | 1a red | 800.00 | 110.00 |

No. 7 was printed from a lithographic transfer made from the original die retouched. The lines of the bust at the lower left are nearly straight and meet in a point.

Diadem includes Maltese Crosses — A7

**1855-64 — Unwmk. — Typo. — *Perf. 14***

**Blue Glazed Paper**

| No. | Type | Description | Unused | Used |
|---|---|---|---|---|
| *9* | A7 | 4a black | 140.00 | 7.75 |
| a | | Imperf., pair | 700.00 | 700.00 |
| b | | Half used as 2a on cover | | *4,150.* |
| *10* | A7 | 8a rose | 125.00 | 8.25 |
| a | | Imperf., pair | 650.00 | 650.00 |
| b | | Half used as 4a on cover | | *4,750.* |

**1855-64 — White Paper**

| No. | Type | Description | Unused | Used |
|---|---|---|---|---|
| *11* | A7 | ½a blue | 4.50 | 50 |
| a | | Imperf., pair | 365.00 | 425.00 |
| *12* | A7 | 1a brown | 7.00 | 1.10 |
| a | | Imperf., pair | 650.00 | 700.00 |
| b | | Vert. pair, imperf between | | |
| c | | Half used as ½a on cover | | *6,500.* |
| *13* | A7 | 2a dull rose | 80.00 | 20.00 |
| a | | Imperf., pair | 600.00 | 600.00 |
| *14* | A7 | 2a yellow green | 650.00 | |
| a | | Imperf., pair | 825.00 | |
| *15* | A7 | 2a buff | 24.00 | 6.25 |
| a | | 2a orange | 40.00 | 6.25 |
| b | | Imperf., pair | 650.00 | 700.00 |
| *16* | A7 | 4a black | 32.50 | 4.00 |
| a | | Imperf., pair | 600.00 | 625.00 |
| b | | Diagonal half used as 2a on cover | | *4,000.* |
| *17* | A7 | 4a green ('64) | 150.00 | 17.50 |
| *18* | A7 | 8a rose | 25.00 | 6.50 |
| a | | Half used as 4a on cover | | *6,500.* |

No. 14 was not regularly issued. See note after No. 25.

### Government Issues

Queen Victoria — A8

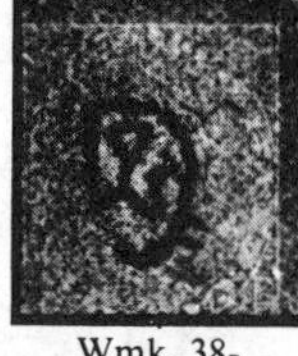
Wmk. 38- Elephant's Head

**1860-64 — Unwmk. — *Perf. 14***

| No. | Type | Description | Unused | Used |
|---|---|---|---|---|
| *19* | A8 | 8p lilac | 7.50 | 4.00 |
| a | | Diagonal half used as 4p on cover | | *8,250.* |
| b | | Imperf., pair | 650.00 | 700.00 |
| *19C* | A8 | 8p lilac, *bluish* | 90.00 | 40.00 |

**1865-67 — Wmk. 38**

| No. | Type | Description | Unused | Used |
|---|---|---|---|---|
| *20* | A7 | ½a blue | 1.40 | 18 |
| a | | Imperf., pair | | 350.00 |
| *21* | A8 | 8p lilac | 5.00 | 3.00 |
| *22* | A7 | 1a brown | 1.50 | 12 |
| *23* | A7 | 2a orange | 10.50 | 65 |
| a | | 2a yellow | 11.50 | 1.65 |
| b | | Imperf., pair | | 650.00 |
| *24* | A7 | 4a green | 87.50 | 15.00 |
| *25* | A7 | 8a rose | 525.00 | 57.50 |

No. 21 was variously surcharged locally, "NINE" or "NINE PIE", to indicate that it was being sold for 9 pies (the soldier's letter rate had been raised from 8 to 9 pies). These surcharges were made without government authorization.

Stamps of types A7 and A9 overprinted with crown and surcharged with new values were for use in Straits Settlements.

A9

A10

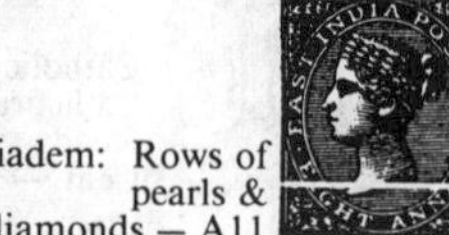

Diadem: Rows of pearls & diamonds — A11

FOUR ANNAS.
Type I. Slanting line at corner of mouth extends downward only. Shading about mouth and chin.
Type II. Line at corner of mouth extends both up and down. Upper lip and chin are defined by a colored line, but there is no shading.

**1866-68**

| No. | Type | Description | Unused | Used |
|---|---|---|---|---|
| *26* | A9 | 4a green, type I | 8.00 | 45 |
| *26B* | A9 | 4a bl grn, type II | 8.00 | 35 |
| *27* | A10 | 6a8p slate | 20.00 | 15.00 |
| a | | Imperf., pair | 850.00 | |
| *28* | A11 | 8a rose ('68) | 8.25 | 3.00 |

Type A11 is a redrawing of type A7. The main difference is in the diadem.

Queen Victoria — A12

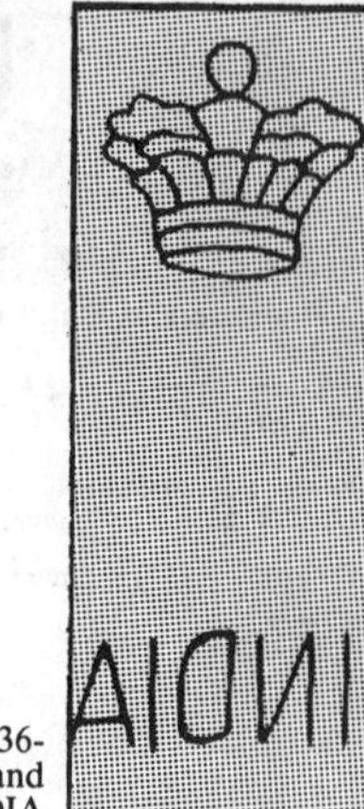

Wmk. 36- Crown and INDIA

SIX ANNAS.
Type I. "POSTAGE" 3½mm high
Type II. "POSTAGE" 2½mm high

**Blue Glazed Paper**
**Green Overprint**
***Perf. 14 Vert.***

**1866, June 28 — Wmk. 36**

| No. | Type | Description | Unused | Used |
|---|---|---|---|---|
| *29* | A12 | 6a violet, type I | 375.00 | 82.50 |
| a | | Inverted overprint | | *5,250.* |
| *30* | A12 | 6a violet, type II | 575.00 | 82.50 |

Nos. 29 and 30 were made from revenue stamps with the labels at top and bottom cut off. Most and sometimes all of the watermark was removed with the labels.

A13

A14


A15


A16

**1873-76 — Wmk. 38 — *Perf. 14***

| No. | Type | Description | Unused | Used |
|---|---|---|---|---|
| *31* | A7 | ½a blue, redrawn | 2.50 | 22 |
| *32* | A13 | 9p lilac ('74) | 5.25 | 4.50 |
| *33* | A14 | 6a bister ('76) | 2.50 | 1.25 |
| *34* | A15 | 12a red brn ('76) | 5.50 | 4.00 |
| *35* | A16 | 1r slate ('74) | 14.00 | 5.50 |

In the redrawn ½ anna the lines of the mouth are more deeply cut, making the lips appear fuller and more open, and the nostril is defined by a curved line.

### Issues of the Empire

A17

A18

A19 A20

A21 A22

A23 A24

A25 A26

A27

Wmk. 39- Star

**1882-87** **Wmk. 39**

| No. | Type | Description | Unused | Used |
|---|---|---|---|---|
| 36 | A17 | ½a green | 18 | 8 |
| a | | Double impression | 175.00 | |
| 37 | A18 | 9p rose | 60 | 1.75 |
| 38 | A19 | 1a maroon | 1.00 | 8 |
| a | | 1a violet brown | 1.00 | 8 |
| 39 | A20 | 1a6p bister brn | 1.25 | 35 |
| 40 | A21 | 2a ultra | 1.10 | 10 |
| a | | Double impression | 300.00 | 300.00 |
| 41 | A22 | 3a brown org | 3.00 | 16 |
| a | | 3a orange | 6.75 | 2.75 |
| 42 | A23 | 4a olive grn | 2.50 | 16 |
| 43 | A24 | 4a6p green | 6.50 | 3.25 |
| 44 | A25 | 8a red violet | 5.75 | 1.00 |
| a | | 8a rose lilac | 5.75 | 1.00 |
| 45 | A26 | 12a violet, *red* | 4.50 | 1.25 |
| 46 | A27 | 1r gray | 6.75 | 1.40 |
| | | *Nos. 36-46 (11)* | 33.13 | 9.58 |

A 6a bister and a 12a Venetian red were prepared but not issued. See Nos. 56-58.

No. 43 Surcharged **2½ As.**

**1891, Jan. 1**

| No. | Type | Description | Unused | Used |
|---|---|---|---|---|
| 47 | A24 | 2½a on 4a6p green | 1.50 | 1.50 |

A28 A29

**1892**

| No. | Type | Description | Unused | Used |
|---|---|---|---|---|
| 48 | A28 | 2a6p green | 50 | 35 |
| 49 | A29 | 1r car rose & grn | 3.25 | 1.90 |

See No. 59.

Queen Victoria

A30 A31

**1895, Sept. 1**

| No. | Type | Description | Unused | Used |
|---|---|---|---|---|
| 50 | A30 | 2r brown & rose | 25.00 | 6.25 |
| 51 | A30 | 3r green & brown | 27.50 | 6.25 |
| 52 | A30 | 5r violet & ultra | 27.50 | 12.50 |

No. 36 Surcharged **¼**

**1898**

| No. | Type | Description | Unused | Used |
|---|---|---|---|---|
| 53 | A17 | ¼a on ½a green | 18 | 18 |
| a | | Double surch. | 70.00 | |
| b | | Dbl. impression of stamp | 140.00 | |

For Nos. 61, 81 with this overprint see Nos. 77 and 105.

**1899**

| No. | Type | Description | Unused | Used |
|---|---|---|---|---|
| 54 | A31 | 3p carmine rose | 9 | 9 |

**1900**

| No. | Type | Description | Unused | Used |
|---|---|---|---|---|
| 55 | A31 | 3p gray | 12 | 12 |
| 56 | A17 | ½a light green | 18 | 7 |
| 57 | A19 | 1a carmine rose | 25 | 7 |
| 58 | A21 | 2a violet | 1.10 | 50 |
| 59 | A28 | 2a6p ultramarine | 3.50 | 3.00 |
| | | *Nos. 55-59 (5)* | 5.15 | 3.76 |

Edward VII — A32 A33

A34 A35

A36 A37

A38 A39

A40 A41

A42 A43

**1902-09**

| No. | Type | Description | Unused | Used |
|---|---|---|---|---|
| 60 | A32 | 3p gray | 8 | 5 |
| 61 | A33 | ½a green | 20 | 5 |
| a | | Booklet pane of 6 ('04) | 35.00 | |
| 62 | A34 | 1a carmine rose | 45 | 5 |
| a | | Booklet pane of 6 ('04) | 100.00 | |
| 63 | A35 | 2a violet | 1.75 | 5 |
| 64 | A36 | 2a6p ultra | 1.75 | 14 |
| 65 | A37 | 3a brn org | 2.25 | 16 |
| 66 | A38 | 4a olive grn | 1.40 | 20 |
| 67 | A39 | 6a bister | 6.25 | 2.00 |
| 68 | A40 | 8a red violet | 2.25 | 70 |
| 69 | A41 | 12a vio, *red* | 4.00 | 2.25 |
| 70 | A42 | 1r car rose & grn | 5.00 | 50 |
| 71 | A43 | 2r brn & rose | 12.00 | 2.75 |
| 72 | A43 | 3r grn & brn ('04) | 19.00 | 14.00 |
| 73 | A43 | 5r violet & ultra ('04) | 45.00 | 37.50 |
| 74 | A43 | 10r carmine rose & green ('09) | 62.50 | 17.50 |
| 75 | A43 | 15r olive gray & ultra ('09) | 115.00 | 35.00 |
| 76 | A43 | 25r ultra & org brn | 525.00 | 500.00 |
| | | Telegraph cancel | | 125.00 |
| | | *Nos. 60-75 (16)* | 278.88 | 112.90 |

No. 61 Surcharged Like No. 53

**1905**

| No. | Type | Description | Unused | Used |
|---|---|---|---|---|
| 77 | A33 | ¼a on ½a green | 20 | 20 |
| a | | Inverted surcharge | 250.00 | |

A44 A45

**1906**

| No. | Type | Description | Unused | Used |
|---|---|---|---|---|
| 78 | A44 | ½a green | 12 | 5 |
| a | | Booklet pane of 4 | 17.50 | |
| 79 | A45 | 1a carmine rose | 18 | 5 |
| a | | Booklet pane of 4 | 25.00 | |

A46 A47

A48 A49

A50 A51

A52 A53

A54 A55

George V — A56



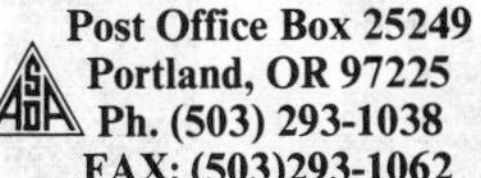

**1911-26** **Wmk. Star (39)**
*80* A46 3p gray 6 5
a Booklet pane of 4 25.00
*81* A47 ½a green 5 5
a Double impression 60.00
b Booklet pane of 4 21.00
*82* A48 1a carmine rose 16 5
a Printed on both sides
b Booklet pane of 4 35.00
*83* A48 1a dk brn ('22) 90 5
a Booklet pane of 4 42.50
*84* A49 2a dull vio 52 5
a Booklet pane of 4 42.50
*85* A50 2a6p ultramarine 1.00 85
*86* A51 3a brn org 1.00 12
*87* A51 3a ultra ('23) 5.25 65
*88* A52 4a olive grn 1.40 12
*89* A53 6a yel bis 2.00 22
*90* A53 6a bister ('15) 5.75 40
*91* A54 8a red vio 2.00 20
*92* A55 12a claret 3.75 50
*93* A56 1r grn & red brn 7.75 24
*94* A56 2r brn & car rose 10.50 50
*95* A56 2r vio & ultra 21.00 1.75
*96* A56 10r car rose & grn 37.50 4.00
*97* A56 15r ol grn & ultra 87.50 7.25
*98* A56 25r ultra & brn org 170.00 20.00
*Nos. 80-98 (19)* 358.09 37.05

See Nos. 106-125.

A57

**1913-26**
*99* A57 2a6p ultramarine 1.10 18
*100* A57 2a6p brn org ('26) 3.25 1.10

"One and Half" — A58

"One and a Half" — A59

**1919**
*101* A58 1½a chocolate 50 20
a Booklet pane of 4 35.00

**1921-26**
*102* A59 1½a chocolate 70 30
*103* A59 1½a rose ('26) 40 10

Type of 1911-26 Surcharged

**NINE**

**PIES**

**1921**
*104* A48 9p on 1a rose 10 8
a Surcharged "NINE-NINE" 30.00 *30.00*
b Surcharged "PIES-PIES" 30.00 *30.00*
c Double surcharge 50.00 55.00
e Booklet pane of 4 27.50

No. 81 Surcharged Like No. 53

**1922**
*105* A47 ¼a on ½a green 10 8
a Inverted surcharge 8.00 8.00
b Pair, one without surcharge 175.00

Wmk. 196-Multiple Stars

Types of 1911-26 Issues

**1926-36** **Wmk. 196**
*106* A46 3p slate 5 5
*107* A47 ½a green 12 5
*108* A48 1a dark brown 18 5
a Tete beche pair 1.50 3.00
b Booklet pane of 4 16.00
*109* A59 1½a car rose ('29) 45 15
*110* A49 2a dull violet 75 20
a Booklet pane of 4 32.50
*111* A49 2a ver ('34) 7.50 90
a Small die ('36) 2.50 60
*112* A57 2a6p buff 38 5
*113* A51 3a ultramarine 5.00 1.25
*114* A51 3a blue ('30) 5.00 15
*115* A51 3a car rose ('32) 52 9
*116* A52 4a olive grn 75 7
*117* A53 6a bister ('35) 13.00 7.75
*118* A54 8a red violet 1.90 6
*119* A55 12a claret 2.25 9
*120* A56 1r grn & brown 1.65 8
*121* A56 2r brn org & car rose 2.50 20
*122* A56 5r dk vio & ultra 13.00 90
*123* A56 10r carmine & grn 37.50 1.75
*124* A56 15r ol grn & ultra 15.00 12.00
*125* A56 25r blue & ocher 82.50 18.00
*Nos. 106-125 (20)* 190.00 43.84

No. 111 measures 19x22½mm, while the small die, No. 111a, measures 18½x22mm.

A60

A61

**1926-32** **Typo.**
*126* A60 2a dull violet 45 5
a Tete beche pair 4.50 4.50
b 2a rose violet 45 6
c Booklet pane of 4 19.00
*127* A60 2a ver ('32) 4.25 1.75
*128* A61 4a olive green 1.40 6

Fortress of Purana Qila — A62

King George V Flanked by Dominion Columns A67

Designs: ½a, War Memorial Arch. 1a, Council Building. 2a, Viceroy's House. 3a, Parliament Building.

**1931, Feb. 9** **Litho.**
*129* A62 ¼a brn & ol grn 28 20
*130* A62 ½a grn & violet 28 12
*131* A62 1a choc & red vio 32 6
*132* A62 2a blue & green 1.00 55
*133* A62 3a car & choc 2.25 1.25
*134* A67 1r violet & grn 8.50 5.00
*Nos. 129-134 (6)* 12.63 7.18

Change of the seat of Government from Calcutta to New Delhi.

A68

A69

A70

**1932, Apr. 22** **Litho.**
*135* A68 9p dark green 28 5
*136* A69 1a3p violet 25 5
*137* A70 3a6p deep blue 1.25 18

No. 135 exists both litho. and typo.

A71

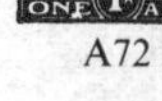

A72

**1934** **Typo.**
*138* A71 ½a green 80 8
*139* A72 1a dark brown 80 6

**Silver Jubilee Issue**

Gateway of India, Bombay A73

Designs: 9p, Victoria Memorial, Calcutta. 1a, Rameswaram Temple, Madras. 1¼a, Jain Temple, Calcutta. 2½a, Taj Mahal, Agra. 3½a, Golden Temple, Amritsar. 8a, Pagoda, Mandalay.

**1935** **Litho.** ***Perf. 13½x14***
*142* A73 ½a light grn & blk 10 5
*143* A73 9p dull grn & blk 15 5
*144* A73 1a brown & blk 10 5
*145* A73 1¼a violet & blk 15 6
*146* A73 2½a brn org & blk 45 18
*147* A73 3½a blue & blk 75 48
*148* A73 8a rose lil & blk 1.90 1.00
*Nos. 142-148 (7)* 3.60 1.87

25th anniv. of the reign of George V.

King George VI
A80 A82

Dak Runner A81

Designs (mail transport): 2a6p, Dak bullock cart. 3a, Dak tonga. 3a6p, Dak camel. 4a, Mail train. 6a, Mail steamer. 8a, Mail truck. 12a, 14a, Mail plane.

**1937-40** **Typo.** **Wmk. 196**
*150* A80 3p slate 18 5
*151* A80 ½a brown 18 5
*152* A80 9p green 30 5
*153* A80 1a carmine 8 5
a Tete beche pair 20 20
b Booklet pane of 4 2.00
*154* A81 2a scarlet 35 6
*155* A81 2a6p purple 15 6
*156* A81 3a yellow green 24 8
*157* A81 3a6p ultramarine 32 20
*158* A81 4a dark brown 32 8
*159* A81 6a peacock bl 42 14
*160* A81 8a bl violet 50 10
*161* A81 12a car lake 75 38
*161A* A81 14a rose vio ('40) 2.00 16
*162* A82 1r brn & slate 35 8
*163* A82 2r dk brn & dk vio 2.75 8
*164* A82 5r dp ultra & dk grn 6.00 12
*165* A82 10r rose car & dk vio 7.50 45
*166* A82 15r dk grn & dk brn 40.00 42.50
*167* A82 25r dk vio & bl vio 27.50 8.75
*Nos. 150-167 (19)* 89.89 53.44

The King's portrait is larger on No. 161A than on other stamps of type A81.

**Catalogue values for unused stamps in this section, from this point to the end of the section, are for Never Hinged items.**

A83

A84

A85

**1941-43** **Typo.** **Wmk. 196**
*168* A83 3p slate ('42) 8 5
*169* A83 ½a rose vio ('42) 8 5
*170* A83 9p light green 18 5
*171* A83 1a car rose ('43) 18 5
*172* A84 1a3p bister 90 6
*172A* A84 1½a dk pur ('42) 20 5
*173* A84 2a scarlet 30 5
*174* A84 3a violet 35 5
*175* A84 3½a ultramarine 52 5
*176* A85 4a chocolate 52 5
*177* A85 6a peacock bl 52 6
*178* A85 8a bl violet 90 8
*179* A85 12a car lake 1.40 20
*Nos. 168-179 (13)* 6.13 85

Early printings of the 1½a and 3a were lithographed.

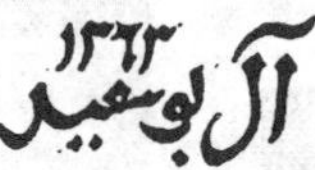


For stamps with this overprint, or a smaller type, see Oman (Muscat).

Symbols of Victory A86

**1946, Jan. 2** **Litho.** ***Perf. 13***
*195* A86 9p green 8 8
*196* A86 1½a dull purple 18 15
*197* A86 3½a ultramarine 22 22
*198* A86 12a brown lake 60 60

Victory of the Allied Nations in WW II.

No. 172 Surcharged With New Value and Bars.

**1946, Aug. 8** ***Perf. 13½x14***
*199* A84 3p on 1a3p bister 5 5

**Dominion of India**

Asoka Pillar — A87

National Flag — A88

Four-Motor Plane A89

*Perf. 14x13½, 13½x14*

**1947 Litho. Wmk. 196**

| | | | | |
|---|---|---|---|---|
| *200* | A87 | 1½a greenish gray | 8 | 6 |
| *201* | A88 | 3½a deep bl, red org & dark grn | 22 | 18 |
| *202* | A89 | 12a ultramarine | 90 | 45 |

Elevation of India to dominion status, Aug. 15, 1947.

Mahatma Gandhi — A90

Design: 10r, Gandhi profile.

*Perf. 11½*

**1948, Aug. 15 Unwmk. Photo.**

**Size: 22x32½mm**

| | | | | |
|---|---|---|---|---|
| *203* | A90 | 1½a brown | 14 | 8 |
| *204* | A90 | 3½a violet | 22 | 8 |
| *205* | A90 | 12a dark gray grn | 90 | 18 |

**Size: 22x37mm**

| | | | | |
|---|---|---|---|---|
| *206* | A90 | 10r rose brn & brn | 55.00 | 25.00 |

Mohandas K. Gandhi, 1869-1948.

Ajanta Panel A91

Konarak Horse A92

Bodhisattva A93

Tomb of Muhammad Adil Shah, Bijapur A95

Sanchi Stupa A94

Victory Tower, Chittorgarh A96

Red Fort, Delhi A97

Satrunjaya Temple, Palitana A98

Designs: 9p, Trimurti. 2a, Nataraja. 3½a, Bodh Gaya Temple. 4a, Bhuvanesvara. 8a, Kandarya Mahadeva Temple. 12a, Golden Temple, Amritsar. 5r, Taj Mahal. 10r, Qutb Minar.

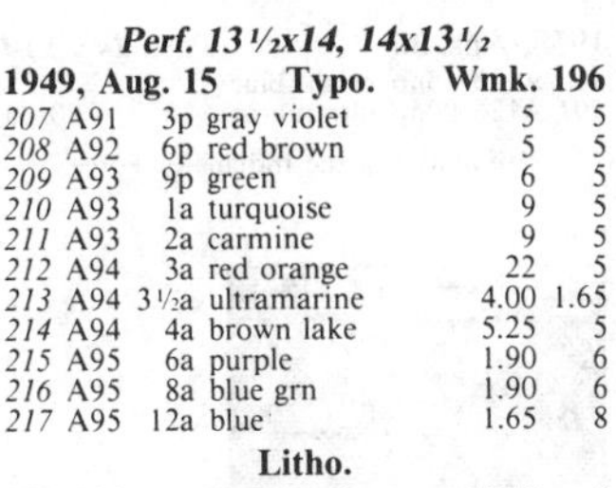

*Perf. 13½x14, 14x13½*

**1949, Aug. 15 Typo. Wmk. 196**

| | | | | |
|---|---|---|---|---|
| *207* | A91 | 3p gray violet | 5 | 5 |
| *208* | A92 | 6p red brown | 5 | 5 |
| *209* | A93 | 9p green | 6 | 5 |
| *210* | A93 | 1a turquoise | 9 | 5 |
| *211* | A93 | 2a carmine | 9 | 5 |
| *212* | A94 | 3a red orange | 22 | 5 |
| *213* | A94 | 3½a ultramarine | 4.00 | 1.65 |
| *214* | A94 | 4a brown lake | 5.25 | 5 |
| *215* | A95 | 6a purple | 1.90 | 6 |
| *216* | A95 | 8a blue grn | 1.90 | 6 |
| *217* | A95 | 12a blue | 1.65 | 8 |

**Litho.**

| | | | | |
|---|---|---|---|---|
| *218* | A96 | 1r dark grn & pur | 10.50 | 6 |
| *219* | A97 | 2r pur & rose red | 4.50 | 9 |
| *220* | A97 | 5r brn car & dk grn | 13.00 | 18 |
| *221* | A96 | 10r dp bl & brn car | 20.00 | 65 |

*Perf. 13½x13*

| | | | | |
|---|---|---|---|---|
| *222* | A98 | 15r dp car & dk brn | 13.00 | 2.75 |
| | | *Nos. 207-222 (16)* | 76.26 | 5.93 |

See Nos. 231, 235-236.

Symbols of UPU and Asoka Pillar — A99

**1949, Oct. Litho. *Perf. 13½x13***

| | | | | |
|---|---|---|---|---|
| *223* | A99 | 9p dull green | 25 | 18 |
| *224* | A99 | 2a carmine rose | 70 | 20 |
| *225* | A99 | 3½a ultramarine | 85 | 45 |
| *226* | A99 | 12a red brown | 1.75 | 60 |

75th anniv. of the formation of the UPU.

## Republic of India

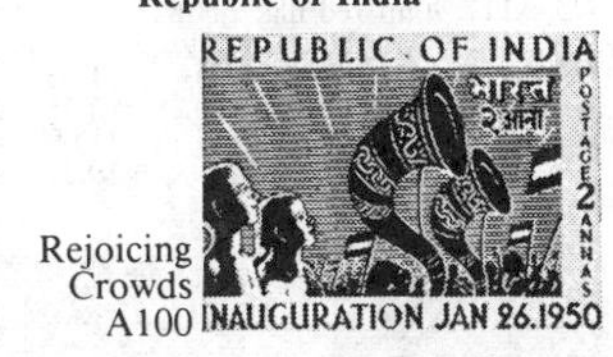

Rejoicing Crowds A100

Designs: 3½a, Quill pen (vert.). 4a, Plow and wheat. 12a, Charkha and cloth.

*Perf. 13½x13*

**1950, Jan. 26 Wmk. 196**

| | | | | |
|---|---|---|---|---|
| *227* | A100 | 2a carmine | 22 | 9 |
| *228* | A100 | 3½a ultramarine | 70 | 30 |
| *229* | A100 | 4a purple | 80 | 15 |
| *230* | A100 | 12a claret | 1.40 | 42 |

Type of 1949 Redrawn

Bodhisattva — A101

**1950, July 15 Typo. *Perf. 13½x14***

| | | | | |
|---|---|---|---|---|
| *231* | A101 | 1a turquoise | 25 | 5 |

Extinct Stegodon Ganesa A102

**1951, Jan. 13 *Perf. 13***

| | | | | |
|---|---|---|---|---|
| *232* | A102 | 2a deep car & blk | 35 | 20 |

Centenary of the foundation of the Geological Survey of India.

Torch and Map — A103

Kabir — A104

**1951, Mar. 4 Typo.**

| | | | | |
|---|---|---|---|---|
| *233* | A103 | 2a red vio & red org | 28 | 10 |
| *234* | A103 | 12a dark brn & ultra | 1.00 | 35 |

First Asian Games, New Delhi.

Temple Type of 1949

Designs: 2½a, Bodh Gaya Temple. 4a, Bhuvanesvara.

*Perf. 13½x14*

**1951, Apr. 30 Wmk. 196**

| | | | | |
|---|---|---|---|---|
| *235* | A94 | 2½a brown lake | 12 | 10 |
| *236* | A94 | 4a ultramarine | 20 | 5 |

*Perf. 14x13½*

**1952, Oct. 1 Photo. Wmk. 196**

Portraits: 1a, Tulsidas, poet and saint. 2a, Meera, Rajput princess. 4a, Surdas, blind poet and saint. 4½a, Ghalib, Urdu poet. 12a, Rabindranath Tagore.

| | | | | |
|---|---|---|---|---|
| *237* | A104 | 9p emerald | 10 | 8 |
| *238* | A104 | 1a crimson | 15 | 8 |
| *239* | A104 | 2a red orange | 22 | 8 |
| *240* | A104 | 4a ultramarine | 30 | 10 |
| *241* | A104 | 4½a red violet | 50 | 18 |
| *242* | A104 | 12a brown | 1.10 | 48 |
| | | *Nos. 237-242 (6)* | 2.37 | 1.00 |

First Locomotive and Streamliner — A105

**1953, Apr. 16 *Perf. 14½x14***

| | | | | |
|---|---|---|---|---|
| *243* | A105 | 2a black | 28 | 10 |

Centenary of India's railroads.

Mt. Everest A106

**1953, Oct. 2**

| | | | | |
|---|---|---|---|---|
| *244* | A106 | 2a violet | 18 | 8 |
| *245* | A106 | 14a brown | 2.75 | 30 |

Conquest of Mt. Everest, May 29, 1953.

Telegraph Poles of 1851 and 1951 A107

**1953, Nov. 1**

| | | | | |
|---|---|---|---|---|
| *246* | A107 | 2a blue green | 18 | 7 |
| *247* | A107 | 12a blue | 2.50 | 28 |

Centenary of the telegraph in India.

Mail Transport, 1854 A108

Designs: 2a and 14a, Pigeon and plane. 4a, Mail transport, 1954.

**1954, Oct. 1**

| | | | | |
|---|---|---|---|---|
| *248* | A108 | 1a rose lilac | 8 | 6 |
| *249* | A108 | 2a rose pink | 14 | 8 |
| *250* | A108 | 4a yellow brown | 1.25 | 12 |
| *251* | A108 | 14a blue | 1.40 | 50 |

Centenary of India's postage stamps.

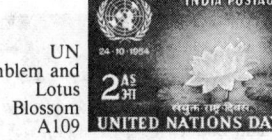

UN Emblem and Lotus Blossom A109

**1954, Oct. 24**

| | | | | |
|---|---|---|---|---|
| *252* | A109 | 2a Prussian grn | 14 | 10 |

United Nations Day.

Forest Research Institute, Dehra Dun A110

**1954, Dec. 11**

| | | | | |
|---|---|---|---|---|
| *253* | A110 | 2a ultra | 12 | 8 |

4th World Forestry Cong., Dehra Dun.

Tractor A111

Charkha Operator A112

Symbols of Malaria Control A113

Designs: 6p, Power looms. 9p, Bullock irrigation pump. 1a, Damodar Valley dam. 3a, Naga woman at hand loom. 4a, Bullock team. 8a, Chittaranjan Locomotive Works. 10a, Plane over Marine Drive, Bombay. 12a, Hindustan aircraft factory. 14a, Plane over Kashmir valley. 1r, Telephone factory worker. 1r2a, Plane over Cape Comorin. 1r8a, Plane over Kanchenjunga Mountains. 2r, Rare earth factory. 5r, Sindri fertilizer factory. 10r, Steel mill.

*Perf. 14x14½, 14½x14*

**1955, Jan. 26 Photo.**

| | | | | |
|---|---|---|---|---|
| *254* | A111 | 3p rose lilac | 6 | 5 |
| *255* | A111 | 6p deep violet | 8 | 5 |
| *256* | A111 | 9p orange brn | 8 | 5 |
| *257* | A111 | 1a deep bl grn | 8 | 5 |
| *258* | A112 | 2a blue | 8 | 5 |
| *259* | A112 | 3a blue green | 14 | 5 |
| *260* | A111 | 4a rose red | 18 | 5 |
| *261* | A113 | 6a yellow brown | 18 | 6 |
| *262* | A111 | 8a deep blue | 45 | 8 |
| *263* | A113 | 10a aquamarine | 40 | 8 |
| *264* | A111 | 12a violet blue | 45 | 6 |
| *265* | A113 | 14a emerald | 45 | 9 |
| *266* | A111 | 1r grnsh blk | 1.25 | 6 |
| *267* | A113 | 1r2a gray | 2.75 | 24 |
| *268* | A113 | 1r8a claret | 3.00 | 25 |
| *269* | A111 | 2r car rose | 2.50 | 7 |
| *270* | A111 | 5r brown | 9.00 | 25 |
| *271* | A111 | 10r orange | 13.00 | 90 |
| | | *Nos. 254-271 (18)* | 34.13 | 2.49 |

See Nos. 316-319.

Values quoted in this catalogue are for stamps graded at Fine-Very Fine and with no faults. An illustrated guide to grade is provided in introductory material, beginning on Page V.

Bodhi Tree — A114

Ornament and Bodhi Tree — A115

**1956, May 24** **Wmk. 196** ***Perf. 13***

| | | | | |
|---|---|---|---|---|
| *272* | A114 | 2a brown | 15 | 7 |
| *273* | A115 | 14a brick red | 1.25 | 45 |

2500th anniv. of the birth of Buddha.

Bal Gangadhar Tilak — A116

Map of India — A117

**1956, July 23** **Photo.**

| | | | | |
|---|---|---|---|---|
| *274* | A116 | 2a orange brown | 15 | 5 |

Centenary of the birth of Bal Gangadhar Tilak, independence leader.

**1957-58** ***Perf. 14x14½***

| | | | | |
|---|---|---|---|---|
| *275* | A117 | 1np blue green | 5 | 5 |
| *276* | A117 | 2np light brown | 5 | 5 |
| *277* | A117 | 3np brown | 5 | 5 |
| *278* | A117 | 5np emerald | 3.50 | 5 |
| *279* | A117 | 6np gray | 12 | 5 |
| *280* | A117 | 8np brt grn ('58) | 35 | 25 |
| *281* | A117 | 10np dark green | 3.50 | 5 |
| *282* | A117 | 13np bright car | 15 | 5 |
| *283* | A117 | 15np vio ('58) | 25 | 5 |
| *284* | A117 | 20np bright blue | 30 | 5 |
| *285* | A117 | 25np ultramarine | 35 | 5 |
| *286* | A117 | 50np orange | 1.50 | 8 |
| *287* | A117 | 75np plum | 1.25 | 12 |
| *288* | A117 | 90np red lil ('58) | 1.75 | 15 |
| | | *Nos. 275-288 (14)* | 13.17 | 1.10 |

Denominations of the 8np, 15np and 90np are inscribed "nP". See Nos. 302-315.

Laxmibai, Rani of Jhansi A118

Banyan Sapling, Arch and Flames — A119

***Perf. 14½x14, 13***

**1957, Aug. 15** **Wmk. 196**

| | | | | |
|---|---|---|---|---|
| *289* | A118 | 15np brown | 18 | 8 |
| *290* | A119 | 90np bright red vio | 90 | 20 |

Centenary of the struggle for independence (Indian Mutiny).

Scott's editorial staff cannot undertake to identify, authenticate or appraise stamps and postal markings.

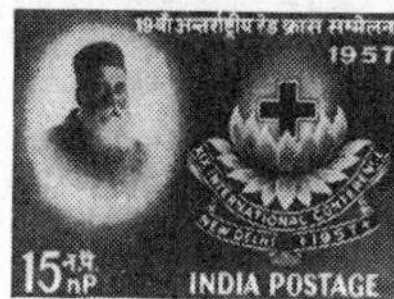

Henri Dunant A120

**1957, Oct. 28** ***Perf. 13½x13***

| | | | | |
|---|---|---|---|---|
| *291* | A120 | 15np car rose & blk | 15 | 5 |

19th Intl. Red Cross Conf., New Delhi.

Boy Eating Banana — A121

Toy Horse — A122

Children's Day: 15np, Girl writing on tablet.

**1957, Nov. 14** ***Perf. 13½***

| | | | | |
|---|---|---|---|---|
| *292* | A121 | 8np rose lilac | 8 | 6 |
| *293* | A121 | 15np aquamarine | 15 | 6 |
| *294* | A122 | 90np light org brn | 55 | 15 |

Madras University A123

University Centenaries: No. 296, Calcutta. No. 297, Bombay (vertical).

**1957, Dec. 31** **Photo.**

**Size: 29½x25mm**

| | | | | |
|---|---|---|---|---|
| *295* | A123 | 10np light brown | 15 | 10 |
| *296* | A123 | 10np gray | 15 | 10 |

**Size: 21½x38mm**

| | | | | |
|---|---|---|---|---|
| *297* | A123 | 10np violet | 15 | 10 |

J. N. Tata and Steel Works, Jamshedpur — A124

**1958, Mar. 1** ***Perf. 14½x14***

| | | | | |
|---|---|---|---|---|
| *298* | A124 | 15np red orange | 15 | 5 |

50th anniv. of Indian steel industry.

Dr. Dhondo Keshav Karve — A125

**1958, Apr. 18** ***Perf. 14x13½***

| | | | | |
|---|---|---|---|---|
| *299* | A125 | 15np orange brown | 15 | 6 |

Cent. of the birth of Karve, educator and pioneer of women's education.

Wapiti and Hunter Planes A126

**1958, Apr. 30** ***Perf. 14½x14***

| | | | | |
|---|---|---|---|---|
| *300* | A126 | 15np bright blue | 15 | 8 |
| *301* | A126 | 90np ultramarine | 90 | 35 |

25th anniv. of the Indian Air Force.

Wmk. 324- Asoka Pillar, Multiple

Map Type of 1957-58 and Industrial Type of 1955

Designs: 1r, Telephone factory worker. 2r, Rare earth factory. 5r, Sindri fertilizer factory. 10r, Steel mill.

***Perf. 14x14½***

**1958-63** **Photo.** **Wmk. 324**

| | | | | |
|---|---|---|---|---|
| *302* | A117 | 1np blue grn ('60) | 5 | 5 |
| *a* | | Imperf., pair | 110.00 | |
| *303* | A117 | 2np light brn | 5 | 5 |
| *304* | A117 | 3np brown | 5 | 5 |
| *305* | A117 | 5np emerald | 5 | 5 |
| *306* | A117 | 6np gray ('63) | 6 | 5 |
| *307* | A117 | 8np bright grn | 6 | 5 |
| *308* | A117 | 10np dark grn | 6 | 5 |
| *309* | A117 | 13np brt car ('63) | 8 | 5 |
| *310* | A117 | 15np vio ('59) | 9 | 5 |
| *311* | A117 | 20np brt blue | 9 | 5 |
| *312* | A117 | 25np ultramarine | 12 | 5 |
| *313* | A117 | 50np orange ('59) | 55 | 5 |
| *314* | A117 | 75np plum ('59) | 38 | 5 |
| *315* | A117 | 90np red lilac ('60) | 50 | 8 |
| *316* | A111 | 1r dark grn ('59) | 70 | 5 |
| *317* | A111 | 2r lil rose ('59) | 1.65 | 8 |
| *318* | A111 | 5r brown ('59) | 3.75 | 20 |
| *319* | A111 | 10r orange ('59) | 11.00 | 48 |
| | | *Nos. 302-319 (18)* | 19.29 | 1.54 |

Bipin Chandra Pal — A128

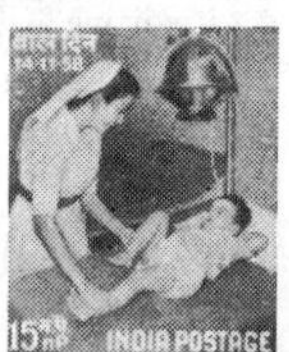

Nurse and Child — A129

**1958, Nov. 7** ***Perf. 13½***

| | | | | |
|---|---|---|---|---|
| *320* | A128 | 15np dull green | 15 | 5 |

Cent. of the birth of Pal, early leader of India's freedom movement.

**1958, Nov. 30**

Portrait: Sir Jagadis Chandra Bose.

| | | | | |
|---|---|---|---|---|
| *321* | A128 | 15np brt grnsh bl | 15 | 5 |

Cent. of the birth of Bose, physicist and plant physiologist.

**1958, Nov. 14** **Wmk. 324**

| | | | | |
|---|---|---|---|---|
| *322* | A129 | 15np violet | 15 | 6 |

Children's Day, Nov. 14.

Exhibition Gate A130

**1958, Dec. 30** ***Perf. 14½x14***

| | | | | |
|---|---|---|---|---|
| *323* | A130 | 15np claret | 15 | 5 |

India 1958 Exhibition at Kampur.

Sir Jamsetjee Jejeebhoy — A131

**1959, Apr. 13** ***Perf. 13½***

| | | | | |
|---|---|---|---|---|
| *324* | A131 | 15np brown | 15 | 5 |

Cent. of the death of Jejeebhoy, philosopher and philanthropist.

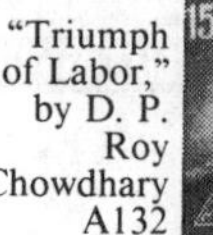

"Triumph of Labor," by D. P. Roy Chowdhary A132

**1959, June 15** ***Perf. 14½x14***

| | | | | |
|---|---|---|---|---|
| *325* | A132 | 15np dull green | 20 | 6 |

40th anniv. of the ILO.

Children Arriving at Institution — A133

***Perf. 14x14½***

**1959, Nov. 14** **Photo.** **Wmk. 324**

| | | | | |
|---|---|---|---|---|
| *326* | A133 | 15np dull green | 15 | 6 |
| *a* | | Imperf., pair | 225.00 | |

Children's Day, Nov. 14.

Farmer Plowing with Bullocks A134

**1959, Dec. 30** ***Perf. 13***

| | | | | |
|---|---|---|---|---|
| *327* | A134 | 15np gray | 15 | 6 |

World Agriculture Fair, New Delhi.

Thiruvalluvar Holding Stylus and Palmyra Leaf — A135

**1960, Feb. 15** ***Perf. 14***

| | | | | |
|---|---|---|---|---|
| *328* | A135 | 15np rose lilac | 15 | 5 |

Honoring the ancient and saintly Tamil poet, Thiruvalluvar.

Scene from Meghduta — A136

Scene from Sakuntala A137

**1960, June 22** *Perf. 13*
*329* A136 15np gray 15 5
*330* A137 1.03r brn & bister 30 15

Honoring Kalidasa, 5th cent. poet and dramatist.

Subramania Bharati A138

Dr. M. Visvesvaraya A139

**1960, Sept. 11** **Photo.** *Perf. 14x13½*
*331* A138 15np bright blue 15 5

Honoring the poet and statesman Subramania Bharati (1882-1921).

**1960, Sept. 15** *Perf. 13x13½*
*332* A139 15np car rose & brn 15 5

Birth cent. of Visvesvaraya, engineer and statesman.

Children Playing and Studying A140

**1960, Nov. 14** *Perf. 13½x13*
*333* A140 15np green 15 6

Children's Day, Nov. 14.

Children and UN Emblem A141

**1960, Dec. 11** **Wmk. 324**
*334* A141 15np ol gray & org brn 15 6

UNICEF Day.

Tyagaraja, Indian musician — A142

**1961, Jan. 6** **Photo.** *Perf. 14*
*335* A142 15np bright blue 15 6

the 114th anniv. of his death.

First Airmail Postmark — A143

Boeing 707 Jetliner — A144

Design: 1r, Humber-Sommer biplane.

*Perf. 14, 13x13½*

**1961, Feb. 18** **Wmk. 324**
*336* A143 5np olive bister 18 6
*337* A144 15np gray & green 45 10
*338* A144 1r gray & claret 2.75 55

50th anniv. of the world's 1st airmail. The flight was from Allahabad to Naini, Feb. 18, 1911.

Chatrapati Sivaji Maharaj (1627-1680) — A145

**1961, Apr. 17** *Perf. 13x13½*
*339* A145 15np gray grn & brn 15 8

Leader of the Maharattas in the fight against the Moguls.

Motilal Nehru — A146

Rabindranath Tagore — A147

**1961, May 6** *Perf. 14x13½*
*340* A146 15np org & ol gray 15 8

Cent. of the birth of Motilal Nehru, leader in India's fight for freedom.

**1961, May 7** *Perf. 13*
*341* A147 15np blue grn & org 20 8

Cent. of the birth of Tagore, poet.

Radio Masts and All India Radio Emblem A148

**1961, June 8** **Photo.** **Wmk. 324**
*342* A148 15np ultramarine 15 6

25th anniv. of All India Radio.

Prafulla Chandra Ray A149

Vishnu Narayan Bhatkhande A150

**1961, Aug. 2** *Perf. 14x13½*
*343* A149 15np gray 15 6

Cent. of the birth of Ray, scientist.

**1961, Sept. 1** *Perf. 13*
*344* A150 15np olive gray 15 6

Bhatkhande (1860-1936), musician.

Boy Making Pottery — A151

Gate at Fair — A152

**1961, Nov. 14** *Perf. 13½*
*345* A151 15np brown 15 6

Children's Day, Nov. 14.

**1961, Nov. 14** *Perf. 14x14½*
*346* A152 15np blue & carmine 15 6

Indian Industries Fair at New Delhi.

Forest and Himalayas — A153

**1961, Nov. 21** *Perf. 13*
*347* A153 15np brown & green 15 6

Cent. of the introduction of scientific forestry in India.

Yaksha, God of Fertility A154

Kalibangan Seal A155

**1961, Dec. 14** **Photo.** *Perf. 14*
*348* A154 15np orange brown 15 6
*349* A155 90np org brn & olive 30 12

Cent. of the Archaeological Survey of India.

Madan Mohan Malaviya A156

Nunmati Refinery, Gauhati A157

**1961, Dec. 25** *Perf. 14x13½*
*350* A156 15np slate 15 6

Cent. of the birth of Malaviya, Pres. of the Indian Natl. Cong. and Vice Chancellor of Benares University.

**1962, Jan. 1** **Photo.** *Perf. 13*
*351* A157 15np blue 15 6

1st Indian oil refinery at Gauhati.

Bhikaiji Cama — A158

Village Council, Banyan Tree, Parliament and Map — A159

**1962, Jan. 26** *Perf. 14*
*352* A158 15np rose lilac 15 6

Cent. of the birth of Madame Cama, a leader in India's fight for independence.

**1962, Jan. 26** *Perf. 13*
*353* A159 15np red lilac 15 6

Panchayati Raj, the system of government by village council.

Dayananda Sarasvati A160

Ganesh Shankar Vidyarthi A161

**1962, Mar. 4** *Perf. 14*
*354* A160 15np brown orange 15 6

135th anniv. of the birth of Sarasvati, reformer of the Vedic religion and founder of the Arya Samaj educational institutions.

**1962, Mar. 25**
*355* A161 15np reddish brown 15 6

Vidvarthi (1890-1931), reformer of community life.

Malaria Eradication Emblem — A162

Dr. Rajendra Prasad — A163

**1962, Apr. 7** *Perf. 13*
*356* A162 15np dk car rose & yel 15 6

WHO drive to eradicate malaria.

**1962, May 13** *Perf. 13*
*357* A163 15np bright red lilac 15 6

Prasad, President of India (1950-62).

High Court, Calcutta A164

**1962 Photo. *Perf. 13½x14***
*358* A164 15np green 15 6
*359* A164 15np Madras 15 6
*360* A164 15np Bombay 15 6

Indian High Courts, cent. No. 358 issued July 1; No. 359, Aug. 8; No. 360, Aug. 14.

Ramabai Ranade — A165

Indian Rhinoceros — A166

**1962, Aug. 15 *Perf. 14***
*361* A165 15np brown orange 15 6

Ramabai Ranade (1862-1924), woman social reformer.

**1962-63 Wmk. 324 *Perf. 14***

Designs: 10np, Gaur. No. 363, Lesser panda (vert.). 30np, Elephant (vert.). 50np, Tiger. 1r, Lion. **Size: 30x26mm**

*361A* A166 10np yellow org & black ('63) 24 6
*362* A166 15np Prus bl & brn 24 6

***Perf. 13x13½, 13½x13***
**Size: 25x36mm, 36x25mm**

*363* A166 15np green & red brown ('63) 35 9
*364* A166 30np bis & sl ('63) 45 8
*365* A166 50np dp grn, ocher & brown ('63) 1.10 25
*366* A166 1r brt bl & pale brown ('63) 1.50 60
*Nos. 361A-366 (6)* 3.88 1.14

Child Reaching for Flag — A167

**1962, Nov. 14 *Perf. 13***
*367* A167 15np lt bluish grn & ver 15 7

Children's Day.

Eye within Lotus Blossom A168

**1962, Dec. 3 Photo.**
*368* A168 15np olive gray 15 6

16th Intl. Cong. of Ophthalmology, New Delhi, Dec. 1962.

Srinivasa Ramanujan A169

Swami Vivekananda A170

**1962, Dec. 22 *Perf. 13½x14***
*369* A169 15np olive gray 15 6

75th anniv. of the birth of Ramanujan (1887-1920), mathematician.

**1963, Jan. 17 *Perf. 14x14½***
*370* A170 15np olive & org brn 12 6

Cent. of the birth of Vivekananda (1863-1902), philosopher.

No. 330 Surcharged with New Value and Two Bars

**1963, Feb. 2 *Perf. 13***
*371* A137 1r on 1.03r brn & bis 30 12

Hands Reaching for "FAO" Emblem A171

Henri Dunant and Centenary Emblem A172

**1963, Mar. 21 Photo.**
*372* A171 15np chalky blue 15 6

UNFAO Freedom from Hunger campaign.

**1963, May 8 *Perf. 13***
*373* A172 15np gray & red 15 8

Centenary of the International Red Cross.

Field Artillery and Helicopter A173

Design: 1r, Soldier guarding frontier and plane dropping supplies.

**1963, Aug. 15 *Perf. 13½x14***
*374* A173 15np dull green 15 6
*375* A173 1r red brown 50 12

Honoring the Armed Forces and the 16th anniv. of independence.

Dadabhoy Naoroji — A174

**1963, Sept. 4 *Perf. 13***
*376* A174 15np gray green 12 6

Honoring Dadabhoy Naoroji (1825-1917), mathematician and statesman.

Annie Besant — A175

School Lunch — A176

**1963, Oct. 1 Photo. *Perf. 14***
*377* A175 15np blue green 12 6

Besant (1847-1933), an English woman devoted to the cause of India's freedom, theosophist and writer. Stamp gives birth date as 1837.

**1963, Nov. 14 Wmk. 324 *Perf. 14***
*378* A176 15np olive bister 12 6

Children's Day.

Eleanor Roosevelt at Spinning Wheel A177

**1963, Dec. 10 *Perf. 13***
*379* A177 15np rose violet 12 6

Honoring Eleanor Roosevelt on the 15th anniv. of the Universal Declaration of Human Rights.

Gopabandhu Das (1877-1928) A178

Lakshmi, Goddess of Wealth A179

**1964, Jan. 4 *Perf. 13***
*380* A178 15np dull purple 12 6

Gopabandhu Das , social reformer.

**1964, Jan. 4 Photo.**
*381* A179 15np dull vio blue 15 8

26th Intl. Cong. of Orientalists, New Delhi, Jan. 4-14.

Purandaradasa Holding Veena and Chipala — A180

**1964, Jan. 14**
*382* A180 15np golden brown 12 6

400th anniv. of the death of Purandaradasa (1484-1564), musician.

Subhas Chandra Bose and INA Emblem A181

Design: 55np, Bose addressing troops.

**1964, Jan. 23 *Perf. 13***
*383* A181 15np olive 12 6
*384* A181 55np red & black 25 18

67th anniv. of the birth of Bose, organizer of the Indian Natl. Army.

Sarojini Naidu (1879-1949) A182

Kasturba Gandhi A183

**1964, Feb. 13 *Perf. 14x13½***
*385* A182 15np dl lil & slate grn 12 6

Mrs. Sarojini Haidu , poet, politician, governor of United Provinces.

**1964, Feb. 22 Photo. Wmk. 324**
*386* A183 15np brown orange 15 8

20th anniv. of the death of Kasturba Gandhi (1869-1944), wife of Mahatma Gandhi.

Dr. Waldemar M. Haffkine (1860-1930) — A184

**1964, Mar. 16 *Perf. 13***
*387* A184 15np violet brn, *buff* 15 8

Haffkine , bacteriologist, who as director of Haffkine Institute introduced inoculations against cholera and plague.

Jawaharlal Nehru (1889-1964) and People A185

**1964, June 12 Unwmk. *Perf. 13***
*388* A185 15p garyish blue 12 5

Prime Minister Jawaharlal Nehru.

Asutosh Mookerjee and High Court, Calcutta A186

**1964, June 29 Wmk. 324**
*389* A186 15p olive grn & brn 12 6

Cent. of the birth of Asutosh Mookerjee (1864-1924), educator, lawyer and judge.

Sri Aurobindo Ghose (1872-1950), Writer and Philosopher — A187

**1964, Aug. 15 Photo.**
*390* A187 15p violet brown 12 6

Raja Rammohun Roy — A188

**1964, Sept. 27 *Perf. 13***
*391* A188 15p reddish brown 12 6

Roy (1772-1833), Hindu religious reformer.

Globe, Lotus, and Calipers — A189

Nehru Medal and Rose — A190

**1964, Nov. 9 Unwmk. Photo.**
*392* A189 15p carmine rose 12 6

6th gen. assembly of the Intl. Organization for Standardization.

**1964, Nov. 14** ***Perf. 13½***
*393* A190 15p blue gray 12 6

Children's Day.

St. Thomas Statue, Ortona, Italy — A191

Globe and Pickax — A192

**1964, Dec. 2 Unwmk.** ***Perf. 13½***
*394* A191 15p rose violet 12 6

Visit of Pope Paul VI, Nov. 30-Dec. 2.

**1964, Dec. 14 Wmk. 324**
*395* A192 15p bright green 15 6

22nd Intl. Geological Cong., New Delhi.

Jamsetji N. Tata — A193

**1965, Jan. 7 Unwmk.** ***Perf. 13***
*396* A193 15p dark brn & org 12 6

125th anniv. of the birth of Tata (1839-1904), founder of India's steel industry.

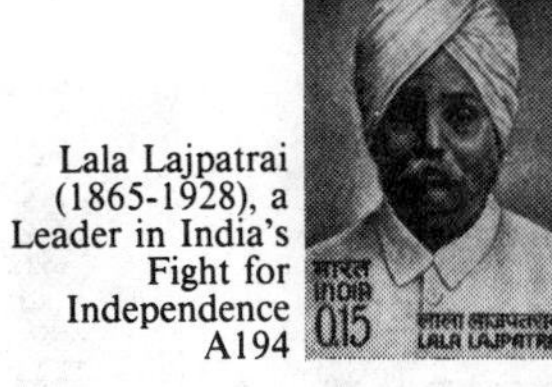

Lala Lajpatrai (1865-1928), a Leader in India's Fight for Independence A194

**1965, Jan. 28 Photo.** ***Perf. 13***
*397* A194 15p brown 12 6

ICC Emblem and Globe A195

**1965, Feb. 8 Litho.**
*398* A195 15p dull grn & car 12 6

20th cong. of the Intl. Chamber of Commerce, New Delhi.

Freighter Jalausha at Visakhapatnam — A196

***Perf. 14½x14***

**1965, Apr. 5 Photo. Wmk. 324**
*399* A196 15p ultramarine 12 6

National Maritime Day.

Centenary of Death of Abraham Lincoln — A197

**1965, Apr. 15** ***Perf. 13***
*400* A197 15p yel & dark brn 15 6

ITU Emblem, Old and New Communication Equipment — A198

**1965, May 17 Photo.** ***Perf. 14½x14***
*401* A198 15p rose violet 15 6

Cent. of the ITU.

Torch and Rose — A199

**1965, May 27 Wmk. 324** ***Perf. 13***
*402* A199 15p carmine & blue 12 6

1st anniv. of the death of Jawaharlal Nehru.

ICY Emblem A200

**1965, June 26 Photo. Unwmk.**
*403* A200 15p bis & dark grn 15 6

International Cooperation Year, 1965.

Indians Raising Flag on Everest — A201

**1965, Aug. 15 Unwmk.** ***Perf. 13***
*404* A201 15p plum 12 6

Success of the Indian Mt. Everest Expedition, May 20, 1965.

Elephant from Konarak Temple, Orissa A202

Tea Picking A203

Woman Writing Letter, Chandella Carving, 11th Century — A204

Trombay Atomic Center A205

Designs: 2p, Vase (bidri ware). 3p, Brass lamp. 4p, Coffee berries. 5p, Family (family planning). 8p, Axis deer (chital). 10p, Electric locomotive, 1961. 20p, Gnat plane. 30p, Male and female figurines. 40p, General Post Office, Calcutta, 1868. 50p, Mangoes. 60p, Somnath Temple. 70p, Stone chariot, Hampi, Mysore. 2r, Dal Lake, Kashmir. 5r, Bhakra Dam, Punjab.

***Perf. 14½x14, 14x14½***

**1965-68 Photo. Wmk. 324**

| | | | | | |
|---|---|---|---|---|---|
| *405* | A202 | 2p | redsh brn ('67) | 5 | 5 |
| *406* | A202 | 3p | olive bis ('67) | 5 | 5 |
| *407* | A203 | 4p | org brn ('68) | 5 | 5 |
| *408* | A202 | 5p | cerise ('67) | 5 | 5 |
| *409* | A202 | 6p | gray ('66) | 5 | 5 |
| *410* | A202 | 8p | red brn ('67) | 16 | 10 |
| *411* | A203 | 10p | bright bl ('66) | 15 | 5 |
| *412* | A203 | 15p | dark yel grn | 6 | 5 |
| *413* | A203 | 20p | plum ('67) | 6 | 5 |
| *414* | A202 | 30p | brown ('67) | 8 | 5 |
| *415* | A203 | 40p | brn vio ('68) | 10 | 5 |
| *416* | A202 | 50p | green ('67) | 12 | 5 |
| *417* | A202 | 60p | dark gray ('67) | 18 | 5 |
| *418* | A203 | 70p | violet ('67) | 60 | 5 |
| *419* | A204 | 1r | deep claret & red brn ('66) | 45 | 5 |
| *420* | A205 | 2r | vio & brt bl ('67) | 1.10 | 10 |
| *421* | A205 | 5r | brn & vio ('67) | 2.00 | 30 |
| *422* | A205 | 10r | green & gray | 5.00 | 75 |
| | | | *Nos. 405-422 (18)* | 10.31 | 1.95 |

See Nos. 623, 666-683.

**1975-76 Wmk. 360** ***Perf. 14½x14***
*423* A202 5p cerise 5 5

**Unwmk.**

*423A* A202 5p cerise ('76) 5 5

Govind Ballabh Pant (1887-1961), Home Minister of India — A206

**1965, Sept. 10 Unwmk.** ***Perf. 13***
*424* A206 15p dark grn & brn 12 6

Vallabhbhai Patel (1875-1950), Deputy Prime Minister of India — A207

**1965, Oct. 31** ***Perf. 14***
*425* A207 15p gray 12 6

Chittaranjan Das (1870-1925) A208

Vidyapati, 15th Cent. Poet A209

**1965, Nov. 5 Photo.** ***Perf. 13***
*426* A208 15p brown 12 6

Das, freedom fighter, pres. of Indian Natl. Cong., mayor of Calcutta.

**1965, Nov. 17** ***Perf. 14x14½***
*427* A209 15p brown 12 6

Tomb of Akbar the Great, Sikandra — A210

**1966, Jan. 24** ***Perf. 14***
*428* A210 15p dark gray 12 6

Pacific Area Travel Assoc. Conf., New Delhi.

Soldier, Planes and Warships — A211

**1966, Jan. 26**
*429* A211 15p bright violet 12 6

Honoring the Indian armed forces.

Lal Bahadur Shastri A212

Kambar A213

**1966, Jan. 26** ***Perf. 13***
*430* A212 15p gray 12 5

Prime Minister Shastri (1904-66).

**1966, Apr. 9** ***Perf. 14x14½***
*431* A213 15p green 12 6

Kambar, 9th century Tamil poet.

B. R. Ambedkar A214

Kunwar Singh A215

**1966, Apr. 14 Unwmk. *Perf. 14***
*432* A214 15p violet brown 12 6

10th anniv. of the death of Dr. Bhimrao R. Ambedkar (1891-1956), lawyer and leader in social reform.

**1966, Apr. 23 Photo.**
*433* A215 15p orange brown 12 6

Kunwar Singh (1777-1858), hero of 1857 War of Independence (1857 Mutiny).

Gopal Krishna Gokhale A216

**1966, May 9 Unwmk. *Perf. 13***
*434* A216 15p vio brn & yel 12 6

Cent. of the birth of Gokhale (1866-1915), professor of history and political economy and leader of the opposition party.

A. M. P. Dvivedi (1864-1938) A217

Ranjit Singh (1780-1839) A218

**1966, May 15 *Perf. 14***
*435* A217 15p ol gray 12 6

Acharya Mahavir Prasad Dvivedi, Hindi writer.

**1966, June 28 Unwmk. *Perf. 14***
*436* A218 15p plum 12 6

Maharaja Ranjit Singh, ruler of Punjab.

Homi Bhabha and Atomic Reactor A219

**1966, Aug. 4 *Perf. 14½x14***
*437* A219 15p brown violet 12 6

Dr. Homi Bhabha (1909-1966), scientist.

Rama Tirtha A220

**1966, Nov. 11 Unwmk. *Perf. 13***
*438* A220 15p greenish blue 12 6

60th anniv. of the death of Swami Rama Tirtha (1873-1906).

Abdul Kalam Azad (1888-1958), President of the All-India Congress A221

**1966, Nov. 11 Photo. *Perf. 13½***
*439* A221 15p dark vio blue 12 6

Child and Dove — A222

**1966, Nov. 14 *Perf. 13***
*440* A222 15p bright rose lil 12 6

Children's Day.

Allahabad High Court, Cent. A223

**1966, Nov. 25 *Perf. 14½x14***
*441* A223 15p violet brown 12 6

Family A224

**1966, Dec. 12 *Perf. 13½x13***
*442* A224 15p brown 12 8

Intl. Conf. for Marriage Guidance, New Delhi, and Family Planning Week.

Hockey A225

**1966, Dec. 31 Unwmk. *Perf. 13***
*443* A225 15p bright blue 12 6

Victory of the Indian hockey team at the 5th Asian Games, Bangkok, Dec. 19.

Grain Harvest — A226

**1967, Jan. 11 *Perf. 13½***
*444* A226 15p yellow green 12 6

1st anniv. of the death of Prime Minister Lal Bahadur Shastri, who advocated self-sufficiency in food production.

Voters — A227

Guru Dwara Shrine, Patna — A228

**1967, Jan. 13 Photo.**
*445* A227 15p light red brn 12 6

General elections, Feb. 1967.

**1967, Jan. 17 *Perf. 14***
*446* A228 15p violet 12 6

300th anniv. of the birth of Gobind Singh (1666-1708), religious leader.

Taj Mahal A229

**1967, Mar. 19 *Perf. 14½x14***
*447* A229 15p brn & org 12 6

International Tourist Year, 1967.

Nandalal Bose and Garuda — A230

**1967, Apr. 16 *Perf. 13½***
*448* A230 15p brown 10 6

Nandalal Bose (1882-1966), painter.

Survey of India Emblem A231

**1967, May 1 Unwmk. *Perf. 13***
*449* A231 15p lilac 10 6

Bicentenary of Survey of India.

Basaveswara, 12th Cent. Statesman and Philosopher, at Work — A232

**1967, May 11 *Perf. 13½x14***
*450* A232 15p dp org 10 5

Narsinha Mehta A233

Maharana Pratap A234

**1967, May 30 *Perf. 13½***
*451* A233 15p gray brown 10 5

Narsina Mehta, 15th cent. musician.

**1967, June 11 *Perf. 14x14½***
*452* A234 15p reddish brown 10 5

Pratap (1540-1597), Mewar ruler.

Narayana Guru A235

Dr. Sarvepalli Radhakrishnan A236

**1967, Aug. 21 Photo. *Perf. 14***
*453* A235 15p brown 10 5

Narayana Guru (1855-1928), religious reformer.

**1967, Sept. 5 Unwmk. *Perf. 13***
*454* A236 15p dull claret 10 5

Radhakrishnan, Pres. of India 1962-67.

Martyrs' Memorial, Patna A237

**1967, Oct. 1 Photo. *Perf. 14½x14***
*455* A237 15p dark carmine 10 5

25th anniv. of the "Quit India" revolt led by Gandhi.

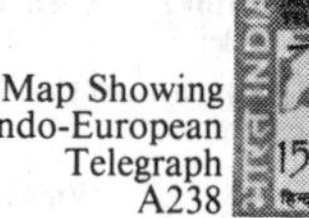

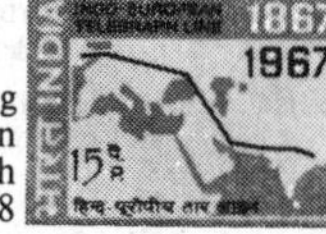


Map Showing Indo-European Telegraph A238

**1967, Nov. 9 Photo. *Perf. 13½***
*456* A238 15p blue & black 10 5

Cent. of the laying of the Indo-European telegraph line.

Wrestlers A239

**1967, Nov. 12**
*457* A239 15p ocher & plum 10 6

World Wrestling Championships, New Delhi, Nov. 1967.

Nehru and Naga Tribesmen A240

Rashbehari Basu A241

**1967, Dec. 4 Photo. *Perf. 13***
*458* A240 15p ultramarine 10 5

**1967, Dec. 26 *Perf. 13½***
*459* A241 15p dull purple 10 5

Basu (1886-1945), Bengali leader.

Bugle, Scout Emblem and Scout Sign A242

**1967, Dec. 27** *Perf. 14½x14*
*460* A242 15p orange brown 10 5

Boy Scout Movement, 60th anniv.

People Encircling the Globe and Human Rights Flame A243

**1968, Jan. 1** *Perf. 13*
*461* A243 15p dark green 10 5

Intl. Human Rights Year 1968.

Conference Emblem and Gopuram Temple — A244

**1968, Jan. 3 Photo. Unwmk.**
*462* A244 15p purple 10 5

2nd Intl. Conf. on Tamil Studies, Madras.

UN Emblem, Plane and Ship A245

**1968, Feb. 1** *Perf. 14½x14*
*463* A245 15p greenish blue 10 5

UN Conference on Trade and Development, New Delhi, Feb. 1968.

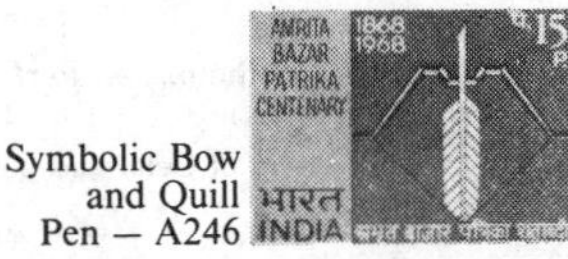
Symbolic Bow and Quill Pen — A246

**1968, Feb. 20** *Perf. 13½x14*
*464* A246 15p ocher & sepia 10 5

Cent. of the newspaper Amrit Bazar Patrika, Calcutta.

Maxim Gorky (1868-1936), Russian Writer — A247

**1968, Mar. 28 Photo.** *Perf. 14*
*465* A247 15p brown violet 10 5

Canceled-to-order stamps are often from remainders. Most collectors of canceled stamps prefer postally used specimens.

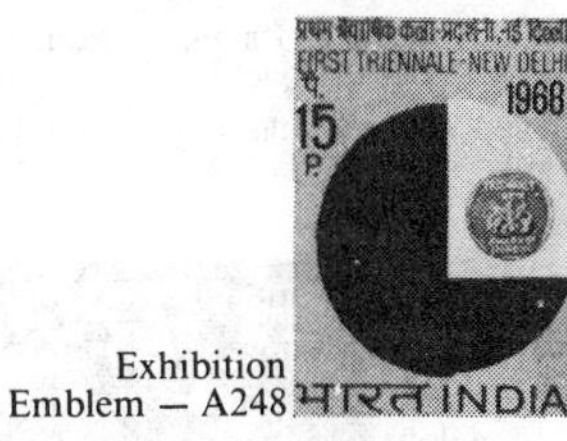
Exhibition Emblem — A248

**1968, Mar. 31** *Perf. 13*
*466* A248 15p dark blue & org 15 8

First Triennial Exhibition, New Delhi.

Symbolic Mail Box — A249

**1968, July 1 Unwmk.** *Perf. 13*
*467* A249 20p ver & blue 10 5

Opening of 100,000th Indian post office.

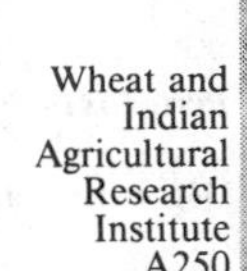

Wheat and Indian Agricultural Research Institute A250

**1968, July 15 Photo.** *Perf. 13*
*468* A250 20p brt grn & brn org 10 5

India's 1968 bumper wheat crop.

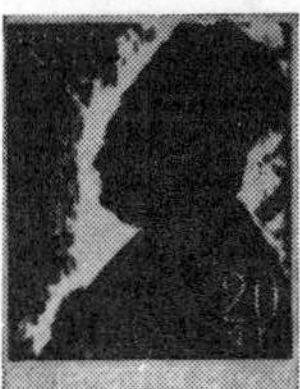
Gaganendranath Tagore (1867-1938), Self-portrait A251

**1968, Sept. 17 Unwmk.** *Perf. 13*
*469* A251 20p ocher & dp cl 10 5

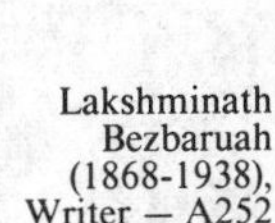

Lakshminath Bezbaruah (1868-1938), Writer — A252

**1968, Oct. 5 Photo.** *Perf. 13½*
*470* A252 20p sepia 10 5

19th Olympic Games, Mexico City A253

**1968, Oct. 12** *Perf. 14½x14*
*471* A253 20p bl gray & red brn 10 5
*472* A253 1r ol gray & dk brn 25 20

Bhagat Singh (1907-1931), Revolutionary — A254

**1968, Oct. 19 Photo.** *Perf. 13½x13*
*473* A254 20p orange brown 10 5

Bose Reading Proclamation A255

Sister Nivedita A256

**1968, Oct. 21** *Perf. 14x14½*
*474* A255 20p dark blue 10 5

25th anniv. of the establishment of the Azad Hind (Free India) government by Subhas Chandra Bose (1897-1945), independence leader.

**1968, Oct. 27**
*475* A256 20p blue green 10 5

Sister Nivedita (Margaret Noble, 1867-1911), Irish-born friend of India.

Marie Curie and Patient Receiving Radiation A257

**1968, Nov. 6** *Perf. 14½x14*
*476* A257 20p purple 10 5

Marie Sklodowska Curie (1867-1934), discoverer of radium and polonium.

World Map A258

Interior of Cochin Synagogue A259

**1968, Dec. 1** *Perf. 13*
*477* A258 20p blue 10 5

21st Intl. Geographical Congress.

*Perf. 13x13½*

**1968, Dec. 15 Photo. Unwmk.**
*478* A259 20p vio bl & car rose 10 5

400th anniv. of Cochin Synagogue.

Frigate Nilgiri A260

**1968, Dec. 15** *Perf. 13½x13*
*479* A260 20p dull vio blue 10 5

Navy Day. The Nilgiri, launched Oct. 23, 1968, was the 1st Indian warship.

Redbilled Blue Magpie A261

Birds: 50p, Brown-fronted pied woodpecker. 1r, Slaty-headed scimitar babbler (vert.). 2r, Yellow-backed sunbirds.

*Perf. 14½x14, 14x14½*

**1968, Dec. 31**
*480* A261 20p pink & multi 10 5
*481* A261 50p multicolor 24 12
*482* A261 1r multicolor 52 24
*483* A261 2r multicolor 1.00 52

Chatterjee A262

Dr. Bhagavan Das A263

**1969, Jan. 1** *Perf. 13½*
*484* A262 20p ultramarine 10 5

Bankim Chandra Chatterjee (1838-1894), writer.

**1969, Jan. 12 Photo.** *Perf. 13½*
*485* A263 20p red brown 10 5

Das (1869-1958), philosopher.

Martin Luther King, Jr. (1929-1968), American Civil Rights Leader — A264

**1969, Jan. 25**
*486* A264 20p olive gray 10 5

Mirza Ghalib A265

**1969, Feb. 17** *Perf. 14½x14*
*487* A265 20p dk gray & salmon 10 5

Mirza Ghalib (Asad Ullah Beg Khan 1797-1869), poet who modernized the Urdu language.

Osmania University, Hyderabad, 50th Avviv. A266

**1969, Mar. 15 Photo.** *Perf. 14½x14*
*488* A266 20p green 10 5

Rafi Ahmed Kidwai A267

**1969, Apr. 1** *Perf. 13*
*489* A267 20p grayish blue 10 5

Minister of communications and food, introduced around-the-clock airmail service.

ILO Emplems A268

**1969, Apr. 11** *Perf. 14½x14*
*490* A268 20p orange brown 10 5

50th anniv. of the ILO.

Memorial Monument and Hands Strewing Flowers — A269

**1969, Apr. 13** *Perf. 13½*
*491* A269 20p rose carmine 10 5

50th anniv. of Jallianwala Bagh, Amritsar, massacre.

Nageswara Rao (1867-1938), Journalist and Congressman A270

**1969, May 1 Photo.** *Perf. 13½x14*
*492* A270 20p brown 10 5

Ardaseer Cursetjee Wadia and Ships A271

**1969, May 27 Photo.** *Perf. 14½x14*
*493* A271 20p blue green 10 5

Wadia (1808-1877), shipbuilder.

Serampore College, 150th Anniv. — A272

**1969, June 7 Photo.** *Perf. 13½*
*494* A272 20p violet brown 10 5

Dr. Zakir Husain (1897-1969), President of India 1967-1969 — A273

**1969, June 11** *Perf. 13*
*495* A273 20p olive gray 10 5

Laxmanrao Kirloskar and Plow A274

**1969, June 20**
*496* A274 20p gray 10 5

Kirloskar (1869-1956), industrialist and social reformer, introduced the iron plow to India.

Mahatma Gandhi (1869-1948) A275

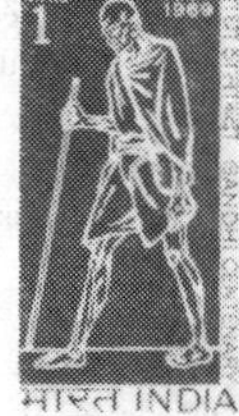

Gandhi on the Dandi March A276

Designs: 20p, Gandhi and his wife Kasturba (horiz.). 5r, Gandhi with spinning wheel (horiz.).

**1969, Oct. 2 Photo. Unwmk.**

**Size: 29x25mm**
*Perf. 13½*
*497* A275 20p sepia 7 6

**Size: 28x38mm**
*Perf. 13*
*498* A275 75p ol gray, sal & brn 28 15

**Size: 20x38mm**
*Perf. 14x14½*
*499* A276 1r bright blue 45 20

**Size: 35½x25½mm**
*Perf. 13*
*500* A275 5r org & sepia 2.00 1.40

Freighter and IMCO Emblem A277

**1969, Oct. 14** *Perf. 13*
*501* A277 20p ultramarine 10 5

10th anniv. of the Intergovernmental Maritime Consultative Organization.

Globe and Parliament, New Delhi A278

**1969, Oct. 30 Photo.** *Perf. 14½x14*
*502* A278 20p bright blue 10 5

57th Interparliamentary Conf., New Delhi.

Astronaut on Moon A279

Nanak Mausoleum, Talwandi, Punjab A280

**1969, Nov. 19** *Perf. 14x14½*
*503* A279 20p olive brown 10 5

See note after US No. C76.

**1969, Nov. 23 Photo.** *Perf. 13½*
*504* A280 20p gray violet 10 5

500th anniv. of the birth of the Guru Nanak, Sikh leader.

Tiger and Globe A281

**1969, Nov. 24** *Perf. 14½x14*
*505* A281 20p ol grn & red brn 12 6

Intl. Union for the Conservation of Nature and Natural Resources.

T. L. Vaswani A282

Thakkar Bapa A283

**1969, Nov. 25** *Perf. 14x14½*
*506* A282 20p dark gray 12 6

of T. L. Vaswani (1879-1966), writer and orator.

**1969, Nov. 29** *Perf. 13½*
*507* A283 20p dark brown 12 6

Thakkar Bapa (1869-1951), statesman who worked to help the untouchables.

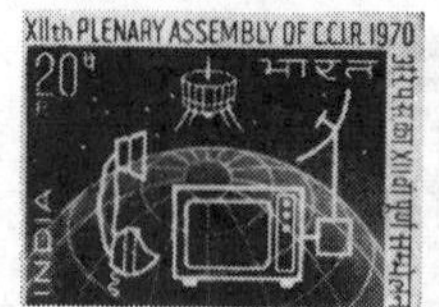

Globe and Telecommunications Symbols — A284

**1970, Jan. 21** *Perf. 13*
*508* A284 20p Prussian blue 12 6

12th Plenary Assembly of the Intl. Radio Consultative Committee.

C. N. Annadurai (1909-1969), Journalist A285

Munshi Newal Kishore and Printing Plant A286

**1970, Feb. 2**
*509* A285 20p dk bl & magenta 12 6

**1970, Feb. 19 Photo.** *Perf. 13x13½*
*510* A286 20p dark carmine 12 6

Kishore (1836-1895), publisher.

Cent. of Nalanda College A287

**1970, Mar. 27 Photo.** *Perf. 14½x14*
*511* A287 20p light red brn 12 6

Swami Shraddhanand (1856-1926), Patriot — A288

**1970, Mar. 30** *Perf. 13½*
*512* A288 20p orange brown 12 6

Lenin A289

**1970, Apr. 22 Photo.** *Perf. 13*
*513* A289 20p multicolor 12 6

UPU Headquarters, Bern — A290

**1970, May 20**
*514* A290 20p black & green 12 6

New UPU Headquarters in Bern.

Sher Shah Suri — A291

**1970, May 22 Photo.** *Perf. 13*
*515* A291 20p blue green 12 6

Suri, 15th cent. ruler of Delhi and postal service reformer.

Vir D. Savarkar and Prison at Port Blair, Andamans A292

**1970, May 28**
*516* A292 20p orange brown 12 6

V. D. Savarkar (1883-1966), patriot.

"UN" and UN Emblem — A293

**1970, June 26 Photo.** *Perf. 13*
*517* A293 20p blue 12 6

25th anniv. of the UN.

Harvest, Crane, Factory and Emblem
A294

**1970, Aug. 18** *Perf. 14½x14*
*518* A294 20p violet 12 6

Asian Productivity Year.

Dr. Maria Montessori and Education Symbol
A295

**1970, Aug. 31** *Perf. 13½x13*
*519* A295 20p dull claret 12 6

Intl. Education Year and Maria Montessori (1870-1952), Italian educator and physician.

Jatindra Nath Mukherjee
A296

**1970, Sept. 9** *Perf. 14½x14*
*520* A296 20p dark red brn 15 8

Mukherjee (1879-1915), revolutionary leader.

Srinivasa Sastri (1869-1946)
A297

Iswar Chandra Vidyasagar
A298

**1970, Sept. 22** **Photo.** *Perf. 13*
*521* A297 20p dark brn & ocher 12 6

V. S. Srinivasa Sastri, statesman.

**1970, Sept. 26**
*522* A298 20p rose lilac & brn 12 6

Vidyasagar (1820-91), educator and writer.

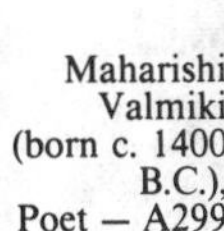

Maharishi Valmiki (born c. 1400 B.C.), Poet — A299

**1970, Oct. 14** **Photo.** *Perf. 13*
*523* A299 20p plum 12 6

Calcutta Harbor
A300

**1970, Oct. 17**
*524* A300 20p blue 12 6

Cent. of Calcutta Port Commissioners.

Jamia Millia Islamia University, 50th Anniv.
A301

**1970, Oct. 29** *Perf. 14½x14*
*525* A301 20p yellow green 12 6

Jamnalal Bajaj (1889-1942), Patriot
A302

**1970, Nov. 4** **Wmk. 324** *Perf. 13*
*526* A302 20p sepia 12 6

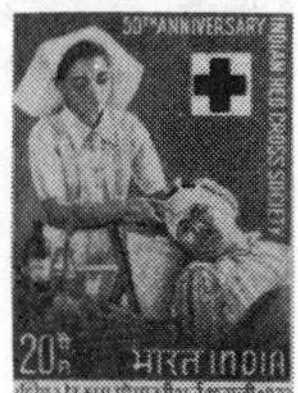

Nurse and Patient
A303

Ludwig van Beethoven
A305

Sant Namdeo (1270-1350), Holy Man — A304

**1970, Nov. 5**
*527* A303 20p Prus blue & red 12 6

50th anniv. of the Indian Red Cross Soc.

**1970, Nov. 9** **Photo.**
*528* A304 20p orange 12 6

**1970, Dec. 16** **Unwmk.** *Perf. 13*
*529* A305 20p dark brn & org 12 6

Children with Stamp Album
A306

Design: 1r, Hands holding magnifying glass over Gandhi stamp.

**1970, Dec. 23** **Photo.** *Perf. 13*
*530* A306 20p dl grn & lt brn 10 5
*531* A306 1r ocher & brown 25 15

INPEX 1970, Indian Natl. Phil. Exhib., New Delhi, Dec. 23, 1970-Jan. 6, 1971.

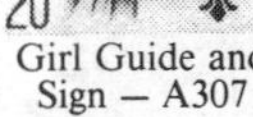
Girl Guide and Sign — A307

Hands Shielding Flame — A308

**1970, Dec. 27**
*532* A307 20p dark brn vio 12 6

Girl Guides, 60th anniv.

**1971, Jan. 11**
*533* A308 20p bister brn & dp cl 12 6

Centenary of Indian Life Insurance.

Kashi Vidyapith, 50th Anniv.
A309

**1971, Feb. 10** *Perf. 14½x14*
*534* A309 20p black brown 12 6

Kashi Vidyapith University, Benares.

Charles Freer Andrews (1871-1940), British Publicist, Friend of Gandhi — A310

**1971, Feb. 12** *Perf. 13x13½*
*535* A310 20p orange brn 12 6

Ravidas, 15th Cent. Poet and Holy Man — A311

**1971, Feb.** *Perf. 13*
*536* A311 20p rose carmine 12 6

Acharya Narendra Deo (1889-1956), Educator, Patriot, Statesman — A312

**1971, Feb. 18** **Photo.** *Perf. 13*
*537* A312 20p olive bis 12 6

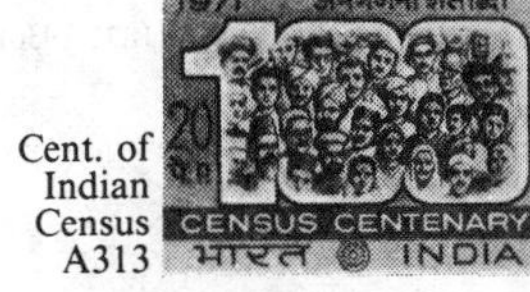
Cent. of Indian Census
A313

**1971, Mar. 10**
*538* A313 20p ultra & sepia 12 6

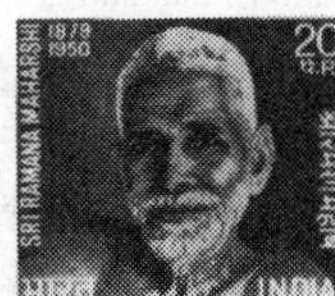
Ramana Maharshi (1879-1950), Holy Man — A314

**1971, Apr. 14** **Photo.** *Perf. 13½x14*
*539* A314 20p ol gray & org 12 6

Raja Ravi Varma (1848-1906) and His Painting, Damayanti and the Swan — A315

**1971, Apr. 29** *Perf. 13x13½*
*540* A315 20p deep yel grn 12 6

Dadasaheb Phalke, Movie Camera
A316

**1971, Apr. 30** *Perf. 13½x13*
*541* A316 20p violet brown 12 6

Dadasaheb Phalke (1870-1944), motion picture pioneer.

Abhisarika, by Abanindranath Tagore
A317

Swami Virjanand
A318

*Perf. 14x14½*
**1971, Aug. 7** **Photo.** **Unwmk.**
*542* A317 20p dark brn & ocher 12 6

Tagore (1871-1951), painter.

**1971, Sept. 14** *Perf. 14x13½*
*543* A318 20p orange brn 12 6

Virjanand (1778-1868), scholar and sage.

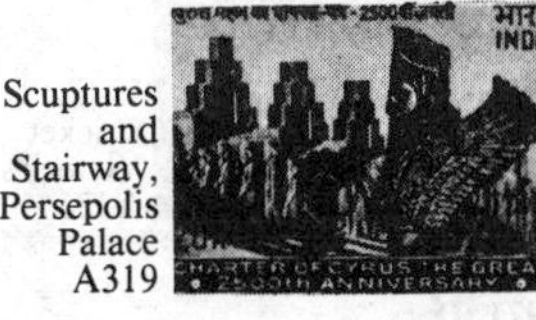
Scuptures and Stairway, Persepolis Palace
A319

**1971, Oct. 12** *Perf. 13*
*544* A319 20p sepia 10 5

2500th anniv. of the founding of the Persian empire by Cyrus the Great.

World Thrift Day
A320

**1971, Oct. 31** *Perf. 14½x14*
*545* A320 20p dark vio bl 10 5

Foreign postal stationery (stamped envelopes, postal cards and air letter sheets) lies beyond the scope of this Catalogue, which is limited to adhesive postage stamps.

Bodhisatva Padampani, from Ajanta Cave
A321

Girls at Work, by Geeta Gupta
A322

**1971, Nov. 4** ***Perf. 13***
*546* A321 20p brown 12 6

25th anniv. of UNESCO.

**1971, Nov. 14** ***Perf. 14x14½***
*547* A322 20p salmon pink 12 6

Chidren's Day.

C. V. Raman
A323

**1971, Nov. 21** ***Perf. 13***
*548* A323 20p brn & deep org 12 6

Sir Chandrasekhara Venkata Raman (1888-1970), physicist, Nobel Prize winner.

Rabindranath Tagore, Visva-Bharati Building — A324

**1971, Dec. 24** ***Perf. 14½x14***
*549* A324 20p blk brn & org brn 12 5

50th anniv. of Visva-Bharati, center for Eastern cultural studies.

Indian Cricket Victories
A325

**1971, Dec. 24**
*550* A325 20p green 12 5

Intelsat 3 over Map of Eastern Hemisphere
A326

**1972, Feb. 26** **Photo.** ***Perf. 13½***
*551* A326 20p dark purple 12 5

Arvi Satellite Earth Station.

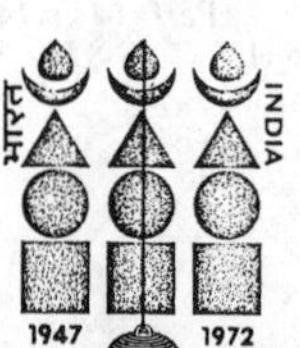

Plumb Line and Symbols
A327

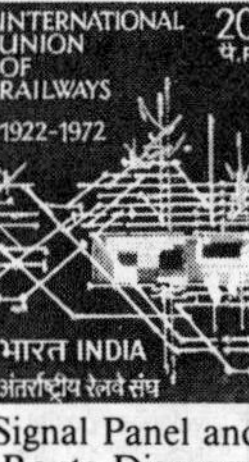

Signal Panel and Route Diagram
A328

**1972, May 29** **Photo.** ***Perf. 13***
*552* A327 20p bluish gray & blk 12 5

India's Bureau of Standards, 25th anniv.

**1972, June 30**
*553* A328 20p black & multi 12 5

50th anniv. of the founding of the Intl. Railroad Union (UIC).

Hockey, Olympic Rings
A329

20th Olympic Games, Munich, Aug. 26-Sept. 11: 1.45r, "1972", Olympic rings, symbols for running, wrestling, shooting and hockey.

**1972, Aug. 10** **Photo.** ***Perf. 13***
*554* A329 20p dull violet 12 5
*555* A329 1.45r bl grn & dk red 32 20

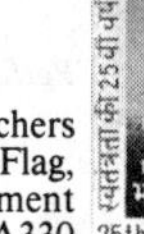

Marchers with Flag, Parliament
A330

**1972, Aug. 15**
*556* A330 20p blue & multi 12 5

25th anniv. of Independence.

Armed Forces' Emblems
A331

Symbol of Aurobindo and Sun
A332

**1972, Aug. 15**
*557* A331 20p blue & multi 12 5

Honoring India's defense forces.

**1972, Aug. 15** ***Perf. 14x13½***
*558* A332 20p yellow & blue 12 5

Sri Aurobindo Ghose (1872-1950).

V.O. Chidambaram Pillai and Ship — A333

***Perf. 13½x13***
**1972, Sept. 5** **Photo.** **Unwmk.**
*559* A333 20p bl & dk red brn 12 5

V.O. Chidambaram Pillai (1872-1936), founder of steamship company, trade union leader, resistance fighter.

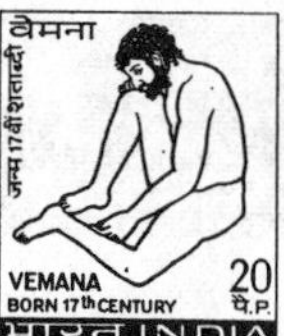

Vemana, 17th-18th Cent. Poet — A334

Bertrand Russell — A335

**1972, Oct. 16** **Wmk. 324** ***Perf. 14***
*560* A334 20p black 12 5

**1972, Oct. 16** **Unwmk.**
*561* A335 1.45r black 32 20

British philosopher and pacifist (1872-1970).

Bhai Vir Singh
A336

T. Prakasam
A337

**1972, Oct. 16** ***Perf. 13½***
*562* A336 20p dull purple 12 5

Singh (1872-1957), poet and scholar.

**1972, Oct. 16**
*563* A337 20p yellow brown 12 5

T. Prakasam (1872-1957), national leader and lawyer.

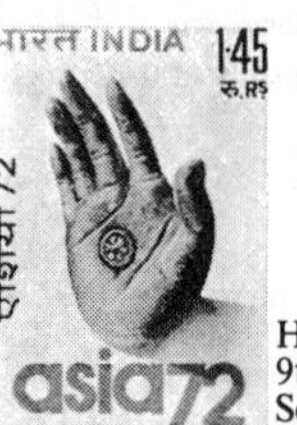

Hand of Buddha, 9th Century Sculpture — A338

Design: 20p, Stylized Hand of Buddha as Fair emblem.

**1972, Nov. 3** **Wmk. 324** ***Perf. 13***
*564* A338 20p orange & blk 12 5
*565* A338 1.45r org, blk & ind 32 20

3rd Asian Intl. Trade Fair, ASIA 72, New Delhi.

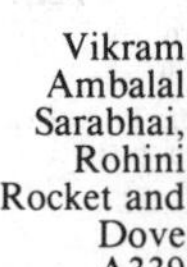

Vikram Ambalal Sarabhai, Rohini Rocket and Dove
A339

**1972, Dec. 30** **Unwmk.**
*566* A339 20p slate grn & brn 12 5

1st anniv. of the death of Dr. Vikram Ambalal Sarabhai (1919-1971), chairman of Natl. Committee for Space Research.

Flag of USSR and Spasski Tower
A340

**1972, Dec. 30** ***Perf. 13***
*567* A340 20p red & yellow 12 5

50th anniv. of the Soviet Union.

INDIPEX 73 Emblem
A341

Wheel of Asoka, Naga (Serpent)
A342

India Gate, Gnat Planes, India's Colors
A343

**1973, Jan. 8** **Photo.** ***Perf. 13***
*568* A341 1.45r blk, pink & gold 28 22

Intl. Phil. Exhib., New Delhi, Nov. 14-23, 1973.
See Nos. 597-599.

**1973, Jan. 26** ***Perf. 13***
*569* A342 20p orange & multi 12 5
***Perf. 14½x14***
*570* A343 1.45r violet & multi 28 22

Republic Day, 25th year of Independence.

Ramakrishna Paramahamsa (1836-86)
A344

Army Postal Service Corps Emblem
A345

**1973, Feb. 18** **Photo.** ***Perf. 13***
*571* A344 20p yellow brown 12 5

Hindu spiritual leader; Ramakrishna Mission founded by his followers.

**1973, Mar. 1**
*572* A345 20p vio blue & red 12 5

1st anniv. of establishment of Army Postal Service Corps.

Flower, Flag, Map — A346

Kumaran Asan — A347

**1973, Apr. 10** **Unwmk.** ***Perf. 13***
*573* A346 20p blue & multi 12 5

1st anniv. of Bangladesh independence.

**1973, Apr. 12**
*574* A347 20p brown 12 5

Kumaran Asan (1873-1924), Kerala social reformer and writer.

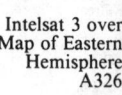

Flame and Flag of India — A348

**1973, Apr. 13**
*575* A348 20p deep bl & multi 12 5

In honor of the martyrs of the massacre of Jallianwala Bagh, Apr. 13, 1919.

B. R. Ambedkar and Parliament Building A349

**1973, Apr. 14** *Perf. 14½x14*
*576* A349 20p olive & plum 12 5

Bhimrao R. Ambedkar (1891-1956), lawyer, reformer of Hindu law and one of the writers of India's Constitution.

Radha-Kishangarh, by Nihal Chand, 1778 — A350

Indian Miniatures: 50p, Dancing Couple, late 17th century. 1r, Lovers on a Camel, by Nasir-ud-Din, c. 1605. 2r, Chained Elephant, by Zain-al-Abidin, 16th century.

**1973, May 5** **Photo.** *Perf. 13½x13*
*577* A350 20p gold & multi 8 5
*578* A350 50p lilac & multi 15 12
*579* A350 1r ocher & multi 60 24
*580* A350 2r gold & multi 1.25 48

Himalayas A351

**1973, May 15** *Perf. 13½x13*
*581* A351 20p blue 12 5

15th anniv. of Indian Mountaineering Foundation.

Air India Jet — A352

**1973, June 8** **Photo.** *Perf. 13*
*582* A352 1.45r multicolored 32 22

Air India, 25 years of intl. service.

Stone Cross on St. Thomas's Mount, Madras — A353

Michael Madhusudan Dutt — A354

**1973, July 3**
*583* A353 20p gray ol & bl gray 12 5

1900th anniv. of the death of St. Thomas.

**1973, July 21** **Photo.** *Perf. 13*
*584* A354 20p ocher & olive 12 5

Dutt (1824-73), writer and poet.

Vishnu Dingambar Paluskar (1872-1931), Musician A355

**1973, July 21**
*585* A355 30p red brown 14 5

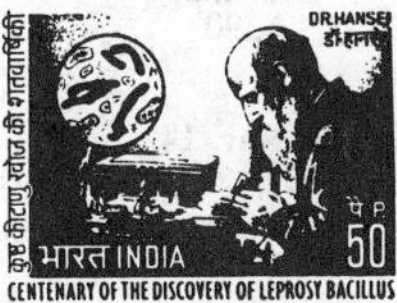

Dr. Armauer G. Hansen, Microscope, Petri Dish with Bacilli A356

**1973, July 21**
*586* A356 50p deep brown 23 12

Cent. of the discovery by Hansen of the Hansen bacillus, the cause of leprosy.

Nicolaus Copernicus, Heliocentric System A357

**1973, July 21**
*587* A357 1r vio bl & red brn 45 25

500th anniv. of the birth of Nicolaus Copernicus (1473-1543), Polish astronomer.

Allan Octavian Hume — A358

**1973, July 31**
*588* A358 20p gray 12 5

Allan Octavian Hume (1829-1912), British civil servant and friend of India, on the 25th anniv. of independence.

Nehru and Gandhi A359

**1973, Aug. 15** **Photo.** *Perf. 13*
*589* A359 20p bl vio & red brn 12 5

25th anniv. of India's independence.

Romesh Chunder Dutt — A360

Ranjit Sinhji — A361

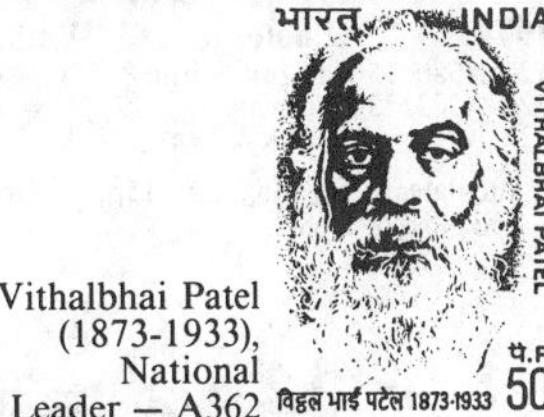

Vithalbhai Patel (1873-1933), National Leader — A362

**1973, Sept. 27** **Photo.** *Perf. 13*
*590* A360 20p brown 6 5
*591* A361 30p dark green 18 8
*592* A362 50p brown 12 10

Birth anniv.: Dutt (1848-1909), economist and pres. of Natl. Cong. in 1890; Sinhji, Maharaja of Nawanagar (1872-1933), cricketer.

President's Body Guard — A363

INTERPOL Emblem — A364

**1973, Sept. 30**
*593* A363 20p multicolored 20 5

Bicentenary of President's Body Guard.

**1973, Oct. 9** **Photo.** *Perf. 13*
*594* A364 20p brown 12 5

50th anniv. of Intl. Criminal Police Org.

Syed Ahmad Khan, Aligarh University A365

**1973, Oct. 17**
*595* A365 20p olive gray 12 5

Khan (1817-1898), founder of Aligarh Muslim Univ.

Child's Drawing A366

**1973, Nov. 14** **Photo.** *Perf. 13*
*596* A366 20p multicolored 12 5

Children's Day.

Elephant with Howdah, and No. 200 — A367

**1973, Nov. 14**
*597* A367 20p Emblem 9 5
*598* A367 1r shown 38 12
*599* A367 2r Peacock, vert. 65 25
*a* Souvenir sheet of 4 2.00 2.00

Intl. Phil. Exhib., INDIPEX 73, New Delhi, Nov. 14-23. No. 599a contains 4 imperf. stamps similar to Nos. 568, 597-599. Bluish gray marginal design and violet blue inscription. Size: 127x127mm. The imperf. stamps from No. 599a were not valid individually.

NCC Emblem A368

Rajagopalachari A369

**1973, Nov. 25**
*600* A368 20p multicolored 12 5

National Cadet Corps, 25th anniv.

**1973, Dec. 25**
*601* A369 20p gray olive 12 5

Chakravarti Rajagopalachari (1878-1972), statesman, governor general (1948-50).

Sun Mask — A370

Narasimha Mask — A371

Designs: Masks.

**1974, Apr. 15** **Photo.** *Perf. 13*
*602* A370 20p *shown* 6 5
*603* A370 50p *Moon* 12 6
*604* A371 1r *shown* 22 22
*605* A371 2r *Ravana* (horiz.) 45 45
*a* Souvenir sheet of 4 1.75 1.75

No. 605a contains one each of Nos. 602-605. Silver ornamental margin and inscription. Size: 108x134mm.

300th Anniv. of the Coronation of Chatrapati Sivaji Maharaj (1627-1680), Military Leader of the Maharattas and Enlightened Ruler — A372

**1974, June 2** **Photo.** *Perf. 13*
*606* A372 25p gold & multi 12 6

Maithili Sharan Gupta — A373

Utkal Gourab Madhusudan Das — A374

Kandukuri Veeresalingam A375

Tipu Sultan A376

Designs: No. 608, Jainarain Vyas. 1r, Max Mueller.

**1974 Photo. *Perf. 13***

*607* A373 25p red brown 7 6
*608* A373 25p brown 7 6
*609* A374 25p olive gray 7 6
*610* A375 25p red brown 7 6
*611* A376 50p violet brn 15 7
*612* A376 1r brown 30 15
*Nos. 607-612 (6)* 73 46

Gupta (1886-1964), poet and patriot; Vyas (1899-1963), writer and member of parliament; Das (1848-1934), writer and patriot. Veeresalingam (1848-1919), reformer; Sultan (1750-99), military leader and reformer; Mueller (1823-1900), German scholar of Sanskrit and Indian culture.

Issue dates: Nos. 607-609, July 3; Nos. 610-612, July 15.

Kamala Nehru — A377

**1974, Aug 1 Photo. *Perf. 14½x14***

*613* A377 25p multicolored 12 6

Kamala Nehru (1899-1936), champion of India's freedom, mother of Indira Gandhi.

WPY Emblem — A378

V. V. Giri — A379

***Perf. 13½***

**1974, Aug. 14 Photo. Unwmk.**

*614* A378 25p buff & plum 12 6

**1974, Aug. 24 *Perf. 13x13½***

*615* A379 25p green & multi 12 6

Vaharagiri Venkata Giri, pres. of India, 1969-74.

Type of 1965-68 and

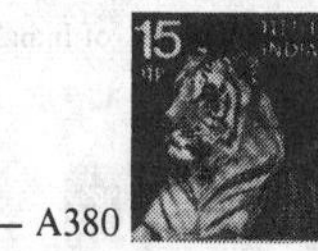

Tiger — A380

Veena A381

Design: 25p, Axis deer (chital).

***Perf. 14½x14***

**1974 Photo. Wmk. 324**

*622* A380 15p dk brn (white "15") 10 5
*623* A202 25p brown 10 5
*624* A381 1r black & brn 28 15

Issue dates: 25p, Aug. 20. 15p, 1r, Oct. 1.
See Nos. 671-682.

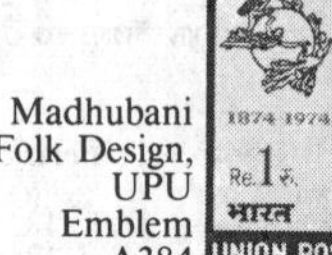

Madhubani Folk Design, UPU Emblem A384

Designs: 25p, UPU emblem. 2r, Arrows circling globe, UPU emblem (vert.).

**Unwmk.**

**1974, Oct. 3 Photo. *Perf. 13***

*634* A384 25p brt bl & gray 12 6
*635* A384 1r olive & multi 50 12
*636* A384 2r ocher & multi 75 25
*a* Souv. sheet of 3, Nos. 634-636 2.00 2.00

Cent. of UPU. No. 636a has Buff margin with dark brown inscription. Size: 107x109mm.

Flute Player — A385 Vidyadhara with Garland — A386

**1974, Oct. 9 Photo. *Perf. 13½***

*637* A385 25p vio brn & red brn 15 10
*638* A386 25p vio brn & red brn 15 10

Cent. of Mathura Museum. Nos. 637-638 printed se-tenant in sheets of 48.

Nicholas Konstantin Roerich, by Henry Dropsy A387

**1974, Oct. 9 *Perf. 13***

*639* A387 1r dark gray & yel 22 12

Roerich (1874-1947), Russian painter and sponsor of Roerich Peace Pact.

Pavapuri Temple, Bihar A388

**1974, Nov. 13 Photo. *Perf. 13***

*640* A388 25p slate 12 6

2500th anniv. of Bhagwan Mahavira's attainment of Nirvana; he was a leader and preacher of Jainism.

Dancers and Musician (Child's Drawing) A389

**1974, Nov. 14 *Perf. 14½x14***

*641* A389 25p multicolored 12 6

UNICEF in India.

Cat (Child's Drawing) A390

Territorial Army Emblem A391

**1974, Nov. 14 *Perf. 13***

*642* A390 25p multicolored 12 6

Children's Day.

**1974, Nov. 16 *Perf. 13***

*643* A391 25p grn, yel & black 12 6

Territorial Army, 25th anniv.

Cows, from Handpainted Rajasthan Cloth — A392

**1974, Dec. 2 *Perf. 14***

*644* A392 25p ocher & maroon 12 6

19th Intl. Dairy Cong., New Delhi, Dec. 2-6.

Symbol of Retardates and Child A393

**1974, Dec. 8 Photo. *Perf. 13½x13***

*645* A393 25p blk & vermilion 12 6

Help the Retardates!

Guglielmo Marconi — A394

**1974, Dec. 12 *Perf. 13x13½***

*646* A394 2r slate 38 38

Marconi (1874-1937), Italian electrical engineer and inventor.

St. Francis Xavier's Tomb and Statue A395

**1974, Dec. 24 *Perf. 13½x13***

*647* A395 25p multicolored 12 6

Showing of the body of St. Francis Xavier, Apostle to the Indies.

Saraswati, Goddess of Language and Learning, Inscription in Hindi — A396

**1975, Jan. 10 Photo. *Perf. 14x14½***

*648* A396 25p dark red & gray 12 6

World Hindi Convention, Nagpur, Jan. 10-14. See No. 654.

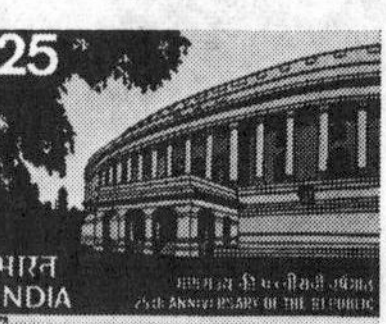

Parliament House A397

**1975, Jan. 26 *Perf. 13***

*649* A397 25p blk, bl & silver 12 6

Republic of India, 25th anniv.

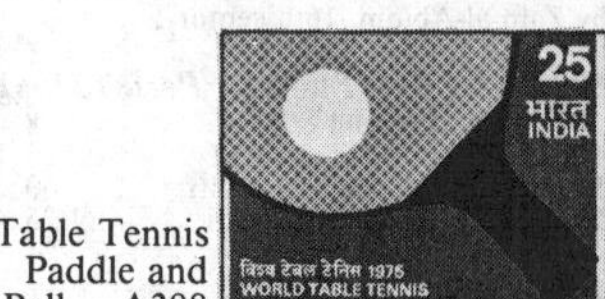

Table Tennis Paddle and Ball — A398

**1975, Feb. 6 *Perf. 13½x13***

*650* A398 25p blk, red & olive 15 6

33rd World Table Tennis Championship, Calcutta.

Woman's Hands Releasing Doves A399

**1975, Feb. 16**

*651* A399 25p yellow & multi 12 6

International Women's Year 1975.

Bicentenary of Army Ordnance Corps — A400

**1975, Apr. 8 Photo.** ***Perf. 13x13½***
*652* A400 25p blk & vermilion 12 6

Flame A401

**1975, Apr. 11** ***Perf. 13½x13***
*653* A401 25p orange & black 12 6

Cent. of the founding of Arya Samaj, a movement dedicated to enlightenment and progress and to a revival of Vedic Law and Aryan culture.

Saraswati Type of 1975

Design: 25p, Saraswati and inscription in Telugu.

**1975, Apr. 12** ***Perf. 14x14½***
*654* A396 25p dp grn & dk gray 12 6

World Telugu Conference, Hyderabad, Apr. 12-18.

Aryabhata Satellite A402

**1975, Apr. 20** ***Perf. 13½x13***
*655* A402 25p multicolored 12 6

Launching of 1st Indian satellite, Apr. 19, 1975.

Bluewinged Pitta — A403

Birds: 50p, Black-headed oriole. 1r, Western tragopan (vert.). 2r, Himalayan monal pheasant (vert.).

***Perf. 13½x13, 13x13½***

**1975, Apr. 28**
*656* A403 25p multicolored 10 6
*657* A403 50p multicolored 25 6
*658* A403 1r multicolored 65 12
*659* A403 2r multicolored 85 25

Quotation from Ram Charit Manas A404

**1975, May 24 Photo.** ***Perf. 13½x13***
*660* A404 25p red, orange & blk 12 6

Ram Charit Manas, Hindi poem by Goswami Tulsidas (1532-1623).

Women and YWCA Emblem — A405

**1975, June 20 Photo.** ***Perf. 13x13½***
*661* A405 25p gray & multi 12 6

YWCA of India, cent.

Creation of Adam, by Michelangelo
A406 A407

Design: Nos. 664-665, Creation of sun, moon and stars, by Michelangelo.

**1975, June 28** ***Perf. 14x13½***
*662* A406 50p multicolored 22 12
*663* A407 50p multicolored 22 12
*664* A406 50p multicolored 22 12
*665* A407 50p multicolored 22 12

Michelangelo Buonarroti (1475-1564), Italian sculptor, painter and architect. Nos. 662-665 printed se-tenant in blocks of 4, sheets of 72.

Types of 1965-1974 Redrawn and

Flying Crane — A408

Jawaharlal Nehru — A409

Mahatma Gandhi — A410

Himalayas A411

Designs: 2p, Bidri vase. 5p, Family. 10p, Electric locomotive. 15p, Tiger. 20p, Wooden toy horse. 30p, Male and female figurines. 60p, Somnath Temple. 1r, Veena. 5r, Bhakra Dam, Punjab. 10r, Trombay Atomic Center.

Three types of 25p Nehru:
I. Size at top, 25mm. Character before NEHRU has 2 lower points.
II. Smaller portrait. Size at top, 23mm. Character has 3 points.
III. Portrait as in type I. Size at top, 25½mm. Character has 3 points.

Without Currency Designation

Design: No. 670A, Electric locomotive, 1961.

***Perf. 14½x14, 14x14½; 14 (#674-676): 11½x12 (#681)***
**Wmk. 324; 360 (#667-668)**

**1975-88** **Photo.**
*666* A202 2(p) redsh brn, wmk. 324 ('76) 5 5
*667* A202 2(p) redsh brn, wmk. 360 ('79) 5 5
*668* A202 5(p) cerise ('76) 5 5
*670* A203 10(p) brt bl ('76) 5 5
*670A* A203 10(p) brt blue, Wmk. 360 ('79) 5 5
*671* A380 15(p) dk brn (brn. "15") 6 5
*672* A408 20(p) green 6 5
*673* A409 25(p) vio, I ('76) 8 5
*674* A409 25(p) vio, II ('76) 8 5
*675* A409 25(p) vio, III ('76) 8 5
*676* A410 25(p) red brn (23x29mm) ('76) 8 5
*677* A410 25(p) red brn (17x20mm) ('78) 8 5
*678* A202 30(p) brown ('79) 9 5
*679* A408 50(p) violet blue 14 5
*680* A202 60(p) dk gray ('76) 9 5
*681* A410 60(p) blk ('88) 10 5
*682* A381 1(r) brn & blk 28 6
*683* A411 2(r) vio & brn 55 12
*684* A205 5(r) brn & vio ('76) 70 20
*685* A205 10(r) dl grn & sl ('76) 1.40 60
*Nos. 666-685 (20)* 4.12 1.78

See Nos. 836-850.

Irrigation Commission Emblem A412

"Educational Television" A413

**Unwmk.**
**1975, July 28 Photo.** ***Perf. 14***
*686* A412 25p multicolored 12 6

9th Intl. Cong. on Irrigation and Drainage, Moscow, and 25th anniv. of the Intl. Commission on Irrigation and Drainage.

**1975, Aug. 1** ***Perf. 13x13½***
*687* A413 25p multicolored 12 6

Inauguration of the Satellite Instructional Television Experiment (SITE).

Arunagirinathar A414

**1975, Aug. 14 Photo.** ***Perf. 13½***
*688* A414 50p rose lilac 22 12

600th birth anniv. of Arunagirinathar, Advaita philosopher, saint and author of Tiruppugazh, a collection of songs.

"Namibia Day" — A415

**1975, Aug. 26 Photo.** ***Perf. 13½***
*689* A415 25p rose & black 12 6

Namibia Day. See note after UN No. 241.

Mir Anees (1803-1874), Urdu Poet — A416

**1975, Sept. 4**
*690* A416 25p slate green 12 6

Chhatri at Maheshwar A417

Bharata Natyam Dance A418

**1975, Sept. 4** ***Perf. 13x13½***
*691* A417 25p red brown 12 6

Queen Ahilyabai Holkar (1725-1795); building shown was place of last rites.

**1975, Oct. 20 Photo.** ***Perf. 13x13½***

Designs: Indian traditional dances.

*692* A418 25p *shown* 8 6
*693* A418 50p *Orissi* 18 6
*694* A418 75p *Kathak* 20 9
*695* A418 1r *Kathakali* 32 12
*696* A418 1.50r *Kuchipudi* 50 18
*697* A418 2r *Manipuri* 65 24
*Nos. 692-697 (6)* 1.93 75

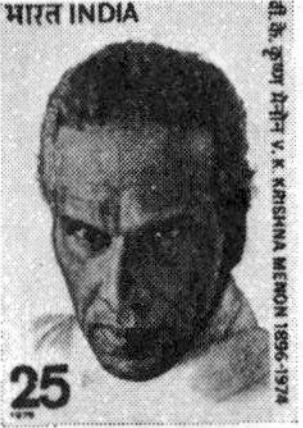

Krishna Menon — A419

Ameer Khusrau — A420

Poem by Bahadur Shah Zafar A421

Design: No. 699, Sardar Vallabhbhai Patel.

**1975** ***Perf. 13x13½, 13½x13***
*698* A419 25p olive 6 6
*699* A419 25p slate 6 6
*700* A420 50p yellow & brn 12 6
*701* A421 1r blk, brn & buff 24 12

Men of India: V. K. Krishna Menon (1896-1974), founder of India League and member of Parliament; Patel (1875-1950), statesman who unified India , birth cent.; Khusrau (1253-1325), poet; Zafar (1775-1862), last Mogul emperor and poet.

Issue dates: No. 699, Oct. 31; others Oct. 24.

Parliament Annex, New Delhi A422

**1975, Oct. 28** ***Perf. 14½x14***
*702* A422 2r gray olive 48 24

21st Commonwealth Parliamentary Conf., New Delhi, Oct. 28-Nov. 4.

Karmavir Nabin Chandra Bardoloi (1875-1936), Writer and Gandhi Associate — A423

**1975, Nov. 3** **Photo.** ***Perf. 13***
*703* A423 25p reddish brown 12 6

Cow, Child's Painting A424

**1975, Nov. 14**
*704* A424 25p multicolored 12 6

Children's Day.

Security Press Building A425

**1975, Dec. 13** **Photo.** ***Perf. 13***
*705* A425 25p multicolored 12 6

India Security Press, 50th anniv.

Gurdwara Sisganj, Chandni Chawk — A426

Theosophical Society Emblem — A427

**1975, Dec. 16**
*706* A426 25p multicolored 12 6

300th anniv. of martyrdom of Tegh Bahadur (1621-75), 9th Sikh Guru; building shown was place of beheading.

**1975, Dec. 20**
*707* A427 25p multicolored 12 6

Centenary of Theosophical Society.

Meteorological Instruments A428

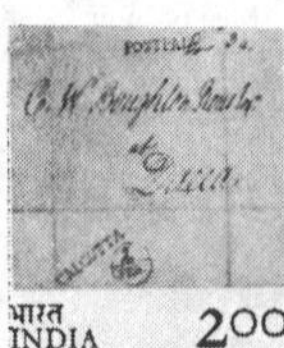

Indian Bishop Mark, 1775 A430

Early Mail Cart A429

**1975, Dec. 24** **Photo.** ***Perf. 13***
*708* A428 25p bl vio, blk & grn 12 6

Indian Meteorological Department, centenary.

**1975, Dec. 25**
*709* A429 25p brown & black 12 6
*710* A430 2r redsh brn & blk 48 24

INPEX 75, Indian Natl. Phil. Exhib., Calcutta, Dec. 25-31.

Lalit Narayan Mishra — A431

Tiger — A432

**1976, Jan. 3**
*711* A431 25p sepia 12 6

Mishra (1923-75), Minister of Railroads.

**1976, Jan. 24**
*712* A432 25p multi 12 6

Jim Corbett (1875-1955), conservationist.

Painted Storks A433

**1976, Feb. 10** **Photo.** ***Perf. 13***
*713* A433 25p sky blue & multi 12 6

Keoladeo Ghana, Bharatpur Water Bird Sanctuary.

Tank A434

**1976, Mar. 4** **Photo.** ***Perf. 13***
*714* A434 25p multicolored 12 6

16th Light Cavalry, senior regiment of Armoured Corps, bicentenary.

Alexander Graham Bell A435

Muthuswami Dikshitar A436

**1976, Mar. 10** **Photo.** ***Perf. 13x13½***
*715* A435 25p yellow & blk 12 6

Cent. of 1st telephone call by Bell, Mar. 10, 1876.

**1976, Mar. 18** ***Perf. 14x13½***
*716* A436 25p dull violet 12 6

Dikshitar (1775-1835), musician, composer.

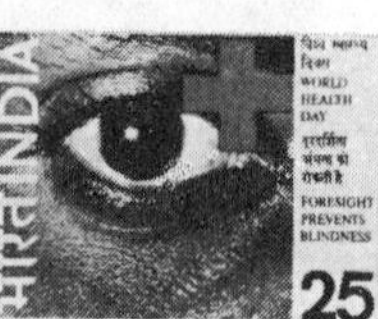

Eye and Red Cross A437

**1976, Apr. 7** ***Perf. 13½x13***
*717* A437 25p dark brn & red 12 6

World Health Day: "Foresight prevents blindness."

"Industries" A438

***Perf. 13x13½***
**1976, Apr. 30** **Unwmk.**
*718* A438 25p multicolored 12 6

Industrial development and progress.

WDM 2 Diesel Locomotive, 1963 — A439

Locomotives: 50p, 1 F/I type, Ajmer, 1895. 1r, 1 WP./1, 4-6-2 Pacific type, 1963. 2r, 1 GIP No. 1, 1853.

**1976, May 15** ***Perf. 15x14***
*719* A439 25p multicolored 8 6
*720* A439 50p multicolored 18 6
*721* A439 1r multicolored 38 12
*722* A439 2r multicolored 75 25

Kumaraswamy Kamaraj (1903-1975), Independence Fighter — A440

**1976, July 15** **Photo.** ***Perf. 13x13½***
*723* A440 25p sepia 12 6

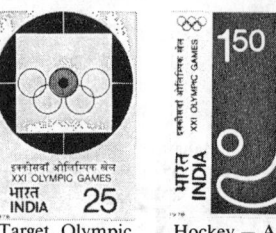

Target, Olympic Rings — A441

Hockey — A442

**1976, July 17**
*724* A441 25p dk bl & car 6 6
*725* A441 1r "Team handball" 28 14
*726* A442 1.50r blk & brt pur 38 22
*727* A441 2.80r "Running" 70 38

21st Olympic Games, Montreal, Canada, July 17-Aug. 1.

Subhadra Kumari Chauhan — A443

Param Vir Chakra Medal — A444

**1976, Aug. 6** **Photo.** ***Perf. 13x13½***
*728* A443 25p grayish blue 12 6

Chauhan (1904-1948), Hindi poetess and member of Legislative Assembly.

**1976, Aug. 15**
*729* A444 25p yellow & multi 12 6

Medal of Honor awarded for bravery to military men.

Women's University, Bombay A445

**1976, Sept. 3** **Photo.** ***Perf. 13½x14***
*730* A445 25p violet 12 6

Indian Women's Univ., 60th anniv.

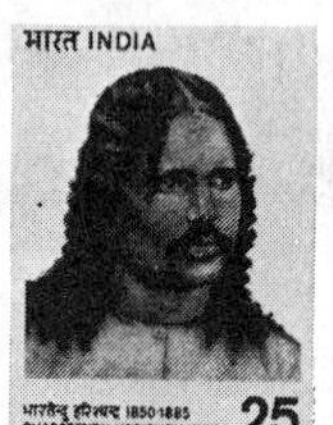

Bharatendu Harishchandra A446

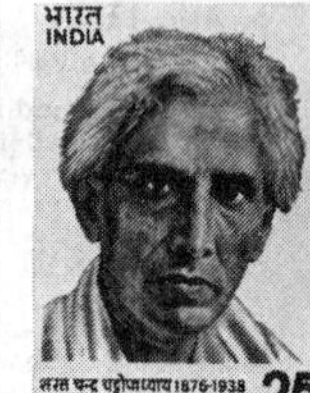

Sarat Chandra Chatterji A447

**1976, Sept. 9** ***Perf. 13***
*731* A446 25p black brown 12 6

Harishchandra (1850-1885), writer, "Father of Modern Hindi."

**1976, Sept. 15** **Unwmk.**
*732* A447 25p dull purple 12 6

Chatterji (1876-1938), writer.

Family Planning — A448

**1976, Sept. 22** **Photo.** ***Perf. 14x14½***
*733* A448 25p multicolored 12 6

Maharaja Agrasen, Coin and Brick Wall A449

**1976, Sept. 24** ***Perf. 13½x13***
*734* A449 25p red brown 12 6

Maharaja Agrasen, legendary ruler of Agra.

India Blood Donation Day — A450

Wildlife Protection
A451

**1976, Oct. 1** *Perf. 13x13½*
*735* A450 25p bis, car & blk 12 6

**1976, Oct. 1** *Perf. 14x14½, 14½x14*

1r and 2r are horiz.

*736* A451 25p Swamp deer 6 6
*737* A451 50p Lion 20 6
*738* A451 1r Leopard 32 14
*739* A451 2r Caracal 70 28

Suryakant Tripathi "Nirala" (1896-1961), Hindi Poet — A452

**1976, Oct. 15** *Perf. 13*
*740* A452 25p dark violet 12 6

Mongoose and Woman
A453

**1976, Nov. 14** **Unwmk.** *Perf. 14*
*741* A453 25p multicolored 12 6

Children's Day.

Hiralal Shastri — A454

Hari Singh Gour — A455

**1976, Nov. 24** *Perf. 13*
*742* A454 25p red brown 12 6

Hiralal Shastri (1899-1974), social worker and political leader.

**1976, Nov. 26**
*743* A455 25p plum 12 6

Hari Singh Gour (1870-1949), University administrator, member Indian Legislative and Constituent Assemblies.

Airbus
A456

**1976, Dec. 1** *Perf. 14½x14*
*744* A456 2r multicolored 48 25

Inauguration of Indian Airlines Airbus.

Hybrid Coconut Palm — A457

**1976, Dec. 27** **Photo.** *Perf. 13x13½*
*745* A457 25p multicolored 12 6

75th anniv. of coconut research in India.

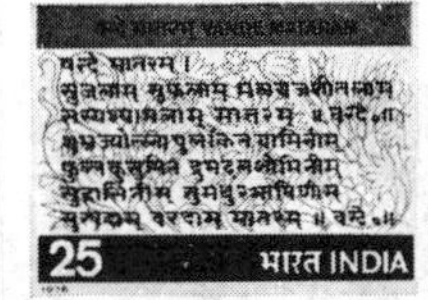

Vande Mataram, First Stanza
A458

**1976, Dec. 30** *Perf. 13*
*746* A458 25p multicolored 12 6

Vande Mataram, national song of India, music by Bankim Chandra Chatterjee, 1896, words by Rabindranath Tagore, 1911.

Film and Globe
A459

**1977, Jan. 3**
*747* A459 2r multicolored 48 25

6th Intl. Film Festival, New Delhi, Jan. 3-16.

Earth's Crust with Fault, Seismograph
A460

**1977, Jan. 10**
*748* A460 2r dull purple 48 25

6th World Conference on Earthquake Engineering, New Delhi, Jan. 10-14.

Tarun Ram Phookun
A461

Paramahansa Yogananda
A462

**1977, Jan. 22** **Photo.** *Perf. 13x13½*
*749* A461 25p sepia 12 6

Phookun (1877-1939), lawyer, Assam political leader.

**1977, Mar. 7** **Photo.** *Perf. 13½*
*750* A462 25p deep orange 10 6

Yogananda (1893-1952), religious leader, founder of Self-realization Society in America.

Red Cross Conference Emblem — A463

Fakhruddin Ali Ahmed (1905-77) — A464

**1977, Mar. 9**
*751* A463 2r multicolored 30 20

1st Asian Regional Red Cross Conference, New Delhi, Mar. 9-16.

**1977, Mar. 22** **Photo.** *Perf. 13½x13*
*752* A464 25p multicolored 10 6

Ahmed, Pres. of India, 1974-77.

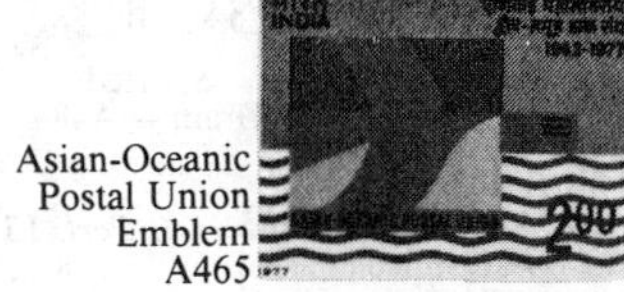

Asian-Oceanic Postal Union Emblem
A465

**1977, Apr. 1** *Perf. 13*
*753* A465 2r silver & multi 30 20

Asian-Oceanic Postal Union, 15th anniv.

"Loyalty" and Morarjee
A466

**1977, Apr. 2** *Perf. 13½x13*
*754* A466 25p blue 10 6

Narottam Morarjee (1877-1929), founder of Scindia Steam Ship Navigation Co.

Makhanlal Chaturvedi
A467

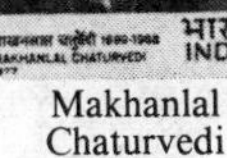

Mahaprabhu Vallabhacharya
A468

**1977, Apr. 4** *Perf. 13*
*755* A467 25p orange brown 10 6

Chaturvedi (1889-1968), Hindi writer.

**1977, Apr. 14**
*756* A468 1r olive brown 15 10

Vallabhacharya (1479-1531), philosopher.

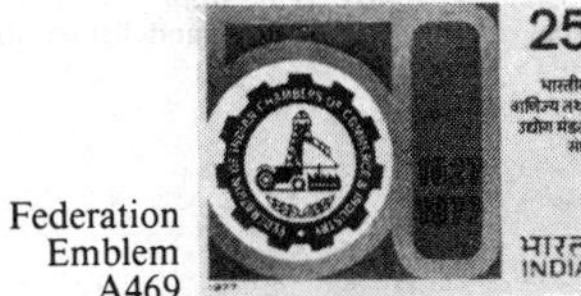

Federation Emblem
A469

**1977, Apr. 23** *Perf. 13½x13*
*757* A469 25p ocher & purple 10 6

Federation of Indian Chambers of Commerce, 50th anniv.

Protection of Environment
A470

**1977, June 5** **Photo.** *Perf. 13*
*758* A470 2r multicolored 30 20

Council of States Chamber
A471

**1977, June 21**
*759* A471 25p multicolored 8 5

Council of States, Rajya Sabha (Parliament), 25th anniv.

Lotus
A472

50p and 1r are vert.

**1977, July 1** *Perf. 15x14, 14x15*
*760* A472 25p shown 5 5
*761* A472 50p Rhododendron 10 8
*762* A472 1r Kadamba 20 10
*763* A472 2r Gloriosa lily 50 20

Berliner Gramaphone — A473

**1977, July 20** *Perf. 13½x13*
*764* A473 2r black & brown 38 20

Centenary of the phonograph.

Ananda Kentish Coomaraswamy (1877-1947) and Dancing Shiva — A474

**1977, Aug. 22** **Photo.** *Perf. 13x13½*
*765* A474 25p multicolored 8 5

Coomaraswamy, art historian and critic.

Ganga Ram (1851-1927) and Hospital, New Delhi
A475

**1977, Sept. 4** *Perf. 14½x14*
*766* A475 25p rose carmine 8 5

Ram, social reformer and philanthropist.

Dr. Samuel Hahnemann and Cinchona
A476

19th Century Postman
A477

Lion and Palm Tree, East India Co. Essay — A478

**1977, Oct. 6 Photo. *Perf. 13***
*767* A476 2r black & green 30 20

32nd Intl. Homeopathic Cong., New Delhi.

**1977, Oct. 12 *Perf. 13***
*768* A477 25p multicolored 8 5

***Perf. 13½***
*769* A478 2r mag & gray, *buff* 30 20

INPEX '77 Phil. Exhib., Bangalore, Oct. 12-16.

Ram Manohar Lohia (1910-67), Founder of Congress Socialist Party, Sec. of Foreign Dept. — A479

**1977, Oct. 12 *Perf. 13x13½***
*770* A479 25p red brown 8 5

Red Scinde Dawks, 1852 — A480

Design: 3r, Foreign mail arriving at Ballard Pier, Bombay, 1927.

**1977, Oct. 19 *Perf. 13½x13***
*771* A480 1r orange & multi 15 10
*772* A480 3r orange & multi 45 32

ASIANA 77, First Asian International Philatelic Exhibition, Bangalore, Oct. 19-23.

Statue of Rani Channamma A481

**1977, Oct. 23**
*773* A481 25p gray green 15 5

Rani Channamma of Kittue (1778-1829), who fought against British rule.

The lack of a price for a listed item does not necessarily indicate rarity.

Mother and Child, Khajuraho Sculpture — A482

**1977, Oct. 23 *Perf. 13x13½***
*774* A482 2r gray & sepia 30 20

15th Intl. Pediatrics Congress.

Sun and National Colors — A483

Stylized Grain — A484

**1977, Nov. 8 Photo. *Perf. 13***
*775* A483 25p multicolored 8 5

Union Public Service Commission, founded 1926.

**1977, Nov. 13**
*776* A484 25p green 8 5

AGRIEXPO '77, Intl. Agriculture Exhib.

Cats — A485

Design: 1r, Friends. Designs are from children's drawings.

**1977, Nov. 14**
*777* A485 25p multicolored 8 5
*778* A485 1r multicolored 15 10

Children's Day.

Jotirao Phooley
A486

Senapati Bapat
A487

**1977, Nov. 28 Wmk. 324**
*779* A486 25p gray olive 8 5

Phooley (1827-90), social reformer.

**1977, Nov. 28**
*780* A487 25p brown orange 8 5

Senapati Bapat (Pandurang Mahadev Bapat, 1880-1967), scholar and fighter for India's independence.

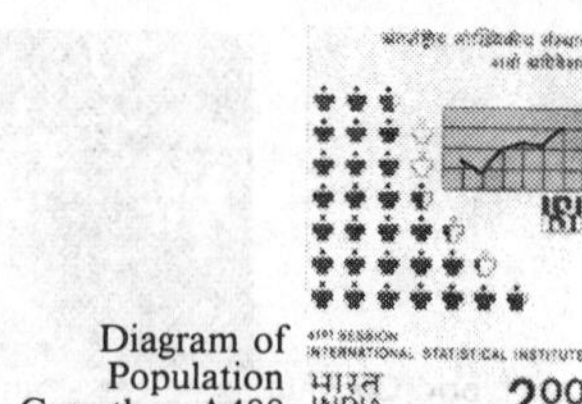


Diagram of Population Growth — A488

***Perf. 13x13½***

**1977, Dec. 13 Photo. Unwmk.**
*781* A488 2r carmine & bl grn 30 20

41st Session of Intl. Statistical Institute, New Delhi, Dec. 5-15.

Kamta Prasad (1875-1947) and Hindi Grammar A489

**1977, Dec. 25 Wmk. 324 *Perf. 14***
*782* A489 25p sepia 8 5

Prasad, compiler of Hindi Grammar.

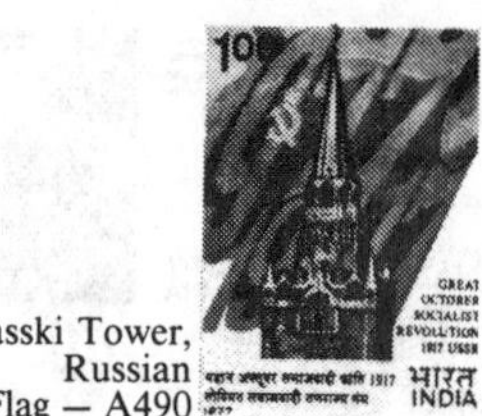


Spasski Tower, Russian Flag — A490

**1977, Dec. 30 Unwmk. *Perf. 13***
*783* A490 1r multicolored 15 10

60th anniv. of Russian October revolution.

Climber Crossing Crevasse — A491

Indian Flag near Summit A492

***Perf. 13½x13, 13x13½***

**1978, Jan. 15 Photo.**
*784* A491 25p multicolored 8 5
*785* A492 1r multicolored 15 10

Conquest of Kanchenjunga (Himalayas), by Indian team under Col. N. Kumar, May 31, 1977.

Tourists in Shikara on Dal Lake — A493

**1978, Jan. 23 *Perf. 13x13½***
*786* A493 1r multicolored 15 10

27th Pacific Area Travel Assoc. Conf., New Delhi, Jan. 23-26.

Children in Library, Fair Emblem A494

**1978, Feb. 11 Photo. *Perf. 13***
*787* A494 1r rose brn & indigo 15 10

3rd World Book Fair, New Delhi, Feb. 1978.

Mother of Pondicherry
A495

Wheat, Globe and Genetic Helix
A496

**1978, Feb. 21**
*788* A495 25p dark & light brn 8 5

Mother of the Sri Aurobindo Ashram, Pondicherry (Mira Richard, 1878-1973, born in Paris).

**1978, Feb. 23**
*789* A496 25p yel & bl grn 8 5

5th Intl. Wheat Genetics Symposium.

Nanalal Dalpatram Kavi — A497

Surjya Sen (1894-1934), Patriot — A498

**Wmk. 324**

**1978, Mar. 16 Photo. *Perf. 13***
*790* A497 25p rose brown 8 5

Kavi (1877-1946), Gujarati poet.

**1978, Mar. 22**
*791* A498 25p ver, blk & brn 8 5

Two Vaishnavas (Vishnu Worshippers) by Jaminy Roy — A499

Modern Indian Paintings: 50p, The Mosque, by Sailoz Mookherjea. 1r, Woman's Head, by Rabindranath Tagore. 2r, Hill Women, by Amrita Sher Gil.

***Perf. 13½x14***

**1978, Mar. 23 Unwmk.**
*792* A499 25p black & multi 8 5
*793* A499 50p black & multi 8 8
*794* A499 1r black & multi 15 8
*795* A499 2r black & multi 30 20

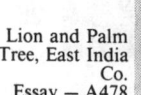

Rubens, Selfportrait A500

**1978, Apr. 4 Photo. *Perf. 13½x13***
*796* A500 2r multicolored 30 20

"The Little Tramp," Charlie Chaplin — A501

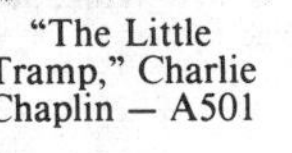
Deendayal Upadhyaya (1916-68) — A502

**1978, Apr. 16 *Perf. 13***
*797* A501 25p gold & indigo 8 5

**1978, May 5 Photo. *Perf. 13***
*798* A502 25p multicolored 8 5

Upadhyaya, social and political reformer.

Syama Prasad Mookerjee (1901-53) — A503

"Airavat," 19th Century Wood Carving — A504

Kushan Gold Coin, 1st Century A505

**1978, July 6 Photo. *Perf. 13***
*799* A503 25p gray olive 8 5

Dr. Mookerjee, educator, member of 1st natl. gov.

**1978, July 27**

Designs: 50p, Wish-fulfilling tree, 2nd century B.C. 2r, Dagger and knife.

*800* A504 25p multicolored 8 5
*801* A504 50p multicolored 8 8
*802* A505 1r multicolored 15 8
*803* A505 2r multicolored 30 20

Treasures from Indian museums.

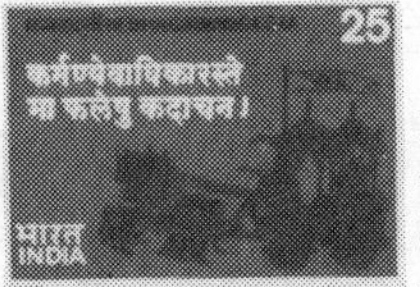
Krishna and Arjuna on Battlefield, Quotation A506

**1978, Aug. 25 Unwmk. *Perf. 13***
*804* A506 25p org red & gold 8 5

Bhagavad Gita, part of Mahabharata Epic, the Divine Song of the Lord.

Bethune College for Women, Calcutta A507

**1978, Sept. 4**
*805* A507 25p green & brown 8 5

E. V. Ramasami A508

Uday Shankar A509

**1978, Sept. 17**
*806* A508 25p black 8 5

E. V. Ramasami (1879-1973), founder of Self-respect Movement, fighting caste system and social injustice.

**1978, Sept. 26**
*807* A509 25p buff & vio brn 8 5

Uday Shankar (1900-77), dancer.

Leo Tolstoi — A510

Vallathol Narayana Menon — A511

**1978, Oct. 2**
*808* A510 1r multicolored 15 10

Tolstoi, novelist and philosopher.

**1978, Oct. 15 Photo. *Perf. 13***
*809* A511 25p multicolored 8 5

Menon (1878-1958), poet.

"Two Friends" A512

**1978, Nov. 14 Photo. *Perf. 13***
*810* A512 25p multicolored 8 5

Children's Day.

Worker at Lathe — A513

**1978, Nov. 17 *Perf. 13½***
*811* A513 25p green 8 5

Small Industries Fair.

Skinner's Horse Soldiers — A514

**1978, Nov. 25 *Perf. 13***
*812* A514 25p multicolored 8 5

175th anniv. of Skinner's Horse Regiment.

Chakravarti Rajagopalachari A515

Mohammad Ali Jauhar A516

**1978, Dec. 10 Photo. *Perf. 13***
*813* A515 25p maroon 8 5

Chakravarti Rajagopalachari (1878-1972), first post-independence Governor General.

**1978, Dec. 10**
*814* A516 25p olive green 8 5

Jauhar (1878-1931), writer and patriot.

Wright Brothers, Flyer — A517

**1978, Dec. 23 *Perf. 13x14***
*815* A517 1r ocher & purple 12 6

75th anniversary of 1st powered flight.

Ravenshaw College, Orissa, Centenary A518

**1978, Dec. 24 *Perf. 14***
*816* A518 25p grn & maroon 8 5

Franz Schubert — A519

**1978, Dec. 25 *Perf. 13***
*817* A519 1r multicolored 12 6

Schubert (1797-1828), Austrian composer.

Punjab Regiment, Uniforms and Crest A520

**Unwmk.**

**1979, Feb. 20 Photo. *Perf. 13***
*818* A520 25p multicolored 8 5

Oldest Indian infantry unit.

Bhai Parmanand (1876-1947) A521

Gandhi and Child A522

**1979, Feb. 24**
*819* A521 25p violet blue 8 5

Parmanand, writer and educator.

**1979, Mar. 5 Photo. *Perf. 13***

Design: 1r, IYC emblem.

*820* A522 25p dk brn & red 8 5
*821* A522 1r dp org & dk brn 12 6

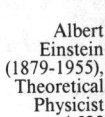

Albert Einstein (1879-1955), Theoretical Physicist A523

**1979, Mar. 14**
*822* A523 1r black 12 6

Rajarshi Shahu Chhatrapati (1874-1922), Ruler of Kolhapur — A524

**1979, May 1 Photo. *Perf. 13x13½***
*823* A524 25p dull purple 6 5

Lotus, India '80 Emblem A525

**1979, July 2 Photo. *Perf. 13***
*824* A525 30p deep org & grn 8 5

India '80 Phil. Exhib., New Delhi, Jan. 25-Feb. 3, 1980.

An enhanced introduction to the Scott Catalogue begins on Page V. A thorough understanding of the material presented there will greatly aid your use of the catalogue itself.

Postal Cards, 1879 and 1979 — A526

Raja Mahendra Pratap (1886-1979), Patriot — A527

**1979, July 2**
*825* A526 50p multicolored 12 8

**1979, Aug. 15 Photo. *Perf. 13***
*826* A527 30p olive gray 8 5

Jatindra Nath Das (1904-29) A528

Early and Modern Light Bulbs A529

**1979, Sept. 13**
*827* A528 30p dark brown 8 5

Das, political martyr.

**1979, Oct. 21 Photo. *Perf. 13***
*828* A529 1r rose magenta 12 6

Centenary of invention of electric light.

Buddhist Text A530

**1979, Oct. 23 *Perf. 14½x14***
*829* A530 30p brn & bister 8 5

National Archives.

Hirakud Dam A531

***Perf. 13½x13***
**1979, Oct. 29 Wmk. 324**
*830* A531 30p brn red & dl grn 8 5

13th Congress (Golden Jubilee) of the Intl. Comm. on Large Dams, New Delhi, Oct. 29-Nov. 2.

Boy and Alphabet Book A532

**1979, Nov. 10 Photo. *Perf. 14½x14***
*831* A532 30p multicolored 8 5

Intl. Children's Book Fair, New Delhi, Nov. 10-19.

Fair Emblem — A533

**1979, Nov. 10 *Perf. 13***
*832* A533 1r black & orange 12 6

India Intl. Trade Fair, New Delhi, Nov. 10-Dec. 9.

Dove, Agency Emblem A534

**1979, Dec. 4 *Perf. 13½x13***
*833* A534 1r multicolored 12 6

23rd Intl. Atomic Energy Agency Conf., New Delhi, Dec. 4-10.

Hindustan Pushpak Plane, Rohini-1 Glider A535

**1979, Dec. 10 *Perf. 13½x13***
*834* A535 30p multicolored 8 5

Gurdwara Baoli Shrine, Goindwal — A536

**1979, Dec. 21 *Perf. 13x13½***
*835* A536 30p multicolored 8 5

Guru Amardas (1469-1574), Sikh spiritual leader.

Types of 1975-79 and Natl. Development Type of 1980

Women in Rice Field A537

Family Planning A537a

Designs: 2p, Adult education. 5p, Fish. 15p, Agricultral technology. 20p, Child nutrition. 25p, Poultry. 1r, Hybrid cotton. 2r, Weaving. 5r, Rubber tapping.

Sizes: 1r, 2r, 17x28mm. 5r, 20x37mm.

***Perf. 14x14½, 14½x14***
**1979-81 Photo. Wmk. 324**
*836* A537 2p violet 5 5
*837* A537 5p blue 5 5
　**a.** Perf. 13 5 5
　**b.** Lithographed, perf. 13 ('82)
*838* A537a 15p bl grn ('80) 5 5
　**a.** Perf. 13 5 5
*839* A537a 20p hn brn ('81) 6 5
　**a.** Perf. 13 6 5
*840* A537 25p brown 6 5
　**a.** Perf. 13 6 5
*840B* A537 25p brt grn ('85) 5 5
*841* A409 30p violet ('80) 8 5
*842* A410 30p red brn ('80) 8 5
*843* A537 30p yel grn 8 5
　**a.** Perf. 13 6 5
*844* A409 35p vio ('80) 10 5
　**a.** Perf. 13 10 5
*845* A410 35p red brn ('80) 10 5
　**a.** Perf. 13 10 5
*846* A537a 35p cerise ('80) 10 5
　**c.** Perf. 13 10 5
*846A* A409 50p violet ('83) 12 6
　**d.** Perf. 13 8 5
*846B* A410 50p red brn ('83) 12 6
　**e.** Perf. 13 8 5
*847* A537a 1r brown ('80) 15 12
　**a.** Perf. 12½x13 20 12
*848* A537a 2r rose vio ('80) 30 15
　**a.** Perf. 13x13½ ('83) 50 25
*849* A537a 5r multi ('80) 45 22
　*Nos. 836-849 (17)* 2.00 1.21

See Nos. 895-900A, 903-914

People Holding Hands, UN Emblem — A538

**1980, Jan. 21 Photo. *Perf. 13***
*851* A538 1r multicolored 12 6

UN Industrial Development Org. (INIDO), 3rd Gen. Conf., New Delhi, Jan. 21-Feb. 8.

Field Post Office, Cancels A539

Money Order Centenary A540

2-Anna Copper Coins, 1774 A541

Rowland Hill, Birthplace, Kidderminster A542

**Wmk. 350, Unwmkd. (1r)**
**1980, Jan. 25**
*852* A539 30p gray olive 8 5
*853* A540 50p brn & citron 6 6
*854* A541 1r bronze 12 6
*855* A542 2r dark gray 25 12

INDIA '80 Intl. Stamp Exhib., New Delhi, Jan. 25-Feb. 3.

India Institution of Engineers, 60th Anniversary A543

Uniforms, 1780 and 1980, Arms and Ribbon A544

***Perf. 13x13½***
**1980, Feb. 17 Unwmk.**
*856* A543 30p dark bl & gold 8 5

**1980, Feb. 26**
*857* A544 30p multicolored 8 5

Madras Sappers bicentennial.

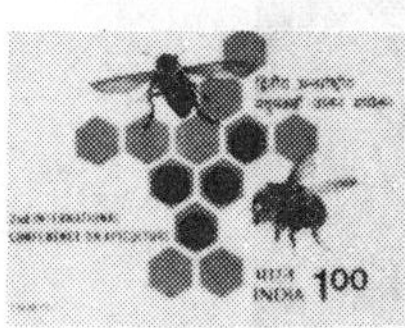

2nd Intl. Apiculture Conf., New Delhi A545

**1980, Feb. 29 *Perf. 13½***
*858* A545 1r multicolored 12 6

4th World Book Fair, New Delhi — A546

**1980, Feb. 29 Wmk. 360**
*859* A546 30p bright blue 8 5

Welthy Fisher (b. 1879), Educator, Literacy House, Lucknow — A547

**1980, Mar. 18 *Perf. 13x13½***
*860* A547 30p bl gray 8 5

Darul Uloom Islamic School, Deoband A548

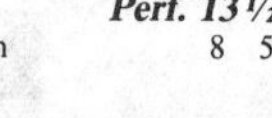

**1980, Mar. 21 *Perf. 13½***
*861* A548 30p gray green 8 5

Keshub Chunder Sen — A549

Sivaji, Raigad Fort — A550

***Perf. 13x13½***
**1980, Apr. 15 Photo. Wmk. 360**
*862* A549 30p brown 8 5

Sen (1838-84), scholar, writer, journalist.

**1980, Apr. 21 Unwmk.**
*863* A550 30p multicolored 8 5

Sivaji (1627-80), Indian patriot.

Narayan Malhar Joshi — A551

Ulloor S. Parameswara Iyer — A552

*Perf. 13x13½*

**1980, June 5 Wmk. 360**

864 A551 30p lilac rose 8 5

Joshi (1879-1955), trade union pioneer.

**1980, June 6**

865 A552 30p dull purple 8 5

Iyer (1877-1949), poet and scholar.

Syed Mohammad Zamin Ali — A553

Helen Keller (1880-1955) — A554

**1980, June 25**

866 A553 30p dark yel grn 8 5

Ali (1880-1955), linguist and educator.

**1980, June 27**

867 A554 30p orange & blk 8 5

Keller, blind and deaf writer and lecturer.

High Jump, Olympic Rings A555

Prem Chand (1880-1936) A556

**1980, July 19 Photo. *Perf. 13½x14***

868 A555 1r *shown* 12 6

869 A555 2.80r *Equestrian* 35 18

22nd Summer Olympic Games, Moscow, July 19-Aug. 3.

**1980, July 31 *Perf. 13***

870 A556 30p red brown 8 5

Pen name of Nawab Rai, writer.

Mother Teresa, Nobel Peace Prize Medallion A557

*Perf. 13½x13*

**1980, Aug. 27 Photo. Wmk. 360**

871 A557 30p violet, *grayish* 8 5

Mother Teresa, founder of Missionaries of Charity, 70th birthday.

Earl Mountbatten of Burma A558

Asian Table Tennis Championship A559

**1980, Aug. 28 *Perf. 13x13½***

872 A558 2.80r multicolored 35 18

Mountbatten (1900-79), 1st governor gen. of India.

**1980, Sept. Photo. *Perf. 13x13½***

873 A559 30p magenta 8 5

Scottish Church College, Calcutta, Sesquicentennial — A560

**1980, Sept. 27 Photo. *Perf. 13½***

874 A560 35p dull purple 10 5

Rajah Annamalai Chettiar (1881-1948), Banker, Founder of Annamalai University — A561

**1980, Sept. 30 Unwmk. *Perf. 14x15***

875 A561 35p dull purple 10 5

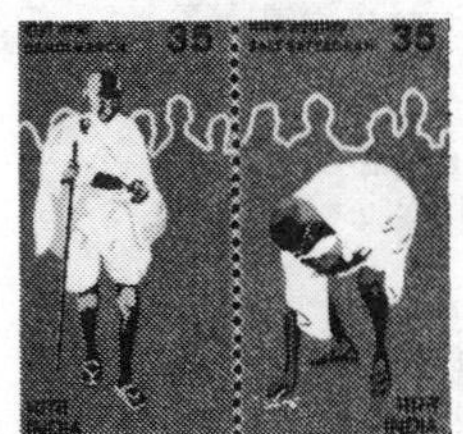

Gandhi on Dandi March — A562

Gandhi Defying Salt Law — A563

**1980, Oct. 2 *Perf. 15x14***

876 A562 35p gold & multi 10 5

877 A563 35p gold & multi 10 5

Se-tenant in sheets of 50.

Jayaprakash Narayan (1902-79), Writer — A564

**1980, Oct. 8 Wmk. 360 *Perf. 14x15***

878 A564 35p red brown 10 5

Great Indian Bustards — A565

Hegira (Pilgrimage Year) — A566

**1980, Nov. 1 Photo. *Perf. 13***

879 A565 2.30r multicolored 30 15

Intl. Symposium on Bustards, Jaipur.

**1980, Nov. 3 *Perf. 13x13½***

880 A566 35p multicolored 10 5

Children's Day — A567

*Perf. 13½x13*

**1980, Nov. 14 Unwmk.**

881 A567 35p multicolored 10 5

Dhyan Chand — A568

Miner, Molten Gold — A569

**1980, Dec. 3 Wmk. 360 *Perf. 14x15***

882 A568 35p dark rose brn 10 5

Chand (1906-79), field hockey player.

*Perf. 13x13½*

**1980, Dec. 20 Unwmk.**

883 A569 1r multicolored 12 6

Kolar gold fields centenary.

Mukhtar Ahmad Ansari (1880-1936), Surgeon — A570

*Perf. 14x15*

**1980, Dec. 25 Wmk. 360**

884 A570 35p olive gray 10 5

Government Mint, Bombay, Sesquicentennial — A571

*Perf. 13½x13*

**1980, Dec. 27 Unwmk.**

885 A571 35p multicolored 10 5

Regional Bridal Outfits — A572

Mazharul Haque (1866-1930), Patriot — A573

**1980, Dec. 30 *Perf. 13x13½***

886 A572 1r *Kashmir* 12 6

887 A572 1r *Bengal* 12 6

888 A572 1r *Rajasthan* 12 6

889 A572 1r *Tamilnada* 12 6

**1981, Jan. 2 Wmk. 360 *Perf. 14x15***

890 A573 35p violet 10 5

St. Stephen's College Centenary — A574

**1981, Feb. 1 Photo. *Perf. 14x14½***

891 A574 35p dull red 10 5

Gommateshwara Statue, Shravanabelgola A575

Ganesh V. Mavalankar (1888-1956) A576

**1981, Feb. 9 Unwmk.**

892 A575 1r multicolored 12 6

**1981, Feb. 27**

893 A576 35p light red brn 10 5

Mavalankar, 1st speaker of parliament.

Type of 1979

*Perf. 14½x14*

**1981-86 Photo. Wmk. 324**

**Size: 19½x37½mm**

| | | | | |
|---|---|---|---|---|
| 895 | A537 2.25r *Cashew* | | 32 | 15 |
| a | Perf. 14x14½ | | 32 | 15 |
| b | Perf. 13 | | 20 | 12 |
| 896 | A537 2.80r *Apples* | | 42 | 20 |
| a | Perf. 14x14½ | | 42 | 20 |
| 897 | A537 3.25r *Oranges* ('83) | | 48 | 24 |
| a | Perf. 13½x13 ('85) | | 30 | 15 |
| b | Perf. 13 | | 30 | 15 |
| 900 | A537 10r *Trees on hill-side* ('84) | | 1.25 | 60 |

*Perf. 13½x13*

900A A537 50r *Windmill* ('86) 4.75 2.50

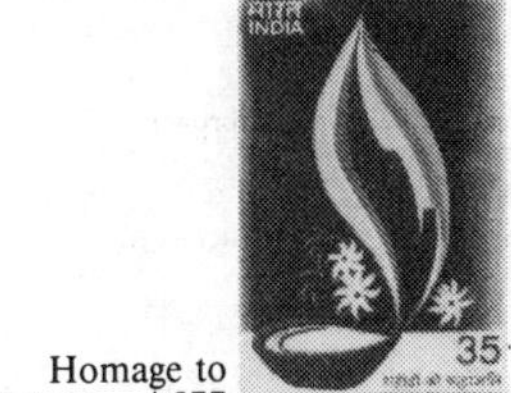

Homage to Martyrs — A577

**1981, Mar. 23 Unwmk. *Perf. 14x15***

901 A577 35p multicolored 10 5

Heinrich von Stephan and UPU Emblem A578

**1981, Apr. 8** *Perf. 15x14*
*902* A578 1r red brn & brt bl 12 6

Type of 1979
***Perf. 14x14½, 14½x14 (15p)***
**1981, Mar. 25 Photo. Wmk. 360**
*903* A537 2p violet 5 5
*904* A537 5p blue 5 5
*905* A537 10p *Irrigation* ('82) 5 5
*a* Perf. 13 5 5
*906* A537a 15p bl grn 5 5
*914* A537 50p *Dairy industry* ('82) 12 6
*a* Perf. 13 12 6

Intl. Year of the Disabled A579

***Perf. 14½x14***
**1981, Apr. 20 Photo. Unwmk.**
*919* A579 1r blue & black 12 6

Khiamngan Naga Tribesman A580

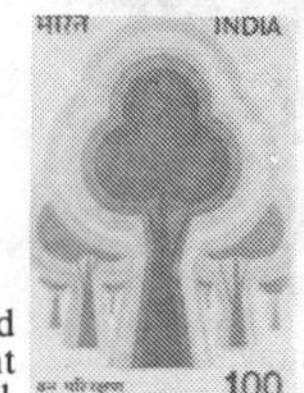
World Environment Day — A581

**1981, May 30** *Perf. 14x14½*
*920* A580 1r shown 12 6
*921* A580 1r Toda 12 6
*922* A580 1r Bhil 12 6
*923* A580 1r Dandami Maria 12 6

**1981, June 15**
*924* A581 1r multicolored 12 6

Nilmoni Phukan (1880-1978), Writer A582

Sanjay Gandhi (1946-1980), Politician A583

**1981, June 22**
*925* A582 35p red brown 10 5

**1981, June 23** *Perf. 13x13½*
*926* A583 35p multicolored 10 5



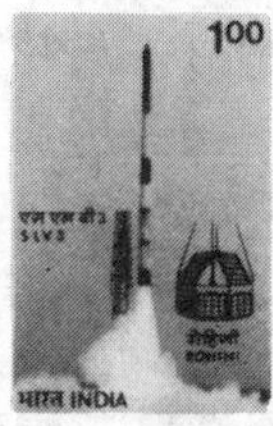
SLV-3 Take-off — A584

**1981, July 18 Photo.** *Perf. 14x15*
*927* A584 1r multicolored 12 6

Launching of India's 1st satellite, 1st anniv.

Mascot, Field Hockey A585

**1981, July 28** *Perf. 13½x13*
*928* A585 1r shown 12 6
*929* A585 1r Emblem 12 6

9th Asian Games, New Delhi, 1982.
See Nos. 942-943.

Flame of the Forest — A586

Designs: Flowering trees.

**1981, Sept. 1 Photo.** *Perf. 13*
*930* A586 35p shown 5 5
*931* A586 50p Crateva 6 6
*932* A586 1r Golden shower 12 6
*933* A586 2r Bauhinia 25 12

World Food Day — A587

Cyrestis Achates — A588

**1981, Oct. 16 Photo.** *Perf. 14x14½*
*934* A587 1r multicolored 12 6

**1981, Oct. 20** *Perf. 13*
*935* A588 35p Stichophthalma camadeva, horiz. 5 5
*936* A588 50p Cethosia biblis, horiz. 6 6
*937* A588 1r shown 12 6
*938* A588 2r Treinopalpus imperialis 25 12

Bellary Raghava (1880-1946), Actor — A589

**1981, Oct. 31** *Perf. 14½x14*
*939* A589 35p olive gray 10 5

40th Anniv. of Mahar Regiment — A590

Children's Day — A591

**1981, Nov. 9** *Perf. 13*
*940* A590 35p multicolored 10 5

**1981, Nov. 14** *Perf. 14x14½*
*941* A591 35p multicolored 10 5

Asian Games Type of 1981
**1981** *Perf. 13½x13*
*942* A585 1r Rajghat Stadium, domed 12 6
*943* A585 1r Nehru Stadium 12 6

Issue dates: No. 942, Nov. 19; No. 943, Dec. 30.

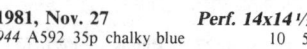

Kashi Prasad Jayaswal (1881-1937), Historian — A592

**1981, Nov. 27** *Perf. 14x14½*
*944* A592 35p chalky blue 10 5

Intl. Palestinian Solidarity Day — A593

**1981, Nov. 29** *Perf. 14½x14*
*945* A593 1r multicolored 12 6

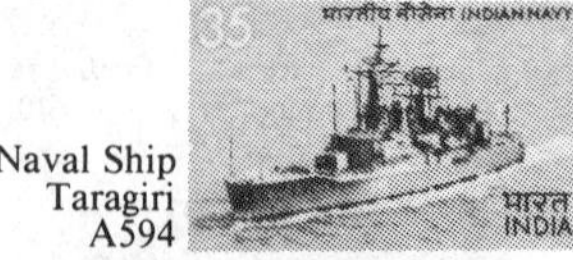
Naval Ship Taragiri A594

**1981, Dec. 4**
*946* A594 35p multicolored 10 5

Henry Heras (1888-1955), Historian — A595

**1981, Dec. 14 Photo.** *Perf. 14½x14*
*947* A595 35p rose violet 10 5

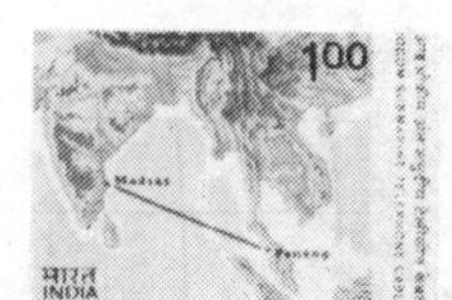
Indian Ocean Commonwealth Submarine Telephone Cable — A596

**1981, Dec. 24** *Perf. 13½*
*948* A596 1r multicolored 12 6

5th World Field Hockey Championship, Bombay — A597

**1981, Dec. 29** *Perf. 13½x13*
*949* A597 1r multicolored 12 6

Telephone Service Centenary — A598

***Perf. 13x13½***
**1982, Jan. 28 Unwmk.**
*950* A598 2r multicolored 25 12

12th Intl. Soil Science Congress, New Delhi, Feb. 8-16 — A599

**1982, Feb. 8** *Perf. 13½x13*
*951* A599 1r multicolored 12 6

Sir Jamsetjee Jejeebhoy School of Art, Bombay — A600

**1982, Mar. 2 Photo.** *Perf. 14x14½*
*952* A600 35p multicolored 10 5

Three Musicians, by Pablo Picasso (1881-1973) — A601

**1982, Mar. 15 Photo.** *Perf. 14*
*953* A601 2.85r multicolored 35 18

Deer, 5th Cent. Bas Relief A602

Radio Telescope, Ooty A603

Festival of India, England: No. 955, Krishna, 9th cent. bronze sculpture.

***Perf. 14x15 (A602), 13***

**1982, Mar. 23**

| | | | | | |
|---|---|---|---|---|---|
| *954* | A602 | 2r | multicolored | 25 | 12 |
| *955* | A602 | 3.05r | multicolored | 38 | 18 |
| *956* | A603 | 3.05r | multicolored | 38 | 18 |

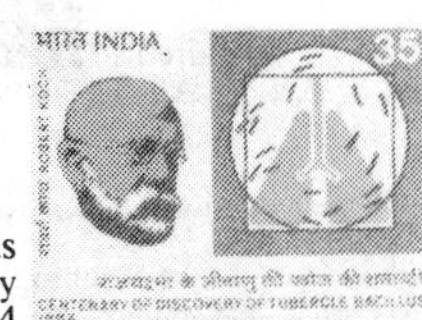
TB Bacillus Centenary A604

**1982, Mar. 24** ***Perf. 13***

*957* A604 35p rose violet 10 5

Durgabai Deshmukh (1909-1981), Social Worker — A605

**1982, May 9 Photo.** ***Perf. 14½x14***

*958* A605 35p blue 10 5

Himalayan Flowers — A606

**1982, May 29** ***Perf. 14x14½***

| | | | | | |
|---|---|---|---|---|---|
| *959* | A606 | 35p | Blue poppies | 5 | 5 |
| *960* | A606 | 1r | Showy inula | 12 | 6 |
| *961* | A606 | 2r | Cobra lily | 25 | 12 |
| *962* | A606 | 2.85r | Brahma kamal | 35 | 18 |

Ariana Passenger Payload Experimental (APPLE) Satellite, First Anniv. — A607

**1982, June 19** ***Perf. 13½x13***

*963* A607 2r multicolored 25 12

Bidhan Chandra Roy (1882-1962), Physician and Politician — A608

**1982, July 1** ***Perf. 14½x14***

*964* A608 50p orange brown 12 6

Telecommunications A608a

**1988 Photo. Wmk. 324** ***Perf. 13***

*970* A608a 40p dull red 8 5

Sagar Samrat Drilling Rig — A609

**1982, Aug. 14 Photo.** ***Perf. 13***

*985* A609 1r multicolored 12 6

Bindu (Cosmic Spirit), by Raza — A610

Kashmir Stag — A611

Paintings: 3.05r, Between the Spider and the Lamp, 1956, by M.F. Husain.

**1982, Sept. 17** ***Perf. 14x14½***

| | | | | | |
|---|---|---|---|---|---|
| *986* | A610 | 2r | multicolored | 25 | 12 |
| *987* | A610 | 3.05r | multicolored | 38 | 18 |

**1982, Oct. 1** ***Perf. 13x13½***

*988* A611 2.85r multicolored 35 18

50th Anniv. of Indian Air Force A612

**1982, Oct. 8** ***Perf. 13½x13***

*989* A612 1r Wapiti, MiG 25 12 6

50th Anniv. of Civil Aviation A613

**1982, Oct. 15**

*990* A613 3.25r J.R.D. Tata and his Puss Moth, 1932 40 20

Police Memorial Day — A614

**1982, Oct. 21**

*991* A614 50p Beat patrol 12 6

Post Office Savings Bank Centenary A615

**1982, Oct. 23**

*992* A615 50p brown 12 6

9th Asian Games — A616

**1982, Oct. 30** ***Perf. 13½x14***

*993* A616 1r Wrestling, by Janaki, 17th cent. 12 6

**1982, Nov. 6 Photo.** ***Perf. 14x13½***

*993A* A616 1r Archery 12 6

Troposcatter, India-USSR Communications Link — A617

**1982, Nov. 2** ***Perf. 13½x13***

*994* A617 3.05r Views 38 18

Children's Day — A618

9th Asian Games A619

**1982, Nov. 14** ***Perf. 14x15***

*995* A618 50p multi 12 6

**1982** ***Perf. 13***

| | | | | | |
|---|---|---|---|---|---|
| *996* | A619 | 50p | Cycling | 6 | 6 |
| *997* | A619 | 2r | Yachting | 25 | 12 |
| *998* | A619 | 2r | Javelin | 25 | 12 |
| *999* | A619 | 2.85r | Rowing | 35 | 18 |
| *1000* | A619 | 2.85r | Discus | 35 | 18 |
| *1001* | A619 | 3.25r | Soccer | 40 | 20 |
| | | | *Nos. 996-1001 (6)* | 1.66 | 86 |

Issue dates: 50p, Nos. 998, 1000-1001 Nov. 19; others Nov. 25.

50th Anniv. of Indian Military Academy, Dehradun A620

**1982, Dec. 10** ***Perf. 13½x13***

*1002* A620 50p multicolored 12 6

Purushot- tamdas Tandon (1882-1962), Politician — A621

**1982, Dec. 15** ***Perf. 13***

*1003* A621 50p bister 12 6

Darjeeling Himalayan Railway Centenary A622

**1982, Dec. 18** ***Perf. 13½x13***

*1004* A622 2.85r multicolored 35 18

Indian Railway Car — A623

Nos. 2 and 201 — A624

**1982, Dec. 30 Photo.** ***Perf. 13, 14***

| | | | | | |
|---|---|---|---|---|---|
| *1005* | A623 | 50p | multicolored | 12 | 6 |
| *1006* | A624 | 2r | multicolored | 25 | 12 |

INPEX '82 Stamp Exhibition.

First Anniv. of Antarctic Expedition A625

**1983, Jan. 9 Photo.** ***Perf. 13½x13***

*1007* A625 1r multicolored 12 6

Pres. Franklin D. Roosevelt (1882-1945) A626

**1983, Jan. 30** ***Perf. 13***

*1008* A626 3.25r brown 40 20

Siberian Cranes — A627

**1983, Feb. 7** *Perf. 13x13½*
*1009* A627 2.85r multicolored 35 18

180th Anniv. of Jat Regiment A628

**1983, Feb. 16** *Perf. 13½x13*
*1010* A628 50p Soldiers, emblem 12 6

7th Non-aligned Summit Conference A629

**1983, Mar. 7**
*1011* A629 1r Emblem 12 6
*1012* A629 2r Jawaharlal Nehru 25 12

Commonwealth Day — A630

**1983, Mar. 14** *Perf. 13*
*1013* A630 1r Shore Temple, Mahabalipuram 12 6
*1014* A630 2r Mountains, Gomukh 25 12

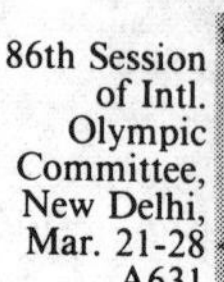

86th Session of Intl. Olympic Committee, New Delhi, Mar. 21-28 A631

**1983, Mar. 25** **Litho.** *Perf. 13½x13*
*1015* A631 1r Acropolis 20 10

St. Francis of Assisi (1182-1226) — A632

**1983, Apr. 4** **Photo.** *Perf. 13*
*1016* A632 1r By Giovanni Collina 20 10

Karl Marx (1818-1883) — A633

**1983, May 5** **Photo.** *Perf. 13x12½*
*1017* A633 1r brown 20 10

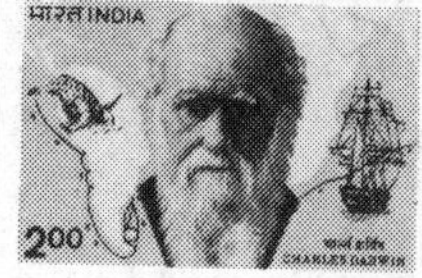

Charles Darwin (1809-1882) A634

**1983, May 18** *Perf. 12½x13*
*1018* A634 2r multicolored 40 20

50th Anniv. of Kanha Natl. Park — A635

**1983, May 30** *Perf. 13½x13*
*1019* A635 1r Barasinga stag 20 10

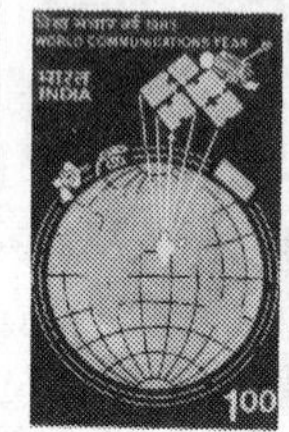

World Communications Year — A636

**1983, July 18** **Photo.** *Perf. 13*
*1020* A636 1r multicolored 20 10

Simon Bolivar (1783-1830) A637

**1983, July 24**
*1021* A637 2r multicolored 40 20

Quit India Resolution, Aug. 8, 1942 — A638

Meera Behn (Madeleine Slade). Disciple of Gandhi, d. 1982 — A639

*Perf. 14, 13½x13*

**1983, Aug. 9** **Photo.**
*1022* A638 50p shown 10 5
*1023* A639 50p shown 10 5
*1024* A639 50p Mahadev Desai (1892-1942) 10 5

Nos. 1023-1024 se-tenant.

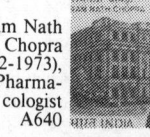

Ram Nath Chopra (1882-1973), Pharmacologist A640

**1983, Aug. 17** *Perf. 13*
*1025* A640 50p brown 10 5

Indian Mountaineering Foundation, 25th Anniv. — A641

**1983, Aug. 27** *Perf. 13½*
*1026* A641 2r Nanda Devi, Himalayas 40 20

Bombay Natural History Society — A642

**1983, Sept. 15** *Perf. 13x13½*
*1027* A642 1r multicolored 20 10

Rock Garden, Chandigarh — A643

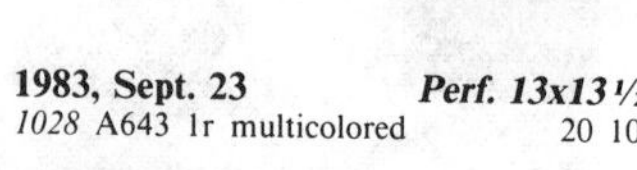

**1983, Sept. 23** *Perf. 13x13½*
*1028* A643 1r multicolored 20 10

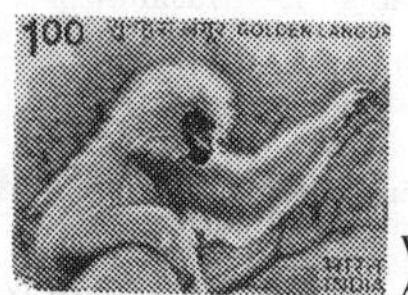

Wildlife A644

**1983, Oct. 1** *Perf. 13½x13*
*1029* A644 1r Golden Langur 20 10
*1030* A644 2r Lion-tailed macaque 40 20

World Tourism, 5th General Assembly — A645

**1983, Oct. 3** **Photo.** *Perf. 14*
*1031* A645 2r Ghats of Varanasi 40 20

Krishna Kanta Handique, Linguist, Sanskritist, Educator and Scholar — A646

**1983, Oct. 7** **Litho.** *Perf. 13*
*1032* A646 50p deep gray vio 10 5

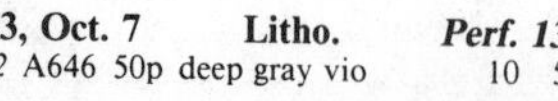

Hemu Kalani, Revolutionary Patriot — A647

**1983, Oct. 18** **Photo.** *Perf. 1*
*1033* A647 50p red brn & multi 10

Children's Day — A648

Painting: Festival, by Kashyap Premswala

**1983, Nov. 14** **Photo.** *Perf. 13*
*1034* A648 50p multicolored 10 5

Acharya Vinoba Bhave (1895-1982), Freedom Fighter — A649

**1983, Nov. 15** **Photo.** *Perf. 13*
*1035* A649 50p dull brn & multi 10 5

Manned Flight Bicentenary — A650

**1983, Nov. 21** **Photo.** *Perf. 13*
*1036* A650 1r 1st Indian Balloon 20 10
*1037* A650 2r Montgolfier Balloon 40 20

Project Tiger — A651

**1983, Nov. 22** **Photo.** *Perf. 13*
*1038* A651 2r multicolored 40 20

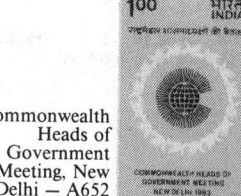

Commonwealth Heads of Government Meeting, New Delhi — A652

Design: 2r, Goanese Couple, 19th century.

**1983, Nov. 23 Photo. *Perf. 13***
*1039* A652 1r lt brnsh bl & multi 20 10
*1040* A652 2r pink & multi 40 20

Nanda Lal Bose (1882-1966), Artist — A653

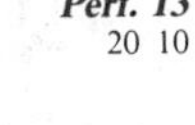

**1983, Dec. 5 Photo. *Perf. 13***
*1041* A653 1r Pratiksha 20 10

Surendranath Banerjee, Journalist A654

7th Light Cavalry Bicentenary A655

**1983, Dec. 28 Photo. *Perf. 13***
*1042* A654 50p multicolored 10 5

**1984, Jan. 7**
*1043* A655 1r Soldier, banner 20 10

Deccan Horse Regiment, 194th Anniv. — A656

**1984, Jan. 9 *Perf. 13x13½***
*1044* A656 1r multicolored 20 10

Asiatic Society Bicentenary A657

Design: Society building, Calcutta; founder William Jones.

**1984, Jan. 15 *Perf. 13***
*1045* A657 1r brt grn & dp lil 20 10

Postal Life Insurance Centenary — A658

**1984, Feb. 1 Photo. *Perf. 13x13½***
*1046* A658 1r Emblem 20 10

Presidential Review of Naval Fleet A659

**1984, Feb. 3 *Perf. 13½x13***
*1047* A659 1r Jet 20 10
*1048* A659 1r Aircraft carrier 20 10
*1049* A659 1r Submarine 20 10
*1050* A659 1r Missile destroyer 20 10

Nos. 1047-1050 se-tenant.

12th Intl. Leprosy Congress, New Delhi A660

**1984, Feb. 10 *Perf. 13x13½***
*1051* A660 1r Globe, emblem 20 10

Vasudeo Balvant Phadke (d. 1884), Freedom Fighter — A661

**1984 *Perf. 13***
*1052* A661 50p Shown 10 5
*1053* A661 50p Baba Kanshi Ram 10 5
*1054* A661 50p Begum Hazrat Mahal 10 5
*1055* A661 50p Mangal Pandey 10 5
*1056* A661 50p Nana Sahib 10 5
*1057* A661 50p Tatya Tope 10 5
*Nos. 1052-1057 (6)* 60 30

Issue dates: No. 1052, Feb. 23. No. 1053, Apr. 23. Nos. 1054-1057, May 10.

Indian-Russian Space Cooperation — A662

**1984, Apr. 3 Photo. *Perf. 14***
*1058* A662 3r Spacecraft 60 30

G. D. Birla (1894-1983), Industrialist A663

Design: Birla, Birla Institute of Technology, Pilani.

**1984, June 11**
*1060* A663 50p sepia 10 5

1984 Summer Olympics A664

Vellore Fort A665

***Perf. 13x12½, 12½x13***
**1984, July 28 Photo.**
*1061* A664 50p Basketball 10 5
*1062* A664 1r High jump 20 10
*1063* A664 2r Gymnastics, horiz. 40 20
*1064* A664 2.50r Weight lifting, horiz. 50 25

**1984, Aug. 3 *Perf. 13½x13, 13x13½***
*1065* A665 50p Gwalior, horiz. 10 5
*1066* A665 1r shown 20 10
*1067* A665 1.50r Simhagad 30 15
*1068* A665 2r Jodhpur, horiz. 40 20

B.V. Paradkar, Editor — A665a

**1984, Sept. 14 Photo. *Perf. 13x13½***
*1068A* A665a 50p sepia 6 5

Dr. D.N. Wadia (1883-1969), Geologist A665b

**1984, Oct. 23 *Perf. 13***
*1068B* A665b 1r multicolored 12 6

Indira Gandhi — A666

**1984, Nov. 19 Photo. *Perf. 15x14***
*1069* A666 50p multicolored 10 5

Children's Day A667

12th World Mining Congress A668

**1984, Nov. 14 Photo. *Perf. 13***
*1070* A667 50p Birds in trees 10 5

**1984, Nov. 20 Photo. *Perf. 13***
*1071* A668 1r Congress emblem 20 10

Dr. Rajendra Prasad (1884-1963), 1st, Pres. — A669

**1984, Dec. 3 Photo. *Perf. 13***
*1072* A669 50p multicolored 6 5

Roses — A670

**1984, Dec. 23 Litho. *Perf. 13***
*1073* A670 1.50r Mrinalini 18 10
*1074* A670 2r Sugandha 24 12

Fergusson College Centenary A671

**1985, Jan. 2 Photo. *Perf. 13x13½***
*1076* A671 100p multicolored 20 10

Narhar Vishnu Gadgil (1896-1966), Freedom Fighter — A672

**1985, Jan. 10 Photo. *Perf. 13***
*1077* A672 50p org, grn & brn 6 5

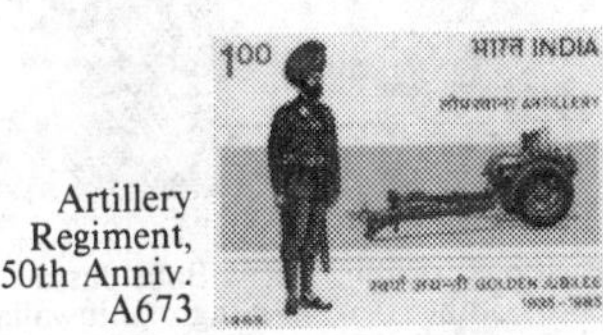


Artillery Regiment, 50th Anniv. A673

**1985, Jan. 15 *Perf. 13½x13***
*1078* A673 1r Gunner, howitzer 12 6

Indira Gandhi (1917-1984) — A674

**1985, Jan. 31 *Perf. 14***
*1079* A674 2r Addressing UN General Assembly 24 12

See Nos. 1098-1099.

Minicoy Lighthouse Cent. — A675

**1985, Feb. 2** *Perf. 13*
*1080* A675 1r multicolored 12 6

Bengal Medical College, 150th Anniv. A676

**1985, Feb. 20** *Perf. 13½x13*
*1081* A676 1r multicolored 12 6

Madras Medical College, 150th Anniv. A677

**1985, Mar. 8** *Perf. 13½x13*
*1082* A677 1r multicolored 12 6

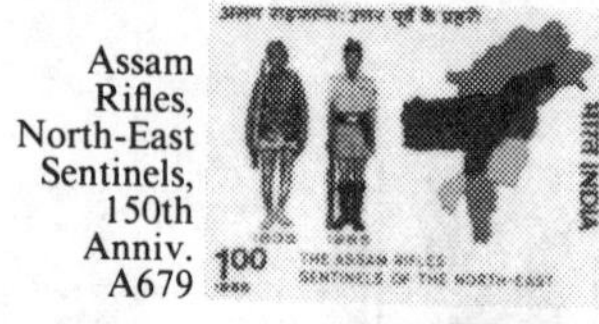
Assam Rifles, North-East Sentinels, 150th Anniv. A679

**1985, Mar. 29**
*1084* A679 1r multicolored 16 8

Potato Research, 50th Anniv. — A680

Baba Jassa Singh Ahluwalia, 1718-1783, Sikh Leader — A681

**1985, Apr. 1** *Perf. 13*
*1085* A680 50p brn & pale brn 8 5

**1985, Apr. 4**
*1086* A681 50p rose violet 8 5

St. Xavier's College, 125th Anniv. A682

Design: College, emblem, statue of St. Xavier.

**1985, Apr. 12**
*1087* A682 1r multicolored 16 8

White-winged Wood Duck A683

Bougainvillea A684

**1985, May 18** *Perf. 14*
*1088* A683 2r multicolored 32 16

**1985, June 5** *Perf. 13*
*1089* A684 50p multicolored 8 5
*1090* A684 1r multicolored 16 8

Statue of Didarganj Yakshi, Indian Deity — A685

Yaudheya Tribal Republic Copper Coin, c. 200 B.C. — A686

**1985**
*1091* A685 1r multicolored 16 8
*1092* A686 2r multicolored 32 16

Festival of India, festival in France and the US for cultural exchange.
Issue dates: 1r, June 7. 2r, June 13.

Jairamdas Doulatram, 1891-1979, Journalist and Politician — A687

**1985, July 21**
*1093* A687 50p org, grn & dl red brn 8 5

Nellie (1909-1973) & Jatindra Mohan (d. 1933) Sengupta, Political Activists — A688

**1985, July 22**
*1094* A688 50p org, grn & fawn 8 5

Swami Haridas (1478-1573), Philosopher — A689

**1985, Sept. 19** **Photo.** *Perf. 13½x13*
*1095* A689 1r multicolored 16 8

Border Roads Org., 25th Anniv. A690

**1985, Oct. 10** *Perf. 13x14*
*1096* A690 2r multicolored 16 8

Prime Minister Nehru at Podium A691

**1985, Oct. 24** *Perf. 13x13½*
*1097* A691 2r multicolored 32 16

UN, 40th anniv.

Indira Gandhi Memorial Type of 1985

**1985** *Perf. 14*
*1098* A674 2r Gandhi addressing crowd 32 16
*1099* A674 3r Portrait 48 25

Issue dates: 2r, Oct. 31. 3r, Nov. 19.

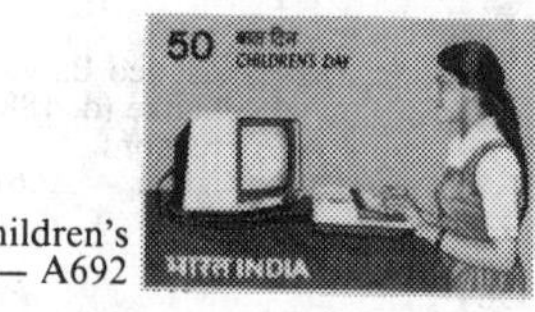
Children's Day — A692

**1985, Nov. 14** *Perf. 13½x13*
*1100* A692 50p multicolored 8 5

Halley's Comet — A693

**1985, Nov. 19** *Perf. 13x13½*
*1101* A693 1r multicolored 16 8

Intl. Astronomical Union, 19th General Assembly, New Delhi, Nov. 19-28.

St. Stephen's Hospital, Delhi, Cent. A694

**1985, Nov. 25** *Perf. 13*
*1102* A694 1r multicolored 16 8

Kakasaheb Kalelkar (1885-1981), Author — A695

**1985, Dec. 2**
*1103* A695 50p org, grn & brn 8 5

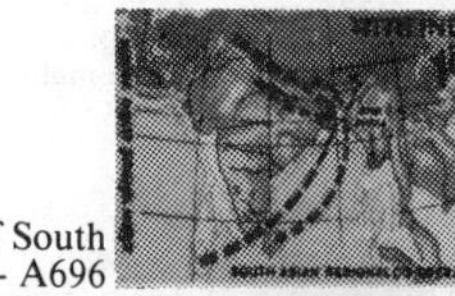
Map of South Asia — A696

Flags of India, Pakistan, Bangladesh, Nepal, Bhutan, Sri Lanka and the Maldive Islands — A697

**1985, Dec. 8** *Perf. 13½x13, 14*
*1104* A696 1r multicolored 16 8
*1105* A697 3r multicolored 48 25

South Asian Regional Cooperation, SARC.

Shyama Shastri (1762-1827), Composer A698

Master Tara Singh (1885-1967), Sikh Leader A699

**1985, Dec. 21** *Perf. 13½x13*
*1106* A698 1r multicolored 16 8

**1985, Dec. 23**
*1107* A699 50p multicolored 8 5

Intl. Youth Year A700

**1985, Dec. 24**
*1108* A700 2r multicolored 32 16

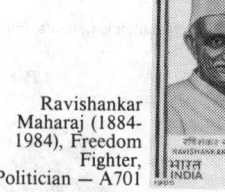

Ravishankar Maharaj (1884-1984), Freedom Fighter, Politician — A701

**1985, Dec. 24**
*1109* A701 50p org, grn & slate 8 5

Handel and Bach — A702

**1985, Dec. 27** *Perf. 13x13½*
*1110* A702 5r multicolored 80 40

Congress Presidents, 1924-1985 A703

**1985, Dec. 28** *Perf. 14*
*1111* Block of 4
***a.-d*** A703 1r. any single

Indian Natl. Congress, cent. Withdrawn on day of issue.

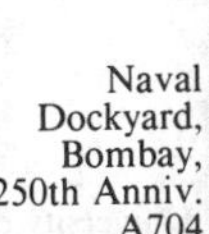

Naval Dockyard, Bombay, 250th Anniv. A704

**1986, Jan. 11** **Photo.** *Perf. 13½*
*1112* A704 2.50r multicolored 38 20

INPEX '86, Jaipur, Feb. 14-19 A705

Designs: 50p, Hawa Mahal Palace, Jaipur No. 3. 2r, Khar Desert mobile post office.

**1986, Feb. 14** *Perf. 13½x13*
*1113* A705 50p multicolored 8 5
*1114* A705 2r multicolored 30 15

Vikrant Aircraft Carrier, 25th Anniv. — A706

**1986, Feb. 16** *Perf. 13x13½*
*1115* A706 2r multicolored 32 16

Inaugural Airmail Flight, 75th Anniv. A707

*Perf. 13½x13, 13x13½*
**1986, Feb. 18**
*1116* A707 50p Biplane 8 5
**Size: 41x28mm**
*1117* A707 3r Jet 48 24

Sixth Triennale of the Arts, Lalit Kala Academy A708

Sri Chaitanya Mahaprabhu A709

**1986, Feb. 22** *Perf. 13x13½*
*1118* A708 1r multicolored 16 8

**1986, Mar. 3** *Perf. 13*
*1119* A709 2r multicolored 28 14

Mayo College, Ajmer, 111th Anniv. A710

**1986, Apr. 12** *Perf. 13½x13*
*1120* A710 1r multicolored 15 8

1986 World Cup Soccer Championships, Mexico A711

**1986, May 31** **Photo.** *Perf. 13*
*1121* A711 5r multicolored 75 38

Bhim Sen Sachar (1894-1978), Freedom Fighter — A712

**1986, Aug. 14** **Photo.** *Perf. 13½x13*
*1122* A712 50p org, grn & sepia 8 5

Swami Sivananda (1887-1963), Religious Author — A713

10th Asian Games — A714

**1986, Sept. 8** **Photo.** *Perf. 13½x13*
*1123* A713 2r multicolored 32 16

**1986, Sept. 16** *Perf. 13x13½*
*1124* A714 1.50r Women's volleyball 24 12
*1125* A714 3r Hurdling 48 24

Madras Post Office, Bicent. A715

**1986, Oct. 9** **Photo.** *Perf. 13x13½*
*1126* A715 5r blk & brn org 80 40

1st Battalion of Parachutists Regiment, 225th Anniv. — A716

Indian Police Force, 125th Anniv. — A717

**1986, Oct. 17**
*1127* A716 3r multicolored 48 24

**1986, Oct. 21** *Perf. 13½*

Uniforms, 1861-1986. Nos. 1129, 1128 printed se-tenant in a continuous design.

*1128* A717 1.50r multicolored 24 12
*1129* A717 2r multicolored 32 16

Intl. Peace Year A718

**1986, Oct. 24**
*1130* A718 5r sage grn, bl & rose 80 40

Children's Day — A719

**1986, Nov. 14** **Photo.** *Perf. 13x13½*
*1131* A719 50p multicolored 8 5

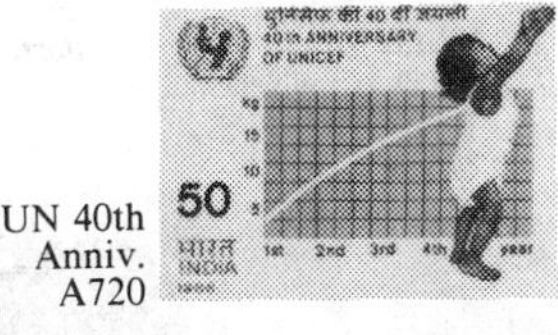

UN 40th Anniv. A720

**1986, Dec. 11** *Perf. 13½x13*
*1132* A720 50p Growth monitoring 8 5
*1133* A720 5r Immunization 80 40

Child Survival Campaign.

Miyan Tansen, 17th Cent. Dhrupad Singer, Playing the Surbahar — A721

**1986, Dec. 12**
*1134* A721 1r multicolored 16 8

Corbett Natl. Park, 50th Anniv. A722

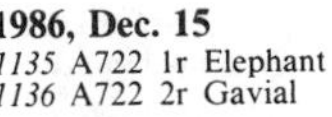

**1986, Dec. 15**
*1135* A722 1r Elephant 16 8
*1136* A722 2r Gavial 32 16

Alluri Seetarama Raju (b. 1897), Freedom Fighter — A723

Freedom Fighters: No. 1138, Shri Sagarmal Gopa (b. 1900). No. 1139, Veer Surendra Sai (b. 1809).

**1986** *Perf. 13*
*1137* A723 50p red, grn & sep 8 5
*1138* A723 50p red, grn & sl bl 8 5
*1139* A723 50p red, grn & dp red brn 8 5

Issue dates: No. 1137, Dec. 26. No. 1138, Dec. 29. No. 1139, Dec. 30.

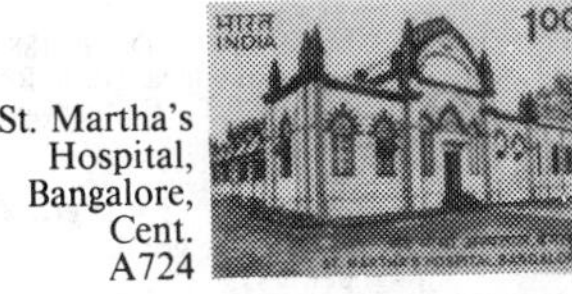

St. Martha's Hospital, Bangalore, Cent. A724

**1986, Dec. 30** *Perf. 13½*
*1140* A724 1r multicolored 16 8

Yacht Trishna A725

**1987, Jan. 10**
*1141* A725 6.50r multicolored 1.05 52

1st Indian Army circumnavigation of the world, Sept. 28, 1985 to 1987.

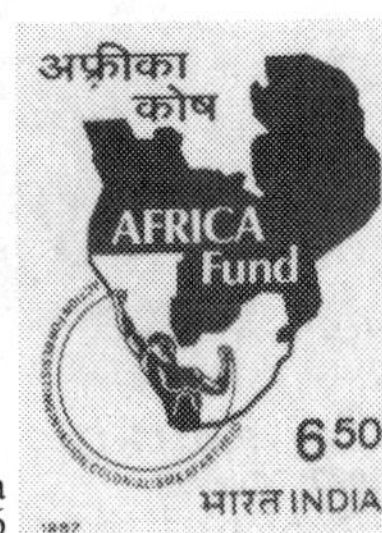

Africa Fund — A726

**1987, Jan. 25** **Photo.** *Perf. 14x14½*
*1142* A726 6.50r black 1.05 52

ICC 29th Congress, New Delhi A727

Hakim Ajmal Khan (1864-1927), Physician, Politician A728

**1987, Feb. 11** *Perf. 13½*
*1143* A727 5r multicolored 80 40

**1987, Feb. 13** *Perf. 13½x13*
*1144* A728 60p org, sage grn & brn 10 5

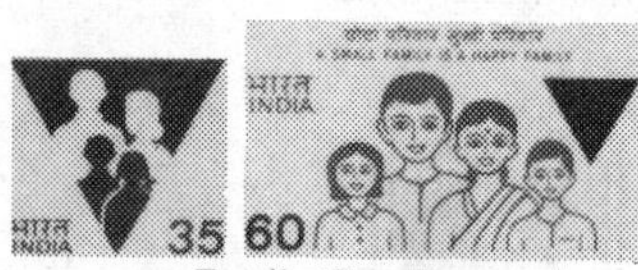

Family Planning
A729 A730

**1987, Feb. 27** *Perf. 13, 13x13½*
*1145* A729 35p dark red 6 5
*1146* A730 60p grn & dark red 10 5

Independence Leaders — A731

Portraits: No. 1147, Lala Har Dayal (1884-1939). No. 1148, Manabendra Nath Roy (1887-1954). No. 1149, T. Ramaswamy Chowdary (1887-1943).

**1987** **Photo.** *Perf. 13*
*1147* A731 60p brt red, sage grn & pur 10 5
*1148* A731 60p brt red, sage grn & red brn 10 5
*1149* A731 60p brt red, sage grn & brt blue 10 5

Issue dates: No. 1147, Mar. 18. No. 1148, Mar. 21. Nos. 1149, Apr. 25.

SER Emblem, Blast Furnaces — A732

Electric Train Crossing Bridge — A734

Steam Locomotive No. 691 — A733

*Perf. 13x13½, 13½x13*
**1987, Mar. 28**
*1150* A732 1r shown 16 8
*1151* A733 1.50r shown 24 12
*1152* A734 2r shown 32 16
*1153* A733 4r Steam locomotive, c. 1890 65 32

Southeastern Railway, cent.

Kalia Bhomora Bridge, Assam A735

**1987, Apr. 14** *Perf. 13½*
*1154* A735 2r multicolored 32 16

Madras Christian College, 150th Anniv. A736

**1987, Apr. 16** *Perf. 13x13½*
*1155* A736 1.50r blk & rose lake 24 12

Shree Shree Ma Anandamayee (1896-1982), Spiritualist A737

**1987, May 1** *Perf. 13½*
*1156* A737 1r dull brown 16 8

Rabindranath Tagore (1861-1941), 1913 Nobel Laureate for Literature — A738

**1987, May 8** *Perf. 14*
*1157* A738 2r multicolored 32 16

Garhwal Rifles and Garhwal Scouts, Cent. — A739

**1987, May 10** *Perf. 13½*
*1158* A739 1r multicolored 16 8

J. Krishnamurti (1895-1986), Mystic — A740

**1987, May 11**
*1159* A740 60p blk brn & buff 10 5

7th Battalion, Mechanised Infantry Regiment, Cent. A741

**1987, June 3** *Perf. 13½x13*
*1160* A741 1r multicolored 16 8

INDIA '89, New Delhi, Jan. 20-29, 1989 A742

**1987, June 15**
*1161* A742 50p Swan emblem 8 5
*1162* A742 5r Hall of Nations, New Delhi 80 40
*a* Souv. sheet, #1161-1162 1.25 1.25

Inscribed 1986. No. 1162a has inscribed decorative margin. Sold for 8r. Size: 157x58mm.

Kailas Nath Katju (1887-1968), Chief Minister A743

Sadyah-Snata, Sanghol Sculpture, c. 2000 B.C. A744

**1987, June 17** *Perf. 13*
*1163* A743 60p orange, sage grn & yellow brn 10 5

**1987, July 3**
*1164* A744 6.50r multicolored 1.05 52

Festival of India in the USSR, July 3, 1987-88.

Natl. Independence, 40th Anniv. — A745

**1987, Aug. 15** **Photo.** *Perf. 13x13½*
*1165* A745 60p org, bright blue & dark grn 10 5

Sant Harchand Singh Longowal (1932-1985), Social Reformer A746

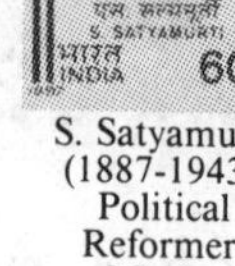

S. Satyamurti (1887-1943), Political Reformer, Martyr A747

**1987, Aug. 20** *Perf. 13½*
*1166* A746 1r multicolored 16 8

**1987, Aug. 22** *Perf. 13½x13*
*1167* A747 60p org, grn & brn 10 5

Guru Ghasidas (1756-1837), Founder of the Saman Sect — A748

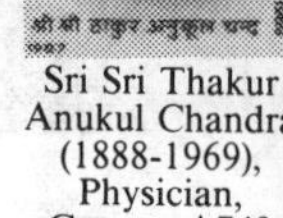
Sri Sri Thakur Anukul Chandra (1888-1969), Physician, Guru — A749

**1987, Sept. 1**
*1168* A748 60p henna brown 10 5

**1987, Sept. 2** *Perf. 13½*
*1169* A749 1r multicolored 16 8

University of Allahabad, Cent. A750

**1987, Sept. 23** *Perf. 13½x13*
*1170* A750 2r multicolored 32 16

Phoolwalon Ki Sair — A751

Maharaja Chhatrasal — A752

**1987, Oct. 1** *Perf. 13x13½*
*1171* A751 2r Pankha (embroidered apron) 32 16

Festival of thanksgiving for fulfilled prayers.

**1987, Oct. 2** *Perf. 14*
*1172* A752 60p henna brown 10 5

Chhatrasal (1649-1731), military commander during the war against the Moguls.

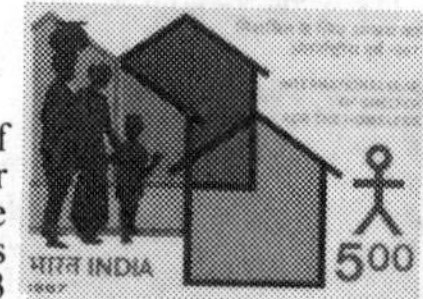

Intl. Year of Shelter for the Homeless A753

**1987, Oct. 5** *Perf. 13½x13*
*1173* A753 5r multicolored 80 40

Asia Regional Conference of Rotary Intl. — A754

**1987, Oct. 14**
*1174* A754 60p shown 10 5
*1175* A754 6.50r Polio immunization 1.05 52

Service to the Blind, Cent. A755

**1987, Oct. 15**

*1176* A755 1r shown 16 8
*1177* A755 2r Eye donation 32 16

World White Cane Day.

INDIA '89 — A756

Designs: 60p, The Iron Pillar, Quwwat-ul-Islam Mosque courtyard, 5th cent., Delhi. 1.50r, The India Gate, New Delhi, war memorial by Luytens, 1921. 5r, The Dewan-E-Khas, Hall of Private Audience, Red Fort, Delhi, c. 1648. 6.50r, Purana Qila, Old Fort, Delhi, c. 1540.

**1987, Oct. 17**

*1178* A756 60p multicolored 10 5
*1179* A756 1.50r multicolored 24 12
*1180* A756 5r multicolored 80 40
*1181* A756 6.50r multicolored 1.05 52
*a.* Souv. sheet of 4, #1178-1181 2.50 1.25

No. 1181a has claret brown inscribed margin picturing exhib. emblem. Sold for 15s. Size: 101x88mm.

Tyagmurti Goswami Ganeshdutt (1889-1959), Educator, Social Activist — A757

**1987, Nov. 2** ***Perf. 13½***

*1182* A757 60p terra cotta 10 5

Children's Day — A758

**1987, Nov. 14**

*1183* A758 60p multicolored 10 5

Trees A759

**1987, Nov. 19** **Photo.** ***Perf. 13½***

*1184* A759 60p Chinar, vert. 10 5
*1185* A759 1.50r Pipal 24 12
*1186* A759 5r Sal, vert. 80 40
*1187* A759 6.50r Banyan 1.05 52

Festival of the USSR in India — A760

Votive coin based on The Worker and the Peasant Woman, by Soviet sculptor Mukhina.

**1987, Nov. 21** ***Perf. 14***

*1188* A760 5r multi 80 40

White Tiger — A761

Rameshwari Nehru (1886-1966), Human Rights and World Peace Activist — A762

**1987, Nov. 29** **Photo.** ***Perf. 13½***

*1189* A761 1r shown 16 8
*1190* A761 5r Snow leopard, horiz. 80 40

**1987, Dec. 10**

*1191* A762 60p red brn 10 5

Execution of Veer Narayan Singh (1795-1857), Sikh Uprising Leader A763

**1987, Dec. 10**

*1192* A763 60p dark brn 10 5

Father Kuriakose Elias Chavara (1806-1871), Theologian Beatified by Pope John Paul II Feb. 8, 1986 — A764

**1987, Dec. 20**

*1193* A764 60p dark brn olive 10 5

Dr. Rajah Sir M.A. Muthiah Chettiar (1905-1984), Politician, Pro-chancellor of Annamalai University — A765

**1987, Dec. 21** ***Perf. 13***

*1194* A765 60p chalky blue blk 10 5

Sri Harmandir Sahib (Gold Temple), Amritsar, 400th Anniv. — A766

**1987, Dec. 26** ***Perf. 13½***

*1195* A766 60p multi 10 5

Rukmini Devi (1904-1986), Dancer, Choreographer — A767

**1987, Dec. 27**

*1196* A767 60p dark red 10 5

Dr. Hiralal (1867-1934), Historian A768

Pandit Hriday Nath Kunzru (1887-1978), Human Rights Activist, Statesman A769

**1987, Dec. 31**

*1197* A768 60p dark blue 10 5

**1987, Dec. 31** ***Perf. 13***

*1198* A769 60p org, brt grn & red brn 10 5

75th Session of the Indian Science Congress Assoc. A770

**1988, Jan. 1**

*1199* A770 4r multi 65 32

Solar Energy A771

13th Asia Pacific Dental Congress, New Delhi, Jan. 28-Feb.2 A772

**Wmk. 324**

**1988, Jan. 1** **Photo.** ***Perf. 13***

*1200* A771 5r deep org & sepia 80 40

**1988, Jan. 28** **Unwmk.** ***Perf.***

*1201* A772 4r multi 65 32

Social and Political Reformers A773

U. Tirot Sing (1800-1833), Patriot A774

Designs: No. 1202, Mohan Lal Sukhadia (1916-82). No. 1203, Dr. S.K. Sinha (1887-1961). No. 1204, Chandra Shekhar Azad (1906-31). No. 1205, Govind Ballabh Pant (1887-1961).

**1988** ***Perf. 13***

*1202* A773 60p org, grn & bluish blk 10 5
*1203* A773 60p org, grn & org brn 10 5
*1204* A773 60p org, grn & rose red 10 5
*1205* A773 60p org, grn & pur 10 5

Issue dates: Nos. 1202, Feb. 2; No. 1203, Feb. 4; No. 1204, Feb. 27; No. 1205, Mar. 7.

**1988, Feb. 3**

*1206* A774 60p dull brn 10 5

Kumaon Regiment 4th Battalion, Bicent. A775

Balgandharva (1888-1967), Musician A776

**1988, Feb. 19** ***Perf. 14***

*1207* A775 1r Uniforms of 1788, 1947, 1988 16 8

**1988, Feb. 22** ***Perf. 13x13½***

*1208* A776 60p brn 10 5

Mechanised Infantry Regiment A777

**1988, Feb. 24** ***Perf. 13½x13***

*1209* A777 1r multi 16 8

Sir B.N. Rau (1887-1953), Constitutional Advisor — A778

**1988, Feb. 26** ***Perf. 13***

*1210* A778 60p bluish blk 10 5

Mohindra College, Patiala — A779

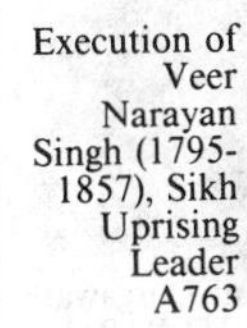

**1988, Mar. 14 Photo.** ***Perf. 13x13½***
*1211* A779 1r brt rose 16 8

Mohindra College, founded in 1875 by Maharaja Mohinder Singh, is now part of Punjabi University.

Dr. D.V. Gundappa (1887-1975), Journalist, and Gikhala Institute of Public Affairs
A780

**1988, Mar. 17** ***Perf. 13½x13***
*1212* A780 60p slate blue 10 5

Woman Warrior Riding into Battle — A781

**1988, Mar. 20** ***Perf. 13x13½***
*1213* A781 60p brt rose 10 5

Rani Avantibai (d. 1858), heroine of the 1857 independence war.

Malayala Manorama Newspaper, Cent.
A782

**1988, Mar. 23**
*1214* A782 1r blue & blk 16 8

Malayala Manorama, published in Kottayam, is the largest circulated daily newspaper in India.

Maharshi Dadhichi, Vedic Period Saint Purported to Have Introduced Fire to Man — A783

**1988, Mar. 26**
*1215* A783 60p deep org 10 5

Mohammad Iqbal (1877-1938), Poet
A784

**1988, Apr. 21**
*1216* A784 60p car & gold 10 5

The indexes in each volume of the Scott Catalogue contain many listings which help to identify stamps.

Samarth Ramdas (1608-1682), Philosopher
A785

Swati Tirunal Rama Varma (1813-1846), Carnatic Composer
A786

**1988, May 1** ***Perf. 13***
*1217* A785 60p dark yel grn 10 5

**1988, May 2** ***Perf. 13x13½***
*1218* A786 60p brt vio 10 5

1st War of Independence, the "Indian Mutiny of 1857" — A787

Painting: Rani Laxmi Bai transformed from a queen into a warrior fighting for justice, by M.F. Husain.

**1988, May 9 Photo.** ***Perf. 13x13½***
*1219* A787 60p multi 10 5

Bhaurao Patil (b. 1887), Educator
A788

**1988, May 9** ***Perf. 13½x13***
*1220* A788 60p red brn 10 5

Himalayan Peaks
A789

**1988, May 19**

| | | | | |
|---|---|---|---|---|
| *1221* | A789 | 1.50r Broad Peak | 24 | 12 |
| *1222* | A789 | 4r Godwin Austin | 65 | 32 |
| *1223* | A789 | 5r Kanchenjunga | 75 | 38 |
| *1224* | A789 | 6.50r Nandadevi | 1.00 | 50 |

Care for the Elderly — A790

**1988, May 24** ***Perf. 13x13½***
*1225* A790 60p multi 10 5

Victoria Terminal, Bombay, Cent.
A791

**1988, May 30** ***Perf. 13½x13***
*1226* A791 1r multi 16 8

Lawrence School, Lovedale, 130th Anniv.
A792

**1988, May 31** ***Perf. 13***
*1227* A792 1r dark grn & red brn 16 8

World Environment Day — A793

**1988, June 5** ***Perf. 14***
*1228* A793 60p Khejri tree 10 5

Dr. Anugrah Narain Singh (1887-1957), Statesman
A794

Rani Durgawati (d. 1564), Ruler of Gondwana
A795

Famous men: No. 1230, Kuladhor Chaliha (1886-1963), political and social reformer. No. 1231, Shivprasad Gupta (1883-1944), freedom fighter.

**1988** ***Perf. 13***
*1229* A794 60p org, sage grn & rose vio 10 5
*1230* A794 60p org, sage grn & gray blk 10 5
*1231* A794 60p org, sage grn & dark vio 10 5

Issue dates: No. 1229, June 18. No. 1230, June 19. No. 1231, June 28.

**1988, June 24**
*1232* A795 60p red 10 5

Acharya Shanti Dev (687-765), Sanskrit and Pali Scholar — A796

Yashwant Singh Parmar (1906-1981), Administrator of Himachal Pradesh State — A797

**1988, July 28 Photo.** ***Perf. 13x13½***
*1233* A796 60p red brn 10 5

**1988, Aug. 4**
*1234* A797 60p blue vio 10 5

A798

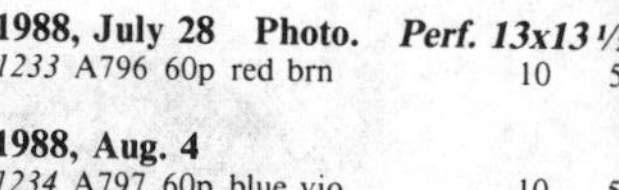

A798a
Painting by M.F. Husain

**1988, Aug. 16 Photo.** ***Perf. 13x13½***
*1235* A798 60p multi 10 5
*1236* A798a 60p multi 10 5

Natl. Independence 40th anniv.

Durgadas Rathore (1638-1718), Guardian of King Ajit Singh
A799

Sarat Chandra Bose (1889-1950), Politician, Lawyer, Publisher
A800

**1988, Aug. 26** ***Litho.***
*1237* A799 60p dark red brn 10 5

**1988, Sept. 6 Photo.** ***Perf. 13***
*1238* A800 60p org, sage grn & dark blue grn 10 5

Gopinath Kaviraj (1887-1976), Scholar — A801

**1988, Sept. 7** ***Perf. 13x13½***
*1239* A801 60p brn olive 10 5

Hindi Language Day, Sept. 14
A802

Indian Olympic Association Emblem
A803

Glory of Sport, Independence 40th Anniv. — A804

**1988, Sept. 14 Photo. *Perf. 13x13½***
*1240* A802 60p ver & dark olive grn 10 5

***Perf. 13½x13, 13x13½***
**1988, Sept. 17**
*1241* A803 60p deep claret 8 5
*1242* A804 5r multi 80 40

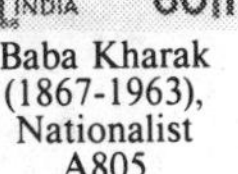

Baba Kharak (1867-1963), Nationalist A805

Jerdon's Courser A806

**1988, Oct. 6 *Perf. 13½x13***
*1243* A805 60p org, grn & org brn 10 5

**1988, Oct. 7 *Perf. 13½***
*1244* A806 1r multi 16 8

*The Times of India,* Newspaper, 150th Anniv. — A807

**1988, Nov. 3 *Perf. 13½x14***
*1245* A807 1.50r blk & gold 25 12

## AIR POST STAMPS

De Havilland Hercules over Lake AP1

**1929-30 Typo. Wmk. 196 *Perf. 14***
*C1* AP1 2a dull green 55 28
*C2* AP1 3a deep blue 80 55
*C3* AP1 4a gray olive 2.25 1.10
*a.* 4a olive green ('30) 2.75 1.10
*C4* AP1 6a bister 2.75 70
*C5* AP1 8a red violet 3.25 3.25
*C6* AP1 12a brown red 9.75 9.75
*Nos. C1-C6 (6)* 19.35 15.63

**Catalogue values for unused stamps in this section, from this point to the end of the section, are for Never Hinged items.**

### Dominion of India

Lockheed Constellation — AP2

***Perf. 13½x14***
**1948, May 29 Litho. Wmk. 196**
*C7* AP2 12a ultra & slate blk 55 28

Bombay-London flight of June 8, 1948.

### Republic of India

The Spirit of '76, by Archibald M. Willard — AP3

**1976, May 29 *Perf. 13x13½***
*C8* AP3 2.80r multicolored 75 55

American Bicentennial.

INDIA '80 Emblem, De Havilland Puss Moth AP4

**1979, Oct. 15 Photo. *Perf. 14½x14***
*C9* AP4 30p shown 5 5
*C10* AP4 50p Chetak helicopter 7 6
*C11* AP4 1r Boeing 737 14 7
*C12* AP4 2r Boeing 747 28 14

INDIA '80 Intl. Stamp Exhib., New Delhi, Jan. 25-Feb. 3, 1980.

## MILITARY STAMPS

### China Expeditionary Force

Regular Issues of India, 1882-99, Overprinted **C. E. F.**

**1900 Wmk. Star. (39) *Perf. 14.***
*M1* A31 3p car rose 18 18
*M2* A17 ½a dk grn 38 70
*M3* A19 1a maroon 45 75
*M4* A21 2a ultra 1.40 *3.00*
*M5* A28 2a6p green 1.10 *3.75*
*M6* A22 3a orange 3.00 *7.75*
*M7* A23 4a ol grn 1.90 3.00
*M8* A25 8a red vio 1.90 4.50
*M9* A26 12a vio, *red* 3.50 *12.00*
*M10* A29 1r car rose & grn 4.00 *6.00*
*a.* Double overprint
*Nos. M1-M10 (10)* 17.81 41.63

The 1a6p of this set was overprinted, but not issued. Value $100.

Overprinted on 1900 Issue of India

**1904**
*M11* A19 1a car rose 16.00 *10.50*

Overprinted on 1902-09 Issue of India.

**1904-11**
*M12* A32 3p gray 55 55
*M13* A34 1a car rose 2.25 2.25
*M14* A35 2a violet 2.00 1.50
*M15* A36 2a6p ultra 1.90 2.00
*M16* A37 3a brn org 2.00 2.50
*M17* A38 4a ol grn 5.25 *7.75*
*M18* A40 8a red vio 5.25 *6.75*
*M19* A41 12a vio, *red* 7.75 *15.00*
*M20* A42 1r car rose & grn 10.50 *21.00*
*Nos. M12-M20 (9)* 37.45 59.30

Overprinted on 1906 Issue of India

**1909**
*M21* A44 ½a green 1.00 1.00
*M22* A45 1a car rose 65 40

Overprinted on 1911-19 Issues of India

**1914-21**
*M23* A46 3p gray 1.00 *1.90*
*M24* A47 ½a green 1.40 *2.00*
*M25* A48 1a car rose 1.50 55
*M26* A58 1½a chocolate 5.25 *15.00*
*M27* A49 2a violet 2.50 *7.00*
*M28* A57 2a6p ultra 3.25 *4.50*
*M29* A51 3a brn org 7.75 *11.00*
*M30* A52 4a ol grn 13.00 *27.50*
*M31* A54 8a red vio 14.00 *30.00*
*M32* A55 12a claret 15.00 *35.00*
*M33* A56 1r grn & red brn 40.00 *77.50*
*Nos. M23-M33 (11)* 104.65 211.95

### Indian Expeditionary Force

Regular Issues of India, 1911-13, Overprinted **I. E. F.**

**1914 Wmk. 39 *Perf. 14.***
*M34* A46 3p gray 10 10
*a.* Double overprint 17.50 17.50
*M35* A47 ½a green 15 15
*M36* A48 1a car rose 15 15
*M37* A49 2a violet 30 25
*M38* A57 2a6p ultra 32 25
*M39* A51 3a brn org 60 60
*M40* A52 4a ol grn 65 65
*M41* A54 8a red vio 1.00 1.00
*M42* A55 12a claret 1.75 1.75
*a.* Double overprint
*M43* A56 1r grn & red brn 3.25 3.50
*Nos. M34-M43 (10)* 8.27 8.40

**Catalogue values for unused stamps in this section, from this point to the end of the section, are for Never Hinged items.**

### Korea Custodial Unit

Regular Issues of India Overprinted in Black **भारतीय संरक्षा कटक कोरिया**

***Perf. 13½x14, 14x13½.***
**1953 Wmk. 196**
*M44* A91 3p gray vio 14 25
*M45* A92 6p red brn 14 25
*M46* A91 9p green 25 40
*M47* A101 1a turquoise 32 50
*M48* A93 2a carmine 55 80
*M49* A94 2½a brn lake 1.10 95
*M50* A94 3a red org 1.25 1.40
*M51* A94 4a ultra 1.40 1.65
*M52* A95 6a purple 5.50 5.00
*M53* A95 8a bl grn 3.75 4.50
*M54* A95 12a blue 5.50 7.25
*M55* A96 1r dk grn & pur 8.25 11.00
*Nos. M44-M55 (12)* 28.15 33.95

Hindi overprint reads "Indian Custodial Unit, Korea."

### Indian U.N. Force in Congo

Nos. 302-303, 305, 307, 282 and 313 Overprinted: "U.N. FORCE (INDIA) CONGO"

***Perf. 14x14½***
**1962, Jan. 15 Photo. Wmk. 324**
*M56* A117 1np bl grn 8 8
*M57* A117 2np lt brn 8 8
*M58* A117 5np emerald 8 8
*M59* A117 8np brt grn 20 20

**Wmk. 196**
*M60* A117 13np brt car 35 35

**Wmk. 324**
*M61* A117 50np orange 80 80
*Nos. M56-M61 (6)* 1.59 1.59

### Indian U.N. Force in Gaza

No. 393 Overprinted in Carmine **UNEF**

**1965, Jan. 15 Unwmk. *Perf. 13½***
*M62* A190 15p bl gray 12 12

Overprint letters stand for "United Nations Emergency Force."

## INTERNATIONAL COMMISSION IN INDO-CHINA

**Catalogue values for all unused stamps in this section are for Never Hinged items.**

### Cambodia

India Nos. 207, 231, 211, 216 and 217 Overprinted in Black **अन्तर्राष्ट्रीय आयोग कम्बोज**

**1954 Wmk. 196 *Perf. 13½x14***
*1* A91 3p gray vio 15 15
*2* A101 1a turquoise 22 22
*3* A93 2a carmine 38 38
*4* A95 8a bl grn 1.25 1.50
*5* A95 12a blue 1.90 2.25
*Nos. 1-5 (5)* 3.90 4.50

The overprint reads "International Commission Cambodia." Top line is 18mm. on Nos. 4-5; 15½ mm. on Nos. 1-3, 6-12.

Same Overprint on India Nos. 276, 279, 282, 286 and 287.

**1957 *Perf. 14x14½***
*6* A117 2np lt brn 6 6
*7* A117 6np gray 8 8
*8* A117 13np brt car 22 22
*9* A117 50np orange 55 65
*10* A117 75np plum 1.10 1.40
*Nos. 6-10 (5)* 2.01 2.41

Same Overprint on India No. 303.

**1962 Wmk. 324**
*12* A117 2np lt brn 65 65

### Laos

India Nos. 207, 231, 211, 216 and 217 Overprinted in Black **अन्तर्राष्ट्रीय आयोग लाओस**

**1954 Wmk. 196 *Perf. 13½x14***
*1* A91 3p gray vio 15 15
*2* A101 1a turquoise 22 22
*3* A93 2a carmine 38 38
*4* A95 8a bl grn 1.25 1.50
*5* A95 12a blue 1.90 2.25
*Nos. 1-5 (5)* 3.90 4.50

The overprint reads "International Commission Laos." Top line is 18mm. on Nos. 4-5; 15½mm. on Nos. 1-3, 6-16.

Same Overprint on India Nos. 276, 279, 282, 286 and 287.

**1957 *Perf. 14x14½***
*6* A117 2np lt brn 6 6
*7* A117 6np gray 8 8
*8* A117 13np brt car 22 22
*9* A117 50np orange 55 65
*10* A117 75np plum 1.10 1.40
*Nos. 6-10 (5)* 2.01 2.41

Same Overprint on India Nos. 303-305, 313-314.

**1962-65 Wmk. 324**
*12* A117 2np lt bl 85 1.00
*13* A117 3np brn ('63) 18 18
*14* A117 5np emer ('63) 20 20
*15* A117 50np org ('65) 65 75
*16* A117 75np plum ('65) 1.40 1.65
*Nos. 12-16 (5)* 3.28 3.78

### Laos and Viet Nam

No. 393 Overprinted in Carmine **ICC**

**1965, Jan. 15 Unwmk. *Perf. 13½***
*1* A190 15p bl gray 32 32

Overprint letters stand for "International Control Commission."

Nos. 406-408, 411-412, 417 and 419-420 Overprinted in Carmine **अंनिआ ICC**

***Perf. 14½x14, 14x14½***
**1968, Oct. 2 Photo. Wmk. 324**
*2* A202 2p redsh brn 5 5
*3* A202 3p ol bis 5 5
*4* A202 5p cerise 5 5
*5* A203 10p brt bl 5 5
*6* A203 15p green 10 10
*7* A202 60p dk gray 45 45
*8* A204 1r dp cl & red brn 75 95
*9* A205 2r vio & brt bl 1.65 2.25
*Nos. 2-9 (8)* 3.15 3.95

The arrangement of the lines of the overprint varies on each denomination.

### Viet Nam

India Nos. 207, 231, 211, 216 and 217 Overprinted in Black

अन्तर्राष्ट्रीय आयोग
वियत नाम

**1954 Wmk. 196 *Perf. 13½x14***

*1* A91 3p gray vio 15 15
*2* A101 1a turquoise 22 22
*3* A93 2a carmine 38 38
*4* A95 8a bl grn 1.25 1.50
*5* A95 12a blue 1.90 2.25
*Nos. 1-5 (5)* 3.90 4.50

The overprint reads "International Commission Viet Nam." Top line of overprint is 18mm. on Nos. 4-5; 15½mm. on Nos.m 1-3, 6-16.

Same Overprint on India Nos. 276, 279, 282, 286 and 287.

**1957 *Perf. 14x14½***

*6* A117 2np lt brn 6 6
*7* A117 6np gray 8 8
*8* A117 13np brt car 22 22
*9* A117 50np orange 55 65
*10* A117 75np plum 1.10 1.40
*Nos. 6-10 (5)* 2.01 2.41

Same Overprint on India Nos. 302-305, 313-314.

**1961-65 Wmk. 324**

*11* A117 1np bl grn 55 65
*12* A117 2np lt brn ('62) 1.10 1.10
*13* A117 3np brn ('63) 38 38
*14* A117 5np emer ('63) 22 32
*15* A117 50np org ('65) 85 1.10
*16* A117 75np plum ('65) 1.65 1.90
*Nos. 11-16 (6)* 4.75 5.45

## OFFICIAL STAMPS

Regular Issues Overprinted in Black **Service.**

**1866, Aug. 1 Unwmk. *Perf. 14***

*O1* A7 ½a blue 65.00
*a.* Inverted overprint
*O3* A7 1a brown 65.00
*O4* A7 8a rose 6.50 *10.50*

The 8p lilac unwatermarked (No. 19) with "Service" overprint was not officially issued.

**Wmk. Elephant's Head. (38)**

*O5* A7 ½a blue 75.00 10.00
*a.* Inverted overprint
*b.* Without period 165.00
*O6* A8 8p lilac 12.00 16.00
*O7* A7 1a brown 85.00 14.00
*a.* Inverted overprint
*O8* A7 2a yellow 62.50 21.50
*a.* Imperf.
*b.* Inverted overprint
*O9* A7 4a green 60.00 52.50
*a.* Inverted overprint
*O10* A9 4a grn (I) 450.00 140.00

*Reprints were made of Nos. O5, O7 and O10 (type II).*

Revenue Stamps Surcharged or Overprinted.

Queen Victoria — O1

Blue Glazed Paper
Black Surcharge

**Wmk. Crown and INDIA. (36)**

**1866 *Perf. 14 Vertically.***

*O11* O1 2a violet 350.00 115.00

*Reprints of No. O11 are surcharged in either black or green, and have the word "SERVICE" 16½x2½mm., instead of 16½x2¼mm. and "TWO ANNAS" 18x3mm., instead of 20x3¼mm.*

O2

O3

O4

**1866**

**Green Overprint**

*O12* O2 2a violet 465.00 225.00
*O13* O3 4a violet 1,150. 400.00
*O14* O4 8a violet 4,000. 2,150.

The note after No. 30 will apply here also.

*Reprints of No. O12 have the overprint in sans-serif letters 2¼mm. high, instead of Roman letters 2½mm. high. On the reprints of No. O13 "SERVICE" measures 16½x2¼mm., instead of 20¼x3mm. and "POSTAGE" 18x2¼mm., instead of 22x3 mm.*

*On No. O14 "SERVICE" is 20½mm. long, instead of 20mm. and "POSTAGE" is 23mm. long, instead of 22mm. All three overprints are in a darker green than on the original stamps.*

O5

Wmk. 40

Green Overprint

**1866 Wmk. 40 *Perf. 15½x15***

**Lilac Paper**

*O15* O5 ½a violet 200.00 67.50
*a.* Double overprint 2,100.

Regular Issues Overprinted in Black **Service.**

**1866-73 Wmk. 38 *Perf. 14***

*O16* A7 ½a blue 3.25 20
*O17* A7 ½a bl, re-engraved 125.00 30.00
*a.* Double overprint
*O18* A7 1a brown 3.50 18
*O19* A7 2a orange 2.25 18
*a.* 2a yel 2.50 60
*O20* A9 4a grn (I) 90 10
*O21* A11 8a rose 1.40 15

The 6a8p with this overprint was not issued. Value $25.

Overprinted in Black **On H. M. S.**

**1874-82**

*O22* A7 ½a bl, re-engraved 1.75 18
*a.* Blue overprint 185.00 37.50
*O23* A7 1a brown 2.00 12
*a.* Blue overprint 375.00 75.00
*O24* A7 2a orange 9.00 3.00
*O25* A9 4a grn (I) 4.00 50
*O26* A11 8a rose 3.00 2.00

**1883-97 Wmk. Star. (39)**

*O27* A17 ½a green 12 6
*a.* Pair, one without overprint
*b.* Double overprint 75.00
*O28* A19 1a maroon 10 6
*a.* Inverted overprint 75.00 85.00
*b.* Double overprint 100.00
*c.* 1a vio brn 10 6
*O29* A21 2a ultra 30 7
*O30* A23 4a ol grn 2.00 8
*O31* A25 8a red vio 90 18
*O32* A29 1r car rose & grn 3.25 50
*Nos. O27-O32 (6)* 6.67 95

**1899**

*O33* A31 3p car rose 50 10

**1900**

*O34* A17 ½a lt grn 30 5
*O35* A19 1a car rose 90 5
*a.* Double overprint 150.00
*b.* Inverted overprint 100.00
*O36* A21 2a violet 2.50 6

**1902-09**

*O37* A32 3p gray 20 5
*O38* A33 ½a green 45 5
*O39* A34 1a car rose 12 5
*O40* A35 2a violet *1.40* 5
*O41* A38 4a ol grn *1.75* 5
*O42* A39 6a bister *2.00* 5
*O43* A40 8a red lil *3.75* 10
*O44* A42 1r car rose & grn ('05) *4.25* 10
*Nos. O37-O44 (8)* 13.92 50

**1906-07**

*O45* A44 ½a green 15 5
*O46* A45 1a car rose 90 5
*a.* Pair, one without overprint
*b.* Overprint on back

**1909**

*O47* A43 2r brn & rose *6.00* 20
*O48* A43 5r vio & ultra *15.00* 65
*O49* A43 10r car rose & grn *18.00* 3.00
*a.* 10r red & grn 25.00 3.00
*O50* A43 15r ol gray & ultra 60.00 22.50
*O51* A43 25r ultra & org brn 125.00 47.50
*Nos. O47-O51 (5)* 224.00 73.85

Regular Issues Overprinted in Black **SERVICE**

**1912-22**

*O52* A41 3p gray 10 5
*O53* A47 ½a green 10 5
*a.* Double ovpt. 82.50
*O54* A48 1a car rose 10 5
*a.* Double overprint 110.00
*O55* A48 1a dk brn ('22) 20 5
*a.* Imperf., pair 75.00
*O56* A49 2a violet 18 5
*O57* A52 4a ol grn 18 6
*O58* A53 6a bister 1.40 90
*O59* A54 8a red vio 1.40 9

Overprinted in Black **SERVICE**

*O60* A56 1r grn & red brn 2.25 8
*O61* A56 2r yel brn & car rose 2.75 90
*O62* A56 5r vio & ultra 15.00 6.00
*O63* A56 10r car rose & grn 35.00 15.00
*O64* A56 15r ol grn & ultra 57.50 42.50
*O65* A56 25r ultra & brn org 115.00 45.00
*Nos. O52-O65 (14)* 231.16 110.78

O6

O7

**1921 Black Surcharge**

*O66* O6 9p on 1a rose 20 10

Official Stamps of 1909 Surcharged **ONE RUPEE**

**1925**

*O67* A43 1r on 15r ol gray & ultra 4.00 1.90
*O68* A43 1r on 25r ultra & org brn 16.00 *25.00*
*O69* A43 2r on 10r red & grn 2.50 2.50
*a.* 2r on 10r car rose & grn 150.00 35.00
*b.* Surcharge on No. O63 (error) 750.00

Official Stamps of 1912-13 Surcharged **ONE RUPEE**

*O70* A56 1r on 15r ol grn & ultra 17.00 21.00
*a.* Inverted surcharge
*O71* A56 1r on 25r ultra & brn org 5.00 4.25
*a.* Inverted surcharge 350.00

**1926**

*O73* O7 1a on 6a bis 30 25

Regular Issues of 1911-26 Surcharged **SERVICE ONE ANNA**

*O74* A48 1a on 1a dk brn (error) 200.00 200.00
*O75* A58 1a on 1½a choc 18 5
*a.* Inverted surcharge
*O76* A59 1a on 1½a choc 25 18
*a.* Inverted surcharge
*b.* Double surcharge 30.00
*O77* A57 1a on 2a6p ultra 40 25

Nos. O74, O75 and O76 have short bars over the numerals in the upper corners.

Regular Issues of 1926-35 Overprinted

a **SERVICE**

**1926-35 Wmk. 196**

*O78* A46 3p sl ('29) 8 5
*O79* A47 ½a grn ('31) 50 5
*O80* A48 1a dk brn 8 5
*a.* Overprint as on No. O55 35.00 4.75
*O81* A49 2a ver ('35) 75 10
*a.* Small die 50 5
*O82* A60 2a dl vio 12 5
*O83* A60 2a ver ('32) 60 8
*O84* A57 2a6p buff ('32) 14 5
*O85* A52 4a ol grn ('35) 1.00 6
*O86* A61 4a ol grn 24 6
*O87* A53 6a bis ('35) 3.00 3.50
*O88* A54 8a red vio 35 5
*O89* A55 12a claret 45 12

Overprinted

b **SERVICE**

*O90* A56 1r grn & brn ('30) 1.25 8
*O91* A56 2r brn org & car rose ('30) 5.25 2.00
*O92* A56 10r car & grn ('31) 52.50 40.00
*Nos. O78-O92 (15)* 66.31 46.30

Regular Issues of 1932-34 Overprinted Type "a"

**1932-35**

*O93* A71 ½a grn ('35) 30 5
*O94* A68 9p dk grn 28 5
*O95* A72 1a dk brn ('35) 28 5
*O96* A69 1a3p violet 10 5

Regular Issue of 1937 Overprinted Type "a"

**1937-39 *Perf. 13½x14.***

*O97* A80 ½a brn ('38) 2.00 5
*O98* A80 9p green 4.25 5
*O99* A80 1a carmine 55 5

### Type "b" Overprint

| | | | | |
|---|---|---|---|---|
| O100 | A82 | 1r brn & sl ('38) | 32 | 6 |
| O101 | A82 | 2r dk brn & dk vio ('38) | 3.50 | 20 |
| O102 | A82 | 5r dp ultra & dk grn ('38) | 4.25 | 1.65 |
| O103 | A82 | 10r rose car & dk vio ('39) | 14.00 | 3.75 |
| | | *Nos. O97-O103 (7)* | 28.87 | 5.81 |

No. 136 Surcharged in Black — SERVICE 1A

**1939 Wmk. 196 *Perf. 14.***

| | | | | |
|---|---|---|---|---|
| O104 | A69 | 1a on 1a3p vio | *1.50* | 8 |

King George VI — O8

**1939-43 Typo. *Perf. 13½x14***

| | | | | |
|---|---|---|---|---|
| O105 | O8 | 3p slate | 5 | 5 |
| O106 | O8 | ½a brown | 10 | 5 |
| O106A | O8 | ½a dk rose vio ('43) | 7 | 5 |
| O107 | O8 | 9p green | 7 | 5 |
| O108 | O8 | 1a car rose | 7 | 5 |
| O108A | O8 | 1a3p bis ('41) | *3.25* | *65* |
| O108B | O8 | 1½a dl pur ('43) | 15 | 5 |
| O109 | O8 | 2a scarlet | 10 | 5 |
| O110 | O8 | 2½a purple | 12 | 5 |
| O111 | O8 | 4a dk brn | 20 | 5 |
| O112 | O8 | 8a bl vio | 30 | 5 |
| | | *Nos. O105-O112 (11)* | *4.48* | *1.15* |

Stamps overprinted "Postal Service" or "I. P. N." were not used as postage stamps.

**Catalogue values for unused stamps in this section, from this point to the end of the section, are for Never Hinged items.**

Nos. 203-206 (Gandhi Issue) Overprinted Type "a"

**1948 Unwmk. Photo. *Perf. 11½***

| | | | | |
|---|---|---|---|---|
| O112A | A90 | 1½a brown | *32.50* | *25.00* |
| O112B | A90 | 3½a violet | *325.00* | *325.00* |
| O112C | A90 | 12a dk gray grn | *1,000.* | *1,000.* |
| O112D | A90 | 10r rose brn & brn | *5,000.* | |

Overprint forgeries exist.

Capital of Asoka Pillar O9 O10

***Perf. 13½x14***

**1950 Wmk. 196 Typo.**

| | | | | |
|---|---|---|---|---|
| O113 | O9 | 3p vio bl | 5 | 5 |
| O114 | O9 | 6p chocolate | 5 | 5 |
| O115 | O9 | 9p green | 6 | 5 |
| O116 | O9 | 1a turquoise | 6 | 5 |
| O117 | O9 | 2a red | 6 | 5 |
| O118 | O9 | 3a vermilion | 10 | 5 |
| O119 | O9 | 4a brn car | 3.75 | 6 |
| O120 | O9 | 6a purple | 15 | 5 |
| O121 | O9 | 8a org brn | 20 | 5 |

**Litho. *Perf. 14x13½***

| | | | | |
|---|---|---|---|---|
| O122 | O10 | 1r dk pur | 40 | 6 |
| O123 | O10 | 2r brn red | 65 | 15 |
| O124 | O10 | 5r dk grn | 1.50 | 70 |
| O125 | O10 | 10r red brn | 4.50 | 1.45 |
| | | *Nos. O113-O125 (13)* | 11.53 | 2.82 |

**1951 Typo.**

| | | | | |
|---|---|---|---|---|
| O126 | O9 | 4a vio bl | 12 | 5 |

Type of 1949-50 Redrawn; Denomination in Naye Paise.

**Typo. or Litho.**

**1957-58 *Perf. 13½x14***

| | | | | |
|---|---|---|---|---|
| O127 | O9 | 1np sl bl | 5 | 5 |
| O128 | O9 | 2np bl vio | 5 | 5 |
| O129 | O9 | 3np chocolate | 5 | 5 |
| O130 | O9 | 5np yel grn | 5 | 5 |
| O131 | O9 | 6np turquoise | 6 | 5 |
| O132 | O9 | 13np red | 6 | 5 |
| O133 | O9 | 15np dk pur ('58) | 12 | 5 |
| O134 | O9 | 20np vermilion | 15 | 6 |
| O135 | O9 | 25np vio bl | 20 | 6 |
| O136 | O9 | 50np redsh brn | 35 | 10 |
| | | *Nos. O127-O136 (10)* | 1.14 | 57 |

Redrawn Type of 1957-58.

**Typo. or Litho.**

**1958-71 Wmk. 324 *Perf. 13½x14***

| | | | | |
|---|---|---|---|---|
| O137 | O9 | 1np sl bl ('59) | 5 | 5 |
| O138 | O9 | 2np bl vio ('59) | 5 | 5 |
| O139 | O9 | 3np chocolate | 5 | 5 |
| O140 | O9 | 5np yel grn | 5 | 5 |
| O141 | O9 | 6np turq ('59) | 15 | 6 |
| O142 | O9 | 10np dk grn ('63) | 15 | 9 |
| O142A | O9 | 13np red ('63) | 5 | 5 |
| O143 | O9 | 15np dk pur | 5 | 5 |
| O144 | O9 | 20np ver ('59) | 5 | 5 |
| O145 | O9 | 25np vio bl ('59) | 8 | 5 |
| O146 | O9 | 50np redsh brn ('59) | 9 | 5 |

**Litho.**

***Perf. 14***

| | | | | |
|---|---|---|---|---|
| O147 | O10 | 1r rose vio ('59) | 20 | 5 |
| O148 | O10 | 2r rose red ('60) | 35 | 9 |
| *a.* | | Watermark sideways ('69) | 35 | 12 |
| O149 | O10 | 5r green ('59) | 90 | 28 |
| *a.* | | Watermark sideways ('69) | 90 | 30 |
| O150 | O10 | 10r rose lake ('59) | 1.75 | 75 |
| *a.* | | Watermark sideways ('71) | 1.75 | 90 |
| | | *Nos. O137-O150 (15)* | 4.02 | 1.77 |

Capital of Asoka Pillar O11 O12

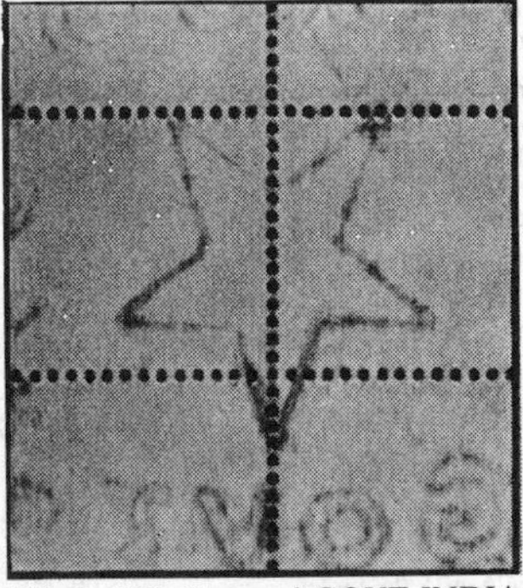

Wmk. 360- Star and GOVT INDIA

**1967-76 Photo. Wmk. 360 *Perf. 14***

**Without Gum**

| | | | | |
|---|---|---|---|---|
| O151 | O11 | 2p vio blk | 5 | 5 |
| O152 | O11 | 3p dk red brn | 5 | 5 |
| O153 | O11 | 5p brt grn | 5 | 5 |
| O154 | O11 | 6p Prus bl | 5 | 5 |
| O155 | O11 | 10p sl grn | 5 | 5 |
| O156 | O11 | 15p purple | 5 | 5 |
| O157 | O11 | 20p org ver | 6 | 5 |
| O158 | O11 | 25p dp car ('76) | 8 | 5 |
| O159 | O11 | 30p vio bl | 10 | 5 |
| O160 | O11 | 50p red brn | 16 | 5 |
| | | *Nos. O151-O160 (10)* | 70 | 50 |

No. O153 Overprinted शरणार्थी सहायता REFUGEE RELIEF

**1971, Nov. 15 Wmk. 360**

**Without Gum**

| | | | | |
|---|---|---|---|---|
| O161 | O11 | 5p green | 5 | 5 |

**No. O153 Overprinted "Refugee / Relief"**

| | | | | |
|---|---|---|---|---|
| O162 | O11 | 5p green | 5 | 5 |

No. O162 was used in Maharashtra state.

**1971, Dec. 1(?)**

**Without Gum**

| | | | | |
|---|---|---|---|---|
| O163 | O12 | 5p green | 5 | 5 |

Nos. O161-O163 were obligatory on all official mail as a postal tax to benefit refugees from East Pakistan. The tax was paid out of the various governmental departments' budgets.

Type of 1968

**1967-74 Wmk. 324 *Perf. 14½x14***

| | | | | |
|---|---|---|---|---|
| O164 | O11 | 2p violet | 5 | 5 |
| O165 | O11 | 5p brt grn ('74) | 5 | 5 |
| O166 | O11 | 10p sl grn ('74) | 5 | 5 |
| O167 | O11 | 15p pur ('73) | 5 | 5 |
| O168 | O11 | 20p dp org ('74) | 6 | 5 |
| O169 | O11 | 30p ultra | 5 | 5 |
| O170 | O11 | 50p red brn ('73) | 16 | 5 |
| O171 | O11 | 1r dl pur | 32 | 8 |
| | | *Nos. O164-O171 (8)* | 79 | 43 |

Without Currency Designation

O13 O14

**Wmk. 360 (2p, 5p, 20p, 25p); Wmk. 324 (others).**

**1976-80 Litho. *Perf. 14½x14***

**Without Gum**

| | | | | |
|---|---|---|---|---|
| O172 | O13 | 2p vio blk | 5 | 5 |
| O173 | O13 | 5p brt grn | 5 | 5 |
| O174 | O13 | 10p sl grn | 5 | 5 |
| O175 | O13 | 15p purple | 5 | 5 |
| O176 | O13 | 20p brn org | 5 | 5 |
| O177 | O13 | 25p car rose | 5 | 5 |
| O178 | O13 | 30p bl ('79) | 8 | 5 |
| O179 | O13 | 35p vio ('80) | 8 | 5 |
| O180 | O13 | 50p red brn | 10 | 5 |
| O181 | O13 | 1r dl pur, wmk. 360 ('80) | 25 | 12 |
| O182 | O13 | 1r dl pur, wmk. 324 | 20 | 5 |

***Perf. 14x13½***

| | | | | |
|---|---|---|---|---|
| O183 | O14 | 2r sal rose | 45 | 15 |
| O184 | O14 | 5r dp grn | 1.10 | 35 |
| O185 | O14 | 10r red brn | 2.25 | 75 |
| | | *Nos. O172-O185 (14)* | 4.81 | 1.87 |

O15

**1981 Litho. Wmk. 360 *Perf. 15x14***

**Without Gum**

| | | | | |
|---|---|---|---|---|
| O186 | O15 | 2r org ver | 50 | 25 |
| O187 | O15 | 5r dk grn | 1.25 | 62 |
| O188 | O15 | 10r dk red brn | 2.50 | 1.25 |

**Unwmk.**

**1981, Dec. 10 Litho. *Imperf.***

**Cream Paper**

| | | | | |
|---|---|---|---|---|
| O189 | O13 | 5p brt grn | 5 | 5 |
| O190 | O13 | 10p sl grn | 5 | 5 |
| O191 | O13 | 15p purple | 5 | 5 |
| O192 | O13 | 20p brn org | 5 | 5 |
| O193 | O13 | 25p car rose | 6 | 5 |
| O194 | O13 | 35p violet | 8 | 5 |
| O195 | O13 | 50p brown | 12 | 6 |
| O196 | O13 | 1r dl pur | 25 | 12 |
| O197 | O15 | 2r sal rose | 50 | 25 |
| O198 | O15 | 5r dp grn | 1.25 | 62 |
| O199 | O15 | 10r red brn | 2.50 | 1.25 |
| | | *Nos. O189-O199 (11)* | 4.96 | 2.60 |

***Perf. 12½x13***

**1982 Photo. Wmk. 360**

**Without Gum**

| | | | | |
|---|---|---|---|---|
| O200 | O13 | 5p brt grn | 5 | 5 |
| O201 | O13 | 10p sl grn | 5 | 5 |
| O202 | O13 | 15p purple | 5 | 5 |
| O203 | O13 | 20p fawn | 6 | 5 |
| O204 | O13 | 25p car rose | 5 | 5 |
| O205 | O13 | 30p dk bl | 6 | 5 |
| O206 | O13 | 35p violet | 8 | 5 |
| O207 | O13 | 50p lt brn | 12 | 6 |
| O208 | O13 | 1r dl pur | 25 | 12 |
| O209 | O15 | 2r sal rose | 50 | 25 |
| O210 | O15 | 5r dp grn | 1.25 | 62 |
| O211 | O15 | 10r red brn | 2.50 | 1.25 |
| | | *Nos. O200-O211 (12)* | 5.02 | 2.65 |

***Perf. 12½x13***

**1984, Apr. 16 Photo. Wmk. 324**

| | | | | |
|---|---|---|---|---|
| O212 | O13 | 5p green | 5 | 5 |
| O213 | O13 | 10p dk grn | 5 | 5 |
| O214 | O13 | 15p rose lake | 5 | 5 |
| O215 | O13 | 20p fawn | 5 | 5 |
| O216 | O13 | 30p blue | 6 | 5 |
| O217 | O13 | 35p purple | 8 | 5 |
| O218 | O13 | 50p brown | 10 | 5 |
| O219 | O15 | 1r vio brn | 20 | 10 |
| O220 | O15 | 2r org ver | 40 | 20 |
| O221 | O15 | 5r gray grn | 1.00 | 50 |
| O222 | O15 | 10r red brn | 2.00 | 1.00 |
| | | *Nos. O212-O222 (11)* | 4.04 | 2.15 |

## POSTAL TAX STAMPS

**Catalogue values for unused stamps in this section, from this point to the end of the section, are for Never Hinged items.**

No. 408 Overprinted शरणार्थी सहायता REFUGEE RELIEF

***Perf. 14½x14***

**1971, Nov. 15 Photo. Wmk. 324**

| | | | | |
|---|---|---|---|---|
| RA1 | A202 | 5p cerise | 5 | 5 |

**No. 408 Overprinted "Refugee/Relief"**

| | | | | |
|---|---|---|---|---|
| RA2 | A202 | 5p cerise | 5 | 5 |

No. RA2 was used in Maharashtra. In order to make the obligatory tax stamps available immediately throughout India postmasters were authorized to overprint locally No. 408. This resulted in a great variety of mostly handstamped overprints of various types and sizes.

Refugees — PT1

***Perf. 14x14½***

**1971, Dec. 1 Photo. Wmk. 324**

| | | | | |
|---|---|---|---|---|
| RA3 | PT1 | 5pa cerise | 5 | 5 |

Nos. RA1-RA3 were obligatory on all mail. The tax was for refugees from East Pakistan.

See also Nos. O161-O163.

**CONVENTION STATES OF THE BRITISH EMPIRE IN INDIA.**

**Stamps of British India overprinted for use in the States of Chamba, Faridkot, Gwalior, Jhind, Nabha and Patiala.**

**These stamps had franking power throughout all British India.**

## CHAMBA

LOCATION — A State of India located in the north Punjab, south of Kashmir.

AREA — 3,127 sq. mi.

POP. — 168,908 (1941).

CAPITAL — Chamba

The varieties with small letters in the overprint are not listed as the letters are merely broken and not from another font of type.

Indian Stamps Overprinted in Black — CHAMBA STATE

**1886-95 Wmk. Star. (39) *Perf. 14.***

| | | | | |
|---|---|---|---|---|
| 1 | A17 | ½a green | 16 | 20 |
| *a.* | | "CHMABA" | 100.00 | *100.00* |
| *c.* | | Double overprint | | |
| 2 | A19 | 1a vio brn | 16 | 24 |
| *a.* | | "CHMABA" | 200.00 | |
| 3 | A20 | 1a6p bis brn ('95) | 1.25 | 2.00 |
| 4 | A21 | 2a ultra | 24 | 28 |
| *a.* | | "CHMABA" | 550.00 | |

5 A28 2a6p grn ('95) 16.00 *30.00*
6 A22 3a brn org 60 80
 a. 3a org 4.00 *8.00*
 b. Invtd. ovpt.
 c. "CHMABA" 1,600.
7 A23 4a ol grn 48 *1.25*
 a. "CHMABA" 600.00
8 A25 8a red vio 1.65 *3.25*
 a. "CHMABA" 1,200.
9 A26 12a vio, *red* ('90) 1.25 1.40
 a. "CHMABA" 1,600.
 b. 1st "T" of "STATE" invtd. 2,400.
10 A27 1r gray 22.00 *40.00*
 a. "CHMABA" 3,000.
11 A29 1r car rose & grn ('95) 1.75 *2.75*
12 A30 2r brn & rose ('95) 45.00 *72.50*
13 A30 3r grn & brn ('95) 55.00 *80.00*
14 A30 5r vio & bl ('95) 65.00 *87.50*

**Wmk. Elephant's Head. (38)**

15 A14 6a bis ('90) 65 1.00
 *Nos. 1-15 (15)* 211.19 323.17

**1900** **Wmk. Star. (39)**

15B A31 3p car rose 6 7

**1902-04**

16 A31 3p gray ('04) 7 7
 a. Invtd. ovpt. 45.00
17 A17 ½a lt grn 7 10
18 A19 1a car rose 7 10
19 A21 2a vio ('03) 6.25 7.75

**1903-05**

20 A32 3p gray 7 8
21 A33 ½a green 10 14
22 A34 1a car rose 12 14
23 A35 2a violet 22 25
24 A37 3a brn org ('05) 55 70
25 A38 4a ol grn ('04) 60 75
26 A39 6a bis ('05) 40 48
27 A40 8a red vio ('04) 52 60
28 A41 12a vio, *red* 70 85
29 A42 1r car rose & grn ('05) 2.50 2.75
 *Nos. 20-29 (10)* 5.78 6.74

**1907**

30 A44 ½a green 9 12
31 A45 1a car rose 18 22

**1913-24**

32 A46 3p gray 5 5
33 A47 ½a green 6 10
34 A48 1a car rose 15 18
35 A48 1a dk brn ('22) 15 15
36 A49 2a violet 80 95
37 A51 3a brn org 80 95
38 A51 3a ultra ('24) 1.25 *2.50*
39 A52 4a ol grn 25 32
40 A53 6a bister 32 38
41 A54 8a red vio 95 1.10
42 A55 12a claret 95 1.10
43 A56 1r grn & red brn 80 95
 *Nos. 32-43 (12)* 6.53 8.73

India No. 104 Overprinted

**1921**

44 A48 9p on 1a rose 55 60

India Stamps of 1913-26 Overprinted CHAMBA STATE

**1922-27**

45 A58 1½a chocolate 14.00 *32.50*
46 A59 1½a chocolate 38 45
47 A59 1½a rose 38 45
48 A57 2a6p ultra 60 80
49 A57 2a6p brn org 38 45
 *Nos. 45-49 (5)* 15.74 34.65

India Stamps of 1926 Overprinted CHAMBA STATE

**1927-28** **Wmk. 196**

50 A46 3p slate 5 5
51 A47 ½a green 5 5
52 A48 1a dk brn 8 8
53 A60 2a dl vio 16 22
54 A51 3a ultra 65 *1.25*
55 A61 4a ol grn 22 32
57 A54 8a red vio 32 *1.25*
58 A55 12a claret 1.00 *2.00*

Overprinted CHAMBA STATE

59 A56 1r grn & brn 2.00 *3.25*
 *Nos. 50-55,57-59 (9)* 4.53 8.47

India Stamps of 1926-35 Overprinted CHAMBA STATE

**1932-37**

60 A71 ½a green 60 65
61 A68 9p dk grn 22 26
62 A72 1a dk brn 35 32
63 A69 1a3p violet 12 16
64 A59 1½a car rose 16 22
65 A49 2a vermilion 42 55
 a. Small die 47.50 *85.00*
66 A57 2a6p buff 20 22
67 A51 3a car rose 65 *1.65*
68 A52 4a ol grn ('36) 3.25 3.50
69 A53 6a bis ('37) 45.00 52.50
 *Nos. 60-69 (10)* 50.97 60.03

Same Overprint on India Stamps of 1937

**1938** **Wmk. 196** ***Perf. 13½x14.***

70 A80 3p slate 60 1.25
71 A80 ½a brown 28 32
72 A80 9p green 70 *1.90*
73 A80 1a carmine 70 60

Overprinted CHAMBA STATE

74 A81 2a scarlet 38 *1.50*
75 A81 2a6p purple 28 *2.50*
76 A81 3a yel grn 3.00 *5.50*
77 A81 3a6p ultra 1.25 *3.00*
78 A81 4a dk brn 1.40 2.75
79 A81 6a pck bl 6.25 *10.00*
80 A81 8a bl vio 1.25 *3.00*
81 A81 12a car lake 2.50 *6.25*

Overprinted CHAMBA STATE

82 A82 1r brn & sl 6.25 *7.75*
83 A82 2r dk brn & dk vio 15.00 *25.00*
84 A82 5r dp ultra & dk grn 37.50 *45.00*
85 A82 10r rose car & dk vio 95.00 95.00
86 A82 15r dk grn & dk brn 140.00 *190.00*
87 A82 25r dk vio & bl vio 190.00 *275.00*
 *Nos. 70-87 (18)* 502.34 676.32

India Nos. 151 and 153 Overprinted CHAMBA

**1942**

87B A80 ½a brown 3.50 *4.25*
88 A80 1a carmine 4.25 *5.00*

Same Overprint on India Stamps of 1941-42

**1942-44**

89 A83 3p slate 10 10
90 A83 ½a rose vio ('43) 10 10
91 A83 9p lt grn ('43) 12 12
92 A83 1a car rose ('43) 12 12
93 A84 1½a dk pur ('44) 14 14
94 A84 2a scar ('43) 14 95
95 A84 3a vio ('43) 22 *1.10*
96 A84 3½a ultra ('43) 95 *3.25*
97 A85 4a choc ('43) 65 *95*
98 A85 6a pck bl ('43) 1.90 *4.75*
99 A85 8a bl vio ('43) 2.50 *6.50*
100 A85 12a car lake ('43) 3.75 *9.50*
 *Nos. 89-100 (12)* 10.69 27.58

India Nos. 162-167 Overprinted CHAMBA

**1943** **Wmk. 196** ***Perf. 13½x14.***

101 A82 1r brn & sl 15.00 15.00
102 A82 2r dk brn & dk vio 19.00 *27.50*
103 A82 5r dp ultra & dk grn 37.50 *45.00*
104 A82 10r rose car & dk vio 50.00 *77.50*
105 A82 15r dk grn & dk brn 140.00 *190.00*
106 A82 25r dk vio & bl vio 225.00 *300.00*
 *Nos. 101-106 (6)* 486.50 655.00

India No. 161A Overprinted CHAMBA

**1948**

107 A81 14a rose vio 6.25 7.75

## OFFICIAL STAMPS

SERVICE

Indian Stamps Overprinted in Black CHAMBA STATE

**1886-98** **Wmk. Star. (39)** ***Perf. 14.***

O1 A17 ½a green 38 6
 a. "CHMABA" 45.00 45.00
 c. "SERV CE" 150.00
O2 A19 1a vio brn 15 10
 a. "CHMABA" 77.50 92.50
 c. "SERV CE" *225.00*
 d. "SERVICE" double 125.00 125.00
O3 A21 2a ultra 22 26
 a. "CHMABA" 350.00 375.00
O4 A22 3a brn org 1.10 1.25
 a. 3a org 12.50 16.00
 b. "CHMABA" 625.00 725.00
O5 A23 4a ol grn 50 55
 a. "CHMABA" 375.00 400.00
 c. "SERV CE" 925.00
O6 A25 8a red vio 55 55
 a. "CHMABA" 1,100. 1,250.
O7 A26 12a vio, *red* ('90) 3.75 4.00
 a. "CHMABA" 1,400.
 b. 1st "T" of "STATE" invtd.
O8 A27 1r gray ('90) 4.00 4.50
 a. "CHMABA" 1,250.
O9 A29 1r car rose & grn ('98) 4.00 5.25

**Wmk. Elephant's Head. (38)**

O10 A14 6a bister 95 1.10
 *Nos. O1-O10 (10)* 15.60 17.62

**1902-04** **Wmk. Star. (39)**

O11 A31 3p gray ('04) 9 9
O12 A17 ½a lt grn 9 9
O13 A19 1a car rose 15 15
O14 A21 2a violet 3.00 *6.25*

**1903-05**

O15 A32 3p gray 6 6
O16 A33 ½a green 7 5
O17 A34 1a car rose 12 12
O18 A35 2a violet 18 12
O19 A38 4a ol grn ('05) 60 *1.10*
O20 A40 8a red vio ('05) 60 *1.25*
O21 A42 1r car rose & grn ('05) 60 *1.50*
 *Nos. O15-O21 (7)* 2.23 4.20

**1907**

O22 A44 ½a green 32 25
 a. Inverted ovpt. 925.00
O23 A45 1a car rose 7 60

**1913**

O24 A49 2a violet 7.50
O25 A52 4a olive green 13.00

India No. 63 Overprinted

On
CHAMBA
STATE
H. S
M.

O26 A35 2a violet 75.00

No. O26 was never placed in use.

India Stamps of 1911-29 Overprinted:

CHAMBA STATE SERVICE — a
CHAMBA STATE SERVICE — b

**1913-25**

O27 A46 (a) 3p gray 5 5
O28 A47 (a) ½a green 5 5
O29 A48 (a) 1a car rose 6 5
O30 A48 (a) 1a dk brn ('25) 1.50 60
O31 A49 (a) 2a vio ('14) 9 9
O32 A52 (a) 4a ol grn 18 18
O33 A54 (a) 8a red vio 25 25
O34 A56 (b) 1r grn & red brn 38 38
 *Nos. O27-O34 (8)* 2.56 1.65

India No. O66 Overprinted

**1921**

O35 O6 9p on 1a rose 25 32

India Stamps of 1926-35 CHAMBA STATE SERVICE

**1927-39** **Wmk. 196**

O36 A46 3p slate 5 5
O37 A47 ½a green 5 5
O38 A68 9p dk grn ('32) 28 28
O39 A48 1a dk brn 10 5
O40 A69 1a3p vio ('32) 22 12
O41 A60 2a dl vio 12 18
O42 A61 4a ol grn 18 21
O43 A54 8a red vio 50 60
O44 A55 12a claret 1.00 60

Overprinted CHAMBA STATE SERVICE

O45 A56 1r grn & brn 1.75 *3.50*
O45A A56 2r brn org & car rose ('39) 8.75
O45B A56 5r dk vio & ultra ('39) 17.50
O45C A56 10r car & grn ('39) 32.50
 *Nos. O36-O45C (13)* 63.00

India Stamps of 1926-35 Overprinted CHAMBA STATE SERVICE

**1935-36**

O46 A71 ½a green 20 24
O47 A72 1a dk brn 12 7
O48 A49 2a vermilion 24 24
 a. Small die 24 24
O49 A52 4a ol grn ('36) 1.10 1.25

Same Overprint on India Stamps of 1937.

**1938** ***Perf. 13½x14.***

O50 A80 9p green 75 75
O51 A80 1a carmine 75 75

India Stamps of 1937 Overprinted CHAMBA STATE SERVICE

**1940-41**

O51A A82 1r brn & sl ('41) 425.00 *525.00*
O52 A82 2r dk brn & dk vio 18.50 *32.50*
O53 A82 5r dp ultra & dk grn 32.50 *50.00*
O54 A82 10r rose car & dk vio 65.00 *90.00*

India Official Stamps of 1939-43 Overprinted CHAMBA

**1941-46** **Wmk. 196**

O55 O8 3p sl ('44) 7 5
O56 O8 ½a brown 2.00 1.75
O57 O8 ½a dk rose vio ('44) 10 7
O58 O8 9p green 10 10
O59 O8 1a car rose 12 8
O60 O8 1a3p bis ('46) 17.50 7.00
O61 O8 1½a dl pur ('46) 50 25
O62 O8 2a scar ('44) 70 70
O63 O8 2½a pur ('44) 1.00 *1.75*
O64 O8 4a dk brn ('44) 1.75 *2.75*
O65 O8 8a bl vio ('41) 2.50 *3.50*
 *Nos. O55-O65 (11)* 26.34 18.00

India Nos. 162-165 Overprinted CHAMBA SERVICE

**1944**

O66 A82 1r brn & sl 10.50 *14.00*
O67 A82 2r dk brn & dk vio 14.00 *17.50*
O68 A82 5r dp ultra & dk grn 35.00 *42.50*
O69 A82 10r rose car & dk vio 52.50 *70.00*

## FARIDKOT

LOCATION — A State of India lying northeast of Nabha in the central Punjab.
AREA — 638 sq. mi.
POP. — 164,364
CAPITAL — Faridkot

Previous stamp issues are listed under Feudatory States. Stamps of Faridkot were superseded by those of India in 1901.

The varieties with small letters in the overprint are not listed as the letters are merely broken and not from another font.

India Stamps Overprinted in Black

FARIDKOT STATE

**1887-93 Wmk. Star. (39) *Perf. 14***

4 A17 ½a green 70 *1.65*
a. "ARIDKOT"
5 A19 1a vio brn 42 *70*
6 A21 2a ultra 85 *1.65*
7 A22 3a orange 85 *1.65*
8 A23 4a ol grn 1.10 *1.90*
a. "ARIDKOT" 250.00
9 A25 8a red vio 1.50 *3.25*
a. "ARIDKOT" 450.00
10 A27 1r gray 27.50 *42.50*
a. "ARIDKOT" *1,050.*
11 A29 1r car rose & grn ('93) 7.50 *11.00*

**Wmk. Elephant's Head. (38)**

12 A14 6a bister 1.40 *2.75*
a. "ARIDKOT" 250.00
*Nos. 4-12 (9)* 41.82 67.05

**1900 Wmk. Star. (39)**

13 A31 3p car rose 52 *1.10*
14 A27 12a vio, *red* 22.50 *52.50*

**OFFICIAL STAMPS**

SERVICE

India Stamps Overprinted in Black

FARIDKOT STATE

**1886 Wmk. Star. (39) *Perf. 14***

O1 A17 ½a green 18 *45*
a. "SERV CE" 250.00
O2 A19 1a vio brn 25 *60*
a. "SERV CE" 275.00
O3 A21 2a ultra 1.25 *3.00*
a. "SERV CE" 350.00
O4 A22 3a orange 1.25 *3.50*
O5 A23 4a ol grn 1.75 *3.50*
a. "SERV CE" 525.00
O6 A25 8a red lil 2.00 *3.50*
a. "SERV CE" 600.00
O7 A27 1r gray 22.50 *30.00*

**Wmk. Elephant's Head. (38)**

O8 A14 6a bister 6.00 *9.25*
a. "ARIDKOT" 275.00
b. "SERVIC" 425.00
*Nos. O1-O8 (8)* 35.18 53.80

**1896 Wmk. Star. (39)**

O9 A29 1r car rose & grn 32.50 *47.50*

Obsolete March 31, 1901.

## GWALIOR

LOCATION — One of the Central Provinces of India.
AREA — 26,008 sq. mi.
POP. — 4,006,159 (1941)
CAPITAL — Lashkar

The varieties with small letters in the overprint are not listed as the letters are merely broken and not from another font.

गवालियर

India Stamps Overprinted in Black

GWALIOR

Lines Spaced 16-17mm.

**1885 Wmk. Star (39) *Perf. 14***

1 A17 ½a green 12.50 12.50
2 A19 1a vio brn 12.50 15.00
3 A20 1a6p bis brn 12.50 12.50
4 A21 2a ultra 12.50 9.25
5 A25 8a red lil 25.00
6 A27 1r gray 32.50

**Wmk. Elephant's Head. (38)**

7 A9 4a green 22.50
8 A14 6a bister 22.50

The Hindi overprint measures 13½to 14x2 mm. and 15 to 15½x2½mm.

The two sizes are found in the same sheet in the proportion of one of the smaller to three of the larger.

The ½a, 1a, 2a, also exist with lines 13mm. apart and the short Hindi overprint.

*Reprints of the ½a and 1a have the 13mm. spacing, the short Hindi overprint and usually carry the overprint "Specimen".*

India Stamps Overprinted

GWALIOR गवालियर

Red Overprint.

**1885 Wmk. Star. (39)**

9 A17 ½a green 24 32
10 A21 2a ultra 7.50 3.75
11 A27 1r gray 6.25 6.25

**Wmk. Elephant's Head. (38)**

12 A9 4a green 8.00 8.00

*Nos. 9 to 12 inclusive have been reprinted. They have the short Hindi overprint. Most copies bear the word "Reprint". Those without it cannot be distinguished from the originals.*

Black Overprint.

**1885-91 Wmk. Star. (39)**

13 A17 ½a green 6 5
a. "GWALICR" 75.00 80.00
b. Double ovpt. 200.00
14 A18 9p rose 24.00 *35.00*
15 A19 1a vio brn 22 6
16 A20 1a6p bis brn 12 12
17 A21 2a ultra 30 15
18 A22 3a orange 30 15
19 A23 4a ol grn 45 30
20 A25 8a red vio 60 45
21 A26 12a vio, *red* 60 30
22 A27 1r gray 75 60

**Wmk. Elephant's Head. (38)**

23 A14 6a bister 48 48
*Nos. 13-23 (11)* 27.88 37.66

The Hindi overprint measures 13½to 14x2 mm. and 15 to 15½x2½mm. as in the preceding issue.

**1896 Wmk. Star. (39)**

24 A28 2a6p green 3.25 3.50
a. "GWALICR" 275.00
25 A29 1r car rose & grn 6.00 6.75
a. "GWALICR" 325.00
26 A30 2r bis brn & rose 6.00 3.50
27 A30 3r grn & brn 13.00 10.00
28 A30 5r vio & bl 17.50 7.50
*Nos. 24-28 (5)* 45.75 31.25

The Hindi inscription varies from 13 to 15½mm. long.

**1899**

29 A31 3p car rose 6 5
a. Invtd. ovpt. 200.00 165.00

**1901-04**

30 A31 3p gray ('04) 4.25 *11.00*
31 A17 ½a lt grn 10 7
32 A19 1a car rose 14 14
33 A21 2a violet 20 20
34 A28 2a6p ultra ('03) 28 28
*Nos. 30-34 (5)* 4.97 11.69

**1903-08**

35 A32 3p gray 6 5
36 A33 ½a green 45 7
37 A34 1a car rose 25 6
38 A35 2a violet 55 15
39 A36 2a6p ultra ('05) 80 60
40 A37 3a brn org ('04) 95 18
41 A38 4a ol grn 60 18
42 A39 6a bis ('06) 32 32
43 A40 8a red vio 95 55
44 A41 12a vio, *red* ('05) 1.40 60
45 A42 1r car rose & grn ('05) 80 60
46 A43 2r brn & rose 5.00 5.00
47 A43 3r grn & brn ('08) 16.00 22.50
48 A43 5r vio & bl ('08) 14.00 17.00
*Nos. 35-48 (14)* 42.13 47.86

There are two settings of the overprint on Nos. 35, 37-46. In the first (1903), "GWALIOR" is 14mm. long and lines are spaced 1¾mm. In the second (1908), "GWALIOR" is 13mm long and lines are 2¾mm apart. No. 36 exists only with first overprint, Nos. 47-48 only with second.

**1907**

49 A44 ½a green 95 5
50 A45 1a car rose 38 25

No. 49 exists with both settings of overprint. See note below No. 48.

**1912-23**

51 A46 3p gray 25 5
52 A47 ½a green 25 5
a. Invtd. overprint
53 A48 1a car rose 9 5
a. Double overprint 37.50
54 A48 1a dk brn ('23) 9 5
55 A49 2a violet 45 5
56 A51 3a brn org 75 5
57 A52 4a ol grn ('13) 22 5
58 A53 6a bister 22 18
59 A54 8a red vio ('13) 80 60
60 A55 12a cl ('14) 38 38
61 A56 1r grn & red brn 70 70
62 A56 2r brn & car rose 4.75 1.10
63 A56 5r vio & ultra 16.00 3.50
*Nos. 51-63 (13)* 24.95 6.81

India No. 104 Overprinted

**1921**

64 A48 9p on 1a rose 10 10
a. Invtd. overprint 50.00

India Stamps of 1911-26 Overprinted

GWALIOR गवालियर

Hindi Overprint 15mm. Long.

**1923-27**

66 A59 1½a choc ('25) 20 20
67 A59 1½a rose ('27) 10 14
a. Inverted ovpt. 13.00 13.00
68 A57 2a6p ultra ('25) 50 50
69 A57 2a6p brn org ('27) 20 24
70 A51 3a ultra ('24) 20 20
*Nos. 66-70 (5)* 1.20 1.28

Similar Overprint on India Stamps of 1926-35.

Hindi Overprint 13½mm. Long.

**1928-32 Wmk. 196**

71 A46 3p sl ('32) 65 10
72 A47 ½a grn ('30) 12 5
73 A48 1a dk brn 5 5
74 A60 2a dl vio 7 7
75 A51 3a ultra 18 5
76 A61 4a ol grn 22 7
77 A54 8a red vio 28 18
78 A55 12a claret 35 35

Overprinted

GWALIOR गवालियर

79 A56 1r grn & brn 42 38
80 A56 2r brn org & car rose 1.00 48
81 A56 5r dk vio & ultra ('29) 11.00 12.00
82 A56 10r car & grn ('30) 21.00 21.00
83 A56 15r ol grn & ultra ('30) 42.50 47.50
84 A56 25r bl & ocher ('30) 62.50 77.50
*Nos. 71-84 (14)* 140.34 159.78

India Stamps of 1932-35 Overprinted in Black

GWALIOR गवालियर

Hindi Overprint 13½mm. Long.

**1933-36**

85 A71 ½a grn ('36) 10 10
86 A68 9p dk grn ('33) 55 30
87 A72 1a dk brn ('36) 12 6
88 A69 1a3p vio ('36) 18 12
89 A49 2a ver ('36) 90 1.10
*Nos. 85-89 (5)* 1.85 1.68

Same Overprinted on India Stamps of 1937.

**1938-40 *Perf. 13½x14.***

90 A80 3p sl ('40) 1.40 22
91 A80 ½a brown 1.40 5
92 A80 9p grn ('40) 24.00 10.00
93 A80 1a carmine 1.75 6
94 A81 3a yel grn ('39) 2.00 2.00
95 A81 4a dk brn 15.00 5.00
96 A81 6a pck bl ('39) 2.00 2.00
*Nos. 90-96 (7)* 47.55 19.33

Same Overprinted on India Stamps of 1941-43.

**1942-49**

100 A83 3p sl ('44) 12 5
101 A83 ½a rose vio ('46) 20 5
102 A83 9p lt grn 8 5
103 A83 1a car rose ('44) 22 5
104 A84 1½a dk pur ('44) 45 5
105 A84 2a scar ('44) 20 5
106 A84 3a vio ('44) 26 16
108 A85 4a choc ('44) 26 8
109 A85 6a pck bl ('48) 7.50 7.50
110 A85 8a bl vio 3.25 3.75
111 A85 12a car lake 5.50 6.50

India Nos. 162-167 Overprinted

GWALIOR गवालियर

***Perf. 13½x14***

112 A82 1r brn & sl ('45) 9.25 60
113 A82 2r dk brn & dk vio ('49) 6.25 6.25
114 A82 5r dp ultra & dk grn ('49) 30.00 21.00
115 A82 10r rose car & dk vio ('49) 37.50 37.50
116 A82 15r dk grn & dk brn ('48) 87.50 77.50
117 A82 25r dk vio & bl vio ('48) 92.50 87.50
*Nos. 100-106,108-117 (17)* 281.04 248.64

India Stamps of 1941-43 Overprinted

GWALIOR गवालियर

**1949**

118 A83 3p slate 35 35
119 A83 ½a rose vio 48 48
120 A83 1a car rose 55 55
121 A84 2a scarlet 2.25 2.25
122 A84 3a violet 11.00 7.50
123 A85 4a chocolate 2.25 1.50
124 A85 6a pck bl 19.00 25.00
125 A85 8a bl vio 47.50 45.00
126 A85 12a car lake 140.00 95.00
*Nos. 118-126 (9)* 223.38 177.63

**OFFICIAL STAMPS.**

गवालियर

India Stamps Overprinted in Black

सरविस

**1895 Wmk. Star (39) *Perf. 14***

O1 A17 ½a green 6 5
a. Double ovpt. 200.00
O2 A19 1a maroon 10 5
O3 A21 2a ultra 16 6
O4 A23 4a ol grn 80 80
O5 A25 8a red vio 42 42
O6 A29 1r car rose & grn 2.00 2.00
*Nos. O1-O6 (6)* 3.54 3.38

Nos. O1 to O6 inclusive are known with the last two characters of the lower word transposed.

**1901-04**

O7 A31 3p gray ('04) 1.25 *1.90*
O8 A17 ½a lt grn 15 5
O9 A19 1a car rose 1.10 6
O10 A21 2a vio ('03) 60 *1.25*

**1902**

O11 A31 3p car rose 25 25

**1903-05**

O12 A32 3p gray 6 5
O13 A33 ½a green 20 5
O14 A34 1a car rose 12 5
O15 A35 2a violet 18 9
O16 A38 4a ol grn ('05) 75 60
O17 A40 8a red vio 50 30
O18 A42 1r car rose & grn ('05) 1.75 75
*Nos. O12-O18 (7)* 3.56 1.89

**1907**

O19 A44 ½a green 14 5
O20 A45 1a car rose 1.10 5

Two spacings of the overprint lines, 10mm. and 8mm., are found on Nos. O12-O20.

**1913**

O21 A46 3p gray 5 5
O22 A47 ½a green 5 5
O23 A48 1a car rose 6 5
a. Double overprint 57.50
O24 A49 2a violet 8 5
O25 A52 4a ol grn 18 6
O26 A54 8a red vio 35 18
O27 A56 1r grn & red brn 3.50 3.50
*Nos. O21-O27 (7)* 4.27 3.94

India No. O66 Overprinted

**1921**

O28 O6 9p on 1a rose 7 5

गवालियर

India No. 83 Overprinted

सरविस

**1923**

*O29* A48 1a dk brn 5 5

Similar Overprint on India Stamps of 1926-35.

**1927-35** **Wmk. 196**

*O30* A46 3p slate 5 5
*O31* A47 ½a green 5 5
*O32* A48 1a dk brn 5 5
*O33* A60 2a dl vio 9 5
*O34* A61 4a ol grn 15 15
*O35* A54 8a red vio 30 12

गवालियर

Overprinted

सरविस

*O36* A56 1r grn & brn 40 35
*O37* A56 2r brn org & car rose ('35) 1.25 *2.00*
*O38* A56 5r dk vio & ultra ('32) 12.00 *24.00*
*O39* A56 10r car & grn ('32) 24.00 *30.00*
*Nos. O30-O39 (10)* 38.34 56.82

गवालियर

India Stamps of 1926-35 Overprinted

सरविस

**1933-37** ***Perf. 13½x14, 14.***

*O40* A71 ½a grn ('36) 35 25
*O41* A68 9p dk grn ('35) 15 25
*O42* A72 1a dk brn ('36) 20 8
*O43* A69 1a3p vio ('33) 50 8
*O44* A49 2a ver ('36) 12 8
*a.* Small die ('36) 12 5
*O45* A52 4a ol grn ('37) 40 20
*Nos. O40-O45 (6)* 1.72 94

Same Overprint on India Stamps of 1937-40.

**1938** ***Perf. 13½x14.***

*O46* A80 ½a brown 75 22
*O47* A80 1a carmine 75 14

गवालियर

India Nos. 162-165 Overprinted

सरविस

**1945-48** **Wmk. 196** ***Perf. 13½x14.***

*O48* A82 1r brn & sl 1.25 1.25
*O49* A82 2r dk brn & dk vio 12.00 *17.00*
*O50* A82 5r dp ultra & dk grn ('46) 37.50 *62.50*
*O51* A82 10r rose car & dk vio ('48) 60.00 *110.00*

India Official Stamps of 1939-43 Overprinted गवालियर

**1940-44** **Wmk. 196** ***Perf. 13½x14.***

*O52* O8 3p slate 14 10
*O53* O8 ½a brown 2.00 1.40
*O54* O8 ½a dk rose vio ('43) 14 12
*O55* O8 9p grn ('43) 14 18
*O56* O8 1a car rose ('41) 12 10
*O57* O8 1a3p bis ('42) 2.50 1.00
*O58* O8 1½a dl pur ('43) 70 12
*O59* O8 2a scar ('41) 14 14
*O60* O8 4a dk brn ('44) 45 45
*O61* O8 8a bl vio ('44) 1.00 1.00
*Nos. O52-O61 (10)* 7.33 4.61

Gwalior No. O43 with Additional Surcharge in Black 1A 1A

**1942**

*O62* A69 1a on 1a3p vio 6.25 1.90

## JIND

## (Jhind)

LOCATION — A State of India in the north Punjab.
AREA — 1,299 sq. mi.
POP. — 361,812 (1941)
CAPITAL — Sangrur

Previous stamp issues are listed under Feudatory States.

The varities with small letters are not listed as the letters are merely broken and not from another font.

India Stamps Overprinted in Black JHIND STATE

**1885** **Wmk. Star (39)** ***Perf. 14***

*33* A17 ½a green 75 75
*a.* Ovpt. reading down 52.50 52.50
*34* A19 1a vio brn 6.00 *7.50*
*a.* Ovpt. reading down 275.00
*35* A21 2a ultra 4.25 4.25
*a.* Ovpt. reading down 150.00
*36* A25 8a red lil 130.00
*a.* Ovpt. reading down 1,750.
*37* A27 1r gray 130.00
*a.* Ovpt. reading down 1,750.

**Wmk. Elephant's Head. (38)**

*38* A9 4a green 19.00 *26.00*

*On the reprints of Nos. 33 to 38 "Jhind" measures 8mm. instead of 9mm and "State" 9mm instead of 9½mm.*

India Stamps Overprinted in Red or Black JEEND STATE

**1885** **Wmk. Star. (39)**

*39* A17 ½a grn (R) 37.50
*40* A19 1a vio brn 37.50
*41* A21 2a ultra (R) 42.50
*42* A25 8a red lil 50.00
*43* A27 1r gray (R) 57.50

**Wmk. Elephant's Head. (38)**

*44* A9 4a grn (R) 45.00
*Nos. 39-44 (6)* 270.00

India Stamps Overprinted JHIND STATE

Red Overprint.

**1886** **Wmk. Star. (39)**

*45* A17 ½a green 10.50
*a.* "JEIND" 225.00
*46* A21 2a ultra 12.50
*a.* "JEIND" 275.00
*47* A27 1r gray 27.50
*a.* "JEIND" 1,050.

**Wmk. Elephant's Head. (38)**

*48* A9 4a green 14.00

Nos. 46, 47 and 48 were not placed in use.

Black Overprint.

**1886-98** **Wmk. Star. (39)**

*49* A17 ½a grn ('88) 5 5
*a.* Invtd. ovpt. 150.00
*50* A19 1a vio brn 14 12
*a.* "JEIND" 175.00
*51* A20 1a6p bis brn ('97) 75 75
*52* A21 2a ultra 30 24
*53* A22 3a orange 24 20
*54* A23 4a ol grn 35 30
*55* A25 8a red vio 60 75
*a.* "JEIND" 750.00
*56* A26 12a vio, *red* ('97) 60 75
*57* A27 1r gray ('91) 6.00 *8.75*
*58* A29 1r car rose & grn ('98) 4.50 *7.50*
*59* A30 2r brn & rose ('97) 110.00 *135.00*
*60* A30 3r grn & brn ('97) 110.00 *135.00*
*61* A30 5r vio & bl ('97) 180.00 *225.00*

**Wmk. Elephant's Head. (38)**

*62* A14 6a bister 90 1.00
*Nos. 49-62 (14)* 414.43 515.41

**1900** **Wmk. Star. (39)**

*63* A31 3p car rose 12 15

**1902-04**

*64* A31 3p gray ('04) 18 20
*65* A17 ½a lt grn 26 30
*66* A19 1a car rose 30 35

**1903-09**

*67* A32 3p gray 12 5
*a.* Double overprint
*68* A33 ½a green 14 12
*69* A34 1a car rose ('09) 18 6
*a.* Double overprint
*70* A35 2a vio ('06) 20 15
*70A* A36 2a6p ultra ('09) 30 35
*71* A37 3a brn org 24 24
*a.* Double overprint 87.50
*72* A38 4a ol grn 32 35
*73* A39 6a bis ('05) 42 48
*74* A40 8a red vio 42 48
*75* A41 12a vio, *red* ('05) 60 75
*76* A42 1r car rose & grn ('05) 75 90
*Nos. 67-76 (11)* 3.69 3.93

**1907**

*77* A44 ½a green 9 9
*78* A45 1a car rose 24 9

**1913**

*80* A46 3p gray 12 15
*81* A47 ½a green 9 12
*82* A48 1a car rose 12 15
*83* A49 2a violet 24 26
*84* A51 3a brn org 85 1.00
*85* A53 6a bister 2.00 2.25
*Nos. 80-85 (6)* 3.42 3.93

India Stamps of 1911-26 Overprinted JIND STATE

**1913-14**

*88* A46 3p gray 5 6
*89* A47 ½a green 9 9
*90* A48 1a car rose 6 5
*91* A49 2a violet 9 9
*92* A51 3a brn org 15 15
*93* A52 4a ol grn 15 18
*94* A53 6a bister 18 20
*95* A54 8a red vio 24 26
*96* A55 12a claret 30 35
*97* A56 1r grn & red brn 48 48
*Nos. 88-97 (10)* 1.79 1.91

India No. 104 Overprinted

**1921**

*98* A48 9p on 1a rose 2.00 2.25

India Stamps of 1913-19 Overprinted JIND STATE

**1922**

*99* A58 1½a chocolate 70 80
*100* A57 2a6p ultra 38 45

Same Overprint on India Stamps of 1911-26.

**1924**

*101* A48 1a dk brn 12 6
*102* A59 1½a chocolate 38 45

Same Overprint on India No. 87.

**1925**

*103* A51 3a ultra 20 22

Same Overprint on India Stamps of 1911-26.

**1927**

*104* A59 1½a rose 15 18
*105* A57 2a6p brn org 15 18
*106* A56 2r yel brn & car rose 5.25 *6.25*
*107* A56 5r vio & ultra 24.00 *27.50*

India Stamps of 1926-35 Overprinted JIND STATE

**1927-32** **Wmk. 196**

*108* A46 3p slate 5 5
*109* A47 ½a green 5 6
*110* A68 9p dk grn ('32) 32 45
*111* A48 1a dk brn 6 5
*112* A69 1a3p vio ('32) 26 38
*113* A59 1½a car rose 18 22
*114* A60 2a dl vio 12 5
*115* A57 2a6p buff 12 14
*116* A51 3a ultra 32 38
*117* A61 4a ol grn 18 22
*118* A54 8a red vio 1.00 1.25
*119* A55 12a claret 60 1.50

Overprinted JIND STATE

*120* A56 1r grn & brn 75 *1.90*
*121* A56 2r buff & car rose 9.50 11.00
*122* A56 5r dk vio & ultra 10.50 14.00
*123* A56 10r car rose & grn 21.00 *27.50*
*124* A56 15r ol grn & bl 37.50 *82.50*
*125* A56 25r bl & ocher 52.50 *110.00*
*Nos. 108-125 (18)* 135.01 251.65

India Stamps of 1926-35 Overprinted JIND STATE

**1934-37**

*126* A71 ½a green 6 5
*127* A72 1a dk brn 12 5
*128* A49 2a vermilion 9 5
*129* A51 3a car rose 12 9
*130* A70 3a6p dp bl ('37) 15 15
*131* A52 4a ol grn 22 22
*132* A53 6a bis ('37) 22 22
*Nos. 126-132 (7)* 98 83

Same Overprint on India Stamps of 1937.

**1937-38** **Wmk. 196** ***Perf. 13½x14.***

*133* A80 3p sl ('38) 14 18
*134* A80 ½a brn ('38) 18 22
*135* A80 9p green 26 22
*136* A80 1a carmine 9 6
*137* A81 2a scar ('38) 12 14
*138* A81 2a6p pur ('38) 14 14
*139* A81 3a yel grn ('38) 18 15
*140* A81 3a6p ultra ('38) 22 22
*141* A81 4a dk brn ('38) 22 22
*142* A81 6a pck bl ('38) 32 38
*143* A81 8a bl vio ('38) 45 *1.10*
*144* A81 12a car lake ('38) 65 *1.50*

Overprinted JIND STATE

**1938**

*145* A82 1r brn & sl 5.25 5.50
*146* A82 2r dk brn & dk vio 9.50 9.50
*147* A82 5r dp ultra & dk grn 26.00 30.00
*148* A82 10r rose car & dk vio 55.00 55.00
*149* A82 15r dk grn & dk brn 110.00 *190.00*
*150* A82 25r dk vio & bl vio 120.00 *225.00*
*Nos. 133-150 (18)* 328.72 519.53

India Stamps of 1937 Overprinted JIND

**1942-43** **Wmk. 196** ***Perf. 13½x14***

*155* A80 3p slate 2.75 2.75
*156* A80 ½a brown 2.75 2.75
*157* A80 9p green 2.75 2.75
*158* A80 1a carmine 2.75 2.75
*159* A82 1r brn & sl 3.00 8.25
*160* A82 2r dk brn & dk vio 9.25 15.00
*161* A82 5r dp ultra & dk grn 37.50 62.50
*162* A82 10r rose car & dk vio ('43) 62.50 100.00
*163* A82 15r dk grn & dk brn ('43) 92.50 140.00
*164* A82 25r dk vio & bl vio 140.00 225.00
*Nos. 155-164 (10)* 355.75 561.75

Same Overprint on India Stamps of 1941-43.

*165* A83 3p slate 30 30
*166* A83 ½a rose vio ('43) 12 12
*167* A83 9p lt grn 12 12
*168* A83 1a car rose ('43) 12 6
*169* A84 1a3p bis ('43) 45 45
*170* A84 1½a dk pur 1.90 1.90
*171* A84 2a scarlet 18 7
*172* A84 3a vio ('43) 1.10 1.10
*173* A84 3½a ultra 38 38
*174* A85 4a chocolate 38 38
*175* A85 6a pck bl 45 38
*176* A85 8a bl vio 1.90 *2.25*
*177* A85 12a car lake 4.50 *5.25*
*Nos. 165-177 (13)* 11.90 12.76

## OFFICIAL STAMPS.

India Stamps Overprinted in Black JHIND STATE SERVICE

**1885 Wmk. Star. (39) *Perf. 14.***
*O1* A17 ½a green 14 14
a. "JHIND STATE" reading down 52.50 32.50
*O2* A19 1a vio brn 25 18
a. "JHIND STATE" reading down 7.00 7.00
*O3* A21 2a ultra 17.50 17.50
a. "JHIND STATE" reading down 275.00

*The reprints may be distinguished by the same measurements as the reprints of the corresponding regular issue.*

India Stamps Overprinted in Red or Black
SERVICE
JEEND STATE

**1885**
*O4* A17 ½a grn (R) 35.00
*O5* A19 1a vio brn 35.00
*O6* A21 2a ultra (R) 42.50

India Stamps Overprinted
SERVICE
JHIND STATE

**1886**
**Red Overprint.**
*O7* A17 ½a green 14.00
a. "JEIND" 190.00
b. "ERVICE"
*O8* A21 2a ultra 14.00
a. "JEIND" 350.00
b. "ERVICE"

No. O8 was not placed in use.

**1886-96**
**Black Overprint.**
*O9* A17 ½a grn ('88) 35 22
*O10* A19 1a vio brn 2.25 22
a. "JEIND" 190.00
b. "ERVICE"
*O11* A21 2a ultra 28 22
*O12* A23 4a ol grn 65 42
*O13* A25 8a red vio 1.90 1.90
*O14* A29 1r car rose & grn ('96) 5.50 10.50
*Nos. O9-O14 (6)* 10.93 13.48

**1902**
*O15* A17 ½a lt grn 25 22

**1903-06**
*O16* A32 3p gray 14 6
*O17* A33 ½a green 1.25 6
a. "HIND" 175.00
*O18* A34 1a car rose 1.75 8
a. "HIND" 175.00
*O19* A35 2a violet 28 10
*O20* A38 4a ol grn 60 35
*O21* A40 8a red vio 2.50 2.00
*O22* A42 1r car rose & grn ('06) 2.75 2.50
*Nos. O16-O22 (7)* 9.27 5.15

**1907**
*O23* A44 ½a green 20 5
*O24* A45 1a car rose 32 5

Indian Stamps of 1911-26 Overprinted

JIND STATE SERVICE — a
JIND STATE SERVICE — b

**1914-27**
*O25* A46(a) 3p gray 7 5
*O26* A47(a) ½a green 42 5
*O27* A48(a) 1a car rose 42 5
*O28* A49(a) 2a violet 22 5
*O29* A52(a) 4a ol grn 22 7
a. Dbl. overprint
*O30* A54(a) 8a red vio 42 42
*O31* A56(b) 1r grn & red brn 65 42
*O32* A56(b) 2r yel brn & car rose ('27) 7.75 10.50
*O33* A56(b) 5r vio & ultra ('27) 19.00 21.00
*Nos. O25-O33 (9)* 29.17 32.61

India Nos. 83 and 89 Overprinted Type "a".

**1924-27**
*O34* A48 1a dk brn 14 5
*O35* A53 6a bis ('27) 28 32

India Stamps of 1926-35 Overprinted
c JIND STATE SERVICE

**1927-32**
*O36* A46 3p slate 5 5
*O37* A47 ½a green 10 10
*O38* A68 9p dk grn ('32) 8 8
*O39* A48 1a dk brn 8 5
*O40* A69 1a3p vio ('32) 20 22
*O41* A60 2a dl vio 10 6
*O42* A61 4a ol grn 12 12
*O43* A54 8a red vio 26 26
*O44* A55 12a claret 32 40

Overprinted
d JIND STATE SERVICE

*O45* A56 1r grn & brn 1.75 1.90
*O46* A56 2r buff & car rose 5.75 6.50
*O47* A56 5r dk vio & ultra 12.00 13.00
*O48* A56 10r car rose & grn 19.00 26.00
*Nos. O36-O48 (13)* 39.81 48.74

India Stamps of 1926-35 Overprinted Type "c".

**1934-37**
*O49* A71 ½a green 25 5
*O50* A72 1a dk brn 10 8
*O51* A49 2a vermilion 15 15
*O52* A57 2a6p buff ('37) 1.10 1.10
*O53* A52 4a ol grn 1.25 1.25
*O54* A53 6a bis ('37) 1.25 1.25
*Nos. O49-O54 (6)* 4.10 3.88

India Nos. 151-153 Overprinted Type "c".

**1937-42 *Perf. 13½x14.***
*O55* A80 ½a brn ('42) 15.00 45
*O56* A80 9p green 38 12
*O57* A80 1a carmine 42 9

India Nos. 162-165 Overprinted Type "d".

*O58* A82 1r brn & sl ('40) 10.00 11.00
*O59* A82 2r dk brn & dk vio ('40) 22.50 37.50
*O60* A82 5r dp ultra & dk grn ('40) 45.00 67.50
*O61* A82 10r rose car & dk vio ('40) 67.50 110.00
*Nos. O55-O61 (7)* 160.80 226.66

India Official Stamps of 1939-43 Overprinted JIND

**1940-43**
*O62* O8 3p slate 5 5
*O63* O8 ½a brown 2.50 1.25
*O64* O8 ½a dk rose vio ('43) 24 15
*O65* O8 9p green 7 7
*O66* O8 1a car rose 6 5
*O67* O8 1½a dl pur ('43) 90 75
*O68* O8 2a scarlet 7 7
*O69* O8 2½a purple 24 24
*O70* O8 4a dk brn 24 22
*O71* O8 8a bl vio 90 90

India Nos. 162-165 Overprinted
JIND SERVICE

**1942 Wmk. 196 *Perf. 13½x14***
*O72* A82 1r brn & sl 10.50 12.00
*O73* A82 2r dk brn & dk vio 21.00 20.00
*O74* A82 5r dp ultra & dk grn 45.00 60.00
*O75* A82 10r rose car & dk vio 75.00 90.00
*Nos. O62-O75 (14)* 156.77 185.75

## NABHA

LOCATION — A State of India in the eastern and southeastern Punjab.
AREA — 966 sq. mi.
POP. — 340,044 (1941)
CAPITAL — Nabha

The varieties with small letters in the overprint are not listed as the letters are merely broken and not from another font.

Indian Stamps Overprinted in Black
NABHA STATE

**1885 Wmk. Star. (39) *Perf. 14.***
*1* A17 ½a green 45 55
*2* A19 1a vio brn 19.00 30.00
*3* A21 2a ultra 9.50 11.00
*4* A25 8a red lil 150.00
*5* A27 1r gray 150.00

**Wmk. Elephant's Head. (38)**
*6* A9 4a green 37.50 45.00

*On the reprints "Nabha" and "State" each measure 9½mm. On the originals they measure 11 and 10 mm. respectively.*

Indian Stamps Overprinted NABHA STATE

Red Overprint.

**1885 Wmk. Star. (39)**
*7* A17 ½a green 50 52
*8* A21 2a ultra 80 85
*9* A27 1r gray 60.00 80.00

**Wmk. Elephant's Head. (38)**
*10* A9 4a green 17.50 32.50

Black Overprint.

**1885-97 Wmk. Star. (39)**
*11* A17 ½a green 20 15
*12* A18 9p rose ('92) 60 70
*13* A19 1a vio brn 15 15
*14* A20 1a6p bis brn 48 48
a. "ABHA" 150.00
*15* A21 2a ultra 48 40
*16* A22 3a orange 1.50 1.50
*17* A23 4a ol grn 60 40
*18* A25 8a red lil 1.50 1.50
*19* A26 12a vio, *red* ('89) 95 1.25
*20* A27 1r gray 10.00 20.00
*21* A29 1r car rose & grn ('93) 1.75 2.00
a. "N BHA"
*22* A30 2r brn & rose ('97) 65.00 105.00
*23* A30 3r grn & brn ('97) 65.00 105.00
*24* A30 5r vio & blk ('97) 77.50 110.00

**Wmk. Elephant's Head. (38)**
*25* A14 6a bis ('89) 1.75 2.00
*Nos. 11-25 (15)* 227.46 350.53

*Nos. 7, 8, 9, 10, 13, and 18 have been reprinted. They usually bear the overprint "Specimen."*

**1900 Wmk. Star. (39)**
*26* A31 3p car rose 10 15

**1903-09**
*27* A32 3p gray 7 5
*28* A33 ½a green 24 24
a. "NABH" 165.00
*29* A34 1a car rose 42 35
*30* A35 2a violet 42 42
*30A* A36 2a6p ultra 27.50 42.50
*31* A37 3a brn org 70 70
*32* A38 4a ol grn 70 70
*33* A39 6a bister 90 90
*34* A40 8a red vio 70 90
*35* A41 12a vio, *red* 1.75 1.90
*36* A42 1r car rose & grn 1.75 1.90
*Nos. 27-36 (11)* 35.15 50.56

**1907**
*37* A44 ½a green 10 7
*38* A45 1a car rose 22 14

**1913**
*40* A46 3p gray 5 5
*41* A47 ½a green 5 5
*42* A48 1a car rose 6 5
*43* A49 2a violet 9 9
*44* A51 3a brn org 14 12
*45* A52 4a ol grn 30 30
*46* A53 6a bister 18 22
*47* A54 8a red vio 30 32
*48* A55 12a claret 35 42
*49* A56 1r grn & red brn 1.50 1.50
*Nos. 40-49 (10)* 3.02 3.12

**1924**
*50* A48 1a dk brn 8 6

India Stamps of 1926-35 Overprinted NABHA STATE

**1927-32 Wmk. 196**
*51* A46 3p sl ('32) 9 9
*52* A47 ½a green 9 9
*53* A48 1a dk brn 6 6
*54* A60 2a dl vio ('32) 18 18
*55* A57 2a 6p buff ('32) 22 22
*56* A51 3a bl ('30) 25 25
*57* A61 4a ol grn ('32) 80 80

Overprinted NABHA STATE

*58* A56 2r brn org & car rose ('32) 5.75 7.75
*59* A56 5r dk vio & ultra ('32) 24.00 27.50
*Nos. 51-59 (9)* 31.44 36.94

India Stamps of 1926-35 Overprinted NABHA STATE

**1936-37**
*63* A71 ½a green 12 12
*64* A68 9p dk grn ('37) 15 15
*65* A72 1a dk brn 15 15
*66* A69 1a3p vio ('37) 10 10
*67* A51 3a car rose ('37) 48 55
*68* A52 4a ol grn ('37) 52 60
*Nos. 63-68 (6)* 1.52 1.67

Same Overprint in Black on 1937 Stamps of India.

**1938-39 *Perf. 13½x14***
*69* A80 3p slate 3.50 1.10
*70* A80 ½a brown 52 52
*71* A80 9p green 14.00 9.50
*72* A80 1a carmine 28 28
*73* A81 2a scarlet 24 24
*74* A81 2a6p purple 28 28
*75* A81 3a yel grn 55 65
*76* A81 3a6p ultra 48 52
*77* A81 4a dk brn 1.40 2.00
*78* A81 6a pck bl 1.50 2.75
*79* A81 8a bl vio 2.75 3.25
*80* A81 12a car lake 3.25 4.75

Overprinted NABHA STATE

*81* A82 1r brn & sl 5.75 8.00
*82* A82 2r dk brn & dk vio 13.00 20.00
*83* A82 5r dp ultra & dk grn 45.00 57.50
*84* A82 10r rose car & dk vio ('39) 80.00 100.00
*85* A82 15r dk grn & dk brn ('39) 125.00 200.00
*86* A82 25r dk vio & bl vio ('39) 150.00 225.00
*Nos. 69-86 (18)* 447.50 636.34

India Stamps of 1937 Overprinted in Black NABHA

**1942 *Perf. 13½x14***
*87* A80 3p slate 22.50 4.00
*88* A80 ½a brown 42.50 17.50
*89* A80 9p green 17.50 4.50
*90* A80 1a carmine 17.50 2.50

Same on India Nos. 168-179.

**1942-46 Wmk. 196**
*100* A83 3p slate 24 24
*101* A83 ½a rose vio ('43) 38 38
*102* A83 9p lt grn ('43) 48 48
*103* A83 1a car rose ('46) 38 38
*104* A84 1a3p bis ('44) 38 38
*105* A84 1½a dk pur ('43) 48 48
*106* A84 2a scar ('44) 65 65
*107* A84 3a vio ('44) 95 95
*108* A84 3½a ultra 1.40 1.40
*109* A85 4a choc ('43) 1.50 1.50
*110* A85 6a pck bl ('44) 1.50 1.50
*111* A85 8a bl vio ('44) 2.00 2.00
*112* A85 12a car lake ('44) 3.75 3.75
*Nos. 100-112 (13)* 14.09 14.09

### OFFICIAL STAMPS.

Indian Stamps Overprinted in Black
NABHA STATE SERVICE

**1885 Wmk. Star. (39) *Perf. 14.***

*O1* A17 ½a green 60 60
*O2* A19 1a vio brn 42 42
*O3* A21 2a ultra 37.50 *57.50*

*The reprints have the same measurements as the reprints of the regular issue of the same date.*

SERVICE

Indian Stamps Overprinted NABHA STATE

**1885**

**Red Overprint.**

*O4* A17 ½a green 70 95
*O5* A21 2a ultra 52 55

**1885-97**

**Black Overprint.**

*O6* A17 ½a green 10 8
*a.* Period after "SERVICE" 40.00 1.50
*O7* A19 1a vio brn 20 16
*a.* "NABHA STATE" double *165.00*
*b.* Period after "SERVICE" 4.50 1.75
*O8* A21 2a ultra 40 40
*O9* A22 3a orange 5.00 *8.50*
*O10* A23 4a ol grn 45 16
*O11* A25 8a red vio ('89) 85 1.00
*O12* A26 12a vio, *red* ('89) 4.00 4.25
*O13* A27 1r gray ('89) 13.00 *24.00*
*O14* A29 1r car rose & grn ('97) 12.00 *15.00*

**Wmk. Elephant's Head. (38)**

*O15* A14 6a bis ('89) 2.50 2.75
*Nos. O6-O15 (10)* 38.50 56.30

*Nos. O4, O5, and O7 have been reprinted. They usually bear the overprint "Specimen".*

**1903-06 Wmk. Star. (39)**

*O16* A32 3p gray ('06) 20 20
*O17* A33 ½a green 10 8
*O18* A34 1a car rose 14 14
*O19* A35 2a violet 32 32
*O20* A38 4a ol grn 32 22
*a.* Double overprint
*O21* A40 8a red vio 48 42
*O22* A42 1r car rose & grn 80 1.00
*Nos. O16-O22 (7)* 2.36 2.38

**1907**

*O23* A44 ½a green 8 8
*O24* A45 1a carmine rose 10 10

**1913**

*O25* A52 4a ol grn 17.50
*O26* A56 1r grn & red brn 92.50

Indian Stamps of 1911-26 Overprinted:

NABHA STATE SERVICE
a

NABHA STATE SERVICE
b

**1913**

*O27* A46 (a) 3p gray 10 10
*O28* A47 (a) ½a green 12 5
*O29* A48 (a) 1a car rose 8 8
*O30* A49 (a) 2a violet 10 10
*O31* A52 (a) 4a ol grn 16 16
*O32* A54 (a) 8a red vio 26 26
*O33* A56 (b) 1r grn & red brn 52 52
*Nos. O27-O33 (7)* 1.34 1.27

India Stamps of 1926-35 Overprinted NABHA STATE SERVICE

**Wmk. Multiple Stars. (196)**

**1932-45 *Perf. 13½x14, 14.***

*O34* A46 3p slate 6 6
*O35* A72 1a dk brn ('35) 15 15
*O36* A52 4a ol grn ('45) 7.00 1.75
*O37* A54 8a red vio ('37) 70 80

Same Overprint in Black on India Stamps of 1937.

**1938**

*O38* A80 9p green 2.25 2.25
*O39* A80 1a carmine 65 65

Official Stamps of India 1939-43 Overprinted in Black NABHA

**1942-44 *Perf. 13½x14.***

*O40* O8 3p slate 6 6
*O41* O8 ½a brn ('43) 7 7
*O42* O8 ½a dk rose vio ('44) 1.10 1.10
*O43* O8 9p grn ('43) 7 7
*O44* O8 1a car rose ('43) 7 6
*O45* O8 1½a dl pur ('43) 18 18
*O46* O8 2a scar ('43) 12 9
*O47* O8 4a dk brn ('43) 95 1.40
*O48* O8 8a bl vio ('43) 95 1.40

India Nos. 162-164 Overprinted in Black NABHA SERVICE

*O49* A82 1r brn & sl 9.25 *12.00*
*O50* A82 2r dk brn & dk vio 25.00 *45.00*
*O51* A82 5r dp ultra & dk grn 62.50 *92.50*
*Nos. O40-O51 (12)* 100.32 153.93

## PATIALA

LOCATION — A State of India in the central Punjab.
AREA — 5,942 sq. mi.
POP. — 1,936,259 (1941)
CAPITAL — Patiala

The varities with small letters in the overprint are not listed as the letters are merely broken and not from another font.

Indian Stamps Overprinted in Red PUTTIALLA STATE

**1884 Wmk. Star. (39) *Perf. 14.***

*1* A17 ½a green 85 90
*a.* Double overprint, one horizontal 250.00 175.00
*2* A19 1a vio brn 14.00 14.00
*a.* Double overprint
*b.* Double overprint, one in blk 250.00
*c.* Pair, one as "b", one without overprint
*3* A21 2a ultra 5.25 5.75
*4* A25 8a red lil 125.00 *180.00*
*a.* Double overprint, one in blk 37.50
*c.* Ovpt. reversed
*d.* Pair like "a", one with overprint reversed
*5* A27 1r gray 90.00 100.00

**Wmk. Elephant's Head. (38)**

*6* A9 4a green 14.00 16.00
*Nos. 1-6 (6)* 249.10 316.65

Indian Stamps Overprinted in Red PUTTIALLA STATE

**1885 Wmk. Star. (39)**

*7* A17 ½a green 42 35
*a.* "AUTTIALLA" 8.50
*c.* "STATE" only
*8* A21 2a ultra 85 45
*a.* "AUTTIALLA" 15.00
*9* A27 1r gray 5.00 *10.50*
*a.* "AUTTIALLA" 170.00

**Wmk. Elephant's Head. (38)**

*10* A9 4a green 1.10 1.10
*a.* Double overprint, one in blk 125.00
*b.* Pair, one as "a", one with blk overprint

Same, Overprinted in Black.

**Wmk. Star. (39)**

*11* A19 1a vio brn 25 25
*a.* "AUTTIALLA" 20.00
*c.* Double overprint, one in red 4.00
*d.* Pair, one as "c", one without ovpt.
*12* A25 8a red lil 4.50 4.50
*a.* "AUTTIALLA" 140.00

*Nos. 7 to 12 inclusive have been reprinted. Most of them bear the word "Reprint". The few copies that escaped the overprint cannot be distinguished from the originals.*

*The error "AUTTIALLA" has been reprinted in entire sheets, in red on the ½, 2, 4a and 1r and in black on the ½, 1, 2, 4, 8a and 1r. "STATE" is 7¾mm. long, instead of 8½mm. Most copies are overprinted "Reprint".*

Same, Overprinted in Black PATIALA STATE

**1891-96**

*13* A17 ½a green 12 9
*14* A18 9p rose 28 32
*15* A19 1a vio brn 20 12
*a.* "STATE" only 100.00 100.00
*16* A20 1a6p bis brn 40 45
*17* A21 2a ultra 60 16
*18* A22 3a orange 32 32
*19* A23 4a ol grn ('96) 24 20
*a.* "STATE" only 160.00 125.00
*20* A25 8a red vio ('96) 60 60
*21* A26 12a vio, *red* 50 60
*22* A29 1r car rose & grn ('96) 4.75 *7.75*
*23* A30 2r brn & rose ('95) 77.50
*24* A30 3r grn & brn ('95) 100.00
*25* A30 5r vio & bl ('95) 120.00

**Wmk. Elephant's Head. (38)**

*26* A14 6a bister 40 32
*Nos. 13-26 (14)* 305.91

**1899 Wmk. Star. (39)**

*27* A31 3p car rose 7 6

**1902**

*28* A17 ½a lt grn 15 12
*29* A19 1a car rose 15 12

**1903-06**

*31* A32 3p gray 7 5
*32* A33 ½a green 8 5
*33* A34 1a car rose 12 7
*34* A35 2a violet 16 8
*35* A37 3a brn org 24 24
*36* A38 4a ol grn ('06) 65 40
*37* A39 6a bis ('05) 50 50
*38* A40 8a red vio ('06) 40 40
*39* A41 12a vio, *red* ('06) 1.10 1.25
*40* A42 1r car rose & grn ('05) 60 75
*Nos. 31-40 (10)* 3.92 3.79

**1908**

*41* A44 ½a green 10 10
*42* A45 1a car rose 12 12

**1912-14**

*43* A46 3p gray 5 5
*44* A47 ½a green 8 5
*45* A48 1a car rose 10 10
*46* A49 2a violet 14 8
*47* A51 3a brn org 26 26
*48* A52 4a ol grn 26 16
*49* A53 6a bister 32 32
*50* A54 8a red vio 45 26
*51* A55 12a claret 65 40
*52* A56 1r grn & red brn 2.50 2.50
*Nos. 43-52 (10)* 4.81 4.18

**1922-26**

*53* A48 1a dk brn ('23) 22 7
*54* A58 1½a chocolate 28 32
*55* A51 3a ultra ('26) 22 22
*56* A56 2r yel brn & car rose ('26) 6.75 7.25
*57* A56 5r vio & ultra ('26) 14.00 15.00
*Nos. 53-57 (5)* 21.47 22.86

India Stamps of 1926-35 Overprinted PATIALA STATE

**1928-34 Wmk. 196**

*60* A46 3p slate 5 5
*61* A47 ½a green 6 5
*62* A68 9p dk grn 8 6
*63* A48 1a dk brn 8 5
*64* A69 1a3p violet 10 6
*65* A60 2a dl vio 12 8
*66* A57 2a6p buff 1.50 1.50
*67* A51 3a blue 90 90
*68* A61 4a ol grn 30 30
*69* A54 8a red vio 40 40

Overprinted PATIALA STATE

*70* A56 1r grn & brn 1.00 1.25
*71* A56 2r buff & car rose 1.75 2.00
*Nos. 60-71 (12)* 6.34 6.70

India Stamps of 1926-35 Overprinted PATIALA STATE

**1935-37 *Perf. 14.***

*75* A71 ½a grn ('37) 10 10
*76* A72 1a dk brn ('36) 8 6
*77* A49 2a ver ('36) 12 10
*78* A51 3a car rose ('37) 1.50 1.50
*79* A52 4a ol grn 50 50
*Nos. 75-79 (5)* 2.30 2.26

Same Overprint in Black on Stamps of India, 1937.

**1937-38 *Perf. 13½x14.***

*80* A80 3p sl ('38) 21.00 3.00
*81* A80 ½a brn ('38) 4.50 80
*82* A80 9p green 2.25 50
*83* A80 1a carmine 35 28
*84* A81 2a scar ('38) 24 24
*85* A81 2a6p pur ('38) 28 28
*86* A81 3a yel grn ('38) 28 28
*87* A81 3a6p ultra ('38) 42 42
*88* A81 4a dk brn ('38) 35 35
*89* A81 6a pck bl ('38) 45 50
*90* A81 8a bl vio ('38) 1.10 1.40
*91* A81 12a car lake ('38) 1.10 1.40

Overprinted PATIALA STATE

**1938**

*92* A82 1r brn & sl 9.25 9.25
*93* A82 2r dk brn & dk vio 15.00 18.00
*94* A82 5r dp ultra & dk grn 27.50 *35.00*
*95* A82 10r rose car & dk vio 45.00 *75.00*
*96* A82 15r dk grn & dk brn 75.00 *140.00*
*97* A82 25r dk vio & bl vio 110.00 *190.00*
*Nos. 80-97 (18)* 314.07 476.70

India Nos. 150-153 Overprinted in Black PATIALA

**1942-43 *Perf. 13½x14.***

*98* A80 3p slate 12.00 1.50
*99* A80 ½a brn ('43) 5.50 1.10
*100* A80 9p grn ('43) 57.50 3.75
*101* A80 1a carmine 9.50 1.50

India Stamps of 1941-43 with same Overprint in Black.

**1942-47 *Perf. 13½x14***

*102* A83 3p slate 5 5
*103* A83 ½a rose vio ('43) 6 6
*104* A83 9p lt grn ('43) 8 8
*a.* Pair, one without overprint *2,400.*
*105* A83 1a car rose ('46) 12 6
*106* A84 1a3p bis ('43) 1.65 1.65
*107* A84 1½a dk pur ('43) 16 10
*108* A84 2a scar ('46) 24 12
*109* A84 3a vio ('46) 40 40
*110* A84 3½a ultra ('46) 2.75 *4.00*
*111* A85 4a choc ('46) 40 40
*112* A85 6a pck bl ('46) 48 48
*113* A85 8a bl vio ('46) 2.50 3.25
*114* A85 12a car lake ('45) 5.25 *10.00*

India No. 162 Overprinted in Black PATIALA

*115* A82 1r brn & sl ('47) 8.00 *14.00*
*Nos. 102-115 (14)* 22.14 34.65

**OFFICIAL STAMPS.**

Indian Stamps Overprinted in Black and Red PUTTIALLA SERVICE STATE

**1884 Wmk. Star. (39) *Perf. 14.***

*O1* A17 ½a green 3.00 22
*O2* A19 1a vio brn 45 12
*a.* "SERVICE" double 300.00 175.00
*b.* "SERVICE" inverted 500.00
*c.* "PUTTIALLA STATE" double 65.00
*d.* "PUTTIALLA STATE" inverted 100.00 65.00
*O3* A21 2a ultra *2,250.* 200.00

Same, Overprinted in Red or Black:

SERVICE PUTTIALLA STATE
a

SERVICE PUTTIALLA STATE
b

**1885-90**

*O4* A17 (a) ½a grn (R & Bk) 55 12
*a.* "AUTTIALLA" 45.00 15.00
*d.* "SERVICE" double 110.00

*O5* A17 (b) ½a grn (Bk) 45 9
*O6* A19 (a) 1a vio brn (Bk) 22 6
**a.** "AUTTILLA" 150.00 37.50
**c.** "SERVICE" double, one inverted 275.00
**d.** "SERVICE" double 190.00 190.00
*O7* A21 (b) 2a ultra (R) 18 15
**c.** "SERVICE" double, one invt. 57.50

*There are reprints of Nos. O4, O6 and O7. That of No. O4 has "SERVICE" overprinted in red in large letters and that of No. O6 has the same overprint in black. The originals have the word in small black letters. The reprints of No. O7, except those overprinted "Reprint", cannot be distinguished from the originals. These three reprints also exist with the error "AUTTIALLA".*

Same, Overprinted in Black

SERVICE

PATIALA
STATE

**1891-1900**

*O8* A17 ½a grn ('95) 12 5
**b.** "SERVICE" inverted 67.50
*O9* A19 1a vio brn ('00) 2.25 8
**a.** "SERVICE" inverted 72.50
*O10* A21 2a ultra 95 45
**a.** "SERVICE" inverted 72.50
*O11* A22 3a orange 35 24
*O12* A23 4a ol grn 18 12
*O13* A25 8a red vio 30 22
*O14* A26 12a vio, *red* 48 32
*O15* A27 1r gray 55 32

**Wmk. Elephant's Head. (38)**

*O16* A14 6a bister 45 38
*Nos. O8-O16 (9)* 5.63 2.18

**1902** **Wmk. Star. (39)**

*O17* A19 1a car rose 22 6

**1903**

*O18* A29 1r car rose & grn 5.25 5.50

**1903-09**

*O19* A32 3p gray 8 8
*O20* A33 ½a green 6 5
*O21* A34 1a car rose 9 5
*O22* A35 2a violet 15 15
*O23* A37 3a brn org 75 75
*O24* A38 4a ol grn ('05) 22 8
*O25* A40 8a red vio 30 18
*O26* A42 1r car rose & grn ('06) 85 85
*Nos. O19-O26 (8)* 2.50 2.19

**1907**

*O27* A44 ½a green 5 5
*O28* A45 1a car rose 8 5

India Stamps of 1911-26 Overprinted:

PATIALA
STATE

PATIALA
STATE

SERVICE
a

SERVICE
b

**1913-26**

*O29* A46 (a) 3p gray 9 6
*O30* A47 (a) ½a green 1.10 6
*O31* A48 (a) 1a car rose 12 6
*O32* A49 (a) 2a violet 12 6
*O33* A52 (a) 4a ol grn 18 12
*O34* A54 (a) 8a red vio 26 18
*O35* A56 (b) 1r grn & red brn 55 45
*O36* A56 (b) 2r yel brn & car rose ('26) 5.50 *9.25*
*O37* A56 (b) 5r vio & ultra ('26) 11.00 *22.50*
*Nos. O29-O37 (9)* 18.92 32.74

Same Overprint on India Nos. 83 and 89.

**1925-26**

*O38* A48 (a) 1a dk brn 15 8
*O39* A53 (a) 6a bis ('26) 22 18

India Stamps of 1926-35 Overprinted

PATIALA STATE
SERVICE

**1927-36** **Wmk. 196**

*O40* A46 3p slate 5 5
*O41* A47 ½a green 5 5
*O42* A48 1a dk brn 5 5
*O43* A69 1a3p violet 5 5
*O44* A60 2a dl vio 9 5
*O45* A60 2a vermilion 7 7
*O46* A57 2a6p buff 9 9
*O47* A61 4a ol grn 12 6
*O48* A54 8a red vio 24 24

Overprinted

PATIALA STATE
SERVICE

*O49* A56 1r grn & brn 75 32
*O50* A56 2r brn org & car rose ('36) 3.00 3.25
*Nos. O40-O50 (11)* 4.56 4.28

India Stamps of 1926-34 Overprinted

PATIALA STATE
SERVICE

**1935-36**

*O51* A71 ½a grn ('36) 8 5
*O52* A72 1a dk brn ('36) 12 8
*O53* A49 2a vermilion 28 5
**a.** Small die 22 12
*O54* A52 4a ol grn ('36) 30 10

Same Overprint on India Nos. 151-153.

**1938-39** ***Perf. 13½x14.***

*O55* A80 ½a brn ('39) 60 6
*O56* A80 9p grn ('39) 21.00 27.50
*O57* A80 1a carmine 60 9

India No. 136 Surcharged in Black

PATIALA STATE
1A SERVICE 1A

**1939** ***Perf. 14.***

*O58* A69 1a on 1a3p vio 2.00 70

"SERVICE" measures 9¼mm.

No. 64 Surcharged in Black

1A SERVICE 1A

**1940**

*O59* A69 1a on 1a3p vio 2.00 1.40

"SERVICE" measures 8½ mm.

India Nos. 162-164 Overprinted

PATIALA STATE
SERVICE

***Perf. 13½x14.***

*O60* A82 1r brn & sl 2.75 2.75
*O61* A82 2r dk brn & dk vio 14.00 14.00
*O62* A82 5r dp ultra & dk grn 27.50 27.50

India Official Stamps of 1939-43 Overprinted

PATIALA

**1940-45**

*O63* O8 3p sl ('41) 5 5
*O64* O8 ½a brown 9 5
*O65* O8 ½a dk rose vio ('43) 5 5
*O66* O8 9p green 5 5
*O67* O8 1a car rose 24 5
*O68* O8 1a3p bis ('41) 6 5
*O69* O8 1½a dl pur ('45) 42 5
*O70* O8 2a scar ('41) 5 5
*O71* O8 2½a pur ('41) 6 6
*O72* O8 4a dk brn ('45) 30 30
*O73* O8 8a bl vio ('45) 90 *1.25*

India Nos. 162-164 Overprinted in Black

PATIALA
SERVICE

*O74* A82 1r brn & sl ('43) 4.50 4.50
*O75* A82 2r dk brn & dk vio ('45) 8.50 *12.00*
*O76* A82 5r dp ultra & dk grn ('45) 15.00 *18.00*
*Nos. O63-O76 (14)* 37.27 36.51

**NATIVE FEUDATORY STATES. These stamps had franking power solely in the states in which they were issued, except for Cochin and Travancore which had a reciprocal postal agreement.**

## ALWAR

LOCATION — A Feudatory State of India, lying southwest of Delhi in the Jaipur Residency
AREA — 3,158 sq. mi.
POP. — 749,751.
CAPITAL — Alwar.

Katar (Indian Dagger) — A1

**1877** **Unwmk.** **Litho.** ***Rouletted.***

*1* A1 ¼a ultra 1.00 75
**a.** ¼a bl 1.00 75
**b.** Horiz. pair, imperf. vert. 32.50
*2* A1 1a brown 1.00 1.00
**a.** 1a yel brn 1.00 1.00
**b.** 1a red brn 1.00 1.00
**c.** Horiz. pair, imperf. vert. 55.00 55.00

Redrawn.

**1899-1901** ***Pin-perf. 12***

*3* A1 ¼a sl bl, wide margins 6.00 3.50
*4* A1 ¼a yel grn, narrow margins ('01) 5.25 3.50
**a.** Horiz. pair, imperf. btwn. 265.00
**b.** ¼a emer, wide margins ('99) 825.00
**c.** ¼a emer, narrow margins 5.25 4.75

Nos. 3 and 4b are printed farther apart in the sheet.

On Nos. 3 and 4, the shading of the left border line is missing.

Nos. 1 to 4 occasionally show portions of the papermaker's watermark, W. T. & Co.

Alwar stamps became obsolete in 1902.

## BAMRA

LOCATION — A Feudatory State in the Eastern States, Orissa States Agency, Bengal.
AREA — 1,988 sq. mi.
POP. — 151,259.
CAPITAL — Deogarh.

Stamps of Bamra were issued without gum.

BAMRA
postage

A1

**1888** **Unwmk.** **Typeset** ***Imperf.***

*1* A1 ¼a *yellow* 80.00
**a.** "g" inverted *2,000.*
*2* A1 ½a *rose* 52.50
**a.** "g" inverted *1,750.*
*3* A1 1a *blue* 32.50
**a.** "g" inverted *1,350.*
**b.** "postge"
*4* A1 2a *green* 40.00
**a.** "postge" *1,750.*
*5* A1 4a *yellow* 27.50
**a.** "postge" *1,500.*
*6* A1 8a *rose* 25.00
**a.** "postge" *1,350.*

All values may be found with the scroll inverted, and with the long end of the scroll pointing to the right or left.

*Nos. 1 and 2 have been reprinted in blocks of eight and Nos. 1 to 6 in blocks of twenty. In the reprints the fourth character of the native inscription often has the curved upper line broken at the left, but in many instances comparison with photographic reproductions of the original settings is the only certain test.*

A2

**1890**

*7* A2 ¼a *rose lil* 1.00 1.00
**a.** "Quatrer" 10.00 10.00
**b.** "e" of "Postage" inverted 10.00 10.00
**c.** "Eeudatory" 10.00 10.00
*8* A2 ½a *green* 1.40 1.40
**a.** "Eeudatory" 16.00 16.00
**b.** "postage" with small "p" 1.40 1.40
**c.** First "a" of "anna" inverted 14.00
*9* A2 1a *yellow* 3.25 3.25
**a.** "Eeudatory" 35.00 40.00
**b.** "postage" with small "p" 2.00 2.00
**c.** "annas" 65.00 65.00
*10* A2 2a *rose lil* 4.75 4.75
**a.** "Eeudatory" 60.00 67.50
*11* A2 4a *rose lil* 36.00 36.00
**a.** "Eeudatory" 150.00 150.00
*12* A2 8a *rose lil* 10.00 10.00
**a.** "BAMBA" 100.00 100.00
**b.** "Foudatory" & "Postage" 100.00 100.00
**c.** "postage" with small "p" 10.00 10.00
*13* A2 1r *rose lil* 32.50 32.50
**a.** "BAMBA" 135.00 135.00
**b.** "Eeudatory" 150.00 150.00
**c.** "postage" with small "p" 32.50 32.50

**1893**

*14* A2 ¼a *rose* 90 90
**a.** "postage" with small "p" 90 90
*15* A2 ¼a *magenta* 90 90
**a.** "postage" with small "p" 90 90
**b.** "AM" of "BAMRA" invtd.
**c.** "M" OF "BAMRA" invtd.
**d.** "AMRA" of "BAMRA" inverted 22.50
**e.** "M" and 2nd "A" of "BAMRA" inverted 52.50 52.50
**f.** First "a" of "anna" inverted 27.50 27.50
*16* A2 2a *rose* 1.40 1.40
**a.** "postage" with small "p" 1.40 1.40
*17* A2 4a *rose* 3.25 3.25
**a.** "postage" with small "p" 3.25 3.25
**b.** "BAMBA" 210.00 210.00
*18* A2 8a *rose* 5.00 5.00
**a.** "postage" with small "p" 5.00 5.00
*19* A2 1r *rose* 18.00 20.00
**a.** "postage" with small "p" 30.00 30.00

The central ornament varies in size and may be found in various positions.

Bamra stamps became obsolete Dec. 31, 1894.

## BARWANI

LOCATION — A Feudatory State of Central India, in the Malwa Agency.
AREA — 1,178 sq. mi.
POP. — 141,110
CAPITAL — Barwani

The stamps of Barwani were all typographed and normally issued in booklets containing panes of four. Exceptions are noted (Nos. 14-15, 20-25). The majority were completely perforated, but some of the earlier printings were perforated only between the stamps, leaving one or two sides imperf. Nos. 1-25 were issued without gum. Many shades exist.

Rana Ranjit Singh
A1 A2

**1921, April (?)** **Unwmk.** ***Pin-Perf. 7***

**Toned Medium Wove Paper**

**Clear Impression**

*1* A1 ¼a dl Prus grn 65.00 *100.00*
*2* A1 ½a dl bl 105.00 *150.00*

**1921** ***Coarse Perf. 7xImperf.***

**White Thin Wove Paper**

**Blurred Impression**

*3* A1 ¼a dl grn 12.00 21.00
*4* A1 ½a pale bl 12.00 18.00

**1921** **Toned Laid Paper** ***Imperf.***

*5* A1 ¼a lt grn 7.25
*6* A1 ½a lt grn 3.00
**a.** Perf. 11, top or bottom only 5.50

**1921** ***Coarse Perf. 7, 7xImperf.***

**Thick Wove Paper**

**Very Blurred Impression**

*7* A1 ¼a dl bl 5.00
*8* A1 ½a dl grn 13.00

In 1927 Nos. 7-8 were printed on thin hard paper.

**1922** ***Perf. 7xImperf.***

**Thick Glazed Paper**

*9* A1 ¼a dl ultra 1.75

***Rough Perf. 11xImperf.***

*10* A2 1a vermilion 1.65
*11* A2 2a violet 2.00 *4.00*
*a.* Double impression 90.00

Shades of No. 11 include purple. No. 11 was also printed on thick dark toned paper.

**1923-26** ***Perf.***
**Wove, Laid Paper**

*12* A1 ¼a grysh ultra, perf. 8½ 1.50
*13* A1 ¼a blk, perf. 7 x imperf. 27.50 *35.00*
*14* A1 ¼a dl rose, perf. 11½-12 1.25
*15* A1 ¼a dk bl, perf. 11 ('26) 1.50
*16* A1 ½a grn, perf. 11 x imperf. 1.10

No. 12 was also printed on pale gray thin toned paper.

No. 14 was printed on horizontally laid paper in horizontal sheets of 12 containing three panes of 4.

No. 15 was printed on vertically laid paper in horizontal sheets of 8.

Rana Ranjit Singh — A3

**1927-28** ***Perf. 7***
**Thin Wove Paper**

*17* A3 4a dl org 35.00

No. 17 was also printed in light brown on thick paper, pin-perf. 6, and in orange brown on thick paper, rough perf. 7.

**1928** ***Coarse Perf. 7***
**Thick Glazed Paper**

*18* A1 ¼a brt bl 1.75
*19* A1 ½a brt yel grn 1.75

**1928, Nov.** ***Rough Perf. 10½***

*20* A1 ¼a dp ultra 1.25
*a.* Tete beche pair 6.50
*21* A1 ½a yel grn 1.75
*a.* Tete beche pair 10.00

**1929-31** ***Perf. 11***

*22* A1 ¼a blue 90 1.25
*a.* ¼a ultra 90 1.25
*23* A1 ½a emer grn 90 1.25
*24* A2 1a car pink ('31) 5.00
*25* A3 4a salmon 25.00

Nos. 20-25 were printed in sheets of 8 (4x2).

No. 22 had five printings in various shades (bright to deep blue) in horizontal or vertical format.

No. 23 also printed in dark myrtle green.

Rana Devi Singh — A4

**1932-48** ***Perf. 11, 12***
**Glazed Paper**

*26* A4 ¼a dk gray 1.40 4.25
*27* A4 ½a bl grn 1.40 1.75
*28* A4 1a brown 1.50 3.00
*a.* 1a choc, perf. 8½ ('48) 7.50
*29* A4 2a dp red vio 2.75 5.50
*a.* Perf. 12 x 11
*b.* 2a red lil 12.50
*30* A4 4a ol grn 8.50 12.50
*Nos. 26-30 (5)* 15.55 27.00

Types of 1921-27

**1934-48** ***Perf. 11***

*31* A1 ¼a sl gray 1.10 2.75
*32* A1 ½a green 2.25 3.75
*33* A2 1a dk brn 2.00 3.75
*a.* 1a brn, perf. 8½ ('48) 6.00
*34* A2 2a brt pur ('38) 42.50
*35* A2 2a rose car ('46) 20.00
*36* A3 4a ol grn 8.50 10.00
*Nos. 31-36 (6)* 76.35

In the nine printings of Nos. 26-36, several plate settings spaced the cliches from 2 to 9 mm. apart. Hence the stamps come in different overall sizes. Not all values were in each printing. Values are for the commonest varieties.

No. 36 was also printed in pale sage green.

Rana Devi Singh — A5

**1938**

*37* A5 1a dark brown 12.50
*a.* Booklet pane of 4 50.00

Stamps of type A5 in red are revenues.

Barwani stamps became obsolete July 1, 1948.

## BHOPAL

LOCATION — A Feudatory State of Central India, in the Bhopal Agency.
AREA — 6,924 sq. mi.
POP. — 995,745
CAPITAL — Bhopal

Inscription in Urdu in an octagon embossed on Nos. 1-83.

The embossed issues may be found with embossing inverted or sideways.

Inscriptions and Values
A1 A2

Double Lined Frame

**Lithographed Frame, Embossed Center**

**1876** **Unwmk.** ***Imperf.***

*1* A1 ¼a black 300.00 300.00
*a.* "EGAM" 1,750. 1,750.
*b.* "BFGAM" 1,500. 1,500.
*c.* "BEGAN" 1,000. 1,000.
*2* A1 ½a red 17.50 17.50
*a.* "EGAM" 100.00 100.00
*b.* "BFGAM" 65.00 75.00
*c.* "BEGAN" 100.00 100.00

Single Lined Frame.

**1877**

*3* A2 ¼a black *3,500.*
*a.* "NWAB"
*4* A2 ½a red 6.75 7.50
*a.* "NWAB" 30.00 37.50

A3

A4

**1878**

*5* A3 ¼a black 42 42
*a.* "J" diagonal, plate II 42 42

All stamps of type A3 are lettered "EEGAM" for "BEGAM".

**1878** **Litho.**

*6* A4 ½a pale red 2.00 2.00
*a.* ½a brn red 7.25 7.25
*b.* "NWAB" 10.50 10.50
*c.* "JAHN" 10.50 10.50
*d.* "EECAM" 10.50 10.50

A5

A6

**1879-80**

*7* A5 ¼a green 4.00 5.00
*8* A5 ½a red 4.00 13.00

***Perf.***

*9* A5 ¼a green 2.00 2.00
*10* A5 ½a red 2.00 2.00

Nos. 7 and 9 have the value in parenthesis; Nos. 8 and 10 are without parenthesis.

**1881** ***Imperf.***

*11* A6 ¼a green 1.75
*a.* "NAWA" 12.00
*b.* "CHAH" 12.00

***Perf.***

*12* A6 ¼a green 2.00 2.00
*a.* "NAWA" 13.00 13.00
*b.* "CHAH" 13.00 13.00

A7

**1881-89** ***Imperf.***

*13* A7 ¼a black 35 90
*a.* "NWAB" 3.00
*14* A7 ½a red 60 1.40
*a.* "NWAB" 4.75
*15* A7 1a brown 60 1.40
*a.* "NWAB" 4.75
*16* A7 2a blue 75 1.50
*a.* "NWAB" 5.50
*17* A7 4a yellow 4.50 4.75
*a.* "NWAB" 16.00

A8

A9

**1884** ***Perf.***

*19* A8 ¼a green 110.00 135.00
*a.* "JAN" 195.00
*b.* "BEGM" 325.00
*c.* "NWAB" 550.00
*d.* "SHAHAN" 550.00
*e.* "JN" 375.00
*f.* "JAHA" 250.00
*20* A9 ¼a green 2.25
*a.* "ANAWAB" 16.00

On type A9 there is a dash at the left of "JA" of "JAHAN" instead of a character like a comma as on types A5 and A6.

Imitations of No. 19 were printed about 1904 in black on wove paper and in red on laid paper, both imperf. and pin-perf.

A10

**1884** **Laid Paper** ***Imperf.***

*21* A10 ¼a bl grn 25.00 25.00
*a.* "NWAB" 75.00
*b.* "NAWAJANAN" 150.00
*c.* "SAH" 75.00
*22* A10 ½a black 40 50
*a.* "NWAB" 2.00
*b.* "NAWAJANAN" 4.00
*c.* "SAH" 2.00

***Perf.***

*23* A10 ¼a bl grn 28 32
*a.* "NWAB" 1.40
*b.* "NAWAJANAN" 2.75
*c.* "SAH" 1.40
*24* A10 ½a black 18 25
*a.* "NWAB" 80
*b.* "NAWAJANAN" 1.65
*c.* "SAH" 80

Type Redrawn.

**1886** **Wove Paper.** ***Imperf.***

*25* A10 ¼a grysh grn 18 20
*a.* ¼a grn 18 20
*b.* "NWAB" 1.40
*c.* "NAWA" 1.40
*d.* "NAWAA" 1.40
*e.* "NAWABABEGAAM" 2.75
*f.* "NWABA" 1.40
*26* A10 ½a red 28 30
*a.* "SAH" 1.40
*b.* "NAWABA" 1.40

***Perf.***

*27* A10 ¼a green 18 32
*a.* "NWAB" 1.65
*b.* "NAWA" 1.65
*c.* "NAWAA" 1.65
*d.* "NAWABABEGAAM" 2.25
*e.* "NWABA" 2.25
*28* A10 ½a red 2.50 2.50
*a.* "SAH" 12.00
*b.* "NAWABA" 12.00

On Nos. 25 to 28 the inscriptions are closer to the value than on Nos. 21 to 24.

A11

A12

**1886** ***Imperf.***

*29* A11 ½a red 75 1.10
*a.* "BEGAM" 4.50
*b.* "NWAB" 4.50

**Laid Paper**

*30* A12 4a yellow 3.25
*a.* "EEGAM" 16.00
*b.* Wove paper 6.50
*c.* As "a," wove paper 32.50

***Perf.***

*31* A12 4a yellow 1.50
*a.* "EEGAM" 7.50

A13

A14

**1889** **Wove Paper** ***Imperf.***

*32* A13 ¼a green 30 30
*a.* "SAH" 3.00
*b.* "NAWA" 3.00
*33* A14 ¼a black 1.10 1.25
*a.* "EEGAN" 7.25

***Perf.***

*34* A13 ¼a green 32 32
*a.* "SAH" 3.25
*b.* "NAWA" 3.25
*c.* Imperf. vertically
*35* A14 ¼a black 75 75
*a.* "EEGAN" 5.00
*b.* Horizontal pair, imperf. between

Type A13 has smaller letters in the upper corners than Type A10.

A15

A16

**1890** ***Imperf.***

*36* A15 ¼a black 35 35
*37* A15 1a brown 75 85
*a.* "EEGAM" 5.75
*b.* "BBGAM" 5.75
*38* A7 2a grnsh bl 1.10 75
*a.* "BBEGAM" 8.00
*b.* "NAWAH" 8.00
*39* A7 4a yellow 1.10 1.10
*40* A16 8a blue 18.00 18.00
*a.* "HAH" 42.50
*b.* "JABAN" 42.50

An imperf. imitation of Nos. 36 and 41 was printed about 1904 in black on wove paper.

***Perf.***

*41* A15 ¼a black 75 75
*a.* Pair, imperf. between 7.50

42 A15 1a brown 90 1.10
a. "EECAM" 7.50
b. "BBGAM" 7.50
43 A7 2a grnsh bl 1.25 1.50
a. "BBEGAM" 12.50
b. "NAWAH" 12.50
44 A7 4a yellow 1.90 1.90
45 A16 8a blue 20.00 20.00
a. "HAH" 47.50
b. "JABAN" 47.50

Nos. 40 and 45 have a frame line around each stamp.

***Imperf***

46 A12 ½a red (BECAM) 90 1.10
47 A13 ½a red (NWAB) 75 60
a. Inverted "N"
b. "SAH" 7.50

***Perf.***

48 A12 ½a red (BECAM) 55 60
a. Without embossing
49 A13 ½a red (NWAB) 75 85
a. Inverted "N"
b. "SAH" 7.50

**1891-93 Laid Paper. *Imperf.***
50 A16 8a dp grn 18.00 18.00
a. "HAH" 42.50 42.50
b. "JABAN" 42.50 42.50

***Perf.***

51 A16 8a dp grn 18.00 18.00
a. "HAH" 42.50 42.50
b. "JABAN" 42.50 42.50

**1894 Redrawn *Imperf.***
53 A10 ¼a green 42 42
a. "NAWAH" 5.00
54 A11 ½a brick red 2.00 2.25
55 A16 8a bl blk 13.00 13.00
a. Laid paper 27.50

***Perf.***

56 A10 ¼a green 42 42
a. "NAWAH" 5.00
57 A11 ½a brick red 2.00 2.25
58 A16 8a bl blk 15.00 15.00

The ¼a redrawn has letters in corners larger; value in very small characters.

The 8a redrawn has no frame to each stamp but a frame to the sheet.

**1898 *Imperf.***
60 A16 8a black 18.00 18.00
b. "E" of "BEGAM" inverted 42.50

A17

A18

A19

A20

A21

**1895**

**Laid Paper.**

61 A17 ¼a green 1.50 1.50
62 A18 ¼a red 1.75 1.75
63 A19 ¼a black 75 75
a. "NAWB" 4.25 4.25
64 A20 ½a black 75 75
65 A21 ½a red 90 1.10

***Perf.***

66 A17 ¼a green 3.25 3.25
67 A18 ¼a red 1.65 1.65
68 A19 ¼a black 2.50 2.50
a. "NAWB" 18.00
69 A20 ½a black 1.65 1.65
70 A21 ½a red

Imperf. imitations of Nos. 65 and 70 were printed about 1904 in deep red on laid paper and in black on wove paper.

**Wove Paper.**

***Small Pin-perf.***

71 A16 8a bl blk

A22

A23

**1898 *Imperf.***
72 A22 ¼a black 32 32
a. "SHAN" 3.25 3.25
73 A22 ¼a green 32 32
a. "SHAN" 3.25 3.25
74 A23 ¼a black 1.50 50

**1899**
75 A13 ½a blk ("NWAB") 60 60
a. "SHN" 6.00
b. "NWASBAHJAHNJ" 6.00
c. "SIIAN" 6.00
d. "SBAH" 6.00
e. "SBAN" 6.00
f. "NWIB" 6.00
g. "BEIAM" 6.00

A24

Coat of Arms — A25

**1902**
76 A24 ¼a red 1.75 1.75
77 A24 ½a black 2.00 2.00
a. Printed on both sides 365.00
78 A24 1a brown 2.00 2.00
79 A24 2a blue 6.00 7.50
80 A24 4a orange 27.50 32.50
81 A24 8a violet 35.00 45.00
82 A24 1r rose 60.00 75.00
*Nos. 76-82 (7)* 134.25 165.75

No. 50 Overprinted in Red

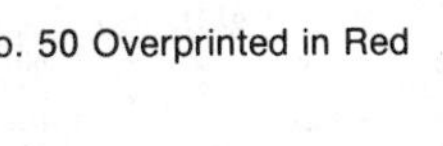

**1903**
83 A16 8a dp grn 20.00 20.00
a. Inverted ovpt. 47.50 47.50

There are two types of the overprint which is the Arabic S, initial of the Begum.

Inscription in Circle
Embossed on Each Stamp

**1903**
84 A24 ¼a red 35 35
85 A24 ½a black 45 45
86 A24 1a brown 55 55
87 A24 2a blue 1.50 1.50
88 A24 4a orange 16.00 16.00
89 A24 8a violet 27.50 35.00
90 A24 1r rose 35.00 47.50
*Nos. 84-90 (7)* 81.35 101.35

*The embossing in a circle, which was first used in 1903, has been applied to many early stamps and impressions from redrawn plates of early issues. So far as is now known, these should be classed as reprints.*

**1908 Engr. *Perf. 13½.***
99 A25 1a yel grn 3.00 60
a. Printed on both sides 120.00

## OFFICIAL STAMPS

O1

Size: 20½x25mm

Overprinted **SERVICE**

**1908 Unwmk. Engr. *Perf. 13½.***
O1 O1 ½a yel grn 1.75 6
a. Pr., one without overprint 120.00
b. Inverted ovpt. 80.00
c. Dbl. ovpt., one invtd. 80.00
O2 O1 1a carmine 1.75 6
a. Inverted ovpt. 60.00
O3 O1 2a blue 10.50 6
O4 O1 4a red brn 7.50 9

Overprinted **SERVICE**

O5 O1 ½a yel grn 2.50 7
O6 O1 1a carmine 6.00 90
O7 O1 2a blue 3.00 20
a. Inverted ovpt. 35.00
O8 O1 4a red brn 45.00 20
a. Inverted overprint 27.50

The difference in the two overprints is in the shape of the letters, most noticeable in the "R".

Type of 1908 Issue
Size: 25½x30½mm

Overprinted **SERVICE**

**1930-31 Litho. *Perf. 14***
O9 O1 ½a gray grn ('31) 1.10 70
O10 O1 1a carmine 1.25 7
O11 O1 2a blue 1.50 9
O12 O1 4a brown 1.75 42

Nos. O9, O11 and O12 are inscribed "POSTAGE" on the left side; No. O10 is inscribed "POSTAGE AND REVENUE".

Similar to Type O1
Size: 21x25mm
"POSTAGE" at left
"BHOPAL STATE" at right

**1932-33 *Perf. 11½, 13, 13½, 14***
O13 O1 ¼a org yel 1.65 12
a. Pair, one without overprint 65.00
b. Perf. 13½ 5.25 2.75
c. Perf. 14 8.00 12

**"BHOPAL GOVT." at right**

***Perf. 13½***

O14 O1 ½a yel grn 1.25 6
O15 O1 1a brn red 2.00 6
O16 O1 2a blue 2.25 12
O17 O1 4a brown 2.75 50

Official Stamps of 1932-33 Surcharged in Red, Violet, Black or Blue:

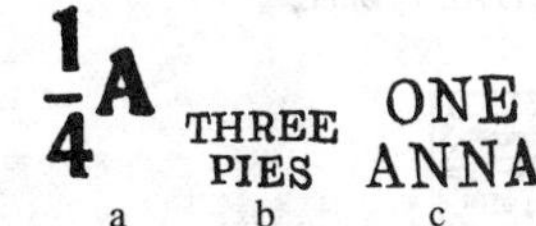

a b c

**1935-36 *Perf. 13½***
O18 O1(a) ¼a on ½a yel grn (R) 3.50 1.75
a. Inverted surcharge 125.00 60.00
O19 O1(b) 3p on ½a yel grn (R) 48 24
O20 O1(a) ¼a on 2a bl (R) 3.50 1.75
a. Inverted surcharge 75.00 60.00
O21 O1(b) 3p on 2a bl (R) 48 48
a. Invt. surch. 45.00 35.00
O22 O1(a) ¼a on 4a brn (R) 135.00 35.00
O23 O1(a) ¼a on 4a brn (Bk) ('36) 14.00 10.50
O24 O1(b) 3p on 4a brn (R) 35.00 18.00
O25 O1(b) 3p on 4a brn (Bk) ('36) 1.75 1.10
O26 O1(c) 1a on ½a yel grn (V) 35 35
a. Inverted surcharge 40.00 40.00
O27 O1(c) 1a on 2a bl (R) 35 28
a. Inverted surcharge 40.00 40.00
O28 O1(c) 1a on 2a bl (Bk) ('36) 60 28
O29 O1(c) 1a on 4a brn (Bl) 40 28

Nos. O18 to O25 are arranged in composite sheets of 100. The two top horizontal rows of each value are surcharged "a" and the next five rows as "b". The next three rows as "b" but in a narrower setting.

Various errors of spelling or inverted letters are found on Nos. O18-O29.

Arms of Bhopal — O2

**1935 Litho.**
O30 O2 1a3p cl & bl 24 20
a. Ovpt. omitted 45.00 45.00

Inscribed: "Bhopal State Postage"
Ovptd. "SERVICE" 11mm long

**1937 *Perf. 12.***
O31 O2 1a6p dk cl & bl 28 24
a. Ovpt. omitted 60.00 60.00

See Nos. O42, O45.

Arms of Bhopal — O3

Brown or Black Overprint.

**1936-38 Typo.**
O32 O3 ¼a org (B) 60 6
a. Black overprint 12.00 12.00
c. Inverted ovpt. 65.00 65.00
d. As "a," inverted 85.00 85.00
O32B O3 ¼a yel (Br) ('38) 1.25 15
O33 O3 1a carmine 90 10

Moti Mahal — O4

Overprinted "SERVICE"

**1936 *Perf. 11½.***
O34 O4 ½a grn & choc 9 6
a. Double impression of stamp 24.00 9.00

Moti Masjid O5

Design: 4a, Taj Mahal and Be-Nazir Palaces.

Overprinted "SERVICE"

**1937 *Perf. 11½***
O35 O5 2a dk bl & brn 18 9
a. Inverted ovpt. 60.00 60.00
O36 O5 4a bis brn & bl 55 30

Types of 1937.
Overprinted "SERVICE" in Black or Brown

**1938-44**

Designs: 4a, Taj Mahal. 8a, Ahmadabad Palace. 1r, Rait-Ghat.

O37 O4 ½a dp grn & brn 9 8
O38 O5 2a vio & dp grn 9 8
O39 O5 4a red brn & brt bl 1.25 35
O40 O5 8a red vio & bl 75 35
a. "SERAICE" 120.00 120.00
b. Ovpt. omitted 65.00 65.00
c. Double ovpt. 65.00 65.00
O41 O5 1r bl & red vio (Br) 1.25 60
a. Black ovpt. ('44) 12.00 9.00
b. "SREVICE" 75.00 85.00
c. Ovpt. omitted
d. Double ovpt. 55.00 55.00
*Nos. O37-O41 (5)* 3.43 1.46

No. O39 measures 36½x22½mm. No. O40 measures 39x24 mm. No. O41 measures 45½x27¾ mm.

Type of 1935.

**1939 *Perf. 12.***
O42 O2 1a6p dk cl 45 25

Tiger — O6

Design: 1a, Deer.

**1940 Typo. *Perf. 11½***
O43 O6 ¼a ultra 1.25 24
O44 O6 1a red vio 3.25 48

Type of 1935.
Inscribed: "Bhopal State Postage"

**1941**
*O45* O2 1a3p emerald 24 9

Moti Palace — O7

Coat of Arms — O8

Designs: 2a, Moti Mosque. 4a, Be-Nazir Palaces.

***Perf. 11½, 12.***

**1944-46 Unwmk. Typo.**

| | | | | |
|---|---|---|---|---|
| *O46* | O8 | 3p ultra | 6 | 5 |
| *O47* | O7 | ½a lt grn | 24 | 10 |
| *O48* | O8 | 9p org brn ('46) | 1.75 | 48 |
| *a.* | | Imperf., pair | | 60.00 |
| *O49* | O8 | 1a brt red vio ('45) | 60 | 9 |
| *O50* | O8 | 1½a dp plum | 24 | 8 |
| *O51* | O7 | 2a red vio ('45) | 42 | 32 |
| *O52* | O8 | 3a yel ('46) | 60 | 60 |
| *a.* | | Imperf., pair | | 60.00 |
| *O53* | O7 | 4a brn ('45) | 75 | 48 |
| *O54* | O8 | 6a brt rose ('46) | 4.75 | 7.50 |
| *a.* | | Imperf., pair | | 75.00 |
| | | *Nos. O46-O54 (9)* | 9.41 | 9.70 |

**1946-47 Unwmk. *Perf. 11½***

| | | | | |
|---|---|---|---|---|
| *O55* | O8 | 1a violet | 35 | 20 |
| *O56* | O7 | 2a vio ('47) | 1.75 | 60 |
| *O57* | O8 | 3a dp org | 24.00 | 24.00 |
| *a.* | | Imperf., pair | | |

No. 050 Surcharged "2 As." and Bars

**1949 *Perf. 12.***

| | | | | |
|---|---|---|---|---|
| *O58* | O8 | 2a on 1½a dp plum | 75 | 60 |
| *a.* | | Inverted surcharge | | |
| *b.* | | Double surcharge | | |
| *c.* | | Imperf., pair | 77.50 | 77.50 |

Same Surcharged "2 As." and Rosettes.

**1949 *Perf. 12, Imperf.***
*O59* O8 2a on 1½a dp plum 225.00 225.00

Three or more types of "2" in surcharge. Bhopal stamps became obsolete in 1950.

## BHOR

LOCATION — A Feudatory State in the Kolhapur Residency and Deccan States Agency.
AREA — 910 sq. mi.
POP. — 141,546
CAPITAL — Bhor

A1

A2

**Handstamped.**

**1879 Unwmk. *Imperf.***

| | | | | |
|---|---|---|---|---|
| *1* | A1 | ½a carmine | 1.75 | 2.00 |
| *2* | A2 | 1a carmine | 1.75 | 2.00 |

Pant Sachiv Shankarrao — A3

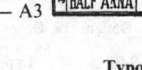

**1901 Typo.**
*3* A3 ½a red 5.50 *27.50*

## BIJAWAR

LOCATION — A Feudatory State in the Bundelkhand Agency of Central India.
AREA — 973 sq. mi.
POP. — 115,852
CAPITAL — Bijawar

Maharaja Sir Sawant Singh
A1 A2

**1935-36 Typo. Unwmk. *Perf. 10½***

| | | | | |
|---|---|---|---|---|
| *1* | A1 | 3p brown | 50 | 50 |
| *a.* | | Imperf., pair | 14.00 | |
| *b.* | | Rouletted 7 ('36) | 60 | 75 |
| *2* | A1 | 6p carmine | 50 | 50 |
| *a.* | | Rouletted 7 ('36) | 75 | 1.25 |
| *3* | A1 | 9p purple | 60 | 60 |
| *a.* | | Rouletted 7 ('36) | 1.50 | 2.50 |
| *4* | A1 | 1a dk bl | 80 | 80 |
| *a.* | | Rouletted 7 ('36) | 2.00 | 3.50 |
| *5* | A1 | 2a sl grn | 1.40 | 1.40 |
| *a.* | | Rouletted 7 ('36) | 4.00 | 7.50 |

**1937 *Perf. 9***

| | | | | |
|---|---|---|---|---|
| *6* | A2 | 4a red org | 2.50 | *4.50* |
| *7* | A2 | 6a yellow | 4.50 | *9.00* |
| *8* | A2 | 8a emerald | 5.50 | *10.50* |
| *9* | A2 | 12a turq bl | 6.75 | *9.00* |
| *10* | A2 | 1r purple | 17.50 | *22.50* |
| *a.* | | "1Rs" instead of "1R" | 45.00 | *67.50* |
| | | *Nos. 1-10 (10)* | 40.55 | 59.30 |

Bijawar stamps became obsolete in 1939.

## BUNDI

LOCATION — A Feudatory State in the Rajputana Agency of India.
AREA — 2,220 sq. mi.
POP. — 216,722
CAPITAL — Bundi

Katar (Indian Dagger) — A1

A2

A3

Laid Paper.

**1894 Unwmk. Litho. *Imperf.***

**Gutters between Stamps.**

*1* A1 ½a slate 2,750. *2,000.*

**Redrawn; Blade Does Not Touch Oval.**

**No Gutters between Stamps.**

**Wove Paper.**

| | | | | |
|---|---|---|---|---|
| *1A* | A1 | ½a slate | 15.00 | 13.00 |
| *b.* | | Value above, name below | 180.00 | 180.00 |
| *c.* | | Top right ornament omitted | 500.00 | 500.00 |

On No. 1A, the dagger is thinner and its point does not touch the oval inner frame.

**1896**

**Laid Paper.**

*2* A2 ½a slate 5.00 5.25

**1897-98**

| | | | | |
|---|---|---|---|---|
| *3* | A3 | 1a red | 6.50 | 6.00 |
| *4* | A3 | 2a yel grn | 8.00 | 10.00 |
| *5* | A3 | 4a yel grn | 17.00 | 18.00 |
| *6* | A3 | 8a red | 32.50 | 40.00 |
| *7* | A3 | 1r yel, *bl* | 50.00 | 52.50 |

A4

A5

Redrawn; Blade Wider and Diamond-shaped.

**1898-1900**

| | | | | |
|---|---|---|---|---|
| *8* | A3 | ½a slate | 40 | 40 |
| *9* | A3 | 1a red | 75 | 60 |
| *10* | A3 | 2a emerald | 4.50 | 4.50 |
| *a.* | | First 2 characters of value omitted | 300.00 | 300.00 |
| *11* | A3 | 4a emer (value above) | 8.00 | 8.00 |
| *12* | A4 | 8a red | 8.00 | 9.50 |
| *13* | A5 | 1r yel, *bl* | 5.00 | 10.00 |
| *a.* | | Wove paper | 8.50 | 8.50 |

On Nos. 9-10, the blade is wider and nearly diamond-shaped.

Point of Dagger to Left.

*14* A3 4a green 5.00 5.00

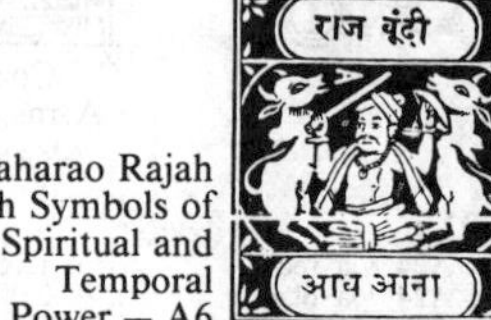
Maharao Rajah with Symbols of Spiritual and Temporal Power — A6

Without Gum

***Rouletted 11 to 13 in Color.***

**1915 Typo.**

**"Bundi" in 3 Characters (word at top right).**

| | | | | |
|---|---|---|---|---|
| *15* | A6 | ¼a blue | 60 | 60 |
| *a.* | | Laid paper | 7.25 | 6.25 |
| *16* | A6 | ½a black | 85 | 85 |
| *17* | A6 | 1a vermilion | 1.10 | 1.10 |
| *a.* | | Laid paper | 9.25 | 9.25 |
| *18* | A6 | 2a emerald | 1.25 | 1.25 |
| *19* | A6 | 2½a yellow | 3.50 | 4.25 |
| *20* | A6 | 3a brown | 2.00 | 4.25 |
| *21* | A6 | 4a yel grn | 4.25 | 4.25 |
| *23* | A6 | 6a ultra | 8.50 | *21.00* |
| *a.* | | 6a deep blue | 8.50 | |
| *24* | A6 | 8a orange | 6.25 | 6.25 |
| *25* | A6 | 10a olive | 7.75 | 7.75 |
| *26* | A6 | 12a dk grn | 11.50 | 11.50 |
| *27* | A6 | 1r violet | 27.50 | *35.00* |
| *28* | A6 | 2r car brn & blk | 35.00 | *42.50* |
| *29* | A6 | 3r bl & brn | 85.00 | *130.00* |
| *30* | A6 | 4r pale grn & red brn | 235.00 | *250.00* |
| *31* | A6 | 5r ver & pale grn | 250.00 | *340.00* |

Minor differences in lettering in top and bottom panels may be divided into 8 types, but not all values come in each type. In one sub-type the top appears as one word. Nos. 30-31 have an ornamental frame around the design.

**1941 *Perf. 11***

**"Bundi" in 4 Characters (word at top right).**

| | | | | |
|---|---|---|---|---|
| *32* | A6 | ¼a lt bl | 4.50 | 4.50 |
| *33* | A6 | ½a black | 37.50 | 37.50 |
| *34* | A6 | 1a carmine | 17.50 | 27.50 |
| *35* | A6 | 2a yel grn | 32.50 | |

The 4-character spelling of "Bundi" is found also on stamps rouletted in color: on ½a and 4a in small characters, and on ¼a, ½a, 1a, 4a, 4r and 5r in large characters like those on Nos. 32-35.

Arms of Bundi — A7

**1941-45 Typo. *Perf. 11***

| | | | | |
|---|---|---|---|---|
| *36* | A7 | 3p brt ultra | 16 | 30 |
| *37* | A7 | 6p indigo | 28 | 50 |
| *38* | A7 | 1a red org | 50 | *1.00* |
| *39* | A7 | 2a fawn | 4.75 | *8.00* |
| *a.* | | 2a brown ('45) | 4.75 | *10.50* |
| *40* | A7 | 4a brt yel grn | 5.25 | *12.00* |
| *41* | A7 | 8a dull green | 9.00 | *19.00* |
| *42* | A7 | 1r royal blue | 11.00 | *30.00* |
| | | *Nos. 36-42 (7)* | 30.94 | 70.80 |

The 1st printing of Nos. 36-42 was gummed. All later printings were without gum. Values are for copies without gum.

Maj. Maharao Rajah Bahadur Singh
A8 A9

View of Bundi — A10

**1947 *Perf. 11***

| | | | |
|---|---|---|---|
| *43* | A8 | ¼a dp grn | 24 |
| *44* | A8 | ½a purple | 24 |
| *45* | A8 | 1a yel grn | 24 |
| *46* | A9 | 2a red | 42 |
| *47* | A9 | 4a dp org | 1.25 |
| *48* | A10 | 8a vio bl | 2.00 |
| *49* | A10 | 1r chocolate | 4.50 |
| | | *Nos. 43-49 (7)* | 8.89 |

For later issues see Rajasthan.

### OFFICIAL STAMPS

Regular Issue of 1915 Handstamped in Black, Red or Green

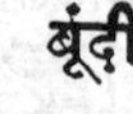
बूंदी
a
सरविस

***Rouletted 11 to 13 in Color.***

**1918 Unwmk.**

| | | | |
|---|---|---|---|
| *O1* | A6 | ¼a dk bl | 45 |
| *O2* | A6 | ½a black | 2.50 |
| *O3* | A6 | 1a vermilion | 1.10 |
| *O4* | A6 | 2a emerald | 2.50 |
| *O5* | A6 | 2½a yellow | 3.00 |
| *O6* | A6 | 3a brown | 3.00 |
| *O7* | A6 | 4a yel grn | 6.00 |
| *O8* | A6 | 6a blue | 4.75 |
| *O9* | A6 | 8a orange | 9.00 |
| *O10* | A6 | 10a ol grn | 9.00 |
| *O11* | A6 | 12a dk grn | 11.00 |
| *O12* | A6 | 1r violet | 15.00 |
| *O13* | A6 | 2r car brn & blk | 90.00 |
| *O14* | A6 | 3r bl & brn | 150.00 |
| *O15* | A6 | 4r pale grn & red brn | 240.00 |
| *O16* | A6 | 5r ver & pale grn | 240.00 |

All values come with black handstamp and most exist in red. The overprint is found in various positions, double, inverted, etc.

Several denominations exist in two or more types. See notes following Nos. 31 and 35.

Regular Issue of 1915 Handstamped in Black, Red or Green

BUNDI
b
SERVICE

**1919**

| | | | |
|---|---|---|---|
| *O17* | A6 | ¼a dk bl | 1.50 |
| *O18* | A6 | ½a black | 3.00 |
| *O19* | A6 | 1a vermilion | 3.50 |
| *O20* | A6 | 2a emerald | 6.00 |
| *O21* | A6 | 2½a yellow | 15.00 |

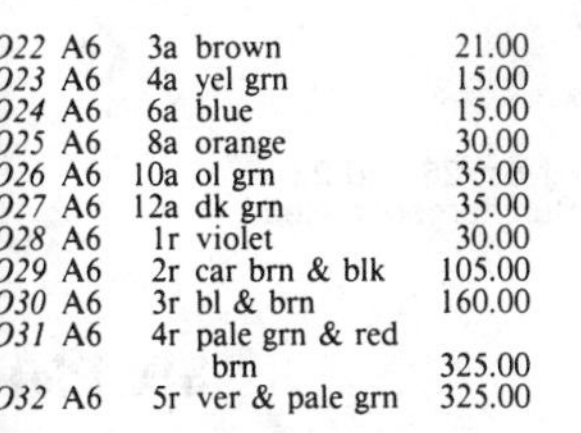

| | | | | |
|---|---|---|---|---|
| O22 | A6 | 3a brown | 21.00 | |
| O23 | A6 | 4a yel grn | 15.00 | |
| O24 | A6 | 6a blue | 15.00 | |
| O25 | A6 | 8a orange | 30.00 | |
| O26 | A6 | 10a ol grn | 35.00 | |
| O27 | A6 | 12a dk grn | 35.00 | |
| O28 | A6 | 1r violet | 30.00 | |
| O29 | A6 | 2r car brn & blk | 105.00 | |
| O30 | A6 | 3r bl & brn | 160.00 | |
| O31 | A6 | 4r pale grn & red brn | 325.00 | |
| O32 | A6 | 5r ver & pale grn | 325.00 | |

Note following No. O16 will apply to this issue, too.

Regular Issue of 1915 Handstamped in Carmine or Black

**BUNDI**

c

**SERVICE**

**1919** *Rouletted in Color.*

| | | | | |
|---|---|---|---|---|
| O33 | A6 | ¼a blue | 5.00 | 5.00 |
| O34 | A6 | ½a black | 3.50 | |
| O35 | A6 | 1a vermilion | 7.50 | |
| O36 | A6 | 2a yel grn | 9.00 | |
| O37 | A6 | 8a orange | 45.00 | |
| O38 | A6 | 10a olive | 45.00 | |
| O39 | A6 | 12a dk grn | 75.00 | |

Nos. 33 and 35 Handstamped Type "a" in Black or Carmine

**1941** *Perf. 11*

| | | | |
|---|---|---|---|
| O41 | A6 | ½a black | 55.00 |
| O42 | A6 | 2a yel grn | 55.00 |

Nos. 32 and 35 Handstamped Type "b" in Black or Carmine

| | | | |
|---|---|---|---|
| O43 | A6 | ¼a lt bl | 47.50 |
| O44 | A6 | 2a yel grn | 80.00 |

Nos. 32-35 Handstamped Type "c" in Black or Carmine

**1941**

| | | | |
|---|---|---|---|
| O45 | A6 | ¼a lt bl | 65.00 |
| O46 | A6 | ½a black | 65.00 |
| O47 | A6 | 1a carmine | 75.00 |
| O48 | A6 | 2a yel grn | 27.50 |

Nos. 36 to 42 Overprinted in Black or Carmine **SERVICE**

**1941** *Perf. 11*

| | | | | |
|---|---|---|---|---|
| O49 | A7 | 3p brt ultra (C) | 1.25 | 1.75 |
| O50 | A7 | 6p ind (C) | 3.00 | 3.50 |
| O51 | A7 | 1a red org | 3.50 | 4.75 |
| O52 | A7 | 2a fawn | 6.00 | 9.00 |
| O53 | A7 | 4a brt yel grn | 24.00 | 30.00 |
| O54 | A7 | 8a dl grn | 35.00 | 45.00 |
| O55 | A7 | 1r ryl bl (C) | 45.00 | 60.00 |
| | | *Nos. O49-O55 (7)* | 117.75 | 154.00 |

## BUSSAHIR

## (Bashahr)

LOCATION — A Feudatory State in the Punjab Hill States Agency
AREA — 3,439 sq. mi.
POP. — 100,192
CAPITAL — Bashahr

Tiger

A1 A2

A3 A4

A5 A6

A7 A8

Overprinted "R S" in Violet (V), Rose (R), or Blue Green (G)

Laid Paper

**1895** **Unwmk.** **Litho.** *Imperf.*

| | | | | |
|---|---|---|---|---|
| 1 | A1 | ¼a pink (V) | 82.50 | |
| 2 | A2 | ½a sl (R) | 100.00 | |
| 3 | A3 | 1a red (V) | 50.00 | |
| 4 | A4 | 2a yel (V,R) | 10.50 | 50.00 |
| 5 | A5 | 4a vio (V,R) | 27.50 | |
| 6 | A6 | 8a brn (V,G) | 27.50 | 40.00 |
| a. | | Without overprint | 65.00 | |
| 7 | A7 | 12a grn (R) | 50.00 | |
| 8 | A8 | 1r ultra (R) | 27.50 | |

*Perf. 7 to 14*

| | | | | |
|---|---|---|---|---|
| 9 | A1 | ¼a pink (V,G) | 20.00 | 40.00 |
| 10 | A2 | ½a sl (R) | 13.00 | 40.00 |
| 11 | A3 | 1a red (V) | 16.00 | 40.00 |
| a. | | Pin-perf. | 65.00 | 100.00 |
| 12 | A4 | 2a yel (V,R,G) | 20.00 | 50.00 |
| a. | | Pin-perf. (V,R) | 25.00 | 50.00 |
| 13 | A5 | 4a vio (V,R,G) | 15.00 | 50.00 |
| a. | | Pin-perf. (R) | 50.00 | |
| 14 | A6 | 8a brn (V,G) | 14.00 | 50.00 |
| 15 | A7 | 12a grn (V,R) | 22.50 | 47.50 |
| a. | | Pin-perf. (R) | 65.00 | |
| b. | | Without ovpt. | 47.50 | |
| 16 | A8 | 1r ultra (V,R) | 14.00 | 40.00 |
| a. | | Pin-perf. (R) | 65.00 | |

"R. S." are the initials of Tika Raghunath Singh, son of the Raja.

A9 A10

A11 A12

A13 A14

Overprinted "R S" Like Nos. 1-16
Wove Paper

**1896** **Engr.** *Pin-perf.*

| | | | | |
|---|---|---|---|---|
| 17 | A9 | ¼a dk gray vio (R) | *200.00* | 165.00 |
| 18 | A10 | ½a bl gray (R) | 325.00 | 90.00 |

**1900** **Litho.** *Imperf.*

| | | | | |
|---|---|---|---|---|
| 19 | A9 | ¼a red (V,G) | 2.25 | |
| 20 | A9 | ¼a vio (V,R) | 3.00 | |
| 21 | A10 | ½a bl (V,R) | 2.75 | |
| 22 | A11 | 1a ol (R) | 9.00 | 20.00 |
| 23 | A11 | 1a red (V,G) | 2.75 | |
| 24 | A12 | 2a yel (V) | 8.50 | |
| a. | | 2a ocher (R) | 8.50 | |
| 25 | A13 | 2a yel (V) | 6.50 | |
| a. | | 2a ocher (V) | 6.50 | |
| 26 | A14 | 4a brn vio (V,R,G) | 17.50 | |

*Pin-perf.*

| | | | | |
|---|---|---|---|---|
| 27 | A9 | ¼a red (V,G) | 2.75 | |
| 28 | A9 | ¼a vio (R) | 3.00 | |
| 29 | A10 | ½a bl (V,R) | 2.75 | |
| 30 | A11 | 1a ol (V,R) | 9.25 | |
| 31 | A11 | 1a red (V) | | |
| 32 | A11 | 1a ver (G) | 2.00 | |
| 33 | A12 | 2a yel (G) | 50.00 | 75.00 |
| 34 | A13 | 2a yel (V,R) | 12.00 | |
| a. | | 2a ocher (V) | 12.00 | |
| 35 | A14 | 4a brn vio (V,R,G) | 22.50 | |

Obsolete March 31, 1901.

*Stamps overprinted with the monogram above (RNS) or with the monogram "PS" were never issued for postal purposes. They are either reprints or remainders to which this overprint has been applied. Many other varieties have appeared since the stamps became obsolete. It is probable that all or nearly all of them are reprints.*

## CHARKHARI

LOCATION — A Feudatory State in the Bundelkhand Agency in Central India.
AREA — 880 sq. mi.
POP. — 120,351
CAPITAL — Maharajnagar

A1

Thin White or Blue Wove Paper.

**1894** **Unwmk.** **Typo.** *Imperf.*

**Value in the Plural**

| | | | | |
|---|---|---|---|---|
| 1 | A1 | 1a green | 2,250. | 2,750. |
| 2 | A1 | 2a green | 2,750. | |
| 3 | A1 | 4a green | 1,850. | |

**1897**

**Value in the Singular.**

| | | | | |
|---|---|---|---|---|
| 3A | A1 | ¼a rose | 1,500. | 1,150. |
| 4 | A1 | ¼a purple | 2.50 | 2.25 |
| 5 | A1 | ½a purple | 2.50 | 2.25 |
| 6 | A1 | 1a green | 5.00 | 4.50 |
| 7 | A1 | 2a green | 7.00 | 6.25 |
| 8 | A1 | 4a green | 7.00 | 6.25 |

In a later printing, the numerals of Nos. 4-8 are smaller or of different shape.

Proofs are known on paper of various colors.

A2 A3

Size: 19½x23mm.

**1909** **Litho.** *Perf. 11*

| | | | | |
|---|---|---|---|---|
| 9 | A2 | 1p red brn | 2.25 | 8.25 |
| 10 | A2 | 1p pale bl | 22 | 22 |
| 11 | A2 | ½a scarlet | 55 | 55 |
| 12 | A2 | 1a lt grn | 70 | 70 |
| 13 | A2 | 2a ultra | 1.10 | 1.10 |
| 14 | A2 | 4a dp grn | 1.10 | 1.10 |
| 15 | A2 | 8a brick red | 2.75 | 4.50 |
| 16 | A2 | 1r red brn | 6.50 | 11.00 |
| | | *Nos. 10-16 (7)* | 12.92 | |

See Nos. 22-27, 39-43.

**1919** **Handstamped** *Imperf.*

| | | | | |
|---|---|---|---|---|
| 21 | A3 | 1p violet | 14.00 | 5.50 |
| c. | | Dbl. frameline | 27.50 | |

The 1p black, type A3, is a proof.

A3a

Wove Paper

**1922** **Handstamped.** *Imperf.*

| | | | | |
|---|---|---|---|---|
| 21A | A3a | 1a violet | 55.00 | 55.00 |
| b. | | Perf. 11, laid paper | 65.00 | 65.00 |

Type of 1909 Issue. Redrawn.
Size: 20x23½mm

**1930-40** **Typo.**

| | | | | |
|---|---|---|---|---|
| 22 | A2 | 1p dk bl | 15 | 65 |
| 23 | A2 | ½a ol grn | 30 | 2.00 |
| 23A | A2 | ½a cop brn ('40) | 65 | |
| 24 | A2 | 1a lt grn | 85 | 2.00 |
| 25 | A2 | 1a chocolate | 2.00 | 3.25 |
| 25A | A2 | 1a dl red ('40) | 40.00 | 40.00 |
| 26 | A2 | 2a lt bl | 55 | 1.25 |
| a. | | Tete beche pair | 4.50 | |
| 27 | A2 | 4a carmine | 3.25 | 6.50 |
| a. | | Tete beche pair | 10.00 | |

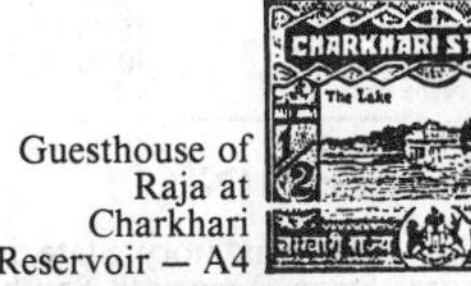

Guesthouse of Raja at Charkhari Reservoir — A4

Imlia Palace — A5

Industrial School — A6

View of City — A7

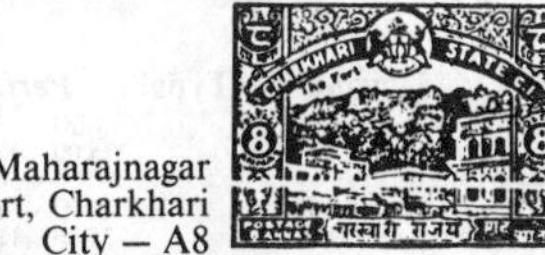

Maharajnagar Fort, Charkhari City — A8

Guesthouse A9

Palace Gate — A10

Temples at Rampur — A11

Govordhan Temple — A12

**1931** *Perf. 11, 11½, 12.*

| | | | | |
|---|---|---|---|---|
| 28 | A4 | ½a dl grn | 6 | 6 |
| 29 | A5 | 1a blk brn | 8 | 6 |
| 30 | A6 | 2a purple | 8 | 6 |
| 31 | A7 | 4a ol grn | 9 | 8 |
| 32 | A8 | 8a magenta | 15 | 8 |
| 33 | A9 | 1r rose & grn | 20 | 14 |
| 34 | A10 | 2r brn & red | 45 | 14 |
| 35 | A11 | 3r bl grn & choc | 90 | 14 |
| 36 | A12 | 5r vio & bl | 65 | 20 |
| | | *Nos. 28-36 (9)* | 2.66 | 96 |

Size range of A4-A12: 30-31x19½-24mm.

Many errors of perforation and printing exist. Used values are for canceled to order copies.

Nos. 15-16 Surcharged in Black **½ As.**

**1940** *Perf. 11*

37 A2 ½a on 8a brick red 18.00 *35.00*
- *a.* Surcharge inverted 240.00
- *b.* "1" of "½" inverted 175.00

38 A2 1a on 1r red brn 35.00 *60.00*
- *b.* Surcharge inverted 240.00

38A A2 "1 ANNA" on 1r red brn 275.00

Type of 1930.

**1943 Unwmk. Typo.** *Imperf.*

**Size: 20x23½mm.**

39 A2 1p violet 9.00 *18.00*
- *a.* Tete beche pair 35.00

40 A2 1p ap grn 30.00 *45.00*
41 A2 ½a org red 7.50 *8.50*
42 A2 ½a black 35.00 *45.00*
43 A2 2a grysh grn 30.00 *32.50*
- *a.* Tete beche pair 75.00

## COCHIN

LOCATION — A Feudatory State in the Madras States Agency in Southern India.
AREA — 1,480 sq. mi.
POP. — 1,422,875 (1941)
CAPITAL — Ernakulam

See also the United State of Travancore and Cochin.

6 Puttans = 5 Annas
12 Pies = 1 Anna
16 Annas = 1 Rupee

State Seal — A1

**1892 Unwmk. Typo.** *Perf. 12*

1 A1 ½p yellow 3.00 1.50
- *a.* Imperf., pair 325.00 325.00
- *b.* Laid paper 360.00 360.00

2 A1 1p red vio 3.50 2.75
- *a.* 1p pur (error) 125.00 110.00

3 A1 2p purple 1.75 1.75
- *a.* Imperf.

Nos. 1 to 3 sometimes have watermark large umbrella in the sheet.

A1a

Wmk. 43

**Wmk. Coat of Arms and Inscription in Sheet.**

**1896**

4 A1a 1p violet 32.50 40.00

**Wmk. Shell. (43)**

4A A1a 1p violet 20.00 20.00

Originally intended for revenue use, Nos. 4-4A were later authorized for postal use.

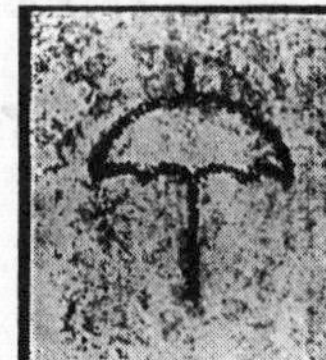

Wmk. 41

Common Design Types are pictured in section before Great Britain.

**1897 Wmk. Small Umbrella (41)**

**Thin Paper**

5 A1 ½p orange 1.50 1.50
- *a.* Imperf., pair

6 A1 1p magenta 1.90 1.75
7 A1 2p purple 3.75 3.25
- *a.* Imperf., pair 25.00 25.00

A2

A3

A4 A5

Thin (1898) or Thick (1903) Paper.

**1898-1903**

8 A2 3p ultra 20 8
9 A3 ½p gray grn 55 10
- *a.* Pair, one sideways 650.00 650.00

10 A4 1p rose 1.35 25
- *a.* Laid paper 1,750.
- *b.* Tete beche pair 1,750. 1,750.
- *c.* As "a," tete beche pair *6,500.*

11 A5 2p purple 2.00 40
- *a.* Double impression 100.00

Type of 1898 Surcharged

**1909**

13 A2 2p on 3p red vio 35 30
- *a.* Inverted surcharge 72.50 72.50
- *b.* Pair, stamps tete beche 130.00 130.00
- *c.* Pair, stamps & surch. tete beche 165.00 165.00

The surcharge is also known in a thin "2" measuring 5½x7mm, with curving foot. Value $125.

Sri Rama Varma I — A6

**1911-14 Engr.** *Perf. 14*

14 A6 2p brown 32 7
- *a.* Imperf., pair

15 A6 3p blue 80 6
- *a.* Perf. 14x12½ 15.00 9.00

16 A6 4p yel grn 55 6
17 A6 9p car rose 40 7
18 A6 1a org buff 1.75 6
19 A6 1½a lilac 1.75 10
20 A6 2a gray 9.00 25
21 A6 3a vermilion 37.50 27.50
*Nos. 14-21 (8)* 52.07 28.17

Sri Rama Varma II
A7 A8

**1918-23 Engr.** *Perf. 14*

23 A7 2p brown 45 6
24 A7 4p green 1.40 6
25 A7 6p red brn ('22) 1.50 5
26 A7 8p blk brn ('23) 1.75 8
27 A7 9p car rose 8.00 42
28 A7 10p dp bl 1.50 8
29 A8 1a brn org 90 8
30 A7 1½a red vio ('21) 5.75 8
31 A7 2a gray 7.00 8
32 A7 2¼a yel grn ('22) 3.75 40
33 A7 3a vermilion 7.50 40
*Nos. 23-33 (11)* 39.50 1.79

The 1a is found in two types, the difference lying in the first of the three characters directly above the maharaja's head.

No. 15 Surcharged

**2**

**Two pies**

Type I. Numeral 8mm high. Curved foot. Top begins with a ball. (As illustrated.)
Type II. Numeral 9mm high. Curved foot. Top begins with a curved line.
Type III. Numeral 6mm high. Straight foot. "Two pies" 15mm wide.
Type IV. "2" as in type III. Capital "P" in "Pies". "Two Pies" 13mm wide.
Type V. Heavy gothic numeral. Capital "P" in "Pies".

**1922-29**

34 A6 2p on 3p bl (Type I) 40 6
- *a.* Type II 90 6
- *b.* Type III 35 15
- *c.* Type IV 30 15
- *d.* Type V 35.00 35.00
- *e.* Dbl. surch., I 45.00
- *f.* Dbl. surch. II 45.00

Types II and III exist with a capital "P" in "Pies". It occurs once in each sheet of the second and third settings. There are four settings.

Type V is the first stamp, fourth row, of the fourth setting.

No. 32 Surcharged

**ONE ANNA**
**ഒരു അണ**
**ANCHAL & REVENUE**

**1928**

36 A7 1a on 2¼a yel grn 5.00 9.00
- *a.* Dbl. surch. 125.00 125.00

Nos. 24, 26 and 28 Surcharged in Black

**Three Pies**
**ന 3**
**മൂന്നു പൈ**

**1932-33**

38 A7 3p on 4p grn 1.25 55
39 A7 3p on 8p blk brn 1.25 55
40 A7 9p on 10p dp bl 3.25 45

Sri Rama Varma III
A9 A10

**1933-38 Engr.** *Perf. 13x13½.*

41 A9 2p brn ('36) 55 6
42 A9 4p green 1.40 6
43 A9 6p red brn 95 6
44 A10 1a brn org ('34) 48 8
45 A9 1a8p rose red 5.25 2.25
46 A9 2a gray blk ('38) 1.25 8
47 A9 2¼a yel grn 1.25 8
48 A9 3a red org ('38) 2.25 8
49 A9 3a4p violet 95 8
50 A9 6a8p blk brn 3.50 2.25
51 A9 10a dp bl 3.50 2.25
*Nos. 41-51 (11)* 21.33 7.33

Nos. 26 and 28 Surcharged in Red

**6**

**Six Pies**

**1934** *Perf. 13½.*

52 A7 6p on 8p blk brn 2.25 1.25
53 A7 6p on 10p dk bl 2.25 80

No. 44 Overprinted in Black

a **ANCHAL**

**1939** **Engr.**

54 A10 1a brn org 1.50 12

Types of 1933-38.

**1938-41 Litho.** *Perf. 11, 13*

55 A9 2p dl brn 85 12
56 A9 4p dl grn ('41) 2.25 8
57 A9 6p red brn 2.75 8
- *c.* Perf. 13 15.00

57A A10 1a brn org 20.00 *25.00*
58 A10 2¼a yel grn 3.50 15

Type of 1934 Overprinted in Black Type "a" or

b **ANCHAL**

**1941-42** *Perf. 11 (#59), 13 (#60)*

59 A10(a) 1a brown orange 12.50 10
- *a.* Perf. 13 15.00 15.00

60 A10(b) 1a brn org ('42) 5.50 65
- *a.* Perf. 11 5.50 1.75

No. 45 Surcharged in Black

**SURCHARGED**

c

**THREE PIES**

**1943-44 Engr.** *Perf. 13x13½*

61 A9 3p on 1a8p rose red ('44) 4.50 1.75
62 A9 1a3p on 1a8p rose red 1.65 18

Maharaja Sri Kerala Varma
A11 A12

Wmk. 294- Letters and Ornaments in Sheet (size reduced)

**1943 Litho. Wmk. 294** *Perf. 11, 13*

63 A11 2p dl gray brn 3.00 8
- *a.* Wmk. 41 65 9

64 A11 4p gray grn 3.00 55
- *a.* Wmk. 41 80.00 45.00

65 A11 6p red brn 1.50 6
66 A11 9p ultra 5.50 1.25
67 A12 1a brn org 22.50 12.00
- *a.* Wmk. 41 75.00 30.00

68 A11 2¼a lt ol grn 4.50 9
*Nos. 63-68 (6)* 40.00 14.03

No. 64 Surcharged Type "c"

69 A11 3p on 4p gray grn 48 6

Nos. 64, 64a and 65 Surcharged in Black

d

THREE PIES

**1944-48** **Wmk. 294**
70 A11 2p on 6p red brn 40 5
71 A11 3p on 4p gray grn 85 5
*a.* Wmk. 41 30.00 2.75
72 A11 3p on 6p red brn 35 6
73 A11 4p on 6p red brn 4.50 2.50

ANCHAL

Nos. 57A, 67a, 67 Surcharged in Black

NINE PIES

**1944** **Litho.** **Wmk. 41**
*73A* A10 6p on 1a brn org 12.50 7.00
*74* A10 9p on 1a brn org 50.00 11.00
*75* A12 9p on 1a brn org 5.50 12
*a.* Wmk. 294

No. 56 Surcharged Type "c" in Black.
*76* A9 3p on 4p dl grn 4.00 18

ANCHAL

Nos. 57A, 67a, 67 Surcharged in Black

SURCHARGED NINE PIES

*77* A10 9p on 1a brn org 7.00 15
*78* A12 9p on 1a brn org, wmk. 41 30 6
*a.* Wmk. 294

No. 67a Surcharged Type "c"

**1944** **Wmk. 41**
*78B* A12 1a3p on 1a brn org

Maharaja Ravi Varma
A13 A15

**1944-46** **Wmk. 294** ***Perf. 13***
*79* A13 9p ultra ('46) 2.50 9
*a.* Perf. 11 7.25 1.90
*80* A13 1a3p magenta 8.50 18
*81* A13 1a9p ultra ('46) 12.50 1.10

**1946-50** **Litho.** ***Perf. 13***
*82* A15 2p dl brn 50 6
*a.* Perf. 11 13.00 75
*b.* Perf. 11x13 90.00 27.50
*83* A15 3p car rose 3.25 5
*83A* A15 4p gray grn ('50) 60.00 7.50
*84* A15 6p red brn ('47) 4.25 45
*a.* Perf. 11 42.50 8
*85* A15 9p ultra 2.25 6
*86* A15 1a dp org ('47) 5.50 3.50
*a.* Perf. 11 225.00
*87* A15 2a gray ('47) 12.00 9
*a.* Perf. 11 45.00 18
*88* A15 3a vermilion 15.00 24
*Nos. 82-88 (8)* 102.75 11.95

Nos. 45, 57A Surcharged Type "d"

***Perf. 13x13½***

**1947-48** **Wmk. 41** **Engr.**
*89* A9 6p on 1a8p rose red 2.75 1.40

**Litho.** ***Perf. 11.***
*89A* A10 6p on 1a org brn

Maharaja Sri Kerala Varma II — A16

**1948-49** **Wmk. 294** ***Perf. 11***
*90* A16 2p ol brn 4.25 6
*91* A16 3p car ('49) 2.00 6
*92* A16 4p gray grn 3.25 6
*a.* Imperf. vert., pair 360.00
*93* A16 6p red brn 2.50 6
*94* A16 9p ultra ('49) 1.65 8
*95* A16 2a black 9.50 8
*96* A16 3a ver ('49) 12.00 15
*97* A16 3a4p vio ('49) 32.50 32.50
*Nos. 90-97 (8)* 67.65 33.05

No. 86 Surcharged Type "d" in Black

**1949**
*98* A15 6p on 1a dp org 47.50 47.50
*99* A15 9p on 1a dp org 32.50 32.50

Dutch Palace — A17

Design: 2a, Chinese fishing net.

**1949** **Unwmk.** ***Perf. 11***
*100* A17 2a gray 75 75
*a.* Imperf. vert., horiz. pair 425.00
*101* A17 2¼a gray grn 75 75

See Travancore-Cochin for succeeding issues.

---

## OFFICIAL STAMPS

Stamps and Type of 1911-14 Overprinted

h

ON
C G
S

**1913-14** **Wmk. 41** **Engr.** ***Perf. 14***
*O1* A6 2p brown
*O2* A6 4p yel grn 9.00 6
*a.* Invt. overprint 750.00 350.00
*b.* Double inverted overprint
*O3* A6 9p car rose 13.00 6
*O4* A6 1½a red vio 20.00 10
*a.* Double overprint 375.00
*O5* A6 2a gray 15.00 8
*O6* A6 3a vermilion 21.00 22
*O7* A6 6a violet 18.00 1.10
*O8* A6 12a blue 30.00 3.25
*O9* A6 1½r dp grn 22.50 18.00

Stamps and Type of 1918-23 with Similar Overprint.

**1918-34**
*O10* A7 4p green 4.75 5
*a.* Double overprint 210.00
*O11* A7 6p red brn ('22) 4.25 5
*a.* Double ovpt. 210.00
*O12* A7 8p blk brn ('26) 4.25 5
*O13* A7 9p car rose 18.00 6
*O14* A7 10p dp bl ('23) 8.00 6
*O16* A7 1½a red vio ('21) 4.75 6
*a.* Double overprint 200.00
*O17* A7 2a gray 18.00 9
*O18* A7 2¼a yel grn ('22) 4.25 8
*b.* Double ovpt. 300.00
*O19* A7 3a ver ('22) 18.00 55
*a.* Double overprint 325.00
*O20* A7 6a vio ('22) 22.50 85
*O21* A7 12a bl ('29) 25.00 4.25
*O22* A7 1½r dk grn ('34) 30.00 35.00

On Nos. O1-O22, width of overprint varies from 14¾mm. to 16½mm.

No. 15 Overprinted in Red

j

On
C G
S

**1921**
*O23* A6 3p blue 21.00 8

Nos. O3 and O13 Surcharged with New Values.

**1923-29**
*O24* A6 8p on 9p car rose 135.00 15
*O25* A7 8p on 9p car rose 70.00 12
*a.* Double surcharge 210.00
*O26* A7 10p on 9p car rose ('25) 70.00 8
*a.* Double surcharge 210.00
*O27* A6 10p on 9p car rose ('29) 200.00 13.00

Regular Issue of 1918-23 Overprinted

k

ON
C G
S

**1933-34**
*O28* A7 4p green 35.00 3.25
*O29* A7 6p red brn ('34) 7.25 5
*O30* A7 8p blk brn 7.25 6
*O31* A7 10p dp bl 7.25 6
*O32* A7 2a gray ('34) 11.00 6
*O33* A7 3a vermilion 13.00 12
*O34* A7 6a dk vio ('34) 85.00 3.75

6

Same with Additional Surcharge on Type of Regular Issue of 1918-23 in Red

Six Pies

*O35* A7 6p on 8p blk brn 1.25 10
*O36* A7 6p on 10p dk bl ('34) 6.00 6

Regular Issue of 1933 Overprinted Type "k" in Black as in 1933-34.

**1933-35** ***Perf. 13x13½***
*O37* A9 4p green 90 8
*O38* A9 6p red brn 1.10 5
*O39* A10 1a brn org 4.75 5
*O40* A9 1a8p rose red 2.50 8
*O41* A9 2a gray 5.50 8
*O42* A9 2¼a yel grn 1.90 6
*O43* A9 3a vermilion 8.25 6
*O44* A9 3a4p violet 5.50 8
*O45* A9 6a8p blk brn 5.50 10
*O46* A9 10a dp bl 5.50 22

Regular Stamps of 1934-38 Overprinted in Black

m

ON
C G
S

**1939-41** ***Perf. 11, 13x13½***
*O47* A10 1a brn org 90.00 6
*O48* A9 2a gray blk 25.00 22
*O49* A9 3a red org 6.00 22

Similar Overprint on Types of 1933-36.

***Perf. 11, 13 x 13½.***

**1939-41** **Litho.** **Wmk. 294**
*O50* A9 4p dl grn ('41) 2.25 28
*O51* A9 6p red brn ('41) 32.50 1.10
*a.* Wmk. 41 1.65 8
*O52* A10 1a brn org 2.25 28
*a.* Wmk. 41 1.40 5
*O53* A9 3a org ('40) 10.00 1.50
*b.* Wmk. 41 3.50 6

Similar Overprint in Narrow Serifed Capitals on No. 57

**Wmk. 41** ***Perf. 11***
*O53A* A9 6p red brn 425.00 250.00

Type of 1933-36 Overprinted in Black

o

ON
C G
S

***Perf. 10½, 11, 13x13½.***
*O54* A9 4p dl grn ('41) 4.50 1.10
*O55* A9 6p red brn ('41) 3.00 6
*O56* A9 2a gray blk 3.00 8

Type of 1934 Overprinted in Black

p

ON
C G
S

**1941** ***Perf. 11.***
*O57* A10 1a brn org 110.00 3.75

Stamps and Types of 1944 Overprinted in Black

q

ON
C G
S

***Perf. 11, 13x13½.***

**1944-48** **Wmk. 294**
*O58* A11 4p gray grn 1.65 6
*a.* Perf. 11 22.50 70
*O59* A11 6p red brn 30 5
*O60* A11 2a gray blk 40 5
*O61* A11 2¼a dl yel grn 1.25 55
*a.* Additional ovpt. on back 75.00
*O62* A11 3a red org 1.00 18

Same Overprint with Additional Surcharge

THREE PIES

*O63* A11 3p on 4p gray grn 80 6
*a.* Additional ovpt. on back
*O64* A12 3p on 1a brn org 3.50 6
*O65* A11 9p on 6p red brn 1.50 6
*O66* A12 1a3p on 1a brn org 3.50 6

Same Overprint in Black on Types of 1944 Surcharged Type "c"

*O67* A11 3p on 4p gray grn 2.75 32
*O68* A11 9p on 6p red brn 20 6
*O69* A12 1a3p on 1a brn org 3.50 8

Nos. O52 and O16 Surcharged Type "d"

***Perf. 11, 13x13½, 14.***

**1944** **Wmk. 41**
*O70* A10 3p on 1a brn org 1.75 8
*O71* A10 9p on 1a brn org 32.50 1.10

**Engr.**
*O71A* A7 9p on 1½a red vio 82.50 5.50

No. O52 Surcharged Type "c"
*O72* A10 1a3p on 1a brn org 40.00 30.00

No. 76 Overprinted in Black

ON
C G
S

***Perf. 13***
*O72A* A9 3p on 4p dl grn 67.50 24.00

No. 45 Overprinted Type "k" and Surcharged Type "d"

**1944-48 Wmk. 41** *Perf. 13x13½.*
*O73* A9 9p on 1a8p rose red 40.00 11.50
*O74* A9 1a9p on 1a8p rose red 1.10 10

No. 45 Overprinted Type "k" and Surcharged Type "c"

*O75* A9 3p on 1a8p rose red 32 6
*O76* A9 1a9p on 1a8p rose red 80 12

Type of 1939-41 Overprinted in Black — ON C G S

**1946 Wmk. 294** *Perf. 11*
*O77* A9 2a gray 80.00 1.25
*O77A* A9 2¼a yel grn 275.00 19.00

Same Overprint in Black on Nos. 79-81.

**1946 Litho.** *Perf. 13*
*O78* A13 9p ultra 25 5
*O79* A13 1a3p magenta 28 6
*a.* Double ovpt. 24.00 18.00
*O80* A13 1a9p ultra 65 14

Types and Stamps of 1946-48 Overprinted Type "h"

**1946-48**
*O81* A15 3p car rose 8 5
*O82* A15 4p gray grn 18.00 1.65
*O83* A15 6p red brn 75 6
*O84* A15 9p ultra 1.25 7
*O85* A15 1a3p magenta 55 6
*O86* A15 1a9p ultra 1.10 25
*O87* A15 2a gray blk 2.25 6
*O88* A15 2¼a ol grn 1.10 14
*Nos. O81-O88 (8)* 25.08 2.34

No. 56 Overprinted Type "q" and Surcharged Type "d"

*Perf. 13x13½.*
**1947 Wmk. 41 Engr.**
*O89* A9 3p on 4p dl grn 6.75 1.40

Stamps and Type of 1948-49 Overprinted Type "o"

**1948-49 Wmk. 294 Litho.** *Perf. 11.*
*O90* A16 3p car ('49) 55 5
*O91* A16 4p gray grn 55 5
*O92* A16 6p red brn 55 5
*O93* A16 9p ultra 70 6
*O94* A16 2a blk ('49) 55 6
*O95* A16 2¼a lt ol grn ('49) 1.10 6
*O96* A16 3a ver ('49) 80 6
*O97* A16 3a4p dp pur ('49) 8.25 8.25
*Nos. O90-O97 (8)* 13.05 8.64

See Travancore-Cochin for succeeding issues.

## DHAR

LOCATION — A Feudatory State in the Malwa Agency in Central India.
AREA — 1,800 sq. mi.
POP. — 243,521
CAPITAL — Dhar

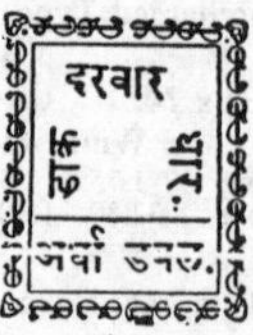

A1

Arms of Dhar — A2

The stamps of type A1 have an oval control mark handstamped in black.

**Unwmk.**
**1897-1900 Typeset** *Imperf.*
*1* A1 ½p *red* 70 70
*a.* Characters for "pice" transposed 15.00
*b.* Five characters in first word 75
*c.* Without control mark 82.50
*2* A1 ¼a *org red* ('00) 1.00 65
*a.* Without control mark 100.00
*3* A1 ½a *lil rose* 1.00 65
*4* A1 1a *bl grn* 4.50 3.00
*5* A1 2a *yel* ('00) 17.50 *22.50*

**1898-1900 Typo.** *Perf. 11½.*
*6* A2 ½a red 85 85
*7* A2 ½a rose ('00) 1.50 1.50
*a.* Imperf., pair 35.00
*8* A2 1a maroon 1.00 1.00
*9* A2 1a vio ('00) 1.25 1.25
*10* A2 1a cl ('00) 1.00 1.00
*11* A2 2a dk grn ('00) 3.25 *5.00*

Obsolete March 31, 1901.

## DUTTIA

## (Datia)

LOCATION — A Feudatory State in the Bundelkhand Agency in Central India.
AREA — 912 sq. mi.
POP. — 158,834
CAPITAL — Datia

Ganesh, Elephant-headed God
A1 A2

All Duttia stamps have a circular control mark, about 23mm. in diameter, handstamped in blue or black. All were issued without gum.

**1893 Typeset Unwmk.** *Imperf.*
*1* A1 ¼a *org red* 2,250.
*2* A1 ½a *grysh grn* 2,250.
*3* A2 1a *red* 2,250.
*4* A1 2a *yellow* 2,000.
*5* A1 4a *rose* 1,750.

Type A2 with Frameline around God, Rosettes in Lower Corners

**1896 (?)**
*5A* A2 ½ *green* *2,750.*
*5C* A2 2a dk bl, *lem* *2,000.*

A 1a in this revised type has been reported.

**1897**
*6* A2 ½a *green* 12.00 *35.00*
*7* A2 1a black 24.00 *45.00*
*a.* Laid paper 8.50
*8* A2 2a *yellow* 16.00 *35.00*
*9* A2 4a *rose* 16.00 *32.50*

A3

*10* A3 ½a *green* 55.00
*11* A3 1a black 75.00
*12* A3 2a *yellow* 55.00
*13* A3 4a *rose* 50.00

A4

Rouletted in Colored Lines on 2 or 3 Sides

**1899-1900**
*14* A4 ¼a red (shades) 55
*b.* Tete beche pair *2,000.*
*15* A4 ½a *green* 65
*16* A4 1a black 55
*17* A4 2a *yellow* 90
*18* A4 4a *rose red* 1.25
*a.* Tete beche pair

**1904** *Imperf.*
*22* A4 ¼a carmine 1.25
*23* A4 ½a *green* 7.00
*24* A4 1a black 3.00

**1911** *Perf. 13½.*
*25* A4 ¼a carmine 2.25 2.25

**1916** *Imperf.*
*26* A4 ¼a dl bl 1.50 *3.25*
*27* A4 ½a green 3.00 *6.50*
*28* A4 1a violet 3.50 *6.50*
*a.* Tete beche pair 20.00
*29* A4 2a brown 6.50 *13.00*
*29A* A4 4a brick red 40.00

A5

**1917 Handstamped in Water Color**
*30* A5 1a blue

Ganesh Type of 1899-1900

**1918**
*31* A4 ½a ultra 3.00
*32* A4 1a rose 75
*33* A4 2a violet 4.00

*Perf. 12*
*34* A4 ¼a black 4.00

**1920** *Rouletted*
*35* A4 ¼a blue 1.50 1.50
*36* A4 ½a rose 3.00 3.00

*Perf. 7*
*37* A4 ½a dl red 6.00

Duttia stamps became obsolete in 1921.

## FARIDKOT

LOCATION — A Feudatory State in the Punjab Agency of India.
AREA — 638 sq. mi.
POP. — 164,364.
CAPITAL — Faridkot

4 FOLUS OR PAISAS = 1 ANNA

A1

A2

A3

Handstamped.

**1879-86 Unwmk.** *Imperf.*
*1* A1 1f ultra 75 75
*a.* Laid paper 16.00 16.00
*b.* Tete beche pair 45.00
*2* A2 1p ultra 75 75
*a.* Laid paper 37.50 37.50
*3* A3 1p ultra 2.25
*a.* Tete beche pair 45.00

Several other varieties exist, but it is believed that only the stamps listed here were issued for postal use. They became obsolete Dec. 31, 1886. See Faridkot under Convention States for issues of 1887-1900.

## HYDERABAD (DECCAN)

LOCATION — Central India
AREA — 82,313 sq. mi.
POP. — 16,338,534 (1941)
CAPITAL — Hyderabad

This independent princely state was occupied and annexed by India in 1948.

A1

A2

**1869-71 Engr. Unwmk.** *Perf. 11½*
*1* A1 ½a brn ('71) 5.50 6.00
*2* A2 1a ol grn 10.00 5.50
*a.* Imperf. horiz., pair 105.00 85.00
*3* A1 2a grn ('71) 27.50 24.00

*The reprints are perforated 12½.*

A3

A4

Wove Paper

**1871-1909** *Perf. 12½*
*4* A3 ½a org brn 18 5
*a.* ½a red brn 18 6
*b.* ½a mag (error) 25.00 11.00
*c.* Perf. 11½ 15.00 15.00
*d.* ½a rose 12 5
*e.* ½a brt ver 10 5
*5* A3 1a dk brn 50 38
*a.* Imperf., pair 25.00
*b.* Pair, imperf. between 50.00
*c.* Perf. 11½ 37.50 37.50
*6* A3 1a blk ('09) 95 8
*7* A3 2a green 14 8
*a.* 2a ol grn ('09) 18 8
*b.* Perf. 11½ 110.00
*8* A3 3a yel brn 30 18
*a.* Perf. 11½ 22.50 22.50
*9* A3 4a slate 40 30
*a.* Imperf. horiz., pair 200.00 200.00
*b.* Perf. 11½ 50.00 50.00
*10* A3 4a dp grn 80 45
*a.* 4a ol grn 2.50 2.25
*11* A3 8a bis brn 95 55
*a.* Perf. 11½
*12* A3 12a blue 1.40 1.40
*a.* Perf. 11½ 95.00 95.00
*b.* 12a sl grn 1.25 1.25

Surcharged

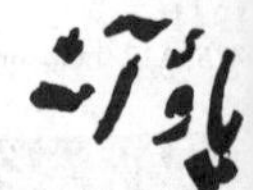

**1900**
*13* A3 ¼a on ½a brt ver 1.00 1.10
*a.* Invtd. surcharge 27.50 19.00

**1902**
*14* A4 ¼a blue 2.00 1.90

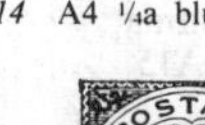

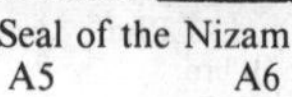

Seal of the Nizam
A5 A6

Wmk. 42

**Engraved by A. G. Wyon**

**1905 Wmk. Urdu Characters (42)**
*17* A5 ¼a blue 2.00 8
*18* A5 ½a red 4.75 10
*19* A5 ½a orange 4.75 8

***Perf. 11, 11½, 12½, 13½ and Compound***

**1908-11**
*20* A5 ¼a gray 40 5
*21* A5 ½a green 85 5
*22* A5 1a carmine 50 6
*23* A5 2a lilac 35 6
*24* A5 3a brn org ('09) 85 6

*25* A5 4a ol grn ('09) 85 22
*26* A5 8a vio ('11) 52 6
*27* A5 12a bl grn ('11) 6.00 2.75
*Nos. 20-27 (8)* 10.32 3.31

**Engraved by Bradbury, Wilkinson & Co.**

**1912**
*28* A5 ¼a brn vio 15 5
*29* A5 ½a dp grn 2.00 5
***a.*** Imperf., pair 20.00

The frame of type A5 differs slightly in each denomination.
Nos. 20-21 measure 19½x20½mm.
Nos. 28-29 measure 20x21½mm.

**1915-16**
*30* A6 ½a green 60 5
*31* A6 1a car rose 60 5
*32* A6 1a red 6.00 8

Unless used, imperf. stamps of types A5 and A6 are from plate proof sheets.
See also No. 58.

A7

Wmk. 211

**Wmk. Urdu Characters. (211)**
**1927** ***Perf. 13½.***
*36* A7 1r yellow 6.00 5.75

Stamps of 1912-16 Surcharged in Red

(4 pies) (8 pies)

**1930**
*37* A5 4p on ¼a brn vio 20 5
***a.*** Perf. 11 130.00
***b.*** Dbl. surch.
*38* A6 8p on ½a grn 20 5
***a.*** Perf. 11 130.00 90.00

Seal of Nizam — A8

Char Minar — A9

High Court of Justice — A10

Reservoir for City of Hyderabad A11

Bidar College — A13

Entrance to Ajanta Caves — A12

Victory Tower at Daulatabad — A14

**Wmk. 211**
**1931-48** **Engr.** ***Perf. 13½***
*39* A8 4p black 8 5
***a.*** Laid paper ('47) 5.25 3.25
*39B* A8 6p car lake ('48) 1.00 60
*40* A8 8p green 8 5
***a.*** 8p yel grn, laid paper ('47) 5.25 3.25
***b.*** Imperf., pair 47.50
*41* A9 1a dk brn 15 5
*42* A10 2a dk vio 22 5
***a.*** Imperf., pair 100.00
*43* A11 4a ultra 60 8
***a.*** Imperf. pair 130.00
*44* A12 8a dp org 1.00 60
*45* A13 12a scarlet 2.00 2.50
*46* A14 1r yellow 2.75 2.75
*Nos. 39-46 (9)* 7.88 6.73

On No. 39B, "POSTAGE" has been moved to ribbon at bottom of design.
Nos. 39a and 40a are printed from worn plates. The background of the design is unshaded.
See No. 59.

Unani General Hospital A15

Osmania General Hospital A16

Osmania University A17

Osmania Jubilee Hall — A18

**1937** **Litho.** **Unwmk.** ***Perf. 13½x14***
*47* A15 4p vio & blk 7 6
*48* A16 8p brn & blk 10 6
*49* A17 1a dl org & gray 16 7
*50* A18 2a dl grn & gray 52 52

The Nizam's Silver Jubilee.

**Catalogue values for unused stamps in this section, from this point to the end of the section, are for Never Hinged items.**

Returning Soldier — A19

**1946** **Typo.** ***Perf. 13½.***
*51* A19 1a dk bl 12 8

**Wmk. 211**
*52* A19 1a blue 12 10

**Wmk. Nizam's Seal in Sheet.**
**Laid Paper.**
*53* A19 1a dk bl 50 35

Victory of the Allied Nations in WW II.

Town Hall, Hyderabad A20

**1947** **Litho.** **Wove Paper**
*54* A20 1a black 12 10

Inauguration of the Reformed Legislature, Feb. 17th, 1947.

Power House, Hyderabad A21

Designs: 3a, Kaktyai Arch, Warangal Fort. 6a, Golkunda Fort.

***Perf. 13½x14.***
**1947-49** **Typo.** **Wmk. 211**
*55* A21 1a4p dk grn 15 10
*56* A21 3a blue 15 12
*57* A21 6a ol brn 4.00 4.00
***a.*** 6a red brn ('49) 35.00 35.00
***b.*** Imperf., pair 90.00

Seal Type of 1915

**1947** **Engr.** ***Perf. 13½***
*58* A6 ½a rose lake 35 18

Seal Type of 1931

**1949** **Litho.**
*59* A8 2p brown 1.25 18

## OFFICIAL STAMPS

Regular Issues of 1869-71 Overprinted

**1873** **Unwmk.** ***Perf. 11½, 12½.***

**Red Overprint**
*O1* A1 ½a brown 21.00
*O2* A2 1a ol grn 50.00 25.00
*O3* A1 2a green 35.00
*O4* A3 ½a red brn 3.50 3.50
*O5* A3 1a dk brn 6.50 4.25
*O6* A3 2a green 6.50 4.00
*O7* A3 3a yel brn 8.50 7.00
*O8* A3 4a slate 7.00 6.25
*O9* A3 8a bister 8.50 8.50
*O10* A3 12a blue 11.00 9.00

**Black Overprint.**
*O11* A1 ½a brown 15.00
*O12* A2 1a ol grn 20.00
*O13* A1 2a green 27.50
*O14* A3 ½a red brn 3.00 1.75
*O15* A3 1a dk brn 2.00 1.75
*O16* A3 2a green 2.25 60
*O17* A3 3a yel brn 2.00 1.00
*O18* A3 4a slate 2.75 2.75
*O19* A3 8a bister 5.00 5.00
*O20* A3 12a blue 8.00 8.00

*The above official stamps became obsolete in August, 1878. Since that date the "Official" overprint has been applied to the reprints and probably to original stamps. Two new varieties of the overprint have also appeared, both on the reprints and on the current stamps. These are overprinted in various colors, positions and combinations.*

Same Overprint On Regular Issues of 1905-11.

**1908** **Wmk. Urdu Characters. (42)**
*O21* A5 ½a green 2.00 6
*O22* A5 1a carmine 2.00 6
*O23* A5 2a lilac 3.25 18

***Perf. 11, 11½, 12½, 13½ and Compound.***
**1909-11**
*O24* A5 ½a red 1.75 8
*O25* A3 1a black 1.00 6
*O26* A3 2a ol grn 1.75 30
*O27* A5 3a brn org 10.00 5.00
*O28* A5 4a ol grn ('11) 1.50 30
*O29* A5 8a vio ('11) 1.75 35
*O30* A5 12a bl grn ('11) 2.50 35
*Nos. O24-O30 (7)* 20.25 6.44

Regular Issue of 1908-11 Overprinted

**1911-12**
*O31* A5 ¼a gray 18 5
*O32* A5 ½a green 30 5
*O33* A5 1a carmine 15 5
*O34* A5 2a lilac 20 5
*O35* A5 3a brn org 1.00 10
*O36* A5 4a ol grn 75 8
*O37* A5 8a violet 1.00 18
*O38* A5 12a bl grn 2.25 50
*Nos. O31-O38 (8)* 5.83 1.06

Same Overprint on Regular Issue of 1912.

**1912**
*O39* A5 ¼a brn vio 15 5
***a.*** ¼a gray vio 15 5
*O40* A5 ½a dp grn 20 5

Same Overprint On Regular Issue of 1915-16.

**1917**
*O41* A6 ½a green 60 5
*O42* A6 1a car rose 1.00 5
*O43* A6 1a red 1.00 6

Same Overprint on Nos. 37 and 38.

**1930**
*O44* A5 4p on ¼a brn vio 80 6
*O45* A6 8p on ½a grn 80 6

Same Overprint on Regular Issue of 1931.

**1934-47** **Wmk. 211** ***Perf. 13½***
*O46* A8 4p black 10 5
***a.*** Laid paper ('47) 30
***b.*** Imperf., pair 50.00
*O47* A8 8p green 20 5
***a.*** 8p yel grn, laid paper ('47) 2.00 30
***b.*** Inverted ovpt. 145.00 145.00
*O48* A9 1a dk brn 25 5
*O49* A10 2a dk vio 25 5
*O50* A11 4a ultra 65 8
*O51* A12 8a dp org 2.00 20
*O52* A13 12a scarlet 2.00 25
*O53* A14 1r yellow 2.75 32
*Nos. O46-O53 (8)* 8.20 1.05

**Catalogue values for unused stamps in this section, from this point to the end of the section, are for Never Hinged items.**

Same Overprint on Nos. 58-59, 39B

**1947-50** ***Perf. 13½***
*O54* A6 ½a rose lake 3.25 1.00
*O55* A8 2p brn ('49) 2.50 1.25
*O56* A8 6p car lake ('50) 4.00 3.00

## IDAR

LOCATION — A Feudatory State in the Western India States Agency.
AREA — 1,669 sq. mi.
POP. — 262,660
CAPITAL — Himmatnagar

Stamps of Idar are in booklet panes of four. All stamps have one or two straight edges.

Maharaja Shri Himatsinhji
A1 A2

**1939 Unwmk. Typo. *Perf. 11.***
*1* A1 ½a light green 2.75 *14.00*

**1941 Same Redrawn**
*2* A1 ½a green 4.50

The panels containing denomination and name of state are shaded.

**1944 Unwmk. *Perf. 12***
*3* A2 ½a green 75 *14.00*
*4* A2 1a purple 40
*a.* Imperf., pair 135.00
*5* A2 2a blue 48
*6* A2 4a red 1.40

## INDORE
## (Holkar)

LOCATION — A Feudatory State in the Indore Agency in Central India.
AREA — 9,902 sq. mi.
POP. — 1,513,966
CAPITAL — Indore

Maharaja Tukoji Rao II — A1

A2

**1886 Unwmk. Litho. *Perf. 15.***
*1* A1 ½a lilac 1.65 1.50

**1889 Handstamped. *Imperf.***
*3* A2 ¼a blk, *rose* 1.75 1.90

No. 3 exists in two types.
*The originals of this stamp are printed in water color. The reprints are in oil color and on paper of a deeper shade of rose.*

Maharaja Shivaji Rao — A3

**1889-92 Engr. *Perf. 15.***
*4* A3 ¼a orange 9 6
*5* A3 ½a brn vio 18 18
*6* A3 1a green 50 50
*7* A3 2a vermilion 1.25 65

Maharaja Tukoji Rao III
A4 A5

**1904-08 *Perf. 13½, 14***
*8* A4 ¼a orange 6 5
*9* A5 ½a lake ('08) 5.00 5
*a.* Imperf., pair 17.50
*10* A5 1a grn ('07) 3.75 8
*a.* Imperf., pair 100.00
*11* A5 2a brn ('05) 2.50 12
*a.* Imperf., pair 62.50
*12* A5 3a violet 2.25 45
*13* A5 4a ultra 2.50 45
*Nos. 8-13 (6)* 16.06 1.20

No. 5 Surcharged पाव आना.

**1905 *Perf. 15.***
*14* A3 ¼a on ½a brn vio 1.75 1.65

Maharaja Yeshwant Rao II
A6 A7

**1928-38 Engr. *Perf. 13½.***
*15* A6 ¼a orange 5 6
*16* A6 ½a claret 15 6
*17* A6 1a green 15 6
*18* A6 1¼a grn ('33) 38 8
*19* A6 2a dk brn 90 65
*20* A6 2a Prus bl ('36) 50 30
*21* A6 3a dl vio 90 90
*22* A6 3½a dl vio ('34) 1.00 1.00
*23* A6 4a ultra 1.00 1.00
*24* A6 4a bis ('38) 1.75 50
*25* A6 8a gray 2.00 2.00
*26* A6 8a red org ('38) 7.50 3.25
*27* A6 12a rose red ('34) 7.00 7.00

***Perf. 14***
*28* A7 1r lt bl & blk 8.25 9.50
*29* A7 2r car lake & blk 20.00 25.00
*30* A7 5r org brn & blk 25.00 30.00
*Nos. 15-30 (16)* 76.53 81.36

Imperforates of types A6 and A7 were used with official sanction at Indore City during a stamp shortage in 1938. They were from sheets placed by the printers (Perkins, Bacon) on top of packets of 100 perforated sheets as identification.

Stamps of 1929-33 Surcharged in Black

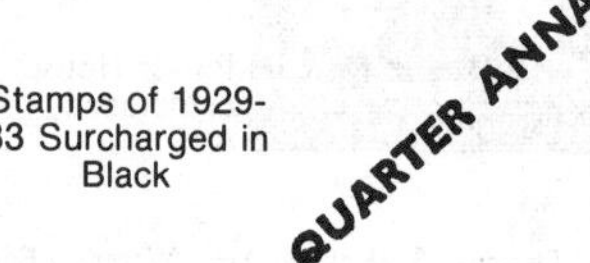

**1940 *Perf. 13, 14***
*31* A7 ¼a on 5r org brn & blk 65 15
*a.* Dbl. surch., blk over grn 185.00
*32* A7 ½a on 2r car lake & blk 1.00 20
*33* A6 1a on 1¼a grn 1.10 18
*a.* Inverted surch. 75.00

Stamps with green surcharge only are proofs.

A8

**1941-47 Typo. *Perf. 11.***
*34* A8 ¼a orange 10 6
*35* A8 ½a rose lil 50 6
*36* A8 1a dk ol grn 65 6
*37* A8 1¼a yel grn 75 18
*a.* Imperf., pair 125.00
*38* A8 2a turq bl 6.00 1.75
*39* A8 4a bis ('47) 16.00 16.00

**Size: 23x28¼mm**
*40* A8 2r car lake, & blk ('47) 12.50 25.00
*41* A8 5r brn org & blk 14.00 30.00
*Nos. 34-41 (8)* 50.50 73.11

Stamps and Type of 1904-08 Overprinted **SERVICE**

**1904-06 *Perf. 13½, 14***
*O1* A5 ½a lake 6 5
*a.* Inverted ovpt. 14.00
*b.* Double overprint 14.00
*c.* Imperf., pair 20.00
*O2* A5 1a green 6 5
*O3* A5 2a brn ('05) 15 10
*O4* A5 3a vio ('06) 75 75
*a.* Imperf., pair 110.00
*O5* A5 4a ultra ('05) 1.25 1.25
*Nos. O1-O5 (5)* 2.27 2.20

Same Overprint on No. 8

**1907**
*O6* A4 ¼a orange 6 6

No. 9 Overprinted **SERVICE**

*O7* A5 ½a lake 8 8

Nos. O1 and O7 differ mainly in the shape of the "R."

## JAIPUR

LOCATION — A Feudatory State in the Jaipur Residency of India.
AREA — 15,610 sq. mi.
POP. — 3,040,876
CAPITAL — Jaipur

Chariot of Surya, Sun God
A1 A1a

***Pin-perf. 14x14½***
**1904 Typo. Unwmk.**
*1* A1 ½a ultra 6.25 6.25
*a.* ½a pale bl 16.00 16.00
*b.* ½a gray bl 250.00
*c.* As "b," imperf. 325.00 375.00
*1D* A1a ½a blue 1.75 2.00
*e.* ½a ultra 1.75 2.00
*f.* Imperf.
*2* A1 1a dl red 1.75 1.90
*a.* 1a chnt 12.50 12.50
*3* A1 2a pale grn 2.75 2.75
*a.* 2a emer 4.25 4.50

No. 1 has 36 varieties (on 2 plates), differing in minor details. Nos. 1b and 1c are from plate II. No. 1D has 24 varieties (one plate).

Chariot of Surya — A2

***Perf. 12½x12 and 13½***
**1904-06 Engr.**
*4* A2 ¼a ol grn ('06) 12 10
*5* A2 ½a dp bl 15 10
*6* A2 1a carmine 38 32
*7* A2 2a dk grn 75 65
*8* A2 4a red brn 3.75 2.00
*9* A2 8a violet 2.50 1.90
*10* A2 1r yellow 3.75 4.00
*Nos. 4-10 (7)* 11.40 9.07

A3 A4

**1911 Typo. *Imperf.***
*11* A3 ¼a yel grn 1.50 1.75
*a.* ¼a ol grn 1.50 1.75
*b.* "¼" inverted 2.00 2.00
*12* A3 ¼a ol yel 20 20
*b.* ¼a bl (error)
*13* A3 ½a ultra 20 20
*a.* ½a dl bl 20 20
*b.* "⅓" for "½" 5.00
*14* A3 1a carmine 30 30
*15* A3 2a dp grn 2.50 2.75
*a.* 2a gray grn 2.50 2.75
*Nos. 11-15 (5)* 4.70 5.20

There are six types for each value and several settings of the ¼a and ½a in the 1911 issue.

**Wmk. "Dorling & Co., London" in Sheet.**
**1913-18 *Perf. 11.***
*16* A4 ¼a ol bis 9 9
*a.* Pair, imperf. between 75.00 75.00
*17* A4 ½a ultra 15 15
*18* A4 1a car ('18) 20 15
*a.* 1a scar 20 15
*b.* Vertical pair, imperf. between 87.50 87.50
*19* A4 2a grn ('18) 2.00 2.00
*20* A4 4a red brn 60 60
*Nos. 16-20 (5)* 3.04 2.99

Stamps of 1904-06 Surcharged

**1926 Unwmk. Engr. *Perf. 13½.***
*21* A2 3a on 8a vio 75 85
*a.* Invtd. surch. 125.00 125.00
*22* A2 3a on 1r yel 75 85
*a.* Invtd. surch. 125.00 125.00

**Wmk. "Overland Bank" in Sheet.**
**1928 Typo. *Perf. 12***
*17a* A4 ½a ultra 4.75 4.75
*18c* A4 1a rose red 12.50 7.50
*18d* A4 1a scarlet 12.50 7.50
*19a* A4 2a green 24.00 18.00
*20a* A4 4a pale brn
*23* A4 8a violet
*23A* A4 1r red org 125.00 125.00

**Durbar Commemorative Issue.**

Chariot of Surya, Sun God — A5

Maharaja Man Singh II — A6

Elephant with Standard — A7

Sowar in Armor — A8

Blue Peafowl — A9

Royal Bullock Carriage — A10

Royal Elephant Carriage — A11

Albert Museum — A12

Sireh-Deorhi Gate — A13

Chandra Palace — A14

Amber Palace — A15

Rajas Jai Singh II and Man Singh II — A16

*Perf. 13½x14, 14, 14x13½*

**1931 Typo. Unwmk.**

24 A5 ¼a red brn & blk 22 10
25 A6 ½a dl vio & blk 38 10
26 A7 1a bl & blk 1.90 90
27 A8 2a ocher & blk 1.90 90
28 A9 2½a rose & blk 8.50 15.00
29 A10 3a dk grn & blk 8.50 14.00
30 A11 4a dl grn & blk 5.50 11.50
31 A12 6a dk bl & blk 5.50 11.50
32 A13 8a brn & blk 6.50 *14.00*
33 A14 1r ol & blk 10.00 *22.50*
34 A15 2r lt grn & blk 10.00 *27.50*
35 A16 5r vio & blk 14.00 *32.50*
*Nos. 24-35 (12)* 72.90 150.50

Issued in commemoration of the investiture of the Maharaja Man Singh II with full ruling powers.

Eighteen sets of this issue were overprinted in red "INVESTITURE—MARCH 14, 1931" for presentation to distinguished personages.

Raja Man Singh II — A18

**1932-46** *Perf. 14.*

36 A6 ¼a red brn & blk 12 5
36A A6 ¾a brn org & blk ('43) 12 5
37 A18 1a bl & blk 15 6
37A A6 1a bl & blk 50 5
38 A18 2a ocher & blk 15 12
38A A6 2a ocher & blk ('45) 75 8
39 A6 2½a dk car & blk 20 12
40 A6 3a grn & blk 25 12
41 A18 4a gray grn & blk 75 75
41A A6 4a gray grn & blk ('45) 1.25 75
42 A6 6a bl & blk 65 65
43 A18 8a choc & blk 65 65
43A A6 8a choc & blk ('45) 2.00 3.00
44 A18 1r bis & gray blk 7.50 *10.00*
44A A6 1r bis & gray blk ('46) 7.50 *10.00*
45 A18 2r yel grn & blk 37.50 *50.00*
*Nos. 36-45 (16)* 60.04 76.45

Stamps of 1931-32 Surcharged in Red or Black — **One Rupee**

**1936** *Perf. 14x13½, 13½x14*

46 A18 1r on 2r rel grn & blk (R) 2.25 *3.75*
47 A16 1r on 5r vio & blk 2.00 *3.75*

No. 25 Surcharged in Red — **पाच आना**

**1938** *Perf. 14x13½*

48 A6 ¼a on ½a dl vio & blk 2.25 2.25

**Catalogue values for unused stamps in this section, from this point to the end of the section, are for Never Hinged items.**

Amber Palace A19

Designs: ¼a, Palace gate. ¾a, Map of Jaipur. 1a, Observatory. 2a, Palace of the Winds. 3a, Arms of the Raja. 4a, Gate of Amber Fort. 8a, Chariot of the Sun. 1r, Raja Man Singh II.

**1947-48 Unwmk. Engr.** *Perf. 14.*

49 A19 ¼a dk grn & red brn ('48) 6 18
50 A19 ½a bl vio & dp grn 8 18
51 A19 ¾a dk car & blk ('48) 10 25
52 A19 1a dp ultra & choc 25 35
53 A19 2a car & bl vio 20 35
54 A19 3a dk gray & grn ('48) 30 52
55 A19 4a choc & dp ultra 40 70
56 A19 8a dk brn & red 50 70
57 A19 1r dk red vio & bl grn ('48) 1.25 2.25
*Nos. 49-57 (9)* 3.14 5.48

Issued to commemorate the 25th anniversary of the enthronement of Raja Man Singh II.

No. 25 Surcharged in Carmine with New Value and Bars.

**1947**

58 A6 3p on ½a dl vio & blk 15.00 15.00
a. "3 PIE" 50.00 50.00
b. Inverted surch. 52.50 52.50
c. Double surch., one inverted 100.00 100.00
d. As "a", inverted surch. 225.00 225.00

## OFFICIAL STAMPS

Regular Issue of 1913-22 Overprinted in Black or Red — **SERVICE**

**1929 Unwmk.** *Perf. 12½x12, 11.*

O1 A4 ¼a ol grn 35 18
O2 A4 ½a ultra 35 6
a. Inverted ovpt. 90.00
O3 A4 ½a ultra (R) 35 8
O4 A4 1a red 50 8
O5 A4 2a green 45 24
O6 A4 4a red brn 2.25 90
O7 A4 8a pur (R) 18.00 18.00
O8 A4 1r red org 35.00 35.00
*Nos. O1-O8 (8)* 57.25 54.54

The 8a and 1r not issued without overprint.

Regular Issue of 1913-22 Overprinted in Black or Red

b **SERVICE**

**1931** *Perf. 11, 12½x12.*

O9 A4 ½a ultra 75.00 9
O10 A4 ½a ultra (R) 90.00 6
O10A A4 8a purple 150.00 150.00
O10B A4 1r red org 150.00 150.00

No. O5 Surcharged — **आध आना**

**1932**

O11 A4 ½a on 2a grn 120.00 24

Regular Issue of 1931 Overprinted in Red — **SERVICE**

**1931-37** *Perf. 13½x14, 14.*

O12 A6 ¼a red brn & blk ('36) 15 7
O13 A6 ½a dl vio & blk 8 5
O14 A7 1a bl & blk 180.00 1.50
O15 A8 2a ocher & blk ('36) 90 45
O16 A11 4a dl grn & blk ('37) 7.50 3.00

Same on Regular Issue of 1932 in Red.

**1932-37** *Perf. 14*

O17 A18 1a bl & blk 18 6
O18 A18 2a ocher & blk 32 6
O19 A18 4a gray grn & blk ('37) 3.00 2.00
O20 A18 8a choc & blk 1.40 1.25
O21 A18 1r bis & gray blk 3.00 3.00
*Nos. O17-O21 (5)* 7.90 6.37

No. 36 Overprinted Type "b" in Black

**1939** *Perf. 14*

O22 A6 ¼a red brn & blk 45.00 35.00

Nos. 36A, 38A, 39, 41A, 43A, 44A and Type of 1931 Overprinted in Carmine — **SERVICE**

**1941-46 Unwmk.** *Perf. 13½, 14.*

O23 A6 ¾a brn org & blk ('43) 12 6
O24 A6 1a bl & blk ('41) 32 8
O25 A6 2a ocher & blk 45 10
O26 A6 2½a dk car & blk ('46) 1.20 *4.50*
O27 A6 4a gray grn & blk ('46) 60 35
O28 A6 8a choc & blk 1.20 60
O29 A6 1r bis & gray blk *120.00*
*Nos. O23-O28 (6)* 3.89 5.69

**Catalogue values for unused stamps in this section, from this point to the end of the section, are for Never Hinged items.**

No. O24 Surcharged with New Value and Bars in Carmine.

**1947** *Perf. 13½.*

O30 A6 9p on 1a bl & blk 25 25

**No. 58 Overprinted in Red "SERVICE"**

***Perf. 14.***

O31 A6 3p on ½a dl vio & blk 3.50 5.00
a. Inverted surch. 1,200. 1,100.
b. Double surch., one inverted 65.00 65.00
c. "3 PIE" 300.00 300.00

No. O13 Surcharged "Three-quarter Anna" in Devanagari, similar to surcharge on No. 48, and Bars in Carmine.

**1949** *Perf. 14x13½.*

O32 A6 ¾a on ½a dl vio & blk 10.00 6.00

For later issues see Rajasthan.

## JAMMU AND KASHMIR

LOCATION — A Feudatory State in the Kashmir Residency in the extreme north of India.
AREA — 82,258 sq. mi.
POP. — 4,021,616 (1941)
CAPITAL — Srinagar

½ Anna — A1

1 Anna — A2

¼ Rupee — A3

Native Grayish Laid Paper.

**Handstamped.**

**1866-67 Unwmk.** ***Imperf.***

**Printed in Water Colors.**

1 A1 ½a gray blk 37.50 27.50
Cut to shape 6.50 2.75
2 A2 1a dl bl 55.00 45.00
a. 1a ultra 55.00 45.00
b. 1a ryl bl 82.50 62.50
Cut to shape 14.00 11.00
3 A2 1a black 75.00 75.00
Cut to shape 19.00 14.00
4 A3 ¼r dl bl 55.00 42.50
a. ¼r ultra 55.00 42.50
b. ¼r ind 425.00 *325.00*
c. ¼r ryl bl 150.00 100.00
Cut to shape 17.50 11.00
5 A3 ¼r black 22.50 17.50
Cut to shape 5.50 4.00

It has now been proved by the leading authorities on Indian stamps that all stamps of ½ anna and 1 anna printed from the so-called Die A are forgeries and that no such die was ever in use.

See Nos. 24-59.

### Jammu

A part of the Feudatory State of Jammu & Kashmir, both being ruled by the same sovereign.

½ Anna — A4

1 Anna — A5

Printed in blocks of four, three types of the ½a and one of the 1a.

Native Grayish Laid Paper.

**Printed in Water Colors.**

**1867-77 Unwmk.** ***Imperf.***

6 A4 ½a black 100.00 32.50
7 A4 ½a indigo 20.00 17.50
a. ½a dp ultra 27.50 25.00
b. ½a dp vio bl 27.50 25.00
8 A4 ½a car red 2.25 1.90
a. ½a org red 32.50 16.00
b. ½a org 47.50 47.50
9 A5 1a black 375.00 250.00
10 A5 1a indigo 55.00 40.00
a. 1a dp ultra 55.00 45.00
b. 1a dp vio bl 70.00 45.00
11 A5 1a car red 2.75 2.75
a. 1a org red 16.00 17.50
b. 1a org 425.00

No. 11b is known only used.

**1876**

12 A4 ½a emerald 275.00 190.00
13 A4 ½a brt bl 80.00
14 A5 1a emerald 425.00 250.00
15 A5 1a brt bl 80.00 80.00

Native Grayish Laid Paper.

**1877 Printed in Oil Colors.**

16 A4 ½a red 7.00 7.00
a. ½a brn red 20.00 16.00

*17* A4 ½a black 275.00 160.00
*18* A5 1a red 20.00 20.00
*a.* 1a brn red 50.00 27.50
*19* A5 1a black 500.00 250.00

*The formerly listed ½a dark blue, ½a dark green, 1a dark blue and 1a dark green are believed to be reprints.*

**European White Laid Paper**

*20* A4 ½a red 350.00 310.00
*a.* Thin laid batonné paper 400.00
*21* A5 1a red 310.00
*a.* Thin laid batonné aper 625.00

**European White Wove Paper**

*22* A4 ¼a red 250.00
*23* A5 1a red 375.00

**RE-ISSUES**

**For Jammu Only**

Native Grayish Laid Paper

**Printed in Water Colors.**

**1869-76** ***Imperf.***

*24* A1 ½a dp blk 4.50 4.50
*25* A1 ½a brt bl 11.00 11.00
*26* A1 ½a org red 5.75 5.75
*a.* ½a org 7.00 7.00
*b.* ½a car 7.00 7.00
*27* A1 ½a emerald 32.50 32.50
*28* A1 ½a yellow 62.50 62.50
*29* A2 1a dp blk 15.00
*30* A2 1a brt bl 11.00
*31* A2 1a org red 32.50 32.50
*a.* 1a org 32.50 32.50
*b.* 1a car 32.50 32.50
*32* A2 1a emerald 37.50 37.50
*33* A2 1a yellow 55.00 55.00
*34* A3 ¼r dp blk 30.00
*35* A3 ¼r brt bl 6.75
*a.* ¼r ind 14.00
*36* A3 ¼r org red 9.00
*a.* ¼r org 9.00
*b.* ¼r car 9.00
*37* A3 ¼r emerald 37.50 37.50
*38* A3 ¼r yellow 55.00 55.00

Native Grayish Laid Paper

**1877** **Printed in Oil Colors.**

*39* A1 ½a org red 6.00 4.50
*a.* ½a brn red 6.00 4.50
*b.* ½a car 6.00 4.50
*40* A1 ½a black 3.75 3.75
*41* A1 ½a sl bl 19.00 19.00
*42* A1 ½a sage grn 50.00 50.00
*43* A2 1a red 20.00 20.00
*a.* 1a brn red 20.00 20.00
*45* A2 1a sl bl 6.75 6.75
*46* A2 1a sage grn 62.50 62.50
*47* A3 ¼r org red 6.00
*a.* ¼r brn red 6.00
*48* A3 ¼r black 14.00
*49* A3 ¼r sl bl 6.00
*50* A3 ¼r sage grn 50.00

**European White Laid Paper**

*51* A1 ½a red 110.00 110.00
*52* A1 ½a black 4.50 4.50
*53* A1 ½a sl bl 4.50 4.50
*54* A1 ½a yellow 55.00
*55* A2 1a red 22.50
*56* A2 1a sl bl 22.50 22.50
*57* A3 ¼r red 50.00 50.00
*58* A3 ¼r sage grn 500.00

**European Brownish Wove Paper**

*59* A1 ½a red 190.00

It is probable that the issues of 1876, 1877 and the re-issues of the circular stamps were made to supply the demands of philatelists more than for postal needs. They were, however, available for postage.

There exist also reprints, printed in a variety of colors, on native and European thin wove paper. Collectors are warned against official imitations, which are very numerous. They are printed on several kinds of paper and in a great variety of colors.

A5a

**Handstamped in Oil Color**

**1877, Nov.**

*60* A5a (½a) red 300.00

This provisional, made with a canceling device, was used only in November, 1877, at Jammu city.

**Kashmir**

A part of the Feudatory State of Jammu & Kashmir, both being ruled by the same sovereign.

½ Anna — A6

Printed in Water Colors
Native Grayish Laid Paper
Printed from a Single Die

**1866** **Unwmk.** ***Imperf.***

*62* A6 ½a black 750.00 340.00

¼ Anna — A7 ½ Anna — A8

1 Anna — A9 2 Annas — A10

4 Annas — A11 8 Annas — A12

The ¼a, 1a and 2a are printed in strips of five varieties, the ½a in sheets of twenty varieties and the 4a and 8a from single dies.

**1866-70**

*63* A7 ¼a black 50 50
*64* A8 ½a black 350.00 140.00
*65* A8 ½a ultra 1.10 1.10
*a.* ½a bl 1.50 1.50
*66* A9 1a black 175.00
*67* A9 1a red org 3.50 3.50
*68* A9 1a ven red 3.50 3.00
*69* A9 1a org brn 3.50 2.25
*70* A9 1a ultra 2,000. 750.00
*71* A10 2a ol yel 5.50 4.50
*72* A11 4a emerald 8.75 8.75
*73* A12 8a red 8.75 8.75

*All the stamps printed in oil colors are reprints.*

*As in Jammu, official imitations are numerous and are found in many colors and on various papers.*

**JAMMU AND KASHMIR**

¼ Anna — A13 ½ Anna — A14

1 Anna — A15 2 Annas — A16

4 Annas — A17 8 Annas — A18

Laid Paper

**Printed in Oil Colors.**

**1878** ***Rough Perf. 10-14***

*74* A13 ¼a red 190.00 190.00
*75* A14 ½a red 3.00 3.00
*a.* Wove paper 65.00
*76* A14 ½a sl bl 19.50 17.00
*77* A15 1a red 225.00 225.00
*78* A15 1a brt vio 300.00 300.00

**1878-80** ***Imperf.***

*79* A13 ¼a red 7.50 6.00
*80* A14 ½a red 2.25 2.25
*81* A14 ½a slate 7.50 7.50
*82* A15 1a red 2.75 2.75
*83* A15 1a violet 11.00 11.00
*a.* 1a dl pur 11.00 11.00
*84* A16 2a red 22.50 22.50
*85* A16 2a brt vio 11.00 11.00
*86* A16 2a dl ultra 75.00
*87* A17 4a red 22.50 17.50

**Thick Wove Paper**

*88* A14 ½a red 11.00 11.00
*89* A15 1a red 5.50 5.50
*90* A16 2a red 6.00 6.00

Thin Toned Wove Paper

**1879-80**

*91* A13 ¼a red 50 50
*92* A14 ½a red 25 25
*93* A15 1a red 50 50
*94* A16 2a red 1.00 1.00
*95* A17 4a red 1.25 1.25
*96* A18 8a red 2.00 2.00

Thin Laid Batonné Paper.

**1880** **Printed in Water Color.**

*97* A13 ¼a ultra 150.00

Thin Toned Wove Paper.

**1881** **Printed in Oil Colors.**

*98* A13 ¼a orange 3.00 3.00
*99* A14 ½a orange 11.00 11.00
*100* A15 1a orange 7.50 7.50
*101* A16 2a orange 10.00 10.00
*102* A17 4a orange 16.00 16.00
*103* A18 8a orange 22.50 22.50

⅛ Anna — A19

Thin White or Yellowish Wove Paper

**1883-94**

*104* A19 ⅛a yel brn 8 8
*a.* ⅛a yel 8 8
*105* A13 ¼a brown 10 10
*a.* Dbl. impression 500.00
*106* A14 ½a red 8 8
*a.* ½a rose 1.10 50
*106B* A19 ½a brt bl 1.75 1.75
*c.* ½a dl bl 1.75 1.75
*107* A15 1a brnz grn 38 38
*108* A15 1a yel grn 12 12
*109* A15 1a bl grn 50 50
*110* A15 1a bister 38 38
*111* A17 4a green 1.00 1.00
*112* A17 4a ol grn 4.00 4.00
*113* A18 8a dp bl 3.00 3.00
*114* A18 8a dk ultra 3.00 3.00
*115* A18 8a gray vio 6.00 6.00

**Printed in Water Color**

*116* A18 8a gray bl 11.00 11.00

**Printed in Oil Colors**

**Yellow Pelure Paper**

*117* A16 2a red 2.25 2.25

**Yellow Green Pelure Paper**

*118* A16 2a red 3.00 3.00

**Deep Green Pelure Paper**

*119* A16 2a red 6.00 6.00

**Coarse Yellow Wove Paper**

*120* A16 2a red 38 38

Thin Creamy Laid Paper

**1886-94**

*121* A19 ⅛a yellow 10.00 10.00
*122* A13 ¼a brown 3.75 4.00
*123* A14 ½a vermilion 3.75 3.75
*124* A14 ½a rose red 6.00 6.00
*125* A15 1a green 75.00 80.00
*126* A17 4a green 87.50 87.50

**Printed in Water Color**

*127* A18 8a gray bl 100.00 100.00

Impressions of types A13 to A19 in colors other than the issued stamps are proofs. Forgeries to defraud the post exist, and some are common.

1/4 Anna

Stamps of the above type, printed in red or black, were never placed in use.

**OFFICIAL STAMPS**

Same Types as Regular Issues
White Laid Paper

**1878** **Unwmk.** ***Rough Perf. 10-14.***

*O1* A14 ½a black 500.00

***Imperf***

*O2* A13 ¼a black 15.00 15.00
*O3* A14 ½a black 2.25 2.25
*O4* A15 1a black 2.25 2.25
*O5* A16 2a black 6.00 3.10

Thin White or Yellowish Wove Paper

**1880**

*O6* A13 ¼a black 5 5
*O7* A14 ½a black 8 8
*O8* A15 1a black 12 12
*O9* A16 2a black 15 15
*O10* A17 4a black 38 38
*O11* A18 8a black 38 38

Thin Creamy Laid Paper

**1890-91**

*O12* A13 ¼a black 3.50 3.50
*O13* A14 ½a black 3.50 3.50
*O14* A15 1a black 3.50 3.50
*O15* A16 2a black 55.00 55.00
*O16* A17 4a black 22.50 15.00
*O17* A18 8a black 22.50 15.00

Obsolete October 31, 1894.

## JASDAN

LOCATION — A Feudatory State in the Kathiawar Agency in Western India.
AREA — 296 sq. mi.
POP. — 34,056 (1931)
CAPITAL — Jasdan

In 1948 Jasdan was incorporated in the United State of Saurashtra (see Soruth).

**Catalogue values for all unused stamps in this state are for Never Hinged items.**

Sun — A1

***Perf. 8½ to 10½***

**1942** **Unwmk.** **Typo.**

*1* A1 1a green 2.75

Issued in booklet panes of 4 and 8.
The 1a carmine is a revenue stamp.
Jasdan's stamp became obsolete Feb. 15, 1948.

## JHALAWAR

LOCATION — A Feudatory State in the Rajputana Agency of India.
AREA — 813 sq. mi.
POP. — 107,890
CAPITAL — Jhalrapatan

Apsaras, Hindu Nymph
A1 A2

Laid Paper

**1887-90 Unwmk. *Imperf.***

| | | | | |
|---|---|---|---|---|
| 1 | A1 | 1p yel grn | 2.00 | 3.25 |
| 2 | A2 | ¼a green | 75 | 1.25 |

Obsolete October 31, 1900.

## JIND

## (Jhind)

LOCATION — A Feudatory State in the north Punjab District of India.
AREA — 1,299 sq. mi.
POP. — 324,679
CAPITAL — Sangrur

Subsequent stamp issues are listed under Convention States.

A1

A2

A3

A4

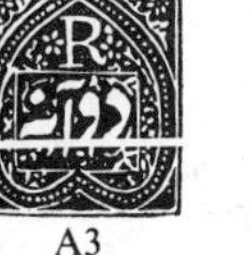

A5

**1874 Unwmk. Litho. *Imperf.***

**Thin White Wove Paper**

| | | | | |
|---|---|---|---|---|
| 1 | A1 | ½a blue | 5.50 | 3.50 |
| 2 | A2 | 1a lilac | 7.50 | 7.50 |
| 3 | A3 | 2a yellow | 1.25 | 1.25 |
| 4 | A4 | 4a green | 27.50 | 5.50 |
| 5 | A5 | 8a dk vio | 125.00 | 32.50 |

**1875**

**Thick Blue Laid Paper**

| | | | | |
|---|---|---|---|---|
| 6 | A1 | ½a blue | 22 | 22 |
| 7 | A2 | 1a red vio | 50 | 50 |
| 8 | A3 | 2a brn org | 75 | 75 |
| 9 | A4 | 4a green | 85 | 85 |
| 10 | A5 | 8a purple | 4.25 | 4.25 |

**1885 *Perf. 12***

| | | | | |
|---|---|---|---|---|
| 11 | A1 | ½a blue | 4.25 | 4.25 |

A6

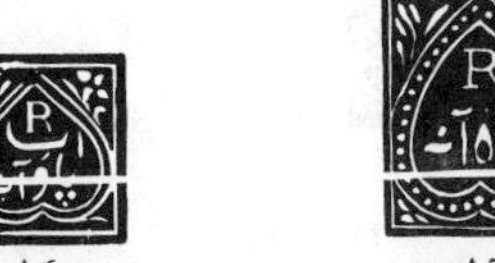

A7

A8 A9

A10 A11

**1882-84 *Imperf.***

**Thin Yellowish Wove Paper**

| | | | | |
|---|---|---|---|---|
| 12 | A6 | ¼a buff | 12 | 12 |
| *a.* | | Dbl. impression | | |
| 13 | A7 | ½a yellow | 55 | 55 |
| 14 | A8 | 1a brown | 1.40 | 1.40 |
| 15 | A9 | 2a blue | 55 | 55 |
| 16 | A10 | 4a green | 65 | 65 |
| 17 | A11 | 8a red | 2.00 | 1.40 |

***Perf. 12***

| | | | | |
|---|---|---|---|---|
| 18 | A6 | ¼a buff | 28 | 28 |
| 19 | A7 | ½a yellow | 38 | 38 |
| 20 | A8 | 1a brown | 85 | 85 |
| 21 | A9 | 2a blue | 1.50 | 1.75 |
| 22 | A10 | 4a green | 2.75 | 2.75 |
| 23 | A11 | 8a red | 6.75 | 6.75 |
| *a.* | | Thick white paper | 6.75 | 6.75 |

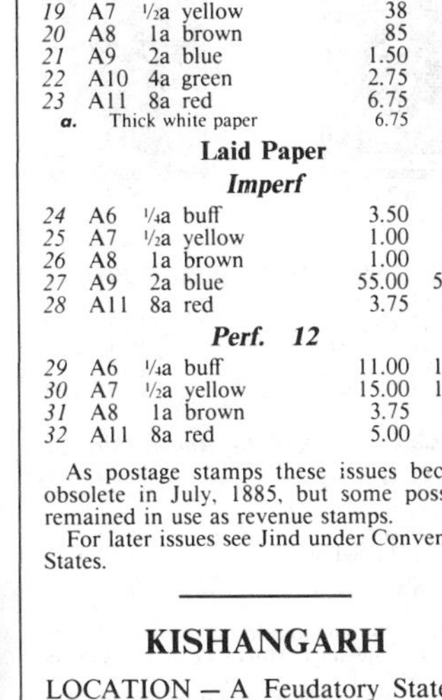

**Laid Paper**

***Imperf***

| | | | | |
|---|---|---|---|---|
| 24 | A6 | ¼a buff | 3.50 | 3.50 |
| 25 | A7 | ½a yellow | 1.00 | 1.00 |
| 26 | A8 | 1a brown | 1.00 | 1.00 |
| 27 | A9 | 2a blue | 55.00 | 55.00 |
| 28 | A11 | 8a red | 3.75 | 3.75 |

***Perf. 12***

| | | | | |
|---|---|---|---|---|
| 29 | A6 | ¼a buff | 11.00 | 11.00 |
| 30 | A7 | ½a yellow | 15.00 | 11.00 |
| 31 | A8 | 1a brown | 3.75 | 3.75 |
| 32 | A11 | 8a red | 5.00 | 5.00 |

As postage stamps these issues became obsolete in July, 1885, but some possibly remained in use as revenue stamps.

For later issues see Jind under Convention States.

## KISHANGARH

LOCATION — A Feudatory State in the Jaipur Residency of India.
AREA — 858 sq. mi.
POP. — 85,744
CAPITAL — Kishangarh

Kishangarh was incorporated in Rajasthan in 1947-49.

Stamps were issued without gum except Nos. 27-35.

Coat of Arms — A1

**1899-1900 Unwmk. Typo. *Imperf.***

**Soft Porous Paper**

| | | | | |
|---|---|---|---|---|
| 1 | A1 | 1a green | 21.00 | 21.00 |
| 2 | A1 | 1a bl ('00) | 300.00 | |

***Pin-perf***

| | | | | |
|---|---|---|---|---|
| 3 | A1 | 1a green | 47.50 | 47.50 |

A2

A3

Coat of Arms — A4

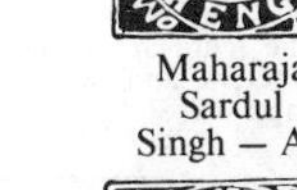

Maharaja Sardul Singh — A5

A6

A7

Coat of Arms
A8 A9

Thin Wove Paper

**1899-1900 Handstamped *Imperf.***

| | | | | |
|---|---|---|---|---|
| 4 | A2 | ¼a carmine | 45 | 45 |
| 5 | A2 | ¼a green | 75.00 | |
| 6 | A3 | ½a blue | 90 | 60 |
| 7 | A3 | ½a green | 13.00 | 13.00 |
| 8 | A3 | ½a carmine | 13.00 | 13.00 |
| 9 | A3 | ½a violet | 30.00 | *35.00* |
| 10 | A4 | 1a gray vio | 60 | 45 |
| *a.* | | 1a gray | 60 | 45 |
| 11 | A4 | 1a rose | 60.00 | 65.00 |
| 11A | A5 | 2a orange | 4.00 | 4.00 |
| 12 | A6 | 4a chocolate | 1.90 | 1.90 |
| *a.* | | Laid paper | 45.00 | 45.00 |
| 13 | A7 | 1r dl grn | 18.00 | |
| 13A | A7 | 1r lt brn | 50.00 | 45.00 |
| 14 | A8 | 2r brn red | 70.00 | |
| *a.* | | Laid paper | 55.00 | |
| 15 | A9 | 5r violet | 45.00 | |
| *a.* | | Laid paper | 75.00 | |

***Pin-perf***

| | | | | |
|---|---|---|---|---|
| 16 | A2 | ¼a magenta | 25 | 25 |
| *a.* | | ¼a rose | 25 | |
| 17 | A2 | ¼a green | 50.00 | 65.00 |
| *a.* | | Imperf. vertically | 180.00 | 180.00 |
| 18 | A3 | ½a blue | 32 | 32 |
| *a.* | | ½a dk bl | 60 | 60 |
| 19 | A3 | ½a green | 12.00 | 12.00 |
| *a.* | | Imperf. vert., pair | 60.00 | 60.00 |
| 20 | A4 | 1a gray vio | 55 | 45 |
| *a.* | | 1a gray | 75 | 75 |
| *b.* | | 1a red lil | | 6.00 |
| *d.* | | As "b", laid paper | 30.00 | 22.50 |
| 20E | A4 | 1a rose | 27.50 | 27.50 |
| 21 | A5 | 2a orange | 7.00 | 4.50 |
| 21B | A6 | 4a pale red brn | 1.50 | 1.25 |
| *c.* | | 4a choc | 1.50 | 1.25 |
| 22 | A7 | 1r dl grn | 14.00 | 19.00 |
| *b.* | | Laid paper | 100.00 | |
| 23 | A8 | 2r brn red | 42.50 | 42.50 |
| *b.* | | Laid paper | 60.00 | |
| 24 | A9 | 5r red vio | 32.50 | |
| *d.* | | Laid paper | 90.00 | |

Nos. 4-24 exist tête bêche and sell for a slight premium.

A9a

A9b

Soft Porous Paper

**1901 Typo.**

| | | | | |
|---|---|---|---|---|
| 24A | A9a | ½a rose | 10.00 | 10.00 |
| 24B | A9b | 1a dl vio | 18.00 | 18.00 |

A10

A11

**1903 Stout Hard Paper. *Imperf.***

| | | | | |
|---|---|---|---|---|
| 25 | A10 | ½a pink | 6.50 | 5.25 |
| *a.* | | Printed on both sides | | *1,000.* |

**1904 Thin Wove Paper *Pin-perf.***

| | | | | |
|---|---|---|---|---|
| 25B | A11 | 8a gray | 6.50 | 6.50 |

Exists tête bêche. Slight premium.

A11a

Maharaja Sardul Singh — A12

| | | | | |
|---|---|---|---|---|
| 25D | A11a | 1r green | 27.50 | 27.50 |

**1903 *Imperf.***

**Stout Hard Paper**

| | | | | |
|---|---|---|---|---|
| 26 | A12 | 2a yellow | 4.50 | 4.50 |

Maharaja Madan Singh
A13 A14

**1904-05 Engr. *Perf. 12½, 13½***

| | | | | |
|---|---|---|---|---|
| 27 | A13 | ¼a carmine | 35 | 16 |
| 28 | A13 | ½a chestnut | 35 | 16 |
| 29 | A13 | 1a dp bl | 1.50 | 50 |
| 30 | A13 | 2a orange | 13.50 | 13.50 |
| 31 | A13 | 4a dk brn | 4.00 | 4.00 |
| 32 | A13 | 8a pur ('05) | 8.00 | 8.00 |
| 33 | A13 | 1r dk grn | 11.00 | 11.00 |
| 34 | A13 | 2r lem yel | 17.00 | *27.50* |
| 35 | A13 | 5r pur brn | 22.50 | *42.50* |
| | | *Nos. 27-35 (9)* | 78.20 | 107.32 |

Thin Wove Paper

**1913 Typo. *Rouletted 9½***

| | | | | |
|---|---|---|---|---|
| 37 | A14 | 2 "ANNA" vio | 2.50 | 2.50 |

Exists tête bêche. Slight premium.

See also Nos. 40-50.

Maharaja Madan Singh
A15 A16

Thick, Chalk-surfaced Paper

**1913 *Rouletted 6½, 12***

| | | | | |
|---|---|---|---|---|
| 38 | A15 | ¼a pale bl | 12 | 12 |
| *a.* | | "Kishangahr" | 3.25 | 3.25 |
| *b.* | | Imperf., pair | 4.50 | |
| 39 | A16 | 2a purple | 13.00 | 13.00 |
| *a.* | | "Kishangahr" | 85.00 | 85.00 |

**1913-16 *Rouletted 12, 14½.***

| | | | | |
|---|---|---|---|---|
| 40 | A14 | ¼a pale bl | 15 | 15 |
| 41 | A14 | ½a grn ('15) | 20 | 20 |
| *a.* | | Printed on both sides | 140.00 | |
| 42 | A14 | 1a carmine | 90 | 90 |
| 43 | A14 | 2 "ANNAS" pur | 2.75 | 3.50 |
| 44 | A14 | 4a ultra | 5.75 | *9.00* |
| 45 | A14 | 8a brown | 5.75 | *12.00* |
| 46 | A14 | 1r rose lil | 12.00 | *24.00* |
| 47 | A14 | 2r dk grn | 30.00 | *35.00* |
| 48 | A14 | 5r brown | 45.00 | *60.00* |
| | | *Nos. 40-48 (9)* | 102.50 | 144.75 |

On Nos. 40-48 the halftone screen covers the entire design.

Nos. 41-48 have ornaments on both sides of value in top panel.

Type of 1913-16 Redrawn

**1918 *Rouletted***

| | | | | |
|---|---|---|---|---|
| 50 | A14 | 1a rose red | 90 | 90 |

The redrawn stamp is 24¾mm. wide instead of 26mm. There is a white oval around the portrait with only traces of the red line. There is less shading outside the wreath.

A particular stamp may be scarce, but if few collectors want it, its market value may remain relatively low.

Maharaja Jagjanarajan Singh
A17 A18

Thick Glazed Paper

**1928-29** ***Pin-perf. 14½ to 16***

52 A17 ¼a lt bl 9 9
53 A17 ½a lt yel grn 28 28
a. Imperf., pair 35.00 35.00
54 A18 1a car rose 55 55
55 A18 2a red vio 2.00 2.00
56 A17 4a yel brn 1.50 1.50
57 A17 8a purple 4.00 4.00
58 A17 1r green 4.00 4.00
59 A17 2r lemon 15.00 *24.00*
60 A17 5r red brn 30.00 *35.00*
a. Imperf., pair 105.00
*Nos. 52-60 (9)* 57.42 71.42

Thick Soft Unglazed Paper

**1945-47**

52a A17 ¼a gray bl 1.25 1.25
b. ¼a grnsh bl ('47) 1.25 1.25
53b A17 ½a dp grn 1.25 1.25
54a A18 1a dl car 2.50 2.50
b. 1a dk vio bl
55a A18 2a dp red vio 5.00 5.00
b. 2a vio brn, imperf. 20.00
56a A17 4a brown 25.00 25.00
57a A17 8a violet 32.50 *40.00*
58a A17 1r dp grn 40.00 *55.00*

The 2r and 2r exist on same paper.
For later issues see Rajasthan.

### OFFICIAL STAMPS

Used values are for CTO copies.

Regular Issues of 1899-1916 Handstamped

ON
K S
D

Black Handstamp
On Issue of 1899-1900

**1918** **Unwmk.** ***Imperf.***

O1 A2 ¼a carmine 8.50
O2 A4 1a gray vio 3.50 2.25
O3 A6 4a chocolate 17.00 17.00

***Pin-perf***

O4 A2 ¼a carmine 50 50
O4B A3 ½a blue 27.50
O5 A3 ½a green 8.50 8.50
O6 A4 1a gray vio 3.50 1.50
O7 A5 2a orange
O8 A6 4a chocolate 15.00 15.00
O9 A7 1r dl grn 60.00 60.00
O10 A8 2r brn red 105.00 105.00
O11 A9 5r red vio 150.00 150.00

See tete beche note after No. 24.

**On Issue of 1901.**

O12 A9b 1a dl vio

**On Issue of 1904**

O13 A11 8a gray 32.50 32.50
O13A A11a 1r green

***Imperf.***

O14 A12 2a yellow 17.00 17.00

**On Issue of 1904-05.**
***Perf. 12½, 13***

O15 A13 ¼a carmine 15.00 12.50
O16 A13 ½a chestnut 60 50
O17 A13 1a dp bl 9.25 4.00
O18 A13 2a orange
O19 A13 4a dk brn 15.00 15.00
O20 A13 8a purple 60.00 50.00
O21 A13 1r dk grn 195.00 150.00
O22 A13 5r pur brn

**On Issue of 1913**
***Rouletted***

O23 A15 ¼a pale bl 8.50

**On Issue of 1913-16.**

O24 A14 ¼a pale bl 75 35
O25 A14 ½a green 1.35 60
O26 A14 1a carmine 1.35 65
O27 A14 2a purple 2.00 2.00
O28 A14 4a ultra 22.50 22.50
O29 A14 8a brown 42.50 42.50
O30 A14 1r rose lil 85.00 85.00
O31 A14 2r dk grn 250.00
O32 A14 5r brown 340.00

**Red Handstamp**
**On Issue of 1904**
***Pin-perf***

O33 A11 8a gray 42.50 42.50

***Imperf***

O34 A12 2a yellow 35.00 35.00

**On Issue of 1904-05**
***Perf. 12½, 13***

O35 A13 1a dp blue 12.00 12.00
O36 A13 4a dk brn 15.00 15.00
O37 A13 8a purple 25.00 35.00
O38 A13 1r dk grn 45.00 72.50

**On Issue of 1913-16**
***Rouletted***

O39 A14 ¼a pale bl 8.50 8.50
O40 A14 ½a green 8.50 8.50
O41 A14 2a purple 22.50 22.50
O42 A14 4a ultra 42.50 42.50
O43 A14 8a brown 42.50 42.50

**On Issue of 1918**
**Redrawn**

O44 A14 1a rose red

The overprint on Nos. O1 to O44 is handstamped and, as usual with that style of overprint, is found inverted, double, etc., etc. In this instance there is evidence that many of the varieties were deliberately made.

## LAS BELA

LOCATION — A Feudatory State in the Baluchistan District.
AREA — 7,132 sq. mi.
POP. — 63,008
CAPITAL — Bela

A1 A2

**1897-98** **Unwmk.** **Typo.** ***Perf. 12.***

1 A1 ½a *white* 9.75 9.75
2 A1 ½a *gray* 2.75 2.50
3 A1 ½a *bl* ('98) 5.50 5.50

**1901**

4 A2 1a *red org* 9.75 9.75

**1904** ***Pin-perf***

5 A1 ½a *lt bl* 6.00 6.00
6 A1 ½a *grnsh gray, granite paper* 3.75 3.75

Las Bela stamps became obsolete in March, 1907.

## MORVI

LOCATION — A Feudatory State in the Kathiawar Agency, Western India.
AREA — 822 sq. mi.
POP. — 113,023
CAPITAL — Morvi

In 1948 Morvi was incorporated in the United State of Saurashtra (see Soruth).

Sir Lakhdhirji Waghji
The Thakur Sahib of
Morvi — A1

**1931** **Unwmk.** **Typo.** ***Perf. 12***
**Size: 21½x26½mm**

1 A1 3p red 95 1.10
a. 3p dp bl (error) 6.00
2 A1 ½a dp bl 1.50 1.25
3 A1 1a red brn 2.00 2.50
4 A1 2a yel brn 4.00 4.75

Nos. 1-4 and 1a were printed in two blocks of four, with stamps 5½mm. apart, and perforated on four sides. Nos. 1 and 2 were also printed in blocks of four, with stamps 10mm. apart, and perforated on two or three sides.

A2 A3

**1932** **Size: 21x25½mm** ***Perf. 11***

5 A2 3p rose 35 75
6 A2 6p gray grn 1.25 1.50
7 A2 6p emerald 1.25 2.50
8 A2 1a ultra 1.10 1.65
9 A2 2a violet 7.25 9.00

**1934-48** ***Perf. 14, Rough Perf. 11***

10 A3 3p car rose 24 28
a. 3p red 30 28
11 A3 6p emerald 28 60
a. 6p grn 28 60
12 A3 1a red brn 1.10 1.50
a. 1a brn 1.25 1.75
13 A3 2a violet 1.10 1.50

The 1934 London printing of Nos. 10-13 is perf. 14; the later Morvi Press printing is rough perf. 11.

Morvi stamps became obsolete Feb. 15, 1948.

## NANDGAON

LOCATION — A Feudatory State in the Chhattisgarh States Agency in Central India.
AREA — 871 sq. mi.
POP. — 182,380
CAPITAL — Rajnandgaon

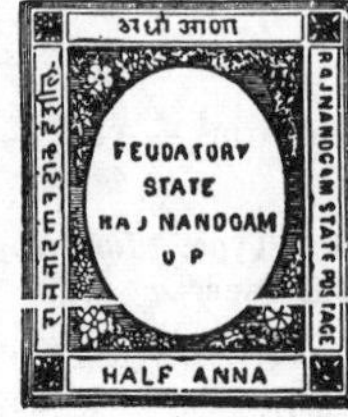

A1 A2

White Paper

**1892, Feb.** **Unwmk.** **Typo.** ***Imperf.***

1 A1 ½a blue 2.50
2 A1 2a rose 12.00

Some authorities claim that No. 2 was a revenue stamp.

**1893**

4 A2 ½a green 9.00
5 A2 2a rose 10.50

Same Redrawn

**1894**

6 A2 ½a yellow green 13.00 9.50
7 A2 1a rose 30.00 30.00
a. Laid paper 120.00

The redrawn stamps have smaller value characters and wavy lines between the stamps.

### OFFICIAL STAMPS

Regular Issues Handstamped in Violet

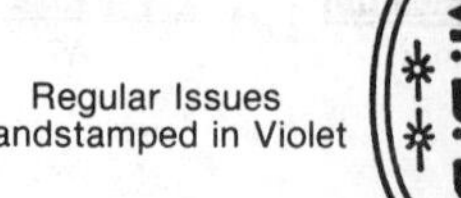


**1893-94** **Unwmk.** ***Imperf***

O1 A1 ½a blue 50.00
O2 A1 2a red 65.00
O3 A2 ½a yellow green 55 55
O4 A2 1a rose 2.00
a. Laid paper 6.50
O5 A2 2a rose 3.00 3.00

Some authorities believe that this handstamp was used as a control mark, rather than to indicate a stamp for official mail.

*The 1 anna has been reprinted in brown and in blue.*

Nandgaon stamps became obsolete in July, 1895.

## NOWANUGGUR
## (Navanagar)

LOCATION — A Feudatory State in the Kathiawar Agency, Western India.
AREA — 3,791 sq. mi.
POP. — 402,192
CAPITAL — Navanagar

Stamps of Nowanuggur were superseded by those of India.

6 Dokra = 1 Anna
16 Annas = 1 Rupee

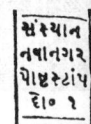

Kandjar (Indian Dagger) — A1

સંસ્થાન
નવાનગર
પોષ્ટસ્ટાંપ
દો॰ ૧

A2

**1877** **Unwmk.** **Typo.** ***Imperf.***
**Laid Paper**

1 A1 1d dl bl 50 10.00
a. 1d ultra 50 1.50
b. Tete beche pair 1,150.

***Perf. 12½***

2 A1 1d slate 65.00 65.00
a. Tete beche pair 1,650.
b. Wove paper

**1877-88** ***Imperf.***
**Wove Paper**

3 A2 1d *red vio* 45 90
a. 1d *rose* 45 90
b. Characters at beginning of 3rd line read "4102" instead of "418"
4 A2 2d *green* 60 90
a. 2d *bl grn* 75 1.20
b. "4102" instead of "418"
5 A2 3d *yellow* 1.10 1.50
a. 3d *org yel* 1.20 1.75
b. "4102" instead of "418"
c. Laid paper 32.50
d. 2d *yel* (error in sheet of 3d) 325.00

Nos. 3-5 range in width from 14 to 19mm.

Seal of the State — A3

**1893** **Thick Paper** ***Imperf.***

6 A3 1d black 60.00

***Perf. 12***

7 A3 1d black 7.50
8 A3 3d orange 4.50

***Imperf***
**Thin Paper**

9 A3 1d black 50.00
10 A3 2d dk grn 50.00
11 A3 3d orange 42.50

***Perf. 12***

12 A3 1d black 18 30
13 A3 2d green 45 45
14 A3 3d orange 60 60
a. Imperf. vert., pair

Obsolete at end of 1895.

## ORCHHA

LOCATION — A Feudatory State in the Bundelkhand Agency in Central India.
AREA — 2,080 sq. mi.
POP. — 314,661
CAPITAL — Tikamgarh

Seal of Orchha — A1

| 1913-17 | Unwmk. | Litho. | Imperf. |
|---|---|---|---|
| 1 | A1 ¼a ultra ('15) | 18 | 22 |
| 2 | A1 ½a emer ('14) | 20 | 28 |
| a. | Background of arms unshaded | 20.00 | 30.00 |
| 3 | A1 1a car ('14) | 1.65 | 2.25 |
| a. | Background of arms unshaded | 20.00 | |
| 4 | A1 2a brn ('17) | 4.50 | 5.50 |
| 5 | A1 4a org ('14) | 7.50 | 8.25 |
| | *Nos. 1-5 (5)* | 14.03 | 16.50 |

Essays similar to Nos. 2-5 are in different colors.

Maharaja Singh Dev
A2 A3

| 1939-40 | | Perf. 13½, 13½x14. | |
|---|---|---|---|
| 6 | A2 ¼a chocolate | 6 | *8.25* |
| 7 | A2 ½a yel grn | 8 | *6.75* |
| 8 | A2 ¾a ultra | 8 | *11.00* |
| 9 | A2 1a rose red | 12 | *6.75* |
| 10 | A2 1¼a dp bl | 14 | *11.00* |
| 11 | A2 1½a lilac | 14 | *10.00* |
| 12 | A2 2a vermilion | 80 | *8.25* |
| 13 | A2 2½a turq grn | 1.10 | *6.75* |
| 14 | A2 3a dl vio | 1.10 | *9.75* |
| 15 | A2 4a bl gray | 1.65 | *11.00* |
| 16 | A2 8a rose lil | 4.00 | *22.50* |
| 17 | A3 1r sage grn | 6.75 | *32.50* |
| 18 | A3 2r lt vio ('40) | 16.00 | *50.00* |
| 19 | A3 5r yel org ('40) | 55.00 | *135.00* |
| 20 | A3 10r blue | 110.00 | *200.00* |
| | *Nos. 6-20 (15)* | 197.02 | 529.50 |

## POONCH

LOCATION — A Feudatory State in the Kashmir Residency in India.
AREA — 1,627 sq. mi.
POP. — 287,000 (estimated)
CAPITAL — Poonch

Poonch was feudatory to Jammu and Kashmir. Cancellations of Jammu and Kashmir are found on Poonch stamps, which became obsolete in 1894. The stamps are all printed in watercolor and handstamped from single dies. They may be found on various papers, including wove, laid, wove batonne, laid batonne and ribbed, in various colors and tones. Nearly all Poonch stamps exist tete beche and impressed sideways. Issued without gum.

A1

**White Paper**

**Handstamped.**

| 1876 | Unwmk. | Imperf. |
|---|---|---|
| | **Size 22x21 mm** | |
| 1 | A1 6p red | 105.00 |

| 1877 | | |
|---|---|---|
| | **Size 19x17 mm** | |
| 1A | A1 ½a red | 4,500. *1,250.* |

| 1879 | | |
|---|---|---|
| | **Size 21x19 mm** | |
| 1B | A1 ½a red | 650.00 |

A2

A3

A4 A5

A6

**1880-88**

| | White Paper | | |
|---|---|---|---|
| 2 | A2 1p red ('84) | 12.00 | 10.50 |
| 3 | A3 ½a red | 4.75 | 3.00 |
| 4 | A4 1a red | 4.25 | 4.25 |
| 5 | A5 2a red | 10.50 | 10.50 |
| 6 | A6 4a red | 10.50 | |
| | **Yellow Paper** | | |
| 7 | A2 1p red | 1.50 | 1.50 |
| 8 | A3 ½a red | 1.90 | 1.50 |
| 9 | A4 1a red | 3.75 | 3.50 |
| 10 | A5 2a red | 1.90 | 2.75 |
| 11 | A6 4a red | 1.10 | 1.10 |
| | **Blue Paper** | | |
| 12 | A2 1p red | 7.75 | 7.75 |
| 13 | A4 1a red | 2.00 | 2.00 |
| | **Orange Paper** | | |
| 14 | A2 1p red | 30 | 30 |
| 15 | A3 ½a red | 4.75 | 4.75 |
| 16 | A5 2a red | 10.50 | 10.50 |
| 17 | A6 4a red | 6.50 | 6.50 |
| | **Green Paper** | | |
| 18 | A3 ½a red | 5.50 | 5.50 |
| 19 | A4 1a red | 2.75 | 2.75 |
| 20 | A5 2a red | 2.50 | 3.75 |
| 21 | A6 4a red | 10.00 | 12.00 |
| | **Lavender Paper** | | |
| 22 | A2 1p red | 24.00 | 24.00 |
| 23 | A4 1a red | 12.00 | 12.00 |
| 24 | A5 2a red | 90 | 90 |

### OFFICIAL STAMPS

White Paper

**Handstamped**

| 1888 | Unwmk. | Imperf. | |
|---|---|---|---|
| O1 | A2 1p black | 35 | 60 |
| O2 | A3 ½a black | 50 | 75 |
| O3 | A4 1a black | 75 | 75 |
| O4 | A5 2a black | 1.00 | 1.00 |
| O5 | A6 4a black | 1.50 | 1.50 |

**1890**

| | Yellowish Paper | | |
|---|---|---|---|
| O6 | A2 1p black | 1.10 | |
| O7 | A3 ½a black | 4.25 | 4.25 |
| O8 | A4 1a black | 10.00 | 7.00 |
| O9 | A5 2a black | 3.50 | 3.75 |
| O10 | A6 4a black | 10.00 | |

Obsolete since 1894.

## RAJASTHAN

### (Greater Rajasthan Union)

LOCATION — India
AREA — 128,424 sq. miles
POP. — 13,085,000

The Rajasthan Union was formed in 1947-49 by 14 Indian States, including the stamp-issuing States of Bundi, Jaipur and Kishangarh.

**Catalogue values for all unused stamps in this state are for Never Hinged items.**

Bundi Nos. 43 to 49 Overprinted

a

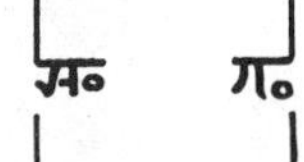


| 1948 | Unwmk. | Perf. 11 |
|---|---|---|
| | **Handstamped in Black, Violet or Blue** | |
| 1 | A8 ¼a dp grn | 1.10 |
| a. | violet overprint | 1.50 |
| 2 | A8 ½a purple | 55 |
| a. | violet overprint | 70 |
| 3 | A8 1a yel grn | 40 |
| 4 | A9 2a red | 2.75 |
| 5 | A9 4a dp org (V) | 2.75 |
| a. | black overprint | 6.75 |
| 6 | A10 8a vio bl | 1.50 |
| 7 | A10 1r choc (Bl) | 22.50 |
| a. | black overprint | |
| b. | violet overprint | 55.00 |
| | *Nos. 1-7 (7)* | 31.55 |
| | **Typo. in Black** | |
| 12 | A9 4a dp org | 1.75 |
| 13 | A10 8a vio bl | 16.00 |
| 14 | A10 1r chocolate | 4.00 |

राजस्थान

Stamps of Jaipur, 1931-47, Overprinted in Blue or Carmine

RAJASTHAN

| 1949 | Center in Black | Perf. 14 | |
|---|---|---|---|
| 15 | A6 ¼a red brn (Bl) | 1.25 | *2.50* |
| 16 | A6 ½a dl vio | 1.25 | *2.50* |
| 17 | A6 ¾a brn org (Bl) | 1.25 | *2.50* |
| 18 | A6 1a blue | 1.50 | *3.25* |
| 19 | A6 2a ocher | 1.50 | *3.25* |
| 20 | A6 2½a rose (Bl) | 1.50 | *3.25* |
| 21 | A6 3a green | 2.00 | *4.00* |
| 22 | A6 4a gray grn | 2.50 | *4.75* |
| 23 | A6 6a blue | 3.25 | *6.50* |
| 24 | A6 8a chocolate | 8.00 | *20.00* |
| 25 | A6 1r bister | 12.00 | *27.50* |
| | *Nos. 15-25 (11)* | 36.00 | 80.00 |

Kishangarh Stamps and Types of 1899-1904 Handstamped Type "a" in Rose

| 1949 | Pin-perf., Rouletted |
|---|---|
| 26 | A3 ½a bl (#18) 25.00 |
| 27 | A4 1a dl lil (#20) 11.00 |
| 28 | A6 4a pale red brn (#21B) 15.00 |
| 29 | A11 8a gray (#25B) 27.50 |
| 30 | A7 1r dl grn (#22) 22.50 |
| 31 | A8 2r brn red (#23) 25.00 |
| 32 | A9 5r red vio (#24) 30.00 |
| | *Nos. 26-32 (7)* 156.00 |

Kishangarh Nos. 28, 31-36 Handstamped Type "a" in Rose or Green

| 1949 | Engr. | Perf. 13½, 12½ |
|---|---|---|
| 33 | A13 ½a chnt (R) | 10.50 |
| 34 | A13 4a dk brn (G) | 13.00 |
| 35 | A13 4a dk brn (R) | 13.00 |
| 36 | A13 8a pur (R) | 13.00 |
| 37 | A13 1r dk grn (R) | 21.00 |
| 38 | A13 2r lem yel (R) | 21.00 |
| 39 | A13 5r pur brn (R) | 25.50 |
| | *Nos. 33-39 (7)* | 117.00 |

Kishangarh Nos. 40-42, 37, 43, 46-48 Handstamped Type "a" in Rose

| 1949 | Typo. | Rouletted | |
|---|---|---|---|
| 40 | A14 ¼a pale bl | 8.00 | 8.00 |
| 41 | A14 ½a green | 8.00 | 8.00 |
| 42 | A14 1a carmine | 7.50 | 7.50 |
| 43 | A14 2 "anna" vio | 7.50 | 7.50 |
| 44 | A14 2 "annas" pur | 7.50 | 7.50 |
| 45 | A14 8a brown | 7.50 | 7.50 |
| 46 | A14 1r rose lil | 9.00 | 9.00 |
| 47 | A14 2r dk grn | 12.00 | 12.00 |
| 48 | A14 5r brown | 32.50 | 32.50 |
| | *Nos. 40-48 (9)* | 99.50 | 99.50 |

Kishangarh Stamps and Types of 1928-29 Handstamped Type "a" in Rose

| 1949 | | Pin-perf | |
|---|---|---|---|
| 49 | A17 ¼a grnsh bl | 13.00 | 13.00 |
| 50 | A17 ½a yel grn | 6.50 | 6.50 |
| 51 | A18 1a car rose | 9.00 | 9.00 |
| 52 | A18 2a red vio | 12.00 | 12.00 |
| 53 | A17 4a yel brn | 2.50 | 2.50 |
| 54 | A17 8a purple | 7.25 | 7.25 |
| 55 | A17 1r dp grn | 7.50 | 7.50 |
| 56 | A17 2r lemon | 24.00 | 24.00 |
| 57 | A17 5r red brn | 25.00 | 25.00 |
| | *Nos. 49-57 (9)* | 106.75 | 106.75 |

Type of Kishangarh 1928-29, Handstamped Type "a" in Rose

| 1949 | Pin-perf |
|---|---|
| 58 | A18 1a dk vio bl |

No. 58 exists imperf.

Rajasthan stamps became obsolete Apr. 1, 1950.

## RAJPEEPLA

### (Rajpipla)

LOCATION — A Feudatory State near Bombay in the Gujarat States Agency in India.
AREA — 1,517 sq. mi.
POP. — 206,086
CAPITAL — Nandod

4 Paisas = 1 Anna

Kandjar (Indian Daggers) — A1

| 1880 | Unwmk. Litho. | Perf. 11, 12½ | |
|---|---|---|---|
| 1 | A1 1pa ultra | 1.00 | 4.75 |

A2

A3

| | | | |
|---|---|---|---|
| 2 | A2 2a green | 6.25 | 6.75 |
| a. | Horiz. pair, imperf. btwn. | 625.00 | 625.00 |
| 3 | A3 4a red | 4.50 | 4.50 |

The stamps of Rajpeepla have been obsolete since 1886.

## SIRMOOR

### (Sirmur)

LOCATION — A Feudatory State in the Punjab District of India.
AREA — 1,046 sq. mi.
POP. — 148,568
CAPITAL — Nahan

A1

Raja Sir Shamsher Prakash — A2

| 1879 | Unwmk. | Perf. 11½. | |
|---|---|---|---|
| | **Wove Paper** | | |
| 1 | A1 1pa green | 6.00 | 6.00 |
| a. | Imperf., pair | | |
| | **Laid Paper** | | |
| 2 | A1 1pa blue | 3.00 | *30.00* |
| a. | Imperf., pair | | |

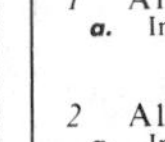

**1885-88 Litho. *Perf. 14 and 14½.***

*3* A2 3p brown 12 12
*4* A2 3p orange 12 8
*5* A2 6p green 60 60
*6* A2 1a blue 45 45
*7* A2 2a carmine 2.00 2.00
*Nos. 3-7 (5)* 3.29 3.25

There are several printings, dies and minor variations of this issue.

A3

Elephant — A4

**1893 *Perf. 11½***

*9* A3 1pa yel grn 30 30
*a.* 1pa dk bl grn 28 28
*10* A3 1pa ultra 48 48
*b.* Imperf., pair 60.00

Nos. 9 and 10 are re-issues, which were available for postage.

The printed perforation, which is a part of the design, is in addition to the regular perforation.

**1895-99 Engr. *Perf. 14***

*11* A4 3p orange 60 18
*12* A4 6p green 90 24
*13* A4 1a dl bl 1.10 30
*14* A4 2a dl red 1.10 45
*15* A4 3a yel grn 2.00 2.00
*16* A4 4a dk grn 2.00 2.00
*17* A4 8a dp bl 5.50 7.50
*18* A4 1r vermilion 7.50 *9.00*
*Nos. 11-18 (8)* 20.70 21.67

Sir Surendar Bikram Prakash — A5

**1899**

*19* A5 3a yel grn 2.75 *6.00*
*20* A5 4a dk grn 3.50 *7.25*
*21* A5 8a blue 4.00 *7.75*
*22* A5 1r vermilion 6.50 *15.00*

**OFFICIAL STAMPS**

Regular Stamps Overprinted

On

S. S.

S.

Black Overprint

**1890-91 Unwmk. *Perf. 14, 14½***

*O1* A2 3p orange 1.40
*O2* A2 6p green 1.40 90
*a.* Double overprint
*b.* Double ovpt., one in red 1,050.
*O3* A2 1a blue 12.00 12.00
*O4* A2 2a carmine 9.00 9.00

**1890-92**

**Red Overprint**

*O5* A2 6p green 4.50 4.00
*O6* A2 1a blue 17.00 9.00

On

S. S.

S.

*O7* A2 6p green 2.50 1.60
*a.* Double overprint
*b.* Inverted overprint
*O8* A2 1a blue 6.00 2.00
*a.* Inverted overprint 200.00
*b.* Double ovpt. 200.00

**1892**

**Black Overprint**

*O9* A2 3p orange 18 18
*a.* Inverted overprint 75.00
*O10* A2 6p green 75 75
*O11* A2 1a blue 3.25 3.25
*a.* Double ovpt. 125.00
*O12* A2 2a carmine 2.50 2.50
*a.* Inverted overprint 125.00 105.00

On

S. S.

S.

**Black Overprint**

*O13* A2 3p orange 3.25 1.50
*a.* Inverted overprint
*O14* A2 6p green 2.75 48
*O15* A2 1a blue 1.90 75
*O16* A2 2a carmine 4.75 4.25

There are several settings of some of these overprints, differing in the sizes and shapes of the letters, the presence or absence of the periods, etc.

The overprints on Nos. O1-O16 are press printed. In addition, nine varieties of handstamped overprints were applied in 1894-96. Most of the handstamps are very similar to the press printed overprints.

Obsolete March 31, 1901.

## SORUTH

(Sorath)
(Junagarh)
(Saurashtra)

LOCATION — A Feudatory State near Bombay in the Western India States Agency in India.
AREA — 3,337 sq. mi.
POP. — 670,719
CAPITAL — Junagarh

The United State of Saurashtra (area 31,885 sq. mi.; population 2,900,000) was formed in 1948 by 217 States, including the stamp-issuing States of Jasdan, Morvi, Nowanuggur and Wadhwan.

Nos. 1-27 were issued without gum.

A1

A2

**Handstamped in Watercolor.**

**1864 Unwmk. *Imperf.***

**Laid Paper**

*1* A1 (1a) *bluish* 360.00 24.00
*a.* Wove paper 80.00
*1B* A1 (1a) *gray* 360.00 24.00

**Wove Paper**

*2* A1 (1a) *cream* 100.00

**1868 Typo. *Imperf.***

**Wove Paper**

*3* A2 1a *yellowish*
*4* A2 1a red, *grn* 1,200.
*5* A2 1a red, *bl* 1,200.
*6* A2 1a *pink* 175.00 42.00
*7* A2 2a *yellow* 1,750.

**Laid Paper**

*8* A2 1a *blue* 25.00 10.00
*a.* Left character, 3rd line, omitted
*9* A2 1a red 20.00 20.00
*a.* Left character, 3rd line, omitted
*10* A2 4a black 105.00 *125.00*
*a.* Left character, 3rd line, omitted

A 1a black on white laid paper exists in type A2.

*In 1890 official imitations of 1a and 4a stamps, type A2, were printed in sheets of 16 and 4. Original sheets have 20 stamps. Four of these imitations are perf. 12, six are imperf.*

A3

A4

**1877-86 Laid Paper *Imperf.***

*11* A3 1a green 15 15
*a.* Printed on both sides 210.00
*12* A4 4a vermilion 75 75
*a.* Printed on both sides 210.00
*13* A4 4a scar, *bluish* 90 90

***Perf. 12***

*14* A3 1a green 18 18
*a.* 1a bl (error) 550.00 550.00
*c.* Imperf., pair 6.50 6.50
*d.* Wove paper 75 75
*e.* As "a," wove paper 550.00 550.00
*f.* As "d," imperf. btwn., pair 10.50 10.50
*15* A3 1a grn, *bluish* 80 80
*a.* Pair, imperf. btwn. 42.50 42.50
*16* A4 4a red 90 90
*a.* 4a car 90 90
*c.* Wove paper 1.75 1.75
*d.* As "c," imperf., pair 12.00 12.00
*17* A4 4a scar, *bluish* 1.50 1.50

Nos. 14d and 16c Surcharged

Three pies. One Anna.
ત્રણ પાઇ. એક આનો.

**1913-14 *Perf. 12***

*18* A3 3p on 1a grn 9 9
*a.* Laid paper 30.00
*b.* Inverted surcharge 20.00
*c.* Imperf., pair
*19* A4 1a on 4a red 1.00 1.00
*a.* Laid paper 5.00 5.00
*b.* Imperf., pair
*c.* Double surcharge 175.00

A5

A6

**1914 *Perf. 12***

*20* A5 3p green 50 50
*a.* Imperf., pair 1.00 1.00
*21* A6 1a rose car 50 60
*a.* Imperf., pair 4.00 4.00
*b.* Laid paper 20.00 15.00

Nawab Mahabat Khan III
A7 A8

**1923-29 Wove Paper *Perf. 12***

*22* A7 3p violet 45 45
*a.* Imperf.
*b.* Laid paper ('29) 75 75
*c.* As "b," imperf. ('29) 1.40 1.40
*d.* As "b," horiz. pair, imperf. between 30.00
*23* A8 1a red 1.50 1.50
*a.* Imperf., pair
*b.* Laid paper 2.00 2.00

Surcharged with New Value.

*27* A8 3p on 1a red 1.50 1.50

Two types of surcharge.

Junagarh City and The Girnar
A9

Gir Lion — A10

Nawab Mahabat Khan III — A11

Kathi Horse
A12

**1929 *Perf. 14***

*30* A9 3p dk grn & blk 1.00 16
*31* A10 ½a dk bl & blk 3.75 14
*32* A11 1a cl & blk 2.25 60
*33* A12 2a org buff & blk 9.00 35
*34* A9 3a car rose & blk 2.50 24
*35* A10 4a dl vio & blk 10.50 28
*36* A12 8a ap grn & blk 12.00 *8.75*
*37* A11 1r dl bl & blk 3.50 *7.00*
*Nos. 30-37 (8)* 44.50 17.52

Type of 1929
Inscribed "Postage and Revenue"

**1937**

*38* A11 1a cl & blk 2.00 48

**Catalogue values for unused stamps in this section, from this point to the end of the section, are for Never Hinged items.**

**United State of Saurashtra.**

A13

Bhavnagar Court Fee Stamp Overprinted in Black "U.S.S. Revenue & Postage Saurashtra."

**1949 Unwmk. Typo. *Perf. 11***

*39* A13 1a dp cl 1.75 1.75
*a.* "POSTAGE" omitted 100.00 100.00
*b.* Double ovpt. 100.00 100.00
*c.* "REVENUE & POSTAGE" omitted 100.00 100.00

Nos. 30, 31 Surcharged in Black or Carmine "POSTAGE & REVENUE ONE ANNA"

**1949-50 *Perf. 14***

*40* A9 1a on 3p dk grn & blk (bl) ('50) 10.00 10.00
*a.* "OSTAGE" 110.00 110.00
*41* A10 1a on ½a dk bl & blk (C) 7.00 1.40
*a.* Double surch. 100.00 100.00

No. 33 Surcharged in Green "Postage & Revenue ONE ANNA"

**1949**

*42* A12 1a on 2a org buff & blk 5.75 2.00

**OFFICIAL STAMPS**

Regular Issue of 1929 Overprinted in Red

a SARKARI

**1929 Unwmk. Perf. 14.**

O1 A9 3p dk grn & blk 10 7
O2 A10 ½a dk bl & blk 40 8
O3 A11 1a cl & blk 12 10
O4 A12 2a org buff & blk 75 10
O5 A9 3a car rose & blk 40 10
O6 A10 4a dl vio & blk 75 12
O7 A12 8a ap grn & blk 1.25 18
O8 A11 1r dl bl & blk 1.90 2.00
*Nos. O1-O8 (8)* 5.67 2.75

Regular Issue of 1929 Overprinted in Red

b **SARKARI**

**1933-49**

O9 A9 3p dk grn & blk ('49) 210.00 4.25
O10 A10 ½a dk bl & blk ('49) 210.00 4.25
O11 A9 3a car rose & blk 9.50 4.50
O12 A10 4a dl vio & blk 22.50 13.00
O13 A12 8a ap grn & blk 22.50 15.00
O14 A11 1r dl bl & blk 25.00 20.00

The 3p is also known with ms. "SARKARI" overprint in carmine.

No. 38 Overprinted Type "a" in Red.

**1938**

O15 A11 1a cl & blk 2.50 50

**Catalogue values for unused stamps in this section, from this point to the end of the section, are for Never Hinged items.**

**United State of Saurashtra.**

No. 41 with Manuscript "Service" in Carmine.

**1949**

O19 A10 1a on ½a dk bl & blk (C) 27.50

No. 42 is also known with carmine ms. "Service" overprint in English or Gujarati.

Nos. O4-O8 and O14 Surcharged "ONE ANNA" in Blue or Black.

**1949**

**Surcharge 2¼mm. high.**

O20 A12 1a on 2a org buff & blk (Bl) 850.00 16.00
O21 A9 1a on 3a car rose & blk 850.00 16.00
O22 A10 1a on 4a dl vio & blk 125.00 15.00
O23 A12 1a on 8a ap grn & blk 125.00 15.00

**Surcharge 4mm. high, Handstamped**

O24 A11 1a on 1r dl bl & blk (#O8) 195.00 10.00
O25 A11 1a on 1r dl bl & blk (#O14) 110.00 19.00

No. 42 Overprinted Type "b" in Carmine.

**1949 Unwmk. Perf. 14**

O26 A12 1a on 2a org buff & blk 20.00 6.75

## TRAVANCORE

LOCATION — A Feudatory State in the Madras States Agency, on the extreme southwest coast of India.
AREA — 7,662 sq. mi.
POP. — 6,070,018 (1941)
CAPITAL — Trivandrum

16 Cash = 1 Chuckram
2 Chuckrams = 1 Anna

Conch Shell (State Seal)
A1 A2

**1888 Unwmk. Typo. Perf. 12**
**Laid Paper**

1 A1 1ch ultra 6.00 4.50
2 A1 2ch org red 5.50 4.75
3 A1 4ch green 22.50 22.50

The frame and details of the central medallion differ slightly on each denomination of type A1.
Laid paper printings of Nos. 1-3, 5-7 in completely different colors are essays.

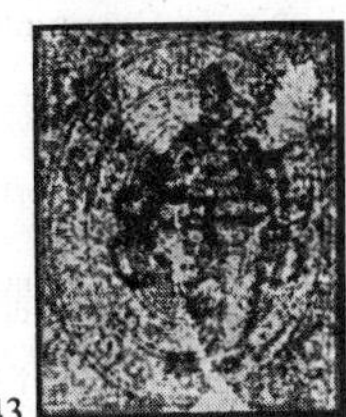

Wmk.43

**1889-99 Wmk. Shell. (43)**
**Wove Paper.**

4 A1 ½ch violet 9 5
5 A1 1ch ultra 9 5
*a.* Vertical pair, imperf. between
6 A1 2ch scarlet 90 10
*a.* Horizontal pair, imperf. between 75.00
7 A1 4ch dk grn 1.25 28

Shades exist for each denomination.

**1901-32**

8 A2 ¾ch blk ('01) 1.25 6
9 A2 ¾ch brt vio ('32) 1.25 5
*a.* Horizontal pair, imperf. between

Surcharged with New Values **1/4**

**1906**

10 A1 ¼ch on ½ch vio 45 5
*a.* Invtd. surch. 35.00 35.00
11 A1 ⅜ch on ½ch vio 20 8
*a.* Pair, one without surcharge
*b.* Inverted surcharge
*c.* Double surch.

A3 A4

**1908-11**

12 A3 4ca rose 9 5
13 A1 6ca red brn ('10) 90 5
*a.* Printed on both sides
14 A4 3ch pur ('11) 75 5

A5 A6

**1916**

15 A5 7ch red vio 1.90 28
16 A6 14ch orange 4.00 2.50

A7 A8

**1920-33**

17 A7 1¼ch claret 1.25 5
18 A7 1½ch lt red ('33) 1.25 5

No. 12 and Type of 1888 Surcharged **1 C**

**1921**

19 A3 1ca on 4ca rose 8 5
*a.* Invtd. surcharge 10.50 6.50
20 A1 5ca on 1ch dl bl (R) 12 5
*a.* Invtd. surcharge 13.00 4.00
*b.* Double surcharge 18.00 13.00

**1921-32**

21 A8 5ca bister 10 5
22 A8 5ca brn ('32) 1.25 5
23 A8 10ca rose 9 5

Sri Padmanabha Shrine at Trivandrum
A9

State Chariot
A10

Maharaja Sir Bala Rama Varma
A11

**1931**

24 A9 6ca emer & blk 28 28
25 A10 10ca ultra & blk 28 28
26 A11 3ch vio & blk 55 55

Nos. 24 to 26 were issued to commemorate the investiture of Sir Bala Rama Varma with full ruling powers.

No. 17 Surcharged **2 C**

27 A7 1ca on 1¼ch cl 10 10
*a.* Inverted surcharge 5.00 5.00
*b.* Double surcharge 16.00 16.00
28 A7 2ca on 1¼ch cl 10 5
*a.* Inverted surcharge 5.00 5.00
*b.* Double surch. 16.00 16.00
*c.* Pair, one without surch. 75.00 75.00

Type of 1932 and No. 23 Surcharged like Nos. 19-20.

29 A8 1ca on 5ca vio brn 10 5
*a.* Inverted surcharge 13.00 12.00
*b.* Double surch. 13.00 13.00
*c.* Pair, one without surch. 55.00
30 A8 2ca on 10ca rose 28 5
*a.* Inverted surcharge 9.00 9.00
*b.* Double surcharge 21.00 21.00

Untouchables Entering Temple and Maharaja — A12

Designs: Different temples and frames.

**1937 Litho. Perf. 11½, 12½**

32 A12 6ca carmine 10 8
33 A12 12ca ultra 15 9
34 A12 1½ch lt grn 15 8
35 A12 3ch purple 32 15

Issued in commemoration of the Temple Entry Bill.

Lake Ashtamudi
A13

A14 A15

Sir Bala Rama Varma — A16

Sri Padmanabha Shrine — A17

View of Cape Comerin
A18

Pachipara Reservoir
A19

***Perf. 11, 12, 12½ or Compound.***

**1939 Litho.**

36 A13 1ch yel grn 10 6
37 A14 1½ch carmine 45 12
*a.* Perf. 13½ 18.00 18.00
38 A15 2ch orange 20 10
39 A16 3ch chocolate 24 8
40 A17 4ch hn brn 32 15
41 A18 7ch lt bl 1.50 1.10
42 A19 14ch turq grn 3.00 2.00
*Nos. 36-42 (7)* 5.81 3.61

Issued in honor of the 27th birthday of Maharaja Sir Bala Rama Varma.

Maharaja Sir Bala Rama Varma and Aruvikara Falls
A20

Maharaja and Marthanda Varma Bridge, Alwaye
A21

**1941 Typo.**

43 A20 6ca vio blk 9 8
44 A21 ¾ch dl brn 30 8

Issued in commemoration of the 29th birthday of the Maharaja, October 20, 1941.

Stamps and Types of 1939-41 Surcharged in Black **2 CASH**

**1943 Wmk. 43 Perf. 11, 12½**

45 A14 2ca on 1½ch car 12 10
46 A21 4ca on ¾ch dl brn 18 8
47 A20 8ca on 6ca red 45 8

Maharaja Sir Bala Rama Varma — A22

**1946 Typo. *Perf. 11, 12***
*48* A22 8ca rose red 1.25 50

No. O54 Overprinted "SPECIAL" Vertically in Orange

**1946 *Perf. 12½***
*49* A20 6ca vio blk 6.50 6.00

## OFFICIAL STAMPS

Nos. O1-O60 were issued without gum.

Regular Issues of 1889-1911 Overprinted in Red or Black

On
S S

**1911 Wmk. 43 *Perf. 12, 12½***
*O1* A1 1ch ind (R) 38 5
a. Invtd. ovpt. 8.75 5.50
b. "nO" for "On" 50.00 50.00
c. Double ovpt. 37.50 37.50
*O2* A1 2ch scarlet 50 5
a. Invtd. overprint 11.00 10.00
*O3* A4 3ch purple 38 5
a. Invtd. overprint 11.00 10.00
b. Double ovpt. 40.00 40.00
*O4* A1 4ch dk grn 50 5
a. Invtd. overprint 12.50 11.00
b. Dbl. overprint 40.00 40.00

Same Overprint on Regular Issues of 1889-1920.

**1918-20**
*O5* A3 4ca rose 10 5
a. Imperf., pair 37.50 37.50
b. Invtd. overprint 12.50 7.50
c. Dbl. overprint 17.50 5.50
*O6* A1 ½ch vio (R) 15 5
a. Invtd. overprint 7.00 3.50
*O7* A7 1¼ch claret 30 5
a. Inverted ovpt. 12.50 7.50
b. Double ovpt. 21.00 17.50

Same Overprint on Regular Issues of 1909-21

**1921**
*O8* A1 6ca red brn 25 15
a. Invtd. overprint 8.75 7.50
*O9* A8 10ca rose 50 5
a. Invtd. overprint 22.50 12.50
b. Double overprint 27.50 17.50

Same Overprint on Regular Issue of 1921.

**1922**
*O10* A8 5ca bister 10 5
a. Invtd. overprint 7.00 3.50

Same Overprint on Regular Issue of 1916

**1925**
*O11* A5 7ch plum 1.10 20
*O12* A6 14ch orange 1.65 20

Same Overprint in Blue on Regular Issues of 1889-1921.

*O13* A3 4ca rose 15.00 1.40
*O14* A8 5ca bister
*O15* A1 6ca red brn 8.50 1.40
*O16* A8 10ca rose 21.00 4.50
*O17* A7 1¼ch claret 24.00 6.50
*O18* A1 4ch dk grn 35.00 9.00

Some authorities question the authenticity of No. O14.

**1930**

**Black Overprint**
*O19* A8 5ca brown 12 5

Regular Issues of 1889-1932 Overprinted in Black or Red

On
S S

**1930-34**
*O20* A3 4ca rose 8.00 6.00
*O21* A8 5ca brown 18.00 13.00
a. Inverted overprint 90.00 90.00
*O22* A1 6ca org brn 8 5
*O23* A8 10ca rose 1.90 24
*O24* A1 ½ch vio ('34) 35 5
*O25* A1 ½ch pur (R) 18 6
*O26* A2 ¾ch blk (R) ('32) 60 8
*O27* A2 ¾ch brt vio ('33) 9 5
*O27B* A1 1ch gray bl (R) ('33) 75 5
*O28* A7 1¼ch claret 1.50 45
*O29* A7 1½ch dl red ('32) 30 5
*O30* A4 3ch pur ('33) 1.50 8
*O31* A4 3ch pur (R) 65 5
*O32* A1 4ch dp grn (R) 1.25 8
*O33* A1 4ch dp grn 2.75 1.40
*O34* A5 7ch maroon 1.75 9
*O35* A6 14ch org ('31) 2.50 40

The overprint on Nos. O22, O26 and O28 is smaller than the illustration. There are two sizes of the overprint on No. O27.

Type of 1921-32 and No. 17 Surcharged and Overprinted

On
S S

**1932**
*O36* A8 6ca on 5ca dk brn 20 12
*O36A* A8 6ca on 5ca bis 75 18
*O37* A8 12ca on 10a rose 35 18
a. New value invtd. 8.50 8.50
*O38* A7 1ch8ca on 1¼ch cl 45 5

Nos. O21, O10, O23 and O28 Surcharged in Black

12 C

*O39* A8 6ca on 5ca dk brn 24 5
a. New value inverted
*O39B* A8 6ca on 5ca bis 60 8
*O40* A8 12ca on 10ca rose 40 5
a. New value invtd. 8.50 8.50
b. "On S S" invtd.
c. Ovpt. & surch. inverted 21.00 21.00
*O41* A7 1ch8ca on 1¼ch cl 60 5
a. New value inverted

Regular Issue of 1889-94 Overprinted

On
S S

**1933**
*O42* A1 ½ch vio (Bk) 1.75 1.25

Regular Issue of 1901 Overprinted in Red

On
S S

**1933**
*O44* A2 ¾ch black 35 5

Regular Issue of 1939 Overprinted in Black

a SERVICE

**1939 *Perf. 11, 12, 12½***
*O45* A13 1ch yel grn 18 6
a. Invtd. ovpt. 15.00 15.00
b. Double ovpt. 15.00 15.00
*O46* A14 1½ch carmine 35 6
a. "SESVICE" 20.00 20.00
*O47* A15 2ch orange 45 8
a. "SESVICE" 21.00 21.00
*O48* A16 3ch chocolate 35 6
a. "SESVICE" 20.00 20.00
*O49* A17 4ch hn brn 75 24
*O50* A18 7ch lt bl 1.75 40
*O51* A19 14ch turq grn 3.00 50
*Nos. O45-O51 (7)* 6.83 1.40

Issued in honor of the 27th birthday of Maharaja Sir Bala Rama Varma.

No. 9 Overprinted

b SERVICE

**1939 Wmk. 43 *Perf. 12.***
*O52* A2 ¾ch violet 1.75 9

No. 13 Overprinted Type "b."

**1941**
*O53* A1 6ca red brn 50 6

Nos. 43-44 Overprinted Type "a."

**1941 *Perf. 12½.***
*O54* A20 6ca vio blk 30 10
*O55* A21 ¾ch dl brn 30 6

Issued in commemoration of the 29th birthday of the Maharaja, October 20, 1941.

No. 18 Overprinted Type "b."

**1945 *Perf. 12***
*O56* A7 1½ch lt red 65 18

Nos. 45-48 Overprinted Type "a."

**1945-49 *Perf. 11, 12***
*O57* A14 2ca on 1½ch car 8 8
*O58* A21 4ca on ¾ch dl brn 35 8
*O59* A20 8ca on 6ca red 24 8
*O60* A22 8ca rose red ('49) 1.25 80
a. Double impression of stamp 30.00 30.00

Travancore stamps became obsolete June 30, 1949.

## TRAVANCORE-COCHIN

LOCATION — Southern India
AREA — 9,155 sq. mi.
POP. — 7,492,000

The United State of Travancore-Cochin was established July 1, 1949.

**Catalogue values for all unused stamps in this state are for Never Hinged items.**

Travancore Stamps of 1939-47 Surcharged in Red or Black

a HALF ANNA
അര അണ

***Perf. 11, 12, 12½***
**1949, July 1 Wmk. 43**
*1* A20 2p on 6ca vio blk (R) 8 8
*2* A22 4p on 8ca rose red 8 8
*3* A13 ½a on 1ch yel grn 8 8
a. Inverted surch. 8.00 8.00
b. "NANA" 32.50 32.50
*4* A15 1a on 2ch org 14 6
*5* A17 2a on 4ch hn brn 28 12
a. Inverted surch. 40.00 40.00
*6* A18 3a on 7ch lt bl 2.25 70
*7* A19 6a on 14ch turq grn 4.00 2.75
*Nos. 1-7 (7)* 6.91 3.87

Cochin Nos. 80, 91 and Types of 1944-46 Surcharged in Black or Carmine

THREE PIES

b

മൂന്ന പൈ

**1949-50 Wmk. 294 *Perf. 11, 13***
*8* A15 3p on 9p ultra 6.75 3.25
*9* A16 3p on 9p ultra 1.10 14
*10* A16 3p on 9p ultra (C) 1.40 14
*11* A16 6p on 9p ultra (C) 2.75 70
*12* A13 6p on 1a3p mag ('50) 95 8
*13* A15 6p on 1a3p mag 95 18
*14* A13 1a on 1a9p ultra (C) 2.75 12
*15* A15 1a on 1a9p ultra (C) 5.50 5
*Nos. 8-15 (8)* 22.15 4.66

The surcharge exists with line of Hindi characters varying from 16½ to 23mm. wide.

Cochin No. 86 Overprinted

U. S. T. C.

**1949**
*15A* A15 1a dp org 7.50 9.25

Conch Shell — A23

View of River — A24

**Wmk. 196**
**1950, Oct. Litho. *Perf. 14***
*16* A23 2p rose red 40 80
*17* A24 4p ultra 55 1.40

Cochin No. 86 and Type of 1948-50 Overprinted in Black

T.-C.

**1950 Wmk. 294 *Perf. 13, 11.***
*18* A15 1a dp org 3.25 2.75
*19* A16 1a dp org 3.00 2.75

No. 18 Surcharged in Black

SIX PIES

*20* A15 6p on 1a dp org 1.25 1.25
*21* A15 9p on 1a dp org 1.25 1.25

## OFFICIAL STAMPS

Travancore Stamps of 1939-46 Surcharged Type "a" in Red or Black and Overprinted

c SERVICE

**1949 Wmk. 43 *Perf. 11, 12, 12½***
*O1* A20 2p on 6ca vio blk (R) 8 5
*O2* A22 4p on 8ca rose red 20 8
*O3* A13 ½a on 1ch yel grn 20 8
*O4* A15 1a on 2ch org 6.75 5.50
*O5* A17 2a on 4ch hn brn 45 25
*O6* A18 3a on 7ch lt bl 55 28
*O7* A19 6a on 14ch turq grn 1.40 80
*Nos. O1-O7 (7)* 9.63 7.04

Cochin Nos. O90-O91 Surcharged Type "b" in Black

**1950 Wmk. 294 *Perf. 11***
*O8* A16 6p on 3p car 55 8
a. Double surcharge 300.00 300.00
*O9* A16 9p on 4p gray grn 55 14

No. O9 exists with Hindi characters varying from 18 to 22mm. wide.

Travancore-Cochin Nos. 14-15 Overprinted "ON C G S"

***Perf. 13***
*O10* A13 1a on 1a9p ultra 70 6
*O11* A15 1a on 1a9p ultra 4.00 2.00

Nos. 2 to 7 Overprinted in Black

d SERVICE

**1949-51 Wmk. 43 *Perf. 11, 12½.***
*O12* A22 4p on 8ca rose red 6 5
*O13* A13 ½a on 1ch yel grn 28 5
*O14* A15 1a on 2ch org 20 18
*O15* A17 2a on 4ch hn brn 70 50
*O16* A18 3a on 7ch lt bl 70 45
*O17* A19 6a on 14ch turq grn 2.25 1.50
*Nos. O12-O17 (6)* 4.19 2.73

Types of 1949 Overprinted Type "d"

**1951 Wmk. 294**
*O18* A13 ½a on 1ch yel grn 18 14
*O19* A15 1a on 2ch org 30 28

Type of 1949 Overprinted Type "c"

**Unwmk.**
*O20* A22 4p on 8ca rose red 1.40 1.10

No. O20 is not from an unwatermarked part of sheet with wmk. 294 but is printed on paper entirely without watermark.

Nos. 1, 3 and 5 Overprinted Type "c"

**Wmk. 294**

| No. | Type | Description | Unused | Used |
|---|---|---|---|---|
| O21 | A13 | ½a on 1ch yel grn | 25 | 20 |
| O22 | A20 | 2p on 6ca vio blk | 12 | 6 |
| O23 | A17 | 2a on 4ch hn brn | 32 | 8 |

No. 9 Overprinted in Black **SERVICE**

**1951**

| No. | Type | Description | Unused | Used |
|---|---|---|---|---|
| O24 | A16 | 3p on 9p ultra | 1.65 | 28 |

## WADHWAN

LOCATION — A Feudatory State in Kathiawar Agency, Western India.
AREA — 242 sq. mi.
POP. — 44,259
CAPITAL — Wadhwan

Coat of Arms — A1

**1888 Litho. Unwmk. *Pin-perf.***

**Thin Paper**

| No. | Type | Description | Unused | Used |
|---|---|---|---|---|
| 1 | A1 | ½p black | 7.50 | |

***Perf. 12½***

| No. | Type | Description | Unused | Used |
|---|---|---|---|---|
| 2 | A1 | ½p black | 5.00 | |

**1889 *Perf. 12 and 12½***

**Thick Paper**

| No. | Type | Description | Unused | Used |
|---|---|---|---|---|
| 3 | A1 | ½p black | 1.75 | |

## IONIAN ISLANDS

LOCATION — A group of seven islands, of which six-Corfu, Paxos Lefkas (Santa Maura), Cephalonia, Ithaca and Zante-are in the Ionian Sea west of Greece, and a seventh-Kythera (Cerigo)-is in the Mediterranean south of Greece.
GOVT. — Former British Protectorate
AREA — 752 sq. mi.
POP. — 251,000 (approx.)

These islands were acquired by Great Britain in 1815 but in 1864 were ceded to Greece on request of the inhabitants. Postage stamps issued under Italian and German occupation, 1941 to 1944, are listed in Vol. III.

10 Oboli = 1 Penny
12 Pence = 1 Shilling

Queen Victoria — A1

**1859 Unwmk. Engr. *Imperf.***

| No. | Type | Description | Unused | Used |
|---|---|---|---|---|
| 1 | A1 | (½p) orange | 50.00 | |

Wmk.138

Wmk.139

**Wmk. "2" (138)**

| No. | Type | Description | Unused | Used |
|---|---|---|---|---|
| 2 | A1 | (1p) blue | 13.00 | |

**Wmk. "1" (139)**

| No. | Type | Description | Unused | Used |
|---|---|---|---|---|
| 3 | A1 | (2p) lake | 10.50 | |

Forged cancellations are plentiful.

## IRAQ

LOCATION — In western Asia, bounded on the north by Syria and Turkey, on the east by Iran, on the south by Saudi Arabia, and on the west by Jordan.
GOVT. — Republic.
AREA — 167,925 sq. mi.
POP. — 12,029,700 (est. 1982).
CAPITAL — Baghdad.

Iraq, formerly Mesopotamia, a province of Turkey, was mandated to Great Britain in 1920. The mandate was terminated in 1932. For earlier issues, see Mesopotamia.

Although an independent state, Iraq is included in the British section in accordance with established philatelic practice.

16 Annas = 1 Rupee.
1000 Fils = 1 Dinar (1932)

**Catalogue values for unused stamps in this country are for Never Hinged items, beginning with Scott 79 in the regular postage section, Scott C1 in the air post section, Scott CO1 in the air post official section, Scott O90 in the officials section, Scott RA1 in the postal tax section, and Scott RAC1 in the air post postal tax section.**

**Issues under British Mandate**

Sunni Mosque — A1

Gufas on the Tigris — A2

Assyrian Winged Bull — A4

Ctesiphon Arch — A5

Motif of Assyrian Origin — A3

Colors of the Dulaim Camel Corps — A6

Golden Shiah Mosque of Kadhimain — A7

Conventionalized Date Palm or "Tree of Life" — A8

**1923-25 Engr. Wmk. 4 *Perf. 12.***

| No. | Type | Description | Unused | Used |
|---|---|---|---|---|
| 1 | A1 | ½a ol grn | 12 | 10 |
| 2 | A2 | 1a brown | 25 | 10 |
| 3 | A3 | 1½a car lake | 18 | 15 |
| 4 | A4 | 2a brn org | 20 | 10 |
| 5 | A5 | 3a dp bl | 20 | 12 |
| 6 | A6 | 4a dl vio | 25 | 18 |
| 7 | A7 | 6a bl grn | 30 | 15 |
| 8 | A6 | 8a ol bis | 50 | 20 |
| 9 | A8 | 1r grn & brn | 2.50 | 70 |
| 10 | A1 | 2r black | 15.00 | 12.50 |
| 11 | A1 | 2r bis ('25) | 7.00 | 1.50 |
| 12 | A6 | 5r orange | 30.00 | 12.00 |
| 13 | A7 | 10r carmine | 65.00 | 20.00 |
| | | *Nos. 1-13 (13)* | 121.50 | 47.80 |

King Faisal I — A9

**1927**

| No. | Type | Description | Unused | Used |
|---|---|---|---|---|
| 14 | A9 | 1r red brn | 4.00 | 1.00 |

King Faisal I
A10 A11

**1931**

| No. | Type | Description | Unused | Used |
|---|---|---|---|---|
| 15 | A10 | ½a green | 15 | 10 |
| 16 | A10 | 1a chestnut | 15 | 6 |
| 17 | A10 | 1½a carmine | 30 | 25 |
| 18 | A10 | 2a orange | 20 | 12 |
| 19 | A10 | 3a lt bl | 20 | 12 |
| 20 | A10 | 4a pur brn | 75 | 60 |
| 21 | A10 | 6a Prus bl | 1.00 | 18 |
| 22 | A10 | 8a dk grn | 2.75 | 30 |
| 23 | A11 | 1r dk brn | 3.00 | 1.25 |
| 24 | A11 | 2r yel brn | 7.50 | 1.25 |
| 25 | A11 | 5r dp org | 40.00 | 25.00 |
| 26 | A11 | 10r red | 75.00 | 75.00 |
| 27 | A9 | 25r violet | 1,200. | 1,500. |
| | | *Nos. 15-27 (13)* | 1,331. | 1,604. |

**Issues of the Kingdom**

Stamps of 1923-31 Surcharged in "Fils" or "Dinars" in Red, Black or Green:

3 Fils ٣ فلس
a

25Fils ٢٥ فلس
b

100Fils ١٠٠ فلس
c

1 Dinar ١ دينار
d

**1932, Apr. 1**

| No. | Type | Description | Unused | Used |
|---|---|---|---|---|
| 28 | A10(a) | 2f on ½a grn (R) | 12 | 10 |
| 29 | A10(a) | 3f on ½a grn | 12 | 10 |
| *a* | | Dbl. surch. | 250.00 | |
| *b* | | Invtd. surch. | 250.00 | |
| 30 | A10(a) | 4f on 1a chnt (G) | 12 | 12 |
| 31 | A10(a) | 5f on 1a chnt | 12 | 10 |
| *a* | | Dble. surch. | 250.00 | |
| *b* | | Invtd. Arabic "5" | 50.00 | 60.00 |
| 32 | A10(a) | 8f on 1½a car | 30 | 25 |
| *a* | | Invtd. surch. | 200.00 | |
| 33 | A10(a) | 10f on 2a org | 20 | 10 |
| 34 | A10(a) | 15f on 3a lt bl | 40 | 25 |
| 35 | A10(a) | 20f on 4a pur brn | 1.50 | 75 |
| 36 | A6(b) | 25f on 4a dl vio | 75 | 75 |
| *a* | | "Flis" for "Fils" | 550.00 | 650.00 |
| *b* | | Invtd. Arabic "5" | 550.00 | 650.00 |
| 37 | A10(a) | 30f on 6a Prus bl | 75 | 75 |
| 38 | A10(a) | 40f on 8a dk grn | 1.50 | 1.50 |
| 39 | A11(c) | 75f on 1r dk brn | 3.00 | 1.50 |
| 40 | A11(c) | 100f on 2r yel brn | 6.00 | 2.00 |
| 41 | A11(c) | 200f on 5r dp org | 20.00 | 12.50 |
| 42 | A11(d) | ½d on 10r red | 75.00 | 50.00 |
| *a* | | Bar in "½" omitted | 675.00 | 750.00 |
| 43 | A9(d) | 1d on 25r vio | 175.00 | 175.00 |
| | | *Nos. 28-43 (16)* | 284.88 | 245.77 |

King Faisal I
A12 A13

A14

Values in "Fils" and "Dinars"

**1932, May 9 Engr.**

| No. | Type | Description | Unused | Used |
|---|---|---|---|---|
| 44 | A12 | 2f ultra | 10 | 8 |
| 45 | A12 | 3f green | 10 | 8 |
| 46 | A12 | 4f vio brn | 12 | 8 |
| 47 | A12 | 5f gray grn | 12 | 6 |
| 48 | A12 | 8f dp red | 15 | 8 |
| 49 | A12 | 10f yellow | 15 | 8 |
| 50 | A12 | 15f dp bl | 1.50 | 8 |
| 51 | A12 | 20f orange | 50 | 18 |
| 52 | A12 | 25f rose lil | 3.00 | 12 |
| 53 | A12 | 30f ol grn | 50 | 12 |
| 54 | A12 | 40f dk vio | 4.00 | 1.00 |
| 55 | A13 | 50f dp brn | 1.00 | 25 |
| 56 | A13 | 75f lt ultra | 3.00 | 1.50 |
| 57 | A13 | 100f dp grn | 5.00 | 35 |
| 58 | A13 | 200f dk red | 12.50 | 75 |
| 59 | A14 | ½d gray bl | 50.00 | 15.00 |
| 60 | A14 | 1d claret | 100.00 | 100.00 |
| | | *Nos. 44-60 (17)* | 181.74 | 119.81 |

A15

A16

King Ghazi — A17

**1934-38 Unwmk.**

| No. | Type | Description | Unused | Used |
|---|---|---|---|---|
| 61 | A15 | 1f pur ('38) | 15 | 15 |
| 62 | A15 | 2f ultra | 6 | 6 |
| 63 | A15 | 3f green | 8 | 6 |
| 64 | A15 | 4f pur brn | 10 | 6 |
| 65 | A15 | 5f gray grn | 10 | 6 |
| 66 | A15 | 8f dp red | 18 | 6 |
| 67 | A15 | 10f yellow | 20 | 8 |
| 68 | A15 | 15f dp bl | 20 | 8 |
| 69 | A15 | 20f orange | 25 | 8 |
| 70 | A15 | 25f brn vio | 50 | 25 |
| 71 | A15 | 30f ol grn | 50 | 15 |
| 72 | A15 | 40f dk vio | 75 | 20 |
| 73 | A16 | 50f dp brn | 80 | 20 |
| 74 | A16 | 75f ultra | 1.10 | 30 |
| 75 | A16 | 100f dp grn | 1.75 | 35 |
| 76 | A16 | 200f dk red | 3.75 | 60 |
| 77 | A17 | ½d gray bl | 12.50 | 7.50 |
| 78 | A17 | 1d claret | 25.00 | 10.00 |
| | | *Nos. 61-78 (18)* | 47.97 | 20.24 |

**Catalogue values for unused stamps in this section, from this point to the end of the section, are for Never Hinged items.**

Sitt Zubaidah Mosque — A18

Mausoleum of King Faisal I — A19

Lion of Babylon A20

Malwiye of Samarra (Spiral Tower) A21

Oil Wells — A22

Mosque of the Golden Dome, Samarra — A23

***Perf. 14, 13½, 12½, 12x13½, 13½x12, 14x13½***

**1941-42** **Engr.**

| No. | Type | Description | Unused | Used |
|---|---|---|---|---|
| *79* | A18 | 1f dk vio ('42) | 6 | 6 |
| *80* | A18 | 2f choc ('42) | 6 | 6 |
| *81* | A19 | 3f brt grn ('42) | 6 | 6 |
| *82* | A19 | 4f pur ('42) | 8 | 8 |
| *83* | A19 | 5f dk car rose ('42) | 10 | 10 |
| *84* | A20 | 8f carmine | 40 | 25 |
| *85* | A20 | 8f ocher ('42) | 10 | 6 |
| *86* | A20 | 10f ocher | 8.00 | 40 |
| *87* | A20 | 10f car ('42) | 12 | 10 |
| *88* | A20 | 15f dl bl | 50 | 20 |
| *89* | A20 | 15f blk ('42) | 12 | 12 |
| *90* | A20 | 20f black | 3.00 | 45 |
| *91* | A20 | 20f dl bl ('42) | 15 | 10 |
| *92* | A21 | 25f dk vio | 20 | 20 |
| *93* | A21 | 30f dp org | 20 | 20 |
| *94* | A21 | 40f brn org | 2.00 | 30 |
| *95* | A21 | 40f chnt ('42) | 75 | 15 |
| *96* | A21 | 50f ultra | 40 | 20 |
| *97* | A21 | 75f rose vio | 60 | 25 |
| *98* | A22 | 100f ol grn ('42) | 1.00 | 30 |
| *99* | A22 | 200f dp org ('42) | 4.00 | 65 |
| *100* | A23 | ½d lt bl, perf. 12x13½ ('42) | 7.00 | 1.00 |
| *a* | | Perf. 14 | 6.00 | 2.50 |
| *101* | A23 | 1d grnsh bl ('42) | 15.00 | 6.50 |
| | | *Nos. 79-101 (23)* | 43.90 | 11.79 |

Nos. 92-95 measure 17¾x21½mm, Nos. 96-97 measure 21x24mm.

King Faisal II
A24 A25

**Photo.; Frame Litho.**

**1942** ***Perf. 13 x 13½.***

| No. | Type | Description | Unused | Used |
|---|---|---|---|---|
| *102* | A24 | 1f vio & brn | 6 | 5 |
| *103* | A24 | 2f dk bl & brn | 6 | 6 |
| *104* | A24 | 3f lt grn & brn | 6 | 6 |
| *105* | A24 | 4f dl brn & brn | 8 | 6 |
| *106* | A24 | 5f sage grn & brn | 8 | 8 |
| *107* | A24 | 6f red org & brn | 10 | 8 |
| *108* | A24 | 10f dl rose red & lt brn | 15 | 8 |
| *109* | A24 | 12f yel grn & brn | 18 | 8 |
| | | *Nos. 102-109 (8)* | 77 | 55 |

***Perf. 11½x12***

**1948, Jan. 15** **Engr.** **Unwmk.**

**Size: 17¾x20½mm**

| No. | Type | Description | Unused | Used |
|---|---|---|---|---|
| *110* | A25 | 1f slate | 5 | 5 |
| *111* | A25 | 2f sepia | 5 | 5 |
| *112* | A25 | 3f emerald | 5 | 5 |
| *113* | A25 | 4f purple | 6 | 5 |
| *114* | A25 | 5f rose lake | 6 | 5 |
| *115* | A25 | 6f plum | 6 | 5 |
| *116* | A25 | 8f ocher | 1.50 | 7 |
| *117* | A25 | 10f rose red | 8 | 6 |
| *118* | A25 | 12f dk ol | 10 | 7 |
| *119* | A25 | 15f black | 1.50 | 8 |
| *120* | A25 | 20f blue | 12 | 8 |
| *121* | A25 | 25f rose vio | 15 | 10 |
| *122* | A25 | 30f red org | 18 | 8 |
| *123* | A25 | 40f org brn | 25 | 10 |

***Perf. 12x11½***

**Size: 22x27½mm**

| No. | Type | Description | Unused | Used |
|---|---|---|---|---|
| *124* | A25 | 60f dp bl | 75 | 12 |
| *125* | A25 | 75f lil rose | 1.25 | 25 |
| *126* | A25 | 100f ol grn | 2.00 | 35 |
| *127* | A25 | 200f dp org | 3.00 | 45 |
| *128* | A25 | ½d blue | 10.00 | 2.00 |
| *129* | A25 | 1d green | 25.00 | 10.00 |
| | | *Nos. 110-129 (20)* | 46.21 | 14.11 |

Sheets of 6 exist, perforated and imperforate, containing Nos. 112, 117, 120 and 125-127, with arms and Arabic inscription in blue green in upper and lower margins. Value each, $25.

See Nos. 133-138.

Post Rider and King Ghazi — A26

Designs: 40f, Equestrian statue & Faisal I. 50f, UPU symbols & Faisal II.

**1949, Nov. 1** ***Perf. 13x13½***

| No. | Type | Description | Unused | Used |
|---|---|---|---|---|
| *130* | A26 | 20f blue | 40 | 25 |
| *131* | A26 | 40f red org | 80 | 25 |
| *132* | A26 | 50f purple | 1.50 | 50 |

75th anniv. of the UPU.

Type of 1948.

**1950-51** **Unwmk.** ***Perf. 11½x12.***

**Size: 17¾x20½mm.**

| No. | Type | Description | Unused | Used |
|---|---|---|---|---|
| *133* | A25 | 3f rose lake | 3.00 | 25 |
| *134* | A25 | 5f emerald | 5.00 | 40 |
| *135* | A25 | 14f dk ol ('50) | 55 | 12 |
| *136* | A25 | 16f rose red | 2.00 | 40 |
| *137* | A25 | 28f blue | 1.00 | 40 |

***Perf. 12 x 11½.***

**Size: 22x27½mm.**

| No. | Type | Description | Unused | Used |
|---|---|---|---|---|
| *138* | A25 | 50f dp bl ('50) | 1.50 | 50 |
| | | *Nos. 133-138 (6)* | 13.05 | 2.07 |

King Faisal II
A27 A28

**1953, May 2** **Engr.** ***Perf. 12***

| No. | Type | Description | Unused | Used |
|---|---|---|---|---|
| *139* | A27 | 3f dp rose car | 25 | 8 |
| *140* | A27 | 14f olive | 50 | 12 |
| *141* | A27 | 28f blue | 1.00 | 30 |
| *b* | | Souvenir sheet | 60.00 | 40.00 |

Issued to commemorate the coronation of King Faisal II, May 2, 1953.

No. 141b measures 134 x 138 mm., and coutains one each of Nos. 139-141 with crown, flags and palm trees in color and black inscriptions.

**1954-57** ***Perf. 11½x12***

**Size: 18x20½mm.**

| No. | Type | Description | Unused | Used |
|---|---|---|---|---|
| *141A* | A28 | 1f bl ('56) | 15 | 5 |
| *142* | A28 | 2f chocolate | 8 | 5 |
| *143* | A28 | 3f rose lake | 8 | 5 |
| *144* | A28 | 4f violet | 8 | 5 |
| *145* | A28 | 5f emerald | 10 | 5 |
| *146* | A28 | 6f plum | 15 | 5 |
| *147* | A28 | 8f ocher | 12 | 5 |
| *148* | A28 | 10f blue | 12 | 5 |
| *149* | A28 | 15f black | 12 | 6 |
| *149A* | A28 | 16f brt rose ('57) | 2.25 | 1.00 |
| *150* | A28 | 20f olive | 20 | 8 |
| *151* | A28 | 25f rose vio ('55) | 35 | 8 |
| *152* | A28 | 30f ver ('55) | 50 | 10 |
| *153* | A28 | 40f org brn | 30 | 12 |

**Size: 22x27½mm.**

| No. | Type | Description | Unused | Used |
|---|---|---|---|---|
| *154* | A28 | 50f blue | 75 | 15 |
| *155* | A28 | 75f pink | 1.25 | 35 |
| *156* | A28 | 100f ol grn | 1.50 | 75 |
| *157* | A28 | 200f orange | 6.00 | 1.00 |
| | | *Nos. 141A-157 (18)* | 14.10 | 4.09 |

No. 143, 148 and 137 Overprinted in Black

الغاء المعاهدة
٦/٤/٥٥

**1955, Apr. 6** ***Perf. 11½x12***

| No. | Type | Description | Unused | Used |
|---|---|---|---|---|
| *158* | A28 | 3f rose lake | 10 | 8 |
| *159* | A28 | 10f blue | 25 | 15 |
| *160* | A25 | 28f blue | 45 | 30 |

Abrogation of Anglo-Iraq treaty of 1930.

King Faisal II — A29

**1955, Nov. 26** ***Perf. 13½x13***

| No. | Type | Description | Unused | Used |
|---|---|---|---|---|
| *161* | A29 | 3f rose lake | 15 | 8 |
| *162* | A29 | 10f lt ultra | 20 | 15 |
| *163* | A29 | 28f blue | 55 | 45 |

Issued to commemorate the 6th Arab Engineers' Conference, Baghdad, 1955.

Faisal II and Globe — A30

**1956, Mar. 3** ***Perf. 13x13½***

| No. | Type | Description | Unused | Used |
|---|---|---|---|---|
| *164* | A30 | 3f rose lake | 10 | 5 |
| *165* | A30 | 10f lt ultra | 25 | 10 |
| *166* | A30 | 28f blue | 50 | 20 |

Issued to commemorate the Arab Postal Conference, Baghdad, March 3, 1956.

Mechanical Loom A31

Designs: 3f, Dam. 5f, Modern city development. 10f, Pipeline. 40f, Tigris Bridge.

**1957, Apr. 8** **Photo.** ***Perf. 11½***

**Granite Paper**

| No. | Type | Description | Unused | Used |
|---|---|---|---|---|
| *167* | A31 | 1f Prus bl & org yel | 8 | 6 |
| *168* | A31 | 3f multi | 8 | 6 |
| *169* | A31 | 5f multi | 8 | 6 |
| *170* | A31 | 10f lt bl, ocher & red | 28 | 12 |
| *171* | A31 | 40f lt bl, blk & ocher | 60 | 15 |
| | | *Nos. 167-171 (5)* | 1.12 | 45 |

Issued to publicize Development Week, 1957. See Nos. 185-187.

Fair Emblem — A32

**1957, June 1** **Unwmk.**

**Granite Paper.**

| No. | Type | Description | Unused | Used |
|---|---|---|---|---|
| *172* | A32 | 10f brn & buff | 25 | 15 |

Issued to publicize the Agricultural and Industrial Exhibition, Baghdad, June 1.

No. 166 Overprinted in Red

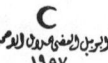

C
اليوبيل الفضي للهلال الاحمر
١٩٥٧

**1957, Nov. 14** ***Perf. 13x13½***

| No. | Type | Description | Unused | Used |
|---|---|---|---|---|
| *173* | A30 | 28f blue | 1.00 | 1.00 |
| *a* | | Dbl. ovpt. | 200.00 | 225.00 |

Issued to commemorate the silver jubilee Iraqi Red Crescent Soc., 25th anniv.

King Faisal II — A33

***Perf. 11½x12***

**1957-58** **Unwmk.** **Engr.**

| No. | Type | Description | Unused | Used |
|---|---|---|---|---|
| *174* | A33 | 1f blue | 10 | 15 |
| *175* | A33 | 2f chocolate | 10 | 15 |
| *176* | A33 | 3f dk car ('57) | 10 | 15 |
| *177* | A33 | 4f dl vio | 10 | 15 |
| *177A* | A33 | 5f emerald | 1.00 | 1.50 |
| *178* | A33 | 6f plum | 15 | 20 |
| *179* | A33 | 8f ocher | 35 | 30 |
| *180* | A33 | 10f blue | 15 | 15 |
| | | *Nos. 174-180 (8)* | 2.05 | 2.75 |

Higher denominations exist without Republic overprint. They were probably not regularly issued.

See note below No. 225.

Tanks — A34

King Faisal II — A35

Designs: 10f, Marching soldiers. 20f, Artillery and planes.

**1958, Jan. 6** ***Perf. 13x13½***

| No. | Type | Description | Unused | Used |
|---|---|---|---|---|
| *181* | A34 | 8f grn & blk | 30 | 12 |
| *182* | A34 | 10f brn & blk | 40 | 20 |
| *183* | A34 | 20f bl & red brn | 50 | 15 |
| *184* | A35 | 30f car & pur | 80 | 30 |

Issued for Army Day, Jan. 6.

Type of 1957.

Designs: 3f, Sugar beet, bag and refining machinery (vert.). 5f, Farm. 10f, Dervendi Khan dam.

**1958, Apr. 26** **Photo.** ***Perf. 11½***

**Granite Paper**

| No. | Type | Description | Unused | Used |
|---|---|---|---|---|
| *185* | A31 | 3f gray vio, grn & lt gray | 12 | 10 |
| *186* | A31 | 5f multi | 18 | 15 |
| *187* | A31 | 10f multi | 35 | 25 |

Issued to publicize Development Week, 1958.

## Republic

Stamps of 1948-51 Overprinted

الجمهورية
العراقية

***Perf. 11½x12, 12x11½***

**1958** **Engr.** **Unwmk.**

**Size: 17¾x20½mm.**

| No. | Type | Description | Unused | Used |
|---|---|---|---|---|
| *188* | A25 | 12f dk ol | 20 | 10 |
| *189* | A25 | 14f olive | 30 | 20 |
| *190* | A25 | 16f rose red | 4.50 | 2.25 |
| *191* | A25 | 28f blue | 1.25 | 45 |

**Size: 22x27½mm.**

| No. | Type | Description | Unused | Used |
|---|---|---|---|---|
| *192* | A25 | 60f dp bl | 1.65 | 45 |
| *193* | A25 | ½d blue | 12.50 | 3.25 |
| *194* | A25 | 1d green | 27.50 | 11.00 |
| | | *Nos. 188-194 (7)* | 47.90 | 17.70 |

Other denominations of type A25 exist with this overprint, but these were probably not regularly issued.

Same Overprint on Stamps of 1954-57.

**Size: 18x20½mm.**

| No. | Type | Description | Unused | Used |
|---|---|---|---|---|
| *195* | A28 | 1f blue | 6 | 6 |
| *196* | A28 | 2f chocolate | 6 | 6 |
| *196A* | A28 | 4f violet | 15 | 15 |
| *196B* | A28 | 5f emerald | 18 | 18 |
| *197* | A28 | 6f plum | 18 | 10 |
| *198* | A28 | 8f ocher | 25 | 25 |
| *199* | A28 | 10f blue | 30 | 10 |

*200* A28 15f black 35 15
*201* A28 16f brt rose 1.40 35
*202* A28 20f olive 50 50
*203* A28 25f rose vio 30 18
*204* A28 30f vermilion 50 25
*205* A28 40f org brn 60 20

**Size: 22½x27½mm.**

*206* A28 50f blue 3.50 2.00
*207* A28 75f pink 2.00 1.50
*208* A28 100f ol grn 2.75 2.00
*209* A28 200f orange 9.00 4.00
*Nos. 195-209 (17)* 22.08 12.03

The lines of this overprint are found transposed on Nos. 195, 196 and 199.

Same Overprint on Stamps and Type of 1957-58

**Size: 18 x 20mm.**

*210* A33 1f blue 6 6
*211* A33 2f chocolate 10 10
*212* A33 3f dk car 20 20
*213* A33 4f dl vio 10 8
*214* A33 5f emerald 10 8
*215* A33 6f plum 15 10
*216* A33 8f ocher 15 10
*217* A33 10f blue 20 12
*218* A33 20f olive 20 10
*219* A33 25f rose vio 60 60
*220* A33 30f vermilion 75 15
*221* A33 40f org brn 2.50 1.00

**Size: 22x27½mm.**

*222* A33 50f rose vio 2.00 50
*223* A33 75f olive 5.00 1.00
*224* A33 100f orange 4.00 1.00
*225* A33 200f blue 7.00 1.50
*Nos. 210-225 (16)* 23.11 6.69

Nos. 218-225 were not issued without the overprint.

The lines of this overprint are found transposed on Nos. 210 and 214.

Many errors of overprint exist of Nos. 188-226.

**Same Overprint on No. 78.**

***Perf. 12***

*226* A17 1d claret 22.50 18.00

No. 163 Surcharged in Red

الجمهورية العراقية
المؤتمر الرابع للمحامين العرب
بغداد ١٩٥٨
10 FILS ١٠ فلوس

**1958, Nov. 26** ***Perf. 13x13½***
*227* A29 10f on 28f bl 75 25

Issued to commemorate the Arab Lawyers' Conference, Baghdad, Nov. 26.

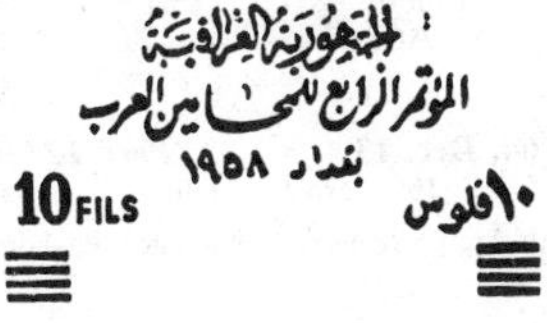
Soldier and Flag — A36

**1959, Jan. 6** **Photo.** ***Perf. 11½***
*228* A36 3f brt bl 8 6
*229* A36 10f ol grn 15 10
*230* A36 40f purple 1.00 35

Issued for Army Day, Jan. 6.

Orange Tree A37

Emblem of Republic A38

**1959, Mar. 21** **Unwmk.** ***Perf. 11½***
*231* A37 10f grn, dk grn & org 50 10

Issued for Arbor Day.

**Litho. and Photo.**

**1959-60 Granite Paper** ***Perf. 11½***

**Emblem in Gold, Red and Blue; Blue Inscriptions.**

*232* A38 1f gray 5 5
*233* A38 2f salmon 5 5
*234* A38 3f pale vio 5 5
*235* A38 4f brt yel 5 5
*236* A38 5f lt bl 6 5
*237* A38 10f brt pink 8 5
*238* A38 15f lt grn 12 6
*239* A38 20f bis brn 15 8
*240* A38 30f lt gray 20 10
*241* A38 40f org yel 25 12
*242* A38 50f yel grn 2.25 15
*243* A38 75f pale grn ('60) 75 20
*244* A38 100f org ('60) 1.75 30
*245* A38 200f lil ('60) 2.75 60
*246* A38 500f bis ('60) 9.00 1.75
*247* A38 1d brt grn ('60) 9.00 3.50
*Nos. 232-247 (16)* 26.56 7.16

See Nos. 305A-305B.

Worker and Buildings — A39

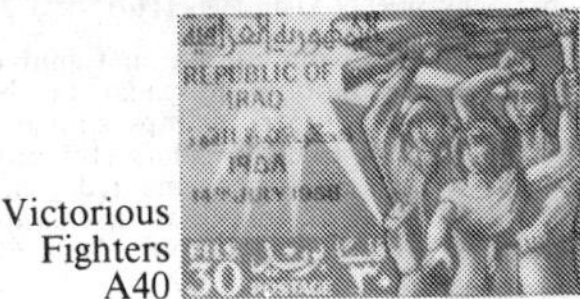
Victorious Fighters A40

***Perf. 12½x13, 13x12½***

**1959, July 14** **Photo.**
*248* A39 10f ocher & bl 35 20
*249* A40 30f ocher & emer 1.00 50

1st anniv. of the Revolution of July 14 (1958), which overthrew the kingdom.

Harvest — A41

**1959, July 14** ***Perf. 11½***
*250* A41 10f lt grn & dk grn 25 10

No. 166 Surcharged in Dark Red

الجمهورية العراقية
يوم الطفل العالمي
١ حزيران ١٩٥٩
10 FILS ١٠ فلوس

**1959, June 1** **Engr.** ***Perf. 13x13½***
*251* A30 10f on 28f bl 50 35

Issued for Children's Day, 1959.

No. 237 Overprinted

اسبوع الصحة والنظافة

**Litho. and Photo.**

**1959, Oct. 23** ***Perf. 11½***
*252* A38 10f brt pink, gold, red & bl 75 35

Health and Sanitation Week.

Abdul Karim Kassem and Army Band — A42

Designs (Abdul Karim Kassem and): 16f, Field maneuvers (horiz.). 30f, Antiaircraft. 40f, Troops at attention, flag and bugler. 60f, Fighters and flag (horiz.).

**1960, Jan. 6** **Photo.** ***Perf. 11½***
*253* A42 10f bl, grn & mar 15 8
*254* A42 16f brt bl & red 50 12
*255* A42 30f ol grn, yel & brn 50 20
*256* A42 40f dp vio & buff 70 25
*257* A42 60f dk brn & buff 1.50 40
*Nos. 253-257 (5)* 3.35 1.05

Issued for Army Day, Jan. 6.

Prime Minister Abdul Karim Kassem — A43

Maroof el Rasafi — A44

**1960, Feb. 1** **Engr.** ***Perf. 12½***
*258* A43 10f lilac 35 6
*259* A43 30f emerald 70 18

Issued to honor Prime Minister Kassem on his recovery from an assassination attempt.

**1960, May 10** **Photo.** ***Perf. 13½x13***
*260* A44 10f mar & blk 75 75
*a* Invtd. ovpt. 75.00 60.00

Exists without overprint.

Symbol of the Republic A45

Unknown Soldier's Tomb and Kassem with Freedom Torch A46

**1960, July 14** ***Perf. 11½***
*261* A45 6f ol grn, red & gold 8 5
*262* A46 10f grn, bl & red 10 6
*263* A46 16f vio, bl & red 12 10
*264* A45 18f ultra, red & gold 18 15
*265* A45 30f brn, red & gold 30 20
*266* A46 60f dk brn, bl & red 1.00 40
*Nos. 261-266 (6)* 1.78 96

2nd anniv. of the July 14, 1958, revolution.

Gen. Kassem and Marching Troops — A47

Gen. Kassem and Arch — A48

**1961, Jan. 6** ***Perf. 11½***

**Granite Paper**

*267* A47 3f gray ol, emer, yel & gold 5 5
*268* A47 6f pur, emer, yel & gold 5 5
*269* A47 10f sl, emer, yel & gold 6 6
*270* A48 20f bl grn, blk & buff 18 12
*271* A48 30f bis brn, blk & buff 45 20
*272* A48 40f ultra, blk & buff 85 25
*Nos. 267-272 (6)* 1.64 73

Issued for Army Day, Jan. 6.

Gen. Kassem and Children A49

**1961, June 1** **Photo.** **Unwmk.**

**Granite Paper**

*273* A49 3f yel & brn 10 5
*274* A49 6f bl & brn 10 5
*275* A49 10f pink & brn 15 6
*276* A49 30f yel & brn 75 20
*277* A49 50f lt grn & brn 75 35
*Nos. 273-277 (5)* 1.85 71

Issued for World Children's Day.

Gen. Kassem and Flag — A50

Design: 5f, 30f, 40f, Gen. Kassem saluting and flags.

**1961, July 14** ***Perf. 11½***

**Granite Paper**

*278* A50 1f pur, emer, blk & gold 5 5
*279* A50 3f vio, emer, blk & gold 5 5
*280* A50 5f multi 5 5
*281* A50 6f ultra, emer, blk & gold 5 5
*282* A50 10f car rose, emer, blk & gold 15 6
*283* A50 30f multi 50 18
*284* A50 40f multi 75 25
*285* A50 50f yel, emer, blk & gold 35 30
*286* A50 100f bl, emer, blk & gold 5.00 2.00
*Nos. 278-286 (9)* 6.95 2.99

3rd anniv. of the July 14, 1958, revolution.

Gen. Kassem and Flag — A51

Gen. Kassem and Symbol of Republic A52

***Perf. 11½***

**1962, Jan. 6** **Unwmk.** **Photo.**

**Granite Paper**

*287* A51 1f multi 5 5
*288* A51 3f multi 5 5
*289* A51 6f multi 5 5
*290* A52 10f blk, lil & gold 10 6
*291* A52 30f blk, org & gold 45 18
*292* A52 50f blk, pale grn & gold 85 30
*Nos. 287-292 (6)* 1.55 69

Issued for Army Day, Jan. 6.

Nos. 234, 237 and 240 Overprinted

مؤتمر
العالم الاسلامى
بغـــداد
١٣٨١هـ-١٩٦٢م

**Litho. and Photo.**

**1962, May 29** *Perf. 11½*

**Emblem in Gold, Red and Blue; Blue Inscriptions.**

*293* A38 3f pale vio 15 6
*294* A38 10f brt pink 20 10
*295* A38 30f lt gray 80 25

Fifth Islamic Congress.

Hands Across Map of Arabia and North Africa — A53

**1962, July 14** **Photo.**

*296* A53 1f brn, org, grn & gold 5 5
*297* A53 3f brn, yel grn, grn & gold 5 5
*298* A53 6f blk, lt brn, grn & gold 6 6
*299* A53 10f brn, lil, grn & gold 15 6
*300* A53 30f brn, rose, grn & gold 45 20
*301* A53 50f brn, gray, grn & gold 85 35
*Nos. 296-301 (6)* 1.61 77

Issued to commemorate the 4th anniversary of the Revolution of July 14, 1958.

al-Kindi A54

Emblem of Republic A54a

Designs: 3f, Horsemen with standards and trumpets. 10f, Old map of Baghdad and Tigris. 40f, Gen. Kassem, modern building and flag.

*Perf. 14x13½*

**1962, Dec. 1** **Litho.** **Unwmk.**

*302* A54 3f multi 10 5
*303* A54 6f multi 15 5
*304* A54 10f multi 35 8
*305* A54 40f multi 1.00 75

Issued to commemorate the millenary of the Round City of Baghdad and in honor of the 9th century Arab philosopher al-Kindi.

*Perf. 13½x14*

**1962, Dec. 20** **Litho.** **Unwmk.**

*305A* A54a 14f brt grn & blk 1.25 25
*305B* A54a 35f ver & blk 1.75 35

Nos. 305A-305B were originally sold affixed to air letter sheets, obliterating the portrait of King Faisal II. They were issued in sheets for general use in 1966.

Tanks on Parade and Gen. Kassem — A55

Malaria Eradication Emblem — A56

**1963, Jan. 6** **Photo.** *Perf. 11½*

*306* A55 3f blk & yel 5 5
*307* A55 5f brn & plum 5 5
*308* A55 6f blk & lt grn 5 5
*309* A55 10f blk & lt bl 20 8
*310* A55 10f blk & pink 20 8
*311* A55 20f blk & ultra 42 15
*312* A55 40f blk & rose lil 60 25
*313* A55 50f brn & brt ultra 85 40
*Nos. 306-313 (8)* 2.42 1.11

Issued for Army Day, Jan. 6.

**1962, Dec. 31** *Perf. 14*

**Republic Emblem in Red, Blue & Gold**

*314* A56 3f yel grn, blk & dk grn 10 5
*315* A56 10f org, blk & dk bl 20 10
*316* A56 40f lil, blk & bl 50 30

Issued for the World Health Organization drive to eradicate malaria.

Gufas on the Tigris A57

Shepherd and Sheep A58

Designs: 2f, 500f, Spiral tower, Samarra. 4f, 15f, Ram's head harp, Ur. 5f, 75f, Map and Republic emblem. 10f, 50f, Lion of Babylon. 20f, 40f, Baghdad University. 30f, 200f, Kadhimain mosque. 100f, 1d, Winged bull, Khorsabad.

**Engr.; Engr. and Photo. (bicolored)**

**1963, Feb. 16** **Unwmk.** *Perf. 12x11*

*317* A57 1f green 5 5
*318* A57 2f purple 5 5
*319* A57 3f black 5 5
*320* A57 4f blk & yel 5 5
*321* A57 5f lil & lt grn 5 5
*322* A57 10f rose red 10 5
*323* A57 15f brn & buff 25 6
*324* A57 20f vio bl 25 8
*325* A57 30f orange 30 8
*326* A57 40f brt grn 40 8
*327* A57 50f dk brn 4.00 15
*328* A57 75f blk & lt grn 2.00 25
*329* A57 100f brt lil 2.00 25
*330* A57 200f brown 4.00 75
*331* A57 500f blue 7.00 1.75
*332* A57 1d dp cl 10.00 3.50
*Nos. 317-332 (16)* 30.55 7.25

**1963, Mar. 21** **Litho.** *Perf. 13½x14*

Designs: 10f, Man holding sheaf. 20f, Date palm grove.

*333* A58 3f emer & gray 15 20
*334* A58 10f dp brn & lil rose 15 25
*335* A58 20f dk bl & red brn 75 50
*a* Souv. sheet of 3 3.50

Issued for the "Freedom from Hunger" campaign of the U.N. Food and Agriculture Organization. No. 335a contains one each of Nos. 333-335; light and dark brown marginal design and inscription. Size: 173x120mm. Sold for 50f.

No. 335a was overprinted in 1970 in black to commemorate the U.N. 25th anniversary. Denominations on the 3 stamps were obliterated, leaving "Price 50 Fils" in the margin.

Centenary Emblem — A59

Design: 30f, Iraqi Red Crescent Society Headquarters (horiz.).

*Perf. 11x11½, 11½x11*

**1963, Dec. 30** **Photo.**

*336* A59 3f vio & red 10 5
*337* A59 10f gray & red 15 10
*338* A59 30f bl & red 50 20

Centenary of International Red Cross.

Rifle, Helmet and Flag — A60

**1964, Jan. 6** **Unwmk.** *Perf. 11½*

**Granite Paper**

*339* A60 3f brn, bl & emer 15 10
*340* A60 10f brn, pink & emer 25 10
*341* A60 30f brn, yel & emer 50 15

Issued for Army Day, Jan. 6.

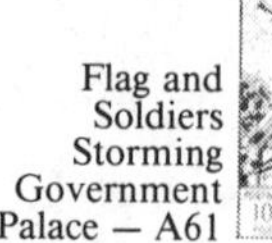

Flag and Soldiers Storming Government Palace — A61

**1964-67** *Perf. 11½*

**Granite Paper**

*342* A61 10f pur, red, grn & blk 15 6
*343* A61 30f red brn, red, grn & blk 40 18
*a* Souv. sheet of 2 5.25 3.50
*b* Souv. sheet of 2 (4th anniv.) ('67) 5.25 3.50

Issued to commemorate the first anniversary of the Revolution of Ramadan 14. No. 343a contains 2 imperf. stamps similar to Nos. 342-343 in changed colors (10f olive, red, grn. & blk.; 30f ultramarine, red, grn. & blk.). Ultramarine marginal inscription. Size: 124x74mm. Sold for 50f. Nos. 342-343, 343a issued Feb. 8, 1964.

No. 343b consists of various block-outs and overprints on No. 343a. It commemorates the 4th anniversary of the Revolution of Ramadan 14. Sold for 70f. Issued Feb. 8, 1967.

Hammurabi and a God from Stele in Louvre — A62

Design: 10f, U.N. emblem and scales.

**1964, June 10** **Litho.** *Perf. 13½*

*344* A62 6f lil & pale grn 15 8
*345* A62 10f org & vio bl 20 12
*346* A62 30f bl & pale grn 80 25

15th anniv. (in 1963) of the Universal Declaration of Human Rights.

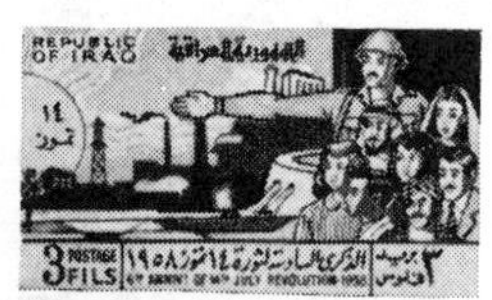

"Industrialization of Iraq" — A63

Soldier Planting New Flag — A64

**1964, July 14** *Perf. 11*

*347* A63 3f gray, org & blk 10 5
*348* A64 10f rose red, blk & emer 15 6
*349* A64 20f rose red, blk & emer 40 15
*350* A63 30f gray, org & blk 80 20

6th anniv. of the July 14, 1958, revolution.

Star and Fighters A65

**1964, Nov. 18** **Photo.** *Perf. 11½*

*351* A65 5f sep & org 15 15
*352* A65 10f lt bl & org 15 15
*353* A65 50f vio & red org 75 30

1st anniv., Revolution of Nov. 18, 1963.

Musician with Lute — A66

*Perf. 13x13½*

**1964, Nov. 28** **Litho.** **Unwmk.**

*354* A66 3f bis & multi 75 50
*355* A66 10f dl grn & multi 75 50
*356* A66 30f dl rose & multi 1.00 75

International Arab Music Conference.

Map of Arab Countries and Emblem A67

**1964, Dec. 13** *Perf. 12½x14*

*357* A67 10f lt grn & rose lil 35 10

9th Arab Engineers' Conference, Baghdad.

Arab Postal Union Emblem A67a

Soldier, Flag and Rising Sun A68

**1964, Dec. 21** **Photo.** *Perf. 11*

*358* A67a 3f sal pink & bl 5 5
*359* A67a 10f brt red lil & brn 10 6
*360* A67a 30f org & bl 75 25

10th anniversary of Permanent Office of Arab Postal Union.

*Perf. 14x12½*

**1965, Jan. 6** **Litho.** **Unwmk.**

*361* A68 5f dl grn & multi 10 6
*362* A68 15f hn brn & multi 15 10
*363* A68 30f blk brn & multi 75 20

Issued for Army Day, Jan. 6.

An imperf. souvenir sheet carries a revised No. 363 with "30 FILS" omitted, and a portrait of Pres. Abdul Salam Arif. Blue marginal background; violet inscriptions including "PRICE 60 FILS." Size: 99x82mm.

Symbols of Agriculture and Industry
A69

**1965, Jan. 8** *Perf. 12½x14*

*364* A69 10f ultra, brn & blk 25 8

Arab Labor Ministers' Conference.

Tanker
A70

**1965, Jan. 30** *Perf. 14*

*365* A70 10f multi 25 8

Inauguration (in 1962) of the deep sea terminal for oil tankers.

Soldier with Flag and Rifle — A71

Tree — A72

**1965, Feb. 8** **Litho.** *Perf. 13½*

*366* A71 10f multi 25 6

Issued to commemorate the second anniversary of the Revolution of Ramadan 14.

**1965, Mar. 6** **Unwmk.** *Perf. 13*

*367* A72 6f multi 10 5
*368* A72 20f multi 75 15

Issued for Tree Week.

Arab Insurance Federation Emblem
A73

Dagger in Map of Palestine
A74

**1965, Mar. 24** **Unwmk.** *Perf. 14*

*369* A73 3f lt bl, vio bl & gold 5 5
*370* A73 10f gray, blk & gold 6 6
*371* A73 30f rose, car & gold 30 30

Arab Federation of Insurance.

**1965, Apr. 9** **Litho.** *Perf. 14x12½*

*372* A74 10f gray & blk 10 6
*373* A74 20f lt brn & dk bl 25 12

Deir Yassin massacre, Apr. 9, 1948.

Smallpox Attacking People — A75

**1965, Apr. 30** **Litho.** *Perf. 14*

*374* A75 3f multi 15 15
*375* A75 10f multi 25 15
*376* A75 20f multi 75 25

World Heath Organization's fight against smallpox. Exist imperf. Value $2.

ITU Emblem, Old and New Telecommunication Equipment. — A76

**1965, May 17** *Perf. 14, Imperf.*

*377* A76 10f multi 30 18
*378* A76 20f multi 75 15
*a* Souv. sheet of 2 5.25 6.00

Issued to commemorate the centenary of the International Telecommunication Union. No. 378a contains one each of Nos. 377-378: light blue margin with black and red inscription. Size: 138x95mm. Exists imperf. Sold for 40f.

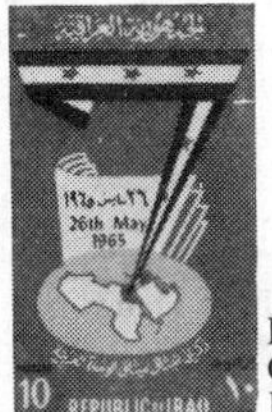

Map of Arab Countries and Banner — A77

**1965, May 26** **Litho.** *Perf. 14x12½*

*379* A77 10f multi 30 15

Issued to commemorate the anniversary of the treaty with the United Arab Republic.

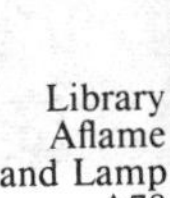

Library Aflame and Lamp
A78

**1965, June** **Photo.** *Perf. 11*

*380* A78 5f blk, grn & red 25 5
*381* A78 10f blk, grn & red 40 6

Issued to commemorate the burning of the Library of Algiers, June 2, 1962.

Revolutionist with Torch, Cannon and Flames — A79

**1965, June 30** **Litho.** *Perf. 13*

*382* A79 5f multi 15 5
*383* A79 10f multi 20 6

45th anniversary, Revolution of 1920.

Mosque — A80

**1965, July 12** **Photo.** *Perf. 12*

*384* A80 10f multi 25 10

Issued in honor of the prophet Mohammed's birthday. A souvenir sheet contains one imperf. stamp similar to No. 384 with blue marginal ornaments and inscription. Sold for 50f. Size: 110x75mm. Value $5

Factories and Grain — A81

Arab Fair Emblem — A82

**1965, July 14** **Litho.** *Perf. 13*

*385* A81 10f multi 15 6

Issued to commemorate the 7th anniversary of the July 14, 1958, Revolution.

**1965, Oct. 22** **Unwmk.** *Perf. 13*

*386* A82 10f multi 15 6

Second Arab Fair, Baghdad.

Pres. Abdul Salam Mohammed Arif — A83

**1965, Nov. 18** **Photo.** *Perf. 11½*

**Granite Paper**

*387* A83 5f org, buff & dk bl 25 15
*388* A83 10f lt ultra, gray & dk brn 35 15
*389* A83 50f lil, pale pink & sl blk 1.50 60

Issued to commemorate the second anniversary of the Revolution of Nov. 18, 1963.

Census Chart and Adding Machine — A84

**1965, Nov. 29** **Litho.** *Perf. 13*

*390* A84 3f gray & plum 30 6
*391* A84 5f brn red & brn 40 6
*392* A84 15f ol bis & dl bl 80 12

Issued to publicize the 1965 census.

Date Palms
A85

Soldiers' Monument
A86

**1965, Dec. 27** **Litho.** *Perf. 13½x14*

*393* A85 3f ol bis & multi 20 10
*394* A85 10f car rose & multi 40 20
*395* A85 15f bl & multi 1.00 30

Issued to commemorate the second FAO International Dates Conference, Baghdad, Dec. 1965.

**1966, Jan. 6** **Photo.** *Perf. 12*

*396* A86 2f car rose & multi 10 5
*397* A86 5f multi 20 5
*398* A86 40f yel grn & multi 1.40 75

Issued for Army Day.

Eagle and Flag of Iraq — A87

*Perf. 12½*

**1966, Feb. 8** **Photo.** **Unwmk.**

*399* A87 5f dl bl & multi 20 5
*400* A87 10f org & multi 40 10

Issued to commemorate the third anniversary of the Revolution of Ramadan 14, which overthrew the Kassem government.

Arab League Emblem — A88

Soccer Players — A89

**1966, March 22** *Perf. 11x11½*

*401* A88 5f org, brn & brt grn 10 10
*402* A88 15f ol, rose lil & ultra 40 15

Arab Publicity Week.

**1966, Apr. 1** *Perf. 12*

Designs: 5f, Player and goal post. 15f, As 2f. 50f, Legs of player, ball and emblem (horiz.).

*403* A89 2f multi 40 10
*404* A89 5f multi 20 10
*405* A89 15f multi 1.25 50

**Miniature Sheet**

***Imperf***

*406* A89 50f vio & multi 6.00 15.00

Issued to commemorate the Third Arab Soccer Cup, Baghdad, Apr. 1-10. No. 406 measures 115x70mm.

Steam Shovel Within Cogwheel A90

**1966, May 1 Litho. *Perf. 13½***

*407* A90 15f multi 12 6

*408* A90 25f red, blk, & sil 25 12

Issued for Labor Day, May 1, 1966.

Queen Nefertari — A91

Facade of Abu Simbel A92

***Perf. 12½x13, 13½***

**1966, May 20 Litho.**

*409* A91 5f ol, yel & blk 15 10

*410* A91 15f bl, yel & brn 22 15

*411* A92 40f bis brn, red & blk 1.65 1.00

Issued to publicize the UNESCO world campaign to save historic monuments in Nubia.

President Arif and Flag — A93

**1966, July 14 Photo. *Perf. 11½***

*412* A93 5f multi 15 8

*413* A93 15f multi 25 10

*414* A93 50f multi 75 25

Issued to commemorate the 8th anniversary of the July 14, 1958, revolution.

A94

**1966, July 22 Litho. *Perf. 12***

**Multicolored Vignette**

*415* A94 5f lt ol grn 5 5

*416* A94 15f lt grnsh bl 10 8

*417* A94 30f lt yel grn 25 18

Mohammed's 1,396th birthday.

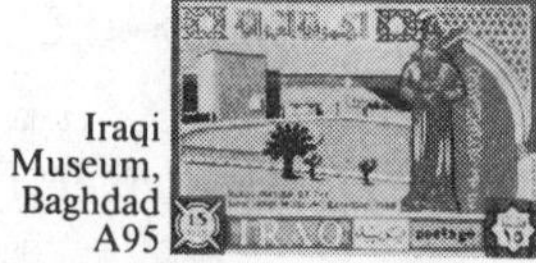


Iraqi Museum, Baghdad A95

Designs: 50f, Golden headdress, Ur. 80f, Carved Sumerian head (vert.).

**1966, Nov. 9 Litho. *Perf. 14***

*418* A95 15f multi 25 10

*419* A95 50f lt bl, blk, gold & pink 1.00 50

*420* A95 80f crim, blk, bl & gold 2.50 75

Opening of New Iraqi Museum, Baghdad.

UNESCO Emblem — A96

**1966, Dec. *Perf. 13½***

*421* A96 5f bl, blk & tan 5 5

*422* A96 15f brt org brn, blk & gray 10 8

20th anniv. of UNESCO.

Iraqi Citizens — A97

**1966, Nov. 18 *Perf. 13½x13***

*423* A97 15f multi 50 35

*424* A97 25f multi 75 85

Issued to commemorate the 3rd anniversary of the Revolution of Nov. 18, 1963.

Rocket Launchers and Soldier A98

**1967, Jan. 6 Photo. *Perf. 11½***

*425* A98 15f cit, dk brn & dp bis 25 10

*426* A98 20f brt lil, dk brn & dp bis 50 20

Issued for Army Day, Jan. 6.

Oil Derrick, Pipeline, Emblem — A99

Design: 15f, 50f, Refinery and emblem (horiz.).

**1967, Mar. 6 Litho. *Perf. 14***

*427* A99 5f ol grn, pale yel & blk 5 5

*428* A99 15f multi 10 8

*429* A99 40f vio, yel & blk 25 20

*430* A99 50f multi 50 35

Issued to commemorate the 6th Arab Petroleum Congress, Baghdad, March 1967.

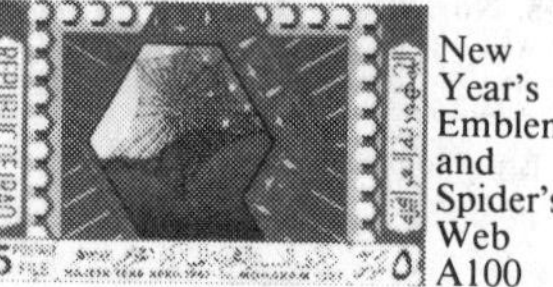


New Year's Emblem and Spider's Web A100

**1967, Apr. 11 Litho. *Perf. 13½***

*431* A100 5f multi 5 5

*432* A100 15f multi 10 8

Issued for the Hajeer Year (New Year)

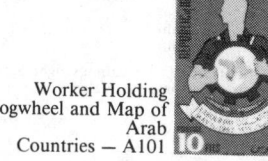

Worker Holding Cogwheel and Map of Arab Countries — A101

**1967, May 1 *Perf. 12½x13***

*433* A101 10f gray & multi 6 5

*434* A101 15f lt ultra & multi 10 8

Issued for Labor Day, 1967.

A102

**1967, June 20 Litho. *Perf. 14***

*435* A102 5f multi 10 5

*436* A102 15f bl & multi 25 8

Mohammed's 1,397th birthday.

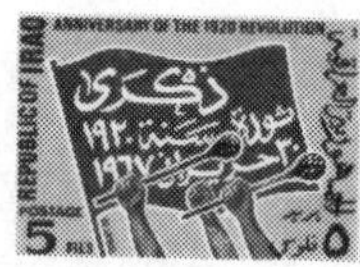

Flag, Hands with Clubs — A103

**1967, July 7 *Perf. 13x13½***

*437* A103 5f multi 5 5

*438* A103 15f multi 10 8

47th anniversary of Revolution of 1920.

Um Qasr Harbor A104

Designs: 10f, 15f, Freighter loading in Um Qasr harbor.

**1967, July 14 Litho. *Perf. 14x13½***

*439* A104 5f multi 15 5

*440* A104 10f multi 15 5

*441* A104 15f multi 50 8

*442* A104 40f multi 1.75 18

Issued to commemorate the 9th anniversary of the July 14, 1958, revolution and the inauguration of the port of Um Qasr.

Iraqi Man — A105

President Arif — A106

Iraqi Costumes: 5f, 15f, 25f, Women's costumes. 10f, 20f, 30f, Men's costumes.

**1967, Nov. 10 Litho. *Perf. 13***

*443* A105 2f pale brn & multi 20 10

*444* A105 5f ver & multi 20 10

*445* A105 10f multi 35 20

*446* A105 15f ultra & multi 42 20

*447* A105 20f lil & multi 85 30

*448* A105 25f lem & multi 85 35

*449* A105 30f fawn & multi 85 45

*Nos. 443-449,C19-C21 (10)* 9.97 3.35

***Perf. 11x11½, 11½x11***

**1967, Nov. 18**

Design: 15f, Pres. Arif and map of Iraq (horiz.).

*450* A106 5f bl, vio blk & yel 15 10

*451* A106 15f rose & multi 50 25

4th anniversary of Nov. 18th revolution.

Ziggurat of Ur — A107

Designs: 5f, Gate with Nimrod statues. 10f, Gate, Babylon. 15f, Minaret of Mosul (vert.). 25f, Arch and ruins of Ctesiphon.

**1967, Dec. 1 Litho. *Perf. 13***

*452* A107 2f org & multi 5 5

*453* A107 5f lil & multi 10 5

*454* A107 10f org & multi 15 6

*455* A107 15f rose red & multi 35 8

*456* A107 25f vio bl & multi 50 12

*Nos. 452-456,C22-C26 (10)* 40.30 19.26

International Tourist Year 1967.

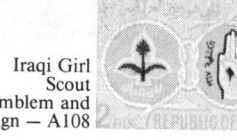


Iraqi Girl Scout Emblem and Sign — A108

Designs: 5f, Girl Scouts at campfire and Girl Scout emblem. 10f, Boy Scout emblem and Boy Scout sign. 15f, Boy Scouts pitching tent and Boy Scout sign.

**1967, Dec. 15**

*457* A108 2f org & multi 95 20

*458* A108 5f bl & multi 1.10 25

*459* A108 10f grn & multi 1.25 40

*460* A108 15f bl & multi 1.25 50

*a* Souv. sheet of 4 6.00 6.00

Issued to honor the Scout movement.

No. 460a contains 4 stamps similar to Nos. 457-460 with simulated perforations. Multicolored decorative border with commemorative inscription. Size: 119x90mm. Sold for 50f.

Soldiers on Maneuvers A109

**1968, Jan. 6 Photo. *Perf. 11½***

*461* A109 5f lt bl, brn & brt grn 15 5

*462* A109 15f lt bl, ind & ol 45 10

Issued for Army Day 1968.

White-cheeked Bulbul — A110

Birds: 10f, Hoopoe. 15f, Eurasian jay. 25f, Peregrine falcon. 30f, White stork. 40f, Black partridge. 50f, Marbled teal.

**1968, Jan. Litho. *Perf. 14***

*463* A110 5f org & blk 20 10
*464* A110 10f bl, blk & brn 25 15
*465* A110 15f pink & multi 50 20
*466* A110 25f dl org & multi 60 40
*467* A110 30f emer, blk & brn 85 20
*468* A110 40f rose lil & multi 2.50 20
*469* A110 50f multi 2.75 45
*Nos. 463-469 (7)* 7.65 1.70

Fighting Soldiers A111

**1968, Feb. 8 *Perf. 11½***

*470* A111 15f blk, org & brt bl 2.25 20

Issued to commemorate the 5th anniversary of the Revolution of Ramadan 14.

Factories, Tractor and Grain A112

**1968, May 1 Litho. *Perf. 13***

*471* A112 15f lt bl & multi 15 6
*472* A112 25f multi 25 12

Issued for Labor Day, 1968.

Soccer A113

Designs: 5f, 25f, Goalkeeper holding ball (vert.).

**1968, June 14 *Perf. 13½***

*473* A113 2f multi 5 5
*474* A113 5f multi 10 8
*475* A113 15f multi 25 12
*476* A113 25f multi 1.75 50
*a* Souv. sheet, 70f 6.00 10.00

Issued to commemorate the 23rd C.I.S.M. (Conseil Internationale du Sports Militaire) Soccer Championships.

No. 476a is imperf. and shows badge of Military Soccer League. Citron margin and multicolored design. Size: 57½x90mm.

Soldier, Flag, Chain and Rising Sun — A114

**1968, July 14 Photo. *Perf. 13½x14***

*478* A114 15f multi 25 10

Issued to commemorate the 10th anniversary of the July 14, 1958, revolution.

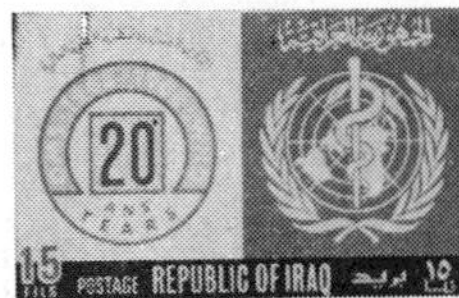


World Health Organization Emblem — A115

Design: 5f, 10f, Staff of Aesculapius over emblem (vert.).

**1968, Nov. 29 Litho. *Perf. 13½***

*479* A115 5f multi 10 5
*480* A115 10f multi 15 5
*481* A115 15f bl, red & blk 25 8
*482* A115 25f yel grn, red & blk 50 12

Issued for the 20th anniversary of the World Health Organization. Exist imperf.

Human Rights Flame — A116

**1968, Dec. 22 Litho. *Perf. 13½***

*483* A116 10f lt bl, yel & car 10 5
*484* A116 25f lt yel grn, yel & car 25 12
*a* Souv. sheet, 100f 3.50 3.50

International Human Rights Year.

No. 484a contains one imperf. design similar to type A116 in lilac, yellow and carmine, with denomination and inscription in carmine on yellow margin. Size: 56x75mm.

Mother and Children — A117

**1968, Dec. 31 Litho. *Perf. 13½***

*485* A117 15f multi 25 8
*486* A117 25f bl & multi 75 15
*a* Souv. sheet, 100f 6.25 4.00

UNICEF (United Nations Children's Fund).

No. 486a contains one imperf. design similar to type A117 in olive, with denomination and inscription in dark blue on greenish margin. Size: 55x74mm.

Tanks A118

**1969, Jan. 6 Photo.**

*487* A118 25f vio, car & brn 2.25 1.00

Issued for Army Day, Jan. 6.

Harvester A119

**1969, Feb. Photo. *Perf. 13½***

*488* A119 15f yel brn & multi 22 15

Issued to commemorate the 6th anniversary of the Revolution of Ramadan 14.

Mosque A119a

**1969, Mar. 19 Photo. *Perf. 13x13½***

*488A* A119a 15f multi 15 10

Issued for Hajeer (pilgrimage) Year.

Emblem A120

**1969, Apr. 12 Litho. *Perf. 12½x12***

*489* A120 10f yel grn & multi 50 10
*490* A120 15f org & multi 75 15

Issued to publicize the first conference of the Arab Veterinary Union, Baghdad, April 1969.

Barbel A121

Fish: 3f, Mahseer. 10f, White pomfret. 100f, Barbel.

**1969, May 9 *Perf. 14***

*491* A121 2f multi 1.10 10
*492* A121 3f multi 1.10 10
*493* A121 10f multi 1.25 10
*494* A121 100f multi 4.25 2.50

Holy Kaaba, Mecca A122

**1969, May 28 Photo. *Perf. 12***

*495* A122 15f bl & multi 15 15

Mohammed's 1,399th birthday.

ILO Emblem A123

**1969, June 6 Litho. *Perf. 13x12½***

*496* A123 5f lt vio, yel & blk 10 5
*497* A123 15f grnsh gray, yel & blk 20 15
*498* A123 50f rose, yel & blk 80 50
*a* Souvenir sheet, 100f 4.50 7.50

50th anniversary of the International Labor Organization.

No. 498a contains one imperf. design similar to type A123 in black, yellow green and red, with denomination and inscription in margin. Size: 75x55mm.

Weight Lifting A124

Coat of Arms, Symbols of Industry A125

Design: 5f, 35f, High jump.

**1969, June 20 *Perf. 13½x13***

*500* A124 3f org yel & multi 5 5
*501* A124 5f bl & multi 5 5
*502* A124 10f rose pink & multi 25 10
*503* A124 35f yel & multi 90 25
*a* Souv. sheet of 4 7.50 7.50

Issued to commemorate the 19th Olympic Games, Mexico City, Oct. 12-27, 1968. No. 503a contains 4 imperf. stamps similar to Nos. 500-503. Light yellow margin with black inscription. Size: 90x116mm. Sold for 100f.

**1969, July 14 Photo. *Perf. 13***

*504* A125 10f brn org & multi 20 5
*505* A125 15f multi 30 8

Issued to commemorate the 11th anniversary of the July 14, 1958, revolution.

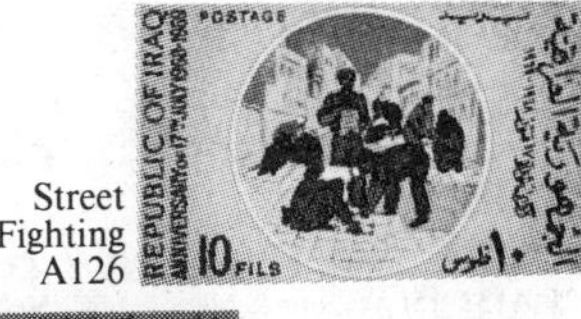


Street Fighting A126

Pres. Ahmed Hassan al-Bakr A127

Wheat and Fair Emblem A128

Design: 20f, Baghdad International Airport.

**1969, July 17 *Perf. 13½***

*506* A126 10f yel & multi 30 15
*507* A126 15f bl & multi 30 15
*508* A126 20f bl & multi 1.00 25
*509* A127 200f gold & multi 10.00 5.00

Issued to commemorate the first anniversary of the coup of July 17, 1968. No. 508 also commemorates the inauguration of Baghdad International Airport.

**1969, Oct. 1 Photo. *Perf. 13½***

*510* A128 10f brt grn, gold & dl red 8 5
*511* A128 15f ultra, gold & red 12 8

6th International Fair, Baghdad.

Motor Ship Al-Waleed A129

Designs: 15f, Floating crane Antara. 30f, Pilot ship Al-Rasheed. 35f, Suction dredge Hillah. 50f, Survey ship Al-Fao.

**1969, Oct. 8 Litho. *Perf. 12½***

*512* A129 15f blk & multi 25 20
*513* A129 20f blk & multi 30 25
*514* A129 30f blk & multi 50 30

*515* A129 35f blk & multi 1.00 60
*516* A129 50f blk & multi 3.00 1.50
*Nos. 512-516 (5)* 5.05 2.85

50th anniversary of Basrah Harbor.

Radio Tower and Map of Palestine
A130

"Search for Knowledge"
A131

**1969, Nov. 9 Litho. *Perf. 12½x13***
*517* A130 15f multi 75 20
*518* A130 50f multi 2.00 50

10th anniversary of Iraqi News Agency.

**1969, Nov. 21 Photo. *Perf. 13***
*519* A131 15f bl & multi 12 8
*520* A131 20f grn & multi 20 10

Campaign against illiteracy.

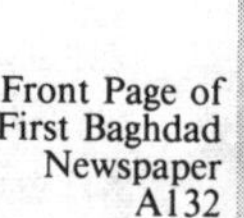

Front Page of First Baghdad Newspaper
A132

**1969, Dec. 26 Litho. *Perf. 13½***
*521* A132 15f yel, org & blk 50 30

Centenary of the Iraqi press.

Soldier, Map of Iraq and Plane — A133

**1970, Jan. 6 Photo. *Perf. 13***
*522* A133 15f lt vio & multi 50 15
*523* A133 20f yel & multi 1.00 30

Issued for Army Day 1970.

Soldier, Farmer and Worker Shoring up Wall in Iraqi Colors
A134

Poppies
A135

**1970, Feb. 8 Photo. *Perf. 13***
*524* A134 10f multi 25 10
*525* A134 15f brick red & multi 50 25

Issued to commemorate the 7th anniversary of the Revolution of Ramadan 14.

**1970, June 12 Litho. *Perf. 13***

Flowers: 3f, Poet's narcissus. 5f, Tulip. 10f, 50f, Carnations. 15f, Rose.

*526* A135 2f emer & multi 5 5
*527* A135 3f bl & multi 8 5
*528* A135 5f multi 12 5
*529* A135 10f lt grn & multi 20 5
*530* A135 15f pale sal & multi 1.00 8
*531* A135 50f lt grn & multi 2.00 75
*Nos. 526-531 (6)* 3.45 1.03

The overprinted sets Nos. 532-543 were released before Nos. 526-531.

Nos. 526-531 Overprinted in Ultramarine

**1970, Mar. 21**
*532* A135 2f emer & multi 10 5
*533* A135 3f lt bl & multi 10 5
*534* A135 5f multi 15 5
*535* A135 10f lt grn & multi 40 8
*536* A135 15f pale sal & multi 80 12
*537* A135 50f lt grn & multi 3.25 1.50
*Nos. 532-537 (6)* 4.80 1.85

Issued for Novrooz (New Year).

Nos. 526-531 Overprinted in Black

**1970, Apr. 18**
*538* A135 2f emer & multi 8 5
*539* A135 3f lt bl & multi 8 5
*540* A135 5f multi 7 5
*541* A135 10f lt grn & multi 25 8
*542* A135 15f pale sal & multi 45 12
*543* A135 50f lt grn & multi 2.25 75
*Nos. 538-543 (6)* 3.18 1.10

Issued for the Spring Festival, Mosul.

Map of Arab Countries, Slogans — A136

Design: 35f, like 15f. 50f, 150f, People, flag, sun and map of Iraq.

**1970, Apr. 7 *Perf. 13x12½***
*544* A136 15f gold & multi 9 7
*545* A136 35f sil & multi 25 20
*546* A136 50f red & multi 50 30
*a* Souvenir sheet, 150f 3.50 3.50

23rd anniversary of Al-Baath Party.

No. 546a contains one imperf. design similar to type A136 with blue denomination and commemorative inscription in margin. Size: 115x76½mm.

Workers and Cogwheel
A137

**1970, May 1**
*547* A137 10f sil & multi 25 12
*548* A137 15f sil & multi 30 12
*549* A137 35f sil & multi 1.00 40

Issued for Labor Day, 1970.

Kaaba, Mecca, and Koran
A138

**1970, May 17 Photo. *Perf. 13***
*550* A138 15f brt bl & multi 10 8
*551* A138 20f org & multi 15 10

Mohammed's 1,400th birthday.

No. 521 Overprinted "1970" and Arabic Inscription in Prussian Blue

**1970, June 15 Litho. *Perf. 13½***
*552* A132 15f yel, org & blk 20 20

Day of Iraqi press.

Revolutionists and Guns — A139

Designs: 35f, Revolutionist and rising sun.

**1970, June 30 Litho. *Perf. 13***
*553* A139 10f blk & ap grn 6 5
*554* A139 15f blk & gold 10 8
*555* A139 35f blk & red org 50 20
*a* Souvenir sheet, 100f 3.00 3.00

50th anniversary, Revolution of 1920.

No. 555a contains two imperf. designs similar to Nos. 553 and 555. Denomination and commemorative inscription in red orange on yellow green background in margin. Size: 109x62mm.

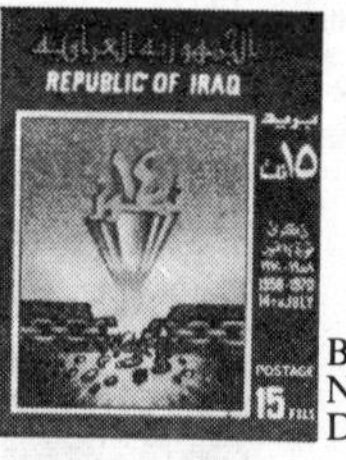

Broken Chain and New Dawn — A140

**1970, July 14 *Perf. 13x13½***
*557* A140 15f vio bl, org, yel & gold 10 7
*558* A140 20f emer, org, yel & gold 15 10

Issued to commemorate the 12th anniversary of the July 14, 1958, revolution.

Map of Arab Countries and Hands
A141

**1970, July 17 *Perf. 13***
*559* A141 15f gold & multi 10 7
*560* A141 25f gold & multi 20 15

2nd anniversary of coup of July 17, 1968.

Pomegranates
A142

Fruits: 5f, Grapefruit. 10f, Grapes. 15f, Oranges. 35f, Dates.

**1970, Aug. 21 *Perf. 14***
*561* A142 3f bl grn & multi 5 5
*562* A142 5f brt bl & multi 10 5
*563* A142 10f lt vio & multi 15 5
*564* A142 15f red & multi 50 7
*565* A142 35f org & multi 1.00 30
*Nos. 561-565 (5)* 1.80 52

The Latin inscriptions on the 5f and 10f have been erroneously transposed.

Kaaba, Mecca, Moon over Mountain and Spider Web — A143

**1970, Sept. 4 Photo. *Perf. 13***
*566* A143 15f blk, grn, gold & brn 10 7
*567* A143 25f blk, vio bl, gold & brn 20 15

Issued for Hajeer (Pilgrimage) Year.

Nos. 510-511 Overprinted in Red

**1970, Sept. Photo. *Perf. 13½***
*567A* A128 10f brt grn, gold & dl red 1.25 1.25
*567B* A128 15f ultra, gold & red 1.75 2.25

7th International Fair, Baghdad.

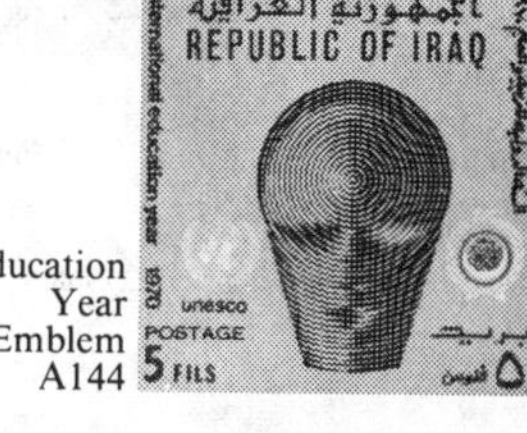

Education Year Emblem
A144

**1970, Nov. 13 Photo. *Perf. 13***
*568* A144 5f yel grn & multi 5 5
*569* A144 15f brick red & multi 15 10

Issued for International Education Year.

Flag and Map of Arab League Countries
A145

**1970 *Perf. 11***
*570* A145 15f ol & multi 10 7
*571* A145 35f gray & multi 25 20

25th anniversary of the Arab League.

Baghdad Hospital and Emblem
A146

**1970, Dec. 7 Litho. *Perf. 12***
*572* A146 15f yel & multi 15 7
*573* A146 40f lt grn & multi 50 25

Iraqi Medical Society, 50th anniversary.

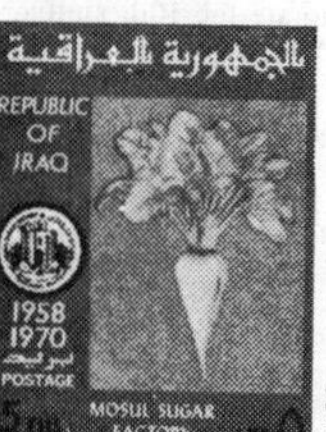

Sugar Beet — A147

Designs: 15f, Sugar factory (horiz.). 30f, like 5f.

***Perf. 13x13½, 13½x13***

**1970, Dec. 25 Photo.**

*574* A147 5f ocher, grn & blk 5 5
*575* A147 15f blk & multi 9 7
*576* A147 30f org ver, grn & blk 18 15

Publicity for Mosul sugar factory.

OPEC Emblem A148

**1970, Dec. 30 Litho. *Perf. 13x13½***

*577* A148 10f rose cl, bis & bl 50 20
*578* A148 40f emer, bis & bl 2.00 70

Organization of Petroleum Exporting Countries (OPEC), 10th anniversary.

REPUBLIC OF IRAQ Soldiers — A149

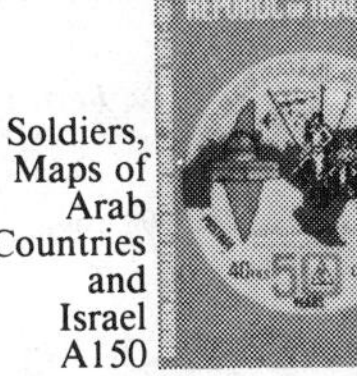

Soldiers, Maps of Arab Countries and Israel A150

***Perf. 13½x14, 11½x12½***

**1971, Jan. 6**

*579* A149 15f blk, brt pink & gold 35 15
*580* A150 40f red org & multi 2.00 50
*a* Souvenir sheet of 2 4.50 7.00

Army Day, 50th anniversary.

No. 580a contains 2 imperf. stamps similar to Nos. 579-580. Black marginal inscription. Size: 122x90mm. Sold for 100f.

Marchers and Map of Arab Countries A151

**1971, Feb. 8 Litho. *Perf. 11½x12½***

*581* A151 15f yel & multi 25 10
*582* A151 40f pink & multi 75 30

Revolution of Ramadan 14, 8th anniversary.

Spider Web, Pilgrims A152

**1971, Feb. 26 Photo. *Perf. 13***

*583* A152 10f pink & multi 10 5
*584* A152 15f buff & multi 15 7

Hajeer (New) Year.

President al-Bakr A153

**1971, March 11 Litho. *Perf. 14***

*585* A153 15f org & multi 60 15
*586* A153 100f emer & multi 3.25 85

First anniversary of March 11th Manifesto.

Marshland A154

Designs: 10f, Stork flying over Baghdad. 15f, "Summer Resorts." 100f, Return of Sindbad the Sailor.

**1971, March 15 *Perf. 13***

*587* A154 5f multi 30 5
*588* A154 10f lt grn & multi 40 10
*589* A154 15f pink & multi 85 50
*590* A154 100f multi 6.00 3.00

Tourist publicity.

Blacksmith Taming Serpent — A155

**1971, March 21 *Perf. 11½x12***

*591* A155 15f multi 60 15
*592* A155 25f yel & multi 1.25 40

Novrooz Festival.

No. 455 Overprinted

يوم الأنواء
W.M. DAY
1971

**1971, March 23 Litho. *Perf. 13***

*593* A107 15f rose red & multi 4.50 3.00

World Meteorological Day. See No. C39.

Workers, Soldier, Map of Arab Countries A156

**1971, Apr. 7**

*594* A156 15f yel & multi 85 15
*595* A156 35f multi 1.65 45
*596* A156 250f multi 12.50 7.50

24th anniversary of the Al Baath Party. No. 596 has circular perforation around vignette set within a white square of paper, perforated on 4 sides. The design of No. 596 is similar to Nos. 594-595, but with denomination within the circle and no inscriptions in margin.

Nos. 443-444, 448 Overprinted

مهرجان الربيع
1971

**1971, Apr. 14**

*597* A105 2f pale brn & multi 50 15
*598* A105 5f ver & multi 50 15
*599* A105 25f lem & multi 2.00 1.00

Mosul Festival.

Worker, Farm Woman with Torch A157

**1971, May 1 Litho. *Perf. 13***

*600* A157 15f ocher & multi 15 7
*601* A157 40f ol & multi 75 20

Labor Day, 1971.

Muslim Praying in Mecca A158

**1971, May 7**

*602* A158 15f yel & multi 25 10
*603* A158 100f pink & multi 3.00 1.00

Mohammed's 1,401st birthday.

People, Fists, Map of Iraq A159

**1971, July 14 Photo. *Perf. 14***

*604* A159 25f grn & multi 20 12
*605* A159 50f lt bl & multi 40 25

13th anniversary of the July 14, 1958, revolution.

Surveyor, Preacher, Rising Sun A160

**1971, July 17 *Perf. 13***

*606* A160 25f multi 25 15
*607* A160 70f org & multi 75 45

3rd anniversary of July 17, 1968, coup.

For unused stamps, more recent issues are valued as never hinged, with the beginning point determined on a country-by-country basis. Notes to show the beginning points are prominently placed in the text.

Rafidain Bank Emblem A161

**1971, Sept. 24 Photo. *Perf. 13½***

**Diameter: 27mm.**

*608* A161 10f org, grn & multi 50 1.00
*609* A161 15f multi 1.00 1.00
*610* A161 25f multi 2.00 3.00

**Diameter: 32mm.**

*611* A161 65f multi 10.00 5.00
*612* A161 250f multi 25.00 15.00
*Nos. 608-612 (5)* 38.50 25.00

30th anniversary of Rafidain Bank. Nos. 608-612 have circular perforation around design within a white square of paper, perforated on 4 sides.

Nos. 561, 564-565 Overprinted

التعداد الزراعى العام
١٩٧١/١٠/١٥

**1971, Oct. 15 Litho. *Perf. 14***

*613* A142 3f bl grn & multi 30 10
*614* A142 15f red & multi 1.00 50
*615* A142 35f org & multi 2.00 75

Agricultural census, Oct. 15, 1971.

Soccer A162

Designs: 25f, Track and field. 35f, Table tennis. 75f, Gymnastics. 95f, Volleyball and basketball.

**1971, Nov. 17 Litho. *Perf. 13½***

*616* A162 15f grn & multi 30 15
*617* A162 25f pink & multi 55 30
*618* A162 35f lt bl & multi 85 70
*619* A162 70f lt grn & multi 3.50 1.00
*620* A162 95f yel grn & multi 5.75 2.00
*a* Souvenir sheet of 5 12.50 5.50
*Nos. 616-620 (5)* 10.95 4.15

4th Pan-Arab Schoolboys Sports Games, Baghdad (1971). No. 620a contains 5 stamps similar to Nos. 616-620 with simulated perforations. Black marginal inscription. Size: 193½x145mm. Sold for 200f.

**70 Fils** 

Nos. 527-528, 530 Overprinted and Surcharged

يوم الطالب
٢٣ تشرين الثانى
٩٦١ - ٩٧١
٧٠ فلسا

**1971, Nov. 23 Litho. *Perf. 13***

*621* A135 15f multi 1.00 25
*622* A135 25f on 5f multi 2.00 75
*623* A135 70f on 3f multi 7.00 2.00

Students' Day. The 15f has only first 3 lines of Arabic overprint.

Nos. 485-486 Overprinted

**25th Anniversary 971**

**1971, Dec. 11 Litho. *Perf. 13½***

*624* A117 15f multi 2.25 75
*625* A117 25f bl & multi 5.25 2.00

25th anniv. UNICEF.

Children Crossing Street A162a

**1971, Dec. 17 Litho.** ***Perf. 13x12½***
*625A* A162a 15f yel & multi 1.25 50
*625B* A162a 25f brt rose & multi 2.50 1.00

2nd Traffic Week.

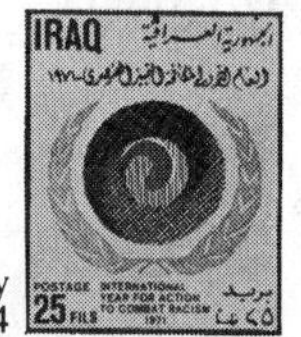
Arab Postal Union Emblem A163

**1971, Dec. 24 Photo.** ***Perf. 11½***
*626* A163 25f emer, yel & brn 30 15
*627* A163 70f vio bl, yel & red 1.10 45

25th anniv. of the Conf. of Sofar, Lebanon, establishing Arab Postal Union.

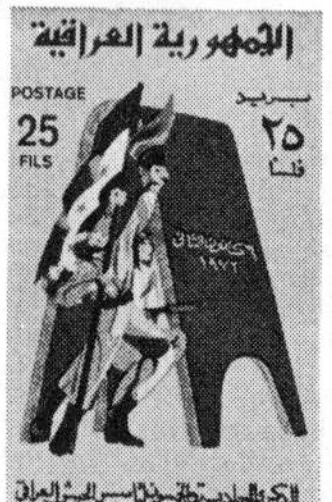
Racial Equality Emblem — A164

**1971, Dec. 31** ***Perf. 13½x14***
*628* A164 25f brt grn & multi 25 13
*629* A164 70f org & multi 65 35

Intl. Year Against Racial Discrimination.

Soldiers with Flag and Torch — A165

**1972, Jan. 6 Photo.** ***Perf. 14x13½***
*630* A165 25f bl & multi 90 50
*631* A165 70f brt grn & multi 3.50 2.00

Army Day, Jan. 6.

Workers — A166

**1972, Feb. 8**
*632* A166 25f brt grn & multi 1.10 50
*633* A166 95f lil & multi 7.75 2.00

9th anniversary of the Revolution of Ramadan 14.

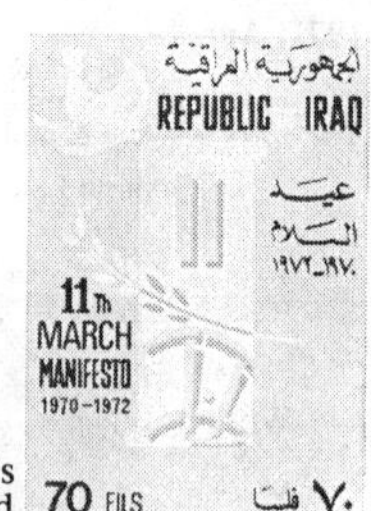
Mosque, Minaret, Crescent and Caravan A167

**1972, Feb. 26 Litho.** ***Perf. 12½x13***
*634* A167 25f bl grn & multi 25 13
*635* A167 35f pur & multi 35 18

Hajeer (Pilgrimage) Year.

Peace Symbols and "11" — A168

**1972, Mar. 11 Photo.** ***Perf. 11x12½***
*636* A168 25f lt bl & blk 1.00 25
*637* A168 70f brt lil & blk 3.00 75

2nd anniversary of March 11 Manifesto.

Mountain Range and Flowers — A169

**1972, March 21** ***Perf. 11½x11***
*638* A169 25f vio bl & multi 1.10 20
*639* A169 70f vio bl & multi 3.25 1.00

Novrooz, New Year Festival.

Party Emblem A170

Symbolic Design — A171

***Perf. 14 (A170), 13 (A171)***
**1972 Litho.**
*640* A170 10f brn org & multi 15 10
*641* A171 25f bis & multi 30 25
*642* A170 35f brn org & multi 50 50
*643* A171 70f red & multi 3.00 75

25th anniversary of the Iraqi Arab Baath Socialist Party.
Issue dates: 25f, 70f, Mar. 23; 10f, 35f, Apr. 7.

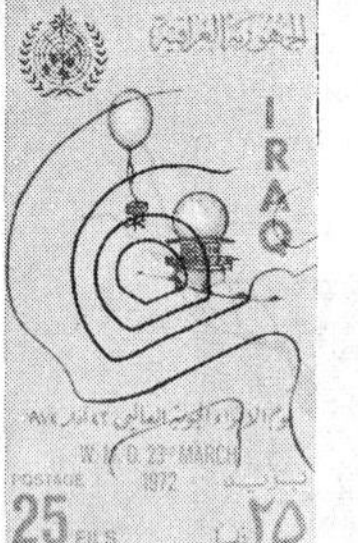
Emblem, Map, Weather Balloons and Chart — A172

Cogwheel and Ship — A173

**1972, Mar. 23 Photo.** ***Perf. 14x13½***
*644* A172 25f multi 75 15
*645* A172 35f yel & multi 1.05 25

12th World Meteorological Day.

**1972, March 25** ***Perf. 11x11½***
*646* A173 25f ocher & multi 25 13
*647* A173 35f pink & multi 40 15

Arab Chamber of Commerce.

Derrick and Flame A174

Quill Pens, Map of Arab Countries A175

**1972, Apr. 7** ***Perf. 13x13½***
*648* A174 25f multi 60 25
*649* A174 35f multi 85 30

Opening of North Rumaila (INOC, North Iraq Oil Fields).

**1972, Apr. 17 Photo.** ***Perf. 11x11½***
*650* A175 25f org & multi 35 13
*651* A175 35f bl & multi 60 18

3rd Congress of Arab Journalists.

Women's Federation Emblem A176

**1972, Apr. 22 Litho.** ***Perf. 13½***
*652* A176 25f grn & multi 35 13
*653* A176 35f lil & multi 60 18

Iraqi Women's Federation, 4th anniversary.

Hand Holding Globe-shaped Wrench — A177

**1972, May 1 Photo.** ***Perf. 11½***
*654* A177 25f yel grn & multi 35 13
*655* A177 35f org & multi 60 18

Labor Day 1972.

Kaaba, Mecca, and Crescent — A178

**1972, May 26**
*656* A178 25f grn & multi 35 13
*657* A178 35f pur & multi 60 18

Mohammed's 1,402nd birthday.

Soldier, Civilian and Guns — A179

**1972, July 14 Photo.** ***Perf. 13½x14***
*658* A179 35f multi 75 25
*659* A180 70f lil & multi 2.25 75

14th anniv. of July 14, 1958, revolution.

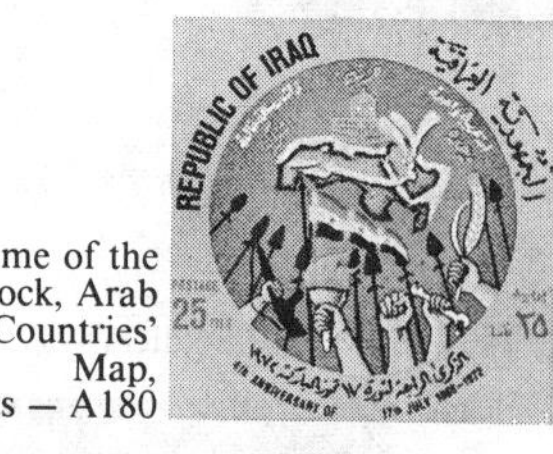
Dome of the Rock, Arab Countries' Map, Fists — A180

**1972, July 17** ***Perf. 13***
*660* A180 25f cit & multi 75 15
*661* A180 95f bl & multi 2.25 75

4th anniversary of July 17, 1968, coup.

Congress Emblem, Scout Saluting Iraqi Flag — A182

**1972, Aug. 12 Photo.** ***Perf. 13½x14***
*664* A182 20f multi 1.25 70
*665* A182 25f lil & multi 2.50 1.00

10th Arab Boy Scouts Jamboree and Conference, Mosul, Aug. 10-19.

**1972, Aug. 24**

Design: Congress emblem and Girl Guide in camp.

*666* A182 10f yel & multi 1.10 50
*667* A182 45f multi 3.25 1.00

4th Arab Guides Camp and Conference, Mosul, Aug. 24-30.

No. 625A Overprinted and Surcharged, No. 625B Overprinted with New Date:

1972 ١٩٧٢

●● 70 Fils ٧٠ ●●

**1972, Oct. 4 Photo.** ***Perf. 13x12½***
*668* A162a 25f brt rose & multi 4.25 2.00
*669* A162a 70f on 15f multi 5.50 5.00

Third Traffic Week.

Central Bank of Iraq — A183

**1972, Nov. 16 Photo. *Perf. 13***

| | | |
|---|---|---|
| *670* A183 25f lt bl & multi | 40 | 30 |
| *671* A183 70f lt grn & multi | 1.10 | 70 |

25th anniversary, Central Bank of Iraq.

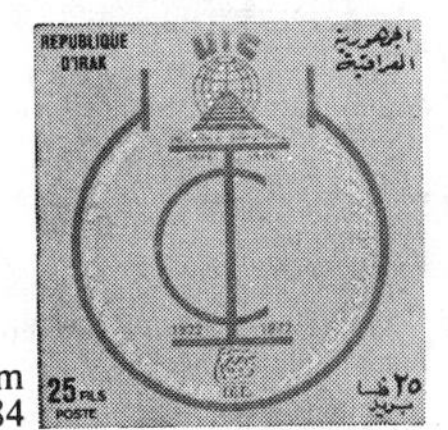

UIC Emblem A184

**1972, Dec. 29**

| | | |
|---|---|---|
| *672* A184 25f dp rose & multi | 75 | 20 |
| *673* A184 45f brt vio & multi | 1.50 | 50 |

50th anniversary, International Railroad Union (UIC).

Nos. 148-149, 151, 180 and Type of 1957-58 Overprinted with 3 Bars

**1973, Jan. 29 Engr. *Perf. 11½x12***

| | | |
|---|---|---|
| *674* A28 10f blue | 50 | 20 |
| *675* A33 10f blue | 50 | 20 |
| *676* A28 15f black | 1.00 | 35 |
| *677* A33 15f black | 1.00 | 35 |
| *678* A28 25f rose vio | 2.00 | 50 |
| *679* A33 25f rose vio | 2.00 | 50 |
| *Nos. 674-679 (6)* | 7.00 | 2.10 |

The size and position of the bottom bar of overprint differs; the bar can be same size as 2 top bars, short and centered or moved to the right.

No. 455 Overprinted

المؤتمر الدولي
للتاريخ/١٩٧٣

**1973, Mar. 25 Litho. *Perf. 13***

| | | |
|---|---|---|
| *680* A186 15f rose red & multi | 7.50 | 3.00 |

Intl. History Cong. See Nos. C52-C53.

Workers and Oil Wells A185

Ram's-head Harp A186

**1973, June 1 Litho. *Perf. 13***

| | | |
|---|---|---|
| *681* A185 25f yel & multi | 1.50 | 50 |
| *682* A185 70f rose & multi | 7.00 | 2.00 |

1st anniv. of nationalization of oil industry.

**1973, June Litho. *Perf. 13x12½***

Designs: 25f, 35f, 45f, Minaret, Mosul. 50f, 70f, 95f, Statue of goddess. 10f, 20f, like 5f.

| | | |
|---|---|---|
| *683* A186 5f org & blk | 5 | 5 |
| *684* A186 10f bis & blk | 8 | 6 |
| *685* A186 20f brt rose & blk | 16 | 10 |
| *686* A186 25f ultra & blk | 20 | 13 |
| *687* A186 35f emer & blk | 27 | 18 |
| *688* A186 45f bl & blk | 35 | 23 |
| *689* A186 50f ol & yel | 40 | 25 |
| *690* A186 70f vio & yel | 54 | 36 |
| *691* A186 95f brn & yel | 75 | 48 |
| *Nos. 683-691 (9)* | 2.80 | 1.84 |

People with Flags, Grain A187

**1973, July 14**

| | | |
|---|---|---|
| *692* A187 25f multi | 25 | 25 |
| *693* A187 35f multi | 50 | 30 |

July Festivals.

Nos. 393 and 395 Surcharged

مهرجان النخيل
وعيد التموز
١٩٧٢
25 Fils ٢٥

**1973 Litho. *Perf. 13½x14***

| | | |
|---|---|---|
| *694* A85 25f on 3f multi | 3.00 | 1.50 |
| *695* A85 70f on 15f multi | 8.00 | 4.00 |

Festival of Date Trees.

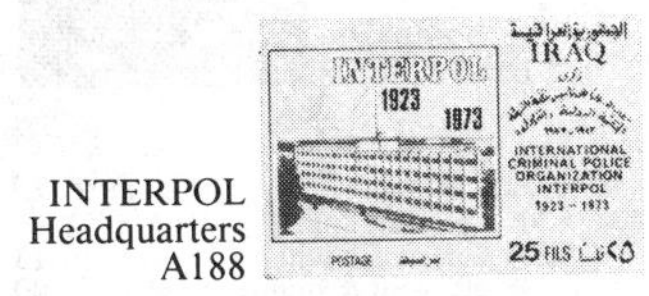

INTERPOL Headquarters A188

**1973, Sept. 20 Litho. *Perf. 12***

| | | |
|---|---|---|
| *696* A188 25f multi | 30 | 13 |
| *697* A188 70f brt bl & multi | 65 | 35 |

50th anniversary of International Criminal Police Organization.

Nos. 517-518 Overprinted in Silver

I.O.J.
SEPTEMBER
26-29. 1973

**1973, Sept. 29 Litho. *Perf. 12½x13***

| | | |
|---|---|---|
| *698* A130 15f multi | 4.00 | 1.00 |
| *699* A130 50f multi | 7.00 | 3.00 |

Meeting of International Organization of Journalists' Executive Committee, Sept. 26-29.

Flags and Fair Emblem A189

WMO Emblem A190

**1973, Oct. 10 Photo. *Perf. 11***

| | | |
|---|---|---|
| *700* A189 10f brt grn & dk brn | 15 | 7 |
| *701* A189 20f ocher & multi | 35 | 12 |
| *702* A189 65f bl & multi | 90 | 55 |

10th International Baghdad Fair, Oct. 1-21.

**1973, Nov. 15 Litho. *Perf. 12***

| | | |
|---|---|---|
| *703* A190 25f org, blk & grn | 50 | 20 |
| *704* A190 35f brt rose, blk & grn | 70 | 25 |

Centenary of international meteorological cooperation.

Flags of Arab League and Iraq, Maghreb Emblem A191

**1973, Dec. 1 Photo. *Perf. 14***

| | | |
|---|---|---|
| *705* A191 20f dl org & multi | 25 | 13 |
| *706* A191 35f bl & multi | 35 | 18 |

11th session of Civil Aviation Council of Arab States, Baghdad, Dec. 1973.

No. 360 Overprinted

المجلس التنفيذي
بغداد/١٩٧٣

**1973, Dec. 12 Photo. *Perf. 11***

| | | |
|---|---|---|
| *707* A67a 30f org & bl | 3.50 | 2.75 |

6th Executive Council Meeting of Arab Postal Union.

Human Rights Flame — A192

**1973, Dec. 25 *Perf. 11½***

| | | |
|---|---|---|
| *708* A192 25f multi | 25 | 13 |
| *709* A192 70f ultra & multi | 65 | 35 |

25th anniversary of Universal Declaration of Human Rights.

Military College Crest and Cadets A193

**1974, Jan. 6 *Perf. 12x11½***

| | | |
|---|---|---|
| *710* A193 25f ocher & multi | 25 | 13 |
| *711* A193 35f ultra & multi | 35 | 18 |

50th anniversary of the Military College.

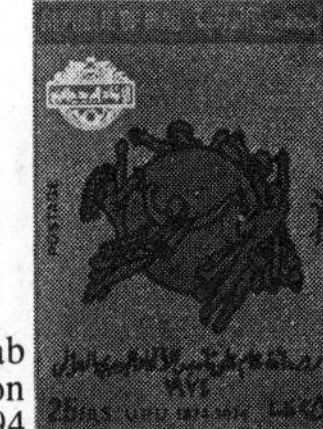
UPU and Arab Postal Union Emblems — A194

**1974, May 28 Photo. *Perf. 11½x12***

| | | |
|---|---|---|
| *712* A194 25f gold & multi | 50 | 15 |
| *713* A194 35f gold & multi | 50 | 30 |
| *714* A194 70f gold & multi | 1.00 | 75 |

Centenary of the Universal Postal Union.

Symbols of Ancient Mesopotamia and Oil Industry — A195

**1974, June 1 Litho. *Perf. 12½***

| | | |
|---|---|---|
| *715* A195 10f bl & multi | 10 | 10 |
| *716* A195 25f ocher & multi | 30 | 25 |
| *717* A195 70f rose & multi | 1.25 | 75 |

2nd anniversary of the nationalization of the oil industry.

Festival — A196

**1974, July 17 Litho. *Perf. 11½x12***

| | | |
|---|---|---|
| *718* A196 20f lil & multi | 20 | 10 |
| *719* A196 35f dl org & multi | 35 | 18 |

July Festivals.

National Front Emblem and People A197

**1974, July 17 *Perf. 12x11½***

| | | |
|---|---|---|
| *720* A197 25f bl & multi | 25 | 13 |
| *721* A197 70f brt grn & multi | 65 | 36 |

1st anniv. of Progressive National Front.

Cement Plant and Brick Wall — A198

**1974, Oct. 19 *Perf. 11½x12***

| | | |
|---|---|---|
| *722* A198 20f gray bl & multi | 25 | 12 |
| *723* A198 25f red & multi | 30 | 13 |
| *724* A198 70f emer & multi | 1.00 | 55 |

25th anniversary of Iraqi Cement Plant.

Nos. 561 and 527 Surcharged

١٠ فلوس
10 Fils

a

Common Design Types are pictured in section before Great Britain.

٢٥ فلسا
25 Fils

b

**1975, Jan. 9 Litho. Perf. 13, 14**

| | | | | |
|---|---|---|---|---|
| 725 | A142 (a) 10f on 3f multi | | 3.00 | 1.50 |
| 726 | A135 (b) 25f on 3f multi | | 9.00 | 6.00 |

Globe and WPY Emblem — A199

**1975, Jan. 30 Perf. 11½x12**

| | | | | |
|---|---|---|---|---|
| 727 | A199 | 25f dl bl & blk | 35 | 15 |
| 728 | A199 | 35f brt pink & ind | 75 | 25 |
| 729 | A199 | 70f yel grn & vio | 2.00 | 75 |

World Population Year 1974.

Festival Symbols — A200

**1975, July 17 Litho. Perf. 12x11½**

| | | | | |
|---|---|---|---|---|
| 730 | A200 | 5f lt brn & multi | 10 | 5 |
| 731 | A200 | 10f lt brn & multi | 15 | 10 |
| 732 | A200 | 35f lt brn & multi | 1.00 | 75 |

Festivals, July 1975.

Map of Arab Countries A201

**1975, Aug. 5 Photo. Perf. 13**

| | | | | |
|---|---|---|---|---|
| 733 | A201 | 25f rose & multi | 30 | 15 |
| 734 | A201 | 35f multi | 32 | 25 |
| 735 | A201 | 45f multi | 52 | 35 |

Arab Working Organization, 10th anniversary.

Symbols of Women, Oil Industry and Agriculture A202

**1975, Aug. 15 Perf. 14**

| | | | | |
|---|---|---|---|---|
| 736 | A202 | 10f lil & multi | 40 | 15 |
| 737 | A202 | 35f multi | 80 | 50 |
| 738 | A202 | 70f bl & multi | 3.25 | 1.00 |
| a | | Souvenir sheet, 100f | 11.00 | 13.00 |

International Women's Year 1975. No. 738a contains an imperf. design similar to type A202; greenish blue denomination, inscription and IWY emblem in margin. Size: 100x82mm.

Euphrates Dam and Causeway A203

**1975, Sept. 5 Litho. Perf. 12x11½**

| | | | | |
|---|---|---|---|---|
| 739 | A203 | 3f org & multi | 5 | 5 |
| 740 | A203 | 25f pur & multi | 50 | 15 |
| 741 | A203 | 70f rose red & multi | 2.00 | 50 |

25th anniversary of the International Commission on Irrigation and Drainage.

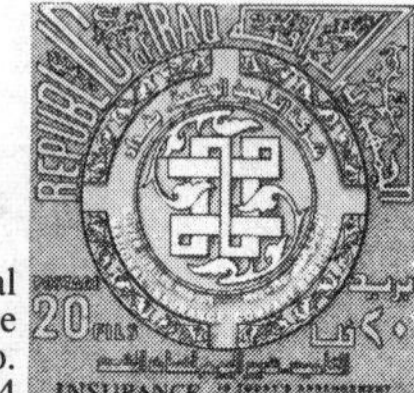

National Insurance Co. Seal — A204

**1975, Oct. 11 Photo. Perf. 13**

| | | | | |
|---|---|---|---|---|
| 742 | A204 | 20f brt bl & multi | 60 | 15 |
| 743 | A204 | 25f crim & multi | 80 | 30 |
| a | | Souvenir sheet, 100f | 9.00 | 11.00 |

National Insurance Company, Baghdad, 25th anniversary. No. 743a contains an imperf. design, type A204; emerald denomination and inscription in margin. Size: 71x71mm.

Musician Entertaining King — A205

**1975, Nov. 21 Perf. 14**

| | | | | |
|---|---|---|---|---|
| 744 | A205 | 25f sil & multi | 30 | 13 |
| 745 | A205 | 45f gold & multi | 55 | 22 |

Baghdad International Music Conference, Nov. 1975.

Telecommunications Center — A206

**1975, Dec. 22 Litho. Perf. 12½**

| | | | | |
|---|---|---|---|---|
| 746 | A206 | 5f lil rose & multi | 15 | 5 |
| 747 | A206 | 10f bl & multi | 20 | 10 |
| 748 | A206 | 60f grn & multi | 1.10 | 50 |

Inauguration of Telecommunications Center Building during July 1975 Festival.

Diesel Locomotive — A207

Designs (Conference Emblem and): 30f, Diesel passenger locomotive # 511. 35f, 0-3-0 steam tank locomotive with passenger train. 50f, 2-3-0 German steam locomotive, c. 1914.

**1975, Dec. 22 Photo. Perf. 14**

| | | | | |
|---|---|---|---|---|
| 749 | A207 | 25f tan & multi | 3.00 | 50 |
| 750 | A207 | 30f tan & multi | 4.00 | 1.00 |
| 751 | A207 | 35f yel grn & multi | 5.50 | 2.00 |
| 752 | A207 | 50f yel grn & multi | 8.00 | 5.50 |

15th Taurus Railway Conference, Baghdad.

Soldier on Guard — A208

**1976, Jan. 6 Perf. 13**

| | | | | |
|---|---|---|---|---|
| 753 | A208 | 5f sil & multi | 5 | 5 |
| 754 | A208 | 25f sil & multi | 30 | 13 |
| 755 | A208 | 50f gold & multi | 90 | 40 |

55th Army Day.

Fingerprint Crossed Out, Arab World — A209

**1976, Jan. 8 Photo. Perf. 13½x13**

| | | | | |
|---|---|---|---|---|
| 756 | A209 | 5f vio & multi | 5 | 5 |
| 757 | A209 | 15f bl & multi | 35 | 15 |
| 758 | A209 | 35f grn & multi | 1.10 | 75 |

Statue of Goddess A210

Iraq Earth Station A211

Designs: 10f, 15f, like 5f. 20f, 25f, 30f, Two female figures forming column. 35f, 50f, 75f, Head of bearded man.

**1976, Jan. 1 Litho. Perf. 13x12½**

| | | | | |
|---|---|---|---|---|
| 759 | A210 | 5f lil & multi | 5 | 5 |
| 760 | A210 | 10f rose & multi | 8 | 5 |
| 761 | A210 | 15f yel & multi | 12 | 7 |
| 762 | A210 | 20f bis & multi | 16 | 10 |
| 763 | A210 | 25f lt grn & multi | 20 | 13 |
| 764 | A210 | 30f bl & multi | 24 | 14 |
| 765 | A210 | 35f lil rose & multi | 25 | 18 |
| 766 | A210 | 50f cit & multi | 40 | 25 |
| 767 | A210 | 75f vio & multi | 60 | 40 |
| | | *Nos. 759-767 (9)* | 2.10 | 1.37 |

**1976, Feb. 8 Perf. 13x13½**

| | | | | |
|---|---|---|---|---|
| 768 | A211 | 10f sil & multi | 32 | 15 |
| 769 | A211 | 25f sil & multi | 1.00 | 30 |
| 770 | A211 | 75f gold & multi | 4.00 | 1.25 |

Revolution of Ramadan 14, 13th anniversary.

Telephones 1876 and 1976 — A212

Map of Maghreb, ICATU Emblem — A213

**1976, Mar. 17 Litho. Perf. 12x12½**

| | | | | |
|---|---|---|---|---|
| 771 | A212 | 35f multi | 1.00 | 30 |
| 772 | A212 | 50f multi | 2.00 | 50 |
| 773 | A212 | 75f multi | 3.00 | 75 |

Centenary of first telephone call by Alexander Graham Bell, Mar. 10, 1876.

**1976, Mar. 24 Photo. Perf. 13½**

| | | | | |
|---|---|---|---|---|
| 774 | A213 | 5f grn & multi | 5 | 5 |
| 775 | A213 | 10f multi | 25 | 15 |

20th International Conference of Arab Trade Unions. See No. C54.

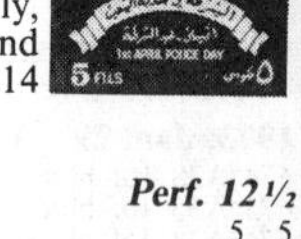

Map of Iraq, Family, Torch and Wreath — A214

**1976, Apr. 1 Perf. 12½**

| | | | | |
|---|---|---|---|---|
| 776 | A214 | 5f multi | 5 | 5 |
| 777 | A214 | 15f lil & multi | 24 | 10 |
| 778 | A214 | 35f multi | 50 | 25 |

Police Day.

Pipe Line, Map of Iraq — A215

Pres. A. H. al-Bakr Embracing Vice Pres. Saddam Hussain — A216

**1976, June 1 Photo. Perf. 13**

| | | | | |
|---|---|---|---|---|
| 779 | A215 | 25f multi | 2.00 | 75 |
| 780 | A215 | 75f multi | 6.00 | 2.00 |

**Souvenir Sheet**

***Imperf***

| | | | | |
|---|---|---|---|---|
| 781 | A216 | 150f multi | 25.00 | 30.00 |

4th anniversary of oil nationalization No. 781 contains one stamp; gold and red ornamental margin. Size: 80x90mm.

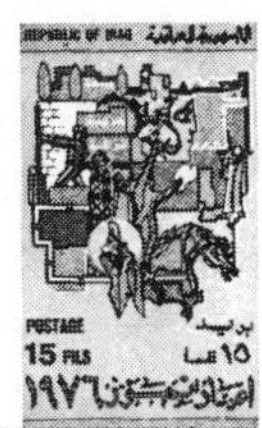


"Festival" — A217

**1976, July 17** ***Perf. 14***

| | | | |
|---|---|---|---|
| *782* | A217 15f org & multi | 25 | 15 |
| *783* | A217 35f org & multi | 75 | 50 |

Festivals, July 1976.

Archbishop Capucci, Map of Palestine A218

**1976, Aug. 18** **Litho.** ***Perf. 12***

| | | | |
|---|---|---|---|
| *784* | A218 25f multi | 50 | 18 |
| *785* | A218 35f multi | 75 | 18 |
| *786* | A218 75f multi | 2.50 | 1.00 |

Detention of Archbishop Hilarion Capucci in Israel, Aug. 18, 1974.

Common Kingfisher A219

"15" A220

Birds: 10f, Turtle dove. 15f, Pin-tailed sandgrouse. 25f, Blue rock thrush. 50f, Purple and gray herons.

**1976, Sept. 15** **Litho.** ***Perf. 13½x14***

| | | | |
|---|---|---|---|
| *787* | A219 5f multi | 10 | 5 |
| *788* | A219 10f multi | 20 | 15 |
| *789* | A219 15f multi | 35 | 15 |
| *790* | A219 25f multi | 50 | 25 |
| *791* | A219 50f multi | 2.00 | 35 |
| | *Nos. 787-791 (5)* | 3.15 | 95 |

**1976, Nov. 23** **Photo.** ***Perf. 13½***

| | | | |
|---|---|---|---|
| *792* | A220 30f multi | 1.10 | 50 |
| *793* | A220 70f multi | 3.25 | 75 |

15th anniversary of National Students Union.

Oil Tanker and Emblems A221

Designs: 15f, like 10f. 25f, 50f, Pier, refinery, pipeline.

**1976, Dec. 25** ***Perf. 12½x12***

| | | | |
|---|---|---|---|
| *794* | A221 10f multi | 50 | 15 |
| *795* | A221 15f multi | 80 | 25 |
| *796* | A221 25f multi | 2.25 | 50 |
| *797* | A221 50f multi | 3.00 | 75 |

1st Iraqi oil tanker (10f, 15f) and Nationalization of Basrah Petroleum Co. Ltd., 1st anniversary (25f, 50f).

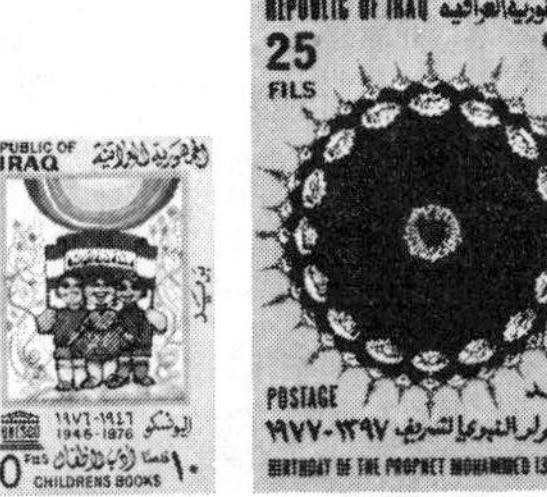


Happy Children A222

Ornament A223

Designs (UNESCO Emblem and): 25f, Children with flowers and butterflies. 75f, Children planting flowers around flagpole.

**1976, Dec. 25** ***Perf. 12x12½***

| | | | |
|---|---|---|---|
| *798* | A222 10f multi | 15 | 15 |
| *799* | A222 25f multi | 2.00 | 25 |
| *800* | A222 75f multi | 3.00 | 75 |

30th anniv. of UNESCO, and Books for Children Campaign.

**1977, Mar. 2** **Photo.** ***Perf. 13½***

| | | | |
|---|---|---|---|
| *801* | A223 25f gold & multi | 60 | 20 |
| *802* | A223 35f gold & multi | 85 | 25 |

Birthday of Mohammed (570-632).

Peace Dove — A224

Dahlia — A225

**1977, Mar. 11** ***Perf. 14x13½***

| | | | |
|---|---|---|---|
| *803* | A224 25f lt bl & multi | 30 | 12 |
| *804* | A224 30f buff & multi | 35 | 15 |

Peace Day 1977.

**1977, Mar. 21** **Litho.** ***Perf. 12½***

Flowers: 10f, Sweet peas. 35f, Chrysanthemums. 50f, Verbena.

| | | | |
|---|---|---|---|
| *805* | A225 5f multi | 25 | 5 |
| *806* | A225 10f multi | 30 | 10 |
| *807* | A225 35f multi | 1.00 | 25 |
| *808* | A225 50f multi | 2.00 | 50 |

Spring Festivals, Baghdad.

Emblem with Doves A226

Designs: 75f, Emblem with flame. 100f, Dove with olive branch.

**1977, Apr. 7** **Photo.** ***Perf. 13***

| | | | |
|---|---|---|---|
| *809* | A226 25f yel & multi | 65 | 12 |
| *810* | A226 75f yel & multi | 2.50 | 40 |

**Souvenir Sheet**

***Imperf***

| | | | |
|---|---|---|---|
| *811* | A227 100f multi | 6.00 | 8.00 |

Al Baath Party, 30th anniversary. No. 811 contains one stamp (49x35mm.). Gold and light green margin with black inscription and control number. Size: 80x60mm.

APU Emblem, Members' Flags — A227

**1977, Apr. 12** **Litho.** ***Perf. 14***

| | | | |
|---|---|---|---|
| *812* | A227 25f org & multi | 35 | 12 |
| *813* | A227 35f gray & multi | 45 | 18 |

25th anniversary of Arab Postal Union.

Cogwheel, Globe and "1" — A228

**1977, May 1** **Litho.** ***Perf. 14½x14***

| | | | |
|---|---|---|---|
| *814* | A228 10f multi | 10 | 5 |
| *815* | A228 30f multi | 35 | 15 |
| *816* | A228 35f multi | 42 | 18 |

Labor Day.

Weight Lifting A229

Designs: 75f, Weight lifter, standing up. 100f, Symbolic weight lifter with Iraqi coat of arms, laurel wreath.

**1977, May 8** **Photo.** ***Perf. 14***

| | | | |
|---|---|---|---|
| *817* | A229 25f multi | 75 | 75 |
| *818* | A229 75f multi | 1.50 | 1.00 |

**Souvenir Sheet**

***Imperf***

| | | | |
|---|---|---|---|
| *819* | A229 100f multi | 7.50 | 8.50 |

8th Asian Weight Lifting Championship, Baghdad, May 1977. No. 819 contains one stamp, size: 42x52mm.; tan, blue and black margin with black control number. Size: 60x80mm.

Arabian Garden — A230

Grain and Dove — A231

Designs Tourist Year Emblem and): 10f, View of town with minarets (horiz.). 30f, Landscape with bridge and waterfall. 50f, Hosts welcoming tourists, and drum (horiz.).

***Perf. 11½x12, 12x11½***

**1977, June 15** **Litho.**

| | | | |
|---|---|---|---|
| *820* | A230 5f multi | 10 | 5 |
| *821* | A230 10f multi | 15 | 10 |
| *822* | A230 30f multi | 90 | 20 |
| *823* | A230 50f multi | 2.50 | 1.25 |

Arab Tourist Year.

**1977, July 17** **Photo.** ***Perf. 14***

| | | | |
|---|---|---|---|
| *824* | A231 25f multi | 30 | 12 |
| *825* | A231 30f multi | 38 | 15 |

Festivals, July 1977.

Map of Arab Countries A232

**1977, Sept. 9** **Photo.** ***Perf. 13½x14***

| | | | |
|---|---|---|---|
| *826* | A232 30f multi | 45 | 25 |
| *827* | A232 70f multi | 2.00 | 50 |

U.N. Conference on Desertification, Nairobi, Kenya, Aug. 29-Sept. 9.

Census Emblem A233

Festival Emblem A234

**1977, Oct. 17** **Litho.** ***Perf. 14x14½***

| | | | |
|---|---|---|---|
| *828* | A233 20f ultra & multi | 25 | 10 |
| *829* | A233 30f brn & multi | 38 | 15 |
| *830* | A233 70f gray & multi | 80 | 35 |

Population Census Day, Oct. 17.

**1977, Nov. 1** **Photo.** ***Perf. 14***

| | | | |
|---|---|---|---|
| *831* | A234 25f sil & multi | 30 | 12 |
| *832* | A234 50f gold & multi | 60 | 24 |

Al Mutanabby Festival, Nov. 1977.

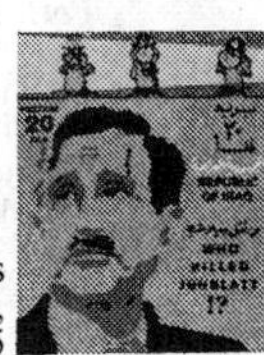

Junblatt, Caricatures of Britain, USA, Israel — A235

**1977, Nov. 16** **Photo.** ***Perf. 14***

| | | | |
|---|---|---|---|
| *833* | A235 20f multi | 24 | 10 |
| *834* | A235 30f multi | 35 | 15 |
| *835* | A235 70f multi | 80 | 35 |

Kemal Junblatt, Druse leader, killed in Lebanese war.

Ornament — A236

**1977, Dec. 12** **Photo.** ***Perf. 14***

| | | | |
|---|---|---|---|
| *836* | A236 30f gold & multi | 40 | 15 |
| *837* | A236 35f sil & multi | 50 | 18 |

Hajeer (Pilgrimage) Year.

Young People and Flags — A237

Coins and Coin Bank — A238

**1978, Apr. 7 Photo. *Perf. 11½x11***
*838* A237 10f multi 10 5
*839* A237 15f multi 25 8
*840* A237 35f multi 55 18

Youth Day.

**1978, Apr. 15**
*841* A238 15f multi 15 8
*842* A238 25f multi 30 12
*843* A238 35f multi 42 18

6th anniversary of postal savings law.

Microwave Transmission and Receiving A239

Emblems and Flags of Participants A240

**1978, May 17 Photo. *Perf. 14***
*844* A239 25f org & multi 22 12
*845* A239 35f lil & multi 30 18
*846* A239 75f emer & multi 65 35

10th World Telecommunications Day and 1st anniversary of commissioning of national microwave network.

***Perf. 12½x11½***
**1978, June 19 Litho.**
*847* A240 25f multi 55 12
*848* A240 35f multi 85 18

Conference of Postal Ministers of Arabian Gulf Countries, Baghdad (Saudi Arabia, United Arab Emirates, Qatar, Bahrain, Kuwait, Oman, People's Republic or Yemen).

Ancient Coin — A241

Designs: Ancient Iraqi coins. 75f vertical.

***Perf. 11½x12½***
**1978, June 25 Photo.**
*849* A241 1f cit & multi 8 5
*850* A241 2f bl & multi 8 5
*851* A241 3f sal & multi 8 5
*852* A241 4f sal & multi 8 5
*853* A241 75f bl grn & multi 2.25 40
*Nos. 849-853 (5)* 2.57 60

Festival Emblem — A242

Festival Poster — A243

**1978, July 17 *Perf. 13½x13***
*854* A242 25f multi 20 12
*855* A242 35f multi 28 18

**Souvenir Sheet**
***Perf. 13x13½***
*856* A243 100f multi 5.00 6.00

Festivals, July 1978. No. 856 has yellow margin with black inscription. Size: 79x60mm.

WHO Emblem, Nurse, Hospital, Sick Child A244

**1978, Aug. 18 Photo. *Perf. 14***
*857* A244 25f multi 30 12
*858* A244 35f multi 40 18
*859* A244 75f multi 90 35

Eradication of smallpox.

Maritime Union Emblem A245

**1978, Aug. 30 Photo. *Perf. 11½x12***
*860* A245 25f multi 30 12
*861* A245 75f multi 90 35

1st World Maritime Day.

Workers A246

**1978, Sept. 12 *Perf. 14***
*862* A246 10f multi 20 5
*863* A246 25f multi 45 12
*864* A246 35f multi 75 18

10th anniversary of People's Work Groups.

Fair Emblem with Atom Symbol — A247

Map of Iraq, Ruler and Globe — A248

**1978, Oct. 1**
*865* A247 25f multi 30 12
*866* A247 35f multi 40 18
*867* A247 75f multi 90 35

15th International Fair, Baghdad, Oct. 1-15.

**1978, Oct. 14**
*868* A248 25f multi 30 12
*869* A248 35f multi 40 18
*870* A248 75f multi 90 35

World Standards Day.

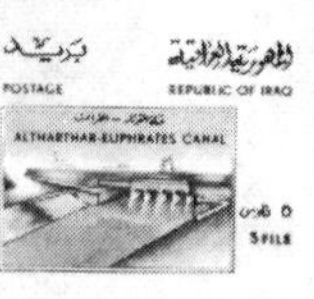

Altharthar-Euphrates Dam — A249

**1978 Photo. *Perf. 11½***
*871* A249 5f multi 5 5
*872* A249 10f multi 10 5
*873* A249 15f multi 15 18
*874* A249 25f multi 30 12
*875* A249 35f multi 45 18
*876* A251 50f multi 65 25
*Nos. 871-876 (6)* 1.70 83

Arab Summit Conference A250

Surgeons' Conference Emblem A251

**1978, Nov. 2 Photo. *Perf. 14***
*890* A250 25f multi 25 15
*891* A250 35f multi 50 25
*892* A250 75f multi 1.00 50

9th Arab Summit Conference, Baghdad, Nov. 2-5.

**1978, Nov. 8 Litho. *Perf. 12x11½***
*893* A251 25f multi 25 12
*894* A251 75f multi 80 35

4th Congress of the Association of Thoracic and Cardiovascular Surgeons of Asia, Baghdad, Nov. 6-10.

Pilgrims at Mt. Arafat and Holy Kaaba A252

**1978, Nov. 9 Photo. *Perf. 14***
*895* A252 25f multi 25 12
*896* A252 35f multi 35 18

Pilgrimage to Mecea.

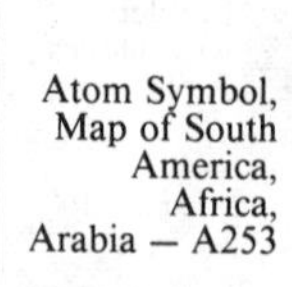
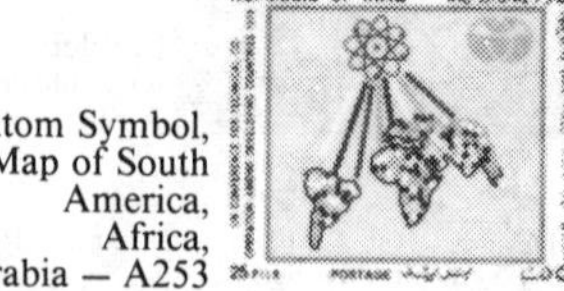

Atom Symbol, Map of South America, Africa, Arabia — A253

**1978, Nov. 11 *Perf. 13½***
*897* A253 25f multi 65 12
*898* A253 50f multi 55 25
*899* A253 75f multi 80 35

Technical Cooperation Among Developing Countries Conference, Buenos Aires, Argentina, Sept. 1978.

Hands Holding Emblem — A254


Globe and Flame Emblem — A255

**1978, Nov. 30 Litho. *Perf. 13½x13***
*900* A254 25f multi 35 12
*901* A254 50f multi 75 25
*902* A254 75f multi 1.10 35

Anti-Apartheid Year.

**1978, Dec. 20 *Perf. 14***
*903* A255 25f multi 20 12
*904* A255 75f multi 60 35

Declaration of Human Rights, 30th anniversary.

Candle and Emblem — A256

Book, Pencil and Flame — A257

**1979, Jan. 9 Photo. *Perf. 14***
*905* A256 10f multi 8 6
*906* A256 25f multi 20 12
*907* A256 35f multi 28 18

Police Day.

**1979, Feb. 15 Photo. *Perf. 14***
*908* A257 15f multi 25 8
*909* A257 25f multi 35 12
*910* A257 35f multi 65 18

Application of Compulsory Education Law, anniversary.

Pupils, School and Teacher — A258

**1979, Mar. 1 *Perf. 13***
*911* A258 10f multi 10 5
*912* A258 15f multi 20 8
*913* A258 50f multi 80 25

Teacher's Day.

Pupils, Flag, Pencil — A259

**1979, Mar. 10 *Perf. 13½x13***
*914* A259 15f multi 15 8
*915* A259 25f multi 25 12
*916* A259 35f multi 50 18

National Comprehensive Compulsory Literacy Campaign.

Book, World Map, Arab Achievements A260

**1979, Mar. 22** *Perf. 13*
*917* A260 35f multi 28 18
*918* A260 75f multi 60 38

Achievements of the Arabs.

Girl Playing Flute — A261

**1979, Apr. 15** **Litho.** *Perf. 13½*
*919* A261 15f multi 22 10
*920* A261 25f multi 35 15
*921* A261 35f multi 75 30

Mosul Spring Festival 1979.

Iraqi Flag, Globe, UPU Emblem A262

**1979, Apr. 22** **Photo.** *Perf. 13x13½*
*922* A262 25f multi 40 12
*923* A262 35f multi 45 18
*924* A262 75f multi 1.00 50

50th anniversary of Iraq's admission to the Universal Postal Union.

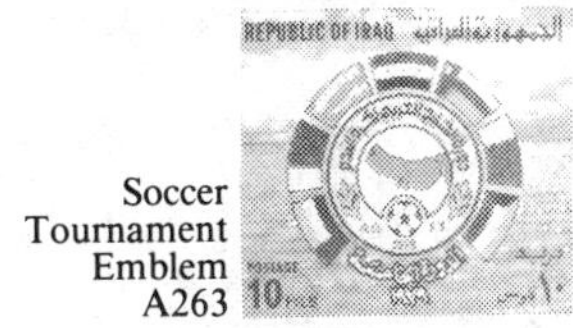
Soccer Tournament Emblem A263

**1979, May 4** **Photo.** *Perf. 13*
*925* A263 10f multi 15 6
*926* A263 15f multi 30 8
*927* A263 50f multi 1.00 50

5th Arabian Gulf Soccer Championship.

Child With Globe and Candle A264

Design: 100f, IYC emblem, boy and girl reaching for U.S. emblem, vert.

**1979, June 1** **Photo.** *Perf. 13x13½*
*928* A264 25f multi 38 18
*929* A264 75f multi 1.25 65

**Souvenir Sheet**

*930* A264 100f multi 30.00 25.00

International Year of the Child.
No. 930 contains one stamp (30x42mm.). Multicolored margin, silver inscription. Size: 68x80mm.

Leaf and Flower — A265

**1979, July 17** **Litho.** *Perf. 12½*
*931* A265 15f multi 12 8
*932* A265 25f multi 20 12
*933* A265 35f multi 28 18

July festivals.

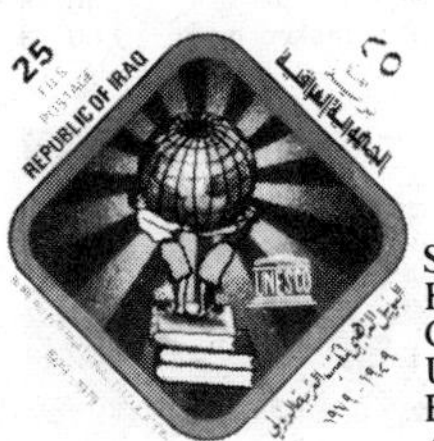
Students Holding Globe, UNESCO Emblem A266

**1979, July 25**
*934* A266 25f multi 40 15
*935* A266 40f multi 70 25
*936* A266 100f multi 2.00 50

International Bureau of Education, Geneva, 50th anniversary.

S. al Hosari, Philosopher A267

Designs: No. 938, Mustapha Jawad, historian. No. 939, Jawad Selim, sculptor.

**1979, Oct. 15** **Litho.** *Perf. 12½*
*937* A267 25f multi 30 12
*938* A267 25f multi 30 12
*939* A267 25f multi 30 12

Pilgrimage to Mecca A268

**1979, Oct. 25** **Litho.** *Perf. 12½*
*940* A268 25f multi 30 12
*941* A268 50f multi 60 24

Iraqi News Agency, 20th Anniversary A269

Telecom 79 A270

**1979, Nov. 9** **Photo.** *Perf. 11½*
*942* A269 25f multi 20 12
*943* A269 50f multi 40 25
*944* A269 75f multi 60 35

**1979, Nov. 20** **Litho.** *Perf. 11½*
*945* A270 25f multi 25 15
*946* A270 50f multi 50 35
*947* A270 75f multi 75 50

3rd World Telecommunications Exhibition, Geneva, Sept. 20-26.

International Palestinian Solidarity Day — A271

**1979, Nov. 29** **Photo.** *Perf. 11½x12*
*948* A271 25f multi 75 15
*949* A271 50f multi 1.25 35
*950* A271 75f multi 1.75 50

Ahmad Hassan Al-Bakir — A272

**1979, Dec. 1** **Photo.** *Perf. 13x13½*
*951* A272 25f *shown* 25 12
*952* A272 35f *Pres. Saddam Hussain* 35 18
*953* A272 75f *Like No. 951* 75 35
*954* A272 100f *Like No. 952* 3.00 2.00

Vanguard Emblem — A273

Vanguard Emblem and: 10f, Boy and violin. 15f, Children, map of Iraq. 25f, Youths.

**1979, Dec. 10** *Perf. 14*
*955* A273 10f multi 10 5
*956* A273 15f multi 16 8
*957* A273 25f multi 25 12
*958* A273 35f multi 35 18

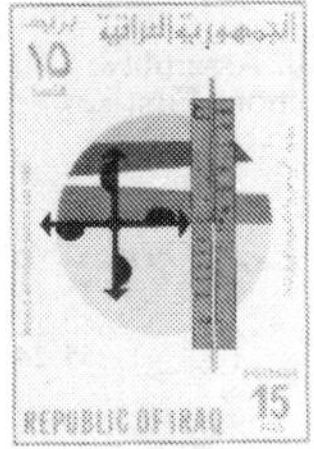
World Meteorological Day — A274

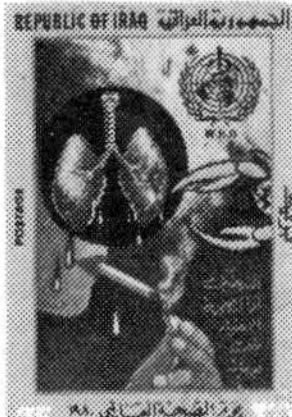
World Health Day — A275

**1980, Mar. 23** **Photo.** *Perf. 14*
*959* A274 15f multi 16 8
*960* A274 25f multi 25 12
*961* A274 35f multi 35 18

**1980, Apr. 7** **Photo.** *Perf. 14*
*962* A275 25f multi 30 12
*963* A275 35f multi 42 18
*964* A275 75f multi 1.50 38

Festivals Emblem — A276

Pres. Hussein — A277

*Perf. 13½x13, 13½ (100f)*

**1980, July 17** **Photo.**
*965* A276 25f multi 25 12
*966* A276 35f multi 35 18

**Souvenir Sheet**

*967* A278 100f multi 4.50 4.50

July Festivals. No. 967 has multicolored decorative margin. Size: 60x80mm.

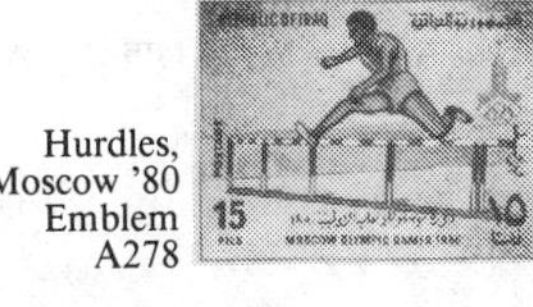
Hurdles, Moscow '80 Emblem A278

**1980, July 30** **Photo.** *Perf. 14*
*968* A278 15f *shown* 18 10
*969* A278 20f *Weight lifting, vert.* 28 25
*970* A278 30f *Boxing* 55 35
*971* A278 35f *Soccer, vert* 1.10 55

**Souvenir Sheet**

*972* A278 100f *Wrestling* 6.00 6.00

22nd Summer Olympic Games, Moscow, July 19-Aug. 3. No. 972 has multicolored margin showing Moscow "80 emblem, flag of Iraq. Size: 80x61mm.

Fruits — A279

**1980, Aug. 15**
*973* A279 5f Blackberries 12 5
*974* A279 15f Apricots 20 10
*975* A279 20f Pears 35 15
*976* A279 25f Apples 50 15
*977* A279 35f Plums 1.00 25
*Nos. 973-977 (5)* 2.17 70

World Tourism Conference, Manila, Sept. 27 — A279a

**1980, Aug. 30** **Litho.** *Perf. 12½*
*978* A279a 25f multi 28 15
*979* A279a 50f multi 55 25
*980* A279a 100f multi 1.10 55

The only foreign revenue stamps listed in this Catalogue are those authorized for prepayment of postage.

Postal Union Emblem, Posthorn, Map of Arab States — A280

**1980, Sept. 8** *Perf. 12*

| | | | | |
|---|---|---|---|---|
| *981* | A280 | 10f multi | 10 | 5 |
| *982* | A280 | 30f multi | 35 | 16 |
| *983* | A280 | 35f multi | 40 | 18 |

Arab Postal Union, 11th Congress, Baghdad.

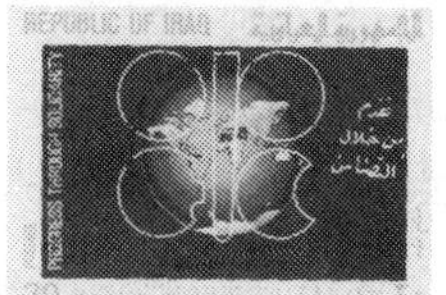

20th Anniversary of OPEC — A281

**1980, Sept. 30**

| | | | | |
|---|---|---|---|---|
| *984* | A281 | 30f multi | 1.00 | 25 |
| *985* | A281 | 75f multi | 1.50 | 50 |

Papilio Machaon A282

**1980, Oct. 20 Photo.** *Perf. 13½x14*

| | | | | |
|---|---|---|---|---|
| *987* | A282 | 10f shown | 35 | 15 |
| *988* | A282 | 15f Danaus chrysippus | 45 | 20 |
| *989* | A282 | 20f Vanessa atalanta | 60 | 25 |
| *990* | A282 | 30f Colias croceus | 1.00 | 25 |

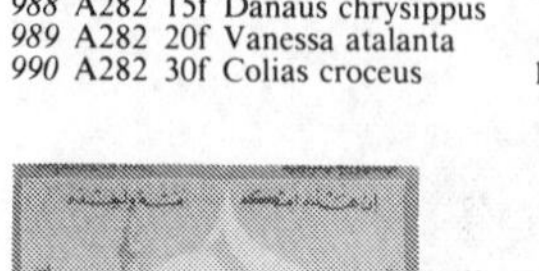

Hegira, 1,500th Anniv. A283

**1980, Nov. 9 Litho.** *Perf. 11½x12*

| | | | | |
|---|---|---|---|---|
| *991* | A283 | 15f multi | 18 | 8 |
| *992* | A283 | 25f multi | 30 | 12 |
| *993* | A283 | 35f multi | 40 | 18 |

International Palestinian Solidarity Day — A284

**1980, Nov. 29**

| | | | | |
|---|---|---|---|---|
| *994* | A284 | 25f multi | 30 | 12 |
| *995* | A284 | 35f multi | 40 | 18 |
| *996* | A284 | 75f multi | 80 | 38 |

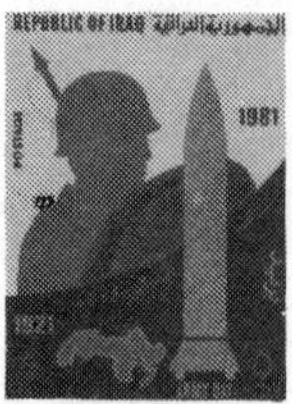

Army Day A285

February Revolution, 18th Anniversary A286

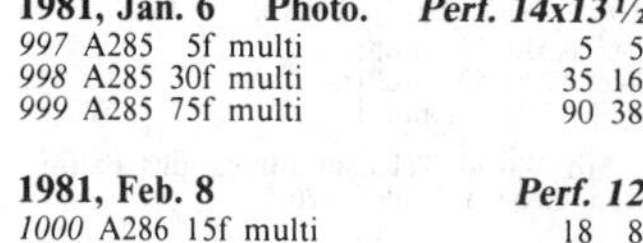

**1981, Jan. 6 Photo.** *Perf. 14x13½*

| | | | | |
|---|---|---|---|---|
| *997* | A285 | 5f multi | 5 | 5 |
| *998* | A285 | 30f multi | 35 | 16 |
| *999* | A285 | 75f multi | 90 | 38 |

**1981, Feb. 8** *Perf. 12*

| | | | | |
|---|---|---|---|---|
| *1000* | A286 | 15f multi | 18 | 8 |
| *1001* | A286 | 30f multi | 30 | 16 |
| *1002* | A286 | 35f multi | 40 | 18 |

Map of Arab Countries A287

**1981, Mar. 22 Litho.** *Perf. 12½*

| | | | | |
|---|---|---|---|---|
| *1003* | A287 | 5f multi | 5 | 5 |
| *1004* | A287 | 25f multi | 30 | 12 |
| *1005* | A287 | 35f multi | 40 | 18 |

Saddam's Battle of Qadisiya — A288

**1981, Apr. 7 Photo.** *Perf. 13½x13*

| | | | | |
|---|---|---|---|---|
| *1006* | A288 | 30f multi | 35 | 16 |
| *1007* | A288 | 35f multi | 40 | 18 |
| *1008* | A288 | 75f multi | 80 | 38 |

**Souvenir Sheet**

| | | | | |
|---|---|---|---|---|
| *1009* | A288 | 100f multi | 4.50 | 5.50 |

No. 1009 contains one horiz. stamp. Size: 80x60mm.

Helicopters and Tank A289

**1981, June 1** **Photo.**

| | | | | |
|---|---|---|---|---|
| *1010* | A289 | 5f shown | 15 | 5 |
| *1011* | A289 | 10f Plane | 25 | 10 |
| *1012* | A289 | 15f Rocket | 50 | 15 |

Air Force, 50th anniv. See No. C66.

Natl. Assembly Election, First Anniv. — A290

**1981, June 20** *Perf. 12½*

| | | | | |
|---|---|---|---|---|
| *1013* | A290 | 30f multi | 35 | 16 |
| *1014* | A290 | 35f multi | 40 | 18 |
| *1015* | A290 | 45f multi | 55 | 24 |

July Festivals 1981 — A291

**1981, July 17** **Photo.**

| | | | | |
|---|---|---|---|---|
| *1016* | A291 | 15f multi | 15 | 8 |
| *1017* | A291 | 25f multi | 30 | 14 |
| *1018* | A291 | 35f multi | 40 | 18 |

Pottery Maker — A292

Designs: Popular industries.

**1981, Aug. 15** *Perf. 14*

| | | | | |
|---|---|---|---|---|
| *1019* | A292 | 5f Straw weaver | 5 | 5 |
| *1020* | A292 | 30f Metal worker | 35 | 16 |
| *1021* | A292 | 35f shown | 40 | 18 |
| *1022* | A292 | 50f Rug maker, horiz. | 1.00 | 28 |

Islamic Pilgrimage A293

**1981, Oct. 7 Photo.** *Perf. 12x11½*

| | | | | |
|---|---|---|---|---|
| *1023* | A293 | 25f multi | 30 | 14 |
| *1024* | A293 | 45f multi | 55 | 24 |
| *1025* | A293 | 50f multi | 60 | 30 |

World Food Day A294

**1981, Oct. 16 Photo.** *Perf. 14*

| | | | | |
|---|---|---|---|---|
| *1026* | A294 | 30f multi | 35 | 16 |
| *1027* | A294 | 45f multi | 50 | 24 |
| *1028* | A294 | 75f multi | 80 | 45 |

Intl. Year of the Disabled — A295

**1981, Nov. 15**

| | | | | |
|---|---|---|---|---|
| *1029* | A295 | 30f multi | 30 | 16 |
| *1030* | A295 | 45f multi | 50 | 24 |
| *1031* | A295 | 75f multi | 70 | 45 |

5th Anniv. of United Arab Shipping Co. — A296

**1981, Dec. 2** *Perf. 13x13½*

| | | | | |
|---|---|---|---|---|
| *1032* | A296 | 50f multi | 75 | 30 |
| *1033* | A296 | 120f multi | 2.25 | 75 |

Saddam Hussein Gymnasium A297

**1981, Sept. 26 Litho.** *Perf. 12x12½*

| | | | | |
|---|---|---|---|---|
| *1034* | A297 | 45f shown | 48 | 24 |
| *1035* | A297 | 50f Palace of Conferences | 52 | 30 |
| *1036* | A297 | 120f like #1035 | 1.25 | 75 |
| *1037* | A297 | 150f like #1034 | 1.40 | 90 |

35th Anniv. of Al Baath Party — A298

**1982, Apr. 7 Photo.** *Perf. 13½x13*

| | | | | |
|---|---|---|---|---|
| *1038* | A298 | 25f Pres. Hussein, flowers | 22 | 14 |
| *1039* | A298 | 30f "7 7 7" | 26 | 16 |
| *1040* | A298 | 45f like 25f | 40 | 24 |
| *1041* | A298 | 50f like 30f | 45 | 30 |

**Souvenir Sheet**
**Imperf.**

| | | | | |
|---|---|---|---|---|
| *1042* | A298 | 150f multi | 1.75 | 1.25 |

Margin shows battle scenes. Size 100x53mm.

Mosul Spring Festival — A299

**1982, Apr. 15 Litho.** *Perf. 11½x12*

| | | | | |
|---|---|---|---|---|
| *1043* | A299 | 25f Birds | 30 | 14 |
| *1044* | A299 | 30f Girl | 35 | 16 |
| *1045* | A299 | 45f like 25f | 55 | 24 |
| *1046* | A299 | 50f like 30f | 60 | 30 |

Intl. Workers' Day A300

**1982, May 1** *Perf. 12½*

| | | | | |
|---|---|---|---|---|
| *1047* | A300 | 25f multi | 20 | 14 |
| *1048* | A300 | 45f multi | 36 | 24 |
| *1049* | A300 | 50f multi | 40 | 30 |

14th World Telecommunications Day — A301

**1982, May 17 Photo.** *Perf. 13x13½*

| | | | | |
|---|---|---|---|---|
| *1050* | A301 | 5f multi | 5 | 5 |
| *1051* | A301 | 45f multi | 36 | 24 |
| *1052* | A301 | 100f multi | 80 | 60 |

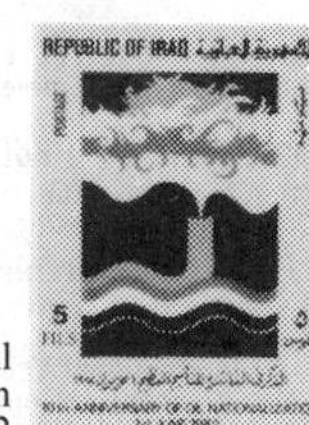

10th Anniv. of Oil Nationalization A302

**1982, June 1 Litho.** *Perf. 12½*

| | | | | |
|---|---|---|---|---|
| *1053* | A302 | 5f Oil gusher | 15 | 5 |
| *1054* | A302 | 25f like 5f | 60 | 14 |
| *1055* | A302 | 45f Statue | 1.25 | 24 |
| *1056* | A302 | 50f like 45f | 1.40 | 30 |

Martyrs' Day — A303

Women's Day — A304

1981, Dec. 1 **Photo.** *Perf. 14*
1057 A303 45f multi 36 24
1058 A303 50f multi 40 30
1059 A303 120f multi 1.00 75

**1982, Mar. 4 Litho.** *Perf. 12½x13*
1060 A304 25f multi 30 14
1061 A304 45f multi 55 24
1062 A304 50f multi 60 30

Arab Postal Union, 30th Anniv. — A305

**1982, Apr. 12** *Perf. 12½*
1063 A305 25f multi 30 14
1064 A305 45f multi 55 24
1065 A305 50f multi 60 30

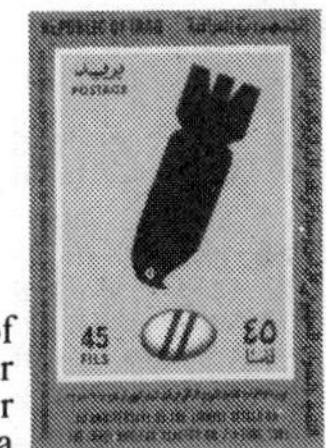
First Anniv. of Attack on Nuclear Power Reactor — A305a

**1982, June 7 Photo.** *Perf. 14*
1065A A305a 30f Nuclear power emblem, lion 50 20
1065B A305a 45f Bomb, natl. colors 75 30
1065C A305a 50f like 30f 90 40
1065D A305a 120f like 45f 2.00 1.00

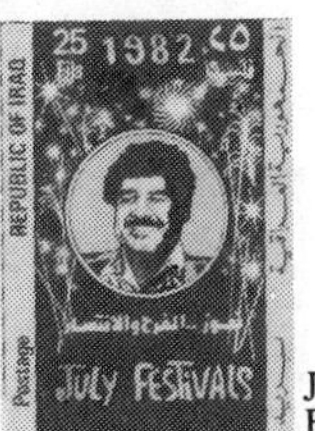
July Festivals — A306

**1982, July 17 Photo.** *Perf. 14½x14*
1066 A306 25f multi 40 14
1067 A306 45f multi 55 24
1068 A306 50f multi 60 30

Lacerta Viridis A307

**1982, Aug. 20 Litho.** *Perf. 12½*
1069 A307 25f shown 30 14
1070 A307 30f Vipera aspis 35 16
1071 A307 45f Lacerta virdis, diff. 55 24
1072 A307 50f Natrix tessellata 60 30

7th Non-aligned Countries Conference, Baghdad, Sept. — A308

Designs: No. 1073, Tito. No. 1074, Nehru. No. 1075, Nasser. No. 1076, Kwame Nkrumah. No. 1077, Pres. Hussein.

**1982, Sept. 6 Photo.** *Perf. 13x13½*
1073 A308 50f multi 55 40
1074 A308 50f multi 55 40
1075 A308 50f multi 55 40
1076 A308 50f multi 55 40
1077 A308 100f multi 1.10 55
*Nos. 1073-1077 (5)* 3.30 2.15

TB Bacillus Centenary A309

**1982, Oct. 1** *Perf. 14x14½*
1078 A309 20f multi 20 10
1079 A309 50f multi 55 30
1080 A309 100f multi 1.10 40

1982 World Cup — A310

Designs: Various soccer players. 150f horiz.

**1982, July 1 Litho.** *Perf. 11½x12*
1081 A310 5f multi 5 5
1082 A310 45f multi 50 24
1083 A310 50f multi 55 30
1084 A310 100f multi 1.10 60

**Souvenir Sheet**
*Perf. 12½*
1085 A310 150f multi 1.75 1.25

No. 1085 has multicolored margin showing soccer players. Size: 85x60mm.

13th UPU Day A311

**1982, Oct. 9** *Perf. 12x11½*
1086 A311 5f multi 5 5
1087 A311 45f multi 40 24
1088 A311 100f multi 90 60

Musical Instruments A312

**1982, Nov. 15** *Perf. 12½x13*
1089 A312 5f Drums 10 5
1090 A312 10f Zither 20 10
1091 A312 35f Stringed instrument 65 35
1092 A312 100f Lute 1.75 85

Birth Anniv. of Mohammed A313

Mecca Mosque views.

**1982, Dec. 27 Litho.** *Perf. 12x11½*
1093 A313 25f multi 20 15
1094 A313 30f multi 28 22
1095 A313 45f multi 36 24
1096 A313 50f multi 40 30

Nos. 1034-1036 Surcharged.

**1983, May 15 Litho.** *Perf. 12x12½*
1097 A297 60f on 50f multi 75 32
1098 A297 70f on 45f multi 90 45
1099 A297 160f on 120f multi 2.00 90

July Festivals A314

**1983, July 17 Litho.** *Perf. 14½x14*
1100 A314 30f multi 35 16
1101 A314 60f multi 75 32
1102 A314 70f multi 90 45

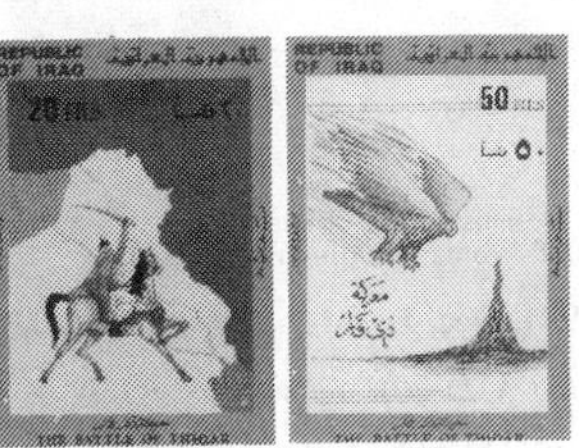
Local Flowers — A315

**1983, June 15 Photo.** *Perf. 15x14*
**Border Color**
1103 A315 10f shown, light blue 8 5
1104 A315 20f Flowers, diff., pale yellow 16 8
1105 A315 30f like 10f, yellow 25 16
1106 A315 40f like 20f, gray 35 25
1107 A315 50f like 10f, pale green 40 30
1108 A315 100f like 20f, pink 80 60
*a* Bklt. pane of 6 (#1103-1108) 3.00
*Nos. 1103-1108 (6)* 2.04 1.44

Nos. 1103-1108 issued in booklets only.

Battle of Thi Qar
A316 A317

**1983, Oct. 30 Photo.** *Perf. 12½x13*
1109 A316 20f sil & multi 24 12
1110 A317 50f sil & multi 60 30
1111 A316 60f gold & multi 70 32
1112 A317 70f gold & multi 1.10 40

World Communications Year — A318

Design: 25f, 70f show emblem and hexagons.

**1983, Oct. 20 Photo.** *Perf. 11½x12*
1113 A318 5f brt yel grn & multi 5 5
1114 A318 25f rose lil & multi 30 15
1115 A318 60f brt org yel & multi 70 34
1116 A318 70f brt bl vio & multi 1.10 40

**Souvenir Sheet**
1117 A318 200f ap grn & multi 3.75 3.75

Margin shows emblems. Black marginal inscription. Size: 81x61mm.

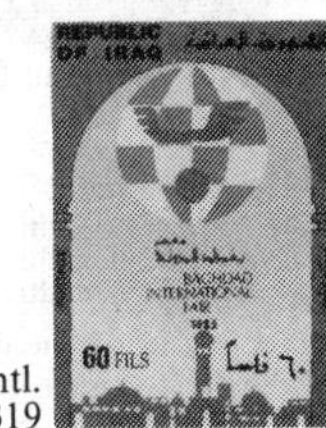
Baghdad Intl. Fair — A319

**1983, Nov. 1 Photo.** *Perf. 12½*
1118 A319 60f multi 48 32
1119 A319 70f multi 56 40
1120 A319 160f multi 1.30 90

Symbolic "9" — A320

9th Natl. Congress of Arab Baath Socialist Party: 30f, 70f, Symbols of development. 60f, 100f, Torch, eagle, globe, open book.

**1983, Nov. 10 Photo.** *Perf. 14*
1121 A320 30f multi 24 16
1122 A320 60f multi 48 32
1123 A320 70f multi 56 40
1124 A320 100f multi 80 55

Festival Crowd — A321

Various Paintings.

**1983, Nov. 20 Litho.** *Perf. 12½*
1125 A321 60f shown 48 32
1126 A321 60f Men hauling boat, vert. 48 32
1127 A321 60f Decorations 48 32
1128 A321 70f Village 56 40
1129 A321 70f Crowd 56 40
*Nos. 1125-1129 (5)* 2.56 1.76

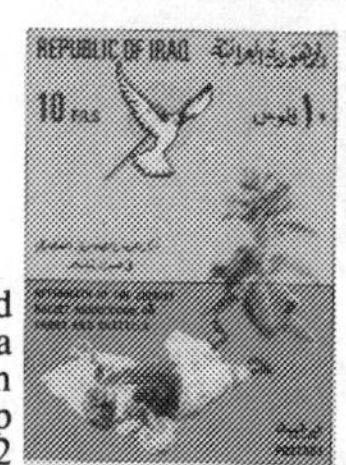

Sabra and Shattela Palestinian Refugee Camp Massacre — A322

Various Victims.

**1983, Nov. 29** *Perf. 11 ½x12*

| | | | | |
|---|---|---|---|---|
| *1130* | A322 | 10f multi | 10 | 5 |
| *1131* | A322 | 60f multi | 1.00 | 32 |
| *1132* | A322 | 70f multi | 1.10 | 40 |
| *1133* | A322 | 160f multi | 2.00 | 92 |

Pres. Hussein, Map — A323

**1983** **Photo.** *Perf. 13 ½x13*

| | | | | |
|---|---|---|---|---|
| *1134* | A323 | 60f multi | 60 | 32 |
| *1135* | A323 | 70f multi | 70 | 40 |
| *1136* | A323 | 250f multi | 2.50 | 1.65 |

Pres. Hussein as head of Al Baath Party, 4th anniv.

Modern Building — A324

Various buildings.

**1983, Dec. 31** **Litho.** *Perf. 14*

| | | | | |
|---|---|---|---|---|
| *1137* | A324 | 60f multi | 48 | 32 |
| *1138* | A324 | 70f multi | 56 | 40 |
| *1139* | A324 | 160f multi | 1.30 | 92 |
| *1140* | A324 | 200f multi | 1.60 | 1.10 |
| | | *Nos. 1137-1140,O340-O341 (6)* | 4.98 | 3.46 |

Medical Congress Emblem A325

**1984, Mar. 10** *Perf. 13x12 ½*

| | | | | |
|---|---|---|---|---|
| *1141* | A325 | 60f multi | 60 | 32 |
| *1142* | A325 | 70f multi | 70 | 40 |
| *1143* | A325 | 200f multi | 2.00 | 1.10 |

25th Intl. Congress of Military Medicine and Pharmacy, Baghdad, Mar. 10-15.

Pres. Hussein's Birthday — A326

Various portraits of Hussein.

**Litho. & Embossed**

**1984, Apr. 28** *Perf. 12 ½x13*

| | | | | |
|---|---|---|---|---|
| *1144* | A326 | 60f multi | 48 | 32 |
| *1145* | A326 | 70f multi | 56 | 40 |
| *1146* | A326 | 160f multi | 1.30 | 92 |
| *1147* | A326 | 200f multi | 1.60 | 1.10 |

**Souvenir Sheet**

| | | | | |
|---|---|---|---|---|
| *1148* | A326 | 250f multi | 2.00 | 1.75 |

Size of No. 1148: 81x62mm.

1984 Summer Olympics, Los Angeles A327

**1984, Aug. 12** **Litho.** *Perf. 12x11 ½*

| | | | | |
|---|---|---|---|---|
| *1149* | A327 | 50f Boxing | 32 | 22 |
| *1150* | A327 | 60f Weight lifting | 38 | 25 |
| *1151* | A327 | 70f like 50f | 45 | 30 |
| *1152* | A327 | 100f like 60f | 65 | 45 |

**Size: 80x60mm.**

***Imperf***

| | | | | |
|---|---|---|---|---|
| *1153* | A327 | 200f Soccer | 1.40 | 95 |
| | | *Nos. 1149-1153 (5)* | 3.20 | 2.17 |

Nos. 1153 contains one perf. 12 ½label (size: 32x41mm) within the stamp.

Pres. Hussein, Flaming Horses Heads, Map — A328

Designs: 50f, 70f, Shown. 60f, 100f, Abstract of woman, sapling, rifle. 200f, Shield, heraldic eagle.

**1984, Sept. 22** *Perf. 11 ½x12*

| | | | | |
|---|---|---|---|---|
| *1154* | A328 | 50f multi | 32 | 22 |
| *1155* | A328 | 60f multi | 38 | 25 |
| *1156* | A328 | 70f multi | 45 | 30 |
| *1157* | A328 | 100f multi | 65 | 45 |

**Size: 80x60mm.**

***Imperf***

| | | | | |
|---|---|---|---|---|
| *1158* | A328 | 200f multi | 1.40 | 95 |
| | | *Nos. 1154-1158 (5)* | 3.20 | 2.17 |

Hussein's Battle of Qadisiya. No. 1158 contains one perf. 12 ½ label (32x41mm) within the stamp.

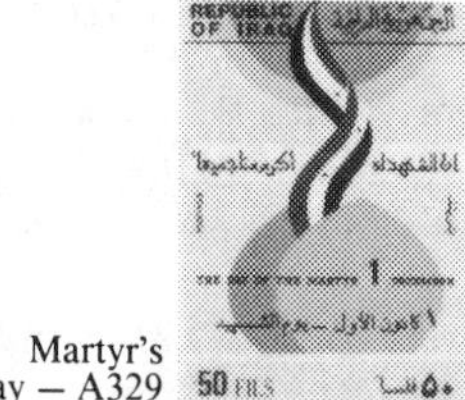

Martyr's Day — A329

Designs: 50f, 70f, Natl. flag as flame. 60f, 100f, Woman holding rifle, medal.

**1984, Dec. 1** *Perf. 13 ½*

| | | | | |
|---|---|---|---|---|
| *1159* | A329 | 50f multi | 32 | 22 |
| *1160* | A329 | 60f multi | 38 | 25 |
| *1161* | A329 | 70f multi | 45 | 30 |
| *1162* | A329 | 100f multi | 65 | 45 |

Pres. Hussein's Visit to Al-Mustansiriyah University, 5th Anniv. — A330

**1985, Apr. 2** **Photo.** *Perf. 12x11 ½*

| | | | | |
|---|---|---|---|---|
| *1163* | A330 | 60f dk bl gray & dk pink | 38 | 25 |
| *1164* | A330 | 70f myr grn & dk pink | 45 | 30 |
| *1165* | A330 | 250f blk & dk pink | 1.75 | 1.15 |

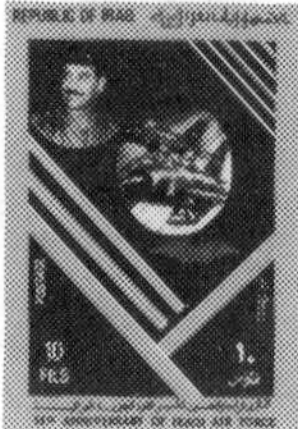

Iraqi Air Force, 54th Anniv. — A331

Pres. Hussein, 48th Birthday — A332

Designs: 10f, 160f, Pres. Hussein, fighter planes, pilot's wings. 60f, 70f, 200f, Planes, flag, "54," horiz.

*Perf. 13x12 ½, 13 ½ (60f, 70f)*

**1985, Apr. 22** **Litho.**

| | | | | |
|---|---|---|---|---|
| *1166* | A331 | 10f multi | 8 | 5 |
| *1167* | A331 | 60f multi | 38 | 25 |
| *1168* | A331 | 70f multi | 45 | 30 |
| *1169* | A331 | 160f multi | 1.05 | 70 |

**Souvenir Sheet**

*Perf. 12 ½*

| | | | | |
|---|---|---|---|---|
| *1170* | A331 | 200f multi | 1.40 | 95 |

No. 1170 has multicolored margin continuing the design and picturing Pres. Hussein. Size: 80x60mm.

**1985, Apr. 28** *Perf. 13 ½*

Designs: 30f, 70f, Pres. Hussein, sunflower. 60f, 100f, Pres., candle and flowers. 200f, Flowers and text.

| | | | | |
|---|---|---|---|---|
| *1171* | A332 | 30f multi | 20 | 12 |
| *1172* | A332 | 60f multi | 38 | 25 |
| *1173* | A332 | 70f multi | 45 | 30 |
| *1174* | A332 | 100f multi | 65 | 45 |

**Souvenir Sheet**

*Perf. 13x12 ½*

| | | | | |
|---|---|---|---|---|
| *1175* | A332 | 200f multi | 1.40 | 95 |

No. 1175 has multicolored decorative margin picturing Pres. Hussein, natl. flag, candles and flowers. Size: 87x60mm.

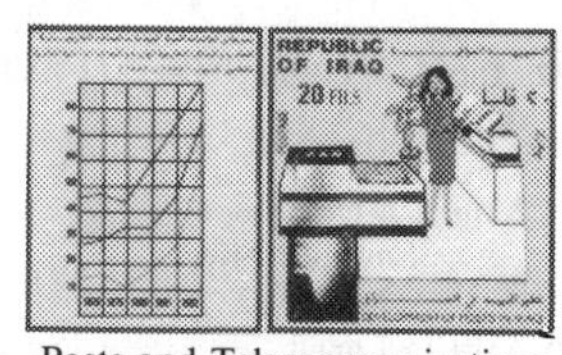

Posts and Telecommunications Development Program — A333

Designs: 20f, 60f, Graph, woman in modern office. 50f, 70f, Satellite dish and graphs.

**1985, June 30** *Perf. 12 ½*

| | | | | |
|---|---|---|---|---|
| *1176* | A333 | 20f multi | 14 | 10 |
| *1177* | A333 | 50f multi | 32 | 22 |
| *1178* | A333 | 60f multi | 38 | 25 |
| *1179* | A333 | 70f multi | 45 | 30 |

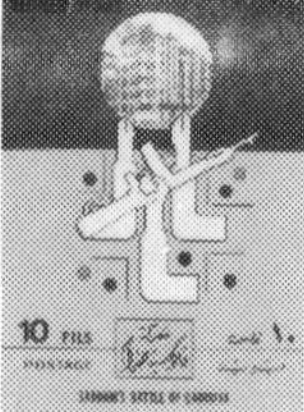

Battle of Qadisiya — A334

Designs: 10f, 60f, Shown. 20f, 70f, Pres. Hussein, Al-Baath Party emblem. 200f, Dove, natl. flag as shield, soldier.

**1985, Sept. 4** *Perf. 11 ½x12*

| | | | | |
|---|---|---|---|---|
| *1180* | A334 | 10f multi | 8 | 5 |
| *1181* | A334 | 20f multi | 14 | 10 |
| *1182* | A334 | 60f multi | 38 | 25 |
| *1183* | A334 | 70f multi | 45 | 30 |

**Souvenir Sheet**

*Perf. 12x12 ½*

| | | | | |
|---|---|---|---|---|
| *1184* | A334 | 200f multi | 1.40 | 95 |

No. 1184 contains one stamp (size: 30x45mm); multicolored margin pictures Pres. Hussein and flags. Size: 80x60mm.

Solar Energy Research Center A335

**1985, Sept. 19** *Perf. 13 ½*

| | | | | |
|---|---|---|---|---|
| *1185* | A335 | 10f multi | 8 | 5 |
| *1186* | A335 | 50f multi | 32 | 22 |
| *1187* | A335 | 100f multi | 65 | 45 |

UN Child Survival Campaign A336

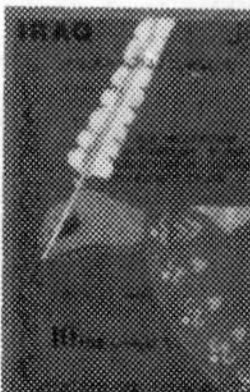

Al Sharif, Poet, Death Millennium A337

Designs: 10f, 50f, Stop Polio Campaign. 15f, 100f, Girl, infant.

**1985, Oct. 10**

| | | | | |
|---|---|---|---|---|
| *1188* | A336 | 10f multi | 8 | 5 |
| *1189* | A336 | 15f multi | 10 | 8 |
| *1190* | A336 | 50f multi | 32 | 22 |
| *1191* | A336 | 100f multi | 65 | 45 |

**1985, Oct. 20**

| | | | | |
|---|---|---|---|---|
| *1192* | A337 | 10f multi | 8 | 5 |
| *1193* | A337 | 50f multi | 32 | 22 |
| *1194* | A337 | 100f multi | 65 | 45 |

UN 40th Anniv. A338

**1985, Oct. 24**

| | | | | |
|---|---|---|---|---|
| *1195* | A338 | 10f multi | 8 | 5 |
| *1196* | A338 | 40f multi | 28 | 18 |
| *1197* | A338 | 100f multi | 65 | 45 |

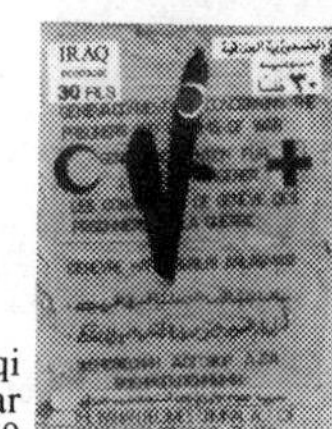

Death of Iraqi Prisoners of War in Iran — A339

Designs: 30f, 100f, Knife, Geneva Convention declaration, red crescent, red cross. 70f, 200f, POWs, gun shell, natl. flag, cherub and dove.

**1985, Nov. 10** *Perf. 14*

| | | | | |
|---|---|---|---|---|
| *1198* | A339 | 30f multi | 20 | 14 |
| *1199* | A339 | 70f multi | 45 | 30 |
| *1200* | A339 | 100f multi | 65 | 45 |
| *1201* | A339 | 200f multi | 1.40 | 95 |

**Size: 110x80mm.**

***Imperf***

| | | | | |
|---|---|---|---|---|
| *1202* | A339 | 250f multi | 2.75 | 1.15 |
| | | *Nos. 1198-1202 (5)* | 5.45 | 2.99 |

No. 1202 contains 2 perf. 14 labels similar to 100f and 200f designs within the stamp.

Intl. Palestinian Solidarity Day — A341

**1985, Nov. 29 Litho. *Perf. 13½***
*1207* A341 10f multi 8 6
*1208* A341 50f multi 50 25
*1209* A341 100f multi 1.00 50

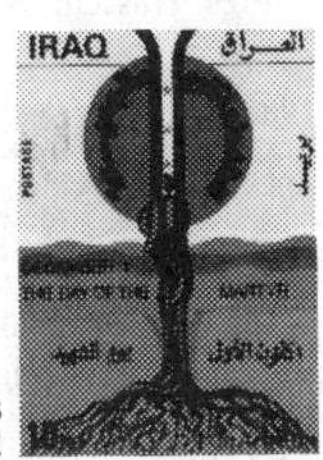

Martyr's Day — A342

**1985, Dec. 1 *Perf. 11½x12***
*1210* A342 10f multi 8 6
*1211* A342 40f multi 28 18
*1212* A342 100f multi 70 50

Intl. Youth Year — A343

IYY emblem and: 40f, 100f, Soldier holding flag. 50f, 200f, Youths, flag. 250f, Flag, cogwheel, rifle muzzle, symbols of industry.

**1985, Dec. 12 Litho. *Perf. 11½x12***
*1213* A343 40f multi 40 18
*1214* A343 50f multi 45 22
*1215* A343 100f multi 90 45
*1216* A343 200f multi 2.00 95

**Souvenir Sheet**
***Perf. 12x12½***
*1217* A343 250f multi 2.50 1.15

No. 1217 contains one stamp (size: 30x45mm); multicolored margin continues the design. Exists imperf. Size: 80x60mm.

Army Day A344

Pres. Hussein, "6" and: 10f, 50f, Soldier, flowers, vert. 40f, 100f, Flag, cogwheel, rockets. 200f, Al-Baath Party emblem, rifle, waves.

**1986, Jan. 6 *Perf. 11½x12, 12x11½***
*1218* A344 10f multi 8 5
*1219* A344 40f multi 40 18
*1220* A344 50f multi 45 22
*1221* A344 100f multi 90 45

**Miniature Sheet**
***Perf. 12½x11½***
*1222* A344 200f multi 2.00 95

No. 1222 contains one stamp (size: 52x37mm); gold margin. Size: 80x60mm.

Women's Day A345

Designs: 30f, 100f, Women in traditional and modern occupations, vert. 50f, 150f, Emblem, green flag, battle scene, grapes.

***Perf. 11½x12, 12x11½***
**1986, Mar. 8 Litho.**
*1223* A345 30f multi 22 14
*1224* A345 50f multi 35 24
*1225* A345 100f multi 70 48
*1226* A345 150f multi 1.05 70

Pres. Hussein, 49th Birthday — A346

Designs: 30f, 100f, Children greeting Pres. 50f, 150f, Portrait. 250f, Portrait, flag, flowers.

**1986, Apr. 28 Litho. *Perf. 11½x12***
*1227* A346 30f multi 28 12
*1228* A346 50f multi 45 22
*1229* A346 100f multi 90 45
*1230* A346 150f multi 1.25 65

**Size: 80x60mm.**
***Imperf***
*1231* A346 250f multi 2.50 1.15
*Nos. 1227-1231 (5)* 5.38 2.59

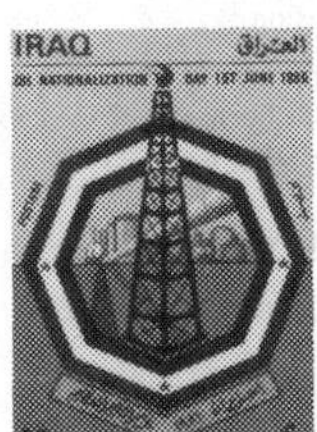

Oil Nationalization Day, June 1 — A347

1st May Labor Day — A348

Designs: 10f, 100f, Symbols of industry, horiz. 40f, 150f, Oil well, pipeline to refinery.

***Perf. 12x11½, 11½x12***
**1986, July 25 Litho.**
*1232* A347 10f multi 8 5
*1233* A347 40f multi 45 18
*1234* A347 100f multi 85 45
*1235* A347 150f multi 1.25 65

**1986, July 28 *Perf. 11½x12***

Designs: 10f, 100f, Laborer, cog wheel. 40f, 150f, 1st May Day emblem.

*1236* A348 10f multi 8 5
*1237* A348 40f multi 28 18
*1238* A348 100f multi 65 45
*1239* A348 150f multi 95 65

Iraqi Air Force, 55th Anniv. A349

Designs: 30f, 100f, Fighter plane, pilot's wings, natl. flag. 50f, 150f, Fighter planes. 250f, Medal, aircraft in flight.

**1986, July 28 *Perf. 12x11½***
*1240* A349 30f multi 30 8
*1241* A349 50f multi 42 22
*1242* A349 100f multi 85 45
*1243* A349 150f multi 1.25 65

**Size: 81x61mm.**
***Imperf***
*1244* A349 250f multi 2.50 1.10
*Nos. 1240-1244 (5)* 5.32 2.50

No. 1244 also exists perf.

July Festivals — A350

Pres. Hussein and: 20f, 100f, Flag. 30f, 150f, "17." 250f, Inscription, portrait inside medal of honor.

**1986, July 29 *Perf. 11½x12***
*1245* A350 20f multi 14 8
*1246* A350 30f multi 22 8
*1247* A350 100f multi 65 45
*1248* A350 150f multi 95 65

Size: 81x61mm.
***Imperf.***
*1249* A350 250f multi 1.60 1.10
*Nos. 1245-1249 (5)* 3.56 2.36

1st Qadisiya Battle — A351

Designs: 20f, 70f, Warrior, shield, vert. 60f, 100f, Pres. Hussein, star, battle scene.

***Perf. 13x13½, 13½x13***
**1986, Sept. 4 Litho.**
*1250* A351 20f multi 14 10
*1251* A351 60f multi 42 28
*1252* A351 70f multi 50 35
*1253* A351 100f multi 70 48

Battle between the Arabs and Persian Empire.

Hussein's Battle of Qadisiya — A352

Designs: 30f, 100f, Pres. Hussein, soldiers saluting peace, vert. 40f, 150f, Pres., armed forces. 250f, Pres., soldiers, flags, military scenes.

***Perf. 11½x12½, 12½x11½***
**1986, Sept. 4**
*1254* A352 30f multi 22 14
*1255* A352 40f multi 28 20
*1256* A352 100f multi 70 48
*1257* A352 150f multi 1.05 70

Souvenir Sheet
***Imperf.***
*1258* A352 250f multi 1.75 1.15

Size of No. 1258: 80x60mm.

Intl. Peace Year — A353

**1986, Nov. 15 Litho. *Perf. 11½x12***
*1259* A353 50f Dove, flag, G clef 32 24
*1260* A353 100f Globe, dove, rifle 65 48
*1261* A353 150f like 50f 1.00 70
*1262* A353 250f like 100f 1.60 1.10

Size: 80x69mm.
***Imperf.***
*1263* A353 200f Emblem, flag, map, fist 1.30 1.00
*Nos. 1259-1263 (5)* 4.87 3.52

Pres. Hussein — A354

A355

**1986 *Perf. 12½x12***
*1264* A354 30f multi 20 14
*1265* A355 30f multi 20 14
*1266* A354 50f multi 32 22
*1267* A355 50f multi 32 22
*1268* A354 100f multi 65 45
*1269* A355 100f multi 65 45
*1270* A354 150f multi 1.00 68
*1271* A355 150f multi 1.00 68
*1272* A354 250f multi 1.60 1.05
*1273* A354 350f multi 2.25 1.50
*Nos. 1264-1273 (10)* 8.19 5.53

Army Day — A356

**1987, Jan. 6 Litho. *Perf. 12x12½***
*1274* A356 20f shown 14 14
*1275* A356 40f Hussein, armed forces 25 25
*1276* A356 90f like 20f 58 58
*1277* A356 100f like 40f 65 65

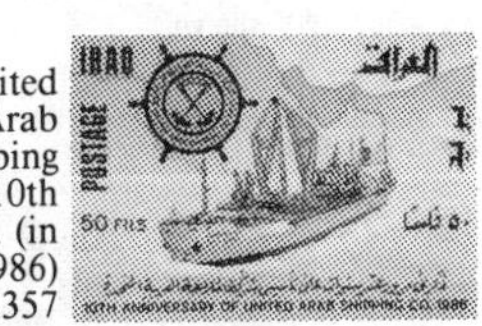

United Arab Shipping Co., 10th Anniv. (in 1986) A357

**1987, Apr. 3 Litho. *Perf. 12½***
*1278* A357 50f Cargo ship 32 22
*1279* A357 100f Container ship Chaleb Ibn Al Waleeb 65 45
*1280* A357 150f like 50f 1.00 68
*1281* A357 250f like 100f 1.60 1.05

**Size: 102x91mm.**
***Imperf***
*1282* A357 200f Loading cargo aboard the Waleeb 1.30 1.00

Arab Baath Socialist Party, 40th Anniv. — A358

**1987, Apr. 7** **Litho.** ***Perf. 12x12½***

*1283* A358 20f shown 14 14
*1284* A358 40f Hussein, "7," map 25 25
*1285* A358 90f like 20f 58 58
*1286* A358 100f like 40f 65 65

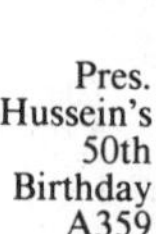

Pres. Hussein's 50th Birthday A359

**1987, Apr. 28** ***Perf. 12½x12***

*1287* A359 20f shown 14 14
*1288* A359 40f Portrait 25 25
*1289* A359 90f like 20f 58 58
*1290* A359 100f like 40f 65 65

July Festivals — A360

UNICEF, 40th Anniv. — A361

***Perf. 12½x12, 12x12½***

**1987, July 17**

*1291* A360 20f Hussein, star, flag, horiz. 14 14
*1292* A360 40f shown 25 25
*1293* A360 90f like 20f, horiz. 58 58
*1294* A360 100f like 40f 65 65

**1987, Oct. 4** ***Perf. 12x12½, 12½x12***

*1295* A361 20f shown 14 14
*1296* A361 40f "40," horiz. 25 25
*1297* A361 90f like 20f 58 58
*1298* A361 100f like 40f, horiz. 65 65

Census Day A362

**1987, Nov. 1** ***Perf. 12x11½***

*1299* A362 20f shown 14 14
*1300* A362 30f Graph, Arabs, diff. 20 20
*1301* A362 50f like 30f 35 35
*1302* A362 500f like 20f 3.25 3.25

Army Day A363

***Perf. 11½x12, 12x11½***

**1988, Jan. 6** **Litho.**

*1303* A363 20f "6," Hussein, troops, vert. 14 5
*1304* A363 30f shown 20 6
*1305* A363 50f like 20f, vert. 35 12
*1306* A363 150f like 30f 1.00 38

Art Day — A364

Anniversaries A365

**1988, Jan. 8** **Litho.** ***Perf. 11½x12***

*1307* A364 20f shown 15 5
*1308* A364 30f Hussein, rainbow, gun barrel, music 22 8
*1309* A364 50f like 20f 38 12
*1310* A364 100f like 30f 75 25

**Size: 60x80mm**

***Imperf***

*1311* A364 150f Notes, musical instruments, floral ornament 1.20 80

**1988, Feb. 8** ***Perf. 11½x12, 12x11½***

*1312* A365 20f "8," troops, Hussein, horiz. 15 5
*1313* A365 30f "8," Hussein, eagle 22 8
*1314* A365 50f like 20f, horiz. 38 12
*1315* A365 150f like 30f 1.20 40

Popular Army, 18th anniv. (20f, 50f); Feb. 8th Revolution, 25th anniv. (30f, 150f).

Al-Baath Arab Socialist Party, 50th Anniv. A366

President Hussein's 50th Birthday A367

**1988, Apr. 7** ***Perf. 12x12½, 12½x12***

*1316* A366 20f Natl. flag, grain, convention, horiz. 15 5
*1317* A366 30f shown 22 8
*1318* A366 50f like 20f, horiz. 38 12
*1319* A366 150f like 30f 1.20 40

**1988, Apr. 28** ***Perf. 12x12½***

*1320* A367 20f shown 15 5
*1321* A367 30f Hussein, 3 hands, flowers 22 8
*1322* A367 50f like 20f 38 12
*1323* A367 100f like 50f 75 25

**Size: 90x99mm**

***Imperf***

*1324* A367 150f Sun, Hussein, natl. colors, heart, flowers 1.20 80

World Health Organization, 40th Anniv. — A368

Regional Marine Environment Day, Apr. 24 — A369

**1988, June 1** ***Perf. 12½x12, 12x12½***

*1325* A368 20f WHO anniv. emblem, horiz. 15 5
*1326* A368 40f shown 30 10
*1327* A368 90f like 20f, horiz. 68 22
*1328* A368 100f like 40f 75 25

***Perf. 12x12½, 12½x12***

**1988, Apr. 24**

*1329* A369 20f shown 15 5
*1330* A369 40f Flag in map, fish, horiz. 30 10
*1331* A369 90f like 20f 68 22
*1332* A369 100f like 40f, horiz. 75 25

Shuhada School Victims Memorial A370

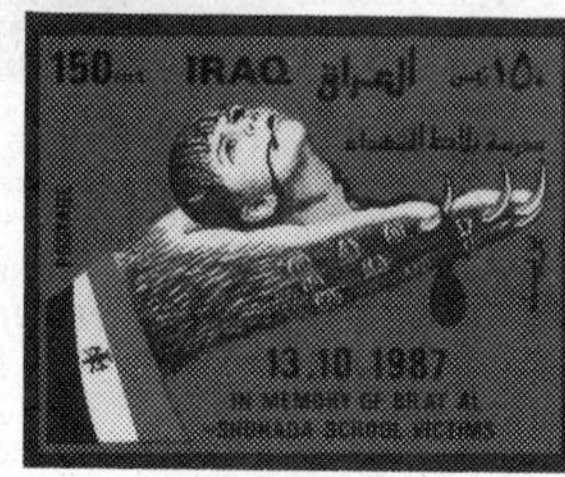

A371

**1988, June 1** ***Perf. 11½x12, 12x11½***

*1333* A370 20f shown 15 5
*1334* A370 40f Girl caught in explosion, horiz. 30 10
*1335* A370 90f like 20f 68 22
*1336* A370 100f like 40f, horiz. 75 25

**Souvenir Sheet**

***Perf. 12½***

*1337* A371 150f red, blk & brt grn 1.15 75

No. 1337 has pale gray margin. Size: 80x60mm.

Pilgrimage to Mecca — A372

**1988** **Litho.** ***Perf. 13½***

*1338* A372 90f multi 70 22
*1339* A372 100f multi 80 28
*1340* A372 150f multi 1.20 40

Basra, 1350th Anniv. A373

**1988** ***Perf. 12x11½***

*1341* A373 100f multi 75 25

Natl. Flag, Grip on Lightning — A374

Pres. Hussein, Natl. Flag — A375

**1988** ***Perf. 12x12½***

*1342* A374 50f shown 38 14
*1343* A374 90f Map, Hussein, desert 68 22
*1344* A374 100f like 50f 75 25
*1345* A374 150f like 90f 1.15 35

**Size: 90x70mm**

***Imperf***

*1346* A375 250f shown 1.90 65

July Festivals and 9th anniv. of Pres. Hussein's assumption of office.

Nos. 1272-1273 Overprinted

انتصر العراق
١٩٨٨/٨/٨

**1988** **Litho.** ***Perf. 12½x12***

*1347* A354 250f multi 2.90 95
*1348* A354 350f multi 4.00 1.35

Victory.

Navy Day — A376

**1988** ***Perf. 12x12½***

*1349* A376 50f shown 58 20
*1350* A376 90f Map, boats 1.05 35
*1351* A376 100f like 50f 1.15 38
*1352* A376 150f like 90f 1.75 58

**Size: 91x70mm.**

***Imperf***

*1353* A376 250f Emblem, Pres. Hussein decorating officers 3.50 1.15

1988 Summer Olympics, Seoul — A377

**1988** ***Perf. 12x12½***

*1354* A377 100f Boxing, character trademark 1.15 38
*1355* A377 150f Flag, emblems 1.75 58

**Size: 101x91mm**

***Imperf***

*1356* A377 500f Emblem, trademark, Hussein presenting trophy 7.00 2.35

FAO Liberation A378

**1988** *Perf. 12x11 ½*
*1357* A378 100f multi 1.15 38
*1358* A378 150f multi 1.75 58

**Size: 60x80mm**

***Imperf***

*1359* A378 500f Hussein, text 7.00 2.35

Mosul A379

Baghdad — A380

Ancient cities.

**1988** *Perf. 12x11 ½, 11 ½x12*
*1360* A379 50f Fortress 58 20
*1361* A380 150f Astrolabe, modern architecture 1.75 58

Al-Hussein Missile — A381

**1988** *Perf. 11 ½x12*
*1362* A381 100f multi 80 28
*1363* A381 150f multi 1.20 40

**Size: 80x60mm**

***Imperf***

*1364* A381 500f Hussein, map, missile 3.75 1.25

2nd Intl. Festival, Babylon — A382

**1988** *Perf. 11 ½x12*
*1365* A382 100f multi 78 25
*1366* A382 150f multi 1.15 38

**Size: 60x80mm**

***Imperf***

*1367* A382 500f Medallions 3.75 1.25

A383

**1988, Aug. 8** **Litho.** *Perf. 12x11 ½*
*1368* A383 50f multi 40 14
*1369* A383 100f multi 80 28
*1370* A383 150f multi 1.20 40

## AIR POST STAMPS

**Catalogue values for unused stamps in this section, from this point to the end of the section, are for Never Hinged items.**

Basrah Airport — AP1

Diyala Railway Bridge — AP2

Designs (Vickers Viking over): 4f, 20f, Kut Dam. 5f, 35f, Faisal II Bridge.

*Perf. 11 ½, 11 ½x12*

**1949, Feb. 1** **Engr.** **Unwmk.**
*C1* AP1 3f bl grn 5 5
*C2* AP1 4f red vio 8 8
*C3* AP1 5f red brn 6 6
*C4* AP1 10f carmine 15 15
*C5* AP1 20f blue 15 12
*C6* AP1 35f red org 25 15
*C7* AP2 50f olive 1.50 18
*C8* AP2 100f violet 2.00 25
*Nos. C1-C8 (8)* 4.24 1.04

Sheets exist, perf. and imperf., containing one each of Nos. C1-C8, with arms and Arabic inscription in blue green in upper and lower margin. Value (2 sheets) $40.

**Republic**

ICY Emblem — AP3

**1965, Aug. 13** **Litho.** *Perf. 13 ½*
*C9* AP3 5f brn org blk 50 10
*C10* AP3 10f cit & dk brn 75 15
*C11* AP3 30f ultra & blk 2.00 50

International Cooperation Year, 1965.

Trident 1E Jet Plane — AP4

**1965, Dec. 1** **Photo.** *Perf. 11 ½*

**Granite Paper**

*C12* AP4 5f multi 15 5
*C13* AP4 10f multi 25 8
*C14* AP4 40f multi 3.00 50

Issued to commemorate the introduction by Iraqi Airways of Trident 1E jet planes.

Arab International Tourist Union Emblem — AP5

Travelers on Magic Carpet AP6

**1966, Dec. 3** **Litho.** *Perf. 13 ½, 14*
*C15* AP5 2f multi 10 5
*C16* AP6 5f yel & multi 20 6
*C17* AP5 15f bl & multi 25 10
*C18* AP6 50f multi 1.00 35

Issued to commemorate the meeting of the Arab International Tourist Union, Baghdad.

**Costume Type of Regular Issue**

Iraqi Costumes: 40f, Woman's head. 50f, Woman's costume. 80f, Man's costume.

**1967, Nov. 10** **Litho.** *Perf. 13*
*C19* A105 40f multi 50 25
*C20* A105 50f bl & multi 75 40
*C21* A105 80f grn & multi 5.00 1.00

**International Tourist Year Type of Regular Issue**

Designs: 50f, Female statue, Temples of Hatra. 80f, Spiral Tower (Malwiye of Samarra). 100f, Adam's Tree. 200f, Aladdin's Cave. 500f, Golden Shiah Mosque of Kadhimain. (50f, 80f, 100f and 200f are vertical)

**1967, Dec. 1** **Litho.**
*C22* A107 50f multi 75 30
*C23* A107 80f multi 1.40 50
*C24* A107 100f multi 2.75 60
*C25* A107 200f ver & multi 4.25 2.50
*C26* A107 500f brn & multi 30.00 15.00
*Nos. C22-C26 (5)* 39.15 18.90

Arabian AP7

Animals: 2f, Striped hyena. 3f, Leopard. 5f, Mountain gazelle. 200f, Arabian stallion.

**1969, Sept. 1** **Litho.** *Perf. 14*
*C27* AP7 2f multi 5 5
*C28* AP7 3f multi 5 5
*C29* AP7 5f multi 12 12
*C30* AP7 10f multi 25 18
*C31* AP7 200f multi 8.50 4.75
*Nos. C27-C31 (5)* 8.97 5.15

Ross Smith's Vickers Vimy AP8

**1969, Dec. 4** **Litho.** *Perf. 14*
*C32* AP8 15f dk bl & multi 1.00 35
*C33* AP8 35f multi 2.00 50
*a* Souv. sheet of 2 10.00 8.00

Issued to commemorate the 50th anniversary of the first England to Australia flight of Capt. Ross Smith and Lt. Keith Smith. No. C33a contains 2 imperf. stamps similar to Nos. C32-C33, black marginal inscriptions and map of flight route. Size: 80x100mm. Sold for 100f.

View Across Euphrates — AP9

Iraqi Banknotes and Pres. Hassan al-Bakr AP10

**1970, Oct. 30** **Litho.** *Perf. 13*
*C34* AP9 10f brt bl & multi 1.00 15
*C35* AP9 15f multi 1.00 15
*C36* AP10 1d multi 25.00 10.00

National Development Plan.

Telecommunications Emblem — AP11

**1970, Dec. 15** **Litho.** *Perf. 14x13 ½*
*C37* AP11 15f gray & multi 25 15
*C38* AP11 25f lt bl & multi 50 35

Tenth Conference of Arab Telecommunications Union.

No. C23 Overprinted **يوم الأنواء W.M. DAY 1971**

**1971, Apr. 23** *Perf. 13*
*C39* A107 80f multi 7.00 5.00

World Meteorological Day.

Iraqi Philatelic Society Emblem — AP12

**1972, Feb. 25** **Litho.** *Perf. 13*
*C40* AP12 25f multi 1.00 50
*C41* AP12 70f pink & multi 3.00 1.50

Iraqi Philatelic Society, 20th anniversary.

Nos. C34-C35 Overprinted

**المؤتمر التاسع للاتحاد الوطني**
**لطلبة العراق**
**٢٥ شباط ـ ٢ آذار / ١٩٧٢**

**1972, Feb. 25**

| | | | | |
|---|---|---|---|---|
| *C42* | AP9 | 10f brt bl & multi | 1.00 | 25 |
| *C43* | AP9 | 15f multi | 2.00 | 1.00 |

9th Cong. of Natl. Union of Iraqi Students.

IRAQ AIRMAIL الجمهورية العراقية 10 FILS

Soccer and C.I.S.M. Emblem AP13

Designs: 20f, 35f, Players, soccer ball, C.I.S.M. emblem. 100f, Winged lion, Olympic and C.I.S.M. emblems.

**1972, June 9 Litho. *Perf. 13½***

| | | | | |
|---|---|---|---|---|
| *C46* | AP13 | 10f lt bl & multi | 50 | 8 |
| *C47* | AP13 | 20f dp bl & multi | 1.00 | 15 |
| *C48* | AP13 | 25f grn & multi | 1.00 | 20 |
| *C49* | AP13 | 35f brt bl & multi | 4.00 | 50 |
| *a.* | | Souvenir sheet, 100f | 10.50 | 10.50 |

25th Military Soccer Championships (C.I.S.M.), Baghdad, June 9-19.

No. C49a contains one imperf. stamp. Blue border with black inscription. Size: 76x63mm.

Statue of Athlete — AP14

Design: 70f, Mesopotamian archer on horseback, ancient and modern athletes.

**1972, Nov. 15 Photo. *Perf. 14x13½***

| | | | | |
|---|---|---|---|---|
| *C50* | AP14 | 25f multi | 1.00 | 50 |
| *C51* | AP14 | 70f multi | 3.00 | 1.50 |

Cong. of Asian and World Body Building Championships, Baghdad, Nov. 15-23, 1972.

Nos. C23, C26 Overprinted

المؤتمر الدولي
للتاريخ/١٩٧٣

**1973, Mar. 25 Litho. *Perf. 13***

| | | | | |
|---|---|---|---|---|
| *C52* | A107 | 80f multi | 15.00 | 6.00 |
| *C53* | A107 | 500f multi | 50.00 | *70.00* |

International History Congress.

ICATU Type of 1976

**1976, Mar. 24 Photo. *Perf. 13½***

| | | | | |
|---|---|---|---|---|
| *C54* | A213 | 75f bl & multi | 5.00 | 2.00 |

Symbolic Eye AP15

Basketball AP16

**1976, June 20 Photo. *Perf. 14***

| | | | | |
|---|---|---|---|---|
| *C55* | AP15 | 25f ultra & dk brn | 20 | 13 |
| *C56* | AP15 | 35f brt grn & dk brn | 25 | 18 |
| *C57* | AP15 | 50f org & multi | 40 | 25 |

World Health Day: Foresight prevents blindness.

**1976, July 30 Litho. *Perf. 12x12½***

Designs (Montreal Olympic Games Emblem and): 35f, Volleyball. 50f, Wrestling. 75f, Boxing. 100f, Target shooting (horiz.).

| | | | | |
|---|---|---|---|---|
| *C58* | AP16 | 25f yel & multi | 50 | 15 |
| *C59* | AP16 | 35f bl & multi | 75 | 25 |
| *C60* | AP16 | 50f ver & multi | 1.00 | 50 |
| *C61* | AP16 | 75f yel grn & multi | 1.50 | 70 |

**Souvenir Sheet**

***Imperf***

| | | | | |
|---|---|---|---|---|
| *C62* | AP16 | 100f grn & multi | 6.00 | 6.00 |

21st Olympic Games, Montreal, Canada, July 17-Aug. 1. No. C62 has yellow margin with green inscription. Size: 120x90mm.

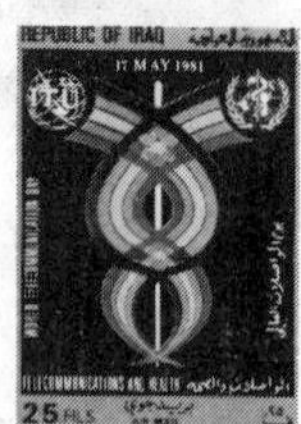


13th World Telecommunications Day — AP17

**1981, May 17 Photo. *Perf. 12½***

| | | | | |
|---|---|---|---|---|
| *C63* | AP17 | 25f multi | 20 | 12 |
| *C64* | AP17 | 50f multi | 40 | 25 |
| *C65* | AP17 | 75f multi | 60 | 38 |

Air Force Type of 1981

**1981, June 1 Photo. *Perf. 14x13½***

| | | | | |
|---|---|---|---|---|
| *C66* | A289 | 120f Planes, vert. | 1.00 | 75 |

## AIR POST OFFICIAL STAMP

**Catalogue values for all unused stamps in this country are for Never Hinged items.**

Nos. C19-C22 Overprinted

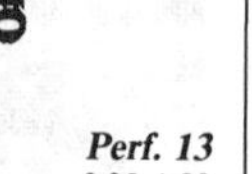

**1971 Litho. *Perf. 13***

| | | | | |
|---|---|---|---|---|
| *CO1* | A105 | 40f multi | 3.25 | 1.00 |
| *CO2* | A105 | 50f multi | 4.25 | 1.00 |
| *CO3* | A105 | 80f multi | 4.00 | 1.00 |

**"Official" Reading Down**

| | | | | |
|---|---|---|---|---|
| *CO4* | A107 | 50f multi | 3.50 | 2.25 |

Nos. C27-C28, C30 Overprinted or Surcharged

**Official** رسمي

**25 Fils** ٢٥

**1971 *Perf. 14***

| | | | | |
|---|---|---|---|---|
| *CO5* | AP7 | 10f multi | 55 | 25 |
| *CO6* | AP7 | 15f on 3f multi | 80 | 50 |
| *CO7* | AP7 | 25f on 2f multi | 1.65 | 1.00 |

No bar and surcharge on No. CO5.

## OFFICIAL STAMPS

### British Mandate

Regular Issue of 1923 Overprinted:

ON STATE SERVICE
k

ON STATE SERVICE
l

**1923 Wmk. 4 *Perf. 12***

| | | | | |
|---|---|---|---|---|
| *O1* | A1(k) | ½a ol grn | 15 | 10 |
| *O2* | A2(k) | 1a brown | 15 | 10 |
| *O3* | A3(l) | 1½a car lake | 35 | 10 |
| *O4* | A4(k) | 2a brn org | 25 | 10 |
| *O5* | A5(k) | 3a dp bl | 35 | 10 |
| *O6* | A6(l) | 4a dl vio | 25 | 15 |
| *O7* | A7(k) | 6a bl grn | 30 | 25 |
| *O8* | A6(l) | 8a ol bis | 35 | 35 |
| *O9* | A8(l) | 1r grn & brn | 5.00 | 85 |
| *O10* | A1(k) | 2r blk (R) | 15.00 | 1.50 |
| *O11* | A6(l) | 5r orange | 45.00 | 15.00 |
| *O12* | A7(k) | 10r carmine | 75.00 | 40.00 |
| | | *Nos. O1-O12 (12)* | 142.15 | 58.60 |

Regular Issue of 1923-25 Overprinted:

m ON STATE SERVICE رسمي

n ON STATE SERVICE رسمي

**1924-25**

| | | | | |
|---|---|---|---|---|
| *O13* | A1(m) | ½a ol grn | 8 | 7 |
| *O14* | A2(m) | 1a brown | 15 | 6 |
| *O15* | A3(n) | 1½a car lake | 10 | 8 |
| *O16* | A4(m) | 2a brn org | 15 | 5 |
| *O17* | A5(m) | 3a dp bl | 20 | 8 |
| *O18* | A6(n) | 4a dl vio | 30 | 8 |
| *O19* | A7(m) | 6a bl grn | 35 | 12 |
| *O20* | A6(n) | 8a ol bis | 50 | 12 |
| *O21* | A8(n) | 1r grn & brn | 3.00 | 75 |
| *O22* | A1(m) | 2r bis ('25) | 10.00 | 5.00 |
| *O23* | A6(n) | 5r orange | 45.00 | 20.00 |
| *O24* | A7(m) | 10r brn red | 75.00 | 30.00 |
| | | *Nos. O13-O24 (12)* | 134.83 | 56.41 |

No. 14 Overprinted Type "n"

**1927**

| | | | | |
|---|---|---|---|---|
| *O25* | A9 | 1r red brn | 3.00 | 60 |

Regular Issue of 1931 Overprinted Vertically

o ON STATE SERVICE رسمي

**1931**

| | | | | |
|---|---|---|---|---|
| *O26* | A10 | ½a green | 12 | 8 |
| *O27* | A10 | 1a chestnut | 10 | 6 |
| *O28* | A10 | 1½a carmine | 20.00 | 7.50 |
| *O29* | A10 | 2a orange | 25 | 8 |
| *O30* | A10 | 3a lt bl | 30 | 10 |
| *O31* | A10 | 4a pur brn | 50 | 10 |
| *O32* | A10 | 6a Prus bl | 25.00 | 2.00 |
| *O33* | A10 | 8a dk grn | 18.00 | 2.25 |

Overprinted Horizontally

ON STATE SERVICE

p

| | | | | |
|---|---|---|---|---|
| *O34* | A11 | 1r dk brn | 5.00 | 1.75 |
| *O35* | A11 | 2r yel brn | 9.00 | 9.00 |
| *O36* | A11 | 5r dp org | 45.00 | 45.00 |
| *O37* | A11 | 10r red | 75.00 | 75.00 |
| | | *Nos. O26-O37 (12)* | 198.27 | 142.92 |

**Overprinted Vertically Reading Up**

| | | | | |
|---|---|---|---|---|
| *O38* | A9(p) | 25r violet | 1,100. | 1,200. |

### Kingdom

Official Stamps of 1924-31 Surcharged with New Values in Fils and Dinars, like Nos. 28 to 43.

**1932, Apr. 1**

| | | | | |
|---|---|---|---|---|
| *O39* | A10 | 3f on ½a grn | 35 | 35 |
| *O40* | A10 | 4f on 1a chnt (G) | 15 | 6 |
| *O41* | A10 | 5f on 1a chnt | 18 | 8 |
| *a.* | | Invtd. Arabic "5" | *40.00* | *35.00* |
| *O42* | A3 | 8f on 1½a car lake | 70 | 8 |
| *O43* | A10 | 10f on 2a org | 25 | 6 |
| *O44* | A10 | 15f on 3a lt bl | 40 | 12 |
| *O45* | A10 | 20f on 4a pur brn | 45 | 15 |
| *O46* | A10 | 25f on 4a pur brn | 50 | 25 |
| *O47* | A7 | 30f on 6a bl grn | 60 | 35 |
| *O48* | A10 | 40f on 8a dk grn | 1.65 | 35 |
| *a.* | | "Flis" for "Fils" | *300.00* | *450.00* |
| *O49* | A11 | 50f on 1r dk brn | 2.50 | 1.00 |
| *O50* | A11 | 75f on 1r dk brn | 4.25 | 3.50 |
| *O51* | A1 | 100f on 2r bis | 8.50 | 1.25 |
| *O52* | A6 | 200f on 5r org | 17.00 | 10.00 |
| *O53* | A7 | ½d on 10r brn red | 50.00 | 42.50 |
| *a.* | | Bar in "½" omitted | *700.00* | |
| *O54* | A9 | 1d on 25r vio | 125.00 | 110.00 |
| | | *Nos. O39-O54 (16)* | 212.48 | 170.10 |

Regular Issue of 1932 Overprinted Vertically like Nos. O26 to O33.

**1932, May 9**

| | | | | |
|---|---|---|---|---|
| *O55* | A12 | 2f ultra | 6 | 5 |
| *O56* | A12 | 3f green | 6 | 5 |
| *O57* | A12 | 4f vio brn | 8 | 5 |
| *O58* | A12 | 5f gray | 8 | 6 |
| *O59* | A12 | 8f dp red | 10 | 5 |
| *O60* | A12 | 10f yellow | 12 | 5 |
| *O61* | A12 | 15f dp bl | 2.00 | 8 |
| *O62* | A12 | 20f orange | 25 | 10 |
| *O63* | A12 | 25f rose lil | 5.00 | 40 |
| *O64* | A12 | 30f ol grn | 75 | 40 |
| *O65* | A12 | 40f dk vio | 2.00 | 40 |

**Overprinted Horizontally Like Nos. O34 to O37.**

| | | | | |
|---|---|---|---|---|
| *O66* | A13 | 50f dp brn | 2.00 | 50 |
| *O67* | A13 | 75f lt ultra | 3.00 | 25 |
| *O68* | A13 | 100f dp grn | 7.50 | 50 |
| *O69* | A13 | 200f dk red | 20.00 | 2.75 |

**Overprinted Vertically like No. O38.**

| | | | | |
|---|---|---|---|---|
| *O70* | A14 | ½d gray bl | 20.00 | 3.50 |
| *O71* | A14 | 1d claret | 50.00 | 50.00 |
| | | *Nos. O55-O71 (17)* | 113.00 | 59.19 |

Regular Issue of 1934-38 Overprinted Type "o" Vertically Reading up in Black.

**1934-38 Unwmk.**

| | | | | |
|---|---|---|---|---|
| *O72* | A15 | 1f pur ('38) | 1.00 | 5 |
| *O73* | A15 | 2f ultra | 30 | 5 |
| *O74* | A15 | 3f green | 15 | 5 |
| *O75* | A15 | 4f pur brn | 7 | 5 |
| *O76* | A15 | 5f gray grn | 9 | 5 |
| *O77* | A15 | 8f dp red | 1.00 | 5 |
| *O78* | A15 | 10f yellow | 15 | 6 |
| *O79* | A15 | 15f dp bl | 5.00 | 12 |
| *O80* | A15 | 20f orange | 25 | 6 |
| *O81* | A15 | 25f brn vio | 10.00 | 2.50 |
| *O82* | A15 | 30f ol grn | 55 | 18 |
| *O83* | A15 | 40f dk vio | 1.25 | 18 |

**Overprinted Type "p".**

| | | | | |
|---|---|---|---|---|
| *O84* | A16 | 50f dp brn | 55 | 20 |
| *O85* | A16 | 75f ultra | 80 | 80 |
| *O86* | A16 | 100f dp grn | 2.00 | 70 |
| *O87* | A16 | 200f dk red | 4.00 | 1.00 |

**Overprinted Type "p" Vertically Reading Up.**

| | | | | |
|---|---|---|---|---|
| *O88* | A17 | ½d gray bl | 15.00 | 10.00 |
| *O89* | A17 | 1d claret | 30.00 | 20.00 |
| | | *Nos. O72-O89 (18)* | 72.16 | 36.10 |

**Catalogue values for unused stamps in this section, from this point to the end of the section, are for Never Hinged items.**

Stamps of 1941-42 Overprinted in Black or Red:

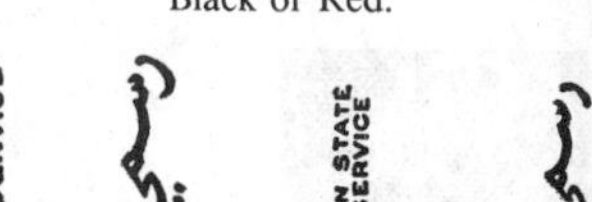

r s

***Perf. 11½x13½, 13 to 14 and compound.***

**1941-42**

| | | | | |
|---|---|---|---|---|
| *O90* | A18(r) | 1f dk vio ('42) | 6 | 6 |
| *O91* | A18(r) | 2f choc ('42) | 6 | 6 |
| *O92* | A19(r) | 3f brt grn ('42) | 8 | 8 |
| *O93* | A19(r) | 4f pur (R) ('42) | 8 | 8 |
| *O94* | A19(r) | 5f dk car rose ('42) | 10 | 8 |
| *O95* | A20(s) | 8f carmine | 50 | 8 |
| *O96* | A20(s) | 8f ocher ('42) | 15 | 6 |
| *O97* | A20(s) | 10f ocher | 2.00 | 8 |
| *O98* | A20(s) | 10f car ('42) | 20 | 8 |
| *O99* | A20(s) | 15f dl bl | 5.50 | 35 |
| *O100* | A20(s) | 15f blk (R) ('42) | 20 | 9 |
| *O101* | A20(s) | 20f blk (R) | 1.00 | 20 |
| *O102* | A20(s) | 20f dl bl ('42) | 40 | 8 |
| *O103* | A21(s) | 25f dk vio | 1.50 | 18 |
| *O104* | A21(r) | 25f dk vio ('42) | 30 | 15 |
| *O105* | A21(s) | 30f dp org | 1.10 | 15 |
| *O106* | A21(r) | 30f dk org ('42) | 25 | 15 |
| *O107* | A21(s) | 40f brn org | 1.10 | 25 |
| *O108* | A21(r) | 40f chnt ('42) | 50 | 25 |
| *O109* | A21(r) | 50f ultra | 1.00 | 18 |

O110 A21(r) 75f rose vio 40 30
O111 A22(s) 100f ol grn ('42) 60 40
O112 A22(s) 200f dp org ('42) 1.65 1.65
O113 A23(r) ½d bl ('42) 8.00 5.00
O114 A23(r) 1d grnsh bl ('42) 16.00 12.50
*Nos. O90-O114 (25)* 42.73 22.54

The space between the English and Arabic on overprints "r" and "s" varies with the size of the stamps.

Stamps of 1942 Overprinted in Black — ON STATE SERVICE

**1942 Unwmk. *Perf. 13x13½***

O115 A24 1f vio & brn 6 6
O116 A24 2f dk bl & brn 8 6
O117 A24 3f lt grn & brn 8 5
O118 A24 4f dl brn & brn 10 6
O119 A24 5f sage grn & brn 12 6
O120 A24 6f red org & brn 12 5
O121 A24 10f dl rose red & brn 15 6
O122 A24 12f yel grn & brn 20 5
*Nos. O115-O122 (8)* 91 45

Stamps of 1948 Overprinted in Black — ON STATE SERVICE

**1948, Jan. 15 *Perf. 11½x12***

**Size: 17¾x20½mm.**

O123 A25 1f slate 5 5
O124 A25 2f sepia 5 5
O125 A25 3f emerald 5 5
O126 A25 4f purple 6 5
O127 A25 5f rose lake 6 5
O128 A25 6f plum 6 5
O129 A25 8f ocher 8 5
O130 A25 10f rose red 6 5
O131 A25 12f dk ol 10 6
O132 A25 15f black 25 75
O133 A25 20f blue 15 10
O134 A25 25f rose vio 18 12
O135 A25 30f red org 20 15
O136 A25 40f org brn 25 15

***Perf. 12x11½***

**Size: 22x27½mm.**

O137 A25 60f dp bl 35 25
O138 A25 75f lil rose 40 40
O139 A25 100fol grn 55 35
O140 A25 200fdp org 1.15 1.00
O141 A25 ½d blue 5.00 2.75
O142 A25 1d green 10.00 5.50
*Nos. O123-O142 (20)* 19.05 11.98

Same Overprint on Nos. 133-138

**1949-51 *Perf. 11½x12***

**Size: 17¾x20½mm.**

O143 A25 3f rose lake ('51) 1.00 35
O144 A25 5f emer ('51) 1.00 35
O145 A25 14f dk ol ('50) 1.00 8
O146 A25 16f rose red ('51) 1.00 35
O147 A25 28f bl ('51) 1.00 25

***Perf. 12x11½***

**Size: 22x27½mm.**

O148 A25 50f dp bl 1.50 50
*Nos. O143-O148 (6)* 6.50 1.88

Same Overprint in Black on Stamps and Type of 1954-57.

**1955-59 *Perf. 11½x12***

O148A A28 1f bl ('56) 15 5
O149 A28 2f chocolate 5 5
O150 A28 3f rose lake 5 5
O151 A28 4f violet 5 5
O152 A28 5f emerald 5 5
O153 A28 6f plum ('56) 8 6
O154 A28 8f ocher ('56) 8 6
O155 A28 10f blue 8 6
O155A A28 16f brt rose ('57) 12.50 11.00
O156 A28 20f olive 15 8
O157 A28 25f rose vio 80 45
O158 A28 30f vermilion 20 12
O159 A28 40f org brn 30 20

**Size: 22½x27½mm.**

O160 A28 50f blue 2.00 30
O161 A28 60f pale pur 7.00 3.00
O161A A28 100f ol grn ('59) 15.00 3.00
*Nos. O148A-O161A (16)* 38.54 18.58

Dates of issue for Nos. O155A and O161A are suppositional.

Same Ovpt. on Stamps of 1957-58.

O162 A33 1f blue 2.50 60
O162A A33 2f chocolate 3.00 1.00
O162B A33 3f dk car 3.75 1.50
O162C A33 4f dl vio 4.50 80
O162D A33 5f emerald 2.50 80
O163 A33 6f plum 2.50 80
O164 A33 10f blue 2.50 80
*Nos. O162-O164 (7)* 21.25 6.30

**Republic**

Official Stamps of 1942-51 with Additional Overprint — الجمهورية العراقية

***Perf. 13½x14***

**1958-59 Engr. Unwmk.**

O165 A22 200f dp org 4.00 3.00

***Perf. 11½x12, 12x11½***

O166 A25 12f dk ol 60 45
O167 A25 14f olive 60 55
O168 A25 15f black 35 25
O169 A25 16f rose red 1.75 1.75
O170 A25 25f rose vio 2.50 1.50
O171 A25 28f blue 1.25 1.25
O172 A25 40f org brn 60 60
O173 A25 60f dp bl 2.00 1.75
O174 A25 75f lil rose 1.50 1.25
O175 A25 200f dp org 2.00 2.00
O176 A25 ½d blue 12.50 4.50
O177 A25 1d green 20.00 9.00
*Nos. O166-O177 (12)* 45.65 24.85

Other denominations of types A22 and A25 exist with this overprint, but these were probably not regularly issued.

Same Ovpt. on Nos. O148A-O161A

O178 A28 1f blue 10 6
O179 A28 2f chocolate 10 8
O180 A28 3f rose lake 15 8
O181 A28 4f violet 10 8
O181A A28 5f emerald 40 15
O182 A28 6f plum 12 8
O183 A28 8f ocher 30 12
O183A A28 10f blue 1.00 25
O184 A28 16f brt rose 4.00 2.50
O185 A28 20f olive 30 15
O186 A28 25f rose vio 30 20
O187 A28 30f vermilion 40 20
O188 A28 40f org brn 50 25
O189 A28 50f blue 60 40
O190 A28 60f pale pur 75 55
O191 A28 100f ol grn 1.00 50
*Nos. O178-O191 (16)* 10.12 5.65

Same Overprints on #O162-O164, 216

O192 A33 1f blue 8 5
O193 A33 2f chocolate 8 5
O194 A33 3f dk car 15 10
O195 A33 4f dl vio 8 5
O196 A33 5f emerald 8 5
O197 A33 6f plum 15 6
O198 A33 8f ocher 15 12
O199 A33 10f blue 15 8
*Nos. O192-O199 (8)* 92 56

Nos. 232-233, 235-237, 242 Overprinted — On State Service

**Litho. and Photo.**

**1961, Apr. 1 Unwmk. *Perf. 11½***

**Emblem in Gold, Red and Blue; Blue Inscriptions.**

O200 A38 1f gray 8 6
O201 A38 2f salmon 10 8
O202 A38 4f brt yel 18 12
O203 A38 5f lt bl 25 10
O204 A38 10f brt pink 45 35
O205 A38 50f yel grn 5.00 2.00
*Nos. O200-O205 (6)* 6.06 2.71

Nos. 232-247 Overprinted — ON STATE SERVICE

**1961**

**Emblem in Gold, Red and Blue; Blue Inscriptions.**

O206 A38 1f gray 5 5
O207 A38 2f salmon 5 5
O208 A38 3f pale vio 5 5
O209 A38 4f brt yel 5 5
O210 A38 5f lt bl 5 5
O211 A38 10f brt pink 6 5
O212 A38 15f lt grn 9 8
O213 A38 20f bis brn 12 8
O214 A38 30f lt gray 25 10
O215 A38 40f org yel 24 12
O216 A38 50f yel grn 30 15
O217 A38 75f pale grn 45 25
O218 A38 100f orange 75 40
O219 A38 200f lilac 1.50 75
O220 A38 500f bister 10.00 5.00
O221 A38 1d brt grn 20.00 10.00
*Nos. O206-O221 (16)* 34.01 17.23

Nos. 480-482 Overprinted — Official

**1971 Litho. *Perf. 13½***

O222 A115 10f multi 50 1.00
O223 A115 15f bl & multi 5.00 1.00
O224 A115 25f multi 5.00 2.00

Overprint lines are spaced 16mm. on No. O222, 32½mm. on Nos. O223-O224.

Same Overprint on Nos. 453, 455-456

**1971 *Perf. 13***

O225 A107 5f lil & multi 5.00 18
O226 A107 15f rose red & multi 5.00 35
O227 A107 25f vio bl & multi 8.00 1.00

Overprint horizontal on Nos. O225 and O227; vertical, reading down on No. O226. Distance between English and Arabic words: 8mm.

Nos. 446, 448-449 Overprinted — Official

**1971 Litho. *Perf. 13***

O228 A105 15f multi 1.00 50
O229 A105 15f multi 45.00 5.00
O230 A105 25f multi 8.00 2.00
O231 A105 30f multi 8.00 2.00

No. O229 overprinted "Official" horizontally

Same Overprint on Nos. 483-486

**1972 *Perf. 13½***

O232 A116 10f multi 1.50 50
O233 A116 25f multi 3.00 1.00

**1972**

O234 A117 15f multi 2.00 50
O235 A117 25f multi 3.00 1.00

Same Overprint, "Official" Reading Down on Nos. 562-565

**1972**

O240 A142 5f multi 50 25
O241 A142 10f multi 2.00 50
O242 A142 15f multi 5.00 50
O243 A142 35f multi 6.00 1.00

Latin inscription on Nos. O240-O241 obliterated with heavy bar.

No. 487 Overprinted "Official" like No. CO5

**1972 Photo. *Perf. 13½***

O244 A118 25f multi 20 12

#O134, O148 Ovptd. with 3 Bars

***Perf. 11½x12, 12x11½***

**1973, Jan. 29 Engr.**

O257 A25 25f rose vio 6.00 2.00
O258 A25 50f dp bl 6.00 5.00

Same on Nos. O157 and O160

O259 A28 25f rose vio 6.00 6.00
O260 A28 50f blue 6.00 6.00

Type of 1957 Overprinted with 3 Bars and — ON STATE SERVICE

**Size: 22x27½mm**

O261 A33 50f rose vio 6.00 6.00

See note after No. 679. No. O261 not issued without overprints.

King Faisal Issues Overprinted — Official

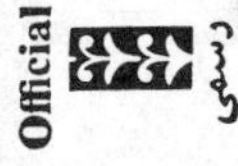

Two sizes of overprint: Arabic 6½mm or 9mm.

**1973**

O263 A28 15f blk (#149) 6.00 6.00
O264 A33 15f black 6.00 1.00
O265 A25 25f rose vio (#121) 8.50 2.00
O266 A28 25f rose vio (#151) 8.50 2.00
O267 A33 25f rose vio 8.50 2.00

Same Overprint on Nos. 674-677

O268 A28 10f blue 1.50 50
O269 A33 10f blue 1.50 50
O270 A28 15f black 6.00 1.00
O271 A33 15f black 6.00 1.00

Official Stamps of 1948-51 Overprinted

Overprint design faces left or right.

**1973**

O272 A25 12f dk ol (#O131) 75 20
O273 A25 14f dk ol (#O145) 75 30
O274 A25 15f blk (#O132) 75 30
O275 A25 16f rose red (#O146) 2.00 50
O276 A25 28f bl (#O147) 4.00 75
O277 A25 30f red org (#O135) 4.00 50
O278 A25 40f org brn (#O136) 4.00 90
O279 A25 60f dp bl (#O137) 4.00 3.00
O280 A25 100fol grn (#O139) 13.00 5.00
O281 A25 ½d bl (#O141) 32.50 13.00
O282 A25 1d grn (#O142) 67.50 67.50
*Nos. O272-O282 (11)* 133.25 91.95

Same Overprint on Official Stamps of 1955-59

O283 A28 3f rose lake (#O150) 20 10
O284 A28 6f plum (#O153) 20 12
O285 A28 8f ocher (#O154) 20 14
O286 A28 16f brt rose (#O155A) *10.00 10.00*
O287 A28 20f ol (#O156) 1.00 32
O288 A28 30f ver (#O158) 1.00 50
O289 A28 40f org brn (#O159) 1.00 1.00
O290 A28 60f pale pur (#O161) *8.75 2.00*
O291 A28 100f ol grn (#O161A) *17.50 5.00*

Same Overprint on 1957-58 Issues

O292 A33 3f dk car (#O162B) 20 20
O293 A33 6f plum (#O163) 20 20
O294 A33 8f ocher (#179) 20 20
O295 A33 30f red org 1.00 1.00

The overprint on Nos. O294-O295 includes the "On State Service" overprint; No. O295 was not issued without overprints. The overprint leaf design faces left or right and varies in size.

Nos. 403, 497, 681 Overprinted — رسمي **Official**

***Perf. 12½, 13x12½, 13½***

**1974 (?) Photo., Litho.**

O296 A89 2f multi 1.00
O297 A123 15f multi 1.00 50
O298 A185 25f multi 3.00 1.00

Size of "Official" on Nos. O297-O298 9mm.

Nos. 683-691 Overprinted — OFFICIAL

**1974 Litho. *Perf. 13x12½***

O299 A186 5f org & blk 10 10
O300 A186 10f bis & blk 15 10
O301 A186 20f brt rose & blk 35 20
O302 A186 25f ultra & blk 75 75
O303 A186 35f emer & blk 75 28
O304 A186 45f bl & blk 75 35
O305 A186 50f ol & yel 1.00 40
O306 A186 70f vio & yel 1.00 55
O307 A186 95f brn & yel 1.50 75
*Nos. O299-O307 (9)* 6.35 3.48

Nos. 455 and 467 Overprinted — رسمي **Official**

**1975 Litho. *Perf. 13, 14***

| | | |
|---|---|---|
| *O308* A107 15f multi | 1.00 | 35 |
| *O311* A110 30f multi | 4.00 | 60 |

Space between Arabic and English lines of overprint is 4mm. on No. O308, 13mm. on No. O311.

Nos. 491-493 Overprinted or Surcharged like Nos. CO5-CO7.

**1975 *Perf. 14***

| | | |
|---|---|---|
| *O312* A121 10f multi | 1.50 | 70 |
| *O312A* A121 15f on 3f multi | 6.00 | 1.00 |
| *O313* A121 25f on 2f multi | 5.00 | 1.00 |

Nos. 322-325 Overprinted رسمي Official

**Engr.; Engr. & Photo.**

**1975 *Perf. 12x11***

| | | |
|---|---|---|
| *O314* A57 10f rose red | 8.00 | 60 |
| *O315* A57 15f brn & buff | 8.00 | 75 |
| *O316* A57 20f vio bl | 8.00 | 75 |
| *O317* A57 30f orange | 15.00 | 80 |

Arms of Iraq — O1

Altharthar - Euphrates Canal — O2

**1975 Photo. *Perf. 14***

| | | |
|---|---|---|
| *O318* O1 5f multi | 5 | 5 |
| *O319* O1 10f bl & multi | 8 | 8 |
| *O320* O1 15f yel & multi | 24 | 24 |
| *O321* O1 20f ultra & multi | 32 | 32 |
| *O322* O1 25f org & multi | 40 | 40 |
| *O323* O1 30f rose & multi | 50 | 50 |
| *O324* O1 50f multi | 80 | 80 |
| *O325* O1 100f multi | 1.65 | 1.65 |
| *Nos. O318-O325 (8)* | 4.04 | 4.04 |

Nos. 787-791 Overprinted "OFFICIAL" in English and Arabic.

**1976 Litho. *Perf. 13½x14***

| | | |
|---|---|---|
| *O327* A219 5f multi | 8 | 8 |
| *O328* A219 10f multi | 12 | 8 |
| *O329* A219 15f multi | 80 | 15 |
| *O330* A219 25f multi | 1.00 | 35 |
| *O331* A219 50f multi | 2.25 | 75 |
| *Nos. O327-O331 (5)* | 4.25 | 1.41 |

**1978 Photo. *Perf. 11½***

| | | |
|---|---|---|
| *O332* O2 5f multi | 5 | 5 |
| *O333* O2 10f multi | 8 | 8 |
| *O334* O2 15f multi | 15 | 12 |
| *O335* O2 25f multi | 40 | 20 |

Baghdad University Entrance — O3

**1981, Oct. 21 Litho. *Perf. 12x12½***

| | | |
|---|---|---|
| *O336* O3 45f multi | 36 | 24 |
| *O337* O3 50f multi | 40 | 30 |

Nos. O336-O337 Surcharged.

**1983, May 15 Litho. *Perf. 12x12½***

| | | |
|---|---|---|
| *O338* O3 60f on 45f multi | 50 | 32 |
| *O339* O3 70f on 50f multi | 60 | 45 |

Martyrs Type of 1981

**1981 Photo. *Perf. 14***

| | | |
|---|---|---|
| *O339A* A303 45f silver border | 36 | 24 |
| *O339B* A303 50f gold border | 40 | 30 |
| *O339C* A303 120f silver border | 96 | 64 |

Building Type of 1983

**1982, Dec. 31 Litho. *Perf. 14***

| | | |
|---|---|---|
| *O340* A324 60f multi | 48 | 32 |
| *O341* A324 70f multi | 56 | 40 |

Martyr Type of 1984

**1984, Dec. 1**

| | | |
|---|---|---|
| *O342* A329 20f multi | 14 | 10 |
| *O343* A329 30f multi | 20 | 12 |
| *O344* A329 50f multi | 32 | 22 |
| *O345* A329 60f multi | 38 | 25 |

No. RA22 Ovptd. "OFFICIAL POSTAGE" in Arabic.

**1985 (?) Litho. *Perf. 13x12½***

| | | |
|---|---|---|
| *O346* PT2 5f bis, blk & yel | 30 | 30 |

---

## POSTAL TAX STAMPS

**Catalogue values for unused stamps in this section, from this point to the end of the section, are for Never Hinged items.**

Nos. O125 and 115 Surcharged in Carmine or Black

مالية
فلسان
انقاذ فلسطين

**1949 Unwmk. *Perf. 11½x12***

| | | |
|---|---|---|
| *RA1* A25 2f on 3f emer (C) | 24.00 | 15.00 |
| *RA2* A25 2f on 6f plum | 60.00 | 10.00 |

Similar Overprint in Carmine or Black on Nos. O124, O127 and O94. Middle Arabic Line Omitted.

***Perf. 11½x12***

| | | |
|---|---|---|
| *RA3* A25 2f sep (C) | 22.50 | 4.50 |
| *RA4* A25 5f rose lake | 65.00 | 10.00 |

***Perf. 12x13½, 14***

| | | |
|---|---|---|
| *RA5* A19 5f dk car rose | 16.00 | 5.00 |

Larger overprint on No. RA5, 20½mm wide.

No. 115 Surcharged in Black

مالية
٥ فلوس
انقاذ فلسطين

***Perf. 11½x12***

| | | |
|---|---|---|
| *RA6* A25 5f on 6f plum | 72.50 | 27.50 |

The tax on Nos. RA1 to RA6 was to aid the war in Palestine.

Nos. 317, 322-326 Surcharged

دفاع وطني
٥ فلوس

**Engraved; Engraved and Photogravure**

**1963 *Perf. 12x11***

| | | |
|---|---|---|
| *RA7* A57 5f on 1f grn | 60 | 60 |
| *RA8* A57 5f on 10f rose red | 60 | 60 |
| *RA9* A57 5f on 15f brn & buff | 60 | 60 |
| *RA10* A57 5f on 20f vio bl | 60 | 60 |
| *RA11* A57 5f on 30f org | 60 | 60 |
| *RA12* A57 5f on 40f brt grn | 60 | 60 |
| *Nos. RA7-RA12 (6)* | 3.60 | 3.60 |

Surtax was for the Defense Fund.

PT1

دفاع
وطني
b

**1967, Aug. Photo. *Perf. 13½***

| | | |
|---|---|---|
| *RA13* PT1 5f brown | 35 | 10 |

Surtax was for flood victims.

Same Overprinted "b"

**1967, Nov.**

| | | |
|---|---|---|
| *RA14* PT1 5f brown | 1.00 | 1.00 |

Surtax was for Defense Fund.

Nos. 305A-305B with Surcharge Similar to Nos. RA7-RA12

**1972 Litho. *Perf. 13½x14***

| | | |
|---|---|---|
| *RA15* A54a 5f on 14f brt grn & blk | 5.25 | 3.75 |
| *RA16* A54a 5f on 35f ver & blk | 5.25 | 3.75 |

Surtax was for the Defense Fund. The 2 disks obliterating old denominations are on one line at the bottom. Size of Arabic inscription: 17x12mm.

No. 452 with Surcharge Similar to Nos. RA7-RA12 and Nos. 443, 457 and 526 Surcharged

دفاع وطني
٥ فلوس

**1973 Litho. *Perf. 13***

| | | |
|---|---|---|
| *RA17* A105 5f on 2f multi | 5.75 | 40 |
| *RA18* A107 5f on 2f multi | 5.75 | 40 |
| *RA19* A108 5f on 2f multi | 5.75 | 40 |
| *RA20* A135 5f on 2f multi | 5.75 | 40 |

Surtax was for the Defense Fund. Surcharges on Nos. RA17-RA20 are adjusted to fit shape of stamps and to obliterate old denominations.

No 683 Overprinted

دفاع
وطني

**1974 Litho. *Perf. 13x12½***

| | | |
|---|---|---|
| *RA21* A186 5f org & blk | 2.50 | 2.50 |

Soldier PT2

Dome of the Rock, Jerusalem PT3

**1974**

| | | |
|---|---|---|
| *RA22* PT2 5f bis, blk & yel | 50 | 30 |

Surtax of Nos. RA21-RA22 was for the Defense Fund.

**1977 Photo. *Perf. 14***

| | | |
|---|---|---|
| *RA23* PT3 5f multi | 2.00 | 5 |

Surtax was for families of Palestinians.

---

## AIR POST POSTAL TAX STAMPS

**Catalogue values for unused stamps in this section, from this point to the end of the section, are for Never Hinged items.**

No. C15 Surcharged

دفاع وطني
٥ فلوس

**1973 Litho. *Perf. 13½***

| | | |
|---|---|---|
| *RAC1* AP5 5f on 2f multi | 5.00 | 5.00 |

Surtax was for the Defense Fund.

---

# IRELAND

## (Eire)

LOCATION — Comprises the entire island of Ireland, except 5,237 square miles at the extreme north.
GOVT. — Republic.
AREA — 27,136 sq. mi.
POP. — 3,443,405 (1981).
CAPITAL — Dublin.

12 Pence = 1 Shilling
100 Pence = 1 Pound (1971)

**Catalogue values for unused stamps in this country are for Never Hinged items, beginning with Scott 99 in the regular postage section, Scott C1 in the air post section, and Scott J5 in the postage due section.**

**Printed by Dollard, Ltd.**

Stamps of Great Britain, 1912-19, Overprinted

Rialtap Sealadac na hÉireann 1922

Overprint measures 15x17½mm.

This overprint means "Provisional Government of Ireland".

Black or Gray Black Overprint

**1922, Feb. 17 Wmk. 33 *Perf. 15x14***

| | | | |
|---|---|---|---|
| *1* A82 | ½p green | 18 | 12 |
| *a* | Invtd. ovpt. | 350.00 | 450.00 |
| *2* A83 | 1p scarlet | 20 | 12 |
| *a* | Invted. ovpt. | 225.00 | 275.00 |
| *3* A86 | 2½p ultra | 85 | 2.75 |
| *4* A87 | 3p violet | 1.75 | 2.75 |
| *5* A88 | 4p slate grn | 1.75 | 4.75 |
| *6* A89 | 5p yel brown | 3.50 | 8.00 |
| *7* A90 | 9p black brn | 9.00 | 13.00 |
| *8* A90 | 10p light bl | 6.00 | 12.00 |
| | *Nos. 1-8 (8)* | 23.23 | 43.49 |

The ½p with red overprint is a trial printing. Value $180.

Red or Carmine Overprint

**1922, Apr.-July**

| | | | |
|---|---|---|---|
| *9* A86 | 2½p ultra | 1.25 | 2.75 |
| *10* A88 | 4p slate grn (R) | 7.25 | 8.25 |
| *10A* A88 | 4p slate grn (C) | 40.00 | 50.00 |
| *11* A90 | 9p black brown | 12.00 | 11.50 |

Overprinted in Black

Rialtap Sealadac na hÉireann 1922

Overprint measures 21½x14mm.

**1922, Feb. 17 Wmk. 34 *Perf. 11x12***

| | | | |
|---|---|---|---|
| *12* A91 | 2sh6p brown | 22.50 | 50.00 |
| *13* A91 | 5sh car rose | 40.00 | 95.00 |
| *14* A91 | 10sh gray bl | 110.00 | 225.00 |

**Printed by Alex. Thom & Co.**

Overprinted in Black

Rialtap Sealadac na hÉireann 1922.

Overprint measures 14½x16mm.

TWO PENCE

Die I - Four horizontal lines above the head. Heavy colored lines above and below the bottom tablet.

Die II - Three lines above the head. Thinner lines above and below the bottom tablet.

**1922, Feb. 17 Wmk. 33 *Perf. 15x14***

| | | | | |
|---|---|---|---|---|
| *15* | A84 | 1½p red brown | 85 | 70 |
| *a* | | "PENCF" | 700.00 | 650.00 |
| *16* | A85 | 2p orange (II) | 1.65 | 35 |
| *a* | | Inverted overprint (II) | 525.00 | 675.00 |
| *b* | | 2p orange (I) | 1.25 | 28 |
| *c* | | Inverted overprint (I) | 110.00 | 150.00 |
| *17* | A89 | 6p red violet | 6.50 | 4.25 |
| *18* | A90 | 1sh bister | 13.00 | 7.75 |

**Printed by Harrison & Sons**

Coil Stamps

Overprint similar to the preceding,* in glossy black ink

Overprint measures 15¼x17mm.

**1922, June**

| | | | | |
|---|---|---|---|---|
| *19* | A82 | ½p green | 3.25 | 5.75 |
| *20* | A83 | 1p scarlet | 1.50 | 3.25 |
| *21* | A84 | 1½p red brown | 5.25 | 9.25 |
| *22* | A85 | 2p orange (I) | 10.00 | 12.50 |
| *a* | | 2p orange (II) | 14.50 | 16.00 |

* In Harrison overprint, "i" of "Rialtas" extends below the base of the other letters.

The Harrison stamps were issued in coils, either horizontal or vertical. The paper is double where the ends of the strips were overlapped. The perforations are often clipped.

**Printed by Alex. Thom & Co.**

Stamps of Great Britain, 1912-22 Overprinted as Nos. 15 to 18, in Shiny to Dull Blue Black, or Red

Overprint measures 14½x16mm.

**1922, July-Nov. *Perf. 15x14***

| | | | | |
|---|---|---|---|---|
| *23* | A82 | ½p green | 1.40 | 90 |
| *24* | A83 | 1p scarlet | 45 | 20 |
| *25* | A84 | 1½p red brown | 5.25 | 2.50 |
| *26* | A85 | 2p orange (II) | 1.75 | 60 |
| *a* | | Inverted overprint (II) | 275.00 | 350.00 |
| *b* | | 2p orange (I) | 17.00 | 2.00 |
| *27* | A86 | 2½p ultra (R) | 5.50 | 11.50 |
| *28* | A87 | 3p violet | 1.25 | 1.40 |
| *29* | A88 | 4p slate grn (R) | 2.50 | 2.75 |
| *30* | A89 | 5p yel brown | 3.50 | 6.00 |
| *31* | A89 | 6p red violet | 5.25 | 4.50 |
| *32* | A90 | 9p blk brown (R) | 10.50 | 12.00 |
| *33* | A90 | 9p ol green (R) | 5.50 | 10.50 |
| *34* | A90 | 10p light blue | 27.50 | 30.00 |
| *35* | A90 | 1sh bister | 12.50 | 9.00 |
| | | *Nos. 23-35 (13)* | 82.85 | 91.85 |

Overprinted as Nos. 12 to 14 in Blue Black (Shiny to Dull)

Overprint measures 21x13½mm.

**1922 Wmk. 34 *Perf. 11x12***

| | | | | |
|---|---|---|---|---|
| *36* | A91 | 2sh6p gray brown | 175.00 | 225.00 |
| *37* | A91 | 5sh car rose | 175.00 | 250.00 |
| *38* | A91 | 10sh gray blue | 975. | 1,200. |

Overprinted in Blue Black

Rialtaṡ Sealadaċ na hÉireann 1922.

Overprint measures 15¾x16mm.

**1922, Dec. Wmk. 33 *Perf. 15x14***

| | | | | |
|---|---|---|---|---|
| *39* | A82 | ½p green | 35 | 45 |
| *40* | A83 | 1p scarlet | 80 | 75 |
| *41* | A84 | 1½p red brown | 2.00 | 4.50 |
| *42* | A85 | 2p orange (II) | 8.50 | 8.50 |
| *43* | A90 | 1sh bister | 24.00 | 30.00 |
| | | *Nos. 39-43 (5)* | 35.65 | 44.20 |

Stamps of Great Britain, 1912-22, Overprinted in Shiny to Dull Blue Black or Red

Saorstát Éireann 1922

This overprint means the "Free State of Ireland".

Overprint measures 15x8½mm.

"1922" is 6¼mm. long

There were five plates for printing the overprint on Nos. 44 to 55. In the impressions from plate I the twelfth stamp in the fifteenth row has no accent on the second "A" of "SAORSTAT". To correct this an accent was inserted by hand, sometimes this was in a reversed position. On Nos. 56 to 58 the accent was omitted on the second stamp in the third and eighth rows and was inserted by hand.

**1922-23 Wmk. 33 *Perf. 15x14***

| | | | | |
|---|---|---|---|---|
| *44* | A82 | ½p green | 15 | 15 |
| *a* | | Accent omitted | 950. | 800. |
| *b* | | Accent added | 80.00 | 95.00 |
| *45* | A83 | 1p scarlet | 20 | 15 |
| *a* | | Accent omitted | 8,000. | 8,000. |
| *b* | | Accent added | 95.00 | 125.00 |
| *c* | | Accent and final "t" omitted | 8,000. | 7,000. |
| *d* | | Accent and final "t" added | 150.00 | 200.00 |
| *46* | A84 | 1½p red brown | 2.25 | 4.00 |
| *47* | A85 | 2p orange (II) | 1.00 | 1.00 |
| *48* | A86 | 2½p ultra (R) | 1.50 | 3.50 |
| *a* | | Accent omitted | 100.00 | 150.00 |
| *49* | A87 | 3p violet | 6.00 | 7.00 |
| *a* | | Accent omitted | 250.00 | 285.00 |
| *50* | A88 | 4p sl green (R) | 1.50 | 2.00 |
| *a* | | Accent omitted | 125.00 | 165.00 |
| *51* | A89 | 5p yel brown | 2.25 | 3.50 |
| *52* | A89 | 6p dl violet | 2.00 | 2.00 |
| *a* | | Accent added | 1,000. | 1,000. |
| *53* | A90 | 9p ol grn (R) | 2.75 | 3.75 |
| *a* | | Accent omitted | 225.00 | 285.00 |
| *54* | A90 | 10p lt blue | 13.00 | 22.50 |
| *55* | A90 | 1sh bister | 8.25 | 9.25 |
| *a* | | Accent omitted | 8,000. | 8,500. |
| *b* | | Accent added | 875. | 800. |

***Perf. 11x12***

**Wmk. 34**

| | | | | |
|---|---|---|---|---|
| *56* | A91 | 2sh6p lt brn | 30.00 | 45.00 |
| *a* | | Accent omitted | 350.00 | 400.00 |
| *b* | | Accent reversed | 415.00 | 475.00 |
| *57* | A91 | 5sh car rose | 55.00 | 95.00 |
| *a* | | Accent omitted | 500.00 | 575.00 |
| *b* | | Accent reversed | 450.00 | 500.00 |
| *58* | A91 | 10sh gray bl | 130.00 | 225.00 |
| *a* | | Accent omitted | 2,750. | 3,250. |
| *b* | | Accent reversed | 3,250. | 3,500. |
| | | *Nos. 44-58 (15)* | 255.85 | 423.80 |

See Nos. 77b, 78b and 79b.

**Printed by Harrison & Sons**

Coil Stamps

Same Overprint in Black or Blue Black

**1923 Wmk. 33 *Perf. 15x14***

| | | | | |
|---|---|---|---|---|
| *59* | A82 | ½p green | 1.50 | 3.50 |
| *a* | | Tall "1" | 13.00 | 20.00 |
| *60* | A83 | 1p scarlet | 2.75 | 6.75 |
| *a* | | Tall "1" | 52.50 | 90.00 |
| *61* | A84 | 1½p red brown | 3.25 | 14.00 |
| *a* | | Tall "1" | 77.50 | 150.00 |
| *62* | A85 | 2p orange (II) | 1.75 | 4.50 |
| *a* | | Tall "1" | 15.00 | 27.50 |

These stamps were issued in coils, made by joining horizontal or vertical strips of the stamps. In each strip there were two stamps with the "1" of "1922" 2½mm. high and with serif at foot.

In this setting the middle "e" of "eireann" is a trifle above the line of the other letters, making the word appear slightly curved. The lower end of the "1" of "1922" is rounded instead of flat.

**Printed by the Government Printing Office, Dublin Castle**

"Sword of Light" A1

Map of Ireland A2

Coat of Arms — A3

Celtic Cross — A4

Wmk. 44 - SE in Monogram

The letters "SE" are the initials of "Saorstat Eireann" (Free State Ireland).

***Perf. 15x14***

**1922-23 Typo. Wmk. 44**

| | | | | |
|---|---|---|---|---|
| *65* | A1 | ½p emerald | 16 | 9 |
| *a* | | Booklet pane of 6 | 175.00 | |
| *66* | A2 | 1p car rose | 7 | 5 |
| *a* | | Booklet pane of 6 | 150.00 | |
| *b* | | Booklet pane of 3 + 3 labels | 250.00 | |
| *67* | A2 | 1½p claret | 1.50 | 75 |
| *68* | A2 | 2p deep green | 10 | 5 |
| *a* | | Booklet pane of 6 | 150.00 | |
| *b* | | Perf. 15 horiz. | 15,000. | 1,700. |
| *69* | A3 | 2½p chocolate | 3.00 | 1.50 |
| *70* | A4 | 3p ultra | 1.75 | 22 |
| *71* | A3 | 4p slate | 2.00 | 48 |
| *72* | A1 | 5p deep violet | 8.50 | 7.50 |
| *73* | A1 | 6p red violet | 3.00 | 3.00 |
| *74* | A3 | 9p violet | 10.50 | 10.50 |
| *75* | A4 | 10p brown | 8.50 | 13.00 |
| *76* | A1 | 1sh light blue | 27.50 | 5.75 |
| | | *Nos. 65-76 (12)* | 66.58 | 42.89 |

The 2p was issued in 1922; other denominations in 1923.

No. 68b is a vertical coil stamp.

See Nos. 87, 91-92, 105-117, 137-138, 225-226, 326.

Stamps of Great Britain, 1919, Overprinted as Nos. 56 to 58 in Black or Gray Black

"1922" is 5½mm. long

**1925-27 Wmk. 34 *Perf. 11x12***

| | | | | |
|---|---|---|---|---|
| *77* | A91 | 2sh6p gray brown | 30.00 | 50.00 |
| *a* | | Pair with "1922" wide and narrow ('27) | 225.00 | |
| *b* | | Wide "1922" ('27) | 27.50 | 30.00 |
| *78* | A91 | 5sh rose red | 40.00 | 60.00 |
| *a* | | Pair with "1922" wide and narrow ('27) | 450.00 | |
| *b* | | Wide "1922" ('27) | 60.00 | 65.00 |
| *79* | A91 | 10sh gray blue | 115.00 | 200.00 |
| *a* | | Pair with "1922" wide and narrow ('27) | 1,250. | |
| *b* | | Wide "1922" ('27) | 150.00 | 165.00 |

In 1927 the 2sh 6p, 5sh and 10sh stamps were overprinted from a plate in which the Thom and Castle cliches were combined, thus including the wide and narrow "1922" in the same setting.

Daniel O'Connell — A5

**1929, June 22 Wmk. 44 *Perf. 15x14***

| | | | | |
|---|---|---|---|---|
| *80* | A5 | 2p dark green | 25 | 18 |
| *81* | A5 | 3p dark blue | 2.75 | 8.50 |
| *82* | A5 | 9p dark violet | 3.00 | 8.00 |

Catholic Emancipation in Ireland, centenary.

Shannon River Hydroelectric Station — A6

**1930, Oct. 15**

| | | | | |
|---|---|---|---|---|
| *83* | A6 | 2p black brown | 48 | 28 |

Opening of the hydroelectric development of the River Shannon.

Farmer with Scythe — A7

Cross of Cong and Chalice — A8

**1931, June 12**

| | | | | |
|---|---|---|---|---|
| *84* | A7 | 2p pale blue | 75 | 22 |

Bicentenary of Royal Dublin Society.

**1932, May 12**

| | | | | |
|---|---|---|---|---|
| *85* | A8 | 2p dark green | 80 | 25 |
| *86* | A8 | 3p bright blue | 2.00 | 4.50 |

International Eucharistic Congress.

Coil Stamp

Type of 1922-23 Issue.

**1933-34 *Perf. 15 Horizontally***

| | | | | |
|---|---|---|---|---|
| *87* | A2 | 1p rose ('34) | 21.00 | 35.00 |
| *a* | | 1p carmine rose | 85.00 | 150.00 |

No. 87a has a single perforation at each side near the top, while No. 87 is perforated top and bottom only.

See also No. 68b.

Adoration of the Cross A9

Hurling A10

**1933, Sept. 18** *Perf. 15x14*

*88* A9 2p slate green 45 25
*89* A9 3p deep blue 2.50 3.75

Holy Year.

**1934, July 27**

*90* A10 2p green 90 30

50th anniv. of the Gaelic Athletic Assoc.

Coil Stamps

Types of 1922-23

**1934** *Perf. 14 Vertically*

*91* A1 ½p green 27.50 37.50
*92* A2 2p gray green 42.50 52.50

Stamps of Great Britain, 1934, Overprinted in Black

SAORSTÁT ÉIREANN 1922

**1935** **Wmk. 34** *Perf. 11x12*

*93* A91 2sh6p brown 30.00 30.00
*94* A91 5sh carmine 90.00 100.00
*95* A91 10sh dark blue 375.00 375.00

Waterlow printing can be distinguished by the crossed lines in the background of portrait. Previous issues have horizontal lines only.

St. Patrick and Paschal Fire — A11

**1937, Sept. 8** **Wmk. 44** *Perf. 14x15*

*96* A11 2sh6p bright grn 50.00 75.00
*97* A11 5sh brn violet 55.00 85.00
*98* A11 10sh dark blue 42.50 65.00

See Nos. 121-123.

**Catalogue values for unused stamps in this section, from this point to the end of the section, are for Never Hinged items.**

Allegory of Ireland and Constitution A12

**1937, Dec. 29** *Perf. 15x14*

*99* A12 2p plum 1.25 25
*100* A12 3p deep blue 5.75 2.75

Constitution Day.

See Nos. 169-170.

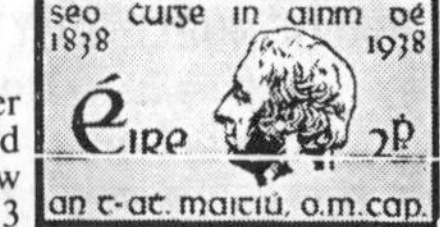

Father Theobald Mathew A13

**1938, July 1**

*101* A13 2p black brown 95 15
*102* A13 3p ultramarine 10.50 5.50

Temperance Crusade by Father Mathew, centenary.

Washington, US Eagle and Harp — A14

**1939, Mar. 1**

*103* A14 2p bright car 85 28
*104* A14 3p deep blue 8.50 6.50

US Constitution, 150th anniv.

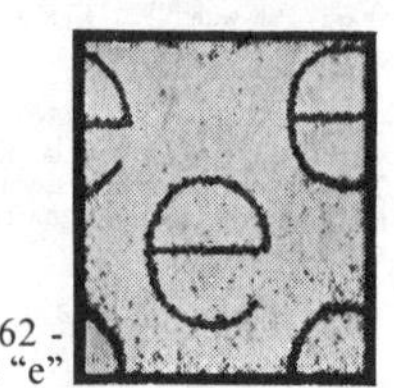

Wmk. 262 - Multiple "e"

Coil Stamp

Type of 1922-23

**1940-46** **Wmk. 262** *Perf. 15 Horiz.*

*105* A2 1p car rose ('46) 22.50 18.00
*a* Perf. 14 horiz. 47.50 45.00

Types of 1922-23

**1940-42** *Perf. 15x14*

**Size: 18x22mm.**

*106* A1 ½p emerald ('41) 1.75 16
*a* Booklet pane of 6 200.00
*107* A2 1p car rose ('41) 12 5
*a* Booklet pane of 6 3.75
*b* Bklt. pane of 3 + 3 labels 625.00
*108* A2 1½p claret ('41) 9.50 20
*a* Booklet pane of 6 85.00
*109* A2 2p deep green 22 5
*a* Booklet pane of 6 6.00
*110* A3 2½p choc ('41) 6.50 6
*a* Booklet pane of 6 57.50
*111* A4 3p dull bl ('41) 30 5
*a* Booklet pane of 6 24.00
*112* A3 4p slate 35 5
*a* Bklt. pane of 6 40.00
*113* A1 5p deep violet 48 5
*114* A1 6p red vio ('42) 60 15
*115* A3 9p violet 70 20
*116* A4 10p olive brown 1.75 30
*117* A1 1sh blue 100.00 7.25
*Nos. 106-117 (12)* 122.27 8.57

Types of 1922-23 Overprinted in Green or Violet

1941 I gCUIMNE AISÉIRGHE 1916

**1941, April** *Perf. 15x14*

*118* A2 2p yellow orange 2.25 50
*119* A4 3p blue (V) 37.50 16.00

Overprint reads: "In memory of the Rebellion of 1916."

Volunteer Soldier and Dublin Post Office A15

**1941, Oct. 27**

*120* A15 2½p bluish black 90 30

Nos. 118-120 commemorate the 25th anniv. of the Easter Rebellion.

St. Patrick Type of 1937

**1943-45** **Wmk. 262** *Perf. 14x15*

*121* A11 2sh6p bright green 5.00 65
*122* A11 5sh brown violet 7.75 1.25
*123* A11 10sh dark bl ('45) 17.00 3.50

Dr. Douglas Hyde A16

Sir Rowan Hamilton A17

**1943, July 31** *Perf. 15x14*

*124* A16 ½p green 50 25
*125* A16 2½p red lilac 95 60

50th anniv. of the Gaelic League.

*Perf. 15x14*

**1943, Nov. 13** **Typo.** **Wmk. 262**

*126* A17 ½p deep green 1.75 22
*127* A17 2½p dk red brown 1.65 60

Centenary of discovery of the mathematical formula of Quaternions by William Rowan Hamilton.

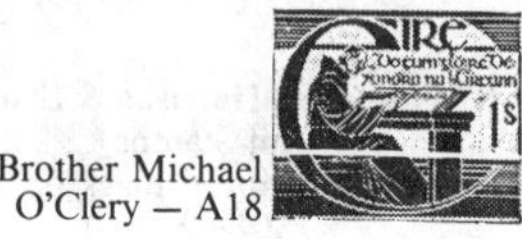

Brother Michael O'Clery — A18

**1944, June 30** *Perf. 14x15*

*128* A18 ½p emerald 20 5
*a* Booklet pane of 6 20.00
*129* A18 1sh reddish brown 1.00 16

300th anniv. of the death of Michael O'Clery, Irish historian.

Edmund Rice A19

Sower A20

**1944, Aug. 29** *Perf. 15x14*

*130* A19 2½p slate 85 16

Death centenary of Edmund Ignatius Rice, founder of the Christian Brothers of Ireland.

**1945, Sept. 15**

*131* A20 2½p ultramarine 1.25 15
*132* A20 6p red violet 5.75 3.25

Commemorates the work of the Young Irelanders and the death centenary of Thomas Davis, September 16, 1845.

Plowman A21

**1946, Sept. 16** **Typo.**

*133* A21 2½p red 1.50 18
*134* A21 3p dark blue 4.25 3.25

Birth centenary of Charles Stewart Parnell and Michael Davitt, leaders in the struggle for Irish political independence.

Theobald Wolfe Tone A22

*Perf. 15x14*

**1948, Nov. 19** **Wmk. 262**

*135* A22 2½p deep plum 1.50 14
*136* A22 3p deep violet 6.75 4.00

Insurrection of 1798, 150th anniversary.

Types of 1922-23

**1949**

*137* A1 8p bright red 75 25
*138* A4 11p carmine rose 1.40 1.00

Leinster House, Dublin A23

**1949, Nov. 21**

*139* A23 2½p red brown 80 40
*140* A23 3p violet blue 4.25 2.75

International recognition of the Republic, Easter Monday, 1949.

James Clarence Mangan — A24

Statue of St. Peter — A25

**1949, Dec. 5**

*141* A24 1p dark green 4.00 38

Mangan (1803-49), poet.

**Wmk. 262**

**1950, Sept. 11** **Engr.** *Perf. 12½*

*142* A25 2½p violet 58 8
*143* A25 3p blue 11.00 7.25
*144* A25 9p brown 12.00 6.00

Holy Year, 1950.

Thomas Moore — A26

Irish Harp — A27

**1952, Nov. 10** *Perf. 13*

*145* A26 2½p deep plum 20 15
*146* A26 3½p dark ol green 4.00 2.00

Death centenary of Thomas Moore (1779-1852), poet.

**1953, Feb. 9** **Typo.** *Perf. 14x15*

*147* A27 2½p bright green 95 12
*148* A27 1sh4p bright blue 27.50 18.00

Ireland's National festival "An Tostal."

Robert Emmet — A28

Madonna by della Robbia — A29

**1953, Sept. 21** **Engr.** *Perf. 12½x13*

*149* A28 3p deep green 2.75 40
*150* A28 1sh3p car rose 45.00 9.50

150th anniv. of the execution of Robert Emmet (1778-1803), Irish nationalist.

**1954, May 24** ***Perf. 15***
*151* A29 3p blue 1.10 6
*152* A29 5p deep green 9.25 4.50

Marian Year, 1953-54.

John Henry Cardinal Newman A30

Statue of John Barry A31

**1954, July 19** **Typo.** ***Perf. 15x14***
*153* A30 2p rose lilac 2.00 18
*154* A30 1sh3p blue 16.00 7.25

Opening of the Catholic University of Ireland, centenary.

**1956, Sept. 16** **Engr.** ***Perf. 15***
*155* A31 3p dull purple 75 8
*156* A31 1sh3p blue 10.50 5.50

John Barry (1745-1803), "Father of the American Navy," on the occasion of the unveiling of a statue in Wexford, Ireland, his birthplace.

John Redmond A32

Thomas O'Crohan A33

***Perf. 14x15***
**1957, June 11** **Wmk. 262**
*157* A32 3p dark blue 75 7
*158* A32 1sh3p rose lake 12.00 6.25

Birth cent. of John Edward Redmond (1856-1918), Irish political leader.

**1957, July 1**
*159* A33 2p dull purple 2.25 8
*160* A33 5p violet 7.25 4.00

Birth cent. of Thomas O'Crohan (Tomas O'Criomhthain) (1856-1937), fisherman and author.

Admiral Brown A34

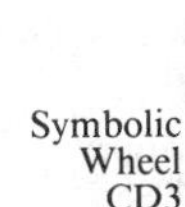

Father Luke Wadding A35

**1957, Sept. 23** **Typo.** ***Perf. 15x14***
*161* A34 3p blue 2.25 32
*162* A34 1sh3p car rose 40.00 12.50

Adm. William (Guillermo) Brown (1777-1857), founder of the Argentine Navy.

**1957, Nov. 25** **Engr.** ***Perf. 15***
*163* A35 3p dark blue 1.00 22
*164* A35 1sh3p dp claret 15.00 5.75

Luke Wadding (1588-1657), Irish Franciscan friar and historian.

Thomas J. Clarke A36

Mother Mary Aikenhead A37

**1958, July 28** **Wmk. 262**
*165* A36 3p deep green 95 8
*166* A36 1sh3p red brown 15.00 5.50

Tom Clarke (1858-1916), patriot.

**1958, Oct. 20** ***Perf. 15x14***
*167* A37 3p blue 1.00 10
*168* A37 1sh3p carmine 15.00 6.25

Mother Mary Aikenhead (1787-1858), founder of the Irish Sisters of Charity.

Constitution Type of 1937

**1958, Dec. 29** **Typo.** **Wmk. 262**
*169* A12 3p brown 95 16
*170* A12 5p bright green 6.00 3.78

21st anniv. of the constitution.

Arthur Guinness — A38

**1959, July 20** **Engr.** ***Perf. 15***
*171* A38 3p rose lake 1.40 12
*172* A38 1sh3p dark blue 16.00 6.00

Bicentenary of Guinness Brewery.

Flight of the Holy Family A39

**1960, June 20** ***Perf. 15***
*173* A39 3p rose violet 25 20
*174* A39 1sh3p sepia 1.00 1.65

World Refugee Year, July 1, 1959-June 30, 1960.

**Europa Issue, 1960**

Symbolic Wheel CD3

**1960, Sept. 19** **Engr.** ***Perf. 15***
*175* CD3 6p orange brown 1.90 1.90
*176* CD3 1sh3p violet 11.00 10.50

De Havilland Dragon, Boeing 707 Jet and Dublin Airport A41

**1961, June 26** ***Perf. 15***
*177* A41 6p dull blue 1.90 1.40
*178* A41 1sh3p green 4.25 3.25

25th anniv. of the founding of Aer Lingus, Irish International Airlines.

St. Patrick — A42

**1961, Sept. 25** ***Perf. 14½***
*179* A42 3p blue 52 16
*180* A42 8p pale purple 1.90 2.25
*181* A42 1sh3p green 1.90 1.90

1,500th anniv. of St. Patrick's death.

John O'Donovan and Eugene O'Curry A43

**1962, Mar. 26** ***Perf. 15***
*182* A43 3p crimson 38 10
*183* A43 1sh3p purple 4.75 2.75

Death centenaries of John O'Donovan (1806-1861) and Eugene O'Curry (1794-1862), Gaelic scholars and translators.

**Europa Issue, 1962**

19 Leaves on Young Tree — CD5

**1962, Sept. 17** **Engr.** **Wmk. 262**
*184* CD5 6p pink & dk red 32 35
*185* CD5 1sh3p bluish grn & dk bl grn 1.25 1.40

Wheat Emblem and Globe A45

**1963, Mar. 21** **Wmk. 262**
*186* A45 4p violet 22 12
*187* A45 1sh3p red 1.90 1.75

"Freedom from Hunger" campaign of the FAO.

Common Design Types in section before Great Britain.

**Europa Issue, 1963**

Stylized Links, Symbolizing Unity CD6

**1963, Sept. 16** ***Perf. 15***
*188* CD6 6p rose carmine 65 55
*189* CD6 1sh3p dark blue 3.75 3.50

Centenary Emblem A47

**1963, Dec. 2** **Photo.** ***Perf. 14½x14***
*190* A47 4p gray & red 20 15
*191* A47 1sh3p brt grn, gray & red 1.10 1.40

Centenary of the International Red Cross.

Wolfe Tone — A48

**1964, Apr. 13** **Engr.** ***Perf. 15***
*192* A48 4p black 70 20
*193* A48 1sh3p dark blue 4.00 3.50

Birth bicentenary of Theobald Wolfe Tone (1763-1798), Irish revolutionist.

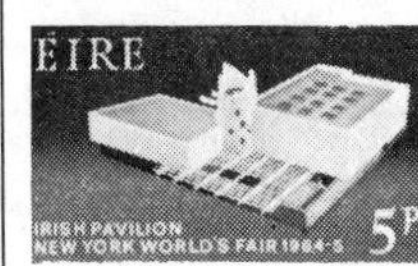

Irish Pavilion A49

**1964, July 20** **Photo.** ***Perf. 14½x14***
*194* A49 5p multicolored 65 15
*195* A49 1sh5p multicolored 4.00 3.50

New York World's Fair, 1964-65.

**Europa Issue, 1964**

CEPT Daisy (22 Petals) — CD7

***Perf. 14x14½***
**1964, Sept. 14** **Litho.** **Wmk. 262**
*196* CD7 8p dl grn & ultra 85 75
*197* CD7 1sh5p red brn & org 3.50 3.50

ITU Emblem, Globe and Communication Waves — A51

**1965, May 17** **Photo.** ***Perf. 14½x14***
*198* A51 3p dp bl & emer 32 22
*199* A51 8p black & emer 1.75 1.90

ITU, cent.

William Butler Yeats — A52

**1965, June 14** ***Perf. 15***
*200* A52 5p org brn & blk 95 24
*201* A52 1sh5p gray grn, brn & black 4.75 3.75

Birth centenary of William Butler Yeats (1865-1939), poet and dramatist.

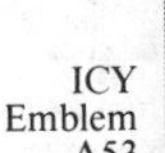

ICY Emblem A53

**1965, Aug. 16 Photo. *Perf. 15***

| | | | | |
|---|---|---|---|---|
| *202* | A53 | 3p brt bl & vio bl | 75 | 16 |
| *203* | A53 | 10p redsh brn & dk brn | 3.75 | 5.00 |

International Cooperation Year, 1965.

**Europa Issue, 1965**

Leaves and Fruit CD8

**1965, Sept. 27 *Perf. 15***

| | | | | |
|---|---|---|---|---|
| *204* | CD8 | 8p brick red & blk | 85 | 85 |
| *205* | CD8 | 1sh5p lt bl & claret | 4.25 | 3.75 |

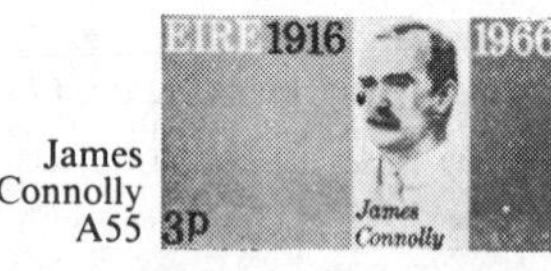

James Connolly A55

Designs: No. 207, Thomas J. Clarke. No. 208, Patrick Henry Pearse. No. 209, Symbolic of lives lost in fight for independence, and of Ireland marching into freedom. No. 210, Eamonn Ceannt. No. 211, Sean MacDiarmada. No. 212, Thomas MacDonagh. No. 213, Joseph Plunkett.

**1966, Apr. 12 Wmk. 262 *Perf. 15***

| | | | | |
|---|---|---|---|---|
| *206* | A55 | 3p blue & black | 75 | 35 |
| *207* | A55 | 3p olive green | 75 | 35 |
| *208* | A55 | 5p olive & black | 80 | 35 |
| *209* | A55 | 5p brt grn, blk & orange | 80 | 35 |
| *210* | A55 | 7p dull org & blk | 1.75 | 1.40 |
| *211* | A55 | 7p blue grn & blk | 1.75 | 1.40 |
| *212* | A55 | 1sh5p grnsh bl & blk | 2.25 | 1.75 |
| *213* | A55 | 1sh5p emerald & blk | 2.25 | 1.75 |
| | | *Nos. 206-213 (8)* | 11.10 | 7.70 |

50th anniv. of the Easter Week Rebellion, and to honor the signers of the Proclamation of the Irish Republic.

Stamps of same denomination are printed alternately in sheets of 120. Value of se-tenant pairs is about three times that of a single.

Roger Casement A56

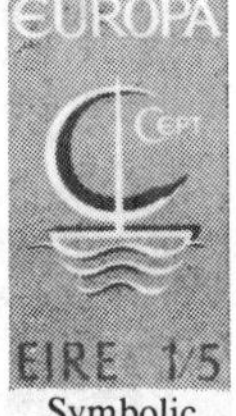

Symbolic Sailboat CD9

**1966, Aug. 3 *Perf. 15***

| | | | | |
|---|---|---|---|---|
| *214* | A56 | 5p black | 20 | 10 |
| *215* | A56 | 1sh dark red brn | 90 | 80 |

50th anniversary of the death of Roger Casement (1864-1916), British consular agent and Irish rebel who was executed for treason.

**Europa Issue, 1966**

**1966, Sept. 26 Photo. *Perf. 15***

| | | | | |
|---|---|---|---|---|
| *216* | CD9 | 7p org & green | 65 | 24 |
| *217* | CD9 | 1sh5p gray & green | 1.60 | 1.10 |

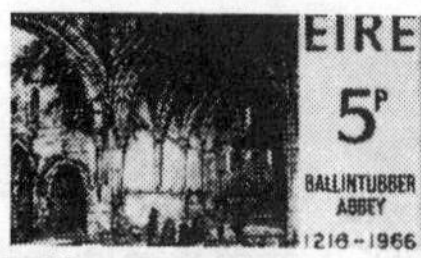

Ballintubber Abbey — A58

**1966, Nov. 8 *Perf. 15***

| | | | | |
|---|---|---|---|---|
| *218* | A58 | 5p red brown | 20 | 10 |
| *219* | A58 | 1sh black | 60 | 55 |

750th anniversary of Ballintubber Abbey.

Cross and Sword Types of 1922

**1966-67 Photo. *Perf. 15***

**Size: 17x20½mm**

| | | | | |
|---|---|---|---|---|
| *225* | A4 | 3p blue ('67) | 1.25 | 25 |
| *226* | A1 | 5p brt vio, type II ('68) | 2.25 | 30 |
| *a* | | Booklet pane of 6, No. 226b | 19.00 | |
| *b* | | Type I ('66) | 2.25 | 38 |

Type I has irregularly spaced lines in shading behind sword.

Cogwheels — CD10

**1967, May 2**

| | | | | |
|---|---|---|---|---|
| *232* | CD10 | 7p green & gold | 42 | 60 |
| *233* | CD10 | 1sh5p dk red & gold | 1.10 | 90 |

Maple Leaves A60

**1967, Aug. 28 Photo.**

| | | | | |
|---|---|---|---|---|
| *234* | A60 | 5p multicolored | 15 | 14 |
| *235* | A60 | 1sh5p multicolored | 55 | 60 |

Centenary of the Canadian Confederation.

Rock of Cashel A61

**1967, Sept. 25 Wmk. 262 *Perf. 15***

| | | | | |
|---|---|---|---|---|
| *236* | A61 | 7p sepia | 20 | 28 |
| *237* | A61 | 10p Prus blue | 40 | 55 |

International Tourist Year, 1967.

One Cent Fenian Essay — A62

Swift's Bust and St. Patrick's Cathedral, Dublin — A63

Design: 1sh, 24c Fenian essay.

**1967, Oct. 23 Photo. *Perf. 15***

| | | | | |
|---|---|---|---|---|
| *238* | A62 | 5p lt green & sl grn | 14 | 15 |
| *239* | A62 | 1sh pale pink & gray | 40 | 60 |

Fenian Rising, centenary. The Fenian essays were prepared in the U.S. to be used after the success of the uprising.

**1967, Nov. 30 *Perf. 15***

Design: 1sh5p, Gulliver, Lilliputian army.

| | | | | |
|---|---|---|---|---|
| *240* | A63 | 3p gray & sepia | 15 | 12 |
| *241* | A63 | 1sh5p lt bl & sepia | 40 | 48 |

Birth tercentenary of Jonathan Swift (1667-1745), author of Gulliver's Travels.

**Europa Issue, 1968**

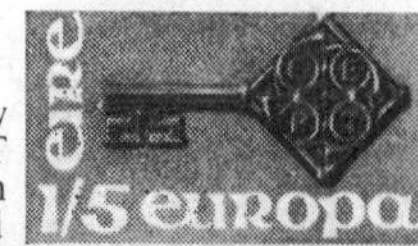

Golden Key with CEPT Emblem CD11

**1968, Apr. 29 Photo. Wmk. 262**

| | | | | |
|---|---|---|---|---|
| *242* | CD11 | 7p multi | 42 | 42 |
| *243* | CD11 | 1sh5p multi | 90 | 90 |

St. Mary's Cathedral, Limerick A65

**1968, Aug. 26 Engr. *Perf. 15***

| | | | | |
|---|---|---|---|---|
| *244* | A65 | 5p dull blue | 20 | 12 |
| *245* | A65 | 10p olive | 60 | 80 |

800th anniv. of the founding of St. Mary's Cathedral by Donal Mor O'Brien, last King of Munster.

Countess Markievicz A66

**1968, Sept. 23 Photo. Wmk. 262**

| | | | | |
|---|---|---|---|---|
| *246* | A66 | 3p black | 8 | 10 |
| *247* | A66 | 1sh5p dark blue | 45 | 65 |

Birth centenary of Countess Constance Markievicz (1868-1927), champion of Irish Independence and first Minister of Labor.

James Connolly — A67

**1968, Sept. 23 *Perf. 15***

| | | | | |
|---|---|---|---|---|
| *248* | A67 | 6p brn, dk brn & blk | 15 | 20 |
| *249* | A67 | 1sh dl grn, grn & blk | 40 | 50 |

Birth centenary of James Connolly (1868-1916), founder of the Irish Socialist Party, editor of "Workers' Republic" and Commander of the Irish Citizen Army.

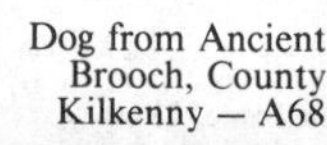

Dog from Ancient Brooch, County Kilkenny — A68

Winged Ox from Lichfield Gospel Book — A69

Designs: ½p, 1p, 2p, 3p, 4p, 5p, 6p, Dog. 7p, 8p, 9p, 10p, 1sh, 1sh9p, Stag from ancient bowl, Kent. 2sh6p, 5sh, Winged ox. 10sh, Eagle, from ancient manuscript.

**1968-70 Photo. Wmk. 262 *Perf. 15***

| | | | | |
|---|---|---|---|---|
| *250* | A68 | ½p orange ('69) | 12 | 6 |
| *251* | A68 | 1p yel green ('69) | 6 | 6 |
| *a* | | Perf. 14x15 | 90 | 2.65 |
| *252* | A68 | 2p ocher | 12 | 6 |
| *a* | | Perf. 14x15 | 90 | 2.65 |
| *253* | A68 | 3p brt blue ('69) | 12 | 6 |
| *a* | | Perf. 14x15 | 90 | 2.65 |
| *254* | A68 | 4p dark red ('69) | 18 | 7 |
| *255* | A68 | 5p deep grn ('69) | 22 | 22 |
| *256* | A68 | 6p brown ('69) | 24 | 14 |
| *a* | | Booklet pane of 6 ('70) | 25.00 | |
| *257* | A68 | 7p yel & brn ('69) | 1.00 | 1.00 |
| *258* | A68 | 8p red org & blk | 65 | 70 |
| *259* | A68 | 9p olive grn & dk bl ('69) | 1.00 | 45 |
| *260* | A68 | 10p violet & dk brn ('69) | 1.00 | 1.00 |
| *261* | A68 | 1sh dk red brn & brn ('69) | 1.00 | 45 |
| *262* | A68 | 1sh9p grnsh bl & dk brn ('69) | 2.00 | 2.50 |
| *263* | A69 | 2sh6p red org, bl, ol & dl yel | 4.00 | 55 |
| *264* | A69 | 5sh ol, gray, bis & yel ('69) | 8.25 | 1.25 |
| *265* | A69 | 10sh dk red brn, yel & dp org | 16.00 | 3.50 |
| | | *Nos. 250-265 (16)* | 35.96 | 12.07 |

Issue dates: 2p, 8p, 2sh6p, 10sh, Oct. 14, 1968. 6p, 9p, 1sh9p, 5sh, Feb. 24, 1969. 4p, 5p, 10p, 1sh, Mar. 31, 1969. ½p, 1p, 3p, 7p, June 9, 1969.

Nos. 251a, 252a and 253a are coil stamps.

See Nos. 290-304, 343-359, 395-402, 466-475.

Human Rights Flame — A70

**1968, Nov. 4 Wmk. 262 *Perf. 15***

| | | | | |
|---|---|---|---|---|
| *266* | A70 | 5p blk, ocher & gold | 12 | 10 |
| *267* | A70 | 7p crim, ocher & gold | 42 | 50 |

International Human Rights Year.

First Meeting of Irish Parliament A71

**1969, Jan. 21 *Perf. 15x14½***

| | | | | |
|---|---|---|---|---|
| *268* | A71 | 6p dk sl green | 9 | 9 |
| *269* | A71 | 9p dk blue gray | 50 | 60 |

50th anniv. of the first meeting of the Dail Eireann at the Mansion House, Dublin, Jan. 21, 1919.

**Europa Issue, 1969**

"EUROPA" and "CEPT" CD12

**1969, Apr. 28 Photo. *Perf. 15***

| | | | | |
|---|---|---|---|---|
| *270* | CD12 | 9p ultra, gray & ocher | 60 | 1.10 |
| *271* | CD12 | 1sh9p car, gray & gold | 1.75 | 1.10 |

CEPT, 10th anniv.

ILO Emblem — A73

**1969, July 14 *Perf. 15***

| | | | | |
|---|---|---|---|---|
| *272* | A73 | 6p gray & black | 10 | 10 |
| *273* | A73 | 9p yellow & blk | 40 | 42 |

ILO, 50th anniv.

Last Supper and Crucifixion, by Evie Hone — A74

*Perf. 15x14½*

**1969, Sept. 1 Photo. Wmk. 262**

*274* A74 1sh multicolored 70 1.25

The design is after a stained-glass window by Evie Hone (1894-1955) in the Eton College Chapel.

Mahatma Gandhi A75

**1969, Oct. 2** ***Perf. 15***

*275* A75 6p dk yel grn & blk 14 6
*276* A75 1sh9p yel, grn & black 55 60

Birth centenary of Mohandas K. Gandhi (1869-1948), leader in India's fight for independence.

Stylized Bird, Tree and Shamrock A76

**1970, Feb. 23** ***Perf. 15***

*277* A76 6p ol bister & blk 18 12
*278* A76 9p violet & black 75 60

Nature Conservation Year, 1970.

**Europa Issue, 1970**

Interwoven Threads CD13

**1970, May 4 Photo.** ***Perf. 15***

*279* CD13 6p pur & silver 30 7
*280* CD13 9p yel brn & sil 1.10 65
*281* CD13 1sh9p dk gray & sil 2.00 1.00

Sailing Boats, by Peter Monamy (1670-1749) A78

**1970, July 13** ***Perf. 15***

*282* A78 4p gold & multi 18 18

250th anniv. of the Royal Cork Yacht Club.

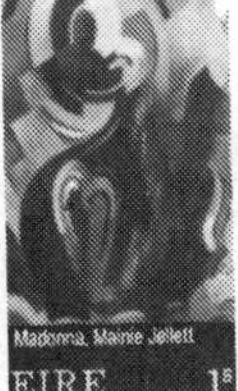


Madonna of Eire, by Mainie Jellett (1896-1943) A79

Tomas MacCurtain A80

**1970, Sept. 1 Photo.** ***Perf. 15***

*283* A79 1sh vio blue & multi 65 50

**1970, Oct. 26** ***Perf. 15***

Designs: Nos. 285, 287, Terence MacSwiney.

*284* A80 9p violet & blk 1.10 90
*285* A80 9p violet & blk 1.10 90
*286* A80 2sh9p brt bl & blk 3.00 2.25
*287* A80 2sh9p brt bl & blk 3.00 2.25

50th anniv. of the deaths of Tomás MacCurtain (1884-1920) and Terence MacSwiney (1879-1920), lord mayors of Cork, who died during the Irish war of independence.

Stamps of same denomination are printed alternately in sheets of 120.

Kevin Barry A81

**1970, Nov. 2**

*288* A81 6p olive grn 20 12
*289* A81 1sh2p violet bl 65 60

50th anniv. of the death of Kevin Barry (1902-1920), who was hanged during the Irish war of independence.

**Decimal Currency Issue**

Types of 1968-69 (Numerals only)

Designs: ½p, 1p, 1½p, 2p, 2½p, 3p, 3½p, 4p, No. 298A, Dog. No. 298, 6p, 7p, 7½p, 9p, Stag. 10p, 12p, 20p, Winged ox. 50p, Eagle.

Two types of 10p:
I. Ox outlined in brown
II. Outlined in dull lilac

**1971-75 Wmk. 262 Photo.** ***Perf. 15***

*290* A68 ½p yellow grn 8 5
*a* Booklet pane of 6 32.50
*291* A68 1p brt blue 62 12
*a* Booklet pane of 6 2.25
*c* Bklt. pane of 5 + label ('74) 75
*292* A68 1½p brown red 22 30
*293* A68 2p dark green 22 5
*b* Booklet pane of 5 + label ('75) 1.25
*294* A68 2½p sepia 40 10
*a* Booklet pane of 6 9.50
*295* A68 3p yel orange 30 15
*296* A68 3½p deep orange 50 20
*297* A68 4p violet 22 10
*298* A68 5p ap grn & brn 1.50 40
*298A* A68 5p ap grn ('74) 1.75 40
*c* Booklet pane of 6 ('74) 10.50
*d* Bklt. pane of 5 + label ('74) 2.25
*299* A68 6p bl grn & dk brown 2.75 50
*299A* A68 7p ol green & ind ('74) 5.00 3.25
*300* A68 7½p rose vio & dk brown 50 45
*301* A68 9p bl grn & blk 2.50 62
*302* A69 10p lil & multi (II) 8.00 85
*b* Type I 13.00 3.75
*302A* A69 12p multi ('74) 1.00 30
*303* A69 20p sl & multi 4.25 75
*304* A69 50p rose brn & multi 12.50 1.25
*Nos. 290-304 (18)* 42.31 9.84

Booklet panes have watermark sideways.

Issue dates: No. 298A, 7p, 12p, Jan. 29, 1974. Others, Feb. 15, 1971.

See Nos. 343-359, 395-402, 466-475.

Coil Stamps

**1971-74** ***Perf. 14x15***

*291b* A68 1p bright blue 90 45
*292a* A68 1½p brown red 30 18
*293a* A68 2p dark green ('72) 35 18
*294b* A68 2½p sepia 30 12
*297a* A68 4p violet ('72) 1.25 70
*298b* A68 5p apple grn ('74) 1.25 80
Strip of 3 (1p, 1½p, 2½p) 1.50
Strip of 4 (1½p, 2p, 2½p, 4p) ('72) 2.25
Strip of 4 (2x1½p, 2p, 5p) ('74) 2.25

**Europa Issue, 1971**

Common Design Type

Size: 36½x21mm.

**1971, May 3 Wmk. 262** ***Perf. 15***

*305* CD14 4p ap grn & blk 40 20
*306* CD14 6p blue & black 2.50 1.75

John M. Synge — A82

An Island Man, by Jack B. Yeats — A83

**1971, July 19 Photo.** ***Perf. 15***

*307* A82 4p gray, blk & gold 28 16
*308* A82 10p org, blk & gold 1.10 90

Birth cent. of John Millington Synge (1871-1909), poet and dramatist.

**1971, Aug. 30** ***Perf. 15***

*309* A83 6p multicolored 75 60

Birth cent. of Jack Butler Yeats (1871-1957), painter.

Racial Equality Emblem A84

Madonna, by John Hughes, Loughrea Cathedral A85

*Perf. 14x14½*

**1971, Oct. 18 Litho. Unwmk.**

*310* A84 4p red 25 16
*311* A84 10p black 95 80

Intl. Year Against Racial Discrimination.

**1971, Nov. 15 Photo.** ***Perf. 15***

*312* A85 2½p dp bl grn, gold & slate 24 15
*313* A85 6p ultra, gold & sl 75 90

Christmas.

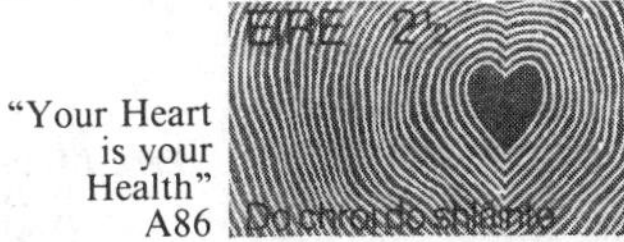


"Your Heart is your Health" A86

**1972, Apr. 7 Photo. Wmk. 262**

*314* A86 2½p gold & brown 55 22
*315* A86 12p silver & blk 2.50 2.25

World Health Day.

**Europa Issue 1972**

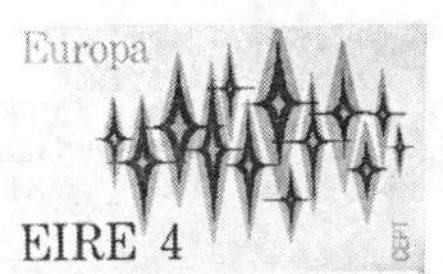


Sparkles, Symbolic of Communications — CD15

**1972, May 1** ***Perf. 15***

*316* CD15 4p red, blk & sil 2.00 48
*317* CD15 6p blue, blk & sil 6.25 3.25

Dove Soaring Past Rising Moon — A88

**1972, June 1 Photo.**

*318* A88 4p gray bl, org & dk bl 22 24
*319* A88 6p olive, yel & dk grn 75 55

The patriot dead of 1922-23.

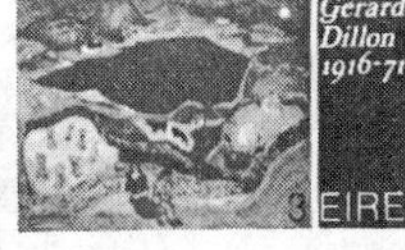


Black Lake, by Gerard Dillon A89

**1972, July 10** ***Perf. 15***

*320* A89 3p indigo & multi 45 40

Rider from Clonmacnoise Slab and Olympic Rings — A90

Madonna and Child — A91

**1972, Aug. 28 Photo. Wmk. 262**

*321* A90 3p yel, blk & gold 24 18
*322* A90 6p sal, blk & gold 75 55

20th Olympic Games, Munich, Aug. 26-Sept. 11, and 50th anniversary of the Olympic Council of Ireland.

**1972, Oct. 16 Unwmk.** ***Perf. 15***

*323* A91 2½p dk grn & multi 20 12
*324* A91 4p tan & multi 95 30
*325* A91 12p multicolored 1.25 85

Christmas. The design is after a miniature in the Book of Kells, 9th century.

Ireland No. 68 — A92

**1972, Dec. 6 Photo.**

*326* A92 6p bl gray & dp grn 40 85
*a* Souvenir sheet of 4 12.00 18.00

50th anniversary of first Irish postage stamp. No. 326a contains 4 No. 326. Green marginal inscription and date. Size: 72x107mm.

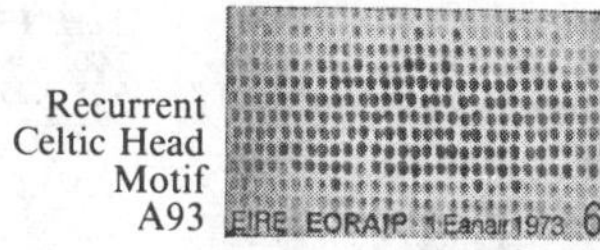

Recurrent Celtic Head Motif
A93

**1973, Jan. 1** **Unwmk.**
*327* A93 6p orange & multi 45 30
*328* A93 12p green & multi 1.65 1.75

Ireland's entry into the European Community.

**Europa Issue 1973**

Post Horn of Arrows
CD16

**1973, Apr. 30**
*329* CD16 4p bright ultra 55 18
*330* CD16 6p black 2.50 1.50

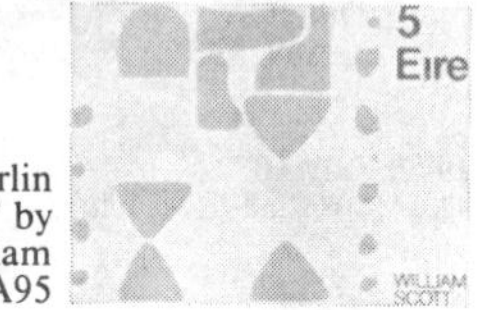


"Berlin Blues I," by William Scott – A95

***Perf. 15x14½***
**1973, Aug. 9** **Photo.** **Unwmk.**
*331* A95 5p lt bl, bl & dk brn 65 32

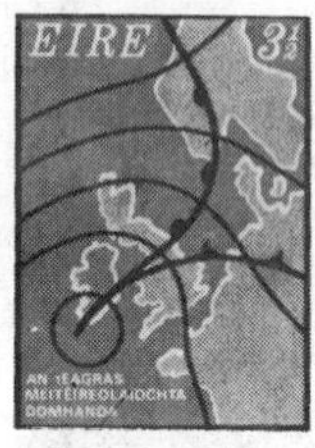


Weather Map of Northwest Europe – A96

**1973, Sept. 4** ***Perf. 14½x15***
*332* A96 3½p ultra & multi 24 20
*333* A96 12p lilac & multi 2.00 1.10

Intl. meteorological cooperation, cent.

Tractor Plowing and Birds – A97

**1973, Oct. 5** ***Perf. 15x14½***
*334* A97 5p emer & multi 35 20
*335* A97 7p emer & multi 1.40 70

World Plowing Championships, Wellington Bridge, County Wexford, Oct. 1-7.

Flight into Egypt, by Jan de Cock – A98

**1973, Nov. 1** ***Perf. 15***
*336* A98 3½p black & multi 22 12
*337* A98 12p gold & multi 1.50 85

Christmas.

Rescue, by Bernard Gribble
A99

Design: Ballycotton lifeboat rescuing crew of Daunt Rock Lightship, 1936.

**1974, Mar. 28** **Photo.** **Wmk. 262**
*338* A99 5p multicolored 60 32

Sesquicentennial of the founding of the Royal National Lifeboat Institution.

Edmund Burke, by John Henry Foley – A100

Oliver Goldsmith, by John Henry Foley – A101

**Europa Issue 1974**
***Perf. 14½x15***

**1974, Apr. 29** **Unwmk.**
*339* A100 5p lt ultra & blk 70 15
*340* A100 7p lt green & blk 2.75 1.25

**1974, June 24** **Photo.**
*341* A101 3½p brt cit & blk 40 15
*342* A101 12p emerald & blk 2.00 1.25

Death bicent. of Oliver Goldsmith (1728-1774), writer.

Types of 1968-69

Designs: ½p, 1p, 2p, 3p, 3½p, 5p, Nos. 350, 352, Dog. Nos. 349, 351, 8p, 9p, Stag. 10p, 15p, 20p, Winged ox. 50p, £1, Eagle.

**1974-78** **Unwmk.** ***Perf. 15***
*343* A68 ½p yel green ('78) 6 6
*344* A68 1p bright bl ('75) 5 5
*345* A68 2p dark green ('76) 6 5
*346* A68 3p ocher ('75) 10 6
*347* A68 3½p deep orange 4.00 2.50
*348* A68 5p apple green 30 16
*349* A68 6p bl gray & dk brn 2.75 1.10
*350* A68 6p blue gray ('75) 20 8
*351* A68 7p ol grn & indigo 3.25 45
*352* A68 7p olive grn ('75) 50 10
*a* Bklt. pane of 5 + label ('77) 14.00
*353* A68 8p brown & dk brn ('75) 65 22
*354* A68 9p bl grn & black ('75) 65 16
*355* A69 10p lil & multi ('75) 3.25 35
*356* A69 15p multi ('75) 48 16
*357* A69 20p slate & multi 60 22
*358* A69 50p rose brown & multi ('75) 2.00 80
*359* A69 £1 multi ('75) 3.00 1.65
*Nos. 343-359 (17)* 21.90 8.17

Two types of No. 358 differ in clarity of screening, date on tail, etc.

Coil Stamps

**1977, Mar. 21** ***Perf. 14x15***
*344b* A68 1p bright blue 35 25
*345b* A68 2p dark green 25 18
*348b* A68 5p apple green 75 55
Strip of 4 (1p, 2x2p, 5p) 1.10

Kitchen Table, by Norah McGuinness
A102

**1974, Aug. 19** **Photo.** ***Perf. 14x15***
*360* A102 5p multicolored 60 18

Rugby
A103

**1974, Sept. 2** **Engr.** ***Perf. 15x14***
*361* A103 3½p slate green 60 15
*362* A103 12p multicolored 2.50 1.25

Centenary of Irish Rugby Union.

UPU "Postmark"
A104

Virgin and Child, by Bellini
A105

**1974, Oct. 9** **Photo.** ***Perf. 14½x15***
*363* A104 5p emerald & blk 40 20
*364* A104 7p ultra & multi 1.25 55

Centenary of Universal Postal Union.

**1974, Nov. 14**
*365* A105 5p multicolored 30 10
*366* A105 15p multicolored 2.25 90

Christmas.

"Peace" – A106

**1975, Mar. 25** **Photo.** ***Perf. 14½x15***
*367* A106 8p dp rose lil & ultra 30 22
*368* A106 15p ultra & emerald 1.10 90

International Women's Year.

**Europa Issue 1975**

Castletown Hunt (detail), by Robert Healy
A107

**1975, Apr. 28** **Photo.** ***Perf. 15x14½***
*369* A107 7p black 60 30
*370* A107 9p green 1.65 1.10

Chipping from the Fringe
A108

**1975, June 26** **Photo.** ***Perf. 15x14½***
*371* A108 6p shown 40 15
*372* A108 9p Putting 1.40 1.25

9th European Amateur Golf Team Championships, Killarney.

Bird of Prey, by Oisin Kelly
A109

**1975, July 28**
*373* A109 15p ocher 80 1.10

Nano Nagle and Pupils, Engraving by Charles Turner – A110

Clock Tower, St. Ann's Church, Shandon – A111

**1975, Sept. 1** **Photo.** ***Perf. 14½x15***
*374* A110 5p light bl & blk 22 9
*375* A110 7p buff & black 60 35

Presentation Order of Nuns, bicentenary.

**1975, Oct. 6** **Photo.** ***Perf. 12½***

Designs: 6p, like 5p. 7p, 9p, Holycross Abbey.

*376* A111 5p sepia 30 12
*377* A111 6p ultra & multi 60 80
*378* A111 7p sapphire 75 32
*379* A111 9p multicolored 1.10 70

European Architectural Heritage Year.

St. Oliver Plunkett, by Imogen Stuart
A112

Madonna and Child, by Fra Filippo Lippi
A113

**1975, Oct. 13** **Engr.** ***Perf. 14x14½***
*380* A112 7p black 30 22
*381* A112 15p dull red 1.10 85

Canonization of Oliver Plunkett (1625-1681), Primate of Ireland.

**1975, Nov. 18** **Photo.** ***Perf. 15***
*382* A113 5p multicolored 18 6
*383* A113 7p multicolored 32 20
*384* A113 10p gold & multi 65 48

Christmas.

James Larkin – A114

Bell Making First Call – A115

**1976 Jan. 21** **Photo.** ***Perf. 14½x15***
*385* A114 7p gray & sl grn 20 20
*386* A114 11p ocher & brown 1.25 65

James Larkin (1876-1947), trade union leader.

**1976, Mar. 10 Photo. *Perf. 14½x15***

| | | | | |
|---|---|---|---|---|
| *387* | A115 | 9p multicolored | 28 | 25 |
| *388* | A115 | 15p multicolored | 1.25 | 60 |

Centenary of first telephone call by Alexander Graham Bell, March 10, 1876.

13 Stars and Stripes A116

Designs: 8p, 50 stars, and stripes. 9p, 15p, Benjamin Franklin on Albany essay of 1847.

**1976, May 17 Litho. *Perf. 15x14***

| | | | | |
|---|---|---|---|---|
| *389* | A116 | 7p ultra, sil & red | 25 | 15 |
| *a* | | Silver (inscription) omitted | | *275.00* |
| *390* | A116 | 8p ultra, sil & red | 40 | 62 |
| *391* | A116 | 9p bl, sil & ocher | 70 | 38 |
| *392* | A116 | 15p red, sil & blue | 80 | 75 |
| *a* | | Souvenir sheet of 4 | 7.25 | 7.50 |
| *b* | | Silver (inscription) omitted, #392 | *800.00* | *900.00* |

American Bicentennial. No. 392a contains one each of Nos. 389-392. Blue marginal inscription. Size: 95x75mm. No. 392a exists with silver omitted.

**Europa Issue 1976**

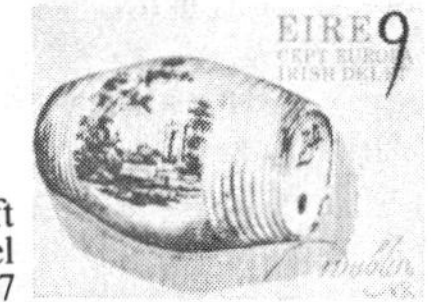

Irish Delft Spirit Barrel A117

Design: 11p, Bowl, Irish Delft. Designs show mark of Henry Delamain's Factory, Dublin, both pieces c. 1756.

**1976, July 1 Photo. *Perf. 15x14½***

| | | | | |
|---|---|---|---|---|
| *393* | A117 | 9p gray & mag | 45 | 28 |
| *394* | A117 | 11p gray & blue | 70 | 70 |

Types of 1968

Designs: 8p, 9p, No. 399, Dog. No. 398, 11p, 12p, Stag. 17p, Winged ox.

**1976-79 Photo. Unwmk. *Perf. 15***

| | | | | |
|---|---|---|---|---|
| *395* | A68 | 8p brown | 35 | 6 |
| *396* | A68 | 9p blue green | 55 | 6 |
| *397* | A68 | 9½p red ('79) | 55 | 20 |
| *398* | A68 | 10p lilac & black | 1.50 | 32 |
| *399* | A68 | 10p purple ('77) | 65 | 10 |
| *400* | A68 | 11p carmine & black | 90 | 22 |
| *401* | A68 | 12p emer & black ('77) | 90 | 14 |
| *402* | A69 | 17p ol, bl & ocher ('77) | 80 | 16 |
| | | *Nos. 395-402 (8)* | 6.20 | 1.26 |

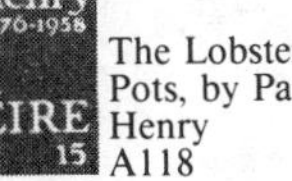

The Lobster Pots, by Paul Henry A118

**1976, Aug. 30 Photo. *Perf. 15***

| | | | | |
|---|---|---|---|---|
| *405* | A118 | 15p gold & multi | 75 | 50 |

Paul Henry (1876-1958), birth centenary.

Radio Waves A119

Radio Tower and Waves, Globe — A120

***Perf. 14½x14, 14x14½***

**1976, Oct. 5 Litho.**

| | | | | |
|---|---|---|---|---|
| *406* | A119 | 9p brt bl & blk | 18 | 10 |
| *407* | A120 | 11p black & multi | 1.10 | 1.25 |

Irish broadcasting, 50th anniversary.

Nativity, by Lorenzo Monaco A121

**1976, Nov. 11 *Perf. 15x14½***

| | | | | |
|---|---|---|---|---|
| *408* | A121 | 7p multicolored | 25 | 18 |
| *409* | A121 | 9p multicolored | 50 | 22 |
| *410* | A121 | 15p multicolored | 1.00 | 60 |

Christmas.

Irish Manuscript, 16th Century A122

Stone from Newgrange Burial Mound A123

**1977, May 9 Photo. *Perf. 15x14½***

| | | | | |
|---|---|---|---|---|
| *411* | A122 | 8p multicolored | 30 | 16 |
| *412* | A123 | 10p multicolored | 65 | 60 |

Centenaries of National Library (8p) and National Museum (10p).

**Europa Issue 1977**

View of Ballynahinch A124

Lugalla Lake A125

**1977, June 27 Litho. *Perf. 14x14½***

| | | | | |
|---|---|---|---|---|
| *413* | A124 | 10p multicolored | 60 | 32 |
| *414* | A125 | 12p multicolored | 1.25 | 95 |

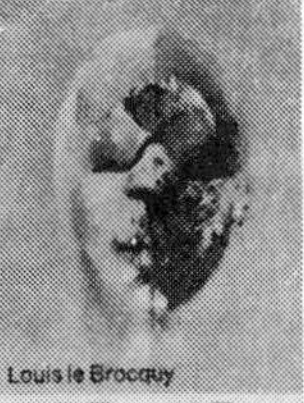

Head, by Louis le Brocquy, 1973 — A126

**1977, Aug. 8 *Perf. 14x14½***

| | | | | |
|---|---|---|---|---|
| *415* | A126 | 17p multicolored | 1.00 | 85 |

Girl Guide and Tents A127

Design: 17p, Boy Scout and tents.

**1977, Aug. 22 Photo. *Perf. 15x14½***

| | | | | |
|---|---|---|---|---|
| *416* | A127 | 8p multicolored | 45 | 25 |
| *417* | A127 | 17p multicolored | 1.00 | 1.25 |

European Scout and Guide Conference, Ireland, 1977, and 50th anniversary of Catholic Boy Scouts of Ireland.

The Shanachie, by Jack B. Yeats — A128

Eriugena A129

***Perf. 14x14½, 14½x14***

**1977, Sept. 12 Litho.**

| | | | | |
|---|---|---|---|---|
| *418* | A128 | 10p black | 40 | 30 |
| *419* | A129 | 12p black | 1.10 | 1.25 |

Folklore of Ireland Society, 50th anniv. and 1100th death anniv. of Johannes Scottus Eriugena, philospher, poet and mystic.

"Electricity," Mural by Robert Ballagh — A130

Bulls, from Contemporary Coin — A131

Greyhound — A132

**Litho. (10p, 17p); Photo. (12p)**

***Perf. 14½x14; 15x14½(12p)***

**1977, Oct. 10**

| | | | | |
|---|---|---|---|---|
| *420* | A130 | 10p multicolored | 32 | 20 |
| *421* | A131 | 12p multicolored | 70 | 1.10 |
| *422* | A132 | 17p multicolored | 55 | 70 |

50th anniversaries of: Electricity Supply Board (10p); Agricultural Credit Act (12p); introduction of greyhound racing (17p).

*Ireland stamps can be mounted in Scott's annually supplemented Ireland Album.*

Holy Family, by Giorgione A133

Bremen, Junkers Monoplane A134

**1977, Nov. 3 Photo. *Perf. 14½x15***

| | | | | |
|---|---|---|---|---|
| *423* | A133 | 8p multicolored | 35 | 18 |
| *424* | A133 | 10p multicolored | 55 | 30 |
| *425* | A133 | 17p multicolored | 95 | 48 |

Christmas.

**1978, Apr. 13 Litho. *Perf. 14***

| | | | | |
|---|---|---|---|---|
| *426* | A134 | 10p ultra & black | 32 | 30 |
| *427* | A134 | 17p lt brn & black | 80 | 60 |

50th anniversary of first East-West transatlantic flight from Baldonnel, County Dublin, to Greenly Island, Gulf of St. Lawrence.

Spring Gentian — A135

Wild flowers: 10p, Strawberry tree. 11p, Large-flowered butterwort. 17p, St. Daboec's heath.

**1978, June 12 Litho. *Perf. 14x14½***

| | | | | |
|---|---|---|---|---|
| *428* | A135 | 8p multicolored | 20 | 18 |
| *429* | A135 | 10p multicolored | 45 | 28 |
| *430* | A135 | 11p multicolored | 62 | 80 |
| *431* | A135 | 17p multicolored | 75 | 90 |

Catherine McAuley — A136

Vaccination, lithograph by Manigaud — A137

William Orpen, Self-portrait A138

**1978, Sept. 18 Litho. *Perf. 14***

| | | | | |
|---|---|---|---|---|
| *432* | A136 | 10p multicolored | 28 | 14 |
| *433* | A137 | 11p multicolored | 50 | 40 |
| *434* | A138 | 17p multicolored | 1.00 | 80 |

Catherine McAuley (1778-1841), founder of Sisters of Mercy (10p); eradication of smallpox (11p); William Orpen (1878-1931), painter (17p).

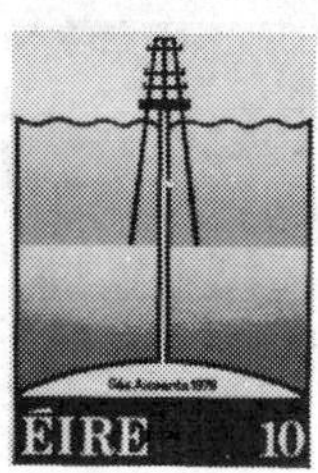

Offshore Oil Well — A139

**1978, Oct. 18 Litho. *Perf. 14***
*435* A139 10p multicolored 40 18

First natural gas coming in off the Irish Coast at Kinsale.

Woodcock on Farthing A140

Coins: 10p, Salmon on florin. 11p, Hen and chicks on penny. 17p, Horse on half crown.

**1978, Oct. 26 Photo. *Perf. 15x14½***
*436* A140 8p multicolored 28 12
*437* A140 10p multicolored 38 18
*438* A140 11p multicolored 40 42
*439* A140 17p multicolored 55 55

Irish currency, 50th anniversary.

Virgin and Child, by Guercino — A141

**1978, Nov. 16 Photo. *Perf. 14½x15***
*440* A141 8p multicolored 30 12
*441* A141 10p multicolored 38 15
*442* A141 17p multicolored 65 60

Christmas.

**Europa Issue 1978**

Conolly Folly, Castletown A142

Design: 11p, Belvedere on Tower Hill at Dromoland.

**1978, Dec. 6 *Perf. 15x14½***
*443* A142 10p brown 45 24
*444* A142 11p dull green 65 42

Cross-country Runners — A143

**1979, Aug. 20 Litho. *Perf. 14½x14***
*445* A143 8p multicolored 28 25

7th World Cross-country Championships, Greenpark Racecourse, Limerick, March 25.

Rowland Hill, Bronze Statue A144

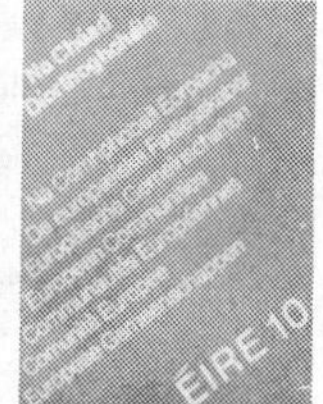

"European Communities" (7 Languages) A145

**1979, Aug. 20 *Perf. 14x14½***
*446* A144 17p multicolored 50 55

Sir Rowland Hill (1795-1879), originator of penny postage.

**1979, Aug. 20 Photo. *Perf. 14½x15***
*447* A145 10p lt grnsh gray 38 38
*448* A145 11p rose lilac 45 45

European Parliament, first direct elections, June 7-10.

Wren A146

Birds: 10p, Great crested grebe. 11p, Greenland white-fronted geese. 17p, Peregrine falcon.

**1979, Aug. 30 Litho. *Perf. 14½x14***
*449* A146 8p multicolored 32 15
*450* A146 10p multicolored 40 35
*451* A146 11p multicolored 45 40
*452* A146 17p multicolored 85 1.00

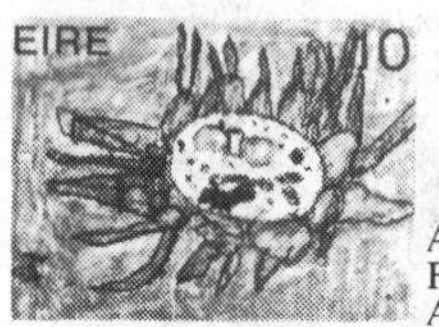

A Happy Flower A147

Children's Drawings: 11p, "Me and my skipping rope" (vert.). 17p, "Swans on a lake."

***Perf. 14½x14, 14x14½***
**1979, Sept. 13 Litho.**
*453* A147 10p multicolored 28 28
*454* A147 11p multicolored 35 45
*455* A147 17p multicolored 50 60

International Year of the Child.

Pope John Paul II A148

**1979, Sept. 29 Litho. *Perf. 14½x14***
*456* A148 12p multicolored 40 18

Visit of Pope John Paul II to Ireland.

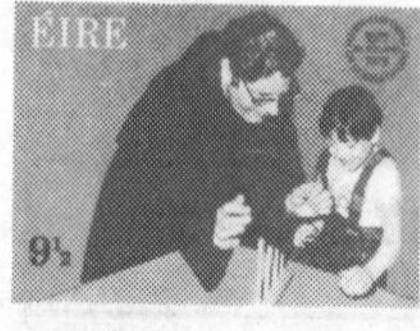

Hospitaller Brother Teaching Child A149

**1979, Oct. 4**
*457* A149 9½p rose & black 28 28

Hospitaller Order of St. John of God, centenary in Ireland.

Windmill and Sun — A150

**1979, Oct. 4 Photo. *Perf. 14½x15***
*458* A150 11p multicolored 38 42

Energy conservation.

"Seated Figure," by F.E. McWilliam A151

**1979, Oct. 4 Litho. *Perf. 14½x14***
*459* A151 20p multicolored 60 70

Patrick Pearse A152

**1979, Nov. 10 Photo. *Perf. 15x14½***
*460* A152 12p multicolored 40 18

Patrick Henry Pearse (1879-1916), Irish writer and leader of Easter Rebellion.

Mother and Child, Panel, Domnach Argid Shrine — A153

**1979, Nov. 15 Photo. *Perf. 14½x15***
*461* A153 9½p multicolored 28 18
*462* A153 20p multicolored 60 35

Christmas.

**Europa Issue 1979**

Bianconi Long Car, 1836 A154

Laying Transatlantic Cable, Steamer William Cory, 1866 — A155

**1979, Dec. 6 Litho. *Perf. 15x14***
*463* A154 12p multicolored 25 18
*464* A155 13p multicolored 45 60

**Type of 1968**

Design: 12p, 15p, 18p, 19p, 22p, 24p, 26p, 29p, Dog. 13p, 16p, Stag.

**1980-82 Photo. *Perf. 15***
*466* A68 12p green 55 22
*467* A68 13p red brn & dk brn 65 38
*468* A68 15p ultra 60 22
*469* A68 16p olive grn & blk 80 38

**Litho.**
*470* A68 18p dl red brn ('81) 60 22
*471* A68 19p dull blue ('81) 75 45
*472* A68 22p gray blue ('81) 75 18
*473* A68 24p brn olive ('81) 85 50
*474* A68 26p bluish grn ('82) 85 22
*475* A68 29p dp rose lil ('82) 1.25 75
*Nos. 466-475 (10)* 7.65 3.52

St. Jean Baptiste de la Salle — A156

**1980, Mar. 19 Litho. *Perf. 14x15***
*477* A156 12p multicolored 40 18

Salesian Order (founded by St. Jean Baptiste), centenary in Ireland.

**Europa Issue 1980**

George Bernard Shaw, by Alick Ritchie A157

Oscar Wilde, by Toulouse-Lautrec A158

**1980, May 7 Litho. *Perf. 14x15***
*478* A157 12p multicolored 35 35
*479* A158 13p multicolored 45 45

Irish Ermine — A159

**1980, July 30 Litho. *Perf. 14x15***
*480* A159 12p shown 32 18
*481* A159 15p Irish hare 40 14
*482* A159 16p Fox 42 32
*483* A159 25p Red deer 85 60
*a* Miniature sheet of 4 3.25 4.50

No. 483a contains Nos. 480-483. Size: 74x97mm.

Bodhran Drum and Whistle Players — A160

**1980, Sept. 25 Photo. *Perf. 14x15***

*484* A160 12p shown 35 25
*485* A160 15p Piper, Uilleann pipes 40 30
*486* A160 25p Irish jig 65 50

Sean O'Casey — A161

Patrick Scott
ÉIRE 25

Gold Painting No. 57, by Patrick Scott — A162

**1980, Oct. 23 Litho. *Perf. 14x14½***

*487* A161 12p multicolored 35 25

Sean O'Casey (1880-1964), playwright.

**1980, Oct. 23 *Perf. 14x15***

*488* A162 25p multicolored 70 55

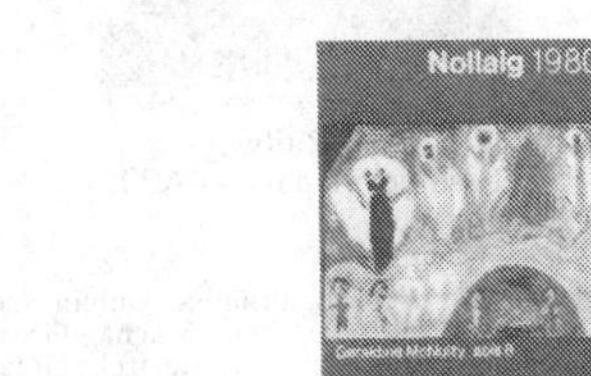


Christmas — A163

**1980, Dec. 4 Photo. *Perf. 15x14½***

*489* A163 12p multicolored 30 14
*490* A163 15p multicolored 42 28
*491* A163 25p multicolored 70 52

Robert Boyle (1627-91), and Air Pump, 1659 — A164

Scientists and Inventions: 15p, Harry Ferguson (1884-1960), hydraulic tractor, 1936. 16p, Charles Parsons (1854-1931), Parsons' turbine, 1884. 25p, John Holland (1841-1914), Holland submarine, 1878.

**1981, Mar. 12 Litho. *Perf. 14x14½***

*492* A164 12p multicolored 28 20
*493* A164 15p multicolored 32 25
*494* A164 16p multicolored 35 26
*495* A164 25p multicolored 55 70

**Europa Issue 1981**

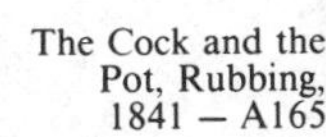

The Cock and the Pot, Rubbing, 1841 — A165

Design: 19p, The Scales of Judgment, rubbing, 1827.

**1981, May 4 Litho. *Perf. 14½x15***

*496* A165 18p multicolored 45 30
*497* A165 19p multicolored 48 50

Hiking A166

***Perf. 14x15, 15x14***

**1981, June 24 Litho.**

*498* A166 15p Bicycling, vert. 35 15
*499* A166 18p shown 45 32
*500* A166 19p Mountain climbing 45 42
*501* A166 30p Rock climbing, vert. 75 62

Youth Hostel Assn., 50th anniv.

Jeremiah O'Donovan Rossa (1831-1915), Journalist — A167

Railway Embankment, by William John Leech (1881-1968) — A168

***Perf. 14½x15, 15x14½***

**1981, Aug. 31**

*502* A167 15p multicolored 35 28
*503* A168 30p multicolored 75 70

James Hoban (1762-1831), White House Architect A169

**1981, Sept. 29 *Perf. 15x14***

*504* A169 18p multicolored 55 28

Same design used for U.S. Nos. 1935-1936.

Draft Horse King of Diamonds A170

Famous Horses: No. 505, Show-jumper Boomerang. No. 506, Steeplechaser Arkle. 24p, Flat racer Ballymoss. 36p, Connemara pony Coosheen Finn. Nos. 505-506 se-tenant.

**1981, Oct. 23 Litho. *Perf. 15x14***

*505* A170 18p multicolored 52 35
*506* A170 18p multicolored 52 35
*507* A170 22p multicolored 50 32
*508* A170 24p multicolored 52 70
*509* A170 36p multicolored 85 70
*Nos. 505-509 (5)* 2.91 2.42

Nativity, by Federico Barocci (Christmas 1981) — A171

**1981, Nov. 19 Litho. *Perf. 14x15***

*510* A171 18p multicolored 45 20
*511* A171 22p multicolored 55 24
*512* A171 36p multicolored 90 60

Land Law Act Centenary — A172

**1981, Dec. 10 Litho. *Perf. 14x14½***

*513* A172 18p multicolored 48 20

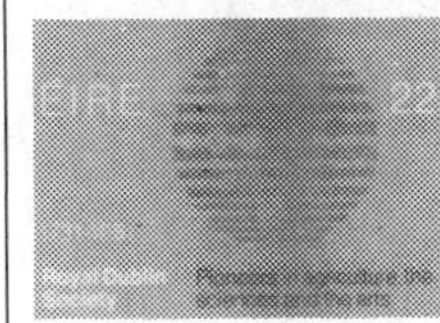


250th Anniv. of Royal Dublin Society A173

**1981, Dec. 10 *Perf. 14½x14***

*514* A173 22p multicolored 58 55

50th Anniv. of Killarney Natl. Park A174

**1982, Feb. 26 Litho. *Perf. 14½x14***

*515* A174 18p Upper Lake 48 28
*516* A174 36p Eagle's Nest 85 70

The Stigmatization of St. Francis, by Sassetta — A175

Francis Makemie, Old Presbyterian Church, Ramelton — A176

***Perf. 14x15, 15x14***

**1982, Apr. 2 Litho.**

*517* A175 22p multicolored 52 35
*518* A176 24p brown 70 50

800th birth anniv. of St. Francis of Assisi; 300th anniv. of Francis Makemie's ordination (father of American Presbyterianism).

**Europa Issue 1982**

Great Famine of 1845-50 — A177

Conversion of Ireland to Christianity (St. Patrick and his Followers, by Vincenzo Valdre) — A178

***Perf. 14x15, 15x14***

**1982, May 4 Litho.**

*519* A177 26p tan & brn 60 45
*520* A178 29p multicolored 75 55

Padraic O'Connaire (1882-1928), Writer — A179

Designs: 26p, James Joyce (1882-1941), writer and poet, by Brancusi. 29p, John Field (1782-1837), Composer and pianist, Nocturne score. 44p, Charles Joseph Kickham (1828-1882), journalist and writer. 29p, 44p by Colin Harrison.

**1982, June 16 Litho. *Perf. 14x15***

*521* A179 22p blue & black 50 30
*522* A179 26p black & brown 65 52
*523* A179 29p black & blue 75 60
*524* A179 44p gray grn & blk 1.10 95

Porbeagle Shark A180

**1982, July 29 *Perf. 15x14***

*525* A180 22p shown 50 38
*526* A180 22p Oyster 50 38
*527* A180 26p Salmon 70 35
*528* A180 29p Dublin Bay prawn 80 70

Currach A181

**1982, Sept. 21 *Perf. 15x14, 14x15***

*529* A181 22p shown 65 32
*530* A181 22p Galway hooker, vert. 65 32
*531* A181 26p Asgard II training ship 90 30
*532* A181 29p Howth 17-footer, vert. 1.10 65

The Irish House of Commons, by Francis Wheatley
A182

**1982, Oct. 14 Litho. *Perf. 14½x14***
*533* A182 22p multicolored 55 28

Bicentenary of Grattan's Parliament.

Eamon de Valera (1882-1975), Former President, by Robert Ballagh — A183

**1982, Oct. 14 *Perf. 14x14½***
*534* A183 26p multicolored 70 28

Christmas — A184

Design: Madonna and Child, by Andrea della Robbia (1435-1525).

**1982, Nov. 11 Litho. *Perf. 14½x15***
*535* A184 22p lt vio & multi 50 28
*536* A184 26p gray & multi 70 40

Central Pavilion, Dublin Botanical Gardens
A184a

Aughnanure Castle, Oughterard, 16th Cent.
A185

Killarney Cathedral, 1855 — A186

Designs: 6p, 7p, 10p, 12p, Dr. Steeven's Hospital, Dublin. 23p, 26p, Cormac's Chapel, 1134. 29p, 30p, St. Mac Dara's Church. 50p, Casino, Marino. £1, Cahir Castle, 15th century. £5 Central Bus Station, Dublin, 1953.

**1982-83 Litho. *Perf. 14x15, 15x14***
*537* A184a 1p dull blue 5 5
*538* A184a 2p gray green 8 5
*539* A184a 3p black 8 6
*540* A184a 4p rose lake ('83) 10 8
*541* A184a 5p brown ('83) 12 8
*542* A184a 6p dull blue ('83) 14 8
*543* A184a 7p gray green ('83) 16 10
*544* A184a 10p black ('83) 24 14
*545* A184a 12p rose lake ('83) 32 16
*546* A185 15p gray green ('83) 38 22
*547* A185 20p rose lake ('83) 52 32
*548* A185 22p dull blue 55 32
*549* A185 23p gray green ('83) 55 35
*550* A185 26p black 60 38
*a* Bklt. pane of 6 (2 each 2p, 22p, 26p) 2.25
*b* Bklt. pane of 12 (4 each 2p, 22p, 26p) 4.50
*551* A184a 29p gray green 70 42
*552* A184a 30p black ('83) 70 45

***Perf. 14x15***
*553* A186 44p gray & black 1.10 70

***Perf. 15x14***
*554* A186 50p gray & dl bl, horiz. ('83) 1.25 75
*555* A186 £1 gray & brn, horiz. 6.25 2.75
*556* A186 £5 gray & rose lake, horiz. 12.00 7.25
*Nos. 537-556 (20)* 25.89 14.71

See Nos. 638-645.

Dublin Chamber of Commerce Bicentenary
A187

Bank of Ireland Bicentenary — A188

**1983, Feb. 23 Litho.**
*557* A187 22p Ouzel Galley goblet 60 30
*558* A188 26p Bank 75 45

Padraig Siochfhradha (1883-1964), Writer — A189

Boys' Brigade Centenary — A190

**1983, Apr. 7 Litho. *Perf. 14x14½***
*559* A189 26p multicolored 65 32
*560* A190 29p multicolored 85 55

Europa
A191

Designs: 26p, Newgrange Winter Solstice, neolithic pattern drawing by Louis le Brocquy. 29p, Quaternion formula, by William Rowan Hamilton (1805-1865).

**1983, May 4 Litho. *Perf. 14½x14***
*561* A191 26p black & gold 90 40
*562* A191 29p multicolored 1.10 55

Kerry Blue Terrier
A192

Drawings of dogs by Wendy Walsh.

**1983, June 23**
*563* A192 22p shown 55 38
*564* A192 26p Irish wolfhound 65 38
*565* A192 26p Irish water spaniel 65 38
*566* A192 29p Irish terrier 75 70
*567* A192 44p Irish setters 1.10 1.10
*a* Miniature sheet of 5 (#563-567) 5.00 4.25
*Nos. 563-567 (5)* 3.70 2.94

Sean Mac Diarmada (1883-1916), Nationalist
A193

Society for the Prevention of Cruelty to Animals
A194

Society of St. Vincent de Paul Sesquicentennial
A195

Industrial Credit Co., 50th Anniv.
A196

US Pres. Andrew Jackson (1767-1845)
A197

***Perf. 14x14½, 14½x14***
**1983, Aug. 11**
*568* A193 22p multicolored 45 45
*569* A194 22p multicolored 45 45
*570* A195 26p multicolored 60 52
*571* A196 26p multicolored 60 52
*572* A197 44p gray 1.10 1.00
*Nos. 568-572 (5)* 3.20 2.94

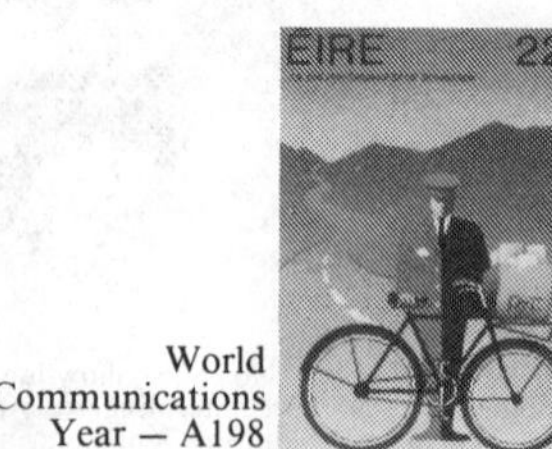

World Communications Year — A198

**1983, Sept. 15 Litho. *Perf. 14x15***
*573* A198 22p Mailman 48 35
*574* A198 29p Dish antenna 70 52

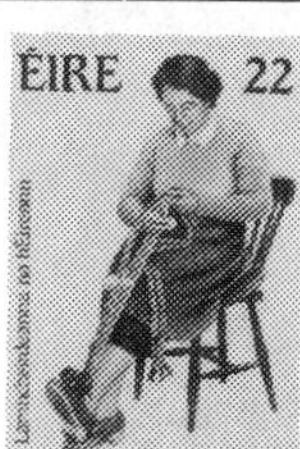

Handicrafts
A199

**1983, Oct. 13 Litho. *Perf. 14x15***
*575* A199 22p Weaving 50 35
*576* A199 26p Basketweaving 60 40
*577* A199 29p Irish crochet 70 65
*578* A199 44p Harpmaking 1.00 95

La Natividad by Rogier van der Weyden — A200

**1983, Nov. 30 Litho. *Perf. 14x14½***
*579* A200 22p multicolored 52 35
*580* A200 26p multicolored 60 48

Christmas.

Irish Railways Sesquicentenary — A201

Locomotives: 23p, Princess, Dublin and Kingstown Railway. 26p, Macha, Great Southern Railways. 29p, Kestrel, Great Northern Railway. 44p, Link-Hoffman railcar, Coras Iompair Eireann.

**1984, Jan. 30 *Perf. 14½x14***
*581* A201 23p multicolored 52 70
*582* A201 26p multicolored 55 38
*583* A201 29p multicolored 52 80
*584* A201 44p multicolored 90 95
*a* Souvenir sheet of 4 4.75 4.25

No. 584a contains Nos. 581-584; multicolored margin shows Listowel-Ballybunion Railway and O71 Class modern diesel.

Local Trees
A202

**1984, Mar. 1 Litho. *Perf. 15x14***
*585* A202 22p Irish whitebeam 50 38
*586* A202 26p Irish yew 65 48
*587* A202 29p Irish willow 72 55
*588* A202 44p Birch 1.10 80

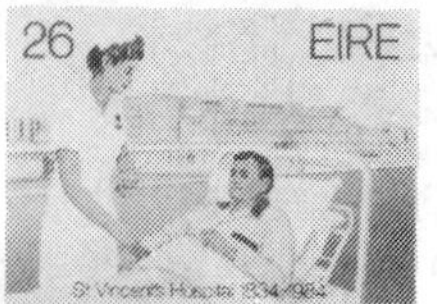

St. Vincent's Hospital, Dublin, Sesquicentenary — A203

Royal College of Surgeons in Ireland Bicentenary — A204

**1984, Apr. 12** **Litho.**
589 A203 26p multicolored 65 48
590 A204 44p multicolored 1.10 80

2nd European Parliament Election A205

**1984, May 10** **Litho.** ***Perf. 15x14***
591 A205 26p multicolored 85 42

Europa (1959-84) A206

**1984, May 10**
592 A206 26p multicolored 80 70
593 A206 29p multicolored 85 80

John McCormack (1884-1945), Singer — A207

**1984, June 6** **Litho.** ***Perf. 14x14½***
594 A207 22p multicolored 55 35

See US No. 2090.

1984 Summer Olympics A208

Gaelic Athletic Assoc. Centenary A209

**1984, June 21** **Litho.** ***Perf. 14½x14***
595 A208 22p Hammer throw 50 42
596 A208 26p Hurdles 65 55
597 A208 29p Running 70 60

**1984, Aug. 23** **Litho.** ***Perf. 14x15***
598 A209 22p Hurlers 50 35
599 A209 26p Soccer, vert. 65 45

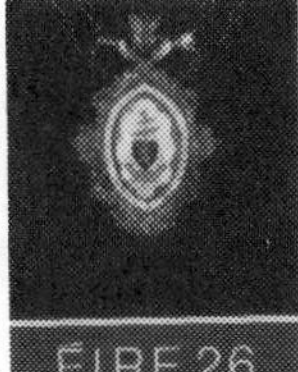

Mayoral City of Galway, 500th Anniv. — A210

St. Brendan (484-577) A211

**1984, Sept. 18** ***Perf. 14x15, 15x14***
600 A210 26p Medal 65 55
601 A211 44p Portrait, manuscript 1.00 90

Post Office Bicentenary A212

**1984, Oct. 19** ***Perf. 15x14***
602 A212 26p Handing sealed letter 70 35

A213

Virgin And Child by Sassoferrato A214

***Perf. 14½x14, 14x14½***
**1984, Nov. 26** **Litho.**
603 A213 17p multicolored 42 22
604 A214 22p multicolored 55 28
605 A214 26p multicolored 75 35

Christmas.

Love A215

A216

**1985, Jan. 31** **Litho.** ***Perf. 15x14***
606 A215 22p Heart-shaped balloon 50 30
607 A216 26p Bouquet of hearts 65 35

Dunsink Observatory, 200th Anniv. — A217

Cork City Charter, 800th Anniv. A218

Royal Irish Academy, 200th Anniv. — A219

1st Manned Flight in Ireland, 200th Anniv. — A220

**1985, Mar. 14** **Litho.**
608 A217 22p black 50 45
609 A218 26p multicolored 65 52
610 A219 37p multicolored 85 70
611 A220 44p multicolored 1.00 85

Butterflies — A221

**1985, Apr. 11** **Litho.** ***Perf. 14x15***
612 A221 22p Common blue 50 48
613 A221 26p Red admiral 60 55
614 A221 28p Brimstone 65 60
615 A221 44p Marsh fritillary 1.00 90

Europa A222

Composers: 26p, Charles Villiers Stanford (1852-1924). 37p, Turlough O'Carolan (1670-1738).

**1985, May 16** **Litho.** ***Perf. 15x14***
616 A222 26p multicolored 80 60
617 A222 37p multicolored 1.10 85

European Music Year — A223

Composers: No. 618, Giuseppe Domenico Scarlatti (1685-1757). No. 619, George Frideric Handel (1685-1759). No. 620, Johann Sebastian Bach (1685-1750).

**1985, May 16** **Litho.** ***Perf. 14x15***
618 A223 22p multicolored 30 30
619 A223 22p multicolored 30 30
*a* Se-tenant pair 65 65
620 A223 26p multicolored 35 35

Irish UN Defense Forces in the Congo, 1960 A224

Thomas Ashe (1885-1917), Patriot and Educator — A225

Bishop George Berkeley (1685-1753), Philosopher and Educator — A226

***Perf. 15x14, 14x15***
**1985, June 20** **Litho.**
621 A224 22p multicolored 55 45
622 A225 26p multicolored 65 55
623 A226 44p multicolored 1.10 90

Irish forces as part of the UN Defense Forces, 25th anniv. (22p).

Intl. Youth Year — A227

**1985, Aug. 1** **Litho.**
624 A227 22p multi, horiz. 55 45
625 A227 26p multi 65 52

Architecture Type of 1982

Designs: 24p, 39p, Aughnanure Castle. 28p, 32p, 37p, St. Mac Dara's Church. 46p, Cahir Castle. £1, Killarney Cathedral. £2, Casino, Marino.

***Perf. 15x14, 14x15 (A184a, No. 644)***
**1985-88** **Litho.**
638 A185 24p brown 45 28
639 A184a 28p rose lake 52 32
640 A184a 32p brown ('86) 65 40
641 A184a 37p dull blue 75 45
642 A185 39p rose lake ('86) 80 50
643 A186 46p gray & gray grn, horiz. ('86) 95 60
644 A186 £1 gray & dl bl 1.90 1.10
645 A186 £2 gray & gray grn, horiz. ('88) 6.00 3.00
*Nos. 638-645 (8)* 12.02 6.65

Industrial Innovations — A228

Institution of Engineers, 150th Anniv. A229

**1985, Oct. 3 Litho. *Perf. 15x14***

*646* A228 22p Computer technology 55 50
*647* A228 26p Peat production 70 65
*648* A229 44p The Key Man, by Sean Keating 1.10 1.00

Candle, Holly A230

Virgin and Child in a Landscape, by Adrian van Ijsenbrandt A231

Designs: No. 651, The Holy Family, by Murillo. 26p, Adoration of the Shepherds, by Louis Le Nain, horiz.

***Perf. 14x15, 15x14***

**1985, Nov. 26 Litho.**

*649* A230 22p shown 55 28
*650* A231 22p shown 55 28
*651* A231 22p multicolored 55 28
*652* A231 26p multicolored 65 32

Christmas. No. 649 issued in sheets of 16. Nos. 650-651 printed se-tenant.

Love — A232

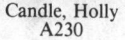

**1986, Jan. 30 *Perf. 14x15***

*653* A232 22p shown 55 28
*654* A232 26p Heart-shaped mailbox 68 35

Ferns — A233

Europa — A234

**1986, Mar. 20 Litho. *Perf. 14½x15***

*655* A233 24p Hart's tongue 65 32
*656* A233 28p Rusty-back 75 38
*657* A233 46p Killarney 1.25 62

**1986, May 1 *Perf. 14x15, 15x14***

*658* A234 28p Industry and nature 80 40
*659* A234 39p Hedgerows, horiz. 1.10 55

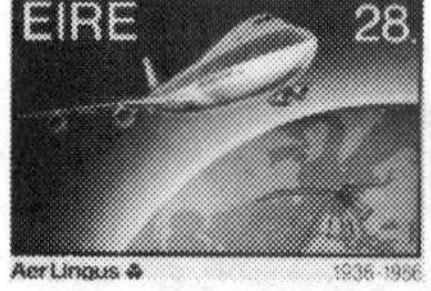


Aer Lingus, 50th Anniv. A235

**1986, May 27 *Perf. 15x14***

*660* A235 28p Jet, 1986 75 38
*661* A235 46p The Eagle, 1936 1.25 62

Inland Waterways A236

**1986, May 27 *Perf. 15x14, 14x15***

*662* A236 24p Robertstown Grand Canal 65 32
*663* A236 28p Fishing, County Mayo, vert. 75 38
*664* A236 30p Yachting, River Shannon 80 40

British & Irish Steam Packet Co., 150th Anniv. A237

**1986, July 10 *Perf. 15x14***

*665* A237 24p Steamer Severn, 1836 68 50
*666* A237 28p M.V. Leinster, 1986 80 55

Lighthouses A238

**1986, July 10 *Perf. 14½x15***

*667* A238 24p Kish, helicopter 68 55
*668* A238 30p Fastnet 85 65

Dublin Council of Trade Unions, Cent. A239

Arthur Griffith (1871-1922), Statesman A240

Women in Society, Construction Surveyor A241

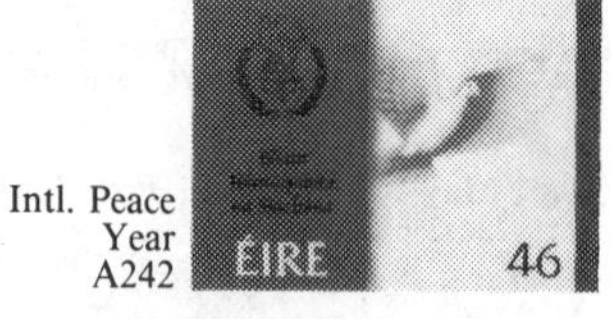


Intl. Peace Year A242

***Perf. 14½x15, 14x15 (#670, 672), 15x14½, 15x14***

**1986, Aug. 21**

*669* A239 24p multicolored 60 55
*670* A240 28p multicolored 70 60
*671* A241 28p multicolored 70 60
*672* A242 30p multi, vert. 75 65
*673* A242 46p shown 1.10 1.00
*Nos. 669-673 (5)* 3.85 3.40

See Nos. 699, 711.

William Mulready (1786-1863), Letter Sheet Designer A243

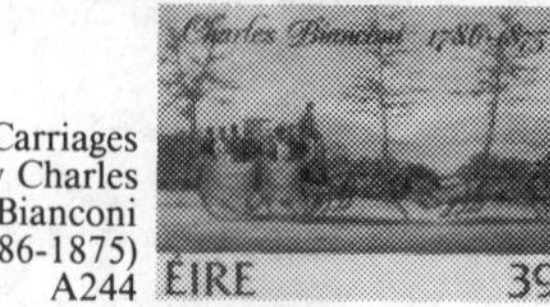


Carriages by Charles Bianconi (1786-1875) A244

***Perf. 15x14, 14x15***

**1986, Oct. 2 Litho.**

*674* A243 24p multicolored 68 52
*675* A244 28p multi, vert. 78 60
*676* A244 39p shown 1.10 80

Adoration of the Shepherds, by Francesco Pascucci A245

Adoration of the Magi, by Frans Francken III (1542-1616) A246

**1986, Nov. 20 *Perf. 15x14, 14½x15***

*677* A245 21p multicolored 95 45
*678* A246 28p multicolored 1.25 60

Christmas.

Love A247

***Perf. 15x14, 14x15***

**1987, Jan. 27 Litho.**

*679* A247 24p Flowers, butterfly 68 35
*680* A247 28p Postman, vert. 78 40

Trolleys A248

**1987, Mar. 4 Litho. *Perf. 15x14***

*681* A248 24p Cork Electric 72 35
*682* A248 28p Dublin Standard 85 42
*683* A248 30p Howth (G.N.R.) 90 45
*684* A248 46p Galway Horse 1.40 70
*a* Miniature sheet of 4, Nos. 681-684 3.90 3.90

No. 684a has inscribed margin picturing the Dublin Luxury and Dublin Balcony trams. Size: 131x85mm.

Waterford Chamber of Commerce, 200th Anniv. — A249

Muintir Na Tire, 50th Anniv. A250

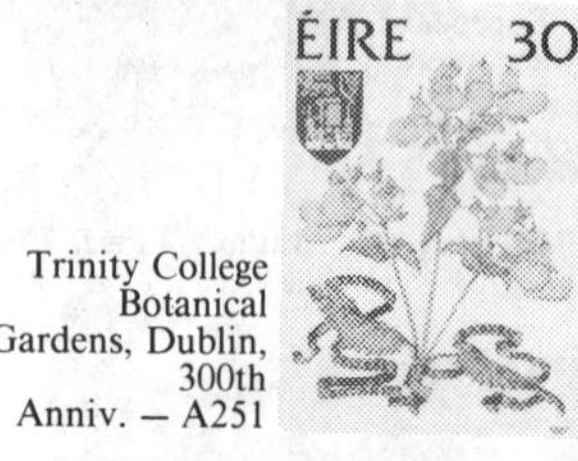


Trinity College Botanical Gardens, Dublin, 300th Anniv. — A251

Medical Missionaries of Mary, 50th Anniv. — A252

Anniversaries and events: 24p, Three ships, Chamber crest. 28p, Canon Hayes (1887-1957), founder, and symbols of Muintir Na Tire activities. 30p, College crest, Calceolaria burbidgei. 39p, Intl. Missionary Training Hospital, Drogheda, and Mother Mary Martin.

***Perf. 15x14, 14x15***

**1987, Apr. 9 Litho.**

*685* A249 24p vio blue, blk & dark grn 75 38
*686* A250 28p multicolored 85 42
*687* A251 30p multicolored 90 45
*688* A252 39p multicolored 1.20 60

Europa A253

Modern architecture, art: 28p, Borda na Mona headquarters, Dublin, and The Turf Cutter, by sculptor John Behan. 39p, St. Mary's Church and ruins of Romanesque monastery at Cong.

**1987, May 14 *Perf. 15x14***

*689* A253 28p multicolored 85 42
*690* A253 39p multicolored 1.20 60

Cattle A254

**1987, July 2**

*691* A254 24p Kerry 72 35
*692* A254 28p Friesian 85 42
*693* A254 30p Hereford 90 45
*694* A254 39p Shorthorn 1.15 58

Festivals A255

**1987, Aug. 27** ***Perf. 14x15***

*695* A255 24p Fleadh Nua, Ennis 72 35
*696* A255 28p Festival Queen, Tralee 85 42
*697* A255 30p Wexford opera festival 90 45
*698* A255 46p Ballinasloe horse fair 1.40 70

Nos. 695-696 vert.

Statesmen Type of 1986 and

Company of Goldsmiths of Dublin, 350th Anniv. — A256

Irish Constitution, 50th Anniv. — A257

Women in Society — A258

Designs: No. 699, Cathal Brugha, vert. No. 700, Ewer and chalice, company crest. 28p, Harp in shield, excerpt from preamble. 46p, Woman chairing a board meeting.

***Perf. 14x15, 15x14***

**1987, Oct. 1** **Litho.**

*699* A240 24p black 75 38
*700* A256 24p multicolored 75 38
*701* A257 28p multicolored 88 45
*702* A258 46p multicolored 1.40 70

A259

Christmas A260

Designs: 21p, Twelve Days of Christmas (first three days). 24p, Embroidery (detail), Waterford Vestments, 15th cent. 28p, Neapolitan creche (detail), 1850.

***Perf. 15x14, 14x15***

**1987, Nov. 17** **Litho.**

*703* A259 21p multicolored 67 35
*704* A260 24p multicolored 78 40
*705* A260 28p multicolored 90 45

No. 703 issued in discount sheets of 14 + center label; sheet sold for £2.90.

Love A261

***Perf. 15x14½, 14½x15***

**1988, Jan. 27** **Litho.**

*706* A261 24p shown 78 40
*707* A261 28p Pillar box, vert. 90 45

Dublin Millennium A262

A263

Impact of the Irish Abroad A264

Designs: No. 709, Portrait of explorer Robert O'Hara Burke (1820-61), by Sir Sidney Nolan, and a 19th cent. map of Australia, Burke-Wills expedition route highlighted. 46p, Mural (detail) of the Eureka Stockade by Nolan.

**1988, Mar. 1** ***Perf. 15x14***

*708* A262 28p multi 90 45
*a.* Bklt. pane of 4, Gaelic 3.60
*b.* Bklt. pane of 4, English 3.60
*709* A263 28p multi 90 45
*710* A264 46p multi 1.50 75

Nos. 708a, 708b consist of two vert. pairs separated by a history in Gaelic or English.

Statesmen Type of 1986 and

1988 Summer Olympics, Seoul — A265

Order of Malta Ambulance Corps, 50th Anniv. — A266

Barry Fitzgerald (1888-1961), Actor — A267

Designs: 24p, William T. Cosgrave (1880-1965), president of the United Ireland and Fine Gael party. No. 712, Equestrian. No. 713, Cycling. 30p, Emergency service. Nos. 712-713 printed se-tenant.

***Perf. 15x14 (28p)***

**1988, Apr. 7** **Litho.**

*711* A240 24p black 78 40
*712* A265 28p multi 90 45
*713* A265 28p multi 90 45
*a.* Miniature sheet of 10+2 labels, 5 each Nos. 712-713 9.00
*714* A266 30p multi 98 50
*715* A267 50p multi 1.60 80
*Nos. 711-715 (5)* 5.16 2.60

Labels contained in No. 713a picture 5-ring Olympic emblem. Size of No. 713a: 190x119mm.

Historic Transatlantic Crossings — A268

Europa 1988 A269

Transport and communications: 24p, Sirius sailing from Passage West, County Cork. 28p, Air traffic controllers and A320 Airbus. 39p, Europe on globe, letters. 46p, Maia and Mercury flying boats in Foynes Harbor.

***Perf. 15x14 (Nos. 717-718)***

**1988, May 12** **Litho.**

*716* A268 24p multi 78 40
*717* A269 28p multi 90 45
*718* A269 39p multi 1.25 62
*719* A268 46p multi 1.50 75

1st scheduled transatlantic crossing by steamship, sesquicentennial (24p); 1st east-west transatlantic crossing by seaplane, 50th anniv. (46p).

Wildlife Conservation: Flora — A270

**1988, June 21** **Litho.** ***Perf. 14x15***

*720* A270 24p Otanthus maritimus 72 35
*721* A270 28p Saxifraga hartii 85 42
*722* A270 46p Astragalus danicus 1.40 70

Irish Security Forces A271

**1988, Aug. 23** **Litho.** ***Perf. 15x14***

*723* A271 28p Garda Siochana (police) 82 40
*724* A271 28p Army 82 40
*725* A271 28p Navy, air corps 82 40
*726* A271 28p FCA, Slua Muiri 82 40

Printed se-tenant in sheets of 20.

Institute of Chartered Accountants, Cent. — A272

Defeat of the Spanish Armada, 400th Anniv. A273

***Perf. 14x15, 15x14***

**1988, Oct. 6** **Litho.**

*727* A272 24p multi 72 35
*728* A273 46p *Duquesa Santa Ana* off Donegal Coast 1.35 68

John F. Kennedy, Portrait by James Wyeth
A274

**1988, Nov. 24 Litho. *Perf. 15x14***

| | | | | |
|---|---|---|---|---|
| *729* | A274 | 28p multi | 90 | 45 |

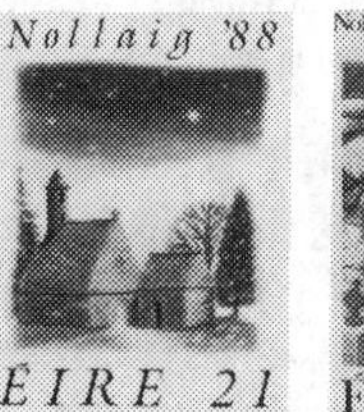

Christmas
A275 A276

**1988, Nov. 24 *Perf. 14x15***

| | | | | |
|---|---|---|---|---|
| *730* | A275 | 21p St. Kevin's Church, Glendalough | 65 | 32 |
| *731* | A276 | 24p Adoration of the Magi | 75 | 38 |
| *732* | A276 | 28p Flight into Egypt | 90 | 45 |
| *733* | A276 | 46p Holy Family | 1.45 | 72 |

No. 730 issued only in discount sheets of 14. Sheet sold for £2.90.

## AIR POST STAMPS

**Catalogue values for unused stamps in this section, from this point to the end of the section, are for Never Hinged items.**

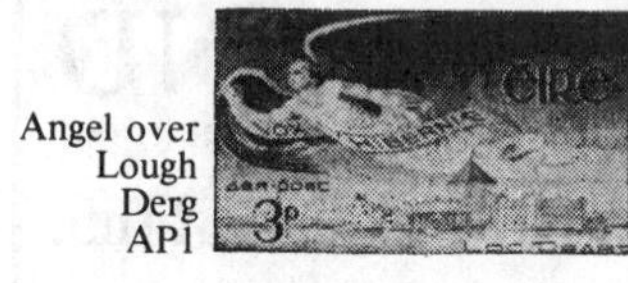

Angel over Lough Derg
AP1

Designs: 1p, 1sh3p, 1sh5p, Rock of Cashel. 6p, Croagh Patrick. 1sh, Glendalough.

***Perf. 15x14***

**1948-65 Wmk. 262 Engr.**

| | | | | |
|---|---|---|---|---|
| *C1* | AP1 | 1p dk brn ('49) | 4.00 | 2.75 |
| *C2* | AP1 | 3p blue | 6.75 | 4.25 |
| *C3* | AP1 | 6p rose lilac | 70 | 10 |
| *C4* | AP1 | 8p red brn ('54) | 3.50 | 30 |
| *C5* | AP1 | 1sh green ('49) | 1.50 | 42 |
| *C6* | AP1 | 1sh3p ver ('54) | 4.25 | 20 |

***Perf. 15***

| | | | | |
|---|---|---|---|---|
| *C7* | AP1 | 1sh5p dark bl ('65) | 4.25 | 75 |
| | | *Nos. C1-C7 (7)* | 24.95 | 8.77 |

## POSTAGE DUE STAMPS

D1

**1925 Typo. Wmk. 44 *Perf. 14x15***

| | | | | |
|---|---|---|---|---|
| *J1* | D1 | ½p emerald | 19.00 | 17.50 |
| *J2* | D1 | 1p carmine | 11.00 | 7.50 |
| *J3* | D1 | 2p dark green | 21.00 | 9.00 |
| *J4* | D1 | 6p plum | 7.00 | 6.50 |

**Catalogue values for unused stamps in this section, from this point to the end of the section, are for Never Hinged items.**

**1940-70 Wmk. 262**

| | | | | |
|---|---|---|---|---|
| *J5* | D1 | ½p emerald ('43) | 30.00 | 20.00 |
| *J6* | D1 | 1p brt car ('41) | 1.10 | 28 |
| *J7* | D1 | 1½p vermilion ('52) | 2.25 | 3.25 |
| *J8* | D1 | 2p dark green | 95 | 55 |
| *J9* | D1 | 3p blue ('52) | 1.50 | 70 |
| *J10* | D1 | 5p royal pur ('43) | 3.00 | 3.50 |
| *J11* | D1 | 6p plum ('60) | 2.25 | 95 |
| ***a.*** | | Wmkd. sideways ('67) | 2.25 | 1.65 |
| *J12* | D1 | 8p orange ('62) | 6.50 | 3.75 |
| *J13* | D1 | 10p red lilac ('65) | 7.75 | 4.00 |
| *J14* | D1 | 1sh lt yel grn ('69) | 20.00 | 6.00 |
| ***a.*** | | Wmkd. sideways ('70) | 47.50 | 11.00 |
| | | *Nos. J5-J14 (10)* | 75.30 | 42.98 |

**1971, Feb. 15 Typo. Wmk. 262**

| | | | | |
|---|---|---|---|---|
| *J15* | D1 | 1p sepia | 12 | 10 |
| ***a.*** | | Wmkd. sideways | 80 | 80 |
| *J16* | D1 | 1½p bright grn | 14 | 8 |
| *J17* | D1 | 3p gray green | 1.10 | 90 |
| *J18* | D1 | 4p orange | 1.40 | 1.10 |
| *J19* | D1 | 5p bright blue | 2.75 | 1.75 |
| *J20* | D1 | 7p yellow | 32 | 22 |
| *J21* | D1 | 8p scarlet | 32 | 22 |
| | | *Nos. J15-J21 (7)* | 6.15 | 4.37 |

**1978 Unwmk.**

| | | | | |
|---|---|---|---|---|
| *J25* | D1 | 3p gray green | 2.50 | 6.00 |
| *J26* | D1 | 4p orange | 4.00 | *10.50* |
| *J27* | D1 | 5p bright blue | 2.50 | 6.00 |

Celtic Knot — D2

**1980, June 11 Photo. *Perf. 15***

| | | | | |
|---|---|---|---|---|
| *J28* | D2 | 1p brt yel grn | 5 | 5 |
| *J29* | D2 | 2p ultramarine | 8 | 5 |
| *J30* | D2 | 4p dark green | 45 | 40 |
| *J31* | D2 | 6p yel orange | 60 | 55 |
| *J32* | D2 | 8p vio blue | 85 | 80 |
| *J33* | D2 | 18p green | 1.90 | 1.75 |
| *J33A* | D2 | 20p org brown ('85) | 1.50 | 1.40 |
| *J34* | D2 | 24p emerald | 2.50 | 2.25 |
| *J35* | D2 | 30p plum ('85) | 2.00 | 1.80 |
| *J36* | D2 | 50p rose pink ('85) | 3.50 | 3.25 |
| | | *Nos. J28-J36 (10)* | 13.43 | 12.30 |

D3

**1988, Oct. 6 Litho. *Perf.***

| | | | | |
|---|---|---|---|---|
| *J37* | D3 | 1p | 5 | 5 |
| *J38* | D3 | 2p | 6 | 5 |
| *J39* | D3 | 3p | 10 | 5 |
| *J40* | D3 | 4p | 12 | 6 |
| *J41* | D3 | 5p | 15 | 8 |
| *J42* | D3 | 17p | 50 | 25 |
| *J43* | D3 | 20p | 60 | 30 |
| *J44* | D3 | 24p | 70 | 35 |
| *J45* | D3 | 30p | 88 | 45 |
| *J46* | D3 | 50p | 1.50 | 75 |
| *J47* | D3 | £1 | 3.00 | 1.50 |
| | | *Nos. J37-J47 (11)* | 7.66 | 3.89 |

# JAMAICA

LOCATION — In the Caribbean Sea, about 90 miles south of Cuba.
GOVT. — Independent state in the British Commonwealth.
AREA — 4,411 sq. mi.
POP. — 2,230,000 (est. 1982).
CAPITAL — Kingston.

Jamaica became an independent state in the British Commonwealth in August 1962. As a colony, it administered two dependencies: Cayman Islands and Turks and Caicos Islands.

12 Pence = 1 Shilling
20 Shillings = 1 Pound
100 Cents = 1 Dollar (1969)

**Catalogue values for unused stamps in this country are for Never Hinged items, beginning with Scott 129.**

Queen Victoria
A1 A2

A3

A4

A5

A6

Wmk.45

**Wmk. Pineapple. (45)**

**1860-63 Typo. *Perf. 14***

| | | | | |
|---|---|---|---|---|
| *1* | A1 | 1p blue | 37.50 | 6.75 |
| ***a*** | | Diagonal half used as ½p on cover | | 850.00 |
| *2* | A2 | 2p rose | 90.00 | 35.00 |
| ***a*** | | One quarter used as ½p on cover | | |
| *3* | A3 | 3p grn ('63) | 110.00 | 24.00 |
| *4* | A4 | 4p brn org | 150.00 | 16.00 |
| ***a*** | | 4p org | 150.00 | 16.00 |
| *5* | A5 | 6p lilac | 165.00 | 10.00 |
| ***a*** | | 6p dp lil | 750.00 | 30.00 |
| *6* | A6 | 1sh brown | 185.00 | 17.00 |
| ***a*** | | 1sh lil brn | 500.00 | 17.00 |
| ***b*** | | 1sh yel brn | 450.00 | 17.00 |

All except No. 3 exist imperforate.

**1870-71 Wmk. Crown and C. C. (1)**

| | | | | |
|---|---|---|---|---|
| *7* | A1 | 1p blue | 30.00 | 1.00 |
| ***a*** | | Diagonal half used as ½p on cover | | |
| *8* | A2 | 2p rose | 35.00 | 35 |
| ***a*** | | 2p brnsh rose | 75.00 | 35 |
| *9* | A3 | 3p green | 72.50 | 3.50 |
| *10* | A4 | 4p brn org ('72) | 130.00 | 3.50 |
| ***a*** | | 4p red org | 475.00 | 4.50 |
| *11* | A5 | 6p lil ('71) | 47.50 | 2.75 |
| *12* | A6 | 1sh brn ('73) | 21.00 | 5.25 |

The 1p and 4p exist imperf.
See Nos. 17-23, 40, 43, 47-53.

Queen Victoria — A7

**1872, Oct. 29**

| | | | | |
|---|---|---|---|---|
| *13* | A7 | ½p claret | 7.50 | 1.40 |

Exists imperf. See No. 16.

A8

A9

**1875, Aug. 27 *Perf. 12½***

| | | | | |
|---|---|---|---|---|
| *14* | A8 | 2sh red brn | 22.50 | 25.00 |
| *15* | A9 | 5sh violet | 67.50 | 92.50 |

Exist imperf.
See Nos. 29-30, 44, 54.

**1883-90 Wmk. 2 *Perf. 14***

| | | | | |
|---|---|---|---|---|
| *16* | A7 | ½p bl grn ('85) | 38 | 10 |
| ***a*** | | ½p gray grn | 38 | 10 |
| *17* | A1 | 1p bl ('84) | 300.00 | 6.75 |
| *18* | A1 | 1p car ('85) | 7.50 | 70 |
| ***a*** | | 1p rose | 30.00 | 70 |
| *19* | A2 | 2p rose ('84) | 165.00 | 3.50 |
| *20* | A2 | 2p sl ('85) | 24.00 | 28 |
| ***a*** | | 2p gray | 24.00 | 28 |
| *21* | A3 | 3p ol grn ('86) | 1.25 | 70 |
| *22* | A4 | 4p red brn | 1.65 | 28 |
| ***a*** | | 4p org brn | 300.00 | 11.00 |
| *23* | A5 | 6p org yel ('90) | 7.00 | 5.00 |
| ***a*** | | 6p yel | 19.00 | 8.50 |
| | | *Nos. 16-23 (8)* | 506.78 | 17.31 |

Queen Victoria — A10

**1889-91**

| | | | | |
|---|---|---|---|---|
| *24* | A10 | 1p lil & red vio | 70 | 7 |
| *25* | A10 | 2p green | 2.75 | 1.25 |
| *26* | A10 | 2½p lil & ultra ('91) | 2.75 | 60 |

No. 22a Surcharged in Black **TWO PENCE HALF-PENNY**

**1890, June**

| | | | | |
|---|---|---|---|---|
| *27* | A4 | 2½p on 4p org brn | 27.50 | 7.50 |
| ***b*** | | Double surch. | 350.00 | 225.00 |
| ***d*** | | "PFNNY" | 100.00 | 75.00 |
| ***e*** | | "PFNNK" | 190.00 | 140.00 |
| ***f*** | | As "d," double surcharge | | |

Three settings of surcharge.

**1897**

| | | | | |
|---|---|---|---|---|
| *28* | A6 | 1sh brown | 4.75 | 3.25 |
| *29* | A8 | 2sh red brn | 26.00 | 14.00 |
| *30* | A9 | 5sh violet | 32.50 | *60.00* |

Llandovery Falls
A12

Arms of Jamaica
A13

**1900, May 1 Engr. Wmk. 1**

| | | | | |
|---|---|---|---|---|
| *31* | A12 | 1p red | 55 | 12 |

**1901, Sept. 25**

| | | | | |
|---|---|---|---|---|
| *32* | A12 | 1p red & blk | 1.10 | 9 |
| ***a*** | | Imperf. horiz., pair | | |
| ***b*** | | bluish paper | 175.00 | 125.00 |

**1903-04 Typo. Wmk. 2**

| | | | | |
|---|---|---|---|---|
| *33* | A13 | ½p grn & blk | 68 | 14 |
| ***b*** | | "SERv ET" for "SERVIET" | 40.00 | 45.00 |
| *34* | A13 | 1p car & blk ('04) | 2.00 | 5 |
| ***b*** | | "SERv ET" for "SERVIET" | 40.00 | 40.00 |
| *35* | A13 | 2½p ultra & blk | 2.00 | 45 |
| ***a*** | | "SERv ET" for "SERVIET" | 55.00 | 65.00 |
| *36* | A13 | 5p yel & blk ('04) | 14.00 | *22.50* |
| ***a*** | | "SERv ET" for "SERVIET" | 600.00 | *600.00* |

**1905-11 Chalky Paper Wmk. 3**

| | | | | |
|---|---|---|---|---|
| *37* | A13 | ½p grn & blk | 65 | 8 |
| ***b*** | | "SERv ET" for "SERVIET" | 26.00 | 26.00 |
| *38* | A13 | 1p car & blk | 8.50 | 8 |
| *39* | A13 | 2½p ultra & blk ('07) | 1.50 | 65 |
| *40* | A4 | 4p *yel* ('10) | 8.50 | 17.50 |
| *41* | A13 | 5p yel & blk ('07) | 16.00 | 19.00 |
| ***a*** | | "SERv ET" for "SERVIET" | 1,200. | 1,400. |
| *42* | A13 | 6p red vio & vio ('11) | 6.50 | 8.50 |
| *43* | A6 | 1sh *green*('10) | 2.00 | 4.25 |
| *44* | A8 | 2sh vio, *bl*('10) | 4.25 | 2.50 |
| *45* | A13 | 15sh vio & blk | 26.00 | 22.50 |
| | | *Nos. 37-45 (9)* | 73.90 | 75.06 |

**1905-11 Ordinary Paper.**

| | | | | |
|---|---|---|---|---|
| *46* | A13 | 2½p ultra ('10) | 95 | 42 |
| *47* | A3 | 3p ol grn | 1.15 | 25 |
| *48* | A3 | 3p vio, *yel* ('10) | 70 | 45 |
| *49* | A4 | 4p red brn ('08) | 32.50 | 27.50 |
| *50* | A4 | 4p red, *yel* ('11) | 1.25 | 2.75 |
| *51* | A5 | 6p dl vio ('09) | 2.50 | 6.25 |
| *52* | A5 | 6p org yel ('09) | 12.50 | 15.00 |
| ***a*** | | 6p org ('06) | 12.50 | 15.00 |

53 A6 1sh brn ('06) 10.00 4.00
54 A8 2sh red brn ('08) 85.00 87.50
*Nos. 46-54 (9)* 146.55 144.12

Nos. 48 and 51 also come on chalky paper.

A14  A15

**1906**

58 A14 ½p green 32 5
*a* Booklet pane of 6
59 A15 1p carmine 38 5

Edward VII — A16

George V — A17

**1911, Feb. 3**

60 A16 2p gray 2.00 *7.75*

**1912-19**

61 A17 1p scar ('16) 15 5
*a* 1p car ('12) 15 5
*b* Booklet pane of 6
62 A17 1½p brn org ('16) 1.40 6
*a* 1½p yel org 3.25 95
63 A17 2p gray 45 75
64 A17 2½p ultra ('13) 25 15

**Chalky Paper**

65 A17 3p vio, *yel* 45 15
66 A17 4p scar & blk, *yel* ('13) 60 38
67 A17 6p red vio & dl vio 60 1.25
68 A17 1sh *green* 85 55
*a* 1sh *bl grn*, olive back 4.50 3.25
69 A17 2sh ultra & vio, *bl* ('19) 7.75 9.25
70 A17 5sh scar & grn, *yel* ('19) 27.50 30.00

**Surface-colored Paper**

71 A17 3p vio, *yel* ('13) 45 22
72 A17 4p scar & blk, *yel* ('14) 85 1.75
73 A17 1sh *green*('15) 1.75 3.00
*Nos. 61-73 (13)* 43.05 47.56

See Nos. 101-102.

Exhibition Buildings of 1891 A18

Arawak Woman Preparing Cassava A19

World War I Contingent Embarking for Overseas Duty — A20

King's House, Spanish Town — A21

Return of Overseas Contingent, 1919 — A22

Columbus Landing in Jamaica — A23

Cathedral in Spanish Town — A24

Statue of Queen Victoria — A26

Memorial to Admiral Rodney — A27

Monument to Sir Charles Metcalfe — A28

Woodland Scene — A29

King George V — A30

**1919-21 Typo. Wmk. 3 *Perf. 14***

**Chalky Paper**

75 A18 ½p ol grn & dk grn ('20) 16 5
76 A19 1p org & car ('21) 2.00 5

**Engr.**

**Ordinary Paper.**

77 A20 1½p green 16 5
78 A21 2p grn & bl ('21) 1.00 1.50
79 A22 2½p bl & dk bl ('21) 65 52
80 A23 3p bl & grn ('21) 1.00 32
81 A24 4p grn & dk brn ('21) 2.50 *5.00*
83 A26 1sh brt org & org ('20) 2.25 2.25
*a* Frame inverted *22,500. 13,000.*
As "a," revenue cancel *2,500.*
84 A27 2sh brn & bl ('20) 15.00 5.00
85 A28 3sh org & vio ('20) 20.00 *30.00*
86 A29 5sh ocher & bl ('21) 32.50 32.50
87 A30 10sh dk myr grn ('20) 65.00 *130.00*
*Nos. 75-87 (12)* 142.22 207.24

See note after No. 100.

A 6p stamp depicting the abolition of slavery was sent to the Colony but was not issued. "Specimen" copies exist with wmk. 3 or 4. Value $1,250 each.

Without "Specimen", value $20,000.

Port Royal in 1853 A31

**1921-23 Typo. Wmk. 4 *Perf. 14.***

**Chalky Paper.**

88 A18 ½p ol grn & dk grn ('22) 65 6
*a* Booklet pane of 4
89 A19 1p org & car ('22) 42 5
*a* Booklet pane of 6

**Engr.**

**Ordinary Paper.**

90 A20 1½p green 1.65 7
91 A21 2p grn & bl 1.00 18
92 A22 2½p bl & dk bl 60 18
93 A23 3p bl & grn ('22) 35 7
94 A24 4p grn & dk brn 45 15
95 A31 6p bl & blk ('22) 10.00 1.25
96 A26 1sh brn org & dl org 1.25 22
97 A27 2sh brn & bl ('22) 1.65 90
98 A28 3sh org & vio 13.00 12.00
99 A29 5sh ocher & bl ('23) 11.00 10.00
*a* 5sh org & bl 14.00 13.00
100 A30 10sh dk myr grn ('22) 40.00 40.00
*Nos. 88-100 (13)* 82.02 65.13

No. 89 differs from No. 76 in having the words "Postage and Revenue" at the bottom.

On No. 79 the horizontal bar of the flag at the left has a broad white line below the colored line. On No. 92 this has been corrected and the broad white line placed above the colored line.

Watermark is sideways on Nos. 76, 77, 87, 89 and 90.

Type of 1912-19 Issue.

**1921-27 Typo. Wmk. 4**

101 A17 ½p grn ('27) 14 6
*a* Booklet pane of 6
102 A17 6p red vio & dl vio 8.00 3.25

No. 102 is on chalky paper.

A32

Type I

Type II

Type II- Cross shading beneath "Jamaica."

**1929-32 Engr. *Perf. 13½x14, 14***

103 A32 1p red, type I 22 5
*a.* 1p red, type II ('32) 12 5
*b.* Booklet pane of 6, type II
104 A32 1½pbrown 175 8
105 A32 9p vio brn 3.75 1.40

The frames on Nos. 103 to 105 differ.

Coco Palms at Columbus Cove — A33

Scene near Castleton, St. Andrew — A34

Priestman's River, Portland Parish — A35

**1932 *Perf. 12½.***

106 A33 2p grn & gray blk 3.50 45
*a* Vertical pair, imperf. between *3,500.*
107 A34 2½p ultra & sl bl 1.65 60
*a* Vertical pair, imperf. between *4,000. 4,000*
108 A35 6p red vio & gray blk 2.75 1.65

**Silver Jubilee Issue.**

Common Design Type

**1935, May 6 *Perf. 11x12***

109 CD301 1p car & bl 16 16
*a* Bklt. pane of 6 *150.00*
110 CD301 1½p blk & ultra 32 32
111 CD301 6p ind & grn 2.00 2.00
112 CD301 1sh brn vio & ind 2.50 2.50

**Coronation Issue.**

Common Design Type

**1937, May 12 *Perf. 13½x14***

113 CD302 1p carmine 10 6
114 CD302 1½p gray blk 14 10
115 CD302 2½p brt ultra 32 22

King George VI — A36

Coco Palms at Columbus Cove — A37

Scene near Castleton, St. Andrew — A38

Bananas A39

Citrus Grove A40

Priestman's River, Portland Parish — A41

Kingston Harbor A42

Sugar Industry A43

Bamboo Walk — A44

Woodland Scene — A45

King George VI — A46

**1938-51 *Perf. 13½x14.***

116 A36 ½p dk bl grn 5 5
*a* Booklet pane of 6 4.50
*b* Wmkd. sideways
117 A36 1p carmine 5 5
*a* Booklet pane of 6 7.50
118 A36 1½p brown 5 5

*Perf. 12½, 13x13½, 13½x13, 12½x13.*

*119* A37 2p grn & gray blk, perf. 12½ 6 5
*a* Perf. 13x13½ ('39) 8 5
*b* Perf. 12½x13 ('51) 6 5
*120* A38 2½p ultra & sl bl 1.50 1.10
*121* A39 3p grn & lt ultra 10 10
*122* A40 4p grn & yel brn 12 6
*123* A41 6p red vio & gray blk, perf. 13½x13 ('50) 15 5
*a* Perf. 12½ 15 5
*124* A42 9p rose lake 28 22
*125* A43 1sh dk brn & brt grn 28 10
*126* A44 2sh brn & brt bl 1.10 42

*Perf. 13, 14*

*127* A45 5sh ocher & bl, perf. 13 ('50) 2.00 1.00
*a* bluish paper, perf. 13 ('49) 5.00 5.00
*b* Perf. 14 1.50 1.10
Revenue cancel 20
*128* A46 10sh dk myr grn, perf. 14 3.50 2.75
*a* Perf. 13 ('50) 3.50 2.50
*Nos. 116-128 (13)* 9.24 6.00

See Nos. 140, 148, 149, 152.

**Catalogue values for unused stamps in this section, from this point to the end of the section, are for Never Hinged items.**

Courthouse, Falmouth A47

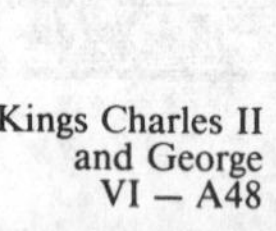

Kings Charles II and George VI — A48

House of Assembly, 1762-1869 A50

Institute of Jamaica — A49

Allegory of Labor and Learning — A51

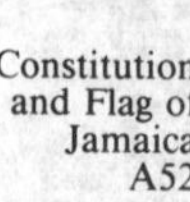

Constitution and Flag of Jamaica A52

**1945-46 Engr. Wmk. 4 *Perf. 12½***

*129* A47 1½p brown 9 5
*a* Booklet pane of 4 27.50
*b* Perf. 12½x13½ ('46) 14 9
*130* A48 2p dp grn, perf. 12½x13½ 14 14
*a* Perf. 12½ 95 48
*131* A49 3p brt ultra 18 16
*a* Perf. 13 ('46) 38 32
*132* A50 4½p sl blk 24 24
*a* Perf. 13 ('46) 42 42
*133* A51 2s chocolate 80 80
*134* A52 5s dp bl 1.00 1.00
*135* A49 10s green 2.25 2.25
*Nos. 129-135 (7)* 4.70 4.64

Issued to commemorate the granting of a new Constitution in 1944.

*Jamaica stamps can be mounted in Scott's annually supplemented British North and West Caribbean Album.*

**Peace Issue.**

Common Design Type

***Perf. 13½x14, 13½***

**1946, Oct. 14 Wmk. 4**

*136* CD303 1½p blk brn, perf. 13½ 12 12
*a* Perf. 13½x14 14 14
*137* CD303 3p dp bl, perf. 13½x14 20 20
*a* Perf. 13½ 35 35

**Silver Wedding Issue.**

Common Design Types

**1948, Dec. 1 Photo. *Perf. 14x14½***

*138* CD304 1½p red brn 12 12

**Engr.; Name Typo.**

***Perf. 11½x11***

*139* CD305 £1 red 20.00 20.00

Type of 1938 and

Tobacco Industry A53

**1949, Aug. 15 Engr. *Perf. 12½***

*140* A39 3p ultra & sl bl 1.00 40
*141* A53 £1 pur & brn 25.00 25.00

**UPU Issue**

Common Design Types

***Perf. 13½, 11x11½***

**1949, Oct. 10 Wmk. 4**

*142* CD306 1½p red brn 28 14
*143* CD307 2p dk grn 38 22
*144* CD308 3p indigo 75 48
*145* CD309 6p rose vio 1.90 1.25

**University Issue**

Common Design Types

**1951, Feb. 16 *Perf. 14x14½***

*146* CD310 2p brn & gray blk 24 10
*147* CD311 6p rose lil & gray blk 65 35

George VI Type of 1938

**1951, Oct. 25 *Perf. 13½x14***

*148* A36 ½p orange 5 5
*a* Booklet pane of 6 5.00
*149* A36 1p bl grn 18 5
*a* Booklet pane of 6 11.00

Boy Scout Emblem with Map — A54

Map and Emblem A55

***Perf. 13½x13, 13x13½.***

**1952, Mar. 5 Typo. Wmk. 4**

*150* A54 2p blk, yel grn & bl 35 16
*151* A55 6p blk, yel grn & dk red 60 40

1st Caribbean Boy Scout Jamboree, 1952.

Banana Type of 1938.

**1952, July 1 Engr. *Perf. 12½***

*152* A39 3p rose red & grn 50 40

**Coronation Issue.**

Common Design Type

**1953, June 2 *Perf. 13½x13***

*153* CD312 2p dk grn & blk 18 12

Type of 1938 with Portrait of Queen Elizabeth II and Inscription: "ROYAL VISIT 1953"

**1953, Nov. 25 *Perf. 13***

*154* A37 2p grn & gray blk 14 14

Visit of Queen Elizabeth II and the Duke of Edinburgh, 1953.

Warship off Port Royal A56

Designs: 2½p, Old Montego Bay. 3p, Old Kingston. 6p, Proclaiming abolition of slavery.

**1955, May 10 Engr. *Perf. 12x12½***

**Center in Black**

*155* A56 2p ol grn 7 6
*156* A56 2½p lt ultra 20 18
*157* A56 3p dp plum 25 20
*158* A56 6p rose red 32 30

300th anniversary of Jamaica's establishment as a British territory.

Palm Trees — A57

Blue Mountain Peak — A58

Arms of Jamaica — A59

Arms of Jamaica — A60

Designs: 1p, Sugar cane. 2p, Pineapple. 2½p, Bananas. 3p, Mahoe flower. 4p, Breadfruit. 5p, Ackee fruit. 6p, Streamer (hummingbird). 1sh, Royal Botanic Gardens, Hope. 1sh6p, Rafting on the Rio Grande. 2sh, Fort Charles.

**1956 Wmk. 4 *Perf. 12½***

*159* A57 ½p org ver & blk 5 5
*a* Booklet pane of 6 32
*160* A57 1p emer & blk 5 5
*a* Booklet pane of 6 50
*161* A57 2p rose red & blk 6 5
*a* Booklet pane of 6 80
*162* A57 2½p lt ultra & blk 10 6
*a* Booklet pane of 6 1.65
*163* A57 3p brn & grn 10 6
*164* A57 4p dk bl & ol grn 14 10
*165* A57 5p ol grn & car 20 10
*166* A57 6p car & blk 24 6

***Perf. 13½***

*167* A58 8p red org & brt ultra 24 16
*168* A58 1sh bl & yel grn 32 14
*169* A58 1sh6p dp cl & ultra 60 20
*170* A58 2sh ol grn & ultra 2.00 40

***Perf. 11½***

*171* A59 3sh bl & blk 1.90 90
*172* A59 5sh car & blk 2.75 1.25
*173* A60 10sh bl grn & blk 6.50 4.00
*174* A60 £1 pur & blk 12.00 6.50
*Nos. 159-174 (16)* 27.25 14.08

**West Indies Federation**

Common Design Type

***Perf. 11½x11***

**1958, Apr. 22 Engr. Wmk. 314**

*175* CD313 2p green 7 7
*176* CD313 5p blue 32 32
*177* CD313 6p car rose 42 32

Britannia Plane over 1860 Packet Boat A61

1sh Stamps of 1860 and 1956 — A62

Design: 6p, Victorian post cart and mail truck.

**1960, Jan. 4 *Perf. 13x13½***

*178* A61 2p lil & bl 8 6
*179* A61 6p ol grn & car rose 28 20

***Perf. 13***

*180* A62 1sh bl, yel grn & brn 52 52

Centenary of Jamaican postal service.

**Independent State**

Zouave Bugler and Map of Jamaica A63

Designs: 1sh6p, Gordon House (Legislature) and hands of three races holding banner. 5sh, Map and symbols of agriculture and industry.

**1962, Aug. 8 Photo. *Perf. 13***

*181* A63 2p multi 6 5
*182* A63 4p multi 15 7
*a* Yellow omitted
*183* A63 1sh6p red, blk & brn 45 24
*184* A63 5sh multi 1.65 1.65

Issue of 1956 Overprinted:

1962 INDEPENDENCE
a

1962 INDEPENDENCE 1962
b

***Perf. 12½***

**1962, Aug. 8 Wmk. 4 Engr.**

*185* A57(a) ½p org ver & blk 5 5
*186* A57(a) 1p emer & blk 5 5
*187* A57(a) 2½p lt ultra & blk 8 5
*188* A57(b) 3p brn & grn 10 7
*189* A57(b) 5p ol grn & car 18 14
*190* A57(b) 6p car & blk 18 9

***Perf. 13½***

*191* A58(b) 8p red org & brt ultra 28 18
*192* A58(b) 1sh bl & yel grn 35 28
*193* A58(b) 2sh ol grn & ultra 1.10 65

***Perf. 11½***

*194* A59(a) 3sh bl & blk 1.75 1.10
*195* A60(a) 10sh bl grn & blk 4.50 3.50
*196* A60(a) £1 pur & blk 9.00 7.50
*Nos. 185-196 (12)* 17.62 13.66

Nos. 181-196 issued to commemorate Jamaica's independence.

The word "Independence" measures 17½x1½mm on Nos. 185-187; it is 18x1mm on Nos. 194-196.

See Nos. 208-216.

Weight Lifting, Soccer, Boxing and Cycling A64

Designs: 6p, Various water sports. 8p, Running and jumping. 2sh, Arms and runner.

***Perf. 14½x14***

**1962, Aug. 11 Photo. Wmk. 314**

*197* A64 1p car & dk brn 6 5
*198* A64 6p bl & brn 14 12
*199* A64 8p ol & dk brn 22 16
*200* A64 2sh multi 75 75

IX Central American and Caribbean Games, Kingston, Aug. 11-25.

A souvenir sheet containing one each of Nos. 197-200, imperf., was sold exclusively by National Sports, Ltd., at 5sh (face 3sh3p). The Jamaican Post Office sold the entire issue of this sheet to National Sports at face value, plus the printing cost. The stamps are postally valid. The sheet has marginal inscriptions and simulated perforations in ultramarine. Size: 152x114mm. Value $3.25.

### Freedom from Hunger Issue

Man Planting Mango Tree and Produce A65

*Perf. 12½*

**1963, June 4 Unwmk. Litho.**

| | | | | |
|---|---|---|---|---|
| *201* | A65 | 1p bl & multi | 10 | 10 |
| *202* | A65 | 8p rose & multi | 60 | 60 |

See note after CD314, Common Design section.

### Red Cross Centenary Issue
Common Design Type

**1963, Sept. 2 Wmk. 314 *Perf. 13***

| | | | | |
|---|---|---|---|---|
| *203* | CD315 | 2p blk & red | 8 | 6 |
| *204* | CD315 | 1sh6p ultra & red | 60 | 50 |

Carole Joan Crawford — A66

**Unwmk.**

**1964, Feb. 14 Photo. *Perf. 13***

| | | | | |
|---|---|---|---|---|
| *205* | A66 | 3p multi | 8 | 6 |
| *206* | A66 | 1sh ol & multi | 30 | 26 |
| *207* | A66 | 1sh6p multi | 40 | 40 |
| *a* | | Souv. sheet of 3 | 90 | 90 |

Issued to honor Carole Joan Crawford, Miss World, 1963.

No. 207a contains one each of Nos. 205-207 with simulated perforations, marginal decorations and inscriptions in blue. Size: 151x102mm. Issued May 25. Sold for 4sh.

### Types of 1956 Overprinted like 1962 Independence Issue

**Wmk. 314**

**1963-64 Engr. *Perf. 12½***

| | | | | |
|---|---|---|---|---|
| *208* | A57 (a) | ½p org ver & blk | 9 | 7 |
| *209* | A57 (a) | 1p emer & blk ('64) | 12 | 7 |
| *210* | A57 (a) | 2½p lt ultra & blk ('64) | 22 | 18 |
| *211* | A57(b) | 3p brn & grn | 35 | 18 |
| *212* | A57(b) | 5p ol grn & car ('64) | 65 | 60 |
| | | ***Perf. 13½*** | | |
| *213* | A58(b) | 8p red org & brt ultra ('64) | 80 | 70 |
| *214* | A58(b) | 1sh bl & yel grn | 2.00 | 1.90 |
| *215* | A58(b) | 2sh ol grn & ultra ('64) | 2.75 | 2.75 |
| | | ***Perf. 11½*** | | |
| *216* | A59 (a) | 3sh bl & blk ('64) | 3.75 | 3.75 |
| | | *Nos. 208-216 (9)* | 10.73 | 10.20 |

Overprint is at bottom on Nos. 214-215, at top on Nos. 192-193.

Lignum Vitae, National Flower, and Map — A67

Wmk.352

Designs: 1½p, Ackee, national fruit, and map. 2p, Blue Mahoe, national tree, and map (vert.). 2½p, Land shells (snails). 3p, Flag over map. 4p, Murex antillarum, sea shell. 6p, Papilio homerus. 8p, Streamer (hummingbird). 9p, Gypsum industry. 1sh, Stadium and statue of runner. 1sh6p, Palisadoes International Airport. 2sh, Bauxite mining. 3sh, Blue marlin and boat. 5sh, Port Royal exploration of sunken city, map, ship and artifacts. 10sh, Coat of arms (vert.). £1, Flag and Queen Elizabeth II.

### Wmk. J and Pineapple, Multiple (352)

*Perf. 14½, 14x14½*

**1964, May 4 Photo.**

**Size: 26x22mm, 22x26mm**

| | | | | |
|---|---|---|---|---|
| *217* | A67 | 1p bis, vio bl & grn | 5 | 5 |
| *a* | | Bklt. pane of 6 | 35 | |
| *218* | A67 | 1½p multi | 7 | 5 |
| *219* | A67 | 2p multi | 8 | 5 |
| *a* | | Booklet pane of 6 | 85 | |
| *220* | A67 | 2½p multi | 10 | 9 |
| *221* | A67 | 3p emer, yel & blk | 10 | 5 |
| *a* | | Bklt. pane of 6 | 1.10 | |
| *222* | A67 | 4p vio & buff | 12 | 7 |
| *223* | A67 | 6p multi | 18 | 5 |
| *a* | | ultra omitted | 30.00 | |
| *224* | A67 | 8p multi | 22 | 10 |
| *a* | | Red omitted | | |

***Perf. 14½x14, 13½x14½, 14x14½***

**Size: 32x26mm, 26x32mm**

| | | | | |
|---|---|---|---|---|
| *225* | A67 | 9p bl & yel | 25 | 9 |
| *226* | A67 | 1sh yel brn & blk | 30 | 9 |
| *a* | | Yellow brn omitted | 200.00 | |
| *b* | | Black omitted | 550.00 | |
| *227* | A67 | 1sh6p sl, buff & bl | 42 | 18 |
| *228* | A67 | 2sh bl, brn red & blk | 65 | 35 |
| *229* | A67 | 3sh grn, saph & dk bl, perf. 14½x14 | 1.10 | 65 |
| *a* | | Perf. 14x14½ | 1.90 | 1.25 |
| *230* | A67 | 5sh bl, blk & bis | 1.50 | 85 |
| *231* | A67 | 10sh multi | 2.25 | 1.75 |
| *a* | | Blue ("Jamaica" etc.) omitted | 150.00 | |
| *232* | A67 | £1 multi | 5.00 | 3.25 |
| | | *Nos. 217-232 (16)* | 12.39 | 7.72 |

See Nos. 306-318.

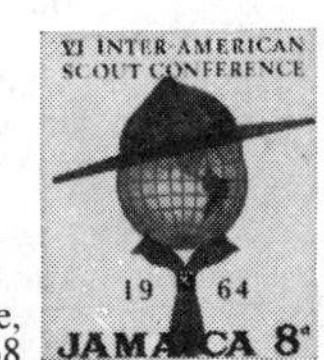


Scout Hat, Globe, Neckerchief — A68

Scout Emblem, American Crocodile — A69

Design: 3p, Scout belt buckle.

*Perf. 14½x14, 14*

**1964, Aug. 27 Wmk. 352**

| | | | | |
|---|---|---|---|---|
| *233* | A68 | 3p pink, blk & red | 9 | 7 |
| *234* | A68 | 8p ultra, blk & ol | 20 | 20 |
| *235* | A69 | 1sh ultra & gold | 35 | 35 |

6th Inter-American Scout Conference, Kingston, Aug. 25-29.

Gordon House, Kingston, and Commonwealth Parliamentary Association Emblem — A70

Designs: 6p, Headquarters House, Kingston. 1sh6p, House of Assembly, Spanish Town.

**1964, Nov. 16 Photo. *Perf. 14½x14***

| | | | | |
|---|---|---|---|---|
| *236* | A70 | 3p yel grn & blk | 8 | 6 |
| *237* | A70 | 6p red & blk | 16 | 12 |
| *238* | A70 | 1sh6p ultra & blk | 38 | 35 |

10th Commonwealth Parliamentary Conf.

---

Common Design Types pictured in section before Great Britain.

---

Eleanor Roosevelt — A71

**1964, Dec. 10 Wmk. 352**

| | | | | |
|---|---|---|---|---|
| *239* | A71 | 1sh lt grn, blk & red | 25 | 22 |

Issued in memory of Eleanor Roosevelt (1884-1962) on the 16th anniversary of the Universal Declaration of Human Rights.

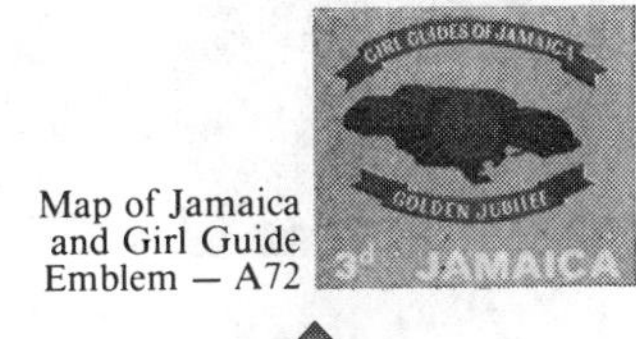


Map of Jamaica and Girl Guide Emblem — A72

Girl Guide Emblems — A73

*Perf. 14x14½, 14*

**1965, May 17 Photo. Wmk. 352**

| | | | | |
|---|---|---|---|---|
| *240* | A72 | 3p lt bl, yel & yel grn | 9 | 6 |
| *241* | A73 | 1sh lt yel grn, blk & bis | 30 | 30 |

50th anniv. of the Girl Guides of Jamaica.

Salvation Army Cap — A74

Design: 1sh6p, Flag bearer, drummer and globe (vert.).

*Perf. 14x14½, 14½x14*

**1965, Aug. 23 Photo. Wmk. 352**

| | | | | |
|---|---|---|---|---|
| *242* | A74 | 3p dp bl, yel, mar & blk | 8 | 6 |
| *243* | A74 | 1sh6p emer & multi | 38 | 38 |

Centenary of the Salvation Army.

> The Scott Catalogue value is a retail price, what you could expect to pay for the stamp in a grade of Fine-Very Fine. The value listed is a reference which reflects recent actual dealer selling price.

Paul Bogle, William Gordon and Morant Bay Court House A75

**1965, Dec. 29 Unwmk. *Perf. 14x13***

| | | | | |
|---|---|---|---|---|
| *244* | A75 | 3p vio bl, blk & brn | 7 | 6 |
| *245* | A75 | 1sh6p yel grn, blk & brn | 35 | 35 |
| *246* | A75 | 3sh pink & brn | 65 | 65 |

Cent. of the Morant Bay rebellion against governor John Eyre.

ITU Emblem, Telstar, Telegraph Key and Man Blowing Horn — A76

*Perf. 14x14½*

**1965, Dec. 29 Photo. Wmk. 352**

| | | | | |
|---|---|---|---|---|
| *247* | A76 | 1sh gray, blk & red | 45 | 45 |

Cent. of the ITU.

Nos. 221, 223, 226-227 Overprinted: "ROYAL VISIT / MARCH 1966"

*Perf. 14½, 14½x14*

**1966, March 3 Photo. Wmk. 352**

**Size: 26x22mm.**

| | | | | |
|---|---|---|---|---|
| *248* | A67 | 3p emer, yel & blk | 12 | 9 |
| *249* | A67 | 6p multi | 22 | 20 |

**Size: 32x26mm.**

| | | | | |
|---|---|---|---|---|
| *250* | A67 | 1sh yel brn & blk | 38 | 32 |
| *251* | A67 | 1sh6p sl, buff & bl | 65 | 65 |

See note after Antigua No. 162.

Winston Churchill A77

**1966, Apr. 18 *Perf. 14, 14x14½***

| | | | | |
|---|---|---|---|---|
| *252* | A77 | 6p ol grn & gray | 30 | 26 |
| *253* | A77 | 1sh vio & sep | 56 | 48 |

Issued in memory of Sir Winston Leonard Spencer Churchill (1874-1965), statesman and World War II leader.

Runner, Flags of Jamaica, Great Britain and Games' Emblem A78

Designs: 6p, Bicyclists and waterfall. 1sh, Stadium. 3sh, Games' Emblem.

*Perf. 14½x14*

**1966, Aug. 4 Photo. Wmk. 352**

| | | | | |
|---|---|---|---|---|
| *254* | A78 | 3p multi | 7 | 6 |
| *255* | A78 | 6p multi | 12 | 10 |
| *256* | A78 | 1sh multi | 28 | 28 |
| *257* | A78 | 3sh gold & dk vio bl | 75 | 75 |
| *a* | | Souv. sheet of 4 | 2.75 | 2.75 |

Issued to publicize the 8th British Empire and Commonwealth Games, August 4-13, 1966.

No. 257a contains 4 imperf. stamps with simulated perforations similar to Nos. 254-257. Light brown margin with gold and black inscription. Size: 126½x101mm. Issued Aug. 25, 1966.

Bolivar Statue, Kingston, Flags of Jamaica and Venezuela — A79

*Perf. 14x14½*

**1966, Dec. 5 Photo. Wmk. 352**

*258* A79 8p multi 25 25

Issued to commemorate the 150th anniversary of the "Bolivar Letter," written by Simon Bolivar, while in exile in Jamaica.

Jamaican Pavilion — A80

**1967, Apr. 28** *Perf. 14½x14*

*259* A80 6p multi 16 14
*260* A80 1sh multi 28 28

Issued to commemorate EXPO '67 International Exhibition, Montreal, Apr. 28-Oct. 27, 1967.

Donald Burns Sangster — A81

*Perf. 13x13½*

**1967, Aug. 28 Photo. Unwmk.**

*261* A81 3p multi 7 7
*262* A81 1sh6p multi 35 35

Issued in memory of Sir Donald Burns Sangster (1911-1967), Prime Minister.

Traffic Police and Post Office A82

Designs: 1sh, Officers representing various branches of police force in front of Police Headquarters. 1sh6p, Constable, 1867, Old House of Assembly, and 1967 constable with New House of Assembly.

*Perf. 13½x14*

**1967, Nov. 28 Photo. Wmk. 352**

**Size: 42x25mm**

*263* A82 3p red brn & multi 12 12

**Size: 56½x20½mm**

*Perf. 13½x14½*

*264* A82 1sh yel & multi 35 35

**Size: 42x25mm**

*Perf. 13½x14*

*265* A82 1sh6p gray & multi 55 55

Centenary of the Constabulary Force.

A Human Rights set of three (3p, 1sh, 3sh) was prepared and announced for release on Jan. 2, 1968. The Crown Agents distributed sample sets, but the stamps were not issued. Designs show bowls of food, an abacus and praying hands. On Dec. 3, Nos. 271-273 were issued instead.

Cricket Type of Guyana

Designs: No. 266, Wicketkeeper and emblem of West Indies Cricket Team. No. 267, Batsman and emblem of Marylebone Cricket Club. No. 268, Bowler and emblem of West Indies Cricket Team.

**1968, Feb. 8 Photo.** *Perf. 14*

*266* A6 6p multi 30 30
*267* A6 6p multi 30 30
*268* A6 6p multi 30 30

Issued to publicize the visit of the Marylebone Cricket Club to the West Indies, Jan.-Feb. 1968. Nos. 266-268 are printed in sheet of 9 (3x3) in horiz. se-tenant strips of 3; sheet has decorative border.

Sir Alexander and Lady Bustamante — A83

**1968, May 23** *Perf. 14½*

*269* A83 3p brt rose & blk 7 7
*270* A83 1sh ol grn & blk 22 22

Issued for Labor Day, May 23, 1968.

Human Rights Flame and Map of Jamaica A84

Designs: 1sh, Hands shielding Human Rights flame (vert.). 3sh, Man kneeling on Map of Jamaica, and Human Rights flame.

**Wmk. 352**

**1968, Dec. 3 Photo.** *Perf. 14½*

*271* A84 3p blk, red, gold & emer 6 5
*a* Gold (flame) omitted 110.00
*272* A84 1sh blk, org, yel & gold 22 22
*273* A84 3sh blk, emer, yel & gold 75 75
*a* Gold (flame) omitted 110.00

International Human Rights Year.

ILO Emblem A85

**Unwmk.**

**1969, May 23 Litho.** *Perf. 14*

*274* A85 6p blk & org yel 12 9
*275* A85 3sh blk & brt grn 60 60

50th anniv. of the ILO.

WHO Emblem, Children and Nurse — A86

Designs: 1sh, Malaria eradication (horiz.). 3sh, Student nurses.

**1969, May 30 Photo.** *Perf. 14*

*276* A86 6p org, blk & brn 12 9
*277* A86 1sh bl grn, blk & brn 22 22
*278* A86 3sh ultra, blk & brn 60 60

20th anniv. of the World Health Organization.

Nos. 217-219, 221-223, 225-232 Surcharged with New Value and: "C-DAY 8th SEPTEMBER 1969"

**1969, Sept. 8 Wmk. 352** *Perf. 14½*

**Size: 26x22mm, 22x26mm**

*279* A67 1c on 1p multi 5 5
*280* A67 2c on 2p multi 7 5
*281* A67 3c on 3p multi 10 5
*282* A67 4c on 4p multi 12 9
*283* A67 5c on 6p multi 16 10
*a* Blue (wing dots) omitted 32.50

*Perf. 14½x14, 13½x14½, 14x14½*

**Size: 32x26mm., 26x32mm.**

*284* A67 8c on 9p multi 25 16
*285* A67 10c on 1sh multi 30 22
*286* A67 15c on 1sh6p multi 42 30
*287* A67 20c on 2sh multi 65 50
*288* A67 30c on 3sh multi 85 65
*289* A67 50c on 5sh multi 1.00 85
*290* A67 $1 on 10sh multi 2.00 1.90
*291* A67 $2 on £1 multi 4.75 3.50
*Nos. 279-291 (13)* 10.72 8.42

Introduction of decimal currency.

The old denomination is obliterated by groups of small rectangles on the 1c and 3c, and with a square on the 2c, 4c and 8c; old denominations not obliterated on others.

Madonna and Child with St. John, by Raphael — A87

Paintings: 2c, The Adoration of the Kings, by Vincenzo Foppa. 8c, The Adoration of the Kings, by Dosso Dossi.

**1969, Oct. 25 Litho.** *Perf. 13*

*292* A87 2c ver & multi 6 6
*293* A87 5c multi 18 18
*294* A87 8c org & multi 30 30

Christmas 1969.

First Jamaica Penny — A88

Design: 3c, First Jamaica halfpenny.

**1969, Oct. 27** *Perf. 12x12½*

*295* A88 3c brt pink, blk & sil 7 7
*296* A88 15c emer, blk & sil 30 30

Centenary of the first Jamaican coinage.

George William Gordon — A89

Crucifixion, by Antonello da Messina — A90

Portraits: 3c, Sir Alexander Bustamante (1884-1977). 5c, Norman W. Manley (1893-1969). 10c, Marcus M. Garvey (1887-1940). 15c, Paul Bogle (1820-1865).

*Perf. 12x12½*

**1970, Mar. 11 Photo. Unwmk.**

*297* A89 1c lt vio & multi 5 5
*298* A89 3c lt bl & multi 7 7
*299* A89 5c lt gray & multi 12 12
*300* A89 10c pale rose & multi 25 25
*301* A89 15c pale grn & multi 48 48
*Nos. 297-301 (5)* 97 97

Issued to honor national heroes connected with Jamaica's independence.

**1970, Mar. 23**

Easter: 3c, Christ Appearing to St. Peter, by Annibale Carracci. 20c, Easter lily.

*302* A90 3c pink & multi 8 8
*303* A90 10c gray grn & multi 30 30
*304* A90 20c gray & multi 60 60

No. 219 Surcharged **2c** 

**1970, July 16 Wmk. 352** *Perf. 14½*

*305* A67 2c on 2p multi 14 10

Type of Regular Issue, 1964
Values in Cents and Dollars

Designs: 1c, Lignum vitae and map. 2c, Blue mahoe and map (vert.). 3c, Flag over map. 4c, Murex antillarum, sea shell. 5c, Papilio homerus. 8c, Gypsum industry. 10c, Stadium and statue of runner. 15c, Palisadoes International Airport. 20c, Bauxite mining. 30c, Blue marlin and boat. 50c, Port Royal exploration of sunken city, map, ship and artifacts. $1, Coat of arms (vert.). $2, Flag and Queen Elizabeth II.

**1970 Wmk. 352 Photo.** *Perf. 14½*

**Size: 26x22mm., 22x26mm.**

*306* A67 1c bis & multi 5 5
*307* A67 2c gray grn & multi 9 5
*308* A67 3c emer, yel & blk 12 5
*309* A67 4c vio & buff 14 5
*310* A67 5c grn & multi 18 7

*Perf. 14½x14, 13½x14½, 14x14½*

**Size: 32x26mm., 26x32mm.**

*311* A67 8c bl & yel 28 14
*312* A67 10c yel brn & blk 40 18
*313* A67 15c multi 60 28
*314* A67 20c multi 80 45
*315* A67 30c multi 90 60
*316* A67 50c multi 1.40 1.00
*317* A67 $1 multi 2.75 1.75
*318* A67 $2 multi 5.50 3.75
*Nos. 306-318 (13)* 13.21 8.42

Issue dates: Nos. 306-312, Sept. 7; Nos. 313-318, Nov. 2.

Bright's Cable Gear on "Dacia" A91

Designs: 3c, Telegraph cable ship "Dacia." 50c, Double current Morse key, 1870, and map of Jamaica.

**1970, Oct. 12 Litho.** *Perf. 14½*

*319* A91 3c red org & multi 10 8
*320* A91 10c bl grn & multi 38 10
*321* A91 50c emer & multi 1.65 1.65

Centenary of telegraph service.

Bananas, Citrus Fruit, Sugar Cane and Tobacco — A92

**1970, Nov. 2 Wmk. 352 *Perf. 14***

322 A92 2c brn & multi 8 6
323 A92 10c blk & multi 38 38

Issued to commemorate the 75th anniversary of the Jamaica Agricultural Society.

"The Projector," 1845 — A93

Locomotives: 15c, Engine 54, 1944. 50c, Engine 102, 1967.

**1970, Nov. 21 Litho. *Perf. 13½***

324 A93 3c grn & multi 20 20
325 A93 15c org brn & multi 1.10 1.10
326 A93 50c multi 4.00 4.00

125th anniv. of the Jamaican railroad.

Kingston Cathedral — A94

Designs: 10c, 20c, like 3c. 30c, Arms of Jamaica Bishopric.

**1971, Feb. 22 *Perf. 14½***

327 A94 3c lt grn & multi 7 6
328 A94 10c dl org & multi 22 22
329 A94 20c ultra & multi 45 45
330 A94 30c gray & multi 75 75

Centenary of the disestablishment of the Church of England.

Henry Morgan, Ships in Port Royal Harbor A95

Designs: 15c, Mary Read, Anne Bonny and pamphlet on their trial. 30c, 18th century merchantman surrendering to pirate schooner.

**1971, May 10 Litho. Wmk. 352**

331 A95 3c red brn & multi 15 15
332 A95 15c gray & multi 90 90
333 A95 30c lil & multi 2.00 2.00

Pirates and buccaneers.

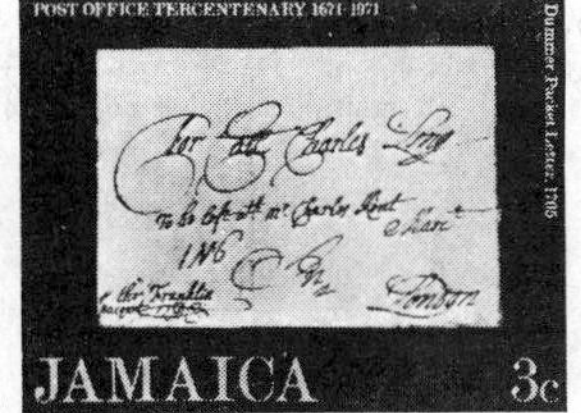


Dummer Packet Letter, 1705 — A96

Designs: 5c, Stampless cover, 1793. 8c, Post office, Kingston, 1820. 10c, Modern date cancellation on No. 312. 20c, Cover with stamps of Great Britain and Jamaica cancellations, 1859. 50c, Jamaica No. 83a (vert.).

**1971, Oct. 30 *Perf. 13½***

334 A96 3c dk car & blk 12 12
335 A96 5c lt ol grn & blk 20 20
336 A96 8c pur & blk 30 30
337 A96 10c sl, blk & brn 38 38
338 A96 20c multi 75 75
339 A96 50c dk gray, blk & org 1.90 1.90
*Nos. 334-339 (6)* 3.65 3.65

Tercentenary of Jamaica Post Office.

Earth Station and Satellite — A97

**1972, Feb. 17 *Perf. 14x13½***

340 A97 3c red & multi 10 9
341 A97 15c gray & multi 60 60
342 A97 50c multi 1.75 1.75

Jamaica's earth satellite station.

Bauxite Industry — A98

National Stadium A99

***Perf. 14½x14, 14x14½***

**1972-79 Litho. Wmk. 352**

343 A98 1c *Pimento (vert.)* 5 5
344 A98 2c *Red ginger* (vert.) 5 5
345 A98 3c *shown* 5 5
346 A98 4c *Kingston harbor* 5 5
347 A98 5c *Oil refinery* 6 5
348 A98 6c *Senate Building, Univ. of the West Indies* 7 6

***Perf. 13½, 14½x14 ($5)***

349 A99 8c *shown* 9 7
350 A99 9c *Devon House, Hope Road* 10 9
351 A99 10c *Stewardess and Air Jamaica plane* 10 9
352 A99 15c *Old Iron Bridge* (vert.) 15 14
353 A99 20c *College of Arts, Science & Technology* 20 18
354 A99 30c *Dunn's River Falls* (vert.) 30 26
355 A99 50c *River raft* 52 42
356 A99 $1 *Jamaica House* 1.00 90
357 A99 $2 *Kings House* 1.50 1.40
358 A99 $5 *Map and arms of Jamaica* ('79) 3.25 3.25
*Nos. 343-358 (16)* 7.54 7.11

Size of No. 358: 37x26½mm.

Nos. 345, 351, 355 Overprinted: "TENTH ANNIVERSARY INDEPENDENCE 1962-1972"

**1972, Aug. 8 *Perf. 14½x14, 13½***

360 A98 3c multi 8 7
361 A99 10c multi 28 28
362 A99 50c multi 1.40 1.40

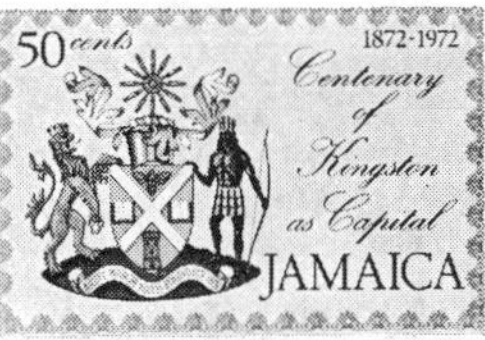


Arms of Kingston — A100

Design: 5c, 30c, Arms of Kingston (vert.).

**1972, Dec. 4 *Perf. 13½x14, 14x13½***

363 A100 5c pink & multi 10 9
364 A100 30c lem & multi 75 75
365 A100 50c lt bl & multi 1.25 1.25

Centenary of Kingston as capital.

Mongoose and Map of Jamaica A101

Designs: 40c, Mongoose and rat. 60c, Mongoose and chicken.

***Perf. 14x14½***

**1973, Apr. 9 Litho. Wmk. 352**

366 A101 8c yel grn & blk 22 22
367 A101 40c bl & blk 1.10 1.10
368 A101 60c sal & blk 1.90 1.90
*a* Souvenir sheet of 3 4.00 4.00

Centenary of the introduction of the mongoose to Jamaica.

No. 368a contains one each of Nos. 366-368 with bicolored marginal decoration and inscriptions. Size: 165x94½mm.

Euphorbia Punicea — A102

Flowers: 6c, Hylocereus triangularis. 9c, Columnea argentea. 15c, Portlandia grandiflora. 30c, Samyda pubescens. 50c, Cordia sebestena.

**1973, July 9 *Perf. 14***

369 A102 1c dp grn & multi 6 6
370 A102 6c vio bl & multi 22 22
371 A102 9c org & multi 35 35
372 A102 15c brn & multi 55 55
373 A102 30c ol & multi 1.10 1.10
374 A102 50c multi 1.90 1.90
*Nos. 369-374 (6)* 4.18 4.18

Broughtonia Sanguinea — A103

Orchids: 10c, Arpophyllum jamaicense (vert.). 20c, Oncidium pulchellum (vert.). $1, Brassia maculata.

**1973, Oct. 8 *Perf. 14x13½, 13½x14***

375 A103 5c multi 22 22
376 A103 10c multi 45 45
377 A103 20c sl & multi 90 90
378 A103 $1 ultra & multi 4.50 4.50
*a* Souvenir sheet of 4 6.50 6.50

No. 378a contains one each of Nos. 375-378, perf. 12. Slate green and purple marginal designs of orchids and inscription. Size: 165x95mm.

Mailboat "Mary" (1808-1815) — A104

Designs: Mailboats.

***Perf. 13½ (5c, 50c), 14½ (10c, 15c)***

**1974, Apr. 8 Wmk. 352**

379 A104 5c *shown* 18 14
*a* Perf. 14½ 7.50 1.25
380 A104 10c *"Queensbury" (1814-27)* 48 38
381 A104 15c *"Sheldrake" (1829-34)* 75 55
382 A104 50c *"Thames" (1842)* 2.25 1.90
*a* Souvenir sheet of 4 6.00 4.50

No. 382a contains one each of Nos. 379-382, perf. 13½. Multicolored margin shows map with route of mailboats and "Ship Letter" cancellation. Size: 132½x157mm.

Jamaican Dancers — A105

Designs: Dancers.

**1974, Aug. 1 Litho. *Perf. 13½***

383 A105 5c grn & multi 12 12
384 A105 10c blk & multi 26 26
385 A105 30c brn & multi 65 65
386 A105 50c lil & multi 1.40 1.40
*a* Souvenir sheet of 4 3.00 3.00

National Dance Theatre.

No. 386a contains one each of Nos. 383-386. Black and lilac margin with inscription telling story of dance company. Size: 163x109mm.

Globe, Letter, UPU Emblem A106

**1974, Oct. 9 *Perf. 14***

387 A106 5c plum & multi 15 15
388 A106 9c ol & multi 30 30
389 A106 50c multi 1.50 1.50

Centenary of Universal Postal Union.

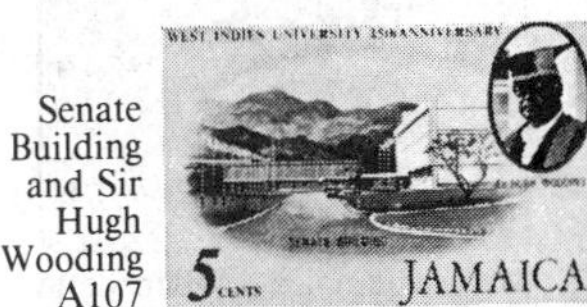


Senate Building and Sir Hugh Wooding A107

Designs: 10c, 50c, Chapel and Princess Alice. 30c, like 5c.

**1975, Jan. 13 Wmk. 352**

390 A107 5c yel & multi 10 10
391 A107 10c sal & multi 20 20
392 A107 30c dl org & multi 55 55
393 A107 50c multi 1.00 1.00

University College of the West Indies, 25th anniversary.

Common Design Types are pictured in section before Great Britain.

Commonwealth Symbol — A108

Commonwealth Symbol and: 10c, Arms of Jamaica. 30c, Dove of peace. 50c, Jamaican flag.

**1975, Apr. 29 Litho. *Perf. 13½***

| | | | | |
|---|---|---|---|---|
| *394* | A108 | 5c buff & multi | 12 | 12 |
| *395* | A108 | 10c rose & multi | 22 | 22 |
| *396* | A108 | 30c vio bl & multi | 80 | 65 |
| *397* | A108 | 50c multi | 1.25 | 1.00 |

Commonwealth Heads of Government Conference, Jamaica, Apr.-May.

Graphium Marcellinus A109

Koo Koo, "Actor-boy" A110

Butterflies: 20c, Papilio thoas melonius. 25c, Papilio thersites. 30c, Papilio homerus.

**1975, Aug. 25 Litho. *Perf. 14***

| | | | | |
|---|---|---|---|---|
| *398* | A109 | 10c lt grn & multi | 60 | 42 |
| *399* | A109 | 20c lt grn & multi | 1.25 | 85 |
| *400* | A109 | 25c lt grn & multi | 1.75 | 1.25 |
| *401* | A109 | 30c lt grn & multi | 2.00 | 1.50 |
| *a* | | Souvenir sheet of 4 | 6.00 | 4.50 |

No. 401a contains one each of Nos. 398-401. Light blue margin with black and magenta inscription. Size: 134x172mm.

See Nos. 423-426, 435-438.

**1975, Nov. 3 Litho. Wmk. 352**

Designs: 10c, Red "set-girls." 20c, French "set-girls." 50c, Jawbone or "House John Canoe." Festival dancers drawn by I. M. Belisario in Kingston, 1837.

| | | | | |
|---|---|---|---|---|
| *402* | A110 | 8c multi | 18 | 18 |
| *403* | A110 | 10c ol & multi | 24 | 24 |
| *404* | A110 | 20c ultra & multi | 45 | 45 |
| *405* | A110 | 50c multi | 1.25 | 1.25 |
| *a* | | Souvenir sheet of 4 | 3.25 | 3.25 |

Christmas 1975. No. 405a contains one each of Nos. 402-405, perf. 13½. Decorative margin with black inscription. Size: 136x140mm.

See Nos. 416-418.

Map of Jamaica, by Benedetto Bordone, 1528 — A111

Maps of Jamaica by: 20c, Tommaso Porcacchi, 1576. 30c, Theodor DeBry, 1594. 50c, Barent Langenes, 1598.

***Perf. 13½x14***

**1976, Mar. 12 Litho. Wmk. 352**

| | | | | |
|---|---|---|---|---|
| *406* | A111 | 10c brn, buff & red | 20 | 20 |
| *407* | A111 | 20c bis & multi | 42 | 42 |
| *408* | A111 | 30c lt bl & multi | 65 | 65 |
| *409* | A111 | 50c multi | 1.25 | 1.25 |

See Nos. 419-422.

Olympic Rings — A112

**1976, June 14 Litho. *Perf. 13½x14***

| | | | | |
|---|---|---|---|---|
| *410* | A112 | 10c blk & multi | 22 | 22 |
| *411* | A112 | 20c bl & multi | 45 | 45 |
| *412* | A112 | 25c red & multi | 55 | 55 |
| *413* | A112 | 50c grn & multi | 1.10 | 1.10 |

21st Olympic Games, Montreal, Canada, July 17-Aug. 1.

### Cricket Types of Barbados 1976

**Unwmk.**

**1976, Aug. 9 Litho. *Perf. 14***

| | | | | |
|---|---|---|---|---|
| *414* | A63 | 10c lt bl & multi | 50 | 50 |
| *415* | A64 | 25c lil rose & blk | 1.25 | 1.25 |

World Cricket Cup, won by West Indies Team, 1975.

### Christmas Type of 1975

Belisario Prints, 1837: 10c, Queen of the "set-girls." 20c, Band of Jawbone John Canoe. 50c, Koo Koo, "actor-boy."

**1976, Nov. 8 Wmk. 352 *Perf. 13½***

| | | | | |
|---|---|---|---|---|
| *416* | A110 | 10c brick red & multi | 20 | 20 |
| *417* | A110 | 20c bis & multi | 40 | 40 |
| *418* | A110 | 50c tan & multi | 1.00 | 1.00 |
| *a* | | Souvenir sheet of 3 | 2.50 | 2.50 |

Christmas 1976. No. 418a contains one each of Nos. 416-418, perf. 14. Decorative margin with black inscription, Size: 110x140mm.

### Map Type of 1976

Maps of Jamaica by: 9c, Edmund Hickeringill, 1661. 10c, John Ogilby, 1671. 25c, House of Visscher, 1680. 40c, John Thornton, 1689.

**1977, Feb. 28 Litho. *Perf. 13***

| | | | | |
|---|---|---|---|---|
| *419* | A111 | 9c lt bl & multi | 20 | 20 |
| *420* | A111 | 10c buff & multi | 24 | 24 |
| *421* | A111 | 25c multi | 60 | 60 |
| *422* | A111 | 40c multi | 1.00 | 1.00 |

### Butterfly Type of 1975

Butterflies: 10c, Eurema elathea. 20c, Dynamine egaea. 25c, Atlantea pantoni. 40c, Hypolimnas misippus.

**Wmk. 352**

**1977, May 9 Litho. *Perf. 13½***

| | | | | |
|---|---|---|---|---|
| *423* | A109 | 10c blk & multi | 60 | 60 |
| *424* | A109 | 20c blk & multi | 1.25 | 1.25 |
| *425* | A109 | 25c blk & multi | 1.50 | 1.50 |
| *426* | A109 | 40c blk & multi | 2.50 | 2.50 |
| *a* | | Souvenir sheet of 4 | 7.00 | 7.00 |

No. 426a contains one each of Nos. 423-426, perf. 14½. Multicolored margin shows butterflies and leaves. Size: 138x122½mm.

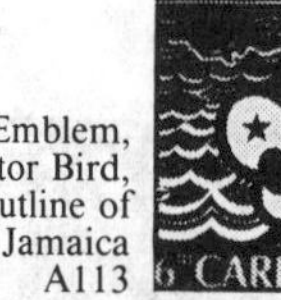

Scout Emblem, Doctor Bird, Outline of Jamaica A113

**1977, Aug. 5 Litho. *Perf. 14***

| | | | | |
|---|---|---|---|---|
| *427* | A113 | 10c multi | 22 | 16 |
| *428* | A113 | 20c multi | 35 | 32 |
| *429* | A113 | 25c multi | 52 | 42 |
| *430* | A113 | 50c multi | 1.10 | 85 |

6th Caribbean Jamboree, Hope Gardens, Kingston, Aug. 3-17.

Trumpeter — A114

Designs: 10c, 3 clarinetists. 20c, 2 kettle drummers (vert.). 25c, Cellist and trumpeter (vert.).

**1977, Dec. 19 Litho. *Perf. 14***

| | | | | |
|---|---|---|---|---|
| *431* | A114 | 9c multi | 32 | 28 |
| *432* | A114 | 10c multi | 40 | 32 |
| *433* | A114 | 20c multi | 80 | 60 |
| *434* | A114 | 25c multi | 1.00 | 80 |
| *a* | | Souvenir sheet of 4 | 3.25 | 2.50 |

Jamaica Military Band, 50th anniversary. No. 434a contains one each of Nos. 431-434; blue and multicolored margin with Military Band banner and descriptive inscription. Size: 120x137mm.

### Butterfly Type of 1975

Butterflies: 10c, Callophrys crethona. 20c, Siproeta stelenes. 25c, Urbanus proteus. 50c, Anaca troglodyta.

**1978, Apr. 17 Litho. *Perf. 14½***

| | | | | |
|---|---|---|---|---|
| *435* | A109 | 10c blk & multi | 42 | 42 |
| *436* | A109 | 20c blk & multi | 85 | 485 |
| *437* | A109 | 25c blk & multi | 1.10 | 1.10 |
| *438* | A109 | 50c blk & multi | 2.00 | 2.00 |
| *a* | | Souvenir sheet of 4 | 5.75 | 4.50 |

No. 438a contains one each of Nos. 435-438. Multicolored margin shows butterflies. Size: 100x125mm.

Half Figure with Canopy — A115

Norman Manley Statue — A116

Arawak Artifacts, found 1792: 20c, Standing figure. 50c, Birdman.

**1978, July 10 Litho. *Perf. 13½x13***

| | | | | |
|---|---|---|---|---|
| *439* | A115 | 10c multi | 20 | 20 |
| *440* | A115 | 20c multi | 42 | 42 |
| *441* | A115 | 50c multi | 1.10 | 1.10 |
| *a* | | Souvenir sheet of 3 | 1.75 | 1.75 |

No. 441a contains one each of Nos. 439-441, perf. 14; multicolored margin shows map of Jamaica and birdman figure. Size: 139x90mm.

**1978, Sept. 25 Litho. Wmk. 352**

Designs: 20c, Alexander Bustamante statue. 25c, Kingston coat of arms. 40c, Gordon House Chamber, House of Representatives.

| | | | | |
|---|---|---|---|---|
| *442* | A116 | 10c multi | 12 | 12 |
| *443* | A116 | 20c multi | 42 | 42 |
| *444* | A116 | 25c multi | 32 | 32 |
| *445* | A116 | 40c multi | 52 | 52 |

24th Commonwealth Parliamentary Conf.

Salvation Army Band A117

Designs: 20c, Trumpeter. 25c, "S" and Cross entwined on pole of Army flag. 50c, William Booth and Salvation Army shield.

**1978, Dec. 4 *Perf. 1***

| | | | | |
|---|---|---|---|---|
| *446* | A117 | 10c multi | 16 | 1 |
| *447* | A117 | 20c multi | 32 | 3 |
| *448* | A117 | 25c multi | 38 | 3 |
| *449* | A117 | 50c multi | 75 | 7 |

Christmas 1978 and Salvation Army centenary.

"Negro Aroused," by Edna Manley — A118

Arawak Grinding Stone, c. 400 B.C. — A119

**1978, Dec. 11 *Perf. 13***

| | | | | |
|---|---|---|---|---|
| *450* | A118 | 10c multi | 20 | 20 |

International Anti-Apartheid Year.

### No. 351 Overprinted: "TENTH / ANNIVERSARY / AIR JAMAICA / 1st APRIL 1979"

**1979, Apr. 2 Litho. *Perf. 13½***

| | | | | |
|---|---|---|---|---|
| *451* | A99 | 10c multi | 20 | 20 |

**1979, Apr. 23 *Perf. 14***

Arawak Artifacts (all A.D.): 10c, Stone implements, c. 500 (horiz.). 20c, Cooking pot, c. 300 (horiz.). 25c, Serving boat, c. 300 (horiz.). 50c, Storage jar fragment, c. 300.

| | | | | |
|---|---|---|---|---|
| *452* | A119 | 5c multi | 6 | 6 |
| *453* | A119 | 10c multi | 12 | 12 |
| *454* | A119 | 20c multi | 22 | 22 |
| *455* | A119 | 25c multi | 28 | 28 |
| *456* | A119 | 50c multi | 55 | 55 |
| | | *Nos. 452-456 (5)* | 1.23 | 1.23 |

Jamaica No. 183, Hill Statue A120

Hill Statue and Stamps of Jamaica: 20c, No. 83a. 25c, No. 5. 50c, No. 271.

**1979, Aug. 13 Litho. *Perf. 14***

| | | | | |
|---|---|---|---|---|
| *457* | A120 | 10c multi | 9 | 9 |
| *458* | A120 | 20c multi | 18 | 18 |
| *a* | | Souvenir sheet | 35 | 35 |
| *459* | A120 | 25c multi | 22 | 22 |
| *460* | A120 | 50c multi | 45 | 45 |

Sir Rowland Hill (1795-1879), originator of penny postage. No. 458a contains No. 458; multicolored margin shows first Jamaican postal card. Size: 147x95mm.

Children, IYC Emblem A121

International Year of the Child: 20c, Doll (vert.). 25c, "The Family." 25c, "House on the Hill." 25c, 50c are children's drawings.

**1979, Oct. 1**

| | | | | |
|---|---|---|---|---|
| *461* | A121 | 10c multi | 9 | 9 |
| *462* | A121 | 20c multi | 18 | 18 |
| *463* | A121 | 25c multi | 22 | 22 |
| *464* | A121 | 50c multi | 42 | 42 |

Tennis, Montego Bay — A122

Jamaican Tody — A123

Designs: 2c, Golfing, Tryall Hanover. 4c, Horseback riding, Negril Beach. 5c, Old Waterwheel, Tryall Hanover. 6c, Fern Gully, Ocho Rios. 7c, Dunn's River Falls, Ocho Rios.

10c, Doctorbird. 12c, Yellow-billed parrot. 15c, Hummingbird. 35c, White-chinned thrush. 50c, Jamaican woodpecker. 65c, Rafting Martha Brae Trelawny. 75c, Blue marlin fishing, Port Antonio. $1, Scuba diving, Ocho Rios. $2, Sail boats, Montego Bay.,

**1979-80 Litho. *Perf. 13½ Wmk. 352***

*465* A122 1c multi 5 5
*466* A122 2c multi 5 5
*467* A122 4c multi 5 5
*468* A122 5c multi 6 6
*469* A122 6c multi 8 8
*470* A122 7c multi 9 9
*472* A123 8c multi 5 5
*473* A123 10c multi 6 6
*474* A123 12c multi 7 7
*475* A123 15c multi 9 9
*476* A123 35c multi 22 22
*477* A123 50c multi 32 32
*478* A122 65c multi 40 40
*479* A122 75c multi 48 48
*480* A122 $1 multi 60 60
*481* A122 $2 multi 1.25 1.25
*Nos. 465-481 (16)* 3.92 3.92

Issue dates: Nos. 465-470, Nov. 26; Nos. 472-481, May 1980.

Institute of Jamaica Centenary — A124

**1980, Feb. 25 Litho. *Perf. 13½***

*484* A124 5c *shown* 5 5
*485* A124 15c *Institute building, 1980* 16 16
*486* A124 35c *"The Ascension" on microfilm reader, vert.* 40 40
*487* A124 50c *Hawksbill and green turtles* 52 52
*488* A124 75c *Jamaican owl, vert.* 80 80
*Nos. 484-488 (5)* 1.93 1.93

Don Quarrie, 1976 Gold Medalist, 200-Meter Race, Moscow '80 Emblem A125

**1980, July 21 Litho. *Perf. 13***

*489* A125 15c *shown* 12 9
*490* Strip of 4, *1952 4x400-meter relay* 2.50 1.25
*a* A125 35c *Arthur Wint* 60 30
*b* A125 35c *Leslie Laing* 60 30
*c* A125 35c *Herbert McKenley* 60 30
*d* A125 35c *George Rhoden* 60 30

22nd Summer Olympic Games, Moscow, July 19-Aug. 3.

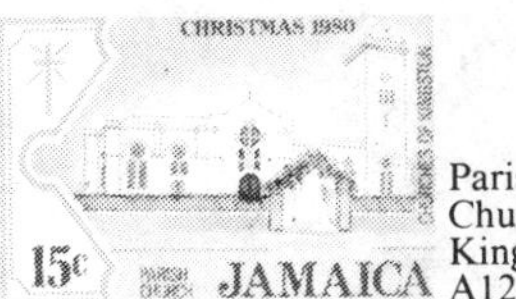


Parish Church, Kingston A126

**1980, Nov. 24 Litho. *Perf. 14***

*491* A126 15c *shown* 12 12
*492* A126 20c *Coke Memorial* 16 16
*493* A126 25c *Church of the Redeemer* 20 20
*494* A126 $5 *Holy Trinity Cathedral* 4.00 4.00
*a* Souvenir sheet of 4 4.50 4.50

Christmas 1980. No. 494a contains Nos. 491-494; multicolored margin shows map of Kingston. Size: 121½x140mm.

Tube Sponge A127

**Wmk. 352**

**1981, Feb. 27 Litho. *Perf. 14***

*495* A127 20c Blood cup sponge, vert. 18 18
*496* A127 45c shown 40 40
*497* A127 60c Black coral, vert. 52 52
*498* A127 75c Tire reef 65 65

See Nos. 523-527.

Indian Coney A128

**Wmk. 352**

**1981, May 25 Litho. *Perf. 14***

*499* Strip of 4 1.00 1.00
*a* A128 20c, any single 25 25

**Royal Wedding Issue**
Common Design Type

**1981, July 29 Litho. *Perf. 13½***

*500* CD331 20c White orchid 16 16
*501* CD331 45c Royal coach 35 35
*502* CD331 60c Couple 45 45
*503* CD331 $5 St. James' Palace 3.75 3.75
*a* Souvenir sheet 3.75 3.75
*b* Booklet pane of 4, perf. 14x14½ 4.75

No. 503a has red and black margin showing heraldic design. Size: 99x86mm.

Intl. Year of the Disabled A129

**Wmk. 352**

**1981, Sept. Litho. *Perf. 13½***

*504* A129 20c Blind weaver 18 18
*505* A129 45c Artist 40 40
*506* A129 60c Learning sign language 52 52
*507* A129 1.50 Basketball players 1.25 1.25

World Food Day A130

***Perf. 13x13½, 13½x13***

**1981, Oct. 16 Litho. Wmk. 352**

*508* A130 20c No. 218 16 16
*509* A130 45c No. 76, vert. 35 35
*510* A130 $2 No. 121 1.65 1.65
*511* A130 $4 No. 125 3.25 3.25

Bob Marley (1945-1981) A131

Designs: Portraits of Bob Marley and song titles.

**1981, Nov. 20 Wmk. 373 *Perf. 14½***

*512* A131 1c multi 5 5
*513* A131 2c multi 5 5
*514* A131 3c multi 6 6
*515* A131 15c multi 30 30
*516* A131 20c multi 42 42
*517* A131 60c multi 1.25 1.25
*518* A131 $3 multi 6.50 6.50
*Nos. 512-518 (7)* 8.63 8.63

**Souvenir Sheet**

*519* A131 $5.25 multi 7.00 7.00

No. 519 has multicolored margin showing record album covers. Size: 134x110mm.

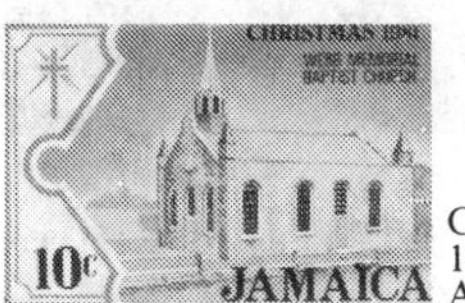


Christmas 1981 A132

**Wmk. 352**

**1981, Dec. 11 Litho. *Perf. 14***

*520* A132 10c Webb Memorial Baptist Church 8 8
*521* A132 45c Church of God 38 38
*522* A132 $5 Bryce United Church 4.00 4.00
*a* Souvenir sheet of 3 4.50 4.50

No. 522a contains Nos. 520-522 (perf. 12½x12); multicolored margin shows map of Jamaica. Size: 120x169mm.

Marine Life Type of 1981

**Wmk. 352**

**1982, Feb. 22 Litho. *Perf. 14***

*523* A127 20c Gorgonian coral, vert. 18 18
*524* A127 45c Hard sponge 40 40
*525* A127 60c Sea cow 52 52
*526* A127 75c Plume worm 65 65
*527* A127 $3 Coral-banded shrimp 2.75 2.75
*Nos. 523-527 (5)* 4.50 4.50

Scouting Year — A133

Princess Diana, 21st Birthday — A134

Designs: 20c, 45c, 60c, Various scouts. $2, Baden-Powell.

**1982, July 12 Litho. *Perf. 13½***

*528* A133 20c multi 18 18
*529* A133 45c multi 38 38
*530* A133 60c multi 48 48
*531* A133 $2 multi 1.75 1.75
*a* Souvenir sheet of 4 3.00 3.00

No. 531a contains Nos. 528-531; green and yellow decorative margin. Size: 80x130mm.

**1982, Sept. 1 *Perf. 14½***

*532* A134 20c Lignum vitae 18 18
*533* A134 45c Couple in coach 42 42
*534* A134 60c Wedding portrait 55 55
*a* Bklt. pane of 3 (#532-534) 1.25
*535* A134 75c Saxifraga longifolia 65 65
*536* A134 $2 Diana 1.90 1.90
*537* A134 $3 Viola gracilis major 2.75 2.75
*a* Bklt. pane of 3 (#535-537) 5.50
*Nos. 532-537 (6)* 6.45 6.45

**Souvenir Sheet**

*538* A134 $5 Honeymoon 5.75 5.75

Nos. 535, 537 in sheets of 5. No. 538 has multicolored floral margin. Size: 106x77mm.

Nos. 532-538 Overprinted: "ROYAL BABY/21.6.82"

**1982, Sept. 13**

*539* A134 20c multi 18 18
*540* A134 45c multi 42 42
*541* A134 60c multi 55 55
*a* Bklt. pane of 3 (#539-541) 1.25
*542* A134 75c multi 65 65
*543* A134 $2 multi 1.90 1.90
*544* A134 $3 multi 2.75 2.75
*a* Bklt. pane of 3 (#542-544) 5.50
*Nos. 539-544 (6)* 6.45 6.45

**Souvenir Sheet**

*545* A134 $5 multi 5.75 5.75

Birth of Prince William of Wales, June 21.

Lizard Cuckoo Capturing Prey — A135

Designs: b. Searching for prey. c. Calling. d. Landing. e. Flying.

**1982, Oct. 25**

*546* Strip of 5 4.50 4.50
*a.-e.* A135 $1 any single 90 90

Christmas Type of 1981

***Perf. 13x13½***

**1982, Dec. 8 Litho. Wmk. 352**

*547* A132 20c United Pentecostal Church 22 22
*548* A132 45c Disciples of Christ Church 45 45
*549* A132 75c Open Bible Church 75 75

Christmas 1982.

Visit of Queen Elizabeth II — A136

**1983, Feb. 14 Litho. *Perf. 14***

*550* A136 $2 Queen Elizabeth II 1.90 1.90
*551* A136 $3 Arms 2.75 2.75

**Commonwealth Day**
Common Design Type

**1983, Mar. 14 Litho. Wmk. 352**

*552* CD334 20c Dancers 18 18
*553* CD334 45c Bauxite mining 38 38
*554* CD334 75c Map 65 65
*555* CD334 $2 Arms, citizens 1.75 1.75



25th Anniv. of Intl. Maritime Org A137

**1983, Mar. 17** **Litho.** ***Perf. 14***
*556* A137 15c Cargo ship 14 14
*557* A137 20c Cruise liner 18 18
*558* A137 45c Container vessel 40 40
*559* A137 $1 Intl. Seabed Headquarters 95 95

21st Anniv. of Independence A138

Prime Ministers Norman Washington Manley and Alexander Bustamante.

**1983, July 25** **Litho.** ***Perf. 14***
*560* A138 15c bl & multi 15 15
*561* A138 20c lt grn & multi 20 20
*562* A138 45c yel & multi 45 45

World Communications Year — A139

**Wmk. 352**
**1983, Oct. 18** **Litho.** ***Perf. 14***
*563* A139 20c Ship-to-shore radio 18 18
*564* A139 45c Postal services 42 42
*565* A139 75c Telephone communication 70 70
*566* A139 $1 TV satellite 95 95

Christmas 1983 A140

Paintings: 15c, Racing at Caymanas, by Sidney McLaren. 20c, Seated Figures, by Karl Parboosingh. 75c, The Petitioner, by Henry Daley (vert.). $2, Banana Plantation, by John Dunkley (vert.).

**1983, Dec. 12** **Litho.** ***Perf. 13½***
*567* A140 15c multi 8 8
*568* A140 20c multi 10 10
*569* A140 75c multi 42 42
*570* A140 $2 multi 1.00 1.00

Alexander Bustamante (1884-1977), First Prime Minister — A141

**1984, Feb. 24** **Litho.** ***Perf. 14***
*571* A141 20c Portrait 15 15
*572* A141 20c Blenheim (birthplace) 15 15

Se-tenant.

Sea Planes A142

**1984, June 11** **Litho.** ***Perf. 14***
*573* A142 25c Gypsy Moth 18 18
*574* A142 55c Consolidated Commodore 42 42
*575* A142 $1.50 Sikorsky S-38 1.15 1.15
*576* A142 $3 Sikorsky S-40 2.25 2.25

1984 Summer Olympics A143

**1984, July 11**
*577* A143 25c Bicycling 18 18
*578* A143 55c Relay race 40 40
*579* A143 $1.50 Running 1.15 1.15
*580* A143 $3 Women's running 2.25 2.25
*a* Souvenir sheet of 4 4.00 4.00

No. 580a contains Nos. 577-580. Size 136x105mm.

Nos. 469, 474 Surcharged.

**1984, Aug.** **Litho.** ***Perf. 13½***
*581* A122 5c on 6c #469 5 5
*582* A123 10c on 12c #474 8 8

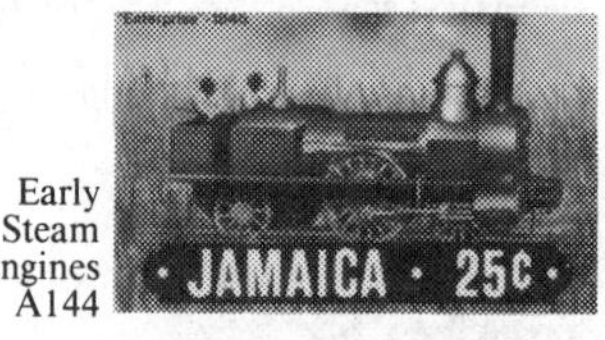

Early Steam Engines A144

**1984, Nov. 16** **Litho.** ***Perf. 13½***
*583* A144 25c Enterprise, 1845 18 18
*584* A144 55c Tank Locomotive, 1880 42 42
*585* A144 $1.50 Kitson-Meyer Tank, 1904 1.15 1.15
*586* A144 $3 Superheater, 1916 2.25 2.25

See Nos. 608-611.

Christmas 1984 — A145

Local sculptures: 20c, Accompong Madonna, by Namba Roy. 25c, Head, by Alvin Marriott. 55c, Moon, by Edna Manley. $1.50, All Women are Five Women, by Mallica Reynolds.

**Wmk. 352**
**1984, Dec. 6** **Litho.** ***Perf. 14***
*587* A145 20c multi 15 15
*588* A145 25c multi 18 18
*589* A145 55c multi 42 42
*590* A145 $1.50 multi 1.10 1.10

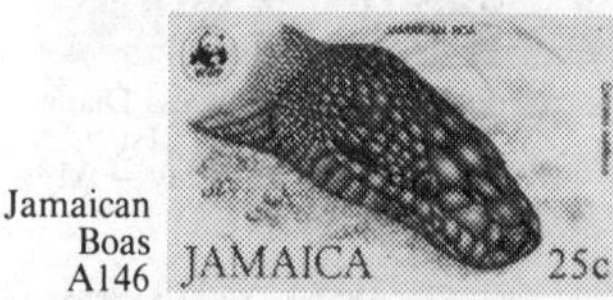

Jamaican Boas A146

**1984, Oct. 22** **Litho.** ***Perf. 14½***
*591* A146 25c Head of boa 12 12
*592* A146 55c Boa over water 28 28
*593* A146 70c Boa with young 35 35
*594* A146 $1 Boa on branch 50 50
*a* Souvenir sheet of 4 1.25 1.25

No. 594a contains Nos. 591-594 with boas in margin. Size: 133x98mm.

Brown Pelicans — A147

**Wmk. 352**
**1985, Apr. 15** **Litho.** ***Perf. 13***
*595* A147 20c multi 8 8
*596* A147 55c multi 22 22
*597* A147 $2 multi 80 80
*598* A147 $5 multi 1.90 1.90
*a* Souvenir sheet of 4 3.00 3.00

Birth bicentenary of artist/naturalist John J. Audubon (1785-1851). No. 598a contains Nos. 595-598 and has a multicolored margin showing brown pelicans and inscribed with historical data. Size: 101x101mm.

**Queen Mother 85th Birthday**
Common Design Type
***Perf. 14½x14***
**1985, June 7** **Litho.** **Wmk. 352**
*599* CD336 25c Holding photograph album, 1963 10 10
*600* CD336 55c With Prince Charles, Windsor Castle, 1983 22 22
*601* CD336 $1.50 At Belfast University 58 58
*602* CD336 $3 Holding Prince Henry 1.15 1.15

**Souvenir Sheet**
*603* CD336 $5 Riding train 1.90 1.90

No. 603 has multicolored margin continuing design. Size: 92x74mm.

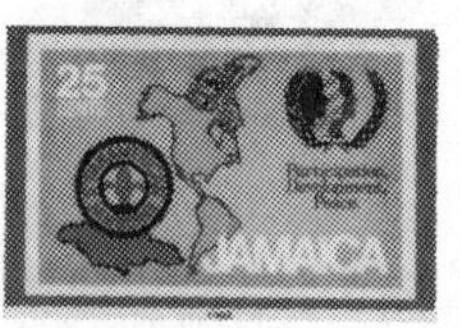

Maps of Americas and Jamaica, IYY and Jamboree Emblems A148

**1985, July 30** **Litho.** ***Perf. 14***
*604* A148 25c multi 10 10
*605* A148 55c multi 22 22
*606* A148 70c multi 28 28
*607* A148 $4 multi 1.50 1.50

Intl. Youth Year and 5th Pan-American Scouting Jamboree.

Locomotives Type of 1984
**1985, Sept.** **Size: 39x25mm**
*608* A144 25c Baldwin 10 10
*609* A144 55c Rogers 22 22
*610* A144 $1.50 Projector 60 60
*611* A144 $4 Diesel 1.50 1.50

The Old Settlement, by Ralph Campbell — A149

Paintings by local artists: 55c, The Vendor, by Albert Hiue, vert. 75c, Road Menders, by Gaston Tabois. $4, Woman, Must I Not Be About My Father's Business? by Carl Abrahams, vert.

**1985, Dec. 9**
*612* A149 20c multi 8 8
*613* A149 55c multi 22 22
*614* A149 75c multi 30 30
*615* A149 $4 multi 1.50 1.50

Christmas 1985.

Birds — A150

**1986, Feb. 10** **Litho.** ***Perf. 14***
*616* A150 25c Chestnut-bellied cuckoo 10 10
*617* A150 55c Jamaican becard 22 22
*618* A150 $1.50 White-eyed thrush 58 58
*619* A150 $5 Rufous-tailed flycatcher 2.00 2.00

**Queen Elizabeth II 60th Birthday**
Common Design Type

Designs: 20c, With Princess Margaret, 1939. 25c, Leaving Liverpool Street Station for Sandringham with Princes Charles and Andrew, 1962. 70c, Visiting the Montego Bay war memorial, Jamaica, 1983. $3, State visit to Luxembourg, 1976. $5, Visiting Crown Agents' offices, 1983.

**1986, Apr. 21** ***Perf. 14½***
*620* CD337 20c scar, blk & sil 8 8
*621* CD337 25c ultra & multi 10 10
*622* CD337 70c grn & multi 28 28
*623* CD337 $3 vio & multi 1.15 1.15
*624* CD337 $5 rose vio & multi 2.00 2.00
*Nos. 620-624 (5)* 3.61 3.61

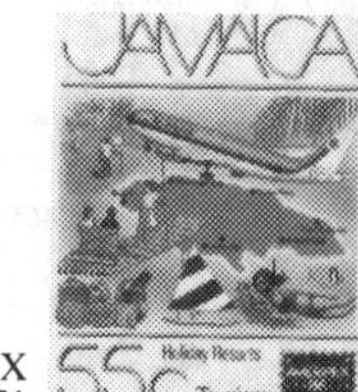

AMERIPEX '86 — A151

Designs: 25c, Bustamante Childrens Hospital. 55c, Vacation cities. $3, Norman Manley Law School. $5, Exports.

**1986, May 19**
*625* A151 25c multi 10 10
*626* A151 55c multi 22 22
*627* A151 $3 multi 1.15 1.15
*628* A151 $5 multi 2.00 2.00
*a* Souvenir sheet of 4, #625-628 3.50 3.50

No. 628a has multicolored decorative margin picturing White House, maps, natl. flags and Statue of Liberty.

**Royal Wedding Issue, 1986**
Common Design Type

Designs: 30c, At the races. $4, Andrew addressing the press.

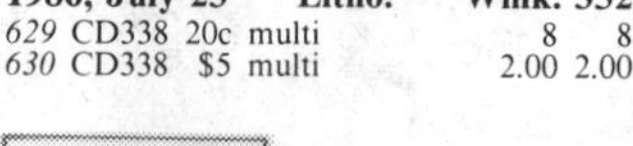

***Perf. 14½x14***
**1986, July 23** **Litho.** **Wmk. 352**
*629* CD338 20c multi 8 8
*630* CD338 $5 multi 2.00 2.00

Boxing Champions — A152

Champions: 45c, Richard "Shrimpy" Clarke, 1986 Commonwealth flyweight. 70c, Michael McCallum, 1984 WBA junior middleweight. $2, Trevor Berbick, 1986 WBC heavyweight. $4, Clarke, McCallum and Berbick.

**1986, Oct. 27** **Litho.** ***Perf. 14***
*631* A152 45c multi 18 18
*632* A152 70c multi 28 28
*633* A152 $2 multi 78 78
*634* A152 $4 multi 1.50 1.50

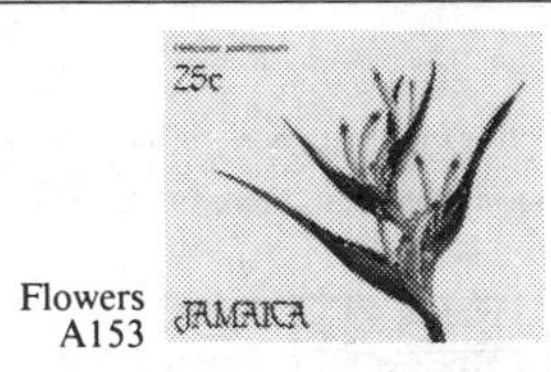
Flowers A153

**1986, Dec. 1** *Perf. 14*
*635* A153 20c Heliconia wagneriana, vert. 8 8
*636* A153 25c Heliconia psittacorum 10 10
*637* A153 55c Heliconia rostrata, vert. 22 22
*638* A153 $5 Strelitzia reginae 2.00 2.00

Christmas. See Nos. 675-678.

Shells — A154

**1987, Feb. 23** **Litho.** *Perf. 15*
*639* A154 35c Crown cone 15 15
*640* A154 75c Measled cowrie 30 30
*641* A154 $1 Trumpet triton 40 40
*642* A154 $5 Rooster-tail conch 2.00 2.00

Prime Ministers A155

Natl. Coat of Arms A156

Designs: 1c-9c, Norman Washington Manley. 10c-90c, Sir Alexander Bustamante.

**1987, May 18** *Perf. 12½x13*
*643* A155 1c dull red 5 5
*644* A155 2c rose pink 5 5
*645* A155 3c lt olive 5 5
*646* A155 4c dull grn 5 5
*647* A155 5c slate blue 5 5
*648* A155 6c ultra 5 5
*649* A155 7c dull mag 5 5
*650* A155 8c red lil 5 5
*651* A155 9c brn olive 5 5
*652* A155 10c deep rose 5 5
*653* A155 20c brt org 8 8
*654* A155 30c emer 12 12
*655* A155 40c lt blue grn 16 16
*656* A155 50c gray olive 20 20
*657* A155 60c lt ultra 24 24
*658* A155 70c pale vio 28 28
*659* A155 80c vio 32 32
*660* A155 90c lt brn 36 36
*661* A156 $1 dull brn & buff 40 40
*662* A156 $2 org 80 80
*663* A156 $5 gray olive & grnh buff 2.00 2.00
*664* A156 $10 royal blue & pale blue 4.00 4.00
*Nos. 643-664 (22)* 9.46 9.46

Nos. 647, 653 reprinted with "1988" imprint.

Nos. 477-478 Surcharged

**1986, Nov. 3** *Perf. 13½*
*665* A123 5c on 50c multi 5 5
*666* A122 10c on 65c multi 5 5

Natl. Independence, 25th Anniv. — A157

**Wmk. 352**

**1987, July 27** **Litho.** *Perf. 14*
*667* A157 55c Flag, sunset 20 20
*668* A157 70c Flag, horiz. 25 25

Marcus Mosiah Garvey (1887-1940), Natl. Hero, and Natl. Colors — A158

**1987, Aug. 17**
*669* A158 25c Portrait 12 12
*670* A158 25c Statue 12 12

Printed se-tenant in a continuous design.

Salvation Army in Jamaica, Cent. A159

Designs: 25c, School for the Blind. 55c, Col. Mary Booth, Bramwell-Booth Memorial Hall. $3, "War Chariot," 1929. $5, Arrival of col. Abram Davey on the S.S. Alene, 1887.

**1987, Oct. 8** *Perf. 13*
*671* A159 25c multi 10 10
*672* A159 55c multi 22 22
*673* A159 $3 multi 1.20 1.20
*674* A159 $5 multi 2.00 2.00
*a* Souv. sheet of 4, Nos. 671-674 3.55 3.55

No. 674a has vermilion and black inscribed margin. Size: 100x80mm.

Flower Type of 1986

**1987, Nov. 30** **Litho.** *Perf. 14½*
*675* A153 20c Hibiscus hybrid 8 8
*676* A153 25c Hibiscus elatus 10 10
*677* A153 $4 Hibiscus cannabinus 1.50 1.50
*678* A153 $5 Hibiscus rosa sinensis 1.85 1.85

Christmas. Nos. 675-678 vert.

Birds — A160

Designs: No. 679, Chestnut-bellied cuckoo, black-billed parrot, Jamaican euphonia. No. 680, Jamaican white-eyed vireo, rufous-throated solitaire, yellow-crowned elaenia. No. 681, Snowy plover, little blue heron, great white heron. No. 682, Common stilt, snowy egret, black-crowned night heron.

**1988, Jan. 22** **Litho.** *Perf. 14*
*679* A160 45c multi 18 18
*680* A160 45c multi 18 18
*681* A160 $5 multi 1.85 1.85
*682* A160 $5 multi 1.85 1.85

Stamps of the same denomination printed se-tenant in continuous designs.

Marine Mammals A161

**1988, Apr. 14** **Litho.** *Perf. 14*
*683* A161 20c Blue whales 8 8
*684* A161 25c Gervais's whales 10 10
*685* A161 55c Killer whales 20 20
*686* A161 $5 Common dolphins 1.80 1.80

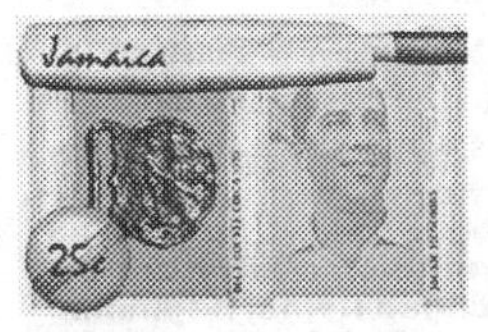
Cricket A162

Bat, wicket posts, ball, 18th cent. belt buckle and batsmen: 25c, Jackie Hendriks. 55c, George Headley. $2, Michael Holding. $3, R.K. Nunes. $4, Allan Rae.

**1988, June 6** **Litho.** *Perf. 14*
*687* A162 25c multi 10 10
*688* A162 55c multi 20 20
*689* A162 $2 multi 75 75
*690* A162 $3 multi 1.10 1.10
*691* A162 $4 multi 1.45 1.45
*Nos. 687-691 (5)* 3.60 3.60

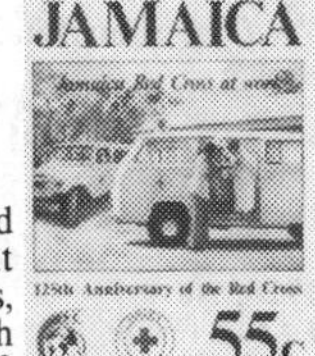
Intl. Red Cross and Red Crescent Organizations, 125th Annivs. — A163

Anniversary emblem, Jamaica Red Cross emblem and: 55c, Ambulances. $5, Jean-Henri Dunant, 1828-1910, treating the wounded after the Battle of Solferino, 1859.

**1988, Aug. 8** **Litho.** *Perf. 14½*
*692* A163 55c multi 20 20
*693* A163 $5 multi 1.85 1.85

1988 Summer Olympics, Seoul A164

**1988, Aug. 24** **Wmk. 352** *Perf. 14*
*694* A164 25c Boxing 10 10
*695* A164 45c Cycling 18 18
*696* A164 $4 Women's running 1.50 1.50
*697* A164 $5 Hurdling 1.90 1.90
*a.* Souv. sheet of 4, Nos. 694-697 3.75 3.75

No. 697a has multicolored decorative margin. Sold for $9.90. Size: 128x88mm.

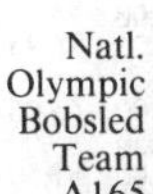

Natl. Olympic Bobsled Team A165

**1988, Nov. 4** **Litho.** *Perf. 14*
*698* A165 25c Team members 10 10
*699* A165 25c Two-man bobsled 10 10
*700* A165 $5 Team members, diff. 1.85 1.85
*701* A165 $5 Four-man bobsled 1.85 1.85

Nos. 698-699 and 700-701 are printed se-tenant in continuous designs.

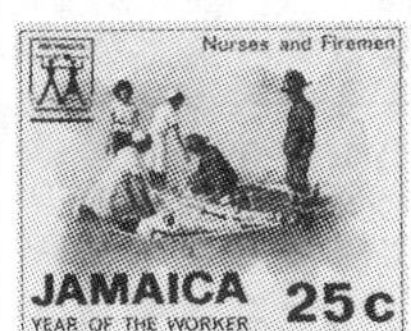
Labor Year — A166

*Perf. 14½x14*

**1988, Nov. 24** **Litho.** **Wmk. 352**
*702* A166 25c Medicine, fire fighting 10 10
*703* A166 55c Handicrafts 20 20
*704* A166 $3 Garment industry 1.10 1.10
*705* A166 $5 Fishing 1.85 1.85

Flower Type of 1986

**1988, Dec. 15**
*706* A153 25c Euphorbia pulcherrima, vert. 10 10
*707* A153 55c Spathodea campanulata 20 20
*708* A153 $3 Hylocereus triangularis, vert. 1.10 1.10
*709* A153 $4 Broughtonia sanguinea 1.50 1.50

Christmas.

Methodist Church in Jamaica, Bicent. — A167

Designs: 25c, Old York Castle School. 45c, Parade Chapel, Kingston, and Rev. Thomas Coke. $5, Fr. Hugh Sherlock and St. John's Church.

**1989, Jan. 19** *Perf.*
*710* A167 25c multi 10 10
*711* A167 45c multi 18 18
*712* A167 $5 multi 1.85 1.85

## SEMI-POSTAL STAMPS

Native Girl — SP1

Native Boy — SP2

Native Boy and Girl — SP3

**1923, Nov. 1** **Engr.** *Perf. 12*
*B1* SP1 ½p grn & blk 2.50 *3.50*
*B2* SP2 1p car & blk 4.75 *7.00*
*B3* SP3 2½p bl & blk 14.00 *20.00*

Each stamp was sold for ½p over face value. The surtax benefited the Child Saving League of Jamaica.

Nos. 694-697 Surcharged "HURRICANE GILBERT RELIEF FUND" and New Value in Black.

**Wmk. 352**

**1988, Nov. 11 Litho. *Perf. 14***

| | | | | |
|---|---|---|---|---|
| *B4* | A164 | 25c +25c multi | 18 | 18 |
| a. | | Red surcharge | 18 | 18 |
| *B5* | A164 | 45c +45c multi | 32 | 32 |
| a. | | Red surcharge | 32 | 32 |
| *B6* | A164 | $4 +$4 multi | 2.90 | 2.90 |
| a. | | Red surcharge | 2.90 | 2.90 |
| *B7* | A164 | $5 +$5 multi | 3.60 | 3.60 |
| a. | | Red surcharge | 3.60 | 3.60 |

## WAR TAX STAMPS

Regular Issues of 1906-19 Overprinted WAR STAMP.

**1916 Wmk. 3 *Perf. 14***

| | | | | |
|---|---|---|---|---|
| *MR1* | A14 | ½p green | 10 | 5 |
| a. | | Without period | 11.00 | 9.50 |
| b. | | Double overprint | 100.00 | 100.00 |
| c. | | Inverted overprint | 62.50 | 62.50 |
| d. | | As "c", without period | 350.00 | |
| *MR2* | A17 | 3p vio, *yel* | 5.50 | 8.25 |
| a. | | Without period | 21.00 | 30.00 |

**Surface-colored Paper**

| | | | | |
|---|---|---|---|---|
| *MR3* | A17 | 3p vio, *yel* | 1.40 | 1.50 |

Regular Issues of 1906-18 Overprinted WAR STAMP.

| | | | | |
|---|---|---|---|---|
| *MR4* | A14 | ½p green | 18 | 10 |
| a. | | Without period | 11.00 | 11.00 |
| b. | | Pair, one without overprint | 475.00 | 375.00 |
| c. | | "R" inserted by hand | 300.00 | 210.00 |
| d. | | "WAR" only | 125.00 | |
| *MR5* | A17 | 1½p orange | 16 | 6 |
| a. | | Without period | 6.75 | 6.50 |
| b. | | "TAMP" | 57.50 | 57.50 |
| c. | | "S" inserted by hand | 225.00 | |
| d. | | "R" omitted | 400.00 | 350.00 |
| e. | | "R" inserted by hand | 250.00 | 200.00 |
| *MR6* | A17 | 3p vio, *yel* | 38 | 40 |
| a. | | Without period | 17.00 | 17.00 |
| b. | | "TAMP" | 225.00 | 140.00 |
| c. | | "S" inserted by hand | 150.00 | 140.00 |
| d. | | Inverted ovpt. | 250.00 | 175.00 |
| e. | | As "a", inverted | | |

Regular Issues of 1906-19 Overprinted WAR STAMP.

**1917, Mar.**

| | | | | |
|---|---|---|---|---|
| *MR7* | A14 | ½p green | 10 | 8 |
| a. | | Without period | 7.50 | 6.00 |
| b. | | Overprinted on back instead of face | 90.00 | |
| c. | | Inverted overprint | 13.00 | 10.00 |
| *MR8* | A17 | 1½p orange | 8 | 5 |
| a. | | Without period | 7.00 | 5.25 |
| b. | | Double overprint | 80.00 | 80.00 |
| c. | | Inverted overprint | 80.00 | 80.00 |
| d. | | As "a", inverted | | |
| *MR9* | A17 | 3p vio, *yel* | 22 | 22 |
| a. | | Without period | 13.00 | 12.00 |
| b. | | Vertical overprint | 225.00 | 225.00 |
| c. | | Inverted overprint | 175.00 | |
| d. | | As "a", inverted | | |

There are many minor varieties of Nos. MR1-MR9.

Regular Issues of 1906-19 Overprinted in Red WAR STAMP

**1919, Oct. 4**

| | | | | |
|---|---|---|---|---|
| *MR10* | A14 | ½p green | 8 | 5 |
| *MR11* | A17 | 3p vio, *yel* | 22 | 18 |

## OFFICIAL STAMPS

No. 16 Overprinted in Black OFFICIAL

Type I. Word 15 to 16mm long.
Type II. Word 17 to 17½mm long.

**1890 Wmk. 2 *Perf. 14***

| | | | | |
|---|---|---|---|---|
| *O1* | A7 | ½p grn (II) | 8.50 | 60 |
| a. | | Type I | 21.00 | 21.00 |
| b. | | Inverted overprint (II) | 95.00 | 95.00 |
| c. | | Double ovpt. (II) | 95.00 | 95.00 |
| d. | | Double overprint one inverted (II) | 425.00 | 425.00 |
| e. | | Double ovpt., one vertical (II) | 1,100. | |
| f. | | Double ovpt. (I) | 650.00 | |

No. 16 and Type of 1889 Overprinted OFFICIAL

**1890-91**

| | | | | |
|---|---|---|---|---|
| *O2* | A7 | ½p green | 95 | 12 |
| *O3* | A10 | 1p car rose | 1.25 | 10 |
| *O4* | A10 | 2p slate | 1.75 | 25 |

# JORDAN

## Trans-Jordan

LOCATION — In the Near East, separated from the Mediterranean Sea by Israel.
GOVT. — Kingdom.
AREA — 38,400 sq. mi.
POP. — 3,750,000 (est. 1982).
CAPITAL — Amman.

The former Turkish territory was mandated to Great Britain following World War I. It became an independent state in 1946.

10 Milliemes = 1 Piastre
1000 Mils = 1 Palestine Pound (1930)
1000 Fils = 1 Jordan Dinar (1951)

**Catalogue values for unused stamps in this country are for Never Hinged items, beginning with Scott 221 in the regular postage section, Scott C1 in the air post section, Scott J47 in the postage due section, Scott RA1 in the postal tax section, Scott N1 in the occupation section, Scott NJ1 in the occupation postage due section, and Scott NRA1 in the occupation postal tax section.**

**British Mandate**

Stamps and Type of Palestine 1918 Overprinted in Black or Silver

شرقي الاردن

***Perf. 14, 15x14***

**1920, Nov. Wmk. 33**

| | | | | |
|---|---|---|---|---|
| *1* | A1 | 1m dk brn | 14 | 28 |
| a | | Inverted ovpt. | 87.50 | 87.50 |
| b | | Perf. 15x14 | 25 | 38 |
| c | | As "b", inverted overprint | 75.00 | 65.00 |
| *2* | A1 | 2m bl grn | 14 | 20 |
| a | | Perf. 15x14 | 1.90 | 2.25 |
| *3* | A1 | 3m lt brn | 20 | 30 |
| a | | Perf. 14 | 2.75 | 3.25 |
| *4* | A1 | 4m scarlet | 30 | 38 |
| a | | Perf. 14 | 5.00 | 6.25 |
| *5* | A1 | 5m orange | 30 | 25 |
| a | | Perf. 15x14 | 50 | 65 |
| *6* | A1 | 1pi dk bl (S) | 35 | 45 |
| *7* | A1 | 2pi ol grn | 90 | 90 |
| a | | Perf. 15x14 | 1.10 | 1.25 |
| *8* | A1 | 5pi plum | 1.00 | 2.00 |
| a | | Perf. 15x14 | 7.50 | 10.00 |
| *9* | A1 | 9pi bister | 2.50 | 3.50 |
| a | | Perf. 15x14 | 875.00 | 875.00 |
| *10* | A1 | 10pi ultra | 2.75 | 5.00 |
| *11* | A1 | 20pi gray | 4.25 | 6.25 |
| | | *Nos. 1-11 (11)* | 12.83 | 19.51 |

The overprint reads "Sharqi al-ardan" (East of Jordan).

Stamps of 1920 Issue Handstamp Surcharged "Ashir el qirsh" (tenth of piaster) and numeral in Black, Red or Violet

**1922**

| | | | | |
|---|---|---|---|---|
| *12* | A1 | 1/10pi on 1m dk brn | 17.50 | 20.00 |
| *13* | A1 | 1/10pi on 1m dk brn (R) | 67.50 | 67.50 |
| *13A* | A1 | 1/10pi on 1m dk brn (V) | 67.50 | 67.50 |
| *14* | A1 | 2/10pi on 2m bl grn | 17.50 | 20.00 |
| a | | 3/10pi on 2m bl grn (error) | 75.00 | 75.00 |
| *15* | A1 | 2/10pi on 2m bl grn (R) | 75.00 | 60.00 |
| *16* | A1 | 2/10pi on 2m bl grn (V) | 75.00 | 75.00 |
| *17* | A1 | 3/10pi on 3m lt brn | 6.25 | 6.25 |
| *17A* | A1 | 3/10pi on 3m lt brn (V) | 165.00 | 165.00 |
| *18* | A1 | 4/10pi on 4m scar | 32.50 | 35.00 |
| *19* | A1 | 5/10pi on 5m org | 100.00 | 87.50 |
| c | | Perf. 15x14 | 140.00 | 140.00 |
| *19A* | A1 | 5/10pi on 5m dp org (R) | 225.00 | |
| *19B* | A1 | 5/10pi on 5m org (V) | 225.00 | |

Handstamp Surcharged "El qirsh" (piaster) and numeral in Black, Red or Violet

| | | | | |
|---|---|---|---|---|
| *20* | A1 | 1pi dk bl (R) | 87.50 | 42.50 |
| *20A* | A1 | 1pi dk bl (V) | 180.00 | 175.00 |
| *21* | A1 | 2pi ol grn (Bk) | 150.00 | 22.50 |
| *22* | A1 | 2pi ol grn (R) | 150.00 | 42.50 |
| *22A* | A1 | 2pi ol grn (V) | 165.00 | 55.00 |
| *23* | A1 | 5pi plum (Bk) | 30.00 | 32.50 |
| *23A* | A1 | 5pi plum (V) | *250.00* | |
| *24* | A1 | 9pi bis (Bk) | 150.00 | 145.00 |
| *25* | A1 | 9pi bis (R) | 60.00 | 62.50 |
| a | | Perf. 14 | 175.00 | 175.00 |
| *26* | A1 | 10pi ultra (Bk) | 625.00 | 625.00 |
| *27* | A1 | 20pi gray (Bk) | 525.00 | 525.00 |
| *27A* | A1 | 20pi gray (V) | 625.00 | 625.00 |

**Same Surcharge in Black on Palestine Nos. 13-14.**

| | | | | |
|---|---|---|---|---|
| *28* | A1 | 10pi on 10pi ultra | *1,750.* | |
| *29* | A1 | 20pi on 20pi gray | *1,750.* | |

Stamps of 1920 Handstamped in Violet, Black or Red

**1922, Dec. *Perf. 15x14, 14***

| | | | | |
|---|---|---|---|---|
| *30* | A1 | 1m dk brn (V) | 15.00 | 15.00 |
| *31* | A1 | 1m dk brn (Bk) | 15.00 | 15.00 |
| *32* | A1 | 1m dk brn (R) | 6.00 | 6.00 |
| *33* | A1 | 2m bl grn (V) | 3.00 | 3.00 |
| *34* | A1 | 2m bl grn (Bk) | 4.50 | 4.50 |
| *35* | A1 | 2m bl grn (R) | 15.00 | 15.00 |
| *36* | A1 | 3m lt brn (V) | 3.75 | 3.75 |
| *37* | A1 | 3m lt brn (Bk) | 4.50 | 4.50 |
| *38* | A1 | 3m lt brn (R) | 17.50 | 17.50 |
| *39* | A1 | 4m scar (V) | 32.50 | 32.50 |
| *39A* | A1 | 4m scar (Bk) | 32.50 | 32.50 |
| *40* | A1 | 4m scar (R) | 32.50 | 32.50 |
| *41* | A1 | 5m org (V) | 8.25 | 8.25 |
| *42* | A1 | 5m org (R) | 22.50 | 19.00 |
| a | | Perf. 14 | 225.00 | 55.00 |
| *43* | A1 | 1pi dk bl (V) | 8.25 | 8.25 |
| *44* | A1 | 1pi dk bl (R) | 14.00 | 14.00 |
| *45* | A1 | 2pi ol grn (V) | 14.00 | 11.50 |
| a | | Perf. 14 | 47.50 | 47.50 |
| *46* | A1 | 2pi ol grn (Bk) | 7.50 | 7.50 |
| *47* | A1 | 2pi ol grn (R) | 40.00 | 40.00 |
| *48* | A1 | 5pi plum (V) | 37.50 | 37.50 |
| a | | Perf. 14 | 67.50 | 67.50 |
| *49* | A1 | 5pi plum (R) | 60.00 | 60.00 |
| *50* | A1 | 9pi bis (V) | 125.00 | 125.00 |
| *50A* | A1 | 9pi bis (Bk) | 45.00 | 45.00 |
| *50B* | A1 | 9pi bis (R) | 225.00 | 225.00 |
| *51* | A1 | 10pi ultra (V) | 725.00 | 750.00 |
| *51A* | A1 | 10pi ultra (R) | *1,350.* | *1,350.* |
| *52* | A1 | 20pi gray (V) | 725.00 | 725.00 |
| *52A* | A1 | 20pi gray (R) | *1,500.* | *1,500.* |

The overprint reads "Hukumat al Sharqi al Arabia" (Arab Government of the East) and date, 1923. The surcharges or overprints on Nos. 12 to 52A inclusive are handstamped and, as usual, are found inverted and double.

Ink pads of several colors were in use at the same time and the surcharges and overprints frequently show a mixture of two colors.

Stamps of 1920 Overprinted in Gold

حكومة الشرق
العربية
نيسان سنة ٩٢١

**1923, Mar. 1 *Perf. 14, 15x14***

| | | | | |
|---|---|---|---|---|
| *53* | A1 | 1m dk brn (G) | 8.75 | 10.00 |
| a | | Perf. 15x14 | 875.00 | 875.00 |
| *54* | A1 | 2m bl grn (G) | 10.00 | 15.00 |
| a | | Double overprint | 200.00 | |
| b | | Inverted ovpt. | 200.00 | |
| *55* | A1 | 3m lt brn (G) | 6.00 | 7.00 |
| a | | blk overprint | 50.00 | 50.00 |
| *56* | A1 | 4m scar (Bk) | 6.00 | 6.00 |
| *57* | A1 | 5m org (Bk) | 6.00 | 6.00 |
| a | | Perf. 15x14 | 25.00 | 25.00 |
| *58* | A1 | 1pi dk bl (G) | 6.00 | 6.00 |
| a | | Double overprint | 300.00 | 300.00 |
| b | | blk ovpt. | *300.00* | *300.00* |
| *59* | A1 | 2pi ol grn (G) | 7.50 | 7.50 |
| a | | blk overprint | 200.00 | |
| b | | Ovpt. on back | 175.00 | |
| *60* | A1 | 5pi plum (G) | 27.50 | 30.00 |
| a | | Invtd. overprint | 225.00 | 175.00 |
| b | | "922" for "921" | | |
| *61* | A1 | 9pi bis (Bk) | 32.50 | 40.00 |
| a | | Perf. 15x14 | *200.00* | *200.00* |
| *62* | A1 | 10pi ultra (G) | 40.00 | 42.50 |
| *63* | A1 | 20pi gray (G) | 40.00 | 42.50 |
| a | | Inverted ovpt. | 300.00 | |
| b | | Double overprint | 350.00 | |

| | | | | |
|---|---|---|---|---|
| c | | Double overprint, one inverted | 500.00 | |

The overprint reads "Hukumat al Sharqi al Arabia, Nissan Sanat 921" (Arab Government of the East, April, 1921).

Coat of Arms (Hejaz A7)

حكومة

Stamps of Hejaz, 1922, Overprinted in Black

الشرق العربيه
٩ شعبان ١٣٤١

**1923, April Unwmk. *Perf. 11½***

| | | | | |
|---|---|---|---|---|
| *64* | A7 | 1/8pi org brn | 1.40 | 1.50 |
| a | | Double ovpt. | 100.00 | |
| *65* | A7 | ½pi red | 1.40 | 50 |
| a | | Inverted ovpt. | 100.00 | |
| *66* | A7 | 1pi dk bl | 28 | 28 |
| a | | Inverted overprint | 105.00 | |
| *67* | A7 | 1½pi violet | 45 | 50 |
| a | | Double ovpt. | 125.00 | |
| *68* | A7 | 2pi orange | 45 | 50 |
| a | | Inverted ovpt. | | |
| b | | Pair, one without overprint | | |
| *69* | A7 | 3pi ol brn | 1.10 | 1.40 |
| a | | Inverted ovpt. | 125.00 | |
| b | | Double ovpt. | 150.00 | |
| c | | Pair, one without overprint | *300.00* | |
| *70* | A7 | 5pi ol grn | 1.90 | 2.25 |
| | | *Nos. 64-70 (7)* | 6.98 | 6.93 |

The overprint is similar to that on the preceding group but is differently arranged. There are numerous varieties in the Arabic letters.

With Additional Surcharge of New Value in Arabic:

a b

| | | | | |
|---|---|---|---|---|
| *71* | A7 (a) | 1/4pi on 1/8pi org brn | 2.50 | 2.75 |
| a | | Inverted surch. | 100.00 | |
| *72* | A7 (b) | 10pi on 5pi ol grn | 5.00 | 6.25 |

**Independence Issue.**

Palestine Stamps and Type of 1918 Overprinted Vertically in Black or Gold

**1923, May Wmk. 33 *Perf. 15x14***

| | | | | |
|---|---|---|---|---|
| *73* | A1 | 1m dk brn (Bk) | 7.00 | 8.00 |
| a | | Double overprint, one reversed | 425.00 | 425.00 |
| *73B* | A1 | 1m dk brn (G) | 190.00 | 190.00 |
| c | | Double overprint, one reversed | 625.00 | 625.00 |
| *74* | A1 | 2m bl grn | 22.50 | 24.50 |
| *75* | A1 | 3m lt brn | 5.00 | 5.50 |
| *76* | A1 | 4m scarlet | 5.00 | 5.50 |
| *77* | A1 | 5m orange | 37.50 | 40.00 |
| *78* | A1 | 1pi dk bl (G) | 37.50 | 40.00 |
| a | | Double overprint | 500.00 | 500.00 |
| *79* | A1 | 2pi ol grn | 37.50 | 40.00 |
| *80* | A1 | 5pi plum (G) | 37.50 | 40.00 |
| a | | Double overprint | *360.00* | |
| *81* | A1 | 9pi bis, perf. 14 | 37.50 | 40.00 |
| *82* | A1 | 10pi ultra, perf. 14 | 37.50 | 40.00 |
| *83* | A1 | 20pi gray | 37.50 | 40.00 |

The overprint reads, "Arab Government of the East (abbreviated), Souvenir of Independence, 25th, May, 1923 ('923')".

There were printed 480 complete sets and a rger number of the 1, 2, 3 and 4m. A large ımber of these sets were distributed to high ficials. The overprint was in a setting of venty-four and the error "933" instead of )23" occurs once in the setting.

The overprint exists reading downward on ll values, as illustrated, and reading upward ı all except the 5m and 2pi.

Stamps of Preceding Issues, Handstamp Surcharged

| No. | Type | Description | Unused | Used |
|---|---|---|---|---|
| 3A | A1 | 2½ /10pi on 5m dp org | 125.00 | 140.00 |
| 3B | A1 | ⁵⁄₁₀pi on 3m lt brn (#17) | 8,000. | |
| 4 | A1 | ⁵⁄₁₀pi on 3m lt brn (#36) | 20.00 | 20.00 |
| 5 | A1 | ⁵⁄₁₀pi on 3m lt brn (#55) | 8.75 | 8.75 |
| 6 | A1 | ⁵⁄₁₀pi on 5pi plum (#23) | 42.50 | 42.50 |
| 7 | A1 | ⁵⁄₁₀pi on 5pi plum (#48) | 4.00 | 4.00 |
| 8 | A1 | 1pi on 5pi plum (#23) | 42.50 | 42.50 |
| 9 | A1 | 1pi on 5pi plum (#48) | 1,500. | |

**Same Surcharge on Palestine Stamp of 1918.**

| No. | Type | Description | Unused | Used |
|---|---|---|---|---|
| 0 | A1 | ⁵⁄₁₀pi on 3m lt brn | 6,500. | |

As is usual with handstamped surcharges these are found double, inverted, etc.

No. 67 Surcharged by Handstamp

نصف قرش

**Unwmk.** *Perf. 11½.*

| No. | Type | Description | Unused | Used |
|---|---|---|---|---|
| 1 | A7 | ½pi on 1½pi vio | 3.50 | 3.75 |
| a. | | Surcharge typographed | 30.00 | 32.50 |

The surcharge reads: "Nusf el qirsh" (half piastre). See note after No. 90.

Stamps of Preceding Issues Surcharged by Handstamp

*Perf. 14, 15x14*

**1923, Nov.** **Wmk. 33**

| No. | Type | Description | Unused | Used |
|---|---|---|---|---|
| 92 | A1 | ½pi on 2pi ol grn (No. 45) | 45.00 | 45.00 |
| 93 | A1 | ½pi on 2pi ol grn (No. 47) | 87.50 | 87.50 |
| 94 | A1 | ½pi on 5pi plum (No. 23) | 27.50 | 27.50 |
| 95 | A1 | ½pi on 5pi plum (No. 48) | 2,250. | 2,000. |
| 96 | A1 | ½pi on 5pi plum (No. 49) | 1,900. | 1,750. |
| 97 | A1 | ½pi on 9pi bis (No. 24) | 6,500. | |
| 98 | A1 | ½pi on 9pi bis (No. 25) | 87.50 | 87.50 |
| 99 | A1 | ½pi on 9pi bis (No. 61) | 165.00 | 165.00 |

Surcharged by Handstamp

| No. | Type | Description | Unused | Used |
|---|---|---|---|---|
| 100 | A1 | 1pi on 10 pi ultra (No. 62) | 2,000. | 2,000. |
| 101 | A1 | 1pi on 10pi ultra (No. 82) | 3,000. | 3,000. |
| 102 | A1 | 2pi on 20pi gray (No. 63) | 22.50 | 24.00 |

Stamp of Hejaz, 1922, Overprinted by Handstamp

**1923, Dec.** **Unwmk.** *Perf. 11½.*

| No. | Type | Description | Unused | Used |
|---|---|---|---|---|
| 103 | A7 | ½pi red | 3.00 | 3.25 |

Stamp of Hejaz, 1922, Overprinted

**1924**

| No. | Type | Description | Unused | Used |
|---|---|---|---|---|
| 104 | A7 | ½pi red | 3.25 | 3.75 |

**King Hussein Issue.**

Stamps of Hejaz, 1922, Overprinted

**1924**

**Gold Overprint.**

| No. | Type | Description | Unused | Used |
|---|---|---|---|---|
| 105 | A7 | ½pi red | 1.25 | 1.25 |
| 106 | A7 | 1pi dk bl | 1.75 | 1.75 |
| 107 | A7 | 1½pi violet | 1.50 | 1.50 |
| 108 | A7 | 2pi orange | 2.00 | 2.00 |

**Black Overprint.**

| No. | Type | Description | Unused | Used |
|---|---|---|---|---|
| 109 | A7 | ½pi red | 65 | 65 |
| 110 | A7 | 1pi dk bl | 75 | 75 |
| 111 | A7 | 1½pi violet | 90 | 90 |
| 112 | A7 | 2pi orange | 1.00 | 1.00 |
| | | *Nos. 105-112 (8)* | 9.80 | 9.80 |

The overprint reads: "Arab Government of the East. In commemoration of the visit of H. M. the King of the Arabs, 11 Jemad el Than i 1342 (17th Jan. 1924)." The overprint was in a setting of thirty-six and the error "432" instead of "342" occurs once in the setting and is found on all values.

Coat of Arms (Hejaz A8)

Stamps of Hejaz, 1922-24, Overprinted in Black or Red

حكومة الشرق العربي ١٣٤٢

**1924**

| No. | Type | Description | Unused | Used |
|---|---|---|---|---|
| 113 | A7 | ⅛pi red brn | 20 | 15 |
| 114 | A7 | ¼pi yel grn | 15 | 15 |
| a. | | Tete beche pair | 2.00 | 2.00 |
| 115 | A7 | ½pi red | 10 | 8 |
| 116 | A7 | 1pi dk bl | 2.50 | 2.50 |
| 117 | A7 | 1½pi violet | 1.40 | 1.40 |
| 118 | A7 | 2pi orange | 75 | 75 |
| 119 | A7 | 3pi red brn | 50 | 50 |
| 120 | A7 | 5pi ol grn | 75 | 75 |
| 121 | A8 | 10pi vio & dk brn (R) | 1.10 | 1.40 |
| a. | | Pair, one without overprint | | |
| | | *Nos. 113-121 (9)* | 7.45 | 7.68 |

The overprint reads: "Hukumat al Sharqi al Arabia, 1342." (Arab Government of the East, 1924).

(Hejaz A9)

(Hejaz A10)

(Hejaz A11)

Stamps of Hejaz, 1925, Overprinted in Black or Red

**1925, Aug.**

| No. | Type | Description | Unused | Used |
|---|---|---|---|---|
| 122 | A9 | ⅛pi chocolate | 12 | 12 |
| 123 | A9 | ¼pi ultra | 12 | 12 |
| 124 | A9 | ½pi car rose | 15 | 15 |
| 125 | A10 | 1pi yel grn | 15 | 15 |
| 126 | A10 | 1½pi orange | 20 | 20 |
| 127 | A10 | 2pi dp bl | 25 | 25 |
| 128 | A11 | 3pi dk grn (R) | 38 | 38 |
| 129 | A11 | 5pi org brn | 75 | 75 |
| | | *Nos. 122-129 (8)* | 2.12 | 2.12 |

The overprint reads: "Hukumat al Sharqi al Arabi. 1343 Sanat." (Arab Government of the East, 1925). Nos. 122-129 exist imperforate, and with overprint inverted or double. Value 75-cents each.

Type of Palestine, 1918, Overprinted in Black

شرق الاردن

**1925, Nov. 1** **Wmk. 4** *Perf 14*

| No. | Type | Description | Unused | Used |
|---|---|---|---|---|
| 130 | A1 | 1m dk brn | 8 | 8 |
| 131 | A1 | 2m yellow | 5 | 5 |
| 132 | A1 | 3m Prus bl | 6 | 6 |
| 133 | A1 | 4m rose | 6 | 6 |
| 134 | A1 | 5m orange | 6 | 6 |
| 135 | A1 | 6m bl grn | 10 | 10 |
| 136 | A1 | 7m yel brn | 10 | 10 |
| 137 | A1 | 8m red | 15 | 15 |
| 138 | A1 | 1pi gray | 20 | 12 |
| 139 | A1 | 13m ultra | 20 | 22 |
| 140 | A1 | 2pi ol grn | 30 | 35 |
| 141 | A1 | 5pi plum | 65 | 75 |
| 142 | A1 | 9pi bister | 2.50 | 2.00 |
| a. | | Perf. 15x14 | 550.00 | 400.00 |
| 143 | A1 | 10pi lt bl | 2.00 | 1.50 |
| a. | | Perf. 15x14 | 45.00 | 50.00 |
| 144 | A1 | 20pi violet | 5.00 | 4.25 |
| a. | | Perf. 15x14 | 750.00 | 500.00 |
| | | *Nos. 130-144 (15)* | 11.51 | 9.85 |

This overprint reads: "Sharqi al-ardan" (East of Jordan).

Amir Abdullah ibn Hussein

A1 A2

**1927-29** **Engr.** *Perf. 14.*

| No. | Type | Description | Unused | Used |
|---|---|---|---|---|
| 145 | A1 | 2(m) Prus bl | 7 | 6 |
| 146 | A1 | 3(m) rose | 10 | 6 |
| 147 | A1 | 4(m) green | 25 | 22 |
| 148 | A1 | 5(m) orange | 12 | 8 |
| 149 | A1 | 10(m) red | 15 | 18 |
| 150 | A1 | 15(m) ultra | 30 | 12 |
| 151 | A1 | 20(m) ol grn | 50 | 65 |
| 152 | A2 | 50(m) claret | 1.00 | 1.10 |
| 153 | A2 | 90(m) bister | 3.00 | 3.00 |
| 154 | A2 | 100(m) lt bl | 3.00 | 2.25 |
| 155 | A2 | 200(m) violet | 6.50 | 5.00 |
| 156 | A2 | 500(m) dp brn ('29) | 30.00 | 20.00 |
| 157 | A2 | 1000(m) gray ('29) | 75.00 | 10.00 |
| | | *Nos. 145-157 (13)* | 119.99 | 42.72 |

Stamps of 1927 Overprinted in Black

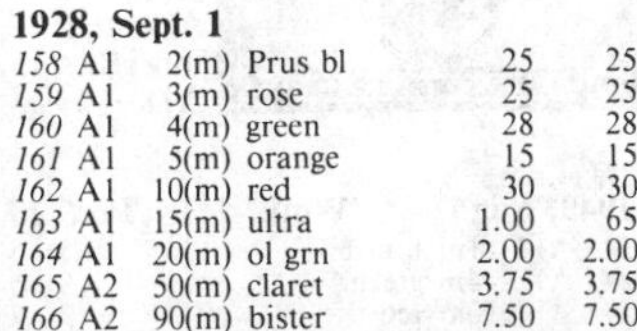

**1928, Sept. 1**

| No. | Type | Description | Unused | Used |
|---|---|---|---|---|
| 158 | A1 | 2(m) Prus bl | 25 | 25 |
| 159 | A1 | 3(m) rose | 25 | 25 |
| 160 | A1 | 4(m) green | 28 | 28 |
| 161 | A1 | 5(m) orange | 15 | 15 |
| 162 | A1 | 10(m) red | 30 | 30 |
| 163 | A1 | 15(m) ultra | 1.00 | 65 |
| 164 | A1 | 20(m) ol grn | 2.00 | 2.00 |
| 165 | A2 | 50(m) claret | 3.75 | 3.75 |
| 166 | A2 | 90(m) bister | 7.50 | 7.50 |
| 167 | A2 | 100(m) lt bl | 10.00 | 10.00 |
| 168 | A2 | 200(m) violet | 25.00 | 25.00 |
| | | *Nos. 158-168 (11)* | 50.48 | 50.13 |

The overprint is the Arabic word "Dastour," meaning "Constitution." The stamps were in commemoration of the enactment of the law setting forth the Constitution.

A3

"MILS" or "L. P." at lower right and Arabic equivalents at upper left.

Size: 17¼x21mm.

**1930-36** **Engr.** *Perf. 14*

| No. | Type | Description | Unused | Used |
|---|---|---|---|---|
| 169 | A3 | 1m red brn ('34) | 8 | 5 |
| 170 | A3 | 2m Prus bl | 6 | 5 |
| 171 | A3 | 3m rose | 8 | 8 |
| 172 | A3 | 3m grn ('34) | 42 | 14 |
| 173 | A3 | 4m green | 9 | 9 |
| 174 | A3 | 4m rose ('34) | 55 | 12 |
| 175 | A3 | 5m orange | 9 | 8 |
| a. | | Perf. 13½x14 (coil) ('36) | 2.00 | 55 |
| 176 | A3 | 10m red | 14 | 14 |
| 177 | A3 | 15m ultra | 25 | 16 |
| a. | | Perf. 13½x14 (coil) ('36) | 2.00 | 70 |
| 178 | A3 | 20m ol grn | 38 | 15 |

**Size: 19¼x23½mm.**

| No. | Type | Description | Unused | Used |
|---|---|---|---|---|
| 179 | A3 | 50m red vio | 38 | 32 |
| 180 | A3 | 90m bister | 55 | 50 |
| 181 | A3 | 100m lt bl | 1.10 | 1.00 |
| 182 | A3 | 200m violet | 1.90 | 1.50 |
| 183 | A3 | 500m dp brn | 8.75 | 4.00 |
| 184 | A3 | £1 gray | 20.00 | 7.50 |
| | | *Nos. 169-184 (16)* | 34.82 | 15.88 |

See also Nos. 199-220, 230-235.

**1939** *Perf. 13½x13*

**Size: 17¼x21mm.**

| No. | Type | Description | Unused | Used |
|---|---|---|---|---|
| 169a | A3 | 1m red brn | 25 | 12 |
| 170a | A3 | 2m Prus bl | 25 | 8 |
| 172a | A3 | 3m green | 65 | 25 |
| 174a | A3 | 4m rose | 3.00 | 2.50 |
| 175b | A3 | 5m orange | 5.00 | 35 |
| 176a | A3 | 10m red | 20.00 | 1.00 |
| 177b | A3 | 15m ultra | 65 | 30 |
| 178a | A3 | 20m ol grn | 9.00 | 3.00 |
| | | *Nos. 169a-178a (8)* | 38.80 | 7.60 |

Mushetta — A4

Nymphaeum, Jerash — A5

Kasr Kharana — A6

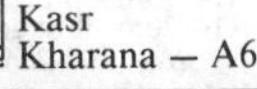

Kerak Castle — A7

Temple of Artemis, Jerash — A8

The first price column gives the catalogue value of an unused stamp, the second that of a used stamp.

Aijalon Castle — A9

Khazneh, Rock-hewn Temple, Petra — A10

Amir Abdullah ibn Hussein — A13

Allenby Bridge, River Jordan — A11

Ancient Threshing Floor — A12

**1933, Feb. 1** ***Perf. 12***

| | | | | |
|---|---|---|---|---|
| *185* | A4 | 1m dk brn & blk | 15 | 20 |
| *186* | A5 | 2m cl & blk | 20 | 25 |
| *187* | A6 | 3m bl grn | 38 | 32 |
| *188* | A7 | 4m bis & blk | 38 | 38 |
| *189* | A8 | 5m org & blk | 40 | 40 |
| *190* | A9 | 10m brn red | 50 | 50 |
| *191* | A10 | 15m dl bl | 1.00 | 65 |
| *192* | A11 | 20m ol grn & blk | 1.25 | 75 |
| *193* | A12 | 50m brn vio & blk | 2.00 | 1.75 |
| *194* | A6 | 90m yel & blk | 3.25 | 2.75 |
| *195* | A8 | 100m bl & blk | 4.00 | 3.25 |
| *196* | A9 | 200m dk vio & blk | 17.50 | 22.50 |
| *197* | A10 | 500m brn & ver | 50.00 | 55.00 |
| *198* | A13 | £1 grn & blk | 225.00 | 275.00 |
| | | *Nos. 185-198 (14)* | 306.01 | 363.70 |

Nos. 194-197 are larger than the lower values in the same designs.

Amir Abdullah ibn Hussein — A14

***Perf. 13x13½***

**1942, May 18** **Litho.** **Unwmk.**

| | | | | |
|---|---|---|---|---|
| *199* | A14 | 1m dl red brn | 10 | 8 |
| *200* | A14 | 2m dl grn | 10 | 8 |
| *201* | A14 | 3m dp yel grn | 12 | 9 |
| *202* | A14 | 4m rose pink | 18 | 10 |
| *203* | A14 | 5m org yel | 20 | 12 |
| *204* | A14 | 10m dl ver | 32 | 20 |
| *205* | A14 | 15m dp bl | 40 | 20 |
| *206* | A14 | 20m dl ol grn | 65 | 50 |
| | | *Nos. 199-206 (8)* | 2.07 | 1.37 |

Type A14 differs from A3 in the redrawn inscription above the head and in the form of the "millieme" character at upper left.

Abdullah Type of 1930-39
White Paper

**1943-44** **Engr.** **Wmk. 4** ***Perf. 12***

**Size: 17¾x21½mm.**

| | | | | |
|---|---|---|---|---|
| *207* | A3 | 1m red brn | 5 | 5 |
| *208* | A3 | 2m Prus grn | 6 | 5 |
| *209* | A3 | 3m bl grn | 6 | 5 |
| *210* | A3 | 4m dp rose | 7 | 6 |
| *211* | A3 | 5m orange | 7 | 6 |
| *212* | A3 | 10m scarlet | 12 | 10 |
| *213* | A3 | 15m blue | 15 | 12 |
| *214* | A3 | 20m ol ('44) | 18 | 10 |

**Size: 20x24mm.**

| | | | | |
|---|---|---|---|---|
| *215* | A3 | 50m red lil ('44) | 22 | 20 |
| *216* | A3 | 90m ocher | 50 | 50 |
| *217* | A3 | 100m dp bl ('44) | 75 | 42 |
| *218* | A3 | 200m dk vio ('44) | 1.50 | 1.00 |
| *219* | A3 | 500m dk brn ('44) | 5.00 | 1.75 |
| *220* | A3 | £1 blk ('44) | 12.50 | 2.50 |
| | | *Nos. 207-220 (14)* | 21.23 | 6.96 |

See Nos. 230-235.

**Catalogue values for unused stamps in this section, from this point to the end of the section, are for Never Hinged items.**

**Independent Kingdom**

Symbols of Peace and Liberty — A15

***Perf. 11½***

**1946, May 25** **Unwmk.** **Litho.**

| | | | | |
|---|---|---|---|---|
| *221* | A15 | 1m sepia | 6 | 5 |
| *222* | A15 | 2m yel org | 6 | 6 |
| *223* | A15 | 3m dl ol grn | 6 | 6 |
| *224* | A15 | 4m lt vio | 6 | 6 |
| *225* | A15 | 10m org brn | 6 | 6 |
| *226* | A15 | 12m rose red | 6 | 6 |
| *227* | A15 | 20m dk bl | 7 | 7 |
| *228* | A15 | 50m ultra | 38 | 30 |
| *229* | A15 | 200m green | 65 | 65 |
| | | *Nos. 221-229 (9)* | 1.46 | 1.37 |

Issued to commemorate the independence of the Kingdom of Trans-Jordan.
Nos. 221 to 229 exist imperforate.

Abdullah Type of 1930-39.

**1947** **Wmk. 4** **Engr.** ***Perf. 12***

| | | | | |
|---|---|---|---|---|
| *230* | A3 | 3m rose car | 5 | 5 |
| *231* | A3 | 4m dp yel grn | 5 | 5 |
| *232* | A3 | 10m violet | 8 | 8 |
| *233* | A3 | 12m dp rose | 50 | 50 |
| *234* | A3 | 15m dl ol grn | 12 | 12 |
| *235* | A3 | 20m dp bl | 14 | 14 |
| | | *Nos. 230-235 (6)* | 94 | 94 |

Parliament Building, Amman A16

**1947, Nov. 1** **Engr.** **Unwmk.**

| | | | | |
|---|---|---|---|---|
| *236* | A16 | 1m purple | 6 | 6 |
| *237* | A16 | 3m red org | 6 | 6 |
| *238* | A16 | 4m yel grn | 6 | 6 |
| *239* | A16 | 10m dk vio brn | 7 | 7 |
| *240* | A16 | 12m carmine | 7 | 7 |
| *241* | A16 | 20m dp bl | 8 | 8 |
| *242* | A16 | 50m red vio | 20 | 20 |
| *243* | A16 | 100m rose | 35 | 35 |
| *244* | A16 | 200m dk grn | 75 | 75 |
| | | *Nos. 236-244 (9)* | 1.70 | 1.70 |

Issued to commemorate the founding of the new Trans-Jordan parliament, 1947.
Nos. 236 to 244 exist imperforate.

Symbols of the UPU A17

King Abdullah ibn Hussein A18

**1949, Aug. 1** **Wmk. 4** ***Perf. 13***

| | | | | |
|---|---|---|---|---|
| *245* | A17 | 1m brown | 5 | 5 |
| *246* | A17 | 4m green | 8 | 6 |
| *247* | A17 | 10m red | 7 | 7 |
| *248* | A17 | 20m ultra | 16 | 16 |
| *249* | A18 | 50m dl grn | 28 | 28 |
| | | *Nos. 245-249 (5)* | 64 | 62 |

75th anniv. of the UPU.

Stamps of 1943-47 Surcharged in Carmine, Black or Green

فلس
FILS

**1952** **Wmk. 4** ***Perf. 12***

**Size: 17¾x21½mm.**

| | | | | |
|---|---|---|---|---|
| *255* | A3 | 1f on 1m red brn | 10 | 7 |
| *256* | A3 | 2f on 2m Prus grn (C) | 8 | 8 |
| *257* | A3 | 3f on 3m rose car | 10 | 10 |
| *258* | A3 | 4f on 4m dp yel grn (C) | 14 | 10 |
| *259* | A3 | 5f on 5m org (G) | 50 | 16 |
| *260* | A3 | 10f on 10m vio (C) | 35 | 35 |
| *261* | A3 | 12f on 12m dp rose | 35 | 35 |
| *262* | A3 | 15f on 15m dl ol grn (C) | 40 | 22 |
| *263* | A3 | 20f on 20m dp bl (C) | 55 | 35 |

**Size: 20x24mm.**

| | | | | |
|---|---|---|---|---|
| *264* | A3 | 50f on 50m red lil (G) | 85 | 50 |
| *265* | A3 | 90f on 90m ocher (G) | 4.25 | 4.00 |
| *266* | A3 | 100f on 100m dp bl (C) | 2.75 | 85 |
| *267* | A3 | 200f on 200m dk vio (C) | 3.50 | 65 |
| *268* | A3 | 500f on 500m dk brn (C) | 6.50 | 2.00 |
| *269* | A3 | 1d on £1 blk (C) | 16.00 | 3.50 |
| | | *Nos. 255-269 (15)* | 36.42 | 13.28 |

Relief Map A19

Amir Abdullah ibn Hussein A20

***Perf. 13½x13***

**1952, Apr. 1** **Engr.** **Wmk. 4**

| | | | | |
|---|---|---|---|---|
| *270* | A19 | 1f red brn & yel grn | 7 | 7 |
| *271* | A19 | 2f dk bl grn & red | 7 | 7 |
| *272* | A19 | 3f car & gray blk | 7 | 7 |
| *273* | A19 | 4f grn & org | 8 | 8 |
| *274* | A19 | 5f choc & rose vio | 10 | 8 |
| *275* | A19 | 10f vio & brn | 12 | 10 |
| *276* | A19 | 20f dk bl & blk | 16 | 16 |
| *277* | A19 | 100f dp bl & brn | 85 | 60 |
| *278* | A19 | 200f pur & org | 1.10 | 1.10 |
| | | *Nos. 270-278 (9)* | 2.62 | 2.33 |

Issued to commemorate the unity of Jordan, April 24, 1950.
See Nos. 297-305.

**1952** **Wmk. 4** ***Perf. 11½.***

| | | | | |
|---|---|---|---|---|
| *279* | A20 | 5f orange | 5 | 5 |
| *280* | A20 | 10f violet | 8 | 7 |
| *281* | A20 | 12f carmine | 28 | 28 |
| *282* | A20 | 15f olive | 10 | 10 |
| *283* | A20 | 20f dp bl | 14 | 10 |

**Size: 20x24½mm.**

***Perf. 12x12½.***

| | | | | |
|---|---|---|---|---|
| *284* | A20 | 50f plum | 35 | 35 |
| *285* | A20 | 90f brn org | 1.00 | 85 |
| *286* | A20 | 100f dp bl | 85 | 40 |
| | | *Nos. 279-286 (8)* | 2.85 | 2.20 |

Nos. RA5-RA7 Overprinted in Black or Carmine

***Perf. 11½x12½***

**1953** **Unwmk.** **Engr.**

| | | | | |
|---|---|---|---|---|
| *286A* | PT1 | 10m carmine | 14.00 | 14.00 |
| *286B* | PT1 | 15m gray (C) | 1.40 | 65 |
| *286C* | PT1 | 20m dk brn | 18.00 | 18.00 |

**Same Overprint on Nos. NRA4-NRA7.**

| | | | | |
|---|---|---|---|---|
| *286D* | PT1 | 5m plum | 18.00 | 18.0 |
| *286E* | PT1 | 10m carmine | 18.00 | 18.0 |
| *286F* | PT1 | 15m gray (C) | 18.00 | 18.0 |
| *286G* | PT1 | 20m dk brn (C) | 18.00 | 18.0 |

In addition a few sheets of Nos. RA9 NRA1, NRA3, NRA8-NRA9 and RA37 RA41 have been reported with this overprint. It is doubtful whether they were regularly issued. See Nos. 344-347.

Same Overprint on Nos. RA28 to RA31 in Black or Carmine.

**1953** **Wmk. 4** ***Perf. 11½x12½***

| | | | | |
|---|---|---|---|---|
| *287* | PT1 | 5f plum | 8 | |
| *288* | PT1 | 10f carmine | 10 | 1 |
| *289* | PT1 | 15f gray (C) | 20 | 1 |
| *290* | PT1 | 20f dk brn (C) | 30 | 2 |

King Hussein A21

**Unwmk.**

**1953, Oct. 1** **Engr.** ***Perf. 12***

**Portrait in Black.**

| | | | | |
|---|---|---|---|---|
| *291* | A21 | 1f dk grn | 5 | 5 |
| *292* | A21 | 4f dp plum | 6 | 5 |
| *293* | A21 | 15f dp ultra | 10 | 8 |
| *294* | A21 | 20f dk pur | 12 | 6 |
| *295* | A21 | 50f dk bl grn | 40 | 18 |
| *296* | A21 | 100f dk bl | 55 | 35 |
| | | *Nos. 291-296 (6)* | 1.28 | 77 |

Accession of King Hussein, May 2, 1953.

Nos. 270 to 278 Overprinted in Black with Two Bars Through Center Inscription

**1953** **Wmk. 4** ***Perf. 13½x13.***

| | | | | |
|---|---|---|---|---|
| *297* | A19 | 1f red brn & yel grn | 5 | 5 |
| *298* | A19 | 2f dk bl grn & red | 5 | 5 |
| *299* | A19 | 3f car & gray blk | 5 | 5 |
| *300* | A19 | 4f grn & org | 6 | 6 |
| *301* | A19 | 5f choc & rose vio | 7 | 7 |
| *302* | A19 | 10f vio & brn | 18 | 8 |
| *303* | A19 | 20f dk bl & blk | 18 | 15 |
| *304* | A19 | 100f dp bl & brn | 75 | 38 |
| *305* | A19 | 200f pur & org | 1.50 | 65 |
| | | *Nos. 297-305 (9)* | 2.89 | 1.54 |

Two main settings of the bars exist on Nos. 297-300 and 304—the "normal" 1½mm spacing, and the "narrow" ½mm spacing.

El Deir Temple, Petra — A22

Dome of the Rock — A23

Designs: 2f, 4f, 500f, 1d, King Hussein. 3f, 5f, Treasury Bldg., Petra. 12f, 50f, 100f, 200f, Al Aqsa Mosque. 20f, as 10f.

**1954** **Unwmk.** **Engr.** ***Perf. 12½***

| | | | | |
|---|---|---|---|---|
| *306* | A22 | 1f dk bl grn & red brn | 6 | 5 |
| *307* | A22 | 2f red & blk | 6 | 6 |
| *308* | A22 | 3f dp plum & vio bl | 6 | 5 |
| *309* | A22 | 4f org brn & dk grn | 6 | 5 |
| *310* | A22 | 5f vio & dk grn | 60 | 5 |
| *311* | A23 | 10f pur & dk grn | 12 | 6 |
| *312* | A23 | 12f car rose & sep | 30 | 20 |
| *313* | A23 | 20f dp bl & dk grn | 14 | 6 |
| *314* | A23 | 50f dk bl & dp rose | 1.10 | 1.10 |
| *315* | A23 | 100f dk grn & dp bl | 55 | 22 |
| *316* | A23 | 200f dp cl & pck bl | 1.75 | 35 |
| *317* | A22 | 500f choc & pur | 4.50 | 2.25 |
| *318* | A22 | 1d dk ol grn & rose brn | 8.75 | 5.00 |
| | | *Nos. 306-318 (13)* | 18.05 | 9.50 |

See Nos. 324-337.

Globe — A23a

*Perf. 13½x13*

**1955, Jan. 1 Photo. Wmk. 195**

*319* A23a 15f green 8 6
*320* A23a 20f violet 10 9
*321* A23a 25f yel brn 12 10

Issued to commemorate the founding of the Arab Postal Union, July 1, 1954.

Princess Dina Abdul Hamid and King Hussein — A24

**1955, Apr. 19** ***Perf. 11x11½***

*322* A24 15f ultra 12 10
*323* A24 100f rose brn 50 50

Marriage of King Hussein and Princess Dina Abdul Hamid.

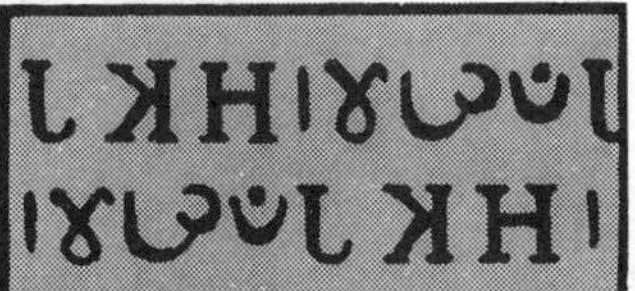

Wmk. 305- Roman and Arabic Initials

Types of 1954

Design: 15f, Dome of the Rock.

**Wmk. 305**

**1955-64 Engr.** ***Perf. 12½***

*324* A22 1f dk bl grn & red brn ('57) 5 5
*325* A22 2f red & blk ('57) 5 5
*326* A22 3f dp plum & vio bl ('56) 5 5
*327* A22 4f org brn & dk grn ('56) 5 5
*328* A22 5f vio & dk grn ('56) 5 5
*329* A23 10f pur & grn ('57) 5 5
*330* A23 12f car rose & sep 5 5
*331* A23 15f dp brn & rose red 6 5
*332* A23 20f dp bl & dk grn ('57) 8 5
*333* A23 50f dk bl & dp rose 15 9
*334* A23 100f dk grn & dp bl ('62) 30 18
*335* A23 200f dp cl & pck bl ('65) 1.00 25
*336* A22 500f choc & pur ('65) 3.75 1.50
*337* A22 1d dk ol grn & rose brn ('65) 10.00 2.00
*Nos. 324-337 (14)* 15.69 4.47

Envelope A25

**Wmk. 305**

**1956, Jan. 15 Engr.** ***Perf. 14***

**"Postmarks" in Black**

*338* A25 1f lt brn 5 5
*339* A25 4f dk car rose 5 5
*340* A25 15f blue 8 6
*341* A25 20f yel ol 9 8
*342* A25 50f sl bl 22 12
*343* A25 100f vermilion 38 22
*Nos. 338-343 (6)* 87 58

1st Arab Postal Congress in Amman.

Nos. RA1, RA3, RA8 and RA33 Overprinted in Carmine or Black

بريد
POSTAGE

**1956 Unwmk.** ***Perf. 11½x12½***

*344* PT1 1m ultra 5 5
*345* PT1 3m emerald 5 5
*346* PT1 50m purple 20 12

**Wmk. 4**

*347* PT1 100f org (Bk) 65 38

Torch of Liberty — A26

King Hussein — A27

**1958 Wmk. 305 Engr.** ***Perf. 12½***

*348* A26 5f bl & red brn 5 5
*349* A26 15f bis brn & blk 9 9
*350* A26 35f bl grn & plum 12 10
*351* A26 45f car & ol grn 16 12

Issued to commemorate the 10th anniversary of the Universal Declaration of Human Rights.

*Perf. 12x11½*

**1959 Wmk. 305 Engr.**

**Centers in Black**

*352* A27 1f dp grn 5 5
*353* A27 2f violet 5 5
*354* A27 3f dp car 5 5
*355* A27 4f brn blk 6 5
*356* A27 7f dk grn 7 7
*357* A27 12f dp car 8 8
*358* A27 15f dk red 8 6
*359* A27 21f green 25 20
*360* A27 25f ocher 14 7
*361* A27 35f dk bl 16 10
*362* A27 40f ol grn 20 10
*363* A27 50f red 28 12
*364* A27 100f bl grn 60 14
*365* A27 200f rose lake 90 30
*366* A27 500f gray bl 2.25 1.00
*367* A27 1d dk pur 5.50 2.75
*Nos. 352-367 (16)* 10.72 5.19

Arab League Center, Cairo, and King Hussein A28

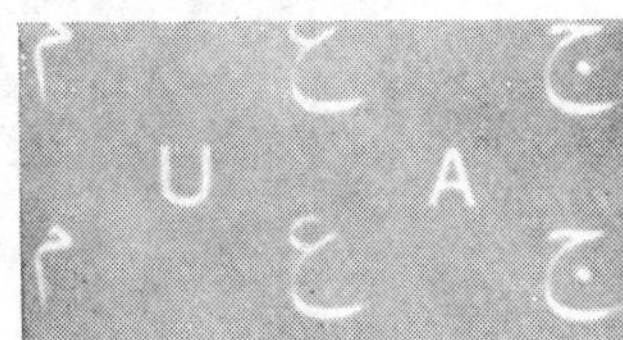


Wmk. 328- UAR

*Perf. 13x13½*

**1960, Mar. 22 Photo. Wmk. 328**

*368* A28 15f dl grn & blk 14 8

Issued to commemorate the opening of the Arab League Center and the Arab Postal Museum in Cairo.

World Refugee Year Emblem A29

**Wmk. 305**

**1960, Apr. 7 Litho.** ***Perf. 13½***

*369* A29 15f pale bl & red 14 10
*370* A29 35f bis & bl 22 22

Issued to publicize World Refugee Year, July 1, 1959-June 30, 1960.

Shah of Iran, King Hussein and Flags A30

*Perf. 13x13½*

**1960, May 15 Wmk. 305**

**Flags in Green, Red & Black.**

*371* A30 15f yel & blk 8 6
*372* A30 35f bl & blk 15 10
*373* A30 50f sal & blk 22 12

Issued to commemorate the visit of Mohammed Riza Pahlavi, Shah of Iran, to Jordan, Nov. 2, 1959.

Oil Refinery, Zarka A31

**1961, May 1 Engr.** ***Perf. 14x13***

*374* A31 15f dl vio & bl 10 7
*375* A31 35f dl vio & brick red 20 14

Opening of oil refinery at Zarka.

Urban and Nomad Families and Chart A32

*Perf. 13x13½*

**1961, Oct. 15 Photo. Unwmk.**

*376* A32 15f org brn 10 7

First Jordanian census, 1961.

Nos. 369-370 Overprinted in English and Arabic, "In Memorial of Dag Hammarskjoeld 1904-1961", and Laurel Leaf Border

**1961 Wmk. 305 Litho.** ***Perf. 13½***

*377* A29 15f pale bl & red 2.00 1.10
*378* A29 35f bis & bl 2.00 1.10

Issued in memory of Dag Hammarskjold, Secretary General of the United Nations, 1953-1961.

Malaria Eradication Emblem — A33

*Perf. 11x11½*

**1962, Apr. 15 Unwmk.**

*379* A33 15f brt pink 8 8
*380* A33 35f blue 18 18

Issued for the World Health Organization drive to eradicate malaria. A souvenir sheet exists with one each of Nos. 379-380. Light blue margin with blue inscription. Size: 75x76mm. Value $2.

Dial and Exchange Building, Amman A34

**1962, Dec. 11 Engr. Wmk. 305**

*381* A34 15f bl & lil 8 8
*382* A34 35f lil & emer 18 18

Issued to commemorate telephone automation in Amman (in 1960).

Port of 'Aqaba A35

**1962, Dec. 11**

*383* A35 15f lil & blk 8 8
*384* A35 35f vio bl & blk 12 12
*a* Souv. sheet of 2 75 75

Opening the port of 'Aqaba.

No. 384a contains Nos. 383-384. Light blue sheet margin, black inscriptions. Size: 80½x93mm. The sheet also exists imperf.

Dag Hammarskjold and UN Headquarters, N.Y. — A36

*Perf. 14x14½*

**1963, Jan. 24 Photo. Unwmk.**

*385* A36 15f ultra, ol grn & brn red 15 12
*386* A36 35f ol, brn red & ultra 32 28
*387* A36 50f brn red, ol & ultra 50 50

17th anniv. of the UN and in memory of Dag Hammarskjold, Secretary General of the UN, 1953-61. An imperf. souvenir sheet contains one each of Nos. 385-387 with simulated perforations. Ultramarine margin and inscription. Size: 132x95mm. Value $2.50.

Imperforates

Starting with No. 385, imperforates exist of many Jordanian stamps.

Church of St. Virgin's Tomb, Jerusalem — A37

Arab League Building, Cairo — A38

Designs: No. 389, Basilica of the Agony, Gethsemane. No. 390, Church of the Holy Sepulcher, Jerusalem. No. 391, Church of the

Nativity, Bethlehem. No. 392, Haram el-Khalil (tomb of Abraham), Hebron. No. 393, Dome of the Rock, Jerusalem. No. 394, Mosque of Omar el-Khatab, Jerusalem. No. 395, Al Aqsa Mosque, Jerusalem.

**1963, Feb. 5** *Perf. 14½x14*

**Center Multicolored**

| | | |
|---|---|---|
| *388* A37 50f blue | 30 | 25 |
| *389* A37 50f dl red | 30 | 25 |
| *390* A37 50f brt bl | 30 | 25 |
| *391* A37 50f ol grn | 30 | 25 |
| *a* Vert. strip of 4 | 1.25 | |
| *392* A37 50f gray | 40 | 25 |
| *393* A37 50f purple | 40 | 25 |
| *394* A37 50f dl red | 40 | 25 |
| *395* A37 50f lt pur | 40 | 25 |
| *a* Vert. strip of 4 | 1.75 | |
| *Nos. 388-395 (8)* | 2.80 | 2.00 |

Nos. 388-391 and 392-395 printed in sheets of 16 (4x4), each design in a horizontal row of 4 stamps. Vertical strips of four contain one each of Nos. 388-391 (No. 391a), and one each of Nos. 392-395 (No. 395a).

**1963, July 16 Photo.** *Perf. 13½x13*

| | | |
|---|---|---|
| *396* A38 15f sl bl | 8 | 5 |
| *397* A38 35f org red | 15 | 10 |

Arab League.

Wheat and U.N. Emblem — A39

*Perf. 11½x12½*

**1963, Sept. Litho. Wmk. 305**

| | | |
|---|---|---|
| *398* A39 15f lt bl, grn & blk | 8 | 6 |
| *399* A39 35f lt grn, grn & blk | 12 | 10 |
| *a* Souv. sheet of 2 | 30 | 30 |

Issued for the "Freedom from Hunger" campaign of the U.N. Food and Agriculture Organization. No. 399a contains Nos. 398-399, pale green margin with dark green inscription. Size: 97x84mm. The sheet also exists imperf. Value 50 cents.

East Ghor Canal, Pylon, Gear Wheel and Wheat — A40

**1963, Sept. 20** *Perf. 14½x14*

| | | |
|---|---|---|
| *400* A40 1f dl yel & blk | 5 | 5 |
| *401* A40 4f bl & blk | 5 | 5 |
| *402* A40 5f lil & blk | 5 | 5 |
| *403* A40 10f brt yel grn & blk | 6 | 6 |
| *404* A40 35f org & blk | 15 | 12 |
| *Nos. 400-404 (5)* | 36 | 33 |

East Ghor Canal Project.

UNESCO Emblem, Scales and Globe — A41

*Perf. 13½x13*

**1963, Dec. 10 Litho. Unwmk.**

| | | |
|---|---|---|
| *405* A41 50f pale vio bl & red | 25 | 25 |
| *406* A41 50f rose red & bl | 25 | 25 |

Issued to commemorate the 15th anniversary of the Universal Declaration of Human Rights.

> Values quoted in this catalogue are for stamps graded at Fine-Very Fine and with no faults. An illustrated guide to grade is provided in introductory material, beginning on Page V.

Red Crescent and King Hussein — A42

**1963, Dec. 24 Photo.** *Perf. 14x14½*

| | | |
|---|---|---|
| *407* A42 1f red & red lil | 5 | 5 |
| *408* A42 2f red & bl grn | 5 | 5 |
| *409* A42 3f red & dk bl | 5 | 5 |
| *410* A42 4f red & dk grn | 5 | 5 |
| *411* A42 5f red & dk brn | 5 | 5 |
| *412* A42 85f red & dp grn | 75 | 75 |

**Design: Red Cross at right, no portrait.**

| | | |
|---|---|---|
| *413* A42 1f red lil & red | 5 | 5 |
| *414* A42 2f bl grn & red | 5 | 5 |
| *415* A42 3f dk bl & red | 5 | 5 |
| *416* A42 4f dk grn & red | 5 | 5 |
| *417* A42 5f dk brn & red | 5 | 5 |
| *418* A42 85f dp grn & red | 3.00 | 3.00 |
| *Nos. 407-418 (12)* | 4.25 | 4.25 |

Issued to commemorate the centenary of the International Red Cross. Two 100f imperf. souvenir sheets, red and red lilac, exist in the Red Crescent and Red Cross designs. Size: 90x64mm. Value $15.

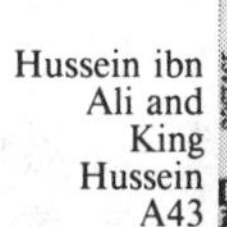

Hussein ibn Ali and King Hussein — A43

*Perf. 11x11½*

**1963, Dec. 25 Litho. Unwmk.**

| | | |
|---|---|---|
| *419* A43 15f yel & multi | 14 | 10 |
| *420* A43 25f multi | 16 | 14 |
| *421* A43 35f brt pink & multi | 35 | 28 |
| *422* A43 50f lt bl & multi | 50 | 50 |

Issued to commemorate Arab Renaissance Day, June 10, 1916. Perf. and imperf. souvenir sheets exist containing one each of Nos. 419-422. Light blue margin and black inscription. Size: 111x92mm. Value for both, $3.

Nos. 359, 312, 357 and 361 Surcharged **1 Fils** ١ فلس

**Wmk. 305, Unwmk.**

*Perf. 12x11½, 12½*

**1963, Dec. 16 Engr.**

| | | |
|---|---|---|
| *423* A27 1f on 21f grn & blk | 7 | 5 |
| *424* A27 2f on 21f grn & blk | 5 | *1.00* |
| *425* A23 4f on 12f car rose & sep | 14 | 7 |
| *a* 4f on 12f dp car & blk (#357) | 6.50 | 5.00 |
| *426* A27 5f on 21f grn & blk | 16 | 12 |
| *427* A27 25f on 35f dk bl & blk | 35 | 10 |
| *Nos. 423-427 (5)* | 77 | *1.34* |

Pope Paul VI, King Hussein and Al Aqsa Mosque, Jerusalem — A44

Designs (Portraits and): 35f, Dome of the Rock. 50f, Church of the Holy Sepulcher. 80f, Church of the Nativity, Bethlehem.

**1964, Jan. 4 Litho.** *Perf. 13x13½*

| | | |
|---|---|---|
| *428* A44 15f emer & blk | 10 | 10 |
| *429* A44 35f car rose & blk | 25 | 25 |
| *430* A44 50f brn & blk | 45 | 45 |
| *431* A44 80f vio bl & blk | 75 | 75 |

Issued to commemorate the visit of Pope Paul VI to the Holy Land, Jan. 4-6. An imperf. souvenir sheet contains 4 stamps similar to Nos. 428-431. Black marginal inscription. Size: 140x108mm. Value $3.

A45

Crown Prince Abdullah ben Al-Hussein — A46

Design: 5f, Crown Prince standing (vert.).

**1964, Mar. 30 Photo.** *Perf. 14*

| | | |
|---|---|---|
| *432* A46 5f multi | 5 | 5 |
| *433* A45 10f multi | 6 | 6 |
| *434* A46 35f multi | 25 | 25 |

Issued to commemorate the second birthday of Crown Prince Abdullah ben Al-Hussein (b. Jan. 30, 1962).

Table Tennis A49

Designs: 1f, Basketball. 2f, Volleyball. 3f, Soccer. 5f, Running (1f, 2, 3f, 5f vertical). 35f, Bicycling. 50f, Fencing. 100f, High jump.

*Perf. 14½x14, 14x14½*

**1964, June 1 Litho. Unwmk.**

| | | |
|---|---|---|
| *446* A49 1f car rose | 5 | 5 |
| *447* A49 2f dk bl | 5 | 5 |
| *448* A49 3f bl grn | 5 | 5 |
| *449* A49 4f org brn | 5 | 5 |
| *450* A49 5f lilac | 7 | 7 |
| *451* A49 35f rose red | 35 | 35 |
| *452* A49 50f emerald | 50 | 50 |
| *453* A49 100f dk red brn | 85 | 85 |
| *Nos. 446-453 (8)* | 1.97 | 1.97 |

Issued for the 1964 Olympic Games, Tokyo, Oct. 10-25. An imperf. 200f greenish blue souvenir sheet in design of 100f exists. Size: 90x64mm. Value $6.

Mother and Child — A50

**1964, June 1 Wmk. 305** *Perf. 14*

| | | |
|---|---|---|
| *454* A50 5f multi | 5 | 5 |
| *455* A50 10f multi | 7 | 5 |
| *456* A50 25f multi | 16 | 10 |

Social Studies Seminar, fourth session.

Pres. John F. Kennedy — A51

**1964, July 15 Unwmk.**

| | | |
|---|---|---|
| *457* A51 1f brt vio | 5 | 5 |
| *458* A51 2f car rose | 5 | 5 |
| *459* A51 3f ultra | 5 | 5 |
| *460* A51 4f org brn | 5 | 5 |
| *461* A51 5f brt grn | 5 | 5 |
| *462* A51 85f rose red | 1.75 | 1.75 |
| *Nos. 457-462 (6)* | 2.00 | 2.00 |

Issued in memory of President John F. Kennedy (1917-63). An imperf. 100f brown souvenir sheet exists. Size of stamp: 58x83mm.; size of sheet: 108x77mm. Value $5.

Ramses II — A52

*Perf. 14½x14*

**1964, July Litho. Wmk. 305**

| | | |
|---|---|---|
| *463* A52 4f lt bl & dk brn | 5 | 5 |
| *464* A52 15f yel & vio | 6 | 5 |
| *465* A52 25f lt yel grn & dk red | 10 | 9 |

UNESCO world campaign to save historic monuments in Nubia.

King Hussein and Map of Jordan and Israel — A53

**1964, Sept. 5 Unwmk.** *Perf. 12*

| | | |
|---|---|---|
| *466* A53 10f multi | 5 | 5 |
| *467* A53 15f multi | 8 | 6 |
| *468* A53 25f multi | 14 | 8 |
| *469* A53 50f multi | 28 | 22 |
| *470* A53 80f multi | 40 | 35 |
| *Nos. 466-470 (5)* | 95 | 76 |

Issued to commemorate the council of the Heads of State of the Arab League (Arab Summit Conference), Cairo, Jan. 13, 1964. An imperf. souvenir sheet contains five stamps similar to Nos. 466-470 with simulated perforations. Bright green border with white inscription. Size: 109x90mm. Value $1.

Pope Paul VI, King Hussein and Patriarch Athenagoras; Church of St. Savior, Church of the Holy Sepulcher and Dome of the Rock — A54

**1964, Aug. 17 Litho.**

| | | |
|---|---|---|
| *471* A54 10f dk grn, sep & org | 7 | 5 |
| *472* A54 15f cl, sep & org | 8 | 7 |
| *473* A54 25f choc, sep & org | 14 | 12 |
| *474* A54 50f bl, sep & org | 28 | 25 |
| *475* A54 80f brt grn, sep & org | 40 | 35 |
| *Nos. 471-475 (5)* | 97 | 84 |

Issued to commemorate the meeting between Pope Paul VI and Patriarch Athenagoras of the Greek Orthodox Church in Jerusalem, Jan. 5, 1964. An imperf. souvenir sheet contains five stamps similar to Nos. 471-475 with simulated perforations. Light blue border with white inscription. Size: 129x100mm. Value $3.

A two-line bilingual overprint, "Papa Paulus VI World Peace Visit to United Nations 1965", was applied to Nos. 471-475 and the souvenir sheet. These overprints were issued Apr. 27, 1966.

Pagoda, Olympic Torch and Emblem — A55

**1964, Nov. 21 Litho. *Perf. 14***

| | | | | |
|---|---|---|---|---|
| *476* | A55 | 1f dk red | 5 | 5 |
| *477* | A55 | 2f brt vio | 5 | 5 |
| *478* | A55 | 3f bl grn | 5 | 5 |
| *479* | A55 | 4f brown | 5 | 5 |
| *480* | A55 | 5f hn brn | 7 | 7 |
| *481* | A55 | 35f indigo | 35 | 35 |
| *482* | A55 | 50f olive | 50 | 50 |
| *483* | A55 | 100f vio bl | 1.00 | 1.00 |
| | | *Nos. 476-483 (8)* | 2.12 | 2.12 |

Issued to commemorate the 18th Olympic Games, Tokyo, Oct. 10-25. An imperf. 100f carmine rose souvenir sheet exists. Size of stamp: 82mm. at the base. Size of sheet: 109x76mm. Value $6.

Scouts Crossing Stream on Log Bridge — A56

Designs: 2f, First aid. 3f, Calisthenics. 4f, Instruction in knot tying. 5f, Outdoor cooking. 35f, Sailing. 50f, Campfire.

**1964, Dec. 7 Unwmk.**

| | | | | |
|---|---|---|---|---|
| *484* | A56 | 1f brown | 12 | 6 |
| *485* | A56 | 2f brt vio | 12 | 6 |
| *486* | A56 | 3f ocher | 12 | 6 |
| *487* | A56 | 4f maroon | 12 | 6 |
| *488* | A56 | 5f yel grn | 12 | 6 |
| *489* | A56 | 35f brt bl | 50 | 50 |
| *490* | A56 | 50f dk sl grn | 90 | 75 |
| | | *Nos. 484-490 (7)* | 2.00 | 1.55 |

Issued to honor the Jordanian Boy Scouts. An imperf. 100f dark blue souvenir sheet in campfire design exists. Size of stamp: 104mm. at the base. Size of sheet: 107x77mm. Value $6.

Yuri A. Gagarin — A57

Russian Astronauts: No. 492, Gherman Titov. No. 493, Andrian G. Nikolayev. No. 494, Pavel R. Popovich. No. 495, Valeri Bykovski. No. 496, Valentina Tereshkova.

**1965, Jan. 20 Litho. *Perf. 14***

| | | | | |
|---|---|---|---|---|
| *491* | A57 | 40f sep & vio bl | 25 | 25 |
| *492* | A57 | 40f pink & dk grn | 25 | 25 |
| *493* | A57 | 40f lt bl & vio blk | 25 | 25 |
| *494* | A57 | 40f ol & dk vio | 25 | 25 |
| *495* | A57 | 40f lt grn & red brn | 25 | 25 |
| *496* | A57 | 40f chlky bl & blk | 25 | 25 |
| | | *Nos. 491-496 (6)* | 1.50 | 1.50 |

Issued to honor Russian astronauts. A blue 100f souvenir sheet exists showing portraits of the six astronauts and space-ship circling globe. This sheet received later an additional overprint honoring the three-men space flight of Komarov, Feoktistov and Yegorov. Size: 115x83mm. Value $10 each.

U.N. Headquarters and Emblem — A58

**1965, Feb. 15 *Perf. 14x15***

| | | | | |
|---|---|---|---|---|
| *497* | A58 | 30f yel brn, pur & lt bl | 12 | 12 |
| *498* | A58 | 70f vio, lt bl & yel brn | 28 | 28 |

Nineteenth anniversary of the United Nations (in 1964). A souvenir sheet contains two imperf. stamps similar to Nos. 497-498. Light blue margin with brown inscription. Size 76x102mm. Value $9.

Dagger in Map of Palestine A59

Volleyball Player and Cup A60

**1965, Apr. 9 Photo. *Perf. 11x11½***

| | | | | |
|---|---|---|---|---|
| *499* | A59 | 25f red & ol | 65 | 20 |

Deir Yassin massacre, Apr. 9, 1948.

**1965, June Litho. *Perf. 14½x14***

| | | | | |
|---|---|---|---|---|
| *500* | A60 | 15f lemon | 8 | 6 |
| *501* | A60 | 35f rose brn | 18 | 15 |
| *502* | A60 | 50f grnsh bl | 25 | 22 |

Issued to commemorate the Arab Volleyball Championships. An imperf. 100f orange brown souvenir sheet exists. Size of stamp: 33x57mm. Size of sheet: 64½x89mm. Value $6.

Cavalry Horsemanship A61

Designs: 10f, Tank. 35f, King Hussein and aides standing in army car.

**1965, May 24**

| | | | | |
|---|---|---|---|---|
| *503* | A61 | 5f green | 5 | 5 |
| *504* | A61 | 10f vio bl | 5 | 5 |
| *505* | A61 | 35f brn red | 22 | 16 |

Issued for Army Day.

John F. Kennedy — A62

**1965, June 1 Wmk. 305 *Perf. 14***

| | | | | |
|---|---|---|---|---|
| *506* | A62 | 10f blk & brt grn | 8 | 6 |
| *507* | A62 | 15f vio & org | 15 | 10 |
| *508* | A62 | 25f brn & lt bl | 15 | 15 |
| *509* | A62 | 50f dp cl & emer | 50 | 30 |

Issued in memory of Pres. John F. Kennedy (1917-63). An imperf. 50f salmon and dark blue souvenir sheet exists. Size: 84x89mm. Value $8.

Pope Paul VI, King Hussein and Dome of the Rock — A63

***Perf. 13½x14***

**1965, June 15 Litho. Wmk. 305**

| | | | | |
|---|---|---|---|---|
| *510* | A63 | 5f brn & rose lil | 5 | 5 |
| *511* | A63 | 10f vio brn & lt yel grn | 15 | 10 |
| *512* | A63 | 15f ultra & sal | 15 | 12 |
| *513* | A63 | 50f blk & rose | 50 | 35 |

Issued to commemorate the first anniversary of the visit of Pope Paul VI to the Holy Land. An imperf. 50f violet and light blue souvenir sheet exists with simulated perforations. Size: 101x75mm. Value $7.50.

Jordan's Pavilion and Unisphere — A64

***Perf. 14x13½***

**1965, Aug. Unwmk. Photo.**

| | | | | |
|---|---|---|---|---|
| *514* | A64 | 15f sil & multi | 6 | 5 |
| *515* | A64 | 25f brnz & multi | 10 | 9 |
| *516* | A64 | 50f gold & multi | 20 | 18 |
| *a* | | Souvenir sheet of 1 | 75 | 75 |

New York World's Fair, 1964-65.

No. 516a contains a 100f gold and multicolored stamp, type A64, imperf. Blue margin with black inscriptions. Size: 114x76mm.

Algiers Library Type of Iraq, 1965

**1965, Aug. Wmk. 305 *Perf. 11½x11***

| | | | | |
|---|---|---|---|---|
| *517* | A78 | 25f blk, grn & red | 15 | 10 |

Issued to commemorate the burning of the Library of Algiers, June 2, 1962.

ITU Emblem, Old and New Telecommunication Equipment — A65

**1965, Aug. Litho. *Perf. 14x13½***

| | | | | |
|---|---|---|---|---|
| *518* | A65 | 25f lt bl & dk bl | 10 | 9 |
| *519* | A65 | 45f grnsh gray & blk | 18 | 15 |

Issued to commemorate the centenary of the International Telecommunication Union. An imperf. 100f salmon and carmine rose souvenir sheet exists with carmine rose border. Size of stamp: 39x32mm.; size of sheet: 60x90mm. Value $1.

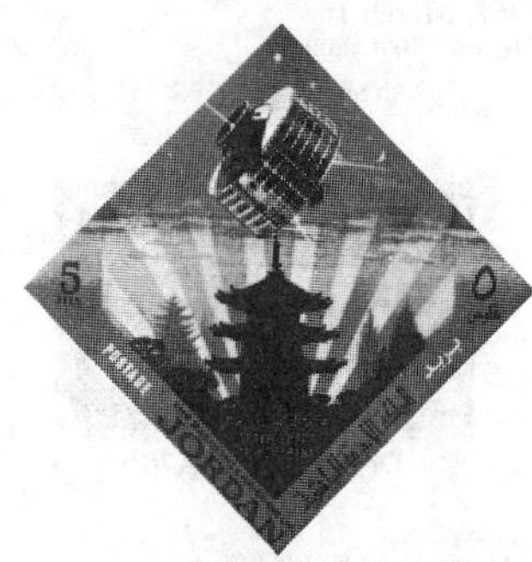


Syncom Satellite over Pagoda — A66

Designs: 10f, 20f, Rocket in space. 15f, Astronauts in cabin.

**1965, Sept. *Perf. 14***

| | | | | |
|---|---|---|---|---|
| *520* | A66 | 5f brt ultra, org & grnsh blk | 5 | 5 |
| *521* | A66 | 10f multi | 8 | 5 |
| *522* | A66 | 15f multi | 12 | 10 |
| *523* | A66 | 20f multi | 15 | 12 |
| *524* | A66 | 50f brt ultra, brt & dp yel grn | 38 | 30 |
| | | *Nos. 520-524 (5)* | 78 | 62 |

Issued to commemorate achievements in space research. A 50f multicolored imperf. souvenir sheet shows earth and Syncom satellite. Size: 102x77mm. Value $5.

King Hussein — A67

***Perf. 14½x14***

**1966, Jan. 15 Photo. Unwmk.**

**Portrait in Slate Blue**

| | | | | |
|---|---|---|---|---|
| *525* | A67 | 1f orange | 5 | 5 |
| *526* | A67 | 2f ultra | 5 | 5 |
| *527* | A67 | 3f dk pur | 5 | 5 |
| *528* | A67 | 4f plum | 5 | 5 |
| *529* | A67 | 7f brn org | 5 | 5 |
| *530* | A67 | 12f cerise | 8 | 5 |
| *531* | A67 | 15f ol brn | 10 | 5 |

**Portrait in Violet Brown**

| | | | | |
|---|---|---|---|---|
| *532* | A67 | 21f green | 15 | 10 |
| *533* | A67 | 25f grnsh bl | 18 | 8 |
| *534* | A67 | 35f yel bis | 25 | 15 |
| *535* | A67 | 40f org yel | 30 | 18 |
| *536* | A67 | 50f ol grn | 38 | 10 |
| *537* | A67 | 100f lt yel grn | 75 | 22 |
| *538* | A67 | 150f violet | 1.25 | 50 |
| | | *Nos. 525-538,C43-C45 (17)* | 12.19 | 5.93 |

Symbolic Water Cycle — A68

***Perf. 14½x14***

**1967, Mar. 1 Litho. Wmk. 305**

| | | | | |
|---|---|---|---|---|
| *539* | A68 | 10f dp org, blk & gray | 5 | 5 |
| *540* | A68 | 15f grnsh bl, blk & gray | 8 | 8 |
| *541* | A68 | 25f brt rose lil, blk & gray | 12 | 12 |

Hydrological Decade (UNESCO), 1965-74.

UNESCO Emblem — A69

**1967, March 16**
542 A69 100f multi 50 50

20th anniv. of UNESCO.

Dromedary — A70

Animals: 2f, Karakul 3f, Angora goat.

***Perf. 14x15***

**1967, Feb. 11 Photo. Unwmk.**
543 A70 1f dk brn & multi 5 5
544 A70 2f yel & multi 5 5
545 A70 3f lt bl & multi 5 5
*Nos. 543-545,C46-C48 (6)* 65 50

A souvenir sheet exists with a 100f in design and colors of No. C47, simulated perforation and marginal animal design. Size: 114x89mm. Value $5.

WHO Headquarters, Geneva — A71

**1967, Apr. 7 Wmk. 305**
546 A71 5f emer & blk 5 5
547 A71 45f dl org & blk 22 22

Inauguration of WHO Headquarters, Geneva.

Arab League Emblem and Hands Reaching for Knowledge — A72

**1968, May 5 Unwmk. *Perf. 11***
548 A72 20f org & sl grn 10 10
549 A72 20f brt pink & dk bl 10 10

Issued to publicize the literacy campaign.

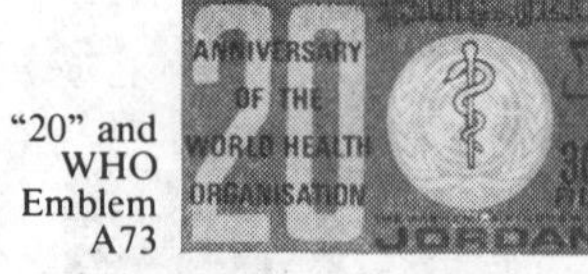

"20" and WHO Emblem A73

***Perf. 14½x14***

**1968, Aug. 10 Wmk. 305**
550 A73 30f multi 15 12
551 A73 100f multi 50 40

20th anniv. of the WHO.

European Goldfinch A74

Protected Game: 10f, Rock partridge (vert.). 15f, Ostriches (vert.). 20f, Sand partridge. 30f, Dorcas gazelle. 40f, Oryxes. 50f, Houbara bustard.

**1968, Oct. 5 Unwmk. *Perf. 13½***
552 A74 5f multi 5 5
553 A74 10f multi 12 5
554 A74 15f multi 14 6
555 A74 20f multi 22 8
556 A74 30f multi 32 12
557 A74 40f multi 40 16
558 A74 50f multi 55 20
*Nos. 552-558,C49-C50 (9)* 3.20 2.12

Human Rights Flame — A75

**1968, Dec. 10 Litho. *Perf. 13***
559 A75 20f dp org, lt org & blk 12 10
560 A75 60f grn, lt bl & blk 38 30

International Human Rights Year.

Dome of the Rock, Jerusalem A76

Designs: 5f, 45f, Holy Kaaba, Mecca, and Dome of the Rock.

**1969, Oct. 8 Photo. *Perf. 12***
**Size: 56x25mm.**
561 A76 5f dl vio & multi 5 5
**Size: 36x25mm.**
562 A76 10f vio bl & multi 12 5
563 A76 20f Prus bl & multi 25 8
**Size: 56x25mm.**
564 A76 45f Prus bl & multi 50 15

ILO Emblem A77

**1969, June 10 *Perf. 13½x14***
565 A77 10f bl & blk 8 5
566 A77 20f bis brn & blk 10 8
567 A77 25f lt ol & blk 12 10
568 A77 45f lil rose & blk 22 20
569 A77 60f org & blk 30 25
*Nos. 565-569 (5)* 82 68

Issued to commemorate the 50th anniversary of the International Labor Organization.

Horses A78

Designs: 20f, White stallion. 45f, Mare and foal.

**1969, July 6 Unwmk. *Perf. 13½***
570 A78 10f dk bl & multi 8 5
571 A78 20f dl grn & multi 12 8
572 A78 45f red & multi 30 20

Prince Hassan and Princess Tharwat A79

Designs: 60f, 100f, Prince Hassan and bride in western bridal gown.

**1969, Dec. 2 Photo. *Perf. 12½***
573 A79 20f gold & multi 10 8
574 A79 60f gold & multi 30 25
575 A79 100f gold & multi 50 50
Strip of 3. #573-575 1.00

Issued to commemorate the wedding of Crown Prince Hassan, Nov. 14, 1968. Nos. 573-575 printed se-tenant.

Pomegranate Flower (inscribed "Desert Scabius") — A80

Oranges — A81

Black Bush Robin — A82

Designs: 15f, Wattle flower ("Caper"). 20f, Melon. 25f, Caper flower ("Pomegranate"). 30f, Lemons. 35f, Morning glory. 40f, Grapes. 45f, Desert scabius ("Wattle"). 50f, Olive-laden branch. 75f, Black iris. 100f, Apples. 180f, Masked shrike. 200f, Palestine sunbird. (Inscriptions incorrect on 5f, 15f, 25f and 45f.)

***Perf. 14x13½ (flowers), 12 (fruit), 13½x14 (birds)***

**1969-70 Photo.**
576 A80 5f yel & multi ('70) 5 5
577 A81 10f bl & multi 9 5
578 A80 15f tan & multi ('70) 14 5
579 A81 20f sep & multi 20 6
580 A80 25f multi ('70) 25 6
581 A81 30f vio bl & multi 28 6
582 A80 35f multi ('70) 30 6
583 A81 40f dl yel & multi 35 6
584 A80 45f gray & multi ('70) 38 8
585 A81 50f car rose & multi 40 9
586 A80 75f multi ('70) 65 15
587 A81 100f dk gray & multi 90 25
588 A82 120f org & multi ('70) 1.25 30
589 A82 180f multi ('70) 1.50 70
590 A82 200f multi ('70) 1.90 85
*Nos. 576-590 (15)* 8.64 2.87

Issue dates: Fruits, Nov. 22; flowers, Mar. 21; birds, Sept. 1.

Rugby — A83

Designs: 10f, Diver. 15f, Boxers. 50f, Runner. 100f, Bicyclist (vert.). 150f, Basketball (vert.).

**1970, Aug. *Perf. 13½x14, 14x13½***
651 A83 5f grn & multi 5 5
652 A83 10f lt bl & multi 6 5
653 A83 15f gray & multi 8 6
654 A83 50f gray & multi 25 20
655 A83 100f yel & multi 50 40
656 A83 150f multi 75 65
*Nos. 651-656 (6)* 1.69 1.41

Boy Fetching Water, UNICEF and Refugee Emblems — A84

Designs (UNICEF and Refugee Emblems) and: 5f, Refugee children (horiz.). 15f, Girl and tents. 20f, Boy in front of tent.

**1970, Aug.**
657 A84 5f multi 5 5
658 A84 10f multi 20 14
659 A84 15f multi 28 14
660 A84 20f multi 40 14

Issued for Childhood Day.

Nativity Grotto, Bethlehem A85

Designs (Church of the Nativity, Bethlehem): 10f, Manger. 20f, Altar. 25f, Interior.

**1970, Dec. 25 Photo. *Perf. 13½***
661 A85 5f bl & multi 5 5
662 A85 10f scar & multi 7 5
663 A85 20f rose lil & multi 14 7
664 A85 25f grn & multi 20 14

Christmas 1970.

Arab League Type of Iraq

**1971, May 10 Photo. *Perf. 11½x11***
665 A145 10f org & multi 7 5
666 A145 20f lt bl & multi 14 7
667 A145 30f ol & multi 20 14

25th anniversary of the Arab League.

Emblem and Doves — A86

Designs: 5f, Emblem and 4 races (vert.). 10f, Emblem as flower (vert.).

**1971, July**
668 A86 5f grn & multi 5 5
669 A86 10f brick red & multi 10 5
670 A86 15f dk bl & multi 14 6

International Year Against Racial Discrimination.

Dead Sea — A87

Views of the Holy Land: 30f, Excavated building, Petra. 45f, Via Dolorosa, Jerusalem (vert.). 60f, Jordan River. 100f, Christmas bell, Bethlehem (vert.).

**1971, Aug.** ***Perf. 14x13½, 13½x14***

*671* A87 5f bl & multi 5 5
*672* A87 30f pink & multi 25 14
*673* A87 45f bl & multi 38 25
*674* A87 60f gray & multi 50 35
*675* A87 100f gray & multi 85 55
*Nos. 671-675 (5)* 2.03 1.34

Tourist publicity.

UPU Headquarters, Bern — A88

**1971, Oct.** ***Perf. 11***

*676* A88 10f brn, brn & yel grn 10 5
*677* A88 20f dk vio, grn & yel grn 20 10

Opening of Universal Postal Union Headquarters, Bern, Switzerland, 1970.

Avicenna (980-1037) A89

Child Learning to Write A90

Arab Scholars: 10f, Averroes (1126-1198). 20f, ibn-Khaldun (1332-1406). 25f, ibn-Tufail (?-1185). 30f, Alhazen (965?-1039?).

**1971, Sept.** ***Perf. 12***

*678* A89 5f gold & multi 5 5
*679* A89 10f gold & multi 10 5
*680* A89 20f gold & multi 20 10
*681* A89 25f gold & multi 22 10
*682* A89 30f gold & multi 30 14
*Nos. 678-682 (5)* 87 44

**1972, Feb. 9 Photo.** ***Perf. 11***

*683* A90 5f ultra, brn & grn 5 5
*684* A90 15f mag, brn & bl 10 7
*685* A90 20f grn, brn & bl 14 10
*686* A90 30f org, brn & bl 20 14

International Education Year 1970.

Mother and Child A91

Pope Paul VI and Holy Sepulcher A92

Mother's Day: 10f, Mothers and children (horiz.). 30f, Arab mother and child.

**1972, Mar.** ***Perf. 14x13½***

*687* A91 10f lt grn & multi 7 5
*688* A91 20f red brn & blk 14 10
*689* A91 30f bl, brn & blk 20 14

**1972, Apr. Photo.** ***Perf. 14x13½***

*690* A92 30f blk & multi 20 14

Easter 1972. See Nos. C51-C52.

UNICEF Emblem, Children A93

Designs (UNICEF Emblem and): 20f, Child playing with blocks spelling "UNICEF" (vert.). 30f, Mother and child.

**1972, May** ***Perf. 11½x11, 11x11½***

*691* A93 10f bl, vio bl & blk 7 5
*692* A93 20f multi 14 9
*693* A93 30f bl & multi 20 14

25th anniv. (in 1971) of UNICEF.

U.N. Emblem, Dove and Grain — A94

**1972, July** ***Perf. 11x11½***

*694* A94 5f vio & multi 5 5
*695* A94 10f multi 8 5
*696* A94 15f blk & multi 14 7
*697* A94 20f grn & multi 16 10
*698* A94 30f multi 28 16
*Nos. 694-698 (5)* 71 43

25th anniv. (in 1970) of the UN.

Al Aqsa Mosque, Jerusalem — A95

Designs: 60f, Al Aqsa Mosque on fire. 100f, Al Aqsa Mosque, interior.

**1972, Aug. 21 Litho.** ***Perf. 14½***

*699* A95 30f grn & multi 18 14
*700* A95 60f bl & multi 35 28
*701* A95 100f ocher & multi 60 40

3rd anniversary of the burning of Al Aqsa Mosque, Jerusalem.

House in Desert — A96

**1972, Nov.** ***Perf. 14x13½, 13½x14***

*702* A96 5f *Falconer* (vert.) 5 5
*703* A96 10f *shown* 10 5
*704* A96 15f *Man on camel* 15 7
*705* A96 20f *Pipe line construction* 20 9
*706* A96 25f *Shepherd* 22 10
*707* A96 30f *Camels at water trough* 35 14
*708* A96 35f *Chicken farm* 40 15
*709* A96 45f *Irrigation canal* 55 28
*Nos. 702-709 (8)* 2.02 93

Life in the Arab desert.

Wasfi el Tell and Dome of the Rock A97

Canceled-to-order stamps are often from remainders. Most collectors of canceled stamps prefer postally used specimens.

Wasfi el Tell, Map of Palestine and Jordan — A98

***Perf. 13x13½, 13½x13***

**1972, Dec. Photo.**

*710* A97 5f cit & multi 5 5
*711* A98 10f red & multi 9 5
*712* A97 20f dl bl & multi 18 12
*713* A98 30f grn & multi 30 18

In memory of Prime Minister Wasfi el Tell, who was assassinated in Cairo by Black September terrorists.

Trapshooting A99

Designs: 75f, Trapshooter facing right (horiz.). 120f, Trapshooter facing left (horiz.).

**1972, Dec.** ***Perf. 14x13½, 13½x14***

*714* A99 25f multi 15 12
*715* A99 75f multi 42 35
*716* A99 120f multi 75 50

World Trapshooting Championships.

Aero Club Emblem A100

**1973, Jan. Photo.** ***Perf. 13½x14***

*717* A100 5f bl, blk & yel 7 5
*718* A100 10f bl, blk & yel 14 7
*Nos. 717-718,C53-C55 (5)* 67 40

Royal Jordanian Aero Club.

Peace Dove and Jordanian Flag — A101

Designs: 10f, Emblem. 15f, King Hussein. 30f, Map of Jordan.

**1973, Mar.** ***Perf. 11½***

*719* A101 5f bl & multi 5 5
*720* A101 10f pale grn & multi 6 5
*721* A101 15f ol & multi 9 5
*722* A101 30f yel grn & multi 18 15

50th anniversary of the Hashemite Kingdom of Jordan.

Battle, Flag and Map of Palestine — A102

Designs: 10f, Two soldiers in combat, map of Palestine. 15f, Map of Palestine, olive branch, soldier on tank.

**1973, Apr. 10 Photo.** ***Perf. 11***

*723* A102 5f crim & multi 8 5
*724* A102 10f crim & multi 15 8
*725* A102 15f grn, bl & brn 25 10

5th anniversary of Karama Battle.

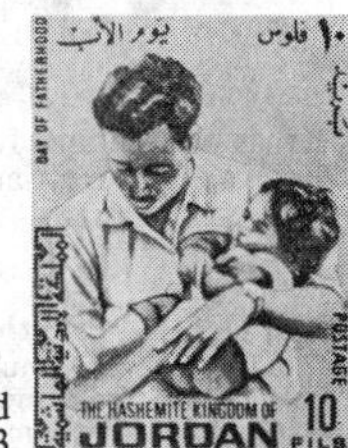

Father and Child — A103

Father's Day: 20f, Father and infant. 30f, Family.

**1973, Apr. 20** ***Perf. 13½***

*726* A103 10f cit & multi 6 5
*727* A103 20f lt bl & multi 10 7
*728* A103 30f multi 15 10

Phosphate Mine — A104

**1973, June 25 Litho.** ***Perf. 13½x14***

*729* A104 5f *shown* 5 5
*730* A104 10f *Cement factory* 5 5
*731* A104 15f *Sharmasil Dam* 8 5
*732* A104 20f *Kafrein Dam* 10 7

Development projects.

Camel Racer — A105

Designs: Camel racing.

**1973, July 21**

*733* A105 5f multi 5 5
*734* A105 10f multi 5 5
*735* A105 15f multi 7 5
*736* A105 20f multi 12 6

Book Year Emblem — A106

**1973, Aug. 25 Photo.** ***Perf. 13x13½***

*737* A106 30f dk grn & multi 22 9
*738* A106 60f pur & multi 45 18

International Book Year.

Family A107

Family Day: 30f, Family around fire. 60f, Large family outdoors.

**1973, Sept. 18 Litho. *Perf. 13½***

| | | | |
|---|---|---|---|
| *739* A107 20f multi | 9 | 6 |
| *740* A107 30f multi | 14 | 9 |
| *741* A107 60f multi | 28 | 18 |

Kings of Iran and Jordan, Tomb of Cyrus the Great and Mosque of Omar — A108

**1973, Oct. Litho. *Perf. 13***

| | | |
|---|---|---|
| *742* A108 5f ver & multi | 5 | 5 |
| *743* A108 10f brn & multi | 5 | 5 |
| *744* A108 15f gray & multi | 8 | 5 |
| *745* A108 30f bl & multi | 15 | 9 |

2500th anniversary of the founding of the Persian Empire by Cyrus the Great.

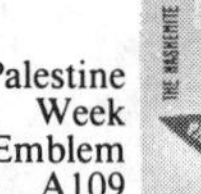

Palestine Week Emblem A109

Designs (Palestine Week Emblem and): 10f, Torch and laurel. 15f, Refugee family behind barbed wire (vert.). 30f, Children, Map of Palestine, globe. Sizes: 5f, 10f, 30f, 38½x22mm. 15f, 25x46mm.

**1973, Nov. 17 Photo. *Perf. 11***

| | | |
|---|---|---|
| *746* A109 5f multi | 5 | 5 |
| *747* A109 10f dl bl & multi | 8 | 5 |
| *748* A109 15f yel grn & multi | 10 | 5 |
| *749* A109 30f brt grn & multi | 22 | 9 |

Palestine Week.

Traditional Harvest A110

Designs: Traditional and modern agricultural methods.

**1973, Dec. 25 *Perf. 13½***

| | | |
|---|---|---|
| *750* A110 5f *shown* | 5 | 5 |
| *751* A110 10f *Harvesting machine* | 6 | 5 |
| *752* A110 15f *Traditional seeding* | 10 | 8 |
| *753* A110 20f *Seeding machine* | 12 | 10 |
| *754* A110 30f *Ox plow* | 18 | 15 |
| *755* A110 35f *Plowing machine* | 20 | 15 |
| *756* A110 45f *Pest control* | 25 | 22 |
| *757* A110 60f *Horticulture* | 38 | 32 |
| *Nos. 750-757,C56 (9)* | 1.79 | 1.42 |

Red Sea Fish A111

Designs: Various Red Sea fishes.

**1974, Feb. 15 Photo. *Perf. 14***

| | | |
|---|---|---|
| *758* A111 5f multi | 5 | 5 |
| *759* A111 10f multi | 8 | 5 |
| *760* A111 15f multi | 12 | 8 |
| *761* A111 20f multi | 15 | 8 |
| *762* A111 25f multi | 18 | 10 |
| *763* A111 30f multi | 20 | 12 |
| *764* A111 35f multi | 22 | 15 |
| *765* A111 40f multi | 25 | 18 |
| *766* A111 45f multi | 30 | 20 |
| *767* A111 50f multi | 35 | 25 |
| *768* A111 60f multi | 50 | 32 |
| *Nos. 758-768 (11)* | 2.40 | 1.58 |

Battle of Muta, 1250 A112

**1974, Mar. 15 Photo. *Perf. 13½***

| | | |
|---|---|---|
| *769* A112 10f *shown* | 6 | 5 |
| *770* A112 20f *Yarmouk Battle, 636* | 12 | 6 |
| *771* A112 30f *Hitteen Battle, 1187* | 18 | 9 |

Clubfooted Boy, by Murillo — A113

Paintings: 10f, Praying Hands, by Dürer. 15f, St. George and the Dragon, by Paolo Uccello. 20f, Mona Lisa, by Da Vinci. 30f, Hope, by Frederic Watts. 40f, Angelus, by Jean F. Millet (horiz.). 50f, The Artist and her Daughter, by Angelica Kauffmann. 60f, Portrait of my Mother, by James Whistler (horiz.). 100f, Master Hare, by Reynolds.

***Perf. 14x13½, 13½x14***

**1974, Apr. 15 Litho.**

| | | |
|---|---|---|
| *772* A113 5f blk & multi | 5 | 5 |
| *773* A113 10f blk & gray | 6 | 5 |
| *774* A113 15f blk & multi | 7 | 5 |
| *775* A113 20f blk & multi | 9 | 6 |
| *776* A113 30f blk & multi | 14 | 9 |
| *777* A113 40f blk & multi | 18 | 10 |
| *778* A113 50f blk & multi | 22 | 15 |
| *779* A113 60f blk & multi | 28 | 18 |
| *780* A113 100f blk & multi | 45 | 30 |
| *Nos. 772-780 (9)* | 1.54 | 1.03 |

Nos. 737-738 Overprinted

المؤتمر الدولي لتاريخ بلاد الشام
٢٠ – ١٩٧٤/٤/٢٥
الجامعة الاردنية

**1974, Apr. 20 Photo. *Perf. 13x13½***

| | | |
|---|---|---|
| *781* A106 30f dk grn & multi | 28 | 16 |
| *782* A106 60f pur & multi | 60 | 40 |

International Conference for Damascus History, Apr. 20-25.

UPU Emblem — A114

**1974 *Perf. 13x12½***

| | | |
|---|---|---|
| *783* A114 10f yel grn & multi | 14 | 5 |
| *784* A114 30f bl & multi | 30 | 14 |
| *785* A114 60f multi | 60 | 30 |

Centenary of Universal Postal Union.

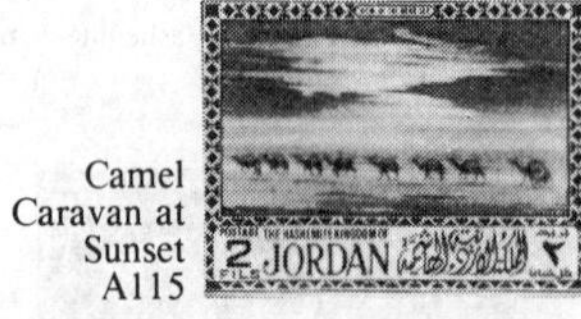

Camel Caravan at Sunset A115

Designs: 3f, 30f, Palm at shore of Dead Sea. 4f, 40f, Hotel at shore. 5f, 50f, Jars from Qumran Caves. 6f, 60f, Copper scrolls (vert.). 10f, 100f, Cracked cistern steps (vert.). 20f, like 2f.

**1974, June 25 Photo. *Perf. 14***

| | | |
|---|---|---|
| *786* A115 2f multi | 5 | 5 |
| *787* A115 3f multi | 5 | 5 |
| *788* A115 4f multi | 5 | 5 |
| *789* A115 5f multi | 5 | 5 |
| *790* A115 6f multi | 5 | 5 |
| *791* A115 10f multi | 5 | 5 |
| *792* A115 20f multi | 15 | 7 |
| *793* A115 30f multi | 22 | 12 |
| *794* A115 40f multi | 30 | 15 |
| *795* A115 50f multi | 35 | 20 |
| *796* A115 60f multi | 50 | 25 |
| *797* A115 100f multi | 75 | 40 |
| *Nos. 786-797 (12)* | 2.57 | 1.49 |

WPY Emblem — A116

Water Skiing — A117

**1974, Aug. 20 Photo. *Perf. 11***

| | | |
|---|---|---|
| *798* A116 5f lt grn, blk & pur | 5 | 5 |
| *799* A116 10f lt grn, blk & car | 10 | 5 |
| *800* A116 20f lt grn, blk & org | 20 | 10 |

World Population Year, 1974.

***Perf. 14x13½, 13½x14***

**1974, Sept. 20**

Water Skiing: 10f, 100f, Side view (horiz.). 20f, 200f, Turning (horiz.). 50f, like 5f.

| | | |
|---|---|---|
| *801* A117 5f multi | 5 | 5 |
| *802* A117 10f multi | 8 | 5 |
| *803* A117 20f multi | 14 | 8 |
| *804* A117 50f multi | 35 | 20 |
| *805* A117 100f multi | 65 | 40 |
| *806* A117 200f multi | 1.40 | 80 |
| *Nos. 801-806 (6)* | 2.67 | 1.58 |

Holy Kaaba, Mecca, and Pilgrims — A118

**1974, Nov. Photo. *Perf. 11***

| | | |
|---|---|---|
| *807* A118 10f bl & multi | 8 | 5 |
| *808* A118 20f yel & multi | 16 | 10 |

Pilgrimage season.

Amrah Palace A119

Ruins: 20f, Hisham Palace. 30f, Kharraneh Castle.

**1974, Nov. 25 Photo. *Perf. 14x13½***

| | | |
|---|---|---|
| *809* A119 10f blk & multi | 5 | 5 |
| *810* A119 20f blk & multi | 12 | 7 |
| *811* A119 30f blk & multi | 18 | 12 |

Jordanian Woman — A120

Designs: Various women's costumes.

**1975, Feb. 1 Photo. *Perf. 12***

| | | |
|---|---|---|
| *812* A120 5f lt grn & multi | 5 | 5 |
| *813* A120 10f yel & multi | 5 | 5 |
| *814* A120 15f lt bl & multi | 7 | 5 |
| *815* A120 20f ultra & multi | 9 | 6 |
| *816* A120 25f grn & multi | 12 | 8 |
| *Nos. 812-816 (5)* | 38 | 29 |

Treasury, Petra — A121

Ommayyad Palace, Amman A122

Designs: 30f, Dome of the Rock, Jerusalem. 40f, Columns, Forum of Jerash.

***Perf. 14x13½, 13½x14 8***

**1975, Mar. 1 Photo.**

| | | |
|---|---|---|
| *824* A121 15f lt bl & multi | 10 | 5 |
| *825* A122 20f pink & multi | 12 | 6 |
| *826* A122 30f yel & multi | 20 | 10 |
| *827* A122 40f lt bl & multi | 25 | 12 |
| *Nos. 824-827,C59-C61 (7)* | 1.52 | 90 |

King Hussein — A123

**1975, Apr. 8 Photo. *Perf. 14***

**Size: 19x23mm.**

| | | |
|---|---|---|
| *831* A123 5f grn & ind | 5 | 5 |
| *832* A123 10f vio & ind | 5 | 5 |
| *833* A123 15f car & ind | 7 | 5 |
| *834* A123 20f brn ol & ind | 9 | 6 |
| *835* A123 25f vio bl & ind | 12 | 8 |
| *836* A123 30f brn & ind | 14 | 9 |
| *837* A123 35f vio & ind | 16 | 10 |
| *838* A123 40f org & ind | 18 | 12 |
| *839* A123 45f red lil & ind | 20 | 14 |
| *840* A123 50f grn & ind | 22 | 15 |
| *Nos. 831-840,C62-C68 (17)* | 8.23 | 5.23 |

Globe, "alia" and Plane — A125

Designs: 30f, Boeing 727 connecting Jordan with world (horiz.). 60f, Globe and "alia."

**1975, June 15 Photo. *Perf. 11***

| | | |
|---|---|---|
| *853* A125 10f multi | 5 | 5 |
| *854* A125 30f multi | 18 | 12 |
| *855* A125 60f multi | 38 | 25 |

Royal Jordanian Airline, 30th anniversary.

Satellite Transmission System, Map of Mediterranean — A126

**1975, Aug. 1 Photo. *Perf. 11***

| | | | | |
|---|---|---|---|---|
| *856* | A126 | 20f vio bl & multi | 16 | 8 |
| *857* | A126 | 30f grn & multi | 22 | 12 |

Opening of satellite earth station.

Chamber of Commerce Emblem — A127

**1975, Oct. 15 Photo. *Perf. 11***

| | | | | |
|---|---|---|---|---|
| *858* | A127 | 10f yel & bl | 8 | 5 |
| *859* | A127 | 15f yel, red & bl | 14 | 6 |
| *860* | A127 | 20f yel, grn & bl | 16 | 8 |

Amman Chamber of Commerce, 50th anniversary.

Hand Holding Wrench, Wall and Emblem — A128

**1975, Nov. Photo. *Perf. 11½***

| | | | | |
|---|---|---|---|---|
| *861* | A128 | 5f grn, car & blk | 5 | 5 |
| *862* | A128 | 10f car, grn & blk | 8 | 5 |
| *863* | A128 | 20f blk, grn & car | 16 | 8 |

Three-year development plan.

Family and IWY Emblem A129

Salt Industry A130

Designs (IWY Emblem and): 25f, Woman scientist with microscope. 60f, Woman graduate.

**1976, Apr. 27 Litho. *Perf. 14x13½***

| | | | | |
|---|---|---|---|---|
| *864* | A129 | 5f multi | 5 | 5 |
| *865* | A129 | 25f multi | 15 | 10 |
| *866* | A129 | 60f multi | 38 | 25 |

International Women's Year 1975.

**1976, June 1 Litho. *Perf. 13½x14***

Designs (Arab Labor Organization Emblem and): 30f, Welders. 60f, Ship at 'Aqaba.

| | | | | |
|---|---|---|---|---|
| *867* | A130 | 10f gray & multi | 5 | 5 |
| *868* | A130 | 30f bis & multi | 18 | 12 |
| *869* | A130 | 60f brn & multi | 38 | 25 |

Arab Labor Organization.

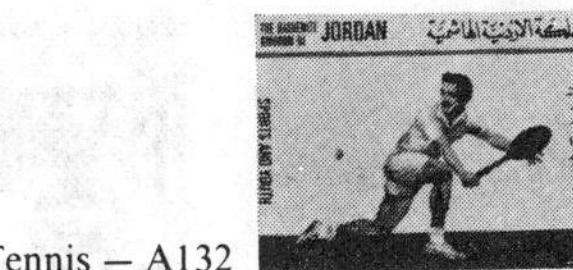

Tennis — A132

Designs: 10f, Athlete and wreath. 15f, Soccer. 20f, Equestrian and Jordanian flag. 30f, Weight lifting. 100f, Stadium, Amman.

**1976, Nov. 1 Litho. *Perf. 14x13½***

| | | | | |
|---|---|---|---|---|
| *990* | A132 | 5f buff & multi | 5 | 5 |
| *991* | A132 | 10f lt bl & multi | 8 | 5 |
| *992* | A132 | 15f grn & multi | 10 | 6 |
| *993* | A132 | 20f grn & multi | 14 | 8 |
| *994* | A132 | 30f grn & multi | 20 | 12 |
| *995* | A132 | 100f multi | 65 | 40 |
| | | *Nos. 990-995 (6)* | 1.22 | 76 |

Sports and youth.

Dam — A133

Telephones, 1876 and 1976 — A134

Designs: Various dams.

**1976, Dec. 7 Litho. *Perf. 14x13½***

| | | | | |
|---|---|---|---|---|
| *996* | A133 | 30f multi | 18 | 12 |
| *997* | A133 | 60f multi | 38 | 25 |
| *998* | A133 | 100f multi | 60 | 40 |

**1977, Feb. 17 Litho. *Perf. 11½x12***

Design: 125f, 1876 telephone and 1976 receiver.

| | | | | |
|---|---|---|---|---|
| *999* | A134 | 75f rose & multi | 40 | 30 |
| *1000* | A134 | 125f bl & multi | 60 | 50 |

Centenary of first telephone call by Alexander Graham Bell, Mar. 10, 1876.

Street Crossing, Traffic Light — A135

Designs: 75f, Traffic circle and light. 125f, Traffic light and signs, motorcycle policeman.

**1977, May 4 Litho. *Perf. 11x12***

| | | | | |
|---|---|---|---|---|
| *1001* | A135 | 5f rose & multi | 5 | 5 |
| *1002* | A135 | 75f blk & multi | 40 | 30 |
| *1003* | A135 | 125f yel & multi | 65 | 50 |

International Traffic Day.

Plane over Ship — A136

Child with Toy Bank — A137

Designs (Coat of Arms and): 25f, Factories and power lines. 40f, Fertilizer plant and trucks. 50f, Ground to air missile. 75f, Mosque and worshippers. 125f, Radar station and TV emblem.

**1977, Aug. 11 Photo. *Perf. 11½x12***

| | | | | |
|---|---|---|---|---|
| *1004* | A136 | 10f sil & multi | 6 | 5 |
| *1005* | A136 | 25f sil & multi | 14 | 10 |
| *1006* | A136 | 40f sil & multi | 20 | 16 |
| *1007* | A136 | 50f sil & multi | 28 | 20 |
| *1008* | A136 | 75f sil & multi | 40 | 30 |
| *1009* | A136 | 125f sil & multi | 75 | 50 |
| | | *Nos. 1004-1009 (6)* | 1.83 | 1.31 |

25th anniv. of the reign of King Hussein.

**1977, Sept. 1 Litho. *Perf. 11½x12***

Postal Savings Bank: 25f, Boy with piggy bank. 50f, Postal Savings Bank emblem. 75f, Boy talking to teller.

| | | | | |
|---|---|---|---|---|
| *1010* | A137 | 10f multi | 6 | 5 |
| *1011* | A137 | 25f multi | 15 | 10 |
| *1012* | A137 | 50f multi | 30 | 20 |
| *1013* | A137 | 75f multi | 45 | 30 |

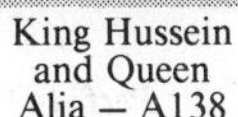

King Hussein and Queen Alia — A138

Queen Alia — A139

**1977, Nov. 1 Litho. *Perf. 11½x12***

| | | | | |
|---|---|---|---|---|
| *1014* | A138 | 10f lt grn & multi | 6 | 5 |
| *1015* | A138 | 25f rose & multi | 15 | 10 |
| *1016* | A138 | 40f yel & multi | 28 | 16 |
| *1017* | A138 | 50f bl & multi | 35 | 20 |

**1977, Dec. 1 Litho. *Perf. 11½x12***

| | | | | |
|---|---|---|---|---|
| *1018* | A139 | 10f grn & multi | 6 | 5 |
| *1019* | A139 | 25f brn & multi | 16 | 10 |
| *1020* | A139 | 40f bl & multi | 28 | 16 |
| *1021* | A139 | 50f yel & multi | 35 | 20 |

Queen Alia, died in 1977 air crash.

Jinnah, Flags of Pakistan and Jordan A140

APU Emblem, Members' Flags A141

**1977, Dec. 20 *Perf. 11½***

| | | | | |
|---|---|---|---|---|
| *1022* | A140 | 25f multi | 15 | 10 |
| *1023* | A140 | 75f multi | 45 | 30 |

Mohammed Ali Jinnah (1876-1948), 1st Governor General of Pakistan.

**1978, Apr. 12 Litho. *Perf. 12x11½***

| | | | | |
|---|---|---|---|---|
| *1024* | A141 | 25f yel & multi | 15 | 10 |
| *1025* | A141 | 40f buff & multi | 25 | 16 |

25th anniv. (in 1977), of Arab Postal Union.

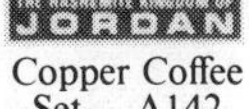

Copper Coffee Set — A142

Roman Amphitheater, Jerash — A143

Handicraft: 40f, Porcelain plate and ashtray. 75f, Vase and jewelry. 125f, Pipe holder.

**1978, May 30 Photo. *Perf. 11½x12***

| | | | | |
|---|---|---|---|---|
| *1026* | A142 | 25f ol & multi | 15 | 10 |
| *1027* | A142 | 40f lil & multi | 25 | 16 |
| *1028* | A142 | 75f ultra & multi | 45 | 30 |
| *1029* | A142 | 125f org & multi | 75 | 50 |

**1978, July 30 Litho. *Perf. 12***

Tourist Views: 20f, Roman Columns, Jerash. 40f, Goat, grapes and man, Roman mosaic, Madaba. 75f, Rock formations, Rum, and camel rider.

| | | | | |
|---|---|---|---|---|
| *1030* | A143 | 5f multi | 5 | 5 |
| *1031* | A143 | 20f multi | 12 | 8 |
| *1032* | A143 | 40f multi | 25 | 16 |
| *1033* | A143 | 75f multi | 45 | 30 |

King Hussein and Pres. Sadat — A144

Designs: No. 1035, King Hussein and Pres. Assad, Jordanian and Syrian flags (horiz.). No. 1036, King Hussein, King Khalid, Jordanian and Saudi Arabian flags (horiz.).

**1978, Aug. 20 *Perf. 11½x12***

| | | | | |
|---|---|---|---|---|
| *1034* | A144 | 40f multi | 24 | 16 |
| *1035* | A144 | 40f multi | 24 | 16 |
| *1036* | A144 | 40f multi | 24 | 16 |

Visits of Arab leaders to Jordan.

Cement Factory A145

Designs: 10f, Science laboratory. 25f, Printing press. 75f, Artificial fertilizer plant.

**1978, Sept. 25 Litho. *Perf. 12***

| | | | | |
|---|---|---|---|---|
| *1037* | A145 | 5f multi | 5 | 5 |
| *1038* | A145 | 10f multi | 7 | 5 |
| *1039* | A145 | 25f multi | 15 | 10 |
| *1040* | A145 | 75f multi | 45 | 30 |

Industrial development.

"UNESCO" Scales and Globe — A146

**1978, Dec. 5 Litho. *Perf. 12x11½***

| | | | | |
|---|---|---|---|---|
| *1041* | A146 | 40f multi | 25 | 18 |
| *1042* | A146 | 75f multi | 52 | 35 |

30th anniversary of UNESCO.

1976-1980 Development Plan — A147

**1979, Oct. 25 Litho. *Perf. 12½x12***

| | | | | |
|---|---|---|---|---|
| *1043* | A147 | 25f multi | 15 | 10 |
| *1044* | A147 | 40f multi | 25 | 16 |
| *1045* | A147 | 50f multi | 30 | 18 |

IYC Emblem, Flag of Jordan — A148

**1979, Nov. 15 Litho. *Perf. 12x12½***

| | | | | |
|---|---|---|---|---|
| *1046* | A148 | 25f multi | 15 | 10 |
| *1047* | A148 | 40f multi | 25 | 16 |
| *1048* | A148 | 50f multi | 30 | 18 |

International Year of the Child.

1979 Population and Housing Census — A149

**1979, Dec. 25 Litho. *Perf. 12½x12***

| | | | | |
|---|---|---|---|---|
| *1049* | A149 | 25f multi | 15 | 10 |
| *1050* | A149 | 40f multi | 25 | 16 |
| *1051* | A149 | 50f multi | 30 | 20 |

King Hussein — A150

**1980 Litho. *Perf. 13½x13***

| | | | | |
|---|---|---|---|---|
| *1052* | A150 | 5f multi | 5 | 5 |
| *1053* | A150 | 10f multi | 7 | 5 |
| *1055* | A150 | 20f multi | 12 | 8 |
| *1056* | A150 | 25f multi | 15 | 10 |
| *a* | | Inscribed 1979 | 15 | 10 |
| *1058* | A150 | 40f multi | 25 | 16 |
| *a* | | Inscribed 1979 | 25 | 16 |
| *1059* | A150 | 50f multi | 30 | 20 |
| *1060* | A150 | 75f multi | 42 | 25 |
| *1061* | A150 | 125f multi | 75 | 50 |
| | | *Nos. 1052-1061 (8)* | 2.11 | 1.39 |

The 5f, 10f, 20f, 25f and 40f also come inscribed 1981.

International Nursing Day — A151

El Deir Temple, Petra — A152

**1980, May 12 Litho. *Perf. 12x12½***

| | | | | |
|---|---|---|---|---|
| *1062* | A151 | 25f multi | 12 | 8 |
| *1063* | A151 | 40f multi | 18 | 12 |
| *1064* | A151 | 50f multi | 22 | 14 |

**1980 Litho. *Perf. 14½***

| | | | | |
|---|---|---|---|---|
| *1065* | A152 | 25f multi | 12 | 8 |
| *1066* | A152 | 40f multi | 18 | 12 |
| *1067* | A152 | 50f multi | 22 | 15 |

World Tourism Conf., Manila, Sept. 27.

Hegira (Pilgrimage Year) — A153

**1980, Nov. 11 Litho. *Perf. 14½***

| | | | | |
|---|---|---|---|---|
| *1068* | A153 | 25f multi | 12 | 8 |
| *1069* | A153 | 40f multi | 20 | 12 |
| *1070* | A153 | 50f multi | 25 | 15 |
| *1071* | A153 | 75f multi | 45 | 22 |
| *1072* | A153 | 100f multi | 45 | 30 |
| | | *Nos. 1068-1072 (5)* | 1.47 | 87 |

**Souvenir Sheet**

***Imperf***

| | | | | |
|---|---|---|---|---|
| *1073* | A153 | 290f multi | 1.40 | 90 |

No. 1073 contains designs of Nos. 1068-1071. Size: 128x89½mm.

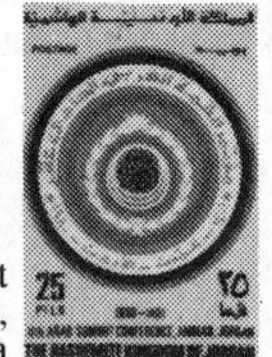

11th Arab Summit Conference, Amman — A153a

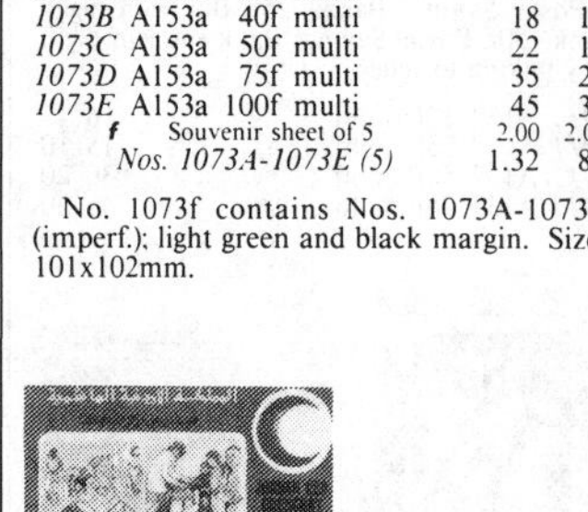

**1980, Nov. 25 Litho. *Perf. 14½***

| | | | | |
|---|---|---|---|---|
| *1073A* | A153a | 25f multi | 12 | 8 |
| *1073B* | A153a | 40f multi | 18 | 12 |
| *1073C* | A153a | 50f multi | 22 | 15 |
| *1073D* | A153a | 75f multi | 35 | 22 |
| *1073E* | A153a | 100f multi | 45 | 30 |
| *f* | | Souvenir sheet of 5 | 2.00 | 2.00 |
| | | *Nos. 1073A-1073E (5)* | 1.32 | 87 |

No. 1073f contains Nos. 1073A-1073E (imperf.); light green and black margin. Size: 101x102mm.

Red Crescent Society — A154

**1981, May 8 Litho. *Perf. 14½***

| | | | | |
|---|---|---|---|---|
| *1074* | A154 | 25f multi | 18 | 12 |
| *1075* | A154 | 40f multi | 30 | 20 |
| *1076* | A154 | 50f multi | 35 | 25 |

13th World Telecommunications Day — A155

**1981, June 17 Litho. *Perf. 14x14½***

| | | | | |
|---|---|---|---|---|
| *1077* | A155 | 25f multi | 18 | 12 |
| *1078* | A155 | 40f multi | 25 | 20 |
| *1079* | A155 | 50f multi | 35 | 25 |

Nos. 174 and 832 — A156

***Perf. 13½x14½, 14½x13½***

**1981, July 1 Litho.**

| | | | | |
|---|---|---|---|---|
| *1080* | A156 | 25f shown | 18 | 12 |
| *1081* | A156 | 40f Nos. 313, 189, vert. | 30 | 20 |
| *1082* | A156 | 50f Nos. 272, 222 | 35 | 25 |

Postal Museum opening.

Khawla Bint El-Azwar, Ancient Warrior — A157

Arab Women: 40f, El-Khansa (d.645), writer. 50f, Rabia El-Adawiyeh, religious leader.

**1981, Aug. 25 Litho. *Perf. 14½x14***

| | | | | |
|---|---|---|---|---|
| *1083* | A157 | 25f multi | 22 | 15 |
| *1084* | A157 | 40f multi | 36 | 24 |
| *1085* | A157 | 50f multi | 45 | 30 |

World Food Day — A158

**1981, Oct. 16 Litho. *Perf. 14x14½***

| | | | | |
|---|---|---|---|---|
| *1086* | A158 | 25f multi | 22 | 15 |
| *1087* | A158 | 40f multi | 36 | 24 |
| *1088* | A158 | 50f multi | 45 | 30 |

Intl. Year of the Disabled A159

Hands Reading Braille A160

**1981, Nov. 14 Litho. *Perf. 14½x14***

| | | | | |
|---|---|---|---|---|
| *1089* | A159 | 25f multi | 22 | 15 |
| *1090* | A159 | 40f multi | 36 | 24 |
| *1091* | A159 | 50f multi | 45 | 30 |

**1981, Nov. 14 *Perf. 14x14½***

| | | | | |
|---|---|---|---|---|
| *1092* | A160 | 25f multi | 22 | 15 |
| *1093* | A160 | 40f multi | 36 | 24 |
| *1094* | A160 | 50f multi | 45 | 30 |

Hand Holding Jug and Stone Tablet — A161

**1982, Mar. 10 Litho. *Perf. 14x14½***

| | | | | |
|---|---|---|---|---|
| *1095* | A161 | 25f multi | 22 | 15 |
| *1096* | A161 | 40f multi | 36 | 24 |
| *1097* | A161 | 50f multi | 45 | 30 |

Nos. 1095-1097 inscribed 1981.

30th Anniv. of Arab Postal Union — A162

**1982, Apr. 12 Litho. *Perf. 14x14½***

| | | | | |
|---|---|---|---|---|
| *1098* | A162 | 10f multi | 10 | 6 |
| *1099* | A162 | 25f multi | 22 | 15 |
| *1100* | A162 | 40f multi | 36 | 24 |
| *1101* | A162 | 50f multi | 45 | 30 |
| *1102* | A162 | 100f multi | 90 | 60 |
| | | *Nos. 1098-1102 (5)* | 2.03 | 1.35 |

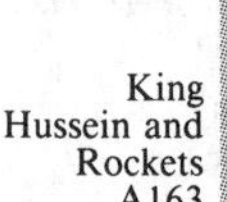

King Hussein and Rockets A163

**1982, May 25 Litho. *Perf. 14½x14***

| | | | | |
|---|---|---|---|---|
| *1103* | A163 | 10f shown | 10 | 6 |
| *1104* | A163 | 25f Tanks crossing bridge | 22 | 15 |
| *1105* | A163 | 40f Jet | 36 | 24 |
| *1106* | A163 | 50f Tanks, diff. | 45 | 30 |
| *1107* | A163 | 100f Raising flag | 90 | 60 |
| | | *Nos. 1103-1107 (5)* | 2.03 | 1.35 |

Independence and Army Day; 30th anniv. of King Hussein's accession to the throne.

Salt Secondary School — A164

**1982, Sept. 12 Litho. *Perf. 14½x14***

| | | | | |
|---|---|---|---|---|
| *1108* | A164 | 10f multi | 10 | 6 |
| *1109* | A164 | 25f multi | 22 | 15 |
| *1110* | A164 | 40f multi | 36 | 24 |
| *1111* | A164 | 50f multi | 45 | 30 |
| *1112* | A164 | 100f multi | 90 | 60 |
| | | *Nos. 1108-1112 (5)* | 2.03 | 1.35 |

International Heritage of Jerusalem — A165

**1982, Nov. 14 Litho. *Perf. 14x14½***

| | | | | |
|---|---|---|---|---|
| *1113* | A165 | 10f Gate to Old City | 10 | 6 |
| *1114* | A165 | 25f Minaret | 28 | 15 |
| *1115* | A165 | 40f Al Aqsa | 45 | 24 |
| *1116* | A165 | 50f Dome of the Rock | 55 | 30 |
| *1117* | A165 | 100f Dome of the Rock, diff. | 1.10 | 60 |
| | | *Nos. 1113-1117 (5)* | 2.48 | 1.35 |

Yarmouk Forces — A166

**1982, Nov. 14 *Perf. 14½x14***

| | | | | |
|---|---|---|---|---|
| *1118* | A166 | 10f multi | 12 | 8 |
| *1119* | A166 | 25f multi | 30 | 20 |
| *1120* | A166 | 40f multi | 48 | 30 |
| *1121* | A166 | 50f multi | 60 | 40 |
| *1122* | A166 | 100f multi | 1.20 | 90 |

**Size: 71x51mm**

***Imperf***

| | | | | |
|---|---|---|---|---|
| *1123* | A166 | 100f Armed Forces emblem | 4.00 | 4.00 |

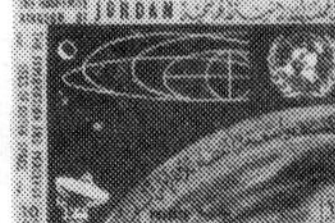

2nd UN Conf. on Peaceful Uses of Outer Space, Vienna, Aug. 9-21 — A167

**1982, Dec. 1 *Perf. 14½x14***

| | | | | |
|---|---|---|---|---|
| *1124* | A167 | 10f multi | 10 | 6 |
| *1125* | A167 | 25f multi | 22 | 15 |
| *1126* | A167 | 40f multi | 36 | 24 |
| *1127* | A167 | 50f multi | 45 | 30 |
| *1128* | A167 | 100f multi | 90 | 60 |
| | | *Nos. 1124-1128 (5)* | 2.03 | 1.35 |

Birth Centenary of Amir Abdullah ibn Hussein — A168

**1982, Dec. 13 Litho. *Perf. 14½***

| | | | | |
|---|---|---|---|---|
| *1129* | A168 | 10f multi | 6 | 5 |
| *1130* | A168 | 25f multi | 12 | 8 |
| *1131* | A168 | 40f multi | 20 | 15 |
| *1132* | A168 | 50f multi | 30 | 35 |
| *1133* | A168 | 100f multi | 70 | 45 |
| | | *Nos. 1129-1133 (5)* | 1.38 | 1.08 |

Roman Ruins of Jerash A169

**1982, Dec. 29 Litho. *Perf. 15***

| | | | | |
|---|---|---|---|---|
| *1134* | A169 | 10f Temple colonnade | 10 | 6 |
| *1135* | A169 | 25f Arch | 22 | 15 |
| *1136* | A169 | 40f Columns | 36 | 24 |
| *1137* | A169 | 50f Ampitheater | 45 | 30 |
| *1138* | A169 | 100f Hippodrome | 90 | 60 |
| | | *Nos. 1134-1138 (5)* | 2.03 | 1.35 |

King Hussein — A170

**1983** **Litho.** ***Perf. 14½x14***
1139 A170 10f multi 6 5
1140 A170 25f multi 12 8
1141 A170 40f multi 20 15
1142 A170 60f multi 30 20
1143 A170 100f multi 50 34
1144 A170 125f multi 60 35
*Nos. 1139-1144 (6)* 1.78 1.17

Issue dates: 10f, 60f, Feb. 1; 40f, Feb. 8; 25f, 100f, 125f, Mar. 3. Inscribed 1982.

Massacre at Shatalla and Sabra Palestinian Refugee Camps A171

Designs: 10f, 25f, 50f, No. 1149, Various victims. 40f, Children. No. 1150, Wounded child.

**1983, Apr. 9** **Litho.** ***Perf. 14½***
1145 A171 10f multi 25 20
1146 A171 25f multi 45 40
1147 A171 40f multi 70 50
1148 A171 50f multi 85 70
1149 A171 100f multi 1.25 1.00

**Souvenir Sheet**

***Imperf***

1150 A171 100f multi 9.00

Size of No. 1150: 80x59mm.

Opening of Queen Alia Intl. Airport A172

**1983, May 25** **Litho.** ***Perf. 12½***
1151 A172 10f Aerial view 10 6
1152 A172 25f Terminal buildings 22 15
1153 A172 40f Hangar 36 24
1154 A172 50f Terminal buildings, diff. 45 30
1155 A172 100f Embarkation Bridge 90 60
*Nos. 1151-1155 (5)* 2.03 1.35

Royal Jordanian Radio Amateurs' Society A173

**1983, Aug. 11** **Litho.** ***Perf. 12***
1156 A173 10f multi 10 6
1157 A173 25f multi 22 15
1158 A173 40f multi 36 24
1159 A173 50f multi 45 30
1160 A173 100f multi 90 60
*Nos. 1156-1160 (5)* 2.03 1.35

Royal Academy for Islamic Cultural Research A174

**1983, Sept. 16** **Litho.** ***Perf. 12***
1161 A174 10f Academy Bldg. 8 5
1162 A174 25f Silk carpet 18 12
1163 A174 40f Mosque, Amman 25 18
1164 A174 50f Dome of the Rock 35 22
1165 A174 100f Islamic city views 70 45
*Nos. 1161-1165 (5)* 1.56 1.02

A 100f souvenir sheet shows letter from Mohammed.

World Food Day — A175

**1983, Oct. 16** **Litho.** ***Perf. 12***
1166 A175 10f Irrigation canal 10 6
1167 A175 25f Greenhouses 25 15
1168 A175 40f Light-grown crops 40 24
1169 A175 50f Harvest 50 30
1170 A175 100f Sheep farm 1.00 60
*Nos. 1166-1170 (5)* 2.25 1.35

World Communications Year — A176

**1983, Nov. 14**
1171 A176 10f Radio switchboard operators 8 5
1172 A176 25f Earth satellite station 20 12
1173 A176 40f Symbols of communication 32 20
1174 A176 50f Emblems 40 25
1175 A176 100f Airmail letter 80 48
*Nos. 1171-1175 (5)* 1.80 1.10

Intl. Palestinian Solidarity Day — A177

Dome of the Rock, Jerusalem.

**1983, Nov. 29** ***Perf. 12***
1176 A177 5f multi 5 5
1177 A177 10f multi 8 5

35th Anniv. of UN Declaration of Human Rights A178

**1983, Dec. 10**
1178 A178 10f multi 8 5
1179 A178 25f multi 18 12
1180 A178 40f multi 25 18
1181 A178 50f multi 35 22
1182 A178 100f multi 70 45
*Nos. 1178-1182 (5)* 1.56 1.02

Anti-Paralysis — A179

**1984, Apr. 7** ***Perf. 13½x11½***
1183 A179 40f multi 40 24
1184 A179 60f multi 60 36
1185 A179 100f multi 1.00 60

Anti-Polio Campaign.

Israeli Bombing of Iraq Nuclear Reactor A180

Various designs.

**1984, June 7** **Litho.** ***Perf. 13½x11½***
1186 A180 40f multi 60 24
1187 A180 60f multi 80 35
1188 A180 100f multi 1.25 60

Independence and Army Day — A181

King Hussein and various armed forces.

**1984, June 10**
1189 A181 10f multi 10 6
1190 A181 25f multi 25 15
1191 A181 40f multi 40 24
1192 A181 60f multi 60 35
1193 A181 100f multi 1.00 60
*Nos. 1189-1193 (5)* 2.35 1.40

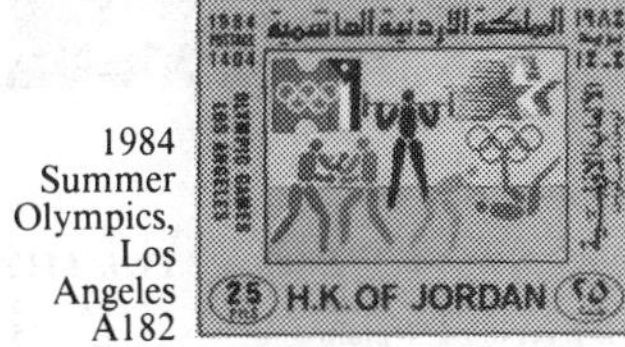


1984 Summer Olympics, Los Angeles A182

**1984, July 28**
1194 A182 25f shown 25 15
1195 A182 40f Swimming 40 24
1196 A182 60f Shooting, archery 60 35
1197 A182 100f Gymnastics 1.00 60

An imperf. 100f souvenir sheet exists picturing pole vaulting.

Water and Electricity Year A183

**1984, Aug. 11**
1198 A183 25f Power lines, factory 25 15
1199 A183 40f Amman Power Station 40 24
1200 A183 60f Irrigation 60 35
1201 A183 100f Hydro-electric dam 1.00 60

Coins A184

**1984, Sept. 26** **Photo.** ***Perf. 13***
1202 A184 40f Omayyad gold dinar 40 24
1203 A184 60f Abbasid gold dinar 60 35
1204 A184 125f Hashemite silver dinar 1.25 75

Royal Society for the Conservation of Nature — A185

**1984, Oct. 18**
1205 A185 25f Four antelopes 25 15
1206 A185 40f Grazing 40 24
1207 A185 60f Three antelopes 60 35
1208 A185 100f King Hussein, Queen Alia, Duke of Edinburgh 1.00 60

Natl. Universities — A186

Designs: 40f, Mu'ta Military University, Karak. 60f, Yarmouk University, Irbib. 125f, Jordan University, Amman.

**1984, Nov. 14** ***Perf. 13x13½***
1209 A186 40f multi 40 24
1210 A186 60f multi 60 35
1211 A186 125f multi 1.25 75

Al Sahaba Tombs A187

Designs: 10f, El Harath bin Omier el-Azdi and Derer bin El-Azwar. 25f, Sharhabil bin Hasna and Abu Obaidah Amer bin el-Jarrah. 40f, Muath bin Jabal. 50f, Zaid bin Haretha and Abdullah bin Rawaha. 60f, Amer bin Abi Waqqas. 100f, Jafar bin Abi Taleb.

**1984, Dec. 5** **Litho.** ***Perf. 13½x11½***
1212 A187 10f multi 10 6
1213 A187 25f multi 25 15
1214 A187 40f multi 40 24
1215 A187 50f multi 50 30
1216 A187 60f multi 60 35
1217 A187 100f multi 1.00 60
*Nos. 1212-1217 (6)* 2.85 1.70

Independence and Army Day — A188

Designs: 25f, King Hussein, soldier descending mountain. 40f, Hussein, Arab revolt flag, globe, King Abdullah. 60f, Flag, natl. arms, equestrian. 100f, Natl. flag, arms, King Abdullah.

**1985, June 10** ***Perf. 13x13½***
1218 A188 25f multi 25 15
1219 A188 40f multi 40 24
1220 A188 60f multi 60 35
1221 A188 100f multi 1.00 60

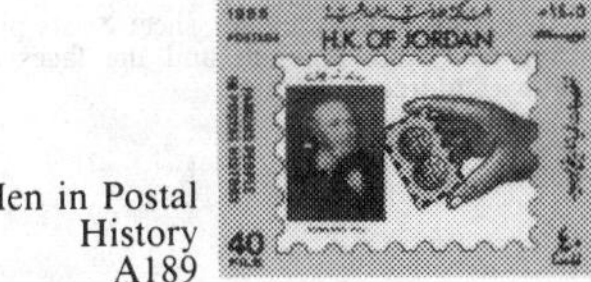


Men in Postal History A189

**1985, July 1**

*1222* A189 40f Sir Rowland Hill 40 24
*1223* A189 60f Heinrich von Stephan 60 35
*1224* A189 125f Yacoub al-Sukkar 1.25 75

1st Convention of Jordanian Expatriates A190

Various designs.

**1985, July 20** **Photo.**

*1225* A190 40f multi 40 24
*1226* A190 60f multi 60 35
*1227* A190 125f multi 1.25 75

Intl. Youth Year — A191

Various designs.

**1985, Aug. 11** **Litho.** ***Perf. 13½x13***

*1228* A191 10f multi 10 6
*1229* A191 25f multi 25 15
*1230* A191 40f multi 40 24
*1231* A191 60f multi 60 35
*1232* A191 125f multi 1.25 75
*Nos. 1228-1232 (5)* 2.60 1.55

World Tourism Organization, 10th Anniv. — A192

**1985, Sept. 13** ***Perf. 13½x13***

*1233* A192 10f Ruins of the Treasury, Petra 10 6
*1234* A192 25f Jerash Temple 25 15
*1235* A192 40f Roman baths 40 24
*1236* A192 50f Jordanian valley town 50 30
*1237* A192 60f Aqaba Bay 60 35
*1238* A192 125f Roman amphitheater 1.25 75
*Nos. 1233-1238 (6)* 3.10 1.85

An imperf. 100f souvenir sheet exists picturing flower, 10 and natl. flag.

UN Child Survival Campaign A193

Various designs.

**1985, Oct. 7**

*1239* A193 25f multi 25 15
*1240* A193 40f multi 40 24
*1241* A193 60f multi 60 35
*1242* A193 125f multi 1.25 75

An imperf. 100f souvenir sheet exists picturing campaign emblem and the faces of healthy children.

5th Jerash Festival A194

**1985, Oct. 21**

*1243* A194 10f Opening ceremony, 1980 10 6
*1244* A194 25f Folk dancers 25 15
*1245* A194 40f Dancers 40 24
*1246* A194 60f Choir, Roman theater 60 35
*1247* A194 100f King and Queen 1.00 60
*Nos. 1243-1247 (5)* 2.35 1.40

UN, 40th Anniv. A195

**1985, Oct. 25** **Photo.** ***Perf. 13x13½***

*1248* A195 60f multi 60 35
*1249* A195 125f multi 1.25 75

King Hussein, 50th Birthday A196

Various photos of King.

**1985, Nov. 14** **Litho.** ***Perf. 14½***

*1250* A196 10f multi 10 6
*1251* A196 25f multi 25 15
*1252* A196 40f multi 40 24
*1253* A196 60f multi 60 35
*1254* A196 100f multi 1.00 60
*Nos. 1250-1254 (5)* 2.35 1.40

An imperf. 200f souvenir sheet exists picturing flags, King Hussein and Dome of the Rock.

Restoration of Al Aqsa Mosque, Jerusalem A196a

**1985, Nov. 25** **Litho.** ***Perf. 13x13½***

*1254A* A196a 5f multi *50 50*
*1254B* A196a 10f multi *1.00 75*

Police A197

**1985, Dec. 18**

*1255* A197 40f Patrol car 22 14
*1256* A197 60f Crossing guard 32 20
*1257* A197 125f Police academy 70 42

Launch of ARABSAT-1, 1st Anniv. — A198

**1986, Feb. 8** **Litho.** ***Perf. 13½x13***

*1258* A198 60f Satellite in orbit 32 20
*1259* A198 100f Over map of Arab countries 55 32

Arabization of the Army, 30th Anniv. — A199

Designs: 40f, King Hussein presenting flag. 60f, Greeting army sergeant. 100f, Hussein addressing army.

**1986, Mar. 1** ***Perf. 11½x12½***

*1260* A199 40f multi 22 14
*1261* A199 60f multi 32 20
*1262* A199 100f multi 55 32

An imperf. souvenir sheet exists with design of 100f.

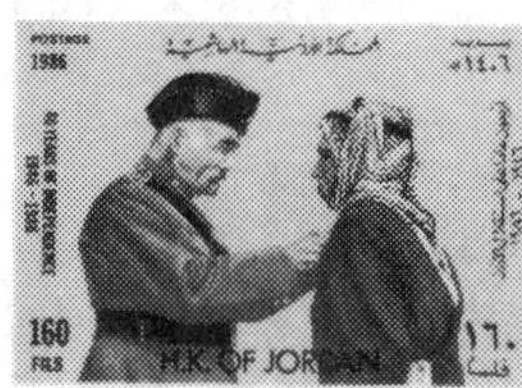

Natl. Independence, 40th Anniv. — A200

Design: King Abdullah decorating soldier.

**1986, May 25** ***Perf. 12½x11½***

*1263* A200 160f multi 88 52

Arab Revolt against Turkey, 70th Anniv. — A201

Unattributed paintings (details): 40f, The four sons of King Hussein, Prince of Mecca, vert. 60f, Abdullah, retainers and bodyguard. 160f, Abdullah and followers on horseback.

***Perf. 12½x11½, 11½x12½***

**1986, June 10**

*1264* A201 40f multi 22 14
*1265* A201 60f multi 32 20
*1266* A201 160f multi 88 52

An imperf. souvenir sheet exists picturing the Arab Revolt flag, King Abdullah and text from independence declaration.

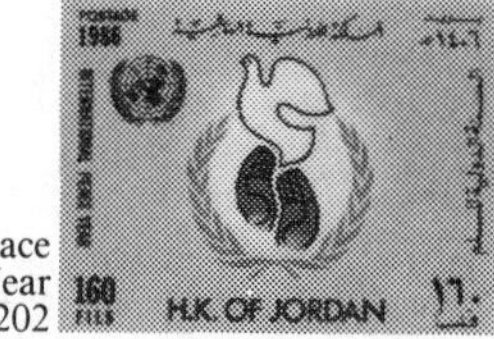


Intl. Peace Year A202

**1986, July 1** **Litho.** ***Perf. 13½x13***

*1267* A202 160f multi 90 55
*1268* A202 240f multi 1.35 80

King Hussein Medical City Cardiac Center A203

**1986, Aug. 11**

*1269* A203 40f Cardiac Center 22 14
*1270* A203 60f Surgery 35 22
*1271* A203 100f Surgery, diff. 55 32

UN, 40th Anniv. — A204

Excerpts from King Hussein's speech: 40f, In Arabic. 80f, Arabic, diff. 100f, English.

**1986, Sept. 27** ***Perf. 12½x11½***

*1272* A204 40f multi 22 12
*1273* A204 80f multi 45 28
*1274* A204 100f multi 55 32

An imperf. 200f stamp (size: 90x70mm) exists picturing speech in Arabic and English, King Hussein at podium.

Arab Postal Union, 35th Anniv. A205

**1987, Apr. 12** **Litho.** ***Perf. 13½x13***

*1275* A205 80f Old post office 45 28
*1276* A205 160f New post office 90 55

Chemical Soc. Emblem and Chemists — A206

Designs: 60f, Jaber ibn Hayyan al-Azdi (720-813). 80f, Abu-al-Qasem al-Majreeti (950-1007). 240f, Abu-Bakr al-Razi (864-932).

**1987, Apr. 24**

*1277* A206 60f multi 35 22
*1278* A206 80f multi 45 28
*1279* A206 240f multi 1.35 80

SOS Children's Village — A207

**1987, May 7**
1280 A207 80f Village in Amman 45 28
1281 A207 240f Child, bird mural 1.35 80

4th Brigade, 40th Anniv. A208

**1987, June 10**
1282 A208 60f shown 35 22
1283 A208 80f Soldiers in armored vehicle 45 28

**Size: 70x91mm.**
***Imperf***

1284 A208 160f Four veterans 90 55

Indigenous Birds A209

**1987, June 24**
1285 A209 10f Hoopoe 8 6
1286 A209 40f Palestine sunbird 30 20
1287 A209 50f Black-headed bunting 38 25
1288 A209 60f Spur-winged plover 45 30
1289 A209 80f Greenfinch 60 40
1290 A209 100f Black-winged stilt 75 50
*Nos. 1285-1290 (6)* 2.56 1.71

King Hussein — A210

**1987, June 24 Litho. *Perf. 13x13½***
1291 A210 60f multi 45 30
1292 A210 80f multi 60 40
1293 A210 160f multi 1.20 40
1294 A210 240f multi 1.80 1.20

Battle of Hittin, 800th Anniv. A211

Dome of the Rock and Saladin (1137-1193), Conqueror of Jerusalem — A212

**1987, July 4**
1295 A211 60f Battle, Jerusalem 35 24
1296 A211 80f Horseman, Jerusalem, Dome of the Rock 45 30
1297 A211 100f Saladin 75 50

**Souvenir Sheet**
***Perf. 12x12½***

1298 A212 100f shown 75 50

No. 1298 exists imperf. Size: 90x70mm.

Natl. Coat of Arms — A213

***Perf. 11½x12½***
**1987, Aug. 11 Litho.**
1299 A213 80f multi 60 40
1300 A213 160f multi 1.20 80

Amman Industrial Park at Sahab — A214

**1987, Aug. 11 *Perf. 13½x13***
1301 A214 80f multi 60 40

University Crest A215

University Entrance — A216

***Perf. 11½x11, 12½x11½***
**1987, Sept. 2**
1302 A215 60f multi 45 30
1303 A216 80f multi 60 40

University of Jordan, 25th anniv.

U.N. Child Survival Campaign A217

**1987, Oct. 5 Litho. *Perf. 13x13½***
1304 A217 60f Oral vaccine 45 30
1305 A217 80f Natl. flag, child 60 40
1306 A217 160f Growth monitoring 1.20 80

Parliament, 40th Anniv. — A218

**1987, Oct. 20 *Perf. 13½x13***
1307 A218 60f Opening ceremony, 1947 45 30
1308 A218 80f In session, 1987 60 40

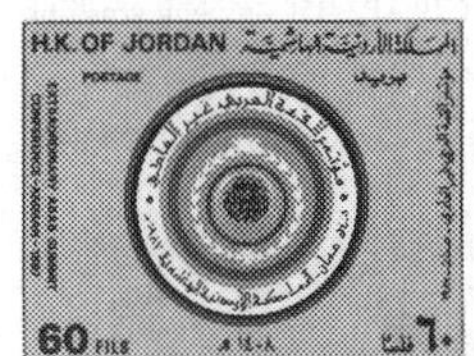

A219

Special Arab Summit Conference, Amman — A220

**1987, Nov. 8**
1309 A219 60f multi 45 30
1310 A219 80f multi 60 40
1311 A219 160f multi 1.20 80
1312 A219 240f multi 1.80 1.20

**Size: 90x66mm.**
***Imperf***

1313 A220 100f multi

King Hussein, Dag Hammarskjold Peace Prize Winner for 1987 — A221

**1988, Feb. 6 Litho. *Perf. 12½***
1314 A221 80f Hussein, woman, vert. 60 40
1315 A221 160f shown 1.20 80

Natl. Victory at the 1987 Arab Military Basketball Championships — A222

**1988, Mar. 1 *Perf. 13½x13***
1316 A222 60f Golden Sword Award 45 30
1317 A222 80f Hussein congratulating team 60 40
1318 A222 160f Jump ball 1.20 80

World Health Organization (WHO), 40th Anniv. — A223

**1988, Apr. 7 Photo. *Perf. 13x13½***
1319 A223 60f multi 55 38
1320 A223 80f multi 72 48

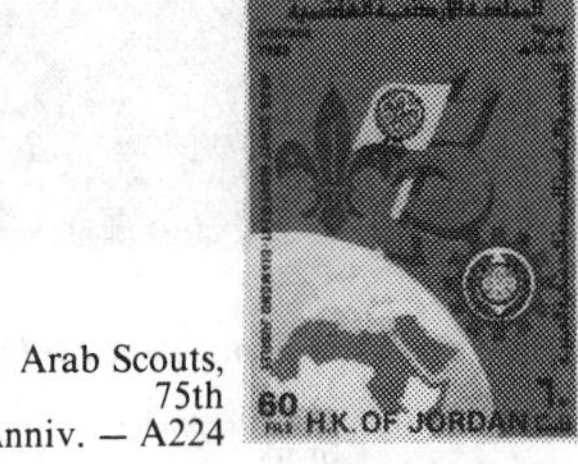

Arab Scouts, 75th Anniv. — A224

**1988, July 2 Litho. *Perf. 13x13½***
1321 A224 60f multi 45 35
1322 A224 80f multi 60 45

Birds A225

**1988, July 21 Litho. *Perf. 11½x12***
1323 A225 10f Crested lark 8 6
1324 A225 20f Stone curlew 15 12
1325 A225 30f Redstart 20 15
1326 A225 40f Blackbird 28 22
1327 A225 50f Rock dove 35 28
1328 A225 160f Smyrna kingfisher 1.10 82

**Size: 71x90mm**
***Imperf***

1328A A225 310f Six species 3.75 2.75
*Nos. 1323-1328A (7)* 5.91 4.40

Prices of premium quality never hinged stamps will be in excess of catalogue price.

Restoration of San'a City, Capital of Yemen Arab Republic
A226

**1988, Aug. 11 Litho. *Perf. 12x11½***

| | | | | |
|---|---|---|---|---|
| *1329* | A226 | 80f multi | 60 | 45 |
| *1330* | A226 | 160f multi | 1.20 | 90 |

Historic Natl. Sites
A227

**1988, Aug. 11 *Perf. 13½x13***

| | | | | |
|---|---|---|---|---|
| *1331* | A227 | 60f Umm Al-rasas | 45 | 35 |
| *1332* | A227 | 80f Umm Qais | 60 | 45 |
| *1333* | A227 | 160f Iraq Al-amir | 1.20 | 90 |

An imperf. souvenir sheet of 3 exists containing one each Nos. 1331-1333.

1988 Summer Olympics, Seoul — A228

**1988, Sept. 17 Litho. *Perf. 13x13½***

| | | | | |
|---|---|---|---|---|
| *1334* | A228 | 10f Tennis | 8 | 6 |
| *1335* | A228 | 60f Character trade-mark | 45 | 35 |
| *1336* | A228 | 80f Running, swimming | 60 | 45 |
| *1337* | A228 | 120f Basketball | 90 | 68 |
| *1338* | A228 | 160f Soccer | 1.20 | 90 |
| | | *Nos. 1334-1338 (5)* | 3.23 | 2.44 |

**Size: 70x91mm**

***Imperf***

| | | | | |
|---|---|---|---|---|
| *1339* | A228 | 100f Emblems | | |

## SEMI-POSTAL STAMPS

### Locust Campaign Issue

Nos. 145-156 Overprinted

**1930, Apr. 1 Wmk. 4 *Perf. 14***

| | | | | |
|---|---|---|---|---|
| *B1* | A1 | 2(m) Prus bl | 1.00 | 1.10 |
| *a.* | | Invtd. ovpt. | 175.00 | |
| *B2* | A1 | 3(m) rose | 1.25 | 1.40 |
| *B3* | A1 | 4(m) green | 18 | 20 |
| *B4* | A1 | 5(m) orange | 5.00 | 5.25 |
| *a.* | | Dbl. ovpt. | 250.00 | |
| *B5* | A1 | 10(m) red | 25 | 30 |
| *B6* | A1 | 15(m) ultra | 30 | 32 |
| *a.* | | Inverted overprint | 150.00 | |
| *B7* | A1 | 20(m) ol grn | 35 | 40 |
| *B8* | A2 | 50(m) claret | 1.40 | 1.50 |
| *B9* | A2 | 90(m) bister | 5.00 | 5.50 |
| *B10* | A2 | 100(m) lt bl | 3.50 | 3.50 |
| *B11* | A2 | 200(m) violet | 15.00 | 15.00 |
| *B12* | A2 | 500(m) brown | 40.00 | 40.00 |
| *a.* | | "C" of "Locust" omittedst | 600.00 | |
| | | *Nos. B1-B12 (12)* | 73.23 | 74.47 |

These stamps were issued to raise funds to help combat a plague of locusts.

## AIR POST STAMPS

**Catalogue values for unused stamps in this section, from this point to the end of the section, are for Never Hinged items.**

Plane and Globe
AP1

Temple of Artemis, Jerash
AP2

***Perf. 13½x13***

**1950, Sept. 16 Engr. Wmk. 4**

| | | | | |
|---|---|---|---|---|
| *C1* | AP1 | 5f org & red vio | 6 | 6 |
| *C2* | AP1 | 10f pur & brn | 8 | 8 |
| *C3* | AP1 | 15f ol grn & rose car | 10 | 10 |
| *C4* | AP1 | 20f dp bl & blk | 15 | 12 |
| *C5* | AP1 | 50f rose pink & dl grn | 20 | 15 |
| *C6* | AP1 | 100f bl & brn | 35 | 35 |
| *C7* | AP1 | 150f blk & red org | 50 | 50 |
| | | *Nos. C1-C7 (7)* | 1.44 | 1.36 |

**1954 Unwmk. *Perf. 12***

| | | | | |
|---|---|---|---|---|
| *C8* | AP2 | 5f bl blk & org | 5 | 5 |
| *C9* | AP2 | 10f vio brn & ver | 5 | 5 |
| *C10* | AP2 | 25f bl grn & ultra | 9 | 9 |
| *C11* | AP2 | 35f dp plum & grnsh bl | 12 | 10 |
| *C12* | AP2 | 40f car rose & blk | 15 | 10 |
| *C13* | AP2 | 50f dp ultra & org yel | 18 | 18 |
| *C14* | AP2 | 100f dk bl & vio brn | 30 | 30 |
| *C15* | AP2 | 150f stl bl & red brn | 42 | 42 |
| | | *Nos. C8-C15 (8)* | 1.36 | 1.29 |

**1958-59 Wmk. 305 *Perf. 12***

| | | | | |
|---|---|---|---|---|
| *C16* | AP2 | 5f bl blk & org | 5 | 5 |
| *C17* | AP2 | 10f vio brn & ver | 5 | 5 |
| *C18* | AP2 | 25f bl grn & ultra | 10 | 8 |
| *C19* | AP2 | 35f dp plum grnsh bl | 10 | 10 |
| *C20* | AP2 | 40f car rose & blk | 12 | 12 |
| *C21* | AP2 | 50f dp ultra & org yel ('59) | 30 | 30 |
| | | *Nos. C16-C21 (6)* | 72 | 70 |

Stadium and Torch
AP3

***Perf. 11x11½***

**1964, July 12 Litho. Wmk. 305**

| | | | | |
|---|---|---|---|---|
| *C22* | AP3 | 1f yel & multi | 5 | 5 |
| *C23* | AP3 | 4f red & multi | 5 | 5 |
| *C24* | AP3 | 10f bl & multi | 5 | 5 |
| *C25* | AP3 | 35f yel grn & multi | 14 | 14 |
| *a.* | | Souv. sheet of 4 | 50 | 50 |

Issued to commemorate the opening of Hussein Sports City. No. C25a contains one each of Nos. C22-C25. Blue margin with black inscription. Size: 121½x93mm. No. C25a also exists imperf.

Gorgeous Bush-Shrike — AP4

Birds: 500f, Ornate hawk-eagle (vert.). 1d, Gray-headed kingfisher (vert.).

***Perf. 14x14½***

**1964, Dec. 18 Photo. Unwmk.**

**Birds in Natural Colors**

| | | | | |
|---|---|---|---|---|
| *C26* | AP4 | 150f lt grn, blk & car | 1.25 | 30 |
| *C27* | AP4 | 500f brt bl, blk & grn | 6.25 | 2.00 |
| *C28* | AP4 | 1d lt ol grn & blk | 12.50 | 6.25 |

Exist imperf.

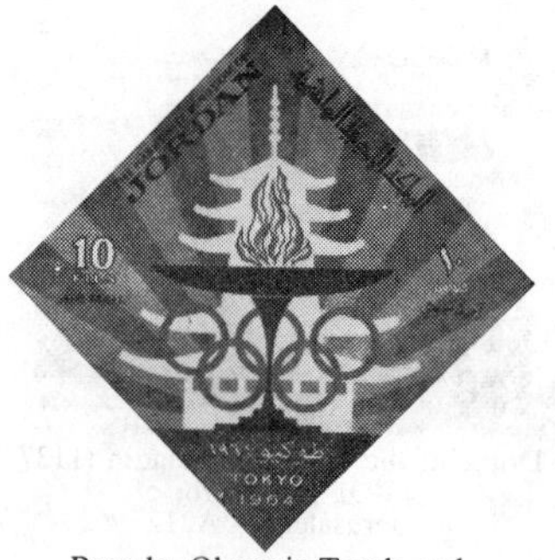


Pagoda, Olympic Torch and Emblem — AP5

**1965, Mar. 5 Litho. *Perf. 14***

| | | | | |
|---|---|---|---|---|
| *C29* | AP5 | 10f dp rose | 5 | 5 |
| *C30* | AP5 | 15f violet | 6 | 6 |
| *C31* | AP5 | 20f blue | 8 | 8 |
| *C32* | AP5 | 30f green | 12 | 12 |
| *C33* | AP5 | 40f green | 18 | 18 |
| *C34* | AP5 | 60f car rose | 25 | 25 |
| | | *Nos. C29-C34 (6)* | 74 | 74 |

Issued to commemorate the 18th Olympic Games, Tokyo, Oct. 10-25, 1964. An imperf. 100f violet blue souvenir sheet exists. Size of stamp: 60x60mm. Size of sheet: 102x102mm. Value $9.

Forum, Jerash
AP6

Antiquities of Jerash: No. C36, South Theater. No. C37, Triumphal arch. No. C38, Temple of Artemis. No. C39, Cathedral steps. No. C40, Artemis Temple, gate. No. C41, Columns. No. C42, Columns and niche, South Theater. Nos. C39-C42 are vertical.

**1965, June 22 Photo. *Perf. 14x15***

**Center Multicolored**

| | | | | |
|---|---|---|---|---|
| *C35* | AP6 | 55f brt pink | 35 | 35 |
| *C36* | AP6 | 55f lt bl | 35 | 35 |
| *C37* | AP6 | 55f green | 35 | 35 |
| *C38* | AP6 | 55f black | 35 | 35 |
| *C39* | AP6 | 55f lt grn | 35 | 35 |
| *C40* | AP6 | 55f car rose | 35 | 35 |
| *C41* | AP6 | 55f gray | 35 | 35 |
| *C42* | AP6 | 55f blue | 35 | 35 |
| | | *Nos. C35-C42 (8)* | 2.80 | 2.80 |

Nos. C35-C38 are printed in horizontal rows of four; Nos. C39-C42 in vertical rows of four; sheets of 16.

### King Hussein Type of Regular Issue

**1966, Jan. 15 Photo. *Perf. 14½x14***

**Portrait in Brown**

| | | | | |
|---|---|---|---|---|
| *C43* | A67 | 200f brt bl grn | 1.00 | 50 |
| *C44* | A67 | 500f lt grn | 2.50 | 1.25 |
| *C45* | A67 | 1d lt ultra | 5.00 | 2.50 |

### Animal Type of Regular Issue, 1967.

Animals: 4f, Striped hyena. 30f, Arabian stallion. 60f, Persian gazelle.

**1967, Feb. 11 Photo. *Perf. 14x15***

| | | | | |
|---|---|---|---|---|
| *C46* | A70 | 4f dk brn & multi | 5 | 5 |
| *C47* | A70 | 30f lt bl & multi | 15 | 10 |
| *C48* | A70 | 60f yel & multi | 30 | 20 |

### Game Type of Regular Issue, 1968

Protected Game: 60f, Nubian ibex (vert.). 100f, Wild ducks.

**1968, Oct. 5 Litho. *Perf. 13½***

| | | | | |
|---|---|---|---|---|
| *C49* | A74 | 60f multi | 50 | 50 |
| *C50* | A74 | 100f multi | 90 | 90 |

### Easter Type of Regular Issue

Designs: 60f, Altar, Holy Sepulcher. 100f, Feet Washing, Holy Gate, Jerusalem.

**1972, Apr. Photo. *Perf. 14x13½***

| | | | | |
|---|---|---|---|---|
| *C51* | A92 | 60f dk bl & multi | 30 | 30 |
| *C52* | A92 | 100f multi | 50 | 50 |

### Aero Club Type of Regular Issue

Designs: 15f, Two Piper 140s. 20f, R.J.A.C. Beechcraft. 40f, Aero Club emblem with winged horse.

**1973, Jan. Photo. *Perf. 13½x14***

| | | | | |
|---|---|---|---|---|
| *C53* | A100 | 15f bl, blk & red | 9 | 5 |
| *C54* | A100 | 20f bl, blk & red | 12 | 8 |
| *C55* | A100 | 40f mag, blk & yel | 25 | 15 |

### Agriculture Type of Regular Issue

Design: 100f, Soil conservation.

**1973, Dec. 25 *Perf. 13½***

| | | | | |
|---|---|---|---|---|
| *C56* | A110 | 100f multi | 45 | 30 |

King Hussein Driving Car — AP7

**1974, Dec. 20 *Perf. 12***

| | | | | |
|---|---|---|---|---|
| *C57* | AP7 | 30f multi | 14 | 9 |
| *C58* | AP7 | 60f multi | 35 | 25 |

Royal Jordanian Automobile Club.

### Building Type of Regular Issue

Designs: 50f, Palms, Aqaba. 60f, Obelisk tomb. 80f, Fort of Wadi Rum.

**1975, Mar. 1 Photo. *Perf. 13½x14***

| | | | | |
|---|---|---|---|---|
| *C59* | A121 | 50f pink & multi | 22 | 15 |
| *C60* | A121 | 60f lt bl & multi | 28 | 20 |
| *C61* | A121 | 80f yel & multi | 35 | 22 |

### Hussein Type of Regular Issue

**1975, Apr. 8 Photo. *Perf. 14x13½***

**Size: 22x27mm.**

| | | | | |
|---|---|---|---|---|
| *C62* | A123 | 60f dk grn & brn | 28 | 18 |
| *C63* | A123 | 100f org brn & brn | 42 | 30 |
| *C64* | A123 | 120f dp bl & brn | 50 | 36 |
| *C65* | A123 | 180f brt mag & brn | 85 | 50 |
| *C66* | A123 | 200f grnsh bl & brn | 90 | 50 |
| *C67* | A123 | 400f pur & brn | 1.75 | 1.10 |
| *C68* | A123 | 500f org & brn | 2.25 | 1.40 |
| | | *Nos. C62-C68 (7)* | 6.95 | 4.34 |

## POSTAGE DUE STAMPS

Stamps of Regular Issue (Nos. 69, 66-68 Surcharged with New Value like No. 91) Overprinted

This overprint reads: "Mustahaq" (Tax or Due)

**1923 Unwmk. *Perf. 11½***

**Typo. Ovpt. "Mustahaq" 10mm long**

| | | | | |
|---|---|---|---|---|
| *J1* | A7 | ½pi on 3pi ol brn | 50.00 | 52.50 |
| *a.* | | Inverted overprint | 120.00 | 120.00 |
| *b.* | | Double overprint | 160.00 | 150.00 |

**Handstamped Overprints "Mustahaq" 12mm long**

| | | | | |
|---|---|---|---|---|
| *J2* | A7 | ½pi on 3pi ol brn | 19.00 | 20.00 |
| *J3* | A7 | 1pi dark buel | 9.00 | 10.00 |
| *J4* | A7 | 1½pi violet | 9.00 | 10.00 |
| *J5* | A7 | 2pi orange | 9.00 | 10.00 |

These overprints are found double, inverted, etc. as is usual with handstamps.

حكومة
الشرق العربية
مستحق
٩ نيسان ١٣٤١

Stamps of Hejaz Handstamped

| | | | | |
|---|---|---|---|---|
| *J6* | A7 | ½pi red | 35 | 35 |
| *J7* | A7 | 1pi dk bl | 40 | 40 |
| *J8* | A7 | 1½pi violet | 50 | 50 |
| *J9* | A7 | 2pi orange | 65 | 65 |
| *J10* | A7 | 3pi ol brn | 1.00 | 1.00 |
| *J11* | A7 | 5pi ol grn | 1.40 | 1.40 |
| | | *Nos. J6-J11 (6)* | 4.30 | 4.30 |

مستحق
شرق الاردن

Type of Regular Issue of 1925 Overprinted

**1925 Wmk. 4 *Perf. 14.***

| | | | | |
|---|---|---|---|---|
| *J12* | A1 | 1m dk brn | 16 | 35 |
| *J13* | A1 | 2m yellow | 20 | 40 |
| *J14* | A1 | 4m rose | 30 | 50 |
| *J15* | A1 | 8m red | 35 | 50 |
| *J16* | A1 | 13m ultra | 50 | 55 |
| *J17* | A1 | 5pi plum | 80 | 1.00 |
| a. | | Perf. 15x14 | 4.00 | 4.25 |
| | | *Nos. J12-J17 (6)* | 2.31 | 3.30 |

The overprint reads: "Mustahaq. Sharqi al'Ardan." (Tax. Eastern Jordan).

مستحق
شرق
الاردن
٤ مليم

Stamps of Regular Issue of 1925 Surcharged

**1926**

| | | | | |
|---|---|---|---|---|
| *J18* | A1 | 1m on 1m dk brn | 50 | 60 |
| *J19* | A1 | 2m on 1m dk brn | 50 | 60 |
| *J20* | A1 | 4m on 3m Prus bl | 95 | 1.10 |
| *J21* | A1 | 8m on 3m Prus bl | 75 | 95 |
| *J22* | A1 | 13m on 13m ultra | 1.10 | 1.40 |
| *J23* | A1 | 5pi on 13m ultra | 1.10 | 1.40 |
| | | *Nos. J18-J23 (6)* | 4.90 | 6.05 |

The surcharge reads "Tax—Eastern Jordan" and New Value.

Stamps of Regular Issue, 1927, Overprinted

**1929**

| | | | | |
|---|---|---|---|---|
| *J24* | A1 | 2m Prus bl | 25 | 18 |
| *J25* | A1 | 10m red | 55 | 30 |
| *J26* | A2 | 50m claret | 1.10 | 90 |

**With Additional Surcharge**

| | | | | |
|---|---|---|---|---|
| *J27* | A1 | 4(m) on 3(m) rose | 18 | 18 |
| *J28* | A1 | 4(m) on 15(m) ultra | 45 | 28 |
| a. | | Invtd. surch. and ovpt. | 90.00 | |
| *J29* | A2 | 20(m) on 100(m) lt bl | 90 | 80 |

D1

D2

**1929 Engr. *Perf. 14***

**Size: 17¼x21mm**

| | | | | |
|---|---|---|---|---|
| *J30* | D1 | 1m brown | 12 | 12 |
| a. | | Perf. 13½x13 | 50.00 | 45.00 |
| *J31* | D1 | 2m orange | 15 | 15 |
| *J32* | D1 | 4m green | 15 | 15 |
| *J33* | D1 | 10m carmine | 30 | 30 |
| *J34* | D1 | 20m ol grn | 30 | 30 |
| *J35* | D1 | 50m blue | 50 | 50 |
| | | *Nos. J30-J35 (6)* | 1.52 | 1.52 |

**1942 Unwmk. Litho. *Perf. 13x13½***

| | | | | |
|---|---|---|---|---|
| *J36* | D2 | 1m dl red brn | 15 | 15 |
| *J37* | D2 | 2m dl org yel | 25 | 25 |
| *J38* | D2 | 10m dk car | 50 | 50 |

Type of 1929
White Paper
Size: 17¾x21¼mm

**1943-44 Engr. Wmk. 4 *Perf. 12***

| | | | | |
|---|---|---|---|---|
| *J39* | D1 | 1m org brn | 6 | 6 |
| *J40* | D1 | 2m yel org | 8 | 8 |
| *J41* | D1 | 4m yel grn | 9 | 9 |
| *J42* | D1 | 10m rose car | 15 | 15 |
| *J43* | D1 | 20m ol grn | 4.50 | 4.50 |
| | | *Nos. J39-J43 (5)* | 4.88 | 4.88 |

**Catalogue values for unused stamps in this section, from this point to the end of the section, are for Never Hinged items.**

Postage Due Stamps and Type of 1929-43 Surcharged "FILS" and its Arabic Equivalent in Black, Green or Carmine

**1952 Wmk. 4 *Perf. 12, 14***

| | | | | |
|---|---|---|---|---|
| *J47* | D1 | 1f on 1m org brn (Bk) | 14 | 10 |
| *J48* | D1 | 2f on 2m yel org (G) | 14 | 10 |
| *J49* | D1 | 4f on 4m yel grn | 14 | 10 |
| *J50* | D1 | 10f on 10m rose car (Bk) | 40 | 35 |
| *J51* | D1 | 20f on 20m ol grn | 50 | 50 |
| *J52* | D1 | 50f on 50m bl | 65 | 65 |
| | | *Nos. J47-J52 (6)* | 1.97 | 1.80 |

D3

Inscribed: "The Hashemite Kingdom of the Jordan"

**1952 Engr. *Perf. 11½***

| | | | | |
|---|---|---|---|---|
| *J53* | D3 | 1f org brn | 5 | 5 |
| *J54* | D3 | 2f yel org | 5 | 5 |
| *J55* | D3 | 4f yel grn | 5 | 5 |
| *J56* | D3 | 10f rose car | 7 | 5 |
| *J57* | D3 | 20f yel brn | 10 | 10 |
| *J58* | D3 | 50f blue | 35 | 20 |
| | | *Nos. J53-J58 (6)* | 67 | 50 |

Type of 1952 Redrawn.

Inscribed: "The Hashemite Kingdom of Jordan"

**1957 Wmk. 305 *Perf. 11½***

| | | | | |
|---|---|---|---|---|
| *J59* | D3 | 1f org brn | 5 | 5 |
| *J60* | D3 | 2f yel org | 5 | 5 |
| *J61* | D3 | 4f yel grn | 5 | 5 |
| *J62* | D3 | 10f rose car | 5 | 5 |
| *J63* | D3 | 20f yel brn | 12 | 8 |
| | | *Nos. J59-J63 (5)* | 32 | 28 |

## OFFICIAL STAMP

(حكومة)
الشرق العربي
١٣٤٢

Saudi Arabia No. L34 Overprinted

**1924, Jan. Typo. *Perf. 11½***

| | | | | |
|---|---|---|---|---|
| *O1* | A7 | ½pi red | 17.50 | |

Overprint reads: "(Government) the Arabian East 1342."

## POSTAL TAX STAMPS

**Catalogue values for unused stamps in this section, from this point to the end of the section, are for Never Hinged items.**

Mosque at Hebron — PT1

Designs: 10m, 15m, 20m, 50m, Dome of the Rock. 100m, 200m, 500m, £1, Acre.

***Perf. 11½x12½.***

**1947 Unwmk. Engr.**

| | | | | |
|---|---|---|---|---|
| *RA1* | PT1 | 1m ultra | 20 | 15 |
| *RA2* | PT1 | 2m carmine | 20 | 20 |
| *RA3* | PT1 | 3m emerald | 28 | 28 |
| *RA4* | PT1 | 5m plum | 38 | 20 |
| *RA5* | PT1 | 10m carmine | 40 | 30 |
| *RA6* | PT1 | 15m gray | 60 | 30 |
| *RA7* | PT1 | 20m dk brn | 75 | 45 |
| *RA8* | PT1 | 50m purple | 1.90 | 1.10 |
| *RA9* | PT1 | 100m org red | 3.75 | 2.50 |
| *RA10* | PT1 | 200m dp bl | 9.00 | 7.50 |
| *RA11* | PT1 | 500m green | 15.00 | 12.50 |
| *RA12* | PT1 | £1 dk brn | 25.00 | 25.00 |
| | | *Nos. RA1-RA12 (12)* | 57.46 | 50.48 |

Issued to help the Welfare Fund for Arabs in Palestine. Required on foreign-bound letters to the amount of half the regular postage.

اعانة

Nos. 211, 232 and 234 Overprinted in Black

Aid

**1950 Wmk. 4 *Perf. 12.***

| | | | | |
|---|---|---|---|---|
| *RA23* | A3 | 5m orange | 6.50 | |
| *RA24* | A3 | 10m violet | 10.00 | |
| *RA25* | A3 | 15m dl ol grn | 12.00 | |

Arch and Colonnade, Palmyra, Syria — PT2

Two types of 5m:

Type I: "A" with serifs. Arabic ovpt. 8mm wide.

Type II: "A" without serifs. Arabic ovpt. 5mm. wide.

Black or Carmine Overprint.

**1950-51 Engr. *Perf. 13½x13***

| | | | | |
|---|---|---|---|---|
| *RA26* | PT2 | 5m org (I) | 6.55 | |
| a. | | Type II ('51) | 20.00 | |
| *RA27* | PT2 | 10m vio (C) | 6.50 | |

The overprint on No. RA27 is similar to that on RA23-RA25 but slightly bolder.

Type of 1947.

Designs: 5f, Hebron Mosque. 10f, 15f, 20f, Dome of the Rock. 100f, Acre.

**1951 Wmk. 4 *Perf. 11½x12½.***

| | | | | |
|---|---|---|---|---|
| *RA28* | PT1 | 5f plum | 6 | 6 |
| *RA29* | PT1 | 10f carmine | 10 | 10 |
| *RA30* | PT1 | 15f gray | 16 | 16 |
| *RA31* | PT1 | 20f dk brn | 22 | 22 |
| *RA33* | PT1 | 100f orange | 1.50 | 1.50 |
| | | *Nos. RA28-RA33 (5)* | 2.04 | 2.04 |

The tax on Nos. RA1-RA33 was for Arab aid in Palestine.

Postal Tax Stamps of 1947 Surcharged "FILS" or "J.D." their Arabic Equivalents and Bars in Carmine or Black.

**1952 Unwmk.**

| | | | | |
|---|---|---|---|---|
| *RA37* | PT1 | 1f on 1m ultra | 25 | 12 |
| *RA38* | PT1 | 3f on 3m emer | 25 | 14 |
| *RA39* | PT1 | 10f on 10m car | 40 | 28 |
| *RA40* | PT1 | 15f on 15m gray | 55 | 40 |
| *RA41* | PT1 | 20f on 20m dk brn | 80 | 55 |
| *RA42* | PT1 | 50f on 50m pur | 2.00 | 1.40 |
| *RA43* | PT1 | 100f on 100m org red | 5.50 | 3.50 |
| *RA44* | PT1 | 200f on 200m dp bl | 14.00 | 4.25 |
| *RA45* | PT1 | 500f on 500m grn | 22.50 | 9.00 |
| *RA46* | PT1 | 1d on £1 dk brn | 37.50 | 21.00 |
| | | *Nos. RA37-RA46 (10)* | 83.75 | 40.64 |

"J.D." stands for Jordanian Dinar.

## OCCUPATION STAMPS

**Catalogue values for unused stamps in this section, from this point to the end of the section, are for Never Hinged items.**

**For Use in Palestine.**

فلسطين
PALESTINE

Stamps of Jordan Overprinted in Red, Black, Dark Green, Green or Orange Red

On No. 200.

**1948 Unwmk. *Perf. 13x13½.***

| | | | | |
|---|---|---|---|---|
| *N1* | A14 | 2m dl grn (R) | 75 | 75 |

On Nos. 207 to 209, 211, 230 to 235 and 215 to 220.

**1948 Wmk. 4 *Perf. 12, 13½x13, 14.***

| | | | | |
|---|---|---|---|---|
| *N2* | A3 | 1m red brn | 20 | 20 |
| *N3* | A3 | 2m Prus grn (R) | 30 | 30 |
| a. | | 2m Prus bl, perf. 13½x13 (R) (#170a) | 30 | 50 |
| *N4* | A3 | 3m bl grn (R) | 50 | 50 |
| *N5* | A3 | 3m rose car | 25 | 25 |
| *N6* | A3 | 4m dp yel grn (R) | 25 | 25 |
| *N7* | A3 | 5m org (G) | 60 | 25 |
| *N8* | A3 | 10m vio (OR) | 75 | 35 |
| *N9* | A3 | 12m dp rose | 60 | 60 |
| *N10* | A3 | 15m dl ol grn (R) | 70 | 50 |
| *N11* | A3 | 20m dp bl (R) | 60 | 60 |
| *N12* | A3 | 50m red lil (Dk G) | 1.25 | 1.25 |
| *N13* | A3 | 90m ocher (Dk G) | 4.00 | 3.50 |
| *N14* | A3 | 100m dp bl (R) | 4.50 | 4.00 |
| *N15* | A3 | 200m dk vio (R) | 8.00 | 7.00 |
| a. | | 200m vio, perf. 14 (R) (#182) | 15.00 | 15.00 |
| *N16* | A3 | 500m dk brn (R) | 13.00 | 5.00 |
| *N17* | A3 | £1 blk (R) | 20.00 | 10.00 |
| | | *Nos. N2-N17 (16)* | 55.50 | 34.55 |

Nos. N7 and N8 are from a second overprinting of Nos. N1, N3, N5, N6 and N9 to N17, in inks differing in shade from the originals.

Many values exist with inverted or double overprint.

فلسطين

Jordan, Nos. 245 to 249, Overprinted in Black or Red

PALESTINE

**1949, Aug. Wmk. 4 *Perf. 13***

| | | | | |
|---|---|---|---|---|
| *N18* | A17 | 1m brn (Bk) | 10 | 10 |
| *N19* | A17 | 4m green | 20 | 20 |
| a. | | "PLAESTINE" | 20.00 | |
| *N20* | A17 | 10m ultra | 30 | 30 |
| *N21* | A17 | 20m ultra | 30 | 30 |
| *N22* | A18 | 50m dl grn | 80 | 80 |
| a. | | "PLAESTINE" | 20.00 | |
| | | *Nos. N18-N22 (5)* | 1.70 | 1.70 |

The overprint is in one line on No. N22.

Issued to commemorate the 75th anniversary of the formation of the Universal Postal Union.

## OCCUPATION POSTAGE DUE STAMPS

**Catalogue values for unused stamps in this section, from this point to the end of the section, are for Never Hinged items.**

فلسطين

Jordan Nos. J39, J30a, J40, J32, J41-J43, J34 and J35 Overprinted in Black, Red or Carmine

PALESTINE

**1948-49 Wmk. 4 *Perf. 12, 14.***

| | | | | |
|---|---|---|---|---|
| *NJ1* | D1 | 1m org brn, perf. 12 | 14 | 14 |
| a. | | Perf. 13½x13 (#J30a) | 15.00 | 10.00 |
| *NJ2* | D1 | 2m yel org | 14 | 14 |
| *NJ3* | D1 | 4m grn (R) (#J32) | 50 | 50 |
| a. | | 4m yel grn (C) (#J41) | 3.75 | |

*NJ5* D1 10m rose car (#J42) ('49) 80 80
*a.* Perf. 14 (#J33) 80.00
*NJ6* D1 20m ol grn (R), perf. 14 50 50
*a.* Perf. 12(R)(#J43) 20.00
*NJ7* D1 50m bl (R) 50 50
*Nos. NJ1-NJ3,NJ5-NJ7 (6)* 2.58 2.58

No. NJ3a is from a second overprinting of Nos. NJ1-NJ3 and NJ5-NJ7, in inks differing in shade from the originals.
Double and inverted overprints exist.

Same Overprint in Black on Jordan Nos. J36-J38.

**1948-49 Unwmk. *Perf. 13x13½***
*NJ8* D2 1m dl red brn 100.00 100.00
*NJ9* D2 2m dl org yel ('49) 5.00 5.00
*NJ10* D2 10m dk car 2.00 2.00

**OCCUPATION POSTAL TAX STAMPS**

**Catalogue values for unused stamps in this section, from this point to the end of the section, are for Never Hinged items.**

Postal Tax Stamps of 1947 Overprinted in Red or Black فلسطين PALESTINE

**1950**
*NRA1* PT1 1m ultra (R) 20 16
*NRA2* PT1 2m carmine 20 16
*NRA3* PT1 3m emer (R) 28 20
*NRA4* PT1 5m plum 40 28
*NRA5* PT1 10m carmine 90 40
*NRA6* PT1 15m gray (R) 1.40 60
*NRA7* PT1 20m dk brn (R) 2.00 75
*NRA8* PT1 50m pur (R) 2.75 1.40
*NRA9* PT1 100m org red 3.50 1.75
*NRA10* PT1 200m dp bl (R) 10.00 4.00
*NRA11* PT1 500m grn (R) 20.00 10.00
*NRA12* PT1 £1 dk brn (R) 37.50 20.00
*Nos. NRA1-NRA12 (12)* 79.13 39.70

## KENYA

LOCATION – East Africa, bordering on the Indian Ocean.
GOVT. – Republic.
AREA – 224,960 sq. mi.
POP. – 18,750,000 (est. 1983).
CAPITAL – Nairobi.

Formerly a part of the British colony of Kenya, Uganda and Tanganyika, Kenya gained independence December 12, 1963.

100 Cents = 1 Shilling

**Catalogue values for all unused stamps in this country are for Never Hinged items.**

Treetop Hotel and Elephants A1

Designs: 5c, Cattle ranching. 10c, Wood carving. 15c, Riveter. 20c, Timber industry. 30c, Jomo Kenyatta facing Mt. Kenya. 40c, Fishing industry. 50c, Flag and emblem. 65c, Pyrethrum industry (daisies). 1sh, National Assembly bldg. 2sh, Harvesting coffee. 5sh, Harvesting tea. 10sh, Mombasa port. 20sh, Royal College, Nairobi.

***Perf. 14x14½***
**1963, Dec. 12 Photo. Unwmk.**
**Size: 21x17½mm.**
*1* A1 5c bl, buff & dk brn 6 5
*2* A1 10c brown 6 5
*a* Bklt. pane of 4 30
*3* A1 15c dp mag 7 5
*a* Bklt. pane of 4 30
*4* A1 20c yel grn & dk brn 8 6
*a* Bklt. pane of 4 40
*5* A1 30c yel & blk 12 5
*a* Bklt. pane of 4 55
*6* A1 40c bl & brn 16 8
*7* A1 50c grn, blk & dp car 20 6
*a* Bklt. pane of 4 1.25
*8* A1 65c stl bl & yel 40 25

***Perf. 14½***
**Size: 41½x25½mm.**
*9* A1 1sh multi 50 7
*10* A1 1.30sh grn, brn & blk 55 8
*11* A1 2sh multi 80 16
*12* A1 5sh ultra, yel grn & brn 1.60 40
*13* A1 10sh brn & dk brn 4.00 1.25
*14* A1 20sh pink & grnsh blk 8.00 2.50
*Nos. 1-14 (14)* 16.60 5.11

President Jomo Kenyatta and Flag of Kenya – A2

Designs (flag and): 15c, Cockerel. 50c, African lion. 1.30sh, Hartlaub's touraco. 2.50sh, Nandi flame flower.

**1964, Dec. 12 Photo. *Perf. 13x12½***
*15* A2 15c lt vio & multi 20 10
*16* A2 30c dk bl & multi 40 12
*17* A2 50c dk brn & multi 65 35
*18* A2 1.30sh multi 2.00 75
*19* A2 2.50sh multi 5.00 3.75
*Nos. 15-19 (5)* 8.25 5.07

Issued to commemorate the establishment of the Republic of Kenya, Dec. 12, 1964.

Greater Kudu A3

Animals: 5c, Thomson's gazelle. 10c, Sable antelope. 15c, Aardvark. 20c, Senegal bush baby. 30c, Warthog. 40c, Zebra. 50c, Buffalo. 65c, Black rhinoceros. 70c, Ostrich. 1.30sh, Elephant. 1.50sh, Bat-eared fox. 2.50sh, Cheetah. 5sh, Vervet monkey. 10sh, Giant pangolin. 20sh, Lion.

***Perf. 14x14½***
**1966-69 Photo. Unwmk.**
**Size: 21x17mm.**
*20* A3 5c gray, blk & org 5 5
*21* A3 10c blk & yel grn 5 5
*22* A3 15c dp org & blk 5 5
*23* A3 20c ultra, lt brn & blk 9 5
*24* A3 30c lt ultra & blk 10 5
*25* A3 40c ocher & blk 16 5
*26* A3 50c dp org & blk 22 5
*27* A3 65c dp yel grn & blk 1.40 90
*28* A3 70c rose lake & blk ('69) 1.40 70

***Perf. 14½***
**Size: 41x25mm.**
*29* A3 1sh gray bl, ol & blk 50 9
*30* A3 1.30sh yel grn & blk 1.40 9
*31* A3 1.50sh brn org, brn & blk ('69) 1.75 90
*32* A3 2.50sh ol bis, yel & blk 2.50 45
*33* A3 5sh brt grn, ultra & blk 2.25 70
*34* A3 10sh red brn, bis & blk 4.50 1.40
*35* A3 20sh ocher, bis, gold & blk 9.00 3.00
*Nos. 20-35 (16)* 25.42 8.58

Issue dates: Nos. 28, 31, Sept. 15, 1969. Others, Dec. 12, 1966.

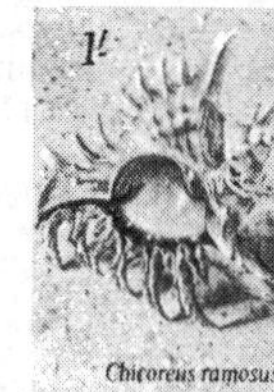

Branched Murex – A4

Sea shells: 5c, Morning pink. 10c, Episcopal miter. 15c, Strawberry-top shell. 20c, Humpback cowrie. 30c, variable abalone. 40c, Flame-top shell. 50c, Violet sailor. 60c, Bull's-mouth helmet. 70c, Pearly nautilus. 1.50sh, Neptune's trumpet. 2.50sh, Mediterranean tulip shell. 5sh, Fluctuating turban. 10sh, Textile cone. 20sh, Scorpion shell.

***Perf. 14½x14***
**1971 Dec. 13 Photo. Unwmk.**
**Size: 17x21mm.**
*36* A4 5c bis & multi 8 5
*37* A4 10c dl grn & multi 10 5
*a* Booklet pane of 4 40
*38* A4 15c tan & multi 10 5
*a* Booklet pane of 4 40
*39* A4 20c tan & multi 12 5
*a* Booklet pane of 4 48
*40* A4 30c yel & multi 20 5
*a* Booklet pane of 4 80
*41* A4 40c gray & multi 20 6
*a* Booklet pane of 4 80
*42* A4 50c buff & multi *(Janthina globosa)* 45 7
*a* Booklet pane of 4 1.80
*43* A4 60c lil & multi 45 10
*44* A4 70c gray grn & multi *(Nautilus pompileus)* 75 12
*a* Booklet pane of 4 2.50

***Perf. 14½***
**Size: 25x41mm.**
*45* A4 1sh ocher & multi 65 12
*46* A4 1.50sh pale grn & multi 90 14
*47* A4 2.50sh vio gray & multi 1.50 *10*
*48* A4 5sh lem & multi 3.00 *25*
*49* A4 10sh multi 5.00 *75*
*50* A4 20sh gray & multi 12.50 *1.75*
*Nos. 36-50 (15)* 26.00 3.71

Used values of Nos. 48-50 are for stamps with printed cancellations.

Revised Inscription

**1974, Jan. 20 *Perf. 14½x14***
*51* A4 50c multi *(Janthina janthina)* 2.00 20
*52* A4 70c multi *(Nautilus pompilius)* 3.50 1.00

Nos. 46-47, 50 Surcharged with New Value and 2 Bars

**1975, Nov. 17 Photo. *Perf. 14½***
*53* A4 2sh on 1.50sh multi 2.50 1.60
*54* A4 3sh on 2.50sh multi 12.00 15.00
*55* A4 40sh on 20sh multi 14.00 14.00

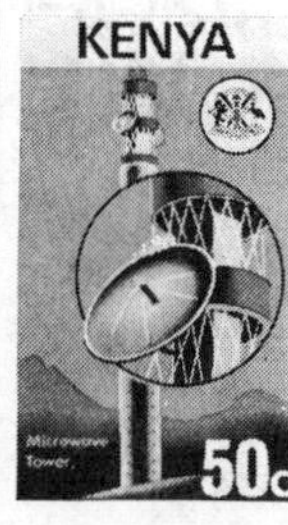

Microwave Tower – A5

Designs: 1sh, Cordless switchboard and operators (horiz.). 2sh, Telephones of 1880, 1930 and 1976. 3sh, Message switching center (horiz.).

**1976, Apr. 15 Litho. *Perf. 14½***
*56* A5 50c bl & multi 15 10
*57* A5 1sh red & multi 30 18
*58* A5 2sh yel & multi 50 35
*59* A5 3sh multi 85 60
*a* Souvenir sheet of 4 2.50 2.25

Telecommunication development in East Africa. No. 59a contains 4 stamps similar to Nos. 56-59 with simulated perforations; dark carmine rose margin with black inscription and white telephones. Size: 120x120mm.

Akii Bua, Ugandan Hurdler A6

Designs: 1sh, Filbert Bayi, Tanzanian runner. 2sh, Steve Muchoki, Kenyan boxer. 3sh, Olympic torch, flags of Kenya, Tanzania and Uganda.

**1976, July 5 Litho. *Perf. 14½***
*60* A6 50c bl & multi 18 1
*61* A6 1sh red & multi 35 2
*62* A6 2sh yel & multi 60 4
*63* A6 3sh bl & multi 1.00 6
*a* Souvenir sheet of 4 12.50 11.0

21st Olympic Games, Montreal, Canada, July 17-Aug. 1. No. 63a contains one each of Nos. 60-63, perf. 13; orange and multicolored margin. Size: 130x154mm.

Tanzania-Zambia Railway – A7

Designs: 1sh, Nile Bridge, Uganda. 2sh, Nakuru Station, Kenya. 3sh, Class A locomotive, 1896.

**1976, Oct. 4 Litho. *Perf. 14½***
*64* A7 50c lil & multi 35 1
*65* A7 1sh emer & multi 65 2
*66* A7 2sh brt rose & multi 1.25 4
*67* A7 3sh yel & multi 2.00 7
*a* Souvenir sheet of 4 8.00 5.0

Rail transport in East Africa. No. 67a contains one each of Nos. 64-67, perf. 13; yellow and multicolored margin showing African scenes with animals and birds. Size: 154x104mm.

Nile Perch – A8

Game Fish: 1sh, Tilapia. 3sh, Sailfish. 5sh, Black marlin.

**1977, Jan. 10 Litho. *Perf. 14½***
*68* A8 50c multi 20 8
*69* A8 1sh multi 40 16
*70* A8 3sh multi 1.50 50
*71* A8 5sh multi 2.00 1.00
*a* Souvenir sheet of 4 7.50 5.00

No. 71a contains one each of Nos. 68-71; multicolored margin shows fishing vessel and sea floor. Size: 153x129mm.

Festival Emblem and Masai Tribesmen Bleeding Cow – A9

Designs (Festival Emblem and): 1sh, Dancers from Uganda. 2sh, Makonde sculpture, Tanzania. 3sh, Tribesmen skinning hippopotamus.

**1977, Jan. 15** *Perf. 13½x14*

*72* A9 50c multi 15 10
*73* A9 1sh multi 35 20
*74* A9 2sh multi 1.25 40
*75* A9 3sh multi 1.40 60
*a* Souvenir sheet of 4 3.50 2.50

2nd World Black and African Festival, Lagos, Nigeria, Jan. 15-Feb. 12. No. 75a contains one each of Nos. 72-75; purple margin with black inscription and decoration. Size: 132x98mm.

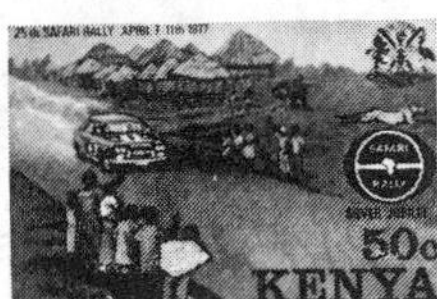


Automobile Passing through Village — A10

Designs (Safari Rally Emblem and): 1sh, Winner at finish line. 2sh, Car going through washout. 5sh, Car, elephants and Mt. Kenya.

**1977, Apr. 5** **Litho.** *Perf. 14*

*76* A10 50c multi 16 12
*77* A10 1sh multi 35 25
*78* A10 2sh multi 70 50
*79* A10 5sh multi 1.60 1.25
*a* Souvenir sheet of 4 5.00 4.00

25th Safari Rally, Apr. 7-11. No. 79a contains one each of Nos. 76-79; blue and multicolored margin showing automobiles and antelopes. Size: 126x93mm.

Rev. Canon Apolo Kivebulaya — A11

Designs: 1sh, Uganda Cathedral. 2sh, Early grass-topped Cathedral. 5sh, Early tent congregation, Kigezi.

**1977, June 20** **Litho.** *Perf. 14*

*80* A11 50c multi 15 12
*81* A11 1sh multi 35 22
*82* A11 2sh multi 65 45
*83* A11 5sh multi 1.50 1.10
*a* Souvenir sheet of 4 3.00 2.50

Church of Uganda, centenary. No. 83a contains one each of Nos. 80-83; ocher and black margin. Size: 125x89mm.

Elizabeth II and Prince Philip at Sagana Lodge — A12

Designs: 5sh, "Treetops" observation hut, Aberdare Forest, and elephants (vert.). 10sh, Pres. Jomo Kenyatta, Elizabeth II, crossed spears and shield. 15sh, Elizabeth II and Pres. Kenyatta in open automobile. 50sh, Elizabeth II and Prince Philip at window in Treetops.

**1977, July 20** **Litho.** *Perf. 14*

*84* A12 2sh multi 40 35
*85* A12 5sh multi 60 75
*86* A12 10sh multi 2.25 1.75
*87* A12 15sh multi 2.75 2.25
*a* Souvenir sheet 5.00 5.00

**Souvenir Sheet**

*88* A12 50sh multi 12.50 10.00

25th anniversary of reign of Queen Elizabeth II. No. 87a contains one No. 87; silver, deep blue and black margin shows "Treetops." Size: 140x60mm. No. 88 contains one stamp; multicolored margin shows "Treetops" and elephant. Size: 153x127mm.

Pancake Tortoise A13

Designs (Wildlife Fund Emblem and): 1sh, Nile crocodile. 2sh, Hunter's hartebeest. 3sh, Red colobus monkey. 5sh, Dugong.

**1977, Sept. 26** **Litho.** *Perf. 14x13½*

*89* A13 50c multi 18 12
*90* A13 1sh multi 40 25
*91* A13 2sh multi 75 50
*92* A13 3sh multi 1.25 70
*93* A13 5sh multi 2.00 1.20
*a* Souvenir sheet of 4 4.00 3.00
*Nos. 89-93 (5)* 4.58 2.77

Endangered species. No. 93a contains one each of Nos. 90-93; multicolored margin shows storks in flight and marsh. Size: 128x102mm.

Kenya-Ethiopia Border Point — A14

Designs: 1sh, Station wagon at Archer's Post. 2sh, Thika overpass. 5sh, Marsabit Game Lodge and elephant.

**1977, Nov. 10** **Litho.** *Perf. 14*

*94* A14 50c multi 20 8
*95* A14 1sh multi 30 18
*96* A14 2sh multi 65 30
*97* A14 5sh multi 1.75 85
*a* Souvenir sheet of 4 4.00 3.50

Opening of Nairobi-Addis Ababa highway. No. 97a contains one each of Nos. 94-97; salmon and dark brown margin shows animals. Size: 145x92mm.

Gypsum — A15

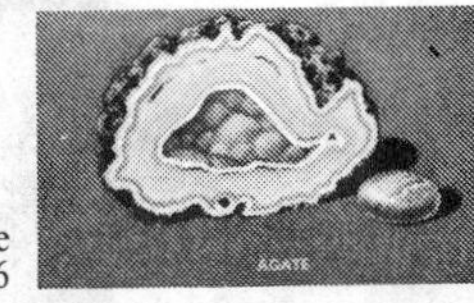

Agate A16

Designs: Minerals found in Kenya.

*Perf. 14½x14, 14½ (A16)*

**1977, Dec. 13** **Photo.**

*98* A15 10c *shown* 5 5
*99* A15 20c *Trona* 6 5
*100* A15 30c *Kyanite* 9 5
*101* A15 40c *Amazonite* 12 6
*102* A15 50c *Galena* 15 8
*103* A15 70c *Silicified wood* 22 10
*104* A15 80c *Fluorite* 25 12
*105* A16 1sh *Amethyst* 30 14
*106* A16 1.50sh *shown* 45 20
*107* A16 2sh *Tourmaline* 60 30
*108* A16 3sh *Aquamarine* 90 45
*109* A16 5sh *Rhodolite garnet* 1.50 75
*110* A16 10sh *Sapphire* 3.00 1.50
*111* A16 20sh *Ruby* 6.00 3.00
*112* A16 40sh *Green grossular garnet* 15.00 6.00
*Nos. 98-112 (15)* 28.69 12.85

The 10c, 20c, 40c, 50c and 80c were also issued in booklet panes of 4.

The 50c was also issued in a booklet pane of 2.

Soccer, Joe Kadenge and World Cup — A17

Designs (World Cup and): 1sh, Mohammed Chuma receiving trophy, and his portrait. 2sh, Shot on goal and Omari S. Kidevu. 3sh, Backfield defense and Polly Ouma.

**1978, Apr. 10** **Litho.** *Perf. 14x13½*

*113* A17 50c grn & multi 15 8
*114* A17 1sh lt brn & multi 30 18
*115* A17 2sh lil & multi 60 35
*116* A17 3sh dk bl & multi 1.00 55
*a* Souvenir sheet of 4 2.50 2.10

World Soccer Cup Championships, Argentina 78, June 1-25. No. 116a contains one each of Nos. 113-116; yellow green and dark green margin shows players with trophy. Size: 135½x82mm.

Boxing and Games' Emblem A18

Designs (Games Emblem and): 1sh, Pres. Kenyatta welcoming 1968 Olympic team. 3sh, Javelin. 5sh, Pres. Kenyatta, boxing team and trophy.

**1978, July 15** **Photo.** *Perf. 13x14*

*117* A18 50c multi 10 8
*118* A18 1sh multi 25 15
*119* A18 3sh multi 75 40
*120* A18 5sh multi 1.25 65

Commonwealth Games, Edmonton, Canada, Aug. 3-12.

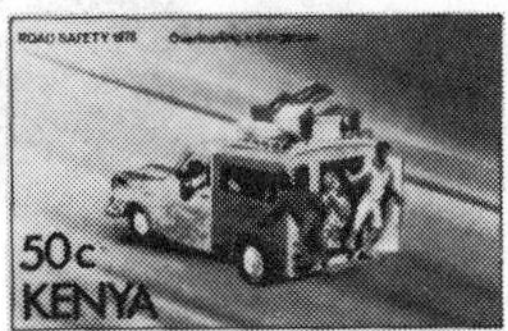


Overloaded Truck — A19

Designs (Accidents): 1sh, Observe speed limit. 1.50sh, Observe traffic lights. 2sh, School crossing. 3sh, Passing. 5sh, Railroad crossing.

**1978, Sept. 18** **Litho.** *Perf. 13½x14*

*121* A19 50c multi 15 8
*122* A19 1sh multi 25 16
*123* A19 1.50sh multi 40 25
*124* A19 2sh multi 50 30
*125* A19 3sh multi 80 50
*126* A19 5sh multi 1.25 75
*Nos. 121-126 (6)* 3.35 2.04

Road safety.

Pres. Kenyatta at Harambee Water Project Opening A20

Kenyatta Day: 1sh, Prince Philip handing over symbol of independence, 1963. 2sh, Pres. Jomo Kenyatta addressing independence rally. 3sh, Stage at 15th independence anniversary celebration. 5sh, Handcuffed Kenyatta led by soldiers, 1952.

**1978, Oct. 16** **Litho.** *Perf. 14*

*127* A20 50c multi 15 8
*128* A20 1sh multi 25 15
*129* A20 2sh multi 40 30
*130* A20 3sh multi 60 40
*131* A20 5sh multi 90 75
*Nos. 127-131 (5)* 2.30 1.68

Soldiers and Emblem A21

Designs (Anti-Apartheid Emblem and): 1sh, Anti-Apartheid Conference. 2sh, Stephen Biko, South African Anti-Apartheid leader. 3sh, Nelson Mandela, jailed since 1961. 5sh, Bishop Lamont, expelled from Rhodesia in 1977.

**1978, Dec. 11** **Litho.** *Perf. 14x14½*

*132* A21 50c multi 15 8
*133* A21 1sh multi 25 15
*134* A21 2sh multi 40 30
*135* A21 3sh multi 60 40
*136* A21 5sh multi 1.10 75
*Nos. 132-136 (5)* 2.50 1.68

Anti-Apartheid Year and Namibia's struggle for independence.

Children on School Playground — A22

Designs (Children's Year Emblem and): 2sh, Boy catching fish. 3sh, Children dancing and singing. 5sh, Children and camel caravan.

**1979, Feb. 5** **Litho.** *Perf. 14*

*137* A22 50c multi 15 6
*138* A22 2sh multi 60 25
*139* A22 3sh multi 85 35
*140* A22 5sh multi 1.50 60

International Year of the Child.

"The Lion and the Jewel" A23

National Theater: 1sh, Dancers and drummers. 2sh, Programs of various productions. 3sh, View of National Theater. 5sh, "Genesis," performed by Nairobi City Players.

**1979, Apr. 6** **Litho.** *Perf. 13½x14*

*141* A23 50c multi 10 8
*142* A23 1sh multi 20 16
*143* A23 2sh multi 40 30
*144* A23 3sh multi 60 50
*145* A23 5sh multi 1.00 80
*Nos. 141-145 (5)* 2.30 1.84

Village Workshop — A24

Salvation Army Emblem and: 50c, Blind telephone operator (vert.). 1sh, Care for the aged (vert.). 5sh, Vocational training (nurse).

**1979, June 4** *Perf. 13½x13, 13x13½*

*146* A24 50c multi 15 8
*147* A24 1sh multi 25 15
*148* A24 3sh multi 75 40
*149* A24 5sh multi 1.10 75

Salvation Army Social Services, 50th anniversary.

Funeral Procession — A25

Kenyatta: 1sh, Taking oath of office. 3sh, Addressing crowd. 5sh, As young man with wooden trying plane.

**1979, Aug. 22 Litho. *Perf. 13½x14***

| No. | Type | Value | Description | Unused | Used |
|---|---|---|---|---|---|
| *150* | A25 | 50c | multi | 18 | 8 |
| *151* | A25 | 1sh | multi | 30 | 18 |
| *152* | A25 | 3sh | multi | 80 | 50 |
| *153* | A25 | 5sh | multi | 1.40 | 80 |

Jomo Kenyatta (1893-1978), first president of Kenya.

British East Africa No. 2, Hill, Signature — A26

Hill, Signature and: 1sh, Kenya, Uganda and Tanzania No. 54. 2sh, Penny Black. 5sh, Kenya No. 19.

**1979, Nov. 27 Litho. *Perf. 14***

| No. | Type | Value | Description | Unused | Used |
|---|---|---|---|---|---|
| *154* | A26 | 50c | multi | 15 | 8 |
| *155* | A26 | 1sh | multi | 25 | 15 |
| *156* | A26 | 2sh | multi | 50 | 30 |
| *157* | A26 | 5sh | multi | 1.10 | 65 |

Sir Rowland Hill (1795-1879), originator of penny postage.

Highways, Globe, Conference Emblem — A27

Conference Emblem and: 1sh, Truck at Athi River, New Weighbridge. 3sh, New Nyali Bridge, Mombasa. 5sh, Jomo Kenyatta Airport Highway.

**1980, Jan. 10 Litho. *Perf. 14***

| No. | Type | Value | Description | Unused | Used |
|---|---|---|---|---|---|
| *158* | A27 | 50c | multi | 12 | 8 |
| *159* | A27 | 1sh | multi | 25 | 20 |
| *160* | A27 | 3sh | multi | 70 | 60 |
| *161* | A27 | 5sh | multi | 1.25 | 1.00 |

4th IRF African Highway Conference, Nairobi, Jan. 20-25.

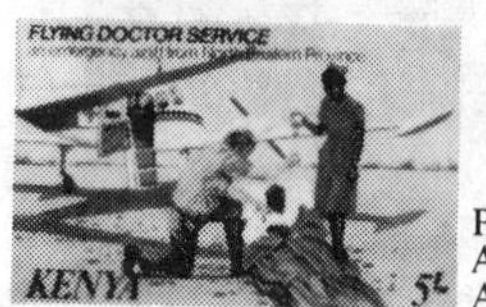


Patient Airlift A28

**1980, Mar. 20 Litho. *Perf. 14½***

| No. | Type | Value | Description | Unused | Used |
|---|---|---|---|---|---|
| *162* | A28 | 50c | *Outdoor clinic* | 12 | 10 |
| *163* | A28 | 1sh | *Mule transport of patient*, vert. | 22 | 18 |
| *164* | A28 | 3sh | *Surgery*, vert. | 70 | 60 |
| *165* | A28 | 5sh | *shown* | 1.10 | 90 |
| *a* | | | Souvenir sheet of 4 | 2.50 | 2.00 |

Flying doctor service. No. 165 contains Nos. 162-165. Multicolored margin shows caduceus and Red Cross. Size: 145½x133mm.

Hill Statue, Kidderminster and Mt. Kenya — A29

**1980, May 6 Litho. *Perf. 14***

| No. | Type | Value | Description | Unused | Used |
|---|---|---|---|---|---|
| *166* | A29 | 25sh | multi | 5.25 | 4.00 |
| *a* | | | Souvenir sheet | 6.00 | 3.50 |

London 1980 International Stamp Exhibition, May 6-14. No. 166a has multicolored margin showing exhibition hall, flags of Kenya and Gt. Britain, London 1980 emblem. Size: 14x101½mm.

Pope John Paul II and Crowd A30

Visit of Pope John Paul II to Kenya: 1sh, Pope, Nairobi Cathedral, papal flag and arms (vert.). 5sh, Pope, papal and Kenya flags, dove (vert.). 10sh, Pres. Arap Moi of Kenya, Pope, flag of Kenya on map of Africa.

**1980, May 8 *Perf. 13½***

| No. | Type | Value | Description | Unused | Used |
|---|---|---|---|---|---|
| *167* | A30 | 50c | multi | 12 | 9 |
| *168* | A30 | 1sh | multi | 22 | 18 |
| *169* | A30 | 5sh | multi | 1.10 | 90 |
| *170* | A30 | 10sh | multi | 2.25 | 1.75 |

Sting Ray — A31

**1980, June 27 Litho. *Perf. 14½***

| No. | Type | Value | Description | Unused | Used |
|---|---|---|---|---|---|
| *171* | A31 | 50c | *shown* | 12 | 10 |
| *172* | A31 | 2sh | *Alkit snapper* | 48 | 40 |
| *173* | A31 | 3sh | *Sea slug* | 75 | 60 |
| *174* | A31 | 5sh | *Hawksbill turtle* | 1.25 | 1.00 |

National Archives, 1904 A32

**1980, Oct. 9 Litho. *Perf. 14***

| No. | Type | Value | Description | Unused | Used |
|---|---|---|---|---|---|
| *175* | A32 | 50c | *shown* | 12 | 10 |
| *176* | A32 | 1sh | *Commissioner's Office, Nairobi, 1913* | 22 | 18 |
| *177* | A32 | 1.50sh | *Nairobi House, 1913* | 35 | 25 |
| *178* | A32 | 2sh | *Norfolk Hotel, 1904* | 45 | 38 |
| *179* | A32 | 3sh | *McMillan Library, 1929* | 70 | 60 |
| *180* | A32 | 5sh | *Kipande House, 1913* | 1.10 | 1.00 |
| | | | *Nos. 175-180 (6)* | 2.94 | 2.51 |

Woman in Wheelchair and Child — A33

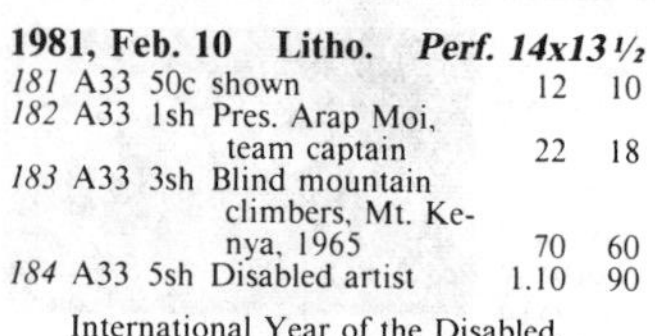

**1981, Feb. 10 Litho. *Perf. 14x13½***

| No. | Type | Value | Description | Unused | Used |
|---|---|---|---|---|---|
| *181* | A33 | 50c | shown | 12 | 10 |
| *182* | A33 | 1sh | Pres. Arap Moi, team captain | 22 | 18 |
| *183* | A33 | 3sh | Blind mountain climbers, Mt. Kenya, 1965 | 70 | 60 |
| *184* | A33 | 5sh | Disabled artist | 1.10 | 90 |

International Year of the Disabled.

Longonot Earth Station Complex — A34

**1981, Apr. 4 Litho. *Perf. 14x14½***

| No. | Type | Value | Description | Unused | Used |
|---|---|---|---|---|---|
| *185* | A34 | 50c | shown | 12 | 10 |
| *186* | A34 | 2sh | Intelsat V | 45 | 35 |
| *187* | A34 | 3sh | Longonot I | 75 | 50 |
| *188* | A34 | 5sh | Longonot II | 1.10 | 90 |

Conference Center, OAU Flag — A35

18th Organization for African Unity Conference, Nairobi: 1sh, Map of Africa showing Panaftel earth stations. 3sh, Parliament Building, Nairobi. 5sh, Jomo Kenyatta Intl. Airport. 10sh, OAU flag.

**Wmk. 373**

**1981, June 24 Litho. *Perf. 13½***

| No. | Type | Value | Description | Unused | Used |
|---|---|---|---|---|---|
| *189* | A35 | 50c | multi | 10 | 8 |
| *190* | A35 | 1sh | multi | 20 | 16 |
| *191* | A35 | 3sh | multi | 60 | 50 |
| *192* | A35 | 5sh | multi | 1.00 | 80 |
| *193* | A35 | 10sh | multi | 2.00 | 1.75 |
| *a* | | | Souvenir sheet | 2.25 | 2.00 |
| | | | *Nos. 189-193 (5)* | 3.90 | 3.29 |

No. 193a contains No. 193 (perf. 14½); multicolored margin shows flags of OAU members. Size: 111x111mm.

St. Paul's Cathedral — A36

**1981, July 29 Litho. *Perf. 14***

| No. | Type | Value | Description | Unused | Used |
|---|---|---|---|---|---|
| *194* | A36 | 50c | Charles, Pres. Arap Moi | 10 | 8 |
| *195* | A36 | 3sh | shown | 60 | 50 |
| *196* | A36 | 5sh | Britannia | 1.00 | 80 |
| *197* | A36 | 10sh | Charles | 2.00 | 1.75 |

**Souvenir Sheet**

| No. | Type | Value | Description | Unused | Used |
|---|---|---|---|---|---|
| *198* | A36 | 25sh | Couple | 9.00 | 8.50 |

Royal Wedding. No. 198 has gray decorative margin. Size: 85x103mm.

Reticulated Giraffe — A37

**1981, Aug. 31 Litho. *Perf. 14½***

| No. | Type | Value | Description | Unused | Used |
|---|---|---|---|---|---|
| *199* | A37 | 50c | shown | 12 | 10 |
| *200* | A37 | 2sh | Bongo | 45 | 35 |
| *201* | A37 | 5sh | Roan antelope | 1.10 | 90 |
| *202* | A37 | 10sh | Mangabey | 2.25 | 1.75 |

World Food Day — A38

**1981, Oct. 16 Litho. *Perf. 14***

| No. | Type | Value | Description | Unused | Used |
|---|---|---|---|---|---|
| *203* | A38 | 50c | Plowing | 10 | 8 |
| *204* | A38 | 1sh | Rice field | 20 | 18 |
| *205* | A38 | 2sh | Irrigation | 40 | 35 |
| *206* | A38 | 5sh | Cattle | 1.00 | 80 |

Ceremonial Tribal Costumes — A39

***Perf. 14½x13½***

**1981, Dec. 18 Litho.**

| No. | Type | Value | Description | Unused | Used |
|---|---|---|---|---|---|
| *207* | A39 | 50c | Kamba | 12 | 10 |
| *208* | A39 | 1sh | Turkana | 25 | 20 |
| *209* | A39 | 2sh | Giriama | 48 | 40 |
| *210* | A39 | 3sh | Masai | 70 | 60 |
| *211* | A39 | 5sh | Luo | 1.25 | 1.00 |
| | | | *Nos. 207-211 (5)* | 2.80 | 2.30 |

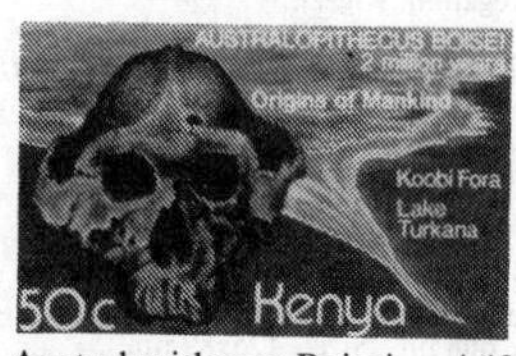


Australopithecus Boisei — A40

**1982, Jan. 16 Litho. *Perf. 14***

| No. | Type | Value | Description | Unused | Used |
|---|---|---|---|---|---|
| *212* | A40 | 50c | shown | 12 | 10 |
| *213* | A40 | 2sh | Homo erectus | 45 | 40 |
| *214* | A40 | 3sh | Homo habilis | 70 | 60 |
| *215* | A40 | 5sh | Proconsul africanus | 1.10 | 90 |

Scouting Year — A41

**1982, June 2 Litho. *Perf. 14½***

| No. | Type | Value | Description | Unused | Used |
|---|---|---|---|---|---|
| *216* | A41 | 70c | Tree planting | 12 | 10 |
| *217* | A41 | 70c | Paying homage | 12 | 10 |
| *218* | A41 | 3.50sh | Be Prepared | 60 | 50 |
| *219* | A41 | 3.50sh | Intl. friendship | 60 | 50 |
| *220* | A41 | 5sh | Helping disabled | 90 | 75 |
| *221* | A41 | 5sh | Community service | 90 | 75 |
| *222* | A41 | 6.50sh | Paxtu Cottage | 1.10 | 90 |
| *223* | A41 | 6.50sh | Lady Baden-Powell | 1.10 | 90 |
| | | | *Nos. 216-223 (8)* | 5.44 | 4.50 |

**Souvenir Sheet**

| No. | Type | Value | Description | Unused | Used |
|---|---|---|---|---|---|
| *224* | | | Sheet of 4 | 3.25 | 2.50 |
| *a* | A41 | 70c | like #216 | 15 | 10 |
| *b* | A41 | 3.50sh | like #218 | 65 | 50 |
| *c* | A41 | 5sh | like #220 | 1.00 | 75 |
| *d* | A41 | 6.50sh | like #222 | 1.40 | 90 |

Stamps of same denomination se-tenant. No. 224 has purple and green margin showing cottage, text, emblem. Size: 113x112mm.

1982 World Cup — A42

Designs: Various soccer players on world map.

**1982, July 5 Litho. *Perf. 12½***
*225* A42 70c multi 15 12
*226* A42 3.50sh multi 65 60
*227* A42 5sh multi 1.00 80
*228* A42 10sh multi 2.00 1.75

**Souvenir Sheet**
***Perf. 13½x14***
*229* A42 20sh multi 4.00 3.50

No. 229 has multicolored margin showing stadium. Size: 102x77mm.

Agricultural Society, 80th Anniv. — A43

ITU Plenipoteniaries Conference, Nairobi, Sept. — A44

**1982, Sept. 28 Litho. *Perf. 14½***
*230* A43 70c Cattle judging 15 12
*231* A43 2.50sh Farm machinery 50 40
*232* A43 3.50sh Musical ride 65 60
*233* A43 6.50sh Emblem 1.40 1.25

**1982, Oct. 27 Photo. *Perf. 11½***
**Granite Paper**
*234* A44 70c Microwave radio system 12 10
*235* A44 3.50sh Ship-to-shore communication 60 50
*236* A44 5sh Rural telecommunication 90 75
*237* A44 6.50sh Emblem 1.25 1.00

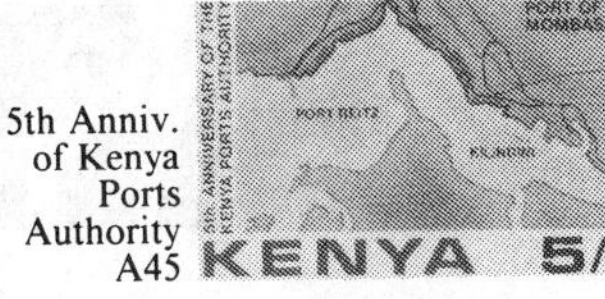


5th Anniv. of Kenya Ports Authority A45

**1983, Jan. 20 Litho. *Perf. 14***
*238* A45 70c Container cranes 18 15
*239* A45 2sh Cranes, diff. 45 38
*240* A45 3.50sh Cranes, diff. 75 70
*241* A45 5sh Mombasa Harbor map 1.10 90
*a* Souvenir sheet of 4 3.50 3.00

No. 241a contains Nos. 238-241; multicolored margin shows map. Size: 125x85mm.

No. 104 Surcharged.

**1983, Jan. Photo. *Perf. 14½x14***
*242* A15 70c on 80c multi 16 14

**Commonwealth Day**
Common Design Type

**1983, Mar. 14 Litho. *Perf. 14½***
*243* CD334 70c Coffee picking, vert. 12 10
*244* CD334 2sh Pres. Arap Moi, vert. 35 30
*245* CD334 5sh Globe 80 65
*246* CD334 10sh Masai dance 1.60 1.40

Dichrostachys Cinerea A46

Dombeya Burgessiae A47

***Perf. 14½x14, 14x14½***
**1983, Feb. 15 Photo.**
*247* A46 10c shown 5 5
*248* A46 20c Rhamphicarpa montana 6 5
*249* A46 30c Barleria eranthemoides 8 6
*250* A46 40c Commelina 9 7
*251* A46 50c Canarina abyssinica 12 8
*252* A46 70c Aspilia mossambicensis 18 15
*253* A47 1sh Dombeya burgessiae 22 18
*254* A47 1.50sh Lantana trifolia 35 28
*255* A47 2sh Adenium obesum 45 38
*256* A47 2.50sh Terminalia orbicularis 60 50
*257* A47 3.50sh Ceropegia ballyana 75 70
*258* A47 5sh Ruttya fruticosa 1.10 90
*259* A47 10sh Pentanisia ouranogyne 1.75 1.50
*260* A47 20sh Brillantaisia nyanzarum 3.00 2.75
*261* A47 40sh Crotalaria axillaris 6.00 4.50
*Nos. 247-261 (15)* 14.80 12.15

See Nos. 350-354.

30th Anniv. of Customs Cooperation Council — A48

**1983, May 11 Litho. *Perf. 14½***
*262* A48 70c Parcel check 15 12
*263* A48 2.50sh Headquarters, Mombasa 50 40
*264* A48 3.50sh Headquarters, Brussels 65 60
*265* A48 10sh Patrol boat 2.00 1.75

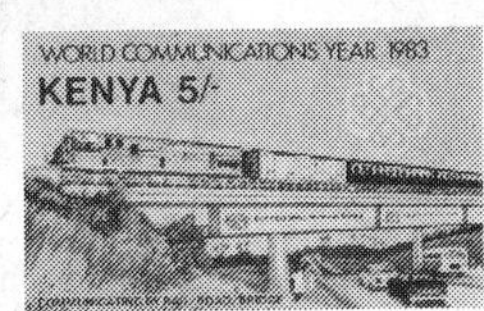


World Communications Year — A49

**1983, July 4 Litho. *Perf. 14½***
*266* A49 70c Satellite, dish antenna, vert. 15 12
*267* A49 2.50sh Mailbox, birthday card, telephone, vert. 50 40
*268* A49 3.50sh Jet, ship 65 60
*269* A49 5sh Railroad bridge, highway 1.00 80

Intl. Maritime Organization, 25th Anniv. — A50

**1983, Sept. 22 Litho. *Perf. 14½***
*270* A50 70c Kilindini Harbor 12 10
*271* A50 2.50sh Life preserver 38 30
*272* A50 3.50sh Mombasa Container Terminal 52 40
*273* A50 10sh Marine Park 1.50 1.25

29th Commonwealth Parliamentary Conference — A51

**1983, Oct. 31 Litho. *Perf. 14***
*274* A51 70c shown 12 10
*275* A51 2.50sh Parliament Bldg., vert. 38 30
*276* A51 5sh State Opening, vert. 75 60
*a* Souvenir sheet of 3 plus label 1.50 1.25

No. 276a has multicolored margin showing Parliament Buildings, Nairobi. Size: 120x141mm.

Royal Visit A52

**1983, Nov. 10 Litho. *Perf. 14***
*277* A52 70c Flags 15 12
*278* A52 3.50sh Sagana State Lodge 65 50
*279* A52 5sh Tree Tops Hotel 90 75
*280* A52 10sh Elizabeth II and Daniel Arap Moi 1.75 1.50

**Souvenir Sheet**
*281* A52 25sh multi 3.75 3.00

No. 281 contains Nos. 277-280 without denominations showing simulated perforations. Marginal inscription. Size: 126x98mm.

President Daniel Arap Moi, Monument — A53

**1983, Dec. 9 Litho. *Perf. 14½***
*282* A53 70c shown 12 10
*283* A53 2sh Tree planting 30 24
*284* A53 3.50sh Map, flag, emblem 52 40
*285* A53 5sh School, milk program 75 60
*286* A53 10sh People, flag, banner 1.50 1.20
*Nos. 282-286 (5)* 3.19 2.54

**Souvenir Sheet**
***Imperf***
*287* A53 25sh multi 3.75 3.00

Independence, 20th Anniv. No. 287 contains Nos. 282-286 without denominations. Size: 127x92mm.

Rare Local Birds — A54

**1984, Feb. 6 Litho. *Perf. 14½x13½***
*288* A54 70c White-backed night heron 12 10
*289* A54 2.50sh Quail plover 38 30
*290* A54 3.50sh Heller's ground thrush 52 40
*291* A54 5sh Papyrus gonolek 75 60
*292* A54 10sh White-winged Apalis 1.50 1.20
*Nos. 288-292 (5)* 3.27 2.60

Intl. Civil Aviation Org., 40th Anniv. A55

**1984, Apr. 2 Litho. *Perf. 14***
*293* A55 70c Radar, vert. 12 10
*294* A55 2.50sh Kenya School of Aviation 38 30
*295* A55 3.50sh Jet, Moi Intl. Airport 52 40
*296* A55 5sh Air traffic control center 75 60

1984 Summer Olympics A56

**1984, May 21 *Perf. 14½***
*297* A56 70c Running 12 10
*298* A56 2.50sh Hurdles 38 30
*299* A56 5sh Boxing 75 60
*300* A56 10sh Field Hockey 1.50 1.20

**Souvenir Sheet**
***Imperf***
*301* A56 25sh Torch bearers 3.50 3.50

No. 301 contains designs of 297-300. Size: 130x122mm.

Bookmobile — A57

**1984, Aug. 10 Litho. *Perf. 14½***
*302* A57 70c Emblem 12 10
*303* A57 3.50sh shown 52 40
*304* A57 5sh Adult library 75 60
*305* A57 10sh Children's library 1.50 1.20

Intl. Federation of Library Associations, 50th Conference.

Kenya Export Year (KEY) A58

**1984, Oct. 1 Litho. *Perf. 14***

*306* A58 70c Emblem, vert. 12 10
*307* A58 3.50sh Airport 52 40
*308* A58 5sh Harbor, vert. 75 60
*309* A58 10sh Exports 1.50 1.25

World Conference on Religion and Peace, Nairobi, August 23-31, 1984 — A59

**1984, Aug. 23 Litho. *Perf. 14x14½***

*310* A59 70c Doves, cross 15 12
*311* A59 2.50sh Doves, Hinduism symbol 50 40
*312* A59 3.50sh Doves, Sikhism symbol 65 50
*313* A59 6.50sh Doves, Islam symbol 1.40 1.10

Tribal Costumes A60

**1984, Nov. 5 Litho. *Perf. 14½x13½***

*314* A60 70c Luhya 10 8
*315* A60 2sh Kikuyu 25 20
*316* A60 3.50sh Pokomo 45 35
*317* A60 5sh Nandi 65 50
*318* A60 10sh Rendile 1.25 1.10
*Nos. 314-318 (5)* 2.70 2.23

60th Anniv., World Chess Federation — A61

**1984, Dec. 21 Litho. *Perf. 14½***

*319* A61 70c Nyayo Stadium, knight 10 8
*320* A61 2.50sh Fort Jesus, rook 32 28
*321* A61 3.50sh National Monument, bishop 48 40
*322* A61 5sh Parliament, queen 65 52
*323* A61 10sh Nyayo Fountain, king 1.25 1.00
*Nos. 319-323 (5)* 2.80 2.28

Energy Conservation — A62

**1985, Jan. 22 Litho. *Perf. 13½***

*324* A62 70c Stove, fire pit 10 8
*325* A62 2sh Solar panel 28 24
*326* A62 3.50sh Biogas tank 48 40
*327* A62 10sh Plowing field 1.25 1.00

***Imperf***

*328* A62 20sh Energy conservation 2.75 2.00

No. 328 contains Nos. 324-327 without denominations. Size: 110x85mm.

Girl Guides, 75th Anniv. A63

**1985, Mar. 27 Litho. *Perf. 13½***

*329* A63 1sh Girl Guide, handicrafts 14 10
*330* A63 3sh Community service 40 30
*331* A63 5sh Lady Baden-Powell, Kenyan leader 65 50
*332* A63 7sh Food project 90 68

Intl. Red Cross Day A64

**1985, May 8 *Perf. 14½***

*333* A64 1sh Emblem 15 12
*334* A64 4sh First Aid 55 45
*335* A64 5sh Blood donation 70 60
*336* A64 7sh Famine relief, cornucopia 1.00 75

7th Intl. Congress on Protozoology, Nairobi, June 22-29 — A65

Diseases caused by microorganisms carried by insects.

**1985, June 25**

*337* A65 1sh Malaria 15 12
*338* A65 3sh Leishmaniasis 45 32
*339* A65 5sh Trypanosomiasis 70 55
*340* A65 7sh Babesiosis 1.00 75

U.N. Decade for Women — A66

**1985, July 15**

*341* A66 1sh Repairing water pipes 14 10
*342* A66 3sh Traditional food processing 40 30
*343* A66 5sh Basket weaving 65 50
*344* A66 7sh Dress making 90 68

43rd Intl. Eucharistic Congress, Nairobi, Aug. 11-18 — A67

**1985, Aug. 15 *Perf. 13½***

*345* A67 1sh The Last Supper 14 10
*346* A67 3sh Afro-Christian family 40 30
*347* A67 5sh Congress altar, Uhuru Park 65 50
*348* A67 7sh St. Peter Claver's Church 90 68

**Souvenir Sheet**

*349* A67 25sh Pope John Paul II 3.25 2.50

No. 349 has split-view multicolored margin picturing a nature preserve and Nairobi. Size: 118x82mm.

Flower Types of 1983

**1985 Photo. *Perf. 14½x14, 14½***

*350* A46 80c like #250 10 8
*351* A46 1sh Dombeya burgessiae 12 10
*352* A47 3sh Calotropis procera 38 28
*353* A47 4sh Momordica foetida 50 38
*354* A47 7sh Oncoba spinosa 85 65
*Nos. 350-354 (5)* 1.95 1.49

Endangered Wildlife — A68

**1985, Dec. 10 Litho. *Perf. 14½***

*355* A68 1sh Diceros bicornis 20 18
*356* A68 3sh Acinonyx jubatus 60 50
*357* A68 5sh Cercopithecus neglectus 1.10 75
*358* A68 10sh Equus greyvi 2.25 1.50

**Size: 130x122mm.**

***Imperf***

*359* A68 25sh Hunter pursuing game 3.00 2.25
*Nos. 355-359 (5)* 7.15 5.18

Trees A69

**1986, Jan. 24 *Perf. 14½***

*360* A69 1sh Borassus aethiopum 14 12
*361* A69 3sh Acacia xanthophloea 45 32
*362* A69 5sh Ficus natalensis 75 55
*363* A69 7sh Spathodea nilotica 1.00 75

**Size: 117x97mm.**

***Imperf***

*364* A69 25sh Glade 3.50 2.75
*Nos. 360-364 (5)* 5.84 4.49

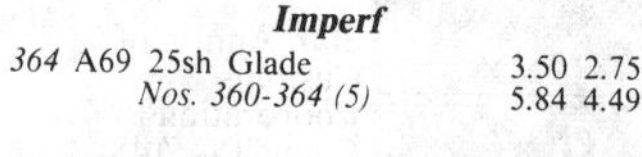

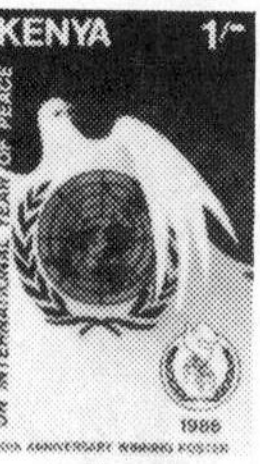

Intl. Peace Year — A70

1986 World Cup Soccer Championships, Mexico — A71

**1986, Apr. 17 *Perf. 14½***

*365* A70 1sh Dove, UN emblem 15 12
*366* A70 3sh UN General Assembly, horiz. 45 35
*367* A70 7sh Mushroom cloud 1.00 75
*368* A70 10sh Isaiah 2:4, horiz. 1.50 1.10

**1986, May 9**

*369* A71 1sh Dribbling 15 12
*370* A71 3sh Penalty shot 45 35
*371* A71 5sh Tackling 80 55
*372* A71 7sh Champions 1.10 75
*373* A71 10sh Heading the ball 1.60 1.25

**Size: 110x86mm.**

***Imperf***

*374* A71 30sh Harambee Stars 4.50 3.50
*Nos. 369-374 (6)* 8.60 6.52

EXPO '86, Vancouver — A72

**1986, June 11 *Perf. 13½x1***

*375* A72 1sh Rural post office 14 1
*376* A72 3sh Container depot, Embakasi 45 3
*377* A72 5sh Plane landing 75 5
*378* A72 7sh Shipping exports 1.00 7
*379* A72 10sh Goods transport 1.40 1.1
*Nos. 375-379 (5)* 3.74 2.7

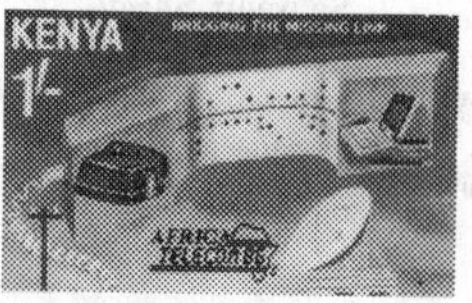

TELECOM '86, Nairobi, Sept. 16-23 — A73

**1986, Sept. 16 Litho. *Perf. 14½***

*380* A73 1sh Telephone-computer links 12 1
*381* A73 3sh Telephones, 1876-1986 38 2
*382* A73 5sh Satellite communications 62 4
*383* A73 7sh Switchboards 85 6

A74

Dhows (Ships) A75

**1986, Oct. 30 Litho. *Perf. 14½***

*384* A74 1sh Mashua 18 15
*385* A74 3sh Mtepe 60 40
*386* A74 5sh Dau La Mwao 1.00 75
*387* A74 10sh Jahazi 2.00 1.50

**Souvenir Sheet**

*388* A75 25sh Lamu, map 3.25 2.50

No. 388 has multicolored margin continuing map of Africa, Middle East and Asia. Size: 118x80mm.

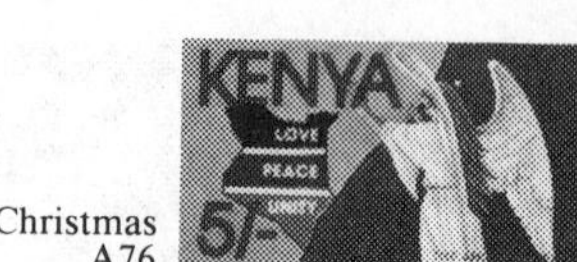

Christmas A76

**1986, Dec. 5 *Perf. 12***

*389* A76 1sh Nativity, vert. 12 10
*390* A76 3sh Shepherd boy, vert. 38 28
*391* A76 5sh Angel, map 62 45
*392* A76 7sh Magi 88 65

UNICEF, 40th Anniv. — A77

Child Survival Campaign: 1sh, Universal immunization by 1990. 3sh, Food and nutrition. 4sh, Oral rehydration. 5sh, Family planning. 10sh, Literacy of women.

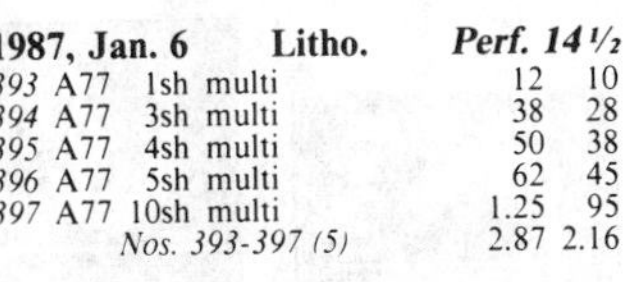

**1987, Jan. 6 Litho. *Perf. 14½***

*393* A77 1sh multi 12 10
*394* A77 3sh multi 38 28
*395* A77 4sh multi 50 38
*396* A77 5sh multi 62 45
*397* A77 10sh multi 1.25 95
*Nos. 393-397 (5)* 2.87 2.16

A78

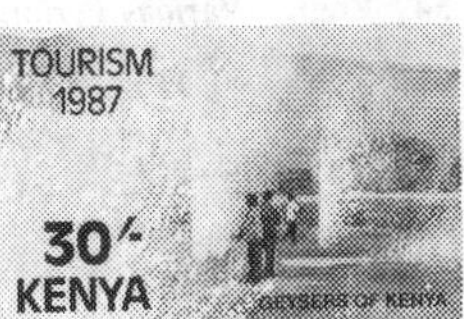


Tourism — A79

**1987, Mar. 25 Litho. *Perf. 14½***

*398* A78 1sh Akamba carvers 12 10
*399* A78 3sh Beach 35 28
*400* A78 5sh Escarpment 60 45
*401* A78 7sh Pride of lions 85 65

**Souvenir Sheet**

*402* A79 30sh Kenya geysers 3.75 3.00

No. 402 has multicolored margin continuing the design. Size: 118x81mm.

Ceremonial Costumes A80

**1987, May 20 *Perf. 14½x13½***

*403* A80 1sh Embu 14 12
*404* A80 3sh Kisii 40 32
*405* A80 5sh Samburu 70 56
*406* A80 7sh Taita 1.00 80
*407* A80 10sh Boran 1.40 1.10
*Nos. 403-407 (5)* 3.64 2.90

Posts & Telecommunications Corp., 10th Anniv. — A81

**1987, July 1 Litho. *Perf. 13½***

*408* A81 1sh Telecommunications satellite 12 10
*409* A81 3sh Rural post office, Kajiado 35 28
*410* A81 4sh Athletics 48 36
*411* A81 5sh Rural communication 60 45
*412* A81 7sh Speedpost 85 65
*Nos. 408-412 (5)* 2.40 1.84

**Souvenir Sheet**

*413* A81 25sh Natl. Flag 3.25 2.50

No. 413 has multicolored decorative margin picturing telephone, dove and letter. Size: 111x80mm.

4th All Africa Games, Nairobi, Aug. 1-12 — A82

**1987, Aug. 5 *Perf. 14½x14***

*414* A82 1sh Volleyball 12 10
*415* A82 3sh Cycling 35 28
*416* A82 4sh Boxing 48 36
*417* A82 5sh Swimming 60 45
*418* A82 7sh Steeple chase 85 65
*Nos. 414-418 (5)* 2.40 1.84

**Souvenir Sheet**

***Perf. 14x14½***

*419* A82 30sh Kasarani Sports Complex 3.75 2.75

Nos. 414-418, vert. No. 419 has orange inscribed margin picturing games emblem. Size: 117x81mm.

Medicinal Herbs — A83

**1987, Oct. 27 Litho. *Perf. 13½x14***

*420* A83 1sh Aloe volkensii 12 10
*421* A83 3sh Cassia didymobotrya 35 28
*422* A83 5sh Erythrina abyssinica 60 45
*423* A83 7sh Adenium obesum 85 65
*424* A83 10sh Herbalist's clinic 1.15 88
*Nos. 420-424 (5)* 3.07 2.36

Butterflies — A84

**1988, Feb. 14 Photo. *Perf. 15x14***

*425* A84 20c Iolaus sidus 5 5
*426* A84 40c Vanessa cardui 5 5
*427* A84 50c Colotis euippe omphale 6 5
*428* A84 70c Precis westermanni 8 6
*429* A84 80c Colias electo 10 8
*430* A84 1sh Eronia leda 12 10

**Size: 25x41mm.**

***Perf. 14½***

*431* A84 2sh Papilio rex 24 18
*432* A84 2.50sh Colotis phisadia 30 22
*433* A84 3sh Papilio desmondi teita 35 28
*434* A84 3.50sh Papilio demodocus 40 30
*435* A84 4sh Papilio phorcas 48 36
*436* A84 5sh Charaxes druceanus teita 58 45
*437* A84 7sh Cymothoe teita 82 60
*438* A84 10sh Charaxes zoolina 1.15 88
*439* A84 20sh Papilio dardanus 2.35 1.75
*440* A84 40sh Charaxes cithaeron kennethi 4.65 3.50
*Nos. 425-440 (16)* 11.78 8.91

Game Lodges A85

**1988, May 31 Litho. *Perf. 14½***

*441* A85 1sh Samburu 14 10
*442* A85 3sh Naro Moru River 40 30
*443* A85 4sh Mara Serena 52 40
*444* A85 5sh Voi Safari 65 48
*445* A85 7sh Kilimanjaro Buffalo Lodge 90 68
*446* A85 10sh Meru Mulika 1.30 1.00
*Nos. 441-446 (6)* 3.91 2.96

World Expo '88, Brisbane A86

EXPO '88 and Australia bicentennial emblems plus: 1sh, Stadium, site of the 1982 Commonwealth Games, and runners. 3sh, Flying Doctor Service aircraft. 4sh, HMS *Sirius*, a 19th cent. immigrant ship. 5sh, Ostrich and emu. 7sh, Pres. Daniel Arap Moi, Queen Elizabeth II and Robert Hawke, prime minister of Australia. 30sh, Kenya Pavilion at EXPO '88.

**1988, June 10**

*447* A86 1sh multi 14 10
*448* A86 3sh multi 40 30
*449* A86 4sh multi 52 40
*450* A86 5sh multi 65 48
*451* A86 7sh multi 90 68
*Nos. 447-451 (5)* 2.61 1.96

**Souvenir Sheet**

*452* A86 30sh multi 3.25 2.50

No. 452 has multicolored margin continuing the design and picturing flags of Kenya and Australia. Size: 117x80mm.

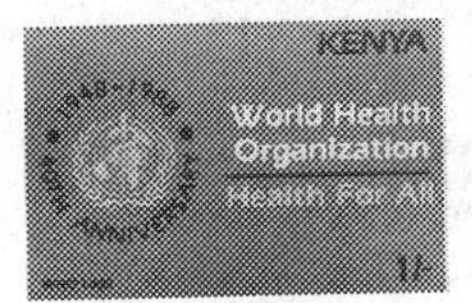


World Health Organization, 40th Anniv. — A87

**1988, July 1 Litho. *Perf. 14½***

*453* A87 1sh shown 14 10
*454* A87 3sh Nutrition 40 30
*455* A87 5sh Immunization 65 48
*456* A87 7sh Water supply 90 68

1988 Summer Olympics, Seoul — A88

**1988, Aug. 1 Litho. *Perf. 14½x14***

*457* A88 1sh Handball 12 10
*458* A88 3sh Judo 38 28
*459* A88 5sh Weight lifting 62 48
*460* A88 7sh Javelin 88 65
*461* A88 10sh 400-meter relay 1.25 95
*Nos. 457-461 (5)* 3.25 2.46

**Souvenir Sheet**

*462* A88 30sh Tennis 3.75 2.75

No. 462 has multicolored inscribed margin picturing emblem. Size: 112x79mm.

Utensils A89

***Perf. 14½x14, 14x14½***

**1988, Sept. 20 Litho.**

*463* A89 1sh Calabashes, vert. 12 10
*464* A89 3sh Milk gourds, vert. 35 25
*465* A89 5sh Cooking pots 60 45
*466* A89 7sh Winnowing trays 85 65
*467* A89 10sh Reed baskets 1.20 90
*Nos. 463-467 (5)* 3.12 2.35

**Souvenir Sheet**

*468* A89 25sh Gourds, calabash, horn 3.25 2.40

No. 468 has decorative multicolored margin. Size: 118x80mm.

10-Year Presidency of Daniel Arap Moi — A90

Designs: 1sh, Swearing-in ceremony, 1978. 3sh, Promoting soil conservation. 3.50sh, Public transportation (bus), Nairobi. 4sh, Jua Kali artisans at market. 5sh, Moi University, Eldoret, established in 1985. 7sh, Hospital ward expansion. 10sh, British Prime Minister Margaret Thatcher and Pres. Moi inaugurating the Kapsabet Telephone Exchange, Jan. 6, 1988.

***Perf. 13½x14½***

**1988, Oct. 13 Litho.**

*469* A90 1sh multi 12 10
*470* A90 3sh multi 35 28
*471* A90 3.50sh multi 42 32
*472* A90 4sh multi 48 35
*473* A90 5sh multi 60 45
*474* A90 7sh multi 85 65
*475* A90 10sh multi 1.20 90
*Nos. 469-475 (7)* 4.02 3.05

Independence, 25th Anniv. — A91

**1988, Dec. 9 Litho. *Perf.***

*476* A91 1sh Natl. flag 12 10
*477* A91 3sh Coffee picking 35 28
*478* A91 5sh Model of postal hq. 60 45
*479* A91 7sh Harambee Star Airbus A310-300 85 65
*480* A91 10sh Locomotive 9401 1.20 90
*Nos. 476-480 (5)* 3.12 2.38

## POSTAGE DUE STAMPS

D1

***Perf. 14x13½, 14, 14x15, 15, 15x14***

**1967-85 Litho. Unwmk.**

*J1* D1 5c dk red 5 5
*J2* D1 10c green 5 5
*J3* D1 20c dk bl 7 7
*J4* D1 30c redsh brn 15 10
*J5* D1 40c brt red lil 16 15
*J6* D1 80c brick red ('78) 35 30

| | | | | |
|---|---|---|---|---|
| J7 | D1 | 1sh orange | 80 | 1.90 |
| J8 | D1 | 2sh pale vio ('85) | 15 | 10 |
| | | *Nos. J1-J8 (8)* | 1.78 | 2.72 |

Issue dates: 80c, 1978. Others, Jan. 3, 1967.

Nos. J1-J5, J7 were reissued Feb. 18, 1970, with perf. 14; in 1971-73 with perf. 14x15; and in 1973 with perf. 15. J6 is perf. 14; J7 is perf. 15x14.

## OFFICIAL STAMPS

Nos. 1-5 and 7 Overprinted **OFFICIAL**

***Perf. 14x14½***

**1964, Oct. 1 Photo. Unwmk.**

**Size: 21x17½mm.**

| | | | | |
|---|---|---|---|---|
| O1 | A1 | 5c bl, buff & dk brn | 10 | 10 |
| O2 | A1 | 10c brown | 25 | 25 |
| O3 | A1 | 15c dp mag | 35 | 35 |
| O4 | A1 | 20c yel grn & dk brn | 50 | 50 |
| O5 | A1 | 30c yel & blk | 75 | 75 |
| O6 | A1 | 50c grn, blk & dp car | 1.25 | 1.25 |
| | | *Nos. O1-O6 (6)* | 3.20 | 3.20 |

# KENYA, UGANDA, TANZANIA

LOCATION — In East Africa, bordering on the Indian Ocean.

GOVT. — States in British Commonwealth.

AREA — 679,802 sq. mi.

POP. — 42,760,000 (est. 1977).

CAPITAL — Nairobi (Kenya), Kampala (Uganda), Dar es Salaam (Tanzania).

Kenya became a crown colony in 1906, including the former East Africa Protectorate leased from the Sultan of Zanzibar and known as the Kenya Protectorate. In 1963 the colony became independent. Its stamps are listed under "Kenya."

The inland Uganda Protectorate, lying west of Kenya Colony, was declared a British Protectorate in 1894. Uganda became independent in 1962.

Tanganyika, a trust territory larger than Kenya or Uganda, was grouped with them postally from 1935 under the East African Posts & Telecommunications Administration. Tanganyika became independent in 1961. When it merged with Zanzibar in 1964, "Zanzibar" was added to the inscriptions on stamps issued under the E.A.P. & T. Administration. In 1965 the multiple inscription was changed to "Kenya, Uganda, Tanzania," variously arranged.

Zanzibar withdrew its own stamps in 1968, and K., U. & T. stamps became valid Jan. 1, 1968.

100 Cents = 1 Rupee
100 Cents = 1 Shilling (1922)
20 Shillings = 1 Pound

**Catalogue values for unused stamps in this country are for Never Hinged items, beginning with Scott 84.**

### East Africa and Uganda Protectorates

King George V
A1 A2

**1921 Typo. Wmk. 4 *Perf. 14***

**Ordinary Paper**

| | | | | |
|---|---|---|---|---|
| 1 | A1 | 1c black | 90 | 38 |
| 2 | A1 | 3c green | 65 | 38 |
| 3 | A1 | 6c rose red | 2.00 | 40 |
| 4 | A1 | 10c orange | 3.00 | 20 |
| 5 | A1 | 12c gray | 4.25 | 12.50 |
| 6 | A1 | 15c ultra | 3.25 | 6.25 |

**Chalky Paper**

| | | | | |
|---|---|---|---|---|
| 7 | A1 | 50c gray lil & blk | 8.75 | 15.00 |
| 8 | A2 | 2r blk & red, *bl* | 30.00 | 50.00 |
| 9 | A2 | 3r grn & vio | 50.00 | 87.50 |
| 10 | A2 | 5r gray lil & ultra | 62.50 | 100.00 |
| 11 | A2 | 50r gray grn & red | 1,250. | 1,600. |
| | | *Nos. 1-10 (10)* | 165.30 | 272.61 |

The name of the colony was changed to Kenya in August, 1920, but stamps of the East Africa and Uganda types were continued in use. Stamps of types A1 and A2 watermarked Multiple Crown and C A (3) are listed under East Africa and Uganda Protectorates.

For stamps of Kenya and Uganda overprinted "G. E. A." used in parts of former German East Africa occupied by British forces, see Tanganyika Nos. 1 to 9.

### Kenya and Uganda

King George V
A3 A4

**1922-27 Wmk. 4**

| | | | | |
|---|---|---|---|---|
| 18 | A3 | 1c brown | 12 | 12 |
| 19 | A3 | 5c violet | 1.10 | 10 |
| 20 | A3 | 5c grn ('27) | 1.40 | 8 |
| 21 | A3 | 10c green | 1.40 | 10 |
| 22 | A3 | 10c blk ('27) | 1.25 | 5 |
| 23 | A3 | 12c black | 1.25 | 1.90 |
| 24 | A3 | 15c car rose | 75 | 8 |
| 25 | A3 | 20c orange | 1.25 | 8 |
| 26 | A3 | 30c ultra | 50 | 10 |
| 27 | A3 | 50c gray | 1.75 | 10 |
| 28 | A3 | 75c ol bis | 2.25 | 1.75 |
| 29 | A4 | 1sh green | 2.25 | 50 |
| 30 | A4 | 2sh gray lil | 3.25 | 1.10 |
| 31 | A4 | 2sh50c brn ('25) | 20.00 | 50.00 |
| 32 | A4 | 3sh gray blk | 8.75 | 6.25 |
| 33 | A4 | 4sh gray ('25) | 25.00 | 55.00 |
| 34 | A4 | 5sh carmine | 17.50 | 15.00 |
| 35 | A4 | 7sh50c org ('25) | 55.00 | 150.00 |
| 36 | A4 | 10sh ultra | 37.50 | 37.50 |
| 37 | A4 | £1 org & blk | 87.50 | 75.00 |
| 38 | A4 | £2 brn vio & grn ('25) | 800.00 | 1,000. |
| 39 | A4 | £3 yel & dl vio ('25) | 1,000. | 1,250. |
| 40 | A4 | £4 rose lil & blk ('25) | 1,800. | 2,500. |
| 41 | A4 | £5 bl & blk | 2,500. | 3,000. |
| | | Revenue cancel | | 50.00 |
| 41A | A4 | £10 grn & blk | 9,000. | |
| 41B | A4 | £20 grn & red ('25) | 12,500. | |
| 41C | A4 | £25 red & blk | 15,000. | |
| | | *Nos. 18-37 (20)* | 269.77 | 394.81 |

Stamps of £50, £75 and £100 also exist. They were theoretically available for postage, but were seldom, if ever, so used. The listed high values are known with revenue cancellations removed and forged postal cancellations added.

### Kenya, Uganda, Tanganyika Silver Jubilee Issue

Common Design Type

**1935, May Engr. *Perf. 13½x14***

| | | | | |
|---|---|---|---|---|
| 42 | CD301 | 20c ol grn & lt bl | 20 | 10 |
| 43 | CD301 | 30c bl & brn | 55 | 50 |
| 44 | CD301 | 65c ind & grn | 1.60 | 1.50 |
| 45 | CD301 | 1sh brt vio & ind | 1.90 | 1.60 |

Kavirondo Cranes — A5

Dhow on Lake Victoria — A6

Lion — A7

Mount Kilimanjaro — A8

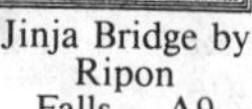

Jinja Bridge by Ripon Falls — A9

Mount Kenya — A10

Lake Naivasha — A11

FIVE CENTS,
Type I. Left rope does not touch sail.
Type II. Left rope touches sail.

***Perf. 13, 14, 11½ x 13, 13 x 11½***

**1935 Engr.; Typo. (10c, £1)**

| | | | | |
|---|---|---|---|---|
| 46 | A5 | 1c red brn & blk | 5 | 5 |
| 47 | A6 | 5c grn & blk (type I) | 6 | 5 |
| a. | | Type II | 75 | 12 |
| b. | | Perf. 13 x 11½ (type I) | 190.00 | 47.50 |
| c. | | Perf. 13 x 11½ (type II) | 175.00 | 37.50 |
| 48 | A7 | 10c blk & yel | 30 | 5 |
| 49 | A8 | 15c red & blk | 30 | 5 |
| 50 | A5 | 20c red org & blk | 15 | 5 |
| 51 | A9 | 30c dk ultra & blk | 18 | 10 |
| 52 | A6 | 50c blk & red vio | 50 | 9 |
| 53 | A10 | 65c yel brn & blk | 1.00 | 1.50 |
| 54 | A11 | 1sh grn & blk | 1.00 | 40 |
| a. | | Perf. 13 x 11½ | 600.00 | 40.00 |
| 55 | A8 | 2sh red vio & rose brn | 5.00 | 2.25 |
| 56 | A11 | 3sh blk & ultra | 5.00 | 3.00 |
| a. | | Perf. 13 x 11½ | 900.00 | |
| 57 | A9 | 5sh car & blk | 15.00 | 17.50 |
| 58 | A5 | 10sh ultra & red vio | 37.50 | 37.50 |
| 59 | A7 | £1 blk & scar | 100.00 | 95.00 |
| | | *Nos. 46-59 (14)* | 166.04 | 157.59 |

### Coronation Issue

Common Design Type

**1937, May 12 Engr. *Perf. 13½x14***

| | | | | |
|---|---|---|---|---|
| 60 | CD302 | 5c dp grn | 8 | 8 |
| 61 | CD302 | 20c dp org | 14 | 14 |
| 62 | CD302 | 30c brt ultra | 22 | 22 |

Kavirondo Cranes — A12

Dhow on Lake Victoria — A13

Lake Naivasha — A14

Jinja Bridge, Ripon Falls — A16

Mt. Kilimanjaro — A15

Lion — A17

FIFTY CENTS:
Type I. Left rope does not touch sail.
Type II. Left rope touches sail.

**1938-54 Engr. *Various Perforations***

| | | | | |
|---|---|---|---|---|
| 63 | A12 | 1c red brn & gray blk, perf. 13 | 5 | 5 |
| a. | | 1c vio brn & blk, perf. 13x13½ ('42) | 5 | 5 |
| 64 | A13 | 5c grn & blk, perf. 13x11½ | 8 | 5 |
| 65 | A14 | 10c org & brn, perf. 13x11½ | 8 | 5 |
| a. | | Perf. 14 ('41) | 20.00 | 2.00 |
| 66 | A15 | 15c car & gray blk, perf. 13½x13 ('43) | 8 | 5 |
| a. | | Booklet pane of 4 | 3.50 | |
| b. | | Perf. 13 | 35 | 5 |
| 67 | A12 | 20c org & gray blk, perf. 13x13½ ('42) | 8 | 5 |
| a. | | Booklet pane of 4 | 6.50 | |
| b. | | Imperf., pair | | |
| c. | | Perf. 13 | 38 | 5 |
| d. | | Perf. 14 ('41) | 4.25 | 2.75 |
| 68 | A16 | 30c dp bl & gray blk, perf. 13x13½ ('42) | 12 | 5 |
| a. | | Perf. 14 ('41) | 35.00 | 5.00 |
| b. | | Perf. 13 | 85 | 7 |
| 69 | A13 | 50c gray blk & red vio, perf. 13x12½ (II) ('49) | 16 | 5 |
| a. | | Perf. 13x11½ (II) | 22 | 5 |
| b. | | Perf. 13x11½ (I) | 200.00 | 100.00 |
| 70 | A14 | 1sh yel brn & gray blk, perf. 13x12½ ('49) | 35 | 6 |
| a. | | Perf. 13x11½ | 35 | 6 |
| 71 | A15 | 2sh red vio & org brn, perf. 13½x13 ('44) | 60 | 28 |
| a. | | Perf. 13 | 5.50 | 1.00 |
| b. | | Perf. 14 ('41) | 8.25 | 3.00 |
| 72 | A14 | 3sh gray blk & ultra, perf. 13x12½ ('50) | 2.00 | 60 |
| a. | | Perf. 13x11½ | 1.75 | 50 |
| 73 | A16 | 5sh car rose & gray blk, perf. 13x13½ ('44) | 2.00 | 65 |
| a. | | Perf. 13 | 11.00 | 3.50 |
| b. | | Perf. 14 ('41) | 8.00 | 1.75 |
| 74 | A12 | 10sh ultra & red vio, perf. 13x13½ ('44) | 4.00 | 1.75 |
| a. | | Perf. 13 | 11.00 | 6.50 |
| b. | | Perf. 14 ('41) | 16.00 | 10.00 |

**Typo.**

| | | | | |
|---|---|---|---|---|
| 75 | A17 | £1 blk & scar, perf. 12½ ('54) | 8.25 | 6.50 |
| a. | | Perf. 11½x13 | 140.00 | 50.00 |
| b. | | Perf. 14 ('41) | 5.50 | 4.75 |
| | | *Nos. 63-75 (13)* | 17.85 | 10.19 |

See Nos. 88-89, 94-100.

South Africa Nos. 48, 57, 60 and 62 Surcharged **5c KENYA TANGANYIKA UGANDA**

Basic stamps of Nos. 76-79 are inscribed alternately in English and Afrikaans.

**1941-42 Wmk. 201 *Perf. 15x14, 14***

| | | | | |
|---|---|---|---|---|
| 76 | A6 | 5c on 1p car & gray | 6 | 6 |
| a. | | Pair | 16 | 22 |
| 77 | A17 | 10c on 3p ultra | 7 | 6 |
| a. | | Pair | 20 | 22 |
| 78 | A7 | 20c on 6p org & grn | 14 | 12 |
| a. | | Pair | 28 | 28 |
| 79 | A11 | 70c on 1sh lt bl & ol brn ('42) | 22 | 10 |
| a. | | Pair | 45 | 40 |

Issue dates: Nos. 76-78, July 1, 1941. No. 79, Apr. 20, 1942.

**Catalogue values for unused stamps in this section, from this point to the end of the section, are for Never Hinged items.**

**Peace Issue**
Common Design Type
***Perf. 13½x14***

**1946, Nov. 11 Engr. Wmk. 4**
84 CD303 20c red org 10 10
85 CD303 30c dp bl 15 15

**Silver Wedding Issue**
Common Design Types

**1948, Dec. 1 Photo. *Perf. 14x14½***
86 CD304 20c orange 20 15

**Engr.; Name Typo.**
***Perf. 11½x11***
87 CD305 £1 red 25.00 25.00

Types of 1938

**1949, June 1 Engr. *Perf. 13x11½***
88 A13 5c red org & brn 12 8
a. Perf. 13 x 12½ ('50) 8 6
89 A14 10c grn & blk 10 5
a. Perf. 13 x 12½ ('50) 10 5

**UPU Issue**
Common Design Types
**Engr.; Typo. on Nos. 91 and 92**

**1949, Oct. 10 *Perf. 13, 11x11½***
90 CD306 20c red org 30 22
91 CD307 30c indigo 45 36
92 CD308 50c gray 80 80
93 CD309 1sh red brn 1.60 1.60

Type of 1949 with Added Inscription: "Royal Visit 1952."

**1952, Feb. 1 Engr. *Perf. 13x12½***
94 A14 10c grn & blk 10 10
95 A14 1sh yel brn & gray blk 65 65

Visit of Princess Elizabeth, Duchess of Edinburgh, and the Duke of Edinburgh, 1952.

Types of 1938-42
***Perf. 13x12½ (10c, 25c), 13½x13 (15c), 13x13½ (30c, 40c)***

**1952**
96 A14 10c gray & red brn 10 5
97 A15 15c grn & blk 10 10
98 A13 25c car & blk 50 30
99 A16 30c brn & pur 18 8
100 A12 40c brt bl & gray blk 25 18
*Nos. 96-100 (5)* 1.13 71

**Coronation Issue**
Common Design Type

**1953, June 2 *Perf. 13½x13***
101 CD312 20c red org & blk 15 10

Owen Falls Dam — A18

**1954, Apr. 28 *Perf. 12½x13***
102 A18 30c dp ultra & blk 20 20

Visit of Queen Elizabeth II and the Duke of Edinburgh, 1954.

Giraffe A19

Elizabeth II A21

Mt. Kilimanjaro A20

Designs: 5c, 30c, Owen Falls dam (without "Royal Visit 1954"). 20c, 40c, 1sh, Lion. 15c, 1.30sh, 5sh, Elephants. 10sh, Royal Lodge, Sagana.

**1954-59 *Perf. 12½x13, 13x12½***
103 A18 5c choc & blk 8 5
a. Booklet pane of 4 50
b. Dam inverted
104 A19 10c carmine 10 5
a. Booklet pane of 4 60
105 A20 15c lt bl & blk (no period below "c") ('58) 35 8
a. Bklt. pane of 4 2.00
106 A20 15c lt bl & blk (period below "c") ('59) 1.25 15
a. Booklet pane of 4 6.00
107 A19 20c org & blk 20 5
a. Booklet pane of 4 80
b. Imperf., pair 800.00
108 A18 30c ultra & blk 20 5
a. Booklet pane of 4 1.00
109 A19 40c brn ('58) 35 6
110 A19 50c dp red lil 45 6
a. Booklet pane of 4 2.00
111 A20 65c brn car & grn ('55) 1.75 65
112 A19 1sh dp mag & blk 50 8
113 A20 1.30sh pur & red org ('55) 1.50 10
114 A20 2sh dp grn & gray 1.75 30
115 A20 5sh blk & org 5.00 75
116 A20 10sh ultra & blk 10.00 1.40
117 A21 £1 blk & ver 15.00 3.25
*Nos. 103-117 (15)* 38.48 7.08

No. 103b is unique and used.

Map Showing Lakes Victoria and Tanganyika A22

***Perf. 12½x13***
**1958, July 30 Engr. Wmk. 314**
118 A22 40c grn & bl 30 30
119 A22 1.30sh vio & grn 75 70

Cent. of the discovery of Lakes Victoria and Tanganyika by Sir Richard F. Burton and Capt. J. H. Speke.

Sisal — A23

A25

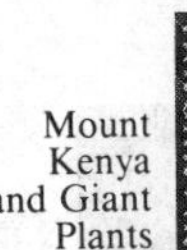

Mount Kenya and Giant Plants A24

Designs: 10c, Cotton. 15c, Coffee. 20c, Gnu. 25c, Ostriches. 30c, Thompson's gazelles. 40c, Manta ray. 50c, Zebras. 65c, Cheetah. 1.30sh, Murchison Falls and hippopotamuses. 2sh, Mt. Kilimanjaro and giraffes. 2.50sh, Candelabra tree and black rhinoceroses. 5sh, Crater Lake and Mountains of the Moon. 10sh, Ngorongoro Crater and buffaloes.

***Perf. 14½x14***
**1960-61 Photo. Wmk. 314**
120 A23 5c dl bl 5 5
121 A23 10c lt ol grn 8 5
a. Bklt. pane of 4 40
122 A23 15c dl pur 8 5
a. Bklt. pane of 4 40
123 A23 20c brt lil rose 12 5
a. Bklt. pane of 4 55
124 A23 25c ol gray 50 25
125 A23 30c brt ver 15 5
a. Bklt. pane of 4 70
126 A23 40c brt bl 25 6
127 A23 50c dl vio 30 6
a. Bklt. pane of 4 1.50
128 A23 65c lemon 75 1.00

**Engr.**
***Perf. 14***
129 A24 1sh vio & red lil 40 6
130 A24 1.30sh choc & dk car 75 12
131 A24 2sh dk bl & dl bl 1.00 25
132 A24 2.50sh ol grn & dl bl 1.25 60
133 A24 5sh rose red & lil 2.50 60
134 A24 10sh sl bl & ol grn 5.00 1.25

***Perf. 13½x13***
135 A25 20sh lake & bluish vio 10.00 4.00
*Nos. 120-135 (16)* 23.18 8.50

Booklets issued in 1961.
On Nos. 120-134, positions of "Kenya," "Uganda" and "Tanganyika" are rotated.

Agricultural Development — A26

Design: 30c, 1.30sh, Farmer picking corn.

**Unwmk.**
**1963, Mar. 21 Photo. *Perf. 14***
136 A26 15c lt ol grn & ultra 10 7
137 A26 30c yel & red brn 20 8
138 A26 50c dp org & ultra 30 16
139 A26 1.30sh lt bl & red brn 60 40

"Freedom from Hunger" campaign of the FAO.

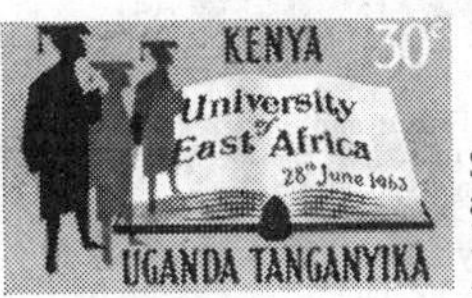

Scholars and Open Book A27

**1963, June 28 Unwmk. *Perf. 14***
140 A27 30c multi 10 7
141 A27 1.30sh multi 35 35

Inauguration of University of East Africa.

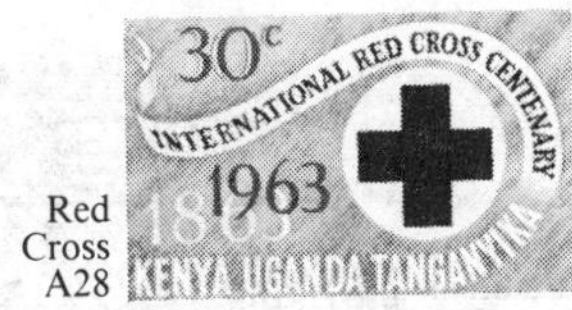

Red Cross A28

**1963, Sept. 2**
142 A28 30c bl & red 18 12
143 A28 50c bis brn & red 60 30

Centenary of International Red Cross.

**Kenya, Uganda, Tanganyika and Zanzibar**
Issued by the East African Common Services Organization. Not used in Zanzibar.

Japanese Crest and Olympic Rings — A29

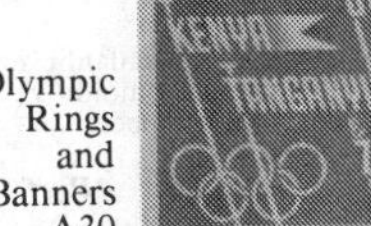

Olympic Rings and Banners A30

**Unwmk.**
**1964, Oct. 25 Photo. *Perf. 14***
144 A29 30c org & dk pur 7 6
145 A29 50c dk pur & org 12 10
146 A30 1.30sh bl, grn & org 32 32
147 A30 2.50sh bl, vio & lil rose 60 60

18th Olympic Games, Tokyo, Oct. 10-25.

**Kenya, Uganda, Tanzania**
Issued by the East African Common Services Organization.

Safari Rally Emblem and Leopard — A31

Design: 1.30sh, Car on road through national park and emblem of the East African Safari Rally.

**1965, Apr. 15 Unwmk. *Perf. 14***
148 A31 30c bl grn, yel & blk 8 7
149 A31 50c brn, yel & blk 16 10
150 A31 1.30sh lt ultra, ocher & grn 35 28
151 A31 2.50sh bl, dk grn & dl red 65 65

Issued to publicize the 13th East African Safari Rally, Apr. 15-19, 1965.

ITU Emblem, Old and Modern Communication Equipment — A32

**1965, May 17 Photo.**
152 A32 30c lil rose, gold & brn 12 6
153 A32 50c gray, gold & brn 15 14
154 A32 1.30sh lt vio bl, gold & brn 35 30
155 A32 2.50sh brt bl grn, gold & brn 75 75

Cent. of the ITU.

ICY Emblem — A33

**1965, Aug. 4 Unwmk. *Perf. 14***
156 A33 30c grn & gold 12 6
157 A33 50c slate blk & gold 15 14
158 A33 1.30sh ultra & gold 35 30
159 A33 2.50sh car & gold 70 70

International Cooperation Year, 1965.

Game Park Lodge A34

Designs: 50c, Murchison Falls, Uganda. 1.30sh, Lake Nakuru, Kenya. 2.50sh, Deep-sea fishing, Tanzania.

**1966, Apr. 4 Photo. *Perf. 14***
160 A34 30c ocher & multi 12 6
161 A34 50c grn & multi 15 14
a. Blue omitted

*162* A34 1.30sh multi 35 30
*163* A34 2.50sh gray & multi 75 75

Tourist publicity.

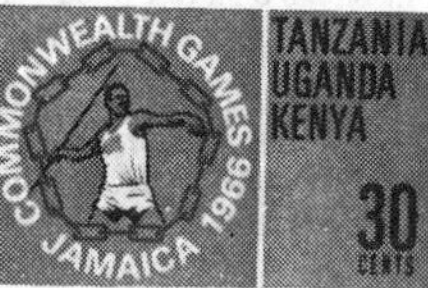


Javelin Thrower and Games' Emblem A35

**1966, Aug. 2 Unwmk. *Perf. 14***

*164* A35 30c multi 12 8
*165* A35 50c multi 15 14
*166* A35 1.30sh multi 35 30
*167* A35 2.50sh multi 75 75

8th British Commonwealth and Empire Games, Jamaica, Aug. 4-13, 1966.

UNESCO Emblem — A36

**1966, Oct. 3 Photo. *Perf. 14***

*168* A36 30c rose red, brt grn & blk 12 6
*169* A36 50c lt brn, brt grn & blk 15 14
*170* A36 1.30sh gray, brt grn & blk 35 30
*171* A36 2.50sh yel, brt grn & blk 75 70

20th anniv. of UNESCO.

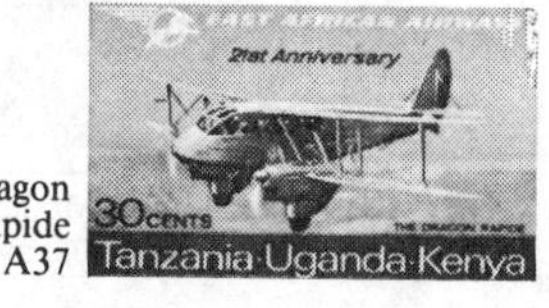


Dragon Rapide A37

Planes: 50c, Super VC10. 1.30sh, Comet 4. 2.50sh, F.27 Friendship.

**1967, Jan. 23 Unwmk.**

*172* A37 30c multi 15 8
*173* A37 50c multi 20 15
*174* A37 1.30sh multi 50 40
*175* A37 2.50sh multi 1.50 1.50

21st anniversary of East African Airways.

Pillar Tomb, East African Coast — A38

Designs: 50c, Man hunting elephant, petroglyph, Tanzania. 1.30sh, Clay head, Luzira, Uganda. 2.50sh, Proconsul skull, Rusinga Island, Kenya.

**1967, May 2 Photo. *Perf. 14***

*176* A38 30c rose lake, blk & yel 12 6
*177* A38 50c gray, blk & ver 15 12
*178* A38 1.30sh grn, yel & blk 35 30
*179* A38 2.50sh cop red, yel & blk 70 65

Archaeological relics of East Africa.

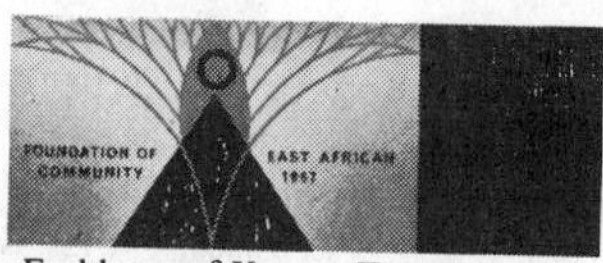


Emblems of Kenya, Tanzania and Tanganyika — A39

**Photo.; Gold Impressed**

**1967, Dec. 1 *Perf. 14½x14***

*180* A39 5sh gray, blk & gold 1.25 1.25

Establishment of East African Community.

Mount Kenya A40

Designs: 30c Mountain climber. 1.30sh, Mount Kilimanjaro. 2.50sh, Ruwenzori Mountains.

***Perf. 14½***

**1968, Mar. 4 Unwmk. Photo.**

*181* A40 30c multi 14 8
*182* A40 50c multi 18 14
*183* A40 1.30sh multi 42 35
*184* A40 2.50sh multi 90 90

Family and Rural Hospital A41

Designs (Family and): 50c, Student nurse. 1.30sh, Microscope. 2.50sh, Mosquito and hand holding hypodermic.

**1968, May 13 Photo. *Perf. 13½***

*185* A41 30c multi 10 7
*186* A41 50c rose vio, blk & brt pink 14 12
*187* A41 1.30sh brn org, blk & brt pink 35 28
*188* A41 2.50sh gray, blk & brt pink 65 65

20th anniv. of the WHO.

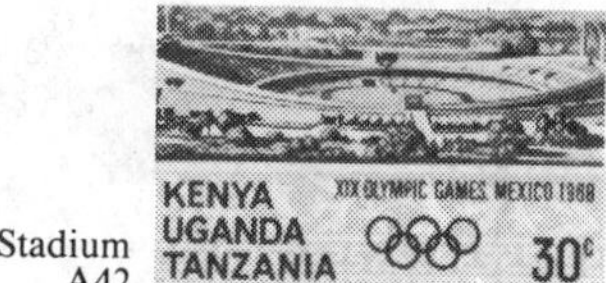


Stadium A42

Designs: 50c, Diving tower. 1.30sh, Pylons and tracks. 2.50sh, Boxing ring (vert.).

***Perf. 14½x14, 14x14½***

**1968, Oct. 14 Photo.**

*189* A42 30c dl pur & gray grn 10 5
*190* A42 50c brt grn, blk & gray 14 10
*191* A42 1.30sh gray grn, blk & dk car 35 28
*192* A42 2.50sh buff, brn org & brn blk 65 65

19th Olympic Games, Mexico City, Oct. 12-27.

Railroad Ferry MV Umoja A43

Water Transport: 50c, Transatlantic liner S.S. Harambee. 1.30sh, Lake motor vessel Victoria. 2.50sh, Ferry St. Michael.

**1969, Jan. 20 Photo. *Perf. 14***

*193* A43 30c bl, gray & dk bl 16 12
*194* A43 50c bl, gray & scar 28 20
*195* A43 1.30sh bl, dk bl & dk grn 70 60
*196* A43 2.50sh bl, dk bl & org 1.60 1.60

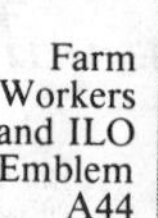

Farm Workers and ILO Emblem A44

Designs (ILO Emblem and); 50c, Construction. 1.30sh, Industry. 2.50sh, Shipping.

**1969, Apr. 14 Photo. *Perf. 14***

*197* A44 30c grn, blk & yel 8 6
*198* A44 50c car rose, blk & car 14 10
*199* A44 1.30sh dp org, blk & org 30 25
*200* A44 2.50sh grnsh bl, blk & ultra 60 60

50th anniv. of the ILO.

Pope Paul VI, Mountains of the Moon, Papal Arms, Crested Crane — A45

Euphorbia Tree in Shape of Africa, Development Bank Emblem — A46

**1969, July 31 Photo. *Perf. 14***

*201* A45 30c dk bl, blk & gold 8 6
*202* A45 70c plum, blk & gold 16 10
*203* A45 1.50sh gray bl, blk & gold 40 35
*204* A45 2.50sh dp vio, blk & gold 65 65

Issued to commemorate the visit of Pope Paul VI to Uganda, July 31-Aug. 2.

***Perf. 14x13½***

**1969, Dec. 8 Litho. Unwmk.**

*205* A46 30c brt grn, dk grn & gold 8 6
*206* A46 70c plum, dk grn & gold 16 10
*207* A46 1.50sh grnsh bl, dk grn & gold 40 30
*208* A46 2.50sh brn org, dk grn & gold 65 65

Issued to commemorate the 5th anniversary of the African Development Bank.

Amadinda, Uganda — A47

Musical Instruments: 30c, Marimba, Tanzania. 1.50sh, Nzomari (trumpet), Kenya. 2.50sh, Adeudeu, Kenya.

**1970, Feb. 16 Litho. *Perf. 11x12***

*209* A47 30c multi 8 6
*210* A47 70c multi 16 10
*211* A47 1.50sh dk rose brn & org 40 30
*212* A47 2.50sh multi 65 65

Satellite Earth Station A48

Designs: 70c, Radar station by day. 1.50sh, Radar station by night. 2.50sh, Satellite transmitting communications to and from earth.

**1970, May 18 Litho. *Perf. 14½***

*213* A48 30c multi 8
*214* A48 70c multi 16 1
*215* A48 1.50sh org, blk & vio 45 3
*216* A48 2.50sh dl bl & multi 65 6

Opening of the East African Satellite Earth Station, Mt. Margaret, Kenya.

Runner — A49

**1970, July 16 Litho. *Perf. 14½***

*217* A49 30c org brn, dk brn & blk 8 5
*218* A49 70c grn, dk brn & blk 16 10
*219* A49 1.50sh dl pur, dk brn & blk 40 30
*220* A49 2.50sh grnsh bl, dk brn & blk 65 65

Issued to publicize the 9th British Commonwealth Games, Edinburgh, July 16-25.

U.N. Emblem and People A50

**1970, Oct. 19 Photo. *Perf. 14½***

*221* A50 30c org brn, gold & blk 8 5
*222* A50 70c bl grn, gold & blk 16 10
*223* A50 1.50sh dl red brn, gold & blk 40 30
*224* A50 2.50sh ol, gold & blk 65 65

25th anniversary of the United Nations.

Conversion from Pounds to Kilograms — A51

Designs: 70c, Conversion from Fahrenheit to centigrade. 1.50sh, Conversion from gallons to liters. 2.50sh, Conversion from miles to kilometers.

**1971, Jan. 4 Photo. *Perf. 14½***

*225* A51 30c sil & multi 8 5
*226* A51 70c sil & multi 16 10
*227* A51 1.50sh sil & multi 40 30
*228* A51 2.50sh sil & multi 65 65

Conversion to metric system of weights and measures.

Locomotive — A52

Designs: Various locomotives.

**1971, Apr. 19 Photo. *Perf. 14½***

*229* A52 30c gold & multi 8 5
*230* A52 70c gold & multi 28 16
*231* A52 1.50sh gold & multi 65 65

| | | | | |
|---|---|---|---|---|
| *232* | A52 | 2.50sh gold & multi | 1.50 | 1.50 |
| *a.* | | Souvenir sheet of 4 | 5.00 | 5.00 |

70th anniversary of the completion of the Mombasa to Kisumu line. No. 232a contains one each of Nos. 229-232; lemon and dark carmine rose margin. Size: 121x89mm.

Bull and Campaign Emblem — A53

Designs: 30c, 1.50sh, Campaign emblem and cow. 2.50sh, like 70c.

**1971, July 5 Photo. *Perf. 14½***

| | | | | |
|---|---|---|---|---|
| *233* | A53 | 30c yel grn, blk & bis | 8 | 5 |
| *234* | A53 | 70c gray bl, blk & bis | 16 | 10 |
| *235* | A53 | 1.50sh mag, blk & bis | 40 | 30 |
| *236* | A53 | 2.50sh red org, blk & bis | 65 | 65 |

Rinderpest campaign by the Organization for African Unity.

Meeting of Stanley and Livingstone — A54

**1971, Oct. 28 Litho. *Perf. 14***

| | | | | |
|---|---|---|---|---|
| *237* | A54 | 5sh multi | 1.50 | 1.50 |

Centenary of the meeting at Ujiji of Dr. David Livingstone, missionary, and Henry M. Stanley, journalist, who had been sent to find Livingstone.

Modern Farming Village — A55

Designs: 30c, Pres. Julius K. Nyerere carried in triumph, 1961 (vert.). 1.50sh, University of Dar es Salaam. 2.50sh, Kilimanjaro International Airport.

**1971, Dec. 9 *Perf. 14***

| | | | | |
|---|---|---|---|---|
| *238* | A55 | 30c bis & multi | 8 | 5 |
| *239* | A55 | 70c lt bl & multi | 16 | 10 |
| *240* | A55 | 1.50sh lt grn & multi | 40 | 30 |
| *241* | A55 | 2.50sh yel & multi | 85 | 85 |

10th anniv. of independence of Tanzania.

Flags of African Nations and Fair Emblem — A56

**1972, Feb. 23 *Perf. 13½x14***

| | | | | |
|---|---|---|---|---|
| *242* | A56 | 30c lt bl & multi | 8 | 5 |
| *243* | A56 | 70c gray & multi | 16 | 10 |
| *244* | A56 | 1.50sh yel & multi | 40 | 30 |
| *245* | A56 | 2.50sh multi | 65 | 65 |

First All-Africa Trade Fair, Nairobi, Kenya, Feb. 23-Mar. 5.

Child Drinking Milk, UNICEF Emblem A57

Designs (UNICEF Emblem and): 70c, Children playing ball. 1.50sh, Child writing on blackboard. 2.50sh, Boy playing with tractor.

**1972, Apr. 24 Litho. *Perf. 14½x14***

| | | | | |
|---|---|---|---|---|
| *246* | A57 | 30c brn org & multi | 12 | 5 |
| *247* | A57 | 70c lt ultra & multi | 25 | 15 |
| *248* | A57 | 1.50sh yel & multi | 55 | 45 |
| *249* | A57 | 2.50sh grn & multi | 1.00 | 1.00 |

25th anniv. (in 1971) of UNICEF.

Hurdles, Olympic and Motion Emblems A58

**1972, Aug. 28**

| | | | | |
|---|---|---|---|---|
| *250* | A58 | 40c *shown* | 8 | 5 |
| *251* | A58 | 70c *Running* | 15 | 8 |
| *252* | A58 | 1.50sh *Boxing* | 25 | 20 |
| *253* | A58 | 2.50sh *Hockey* | 50 | 50 |
| *a.* | | Souvenir sheet of 4 | 6.00 | 6.00 |

20th Olympic Games, Munich, Aug. 26-Sept. 11.

No. 253a contains one each of Nos. 250-253; blue decorative margin and inscription. Size: 130x97mm.

Uganda Kob, Semliki Game Reserve — A59

**1972, Oct. 9 Litho. *Perf. 14***

| | | | | |
|---|---|---|---|---|
| *254* | A59 | 40c *shown* | 15 | 8 |
| *255* | A59 | 70c *International Conference Center* | 25 | 15 |
| *256* | A59 | 1.50sh *Makarere Univ., Kampala* | 55 | 45 |
| *257* | A59 | 2.50sh *Uganda arms* | 1.50 | 1.50 |
| *a.* | | Souvenir sheet of 4 | 6.00 | 6.00 |

10th anniversary of Uganda's independence. No. 256 also commemorate the 50th anniversary of Makarere University, Kampala. No. 257a contains one each of Nos. 254-257, perf. 13x14; green margin with black inscription and multicolored coat of arms. Size: 135x119mm.

Flag of East Africa — A60

**1972, Dec. 1 Litho. *Perf. 14½x14***

| | | | | |
|---|---|---|---|---|
| *258* | A60 | 5sh multi | 2.50 | 2.50 |

5th anniv. of the East African Community.

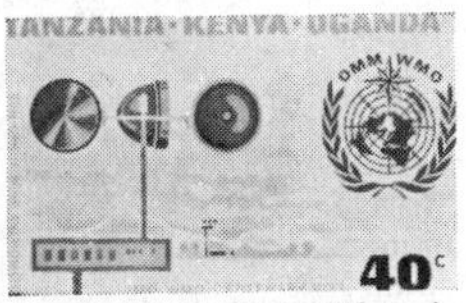

Anemometer, Lake Victoria Station — A61

Designs (WMO Emblem and): 70c, Release of weather balloon (vert.). 1.50sh, Hail suppression by meteorological rocket. 2.50sh, Meteorological satellite receiving antenna.

**1973, Mar. 5 Litho. *Perf. 14***

| | | | | |
|---|---|---|---|---|
| *259* | A61 | 40c multi | 15 | 8 |
| *260* | A61 | 70c ultra & multi | 25 | 15 |
| *261* | A61 | 1.50sh emer & multi | 55 | 45 |
| *262* | A61 | 2.50sh multi | 1.00 | 1.00 |

Cent. of intl. meteorological cooperation.

Scouts Laying Bricks — A62

Designs: 70c, Baden-Powell's gravestone, Nyeri, Kenya. 1.50sh, World Scout emblem. 2.50sh, Lord Baden-Powell.

**1973, July 16 Litho. *Perf. 14***

| | | | | |
|---|---|---|---|---|
| *263* | A62 | 40c ocher & multi | 25 | 15 |
| *264* | A62 | 70c multi | 40 | 30 |
| *265* | A62 | 1.50sh multi | 90 | 75 |
| *266* | A62 | 2.50sh grn & ultra | 2.25 | 1.50 |

24th Boy Scout World Conference (1st in Africa), Nairobi, Kenya, July 16-21.

International Bank for Reconstruction and Development and Affiliates' Emblems — A63

Designs: 40c, Arrows dividing 4 bank affiliate emblems. 70c, Vert. lines dividing 4 emblems. 1.50sh, Kenyatta Conference Center, Nairobi (vert.).

**1973, Sept. 24 Litho. *Perf. 14x13½***

| | | | | |
|---|---|---|---|---|
| *267* | A63 | 40c gray, blk & grn | 20 | 10 |
| *268* | A63 | 70c brn, gray & blk | 32 | 20 |
| *269* | A63 | 1.50sh lem, gray & blk | 75 | 60 |
| *270* | A63 | 2.50sh blk, org & gray | 1.40 | 1.40 |
| *a.* | | Souvenir sheet of 4 | 3.75 | 3.75 |

International Bank for Reconstruction and Development and Affiliate International Monetary Fund Meetings, Nairobi.

No. 270a contains stamps similar to Nos. 267-270 with simulated perforations. Green and orange border, brown inscription. Size: 166x141mm.

INTERPOL Emblem, Policeman and Dog — A64

Designs: 70c, East African policemen and emblem. 1.50sh, INTERPOL emblem. 2.50sh, INTERPOL Headquarters, St. Cloud, France.

**1973-74 Litho. *Perf. 14x14½***

| | | | | |
|---|---|---|---|---|
| *271* | A64 | 40c yel & multi | 22 | 12 |
| *272* | A64 | 70c multi | 38 | 22 |
| *273* | A64 | 1.50sh vio & multi | 80 | 70 |
| *274* | A64 | 2.50sh lem & multi *(St. Clans)* | 1.90 | 1.90 |
| *275* | A64 | 2.50sh lem & multi *(St. Cloud)* ('74) | 1.90 | 1.90 |
| | | *Nos. 271-275 (5)* | 5.20 | 4.84 |

50th anniversary of International Criminal Police Organization.

Issue date of Nos. 271-274, Oct. 24, 1973.

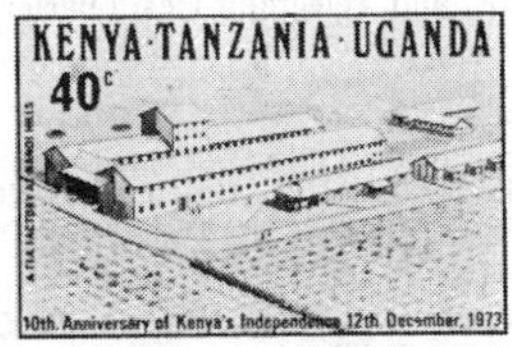

Tea Factory, Nandi Hills — A65

**1973, Dec. 12 Photo. *Perf. 13x14***

| | | | | |
|---|---|---|---|---|
| *276* | A65 | 40c *shown* | 15 | 8 |
| *277* | A65 | 70c *Kenyatta Hospital* | 25 | 15 |
| *278* | A65 | 1.50sh *Nairobi Airport* | 55 | 45 |
| *279* | A65 | 2.50sh *Kindaruma hydroelectric plant* | 1.00 | 1.00 |

10th anniversary of independence.

Afro-Shirazi Party Headquarters — A66

Designs: 70c, Michenzani housing development. 1.50sh, Map of East Africa and television screen with flower. 2.50sh, Amaan Stadium.

**1974, Jan. 12 Litho. *Perf. 13½x14***

| | | | | |
|---|---|---|---|---|
| *280* | A66 | 40c multi | 12 | 8 |
| *281* | A66 | 70c multi | 25 | 15 |
| *282* | A66 | 1.50sh blk & multi | 55 | 45 |
| *283* | A66 | 2.50sh blk & multi | 1.00 | 1.00 |

10th anniversary of Zanzibar revolution.

Symbol of Union A67

Designs: 70c, Map of Tanganyika and Zanzibar, and handshake. 1.50sh, Map of Tanganyika and Zanzibar, and communications symbols. 2.50sh, Flags of Tanu, Tanzania and Afro-Shirazi Party.

**1974, Apr. 24 Litho. *Perf. 14½***

| | | | | |
|---|---|---|---|---|
| *284* | A67 | 40c sep & multi | 15 | 8 |
| *285* | A67 | 70c bl grn & multi | 25 | 15 |
| *286* | A67 | 1.50sh ultra & multi | 65 | 50 |
| *287* | A67 | 2.50sh multi | 1.50 | 1.50 |

10th anniversary of Union of Tanganyika and Zanzibar.

Family and Home A68

Designs: 70c, Drummer at dawn. 1.50sh, Family hoeing, and livestock. 2.50sh, Telephonist, train, plane, telegraph lines.

**1974, July 15 Litho. *Perf. 14½***

| | | | | |
|---|---|---|---|---|
| *288* | A68 | 40c multi | 15 | 8 |
| *289* | A68 | 70c multi | 25 | 15 |
| *290* | A68 | 1.50sh multi | 65 | 50 |
| *291* | A68 | 2.50sh multi | 1.20 | 1.20 |

17th Intl. Conf. on Social Welfare, July 14-20.

Post and Telegraph Headquarters, Kampala — A69

Cent. of the UPU: 70c, Mail train and truck. 1.50sh, UPU Headquarters, Bern. 2.50sh, Loading mail on East African Airways VC-10.

**1974, Oct. 9 Litho. *Perf. 14***

| | | | | |
|---|---|---|---|---|
| *292* | A69 | 40c lt grn & multi | 15 | 8 |
| *293* | A69 | 70c gray & multi | 25 | 15 |
| *294* | A69 | 1.50sh yel & multi | 65 | 50 |
| *295* | A69 | 2.50sh lt bl & multi | 1.20 | 1.20 |

Family Planning Clinic A70

Designs: 70c, "Tug of War." 1.50sh, Scales and world population figures. 2.50sh, World Population Year emblem.

**1974, Dec. 16 Litho. *Perf. 14½***

| | | | | |
|---|---|---|---|---|
| *296* | A70 | 40c multi | 15 | 8 |
| *297* | A70 | 70c pur & multi | 25 | 15 |
| *298* | A70 | 1.50sh multi | 65 | 50 |
| *299* | A70 | 2.50sh bl blk & multi | 1.20 | 1.20 |

World Population Year.

Seronera Wild Life Lodge, Tanzania A71

Designs: 70c, Mweya Safari Lodge, Uganda. 1.50sh, Ark-Aberdare Forest Lodge, Kenya. 2.50sh, Paraa Safari Lodge, Uganda.

**1975, Feb. 24 Litho. *Perf. 14½***

| | | | | |
|---|---|---|---|---|
| *300* | A71 | 40c multi | 20 | 10 |
| *301* | A71 | 70c multi | 32 | 20 |
| *302* | A71 | 1.50sh multi | 90 | 65 |
| *303* | A71 | 2.50sh multi | 1.60 | 1.60 |

Game lodges of East Africa.

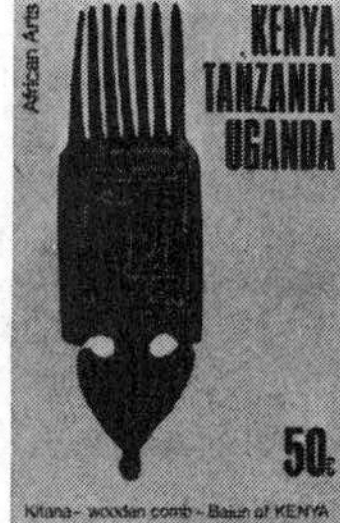


Wooden Comb, Bajun, Kenya — A72

African Artifacts: 1sh, Earring, Chaga, Tanzania. 2sh, Armlet, Acholi, Uganda. 3sh, Kamba gourd, Kenya.

**1975, May 5 Litho. *Perf. 13½***

| | | | | |
|---|---|---|---|---|
| *304* | A72 | 50c gray & multi | 18 | 15 |
| *305* | A72 | 1sh gray & multi | 35 | 30 |
| *306* | A72 | 2sh multi | 75 | 60 |
| *307* | A72 | 3sh multi | 1.20 | 1.20 |

Common Design Types are pictured in section before Great Britain.

Map Showing OAU Members, Ugandan Flag — A73

Elephant, Kenya — A74

Designs (OAU Emblem and): 50c, Entebbe Airport (horiz.). 2sh, Nile Hotel, Kampala (horiz.). 3sh, Ugandan Martyrs' Shrine, Namugongo.

***Perf. 11½x11, 11x11½***

**1975, July 28 Litho.**

| | | | | |
|---|---|---|---|---|
| *308* | A73 | 50c multi | 18 | 15 |
| *309* | A73 | 1sh multi | 35 | 30 |
| *310* | A73 | 2sh multi | 75 | 60 |
| *311* | A73 | 3sh multi | 1.20 | 1.20 |

Organization for African Unity (OAU), Summit Conf., Kampala, July 28-Aug. 1.

**1975, Sept. 11 Litho. *Perf. 11x11½***

Designs: 1sh, Albino buffalo, Uganda. 2sh, Elephant, exhibit in National Museum, Kenya. 3sh, Abbott's duiker, Tanzania.

| | | | | |
|---|---|---|---|---|
| *312* | A74 | 50c multi | 40 | 30 |
| *313* | A74 | 1sh brn & multi | 70 | 60 |
| *314* | A74 | 2sh yel grn & multi | 1.50 | 1.25 |
| *315* | A74 | 3sh bl grn & multi | 2.50 | 2.50 |

Protected animals.

Masai Villagers Bleeding Cow, Masai, Kenya — A75

Designs (Festival Emblem and): 1sh, Ugandan dancers. 2sh, Family, Makonde sculpture, Tanzania. 3sh, Skinning hippopotamus, East Africa.

**1975, Nov. 3 Litho. *Perf. 13½x14***

| | | | | |
|---|---|---|---|---|
| *316* | A75 | 50c org brn & multi | 18 | 15 |
| *317* | A75 | 1sh brt grn & multi | 35 | 30 |
| *318* | A75 | 2sh dk bl & multi | 75 | 60 |
| *319* | A75 | 3sh lil & multi | 1.20 | 1.20 |

2nd World Black and African Festival of Arts and Culture, Lagos, Nigeria, Jan. 5-Feb. 12.

Fokker Friendship, Nairobi Airport — A76

Designs: 1sh, DC-9 Kilimanjaro Airport. 2sh, Super VC10, Entebbe Airport. 3sh, East African Airways emblem.

**1976, Jan. 2 Litho. *Perf. 11½***

| | | | | |
|---|---|---|---|---|
| *320* | A76 | 50c ultra & multi | 25 | 25 |
| *321* | A76 | 1sh rose & multi | 40 | 40 |
| *322* | A76 | 2sh org & multi | 1.00 | 1.00 |
| *323* | A76 | 3sh blk & multi | 1.60 | 1.60 |

East African Airways, 30th anniversary.

## POSTAGE DUE STAMPS

### Kenya and Uganda

Numeral of Value
D1 D2

***Perf. 14½x14***

**1928-33 Typo. Wmk. 4**

| | | | | |
|---|---|---|---|---|
| *J1* | D1 | 5c dp vio | 50 | 75 |
| *J2* | D1 | 10c org red | 75 | 1.00 |
| *J3* | D1 | 20c yel grn | 1.00 | 1.25 |
| *J4* | D1 | 30c ol brn ('31) | 3.00 | *5.00* |
| *J5* | D1 | 40c dl bl | 2.50 | *7.50* |
| *J6* | D1 | 1sh grnsh gray ('33) | 30.00 | *100.00* |
| | | *Nos. J1-J6 (6)* | 37.75 | *115.50* |

### Kenya, Uganda, Tanganyika

**1935, May 1 *Perf. 13½x14***

| | | | | |
|---|---|---|---|---|
| *J7* | D2 | 5c violet | 8 | 12 |
| *J8* | D2 | 10c red | 8 | 8 |
| *J9* | D2 | 20c green | 12 | 14 |
| *J10* | D2 | 30c brown | 20 | *38* |
| *J11* | D2 | 40c ultra | 1.25 | *2.50* |
| *J12* | D2 | 1sh gray | 3.25 | *6.25* |
| | | *Nos. J7-J12 (6)* | 4.98 | 9.47 |

## OFFICIAL STAMPS

The 1959-60 "OFFICIAL" overprints on Kenya-Uganda-Tanganyika stamps are listed under Tanganyika, as they were used by the Tanganyika government.

# KIRIBATI

LOCATION — A group of islands in the Pacific Ocean northeast of Australia.
GOVT. — Republic.
AREA — 264 sq. mi.
POP. — 60,302 (1982).
CAPITAL — Tarawa.

Kiribati, former Gilbert Islands, consists of the Gilbert, Phoenix, Ocean and Line Islands.

**Catalogue values for all unused stamps in this country are for Never Hinged items.**

Kiribati Flag A50

Parliament, London, Assembly, Tarawa — A51

**Wmk. 373**

**1979, July 12 Litho. *Perf. 14***

| | | | | |
|---|---|---|---|---|
| *325* | A50 | 10c multi | 25 | 25 |
| *326* | A51 | 45c multi | 90 | 90 |

Independence.

Training Ship Teraaka A52

Designs: 3c, Passenger launch Tautunu. 5c, Hibiscus. 7c, Cathedral, Tarawa. 10c, House of Assembly, Bikenibeu Island. 12c, Betio harbor. 15c, Reef egret. 20c, Flamboyant tree. 25c, Moorish idol (fish). 30c, Frangipani blossoms. 35c, Chapel, Tangintebu Island. 50c, Hypolimnas bolina elliciana (butterfly). $1, Tarawa Lagoon ferry, Tabakea. $2, Sunset over lagoon. $5, Natl. flag.

**Wmk. 373, Unwmkd.**

**1979, July 12-80**

| | | | | |
|---|---|---|---|---|
| *327* | A52 | 1c multi | 5 | 5 |
| *328* | A52 | 3c multi | 7 | 6 |
| *329* | A52 | 5c multi | 10 | 8 |
| *330* | A52 | 7c multi | 14 | 12 |
| *331* | A52 | 10c multi | 20 | 18 |
| *332* | A52 | 12c multi | 25 | 20 |
| *333* | A52 | 15c multi | 30 | 25 |
| *334* | A52 | 20c multi | 40 | 35 |
| *335* | A52 | 25c multi | 45 | 42 |
| *336* | A52 | 30c multi | 60 | 50 |
| *337* | A52 | 35c multi | 65 | 60 |
| *338* | A52 | 50c multi | 80 | 80 |
| *339* | A52 | $1 multi | 1.40 | 1.00 |
| *340* | A52 | $2 multi | 3.50 | 2.75 |
| *340A* | A52 | $5 multi ('80) | 5.00 | 4.00 |
| | | *Nos. 327-340A (15)* | 13.91 | 11.36 |

Gilbert and Ellice Islands No. 1 — A53

Simulated Cancel and: 20c, Gilbert and Ellice No. 70. 25c, Great Britain No. 139. 45c, Gilbert and Ellice No. 31.

**Wmk. 373**

**1979, Sept. 27 Litho. *Perf. 14***

| | | | | |
|---|---|---|---|---|
| *341* | A53 | 10c multi | 20 | 20 |
| *342* | A53 | 20c multi | 35 | 35 |
| *343* | A53 | 25c multi | 40 | 40 |
| *344* | A53 | 45c multi | 60 | 60 |
| | *a* | Souvenir sheet of 4 | 1.50 | 1.50 |

Sir Rowland Hill (1795-1879), originator of penny postage. No. 344a contains Nos. 341-344. Margin shows dark blue simulated cancel, coat of arms. Size: 113x111½mm.

Boy Climbing Coconut Palm, IYC Emblem — A54

IYC Emblem, Coat of Arms and: 10c, Boy and giant clam shell. 45c, Girl reading book. $1, Boy wearing garlands. All vert.

***Perf. 14x13½, 13½x14***

**1979, Nov. 28 Litho.**

| | | | | |
|---|---|---|---|---|
| *345* | A54 | 10c multi | 20 | 20 |
| *346* | A54 | 20c multi | 35 | 35 |
| *347* | A54 | 45c multi | 50 | 50 |
| *348* | A54 | $1 multi | 1.00 | 1.00 |

International Year of the Child.

Downrange Station A55

National Space Development Agency of Japan (NASDA) Satellite Tracking: 45c, Experimental satellite trajectory (map). $1, Rocket launch, Tanegashima, Japan (vert.).

**1980, Feb. 20 Litho. *Perf. 14½***

| | | | | |
|---|---|---|---|---|
| *349* | A55 | 25c multi | 35 | 35 |
| *350* | A55 | 45c multi | 50 | 50 |
| *351* | A55 | $1 multi | 1.00 | 1.00 |

T.S. Teraaka, London 1980 Emblem A56

**1980, Apr. 30 Litho. Unwmk.**

352 A56 12c *shown* 20 20
353 A56 25c *Air Tungaru plane, Bonriki Airport* 25 25
354 A56 30c *Radio operator* 35 35
355 A56 $1 *Bairiki post office* 1.00 1.00
a Souvenir sheet of 4 2.00 2.00

London 1980 International Stamp Exhibition, May 6-14. No. 355a contains Nos. 352-355; multicolored margin shows Gilbert & Ellice Islands Nos. 2 and 9, Penny Black, London 1980 emblem. Size: 139x116mm.

Achaea Janata A57

**1980, Aug. 27 Litho. Perf. 14**

356 A57 12c shown 18 18
357 A57 25c Ethmia nigroapicella 28 28
358 A57 30c Utetheisa pulchelloides 35 35
359 A57 50c Anua coronata 65 65

Capt. Cook Hotel A58

**Wmk. 373**

**1980, Nov. 19 Litho. Perf. 13½**

360 A58 10c *shown* 14 14
361 A58 20c *Stadium* 22 22
362 A58 25c *Intl. Airport, Bonriki* 28 28
363 A58 35c *National Library* 40 40
364 A58 $1 *Otintai Hotel* 1.00 1.00
*Nos. 360-364 (5)* 2.04 2.04

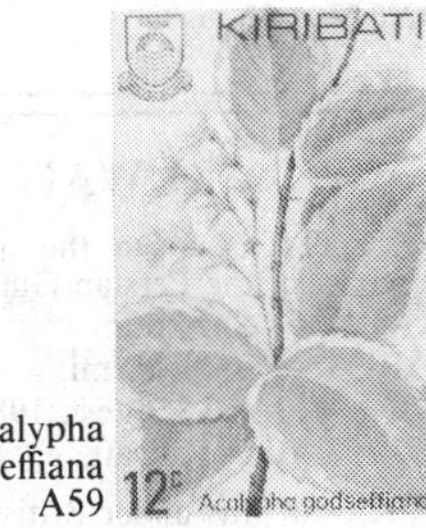


Acalypha Godseffiana A59

***Perf. 14x13½***

**1981, Feb. 18 Litho. Wmk. 373**

365 A59 12c shown 14 14
366 A59 30c Hibiscus schizopetalus 35 35
367 A59 35c Calotropis gigantea 42 42
368 A59 50c Euphorbia pulcherrima 60 60

Abaiang and Marakei Islands, String Figures — A60

**Wmk. 380: "POST OFFICE"**

**1981, May 6 Litho. Perf. 14**

369 A60 12c shown 20 20
370 A60 30c Butaritari, Little Makin, house 35 35
371 A60 35c Maiana, Coral Road 50 50
372 A60 $1 Christmas Isld., Resolution 1.00 1.00

Royal Wedding Types of Montserrat

**Wmk. 380**

**1981, July 29 Litho. Perf. 14**

373 A66 12c Couple, The Katherine 18 18
a Bklt. pane of 4, perf. 12, unwmkd. 75
374 A67 12c Couple 18 18
375 A66 50c The Osborne 75 75
376 A67 50c like #374 75 75
a Bklt. pane of 2, perf. 12, unwmkd. 1.50
377 A66 $2 Britannia 2.75 2.75
378 A67 $2 like #374 2.75 2.75
*Nos. 373-378 (6)* 7.36 7.36

**Souvenir Sheet**

***Perf. 12***

379 A67 $1.20 like #374 2.00 2.00

No. 379 has dull rose decorative margin. Size: 121x109mm.

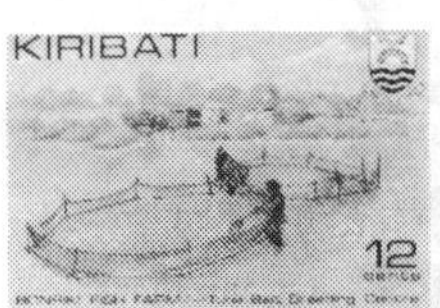


Bonriki Tuna Fish Bait Breeding Center A61

**1981, Nov. 19**

380 A61 12c shown 20 20
381 A61 30c Fishing boat 50 50
382 A61 35c Cold storage, Betio 60 60
383 A61 50c Nei Manganibuka 85 85
a Souvenir sheet of 4 2.25 2.25

No. 383a contains Nos. 380-383.

Pomarine Jaegers A62

**1982, Feb. 18-85 Litho. Perf. 14**

384 A62 1c shown 5 5
385 A62 2c Mallards 5 5
386 A62 4c Collared petrels 7 7
387 A62 5c Blue-faced boobies 8 8
388 A62 7c Friendly quail dove 12 12
389 A62 8c Shovelers 14 14
390 A62 12c Christmas Isld. warblers 20 20
391 A62 15c Pacific plovers 25 25
392 A62 20c Reef herons 35 35
392A A62 25c Brown noddies ('83) 40 40
393 A62 30c Brown boobies 50 50
394 A62 35c Audubon's shearwaters 60 60
395 A62 40c White-throated storm petrels, vert. 65 65
396 A62 50c Bristle-thighed curlews, vert. 85 85
396A A62 55c Fairy tern ('85) 50 50
397 A62 $1 Scarlet-breasted lorikeets, vert. 1.75 1.75
398 A62 $2 Long-tailed cuckoo, vert. 2.25 2.25
399 A62 $5 Great frigate birds, vert. 6.50 6.50
*Nos. 384-399 (18)* 15.31 15.31

Air Tungaru A63

**1982, Feb. 18 Wmk. 380**

400 A63 12c De Havilland DH114 Heron 20 20
401 A63 30c Britten-Norman Trislander 50 50
402 A63 35c Casa 212 Aviocar 60 60
403 A63 50c Boeing 727 85 85

21st Birthday of Princess Diana, July 1 — A64

**1982, May 19**

404 A64 12c Mary of Teck, 1893 20 20
405 A64 50c Teck arms 85 85
406 A64 $1 Diana 1.75 1.75

Nos. 404-406 Overprinted: "ROYAL BABY"

**1982, July 14**

407 A64 12c multi 20 20
408 A64 50c multi 85 85
409 A64 $1 multi 1.75 1.75

Birth of Prince William of Wales, June 21.

Scouting Year — A65

**1982, Aug. 12**

410 A65 12c First aid 20 20
411 A65 25c Repairing boat 40 40
412 A65 30c Saluting 50 50
413 A65 50c Gilbert Islds. #304 85 85

Visit of Queen Elizabeth II and Prince Philip A66

**Wmk. 380**

**1982, Oct. 23 Litho. Perf. 14**

414 A66 12c Couple, dancer 20 20
415 A66 25c Couple, boat 40 40
416 A66 35c Philatelic Bureau 60 60

**Souvenir Sheet**

417 A66 50c Queen Elizabeth II, vert. 85 85

No. 417 has multicolored margin showing map, ship. Size: 89x77mm. Also issued in sheets of 6.

**Commonwealth Day**

Common Design Type

**Wmk. 380**

**1983, Mar. 14 Litho. Perf. 14**

418 CD334 12c Obaia the Feathered legend 20 20
419 CD334 30c Robert Louis Stevenson Hotel, Abemama 50 50
420 CD334 50c Betio Harbor 85 85
421 CD334 $1 Map 1.75 1.75

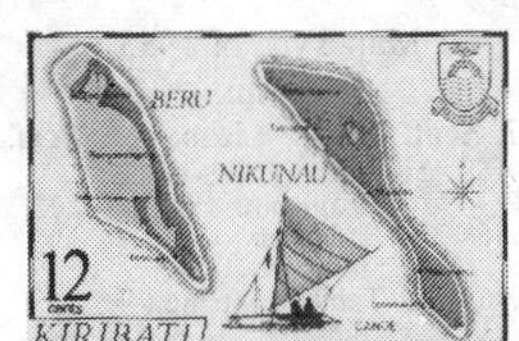


Map of Beru and Nikunau Islds., Canoe — A68

**Wmk. 380**

**1983, May 19 Litho. Perf. 14**

422 A68 12c shown 20 20
423 A68 25c Abemama, Kuria, Aranuka 40 40
424 A68 35c Nonouti, vert. 60 60
425 A68 50c Tarawa, vert. 85 85

See Nos. 436-439, 456-459, 475-479, 487-490.

Copra Industry A69

Designs: 12c, Collecting fallen Coconuts. 25c, Selecting Coconuts for Copra. 30c, Removing Husk from Coconuts. 35c, Drying Copra in the Sun. 50c, Loading Copra, Betio Harbor.

**Wmk. 380**

**1983, Aug. 8 Litho. Perf. 14**

426 A69 12c multi 20 20
427 A69 25c multi 40 40
428 A69 30c multi 50 50
429 A69 35c multi 60 60
430 A69 50c multi 85 85
*Nos. 426-430 (5)* 2.55 2.55

Battle of Tarawa, 40th Anniv. A70

**Wmk. 380**

**1983, Nov. 17 Litho. Perf. 14**

431 A70 12c War memorials 20 20
432 A70 30c Battle map 50 50
433 A70 35c Defense gun 60 60
434 A70 50c Scenes, 1943, 1983 85 85
435 A70 $1 Air craft carrier 1.75 1.75
*Nos. 431-435 (5)* 3.90 3.90

Map Type of 1983

**Wmk. 380**

**1984, Feb. 14 Litho. Perf. 14**

436 A68 12c Teraina 20 20
437 A68 30c Nikumaroro 50 50
438 A68 35c Kanton 60 60
439 A68 50c Banaba 85 85

Local Ships A71

**Wmk. 380**

**1984, May 9 Litho. Perf. 14**

440 A71 12c Tug boat 20 20
441 A71 35c Ferry landing craft 60 60
442 A71 50c Ferry 85 85
443 A71 $1 Cargo and passenger boat 1.75 1.75
a. Souv. sheet of 4, Nos. 440-443, perf. 13½ 5.00 5.00

No. 443a has multicolored inscribed margin picturing shipping corporation emblem and natl. coat of arms. Size: 116x89mm.

Ausipex '84 — A72

Wmk. 380

**1984, Aug. 21 Litho. Perf. 14**

*444* A72 12c South Tarawa sewer & water system 20 20
*445* A72 30c Fishing boat Nouamake 50 50
*446* A72 35c Overseas communications training 60 60
*447* A72 50c Intl. telecommunications link 85 85

Legends A73

Designs: 12c, Tabakea supporting Banaba on his back. 30c, Nakaa, Judge of the Dead. 35c, Naareau and Tiku-Tiku-Tamoamoa. 50c, Whistling Ghosts.

Wmk. 380

**1984, Nov. 21 Litho. Perf. 14**

*448* A73 12c multi 20 20
*449* A73 30c multi 50 50
*450* A73 35c multi 60 60
*451* A73 50c multi 85 85

See Nos. 464-467.

Reef Fish A74

**1985, Feb. 19 Litho. Perf. 14**

*452* A74 12c Tang 12 12
*453* A74 25c White-barred triggerfish 25 25
*454* A74 35c Surgeon fish 40 40
*455* A74 80c Squirrel fish 90 90

See Nos. 480-483, 491-494.

Map Type of 1983

**1985, May 9 Litho. Perf. 13½**

*456* A68 12c Tabuaeran, frigate bird 18 18
*457* A68 35c Rawaki, coconuts 50 50
*458* A68 50c Arorae, xanthid crab 68 68
*459* A68 $1 Tamana, fish hook 1.40 1.40

Intl. Youth Year A76

**1985, Aug. 5**

*460* A76 15c Boys playing soccer 22 22
*461* A76 35c Emblems 50 50
*462* A76 40c Girl processing fruit, vert. 58 58
*463* A76 55c Intl. youth exchange 80 80

Legends Type of 1984

Designs: 15c, Nang Kineia and the Tickling Ghosts. 35c, Myth of Auriaria and Tituabine. 40c, First Coming of Babai at Arorae. 55c, Riiki and the Milky Way.

Wmk. 380

**1985, Nov. 19 Litho. Perf. 14**

*464* A73 15c multi 22 22
*465* A73 35c multi 52 52
*466* A73 40c multi 60 60
*467* A73 55c multi 82 82

Transport and Telecommunications Decade 1985-95 — A77

**1985, Dec. 9 Litho. Perf. 14**

*468* A77 15c Satellite network 22 22
*469* A77 40c Tarawa-Suva feeder service 55 55

**Queen Elizabeth II 60th Birthday**
Common Design Type

Designs: 15c, Review of Girl Guides, Windsor Castle, 1938. 35c, Birthday parade, Buckingham Palace, 1980. 40c, With Prince Philip during royal tour, 1982. 55c, Banquet, Austrian embassy in London, 1966. $1, Visiting Crown Agents' offices, 1983.

**1986, Apr. 21 Perf. 14½x14**

*470* CD337 15c scar, blk & sil 22 22
*471* CD337 35c ultra & multi 52 52
*472* CD337 40c grn & multi 60 60
*473* CD337 55c vio & multi 82 82
*474* CD337 $1 rose vio & multi 1.50 1.50
*Nos. 470-474 (5)* 3.66 3.66

Map Type of 1983
Wmk. 380

**1986, June 17 Litho. Perf. 14**

*475* A68 15c Manra 22 22
*476* A68 30c Birnie, McKean 45 45
*477* A68 35c Orona 52 52
*478* A68 40c Malden 60 60
*479* A68 55c Vostok, Caroline, Flint 82 82
*Nos. 475-479 (5)* 2.61 2.61

Marine Type of 1985
Unwmk.

**1986, Aug. 26 Litho. Perf. 14**

*480* A74 15c Lepidodactylus lugubris 20 20
*481* A74 35c Gehyra mutilata 42 42
*482* A74 40c Hemidactylus frenatus 50 50
*483* A74 55c Gehyra oceanica 70 70

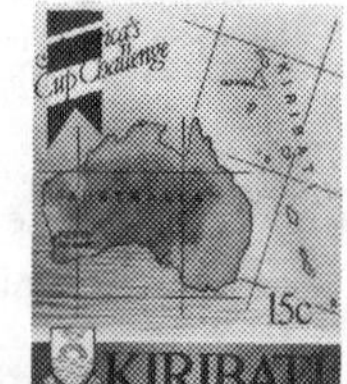


America's Cup — A80

**Perf. 14x14½**

**1986, Dec. 29 Litho. Unwmk.**

*484* Strip of 3 3.00 3.00
*a.* A80 15c Map of Australia 20 20
*b.* A80 55c Course, trophy 75 75
*c.* A80 $1.50 Australia II 2.00 2.00

Nos. 484a-484c printed se-tenant in a continuous design with $1.50 on left and 15c in center.

Transport and Telecommunications Decade (1985-1995) — A81

Designs: 30c, Nei Moamoa, flagship of Kiribati overseas shipping line. 55c, Manual and electronic telephone switching systems.

Unwmk.

**1987, Mar. 31 Litho. Perf. 14**

*485* A81 30c multi 40 40
*486* A81 55c multi 70 70

Map Type of 1983
Unwmk.

**1987, Sept. 22 Litho. Perf. 14**

*487* A68 15c Starbuck, red-tailed tropicbird 22 22
*488* A68 30c Enderbury, white tern 45 45
*489* A68 55c Tabiteuea, pandanus 82 82
*490* A68 $1 Onotoa, Okai house 1.50 1.50

Nos. 487-490 vert.

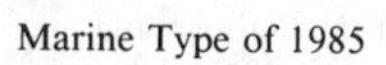

Marine Type of 1985

**1987, Oct. 27 Perf. 15**

*491* A74 15c Emoia nigra 20 20
*492* A74 35c Cryptoblepharus 50 50
*493* A74 40c Emoia cyanura 55 55
*494* A74 $1 Lipinia noctua 1.40 1.40

Nos. 470-474 Overprinted "40TH WEDDING ANNIVERSARY" in Silver

**Perf. 14½x14**

**1987, Nov. 30 Litho. Unwmk.**

*495* CD337 15c scar, blk & sil 22 22
*496* CD337 35c ultra & multi 48 48
*497* CD337 40c grn & multi 55 55
*498* CD337 55c vio & multi 75 75
*499* CD337 $1 rose vio & multi 1.40 1.40
*Nos. 495-499 (5)* 3.40 3.40

Intl. Red Cross and Red Crescent Organizations, 125th Annivs. — A83

Designs: 15c, Jean Henri Dunant (1828-1910), promulgator. 35c, Red Cross volunteers on parade. 40c, Stretcher bearers. 55c, Gilbert and Ellice Islands No. 159.

**1988, May 8 Litho. Unwmk. Perf.**

*500* A83 15c multi 24 24
*501* A83 35c multi 55 55
*502* A83 40c multi 62 62
*503* A83 55c multi 85 85

A84

SYDPEX '88, Australia Bicentennial — A85

Emblem and: 15c, Australia-assisted causeway construction. 35c, Capt. Cook, map of Australia and Kiribati. No. 506, Australia bicentennial banknote obverse. No. 507, Bank note reverse. $2, "Logistic Ace."

**1988, July 30 Litho. Perf. 14½**

*504* A84 15c multi 25 25
*505* A84 35c multi 58 58
*506* A84 $1 multi 1.65 1.65
*507* A84 $1 multi 1.65 1.65

**Souvenir Sheet**

**Perf. 13½x14**

*508* A85 $2 multi 3.25 3.25

Nos. 506-507 printed se-tenant.

*Robert F. Stockton*, 1st propeller-driven steamship, 150th anniv. No. 508 has multicolored inscribed margin picturing the ship. Size: 95x76mm.

Transport and Telecommunications Decade (1985-1995) — A86

**1988 Litho. Wmk. 384 Perf.**

*509* A86 35c Telephone operator, map 62 62
*510* A86 45c Betio-Bairiki Causeway 80 80

**POSTAGE DUE STAMPS**

Natl. Arms — D1

**1981, Aug. 27 Litho. Perf. 14**

*J1* D1 1c brt pink & blk 5 5
*J2* D1 2c greenish blue & blk 5 5
*J3* D1 5c brt yel grn & blk 12 12
*J4* D1 10c lt red brn & blk 22 22
*J5* D1 20c ultra & blk 45 45
*J6* D1 30c yel bister & blk 65 65
*J7* D1 40c brt pur & blk 88 88
*J8* D1 50c grn & blk 1.10 1.10
*J9* D1 $1 red org & blk 2.20 2.20
*Nos. J1-J9 (9)* 5.72 5.72

**OFFICIAL STAMPS**

Nos. 327-340A Overprinted: "O.K.G.S."

**1981 Litho. Perf. 14**

*O1* A52 1c multi 5 5
*O2* A52 3c multi 6 6
*O3* A52 5c multi 8 8
*O4* A52 7c multi 10 10
*O5* A52 10c multi 15 15
*O6* A52 12c multi 18 18
*O7* A52 15c multi 25 25
*O8* A52 20c multi 30 30
*O9* A52 25c multi 40 40
*O10* A52 30c multi 45 45
*O11* A52 35c multi 50 50
*O12* A52 50c multi 75 75
*O13* A52 $1 multi 1.50 1.50
*O14* A52 $2 multi 3.00 3.00
*O15* A52 $5 multi 7.50 7.50
*Nos. O1-O15 (15)* 15.27 15.27

Nos. 390, 393-394, 396, 398 Overprinted "O.K.G.S."

**1983, June 28 Litho. Perf. 14**

*O16* A62 12c multi 18 18
*O17* A62 30c multi 45 45
*O18* A62 35c multi 48 48
*O19* A62 50c multi 75 75
*O20* A62 $2 multi 3.25 3.25
*Nos. O16-O20 (5)* 5.11 5.11

# KUWAIT

LOCATION — On the northwestern coast of the Persian Gulf.
GOVT. — Sheikdom.
AREA — 7,000 sq. mi.
POP. — 1,910,856 (est. 1985).
CAPITAL — Kuwait.

Kuwait was under British protection until June 19, 1961, when it became a fully independent state.

16 Annas = 1 Rupee
100 Naye Paise = 1 Rupee (1957)
1000 Fils = 1 Kuwaiti Dinar (1961)

There was a first or trial setting of the overprint with the word "Koweit". Twenty-four sets of regular and official stamps were printed with this spelling.

**Catalogue values for unused stamps in this country are for Never Hinged items, beginning with Scott 72 in the regular postage section, Scott C5 in the air post section, and Scott J1 in the postage due section.**

Stamps of India, 1911-23, Overprinted

KUWAIT a    KUWAIT b

**1923-24 Wmk. Star. (39) Perf. 14**

| No. | Type | Description | Unused | Used |
|---|---|---|---|---|
| 1 | A47(a) | ½a green | 65 | 85 |
| 2 | A48(a) | 1a dk brn | 65 | 65 |
| 3 | A58(a) | 1½a chocolate | 1.00 | 1.40 |
| 4 | A49(a) | 2a violet | 50 | 50 |
| 5 | A57(a) | 2a6p ultra | 1.10 | 3.00 |
| 6 | A51(a) | 3a brn org | 2.50 | 5.00 |
| a | | Inverted overprint | 35.00 | 37.50 |
| 7 | A51(a) | 3a ultra ('24) | 3.00 | 75 |
| 8 | A52(a) | 4a ol grn | 2.25 | 4.00 |
| 9 | A53(a) | 6a bister | 3.00 | 4.50 |
| 10 | A54(a) | 8a red vio | 4.50 | 5.00 |
| 11 | A55(a) | 12a claret | 5.00 | 6.00 |
| 12 | A56(b) | 1r grn & red brn | 9.00 | 5.00 |
| 13 | A56(b) | 2r brn & car rose | 32.50 | 45.00 |
| 14 | A56(b) | 5r vio & ultra | 80.00 | 100.00 |
| 15 | A56(b) | 10r car & grn | 200.00 | 250.00 |
| | | *Nos. 1-15 (15)* | 345.65 | 431.65 |

Overprint "a" on India No. 102 is generally considered unofficial.

Stamps of India, 1926-35, Overprinted type "a".

**1929-37 Wmk. 196**

| No. | Type | Description | Unused | Used |
|---|---|---|---|---|
| 17 | A47 | ½a green | 75 | 25 |
| 18 | A71 | ½a grn ('34) | 1.00 | 30 |
| 19 | A48 | 1a dk brn | 4.00 | 40 |
| 20 | A72 | 1a dk brn ('34) | 1.75 | 1.00 |
| 21 | A60 | 2a dk vio | 38 | 32 |
| 22 | A60 | 2a vermilion | 25.00 | 37.50 |
| 23 | A49 | 2a ver ('34) | 10.00 | 3.50 |
| a | | Small die | 2.50 | 90 |
| 24 | A51 | 3a ultra | 3.25 | 1.00 |
| 25 | A51 | 3a car rose ('34) | 3.25 | 3.25 |
| 26 | A61 | 4a ol grn | 25.00 | 30.00 |
| 27 | A52 | 4a ol grn ('34) | 6.00 | 6.75 |
| 28 | A53 | 6a bis ('37) | 6.00 | 6.25 |
| 29 | A54 | 8a red vio | 3.25 | 3.75 |
| 30 | A55 | 12a claret | 5.00 | 6.50 |

Overprinted

c    KUWAIT

| No. | Type | Description | Unused | Used |
|---|---|---|---|---|
| 31 | A56 | 1r grn & brn | 4.00 | 4.00 |
| 32 | A56 | 2r buff & car rose | 17.50 | 15.00 |
| 33 | A56 | 5r dk vio & ultra ('37) | 40.00 | 75.00 |
| 34 | A56 | 10r car & grn ('34) | 150.00 | 225.00 |
| 35 | A56 | 15r ol grn & ultra ('37) | 400.00 | 600.00 |
| | | *Nos. 17-35 (19)* | 706.13 | 1,019. |

Stamps of India, 1937, Overprinted type "a" (A80, A81) or "c" (A82)

**1939 Wmk. 196 Perf. 13½x14.**

| No. | Type | Description | Unused | Used |
|---|---|---|---|---|
| 45 | A80 | ½a brown | 35 | 35 |
| 46 | A80 | 1a carmine | 35 | 35 |
| 47 | A81 | 2a scarlet | 65 | 60 |
| 48 | A81 | 3a yel grn | 1.00 | 1.00 |
| 49 | A81 | 4a dk brn | 1.50 | 2.00 |
| 50 | A81 | 6a pck bl | 1.50 | 2.25 |
| 51 | A81 | 8a bl vio | 2.75 | 3.00 |
| 52 | A81 | 12a car lake | 3.00 | 4.25 |
| 53 | A82 | 1r brn & sl | 1.10 | 1.00 |
| 54 | A82 | 2r dk brn & dk vio | 6.50 | 5.00 |
| 55 | A82 | 5r dp ultra & dk grn | 8.00 | 7.50 |
| 56 | A82 | 10r rose car & dk vio | 35.00 | 27.50 |
| a | | Dbl. ovpt. | 350.00 | 350.00 |
| 57 | A82 | 15r dk grn & dk brn | 45.00 | 60.00 |
| | | *Nos. 45-57 (13)* | 106.70 | 114.80 |

Stamps of India 1940-43, Overprinted in Black    KUWAIT

**1945 Wmk. 196 Perf. 13½x14.**

| No. | Type | Description | Unused | Used |
|---|---|---|---|---|
| 59 | A83 | 3p slate | 35 | 35 |
| 60 | A83 | ½a rose vio | 12 | 6 |
| 61 | A83 | 9p lt grn | 16 | 16 |
| 62 | A83 | 1a car rose | 16 | 12 |
| 63 | A84 | 1½a dk pur | 28 | 28 |
| 64 | A84 | 2a scarlet | 25 | 25 |
| 65 | A84 | 3a violet | 35 | 35 |
| 66 | A84 | 3½a ultra | 65 | 65 |
| 67 | A85 | 4a chocolate | 28 | 20 |
| 68 | A85 | 6a pck bl | 5.00 | 10.00 |
| 69 | A85 | 8a bl vio | 65 | 45 |
| 70 | A85 | 12a car lake | 85 | 60 |
| 71 | A81 | 14a rose vio | 4.00 | 10.00 |
| | | *Nos. 59-71 (13)* | 13.10 | 23.47 |

**Catalogue values for unused stamps in this section, from this point to the end of the section, are for Never Hinged items.**

**British Postal Administration**

See Oman (Muscat) for similar stamps with surcharge of new value only.

Great Britain Nos. 258 to 263, 243 and 248 Surcharged in Black    KUWAIT ½ ANNA

**1948-49 Wmk. 251 Perf. 14½x14**

| No. | Type | Description | Unused | Used |
|---|---|---|---|---|
| 72 | A101 | ½a on ½p grn | 25 | 10 |
| 73 | A101 | 1a on 1p ver | 25 | 10 |
| 74 | A101 | 1½a on 1½p lt red brn | 15 | 10 |
| 75 | A101 | 2a on 2p lt org | 15 | 12 |
| 76 | A101 | 2½a on 2½p ultra | 15 | 12 |
| 77 | A101 | 3a on 3p vio | 15 | 12 |
| a | | Pair, one without surcharge | 2,250. | 1,750. |
| 78 | A102 | 6a on 6p rose lil | 25 | 15 |
| 79 | A103 | 1r on 1sh brn | 50 | 40 |

Great Britain Nos. 249A, 250 and 251A Surcharged in Black    KUWAIT 2 RUPEES

**Wmk. 259 Perf. 14.**

| No. | Type | Description | Unused | Used |
|---|---|---|---|---|
| 80 | A104 | 2r on 2sh6p yel grn | 1.75 | 3.00 |
| 81 | A104 | 5r on 5sh dl red | 5.50 | 3.75 |
| 81A | A105 | 10r on 10sh ultra ('49) | 30.00 | 17.50 |
| | | *Nos. 72-81A (11)* | 39.10 | 25.46 |

Issue dates: Nos. 72-81, April, 1948; 10r, July 4, 1949.

Bars of surcharge at bottom on No. 81A.

**Silver Wedding Issue.**

Great Britain Nos. 267 and 268 Surcharged in Black    KUWAIT 2½ ANNAS

**Perf. 14½x14, 14x14½.**

**1948 Wmk. 251**

| No. | Type | Description | Unused | Used |
|---|---|---|---|---|
| 82 | A109 | 2½a on 2½p brt ultra | 10 | 10 |
| 83 | A110 | 15r on £1 dp chlky bl | 35.00 | 50.00 |

Three bars obliterate the original denomination on No. 83.

**Olympic Games Issue.**

Great Britain Nos. 271 to 274 Surcharged "KUWAIT" and New Value in Black.

**1948 Perf. 14½x14**

| No. | Type | Description | Unused | Used |
|---|---|---|---|---|
| 84 | A113 | 2½a on 2½p brt ultra | 20 | 20 |
| 85 | A114 | 3a on 3p dp vio | 35 | 35 |
| 86 | A115 | 6a on 6p red vio | 60 | 60 |
| 87 | A116 | 1r on 1sh dk brn | 1.00 | 1.00 |

A square of dots obliterates the original denomination on No. 87.

**UPU Issue**

Great Britain Nos. 276 to 279 Surcharged "KUWAIT", New Value and Square of Dots in Black.

**1949, Oct. 10 Photo.**

| No. | Type | Description | Unused | Used |
|---|---|---|---|---|
| 89 | A117 | 2½a on 2½p brt ultra | 16 | 16 |
| 90 | A118 | 3a on 3p brt vio | 35 | 35 |
| 91 | A119 | 6a on 6p red vio | 60 | 60 |
| 92 | A120 | 1r on 1sh brn | 1.10 | 1.10 |

Great Britain Nos. 280-285 Surcharged Like Nos.72-79 in Black

**1950-51 Wmk. 251 Perf. 14½x14.**

| No. | Type | Description | Unused | Used |
|---|---|---|---|---|
| 93 | A101 | ½a on ½p lt org | 14 | 14 |
| 94 | A101 | 1a on 1p ultra | 7 | 6 |
| 95 | A101 | 1½a on 1½p grn | 10 | 10 |
| 96 | A101 | 2a on 2p lt red brn | 10 | 10 |
| 97 | A101 | 2½a on 2½p ver | 14 | 14 |
| 98 | A102 | 4a on 4p ultra ('50) | 16 | 14 |

Great Britain Nos. 286-288 Surcharged in Black    KUWAIT 2 RUPEES

**Perf. 11x12**

**Wmk. 259**

| No. | Type | Description | Unused | Used |
|---|---|---|---|---|
| 99 | A121 | 2r on 2sh6p grn | 5.00 | 2.00 |
| 100 | A121 | 5r on 5sh dl red | 10.00 | 5.00 |
| 101 | A122 | 10r on 10sh ultra | 17.50 | 8.00 |
| | | *Nos. 93-101 (9)* | 33.21 | 15.68 |

Longer bars, at lower right, on No. 101.

Issue dates: 4a, Oct. 2, 1950. Others, May 3, 1951.

Stamps of Great Britain, 1952-54 Surcharged "KUWAIT" and New Value in Black or Dark Blue.

**1952-54 Wmk. 298 Perf. 14½x14.**

| No. | Type | Description | Unused | Used |
|---|---|---|---|---|
| 102 | A126 | ½a on ½p red org ('53) | 10 | 5 |
| 103 | A126 | 1a on 1p ultra ('53) | 10 | 5 |
| 104 | A126 | 1½a on 1½p grn | 10 | 6 |
| 105 | A126 | 2a on 2p red brn ('53) | 10 | 7 |
| 106 | A127 | 2½a on 2½p scar | 10 | 8 |
| 107 | A127 | 3a on 3p dk pur (Dk Bl) ('54) | 10 | 10 |
| 108 | A128 | 4a on 4p ultra ('53) | 14 | 10 |
| 109 | A129 | 6a on 6p lil rose ('54) | 22 | 14 |
| 111 | A132 | 12a on 1sh6p dk grn ('53) | 75 | 75 |
| 112 | A131 | 1r on 1sh 6p dk bl ('53) | 85 | 65 |
| | | *Nos. 102-112 (10)* | 2.56 | 2.05 |

**Coronation Issue.**

Great Britain Nos. 313-316 Surcharged "KUWAIT" and New Value in Black.

**1953, June 3**

| No. | Type | Description | Unused | Used |
|---|---|---|---|---|
| 113 | A134 | 2½a on 2½p scar | 50 | 50 |
| 114 | A135 | 4a on 4p brt ultra | 65 | 50 |
| 115 | A136 | 12a on 1sh3p dk grn | 1.50 | 1.10 |
| 116 | A137 | 1r on 1sh6p dk bl | 2.00 | 1.75 |

Squares of dots obliterate the original denominations on Nos. 115 and 116.

Great Britain Stamps of 1955-56 Surcharged "KUWAIT" and New Value in Black.

**1955 Wmk. 308 Engr. Perf. 11x12**

| No. | Type | Description | Unused | Used |
|---|---|---|---|---|
| 117 | A133 | 2r on 2sh6p dk brn | 2.50 | 1.00 |
| 118 | A133 | 5r on 5sh crim | 8.50 | 2.75 |
| 119 | A133 | 10r on 10sh dp ultra | 14.00 | 6.50 |

The surcharge on Nos. 117-119 exists in two types.

**1956 Photo. Perf. 14½x14**

| No. | Type | Description | Unused | Used |
|---|---|---|---|---|
| 120 | A126 | ½a on ½p red org | 22 | 22 |
| 121 | A126 | 1a on 1p ultra | 10 | 10 |
| 122 | A126 | 1½a on 1½p grn | 14 | 8 |
| 123 | A126 | 2a on 2p red brn | 12 | 7 |
| 124 | A127 | 2½a on 2½p scar | 28 | 10 |
| 125 | A128 | 4a on 4p ultra | 1.40 | 65 |
| 126 | A129 | 6a on 6p lil rose | 35 | 18 |
| 127 | A132 | 12a on 1sh3p dk grn | 3.50 | 1.10 |
| 128 | A131 | 1r on 1sh6p dk bl | 85 | 45 |
| | | *Nos. 120-128 (9)* | 6.96 | 2.95 |

Great Britain Nos. 317-325, 328 and 332 Surcharged "KUWAIT" and New Value in Black.

**1957-58 Wmk. 308 Perf. 14½x14**

| No. | Type | Description | Unused | Used |
|---|---|---|---|---|
| 129 | A129 | 1np on 5p lt brn | 10 | 6 |
| 130 | A126 | 3np on ½p red org | 10 | 10 |
| 131 | A126 | 6np on 1p ultra | 10 | 8 |
| 132 | A126 | 9np on 1½p grn | 10 | 8 |
| 133 | A126 | 12np on 2p red brn | 10 | 8 |
| 134 | A127 | 15np on 2½p scar, type I | 20 | 20 |
| a | | Type II ('58) | 30.00 | 30.00 |
| 135 | A127 | 20np on 3p dk pur | 20 | 15 |
| 136 | A128 | 25np on 4p ultra | 55 | 35 |
| 137 | A129 | 40np on 6p lil rose | 35 | 28 |
| 138 | A130 | 50np on 9p dp ol grn | 1.40 | 85 |
| 139 | A132 | 75np on 1sh3p dk grn | 1.75 | 1.00 |
| | | *Nos. 129-139 (11)* | 4.95 | 3.23 |

The arrangement of the surcharge varies on different values; there are three bars through value on No. 138.

Sheik Abdullah A1

Dhow A2

Oil Derrick A3

Designs: 50np, Pipe lines. 75np, Main square, Kuwait. 2r, Dhow, derrick and Sheik. 5r, Mosque and Sheik. 10r, Oil plant at Burgan and Sheik.

**Perf. 12½**

**1959, Feb. 1 Unwmk. Engr.**

| No. | Type | Description | Unused | Used |
|---|---|---|---|---|
| 140 | A1 | 5np green | 15 | 6 |
| 141 | A1 | 10np rose brn | 15 | 8 |
| 142 | A1 | 15np yel brn | 35 | 25 |
| 143 | A1 | 20np gray vio | 20 | 12 |
| 144 | A1 | 25np vermilion | 20 | 15 |
| 145 | A1 | 40np rose cl | 1.75 | 1.00 |

**Perf. 13½x13**

| No. | Type | Description | Unused | Used |
|---|---|---|---|---|
| 146 | A2 | 40np dk bl | 30 | 25 |
| 147 | A2 | 50np carmine | 30 | 25 |
| 148 | A2 | 75np ol grn | 50 | 40 |

**Perf. 14x13½**

| No. | Type | Description | Unused | Used |
|---|---|---|---|---|
| 149 | A3 | 1r claret | 60 | 50 |
| 150 | A3 | 2r red brn & dp bl | 1.25 | 90 |
| 151 | A3 | 5r green | 3.50 | 2.00 |
| 152 | A3 | 10r purple | 11.00 | 6.00 |
| | | *Nos. 140-152 (13)* | 20.25 | 11.96 |

No. 140-141 and 145 were issued in 1958 for local use. They became valid for international mail on Feb. 1, 1959, but No. 145 was withdrawn after two weeks.

Sheik Abdullah and Flag — A4

**1960, Feb. 25 Engr. Perf. 14**

| No. | Type | Description | Unused | Used |
|---|---|---|---|---|
| 153 | A4 | 40np ol grn & red | 30 | 15 |
| 154 | A4 | 60np bl & red | 50 | 25 |

10th anniv. of the accession of Sheik Sir Abdullah As-Salim As-Sabah.

Types of 1959, Redrawn

Designs: 20f, 3d, Mosque and Sheik. 25f, 100f, Vickers Viscount. 30f, 75f, Dhow, derrick and Sheik. 35f, 90f, Shuwaikh secondary school. 45f, 1d, Wara Hill, Burgan oil field.

**1961, April-May Perf. 12½**

| No. | Type | Description | Unused | Used |
|---|---|---|---|---|
| 155 | A1 | 1f green | 10 | 5 |
| 156 | A1 | 2f rose brn | 10 | 5 |
| 157 | A1 | 4f yel brn | 10 | 5 |
| 158 | A1 | 5f gray vio | 10 | 5 |
| 159 | A1 | 8f sal pink | 10 | 5 |
| 160 | A1 | 15f rose cl | 10 | 7 |

**Perf. 14x13½**

| No. | Type | Description | Unused | Used |
|---|---|---|---|---|
| 161 | A3 | 20f green | 10 | 7 |
| 162 | A3 | 25f blue | 10 | 8 |
| 163 | A3 | 30f red brn & dp bl | 20 | 12 |
| 164 | A3 | 35f ver & blk | 35 | 25 |
| 165 | A2 | 40f dk bl, perf. 13½ | 25 | 16 |
| 166 | A3 | 45f vio brn | 20 | 16 |
| 167 | A3 | 75f grn & sep | 30 | 20 |
| 168 | A3 | 90f ultra & brn | 40 | 28 |
| 169 | A3 | 100f rose red | 40 | 30 |
| 170 | A3 | 250f ol grn, perf. 13½ | 2.00 | 65 |
| 171 | A3 | 1d orange | 6.50 | 3.50 |
| 172 | A3 | 3d brick red | 27.50 | 20.00 |
| | | *Nos. 155-172 (18)* | 38.81 | 26.09 |

Nos. 165 and 170 are 32x22mm.

Symbols of Telecommunications — A5

*Perf. 11½*

**1962, Jan. 11 Unwmk. Photo.**

**Granite Paper**

| No. | Type | Description | Unused | Used |
|---|---|---|---|---|
| 173 | A5 | 8f bl & blk | 20 | 10 |
| 174 | A5 | 20f rose & blk | 50 | 25 |

Issued to commemorate the fourth Arab Telecommunications Union Conference.

Mubarakiya School and Sheiks Abdullah and Mubarak — A6

**1962, Apr. 15 Unwmk.** ***Perf. 11½***

| No. | Type | Description | Unused | Used |
|---|---|---|---|---|
| 175 | A6 | 8f gldn brn, blk, org & gold | 20 | 10 |
| 176 | A6 | 20f lt bl, blk, org & gold | 50 | 25 |

50th anniversary of Mubarakiya School.

Arab League Building, Cairo, and Emblem — A7

**1962, Apr. 23** ***Perf. 13½x13***

| No. | Type | Description | Unused | Used |
|---|---|---|---|---|
| 177 | A7 | 20f purple | 15 | 12 |
| 178 | A7 | 45f brown | 50 | 25 |

Arab Publicity Week, Mar. 22-28.

Flag of Kuwait A8

Malaria Eradication Emblem A9

**1962, June 19** ***Perf. 11½***

**Flag in Green, Black & Red**

| No. | Type | Description | Unused | Used |
|---|---|---|---|---|
| 179 | A8 | 8f blk & tan | 16 | 12 |
| 180 | A8 | 20f blk & yel | 32 | 25 |
| 181 | A8 | 45f blk & lt bl | 52 | 40 |
| 182 | A8 | 90f blk & lil | 1.40 | 80 |

Issued for National Day, June 19.

**1962, Aug. 1** ***Perf. 13½x13***

| No. | Type | Description | Unused | Used |
|---|---|---|---|---|
| 183 | A9 | 4f sl grn & yel grn | 15 | 10 |
| 184 | A9 | 25f grn & gray | 50 | 30 |

Issued for the World Health Organization drive to eradicate malaria.

No. 184 has laurel leaves added and inscription rearranged.

Cogwheel, Oil Wells, Camels and Modern Building — A10

*Perf. 11x13*

**1962, Dec. 8 Unwmk. Litho.**

| No. | Type | Description | Unused | Used |
|---|---|---|---|---|
| 185 | A10 | 8f multi | 20 | 10 |
| 186 | A10 | 20f multi | 25 | 20 |
| 187 | A10 | 45f multi | 50 | 35 |
| 188 | A10 | 75f multi | 1.00 | 60 |

Bicentenary of the Sabah dynasty.

Mother and Child — A11

**1963, Mar. 21 Photo.** ***Perf. 14½x14***

| No. | Type | Description | Unused | Used |
|---|---|---|---|---|
| 189 | A11 | 8f yel, red, blk & grn | 12 | 10 |
| 190 | A11 | 20f bl, red, blk & grn | 25 | 18 |
| 191 | A11 | 45f lt ol, red, blk & grn | 50 | 35 |
| 192 | A11 | 75f gray, red, blk & grn | 60 | 60 |

Issued for Mother's Day, March 21, 1963.

Wheat Emblem, Date Palm, Cow and Sheep — A12

**1963, Mar. 21** ***Perf. 14x14½***

| No. | Type | Description | Unused | Used |
|---|---|---|---|---|
| 193 | A12 | 4f red brn, lt bl & grn | 20 | 10 |
| 194 | A12 | 8f brn, yel & grn | 35 | 15 |
| 195 | A12 | 20f red brn, pale vio & grn | 50 | 30 |
| 196 | A12 | 45f red brn, rose & grn | 1.00 | 60 |

Issued for the "Freedom from Hunger" campaign of the U.N. Food and Agriculture Organization.

Test Tube, Oil Drops and Ship — A13

**1963, Apr. 15 Photo.** ***Perf. 14½x14***

| No. | Type | Description | Unused | Used |
|---|---|---|---|---|
| 197 | A13 | 4f brn, yel & bl | 12 | 8 |
| 198 | A13 | 20f grn, yel & bl | 35 | 22 |
| 199 | A13 | 45f brt mag, yel & bl | 65 | 45 |

Issued for Education Day.

Sheik Abdullah, Flags and Map of Kuwait A14

**1963, June 19** ***Perf. 14x13***

**Flags in Black, Bright Green & Red; Denominations in Black**

| No. | Type | Description | Unused | Used |
|---|---|---|---|---|
| 200 | A14 | 4f ultra | 75 | 75 |
| 201 | A14 | 5f ocher | 90 | 90 |
| 202 | A14 | 20f brt lil | 3.50 | 3.50 |
| 203 | A14 | 50f olive | 6.00 | 6.00 |

Second anniversary of National Day.

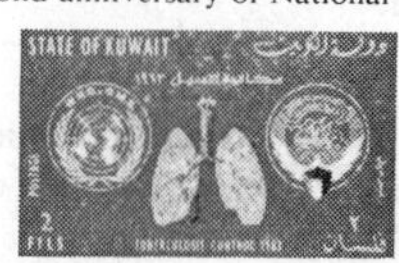

Lungs and Emblems of World Health Organization and Kuwait Tuberculosis Society — A15

**1963, July 27** ***Perf. 13x13½***

**Design in Yellow, Black, Emerald & Red**

| No. | Type | Description | Unused | Used |
|---|---|---|---|---|
| 204 | A15 | 2f ocher | 12 | 8 |
| 205 | A15 | 4f dk grn | 22 | 8 |
| 206 | A15 | 8f lt vio bl | 30 | 10 |
| 207 | A15 | 20f rose brn | 50 | 22 |

Issued to publicize tuberculosis control.

Sheik Abdullah, Scroll and Scales of Justice — A16

**1963, Oct. 29 Photo.** ***Perf. 11x13***

**Center in Gray.**

| No. | Type | Description | Unused | Used |
|---|---|---|---|---|
| 208 | A16 | 4f dp red & red brn | 6 | 5 |
| 209 | A16 | 8f dk grn & red brn | 9 | 5 |
| 210 | A16 | 20f vio brn & red brn | 30 | 14 |
| 211 | A16 | 45f brn org & red brn | 45 | 25 |
| 212 | A16 | 75f pur & red brn | 75 | 45 |
| 213 | A16 | 90f ultra & red brn | 90 | 55 |
| | | *Nos. 208-213 (6)* | 2.55 | 1.49 |

Promulgation of the constitution.

Soccer — A17

Sports: 4f, Basketball. 5f, Swimming (horiz.). 8f, Track. 15f, Javelin (horiz.). 20f, Pole vault (horiz.). 35f, Gymnast on rings (horiz.). 45f, Gymnast on parallel bars.

**1963, Nov. 8 Unwmk.** ***Perf. 14½x14***

| No. | Type | Description | Unused | Used |
|---|---|---|---|---|
| 214 | A17 | 1f multi | 9 | 8 |
| 215 | A17 | 4f multi | 12 | 8 |
| 216 | A17 | 5f multi | 14 | 9 |
| 217 | A17 | 8f multi | 16 | 12 |
| 218 | A17 | 15f multi | 22 | 15 |
| 219 | A17 | 20f multi | 35 | 22 |
| 220 | A17 | 35f multi | 70 | 30 |
| 221 | A17 | 45f multi | 1.40 | 40 |
| | | *Nos. 214-221 (8)* | 3.18 | 1.44 |

Arab School Games of 1963.

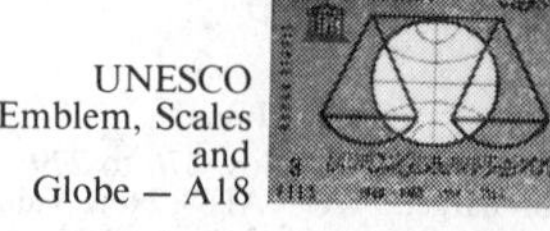

UNESCO Emblem, Scales and Globe — A18

**1963, Dec. 10 Litho.** ***Perf. 13x12½***

| No. | Type | Description | Unused | Used |
|---|---|---|---|---|
| 222 | A18 | 8f vio, blk & pale grn | 8 | 7 |
| 223 | A18 | 20f gray, blk & yel | 16 | 14 |
| 224 | A18 | 25f bl, blk & tan | 25 | 16 |

Issued to commemorate the 15th anniversary of the Universal Declaration of Human Rights.

Sheik Abdullah — A19

*Perf. 12½x13*

**1964-66 Unwmk. Photo.**

**Portrait in Natural Colors**

| No. | Type | Description | Unused | Used |
|---|---|---|---|---|
| 225 | A19 | 1f gray & sil | 12 | 10 |
| a | | Bklt. pane of 6 ('66) | 45 | |
| 226 | A19 | 2f brt bl & sil | 12 | 10 |
| 227 | A19 | 4f ocher & sil | 12 | 10 |
| a | | Bklt. pane of 6 ('66) | 45 | |
| 228 | A19 | 5f fawn & sil | 12 | 10 |
| 229 | A19 | 8f dk brn & sil | 15 | 10 |
| 230 | A19 | 10f cit & sil | 15 | 10 |
| a | | Bklt. pane of 6 ('66) | 75 | |
| 231 | A19 | 15f brt grn & sil | 50 | 50 |
| a | | Bklt. pane of 6 ('66) | 1.10 | |
| 232 | A19 | 20f bl gray & sil | 25 | 12 |
| a | | Bklt. pane of 6 ('66) | 1.50 | |
| 233 | A19 | 25f grn & sil | 30 | 18 |
| 234 | A19 | 30f gray grn & sil | 35 | 20 |
| 235 | A19 | 40f brt vio & sil | 50 | 25 |
| 236 | A19 | 45f vio & sil | 55 | 25 |
| 237 | A19 | 50f ol & sil | 60 | 30 |
| 238 | A19 | 70f red lil & sil | 1.00 | 35 |
| 239 | A19 | 75f rose red & sil | 1.10 | 40 |
| 240 | A19 | 90f ultra & sil | 1.35 | 50 |
| 241 | A19 | 100f pale lil & sil | 1.65 | 55 |

***Perf. 14x14½***

**Size: 25x30mm.**

| No. | Type | Description | Unused | Used |
|---|---|---|---|---|
| 242 | A19 | 250f brn & sil | 3.50 | 1.25 |
| 243 | A19 | 1d brn vio & sil | 14.00 | 5.50 |
| | | *Nos. 225-243 (19)* | 26.43 | 10.95 |

Ramses II Battling the Hittites (from Abu Simbel) — A20

**Engr. and Litho.**

**1964, March 8** ***Perf. 13x12½***

| No. | Type | Description | Unused | Used |
|---|---|---|---|---|
| 244 | A20 | 8f buff, ind & mar | 15 | 10 |
| 245 | A20 | 20f lt bl, ind & vio | 35 | 25 |
| 246 | A20 | 30f bluish grn, ind & vio | 60 | 40 |

UNESCO world campaign to save historic monuments in Nubia.

Mother and Child — A21

**1964, Mar. 21 Litho.** ***Perf. 14x13***

| No. | Type | Description | Unused | Used |
|---|---|---|---|---|
| 247 | A21 | 8f grn, gray & vio blk | 18 | 8 |
| 248 | A21 | 20f grn, red & vio blk | 25 | 15 |
| 249 | A21 | 30f grn, ol bis & vio blk | 35 | 20 |
| 250 | A21 | 45f grn, saph & vio blk | 60 | 40 |

Issued for Mother's Day, March 21, 1964.

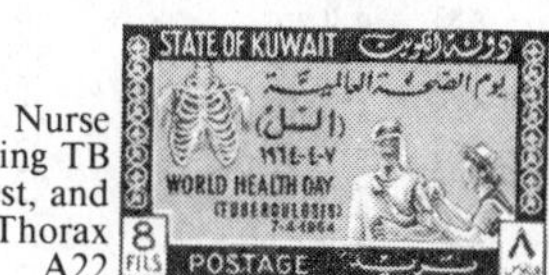

Nurse Giving TB Test, and Thorax A22

*Perf. 13x13½*

**1964, Apr. 7 Photo. Unwmk.**

| No. | Type | Description | Unused | Used |
|---|---|---|---|---|
| 251 | A22 | 8f brn & grn | 22 | 15 |
| 252 | A22 | 20f grn & rose red | 75 | 25 |

Issued for World Health Day (fight against tuberculosis), Apr. 7, 1964.

Microscope and Dhow — A23

**1964, Apr. 15** ***Perf. 12½x13***

| No. | Type | Description | Unused | Used |
|---|---|---|---|---|
| *253* | A23 | 8f multi | 20 | 6 |
| *254* | A23 | 15f multi | 22 | 10 |
| *255* | A23 | 20f multi | 30 | 15 |
| *256* | A23 | 30f multi | 45 | 35 |

Issued for Education Day.

Doves and State Seal — A24

**1964, June 19 Litho.** ***Perf. 13½***

**Seal in Blue, Brown, Black, Red & Green**

| No. | Type | Description | Unused | Used |
|---|---|---|---|---|
| *257* | A24 | 8f blk & bis brn | 30 | 9 |
| *258* | A24 | 20f blk & grn | 45 | 22 |
| *259* | A24 | 30f blk & gray | 75 | 38 |
| *260* | A24 | 45f blk & bl | 1.00 | 65 |

Third anniversary of National Day.

Arab Postal Union Emblem — A25

**1964, Nov. 21 Photo.** ***Perf. 11x11½***

| No. | Type | Description | Unused | Used |
|---|---|---|---|---|
| *261* | A25 | 8f lt bl & brn | 15 | 10 |
| *262* | A25 | 20f yel & ultra | 35 | 15 |
| *263* | A25 | 45f ol & brn | 65 | 40 |

Issued to commemorate the 10th anniversary of the Permanent Office of the Arab Postal Union.

Conference Emblem A26

**1965, Feb. 8 Litho.** ***Perf. 14***

| No. | Type | Description | Unused | Used |
|---|---|---|---|---|
| *264* | A26 | 8f blk, org brn & yel | 20 | 10 |
| *265* | A26 | 20f multi | 40 | 15 |

First Arab Journalists' Conference.

Oil Derrick, Dhow, Sun and Doves A27

Mother and Children A28

**1965, Feb. 25** ***Perf. 13½***

| No. | Type | Description | Unused | Used |
|---|---|---|---|---|
| *266* | A27 | 10f lt grn & multi | 15 | 10 |
| *267* | A27 | 15f pink & multi | 25 | 10 |
| *268* | A27 | 20f gray & multi | 45 | 20 |

Fourth anniversary of National Day.

**1965, Mar. 21 Unwmk.** ***Perf. 13½***

| No. | Type | Description | Unused | Used |
|---|---|---|---|---|
| *269* | A28 | 8f multi | 22 | 15 |
| *270* | A28 | 15f multi | 38 | 15 |
| *271* | A28 | 20f multi | 45 | 22 |

Mother's Day, March 21.

Weather Balloon A29

**1965, Mar. 23 Photo.** ***Perf. 11½x11***

| No. | Type | Description | Unused | Used |
|---|---|---|---|---|
| *272* | A29 | 4f dp ultra & yel | 25 | 10 |
| *273* | A29 | 5f bl & dp org | 50 | 10 |
| *274* | A29 | 20f dk bl & emer | 65 | 15 |

Fifth World Meteorological Day.

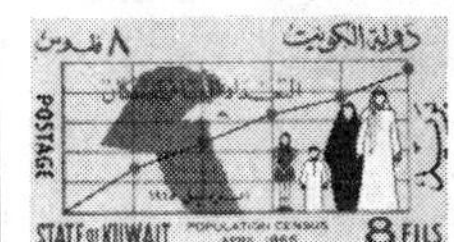

Census Chart, Map and Family A30

**1965, Mar. 28 Litho.** ***Perf. 13½***

| No. | Type | Description | Unused | Used |
|---|---|---|---|---|
| *275* | A30 | 8f multi | 25 | 15 |
| *276* | A30 | 20f multi | 65 | 30 |
| *277* | A30 | 50f multi | 1.25 | 75 |

Issued to publicize the 1965 census.

ICY Emblem A31

**1965, March 7** ***Engr.***

| No. | Type | Description | Unused | Used |
|---|---|---|---|---|
| *278* | A31 | 8f red & blk | 15 | 12 |
| *279* | A31 | 20f lt ultra & blk | 65 | 40 |
| *280* | A31 | 30f emer & blk | 1.20 | 65 |

International Cooperation Year, 1965.

Deir Yassin Type of Iraq, 1965

***Perf. 11x11½***

**1965, Apr. 9 Photo. Unwmk.**

| No. | Type | Description | Unused | Used |
|---|---|---|---|---|
| *281* | A74 | 4f red & ultra | 40 | 25 |
| *282* | A74 | 45f red & emer | 1.10 | 55 |

Deir Yassin massacre, Apr. 9, 1948.

Tower of Shuwaikh School and Atom Symbol — A32

**1965, Apr. 15 Litho.** ***Perf. 14x13***

| No. | Type | Description | Unused | Used |
|---|---|---|---|---|
| *283* | A32 | 4f multi | 20 | 12 |
| *284* | A32 | 20f multi | 45 | 20 |
| *285* | A32 | 45f multi | 80 | 40 |

Issued for Education Day.

ITU Emblem, Old and New Communication Equipment — A33

**1965, May 17** ***Perf. 13½x14***

| No. | Type | Description | Unused | Used |
|---|---|---|---|---|
| *286* | A33 | 8f dk bl, lt bl & red | 35 | 22 |
| *287* | A33 | 20f grn, lt grn & red | 75 | 35 |
| *288* | A33 | 45f red, pink & bl | 1.25 | 65 |

Issued to commemorate the centenary of the International Telecommunication Union.

Library Type of Iraq, 1965

**1965, June 7 Photo.** ***Perf. 11***

| No. | Type | Description | Unused | Used |
|---|---|---|---|---|
| *289* | A78 | 8f blk, grn & red | 45 | 15 |
| *290* | A78 | 15f blk, red & grn | 70 | 15 |

Burning of Library of Algiers, June 2, 1962.

Falcon — A34

Book and Wreath Emblem — A35

**1965, Dec. 1 Engr.** ***Perf. 13***

**Center in Sepia**

| No. | Type | Description | Unused | Used |
|---|---|---|---|---|
| *291* | A34 | 8f red lil | 30 | 9 |
| *292* | A34 | 15f ol grn | 22 | 12 |
| *293* | A34 | 20f dk bl | 38 | 18 |
| *294* | A34 | 25f orange | 50 | 22 |
| *295* | A34 | 30f emerald | 45 | 25 |
| *296* | A34 | 45f blue | 75 | 38 |
| *297* | A34 | 50f claret | 1.00 | 45 |
| *298* | A34 | 90f carmine | 1.90 | 90 |
| | | *Nos. 291-298 (8)* | 5.50 | 2.59 |

**1966, Jan. 10 Photo.** ***Perf. 14x15***

| No. | Type | Description | Unused | Used |
|---|---|---|---|---|
| *299* | A35 | 8f lt vio & multi | 32 | 5 |
| *300* | A35 | 20f brn red & multi | 55 | 15 |
| *301* | A35 | 30f bl & multi | 60 | 25 |

Issued for Education Day.

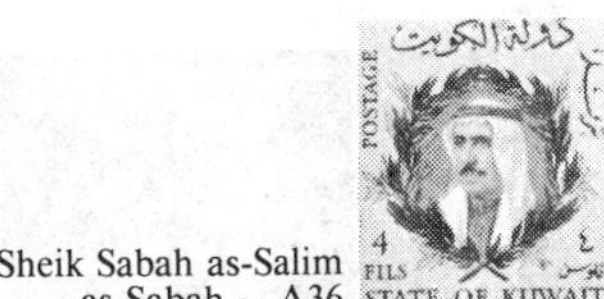

Sheik Sabah as-Salim as-Sabah — A36

**1966, Feb. 1 Photo.** ***Perf. 14x13***

| No. | Type | Description | Unused | Used |
|---|---|---|---|---|
| *302* | A36 | 4f lt bl & multi | 12 | 8 |
| *303* | A36 | 5f pale rose & multi | 12 | 8 |
| *304* | A36 | 20f multi | 40 | 15 |
| *305* | A36 | 30f lt vio & multi | 45 | 20 |
| *306* | A36 | 40f sal & multi | 65 | 30 |
| *307* | A36 | 45f lt gray & multi | 75 | 38 |
| *308* | A36 | 70f yel & multi | 1.10 | 50 |
| *309* | A36 | 90f pale grn & multi | 1.50 | 65 |
| | | *Nos. 302-309 (8)* | 5.09 | 2.34 |

Wheat and Fish — A37

**1966, Feb. 15** ***Perf. 11x11½***

| No. | Type | Description | Unused | Used |
|---|---|---|---|---|
| *310* | A37 | 20f multi | 90 | 50 |
| *311* | A37 | 45f multi | 1.75 | 90 |

"Freedom from Hunger" campaign.

Eagle, Banner, Scales and Emblems A38

**1966, Feb. 25 Litho.** ***Perf. 12½x13***

| No. | Type | Description | Unused | Used |
|---|---|---|---|---|
| *312* | A38 | 20f tan & multi | 70 | 25 |
| *313* | A38 | 25f lt grn & multi | 90 | 28 |
| *314* | A38 | 45f gray & multi | 1.25 | 50 |

Fifth anniversary of National Day.

Wheel of Industry and Map of Arab Countries A39

**1966, March 1** ***Perf. 14x13½***

| No. | Type | Description | Unused | Used |
|---|---|---|---|---|
| *315* | A39 | 20f brt bl, brt grn & blk | 35 | 18 |
| *316* | A39 | 50f lt red brn, brt grn & blk | 75 | 45 |

Issued to publicize the conference on industrial development in Arab countries.

Mother and Children — A40

**1966, March 21** ***Perf. 11½x11***

| No. | Type | Description | Unused | Used |
|---|---|---|---|---|
| *317* | A40 | 20f pink & multi | 35 | 12 |
| *318* | A40 | 45f multi | 75 | 18 |

Mother's Day, March 21.

Medical Conference Emblem — A41

Composite View of a City — A42

**1966, Apr. 1 Photo.** ***Perf. 14½x14***

| No. | Type | Description | Unused | Used |
|---|---|---|---|---|
| *319* | A41 | 15f bl & red | 30 | 15 |
| *320* | A41 | 30f red & bl | 70 | 45 |

Fifth Arab Medical Conference, Kuwait.

**1966, Apr. 7 Litho.** ***Perf. 12½x13***

| No. | Type | Description | Unused | Used |
|---|---|---|---|---|
| *321* | A42 | 8f multi | 30 | 10 |
| *322* | A42 | 10f multi | 75 | 15 |

Issued for World Health Day, Apr. 7, 1966.

WHO Headquarters, Geneva — A43

**1966, May 3 Litho.** ***Perf. 11x11½***

| No. | Type | Description | Unused | Used |
|---|---|---|---|---|
| *323* | A43 | 5f dl sal, ol grn & vio bl | 30 | 5 |
| *324* | A43 | 10f lt grn, ol grn & vio bl | 35 | 8 |

Inauguration of WHO Headquarters, Geneva.

An enhanced introduction to the Scott Catalogue begins on Page V. A thorough understanding of the material presented there will greatly aid your use of the catalogue itself.

Traffic Signal at Night A44

"Blood Transfusion" A45

**1966, May 4**

325 A44 10f grn, red & blk 30 6
326 A44 20f grn, red & blk 40 12

Issued for Traffic Day.

**1966, May 5** ***Perf. 13½***

327 A45 4f multi 30 5
328 A45 8f multi 35 6

Blood Bank Day, May 5, 1966.

Sheik Ahmad and Ship Carrying First Crude Oil Shipment A46

**1966, June 30** ***Perf. 13½***

329 A46 20f multi 55 20
330 A46 45f multi 1.00 32

20th anniv. of the first crude oil shipment, June 30, 1946.

Ministry of Guidance and Information — A47

**1966, July 25 Photo.** ***Perf. 11½x11***

331 A47 4f rose & brn 20 10
332 A47 5f yel brn & brt grn 25 5
333 A47 8f brt grn & pur 30 6
334 A47 20f sal & ultra 35 15

Opening of Ministry of Guidance and Information Building.

Fishing Boat, Lobster, Fish, Crab and FAO Emblem A48

**1966, Oct. 10 Litho.** ***Perf. 13½***

335 A48 4f buff & multi 65 5
336 A48 20f lt lil & multi 75 15

Issued to publicize the Fisheries' Conference of Near East Countries under the sponsorship of the U.N. Food and Agriculture Organization, October, 1966.

United Nations Flag A49

UNESCO Emblem A50

**1966, Oct. 24** ***Perf. 13x14***

337 A49 20f bl, dk bl & pink 65 25
338 A49 45f bl, dk bl & pale grn 1.00 45

Issued for United Nations Day.

**1966, Nov. 4 Litho.** ***Perf. 12½x13***

339 A50 20f multi 50 25
340 A50 45f multi 1.00 55 50

20th anniversary of UNESCO.

Kuwait University Emblem — A51

**1966, Nov. 27 Photo.** ***Perf. 14½***

**Emblem in Yellow, Bright Blue, Green and Gold**

341 A51 8f lt ultra, vio & gold 20 10
342 A51 10f red, brn & gold 45 14
343 A51 20f lt yel grn, sl & gold 55 22
344 A51 45f buff, grn & gold 1.00 60

Opening of Kuwait University.

Jabir al-Ahmad al-Jabir and Sheik Sabah A52

**1966, Dec. 11** ***Perf. 14x13***

345 A52 8f yel grn & multi 30 5
346 A52 20f yel & multi 38 18
347 A52 45f pink & multi 75 45

Issued to commemorate the appointment of the heir apparent, Jabir al-Ahmad al-Jabir.

Scout Badge and Square Knot — A52a

**1966, Dec. 21 Litho.** ***Perf. 14x13***

347A A52a 4f lt ol grn & fawn 50 15
347B A52a 20f yel brn & bl grn 2.25 45

Kuwait Boy Scouts, 30th anniversary.

"Symbols of Science and Peace" — A53

**1967, Jan. 15 Litho.** ***Perf. 13x14***

348 A53 10f multi 20 10
349 A53 45f multi 65 30

Issued for Education Day 1967.

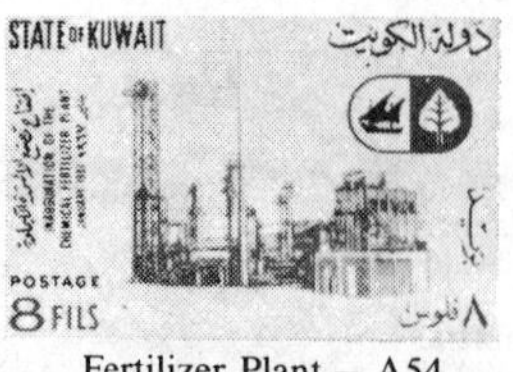
Fertilizer Plant — A54

**1967, Feb. 19 Unwmk.** ***Perf. 13***

350 A54 8f lt bl & multi 30 10
351 A54 20f cr & multi 70 25

Opening of Chemical Fertilizer Plant.

Sun, Dove and Olive Branch — A55

**1967, Feb. 25 Litho.** ***Perf. 13***

352 A55 8f sal & multi 18 8
353 A55 20f yel & multi 50 18

Sixth anniversary of National Day.

Map of Arab States and Municipal Building A56

**1967, March 11** ***Perf. 14½x13***

354 A56 20f gray & multi 80 40
355 A56 30f lt brn & multi 1.25 60

Issued to publicize the first conference of the Arab Cities Organization, Kuwait.

Family — A57

**1967, Mar. 21 Litho.** ***Perf. 13x13½***

356 A57 20f pale rose & multi 65 20
357 A57 45f pale grn & multi 1.40 50

Issued for Family Day, March 21.

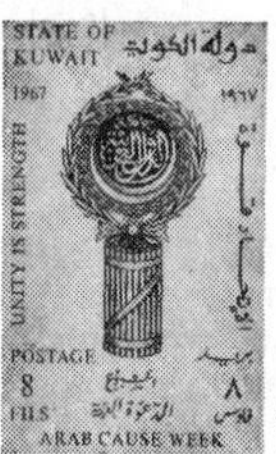
Arab League Emblem — A58

**1967, March 27** ***Perf. 13x14***

358 A58 8f gray & dk bl 40 8
359 A58 10f bis & grn 50 12

Issued for Arab Publicity Week.

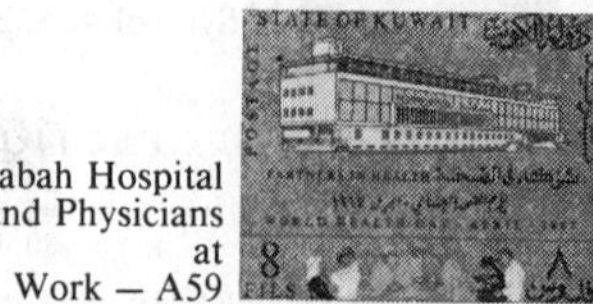
Sabah Hospital and Physicians at Work — A59

**1967, Apr. 7** ***Perf. 14x13***

360 A59 8f dl rose & multi 60 12
361 A59 20f gray & multi 70 30

Issued for World Health Day.

Two Heads of Ramses II — A60

**1967, Apr. 17** ***Perf. 13½***

362 A60 15f cit, grn & brn 40 12
363 A60 20f chlky bl, grn & pur 65 25

Issued for Arab Week to Save the Nubian Monuments.

Traffic Policeman A61

**1967, May 4 Litho.** ***Perf. 14x13***

364 A61 8f lt grn & multi 75 15
365 A61 20f rose lil & multi 80 35

Issued for Traffic Day.

ITY Emblem — A62

**1967, June 4 Photo.** ***Perf. 13***

366 A62 20f Prus bl, lt bl & blk 50 30
367 A62 45f rose lil, lt bl & blk 1.00 60

International Tourist Year, 1967.

Arab League Emblem and Hands Reaching for Knowledge A63

Map of Palestine and U.N. Emblem A64

**1967, Sept. 8 Litho.** ***Perf. 13x14***

368 A63 8f bl & multi 70 9
369 A63 20f dl rose & multi 90 22

Issued to publicize the literacy campaign.

**1967, Oct. 24 Litho.** ***Perf. 13***

370 A64 20f bl & pink 65 28
371 A64 45f org & pink 1.50 60

Issued for United Nations Day.

Factory and Cogwheels — A65

**1967, Nov. 25 Photo.** ***Perf. 13***

372 A65 20f crim & yel 50 15
373 A65 45f gray & yel 1.00 30

Issued to publicize the 3rd Conference of Arab Labor Ministers held in Kuwait.

Flag and Open Book — A66

**1968, Jan. 15 Litho. *Perf. 14***

| | | | | |
|---|---|---|---|---|
| *374* | A66 | 20f brt bl & multi | 45 | 22 |
| *375* | A66 | 45f yel org & multi | 90 | 45 |

Issued for Education Day 1968.

Map of Kuwait and Oil Derrick — A67

**1968, Feb. 23 Litho. *Perf. 12***

| | | | | |
|---|---|---|---|---|
| *376* | A67 | 10f multi | 50 | 25 |
| *377* | A67 | 20f multi | 90 | 50 |

30th anniv. of the discovery of oil in the Greater Burgan Field.

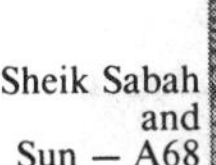

Sheik Sabah and Sun — A68

**1968, Feb. 25 Litho. *Perf. 14x15***

| | | | | |
|---|---|---|---|---|
| *378* | A68 | 8f red lil & multi | 20 | 14 |
| *379* | A68 | 10f lt bl & multi | 28 | 20 |
| *380* | A68 | 15f vio & multi | 40 | 28 |
| *381* | A68 | 20f ver & multi | 50 | 35 |

Seventh anniversary of National Day.

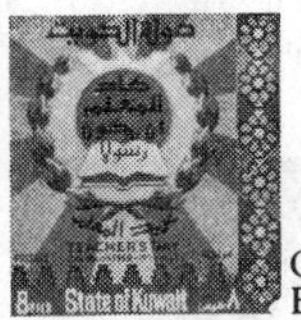


Open Book and Emblem — A69

**1968, Mar. 2 *Perf. 14***

| | | | | |
|---|---|---|---|---|
| *382* | A69 | 8f yel & multi | 30 | 9 |
| *383* | A69 | 20f lil rose & multi | 38 | 18 |
| *384* | A69 | 45f org & multi | 75 | 38 |

Issued for Teachers' Day.

Family Picnic A70

**1968, Mar. 21 *Perf. 13½x13***

| | | | | |
|---|---|---|---|---|
| *385* | A70 | 8f bl & multi | 18 | 5 |
| *386* | A70 | 10f red & multi | 20 | 5 |
| *387* | A70 | 15f lil & multi | 25 | 7 |
| *388* | A70 | 20f dk brn & multi | 28 | 8 |

Issued for Family Day.

Sheik Sabah, Arms of WHO and Kuwait — A71

**1968, Apr. 7 Photo. *Perf. 12***

| | | | | |
|---|---|---|---|---|
| *389* | A71 | 20f brt lil & multi | 45 | 45 |
| *390* | A71 | 45f multi | 90 | 90 |

20th anniv. of WHO.

Dagger in Map of Palestine — A72

**1968, Apr. 9 Litho. *Perf. 14***

| | | | | |
|---|---|---|---|---|
| *391* | A72 | 20f lt bl & ver | 70 | 40 |
| *392* | A72 | 45f lil & ver | 1.40 | 70 |

Issued to commemorate the 20th anniversary of the Deir Yassin massacre.

Street Crossing A74

**1968, May 4 Photo. *Perf. 14x14½***

| | | | | |
|---|---|---|---|---|
| *395* | A74 | 10f dk brn & multi | 50 | 35 |
| *396* | A74 | 15f brt vio & multi | 60 | 50 |
| *397* | A74 | 20f grn & multi | 90 | 60 |

Issued for Traffic Day, 1968.

Map of Palestine and Torch — A75

***Perf. 13½x12½***

**1968, May 15 Litho.**

| | | | | |
|---|---|---|---|---|
| *398* | A75 | 10f lt ultra & multi | 20 | 12 |
| *399* | A75 | 20f yel & multi | 1.00 | 25 |
| *400* | A75 | 45f aqua & multi | 2.00 | 50 |

Issued for Palestine Day.

Palestinian Refugees — A76

**1968, June 5 Litho. *Perf. 13x13½***

| | | | | |
|---|---|---|---|---|
| *401* | A76 | 20f pink & multi | 35 | 10 |
| *402* | A76 | 30f ultra & multi | 50 | 12 |
| *403* | A76 | 45f grn & multi | 65 | 16 |
| *404* | A76 | 90f lil & multi | 1.10 | 35 |

International Human Rights Year.

Museum of Kuwait — A77

***Perf. 12½***

**1968, Aug. 25 Unwmk. Engr.**

| | | | | |
|---|---|---|---|---|
| *405* | A77 | 1f dk brn & brt grn | 5 | 5 |
| *406* | A77 | 2f dp cl & grn | 5 | 5 |
| *407* | A77 | 5f blk & org | 5 | 5 |
| *408* | A77 | 8f dk brn & grn | 5 | 5 |
| *409* | A77 | 10f Prus bl & cl | 12 | 5 |
| *410* | A77 | 20f org brn & bl | 30 | 15 |
| *411* | A77 | 25f dk bl & org | 38 | 18 |
| *412* | A77 | 30f Prus bl & yel grn | 45 | 22 |
| *413* | A77 | 45f plum & vio blk | 60 | 30 |
| *414* | A77 | 50f grn & car | 75 | 38 |
| | | *Nos. 405-414 (10)* | 2.80 | 1.48 |

Man Reading Book, Arab League, UN and UNESCO Emblems A78

**1968, Sept. 8 Litho. *Perf. 12½x13***

| | | | | |
|---|---|---|---|---|
| *415* | A78 | 15f bl gray & multi | 40 | 7 |
| *416* | A78 | 20f pink & multi | 60 | 10 |

Issued for International Literacy Day.

Map of Palestine on U.N. Building and Children with Tent A79

**1968, Oct. 25 Litho. *Perf. 13***

| | | | | |
|---|---|---|---|---|
| *417* | A79 | 20f multi | 20 | 8 |
| *418* | A79 | 30f gray & multi | 40 | 12 |
| *419* | A79 | 45f sal pink & multi | 50 | 16 |

Issued for United Nations Day.

Kuwait Chamber of Commerce A80

**1968, Nov. 6 Litho. *Perf. 13½x12½***

| | | | | |
|---|---|---|---|---|
| *420* | A80 | 10f dp org & dk brn | 15 | 6 |
| *421* | A80 | 15f rose cl & vio bl | 22 | 12 |
| *422* | A80 | 20f brn org & dk grn | 30 | 15 |

Issued to commemorate the opening of the Kuwait Chamber of Commerce Building.

Conference Emblem — A81

**1968, Nov. 10 Litho. *Perf. 13***

**Emblem in Ocher, Blue, Red and Black**

| | | | | |
|---|---|---|---|---|
| *423* | A81 | 10f dk brn & bl | 15 | 6 |
| *424* | A81 | 15f dk brn & org | 20 | 10 |
| *425* | A81 | 20f dk brn & vio bl | 30 | 12 |
| *426* | A81 | 30f dk brn & org brn | 40 | 18 |

Issued to commemorate the 14th Conference of the Arab Chambers of Commerce, Industry and Agriculture.

Shuaiba Refinery — A82

**1968, Nov. 18 *Perf. 13½***

**Emblem in Red, Black and Blue**

| | | | | |
|---|---|---|---|---|
| *427* | A82 | 10f blk & lt bl grn | 22 | 9 |
| *428* | A82 | 20f blk & gray | 45 | 18 |
| *429* | A82 | 30f blk & sal | 60 | 30 |
| *430* | A82 | 45f blk & emer | 90 | 38 |

Opening of Shuaiba Refinery.

Koran, Scales and People A83

**1968, Dec. 19 Photo. *Perf. 14x14½***

| | | | | |
|---|---|---|---|---|
| *431* | A83 | 5f multi | 20 | 12 |
| *432* | A83 | 20f multi | 50 | 30 |
| *433* | A83 | 30f multi | 70 | 40 |
| *434* | A83 | 45f multi | 1.00 | 60 |

The 1400th anniversary of the Koran.

Boeing 707 — A84

**1969, Jan. 1 Litho. *Perf. 13½x14***

| | | | | |
|---|---|---|---|---|
| *435* | A84 | 10f brt yel & multi | 30 | 12 |
| *436* | A84 | 20f grn & multi | 50 | 25 |
| *437* | A84 | 25f multi | 60 | 30 |
| *438* | A84 | 45f lil & multi | 1.00 | 50 |

Issued to commemorate the introduction of Boeing 707 service by Kuwait Airways.

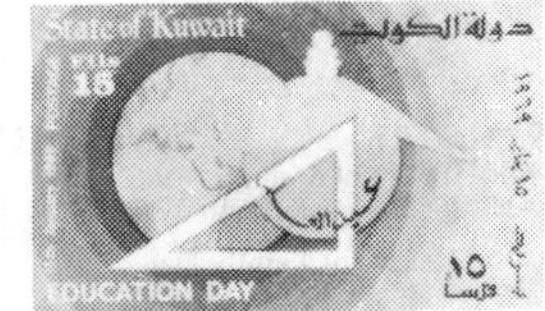


Globe, Retort and Triangle — A85

**1969, Jan. 15 *Perf. 13***

| | | | | |
|---|---|---|---|---|
| *439* | A85 | 15f gray & multi | 60 | 30 |
| *440* | A85 | 20f multi | 90 | 35 |

Issued for Education Day.

Kuwait Hilton Hotel — A86

**1969, Feb. 15 Litho. *Perf. 14x12½***

| | | | | |
|---|---|---|---|---|
| *441* | A86 | 10f brt bl & multi | 26 | 8 |
| *442* | A86 | 20f pink & multi | 60 | 15 |

Opening of the Kuwait Hilton Hotel.

Foreign postal stationery (stamped envelopes, postal cards and air letter sheets) lies beyond the scope of this Catalogue, which is limited to adhesive postage stamps.

Teachers' Society Emblem, Father and Children — A87

**1969, Feb. 15** **Perf. 13**
*443* A87 10f vio & multi 20 12
*444* A87 20f rose & multi 50 25

Issued for Education week.

Wreath, Flags and Dove — A88

Emblem, Teacher and Students — A89

**1969, Feb. 25** **Photo.** **Perf. 14½x14**
*445* A88 15f lil & multi 20 12
*446* A88 20f bl & multi 32 15
*447* A88 30f ocher & multi 40 25

Eighth anniversary of National Day.

**1969, Mar. 8** **Litho.** **Perf. 13x12½**
*448* A89 10f multi 20 6
*449* A89 20f dp red & multi 40 12

Issued for Teachers' Day.

Family A90

**1969, Mar. 21** **Perf. 13½**
*450* A90 10f dk bl & multi 20 5
*451* A90 20f dp car & multi 35 10

Issued for Family Day.

Avicenna, WHO Emblem, Patient and Microscope — A91

**1969, Apr. 7** **Litho.** **Perf. 13½**
*452* A91 15f red brn & multi 35 7
*453* A91 20f lt grn & multi 85 8

Issued for World Health Day, Apr. 7.

Motorized Traffic Police A92

**1969, May 4** **Litho.** **Perf. 12½x13**
*454* A92 10f multi 32 12
*455* A92 20f multi 1.40 28

Issued for Traffic Day.

ILO Emblem A93

**1969, June 1** **Perf. 11½**
*456* A93 10f red, blk & gold 18 5
*457* A93 20f lt bl grn, blk & gold 38 9

50th anniv. of the ILO.

S.S. Al Sabahiah A94

**1969, June 10** **Litho.** **Perf. 13½**
*458* A94 20f multi 52 15
*459* A94 45f multi 1.10 38

4th anniversary of Kuwait Shipping Co.

UNESCO Emblem, Woman, Globe and Book — A95

**1969, Sept. 8** **Litho.** **Perf. 13½**
*460* A95 10f bl & multi 18 5
*461* A95 20f rose red & multi 38 8

International Literacy Day, Sept. 8.

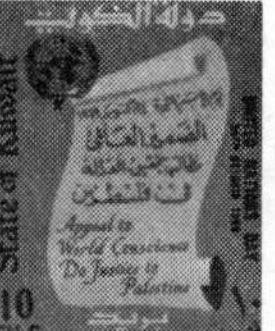

Sheik Sabah — A96

U.N. Emblem and Scroll — A97

**1969-74** **Litho.** **Perf. 14**
*462* A96 8f lt bl & multi 5 5
*463* A96 10f pink & multi 10 10
*464* A96 15f gray & multi 16 8
*465* A96 20f yel & multi 20 12
*466* A96 25f vio & multi 25 16
*467* A96 30f sal & multi 32 20
*468* A96 45f tan & multi 45 28
*469* A96 50f yel grn & multi 52 32
*470* A96 70f multi 70 40
*471* A96 75f ultra & multi 80 45
*472* A96 90f rose & multi 1.00 52
*473* A96 250f lil & multi 3.50 1.65
*473A* A96 500f gray grn & multi ('74) 7.25 5.25
*473B* A96 1d lil rose & multi ('74) 14.00 8.00
*Nos. 462-473B (14)* 29.30 17.58

Nos. 473A-473B issued Jan. 12, 1974; others Oct. 5, 1969.

**1969, Oct. 24** **Litho.** **Perf. 13**
*474* A97 10f emer & multi 8 8
*475* A97 20f bis & multi 28 16
*476* A97 45f rose red & multi 60 35

Issued for United Nations Day.

Radar, Satellite Earth Station, Kuwait A98

Design: 45f, Globe and radar (vert.).

**1969, Dec. 15** **Photo.** **Perf. 14½**
*477* A98 20f sil & multi 60 25
*478* A98 45f sil & multi 1.40 55

Issued to publicize the inauguration of the Kuwait Earth Station for Satellite Communications.

Globe with Science Symbols, and Education Year Emblem — A99

**1970, Jan. 15** **Photo.** **Perf. 13½x13**
*479* A99 20f brt lil & multi 38 18
*480* A99 45f bl & multi 60 42

International Education Year.

Shoue A100

Old Kuwaiti Vessels: 10f, Sambook. 15f, Baghla. 20f, Batteel. 25f, Boom. 45f, Bakkara. 50f, Shipbuilding.

**1970, Feb. 1** **Perf. 14½x14**
*481* A100 8f multi 18 5
*482* A100 10f multi 25 6
*483* A100 15f multi 30 15
*484* A100 20f multi 40 12
*485* A100 25f multi 60 15
*486* A100 45f multi 90 28
*487* A100 50f multi 1.25 30
*Nos. 481-487 (7)* 3.88 1.11

Refugee Father and Children A101

Kuwait Flag, Emblem and Sheik Sabah A102

**1970** **Photo.** **Perf. 14x12½**
*488* A101 20f red brn & multi 1.00 32
*489* A101 45f ol & multi 2.00 80

Issued for Universal Palestinian Refugees Week, Dec. 16-22, 1969.

**1970, Feb. 25** **Perf. 13½x13**
*490* A102 15f sil & multi 25 6
*491* A102 20f gold & multi 35 10

Ninth anniversary of National Day.

Dome of the Rock, Jerusalem, and Boy Commando — A103

Designs: 20f, Dome and man commando. 45f, Dome and woman commando.

**1970, Mar. 4** **Litho.** **Perf. 13**
*492* A103 10f pale vio & multi 52 12
*493* A103 20f lt bl & multi 1.00 32
*494* A103 45f multi 2.00 65

Honoring Palestinian commandos.

Parents and Children A104

**1970, Mar. 21** **Perf. 14**
*495* A104 20f multi 32 12
*496* A104 30f pink & multi 45 20

Issued for Family Day.

Map of Arab League Countries, Flag and Emblem — A104a

**1970, Mar. 22** **Perf. 11½x11**
*497* 104a 20f lt bl, grn & lt brn 25 12
*498* 104a 45f sal, grn & dk pur 55 25

25th anniversary of the Arab League.

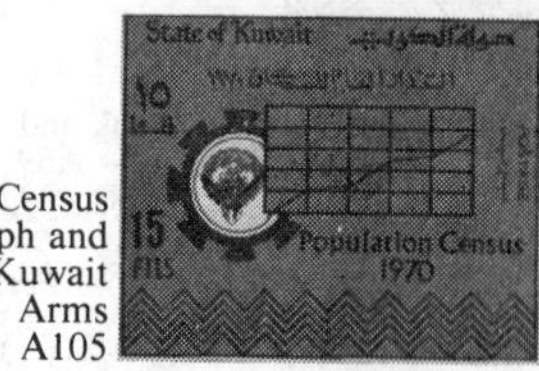

Census Graph and Kuwait Arms A105

**1970, Apr. 1** **Litho.** **Perf. 13½x13**
*499* A105 15f dl org & multi 22 9
*500* A105 20f yel & multi 30 15
*501* A105 30f pink & multi 45 22

Issued to publicize the 1970 census.

"Fight Cancer," Kuwait Arms, WHO Emblem — A106

**1970, Apr. 7** **Perf. 13½x13**
*502* A106 20f bl, vio bl & rose lil 38 15
*503* A106 30f dl yel, vio bl & lil rose 50 22

Issued for World Health Organization Day, Apr. 7, and to publicize the fight against cancer.

Traffic Signs A107

**1970, May 4 Photo. *Perf. 13½***

| | | | |
|---|---|---|---|
| *504* A107 20f multi | | 50 | 20 |
| *505* A107 30f multi | | 80 | 30 |

Issued for Traffic Day.

Red Crescent A108

**1970, May 8 Litho. *Perf. 12½x13½***

| | | |
|---|---|---|
| *506* A108 10f yel & multi | 30 | 5 |
| *507* A108 15f emer & multi | 50 | 12 |
| *508* A108 30f tan & multi | 1.00 | 30 |

Issued for International Red Crescent and Red Cross Day.

UPU Headquarters, Bern — A109

**1970, May 25 Photo. *Perf. 12x11½***

| | | |
|---|---|---|
| *509* A109 20f multi | 50 | 20 |
| *510* A109 30f multi | 70 | 30 |

Opening of the new UPU Headquarters in Bern.

Sheik Sabah — A110

**1970, June 15 Photo. *Perf. 14***

| | | |
|---|---|---|
| *511* A110 20f sil & multi | 45 | 10 |
| *512* A110 45f gold & multi | 1.00 | 22 |
| *a* Miniature sheet of 2 | 3.00 | 1.10 |

Nos. 511-512 have circular perforation around vignette set within a white square of paper, perforated on 4 sides. No. 512a contains 2 imperf. stamps similar to Nos. 511-512. Gold marginal inscription. Size: 127x101½mm.

U.N. Emblem, Symbols of Peace, Progress, Justice — A111

**1970, July 1 Litho. *Perf. 13½x12½***

| | | |
|---|---|---|
| *513* A111 20f lt grn & multi | 35 | 12 |
| *514* A111 45f multi | 65 | 30 |

25th anniversary of the United Nations.

Tanker Loading Crude Oil from Sea Island A112

**1970, Aug. 1 *Perf. 13½x13***

| | | |
|---|---|---|
| *515* A112 20f multi | 65 | 20 |
| *516* A112 45f multi | 1.40 | 45 |

Issued to publicize the artificial "Sea Island" loading facilities in Kuwait.

"Writing," Kuwait and U.N. Emblems A113

**1970, Sept. 8 Photo. *Perf. 13½***

| | | |
|---|---|---|
| *517* A113 10f brt bl & multi | 50 | 5 |
| *518* A113 15f brt grn & multi | 75 | 6 |

International Literacy Day, Sept. 8.

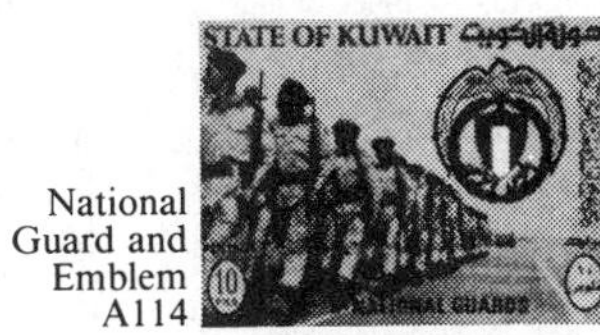

National Guard and Emblem A114

**1970, Oct. 20 Photo. *Perf. 13x13½***

| | | |
|---|---|---|
| *519* A114 10f gold & multi | 32 | 5 |
| *520* A114 20f sil & multi | 65 | 12 |

First National Guard graduation.

Flag of Kuwait, Symbols of Development A115

**1971, Feb. 25 Litho. *Perf. 12***

| | | |
|---|---|---|
| *521* A115 20f gray & multi | 50 | 20 |
| *522* A115 30f multi | 65 | 32 |

Tenth anniversary of National Day.

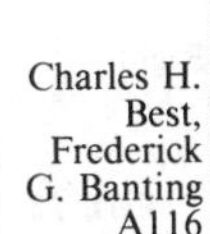

Charles H. Best, Frederick G. Banting A116

**1971, Apr. 7 Litho. *Perf. 14***

| | | |
|---|---|---|
| *523* A116 20f multi | 50 | 18 |
| *524* A116 45f multi | 1.10 | 50 |

World Health Day; discoverers of insulin.

Globe with Map of Palestine A117

**1971, May 3 Litho. *Perf. 12½x13***

| | | |
|---|---|---|
| *525* A117 20f yel grn & multi | 65 | 50 |
| *526* A117 45f lil & multi | 1.35 | 1.00 |

International Palestine Week.

ITU Emblem and Waves A118

**1971, May 17 Photo. *Perf. 13x13½***

| | | |
|---|---|---|
| *527* A118 20f sil, dk red & blk | 40 | 12 |
| *528* A118 45f gold, dk red & blk | 80 | 28 |

3rd World Telecommunications Day.

Men of 3 Races — A119

**1971, June 5 Litho. *Perf. 11½x11***

| | | |
|---|---|---|
| *529* A119 15f red brn & multi | 35 | 15 |
| *530* A119 30f ultra & multi | 60 | 30 |

Intl. Year against Racial Discrimination.

Arab Postal Union Emblem A120

**1971, Aug. 30 *Perf. 13x12½***

| | | |
|---|---|---|
| *531* A120 20f brn & multi | 35 | 20 |
| *532* A120 45f bl & multi | 70 | 30 |

25th anniv. of the Conf. of Sofar, Lebanon, establishing the Arab Postal Union.

Symbols of Learning, UNESCO and Kuwait Emblems — A121

**1971, Sept. 8 *Perf. 12***

| | | |
|---|---|---|
| *533* A121 25f dl yel & multi | 40 | 15 |
| *534* A121 60f lt bl & multi | 90 | 40 |

International Literacy Day, Sept. 8.

Soccer A122

Design: 30f, Soccer (different).

**1971, Dec. 10 *Perf. 13***

| | | |
|---|---|---|
| *535* A122 20f grn & multi | 50 | 20 |
| *536* A122 30f ultra & multi | 75 | 30 |

Regional Sports Tournament, Kuwait, Dec. 1971.

UNICEF Emblem and Arms of Kuwait — A123

***Perf. 11x11½***

**1971, Dec. 11 Litho. Engr.**

| | | |
|---|---|---|
| *537* A123 25f gold & multi | 40 | 20 |
| *538* A123 60f sil & multi | 90 | 50 |

25th anniv. of UNICEF.

Book Year Emblem A124

**1972, Jan. 2 Litho. *Perf. 14x13***

| | | |
|---|---|---|
| *539* A124 20f blk & buff | 30 | 18 |
| *540* A124 45f blk & lt bl grn | 70 | 40 |

International Book Year, 1972.

Kuwait Emblem with 11 Rays, Olive Branch A125

**1972, Feb. 25 Litho. *Perf. 13x13½***

| | | |
|---|---|---|
| *541* A125 20f pink, gold & multi | 45 | 25 |
| *542* A125 45f lt bl, gold & multi | 70 | 50 |

11th anniversary of National Day.

Telecommunications Center — A126

**1972, Feb. 28 *Perf. 13½***

| | | |
|---|---|---|
| *543* A126 20f lt bl & multi | 50 | 22 |
| *544* A126 45f multi | 1.25 | 50 |

Opening of Kuwait Telecommunications Center.

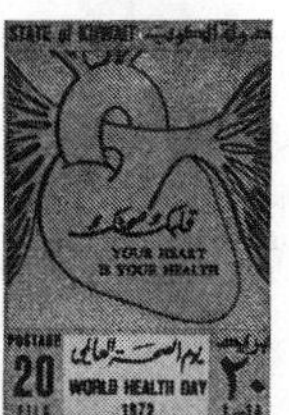

"Your Heart is your Health" — A127

Nurse and Child — A128

**1972, Apr. 7 Photo. *Perf. 14½x14***
*545* A127 20f red & multi 65 25
*546* A127 45f red & multi 1.40 55

World Health Day.

**1972, May 8 Litho. *Perf. 12½x13***
*547* A128 8f vio bl, red & emer 40 5
*548* A128 40f pink & multi 1.20 40

Red Cross and Red Crescent Day.

Soccer, Olympic Emblems A129

**1972, Sept. 2 Litho. *Perf. 14½***
*549* A129 2f *shown* 5 5
*550* A129 4f *Running* 5 5
*551* A129 5f *Swimming* 5 5
*552* A129 8f *Gymnastics* 5 5
*553* A129 10f *Discus* 8 6
*554* A129 15f *Equestrian* 25 10
*555* A129 20f *Basketball* 30 12
*556* A129 25f *Volleyball* 40 15
*Nos. 549-556 (8)* 1.23 63

20th Olympic Games, Munich, Aug. 26-Sept. 11.

FAO Emblem, Vegetables, Fish and Ship — A130

**1972, Sept. 9 Litho. *Perf. 14x13½***
*557* A130 5f bl & multi 6 6
*558* A130 10f emer & multi 20 15
*559* A130 20f org & multi 40 30

11th Food and Agriculture Organization Regional Conference in the Near East, Kuwait, Sept. 1972.

National Bank Emblem A131

**1972, Nov. 15 Photo. *Perf. 13x14***
*560* A131 10f grn & multi 20 15
*561* A131 35f dl red & multi 70 50

20th anniversary of Kuwait National Bank.

Capitals — A132

Relics of Failaka: 5f, View of excavations. 10f, Acanthus leaf capital. 15f, Excavations.

**1972, Dec. 4 Litho. *Perf. 12***
*562* A132 2f lil rose & multi 6 5
*563* A132 5f bis & multi 6 5
*564* A132 10f lt bl & multi 28 7
*565* A132 15f grn & multi 40 10

Flower and Kuwait Emblem A133

INTERPOL Emblem A134

**1973, Feb. 25 Litho. *Perf. 13½x13***
*566* A133 10f lt ol & multi 18 12
*567* A133 20f multi 38 25
*568* A133 30f yel & multi 55 38

12th anniversary of National Day.

**1973, June 3 Litho. *Perf. 12***
*569* A134 10f emer & multi 30 25
*570* A134 15f red org & multi 50 35
*571* A134 20f bl & multi 80 50

50th anniversary of International Criminal Police Organization (INTERPOL).

I.C.M.S. Emblem and Flag of Kuwait A135

Kuwait Airways Building A136

**1973, June 24 *Perf. 13***
*572* A135 30f gray & multi 30 18
*573* A135 40f brn & multi 50 25

International Council of Military Sports, 25th anniversary.

**1973, July 1 Litho. *Perf. 12½x14***
*574* A136 10f lt grn & multi 28 12
*575* A136 15f lil & multi 40 20
*576* A136 20f lt ultra & multi 60 25

Opening of Kuwait Airways Corporation Building.

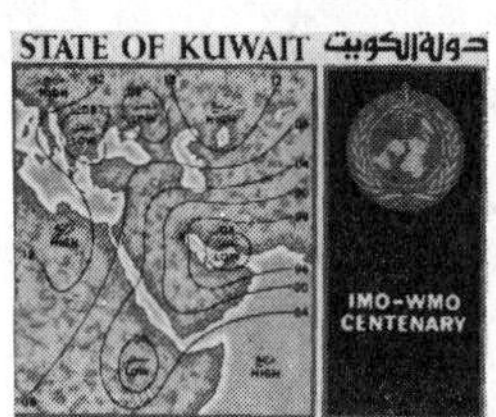
Weather Map of Suez Canal and Persian Gulf Region — A137

**1973, Sept. 4 Photo. *Perf. 14***
*577* A137 5f red & multi 18 5
*578* A137 10f grn & multi 35 8
*579* A137 15f multi 50 12

Centenary of international meteorological cooperation.

Sheiks Ahmad and Sabah — A138

**1973, Nov. 12 Photo. *Perf. 14***
*580* A138 10f lt grn & multi 20 10
*581* A138 20f yel org & multi 40 20
*582* A138 70f lt bl & multi 1.40 80

50th anniversary of stamps overprinted "Kuwait."

Mourning Dove, Eurasian Hoopoe, Rock Dove, Stone Curlew — A139

Designs: Birds and traps.

**1973, Dec. 1 Litho. *Perf. 14***
**Size (single stamp): 32x32mm.**
*583* A139 Block of four 1.00 50
*a* 5f *Mourning dove* 22 12
*b* 5f *Eurasian hoopoe* 22 12
*c* 5f *Rock dove* 22 12
*d* 5f *Stone curlew* 22 12
*584* A139 Block of four 1.25 65
*a* 8f *Great gray shrike* 30 15
*b* 8f *Red-backed shrike* 30 15
*c* 8f *Rufous-backed shrike* 30 15
*d* 8f *Black-naped oriole* 30 15
*585* A139 Block of four 1.50 85
*a* 10f *Willow warbler* 35 20
*b* 10f *Great reed warbler* 35 20
*c* 10f *Blackcap* 35 20
*d* 10f *Common (barn) swallow* 35 20
*586* A139 Block of four 2.50 1.40
*a* 15f *Common rock thrush* 60 30
*b* 15f *European redstart* 60 30
*c* 15f *Wheatear* 60 30
*d* 15f *Bluethroat* 60 30
*587* A139 Block of four 3.00 1.60
*a* 20f *Houbara bustard* 70 35
*b* 20f *Pin-tailed sandgrouse* 70 35
*c* 20f *Ypecaha wood rail* 70 35
*d* 20f *Spotted crake* 70 35
**Size (single stamp): 35x35mm.**
*588* A139 Block of four 3.25 2.00
*a* 25f *American sparrow hawk* 75 45
*b* 25f *Great black-backed gull* 75 45
*c* 25f *Purple heron* 75 45
*d* 25f *Wryneck* 75 45
*589* A139 Block of four 4.50 2.50
*a* 30f *European bee-eater* 1.10 60
*b* 30f *Goshawk* 1.10 60
*c* 30f *Gray wagtail* 1.10 60
*d* 30f *Pied wagtail* 1.10 60
*590* A139 Block of four 6.00 3.50
*a* 45f *Crossbows* 1.50 85
*b* 45f *Tent-shaped net* 1.50 85
*c* 45f *Hand net* 1.50 85
*d* 45f *Rooftop trap* 1.50 85
*Nos. 583-590 (8)* 23.00 13.00

Nos. 583-590 printed in sheets of 100 containing 25 blocks of 4.

Human Rights Flame — A141

**1973, Dec. 10 Litho. *Perf. 12***
*594* A141 10f red & multi 30 8
*595* A141 40f lt grn & multi 75 32
*596* A141 75f lil & multi 1.10 60

25th anniversary of the Universal Declaration of Human Rights.

Promoting Animal Resources A142

Stylized Wheat and Kuwaiti Flag A143

**1974, Feb. 16 Litho. *Perf. 12½***
*597* A142 30f vio bl & multi 50 18
*598* A142 40f rose & multi 70 24

4th Congress of the Arab Veterinary Union, Kuwait.

**1974, Feb. 25 *Perf. 13½x13***
*599* A143 20f lem & multi 15 12
*600* A143 30f bis brn & multi 50 18
*601* A143 70f sil & multi 90 42

13th anniversary of National Day.

Conference Emblem and Sheik Sabah A144

**1974, Mar. 8 *Perf. 12½***
*602* A144 30f multi 50 18
*603* A144 40f yel & multi 75 24

12th Conf. of the Arab Medical Union and 1st Conf. of the Kuwait Medical Soc.

Tournament Emblem — A145

**1974, Mar. 15**
*604* A145 25f multi 75 30
*605* A145 45f multi 1.40 50

Third Soccer Tournament for the Arabian Gulf Trophy, Kuwait, March 1974.

Scientific Research Institute — A146

**1974, Apr. 3 Photo. *Perf. 12½***
*606* A146 15f mag & multi 30 10
*607* A146 20f grn & multi 60 12

Opening of Kuwait Scientific Research Institute.

Arab Postal Union, Kuwait and UPU Emblems A147

**974, May 1** *Perf. 13x14*
*08* A147 20f gold & multi 20 14
*09* A147 30f gold & multi 30 20
*10* A147 60f gold & multi 60 40

Centenary of Universal Postal Union.

Telephone Dial with Communications Symbols and Globe — A148

**974, May 17** *Perf. 14x13½*
*11* A148 10f bl & multi 18 9
*12* A148 30f multi 60 25
*13* A148 40f blk & multi 75 35

World Telecommunications Day, May 17.

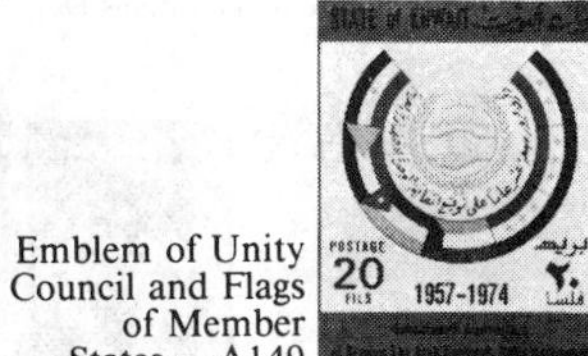

Emblem of Unity Council and Flags of Member States — A149

**1974, June 25 Litho.** *Perf. 13½*
*614* A149 20f red, blk & grn 40 18
*615* A149 30f grn, blk & red 50 25

17th anniversary of the signing of the Arab Economic Unity Agreement.

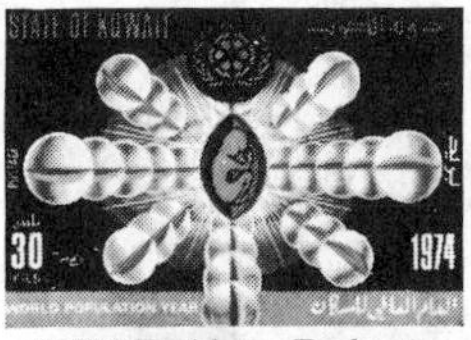

WPY Emblem, Embryo, "Growth" — A150

**1974, Aug. 19 Litho.** *Perf. 14x14½*
*616* A150 30f blk & multi 60 18
*617* A150 70f vio bl & multi 90 42

World Population Year, 1974.

Development Building and Emblem — A151

**1974, Oct. 30 Litho.** *Perf. 13x13½*
*618* A151 10f pink & multi 25 6
*619* A151 20f ultra & multi 45 12

Kuwait Fund for Arab Economic Development.

Emblem of Shuaiba Industrial Area — A152

**1974, Dec. 17 Litho.** *Perf. 12½x12*
*620* A152 10f lt bl & multi 20 8
*621* A152 20f sal & multi 52 15
*622* A152 30f lt grn & multi 65 25

Shuaiba Industrial Area, 10th anniversary.

Arms of Kuwait and "14" — A153

**1975, Feb. 25 Litho.** *Perf. 13x13½*
*623* A153 20f multi 25 12
*624* A153 70f yel grn & multi 85 42
*625* A153 75f rose & multi 1.00 45

14th anniversary of National Day.

Male and Female Symbols — A154

**1975, Apr. 14 Photo.** *Perf. 11½x12*
*626* A154 8f lt grn & multi 5 5
*627* A154 20f rose & multi 22 15
*628* A154 30f bl & multi 40 25
*629* A154 70f yel & multi 1.00 55
*630* A154 100f blk & multi 1.40 80
*Nos. 626-630 (5)* 3.07 1.80

Kuwaiti census 1975.

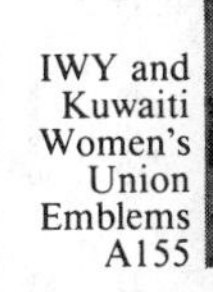

IWY and Kuwaiti Women's Union Emblems A155

**1975, June 10 Litho.** *Perf. 14½*
*631* A155 15f brn org & multi 25 12
*632* A155 20f ol & multi 35 16
*633* A155 30f vio & multi 50 25

International Women's Year 1975.

Classroom and UNESCO Emblem — A156

**1975, Sept. 8 Litho.** *Perf. 12½x12*
*634* A156 20f grn & multi 30 15
*635* A156 30f multi 45 25

International Literacy Day 1975.

Symbols of Measurements A157

UN Flag, Rifle and Olive Branch A158

**1975, Oct. 14 Photo.** *Perf. 14x13*
*636* A157 10f grn & multi 20 10
*637* A157 20f pur & multi 40 20

World Standards Day.

**1975, Oct. 24 Litho.** *Perf. 12x12½*
*638* A158 20f multi 25 12
*639* A158 45f org & multi 55 28

United Nations, 30th anniversary.

Sheik Sabah — A159

**1975, Dec. 22 Litho.** *Perf. 12½x12*
*640* A159 8f yel & multi 22 15
*641* A159 20f lil & multi 35 18
*642* A159 30f buff & multi 45 25
*643* A159 50f sal & multi 75 45
*644* A159 90f lt bl & multi 1.50 80
*645* A159 100f multi 1.60 90
*Nos. 640-645 (6)* 4.87 2.73

"Progress" A160

**1976, Feb. 25 Litho.** *Perf. 12*
*646* A160 10f multi 28 8
*647* A160 20f multi 55 15

15th anniversary of National Day.

Medical Equipment, Emblem and Surgery — A161

Telephones, 1876 and 1976 — A162

**1976, Mar. 1 Litho.** *Perf. 14½*
*648* A161 5f dl grn & multi 5 5
*649* A161 10f bl & multi 30 9
*650* A161 30f gray & multi 90 25

Kuwait Medical Association, second annual conference.

**1976, Mar. 10 Litho.** *Perf. 12*
*651* A162 5f org & blk 10 5
*652* A162 15f lt bl & blk 50 10

Centenary of first telephone call by Alexander Graham Bell, Mar. 10, 1876.

Human Eye — A163

Photo. and Engr.

**1976, Apr. 7** *Perf. 11½*
*653* A163 10f multi 20 10
*654* A163 20f blk & multi 40 20
*655* A163 30f multi 65 30

World Health Day: "Foresight prevents blindness."

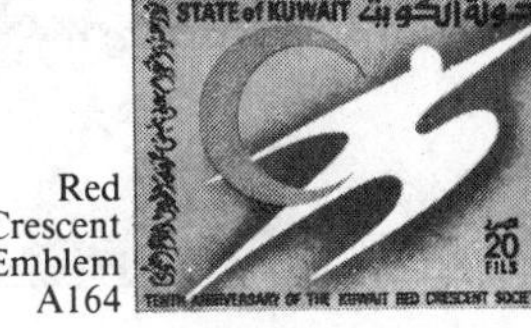

Red Crescent Emblem A164

**1976, May 8 Litho.** *Perf. 12x11½*
*656* A164 20f brt grn, blk & red 25 15
*657* A164 30f vio bl, blk & red 50 20
*658* A164 45f yel, blk & red 60 35
*659* A164 75f lil rose, blk & red 1.10 55

Kuwait Red Crescent Society, 10th anniversary.

Modern Suburb of Kuwait A165

**1976, June 1 Photo.** *Perf. 13x13½*
*660* A165 10f lt grn & multi 25 6
*661* A165 20f sal & multi 45 12

Habitat, U. N. Conference on Human Settlements, Vancouver, Canada, May 31-June 11.

Basketball, Kuwait Olympic Emblem A166

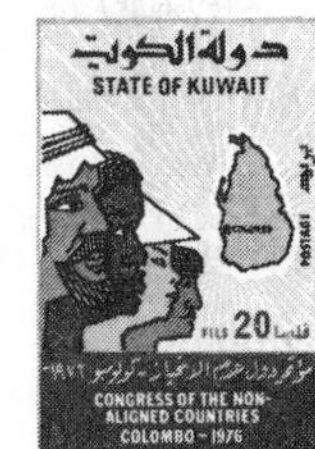

Various Races, Map of Sri Lanka A167

Designs: 8f, Running. 10f, Judo. 15f, Fieldball. 20f, Gymnastics. 30f, Water polo. 45f, Soccer. 70f, Swimmers at start.

**1976, July 17 Litho.** *Perf. 14½*
*662* A166 4f blk & multi 5 5
*663* A166 8f red & multi 5 5
*664* A166 10f grn & multi 10 6
*665* A166 15f lem & multi 15 10
*666* A166 20f bl & multi 20 12
*667* A166 30f lil & multi 30 18
*668* A166 45f multi 45 28
*669* A166 70f brn & multi 70 42
*Nos. 662-669 (8)* 2.00 1.26

21st Olympic Games, Montreal, Canada, July 17-Aug. 1.

**1976, Aug. 16 Photo.** *Perf. 14*
*670* A167 20f dk bl & multi 20 12
*671* A167 30f pur & multi 30 18
*672* A167 45f grn & multi 50 28

5th Summit Conference of Non-aligned Countries, Colombo, Sri Lanka, Aug. 9-19.

"UNESCO," Torch and Kuwait Arms — A168

**1976, Nov. 4 Litho.** *Perf. 12x11½*
*673* A168 20f yel grn & multi 25 12
*674* A168 45f scar & multi 55 28

30th anniversary of United Nations Educational, Scientific and Cultural Organization.

Blindman's Buff — A169

Designs: Popular games. 5f, 15f, 30f, vertical.

**Perf. 14½x14, 14x14½**

**1977, Jan. 10 Litho.**

675 A169 5f *Pot throwing* 10 10
676 A169 5f *Kite flying* 10 10
677 A169 5f *Balancing sticks* 10 10
678 A169 5f *Spinning tops* 10 10
679 A169 10f *shown* 15 12
680 A169 10f *Rowing* 15 12
681 A169 10f *Hoops* 15 12
682 A169 10f *Ropes* 15 12
683 A169 15f *Rope skipping* 25 20
684 A169 15f *Marbles* 25 20
685 A169 15f *Cart steering* 25 20
686 A169 15f *Teetotum* 25 20
687 A169 20f *Halma* 35 25
688 A169 20f *Model boats* 35 25
689 A169 20f *Pot and candle* 35 25
690 A169 20f *Hide and seek* 35 25
691 A169 30f *Throwing bones* 50 35
692 A169 30f *Mystery gifts* 50 35
693 A169 30f *Hopscotch* 50 35
694 A169 30f *Catch as catch can* 50 35
695 A169 40f *Bowls* 75 50
696 A169 40f *Sword fighting* 75 50
697 A169 40f *Mother and child* 75 50
698 A169 40f *Fivestones* 75 50
699 A169 60f *Hiding a cake* 1.10 75
700 A169 60f *Chess* 1.10 75
701 A169 60f *Dancing* 1.10 75
702 A169 60f *Treasure hunt* 1.10 75
703 A169 70f *Hobby-horses* 1.25 85
704 A169 70f *Hide and seek* 1.25 85
705 A169 70f *Catch* 1.25 85
706 A169 70f *Storytelling* 1.25 85
*Nos. 675-706 (32)* 17.80 12.48

Stamps of same denomination printed se-tenant in blocks of 4, sheets of 100.

Diseased Knee — A170

**1977, Feb. 15 Perf. 13x13½**

707 A170 20f yel & multi 20 12
708 A170 30f multi 35 18
709 A170 45f red & multi 45 28
710 A170 75f blk & multi 80 45

World Rheumatism Year.

Sheik Sabah A171

**1977, Feb. 25 Photo. Perf. 13½x13**

711 A171 10f multi 12 6
712 A171 15f multi 18 10
713 A171 30f multi 30 18
714 A171 80f multi 75 48

16th National Day.

Kuwait Tower — A172

APU Emblem — A173

**1977, Feb. 26 Perf. 14x13½**

715 A172 30f multi 25 12
716 A172 80f multi 65 30

Inauguration of Kuwait Tower.

**1977, Apr. 12 Litho. Perf. 13½x14**

717 A173 5f yel & multi 5 5
718 A173 15f pink & multi 15 8
719 A173 30f lt bl & multi 28 15
720 A173 80f lil & multi 70 40

Arab Postal Union, 25th anniversary.

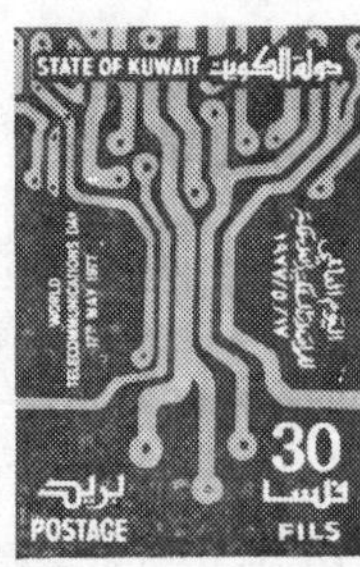

Electronic Tree — A174

**1977, May 17 Litho. Perf. 12x12½**

721 A174 30f brn & red 40 18
722 A174 80f grn & red 1.00 48

World Telecommunications Day.

Sheik Sabah A175

Games Emblem A176

**1977, June 1 Photo. Perf. 11½x12**

723 A175 15f bl & multi 12 15
724 A175 25f yel & multi 22 15
725 A175 30f red & multi 30 18
726 A175 80f vio & multi 90 50
727 A175 100f dp org & multi 1.00 60
728 A175 150f ultra & multi 1.50 90
729 A175 200f ol & multi 2.00 1.20
*Nos. 723-729 (7)* 6.04 3.68

**1977, Oct. 1 Litho. Perf. 12**

730 A176 30f multi 25 25
731 A176 80f multi 65 50

4th Asian Basketball Youth Championship, Oct. 1-15.

Dome of the Rock, Bishop Capucci, Fatima Bernawi, Sheik Abu Tair — A177

**1977, Nov. 1 Perf. 14**

732 A177 30f multi 50 25
733 A177 80f multi 1.00 60

Struggle for the liberation of Palestine.

Children and Houses A178

Children's Paintings: No. 735, Women musicians. No. 736, Boats. No. 737, Women preparing food (vert.). No. 738, Women and children (vert.). No. 739, Seated woman (vert.).

**1977, Nov. Photo. Perf. 13½x13**

734 A178 15f lt grn & multi 12 10
735 A178 15f yel & multi 12 10
736 A178 30f brt yel & multi 25 18
737 A178 30f lt vio & multi 25 18
738 A178 80f blk & multi 65 50
739 A178 80f rose & multi 65 50
*Nos. 734-739 (6)* 2.04 1.56

Dentist Treating Patient A179

**1977, Dec. 3**

740 A179 30f grn & multi 25 25
741 A179 80f vio & multi 75 50

10th Arab Dental Union Congress, Kuwait, Dec. 3-6.

Ships Unloading Water A180

Designs: Water resources in Kuwait. 30f, 80f, 100f, vertical.

**Perf. 14x13½, 13½x14**

**1978, Jan. 25 Litho.**

742 A180 Block of four 50 28
a 5f *shown* 10 6
b 5f *Home delivery by camel* 10 6
c 5f *Man with water bags* 10 6
d 5f *Man with wheelbarrow* 10 6
743 A180 Block of four 75 35
a 10f *Well* 16 8
b 10f *Trough* 16 8
c 10f *Water hole* 16 8
d 10f *Irrigation* 16 8
744 A180 Block of four 1.10 50
a 15f *Sheep drinking* 25 12
b 15f *Laundresses* 25 12
c 15f *Sheep and camels drinking* 25 12
d 15f *Water stored in skins* 25 12
745 A180 Block of four 1.25 65
a 20f *Animals at well* 30 15
b 20f *Water in home* 30 15
c 20f *Water pot* 30 15
d 20f *Communal fountain* 30 15
746 A180 Block of four 1.50 85
a 25f *Distillation plant* 35 20
b 25f *Motorized delivery* 35 20
c 25f *Water trucks* 35 20
d 25f *Water towers* 35 20
747 A180 Block of four 1.75 1.00
a 30f *Shower bath* 42 22
b 30f *Water tower* 42 22
c 30f *Gathering rain water* 42 22
d 30f *2 water towers* 42 22
748 A180 Block of four 5.25 2.75
a 80f *Donkey with water bags* 1.25 65
b 80f *Woman with water can* 1.25 65
c 80f *Woman with water skin* 1.25 65
d 80f *Loading tank car* 1.25 65
749 A180 Block of four 6.25 3.50
a 100f *Truck delivering water* 1.50 85
b 100f *Barnyard water supply* 1.50 85
c 100f *Children at water basin* 1.50 85
d 100f *Well in courtyard* 1.50 85
*Nos. 742-749 (8)* 18.35 9.88

Radar, Torch, Minarets A181

**1978, Feb. 25 Litho. Perf. 14x14½**

750 A181 30f multi 25 18
751 A181 80f multi 75 50

17th National Day.

Man with Smallpox, Target — A182

**1978, Apr. 17 Litho. Perf. 12½**

752 A182 30f vio & multi 25 18
753 A182 80f grn & multi 75 50

Global eradication of smallpox.

Antenna and ITU Emblem A183

**1978, May 17 Perf. 14**

754 A183 30f sil & multi 25 18
755 A183 80f sil & multi 75 50

10th World Telecommunications Day.

Sheik Sabah — A184

**1978, June 28 Litho. Perf. 13x14**

**Portrait in Brown**

**Size: 21½x27mm.**

756 A184 15f grn & gold 10 10
757 A184 30f org & gold 20 20
758 A184 80f rose lil & gold 50 50
759 A184 100f lt grn & gold 60 60
760 A184 130f lt brn & gold 80 80
761 A184 180f vio & gold 1.25 1.10

**Size: 23½x29mm.**

762 A184 1d red & gold 6.50 6.00
763 A184 4d bl & gold 26.00 24.00
*Nos. 756-763 (8)* 35.95 33.30

Mt. Arafat, Pilgrims, Holy Kaaba A185

**1978, Nov. 9 Photo. Perf. 11½**

764 A185 30f multi 25 20
765 A185 80f multi 65 50

Pilgrimage to Mecca.

UN and Anti-Apartheid Emblems — A186

**1978, Nov. 27 Litho. Perf. 12**

766 A186 30f multi 20 16
767 A186 80f multi 48 40
768 A186 180f multi 1.25 90

Anti-Apartheid Year.

Refugees, Human Rights Emblems A187

**1978, Dec. 10 Photo. *Perf. 13x13½***

*769* A187 30f multi 25 20
*770* A187 80f multi 75 50
*771* A187 100f multi 1.00 60

Declaration of Human Rights, 30th anniversary.

Information Center — A188

**1978, Dec. 26 Photo. *Perf. 13***

*772* A188 5f multi 5 5
*773* A188 15f multi 12 8
*774* A188 30f multi 25 16
*775* A188 80f multi 60 40

New Kuwait Information Center.

Kindergarten A189

**1979, Jan. 24 Photo. *Perf. 13½x14***

*776* A189 30f multi 25 20
*777* A189 80f multi 65 50

International Year of the Child.

Flag and Peace Doves — A190

**1979, Feb. 25 *Perf. 14½x14***

*778* A190 30f multi 25 20
*779* A190 80f multi 65 50

18th National Day.

Modern Agriculture in Kuwait — A191

**1979, Mar. 13 Photo. *Perf. 14***

*780* A191 30f multi 25 20
*781* A191 80f multi 65 50

4th Congress of Arab Agriculture Ministers of the Gulf and Arabian Peninsula.

World Map, Book, Symbols of Learning A192

**1979, Mar. 22**

*782* A192 30f multi 25 20
*783* A192 80f multi 65 50

Cultural achievements of the Arabs.

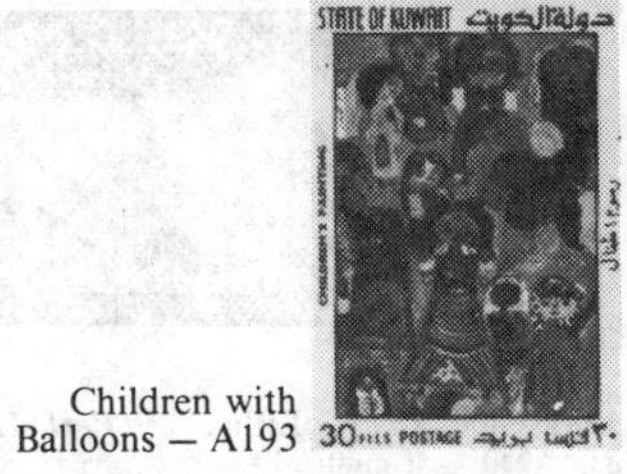

Children with Balloons — A193

Children's Paintings: No. 785, Boys flying kites. No. 786, Girl and doves. No. 787, Children and houses (horiz.). No. 788, Four children (horiz.). No. 789, Children sitting in circle (horiz.).

**1979, Apr. 18 Photo. *Perf. 14***

*784* A193 30f yel & multi 20 16
*785* A193 30f buft & multi 20 16
*786* A193 30f pale yel & multi 20 16
*787* A193 80f lt bl & multi 52 45
*788* A193 80f yel grn & multi 52 45
*789* A193 80f lil & multi 52 45
*Nos. 784-789 (6)* 2.16 1.83

Cables, ITU Emblem, People A194

**1979, May 17**

*790* A194 30f multi 25 20
*791* A194 80f multi 70 55

World Telecommunications Day.

Military Sports Council Emblem — A195

**1979, June 1 Photo. *Perf. 14***

*792* A195 30f multi 25 20
*793* A195 80f multi 65 55

29th International Military Soccer Championship.

Child, Industrial Landscape, Environmental Emblems — A196

**1979, June 5 *Perf. 12x11½***

*794* A196 30f multi 25 20
*795* A196 80f multi 65 55

World Environment Day, June 5.

Children Holding Globe, UNESCO Emblem — A197

**1979, July 25 Litho. *Perf. 11½x12***

*796* A197 30f multi 25 20
*797* A197 80f multi 65 55
*798* A197 130f multi 1.00 80

International Bureau of Education, Geneva, 50th anniversary.

Kuwait Kindergartens, 25th Anniversary A198

Children's Drawings: 80f, Children waving flags.

**1979, Sept. 15 Litho. *Perf. 12½***

*799* A198 30f multi 40 28
*800* A198 80f multi 1.00 70

Pilgrims at Holy Ka'aba, Mecca Mosque A199

**1979, Oct. 29 *Perf. 14x14½***

*801* A199 30f multi 25 20
*802* A199 80f multi 75 55

Hegira (Pilgrimage Year).

International Palestinian Solidarity Day — A200

**1979, Nov. 29 Photo. *Perf. 11½x12***

*803* A200 30f multi 1.00 50
*804* A200 80f multi 2.25 1.00

Kuwait Airways 25th Anniversary A201

**1979, Dec. 24 Photo. *Perf. 13x13½***

*805* A201 30f multi 38 30
*806* A201 80f multi 1.00 80

19th National Day — A202

**1980, Feb. 25 Litho. *Perf. 14x14½***

*807* A202 30f multi 25 20
*808* A202 80f multi 65 55

1980 Population Census A203

**1980, Mar. 18 *Perf. 13½x14***

*809* A203 30f multi 30 20
*810* A203 80f multi 85 55

World Health Day A204

**1980, Apr. 7**

*811* A204 30f multi 30 20
*812* A204 80f multi 85 55

Kuwait Municipality, 50th Anniversary A205

**1980, May 1 Photo. *Perf. 14***

*813* A205 15f multi 15 10
*814* A205 30f multi 30 20
*815* A205 80f multi 85 55

Citizens of Kuwait A206

Future Kuwait (Children's Drawings): 80f, Super highway.

**1980, May 14 Litho. *Perf. 14x14½***

*816* A206 30f multi 30 20
*817* A206 80f multi 85 55

World Environment Day — A207

**1980, June 5 Litho. *Perf. 12x11½***

*818* A207 30f multi 30 20
*819* A207 80f multi 85 55

Swimming, Moscow '80 and Kuwait Olympic Committee Emblems — A208

**1980, July 19 Litho. *Perf. 12x12½***

*820* A208 15f *Volleyball* 12 10
*821* A208 15f *Tennis* 12 10
*822* A208 30f *shown* 25 20
*823* A208 30f *Weight lifting* 25 20

*824* A208 30f *Basketball* 25 20
*825* A208 30f *Judo* 25 20
*826* A208 80f *Gymnast* 80 55
*827* A208 80f *Badminton* 80 55
*828* A208 80f *Fencing* 80 55
*829* A208 80f *Soccer* 80 55
*Nos. 820-829 (10)* 4.44 3.20

22nd Summer Olympic Games, Moscow, July 19-Aug. 3. Stamps of same denomination se-tenant.

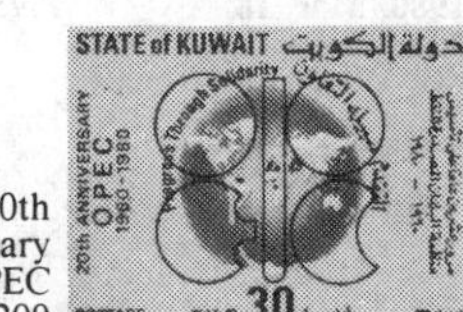


20th Anniversary of OPEC A209

**1980, Sept. 16 Litho. *Perf. 14x14½***
*830* A209 30f multi 30 20
*831* A209 80f multi 85 55

Hegira (Pilgrimage Year) — A210

**1980, Nov. 9 Photo. *Perf. 12x11½***
*832* A210 15f multi 15 10
*833* A210 30f multi 30 20
*834* A210 80f multi 85 55

Dome of the Rock, Jerusalem A211

**1980, Nov. 29 *Perf. 12x11½***
*835* A211 30f multi 50 20
*836* A211 80f multi 1.25 55

International Palestinian Solidarity Day.

Avicenna (980-1037), Philosopher and Physician A212

Conference Emblem A213

**1980, Dec. 7 *Perf. 12x12½***
*837* A212 30f multi 50 20
*838* A212 80f multi 1.00 55

**1981, Jan. 12 Photo. *Perf. 13½x13***
*839* A213 30f multi 30 20
*840* A213 80f multi 85 55

First Islamic Medical Conference.

Girl in Wheelchair A214

International Year of the Disabled: 30f, Man in wheelchair playing billiards (vert.).

***Perf. 13½x13, 13x13½***
**1981, Jan. 26 Photo.**
*841* A214 30f multi 30 20
*842* A214 80f multi 85 55

20th National Day — A215

**1981, Feb. 25 Litho. *Perf. 13x13½***
*843* A215 30f multi 30 20
*844* A215 80f multi 85 55

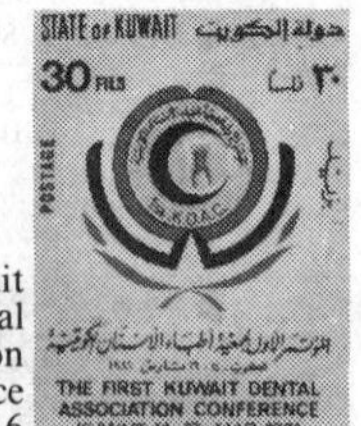


First Kuwait Dental Association Conference A216

**1981, Mar. 14 *Perf. 11½x12***
*845* A216 30f multi 38 25
*846* A216 80f multi 1.10 70

International Red Cross Day — A217

**1981, May 8 Photo. *Perf. 14***
*847* A217 30f multi 38 25
*848* A217 80f multi 1.10 70

13th World Telecommunications Day — A218

**1981, May 17 Litho. *Perf. 14½x14***
*849* A218 30f multi 30 20
*850* A218 80f multi 85 55

World Environment Day — A219

**1981, June 5 Photo. *Perf. 12***
*851* A219 30f multi 38 25
*852* A219 80f multi 1.10 70

Sief Palace — A220

A221

**1981, Sept. 16 Litho. *Perf. 12***
*853* A220 5f multi 5 5
*854* A220 10f multi 10 10
*855* A220 15f multi 12 15
*856* A220 25f multi 20 20
*857* A220 30f multi 25 20
*858* A220 40f multi 30 20
*859* A220 60f multi 45 25
*860* A220 80f multi 60 40
*861* A220 100f multi 75 60
*862* A220 115f multi 90 70
*863* A220 130f multi 1.00 90
*864* A220 150f multi 1.25 90
*865* A220 180f multi 1.50 1.00
*866* A220 250f multi 2.00 1.15
*867* A220 500f multi 4.00 1.50
*868* A221 1d multi 7.50 2.00
*869* A221 2d multi 15.00 3.00
*870* A221 3d multi 22.50 9.00
*871* A221 4d multi 30.00 11.00
*Nos. 853-871 (19)* 88.47 33.30

Islamic Pilgrimage A222

**1981, Oct. 7 Photo. *Perf. 13x13½***
*872* A222 30f multi 32 25
*873* A222 80f multi 1.10 70

World Food Day — A223

**1981, Oct. 16 Litho. *Perf. 13***
*874* A223 30f multi 38 25
*875* A223 80f multi 1.10 70

20th Anniv. of Natl. Television — A224

**1981, Dec. 30 Photo. *Perf. 14***
*876* A224 30f multi 38 25
*877* A224 80f multi 1.10 70

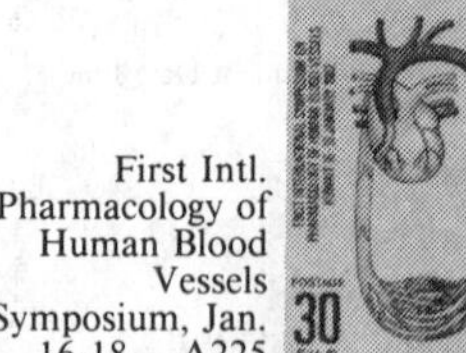


First Intl. Pharmacology of Human Blood Vessels Symposium, Jan. 16-18 — A225

**1982, Jan. 16 Photo. *Perf. 14***
*878* A225 30f multi 38 50
*879* A225 80f multi 1.10 70

21st Natl. Day — A226

**1982, Feb. 25 *Perf. 13½x13***
*880* A226 30f multi 38 25
*881* A226 80f multi 1.10 70

Scouting Year A227

**1982, Mar. 22 Photo. *Perf. 12x11½***
*882* A227 30f multi 45 30
*883* A227 80f multi 1.25 80

Arab Pharmacists' Day — A228

**1982, Apr. 2 Litho. *Perf. 12x11½***
*884* A228 30f lt grn & multi 38 25
*885* A228 80f pink & multi 1.10 70

World Health Day — A229

Arab Postal Union, 30th Anniv. — A230

**1982, Apr. 7 Litho. *Perf. 13½x13***
*886* A229 30f multi 38 25
*887* A229 80f multi 1.10 70

**1982, Apr. 12 Photo. *Perf. 13½x13***
*888* A230 30f multi 30 20
*889* A230 80f multi 85 55

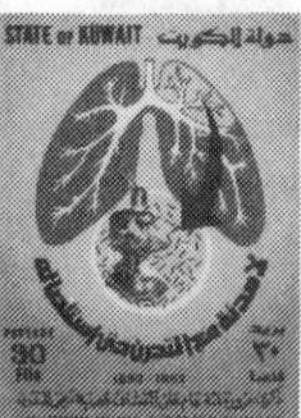


TB Bacillus Centenary A231

**1982, May 24 Litho. *Perf. 11½x12***
*890* A231 30f multi 30 20
*891* A231 80f multi 85 55

1982 World Cup A232

**1982, June 17 Photo. *Perf. 14***

| | | |
|---|---|---|
| *892* A232 30f multi | 30 | 20 |
| *893* A232 80f multi | 85 | 55 |

10th Anniv. of Science and Natural History Museum — A233

**1982, July 14 *Perf. 14***

| | | |
|---|---|---|
| *894* A233 30f multi | 30 | 20 |
| *895* A233 80f multi | 85 | 55 |

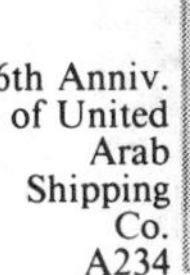

6th Anniv. of United Arab Shipping Co. A234

Designs: Freighters.

**1982, Sept. 1 *Perf. 13***

| | | |
|---|---|---|
| *896* A234 30f multi | 40 | 20 |
| *897* A234 80f multi | 1.00 | 55 |

Arab Day of the Palm Tree — A235

**1982, Sept. 15 *Perf. 14***

| | | |
|---|---|---|
| *898* A235 30f multi | 30 | 20 |
| *899* A235 80f multi | 85 | 55 |

Islamic Pilgrimage A236

**1982, Sept. 26 Litho.**

| | | |
|---|---|---|
| *900* A236 15f multi | 15 | 10 |
| *901* A236 30f multi | 30 | 20 |
| *902* A236 80f multi | 85 | 55 |

Desert Flowers & Plants — A237

**1983, Jan. 25 Litho. *Perf. 12***

| | | | |
|---|---|---|---|
| *903* | Strip of 10 | 1.00 | 80 |
| *a.-j* | A237 10f. Any single | 10 | 8 |
| *904* | Strip of 10 | 1.25 | 1.00 |
| *a.-j* | A237 15f. Any single | 12 | 10 |
| *905* | Strip of 10 | 2.50 | 2.00 |
| *a.-j* | A237 30f. Any single | 25 | 20 |
| *906* | Strip of 10 | 3.00 | 2.50 |
| *a.-j* | A237 40f. Any single | 30 | 25 |
| *907* | Strip of 10 | 6.25 | 5.25 |
| *a.-j* | A237 80f. Any single | 60 | 52 |
| | *Nos. 903-907 (5)* | 14.00 | 11.55 |

22nd Natl. Day — A238

**1983, Feb. 25 Litho. *Perf. 12½***

| | | |
|---|---|---|
| *908* A238 30f multi | 30 | 20 |
| *909* A238 80f multi | 85 | 55 |

25th Anniv. of Intl. Maritime Org. A239

**1983, Mar. 17 Photo. *Perf. 14***

| | | |
|---|---|---|
| *910* A239 30f multi | 30 | 20 |
| *911* A239 80f multi | 85 | 55 |

Map of Middle East and Africa, Conference Emblem — A240

**1983, Mar. 19 *Perf. 13***

| | | |
|---|---|---|
| *912* A240 15f multi | 15 | 10 |
| *913* A240 30f multi | 30 | 20 |
| *914* A240 80f multi | 85 | 55 |

3rd Intl. Conference on the Impact of Viral Diseases on the Development of the Middle East and Africa, Mar. 19-27.

World Health Day A241

**1983, Apr. 7 *Perf. 12x11½***

| | | |
|---|---|---|
| *915* A241 15f multi | 15 | 10 |
| *916* A241 30f multi | 30 | 20 |
| *917* A241 80f multi | 85 | 55 |

World Communications Year — A242

**1983, May 17 Photo. *Perf. 13x13½***

| | | |
|---|---|---|
| *918* A242 15f multi | 15 | 10 |
| *919* A242 30f multi | 30 | 20 |
| *920* A242 80f multi | 85 | 55 |

World Environment Day — A243

**1983, June 5 Litho. *Perf. 12½***

| | | |
|---|---|---|
| *921* A243 15f multi | 15 | 10 |
| *922* A243 30f multi | 30 | 20 |
| *923* A243 80f multi | 85 | 55 |

Wall of Old Jerusalem A244

**1983, July 25 Litho. *Perf. 12***

| | | |
|---|---|---|
| *924* A244 15f multi | 30 | 10 |
| *925* A244 30f multi | 55 | 20 |
| *926* A244 80f multi | 85 | 55 |

World Heritage Year.

Islamic Pilgrimage A245

**1983, Sept. 15 Photo. *Perf. 11½***

| | | |
|---|---|---|
| *927* A245 15f multi | 15 | 10 |
| *928* A245 30f multi | 30 | 20 |
| *929* A245 80f multi | 85 | 55 |

Intl. Palestinian Solidarity Day A246

**1983, Nov. 29 Photo. *Perf. 14***

| | | |
|---|---|---|
| *930* A246 15f multi | 25 | 10 |
| *931* A246 30f multi | 50 | 20 |
| *932* A246 80f multi | 85 | 55 |

21st Pan Arab Medical Congress, Jan. 30-Feb. 2 — A247

**1984, Jan. 30 Litho. *Perf. 14½x14***

| | | |
|---|---|---|
| *933* A247 15f pur & multi | 15 | 10 |
| *934* A247 30f bl grn & multi | 30 | 20 |
| *935* A247 80f pink & multi | 85 | 55 |

Key, Natl. Emblem, and Health Establishments Emblem A248

**1984, Feb. 20 Photo. *Perf. 13x13½***

| | | |
|---|---|---|
| *936* A248 15f multi | 15 | 10 |
| *937* A248 30f multi | 30 | 20 |
| *938* A248 80f multi | 85 | 55 |

Inauguration of Amiri and Al-Razi Hospitals, Allergy Center and Medical Stores Center.

23rd National Day — A249

**1984, Feb. 25 Litho. *Perf. 13½***

| | | |
|---|---|---|
| *939* A249 15f multi | 15 | 10 |
| *940* A249 30f multi | 30 | 20 |
| *941* A249 80f multi | 85 | 55 |

2nd Kuwait Intl. Medical Science Conference, Mar. 4-8 — A250

**1984, Mar. 4 Photo. *Perf. 12***
**Granite Paper**

| | | |
|---|---|---|
| *942* A250 15f multi | 15 | 10 |
| *943* A250 30f multi | 30 | 20 |
| *944* A250 80f multi | 85 | 55 |

30th Anniv. of Kuwait Airways Corp. A251

**1984, Mar. 15 *Perf. 13½***

| | | |
|---|---|---|
| *946* A251 30f multi | 30 | 20 |
| *947* A251 80f multi | 85 | 55 |

Al-Arabi Magazine, 25th Anniv. — A252

**1984, Mar. 20 *Perf. 14½x14***

| | | |
|---|---|---|
| *948* A252 15f multi | 15 | 10 |
| *949* A252 30f multi | 30 | 20 |
| *950* A252 80f multi | 85 | 55 |

World Health Day — A253

**1984, Apr. 7 *Perf. 12***

| | | |
|---|---|---|
| *951* A253 15f multi | 15 | 10 |
| *952* A253 30f multi | 30 | 20 |
| *953* A253 80f multi | 85 | 55 |

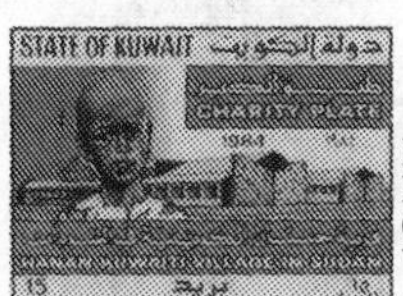
Hanan Kuwaiti Orphan Village, Sudan A254

**1984, May 15 Litho. *Perf. 12***

| | | |
|---|---|---|
| *954* A254 15f multi | 15 | 10 |
| *955* A254 30f multi | 30 | 20 |
| *956* A254 80f multi | 85 | 55 |

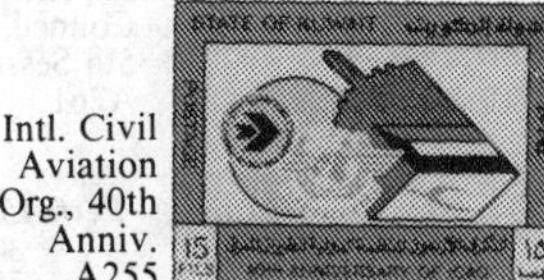
Intl. Civil Aviation Org., 40th Anniv. A255

**1984, June 12**

| | | | |
|---|---|---|---|
| *957* A255 15f multi | | 15 | 10 |
| *958* A255 30f multi | | 30 | 20 |
| *959* A255 80f multi | | 85 | 55 |

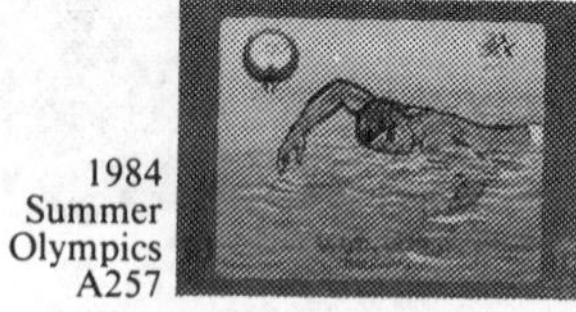

Arab Youth Day — A256

**1984, July 5** ***Perf. 13½***

| | | |
|---|---|---|
| *960* A256 30f multi | 30 | 20 |
| *961* A256 80f multi | 85 | 55 |

1984 Summer Olympics A257

**1984, July 28** ***Perf. 15x14***

| | | |
|---|---|---|
| *962* A257 30f Swimming | 25 | 20 |
| *963* A257 30f Hurdles | 25 | 20 |
| *964* A257 80f Judo | 65 | 55 |
| *965* A257 80f Equestrian | 65 | 55 |

Stamps of same denomination se-tenant.

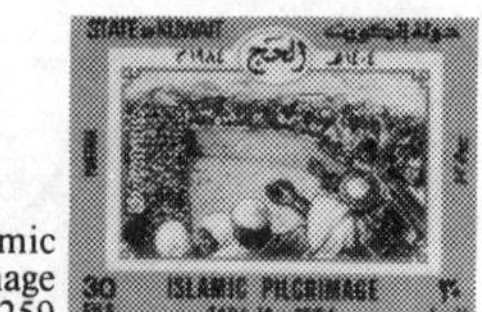

10th Anniv. of the Science Club A258

**1984, Aug. 11 Photo.** ***Perf. 13½x13***

| | | |
|---|---|---|
| *966* A258 15f multi | 15 | 10 |
| *967* A258 30f multi | 30 | 20 |
| *968* A258 80f multi | 75 | 55 |

Islamic Pilgrimage A259

**1984, Sept. 4 Photo.** ***Perf. 12x11½***

| | | |
|---|---|---|
| *969* A259 30f multi | 30 | 20 |
| *970* A259 80f multi | 75 | 55 |

INTELSAT '84, 20th Anniv. — A260

**1984, Oct. 1 Litho.** ***Perf. 13½x14***

| | | |
|---|---|---|
| *971* A260 30f multi | 30 | 20 |
| *972* A260 80f multi | 75 | 55 |

G.C.C. Supreme Council, 5th Session A261

**1984, Nov. 24 Litho.** ***Perf. 15x14***

| | | |
|---|---|---|
| *973* A261 30f multi | 30 | 20 |
| *974* A261 80f multi | 75 | 55 |

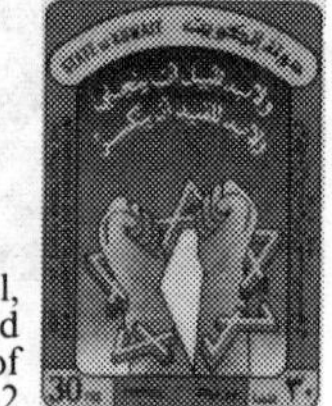

Map of Israel, Fists, Shattered Star of David — A262

**1984, Nov. 29 Photo.** ***Perf. 12***

| | | |
|---|---|---|
| *975* A262 30f multi | 30 | 20 |
| *976* A262 80f multi | 75 | 55 |

Intl. Palestinian Solidarity Day.

Globe, Emblem A263

**1984, Dec. 24** ***Perf. 12x11½***
**Granite Paper**

| | | |
|---|---|---|
| *977* A263 30f multi | 40 | 15 |
| *978* A263 80f multi | 1.25 | 50 |

Kuwait Oil Co., 50th anniv.

Intl. Youth Year — A264

**1985, Jan. 15** ***Perf. 13½***

| | | |
|---|---|---|
| *979* A264 30f multi | 25 | 15 |
| *980* A264 80f multi | 75 | 50 |

24th National Day — A265

**1985, Feb. 25 Litho.** ***Perf. 14x15***

| | | |
|---|---|---|
| *981* A265 30f multi | 25 | 15 |
| *982* A265 80f multi | 75 | 50 |

Intl. Program for the Development of Communications — A266

**1985, Mar. 4 Photo.** ***Perf. 11½***
**Granite Paper**

| | | |
|---|---|---|
| *983* A266 30f multi | 25 | 15 |
| *984* A266 80f multi | 75 | 50 |

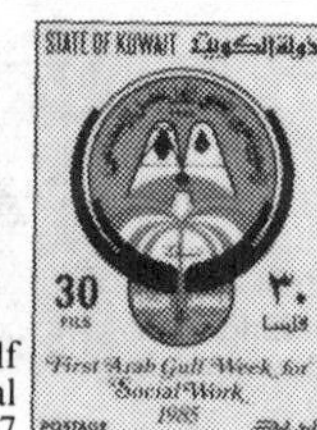

1st Arab Gulf Week for Social Work — A267

**1985, Mar. 13 Photo.** ***Perf. 13½x13***

| | | |
|---|---|---|
| *985* A267 30f multi | 30 | 20 |
| *986* A267 80f multi | 75 | 50 |

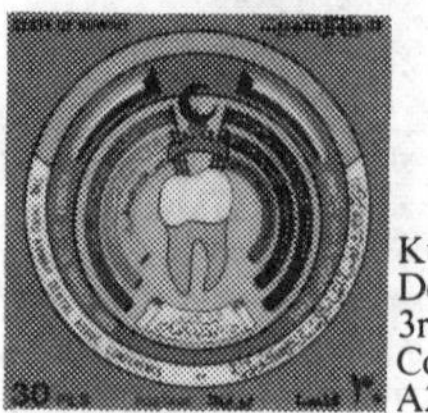

Kuwait Dental Assoc. 3rd Conference A268

**1985, Mar. 23 Litho.** ***Perf. 13½***

| | | |
|---|---|---|
| *987* A268 30f multi | 25 | 15 |
| *988* A268 80f multi | 75 | 50 |

1985 Census — A269

**1985, Apr. 1** ***Perf. 14x13½***

| | | |
|---|---|---|
| *989* A269 30f multi | 25 | 15 |
| *990* A269 80f multi | 75 | 50 |

World Health Day — A270

**1985, Apr. 7 Photo.** ***Perf. 13½x13***

| | | |
|---|---|---|
| *991* A270 30f multi | 25 | 15 |
| *992* A270 80f multi | 75 | 50 |

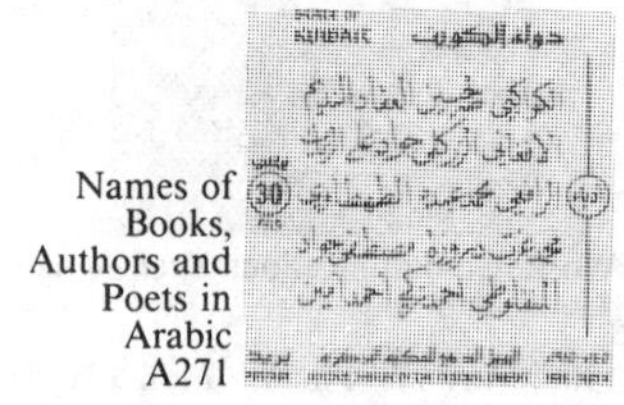

Names of Books, Authors and Poets in Arabic A271

**1985, May 20** ***Perf. 12***
**Granite Paper**

| | | |
|---|---|---|
| *993* Block of 4 | 1.10 | 75 |
| *a.-d* A271 30f. Any single | 27 | 27 |
| *994* Block of 4 | 3.00 | 2.00 |
| *a.-d* A271 80f. Any single | 75 | 50 |

Central Library, 50th anniv.

World Environment Day — A272

**1985, June 5** ***Perf. 11½***

| | | |
|---|---|---|
| *995* A272 30f multi | 30 | 20 |
| *996* A272 80f multi | 75 | 50 |

Org. of Petroleum Exporting Countries, 25th Anniv. A273

**1985, Sept. 1** ***Perf. 13x13½***

| | | |
|---|---|---|
| *997* A273 30f multi | 30 | 20 |
| *998* A273 80f multi | 75 | 50 |

Inauguration of Civil Information System — A274

**1985, Oct. 1 Photo.** ***Perf. 12x11½***

| | | |
|---|---|---|
| *999* A274 30f multi | 30 | 20 |
| *1000* A274 80f multi | 75 | 50 |

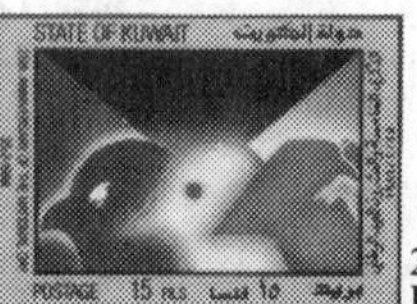

Intl. Day of Solidarity with Palestinian People — A275

**1985, Nov. 29 Photo.** ***Perf. 12***

| | | |
|---|---|---|
| *1001* A275 15f multi | 25 | 10 |
| *1002* A275 30f multi | 45 | 20 |
| *1003* A275 80f multi | 80 | 50 |

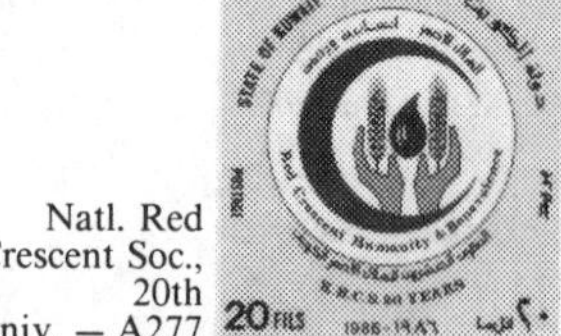

25th Natl. Day — A276

**1986, Feb. 25 Litho.** ***Perf. 15x14***

| | | |
|---|---|---|
| *1004* A276 15f multi | 15 | 10 |
| *1005* A276 30f multi | 35 | 20 |
| *1006* A276 80f multi | 85 | 50 |

Natl. Red Crescent Soc., 20th Anniv. — A277

**1986, Mar. 26 Photo.** ***Perf. 13½***

| | | |
|---|---|---|
| *1007* A277 20f multi | 15 | 12 |
| *1008* A277 25f multi | 20 | 16 |
| *1009* A277 70f multi | 60 | 45 |

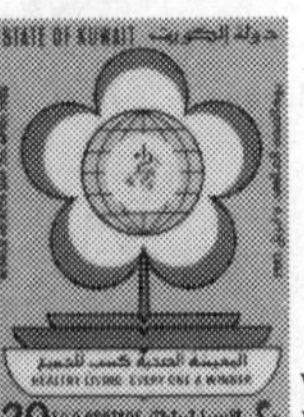

World Health Day — A278

**1986, Apr. 7** *Perf. 13½x13*
*1010* A278 20f multi 15 12
*1011* A278 25f multi 20 16
*1012* A278 70f multi 60 45

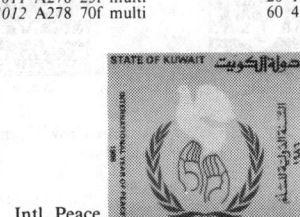

Intl. Peace Year A279

**1986, June 5 Litho.** *Perf. 13½*
*1013* A279 20f multi 15 12
*1014* A279 25f multi 25 16
*1015* A279 70f multi 65 45

United Arab Shipping Co., 10th Anniv. A280

**1986, July 1 Photo.** *Perf. 12x11½*
*1016* A280 20f Al Mirqab 15 12
*1017* A280 70f Al Mubarakiah 60 45

Gulf Bank, 25th Anniv. A281

**1986, Oct. 1 Photo.** *Perf. 12½*
*1018* A281 20f multi 14 10
*1019* A281 25f multi 18 14
*1020* A281 70f multi 50 35

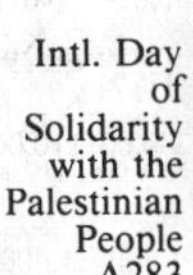
Sadu Art — A282

Various tapestry weavings.

**1986, Nov. 5 Photo.** *Perf. 12x11½*
**Granite Paper**
*1021* A282 20f multi 14 10
*1022* A282 70f multi 50 35
*1023* A282 200f multi 1.40 1.00

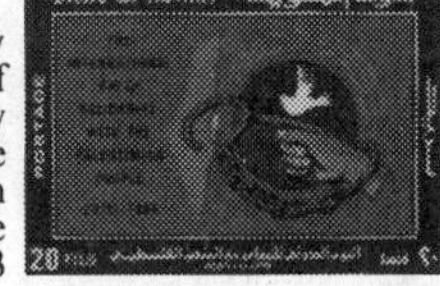
Intl. Day of Solidarity with the Palestinian People A283

**1986, Nov. 29** *Perf. 14*
*1024* A283 20f multi 14 10
*1025* A283 25f multi 18 14
*1026* A283 70f multi 50 35

5th Islamic Summit Conference — A284

**1987, Jan. 26 Litho.** *Perf. 14½*
*1027* A284 25f multi 18 14
*1028* A284 50f multi 35 25
*1029* A284 150f multi 1.10 80

26th Natl. Day A285

**1987, Feb. 25** *Perf. 13½x14*
*1030* A285 50f multi 35 25
*1031* A285 150f multi 1.10 80

Natl. Health Sciences Center A286

**1987, Mar. 15 Photo.** *Perf. 12x11½*
**Granite Paper**
*1032* A286 25f multi 18 14
*1033* A286 150f multi 1.10 80

3rd Kuwait Intl. Medical Sciences Conference on Infectious Diseases in Developing Countries.

World Health Day — A287

**1987, Apr. 7 Photo.** *Perf. 13x13½*
*1034* A287 25f multi 18 14
*1035* A287 50f multi 38 25
*1036* A287 150f multi 1.10 80

Day of Ghods (Jerusalem) — A288

**1987, June 7 Photo.** *Perf. 12x11½*
*1037* A288 25f multi 20 15
*1038* A288 50f multi 40 30
*1039* A288 150f multi 1.20 90

Islamic Pilgrimage to Miqat Wadi Mihrim — A289

**1987, Aug. Photo.** *Perf. 13½x14½*
*1040* A289 25f multi 20 15
*1041* A289 50f multi 40 30
*1042* A289 150f multi 1.20 90

Arab Telecommunications Day — A290

**1987, Sept. 9 Litho.** *Perf. 14x13½*
*1043* A290 25f multi 20 15
*1044* A290 50f multi 40 30
*1045* A290 150f multi 1.20 70

World Maritime Day A291

**1987, Sept. 24** *Perf. 12x11½*
**Granite Paper**
*1046* A291 25f multi 20 15
*1047* A291 50f multi 40 30
*1048* A291 150f multi 1.25 90

Al Qurain Housing Project — A292

**1987, Oct. 5** *Perf. 13x13½*
*1049* A292 25f multi 20 15
*1050* A292 50f multi 40 30
*1051* A292 150f multi 1.25 90

Port Authority, 10th Anniv. — A293

**1987, Nov. 16 Litho.** *Perf. 14½*
*1052* A293 25f multi 20 15
*1053* A293 50f multi 40 30
*1054* A293 150f multi 1.25 90

Intl. Day of Solidarity with the Palestinian People — A294

**1987, Nov. 29** *Perf. 14x13½*
*1055* A294 25f multi 20 15
*1056* A294 50f multi 40 30
*1057* A294 150f multi 1.25 90

Women's Cultural and Social Soc., 25th Anniv. — A295

National Day, 27th Anniv. — A296

**1988, Feb. 3 Photo.** *Perf. 14*
*1058* A295 25f multi 20 20
*1059* A295 50f multi 40 40
*1060* A295 150f multi 1.25 1.25

**1988, Feb. 25**
*1061* A296 25f multi 20 20
*1062* A296 50f multi 40 40
*1063* A296 150f multi 1.25 1.25

World Health Day, WHO 40th Anniv. — A297

**1988, Apr. 7 Litho.** *Perf. 14x15*
*1064* A297 25f multi 20 20
*1065* A297 50f multi 40 40
*1066* A297 150f multi 1.25 1.25

Regional Marine Environment Day — A298

**1988, Apr. 24 Photo.** *Perf. 12*
**Granite Paper**
*1067* A298 35f brt ultra, beige & lt blue 30 30
*1068* A298 50f brt ultra, pale yel grn & lt blue 45 45
*1069* A298 150f brt ultra, pale lil rose & lt blue 1.30 1.30

Kuwait Regional Convention on the Marine Environment, 10th anniv. See Iraq Nos. 1333-1336.

Kuwait Teachers Soc., 25th Anniv. — A299

**1988, July 10 Photo. *Perf. 14***

| | | | | |
|---|---|---|---|---|
| *1070* | A299 | 25f multi | 20 | 14 |
| *1071* | A299 | 50f multi | 40 | 25 |
| *1072* | A299 | 150f multi | 1.25 | 85 |

Pilgrimage to Mecca A300

**1988, July Litho. *Perf. 13½x14***

| | | | | |
|---|---|---|---|---|
| *1073* | A300 | 25f multi | 20 | 14 |
| *1074* | A300 | 50f multi | 40 | 25 |
| *1075* | A300 | 150f multi | 1.25 | 85 |

Uprising in Occupied Palestine A301

Design: Palestinian "Children of Stone" in struggle with occupying Zionists.

**1988, Sept. 15 Photo. *Perf. 13x13½***

| | | | | |
|---|---|---|---|---|
| *1076* | A301 | 50f multi | 48 | 32 |
| *1077* | A301 | 150f multi | 1.40 | 95 |

Dated 1987.

Arab Housing Day — A302

**1988, Oct. 3**

| | | | | |
|---|---|---|---|---|
| *1078* | A302 | 50f multi | 42 | 28 |
| *1079* | A302 | 100f multi | 82 | 55 |
| *1080* | A302 | 150f multi | 1.25 | 85 |

## AIR POST STAMPS

Air Post Stamps of India, 1929-30, Overprinted type "c"

**1933-34 Wmk. 196 *Perf. 14***

| | | | | |
|---|---|---|---|---|
| *C1* | AP1 | 2a dull green | 5.50 | *12.50* |
| *C2* | AP1 | 3a deep blue | 1.25 | 1.75 |
| *C3* | AP1 | 4a gray olive | 75.00 | *150.00* |
| *C4* | AP1 | 6a bister ('34) | 2.75 | 3.75 |

Counterfeits of Nos. C1-C4 exist.

**Catalogue values for unused stamps in this section, from this point to the end of the section, are for Never Hinged items.**

Dakota and Comet Planes AP1

***Perf. 11x11½***

**1964, Nov. 29 Litho. Unwmk.**

| | | | | |
|---|---|---|---|---|
| *C5* | AP1 | 20f multicolored | 15 | 22 |
| *C6* | AP1 | 25f multicolored | 50 | 30 |
| *C7* | AP1 | 30f multicolored | 70 | 30 |
| *C8* | AP1 | 45f multicolored | 80 | 40 |

10th anniversary of Kuwait Airways.

## POSTAGE DUE STAMPS

**Catalogue values for unused stamps in this section, from this point to the end of the section, are for Never Hinged items.**

D1

***Perf. 14x15***

**1963, Oct. 19 Unwmk. Litho.**

**Inscriptions in Black**

| | | | | |
|---|---|---|---|---|
| *J1* | D1 | 1f ocher | 30 | 10 |
| *J2* | D1 | 2f lilac | 35 | 15 |
| *J3* | D1 | 5f blue | 45 | 20 |
| *J4* | D1 | 8f pale grn | 50 | 25 |
| *J5* | D1 | 10f yellow | 55 | 30 |
| *J6* | D1 | 25f brick red | 95 | 50 |
| | | *Nos. J1-J6 (6)* | 3.10 | 1.50 |

D2

**1965, Apr. 1 *Perf. 13***

| | | | | |
|---|---|---|---|---|
| *J7* | D2 | 4f rose & yel | 15 | 15 |
| *J8* | D2 | 15f dp rose & bl | 30 | 25 |
| *J9* | D2 | 40f bl & brt yel grn | 75 | 60 |
| *J10* | D2 | 50f grn & pink | 1.00 | 75 |
| *J11* | D2 | 100f dk bl & yel | 1.75 | 1.50 |
| | | *Nos. J7-J11 (5)* | 3.95 | 3.25 |

## OFFICIAL STAMPS

Stamps of India, 1911-23, Overprinted

KUWAIT KUWAIT

SERVICE SERVICE
d e

**1923-24 Wmk. Star. (39) *Perf. 14***

| | | | | |
|---|---|---|---|---|
| *O1* | A47(d) | ½a green | 10 | *55* |
| *O2* | A48(d) | 1a brown | 12 | *55* |
| *O3* | A58(d) | 1½a chocolate | 40 | *1.60* |
| *O4* | A49(d) | 2a violet | 32 | *1.75* |
| *O5* | A57(d) | 2a 6p ultra | 32 | *2.75* |
| *O6* | A51(d) | 3a brn org | 2.25 | *8.00* |
| *O7* | A51(d) | 3a ultra ('24) | 75 | *2.25* |
| *O8* | A52(d) | 4a ol grn | 1.25 | *4.00* |
| *O9* | A54(d) | 8a red vio | 2.00 | *8.00* |
| *O10* | A56(e) | 1r grn & brn | 5.00 | *14.00* |
| *O11* | A56(e) | 2r brn & car rose | 7.50 | *27.50* |
| *O12* | A56(e) | 5r vio & ultra | 40.00 | *110.00* |
| *O13* | A56(e) | 10r car & grn | 62.50 | *150.00* |
| *O14* | A56(e) | 15r ol grn & ultra | 100.00 | *250.00* |
| | | *Nos. O1-O14 (14)* | 222.51 | |

Stamps of India, 1926-30, Overprinted

KUWAIT KUWAIT

SERVICE SERVICE
f g

**1929-33 Wmk. 196**

| | | | | |
|---|---|---|---|---|
| *O15* | A48 (f) | 1a dk brn | 30 | *1.40* |
| *O16* | A60 (f) | 2a violet | 15.00 | *22.50* |
| *O17* | A51 (f) | 3a blue | 45 | *1.75* |
| *O18* | A61 (f) | 4a ol grn | 2.50 | *4.25* |
| *O19* | A54 (f) | 8a red vio | 1.50 | *5.00* |
| *O20* | A55 (f) | 12a claret | 6.25 | *10.00* |
| *O21* | A56 (g) | 1r grn & brn | 3.75 | *15.00* |
| *O22* | A56 (g) | 2r buff & car rose | 5.00 | *30.00* |
| *O23* | A56 (g) | 5r dk vio & ultra | 15.00 | *100.00* |
| *O24* | A56 (g) | 10r car & grn | 50.00 | *140.00* |
| *O25* | A56 (g) | 15r ol grn & ultra | 100.00 | *325.00* |
| | | *Nos. O15-O25 (11)* | 199.75 | |

# LABUAN

LOCATION — An island in the East Indies, about six miles off the northwest coast of Borneo.

GOVT. — A British possession, administered as a part of the North Borneo Colony.

AREA — 35 sq. mi.

POP. — 8,963 (estimated).

CAPITAL — Victoria.

The stamps of Labuan were replaced by those of Straits Settlements in 1906.

100 Cents = 1 Dollar

Queen Victoria — A1

Wmk. 46- C A over Crown

On Nos. 1, 2, 3, 4 and 11 the watermark is 32mm high. It is always placed sideways and extends over two stamps.

**1879, May Engr. Wmk. 46 *Perf. 14***

| | | | | |
|---|---|---|---|---|
| *1* | A1 | 2c green | 575.00 | 575.00 |
| *2* | A1 | 6c orange | 110.00 | 100.00 |
| *3* | A1 | 12c carmine | 675.00 | 375.00 |
| *4* | A1 | 16c blue | 27.50 | 30.00 |

**1880-82 Wmk. Crown and C. C. (1)**

| | | | | |
|---|---|---|---|---|
| *5* | A1 | 2c green | 6.75 | 8.25 |
| *6* | A1 | 6c orange | 27.50 | 25.00 |
| *7* | A1 | 8c car ('82) | 32.50 | 35.00 |
| *8* | A1 | 10c yel brn | 30.00 | 32.50 |
| *9* | A1 | 12c carmine | 85.00 | 72.50 |
| *10* | A1 | 16c bl ('81) | 30.00 | 30.00 |

A2

A3

A3a

A4

**1880 Wmk. C. A. over Crown. (46)**

| | | | | |
|---|---|---|---|---|
| *11* | A2 | 6c on 16c bl (with additional "6" across original value) (R) | 1,000. | 575.00 |

**1880-83 Wmk. Crown and C. C. (1)**

| | | | | |
|---|---|---|---|---|
| *12* | A2 | 8c on 12c car ('80) | 450.00 | 400.00 |
| *a.* | | Original value not obliterated | 575.00 | 450.00 |
| *b.* | | Additional surcharge "8" across original value | 525.00 | 400.00 |
| *c.* | | "8" inverted | 525.00 | 400.00 |
| *13* | A3 | 8c on 12c car ('81) | 110.00 | 125.00 |
| *14* | A3a | 8c on 12c car ('81) | 26.00 | 32.50 |
| *a.* | | "Eighr" | *3,250.* | |
| *b.* | | Inverted surcharge | 1,000. | |
| *c.* | | Double surch. | 325.00 | 325.00 |
| *15* | A4 | $1 on 16c bl (R) ('83) | 2,250. | |

On No. 12 the original value is obliterated by a pen mark in either black or red.

**1883-86 Wmk. Crown and C. A. (2)**

| | | | | |
|---|---|---|---|---|
| *16* | A1 | 2c green | 10.00 | 10.00 |
| *a.* | | Horiz. pair, imperf. btwn. | 1,600. | |
| *17* | A1 | 2c rose red ('85) | 1.65 | 1.65 |
| *18* | A1 | 8c carmine | 90.00 | 42.50 |
| *19* | A1 | 8c dk vio ('85) | 4.25 | 4.25 |
| *20* | A1 | 10c yel brn | 9.00 | 10.50 |
| *21* | A1 | 10c blk brn ('86) | 4.50 | 4.50 |
| *22* | A1 | 16c blue | 37.50 | 40.00 |
| *23* | A1 | 16c gray bl ('86) | 32.50 | 35.00 |
| *24* | A1 | 40c ocher | 8.00 | 9.00 |
| | | *Nos. 16-24 (9)* | 197.40 | 157.40 |

Nos. 1-10, 16-24 are in sheets of 10.

A5

A6

A7

A8

**1885 Wmk. Crown and C. C. (1)**

| | | | | |
|---|---|---|---|---|
| *25* | A5 | 2c on 16c bl | 675.00 | 575.00 |

**Wmk. Crown and C. A. (2)**

| | | | | |
|---|---|---|---|---|
| *26* | A5 | 2c on 8c car | 47.50 | 47.50 |
| *a.* | | Double surcharge | | |
| *27* | A6 | 2c on 16c bl | 37.50 | 37.50 |
| *a.* | | Double surcharge of | | *2,000.* |
| *28* | A7 | 2c on 8c car | 17.50 | 17.50 |

**1891**

**Black or Red Surcharge.**

| | | | | |
|---|---|---|---|---|
| *29* | A8 | 6c on 8c vio | 2.00 | 2.00 |
| *a.* | | 6c on 8c dk vio | 14.00 | 14.00 |
| *b.* | | Double surcharge | 130.00 | 130.00 |
| *c.* | | "Cents" omitted | 250.00 | 250.00 |
| *d.* | | Inverted surcharge | 25.00 | 25.00 |
| *e.* | | Double surcharge, one inverted | 190.00 | 190.00 |
| *f.* | | Double surcharge, both inverted | 190.00 | 190.00 |
| *g.* | | "6" omitted | 175.00 | |
| *30* | A8 | 6c on 8c dk vio (R) | 200.00 | 110.00 |
| *a.* | | Inverted surcharge | 200.00 | 110.00 |

**Wmk. 46**

| | | | | |
|---|---|---|---|---|
| *31* | A8 | 6c on 16c bl | 1,600. | 1,400. |
| *a.* | | Inverted surch. | 2,100. | 1,800. |

**Wmk. 2**

| | | | | |
|---|---|---|---|---|
| *32* | A8 | 6c on 40c ocher | 1,600. | 1,800. |
| *a.* | | Inverted surch. | 2,250. | 2,000. |

From Jan. 1, 1890, to Jan. 1, 1906, Labuan was administered by the British North Borneo Co. During that period Nos. 33-39, 42-83, 53a, 63a, 64a, 65a, 85, 96-118, 103a, 107a, Ji-J9, J3a and J6a were canceled to order by bars forming an oval. Values for these stamps used are for those with this form of cancellation. These stamps with dated town cancellation sell for three to five times as such as those with with bar cancellation.

**1892 Engr. Unwmk.**

| No. | Type | Description | Unused | Used |
|---|---|---|---|---|
| *33* | A1 | 2c rose | 50 | 30 |
| *34* | A1 | 6c yel grn | 2.25 | 30 |
| *35* | A1 | 8c violet | 1.25 | 30 |
| *36* | A1 | 10c brown | 1.00 | 30 |
| *37* | A1 | 12c dp ultra | 1.65 | 30 |
| *38* | A1 | 16c gray | 1.65 | 30 |
| *39* | A1 | 40c ocher | 4.50 | 32 |
| | | *Nos. 33-39 (7)* | 12.80 | 2.12 |

The 2c, 8c and 10c are in sheets of 30; others in sheets of 10.

Nos. 39 and 38 Surcharged

Two
CENTS

**1893**

| No. | Type | Description | Unused | Used |
|---|---|---|---|---|
| *40* | A1 | 2c on 40c ocher | 40.00 | 35.00 |
| *a.* | | Inverted surcharge | 125.00 | 130.00 |
| *41* | A1 | 6c on 16c gray | 82.50 | 77.50 |
| *a.* | | Inverted surcharge | 150.00 | 150.00 |
| *b.* | | Surcharge sideways | 110.00 | 110.00 |
| *c.* | | "Six" omitted | | |
| *d.* | | "Cents" omitted | | |

Surcharges on Nos. 40-41 each exist in 10 types. Counterfeits exist.

**1894, April Litho.**

| No. | Type | Description | Unused | Used |
|---|---|---|---|---|
| *42* | A1 | 2c brt rose | 85 | 14 |
| *43* | A1 | 6c yel grn | 3.00 | 30 |
| *a.* | | Horizontal pair, imperf. between | 1,300. | |
| *44* | A1 | 8c brt vio | 5.00 | 30 |
| *45* | A1 | 10c brown | 6.75 | 30 |
| *46* | A1 | 12c lt ultra | 6.75 | 30 |
| *47* | A1 | 16c gray | 6.75 | 30 |
| *48* | A1 | 40c orange | 8.50 | 50 |
| | | *Nos. 42-48 (7)* | 37.60 | 2.14 |

Counterfeits exist.

Dyak Chieftain — A9

Malayan Sambar — A10

Sago Palm — A11

Argus Pheasant — A12

Arms of North Borneo — A13

Dhow — A14

Saltwater Crocodile — A15

Mt. Kinabalu — A16

Arms of North Borneo — A17

**1894 Engr.**

| No. | Type | Description | Unused | Used |
|---|---|---|---|---|
| *49* | A9 | 1c lil & blk | 1.10 | 32 |
| *a.* | | Vert. pair, imperf. btwn. | 300.00 | 190.00 |
| *50* | A10 | 2c bl & blk | 2.75 | 28 |
| *a.* | | Imperf. pair | 275.00 | |
| *51* | A11 | 3c bis & blk | 2.75 | 28 |
| *52* | A12 | 5c grn & blk | 3.25 | 28 |
| *53* | A13 | 6c brn, red & blk | 3.75 | 28 |
| *a.* | | Imperf., pair | | 250.00 |
| *54* | A14 | 8c red & blk | 1.90 | 28 |
| *55* | A15 | 12c org & blk | 5.00 | 32 |
| *56* | A16 | 18c ol bis & blk | 5.00 | 32 |
| *57* | A17 | 24c lil & bl | 4.75 | 32 |
| | | *Nos. 49-57 (9)* | 30.25 | 2.68 |

A18

A19

A20

A21

**1895, June Litho.**

| No. | Type | Description | Unused | Used |
|---|---|---|---|---|
| *58* | A18 | 4c on $1 red | 95 | 35 |
| *59* | A18 | 10c on $1 red | 1.50 | 35 |
| *60* | A18 | 20c on $1 red | 3.00 | 35 |
| *61* | A18 | 30c on $1 red | 2.75 | 35 |
| *62* | A18 | 40c on $1 red | 4.00 | 35 |
| | | *Nos. 58-62 (5)* | 12.20 | 1.75 |

**1896**

| No. | Type | Description | Unused | Used |
|---|---|---|---|---|
| *63* | A19 | 25c bl grn | 15.00 | 80 |
| *a.* | | Without overprint | 6.25 | 2.00 |
| *b.* | | As "a" imperf., pair | 30.00 | |
| *64* | A20 | 50c claret | 17.50 | 80 |
| *a.* | | Without overprint | 7.50 | 2.00 |
| *b.* | | As "a" imperf., pair | 30.00 | |
| *65* | A21 | $1 dk bl | 19.00 | 80 |
| *a.* | | Without overprint | 9.50 | 2.00 |
| *b.* | | As "a" imperf., pair | 30.00 | |

Nos. 49-54 Overprinted

1846
JUBILEE
1896

**1896**

| No. | Type | Description | Unused | Used |
|---|---|---|---|---|
| *66* | A9 | 1c lil & blk | 4.25 | 70 |
| *a.* | | Orange ovpt. | 82.50 | 82.50 |
| *b.* | | Double ovpt. | 100.00 | 100.00 |
| *c.* | | "JEBILEE" | | 200.00 |
| *67* | A10 | 2c bl & blk | 5.25 | 70 |
| *a.* | | Vertical pair, imperf. btwn. | 175.00 | |
| *b.* | | "JEBILEE" | 375.00 | |
| *68* | A11 | 3c bis & blk | 5.25 | 70 |
| *a.* | | Double ovpt. | 77.50 | 35.00 |
| *b.* | | Triple ovpt. | 800.00 | |
| *c.* | | "JEBILEE" | | 725.00 |
| *69* | A12 | 5c grn & blk | 7.00 | 70 |
| *a.* | | Double ovpt. | 72.50 | 72.50 |
| *70* | A13 | 6c brn red & blk | 5.50 | 70 |
| *a.* | | Double ovpt. | 95.00 | 95.00 |
| *71* | A14 | 8c rose & blk | 7.00 | 70 |
| | | *Nos. 66-71 (6)* | 34.25 | 4.20 |

Cession of Labuan to Great Britain, 50th anniversary.

Dyak Chieftain — A22

Malayan Sambar — A23

Sago Palm — A24

Argus Pheasant — A25

A26

Dhow — A27

Saltwater Crocodile — A28

Mt. Kinabalu "Postal Revenue" — A29

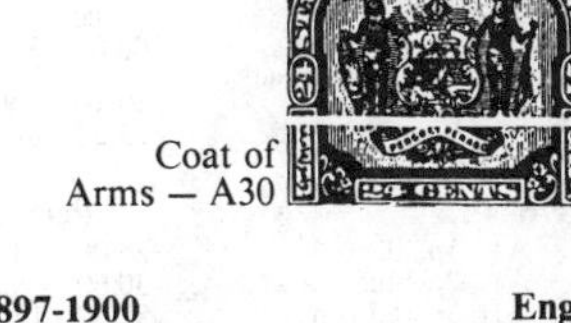
Coat of Arms — A30

**1897-1900 Engr.**

| No. | Type | Description | Unused | Used |
|---|---|---|---|---|
| *72* | A22 | 1c lil & blk | 1.65 | 20 |
| *72A* | A22 | 1c red brn & blk | 5.00 | 20 |
| *73* | A23 | 2c bl & blk | 5.00 | 20 |
| *74* | A23 | 2c grn & blk ('00) | 4.50 | 20 |
| *75* | A24 | 3c bis & blk | 5.00 | 20 |
| *76* | A25 | 5c grn & blk | 6.00 | 30 |
| *77* | A25 | 5c lt bl & blk ('00) | 6.00 | 20 |
| *78* | A26 | 6c brn red & blk | 4.75 | 30 |
| *79* | A27 | 8c red & blk | 5.00 | 35 |
| *80* | A28 | 12c red & blk | 17.00 | 50 |
| *81* | A29 | 18c ol bis & blk | 5.00 | 50 |
| *82* | A30 | 24c gray lil & bl | 5.00 | 50 |
| | | *Nos. 72-82 (12)* | 69.90 | 3.65 |

The 2c, 3c 6c and 18c exist in pairs, imperf. between.

"Postage & Revenue" — A31

"Postage & Revenue" — A32

**1897**

| No. | Type | Description | Unused | Used |
|---|---|---|---|---|
| *83* | A31 | 18c bis & blk | 30.00 | 1.00 |
| *84* | A32 | 24c brn lil & bl | 10.50 | 65 |

A33

A34

**1898**

| No. | Type | Description | Unused | Used |
|---|---|---|---|---|
| *85* | A33 | 12c red & blk | 9.50 | 52 |
| *86* | A34 | 18c bis & blk | 9.50 | 60 |

Nos. 83-86 are inscribed "Postage & Revenue."

Regular Issue Surcharged in Black

4
CENTS

**1899**

| No. | Type | Description | Unused | Used |
|---|---|---|---|---|
| *87* | A25 | 4c on 5c grn & blk | 7.00 | 6.75 |
| *88* | A26 | 4c on 6c brn red & blk | 7.00 | 6.75 |
| *89* | A27 | 4c on 8c red & blk | 7.00 | 6.25 |
| *90* | A33 | 4c on 12c red & blk | 7.00 | 7.00 |
| *91* | A34 | 4c on 18c bis & blk | 7.00 | 7.00 |
| *a.* | | Double surch. | 225.00 | 225.00 |
| *92* | A32 | 4c on 24c lil & bl | 6.50 | 5.50 |
| *93* | A19 | 4c on 25c bl grn | 5.50 | 5.50 |
| *94* | A20 | 4c on 50c cl | 5.50 | 5.50 |
| *95* | A21 | 4c on $1 dk bl | 5.50 | 5.50 |
| | | *Nos. 87-95 (9)* | 58.00 | 55.75 |

Orangutan A35

Sun Bear A36

Railroad Train — A37

Crown — A38

**1899-1901**

| No. | Type | Description | Unused | Used |
|---|---|---|---|---|
| *96* | A35 | 4c yel brn & blk | 3.25 | 18 |
| *a.* | | Vertical pair, imperf. between | 165.00 | |
| *97* | A35 | 4c car & blk ('00) | 7.50 | 22 |
| *98* | A36 | 10c gray vio & dk brn ('01) | 9.50 | 35 |
| *99* | A37 | 16c org brn & grn (G) ('01) | 9.50 | 35 |

***Perf. 12½ to 16 and Compound.***

**1902-03 Engr.**

| No. | Type | Description | Unused | Used |
|---|---|---|---|---|
| *99A* | A38 | 1c vio & blk | 1.40 | 25 |
| *100* | A38 | 2c grn & blk | 80 | 25 |
| *100A* | A38 | 3c sep & blk | 1.40 | 25 |
| *101* | A38 | 4c car & blk | 42 | 25 |
| *102* | A38 | 8c org & blk | 45 | 25 |
| *103* | A38 | 10c sl bl & brn | 45 | 25 |
| *a.* | | Vert. pair, imperf. between | | 325.00 |
| *104* | A38 | 12c yel & blk | 1.00 | 25 |
| *105* | A38 | 16c org brn & grn | 1.00 | 25 |
| *106* | A38 | 18c bis brn & blk | 1.00 | 25 |
| *107* | A38 | 25c grnsh bl & grn | 1.10 | 25 |
| *a.* | | 25c grnsh bl & blk | | 125.00 |

| No. | Type | Description | Unused | Used |
|---|---|---|---|---|
| *108* | A38 | 50c gray lil & vio | 1.00 | 32 |
| *109* | A38 | $1 org & red brn | 1.40 | 40 |
| | | *Nos. 99A-109 (12)* | 11.42 | 3.22 |

Part perforate examples exist of 12c (vert. strip of 3 imperf. between) and 16c (vert. pair, imperf. between).

Regular Issue of 1896-97 Surcharged in Black

**4 cents**

**1904**

| No. | Type | Description | Unused | Used |
|---|---|---|---|---|
| *110* | A25 | 4c on 5c grn & blk | 7.00 | 90 |
| *111* | A26 | 4c on 6c brn red & blk | 7.00 | 90 |
| *112* | A27 | 4c on 8c red & blk | 7.00 | 90 |
| *113* | A33 | 4c on 12c red & blk | 7.00 | 90 |
| *114* | A34 | 4c on 18c bis & blk | 7.00 | 90 |
| *115* | A32 | 4c on 24c brn lil & bl | 7.00 | 90 |
| *116* | A19 | 4c on 25c bl grn | 7.00 | 90 |
| *117* | A20 | 4c on 50c cl | 7.00 | 90 |
| *a.* | | Double surch. | 200.00 | |
| *118* | A21 | 4c on $1 dk bl | 7.00 | 90 |
| | | *Nos. 110-118 (9)* | 63.00 | 8.10 |

Stamps of North Borneo, 1893, and Labuan No. 65a Overprinted in Black:

LABUAN a — LABUAN b — LABUAN c

**1905**

| No. | Type | Description | Unused | Used |
|---|---|---|---|---|
| *119* | A30 (a) | 25c sl bl | 650.00 | 425.00 |
| *120* | A21 (c) | $1 blue | | 425.00 |
| *121* | A33 (b) | $2 gray grn | 2,750. | 950.00 |
| *122* | A34 (c) | $5 red vio | 3,250. | 850.00 |
| *123* | A35 (c) | $10 brown | | *3,000.* |

### POSTAGE DUE STAMPS

Regular Issues Overprinted

POSTAGE DUE

**1901** **Unwmk.** ***Perf. 14.***

| No. | Type | Description | Unused | Used |
|---|---|---|---|---|
| *J1* | A23 | 2c grn & blk | 9.00 | 25 |
| *a.* | | Double overprint | 140.00 | |
| *J2* | A24 | 3c bis & blk | 9.00 | 25 |
| *J3* | A35 | 4c car & blk | 10.50 | 25 |
| *a.* | | Double ovpt. | | 77.50 |
| *J4* | A25 | 5c lt bl & blk | 9.00 | 25 |
| *J5* | A26 | 6c brn red & blk | 10.50 | 35 |
| *J6* | A27 | 8c red & blk | 10.50 | 25 |
| *a.* | | Center inverted, ovpt. reading down | | *3,000.* |
| *J7* | A33 | 12c red & blk | 18.00 | 1.25 |
| *J8* | A34 | 18c ol bis & blk | 6.00 | 35 |
| *J9* | A32 | 24c brn lil & bl | 9.00 | 48 |
| | | *Nos. J1-J9 (9)* | 91.50 | 3.68 |

The stamps of Labuan were superseded by those of Straits Settlements in 1907.

## LAGOS

LOCATION — In West Africa bordering on the former Southern Nigeria Colony.
GOVT. — Former British Crown Colony and Protectorate.
AREA — 3,460 sq. mi. (approx.)
POP. — 1,500,000 (1901).
CAPITAL — Lagos.

This territory was purchased by the British in 1861 and placed under the Governor of Sierra Leone. In 1874 it was detached and formed part of the Gold Coast Colony until 1886 when the Protectorate of Lagos was established. It was chartered to the Royal Niger Company until 1899 when all territories of this Company were surrendered to the Crown of Great Britain and formed into the Northern and Southern Nigeria Protectorates. In 1906 Lagos and Southern Nigeria were united to form the Colony and Protectorate of Southern Nigeria.

12 Pence = 1 Shilling

Queen Victoria — A1

**Wmk. Crown and C. C. (1)**

**1874-75** **Typo.** ***Perf. 12½***

| No. | Type | Description | Unused | Used |
|---|---|---|---|---|
| *1* | A1 | 1p lilac | 32.50 | 32.50 |
| *2* | A1 | 2p blue | 32.50 | 25.00 |
| *3* | A1 | 3p red brn ('75) | 77.50 | 27.50 |
| *a.* | | Value in chnt | 77.50 | 27.50 |
| *4* | A1 | 4p rose | 55.00 | 32.50 |
| *5* | A1 | 6p bl grn | 55.00 | 14.00 |
| *a.* | | Value in yel grn | 55.00 | 14.00 |
| *6* | A1 | 1sh org ('75) | 200.00 | 50.00 |
| *a.* | | Value 15½mm instead of 16½mm long | 260.00 | 140.00 |
| | | *Nos. 1-6 (6)* | 452.50 | 181.50 |

**1876** ***Perf. 14***

| No. | Type | Description | Unused | Used |
|---|---|---|---|---|
| *7* | A1 | 1p lilac | 25.00 | 4.50 |
| *8* | A1 | 2p blue | 30.00 | 6.25 |
| *9* | A1 | 3p red brn | 82.50 | 12.50 |
| *10* | A1 | 4p rose | 140.00 | 6.25 |
| *11* | A1 | 6p green | 47.50 | 7.75 |
| *12* | A1 | 1sh orange | 575.00 | 77.50 |
| | | *Nos. 7-12 (6)* | 900.00 | 114.75 |

The 4p exists with watermark sideways.

**1882-1902** **Wmk. 2**

| No. | Type | Description | Unused | Used |
|---|---|---|---|---|
| *13* | A1 | ½p grn ('86) | 30 | 30 |
| *14* | A1 | 1p lilac | 15.00 | 7.50 |
| *15* | A1 | 1p car rose | 35 | 28 |
| *16* | A1 | 2p blue | 90.00 | 7.50 |
| *17* | A1 | 2p gray | 16.00 | 3.25 |
| *18* | A1 | 2p lil & bl ('87) | 1.10 | 65 |
| *19* | A1 | 2½p ultra ('91) | 60 | 38 |
| *a.* | | 2½p bl | 65.00 | 32.50 |
| *20* | A1 | 3p org brn | 7.25 | 5.75 |
| *21* | A1 | 3p lil & brn org ('91) | 1.50 | 1.65 |
| *22* | A1 | 4p rose | 65.00 | 6.50 |
| *23* | A1 | 4p violet | 27.50 | 5.25 |
| *24* | A1 | 4p lil & blk ('87) | 1.50 | 1.50 |
| *25* | A1 | 5p lil & grn ('94) | 3.00 | *10.00* |
| *26* | A1 | 6p ol grn | 3.00 | *6.25* |
| *27* | A1 | 6p lil & red vio ('87) | 1.90 | 2.50 |
| *28* | A1 | 6p lil & car rose ('02) | 7.50 | *15.00* |
| *29* | A1 | 7½p lil & car rose ('94) | 1.90 | *7.50* |
| *30* | A1 | 10p lil & yel ('94) | 1.90 | *6.25* |
| *31* | A1 | 1sh org ('85) | 5.00 | *7.50* |
| *32* | A1 | 1sh grn & blk ('87) | 3.00 | *5.00* |
| *33* | A1 | 2sh6p ol brn ('86) | 275.00 | 225.00 |
| *34* | A1 | 2sh6p grn & car rose ('87) | 16.00 | *27.50* |
| *35* | A1 | 5sh bl ('86) | 800.00 | 350.00 |
| *36* | A1 | 5sh grn & ultra ('87) | 27.50 | *42.50* |
| *37* | A1 | 10sh brn vio ('86) | 15.00 | 950.00 |
| *38* | A1 | 10sh grn & brn ('87) | 52.50 | *95.00* |

Excellent forgeries exist of Nos. 33, 35 and 37 on paper with genuine watermark.

No. 24 Surcharged in Black

HALF PENNY

**1893**

| No. | Type | Description | Unused | Used |
|---|---|---|---|---|
| *39* | A1 | ½p on 4p lil & blk | 1.50 | 2.00 |
| *a.* | | Double surcharge | 65.00 | 65.00 |
| *b.* | | Triple surcharge | 95.00 | |
| *c.* | | ½p on 2p lil & bl (#18) | | |

Four settings of surcharge.

King Edward VII — A3

**1904, Jan. 22**

| No. | Type | Description | Unused | Used |
|---|---|---|---|---|
| *40* | A3 | ½p grn & bl grn | 2.25 | *4.50* |
| *41* | A3 | 1p vio & blk, *red* | 60 | 18 |
| *42* | A3 | 2p vio & ultra | 6.25 | *9.25* |
| *43* | A3 | 2½p vio & ultra, *bl* | 1.90 | *2.75* |
| *44* | A3 | 3p vio & org brn | 1.40 | 2.50 |
| *45* | A3 | 6p vio & red vio | 11.00 | 4.50 |
| *46* | A3 | 1sh grn & blk | 27.50 | 25.00 |
| *47* | A3 | 2sh6p grn & car rose | 82.50 | *175.00* |
| *48* | A3 | 5sh grn & ultra | 150.00 | *225.00* |
| *49* | A3 | 10sh grn & brn | 375.00 | *775.00* |
| | | *Nos. 40-49 (10)* | 658.40 | 1,223. |

**1904-05** **Wmk. 3**

| No. | Type | Description | Unused | Used |
|---|---|---|---|---|
| *50* | A3 | ½p grn & bl grn | 60 | 60 |
| *51* | A3 | 1p vio & blk, *red* | 42 | 14 |
| *52* | A3 | 2p vio & ultra | 90 | 70 |
| *53* | A3 | 2½p vio & ultra, *bl* | 2.50 | 1.10 |
| *54* | A3 | 3p vio & org brn | 70 | 1.10 |
| *55* | A3 | 6p vio & red vio | 1.65 | 90 |
| *56* | A3 | 1sh grn & blk | 2.75 | 1.65 |
| *57* | A3 | 2sh6p grn & car rose | 8.50 | *20.00* |
| *58* | A3 | 5sh grn & ultra | 8.50 | *22.50* |
| *59* | A3 | 10sh grn & brn | 40.00 | *85.00* |
| | | *Nos. 50-59 (10)* | 66.52 | *133.69* |

The 2½p is on chalky paper, the other values are on both ordinary and chalky.

The stamps of Lagos were superseded by those of Southern Nigeria.

## LEEWARD ISLANDS

LOCATION — A group of islands in the West Indies, southeast of Puerto Rico.
GOVT. — Former British Colony.
AREA — 423 sq. mi.
POP. — 108,847 (1946).
CAPITAL — St. John.

While stamps inscribed "Leeward Islands" were in use, 1890-1956, the colony consisted of the presidencies (now colonies) of Antigua, Montserrat, St. Christopher (St. Kitts) with Nevis and Anguilla, the British Virgin Islands and Dominica (which became a separate colony in 1940).

Each presidency issued its own stamps, using them along with the Leeward Islands general issues. The Leeward Islands federation was abolished in 1956.

12 Pence = 1 Shilling
20 Shillings = 1 Pound
100 Cents = 1 Dollar

**Catalogue values for unused stamps in this country are for Never Hinged items, beginning with Scott 116.**

Queen Victoria — A1

*Leeward Islands stamps can be mounted in Scott's British Leeward Islands Album.*

**Wmk. Crown and C. A. (2)**

**1890** **Typo.** ***Perf. 14.***

| No. | Type | Description | Unused | Used |
|---|---|---|---|---|
| *1* | A1 | ½p lil & grn | 30 | 18 |
| *2* | A1 | 1p lil & car | 45 | 12 |
| *3* | A1 | 2½p lil & ultra | 2.75 | 30 |
| *4* | A1 | 4p lil & org | 3.50 | 3.00 |
| *5* | A1 | 6p lil & brn | 3.50 | *3.50* |
| *6* | A1 | 7p lil & sl | 2.75 | *5.00* |
| *7* | A1 | 1sh grn & car | 16.00 | *17.50* |
| *8* | A1 | 5sh grn & ultra | 105.00 | *135.00* |
| | | *Nos. 1-8 (8)* | 134.25 | 164.60 |

Denomination of Nos. 7-8 are in color on plain tablet: "ONE SHILLING" or "FIVE SHILLINGS."

**Jubilee Issue.**

Regular Issue of 1890 Handstamp Overprinted

**1897**

| No. | Type | Description | Unused | Used |
|---|---|---|---|---|
| *9* | A1 | ½p lil & grn | 5.00 | *12.50* |
| *10* | A1 | 1p lil & car | 5.00 | *11.50* |
| *11* | A1 | 2½p lil & ultra | 5.50 | 11.00 |
| *12* | A1 | 4p lil & org | 13.00 | 20.00 |
| *13* | A1 | 6p lil & brn | 22.50 | 30.00 |
| *14* | A1 | 7p lil & sl | 22.50 | 30.00 |
| *15* | A1 | 1sh grn & car | 100.00 | 140.00 |
| *16* | A1 | 5sh grn & ultra | 475.00 | 650.00 |
| | | *Nos. 9-15 (7)* | 173.50 | 255.00 |

60th year of Queen Victoria's reign.

Excellent counterfeits of Nos. 9 to 16 exist.

All values exist with double overprint, the ½p with inverted overprint.

Stamps of 1890 Surcharged in Black or Red:

One Penny b — One Penny c

**1902**

| No. | Type | Description | Unused | Used |
|---|---|---|---|---|
| *17* | A1(b) | 1p on 4p lil & org | 1.00 | 1.90 |
| *a.* | | Tall narrow "O" in "One" | 15.00 | 16.00 |
| *b.* | | Double surch. | | |
| *18* | A1(b) | 1p on 6p lil & brn | 1.00 | 1.90 |
| *a.* | | Tall narrow "O" in "One" | 21.00 | 21.00 |
| *19* | A1(c) | 1p on 7p lil & sl | 1.25 | 2.50 |

King Edward VII — A4

Numerals of ¼p, 2p, 3p and 2sh6p of type A4 are in color on plain tablet. The 1sh and 5sh denominations are expressed as "ONE SHILLING" and "FIVE SHILLINGS" on plain tablet.

**1902**
20 A4 ½p vio & grn 45 40
21 A4 1p vio & car rose 45 18
22 A4 2p vio & bis 2.00 3.00
23 A4 2½p vio & ultra 4.50 1.25
24 A4 3p vio & blk 2.00 3.50
25 A4 6p vio & brn 1.65 6.00
26 A4 1sh grn & car rose 6.00 7.50
27 A4 2sh6p grn & blk 22.50 40.00
28 A4 5sh grn & ultra 27.50 50.00
*Nos. 20-28 (9)* 67.05 111.83

**1905-11** **Wmk. 3**

**Chalky Paper**
29 A4 ½p vio & grn ('06) 90 1.40
30 A4 1p vio & car rose 2.25 35
31 A4 2p vio & bis ('08) 3.50 7.00
32 A4 2½p vio & ultra 21.00 21.00
33 A4 3p vio & blk 3.75 7.00
34 A4 3p vio, *yel* ('10) 2.25 3.25
35 A4 6p vio & brn ('08) 17.50 27.50
36 A4 6p vio & red vio ('11) 2.50 3.25
37 A4 1sh grn & car rose ('08) 25.00 37.50
38 A4 1sh blk, *grn* ('11) 5.25 8.75
39 A4 2sh 6p blk & red, *bl* ('11) 27.50 50.00
40 A4 5sh grn & red, *yel* ('11) 40.00 60.00
*Nos. 29-40 (12)* 151.40 227.00

Nos. 29 and 33 are also on ordinary paper.

**1907-11**

**Ordinary Paper**
41 A4 ¼p brn ('09) 12 25
42 A4 ½p green 28 22
43 A4 1p carmine 70 15
44 A4 2p gray ('11) 85 5.00
45 A4 2½p ultra 1.40 1.00
*Nos. 41-45 (5)* 3.35 6.62

King George V
A5 A6

Dies I and II, type A5, described at back of volume.

The ½p, 1p, 2½p and 6p denominations of type A5 show the numeral on horizontally-lined tablet. The 1sh and 5sh denominations are expressed as "ONE SHILLING" and "FIVE SHILLINGS" on plain tablet.

Die I.

**1912**

**Ordinary Paper**
46 A5 ¼p brown 12 10
47 A5 ½p green 35 8
48 A5 1p scarlet 32 6
**a.** 1p car 45 6
49 A5 2p gray 2.10 2.00
50 A5 2½p ultra 1.25 1.20

**1912-22**

**Chalky Paper**
51 A5 3p vio, *yellow* 50 62
52 A5 4p blk & red, *yel* (Die II) ('22) 75 2.00
53 A5 6p vio & red vio 1.25 3.75
54 A5 1sh *bl grn*, ol back 1.25 3.50
**a.** 1sh *grn* 3.50 3.00
55 A5 2sh vio & ultra, *bl* (Die II) ('22) 3.50 5.50
56 A5 2sh6p blk & red, *bl* ('14) 8.75 17.50
57 A5 5sh grn & red, *yel* ('14) 7.50 15.00
*Nos. 46-57 (12)* 27.64 51.31

**1914**

**Surface-colored Paper**
58 A5 3p vio, *yel* 35.00 35.00
59 A5 1sh blk, *green* 26.00 35.00
60 A5 5sh grn & red, *yel* 26.00 37.50

Die II

**1921-32** **Wmk. 4**

**Ordinary Paper**
61 A5 ¼p dk brn ('22) 6 6
**a.** ¼p dk brn (I) ('32) 12 20
62 A5 ½p green 10 10
**a.** ½p grn (I) ('32) 75 2.50
63 A5 1p carmine 25 12
**a.** 1p rose red (I) ('32) 80 80
64 A5 1p dp vio ('22) 38 10
65 A5 1½p rose red ('26) 85 15
66 A5 1½p red brn ('29) 42 12
**a.** 1½p red brn (I) ('32) 1.50 2.50
68 A5 2p gray ('22) 85 50
69 A5 2½p org ('23) 5.00 12.50
70 A5 2½p ultra ('27) 42 32
**a.** Die I ('32) 3.00 3.00
71 A5 3p ultra ('23) 5.00 10.00

**Chalky Paper**
72 A5 3p vio, *yel* 55 1.25
73 A5 4p blk & red, *yel* ('23) 1.00 3.75
74 A5 5p vio & ol grn ('22) 38 1.25
75 A5 6p vio & red vio ('23) 3.75 7.50
**a.** Die I ('32) 6.25 10.00
76 A5 1sh blk, *emer* ('23) 1.25 3.75
**a.** 1sh blk, *grn* (I) ('32) 17.50 22.50
77 A5 2sh vio & ultra, *bl* ('22) 5.00 7.50
78 A5 2sh6p blk & red, *bl* ('23) 6.25 7.50
79 A5 3sh grn & vio 6.25 10.00
80 A5 4sh blk & scar 8.75 15.00
81 A5 5sh grn & red, *yel* 20.00 27.50
82 A6 10sh red & grn, *emer* ('28) 40.00 50.00

**Wmk. 3**
83 A6 £1 blk & vio, *red* ('28) 180.00 175.00
*Nos. 61-66,68-83 (22)* 286.51 333.97

**Silver Jubilee Issue.**
Common Design Type
***Perf. 11x12***

**1935, May 6** **Engr.** **Wmk. 4**
96 CD301 1p car & dk bl 32 32
97 CD301 1½p blk & ultra 80 80
98 CD301 2½p ultra & brn 1.40 1.40
99 CD301 1sh brn vio & ind 4.00 4.00

**Coronation Issue.**
Common Design Type

**1937, May 12** ***Perf. 13½x14***
100 CD302 1p carmine 20 20
101 CD302 1½p brown 25 25
102 CD302 2½p brt ultra 40 40

Common Design Types pictured in section before Great Britain.

King George VI
A7 A8

**1938-51** **Typo.** ***Perf. 14.***
103 A7 ¼p brown 6 5
104 A7 ½p green 8 6
105 A7 1p scarlet 12 8
**a.** 1p car ('42) 22 34
106 A7 1½p red brn 12 10
107 A7 2p gray 12 10
108 A7 2½p ultra 14 12
109 A7 3p dl org ('42) 18 12
**a.** 3p brn org 3.50 90
110 A7 6p vio & red vio 25 25
111 A7 1sh blk, *emerald* 70 48
**a.** 1sh blk, *emer*, ol grn back 1.40 1.40
112 A7 2sh vio & ultra, *bl* 1.65 1.10
113 A7 5sh grn & red, *yel* 5.50 5.50
114 A8 10sh red & grn, *emer* 22.50 15.00

Two dies were used for the 1p, differing in thickness of shading line at base of "1."

See Nos. 120-125.

**Wmk. Multiple Crown and C. A. (3)**
***Perf. 13***
115 A8 £1 blk & vio, *scar* 12.50 13.75
**a.** £1 blk & brn pur, *red*, perf. 14 165.00 130.00
**b.** £1 blk & pur, *car*, perf. 14 ('41) 27.50 30.00
**c.** £1 blk & brn pur, *sal*, perf. 14 ('43) 12.50 13.75
**d.** Wmkd. sideways (as #115, perf. 13) *2,000.*
*Nos. 103-115 (13)* 43.92 36.71

**Catalogue values for unused stamps in this section, from this point to the end of the section, are for Never Hinged items.**

**Peace Issue**
Common Design Type
***Perf. 13½x14***

**1946, Nov. 1** **Wmk. 4** **Engr.**
116 CD303 1½p brown 10 10
117 CD303 3p dp org 15 15

**Silver Wedding Issue**
Common Design Types

**1949, Jan. 2** **Photo.** ***Perf. 14x14½***
118 CD304 2½p brt ultra 14 14

**Engraved; Name Typographed**
***Perf. 11½x11***
119 CD305 5sh green 5.75 5.75

George VI Type of 1938.

**1949** **Typo.** ***Perf. 13½x14***
120 A7 ½p gray 6 5
121 A7 1p green 10 6
122 A7 1½p org & blk 14 9
123 A7 2p crim rose 24 15
124 A7 2½p blk & plum 24 15
125 A7 3p ultra 24 15
*Nos. 120-125 (6)* 1.02 65

**UPU Issue**
Common Design Types
**Engr.; Name Typo. on 3p and 6p**

**1949, Oct. 10** ***Perf. 13½, 11x11½***
126 CD306 2½p slate 40 40
127 CD307 3p indigo 60 60
128 CD308 6p red lil 1.25 1.25
129 CD309 1sh bl grn 1.50 1.50

**University Issue**
Common Design Types
***Perf. 14x14½***

**1951, Feb. 16** **Engr.** **Wmk. 4**
130 CD310 3c gray blk & org 30 30
131 CD311 12c lil & rose car 95 95

**Coronation Issue.**
Common Design Type

**1953, June 2** ***Perf. 13½x13***
132 CD312 3c dk grn & blk 25 25

Queen Elizabeth II
A9 A10

**1954, Feb. 22** **Typo.** ***Perf. 14***
133 A9 ½c brown 6 6
134 A9 1c gray 8 8
135 A9 2c green 8 8
136 A9 3c org & blk 12 12
137 A9 4c rose red 16 16
138 A9 5c blk & cl 18 18
139 A9 6c orange 22 22
140 A9 8c dp ultra 25 25
141 A9 12c rose vio & mag 38 38
142 A9 24c blk & grn 60 60
143 A9 48c rose vio & ultra 1.25 1.25
144 A9 60c brn & grn 1.65 1.65
145 A9 $1.20 yel grn & rose red 3.25 3.25

***Perf. 13***
146 A10 $2.40 red & bl grn 5.00 8.00
147 A10 $4.80 blk & cl 9.50 15.00
*Nos. 133-147 (15)* 22.78 31.28

# LESOTHO

LOCATION — An enclave within the Republic of South Africa.

GOVT. — Independent state in British Commonwealth.

AREA — 11,720 sq. mi.

POP. — 1,470,000 (est. 1984).

CAPITAL — Maseru.

Basutoland, the British Crown Colony, became independent October 4, 1966, taking the name Lesotho.

100 Cents = 1 Rand
100 Sente = 1 Maloti (1979)

**Catalogue values for all unused stamps in this country are for Never Hinged items.**

Moshoeshoe I and II — A1

***Perf. 12½x13***

**1966, Oct. 4** **Photo.** **Unwmk.**
1 A1 2½c red brn, blk & red 6 6
2 A1 5c red brn, blk & brt bl 12 12
3 A1 10c red brn, blk & brt grn 25 25
4 A1 20c red brn, blk & red lil 45 45

Issued to commemorate Lesotho's independence, Oct. 4, 1966.

Basutoland Nos. 72-74, 76-82 Overprinted **LESOTHO**

***Perf. 13½***

**1966, Nov. 1** **Wmk. 4** **Engr.**
5 A7 ½c dk brn & gray 5 5
6 A7 1c dp grn & gray blk 6 6
7 A7 2c org & dp bl 8 8
8 A7 3½c dp bl & ind 12 12
9 A7 5c dk grn & org brn 16 16
10 A7 10c rose vio & dk ol 32 32
11 A7 12½c aqua & brn 40 40
12 A7 25c lil rose & dp ultra 80 80
13 A7 50c dp car & blk 1.60 1.60

***Perf. 11½***
14 A8 1r dp cl & blk 4.40 4.40
**a** "Lseotho" 100.00
*Nos. 5-14 (10)* 7.99 7.99

Same Overprint on Nos. 87-91 and Type of 1954

**Wmk. 314** ***Perf. 13½***
15 A7 1c grn & gray blk 6 6
16 A7 2½c car & ol grn 10 10
17 A7 5c dk grn & org brn 20 20
18 A7 12½c aqua & brn 40 40
19 A7 50c dp car & blk 1.40 1.40

***Perf. 11½***
20 A8 1r dp cl & blk 2.75 2.75
**a** "Lseotho" 50.00
*Nos. 15-20 (6)* 4.91 4.91

UNESCO Emblem, Microscope, Book, Violin and Retort — A2

**Unwmk.**

**1966, Dec. 1** **Litho.** ***Perf. 14***
21 A2 2½c grn & ocher 7 7
22 A2 5c ol & brt grn 14 14
23 A2 12½c ver & lt bl 40 40
24 A2 25c dl bl & org 65 65

20th anniv. of UNESCO.

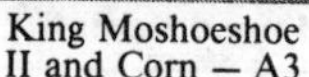

King Moshoeshoe II and Corn — A3

King Moshoeshoe II — A4

Designs: 1c, Bull. 2c, Aloes. 2½c, Basotho hat. 3½c, Merino sheep. 5c, Basotho pony. 10c, Wheat. 12½c, Angora goat. 25c, Maletsunyane Falls. 50c, Diamonds. 1r, Coat of Arms.

***Perf. 13½x14½***

**1967, Apr. 1 Photo. Unwmk.**

*25* A3 ½c vio & grn 5 5
*26* A3 1c dk red & brn 6 5
*27* A3 2c grn & yel 8 6
*28* A3 2½c yel bis & blk 10 8
*29* A3 3½c yel & blk 12 10
*30* A3 5c brt bl & yel bis 18 10
*31* A3 10c gray & ocher 30 20
*32* A3 12½c org & blk 35 30
*33* A3 25c ultra & blk 75 75
*34* A3 50c Prus grn & blk 1.50 1.50
*35* A3 1r gray & multi 2.25 2.25

***Perf. 14½x13½***

*36* A4 2r mag, blk & gold 5.00 5.00
*Nos. 25-36 (12)* 10.74 10.44

See Nos. 47-59.

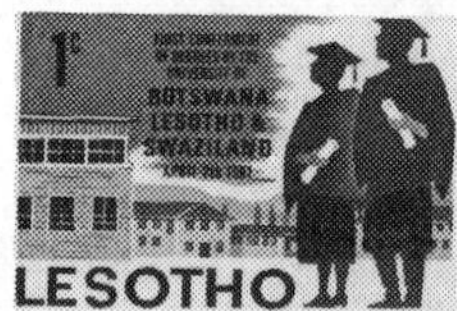

University Buildings and Graduates A4a

**1967, Apr. 7** ***Perf. 14x14½***

*37* A3 1c yel, sep & dp bl 5 5
*38* A3 2½c bl, sep & dp bl 6 6
*39* A3 12½c dl rose, sep & dp bl 25 25
*40* A3 25c lt vio, sep & dp bl 45 45

1st conferment of degrees by the Univ. of Botswana, Lesotho and Swaziland at Roma, Lesotho.

Statue of Moshoeshoe I — A5

Designs: 12½c, Flag of Lesotho. 25c, Crocodile.

**1967, Oct. 4 Photo.** ***Perf. 14***

*41* A5 2½c ap grn & blk 7 7
*42* A5 12½c multi 35 35
*43* A5 25c tan, blk & dp grn 65 65

First anniversary of independence.

Boy Scout and Lord Baden-Powell — A6

***Perf. 14x14½***

**1967, Nov. 1 Photo. Unwmk.**

*44* A6 15c lt ol grn, dk grn & brn 50 50

60th anniversary of the Boy Scouts.

The lack of a price for a listed item does not necessarily indicate rarity.

World Map and WHO Emblem A7

Design: 25c, Nurse and child, arms of Lesotho and WHO emblem.

**1968, Apr. 8 Photo.** ***Perf. 14x14½***

*45* A7 2½c dp bl, car rose & gold 6 5
*46* A7 25c gold, gray grn & redsh brn 45 40

20th anniv. of WHO.

Types of 1967

Wmk. 362- Basotho Hat Multiple

Design: 3c, Sorghum. Others as before.

***Perf. 13½x14½***

**1968-69 Photo. Wmk. 362**

*47* A3 ½c vio & grn 5 5
*48* A3 1c dk red & brn 6 6
*49* A3 2c grn & yel 10 10
*50* A3 2½c yel bis & blk 12 12
*51* A3 3c lt brn, dk brn & grn 18 18
*52* A3 3½c yel & blk 18 18
*53* A3 5c brt bl & yel bis 22 18
*54* A3 10c gray & ocher 55 45
*55* A3 12½c org & blk ('69) 90 75
*56* A3 25c ultra & blk ('69) 1.60 1.25
*57* A3 50c Prus grn & blk ('69) 3.50 2.75
*58* A3 1r gray & multi 6.00 5.50

***Perf. 14½x13½***

*59* A4 2r mag, blk & gold ('69) 15.00 11.50
*Nos. 47-59 (13)* 28.46 23.07

Hunters, Rock Painting A8

Rock Paintings: 3½c, Baboons. 5c, Javelin thrower (vert.). 10c, Archers. 15c, Cranes (vert.). 20c, Eland. 25c, Hunting scene.

***Perf. 14½x14, 14x14½***

**1968, Nov. 1 Photo. Wmk. 362**

*60* A8 3c dk & lt grn & brn 12 12
*61* A8 3½c dk brn & yel 15 15
*62* A8 5c sep, yel & red brn 20 20
*63* A8 10c blk, brt rose & org 45 45
*64* A8 15c ol brn & buff 75 75
*65* A8 20c blk, yel & lt grn 1.00 1.00
*66* A8 25c dk brn, yel & org 1.25 1.25
*Nos. 60-66 (7)* 3.92 3.92

Protection for Lesotho's rock paintings.

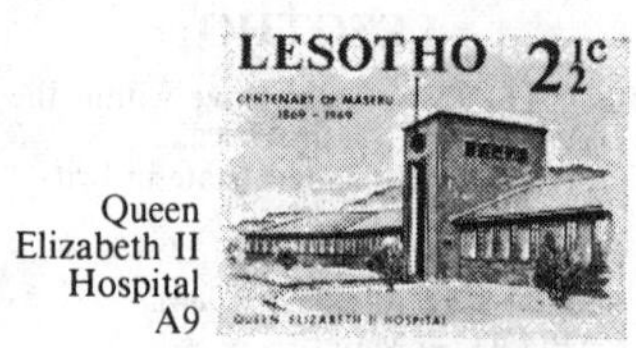

Queen Elizabeth II Hospital A9

Designs: 10c, Radio Lesotho. 12½c, Leabua Jonathan Airport. 25c, Royal Palace.

***Perf. 14x13½***

**1969, Mar. 11 Litho. Wmk. 362**

*67* A9 2½c multi 7 7
*68* A9 10c multi 25 25
*69* A9 12½c multi 28 28
*70* A9 25c multi 65 65

Centenary of Maseru, capital of Lesotho.

Mosotho Horseman and Car — A10

Designs: 12½c, Car on mountain pass. 15c, View from Sani Pass and signal flags. 20c, Map of Lesotho and Independence Trophy.

***Perf. 14½x14***

**1969, Sept. 26 Photo. Wmk. 362**

*71* A10 2½c brn & multi 5 5
*72* A10 12½c multi 28 28
*73* A10 15c multi 35 35
*74* A10 20c yel & multi 50 50

Issued to commemorate the Roof of Africa Automobile Rally, Sept. 19-20.

Plateosauravus and Footprints — A11

Prehistoric Reptile Footprints, Moyeni: 3c, Dinosaur. 5c, Gryponyx. 15c, Tritylodon. 25c, Massospondylus.

***Perf. 14½x14***

**1970, Jan. 5 Photo. Wmk. 362**

**Size: 60x23mm.**

*75* A11 3c brn, yel & blk 15 15

***Perf. 15x14***

**Size: 40x23mm.**

*76* A11 5c mar, blk & pink 32 32
*77* A11 10c sep, blk & yel 65 65
*78* A11 15c sl grn, blk & yel 1.10 1.10
*79* A11 25c gray bl, blk & bl 1.50 1.50
*Nos. 75-79 (5)* 3.72 3.72

Moshoeshoe I — A12

Design: 25c, Moshoeshoe I with top hat.

***Perf. 14x13½***

**1970, Mar. 11 Litho. Wmk. 362**

*80* A12 2½c brt grn & car rose 8 8
*81* A12 25c lt bl & org brn 65 65

Cent. of the death of Moshoeshoe I, chief of the Bakoena clan of the Basothos.

UN Headquarters, New York — A13

Designs: 2½c, UN emblem. 12½c, UN emblem and people. 25c, UN emblem and peace dove.

***Perf. 14½x14***

**1973, June 26 Litho. Wmk. 362**

*82* A13 2½c pink, red brn & bl 7 5
*83* A13 10c bl & multi 25 20
*84* A13 12½c ol, ver & lt bl 25 22
*85* A13 25c tan & multi 60 50

25th anniversary of the United Nations.

Basotho Hat Gift Shop, Maseru A14

Tourism: 5c, Trout fishing. 10c, Horseback riding. 12½c, Skiing, Maluti Mountains. 20c, Holiday Inn, Maseru.

**1970, Oct. 27** ***Perf. 14x14½***

*86* A14 2½c multi 10 10
*87* A14 5c multi 20 20
*88* A14 10c multi 45 45
*89* A14 12½c multi 45 45
*90* A14 20c multi 65 65
*Nos. 86-90 (5)* 1.85 1.85

Corn — A15

Designs: 1c, Bull. 2c, Aloes. 2½c, Basotho hat. 3c, Sorghum. 3½c, Merino sheep. 4c, National flag. 5c, Basotho pony. 10c, Wheat. 12½c, Angora goat. 25c, Maletsunyane Falls. 50c, Diamonds. 1r, Coat of Arms. 2r, Statue of King Moshoeshoe I in Maseru (vert.).

**1971 Litho. Wmk. 362** ***Perf. 14***

*91* A15 ½c lil & grn 5 5
*92* A15 1c brn red & brn 5 5
*93* A15 2c yel brn & yel 8 8
*94* A15 2½c dl yel & blk 8 8
*95* A15 3c bis, brn & grn 9 9
*96* A15 3½c yel & blk 12 12
*97* A15 4c ver & multi 12 12
*98* A15 5c bl & brn 15 15
*99* A15 10c gray & ocher 28 28
*100* A15 12½c org & brn 32 32
*101* A15 25c ultra & blk 70 70
*102* A15 50c lt bl grn & blk 1.40 1.40
*103* A15 1r gray & multi 2.00 2.00
*104* A15 2r ultra & brn 4.75 4.75
***a*** Unwmk. ('80) 4.25 4.25
*Nos. 91-104 (14)* 10.19 10.19

Issue dates: 4c, Apr. 1; others, Jan. 4.

Lammergeier A16

Birds: 5c, Bald ibis. 10c, Rufous rock jumper. 12½c, Blue korhaan (bustard). 15c, Painted snipe. 20c, Golden-breasted bunting. 25c, Ground woodpecker.

**1971, Mar. 1** ***Perf. 14***

*105* A16 2½c multi 32 15
*106* A16 5c multi 70 32
*107* A16 10c multi 1.10 80
*108* A16 12½c multi 1.60 1.00
*109* A16 15c multi 2.00 1.40
*110* A16 20c multi 2.75 1.75
*111* A16 25c multi 3.00 2.25
*Nos. 105-111 (7)* 11.47 7.67

Lionel Collett Dam A17

Designs: 10c, Contour farming. 15c, Earth dams. 25c, Beaver dams.

**1971, July 15 Litho. Wmk. 362**

| | | | | |
|---|---|---|---|---|
| *112* | A17 | 4c multi | 12 | 12 |
| *113* | A17 | 10c multi | 32 | 32 |
| *114* | A17 | 15c multi | 45 | 45 |
| *115* | A17 | 25c multi | 75 | 75 |

Soil conservation and erosion control.

Diamond Mining A18

Designs: 10c, Potter. 15c, Woman weaver at loom. 20c, Construction worker and new buildings.

**1971, Oct. 4**

| | | | | |
|---|---|---|---|---|
| *116* | A18 | 4c ol & multi | 12 | 12 |
| *117* | A18 | 10c ocher & multi | 28 | 28 |
| *118* | A18 | 15c red & multi | 45 | 45 |
| *119* | A18 | 20c dk brn & multi | 60 | 60 |

Mail Cart, 19th Century A19

Designs: 10c, Postal bus. 15c, Cape of Good Hope No. 17 (vert.). 20c, Maseru Post Office.

**1972, Jan. 3**

| | | | | |
|---|---|---|---|---|
| *120* | A19 | 5c pink & blk | 15 | 15 |
| *121* | A19 | 10c lt bl & multi | 35 | 35 |
| *122* | A19 | 15c gray, blk & bl | 50 | 50 |
| *123* | A19 | 20c yel & multi | 90 | 90 |

Centenary of mail service between Maseru and Aliwal North in Cape Colony.

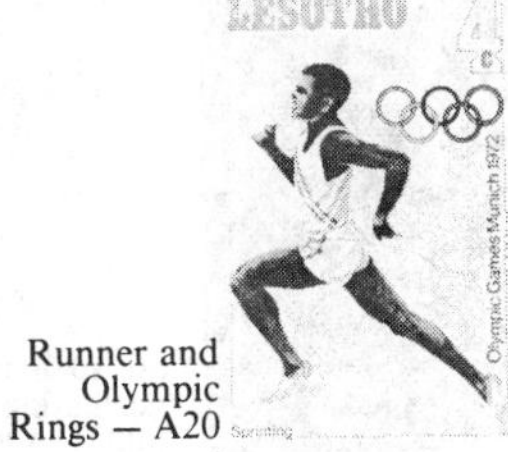


Runner and Olympic Rings — A20

**1972, Sept. 1**

| | | | | |
|---|---|---|---|---|
| *124* | A20 | 4c *shown* | 8 | 8 |
| *125* | A20 | 10c *Shot put* | 25 | 25 |
| *126* | A20 | 15c *Hurdles* | 35 | 35 |
| *127* | A20 | 25c *Broad jump* | 75 | 75 |

20th Olympic Games, Munich, Aug. 26-Sept. 11.

Adoration of the Shepherds, by Matthias Stomer — A21

**1972, Dec. 1 Litho. Perf. 14**

| | | | | |
|---|---|---|---|---|
| *128* | A21 | 4c bl & multi | 12 | 12 |
| *129* | A21 | 10c red & multi | 35 | 35 |
| *130* | A21 | 25c emer & multi | 90 | 90 |

Christmas 1972.

WHO Emblem — A22

**1973, Apr. 7 Litho. *Perf. 13½***

| | | | | |
|---|---|---|---|---|
| *131* | A22 | 20c bl & yel | 50 | 50 |

25th anniversary of the World Health Organization.

Nos. 94, 97-99 overprinted: "O.A.U. / 10th Anniversary / Freedom in Unity"

**1973, May 25 Wmk. 362 *Perf. 14***

| | | | | |
|---|---|---|---|---|
| *132* | A15 | 2½c dl yel & blk | 12 | 12 |
| *133* | A15 | 4c ver & multi | 20 | 20 |
| *134* | A15 | 5c bl & brn | 25 | 25 |
| *135* | A15 | 10c gray & ocher | 50 | 50 |

Basotho Hat, WFP/FAO Emblem — A23

Designs: 15c, School lunch. 20c, Child drinking milk and cow. 25c, Map of mountain roads and farm workers.

**1973, June 1 *Perf. 13½***

| | | | | |
|---|---|---|---|---|
| *136* | A23 | 4c ultra & multi | 10 | 10 |
| *137* | A23 | 15c buff & multi | 30 | 30 |
| *138* | A23 | 20c yel & multi | 40 | 40 |
| *139* | A23 | 25c vio & multi | 60 | 60 |

World Food Program, 10th anniversary.

Christmas Butterfly A24

Designs: Butterflies of Lesotho.

**1973, Sept. 3 *Perf. 14x14½***

| | | | | |
|---|---|---|---|---|
| *140* | A24 | 4c *Mountain Beauty* | 30 | 30 |
| *141* | A24 | 5c *shown* | 45 | 45 |
| *142* | A24 | 10c *Painted lady* | 90 | 90 |
| *143* | A24 | 15c *Yellow pansy* | 1.25 | 1.25 |
| *144* | A24 | 20c *Blue pansy* | 1.75 | 1.75 |
| *145* | A24 | 25c *African monarch* | 2.50 | 2.50 |
| *146* | A24 | 30c *Orange tip* | 3.50 | 3.50 |
| | | *Nos. 140-146 (7)* | 10.65 | 10.65 |

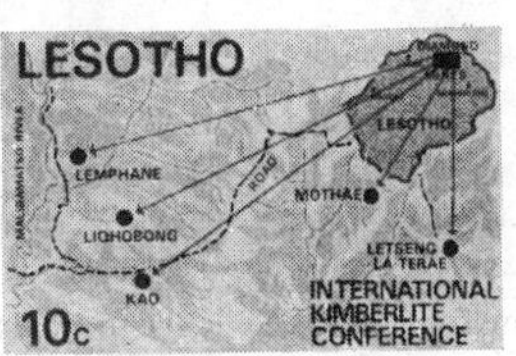


Map of Northern Lesotho and Location of Diamond Mines — A25

Designs: 15c, Kimberlite (diamond-bearing) rocks. 20c, Diagram of Kimberlite volcano (vert.). 30c, Diamond prospector (vert.).

***Perf. 13½x14, 14x13½***

**1973, Oct. 1 Litho. Wmk. 362**

| | | | | |
|---|---|---|---|---|
| *147* | A25 | 10c gray & multi | 75 | 50 |
| *148* | A25 | 15c multi | 1.00 | 75 |
| *149* | A25 | 20c multi | 1.25 | 1.00 |
| *150* | A25 | 30c multi | 2.50 | 1.50 |

International Kimberlite Conference.

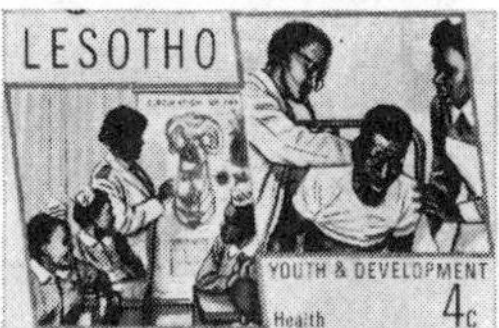


Nurses' Training and Medical Care — A26

Designs: 10c, Classroom, student with microscope. 20c, Farmers with tractor and bullock team and crop instruction. 25c, Potter and engineers with lathe. 30c, Boy scouts and young bricklayers.

**1974, Feb. 18 Litho. *Perf. 13½x14***

| | | | | |
|---|---|---|---|---|
| *151* | A26 | 4c lt bl & multi | 10 | 10 |
| *152* | A26 | 10c ocher & multi | 20 | 20 |
| *153* | A26 | 20c multi | 40 | 40 |
| *154* | A26 | 25c bis & multi | 60 | 60 |
| *155* | A26 | 30c yel & multi | 75 | 75 |
| | | *Nos. 151-155 (5)* | 2.05 | 2.05 |

Youth and development.

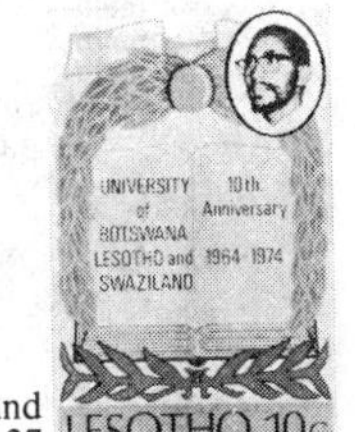


Open Book and Wreath — A27

Designs: 15c, Flags of Botswana, Lesotho and Swaziland; cap and diploma. 20c, Map of Africa and location of Botswana, Lesotho and Swaziland. 25c, King Moshoeshoe II, Chancellor of UBLS, capping graduate.

**1974, Apr. 7 Litho. *Perf. 14***

| | | | | |
|---|---|---|---|---|
| *156* | A27 | 10c multi | 30 | 30 |
| *157* | A27 | 15c multi | 50 | 50 |
| *158* | A27 | 20c multi | 60 | 60 |
| *159* | A27 | 25c multi | 75 | 75 |

10th anniversary of the University of Botswana, Lesotho and Swaziland.

Senqunyane River Bridge, Marakabei — A28

Designs: 5c, Tsoelike River Bridge. 10c, Makhaleng River Bridge. 15c, Seaka Bridge, Orange/Senqu River. 20c, Masianokeng Bridge, Phuthiatsana River. 25c, Mahobong Bridge, Hlotse River.

**1974, June 26 Wmk. 362 *Perf. 14***

| | | | | |
|---|---|---|---|---|
| *160* | A28 | 4c multi | 10 | 10 |
| *161* | A28 | 5c multi | 12 | 12 |
| *162* | A28 | 10c multi | 25 | 25 |
| *163* | A28 | 15c multi | 50 | 40 |
| *164* | A28 | 20c multi | 65 | 50 |
| *165* | A28 | 25c multi | 80 | 60 |
| | | *Nos. 160-165 (6)* | 2.42 | 1.97 |

Bridges and rivers of Lesotho.

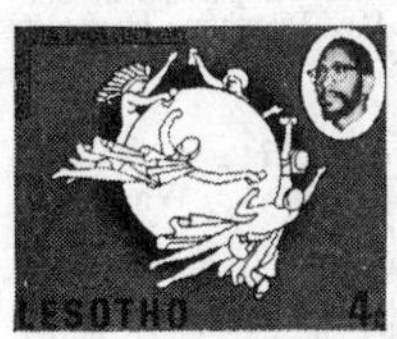


UPU Emblem A29

**1974, Sept. 6 Litho. *Perf. 14x13***

| | | | | |
|---|---|---|---|---|
| *166* | A29 | 4c *shown* | 10 | 10 |
| *167* | A29 | 10c *Map of Lesotho* | 25 | 25 |
| *168* | A29 | 15c *GPO, Maseru* | 40 | 40 |
| *169* | A29 | 20c *Rural mail delivery* | 60 | 60 |

Centenary of Universal Postal Union.

Siege of Thaba-Bosiu — A30

King Moshoeshoe I — A31

Designs: 5c, King Moshoeshoe II laying wreath at grave of Moshoeshoe I. 20c, Makoanyane, warrior hero.

***Perf. 12½x12, 12x12½***

**1974, Nov. 25**

| | | | | |
|---|---|---|---|---|
| *170* | A30 | 4c multi | 15 | 15 |
| *171* | A30 | 5c multi | 18 | 18 |
| *172* | A31 | 10c multi | 35 | 35 |
| *173* | A31 | 20c multi | 85 | 85 |

Sesquicentennial of the siege of Thaba-Bosiu, which established independence for Basuto nation.

Mamokhorong — A32

Musical Instruments of the Basotho: 10c, Lesiba. 15c, Setolotolo. 20c, Meropa (drums).

***Perf. 14x14½***

**1975, Jan. 25 Wmk. 362**

| | | | | |
|---|---|---|---|---|
| *174* | A32 | 4c multi | 15 | 15 |
| *175* | A32 | 10c multi | 40 | 40 |
| *176* | A32 | 15c multi | 60 | 60 |
| *177* | A32 | 20c multi | 80 | 80 |
| | *a* | Souvenir sheet of 4 | 2.50 | 2.50 |

No. 177a contains one each of Nos. 174-177, green margin with white design and inscription. Size: 113x91½mm.

View, Sehlabathebe National Park — A33

Designs: 5c, Natural arch. 15c, Mountain stream. 20c, Lake and mountains. 25c, Waterfall.

**1975, Apr. 8 Litho. *Perf. 14***

| | | | | |
|---|---|---|---|---|
| *178* | A33 | 4c multi | 15 | 15 |
| *179* | A33 | 5c multi | 20 | 20 |
| *180* | A33 | 15c multi | 60 | 60 |
| *181* | A33 | 20c multi | 80 | 80 |
| *182* | A33 | 25c multi | 1.00 | 1.00 |
| | | *Nos. 178-182 (5)* | 2.75 | 2.75 |

Schlabathebe National Park.

Moshoeshoe I (1824-1870) A34

Mofumahali Mantsebo Seeiso (1940-1960) A35

Leaders of Lesotho: 4c, Moshoeshoe II. 5c, Letsie I (1870-1891). 6c, Lerotholi (1891-1905). 10c, Letsie II (1905-1913). 15c, Griffith (1913-1939). 20c, Seeiso Griffith Lerotholi (1939-1940).

**1975, Sept. 10 Litho. Wmk. 362**

| | | | | |
|---|---|---|---|---|
| *183* | A34 | 3c dl bl & blk | 6 | 6 |
| *184* | A34 | 4c lil rose & blk | 10 | 10 |
| *185* | A34 | 5c pink & blk | 12 | 12 |
| *186* | A34 | 6c brn & blk | 15 | 15 |
| *187* | A34 | 10c rose car & blk | 25 | 25 |
| *188* | A34 | 15c org & blk | 35 | 35 |
| *189* | A34 | 20c ol & blk | 45 | 45 |
| *190* | A35 | 25c lt bl & blk | 60 | 60 |
| | | *Nos. 183-190 (8)* | 2.08 | 2.08 |

No. 190 issued for International Women's Year 1975.

Mokhibo, Women's Dance A36

Traditional Dances: 10c, Ndlamo, men's dance. 15c, Raleseli, men and women. 20c, Mohobelo, men's dance.

**1975, Dec. 17 *Perf. 14x14½***

| | | | | |
|---|---|---|---|---|
| *191* | A36 | 4c bl & multi | 15 | 15 |
| *192* | A36 | 10c blk & multi | 35 | 35 |
| *193* | A36 | 15c blk & multi | 50 | 50 |
| *194* | A36 | 20c bl & multi | 75 | 75 |
| *a* | | Souvenir sheet of 4 | 3.00 | 3.00 |

No. 194a contains one each of Nos. 191-194; deep orange and black margin. Size: 110x100mm.

Enrollment in Junior Red Cross — A37

Designs: 10c, First aid team and truck. 15c, Red Cross nurse on horseback in rural area. 25c, Supplies arriving by plane.

**1976, Feb. 20 Litho. *Perf. 14***

| | | | | |
|---|---|---|---|---|
| *195* | A37 | 4c red & multi | 15 | 15 |
| *196* | A37 | 10c red & multi | 35 | 35 |
| *197* | A37 | 15c red & multi | 50 | 50 |
| *198* | A37 | 25c red & multi | 80 | 80 |

Lesotho Red Cross, 25th anniversary.

Mosotho Horseman A38

King Moshoeshoe II — A39

Designs: 2c, Tapestry (weavers and citation). 4c, Map of Lesotho. 5c, Hand holding Lesotho brown diamond. 10c, Lesotho Bank. 15c, Flags of Lesotho and Organization of African Unity. 25c, Sehlabathebe National Park. 40c, Pottery. 50c, Pre-historic rock painting.

**1976, June 2 *Perf. 14***

| | | | | |
|---|---|---|---|---|
| *199* | A38 | 2c multi | 6 | 6 |
| *200* | A38 | 3c multi | 9 | 9 |
| *201* | A38 | 4c multi | 12 | 12 |
| *202* | A38 | 5c multi | 15 | 15 |
| *203* | A38 | 10c multi | 30 | 30 |
| *204* | A38 | 15c multi | 45 | 45 |
| *205* | A38 | 25c multi | 75 | 75 |
| *206* | A38 | 40c multi | 1.20 | 1.20 |
| *207* | A38 | 50c multi | 1.50 | 1.50 |
| *208* | A39 | 1r multi | 2.00 | 2.00 |
| | | *Nos. 199-208 (10)* | 6.62 | 6.62 |

Soccer A40

Rising Sun of Independence A41

Designs (Olympic Rings and): 10c, Weight lifting. 15c, Boxing. 25c, Discus.

**1976, Aug. 9 Litho. Wmk. 362**

| | | | | |
|---|---|---|---|---|
| *209* | A40 | 4c cit & multi | 12 | 10 |
| *210* | A40 | 10c lil & multi | 28 | 25 |
| *211* | A40 | 15c sal & multi | 40 | 35 |
| *212* | A40 | 25c bl & multi | 80 | 65 |

21st Olympic Games, Montreal, Canada, July 17-Aug. 1.

**1976, Oct. 4 *Perf. 14***

Designs: 10c, Opening gates. 15c, Broken chain. 25c, Plane over Molimo Restaurant.

| | | | | |
|---|---|---|---|---|
| *213* | A41 | 4c yel & multi | 12 | 12 |
| *214* | A41 | 10c pink & multi | 30 | 30 |
| *215* | A41 | 15c bl & multi | 45 | 45 |
| *216* | A41 | 25c dl bl & multi | 75 | 75 |

Lesotho's independence, 10th anniversary.

Telephones, 1876 and 1976 — A42

Designs: 10c, Woman using telephone, and 1895 telephone. 15c, Telephone operators and wall telephone. 25c, A.G. Bell and 1905 telephone.

***Perf. 13x13½***

**1976, Dec. 6 Litho. Wmk. 362**

| | | | | |
|---|---|---|---|---|
| *217* | A42 | 4c multi | 10 | 10 |
| *218* | A42 | 10c multi | 22 | 22 |
| *219* | A42 | 15c multi | 35 | 35 |
| *220* | A42 | 25c multi | 60 | 60 |

Centenary of first telephone call by Alexander Graham Bell, Mar. 10, 1876.

Aloe Striatula — A43

Aloes and Succulents: 4c, Aloe aristata. 5c, Kniphofia caulescens. 10c, Euphorbia pulvinata. 15c, Aloe saponaria. 20c, Caralluma lutea. 25c, Aloe polyphylla.

**1977, Feb. 14 Litho. *Perf. 14***

| | | | | |
|---|---|---|---|---|
| *221* | A43 | 3c multi | 18 | 12 |
| *222* | A43 | 4c multi | 22 | 15 |
| *223* | A43 | 5c multi | 25 | 20 |
| *224* | A43 | 10c multi | 50 | 40 |
| *225* | A43 | 15c multi | 90 | 50 |
| *226* | A43 | 20c multi | 1.10 | 75 |
| *227* | A43 | 25c multi | 1.25 | 1.00 |
| | | *Nos. 221-227 (7)* | 4.40 | 3.12 |

Rock Rabbits A44

***Perf. 14x14½***

**1977, Apr. 25 Litho. Wmk. 362**

| | | | | |
|---|---|---|---|---|
| *228* | A44 | 4c shown | 20 | 15 |
| *229* | A44 | 5c Porcupine | 25 | 20 |
| *230* | A44 | 10c Polecat | 50 | 40 |
| *231* | A44 | 15c Klipspringers | 80 | 60 |
| *232* | A44 | 25c Baboons | 1.50 | 1.00 |
| | | *Nos. 228-232 (5)* | 3.25 | 2.35 |

Man with Cane, Concentric Circles — A45

Designs (Man with Cane): 10c, Surrounded by flames of pain. 15c, Surrounded by chain. 25c, Man and globe.

**1977, July 4 Litho. *Perf. 14***

| | | | | |
|---|---|---|---|---|
| *233* | A45 | 4c red & yel | 12 | 10 |
| *234* | A45 | 10c dk & lt bl | 28 | 15 |
| *235* | A45 | 15c bl grn & yel | 48 | 35 |
| *236* | A45 | 25c blk & org | 80 | 60 |

World Rheumatism Year.

Small-mouthed Yellow-fish — A46

Fresh-water Fish: 10c, Orange River mud fish. 15c, Rainbow trout. 25c, Oreodaimon quathlambae.

**1977, Sept. 28 Wmk. 362 *Perf. 14***

| | | | | |
|---|---|---|---|---|
| *237* | A46 | 4c multi | 15 | 10 |
| *238* | A46 | 10c multi | 32 | 25 |
| *239* | A46 | 15c multi | 48 | 35 |
| *240* | A46 | 25c multi | 80 | 60 |

White and Black Equal — A47

Designs: 10c, Black and white jigsaw puzzle. 15c, White and black cogwheels. 25c, Black and white handshake.

**1977, Dec. 12 Litho. *Perf. 14***

| | | | | |
|---|---|---|---|---|
| *241* | A47 | 4c lil rose & blk | 10 | 10 |
| *242* | A47 | 10c brt bl & blk | 22 | 22 |
| *243* | A47 | 15c org & blk | 35 | 35 |
| *244* | A47 | 25c lt grn & blk | 60 | 60 |

Action to Combat Racism Decade.

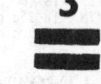

No. 99 Surcharged

3

**1977, Dec. 7**

| | | | | |
|---|---|---|---|---|
| *245* | A15 | 3c on 10c gray & ocher | 1.60 | 1.40 |

Poppies — A48

Edward Jenner Vaccinating Child — A49

Flowers of Lesotho: 3c, Diascia integerrima. 4c, Helichrysum trilineatum. 5c, Zaluzianskya maritima. 10c, Gladioli. 15c, Chironia krebsii. 25c, Wahlenbergia undulata. 40c, Brunsvigia radulosa.

**1978, Feb. 13 Litho. Wmk. 362**

| | | | | |
|---|---|---|---|---|
| *246* | A48 | 2c multi | 6 | 6 |
| *247* | A48 | 3c multi | 8 | 8 |
| *248* | A48 | 4c multi | 10 | 10 |
| *249* | A48 | 5c multi | 12 | 12 |
| *250* | A48 | 10c multi | 25 | 25 |
| *251* | A48 | 15c multi | 40 | 40 |
| *252* | A48 | 25c multi | 65 | 65 |
| *253* | A48 | 40c multi | 1.00 | 1.00 |
| | | *Nos. 246-253 (8)* | 2.66 | 2.66 |

***Perf. 13½x13***

**1978, May 8 Litho. Wmk. 362**

Design: 25c, Child's head and World Health Organization emblem.

| | | | | |
|---|---|---|---|---|
| *254* | A49 | 5c multi | 15 | 15 |
| *255* | A49 | 25c multi | 75 | 75 |

Global eradication of smallpox.

Tsoloane Falls — A50

Lesotho Waterfalls: 10c, Qiloane Falls. 15c, Tsoelikana Falls. 25c, Maletsunyane Falls.

**1978, July 28 Litho. *Perf. 14***

| | | | |
|---|---|---|---|
| *256*A50 | 4c multi | 12 | 12 |
| *257*A50 | 10c multi | 32 | 32 |
| *258*A50 | 15c multi | 50 | 50 |
| *259*A50 | 25c multi | 80 | 80 |

Flyer 1 — A51

Design: 25c, Orville and Wilbur Wright, Flyer 1.

**Wmk. 362**

**1978, Oct. 9 Litho. *Perf. 14½***

| | | | |
|---|---|---|---|
| *260*A51 | 5c multi | 10 | 10 |
| *261*A51 | 25c multi | 50 | 50 |

75th anniversary of 1st powered flight.

Dragonflies A52

Leucosidea Sericea A53

Insects: 10c, Winged grasshopper. 15c, Wasps. 25c, Praying mantis.

**1978, Dec. 18 Litho. *Perf. 14***

| | | | |
|---|---|---|---|
| *262*A52 | 4c multi | 12 | 12 |
| *263*A52 | 10c multi | 30 | 30 |
| *264*A52 | 15c multi | 45 | 45 |
| *265*A52 | 25c multi | 75 | 75 |

**1979, Mar. 26 Litho. *Perf. 14***

Trees: 10c, Wild olive. 15c, Blinkblaar. 25c, Cape holly.

| | | | |
|---|---|---|---|
| *266*A53 | 4c multi | 12 | 12 |
| *267*A53 | 10c multi | 30 | 30 |
| *268*A53 | 15c multi | 45 | 45 |
| *269*A53 | 25c multi | 75 | 75 |

Agama Lizard A54

Reptiles: 10c, Berg adder. 15c, Rock lizard. 25c, Spitting snake.

**Wmk. 362**

**1979, June 4 Litho. *Perf. 14***

| | | | |
|---|---|---|---|
| *270*A54 | 4s multi | 12 | 12 |
| *271*A54 | 10s multi | 30 | 30 |
| *272*A54 | 15s multi | 45 | 45 |
| *273*A54 | 25s multi | 75 | 75 |

Basutoland No. 2 — A55

**1979, Oct. 22 Litho. *Perf. 14½***

| | | | | |
|---|---|---|---|---|
| *274* A55 | 4s | shown | 8 | 8 |
| *275* A55 | 15s | Basutoland No. 72 | 30 | 30 |
| *276* A55 | 25s | Penny Black | 50 | 50 |

**Souvenir Sheet**

| | | | | |
|---|---|---|---|---|
| *277* A55 | 50s | Lesotho No. 122 | 1.25 | 1.25 |

Sir Rowland Hill (1795-1879), originator of penny postage. No. 277 has multicolored margin showing Hill portrait. Size: 118x94½mm.

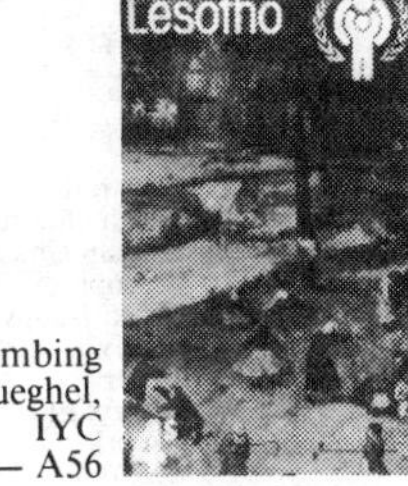


Children Climbing Tree, by Brueghel, IYC Emblem — A56

Children's Games, by Brueghel the Elder, and IYC emblem: 10c, Follow the leader. 15c, Three cup montie. 25c, Entire painting.

**Wmk. 362**

**1979, Dec. 10 Litho. *Perf. 14½***

| | | | |
|---|---|---|---|
| *278*A56 | 4s multi | 10 | 10 |
| *279*A56 | 10s multi | 22 | 22 |
| *280*A56 | 15s multi | 35 | 35 |

**Souvenir Sheet**

| | | | |
|---|---|---|---|
| *281*A56 | 25s multi | 60 | 60 |

International Year of the Child. Size of No. 281: 114x89mm.

Beer Strainer, Brooms and Mat A57

**1980, Feb. 18 Litho. *Perf. 14½***

| | | | | |
|---|---|---|---|---|
| *282*A57 | 4s | shown | 8 | 8 |
| *283*A57 | 10s | Winnowing basket | 20 | 20 |
| *284*A57 | 15s | Basotho hat | 30 | 30 |
| *285*A57 | 25s | Grain storage pots | 50 | 50 |

Qalabane Ambush A58

Gun War Centenary: 4s, Praise poet, text. 5s, Basotho army commander Lerotholi. 15s, Snider and Martini-Henry rifles. 25s, Map of Basutoland showing battle sites.

**1980, May 6 Litho. *Perf. 14***

| | | | |
|---|---|---|---|
| *286*A58 | 4s multi | 10 | 10 |
| *287*A58 | 5s multi | 12 | 12 |
| *288*A58 | 10s multi | 25 | 25 |
| *289*A58 | 15s multi | 35 | 35 |
| *290*A58 | 25s multi | 60 | 60 |
| | *Nos. 286-290 (5)* | 1.42 | 1.42 |

St. Basil's, Moscow, Olympic Torch A59

**1980, Sept. 20 Litho. *Perf. 14½***

| | | | | |
|---|---|---|---|---|
| *291* A59 | 25s | *shown* | 55 | 55 |
| *292* A59 | 25s | *Torch and flags* | 55 | 55 |
| *293* A59 | 25s | *Soccer* | 55 | 55 |
| *294* A59 | 25s | *Running* | 55 | 55 |
| *295* A59 | 25s | *Misha and stadium* | 55 | 55 |
| | | *Nos. 291-295 (5)* | 2.75 | 2.75 |

**Souvenir Sheet**

| | | | | |
|---|---|---|---|---|
| *296* A59 | 1.40m | *Classic and modern torch bearers* | 3.25 | 3.25 |

22nd Summer Olympic Games, Moscow, July 19-Aug. 3. Nos. 291-295 se-tenant. No. 296 has multicolored margin showing St. Basil's Cathedral, Olympic flame and emblem, flags. Size: 110x85mm.

Beer Mug and Man Drinking A60

Prince Philip — A61

**Wmk. 362**

**1980, Oct. 1 Litho. *Perf. 14***

| | | | | |
|---|---|---|---|---|
| *297* A60 | 4s | *shown* | 8 | 8 |
| *298* A60 | 10s | *Beer brewing pot* | 22 | 22 |
| *299* A60 | 15s | *Water pot* | 35 | 35 |
| *300* A60 | 25s | *Pots and jugs* | 60 | 60 |

**Souvenir Sheet**

***Perf. 14x14½***

| | | | |
|---|---|---|---|
| *301* | Sheet of 4 | 3.50 | 2.25 |
| *a* | A61 40s *shown* | 70 | 50 |
| *b* | A61 40s *Queen Elizabeth* | 70 | 50 |
| *c* | A61 40s *Prince Charles* | 70 | 50 |
| *d* | A61 40s *Princess Anne* | 70 | 50 |

Traditional pottery/ 250th birth anniversary of Josiah Wedgewood, potter. No. 301 has multicolored margin showing portrait of Wedgewood. Size: 150x110mm.

Nos. 104, 199-208 Surcharged

**Wmk. 362**

**1980, Oct. 20 Litho. *Perf. 14***

| | | | | |
|---|---|---|---|---|
| *302* A38 | 2s | on 2c multi | 5 | 5 |
| *303* A38 | 3s | on 3c multi | 6 | 6 |
| *304* A38 | 5s | on 5c multi | 8 | 8 |
| *a* | | 5s on 6s on 5c | 8 | 8 |
| *305* A38 | 6s | on 4c multi | 10 | 10 |
| *306* A38 | 10s | on 10c multi | 18 | 18 |
| *307* A38 | 25s | on 25s multi | 40 | 40 |
| *308* A38 | 40s | on 40c multi | 65 | 65 |
| *309* A38 | 50s | on 50c multi | 90 | 90 |
| *310* A38 | 75s | on 15c multi | 1.75 | 1.75 |
| *311* A38 | 1m | on 1r multi | 2.25 | 2.25 |
| *312* A38 | 2m | on 2r multi | 4.00 | 4.00 |
| | | *Nos. 302-312 (11)* | 10.42 | 10.42 |

Souvenir Sheet

Queen Mother Elizabeth and Prince Charles — A62

Basutoland No. 36, Flags of Lesotho and Britain — A63

**1980, Dec. 1 *Perf. 14½***

| | | | |
|---|---|---|---|
| *313* | Sheet of 9 | 5.00 | 5.00 |
| *a* | A62 5s *shown* | 10 | 10 |
| *b* | A62 10s *Portrait* | 20 | 20 |
| *c* | A63 1m *shown* | 2.00 | 2.00 |

Queen Mother Elizabeth, 80th birthday. No. 313 contains 3 each Nos. 313a-313c; multicolored decorative margin. Size: 145x172mm.

St. Agnes' Anglican Church, Teyateyaneng — A63a

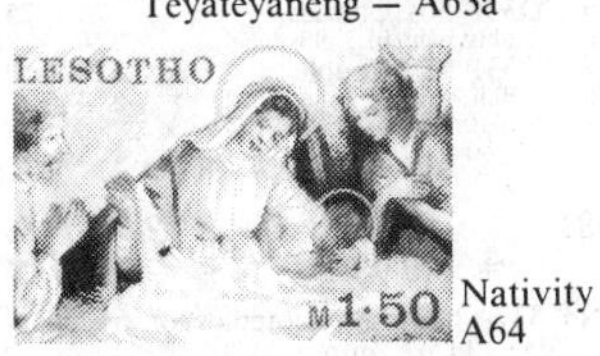


Nativity A64

**1980, Dec. 8 *Perf. 14x14½***

| | | | | |
|---|---|---|---|---|
| *314* A63a | 4s | *Lesotho Evangelical Church, Morija* | 10 | 10 |
| *315* A63a | 15s | *shown* | 35 | 35 |
| *316* A63a | 25s | *Our Lady's Victory Cathedral, Maseru* | 60 | 60 |
| *317* A63a | 75s | *University Chapel, Roma* | 1.75 | 1.75 |

**Souvenir Sheet**

| | | | | |
|---|---|---|---|---|
| *318* A64 | 1.50m | *shown* | 3.25 | 2.00 |

Christmas 1980. No. 318 has multicolored margin showing Nativity. Size: 111x85mm.

Voyager Satellite and Saturn A65

**1981, Mar. 15 Litho. *Perf. 14***

| | | | |
|---|---|---|---|
| *319* | Strip of 5 | 2.75 | 2.75 |
| *a* | A65 25s Voyager, planet | 55 | 55 |
| *b* | A65 25s shown | 55 | 55 |
| *c* | A65 25s Voyager, Saturn's rings | 55 | 55 |
| *d* | A65 25s Columbia space shuttle | 55 | 55 |
| *e* | A65 25s Columbia, diff. | 55 | 55 |

**Souvenir Sheet**

| | | | | |
|---|---|---|---|---|
| *320* A65 | 1.40m | Saturn | 3.25 | 3.25 |

Voyager expedition to Saturn and flight of Columbia space shuttle. No. 315 has multicolored margin showing Voyager and Saturn's moons. Size: 112x86mm.

Rock Pigeons A66

**1981, Apr. 20** *Perf. 14½*

| | | | | |
|---|---|---|---|---|
| *321* | A66 | 1s Greater kestrel, vert. | 5 | 5 |
| *322* | A66 | 2s shown | 6 | 6 |
| *323* | A66 | 3s Crowned cranes, vert. | 8 | 8 |
| *324* | A66 | 5s Bokmakierie, vert. | 12 | 12 |
| *325* | A66 | 6s Cape robins, vert. | 15 | 15 |
| *326* | A66 | 7s Yellow canary, vert. | 18 | 18 |
| *327* | A66 | 10s Red-billed teal | 25 | 25 |
| *328* | A66 | 25s Malachite kingfisher, vert. | 60 | 60 |
| *329* | A66 | 40s Malachite sunbirds | 1.00 | 1.00 |
| *330* | A66 | 60s Orange-throated longclaw | 1.50 | 1.50 |
| *331* | A66 | 75s African hoopoe | 1.75 | 1.75 |
| *332* | A66 | 1m Red bishops | 2.50 | 2.50 |
| *333* | A66 | 2m Egyptian goose | 4.75 | 4.75 |
| *334* | A66 | 5m Lilac-breasted rollers | 10.00 | 10.00 |
| | | *Nos. 321-334 (14)* | 22.99 | 22.99 |

Nos. 321-334 reprinted and inscribed 1982.

**Royal Wedding Issue**
Common Design Type

Royal Wedding — A66a

**1981, July 22** **Litho.** *Perf. 14*

| | | | | |
|---|---|---|---|---|
| *335* | CD331 | 25s Bouquet | 40 | 40 |
| *a* | | Bklt. pane of 3 plus label | 1.25 | |
| *336* | CD331 | 50s Charles | 75 | 75 |
| *a* | | Bklt. pane of 3 plus label | 2.50 | |
| *337* | CD331 | 75s Couple | 1.10 | 1.10 |
| *b* | | Bklt. pane of 3 plus label | 3.50 | |
| *c* | | Bklt. pane of 3, #335-337 plus label | 2.75 | |

**1981** **Litho.** *Perf. 14½*

| | | | | |
|---|---|---|---|---|
| *337A* | A66a | 1.50m Couple | 3.00 | 3.00 |

No. 337A has multicolored decorative margin. Size: 115x91mm.
Nos. 335-337A exist imperf.

Tree Planting A67

**1981, Oct. 30** **Litho.** *Perf. 14½*

| | | | | |
|---|---|---|---|---|
| *338* | A67 | 6s Duke of Edinburgh | 12 | 12 |
| *339* | A67 | 7s shown | 15 | 22 |
| *340* | A67 | 25s Digging | 50 | 50 |
| *341* | A67 | 40s Mountain climbing | 80 | 80 |
| *342* | A67 | 75s Emblem | 1.50 | 1.50 |
| | | *Nos. 338-342 (5)* | 3.07 | 3.14 |

**Souvenir Sheet**

| | | | | |
|---|---|---|---|---|
| *343* | A67 | 1.40m Duke of Edinburgh, diff. | 2.75 | 2.75 |

Duke of Edinburgh's Awards, 25th anniv. No. 343 contains one stamp (45x29mm.; perf. 13½); multicolored margin shows people tending fields. Size: 111x86mm.

Santa Claus at Globe, by Norman Rockwell A68

The Mystic Nativity, by Botticelli — A69

Designs: Saturday Evening Post covers by Norman Rockwell.

**1981, Oct. 5** *Perf. 13½x14*

| | | | | |
|---|---|---|---|---|
| *344* | A68 | 6s multi | 12 | 12 |
| *345* | A68 | 10s multi | 20 | 20 |
| *346* | A68 | 15s multi | 30 | 30 |
| *347* | A68 | 20s multi | 40 | 40 |
| *348* | A68 | 25s multi | 50 | 50 |
| *349* | A68 | 60s multi | 1.25 | 1.25 |
| | | *Nos. 344-349 (6)* | 2.77 | 2.77 |

**Souvenir Sheet**

| | | | | |
|---|---|---|---|---|
| *350* | A69 | 1.25m multi | 2.50 | 2.50 |

Christmas 1981. No. 350 has multicolored margin showing entire painting and floral wreath. Size: 112x86mm.

Chacma Baboons A70

***Perf. 14x13½, 14½ (20s, 40s, 50s)***

**1982, Jan. 15** **Litho.**

| | | | | |
|---|---|---|---|---|
| *351* | A70 | 6s African wild cat | 12 | 12 |
| *352* | A70 | 20s shown | 40 | 40 |
| *353* | A70 | 25s Cape eland | 50 | 50 |
| *354* | A70 | 40s Porcupine | 80 | 80 |
| *355* | A70 | 50s Oribi | 1.00 | 1.00 |
| | | *Nos. 351-355 (5)* | 2.82 | 2.82 |

**Souvenir Sheet**
*Perf. 14*

| | | | | |
|---|---|---|---|---|
| *356* | A70 | 1.50m Black-backed jackal | 3.00 | 3.00 |

6s, 25s; 50x37mm. No. 356 contains one stamp (48x31mm.); multicolored margin continues design. Size: 112x86mm.

Scouting Year — A71

**1982, Mar. 5** **Litho.** *Perf. 14x13½*

| | | | | |
|---|---|---|---|---|
| *357* | A71 | 6s Bugle call | 12 | 12 |
| *358* | A71 | 30s Hiking | 60 | 60 |
| *359* | A71 | 40s Drawing | 80 | 80 |
| *360* | A71 | 50s Holding flag | 1.00 | 1.00 |
| *361* | A71 | 75s Salute | 1.50 | 1.50 |
| *a* | | Bklt. pane of 10 + sheet | 12.50 | |
| | | *Nos. 357-361 (5)* | 4.02 | 4.02 |

**Souvenir Sheet**

| | | | | |
|---|---|---|---|---|
| *362* | A71 | 1.50m Baden-Powell | 2.75 | 2.75 |

No. 361a contains 2 each Nos. 357-361 with gutter and No. 362.
No. 362 has multicolored margin showing flags, emblem. Size: 118x93mm. Issued in sheets of 8 with gutter.

1982 World Cup Soccer A72

Championships, 1930-1978: a. Uruguay, 1930. b. Italy, 1934. c. France, 1938. d. Brazil, 1950. e. Switzerland, 1954. f. Sweden, 1958. g. Chile, 1962. h. England, 1966. i. Mexico, 1970. j. Germany, 1974. k. Argentina, 1978. l. World Cup.

**1982, Apr. 14** *Perf. 14½*

| | | | | |
|---|---|---|---|---|
| *363* | | Sheet of 12 | 3.25 | 3.25 |
| *a-l* | | A72 15s, any single | 25 | 25 |

**Souvenir Sheet**

| | | | | |
|---|---|---|---|---|
| *364* | A72 | 1.25m Stadium | 2.50 | 2.50 |

No. 364 has multicolored margin showing Cup. Size: 118x93mm.

George Washington's Birth Bicentenary — A73

Designs: Paintings.

**1982, June 7**

| | | | | |
|---|---|---|---|---|
| *365* | A73 | 6s Portrait | 12 | 12 |
| *366* | A73 | 7s With children | 15 | 15 |
| *367* | A73 | 10s Indian Chief's Prophecy | 20 | 20 |
| *368* | A73 | 25s With troops | 50 | 50 |
| *369* | A73 | 40s Arriving at New York | 80 | 80 |
| *370* | A73 | 1m Entry into New York | 2.00 | 2.00 |
| | | *Nos. 365-370 (6)* | 3.77 | 3.77 |

**Souvenir Sheet**

| | | | | |
|---|---|---|---|---|
| *371* | A73 | 1.25m Crossing Delaware | 2.50 | 2.50 |

No. 371 has multicolored margin showing entire painting. Size: 118x93mm.

**Princess Diana Issue**
Common Design Type
**Wmk. 373**

**1982, July 1** **Litho.** *Perf. 14*

| | | | | |
|---|---|---|---|---|
| *372* | CD333 | 30s Arms | 45 | 45 |
| *373* | CD333 | 50s Diana | 75 | 75 |
| *374* | CD333 | 75s Wedding | 1.10 | 1.10 |
| *375* | CD333 | 1m Portrait | 1.50 | 1.50 |

Sesotho Bible Centenary — A74

Birth of Prince William of Wales, June 21 — A75

**1982, Aug. 20** **Litho.** *Perf. 14½*

| | | | | |
|---|---|---|---|---|
| *376* | A74 | 6s Man reading bible | 10 | 10 |
| *377* | A74 | 15s Angels, bible | 25 | 25 |

**Size: 59½x40½mm**

| | | | | |
|---|---|---|---|---|
| *378* | A74 | 1m Bible, Maseru Cathedral | 1.75 | 1.75 |

Issued in sheets of 9 (3 each Nos. 376-378).

**1982, Sept. 30**

| | | | | |
|---|---|---|---|---|
| *379* | A75 | 6s Congratulation | 10 | 10 |
| *380* | A75 | 60s Diana, William | 1.10 | 1.10 |

Issued in sheets of 6 (No. 379, 5 No. 380).

Christmas 1982 — A76

Designs: Scenes from Walt Disney's The Twelve Days of Christmas. Stamps of same denomination se-tenant.

**1982, Dec. 1** **Litho.** *Perf. 11*

| | | | | |
|---|---|---|---|---|
| *381* | A76 | 2s multi | 6 | 6 |
| *382* | A76 | 2s multi | 6 | 6 |
| *383* | A76 | 3s multi | 8 | 8 |
| *384* | A76 | 3s multi | 8 | 8 |
| *385* | A76 | 4s multi | 10 | 10 |
| *386* | A76 | 4s multi | 10 | 10 |
| *387* | A76 | 75s multi | 1.50 | 1.50 |
| *388* | A76 | 75s multi | 1.50 | 1.50 |
| | | *Nos. 381-388 (8)* | 3.48 | 3.48 |

**Souvenir Sheet**
***Perf. 14x13½***

| | | | | |
|---|---|---|---|---|
| *389* | A76 | 1.50m multi | 3.25 | 3.25 |

No. 389 has multicolored margin continuing design.

Local Mushrooms — A77

**1982, Jan. 11** *Perf. 14½*

| | | | | |
|---|---|---|---|---|
| *390* | A77 | 10s Lepista caffrorum | 20 | 20 |
| *391* | A77 | 30s Broomexia congregate | 60 | 60 |
| *a* | | Bklt. pane of 2 (#390, 391) | 85 | |
| *392* | A77 | 50s Afroboletus luteolus | 1.00 | 1.00 |
| *393* | A77 | 75s Lentinus tuberregium | 1.50 | 1.50 |
| *a* | | Bklt. pane of 4 (#390-393) | 3.50 | |

Commonwealth Day — CD334

**1983, Mar. 14** **Litho.** *Perf. 14½*

| | | | | |
|---|---|---|---|---|
| *394* | CD334 | 5s Ba-Leseli dance | 10 | 10 |
| *395* | CD334 | 30s Tapestry weaving | 50 | 50 |
| *396* | CD334 | 60s Elizabeth II | 1.00 | 1.00 |
| *397* | CD334 | 75s Moshoeshoe II | 1.10 | 1.10 |

Trance Dancers A79

Hunters — A79a

Rock Paintings: 25s, Baboons, Sehonghong Thaba Tseka. 60s, Hunter attacking mountain reedbuck, Makhetha Berera. 75s, Eland, Leribe.

**1983, May 20 Litho. *Perf. 14½***

*398* A79 6s multi 12 12
*399* A79 25s multi 50 50
*400* A79 60s multi 1.25 1.25
*401* A79 75s multi 1.50 1.50

**Souvenir Sheet**

*402* Sheet of 5 3.75 3.75
*a* A79a 10s multi 20 20

No. 402 contains Nos. 398-401, 402a.

Manned Flight Bicentenary — A80

**1983, July 11 Litho. *Perf. 14½***

*403* A80 7s Montgolfier, 1783 15 15
*404* A80 30s Wright brothers 40 40
*405* A80 60s 1st airmail plane 1.20 1.20
*406* A80 1m Concorde 2.00 2.00

**Souvenir Sheet**

*407* Sheet of 5 4.00 4.00
*a* A80 6s Dornier 228 12 12

No. 407 contains Nos. 403-406, 407a (60x60mm.). Size: 180x92mm.

Sesquicentennial of French Missionaries' Arrival — A81

**1983, Sept. 5 Litho. *Perf. 13½x14***

*408* A81 6s Rev. Eugene Casalis, flags 12 12
*409* A81 25s Morija, 1833 50 50
*410* A81 40s Baptism of Libe 80 80
*411* A81 75s Map of Basutoland, 1834 1.50 1.50

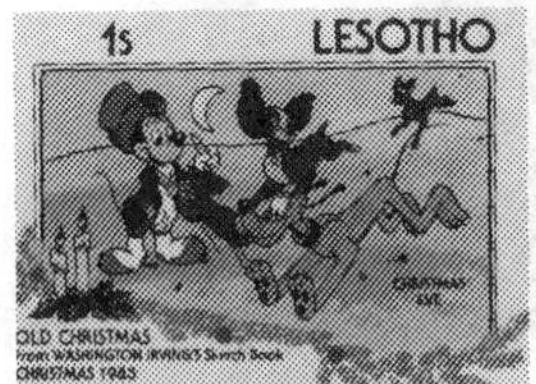


Christmas 1983 — A82

Scenes from Disney's Old Christmas, from Washington Irving's Sketch Book.

**1983, Dec. Litho. *Perf. 14***

*412* A82 1s shown 5 5
*413* A82 2s Christmas eve, diff. 6 6
*414* A82 3s Christmas day 7 7
*415* A82 4s Christmas day, diff. 10 10
*416* A82 5s Christmas dinner 12 12
*417* A82 6s Christmas dinner, diff. 14 14
*418* A82 75s Christmas games 1.50 1.50
*419* A82 1m Christmas dancers 2.00 2.00
*Nos. 412-419 (8)* 4.04 4.04

**Souvenir Sheet**

*420* A82 1.75m Christmas eve 3.50 3.50

African Monarch A83

Bufferflies.

**1984, Jan. 20 Litho.**

*421* A83 1s shown 5 5
*422* A83 2s Mountain Beauty 6 6
*423* A83 3s Orange Tip 7 7
*424* A83 4s Blue Pansy 8 8
*425* A83 5s Yellow Pansy 10 10
*426* A83 6s African Migrant 12 12
*427* A83 7s African Leopard 15 15
*428* A83 10s Suffused Acraea 20 20
*429* A83 15s Painted Lady 30 30
*430* A83 20s Lemon Traveller 40 40
*431* A83 30s Foxy Charaxes 60 60
*432* A83 50s Broad-Bordered Grass Yellow 1.00 1.00
*433* A83 60s Meadow White 1.25 1.25
*434* A83 75s Queen Purple Tip 1.50 1.50
*435* A83 1m Daidem 2.00 2.00
*436* A83 5m Christmas Butterfly 10.00 10.00
*Nos. 421-436 (16)* 17.88 17.88

Easter 1984 A84

Designs: No. 437a-437j, The Ten Commandments. 1.50m, Moses holding tablets.

**1984, Mar. 30 Litho. *Perf. 14***

*437* Sheet of 10 + 2 labels 3.50 3.50
*a.-j.* A84 20s, any single 35 35

**Souvenir Sheet**

*438* A84 1.50m multi 2.50 2.50

No. 438 contains one stamp (45x29mm.); multicolored decorative margin. Size: 104x73mm. Size of No. 437: 161x231mm.

1984 Summer Olympics — A85

**1984, May 5 Litho. *Perf. 13½***

*439* A85 10s Torch bearer 15 15
*440* A85 30s Equestrian 45 45
*441* A85 50s Swimming 75 75
*442* A85 75s Basketball 1.25 1.25
*443* A85 1m Running 1.50 1.50
*Nos. 439-443 (5)* 4.10 4.10

**Souvenir Sheet**

*444* A85 1.50m Flags, flame, stadium 2.50 2.50

Size of No. 444: 103x72mm.

Prehistoric Footprints — A86

**1984, July 2 Litho. *Perf. 13½***

*445* A86 10s Sauropodomorph 18 18
*446* A86 30s Lesothosaurus 50 50
*447* A86 50s Carnivorous dinosaur 90 90

Common Design Types are pictured in section before Great Britain.

Mail Coach Bicentenary and Ausipex '84 — A87

**1984, Sept. 5 Litho. *Perf. 14***

*448* A87 6s Wells Fargo, 1852 18 18
*449* A87 7s Basotho mail cart, 1900 22 22
*450* A87 10s Bath mail coach, 1784 30 30
*451* A87 30s Cobb coach, 1853 90 90

**Size: 82x26mm.**

*451A* A87 50s Exhibition buildings 1.50 1.50

**Souvenir Sheet**

*452* A87 1.75m Penny Black, Basutoland #04, Western Australia #3 3.00 3.00

No. 452 contains one stamp (82x26mm.); multicolored margin shows flags, Australian wildlife, mail coach. Size: 147x98mm.

Trains A88

**1984, Nov. 5 Litho. *Perf. 13½***

*453* A88 6s Orient Express, 1900 8 8
*454* A88 15s 05.001, Class 5, 1935 20 20
*455* A88 30s Cardean, Caledonian, 1906 40 40
*456* A88 60s Santa Fe, Super Chief, 1940 75 75
*457* A88 1m Flying Scotsman, 1934 1.40 1.40
*Nos. 453-457 (5)* 2.83 2.83

**Souvenir Sheet**

***Perf. 14x13½***

*458* A88 2m The Blue Train, 1972 3.00 3.00

No. 458 has multicolored margin continuing the design. Size: 108x83mm.

Indigenous Young Animals A89

**1984, Dec. 20 *Perf. 14½***

*459* A89 15s Cape Eland calf 20 20
*460* A89 20s Chacma baboons 25 25
*461* A89 30s Oribo calf 35 35
*462* A89 75s Red rock hares 90 90

**Size: 47x28mm.**

***Perf. 13½***

*463* A89 1m Black-backed jackals 1.25 1.25
*Nos. 459-463 (5)* 2.95 2.95

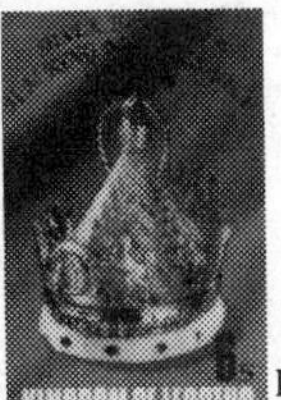


King Moshoeshoe II — A90

**1985, Jan. 30 Litho. *Perf. 15***

*464* A90 6s Royal crown, 1974 9 9
*465* A90 30s Moshoeshoe II, 1966 45 45
*466* A90 75s In Basotho dress 1.10 1.10
*467* A90 1m In military uniform 1.50 1.50

25th anniversary of reign.

**Miniature Sheet**

Easter 1985 — A91

Stations of the Cross: a, Condemned to death. b, Bearing cross. c, Falls the first time. d, Meets his mother. e, Cyrenean helps carry cross. f, Veronica wipes His face. g, Second fall. h, Consoles women of Jerusalem. i, Third fall. j, Stripped. k, Nailed to cross. l, Dies on cross. m, Taken down from cross. n, Laid in sepulchre. No. 469, The Crucifixion, detail, by Mathias Grunewald (c. 1460-1528).

**1985, Mar. 8 *Perf. 11***

*468* Sheet of 14 + label 4.25
*a.-n* A91 20s any single 30 30

**Souvenir Sheet**

***Perf. 14***

*469* A91 2m multi 3.00 3.00

No. 469 has multicolored margin continuing the painting. Size: 139x99mm.

Queen Mother, 85th Birthday — A92

Photographs: 10s, Queen Mother, Princess Elizabeth, 1931. 30s, 75th birthday portrait. 60s With Queen Elizabeth II and Princess Margaret, 80th birthday. No. 473, With Queen Elizabeth II, Princess Diana, Princes Henry and Charles, christening of Prince Henry. No. 474, like No. 473, with Prince William.

**1985, May 30 *Perf. 13½x14***

*470* A92 10s multi 12 12
*471* A92 30s multi 40 40
*472* A92 60s multi 1.00 1.00
*473* A92 2m multi 2.50 2.50

**Souvenir Sheet**

*474* A92 2m multi 3.00 3.00

No. 474 contains one stamp (38x51mm); multicolored decorative margin completes the portrait. Size: 139x98mm.

Automobile Centenary — A93

Luxury cars.

**1985, June 10 *Perf. 14***

*475* A93 6s BMW 732i 9 9
*476* A93 10s Ford LTD Crown Victoria 15 15
*477* A93 30s Mercedes-Benz 500SE 45 45
*478* A93 90s Cadillac Eldorado Biarritz 1.25 1.25

*479* A93 2m Rolls Royce Silver Spirit 3.00 3.00
*Nos. 475-479 (5)* 4.94 4.94

**Souvenir Sheet**

*480* A93 2m 1907 Rolls Royce Silver Ghost Tourer, vert. 3.00 3.00

No. 480 contains one stamp (38x51mm); multicolored margin continues the design. Size: 139x99mm.

Audubon Birth Bicentenary — A94

Illustrations of North American bird species by artist/naturalist John J. Audubon.

**1985, Aug. 5** ***Perf. 14½***

*481* A94 5s Cliff swallow, vert. 6 6
*482* A94 6s Great crested grebe 9 9
*483* A94 10s Vesper sparrow 15 15
*484* A94 30s Greenshank 45 45
*485* A94 60s Stilt sandpiper 90 90
*486* A94 2m Glossy ibis 3.00 3.00
*Nos. 481-486 (6)* 4.65 4.65

Nos. 481-486 printed in sheets of 5 with labels picturing various birds.

Intl. Youth Year, Girl Guides 75th Anniv. — A95

**1985, Sept. 26** ***Perf. 15***

*487* A95 10s Mountain climbing 15 15
*488* A95 30s Medical research 45 45
*489* A95 75s Guides on parade 1.10 1.10
*490* A95 2m Guide saluting 3.00 3.00

**Souvenir Sheet**

*491* A95 2m Lady Baden-Powell, World Chief Guide 3.00 3.00

No. 491 has multicolored margin continuing the portrait of Lady Baden-Powell, by Grace Wheatley.

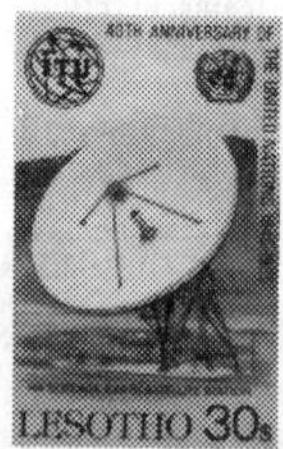


UN, 40th Anniv. A96

Wildflowers A97

Designs: 10s, UN No. 1, flag, horiz. 30s, Dish satellite, Ha Sofonia Earth Satellite Station, ITU emblem. 50s, Aircraft, Maseru Airport, ICAO emblem, horiz. 2m, Maimonides (1135-1204), medieval Jewish scholar, WHO emblem.

**1985, Oct. 15** **Litho.** ***Perf. 15***

*492* A96 10s multi 12 12
*493* A96 30s multi 35 35
*494* A96 50s multi 65 65
*495* A96 2m multi 2.50 2.50

**1985, Nov. 11** ***Perf. 11***

*496* A97 6s Cosmos 6 6
*497* A97 10s Small agapanthus 12 12
*498* A97 30s Pink witchweed 35 35
*499* A97 60s Small iris 75 75
*500* A97 90s Wild geranium 1.10 1.10
*501* A97 1m Large spotted orchid 1.25 1.25
*Nos. 496-501 (6)* 3.63 3.63

Mark Twain, Author, Jacob and Wilhelm Grimm, Fabulists A98

Disney characters acting out Mark Twain quotes or portraying characters from The Wishing Table, by the Grimm Brothers.

**1985, Dec. 2** ***Perf. 11***

*502* A98 6s multi 6 6
*503* A98 10s multi 12 12
*504* A98 50s multi 60 60
*505* A98 60s multi 75 75
*506* A98 75s multi 90 90
*507* A98 90s multi 1.10 1.10
*508* A98 1m multi 1.25 1.25
*509* A98 1.50m multi 2.00 2.00
*Nos. 502-509 (8)* 6.78 6.78

**Souvenir Sheets**
***Perf. 14***

*510* A98 1.25m multi 1.50 1.50
*511* A98 1.50m multi 2.00 2.00

Christmas 1985. Nos. 505, 507 printed in sheets of 8. Nos. 510-511 have multicolored margins continuing the designs. Sizes: 127x102mm.

World Wildlife Fund — A99

Flora and Fauna — A100

Lammergeier vulture.

**1986, Jan. 20** ***Perf. 15***

*512* A99 7s Male 8 8
*513* A99 15s Male, female 15 15
*514* A99 50s Male in flight 50 50
*515* A99 1m Adult, young 1.00 1.00

**1986, Jan. 20**

*516* A100 9s Prickly pear 10 10
*517* A100 12s Stapelia 12 12
*518* A100 35s Pig's ears 35 35
*519* A100 2m Columnar cereus 2.00 2.00

**Souvenir Sheet**

*520* A100 2m Black eagle 2.00 2.00

No. 520 has multicolored margin picturing cacti. Size: 126x106mm.

1986 World Cup Soccer Championships, Mexico — A101

Various soccer plays.

**1986, Mar. 17** ***Perf. 14***

*521* A101 35s multi 35 35
*522* A101 50s multi 50 50
*523* A101 1m multi 1.00 1.00
*524* A101 2m multi 2.00 2.00

**Souvenir Sheet**

*525* A101 3m multi 3.00 3.00

Nos. 525 has multicolored margin picturing crowded stadium. Size: 104x74mm.

A102

Halley's Comet A103

Designs: 9s, Hale Telescope, Mt. Palomar, Galileo. 15s, Venus 2 probe, 1985 sighting. 70s, 684 sighting illustration, Nuremberg Chronicles. 3m, 1066 sighting, Norman conquest of England. 4m, Comet over Lesotho.

**1986, Apr. 5**

*526* A102 9s multi 10 10
*527* A102 15s multi 15 15
*528* A102 70s multi 70 70
*529* A102 3m multi 3.00 3.00

**Souvenir Sheet**

*530* A103 4m multi 4.00 4.00

No. 530 has multicolored margin continuing landscape. Size: 102x70mm.

**Queen Elizabeth II, 60th Birthday**
Common Design Type

Designs: 90s, In pantomime during youth. 1m, At Windsor Horse Show, 1971. 2m, At Royal Festival Hall, 1971. 4m, Age 8.

**1986, Apr. 21**

*531* CD339 90s lt yel bis & blk 90 90
*532* CD339 1m pale grn & multi 1.00 1.00
*533* CD339 2m dl vio & multi 2.00 2.00

**Souvenir Sheet**

*534* CD339 4m tan & blk 4.00 4.00

No. 534 has tan and gray inscribed margin. Size: 120x85mm.

Statue of Liberty, Cent. A104

Statue and famous emigrants: 15s, Bela Bartok (1881-1945), composer. 35s, Felix Adler (1857-1933), philosopher. 1m, Victor Herbert (1859-1924), composer. No. 538, David Niven (1910-1983), actor. No. 539, Statue, vert.

**1986, May 1**

*535* A104 15s multi 15 15
*536* A104 35s multi 35 35
*537* A104 1m multi 1.00 1.00
*538* A104 3m multi 3.00 3.00

**Souvenir Sheet**

*539* A104 3m multi 3.00 3.00

No. 539 has multicolored margin picturing aerial view of New York City and: Henry E. Steinway (1797-1891), piano manufacturer; Yul Brynner (1920-1985), actor; Samuel Gompers (1850-1924), labor leader; Ernestine Schumann-Heink (1861-1936), opera singer. Size: 103x75mm.

AMERIPEX '86 — A105

Walt Disney characters.

**1986, May 22** ***Perf. 11***

*540* A105 15s Goofy, Mickey 15 15
*541* A105 35s Mickey, Pluto 35 35
*542* A105 1m Goofy 1.00 1.00
*543* A105 2m Donald, Pete 2.00 2.00

**Souvenir Sheet**
***Perf. 14***

*544* A105 4m Goofy, Chip-n-Dale 4.00 4.00

No. 544 has multicolored margin continuing the design. Size: 128x102mm.

**Royal Wedding Issue, 1986**
Common Design Type

Designs: 50s, Prince Andrew and Sarah Ferguson. 1m, Andrew. 3m, Andrew at helicopter controls. 4m, Couple, diff.

**1986, July 23** ***Perf. 14***

*545* CD340 50s multi 50 50
*546* CD340 1m multi 1.00 1.00
*547* CD340 3m multi 3.00 3.00

**Souvenir Sheet**

*548* CD340 4m multi 4.00 4.00

No. 548 has multicolored margin picturing Andrew in helicopter. Size: 88x88mm.

Natl. Independence, 20th Anniv. — A106

**1986, Oct. 20** **Litho.** ***Perf. 15***

*549* A106 9s Basotho pony, rider 10 10
*550* A106 15s Mohair spinning 15 15
*551* A106 35s River crossing 35 35
*552* A106 3m Thaba Tseka P.O. 3.00 3.00

**Souvenir Sheet**

*553* A106 4m Moshoeshoe I 4.00 4.00

No. 553 has multicolored decorative margin picturing cosmos. Size: 109x78mm.

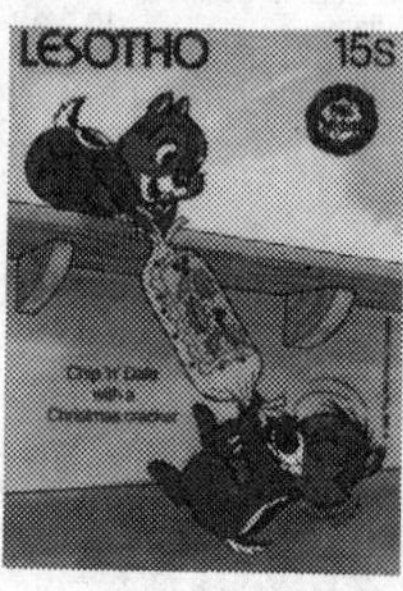


Christmas A107

Walt Disney characters.

**1986, Nov. 4** **Litho.** ***Perf. 11***

*554* A107 15s Chip-n-Dale 15 15
*555* A107 35s Mickey, Minnie 35 35
*556* A107 1m Pluto 1.00 1.00
*557* A107 2m Aunt Matilda 2.00 2.00

**Souvenir Sheet**
***Perf. 14***

*558* A107 5m Huey and Dewey 5.00 5.00

No. 558 has multicolored margin continuing the design and picturing Louie, Grandma Duck and gingerbread house. Size: 127x102mm.

Butterfly and Bird Type of 1981-84
Surcharged

**1986** **Litho.** ***Perf. 14, 14½***

*559* A83 9s on 30s No. 431 10 10
*560* A83 9s on 60s No. 433 10 10
*561* A66 15s on 1s No. 321 15 15
*562* A66 15s on 2s No. 322 15 15
*563* A66 15s on 60s No. 330 15 15
*564* A83 15s on 2s No. 422 15 15
*565* A83 15s on 3s No. 423 15 15
*566* A83 35s on 75s No. 434 35 35
*Nos. 559-566 (8)* 1.30 1.30

Issue dates: Nos. 559-560, July 1. Nos. 561-563, Aug. 22. Nos. 564-566, June 25.

Roof of Africa Rally — A108

**1987, Apr. 28 Litho. Perf. 14**
*567* A108 9s White car 10 10
*568* A108 15s Motorcycle #26 15 15
*569* A108 35s Motorcycle #25 35 35
*570* A108 4m Red car 4.00 4.00

1988 Summer Olympics, Seoul — A109

**1987, May 29 Perf. 14**
*571* A109 9s Tennis 10 10
*572* A109 15s Judo 15 15
*573* A109 20s Running 20 20
*574* A109 35s Boxing 35 35
*575* A109 1m Diving 1.00 1.00
*576* A109 3m Bowling 3.00 3.00
*Nos. 571-576 (6)* 4.80 4.80

**Souvenir Sheet**
*577* A109 2m Tennis, diff. 2.00 2.00

No. 577 has multicolored margin continuing the design. Size: 75x105mm.

See Nos. 606-611. The only difference in the designs of Nos. 571-576 and Nos. 606-611 is the configuration of the Lesotho flag. Nos. 571-576 show green and white colors reversed.

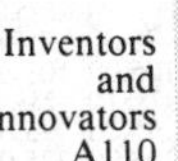
Inventors and Innovators A110

Designs: 5s, Sir Isaac Newton, reflecting telescope. 9s, Alexander Graham Bell, telephone. 75s, Robert H. Goddard, liquid fuel rocket. 4m, Chuck Yeager (b. 1923), test pilot. No. 582, Mariner 10 spacecraft.

**1987, June 30 Perf. 15**
*578* A110 5s multi 5 5
*579* A110 9s multi 10 10
*580* A110 75s multi 75 75
*581* A110 4m multi 4.00 4.00

**Souvenir Sheet**
*582* A110 4m multi 4.00 4.00

No. 582 has multicolored margin continuing the design. Size: 99x69mm.

Fauna and Flora A111

**1987, Aug. 14**
*583* A111 5s Gray rhebuck 5 5
*584* A111 9s Cape clawless otter 10 10
*585* A111 15s Cape gray mongoose 15 15
*586* A111 20s Free state daisy 20 20
*587* A111 35s River bells 35 35
*588* A111 1m Turkey flower 1.00 1.00
*589* A111 2m Sweet briar 2.00 2.00
*590* A111 3m Mountain reedbuck 3.00 3.00
*Nos. 583-590 (8)* 6.85 6.85

**Souvenir Sheet**
*591* A111 2m Pig-lily 2.00 2.00
*592* A111 4m Cape wildebeest 4.00 4.00

Nos. 586-589 and 591 vert. Nos. 591-592 have multicolored margins picturing flora or fauna shown. Sizes: 115x98mm (#591) and 114x97mm.

16th World Scout Jamboree, Australia, 1987-88 — A112

**1987, Sept. 10 Litho. Perf. 14**
*593* A112 9s Orienteering 10 10
*594* A112 15s Playing soccer 15 15
*595* A112 35s Kangaroos 35 35
*596* A112 75s Salute, flag 75 75
*597* A112 4m Windsurfing 4.00 4.00
*Nos. 593-597 (5)* 5.35 5.35

**Souvenir Sheet**
*598* A112 4m Map, flag of Australia 4.00 4.00

No. 598 has multicolored margin picturing previous jamboree emblems. Size: 96x66mm.

Nos. 324, 425, 424, 328 and 427 Surcharged
15s

**1987 Litho. Perf. 14½, 14**
*598A* A66 9s on 5s No. 324 10 10
*599* A66 15s on 5s No. 324 15 15
*600* A83 15s on 5s No. 425 15 15
*600A* A83 20s on 4s No. 424 20 20
*600B* A66 35s on 25s No. 328 35 35
*600D* A83 40s on 7s No. 427 40 40
*Nos. 598A-600D (6)* 1.35 1.35

Issue dates: Nos. 599-600, Nov. 16. No. 600B, Dec. 15. No. 598A, 600A and 600D, Dec. 30.

A113

A114

Religious paintings (details) by Raphael: 9s, Madonna and Child. 15s, Marriage of the Virgin. 35s, Coronation of the Virgin. 90s, Madonna of the Chair. 3m, Madonna and Child Enthroned with Five Saints.

**1987, Dec. 21 Perf. 14**
*601* A113 9s multi 10 10
*602* A113 15s multi 18 18
*603* A113 35s multi 40 40
*604* A113 90s multi 1.05 1.05

**Souvenir Sheet**
*605* A114 3m multi 3.25 3.25

Christmas. No. 605 has multicolored margin continuing the painting. Size: 75x100mm.

Summer Olympics Type of 1987

**1987, Nov. 30 Litho. Perf. 14**
*606*A109 5s like 9s 5 5
*607*A109 10s like 15s 10 10
*608*A109 25s like 20s 25 25
*609*A109 40s like 35s 40 40
*610*A109 50s like 1m 50 50
*611*A109 3.50m like 3m 3.50 3.50
*Nos. 606-611 (6)* 4.80 4.80

**Souvenir Sheet**
*612*A109 4m Soccer 4.00 4.00

The only difference in the designs of Nos. 571-576 and Nos. 606-611 is the configuration of the Lesotho flag. Nos. 571-576 show green and white colors reversed.

Discovery of America, 500th Anniv. (in 1992) A115

Columbus's fleet and marine life: 9s, Spotted trunkfish. 15s, Green sea turtle. 35s, Common dolphin. 5m, White-tailed tropicbird. 4m, Ship.

**1987, Dec. 14 Litho. Perf. 14**
*613*A115 9s multi 8 8
*614*A115 15s multi 15 15
*615*A115 35s multi 35 35
*616*A115 5m multi 5.00 5.00

**Souvenir Sheet**
*617*A115 4m multi 4.00 4.00

No. 617 has multicolored margin continuing the design and picturing Cuban Amazon parrot and ground iguana. Size: 105x75mm.

Birds A116

**1988, Apr. 5 Litho. Perf. 15**
*618* A116 2s Pied kingfisher 5 5
*619* A116 3s Three-banded plover 5 5
*620* A116 5s Spurwing goose 5 5
*621* A116 10s Clapper lark 10 10
*622* A116 12s Red-eyed bulbul 12 12
*623* A116 16s Cape weaver 16 16
*624* A116 20s Red-headed finch 20 20
*625* A116 30s Mountain chat 30 30
*626* A116 40s Stone chat 40 40
*627* A116 55s Pied barbet 55 55
*628* A116 60s Cape glossy starling 60 60
*629* A116 75s Cape sparrow 75 75
*630* A116 1m Cattle egret 1.00 1.00
*631* A116 3m Giant kingfisher 3.00 3.00
*632* A116 10m Crowned guinea fowl 10.00 10.00
*Nos. 618-632 (15)* 17.33 17.33

Nos. 531-534 Overprinted "40th WEDDING ANNIVERSARY H.M. Queen ELIZABETH II H.R.H. THE DUKE OF EDINBURGH" in Silver

**1988, May 3 Perf. 14**
*636* CD339 90s lt yel bis & blk 90 90
*637* CD339 1m pale grn & multi 1.00 1.00
*638* CD339 2m dull vio & multi 2.00 2.00

**Souvenir Sheet**
*639* CD339 4m tan & blk 4.00 4.00

FINLANDIA '88, Helsinki, June 1-12 — A117

Disney animated characters and Helsinki sights.

**1988, June 2 Litho. Perf. 14x13½**
*640* A117 1s Touring President's Palace 5 5
*641* A117 2s Sauna 5 5
*642* A117 3s Lake Country fishing 5 5
*643* A117 4s Finlandia Hall 5 5
*644* A117 5s Photographing Sibelius Monument 5 5
*645* A117 10s Pony trek, youth hostel 10 10
*646* A117 3m Olympic Stadium 3.00 3.00
*647* A117 5m Santa Claus, Arctic Circle 5.00 5.00
*Nos. 640-647 (8)* 8.35 8.35

**Souvenir Sheets**
**Perf. 14x13½, 13½x14**
*648* A117 4m Market Square 4.00 4.00
*649* A117 4m Lapp encampment, vert. 4.00 4.00

Mickey Mouse, 60th anniv. Nos. 648-649 have multicolored margins continuing the designs. Sizes: 127x102mm.

Visit of Pope John Paul II, Sept. 14-16 — A118

**1988, Sept. 1 Litho. Perf. 14**
*650* A118 55s Pope giving communion 55 55
*651* A118 2m Leading procession 2.00 2.00
*652* A118 3m Walking in garden 3.00 3.00
*653* A118 4m Wearing scullcap 4.00 4.00

**Souvenir Sheet**
*654* A118 5m Pope, Archbishop Morapeli of Lesotho, horiz. 5.00 5.00

No. 654 has multicolored decorative margin picturing the Vatican. Size: 98x78mm.

Small Indigenous Mammals — A119

**1988, Oct. 13 Litho. Perf. 14**
*655* A119 16s Rock hyrax 16 16
*656* A119 40s Honey badger 40 40
*657* A119 75s Genet 75 75
*658* A119 3m Yellow mongoose 3.00 3.00

**Souvenir Sheet**
*659* A119 4m Meerkat 4.00 4.00

No. 659 has multicolored decorative margin continuing the design. Size: 110x78mm.

*Birth of Venus*, 1480, by Botticelli A120

Paintings: 25s, *View of Toledo*, 1608, by El Greco. 40s, *Maids of Honor*, 1656, by Diego Velazquez. 50s, *The Fifer*, 1866, by Manet. 55s, *The Starry Night*, 1889, by Van Gogh. 75s, *Prima Ballerina*, 1876, by Degas. 2m, *Bridge over Water Lilies*, 1899, by Monet. 3m, *Guernica*, 1937, by Picasso. No. 668, *The Presentation of the Virgin in the Temple*, c. 1534, by Titian. No. 669, *The Miracle of the Newborn Infant*, 1511, by Titian.

**1988, Oct. 17 Litho. *Perf. 13½x14***
660 A120 15s multi 15 15
661 A120 25s multi 25 25
662 A120 40s multi 40 40
663 A120 50s multi 50 50
664 A120 55s multi 55 55
665 A120 75s multi 75 75
666 A120 2m multi 2.00 2.00
667 A120 3m multi 3.00 3.00
*Nos. 660-667 (8)* 7.60 7.60

**Souvenir Sheets**

668 A120 4m multi 4.00 4.00
669 A120 4m multi 4.00 4.00

Nos. 668-669 have multicolored margins continuing the paintings. Sizes: 111x95mm.

1988 Summer Olympics, Seoul — A121

Intl. Tennis Federation, 75th Anniv. — A122

**1988, Nov. 11 Litho. *Perf. 14***
670 A121 12s Wrestling, horiz. 12 12
671 A121 16s Equestrian 16 16
672 A121 55s Shooting, horiz. 55 55
673 A121 3.50m like 16s 3.50 3.50

**Souvenir Sheet**

674 A121 4m Eternal flame 4.00 4.00

No. 674 has multicolored margin picturing flags. Size: 108x77mm.

**1988, Nov. 18**

Tennis champions, views of cities or landmarks: 12s, Yannick Noah, Eiffel Tower, horiz. 20s, Rod Laver, Sydney Opera House and Harbor Bridge, horiz. 30s, Ivan Lendl, Prague, horiz. 65s, Jimmy Connors, Tokyo. 1m, Arthur Ash, Barcelona. 1.55m, Althea Gibson, NYC. 2m, Chris Evert, Vienna. 2.40m, Boris Becker, London. 3m, Martina Navratilova, Golden Gate Bridge, horiz. 4m, Steffi Graf, Berlin, West Germany.

675 A122 12s multi 12 12
676 A122 20s multi 20 20
677 A122 30s multi 30 30
678 A122 65s multi 65 65
679 A122 1m multi 1.00 1.00
680 A122 1.55m multi 1.55 1.55
681 A122 2m multi 2.00 2.00
682 A122 2.40m multi 2.40 2.40
683 A122 3m multi 3.00 3.00
*Nos. 675-683 (9)* 11.22 11.22

**Souvenir Sheet**

684 A122 4m multi 4.00 4.00

No. 684 has multicolored margin continuing the design. Size: 98x72mm.
No. 676 has "Sidney" instead of "Sydney."

Paintings by Titian A123

Designs: 12s, *The Averoldi Polyptych.* 20s, *Christ and the Adulteress* (Christ). 35s, *Christ and the Adulteress* (adultress). 45s, *Angel of the Annunciation.* 65s, *Saint Dominic.* 1m, *The Vendramin Family.* 2m, *Mary Magdalen.* 3m, *The Tribute Money.* No. 693, *Christ and the Woman Taken in Adultery.* No. 694, *The Mater Dolorosa.*

**1988, Dec. 1 *Perf. 14x13½***
685 A123 12s multi 12 12
686 A123 20s multi 20 20
687 A123 35s multi 35 35
688 A123 45s multi 45 45
689 A123 65s multi 65 65
690 A123 1m multi 1.00 1.00
691 A123 2m multi 2.00 2.00
692 A123 3m multi 3.00 3.00
*Nos. 685-692 (8)* 7.77 7.77

**Souvenir Sheets**

693 A123 5m multi 5.00 5.00
694 A123 5m multi 5.00 5.00

Birth of Titian, 500th anniv. Nos. 685-693 inscribed "Christmas 1988."
Nos. 693-694 have multicolored margins continuing the designs. Size: 95x110mm.

Intl. Red Cross, 125th Anniv. A124

Anniv. emblem, supply and ambulance planes: 12s, Pilatus PC-6 Turbo Porter. 20s, Cessna Caravan. 55s, De Havilland DHC-6 Otter. 3m, Douglas DC-3 in thunderstorm. 4m, Douglas DC-3, diff.

**1988 Litho. *Perf.***
695 A124 12s multi 12 12
696 A124 20s multi 20 20
697 A124 55s multi 55 55
698 A124 3m multi 3.00 3.00

**Souvenir Sheet**

699 A124 4m multi, vert. 4.00 4.00

No. 699 has multicolored margin continuing the design and picturing national and Red Cross flags.

## POSTAGE DUE STAMPS

Basutoland Nos. J9-J10 Overprinted: "LESOTHO"

**Wmk. 314**

**1966, Nov. 1 Typo. *Perf. 14***
J1 D2 1c carmine 20 25
a. "Lseotho" 50.00
J2 D2 5c dk pur 75 60
a. "Lseotho" 85.00

D1

***Perf. 13½***

**1967, Apr. 1 Unwmk. Litho.**
J3 D1 1c dk bl 10 12
J4 D1 2c dl rose 24 28
J5 D1 5c emerald 60 70

**1976, Nov. 30 Wmk. 362**
J7 D1 2c dl rose 10 10
J8 D1 5c emerald 20 20

# MADAGASCAR

**British Consular Mail.**

Postage stamps issued by the British Consulate in Madagascar were in use for a short period until the British relinquished all claims to this territory in favor of France in return for which France recognized Great Britain's claims in Zanzibar.

12 Pence = 1 Shilling

Most Madagascar stamps are found with small faults, expecially used. Values are for stamps with small faults.
The stamps were issued with gum in one corner only. Unused values are for stamps without gum. Copies having original corner gum will sell for more.

"B.C.M." and Arms A1

Handstamped "British Vice-Consulate"

**Black Seal Handstamped.**

**1884 Unwmk. Typo. *Rouletted***
1 A1 1p violet 125.00 125.00
b. Seal omitted 875.00 875.00
2 A1 2p violet 150.00 150.00
3 A1 3p violet 125.00 *125.00*
4 A1 4p vio 1 oz. 2,250. 2,250.
a. "1 oz." corrected to "4 oz." in mss. 550.00 550.00
b. Seal omitted *1,600.*
5 A1 6p violet 225.00 225.00
6 A1 1sh violet 200.00 200.00
7 A1 1sh6p violet 225.00 225.00
8 A1 2sh violet 300.00 300.00
9 A1 1p on 1sh vio
10 A1 4½ on 1sh vio
11 A1 6p red 200.00 200.00

**1886**

**Violet Seal Handstamped.**

12 A1 4p violet 950.00 950.00
13 A1 6p violet 1,350. 1,350.

**Handstamped "British Consular Mail" as on A3**

**Black Seal Handstamped.**

14 A1 4p violet 1,600. 1,600.

**Violet Seal Handstamped.**

15 A1 4p violet 1,750. 1,750.

The 1, 2, 3 and 4 pence are inscribed "POSTAL PACKET", the other values of the series are inscribed "LETTER".

"British Vice-Consulate" — A2

Three types of A2 and A3:
I. "POSTAGE" 29 ½mm. Periods after "POSTAGE" and value.
II. "POSTAGE" 29½mm. No periods.
III. "POSTAGE" 24½mm. Period after value.

**1886**

**Violet Seal Handstamped.**

16 A2 1p rose, I 140.00 140.00
a. Type II 900.00 900.00
17 A2 1½p rose, I 265.00 265.00
a. Type II 1,000. 1,000.
18 A2 2p rose, I 265.00 265.00
19 A2 3p rose, I 265.00 265.00
a. Type II 1,250. 1,250.
20 A2 4p rose, III 225.00 225.00
21 A2 4½p rose, I 275.00 275.00
a. Type II 900.00 900.00
22 A2 6p rose, II 275.00 275.00
23 A2 8p rose, I 750.00 750.00
a. Type III 300.00. 300.00
24 A2 9p rose 525.00 525.00
24A A2 1sh rose, III 1,000.
24B A2 1sh6p rose, III 2,250. 2,250.
25 A2 2sh rose, III 1,000. 1,000.

**Black Seal Handstamped.**

Type I

26 A2 1p rose 60.00 60.00
27 A2 1½p rose 400.00 400.00
28 A2 2p rose 65.00 65.00
29 A2 3p rose 625.00 625.00
30 A2 4½p rose 625.00 625.00
31 A2 8p rose 750.00 750.00
32 A2 9p rose 2,700.
32A A2 2sh rose, III

"British Consular Mail" — A3

**Violet Seal Handstamped.**

**1886**
33 A3 1p rose, II 55.00 55.00
34 A3 1½p rose, II 60.00 60.00
35 A3 2p rose, II 60.00 60.00
36 A3 3p rose, II 60.00 60.00
37 A3 4p rose, III 120.00 120.00
38 A3 4½p rose, II 65.00 65.00
39 A3 6p rose, II 120.00 120.00
40 A3 8p rose, III 315.00 315.00
a. Type I 825.00 825.00
41 A3 9p rose, I 105.00 105.00
42 A3 1sh rose, III 800.00 800.00
43 A3 1sh6p rose, III 900.00 900.00
44 A3 2sh rose, III 1,150. 1,150.

**Black Seal Handstamped**

45 A3 1p rose, I 60.00 60.00
a. Type II 60.00 60.00
46 A3 1½p rose, I 60.00 60.00
a. Type II 60.00 60.00
47 A3 2p rose, I 60.00 60.00
a. Type II 60.00 60.00
48 A3 3p rose, I 75.00 75.00
a. Type II 75.00 75.00
49 A3 4p rose, III 175.00 175.00
50 A3 4½p rose, I 75.00 75.00
a. Type II 75.00 75.00
51 A3 6p rose, II 75.00 75.00
52 A3 8p rose, I 105.00 105.00
a. Type III 285.00 285.00
53 A3 9p rose, I 95.00 95.00
54 A3 1sh rose, III 225.00 225.00
55 A3 1sh6p rose, III 175.00 175.00
56 A3 2sh rose, III 225.00 225.00

**Seal Omitted**

45b A3 1p rose, II 380.00
46b A3 1½p rose, II 380.00
48b A3 3p rose, II 825.00
49a A3 4p rose, III 1,000.
50b A3 4½p rose, II 1,100.
51a A3 6p rose, II 1,250.
52b A3 8p rose, III 1,000.
53a A3 9p rose, I 1,250.
54a A3 1sh rose, III 1,100.
55a A3 1sh6p rose, III 1,100.
56a A3 2sh rose, III 1,100.

Some students of these issues doubt that the 1886 "seal omitted" varieties were regularly issued.

**Red Seal Handstamped.**

57 A3 3p rose, I *2,500.*
58 A3 4½p rose, I *2,250.*

# MALAWI

LOCATION — Southeast Africa.
GOVT. — Republic in British Commonwealth.
AREA — 36,100 sq. mi.
POP. — 5,530,000 (est. 1977).
CAPITAL — Lilongwe.

The British Protectorate of Nyasaland became the independent state of

Malawi on July 6, 1964, and a republic on July 6, 1966.

12 Pence = 1 Shilling
20 Shillings = 1 Pound
100 Tambalas = 1 Kwacha (1970)

**Catalogue values for all unused stamps in this country are for Never Hinged items.**

Dr. H. Kamuzu Banda and Independence Monument — A1

Designs (Prime Minister Banda and): 6p, Sun rising from lake. 1sh3p, National flag. 2sh6p, Coat of Arms.

*Perf. 14½*

**1964, July 6 Unwmk. Photo.**

*1* A1 3p dk gray & lt ol grn 5 5
*2* A1 6p car rose, red, gold & bl 8 8
*3* A1 1sh3p dl vio, blk, red & grn 18 18
*4* A1 2sh6p multi 40 40

Malawi's independence, July 6, 1964.

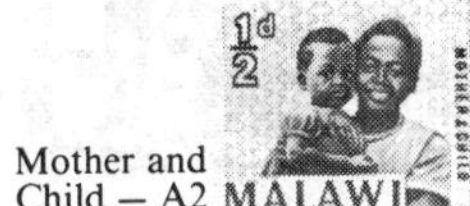


Mother and Child — A2

Designs: 1p, Chambo fish. 2p, Zebu bull. 3p, Peanuts. 4p, Fishermen in boat. 6p, Harvesting tea. 9p, Tung nut, flower and leaves. 1sh, Lumber and tropical pine branch. 1sh3p, Tobacco drying and Turkish tobacco plant. 2sh6p, Cotton industry. 5sh, Monkey Bay, Lake Nyasa. 10sh, Afzelia tree (pod mahogany). £1, Nyala antelope (vert.).

**1964, July 6**

**Size: 23x19mm.**

*5* A2 ½p lilac 7 5
*6* A2 1p grn & blk 7 5
*7* A2 2p red brn 8 5
*8* A2 3p pale brn, brn red & grn 12 5
*9* A2 4p org yel & ind 15 6

**Size: 41½x25, 25x41½mm.**

*10* A2 6p bl, vio bl & brt yel grn 25 15
*11* A2 9p grn, yel & brn 30 25
*12* A2 1sh yel, brn & dk grn 35 25
*13* A2 1sh3p red brn & ol 45 30
*14* A2 2sh6p bl & brn 75 60
*15* A2 5sh grn, bl, sep & yel *(Monkey Bay-Lake Nyasa)* 2.75 2.25
*16* A2 10sh org brn, grn & gray 3.00 2.50
*17* A2 £1 yel & dk brn 6.75 4.75
*Nos. 5-17 (13)* 15.09 11.31

See Nos. 26, 41-51.

Sixpence, Shilling, Florin and Half-Crown Coins — A4

John Chilembwe, Rebels and Church at Mbwombwe — A5

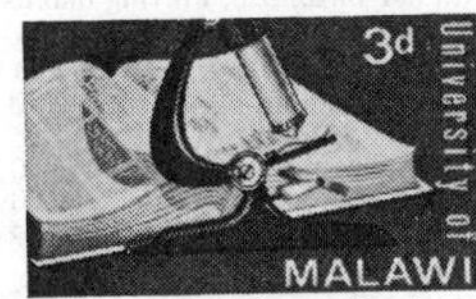


Microscope and Open Book — A6

African Danaine A7

Designs: Various butterflies.

Star of Bethlehem over World — A3

**1964, Dec. 1 Photo. *Perf. 14½***

*18* A3 3p brt grn & gold 8 8
*19* A3 6p lil rose & gold 15 15
*20* A3 1sh3p lil & gold 35 35
*21* A3 2sh6p ultra & gold 65 65
*a* Souv. sheet of 4 2.25 2.00

Christmas 1964.

No. 21a contains one each of Nos. 18-21 with simulated perforations; blue border with gold inscription. Size: 82x126mm.

*Perf. 13x13½*

**1965, Mar. 1 Unwmk.**

**Coins in Silver and Black**

*22* A4 3p green 8 8
*23* A4 9p rose 18 18
*a* Silver omitted
*24* A4 1sh6p rose vio 35 35
*25* A4 3sh dk bl 65 65
*a* Souv. sheet of 4 1.50 1.40

Issued to commemorate the first coinage of Malawi. No. 25a contains one each of Nos. 22-25 with simulated perforations; lilac border with silver inscription. Size: 128x104mm. Sold for 6sh.

**Type of 1964 Redrawn**

**1965, June 1 Photo. *Perf. 14½***

*26* A2 5sh grn bl, sep & yel *(Monkey Bay-Lake Malawi)* 1.75 1.75

**Nos. 13-14 Surcharged with New Value and Two Bars**

**1965, June 14**

*27* A2 1sh6p on 1sh3p red brn & ol 35 35
*28* A2 3sh on 2sh6p bl & brn 65 65

**1965, Aug. 20 Photo. *Perf. 14½***

*29* A5 3p yel grn & pur 6 6
*30* A5 9p red org & ol 15 15
*31* A5 1sh6p dk bl & red brn 30 30
*32* A5 3sh dl bl & grn 60 60
*a* Souv. sheet of 4 6.25 5.25

Issued to commemorate the 50th anniversary of the revolution of Jan. 23, 1915, led by John Chilembwe (1871-1915), missionary.

No. 32a contains one each of Nos. 29-32. Blue margin with white inscription. Size: 126x83mm.

**1965, Oct. 6 *Perf. 14***

*33* A6 3p emer & sl 7 5
*34* A6 9p brt rose & sl 15 12
*35* A6 1sh6p pur & sl 35 25
*36* A6 3sh ultra & sl 60 40
*a* Souv. sheet of 4 6.25 5.75

Issued to commemorate the opening of the University of Malawi in temporary quarters in Chichiri secondary school, Blantyre. The University will be located in Zomba.

No. 36a contains one each of Nos. 33-36. Ultramarine margin. Size: 126x84mm.

*Perf. 13x13½*

**1966, Feb. 15 Photo. Unwmk.**

*37* A7 4p multi 25 15
*38* A7 9p multi 60 50
*39* A7 1sh6p lil, blk & bl 1.25 1.00
*40* A7 3sh bl, dk brn & bis 2.50 2.00
*a* Souv. sheet of 4 10.00 8.50

No. 40a contains one each of Nos. 37-40. Pink margin with black inscription and design. Size: 130x100mm.

See No. 51.

**Type of 1964**

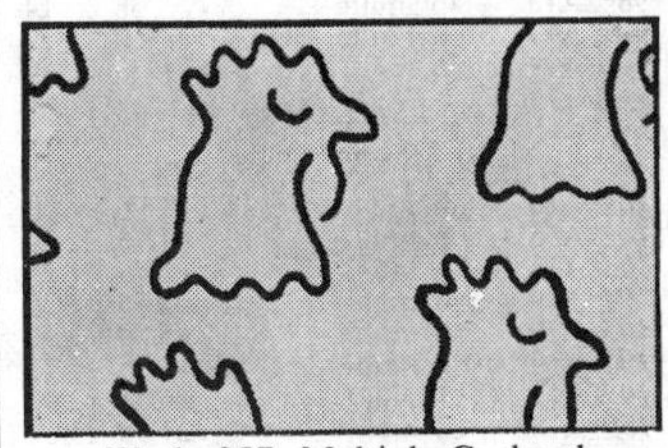

Wmk. 357- Multiple Cockerel

Designs: 1sh6p, Curing tobacco and Burley tobacco plant. £2, Cyrestis camillus sublineatus (butterfly). Other designs as in 1964.

**Wmk. 357**

**1966-67 Photo. *Perf. 14½***

**Size: 23x19mm**

*41* A2 ½p lilac 5 5
*42* A2 1p grn & blk 5 5
*43* A2 2p red brn ('67) 12 5
*44* A2 3p multi ('67) 20 8

**Size: 41½x25mm**

*45* A2 6p bl, vio bl & brt yel grn ('67) 50 12
*46* A2 9p grn, yel & brn ('67) 60 30
*47* A2 1sh yel, brn & dk grn 65 32
*48* A2 1sh6p choc & emer 1.10 65
*49* A2 5sh multi ('67) 7.50 2.50
*50* A2 10sh org brn, grn & gray ('67) 12.00 6.00
*51* A2 £2 dl vio, yel & blk 32.50 25.00
*Nos. 41-51 (11)* 55.27 35.12

British Central Africa Stamp 1891 — A8

President Kamuzu Banda — A9

**1966, May 4 *Perf. 14½***

*54* A8 4p yel grn & sl bl 8 8
*55* A8 9p dl rose & sl bl 20 20
*56* A8 1sh6p lil & sl bl 35 35
*57* A8 3sh bl & sl bl 65 65
*a* Souv. sheet of 4 4.00 3.00

Postal service, 75th anniversary.

No. 57a contains one each of Nos. 54-57. Blue marginal inscription. Size: 83x127mm.

*Perf. 14x14½*

**1966, July 6 Photo. Wmk. 357**

*58* A9 4p grn, sil & brn 6 6
*59* A9 9p mag, sil & brn 12 12
*60* A9 1sh6p vio, sil & brn 25 25
*61* A9 3sh bl, sil & brn 50 50
*a* Souv. sheet of 4 2.50 1.75

Issued to commemorate Republic Day, July 6, 1966, and the second anniversary of Independence. No. 61a contains one each of Nos. 58-61. Green Margin. Size: 82½x127mm.

Star over Bethlehem — A10

*Perf. 14½x14*

**1966, Oct. 12 Photo. Wmk. 357**

*63* A10 4p dp grn & gold 10 8
*64* A10 9p plum & gold 25 25
*65* A10 1sh6p org & gold 50 50
*66* A10 3sh dp bl & gold 1.00 1.00

Christmas 1966.

Ilala I, 1875 A11

Steamers on Lake Malawi: 9p, Dove, 1892. 1sh6p, Chauncey Maples, 1901. 3sh, Guendolen, 1899.

**1967, Jan. 4 *Perf. 14½x14***

*67* A11 4p emer, blk & yel 12 10
*a* Yellow omitted
*68* A11 9p car rose, blk & yel 28 25
*69* A11 1sh6p lt. vio, blk & red 60 50
*70* A11 3sh ultra, blk & red 1.50 1.00

Pseudotropheus Auratus — A12

Fish of Lake Malawi: 9p, Labeotropheus trewavasae. 1sh6p, Pseudotropheus zebra. 3sh, Pseudotropheus tropheops.

**1967, May 3 Photo. *Perf. 12½x12***

*71* A12 4p grn & multi 18 15
*72* A12 9p ocher & multi 40 35
*73* A12 1sh6p multi 85 75
*74* A12 3sh ultra & multi 1.75 1.50

Rising Sun and Cogwheel A13

*Perf. 13½x13*

**1967, July 5 Litho. Unwmk.**

*75* A13 4p blk & brt grn 6 6
*76* A13 9p blk & car rose 15 15
*77* A13 1sh6p blk & brt pur 30 30
*78* A13 3sh blk & brt ultra 60 60
*a* Souv. sheet of 4 1.75 1.75

Issued to publicize Malawi industrial development. No. 78a contains one each of Nos. 75-78. Blue margin with black inscription and perforations extending into margins. Size: 133x107mm.

Nativity A14

*Perf. 14x14½*

**1967, Oct. 12 Photo. Wmk. 357**

| | | | | |
|---|---|---|---|---|
| *79* | A14 | 4p vio bl & grn | 6 | 6 |
| *80* | A14 | 9p vio bl & red | 15 | 15 |
| *81* | A14 | 1sh6p vio bl & yel | 30 | 30 |
| *82* | A14 | 3sh brt bl | 60 | 60 |
| *a* | | Souvenir sheet of 4 | 3.00 | 2.50 |

Christmas 1967.

No. 82a contains one each of Nos. 79-82, but perf. 14x13½. Violet blue margin. Size: 114x101mm.

Calotropis Procera — A15

Wild Flowers: 9p, Borreria dibrachiata. 1sh6p, Hibiscus rhodanthus. 3sh, Bidens pinnatipartita.

*Perf. 13½x13*

**1968, Apr. 24 Litho. Wmk. 357**

| | | | | |
|---|---|---|---|---|
| *83* | A15 | 4p grn & multi | 10 | 10 |
| *84* | A15 | 9p pale grn & multi | 28 | 28 |
| *85* | A15 | 1sh6p lt grn & multi | 55 | 55 |
| *86* | A15 | 3sh brt bl & multi | 1.10 | 1.10 |
| *a* | | Souv. sheet of 4 | 3.75 | 3.50 |

No. 86a contains one each of Nos. 83-86. Bright green decorative border and inscription. Size: 135x93mm.

Thistle No. 1, 1902 A16

Locomotives: 9p, G-class steam engine, 1954. 1sh6p, "Zambesi" diesel locomotive No. 202, 1963. 3sh, Diesel rail car No. 1, 1955.

*Perf. 14x14½*

**1968, July 24 Photo. Wmk. 357**

| | | | | |
|---|---|---|---|---|
| *87* | A16 | 4p gray grn & multi | 22 | 22 |
| *88* | A16 | 9p red & multi | 55 | 55 |
| *89* | A16 | 1sh6p cr & multi | 1.10 | 1.10 |
| *90* | A16 | 3sh lt ultra & multi | 2.25 | 2.25 |
| *a* | | Souv. sheet of 4 | 5.50 | 5.00 |

No. 90a contains one each of Nos. 87-90, but perf. 14. Light ultramarine margin with tracks and trestle design. Size: 120x89mm.

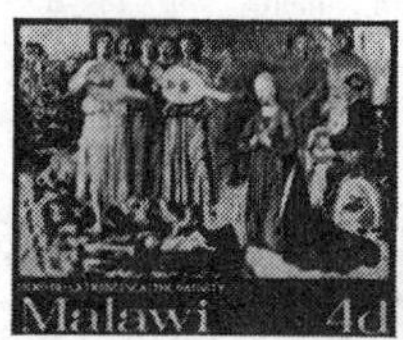


Nativity, by Piero della Francesca A17

Paintings: 9p, Adoration of the Shepherds, by Murillo. 1sh6p, Adoration of the Shepherds, by Guido Reni. 3sh, Nativity with God the Father and the Holy Ghost, by Giovanni Batista Pittoni.

**1968, Nov. 6 Photo. Wmk. 357**

| | | | | |
|---|---|---|---|---|
| *91* | A17 | 4p blk & multi | 8 | 8 |
| *92* | A17 | 9p multi | 20 | 20 |
| *93* | A17 | 1sh6p multi | 40 | 40 |
| *94* | A17 | 3sh bl & multi | 90 | 90 |
| *a* | | Souv. sheet of 4 | 2.75 | 2.50 |

Christmas 1968.

No. 94a contains one each of Nos. 91-94, but perf. 14x13½. Dull lilac margin with star design. Size: 115x102mm.

The Catalogue editors cannot undertake to appraise, identify or judge the genuineness or condition of stamps.

Scarlet-chested Sunbird A18

Nyasa Lovebird A19

Birds: 2p, Violet-backed starling. 3p, White-browed robin-chat. 4p, Red-billed firefinch. 9p, Yellow bishop. 1sh, Southern carmine bee-eater. 1sh6p, Grayheaded bush shrike. 2sh, Paradise whydah. 3sh, African paradise flycatcher. 5sh, Bateleur. 10sh, Saddlebill. £1, Purple heron. £2, Livingstone's lorie.

**1968, Nov. 13** *Perf. 14½*

**Size: 23x19, 19x23mm.**

| | | | | |
|---|---|---|---|---|
| *95* | A18 | 1p multi | 14 | 5 |
| *96* | A18 | 2p multi | 20 | 5 |
| *97* | A18 | 3p multi | 25 | 14 |
| *98* | A18 | 4p multi | 38 | 14 |
| *99* | A19 | 6p multi | 60 | 22 |
| *100* | A19 | 9p multi | 75 | 30 |

*Perf. 14*

**Size: 42x25, 25x42mm.**

| | | | | |
|---|---|---|---|---|
| *101* | A18 | 1sh multi | 90 | 50 |
| *102* | A18 | 1sh6p multi | 1.75 | 80 |
| *103* | A18 | 2sh multi | 2.75 | 1.25 |
| *104* | A19 | 3sh multi | 3.75 | 2.25 |
| *105* | A19 | 5sh multi | 5.00 | 3.50 |
| *106* | A19 | 10sh multi | 8.25 | 5.75 |
| *107* | A19 | £1 multi | 16.50 | 12.00 |
| *109* | A18 | £2 multi | 27.50 | 25.00 |
| | | *Nos. 95-109 (14)* | 68.72 | 51.95 |

No. 104 was surcharged "30t Special United Kingdom Delivery Service" in 5 lines and issued Feb. 8, 1971, during the British postal strike. The 30t was to pay a private postal service.

ILO Emblem A20

**Photo., Gold Impressed (Emblem)**

*Perf. 14x14½*

**1969, Feb. 5 Wmk. 357**

| | | | | |
|---|---|---|---|---|
| *110* | A20 | 4p dp grn | 6 | 6 |
| *111* | A20 | 9p dk rose brn | 15 | 15 |
| *112* | A20 | 1sh6p dk gray | 30 | 30 |
| *113* | A20 | 3sh dk bl | 60 | 60 |
| *a* | | Souv. sheet of 4 | 9.00 | 9.00 |

Issued to commemorate the 50th anniversary of the International Labor Organization. No. 113a contains one each of Nos. 110-113, light green margin with commemorative inscription. Size: 127x89mm.

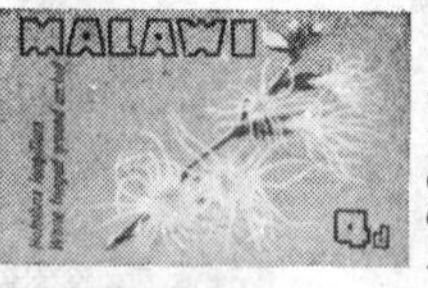


White Fringed Ground Orchid A21

Malawi Orchids: 9p, Red ground orchid. 1sh6p, Leopard tree orchid. 3sh, Blue ground orchid.

**1969, July 9 Litho.** *Perf. 13½*

| | | | | |
|---|---|---|---|---|
| *114* | A21 | 4p gray & multi | 20 | 15 |
| *115* | A21 | 9p gray & multi | 45 | 35 |
| *116* | A21 | 1sh6p gray & multi | 90 | 75 |
| *117* | A21 | 3sh gray & multi | 2.00 | 1.50 |
| *a* | | Souvenir sheet of 4 | 3.75 | 3.00 |

No. 117a contains one each of Nos. 114-117. Green ornaments and black inscription in margin. Size: 119x87mm.

African Development Bank Emblem — A22

**1969, Sept. 10** *Perf. 14*

| | | | | |
|---|---|---|---|---|
| *118* | A22 | 4p ocher, org yel & dk brn | 7 | 7 |
| *119* | A22 | 9p ocher, org yel & dk grn | 15 | 15 |
| *120* | A22 | 1sh6p ocher, org yel & blk | 30 | 30 |
| *121* | A22 | 3sh ocher, org yel & dk bl | 60 | 60 |
| *a* | | Souv. sheet of 4 | 1.75 | 1.75 |

Issued to commemorate the 5th anniversary of the African Development Bank. No. 121a contains one each of Nos. 118-121. Black marginal inscription and ornamental border. Size: 92x135mm.

"Peace on Earth" — A23

*Perf. 14x14½*

**1969, Nov. 5 Photo. Wmk. 357**

| | | | | |
|---|---|---|---|---|
| *122* | A23 | 2p cit & blk | 5 | 5 |
| *123* | A23 | 4p Prus bl & blk | 10 | 10 |
| *124* | A23 | 9p scar & blk | 25 | 25 |
| *125* | A23 | 1sh6p pur & blk | 45 | 45 |
| *126* | A23 | 3sh ultra & blk | 90 | 90 |
| *a* | | Souv. sheet of 5 | 2.75 | 2.75 |
| | | *Nos. 122-126 (5)* | 1.75 | 1.75 |

Christmas 1969.

No. 126a contains one each of Nos. 122-126. Dark blue decorative margin. Size: 130x74mm.

Elegant Grasshopper A24

Runner A25

Insects: 9p, Bean blister beetle. 1sh6p, Pumpkin ladybird. 3sh, Praying mantis.

**1970, Feb. 4 Litho.** *Perf. 14x14½*

| | | | | |
|---|---|---|---|---|
| *127* | A24 | 4p multi | 10 | 10 |
| *128* | A24 | 9p multi | 25 | 25 |
| *129* | A24 | 1sh6p multi | 50 | 50 |
| *130* | A24 | 3sh multi | 1.00 | 1.00 |
| *a* | | Souvenir sheet of 4 | 2.75 | 2.75 |

No. 130a contains one each of Nos. 127-130. Blue gray decorative margin with black inscription. Size: 85x136mm.

No. 102 Overprinted: "Rand Easter Show / 1970"

**1970, Mar. 18 Photo.** *Perf. 14*

| | | | | |
|---|---|---|---|---|
| *131* | A18 | 1sh6p multi | 50 | 50 |

Issued to publicize the 75th Anniversary Rand Easter Show, Johannesburg, South Africa, Mar. 24-Apr. 6.

**1970, June 3 Litho.** *Perf. 13*

| | | | | |
|---|---|---|---|---|
| *132* | A25 | 4p grn & dk bl | 8 | 8 |
| *133* | A25 | 9p rose & dk bl | 18 | 18 |
| *134* | A25 | 1sh6p dl yel & dk bl | 35 | 35 |
| *135* | A25 | 3sh bl & dk bl | 65 | 65 |
| *a* | | Souvenir sheet of 4 | 1.75 | 1.75 |

Issued to publicize the 9th Commonwealth Games, Edinburgh, Scotland, July 16-25. No. 135a contains one each of Nos. 132-135, violet blue margin. Size: 153x95mm.

**Dual Currency Issue**

Bird Type of 1968 with Denominations in Tambalas

Designs: 10t/1sh, Southern carmine bee-eater. 20t/2sh, Paradise whydah.

**1970, Sept. 2 Photo.** *Perf. 14½*

**Size: 42x25mm.**

| | | | | |
|---|---|---|---|---|
| *136* | A18 | 10t/1sh multi | 35 | 35 |
| *137* | A18 | 20t/2sh /multi | 75 | 75 |

Aegocera Trimenii A26

Moths of Malawi: 9p, Epiphora bauhiniae. 1sh6p, Parasa karschi. 3sh, Teracotona euprepia.

*Perf. 11x11½*

**1970, Sept. 30 Photo. Wmk. 357**

| | | | | |
|---|---|---|---|---|
| *138* | A26 | 4p multi | 16 | 14 |
| *139* | A26 | 9p multi | 35 | 30 |
| *140* | A26 | 1sh6p lt vio & multi | 70 | 65 |
| *141* | A26 | 3sh multi | 1.75 | 1.25 |
| *a* | | Souvenir sheet of 4 | 3.25 | 3.25 |

Nos. 141a contains one each of Nos. 138-141, bluish black margin. Size: 111x92½mm.

Mother and Child A27

**1970, Nov. 4 Litho.** *Perf. 14½*

| | | | | |
|---|---|---|---|---|
| *142* | A27 | 2p blk & yel | 6 | 6 |
| *143* | A27 | 4p blk & emer | 10 | 10 |
| *144* | A27 | 9p blk & dp org | 25 | 25 |
| *145* | A27 | 1sh6p blk & red lil | 50 | 50 |
| *146* | A27 | 3sh blk & ultra | 1.00 | 1.00 |
| *a* | | Souvenir sheet of 5 | 2.50 | 2.50 |
| | | *Nos. 142-146 (5)* | 1.91 | 1.91 |

Christmas 1970.

No. 146a contains one each of Nos. 142-146 and one label inscribed "PAX." Yellow margin with black inscription. Size: 164x99m.

**Decimal Currency Issue**

Greater Kudu A28

Eland A29

Antelopes: 2t, Nyala. 3t, Reedbuck. 5t, Puku. 8t, Impala. 15t, Klipspringer. 20t, Livingstone's suni. 30t, Roan antelope. 50t, Waterbuck. 1k, Bushbuck. 2k, Red duiker. 4k, Gray bush duiker.

*Perf. 13½x14 (A28), 14x14½ (A29)*

**1971, Feb. 15 Litho. Wmk. 357**

| | | | | |
|---|---|---|---|---|
| *148* | A28 | 1t dl vio & multi | 5 | 5 |
| *a* | | Perf. 14½x14, coil | 12 | 12 |
| *b* | | Perf. 14 ('74) | 16 | 12 |
| *149* | A28 | 2t dp yel & multi | 5 | 5 |
| *150* | A28 | 3t ap grn & multi | 12 | 6 |
| *a* | | Perf. 14 ('74) | 28 | 22 |
| *151* | A28 | 5t multi | 16 | 14 |
| *a* | | Perf. 14 ('74) | 38 | 32 |
| *152* | A28 | 8t org red & multi | 28 | 22 |
| *153* | A29 | 10t grn & multi | 32 | 28 |
| *154* | A29 | 15t brt pur & multi | 55 | 55 |
| *155* | A29 | 20t bl gray & multi | 70 | 70 |
| *156* | A29 | 30t dl bl & multi | 1.10 | 1.10 |
| *157* | A29 | 50t multi | 1.90 | 1.90 |
| *158* | A29 | 1k multi | 2.75 | 2.75 |

159 A29 2k gray & multi 5.50 5.50
160 A29 4k multi 13.50 12.00
*Nos. 148-160 (13)* 26.98 25.30

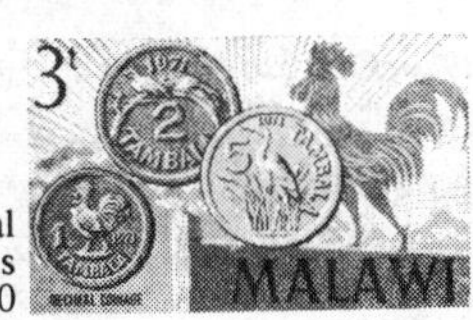

Decimal Coins A30

**1971, Feb. 15** *Perf. 14½*

*161* A30 3t multi 7 7
*162* A30 8t dl red & multi 18 18
*163* A30 15t pur & multi 35 35
*164* A30 30t brt bl & multi 65 65
*a* Souvenir sheet of 4 1.75 1.75

Introduction of decimal currency and coinage. No. 164a contains one each of Nos. 161-164. Multicolored decorative margin. Size: 140x101mm.

Christ on the Cross, by Dürer — A31

Design: Nos. 166, 168, 170, 172, The Resurrection, by Albrecht Dürer.

*Perf. 14x13½*

**1971, Apr. 7 Litho. Wmk. 357**

*165* A31 3t emer & blk 6 6
*166* A31 3t emer & blk 6 6
*167* A31 8t org & blk 18 18
*168* A31 8t org & blk 18 18
*169* A31 15t red lil & blk 35 35
*170* A31 15t red lil & blk 35 35
*171* A31 30t bl & blk 65 65
*a* Souvenir sheet of 4 1.75 1.75
*172* A31 30t bl & blk 65 65
*a* Souvenir sheet of 4 1.75 1.75
*Nos. 165-172 (8)* 2.48 2.48

Easter 1971. The 2 designs of each denomination are printed se-tenant, arranged checkerwise, in sheets of 25. No. 171a contains one each of Nos. 165, 167, 169 and 171; No. 172a contains one each of Nos. 166, 168, 170 and 172. Black marginal inscriptions. Size: 95x145mm.

Holarrhena Febrifuga — A32 Drum Major — A33

Flowering Shrubs and Trees: 8t, Brachystegia spiciformis. 15t, Securidaca longepedunculata. 30t, Pterocarpus rotundifolius.

**1971, July 14 Litho. Wmk. 357**

*173* A32 3t gray & multi 6 6
*174* A32 8t gray & multi 18 18
*175* A32 15t gray & multi 35 35
*176* A32 30t gray & multi 65 65
*a* Souvenir sheet of 4 2.25 2.25

No. 176a contains one each of Nos. 173-176. Yellow margin with gray ornament, brown inscription. Size: 101½x135mm.

**1971, Oct. 5** *Perf. 14x14½*

*177* A33 30t lt bl & multi 90 90

50th anniversary of Malawi Police Force.

Madonna and Child, by William Dyce — A34

Paintings of Holy Family by: 8t, Martin Schongauer. 15t, Raphael. 30t, Bronzino.

**1971, Nov. 10** *Perf. 14½*

*178* A34 3t grn & multi 8 8
*179* A34 8t car & multi 20 20
*180* A34 15t dp cl & multi 40 40
*181* A34 30t dl bl & multi 90 90
*a* Souvenir sheet of 4 2.75 2.75

Christmas 1971. No. 181a contains one each of Nos. 178-181. Deep carmine ornamental margin. Size: 101x139mm.

Vickers Viscount — A35

Airplanes: 8t, Hawker Siddeley 748. 15t, Britten Norman Islander. 30t, B.A.C. One Eleven.

*Perf. 13½x14*

**1972, Feb. 9 Litho. Wmk. 357**

*182* A35 3t brt grn, blk & red 8 8
*183* A35 8t red org & blk 25 25
*184* A35 15t dp rose lil, red & blk 50 50
*185* A35 30t vio bl & multi 1.00 1.00
*a* Souvenir sheet of 4 4.00 4.00

Publicity for Air Malawi. No. 185a contains one each of Nos. 182-185. Red orange and black margin. Size: 143½x94mm.

Figures, Chencherere Hill — A36

Rock Paintings: 8t, Lizard and cat, Chencherere Hill. 15t, Symbols, Diwa Hill. 30t, Sun behind rain, Mikolongwe Hill.

**1972, May 10** *Perf. 13½*

*186* A36 3t blk & yel grn 8 8
*187* A36 8t blk & dp car 20 20
*188* A36 15t blk, vio & car 40 40
*189* A36 30t blk, bl & yel 90 90
*a* Souvenir sheet of 4 2.25 2.25

No. 189a contains one each of Nos. 186-189, but perf. 15. Yellow green and black decorative margin. Size: 121x96mm.

Athlete and Olympic Rings — A37

**1972, Aug. 9** *Perf. 14x14½*

*190* A37 3t gray, blk & grn 7 7
*191* A37 8t gray, blk & scar 18 18
*192* A37 15t gray, blk & lil 32 32
*193* A37 30t gray, blk & bl 65 65
*a* Souvenir sheet of 4 2.00 2.00

20th Olympic Games, Munich, Aug. 26-Sept. 10.

No. 193a contains one each of Nos. 190-193. Deep carmine margin with black inscription. Size: 110x91mm.

Malawi Coat of Arms — A38

**1972, Oct. 20 Litho.** *Perf. 13½x14*

*194* A38 15t bl & multi 50 50

18th Commonwealth Parliamentary Conference, Malawi, Oct. 1972.

Adoration of the Kings, by Orcagna — A39

Paintings of the Florentine School: 8t, Madonna and Child Enthroned, anonymous. 15t, Madonna and Child with Sts. Bonaventura and Louis of Toulouse, by Carlo Crivelli. 30t, Madonna and Child with St. Anne, by Jean de Bruges.

*Perf. 14½x14*

**1972, Nov. 8 Wmk. 357**

*195* A39 3t lt ol & multi 8 8
*196* A39 8t car & multi 20 20
*197* A39 15t pur & multi 40 40
*198* A39 30t bl & multi 90 90
*a* Souvenir sheet of 4 2.50 2.50

Christmas 1972. No. 198a contains one each of Nos. 195-198. Multicolored margin. Size: 95x122mm.

Charaxes Bohemani — A40

**1973** *Perf. 13½x14*

*199* A40 3t shown 20 16
*200* A40 8t Uranothauma crawshayi 60 50
*201* A40 15t Charaxes acuminatus 1.25 1.00
*202* A40 30t "euphaedra zaddachi" 3.25 2.00
*a* Souvenir sheet of 4 9.00 2.50
*203* A40 30t amauris ansorgei 2.75 2.00
*Nos. 199-203 (5)* 8.05 5.66

No. 202a contains one each of Nos. 199-202. Green and blue margin with scarlet inscription. Size: 143½x95mm.

Issue dates: Nos. 199-202, Feb. 7. No. 203, Apr. 5.

Dr. Livingstone and Map of West Africa — A41

Livingstone Choosing Site for Mission — A42

**1973 Litho.** *Perf. 13½x14*

*204* A41 3t ap grn & multi 10 10
*205* A41 8t red org & multi 30 30
*206* A41 15t multi 60 60
*207* A41 30t bl & multi 1.25 1.25
*a* Souvenir sheet of 4 2.25 2.25
*208* A42 50t blk & multi 1.25 1.25
*a* Souvenir sheet of 4 2.00 2.00
*Nos. 204-208 (5)* 3.50 3.50

Centenary of the death of Dr. David Livingstone (1813-1873), medical missionary and explorer. No. 207a contains one each of Nos. 204-207. Multicolored margin with black inscription. Size: 144x95mm.

No. 208a contains one stamp with design extending into black margin showing stained glass window at Livingstonia Mission. Size: 70x76mm.

Issue dates: May 1, Nos. 204-207, 207a; Dec. 12, No. 208, 208a.

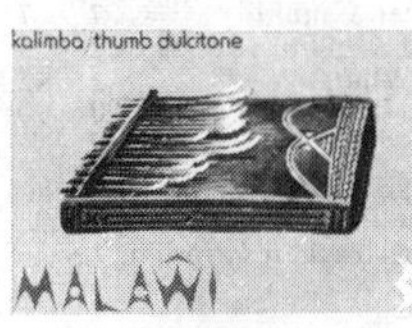

Thumb Dulcitone (Kalimba) A43

African Musical Instruments: 8t, Hand zither (bangwe; vert.). 15t, Hand drum (ng'oma; vert.). 30t, One-stringed fiddle (kaligo).

**1973, Aug. 8 Wmk. 357** *Perf. 14*

*209* A43 3t brt grn & multi 8 8
*210* A43 8t red & multi 25 25
*211* A43 15t vio & multi 48 48
*212* A43 30t bl & multi 1.00 1.00
*a* Souvenir sheet of 4 2.25 2.25

No. 212a contains one each of Nos. 209-212. Multicolored border and marginal inscription. Size: 119x103mm.

The Three Kings A44

**1973, Nov. 8** *Perf. 13½x14*

*213* A44 3t bl & multi 7 7
*214* A44 8t ver & multi 20 20
*215* A44 15t multi 40 40
*216* A44 30t org & multi 80 80
*a* Souvenir sheet of 4 2.00 2.00

Christmas 1973. No. 216a contains one each of Nos. 213-216, multicolored border. Size: 159x113½mm.

Largemouth Black Bass — A45

Designs: Game fish.

**1974, Feb. 20 Litho.** *Perf. 14x14½*

*217* A45 3t *shown* 15 15
*218* A45 8t *Rainbow trout* 40 40
*219* A45 15t *Lake salmon* 90 90
*220* A45 30t *Triggerfish* 1.60 1.60
*a* Souvenir sheet of 4 3.00 3.00

30th anniversary of Angling Society of Malawi. No. 220a contains one each of Nos. 217-220; multicolored margin with emblem of Angling Society and fishermen. Size: 168x92mm.

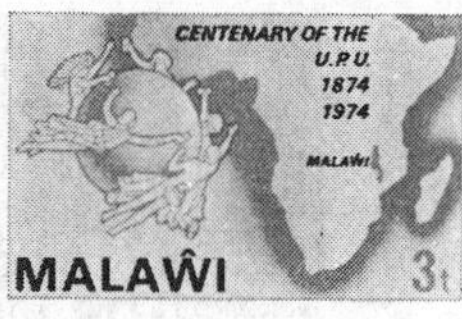


UPU Emblem, Map of Africa with Malawi
A46

**1974, Apr. 24** *Perf. 13½*

| | | | | |
|---|---|---|---|---|
| *221* | A46 | 3t grn & bis | 8 | 8 |
| *222* | A46 | 8t ver & bis | 20 | 20 |
| *223* | A46 | 15t lil & bis | 40 | 40 |
| *224* | A46 | 30t gray & bis | 85 | 85 |
| *a* | | Souvenir sheet of 4 | 2.25 | 2.00 |

Centenary of Universal Postal Union. No. 224a contains one each of Nos. 221-224; multicolored margin with globes and commemorative inscription. Size: 115x145mm.

Capital Hill, Lilongwe and Pres. Kamuzu Banda
A47

**1974, July 3** **Litho.** *Perf. 14*

| | | | | |
|---|---|---|---|---|
| *225* | A47 | 3t emer & multi | 7 | 7 |
| *226* | A47 | 8t red & multi | 22 | 22 |
| *227* | A47 | 15t lil & multi | 45 | 45 |
| *228* | A47 | 30t vio bl & multi | 90 | 90 |
| *a* | | Souvenir sheet of 4 | 1.40 | 1.40 |

10th anniversary of independence. No. 228a contains one each of Nos. 225-228, pale lilac margin and black inscription. Size: 120x85mm.

Madonna of the Meadow, by Giovanni Bellini — A48

Paintings: 8t, Holy Family, by Jacob Jordaens. 15t, Nativity, by Peter F. de Grebber. 30t, Adoration of the Shepherds, by Lorenzo di Credi.

**1974, Dec. 4** **Litho.** *Perf. 13½x14*

| | | | | |
|---|---|---|---|---|
| *229* | A48 | 3t dk grn & multi | 7 | 7 |
| *230* | A48 | 8t multi | 20 | 20 |
| *231* | A48 | 15t pur & multi | 40 | 40 |
| *232* | A48 | 30t dk bl & multi | 85 | 85 |
| *a* | | Souvenir sheet of 4 | 1.75 | 1.75 |

Christmas 1974. No. 232a contains one each of Nos. 229-232. Yellow and dark brown margin. Size: 117x106mm.

African Snipe
A49

Double-banded Sandgrouse
A50

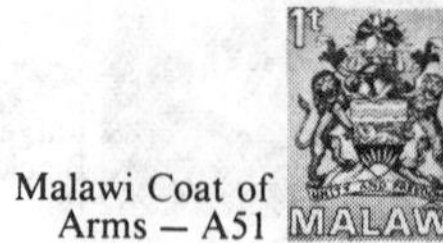


Malawi Coat of Arms — A51

Birds: 3t, Blue quail. 5t, Red-necked francolin. 8t, Harlequin quail. 10t, Spurwing goose. 15t, Denham's bustard. 20t, Knob-billed duck. 30t, Helmeted guinea fowl. 50t, Pigmy goose. 1k, Garganey. 2k, White-faced tree duck. 4k, Green pigeon.

**Wmk. 357**

**1975, Feb. 19** **Litho.** *Perf. 14*

**Size: 17x21, 21x17mm.**

| | | | | |
|---|---|---|---|---|
| *233* | A49 | 1t multi | 8 | 5 |
| *234* | A50 | 2t multi | 12 | 5 |
| *235* | A50 | 3t multi | 16 | 12 |
| *236* | A49 | 5t multi | 20 | 14 |
| *237* | A50 | 8t multi | 32 | 22 |

*Perf. 14½*

**Size: 25x41, 41x25mm.**

| | | | | |
|---|---|---|---|---|
| *238* | A49 | 10t multi | 55 | 38 |
| *239* | A49 | 15t multi | 75 | 55 |
| *240* | A49 | 20t multi | 90 | 65 |
| *241* | A49 | 30t multi | 1.40 | 1.00 |
| *242* | A50 | 50t multi | 2.25 | 55 |
| *243* | A50 | 1k multi | 4.25 | 3.25 |
| *244* | A49 | 2k multi | 8.75 | 7.00 |
| *245* | A50 | 4k multi | 14.00 | 11.00 |
| | | *Nos. 233-245 (13)* | 33.73 | 24.96 |

See Nos. 270-279.

Coil Stamp

**1975-85** *Perf. 14½x14*

| | | | | |
|---|---|---|---|---|
| *246* | A51 | 1t dk vio bl | 6 | 6 |
| *247* | A51 | 5t red ('85) | 8 | 8 |

"Mpasa"
A52

Designs: Lake Malawi ships.

**Wmk. 357**

**1975, Mar. 12** **Litho.** *Perf. 13½*

| | | | | |
|---|---|---|---|---|
| *251* | A52 | 3t *shown* | 10 | 10 |
| *252* | A52 | 8t *"Ilala II"* | 30 | 30 |
| *253* | A52 | 15t *"Chauncy Maples"* | 60 | 60 |
| *254* | A52 | 30t *"Nkwazi"* | 1.25 | 1.25 |
| *a* | | Souvenir sheet of 4 | 2.75 | 2.75 |

No. 254a contains one each of Nos. 251-254, perf. 14½. Light blue and black margin showing map of Lake Malawi, ships and their descriptions. Size: 105x142mm.

Habenaria Splendens
A53

Bush Baby
A54

Orchids of Malawi: 10t, Eulophia cucullata. 20t, Disa welwitschii. 40t, Angraecum conchiferum.

**1975, June 6** **Litho.** *Perf. 14½*

| | | | | |
|---|---|---|---|---|
| *255* | A53 | 3t lt grn & multi | 14 | 14 |
| *256* | A53 | 10t red org & multi | 42 | 42 |
| *257* | A53 | 20t dl vio & multi | 90 | 90 |
| *258* | A53 | 40t multi | 1.75 | 1.75 |
| *a* | | Souvenir sheet of 4 | 2.75 | 2.75 |

No. 258a contains one each of Nos. 255-258; brief descriptions of orchids. Size: 127x111mm.

**1975, Sept. 3** **Litho.** *Perf. 14*

| | | | | |
|---|---|---|---|---|
| *259* | A54 | 3t *shown* | 14 | 14 |
| *260* | A54 | 10t *Leopard* | 42 | 42 |
| *261* | A54 | 20t *Roan antelope* | 90 | 90 |
| *262* | A54 | 40t *Burchell's zebra* | 1.75 | 1.75 |
| *a* | | Souvenir sheet of 4 | 3.75 | 3.75 |

Animals of Malawi. No. 262a contains one each of Nos. 259-262; bister margin with green description and animal design. Size: 87x127½mm.

No. 242 Overprinted: "10th ACP / Ministerial / Conference / 1975"

**1975, Dec. 9** **Litho.** *Perf. 14½*

| | | | | |
|---|---|---|---|---|
| *263* | A50 | 50t multi | 1.25 | 1.25 |

10th African, Caribbean and Pacific Ministerial Conference.

Adoration of the Kings, French
A55

Designs: 10t, Nativity, 16th century, Spanish. 20t, Nativity, by Pierre Raymond, 16th century. 40t, Angel Appearing to the Shepherds, 14th century, English.

**1975, Dec. 12** *Perf. 13x13½*

| | | | | |
|---|---|---|---|---|
| *264* | A55 | 3t multi | 8 | 8 |
| *265* | A55 | 10t multi | 25 | 25 |
| *266* | A55 | 20t pur & multi | 50 | 50 |
| *267* | A55 | 40t bl & multi | 1.00 | 1.00 |
| *a* | | Souvenir sheet of 4 | 1.90 | 1.90 |

Christmas 1975. No. 267a contains one each of Nos. 264-267, perf. 14. Lilac margin with black inscriptions giving details about designs. Size: 97x166mm.

Bird Types of 1975

**1975** **Litho.** **Unwmk.** *Perf. 14*

**Size: 21x17mm.**

| | | | | |
|---|---|---|---|---|
| *270* | A50 | 3t multi | 6 | 6 |

*Perf. 14½*

**Size: 25x41mm.**

| | | | | |
|---|---|---|---|---|
| *273* | A49 | 10t multi | 22 | 22 |
| *274* | A49 | 15t multi | 45 | 45 |
| *279* | A49 | 2k multi | 7.50 | 5.50 |

Alexander Graham Bell — A56

President Kamuzu Banda — A57

*Perf. 14x14½*

**1976, Mar. 24** **Litho.** **Wmk. 357**

| | | | | |
|---|---|---|---|---|
| *281* | A56 | 3t grn & blk | 6 | 6 |
| *282* | A56 | 10t dp lil rose & blk | 22 | 22 |
| *283* | A56 | 20t brt pur & blk | 45 | 45 |
| *284* | A56 | 40t brt bl & blk | 90 | 90 |
| *a* | | Souvenir sheet of 4 | 1.90 | 1.90 |

Centenary of first telephone call by Alexander Graham Bell, Mar. 10, 1876. No. 284a contains one each of Nos. 281-284; Bell's telephone and inscription in purple and black in margin. Size: 137x114mm.

**1976, July 1** **Photo.** *Perf. 13*

| | | | | |
|---|---|---|---|---|
| *285* | A57 | 3t brt grn & multi | 6 | 6 |
| *286* | A57 | 10t multi | 16 | 16 |
| *287* | A57 | 20t vio & multi | 35 | 35 |
| *288* | A57 | 40t dl bl & multi | 65 | 65 |
| *a* | | Souvenir sheet of 4 | 2.00 | 2.00 |

10th anniversary of the Republic. No. 288a contains one each of Nos. 285-288; violet decorative margin. Size: 102x112mm.

Bagnall Diesel No. 100
A58

Diesel Locomotives: 10t, Shire class No. 503. 20t, Nippon Sharyo No. 301. 40t, Hunslet No. 110.

**1976, Oct. 1** **Litho.** *Perf. 14½*

| | | | | |
|---|---|---|---|---|
| *289* | A58 | 3t emer & multi | 12 | 7 |
| *290* | A58 | 10t red & multi | 40 | 25 |
| *291* | A58 | 20t lil & multi | 75 | 50 |
| *292* | A58 | 40t bl & multi | 1.60 | 1.00 |
| *a* | | Souvenir sheet of 4 | 2.75 | 2.50 |

Malawi Railways. No. 292a contains one each of Nos. 289-292; multicolored margin showing locomotive. Size: 130x117mm.

Nos. 274 and 241 Overprinted: **Blantyre Mission Centenary 1876-1976**

**1976, Oct. 22** **Litho.** **Unwmk.**

| | | | | |
|---|---|---|---|---|
| *293* | A49 | 15t multi | 45 | 45 |

**Wmk. 357**

| | | | | |
|---|---|---|---|---|
| *294* | A49 | 30t multi | 90 | 90 |

Blantyre Mission centenary.

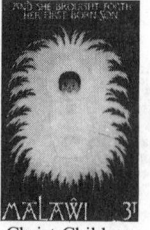

Christ Child on Straw Bed — A59

Ebony Ancestor Figures — A60

**1976, Dec. 6** **Wmk. 357** *Perf. 14*

| | | | | |
|---|---|---|---|---|
| *295* | A59 | 3t grn & multi | 8 | 8 |
| *296* | A59 | 10t mag & multi | 22 | 22 |
| *297* | A59 | 20t pur & multi | 45 | 45 |
| *298* | A59 | 40t dk bl & multi | 90 | 90 |
| *a* | | Souvenir sheet of 4 | 1.75 | 1.75 |

Christmas 1976. No. 298a contains one each of Nos. 295-298 violet blue and black margin with kneeling Mary and Jesus. Size: 135x96mm.

**1977, Apr. 1** **Litho.** **Wmk. 357**

Handicrafts: 10t, Ebony elephant (horiz.). 20t, Ebony rhinoceros (horiz.). 40t, Wooden antelope.

| | | | | |
|---|---|---|---|---|
| *299* | A60 | 4t yel & multi | 8 | 8 |
| *300* | A60 | 10t blk & multi | 20 | 20 |
| *301* | A60 | 20t ocher & multi | 40 | 40 |
| *302* | A60 | 40t ver & multi | 85 | 85 |
| *a* | | Souvenir sheet of 4 | 2.25 | 2.25 |

No. 302a contains one each of Nos. 299-302; vermilion margin with black inscription and coat of arms. Size: 151x101mm.

Chileka Airport, Blantyre, and VC10
A61

Designs: 10t, Leyland bus on Blantyre-Lilongwe Road. 20t, Ilala II on Lake Malawi. 40t, Freight train of Blantyre-Nacala line on overpass.

**1977, July 12** **Litho.** *Perf. 14½*

| | | | | |
|---|---|---|---|---|
| *303* | A61 | 4t multi | 8 | 8 |
| *304* | A61 | 10t multi | 20 | 20 |
| *305* | A61 | 20t multi | 40 | 40 |
| *306* | A61 | 40t multi | 85 | 85 |
| *a* | | Souvenir sheet of 4 | 2.75 | 2.75 |

Transportation in Malawi. No. 306a contains one each of Nos. 303-306; multicolored margin shows landscape and plane. Size: 127x83mm.

Pseudotropheus Johanni — A62

Lake Malawi Fish: 10t, Pseudotropheus livingstoni. 20t, Pseudotropheus zebra. 40t, Genyochromis mento.

**Wmk. 357, Unwmkd.**

**1977, Oct. 4** **Litho.** *Perf. 13½x14*

| | | | | |
|---|---|---|---|---|
| *307* | A62 | 4t multi | 10 | 10 |
| *308* | A62 | 10t multi | 25 | 25 |
| *309* | A62 | 20t multi | 50 | 50 |

*310* A62 40t multi 1.00 1.00
*a* Souvenir sheet of 4 2.00 2.00

No. 310a contains one each of Nos. 307-310; multicolored margin shows various fish and map of Lake Malawi. Size: 149x98mm.

Virgin and Child, by Bergognone A63

Entry into Jerusalem, by Giotto A64

Virgin and Child: 10t, with God the Father and Angels, by Ambrogio Bergognone. 20t, detail from Bottigella altarpiece, by Vincenzo Foppa. 40t, with the fountain, by Jan Van Eyck.

***Perf. 14x13½***

**1977, Nov. 21 Litho. Unwmk.**

*311* A63 4t multi 8 8
*312* A63 10t red & multi 20 20
*313* A63 20t lil & multi 40 40
*314* A63 40t vio bl & multi 85 85
*a* Souvenir sheet of 4 2.00 2.00

Christmas 1977. No. 314a contains one each of Nos. 311-314; multicolored margin shows Angel. Size: 150x116mm.

**1978, Mar. 1 Litho. *Perf. 12x12½***

Giotto Paintings: 10t, Crucifixion. 20t, Descent from the Cross. 40t, Jesus Appearing to Mary.

*315* A64 4t multi 8 8
*316* A64 10t multi 20 20
*317* A64 20t multi 40 40
*318* A64 40t multi 85 85
*a* Souvenir sheet of 4 2.75 1.75

Easter 1978. No. 318a contains one each of Nos. 315-318; multicolored margin shows angel with cross. Size: 149x100mm.

Lions, Wildlife Fund Emblem A65

Animals and Wildlife Fund Emblem: 4t, Nyala (vert.). 20t, Burchell's zebras. 40t, Reedbuck (vert.).

***Perf. 13x13½***

**1978, June 1 Litho. Unwmk.**

*319* A65 4t multi 15 15
*320* A65 10t multi 35 35
*321* A65 20t multi 75 75
*322* A65 40t multi 1.50 1.50
*a* Souvenir sheet of 4 3.00 3.00

Nos. 322a contains Nos. 319-322, perf. 13½; yellow and multicolored margin with cheetah and Wildlife Fund Emblem. Size: 173x113½mm.

Malamulo Seventh Day Adventist Church — A66

Designs (Virgin and Child and): 10t, Likoma Cathedral. 20t, St. Michael's and All Angel's, Blantyre. 40t, Zomba Catholic Cathedral.

**1978, Nov. 15 Wmk. 357 *Perf. 14***

*323* A66 4t multi 8 8
*324* A66 10t multi 22 22
*325* A66 20t multi 45 45
*326* A66 40t multi 90 90
*a* Souvenir sheet of 4 1.75 1.75

Christmas 1978. No. 326a contains Nos. 323-326. Green margin shows Virgin and Child. Size: 190x105mm.

Vanilla Polylepis — A67

Brachystegia Spiciformis — A68

Orchids of Malawi: 2t, Cirrhopetalum umbellatum. 5t, Calanthe natalensis. 7t, Ansellia gigantea. 8t, Tridactyle bicaudata. 10t, Acampe pachyglossa. 15t, Eulophia quartiniana. 20t, Cyrtorchis arcuata. 30t, Eulophia tricristata. 50t, Disa hamatopetala. 75t, Cynorchis glandulosa. 1k, Aerangis kotschyana. 1.50k, Polystachya dendrobiiflora. 2k, Disa ornithantha. 4k, Cytorchis praetermissa.

**1979, Jan. 2 Litho. *Perf. 13½***

*327* A67 1t multi 5 5
*328* A67 2t multi 5 5
*329* A67 5t multi 10 10
*330* A67 7t multi 12 12
*331* A67 8t multi 14 14
*332* A67 10t multi 18 18
*333* A67 15t multi 28 28
*334* A67 20t multi 35 35
*335* A67 30t multi 50 50
*336* A67 50t multi 90 90
*337* A67 75t multi 1.40 1.40
*338* A67 1k multi 1.75 1.75
*339* A67 1.50k multi 2.50 2.50
*340* A67 2k multi 3.25 3.25
*341* A67 4k multi 7.50 7.50
*Nos. 327-341 (15)* 19.07 19.07

**1979, Jan. 21 *Perf. 14x13½***

Trees: 10t, Widdringtonia nodiflora. 20t, Sandalwood. 40t, African mahogany.

*342* A68 5t multi 12 12
*343* A68 10t multi 22 22
*344* A68 20t multi 45 45
*345* A68 40t multi 90 90
*a* Souvenir sheet of 4 1.75 1.75

National Tree Planting Day. No. 345a contains Nos. 342-345; dark green and yellow green margin showing leaves. Size: 108x153mm.

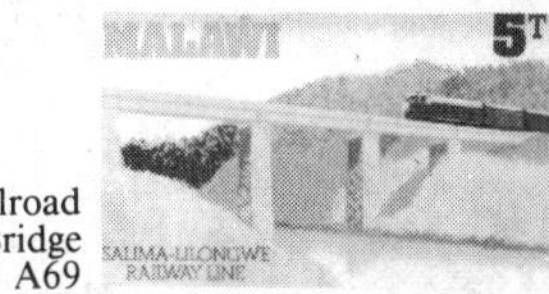

Railroad Bridge A69

Designs: 10t, Station and train. 20t, 40t, Train passing through man-made pass (diff.).

**1979, Feb. 17 Litho. *Perf. 14½***

*346* A69 5t multi 12 12
*347* A69 10t multi 25 25
*348* A69 20t multi 52 52
*349* A69 40t multi 1.05 1.05
*a* Souvenir sheet of 4 1.75 1.75

Inauguration of Salima-Lilongwe Railroad. No. 349a contains Nos. 346-349; blue and violet blue margin shows tracks and train. Size: 155x102mm.

Malawi Boy and IYC Emblem — A70

Designs: Malawi children and IYC emblem.

**Wmk. 357**

**1979, July 10 Litho. *Perf. 14***

*350* A70 5t multi 8 8
*351* A70 10t multi 18 18
*352* A70 20t multi 35 35
*353* A70 40t multi 75 75

International Year of the Child.

Malawi No. 1 — A71

Stamps of Malawi: 10t, No. 2. 20t, No. 3. 40t, No. 4.

***Perf. 13½x14***

**1979, Sept. 17 Litho. Wmk. 357**

*354* A71 5t multi 8 8
*355* A71 10t multi 20 20
*356* A71 20t multi 35 35
*357* A71 40t multi 65 65
*a* Souvenir sheet of 4 2.25 2.25

Sir Rowland Hill (1795-1879), originator of penny postage. No. 357a contains Nos. 354-357. Tan and black margin shows Hill's portrait and signature. Size: 162x107½mm.

Christmas 1979 — A72

Designs: Landscapes.

**1979, Nov. 15 Litho. *Perf. 13½x14***

*358* A72 5t multi 8 8
*359* A72 10t multi 18 18
*360* A72 20t multi 35 35
*361* A72 40t multi 65 65

Limbe Rotary Club Emblem — A73

Malawi Rotary Club Emblems: 10t, Blantyre. 20t, Lilongwe. 40t, Rotary International.

**1980, Feb. 23 Litho. *Perf. 13½***

*362* A73 5t multi 8 8
*363* A73 10t multi 18 18
*364* A73 20t multi 35 35
*365* A73 40t multi 65 65
*a* Souvenir sheet of 4 1.50 1.50

Rotary International, 75th anniversary. No. 365a contains Nos. 362-365; light violet and gold margin shows Rotary emblem. Size: 105x144mm.

Mangochi District Post Office, 1976, London 1980 Emblem — A74

London 1980 Emblem and: 10t, New Blantyre sorting office, 1979. 20t, Mail transfer hut, Walala. 1k, Nyasaland Post Office, Chiromo, 1891.

**Wmk. 357**

**1980, May 6 Litho. *Perf. 14½***

*366* A74 5t bl grn & blk 7 7
*367* A74 10t red & blk 15 15
*368* A74 20t dp vio & blk 30 30
*369* A74 1k dk bl & blk 1.40 1.40
*a* Souvenir sheet of 4 2.50 2.50

London 1980 International Stamp Exhibition, May 6-14. No. 369a contains Nos. 366-369; light and dark blue margin shows London 1980 emblem. Size: 115x89½mm.

Agate Nodule — A75

**1980, Aug. 20 Litho. *Perf. 13½***

*370* A75 5t *shown* 12 12
*371* A75 10t *Sunstone* 25 25
*372* A75 20t *Smoky Quartz* 50 50
*373* A75 1k *Kyanite crystal* 2.50 2.50

Elephants Drinking (Christmas 1980) — A76

**1980, Nov. 10 Litho. *Perf. 13***

*374* A76 5t *shown* 8 8
*375* A76 10t *Flowers* 16 16
*376* A76 20t *Train* 35 35
*377* A76 1k *Bird* 1.75 1.75

Livingstone's Suni — A77

**1981, Feb. 4 Litho. *Perf. 14½***

*378* A77 7t shown 15 15
*379* A77 10t Blue duikers 18 18
*380* A77 20t African buffalo 40 40
*381* A77 1k Lichtenstein's hartebeests 1.90 1.90

Standard A Earth Station A78

**1981, Apr. 24 Litho. *Perf. 14½***

*382* A78 7t shown 12 12
*383* A78 10t Blantyre International Gateway Exchange 16 16
*384* A78 20t Standard B Earth Station 35 35

*385* A78 1k Satellite and earth 1.75 1.75
*a* Souvenir sheet of 4 2.50 2.50

International communications. No. 385a contains Nos. 382-385; multicolored margin shows rocket take-off. Size: 102x151mm.

World Food Day A79

**1981, Sept. 11 Litho. *Perf. 14***
*386* A79 7t Corn 12 12
*387* A79 10t Rice 16 16
*388* A79 20t Finger millet 35 35
*389* A79 1k Wheat 1.75 1.75

Holy Family, by Lippi A80

Christmas 1981 (Paintings): 7t, Adoration of the Shepherds, by Murillo (vert.). 20t, Adoration of the Shepherds, by Louis Le Nain. 1k, Virgin and Child, St. John the Baptist and Angel, by Paolo Morando (vert.).

***Perf. 13½x13, 13x13½***
**1981, Nov. 26 Litho.**
*390* A80 7t multi 12 12
*391* A80 10t multi 16 16
*392* A80 20t multi 35 35
*393* A80 1k multi 1.75 1.75

Wildlife in Natl. Parks A81

**1982, Mar. 15 Litho. *Perf. 14½x14***
*394* A81 7t Impalas 12 12
*395* A81 10t Lions 16 16
*396* A81 20t Kudus 35 35
*397* A81 1k Flamingos 1.75 1.75

Kamuzu Academy — A82

Designs: Academy views.

**1982, July 1 Litho. *Perf. 14½***
*398* A82 7t multi 10 10
*399* A82 20t multi 28 28
*400* A82 30t multi 40 40
*401* A82 1k multi 1.40 1.40

1982 World Cup — A83

**1982, Sept. *Perf. 14x14½***
*402* A83 7t Players 15 15
*403* A83 20t World Cup 40 40
*404* A83 30t Stadium 55 55

**Souvenir Sheet**
*405* A83 1k Emblem on field 2.00 2.00

No. 405 has multicolored margin continuing design. Size: 81x60mm.

Remembrance Day — A84

Designs: War Memorials.

**1982, Nov. 5 *Perf. 14½***
*406* A84 7t Blantyre 12 12
*407* A84 20t Zomba 35 35
*408* A84 30t Chichiri, badges 50 50
*409* A84 1k Lilongwe 1.75 1.75

**Commonwealth Day**
Common Design Type
**Wmk. 357**
**1983, Mar. 14 Litho. *Perf. 14***
*410* CD334 7t Kwacha Intl. Conf. Ctr. 12 12
*411* CD334 20t Tea picking, Mulanje 35 35
*412* CD334 30t Map 50 50
*413* CD334 1k Pres. Banda, flag 1.75 1.75

The Miraculous Draught of Fishes, by Raphael (1483-1517) — A86

Designs: 7t, 20t, 30t, Details. 1k, Entire painting. 7t, 20t vert.

**1983, Apr. 4 Litho. Wmk. 357**
*414* A86 7t multi 12 12
*415* A86 20t multi 35 35
*416* A86 30t multi 50 50

**Souvenir Sheet**
*417* A86 1k multi 1.50 1.50

Fish Eagles — A87

Designs: a. Lakeside sentinel. b. Gull-like, far-carrying call. c. Diving on its fish prey. d. Prey captured. e. Feeding on its catch. Nos. 418a-418e in continuous design.

**Wmk. 357**
**1983, July 11 Litho. *Perf. 14½***
*418* Strip of 5 2.75 2.75
*a.-e.* A87 30t, multi 55 55

Manned Flight Bicentenary — A88

Kamuzu Intl. Airport.

**1983, Aug. 31 Litho. *Perf. 14***
*419* A88 7t multi 12 12
*420* A88 20t multi 35 35
*421* A88 30t multi 50 50
*422* A88 1k multi 1.75 1.75
*a* Souvenir sheet of 4 2.75 2.75

No. 422a contains Nos. 419-422; margin shows runway. Size: 102x121mm.

Christmas 1983 — A89

Local flowers.

**Wmk. 357**
**1983, Nov. 1 Litho. *Perf. 14***
*423* A89 7t Clerodendium myricoides 12 12
*424* A89 20t Gloriosa superba 35 35
*425* A89 30t Gladiolus laxiflorus 50 50
*426* A89 1k Aframomum angustifolium 1.75 1.75

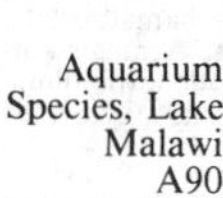

Aquarium Species, Lake Malawi A90

***Perf. 14½x14***
**1984, Feb. 2 Litho. Wmk. 373**
*427* A90 1t Melanochromis auratus 5 5
*428* A90 2t Haplochromis compressiceps 5 5
*429* A90 5t Labeotropheus fuelleborni 7 7
*430* A90 7t Pseudotropheus lombardoi 9 9
*431* A90 8t Gold pseudotropheus zebra 10 10
*432* A90 10t Trematocranus jacobfreibergi 12 12
*433* A90 15t Melanochromis crabro 18 18
*434* A90 20t Marbled pseadotropheus 25 25
*435* A90 30t Labidochromis caeruleus 38 38
*436* A90 40t Haplochromis venustus 50 50
*437* A90 50t Aulonacara of Thumbi 65 65
*438* A90 75t Melanochromis vermivorus 1.00 1.00
*439* A90 1k Pseudotropheus zebra 1.25 1.25
*440* A90 2k Trematocranus spp. 2.50 2.50
*441* A90 4k Aulonacara of Mbenje 5.00 5.00
*Nos. 427-441 (15)* 12.19 12.19

Nyika Red Hare A91

**Wmk. 357**
**1984, Feb. 2 Litho. *Perf. 14***
*442* A91 7t shown 14 14
*443* A91 20t Sun squirrel 38 38
*444* A91 30t Hedgehog 55 55
*445* A91 1k Genet 1.75 1.75

1984 Summer Olympics A92

Local Butterflies A93

**1984, June 1 Photo. *Perf. 14***
*446* A92 7t Running 12 12
*447* A92 20t Boxing 30 30
*448* A92 30t Bicycling 45 45
*449* A92 1k Long jump 1.50 1.50
*a* Souvenir sheet of 4 2.25 2.25

No. 449a contains Nos. 446-449. Size: 91x128mm.

**1984, Aug. 1 Photo. *Perf. 11½***
**Granite Paper**
*450* A93 7t Euphaedra neophron 12 12
*451* A93 20t Papilio dardanus 30 30
*452* A93 30t Antanartia schaeneia 45 45
*453* A93 1k Spindasis 1.50 1.50

Christmas — A94

Virgin and Child Paintings.

**Wmk. 357**
**1984, Oct. 15 Litho. *Perf. 14½***
*454* A94 7t Duccio 12 12
*455* A94 20t Raphael 30 30
*456* A94 30t Lippi 45 45
*457* A94 1k Wilton diptych 1.50 1.50

Fungi A94a

**1985, Jan. 23 *Perf. 14½x14***
*458* A94a 7t Leucopaxillus gracillimus 15 15
*459* A94a 20t Limacella guttata 35 35
*460* A94a 30t Termitomyces eurhizles 55 55
*461* A94a 1k Xerulina asprata 1.75 1.75

Southern African Development Coordination Conference — A95

**1985, Apr. 1 Litho. *Perf. 14***
*462* A95 7t Forestry 8 8
*463* A95 15t Communications 18 18
*464* A95 20t Transportation 24 24
*465* A95 1k Fishing 1.20 1.20

Ships on Lake Malawi
A96

**1985, June 3** *Perf. 13½x13*
*466* A96 7t Ufulu 8 8
*467* A96 15t Chauncy Maples 18 18
*468* A96 20t Mtendere 24 24
*469* A96 1k Ilala 1.20 1.20
*a* Souvenir sheet of 4 1.90 1.90

No. 469a contains Nos. 466-469, perf. 13x12; light blue margin pictures lake and ships. Size: 120x85mm.

Audubon Birth Bicent. — A97

**1985, Aug. 1** **Litho.** *Perf. 14*
*470* A97 7t Stierling's wood-pecker 8 8
*471* A97 15t Lesser seed-cracker 18 18
*472* A97 20t Gunning's akalat 24 24
*473* A97 1k Boehm's bee-eater 1.20 1.20
*a* Souv. sheet of 4, #470-473 1.90 1.90

No. 473a has multicolored inscribed margin picturing a yellow-billed hornbill. Size: 130x90mm.

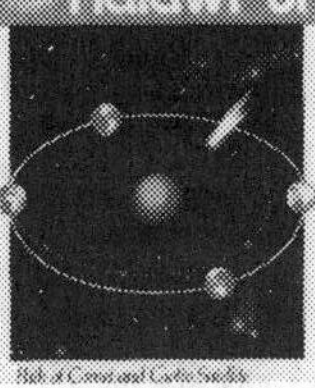

Christmas A98 — Halley's Comet A99

Paintings: 7t, The Virgin of Humility, by Jaime Serra. 15t, Adoration of the Magi, by Stefano da Zevio. 20t, Madonna and Child, by Gerard van Honthorst. 1k, Virgin of Zbraslav, by a Master of Vissi Brod.

*Perf. 11½x12*
**1985, Oct. 14** **Unwmk.**
*474* A98 7t multi 9 9
*475* A98 15t multi 20 20
*476* A98 20t multi 25 25
*477* A98 1k multi 1.40 1.40

**1986, Feb. 10** **Wmk. 357** *Perf. 14½*
*478* A99 8t Earth, comet and Giotto trajectories 10 10
*479* A99 15t Comet over Earth 18 18
*480* A99 20t Over Malawi 24 24
*481* A99 1k Giotto probe 1.20 1.20

1986 World Cup Soccer Championships, Mexico — A100

Various soccer plays.

*Perf. 12x11½*
**1986, May 26** **Unwmk.**
**Granite Paper**
*482* A100 8t multi 10 10
*483* A100 15t multi 18 18
*484* A100 20t multi 24 24
*485* A100 1k multi 1.20 1.20
*a* Souvenir sheet of 4, #482-485 1.75 1.75

No. 485a has grayish black inscribed margin bearing control number. Size: 109x77mm.

Natl. Independence, 20th Anniv. — A101

**Unwmk.**
**1986, June 30** **Litho.** *Perf. 14*
*486* A101 8t Pres. Banda 10 10
*487* A101 15t Natl. flag 18 18
*488* A101 20t Natl. crest 24 24
*489* A101 1k Natl. airline 1.20 1.20

Christmas — A102

Paintings: 8t, Virgin and Child, Galerie Liechtenstein, Vienna, by Botticelli (1445-1510). 15t, Adoration of the Shepherds, Galerie Liechtenstein, by Guido Reni (1575-1642). 20t, Madonna of the Veil, Corsini Gallery, Rome, by Carlo Dolci (161

*Perf. 11½*
**1986, Dec. 15** **Litho.** **Unwmk.**
*490* A102 8t multi 8 8
*491* A102 15t multi 16 16
*492* A102 20t multi 22 22
*493* A102 1k multi 1.05 1.05

World Wildlife Fund
A103

Bugeranus carunculatus.

**Wmk. 357**
**1987, Jan. 30** **Litho.** *Perf. 14½*
*494* A103 8t Wattled crane 10 10
*a.* Wmk. 373 ('88) 6 6
*495* A103 15t Two cranes 18 18
*a.* Wmk. 373 ('88) 12 12
*496* A103 20t Nesting 24 24
*a.* Wmk. 373 ('88) 15 15
*497* A103 75t Crane in water 90 90
*a.* Wmk. 373 ('88) 58 58

British Steam Locomotives — A104

**1987, May 25** **Litho.** *Perf. 14x13½*
*498* A104 10t Shamrock No. 2, 1902 10 10
*499* A104 25t D Class No. 8, 1914 22 22
*500* A104 30t Thistle No. 1, 1902 28 28
*501* A104 1k Kitson No. 6, 1903 90 90

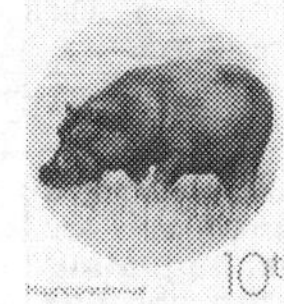

Hippopotamus
A105

**1987, Aug. 24** **Photo.** *Perf. 12½*
**Granite Paper**
*502* A105 10t Feeding 10 10
*503* A105 25t Swimming, roaring 22 22
*504* A105 30t Mother and young swimming 28 28
*505* A105 1k At rest, egret 90 90
*a* Souv. sheet of 4, Nos. 502-505 1.50 1.50

No. 505 has multicolored decorative margin. Size: 78x102mm.

Wild Flowers — A106

**Unwmk.**
**1987, Oct. 19** **Litho.** *Perf. 14*
*506* A106 10t Stathmostelma spectabile 10 10
*507* A106 25t Pentanisia schweinfurthii 22 22
*508* A106 30t Chironia krebsii 28 28
*509* A106 1k Ochna macrocalyx 90 90

Chess — A107

Locally carved and Staunton chessmen: 15t, Knights. 35t, Bishops. 50t, Rooks. 2k, Queens.

**Wmk. 384**
**1988, Feb. 8** **Litho.** *Perf. 14½*
*510* A107 15t multi 12 12
*511* A107 35t multi 28 28
*512* A107 50t multi 40 40
*513* A107 2k multi 1.60 1.60

1988 Summer Olympics, Seoul — A108 — Birds — A109

**Unwmk.**
**1988, June 13** **Litho.** *Perf. 14*
*514* A108 15t High jump 15 15
*515* A108 35t Javelin 35 35
*516* A108 50t Women's tennis 48 48
*517* A108 2k Shot put 1.90 1.90
*a.* Souv. sheet of 4, Nos. 514-517 2.90 2.90

No. 517a has multicolored margin picturing track and grandstand. Size: 91x121mm.

**1988, July 25** **Photo.** *Perf. 14x14½*
**Granite Paper (1t-4k)**
*518* A109 1t Eastern forest scrub-warbler 5 5
*519* A109 2t Yellow-throated warbler 5 5
*520* A109 5t Moustached green tinkerbird 5 5
*521* A109 7t Waller's chest-nut-wing star-ling 5 5
*522* A109 8t Oriole finch 6 6
*523* A109 10t Starred robin 8 8
*524* A109 15t Bar-tailed trogon 12 12
*525* A109 20t Green twinspot 16 16
*526* A109 30t Gray cuckoo shrike 25 25
*527* A109 40t Black-fronted bush shrike 32 32
*528* A109 50t White-tailed crested fly-catcher 40 40
*529* A109 75t Green barbet 62 62
*530* A109 1k Cinnamon dove 82 82
*531* A109 2k Silvery-cheeked hornbill 1.65 1.65
*532* A109 4k Crowned eagle 3.25 3.25
*533* A109 10k Red-and-blue sunbird 8.15 8.15
*Nos. 518-533 (16)* 16.08 16.08

**Lloyds of London, 300th Anniv.**
Common Design Type

Designs: 15t, Royal Exchange, 1844. 35t, Opening of the Nkula Falls hydroelectric power station, horiz. 50t, Air Malawi passenger jet, horiz. 2k, Cruise ship *Queen Elizabeth (Seawise University)* on fire, Hong Kong, 1972.

**Wmk. 373**
**1988, Oct. 24** **Litho.** *Perf. 14*
*534* CD341 15t multi 12 12
*535* CD341 35t multi 28 28
*536* CD341 50t multi 38 38
*537* CD341 2k multi 1.50 1.50

Christmas — A110

Paintings: 15t, *Madonna in the Church*, by Jan Van Eyck (d. 1441). 35t, *Virgin, Infant Jesus and St. Anne*, by Leonardo da Vinci. 50t, *Virgin and Angels*, by Cimabue (c. 1240-1302). 2k, *Virgin and Child*, by Alesso Baldovinetti (c. 1425-1499).

**Unwmk.**
**1988, Nov. 28** **Litho.** *Perf. 14*
*538* A110 15t multi 12 12
*539* A110 35t multi 25 25
*540* A110 50t multi 38 38
*541* A110 2k multi 1.50 1.50

---

## POSTAGE DUE STAMPS

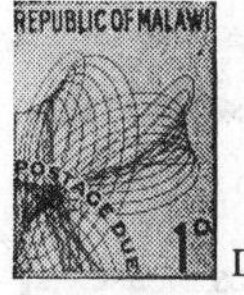

D1

**Wmk. 357**
**1967, Sept. 1** **Litho.** *Perf. 11½*
*J1* D1 1p dp lil rose 20 20
*J2* D1 2p sepia 30 30
*J3* D1 4p lilac 60 60
*J4* D1 6p dk bl 75 75
*J5* D1 8p emerald 1.25 1.25
*J6* D1 1sh black 1.50 1.50
*Nos. J1-J6 (6)* 4.60 4.60

Values in Decimal Currency

**1971, Feb. 15**
**Size: 18x23mm.**
*J7* D1 2t sepia 15 15
*J8* D1 4t lilac 20 20
*J9* D1 6t dk bl 30 30

| | | | | |
|---|---|---|---|---|
| *J10* | D1 | 8t green | 40 | 40 |
| *J11* | D1 | 10t black | 50 | 50 |
| | | *Nos. J7-J11 (5)* | 1.55 | 1.55 |

Type of 1971 Redrawn

**1975 Wmk. 357 *Perf. 14***

**Size: 17x21mm.**

| | | | | |
|---|---|---|---|---|
| *J12* | D1 | 2t brown | 20 | 20 |

No. J12 has accent mark over "W".

**1977-78 Litho. Unwmk. *Perf. 14***

**Size: 18x21mm.**

| | | | | |
|---|---|---|---|---|
| *J13* | D1 | 2t sep ('77) | 5 | 5 |
| *a.* | | Wmk 357, sideways ('82) | 5 | 5 |
| *J14* | D1 | 4t rose lil ('77) | 10 | 10 |
| *a.* | | Wmk 357, sideways ('82) | 10 | 10 |
| *J15* | D1 | 8t brt grn ('78) | 20 | 20 |
| *J16* | D1 | 10t blk ('77) | 25 | 25 |
| *a.* | | Wmk 357, sideways ('82) | 25 | 25 |

## MALAYA

### Federated Malay States

LOCATION — Malay peninsula.
GOVT. — Former British Protectorate.
AREA — 27,585 sq. mi.
CAPITAL — Kuala Lumpur.

The Federated Malay States consisted of the sultanates of Negri Sembilan, Pahang, Perak and Selangor.

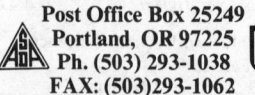

Stamps of the Federated Malay States replaced those of the individual states and were used until 1935, when individual issues were resumed.

100 Cents = 1 Dollar

**Catalogue values for unused stamps in this country are for Never Hinged items, beginning with Scott 80 in the regular postage section, Scott J20 in the postage due section, Scott 128 in Johore, Scott 55 in Kedah, Scott 44 in Kelantan, Scott 1 in Malacca, Scott 36 in Negri Sembilan, Scott 44 in Pahang, Scott 1 in Penang, Scott 99 in Perak, Scott 1 in Perlis, Scott 74 in Selangor, and Scott 47 in Trengganu.**

Stamps and Type of Negri Sembilan Overprinted in Black **FEDERATED MALAY STATES**

**1900 Wmk. 2 *Perf. 14***

| | | | | |
|---|---|---|---|---|
| *1* | A2 | 1c lil & grn | 90 | *1.50* |
| *2* | A2 | 2c lil & brn | 14.00 | *18.00* |
| *3* | A2 | 3c lil & blk | 1.50 | *2.25* |
| *4* | A2 | 5c lil & ol | 22.50 | 22.50 |
| *5* | A2 | 10c lil & org | 1.10 | *3.50* |
| *6* | A2 | 20c grn & ol | 22.50 | *32.50* |
| *7* | A2 | 25c grn & car rose | 50.00 | *75.00* |
| *8* | A2 | 50c grn & blk | 27.50 | *35.00* |
| | | *Nos. 1-8 (8)* | 140.00 | 190.25 |

Overprinted on 1895-99 Issue of Perak

**1900**

| | | | | |
|---|---|---|---|---|
| *9* | A9 | 5c lil & ol | 12.00 | *30.00* |
| *10* | A9 | 10c lil & org | 24.00 | *30.00* |
| *a.* | | Bar omitted | 450.00 | |

**Wmk. Crown and C. C. (1)**

| | | | | |
|---|---|---|---|---|
| *11* | A10 | $1 grn & lt grn | 65.00 | 72.50 |
| *12* | A10 | $2 grn & car rose | 57.50 | 72.50 |
| *13* | A10 | $5 grn & ultra | 120.00 | 130.00 |
| *13A* | A10 | $25 grn & org | *3,750.* | |
| | | Revenue cancel | | 200.00 |

Elephants and Howdah — A3

Tiger — A4

Stamps of type A4 are watermarked sideways.

**1900 Typo.**

| | | | | |
|---|---|---|---|---|
| *14* | A3 | $1 grn & lt grn | 37.50 | 37.50 |
| *15* | A3 | $2 grn & car rose | 42.50 | 47.50 |
| *16* | A3 | $5 grn & ultra | 72.50 | 65.00 |
| *17* | A3 | $25 grn & org | 725.00 | 375.00 |

High values with revenue cancellations are plentiful and inexpensive.

**1901 Wmk. 2**

| | | | | |
|---|---|---|---|---|
| *18* | A4 | 1c bl grn & blk | 12 | 10 |
| *19* | A4 | 3c brn & gray | 1.25 | 10 |
| *20* | A4 | 4c rose & blk | 1.50 | 30 |
| *21* | A4 | 5c scar & grn, *yel* | 1.00 | 90 |
| *22* | A4 | 8c ultra & blk | 14.00 | 2.50 |
| *23* | A4 | 10c vio & blk | 12.50 | 75 |
| *24* | A4 | 20c blk & gray vio | 12.50 | 2.50 |
| *25* | A4 | 50c brn org & blk | 37.50 | 17.50 |
| | | *Nos. 18-25 (8)* | 80.37 | 24.65 |

**Wmk. Multiple Crown and C. A. (3)**

**1904-10**

| | | | | |
|---|---|---|---|---|
| *26* | A4 | 1c grn & blk | 4.25 | 42 |
| *27* | A4 | 3c brn & gray | 5.25 | 20 |
| *28* | A4 | 4c rose & blk | 2.75 | 22 |
| *29* | A4 | 5c scar & grn, *yel* | 1.10 | 42 |
| *30* | A4 | 8c ultra & blk ('05) | 4.50 | 2.75 |
| *31* | A4 | 10c vio & blk | 3.00 | 12 |
| *32* | A4 | 20c blk & gray vio ('05) | 2.25 | 20 |
| *33* | A4 | 50c brn org & blk ('05) | 14.00 | 1.65 |

The 1c and 4c are on ordinary paper, the other values on both ordinary and chalky papers.

**Chalky Paper**

| | | | | |
|---|---|---|---|---|
| *34* | A3 | $1 grn & lt grn ('07) | 25.00 | 16.00 |
| *35* | A3 | $2 grn & car rose ('06) | 47.50 | 47.50 |
| *36* | A3 | $5 grn & ultra ('06) | 70.00 | *77.50* |
| *37* | A3 | $25 grn & org ('10) | 675.00 | 350.00 |
| | | *Nos. 26-36 (11)* | 179.60 | 146.98 |

High values with revenue cancellations are plentiful and inexpensive.

**1906-22 Ordinary Paper**

Two dies for Nos. 38 and 44:
I. Thick line under "Malay."
II. Thin line under "Malay."

| | | | | |
|---|---|---|---|---|
| *38* | A4 | 1c dl grn, die II | 1.90 | 10 |
| *b.* | | Die I | 1.90 | 1.40 |
| *39* | A4 | 1c brn ('19) | 1.65 | 1.10 |
| *40* | A4 | 2c grn ('19) | 30 | 10 |
| *41* | A4 | 3c brown | 2.75 | 14 |
| *42* | A4 | 3c car ('09) | 2.25 | 6 |
| *43* | A4 | 3c dp gray ('19) | 1.10 | 14 |
| *44* | A4 | 4c scar, die I ('19) | 1.40 | 1.10 |
| *b.* | | Die II | 1.10 | 32 |
| *45* | A4 | 6c org ('19) | 1.65 | 85 |
| *46* | A4 | 8c ultra ('09) | 4.25 | 55 |
| *47* | A4 | 10c ultra ('19) | 5.50 | 48 |
| *48* | A4 | 35c red, *yel* | 11.00 | 14.00 |
| | | *Nos. 38-48 (11)* | 33.75 | 18.62 |

**1922-32 Wmk. 4**

**Ordinary Paper**

| | | | | |
|---|---|---|---|---|
| *49* | A4 | 1c brn ('22) | 1.75 | 1.75 |
| *50* | A4 | 1c blk ('23) | 18 | 8 |
| *51* | A4 | 2c dk brn ('25) | 3.00 | 1.75 |
| *52* | A4 | 2c grn ('26) | 20 | 14 |
| *53* | A4 | 3c dp gray ('23) | 3.50 | 4.25 |
| *54* | A4 | 3c grn ('24) | 4.75 | 1.75 |
| *55* | A4 | 3c brn ('27) | 35 | 14 |
| *56* | A4 | 4c scar (II) ('23) | 50 | 12 |
| *57* | A4 | 4c org ('26) | 26 | 6 |
| *c.* | | Unwmkd. | *200.00* | *87.50* |
| *58* | A4 | 5c vio, *yel* ('22) | 32 | 12 |
| *59* | A4 | 5c dk brn ('32) | 1.25 | 12 |
| *60* | A4 | 6c org ('22) | 30 | 18 |
| *61* | A4 | 6c scar ('26) | 32 | 8 |
| *62* | A4 | 10c ultra ('23) | 1.25 | 1.75 |
| *63* | A4 | 10c ultra & blk ('23) | 1.75 | 38 |
| *64* | A4 | 10c vio, *yel* ('31) | 5.75 | 38 |
| *65* | A4 | 12c ultra ('22) | 1.00 | 12 |
| *66* | A4 | 20c blk & vio ('23) | 2.50 | 14 |

**Chalky Paper**

| | | | | |
|---|---|---|---|---|
| *67* | A4 | 25c red vio & ol vio ('29) | 1.75 | 60 |
| *68* | A4 | 30c yel & dl vio ('29) | 2.25 | 65 |
| *69* | A4 | 35c red, *yel* ('28) | 5.75 | 8.75 |
| *70* | A4 | 35c dk vio & car ('31) | 12.00 | 10.50 |
| *71* | A4 | 50c org & blk ('24) | 12.00 | 3.00 |
| *72* | A4 | 50c blk, *bl grn* ('31) | 4.00 | 90 |
| *73* | A3 | $1 gray grn & yel grn ('26) | 12.00 | 12.00 |
| *a.* | | $1 grn & bl grn | 17.50 | 17.50 |
| *74* | A3 | $2 grn & car ('26) | 12.00 | 16.00 |
| *75* | A3 | $5 grn & ultra ('25) | 50.00 | 57.50 |
| *76* | A3 | $25 grn & org ('28) | 575.00 | 300.00 |
| | | *Nos. 49-75 (27)* | 140.68 | 123.21 |

No. 64 is on chalky paper; No. 66 exists on both ordinary and chalky paper; No. 69 is on ordinary paper.

**1931-34**

| | | | | |
|---|---|---|---|---|
| *77* | A4 | $1 red & blk, *bl* | 9.00 | 1.65 |
| *78* | A4 | $2 car & grn, *yel* ('34) | 30.00 | 27.50 |
| *79* | A4 | $5 car & grn, *emer* ('34) | 120.00 | *130.00* |

## FEDERATION OF MALAYA

GOVT. — Sovereign state in British Commonwealth of Nations.
AREA — 50,700 sq. mi.
POP. — 7,139,000 (est. 1961).
CAPITAL — Kuala Lumpur.

The Federation comprised the nine states of Johore, Pahang, Negri Sembilan, Selangor, Perak, Kedah, Perlis, Kelantan and Trengganu and the settlements of Penang and Malacca.

Malaya joined the Federation of Malaysia in 1963.

100 Sen (Cents) = 1 Dollar (1957)

**Catalogue values for unused stamps in this section, from this point to the end of the section, are for Never Hinged items.**

Rubber Tapping A5

Map of Federation A6

Designs: 12c, Federation coat of arms. 25c, Tin dredge and flag.

***Perf. 13x12½, 12½***

**Engr., Litho.**

**1957, May 5 Wmk. 314**

| | | | | |
|---|---|---|---|---|
| *80* | A5 | 6c bl, red & yel | 6 | 5 |
| *a.* | | Yellow omitted | 40.00 | |
| *81* | A5 | 12c car & multi | 15 | 6 |
| *82* | A5 | 25c multi | 24 | 6 |
| *83* | A6 | 30c dp cl & red org | 38 | 5 |

Chief Minister Tunku Abdul Rahman and People of Various Races — A7

***Perf. 12½***

**1957, Aug. 31 Wmk. 4 Engr.**

| | | | | |
|---|---|---|---|---|
| *84* | A7 | 10c brown | 14 | 7 |

Independence Day, Aug. 31.

United Nations Emblem — A8

Design: 30c, U.N. emblem (vert.).

***Perf. 13½, 12½***

**1958, Mar. 5 Wmk. 314**

| | | | | |
|---|---|---|---|---|
| *85* | A8 | 12c rose red | 38 | 24 |
| *86* | A8 | 30c plum | 42 | 28 |

Conf. of the Economic Commission for Asia and the Far East (ECAFE), Kuala Lumpur, Mar. 5-15.

Merdeka Stadium and Flag — A9

Tuanku Abdul Rahman, Paramount Ruler of Malaya — A10

***Perf. 13½x14½, 14½x13½***

**1958, Aug. 31 Photo. Wmk. 314**

| | | | | |
|---|---|---|---|---|
| *87* | A9 | 10c multi | 12 | 6 |
| *88* | A10 | 30c multi | 42 | 28 |

1st anniv. of the Independence of the Federation of Malaya.

Torch of Freedom and Broken Chain

A11 A12

*Perf. 12½x13, 13x12½*

**1958, Dec. 10 Litho. Wmk. 314**

*89* A11 10c multi 14 7

**Photo.**

*90* A12 30c green 52 35

10th anniv. of the signing of the Universal Declaration of Human Rights.

Mace and People — A13

*Perf. 12½x13½*

**1959, Sept. 12 Photo. Unwmk.**

*91* A13 4c rose red 10 8
*92* A13 10c violet 16 8
*93* A13 25c yel grn 38 32

Issued to commemorate the inauguration of the first Federal Parliament of Malaya.

WRY Emblem — A14

Design: 30c, Similar to 12c, vertical.

*Perf. 13½, 13*

**1960, Apr. 7 Engr. Wmk. 314**

*94* A14 12c lilac 28 24
*95* A14 30c dk grn 30 20

Issued to publicize World Refugee Year, July 1, 1959-June 30, 1960.

Rubber Tree Seedling on Map of Malaya — A15

Tuanku Syed Putra — A16

*Perf. 13x13½*

**1960, Sept. 19 Litho. Unwmk.**

*96* A15 6s red brn, brn & blk 15 7
*97* A15 30s ultra, yel grn & blk 55 38

15th meeting of the Intl. Rubber Study Group and the Natural Rubber Research Conference, Kuala Lumpur, Sept. 26-Oct. 1.

*Perf. 13½x14½*

**1961, Jan. 4 Photo. Wmk. 314**

*98* A16 10s bl & blk 15 7

Installation of Tuanku Syed Putra of Perlis as Paramount Ruler (Yang di-Pertuan Agong.)

Colombo Plan Emblem A17

Malaria Eradication Emblem A18

**1961, Oct. 30 Unwmk. *Perf. 13½***

*99* A17 12s rose pink & blk 24 18
*100* A17 25s brt yel & blk 32 24
*101* A17 30s brt bl & blk 38 18

Issued to commemorate the 13th meeting of the Consultative Committee for Technical Co-operation in South and South East Asia, Kuala Lumpur, Oct. 30-Nov. 18.

**Wmk. PTM Multiple (338)**

**1962, Apr. 7 *Perf. 14x14½***

*102* A18 25s org brn 26 10
*103* A18 30s dl vio 30 16
*104* A18 50s ultra 48 35

Issued for the World Health Organization drive to eradicate malaria.

Palmyra Leaf A19

**1962, July 21 Photo. *Perf. 13½***

*105* A19 10s vio & gldn brn 8 5
*106* A19 20s bluish grn & gldn brn 20 14
*107* A19 50s car rose & gldn brn 42 32

National Language Month. Watermark inverted on alternating stamps.

Children and their Future Shadows — A20

**1962, Oct. 1 Wmk. 338 *Perf. 13½***

*108* A20 10s brt rose lil 10 5
*109* A20 25s ocher 35 30
*110* A20 30s brt grn 40 26

Issued to publicize free primary education introduced January 1962.

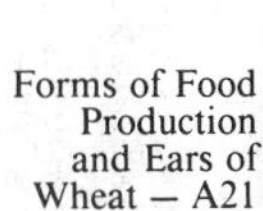

Forms of Food Production and Ears of Wheat — A21

**1963, Mar. 21 Unwmk. *Perf. 11½***

**Granite Paper**

*111* A21 25s lt ol grn & lil rose 32 24
*112* A21 30s dk car & lil rose 42 18
*113* A21 50s ultra & lil rose 52 28

"Freedom from Hunger" campaign of the FAO.

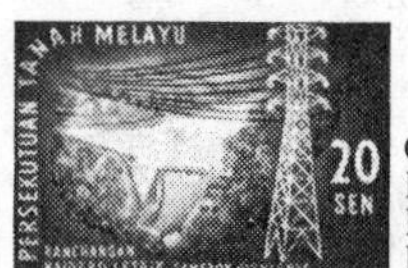

Cameron Highlands Dam and Pylon — A22

**1963, June 26 Wmk. 338 *Perf. 14***

*114* A22 20s pur & brt grn 45 30
*115* A22 30s ultra & brt grn 65 45

Issued to commemorate the opening of the Cameron Highlands hydroelectric plant.

## POSTAGE DUE STAMPS

D1

D2

*Perf. 14½x14*

**1924-26 Typo. Wmk. 4**

| | | | | |
|---|---|---|---|---|
| *J1* | D1 | 1c violet | 1.90 | 1.90 |
| *J2* | D1 | 2c black | 1.25 | 1.50 |
| *J3* | D1 | 4c grn ('26) | 5.00 | *7.75* |
| *J4* | D1 | 8c red | 4.50 | *9.25* |
| *J5* | D1 | 10c orange | 5.00 | *9.25* |
| *J6* | D1 | 12c ultra | 7.50 | *15.00* |
| | | *Nos. J1-J6 (6)* | 25.15 | 44.65 |

**1936-38 *Perf. 14½x14***

| | | | | |
|---|---|---|---|---|
| *J7* | D2 | 1c dk vio ('38) | 1.50 | 50 |
| *J8* | D2 | 4c yel grn | 2.50 | 1.00 |
| *J9* | D2 | 8c scarlet | 1.75 | *4.25* |
| *J10* | D2 | 10c yel org | 1.75 | 45 |
| *J11* | D2 | 12c bl vio | 2.25 | *5.00* |
| *J12* | D2 | 50c blk ('38) | 7.50 | *12.50* |
| | | *Nos. J7-J12 (6)* | 17.25 | 23.70 |

Nos. J7 to J12 were also used in Straits Settlements.

**1945-49**

| | | | | |
|---|---|---|---|---|
| *J13* | D2 | 1c redsh vio | 1.50 | 1.50 |
| *J14* | D2 | 3c yel grn | 7.25 | 10.00 |
| *J15* | D2 | 5c org scar | 10.00 | *12.00* |
| *J16* | D2 | 8c yel org ('49) | 20.00 | 10.00 |
| *J17* | D2 | 9c yel org | 45.00 | 30.00 |
| *J18* | D2 | 15c bl vio | 50.00 | 35.00 |
| *J19* | D2 | 20c dk bl ('48) | 10.00 | 12.00 |
| | | *Nos. J13-J19 (7)* | 143.75 | 110.50 |

**Catalogue values for unused stamps in this section, from this point to the end of the section, are for Never Hinged items.**

**1951-62 Wmk. 4 *Perf. 14***

| | | | | |
|---|---|---|---|---|
| *J20* | D2 | 1c dl vio ('52) | 25 | 25 |
| *J21* | D2 | 2c dk gray ('53) | 30 | 30 |
| | *a.* | Perf. 12½ ('60) | 30 | *3.50* |
| *J22* | D2 | 3c grn ('52) | 10.00 | 10.00 |
| *J23* | D2 | 4c dk brn ('53) | 30 | 30 |
| | *a.* | Perf. 12½ ('60) | 1.00 | *7.50* |
| *J24* | D2 | 5c vermilion | 20.00 | 10.00 |
| *J25* | D2 | 8c yel org | 2.00 | 2.50 |
| *J26* | D2 | 12c mag ('54) | 1.00 | 1.00 |
| | *a.* | Perf. 12½ ('62) | 3.00 | *12.50* |
| *J27* | D2 | 20c dp bl | 5.00 | 6.00 |
| | *a.* | Perf. 12½ ('57) | 5.00 | *25.00* |
| | | *Nos. J20-J27 (8)* | 38.85 | 30.35 |

Nos. J13-J27 were used throughout the Federation and in Singapore, later in Malaysia.

**1964-65 Wmk. 314 *Perf. 12***

| | | | | |
|---|---|---|---|---|
| *J28* | D2 | 1c plum ('65) | 20 | *2.00* |
| | *a.* | Perf. 12½ | 20 | *2.00* |
| *J29* | D2 | 2c bluish blk ('65) | 25 | *5.00* |
| | *a.* | Perf. 12½ | 30 | *7.50* |
| *J30* | D2 | 4c brn ('65) | 30 | *7.50* |
| | *a.* | Perf. 12½ | 65 | *7.00* |
| *J31* | D2 | 8c yel org ('65) | 4.50 | *10.00* |
| *J32* | D2 | 12c mag ('65) | 2.50 | *20.00* |
| | *a.* | Perf. 12½ | 1.50 | *12.50* |
| *J33* | D2 | 20c dk bl ('65) | 3.50 | *27.50* |
| | *a.* | Perf. 12½ | 5.00 | *25.00* |
| | | *Nos. J28-J33 (6)* | 11.25 | 72.00 |
| | | *Nos. J28a-J33a (5)* | 7.65 | 54.00 |

Nos. J28-J33 were used in Malaysia.

No. J16 Surcharged **10 cents**

**1965, Jan. Wmk. 4**

*J34* D2 10c on 8c yel org 50 *1.00*

## OCCUPATION STAMPS

**Issued Under Japanese Occupation**

Malayan Fruit and Fronds OS1

Tin Dredging OS2

Monument to Japanese War Dead OS3

Malayan Plowman OS4

**1943 Unwmk. Litho. *Perf. 12½***

| | | | | |
|---|---|---|---|---|
| *N30* | OS1 | 2c emerald | 25 | 25 |
| | *a.* | Rouletted | 1.25 | 1.25 |
| | *b.* | Imperf., pair | 3.75 | 3.75 |
| *N31* | OS2 | 4c rose red | 25 | 25 |
| | *a.* | Rouletted | 1.25 | 1.25 |
| | *b.* | Imperf., pair | 3.50 | 3.50 |
| *N32* | OS3 | 8c olive blue | 25 | 25 |

**1943, Sept. 1**

*N33* OS4 8c violet 5.00 2.50
*N34* OS4 15c car red 5.00 2.50

Publicity for Postal Savings which had reached a $10,000,000 total in Malaya.

Rubber Tapping OS5

Seaside Houses OS6

Japanese Shrine, Singapore OS7

Sago Palms OS8

Johore Bahru and Strait of Johore OS9

Malay Mosque, Kuala Lumpur OS10

**1943, Oct. 1**

| | | | | |
|---|---|---|---|---|
| *N35* | OS5 | 1c gray grn | 38 | 30 |
| *N36* | OS5 | 3c ol gray | 38 | 30 |
| *N37* | OS6 | 10c red brn | 38 | 30 |
| *N38* | OS7 | 15c violet | 50 | 50 |
| *N39* | OS8 | 30c ol grn | 50 | 50 |
| *N40* | OS9 | 50c blue | 1.00 | 1.00 |
| *N41* | OS10 | 70c dull blue | 10.00 | 15.00 |
| | | *Nos. N35-N41 (7)* | 13.14 | 17.90 |

Rice Planting and Map of Malaysia — OS11

**1944, Feb. 15**

| No. | Type | Description | Unused | Used |
|---|---|---|---|---|
| *N42* | OS11 | 8c carmine | 4.50 | 3.50 |
| *N43* | OS11 | 15c violet | 4.50 | 3.50 |

Issued on the anniversary of the fall of Singapore to commemorate the "Birth of New Malaya".

---

## OCCUPATION POSTAGE DUE STAMPS

Stamps and Type of Postage Due Stamps of 1936-38 Handstamped in Black, Red or Brown

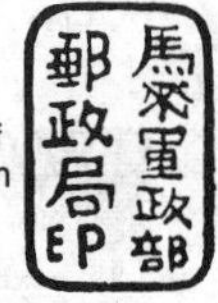


**1942 Wmk. 4 *Perf. 14½x14***

| No. | Type | Description | Unused | Used |
|---|---|---|---|---|
| *NJ1* | D2 | 1c violet | 7.50 | 7.50 |
| *NJ2* | D2 | 3c yel grn | 7.50 | 7.50 |
| *NJ3* | D2 | 4c yel grn | 10.00 | 10.00 |
| *NJ4* | D2 | 8c red | 15.00 | 15.00 |
| *NJ5* | D2 | 10c yel org | 8.00 | 10.00 |
| *NJ6* | D2 | 12c bl vio | 10.00 | 12.50 |
| *NJ7* | D2 | 50c black | 20.00 | 25.00 |
| | | *Nos. NJ1-NJ7 (7)* | 78.00 | 87.50 |

Overprinted in Black

**DAI NIPPON**
**2602**
**MALAYA**

**1942**

| No. | Type | Description | Unused | Used |
|---|---|---|---|---|
| *NJ8* | D2 | 1c violet | 1.00 | 1.00 |
| *NJ9* | D2 | 3c yel grn | 1.40 | 1.65 |
| *NJ10* | D2 | 4c yel grn | 2.50 | 3.00 |
| *NJ11* | D2 | 8c red | 3.75 | 5.00 |
| *NJ12* | D2 | 10c yel org | 1.25 | 1.90 |
| *NJ13* | D2 | 12c bl vio | 1.25 | 1.90 |
| | | *Nos. NJ8-NJ13 (6)* | 11.15 | 14.45 |

The 9c and 15c with this overprint were not regularly issued.

Postage Due Stamps of 1936-45 Overprinted

**大日本郵便**

**1943**

| No. | Type | Description | Unused | Used |
|---|---|---|---|---|
| *NJ14* | D2 | 1c redsh vio | 1.00 | 1.75 |
| *NJ15* | D2 | 3c yel grn | 1.00 | 1.75 |
| *NJ15A* | D2 | 4c yel grn | 25.00 | 20.00 |
| *NJ16* | D2 | 5c scarlet | 1.00 | 2.50 |
| *NJ17* | D2 | 9c yel org | 1.50 | 1.75 |
| *NJ18* | D2 | 10c yel org | 1.50 | 1.75 |
| *NJ19* | D2 | 12c bl vio | 1.50 | 1.75 |
| *NJ20* | D2 | 15c bl vio | 1.50 | 1.75 |
| | | *Nos. NJ14-NJ20 (8)* | 34.00 | 33.00 |

No. NJ15A is said to have been extensively forged.

---

## ISSUED UNDER THAI OCCUPATION

**For use in Kedah, Kelantan, Perlis and Trengganu**

War Memorial — OS1

***Perf. 12½***
**1943, Dec. Unwmk. Litho.**

| No. | Type | Description | Unused | Used |
|---|---|---|---|---|
| *2N1* | OS1 | 1c pale yel | 2.50 | 3.75 |
| *2N2* | OS1 | 2c buff | 2.00 | 2.00 |
| *2N3* | OS1 | 3c pale grn | 3.75 | 4.50 |
| *a.* | | Imperf., pair | 175.00 | |
| *2N4* | OS1 | 4c dl lil | 2.00 | 3.50 |
| *2N5* | OS1 | 8c rose | 2.00 | 3.50 |
| *2N6* | OS1 | 15c lt bl | 5.00 | 7.50 |
| | | *Nos. 2N1-2N6 (6)* | 17.25 | 24.75 |

These stamps, in cent denominations, were for use only in the four Malayan states ceded to Thailand by the Japanese. The states reverted to British rule in September, 1945.

---

## JOHORE

LOCATION — At the extreme south of the Malay Peninsula.
AREA — 7,330 sq. mi.
POP. — 1,009,649 (1960).
CAPITAL — Johore Bahru.

Stamps of the Straits Settlements Overprinted in Black

Overprinted

**1876 Wmk. 1 *Perf. 14***

| No. | Type | Description | Unused | Used |
|---|---|---|---|---|
| *1* | A2 | 2c brown | 5,500. | 3,750. |

Overprinted **JOHORE.**

**Overprint 13 to 14mm Wide**

**1884-86 Wmk. Crown and C. A. (2)**

| No. | Type | Description | Unused | Used |
|---|---|---|---|---|
| *1A* | A2 | 2c rose | 42.50 | 50.00 |

**Without Period**

**Overprint 16 to 17x2mm.**

| No. | Type | Description | Unused | Used |
|---|---|---|---|---|
| *2* | A2 | 2c rose | 250.00 | 130.00 |
| *a.* | | Double overprint | 600.00 | |

Overprinted **JOHORE**

**Overprint 11x2½mm.**

| No. | Type | Description | Unused | Used |
|---|---|---|---|---|
| *3* | A2 | 2c rose | 27.50 | 32.50 |

Overprinted **JOHORE**

**Overprint 17½x2¾mm.**

| No. | Type | Description | Unused | Used |
|---|---|---|---|---|
| *4* | A2 | 2c rose | *675.00* | *675.00* |

Overprinted **JOHOR**

**Overprint 12½ to 15x2¾mm.**

| No. | Type | Description | Unused | Used |
|---|---|---|---|---|
| *5* | A2 | 2c rose | 3.75 | *5.00* |

Overprinted **JOHOR**

**Overprint 9x2½mm.**

| No. | Type | Description | Unused | Used |
|---|---|---|---|---|
| *6* | A2 | 2c brown | | |
| *7* | A2 | 2c rose | 12.00 | *16.00* |

Overprinted **JOHOR**

**Overprint 9x3mm.**

| No. | Type | Description | Unused | Used |
|---|---|---|---|---|
| *8* | A2 | 2c rose | 16.00 | 16.00 |

Overprinted **JOHOR**

**Overprint 14 to 15x3mm.**

| No. | Type | Description | Unused | Used |
|---|---|---|---|---|
| *9* | A2 | 2c rose | 3.00 | 2.25 |

**Tall "J" 3½ mm. High.**

| No. | Type | Description | Unused | Used |
|---|---|---|---|---|
| *10* | A2 | 2c rose | 40.00 | 40.00 |

Overprinted **JOHOR**

**Overprint 15 to 15½x3mm.**

| No. | Type | Description | Unused | Used |
|---|---|---|---|---|
| *11* | A2 | 2c rose | 27.50 | 27.50 |

Overprinted **JOHOR**

**1891**

**Overprint 12½ to 13x2½mm.**

| No. | Type | Description | Unused | Used |
|---|---|---|---|---|
| *12* | A2 | 2c rose | 10.00 | 5.00 |

**Overprint 12x2¾mm.**

| No. | Type | Description | Unused | Used |
|---|---|---|---|---|
| *13* | A2 | 2c rose | *3,500.* | |

Surcharged in Black:

| | |
|---|---|
| JOHOR<br>Two<br>CENTS<br>a | JOHOR<br>*Two*<br>CENTS<br>b |
| JOHOR<br>*Two*<br>CENTS<br>c | JOHOR<br>Two<br>CENTS<br>d |

**1891**

| No. | Type | Description | Unused | Used |
|---|---|---|---|---|
| *14* | A3 (a) | 2c on 24c grn | 19.00 | 26.00 |
| *15* | A3 (b) | 2c on 24c grn | 37.50 | 32.50 |
| *16* | A3 (c) | 2c on 24c grn | 16.00 | 16.00 |
| *a.* | | "CENST" | 300.00 | 225.00 |
| *17* | A3 (d) | 2c on 24c grn | 35.00 | 35.00 |

Sultan Abubakar — A5

**1892-94 Typo. Unwmk.**

| No. | Type | Description | Unused | Used |
|---|---|---|---|---|
| *18* | A5 | 1c lil & vio ('94) | 38 | 38 |
| *19* | A5 | 2c lil & yel | 60 | *1.25* |
| *20* | A5 | 3c lil & car rose ('94) | 70 | 48 |
| *21* | A5 | 4c lil & blk | 2.75 | 1.75 |
| *22* | A5 | 5c lil & grn | 6.50 | 6.50 |
| *23* | A5 | 6c lil & bl | 8.00 | 13.00 |
| *24* | A5 | $1 grn & car rose | 20.00 | *32.50* |
| | | *Nos. 18-24 (7)* | 38.93 | 55.86 |

Stamps of 1892-94 Surcharged in Black — 26

**3 cents.**

**1894**

| No. | Type | Description | Unused | Used |
|---|---|---|---|---|
| *26* | A5 | 3c on 4c lil & blk | 95 | 95 |
| *a.* | | No period after "Cents" | 17.50 | 17.50 |
| *27* | A5 | 3c on 5c lil & grn | 95 | 95 |
| *a.* | | No period after "Cents" | 17.50 | 21.00 |
| *28* | A5 | 3c on 6c lil & bl | 95 | 1.25 |
| *a.* | | No period after "Cents" | 17.50 | 21.00 |
| *29* | A5 | 3c on $1 grn & car | 7.00 | 12.00 |
| *a.* | | No period after "Cents" | 47.50 | 57.50 |

**Coronation Issue**

Stamps of 1892-94 Overprinted "KEMAHKOTAAN"

**1896**

| No. | Type | Description | Unused | Used |
|---|---|---|---|---|
| *30* | A5 | 1c lil & vio | 40 | 48 |
| *a.* | | "KETAHKOTAAN" | 2.25 | 3.50 |
| *31* | A5 | 2c lil & yel | 38 | 48 |
| *a.* | | "KETAHKOTAAN" | 2.25 | 3.50 |
| *32* | A5 | 3c lil & car rose | 95 | 95 |
| *a.* | | "KETAHKOTAAN" | 2.50 | *6.00* |
| *33* | A5 | 4c lil & blk | 80 | 80 |
| *a.* | | "KETAHKOTAAN" | 1.75 | *4.50* |
| *34* | AA5 | 5c lil & grn | 3.25 | 3.75 |
| *a.* | | "KETAHKOTAAN" | 3.50 | 5.00 |
| *35* | A5 | 6c lil & bl | 1.25 | *3.25* |
| *a.* | | "KETAHKOTAAN" | 1.75 | *4.50* |
| *36* | A5 | $1 grn & car rose | 32.50 | 35.00 |
| *a.* | | "KETAHKOTAAN" | 35.00 | *60.00* |
| | | *Nos. 30-36 (7)* | 39.53 | 44.71 |
| | | *Nos. 30a-36a (7)* | 49.00 | 87.00 |

Coronation of Sultan Ibrahim.

Sultan Ibrahim — A7

Wmk. 71- Rosette

**1896-99 Typo. Wmk. 71**

| No. | Type | Description | Unused | Used |
|---|---|---|---|---|
| *37* | A7 | 1c green | 22 | 1 |
| *38* | A7 | 2c grn & bl | 22 | 2. |
| *39* | A7 | 3c grn & vio | 42 | 1 |
| *40* | A7 | 4c grn & car rose | 28 | 2. |
| *41* | A7 | 4c yel & red ('99) | 30 | 2. |
| *42* | A7 | 5c grn & brn | 40 | 2 |
| *43* | A7 | 6c grn & yel | 52 | 5 |
| *44* | A7 | 10c grn & blk | 7.50 | *15.0* |
| *45* | A7 | 25c grn & vio | 7.50 | *15.0* |
| *46* | A7 | 50c grn & car rose | 15.00 | *18.0* |
| *47* | A7 | $1 lil & grn | 15.00 | *27.5* |
| *48* | A7 | $2 lil & car rose | 16.00 | *30.0* |
| *49* | A7 | $3 lil & bl | 27.50 | *40.0* |
| *50* | A7 | $4 lil & brn | 30.00 | *45.0* |
| *51* | A7 | $5 lil & org | 65.00 | *90.0* |
| | | *Nos. 37-51 (15)* | 185.86 | 282.2 |

On Nos. 44-46 the numerals are on white tablets. Numerals of Nos. 48-51 are on tablets of solid color.

Stamps of 1896-1926 with revenue cancellations sell for a fraction of those used postally.

Stamps of 1896-99 Surcharged in Black **3 cents.**

**1903**

| No. | Type | Description | Unused | Used |
|---|---|---|---|---|
| *52* | A7 | 3c on 4c yel & red | 52 | 5 |
| *a.* | | Without bars | 2.50 | *4.2* |
| *53* | A7 | 10c on 4c grn & car rose | 2.00 | 3.0 |
| *a.* | | Without bars | 24.00 | *35.0* |

Bars on Nos. 52-53 were handruled with pen and ink.

Surcharged **50 Cents**

| No. | Type | Description | Unused | Used |
|---|---|---|---|---|
| *54* | A7 | 50c on $3 lil & bl | 17.00 | *27.5* |

Surcharged **One Dollar**

| No. | Type | Description | Unused | Used |
|---|---|---|---|---|
| *55* | A7 | $1 on $2 lil & car rose | 55.00 | *67.5* |
| *a.* | | Inverted "e" in "one" | 1,000. | |

Surcharged **10 CENTS**

**1904**

| No. | Type | Description | Unused | Used |
|---|---|---|---|---|
| *56* | A7 | 10c on 4c yel & red | 27.50 | 32.50 |
| *a.* | | Double surcharge | *5,000.* | |
| *57* | A7 | 10c on 4c grn & car rose | 6.00 | *10.50* |
| *58* | A7 | 50c on $5 lil & org | 50.00 | 50.00 |

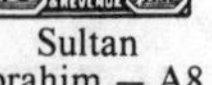

Sultan Ibrahim — A8

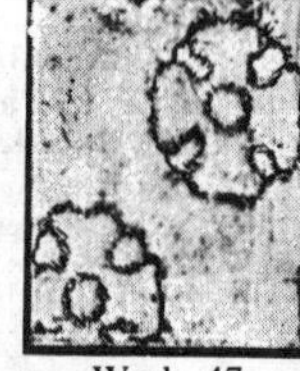

Wmk. 47- Multiple Rosettes

The 10c, 21c, 25c, 50c, and $10 to $500 denominations of type A8 show the numerals on white tablets. The numerals of the 8c, 30c, 40c, and $2 to $5 demonimations are shown on tablets of solid colors.

**1904-08 Typo. Wmk. 71**

| No. | Type | Description | Unused | Used |
|---|---|---|---|---|
| *59* | A8 | 1c vio & grn | 10 | 10 |
| *60* | A8 | 2c vio & brn org | 35 | 18 |
| *61* | A8 | 3c vio & blk | 38 | 18 |
| *62* | A8 | 4c vio & red | 2.25 | 45 |
| *63* | A8 | 5c vio & ol grn | 85 | 1.65 |

| | | | | |
|---|---|---|---|---|
| 64 | A8 | 8c vio & bl | 1.25 | 1.65 |
| 65 | A8 | 10c vio & blk | 4.00 | 3.75 |
| 66 | A8 | 25c vio & grn | 2.75 | 5.25 |
| 67 | A8 | 50c vio & red | 8.00 | 8.00 |
| 68 | A8 | $1 grn & vio | 13.00 | 19.00 |
| 69 | A8 | $2 grn & car | 16.00 | 26.00 |
| 70 | A8 | $3 grn & bl | 17.00 | 32.50 |
| 71 | A8 | $4 grn & brn | 21.00 | 37.50 |
| 72 | A8 | $5 grn & org | 32.50 | 45.00 |
| 73 | A8 | $10 grn & blk | 47.50 | 80.00 |
| 74 | A8 | $50 grn & bl | 160.00 | 240.00 |
| 75 | A8 | $100 grn & scar | 400.00 | 450.00 |
| | | Revenue cancel | | 32.50 |
| | | *Nos. 59-73 (15)* | 166.93 | 261.21 |

The 1c, 2c and 10c also exist on chalky paper.

Nos. 74 and 75 were theoretically available for postage but were mostly used for revenue purposes.

**1910-18 Wmk. 47**

**Chalky Paper**

| | | | | |
|---|---|---|---|---|
| 76 | A8 | 1c vio & grn | 55 | 12 |
| 77 | A8 | 2c vio & org | 95 | 18 |
| 78 | A8 | 3c vio & blk | 1.75 | 12 |
| 79 | A8 | 4c vio & red | 95 | 18 |
| 80 | A8 | 5c vio & ol grn | 95 | 18 |
| 81 | A8 | 8c vio & bl | 2.50 | 3.25 |
| 82 | A8 | 10c vio & blk | 3.75 | 1.25 |
| 83 | A8 | 25c vio & grn | 2.50 | 3.25 |
| 84 | A8 | 50c vio & red | 25.00 | 32.50 |
| 85 | A8 | $1 grn & vio | 40.00 | 47.50 |
| | | *Nos. 76-85 (10)* | 78.90 | 88.53 |

Nos. 78-79 and 82 exist with horizontal watermark.

No. 64 Surcharged **3 CENTS.**

**1912 Wmk. 71**

| | | | | |
|---|---|---|---|---|
| 86 | A8 | 3c on 8c vio & bl | 1.50 | 1.50 |
| *a.* | | "T" of "CENTS" omitted | 400.00 | |

**1918-19 Typo. Wmk. 3**

**Chalky Paper**

| | | | | |
|---|---|---|---|---|
| 87 | A8 | 2c vio & org | 60 | 45 |
| 88 | A8 | 2c vio & grn ('19) | 24 | 12 |
| 89 | A8 | 4c vio & red | 30 | 12 |
| 90 | A8 | 5c vio & ol grn ('19) | 1.25 | 1.75 |
| 91 | A8 | 10c vio & bl | 1.25 | 1.25 |
| 92 | A8 | 21c vio & org | 2.25 | 3.50 |
| 93 | A8 | 25c vio & grn ('19) | 5.75 | 5.75 |
| 94 | A8 | 50c vio & red ('19) | 5.75 | 5.75 |
| 95 | A8 | $1 grn & red vio | 8.75 | 8.75 |
| 96 | A8 | $2 grn & scar | 14.00 | 17.50 |
| 97 | A8 | $3 grn & bl | 22.50 | 30.00 |
| 98 | A8 | $4 grn & brn | 22.50 | 30.00 |
| 99 | A8 | $5 grn & org | 35.00 | 42.50 |
| 100 | A8 | $10 grn & blk | 87.50 | 100.00 |
| | | *Nos. 87-100 (14)* | 207.64 | 247.44 |

**1921-40 Wmk. 4**

| | | | | |
|---|---|---|---|---|
| 101 | A8 | 1c vio & blk | 14 | 8 |
| 102 | A8 | 2c vio & brn | 55 | 1.10 |
| 103 | A8 | 2c grn & dk grn ('28) | 14 | 10 |
| 104 | A8 | 3c grn ('25) | 1.40 | 2.75 |
| 105 | A8 | 3c dl vio & brn ('28) | 55 | 32 |
| 106 | A8 | 4c vio & red | 1.40 | 10 |
| 107 | A8 | 5c vio & ol grn | 28 | 10 |
| 108 | A8 | 6c vio & red brn | 22 | 8 |
| 109 | A8 | 10c vio & bl | 6.75 | 5.50 |
| 110 | A8 | 10c vio & yel ('22) | 28 | 14 |
| 111 | A8 | 12c vio & bl | 1.40 | 22 |
| 111A | A8 | 12c ultra ('40) | 14.00 | 9.50 |
| 112 | A8 | 21c dl vio & org ('28) | 2.25 | 2.25 |
| 113 | A8 | 25c vio & grn | 48 | 38 |
| 114 | A8 | 30c dl vio & org ('36) | 80 | 80 |
| 115 | A8 | 40c dl vio & brn ('36) | 95 | 3.25 |
| 116 | A8 | 50c vio & red | 95 | 55 |
| 117 | A8 | $1 grn & red vio | 2.25 | 70 |
| 118 | A8 | $2 grn & red | 8.00 | 3.50 |
| 119 | A8 | $3 grn & bl | 22.50 | 27.50 |
| 120 | A8 | $4 grn & brn ('26) | 30.00 | 27.50 |
| 121 | A8 | $5 grn & org | 30.00 | 27.50 |
| 122 | A8 | $10 grn & blk | 67.50 | 110.00 |
| 123 | A8 | $50 grn & ultra | 400.00 | |
| 124 | A8 | $100 grn & red | 1,300. | |
| 125 | A8 | $500 ultra & org brn ('26) | 16,000. | |
| | | Revenue cancel | | 140.00 |
| | | *Nos. 101-122 (23)* | 192.79 | 223.92 |

Nos. 123, 124 and 125 were available for postage but were probably used only fiscally.

Sultan Ibrahim and Sultana — A9

**1935, May 15 Engr. *Perf. 12½***

| | | | | |
|---|---|---|---|---|
| 126 | A9 | 8c blk & vio | 85 | 55 |

Sultan Ibrahim
A10 A11

**1940, Feb. *Perf. 13½***

| | | | | |
|---|---|---|---|---|
| 127 | A10 | 8c bl & blk | 85 | 28 |

**Catalogue values for unused stamps in this section, from this point to the end of the section, are for Never Hinged items.**

**Silver Wedding Issue**

Common Design Types

Inscribed: "Malaya Johore"

***Perf. 14x14½***

**1948, Dec. 1 Wmk. 4 Photo.**

| | | | | |
|---|---|---|---|---|
| 128 | CD304 | 10c purple | 18 | 18 |

***Perf. 11½x11***

**Engraved; Name Typographed**

| | | | | |
|---|---|---|---|---|
| 129 | CD305 | $5 green | 24.00 | 24.00 |

**1949-55 Wmk. 4 Typo. *Perf. 18***

| | | | | |
|---|---|---|---|---|
| 130 | A11 | 1c black | 22 | 15 |
| 131 | A11 | 2c orange | 22 | 15 |
| 132 | A11 | 3c green | 65 | 35 |
| 133 | A11 | 4c chocolate | 20 | 10 |
| 134 | A11 | 5c rose vio ('52) | 28 | 12 |
| 135 | A11 | 6c gray | 40 | 18 |
| *a.* | | Wmk. 4a (error) | 425.00 | |
| 136 | A11 | 8c rose red | 1.25 | 90 |
| 137 | A11 | 8c grn ('52) | 65 | 50 |
| 138 | A11 | 10c plum | 40 | 6 |
| *a.* | | Imperf., pair | 850.00 | |
| 139 | A11 | 12c rose red ('52) | 80 | 60 |
| 140 | A11 | 15c ultra | 1.25 | 42 |
| 141 | A11 | 20c dk grn & blk | 1.25 | 60 |
| 142 | A11 | 20c ultra ('52) | 85 | 25 |
| 143 | A11 | 25c org & rose lil | 1.00 | 18 |
| 144 | A11 | 30c plum & rose red ('55) | 2.50 | 90 |
| 145 | A11 | 35c dk vio & rose red ('52) | 2.00 | 1.40 |
| 146 | A11 | 40c dk vio & rose red | 2.50 | 2.00 |
| 147 | A11 | 50c ultra & blk | 1.75 | 25 |
| 148 | A11 | $1 vio brn & ultra | 3.25 | 1.25 |
| 149 | A11 | $2 rose red & emer | 12.00 | 4.00 |
| 150 | A11 | $5 choc & emer | 24.00 | 8.50 |
| | | *Nos. 130-150 (21)* | 57.42 | 22.86 |

**UPU Issue**

Common Design Types

Inscribed: "Malaya-Johore"

**Engr.; Name Typo. on 15c, 25c**

**1949, Oct. 10 *Perf. 13½, 11x11½***

| | | | | |
|---|---|---|---|---|
| 151 | CD306 | 10c rose vio | 30 | 30 |
| 152 | CD307 | 15c indigo | 50 | 50 |
| 153 | CD308 | 25c orange | 1.00 | 1.00 |
| 154 | CD309 | 50c slate | 2.00 | 2.00 |

**Coronation Issue**

Common Design Type

**1953, June 2 Engr. *Perf. 13½x13***

| | | | | |
|---|---|---|---|---|
| 155 | CD312 | 10c mag & blk | 26 | 15 |

Sultan Ibrahim
A12

**1955, Nov. 1 Wmk. 4 *Perf. 14***

| | | | | |
|---|---|---|---|---|
| 156 | A12 | 10c car lake | 26 | 10 |

Sultan Ibrahim's Diamond Jubilee.

Sultan Ismail and Johore State Crest Seal — A13

***Perf. 11½***

**1960, Feb. 10 Unwmk. Photo.**

**Granite Paper**

| | | | | |
|---|---|---|---|---|
| 157 | A13 | 10c multi | 26 | 12 |

Coronation of Sultan Ismail.

Types of Kedah 1957 with Portrait of Sultan Ismail

**1960 Wmk. 314 Engr. *Perf. 13***

| | | | | |
|---|---|---|---|---|
| 158 | A8 | 1c black | 9 | 9 |
| 159 | A8 | 2c red org | 9 | 7 |
| 160 | A8 | 4c dk brn | 9 | 7 |
| 161 | A8 | 5c dk car rose | 12 | 7 |
| 162 | A8 | 8c dk grn | 75 | 28 |
| 163 | A7 | 10c chocolate | 18 | 6 |
| 164 | A7 | 20c blue | 28 | 9 |
| 165 | A7 | 50c ultra & blk | 70 | 14 |
| 166 | A8 | $1 plum & ultra | 1.40 | 55 |
| 167 | A8 | $2 red & grn | 2.75 | 2.00 |
| 168 | A8 | $5 ol & grn & brn | 11.00 | 8.50 |
| | | *Nos. 158-168 (11)* | 17.45 | 11.92 |

Starting in 1965, issues of Johore are listed with Malaysia.

## POSTAGE DUE STAMPS

D1

***Perf. 12½***

**1938, Jan. 1 Typo. Wmk. 4**

| | | | | |
|---|---|---|---|---|
| J1 | D1 | 1c rose red | 3.25 | 8.25 |
| J2 | D1 | 4c green | 8.25 | 16.00 |
| J3 | D1 | 8c dl yel | 12.50 | 22.50 |
| J4 | D1 | 10c bis brn | 16.00 | 22.50 |
| J5 | D1 | 12c rose vio | 19.00 | 35.00 |
| | | *Nos. J1-J5 (5)* | 59.00 | 104.25 |

## OCCUPATION POSTAGE DUE STAMPS

**Issued under Japanese Occupation**

Johore Nos. J1-J5 Overprinted in Black, Brown or Red

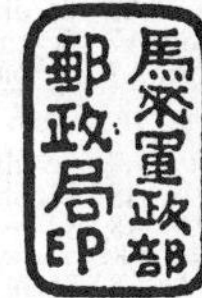


**1942 Wmk. 4 *Perf. 12½***

| | | | | |
|---|---|---|---|---|
| NJ1 | D1 | 1c rose red | 42.50 | 50.00 |
| NJ2 | D1 | 4c green | 42.50 | 55.00 |
| NJ3 | D1 | 8c dl yel | 50.00 | 57.50 |
| NJ4 | D1 | 10c bis brn | 15.00 | 20.00 |
| NJ5 | D1 | 12c rose vio | 25.00 | 30.00 |
| | | *Nos. NJ1-NJ5 (5)* | 175.00 | 212.50 |

Johore Nos. J1-J5 Overprinted in Black 大日本郵便

**1943**

| | | | | |
|---|---|---|---|---|
| NJ6 | D1 | 1c rose red | 1.00 | 2.50 |
| NJ7 | D1 | 4c green | 1.00 | 2.50 |
| NJ8 | D1 | 8c dl yel | 3.50 | 10.00 |
| NJ9 | D1 | 10c bis brn | 2.50 | 10.00 |
| NJ10 | D1 | 12c rose vio | 2.50 | 10.00 |
| | | *Nos. NJ6-NJ10 (5)* | 10.50 | 35.00 |

Nos. NJ6-NJ10 exist with second character sideways.

# KEDAH

LOCATION — On the west coast of the Malay Peninsula.
AREA — 3,660 sq. mi.
POP. — 752,706 (1960).
CAPITAL — Alor Star.

Sheaf of Rice — A1

Native Plowing — A2

Council Chamber — A3

**Wmk. Multiple Crown and C. A. (3)**

**1912-21 Engr. *Perf. 14***

| | | | | |
|---|---|---|---|---|
| 1 | A1 | 1c grn & blk | 18 | 14 |
| 2 | A1 | 1c brn ('19) | 35 | 28 |
| 3 | A1 | 2c grn ('19) | 35 | 10 |
| 4 | A1 | 3c car & blk | 22 | 14 |
| 5 | A1 | 3c dk vio ('19) | 22 | 42 |
| 6 | A1 | 4c sl & car | 3.75 | 22 |
| 7 | A1 | 4c scar ('19) | 38 | 14 |
| 8 | A1 | 5c org brn & grn | 1.40 | 2.25 |
| 9 | A1 | 8c ultra & blk | 55 | 1.65 |
| 10 | A2 | 10c blk brn & bl | 52 | 28 |
| 11 | A2 | 20c yel grn & blk | 1.50 | 2.25 |
| 12 | A2 | 21c red vio & vio ('19) | 5.00 | 13.00 |
| 13 | A2 | 25c red vio & bl ('21) | 1.65 | 8.00 |
| 14 | A2 | 30c car & blk | 1.65 | 5.50 |
| 15 | A2 | 40c lil & blk | 2.75 | 6.75 |
| 16 | A2 | 50c dl bl & brn | 4.25 | 8.00 |
| 17 | A3 | $1 scar & blk, *yel* | 6.50 | 11.00 |
| 18 | A3 | $2 dk brn & dk grn | 11.00 | 27.50 |
| 19 | A3 | $3 dk bl & blk, *bl* | 32.50 | 55.00 |
| 20 | A3 | $5 car & blk | 45.00 | 60.00 |
| | | *Nos. 1-20 (20)* | 119.72 | 202.62 |

There are two types of No. 7, one printed from separate plates for frame and center, the other printed from a single plate.

Stamps of 1912 Surcharged

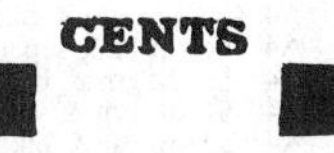


**1919**

| | | | | |
|---|---|---|---|---|
| 21 | A3 | 50c on $2 dk brn & dk grn | 42.50 | 57.50 |
| *a.* | | "C" of ovpt. inserted by hand | 1,000. | 725.00 |
| 22 | A3 | $1 on $3 dk bl & blk, *bl* | 30.00 | 45.00 |

**1921-36 Wmk. 4**

Two types of 1c:

I. The 1's have rounded corners, small top serif. Small letters "c."

II. The 1's have square-cut corners, large top serif. Large letters "c."

Two types of 2c:

I. The 2's have oval drops. Letters "c" are fairly thick and rounded.

The indexes in each volume of the Scott Catalogue contain many listings which help to identify stamps.

II. The 2's have round drops. Letters "c" thin and slightly larger.

| No. | Type | Description | Unused | Used |
|---|---|---|---|---|
| 23 | A1 | 1c brown | 10 | 10 |
| 24 | A1 | 1c blk (I) ('22) | 10 | 10 |
| a. | | 1c blk (II) ('39) | 10.50 | 6.75 |
| 25 | A1 | 2c grn (I) | 7 | 7 |
| a. | | 2c grn (II) ('40) | 55.00 | 10.00 |
| 26 | A1 | 3c dk vio | 55 | 35 |
| 27 | A1 | 3c grn ('22) | 26 | 20 |
| 28 | A1 | 4c carmine | 2.50 | 10 |
| 29 | A1 | 4c dl vio ('26) | 25 | 10 |
| 30 | A1 | 5c yel ('22) | 1.00 | 35 |
| 31 | A1 | 6c scar ('26) | 25 | 20 |
| 32 | A1 | 8c gray ('36) | 5.00 | 50 |
| 33 | A2 | 10c blk brn & bl | 1.00 | 35 |
| 34 | A2 | 12c dk ultra & blk ('26) | 1.00 | *3.75* |
| 35 | A2 | 20c grn & blk | 1.00 | 60 |
| 36 | A2 | 21c red vio & vio | 2.50 | *7.75* |
| 37 | A2 | 25c red vio & bl | 1.10 | *2.00* |
| 38 | A2 | 30c red & blk ('22) | 2.00 | *1.50* |
| 39 | A2 | 35c cl ('26) | 5.00 | *10.00* |
| 40 | A2 | 40c red vio & blk | 2.00 | *7.25* |
| 41 | A2 | 50c dp bl & brn | 85 | 75 |
| 42 | A3 | $1 scar & blk, *yel* ('22) | 5.00 | 5.00 |
| 43 | A3 | $2 brn & grn | 10.00 | *30.00* |
| 44 | A3 | $3 dk bl & blk, *bl* | 25.00 | *37.50* |
| 45 | A3 | $5 car & blk | 37.50 | *60.00* |
| | | *Nos. 23-45 (23)* | 104.03 | 168.52 |

Stamps of 1912-21 Overprinted in Black: "MALAYA-BORNEO EXHIBITION." in Three Lines

**1922** **Wmk. 3**

| No. | Type | Description | Unused | Used |
|---|---|---|---|---|
| 3a | A1 | 2c green | 6.75 | *17.00* |
| 12a | A2 | 21c red vio & vio | 17.00 | *67.50* |
| 13a | A2 | 25c red vio & bl | 24.00 | *67.50* |
| b. | | Inverted overprint | 1,500. | |
| 16a | A2 | 50c dl bl & brn | 24.00 | *85.00* |

**Wmk. 4**

| No. | Type | Description | Unused | Used |
|---|---|---|---|---|
| 23a | A1 | 1c brown | 2.50 | *14.00* |
| 26a | A1 | 3c dk vio | 2.50 | *20.00* |
| 28a | A1 | 4c carmine | 3.50 | *24.00* |
| 33a | A2 | 10c blk brn & bl | 6.75 | *35.00* |
| | | *Nos. 3a-33a (8)* | 87.00 | 330.00 |

Industrial fair at Singapore, Mar. 31-Apr. 15, 1922.

On Nos. 12a, 13a and 16a, "BORNEO" exists both 14mm and 15mm wide.

Sultan of Kedah, Sir Abdul Hamid Halim Shah — A4

**1937, July** **Wmk. 4** ***Perf. 12½***

| No. | Type | Description | Unused | Used |
|---|---|---|---|---|
| 46 | A4 | 10c sep & ultra | 50 | 26 |
| 47 | A4 | 12c gray vio & blk | 7.25 | *13.00* |
| 48 | A4 | 25c brn vio & ultra | 2.50 | *4.25* |
| 49 | A4 | 30c dp car & yel grn | 5.00 | *7.25* |
| 50 | A4 | 40c brn vio & blk | 85 | *7.75* |
| 51 | A4 | 50c dp bl & sep | 1.25 | *3.00* |
| 52 | A4 | $1 dk grn & blk | 1.25 | *5.00* |
| 53 | A4 | $2 dk brn & yel grn | 50.00 | 52.50 |
| 54 | A4 | $5 dp car & blk | 17.00 | *42.50* |
| | | *Nos. 46-54 (9)* | 85.60 | 135.51 |

**Catalogue values for unused stamps in this section, from this point to the end of the section, are for Never Hinged items.**

**Silver Wedding Issue**

Common Design Types

Inscribed: "Malaya Kedah"

**1948, Dec. 1** **Photo.** ***Perf. 14x14½***

| No. | Type | Description | Unused | Used |
|---|---|---|---|---|
| 55 | CD304 | 10c purple | 18 | 18 |

***Perf. 11½x11***

**Engraved; Name Typographed**

| No. | Type | Description | Unused | Used |
|---|---|---|---|---|
| 56 | CD305 | $5 rose car | 24.00 | 24.00 |

**UPU Issue**

Common Design Types

Inscribed: "Malaya-Kedah"

**Engr.; Name Typo. on 15c, 25c**

**1949, Oct. 10** ***Perf. 13½, 11x11½***

| No. | Type | Description | Unused | Used |
|---|---|---|---|---|
| 57 | CD306 | 10c rose vio | 18 | 18 |
| 58 | CD307 | 15c indigo | 42 | 42 |
| 59 | CD308 | 25c orange | 70 | 70 |
| 60 | CD309 | 50c slate | 1.50 | 1.50 |

Sheaf of Rice — A5

Sultan Tungku Badlishah — A6

**1950-55** **Wmk. 4** **Typo.** ***Perf. 18***

| No. | Type | Description | Unused | Used |
|---|---|---|---|---|
| 61 | A5 | 1c black | 6 | 5 |
| 62 | A5 | 2c orange | 8 | 5 |
| 63 | A5 | 3c green | 30 | 32 |
| 64 | A5 | 4c chocolate | 9 | *20* |
| 65 | A5 | 5c rose vio ('52) | 12 | 9 |
| 66 | A5 | 6c gray | 16 | 12 |
| 67 | A5 | 8c rose red | 45 | *1.25* |
| 68 | A5 | 8c grn ('52) | 30 | *1.25* |
| 69 | A5 | 10c plum | 14 | 5 |
| 70 | A5 | 12c rose red ('52) | 24 | *2.50* |
| 71 | A5 | 15c ultra | 90 | *85* |
| 72 | A5 | 20c dk grn & blk | 90 | *2.50* |
| 73 | A5 | 20c ultra ('52) | 38 | 25 |
| 74 | A6 | 25c org & rose lil | 50 | 45 |
| 75 | A6 | 30c plum & rose red ('55) | 2.00 | *85* |
| 76 | A6 | 35c dk vio & rose red ('52) | 60 | *1.65* |
| 77 | A6 | 40c dk vio & rose red | 1.25 | *5.50* |
| 78 | A6 | 50c ultra & blk | 65 | 20 |
| 79 | A6 | $1 yel brn & ultra | 4.50 | 1.65 |
| 80 | A6 | $2 rose red & emer | 17.00 | *21.00* |
| 81 | A6 | $5 choc & emer | 22.50 | *27.50* |
| | | *Nos. 61-81 (21)* | 53.12 | 68.28 |

**Coronation Issue**

Common Design Type

**1953, June 2** **Engr.** ***Perf. 13½x13***

| No. | Type | Description | Unused | Used |
|---|---|---|---|---|
| 82 | CD312 | 10c mag & blk | 28 | 15 |

Fishing Craft — A7

Weaving and Sultan — A8

Portrait of Sultan Tungku Badlishah and: 1c, Copra. 2c, Pineapples. 4c, Rice field. 5c, Mosque. 8c, East Coast Railway. 10c, Tiger. 50c, Aborigines with blowpipes. $1, Government offices. $2, Bersilat.

***Perf. 13x12½, 12½x13***

**1957** **Engr.** **Wmk. 314**

| No. | Type | Description | Unused | Used |
|---|---|---|---|---|
| 83 | A8 | 1c black | 6 | 5 |
| 84 | A8 | 2c red org | 6 | 5 |
| 85 | A8 | 4c dk brn | 8 | 5 |
| 86 | A8 | 5c dk car rose | 10 | 5 |
| 87 | A8 | 8c dk grn | 2.00 | 2.00 |
| 88 | A7 | 10c chocolate | 20 | 5 |
| 89 | A7 | 20c blue | 50 | 20 |

***Perf. 12½, 13½ ($1)***

| No. | Type | Description | Unused | Used |
|---|---|---|---|---|
| 90 | A7 | 50c ultra & blk | 1.00 | 50 |
| 91 | A8 | $1 plum & ultra | 1.65 | 80 |
| 92 | A8 | $2 red & grn | 8.25 | 3.75 |
| | | Revenue cancel | | 15 |
| 93 | A8 | $5 ol grn & brn | 12.50 | 5.75 |
| | | Revenue cancel | | 30 |
| | | *Nos. 83-93 (11)* | 26.40 | 13.25 |

Sultan Abdul Halim — A9

***Perf. 14x14½***

**1959, Feb. 20** **Photo.** **Wmk. 314**

| No. | Type | Description | Unused | Used |
|---|---|---|---|---|
| 94 | A9 | 10c ultra, red & yel | 18 | 12 |

Issued to commemorate the installation of the Sultan of Kedah, Abdul Halim.

Types of 1957

Designs as before with portrait of Sultan Abdul Halim.

***Perf. 13x12½, 12½x13, 12½, 13½***

**1959-62** **Engr.** **Wmk. 314**

| No. | Type | Description | Unused | Used |
|---|---|---|---|---|
| 95 | A8 | 1c black | 7 | 5 |
| 96 | A8 | 2c red org | 7 | 5 |
| 97 | A8 | 4c dk brn | 7 | 5 |
| 98 | A8 | 5c dk car rose | 9 | 5 |
| 99 | A8 | 8c dk grn | 10 | 7 |
| 100 | A7 | 10c chocolate | 32 | 5 |
| 101 | A7 | 20c blue | 28 | 9 |
| 102 | A7 | 50c ultra & blk, perf. 12½ x 13 ('60) | 55 | 14 |
| a. | | Perf. 12½ | 65 | 28 |
| 103 | A8 | $1 plum & ultra | 1.65 | 60 |
| 104 | A8 | $2 red & grn | 4.00 | 2.25 |
| 105 | A8 | $5 ol grn & brn perf. 13 x 12½ ('62) | 9.00 | 3.75 |
| a. | | Perf. 12½ | 8.25 | 3.75 |
| | | *Nos. 95-105 (11)* | 16.20 | 7.15 |

Starting in 1965, issues of Kedah are listed with Malaysia.

## OCCUPATION STAMPS

**Issued Under Japanese Occupation**

Stamps of Kedah 1922-36, Overprinted in Red or Black

DAI NIPPON

2602

**1942, May 13** **Wmk. 4** ***Perf. 14***

| No. | Type | Description | Unused | Used |
|---|---|---|---|---|
| N1 | A1 | 1c blk (R) | 1.25 | 1.75 |
| N2 | A1 | 2c grn (R) | 15.00 | 15.00 |
| N3 | A1 | 4c dl vio (R) | 1.25 | 1.75 |
| N4 | A1 | 5c yel (R) | 1.00 | 1.10 |
| a. | | Black ovpt. | 110.00 | 110.00 |
| N5 | A1 | 6c scar (Bk) | 1.25 | 1.50 |
| N6 | A1 | 8c gray (R) | 1.75 | 1.75 |

Nos. 46 to 54 Overprinted in Red

DAI NIPPON

2602

***Perf. 12½***

| No. | Type | Description | Unused | Used |
|---|---|---|---|---|
| N7 | A4 | 10c sep & ultra | 2.50 | 3.75 |
| N8 | A4 | 12c gray vio & blk | 7.50 | 8.75 |
| N9 | A4 | 25c brn vio & ultra | 5.00 | 5.00 |
| a. | | Black overprint | 87.50 | 87.50 |
| N10 | A4 | 30c dp car & yel grn | 25.00 | 30.00 |
| N11 | A4 | 40c brn vio & blk | 12.50 | 17.50 |
| N12 | A4 | 50c dp bl & sep | 12.50 | 17.50 |
| N13 | A4 | $1 dk grn & blk | 87.50 | 87.50 |
| a. | | Inverted ovpt. | 225.00 | 225.00 |
| N14 | A4 | $2 dk brn & yel grn | 87.50 | 87.50 |
| N15 | A4 | $5 dp car & blk | 25.00 | 25.00 |
| a. | | Black overprint | 200.00 | 225.00 |
| | | *Nos. N1-N15 (15)* | 286.50 | 305.35 |

# KELANTAN

LOCATION — On the eastern coast of the Malay Peninsula.
AREA — 5,750 sq. mi.
POP. — 545,620 (1960)
CAPITAL — Kota Bharu

Symbols of Government — A1

**Wmk. Multiple Crown and C. A. (3)**

**1911-15** **Typo.** ***Perf. 14.***

**Ordinary Paper**

| No. | Type | Description | Unused | Used |
|---|---|---|---|---|
| 1 | A1 | 1c gray grn | 14 | 10 |
| a. | | 1c grn | 14 | 6 |
| 2 | A1 | 3c rose red | 22 | 6 |
| 3 | A1 | 4c blk & red | 26 | 8 |
| 4 | A1 | 5c grn & red, *yel* | 80 | 10 |
| 5 | A1 | 8c ultra | 2.75 | 1.10 |
| 6 | A1 | 10c blk & vio | 3.50 | 22 |

**Chalky Paper**

| No. | Type | Description | Unused | Used |
|---|---|---|---|---|
| 7 | A1 | 30c vio & red | 5.25 | 45 |
| 8 | A1 | 50c blk & org | 3.25 | 2.75 |
| 9 | A1 | $1 grn & emer | 26.00 | 40.00 |
| 10 | A1 | $1 grn & brn ('15) | 16.00 | 5.25 |
| 11 | A1 | $2 grn & car rose | 1.40 | *5.25* |
| 12 | A1 | $5 grn & ultra | 10.50 | *13.00* |
| 13 | A1 | $25 grn & org | 40.00 | *67.50* |
| | | *Nos. 1-13 (13)* | 110.07 | 135.86 |

**1921-28** **Wmk. 4**

**Ordinary Paper**

| No. | Type | Description | Unused | Used |
|---|---|---|---|---|
| 14 | A1 | 1c green | 2.75 | 1.10 |
| 15 | A1 | 1c blk ('23) | 18 | 16 |
| 16 | A1 | 2c brown | 2.75 | *3.50* |
| 17 | A1 | 2c grn ('26) | 26 | 10 |
| 18 | A1 | 3c brn ('27) | 1.10 | 1.40 |
| 19 | A1 | 4c blk & red | 18 | 10 |
| 20 | A1 | 5c grn & red, *yel* | 22 | 10 |
| 21 | A1 | 6c claret | 1.90 | *2.75* |
| 22 | A1 | 6c rose red ('28) | 3.75 | 3.75 |
| 23 | A1 | 10c blk & vio | 1.10 | 18 |

**Chalky Paper**

| No. | Type | Description | Unused | Used |
|---|---|---|---|---|
| 24 | A1 | 30c dl vio & red ('26) | 2.25 | *3.75* |
| 25 | A1 | 50c blk & org | 4.00 | *13.00* |
| 26 | A1 | $1 grn & brn | 20.00 | *32.50* |
| | | *Nos. 14-26 (13)* | 40.44 | 62.39 |

Stamps of 1911-21 Overprinted in Black: "MALAYA BORNEO EXHIBITION" in Three Lines

**1922** **Wmk. 3**

| No. | Type | Description | Unused | Used |
|---|---|---|---|---|
| 3a | A1 | 4c blk & red | 2.50 | *15.00* |
| 4a | A1 | 5c grn & red, *yel* | 3.75 | *16.00* |
| 7a | A1 | 30c vio & red | 5.00 | *27.50* |
| 8a | A1 | 50c blk & org | 6.25 | *32.50* |
| 10a | A1 | $1 grn & brn | 20.00 | *62.50* |
| 11a | A1 | $2 grn & car rose | 50.00 | *110.00* |
| 12a | A1 | $5 grn & ultra | 125.00 | *275.00* |

**Wmk. 4**

| No. | Type | Description | Unused | Used |
|---|---|---|---|---|
| 14a | A1 | 1c green | 1.75 | *12.50* |
| 23a | A1 | 10c blk & vio | 4.25 | *22.50* |
| | | *Nos. 3a-23a (9)* | 218.50 | |

Industrial fair at Singapore. Mar. 31-Apr. 15, 1922.

Sultan Ismail

A2 A2a

**1928-33** **Engr.** ***Perf. 12***

**Size: 21½x30mm.**

| No. | Type | Description | Unused | Used |
|---|---|---|---|---|
| 27 | A2 | $1 ultra | 14.00 | *35.00* |

***Perf. 14***

| No. | Type | Description | Unused | Used |
|---|---|---|---|---|
| 28 | A2 | $1 bl ('33) | 40.00 | *47.50* |

**1937-40** ***Perf. 12***

**Size: 22½x34½mm.**

| No. | Type | Description | Unused | Used |
|---|---|---|---|---|
| 29 | A2a | 1c yel & ol grn | 10 | 7 |
| 30 | A2a | 2c dp grn | 12 | 12 |
| 31 | A2a | 4c brick red | 32 | 20 |
| 32 | A2a | 5c red brn | 65 | 12 |
| 33 | A2a | 6c car lake | 1.50 | 35 |
| 34 | A2a | 8c gray grn | 85 | 20 |
| 35 | A2a | 10c dk vio | 2.50 | 95 |
| 36 | A2a | 12c dp bl | 85 | *3.00* |
| 37 | A2a | 25c vio & red org | 1.90 | *3.75* |
| 38 | A2a | 30c scar & dk vio | 11.00 | *12.00* |
| 39 | A2a | 40c dk grn & org | 3.50 | *7.25* |
| 40 | A2a | 50c org & ol grn | 9.50 | *12.00* |
| 41 | A2a | $1 dp grn & dk vio | 3.75 | *7.25* |
| 42 | A2a | $2 red & red brn ('40) | 110.00 | *225.00* |
| 43 | A2a | $5 rose lake & org ('40) | 190.00 | *275.00* |
| | | *Nos. 29-43 (15)* | 336.54 | 547.26 |

**Catalogue values for unused stamps in this section, from this point to the end of the section, are for Never Hinged items.**

**Silver Wedding Issue**

Common Design Types

Inscribed: "Malaya Kelantan"

***Perf. 14x14½***

**1948, Dec. 1** **Wmk. 4** **Photo.**

| No. | Type | Description | Unused | Used |
|---|---|---|---|---|
| 44 | CD304 | 10c purple | 18 | 18 |

***Perf. 11½x11***

**Engraved; Name Typographed**

| No. | Type | Description | Unused | Used |
|---|---|---|---|---|
| 45 | CD305 | $5 rose car | 24.00 | *30.00* |

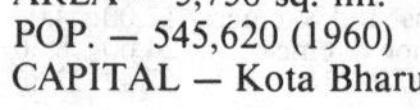

### UPU Issue
Common Design Types
Inscribed: "Malaya-Kelantan"
**Engr.; Name Typo. on 15c, 25c**

**1949, Oct. 10** *Perf. 13½, 11x11½*
*46* CD306 10c rose vio 30 30
*47* CD307 15c indigo 60 60
*48* CD308 25c orange 85 85
*49* CD309 50c slate 1.50 1.50

Sultan Ibrahim — A3

**Wmk. 4**

**1951, July 11** **Typo.** *Perf. 18*
*50* A3 1c black 10 6
*51* A3 2c orange 16 10
*52* A3 3c green 38 35
*53* A3 4c chocolate 22 10
*54* A3 6c gray 22 15
*55* A3 8c rose red 95 *2.00*
*56* A3 10c plum 30 5
*57* A3 15c ultra 1.00 70
*58* A3 20c dk grn & blk 1.90 1.25
*59* A3 25c org & plum 1.50 1.00
*60* A3 40c vio brn & rose red 2.75 2.75
*61* A3 50c dp ultra & blk 1.90 1.25
*62* A3 $1 vio brn & ultra 3.75 2.50
*63* A3 $2 rose red & emer 9.50 7.50
*64* A3 $5 choc & emer 25.00 17.50

**1952-55**
*65* A3 5c rose vio 35 25
*66* A3 8c green 1.40 *3.50*
*67* A3 12c rose red 1.40 *3.50*
*68* A3 20c ultra 1.25 *3.50*
*69* A3 30c plum & rose red ('55) 2.75 2.00
*70* A3 35c dk vio & rose red 1.75 *3.00*
*Nos. 50-70 (21)* 58.53 53.01

### Coronation Issue
Common Design Type

**1953, June 2** **Engr.** *Perf. 13½x13*
*71* CD312 10c mag & blk 25 20

Fishing Craft — A4

Government Offices and Sultan — A5

Portrait of Sultan Ibrahim and: 1c, Copra. 2c, Pineapples. 4c, Rice field. 5c, Mosque. 8c, East Coast Railway. 10c, Tiger. 50c, Aborigines with blowpipes. $2, Bersilat. $5, Weaving.

*Perf. 13x12½, 12½x13, 13½ ($1)*
**1957-63** **Engr.** **Wmk. 314**
*72* A5 1c black 6 5
*73* A5 2c red org 6 5
*74* A5 4c dk brn 9 6
*75* A5 5c dk car rose 9 6
*76* A5 8c dk grn 26 18
*77* A4 10c chocolate 14 5
*78* A4 20c blue 18 12
*79* A4 50c ultra & blk ('60) 48 22
*a.* Perf 12½ 60 22
*80* A5 $1 plum & ultra 1.65 95
*81* A5 $2 red & grn ('63) 3.75 *6.00*
*a.* Perf. 12½ 3.25 *7.50*
*82* A5 $5 ol grn & brn ('63) 8.25 *11.00*
*a.* Perf. 12½ 7.50 *11.00*
*Nos. 72-82 (11)* 15.01 18.74

Common Design Types pictured in section before Great Britain.

Sultan Yahya Petra — A6

**1961, July 17** **Photo.** *Perf. 14½x14*
*83* A6 10s multicolored 18 16

Installation of Sultan Yahya Petra.

Types of 1957 with Portrait of Sultan Yahya Petra.

Designs as before.

*Perf. 13x12½, 12½x13*
**1961-62** **Engr.** **Wmk. 338**
*84* A5 1c black 5 5
*85* A5 2c red org 5 5
*86* A5 4c dk brn 6 5
*87* A5 5c dk car rose 6 5
*88* A5 8c dk grn 70 70
*89* A4 10c choc ('61) 14 5
*90* A4 20c blue 28 25
*Nos. 84-90 (7)* 1.34 1.20

Starting in 1965, issues of Kelantan are listed with Malaysia.

## OCCUPATION STAMPS

### Issued Under Japanese Occupation

Kelantan No. 35 Handstamped in Black

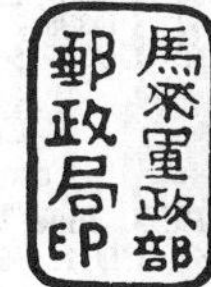

**1942** **Wmk. 4** *Perf. 12*
*N1* A2a 10c dk vio 200.00 200.00

Some authorities believe No. N1 was not regularly issued.

Kelantan Nos. 29-40 Surcharged in Black or Red and Handstamped with Oval Seal "a" in Red

1 Cents

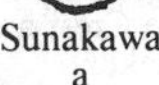
Sunakawa
a

Handa
b

**1942**
*N2* 1c on 50c org & ol grn 50.00 50.00
*a.* With "b" seal 37.50 37.50
*N3* 2c on 40c bl grn & org 37.50 37.50
*a.* With "b" seal 32.50 37.50
*N4* 5c on 12c dp bl (R) 37.50 37.50
*N5* 8c on 5c red brn (R) 37.50 37.50
*a.* With "b" seal (R) 32.50 37.50
*N6* 10c on 6c car lake 27.50 27.50
*a.* With "b" seal 32.50 37.50
*N7* 12c on 8c gray grn (R) 27.50 32.50
*N8* 30c on 4c brick red 250.00 250.00
*N9* 40c on 2c dp grn (R) 30.00 30.00
*N10* 50c on 1c yel & ol grn 100.00 100.00

Surcharged in Black or Red and Handstamped with Oval Seal "a" in Red

2 CENTS

*N10A* 1c on 50c org & ol grn 75.00 87.50
*N11* 2c on 40c bl grn & org 125.00 140.00
*N11A* 4c on 30c scar & dk vio 225.00 250.00
*N12* 5c on 12c dp bl (R) 50.00 45.00
*N13* 6c on 25c vio & red org 62.50 75.00
*N14* 8c on 5c red brn (R) 50.00 60.00
*N15* 10c on 6c car lake 37.50 45.00
*N16* 12c on 8c gray grn (R) 22.50 30.00
*a.* With "b" seal (R) 45.00 60.00
*N17* 25c on 10c dk vio 375.00 *450.00*
*N17A* 30c on 4c brick red 450.00 *500.00*
*N18* 40c on 2c dp grn (R) 30.00 37.50
*N19* 50c on 1c yel & ol grn 150.00 190.00

Kelantan Nos. 4-6 Surcharged in Red or Black and Handstamped with Oval Seal "a" in Red

$1.00

*Perf. 14*
*N20* A1 $1 on 4c blk & red (R) 37.50 45.00
*N21* A1 $2 on 5c grn & red, *yel* 37.50 45.00
*N22* A1 $5 on 6c rose red 37.50 45.00

Examples of Nos. N2-N22 without handstamped seal are from the remainder stocks sent to Singapore after Kelantan was ceded to Thailand. Some authorities believe stamps without seals were used before June 1942.

### Issued under Thai Occupation

OS1

**1943, Nov. 15** *Perf. 11*
*2N1* OS1 1c vio & blk 37.50 50.00
*2N2* OS1 2c vio & blk 37.50 50.00
*2N3* OS1 4c vio & blk 37.50 50.00
*2N4* OS1 8c vio & blk 25.00 37.50
*2N5* OS1 10c vio & blk 37.50 *75.00*
*Nos. 2N1-2N5 (5)* 175.00 262.50

Stamps with centers in red are revenues.

## MALACCA

**Catalogue values for unused stamps in this section, from this point to the end of the section, are for Never Hinged items.**

LOCATION — On the west coast of the Malay peninsula.
AREA — 640 sq. mi.
POP. — 318,110 (1960)
CAPITAL — Malacca

### Silver Wedding Issue
Common Design Types
Inscribed: "Malaya Malacca"
*Perf. 14x14½*

**1948, Dec. 1** **Wmk. 4** **Photo.**
*1* CD304 10c purple 22 22

**Engraved; Name Typographed**
*Perf. 11½x11*
*2* CD305 $5 lt brn 22.50 25.00

Type of Straits Settlements, 1937-41, Inscribed "Malacca".

**Wmk. 4**

**1949, Mar. 1** **Typo.** *Perf. 18*
*3* A29 1c black 12 15
*4* A29 2c orange 15 20
*5* A29 3c green 30 *60*
*6* A29 4c chocolate 18 18
*7* A29 6c gray 18 25
*8* A29 8c rose red 70 *3.00*
*9* A29 10c plum 30 8
*10* A29 15c ultra 80 75
*11* A29 20c dk grn & blk 70 *2.50*
*12* A29 25c org & rose lil 75 75
*13* A29 40c dk vio & rose red 2.25 *8.00*
*14* A29 50c ultra & blk 1.25 75
*15* A29 $1 vio brn & ultra 4.75 *6.75*
*16* A29 $2 rose red & emer 9.50 *19.00*
*17* A29 $5 choc & emer 26.00 *42.50*
*Nos. 3-17 (15)* 47.93 85.46

See Nos. 22-26.

### UPU Issue
Common Design Types
Inscribed: "Malaya-Malacca"
**Engr.; Name Typo. on 15c, 25c**
*Perf. 13½, 11x11½*

**1949, Oct. 10** **Wmk. 4**
*18* CD306 10c rose vio 22 22
*19* CD307 15c indigo 55 *1.10*
*20* CD308 25c orange 75 *1.50*
*21* CD309 50c slate 1.25 *3.75*

Type of Straits Settlements, 1937-41, Inscribed "Malacca"

**1952, Sept. 1** **Wmk. 4** *Perf. 18*
*22* A29 5c rose vio 25 *50*
*23* A29 8c green 50 *1.00*
*24* A29 12c rose red 50 *2.00*
*25* A29 20c ultra 1.00 75
*26* A29 35c dk vio & rose red 1.00 *2.00*
*Nos. 22-26 (5)* 3.25 6.25

### Coronation Issue
Common Design Type

**1953, June 2** **Engr.** *Perf. 13½x13*
*27* CD312 10c multi & blk 42 15

Queen Elizabeth II — A1

**1954-55** **Wmk. 4** **Typo.** *Perf. 18*
*29* A1 1c black 9 5
*30* A1 2c orange 10 7
*31* A1 4c chocolate 12 7
*32* A1 5c rose vio 15 7
*33* A1 6c gray 20 12
*34* A1 8c green 38 30
*35* A1 10c plum 22 5
*36* A1 12c rose red 38 25
*37* A1 20c ultra 65 42
*38* A1 25c org & plum 60 18
*39* A1 30c plum & rose red ('55) 85 38
*40* A1 35c vio brn & rose red 95 52
*41* A1 50c ultra & blk 1.10 45
*42* A1 $1 vio brn & ultra 2.00 1.10
*43* A1 $2 rose red & grn 6.00 3.50
*44* A1 $5 choc & emer 17.00 8.50
*Nos. 29-44 (16)* 30.79 16.03

Types of Kedah with Portrait of Queen Elizabeth II
*Perf. 13x12½, 12½x13*

**1957** **Engr.** **Wmk. 314**
*45* A8 1c black 8 5
*46* A8 2c red org 12 6
*47* A8 4c dk brn 12 6
*48* A8 5c dk car rose 12 5
*49* A8 8c dk grn 48 24
*50* A7 10c chocolate 35 5
*51* A7 20c blue 52 10

*Perf. 12½, 13½ ($1)*
*52* A7 50c ultra & blk 80 16
*53* A8 $1 plum & ultra 1.65 1.00
*54* A8 $2 red & grn 5.25 3.00
*55* A8 $5 ol grn & brn 11.00 6.00
*Nos. 45-55 (11)* 20.49 10.77

Types of Kedah, 1957, With Melaka Tree and Mouse Deer Replacing Portrait of Queen Elizabeth II
*Perf. 13x12½, 12½x13, 13½ ($1)*

**1960, Mar. 15** **Engr.** **Wmk. 314**
*56* A8 1c black 7 5
*57* A8 2c red org 9 5
*58* A8 4c dk brn 10 5
*59* A8 5c dk car rose 14 7
*60* A8 8c dk grn 45 22
*61* A7 10c chocolate 18 5
*62* A7 20c blue 40 10
*63* A7 50c ultra & blk 90 18
*64* A8 $1 plum & ultra 1.50 65
*65* A8 $2 red & grn 3.50 1.50
*66* A8 $5 ol grn & brn 9.00 2.75
*Nos. 56-66 (11)* 16.33 5.67

Starting in 1965, issues of Malacca (Melaka) are listed with Malaysia.

### OCCUPATION STAMPS

**Issued Under Japanese Occupation**

Stamps of Straits Settlements, 1937-41 Handstamped in Carmine

The handstamp covers four stamps. Values are for single stamps. Blocks of four showing complete handstamp sell for six times the price of singles.

**1942 Wmk. 4 *Perf. 14***

*N1* A29 1c black 37.50 45.00
*N2* A29 2c brn org 25.00 25.00
*N3* A29 3c green 37.50 37.50
*N4* A29 5c brown 50.00 50.00
*N5* A29 8c gray 62.50 75.00
*N6* A29 10c dl vio 62.50 62.50
*N7* A29 12c ultra 75.00 75.00
*N8* A29 15c ultra 62.50 62.50
*N9* A29 30c org & vio *1,500. 1,500.*
*N10* A29 40c dk vio & rose red 140.00 140.00
*N11* A29 50c blk, *emerald* 350.00 350.00
*N12* A29 $1 red & blk, *bl* 400.00 400.00
*N13* A29 $2 rose red & gray grn *1,250. 1,000.*
*N14* A29 $5 grn & red, *grn* *1,500. 1,750.*

Some authorities believe Nos. N9, N13, and N14 were not regularly issued.

### OCCUPATION POSTAGE DUE STAMPS

Malaya Postage Due Stamps and Type of 1936-38, Handstamped Like Nos. N1-N14 in Carmine

**1942 Wmk. 4 *Perf. 14½x14***

*NJ1* D2 1c violet 37.50 37.50
*NJ2* D2 4c yel grn 50.00 50.00
*NJ3* D2 8c red *150.00 150.00*
*NJ4* D2 10c yel org 75.00 75.00
*NJ5* D2 12c bl vio 100.00 100.00
*NJ6* D2 50c black *375.00 300.00*

Pricing note above No. N1 also applies to Nos. NJ1-NJ6.

## NEGRI SEMBILAN

LOCATION — South of Selangor on the west coast of the Malay Peninsula, bordering on Pahang on the east and Johore on the south.
AREA — 2,580 sq. mi.
POP. — 401,742 (1960)
CAPITAL — Seremban

Stamps of the Straits Settlements Overprinted in Black **Negri Sembilan**

**1891 Wmk. 2 *Perf. 14***

**Overprint 14½ to 15mm Wide**

*1* A2 2c rose 2.00 3.00

Tiger — A1

Tiger Head — A2

**1891-94 Typo.**

*2* A1 1c grn ('93) 1.65 1.10
*3* A1 2c rose 2.50 1.90
*4* A1 5c bl ('94) 13.00 *16.00*

**1895-99**

*5* A2 1c lil & grn 4.00 4.50
*6* A2 2c lil & brn 10.00 *13.00*
*7* A2 3c lil & car rose 2.00 65
*8* A2 5c lil & ol 4.00 3.00
*9* A2 8c lil & bl 10.00 8.25
*10* A2 10c lil & org 13.00 10.00
*11* A2 15c grn & vio 22.50 26.00
*12* A2 20c grn & ol ('99) 22.50 *26.00*
*13* A2 25c grn & car rose 32.50 *35.00*
*14* A2 50c grn & blk 42.50 50.00
*Nos. 5-14 (10)* 163.00 176.40

Stamps of 1891-99 Surcharged **Four cents.**

**1899 Green Surcharge**

*15* A2 4c on 8c lil & bl 1.65 2.50
***a.*** Double surcharge 600.00 600.00
***b.*** Pair, one without surcharge 1,000. 825.00
***c.*** Dbl. surch., one grn, one red 750.00 750.00

**Black Surcharge**

*16* A2 4c on 8c lil & bl 325.00 *400.00*

**Same Surcharge and Bar in Black**

*17* A1 4c on 1c grn 80 *2.75*
*18* A1 4c on 5c bl 60 *2.75*
*19* A2 4c on 3c lil & car rose 2.75 *7.00*
***a.*** Dbl. surcharge 400.00 350.00
***b.*** Pair, one without surcharge 1,000. *1,200.*
***d.*** Bar double 600.00

Bar at bottom on #17-18, at top on #19.

No. 11 Surcharged in Black **One cent.**

**1900**

*20* A2 1c on 15c grn & vio 87.50 *100.00*
***a.*** Inverted period 250.00 250.00

Arms of Negri Sembilan
A4 A5

**1935-41 Typo. Wmk. 4**

*21* A4 1c blk ('36) 75 8
*22* A4 2c dp grn ('36) 52 8
*22A* A4 2c brn org ('41) 14 *7.00*
*22B* A4 3c grn ('41) 18 *3.50*
*23* A4 4c brn org 52 7
*24* A4 5c chocolate 52 6
*25* A4 6c rose red 2.75 90
*25A* A4 6c gray ('41) 1.90 *19.00*
*26* A4 8c gray 1.25 25
*27* A4 10c dl vio ('36) 1.25 28
*28* A4 12c ultra ('36) 1.50 45
*28A* A4 15c ultra ('41) 2.00 *17.00*
*29* A4 25c rose red & dl vio ('36) 1.50 1.50
*30* A4 30c org & dl vio ('36) 2.00 2.75
*31* A4 40c dl vio & car 90 *3.50*
*32* A4 50c blk, *emer* ('36) 3.75 90
*33* A4 $1 red & blk, *bl* ('36) 1.50 2.00
*34* A4 $2 rose red & grn ('36) 22.50 26.00
*35* A4 $5 brn red & grn, *emer* ('36) 17.50 *35.00*
*Nos. 21-35 (19)* 62.93 120.32

**Catalogue values for unused stamps in this section, from this point to the end of the section, are for Never Hinged items.**

**Silver Wedding Issue**
Common Design Types
Inscribed: "Malaya Negri Sembilan"

**1948, Dec. 1 Photo. *Perf. 14x14½***

*36* CD304 10c purple 18 18

***Perf. 11½x11***

**Engraved; Name Typographed**

*37* CD305 $5 green 24.00 25.00

**1949-55 Wmk. 4 Typo. *Perf. 18***

*38* A5 1c black 6 5
*39* A5 2c orange 10 8
*40* A5 3c green 35 30
*41* A5 4c chocolate 14 12
*42* A5 5c rose vio 20 15
*43* A5 6c gray 28 15
*44* A5 8c rose red 55 60
*45* A5 8c green 2.00 2.00
*46* A5 10c plum 28 5
*47* A5 12c rose red 2.00 2.00
*48* A5 15c ultra 1.50 40
*49* A5 20c dk grn & blk 80 85
*50* A5 20c ultra 1.00 30
*51* A5 25c org & rose lil 45 25
*52* A5 30c plum & rose red ('55) 2.50 1.50
*53* A5 35c dk vio & rose red 1.00 2.00
*54* A5 40c dk vio & rose red 1.10 *4.00*
*55* A5 50c ultra & blk 1.10 40
*56* A5 $1 vio brn & ultra 2.50 1.00
*57* A5 $2 rose red & emer 8.00 6.00
*58* A5 $5 choc & emer 30.00 25.00
*Nos. 38-58 (21)* 55.91 47.20

**UPU Issue**
Common Design Types
Inscribed: "Malaya-Negri Sembilan"

**Engr.; Name Typo. on 15c, 25c**

**1949, Oct. 10 *Perf. 13½, 11x11½***

*59* CD306 10c rose vio 20 20
*60* CD307 15c indigo 38 38
*61* CD308 25c orange 75 75
*62* CD309 50c slate 1.50 2.25

**Coronation Issue**
Common Design Type

**1953, June 2 Engr. *Perf. 13½x13***

*63* CD312 10c mag & blk 28 15

Types of Kedah with Arms of Negri Sembilan

***Perf. 13x12½, 12½x13, 13½ ($1)***

**1957-63 Engr. Wmk. 314**

*64* A8 1c black 6 5
*65* A8 2c red org 6 5
*66* A8 4c dk brn 8 5
*67* A8 5c dk car rose 8 5
*68* A8 8c dk grn 22 16
*69* A7 10c chocolate 12 5
*70* A7 20c blue 22 8
*71* A7 50c ultra & blk ('60) 65 20
***a.*** Perf. 12½ 65 20
*72* A8 $1 plum & ultra 1.50 50
*73* A8 $2 red & grn ('63) 3.50 4.25
***a.*** Perf. 12½ 3.50 4.25
*74* A8 $5 ol grn & brn ('62) 8.25 5.75
***a.*** Perf. 12½ 8.25 5.75
*Nos. 64-74 (11)* 14.74 11.19

Negri Sembilan State Crest and Tuanku Munawir — A6

**1961, Apr. 17 Unwmk. *Perf. 14x13***

*75* A6 10s bl & multi 18 14

Installation of Tuanku Munawir as ruler (Yang di-Pertuan Besar) of Negri Sembilan.
Starting in 1965, issues of Negri (Negeri) Sembilan are listed with Malaysia.

### OCCUPATION STAMPS

**Issued under Japanese Occupation**

Stamps and Type of Negri Sembilan, 1935-41, Handstamped in Red, Black, Brown or Violet

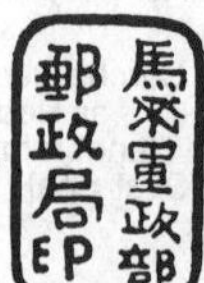


**1942 Wmk. 4 *Perf. 14***

*N1* A4 1c black 15.00 20.00
*N2* A4 2c brn org 10.00 12.50
*N3* A4 3c green 15.00 15.00
*N4* A4 5c chocolate 12.50 10.00
*N5* A4 6c rose red 450.00 450.00
*N6* A4 6c gray 75.00 75.00
*N7* A4 8c gray 65.00 65.00
*N8* A4 8c rose red 17.50 25.00
*N9* A4 10c dk vio 32.50 37.50
*N10* A4 12c ultra 375.00 375.00
*N11* A4 15c ultra 12.50 12.50
*N12* A4 25c rose red & dk vio 25.00 25.00
*N13* A4 30c org & dk vio 75.00 87.50
*N14* A4 40c dk vio & car 250.00 250.00
*N15* A4 $1 red & blk, *bl* 50.00 50.00
*N16* A4 $5 brn red & grn, *emer* 200.00 250.00

The 8c rose red is not known to have been issued without overprint.
Some authorities believe Nos. N5 and N7 were not regularly issued.

Stamps of Negri Sembilan, 1935-41, Overprinted in Black **DAI NIPPON 2602 MALAYA**

*N17* A4 1c black 1.00 1.00
***a.*** Inverted overprint 12.50 20.00
***b.*** Dbl. ovpt., one invtd. 35.00 *50.00*
*N18* A4 2c brn org 1.25 1.00
*N19* A4 3c green 1.00 75
*N20* A4 5c chocolate 65 65
*N21* A4 6c gray 1.50 1.50
***a.*** Inverted overprint *500.00*
*N22* A4 8c rose red 2.00 2.00
*N23* A4 10c dk vio 6.00 6.00
*N24* A4 15c ultra 5.00 5.00
*N25* A4 25c rose red & dk vio 1.50 *5.00*
*N26* A4 30c org & dk vio 3.00 *3.75*
*N27* A4 $1 red & blk, *bl* 125.00 125.00
*Nos. N17-N27 (11)* 147.90 151.65

The 8c rose red is not known to have been issued without overprint.

Negri Sembilan, Nos. 21, 24 and 29, Overprinted or Surcharged in Black:

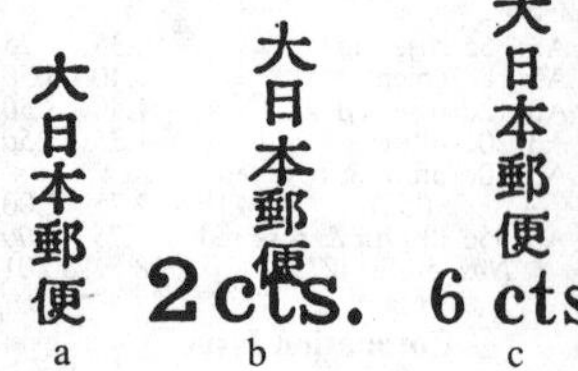


a b c

**1943**

*N28* A4 1c black 50 50
***a.*** Inverted overprint 12.50 17.50
*N29* A4 2c on 5c choc 38 50
*N30* A4 6c on 5c choc 50 65
***a.*** "6 cts." invtd. 250.00 *300.00*
*N31* A4 25c rose red & dk vio 1.50 2.00

The Japanese characters read: "Japanese Postal Service."

## PAHANG

LOCATION — On the east coast of the Malay Peninsula.
AREA — 13,820 sq. mi.
POP. — 338,210 (1960)
CAPITAL — Kuala Lipis

Stamps of the Straits Settlements Overprinted in Black

Overprinted **PAHANG**

**Overprint 16x2¾mm**

**1889 Wmk. 2 *Perf. 14***

*1* A2 2c rose 37.50 20.00
*2* A3 8c orange 1,700. 1,500.
*3* A7 10c slate 250.00 225.00

Overprinted **PAHANG**

**Overprint 12½x2mm.**

*4* A2 2c rose 3.00 3.75

Overprinted **PAHANG**

**1890 Overprint 15x2½mm.**

*5* A2 2c rose 1,000. 850.00

Overprinted **PAHANG**

**Overprint 16x2¾mm.**

*6* A2 2c rose 37.50 14.00

Surcharged in Black:

| a | b |
|---|---|
| PAHANG *Two* CENTS | PAHANG Two CENTS |

| c | d |
|---|---|
| PAHANG *Two* CENTS | PAHANG Two CENTS |

**1891**

| No. | Type | Description | Unused | Used |
|---|---|---|---|---|
| | A3 (a) | 2c on 24c grn | 175.00 | 175.00 |
| | A3 (b) | 2c on 24c grn | 175.00 | 175.00 |
| | A3 (c) | 2c on 24c grn | 30.00 | 35.00 |
| 0 | A3 (d) | 2c on 24c grn | 60.00 | 60.00 |

A5

A6

**1892-95** **Typo.**

| No. | Type | Description | Unused | Used |
|---|---|---|---|---|
| 11 | A5 | 1c green | 3.00 | 2.25 |
| 12 | A5 | 2c rose | 80 | 80 |
| 13 | A5 | 5c blue | 3.75 | *7.50* |

**1895-99**

| No. | Type | Description | Unused | Used |
|---|---|---|---|---|
| 14 | A6 | 3c lil & car rose | 1.25 | 85 |
| 14A | A6 | 4c lil & car rose ('99) | 2.50 | 2.50 |
| 15 | A6 | 5c lil & olive | 10.00 | *11.00* |

Stamps of Perak, 1895-99, Overprinted **Pahang.**

**1898-99**

| No. | Type | Description | Unused | Used |
|---|---|---|---|---|
| 16 | A9 | 10c lil & org | 12.50 | *12.50* |
| 17 | A9 | 25c grn & car rose | 21.00 | *32.50* |
| 18 | A9 | 50c grn & blk | 25.00 | *32.50* |
| 18A | A9 | 50c lil & blk | 80.00 | 80.00 |

Overprinted **Pahang.**

**Wmk. Crown and C. C. (1)**

| No. | Type | Description | Unused | Used |
|---|---|---|---|---|
| 19 | A10 | $1 grn & lt grn | 45.00 | 45.00 |
| 20 | A10 | $5 grn & ultra | 165.00 | 165.00 |

No. 13 Cut in Half and Surcharged With New Value and Initials in ms.

**1897** **Wmk. 2**

**Red Surcharge**

| No. | Type | Description | Unused | Used |
|---|---|---|---|---|
| 21 | A5 | 2c on half of 5c bl | 600.00 | 200.00 |
| *a.* | | Black surcharge | 2,000. | 1,000. |
| 22 | A5 | 3c on half of 5c bl | 600.00 | 200.00 |
| *a.* | | Black surcharge | 2,000. | 1,000. |

Perak No. 52 Surcharged **Pahang Four cents**

**1899**

| No. | Type | Description | Unused | Used |
|---|---|---|---|---|
| 25 | A9 | 4c on 8c lil & bl | 3.00 | 4.00 |
| *b.* | | Inverted surcharge | 1,000. | 800.00 |

Same Surcharge on pieces of White Paper

**1898** **Without Gum** ***Imperf.***

| No. | Description | Unused | Used |
|---|---|---|---|
| 26 | 4c black | | 600.00 |
| 27 | 5c black | 400.00 | |

Pahang No. 15 Surcharged **Four cents.**

**1899** ***Perf. 14***

| No. | Type | Description | Unused | Used |
|---|---|---|---|---|
| 28 | A6 | 4c on 5c lil & ol | 8.50 | *12.50* |

Sultan Abu Bakar
A7 A8

**1935-41** **Typo.** **Wmk. 4** ***Perf. 14***

| No. | Type | Description | Unused | Used |
|---|---|---|---|---|
| 29 | A7 | 1c blk ('36) | 12 | 12 |
| 30 | A7 | 2c dp grn ('36) | 65 | 14 |
| 30A | A7 | 3c grn ('41) | 12 | *1.90* |
| 31 | A7 | 4c brn org | 32 | 5 |
| 32 | A7 | 5c chocolate | 38 | 5 |
| 33 | A7 | 6c rose red ('36) | 1.40 | *3.50* |
| 34 | A7 | 8c gray | 95 | 12 |
| 34A | A7 | 8c rose red ('41) | 24 | *9.50* |
| 35 | A7 | 10c dk vio ('36) | 35 | 7 |
| 36 | A7 | 12c ultra ('36) | 1.25 | 1.10 |
| 36A | A7 | 15c ultra ('41) | 85 | *12.00* |
| 37 | A7 | 25c rose red & pale vio ('36) | 95 | 40 |
| 38 | A7 | 30c org & dk vio ('36) | 60 | 60 |
| 39 | A7 | 40c dk vio & car | 85 | 95 |
| 40 | A7 | 50c blk, *emer* ('36) | 3.50 | 85 |
| 41 | A7 | $1 red & blk, *bl* ('36) | 1.90 | 2.25 |
| 42 | A7 | $2 rose red & grn ('36) | 16.00 | *27.50* |
| 43 | A7 | $5 brn red & grn, *emer* ('36) | 5.75 | *27.50* |
| | | *Nos. 29-43 (18)* | 36.18 | 88.60 |

The 3c was printed on both ordinary and chalky paper; the 15c only on ordinary paper; other values only on chalky paper.

A 2c brown orange and 6c gray, type A7, exist, but are not known to have been regularly issued.

**Catalogue values for unused stamps in this section, from this point to the end of the section, are for Never Hinged items.**

**Silver Wedding Issue**

Common Design Types

Inscribed: "Malaya Pahang"

***Perf. 14x14½***

**1948, Dec. 1** **Photo.** **Wmk. 4**

| No. | Type | Description | Unused | Used |
|---|---|---|---|---|
| 44 | CD304 | 10c purple | 20 | 20 |

***Perf. 11½x11***

**Engraved; Name Typopgraphed**

| No. | Type | Description | Unused | Used |
|---|---|---|---|---|
| 45 | CD305 | $5 green | 24.00 | 27.50 |

**UPU Issue**

Common Design Types

Inscribed: "Malaya-Pahang"

**Engr.; Name Typo. on 15c, 25c**

**1949, Oct. 10** ***Perf. 13½, 11x11½***

| No. | Type | Description | Unused | Used |
|---|---|---|---|---|
| 46 | CD306 | 10c rose vio | 20 | 20 |
| 47 | CD307 | 15c indigo | 28 | 28 |
| 48 | CD308 | 25c orange | 80 | 80 |
| 49 | CD309 | 50c slate | 1.40 | 1.40 |

**Wmk. 4**

**1950, June 1** **Typo.** ***Perf. 18***

| No. | Type | Description | Unused | Used |
|---|---|---|---|---|
| 50 | A8 | 1c black | 8 | 10 |
| 51 | A8 | 2c orange | 15 | 15 |
| 52 | A8 | 3c green | 35 | 60 |
| 53 | A8 | 4c chocolate | 12 | 8 |
| 54 | A8 | 6c gray | 22 | 18 |
| 55 | A8 | 8c rose red | 35 | *1.50* |
| 56 | A8 | 10c plum | 18 | 5 |
| 57 | A8 | 15c ultra | 50 | 35 |
| 58 | A8 | 20c dk grn & blk | 85 | *3.50* |
| 59 | A8 | 25c org & rose lil | 35 | 30 |
| 60 | A8 | 40c dk vio & rose red | 2.00 | *7.50* |
| 61 | A8 | 50c dp ultra & blk | 75 | 55 |
| 62 | A8 | $1 vio brn & ultra | 2.00 | 1.80 |
| 63 | A8 | $2 rose red & emer | 7.50 | 10.00 |
| 64 | A8 | $5 choc & emer | 22.50 | *30.00* |

**1952-55**

| No. | Type | Description | Unused | Used |
|---|---|---|---|---|
| 65 | A8 | 5c rose vio | 20 | 8 |
| 66 | A8 | 8c green | 85 | 1.00 |
| 67 | A8 | 12c rose red | 1.00 | 2.00 |
| 68 | A8 | 20c ultra | 50 | 50 |
| 69 | A8 | 30c plum & rose red ('55) | 2.50 | 1.50 |
| 70 | A8 | 35c dk vio & rose red | 1.25 | 2.00 |
| | | *Nos. 50-70 (21)* | 44.20 | 63.74 |

**Coronation Issue**

Common Design Type

**1953, June 2** **Engr.** ***Perf. 13½x13***

| No. | Type | Description | Unused | Used |
|---|---|---|---|---|
| 71 | CD312 | 10c mag & blk | 18 | 16 |

Types of Kedah with Portrait of Sultan Abu Bakar

***Perf. 13x12½, 12½x13, 13½ ($1)***

**1957-62** **Engr.** **Wmk. 314**

| No. | Type | Description | Unused | Used |
|---|---|---|---|---|
| 72 | A8 | 1c black | 9 | 5 |
| 73 | A8 | 2c red org | 9 | 5 |
| 74 | A8 | 4c dk brn | 10 | 5 |
| 75 | A8 | 5c dk car rose | 10 | 5 |
| 76 | A8 | 8c dk grn | 26 | 18 |
| 77 | A7 | 10c chocolate | 18 | 5 |
| 78 | A7 | 20c blue | 40 | 14 |
| 79 | A7 | 50c ultra & blk ('60) | 65 | 26 |
| *a.* | | Perf. 12½ | 65 | 26 |
| 80 | A8 | $1 plum & ultra | 1.50 | 65 |
| 81 | A8 | $2 red & grn ('62) | 3.50 | 2.00 |
| *a.* | | Perf. 12½ | 3.50 | 2.00 |
| 82 | A8 | $5 ol grn & brn ('60) | 8.75 | 5.00 |
| *a.* | | Perf. 12½ | 8.75 | 5.00 |
| | | *Nos. 72-82 (11)* | 15.62 | 8.48 |

Starting in 1965, issues of Pahang are listed with Malaysia.

**OCCUPATION STAMPS**

**Issued under Japanese Occupation**

Stamps of Pahang, 1935-41, Handstamped in Black, Red, Brown or Violet

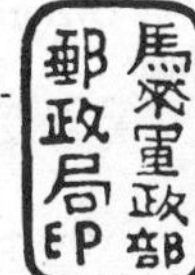


**1942** **Wmk. 4** ***Perf. 14***

| No. | Type | Description | Unused | Used |
|---|---|---|---|---|
| N1 | A7 | 1c black | 25.00 | 30.00 |
| N1A | A7 | 3c green | 50.00 | 60.00 |
| N2 | A7 | 5c chocolate | 10.00 | 12.50 |
| N3 | A7 | 8c rose red | 12.50 | 5.50 |
| N3A | A7 | 8c gray | 175.00 | 175.00 |
| N4 | A7 | 10c dk vio | 22.50 | 25.00 |
| N5 | A7 | 12c ultra | 400.00 | 400.00 |
| N6 | A7 | 15c ultra | 37.50 | 37.50 |
| N7 | A7 | 25c rose red & pale vio | 14.00 | 17.50 |
| N8 | A7 | 30c org & dk vio | 12.50 | 15.00 |
| N9 | A7 | 40c dk vio & car | 10.00 | 12.50 |
| N10 | A7 | 50c blk, *emerald* | 125.00 | 125.00 |
| N11 | A7 | $1 red & blk, *bl* | 50.00 | 50.00 |
| N12 | A7 | $5 brn red & grn, *emer* | 300.00 | 300.00 |

Some authorities claim the 2c green, 4c brown orange, 6c rose red and $2 rose red and green were not regularly issued with this overprint.

Stamps of Pahang, 1935-41, Overprinted in Black **DAI NIPPON 2602 MALAYA**

| No. | Type | Description | Unused | Used |
|---|---|---|---|---|
| N13 | A7 | 1c black | 1.00 | 50 |
| N14 | A7 | 5c chocolate | 1.00 | 1.00 |
| N15 | A7 | 8c rose red | 17.50 | 1.75 |
| N16 | A7 | 10c vio brn | 10.00 | 4.25 |
| N17 | A7 | 12c ultra | 1.00 | 1.50 |
| N18 | A7 | 25c rose red & pale vio | 3.50 | *5.00* |
| N19 | A7 | 30c org & dk vio | 1.25 | *2.50* |
| | | *Nos. N13-N19 (7)* | 35.25 | 16.50 |

Pahang No. 32 Overprinted and Surcharged in Black

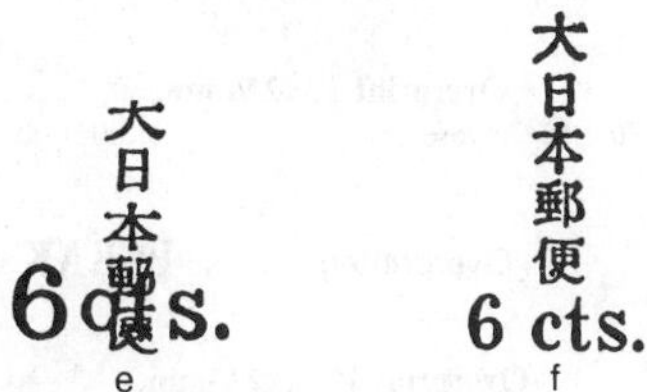


e f

**1943**

| No. | Type | Description | Unused | Used |
|---|---|---|---|---|
| N20 | A7(e) | 6c on 5c choc | 1.00 | 1.00 |
| N21 | A7(f) | 6c on 5c choc | 1.50 | 1.10 |

The Japanese characters read: "Japanese Postal Service."

## PENANG

**Catalogue values for unused stamps in this section, from this point to the end of the section, are for Never Hinged items.**

LOCATION — An island off the west coast of the Malay Peninsula, plus a coastal strip called Province Wellesley.
AREA — 400 sq. mi.
POP. — 616,254 (1960)
CAPITAL — Georgetown

**Silver Wedding Issue**

Common Design Types

Inscribed: "Malaya Penang"

***Perf. 14x14½***

**1948, Dec. 1** **Wmk. 4** **Photo.**

| No. | Type | Description | Unused | Used |
|---|---|---|---|---|
| 1 | CD304 | 10c purple | 18 | 18 |

***Perf. 11½x11***

**Engraved; Name Typographed**

| No. | Type | Description | Unused | Used |
|---|---|---|---|---|
| 2 | CD305 | $5 lt brn | 24.00 | 24.00 |

Type of Straits Settlements, 1937-41, Inscribed "Penang"

**1949-52** ***Perf. 18***

| No. | Type | Description | Unused | Used |
|---|---|---|---|---|
| 3 | A29 | 1c black | 6 | 5 |
| 4 | A29 | 2c orange | 7 | 6 |
| 5 | A29 | 3c green | 20 | 18 |
| 6 | A29 | 4c chocolate | 9 | 7 |
| 7 | A29 | 5c rose vio ('52) | 20 | 10 |
| 8 | A29 | 6c gray | 28 | 12 |
| 9 | A29 | 8c rose red | 38 | *2.00* |
| 10 | A29 | 8c grn ('52) | 38 | 55 |
| 11 | A29 | 10c plum | 55 | 5 |
| 12 | A29 | 12c rose red ('52) | 55 | 60 |
| 13 | A29 | 15c ultra | 65 | *2.00* |
| 14 | A29 | 20c dk grn & blk | 75 | 1.00 |
| 15 | A29 | 20c ultra ('52) | 60 | 35 |
| 16 | A29 | 25c org & rose lil | 45 | 15 |
| 17 | A29 | 35c dk vio & rose red ('52) | 90 | 80 |
| 18 | A29 | 40c dk vio & rose red | 1.40 | *6.00* |
| 19 | A29 | 50c ultra & blk | 1.10 | 15 |
| 20 | A29 | $1 vio brn & ultra | 2.25 | 40 |
| 21 | A29 | $2 rose red & emer | 4.75 | 90 |
| 22 | A29 | $5 choc & emer | 20.00 | 1.25 |
| | | *Nos. 3-22 (20)* | 35.61 | 16.78 |

**UPU Issue**

Common Design Types

Inscribed: "Malaya-Penang"

**Engr.; Name Typo. on 15c, 25c**

**1949, Oct. 10** ***Perf. 13½, 11x11½***

| No. | Type | Description | Unused | Used |
|---|---|---|---|---|
| 23 | CD306 | 10c rose vio | 22 | 22 |
| 24 | CD307 | 15c indigo | 32 | 32 |
| 25 | CD308 | 25c orange | 70 | 70 |
| 26 | CD309 | 50c slate | 1.40 | 1.40 |

**Coronation Issue**

Common Design Type

**1953, June 2** **Engr.** ***Perf. 13½x13***

| No. | Type | Description | Unused | Used |
|---|---|---|---|---|
| 27 | CD312 | 10c mag & blk | 28 | 15 |

Type of Malacca, 1954

**1954-55** **Wmk. 4** **Typo.** ***Perf. 18***

| No. | Type | Description | Unused | Used |
|---|---|---|---|---|
| 29 | A1 | 1c black | 5 | 5 |
| 30 | A1 | 2c orange | 6 | 6 |
| 31 | A1 | 4c chocolate | 12 | 6 |
| 32 | A1 | 5c rose vio | 9 | 5 |
| 33 | A1 | 6c gray | 26 | 16 |
| 34 | A1 | 8c green | 24 | *85* |
| 35 | A1 | 10c plum | 24 | 5 |
| 36 | A1 | 12c rose red | 26 | 16 |
| 37 | A1 | 20c ultra | 32 | 10 |
| 38 | A1 | 25c org & plum | 40 | 8 |
| 39 | A1 | 30c plum & rose red ('55) | 1.00 | 50 |
| 40 | A1 | 35c vio brn & rose red | 85 | 50 |
| 41 | A1 | 50c ultra & blk | 85 | 35 |
| 42 | A1 | $1 vio brn & ultra | 1.65 | 35 |
| 43 | A1 | $2 rose red & grn | 3.25 | 1.40 |
| 44 | A1 | $5 choc & emer | 15.00 | 3.25 |
| | | *Nos. 29-44 (16)* | 24.64 | 7.97 |

Types of Kedah with Portrait of Queen Elizabeth II

***Perf. 13x12½, 12½x13***

**1957** **Engr.** **Wmk. 314**

| No. | Type | Description | Unused | Used |
|---|---|---|---|---|
| 45 | A8 | 1c black | 6 | 5 |
| 46 | A8 | 2c red org | 6 | 5 |
| 47 | A8 | 4c dk brn | 10 | 6 |
| 48 | A8 | 5c dk car rose | 10 | 5 |
| 49 | A8 | 8c dk grn | 60 | 22 |
| 50 | A7 | 10c chocolate | 18 | 5 |
| 51 | A7 | 20c blue | 42 | 12 |

*Perf. 12½, 13½ ($1)*

52 A7 50c ultra & blk 70 20
53 A8 $1 plum & ultra 1.10 26
54 A8 $2 red & grn 4.50 1.90
55 A8 $5 ol grn & brn 9.00 2.25
*Nos. 45-55 (11)* 16.82 5.21

Types of Kedah, 1957 with Penang State Crest and Areca-nut Palm Replacing Portrait of Elizabeth II

***Perf. 13x12½, 12½x13, 13½ ($1)***

**1960, Mar. 15 Engr. Wmk. 314**

56 A8 1c black 6 5
57 A8 2c red org 8 5
58 A8 4c dk brn 8 5
59 A8 5c dk car rose 8 5
60 A8 8c dk grn 60 40
61 A7 10c chocolate 12 5
62 A7 20c blue 20 7
63 A7 50c ultra & blk 48 10
64 A8 $1 plum & ultra 1.00 28
65 A8 $2 red & grn 2.50 70
Revenue cancel 20
66 A8 $5 ol grn & brn 7.00 1.25
*Nos. 56-66 (11)* 12.20 3.05

Starting in 1965, issues of Penang (Pulau Pinang) are listed with Malaysia.

## OCCUPATION STAMPS

**Issued under Japanese Occupation**

Stamps of Straits Settlements, 1937-41, Overprinted in Red or Black

DAI NIPPON
2602
PENANG

**1942 Wmk. 4 *Perf. 14***

N1 A29 1c blk (R) 1.00 1.00
N2 A29 2c brn org 5.00 2.50
N3 A29 3c grn (R) 1.00 1.00
N4 A29 5c brn (R) 1.00 1.00
N5 A29 8c gray (R) 2.50 1.00
N6 A29 10c dl vio (R) 1.50 1.50
N7 A29 12c ultra (R) 2.00 1.50
N8 A29 15c ultra (R) 1.50 1.50
N9 A29 40c dk vio & rose red 2.50 *4.00*
N10 A29 50c *emerald* (R) 4.00 *6.00*
N11 A29 $1 red & blk, *bl* 10.00 *12.50*
N12 A29 $2 rose red & gray grn 17.50 20.00
N13 A29 $5 grn & red, *grn* 250.00 275.00
*Nos. N1-N13 (13)* 299.50 328.50

Stamps of Straits Settlements Handstamped in Red

Okugawa Seal

**1942 Wmk. 4 *Perf. 14***

N14 A29 1c black 12.50 12.50
N15 A29 2c brn org 15.00 12.50
N16 A29 3c green 25.00 10.00
N17 A29 5c brown 10.00 10.00
N18 A29 8c gray 12.50 12.50
N19 A29 10c dl vio 12.50 12.50
N20 A29 12c ultra 12.50 12.50
N21 A29 15c ultra 12.50 12.50
N22 A29 40c dk vio & rose red 37.50 37.50
N23 A29 50c *emerald* 62.50 75.00
N24 A29 $1 red & blk, *bl* 100.00 100.00
N25 A29 $2 rose red & gray grn 150.00 200.00
N26 A29 $5 grn & red, *grn* 425.00 450.00
*Nos. N14-N26 (13)* 887.50 957.50

Handstamped in Red

Uchibori Seal

**Same Colors**

N14a A29 1c 20.00 30.00
N15a A29 2c 20.00 30.00
N16a A29 3c 20.00 30.00
N17a A29 5c 250.00 250.00
N18a A29 8c 20.00 25.00
N19a A29 10c 25.00 35.00
N20a A29 12c 25.00 35.00
N21a A29 15c 25.00 30.00
*Nos. N14a-N21a (8)* 405.00 465.00

## PERAK

LOCATION — On the west coast of the Malay Peninsula.
AREA — 7,980 sq. mi.
POP. — 1,327,120 (1960)
CAPITAL — Taiping

Straits Settlements No. 10 Handstamped in Black

**1878 Wmk. 1 *Perf. 14***

1 A2 2c brown 1,100. 825.00

Overprinted PERAK

**Overprint 17x3½mm. Wide**

**1880**

2 A2 2c brown 17.50 17.50

Overprinted PERAK

**Overprint 10 to 14½ mm. Wide**

3 A2 2c brown 40.00 40.00

Same Overprint on Straits Settlements Nos. 40, 41a

**1883 Wmk. Crown and C. A. (2)**

4 A2 2c brown 8.00 9.25
5 A2 2c rose 7.25 7.25

Overprinted PERAK

**Overprint 14 to 15½ mm. Wide**

6 A2 2c rose 1.00 90
a. Inverted overprint 175.00 165.00
b. Double overprint 575.00

Overprinted PERAK

**Overprint 12¾ to 14 mm. Wide**

**1886-90**

7 A2 2c rose 1.10 1.10
a. "FERAK" corrected by pen 165.00 175.00

Overprinted PERAK

**Overprint 10x1¾mm.**

8 A2 2c rose 12.00 15.00

Overprinted PERAK

**Overprint 13x2¾mm.**

10 A2 2c rose 1.00 1.00

Overprinted PERAK

**Overprint 10¾x2½mm.**

11 A2 2c rose 30.00 32.50

Straits Settlements Nos. 42, 41a Surcharged in Black or Blue

2 CENTS PERAK q

ONE CENT PERAK. r

ONE CENT PERAK s

PERAK ONE CENT t

12 A2(q) 2c on 4c rose 275.00 200.00
13 A2(t) 1c on 2c rose 37.50 28.00
14 A2(r) 1c on 2c rose 17.50 18.50
a. Without period after "PERAK" 275.00
15 A2(s) 1c on 2c rose (Bl) 14.00 15.00
15A A2(s) 1c on 2c rose (Bk) 1,000. 925.00

In type "r" PERAK is 11½ to 14mm. wide.

Surcharged in Black 1 CENT PERAK

16 A2 1c on 2c rose 20.00 20.00
a. Double surch.

Surcharged 1 CENT PERAK

17 A2 1c on 2c rose

Some authorities question the status of No. 17.

Surcharged 1 CENT PERAK

18 A2 1c on 2c rose 725.00 425.00
b. Double surcharge, one inverted
c. "PREAK"

Surcharged 1 CENT PERAK

18A A2 1c on 2c rose 225.00 225.00

Surcharged One CENT PERAK

19 A2 1c on 2c rose 75 2.50
a. Double surcharge, one inverted
b. Invtd. surcharge
c. "One" inverted 450.00
d. Double surch

Straits Settlements No. 41a Surcharged

One CENT PERAK u
One CENT PERAK v
One CENT PERAK w

One CENT PERAK x
One CENT PERAK y
One CENT PERAK z

One CENT PERAK h

**1889-90**

20 A2(u) 1c on 2c rose 50 85
a. Italic Roman "K" in "PERAK" 60.00 75.00
b. Double surch
21 A2(v) 1c on 2c rose 275.00 275.00
23 A2(w) 1c on 2c rose 5.00 9.00
a. "PREAK" 200.00 200.00
24 A2(x) 1c on 2c rose 35.00 45.00
25 A2(y) 1c on 2c rose 4.25 4.00
26 A2(z) 1c on 2c rose 3.00 3.00
27 A2(h) 1c on 2c rose 14.00 14.00

Straits Settlements Nos. 41a, 48, 54 Surcharged in Black:

PERAK One CENT a
PERAK Two CENTS b

PERAK One CENT c
PERAK One CENT d

PERAK One CENT e
PERAK One CENT f

PERAK One CENT g

**1891 Wmk. Crown and C. A. (2)**

28 A2(a) 1c on 2c rose 38 45
a. Bar omitted 100.00
29 A2(a) 1c on 6c vio 6.75 7.25
30 A3(b) 2c on 24c grn 2.75 2.75
31 A2(c) 1c on 2c rose 1.65 1.75
a. Bar omitted 325.00
32 A2(d) 1c on 2c rose 38 45
a. Bar omitted 150.00
33 A2(d) 1c on 6c vio 20.00 16.00
34 A3(d) 2c on 24c grn 14.00 15.00
35 A2(e) 1c on 2c rose 2.75 3.00
a. Bar omitted 325.00
36 A2(e) 1c on 6c vio 15.00 16.00
37 A3(e) 2c on 24c grn 14.00 14.00
38 A2(f) 1c on 6c vio 14.00 14.00
39 A3(f) 2c on 24c grn 16.00 10.50
40 A2(g) 1c on 6c vio 21.00 16.00
41 A3(g) 2c on 24c grn 20.00 21.00

A7

**1892-95 Typo. *Perf. 14***

42 A7 1c green 48 10
43 A7 2c rose 48 10
44 A7 2c org ('95) 30 *90*
45 A7 5c blue 1.25 80

Type of 1892 Surcharged in Black 3 CENTS

**1895**

46 A7 3c on 5c rose 30 *60*

Common Design Types Pictured in section before Great Britain.

A9

A10

**1895-99 Wmk. 2 *Perf. 14***

47 A9 1c lil & grn 32 28
48 A9 2c lil & brn 32 22
49 A9 3c lil & car rose 1.40 12
50 A9 4c lil & car rose ('99) 1.65 *3.25*
51 A9 5c lil & ol 95 38
52 A9 8c lil & bl 8.25 30

3 A9 10c lil & org 3.25 30
4 A9 25c grn & car rose ('96) 55.00 8.25
5 A9 50c lil & blk 21.00 14.00
6 A9 50c grn & blk ('99) 55.00 55.00

**Wmk. Crown and C. C. (1)**

7 A10 $1 grn & lt grn 55.00 32.50
8 A10 $2 grn & car rose ('96) 60.00 42.50
9 A10 $3 grn & ol ('96) 60.00 60.00
0 A10 $5 grn & ultra 190.00 175.00
1 A10 $25 grn & org ('96) 1,250. 350.00
*Nos. 47-57 (11)* 202.14 114.60

Stamps of 1895-99 Surcharged in Black:

One Cent. i — ONE CENT. k

Three Cent. m

**1900 Wmk. 2**

2 A9(i) 1c on 2c lil & brn 32 45
3 A9(k) 1c on 4c lil & car rose 32 60
54 A9(i) 1c on 5c lil & ol 38 70
55 A9(i) 3c on 8c lil & bl 85 85
a. No period after "Cent" 55.00 55.00
b. Double surcharge 110.00 110.00
56 A9(i) 3c on 50c grn & blk 70 70
a. No period after "Cent" 55.00 55.00

**Wmk. 1**

57 A10(m) 3c on $1 grn & lt grn 42.50 *50.00*
58 A10(m) 3c on $2 grn & car rose 12.50 *19.00*
*Nos. 62-68 (7)* 57.57 72.30

Sultan Iskandar
A14 A15

**1935-37 Typo. Wmk. 4**
**Chalky Paper**

69 A14 1c blk ('36) 7 6
70 A14 2c dp grn ('36) 7 6
71 A14 4c brn org 16 8
72 A14 5c chocolate 7 5
73 A14 6c rose red ('37) 1.40 1.10
74 A14 8c gray 1.00 16
75 A14 10c dk vio ('36) 20 7
76 A14 12c ultra ('36) 90 55
77 A14 25c rose red & pale vio ('36) 48 60
78 A14 30c org & dk vio ('36) 52 95
79 A14 40c dk vio & car 2.00 2.00
80 A14 50c blk, *emerald* ('36) 1.25 85
81 A14 $1 red & blk, *bl* ('36) 1.00 95
82 A14 $2 rose red & grn ('36) 7.00 5.50
83 A14 $5 brn red & grn, *emer* ('36) 14.00 12.50
*Nos. 69-83 (15)* 30.12 25.48

**1938-41**

84 A15 1c blk ('39) 7 5
85 A15 2c dp grn ('39) 1.00 5
85A A15 2c brn org ('41) 30 *1.50*
85B A15 3c grn ('41) 30 38
86 A15 4c brn org ('39) 1.50 7
87 A15 5c choc ('39) 12 5
88 A15 6c rose red ('39) 10.00 12
89 A15 8c gray 5.00 7
89A A15 8c rose red ('41) 25 *5.00*
90 A15 10c dk vio 1.50 6
91 A15 12c ultra 3.50 2.25
91A A15 15c ultra ('41) 1.00 *11.00*
92 A15 25c rose red & pale vio ('39) 15.00 3.00
93 A15 30c org & dk vio 50 2.00
94 A15 40c dk vio & rose red 5.00 2.00
95 A15 50c blk, *emerald* 3.00 50
96 A15 $1 red & blk, *bl* ('40) 20.00 15.00
97 A15 $2 rose red & grn ('40) 37.50 30.00
98 A15 $5 red, *emer* ('40) 100.00 *175.00*
*Nos. 84-98 (19)* 205.54 248.10

**Catalogue values for unused stamps in this section, from this point to the end of the section, are for Never Hinged items.**

**Silver Wedding Issue**
Common Design Types
Inscribed: "Malaya Perak"

**1948, Dec. 1 Photo. *Perf. 14x14½***
99 CD304 10c purple 18 18

***Perf. 11½x11***
**Engraved; Name Typographed**
100 CD305 $5 green 24.00 24.00

**UPU Issue**
Common Design Types
Inscribed: "Malaya-Perak"
**Engr.; Name Typo. on 15c, 25c**
***Perf. 13½, 11x11½***

**1949, Oct. 10 Wmk. 4**
101 CD306 10c rose vio 24 24
102 CD307 15c indigo 38 38
103 CD308 25c orange 80 80
104 CD309 50c slate 1.40 1.40

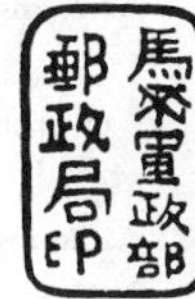

Sultan Yussuf Izuddin Shah — A16

**1950, Aug. 17 Typo. *Perf. 18***
105 A16 1c black 10 5
106 A16 2c orange 15 8
107 A16 3c green 85 50
108 A16 4c chocolate 24 8
109 A16 6c gray 32 12
110 A16 8c rose red 52 40
111 A16 10c plum 32 5
112 A16 15c ultra 70 25
113 A16 20c dk grn & blk 90 45
114 A16 25c org & plum 60 10
115 A16 40c vio brn & rose red 1.65 90
116 A16 50c dp ultra & blk 95 15
117 A16 $1 vio brn & ultra 2.50 40
118 A16 $2 rose red & emer 7.75 90
119 A16 $5 choc & emer 26.00 3.75

**1952-55**
120 A16 5c rose vio 26 6
121 A16 8c green 65 50
122 A16 12c rose red 60 50
123 A16 20c ultra 60 15
124 A16 30c plum & rose red ('55) 1.25 55
125 A16 35c dk vio & rose red 1.00 60
*Nos. 105-125 (21)* 47.91 10.54

**Coronation Issue**
Common Design Type

**1953 Engr. *Perf. 13½x13***
126 CD312 10c mag & blk 22 12

Types of Kedah with Portrait of Sultan Yussuf Izuddin Shah
***Perf. 13x12½, 12½x13, 13½ ($1)***

**1957-61 Engr. Wmk. 314**
127 A8 1c black 7 5
128 A8 2c red org 7 5
129 A8 4c dk brn 9 5
130 A8 5c dk car rose 10 5
131 A8 8c dk grn 90 22
132 A7 10c chocolate 14 5
133 A7 20c blue 22 5
134 A7 50c ultra & blk ('60) 52 16
a. Perf. 12½ 52 16
135 A8 $1 plum & ultra 1.10 22
136 A8 $2 red & grn ('61) 2.75 65
a. Perf. 12½ 2.75 90
137 A8 $5 ol grn & brn ('60) 9.00 2.00
a. Perf. 12½ 9.00 2.75
*Nos. 127-137 (11)* 14.96 3.55

Starting with 1963, issues of Perak are listed with Malaysia.

### OFFICIAL STAMPS

Stamps of Straits Settlements Overprinted in Black — P.G.S.

**1890 Wmk. 1 *Perf. 14***
O1 A3 12c blue 82.50 110.00
O2 A3 24c green 300.00 *300.00*

**Wmk. Crown and C. A. (2)**
O3 A2 2c rose 2.25 2.25
a. No period after "S" 40.00 40.00
b. Double overprint 1,100. 1,100.
O4 A2 4c brown 5.00 6.75
a. No period after "S" 72.50 *100.00*
O5 A2 6c violet 16.00 18.00
O6 A3 8c orange 27.50 30.00
O7 A7 10c slate 42.50 42.50
O8 A3 12c vio brn 125.00 125.00
O9 A3 24c green 72.50 *82.50*

P.G.S. stands for Perak Government Service.

Perak No. 45 Overprinted — Service.

**1894**
O10 A7 5c blue 10.00 50
a. Inverted overprint 110.00 110.00

Same Overprint on No. 51

**1897**
O11 A9 5c lil & ol 85 20
a. Double overprint 100.00 100.00

### OCCUPATION STAMPS

**Issued under Japanese Occupation**

Stamps of Perak, 1938-41, Handstamped in Black, Red, Brown or Violet

馬來軍政部 郵政局 EP

**1942 Wmk. 4 *Perf. 14***
N1 A15 1c black 20.00 25.00
N2 A15 2c brn org 12.50 15.00
N3 A15 3c green 22.50 25.00
N4 A15 5c chocolate 7.50 7.50
N5 A15 8c gray 22.50 25.00
N6 A15 8c rose red 10.00 25.00
N7 A15 10c dk vio 12.50 25.00
N8 A15 12c ultra 50.00 62.50
N9 A15 15c ultra 20.00 25.00
N10 A15 25c rose red & pale vio 10.00 15.00
N11 A15 30c org & dk vio 20.00 25.00
N12 A15 40c dk vio & rose red 100.00 125.00
N13 A15 50c blk, *emerald* 30.00 *35.00*
N14 A15 $1 red & blk, *bl* 125.00 150.00
N15 A15 $2 rose red & grn 500.00 500.00
N16 A15 $5 red, *emer* 450.00 450.00

Some authorities claim No. N6 was not regularly issued. This overprint also exists on No. 85

Stamps of Perak, 1938-41, Overprinted in Black — DAI NIPPON 2602 MALAYA

N16A A15 1c black 25.00 25.00
N17 A15 2c brn org 1.00 1.00
a. Inverted overprint 17.50 19.00
N18 A15 3c green 75 1.00
a. Inverted overprint 20.00 22.50
N18B A15 5c chocolate 25.00
N19 A15 8c rose red 75 50
a. Inverted overprint 7.50 7.50
b. Dbl. ovpt., one invtd. 125.00 150.00
c. Pair, one without ovpt. 200.00 200.00
N20 A15 10c dk vio 5.00 6.00
N21 A15 15c ultra 3.75 4.50
N21A A15 30c org & dk vio 20.00 20.00
N22 A15 50c blk, *emerald* 4.50 5.00
N23 A15 $1 red & blk, *bl* 175.00 *200.00*
N24 A15 $5 red, *emer* 37.50 45.00
a. Inverted overprint 250.00 *300.00*

Some authorities claim Nos. N16A, N18B and N21A were not regularly issued.

Overprinted on Perak No. 87 and Surcharged in Black "2 Cents"

N25 A15 2c on 5c choc 1.50 1.00

Perak Nos. 84 and 89A Overprinted in Black — DAI NIPPON YUBIN

N26 A15 1c black 2.50 3.00
a. Inverted overprint 25.00 30.00
N27 A15 8c rose red 2.50 1.50
a. Inverted overprint 15.00 17.50

Overprinted on Perak No. 87 and Surcharged in Black "2 Cents"

N28 A15 2c on 5c choc 3.75 3.75
a. Inverted overprint 25.00 35.00
b. As "a", "2 Cents" omitted 37.50 42.50

Stamps of Perak, 1938-41, Overprinted or Surcharged in Black:

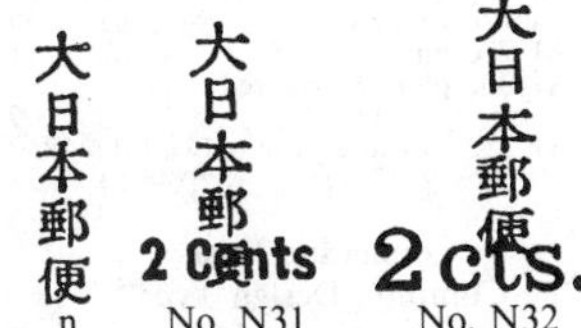


n — No. N31 — No. N32

**1943**
N29 A15 1c black 50 50
N30 A15 2c brn org 26.00 26.00
N31 A15 2c on 5c choc 75 75
a. "2 Cents" inverted 25.00 30.00
b. Entire surcharge inverted 25.00 30.00
N32 A15 2c on 5c choc 1.00 1.00
a. Vertical characters invtd. 25.00 30.00
b. Entire surcharge inverted 25.00 30.00
N33 A15 3c green 27.50 27.50
N34 A15 5c chocolate 75 75
a. Inverted overprint 37.50 45.00
N35 A15 8c gray 25.00 25.00
N36 A15 8c rose red 75 75
a. Inverted overprint 25.00 30.00
N37 A15 10c dk vio 90 90
N38 A15 30c org & dk vio 2.00 3.00
N39 A15 50c blk, *emerald* 4.00 5.00
N40 A15 $5 red, *emer* 50.00 62.50

No. N34 was also used in the Shan States of Burma. The Japanese characters read: "Japanese Postal Service."

Some authorities claim Nos. N30, N33 and N35 were not regularly issued.

## PERLIS

**Catalogue values for unused stamps in this section, from this point to the end of the section, are for Never Hinged items.**

LOCATION — On the west coast of the Malay peninsula, adjoining Siam and Kedah.
AREA — 310 sq. mi.
POP. — 97,645 (1960)
CAPITAL — Kangar

**Silver Wedding Issue**
Common Design Types
Inscribed: "Malaya Perlis"
***Perf. 14x14½***

**1948, Dec. 1 Photo. Wmk. 4**
1 CD304 10c purple 18 18

**Engraved; Name Typographed**
***Perf. 11½x11***
2 CD305 $5 lt brn 27.50 30.00

**UPU Issue**
Common Design Types
Inscribed: "Malaya-Perlis"
**Engr.; Name Typo. on 15c, 25c**

**1949, Oct. 10 *Perf. 13½, 11x11½***
3 CD306 10c rose vio 25 25
4 CD307 15c indigo 50 50
5 CD308 25c orange 85 85
6 CD309 50c slate 1.90 1.90

Raja Syed Putra — A1

**Wmk. 4**

**1951, Mar. 26 Typo. *Perf. 18***

*7* A1 1c black 6 *10*
*8* A1 2c orange 10 *15*
*9* A1 3c green 85 *2.00*
*10* A1 4c chocolate 20 25
*11* A1 6c gray 22 30
*12* A1 8c rose red 65 2.00
*13* A1 10c plum 35 15
*14* A1 15c ultra 1.00 3.00
*15* A1 20c dk grn & blk 2.00 3.50
*16* A1 25c org & rose lil 85 85
*17* A1 40c dk vio & rose red 2.00 *4.00*
*18* A1 50c ultra & blk 1.65 1.15
*19* A1 $1 vio brn & ultra 5.25 4.25
*20* A1 $2 rose red & emer 7.50 *15.00*
*21* A1 $5 choc & emer 18.00 *25.00*

**1952-55**

*22* A1 5c rose vio 16 30
*23* A1 8c green 42 *2.00*
*24* A1 12c rose red 42 *2.50*
*25* A1 20c ultra 60 75
*26* A1 30c plum & rose red ('55) 3.25 *5.00*
*27* A1 35c dk vio & rose red 1.00 *3.00*
*Nos. 7-27 (21)* 46.53 75.25

**Coronation Issue**
Common Design Type

**1953, June 2 Engr. *Perf. 13½x13***

*28* CD312 10c mag & blk 35 35

Types of Kedah with Portrait of Raja Syed Putra

***Perf. 13x12½, 12½x13, 12½ ($2, $5), 13½ ($1)***

**1957-62 Engr. Wmk. 314**

*29* A8 1c black 5 5
*30* A8 2c red org 5 7
*31* A8 4c dk brn 6 5
*32* A8 5c dk car rose 8 5
*33* A8 8c dk grn 1.00 32
*34* A7 10c chocolate 10 7
*35* A7 20c blue 16 14
*36* A7 50c ultra & blk ('62) 60 48
*a.* Perf. 12½ 48 40
*37* A8 $1 plum & ultra 1.25 *1.50*
*38* A8 $2 red & grn 3.00 *2.50*
*39* A8 $5 ol grn & brn 10.00 *5.50*
*Nos. 29-39 (11)* 16.35 10.73

Starting in 1965, issues of Perlis are listed with Malaysia.

## SELANGOR

LOCATION — South of Perak on the west coast of the Malay Peninsula.
AREA — 3,160 sq. mi.
POP. — 1,012,891 (1960)
CAPITAL — Kuala Lumpur

Stamps of the Straits Settlements Overprinted

Handstamped in Black or Red

**1878 Wmk. 1 *Perf. 14***

*1* A2 2c brn (Bk)
*2* A2 2c brn (R)

The authenticity of Nos. 1-2 and the 2c brown, watermarked Crown and CA, is questioned.

Overprinted in Black **S.**

**1882 Wmk. Crown and C. A. (2)**

*3* A2 2c brown 1,000.
*4* A2 2c rose

Overprinted **SELANGOR**

**Overprint 16 to 16¾mm. Wide**

**1881 Wmk. Crown and C. C. (1)**

*5* A2 2c brown 12.00 14.00
*a.* Double overprint

**Overprint 16 to 17mm. Wide**

**1882-83 Wmk. Crown and C. A. (2)**

*6* A2 2c brown 22.50 25.00
*7* A2 2c rose 12.00 12.00

Overprinted **SELANGOR**

**Overprint 14¼x3mm.**

*8* A2 2c rose 3.00 3.75
*a.* Double overprint

Overprinted **SELANGOR**

**Overprint 14½ to 15½mm. Wide**

**1886-89**

*9* A2 2c rose 4.25 4.25

Overprinted **SELANGOR**

**Overprint 16½x1¾mm.**

*9A* A2 2c rose 22.50 25.00

Overprinted **SELANGOR**

**Overprint 15½ to 17mm. Wide With Period**

*10* A2 2c rose 12.00 12.00

**Without Period**

*11* A2 2c rose 4.00 1.10

**Same Overprint, but Vertically**

*12* A2 2c rose 10.50 12.50

Overprinted **SELANGOR**

*12A* A2 2c rose 25.00 2.25

Overprinted ***Selangor***

**Overprint 17mm. Wide**

*13* A2 2c rose 500.00 *550.00*

Overprinted ***SELANGOR***

*14* A2 2c rose 325.00 325.00

Overprinted Vertically **SELANGOR**

**1889**

*15* A2 2c rose 82.50 16.00

Overprinted Vertically ***SELANGOR***

**Overprint 19 to 20¾mm. Wide**

*16* A2 2c rose 42.50 30.00

**Similar Overprint, but Diagonally**

*17* A2 2c rose 825.00

Overprinted Vertically **SELANGOR**

*18* A2 2c rose 9.50 2.00

**Same Overprint Horizontally**

*18A* A2 2c rose 2,000.

Surcharged in Black:

SELANGOR Two CENTS — a
SELANGOR Two CENTS — b
SELANGOR Two CENTS — c
SELANGOR Two CENTS — d
SELANGOR Two CENTS — e

**1891**

*19* A3 (a) 2c on 24c grn 5.50 7.75
*20* A3 (b) 2c on 24c grn 65.00
*21* A3 (c) 2c on 24c grn 65.00
*22* A3 (d) 2c on 24c grn 65.00
*23* A3 (e) 2c on 24c grn 65.00

A6

**1891-95 Typo. Wmk. 2**

*24* A6 1c green 60 10
*25* A6 2c rose 1.10 18
*26* A6 2c org ('95) 45 18
*27* A6 5c blue 2.75 95

Type of 1891 Surcharged **3 CENTS**

**1894**

*28* A6 3c on 5c rose 26 26

A8 A9

**1895-99 Wmk. 2 *Perf. 14***

*29* A8 3c lil & car rose 1.90 9
*30* A8 5c lil & ol 30 25
*31* A8 8c lil & bl 25.00 5.00
*32* A8 10c lil & org 6.00 50
*33* A8 25c grn & car rose 32.50 17.50
*34* A8 50c lil & blk 25.00 12.50
*35* A8 50c grn & blk 110.00 37.50

**Wmk. 1**

*36* A9 $1 grn & lt grn 24.00 15.00
*37* A9 $2 grn & car rose 50.00 45.00
*38* A9 $3 grn & ol 100.00 75.00
*39* A9 $5 grn & ultra 50.00 50.00
*40* A9 $10 grn & brn vio 200.00 100.00
*41* A9 $25 grn & org 500.00

High values with revenue cancellations are plentiful and inexpensive.

Surcharged in Black:

One cent. Three cents.

**1900 Wmk. 2**

*42* A8 1c on 5c lil & ol 32.50 40.00
*43* A8 1c on 50c grn & blk 1.00 1.25
*a.* Double surcharge 950.00
*44* A8 3c on 50c grn & blk 6.50 *9.50*

Mosque at Klang A12 Sultan Sulaiman A13

**1935-41 Typo. Wmk. 4 *Perf. 14***

*45* A12 1c blk ('36) 6 5
*46* A12 2c dp grn ('36) 10 5
*46A* A12 2c org brn ('41) 14 *1.00*
*46B* A12 3c grn ('41) 14 *1.25*
*47* A12 4c org brn 26 5
*48* A12 5c chocolate 20 5
*49* A12 6c rose red 1.50 14
*50* A12 8c gray 32 9
*51* A12 10c dk vio ('36) 32 5
*52* A12 12c ultra ('36) 3.25 16
*52A* A12 15c ultra ('41) 1.50 *15.00*
*53* A12 25c rose red & pale vio ('36) 45 52
*54* A12 30c org & dk vio ('36) 65 80
*55* A12 40c dk vio & car 1.10 1.00
*56* A12 50c blk, *emer* ('36) 1.25 42
*57* A13 $1 red & blk, *bl* ('36) 4.00 65
*58* A13 $2 rose red & grn ('36) 13.00 4.25
*59* A13 $5 brn red & grn, *emer* ('36) 37.50 *26.00*
*Nos. 45-59 (18)* 65.74 51.53

Nos. 46A-46B were printed on both ordinary and chalky paper; 15c only on ordinary paper; other values only on chalky paper.

An 8c rose red was prepared but not issued.

Sultan Hisam-ud-Din Alam Shah
A14 A15

**1941**

*72* A14 $1 red & blk, *blue* 3.25 4.25
*73* A14 $2 car & grn 24.00 *32.50*

A $5 stamp of type A14, issued during the Japanese occupation with different overprints, also exists without overprint. The unoverprinted stamp was not issued before or after the occupation.

**Catalogue values for unused stamps in this section, from this point to the end of the section, are for Never Hinged items.**

**Silver Wedding Issue**
Common Design Types
Inscribed: "Malaya Selangor"

***Perf. 14x14½***

**1948, Dec. 1 Photo. Wmk. 4**

*74* CD304 10c purple 20 20

***Perf. 11½x11***

**Engraved; Name Typographed**

*75* CD305 $5 green 26.00 25.00

**UPU Issue**
Common Design Types
Inscribed: "Malaya-Selangor"

**Engr.; Name Typo. on Nos. 77 and 78**

**1949, Oct. 10 *Perf. 13½, 11x11½***

*76* CD306 10c rose vio 32 32
*77* CD307 15c indigo 38 38
*78* CD308 25c orange 65 65
*79* CD309 50c slate 1.25 1.25

**1949, Sept. 12 Typo. *Perf. 18***

*80* A15 1c black 14 5
*81* A15 2c orange 14 6
*82* A15 3c green 28 18
*83* A15 4c chocolate 18 5
*84* A15 6c gray 22 10
*85* A15 8c rose red 65 1.25
*86* A15 10c plum 22 5
*87* A15 15c ultra 80 10
*88* A15 20c dk grn & blk 1.40 40
*89* A15 25c org & rose lil 8.50 8
*90* A15 40c dk vio & rose red 1.75 3.00
*91* A15 50c ultra & blk 1.50 12
*92* A15 $1 vio brn & ultra 2.00 18
*93* A15 $2 rose red & emer 8.00 75
*94* A15 $5 choc & emer 16.00 1.50

**1952-55**

*95* A15 5c rose vio 20 8
*96* A15 8c green 28 18
*97* A15 12c rose red 50 30
*98* A15 20c ultra 1.00 18
*99* A15 30c plum & rose red ('55) 2.25 30
*100* A15 35c dk vio & rose red 1.25 40
*Nos. 80-100 (21)* 47.26 9.31

**Coronation Issue**
Common Design Type

**1953, June 2 Engr. *Perf. 13½x13***

*101* CD312 10c mag & blk 25 15

Sultan Hisam-ud-Din Alam Shah
A16 A17

Designs as in Kelantan, 1957.

***Perf. 13x12½, 12½x13, 13½ ($1)***

**1957-60 Engr. Wmk. 314**

| | | | | |
|---|---|---|---|---|
| *102* | A17 | 1c black | 6 | 5 |
| *103* | A17 | 2c red org | 6 | 5 |
| *104* | A17 | 4c dk brn | 8 | 5 |
| *105* | A17 | 5c dk car rose | 10 | 5 |
| *106* | A17 | 8c dk grn | 1.00 | 25 |
| *107* | A16 | 10c chocolate | 14 | 5 |
| *108* | A16 | 20c blue | 22 | 8 |
| *109* | A16 | 50c ultra & blk ('60) | 55 | 8 |
| **a.** | | Perf. 12½ | 55 | 18 |
| *110* | A17 | $1 plum & ultra | 1.10 | 30 |
| *111* | A17 | $2 red & grn ('60) | 3.00 | 1.00 |
| **a.** | | Perf. 12½ | 3.00 | 1.25 |
| *112* | A17 | $5 ol grn & brn ('60) | 6.25 | 2.00 |
| **a.** | | Perf. 12½ | 8.00 | 2.75 |
| | | *Nos. 102-112 (11)* | 12.56 | 3.96 |

See Nos. 114-120.

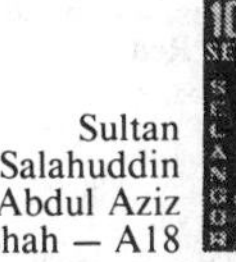

Sultan Salahuddin Abdul Aziz Shah — A18

**1961, June 28 Photo. *Perf. 14½x14***

| | | | | |
|---|---|---|---|---|
| *113* | A18 | 10s multi | 18 | 12 |

Issued to commemorate the installation of Sultan Salahuddin Abdul Aziz Shah.

Types of 1957 with Portrait of Sultan Salahuddin Abdul Aziz Shah

Wmk. 338- PTM Multiple

(PTM stands for Persekutuan Tanah Melayu, or Federation of Malaya.)
Designs as before.

***Perf. 13x12½, 12½x13***

**1961-62 Engr. Wmk. 338**

| | | | | |
|---|---|---|---|---|
| *114* | A17 | 1c black | 7 | 7 |
| *115* | A17 | 2c red org | 7 | 7 |
| *116* | A17 | 4c dk brn | 7 | 7 |
| *117* | A17 | 5c dk car rose | 14 | 7 |
| *118* | A17 | 8c dk grn | 38 | 38 |
| *119* | A16 | 10c choc ('61) | 30 | 9 |
| *120* | A16 | 20c blue | 45 | 18 |
| | | *Nos. 114-120 (7)* | 1.48 | 93 |

Starting in 1965, issues of Selangor are listed with Malaysia.

---

## OCCUPATION STAMPS

### Issued under Japanese Occupation

Stamps of Selangor 1935-41 Handstamped Vertically or Horizontally in Black, Red, Brown or Violet

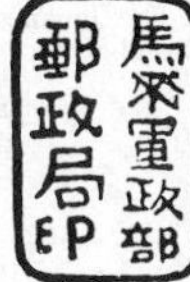

**1942, Apr. 3 Wmk. 4 *Perf. 14***

| | | | | |
|---|---|---|---|---|
| *N1* | A12 | 1c black | 7.50 | 7.50 |
| *N2* | A12 | 2c dp grn | 300.00 | 300.00 |
| *N3* | A12 | 2c org brn | 30.00 | 30.00 |
| *N4* | A12 | 3c green | 12.50 | 12.50 |
| *N5* | A12 | 5c chocolate | 7.50 | 7.50 |
| *N6* | A12 | 6c rose red | 125.00 | 125.00 |
| *N7* | A12 | 8c gray | 20.00 | 20.00 |
| *N8* | A12 | 10c dk vio | 15.00 | 20.00 |
| *N9* | A12 | 12c ultra | 15.00 | 25.00 |
| *N10* | A12 | 15c ultra | 12.50 | 15.00 |
| *N11* | A12 | 25c rose red & pale vio | 50.00 | 62.50 |
| *N12* | A12 | 30c org & dk vio | 17.50 | 22.50 |
| *N13* | A12 | 40c dk vio & car | 37.50 | 45.00 |
| *N14* | A12 | 50c blk, *emerald* | 30.00 | 35.00 |
| *N15* | A13 | $5 brn red & grn, *emer* | 200.00 | 200.00 |

Some authorities believe N15 was not issued regularly.

Handstamped Vertically on Stamps and Type of Selangor 1941 in Black or Red

| | | | | |
|---|---|---|---|---|
| *N16* | A14 | $1 red & blk, *bl* | 50.00 | 60.00 |
| *N17* | A14 | $2 car & grn | 30.00 | 30.00 |
| *N18* | A14 | $5 brn red & grn, *emer* | 37.50 | 37.50 |

Stamps of Selangor, 1935-41, Overprinted in Black

DAI NIPPON
2602
MALAYA

**1942, May**

| | | | | |
|---|---|---|---|---|
| *N18A* | A12 | 1c black | 25.00 | 25.00 |
| *N19* | A12 | 3c green | 75 | 75 |
| *N19A* | A12 | 5c chocolate | 25.00 | 25.00 |
| *N20* | A12 | 10c dk vio | 25.00 | 25.00 |
| *N21* | A12 | 12c ultra | 2.50 | 3.75 |
| *N22* | A12 | 15c ultra | 3.75 | 3.00 |
| *N23* | A12 | 30c org & dk vio | 25.00 | 25.00 |
| *N24* | A12 | 40c dk vio & car | 5.00 | 5.00 |
| *N24A* | A14 | $1 red & blk, *bl* | 25.00 | 25.00 |
| *N25* | A14 | $2 car & grn | 17.50 | 22.50 |
| *N25A* | A14 | $5 red & grn, *emer* | 40.00 | 40.00 |

Overprint is horizontal on $1, $2, $5.
On Nos. N18A and N19 the overprint is known reading up, instead of down.
Some authorities claim Nos. N18A, N19A, N20, N23, N24A and N25A were not regularly issued.

Selangor No. 46B Overprinted in Black

DAI NIPPON
YUBIN

**1942, Dec.**

| | | | | |
|---|---|---|---|---|
| *N26* | A12 | 3c green | 300.00 | 300.00 |

Stamps and Type of Selangor, 1935-41, Overprinted or Surcharged in Black or Red:

大日本郵便 i　大日本郵便 k
大日本郵便　大日本郵便
6 cts. l　6 cts. m

**1943**

| | | | | |
|---|---|---|---|---|
| *N27* | A12(i) | 1c black | 1.00 | 1.00 |
| *N28* | A12(k) | 1c blk (R) | 65 | 65 |
| *N29* | A12(l) | 2c on 5c choc (R) | 65 | 65 |
| *N30* | A12(i) | 3c green | 75 | 75 |
| *N31* | A12(l) | 3c on 5c choc | 50 | 75 |
| *N32* | A12(k) | 5c choc (R) | 50 | 75 |
| *N33* | A12(l) | 6c on 5c choc | 25 | *65* |
| *N34* | A12(m) | 6c on 5c choc | 25 | 75 |
| *N35* | A12(i) | 12c ultra | 1.00 | 1.25 |
| *N36* | A12(i) | 15c ultra | 5.00 | 7.50 |
| *N37* | A12(k) | 15c ultra | 10.00 | 10.00 |
| *N38* | A12(m) | $1 on 10c dk vio | 38 | *1.00* |
| *N39* | A12(m) | $1.50 on 30c org & dk vio | 38 | *1.00* |
| *N40* | A14(i) | $1 red & blk, *bl* | 5.00 | 6.25 |
| *N41* | A14(i) | $2 car & grn | 17.50 | 17.50 |
| *N42* | A14(i) | $5 brn red & grn, *emer* | 37.50 | 40.00 |
| | | *Nos. N27-N42 (16)* | 81.31 | 90.45 |

The "i" overprint is vertical on Nos. N40-N42 and is also found reading in the opposite direction on Nos. N30, N35 and N36.
The overprint reads: "Japanese Postal Service."

---

**Singapore is listed following Sierra Leone.**

---

## SUNGEI UJONG

Formerly a nonfederated native state on the Malay Peninsula, which in 1895 was consolidated with the Federated State of Negri Sembilan.

Stamps of the Straits Settlements Overprinted in Black

Overprinted

**1878 Wmk. 1 *Perf. 14***

| | | | | |
|---|---|---|---|---|
| *2* | A2 | 2c brown | 2,500. | 2,250. |

Overprinted S.U.

**1881-83**

| | | | | |
|---|---|---|---|---|
| *3* | A2 | 2c brown | | |

Overprinted SUNGEI UJONG

| | | | | |
|---|---|---|---|---|
| *4* | A2 | 2c brown | 42.50 | |
| *5* | A2 | 4c rose | 675.00 | |

Overprinted S.U.

**1882-83 Wmk. Crown and C. A. (2)**

| | | | | |
|---|---|---|---|---|
| *6* | A2 | 2c brown | 82.50 | 82.50 |
| *7* | A2 | 4c rose | 1,600. | 1,800. |

Overprinted SU

| | | | | |
|---|---|---|---|---|
| *11* | A2 | 2c brown | 57.50 | 57.50 |

Overprinted SUNGEI UJONG

**1881-84**

| | | | | |
|---|---|---|---|---|
| *14* | A2 | 2c brown | 165.00 | 150.00 |
| *15* | A2 | 2c rose | 14.00 | 15.00 |
| **a.** | | "Ujong" printed sideways | | |
| **b.** | | "Sungei" printed twice | | |
| *16* | A2 | 4c brown | 72.50 | 72.50 |
| *17* | A3 | 8c orange | 825.00 | 550.00 |
| *18* | A7 | 10c slate | 250.00 | 250.00 |

Overprinted SUNGEI UJONG.

| | | | | |
|---|---|---|---|---|
| *19* | A2 | 2c brown | 16.00 | 18.00 |

Overprinted *SUNGEI UJONG*

**1885-90**

**Without Period**

| | | | | |
|---|---|---|---|---|
| *20* | A2 | 2c rose | 16.00 | 17.00 |

**With Period**

| | | | | |
|---|---|---|---|---|
| *21* | A2 | 2c rose | 30.00 | 32.50 |
| **a.** | | "UNJOG" | 1,350. | 1,350. |

Overprinted *Sungei Ujong*

| | | | | |
|---|---|---|---|---|
| *22* | A2 | 2c rose | 17.00 | 17.00 |
| **a.** | | Double overprint | 325.00 | 325.00 |

Overprinted SUNGEI UJONG

| | | | | |
|---|---|---|---|---|
| *23* | A2 | 2c rose | 35.00 | 37.50 |

Overprinted SUNGEI UJONG

| | | | | |
|---|---|---|---|---|
| *24* | A2 | 2c rose | 9.00 | 10.00 |
| **a.** | | Double overprint | | |

Overprinted SUNGEI UJONG

| | | | | |
|---|---|---|---|---|
| *25* | A2 | 2c rose | 27.50 | 30.00 |

Overprinted SUNGEI UJONG

| | | | | |
|---|---|---|---|---|
| *26* | A2 | 2c rose | 45.00 | 47.50 |
| **c.** | | Double overprint | | |

Overprinted SUNGEI UJONG

**Overprint 14-16x3mm**

| | | | | |
|---|---|---|---|---|
| *26A* | A2 | 2c rose | 4.50 | 5.00 |

Overprinted SUNGEI UJONG

| | | | | |
|---|---|---|---|---|
| *26B* | A2 | 2c rose | 25.00 | 5.00 |

Stamp of 1883-91 Surcharged:

SUNGEI UJONG *Two* CENTS — a
SUNGEI UJONG Two CENTS — b
SUNGEI UJONG Two CENTS — c
SUNGEI UJONG *Two* CENTS — d

**1891**

| | | | | |
|---|---|---|---|---|
| *27* | A3 (a) | 2c on 24c grn | 65.00 | 82.50 |
| *28* | A3 (b) | 2c on 24c grn | 225.00 | 225.00 |
| *29* | A3 (c) | 2c on 24c grn | 82.50 | 92.50 |
| *30* | A3 (d) | 2c on 24c grn | 130.00 | 165.00 |

On Nos. 27-28, SUNGEI is 14½mm, UJONG 12¾x2½mm.

A3

A4

**1891-94** **Typo.** ***Perf. 14***
*31* A3 2c rose 6.00 3.00
*32* A3 2c orange ('94) 1.75 4.50
*33* A3 5c blue ('93) 1.75 4.50

Type of 1891 Surcharged in Black **1 CENT**

**1894**
*34* A3 1c on 5c green 80 80
*35* A3 3c on 5c rose 1.40 1.40

**1895**
*36* A4 3c lil & car rose 1.00 1.25

Stamps of Sungei Ujong were superseded by those of Negri Sembilan in 1895.

---

## TRENGGANU

LOCATION — On the eastern coast of the Malay Peninsula.
AREA — 5,050 sq. mi.
POP. — 302,171 (1960)
CAPITAL — Kuala Trengganu

Sultan Zenalabidin
A1 A2

**Wmk. Multiple Crown and C. A. (3)**
**1910-19** **Typo.** ***Perf. 14***
**Ordinary Paper**
*1* A1 1c gray grn 28 25
*2* A1 2c red vio & brn ('15) 55 35
*3* A1 3c rose red 1.10 1.10
*4* A1 4c brn org 1.25 *2.75*
*5* A1 4c grn & org brn ('15) 1.65 *2.75*
*6* A1 4c scar ('19) 28 *85*
*7* A1 5c gray 70 *1.40*
*8* A1 5c choc & gray ('15) 1.65 1.10
*9* A1 8c ultra 70 1.10
*10* A1 10c red & grn, *yel* ('15) 1.65 2.25
**Chalky Paper**
*11* A1 10c vio, *yel* 1.10 98
*12* A1 20c red vio & vio 1.10 *2.25*
*13* A1 25c dl vio & grn ('15) 2.25 *5.50*
*14* A1 30c blk & dl vio ('15) 2.25 *5.50*
*15* A1 50c blk & sep, *grn* 1.65 *2.00*
*16* A1 $1 red & blk, *bl* 10.00 *17.00*
*17* A1 $3 red & grn, *grn*('15) 42.50 *55.00*
*18* A2 $5 lil & bl grn 85.00 *140.00*
*19* A2 $25 grn & car 725.00
*Nos. 1-18 (18)* 155.66 242.13

On No. 19 the numerals and Arabic inscriptions at top, left and right are in color on a colorless background.

Sultan Badaru'l-alam
A3 A4

**1921-38** **Wmk. 4** ***Perf. 14***
**Chalky Paper**
*20* A3 1c blk ('25) 30 15
*21* A3 2c dp grn 15 15
*22* A3 3c dp grn ('25) 60 60
*23* A3 3c lt brn ('38) 4.50 *4.50*
*24* A3 4c rose red 24 15
*25* A3 5c choc & gray 1.50 60
*26* A3 5c vio, *yel* ('25) 95 22
*27* A3 6c org ('24) 2.50 60
*28* A3 8c gray ('38) 3.00 75
*29* A3 10c ultra 95 25
*30* A3 12c ultra ('25) 3.00 *4.50*
*31* A3 20c org & dl vio 95 60
*32* A3 25c dk vio & grn 1.25 *2.50*
*33* A3 30c blk & dl vio 2.00 60
*34* A3 35c red, *yel* ('25) 2.50 *6.00*
*35* A3 50c car & grn 3.00 75
*36* A3 $1 ultra & vio, *bl* ('29) 9.00 4.50
*37* A3 $3 red & green, *emer* ('25) 30.00 *47.50*
*38* A4 $5 red & grn, *yel* ('38) 200.00 *475.00*
*39* A4 $25 bl & lil 450.00 *500.00*
*40* A4 $50 org & grn 1,200. *1,600.*
*41* A4 $100 red & grn 3,750.
*Nos. 20-37 (18)* 66.39 74.92

On Nos. 39 to 41 the numerals and Arabic inscriptions at top, left and right are in color on a colorless background.

A 2c orange, 6c gray, 8c rose red and 15c ultramarine, type A3, exist, but are not known to have been regularly issued.

Stamps of 1910-21 Overprinted in Black: "MALAYA BORNEO EXHIBITION" in THREE LINES

**1922, Mar.** **Wmk. 3**
*8a* A1 5c choc & gray 3.50 *12.00*
*10a* A1 10c red & grn, *yel* 3.50 *16.00*
*12a* A1 20c red vio & vio 1.75 *17.50*
*13a* A1 25c dl vio & grn 2.25 *17.50*
*14a* A1 30c blk & dl vio 2.75 *19.00*
*15a* A1 50c blk & sep, *grn* 3.00 *21.00*
*16a* A1 $1 red & blk, *bl* 17.50 *45.00*
*17a* A1 $3 red & grn, *grn* 130.00 *300.00*
*18a* A1 $5 lil & bl grn 275.00 *450.00*
**Wmk. 4**
*21a* A3 2c dp grn 60 *7.50*
*24a* A3 4c rose red 3.00 *8.75*
*Nos. 8a-24a (11)* 442.85 914.25

Industrial fair at Singapore, Mar. 31-Apr. 15, 1922.

**1921** **Wmk. 3**
**Chalky Paper**
*42* A3 $1 ultra & vio, *bl* 11.00 *13.00*
*43* A3 $3 red & grn, *emer* 35.00 *47.50*
*44* A4 $5 red & grn, *yel* 55.00 *65.00*

Types of 1921-25 Surcharged in Black **8 CENTS**

**1941, May 1** **Wmk. 4** ***Perf. 13½x14***
*45* A3 2c on 5c mag, *yel* 3.75 *2.25*
*46* A3 8c on 10c lt ultra 6.25 *3.75*

**Catalogue values for unused stamps in this section, from this point to the end of the section, are for Never Hinged items.**

**Silver Wedding Issue**
Common Design Types
Inscribed: "Malaya Trengganu"
**1948, Dec. 1** **Photo.** ***Perf. 14x14½***
*47* CD304 10c purple 18 18
**Engraved; Name Typographed**
***Perf. 11½x11***
*48* CD305 $5 rose car 24.00 25.00

**UPU Issue**
Common Design Types
Inscribed: "Malaya-Trengganu"
**Engr.; Name Typo. on 15c, 25c**
***Perf. 13½, 11x11½***
**1949, Oct. 10** **Wmk. 4**
*49* CD306 10c rose vio 35 35
*50* CD307 15c indigo 45 45
*51* CD308 25c orange 75 75
*52* CD309 50c slate 1.25 1.25

Sultan Ismail Nasiruddin Shah — A5

**1949, Dec. 27** **Typo.** ***Perf. 18***
*53* A5 1c black 20 12
*54* A5 2c orange 20 12
*55* A5 3c green 55 45
*56* A5 4c chocolate 26 15
*57* A5 6c gray 55 35
*58* A5 8c rose red 75 60
*59* A5 10c plum 32 8
*60* A5 15c ultra 80 50
*61* A5 20c dk grn & blk 1.10 1.50
*62* A5 25c org & rose lil 95 60
*63* A5 40c dk vio & rose red 3.50 2.75
*64* A5 50c dp ultra & blk 1.25 80
*65* A5 $1 vio brn & ultra 3.50 2.25
*66* A5 $2 rose red & emer 8.25 5.75
*67* A5 $5 choc & emer 27.50 20.00

**1952-55**
*68* A5 5c rose vio 20 12
*69* A5 8c green 75 1.00
*70* A5 12c rose red 75 *2.00*
*71* A5 20c ultra 75 45
*72* A5 30c plum & rose red ('55) 4.25 2.00
*73* A5 35c dk vio & rose red 1.65 2.00
*Nos. 53-73 (21)* 58.03 43.59

**Coronation Issue**
Common Design Type
**1953, June 2** **Engr.** ***Perf. 13½x13***
*74* CD312 10c mag & blk 28 18

Types of Kedah with Portrait of Sultan Ismail
***Perf. 13x12½, 12½x13, 13½ ($1), 12½ ($2)***
**1957-63** **Engr.** **Wmk. 314**
*75* A8 1c black 7 5
*76* A8 2c red org 9 5
*77* A8 4c dk brn 10 5
*78* A8 5c dk car rose 12 5
*79* A8 8c dk grn 1.75 22
*80* A7 10c chocolate 14 5
*81* A7 20c blue 28 22
*82* A7 50c ultra & blk ('62) 80 60
  **a.** Perf. 12½ 80 60
*83* A8 $1 plum & ultra 1.75 1.25
*84* A8 $2 red & grn 4.50 3.00
*85* A8 $5 ol grn & brn ('63) 10.50 6.50
  **a.** Perf. 12½ 10.50 6.25
*Nos. 75-85 (11)* 20.10 12.04

Starting in 1965, issues of Trengganu are listed with Malaysia.

---

### SEMI-POSTAL STAMPS

Nos. 3, 4 and 9 Surcharged **RED CROSS** **2c.**

**1917** **Wmk. 3** ***Perf. 14***
*B1* A1 3c + 2c rose red 24 *2.25*
  **a.** "CSOSS" 40.00 *65.00*
  **b.** Comma after "2c" 2.50 *6.50*
  **c.** Pair, one without surcharge 1,000. 1,000.
*B2* A1 4c + 2c brn org 40 *3.25*
  **a.** "CSOSS" 150.00 *165.00*
  **b.** Comma after "2c" 10.00 *26.00*
*B3* A1 8c + 2c ultra 65 *6.50*
  **a.** "CSOSS" 100.00 *125.00*
  **b.** Comma after "2c" 8.25 *32.50*

Same Surcharge on No. 5
**1918**
*B4* A1 4c + 2c grn & org brn 85 6.50
  **a.** Pair, one without surcharge *650.00*

---

### POSTAGE DUE STAMPS

D1

**Wmk. 4**
**1937, Aug. 10** **Typo.** ***Perf. 14***
*J1* D1 1c rose red 7.25 *25.00*
*J2* D1 4c green 7.25 *25.00*
*J3* D1 8c lemon 50.00 *130.00*
*J4* D1 10c lt brn 52.50 *72.50*

---

### OCCUPATION STAMPS

**Issued under Japanese Occupation**

Stamps of Trengganu, 1921-38, Handstamped in Black or Brown

**1942** **Wmk. 4** ***Perf. 14***
*N1* A3 1c black 50.00 62.50
*N2* A3 2c dp grn 70.00 70.00
*N3* A3 3c lt brn 45.00 45.00
*N4* A3 4c rose red 75.00 87.50
*N5* A3 5c vio, *yel* 6.00 10.00
*N6* A3 6c orange 10.00 15.00
*N7* A3 8c gray 10.00 12.50
*N8* A3 10c ultra 10.00 15.00
*N9* A3 12c ultra 7.50 12.50
*N10* A3 20c org & dl vio 10.00 15.00
*N11* A3 25c dk vio & grn 10.00 15.00
*N12* A3 30c blk & dl vio 10.00 15.00
*N13* A3 35c red, *yel* 10.00 15.00
*N14* A3 50c car & grn 42.50 50.00
*N15* A3 $1 ultra & vio, *bl* 600.00 600.00
*N16* A3 $3 red & grn, *emer* 37.50 37.50
*N17* A4 $5 red & grn, *yel* 100.00 100.00
*N17A* A4 $25 bl & lil 375.00
*N17B* A4 $50 org & grn *1,000.*
*N17C* A4 $100 red & grn 450.00

**Handstamped in Red**
*N18* A3 1c black 55.00 62.50
*N19* A3 2c dp grn 70.00 87.50
*N20* A3 5c vio, *yel* 10.00 10.00
*N21* A3 6c orange 10.00 10.00
*N22* A3 8c gray 17.50 12.50
*N23* A3 10c ultra 17.50 17.50
*N24* A3 12c ultra 17.50 17.50
*N25* A3 20c org & dl vio 10.00 10.00
*N26* A3 25c dk vio & grn 10.00 10.00
*N27* A3 30c blk & dl vio 10.00 10.00
*N28* A3 35c red, *yel* 10.00 10.00
*N29* A3 $3 red & grn, *emer* 30.00 30.00
*N29A* A3 $25 bl & lil 500.00 500.00

**Handstamped on Nos. 45 and 46 in Black or Red**
*N30* A3 2c on 5c mag, *yel* (Bk) 50.00 50.00
*N31* A3 2c on 5c mag, *yel* (R) 30.00 30.00
*N32* A3 8c on 10c lt ultra (Bk) 12.50 17.50
*N33* A3 8c on 10c lt ultra (R) 17.50 25.00

Stamps of Trengganu, 1921-38, Overprinted in Black **DAI NIPPON 2602 MALAYA**

**1942**
*N34* A3 1c black 5.00 4.50
*N35* A3 2c dp grn 75.00 *100.00*
*N36* A3 3c lt brn 10.00 12.50
*N37* A3 4c rose red 10.00 15.00
*N38* A3 5c vio, *yel* 10.00 15.00
*N39* A3 6c orange 10.00 12.50
*N40* A3 8c gray 50.00 15.00
*N41* A3 12c ultra 7.50 10.00
*N42* A3 20c org & dl vio 10.00 12.50
*N43* A3 25c dk vio & grn 10.00 12.50
*N44* A3 30c blk & dl vio 10.00 15.00
*N45* A3 $3 red & grn, *emer* 37.50 50.00

**Overprinted on Nos. 45 and 46 in Black**
*N46* A3 2c on 5c mag, *yel* 12.50 20.00
*N47* A3 8c on 10c lt ultra 12.50 20.00

Stamps of Trengganu, 1921-38, Overprinted in Black **大日本郵便**

**1943**
*N48* A3 1c black 7.50 12.50
*N49* A3 2c dp grn 10.00 20.00
*N50* A3 5c vio, *yel* 12.50 20.00
*N51* A3 6c orange 10.00 20.00
*N52* A3 8c gray 50.00 40.00
*N53* A3 10c ultra 75.00 87.50
*N54* A3 12c ultra 10.00 *37.50*
*N55* A3 20c org & dl vio 10.00 *25.00*
*N56* A3 25c dl vio & grn 10.00 *25.00*
*N57* A3 30c blk & dl vio 10.00 *25.00*
*N58* A3 35c red, *yel* 10.00 *25.00*

**Overprinted on Nos. 45 and 46 in Black**
*N59* A3 2c on 5c mag, *yel* 4.50 *12.50*
*N60* A3 8c on 10c lt ultra 10.00 *25.00*

The Japanese characters read: "Japanese Postal Service."

---

## OCCUPATION POSTAGE DUE STAMPS

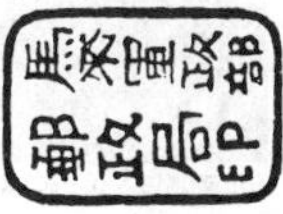

Trengganu Nos. J1-J4 Handstamped in Black or Brown

| 1942 | | Wmk. 4 | | Perf. 14 |
|---|---|---|---|---|
| NJ1 | D1 | 1c rose red | 20.00 | 37.50 |
| NJ2 | D1 | 4c green | 30.00 | 50.00 |
| NJ3 | D1 | 8c lemon | 10.00 | 50.00 |
| NJ4 | D1 | 10c lt brn | 10.00 | 62.50 |

The handstamp reads: "Seal of Post Office of Malayan Military Department."

## MALAYSIA

LOCATION — Malay peninsula and northwestern Borneo.
GOVT. — Federation within the British Commonwealth.
AREA — 128,328 sq. mi.
POP. — 15,070,000 (est. 1984).
CAPITAL — Kuala Lampur.

The Federation of Malaysia was formed September 16, 1963, by a merger of the former Federation of Malaya, Singapore, Sarawak, and North Borneo (renamed Sabah), totaling 14 states. Singapore withdrew in 1965.

Sabah and Sarawak, having different rates than mainland Malaysia, continued to issue their own stamps after joining the federation. The system of individual state issues was extended to Perak in October 1963, and to the 10 other members in November 1965.

100 Cents (Sen) = 1 Dollar

**Catalogue values for all unused stamps in this country are for Never Hinged items.**

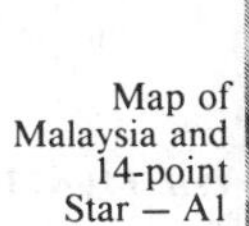

Map of Malaysia and 14-point Star — A1

**Wmk. PTM Multiple (338)**

| 1963, Sept. 16 | | Photo. | | Perf. 14 |
|---|---|---|---|---|
| 1 | A1 | 10s vio & yel | 12 | 5 |
| a. | | Yellow omitted | 100.00 | |
| 2 | A1 | 12s grn & yel | 40 | 28 |
| 3 | A1 | 50s dk red brn & yel | 55 | 28 |

Formation of the Federation of Malaysia.

Orchids — A2

| 1963, Oct. 3 | | Unwmk. | | Perf. 13x14 |
|---|---|---|---|---|
| 4 | A2 | 6s red & multi | 26 | 7 |
| 5 | A2 | 25s blk & multi | 1.40 | 40 |

Issued to publicize the 4th World Orchid Conference, Singapore, Oct. 8-11.

Parliament and Commonwealth Parliamentary Association Emblem — A4

| 1963, Nov. 4 | | | | Perf. 13½ |
|---|---|---|---|---|
| 7 | A4 | 20s dk car rose & gold | 25 | 16 |
| 8 | A4 | 30s dk grn & gold | 50 | 25 |

9th Commonwealth Parliamentary Assoc. Conf.

Globe, Torch, Snake and Hands — A5

| 1964, Oct. 10 | | Photo. | | Perf. 14x13 |
|---|---|---|---|---|
| 9 | A5 | 25s Prus grn, red & blk | 15 | 8 |
| 10 | A5 | 30s lt vio, red & blk | 26 | 12 |
| 11 | A5 | 50s dl yel, red & blk | 50 | 22 |

Eleanor Roosevelt, 1884-1962.

ITU Emblem and Radar Tower — A6

| 1965, May 17 | | Photo. | | Perf. 11½ |
|---|---|---|---|---|
| | | **Granite Paper** | | |
| 12 | A6 | 2c vio, blk & org | 6 | 5 |
| 13 | A6 | 25c brn, blk & org | 42 | 20 |
| 14 | A6 | 50c emer, blk & brn | 1.00 | 30 |

Cent. of the ITU.

National Mosque, Kuala Lumpur — A7

| 1965, Aug. 27 | | Wmk. 338 | | Perf. 14½ |
|---|---|---|---|---|
| 15 | A7 | 6c dk car rose | 8 | 8 |
| 16 | A7 | 15c dk red brn | 16 | 8 |
| 17 | A7 | 20c Prus grn | 24 | 16 |

Issued to commemorate the opening of the National Mosque at Kuala Lumpur.

Control Tower and Airport A8

Crested Wood Partridge A9

| 1965, Aug. 30 | | | | Perf. 14½x14 |
|---|---|---|---|---|
| 18 | A8 | 15c bl, blk & grn | 15 | 6 |
| a. | | Green omitted | 18.00 | |
| 19 | A8 | 30c brt pink, blk & grn | 32 | 15 |

Issued to commemorate the opening of the International Airport at Kuala Lumpur.

| 1965, Sept. 9 | Photo. | Perf. 14½ |
|---|---|---|

Birds: 30c, Fairy bluebird. 50c, Blacknaped oriole. 75c, Rhinoceros hornbill. $1, Zebra dove. $2, Argus pheasant. $5, Indian paradise flycatcher. $10, Banded pitta.

| | | | | |
|---|---|---|---|---|
| 20 | A9 | 25c org & multi | 35 | 5 |
| 21 | A9 | 30c tan & multi | 42 | 5 |
| a. | | Blue omitted | 87.50 | |
| 22 | A9 | 50c rose & multi | 65 | 7 |
| a. | | Rose omitted | 42.50 | |
| 23 | A9 | 75c yel grn & multi | 1.25 | 10 |
| 24 | A9 | $1 ultra & multi | 1.75 | 14 |
| 25 | A9 | $2 mar & multi | 5.25 | 42 |
| 26 | A9 | $5 dk grn & multi | 13.00 | 1.25 |
| 27 | A9 | $10 brt red & multi | 26.00 | 4.25 |
| | | *Nos. 20-27 (8)* | 48.67 | 6.33 |

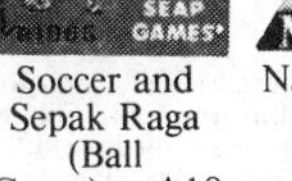

Soccer and Sepak Raga (Ball Game) — A10

National Monument, Kuala Lumpur — A11

Designs: 30c, Runner. 50c, Diver.

| 1965, Dec. 14 | | Unwmk. | | Perf. 13 |
|---|---|---|---|---|
| 28 | A10 | 25c lt ol grn & blk | 22 | 18 |
| 29 | A10 | 30c red lil & blk | 45 | 22 |
| 30 | A10 | 50c aqua & blk | 80 | 55 |

3rd South East Asia Peninsular Games, Kuala Lumpur, Dec. 14-21.

| 1966, Feb. 8 | | Wmk. 338 | | Perf. 13½ |
|---|---|---|---|---|
| 31 | A11 | 10c yel & multi | 10 | 6 |
| a. | | Blue omitted | 52.50 | |
| 32 | A11 | 20c ultra & multi | 50 | 35 |

The National Monument by U.S. Sculptor Felix W. de Weldon commemorates the struggle of the people of Malaysia for peace and for freedom from communism.

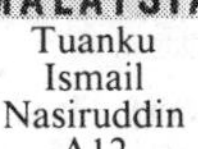

Tuanku Ismail Nasiruddin A12

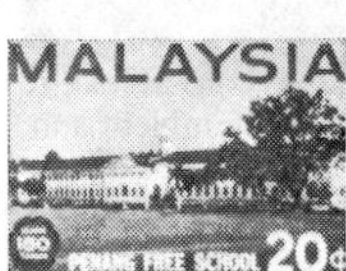


Penang Free School A13

| 1966, Apr. 11 | | Unwmk. | | Perf. 13½ |
|---|---|---|---|---|
| 33 | A12 | 15c yel & blk | 16 | 8 |
| 34 | A12 | 50c bl & blk | 55 | 42 |

Issued to commemorate the installation of Tuanku Ismail Nasiruddin of Trengganu as Paramount Ruler (Yang di-Pertuan Agong).

*Perf. 13x12½*

**1966, Oct. 21 Photo. Wmk. 338**

Design: 50c, like 20c with Malayan inscription and school crest added.

| | | | | |
|---|---|---|---|---|
| 35 | A13 | 20c multi | 22 | 12 |
| 36 | A13 | 50c multi | 65 | 42 |

Penang Free School, 150th anniversary.

Mechanized Plowing and Palms — A14

Designs: No. 38, Rural health nurse, mother and child, dispensary. No. 39, Communication: train, plane, ship, cars and radio tower. No. 40, School children. No. 41, Dam and rice fields.

| 1966, Dec. 1 | | Unwmk. | | Perf. 13 |
|---|---|---|---|---|
| 37 | A14 | 15c bis brn & multi | 42 | 16 |
| 38 | A14 | 15c bl & multi | 42 | 16 |
| 39 | A14 | 15c crim & multi | 42 | 16 |
| 40 | A14 | 15c ol grn & multi | 42 | 16 |
| 41 | A14 | 15c yel & multi | 42 | 16 |
| | | *Nos. 37-41 (5)* | 2.10 | 80 |

Malaysia's First Development Plan.

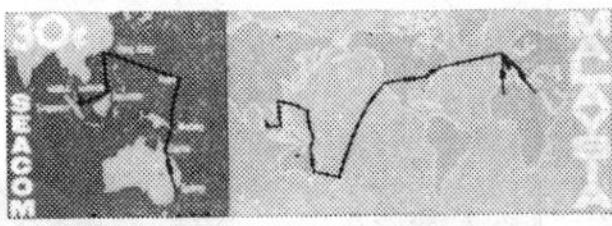


Maps Showing International and South East Asia Telephone Links — A15

| 1967, Mar. 30 | | Photo. | | Perf. 13 |
|---|---|---|---|---|
| 42 | A15 | 30c multi | 45 | 24 |
| 43 | A15 | 75c multi | 2.00 | 90 |

Issued to commemorate the completion of the Hong Kong-Malaysia link of the South East Asia Commonwealth Cable, SEACOM.

Hibiscus and Rulers of Independent Malaysia — A16

| 1967, Aug. 31 | | Wmk. 338 | | Perf. 14 |
|---|---|---|---|---|
| 44 | A16 | 15c yel & multi | 14 | 9 |
| 45 | A16 | 50c bl & multi | 60 | 35 |

10th anniversary of independence.

Arms of Sarawak and Council Mace — A17

| 1967, Sept. 8 | | | | Photo. |
|---|---|---|---|---|
| 46 | A17 | 15c yel grn & multi | 10 | 7 |
| 47 | A17 | 50c multi | 45 | 35 |

Issued to commemorate the centenary of the Representative Council of Sarawak.

Straits Settlements No. 13 and Malaysia No. 20 A18

Designs: 30c, Straits Settlements No. 15 and Malaysia No. 21. 50c, Straits Settlements No. 17 and Malaysia No. 22.

| 1967, Dec. 2 | | Unwmk. | | Perf. 11½ |
|---|---|---|---|---|
| 48 | A18 | 25c brt bl & multi | 50 | 32 |
| 49 | A18 | 30c dl grn & multi | 55 | 32 |
| 50 | A18 | 50c yel & multi | 1.10 | 75 |

Cent. of the Malaysian (Straits Settlements) postage stamps.

Tapped Rubber Tree and Molecular Unit — A20

Designs (Tapped Rubber Tree and): 30c, Rubber packed for shipment. 50c, Rubber tires for Vickers VC 10 plane.

**Wmk. 338**

**1968, Aug. 29 Litho. *Perf. 12***

| No. | Type | Description | Unused | Used |
|---|---|---|---|---|
| *53* | A20 | 25c brick red, blk & org | 26 | 18 |
| *54* | A20 | 30c yel, blk & org | 40 | 22 |
| *55* | A20 | 50c ultra, blk & org | 65 | 48 |

Natural Rubber Conference, Kuala Lumpur.

Olympic Rings, Mexican Hat and Cloth — A21

Tunku Abdul Rahman Putra Al-Haj — A22

Designs: 75c, Olympic rings and Malaysian batik cloth.

**1968, Oct. 12 Wmk. 338 *Perf. 12***

| No. | Type | Description | Unused | Used |
|---|---|---|---|---|
| *56* | A21 | 30c rose red & multi | 32 | 20 |
| *57* | A21 | 75c ocher & multi | 80 | 60 |

Issued to commemorate the 19th Olympic Games, Mexico City, Oct. 12-27.

***Perf. 13½***

**1969, Feb. 8 Photo. Unwmk.**

Designs: Various portraits of Prime Minister Tunku Abdul Rahman Putra Al-Haj with woven pandanus patterns as background. 50c is horiz.

| No. | Type | Description | Unused | Used |
|---|---|---|---|---|
| *58* | A22 | 15c gold & multi | 18 | 7 |
| *59* | A22 | 20c gold & multi | 24 | 14 |
| *60* | A22 | 50c gold & multi | 60 | 45 |

Issued for Solidarity Week, 1969.

Malaysian Girl Holding Sheaves of Rice — A23

**1969, Dec. 8 Wmk. 338 *Perf. 13½***

| No. | Type | Description | Unused | Used |
|---|---|---|---|---|
| *61* | A23 | 15c sil & multi | 20 | 10 |
| *62* | A23 | 75c gold & multi | 1.00 | 80 |

International Rice Year.

Kuantan Radar Station A24

Intelsat III Orbiting Earth A25

***Perf. 14x13***

**1970, Apr. 6 Photo. Unwmk.**

| No. | Type | Description | Unused | Used |
|---|---|---|---|---|
| *63* | A24 | 15c multi | 38 | 8 |
| *64* | A25 | 30c multi | 75 | 55 |
| *65* | A25 | 30c gold & multi | 65 | 30 |

Issued to publicize the Satellite Communications Earth Station at Kuantan, Pahang, Malaysia.

No. 63 was printed tête bêche (50 pairs) in sheet of 100 (10x10).

Blue-branded King Crow — A26

ILO Emblem — A27

Butterflies: 30c, Saturn. 50c, Common Nawab. 75c, Great Mormon. $1, Orange albatross. $2, Raja Brooke's birdwing. $5, Centaur oakblue. $10, Royal Assyrian.

**1970, Aug. 31 Litho. *Perf. 13x13½***

| No. | Type | Description | Unused | Used |
|---|---|---|---|---|
| *66* | A26 | 25c multi | 32 | 5 |
| *67* | A26 | 30c multi | 42 | 5 |
| *68* | A26 | 50c multi | 60 | 6 |
| *69* | A26 | 75c multi | 1.00 | 12 |
| *70* | A26 | $1 multi | 1.25 | 15 |
| *71* | A26 | $2 multi | 2.50 | 50 |
| *72* | A26 | $5 multi | 5.75 | 1.40 |
| *73* | A26 | $10 multi | 12.50 | 4.00 |
| | | *Nos. 66-73 (8)* | 24.34 | 6.33 |

**1970, Sept. 7 *Perf. 14½x13½***

| No. | Type | Description | Unused | Used |
|---|---|---|---|---|
| *74* | A27 | 30c gray & bl | 40 | 24 |
| *75* | A27 | 75c rose & bl | 1.00 | 80 |

50th anniv. of the ILO.

U.N. Emblem and Doves — A28

Sultan Abdul Halim — A29

Designs: 25c, Doves in elliptical arrangement. 30c, Doves arranged diagonally.

**1970, Oct. 24 Litho. *Perf. 13x12½***

| No. | Type | Description | Unused | Used |
|---|---|---|---|---|
| *76* | A28 | 25c lt brn, blk & yel | 28 | 20 |
| *77* | A28 | 30c lt bl, yel & blk | 35 | 24 |
| *78* | A28 | 50c lt ol grn & blk | 60 | 52 |

25th anniversary of the United Nations.

***Perf. 14½x14***

**1971, Feb. 20 Photo. Unwmk.**

| No. | Type | Description | Unused | Used |
|---|---|---|---|---|
| *79* | A29 | 10c yel, blk & gold | 14 | 10 |
| *80* | A29 | 15c pur, blk & gold | 24 | 18 |
| *81* | A29 | 50c bl, blk & gold | 85 | 80 |

Installation of Sultan Abdul Halim of Kedah as Paramount Ruler.

Bank Building and Crescent — A30

**1971, May 15 Photo. *Perf. 14***

| No. | Type | Description | Unused | Used |
|---|---|---|---|---|
| *82* | A30 | 25c sil & blk | 65 | 52 |
| *83* | A30 | 50c gold & brn | 1.25 | 1.25 |

Opening of Main office of the Negara Malaysia Bank. Nos. 82-83 have circular perforations around vignette set within a white square of paper, perf. on 4 sides.

A particular stamp may be scarce, but if few collectors want it, its market value may remain relatively low.

Malaysian Parliament — A31

Malaysian Parliament, Kuala Lumpur — A32

**1971, Sept. 13 Litho. *Perf. 13½***

| No. | Type | Description | Unused | Used |
|---|---|---|---|---|
| *84* | A31 | 25c multi | 52 | 26 |

***Perf. 12½x13***

| No. | Type | Description | Unused | Used |
|---|---|---|---|---|
| *85* | A32 | 75c multi | 1.25 | 95 |

17th Commonwealth Parliamentary Conference, Kuala Lumpur.

Malaysian Festival — A33

**1971, Sept. 18 *Perf. 14½***

| No. | Type | Description | Unused | Used |
|---|---|---|---|---|
| *86* | A33 | Strip of 3 | 1.90 | 1.90 |
| *a.* | | 30c *Dancing couple* | 60 | 50 |
| *b.* | | 30c *Dragon* | 60 | 50 |
| *c.* | | 30c *Flags and stage horse* | 60 | 50 |

Visit ASEAN (Association of South East Asian Nations) Year.

Elephant and Tiger — A34

Children's Drawings: No. 88, Cat and kittens. No. 89, Sun, flower and chick. No. 90, Monkey, elephant and lion in jungle. No. 91, Butterfly and flowers.

**1971, Oct. 2 *Perf. 12½***

**Size: 35x28mm**

| No. | Type | Description | Unused | Used |
|---|---|---|---|---|
| *87* | A34 | 15c pale yel & multi | 45 | 30 |
| *88* | A34 | 15c pale yel & multi | 45 | 30 |

**Size: 21x28mm**

| No. | Type | Description | Unused | Used |
|---|---|---|---|---|
| *89* | A34 | 15c pale yel & multi | 45 | 30 |

**Size: 35x28mm**

| No. | Type | Description | Unused | Used |
|---|---|---|---|---|
| *90* | A34 | 15c pale yel & multi | 45 | 30 |
| *91* | A34 | 15c pale yel & multi | 45 | 30 |
| | | Strip of 5 | 2.50 | 2.50 |

25th anniv. of UNICEF. Nos. 87-91 printed se-tenant.

Track and Field — A35

Designs: 30c, Sepak Raga (a ball game). 50c, Hockey.

**1971, Dec. 11 *Perf. 14½***

| No. | Type | Description | Unused | Used |
|---|---|---|---|---|
| *92* | A35 | 25c org & multi | 52 | 45 |
| *93* | A35 | 30c vio & multi | 65 | 60 |
| *94* | A35 | 50c grn & multi | 1.25 | 1.12 |

6th South East Asia Peninsular Games, Kuala Lumpur, Dec. 11-18.

South East Asian Tourist Attractions — A36

Designs include stylized map.

**1972, Jan. 31 Litho. *Perf. 14½***

| No. | Type | Description | Unused | Used |
|---|---|---|---|---|
| *95* | A36 | Strip of 3 | 2.50 | 2.50 |
| *a.* | | 30c *Flag at left* | 80 | 50 |
| *b.* | | 30c *High rise building* | 80 | 50 |
| *c.* | | 30c *Horse & rider* | 80 | 50 |

Pacific Area Tourist Assn. Conference.

Secretariat Building — A37

Design: 50c, Kuala Lumpur Secretariat Building by night.

**1972, Feb. 1 *Perf. 14½x14***

| No. | Type | Description | Unused | Used |
|---|---|---|---|---|
| *96* | A37 | 25c lt bl & multi | 52 | 38 |
| *97* | A37 | 50c blk & multi | 1.10 | 80 |

Achievement of city status by Kuala Lumpur.

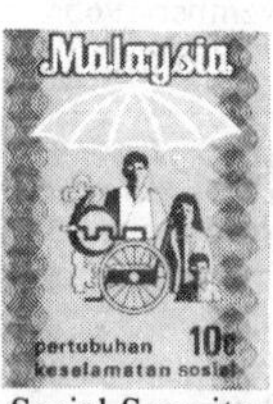


Social Security Emblem A38

WHO Emblem A39

**1973, July 2 Litho. *Perf. 14½x13½***

| No. | Type | Description | Unused | Used |
|---|---|---|---|---|
| *98* | A38 | 10c org & multi | 18 | 15 |
| *99* | A38 | 15c yel & multi | 30 | 15 |
| *100* | A38 | 50c gray & multi | 1.00 | 75 |

Introduction of Social Security System.

**1973, Aug. 1 *Perf. 13x12½, 12½x13***

Design: 30c, World Health Organization emblem (horiz.).

| No. | Type | Description | Unused | Used |
|---|---|---|---|---|
| *101* | A39 | 30c yel & multi | 38 | 35 |
| *102* | A39 | 75c bl & multi | 1.10 | 1.10 |

25th anniv. of WHO.

Flag of Malaysia, Fireworks, Hibiscus — A40

**1973, Aug. 31 Litho. *Perf. 14½***

| No. | Type | Description | Unused | Used |
|---|---|---|---|---|
| *103* | A40 | 10c ol & multi | 18 | 14 |
| *104* | A40 | 15c brn & multi | 20 | 18 |
| *105* | A40 | 50c gray & multi | 1.00 | 1.00 |

10th anniversary of independence.

INTERPOL and Malaysian Police Emblems A41

Design: 75c, "50" with INTERPOL and Malaysian police emblems.

**1973, Sept. 15** *Perf. 12½*

| | | | | |
|---|---|---|---|---|
| *106* | A41 | 25c brn org & multi | 65 | 42 |
| *107* | A41 | 75c dp vio & multi | 1.90 | 1.50 |

50th anniversary of the International Criminal Police Organization (INTERPOL).

MAS Emblem and Plane A42

**1973, Oct. 1** **Litho.** *Perf. 14½*

| | | | | |
|---|---|---|---|---|
| *108* | A42 | 15c grn & multi | 20 | 14 |
| *109* | A42 | 30c bl & multi | 48 | 42 |
| *110* | A42 | 50c brn & multi | 80 | 80 |

Inauguration of Malaysian Airline System.

View of Kuala Lumpur — A43

**1974, Feb. 1** **Litho.** *Perf. 12½x13*

| | | | | |
|---|---|---|---|---|
| *111* | A43 | 25c multi | 60 | 52 |
| *112* | A43 | 50c multi | 1.25 | 1.25 |

Establishment of Kuala Lumpur as a Federal Territory.

Development Bank Emblem and Projects — A44

**1974, Apr. 25** **Litho.** *Perf. 13½*

| | | | | |
|---|---|---|---|---|
| *113* | A44 | 30c gray & multi | 75 | 60 |
| *114* | A44 | 75c bis & multi | 2.00 | 2.00 |

7th annual meeting of the Board of Governors of the Asian Development Bank.

Map of Malaysia and Scout Emblem — A45

Scout Saluting, Malaysian and Scout Flags — A46

Design: 50c, Malaysian Scout emblem.

*Perf. 14x13½, 13x13½ (15c)*

**1974, Aug. 1** **Litho.**

| | | | | |
|---|---|---|---|---|
| *115* | A45 | 10c multi | 20 | 10 |
| *116* | A46 | 15c multi | 42 | 20 |
| *117* | A45 | 50c multi | 2.00 | 95 |

Malaysian Boy Scout Jamboree.

Power Installations, NEB Emblem — A47

National Electricity Board Building A48

*Perf. 14x14½, 13½x14½*

**1974, Sept. 1** **Litho.**

| | | | | |
|---|---|---|---|---|
| *118* | A47 | 30c multi | 50 | 40 |
| *119* | A48 | 75c multi | 1.25 | 1.25 |

National Electricity Board, 25th anniversary.

"100," UPU and P.O. Emblems A49

**1974, Oct. 9** **Litho.** *Perf. 14½x13½*

| | | | | |
|---|---|---|---|---|
| *120* | A49 | 25c ol, red & yel | 30 | 25 |
| *121* | A49 | 30c bl, red & yel | 38 | 32 |
| *122* | A49 | 75c ocher, red & yel | 1.00 | 1.00 |

Centenary of Universal Postal Union.

Gravel Pump Tin Mine — A50

Designs: 20c, Open cast mine. 50c, Silver tin ingot and tin dredge.

**1974, Oct. 31** **Litho.** *Perf. 14*

| | | | | |
|---|---|---|---|---|
| *123* | A50 | 15c sil & multi | 22 | 16 |
| *124* | A50 | 20c sil & multi | 35 | 30 |
| *125* | A50 | 50c sil & multi | 1.25 | 85 |

4th World Tin Conference, Kuala Lumpur.

Hockey, Cup and Emblem A51

**1975, Mar. 1** **Litho.** *Perf. 14*

| | | | | |
|---|---|---|---|---|
| *126* | A51 | 30c yel & multi | 48 | 38 |
| *127* | A51 | 75c bl & multi | 1.65 | 1.25 |

Third World Cup Hockey Tournament, Kuala Lumpur, Mar. 1-15.

Trade Union Emblem and Workers — A52

**1975, May 1** **Litho.** *Perf. 14x14½*

| | | | | |
|---|---|---|---|---|
| *128* | A52 | 20c org & multi | 35 | 30 |
| *129* | A52 | 25c lt grn & multi | 45 | 35 |
| *130* | A52 | 30c ultra & multi | 52 | 52 |

Malaysian Trade Union Congress, 25th anniversary.

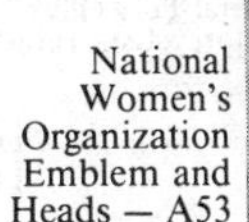

National Women's Organization Emblem and Heads — A53

**1975, Aug. 25** **Litho.** *Perf. 14*

| | | | | |
|---|---|---|---|---|
| *131* | A53 | 10c emer & multi | 14 | 10 |
| *132* | A53 | 15c lil rose & multi | 25 | 15 |
| *133* | A53 | 50c bl & multi | 1.00 | 75 |

International Women's Year 1975.

Ubudiah Mosque, Perak — A54

Designs (from left to right): Zahir Mosque, Kedah; National Mosque, Kuala Lumpur; Sultan Abu Bakar Mosque, Johore; Kuching State Mosque, Sarawak.

**1975, Sept. 22** **Litho.** *Perf. 14½x14*

| | | | | |
|---|---|---|---|---|
| *134* | | Strip of 5 | 2.00 | 2.00 |
| *a.* | | A54 15c, single stamp | 40 | 24 |

Koran reading competition 1975, Malaysia.

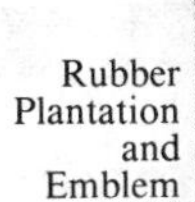

Rubber Plantation and Emblem A55

Designs: 30c, "50" in form of latex cup and tire with emblem. 75c, Six test tubes showing various aspects of natural rubber.

**1975, Oct. 22** **Litho.** *Perf. 14x14½*

| | | | | |
|---|---|---|---|---|
| *135* | A55 | 10c gold & multi | 18 | 14 |
| *136* | A55 | 30c gold & multi | 45 | 45 |
| *137* | A55 | 75c gold & multi | 1.10 | 1.10 |

Rubber Research Institute of Malaysia, 50th anniversary.

Butterflies A55a

### Coil Stamps

**1976, Feb. 6** *Perf. 14*

| | | | | |
|---|---|---|---|---|
| *137A* | A55a | 10c Hebomoia glaucippe aturia | 22 | 22 |
| *137B* | A55a | 15c Precis orithya wallacei | 28 | 28 |

Scrub Typhus — A56

Sultan Jahya Petra — A57

Designs: 25c, Malaria (microscope, blood cells, slides). $1, Beri-beri (grain and men).

**1976, Feb. 6** **Litho.** *Perf. 14*

| | | | | |
|---|---|---|---|---|
| *138* | A56 | 20c red org & multi | 20 | 20 |
| *139* | A56 | 25c ultra & multi | 24 | 24 |
| *140* | A56 | $1 yel & multi | 1.40 | 1.00 |

Institute for Medical Research, Kuala Lumpur, 75th anniversary.

*Perf. 14½x13½*

**1976, Feb. 28** **Photo.**

| | | | | |
|---|---|---|---|---|
| *141* | A57 | 10c yel, blk & bis | 25 | 12 |
| *142* | A57 | 15c lil, blk & bis | 32 | 18 |
| *143* | A57 | 50c bl, blk & bis | 1.90 | 95 |

Installation of Sultan Jahya Petra of Kelantan as Paramount Ruler (Yang di-Pertuan Agong).

Council and Administrative Buildings — A58

**1976, Aug. 17** **Litho.** *Perf. 12½*

| | | | | |
|---|---|---|---|---|
| *144* | A58 | 15c org & blk | 26 | 22 |
| *145* | A58 | 20c brt red lil & blk | 32 | 26 |
| *146* | A58 | 50c bl & blk | 80 | 80 |

Opening of the State Council Complex and Administrative Building, Sarawak.

Provident Fund Building — A59

Provident Fund Emblems — A60

Design: 50c, Provident Fund Building at night.

*Perf. 13½x14½, 14½ (A60)*

**1976, Oct. 18** **Litho.**

| | | | | |
|---|---|---|---|---|
| *147* | A59 | 10c bl & multi | 12 | 9 |
| *148* | A60 | 25c gray & multi | 26 | 22 |
| *149* | A59 | 50c vio & multi | 60 | 60 |

Employees' Provident Fund, 25th anniversary.

Rehabilitation of the Blind — A61

Design: 75c, Blind man casting large shadow.

**1976, Nov. 20** *Perf. 13½x14½*

| | | | | |
|---|---|---|---|---|
| *150* | A61 | 10c multi | 18 | 14 |
| *151* | A61 | 75c multi | 1.50 | 1.25 |

25th anniv. of the Malaysian Assoc. for the Blind.

Abdul Razak and Crowd — A62

Designs (from left to right): Abdul Razak in cap and gown at lectern; Abdul Razak pointing to new roads and bridges on map; new constitution; Abdul Razak addressing Association of Southeast Asian Countries.

**1977, Jan. 14** **Photo.** *Perf. 14x14½*

| | | | | |
|---|---|---|---|---|
| *152* | | Strip of 5 | 1.75 | 1.75 |
| *a.* | | A62 15c, single stamp | 26 | 26 |

Prime Minister Tun Haji Abdul Razak bi Dato Hussein (1922-1976).

FELDA Housing Development A63

Design: 30c, View of oil palm settlement area and FELDA emblem.

**1977, July 7 Litho. *Perf. 13½x14½***

| | | | | |
|---|---|---|---|---|
| *153* | A63 | 15c multi | 22 | 16 |
| *154* | A63 | 30c multi | 55 | 32 |

Federal Land Development Authority (FELDA), 21st anniversary.

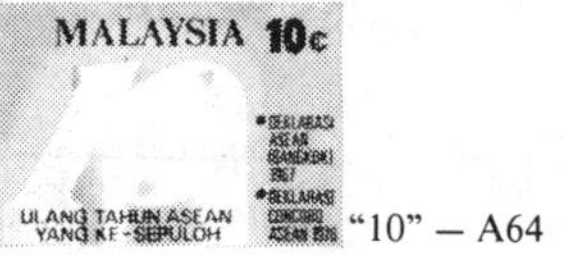


"10" – A64

ASEAN, 10th anniv.: 75c, Flags of ASEAN members: Malaysia, Philippines, Singapore, Thailand and Indonesia.

**1977, Aug. 8 Litho. *Perf. 13½x14½***

| | | | | |
|---|---|---|---|---|
| *155* | A64 | 10c multi | 12 | 10 |
| *156* | A64 | 75c multi | 1.10 | 80 |

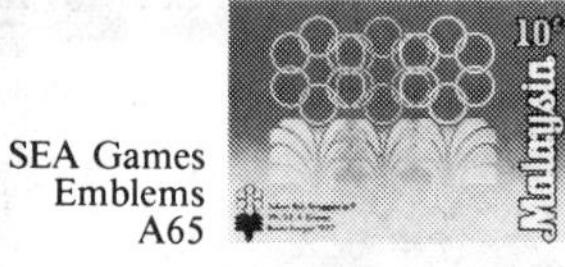


SEA Games Emblems A65

Designs: 20c, Ball, symbolic of 9 participating nations. 75c, Running.

***Perf. 13½x14½***

**1977, Nov. 19 Litho.**

| | | | | |
|---|---|---|---|---|
| *157* | A65 | 10c multi | 12 | 10 |
| *158* | A65 | 20c multi | 25 | 20 |
| *159* | A65 | 75c multi | 1.25 | 75 |

9th South East Asia Games, Kuala Lumpur.

Bank Emblem A66

**1978, Mar. 15 Litho. *Perf. 14***

| | | | | |
|---|---|---|---|---|
| *160* | A66 | 30c multi | 30 | 30 |
| *161* | A66 | 75c multi | 1.00 | 75 |

2nd annual meeting of Islamic Development Bank Governors, Kuala Lumpur, March 1978.

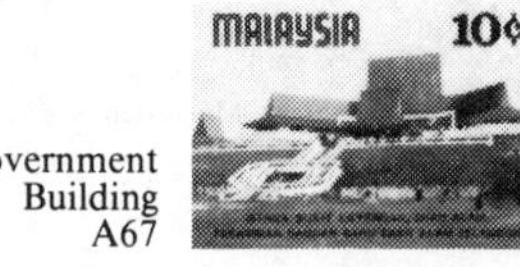


Government Building A67

Designs: Views of Shah Alam.

**1978, Dec. 7 Litho. *Perf. 13½x14½***

| | | | | |
|---|---|---|---|---|
| *162* | A67 | 10c multi | 8 | 8 |
| *163* | A67 | 30c multi | 25 | 25 |
| *164* | A67 | 75c multi | 70 | 70 |

Inauguration of Shah Alam as state capital of Selangor.

Mobile Post Office in Village – A68

Designs: 25c, General Post Office, Kuala Lumpur. 50c, Motorcyclist, rural mail delivery.

**1978, July 10 *Perf. 13***

| | | | | |
|---|---|---|---|---|
| *165* | A68 | 10c multi | 14 | 14 |
| *166* | A68 | 25c multi | 35 | 35 |
| *167* | A68 | 50c multi | 70 | 70 |

4th Conference of Commonwealth Postal Administrators.

Jamboree Emblem A69

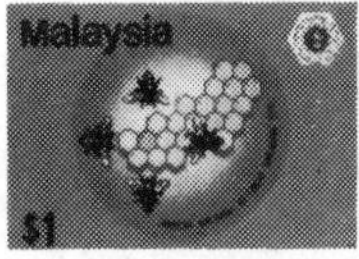


Bees and Honeycomb A70

**1978, July 26 Litho. *Perf. 13½***

| | | | | |
|---|---|---|---|---|
| *168* | A69 | 15c multi | 18 | 18 |
| *169* | A70 | $1 multi | 1.25 | 1.25 |

4th Boy Scout Jamboree, Sarawak.

Globe, Crest and WHO Emblem – A71

**1978, Sept. 30 *Perf. 13½x14½***

| | | | | |
|---|---|---|---|---|
| *170* | A71 | 15c bl, red & blk | 18 | 18 |
| *171* | A71 | 30c grn, red & blk | 35 | 35 |
| *172* | A71 | 50c pink, red & blk | 60 | 60 |

Global eradication of smallpox.

Dome of the Rock A72

**1978, Aug. 21 Litho. *Perf. 12½***

| | | | | |
|---|---|---|---|---|
| *173* | A72 | 15c red & multi | 32 | 26 |
| *174* | A72 | 30c bl & multi | 85 | 52 |

For Palestinian fighters and their families.

Tiger – A73

Wmk. 378 - Multiple POS in Octagonal Frame

Designs: 40c, Cobego. 50 Chevrotain. 75c, Pangolin. $1, Leatherback turtle. $2, Tapir. $5, Gaur. $10, Orangutan (vert.).

***Perf. 15x14½, 14½x15***

**1979, Jan. 4 Litho. Wmk. 378**

| | | | | |
|---|---|---|---|---|
| *175* | A73 | 30c multi | 22 | 22 |
| *a.* | | Unwmkd. ('84) | 72 | 72 |
| *176* | A73 | 40c multi | 28 | 28 |
| *a.* | | Unwmkd. ('84) | 98 | 98 |
| *177* | A73 | 50c multi | 35 | 35 |
| *a.* | | Unwmkd. ('84) | 1.20 | 1.20 |
| *178* | A73 | 75c multi | 55 | 55 |
| *a.* | | Unwmkd. ('87) | 1.80 | 1.80 |
| *179* | A73 | $1 multi | 75 | 75 |
| *a.* | | Unwmkd. ('83) | 2.40 | 2.40 |
| *180* | A73 | $2 multi | 1.40 | 1.40 |
| *a.* | | Unwmkd. ('83) | 4.75 | 4.75 |
| *181* | A73 | $5 multi | 3.50 | 3.50 |
| *a.* | | Unwmkd. ('85) | 12.00 | 12.00 |
| *182* | A73 | $10 multi | 7.25 | 7.25 |
| *a.* | | Unwmkd. ('86) | 25.00 | 25.00 |
| | | *Nos. 175-182 (8)* | 14.30 | 14.30 |
| | | *Nos. 175a-182a (8)* | 48.85 | 48.85 |

Central Bank of Malaysia A74

Year of the Child Emblem A75

Design: 10c, Central Bank of Malaysia and emblem (horiz.).

***Perf. 13½***

**1979, Jan. 26 Litho. Unwmk.**

| | | | | |
|---|---|---|---|---|
| *183* | A74 | 10c multi | 12 | 9 |
| *184* | A74 | 75c multi | 85 | 85 |

Central Bank of Malaysia, 30th anniversary.

**1979, Feb. 24 *Perf. 14***

Designs: 15c, Children of the world, globe and ICY emblem. $1, Children at play, ICY emblem.

| | | | | |
|---|---|---|---|---|
| *185* | A75 | 10c multi | 12 | 9 |
| *186* | A75 | 15c multi | 18 | 14 |
| *187* | A75 | $1 multi | 1.50 | 1.10 |

International Year of the Child.

Symbolic Rubber Plant – A76

Designs: 10c, Symbolic palm. 75c, Symbolic rubber products.

**1979, Apr. 30 Litho. *Perf. 13***

| | | | | |
|---|---|---|---|---|
| *188* | A76 | 10c brt grn & gold | 10 | 8 |
| *189* | A76 | 20c multi | 20 | 15 |
| *190* | A76 | 75c brt grn & gold | 75 | 75 |

Centenary of rubber production.

Rafflesia Hasseltii A77

Flowers: 2c, Pterocarpus indicus. 5c, Lagerstroemia speciosa. 10c, Durio zibethinus. 15c, Hibiscus. 20c, Rhododendron scortechinii. 25c, Phaeomeria speciosa.

**Wmk. 378**

**1979, Apr. 30 Litho. *Perf. 14½***

| | | | | |
|---|---|---|---|---|
| *191* | A77 | 1c multi | 5 | 5 |
| *192* | A77 | 2c multi | 5 | 5 |
| *193* | A77 | 5c multi | 5 | 5 |
| *194* | A77 | 10c multi | 9 | 5 |
| *a.* | | White flowers ('84) | 9 | 5 |
| *195* | A77 | 15c multi | 14 | 7 |
| *a.* | | Yel & multi ('84) | 14 | 7 |
| *196* | A77 | 20c multi | 18 | 9 |
| *a.* | | Grnsh & multi ('84) | 18 | 9 |
| *197* | A77 | 25c multi | 24 | 12 |
| *a.* | | Unwmkd. ('85) | 5.00 | |
| | | *Nos. 191-197 (7)* | 80 | 48 |

Temengor Hydroelectric Dam – A78

Designs: 25c, 50c, Dam and river (diff.).

***Perf. 13½x14½***

**1979, Sept. 19 Litho**

| | | | | |
|---|---|---|---|---|
| *198* | A78 | 15c multi | 14 | 8 |
| *199* | A78 | 25c multi | 24 | 12 |
| *200* | A78 | 50c multi | 48 | 24 |

"TELECOM 79" – A79

Telecom Emblem and: 15c, Telephone receiver and globes. 50c, Modes of communication.

**1979, Sept. 20 *Perf. 13½***

**Size: 34x25mm.**

| | | | | |
|---|---|---|---|---|
| *201* | A79 | 10c multi | 12 | 5 |
| *202* | A79 | 15c multi | 16 | 8 |

***Perf. 14***

**Size: 29x28mm.**

| | | | | |
|---|---|---|---|---|
| *203* | A79 | 50c multi | 55 | 28 |

3rd World Telecommunications Exhibition, Geneva, Sept. 20-26.

Haji Ahmad Shah – A80

**1980, July 10 Litho. *Perf. 14½***

| | | | | |
|---|---|---|---|---|
| *204* | A80 | 10c multi | 12 | 5 |
| *205* | A80 | 15c multi | 16 | 8 |
| *206* | A80 | 50c multi | 55 | 28 |

Installation of Sultan Haji Ahmad Shah of Pahang as Paramount Ruler (Yang di-Pertuan Agong).

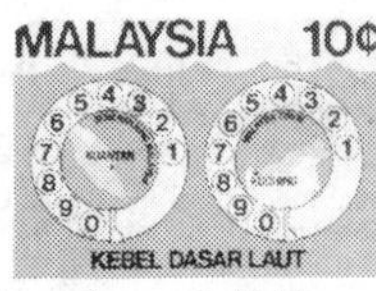


Pahang-Sarawak Cable – A81

**1980, Aug. 31 Litho. *Perf. 13½***

| | | | | | |
|---|---|---|---|---|---|
| *207* | A81 | 10c | *shown* | 10 | 5 |
| *208* | A81 | 15c | *Dial with views of Kuantan and Kuching* | 16 | 6 |
| *209* | A81 | 50c | *Telephone and maps* | 52 | 22 |

National University of Malaysia, 10th Anniversary A82

**1980, Sept. 2 Litho. *Perf. 13½***

| | | | | | |
|---|---|---|---|---|---|
| *210* | A82 | 10c | *shown* | 9 | 5 |
| *211* | A82 | 15c | *Jalan Pantai Baru campus* | 14 | 6 |
| *212* | A82 | 75c | *Great Hall and Tun Haji Abdul Razak (1st chancellor)* | 70 | 35 |

Hegira (Pilgrimage Year) — A83

**1980, Nov. 9**

*213* A83 15c multi 20 6
*214* A83 50c multi 70 35

Child Learning to Walk, IYD Emblem — A84

**1981, Feb. 14 Litho. *Perf. 13½***

*215* A84 10c shown 10 5
*216* A84 15c Seamstress 15 6
*217* A84 15c Athlete 80 40

International Year of the Disabled.

Installation of Sultan Mahmud of Trengganu — A85

**1981, Mar. 21 Litho. *Perf. 14½***

*218* A85 10c multi 12 5
*219* A85 15c multi 18 6
*220* A85 50c multi 60 30

Industrial Training Seminar — A86

Designs: Various workers.

**1981, May 2 Litho. *Perf. 13½***

*221* A86 10c multi 6 5
*222* A86 15c multi 10 5
*223* A86 30c multi 20 10
*224* A86 75c multi 50 25

Sources of Energy — A87

**1981, June 17 Litho. *Perf. 13½***

*225* A87 10c "25" 10 5
*226* A87 15c shown 16 8
*227* A87 75c Non-renewable energy 80 40

World Energy Conference, 25th anniv.

Centenary of Sabah — A88

**1981, Aug. 31 Litho. *Perf. 12***

*228* A88 15c Views, 1881 and 1981 15 7
*229* A88 80c Traditional and modern farming 80 40

Rain Tree — A89

**1981, Dec. 16 Litho. *Perf. 14***

*230* A89 15c shown 15 8
*231* A89 50c Simber tree, vert. 52 26
*232* A89 80c Borneo camphor-wood, vert. 1.00 50

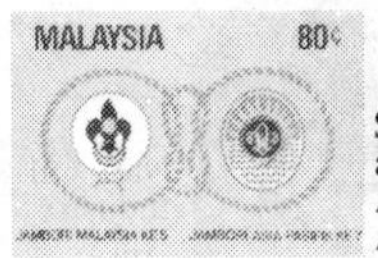


Scouting Year and Jamboree, Apr. 9- 16 A90

**1982, Apr. 10 Litho. *Perf. 13½x13***

*233* A90 15c Jamboree emblem 12 6
*234* A90 50c Flag, emblem 42 22
*235* A90 80c Emblems, knot 70 35

15th Anniv. of Assoc. of South East Asian Nations (ASEAN) A91

**1982, Aug. 8 Litho. *Perf. 14***

*236* A91 15c Meeting Center 16 8
*237* A91 $1 Flags 1.10 55

For the Freedom of Palestine A92

Designs: Dome of the Rock, Jerusalem.

**1982, Aug. 21 *Perf. 13½***

*238* A92 15c multi 16 8
*239* A92 $1 multi 1.10 55

25th Anniv. of Independence — A93

**1982, Aug. 31 Litho. *Perf. 14***

*240* A93 10c Kuala Lumpur 10 5
*241* A93 15c Independence celebration 15 7
*242* A93 50c Parade 52 26
*243* A93 80c Independence ceremony 70 35
*a.* Souv. sheet of 4, #240-243 1.50 75

Traditional Games — A94

**1982, Oct. 30 *Perf. 13½***

*244* A94 10c Shadow play 10 5
*245* A94 15c Cross top 15 7
*246* A94 75c Kite flying 75 38

Handicrafts — A95

**1982, Nov. 26 Litho. *Perf. 13x13½***

*247* A95 10c Sabah hats 9 5
*248* A95 15c Gold-threaded cloth 14 7
*249* A95 75c Sarawak pottery 70 35

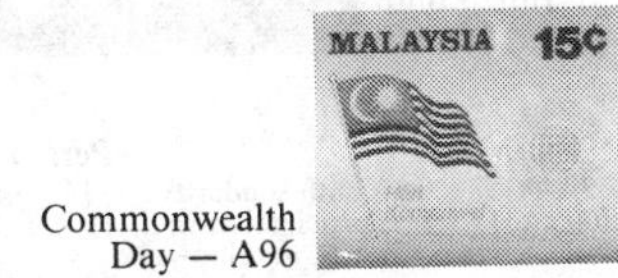


Commonwealth Day — A96

**1983, Mar. 14 Litho. *Perf. 14***

*250* A96 15c Flag 10 5
*251* A96 20c Seri Paduka Baginda 15 7
*252* A96 40c Oil palm refinery 30 15
*253* A96 $1 Globe 75 38

First Shipment of Natural Gas, Bintulu, Sarawak A97

**1983, Jan. 22 Litho. *Perf. 13½***

*254* A97 15c Bintulu Port Authority emblem 12 6
*255* A97 20c Freighter Tenaga Satu 16 8
*256* A97 $1 Gas plant 85 42

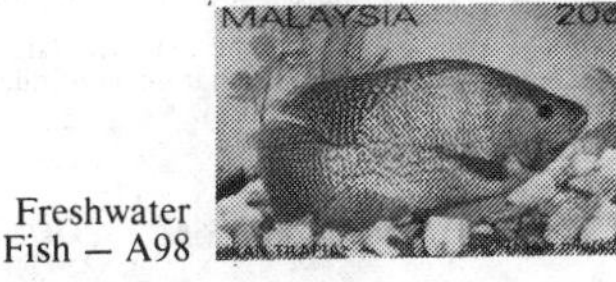


Freshwater Fish — A98

**1983, June 15 *Perf. 12x12½***

*257* Pair 38 18
*a.* A98 20c Tilapia nilotica 18 9
*b.* A98 20c Cyprinus carpio 18 9
*258* Pair 75 38
*a.* A98 40c Puntius gonionotus 35 18
*b.* A98 40c Ctenopharyngodon idellus 35 18

Opening of East-West Highway — A99

**1983, July 1 *Perf. 14x13½***

*259* A99 15c Lower Sungei Pergau Bridge 12 6
*260* A99 20c Sungei Perak Reservoir Bridge 16 8
*261* A99 $1 Map 85 42

Demand, as well as supply, determines a stamp's market value. One is as important as the other.

Armed Forces, 50th Anniv. A100

Designs: 15c, Royal Malaysian Aircraft. 20c, Navy vessel firing missile. 40c, Battle at Pasir Panjang. 80c, Trooping of the Royal colors.

**1983, Sept. 16 Litho. *Perf. 13½***

*262* A100 15c multi 14 7
*263* A100 20c multi 18 9
*264* A100 40c multi 35 18
*265* A100 80c multi 75 38
*a.* Souvenir sheet of 4 (#262-265) 1.50 75

Helmeted Hornbill — A101

Various hornbills.

**1983, Oct. 26 Litho. *Perf. 13½***

*266* A101 15c shown 14 7
*267* A101 20c Wrinkled 18 9
*268* A101 50c White crested 45 22
*269* A101 $1 Rhinoceros hornbill 90 45

25th Anniv. of Begara Bank A102

Branch offices.

**1984, Jan. 26 Litho. *Perf. 13½x14***

*270* A102 20c Ipoh 16 8
*271* A102 $1 Alor Setar 85 42

10th Anniv. of Federal Territory A103

Views of Kuala Lumpur. 20c, 40c vert.

***Perf. 14x13½, 13½x14***

**1984, Feb. 1 Litho.**

*272* A103 20c multi 16 8
*273* A103 40c multi 32 16
*274* A103 80c multi 70 35

Labuan Federal Territory A104

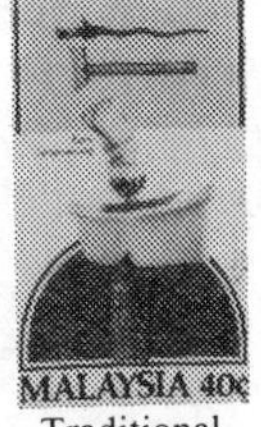


Traditional Weapons A105

**1984, Apr. 16 Litho. *Perf. 13½x14***

*275* A104 20c Development symbols, map, arms 16 8
*276* A104 $1 Flag, map 85 42

**1984, May 30 *Perf. 13x14***

*277* A105 40c Keris Semenanjung 35 18
*278* A105 40c Keris Pekakak 35 18

*279* A105 40c Keris Jawa 35 18
*280* A105 40c Tumbuk Lada 35 18

Nos. 277-280 se-tenant.

Asia-Pacific Broadcasting Union, 20th Anniv. — A106

**1984, June 23** ***Perf. 14x14½***
*281* A106 20c Map, waves 16 8
*282* A106 $1 "20" 75 38

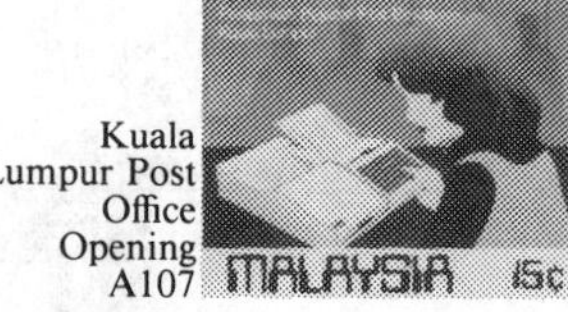


Kuala Lumpur Post Office Opening A107

**1984, Oct. 29** ***Perf. 12x11½***
*283* A107 15c Facsimile transmission 15 7
*284* A107 20c Building 20 10
*285* A107 $1 Mail bag conveyor 1.00 50

Installation of Sultan of Jahore as 8th King of Malaysia — A108

Sultan Mahmood, Arms — A109

**1984, Nov. 15** **Litho.** ***Perf. 12***
*286* A108 15c multi 12 6
*287* A108 20c multi 16 8
*288* A109 40c multi 32 16
*289* A109 80c multi 64 32

Malaysian Hibiscus — A110

**1984, Dec. 12** **Litho.** ***Perf. 13½***
*290* A110 10c White hibiscus 8 5
*291* A110 20c Red hibiscus 16 8
*292* A110 40c Pink hibiscus 32 16
*293* A110 $1 Orange hibiscus 80 40

Parliament, 25th Anniv. — A111

***Perf. 13½x14, 14x13½***
**1985, Mar. 30** **Litho.**
*294* A111 20c Badge, vert. 16 8
*295* A111 $1 Parliament, Kuala Lumpur 75 38

Protected Wildlife A112

**1985, Apr. 25** ***Perf. 14***
*296* A112 10c Prionodon linsang 8 5
*297* A112 40c Nycticebus coucang, vert. 32 16
*298* A112 $1 Petaurista elegans, vert. 80 40

Intl. Youth Year — A113

**1985, May 15** ***Perf. 13***
*299* A113 20c Youth solidarity 16 8
*300* A113 $1 Participation in natl. development 80 40

Malaya Railways Centenary A114

Locomotives.

**1985, June 1** ***Perf. 13***
*301* A114 15c Steam engine, 1885 12 6
*302* A114 20c Diesel-electric, 1957 18 9
*303* A114 $1 Diesel, 1963 85 42

**Souvenir Sheet**

***Perf. 14x13***
*304* A114 80c Train leaving Kuala Lumpur Station, 1938 80 40

No. 304 contains one stamp (size: 48x32mm); multicolored margin continues the design. Size: 120x60mm.

MALAYSIA 20c

Proton Saga A115

**1985, July 9** ***Perf. 14***
*305* A115 20c multi 16 8
*306* A115 40c multi 32 16
*307* A115 $1 multi 80 40

Inauguration of natl. automotive industry.

Sultan Salahuddin Abdul Aziz, Selangor Coat of Arms — A116

**1985, Sept. 5** ***Perf. 13***
*308* A116 15c multi 12 6
*309* A116 20c multi 16 8
*310* A116 $1 multi 80 40

25th anniv. of coronation.

Penang Bridge Opening A117

**1985, Sept. 15** **Litho.** ***Perf. 13½x13***
*311* A117 20c shown 16 8
*312* A117 40c Bridge, map 35 18

**Size: 44x28mm.**

***Perf. 12½***
*313* A117 $1 Map 85 42

Natl. Oil Industry A118

**1985, Nov. 4** ***Perf. 12½***
*314* A118 15c Offshore rig, vert. 14 7
*315* A118 20c 1st refinery 18 9
*316* A118 $1 Map of oil and gas fields 90 45

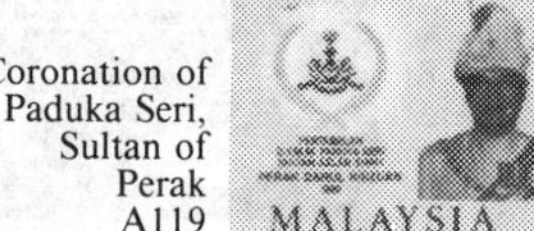


Coronation of Paduka Seri, Sultan of Perak A119

**1985, Dec. 9** ***Perf. 14***
*317* A119 15c lt bl & multi 12 6
*318* A119 20c lil & multi 16 8
*319* A119 $1 gold & multi 80 40

Birds A120

**1986, Mar. 11** **Litho.** ***Perf. 13½***
*320* A120 20c Lophura ignita, vert. 18 9
*321* A120 20c Pavo malacense, vert. 18 9
*322* A120 40c Lophura bulweri 35 18
*323* A120 40c Argusianus argus 35 18

Stamps of same denomination printed se-tenant.

PATA '86, Pacific Area Travel Assoc. Conference, Persidangan — A121

Designs: No. 324a, Two women dancing. No. 324b, Woman in red. No. 324c, Man and woman. No. 325a, Woman in gold. No. 325b, Woman holding fan. No. 325c, Woman in violet.

**1986, Apr. 14** **Litho.** ***Perf. 15x14½***
*324* Strip of 3 45 22
***a.-c.*** A121 20c, any single 15 7
*325* Strip of 3 90 45
***a.-c.*** A121 40c, any single 30 15

Malaysia Games A122

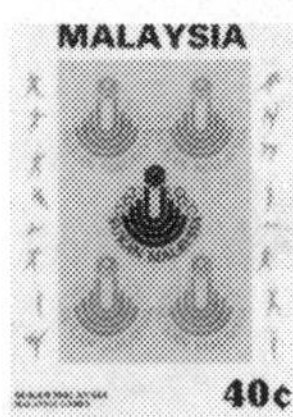


Games Emblem — A123

Flags — A124

**1986, Apr. 14** **Litho.** ***Perf. 12***
*326* A122 20c multi 15 7
*327* A123 40c multi 28 14
*328* A124 $1 multi 75 38

Nephelium Lappaceum A125

Malaysia $2

Averrhoa Carambola A126

**1986, June 5**
*329* A125 40c shown 32 16
*330* A125 50c Ananas comosus 40 20
*331* A125 80c Durio zibethinus 65 32
*332* A125 $1 Garcinia mangostana 80 40

***Perf. 13½***
*333* A126 $2 shown 1.60 80
*334* A126 $5 Musa sapientum 4.00 2.00
*335* A126 $10 Mangifera odorata 8.00 4.00
*336* A126 $20 Carica papaya 16.00 8.00
*Nos. 329-336 (8)* 31.77 15.88

Natl. Assoc. for the Prevention of Drug Abuse, 10th Anniv. A127

**1986, June 26** ***Perf. 13***
*337* A127 20c Skull 16 8
*338* A127 40c Dove 32 16
*339* A127 $1 Addict, vert. 80 40

Malaysian Airlines Kuala Lumpur-Los Angeles Inaugural Flight — A128

**1986, July 31** ***Perf. 14x13½***
*340* A128 20c Flight routes map 16 8
*341* A128 40c MAS emblem, new route 32 16
*342* A128 $1 Emblem, stops 80 40

Industrial Productivity A129

**1986, Nov. 3** **Litho.** ***Perf. 14***
*343* A129 20c Construction, vert. 16 8
*344* A129 40c Industry 32 16
*345* A129 $1 Automobile factory 80 40

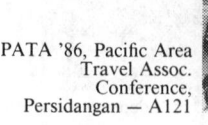

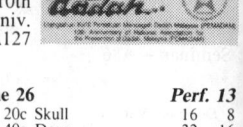

Historic Buildings A130

Designs: 15c, Istana Lama Seri Menanti, Negri Sembilan. 20c, Istana Kenangan, Perak. 40c, Bangunan Stadthuys, Malacca. $1, Istana Kuching, Sarawak.

**1986, Dec. 20** — *Perf. 13*

*346* A130 15c multi 12 6
*347* A130 20c multi 16 8
*348* A130 40c multi 32 16
*349* A130 $1 multi 80 40

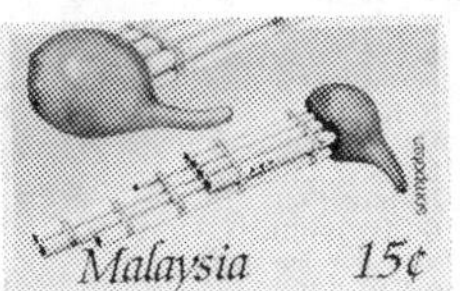


Folk Music Instruments — A131

**1987, Mar. 7 Litho.** — *Perf. 12*

*350* A131 15c Sompotan 12 6
*351* A131 20c Sapih 16 8
*352* A131 50c Serunai, vert. 40 20
*353* A131 80c Rebab, vert. 65 32

Intl. Year of Shelter for the Homeless — A132

**1987, Apr. 6 Litho.** — *Perf. 12*

*354* A132 20c Model village 16 8
*355* A132 $1 Symbols of family, shelter 85 42

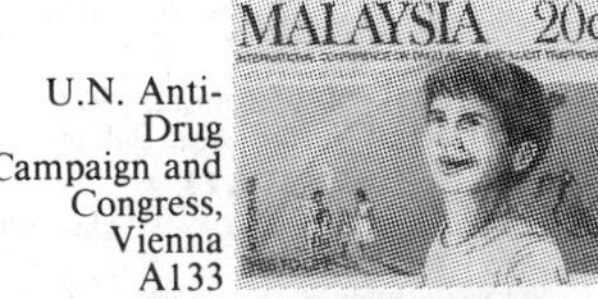


U.N. Anti-Drug Campaign and Congress, Vienna A133

**1987, June 8 Litho.** — *Perf. 13½x13*

*356* A133 20c Health boy, family, rainbow 16 8
*357* A133 20c Holding drugs 16 8
*358* A133 40c Child warding off drugs 32 16
*359* A133 40c Drugs, damaged body in capsule 32 16

Stamps of same denomination printed se-tenant in continuous design.

Kenyir Hydroelectric Power Station Inauguration — A134

**1987, July 13** — *Perf. 12*

*360* A134 20c Power facility, dam 16 8
*361* A134 $1 Side view 85 42

33rd Commonwealth Parliamentary Conference — A135

**1987, Sept. 1 Litho.** — *Perf. 12*

*362* A135 20c Maces, parliament 16 8
*363* A135 $1 Parliament, maces, diff. 85 42

Transportation and Communications Decade in Asia and the Pacific (1985-94) — A136

Designs: 15c, Satellites, Earth, satellite dish. 20c, Car, diesel train, Kuala Lumpur Station. 40c, MISC container ship. $1, Malaysia Airlines jet, Kuala Lumpur Airport.

**1987, Oct. 26** — *Perf. 13½x13*

*364* A136 15c multi 12 6
*365* A136 20c multi 16 8
*366* A136 40c multi 35 18
*367* A136 $1 multi 85 42

Protected Wildcats A137

**1987, Nov. 14**

*368* A137 15c Felis temminckii 12 6
*369* A137 20c Felis planiceps 16 8
*370* A137 40c Felis marmorata 35 18
*371* A137 $1 Neofelis nebulosa 85 42

ASEAN, 20th Anniv. A138

**1987, Dec. 14 Litho.** — *Perf. 13*

*372* A138 20c "20," flags 15 8
*373* A138 $1 Flags, Earth 85 42

Opening of Sultan Salahuddin Abdul Aziz Shah Mosque, Selangor A139

Dome, minarets and: 15c, Arches. 20c, Sultan Abdul Aziz Shah, Selangor crest. $1, Interior, vert.

**1988, Mar. 11 Litho.** — *Perf. 12*

*374* A139 15c multi 12 6
*375* A139 20c multi 16 8
*376* A139 $1 multi 80 40

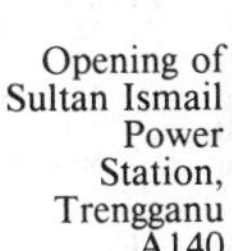

Opening of Sultan Ismail Power Station, Trengganu A140

**1988, Apr. 4** — *Perf. 13*

*377* A140 20c shown 16 8
*378* A140 $1 Station, diff. 80 40

Wildlife Protection A141

Birds.

**1988, June 30 Litho.** — *Perf. 13*

*379* A141 20c Hypothymis azurea 16 8
*380* A141 20c Dicaeum cruentatum 16 8
*381* A141 50c Aethopyga siparaja 40 20
*382* A141 50c Cymbirhynchus macrorhynchos 40 20

Stamps of the same denomination printed se-tenant.

A142 A143

**1988, Aug. 31 Litho.** — *Perf. 13x13½*

*383* A142 20c Sabah 16 8
*384* A142 20c Sarawak 16 8
*385* A143 $1 State and natl. symbols 80 40

Nos. 383-384 printed se-tenant.

### POSTAGE DUE STAMPS

Until 1966 Malaysia used postage due stamps of the Malayan Postal Union. See listings under Malaya.

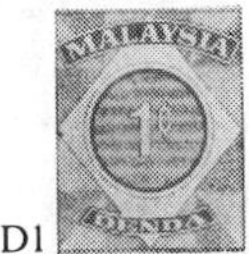


D1

**Wmk. 338 Upright**

**1966, Aug. 15 Litho.** — *Perf. 14½x14*

*J1* D1 1c pink 5 5
*J2* D1 2c slate 5 5
*J3* D1 4c lt yel grn 5 5
*J4* D1 8c brt grn 15 15
*J5* D1 10c ultra 15 15
*J6* D1 12c purple 9 9
*J7* D1 20c brown 40 40
*J8* D1 50c ol bis 1.10 1.10
*Nos. J1-J8 (8)* 2.04 2.04

**1972** — **Wmk. 338 Sideways**

*J4a* D1 8c brt grn 50 50
*J5a* D1 10c ultra 75 75
*J7a* D1 20c brown 1.00 1.00
*J8a* D1 50c ol bis 2.50 2.50

**1981 Litho. Unwmk.** — *Perf. 15x14*

*J9* D1 2c slate 5 5
*J10* D1 8c brt grn 10 5
*J11* D1 10c blue 10 6
*J12* D1 20c brown 20 10
*J13* D1 50c ol bis 50 30
*Nos. J9-J13 (5)* 95 56

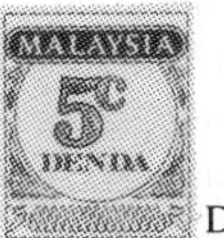


D2

**1988, Sept. 15 Litho.** — *Perf. 12*

*J14* D2 5c brt rose & lil rose 5 5
*J15* D2 10c blk & gray 8 8
*J16* D2 20c deep org & yel org 16 16
*J17* D2 50c blue grn & lt blue grn 40 40
*J18* D2 $1 brt blue & lt ultra 80 80
*Nos. J14-J18 (5)* 1.49 1.49

## JOHORE

Vanda Hookeriana and Sultan Ismail — A14

Orchids: 2c, Arundina graminifolia. 5c, Paphiopedilum niveum. 6c, Spathoglottis plicata. 10c, Arachnis flosaeris. 15c, Rhyncostylis retusa. 20c, Phalaenopsis violacea.

**Wmk. 338**

**1965, Nov. 15 Photo.** — *Perf. 14½*

**Flowers in Natural Colors**

*169* A14 1c blk & lt grnsh bl 10 5
a. Black omitted 50.00
b. Watermark sideways ('70) 12 12
*170* A14 2c blk, red & gray 10 5
*171* A14 5c blk & Prus bl 20 5
a. Yellow omitted 24.00
*172* A14 6c blk & lt lil 24 5
*173* A14 10c blk & lt ultra 35 5
a. Watermark sideways ('70) 65 55
*174* A14 15c blk, lil rose & grn 48 28
*175* A14 20c blk & brn 75 48
*Nos. 169-175 (7)* 2.22 1.01

Malayan Jezebel and Sultan Ismail — A15

Butterflies: 2c, Black-veined tiger. 5c, Clipper. 6c, Lime butterfly. 10c, Great orange tip. 15c, Blue pansy. 20c, Wanderer.

*Perf. 13½x13*

**1971, Feb. 1 Litho. Unwmk.**

*176* A15 1c multi 10 7
a. Photo. ('77) 38 18
*177* A15 2c multi 10 7
a. Photo. ('77) 38 18
*178* A15 5c multi 10 7
a. Photo. ('77) 38 18
*179* A15 6c multi 25 7
*180* A15 10c multi 38 12
a. Photo. ('77) 55 28
*181* A15 15c multi 60 18
a. Photo. ('77) 1.25 45
*182* A15 20c multi 80 30
a. Photo. ('77) 1.50 55
*Nos. 176-182 (7)* 2.33 88
*Nos. 176a-182a (6)* 4.44 1.82

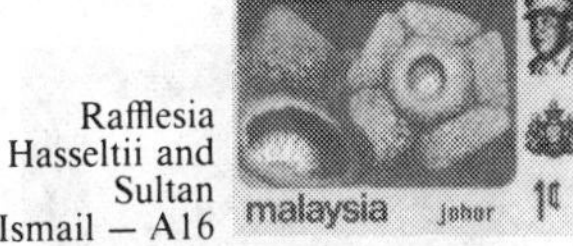


Rafflesia Hasseltii and Sultan Ismail — A16

Flowers: 2c, Pterocarpus indicus. 5c, Lagerstroemia speciosa. 10c, Durio zibethinus. 15c, Hibiscus. 20c, Rhododendron scortechinii. 25c, Phaeomeria speciosa.

**Wmk. 378**

**1979, Apr. 30 Litho. *Perf. 14½***

*183* A16 1c multi 6 5
*184* A16 2c multi 8 5
*185* A16 5c multi 10 5
**a.** "Johor" in round type ('84) 10 5
*186* A16 10c multi 16 5
**a.** "Johor" in round type ('84) 16 5
*187* A16 15c multi 25 6
**a.** "Johor" in round type ('84) 25 6
*188* A16 20c multi 32 8
**a.** "Johor" in round type ('84) 32 8
*189* A16 25c multi 40 10
*Nos. 183-189 (7)* 1.37 44

Agriculture, State Arms and Sultan Mahmood Iskandar Al-Haj, Regent — A19

**Wmk. 388**

**1986, Oct. 25 Litho. *Perf. 12***

*190* A19 1c Coffea liberica 5 5
*191* A19 2c Cocos nucifera 5 5
*192* A19 5c Theobroma cacao 5 5
*193* A19 10c Piper nigrum 8 5
*194* A19 15c Hevea brasiliensis 12 6
*195* A19 20c Elaeis guineensis 16 8
*196* A19 30c Oryza sativa 24 12
*Nos. 190-196 (7)* 75 46

## KEDAH

Orchid Type of Johore, 1965, with Portrait of Sultan Abdul Halim

**Wmk. 338**

**1965, Nov. 15 Photo. *Perf. 14½***

**Flowers in Natural Colors**

*106* A14 1c blk & lt grnsh bl 5 5
**a.** Black omitted 50.00
**b.** Watermark sideways ('70) 75 75
*107* A14 2c blk, red & gray 7 5
*108* A14 5c blk & Prus bl 12 5
*109* A14 6c blk & lt lil 14 5
*110* A14 10c blk & lt ultra 22 6
**a.** Watermark sideways ('70) 3.25 2.50
*111* A14 15c blk, lil rose & grn 28 18
*112* A14 20c blk & brn 42 28
*Nos. 106-112 (7)* 1.30 72

Butterfly Type of Johore, 1971, with Portrait of Sultan Abdul Halim

***Perf. 13½x13***

**1971, Feb. 1 Litho. Unwmk.**

*113* A15 1c multi 5 5
*114* A15 2c multi 8 5
**a.** Photo. ('77) 2.50 1.00
*115* A15 5c multi 20 5
**a.** Photo. ('77) 18 10
*116* A15 6c multi 24 8
*117* A15 10c multi 35 10
**a.** Photo. ('77) 30 15
*118* A15 15c multi 60 18
**a.** Photo. ('77) 60 30
*119* A15 20c multi 75 20
**a.** Photo. ('77) 85 40
*Nos. 113-119 (7)* 2.27 71
*Nos. 114a-119a (5)* 4.43 1.95

Flower Type of Johore, 1979, with Portrait of Sultan Abdul Halim

**Wmk. 378**

**1979, Apr. 30 Litho. *Perf. 14½***

*120* A16 1c multi 5 5
*121* A16 2c multi 5 5
*122* A16 5c multi 6 5
*123* A16 10c multi 14 7
*124* A16 15c multi 20 10
**a.** Unwmkd. ('84) 3.25
*125* A16 20c multi 26 14
**a.** pale yellow flowers ('84) 26 14
*126* A16 25c multi 32 16
*Nos. 120-126 (7)* 1.08 62

25th Anniv. of Installation of Sultan Abdul Halim — A10

**1983, July 15 Litho. *Perf. 13½***

*127* A10 20c Portrait, vert. 24 12
*128* A10 40c View from Mt. Gunung Jerai 50 25
*129* A10 50c Rice fields, Mt. Gunung Jerai 60 30

Agriculture and State Arms Type of Johore with Sultan Abdul Halim

**Wmk. 388**

**1986, Oct. 25 Litho. *Perf. 12***

*130* A19 1c multi 5 5
*131* A19 2c multi 5 5
*132* A19 5c multi 5 5
*133* A19 10c multi 8 5
*134* A19 15c multi 12 6
*135* A19 20c multi 16 8
*136* A19 30c multi 24 12
*Nos. 130-136 (7)* 75 46

## KELANTAN

Orchid Type of Johore, 1965, with Portrait of Sultan Yahya Petra

**Wmk. 338**

**1965, Nov. 15 Photo. *Perf. 14½***

**Flowers in Natural Colors**

*91* A14 1c blk & lt grnsh bl 5 5
**a.** Watermark sideways ('70) 32 32
*92* A14 2c blk, red & gray 10 5
*93* A14 5c blk & Prus bl 22 10
*94* A14 6c blk & lt lil 28 12
*95* A14 10c blk & lt ultra 40 18
**a.** Watermark sideways ('70) 1.40 1.10
*96* A14 15c blk, lil rose & grn 55 35
*97* A14 20c blk & brn 85 60
*Nos. 91-97 (7)* 2.45 1.45

Butterfly Type of Johore, 1971, with Portrait of Sultan Yahya Petra

***Perf. 13½x13***

**1971, Feb. 1 Litho. Unwmk.**

*98* A15 1c multi 5 5
**a.** Photo. ('77) 60 30
*99* A15 2c multi 8 5
*100* A15 5c multi 20 10
**a.** Photo. ('77) 60 30
*101* A15 6c multi 24 12
*102* A15 10c multi 35 18
**a.** Photo. ('77) 1.25 45
*103* A15 15c multi 60 30
**a.** Photo. ('77) 3.00 1.00
*104* A15 20c multi 75 38
*Nos. 98-104 (7)* 2.27 1.18

Flower Type of Johore, 1979, with Portrait of Sultan Yahya Petra

**Wmk. 378**

**1979, Apr. 30 Litho. *Perf. 14½***

*105* A16 1c multi 5 5
*106* A16 2c multi 5 5
*107* A16 5c multi 6 5
**a.** Unwmkd. ('86) 1.05
*108* A16 10c multi 12 6
**a.** White flowers ('84) 12 6
*109* A16 15c multi 18 9
*110* A16 20c multi 24 12
**a.** Pale yellow flowers ('84) 24 12
*111* A16 25c multi 30 15
*Nos. 105-111 (7)* 1.00 57

Sultan Tengku Ismail Petra, Installation — A7

**1980, Mar. 30 Litho. *Perf. 14½***

*112* A7 10c multi 8 5
*113* A7 15c multi 12 6
*114* A7 50c multi 42 22

Agriculture and State Arms Type of Johore with Sultan Ismail Petra

**Wmk. 388**

**1986, Oct. 25 Litho. *Perf. 12***

*115* A19 1c multi 5 5
*116* A19 2c multi 5 5
*117* A19 5c multi 5 5
*118* A19 10c multi 8 5
*119* A19 15c multi 12 6
*120* A19 20c multi 16 8
*121* A19 30c multi 24 12
*Nos. 115-121 (7)* 75 46

## MALACCA

## (Melaka)

Orchid Type of Johore, 1965, with State Crest

**Wmk. 338**

**1965, Nov. 15 Photo. *Perf. 14½***

**Flowers in Natural Colors**

*67* A14 1c blk & lt grnsh bl 5 5
**a.** Watermark sideways ('70) 24 24
*68* A14 2c blk, red & gray 10 5
*69* A14 5c blk & Prus bl 25 6
*70* A14 6c blk & lt lil 32 8
*71* A14 10c blk & lt ultra 48 12
**a.** Watermark sideways ('70) 1.00 80
*72* A14 15c blk, lil rose & grn 65 26
*73* A14 20c blk & brn 95 45
*Nos. 67-73 (7)* 2.80 1.07

Butterfly Type of Johore, 1971, with State Crest

***Perf. 13½x13***

**1971, Feb. 1 Litho. Unwmk.**

*74* A15 1c multi 5 5
**a.** Photo. ('77) 60 32
*75* A15 2c multi 8 5
*76* A15 5c multi 18 8
**a.** Photo. ('77) 48 28
*77* A15 6c multi 25 14
*78* A15 10c multi 38 18
**a.** Photo. ('77) 80 50
*79* A15 15c multi 60 32
**a.** Photo. ('77) 1.65 85
*80* A15 20c multi 75 35
**a.** Photo. ('77) 2.00 1.10
*Nos. 74-80 (7)* 2.29 1.17
*Nos. 74a-80a (5)* 5.53 3.05

Flower Type of Johore, 1979, with State Crest

**Wmk. 378**

**1979, Apr. 30 Litho. *Perf. 14½***

*81* A16 1c multi 5 5
*82* A16 2c multi 5 5
*83* A16 5c multi 6 5
*84* A16 10c multi 12 6
**a.** Unwmkd. ('85) 2.15
*85* A16 15c multi 18 9
**a.** Unwmkd. ('86) 3.25
*86* A16 20c multi 24 12
**a.** Unwmkd. ('85) 4.25
*87* A16 25c multi 30 15
*Nos. 81-87 (7)* 1.00 57

Agriculture and State Arms Type of Johore

**Wmk. 388**

**1986, Oct. 25 Litho. *Perf. 12***

*88* A19 1c multi 5 5
*89* A19 2c multi 5 5
*90* A19 5c multi 5 5
*91* A19 10c multi 8 5
*92* A19 15c multi 12 6
*93* A19 20c multi 16 8
*94* A19 30c multi 24 12
*Nos. 88-94 (7)* 75 46

## NEGRI SEMBILAN

## (Negeri Sembilan)

Orchid Type of Johore, 1965, with State Crest

**Wmk. 338**

**1965, Nov. 15 Photo. *Perf. 14½***

**Flowers in Natural Colors**

*76* A14 1c blk & lt grnsh bl 5 5
**a.** Watermark sideways ('70) 55 55
*77* A14 2c blk, red & gray 9 5
*78* A14 5c blk & Prus bl 22 5
*79* A14 6c blk & lt lil 28 6
*80* A14 10c blk & lt ultra 42 8
*81* A14 15c blk, lil rose & grn 55 16
*82* A14 20c blk & brn 85 28
*Nos. 76-82 (7)* 2.46 73

Tuanku Ja'afar and Crest of Negri Sembilan A7

**1968, Apr. 8 Photo. *Perf. 13½***

*83* A7 15c brt bl & multi 15 10
*84* A7 50c yel & multi 50 50

Installation of Tuanku Ja'afar ibni Al-Marhum as ruler (Yang di-Pertuan Besar) of Negri Sembilan.

Butterfly Type of Johore, 1971, with State Crest

***Perf. 13½x13***

**1971, Feb. 1 Litho. Unwmk.**

*85* A15 1c multi 5
*86* A15 2c multi 9
**a.** Photo. ('77) 52 2
*87* A15 5c multi 20
**a.** Photo. ('77) 52 2
*88* A15 6c multi 26 1
*89* A15 10c multi 40 1
**a.** Photo. ('77) 1.00 4
*90* A15 15c multi 65 2
**a.** Photo. ('77) 1.90 7
*91* A15 20c multi 80 2.
**a.** Photo. ('77) 2.50 1.1
*Nos. 85-91 (7)* 2.45 8
*Nos. 86a-91a (5)* 6.44 2.7

Flower Type of Johore, 1979, with State Crest

**Wmk. 378**

**1979, Apr. 30 Litho. *Perf. 14½***

*92* A16 1c multi 5
*93* A16 2c multi 5
*94* A16 5c multi 6
**a.** Unwmkd. ('85) 1.05
*95* A16 10c multi 12
**a.** White flowers ('84) 12
*96* A16 15c multi 18
**a.** Unwmkd. ('84) 3.25
*97* A16 20c multi 24 1
**a.** Pale yellow flowers ('84) 24 1
*98* A16 25c multi 30 1
*Nos. 92-98 (7)* 1.00 5

Agriculture and State Arms Type of Johore

**Wmk. 388**

**1986, Oct. 25 Litho. *Perf. 12***

*99* A19 1c multi 5 5
*100* A19 2c multi 5 5
*101* A19 5c multi 5 5
*102* A19 10c multi 8 5
*103* A19 15c multi 12 6
*104* A19 20c multi 16 8
*105* A19 30c multi 24 12
*Nos. 99-105 (7)* 75 46

## PAHANG

Orchid Type of Johore, 1965, with Portrait of Sultan Abu Bakar

**Wmk. 338**

**1965, Nov. 15 Photo. *Perf. 14½***

**Flowers in Natural Colors**

*83* A14 1c blk & lt grnsh bl 5 5
**a.** Watermark sideways ('70) 12 12
*84* A14 2c blk, red & gray 6 5
*85* A14 5c blk & Prus bl 16 6
*86* A14 6c blk & lt lil 20 6
*87* A14 10c blk & lt ultra 30 10
**a.** Watermark sideways ('70) 50 40
*88* A14 15c blk, lil rose & grn 40 16
*89* A14 20c blk & brn 60 26
*Nos. 83-89 (7)* 1.77 74

Butterfly Type of Johore, 1971, Portrait of Sultan Abu Bakar

***Perf. 13½x13***

**1971, Feb. 1 Litho. Unwmk.**

*90* A15 1c multi 5 5
*91* A15 2c multi 6 5
*92* A15 5c multi 14 5
**a.** Booklet pane of 4 ('73) 60
*93* A15 6c multi 20 8
*94* A15 10c multi 32 10
**a.** Booklet pane of 4 (73) 1.30
*95* A15 15c multi 52 20
**a.** Booklet pane of 4 (73) 2.25
*96* A15 20c multi 65 22
*Nos. 90-96 (7)* 1.94 75

Sultan Haji Ahmad Shah — A9

**1975, May 8 Litho. *Perf. 14x14½***

*97* A9 10c lil, gold & blk 10 10
*98* A9 15c yel, grn & blk 22 18
*99* A9 50c ultra, dk bl & blk 65 65

Installation of Sultan Haji Ahmad Shah as ruler of Pahang.

A18

**1977-78**

| No. | Type | Description | Unused | Used |
|---|---|---|---|---|
| 100 | A18 | 2c multi ('78) | 22.50 | 22.50 |
| 101 | A18 | 5c multi | 24 | 24 |
| 102 | A18 | 10c multi ('78) | 35 | 35 |
| 103 | A18 | 15c multi ('78) | 70 | 70 |
| 104 | A18 | 20c multi ('78) | 1.25 | 1.25 |
| | | *Nos. 100-104 (5)* | 25.04 | 25.04 |

Flower Type of Johore, 1979, with Portrait of Sultan Haji Ahmad Shah

**Wmk. 378**

**1979, Apr. 30 Litho. *Perf. 14½***

| No. | Type | Description | Unused | Used |
|---|---|---|---|---|
| 105 | A16 | 1c multi | 5 | 5 |
| 106 | A16 | 2c multi | 5 | 5 |
| 107 | A16 | 5c multi | 6 | 5 |
| a. | | Brt rose pink & yel flowers ('84) | 6 | 5 |
| 108 | A16 | 10c multi | 12 | 6 |
| a. | | Unwmkd. ('85) | 2.15 | |
| 109 | A16 | 15c multi | 18 | 9 |
| 110 | A16 | 20c multi | 25 | 12 |
| 111 | A16 | 25c multi | 32 | 16 |
| | | *Nos. 105-111 (7)* | 1.03 | 58 |

Agriculture and State Arms Type of Johore with Sultan Haji Ahmad Shah

**Wmk. 388**

**1986, Oct. 25 Litho. *Perf. 12***

| No. | Type | Description | Unused | Used |
|---|---|---|---|---|
| 112 | A19 | 1c multi | 5 | 5 |
| 113 | A19 | 2c multi | 5 | 5 |
| 114 | A19 | 5c multi | 5 | 5 |
| 115 | A19 | 10c multi | 8 | 5 |
| 116 | A19 | 15c multi | 12 | 6 |
| 117 | A19 | 20c multi | 16 | 8 |
| 118 | A19 | 30c multi | 24 | 12 |
| | | *Nos. 112-118 (7)* | 75 | 46 |

## PENANG
## (Pulau Pinang)

Orchid Type of Johore, 1965, with State Crest

**Wmk. 338**

**1965, Nov. 15 Photo. *Perf. 14½***

**Orchids in Natural Colors**

| No. | Type | Description | Unused | Used |
|---|---|---|---|---|
| 67 | A14 | 1c blk & lt grnsh bl | 5 | 5 |
| a. | | Watermark sideways ('70) | 32 | 32 |
| 68 | A14 | 2c blk, red & gray | 5 | 5 |
| 69 | A14 | 5c blk & Prus bl | 12 | 5 |
| a. | | Prus. bl omitted | | |
| b. | | Yellow omitted | | |
| 70 | A14 | 6c blk & lt lil | 14 | 5 |
| 71 | A14 | 10c blk & lt ultra | 22 | 5 |
| a. | | Watermark sideways ('70) | 1.40 | 1.10 |
| 72 | A14 | 15c blk, lil rose & grn | 28 | 12 |
| 73 | A14 | 20c blk & brn | 42 | 20 |
| | | *Nos. 67-73 (7)* | 1.28 | 57 |

Butterfly Type of Johore, 1971, with State Crest

***Perf. 13½x13***

**1971, Feb. 1 Litho. Unwmk.**

| No. | Type | Description | Unused | Used |
|---|---|---|---|---|
| 74 | A15 | 1c multi | 5 | 5 |
| a. | | Photo. ('77) | 3.25 | 1.25 |
| 75 | A15 | 2c multi | 8 | 5 |
| 76 | A15 | 5c multi | 20 | 6 |
| a. | | Photo. ('77) | 28 | 10 |
| 77 | A15 | 6c multi | 24 | 7 |
| 78 | A15 | 10c multi | 35 | 12 |
| a. | | Photo. ('77) | 40 | 15 |
| 79 | A15 | 15c multi | 60 | 18 |
| a. | | Photo. ('77) | 1.10 | 40 |
| 80 | A15 | 20c multi | 75 | 22 |
| a. | | Photo. ('77) | 1.40 | 50 |
| | | *Nos. 74-80 (7)* | 2.27 | 75 |
| | | *Nos. 74a-80a (5)* | 6.43 | 2.40 |

Flower Type of Johore, 1979, with State Crest

**Wmk. 378**

**1979, Apr. 30 Litho. *Perf. 14½***

| No. | Type | Description | Unused | Used |
|---|---|---|---|---|
| 81 | A16 | 1c multi | 5 | 5 |
| 82 | A16 | 2c multi | 5 | 5 |
| 83 | A16 | 5c multi | 6 | 5 |
| 84 | A16 | 10c multi | 12 | 6 |
| 85 | A16 | 15c multi | 18 | 9 |
| a. | | Unwmkd. ('84) | 3.25 | |
| 86 | A16 | 20c multi | 24 | 12 |
| 87 | A16 | 25c multi | 30 | 15 |
| | | *Nos. 81-87 (7)* | 1.00 | 57 |

Agriculture and State Arms Type of Johore

**Wmk. 388**

**1986, Oct. 25 Litho. *Perf. 12***

| No. | Type | Description | Unused | Used |
|---|---|---|---|---|
| 88 | A19 | 1c multi | 5 | 5 |
| 89 | A19 | 2c multi | 5 | 5 |
| 90 | A19 | 5c multi | 5 | 5 |
| 91 | A19 | 10c multi | 8 | 5 |
| 92 | A19 | 15c multi | 12 | 6 |
| 93 | A19 | 20c multi | 16 | 8 |
| 94 | A19 | 30c multi | 24 | 12 |
| | | *Nos. 88-94 (7)* | 75 | 46 |

## PERAK

Sultan Idris Shah — A17

**Wmk. 338**

**1963, Oct. 26 Photo. *Perf. 14***

| No. | Type | Description | Unused | Used |
|---|---|---|---|---|
| 138 | A17 | 10c yel, blk, bl & brn | 18 | 12 |

Installation of Idris Shah as Sultan of Perak.

Orchid Type of Johore, 1965, with Portrait of Sultan Idris Shah

**1965, Nov. 15 Wmk. 338 *Perf. 14½***

**Flowers in Natural Colors**

| No. | Type | Description | Unused | Used |
|---|---|---|---|---|
| 139 | A14 | 1c blk & lt grnsh bl | 5 | 5 |
| a. | | Watermark sideways ('70) | 25 | 25 |
| 140 | A14 | 2c blk, red & gray | 8 | 5 |
| 141 | A14 | 5c blk & Prus bl | 20 | 5 |
| a. | | Yellow omitted | 20.00 | |
| 142 | A14 | 6c blk & lt lil | 25 | 5 |
| 143 | A14 | 10c blk & lt ultra | 38 | 7 |
| a. | | Watermark sideways ('70) | 1.00 | 95 |
| 144 | A14 | 15c blk, lil rose & grn | 50 | 15 |
| a. | | Lilac rose omitted | 80.00 | |
| 145 | A14 | 20c blk & brn | 75 | 25 |
| | | *Nos. 139-145 (7)* | 2.21 | 67 |

Butterfly Type of Johore, 1971, with Portrait of Sultan Idris Shah

***Perf. 13½x13***

**1971, Feb. 1 Litho. Unwmk.**

| No. | Type | Description | Unused | Used |
|---|---|---|---|---|
| 146 | A15 | 1c multi | 5 | 5 |
| a. | | Photo. ('77) | 42 | 12 |
| 147 | A15 | 2c multi | 10 | 5 |
| 148 | A15 | 5c multi | 25 | 8 |
| a. | | Bklt. pane of 4 (73) | 20 | |
| b. | | Photo. (77) | 65 | 18 |
| 149 | A15 | 6c multi | 30 | 10 |
| 150 | A15 | 10c multi | 45 | 14 |
| a. | | Bklt. pane of 4 (73) | 50 | |
| b. | | Photo. (77) | 75 | 22 |
| 151 | A15 | 15c multi | 75 | 22 |
| a. | | Booklet pane of 4 ('73) | 80 | |
| b. | | Photo. (77) | 1.75 | 50 |
| 152 | A15 | 20c multi | 95 | 26 |
| a. | | Photo. ('77) | 2.25 | 60 |
| | | *Nos. 146-152 (7)* | 2.85 | 90 |

Flower Type of Johore, 1979, with Portrait of Sultan Idris Shah

**Wmk. 378**

**1979, Apr. 30 Litho. *Perf. 14½***

| No. | Type | Description | Unused | Used |
|---|---|---|---|---|
| 153 | A16 | 1c multi | 5 | 5 |
| 154 | A16 | 2c multi | 5 | 5 |
| 155 | A16 | 5c multi | 6 | 5 |
| a. | | Brt rose pink & yel flowers ('84) | 6 | 5 |
| 156 | A16 | 10c multi | 12 | 6 |
| a. | | White flowers ('84) | 12 | 6 |
| 157 | A16 | 15c multi | 18 | 9 |
| a. | | Unwmkd. ('85) | 3.25 | |
| 158 | A16 | 20c multi | 24 | 12 |
| 159 | A16 | 25c multi | 30 | 15 |
| | | *Nos. 153-159 (7)* | 1.00 | 57 |

Agriculture and State Arms Type of Johore with Tun Azlan Shah, Raja

**Wmk. 388**

**1986, Oct. 25 Litho. *Perf. 12***

| No. | Type | Description | Unused | Used |
|---|---|---|---|---|
| 160 | A19 | 1c multi | 5 | 5 |
| 161 | A19 | 2c multi | 5 | 5 |
| 162 | A19 | 5c multi | 5 | 5 |
| 163 | A19 | 10c multi | 8 | 5 |
| 164 | A19 | 15c multi | 12 | 6 |
| 165 | A19 | 20c multi | 16 | 8 |
| 166 | A19 | 30c multi | 24 | 12 |
| | | *Nos. 160-166 (7)* | 75 | 46 |

## PERLIS

Orchid Type of Johore, 1965, with Portrait of Regent Yang Teramat Mulia

**Wmk. 338**

**1965, Nov. 15 Photo. *Perf. 14½***

**Flowers in Natural Colors**

| No. | Type | Description | Unused | Used |
|---|---|---|---|---|
| 40 | A14 | 1c blk & lt grnsh bl | 5 | 5 |
| 41 | A14 | 2c blk, red & gray | 6 | 6 |
| 42 | A14 | 5c blk & Prus bl | 16 | 12 |
| 43 | A14 | 6c blk & lt lil | 20 | 16 |
| 44 | A14 | 10c blk & ultra | 30 | 24 |
| 45 | A14 | 15c blk, lil rose & grn | 50 | 50 |
| 46 | A14 | 20c blk & brn | 80 | 80 |
| | | *Nos. 40-46 (7)* | 2.07 | 1.93 |

Butterlfy Type of Johore, 1971, with Portrait of Sultan Syed Putra

***Perf. 13½x13***

**1971, Feb. 1 Litho. Unwmk.**

| No. | Type | Description | Unused | Used |
|---|---|---|---|---|
| 47 | A15 | 1c multi | 5 | 5 |
| 48 | A15 | 2c multi | 8 | 6 |
| 49 | A15 | 5c multi | 18 | 10 |
| a. | | Booklet pane of 4 ('73) | 75 | |
| 50 | A15 | 6c multi | 25 | 18 |
| 51 | A15 | 10c multi | 38 | 22 |
| a. | | Booklet pane of 4 ('73) | 1.65 | |
| b. | | Photo. ('77) | 10.00 | 10.00 |
| 52 | A15 | 15c multi | 65 | 40 |
| a. | | Booklet pane of 4 ('73) | 2.75 | |
| b. | | Photo. ('77) | 1.90 | 1.50 |
| 53 | A15 | 20c multi | 75 | 55 |
| a. | | Photo. ('77) | 8.50 | 8.50 |
| | | *Nos. 47-53 (7)* | 2.34 | 1.56 |

Sultan Syed Putra — A2

**1971, Mar. 28 Litho. *Perf. 13½x13***

| No. | Type | Description | Unused | Used |
|---|---|---|---|---|
| 54 | A2 | 10c sil, yel & blk | 18 | 18 |
| 55 | A2 | 15c sil, bl & blk | 35 | 35 |
| 56 | A2 | 50c sil, lt vio & blk | 1.10 | 1.10 |

25th anniversary of the installation of Syed Putra as Raja of Perlis. Sold throughout Malaysia on March 28, then only in Perlis.

Flower Type of Johore, 1979, with Portrait of Sultan Syed Putra

**Wmk. 378**

**1979, Apr. 30 Litho. *Perf. 14½***

| No. | Type | Description | Unused | Used |
|---|---|---|---|---|
| 57 | A16 | 1c multi | 5 | 5 |
| 58 | A16 | 2c multi | 5 | 5 |
| 59 | A16 | 5c multi | 6 | 5 |
| 60 | A16 | 10c multi | 12 | 6 |
| 61 | A16 | 15c multi | 18 | 9 |
| 62 | A16 | 20c multi | 24 | 12 |
| a. | | Unwmk. ('85) | 4.25 | |
| 63 | A16 | 25c multi | 30 | 15 |
| | | *Nos. 57-63 (7)* | 1.00 | 57 |

Agriculture and State Arms Type of Johore with Tuanku Syed Putra, Raja

**Wmk. 388**

**1986, Oct. 25 Litho. *Perf. 12***

| No. | Type | Description | Unused | Used |
|---|---|---|---|---|
| 64 | A19 | 1c multi | 5 | 5 |
| 65 | A19 | 2c multi | 5 | 5 |
| 66 | A19 | 5c multi | 5 | 5 |
| 67 | A19 | 10c multi | 8 | 5 |
| 68 | A19 | 15c multi | 12 | 6 |
| 69 | A19 | 20c multi | 16 | 8 |
| 70 | A19 | 30c multi | 24 | 12 |
| | | *Nos. 64-70 (7)* | 75 | 46 |

**Sabah, Sarawak**
**Stamps of types A14-A19 issued by Sabah and Sarawak are listed in the "S" section under those states.**

## SELANGOR

Orchid Type of Johore, 1965, with Portrait of Sultan Salahuddin Abdul Aziz Shah

**Wmk. 338**

**1965, Nov. 15 Photo. *Perf. 14½***

**Flowers in Natural Colors**

| No. | Type | Description | Unused | Used |
|---|---|---|---|---|
| 121 | A14 | 1c blk & lt grnsh bl | 5 | 5 |
| a. | | Watermark sideways ('70) | 16 | 12 |
| 122 | A14 | 2c blk, red & gray | 7 | 5 |
| a. | | Rose car omitted | | |
| 123 | A14 | 5c blk & Prus bl | 18 | 5 |
| 124 | A14 | 6c blk & lt lil | 22 | 5 |
| 125 | A14 | 10c blk & lt ultra | 32 | 5 |
| a. | | Watermark sideways ('70) | 52 | 35 |
| 126 | A14 | 15c blk, lil rose & grn | 42 | 12 |
| 127 | A14 | 20c blk & brn | 65 | 20 |
| a. | | Watermark sideways ('70) | 80 | 50 |
| | | *Nos. 121-127 (7)* | 1.91 | 57 |

Butterfly Type of Johore, 1971, with Portrait of Sultan Salahuddin

***Perf. 13½x13***

**1971, Feb. 1 Litho. Unwmk.**

| No. | Type | Description | Unused | Used |
|---|---|---|---|---|
| 128 | A15 | 1c multi | 5 | 5 |
| a. | | Photo. ('77) | 42 | 12 |
| 129 | A15 | 2c multi | 8 | 5 |
| 130 | A15 | 5c multi | 18 | 6 |
| a. | | Booklet pane of 4 ('73) | 75 | |
| b. | | Photo. ('77) | 60 | 20 |
| 131 | A15 | 6c multi | 25 | 7 |
| 132 | A15 | 10c multi | 38 | 12 |
| a. | | Booklet pane of 4 ('73) | 1.65 | |
| b. | | Photo. ('77) | 75 | 22 |
| 133 | A15 | 15c multi | 65 | 16 |
| a. | | Booklet pane of 4 ('73) | 2.75 | |
| b. | | Photo. ('77) | 1.65 | 50 |
| 134 | A15 | 20c multi | 75 | 20 |
| a. | | Photo. ('77) | 2.00 | 65 |
| | | *Nos. 128-134 (7)* | 2.34 | 71 |

Flower Type of Johore, 1979, with Portrait of Sultan Salahuddin Abdul Aziz Shah

**Wmk. 378**

**1979, Apr. 30 Litho. *Perf. 14½***

| No. | Type | Description | Unused | Used |
|---|---|---|---|---|
| 135 | A16 | 1c multi | 5 | 5 |
| 136 | A16 | 2c multi | 5 | 5 |
| 137 | A16 | 5c multi | 6 | 5 |
| a. | | Brt rose pink & yel flowers ('84) | 6 | 5 |
| 138 | A16 | 10c multi | 12 | 6 |
| a. | | Unwmkd. ('85) | 2.15 | |
| 139 | A16 | 15c multi | 20 | 10 |
| a. | | Unwmkd. ('84) | 3.25 | |
| 140 | A16 | 20c multi | 26 | 12 |
| a. | | Pale yel flowers ('84) | 26 | 12 |
| 141 | A16 | 25c multi | 32 | 16 |
| | | *Nos. 135-141 (7)* | 1.06 | 59 |

Agriculture and State Arms Type of Johore with Sultan Salahuddin Abdul Aziz Shah

**Wmk. 388**

**1986, Oct. 25 Litho. *Perf. 12***

| No. | Type | Description | Unused | Used |
|---|---|---|---|---|
| 142 | A19 | 1c multi | 5 | 5 |
| 143 | A19 | 2c multi | 5 | 5 |
| 144 | A19 | 5c multi | 5 | 5 |
| 145 | A19 | 10c multi | 8 | 5 |
| 146 | A19 | 15c multi | 12 | 6 |
| 147 | A19 | 20c multi | 16 | 8 |
| 148 | A19 | 30c multi | 24 | 12 |
| | | *Nos. 142-148 (7)* | 75 | 46 |

## TRENGGANU

Orchid Type of Johore, 1965, with Portrait of Sultan Ismail

**Wmk. 338**

**1965, Nov. 15 Photo. *Perf. 14½***

**Flowers in Natural Colors**

| No. | Type | Description | Unused | Used |
|---|---|---|---|---|
| 86 | A14 | 1c blk & lt grnsh bl | 5 | 5 |
| 87 | A14 | 2c blk, red & gray | 8 | 5 |
| 88 | A14 | 5c blk & Prus bl | 20 | 5 |
| 89 | A14 | 6c blk & lt lil | 25 | 5 |
| 90 | A14 | 10c blk & lt ultra | 35 | 9 |
| 91 | A14 | 15c blk, lil rose & grn | 50 | 18 |
| 92 | A14 | 20c blk & brn | 75 | 30 |
| | | *Nos. 86-92 (7)* | 2.18 | 77 |

Tuanku Ismail Nasiruddin — A6

*Perf. 14½x13½*

**1970, Dec. 16 Photo. Unwmk.**

| | | | | |
|---|---|---|---|---|
| *93* | A6 | 10c multi | 20 | 20 |
| *94* | A6 | 15c brt yel multi | 35 | 35 |
| *95* | A6 | 50c dp plum & multi | 1.10 | 1.10 |

Installation of Tuanku Ismail Nasiruddin Shah as Sultan of Trengganu, 25th anniversary.

Butterfly Type of Johore, 1971, with Portrait of Sultan Ismail Nasiruddin

*Perf. 13½x13*

**1971, Feb. 1 Litho. Unwmk.**

| | | | | |
|---|---|---|---|---|
| *96* | A15 | 1c multi | 5 | 5 |
| *97* | A15 | 2c multi | 8 | 5 |
| *98* | A15 | 5c multi | 20 | 12 |
| *a.* | | Booklet pane of 4 ('73) | 80 | |
| *b.* | | Photo. ('77) | 5.00 | 5.00 |
| *99* | A15 | 6c multi | 28 | 18 |
| *100* | A15 | 10c multi | 40 | 22 |
| *a.* | | Booklet pane of 4 ('73) | 1.65 | |
| *b.* | | Photo. ('77) | 1.25 | 1.25 |
| *101* | A15 | 15c multi | 70 | 38 |
| *a.* | | Booklet pane of 4 ('73) | 3.00 | |
| *b.* | | Photo. ('77) | 1.25 | 1.25 |
| *102* | A15 | 20c multi | 85 | 42 |
| | | *Nos. 96-102 (7)* | 2.56 | 1.42 |

Flower Type of Johore, 1979, with Portrait of Sultan Ismail Nasiruddin

**Wmk. 378**

**1979, Apr. 30 Litho. *Perf. 14½***

| | | | | |
|---|---|---|---|---|
| *103* | A16 | 1c multi | 5 | 5 |
| *104* | A16 | 2c multi | 5 | 5 |
| *105* | A16 | 5c multi | 6 | 5 |
| *106* | A16 | 10c multi | 12 | 6 |
| *107* | A16 | 15c multi | 18 | 9 |
| *a.* | | Unwmkd. ('86) | 3.25 | |
| *108* | A16 | 20c multi | 24 | 12 |
| *a.* | | Unwmkd. (86) | 4.25 | |
| *109* | A16 | 25c multi | 30 | 15 |
| *a.* | | Pale sal flowers ('84) | 30 | 15 |
| | | *Nos. 103-109 (7)* | 1.00 | 57 |

Agriculture and State Arms Type of Johore with Sultan Mahmud Al Marhum

**Wmk. 388**

**1986, Oct. 25 Litho. *Perf. 12***

| | | | | |
|---|---|---|---|---|
| *110* | A19 | 1c multi | 5 | 5 |
| *111* | A19 | 2c multi | 5 | 5 |
| *112* | A19 | 5c multi | 5 | 5 |
| *113* | A19 | 10c multi | 8 | 5 |
| *114* | A19 | 15c multi | 12 | 6 |
| *115* | A19 | 20c multi | 16 | 8 |
| *116* | A19 | 30c multi | 24 | 12 |

## WILAYAH PERSEKUTUAN

Agriculture and State Arms Type of Johore

**Wmk. 388**

**1986, Oct. 25 Litho. *Perf. 12***

| | | | | |
|---|---|---|---|---|
| *1* | A19 | 1c multi | 5 | 5 |
| *2* | A19 | 2c multi | 5 | 5 |
| *3* | A19 | 5c multi | 5 | 5 |
| *4* | A19 | 10c multi | 8 | 5 |
| *5* | A19 | 15c multi | 12 | 6 |
| *6* | A19 | 20c multi | 16 | 8 |
| *7* | A19 | 30c multi | 24 | 12 |
| | | *Nos. 1-7 (7)* | 75 | 46 |

## MALDIVE ISLANDS

LOCATION — A group of 2,000 islands in the Indian Ocean about 400 miles southwest of Ceylon.

GOVT. — Republic.

AREA — 115 sq. mi.

POP. — 168,000 (est. 1983).

CAPITAL — Male.

Maldive Islands was a British Protectorate, first as a dependency of Ceylon, then from 1948 as an independent sultanate, except for a year (1953) as a republic. The islands became completely independent on July 26, 1965, and became a republic again on November 11, 1968.

100 Cents = 1 Rupee

100 Larees = 1 Rupee (1951)

**Catalogue values for unused stamps in this country are for Never Hinged items, beginning with Scott 20.**

Stamps of Ceylon, 1904-05, Overprinted **MALDIVES**

**1906, Sept. 9 Wmk. 3 *Perf. 14***

| | | | | |
|---|---|---|---|---|
| *1* | A36 | 2c org brn | 10.00 | 12.00 |
| *2* | A37 | 3c green | 12.50 | 15.00 |
| *3* | A37 | 4c yel & bl | 25.00 | 37.50 |
| *4* | A38 | 5c dl lil | 5.00 | 5.00 |
| *5* | A40 | 15c ultra | 45.00 | 55.00 |
| *6* | A40 | 25c bister | 55.00 | 62.50 |
| | | *Nos. 1-6 (6)* | 152.50 | 187.00 |

Minaret of Juma Mosque, near Male — A1

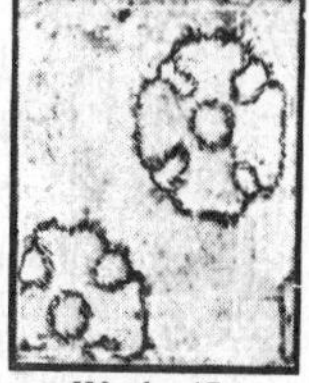

Wmk. 47- Multiple Rosette

**1909 Engr. Wmk. 47**

| | | | | |
|---|---|---|---|---|
| *7* | A1 | 2c org brn | 1.25 | 30 |
| *8* | A1 | 3c green | 35 | 30 |
| *9* | A1 | 5c red vio | 35 | 20 |
| *10* | A1 | 10c carmine | 50 | 35 |

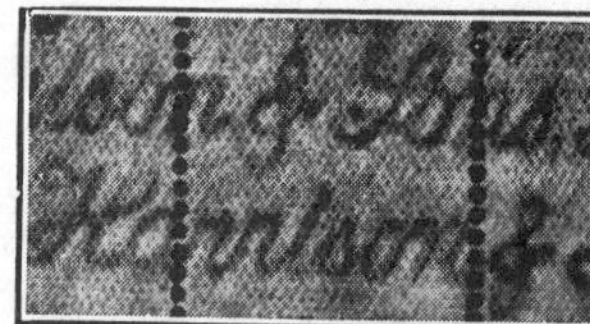

Wmk. 233- "Harrison & Sons, London" in Script

Type of 1909 Issue Redrawn

*Perf. 14½x14*

**1933 Photo. Wmk. 233**

| | | | | |
|---|---|---|---|---|
| *11* | A1 | 2c gray | 75 | 65 |
| *12* | A1 | 3c yel brn | 75 | 75 |
| *13* | A1 | 5c brn lake | 3.25 | 3.75 |
| *14* | A1 | 6c brn red | 2.50 | 2.50 |
| *15* | A1 | 10c green | 65 | 65 |
| *16* | A1 | 15c gray blk | 90 | 90 |
| *17* | A1 | 25c red brn | 1.65 | 1.65 |
| *18* | A1 | 50c red vio | 1.75 | 1.75 |
| *19* | A1 | 1r bl blk | 3.25 | 2.50 |
| | | *Nos. 11-19 (9)* | 15.45 | 15.10 |

On the 6c, 15c, 25c and 50c, the right hand panel carries only the word "CENTS".

Nos. 11-19 exist with watermark vert. or horiz. The 5c with vert. watermark sells for twice the price of the horiz. watermark.

**Catalogue values for unused stamps in this section, from this point to the end of the section, are for Never Hinged items.**

Palm Tree and Seascape — A2

Maldive Fish — A3

**Unwmk.**

**1950, Dec. 24 Engr. *Perf. 13***

| | | | | |
|---|---|---|---|---|
| *20* | A2 | 2 l ol grn | 90 | 90 |
| *21* | A2 | 3 l dp bl | 3.75 | 2.25 |
| *22* | A2 | 5 l dp bl grn | 3.75 | 2.50 |
| *23* | A2 | 6 l red brn | 60 | 60 |
| *24* | A2 | 10 l red | 60 | 60 |
| *25* | A2 | 15 l orange | 70 | 70 |
| *26* | A2 | 25 l rose vio | 75 | 75 |
| *27* | A2 | 50 l vio bl | 1.50 | 1.50 |
| *28* | A2 | 1r dk brn | 6.75 | 6.75 |
| | | *Nos. 20-28 (9)* | 19.30 | 16.55 |

**1952**

Design: 5 l, Urns.

| | | | | |
|---|---|---|---|---|
| *29* | A3 | 3 l dp bl | 30 | 30 |
| *30* | A3 | 5 l dk bl grn | 20 | 20 |

Harbor of Male — A4

Fort and Governor's Palace — A5

*Perf. 13½ (A4), 11½x11 (A5)*

**1956 Engr. Unwmk.**

| | | | | |
|---|---|---|---|---|
| *31* | A4 | 2 l lilac | 5 | 5 |
| *32* | A4 | 3 l gray grn | 5 | 5 |
| *33* | A4 | 5 l redsh brn | 5 | 5 |
| *34* | A4 | 6 l bl vio | 5 | 5 |
| *35* | A4 | 10 l lt grn | 6 | 6 |
| *36* | A4 | 15 l brown | 8 | 8 |
| *37* | A4 | 25 l rose red | 10 | 10 |
| *38* | A4 | 50 l orange | 20 | 20 |
| *39* | A5 | 1r lt grn | 40 | 40 |
| *40* | A5 | 5r ultra | 1.50 | 1.50 |
| *41* | A5 | 10r magenta | 2.50 | 2.50 |
| | | *Nos. 31-41 (11)* | 5.04 | 5.04 |

Bicyclists and Olympic Emblem A6

Design: 25 l, 50 l, 1r, Basketball (vert.).

*Perf. 11½x11, 11x11½*

**1960, Aug. 20 Engr.**

| | | | | |
|---|---|---|---|---|
| *42* | A6 | 2 l rose vio & grn | 5 | 5 |
| *43* | A6 | 3 l grnsh gray & plum | 5 | 5 |
| *44* | A6 | 5 l vio brn & dk bl | 7 | 7 |
| *45* | A6 | 10 l brt grn & brn | 8 | 8 |
| *46* | A6 | 15 l brn & bl | 10 | 10 |
| *47* | A6 | 25 l rose red & ol | 16 | 16 |
| *48* | A6 | 50 l org & dk vio | 30 | 30 |
| *49* | A6 | 1r brt grn & plum | 50 | 50 |
| | | *Nos. 42-49 (8)* | 1.31 | 1.31 |

Issued to commemorate the 17th Olympic Games, Rome, Aug. 25-Sept. 11.

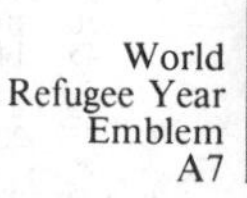

World Refugee Year Emblem A7

**1960, Oct. 15 *Perf. 11½x11***

| | | | | |
|---|---|---|---|---|
| *50* | A7 | 2 l org, vio & grn | 5 | 5 |
| *51* | A7 | 3 l grn, brn & red | 5 | 5 |
| *52* | A7 | 5 l sep, grn & red | 5 | 5 |
| *53* | A7 | 10 l dl pur, grn & red | 5 | 5 |
| *54* | A7 | 15 l gray grn, pur & red | 8 | 8 |
| *55* | A7 | 25 l redsh brn, ultra & ol | 15 | 15 |
| *56* | A7 | 50 l rose, ol & bl | 22 | 22 |
| *57* | A7 | 1r gray, car rose & vio | 35 | 35 |
| | | *Nos. 50-57 (8)* | 1.00 | 1.00 |

Issued to commemorate World Refugee Year, July 1, 1959-June 30, 1960.

Tomb of Sultan — A8

Designs: 3 l, Custom house. 5 l, Cowry shells. 6 l, Old royal palace. 10 l, Road to Minaret, Juma Mosque, Male. 15 l, Council house. 25 l, Government secretariat. 50 l, Prime minister's office. 1r, Tomb and sailboats. 5r, Tomb by the sea. 10r, Port.

**1960, Oct. 15 *Perf. 11½x11***

**Various Frames**

| | | | | |
|---|---|---|---|---|
| *58* | A8 | 2 l lilac | 5 | 5 |
| *59* | A8 | 3 l green | 5 | 5 |
| *60* | A8 | 5 l brn org | 5 | 5 |
| *61* | A8 | 6 l brt bl | 5 | 5 |
| *62* | A8 | 10 l car rose | 5 | 5 |
| *63* | A8 | 15 l sepia | 6 | 6 |
| *64* | A8 | 25 l dl vio | 8 | 8 |
| *65* | A8 | 50 l slate | 16 | 16 |
| *66* | A8 | 1r orange | 35 | 35 |
| *67* | A8 | 5r dk bl | 1.60 | 1.60 |
| *68* | A8 | 10r dl grn | 3.50 | 3.50 |
| | | *Nos. 58-68 (11)* | 6.00 | 6.00 |

Stamps in 25r, 50r and 100r denominations were also issued, but primarily for revenue purposes.

Coconuts — A9

Map of Male Showing Population Distribution A10

*Perf. 14x14½, 14½x14*

**1961, Apr. 20 Photo. Unwmk.**

**Coconuts in Ocher**

| | | | | |
|---|---|---|---|---|
| *69* | A9 | 2 l green | 5 | 5 |
| *70* | A9 | 3 l ultra | 5 | 5 |
| *71* | A9 | 5 l lil rose | 5 | 5 |
| *72* | A9 | 10 l red org | 6 | 6 |
| *73* | A9 | 15 l black | 8 | 8 |
| *74* | A10 | 25 l multi | 12 | 12 |
| *75* | A10 | 50 l multi | 25 | 25 |
| *76* | A10 | 1r multi | 45 | 45 |
| | | *Nos. 69-76 (8)* | 1.11 | 1.11 |

Pigeon and 5c Stamp of 1906 — A11

Designs: 10 l, 15 l, 20 l, Post horn and 3c stamp of 1906. 25 l, 50 l, 1r, Laurel branch and 2c stamp of 1906.

**1961, Sept. 9 *Perf. 14½x14***

| | | | | |
|---|---|---|---|---|
| *77* | A11 | 2 l vio bl & mar | 5 | 5 |
| *78* | A11 | 3 l vio bl & mar | 5 | 5 |
| *79* | A11 | 5 l vio bl & mar | 5 | 5 |
| *80* | A11 | 6 l vio bl & mar | 5 | 5 |
| *81* | A11 | 10 l mar & grn | 5 | 5 |
| *82* | A11 | 15 l mar & grn | 7 | 7 |
| *83* | A11 | 20 l mar & grn | 8 | 8 |
| *84* | A11 | 25 l grn, mar & blk | 10 | 10 |
| *85* | A11 | 50 l grn, mar & blk | 20 | 20 |
| *86* | A11 | 1r grn, mar & blk | 35 | 35 |
| *a* | | Souvenir sheet of 4 | 1.80 | 1.80 |
| | | *Nos. 77-86 (10)* | 1.05 | 1.05 |

55th anniv. of the 1st postage stamps of the Maldive Islands.

No. 86a contains 4 No. 86, with simulated perforations. Gray margins, black inscription. Size: 115x88mm.

Malaria Eradication Emblem — A12

**1962, Apr. 7 Engr. *Perf. 13½x13***

| | | | | |
|---|---|---|---|---|
| *87* | A12 | 2 l org brn | 5 | 5 |
| *88* | A12 | 3 l green | 5 | 5 |
| *89* | A12 | 5 l blue | 5 | 5 |
| *90* | A12 | 10 l vermilion | 6 | 6 |
| *91* | A12 | 15 l black | 10 | 10 |
| *92* | A12 | 25 l dk bl | 15 | 15 |
| *93* | A12 | 50 l green | 25 | 25 |
| *94* | A12 | 1r purple | 45 | 45 |
| | | *Nos. 87-94 (8)* | 1.16 | 1.16 |

WHO drive to eradicate malaria.

Children and Map of Far East and Americas A13

Design: 25 l, 50 l, 1r, 5r, Children and Map of Africa, Europe and Asia.

*Perf. 14½x14*

**1962, Sept. 9 Photo. Unwmk.**

**Children in Multicolor**

| | | | | |
|---|---|---|---|---|
| *95* | A13 | 2 l sepia | 5 | 5 |
| *96* | A13 | 6 l violet | 5 | 5 |
| *97* | A13 | 10 l dk grn | 5 | 5 |
| *98* | A13 | 15 l ultra | 5 | 5 |
| *99* | A13 | 25 l blue | 7 | 7 |
| *100* | A13 | 50 l brt grn | 14 | 14 |
| *101* | A13 | 1r rose cl | 28 | 28 |
| *102* | A13 | 5r emerald | 1.40 | 1.40 |
| | | *Nos. 95-102 (8)* | 2.09 | 2.09 |

15th anniv. of UNICEF.

Sultan Mohamed Farid Didi — A14

**1962, Nov. 29** *Perf. 14x14½*

**Portrait in Orange Brown and Sepia**

| | | | | |
|---|---|---|---|---|
| *103* | A14 | 3 l bluish grn | 5 | 5 |
| *104* | A14 | 5 l slate | 5 | 5 |
| *105* | A14 | 10 l blue | 5 | 5 |
| *106* | A14 | 20 l olive | 8 | 8 |
| *107* | A14 | 50 l dk car rose | 20 | 20 |
| *108* | A14 | 1r dk pur | 40 | 40 |
| | | *Nos. 103-108 (6)* | 83 | 83 |

9th anniv. of the enthronement of Sultan Mohamed Farid Didi.

Regal Angelfish, Sultan's Crest and Skin Diver — A15

Tropical Fish: 10 l, 25 l, Moorish idol. 50 l, Diadem squirrelfish. 1r, Surgeonfish. 5r, Orange butterflyfish.

**1963, Feb. 2** *Perf. 13½*

| | | | | |
|---|---|---|---|---|
| *109* | A15 | 2 l multi | 5 | 5 |
| *110* | A15 | 3 l multi | 5 | 5 |
| *111* | A15 | 5 l multi | 6 | 6 |
| *112* | A15 | 10 l multi | 12 | 12 |
| *113* | A15 | 25 l multi | 30 | 30 |
| *114* | A15 | 50 l multi | 60 | 60 |
| *115* | A15 | 1r multi | 1.25 | 1.25 |
| *116* | A15 | 5r multi | 6.00 | 6.00 |
| | | *Nos. 109-116 (8)* | 8.43 | 8.43 |

Fish in Net — A16

Design: 5 l, 10 l, 50 l, Wheat emblem and hand holding rice (vert.).

**1963, Mar. 21 Photo.** *Perf. 12*

| | | | | |
|---|---|---|---|---|
| *117* | A16 | 2 l grn & lt brn | 5 | 5 |
| *118* | A16 | 5 l dl rose & lt brn | 8 | 8 |
| *119* | A16 | 7 l grnsh bl & lt brn | 10 | 10 |
| *120* | A16 | 10 l bl & lt brn | 15 | 15 |
| *121* | A16 | 25 l brn red & lt brn | 45 | 45 |
| *122* | A16 | 50 l vio & lt brn | 90 | 90 |
| *123* | A16 | 1r rose cl & lt brn | 1.75 | 1.75 |
| | | *Nos. 117-123 (7)* | 3.48 | 3.48 |

Issued for the "Freedom from Hunger" campaign of the U.N. Food and Agriculture Organization.

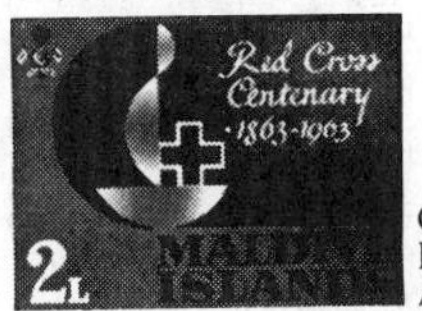

Centenary Emblem A17

**1963, Oct. Unwmk.** *Perf. 14x14½*

| | | | | |
|---|---|---|---|---|
| *124* | A17 | 2 l dl pur & red | 5 | 5 |
| *125* | A17 | 15 l sl grn & red | 6 | 6 |
| *126* | A17 | 50 l brn & red | 25 | 25 |
| *127* | A17 | 1r dk bl & red | 50 | 50 |
| *128* | A17 | 4r dk ol grn & red | 1.75 | 1.75 |
| | | *Nos. 124-128 (5)* | 2.61 | 2.61 |

Centenary of the International Red Cross.

Scout Emblem and Knot — A18

**1963, Dec. 7 Unwmk.** *Perf. 13½*

| | | | | |
|---|---|---|---|---|
| *129* | A18 | 2 l pur & dp grn | 5 | 5 |
| *130* | A18 | 3 l brn & dp grn | 5 | 5 |
| *131* | A18 | 25 l dk bl & dp grn | 10 | 10 |
| *132* | A18 | 1r dp car & dp grn | 40 | 40 |

Issued to commemorate the 11th Boy Scout Jamboree, Marathon, August, 1963. Printed in sheets of 12 (3x4) with ornamental borders and inscriptions.

Mosque at Male — A19

**Wmk. 314**

**1964, Aug. 10 Engr.** *Perf. 11½*

| | | | | |
|---|---|---|---|---|
| *133* | A19 | 2 l rose vio | 5 | 5 |
| *134* | A19 | 3 l green | 5 | 5 |
| *135* | A19 | 10 l car rose | 5 | 5 |
| *136* | A19 | 40 l blk brn | 16 | 16 |
| *137* | A19 | 60 l blue | 24 | 24 |
| *138* | A19 | 85 l org brn | 35 | 35 |
| | | *Nos. 133-138 (6)* | 90 | 90 |

Issued to commemorate the conversion of the Maldive Islanders to Mohammedanism in 1733 (1153 by Islamic calendar).

Shot Put and Maldive Arms A20

Design: 15 l, 25 l, 50 l, 1r, Runner and Maldive arms.

*Perf. 14x13½*

**1964, Oct. 6 Litho. Wmk. 314**

| | | | | |
|---|---|---|---|---|
| *139* | A20 | 2 l grnsh bl & dl vio | 5 | 5 |
| *140* | A20 | 3 l red brn & mar | 5 | 5 |
| *141* | A20 | 5 l dk grn & gray | 5 | 5 |
| *142* | A20 | 10 l plum & ind | 8 | 8 |
| *143* | A20 | 15 l bis brn & dk brn | 10 | 10 |
| *144* | A20 | 25 l dk bl & bluish blk | 16 | 16 |
| *145* | A20 | 50 l ol & blk | 32 | 32 |
| *146* | A20 | 1r gray & dk pur | 60 | 60 |
| *a* | | Souv. sheet of 3 | 2.00 | 2.00 |
| | | *Nos. 139-146 (8)* | 1.41 | 1.41 |

Issued to commemorate the 18th Olympic Games, Tokyo, Oct. 10-25. No. 146a contains 3 imperf. stamps similar to Nos. 144-146. Gray margin with black inscription. Size: 125x140mm.

General Electric Observation Communication Satellite — A21

*Perf. 14½*

**1965, July 1 Photo. Unwmk.**

| | | | | |
|---|---|---|---|---|
| *147* | A21 | 5 l dark blue | 8 | 8 |
| *148* | A21 | 10 l brown | 18 | 18 |
| *149* | A21 | 25 l green | 45 | 45 |
| *150* | A21 | 1r magenta | 1.75 | 1.75 |

Issued to commemorate the Quiet Sun Year, 1964-65. Printed in sheets of 9 (3x3) with ornamental borders and inscriptions.

Queen Nefertari Holding Sistrum and Papyrus — A22

Designs: 3 l, 10 l, 25 l, 1r, Ramses II.

**1965, Sept. 1 Litho. Wmk. 314**

| | | | | |
|---|---|---|---|---|
| *151* | A22 | 2 l dl bl grn & mar | 5 | 5 |
| *152* | A22 | 3 l lake & grn | 5 | 5 |
| *153* | A22 | 5 l grn & lake | 5 | 5 |
| *154* | A22 | 10 l dk bl & ocher | 6 | 6 |
| *155* | A22 | 15 l redsh brn & ind | 9 | 9 |
| *156* | A22 | 25 l dl lil & ind | 15 | 15 |
| *157* | A22 | 50 l grn & brn | 30 | 30 |
| *158* | A22 | 1r brn & grn | 60 | 60 |
| | | *Nos. 151-158 (8)* | 1.35 | 1.35 |

UNESCO world campaign to save historic monuments in Nubia.

John F. Kennedy and Doves A23

Design: 1r, 2r, President Kennedy and hands holding olive branches.

**Unwmk.**

**1965, Oct. 1 Photo.** *Perf. 12*

| | | | | |
|---|---|---|---|---|
| *159* | A23 | 2 l sl & brt pink | 5 | 5 |
| *160* | A23 | 5 l brn & brt pink | 5 | 5 |
| *161* | A23 | 25 l bl blk & brt pink | 7 | 7 |
| *162* | A23 | 1r red lil, yel & grn | 28 | 28 |
| *163* | A23 | 2r sl grn, yel & grn | 55 | 55 |
| *a* | | Souv. sheet of 4 | 3.75 | 3.75 |
| | | *Nos. 159-163 (5)* | 1.00 | 1.00 |

Issued in memory of President John F. Kennedy (1917-63). No. 163a contains four imperf. stamps similar to No. 163. Olive margin with slate green inscription. Size: 149x130mm.

U.N. Flag — A24

**1965, Nov. 24 Photo.** *Perf. 12*

**Flag in Aquamarine**

| | | | | |
|---|---|---|---|---|
| *164* | A24 | 3 l red brn | 5 | 5 |
| *165* | A24 | 10 l violet | 5 | 5 |
| *166* | A24 | 1r dk ol brn | 50 | 50 |

20th anniversary of the United Nations.

ICY Emblem A25

**1965, Dec. 20 Photo.** *Perf. 12*

| | | | | |
|---|---|---|---|---|
| *167* | A25 | 5 l bis & dk brn | 5 | 5 |
| *168* | A25 | 15 l dl vio & dk brn | 7 | 7 |
| *169* | A25 | 50 l ol & dk brn | 22 | 22 |
| *170* | A25 | 1r org & dk brn | 45 | 45 |
| *171* | A25 | 2r bl & dk brn | 90 | 90 |
| *a* | | Souv. sheet of 3 | 2.25 | 2.25 |
| | | *Nos. 167-171 (5)* | 1.69 | 1.69 |

Issued for the International Cooperation Year, 1965. No. 171a contains three imperf. stamps with simulated perforation similar to Nos. 169-171. Bister margin with dark brown inscription. Size: 100x125mm.

Sea Shells — A26

Reinwardtia Trigynia — A27

Designs (Coat of Arms and): 2 l, 10 l, 30 l, No. 181, Conus alicus and cymatium maldiviensis (shells). 5 l, 10r, Conus litteratus and distorsia reticulata (shells). 7 l, No. 182, 2r, India-rubber vine flowers. 15 l, 50 l, 5r, Crab plover and gull. 3 l, 20 l, 1.50r, Reinwardtia trigynia.

**1966, June 1 Unwmk.** *Perf. 12*

| | | | | |
|---|---|---|---|---|
| *172* | A26 | 2 l ol, org & brn | 5 | 5 |
| *173* | A27 | 3 l dk pur, grn & yel | 5 | 5 |
| *174* | A26 | 5 l bl, lil & buff | 5 | 5 |
| *175* | A27 | 7 l brn, grn & rose car | 5 | 5 |
| *176* | A26 | 10 l rose brn, brn & org | 7 | 7 |
| *177* | A26 | 15 l dk sl grn, blk, yel grn & pink | 10 | 10 |
| *178* | A27 | 20 l dk ol grn, grn & yel | 16 | 16 |
| *179* | A26 | 30 l lt brn, brn & org | 22 | 22 |
| *180* | A26 | 50 l multi | 40 | 40 |
| *181* | A26 | 1r rose lil, brn & org | 80 | 80 |
| *182* | A27 | 1r dk bl, grn & rose car | 80 | 80 |
| *183* | A27 | 1.50r rose brn, grn & yel | 1.20 | 1.20 |
| *184* | A27 | 2r dk bl grn, grn & car | 1.60 | 1.60 |
| *185* | A26 | 5r multi | 4.00 | 4.00 |
| *186* | A26 | 10r brn, lil & buff | 8.00 | 8.00 |
| | | *Nos. 172-186 (15)* | 17.55 | 17.55 |

For unused stamps, more recent issues are valued as never hinged, with the beginning point determined on a country-by-country basis. Notes to show the beginning points are prominently placed in the text.

Flag A28

**1966, July 26** *Perf. 14x14½*

| | | | | |
|---|---|---|---|---|
| *187* | A28 | 10 l grnsh bl, red & grn | 5 | 5 |
| *188* | A28 | 1r ocher, brn, red & grn | 50 | 50 |

Issued to commemorate the first anniversary of full independence from Great Britain.

Luna 9 on Moon — A29

Designs: 25 l, 1r, 5r, Gemini 6 and 7, rendezvous in space. 2r, Gemini spaceship as seen from second Gemini spaceship.

**1966, Nov. 1 Litho.** *Perf. 15x14*

| | | | | |
|---|---|---|---|---|
| *189* | A29 | 10 l gray bl, lt brn & ultra | 5 | 5 |
| *190* | A29 | 25 l car rose & grn | 10 | 10 |
| *191* | A29 | 50 l grn & dp org | 20 | 20 |
| *192* | A29 | 1r org brn & grnsh bl | 45 | 45 |
| *193* | A29 | 2r vio & grn | 90 | 90 |
| *194* | A29 | 5r Prus bl & pink | 2.25 | 2.25 |
| *a* | | Souv. sheet of 3 | 4.25 | 4.25 |
| | | *Nos. 189-194 (6)* | 3.95 | 3.95 |

Issued to commemorate the rendezvous in space of Gemini 6 and 7 (U.S.A.), Dec. 4, 1965, and the soft landing on Moon by Luna 9 (U.S.S.R.), Feb. 3, 1966. No. 194a contains 3 imperf. stamps similar to Nos. 192-194 with simulated perforations. Greenish blue margin shows trajectories of space craft and inscription describing rendezvous in space. Size: 108x126mm.

UNESCO Emblem, Owl and Book — A30

20th anniv. of UNESCO: 3 l, 1r, Microscope, globe and communication waves. 5 l, 5r, Palette, violin and mask.

**1966, Nov. 15 Litho.** *Perf. 15x14*

| | | | | |
|---|---|---|---|---|
| *195* | A30 | 2 l grn & multi | 5 | 5 |
| *196* | A30 | 3 l lt vio & multi | 5 | 5 |
| *197* | A30 | 5 l org & multi | 5 | 5 |
| *198* | A30 | 50 l rose & multi | 30 | 30 |
| *199* | A30 | 1r cit & multi | 60 | 60 |
| *200* | A30 | 5r multi | 3.00 | 3.00 |
| | | *Nos. 195-200 (6)* | 4.05 | 4.05 |

Winston Churchill and Coffin on Gun Carriage — A31

Designs: 10 l, 25 l, 1r, Churchill and catafalque.

**1967, Jan. 1** *Perf. 14½x13½*

| | | | | |
|---|---|---|---|---|
| *201* | A31 | 2 l ol grn, red & dk bl | 5 | 5 |
| *202* | A31 | 10 l Prus grn, red & dk bl | 12 | 12 |
| *203* | A31 | 15 l grn, red & dk bl | 15 | 15 |
| *204* | A31 | 25 l vio, red & dk bl | 25 | 25 |
| *205* | A31 | 1r brn, red & dk bl | 1.00 | 1.00 |
| *206* | A31 | 2.50r brn lake, red & dk bl | 2.50 | 2.50 |
| | | *Nos. 201-206 (6)* | 4.07 | 4.07 |

Sir Winston Spencer Churchill (1874-1965), statesman and World War II leader.

Soccer and Jules Rimet Cup — A32

Designs: 3 l, 5 l, 25 l, 50 l, 1r, Various scenes from soccer and Jules Rimet Cup. 2r, British flag, Games' emblem and Big Ben Tower, London.

*Perf. 14x13½*

**1967, Mar. 22 Photo. Unwmk.**

| | | | | |
|---|---|---|---|---|
| *207* | A32 | 2 l ver & multi | 5 | 5 |
| *208* | A32 | 3 l ol & multi | 5 | 5 |
| *209* | A32 | 5 l brt pur & multi | 5 | 5 |
| *210* | A32 | 25 l brt grn & multi | 18 | 18 |
| *211* | A32 | 50 l org & multi | 40 | 40 |
| *212* | A32 | 1r brt bl & multi | 75 | 75 |
| *213* | A32 | 2r brn & multi | 1.50 | 1.50 |
| *a* | | Souvenir sheet of 3 | 2.50 | 2.50 |
| | | *Nos. 207-213 (7)* | 2.98 | 2.98 |

Issued to commemorate England's victory in the World Soccer Cup Championship. No. 213a contains 3 imperf. stamps similar to No. 211-213. Gray margin with black inscription and British flag. Size: 101x126mm.

Clown Butterflyfish — A33

Tropical Fish: 3 l, 1r, Four-saddled puffer. 5 l, Indo-Pacific blue trunkfish. 6 l, Striped triggerfish. 50 l, 2r, Blue angelfish.

**1967, May 1 Photo.** *Perf. 14*

| | | | | |
|---|---|---|---|---|
| *214* | A33 | 2 l brt vio & multi | 5 | 5 |
| *215* | A33 | 3 l emer & multi | 5 | 5 |
| *216* | A33 | 5 l org brn & multi | 5 | 5 |
| *217* | A33 | 6 l brt bl & multi | 5 | 5 |
| *218* | A33 | 50 l ol & multi | 25 | 25 |
| *219* | A33 | 1r rose red & multi | 50 | 50 |
| *220* | A33 | 2r org & multi | 1.00 | 1.00 |
| | | *Nos. 214-220 (7)* | 1.95 | 1.95 |

Plane at Hulule Airport — A34

Designs: 5 l, 15 l, 50 l, 10r, Plane over administration building, Hulule Airport.

**1967, July 26** *Perf. 14x13½*

| | | | | |
|---|---|---|---|---|
| *221* | A34 | 2 l cit & lil | 5 | 5 |
| *222* | A34 | 5 l vio & grn | 5 | 5 |
| *223* | A34 | 10 l lt grn & lil | 5 | 5 |
| *224* | A34 | 15 l yel bis & grn | 7 | 7 |
| *225* | A34 | 30 l sky bl & vio bl | 12 | 12 |
| *226* | A34 | 50 l brt pink & brn | 20 | 20 |
| *227* | A34 | 5r org & vio bl | 1.75 | 1.75 |
| *228* | A34 | 10r lt ultra & dp brn | 3.50 | 3.50 |
| | | *Nos. 221-228 (8)* | 5.79 | 5.79 |

Man and Music Pavilion and EXPO '67 Emblem — A35

Designs: 5 l, 50 l, 2r, Man and his Community Pavilion and EXPO '67 emblem.

*Perf. 14x13½*

**1967, Oct. 1 Photo. Unwmk.**

**EXPO '67 Emblem in Gold**

| | | | | |
|---|---|---|---|---|
| *229* | A35 | 2 l ol gray, ol & brt rose | 5 | 5 |
| *230* | A35 | 5 l ultra, grnsh bl & brn | 5 | 5 |
| *231* | A35 | 10 l brn red, lt grn & red org | 5 | 5 |
| *232* | A35 | 50 l brn, grnsh bl & org | 20 | 20 |
| *233* | A35 | 1r vio, grn & rose lil | 40 | 40 |
| *234* | A35 | 2r dk grn, emer & red brn | 80 | 80 |
| *a* | | Souv. sheet of 2 | 1.50 | 1.50 |
| | | *Nos. 229-234 (6)* | 1.55 | 1.55 |

Issued to commemorate EXPO '67 International Exhibition, Montreal, Apr. 28-Oct. 27. No. 234a contains 2 imperf. stamps similar to Nos. 233-234 with simulated perforations. Green margin contains design and inscription in gold and dark green. Size: 101x135mm.

Nos. 221-228 Overprinted in Gold: "International Tourist Year 1967"

**1967, Dec. 1 Photo.** *Perf. 14x13½*

| | | | | |
|---|---|---|---|---|
| *235* | A34 | 2 l cit & lil | 5 | 5 |
| *236* | A34 | 5 l vio & grn | 5 | 5 |
| *237* | A34 | 10 l lt grn & lil | 5 | 5 |
| *238* | A34 | 15 l yel bis & grn | 7 | 7 |
| *239* | A34 | 30 l sky bl & vio bl | 12 | 12 |
| *240* | A34 | 50 l brt pink & brn | 20 | 20 |
| *241* | A34 | 5r org & vio bl | 1.75 | 1.75 |
| *242* | A34 | 10r lt ultra & dp brn | 3.50 | 3.50 |
| | | *Nos. 235-242 (8)* | 5.79 | 5.79 |

The overprint is in 3 lines on the 2 l, 10 l, 30 l, 5r; one line on the 5 l, 15 l, 50 l, 10r.

Lord Baden-Powell, Wolf Cubs, Campfire and Flag Signals — A36

Designs: 3 l, 1r, Lord Baden-Powell, Boy Scout saluting and drummer.

**1968, Jan. 1 Litho.** *Perf. 14x14½*

| | | | | |
|---|---|---|---|---|
| *243* | A36 | 2 l yel, brn & grn | 5 | 5 |
| *244* | A36 | 3 l lt bl, ultra & rose car | 5 | 5 |
| *245* | A36 | 25 l dp org, red brn & vio bl | 22 | 22 |
| *246* | A36 | 1r yel grn, grn & red brn | 90 | 90 |

Issued to honor the Boy Scouts. Sheets of 12 (4x3) with decorative border.

French Satellites D-1 and A-1 — A37

Designs: 3 l, 25 l, Luna 10, USSR. 7 l, 1r, Orbiter and Mariner, USA. 10 l, 2r, Edward White, Virgil Grissom and Roger Chaffee, USA. 5r, Astronaut V. M. Komarov, USSR.

**1968, Jan. 27 Photo.** *Perf. 14*

| | | | | |
|---|---|---|---|---|
| *247* | A37 | 2 l dp ultra & brt pink | 5 | 5 |
| *248* | A37 | 3 l dk ol bis & vio | 5 | 5 |
| *249* | A37 | 7 l rose car & ol | 5 | 5 |
| *250* | A37 | 10 l blk, gray & dk bl | 5 | 5 |
| *251* | A37 | 25 l pur & brt grn | 10 | 10 |
| *252* | A37 | 50 l brn org bl | 20 | 20 |
| *253* | A37 | 1r dk sl grn & vio brn | 40 | 40 |
| *254* | A37 | 2r blk, bl & dk brn | 80 | 80 |
| *a* | | Souv. sheet of 2 | 1.75 | 1.75 |
| *255* | A37 | 5r blk, tan & lil rose | 2.00 | 2.00 |
| | | *Nos. 247-255 (9)* | 3.70 | 3.70 |

Issued to honor international achievements in space and to honor American and Russian astronauts, who gave their lives during space explorations in 1967. No. 254a contains 2 imperf. stamps similar to Nos. 253-254. Red and black margin showing Apollo rocket and commemorative inscription. Size: 109x154mm.

Shot Put — A38

Design: 6 l, 15 l, 2.50r, Discus.

**1968, Feb. Litho.** *Perf. 14½*

| | | | | |
|---|---|---|---|---|
| *256* | A38 | 2 l emer & multi | 5 | 5 |
| *257* | A38 | 6 l dl yel & multi | 5 | 5 |
| *258* | A38 | 10 l multi | 8 | 8 |
| *259* | A38 | 15 l org & multi | 12 | 12 |
| *260* | A38 | 1r bl & multi | 80 | 80 |
| *261* | A38 | 2.50r rose & multi | 2.00 | 2.00 |
| | | *Nos. 256-261 (6)* | 3.10 | 3.10 |

Issued to publicize the 19th Olympic Games, Mexico City, Oct. 12-27.

On the Adria, by Charles P. Bonington — A39

Seascapes: 1r, Ulysses Deriding Polyphemus (detail), by Joseph M. W. Turner. 2r, Sailboat at Argenteuil, by Claude Monet. 5r, Fishing Boats at Saintes-Maries, by Vincent Van Gogh.

**1968, Apr. 1 Photo.** *Perf. 14*

| | | | | |
|---|---|---|---|---|
| *262* | A39 | 50 l ultra & multi | 25 | 25 |
| *263* | A39 | 1r dk grn & multi | 55 | 55 |
| *264* | A36 | 2r multi | 1.10 | 1.10 |
| *265* | A39 | 5r multi | 2.75 | 2.75 |

Montgolfier Balloon, 1783, and Zeppelin LZ-130, 1928 — A40

History of Aviation: 3 l, 1r, Douglas DC-3, 1933, and Boeing 707, 1958. 5 l, 50 l, Lilienthal's glider, 1892, and Wright brothers' plane, 1905. 7 l, 2r, British-French Concorde and Supersonic Boeing 733, 1968.

**1968, June 1 Photo.** *Perf. 14x13*

| | | | | |
|---|---|---|---|---|
| *266* | A40 | 2 l yel grn, ultra & bis brn | 5 | 5 |
| *267* | A40 | 3 l org brn, grnsh bl & lil | 5 | 5 |
| *268* | A40 | 5 l grnsh bl, sl grn & lil | 5 | 5 |
| *269* | A40 | 7 l org, cl & ultra | 5 | 5 |
| *270* | A40 | 10 l rose lil, bl & brn | 5 | 5 |
| *271* | A40 | 50 l ol, sl grn & mag | 25 | 25 |
| *272* | A40 | 1r ver, bl & emer | 50 | 50 |
| *273* | A40 | 2r ultra, ol & brn vio | 1.50 | 1.00 |
| | | *Nos. 266-273 (8)* | 2.50 | 2.00 |

Issued in sheets of 12.

WHO Headquarters, Geneva — A41

**1968, July 15 Litho. *Perf. 14½x13***

*274* A41 10 l grnsh bl, bl grn & vio 5 5
*275* A41 25 l org, ocher & grn 12 12
*276* A41 1r emer, brt grn & brn 50 50
*277* A41 2r rose lil, dp rose lil & dk bl 1.00 1.00

20th anniv. of WHO.

Nos. 243-246 Overprinted: "International / Boy Scout Jamboree, / Farragut Park, Idaho, / U.S.A. / August 1-9, 1967"

**1968, Aug. 1 *Perf. 14x14½***

*278* A36 2 l yel, brn & grn 5 5
*279* A36 3 l lt bl, ultra & rose car 5 5
*280* A36 25 l dp org, red brn & vio bl 25 25
*281* A36 1r yel grn, grn & red brn 1.00 1.00

1st anniv. of the Intl. Boy Scout Jamboree in Farragut State Park, ID.

Marine Snail Shells — A42

Designs: 2 l, 50 l, Common curlew and redshank. 1r, Angel wings (clam shell) and marine snail shell.

**1968, Sept. 24 Photo. *Perf. 14x13***

*282* A42 2 l ultra & multi 5 5
*283* A42 10 l brn & multi 6 5
*284* A42 25 l multi 20 15
*285* A42 50 l multi 40 30
*286* A42 1r multi 75 60
*287* A42 2r multi 1.50 1.20
*Nos. 282-287 (6)* 2.96 2.35

Discus A43

Designs: 50 l, Runner. 1r, Bicycling. 2r, Basketball.

**1968, Oct. 12 *Perf. 14***

*288* A43 10 l ultra & multi 8 8
*289* A43 50 l multi 40 40
*290* A43 1r plum & multi 80 80
*291* A43 2r vio & multi 1.60 1.60

Issued to commemorate the 19th Olympic Games, Mexico City, Oct. 12-27.

**Republic**

Dhow A44

Design: 1r, Coat of arms, map and flag of Maldive Islands.

***Perf. 14x14½***

**1968, Nov. 11 Photo. Unwmk.**

*292* A44 10 l yel grn, ultra & dk brn 5 5
*293* A44 1r ultra, red & emer 1.10 75

Issued for Republic Day.

The Thinker, by Auguste Rodin — A45

Rodin Sculptures and UNESCO Emblem: 10 l, Hands. 1.50r, Sister and Brother. 2.50r, The Prodigal Son.

**1969, Apr. 10 Photo. *Perf. 13½***

*294* A45 6 l emer & multi 5 5
*295* A45 10 l multi 5 5
*296* A45 1.50r brt bl & multi 50 50
*297* A45 2.50r multi 85 85
*a* Souv. sheet of 2 2.50 2.50

Issued for Intl. Human Rights Year and to honor UNESCO.

No. 297a contains 2 imperf. stamps similar to Nos. 296-297. Gray olive and black margin with white commemorative inscription. Size: 111x130½mm.

Astronaut Gathering Rock Samples on Moon A46

Designs: 6 l, Lunar landing module. 1.50r, Astronaut on steps of module. 2.50r, Astronaut with television camera.

**1969, Sept. 25 Litho. *Perf. 14***

*298* A46 6 l multi 5 5
*299* A46 10 l multi 5 5
*300* A46 1.50r multi 1.00 1.00
*301* A46 2.50r multi 1.60 1.60
*a* Souvenir sheet of 4 2.25 2.25

Issued to commemorate man's first moon landing. See note after U.S. No. C76.

Exist imperf.

No. 301a contains stamps similar to Nos. 298-301, with designs transposed on 10 l and 2.50r. Greenish margin with commemorative inscriptions and U.S. flag. Simulated perfs. Size: 100x129mm.

Nos. 289-290 Overprinted: "REPUBLIC OF MALDIVES" and Commemorative Inscriptions

Designs: 50 l, overprinted "Gold Medal Winner / Mohamed Gammoudi / 5000m. run / Tunisia". 1r, overprinted "Gold Medal Winner / P. Trentin—Cycling / France."

**1969, Dec. 10 Photo. *Perf. 14***

*302* A43 50 l multi 30 30
*303* A43 1r multi 60 60

Issued to honor 2 gold medal winners in the 1968 Olympic Games: Mohamed Gammoudi, Tunisia, 5000m. run, and Pierre Trentin, France, Bicycling.

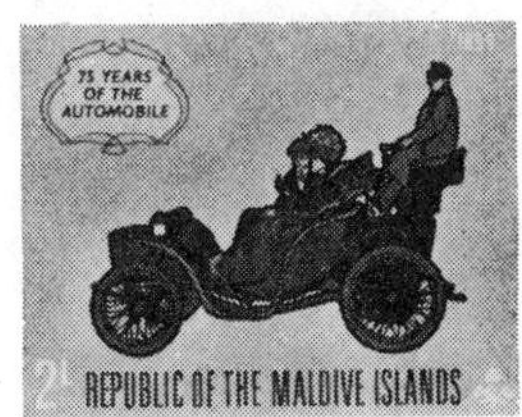


Columbia Daumon Victoria, 1899 — A47

Automobiles (pre-1908): 5 l, 50 l, Duryea Phaeton, 1902. 7 l, 1r, Packard S.24, 1906. 10 l, 2r, Autocar Runabout, 1907. 25 l, like 2 l.

**1970, Feb. 1 Litho. *Perf. 12***

*304* A47 2 l multi 5 5
*305* A47 5 l brt pink & multi 5 5
*306* A47 7 l ultra & multi 5 5
*307* A47 10 l ver & multi 8 5
*308* A47 25 l ocher & multi 15 12
*309* A47 50 l ol & multi 30 25
*310* A47 1r org & multi 62 50
*311* A47 2r multi 1.25 1.00
*a* Souvenir sheet of 2 2.50 2.00
*Nos. 304-311 (8)* 2.55 2.07

Exist imperf.

No. 311a contains stamps similar to Nos. 310-311, perf. 11½. Gray olive margin with black inscription. Size: 95x143 mm.

Orange Butterflyfish — A48

Fish: 5 l, Spotted triggerfish. 25 l, Spotfin turkeyfish. 50 l, Forceps fish. 1r, Imperial angelfish. 2r, Regal angelfish.

**1970, Mar. 1 Litho. *Perf. 10½***

*312* A48 2 l bl & multi 5 5
*313* A48 5 l org & multi 5 5
*314* A48 25 l emer & multi 15 12
*315* A48 50 l brt pink & multi 30 25
*316* A48 1r lt vio bl & multi 62 50
*317* A48 2r ol & multi 1.25 1.00
*Nos. 312-317 (6)* 2.42 1.97

UN Headquarters, New York and UN Emblem — A49

25th anniv. of the UN: 10 l, Surgeons, nurse and WHO emblem. 25 l, Student, performer, musician and UNESCO emblem. 50 l, Children reading and playing, and UNICEF emblem. 1r, Lamb, cock, fish, grain and FAO emblem. 2r, Miner and ILO emblem.

**1970, June 26 Litho. *Perf. 13½***

*318* A49 2 l multi 5 5
*319* A49 10 l multi 5 5
*320* A49 25 l multi 12 12
*321* A49 50 l multi 25 25
*322* A49 1r multi 55 55
*323* A49 2r multi 1.10 1.10
*Nos. 318-323 (6)* 2.12 2.12

IMCO Emblem, Buoy and Ship — A50

EXPO Emblem and Australian Pavilion — A51

Design: 1r, Lighthouse and ship.

**1970, July 26 Litho. *Perf. 13½***

*324* A50 50 l multi 25 20
*325* A50 1r multi 50 40

10th anniv. of the Intergovernmental Maritime Consultative Organization (IMCO).

**1970, Aug. 1 *Perf. 13½x14***

Designs (EXPO Emblem and): 3 l, West German pavilion. 10 l, U.S. pavilion. 25 l, British pavilion. 50 l, Russian pavilion. 1r, Japanese pavilion.

*326* A51 2 l grn & multi 5 5
*327* A51 3 l vio & multi 5 5
*328* A51 10 l brn & multi 5 5
*329* A51 25 l multi 15 15
*330* A51 50 l cl & multi 30 30
*331* A51 1r ultra & multi 60 60
*Nos. 326-331 (6)* 1.20 1.20

EXPO '70 International Exhibition, Osaka, Japan, Mar. 15-Sept. 13, 1970.

Guitar Player, by Watteau — A52

Paintings: 7 l, Guitar Player in Spanish Costume, by Edouard Manet. 50 l, Guitar-playing Clown, by Antoine Watteau. 1r, Mandolin Player and Singers, by Lorenzo Costa (inscribed Ercole Roberti). 2.50r, Guitar Player and Lady, by Watteau. 5r, Mandolin Player, by Frans Hals.

**1970, Aug. 1 Litho. *Perf. 14***

*332* A52 3 l gray & multi 5 5
*333* A52 7 l yel & multi 5 5
*334* A52 50 l multi 20 20
*335* A52 1r multi 40 40
*336* A52 2.50r multi 1.00 1.00
*337* A52 5r multi 2.00 2.00
*a* Souvenir sheet of 2 4.25 4.25
*Nos. 332-337 (6)* 3.70 3.70

No. 337a contains 2 stamps similar to Nos. 336-337 but rouletted 13 and printed se-tenant; pale green decorative margin inscribed "The Guitar Through the Ages." Size: 132x81mm.

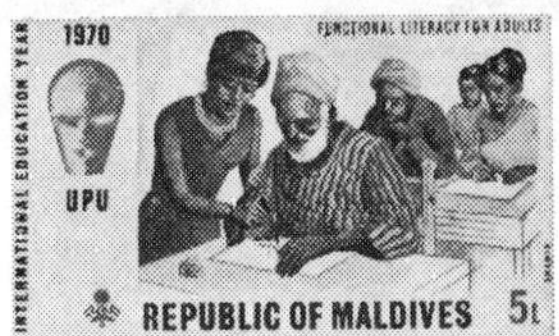


Education Year Emblem and Adult Education — A53

Designs (Education Year Emblem and): 10 l, Teacher training. 25 l, Geography class. 50 l, Classroom. 1r, Instruction by television.

**1970, Sept. 7 Litho. *Perf. 14***

*338* A53 5 l multi 5 5
*339* A53 10 l multi 5 5
*340* A53 25 l multi 15 15
*341* A53 50 l multi 30 30
*342* A53 1r multi 62 62
*Nos. 338-342 (5)* 1.17 1.17

Issued for International Education Year.

Nos. 299-301 Overprinted in Silver: "Philympia / London 1970"

**1970, Sept. 18**

*343* A46 10 l multi 5 5
*344* A46 1.50r multi 75 75
*345* A46 2.50r multi 1.25 1.25

Issued to commemorate Philympia 1970, London Philatelic Exhibition, Sept. 18-26.

This overprint was also applied to No. 301a. Value $2.25.

The only foreign revenue stamps listed in this Catalogue are those authorized for prepayment of postage.

Soccer Play, Rimet Cup — A54

Boy Holding UNICEF Flag — A55

Designs: Various Soccer Scenes, and Rimet Cup.

**1970 Litho. *Perf. 13½***

| | | | | |
|---|---|---|---|---|
| *346* | A54 | 3 l emer & multi | 5 | 5 |
| *347* | A54 | 6 l rose lil & multi | 5 | 5 |
| *348* | A54 | 7 l dp org & multi | 5 | 5 |
| *349* | A54 | 25 l bl & multi | 15 | 15 |
| *350* | A54 | 1r ol & multi | 60 | 60 |
| | | *Nos. 346-350 (5)* | 90 | 90 |

Jules Rimet 9th World Soccer Championships, Mexico City, May 30-June 21.

**1971, Apr. 1 Litho. *Perf. 12***

Design: 10 l, 2r, Girl holding balloon with UNICEF emblem.

| | | | | |
|---|---|---|---|---|
| *351* | A55 | 5 l pink & multi | 5 | 5 |
| *352* | A55 | 10 l lt bl & multi | 5 | 5 |
| *353* | A55 | 1r yel & multi | 50 | 50 |
| *354* | A55 | 2r pale lil & multi | 1.00 | 1.00 |

25th anniv. of UNICEF.

Astronauts Swigert, Lovell and Haise — A56

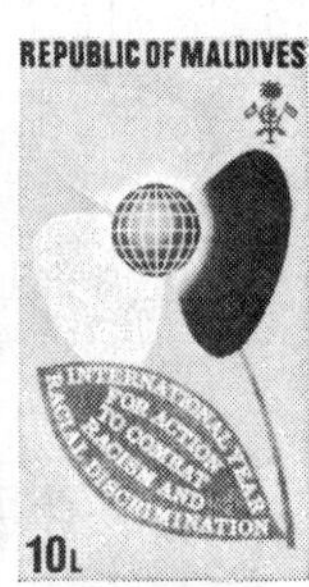

Flowers Symbolizing Races and World — A57

Designs: 20 l, Spacecraft and landing module. 1r, Capsule and boat in Pacific Ocean.

**1971, Apr. 27 *Perf. 14***

| | | | | |
|---|---|---|---|---|
| *355* | A56 | 5 l dl pur & multi | 5 | 5 |
| *356* | A56 | 20 l multi | 20 | 20 |
| *357* | A56 | 1r brt bl & multi | 1.00 | 1.00 |

Safe return of Apollo 13 with U.S. astronauts Capt. James A. Lovell, Jr., Fred W. Haise, Jr. and John L. Swigert, Jr.

**1971, May 3**

| | | | | |
|---|---|---|---|---|
| *358* | A57 | 10 l multi | 6 | 6 |
| *359* | A57 | 25 l gray & multi | 15 | 15 |

Intl. year against racial discrimination.

Mother and Child, by Auguste Renoir A58

Mother and Child Paintings by: 7 l, Rembrandt. 10 l, Titian. 20 l, Degas. 25 l, Berthe Morisot. 1r, Rubens. 3r, Renoir.

**1971, Sept. Litho. *Perf. 12***

| | | | | |
|---|---|---|---|---|
| *360* | A58 | 5 l multi | 5 | 5 |
| *361* | A58 | 7 l multi | 5 | 5 |
| *362* | A58 | 10 l multi | 6 | 6 |
| *363* | A58 | 20 l multi | 12 | 12 |
| *364* | A58 | 25 l multi | 15 | 15 |
| *365* | A58 | 1r multi | 50 | 50 |
| *366* | A58 | 3r multi | 1.50 | 1.50 |
| | | *Nos. 360-366 (7)* | 2.43 | 2.43 |

Capt. Alan B. Shepard, Jr. — A59

Designs: 10 l, Maj. Stuart A. Roosa. 1.50r, Com. Edgar D. Mitchell. 5r, Apollo 14 shoulder patch.

**1971, Nov. 11 Photo. *Perf. 12½***

| | | | | |
|---|---|---|---|---|
| *367* | A59 | 6 l dp grn & multi | 5 | 5 |
| *368* | A59 | 10 l cl & multi | 5 | 5 |
| *369* | A59 | 1.50r ultra & multi | 90 | 90 |
| *370* | A59 | 5r multi | 3.00 | 3.00 |

Apollo 14 U.S. moon landing mission, Jan. 31-Feb. 9.

Ballerina, by Degas A60

Paintings: 10 l, Dancing Couple, by Auguste Renoir. 2r, Spanish Dancer, by Edouard Manet. 5r, Ballerinas, by Degas. 10r, Moulin Rouge, by Henri Toulouse-Lautrec.

**1971, Nov. 19 Litho. *Perf. 14***

| | | | | |
|---|---|---|---|---|
| *371* | A60 | 5 l plum & multi | 5 | 5 |
| *372* | A60 | 10 l grn & multi | 5 | 5 |
| *373* | A60 | 2r org brn & multi | 1.10 | 1.10 |
| *374* | A60 | 5r dk bl & multi | 2.75 | 2.75 |
| *375* | A60 | 10r multi | 5.50 | 5.50 |
| | | *Nos. 371-375 (5)* | 9.45 | 9.45 |

Nos. 371-375 Overprinted Vertically: "ROYAL VISIT 1972"

**1972, Mar. 13 Litho. *Perf. 14***

| | | | | |
|---|---|---|---|---|
| *376* | A60 | 5 l plum & multi | 5 | 5 |
| *377* | A60 | 10 l grn & multi | 5 | 5 |
| *378* | A60 | 2r org brn & multi | 1.10 | 1.10 |
| *379* | A60 | 5r dk bl & multi | 2.75 | 2.75 |
| *380* | A60 | 10r multi | 5.50 | 5.50 |
| | | *Nos. 376-380 (5)* | 9.45 | 9.45 |

Visit of Elizabeth II and Prince Philip.

Book Year Emblem A61

**1972, May 1 *Perf. 13x13½***

| | | | | |
|---|---|---|---|---|
| *381* | A61 | 25 l org & multi | 12 | 12 |
| *382* | A61 | 5r multi | 2.75 | 2.75 |

International Book Year 1972.

National Costume of Scotland A62

National Costumes: 15 l, Netherlands. 25 l, Norway. 50 l, Hungary. 1r, Austria. 2r, Spain.

**1972, May 15 *Perf. 12***

| | | | | |
|---|---|---|---|---|
| *383* | A62 | 10 l gray & multi | 6 | 6 |
| *384* | A62 | 15 l lt brn & multi | 8 | 8 |
| *385* | A62 | 25 l multi | 12 | 12 |
| *386* | A62 | 50 l lt brn & multi | 25 | 25 |
| *387* | A62 | 1r gray & multi | 50 | 50 |
| *388* | A62 | 2r lt ol & multi | 1.00 | 1.00 |
| | | *Nos. 383-388 (6)* | 2.01 | 2.01 |

Stegosaurus — A63

Designs: Prehistoric reptiles.

**1972, May 31 *Perf. 14***

| | | | | |
|---|---|---|---|---|
| *389* | A63 | 2 l *shown* | 5 | 5 |
| *390* | A63 | 7 l *Edaphosaurus* | 5 | 5 |
| *391* | A63 | 25 l *Diplodocus* | 15 | 15 |
| *392* | A63 | 50 l *Triceratops* | 30 | 30 |
| *393* | A63 | 2r *Pteranodon* | 1.20 | 1.20 |
| *394* | A63 | 5r *Tyrannosaurus* | 3.00 | 3.00 |
| | | *Nos. 389-394 (6)* | 4.75 | 4.75 |

A souvenir sheet has five stamps similar to Nos. 389-394 with simulated perforations. It was not regularly issued.

Sapporo '72 Emblem, Longdistance Skiing A64

**1972, June Litho. *Perf. 14***

| | | | | |
|---|---|---|---|---|
| *395* | A64 | 3 l *shown* | 5 | 5 |
| *396* | A64 | 6 l *Bobsledding* | 5 | 5 |
| *397* | A64 | 15 l *Speed skating* | 9 | 9 |
| *398* | A64 | 50 l *Ski jump* | 30 | 30 |
| *399* | A64 | 1r *Figure skating* | 60 | 60 |
| *400* | A64 | 2.50r *Ice hockey* | 1.50 | 1.50 |
| | | *Nos. 395-400 (6)* | 2.59 | 2.59 |

11th Winter Olympic Games, Sapporo, Japan, Feb. 3-13.

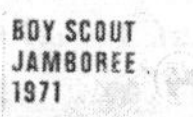

Boy Scout Saluting — A65

Olympic Emblems, Bicycling — A66

Designs (Scout): 15 l, with signal flags. 50 l, Bugler. 1r, Drummer.

**1972, Aug. 1**

| | | | | |
|---|---|---|---|---|
| *401* | A65 | 10 l Prus grn & multi | 7 | 5 |
| *402* | A65 | 15 l dk red & multi | 12 | 10 |
| *403* | A65 | 50 l dp grn & multi | 38 | 30 |
| *404* | A65 | 1r pur & multi | 80 | 62 |

13th International Boy Scout Jamboree, Asagiri Plain, Japan, Aug. 2-11, 1971.

**1972, Oct. Litho. *Perf. 14½x14***

| | | | | |
|---|---|---|---|---|
| *405* | A66 | 5 l *shown* | 5 | 5 |
| *406* | A66 | 10 l *Running* | 5 | 5 |
| *407* | A66 | 25 l *Westling* | 12 | 12 |
| *408* | A66 | 50 l *Hurdles, women's* | 25 | 25 |
| *409* | A66 | 2r *Boxing* | 1.00 | 1.00 |
| *410* | A66 | 5r *Volleyball* | 2.50 | 2.50 |
| | | *Nos. 405-410 (6)* | 3.97 | 3.97 |

**Souvenir Sheet**

***Perf. 15***

| | | | | |
|---|---|---|---|---|
| *411* | A66 | Sheet of 2 | 4.00 | 4.00 |
| *a* | | 3r *like 50 l* | 1.50 | 1.50 |
| *b* | | 4r *like 10 l* | 1.90 | 1.90 |

20th Olympic Games, Munich, Aug. 26-Sept. 11. No. 411 has olive, red and black margin with Olympic motion emblem. Size: 99x127mm.

Globe, Environment Emblem — A67

**1972, Nov. 15 Litho. *Perf. 14½***

| | | | | |
|---|---|---|---|---|
| *412* | A67 | 2 l vio & multi | 5 | 5 |
| *413* | A67 | 3 l brn & multi | 5 | 5 |
| *414* | A67 | 15 l bl & multi | 9 | 9 |
| *415* | A67 | 50 l red & multi | 30 | 30 |
| *416* | A67 | 2.50r grn & multi | 1.50 | 1.50 |
| | | *Nos. 412-416 (5)* | 1.99 | 1.99 |

U.N. Conference on Human Environment, Stockholm, June 5-16.

Nos. 409-411 Overprinted in Violet Blue:

a. LEMECHEV / MIDDLE-WEIGHT /GOLD MEDALLIST

b. JAPAN / GOLD MEDAL / WINNER

c. EHRHARDT / 100 METER / HURDLES / GOLD MEDALLIST

d. SHORTER / MARATHON / GOLD MEDALLIST

**1973, Feb. Litho. *Perf. 14½x14***

| | | | | |
|---|---|---|---|---|
| *417* | A66 (a) | 2r multi | 1.00 | 1.00 |
| *418* | A66 (b) | 5r multi | 2.50 | 2.50 |

**Souvenir Sheet**

| | | | | |
|---|---|---|---|---|
| *419* | A66 | Sheet of 2 | 4.00 | 4.00 |
| *a* | | (c) 3r multi | 1.50 | 1.50 |
| *b* | | (d) 4r multi | 1.90 | 1.90 |

Gold medal winners in 20th Olympic Games: Viatschesiav Lemechev, USSR, middleweight boxing; Japanese team, volleyball. Annelie Ehrhardt, Germany, 100m. hurdles; Frank Shorter, USA, Marathon.

Flowers, by Vincent Van Gogh — A68

Paintings of Flowers by: 2 l, 3 l, 1r, 3r, 5r, Auguste Renoir (each different). 50 l, 5 l, Ambrosius Bosschaert.

**1973, Feb.** *Perf. 13½*

| | | | | |
|---|---|---|---|---|
| *420* | A68 | 1 l bl & multi | 5 | 5 |
| *421* | A68 | 2 l tan & multi | 5 | 5 |
| *422* | A68 | 3 l lil & multi | 5 | 5 |
| *423* | A68 | 50 l ultra & multi | 25 | 25 |
| *424* | A68 | 1r emer & multi | 50 | 50 |
| *425* | A68 | 5r mag & multi | 2.50 | 2.50 |
| | | *Nos. 420-425 (6)* | 3.40 | 3.40 |

**Souvenir Sheet**

*Perf. 15*

| | | | | |
|---|---|---|---|---|
| *426* | A68 | Sheet of 2 | 3.25 | 3.25 |
| *a* | | 2r blk & multi | 1.25 | 1.25 |
| *b* | | 3r blk & multi | 1.75 | 1.75 |

No. 426 has greenish gray decorative border with black inscription and coat of arms. Size: 127x111mm.

Scouts Treating Injured Lamb A69

Designs: 2 l, 1r, Lifesaving. 3 l, 5r, Agricultural training. 4 l, 2r, Carpentry. 5 l, Leapfrog. 3r, Like 1 l.

**1973, Aug.** **Litho.** *Perf. 14½*

| | | | | |
|---|---|---|---|---|
| *427* | A69 | 1 l blk & multi | 5 | 5 |
| *428* | A69 | 2 l blk & multi | 5 | 5 |
| *429* | A69 | 3 l blk & multi | 5 | 5 |
| *430* | A69 | 4 l blk & multi | 5 | 5 |
| *431* | A69 | 5 l blk & multi | 5 | 5 |
| *432* | A69 | 1r blk & multi | 50 | 50 |
| *433* | A69 | 2r blk & multi | 1.00 | 1.00 |
| *434* | A69 | 3r blk & multi | 1.50 | 1.50 |
| | | *Nos. 427-434 (8)* | 3.25 | 3.25 |

**Souvenir Sheet**

| | | | | |
|---|---|---|---|---|
| *435* | A69 | 5r blk & multi | 3.50 | 3.50 |

24th Boy Scout World Conference (1st in Africa), Nairobi, Kenya, July 16-21. No. 435 has olive margin with black inscription. Size: 101½x78mm.

Herschel's Marlin A70

Fish and Ships: 2 l, 4r, Skipjack tuna. 3 l, Bluefin tuna. 5 l, 2.50r, Dolphinfish. 60 l, 75 l, Red snapper. 1.50r, Yellow crescent tail. 3r, Plectropoma maculatum. 5r, Like 1 l. 10r, Spanish mackerel.

**1973, Aug.** *Perf. 14½*

**Size: 38½x24mm**

| | | | | |
|---|---|---|---|---|
| *436* | A70 | 1 l lt grn & multi | 5 | 5 |
| *437* | A70 | 2 l dl org & multi | 5 | 5 |
| *438* | A70 | 3 l brt red & multi | 5 | 5 |
| *439* | A70 | 5 l multi | 5 | 5 |

**Size: 28x22mm**

| | | | | |
|---|---|---|---|---|
| *440* | A70 | 60 l yel & multi | 38 | 38 |
| *441* | A70 | 75 l pur & multi | 45 | 45 |

**Size: 38½x24mm**

| | | | | |
|---|---|---|---|---|
| *442* | A70 | 1.50r vio & multi | 90 | 90 |
| *443* | A70 | 2.50r bl & multi | 1.50 | 1.50 |
| *444* | A70 | 3r multi | 1.90 | 1.90 |
| *445* | A70 | 10r org & multi | 6.25 | 6.25 |
| | | *Nos. 436-445 (10)* | 11.58 | 11.58 |

**Souvenir Sheet**

*Perf. 15*

| | | | | |
|---|---|---|---|---|
| *446* | A70 | Sheet of 2 | 5.25 | 5.25 |
| *a* | | 4r car & multi | 2.00 | 2.00 |
| *b* | | 5r brt grn & multi | 3.00 | 3.00 |

No. 446 has buff and brown margin with ship design. Size: 118x122mm.
Nos. 436-445 exist imperf.

Goldenfronted Leafbird — A71

Designs: 2 l, 3r, Fruit bat. 3 l, 50 l, Indian starred tortoise. 4 l, 5r, Kallima inachus (butterfly). 2r, Like 1 l.

**1973, Oct.** **Litho.** *Perf. 14½*

| | | | | |
|---|---|---|---|---|
| *447* | A71 | 1 l brt pink & multi | 5 | 5 |
| *448* | A71 | 2 l brt bl & multi | 5 | 5 |
| *449* | A71 | 3 l ver & multi | 5 | 5 |
| *450* | A71 | 4 l cit & multi | 5 | 5 |
| *451* | A71 | 50 l emer & multi | 30 | 30 |
| *452* | A71 | 2r lt vio & multi | 1.20 | 1.20 |
| *453* | A71 | 3r multi | 1.75 | 1.75 |
| | | *Nos. 447-453 (7)* | 3.45 | 3.45 |

**Souvenir Sheet**

| | | | | |
|---|---|---|---|---|
| *454* | A71 | 5r yel & multi | 3.25 | 3.25 |

No. 454 has multicolored margin. Size: 65x73mm.

Lantana Camara — A72

Native Flowers: 2 l, Nerium oleander. 3 l, 2r, Rosa polyantha. 4 l, Hibiscus manihot. 5 l, Bougainvillea glabra. 10 l, 3r, Plumera alba. 50 l, Poinsettia pulcherrima. 5r, Ononis natrix.

**1973, Dec. 19** **Litho.** *Perf. 14*

| | | | | |
|---|---|---|---|---|
| *455* | A72 | 1 l ultra & multi | 5 | 5 |
| *456* | A72 | 2 l dp org & multi | 5 | 5 |
| *457* | A72 | 3 l emer & multi | 5 | 5 |
| *458* | A72 | 4 l bl grn & multi | 5 | 5 |
| *459* | A72 | 5 l lem & multi | 5 | 5 |
| *460* | A72 | 10 l lil & multi | 5 | 5 |
| *461* | A72 | 50 l yel grn & multi | 20 | 20 |
| *462* | A72 | 5r red & multi | 2.25 | 2.25 |
| | | *Nos. 455-462 (8)* | 2.75 | 2.75 |

**Souvenir Sheet**

| | | | | |
|---|---|---|---|---|
| *463* | A72 | Sheet of 2 | 3.25 | 3.25 |
| *a* | | 2r lil & multi | 1.10 | 1.10 |
| *b* | | 3r bl & multi | 1.90 | 1.90 |

No. 463 has olive margin with black inscription and coat of arms. Size: 110x100mm.

Tiros Weather Satellite A73

Designs: 2 l, 10r, Nimbus satellite. 3 l, 3r, Nomad weather ("weater") station. 4 l, A.P.T. instant weather picture (radar). 5 l, Richard's electrical wind speed recorder. 2r, like 1 l.

**1974, Jan. 10** *Perf. 14½*

| | | | | |
|---|---|---|---|---|
| *464* | A73 | 1 l ol & multi | 5 | 5 |
| *465* | A73 | 2 l multi | 5 | 5 |
| *466* | A73 | 3 l brt bl & multi | 5 | 5 |
| *467* | A73 | 4 l ocher & multi | 5 | 5 |
| *468* | A73 | 5 l ocher & multi | 5 | 5 |
| *469* | A73 | 2r ultra & multi | 1.00 | 1.00 |
| *470* | A73 | 3r org & multi | 1.50 | 1.50 |
| | | *Nos. 464-470 (7)* | 2.75 | 2.75 |

**Souvenir Sheet**

| | | | | |
|---|---|---|---|---|
| *471* | A73 | 10r lil & multi | 5.50 | 5.50 |

Centenary of World Meteorological Cooperation. No. 471 has green margin with weather vane and WMO emblem. Black inscription. Size: 110x79mm.

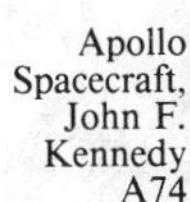

Apollo Spacecraft, John F. Kennedy A74

Designs: 2 l, 3r, Mercury spacecraft and John Glenn. 3 l, Vostok 1 and Yuri Gagarin. 4 l, Vostok 6 and Valentina Tereshkova. 5 l, Soyuz 11 and Salyut spacecrafts. 2r, Skylab. 10r, Like 1 l.

**1974, Feb. 1** **Litho.** *Perf. 14½*

| | | | | |
|---|---|---|---|---|
| *472* | A74 | 1 l multi | 5 | 5 |
| *473* | A74 | 2 l multi | 5 | 5 |
| *474* | A74 | 3 l multi | 5 | 5 |
| *475* | A74 | 4 l multi | 5 | 5 |
| *476* | A74 | 5 l multi | 5 | 5 |
| *477* | A74 | 2r multi | 1.25 | 1.25 |
| *478* | A74 | 3r multi | 1.90 | 1.90 |
| | | *Nos. 472-478 (7)* | 3.40 | 3.40 |

**Souvenir Sheet**

| | | | | |
|---|---|---|---|---|
| *479* | A74 | 10r multi | 6.25 | 6.25 |

Space explorations of US and USSR. No. 479 has greenish blue margin with Icarus design and black inscription. Size: 103x80mm.

Skylab and Copernicus A75

Designs (Copernicus, Various Portraits and): 2 l, 1.50r, Futuristic orbiting station. 3 l, 5r, Futuristic flight station. 4 l, Mariner 2 on flight to Venus. 5 l, Mariner 4 on flight to Mars. 25 l, like 1 l. 10r, Copernicus Orbiting Observatory.

**1974, Apr. 10** **Litho.** *Perf. 14½*

| | | | | |
|---|---|---|---|---|
| *480* | A75 | 1 l multi | 5 | 5 |
| *481* | A75 | 2 l multi | 5 | 5 |
| *482* | A75 | 3 l multi | 5 | 5 |
| *483* | A75 | 4 l multi | 5 | 5 |
| *484* | A75 | 5 l multi | 5 | 5 |
| *485* | A75 | 25 l multi | 12 | 12 |
| *486* | A75 | 1.50r multi | 70 | 70 |
| *487* | A75 | 5r multi | 2.40 | 2.40 |
| | | *Nos. 480-487 (8)* | 3.47 | 3.47 |

**Souvenir Sheet**

| | | | | |
|---|---|---|---|---|
| *488* | A75 | 10r multi | 6.25 | 6.25 |

500th anniversary of the birth of Nicolaus Copernicus (1473-1543), Polish astronomer. No. 488 has brown and buff margin showing Copernicus lecturing in Rome. Size: 105x79mm.

"Motherhood," by Picasso — A76

Picasso Paintings: 2 l, Harlequin and his Companion. 3 l, Pierrot Sitting. 20 l, 2r, Three Musicians. 75 l, L'Aficionada. 3r, 5r, Still life.

**1974, May** *Perf. 14*

| | | | | |
|---|---|---|---|---|
| *489* | A76 | 1 l multi | 5 | 5 |
| *490* | A76 | 2 l multi | 5 | 5 |
| *491* | A76 | 3 l multi | 5 | 5 |
| *492* | A76 | 20 l multi | 15 | 15 |
| *493* | A76 | 75 l multi | 45 | 45 |
| *494* | A76 | 5r multi | 3.00 | 3.00 |
| | | *Nos. 489-494 (6)* | 3.75 | 3.75 |

**Souvenir Sheet**

| | | | | |
|---|---|---|---|---|
| *495* | A76 | Sheet of 2 | 4.00 | 4.00 |
| *a* | | 2r multi | 1.10 | 1.10 |
| *b* | | 3r multi | 1.75 | 1.75 |

Pablo Picasso (1881-1973), painter. No. 495 has details of "Guernica" in sepia margin. Size: 100x100mm.

UPU Emblem, Old and New Trains A77

Designs (UPU Emblem and): 2 l, 2.50r, Old and new ships. 3 l, Zeppelin and jet. 1.50r, Mail coach and truck. 4r, 5r, Like 1 l.

**1974, May** **Litho.** *Perf. 14½, 13½*

| | | | | |
|---|---|---|---|---|
| *496* | A77 | 1 l lt grn & multi | 5 | 5 |
| *497* | A77 | 2 l yel & multi | 5 | 5 |
| *498* | A77 | 3 l rose & multi | 5 | 5 |
| *499* | A77 | 1.50r yel grn & multi | 1.20 | 90 |
| *500* | A77 | 2.50r bl & multi | 1.75 | 1.50 |
| *501* | A77 | 5r ocher & multi | 3.25 | 2.75 |
| | | *Nos. 496-501 (6)* | 6.35 | 5.30 |

**Souvenir Sheet**

| | | | | |
|---|---|---|---|---|
| *502* | A77 | 4r ver & multi | *8.00* | |

Centenary of Universal Postal Union. No. 502 has gray and multicolored margin with 19th century mailman and mailbox. Size: 125x105mm. Exists imperf.

Nos. 496-501 were printed in sheets of 50, perf. 14½, and also in sheets of 5 plus label, perf. 13½. The sheets of 5 have a gray and multicolored margin. The label shows UPU emblem, post horn, globe and carrier pigeon. Marginal inscription on 1 l, 3 l and 1.50r: "U.P.U." multiple; on others: "U.P.U." and "By Air Mail" in 7 languages. Size: 153x85mm.

Capricorn A78

Designs: Zodiac signs and constellations.

**1974, July 3**

| | | | | |
|---|---|---|---|---|
| *503* | A78 | 1 l *shown* | 6 | 5 |
| *504* | A78 | 2 l *Aquarius* | 6 | 5 |
| *505* | A78 | 3 l *Pisces* | 6 | 5 |
| *506* | A78 | 4 l *Aries* | 6 | 5 |
| *507* | A78 | 5 l *Taurus* | 6 | 5 |
| *508* | A78 | 6 l *Gemini* | 6 | 5 |
| *509* | A78 | 7 l *Cancer* | 6 | 5 |
| *510* | A78 | 10 l *Leo* | 7 | 5 |
| *511* | A78 | 15 l *Virgo* | 8 | 5 |
| *512* | A78 | 20 l *Libra* | 10 | 6 |
| *513* | A78 | 25 l *Scorpio* | 10 | 7 |
| *514* | A78 | 5r *Sagittarius* | 2.75 | 1.40 |
| | | *Nos. 503-514 (12)* | 3.52 | 1.98 |

**Souvenir Sheet**

| | | | | |
|---|---|---|---|---|
| *515* | A78 | 10r *Sun* | 5.50 | 5.50 |

The 10r is 50x37mm. No. 515 has multicolored margin with zodiac signs. Size: 127x107mm.

Soccer and Games' Emblem — A79

Designs: Various soccer scenes and games' emblem.

**1974, July 31** **Litho.** *Perf. 14½*

| | | | | |
|---|---|---|---|---|
| *516* | A79 | 1 l brn & multi | 5 | 5 |
| *517* | A79 | 2 l grn & multi | 5 | 5 |
| *518* | A79 | 3 l ultra & multi | 5 | 5 |
| *519* | A79 | 4 l red & multi | 5 | 5 |
| *520* | A79 | 75 l lt bl & multi | 35 | 35 |
| *521* | A79 | 4r ol & multi | 2.00 | 2.00 |
| *522* | A79 | 5r lil & multi | 2.50 | 2.50 |
| | | *Nos. 516-522 (7)* | 5.05 | 5.05 |

**Souvenir Sheet**

| | | | | |
|---|---|---|---|---|
| *523* | A79 | 10r rose & multi | 5.50 | 5.50 |

World Cup Soccer Championship, Munich, June 13-July 7. No. 523 has yellow margin with black inscription and World Soccer Cup in red brown. Size: 87x95mm.

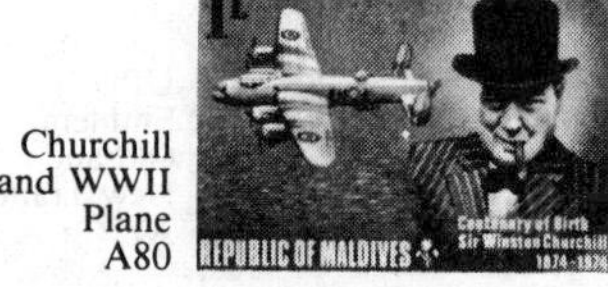


Churchill and WWII Plane A80

Designs (Churchill): 2 l, As pilot. 3 l, First Lord of the Admiralty and battleship. 4 l, Aircraft carrier. 5 l, RAF fighters. 60 l, Anti-aircraft unit. 75 l, Tank. 5r, Seaplane.

**1974, Nov. 30 Litho. *Perf. 14½***

| | | | | |
|---|---|---|---|---|
| *524* | A80 | 1 l multi | 5 | 5 |
| *525* | A80 | 2 l multi | 5 | 5 |
| *526* | A80 | 3 l multi | 5 | 5 |
| *527* | A80 | 4 l multi | 5 | 5 |
| *528* | A80 | 5 l multi | 5 | 5 |
| *529* | A80 | 60 l multi | 30 | 30 |
| *530* | A80 | 75 l multi | 35 | 35 |
| *531* | A80 | 5r multi | 2.50 | 2.50 |
| | | *Nos. 524-531 (8)* | 3.40 | 3.40 |

Sir Winston Churchill (1874-1965), birth centenary.

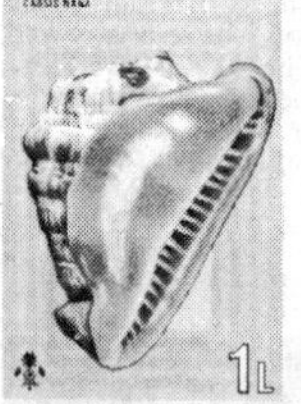


Cassis Nana A81

Cypraea Diliculum A82

**1975, Jan. 25 *Perf. 14½, 14 (A82)***

| | | | | |
|---|---|---|---|---|
| *533* | A81 | 1 l *shown* | 5 | 5 |
| *534* | A81 | 2 l *Murex triremus* | 5 | 5 |
| *535* | A81 | 3 l *Harpa major* | 5 | 5 |
| *536* | A81 | 4 l *Lambis chiragra* | 5 | 5 |
| *537* | A81 | 5 l *Conus pennaceus* | 5 | 5 |
| *538* | A82 | 60 l *shown* | 30 | 30 |
| *539* | A82 | 75 l *Clanculus pharaonis* | 40 | 40 |
| *540* | A81 | 5r *Chicoreus ramosus* | 3.00 | 3.00 |
| | | *Nos. 533-540 (8)* | 3.95 | 3.95 |

**Souvenir Sheet**

***Perf. 13½***

| | | | | |
|---|---|---|---|---|
| *541* | A81 | Sheet of 2 | 2.75 | 2.75 |
| *a.* | | 2r like 3 l | 80 | 80 |
| *b.* | | 3r like 2 l | 1.20 | 1.20 |

Sea shells, including cowries.
No. 541 has violet margin with black inscription. Size: 150x126mm.

Throne — A83

Eid-Miskith Mosque — A84

Designs: 10 l, Ornamental candlesticks (dullisa). 25 l, Tree-shaped lamp. 60 l, Royal umbrellas. 3r, Tomb of Al-Hafiz Abu-al Barakath al-Barubari.

**1975, Feb. 22 Litho. *Perf. 14***

| | | | | |
|---|---|---|---|---|
| *542* | A83 | 1 l multi | 5 | 5 |
| *543* | A83 | 10 l multi | 5 | 5 |
| *544* | A83 | 25 l multi | 12 | 12 |
| *545* | A83 | 60 l multi | 30 | 30 |
| *546* | A84 | 75 l multi | 40 | 40 |
| *547* | A84 | 3r multi | 1.60 | 1.60 |
| | | *Nos. 542-547 (6)* | 2.52 | 2.52 |

Historic relics and monuments.

Guava — A85 Republic of Maldives

**1975, Mar. Litho. *Perf. 14½***

| | | | | |
|---|---|---|---|---|
| *548* | A85 | 1 l *shown* | 5 | 5 |
| *549* | A85 | 4 l *Maldive mulberry* | 5 | 5 |
| *550* | A85 | 5 l *Mountain apples* | 5 | 5 |
| *551* | A85 | 10 l *Bananas* | 5 | 5 |
| *552* | A85 | 20 l *Mangoes* | 10 | 10 |
| *553* | A85 | 50 l *Papaya* | 28 | 28 |
| *554* | A85 | 1r *Pomegranates* | 52 | 52 |
| *555* | A85 | 5r *Coconut* | 2.75 | 2.75 |
| | | *Nos. 548-555 (8)* | 3.85 | 3.85 |

**Souvenir Sheet**

***Perf. 13½***

| | | | | |
|---|---|---|---|---|
| *556* | A85 | Sheet of 2 | 3.50 | 3.50 |
| *a.* | | 2r like 10 l | 1.25 | 1.25 |
| *b.* | | 3r like 2 l | 1.75 | 1.75 |

Tropical fruit. No. 556 has multicolored margin with fruit design and black inscription. Size: 136x102mm.

Phyllangia — A86

Designs: Corals, sea urchins and starfish.

**1975, June 6 Litho. *Perf. 14½***

| | | | | |
|---|---|---|---|---|
| *557* | A86 | 1 l *shown* | 5 | 5 |
| *558* | A86 | 2 l *Madrepora oculata* | 5 | 5 |
| *559* | A86 | 3 l *Acropora gravida* | 5 | 5 |
| *560* | A86 | 4 l *Stylotella* | 5 | 5 |
| *561* | A86 | 5 l *Acropora cervicornis* | 5 | 5 |
| *562* | A86 | 60 l *Strongylocentrotus pupuratus* | 30 | 30 |
| *563* | A86 | 75 l *Pisaster ochraceus* | 40 | 40 |
| *564* | A86 | 5r *Marthasterias glacialis* | 2.50 | 2.50 |
| | | *Nos. 557-564 (8)* | 3.45 | 3.45 |

**Souvenir Sheet**

***Imperf***

| | | | | |
|---|---|---|---|---|
| *565* | A86 | 4r *shown* | 3.25 | 3.25 |

No. 565 has lilac margin with black inscription. Size: 155x98mm.

"10," Clock Tower and Customs House A87

Designs ("10" and): 5 l, Government offices. 7 l, North Eastern waterfront, Male. 15 l, Mosque and Minaret. 10r, Sultan Park and Museum.

**1975, July 26 Litho. *Perf. 14½***

| | | | | |
|---|---|---|---|---|
| *566* | A87 | 4 l sal & multi | 5 | 5 |
| *567* | A87 | 5 l lt bl & multi | 5 | 5 |
| *568* | A87 | 7 l bis & multi | 5 | 5 |
| *569* | A87 | 15 l lil & multi | 6 | 6 |
| *570* | A87 | 10r lt grn & multi | 6.00 | 6.00 |
| | | *Nos. 566-570 (5)* | 6.21 | 6.21 |

10th anniversary of independence.

Nos. 432-435 Overprinted: "14th Boy Scout Jamboree / July 29-Aug. 7, 1975"

**1975, July 26 Litho. *Perf. 14½***

| | | | | |
|---|---|---|---|---|
| *571* | A69 | 1r multi | 50 | 50 |
| *572* | A69 | 2r multi | 1.20 | 1.20 |
| *573* | A69 | 3r multi | 1.80 | 1.80 |

**Souvenir Sheet**

| | | | | |
|---|---|---|---|---|
| *574* | A69 | 5r multi | 3.00 | 3.00 |

Nordjamb 75, 14th World Boy Scout Jamboree, Lillehammer, Norway, July 29-Aug. 7.

Madura-Prau Bedang — A88

Designs (sailing ships, except 5r): 2 l, Ganges patile. 3 l, Indian palla (vert.). 4 l, "Odhi" (vert.). 5 l, Maldivian schooner. 25 l, Cutty Sark. 1r, 10r, Maldivian baggala (vert.). 5r, Freighter Maldive Courage.

**1975, July 26 *Perf. 14½***

| | | | | |
|---|---|---|---|---|
| *575* | A88 | 1 l multi | 5 | 5 |
| *576* | A88 | 2 l multi | 5 | 5 |
| *577* | A88 | 3 l multi | 5 | 5 |
| *578* | A88 | 4 l multi | 5 | 5 |
| *579* | A88 | 5 l multi | 5 | 5 |
| *580* | A88 | 25 l multi | 15 | 15 |
| *581* | A88 | 1r multi | 60 | 60 |
| *582* | A88 | 5r multi | 3.00 | 3.00 |
| | | *Nos. 575-582 (8)* | 4.00 | 4.00 |

**Souvenir Sheet**

***Perf. 13½***

| | | | | |
|---|---|---|---|---|
| *583* | A88 | 10r multi | 6.00 | 6.00 |

No. 583 has green margin showing ship and compass rose, black inscription. Size: 98x84mm.

Brahmaea Wallichii A89

Designs: Butterflies.

**1975, Sept. 7 Litho. *Perf. 14½***

| | | | | |
|---|---|---|---|---|
| *584* | A89 | 1 l *shown* | 5 | 5 |
| *585* | A89 | 2 l *Teoinopalpus imperialis* | 5 | 5 |
| *586* | A89 | 3 l *Cethosia biblis* | 5 | 5 |
| *587* | A89 | 4 l *Hestia jasonia* | 5 | 5 |
| *588* | A89 | 5 l *Apatura* | 5 | 5 |
| *589* | A89 | 25 l *Kallima horsfieldi* | 25 | 12 |
| *590* | A89 | 1.50r *Hebomoia leucippe* | 1.90 | 90 |
| *591* | A89 | 5r *Papilio memnon* | 4.50 | 3.25 |
| | | *Nos. 584-591 (8)* | 6.90 | 4.52 |

**Souvenir Sheet**

***Perf. 13½***

| | | | | |
|---|---|---|---|---|
| *592* | A89 | 10r *like 25 l* | 6.25 | 6.25 |

No. 592 has dull green margin showing butterflies and black inscription. Size: 134x98mm.

Dying Slave by Michelangelo A90

Cup and Vase A91

Works by Michelangelo: 2 l, 4 l, 1r, 5r, paintings from Sistine Chapel. 3 l, Apollo. 5 l, Bacchus. 2r, 10r, David.

**1975, Oct. 9 Litho. *Perf. 14½***

| | | | | |
|---|---|---|---|---|
| *593* | A90 | 1 l bl & multi | 5 | 5 |
| *594* | A90 | 2 l multi | 5 | 5 |
| *595* | A90 | 3 l red & multi | 5 | 5 |
| *596* | A90 | 4 l multi | 5 | 5 |
| *597* | A90 | 5 l emer & multi | 5 | 5 |
| *598* | A90 | 1r multi | 60 | 60 |
| *599* | A90 | 2r red & multi | 1.25 | 1.25 |
| *600* | A90 | 5r multi | 3.25 | 3.25 |
| | | *Nos. 593-600 (8)* | 5.35 | 5.35 |

**Souvenir Sheet**

***Perf. 13½***

| | | | | |
|---|---|---|---|---|
| *601* | A90 | 10r multi | 6.00 | 6.00 |

500th birth anniversary of Michelangelo Buonarotti (1475-1564), Italian sculptor, painter and architect.
No. 601 has multicolored margin with Michelangelo portrait. Size: 123x113mm.

**1975, Dec. Litho. *Perf. 14***

Designs: 4 l, Boxes. 50 l, Vase with lid. 75 l, Bowls with covers. 1r, Worker finishing vases.

| | | | | |
|---|---|---|---|---|
| *602* | A91 | 2 l ultra & multi | 5 | 5 |
| *603* | A91 | 4 l rose & multi | 5 | 5 |
| *604* | A91 | 50 l multi | 30 | 30 |
| *605* | A91 | 75 l bl & multi | 45 | 45 |
| *606* | A91 | 1r multi | 55 | 55 |
| | | *Nos. 602-606 (5)* | 1.40 | 1.40 |

Maldivian lacquer ware.

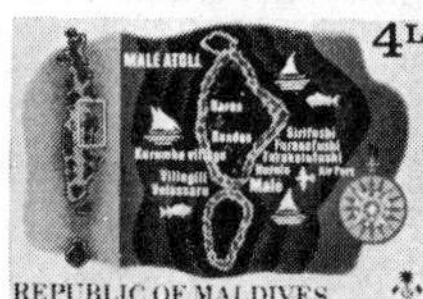


Map of Islands and Atolls A92

Designs: 5 l, Yacht at anchor. 7 l, Sailboats. 15 l, Deep-sea divers and corals. 3r, Hulule Airport. 10r, Cruising yachts.

**1975, Dec. 25 Litho. *Perf. 14***

| | | | | |
|---|---|---|---|---|
| *607* | A92 | 4 l multi | 5 | 5 |
| *608* | A92 | 5 l multi | 5 | 5 |
| *609* | A92 | 7 l multi | 5 | 5 |
| *610* | A92 | 15 l multi | 6 | 6 |
| *611* | A92 | 3r multi | 1.75 | 1.75 |
| *612* | A92 | 10r multi | 5.50 | 5.50 |
| | | *Nos. 607-612 (6)* | 7.46 | 7.46 |

Tourist publicity.

Cross-country Skiing — A93

Gen. Burgoyne, by Joshua Reynolds — A94

Designs (Winter Olympic Games' Emblem): 2 l, Speed skating. 3 l, Figure skating, pair. 4 l, Bobsled. 5 l, Ski jump. 25 l, Figure skating, woman. 1.15r, Slalom. 4r, Ice hockey. 10r, Skiing.

**1976, Jan. 10 Litho. *Perf. 14½***

| | | | | |
|---|---|---|---|---|
| *613* | A93 | 1 l multi | 5 | 5 |
| *614* | A93 | 2 l multi | 5 | 5 |
| *615* | A93 | 3 l multi | 5 | 5 |
| *616* | A93 | 4 l multi | 5 | 5 |
| *617* | A93 | 5 l multi | 5 | 5 |
| *618* | A93 | 25 l multi | 10 | 10 |
| *619* | A93 | 1.15r multi | 65 | 65 |
| *620* | A93 | 4r multi | 2.25 | 2.25 |
| | | *Nos. 613-620 (8)* | 3.25 | 3.25 |

**Souvenir Sheet**

***Perf. 13½***

| | | | | |
|---|---|---|---|---|
| *621* | A93 | 10r multi | 6.25 | 6.25 |

12th Winter Olympic Games, Innsbruck, Austria, Feb. 4-15. No. 621 contains one stamp; multicolored margin with snowman. Size: 92½x117mm.

**1976, Feb. 15 *Perf. 14½***

Paintings: 2 l, John Hancock, by John S. Copley. 3 l, Death of Gen. Montgomery, by

John Trumbull (horiz.). 4 l, Paul Revere, by Copley. 5 l, Battle of Bunker Hill, by Trumbull (horiz.). 2r, Crossing of the Delaware, by Thomas Sully (horiz.). 3r, Samuel Adams, by Copley. 5r, Surrender of Cornwallis, by Trumbull (horiz.). 10r, Washington at Dorchester Heights, by Gilbert Stuart.

*622* A94 1 l multi 5 5
*623* A94 2 l multi 5 5
*624* A94 3 l multi 5 5
*625* A94 4 l multi 5 5
*626* A94 5 l multi 5 5
*627* A94 2r multi 1.25 1.25
*628* A94 3r multi 1.75 1.75
*629* A94 5r multi 3.00 3.00
*Nos. 622-629 (8)* 6.25 6.25

**Souvenir Sheet**

***Perf. 13½***

*630* A94 10r multi 6.25 6.25

American Bicentennial. No. 630 contains one stamp; dull yellow and multicolored margin with portrait of George Washington, 13-star and 50-star US flags. Size: 147½x95mm.

Thomas Alva Edison A95

Designs: 2 l, Alexander Graham Bell and his telephone. 3 l, Telephones of 1919, 1937 and 1972. 10 l, Cable tunnel. 20 l, Equalizer circuit assembly. 1r, Ships laying underwater cable. 4r, Telephones of 1876, 1890 and 1879 Edison telephone. 10r, Intelsat IV-A over earth station.

**1976, Mar. 10 Litho. *Perf. 14½***

*631* A95 1 l multi 5 5
*632* A95 2 l multi 5 5
*633* A95 3 l multi 5 5
*634* A95 10 l multi 5 5
*635* A95 20 l multi 10 10
*636* A95 1r multi 60 60
*637* A95 10r multi 6.00 6.00
*Nos. 631-637 (7)* 6.90 6.90

**Souvenir Sheet**

***Perf. 13½***

*638* A95 4r multi 2.50 2.50

Centenary of first telephone call by Alexander Graham Bell, Mar. 10, 1876. No. 638 contains one stamp, pink and multicolored margin showing globe and telephone. Size: 155x104mm.

Nos. 627-630 Overprinted in Silver or Black: MAY 29TH-JUNE 6TH "INTERPHIL" 1976

**1976, May 29 Litho. *Perf. 14½***

*639* A94 2r multi (S) 1.20 1.20
*640* A94 3r multi (S) 1.80 1.80
*641* A94 5r multi (B) 3.00 3.00

**Souvenir Sheet**

***Perf. 13½***

*642* A94 10r multi (S) 6.25 6.25

Interphil 76 International Philatelic Exhibition, Philadelphia, Pa., May 29-June 6. Overprint on 3r and 10r vertical. Same overprint in one horizontal silver line in margin of No. 642.

Wrestling A96

Bonavist Beans A97

Designs (Olympic Rings and): 2 l, Shot put. 3 l, Hurdles. 4 l, Hockey. 5 l, Women running. 6 l, Javelin. 1.50r, Discus. 5r, Team handball. 10r, Hammer throw.

**1976, June 1 *Perf. 14½***

*643* A96 1 l multi 5 5
*644* A96 2 l multi 5 5
*645* A96 3 l sal & multi 5 5
*646* A96 4 l multi 5 5
*647* A96 5 l pink & multi 5 5
*648* A96 6 l multi 5 5
*649* A96 1.50r bis & multi 90 90
*650* A96 5r lil & multi 3.00 3.00
*Nos. 643-650 (8)* 4.20 4.20

**Souvenir Sheet**

***Perf. 13½***

*651* A96 10r lem & multi 6.25 6.25

21st Olympic Games, Montreal, Canada, July 17-Aug. 1. No. 651 contains one stamp; multicolored margin showing runners and Montreal Olympic Games emblem. Size: 135x106mm.

**1976-77 Litho. *Perf. 14***

Designs: 4 l, 20 l, Beans. 10 l, Eggplant. 50 l, Cucumber. 75 l, 2r, Snake gourd. 1r, Balsam pear.

*652* A97 2 l grn & multi 5 5
*653* A97 4 l lt bl & multi 5 5
*654* A97 10 l ocher & multi 5 5
*655* A97 20 l bl & multi ('77) 10 10
*656* A97 50 l multi 25 25
*657* A97 75 l bis & multi 32 32
*658* A97 1r lil & multi 45 45
*659* A97 2r bis & multi ('77) 90 90
*Nos. 652-659 (8)* 2.17 2.17

Viking I and Mars A98

Design: 20r, Landing craft on Mars.

**1976, Dec. 2 Litho. *Perf. 14***

*660* A98 5r multi 3.00 3.00

**Souvenir Sheet**

*661* A98 20r multi 12.00 12.00

Viking I U.S. Mars Mission. No. 661 has greenish blue and black margin showing rockets and Mars surface. Size: 121x89mm.

Coronation Ceremony — A99

Designs: 2 l, Elizabeth II and Prince Philip. 3 l, Queen, Prince Philip, Princes Edward and Andrew. 1.15r, Queen in procession. 3r, State coach. 4r, Queen, Prince Philip, Princess Anne and Prince Charles. 10r, Queen and Prince Charles.

**1977, Feb. 6 *Perf. 14x13½, 12***

*662* A99 1 l multi 5 5
*663* A99 2 l multi 5 5
*664* A99 3 l multi 5 5
*665* A99 1.15r multi 80 80
*666* A99 3r multi 1.40 1.40
*667* A99 4r multi 2.00 2.00
*Nos. 662-667 (6)* 4.35 4.35

**Souvenir Sheet**

*668* A99 10r multi 5.00 5.00

25th anniv. of the reign of Elizabeth II. No. 668 has multicolored margin showing map of coronation route. Size: 120x77mm.

Nos. 662-667 were printed in sheets of 40 (4x10), perf. 14x13½, and sheets of 5 plus label, perf. 12, in changed colors.

Beethoven in Bonn, 1785 — A100

Designs: 2 l, Moonlight Sonata and portrait, 1801. 3 l, Goethe and Beethoven, Teplitz, 1811. 4 l, Beethoven, 1815, and his string instruments. 5 l, Beethoven House, Heiligenstadt, 1817. 25 l, Composer's hands, gold medal. 2r, Missa Solemnis, portrait, 1823. 4r, Piano, room where Beethoven died, death mask. 5r, Portrait, 1825, hearing aids.

**1977, Mar. 26 Litho. *Perf. 14***

*669* A100 1 l multi 5 5
*670* A100 2 l multi 5 5
*671* A100 3 l multi 5 5
*672* A100 4 l multi 5 5
*673* A100 5 l multi 5 5
*674* A100 25 l multi 10 10
*675* A100 2r multi 1.10 1.10
*676* A100 5r multi 2.75 2.75
*Nos. 669-676 (8)* 4.20 4.20

**Souvenir Sheet**

*677* A100 4r multi 2.10 2.10

Ludwig van Beethoven (1770-1827), composer, 150th death anniversary. No. 677 has light violet and black margin showing Beethoven's grave in Vienna. Size: 120x92mm.

Electronic Tree and ITU Emblem A101

Designs: 90 l, Central Telegraph Office, Maldives. 5r, Intelsat IV over map. 10r, Parabolic antenna, satellite communications earth station.

**1977, May 17 Litho. *Perf. 14***

*678* A101 10 l multi 5 5
*679* A101 90 l multi 45 45
*680* A101 10r multi 5.50 5.50

**Souvenir Sheet**

*681* A101 5r multi 2.50 2.50

Inauguration of Satellite Earth Station and for World Telecommunications Day. No. 681 has pink margin with black inscription. Size: 100x85mm.

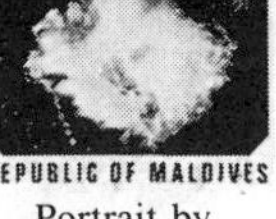

Portrait by Gainsborough A102

REPUBLIC OF MALDIVES 1L

Lesser Frigate Birds A103

Paintings: 2 l, 5 l, 10r, Rubens. 3 l, 95 l, 5r, Titian. 4 l, 1r, Gainsborough.

**1977, May 20**

*682* A102 1 l multi 5 5
*683* A102 2 l multi 5 5
*684* A102 3 l multi 5 5
*685* A102 4 l multi 5 5
*686* A102 5 l multi 5 5
*687* A102 95 l multi 45 45
*688* A102 1r multi 50 50
*689* A102 10r multi 5.00 5.00
*Nos. 682-689 (8)* 6.20 6.20

**Souvenir Sheet**

*690* A102 5r multi 2.50 2.50

Birth anniv. of Thomas Gainsborough; Peter Paul Rubens; Titian. No. 690 contains one stamp showing Titian's self-portrait. Light green and bister margin with black inscription. Size: 152x117mm.

**1977, July 26 Litho. *Perf. 14½***

Birds: 2 l, Crab plovers. 3 l, Long-tailed tropic bird. 4 l, Wedge-tailed shearwater. 5 l, Gray heron. 20 l, White tern. 95 l, Cattle egret. 1.25r, Blacknaped terns. 5r, Pheasant coucals. 10r, Striated herons.

*691* A103 1 l multi 5 5
*692* A103 2 l multi 5 5
*693* A103 3 l multi 5 5
*694* A103 4 l multi 5 5
*695* A103 5 l multi 5 5
*696* A103 20 l multi 15 10
*697* A103 95 l multi 62 50
*698* A103 1.25r multi 90 62
*699* A103 5r multi 3.75 2.50
*Nos. 691-699 (9)* 5.67 3.97

**Souvenir Sheet**

*700* A103 10r multi 5.00 5.00

No. 700 has light and dark green margin showing bird in flight and coat of arms. Size: 125x108mm.

Charles A. Lindbergh — A104

Designs: 2 l, Lindbergh and Spirit of St. Louis. 3 l, Mohawk plane (horiz.). 4 l, Lebaudy I airship, 1902 (horiz.). 5 l, Count Ferdinand von Zeppelin, and Zeppelin in Pernambuco. 1r, Los Angeles, U. S. Navy airship, 1924 (horiz.). 3r, Henry Ford and Lindbergh, 1942. 5r, Spirit of St. Louis, Statue of Liberty and Eiffel Tower (horiz.). 7.50r, German naval airship over battleship (horiz.). 10r, Vickers airship, 1917.

***Perf. 13x13½, 13½x13***

**1977, Oct. 31 Litho.**

*701* A104 1 l multi 5 5
*702* A104 2 l multi 5 5
*703* A104 3 l multi 5 5
*704* A104 4 l multi 5 5
*705* A104 5 l multi 5 5
*706* A104 1r multi 48 48
*707* A104 3r multi 1.50 1.50
*708* A104 10r multi 4.75 4.75
*Nos. 701-708 (8)* 6.98 6.98

**Souvenir Sheet**

*709* A104 Sheet of 2 6.75 6.75
*a* 5r multi 2.50 2.50
*b* 7.50r multi 3.75 3.75

Charles A. Lindbergh's solo transatlantic flight from New York to Paris, 50th anniv., and 75th anniv. of first navigable airship. No. 709 has green and multicolored margin showing Giffard's airship, 1851. Size: 148x114mm.

Boat Building A105

Maldivian Occupations: 15 l, High sea fishing. 20 l, Cadjan weaving. 90 l, Mat weaving. 2r, Lacemaking (vert.).

**1977, Dec. 12**

*710* A105 6 l multi 5 5
*711* A105 15 l multi 6 6
*712* A105 20 l multi 10 10
*713* A105 90 l multi 45 45
*714* A105 2r multi 1.00 1.00
*Nos. 710-714 (5)* 1.66 1.66

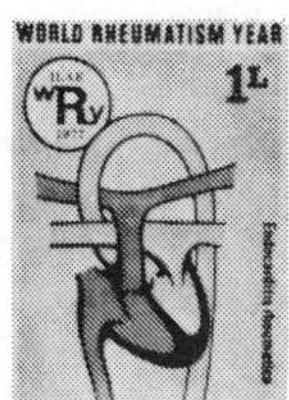


Rheumatic Heart — A106

X-Ray Pictures: 50 l, Shoulder. 2r, Hand. 3r, Knee.

**1978, Feb. 9 *Perf. 14***

*715* A106 1 l multi 5 5
*716* A106 50 l multi 30 30
*717* A106 2r multi 1.25 1.25
*718* A106 3r multi 1.75 1.75

World Rheumatism Year.

Otto Lilienthal's Glider, 1890
A107

Designs: 2 l, Chanute's glider, 1896. 3 l, Wright brothers testing glider, 1900. 4 l, A. V. Roe's plane with paper-covered wings, 1908. 5 l, Wilbur Wright showing his plane to King Alfonso of Spain, 1909. 10 l, Roe's second biplane. 20 l, Alexander Graham Bell and Wright brothers in Washington D.C., 1910. 95 l, Clifton Hadley's triplane, 1910. 5r, British B.E.2 planes, Upavon Field, 1914. 10r, Wilbur Wright flying first motorized plane, 1903.

**1978, Feb. 27 Litho. *Perf. 13x13½***

| | | | | |
|---|---|---|---|---|
| *719* | A107 | 1 l multi | 5 | 5 |
| *720* | A107 | 2 l multi | 5 | 5 |
| *721* | A107 | 3 l multi | 5 | 5 |
| *722* | A107 | 4 l multi | 5 | 5 |
| *723* | A107 | 5 l multi | 5 | 5 |
| *724* | A107 | 10 l multi | 5 | 5 |
| *725* | A107 | 20 l multi | 9 | 9 |
| *726* | A107 | 95 l multi | 45 | 45 |
| *727* | A107 | 5r multi | 2.50 | 2.50 |
| | | *Nos. 719-727 (9)* | 3.34 | 3.34 |

**Souvenir Sheet**

***Perf. 14***

| | | | | |
|---|---|---|---|---|
| *728* | A107 | 10r multi | 4.50 | 4.50 |

75th anniversary of first motorized airplane. No. 728 has olive and black margin showing Wright brothers, sketch of their plane and King Edward VII. Size: 98x82mm.

Edward Jenner, Vaccination Discoverer
A108

TV with Maldives Broadcasting Symbol
A109

Designs: 15 l, Foundling Hospital, London, where children were first inoculated, 1743 (horiz.). 50 l, Newgate Prison, London, where first experiments were carried out, 1721.

**1978, March 15 *Perf. 14***

| | | | | |
|---|---|---|---|---|
| *729* | A108 | 15 l multi | 6 | 6 |
| *730* | A108 | 50 l multi | 20 | 20 |
| *731* | A108 | 2r multi | 80 | 80 |

World eradication of smallpox.

**1978, Mar. 29**

Designs: 25 l, Circuit pattern. 1.50r, Station control panel (horiz.).

| | | | | |
|---|---|---|---|---|
| *732* | A109 | 15 l multi | 10 | 10 |
| *733* | A109 | 25 l multi | 16 | 16 |
| *734* | A109 | 1.50r multi | 1.00 | 1.00 |

Inauguration of Maldive Islands television.

Sailing Ship — A110

The Ampulla — A111

Ships: 1 l, Phoenician. 2 l, Two-master. 5 l, Freighter Maldive Trader. 1r, Trading schooner. 1.25r, 4r, Sailing boat. 3r, Barque Bangala. (1 l, 2 l, 5 l, 1.25r, 4r, horiz.).

**1978, Apr. 27 Litho. *Perf. 14½***

| | | | | |
|---|---|---|---|---|
| *735* | A110 | 1 l multi | 5 | 5 |
| *736* | A110 | 2 l multi | 5 | 5 |
| *737* | A110 | 3 l multi | 5 | 5 |
| *738* | A110 | 5 l multi | 5 | 5 |
| *739* | A110 | 1r multi | 40 | 40 |
| *740* | A110 | 1.25r multi | 50 | 50 |
| *741* | A110 | 3r multi | 1.20 | 1.20 |
| *742* | A110 | 4r multi | 1.60 | 1.60 |
| *a* | | Souvenir sheet of 2 | 2.20 | 2.20 |
| | | *Nos. 735-742 (8)* | 3.90 | 3.90 |

No. 742a contains one each of Nos. 739 and 742; gray blue and slate blue margin shows sailing ship. Size: 152x140mm.

**1978, May 15 *Perf. 14***

Designs: 2 l, Scepter with dove. 3 l, Orb with cross. 1.15r, St. Edward's crown. 2r, Scepter with cross. 5r, Queen Elizabeth II. 10r, Anointing spoon.

| | | | | |
|---|---|---|---|---|
| *743* | A111 | 1 l multi | 5 | 5 |
| *744* | A111 | 2 l multi | 5 | 5 |
| *745* | A111 | 3 l multi | 5 | 5 |
| *746* | A111 | 1.15r multi | 55 | 55 |
| *747* | A111 | 2r multi | 1.00 | 1.00 |
| *748* | A111 | 5r multi | 2.50 | 2.50 |
| | | *Nos. 743-748 (6)* | 4.20 | 4.20 |

**Souvenir Sheet**

| | | | | |
|---|---|---|---|---|
| *749* | A111 | 10r multi | 4.75 | 4.75 |

25th anniversary of coronation of Queen Elizabeth II. No. 749 contains one stamp; multicolored margin shows coronation chair. Size: 109x106mm.

Nos. 743-748 were printed in sheets of 40 (10x4) and in sheets of 3 plus label, in changed colors. Labels show coronation regalia; multicolored margins with coats of arms.

Capt. James Cook — A112

Designs: 2 l, Kamehameha I statue, Honolulu. 3 l, "Endeavour" and boat. 25 l, Capt. Cook and route of his 3rd voyage. 75 l, "Discovery" and "Resolution," map of Hawaiian Islands (horiz.). 1.50r, Capt. Cook's first meeting with Hawaiians (horiz.). 5r, "Endeavour." 10r, Capt. Cook's death (horiz.).

**1978, July 15 Litho. *Perf. 14½***

| | | | | |
|---|---|---|---|---|
| *750* | A112 | 1 l multi | 5 | 5 |
| *751* | A112 | 2 l multi | 5 | 5 |
| *752* | A112 | 3 l multi | 5 | 5 |
| *753* | A112 | 25 l multi | 12 | 12 |
| *754* | A112 | 75 l multi | 35 | 35 |
| *755* | A112 | 1.50r multi | 75 | 75 |
| *756* | A112 | 10r multi | 4.75 | 4.75 |
| | | *Nos. 750-756 (7)* | 6.12 | 6.12 |

**Souvenir Sheet**

| | | | | |
|---|---|---|---|---|
| *757* | A112 | 5r multi | 2.25 | 2.25 |

No. 757 has olive bister and multicolored margin showing ship's prow and Maldives' coat of arms. Size: 100x92mm.

Schizophrys Aspera — A113

Maldivian Crabs and Lobster: 2 l, Atergatis floridus. 3 l, Percnon planissimum. 90 l, Portunus granulatus. 1r, Carpilius maculatus. No. 763, Huenia proteus. No. 765, Panulirus longipes (vert.). 25r, Etisus laevimanus.

**1978, Aug. 30 Litho. *Perf. 14***

| | | | | |
|---|---|---|---|---|
| *758* | A113 | 1 l multi | 5 | 5 |
| *759* | A113 | 2 l multi | 5 | 5 |
| *760* | A113 | 3 l multi | 5 | 5 |
| *761* | A113 | 90 l multi | 48 | 48 |
| *762* | A113 | 1r multi | 55 | 55 |
| *763* | A113 | 2r multi | 1.10 | 1.10 |
| *764* | A113 | 25r multi | 13.50 | 13.50 |
| | | *Nos. 758-764 (7)* | 15.78 | 15.78 |

**Souvenir Sheet**

| | | | | |
|---|---|---|---|---|
| *765* | A113 | 2r multi | 1.00 | 1.00 |

No. 765 has multicolored margin showing podophthalmus vigil (crab). Size: 149x147mm.

Four Apostles, by Dürer — A114

Paintings by Albrecht Dürer: 20 l, Self-portrait, age 27. 55 l, Virgin and Child with Pear. 1r, Rhinoceros (horiz.). 1.80r, Hare. 3r, The Great Piece of Turf. 10r, Columbine.

**1978, Oct. 28 Litho. *Perf. 14***

| | | | | |
|---|---|---|---|---|
| *766* | A114 | 10 l multi | 5 | 5 |
| *767* | A114 | 20 l multi | 12 | 12 |
| *768* | A114 | 55 l multi | 30 | 30 |
| *769* | A114 | 1r multi | 52 | 52 |
| *770* | A114 | 1.80r multi | 1.00 | 1.00 |
| *771* | A114 | 3r multi | 1.60 | 1.60 |
| | | *Nos. 766-771 (6)* | 3.59 | 3.59 |

**Souvenir Sheet**

| | | | | |
|---|---|---|---|---|
| *772* | A114 | 10r multi | 4.75 | 4.75 |

Albrecht Dürer (1471-1528), German painter. No. 772 has multicolored margin showing Dürer's self-portrait as a boy. Size: 141x123mm.

Palms and Fishing Boat
A115

Designs: 5 l, Montessori School. 10 l, TV tower and ITU emblem (vert.). 25 l, Island with beach. 50 l, Boeing 737 over island. 95 l, Walk along the beach. 1.25r, Fishing boat at dawn. 2r, Presidential residence. 3r, Fishermen preparing nets. 5r, Afeefuddin Mosque.

**1978, Nov. 11 Litho. *Perf. 14½***

| | | | | |
|---|---|---|---|---|
| *773* | A115 | 1 l multi | 5 | 5 |
| *774* | A115 | 5 l multi | 5 | 5 |
| *775* | A115 | 1 l multi | 5 | 5 |
| *776* | A115 | 25 l multi | 12 | 12 |
| *777* | A115 | 50 l multi | 25 | 25 |
| *778* | A115 | 95 l multi | 45 | 45 |
| *779* | A115 | 1.25r multi | 62 | 62 |
| *780* | A115 | 2r multi | 1.00 | 1.00 |
| *781* | A115 | 5r multi | 2.50 | 2.50 |
| | | *Nos. 773-781 (9)* | 5.09 | 5.09 |

**Souvenir Sheet**

| | | | | |
|---|---|---|---|---|
| *782* | A115 | 3r multi | 1.75 | 1.75 |

10th anniversary of Republic. No. 782 has multicolored margin with inscription. Size: 119x88mm.

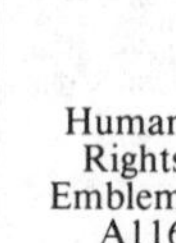

Human Rights Emblem
A116

**1978, Dec. 10 *Perf. 14***

| | | | | |
|---|---|---|---|---|
| *783* | A116 | 30 l multi | 15 | 15 |
| *784* | A116 | 90 l multi | 45 | 45 |
| *785* | A116 | 1.80r multi | 90 | 90 |

Universal Declaration of Human Rights, 30th anniversary.

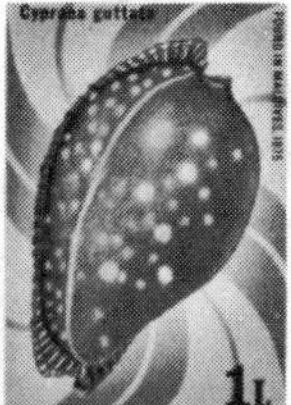


Rare Spotted Cowrie — A117

Sea Shells: 2 l, Imperial cone. 3 l, Green turban. 10 l, Giant spider conch. 1r, Leucodon cowrie. 1.80r, Fig cone. 3r, Glory of the sea. 5r, Top vase.

**1979, Jan. Litho. *Perf. 14***

| | | | | |
|---|---|---|---|---|
| *786* | A117 | 1 l multi | 5 | 5 |
| *787* | A117 | 2 l multi | 5 | 5 |
| *788* | A117 | 3 l multi | 5 | 5 |
| *789* | A117 | 10 l multi | 5 | 5 |
| *790* | A117 | 1r multi | 48 | 48 |
| *791* | A117 | 1.80r multi | 90 | 90 |
| *792* | A117 | 3r multi | 1.40 | 1.40 |
| | | *Nos. 786-792 (7)* | 2.98 | 2.98 |

**Souvenir Sheet**

| | | | | |
|---|---|---|---|---|
| *793* | A117 | 5r multi | 3.00 | 3.00 |

No. 793 has multicolored margin showing shell and coat of arms. Size: 141x111mm.

Bellman Delivering Mail — A118

Designs: 2 l, Royal mail coach, 1840 (horiz.). 3 l, First London letter box, 1855. 1.55r, Great Britain No. 1 and post horn. 5r, Maldive Islands No. 5 and carrier pigeon. 10r, Rowland Hill.

**1979, Feb. 28 Litho. *Perf. 14***

| | | | | |
|---|---|---|---|---|
| *794* | A118 | 1 l multi | 5 | 5 |
| *795* | A118 | 2 l multi | 5 | 5 |
| *796* | A118 | 3 l multi | 5 | 5 |
| *797* | A118 | 1.55r multi | 78 | 60 |
| *798* | A118 | 5r multi | 2.50 | 2.00 |
| | | *Nos. 794-798 (5)* | 3.43 | 2.75 |

**Souvenir Sheet**

| | | | | |
|---|---|---|---|---|
| *799* | A118 | 10r multi | 4.75 | 4.75 |

Sir Rowland Hill (1795-1879), originator of penny postage. No. 799 has blue, black and violet margin showing postilion. Size: 132x107mm.

Girl with Teddy Bear — A119

Designs (IYC Emblem, Boy and): 1.25r, Model boat. 2r, Rocket launcher. 3r, Blimp. 5r, Train.

**1979, May 10 Litho. *Perf. 14***

| | | | | |
|---|---|---|---|---|
| *800* | A119 | 5 l multi | 5 | 5 |
| *801* | A119 | 1.25r multi | 62 | 62 |
| *802* | A119 | 2r multi | 1.00 | 1.00 |
| *803* | A119 | 3r multi | 1.50 | 1.50 |

**Souvenir Sheet**

| | | | | |
|---|---|---|---|---|
| *804* | A119 | 5r multi | 2.50 | 2.50 |

International Year of the Child. No. 804 has multicolored margin showing girl and boy with banner. Size: 118x109mm.

White Feathers, by Matisse A120

Paintings by Henri Matisse: 25 l, Joy of Life. 30 l, Eggplants. 1.50r, Harmony in Red. 4r, Water Pitcher. 5r, Still-life.

**1979, Aug. 20 Litho. *Perf. 14***

| | | | | |
|---|---|---|---|---|
| *805* A120 | 20 l multi | | 10 | 10 |
| *806* A120 | 25 l multi | | 12 | 12 |
| *807* A120 | 30 l multi | | 15 | 15 |
| *808* A120 | 1.50r multi | | 75 | 75 |
| *809* A120 | 5r multi | | 2.50 | 2.50 |
| | *Nos. 805-809 (5)* | | 3.62 | 3.62 |

**Souvenir Sheet**

| | | | |
|---|---|---|---|
| *810* A120 | 4r multi | 2.25 | 2.25 |

Henri Matisse (1869-1954), French painter. No. 810 has multicolored margin with self-portrait. Size: 135x95mm.

Sari and Mosque — A121

National Costumes: 75 l, Sashed apron dress. Male Harbor. 90 l, Serape with necklace, radar station. 95 l, Flowered dress, mosque and minaret.

**1979, Aug. 22 Litho. *Perf. 14***

| | | | |
|---|---|---|---|
| *811* A121 | 50 l multi | 25 | 25 |
| *812* A121 | 75 l multi | 38 | 38 |
| *813* A121 | 90 l multi | 45 | 45 |
| *814* A121 | 95 l multi | 48 | 48 |

Gloriosa Superba — A122

**1979, Oct. 29 Litho. *Perf. 14***

| | | | |
|---|---|---|---|
| *815* A122 | 1 l *shown* | 5 | 5 |
| *816* A122 | 3 l *Hibiscus* | 5 | 5 |
| *817* A122 | 50 l *Barringtonia asiatica* | 25 | 25 |
| *818* A122 | 1r *Abutilon indicum* | 50 | 50 |
| *819* A122 | 5r *Guettarda speciosa* | 2.50 | 2.50 |
| | *Nos. 815-819 (5)* | 3.35 | 3.35 |

**Souvenir Sheet**

| | | | |
|---|---|---|---|
| *820* A122 | 4r *Pandanus odoratissimus* | 2.00 | 2.00 |

Maldive wildflowers. No. 820 has lilac decorative margin. Size: 95x85mm.

Handicraft Exhibition A123

**1979, Nov. 11**

| | | | |
|---|---|---|---|
| *821* A123 | 5 l *shown* | 5 | 5 |
| *822* A123 | 10 l *Jar and cup* | 5 | 5 |
| *823* A123 | 1.30r *Tortoise-shell jewelry* | 65 | 65 |
| *824* A123 | 2r *Wooden boxes* | 1.00 | 1.00 |

**Souvenir Sheet**

| | | | |
|---|---|---|---|
| *825* A123 | 5r *Bracelets, Neckline* | 2.25 | 2.25 |

No. 825 has yellow and black decorative margin. Size: 125½x86½mm.

Postal Scenes A123a

**1979, Dec. Litho. *Perf. 11***

| | | | |
|---|---|---|---|
| *826* A123a | 1 l *Goofy delivering package* | 5 | 5 |
| *827* A123a | 2 l *Mickey at mailbox* | 5 | 5 |
| *828* A123a | 3 l *Goofy buried in letters* | 5 | 5 |
| *829* A123a | 4 l *Minnie Mouse, Pluto* | 5 | 5 |
| *830* A123a | 5 l *Mickey Mouse on skates* | 5 | 5 |
| *831* A123a | 10 l *Donald Duck at mailbox* | 5 | 5 |
| *832* A123a | 15 l *Chip and Dale carrying letter* | 8 | 8 |
| *833* A123a | 1.50r *Donald Duck on unicycle* | 75 | 75 |
| *834* A123a | 5r *Donald Duck wheeling crate* | 2.50 | 2.50 |
| | *Nos. 826-834 (9)* | 3.63 | 3.63 |

**Souvenir Sheet**
**Imperf.**

| | | | |
|---|---|---|---|
| *835* A123a | 4r *Goofy at mailbox* | 12.50 | 12.50 |

No. 835 has multicolored margin showing mountains and path. Size: 128x102mm.

Post Ramadan Dancing A124

Designs: 15 l, Festival of Eeduu. 95 l, Sultan's ceremonial band. 2r, Music festival.

**1980, Jan. 19 Litho. *Perf. 14***

| | | | |
|---|---|---|---|
| *836* A124 | 5 l multi | 5 | 5 |
| *837* A124 | 15 l multi | 8 | 8 |
| *838* A124 | 95 l multi | 48 | 48 |
| *839* A124 | 2r multi | 1.00 | 1.00 |

**Souvenir Sheet**

| | | | |
|---|---|---|---|
| *840* A124 | 5r multi | 3.00 | 3.00 |

National Day. No. 840 has multicolored margin showing drum, horn and flute. Size: 132x99mm.

Leatherback Turtle — A125

**1980, Feb. 17 Litho. *Perf. 14***

| | | | |
|---|---|---|---|
| *841* A125 | 1 l *shown* | 5 | 5 |
| *842* A125 | 2 l *Flatback turtle* | 5 | 5 |
| *843* A125 | 5 l *Hawksbill turtle* | 5 | 5 |
| *844* A125 | 10 l *Loggerhead turtle* | 5 | 5 |
| *845* A125 | 75 l *Olive ridley* | 38 | 38 |
| *846* A125 | 10r *Atlantic ridley* | 5.00 | 5.00 |
| | *Nos. 841-846 (6)* | 5.58 | 5.58 |

**Souvenir Sheet**

| | | | |
|---|---|---|---|
| *847* A125 | 4r *Green turtle* | 2.00 | 2.00 |

No. 847 has multicolored margin showing turtle tracks on beach. Size: 85½x107mm.

Paul Harris in Rotary Emblem — A126

**1980, Mar. Litho. *Perf. 14***

| | | | |
|---|---|---|---|
| *848* A126 | 75 l *shown* | 38 | 38 |
| *849* A126 | 90 l *Family* | 45 | 45 |
| *850* A126 | 1r *Grain* | 50 | 50 |
| *851* A126 | 10r *Caduceus* | 5.00 | 5.00 |

**Souvenir Sheet**

| | | | |
|---|---|---|---|
| *852* A126 | 5r *Anniversary emblem* | 2.50 | 2.50 |

Rotary International, 75th anniversary. No. 852 has multicolored margin showing torch. Size: 110x86mm.

Nos. 797-799 Overprinted "LONDON 1980"

**1980, May 6 Litho. *Perf. 14***

| | | | |
|---|---|---|---|
| *853* A118 | 1.55r multi | 78 | 78 |
| *854* A118 | 5r multi | 2.50 | 2.50 |

**Souvenir Sheet**

| | | | |
|---|---|---|---|
| *855* A118 | 10r multi | 5.00 | 5.00 |

London 1980 International Stamp Exhibition, May 6-14. Sheet margin overprinted "Earls Court—London 6-14 May 1980."

Swimming, Moscow '80 Emblem A127

**1980, June 4 Litho. *Perf. 14***

| | | | |
|---|---|---|---|
| *856* A127 | 10 l *shown* | 5 | 5 |
| *857* A127 | 50 l *Sprinting* | 25 | 25 |
| *858* A127 | 3r *Shot put* | 1.50 | 1.50 |
| *859* A127 | 4r *High Jump* | 2.00 | 2.00 |

**Souvenir Sheet**

| | | | |
|---|---|---|---|
| *860* A127 | 5r *Weight lifting* | 2.50 | 2.50 |

22nd Summer Olympic Games, Moscow, July 19-Aug. 3. No. 860 has multicolored margin showing Moscow '80 emblem. Size: 105½x86mm.

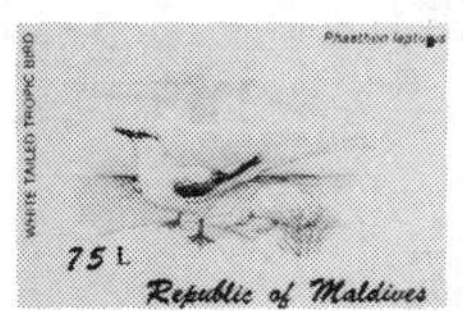
White-tailed Tropic Bird — A128

**1980, July 10 Litho. *Perf. 14***

| | | | |
|---|---|---|---|
| *861* A128 | 75 l *shown* | 38 | 38 |
| *862* A128 | 95 l *Sooty tern* | 48 | 48 |
| *863* A128 | 1r *Brown noddy* | 50 | 50 |
| *864* A128 | 1.55r *Eurasian curlew* | 78 | 78 |
| *865* A128 | 2r *Wilson's petrel* | 1.00 | 1.00 |
| *866* A128 | 4r *Caspian tern* | 2.00 | 2.00 |
| | *Nos. 861-866 (6)* | 5.14 | 5.14 |

**Souvenir Sheet**

| | | | |
|---|---|---|---|
| *867* A128 | 5r *Red-footed & brown boobies* | 2.50 | 2.50 |

No. 867 has light blue and black margin showing bird in flight. Size: 125x86mm.

Common Design Types are pictured in section before Great Britain.

Seal of Sultan Ibrahim II (1720-1750) A129

Sultans' Seals: 2 l, Mohamed Imadudeen II (1704-1720). 5 l, Mohamed Bin Haji Ali (1692-1701). 1r, Kuda Mohamed Rasgefaanu (1687-1691). 2r, Ibrahim Iskander I (1648-1687). 3r, Ibrahim Iskander, second seal.

**1980, July 26**

| | | | |
|---|---|---|---|
| *868* A129 | 1 l vio brn & blk | 5 | 5 |
| *869* A129 | 2 l vio brn & blk | 5 | 5 |
| *870* A129 | 5 l vio brn & blk | 5 | 5 |
| *871* A129 | 1r vio brn & blk | 50 | 50 |
| *872* A129 | 2r vio brn & blk | 1.00 | 1.00 |
| | *Nos. 868-872 (5)* | 1.65 | 1.65 |

**Souvenir Sheet**

| | | | |
|---|---|---|---|
| *873* A129 | 3r vio brn & blk | 1.50 | 1.50 |

No. 873 has violet brown and black margin showing sultans' names and dates in English and Arabic. Size: 131x96mm.

Queen Mother Elizabeth, 80th Birthday — A130

**1980, Sept. 29 *Perf. 14***

| | | | |
|---|---|---|---|
| *874* A130 | 4r multi | 2.00 | 2.00 |

**Souvenir Sheet**
***Perf. 12***

| | | | |
|---|---|---|---|
| *875* A130 | 5r multi | 2.50 | 2.50 |

No. 875 has multi margin showing Queen. Size: 85x110mm.

Munnaaru Tower A131

**1980, Nov. 9 Litho. *Perf. 15***

| | | | |
|---|---|---|---|
| *876* A131 | 5 l *shown* | 5 | 5 |
| *877* A131 | 10 l *Hukuru Miskiiy Mosque* | 5 | 5 |
| *878* A131 | 30 l *Medhuziyaaraiy Shrine* | 15 | 15 |
| *879* A131 | 55 l *Koran verses on wooden tablets* | 28 | 28 |
| *880* A131 | 90 l *Mother teaching son* | 45 | 45 |
| | *Nos. 876-880 (5)* | 98 | 98 |

**Souvenir Sheet**

| | | | |
|---|---|---|---|
| *881* A131 | 2r *Map and arms of Maldives* | 1.00 | 1.00 |

Hegira (Pilgrimage Year). No. 881 has multicolored margin showing map of Holy Land. Size 124½x102mm.

Malaria Eradication Control — A132

**1980, Nov. 30 *Perf. 14***

| | | | |
|---|---|---|---|
| *882* A132 | 15 l *shown* | 8 | 8 |
| *883* A132 | 25 l *Balanced diet* | 12 | 12 |
| *884* A132 | 1.50r *Oral hygiene* | 75 | 75 |
| *885* A132 | 5r *Clinic visit* | 2.50 | 2.50 |

**Souvenir Sheet**

| | | | |
|---|---|---|---|
| *886* A132 | 4r *like #885* | 2.00 | 2.00 |

World Health Day. No. 886 shows design of No. 885 in changed colors. Gray and black margin repeats design. Size: 68½x86mm.

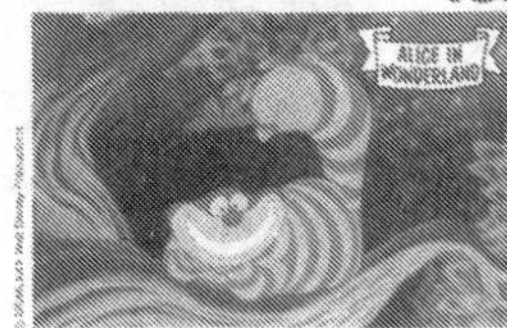


The Cheshire Cat — A133

Designs: Scenes from Walt Disney's Alice in Wonderland. 5r vert.

**1980, Dec. 22** *Perf. 11*

| No. | Type | Description | Unused | Used |
|---|---|---|---|---|
| *887* | A133 | 1 l multi | 5 | 5 |
| *888* | A133 | 2 l multi | 5 | 5 |
| *889* | A133 | 3 l multi | 5 | 5 |
| *890* | A133 | 4 l multi | 5 | 5 |
| *891* | A133 | 5 l multi | 5 | 5 |
| *892* | A133 | 10 l multi | 5 | 5 |
| *893* | A133 | 15 l multi | 8 | 8 |
| *894* | A133 | 2.50r multi | 1.25 | 1.25 |
| *895* | A133 | 4r multi | 2.00 | 2.00 |
| | | *Nos. 887-895 (9)* | 3.63 | 3.63 |

**Souvenir Sheet**

| No. | Type | Description | Unused | Used |
|---|---|---|---|---|
| *896* | A133 | 5r multi | 2.75 | 2.75 |

No. 896 has multicolored margin showing tea party. Size: 127x101½mm.

Ridley Turtle A134

**1980, Dec. 29** **Litho.** *Perf. 14*

| No. | Type | Description | Unused | Used |
|---|---|---|---|---|
| *897* | A134 | 90 l *shown* | 45 | 45 |
| *898* | A134 | 1.25r *Angel flake fish* | 62 | 62 |
| *899* | A134 | 2r *Spiny lobster* | 1.00 | 1.00 |

**Souvenir Sheet**

| No. | Type | Description | Unused | Used |
|---|---|---|---|---|
| *900* | A134 | 4r *Fish* | 2.00 | 2.00 |

No. 900 has multicolored margin showing underwater scene. Size: 140x95mm.

Tomb of Ghaazee Muhammad Thakurufaan — A135

National Day (Furniture and Palace of Muhammad Thakurufaan): 20 l, Hanging lamp, 16th century (vert.). 30 l, Chair (vert.). 95 l, Utheem Palace. 10r, Couch (vert.).

**1981, Jan. 7** *Perf. 15*

| No. | Type | Description | Unused | Used |
|---|---|---|---|---|
| *901* | A135 | 10 l multi | 5 | 5 |
| *902* | A135 | 20 l multi | 10 | 10 |
| *903* | A135 | 30 l multi | 15 | 15 |
| *904* | A135 | 95 l multi | 48 | 48 |
| *905* | A135 | 10r multi | 5.00 | 5.00 |
| | | *Nos. 901-905 (5)* | 5.78 | 5.78 |

**Royal Wedding Issue**

Common Design Type

**1981, June 22** **Litho.** *Perf. 14*

| No. | Type | Description | Unused | Used |
|---|---|---|---|---|
| *906* | CD331 | 1r Couple | 50 | 50 |
| *907* | CD331 | 2r Buckingham Palace | 1.00 | 1.00 |
| *908* | CD331 | 5r Charles | 2.50 | 2.50 |

**Souvenir Sheet**

| No. | Type | Description | Unused | Used |
|---|---|---|---|---|
| *909* | CD331 | 10r Royal state coach | 5.00 | 5.00 |

Nos. 906-908 also printed in sheets of 5 plus label, perf. 12, in changed colors.

Majlis Chamber, 1932 A136

50th Anniv. of Citizens' Majlis (Grievance Rights): 1r, Sultan Muhammed Shamsuddin III (instituted system, 1932) vert. 4r, Constitution, 1932.

**1981, June 27** *Perf. 15*

| No. | Type | Description | Unused | Used |
|---|---|---|---|---|
| *910* | A136 | 95 l multi | 35 | 35 |
| *911* | A136 | 1r multi | 40 | 40 |

**Souvenir Sheet**

| No. | Type | Description | Unused | Used |
|---|---|---|---|---|
| *912* | A136 | 4r multi | 2.00 | 2.00 |

No. 912 has multicolored margin with Arabic inscription. Size: 137x94mm.

Self-portrait with Palette, by Picasso (1881-1973) A137

Child Holding a Dove A138

**1981, Aug. 26** **Litho.** *Perf. 14*

| No. | Type | Description | Unused | Used |
|---|---|---|---|---|
| *913* | A137 | 5 l shown | 5 | 5 |
| *914* | A137 | 10 l Woman in Blue | 5 | 5 |
| *915* | A137 | 25 l Boy with a Pipe | 6 | 6 |
| *916* | A137 | 30 l Card Player | 7 | 7 |
| *917* | A137 | 90 l Sailor | 22 | 22 |
| *918* | A137 | 3r Self-portrait | 75 | 75 |
| *919* | A137 | 5r Harlequin | 1.25 | 1.25 |

***Imperf***

| No. | Type | Description | Unused | Used |
|---|---|---|---|---|
| *920* | A138 | 10r shown | 4.75 | 4.75 |
| | | *Nos. 913-920 (8)* | 7.20 | 7.20 |

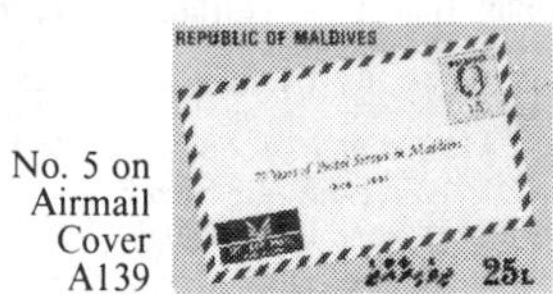


No. 5 on Airmail Cover A139

**1981, Sept. 9** **Litho.** *Perf. 14*

| No. | Type | Description | Unused | Used |
|---|---|---|---|---|
| *921* | A139 | 25 l multi | 12 | 12 |
| *922* | A139 | 75 l multi | 36 | 36 |
| *923* | A139 | 5r multi | 2.50 | 2.50 |

Postal service, 75th anniv.

Hulule Intl. Airport Opening A140

**1981, Nov. 11**

| No. | Type | Description | Unused | Used |
|---|---|---|---|---|
| *924* | A140 | 5 l Jet taking off | 5 | 5 |
| *925* | A140 | 20 l Passengers leaving jet | 10 | 10 |
| *926* | A140 | 1.80r Refueling | 90 | 90 |
| *927* | A140 | 4r shown | 2.00 | 2.00 |

**Souvenir Sheet**

| No. | Type | Description | Unused | Used |
|---|---|---|---|---|
| *928* | A140 | 5r Terminal | 2.00 | 2.00 |

No. 928 has multicolored margin showing aerial view of airport. Size: 107x79mm.

Intl. Year of the Disabled A141

Decade for Women A142

**1981, Nov. 18** **Litho.** *Perf. 14½*

| No. | Type | Description | Unused | Used |
|---|---|---|---|---|
| *929* | A141 | 2 l Homer | 5 | 5 |
| *930* | A141 | 5 l Cervantes | 5 | 5 |
| *931* | A141 | 1r Beethoven | 50 | 50 |
| *932* | A141 | 5r Van Gogh | 2.50 | 2.50 |

**Souvenir Sheet**

| No. | Type | Description | Unused | Used |
|---|---|---|---|---|
| *933* | A141 | 4r Helen Keller, Anne Sullivan | 2.00 | 2.00 |

No. 933 has multicolored margin showing silhouettes, IYD emblems. Size: 111x91mm.

**1981, Nov. 25** *Perf. 14*

| No. | Type | Description | Unused | Used |
|---|---|---|---|---|
| *934* | A142 | 20 l Preparing fish | 10 | 10 |
| *935* | A142 | 90 l 16th cent. woman | 45 | 45 |
| *936* | A142 | 1r Tending yam crop | 50 | 50 |
| *937* | A142 | 2r Making coir rope | 1.00 | 1.00 |

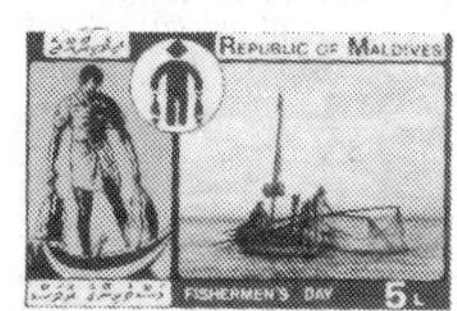


Fishermen's Day — A143

**1981, Dec. 10**

| No. | Type | Description | Unused | Used |
|---|---|---|---|---|
| *938* | A143 | 5 l Collecting bait | 5 | 5 |
| *939* | A143 | 15 l Fishing boats | 8 | 8 |
| *940* | A143 | 90 l Fisherman holding catch | 45 | 45 |
| *941* | A143 | 1.30r Sorting fish | 70 | 70 |

**Souvenir Sheet**

| No. | Type | Description | Unused | Used |
|---|---|---|---|---|
| *942* | A143 | 3r Loading fish for export | 1.50 | 1.50 |

No. 942 has multicolored margin showing world map and fishing boat. Size: 147x101mm.

World Food Day A144

**1981, Dec. 30** **Litho.** *Perf. 14*

| No. | Type | Description | Unused | Used |
|---|---|---|---|---|
| *943* | A144 | 10 l Breadfruit | 5 | 5 |
| *944* | A144 | 25 l Hen, chicks | 12 | 12 |
| *945* | A144 | 30 l Corn | 15 | 15 |
| *946* | A144 | 75 l Skipjack tuna | 38 | 38 |
| *947* | A144 | 1r Pumpkins | 50 | 50 |
| *948* | A144 | 2r Coconuts | 1.00 | 1.00 |
| | | *Nos. 943-948 (6)* | 2.20 | 2.20 |

**Souvenir Sheet**

| No. | Type | Description | Unused | Used |
|---|---|---|---|---|
| *949* | A144 | 5r Eggplants | 2.25 | 2.25 |

No. 949 has multicolored margin showing produce. Size: 110x85mm.

50th Anniv. of Walt Disney's Pluto (1980) A145

**1982, Mar. 29** **Litho.** *Perf. 13½x14*

| No. | Type | Description | Unused | Used |
|---|---|---|---|---|
| *950* | A145 | 4r Scene from Chain Gang, 1930 | 2.25 | 2.25 |

**Souvenir Sheet**

| No. | Type | Description | Unused | Used |
|---|---|---|---|---|
| *951* | A145 | 6r The Pointer, 1939 | 3.75 | 3.75 |

No. 951 has multicolored margin continuing design. Size: 127x102mm.

**Princess Diana Issue**

Common Design Type

**1982, July 15** **Litho.** *Perf. 14½x14*

| No. | Type | Description | Unused | Used |
|---|---|---|---|---|
| *952* | CD332 | 95 l Balmoral | 50 | 50 |
| *953* | CD332 | 3r Honeymoon | 1.50 | 1.50 |
| *954* | CD332 | 5r Diana | 2.50 | 2.50 |

Also issued in sheetlets of 5 + label.

**Souvenir Sheet**

| No. | Type | Description | Unused | Used |
|---|---|---|---|---|
| *955* | CD332 | 8r Diana, diff. | 3.50 | 3.50 |

No. 955 has multicolored margin showing family tree, Noah Webster. Size: 103x76mm.

Scouting Year A146

**1982, Aug. 9** **Litho.** *Perf. 14*

| No. | Type | Description | Unused | Used |
|---|---|---|---|---|
| *956* | A146 | 1.30r Saluting | 65 | 65 |
| *957* | A146 | 1.80r Fire building | 90 | 90 |
| *958* | A146 | 4r Lifesaving | 2.00 | 2.00 |
| *959* | A146 | 5r Map reading | 2.50 | 2.50 |

**Souvenir Sheet**

| No. | Type | Description | Unused | Used |
|---|---|---|---|---|
| *960* | A146 | 10r Flag, emblem | 4.75 | 4.75 |

No. 960 has multicolored margin showing hiking equipment. Size: 128x66m.

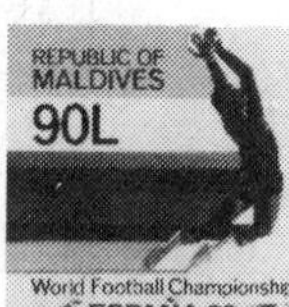


1982 World Cup — A147

Various soccer players.

**1982, Oct. 4** **Litho.** *Perf. 14*

| No. | Type | Description | Unused | Used |
|---|---|---|---|---|
| *961* | A147 | 90 l multi | 45 | 45 |
| *962* | A147 | 1.50r multi | 75 | 75 |
| *963* | A147 | 3r multi | 1.50 | 1.50 |
| *964* | A147 | 5r multi | 2.50 | 2.50 |

**Souvenir Sheet**

| No. | Type | Description | Unused | Used |
|---|---|---|---|---|
| *965* | A147 | 10r multi | 5.00 | 5.00 |

No. 965 has multicolored margin showing ball, banner. Size: 96x64mm.

Nos. 952-955 Overprinted: "ROYAL BABY/21.6.82"

**1982, Oct. 18** *Perf. 14½x14*

| No. | Type | Description | Unused | Used |
|---|---|---|---|---|
| *966* | CD332 | 95 l multi | 50 | 50 |
| *967* | CD332 | 3r multi | 1.50 | 1.50 |
| *968* | CD332 | 5r multi | 2.50 | 2.50 |

Also issued in sheetlets of 5 + label.

**Souvenir Sheet**

| No. | Type | Description | Unused | Used |
|---|---|---|---|---|
| *969* | CD332 | 8r multi | 4.00 | 4.00 |

Birth of Prince William of Wales, June 21.

TB Bacillus Centenary — A148

**1982, Nov. 22** *Perf. 14½*
970 A148 5 l Koch isolating bacillus 5 5
971 A148 15 l Slide, microscope 12 12
972 A148 95 l Koch, 1905 75 75
973 A148 3r Koch, book illus. plates 2.25 2.25

**Souvenir Sheet**

974 A148 5r Koch in lab 2.25 2.25

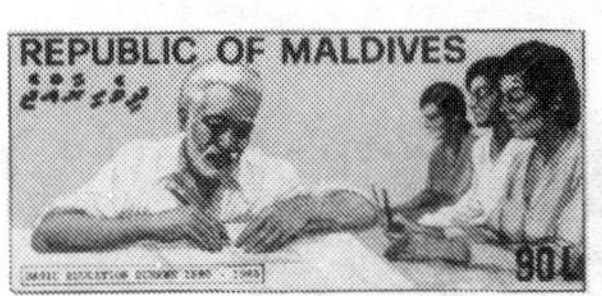


Natl. Education — A149

**1982, Nov. 15**
975 A149 90 l Basic educ. scheme, 1980-85 35 35
976 A149 95 l Formal primary educ. 38 38
977 A149 1.30r Teacher training 55 55
978 A149 2.50r Educational materials production 90 90

**Souvenir Sheet**

979 A149 6r Thanna typewriter 2.75 2.75

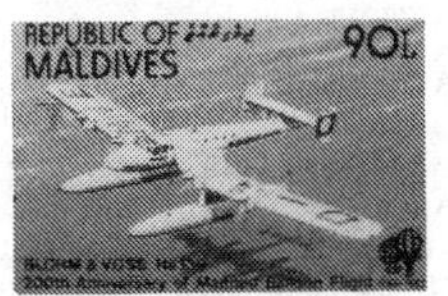


Manned Flight Bicentenary — A150

**1983, July 28** **Litho.** *Perf. 14*
980 A150 90 l Blohm & Voss Ha-139 45 45
981 A150 1.45r Macchi Castoldi MC-72 72 72
982 A150 4r Boeing F4B-3 2.00 2.00
983 A150 5r Le France 2.50 2.50

**Souvenir Sheet**

984 A150 10r Nadar's Le Geant 4.75 4.75

Roughtooth Dolphin — A151

**1983, Sept. 6** **Litho.** *Perf. 14*
985 A151 30 l shown 15 15
986 A151 40 l Indopacific humpback dolphin 20 20
987 A151 4r Finless porpoise 2.00 2.00
988 A151 6r Pygmy sperm whale 3.00 3.00

**Souvenir Sheet**

989 A151 5r Striped dolphins 2.50 2.50
Size: 82x91mm.

Classic Cars A152

**1983, Aug. 15** **Litho.** *Perf. 14½x15*
990 A152 5 l Curved Dash Oldsmobile, 1902 5 5
991 A152 30 l Aston Martin Tourer, 1932 15 15
992 A152 40 l Lamborghini Miura, 1966 20 20
993 A152 1r Mercedes-Benz 300sl, 1954 50 50
994 A152 1.45r Stutz Bearcat, 1913 72 72
995 A152 5r Lotus Elite, 1958 2.50 2.50
*Nos. 990-995 (6)* 4.12 4.12

**Souvenir Sheet**

996 A152 10r Grand Prix Sunbeam, 1924 4.75 4.75
Size of No. 996: 132x103mm.

World Communications Year — A153

**1983, Oct. 9** *Perf. 14*
997 A153 50 l Dish antenna 25 25
998 A153 1r Mail transport 50 50
999 A153 2r Ship-to-shore communications 1.00 1.00
1000 A153 10r Land-air communications 5.00 5.00

**Souvenir Sheet**

1001 A153 20r Telephone calls 9.50 9.50
Size: 90x77mm.

Raphael, 500th Birth Anniv. A154

**1983, Oct. 25** **Litho.** *Perf. 13½x14*
1002 A154 90 l La Donna Gravida 45 45
1003 A154 3r Jean of Aragon 1.50 1.50
1004 A154 4r The Woman with the Unicorn 2.00 2.00
1005 A154 6r La Muta 3.00 3.00

**Souvenir Sheet**

1006 A154 10r The Knights Dream 4.75 4.75
Multicolored margin shows the entire painting. Size: 121x96mm.

Intl. Palestinian Solidarity Day — A155

Various refugees, mosque.

**1983, Nov. 29** **Litho.** *Perf. 14*
1007 A155 4r multi 2.00 2.00
1008 A155 5r multi 2.50 2.50
1009 A155 6r multi 3.00 3.00

Natl. Development Programs — A156

**1983, Dec. 10** **Litho.** *Perf. 13½x14*
1010 A156 7 l Education 5 5
1011 A156 10 l Health care 5 5
1012 A156 5r Food production 2.50 2.50
1013 A156 6r Fishing industry 3.00 3.00

**Souvenir Sheet**

1014 A156 10r Inter-atoll transportation 4.75 4.75

No. 1014 has multicolored margin showing aerial view of atolls. Size: 134x93mm.

23rd Olympic Games, Los Angeles, July 28-Aug. 12 — A157

**1984, Feb.** *Perf. 14*
1015 A157 50 l Baseball 25 25
1016 A157 1.55r Swimming 80 80
1017 A157 3r Judo 1.50 1.50
1018 A157 4r Shot put 2.00 2.00

**Souvenir Sheet**

1019 A157 10r Handball 4.75 4.75

Nos. 982-984 Overprinted: "19th UPU/CONGRESS HAMBURG"

**1984** **Litho.** *Perf. 14*
1020 A150 4r multi 2.00 2.00
1021 A150 5r multi 2.50 2.50

**Souvenir Sheet**

1022 A150 10r multi 4.75 4.75

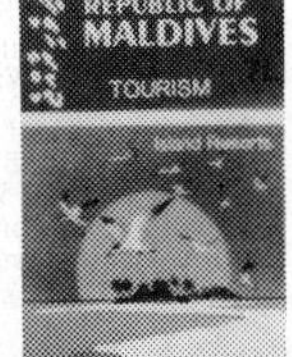


Tourism — A158

**1984, Sept. 21** **Litho.** *Perf. 14½*
1023 A158 7 l Island resorts 5 5
1024 A158 15 l Cruising 5 5
1025 A158 20 l Snorkelling 6 6
1026 A158 2r Wind surfing 55 55
1027 A158 4r Scuba diving 1.10 1.10
1028 A158 6r Night fishing 1.75 1.75
1029 A158 8r Big game fishing 2.25 2.25
1030 A158 10r Nature (turtle) 2.75 2.75
*Nos. 1023-1030 (8)* 8.56 8.56

50th Anniv. of Donald Duck A160

Scenes from various cartoons and movies.

**1984, Nov.** **Litho.** *Perf. 14*
1040 A160 3 l multi 5 5
1041 A160 4 l multi 5 5
1042 A160 5 l multi 5 5
1043 A160 10 l multi 5 5
1044 A160 15 l multi 6 6
1045 A160 25 l multi 8 8
1045A A160 5r multi, perf. 12 x 12½ 1.75 1.75
1046 A160 8r multi 2.75 2.75
1047 A160 10r multi 3.50 3.50
*Nos. 1040-1047 (9)* 8.34 8.34

**Souvenir Sheets**

1048 A160 15r multi 5.00 5.00
1049 A160 15r multi 5.00 5.00

Nos. 1048-1049 have multicolored margins continuing design.

Nos. 952-955, 966-969 Surcharged.

**1984, July** **Litho.** *Perf. 14½x14*
1050 CD332 1.45r on 95l #952 3.00 2.50
1051 CD332 1.45r on 95l #966 3.00 2.50
1052 CD332 1.45r on 3r #953 3.00 2.50
1053 CD332 1.45r on 3r #967 3.00 2.50
1054 CD332 1.45r on 5r #954 3.00 2.50
1055 CD332 1.45r on 5r #968 3.00 2.50
*Nos. 1050-1055 (6)* 18.00 15.00

**Souvenir Sheet**

1056 CD332 1.45r on 8r #955 12.50 10.00
1057 CD332 1.45r on 8r #969 12.50 10.00

Namibia Day A161

**1984, Aug. 26** *Perf. 15*
1058 A161 6r Breaking chain 1.75 1.75
1059 A161 8r Family, rising sun 2.25 2.25

**Souvenir Sheet**

1060 A161 10r Map, sun 2.75 2.75

No. 1060 has multicolored margin continuing design. Size: 129x103mm.

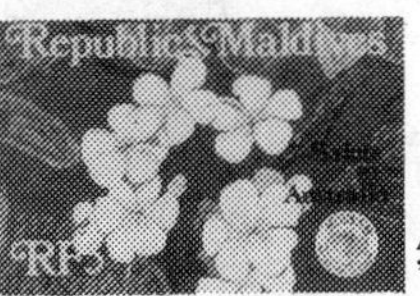


Ausipex '84 — A162

**1984, Sept. 21**
1061 A162 5r Frangipani 2.00 2.00
1062 A162 10r Cooktown orchid 4.00 4.00

**Souvenir Sheet**

1063 A162 15r Sun orchids 6.00 6.00

No. 1063 has multicolored margin continuing design. Size: 106x77mm.

150th Anniv., Birth of Edgar Degas — A163

**1984, Oct.** **Litho.** *Perf. 14*
1064 A163 75 l Portrait of Edmond Iduranty 20 20
1065 A163 2r Portrait of James Tissot 55 55
1066 A163 5r Portrait of Achille Degas 1.40 1.40
1067 A163 10r Lady with Chrysanthemums 2.75 2.75

**Souvenir Sheet**

1068 A163 15r Self-Portrait 4.00 4.00

Nos. 1068 shows portion of painting Dance Lesson in margin. Size: 100x70mm.

Opening of Islamic Center A164

**1984, Nov. 11** **Litho.** *Perf. 15*
1069 A164 2r Mosque 50 50
1070 A164 5r Mosque, minaret, vert. 1.25 1.25

40th Anniv., International Civil Aviation Organization — A165

**1984, Nov. 19** **Litho.** ***Perf. 14***

*1071* A165 7 l Boeing 737 5 5
*1072* A165 4r Lockheed L-1011 1.10 1.10
*1073* A165 6r McDonnell Douglas DC-10 1.75 1.75
*1074* A165 8r Lockheed L-1011 2.25 2.25

**Souvenir Sheet**

*1075* A165 15r Shorts SC7 Skyvan 4.00 4.00

No. 1075 shows several aircraft in margin. Size: 111x93mm.

450th Anniv. of the Death of Correggio — A166

**1984, Dec. 10** **Litho.** ***Perf. 14***

*1076* A166 5r Detail from The Day 1.40 1.40
*1077* A166 10r Detail from The Night 2.75 2.75

**Souvenir Sheet**

*1078* A166 15r Portrait of a Man 4.00 4.00

No. 1078 has design continuing into margin. Size: 61x81mm.

John J. Audubon A167

Illustrations from Audubon's Birds of America.

**1985, Mar. 9** **Litho.** ***Perf. 14***

*1079* A167 3r Flesh-footed shearwater, vert. 90 90
*1080* A167 3.50r Little grebe 2.00 2.00
*1081* A167 4r Great cormorant, vert. 1.10 1.10
*1082* A167 4.50r White-faced storm petrel 1.25 1.25

**Souvenir Sheet**

*1083* A167 15r Red-necked phalarope 4.00 4.00

No. 1083 has multicolored margin continuing design. Size: 109x80mm.

Natl. Security Services — A168

**1985, June 6** **Litho.** ***Perf. 14***

*1084* A168 15 l Drill 5 5
*1085* A168 20 l Combat training 6 6
*1086* A168 1r Fire fighting 30 30
*1087* A168 2r Coast guard 60 60
*1088* A168 10r Parade, vert. 3.00 3.00
*Nos. 1084-1088 (5)* 4.01 4.01

**Souvenir Sheet**

*1089* A168 10r Badge, cannon 3.00 3.00

No. 1089 has multicolored margin picturing harbor police on rescue mission. Size: 129x85mm.

Nos. 1015-1019 Ovptd. with Country or "Gold Medalist," Winner and Nation in 3 Lines.

**1985, July 17**

*1090* A157 50 l Japan 15 15
*1091* A157 1.55r Theresa Andrews 45 45
*1092* A157 3r Frank Wieneke 90 90
*1093* A157 4r Claudia Loch 1.25 1.25

**Souvenir Sheet**

*1094* A157 10r US 3.00 3.00

Queen Mother, 85th Birthday A169

Johann Sebastian Bach, Composer A170

**1985-86** ***Perf. 14, 12 (1r, 4r, 10r)***

*1095* A169 1r Wearing tiara 22 22
*1096* A169 3r like 1r 70 70
*1097* A169 4r At Middlesex Hospital, horiz. 90 90
*1098* A169 5r like 4r 1.10 1.10
*1099* A169 7r Wearing fur stole 1.50 1.50
*1100* A169 10r like 7r 2.25 2.25
*Nos. 1095-1100 (6)* 6.67 6.67

**Souvenir Sheet**

*1101* A169 15r With Prince of Wales 4.25 4.25

Issue dates: 1r, 4r, 10r, Jan. 4, 1986. 3r, 5r, 7r, 15r, Aug. 20, 1985. Nos. 1095, 1097, 1100 printed in sheets of 5 plus label. No. 1101 has multicolored decorative margin picturing Rosa polyantha and Oronis natrix. Size: 57x85mm.

**1985, Sept. 3** ***Perf. 14***

Portrait, Invention No. 1 in C Major and: 15 l, Lira da Braccio. 2r, Tenor oboe. 4r, Serpent. 10r, Table organ.

*1102* A170 15 l multi 5 5
*1103* A170 2r multi 60 60
*1104* A170 4r multi 1.25 1.25
*1105* A170 10r multi 3.00 3.00

**Souvenir Sheet**

*1106* A170 15r Portrait 4.25 4.25

No. 1106 has black margin picturing Bach's signature and St. Thomas Church, Leipzig. Size: 105x76mm.

Ships A171

**1985, Sept. 23**

*1107* A171 3 l Masodi 5 5
*1108* A171 5 l Naalu Baththeli 5 5
*1109* A171 10 l Addu Odi 5 5
*1110* A171 2.60r Masdhoni, 2nd generation 78 78
*1111* A171 2.70r Masdhoni 80 80
*1112* A171 3r Baththeli Dhoni 90 90
*1113* A171 5r Inter 1 1.50 1.50
*1114* A171 10r Yacht Dhoni 3.00 3.00
*Nos. 1107-1114 (8)* 7.13 7.13

World Tourism Org., 10th Anniv. A172

**1985, Oct. 2**

*1115* A172 6r Wind surfing 1.75 1.75
*1116* A172 8r Scuba diving 2.50 2.50

**Souvenir Sheet**

*1117* A172 15r Kuda Hithi Resort 4.25 4.25

No. 1117 has multicolored decorative margin picturing WTO emblem. Size: 171x113mm.

Maldives Admission to UN, 20th Anniv. — A173

**1985, Oct. 24**

*1118* A173 20 l shown 6 6
*1119* A173 15r Flags, UN building 4.25 4.25

UN 40th Anniv., Intl. Peace Year A174

**1985, Oct. 24** **Litho.** ***Perf. 14***

*1120* A174 15 l UN Building 5 5
*1121* A174 2r IPY emblem 60 60
*1122* A174 4r Security Council 1.20 1.20
*1123* A174 10r Lion, lamb 3.00 3.00

**Souvenir Sheet**

*1124* A174 15r UN Building, diff. 4.50 4.50

Nos. 1120-1121, 1123-1124, vert. No. 1124 has multicolored margin continuing design and picturing New York City skyline. Size: 76x92mm.

Intl. Youth Year A175

**1985, Nov. 20** ***Perf. 15***

*1125* A175 90 l Culture 28 28
*1126* A175 6r Games 1.75 1.75
*1127* A175 10r Community service, vert. 3.00 3.00

**Souvenir Sheet**

*1128* A175 15r Youth camp, vert. 4.25 4.25

No. 1128 has multicolored margin picturing emblem and island. Size: 85x84mm.

Summit Nations Flags, Dedication by Pres. Maumoon — A176

**1985, Dec. 8** ***Perf. 14***

*1129* A176 3r multi 90 90

South Asian Regional Cooperation, SARC, 1st Summit, Dec. 7-8, 1985.

Tuna A177

**1985, Dec. 10**

*1130* A177 25 l Frigate 8 8
*1131* A177 75 l Little tuna 22 22
*1132* A177 3r Dogtooth 90 90
*1133* A177 5r Yellowfin 1.50 1.50

**Souvenir Sheet**

*1134* A177 15r Skipjack 4.25 4.25

Fisherman's Day. No. 1134 has multicolored margin picturing fishing boats at sea. Size: 131x90mm.

Mark Twain, American Novelist A178

Disney characters and Twain quotes.

**1985, Dec. 21**

*1135* A178 2 l multi 5 5
*1136* A178 3 l multi 5 5
*1137* A178 4 l multi 5 5
*1138* A178 20 l multi 6 6
*1139* A178 4r multi 1.25 1.25
*1140* A178 13r multi 4.00 4.00
*Nos. 1135-1140 (6)* 5.46 5.46

**Souvenir Sheet**

*1141* A178 15r multi 4.50 4.50

Intl. Youth Year. 4r issued in sheet of 8. No. 1141 has multicolored margin continuing the design. Size: 126x101mm.

The Brothers Grimm — A179

Disney characters in Doctor Knowall.

**1985, Dec. 21**

*1142* A179 1 l multi 5 5
*1143* A179 5 l multi 5 5
*1144* A179 10 l multi 5 5
*1145* A179 15 l multi 5 5
*1146* A179 3r multi 90 90
*1147* A179 14r multi 4.25 4.25
*Nos. 1142-1147 (6)* 5.35 5.35

**Souvenir Sheet**

*1148* A179 15r multi 4.50 4.50

3r issued in sheets of 8. No. 1148 has multicolored margin continuing the design. Size: 127x101mm.

World Disarmament Day — A180

**1986, Feb. 10** ***Perf. 14½x14***

*1149* A180 1.50r shown 45 45
*1150* A180 10r Dove 3.00 3.00

Halley's Comet A181

Designs: 20 l, NASA space telescope. 1.50r, Giotto space probe. 2r, Plant-A probe, Japan. 4r, Edmond Halley, Stonehenge. 5r, Vega probe, USSR. 15r, Comet over Male.

**1986, Apr. 29**

*1151* A181 20 l multi 6 6
*1152* A181 1.50r multi 45 45
*1153* A181 2r multi 60 60
*1154* A181 4r multi 1.20 1.20
*1155* A181 5r multi 1.50 1.50
*Nos. 1151-1155 (5)* 3.81 3.81

**Souvenir Sheet**

*1156* A181 15r multi 4.50 4.50

No. 1156 has multicolored margin continuing design. Size: 102x70mm.

Statue of Liberty, Cent. A182

Detail of statue and: 50 l, Walter Gropius (1883-1969), architect. 70 l, John Lennon (1940-1980), musician. 1r, George Balanchine (1904-1983), choreographer. 10r, Franz Werfel (1890-1945), writer. 15r, Close-up of statue, vert.

**1986, May 5**

*1157* A182 50 l multi 15 15
*1158* A182 70 l multi 20 20
*1159* A182 1r multi 30 30
*1160* A182 10r multi 3.00 3.00

**Souvenir Sheet**

*1161* A182 15r multi 4.50 4.50

No. 1161 has multicolored margin picturing New York skyline and American personalities, John Ericsson (1803-1889), engineer; Stan Laurel (1890-1965), film comedian; David Dubinsky (c. 1895-1982), labor leader; and Vicki Baum (1888-1960), novelist. Size: 100x72mm.

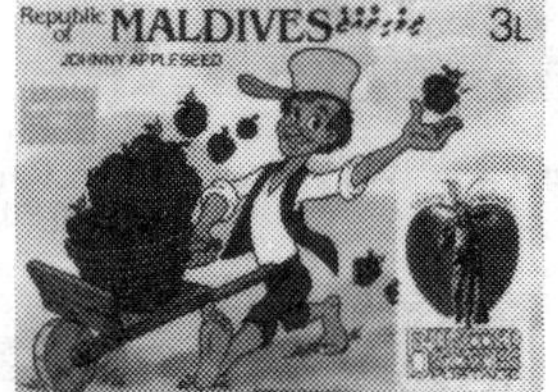


AMERIPEX '86 — A183

US stamps and Disney portrayals of American legends: 3 l, No. 1317, Johnny Appleseed. 4 l, No. 1122, Paul Bunyan. 5 l, No. 1381, Casey at the Bat. 10 l, No. 1548, Tales of Sleepy Hollow. 15 l, No. 922, John Henry. 20 l, No. 1061, Windwagon Smith. 13r, No. 1409, Mike Fink. 14r, No. 993, Casey Jones. No. 1170, Remember the Alamo, No. 1330. No. 1171, Pocahontas, Nos. 328-330.

**1986, May 22** ***Perf. 11***

*1162* A183 3 l multi 5 5
*1163* A183 4 l multi 5 5
*1164* A183 5 l multi 5 5
*1165* A183 10 l multi 5 5
*1166* A183 15 l multi 5 5
*1167* A183 20 l multi 6 6
*1168* A183 13r multi 3.90 3.90
*1169* A183 14r multi 4.20 4.20
*Nos. 1162-1169 (8)* 8.41 8.41

Souvenir Sheets

***Perf. 14***

*1170* A183 15r multi 4.50 4.50
*1171* A183 15r multi 4.50 4.50

Nos. 1170-1171 have multicolored margins continuing the designs. Sizes: 127x102mm.

**Queen Elizabeth II, 60th Birthday**

Common Design Type

**1986, May 29** ***Perf. 14***

*1172* CD339 1r Girl Guides' rally, 1938 30 30
*1173* CD339 2r Canada visit, 1985 60 60
*1174* CD339 12r At Sandringham, 1970 3.60 3.60

**Souvenir Sheet**

*1175* CD339 15r Royal Lodge, 1940 4.50 4.50

No. 1175 has tan and black decorative margin. Size: 120x85mm.

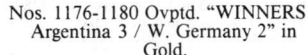

1986 World Cup Soccer Championships, Mexico — A184

Various soccer plays.

**1986, June 18** **Litho.** ***Perf. 14***

*1176* A184 15 l multi 5 5
*1177* A184 2r multi 60 60
*1178* A184 4r multi 1.20 1.20
*1179* A184 10r multi 3.00 3.00

**Souvenir Sheet**

*1180* A184 15r multi 4.50 4.50

No. 1180 has multicolored margin picturing Azteca Stadium interior. Size: 96x115mm.

**Royal Wedding Issue, 1986**

Common Design Type

Designs: 10 l, Prince Andrew and Sarah Ferguson. 2r, Andrew. 12r, Andrew on ship's deck in uniform. 15r, Couple, diff.

**1986, July 23**

*1181* CD340 10 l multi 5 5
*1182* CD340 2r multi 60 60
*1183* CD340 12r multi 3.60 3.60

**Souvenir Sheet**

*1184* CD340 15r multi 4.50 4.50

No. 1184 has multicolored margin picturing Prince Andrew at helicopter controls. Size: 88x88mm.

Marine Life A185

**1986, Sept. 22** **Litho.** ***Perf. 15***

*1185* A185 50 l Sea fan, moorish idol 15 15
*1186* A185 90 l Regal angelfish 28 28
*1187* A185 1r Anemone fish 30 30
*1188* A185 2r Stinging coral, tiger cowrie 60 60
*1189* A185 3r Emperor angelfish, staghorn coral 90 90
*1190* A185 4r Black-naped tern 1.20 1.20
*1191* A185 5r Fiddler crab, staghorn coral 1.50 1.50
*1192* A185 10r Hawksbill turtle 3.00 3.00
*Nos. 1185-1192 (8)* 7.93 7.93

**Souvenir Sheets**

*1193* A185 15r Trumpet fish 4.50 4.50
*1194* A185 15r Long-nosed butterflyfish 4.50 4.50

Nos. 1185-1187, 1189 and 1193 bear the World Wildlife Fund emblem. Nos. 1193-1194 have multicolored margins continuing the designs. Sizes: 107x76mm.

Audubon Type of 1985

**1986, Oct. 9** **Litho.** ***Perf. 14***

*1195* A167 3 l Little blue heron 5 5
*1196* A167 4 l White-tailed kite, vert. 5 5
*1197* A167 5 l Greater shearwater 5 5
*1198* A167 10 l Magnificent frigatebird, vert. 5 5
*1199* A167 15 l Eared grebe, vert. 5 5
*1200* A167 20 l Common merganser, vert. 6 6
*1201* A167 13r Great-footed hawk 4.00 4.00
*1202* A167 14r Greater prairie chicken 4.25 4.25
*Nos. 1195-1202 (8)* 8.56 8.56

**Souvenir Sheets**

*1203* A167 15r White-fronted goose 4.50 4.50
*1204* A167 15r Northern fulmar, vert. 4.50 4.50

Nos. 1197, 1199-1201 printed se-tenant with labels picturing a horned puffin, gray kingbird, downy woodpecker and water pipit, respectively. Nos. 1203-1204 have multicolored margins continuing the designs. Size: 74x104mm.

Nos. 1176-1180 Ovptd. "WINNERS / Argentina 3 / W. Germany 2" in Gold.

**1986, Oct. 25**

*1205* A184 15 l multi 5 5
*1206* A184 2r multi 60 60
*1207* A184 4r multi 1.20 1.20
*1208* A184 10r multi 3.00 3.00

**Souvenir Sheet**

*1209* A184 15r multi 4.50 4.50

Nos. 1151-1156 Printed with Halley's Comet Symbol in Silver.

**1986, Oct. 30**

*1210* A181 20 l multi 6 6
*1211* A181 1.50r multi 45 45
*1212* A181 2r multi 60 60
*1213* A181 4r multi 1.20 1.20
*1214* A181 5r multi 1.50 1.50
*Nos. 1210-1214 (5)* 3.81 3.81

**Souvenir Sheet**

*1215* A181 15r multi 4.50 4.50

UNESCO, 40th Anniv. — A186

**1986, Nov. 4** ***Perf. 15***

*1216* A186 1r Aviation 30 30
*1217* A186 2r Boat-building 60 60
*1218* A186 3r Education 90 90
*1219* A186 5r Research 1.50 1.50

**Souvenir Sheet**

*1220* A186 15r Ocean exploration 4.50 4.50

No. 1220 has multicolored margin picturing UNESCO emblem and traditional sailing ship. Size: 77x101mm.

Mushrooms A187

**1986, Dec. 31** **Litho.** ***Perf. 15***

*1221* A187 15 l Hypholoma fasciculare 5 5
*1222* A187 50 l Kuehneromyces mutabilis 15 15
*1223* A187 1r Amanita muscaria 30 30
*1224* A187 2r Agaricus campestris 60 60
*1225* A187 3r Amanita pantherina 90 90
*1226* A187 4r Coprinus comatus 1.20 1.20
*1227* A187 5r Pholiota spectabilis 1.50 1.50
*1228* A187 10r Pluteus cervinus 3.00 3.00
*Nos. 1221-1228 (8)* 7.70 7.70

**Souvenir Sheets**

*1229* A187 15r Armillaria mellea 4.50 4.50
*1230* A187 15r Stropharia aeruginosa 4.50 4.50

Nos. 1222-1223, 1225-1226 vert. Nos. 1229-1230 have multicolored decorative margins continuing the designs.

Flowers — A188

**1987, Jan. 29** **Litho.** ***Perf. 15***

*1231* A188 10 l Ixora 5 5
*1232* A188 20 l Frangipani 6 6
*1233* A188 50 l Crinum 15 15
*1235* A188 2r Pink rose 60 60
*1236* A188 4r Flamboyant 1.20 1.20
*1238* A188 10r Ground orchid 3.00 3.00
*Nos. 1231-1238 (6)* 5.06 5.06

**Souvenir Sheet**

*1239* A188 15r Gardenia 4.50 4.50
*1240* A188 15r Oleander 4.50 4.50

Nos. 1239-1240 have multicolored margins continuing the designs. Sizes: 100x70mm.

Girl Guides, 75th Anniv. (in 1985) A189

**1987, Apr. 4** **Litho.** ***Perf. 15***

*1241* A189 15 l Nature study 5 5
*1242* A189 2r Guides, rabbits 60 60
*1243* A189 4r Bird-watching 1.20 1.20
*1244* A189 12r Lady Baden-Powell, flag 3.50 3.50

**Souvenir Sheet**

*1245* A189 15r Sailing 4.50 4.50

No. 1245 has multicolored margin picturing maps of the North and South Male atolls. Size: 104x78mm.

Indigenous Trees and Plants A190

**1987, Apr. 22** **Litho.** ***Perf. 14***

*1246* A190 50 l Thespesia populnea, vert. 15 15
*1247* A190 1r Cocos nucifera, vert. 30 30
*1248* A190 2r Calophyllum mophyllum, vert. 60 60
*1249* A190 3r Xyanthosoma indica 90 90
*1250* A190 5r Ipomoea batatas 1.50 1.50
*1251* A190 7r Artocarpus altilis, vert. 2.00 2.00
*Nos. 1246-1251 (6)* 5.45 5.45

**Souvenir Sheet**

*1252* A190 15r Cocos nucifera, diff., vert. 4.50 4.50

No. 1252 has inscribed multicolored margin picturing fruit of Maldivian coconut palm. Size: 74x111mm.

A191

America's Cup — A192

**1987, May 4 Litho. *Perf. 15***

*1253* A191 15 l Intrepid, 1970 5 5
*1254* A191 1r France II, 1974 30 30
*1255* A191 2r Gretel, 1962 60 60
*1256* A191 12r Volunteer, 1887 3.50 3.50

**Souvenir Sheet**

*1257* A192 15r Defender Vs. Valkyrie III, 1895 4.50 4.50

No. 1257 has multicolored margin continuing the design and picturing US flag and trophy. Size: 113x83mm.

Butterflies A193 Scientists A194

**1987, Dec. 16 Litho. *Perf. 15***

*1258* A193 15 l Precis octavia 5 5
*1259* A193 20 l Pachliopta hector 6 6
*1260* A193 50 l Teinopalpus imperialis 15 15
*1261* A193 1r Kallima horsfieldi 30 30
*1262* A193 2r Cethosia biblis 60 60
*1263* A193 4r Hestia jasonia 1.20 1.20
*1264* A193 7r Papilio memnon 2.10 2.10
*1265* A193 10r Meneris tulbaghia 3.00 3.00
*Nos. 1258-1265 (8)* 7.46 7.46

**Souvenir Sheets**

*1266* A193 15r Acraea violae acraeinae 4.50 4.50
*1267* A193 15r Hebomoia leucippe 4.50 4.50

Nos. 1266-1267 have multicolored decorative margins continuing the designs. Sizes: 134x102mm, 135x102mm.

**1988, Jan. 10 *Perf. 14***

Designs: 1.50r, Sir Isaac Newton using prism to demonstrate his Theory of Light, horiz. 3r, Euclid (c. 300 B.C.), mathematician whose Principles of Geometry were the chief source of geometrical reason and method until the 19th cent. 4r, Gregor Johann Mendel (1822-1884), botanist who worked with pea plants; resulting theories of heredity gave rise to genetics. 5r, Galileo, first man to observe four moons of Jupiter, horiz. 15r, Apollo spacecraft orbiting the moon.

*1268* A194 1.50r multi 45 45
*1269* A194 3r multi 90 90
*1270* A194 4r multi 1.15 1.15
*1271* A194 5r multi 1.50 1.50

**Souvenir Sheet**

*1272* A194 15r multi 4.50 4.50

No. 1272 has multicolored decorative margin continuing the design. Size: 101x72mm.

Disney Characters, Space Exploration — A195

**1988, Feb. 15**

*1273* A195 3 l Weather satellite 5 5
*1274* A195 4 l Navigation satellite 5 5
*1275* A195 5 l Communication satellite 5 5
*1276* A195 10 l Moon rover 5 5
*1277* A195 20 l Space shuttle 6 6
*1278* A195 13r Space docking 3.70 3.70
*1279* A195 14r Voyager 2 4.00 4.00
*Nos. 1273-1279 (7)* 7.96 7.96

**Souvenir Sheets**

*1280* A195 15r 1st Man on Moon 4.30 4.30
*1281* A195 15r Space station colony 4.30 4.30

Nos. 1276-1278 and 1281 vert. Nos. 1280-1281 have multicolored decorative margins continuing the designs. Sizes: 127x102mm.

WHO, 40th Anniv. A196

**1988, Apr. 7 Litho. *Perf. 14***

*1282* A196 2r Immunization 58 58
*1283* A196 4r Clean water 1.15 1.15

World Environment Day — A197

**1988, May 9 *Perf. 15***

*1284* A197 15 l Save water 5 5
*1285* A197 75 l Protect the reef 22 22
*1286* A197 2r Conserve nature 58 58

**Souvenir Sheet**

*1287* A197 10r Banyan tree, vert. 3.00 3.00

Nos. 1287 has multicolored inscribed margin continuing the design. Size: 105x76mm.

Nos. 1172-1175 Ovptd. "40th WEDDING ANNIVERSARY/ H.M. QUEEN ELIZABETH II/ H.R.H. THE DUKE OF EDINBURGH" in Gold

**1988, July 7 Litho. *Perf. 14***

*1288* CD339 1r multi 30 30
*1289* CD339 2r multi 58 58
*1290* CD339 12r multi 3.40 3.40

**Souvenir Sheet**

*1291* CD339 15r multi 4.25 4.25

Transportation and Communication Decade for Asia and the Pacific — A198

Globe and: 2r, Postal communications. 3r, Earth satellite telecommunications technology. 5r, Space telecommunications technology. 10r, Automobile, aircraft and ship.

**1988, May 31 Litho. *Perf. 14***

*1292* A198 2r multi 58 58
*1293* A198 3r multi 85 85
*1294* A198 5r multi 1.45 1.45
*1295* A198 10r multi 2.85 2.85

1988 Summer Olympics, Seoul A199 Intl. Year of Shelter for the Homeless A200

**1988, July 16**

*1296* A199 15 l Discus 5 5
*1297* A199 2r 100-Meter sprint 58 58
*1298* A199 4r Gymnastics, horiz. 1.15 1.15
*1299* A199 12r Steeplechase, horiz. 3.45 3.45

**Souvenir Sheet**

*1300* A199 20r Tennis, horiz. 5.25 5.25

No. 1300 has multicolored inscribed margin picturing natl. flag and tennis players in silhouette. Size: 106x76mm.

**1988, July 20**

*1301* A200 50 l Medical clinic 15 15
*1302* A200 3r Prefab housing 90 90

**Souvenir Sheet**

*1303* A200 15r Construction site 4.25 4.25

No. 1303 has multicolored inscribed margin continuing the design. Size: 63x106mm.

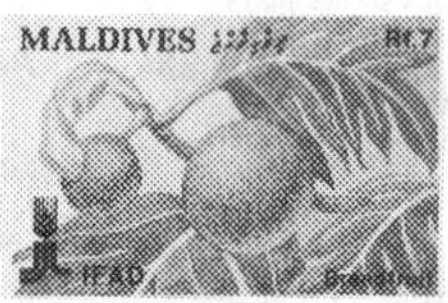

Intl. Fund for Agricultural Development (IFAD), 10th Anniv. — A201

**1988, July 30**

*1304* A201 7r Breadfruit 2.00 2.00
*1305* A201 10r Mango, vert. 2.75 2.75

**Souvenir Sheet**

*1306* A201 15r Coconut palm, yellowtail tuna 4.25 4.25

No. 1306 has multicolored margin continuing the design and picturing lagoon. Size: 103x74mm.

---

## MALTA

LOCATION — A group of islands in the Mediterranean Sea off the coast of Sicily.
GOVT. — Republic within the British Commonwealth.
AREA — 122 sq. mi.
POP. — 329,189 (1983)
CAPITAL — Valletta

The former colony includes the islands of Malta, Gozo, and Comino. It became a republic December 13, 1974.

4 Farthings = 1 Penny
12 Pence = 1 Shilling
20 Shillings = 1 Pound
10 Mils = 1 Cent (1972)
100 Cents = £1 (1972)

**Catalogue values for unused stamps in this country are for Never Hinged items, beginning with Scott 206 in the regular postage section, Scott B1 in the semi-postal section, Scott C2 in the air post section, and Scott J21 in the postage due section.**

Queen Victoria
A1 A2

A3 A4

**1860-61 Unwmk. Typo. *Perf. 14***

*1* A1 ½p buff ('61) 425.00 300.00
*2* A1 ½p buff, *bluish* 950.00 575.00
a Imperf. *11,000.*

**1863-80 Wmk. Crown and C. C. (1)**

*3* A1 ½p org yel ('80) 32.50 14.00
a ½p buff 65.00 50.00
b ½p brn org 110.00 45.00
c ½p yel buff 50.00 40.00
*4* A1 ½p gldn yel ('74) 175.00 200.00

**1865 *Perf. 12½***

*5* A1 ½p buff 60.00 45.00
a ½p yel buff 235.00 225.00

**1878 *Perf. 14x12½***

*6* A1 ½p buff 110.00 85.00
a Perf. 12½x14

**1882 Wmk. 2 *Perf. 14.***

*7* A1 ½p orange 7.50 11.50

**1885, Jan. 1**

*8* A1 ½p green 85 28
*9* A2 1p car rose 1.10 22
a 1p rose 30.00 15.00
*10* A3 2p gray 2.75 1.40
*11* A4 2½p ultra 10.00 50
a 2½p brt ultra 10.00 50
b 2½p dl bl 10.00 50
*12* A3 4p brown 6.00 2.50
a Imperf. (pair) 5,000. 4,750.
*13* A3 1sh violet 16.00 5.50
*Nos. 8-13 (6)* 36.70 10.40

Queen Victoria within Maltese Cross — A5

**1886 Wmk. Crown and C. C. (1)**

*14* A5 5sh rose 77.50 50.00

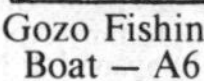

Gozo Fishing Boat — A6 Ancient Galley — A7

**1899, Feb. 4 Engr. Wmk. 2**

*15* A6 4½p blk brn 9.00 5.50
*16* A7 5p brn red 14.00 8.00

See Nos. 42-45.

"Malta" — A8 St. Paul after Shipwreck — A9

**1899 Wmk. Crown and C. C. (1)**

*17* A8 2sh 6p ol gray 20.00 10.50
*18* A9 10sh bl blk 47.50 32.50

See No. 64.

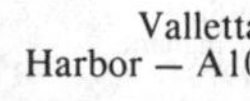

Valletta Harbor — A10

**1901, Jan. 1** **Wmk. 2**
*19* A10 1f red brn 52 52

See Nos. 28-29.

No. 11 Surcharged in Black **One Penny**

**1902, July 4**
*20* A4 1p on 2½p ultra 42 42
*a* "Pney" 18.00 18.00
*b* Double surcharge 4,000. 4,000.

King Edward VII — A12

**1903-04** **Typo.**
*21* A12 ½p dk grn 90 18
*22* A12 1p car & blk 1.50 14
*23* A12 2p gray & red vio 5.75 3.25
*24* A12 2½p ultra & brn vio 6.75 90
*25* A12 3p red vio & gray 65 35
*26* A12 4p brn & blk ('04) 16.00 16.00
*27* A12 1sh vio & gray 6.25 3.50
*Nos. 21-27 (7)* 37.80 24.32

**1904-11** **Wmk. 3**
*28* A10 1f red brn ('05) 1.40 20
*29* A10 1f dk brn ('10) 1.90 25
*30* A12 ½p green 75 8
*31* A12 1p car & blk ('05) 3.75 25
*32* A12 1p car ('07) 70 25
*33* A12 2p gray & red vio ('05) 4.25 1.75
*34* A12 2p gray ('11) 1.25 2.00
*35* A12 2½p ultra & brn vio 2.75 1.00
*36* A12 2½p ultra ('11) 2.75 70
*37* A12 4p brn & blk ('06) 6.25 6.25
*38* A12 4p scar & blk, *yel* ('11) 2.00 2.50
*39* A12 1sh vio & gray 17.50 3.00
*40* A12 1sh blk, *grn* ('11) 3.75 3.75
*41* A12 5sh scar & grn, *yel* ('11) 45.00 52.50

**Engr.**
*42* A6 4½p blk brn ('05) 12.00 5.50
*43* A6 4½p org ('11) 2.75 3.00
*44* A7 5p red ('04) 10.50 5.25
*45* A7 5p ol grn ('10) 3.50 3.50
*Nos. 28-45 (18)* 122.75 91.73

A13

A15

King George V — A16

**1914-21** **Typo.**

**Ordinary Paper.**
*49* A13 ¼p brown 20 9
*50* A13 ½p green 30 9
*51* A13 1p scar ('15) 50 9
*a* 1p car ('14) 50 9
*52* A13 2p gray ('15) 3.25 2.50
*53* A13 2½p ultra 55 28

**Chalky Paper.**
*54* A15 3p vio, *yel* 3.25 4.25
*58* A13 6p dl vio & red vio 4.50 5.50
*59* A15 1sh *green* 5.50 5.50
*a* 1sh *bl grn*, ol back 6.00 6.00
*b* 1sh *emer* ('21) 5.50 5.50
*c* As "b", ol back 6.00 5.50
*60* A16 2sh ultra & dl vio, *bl* 25.00 17.50
*61* A16 5sh scar & grn, *yel* 32.50 35.00

**Surface-colored Paper**
*62* A15 1sh *grn* ('15) 6.00 8.75
*Nos. 49-54,58-62 (11)* 81.55 79.55

See Nos. 66-68, 70-72.

Valletta Harbor — A17

**1915** **Engr.**

**Ordinary Paper**
*63* A17 4p black 8.75 6.00

St. Paul A18

George V A19

**1919**
*64* A8 2sh 6p ol grn 35.00 40.00
*65* A18 10sh black 5,750. *7,500.*
Revenue cancel 70.00

**1921-22** **Typo.** **Wmk. 4**

**Ordinary Paper**
*66* A13 ¼p brown 18 22
*67* A13 ½p green 2.50 3.50
*68* A13 1p rose red 18 14
*69* A19 2p gray 1.75 50
*70* A13 2½p ultra 1.50 2.25

**Chalky Paper**
*71* A13 6p dl vio & red vio 6.50 9.00
*72* A16 2sh ultra & dl vio, *bl* 35.00 45.00

**Engr.**

**Ordinary Paper.**
*73* A18 10sh black 215.00 275.00
*Nos. 66-73 (8)* 262.61 335.61

Stamps of 1914-19 Overprinted in Red or Black

**1922** **Wmk. 3**

**Ordinary Paper**

**Overprint 21mm**
*77* A13 ½p green 8 10
*78* A13 2½p ultra 65 80

**Chalky Paper**
*79* A15 3p vio, *yel* 55 65
*80* A13 6p dl lil & red vio 60 65
*81* A15 1sh blk, *emerald* 80 90

**Overprint 28mm**
*82* A16 2sh ultra & dl vio, *bl* (R) 200.00 275.00

**Ordinary Paper**
*83* A8 2sh 6p ol grn 11.50 13.00

**Chalky Paper**
*84* A16 5sh scar & grn, *yel* 27.50 35.00
*Nos. 77-84 (8)* 241.68 326.10

**Wmk. Crown and C. C. (1)**

**Ordinary Paper**
*85* A9 10sh bl blk (R) 160.00 190.00

Same Overprint on Stamps of 1921

**1922** **Ordinary Paper** **Wmk. 4**

**Overprint 21mm**
*86* A13 ¼p brown 10 14
*87* A13 ½p green 55 80
*88* A13 1p rose red 14 14
*89* A19 2p gray 48 70
*90* A13 2½p ultra 38 38

**Chalky Paper**
*91* A13 6p dl vio & red vio 3.25 3.00

**Overprint 28mm**
*92* A16 2sh ultra & dl vio, *bl* (R) 16.00 19.00

**Ordinary Paper**
*93* A18 10sh blk (R) 67.50 82.50
*Nos. 86-93 (8)* 88.40 106.66

No. 69 Surcharged **One Farthing**

**1922, Apr. 15**
*97* A19 1f on 2p gray 10 10

"Malta" A20

Britannia and Malta A21

**1922-26** **Typo.**

**Chalky Paper**
*98* A20 ¼p brown 50 8
*99* A20 ½p green 18 8
*100* A20 1p buff & plum 45 15
*101* A20 1p vio ('24) 25 12
*102* A20 1½p org brn ('23) 1.25 12
*103* A20 2p ol brn & turq 65 15
*104* A20 2½p ultra ('26) 18 38
*105* A20 3p ultra 60 60
*a* 3p blue 60 60
*106* A20 3p blk, *yel* ('26) 75 1.75
*107* A20 4p yel & ultra 75 75
*108* A20 6p ol grn & vio 60 60
*109* A21 1sh ol brn & bl 2.00 2.00
*110* A21 2sh ultra & ol brn 3.75 5.00
*111* A21 2sh6p blk & red vio 4.00 4.50
*112* A21 5sh ultra & org 7.50 *15.00*
*113* A21 10sh ol brn & gray 16.00 *27.50*

**Engr.**

**Ordinary Paper.**
*114* A20 £1 car red & blk ('25) 62.50 100.00
*a* £1 rose car & blk ('22) 62.50 100.00
*Nos. 98-114 (17)* 101.91 158.78

No. 114a has watermark sideways.

No. 105 Surcharged **Two pence halfpenny**

**1925, Dec.**
*115* A20 2½p on 3p ultramarine 50 65

Stamps of 1922-26 Overprinted **POSTAGE**

**1926**
*116* A20 ¼p brown 10 10
*117* A20 ½p green 9 9
*118* A20 1p violet 10 10
*119* A20 1½p org brn 18 16
*120* A20 2p ol brn & turq 25 25
*121* A20 2½p ultra 25 16
*122* A20 3p blk, *yellow* 32 32
*a* Inverted overprint 150.00 200.00
*123* A20 4p yel & ultra 4.50 5.00
*124* A20 6p ol grn & vio 45 45
*125* A21 1sh ol brn & bl 2.75 3.25
*126* A21 2sh ultra & ol brn 27.50 45.00
*127* A21 2sh6p blk & red vio 7.75 11.50
*128* A21 5sh ultra & org 5.75 9.00
*129* A21 10sh ol brn & gray 5.50 8.00
*Nos. 116-129 (14)* 55.49 83.38

George V — A22

Valletta Harbor — A23

St. Publius — A24

Notabile (Mdina) — A25

Gozo Fishing Boat A26

Statue of Neptune A27

Ruins at Mnaidra A28

St. Paul A29

**1926-27** **Typo.** ***Perf. 14½x14***
*131* A22 ¼p brown 25 8
*132* A22 ½p green 1.25 12
*133* A22 1p red 1.65 20
*134* A22 1½p org brn 1.65 20
*135* A22 2p gray 2.00 2.75
*136* A22 2½p blue 1.90 50
*137* A22 3p dk vio 1.90 2.25
*138* A22 4p org red & blk 3.00 3.25
*139* A22 4½p yel buff & vio 3.00 3.50
*140* A22 6p red & vio 3.25 3.25

**Engr.** ***Perf. 12½***

**Inscribed: "Postage"**

| | | | | |
|---|---|---|---|---|
| *141* | A23 | 1sh black | 3.25 | 3.25 |
| *142* | A24 | 1sh6p grn & blk | 4.50 | *5.00* |
| *143* | A25 | 2sh dp vio & blk | 6.75 | 8.25 |
| *144* | A26 | 2sh6p ver & blk | 11.00 | 14.00 |
| *145* | A27 | 3sh bl & blk | 9.75 | 16.00 |
| *146* | A28 | 5sh grn & blk | 17.50 | *22.50* |
| *147* | A29 | 10sh car & blk | 37.50 | *40.00* |
| | | *Nos. 131-147 (17)* | 110.10 | 125.10 |

See Nos. 167-183.

Stamps and Type of 1926-27 Overprinted in Black

**POSTAGE**

**AND**

**REVENUE**

**1928** ***Perf. 14½x14.***

| | | | | |
|---|---|---|---|---|
| *148* | A22 | ¼p brown | 9 | 6 |
| *149* | A22 | ½p green | 45 | 6 |
| *150* | A22 | 1p red | 52 | 32 |
| *151* | A22 | 1p org brn | 1.25 | 9 |
| *152* | A22 | 1½p yel brn | 28 | 35 |
| *153* | A22 | 1½p red | 45 | 6 |
| *154* | A22 | 2p gray | 1.25 | 1.70 |
| *155* | A22 | 2½p blue | 85 | 28 |
| *156* | A22 | 3p dk vio | 65 | 40 |
| *157* | A22 | 4p org red & blk | 85 | 1.00 |
| *158* | A22 | 4½p yel & vio | 1.40 | 1.00 |
| *159* | A22 | 6p red & vio | 2.00 | 1.60 |

Overprinted in Red

**POSTAGE**

**AND**

**REVENUE.**

***Perf. 12½.***

| | | | | |
|---|---|---|---|---|
| *160* | A23 | 1sh black | 2.25 | 1.90 |
| *161* | A24 | 1sh6p grn & blk | 4.50 | 6.75 |
| *162* | A25 | 2sh dp vio & blk | 5.00 | 12.50 |
| *163* | A26 | 2sh6p ver & blk | 9.00 | 15.00 |
| *164* | A27 | 3sh ultra & blk | 12.50 | 17.00 |
| *165* | A28 | 5sh yel grn & blk | 18.00 | 25.00 |
| *166* | A29 | 10sh car rose & blk | 35.00 | 50.00 |
| | | *Nos. 148-166 (19)* | 96.29 | 135.07 |

Types of 1926-27 Issue

**1930, Oct. 20** **Typo.** ***Perf. 14½x14***

**Inscribed: "Postage & Revenue"**

| | | | | |
|---|---|---|---|---|
| *167* | A22 | ¼p brown | 14 | 6 |
| *168* | A22 | ½p green | 12 | 6 |
| *169* | A22 | 1p yel brn | 32 | 6 |
| *170* | A22 | 1½p red | 32 | 8 |
| *171* | A22 | 2p gray | 55 | 50 |
| *172* | A22 | 2½p blue | 1.25 | 25 |
| *173* | A22 | 3p dk vio | 1.40 | 28 |
| *174* | A22 | 4p org red & blk | 1.65 | 2.50 |
| *175* | A22 | 4½p yel & vio | 2.50 | 3.00 |
| *176* | A22 | 6p red & vio | 2.00 | 2.00 |

**Engr.** ***Perf. 12½***

| | | | | |
|---|---|---|---|---|
| *177* | A23 | 1sh black | 3.25 | 5.50 |
| *178* | A24 | 1sh6p grn & blk | 5.50 | 11.00 |
| *179* | A25 | 2sh dp vio & blk | 6.50 | 14.00 |
| *180* | A26 | 2sh6p ver & blk | 14.00 | 22.50 |
| *181* | A27 | 3sh ultra & blk | 14.00 | 16.00 |
| *182* | A28 | 5sh yel grn & blk | 13.00 | 22.50 |
| *183* | A29 | 10sh car rose & blk | 50.00 | 75.00 |
| | | *Nos. 167-183 (17)* | 116.50 | 175.29 |

**Silver Jubilee Issue**

Common Design Type

**1935, May 6** ***Perf. 11x12***

| | | | | |
|---|---|---|---|---|
| *184* | CD301 | ½p grn & blk | 18 | 20 |
| *185* | CD301 | 2½p ultra & brn | 1.25 | 1.00 |
| *186* | CD301 | 6p ol grn & lt bl | 4.50 | 5.25 |
| *187* | CD301 | 1sh brn vio & ind | 7.50 | 10.50 |

**Coronation Issue**

Common Design Type

***Perf. 13½x14***

**1937, May 12** **Wmk. 4**

| | | | | |
|---|---|---|---|---|
| *188* | CD302 | ½p dp grn | 14 | 14 |
| *189* | CD302 | 1½p carmine | 20 | 20 |
| *190* | CD302 | 2½p brt ultra | 60 | 60 |

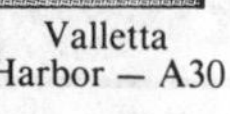


Valletta Harbor — A30

Fort St. Angelo — A31

Verdala Palace — A32

Neolithic Ruins — A33

Victoria and Citadel, Gozo — A34

De l'Isle Adam Entering Mdina — A35

St. John's Co-Cathedral — A36

Mnaidra Temple — A37

Statue of Antonio Manoel de Vilhena — A38

Woman in Faldetta — A39

St. Publius — A40

Mdina Cathedral A41

Statue of Neptune — A42

Palace Square — A43

St. Paul — A44

**1938-43** **Wmk. 4** ***Perf. 12½.***

| | | | | |
|---|---|---|---|---|
| *191* | A30 | 1f brown | 5 | 5 |
| *192* | A31 | ½p green | 12 | 5 |
| *192A* | A31 | ½p chnt ('43) | 10 | 5 |
| *193* | A32 | 1p chestnut | 85 | 20 |
| *193A* | A32 | 1p grn ('43) | 8 | 5 |
| *194* | A33 | 1½p rose red | 20 | 10 |
| *194A* | A33 | 1½p dk gray ('43) | 12 | 10 |
| *195* | A34 | 2p dk gray | 85 | 70 |
| *195A* | A34 | 2p rose red ('43) | 35 | 20 |
| *196* | A35 | 2½p blue | 85 | 55 |
| *196A* | A35 | 2½p vio ('43) | 30 | 30 |
| *197* | A36 | 3p violet | 70 | 50 |
| *197A* | A36 | 3p bl ('43) | 35 | 18 |
| *198* | A37 | 4½p ocher & ol grn | 25 | 25 |
| *199* | A38 | 6p rose red & ol grn | 25 | 25 |
| *200* | A39 | 1sh black | 55 | 50 |
| *201* | A40 | 1sh6p sage grn & blk | 1.00 | 95 |
| *202* | A41 | 2sh dk bl & lt grn | 1.00 | 1.00 |
| *203* | A42 | 2sh6p rose red & blk | 2.75 | 2.75 |
| *204* | A43 | 5sh bl grn & blk | 3.50 | 3.50 |
| *205* | A44 | 10sh dp rose & blk | 8.00 | 8.00 |
| | | *Nos. 191-205 (21)* | 22.22 | 20.23 |

See No. 236a.

**Catalogue values for unused stamps in this section, from this point to the end of the section, are for Never Hinged items.**

**Peace Issue.**

Common Design Type

Inscribed: "Malta" and Crosses

***Perf. 13½x14***

**1946, June 8** **Engr.** **Wmk. 4**

| | | | | |
|---|---|---|---|---|
| *206* | CD303 | 1p brt grn | 10 | 10 |
| *207* | CD303 | 3p dk ultra | 20 | 20 |

Stamps of 1938-43 Overprinted in Black or Carmine

a

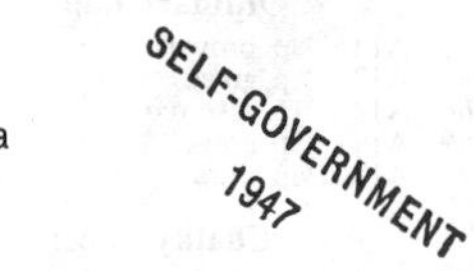


**1948, Nov. 25** ***Perf. 12½***

| | | | | |
|---|---|---|---|---|
| *208* | A30 | 1f brown | 8 | 8 |
| *209* | A31 | ½p chestnut | 12 | 8 |
| *210* | A32 | 1p green | 45 | 8 |
| *211* | A33 | 1½p dk gray (C) | 35 | 12 |
| *212* | A34 | 2p rose red | 50 | 20 |
| *213* | A35 | 2½p vio (C) | 50 | 20 |
| *214* | A36 | 3p bl (C) | 55 | 20 |
| *215* | A37 | 4½p ocher & ol grn | 1.25 | 65 |
| *216* | A38 | 6p rose red & ol grn | 45 | 32 |
| *217* | A39 | 1sh black | 1.25 | 42 |
| *218* | A40 | 1sh6p sage grn & blk | 1.50 | 60 |
| *219* | A41 | 2sh dk bl & lt grn (C) | 2.00 | 90 |
| *220* | A42 | 2sh6p rose red & blk | 3.50 | 2.25 |
| *221* | A43 | 5sh bl grn & blk (C) | 6.25 | 5.25 |
| *222* | A44 | 10sh dp rose & blk | 12.50 | 10.50 |
| | | *Nos. 208-222 (15)* | 31.25 | 21.85 |

The overprint is smaller on No. 208. It reads from lower left to upper right on Nos. 209 and 221.

See Nos. 235-240.

**Silver Wedding Issue.**

Common Design Types

Inscribed: "Malta" and Crosses

**1949, Jan. 4** **Photo.** ***Perf. 14x14½***

| | | | | |
|---|---|---|---|---|
| *223* | CD304 | 1p dk grn | 20 | 20 |

**Engr.** ***Perf. 11½x11.***

| | | | | |
|---|---|---|---|---|
| *224* | CD305 | £1 dk bl | 35.00 | 30.00 |

**UPU Issue**

Common Design Types

Inscribed: "Malta" and Crosses

***Perf. 13½, 11x11½***

**1949, Oct. 10** **Engr.** **Wmk. 4**

| | | | | |
|---|---|---|---|---|
| *225* | CD306 | 2½p violet | 22 | 22 |
| *226* | CD307 | 3p indigo | 60 | 60 |
| *227* | CD308 | 6p dp car | 1.10 | 1.10 |
| *228* | CD309 | 1sh slate | 2.25 | 2.25 |

Princess Elizabeth A45

Madonna and Child A46

**1950, Dec. 1** **Engr.** ***Perf. 12x11½***

| | | | | |
|---|---|---|---|---|
| *229* | A45 | 1p emerald | 14 | 8 |
| *230* | A45 | 3p brt bl | 35 | 32 |
| *231* | A45 | 1sh gray blk | 70 | 70 |

Visit of Princess Elizabeth.

**1951, July 12**

| | | | | |
|---|---|---|---|---|
| *232* | A46 | 1p green | 14 | 10 |
| *233* | A46 | 3p purple | 22 | 18 |
| *234* | A46 | 1sh sl blk | 80 | 80 |

700th anniv. of the presentation of the scapular to St. Simon Stock.

Types of 1938-43 Overprinted Type "a" in Red or Black

**1953, Jan. 8** **Wmk. 4** ***Perf. 12½***

| | | | | |
|---|---|---|---|---|
| *235* | A32 | 1p gray (R) | 12 | 8 |
| *236* | A33 | 1½p green | 20 | 12 |
| *a.* | | Overprint omitted | | *8,000.* |
| *237* | A34 | 2p ocher | 28 | 24 |
| *238* | A35 | 2½p rose red | 48 | 32 |
| *239* | A36 | 3p vio (R) | 35 | 12 |
| *240* | A37 | 4½p ultra & ol grn (R) | 75 | 60 |
| | | *Nos. 235-240 (6)* | 2.18 | 1.48 |

**Coronation Issue.**

Common Design Type

Inscribed: "Malta" and Crosses

**1953, June 3** **Engr.** ***Perf. 13½x13***

| | | | | |
|---|---|---|---|---|
| *241* | CD312 | 1½p dk grn blk | 20 | 15 |

Type of 1938-43 with Portrait of Queen Elizabeth II Inscribed: "Royal Visit 1954."

**1954, May 3** ***Perf. 12½***

| | | | | |
|---|---|---|---|---|
| *242* | A36 | 3p violet | 18 | 12 |

Visit of Elizabeth II and the Duke of Edinburgh, 1954.

Central Altarpiece, Collegiate Parish Church, Cospicua — A47

***Perf. 14½x13½***

**1954, Sept. 8** **Photo.** **Wmk. 4**

| | | | | |
|---|---|---|---|---|
| *243* | A47 | 1½p brt grn | 8 | 6 |
| *244* | A47 | 3p ultra | 18 | 14 |
| *245* | A47 | 1sh gray blk | 70 | 70 |

Cent. of the promulgation of the Dogma of the Immaculate Conception.

Monument of the Great Siege, 1565 — A48

Auberge de Castille — A49

Designs: ½p, Wignacourt Aqueduct Horsetrough. 1p, Victory Church. 1½p, War Memorial. 2p, Mosta Dome. 3p, King's Scroll. 4½p, Roosevelt's Scroll. 6p, Neolithic Temples at Tarxien. 8p, Vedette. 1sh, Mdina Gate. 1sh 6p, Les Gavroches. 2sh, Monument of Christ the King. 2sh 6p, Monument of Nicolas Cottoner. 5sh, Raymond

Perellos Monument. 10sh, St. Paul. £1, Baptism of Christ.

**1956-57 Engr. *Perf. 11½***

| No. | Type | Value | Color | Unused | Used |
|---|---|---|---|---|---|
| *246* | A48 | ¼p | violet | 8 | 6 |
| *247* | A48 | ½p | yel org | 8 | 5 |
| *248* | A48 | 1p | black | 6 | 5 |
| *249* | A48 | 1½p | brt grn | 8 | 6 |
| *250* | A48 | 2p | brown | 10 | 6 |
| *251* | A49 | 2½p | org brn | 14 | 8 |
| *252* | A48 | 3p | rose red | 8 | 6 |
| *253* | A48 | 4½p | blue | 10 | 7 |
| *254* | A49 | 6p | sl bl | 12 | 7 |
| *255* | A48 | 8p | ol bis | 18 | 70 |
| *256* | A48 | 1sh | purple | 35 | 28 |
| *257* | A48 | 1sh6p | Prus grn | 60 | 45 |
| *258* | A48 | 2sh | ol grn | 1.10 | 70 |

***Perf. 13½x13***

| No. | Type | Value | Color | Unused | Used |
|---|---|---|---|---|---|
| *259* | A48 | 2sh6p | cop brn | 2.00 | 1.00 |
| *260* | A48 | 5sh | emerald | 3.75 | 3.00 |
| *261* | A48 | 10sh | dk car | 18.00 | 12.50 |
| *262* | A48 | £1 | yel brn ('57) | 22.50 | 21.00 |
| | | | *Nos. 246-262 (17)* | 49.32 | 40.19 |

See Nos. 296-297.

### First George Cross Issue

Symbol of Malta's War Effort — A50

Searchlights over Malta — A51

Design: 1sh, Bombed houses.

***Perf. 14x14½, 14½x14***

**1957, Apr. 15 Photo.**

**Cross in Silver**

| No. | Type | Value | Color | Unused | Used |
|---|---|---|---|---|---|
| *263* | A50 | 1½p | green | 6 | 5 |
| *264* | A51 | 3p | brt red | 14 | 14 |
| *265* | A50 | 1sh | dk red brn | 38 | 38 |

Award of the George Cross to Malta for its war effort.

See Nos. 269-274.

Symbols of Architecture A52

Designs: 3p, Symbols of Industry (vert.). 1sh, Symbols of electronics and chemistry and Technical School, Paola.

***Perf. 14½x14, 14x14½***

**1958, Feb. 15 Wmk. 314**

| No. | Type | Value | Color | Unused | Used |
|---|---|---|---|---|---|
| *266* | A52 | 1½p | dp grn & blk | 6 | 5 |
| *267* | A52 | 3p | rose red, blk & gray | 14 | 10 |
| *268* | A52 | 1sh | gray, blk & lil | 50 | 50 |

Issued to promote technical education on Malta.

### Second George Cross Issue.

Types of 1957.

Designs: 1½p, Bombed-out family and searchlights. 3p, Convoy entering harbor. 1sh, Searchlight battery.

***Perf. 14½x14, 14x14½***

**1958, Apr. 15**

**Cross in Silver**

| No. | Type | Value | Color | Unused | Used |
|---|---|---|---|---|---|
| *269* | A51 | 1½p | blk & brt grn | 7 | 7 |
| *270* | A50 | 3p | blk & ver | 14 | 10 |
| *271* | A51 | 1sh | blk & brt lil | 55 | 55 |

### Third George Cross Issue

Types of 1957

Designs: 1½p, Air Raid Precautions Organization helping wounded. 3p, Allegory of Malta. 1sh, Mother and child during air raid.

***Perf. 14x14½, 14½x14***

**1959, Apr. 15**

| No. | Type | Value | Color | Unused | Used |
|---|---|---|---|---|---|
| *272* | A50 | 1½p | gold, grn & blk | 7 | 6 |
| *273* | A51 | 3p | gold, lil & blk | 14 | 10 |
| *274* | A50 | 1sh | gold, gray & blk | 65 | 65 |

St. Paul's Shipwreck, Painting in St. Paul's Church, Valletta — A53

Statue of St. Paul, St. Paul's Grotto, Rabat — A54

Designs: 3p, Consecration of St. Publius. 6p, St. Paul leaving Malta; painting, St. Paul's Church, Valletta. 1sh, Angel holding tablet with quotations from Acts of the Apostles. 2sh6p, St. Paul and St. Paul's Bay islets.

**Wmk. 314**

**1960, Feb. 9 Photo. *Perf. 13***

| No. | Type | Value | Color | Unused | Used |
|---|---|---|---|---|---|
| *275* | A53 | 1½ | bis, brt bl & gold | 18 | 12 |
| a | | | Gold dates & crosses omitted | 75.00 | 57.50 |
| *276* | A53 | 3p | lt bl, red lil & gold | 20 | 18 |
| *277* | A53 | 6p | car, gray & gold | 45 | 32 |

***Perf. 14x14½***

| No. | Type | Value | Color | Unused | Used |
|---|---|---|---|---|---|
| *278* | A54 | 8p | blk & gold | 70 | 55 |
| *279* | A54 | 1sh | brt cl & gold | 95 | 70 |
| *280* | A54 | 2sh6p | brt grnsh bl & gold | 4.50 | 3.25 |
| a | | | Gold omitted | 300.00 | |
| | | | *Nos. 275-280 (6)* | 6.98 | 5.12 |

Issued to commemorate the 19th centenary of St. Paul's shipwreck on Malta.

Stamp of 1860 — A55

***Perf. 13x13½***

**1960, Dec. 1 Engr. Wmk. 314**

**1860 ½p in Buff and Pale Blue**

| No. | Type | Value | Color | Unused | Used |
|---|---|---|---|---|---|
| *281* | A55 | 1½p | green | 7 | 7 |
| *282* | A55 | 3p | rose car | 15 | 15 |
| *283* | A55 | 6p | dk bl | 60 | 60 |

Centenary of Malta's first postage stamp.

### Fourth George Cross Issue

George Cross A56

Background designs: 3p, Sun and water. 1sh, Maltese crosses.

**1961, Apr. 15 Photo. *Perf. 14½x14***

| No. | Type | Value | Color | Unused | Used |
|---|---|---|---|---|---|
| *284* | A56 | 1½p | gray, bis & buff | 14 | 12 |
| *285* | A56 | 3p | ol gray, lt & dk grnsh bl | 15 | 8 |
| *286* | A56 | 1sh | ol grn, vio & lil | 1.10 | 1.10 |

19th anniv. of the award of the George Cross to Malta.

Madonna Damascena A57

David Bruce and Themistocles Zammit A58

Designs: 3p, Great Siege Monument by Antonio Sciortino. 6p, Grand Master La Valette (1557-1568). 1sh, Assault on Fort Elmo (old map).

***Perf. 12½x12***

**1962, Sept. 7 Wmk. 314**

| No. | Type | Value | Color | Unused | Used |
|---|---|---|---|---|---|
| *287* | A57 | 2p | ultra | 9 | 9 |
| *288* | A57 | 3p | dk red | 14 | 14 |
| *289* | A57 | 6p | ol grn | 30 | 30 |
| *290* | A57 | 1sh | rose lake | 75 | 75 |

Issued to commemorate the Great Siege of 1565 in which the knights of the Order of St. John and the Maltese Christians defeated the Turks.

### Freedom from Hunger Issue

Common Design Type

**1963, June 4 *Perf. 14x14½***

| No. | Type | Value | Color | Unused | Used |
|---|---|---|---|---|---|
| *291* | CD314 | 1sh 6p | sep | 4.50 | 3.75 |

### Red Cross Centenary Issue

Common Design Type

**1963, Sept. 2 Litho. *Perf. 13***

| No. | Type | Value | Color | Unused | Used |
|---|---|---|---|---|---|
| *292* | CD315 | 2p | blk & red | 28 | 15 |
| *293* | CD315 | 1sh 6p | ultra & red | 3.50 | 3.00 |

Type of 1956

Designs as before.

**1963-64 Engr. *Perf. 11½***

| No. | Type | Value | Color | Unused | Used |
|---|---|---|---|---|---|
| *296* | A48 | 1p | black | 50 | 42 |
| *297* | A48 | 2p | brn ('64) | 85 | 75 |

***Perf. 14x13½***

**1964, Apr. 14 Photo. Wmk. 314**

Design: 1sh6p, Goat and laboratory equipment.

| No. | Type | Value | Color | Unused | Used |
|---|---|---|---|---|---|
| *298* | A58 | 2p | dl grn, blk & brn | 8 | 6 |
| a | | | Black omitted | | |
| *299* | A58 | 1sh6p | rose lake & blk | 1.25 | 1.00 |

Issued to publicize the Anti-Brucellosis (Malta fever) Congress of the U.N. Food and Agriculture Organization, Valletta, June 8-13.

Nicola Cottoner Attending Sick Man and Congress Emblem — A59

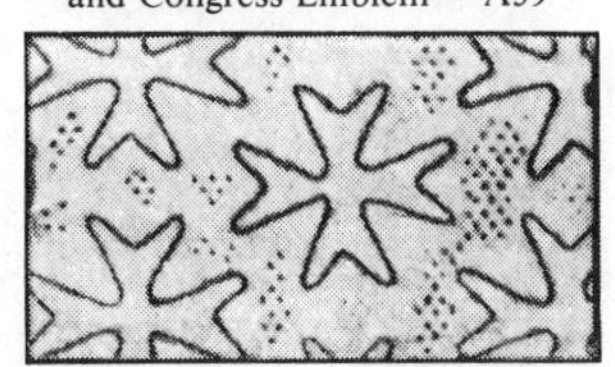

Wmk. 354- Maltese Cross, Multiple

Designs: 6p, Statue of St. Luke and St. Luke's Hospital. 1sh6p, Sacra Infermeria, Valletta.

***Perf. 13½x14***

**1964, Sept. 5 Wmk. 354**

| No. | Type | Value | Color | Unused | Used |
|---|---|---|---|---|---|
| *300* | A59 | 2p | chlky bl, gold, red & blk | 15 | 15 |
| *301* | A59 | 6p | ol bis, gold, red & blk | 52 | 45 |
| *302* | A59 | 1sh6p | dl vio, gold, red & blk | 1.75 | 1.65 |

1st European Cong. of Catholic Physicians, Malta, Sept. 6-10.

### Independent State

Dove, Maltese Cross and British Crown — A60

Nativity — A61

Design (Dove, Maltese Cross and): 3p, 1sh6p, Pope's tiara. 6p, 2sh6p, U.N. Emblem.

***Perf. 14½x13½***

**1964, Sept. 21 Photo.**

| No. | Type | Value | Color | Unused | Used |
|---|---|---|---|---|---|
| *303* | A60 | 2p | gray ol, red & gold | 18 | 14 |
| *304* | A60 | 3p | dk red brn, red & gold | 25 | 20 |
| *305* | A60 | 6p | sl bl, red & gold | 80 | 40 |
| *306* | A60 | 1sh | ultra, red & gold | 1.65 | 60 |
| *307* | A60 | 1sh6p | bl blk, red & gold | 5.00 | 2.75 |
| *308* | A60 | 2sh6p | vio bl, red & gold | 6.50 | 4.50 |
| | | | *Nos. 303-308 (6)* | 14.38 | 8.59 |

Malta's independence.

***Perf. 13x13½***

**1964, Nov. 3 Wmk. 354**

| No. | Type | Value | Color | Unused | Used |
|---|---|---|---|---|---|
| *309* | A61 | 2p | mag & gold | 14 | 12 |
| *310* | A61 | 4p | ultra & gold | 32 | 28 |
| *311* | A61 | 8p | dp grn & gold | 1.40 | 1.25 |

Cippus, Phoenician and Greek Inscriptions — A62

British Arms, Armory, Valletta A63

Designs (History of Malta): ½p, Neolithic (sculpture of sleeping woman). 1½p, Roman (sculpture). 2p, Proto-Christian (lamp, Roman temple, Chrismon). 2½p, Saracen (tomb, 12th cent.). 3p, Siculo Norman (arch, Palazzo Gatto-Murina, Notabile). 4p, Knights of Malta (lamp base, cross, and armor of knights). 4½p, Maltese navy (16th cent. galleons). 5p, Fortifications. 6p, French occupation (Cathedral of Notabile, cap, fasces). 10p, Naval Arsenal.

1sh, Maltese Corps of the British Army (insignia). 1sh3p, International Eucharistic Congress, 1913 (angels adoring Eucharist and map of Malta). 1sh6p, Self Government, 1921 (Knights of Malta Hall, present assembly seat). 2sh, Civic Council, Gozo (Statue of Livia, Gozo City Hall). 2sh6p, State of Malta (seated woman and George Cross). 3sh, Independence (doves, UN emblem, British crown, and Pope's tiara).

5sh, "HAFMED," (headquarters and insigne of Allied Forces, Mediterranean). 10sh, Map of Mediterranean. £1, Catholicism (Sts. Paul, Publius and Agatha).

***Perf. 14x14½, 14½ (A63)***

**1965-70 Photo. Wmk. 354**

| No. | Type | Value | Color | Unused | Used |
|---|---|---|---|---|---|
| *312* | A62 | ½p | vio & yel | 5 | 5 |
| *313* | A62 | 1p | bl, vio & gold | 5 | 5 |
| a | | | Booklet pane of 6 ('70) | 35 | |
| *314* | A62 | 1½p | gray, car, blk, gold & sil | 6 | 5 |
| *315* | A62 | 2p | ultra, pink & gold | 6 | 5 |
| a | | | Gold omitted | 35.00 | |
| b | | | Booklet pane of 6 ('70) | 40 | |
| *316* | A62 | 2½p | dk brn, org red & gold | 9 | 7 |
| a | | | Gold ("SARACENIC") omitted | 55.00 | |

*317* A62 3p blk, vio, gold & sil 8 6
*a* Imperf., pair 400.00
*b* Gold (windows) omitted 42.50
*318* A62 4p dp plum & multi 9 6
*a* Black (arms shading) omitted 47.50
*b* Silver omitted 45.00
*319* A62 4½p gold & multi 15 8
*319A* A62 5p tan, blk & gold ('70) 25 12
*b* Booklet pane of 6 ('71) 1.75
*320* A62 6p dl bl, blk, gold & sil 15 7
*a* Black omitted 60.00
*b* Silver ("MALTA") omitted 60.00
*321* A63 8p gray, vio, red & gold 18 8
*321A* A63 10p gray, blk, mar, red & gold ('70) 35 22
*322* A63 1sh gray, blk, red & gold 35 16
*323* A63 1sh3p gray, ultra, red & gold 75 45
*324* A63 1sh6p gray, pur, red & gold 60 25
*a* Queen's head omitted *275.00*
*325* A63 2sh gray, Prus grn, red & gold 75 45
*326* A63 2sh6p gray, brn, red & gold 90 50
*327* A63 3sh gray, sl, red & gold 1.10 60
*328* A63 5sh gray, Prus grn, red & gold 1.90 1.00
*329* A63 10sh gray, brt pur, red & gold 3.75 2.50
*330* A63 £1 gray, blk, red, pink & gold 7.25 4.50
*a* Pink (shading on figures) omitted 30.00
*Nos. 312-330 (21)* 18.91 11.37

Issue dates: 5p, 10p, Aug. 1, 1970. Others Jan. 7, 1965.

Dante, by Raphael — A64

**1965, July 7 Unwmk. *Perf. 14***
*331* A64 2p dk bl 6 5
*332* A64 6p ol grn 28 22
*333* A64 2sh chocolate 1.00 85

Issued to commemorate the 700th anniversary of the birth of Dante Alighieri.

Turkish Encampment and Fort St. Michael A65

Blockading Turkish Armada A66

Designs: 3p, Knights and Turks in battle. 8p, Arrival of relief force. 1sh, Trophy, arms of Grandmaster Jean de La Valette. 1sh6p, Allegory of Victory, mural by Calabrese from St. John's Co-Cathedral. 2sh6p, Great Siege victory medal; Jean de La Valette on obverse, David slaying Goliath on reverse.

***Perf. 14½x14, 13***
**1965, Sept. 1 Photo. Wmk. 354**
*334* A65 2p ol grn, red & blk 10 8
*335* A65 3p lt gray, red, blk & ol grn 18 14
*336* A66 6p ol grn, red org, cl, blk & gold 40 30
*a* Black omitted *140.00*
*b* Gold omitted *150.00*
*337* A65 8p dk bl, red & gold 55 48
*338* A66 1sh bluish blk, red & gold 1.40 1.10

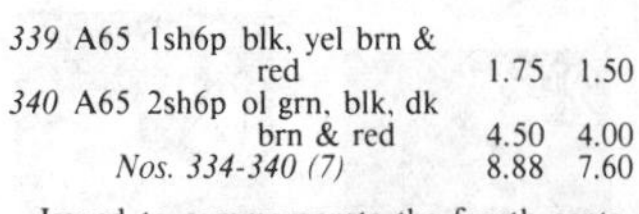

*339* A65 1sh6p blk, yel brn & red 1.75 1.50
*340* A65 2sh6p ol grn, blk, dk brn & red 4.50 4.00
*Nos. 334-340 (7)* 8.88 7.60

Issued to commemorate the fourth centenary of the Great Siege (Turks against Malta).

The Three Wise Men — A67

***Perf. 11x11½***
**1965, Oct. 7 Photo. Wmk. 354**
*341* A67 1p dk pur & red 8 6
*342* A67 4p dk pur & bl 1.10 95
*343* A67 1sh3p dk pur & dp mag 1.25 1.10

Winston Churchill, Map and Cross of Malta — A68

Designs: 3p, 1sh6p, Warships in Valletta Harbor and George Cross.

**1966, Jan. 24 *Perf. 14½x14***
*344* A68 2p blk, gold & red 7 6
*345* A68 3p dk grn, gold & blk 8 8
*346* A68 1sh dp cl, gold & red 38 38
*a* Gold omitted 125.00
*347* A68 1sh6p dk bl, gold & vio 60 50

Sir Winston Spencer Churchill (1874-1965), statesman and World War II leader.

Grand Master Jean Parisot de la Valette — A69

Designs: 3p, Pope St. Pius V. 6p, Map of Valletta. 1sh, Francesco Laparelli, Italian architect. 2sh6p, Girolamo Cassar, Maltese architect.

**1966, March 28 Unwmk. *Perf. 12***
*348* A69 2p gold & multi 8 6
*349* A69 3p gold & multi 10 9
*350* A69 6p gold & multi 15 12
*351* A69 1sh gold & multi 24 18
*352* A69 2sh6p gold & multi 75 75
*Nos. 348-352 (5)* 1.32 1.20

400th anniversary of Valletta.

Kennedy — A70 Trade Fair — A71

***Perf. 15x14***
**1966, May 28 Photo. Wmk. 354**
*353* A70 3p ol gray, blk & gold 9 9
*354* A70 1sh6p dl bl, blk & gold 45 45

Issued in memory of President John F. Kennedy (1917-1963).

**1966, June 16 *Perf. 13x13½***
*355* A71 2p multi 10 8
*356* A71 8p gray & multi 32 32
*357* A71 2sh6p tan & multi 90 90

The 10th Malta Trade Fair.

Nativity — A72

George Cross — A73

**1966, Oct. 7 Photo. Wmk. 354**
*358* A72 1p gray, blk, gold & grnsh bl 8 6
*359* A72 4p gray, blk, gold & vio bl 10 8
*360* A72 1sh3p gray, blk, gold & dp red lil 30 28

**1967, Mar. 1 *Perf. 14½x14***
*361* A73 2p multi 8 6
*362* A73 4p multi 8 7
*363* A73 3sh sl & multi 40 40

Issued to commemorate the 25th anniversary of the award of the George Cross to Malta and Gozo for the war effort.

Crucifixion of St. Peter — A74

Keys, Tiara, Bible, Cross and Sword — A75

Design: 3sh, Beheading of St. Paul.

***Perf. 14½, 13½x14***
**1967, June 28 Photo. Wmk. 354**
*364* A74 2p blk & brn org 8 6
*365* A75 8p blk, gold & lt ol grn 14 12
*366* A74 3sh blk & brt bl 50 45

1900th anniv. of the martyrdom of the Apostles Peter and Paul.

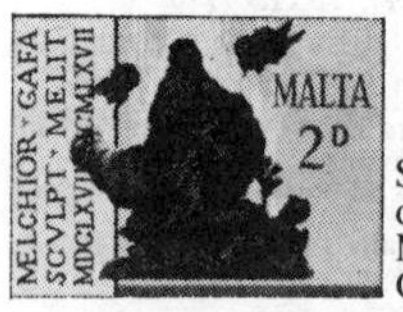

St. Catherine of Siena by Melchior Gafà — A76

Sculptures by Gafà: 4p, St. Thomas from Villanova. 1sh6p, Christ's baptism. 2sh6p, St. John the Baptist.

**1967, Aug. 1 *Perf. 13½***
*367* A76 2p blk, gold, buff & ultra 6 6
*368* A76 4p gold, buff, blk & grn 10 8
*369* A76 1sh6p dl bl, gold, buff, blk & org brn 24 24
*370* A76 2sh6p blk, gold, buff & dp car 45 45

Melchior Gafà (1635-67), Maltese sculptor.

Ruins of Megalithic Temples, Tarxien — A77

Designs: 6p, Facade of Palazzo Falzon, Notabile. 1sh, Facade of Old Parish Church, Birkirkara. 3sh, Entrance to Auberge de Castille.

**1967, Sept. 12 Photo. *Perf. 14½***
*371* A77 2p gold, Prus bl & blk 6 6
*372* A77 6p org brn, blk, gray & gold 10 8
*373* A77 1sh gold, ol, ind & blk 22 22
*374* A77 3sh dk car, rose, blk, gray & gold 42 42

Issued to publicize the 15th Congress of the History of Architecture, Malta, Sept. 12-16.

Nativity
A78 A79

Design: 1sh4p, Angels facing left.

**1967, Oct. 20 *Perf. 13½x14***
*375* A78 1p sl, gold & red 5 5
*a* Red omitted (stars) 50.00
*376* A79 8p sl, gold & red 11 10
*377* A78 1sh4p sl, gold & red 28 28
Triptych (Nos. 375-377) 52 50

Sheets of Nos. 375-377 were arranged in 2 ways: sheets containing 60 stamps of the same denomination arranged tete beche, and sheets containing all 3 denominations in 20 triptychs.

Arms of Malta — A80

Designs: 4p, Queen Elizabeth II in the robes of the Order of St. Michael and St. George (vert.). 3sh, Queen and map of Malta.

***Perf. 14½x14, 14x14½***
**1967, Nov. 13 Photo. Wmk. 354**
*378* A80 2p sl & multi 8 6
*379* A80 4p dp cl, blk & gold 8 8
*380* A80 3sh blk & gold 35 35

Visit of Queen Elizabeth II, Nov. 14-17.

Human Rights Flame and People A81

**1968, May 2 Photo. *Perf. 14½***
**Size: 40x19mm.**
*381* A81 2p sep, dp car, blk & gold 8 6

***Perf. 12x12½***
**Size: 24x24mm.**
*382* A81 6p gray, dk bl, blk & gold 12 10

***Perf. 14½***
**Size: 40x19mm.**
*383* A81 2sh gray, grnsh bl, blk & gold 32 28

International Human Rights Year.

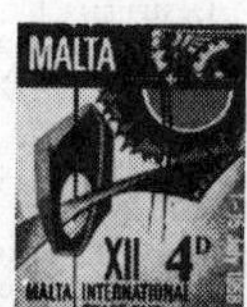

Fair Emblem — A82

*Perf. 14x14½*

**1968, June 1 Photo. Wmk. 354**

*384* A82 4p blk & multi 10 8
*385* A82 8p Prus bl & multi 12 10
*386* A82 3sh dp cl & multi 50 50

12th Malta Intl. Trade Fair, July 1-15.

La Valette in Battle Dress — A83

La Valette's Tomb, Church of St. John, Valletta — A84

Designs: 1p, Arms of Order of St. John of Jerusalem and La Valette's arms (horiz.). 2sh6p, Putti bearing shield with date of La Valette's death, and map of Malta.

*Perf. 13x14, 14x13*

**1968, Aug. 1 Photo. Wmk. 354**

*387* A83 1p blk & multi 6 5
*388* A83 8p dl bl & multi 12 12
*389* A84 1sh6p bl grn & multi 22 22
*390* A83 2sh6p dp cl & multi 45 45

400th anniv. of the death of Grand Master Jean de La Valette (1494-1568).

Star of Bethlehem, Shepherds and Angel A85

Designs: 8p, Nativity. 1sh4p, The Three Wise Men.

*Perf. 14½x14*

**1968, Oct. 3 Wmk. 354**

*391* A85 1p multi 5 5
*392* A85 8p gray & multi 12 12
*393* A85 1sh4p tan & multi 32 32

Christmas 1968. Printed in sheets of 60 with alternate rows inverted.

"Agriculture" A86

Mahatma Gandhi A87

Designs: 1sh, Greek medal and FAO emblem. 2sh6p, Woman symbolizing soil care.

**1968, Oct. 21 Photo. *Perf. 12½x12***

*394* A86 4p ultra & multi 6 6
*395* A86 1sh gray & multi 18 18
*396* A86 2sh6p multi 60 60

Issued to publicize the 6th Regional Congress for Europe of the Food and Agriculture Organization, Malta, Oct. 28-31.

*Perf. 12x12½*

**1969, Mar. 24 Photo. Wmk. 354**

*397* A87 1sh6p gold, blk & sep 35 32

Issued to commemorate the centenary of the birth of Mohandas K. Gandhi (1869-1948), leader in India's struggle for independence.

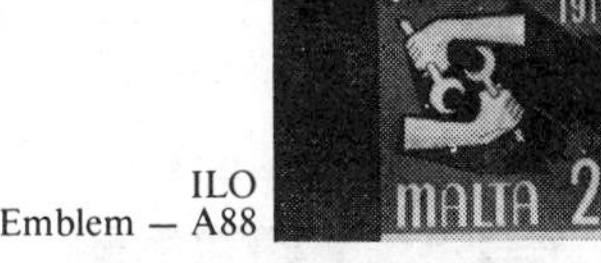

ILO Emblem — A88

*Perf. 13½x14½*

**1969, May 26 Photo. Wmk. 354**

*398* A88 2p ind, bl grn & gold 6 6
*399* A88 6p brn blk, red brn & gold 18 18

50th anniv. of the ILO.

Sea Bed, U.N. Emblem and Dove — A89

Designs: 2p, Robert Samut, bar of music and coat of arms. 10p, Map of Malta and homing birds. 2sh, Grand Master Pinto and arms of Malta University.

**1969, July 26 Photo. *Perf. 13½***

*400* A89 2p vio blk, blk, gold & red 8 8
*401* A89 5p gray, Prus bl, gold & blk 12 12
*402* A89 10p ol, blk & gold 18 18
*403* A89 2sh dk ol, blk, red & gold 40 40

Issued to commemorate the following: Centenary of the birth of Robert Samut, composer of National Anthem (2p); U.N. resolution on peaceful uses of the sea bed (5p); convention of Maltese emigrants (10p), Aug. 3-16; bicentenary of the founding of Malta University (2sh).

June 17, 1919, Uprising Monument A90

"Tourism" A91

Designs: 5p, Maltese flag and 5 doves (horiz.). 1sh6p, Dove and emblems of Malta, U.N. and Council of Euorpe. 2sh6p, Dove and symbols of trade and industry.

*Perf. 13x12½*

**1969, Sept. 20 Photo. Wmk. 354**

*404* A90 2p blk, gray, buff & gold 5 5
*405* A91 5p gray, blk, red & gold 7 7
*406* A91 10p gold, Prus bl, gray & blk 15 15
*407* A91 1sh6p gold, ol & multi 32 32
*408* A91 2sh6p gold, brn ol, gray & blk 55 55
*Nos. 404-408 (5)* 1.14 1.14

Fifth anniversary of independence.

St. John the Baptist in Robe of Knight of Malta A92

Mortar and Jars from Infirmary — A93

Designs: 1p, The Beheading of St. John By Caravaggio. 5p, Interior of St. John's Co-Cathedral. 6p, Allegory depicting functions of the Order. 8p, St. Jerome, by Caravaggio. 1sh6p, St. Gerard Receiving Godfrey de Bouillon, 1093, by Antoine de Favray. 2sh, Sacred vestments.

*Perf. 14x13 (1p, 8p); 13½x14 (2p, 6p, 1sh6p); 13½ (5p) 12x12½ (10p, 2sh)*

**1970, Mar. 21 Photo. Wmk. 354**

*409* A92 1p blk & multi 5 5
*410* A92 2p blk & multi 8 8
*411* A92 5p blk & multi 10 10
*412* A92 6p blk & multi 18 18
*413* A92 8p blk & multi 24 24
*414* A93 10p blk & multi 30 30
*415* A92 1sh6p blk & multi 48 48
*416* A93 2sh blk & multi 65 65
*Nos. 409-416 (8)* 2.08 2.08

13th Council of Europe Art Exhib. in honor of the Order of St. John in Malta, Apr. 2-July 1.

Sizes: 1p, 8p, 54x38mm; 2p, 6p, 44x30mm; 5p, 37x37mm; 10p, 2sh, 60x19mm; 1sh6p, 44x33mm.

EXPO '70 Emblem — A94

**1970, May 29 *Perf. 15***

*417* A94 2p gold & multi 5 5
*418* A94 5p gold & multi 10 10
*419* A94 3sh gold & multi 65 65

Issued to publicize EXPO '70 International Exhibition, Osaka, Japan, Mar. 15-Sept. 13.

U.N. Emblem, Dove, Scales and Symbolic Figure — A95

*Perf. 14x14½*

**1970, Sept. 30 Litho. Wmk. 354**

*420* A95 2p brn & multi 8 8
*421* A95 5p pur & multi 12 12
*422* A95 2sh6p vio bl & multi 65 65

25th anniversary of the United Nations.

Books and Quill — A96

Dun Karm, Books and Pens — A97

*Perf. 13x14*

**1971, Mar. 20 Litho. Wmk. 354**

*423* A96 1sh6p multi 28 28
*424* A97 2sh blk & multi 40 40

No. 423 issued in memory of Canon Gian Pietro Francesco Agius Sultana (De Soldanis; 1712-1770), historian and writer; No. 424 for the centenary of the birth of Mgr. Karm Psaila (Dun Karm, 1871-1961), Maltese poet.

**Europa Issue, 1971**

Common Design Type

**1971, May 3 *Perf. 13½x14½***

**Size: 32x22mm**

*425* CD14 2p ol, org & blk 8 8
*426* CD14 5p ver, org & blk 10 10
*427* CD14 1sh6p gray, org & blk 55 55

St. Joseph, by Giuseppe Cali — A98

Design: 5p, 1sh6p, Statue of Our Lady of Victory. 10p, Like 2p.

*Perf. 13x13½*

**1971, July 24 Litho. Wmk. 354**

*428* A98 2p dk bl & multi 8 8
*429* A98 5p gray & multi 12 12
*430* A98 10p multi 38 38
*431* A98 1sh6p multi 60 60

Centenary (in 1970) of the proclamation of St. Joseph as patron of the Universal Church (2p, 10p), and 50th anniversary of the coronation of the statue of Our Lady of Victory in Senglea, Malta.

Blue Rock Thrush A99

Design: 2p, 1sh6p, Thistle (vert.). 10p, Like 5p.

*Perf. 14x14½, 14½x14*

**1971, Sept. 18**

*432* A99 2p multi 6 6
*433* A99 5p bis & multi 10 10
*434* A99 10p org & multi 32 32
*435* A99 1sh6p bis & multi 60 60

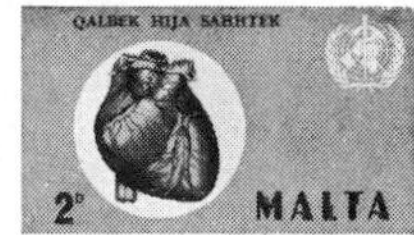

Heart and WHO Emblem A100

**1972, Mar. 20 *Perf. 14***

*436* A100 2p yel grn & multi 8 8
*437* A100 10p lil & multi 20 20
*438* A100 2sh6p lt bl & multi 70 70

World Health Day, Apr. 7.

Coin Showing Mnara (Lampstand) — A101

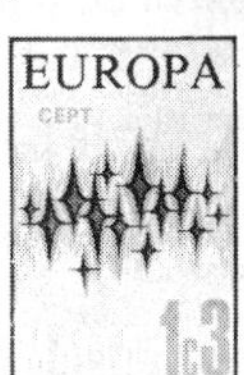

Sparkles, Symbolic of Communications — CD15

Decimal Currency Coins: 2m, Maltese Cross. 3m, Bee and honeycomb. 1c, George Cross. 2c, Penthesilea. 5c, Altar, Megalithic Period. 10c, Grandmaster's Barge, 18th century. 50c, Great Siege Monument, by Antonio Sciortino.

*Perf. 14 (16x21mm.), 2m, 3m, 2c; Perf. 14½x14 (21x26mm), 5m, 1c, 5c*

**1972, May 16**

*439* A101 2m rose red & multi 5 5
*440* A101 3m pink & multi 5 5
*441* A101 5m lil & multi 5 5
*442* A101 1c multi 6 6
*443* A101 2c org & multi 8 8
*444* A101 5c multi 22 22

***Perf. 13½ (27x35mm.)***

*445* A101 10c yel & multi 50 50
*446* A101 50c multi 2.50 2.50
*Nos. 439-446 (8)* 3.51 3.51

Coins to mark introduction of decimal currency.

### Nos. 319A, 321 and 323 Surcharged with New Value and 2 Bars

***Perf. 14x14½, 14½***

**1972, Sept. 30 Photo. Wmk. 354**

*447* A62 1c3m on 5p multi 8 8
*448* A63 3c on 8p multi 15 15
*449* A63 5c on 1sh3p multi 30 30

### Europa Issue 1972

**1972, Nov. 11 Litho. *Perf. 13x13½***

*450* CD15 1c3m yel & multi 7 7
*451* CD15 3c multi 20 20
*452* CD15 5c pink & multi 32 32
*453* CD15 7c5m multi 45 45

Issued in sheets of 10 plus 2 labels (4x3). Labels are in top row.

Archaeology A103

Woman with Grain, FAO Emblem A104

**1973, Mar. 31 Litho. *Perf. 13½***

**Size: 22x24mm.**

*454* A103 2m *shown* 5 5
*455* A103 4m *History (knights)* 5 5
*456* A103 5m *Folklore* 5 5
*457* A103 8m *Industry* 5 5
*458* A103 1c *Fishing* 5 5
*459* A103 1c3m *Pottery* 8 8
*460* A103 2c *Agriculture* 10 10
*461* A103 3c *Sport* 10 10
*462* A103 4c *Marina* 14 14
*463* A103 5c *Fiesta* 16 16
*464* A103 7c5m *Regatta* 25 25
*465* A103 10c *Charity (St. Martin)* 35 35
*466* A103 50c *Education* 1.40 1.40
*467* A103 £1 *Religion* 3.00 3.00

***Perf. 13½x14***

**Size: 32x27mm.**

*468* A103 £2 *Arms of Malta* 12.00 12.00
*Nos. 454-468 (15)* 17.83 17.83

### Europa Issue 1973

### Common Design Type

**1973, June 2 Unwmk. *Perf. 14***

**Size: 36½x19½mm.**

*469* CD16 3c multi 22 22
*470* CD16 5c multi 40 40
*471* CD16 7c5m dk bl & multi 70 70

**1973, Oct. 6 Wmk. 354 *Perf. 13½***

Designs: 7c5m, Mother and child, WHO emblem. 10c, Two heads, Human Rights flame.

*472* A104 1c3m yel grn, blk & gold 8 8
*473* A104 7c5m ultra, blk & gold 45 45
*474* A104 10c cl, blk & gold 60 60

World Food Program, 10th anniv.; WHO, 25th anniv.; Universal Declaration of Human Rights, 25th anniv.

Girolamo Cassar, Architect — A105

Portraits: 3c, Giuseppe Barth, opthalmologist. 5c, Nicolo' Isouard, composer. 7c5m, John Borg, botanist. 10c, Antonio Sciortino, sculptor.

**1974, Jan. 12 Litho. *Perf. 14***

*475* A105 1c3m sl grn & gold 8 8
*476* A105 3c ind & gold 12 12
*477* A105 5c ol gray & gold 22 22
*478* A105 7c5m sl bl & gold 32 32
*479* A105 10c brn vio & gold 55 55
*Nos. 475-479 (5)* 1.29 1.29

Prominent Maltese.

### Europa Issue 1974

Statue of Goddess, 3rd Millenium B.C. A106

Designs (CEPT Emblem and): 3c, Carved door, Cathedral, Mdina, 11th cent. (vert.). 5c, Silver monstrance, 1689. 7c5m, "Vettina" (statue of nude woman), by Antonio Sciortino (1879-1947) (vert.).

***Perf. 13½x14, 14x13½***

**1974, July 13**

*480* A106 1c3m gray bl, blk & gold 10 10
*481* A106 3c ol brn, blk & gold 28 28
*482* A106 5c lil, blk & gold 45 45
*483* A106 7c5m dl grn, blk & gold 90 90

Heinrich von Stephan, Coach and Train, UPU Emblem A107

Designs (UPU Emblem, von Stephan and): 5c, Paddle steamer and ocean liner. 7c5m, Balloon and jet. 50c, UPU Congress Building, Lausanne, and UPU Headquarters, Bern.

**Wmk. 354**

**1974, Sept. Litho. *Perf. 13½***

*484* A107 1c3m multi 8 8
*485* A107 5c multi 22 22
*486* A107 7c5m multi 35 35
*487* A107 50c multi 2.25 2.25
*a* Souvenir sheet of 4 3.25 3.25

Centenary of Universal Postal Union. No. 487a contains one each of Nos. 484-487. Buff sheet margin resembles envelope with blue inscription, red brown 1874 Malta and yellow green 1974 Bern cancels. Size: 125x90mm.

President, Prime Minister, Minister of Justice at Microphone — A108

Designs: 1c3m, President, Prime Minister, Speaker at Swearing-in ceremony. 5c, Flag of Malta.

**1975, Mar. 31 *Perf. 14***

*488* A108 1c3m red & multi 6 6
*489* A108 5c gray, red & blk 40 40
*490* A108 25c red & multi 1.75 1.75

Proclamation of the Republic, Dec. 13, 1974.

IWY Emblem, Mother and Child — A109

Designs: 3c, 20c, Secretary (woman in public life), IWY emblem. 5c, Like 1c3m.

**Wmk. 354**

**1975, May 30 Litho. *Perf. 13***

*491* A109 1c3m vio & gold 15 9
*492* A109 3c bl gray & gold 90 45
*493* A109 5c ol & gold 2.00 1.25
*494* A109 20c red brn & gold 9.00 6.00

International Women's Year 1975.

### Europa Issue 1975

Allegory of Malta, by Francesco de Mura — A110

Painting: 15c, Judith and Holofernes, by Valentin de Boulogne.

**1975, July 15 Litho. *Perf. 14***

*495* A110 5c multi 28 28
*496* A110 15c multi 95 95

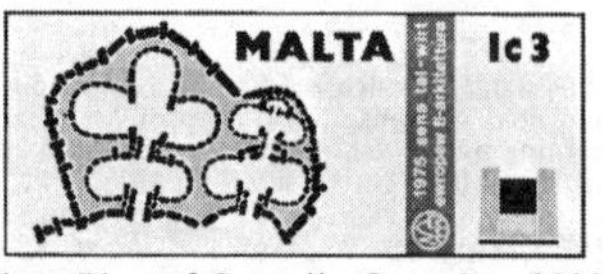


Floor Plan of Ggantija Complex, 3000 B.C. — A111

Designs: 3c, View of Mdina. 5c, Typical Maltese town. 25c, Fort St. Angelo.

**1975, Sept. 16 *Perf. 14***

*497* A111 1c3m blk & org 8 8
*498* A111 3c org, pur & blk 35 30
*499* A111 5c gray, blk & org 60 50
*500* A111 25c org, tan & blk 4.00 2.50

European Architectural Heritage Year 1975.

"Right to Work" — A112

Designs: 5c, Protection of the Environment (Landscape). 25c, Maltese flags.

**1975, Dec. 12 Litho. Wmk. 354**

*501* A112 1c3m multi 8 8
*502* A112 5c multi 45 25
*503* A112 25c multi 2.00 1.25

First anniversary of Malta Republic.

Republic Coat of Arms — A113

***Perf. 13½x14***

**1976, Jan. 28 Litho. Wmk. 354**

*504* A113 £2 blk & multi *9.50* 7.25

Feast of Sts. Peter and Paul — A114

Designs: 1c3m, "Festa" (flags and fireworks; vert.). 7c5m, Carnival. 10c, Good Friday (Christ carrying cross; vert.).

**1976, Feb. 26 Litho. *Perf. 14***

*505* A114 1c3m multi 14 9
*506* A114 5c multi 38 30
*507* A114 7c5m multi 55 40
*508* A114 10c multi 1.90 1.25

Maltese folk festivals.

Water Polo, Olympic Rings A115

Designs (Olympic Rings and): 5c, Yachting. 30c, Running.

**1976, Apr. 28 Litho. *Perf. 13½x14***

*509* A115 1c7m sl grn & red 12 8
*510* A115 5c dp bl & red 38 22
*511* A115 30c sep & red 2.50 1.90

21st Olympic Games, Montreal, Canada, July 17-Aug. 1.

### Europa Issue 1976

Lace-making — A116

Design: 15c, Stone carving.

**1976, July 8 Litho. Wmk. 354**

*512* A116 7c vio & multi 35 35
*513* A116 15c brn & multi 90 80

Grandmaster Nicola Cotoner, Founder — A117

Designs: 5c, Disected arm and hand. 7c, Dr. Fra Giuseppe Zammit, first professor. 11c, School and balustrade.

**1976, Sept. 14 Litho. *Perf. 13½***

*514* A117 2c multi 8 6
*515* A117 5c multi 18 15
*516* A117 7c multi 28 22
*517* A117 11c multi 90 75

School of Anatomy and Surgery, Valletta, 300th anniversary.

Armor of Grand Master Jean de La Valette — A118

Suits of Armor: 7c, Grand Master Aloph de Wignacourt. 11c, Grand Commander Jean Jacques de Verdelin.

**1977, Jan. 20 Litho. Wmk. 354**

*518* A118 2c grn & multi 10 8
*519* A118 7c brn & multi 42 35
*520* A118 11c ultra & multi 75 60

### No. 318 Surcharged with New Value and Bar

**1977, Mar. 24 Photo. *Perf. 14x14½***

*521* A62 1c7m on 4p multi 35 16

Annunciation, Tapestry after Rubens — A119

Nativity — A120

Tapestries after Designs by Rubens: 7c, The Four Evangelists. 20c, Adoration of the Kings. Flemish tapestries commissioned for St. John's Co-Cathedral, Valletta.

**Wmk. 354**

**1977, Mar. 30 Litho. *Perf. 14***

| | | | | |
|---|---|---|---|---|
| *522* | A119 | 2c multi | 8 | 8 |
| *523* | A119 | 7c multi | 35 | 30 |
| *524* | A120 | 11c multi | 65 | 60 |
| *525* | A120 | 20c multi | 1.25 | 1.25 |

**1978, Jan. 26**

Flemish Tapestries: 2c, Jesus' Entry into Jerusalem, by unknown painter. 7c, Last Supper, by Nicholas Poussin. 11c, Crucifixion, by Rubens. 25c, Resurrection, by Rubens.

| | | | | |
|---|---|---|---|---|
| *526* | A120 | 2c multi | 10 | 10 |
| *527* | A120 | 7c multi | 30 | 30 |
| *528* | A120 | 11c multi | 50 | 50 |
| *529* | A120 | 25c multi | 1.25 | 1.25 |

**1979, Jan. 24**

Tapestries after Designs by Rubens (Triumph of): 2c, Catholic Church. 7c, Charity. 11c, Faith. 25c, Truth.

| | | | | |
|---|---|---|---|---|
| *530* | A119 | 2c multi | 10 | 10 |
| *531* | A119 | 7c multi | 30 | 30 |
| *532* | A119 | 11c multi | 45 | 45 |
| *533* | A119 | 25c multi | 1.10 | 1.10 |

Nos. 522-533 commemorate the 400th anniversary of the consecration of St. John's Co-Cathedral, Valetta. Nos. 522-525 are for 400th birth anniversary of Peter Paul Rubens (1577-1640).

Malta Map, Telecommunication — A121

Designs: 1c, 6c, Map of Italy, Sicily, Malta and North Africa, telecommunication tower and waves (vert.). 17c, like 8c.

***Perf. 14x13½, 13½x14***

**1977, May 17 Litho. Wmk. 354**

| | | | | |
|---|---|---|---|---|
| *535* | A121 | 1c grn, red & blk | 6 | 6 |
| *536* | A121 | 6c multi | 22 | 22 |
| *537* | A121 | 8c multi | 35 | 35 |
| *538* | A121 | 17c pur, red & blk | 85 | 85 |

World Telecommunication Day.

**Europa Issue 1977**

View of Ta' L-Isperanza — A122

Design: 20c, Harbor, Is-Salini.

**1977, July Litho. *Perf. 13½***

| | | | | |
|---|---|---|---|---|
| *539* | A122 | 7c multi | 42 | 42 |
| *540* | A122 | 20c multi | 95 | 95 |

Issued in sheets of 10.

Help Given Handicapped Worker — A123

Designs: 7c, Stonemason and shipbuilder. 20c, Mother holding dead son, and Service to the Republic order (horiz.). Sculptures from Workers' Monument.

**1977, Oct. 12 Litho. Wmk. 354**

| | | | | |
|---|---|---|---|---|
| *541* | A123 | 2c red brn & brn | 10 | 10 |
| *542* | A123 | 7c brn & dk brn | 32 | 32 |
| *543* | A123 | 20c multi | 1.00 | 1.00 |

Tribute to Maltese workers.

Lady on Horseback and Soldier, by Dürer A124

Grand Master Nicola Cotoner Monument A125

Dürer Engravings: 8c, Bagpiper. 17c, Madonna with Long-tailed Monkey.

**Wmk. 354**

**1978, Mar. 7 Litho. *Perf. 14***

| | | | | |
|---|---|---|---|---|
| *544* | A124 | 1c7m dk bl, blk & red | 8 | 8 |
| *545* | A124 | 8c gray, blk & red | 35 | 35 |
| *546* | A124 | 17c dk grn, blk & red | 80 | 80 |

Albrecht Dürer (1471-1528), German painter and engraver.

**Europa Issue 1978**

Design: 25c, Grand Master Ramon Perellos monument, by Giuseppe Mazzuoli. The monument on 7c is believed to be the work of Giovanni Batista Foggini.

**1978, Apr. 26 *Perf. 14x13½***

| | | | | |
|---|---|---|---|---|
| *547* | A125 | 7c multi | 35 | 35 |
| *548* | A125 | 25c multi | 1.25 | 1.25 |

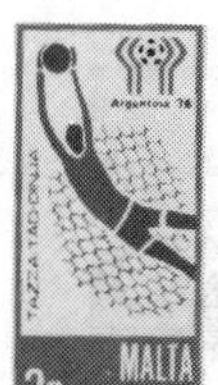


Goalkeeper — A126

Designs (Argentina '78 Emblem and): 11c, 15c, different soccer scenes.

***Perf. 14x13½***

**1978, June 6 Litho. Wmk. 354**

| | | | | |
|---|---|---|---|---|
| *549* | A126 | 2c multi | 10 | 10 |
| *550* | A126 | 11c multi | 50 | 50 |
| *551* | A126 | 15c multi | 80 | 80 |
| *a* | | Souvenir sheet of 3 | 1.75 | 1.75 |

11th World Cup Soccer Championship, Argentina, June 1-25. No. 551a contains Nos. 549-551; multicolored margin shows soccer game. Size: 125x91mm.

Fishing Boat — A127

Maltese Speronara and AirMalta Fuselage — A128

Designs: 5c, 17c Changing of colors. 7c, 20c, British soldier and oranges. 8c, like 2c.

**Wmk. 354**

**1979, Mar. 31 Litho. *Perf. 14***

| | | | | |
|---|---|---|---|---|
| *552* | A127 | 2c cl & multi | 10 | 10 |
| *553* | A127 | 5c cl & multi | 25 | 25 |
| *554* | A127 | 7c cl & multi | 32 | 32 |
| *555* | A127 | 8c dk bl & multi | 40 | 40 |
| *556* | A127 | 17c dk bl & multi | 75 | 75 |
| *557* | A127 | 20c dk bl & multi | 90 | 90 |
| | | *Nos. 552-557 (6)* | 2.72 | 2.72 |

End of military agreement between Malta and Great Britain.

**Europa Issue 1979**

Design: 25c, Coastal watch tower and radio link tower.

**1979, May 9**

| | | | | |
|---|---|---|---|---|
| *558* | A128 | 7c multi | 32 | 32 |
| *559* | A128 | 25c multi | 1.25 | 1.25 |

Children and Globe — A129

Designs: 7c, Children flying kites. 11c, Children in a circle holding hands.

***Perf. 14x13½, 14***

**1979, June 13 Litho. Wmk. 354**

**Size: 20x38mm**

| | | | | |
|---|---|---|---|---|
| *560* | A129 | 2c multi | 12 | 12 |

**Size: 27x33mm**

| | | | | |
|---|---|---|---|---|
| *561* | A129 | 7c multi | 40 | 40 |
| *562* | A129 | 11c multi | 70 | 70 |

International Year of the Child.

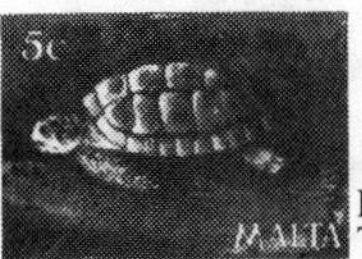


Loggerhead Turtle — A130

Marine Life: 2c, Gibbula nivosa. 7c, Dolphinfish. 25c, Noble pen shell.

**Wmk. 354**

**1979, Oct. 10 Litho. *Perf. 13½***

| | | | | |
|---|---|---|---|---|
| *563* | A130 | 2c multi | 10 | 10 |
| *564* | A130 | 5c multi | 24 | 24 |
| *565* | A130 | 7c multi | 30 | 30 |
| *566* | A130 | 25c multi | 1.25 | 1.25 |

Tapestry Type of 1977-79

Tapestries after Designs by Rubens: 2c, The Institution of Corpus Domini. 8c, The Destruction of Idolatry. 50c, Portrait of Grand Master Perellos. (vert.).

**Wmk. 354**

**1980, Jan. 30 Litho. *Perf. 14***

| | | | | |
|---|---|---|---|---|
| *567* | A120 | 2c multi | 8 | 8 |
| *568* | A120 | 8c multi | 32 | 32 |

**Souvenir Sheet**

| | | | | |
|---|---|---|---|---|
| *569* | A119 | 50c multi | 2.25 | 2.25 |

Multicolored margin of No. 569 shows Sts. Jude and Simon. Size: 114x86mm.

Victoria Citadel, Gozo A131

Monument Restoration (UNESCO Emblem and): 2c5m, Hal Saflieni Catacombs, Paola, 2500 B.C. (vert.). 6c, Vilhena Palace, Mdina, 18th century (vert.). 12c, St. Elmo Fort, Valletta, 16th century.

**1980, Feb. 15**

| | | | | |
|---|---|---|---|---|
| *570* | A131 | 2c5m multi | 10 | 10 |
| *571* | A131 | 6c multi | 30 | 30 |
| *572* | A131 | 8c multi | 38 | 38 |
| *573* | A131 | 12c multi | 60 | 60 |

Don Gorg Preca (1880-1962), Founder of Soc. of Christian Doctrine — A132

**1980, Apr. 12 Litho. *Perf. 14x13½***

| | | | | |
|---|---|---|---|---|
| *574* | A132 | 2c5m gray vio | 15 | 15 |

**Europa Issue 1980**

Ruzar Briffa (1906-1963), Poet, by Vincent Apap — A133

Vincent Apap Sculpture: 30c, Mikiel Anton Vassalli (1764-1829), freedom fighter and scholar.

**1980, Apr. 29 *Perf. 13½x14***

| | | | | |
|---|---|---|---|---|
| *575* | A133 | 8c sl grn & dp bis | 32 | 32 |
| *576* | A133 | 30c brn red & ol | 1.40 | 1.40 |

Chess Pieces A134

Designs: Chess pieces. 30c vert.

**1980, Nov. Litho. *Perf. 14***

| | | | | |
|---|---|---|---|---|
| *577* | A134 | 2c5m multi | 12 | 12 |
| *578* | A134 | 8c multi | 40 | 40 |
| *579* | A134 | 30c multi | 1.50 | 1.50 |

Chess Olypiad, Valletta, Nov. 20-Dec. 8.

Barn Owl — A135

**Wmk. 354**

**1981, Jan. 20 Litho. *Perf. 13½***

| | | | | |
|---|---|---|---|---|
| *580* | A135 | 3c shown | 15 | 15 |
| *581* | A135 | 8c Sardinian warbler | 40 | 40 |
| *582* | A135 | 12c Woodchat shrike | 60 | 60 |
| *583* | A135 | 23c Stormy petrel | 1.10 | 1.10 |

**Europa Issue 1981**

Climbing the Gostra (Greasy Pole) — A136

**1981, Apr. 28 Litho. *Perf. 14***

*584* A136 8c Horse race 38 38
*585* A136 30c shown 1.40 1.40

25th Intl. Fair of Malta, Naxxar, July 1-15 — A137

**Wmk. 354**

**1981, June 12 Litho. *Perf. 13½***

*586* A137 4c multi 18 18
*587* A137 25c multi 1.25 1.25

Disabled Artist — A138

**1981, July 17 Litho. *Perf. 13½***

*588* A138 3c shown 12 12
*589* A138 35c Boy on crutches 1.65 1.65

Intl. Year of the Disabled.

World Food Day — A139

**1981, Oct. 16 Litho. *Perf. 14***

*590* A139 8c multi 40 40
*591* A139 23c multi 1.10 1.10

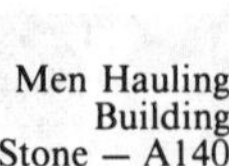

Men Hauling Building Stone — A140

**Wmk. 354**

**1981, Oct. 31 Litho. *Perf. 14***

*592* A140 5m shown 5 5
*593* A140 1c Growing cotton 6 6
*594* A140 2c Ship building 8 8
*595* A140 3c Minting coins 10 10
*596* A140 5c Artistic achievements 20 20
*597* A140 6c Fishing 22 22
*598* A140 7c Farming 25 25
*599* A140 8c Quarrying 30 30
*600* A140 10c Grape pressing 35 35
*601* A140 12c Ship repairing 42 42
*602* A140 15c Energy 52 52
*603* A140 20c Communications 70 70
*604* A140 25c Factories 85 85
*605* A140 50c Water drilling 1.65 1.65
*606* A140 £1 Sea transport 3.25 3.25
*607* A140 £3 Air transport 9.50 9.50
*Nos. 592-607 (16)* 18.50 18.50

Shipbuilding and Repairing, Tarznar Shipyards — A141

**1982, Jan. 29 Litho. *Perf. 13½x14***

*608* A141 3c Assembly sheds 14 14
*609* A141 8c Ships in dry dock 35 35
*610* A141 13c Tanker 60 60
*611* A141 27c Tanker, diff. 1.25 1.25

Man and Home for the Elderly A142

**1982, Mar. 16 Litho. *Perf. 14***

*612* A142 8c shown 35 35
*613* A142 30c Woman, hospital 1.50 1.50

Europa 1982 A143

**1982, Apr. 29 Litho. *Perf. 14***

*614* A143 8c Redemption of the islands, 1428 35 35
*615* A143 30c Declaration of Rights, 1802 1.50 1.50

1982 World Cup — A144

Designs: Various soccer players.

**1982, June 11 Litho. *Perf. 14***

*616* A144 3c multi 18 18
*617* A144 12c multi 72 72
*618* A144 15c multi 90 90
*a.* Souvenir sheet of 3 2.25 2.25

No. 618a contains Nos. 616-618; multicolored margin. Size: 125x90mm.

Brigatine — A145

**1982, Nov. 13 Litho.**

*619* A145 3c shown 15 15
*619A* A145 8c Tartana 45 45
*619B* A145 12c Xebec 60 60
*619C* A145 20c Speronara 1.10 1.10

See Nos. 637-640, 670-673, 686-689, 703-706.

Malta Railway Centenary — A146

**Wmk. 354**

**1983, Jan. 21 Litho. *Perf. 14***

*620* A146 3c Manning Wardle, 1883 14 14
*621* A146 13c Black Hawthorn, 1884 65 65
*622* A146 27c Beyer Peacock, 1895 1.25 1.25

Commonwealth Day — A147

**1983, Mar. 14**

*623* A147 8c Map 35 35
*624* A147 12c Transportation 55 55
*625* A147 15c Beach, vert. 65 65
*626* A147 23c Industry, vert. 1.10 1.10

Europa 1983 A148

**Wmk. 354**

**1983, May 5 Litho. *Perf. 14***

*627* A148 8c Megalithic Temples, Ggantija 40 40
*628* A148 30c Fort St. Angelo 1.50 1.50

World Communications Year — A149

***Perf. 13½x14***

**1983, July 14 Litho. Wmk. 354**

*629* A149 3c Dish antennas 15 15
*630* A149 7c Ships 32 32
*631* A149 13c Trucks 65 65
*632* A149 20c Games emblem 1.00 1.00

25th anniv. of Intl. Maritime Org. (7c); 30th anniv. of Customs Cooperation Council (13c); 9th Mediterranean Games, Casablanca, Sept. 3-17 (20c).

Monsignor Giuseppe De Piro (1877-1933), Founder of Missionary Society of St. Paul — A150

**1983, Sept. 1 Litho. *Perf. 14***

*633* A150 3c multi 14 14

40th Anniv. of General Workers' Union — A151

**1983, Oct. 5 Litho. *Perf. 14x13½***

*634* A151 3c Founding rally 14 14
*635* A151 8c Family, workers 38 38
*636* A151 27c Headquarters 1.25 1.25

**Maltese Ship Type of 1982**

**1983, Nov. 17 Litho. *Perf. 14x13½***

*637* A145 2c Strangier, 1813 10 10
*638* A145 12c Tigre 1839 60 60
*639* A145 13c La Speranza, 1844 65 65
*640* A145 20c Wignacourt 1844 1.00 1.00

Europa (1959-84) A152

**Wmk. 354**

**1984, Apr. 27 Litho. *Perf. 14***

*641* A152 8c multi 36 36
*642* A152 30c multi 1.35 1.35

Police Force, 170th Anniv. — A153

***Perf. 14x13½***

**1984, June 14 Litho. Wmk. 354**

*643* A153 3c Officer, 1880 14 14
*644* A153 8c Mounted policeman 36 36
*645* A153 11c Officer on motorcycle 50 50
*646* A153 25c Traffic duty, firemen 1.15 1.15

1984 Summer Olympics — A154

***Perf. 13½x14***

**1984, July 26 Litho. Wmk. 354**

*647* A154 7c Running 35 35
*648* A154 12c Gymnastics 55 55
*649* A154 23c Swimming 1.10 1.10

10th Anniv. of Republic — A155

**1984, Dec. 12 Litho. Wmk. 354**

*650* A155 3c Dove on map 14 14
*651* A155 8c Fortress 38 38
*652* A155 30c Hands, flag 1.40 1.40

Malta Post Office Centenary A156

**1985, Jan. 2 Litho. *Perf. 14***

*653* A156 3c No. 8 16 16
*654* A156 8c No. 9 40 40
*655* A156 12c No. 11 60 60

*656* A156 20c No. 12 1.00 1.00
*a* Souvenir sheet of 4 2.25 2.25

No. 656a contains Nos. 653-656. Size: 164x90mm.

International Youth Year — A157

**1985, Mar. 7** ***Perf. 14x13½, 13½x14***
*657* A157 2c Males holding vines 10 10
*658* A157 13c Three youths, vert. 54 54
*659* A157 27c Female holding flame 1.10 1.10

Europa 1985 — A158

Composers: 8c, Nicolo Baldacchino (1895-1971). 30c, Francesco Azopardi (1748-1809).

**Wmk. 354**

**1985, Apr. 25** **Litho.** ***Perf. 14***
*660* A158 8c multi 38 38
*661* A158 30c multi 1.50 1.50

Guzeppi Bajada and Manwel Attard, Martyrs A159

Designs: 7c, Karmnu Abela and Wenzu Dyer. 35c, June 7 Uprising Memorial Monument, vert.

**1985, June 7** ***Perf. 14x14½, 14½x14***
*662* A159 3c multi 12 12
*663* A159 7c multi 28 28
*664* A159 35c multi 1.40 1.40

June 7 Uprising, 66th anniv.

UN, 40th Anniv. A160

**1985, July 26** ***Perf. 13½x14***
*665* A160 4c Stylized birds 16 16
*666* A160 11c Arrows 45 45
*667* A160 31c Human figures 1.25 1.25

Famous Men — A161

Portraits: 8c, George Mitrovich (1794-1885), politician and author, novel frontispiece, The Cause of the People of Malta Now Before Parliament. 12c, Pietru Caxaru (1438-1485), scholar, manuscript.

**1985, Oct. 3** ***Perf. 14***
*668* A161 8c multi 32 32
*669* A161 12c multi 48 48

Ships Type of 1982

**1985, Nov. 27**
*670* A145 3c Scotia paddle steamer, 1844 12 12
*671* A145 7c Tagliaferro, 1882 28 28
*672* A145 15c Gleneagles, 1885 60 60
*673* A145 23c L'Isle Adam, 1886 90 90

Intl. Peace Year A162

***Perf. 14x14½, 13½x14 (#675)***
**1986, Jan. 28** **Litho.** **Wmk. 354**
*674* A162 8c John XXIII Peace Laboratory 30 30
*675* A162 11c Unity 40 40
*676* A162 27c Peaceful coexistence 1.00 1.00

Size of No. 675: 43x27mm.

Europa 1986 — A163

**1986, Apr. 3** ***Perf. 14½x14***
*677* A163 8c Butterflies 32 32
*678* A163 35c Earth, air, fire and water 1.40 1.40

1986 World Cup Soccer Championships, Mexico — A164

**Wmk. 354**

**1986, May 30** **Litho.** ***Perf. 14***
*679* A164 3c Heading the ball 12 12
*680* A164 7c Goalie catching ball 28 28
*681* A164 23c Dribbling 92 92
*a* Souvenir sheet of 3, #679-681 1.35 1.35

No. 681a has multicolored decorative margin. Size: 125x90mm.

Philanthropists A165

Designs: 2c, Fra Diegu (1831-1902). 3c, Adelaide Cini (1838-1885). 8c, Alfonso Maria Galea (1861-1941). 27c, Vincenzo Bugeja (1820-1890).

**1986, Aug. 28** ***Perf. 14½x14***
*682* A165 2c multi 8 8
*683* A165 3c multi 12 12
*684* A165 8c multi 32 32
*685* A165 27c multi 1.10 1.10

Ships Type of 1982

**Wmk. 354**

**1986, Nov. 19** **Litho.** ***Perf. 14***
*686* A145 7c San Paul 38 38
*687* A145 10c Knight of Malta 52 52
*688* A145 12c Valetta City 65 65
*689* A145 20c Saver 1.05 1.05

Malta Ornithological Society, 25th Anniv. — A166

**1987, Jan. 26** **Litho.** ***Perf. 14***
*690* A166 3c Erithacus rubecula 14 14
*691* A166 8c Falco peregrinus 38 38
*692* A166 13c Upupa epops 60 60
*693* A166 23c Calonectris diomedea 1.10 1.10

Nos. 691-692 vert.

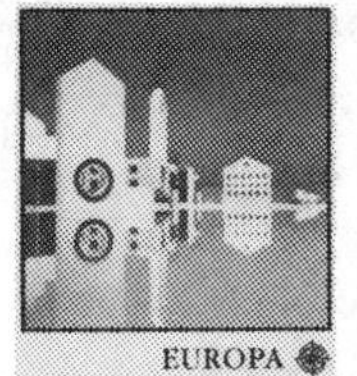

Europa — A167

Limestone buildings.

***Perf. 14½x14***
**1987, Apr. 15** **Litho.** **Wmk. 354**
*694* A167 8c Aquasun Lido 42 42
*695* A167 35c St. Joseph's Church, Manikata 1.85 1.85

Military Uniforms A168

Uniforms of the Order of St. John of Jerusalem (1530-1798).

**Wmk. 354**

**1987, June 10** **Litho.** ***Perf. 14***
*696* A168 3c Soldier, 16th cent. 16 16
*697* A168 7c Officer, 16th cent. 38 38
*698* A168 10c Flag bearer, 18th cent. 52 52
*699* A168 27c General of the galleys, 18th cent 1.40 1.40

See Nos. 723-726.

European Environment Year — A169

Anniversaries and events: 8c, Esperanto movement, cent. 23s, Intl. Year of Shelter for the Homeless.

***Perf. 14½x14***
**1987, Aug. 18** **Litho.** **Wmk. 354**
*700* A169 5c shown 25 25
*701* A169 8c multi 38 38
*702* A169 23c multi 1.10 1.10

Ships Type of 1982

**1987, Oct. 16** **Litho.** ***Perf. 14***
*703* A145 2c Medina, 1969 12 12
*704* A145 11c Rabat, 1974 60 60
*705* A145 13c Ghawdex, 1979 70 70
*706* A145 20c Pinto, 1987 1.10 1.10

A170

Designs: 8c, Dr. Arvid Pardo, representative to U.N. from Malta who proposed the resolution. 12c, U.N. emblem.

**Wmk. 354**

**1987, Dec. 18** **Litho.** ***Perf. 14½***
*707* A170 8c multi 42 42
*708* A170 12c multi 65 65

**Souvenir Sheet**

***Perf. 13x13½***
*709* Sheet of 2 1.10 1.10
*a* A170 8c multi 42 42
*b* A170 12c multi 65 65

U.N. resolution for peaceful use of marine resources, 20th anniv. No. 709 has multicolored decorative margin. Nos. 709a-709b printed in a continuous design. Size of No. 709: 125x90mm.

Nazju Falzon (1813-1865), Clergyman A171

Famous men: 3c, Monsignor Sidor Formosa (1851-1931), benefactor of the poor. 4c, Sir Luigi Preziosi (1888-1965), opthalmologist who developed an operation for the treatment of glaucoma. 10c, Father Anastasju Cuschieri (1876-1962), theologian, poet. 25c, Monsignor Pietru Pawl Saydon (1895-1971), translator, commentator on scripture.

***Perf. 14½x14***
**1988, Jan. 23** **Litho.** **Wmk. 354**
*710* A171 2c shown 12 12
*711* A171 3c multi 16 16
*712* A171 4c multi 22 22
*713* A171 10c multi 52 52
*714* A171 25c multi 1.30 1.30
*Nos. 710-714 (5)* 2.32 2.32

Anniversaries and Events — A172

Designs: 10c, Statue of youth and St. John Bosco in the chapel at St. Patrick's School, Sliema. 12c, Assumption of Our Lady, main altarpiece at Ta' Pinu Sanctuary, Gozo, completed in 1619 by Amodeo Bartolomeo Perugino. 14c, Christ the King monument at the Mall, Floriana, by Antonio Sciortino (1879-1947).

**Wmk. 354**

**1988, Mar. 5 Litho. *Perf. 14***

*715* A172 10c multi 52 52
*716* A172 12c multi 62 62
*717* A172 14c multi 72 72

St. John Bosco (1815-88), educator (10c); Marian Year (12c); Intl. Eucharistic Congress, Malta, Apr. 24-28, 1913, 75th anniv. (14c).

Europa 1988 — A173

Transport and communication: 10c, Land, sea and air transportation. 35c, Telecommunications.

**1988, Apr. 9 *Perf. 14***

*718* A173 10c multi 52 52
*719* A173 35c multi 1.80 1.80

Intl. Anniversaries and Events — A174

Globe picturing hemispheres and: 4c, Red Cross, Red Crescent emblems. 18c, Symbolic design dividing world into north and south regions. 19c, Caduceus, EKG readout.

**Wmk. 354**

**1988, May 25 Litho. *Perf. 14***

*720* A174 4c multi 25 25
*721* A174 18c multi 1.10 1.10
*722* A174 19c multi 1.20 1.20

Intl. Red Cross and Red Crescent Organizations, 125th annivs. (4c); European Public Campaign on North-South Interdependence and Solidarity (18c); WHO, 40th anniv. (19c).

Military Uniforms Type of 1987

Designs: 3c, Light Infantry private, 1800. 4c, Coast Artillery gunner, 1802. 10c, Ist Maltese Provincial Battalion field officer, 1805. 25c, Royal Malta Regiment subaltern, 1809.

**1988, July 23 Litho. Wmk. 354**

*723* A168 3c multi 20 20
*724* A168 4c multi 25 25
*725* A168 10c multi 62 62
*726* A168 25c multi 1.55 1.55

1988 Summer Olympics, Seoul — A175

***Perf. 14x13½***

**1988, Sept. 17 Litho. Wmk. 354**

*727* A175 4c Running 25 25
*728* A175 10c Women's diving 58 58
*729* A175 35c Basketball 2.00 2.00

## SEMI-POSTAL STAMPS

**Catalogue values for unused stamps in this section, from this point to the end of the section, are for Never Hinged items.**

Angels with Trumpet and Harp, Star of Bethlehem and Mdina Cathedral SP1

Designs (Star of Bethlehem and): 1p+1p, Two peasants with tambourine and bagpipe. 1sh6p+3p, Choir boys singing Christmas carols. The background of the 3 stamps together shows the Cathedral of Mdina, Malta, and surrounding countryside.

**Wmk. 354**

**1969, Nov. 8 Litho. *Perf. 12½***

*B1* SP1 1p + 1p multi 6 6
*B2* SP1 5p + 1p multi 10 10
*B3* SP1 1sh6p + 3p multi 35 35
Triptych (Nos. B1-B3) 55 55

Christmas 1969. Nos. B1-B3 were printed singly in sheets of 60 and in sheets containing 20 triptychs.

Christmas Eve Procession — SP2

Designs: 10p+2p, Nativity and Cathedral. 1sh6p+3p, Adoration of the Shepherds and Mdina Cathedral.

**1970, Nov. 7 Photo. *Perf. 14x13½***

*B4* SP2 1p + ½p multi 6 6
*B5* SP2 10p + 2p multi 24 24
*B6* SP2 1sh6p + 3p multi 60 60

Christmas 1970. Surtax for child welfare organizations.

Angel — SP3

Designs: 10p+2p, Madonna and Child. 1sh6p+3p, Shepherd.

**1971, Nov. 8 *Perf. 14***

*B7* SP3 1p + ½p multi 6 6
*B8* SP3 10p + 2p multi 28 28
*B9* SP3 1sh6p + 3p multi 55 55
*a.* Souvenir sheet of 3 1.25 1.25

Christmas 1971. No. B9a contains one each of Nos. B7-B9, Perf. 15. Black and multicolored margin with gold inscription. Size: 137x113mm.

**1972, Dec. Litho. *Perf. 13½***

Designs: 3c+1c, Angel playing tambourine. 7c5m+1c5m, Angel singing.

*B10* SP3 8m + 2m dk gray & gold 6 6
*B11* SP3 3c + 1c dk pur & gold 22 22
*B12* SP3 7c5m + 1c5m sl & gold 60 60
*a.* Souvenir sheet of 3 1.25 1.25

Christmas 1972. No. B12a contains one each of Nos. B10-B12 with purple, gold and gray margin. Size: 136x112mm.

**1973, Nov. 10 Litho. *Perf. 13½***

Designs: 8m+2m, Singers and organ pipes. 3c+1c, Virgin and Child with star. 7c5m+1c5m, Star, candles, buildings, tambourine.

*B13* SP3 8m + 2m multi 8 8
*B14* SP3 3c + 1c multi 40 40
*B15* SP3 7c5m + 1c5m multi 1.00 1.00
*a.* Souvenir sheet of 3 2.00 2.00

Christmas 1973. No. B15a contains one each of Nos. B13-B15 with tan and multicolored margin. Size: 136x112mm.

Star and Holy Family — SP4

Christmas 1974: 3c+1c, Star and two shepherds. 5c+1c, Star and three shepherds. 7c5m+1c5m, Star and Three Kings.

**1974, Nov. 22 Litho. *Perf. 14***

*B16* SP4 8m + 2m multi 8 8
*B17* SP4 3c + 1c multi 20 20
*B18* SP4 5c + 1c multi 45 45
*B19* SP4 7c5m + 1c5m multi 70 70

Nativity, by Maestro Alberto — SP5

Designs: 8m+2m, Shepherds. 7c5m+1c5m, Three Kings.

**1975, Nov. 4 *Perf. 13½***

**Size: 24x23mm. (#B20, B22); 49x23mm. (#B21).**

*B20* SP5 8m + 2m multi 10 10
*B21* SP5 3c + 1c multi 90 65
*B22* SP5 7c5m + 1c5m multi 5.25 4.25
Triptych (Nos. B20-B22) 7.50 7.50

Christmas 1975. Printed singly and as triptychs. Surtax for child welfare.

SP6

Madonna and Saints, by Domenico di Michelino — SP7

Christmas 1976 (Details of Painting): 5c+1c, Virgin and Child. 7c+1c5m, St. Christopher and Bishop.

**1976, Nov. 23 Litho. *Perf. 13½***

*B23* SP6 1c + 5m multi 20 10
*B24* SP6 5c + 1c multi 65 45
*B25* SP6 7c + 1c5m multi 1.10 95

***Perf. 13½x14***

*B26* SP7 10c + 2c multi 2.25 1.40

Nativity SP8

Crèche Figurines: 1c+5m, Annunciation to the Shepherds. 11c+1c5m, Shepherds.

***Perf. 13½x14***

**1977, Nov. 16 Litho. Wmk. 354**

*B27* SP8 1c + 5m multi 8 8
*B28* SP8 7c + 1c multi 30 30
*B29* SP8 11c + 1c5m multi 1.00 1.00
Triptych (Nos. B27-B29) 1.40 1.40

Christmas 1977. Nos. B27-B29 printed singly and as triptychs. Surtax was for child welfare.

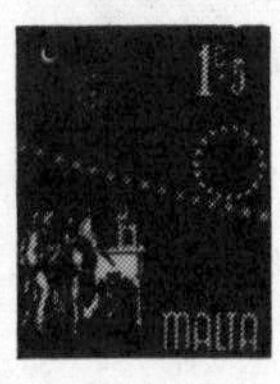


Christmas Decorations, People and Church — SP9

Christmas 1978: 5c+1c, Decorations and angels. 7c+1c5m, Decorations and carolers. 11c+3c, Combined designs of #B30-B32.

**1978, Nov. 9 Litho. *Perf. 14***

**Size: 24x30mm**

*B30* SP9 1c + 5m multi 8 8
*B31* SP9 5c + 1c multi 25 25
*B32* SP9 7c + 1c5m multi 35 35

***Perf. 13½***

**Size: 58x22½mm**

*B33* SP9 11c + 3c multi 65 65

Nativity, by Giuseppe Cali — SP10

Christmas 1979 (Cali Paintings): 5c+1c, 11c+3c, Flight into Egypt. 7c+1c5m, Nativity.

**1979, Nov. 14 Litho. *Perf. 14x13½***

*B34* SP10 1c + 5m multi 8 8
*B35* SP10 5c + 1c multi 32 32
*B36* SP10 7c + 1c5m multi 42 42
*B37* SP10 11c + 3c multi 80 80

Nativity, by Anton Inglott (1915-1945) — SP11

Christmas 1980 (Details of Painting).

**1980, Oct. 7 Litho. *Perf. 14x13½***

**Size: 20x47mm**

*B38* SP11 2c + 5m *Annunciation* 8 8
*B39* SP11 6c + 1c *Angel* 28 28
*B40* SP11 8c + 1c5m *Holy Family* 35 35

***Perf. 14½x14***

**Size: 47x39mm**

*B41* SP11 12c + 3c *shown* 55 55

Christmas 1981 — SP12

**Wmk. 354**

**1981, Nov. 18 Litho. *Perf. 14***

*B42* SP12 2c + 1c Children, vert. 12 12
*B43* SP12 8c + 2c Procession 42 42
*B44* SP12 20c + 3c Service, vert. 1.10 1.10

Christmas 1982 — SP13

Three Kings Following Star: 2c+1c, Star. 8c+2c, Three Kings, 20c+3c. Entire design.

**1982, Oct. 8 Litho. *Perf. 13½***

| | | | | |
|---|---|---|---|---|
| *B45* | SP13 | 2c + 1c multi | 15 | 15 |
| *B46* | SP13 | 8c + 2c multi | 55 | 55 |

***Perf. 14***
**Size: 45x36mm**

| | | | | |
|---|---|---|---|---|
| *B47* | SP13 | 20c + 3c multi | 1.25 | 1.25 |

Christmas 1983 — SP14

Illuminated Manuscripts, Book of Hours, 15th Cent.: 2c+1c, Annunciation. 8c+2c, Nativity. 20c+3c, Three Kings bearing gifts. Surtax was for child welfare.

**1983, Sept. 6 Litho. *Perf. 14***

| | | | | |
|---|---|---|---|---|
| *B48* | SP14 | 2c + 1c multi | 14 | 14 |
| *B49* | SP14 | 8c + 2c multi | 55 | 55 |
| *B50* | SP14 | 20c + 3c multi | 1.30 | 1.30 |

Christmas 1984 — SP15

Paintings by Peter-Paul Caruana, Church of Our Lady of Porto Salvo, Valletta, 1850: 2c+1c, Visitation (vert.). 8c+2c, Epiphany. 20c+3c, Jesus Among the Doctors.

**1984, Oct. 5 Litho. *Perf. 14***

| | | | | |
|---|---|---|---|---|
| *B51* | SP15 | 2c + 1c multi | 14 | 14 |
| *B52* | SP15 | 8c + 2c multi | 45 | 45 |
| *B53* | SP15 | 20c + 3c multi | 1.10 | 1.10 |

Christmas 1985 — SP16

**1985, Oct. 10 Litho. *Perf. 14***

| | | | | |
|---|---|---|---|---|
| *B54* | SP16 | 2c + 1c Adoration of the Magi | 12 | 12 |
| *B55* | SP16 | 8c + 2c Nativity | 40 | 40 |
| *B56* | SP16 | 20c + 3c Trumpeter Angels | 90 | 90 |

Surtax for child welfare organizations.

Christmas — SP17

Paintings by Giuseppe D'Arena (1633-1719).

**Wmk. 354**
**1986, Oct. 10 Litho. *Perf. 14½***

| | | | | |
|---|---|---|---|---|
| *B57* | SP17 | 2c + 1c The Nativity | 12 | 12 |
| *B58* | SP17 | 8c + 2c The Nativity, detail, vert. | 40 | 40 |
| *B59* | SP17 | 20c + 3c The Epiphany | 92 | 92 |

Surtaxed to benefit child welfare organizations.

Christmas — SP18

Illuminated text from choral books of the Veneranda Assemblea of St. John's Conventual Church, Valletta.

**Wmk. 354**
**1987, Nov. 6 Litho. *Perf. 14***

| | | | | |
|---|---|---|---|---|
| *B60* | SP18 | 2c +1c Mary's Visit to Elizabeth | 18 | 18 |
| *B61* | SP18 | 8c +2c Nativity | 55 | 55 |
| *B62* | SP18 | 20c +3c Adoration of the Magi | 1.25 | 1.25 |

Surtaxed to benefit child welfare organizations and the handicapped.

Christmas SP19

***Perf. 14½x14***
**1988, Nov. 5 Wmk. 354 Litho.**

| | | | | |
|---|---|---|---|---|
| *B63* | SP19 | 3c +1c Shepherd | 25 | 25 |
| *B64* | SP19 | 10c +2c Nativity | 70 | 70 |
| *B65* | SP19 | 25c +3c Magi | 1.65 | 1.65 |

Surtax for child welfare organizations and the handicapped.

## AIR-POST STAMPS

No. 140 Overprinted **AIR MAIL**

**1928, Apr. 1 Wmk. 4 *Perf. 14½x14***

| | | | | |
|---|---|---|---|---|
| *C1* | A22 | 6p red & vio | 5.50 | 6.75 |

**Catalogue values for unused stamps in this section, from this point to the end of the section, are for Never Hinged items.**

Jet over Valletta — AP1

Designs: 3c, 5c, 20c, 35c, Winged emblem. 7c5m, 25c, like 4c.

**Wmk. 354**
**1974, Mar. Litho. *Perf. 13½***
**Cross Emblem in Red and Blue**

| | | | | |
|---|---|---|---|---|
| *C2* | AP1 | 3c ol brn & gold | 10 | 10 |
| *C3* | AP1 | 4c dk bl & gold | 16 | 16 |
| *C4* | AP1 | 5c dk vio bl & gold | 22 | 22 |
| *C5* | AP1 | 7c5m sl grn & gold | 32 | 32 |
| *C6* | AP1 | 20c vio brn & gold | 85 | 85 |
| *C7* | AP1 | 25c sl & gold | 1.10 | 1.10 |
| *C8* | AP1 | 35c brn & gold | 1.65 | 1.65 |
| | | *Nos. C2-C8 (7)* | 4.40 | 4.40 |

Jet and Megalithic Temple — AP2

Designs: 7c, 20c, Air Malta Boeing 720B approaching Malta. 11c, 75c, Jumbo jet landing at Luqa Airport. 17c, like 5c.

**1978, Oct. 3 Litho. *Perf. 13½***

| | | | | |
|---|---|---|---|---|
| *C9* | AP2 | 5c multi | 20 | 20 |
| *C10* | AP2 | 7c multi | 28 | 28 |
| *C11* | AP2 | 11c multi | 45 | 45 |
| *C12* | AP2 | 17c multi | 70 | 70 |
| *C13* | AP2 | 20c multi | 90 | 90 |
| *C14* | AP2 | 75c multi | 3.00 | 3.00 |
| | | *Nos. C9-C14 (6)* | 5.53 | 5.53 |

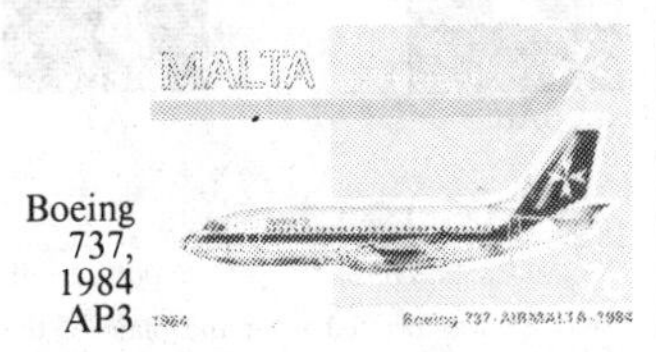

Boeing 737, 1984 AP3

**Wmk. 354**
**1984, Jan. 26 Litho. *Perf. 14***

| | | | | |
|---|---|---|---|---|
| *C15* | AP3 | 7c shown | 32 | 32 |
| *C16* | AP3 | 8c Boeing 720B, 1974 | 36 | 36 |
| *C17* | AP3 | 16c Vickers Vanguard, 1964 | 72 | 72 |
| *C18* | AP3 | 23c Vickers Viscount, 1958 | 1.05 | 1.05 |
| *C19* | AP3 | 27c Douglas DC3 Dakota, 1948 | 1.25 | 1.25 |
| *C20* | AP3 | 38c AW Atlanta, 1936 | 1.75 | 1.75 |
| *C21* | AP3 | 75c Dornier Wal, 1929 | 3.40 | 3.40 |
| | | *Nos. C15-C21 (7)* | 8.85 | 8.85 |

## POSTAGE DUE STAMPS

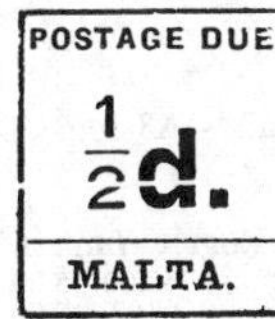

D1

Maltese Cross — D2

**Typeset**
**1925 Unwmk. *Imperf.***

| | | | | |
|---|---|---|---|---|
| *J1* | D1 | ½p blk, *white* | 90 | 1.25 |
| *J2* | D1 | 1p blk, *white* | 90 | 1.65 |
| *J3* | D1 | 1½p blk, *white* | 1.75 | 2.25 |
| *J4* | D1 | 2p blk, *white* | 1.75 | 2.50 |
| *J5* | D1 | 2½p blk, *white* | 2.00 | 3.00 |
| *a.* | | "2" of "½" omitted | 1,200. | 1,350. |
| *J6* | D1 | 3p blk, *gray* | 2.00 | 3.75 |
| *J7* | D1 | 4p blk, *orange* | 2.75 | 3.75 |
| *J8* | D1 | 6p blk, *orange* | 3.50 | 5.00 |
| *J9* | D1 | 1sh blk, *orange* | 6.50 | 12.00 |
| *J10* | D1 | 1sh6p blk, *orange* | 14.00 | 20.00 |
| | | *Nos. J1-J10 (10)* | 36.05 | 55.15 |

These stamps were typeset in groups of 42. In each sheet there were four impressions of a group, two of them being inverted and making tete beche pairs.

Forged examples of No. J5a are known.

**Wmk. 4 Sideways**
**1925 Typo. *Perf. 12***

| | | | | |
|---|---|---|---|---|
| *J11* | D2 | ½p bl grn | 52 | 52 |
| *J12* | D2 | 1p violet | 52 | 24 |
| *J13* | D2 | 1½p yel brn | 75 | 75 |
| *J14* | D2 | 2p gray | 8.75 | 8.75 |
| *J15* | D2 | 2½p orange | 2.50 | 1.50 |
| *J16* | D2 | 3p dk bl | 1.40 | 1.40 |
| *J17* | D2 | 4p ol grn | 7.75 | 7.75 |
| *J18* | D2 | 6p claret | 3.25 | 3.25 |
| *J19* | D2 | 1sh gray blk | 2.00 | 3.50 |
| *J20* | D2 | 1sh 6p dp rose | 4.50 | 6.25 |
| | | *Nos. J11-J20 (10)* | 31.94 | 33.91 |

In 1953-57 six values (½p-2p, 3p, 4p) were reissued on chalky paper in slightly different colors.

**Catalogue values for unused stamps in this section, from this point to the end of the section, are for Never Hinged items.**

**1966 Wmk. 314 *Perf. 12***

| | | | | |
|---|---|---|---|---|
| *J21* | D2 | 2p sepia | 35.00 | 35.00 |

**Wmk. 354 Sideways**
**1967-68 *Perf. 12½***

| | | | | |
|---|---|---|---|---|
| *J22* | D2 | ½p green | 12 | 12 |
| *a.* | | Perf. 12 | 4.00 | 4.00 |
| *J23* | D2 | 1p rose vio | 18 | 18 |
| *a.* | | Perf. 12 | 5.50 | 5.50 |
| *J24* | D2 | 1½p bis brn ('68) | 30 | 30 |
| *J25* | D2 | 2p brn blk | 55 | 55 |
| *a.* | | Perf. 12 | 8.00 | 8.00 |
| *J26* | D2 | 2½p org ('68) | 65 | 65 |
| *J27* | D2 | 3p Prus bl ('68) | 75 | 75 |
| *J28* | D2 | 4p olive | 1.10 | 1.10 |
| *a.* | | Perf. 12 | 135.00 | *180.00* |
| *J29* | D2 | 6p pur ('68) | 1.90 | 1.90 |
| *J30* | D2 | 1sh blk ('68) | 2.00 | 2.00 |
| *J31* | D2 | 1sh6p rose car ('68) | 4.50 | 4.50 |
| | | *Nos. J22-J31 (10)* | 12.05 | 12.05 |

Numeral — D3

***Perf. 13x13½***
**1973, Apr. 28 Litho. Wmk. 354**

| | | | | |
|---|---|---|---|---|
| *J32* | D3 | 2m brown | 5 | 5 |
| *J33* | D3 | 3m brown orange | 5 | 5 |
| *J34* | D3 | 5m carmine | 5 | 5 |
| *J35* | D3 | 1c deep green | 5 | 5 |
| *J36* | D3 | 2c black | 10 | 10 |
| *J37* | D3 | 3c olive | 15 | 15 |
| *J38* | D3 | 5c violet blue | 25 | 25 |
| *J39* | D3 | 10c deep magenta | 52 | 52 |
| | | *Nos. J32-J39 (8)* | 1.22 | 1.22 |

## WAR TAX STAMPS

Nos. 50, 25 Overprinted **WAR TAX**

**1918 Wmk. 3 *Perf. 14***

| | | | | |
|---|---|---|---|---|
| *MR1* | A13 | ½p green | 30 | 30 |

**Wmk. Crown and C. A. (2)**

| | | | | |
|---|---|---|---|---|
| *MR2* | A12 | 3p red vio & gray | 3.00 | 4.00 |

# MAURITIUS

LOCATION — An island in the Indian Ocean about 550 miles east of Madagascar.
GOVT. — Independent State in the British Commonwealth.
AREA — 720 sq. mi.
POP. — 969,191 (est. 1983).
CAPITAL — Port Louis.

12 Pence = 1 Shilling
100 Cents = 1 Rupee

The British Crown Colony of Mauritius was granted self-government in

1967 and became an independent state on March 12, 1968.

Values of early Mauritius stamps vary according to condition. Quotations for Nos. 1-23 are for fine copies. Very fine to superb specimens sell at much higher prices, and inferior or poor copies sell at reduced prices, depending on the condition of the individual specimen.

12 Pence = 1 Shilling
100 Cents = 1 Rupee (1878)

**Catalogue values for unused stamps in this country are for Never Hinged items, beginning with Scott 223 in the regular postage section, Scott J1 in the postage due section.**

Queen Victoria
A1 A2

**1847 Unwmk. Engr. *Imperf.***

| | | | | |
|---|---|---|---|---|
| *1* | A1 | 1p orange | *350,000.* | *225,000.* |
| *2* | A1 | 2p dk bl | *300,000.* | *225,000.* |

Nos. 1 and 2 were engraved and printed in Port Louis. There is but one type of each value. The initials "J. B." on the bust are those of the engraver, J. Barnard.

Earliest Impressions.

**1848**

**Thick Yellowish Paper.**

| | | | | |
|---|---|---|---|---|
| *3* | A2 | 1p orange | *20,000.* | *12,500.* |
| *4* | A2 | 2p dk bl | *25,000.* | *12,500.* |
| *d* | | "PENOE" | *35,000.* | *20,000.* |

**Early Impressions.**

**Yellowish White Paper.**

| | | | | |
|---|---|---|---|---|
| *3a* | A2 | 1p orange | *10,000.* | *5,000.* |
| *4a* | A2 | 2p blue | *14,000.* | *5,500.* |
| *e* | | "PENOE" | *15,000.* | *8,000.* |

**Bluish Paper.**

| | | | | |
|---|---|---|---|---|
| *5* | A2 | 1p orange | *7,500.* | *3,500.* |
| *6* | A2 | 2p blue | *8,000.* | *3,000.* |
| *c* | | "PENOE" | *15,000.* | *6,000.* |

**Intermediate Impressions.**

**Yellowish White Paper.**

| | | | | |
|---|---|---|---|---|
| *3b* | A2 | 1p red org | *3,500.* | 1,350. |
| *4b* | A2 | 2p blue | *2,750.* | 1,250. |
| *f* | | "PENOE" | *5,000.* | *2,750.* |

**Bluish Paper.**

| | | | | |
|---|---|---|---|---|
| *5a* | A2 | 1p red org | *3,000.* | 650.00 |
| *6a* | A2 | 2p blue | *3,000.* | 850.00 |
| *d* | | "PENOE" | *6,000.* | *2,000.* |

**Worn Impressions.**

**Yellowish White Paper.**

| | | | | |
|---|---|---|---|---|
| *3c* | A2 | 1p org red | 950.00 | 300.00 |
| *d* | | 1p brnsh red | 950.00 | 300.00 |
| *4c* | A2 | 2p blue | 1,500. | 500.00 |
| *g* | | "PENOE" | *2,250.* | 1,100. |

**Bluish Paper.**

| | | | | |
|---|---|---|---|---|
| *5b* | A2 | 1p org red | 650.00 | 300.00 |
| *c* | | 1p brnsh red | 650.00 | 400.00 |
| *6b* | A2 | 2p blue | 800.00 | 350.00 |
| *e* | | "PENOE" | 1,500. | 750.00 |

These stamps were printed in sheets of twelve, four rows of three, and all differ in minor details. The "PENOE" error was No. 7 on the plate. They were in use until 1859. Early impressions show the full background of diagonal and vertical lines; as the plate became worn the vertical lines disappeared, giving the intermediate impressions, and, finally, the lines of the background disappeared almost entirely. The paper of the early impressions is usually rather thick, that of the worn impressions is usually thin.

"Britannia"
A3 A4

**1849-58**

| | | | |
|---|---|---|---|
| *7* | A3 | red brn, *blue* | 3.00 |
| *8* | A3 | blue ('58) | 2.00 |

Nos. 7 and 8 were never placed in use.

**1858-59**

| | | | | |
|---|---|---|---|---|
| *9* | A3 | (4p) grn, *bluish* | 300.00 | 150.00 |
| *10* | A3 | (6p) red | 12.50 | *30.00* |
| *11* | A3 | (9p) mag ('59) | 300.00 | 125.00 |

No. 11 was re-issued in November, 1862, as a 1p stamp. When used as such it is always canceled "B53". Same value as No. 11 used.

**1854 Black Surcharge**

| | | | | |
|---|---|---|---|---|
| *12* | A4 | 4p grn, *bluish* | 650.00 | 300.00 |

Queen Victoria — A5

Early Impressions

**1859, Mar.**

| | | | | |
|---|---|---|---|---|
| *14* | A5 | 2p blue, *grysh* | 3,000. | 1,250. |
| *a* | | 2p deep blue, *grysh* | 3,750. | 1,600. |
| *14B* | A5 | 2p blue, *bluish* | 2,250. | 900.00 |
| *c* | | Worn impression | 900.00 | 300.00 |

Type A5 was engraved by Lapirot, in Port Louis, and was printed locally. There were twelve varieties in the sheet.

A6 A7

**1859, Oct.**

| | | | | |
|---|---|---|---|---|
| *15* | A6 | 2p bl, *bluish* | *20,000.* | 2,750. |

No. 15 was printed from the plate of the 1848 issue after it had been entirely re-engraved by Sherwin. It is commonly known as the "fillet head". The plate of the 1p, 1848, was also re-engraved but was never put in use.

**1859, Dec. Litho.**

**Laid Paper**

| | | | | |
|---|---|---|---|---|
| *16* | A7 | 1p red | 1,100. | 375.00 |
| *a* | | 1p dp red | 2,000. | 800.00 |
| *17* | A7 | 2p blue | 900.00 | 300.00 |
| *a* | | 2p sl bl | 2,500. | 700.00 |

Nos. 16 and 17 were lithographed locally by Dardenne.

"Britannia" — A8

**1859 Wove Paper. Engr. *Imperf.***

| | | | | |
|---|---|---|---|---|
| *18* | A8 | 6p blue | 350.00 | 25.00 |
| *19* | A8 | 1sh vermilion | 1,100. | 40.00 |

**1861**

| | | | | |
|---|---|---|---|---|
| *20* | A8 | 6p gray vio | 13.50 | 15.00 |
| *21* | A8 | 1sh green | 135.00 | 60.00 |

**1862 *Perf. 14 to 16.***

| | | | | |
|---|---|---|---|---|
| *22* | A8 | 6p slate | 13.50 | 13.50 |
| *23* | A8 | 1sh dp grn | 1,250. | 275.00 |

A9 A10

**1860-63 Typo. *Perf. 14.***

| | | | | |
|---|---|---|---|---|
| *24* | A9 | 1p brn lil | 60.00 | 8.00 |
| *25* | A9 | 2p blue | 80.00 | 13.50 |
| *26* | A9 | 4p rose | 80.00 | 8.00 |
| *27* | A9 | 6p grn ('62) | 350.00 | 70.00 |
| *28* | A9 | 6p lil ('63) | 100.00 | 35.00 |
| *29* | A9 | 9p dl lil | 55.00 | 22.50 |
| *30* | A9 | 1sh buff ('62) | 125.00 | 27.50 |
| *31* | A9 | 1sh grn ('63) | 350.00 | 80.00 |

**1863-72 Wmk. Crown and C. C. (1)**

| | | | | |
|---|---|---|---|---|
| *32* | A9 | 1p lil brn | 11.00 | 2.00 |
| *a* | | 1p bis brn | 20.00 | 3.50 |
| *33* | A9 | 2p blue | 22.50 | 3.00 |
| *a* | | Imperf., pair | 800.00 | 800.00 |
| *34* | A9 | 3p vermilion | 20.00 | 6.00 |
| *35* | A9 | 4p rose | 35.00 | 1.75 |
| *36* | A9 | 6p lil ('64) | 30.00 | 8.50 |
| *37* | A9 | 6p bl grn ('65) | 32.50 | 2.50 |
| *a* | | 6p yel grn ('65) | 35.00 | 7.50 |
| *38* | A9 | 9p grn ('72) | 95.00 | *165.00* |
| *39* | A9 | 1sh yel ('64) | 55.00 | 4.00 |
| *a* | | 1sh org yel | 55.00 | 4.50 |
| *40* | A9 | 1sh bl ('70) | 57.50 | 7.00 |
| *41* | A9 | 5sh red vio | 65.00 | 12.50 |
| *a* | | 5sh brt vio | 90.00 | 22.50 |

**1872**

| | | | | |
|---|---|---|---|---|
| *42* | A10 | 10p claret | 42.50 | 8.00 |

No. 29 Surcharged in Black or Red:

HALF PENNY
a

½ d
HALF PENNY
b

**1876 Unwmk.**

| | | | | |
|---|---|---|---|---|
| *43* | A9 (a) | ½p on 9p dl lil | 3.00 | *5.50* |
| *a* | | Inverted surcharge | 200.00 | |
| *b* | | Double surcharge | | |
| *44* | A9 (b) | ½p on 9p dl lil | *2,000.* | |
| *45* | A9 (b) | ½p on 9p dl lil (R) | *700.00* | |

Nos. 44 and 45 were never placed in use.

Stamps of 1863-72 Surcharged in Black:

HALF PENNY
c

One Penny
d

**1876-77 Wmk. Crown and C. C. (1)**

| | | | | |
|---|---|---|---|---|
| *46* | A10 (a) | ½p on 10p cl | 1.75 | *8.00* |
| *47* | A10 (c) | ½p on 10p cl ('77) | 3.50 | *8.00* |
| *48* | A9 (d) | 1p on 4p rose ('77) | 4.50 | 7.00 |
| *49* | A9 (d) | 1sh on 5sh red vio ('77) | 135.00 | 60.00 |
| *a* | | 1sh on 5sh vio ('77) | 165.00 | 65.00 |

A16

**1878**

Black Surcharge.

| | | | | |
|---|---|---|---|---|
| *50* | A16 | 2c claret | 2.50 | 3.00 |

Stamps of Type A9 Surcharged in Black

4 CENTS

| | | | | |
|---|---|---|---|---|
| *51* | A9 | 4c on 1p bis brn | 4.00 | 2.75 |
| *52* | A9 | 8c on 2p bl | 16.50 | 1.25 |
| *53* | A9 | 13c on 3p org red | 4.75 | 4.75 |
| *54* | A9 | 17c on 4p rose | 40.00 | 2.00 |
| *55* | A9 | 25c on 6p sl bl | 65.00 | 4.00 |
| *56* | A9 | 38c on 9p vio | 7.00 | 8.00 |
| *57* | A9 | 50c on 1sh grn | 16.50 | 2.50 |
| *58* | A9 | 2r 50c on 5sh vio | 11.50 | 8.00 |
| | | *Nos. 50-58 (9)* | 167.75 | 36.25 |

A18 A19

A20 A21

A22 A23

A24 A25

A26

**1879-80 Wmk. Crown and C. C. (1)**

| | | | | |
|---|---|---|---|---|
| *59* | A18 | 2c red brn ('80) | 9.00 | 6.00 |
| *60* | A19 | 4c orange | 15.00 | 2.50 |
| *61* | A20 | 8c bl ('80) | 7.50 | 1.25 |
| *62* | A21 | 13c sl ('80) | 75.00 | 60.00 |
| *63* | A22 | 17c rose ('80) | 17.00 | 4.00 |
| *64* | A23 | 25c bister | 60.00 | 9.00 |
| *65* | A24 | 38c vio ('80) | 75.00 | 75.00 |
| *66* | A25 | 50c grn ('80) | 3.00 | 3.00 |
| *67* | A26 | 2r 50c brn vio ('80) | 15.00 | 15.00 |
| | | *Nos. 59-67 (9)* | 276.50 | 175.75 |

Nos. 59 to 67 are known imperforate.

**1882-93 Wmk. Crown and C. A. (2)**

| | | | | |
|---|---|---|---|---|
| *68* | A18 | 1c vio ('93) | 15 | 25 |
| *69* | A18 | 2c red brn | 4.25 | 2.00 |
| *70* | A18 | 2c grn ('85) | 1.00 | 30 |
| *71* | A19 | 4c orange | 15.00 | 90 |
| *72* | A19 | 4c rose ('85) | 75 | 15 |
| *73* | A20 | 8c bl ('91) | 75 | 60 |
| *74* | A23 | 25c bis ('83) | 2.50 | 1.00 |
| *75* | A25 | 50c dp org ('87) | 15.00 | 6.00 |
| | | *Nos. 68-75 (8)* | 39.40 | 11.20 |

No. 63 Surcharged in Black:

16 CENTS
f

SIXTEEN CENTS
g

**1883 Wmk. Crown and C. C. (1)**

**Surcharge Measures 14x3½mm**

| | | | | |
|---|---|---|---|---|
| *76* | A22 (f) | 16c on 17c rose | 14.00 | 10.00 |
| *a* | | Double surch. | | |

**Surcharge Measures 15½x3½mm.**

| | | | | |
|---|---|---|---|---|
| *77* | A22 (f) | 16c on 17c rose | 40.00 | 27.50 |

**Surcharge Measures 15½x2¾mm.**

| | | | | |
|---|---|---|---|---|
| *78* | A22 (f) | 16c on 17c rose | *135.00* | *135.00* |

**Wmk. Crown and C. A. (2)**

| | | | | |
|---|---|---|---|---|
| *79* | A22 (g) | 16c on 17c rose | 6.50 | 2.00 |

Queen Victoria — A29

**1885-94**

| | | | | |
|---|---|---|---|---|
| *80* | A29 | 15c org brn ('92) | 50 | 40 |
| *81* | A29 | 15c bl ('94) | 1.25 | 25 |
| *82* | A29 | 16c org brn | 1.25 | 25 |

Various Stamps Surcharged in Black or Red:

2 CENTS
h

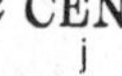

2 CENTS
j

**1885-87 Wmk. Crown and C. C. (1)**

83 A24 (h) 2c on 38c vio 20.00 18.00
- a Inverted surcharge 150.00 150.00
- b Double surcharge 275.00
- c Without bar 55.00

84 A21 (j) 2c on 13c sl (R) ('87) 13.50 16.50
- a Inverted surcharge 55.00 55.00
- b Double surcharge 200.00
- c As "b," one on back 275.00

TWO CENTS k — TWO CENTS l

**1891**

85 A22 (k) 2c on 17c rose 22.50 22.50
- a Inverted surcharge 95.00 95.00
- b Double surcharge 165.00 165.00

86 A24 (k) 2c on 38c vio 2.00 4.00
- a Double surcharge 35.00 35.00
- b Double surcharge, one inverted 35.00 35.00
- c Inverted surcharge 150.00 150.00

87 A9 (e+l) 2c on 38c on 9p vio 1.25 2.50
- a Double surcharge 150.00 150.00
- b Inverted surcharge 65.00 65.00
- c Double surcharge, one inverted 35.00 35.00

**Wmk. Crown and C. A. (2)**

88 A19 (k) 2c on 4c rose 35 30
- a Double surcharge 50.00 40.00
- b Inverted surcharge 42.50 42.50
- c Double surcharge, one inverted 47.50 47.50

ONE CENT m — ONE CENT n

**1893, Jan.**

89 A18 (m) 1c on 2c vio 15 25
90 A29 (n) 1c on 16c org brn 16 30

Coat of Arms — A38

**Wmk. Crown and C. A. (2)**

**1895-1904**

91 A38 1c lil & ultra 25 35
92 A38 1c gray blk & blk ('00) 30 25
93 A38 2c lil & org 85 30
94 A38 2c dl lil & vio ('00) 55 18
95 A38 3c lilac 85 40
96 A38 3c grn & scar, *yel* ('02) 55 30
97 A38 4c lil & grn 65 22
98 A38 4c dl lil & car, *yel* ('00) 1.40 25
99 A38 4c gray grn & pur ('02) 55 55
100 A38 4c blk & car, *bl* ('04) 1.40 15
101 A38 5c lil & vio, *buff* ('02) 3.00 20.00
102 A38 5c lil & blk, *buff* ('02) 1.35 1.35
103 A38 6c grn & rose ('99) 1.50 45
104 A38 6c vio & scar, *red* ('02) 1.35 65
105 A38 8c gray grn & blk, *buff* ('02) 55 85
106 A38 12c blk & car rose ('02) 1.50 1.50
107 A38 15c grn & org ('99) 5.75 8.50
108 A38 15c blk & ultra, *bl* ('04) 11.50 2.00
109 A38 18c gray grn & ultra 6.00 2.75
110 A38 25c grn & car, *grn* ('02) 3.00 6.00
111 A38 50c grn, *yel* ('02) 6.00 12.50
*Nos. 91-111 (21)* 48.85 59.50

The 25c is on both ordinary and chalky paper. Ornaments in lower panel omitted on Nos. 106-111. See Nos. 128-135.

**Diamond Jubilee Issue.**

Arms A39

**1898, May 23 Wmk. 46**

112 A39 36c brn org & ultra 6.00 6.00

60th year of Queen Victoria's reign.

No. 109 Surcharged in Red — 6 CENTS

**1899 Wmk. Crown and C. A. (2)**

113 A38 6c on 18c gray grn & ultra 50 35
- a Inverted surch. 150.00 125.00

No. 112 Surcharged in Blue — 15 CENTS

**Wmk. 46**

114 A39 15c on 36 brn org & ultra 2.00 1.50
- a Without bar 140.00

Admiral Mahe de La Bourdonnais — A40

**1899, Dec. Engr. Wmk. 1**

115 A40 15c ultra 6.50 3.00

Bicentenary of birth of Admiral Mahe de La Bourdonnais, governor of Mauritius, 1734-46.

No. 82 Surcharged in Black — 4 Cents

**1900 Wmk. Crown and C. A. (2)**

116 A29 4c on 16c org brn 50 1.00

No. 109 Surcharged in Black — r 12 CENTS

**1902**

117 A38 12c on 18c grn & ultra 1.40 4.00

Preceding Issues Overprinted in Black — Postage & Revenue.

**1902**

118 A38 4c lil & car, *yel* 70 35
119 A38 6c grn & rose 60 1.20
120 A38 15c grn & org 60 40
121 A23 25c bister 95 1.50

**Wmk. Crown and C. C. (1)**

122 A25 50c green 3.00 2.50
123 A26 2r50c brn vio 35.00 45.00
*Nos. 118-123 (6)* 40.85 50.95

Coat of Arms — A41

**1902 Wmk. Crown and C. C. (1)**

124 A41 1r blk & car rose 20.00 12.50

**Wmk. Crown and C. A. Sideways. (2)**

125 A41 2r50c grn & blk, *bl* 17.50 30.00
126 A41 5r blk & car, *red* 45.00 75.00

No. 112 Surcharged type "r" but longer bar.

**1902 Wmk. 46**

127 A39 12c on 36c brn org & ultra 1.25 2.00
- a Invtd. surch. 200.00 135.00

Arms Type of 1895-1904

**1904-07 Wmk. 3**

**Chalky Paper**

128 A38 1c gray blk & blk ('07) 1.75 50
129 A38 2c dl lil & vio ('05) 1.50 12
130 A38 3c grn & scar, *yel* 12.50 2.00
131 A38 4c blk & car, *bl* 1.90 12
132 A38 6c vio & scar, *red* ('06) 1.25 15
133 A38 15c blk & ultra, *bl* 3.00 80
135 A38 50c grn, *yel* 90 2.00
136 A41 1r blk & car rose ('07) 18.00 18.00
*Nos. 128-136 (8)* 40.80 23.69

The 2c, 4c and 6c also exist on ordinary paper.

Ornaments in lower panel omitted on 15c and 50c.

Arms A42

Edward VII A43

**1910 Wmk. 3**

**Ordinary Paper**

137 A42 1c black 10 10
138 A42 2c brown 14 6
139 A42 3c green 30 18
140 A42 4c ol grn & rose 15 8
141 A43 5c gray & rose 30 1.10
142 A42 6c carmine 65 10
143 A42 8c brn org 40 1.60
144 A43 12c gray 25 25
145 A42 15c ultra 1.75 14

**Chalky Paper**

146 A43 25c blk & scar, *yel* 2.50 6.00
147 A43 50c dl vio & blk 3.00 6.00
148 A43 1r blk, *green* 3.75 6.00
149 A43 2r50c blk & car, *bl* 8.00 17.50
150 A43 5r grn & car, *yel* 12.50 22.50
151 A43 10r grn & car, *grn* 55.00 85.00
*Nos. 137-151 (15)* 88.79 146.61

Numerals of 12c, 25c and 10r of type A43 are in color on plain tablet.
See Nos. 161-178.

King George V — A44

Die I.

For description of dies I and II see back of this section of the Catalogue.

Numeral tablet of 5c, 50c, 1r, 2.50r and 5r of type A44 has lined background with colorless denomination.

**1912-22 Wmk. 3**

**Ordinary Paper**

152 A44 5c gray & rose 1.40 50
153 A44 12c gray 45 42

**Chalky Paper**

154 A44 25c blk & red, *yel* 50 50
- a 25c gray blk & red, *yel*, Die II 75 7.00

155 A44 50c dl vio & blk 12.50 17.50
156 A44 1r *bl grn, ol back* 1.25 1.75
- a 1r *emer, ol back* ('21) 4.00 6.50
- b Die II, *emer* 1.50 3.50

157 A44 2r50c blk & red, *bl* 5.00 6.50
158 A44 5r grn & red, *yel* 12.50 22.50
- a Die II ('22) 50.00 90.00

159 A44 10r grn & red, *grn* 17.50 25.00
- a 10r grn & red, *bl grn, ol back* 550.00
- b 10r grn & red, *emer* 17.50 27.50
- c 10r grn & red, *emer, ol back* 17.50 27.50
- d Die II *emer* ('21) 17.00 37.50

**Surface-colored Paper**

160 A44 25c blk & red, *yel* ('16) 1.50 3.00
*Nos. 152-160 (9)* 52.60 77.67

**1921-26 Wmk. 4**

**Ordinary Paper**

161 A42 1c black 40 25
162 A42 2c brown 50 6
163 A42 2c vio, *yel* ('25) 45 60
164 A42 3c grn ('25) 30 50
165 A42 4c ol grn & rose 1.25 1.50
166 A42 4c green 65 14
167 A42 4c brn ('25) 18 50
168 A42 6c rose red 5.00 4.00
169 A42 6c violet 35 15
170 A42 8c brn org ('25) 1.50 4.00
171 A42 10c gray ('22) 1.75 3.00
172 A42 10c rose red ('25) 30 65
173 A42 12c rose red 30 30
174 A42 12c gray ('25) 50 75
175 A42 15c ultra 4.50 2.50
176 A42 15c dl bl ('25) 45 30
177 A42 20c ultra ('22) 1.75 1.00
178 A42 20c dl vio ('25) 75 1.25
*Nos. 161-178 (18)* 20.88 21.45

Ornaments in lower panel omitted on Nos. 171-178.

Die II

**1922-34**

**Ordinary Paper**

179 A44 1c black 10 14
180 A44 2c brown 10 10
181 A44 3c green 25 45
182 A44 4c ol grn & red ('27) 30 15
- a Die I ('32) 2.50 2.50

183 A44 4c grn, die I ('33) 3.50 7.00
184 A44 5c gray & car 14 5
- a Die I ('32) 65 55

185 A44 6c ol brn ('28) 20 50
186 A44 8c orange 45 1.40
187 A44 10c rose red ('26) 14 10
- a Die I ('32) 25 55

188 A44 12c gray, small "c" ('22) 25 30
189 A44 12c gray, "c" larger & thinner ('34) 4.50 6.50
190 A44 12c rose red 35 70
191 A44 15c dk bl ('28) 60 50
192 A44 20c dl vio 45 55
193 A44 20c dk bl ('34) 2.50 2.25
- a Die I ('27) 2.50 4.00

194 A44 25c blk & red, *yel* 25 15
- a Die I ('32) 75 1.25

**Chalky Paper**

195 A44 50c dl vio & blk 2.75 2.75
196 A44 1r blk, *emerald* 1.00 20
- a Die I ('32) 6.50 20.00

197 A44 2r50c blk & red, *bl* 4.00 4.00
198 A44 5r grn & red, *yel* 11.00 18.00
199 A44 10r grn & red, *emer* ('28) 25.00 40.00
*Nos. 179-199 (21)* 57.83 85.79

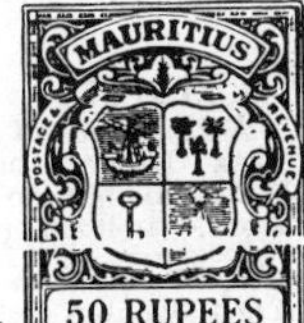

A45

**1924**

200 A45 50r lil & grn 850.00 1,500.

Nos. 166, 173, 177 Surcharged

**10 Cents**

**1925**
201 A42 3c on 4c grn 1.00 1.50
202 A42 10c on 12c rose red 25 70
203 A42 15c on 20c ultra 25 70

**Silver Jubilee Issue.**
Common Design Type

**1935, May 6 Engr. *Perf. 13½x14***
204 CD301 5c gray blk & ultra 20 15
205 CD301 12c ind & grn 50 50
206 CD301 20c bl & brn 1.50 1.00
207 CD301 1r brt vio & ind 12.50 12.50

**Coronation Issue**
Common Design Type
***Perf. 13½x14***

**1937, May 12 Wmk. 4**
208 CD302 5c dk pur 10 10
209 CD302 12c carmine 15 15
210 CD302 20c brt ultra 25 25

King George VI — A46

**1938-43 Typo. *Perf. 14.***
211 A46 2c gray 5 5
a. Perf. 15x14 ('43) 20 20
212 A46 3c rose vio & car 8 8
213 A46 4c green 8 8
214 A46 5c violet 5 5
a. Perf. 15x14 ('43) 4.00 1.00
215 A46 10c carmine 8 8
a. Perf. 15x14 ('43) 3.50 3.00
216 A46 12c sal pink 10 8
a. Perf. 15x14 ('43) 6.50 4.50
217 A46 20c blue 12 10
218 A46 25c maroon 16 10
219 A46 1r brn blk 65 50
220 A46 2.50r pale vio 2.00 2.00
221 A46 5r ol grn 4.00 4.00
222 A46 10r rose vio 5.75 5.75
*Nos. 211-222 (12)* 13.12 12.87

**Catalogue values for unused stamps in this section, from this point to the end of the section, are for Never Hinged items.**

**Peace Issue**
Common Design Type
***Perf. 13½x14***

**1946, Nov. 20 Engr. Wmk. 4**
223 CD303 5c lilac 10 10
224 CD303 20c dp bl 15 15

"Post Office" Stamp of 1847 — A47

**1948, Mar. 22 *Perf. 11½***
225 A47 5c red vio & org 7 7
226 A47 12c grn & org 14 14
227 A47 20c bl & dp bl 16 16
228 A47 1r lt red brn & dp bl 60 60

Issued to commemorate the centenary of the first Mauritius postage stamps.

**Silver Wedding Issue.**
Common Design Types

**1948, Oct. 25 Photo. *Perf. 14x14½***
229 CD304 5c violet 10 10

**Engraved; Name Typographed**
***Perf. 11½x11***
230 CD305 10r lil rose 10.00 17.50

**UPU Issue**
Common Design Types
**Engr.; Name Typo. on 20c, 35c**
***Perf. 13½, 11x11½***

**1949, Oct. 10 Wmk. 4**
231 CD306 12c rose car 30 30
232 CD307 20c indigo 35 35
233 CD308 35c rose vio 40 40
234 CD309 1r sepia 70 60

Sugar Factory — A48

Aloe Plant — A49

Designs: 2c, Grand Port. 4c, Tamarind Falls. 5c, Rempart Mountain. 10c, Transporting cane. 12c, Map and dodo. 20c, "Paul et Virginie." 25c, Statue of MaheLa Bourdonnais. 35c, Government House. 50c, Pieter Both Mountain. 1r, Sambar. 2.50r, Port Louis. 5r, Beach scene. 10r, Arms.

***Perf. 13½x14½, 14½x13½***

**1950, July 1 Photo.**
235 A48 1c red vio 5 5
236 A48 2c cerise 6 6
237 A49 3c yel grn 15 15
238 A49 4c green 6 6
239 A48 5c grnsh bl 8 8
a. Bklt. pane of 4
240 A48 10c red 22 8
241 A48 12c ol grn 15 12
242 A49 20c brt ultra 22 18
243 A49 25c vio brn 45 35
244 A48 35c rose vio 40 25
245 A49 50c emerald 65 45
a. Bklt. pane of 4
246 A48 1r sepia 1.90 1.25
247 A48 2.50r orange 3.25 2.25
248 A48 5r red brn 5.00 4.00
249 A48 10r gray bl 17.50 7.50
*Nos. 235-249 (15)* 30.14 16.83

**Coronation Issue.**
Common Design Type

**1953, June 2 Engr. *Perf. 13½x13***
250 CD312 10c dk grn & blk 25 18
a. Bklt. pane of 4 20.00

Sugar Factory — A50

Tamarind Falls — A51

Designs: 2c, Grand Port. 3c, Aloe plant. 5c, Rempart Mountain. 15c, Museum, Mahebourg. 20c, Statue of MaheLa Bourdonnais. 25c, "Paul et Virginie." 35c, Government House. 50c, Pieter Both Mountain. 60c, Map and dodo. 1r, Sambar. 2.50r, Port Louis. 5r, Beach scene. 10r, Arms.

***Perf. 13½x14½, 14½x13½.***

**1953-54 Photo. Wmk. 4**
251 A50 2c rose car ('54) 6 5
252 A51 3c yel grn ('54) 8 5
253 A50 4c red vio 8 5
254 A50 5c grnsh bl ('54) 10 5
a. Booklet pane of 4 1.50
255 A51 10c dk grn 18 7
a. Booklet pane of 4 2.75
256 A50 15c scarlet 18 8
257 A51 20c vio brn 25 10
a. Imperf., pair
258 A51 25c brt ultra 40 12
259 A50 35c rose vio ('54) 40 15
260 A51 50c emerald 70 20
a. Booklet pane of 4 3.00
261 A50 60c gray grn ('54) 1.75 50
262 A50 1r sepia 1.00 40
a. Imperf., pair
263 A50 2.50r org ('54) 4.00 2.00
264 A50 5r red brn ('54) 6.50 2.75
265 A50 10r gray bl ('54) 10.00 3.75
*Nos. 251-265 (15)* 25.68 10.32

See Nos. 273-275.

King George III and Queen Elizabeth II — A52

**Wmk. 314**

**1961, Jan. 11 Litho. *Perf. 13½***
266 A52 10c dk red & dk brn 12 12
267 A52 20c lt bl & dk bl 18 18
268 A52 35c org yel & brn 35 35
269 A52 1r yel grn & dk brn 75 75

Sesquicentenary of postal service under British administration.

**Freedom from Hunger Issue**
Common Design Type

**1963, June 4 Photo. *Perf. 14x14½***
270 CD314 60c lilac 40 40

**Red Cross Centenary Issue**
Common Design Type

**1963, Sept. 2 Litho. *Perf. 13***
271 CD315 10c blk & red 8 8
272 CD315 60c ultra & red 50 50

Types of 1953-54
***Perf. 14½x13½, 13½x14½***

**1963-64 Photo. Wmk. 314**
273 A51 10c dk grn ('64) 15 10
274 A50 60c gray grn ('64) 65 40
275 A50 2.50r orange 2.00 2.00

Gray White-Eye — A53

Birds of Mauritius: 3c, Rodriguez fody. 4c, Olive white-eye. 5c, Mauritius paradise flycatcher. 10c, Mauritius fody. 15c, Rose-ringed parakeet. 20c, Cuckoo shrike. 25c, Mauritian kestrel. 35c, Pink pigeon. 50c, Mauritius olivaceous bulbul. 60c, Mauritius blue pigeon. 1r, Dodo. 2.50r, Rodriguez solitaire. 5r, Van den Broeck's red rail. 10r, Broad-billed Mauritian parrot.

**Wmk. 314**

**1965, Mar. 16 Photo. *Perf. 14½***
**Birds in Natural Colors**
276 A53 2c brt yel & brn 5 5
a. Gray (leg, etc.) omitted 30.00
277 A53 3c brn & dk brn 6 5
a. Black (eye, beak) omitted 25.00
278 A53 4c dl rose lil & blk 8 5
a. Rose lil omitted 30.00
279 A53 5c gray & ultra 8 5
a. Wmkd. sideways ('66) 10 10
280 A53 10c dl grn & dk brn 8 5
281 A53 15c lt gray & dk brn 10 8
a. Carmine (beak) omitted 25.00
282 A53 20c pale yel & dk brn 12 8
283 A53 25c gray & brn 12 10
284 A53 35c vio bl & blk 16 10
a. Wmkd. sideways ('67) 30 30
285 A53 50c pale yel & blk 18 10
286 A53 60c pale cit & brn 20 15
287 A53 1r lt yel grn & blk 45 20
a. Pale gray (ground) omitted 40.00
b. Pale org omitted 45.00
288 A53 2.50r pale grn & brn 2.00 1.00
289 A53 5r pale bl & blk 4.00 2.00
290 A53 10r pale grn & ultra 7.50 4.00
*Nos. 276-290 (15)* 15.18 8.06

On No. 278 the background was printed in two colors. The rose lilac tint is omitted on No. 278a.
See Nos. 327-332.

**ITU Issue**
Common Design Type
***Perf. 11x11½***

**1965, May 17 Litho. Wmk. 314**
291 CD317 10c dp org & ap grn 8 8
292 CD317 60c yel & vio 45 35

**Intl. Cooperation Year Issue**
Common Design Type

**1965, Oct. 25 *Perf. 14½***
293 CD318 10c lt grn & cl 8 8
294 CD318 60c lt vio grn 35 35

**Churchill Memorial Issue**
Common Design Type

**1966, Jan. 24 Photo. *Perf. 14***
**Design in Black, Gold and Carmine Rose**
295 CD319 2c brt bl 5 5
296 CD319 10c green 8 8
297 CD319 60c brown 45 45
298 CD319 1r violet 1.00 1.00

**UNESCO Anniversary Issue**
Common Design Type

**1966, Dec. 1 Litho. *Perf. 14***
299 CD323 5c "Education" 8 6
300 CD323 10c "Science" 20 10
301 CD323 60c "Culture" 75 60

Red-Tailed Tropic Bird — A54

Birds of Mauritius: 10c, Rodriguez bush warbler. 60c, Newton's parakeet. 1r, Mauritius swiftlet.

**1967, Sept. 1 Photo. *Perf. 14½***
302 A54 2c lt ultra & multi 5 5
303 A54 10c emer & multi 6 6
304 A54 60c sal & multi 40 40
305 A54 1r yel & multi 75 75

Issued to commemorate the attainment of self-government, Sept. 1, 1967.

Bird Issue of 1965-67 and Type Overprinted: "SELF GOVERNMENT 1967"

**1967, Dec. 1 Photo. Wmk. 314**
306 A53 2c multi 5 5
307 A53 3c multi 5 5
308 A53 4c multi 5 5
309 A53 5c multi 5 5
310 A53 10c multi 6 5
311 A53 15c multi 8 6
312 A53 20c multi 10 8
313 A53 25c multi 14 10
314 A53 35c multi 15 14
315 A53 50c multi 25 20
316 A53 60c multi 30 20
317 A53 1r multi 45 35
318 A53 2.50r multi 1.25 1.25
319 A53 5r multi 2.50 2.50
320 A53 10r multi 5.00 5.00
*Nos. 306-320 (15)* 10.48 10.13

The 5c, 10c and 35c have watermark sideways.

**Independent State**

Flag of Mauritius A55

Designs: 3c, 20c, 1r, Dodo emerging from egg and coat of arms.

***Perf. 13½x13***

**1968, Mar. 12 Litho. Unwmk.**
321 A55 2c brt vio & multi 5 5
322 A55 3c red brn & multi 5 5
323 A55 15c brn & multi 8 8
324 A55 20c multi 12 12
325 A55 60c dk grn & multi 40 40
326 A55 1r brt vio & multi 65 65
*Nos. 321-326 (6)* 1.35 1.35

Independence of Mauritius.

Bird Type of 1965 in Changed Background Colors
**Wmk. 314**

**1968, July 12 Photo. *Perf. 14½***
**Birds in Natural Colors**
327 A53 2c lem & brn 8 6
328 A53 3c ultra & dk brn 10 8
329 A53 15c tan & dk brn 20 15
330 A53 20c dl yel & dk brn 28 20
331 A53 60c pink & blk 75 50
332 A53 1r rose lil & blk 1.25 90
*Nos. 327-332 (6)* 2.66 1.89

Domingue Rescuing Paul and Virginie — A56

Designs: 15c, Paul and Virginie crossing river (vert.). 50c, La Bourdonnais visiting Madame de la Tour. 60c, Paul and Virginie (vert.). 1r, Departure of Virginie for Europe. 2.50r, Bernardin de St. Pierre (vert.). The designs are from old prints illustrating "Paul et Virginie."

**Perf. 13½**

**1968, Dec. 2 Unwmk. Litho.**

| | | | | |
|---|---|---|---|---|
| *333* | A56 | 2c multi | 5 | 5 |
| *334* | A56 | 15c multi | 8 | 8 |
| *335* | A56 | 50c multi | 25 | 25 |
| *336* | A56 | 60c multi | 30 | 30 |
| *337* | A56 | 1r multi | 50 | 50 |
| *338* | A56 | 2.50r multi | 1.35 | 1.35 |
| | | *Nos. 333-338 (6)* | 2.53 | 2.53 |

Bicentenary of the visit of Bernardin de St. Pierre (1737-1814), author of "Paul et Virginie."

Batarde Fish A57

Marine Life: 3c, Red reef crab. 4c, Episcopal miter shell. 5c, Bourse fish. 10c, Starfish. 15c, Sea urchin. 20c, Fiddler crab. 25c, Spiny shrimp. 30c, Single and double harp shells. 35c, Argonaut shell. 40c, Nudibranch (sea-slug). 50c, Violet and orange spider shells. 60c, Blue marlin. 75c, Conus clytospira. 1r, Dorad. 2.50r, Spiny lobster. 5r, Sacré chien rouge fish. 10r, Moonfish.

**Wmk. 314 Sideways (#339-344, 351-352), others Upright**

**1969, Mar. 12 Photo. *Perf. 14***

| | | | | |
|---|---|---|---|---|
| *339* | A57 | 2c pink & multi | 5 | 5 |
| *340* | A57 | 3c yel & multi | 5 | 5 |
| *341* | A57 | 4c multi | 5 | 5 |
| *342* | A57 | 5c lt bl & multi | 5 | 5 |
| *343* | A57 | 10c sal & multi | 5 | 5 |
| *344* | A57 | 15c pale bl & multi | 8 | 5 |
| *345* | A57 | 20c pale gray & multi | 8 | 6 |
| *346* | A57 | 25c multi | 10 | 9 |
| *347* | A57 | 30c multi | 12 | 10 |
| *348* | A57 | 35c multi | 15 | 12 |
| *349* | A57 | 40c tan & multi | 20 | 18 |
| *350* | A57 | 50c lt vio & multi | 25 | 22 |
| *351* | A57 | 60c ultra & multi | 30 | 25 |
| *352* | A57 | 75c lem & multi | 38 | 30 |
| *353* | A57 | 1r cr & multi | 45 | 38 |
| *354* | A57 | 2.50r lt vio & multi | 1.90 | 1.90 |
| *355* | A57 | 5r multi | 3.25 | 3.25 |
| *356* | A57 | 10r multi | 6.00 | 6.00 |
| | | *Nos. 339-356 (18)* | 13.51 | 13.15 |

**Wmk. 314 Upright (#339a-344a, 351a-352a), others Sideways**

**1972-74**

| | | | | |
|---|---|---|---|---|
| *339a* | A57 | 2c multi ('74) | 5 | 5 |
| *340a* | A57 | 3c multi ('74) | 5 | 5 |
| *341a* | A57 | 4c multi ('74) | 5 | 5 |
| *342a* | A57 | 5c multi ('74) | 5 | 5 |
| *343a* | A57 | 10c multi | 6 | 5 |
| *344a* | A57 | 15c multi ('74) | 8 | 6 |
| *345a* | A57 | 20c multi | 9 | 8 |
| *346a* | A57 | 25c multi ('73) | 10 | 9 |
| *347a* | A57 | 30c multi | 15 | 12 |
| *348a* | A57 | 35c multi | 18 | 15 |
| *349a* | A57 | 40c multi | 20 | 20 |
| *350a* | A57 | 50c multi ('73) | 20 | 20 |
| *351a* | A57 | 60c multi ('74) | 25 | 22 |
| *352a* | A57 | 75c multi | 35 | 28 |
| *353a* | A57 | 1r multi | 40 | 35 |
| *354a* | A57 | 2.50r multi ('73) | 1.00 | 90 |
| *355a* | A57 | 5r multi ('73) | 1.90 | 1.60 |
| *356a* | A57 | 10r multi | 3.75 | 3.25 |
| | | *Nos. 339a-356a (18)* | 8.91 | 7.75 |

**1975-77 Wmk. 373**

| | | | | |
|---|---|---|---|---|
| *339b* | A57 | 2c multi ('77) | 5 | 5 |
| *340b* | A57 | 3c multi ('77) | 5 | 5 |
| *341b* | A57 | 4c multi ('77) | 5 | 5 |
| *342b* | A57 | 5c multi | 6 | 5 |
| *344b* | A57 | 15c multi | 8 | 6 |
| *345b* | A57 | 20c multi ('76) | 9 | 8 |
| *346b* | A57 | 25c multi | 12 | 9 |
| *347b* | A57 | 30c multi | 14 | 12 |
| *348b* | A57 | 35c multi ('76) | 14 | 12 |
| *349b* | A57 | 40c multi ('76) | 15 | 14 |
| *350b* | A57 | 50c multi ('76) | 18 | 15 |
| *351b* | A57 | 60c multi ('77) | 24 | 20 |
| *352b* | A57 | 75c multi ('77) | 24 | 22 |
| *353b* | A57 | 1r multi ('76) | 38 | 35 |
| *354b* | A57 | 2.50r multi ('77) | 1.50 | 90 |
| *355b* | A57 | 5r multi | 2.50 | 2.00 |
| *356b* | A57 | 10r multi | 6.00 | 4.00 |
| | | *Nos. 339b-356b (17)* | 11.97 | 8.63 |

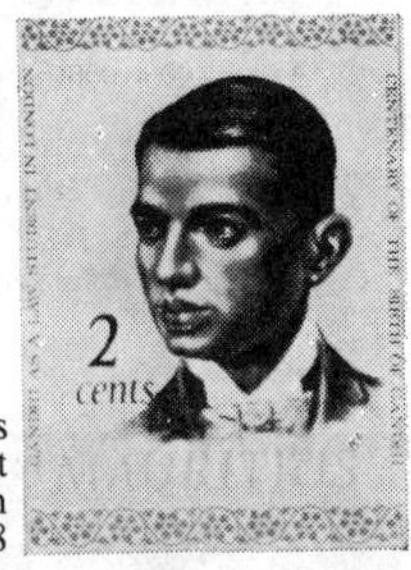


Gandhi as Law Student in London A58

Portraits of Gandhi: 15c, as stretcher bearer during Zulu rebellion. 50c, as member of non-violent movement in South Africa (Satyagrahi). 60c, wearing Indian garment at No. 10 Downing Street, London. 1r, wearing turban in Mauritius, 1901. 2.50r, as old man.

**1969, July 1 Litho. *Perf. 13½***

| | | | | |
|---|---|---|---|---|
| *357* | A58 | 2c dl org & multi | 5 | 5 |
| *358* | A58 | 15c brt bl & multi | 5 | 5 |
| *359* | A58 | 50c multi | 18 | 18 |
| *360* | A58 | 60c brick red & multi | 25 | 25 |
| *361* | A58 | 1r multi | 50 | 50 |
| *362* | A58 | 2.50r ol & multi | 1.25 | 1.25 |
| *a* | | Souv. sheet of 6 | 3.00 | 3.00 |
| | | *Nos. 357-362 (6)* | 2.28 | 2.28 |

Mohandas K. Gandhi (1869-1948), leader in India's struggle for independence. No. 362a contains Nos. 357-362; gray decorative border. Size: 153x153mm.

Vertical Cane Crusher (19th Century) A59

Dr. Charles Telfair (1778-1833) — A60

Designs: 15c, The Frangourinier, 18th century cane crusher. 60c, Beau Rivage sugar factory, 1867, painting by Numa Desjardin. 1r, Mon Desert-Alma sugar factory, 1969.

***Perf. 11x11½, 11½x11***

**1969, Dec. 22 Photo. Wmk. 314**

| | | | | |
|---|---|---|---|---|
| *363* | A59 | 2c multi | 5 | 5 |
| *364* | A59 | 15c multi | 5 | 5 |
| *365* | A59 | 60c multi | 25 | 25 |
| *366* | A59 | 1r multi | 38 | 38 |
| *367* | A60 | 2.50r multi | 90 | 90 |
| *a* | | Souv. sheet of 5 | 2.00 | 2.00 |
| | | *Nos. 363-367 (5)* | 1.63 | 1.63 |

Issued to commemorate the 150th anniversary of Telfair's improvements of the sugar industry.

No. 367a contains one each of Nos. 363-367. The 2.50r in the sheet is imperf., the others are perf. 11x11½. Light blue margin with commemorative inscription. Size: 157x87mm.

Nos. 351 and 353 Overprinted: "EXPO '70 / OSAKA"

**1970, Apr. 7 *Perf. 14***

| | | | | |
|---|---|---|---|---|
| *368* | A57 | 60c ultra & multi | 25 | 25 |
| *369* | A57 | 1r cr & multi | 38 | 38 |

Issued to publicize EXPO '70 International Exhibition, Osaka, Japan, Mar. 15-Sept. 13.

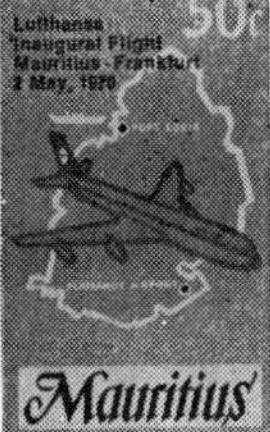


Lufthansa Plane over Mauritius — A61

Design: 25c, Brabant Hotel, Morne Beach (horiz.).

**1970, May 2 Litho. *Perf. 14***

| | | | | |
|---|---|---|---|---|
| *370* | A61 | 25c multi | 14 | 14 |
| *371* | A61 | 50c multi | 25 | 25 |

Issued to commemorate Lufthansa's inaugural flight from Mauritius to Frankfurt, Germany, May 2, 1970.

Lenin as Student, by V. Tsigal — A62

Design: 75c, Bust of Lenin.

**1970, May 15 Photo. *Perf. 12x11½***

| | | | | |
|---|---|---|---|---|
| *372* | A62 | 15c dk sl bl & sil | 6 | 6 |
| *373* | A62 | 75c dk brn & gold | 45 | 45 |

Issued to commemorate the centenary of the birth of Lenin (1870-1924), Russian communist leader.

U.N. Emblem and Symbols of U.N. Activities — A63

**1970, Oct. 24 Litho. *Perf. 14***

| | | | | |
|---|---|---|---|---|
| *374* | A63 | 10c bl blk & multi | 6 | 6 |
| *375* | A63 | 60c bl blk & multi | 28 | 28 |

25th anniversary of the United Nations.

Mauritius No. 2, and Post Office before 1870 A64

Designs: 15c, General Post Office Building, 1870-1970. 50c, Mauritius mail coach, 1870. 75c, Port Louis harbor, 1970. 2.50r, Arrival of Pierre André de Suffren de St. Tropez in Port Louis harbor, 1783.

**1970, Oct. 15 Litho. *Perf. 14***

| | | | | |
|---|---|---|---|---|
| *376* | A64 | 5c multi | 5 | 5 |
| *377* | A64 | 15c multi | 6 | 6 |
| *378* | A64 | 50c multi | 20 | 20 |
| *379* | A64 | 75c multi | 30 | 30 |
| *380* | A64 | 2.50r multi | 1.00 | 1.00 |
| *a* | | Souvenir sheet of 5 | 2.00 | 2.00 |
| | | *Nos. 376-380 (5)* | 1.61 | 1.61 |

Issued to commemorate the centenary of the General Post Office and to show the improvements of Port Louis harbor. No. 380a contains one each of Nos. 376-380 and a label showing map of Mauritius. Light blue margin inscribed: Birthplace of Philately. Size: 168x95mm.

Waterfall A65

Designs: 15c, Trois Mamelles Mountains. 60c, Beach scene with sailboats. 2.50r, Marine life.

**1971, Apr. 12 Litho. *Perf. 14***

| | | | | |
|---|---|---|---|---|
| *381* | A65 | 10c multi | 5 | 5 |
| *382* | A65 | 15c multi | 8 | 8 |
| *383* | A65 | 60c multi | 25 | 25 |
| *384* | A65 | 2.50r multi | 1.25 | 1.25 |

Tourist publicity. Each stamp has a different 6-line message printed in black on back.

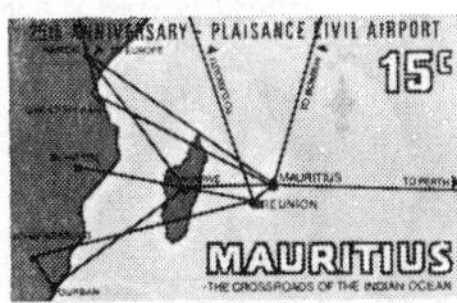


Mauritius at Crossroads of Indian Ocean — A66

Designs: 60c, Plane at Plaisance Airport. 1r, Stewardesses on plane ramp. 2.50r, Roland Garros' airplane, Choisy Airfield, 1937.

**1971, Oct. 23 Wmk. 314 *Perf. 14½***

| | | | | |
|---|---|---|---|---|
| *385* | A66 | 15c multi | 6 | 6 |
| *386* | A66 | 60c multi | 24 | 24 |
| *387* | A66 | 1r multi | 35 | 35 |
| *388* | A66 | 2.50r multi | 1.25 | 1.25 |

25th anniversary of Plaisance Civil Airport.

Princess Margaret Orthopedic Center — A67

Design: 75c, Operating room, National Hospital.

**1971, Nov. 2 *Perf. 14x14½***

| | | | | |
|---|---|---|---|---|
| *389* | A67 | 10c multi | 5 | 5 |
| *390* | A67 | 75c multi | 30 | 30 |

3rd Commonwealth Medical Conference, November 1971.

Elizabeth II and Prince Philip A68

Design: 2.50r, Queen Elizabeth II (vert.)

**1972, Mar. Litho. *Perf. 14½***

| | | | | |
|---|---|---|---|---|
| *391* | A68 | 15c brn & multi | 14 | 14 |
| *392* | A68 | 2.50r ultra & multi | 1.75 | 1.75 |

Visit of Elizabeth II and Prince Philip.

Port Louis Theater and Masks A69

Design: 1r, Interior view and masks of Comedy and Tragedy.

**1972, June 26**

| | | | | |
|---|---|---|---|---|
| *393* A69 10c brn & multi | 5 | 5 |
| *394* A69 1r multi | 30 | 30 |

Sesquicentennial of Port Louis Theater.

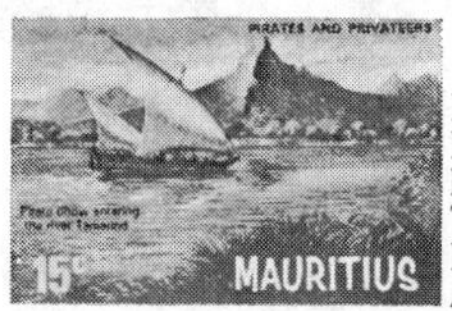
Pirate Dhow Entering Tamarind River A70

***Perf. 14x14½, 14½x14***

**1972, Nov. 17** **Litho.**

| | | |
|---|---|---|
| *395* A70 15c *shown* | 6 | 6 |
| *396* A70 60c *Treasure chest* (vert.) | 20 | 20 |
| *397* A70 1r *Lememe and brig Hirondelle* (vert.) | 38 | 38 |
| *398* A70 2.50r *Robert Surcouf* | 1.75 | 1.75 |

Pirates and privateers.

Mauritius University — A71

Designs: 60c, Tea development plant. 1r, Bank of Mauritius.

**1973, Apr. 10** ***Perf. 14½***

| | | |
|---|---|---|
| *399* A71 15c grn & multi | 5 | 5 |
| *400* A71 60c yel & multi | 20 | 20 |
| *401* A71 1r red & multi | 30 | 30 |

5th anniversary of independence.

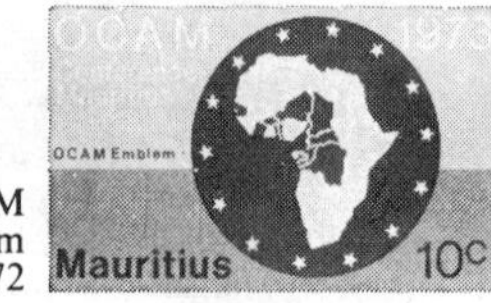
OCAM Emblem A72

Design: 2.50r, Handshake, map of Africa; inscriptions in French (vert.).

**1973, Apr. 25**

| | | |
|---|---|---|
| *402* A72 10c multi | 5 | 5 |
| *403* A72 2.50r lt bl & multi | 90 | 90 |

Conference of the Organisation Commune Africaine, Malgache et Mauricienne (OCAM), Mauritius, Apr. 25-May 6.

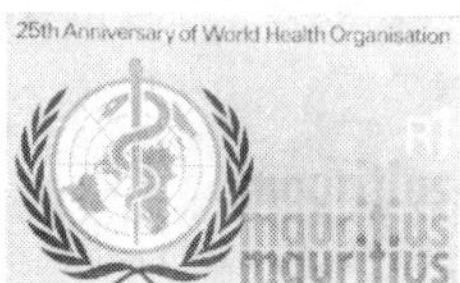
WHO Emblem A73

***Perf. 14½x14***

**1973, Nov. 20** **Wmk. 314**

| | | |
|---|---|---|
| *404* A73 1r grn & multi | 35 | 35 |

25th anniv. of WHO.

Meteorological Station, Vacoas — A74

**1973, Nov. 27**

| | | |
|---|---|---|
| *405* A74 75c multi | 25 | 25 |

Cent. of intl. meteorological cooperation.

Surcouf and Capture of the "Kent" A75

**1974, Mar. 21** **Litho.** ***Perf. 14½x14***

| | | |
|---|---|---|
| *406* A75 60c sep & multi | 38 | 38 |

Bicentenary of the birth of Robert Surcouf (1773-1827), French privateer.

Philibert Commerson and Bougainvillaea A76

**1974, Apr. 18** ***Perf. 14***

| | | |
|---|---|---|
| *407* A76 2.50r sl grn & multi | 90 | 90 |

Philibert Commerson (1727-1773), French physician and naturalist.

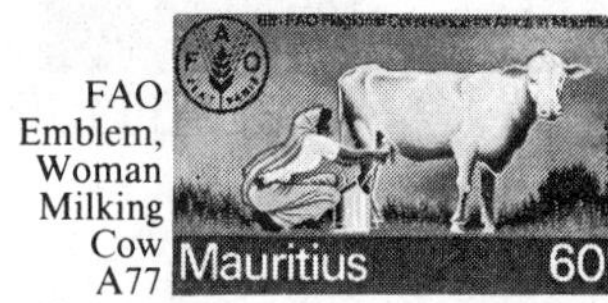
FAO Emblem, Woman Milking Cow A77

**1974, Oct. 23** ***Perf. 14½***

| | | |
|---|---|---|
| *408* A77 60c multi | 25 | 25 |

8th Food and Agriculture Organization Regional Conference, Aug. 1-17.

Mail Train and UPU Emblem A78

Design: 1r, New General Post Office Building, Port Louis, and UPU emblem.

**1974, Dec. 4** **Litho.** ***Perf. 14½***

| | | |
|---|---|---|
| *409* A78 15c multi | 6 | 6 |
| *410* A78 1r multi | 40 | 35 |

Centenary of Universal Postal Union.

Cottage Life, by F. Leroy A79

Paintings: 60c, Milk Seller, by A. Richard (vert.). 1r, Entrance to Port Louis Market, by Thuillier. 2.50r, Washerwomen, by Max Boulle (vert.).

**1975, Mar. 6** **Wmk. 373**

| | | |
|---|---|---|
| *411* A79 15c multi | 6 | 6 |
| *412* A79 60c multi | 25 | 25 |
| *413* A79 1r multi | 40 | 40 |
| *414* A79 2.50r multi | 1.00 | 1.00 |

Artistic views of life on Mauritius.

A little time given to the study of the arrangement of the Scott Catalogue can make it easier to use effectively.

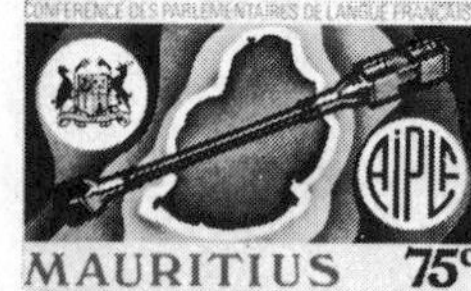
Mace, Map and Arms of Mauritius, Association Emblem — A80

**1975, Nov. 21** **Litho.** **Wmk. 373**

| | | |
|---|---|---|
| *415* A80 75c multi | 25 | 25 |

Conference of the French-speaking Parliamentary Association.

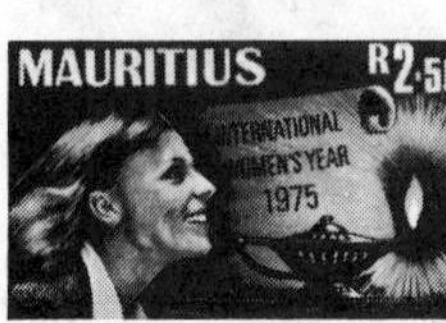
Woman and Aladdin's Lamp A81

**1975, Dec. 5** ***Perf. 14½***

| | | |
|---|---|---|
| *416* A81 2.50r multi | 90 | 90 |

International Women's Year 1975.

Parched Land A82

Drought in Africa: 60c, Map of Africa, carcass and desert (vert.).

**1976, Feb. 26** **Litho.** **Wmk. 373**

| | | |
|---|---|---|
| *417* A82 50c ver & multi | 18 | 18 |
| *418* A82 60c bl & multi | 24 | 24 |

Pierre Loti, 1953-1970 — A83

Mail Carriers: 15c, Secunder, 1907. 50c, Hindoostan, 1842. 60c, St. Geran, 1740. 2.50r, Maen, 1638.

**1976, July 2** **Litho.** **Wmk. 373**

| | | |
|---|---|---|
| *419* A83 10c multi | 5 | 5 |
| *420* A83 15c multi | 6 | 6 |
| *421* A83 50c multi | 25 | 25 |
| *422* A83 60c multi | 30 | 30 |
| *423* A83 2.50r multi | 1.50 | 1.50 |
| a Souvenir sheet of 5 | 2.25 | 2.25 |
| *Nos. 419-423 (5)* | 2.16 | 2.16 |

No. 423a contains one each of Nos. 419-423; multicolored margin with compass rose and description of ships. Size: 143x121mm.

Flame, and "Hindi Carried Across the Sea" A84

Designs: 75c, like 10c. 1.20r, Flame and tablet with Hindi inscription.

**1976, Aug. 28** ***Perf. 14½x14***

| | | |
|---|---|---|
| *424* A84 10c multi | 5 | 5 |
| *425* A84 75c lt bl & multi | 20 | 20 |
| *426* A84 1.20r multi | 35 | 35 |

2nd World Hindi Convention.

Commonwealth Emblem, Map of Mauritius A85

King Priest and Steatite Pectoral A86

Design: 2.50r, Commonwealth emblem twice.

**1976, Sept. 22** **Litho.** ***Perf. 14x14½***

| | | |
|---|---|---|
| *427* A85 1r multi | 30 | 30 |
| *428* A85 2.50r multi | 75 | 75 |

22nd Commonwealth Parliamentary Association Conference, Mauritius, Sept. 17-30.

**1976, Dec. 15** **Wmk. 373** ***Perf. 14***

Designs: 1r, House with well, and goblet. 2.50r, Terracotta goddess and necklace.

| | | |
|---|---|---|
| *429* A86 60c multi | 14 | 14 |
| *430* A86 1r multi | 30 | 30 |
| *431* A86 2.50r multi | 75 | 75 |

UNESCO campaign to save Mohenjo-Daro excavations.

Sega Dance A87

**1977, Jan. 20** **Litho.** ***Perf. 13***

| | | |
|---|---|---|
| *432* A87 1r multi | 25 | 25 |

2nd World Black and African Festival, Lagos, Nigeria, Jan. 15-Feb. 12.

Elizabeth II at Mauritius Legislative Assembly — A88

Designs: 75c, Queen holding scepter and orb. 5r, Presentation of scepter and orb.

**1977, Feb. 7** ***Perf. 14½x14***

| | | |
|---|---|---|
| *433* A88 50c multi | 15 | 15 |
| *434* A88 75c multi | 20 | 20 |
| *435* A88 5r multi | 1.25 | 1.25 |

25th anniv. of the reign of Elizabeth II.

Hugonia Tomentosa — A89

Flowers: 1r, Oehna mauritiana (vert.). 1.50r, Dombeya acuntangula. 5r, Trochetia blackburniana (vert.).

**Wmk. 373**

**1977, Sept. 22** **Litho.** ***Perf. 14***

| | | |
|---|---|---|
| *436* A89 20c multi | 5 | 5 |
| *437* A89 1r multi | 25 | 25 |
| *438* A89 1.50r multi | 38 | 38 |

439 A89 5r multi 1.25 1.25
a Souvenir sheet of 4 2.00 2.00

No. 439a contains one each of Nos. 436-439; yellow green margin with black inscription describing flowers. Size: 130x130mm.

Twin Otter of Air Mauritius A90

Designs: 50c, Air Mauritius emblem (red-tailed tropic bird) and Twin Otter. 75c, Piper Navajo and Boeing 747. 5r, Air Mauritius Boeing 707 in flight.

**1977, Oct. 31 Litho. Perf. 14½**

| | | | |
|---|---|---|---|
| 440 A90 25c multi | 6 | 6 |
| 441 A90 50c multi | 14 | 14 |
| 442 A90 75c multi | 18 | 18 |
| 443 A90 5r multi | 1.25 | 1.25 |
| a Souvenir sheet of 4 | 1.65 | 1.65 |

Air Mauritius International Inaugural Flight. No. 443a contains one each of Nos. 440-443; yellow, black and red margin with description of planes. Size: 110x153mm.

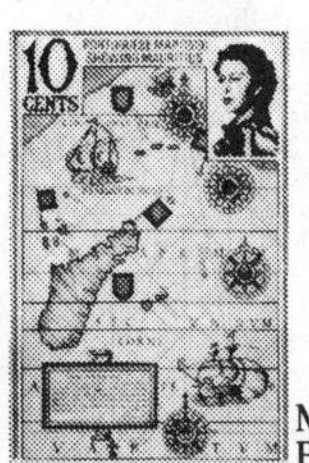
Mauritius, Portuguese Map, 1519 — A91

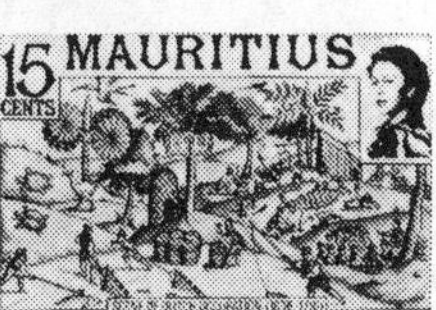
Dutch Occupation, 1638-1710 — A92

Designs: 20c, Mauritius, map by Van Keulen, c. 1700. 25c, 1st settlement of Rodrigues, 1708. 35c, Proclamation, arrival of French settlers, 1715. 50c, Construction of Port Louis, c. 1736. 60c, Pierre Poivre and nutmeg tree. 70c, Map by Belin, 1763. 75c, First coin minted in Mauritius, 1810. 90c, Naval battle of Grand Port, 1810. 1r, Landing of the British, Nov. 1810. 1.20r, Government House, c. 1840. 1.25r, Invitation with No. 1 and ball of Lady Gomm, 1847. 1.50r, Indian immigration in Mauritius, 1835. 2r, Champ de Mars race course, c. 1870. 3r, Place D'Armes, c. 1880. 5r, Postal card commemorating visit of Prince and Princess of Wales, 1901. 10r, Curepipe College, 1914. 15r, Raising flag of Mauritius, 1968. 25r, Raman Osman, first Governor General and Seewoosagur Ramgoolan, first Prime Minister.

**1978, Mar. 12 Litho. Perf. 13½**

| | | |
|---|---|---|
| 444 A92 10c multi | 5 | 5 |
| 445 A92 15c multi | 5 | 5 |
| 446 A92 20c multi | 5 | 5 |
| a Wmk. 384, perf. 14½, "1987" | 5 | 5 |
| 447 A92 25c multi | 5 | 5 |
| a Wmk. 384, perf. 14½, "1987" | 5 | 5 |
| 448 A92 35c multi | 8 | 8 |
| a Wmk. 384 ('85) | 5 | 5 |
| b Wmk. 373, perf. 14½, "1986" | 5 | 5 |
| 449 A92 50c multi | 10 | 10 |
| a Wmk. 384 ('85) | 5 | 5 |
| 450 A92 60c multi | 14 | 14 |
| 451 A92 70c multi | 14 | 14 |
| 452 A92 75c multi | 15 | 15 |
| a Wmk. 384 ('85) | 6 | 6 |
| 453 A92 90c multi | 18 | 18 |
| 454 A92 1r multi | 20 | 20 |
| 455 A92 1.20r multi | 25 | 25 |
| 456 A92 1.25r multi | 25 | 25 |
| 457 A92 1.50r multi | 30 | 30 |
| 458 A92 2r multi | 40 | 40 |
| a Wmk. 384, perf. 14½, "1987" | 14 | 14 |
| 459 A92 3r multi | 60 | 60 |
| 460 A92 5r multi | 1.00 | 1.00 |
| 461 A92 10r multi | 2.00 | 2.00 |
| 462 A92 15r multi | 3.00 | 3.00 |
| 463 A92 25r multi | 5.00 | 5.00 |
| *Nos. 444-463 (20)* | 13.99 | 13.99 |

Nos. 448, 456 reprinted inscribed 1983; Nos. 444, 447-449, 452, 454, 456 reprinted inscribed 1985.

**Elizabeth II Coronation Anniversary Issue**

Common Design Types

**Souvenir Sheet**

**1978, Apr. 21 Unwmk. Perf. 15**

| | | |
|---|---|---|
| 464 Sheet of 6 | 3.75 | |
| a CD326 3r *Antelope of Bohun* | 60 | 60 |
| b CD327 3r *Elizabeth II* | 60 | 60 |
| c CD328 3r *Dodo* | 60 | 60 |

No. 464 contains 2 se-tenant strips of Nos. 464a-464c, separated by horizontal gutter with commemorative and descriptive inscriptions and showing central part of coronation procession with coach. Size: 100x135mm.

Dr. Fleming, WWI Casualty, Bacteria — A93

Designs: 1r, Microscope and 1st mold growth, 1928. 1.50r, Penicillium notatum, close-up. 5r, Alexander Fleming and nurse administering penicillin.

**Wmk. 373**

**1978, Aug. 3 Litho. Perf. 13½**

| | | |
|---|---|---|
| 465 A93 20c multi | 5 | 5 |
| 466 A93 1r multi | 20 | 20 |
| 467 A93 1.50r multi | 30 | 30 |
| 468 A93 5r multi | 1.75 | 1.75 |
| a Souvenir sheet of 4 | 2.75 | 2.75 |

Discovery of penicillin by Dr. Alexander Fleming, 50th anniversary. No. 468a contains Nos. 465-468; gray margin with black inscription and replica of work sheet showing anti-bacterial action of penicillin mold. Size: 150x90mm.

Citrus Butterfly — A94

Designs (Wildlife Fund Emblem and): 1r, Geckos. 1.50r, Flying foxes. 5r, Mauritius kestrels.

***Perf. 13½x14***

**1978, Sept. 21 Litho. Wmk. 373**

| | | |
|---|---|---|
| 469 A94 20c multi | 8 | 8 |
| 470 A94 1r multi | 40 | 40 |
| 471 A94 1.50r multi | 60 | 60 |
| 472 A94 5r multi | 2.00 | 2.00 |
| a Souvenir sheet of 4 | 3.25 | 3.25 |

Wildlife protection. No. 472a contains Nos. 469-472; light blue and black margin with descriptive inscriptions. Size: 154x148mm.

Le Reduit — A95

Designs: 15c, Ornate table. 3r, Reduit gardens.

***Perf. 14½x14***

**1978, Dec. 21 Litho. Wmk. 373**

| | | |
|---|---|---|
| 473 A95 15c multi | 6 | 6 |
| 474 A95 75c multi | 30 | 30 |
| 475 A95 3r multi | 1.00 | 1.00 |

Reconstruction of Chateau Le Reduit, 200th anniversary.

Whitcomb, 1949 — A96

Locomotives: 1r, Sir William, 1922. 1.50r, Kitson, 1930. 2r, Garratt, 1927.

**Wmk. 373**

**1979, Feb. 1 Litho. Perf. 14½**

| | | |
|---|---|---|
| 476 A96 20c multi | 8 | 8 |
| 477 A96 1r multi | 40 | 40 |
| 478 A96 1.50r multi | 60 | 60 |
| 479 A96 2r multi | 80 | 80 |
| a Souvenir sheet of 4 | 2.00 | 2.00 |

No. 479a contains Nos. 476-479; multicolored margin. Size: 128x128mm.

Father Laval and Crucifix — A97

Designs: 1.50r, Jacques DésiréLaval. 5r, Father Laval's sarcophagus (horiz.).

**Wmk. 373**

**1979, Apr. 30 Litho. Perf. 14**

| | | |
|---|---|---|
| 480 A97 20c multi | 6 | 6 |
| 481 A97 1.50r multi | 30 | 30 |
| 482 A97 5r multi | 1.00 | 1.00 |
| a Souvenir sheet of 3 | 1.75 | 1.75 |

Beatification of Father Laval (1803-1864), physician and missionary. No. 482a contains Nos. 480-482; Father Laval's life story in French and English in margin. Size: 159x97mm.

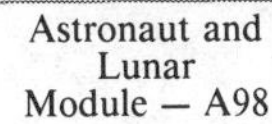
Astronaut and Lunar Module — A98

Rowland Hill and Great Britain No. 23 — A99

Designs: 20c, Neil Armstrong on moon. 5r, Astronaut walking on moon.

***Imperf. x Roulette 5***

**1979, July 20 Litho.**

**Self-adhesive**

| | | |
|---|---|---|
| 483 A98 Souvenir booklet | 5.50 | |
| a Booklet pane of 3 (20c, 5r, 3r) | 2.50 | |
| b Booklet pane of 6 (3 each 20c, 3r) | 2.75 | |

10th anniversary of Apollo 11 moon landing. No. 483 contains 2 booklet panes printed on peelable paper backing showing (a) map of moon and (b) details of uniform and spacecraft. Size of pane: 154x92mm.

**1979, Aug. 29 Perf. 14½**

Designs (Rowland Hill and): 2r, Mauritius No. 261. 3r, Mauritius No. 2. 5r, Mauritius No. 1.

| | | |
|---|---|---|
| 484 A99 25c multi | 5 | 5 |
| 485 A99 2r multi | 40 | 40 |
| 486 A99 5r multi | 1.00 | 1.00 |

***Imperf.***

**Souvenir Sheet**

| | | |
|---|---|---|
| 487 A99 3r multi | 75 | 75 |

Sir Rowland Hill (1795-1879), originator of penny postage. No. 487 contains one stamp. Margin shows 1890 surcharged envelope. Size: 120x88mm.

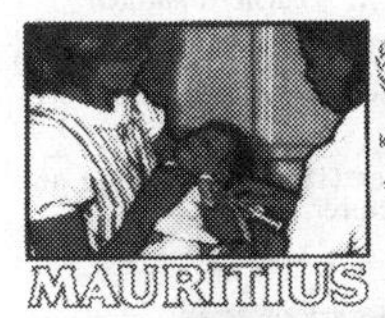
Infant Vaccination — A100

IYC Emblem and: 25c, Children playing. 1r, Coat of arms (vert.). 1.50r, Children in laboratory. 3r, Teacher and student working lathe.

**Wmk. 373**

**1979, Oct. 11 Litho. Perf. 14**

| | | |
|---|---|---|
| 488 A100 15c multi | 5 | 5 |
| 489 A100 25c multi | 6 | 6 |
| 490 A100 1r multi | 20 | 20 |
| 491 A100 1.50r multi | 30 | 30 |
| 492 A100 3r multi | 60 | 60 |
| *Nos. 488-492 (5)* | 1.21 | 1.21 |

International Year of the Child.

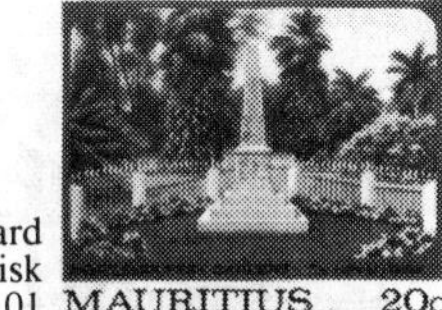
Lienard Obelisk A101

Designs: 25c, Poivre Avenue. 1r, Pandanus. 2r, Giant water lilies. 5r, Mon Plaisir.

***Perf. 14x14½***

**1980, Jan. 24 Litho. Wmk. 373**

| | | |
|---|---|---|
| 493 A101 20c multi | 5 | 5 |
| 494 A101 25c multi | 5 | 5 |
| 495 A101 1r multi | 20 | 20 |
| 496 A101 2r multi | 40 | 40 |
| 497 A101 5r multi | 1.00 | 1.00 |
| a Souvenir sheet of 5 | 1.75 | 1.75 |
| *Nos. 493-497 (5)* | 1.70 | 1.70 |

Pamplemousses Botanical Gardens. No. 497a contains Nos. 493-497; yellow and black decorative margin. Size: 152x106mm.

"Emirne," 19th Century, London 1980 Emblem A102

**1980, May 6 Litho. Perf. 14½**

| | | |
|---|---|---|
| 498 A102 25c *shown* | 5 | 5 |
| 499 A102 1r *Boissevain, 1930's* | 20 | 20 |
| 500 A102 2r *La Boudeuse, 18th cent.* | 40 | 40 |
| 501 A102 5r *Sea Breeze, 19th cent.* | 1.00 | 1.00 |

London 80 Intl. Stamp Exhib., May 6-14.

Helen Keller Reading Braille — A103

**1980, June 27 Litho. *Perf. 14½***

*502* A103 25c *Blind men weaving baskets* 5 5
*503* A103 1r *Teacher and deaf girl* 25 25
*504* A103 2.50r *shown* 50 50
*505* A103 5r *Keller graduating college* 1.00 1.00

Helen Keller (1880-1968), blind and deaf writer and lecturer.

Prime Minister Seewoosagur Ramgoolan, 80th Birthday A104

**Litho.; Gold Embossed**

**1980, Sept. 18 *Perf. 13½***

*506* A104 15r multi 2.75 2.75

Mauritius Institute, Centenary — A105

**1980, Oct. 1 Litho. *Perf. 13***

*507* A105 25c *shown* 5 5
*508* A105 2r *Rare Veda copy* 40 40
*509* A105 2.50r *Rare cone* 50 50
*510* A105 5r *Landscape, by Henri Harpignies* 1.00 1.00

Hibiscus Liliiflorus — A106

**1981, Jan. 15 Litho. *Perf. 14***

*511* A106 25c *shown* 5 5
*512* A106 2r *Erythrospermum monticolum* 45 45
*513* A106 2.50r *Chasalia boryana* 55 55
*514* A106 5r *Hibiscus columnaris* 1.10 1.10

Arms of Curepipe — A107

Designs: City coats of arms.

***Perf. 13½x13***

**1981, Apr. 10 Litho. Wmk. 373**

*515* A107 25c Beau-Bassin/Rose Hill 5 5
*516* A107 1.50r shown 30 30
*517* A107 2r Quatre-Bornes 40 40
*518* A107 2.50r Vacoas/Phoenix 50 50
*519* A107 5r Port Louis 1.00 1.00
*a* Souvenir sheet of 5 2.25 2.25
*Nos. 515-519 (5)* 2.25 2.25

No. 519a contains Nos. 515-519 (perf. 14); blue and gold margin shows drape. Size: 130x130mm.

**Royal Wedding Issue**

Common Design Type

**Wmk. 373**

**1981, July 22 Litho. *Perf. 14***

*520* CD331 25c Bouquet 5 5
*521* CD331 2.50r Charles 50 50
*522* CD331 10r Couple 2.00 2.00

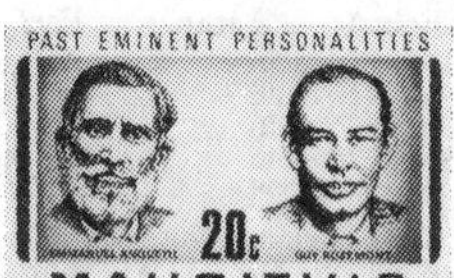


Emmanuel Anquetil and Guy Rozemont — A108

Famous Men: 25c, Remy Ollier, Sookdeo Bissoondoyal. 1.25r, Maurice Cure, Barthelemy Ohsan. 1.50r, Guy Forget, Renganaden Seeneevassen. 2r, Abdul Razak Mohamed, Jules Koenig. 2.50r, Abdoollatiff Mahomed Osman, Dazzi Rama. 5r, Thomas Lewis.

**Wmk. 373**

**1981, Aug. 13 Litho. *Perf. 14½***

*523* A108 20c blk & red 5 5
*524* A108 25c blk & yel 5 5
*525* A108 1.25r blk & grn 25 25
*526* A108 1.50r blk & ver 30 30
*527* A108 2r blk & ultra 40 40
*528* A108 2.50r blk & red brn 50 50
*529* A108 5r blk & bl grn 1.00 1.00
*Nos. 523-529 (7)* 2.55 2.55

Chinese Pagoda A109

**1981, Sept. 16 *Perf. 13½***

*530* A109 20c Tamil Women 5 5
*531* A109 2r Swami Sivananda, vert. 40 40
*532* A109 5r shown 1.00 1.00

World Tamil (Hindu sect) Culture Conference, 1980 (20c).

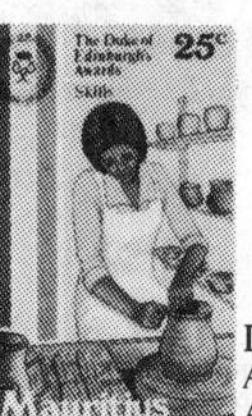


Duke of Edinburgh's Awards, 25th Anniv. — A110

**1981, Oct. 26 Litho. *Perf. 14***

*533* A110 25c Pottery making 5 5
*534* A110 1.25r Dog grooming 25 25
*535* A110 5r Hiking 1.00 1.00
*536* A110 10r Duke of Edinburgh 2.00 2.00

The first price column gives the catalogue value of an unused stamp, the second that of a used stamp.

Hegira 1,500th Anniv. — A111

**Wmk. 373**

**1981, Nov. 26 Litho. *Perf. 14½***

*537* A111 25c Holy Ka'aba, Mecca 5 5
*538* A111 2r Prophet's Mosque 40 40
*539* A111 5r Holy Ka'aba, Prophet's Mosque 1.00 1.00

Scouting Year — A112

***Perf. 14x14½***

**1982, Feb. 25 Litho. Wmk. 373**

*540* A112 25c Emblem 5 5
*541* A112 2r Baden-Powell 40 40
*542* A112 5r Grand howl, sign 1.00 1.00
*543* A112 10r Scouts, mountain 2.00 2.00

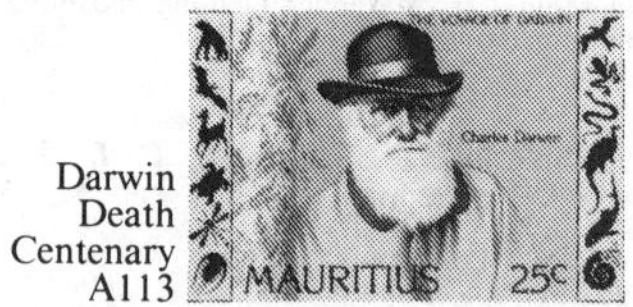


Darwin Death Centenary A113

**1982, Apr. 19 Litho. *Perf. 14***

*544* A113 25c Portrait 5 5
*545* A113 2r Telescope 40 40
*546* A113 2.50r Riding elephant 50 50
*547* A113 10r The Beagle 2.00 2.00

**Princess Diana Issue**

Common Design Type

**1982, July 1 Litho. *Perf. 13***

*548* CD333 25c Arms 5 5
*549* CD333 2.50r Diana 50 50
*550* CD333 5r Wedding 1.00 1.00
*551* CD333 10r Portrait 2.00 2.00

Birth of Prince William of Wales, June 21 — A114

**1982, Sept. 22 Litho. *Perf. 14½***

*552* A114 2.50r Family leaving hospital 60 60

Issued in sheets of 9.

TB Bacillus Centenary — A115

**1982, Dec. 15 *Perf. 14***

*553* A115 25c Aphloia theiformis 5 5
*554* A115 1.25r Central Market, Port Louis 25 25
*555* A115 2r Gaertnera psychotrioides 40 40
*556* A115 5r Selaginella deliquescens 1.00 1.00
*557* A115 10r Koch 2.00 2.00
*Nos. 553-557 (5)* 3.70 3.70

**Commonwealth Day**

Common Design Type

**1983, Mar. 14 *Perf. 13x13½***

*558* CD334 25c Flag, arms 5 5
*559* CD334 2.50r Satellite view 50 50
*560* CD334 5r Sugar cane harvest 1.00 1.00
*561* CD334 10r Port Louis Harbor 2.00 2.00

World Communications Year — A117

**Wmk. 373**

**1983, June 24 Litho. *Perf. 14***

*562* A117 25c Antique telephone, vert. 5 5
*563* A117 1.25r Early telegraph apparatus 25 25
*564* A117 2r Earth satellite station, vert. 40 40
*565* A117 10r 1st hot air balloon in Mauritius, 1784 2.00 2.00

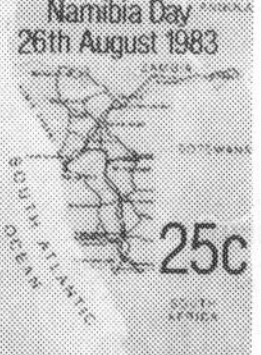


Namibia Day — A118

**1983, Aug. 26**

*566* A118 25c Map 5 5
*567* A118 2.50r Breaking chains 50 50
*568* A118 5r Family, village 1.00 1.00
*569* A118 10r Diamond mining 2.00 2.00

Fishery Resources A119

**1983, Oct. 7**

*570* A119 25c Fish trap, vert. 5 5
*571* A119 1r Fishermen in boat 16 16
*572* A119 5r Game fishing, vert. 80 80
*573* A119 10r Octopus drying 1.75 1.75

Swami Dayananda, Death Centenary — A120

**1983, Nov. 3 Litho. Wmk. 373**

*574* A120 25c shown 5 5
*575* A120 35c Last meeting with father 6 6
*576* A120 2r Receiving instruction 32 32
*577* A120 5r Demonstrating strength 80 80
*578* A120 10r Religious gathering 1.75 1.75
*Nos. 574-578 (5)* 2.98 2.98

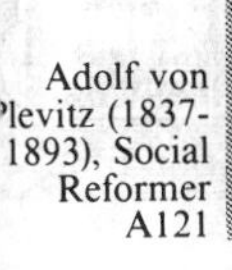

Adolf von Plevitz (1837-1893), Social Reformer
A121

**1983, Dec. 8**

579 A121 25c shown 5 5
580 A121 1.25r Government school 50 50
581 A121 5r Addressing Commission of Enquiry 80 80
582 A121 10r Indian field workers 1.75 1.75

Mauritius Kestrels A122

**Wmk. 373**

**1984, Mar. 26 Litho. *Perf. 14***

583 A122 25c Courtship chase 5 5
584 A122 2r Side view, vert. 32 32
585 A122 2.50r Fledgling 40 40
586 A122 10r Bird, diff., vert. 1.75 1.75

**Lloyd's List Issue**
Common Design Type
***Perf. 14½x14***

**1984, May 23 Litho. Wmk. 373**

587 CD335 25c Tayeb, Port Lewis 5 5
588 CD335 1r Taher 16 16
589 CD335 5r East Indiaman Triton 80 80
590 CD335 10r Astor 1.75 1.75

Palm Trees — A123

Slave Sale — A124

**1984, July 23 Litho. *Perf. 14***

591 A123 25c Blue latan 5 5
592 A123 50c Hyophorbe vaughanii 8 8
593 A123 2.50r Tectiphiala ferox 40 40
594 A123 5r Round Isld. bottle-palm 80 80
595 A123 10r Hyophorbe amaricaulis 1.75 1.75
*Nos. 591-595 (5)* 3.08 3.08

**1984, Aug. *Perf. 14½***

596 A124 25c Woman 5 5
597 A124 1r shown 16 16
598 A124 2r Family, horiz. 32 32
599 A124 10r Immigrant arrival, horiz. 1.75 1.75

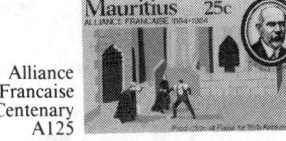

Alliance Francaise Centenary
A125

**1984, Sept. 10 *Perf. 14½***

600 A125 25c Production of Faust, 1959 5 5
601 A125 1.25r Award ceremony 22 22
602 A125 5r Headquarters 80 80
603 A125 10r Lion Mountain 1.75 1.75

**Queen Mother 85th Birthday**
Common Design Type
***Perf. 14½x14***

**1985, June 7 Litho. Wmk. 384**

604 CD336 25c Portrait, 1926 5 5
605 CD336 2r With Princess Margaret 40 40
606 CD336 5r On Clarence House balcony 1.00 1.00
607 CD336 10r Holding Prince Henry 2.00 2.00

**Souvenir Sheet**

608 CD336 15r On Royal Barge, reopening Stratford Canal, 1964 3.00 3.00

No. 608 has multicolored margin continuing the design. Size: 92x74mm.

2nd Annual Indian Ocean Islands Games — A126

Pink Pigeon — A127

***Perf. 14½***

**1985, Aug. 24 Litho. Unwmk.**

609 A126 25c High jump 5 5
610 A126 50c Javelin 10 10
611 A126 1.25r Cycling 25 25
612 A126 10r Wind surfing 2.00 2.00

**1985, Sept. 2 Wmk. 373 *Perf. 14***

613 A127 25c Adult and young 5 5
614 A127 2r Nest site display 40 40
615 A127 2.50r Nesting 50 50
616 A127 5r Preening 1.00 1.00

World Wildlife Fund.

World Tourism Org., 10th Anniv.
A128

**1985, Sept. 20 *Perf. 14½***

617 A128 25c Patates Caverns 5 5
618 A128 35c Colored Earth, Chamarel 8 8
619 A128 5r Serpent Isl. 80 80
620 A128 10r Coin de Mire Isl. 1.75 1.75

Port Louis, 250th Anniv.
A129

**1985, Nov. 22 *Perf. 13½***

621 A129 25c Old Town Hall 5 5
622 A129 1r Al-Aqsa Mosque 20 20
623 A129 2.50r Tamil-speaking Indians, settlement 50 50
624 A129 10r Port Louis Harbor 2.00 2.00

Halley's Comet
A130

**1986, Feb. 21 Wmk. 384 *Perf. 14***

625 A130 25c Halley, map 5 5
626 A130 1.25r Newton's telescope, 1682 sighting 25 25
627 A130 3r Mauritius from space 60 60
628 A130 10r Giotto space probe 2.00 2.00

**Queen Elizabeth II 60th Birthday**
Common Design Type

Designs: 25c, In uniform, Grenadier Guards, 1942. 75c, Investiture of the Prince of Wales, 1969. 2r, State visit with Prince Philip. 3r, State visit to Germany, 1978. 15r, Visiting Crown Agents' offices, 1983.

***Perf. 14½x14***

**1986, Apr. 21 Litho. Wmk. 384**

629 CD337 25c scar, blk & sil 5 5
630 CD337 75c ultra & multi 12 12
631 CD337 2r grn & multi 30 30
632 CD337 3r vio & multi 45 45
633 CD337 15r rose vio & multi 2.15 2.15
*Nos. 629-633 (5)* 3.07 3.07

Intl. Events — A131

Designs: 25c, World Food Day. 1r, African Regional Industrial Property Organization, 10th anniv. 1.25r, Intl. Peace Year. 10r, 1986 World Cup Soccer Championships.

**1986, July 25 Litho. *Perf. 14***

634 A131 25c FAO emblem, corn 5 5
635 A131 1r ARIPO emblem 15 15
636 A131 1.25r IPY emblem 20 20
637 A131 10r Athlete, MFA 1.50 1.50



Orchids — A132

**Wmk. 384**

**1986, Oct. 3 Litho. *Perf. 14½***

638 A132 25c Cryptopus elatus 5 5
639 A132 2r Jumellea recta 28 28
640 A132 2.50r Angraecum mauritianum 35 35
641 A132 10r Bulbophyllum longiflorum 1.40 1.40

Bridges
A133

**1987, May 22 Wmk. 373**

642 A133 25c Hesketh Bell 5 5
643 A133 50c Sir Colville Deverell 8 8
644 A133 2.50r Cavendish 35 35
645 A133 5r Tamarin 70 70
646 A133 10r Grand River North West 1.40 1.40
*Nos. 642-646 (5)* 2.58 2.58

Canceled-to-order stamps are often from remainders. Most collectors of canceled stamps prefer postally used specimens.

The Bar, Bicent.
A134

***Perf. 14x14½***

**1987, June 2 Wmk. 384**

647 A134 25c Port Louis Supreme Court 5 5
648 A134 1r Flacq District Court 14 14
649 A134 1.25r Statue of Justice 18 18
650 A134 10r Barristers, 1787-1987 1.40 1.40

Intl. Festival of the Sea — A135

***Perf. 14x14½***

**1987, Sept. 5 Wmk. 373**

651 A135 25c Dodo mascot, vert. 5 5
652 A135 1.50r Sailboats 22 22
653 A135 3r Water-skier 42 42
654 A135 5r Tall ship Svanen, vert. 70 70

Industrialization — A136

**Wmk. 373**

**1987, Oct. 30 Litho. *Perf. 14***

655 A136 20c Toy 5 5
656 A136 35c Spinning 6 6
657 A136 50c Rattan 8 8
658 A136 2.50r Optical 40 40
659 A136 10r Stone carving 1.55 1.55
*Nos. 655-659 (5)* 2.14 2.14

Art & Architecture
A137

Designs: 25c, Maison Ouvriere. 1r, *Paul and Virginia*, a lithograph. 1.25r, Chateau Rosney. 2r, Old Farmhouse, Boulle. 5r, *Three Peaks*, watercolor.

**1988, June 29 Unwmk. *Perf. 14½***

660 A137 25c multi 5 5
661 A137 1r gray & blk 16 16
662 A137 1.25r multi 20 20
663 A137 2r multi 32 32
664 A137 5r multi 80 80
*Nos. 660-664 (5)* 1.53 1.53

No. 660 pictures emblem of the Intl. Year of Shelter for the Homeless.

Natl. Independence, 20th Anniv. — A138

Designs: 25c, University of Mauritius. 75c, Calisthenics at sunset in stadium. 2.50r, Runners, Sir Maurice Rault Stadium. 5r, Air Mauritius jet at gate. Sir Seewoosagur Ramgoolam Intl. Airport. 10r, Gov.-Gen.

Veerasamy Ringadoo and Prime Minister Anerood Jugnauth.

**1988, Mar. 11 Wmk. 373 *Perf. 14***

| | | | | |
|---|---|---|---|---|
| *665* A138 | 25c multi | | 5 | 5 |
| *666* A138 | 75c multi | | 12 | 12 |
| *667* A138 | 2.50r multi | | 40 | 40 |
| *668* A138 | 5r multi | | 80 | 80 |
| *669* A138 | 10r multi | | 1.60 | 1.60 |
| | *Nos. 665-669 (5)* | | 2.97 | 2.97 |

WHO, 40th Anniv. — A139

**Wmk. 373**

**1988, July 1 Litho. *Perf. 13½***

| | | | |
|---|---|---|---|
| *670* A139 | 20c Breast-feeding | 5 | 5 |
| *671* A139 | 2r Immunization | 32 | 32 |
| *672* A139 | 3r Nutrition | 48 | 48 |
| *673* A139 | 10r Emblem | 1.55 | 1.55 |

Mauritius Commercial Bank, Ltd., 150th Anniv. A140

**Wmk. 373**

**1988, Sept. 1 Litho. *Perf. 14***

| | | | |
|---|---|---|---|
| *674* A140 | 25c Bank, 1981, vert. | 5 | 5 |
| *675* A140 | 1r Bank, 1897 | 15 | 15 |
| *676* A140 | 1.25r Coat of arms, vert. | 18 | 18 |
| *677* A140 | 25r 15-Dollar bank note, 1838 | 3.65 | 3.65 |

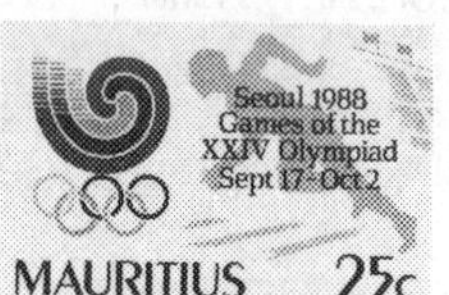


1988 Summer Olympics, Seoul — A141

**1988, Oct. 1**

| | | | |
|---|---|---|---|
| *678* A141 | 25c shown | 5 | 5 |
| *679* A141 | 35c Wrestling | 6 | 6 |
| *680* A141 | 1.50r Running | 25 | 25 |
| *681* A141 | 10r Swimming | 1.55 | 1.55 |

## SPECIAL DELIVERY STAMPS

SD1

**Wmk. Crown and C.C. (1)**

**1903 Red Surcharge *Perf. 14***

| | | | |
|---|---|---|---|
| *E1* SD1 | 15c on 15c ultra | 9.00 | 10.00 |

SD2

SD3

**1904**

| | | | |
|---|---|---|---|
| *E2* SD2 | 15c on 15c ultra | 12.50 | 14.00 |
| **a.** | "INLAND" inverted | 175.00 | 175.00 |
| **b.** | Inverted "A" in "INLAND" | 250.00 | 250.00 |
| *E3* SD3 | 15c on 15c ultra | 6.50 | 2.00 |
| **a.** | Double surcharge | 175.00 | |
| **b.** | Inverted surcharge | | *175.00* |
| **c.** | No period after "c" | 150.00 | 150.00 |

To make No. E2 the word "INLAND" was printed on No. E1. For No. E3 a new setting of the surcharge was made with different spacing between the words.

SD4

SD5

| | | | |
|---|---|---|---|
| *E4* SD4 | 15c grn & red | 4.00 | 2.50 |
| **a.** | Double surcharge | 150.00 | 150.00 |
| **b.** | Inverted surcharge | 100.00 | 100.00 |
| **c.** | "LNIAND." | 125.00 | 125.00 |
| **d.** | As "c", double surch. | *450.00* | |
| *E5* SD5 | 18c grn & blk | 3.50 | 5.00 |
| **a.** | Exclamation point (!) instead of "I" in "FOREIGN" | 200.00 | |

## POSTAGE DUE STAMPS

**Catalogue values for unused stamps in this section, from this point to the end of the section, are for Never Hinged items.**

Numeral — D1

***Perf. 14½x14***

**1933-54 Typo. Wmk. 4**

| | | | |
|---|---|---|---|
| *J1* D1 | 2c black | 15 | 15 |
| *J2* D1 | 4c violet | 14 | 15 |
| *J3* D1 | 6c red | 20 | *70* |
| *J4* D1 | 10c green | 30 | *60* |
| *J5* D1 | 20c ultra | 45 | *1.50* |
| *J6* D1 | 50c dp red lil ('54) | 90 | *2.25* |
| *J7* D1 | 1r org ('54) | 90 | *3.75* |
| | *Nos. J1-J7 (7)* | 3.04 | 9.10 |

**1966-68 Wmk. 314 *Perf. 14***

| | | | |
|---|---|---|---|
| *J8* D1 | 2c blk ('67) | 10 | 10 |

***Perf. 14½x14***

| | | | |
|---|---|---|---|
| *J9* D1 | 4c rose vio ('68) | 10 | 10 |
| *J10* D1 | 6c dp org ('68) | 10 | 10 |
| *J11* D1 | 10c yel grn ('67) | 15 | 15 |
| *J12* D1 | 20c ultra | 25 | 20 |
| *J13* D1 | 50c dp red lil ('68) | 65 | 35 |
| | *Nos. J8-J13 (6)* | 1.35 | 1.00 |

Nos. 445-446, 450, 455, 457, 462 Surcharged "POSTAGE/ DUE" and New Value.

**Wmk. 373**

**1982, Oct. 25 Litho. *Perf. 13½***

| | | | |
|---|---|---|---|
| *J14* A92 | 10c on 15c multi | 5 | 5 |
| *J15* A92 | 20c on 20c multi | 5 | 5 |
| *J16* A91 | 50c on 60c multi | 12 | 12 |
| *J17* A92 | 1r on 1.20r multi | 16 | 16 |
| *J18* A92 | 1.50r on 1.50r multi | 22 | 22 |
| *J19* A91 | 5r on 15r multi | 75 | 75 |
| | *Nos. J14-J19 (6)* | 1.35 | 1.35 |

# MESOPOTAMIA

LOCATION — In Western Asia, bounded on the north by Syria and Turkey, on the east by Persia, on the south by Saudi Arabia and on the west by Trans-Jordan.

GOVT. — A former Turkish Province.

AREA — 143,250 (1918) sq. mi.

POP. — 2,849,282 (1920).

CAPITAL — Baghdad.

During World War I this territory was occupied by Great Britain. It was recognized as an independent state and placed under British Mandate but in 1932 the Mandate was terminated and the country admitted to membership in the League of Nations as the Kingdom of Iraq. Postage stamps of Iraq are now in use.

16 Annas = 1 Rupee

### Issued under British Occupation

### Baghdad Issue

Obelisk of Theodosius, Constantinople A24

Leander's Tower A26

Fenerbahçe (Garden Lighthouse) A28

Castle of Europe on Bosporus — A29

Mosque of Sultan Ahmed — A30

Stamps of Turkey 1901-16 Surcharged

IN BRITISH BAGHDAD OCCUPATION ½ An

The surcharges were printed from slugs which were arranged to fit the various shapes of the stamps.

**1917 Unwmk. *Perf. 12, 13½.***

**On Turkey Nos. 254, 256, 258-260**

| | | | |
|---|---|---|---|
| *N1* A24 | ¼a on 2pa red lil | 100.00 | 105.00 |
| **a.** | "IN BRITISH" omitted | *4,000.* | |
| *N2* A26 | ¼a on 5pa vio brn | 72.50 | 82.50 |
| **a.** | "¼ An" omitted | *3,250.* | |
| *N3* A28 | ½a on 10pa grn | 475.00 | 475.00 |
| *N4* A29 | 1a on 20pa red | 450.00 | 400.00 |
| *N5* A30 | 2a on 1pi bl | 135.00 | 165.00 |
| | *Nos. N1-N5 (5)* | 1,232. | 1,227. |

General Post Office, Constantinople — A22

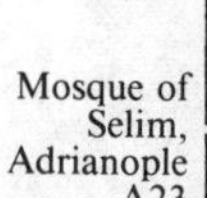

Mosque of Selim, Adrianople A23

On Turkey No. 249 with Overprint ب

| | | | |
|---|---|---|---|
| *N6* A22 | 2a on 1pi ultra | 300.00 | 300.00 |

**On Turkey No. 251**

| | | | |
|---|---|---|---|
| *N7* A23 | ½a on 10pa grn | 1,150. | 900.00 |

On Turkey Nos. 272-273 with Overprint

| | | | |
|---|---|---|---|
| *N8* A29 | 1a on 20pa red | 300.00 | 300.00 |
| **a.** | "OCCUPATION" omitted | *2,600.* | |
| *N9* A30 | 2a on 1pi bl | 4,000. | 4,000. |

Old General Post Office, Constantinople A41

On Turkey Nos. 346-348

| | | | |
|---|---|---|---|
| *N10* A41 | ½a on 10pa car | 200.00 | 200.00 |
| *N11* A41 | 1a on 20pa ultra | 700.00 | 700.00 |
| **a.** | "1 An" omitted | *4,000.* | |
| *N12* A41 | 2a on 1pi vio & blk | 57.50 | 57.50 |
| **a.** | "BAGHDAD" omitted | *2,000.* | |

Tughra, Sultan's Monogram

A17 A18

On Various Issues with Overprint

On Turkey Nos. 297, 300

| | | | |
|---|---|---|---|
| *N13* A17 | ¼a on 5pa pur | *2,500.* | |
| *N14* A17 | 2a on 1pi bl | 140.00 | 140.00 |

**On Turkey No. 306**

| | | | |
|---|---|---|---|
| *N15* A18 | 1a on 20pa car | 200.00 | 200.00 |

**On Turkey Nos. 329-331**

| | | | |
|---|---|---|---|
| *N16* A22 | ½a on 10pa bl grn | 60.00 | 60.00 |
| *N17* A22 | 1a on 20pa car rose | 265.00 | 265.00 |
| **a.** | "1 An" omitted | *2,000.* | *2,000.* |
| *N18* A22 | 2a on 1pi ultra | 100.00 | 100.00 |

On Turkey No. 337 With Overprint

| | | | |
|---|---|---|---|
| *N19* A22 | 1a on 20pa car rose | *4,000.* | *4,000.* |

On Turkey No. P125 with Overprint

and Overprint

| | | | |
|---|---|---|---|
| *N20* A17 | 1a on 20pa car | *2,500.* | *2,600.* |

A21

A11

On Turkey Nos. B1, B8 with Overprint

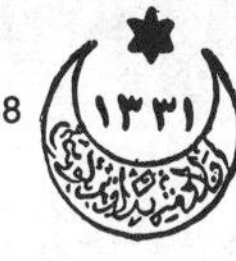

Inscription in crescent is obliterated by another crescent handstamped in violet black on Nos. N21-N27.

*N21* A18 ½a on 10pa dl grn 75.00 75.00
*a.* "OCCUPATION" omitted *3,250.*
*N22* A21 1a on 20pa car rose 250.00 250.00

On Semi-Postal Stamps of 1916 with Overprint

On Turkey No. B29

*N23* A21 2a on 1pi ultra 1,500. 1,500.

**On Turkey Nos. B33-B34**

*N24* A22 1a on 20pa car rose 85.00 85.00
*N25* A22 2a on 1pi ultra 150.00 150.00
*a.* "OCCUPATION" omitted *3,250.*
*b.* "BAGHDAD" omitted *3,250.*

**On Turkey No. B42**

*N26* A41 ½a on 10pa car 150.00 150.00
*a.* "BAGHDAD" double *2,000.*

On Turkey No. B38 with Surcharge

*N27* A11 1a on 10pa on 20pa vio brn 225.00 265.00

**Iraq Issue.**

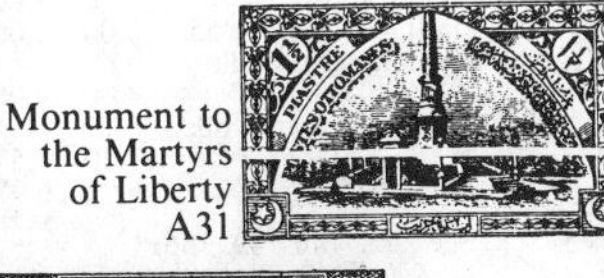
Monument to the Martyrs of Liberty A31

Fountains of Suleiman A32

Cruiser "Hamidie" A33

Kandili on the Bosporus A34

War Ministry A35

Sweet Waters of Europe Park, Constantinople — A36

Mosque of Suleiman A37

The Bosporus A38

Sultan Ahmed's Fountain A39

Turkey Nos. 256, 258-269 Surcharged

IRAQ
IN BRITISH OCCUPATION
1An.

**1918-20** *Perf. 12*

*N28* A26 ¼a on 5pa vio brn 8 8
*N29* A28 ½a on 10pa grn 6 5
*N30* A29 1a on 20pa red 6 6
*N31* A26 1½a on 5pa vio brn 8 8
*N32* A30 2½a on 1pi bl 12 9
*a.* Inverted surcharge *3,250.*
*N33* A31 3a on 1½pi car & blk 12 10
*a.* Double surcharge, red & blk *1,750.*
*N34* A32 4a on 1¾pi sl & red brn 15 15
*a.* Center inverted *10,000.*
*N35* A33 6a on 2pi grn & blk 30 25
*N36* A34 8a on 2½pi org & ol grn 25 18
*N37* A35 12a on 5pi dl vio 1.25 50
*N38* A36 1r on 10pi red brn 1.25 45
*N39* A37 2r on 25pi ol grn 5.50 2.00
*N40* A38 5r on 50pi car 17.50 8.75
*N41* A39 10r on 100pi dp bl 15.00 7.50
*Nos. N28-N41 (14)* 41.72 20.24

See Nos. N50-N53.

**Mosul Issue.**

A13

A14

A15

A16

A17

A18

A19

**1919** **Unwmk.** *Perf. 11½, 12*

*N42* A13 ½a on 1pi grn & brn red 25 30
*N43* A14 1a on 20pa *rose* 50 42
*a.* "POSTAGE" omitted
*N44* A15 1a on 20pa *rose* 75 75
*a.* Double surcharge

Turkish word at right of tughra ("reshad") is large on No. N43, small on No. N44.

**Wmk. Turkish Characters**
***Perf. 12½***

*N45* A16 2½a on 1pi vio & yel 38 30
*N46* A17 3a on 20pa grn & yel 25.00 25.00

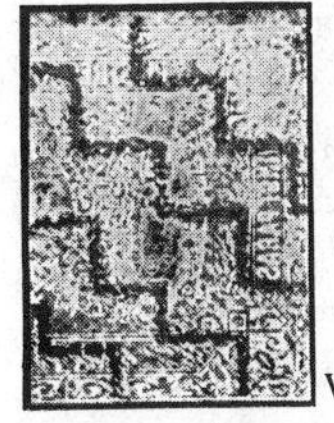
Wmk.48

**Wmk. Diagonal Zigzag Lines. (48)**

*N47* A17 3a on 20pa grn 38 28
*N48* A18 4a on 1pi dl vio 65 50
*a.* Double surcharge
*b.* "4" omitted 1,650.
*c.* As "b", double surch.
*N49* A19 8a on 10pa cl 75 75
*a.* Double surcharge *500.00*
*b.* Inverted surch. *500.00*
*c.* 8a on 1pi dl vio *2,000.*

**Iraq Issue**

Types of 1918-20 Issue

**1921** **Wmk. 4** *Perf. 12*

*N50* A28 ½a on 10pa grn 50 25
*N51* A26 1½a on 5pa dp brn 50 25
*N52* A37 2r on 25pi ol grn 11.00 10.00

Type of 1918-20 without "Reshad".

**1922** **Unwmk.**

*N53* A36 1r on 10pi red brn 100.00 12.50

"Reshad" is the small Turkish word at right of the tughra in circle at top center.

**OFFICIAL STAMPS**

Nos. N29-N41 Overprinted:

ON STATE SERVICE

**1920** **Unwmk.** *Perf. 12*

*NO1* A28 ½a on 10pa grn 18 12
*NO2* A29 1a on 20pa red 25 12
*NO3* A26 1½a on 5pa vio brn 1.10 35
*NO4* A30 2½a on 1pi bl 1.10 60
*NO5* A31 3a on 1½pi car & blk 1.10 38
*NO6* A32 4a on 1¾pi sl & red brn 1.65 50
*NO7* A33 6a on 2pi grn & blk 1.10 38
*NO8* A34 8a on 2½pi org & ol grn 1.10 50
*NO9* A35 12a on 5pi dl vio 2.75 1.65
*NO10* A36 1r on 10pi red brn 2.75 1.10
*NO11* A37 2r on 25pi ol grn 7.25 8.00
*NO12* A38 5r on 50pi car 30.00 15.00
*NO13* A39 10r on 100pi dp bl 27.50 19.00
*Nos. NO1-NO13 (13)* 77.83 47.70

Same Overprint on Types of Regular Issue of 1921

**1921-22** **Wmk. 4**

*NO14* A28 ½a on 10pa grn 14 8
*NO15* A29 1a on 20pa red 14 14
*NO16* A26 1½a on 5pa dp brn 28 28
*NO17* A32 4a on 1¾pi gray & red brn 28 28
*NO18* A33 6a on 2pi grn & blk 3.75 3.25
*NO19* A34 8a on 2½pi org & yel grn 80 55
*NO20* A35 12a on 5pi dl vio 2.75 2.75
*NO21* A37 2r on 25pi ol grn 14.00 14.00
*Nos. NO14-NO21 (8)* 22.14 21.33

Same Overprint on No. N53

**1922** **Unwmk.**

*NO22* A36 1r on 10pi red brn 12.00 5.00

## MONTSERRAT

LOCATION — In the West Indies southeast of Puerto Rico.
GOVT. — British Crown Colony
AREA — 39 sq. mi.
POP. — 12,074 (1980)
CAPITAL — Plymouth

Montserrat was one of the four presidencies of the former Leeward Islands colony until it became a colony itself in 1956.

Montserrat stamps were discontinued in 1890 and resumed in 1903. In the interim, stamps of Leeward Islands were used. In 1903-56, stamps of Montserrat and Leeward Islands were used concurrently.

12 Pence = 1 Shilling
20 Shillings = 1 Pound
100 Cents = 1 Dollar (1951)

**Catalogue values for unused stamps in this country are for Never Hinged items, beginning with Scott 104 in the regular postage section, Scott O45 in the officials section.**

Stamps of Antigua Overprinted in Black — a

MONTSERRAT

**Wmk. Crown and C. C. (1)**

**1876** **Engr.** *Perf. 14*

*1* A1 1p red 15.00 15.00
*a* Vert. or diag. half used as ½p on cover 1,500.
*c* "S" inverted 1,500. 1,500.
*2* A1 6p green 35.00 30.00
*a* Vertical half used as 3p on cover
*b* Vertical third used as 2p on cover
*c* "S" inverted 2,500. 2,500.
*d* 6p bl grn 1,500.
*e* As "d", "S" inverted

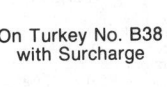

Queen Victoria — A2

**1880** **Typo.**
3 A2 2½p red brn 225.00 200.00
4 A2 4p blue 100.00 60.00

Antigua No. 18 Overprinted type "a" and Type of 1880

**1884-85 Wmk. Crown and C. A. (2)**
5 A2 ½p green 2.00 4.00

**Engr.**
6 A1 1p rose red 7.50 15.00
*a* Vertical half used as ½p on cover 2,000.
*b* "S" inverted 1,500. 1,500.

**Typo.**
7 A2 2½p red brn 175.00 100.00
8 A2 2½p ultra ('85) 6.00 6.00
9 A2 4p blue 3,500. 375.00
10 A2 4p red lil ('85) 4.00 *6.00*

Antigua No. 20 Overprinted type "a"

**1884 Engr.** ***Perf. 12.***
11 A11 1p red 60.00 35.00
*a* "S" inverted 2,500. 2,000.
*b* Vert. half used as ½p on cover 1,500.

Symbol of the Colony A3

King Edward VII A4

**1903 Wmk. 2 Typo.** ***Perf. 14***
12 A3 ½p gray grn 90 1.25
13 A3 1p car & blk 90 30
14 A3 2p brn & blk 4.25 5.00
15 A3 2½p ultra & blk 1.40 1.25
16 A3 3p dk vio & brn org 5.25 6.00
17 A3 6p ol grn & vio 7.00 9.00
18 A3 1sh vio & gray grn 9.50 12.50
19 A3 2sh brn org & gray grn 14.00 20.00
20 A3 2sh 6p blk & gray grn 25.00 *35.00*

**Wmk. Crown and C. C. (1)**
21 A4 5sh car & blk 100.00 *150.00*
*Nos. 12-21 (10)* 168.20 240.30

**1904-08 Wmk. 3**
**Chalky Paper**
22 A3 ½p grn & gray grn 90 1.10
23 A3 1p car & blk ('08) 9.00 9.00
24 A3 2p brn & blk 90 1.50
25 A3 2½p ultra & blk ('06) 2.00 3.00
26 A3 3p dk vio & brn org 1.40 1.65
27 A3 6p ol grn & vio 3.00 *4.50*
28 A3 1sh vio & gray grn ('08) 4.50 6.00
29 A3 2sh brn org & gray grn ('08) 24.00 30.00
30 A3 2sh blk & gray grn 6p ('08) 26.00 30.00
31 A4 5sh car & blk ('07) 90.00 *110.00*
*Nos. 22-31 (10)* 161.70 196.75

The ½, 2, 3 and 6p are also on ordinary paper.

**1908-13**
**Ordinary Paper**
31A A3 ½p dp grn 40 30
32 A3 1p carmine 50 20
33 A3 2p gray 2.50 *4.25*
34 A3 2½p ultra 2.50 4.25

**Chalky Paper**
35 A3 3p vio, *yel* 1.65 7.00
36 A3 6p red vio & gray vio 4.50 10.00
37 A3 1sh *green* 6.00 10.00
38 A3 2sh bl & vio, *bl* 17.50 30.00
39 A3 2sh 6p car & blk, *bl* 30.00 40.00
40 A3 5sh grn & scar, *yel* 55.00 70.00

**Surface-colored Paper**
41 A3 3p vio, *yel* ('13) 3.75 10.00
*Nos. 31A-41 (11)* 124.30 186.00

King George V — A5

**1913**
**Chalky Paper**
42 A5 5sh grn & scar, *yel* 75.00 90.00

King George V and Colonial Device — A6

**Wmk. Multiple Crown and C. A. (3)**
**1916-22 Ordinary Paper.** ***Perf. 14***
43 A6 ½p green 50 50
44 A6 1p scarlet 45 45
45 A6 2p gray 1.75 *3.75*
46 A6 2½p ultra 3.00 *4.50*

**Chalky Paper.**
47 A6 3p vio, *yel* 75 *1.50*
48 A6 4p blk & red, *yel* ('22) 4.50 *6.75*
49 A6 6p dl vio & red vio 2.50 *4.50*
50 A6 1sh *bl grn*, ol back 3.00 *6.00*
51 A6 2sh vio & ultra, *bl* 9.00 12.50
52 A6 2sh 6p blk & red, *bl* 11.50 15.00
53 A6 5sh grn & red, *yel* 22.50 30.00
*Nos. 43-53 (11)* 59.45 85.45

**1922-29 Wmk. 4**
**Ordinary Paper.**
54 A6 ¼p brown 45 60
55 A6 ½p grn ('23) 20 20
56 A6 1p dp vio ('23) 75 28
57 A6 1p car ('29) 1.25 1.10
58 A6 1½p orange 3.00 *6.00*
59 A6 1½p rose red ('23) 50 *1.25*
60 A6 1½p fawn ('29) 1.25 38
61 A6 2p gray 75 *1.25*
62 A6 2½p ultra 75 1.25
63 A6 2½p org ('23) 2.50 *5.00*
64 A6 3p ultra ('23) 75 *2.25*

**Chalky Paper**
65 A6 3p vio, *yel* ('26) 1.75 2.75
66 A6 4p blk & red, *yel* ('23) 1.50 *3.00*
67 A6 5p dl vio & ol grn 4.00 *7.75*
68 A6 6p dl vio & red vio ('23) 1.65 *3.25*
69 A6 1sh *emer* ('23) 2.75 *3.25*
70 A6 2sh vio & ultra, *bl* 4.25 *7.75*
71 A6 2sh 6p blk p red, *bl* ('23) 12.50 18.00
72 A6 3sh grn & vio 12.50 18.00
73 A6 4sh blk & scar 12.50 18.00
74 A6 5sh grn & red, *yel* ('23) 21.00 30.00
*Nos. 54-74 (21)* 86.55 131.31

**Tercentenary Issue.**

New Plymouth and Harbor A7

**1932, Apr. 18 Engr.**
75 A7 ½p green 65 75
76 A7 1p red 65 75
77 A7 1½p org brn 1.65 2.00
78 A7 2p gray 1.90 2.25
79 A7 2½p ultra 1.90 2.25
80 A7 3p orange 3.50 4.00
81 A7 6p violet 5.75 7.75
82 A7 1sh ol grn 10.50 14.00
83 A7 2sh 6p lil rose 42.50 57.50
84 A7 5sh dk brn 85.00 110.00
*Nos. 75-84 (10)* 154.00 201.25

300th anniv. of the colonization of Montserrat.

**Silver Jubilee Issue**
Common Design Type

**1935, May 6** ***Perf. 11x12***
85 CD301 1p car & dk bl 1.00 75
86 CD301 1½p gray blk & ultra 90 *1.50*
87 CD301 2½p ultra & brn 3.50 *5.25*
88 CD301 1sh brn vio & ind 10.00 *15.00*

**Coronation Issue**
Common Design Type

**1937, May 12** ***Perf. 13½x14***
89 CD302 1p carmine 12 20
90 CD302 1½p brown 15 25
91 CD302 2½p brt ultra 25 40

Carr's Bay — A8

Sea Island Cotton — A9

Botanic Station A10

**1938-48** ***Perf. 14***
92 A8 ½p dk grn ('42) 6 6
*a* Perf. 13 8 8
93 A8 1p car ('42) 7 7
*a* Perf. 13 10 10
94 A8 1½p rose vio ('42) 10 10
*a* Perf. 13 2.00 1.65
95 A10 2p red org ('41) 28 22
*a* Perf. 13 1.65 1.65
96 A9 2½p brt ultra ('43) 28 24
*a* Perf. 13 32 40
97 A8 3p brown 35 28
*a* Perf. 13 40 50
98 A10 6p dl vio ('42) 35 22
*a* Perf. 13 35 40
99 A8 1sh brn lake ('42) 70 55
*a* Perf. 13 2.00 2.00
100 A10 2sh6p sl bl ('43) 2.75 2.50
*a* Perf. 13 2.00 2.00
101 A8 5sh car rose ('42) 3.00 3.00
*a* Perf. 13 3.25 6.50

***Perf. 12***
102 A10 10sh blue ('48) 7.00 12.50
103 A8 £1 blk ('48) 10.50 17.50
*Nos. 92-103 (12)* 25.44 37.24
*Nos. 92a-101a (10)* 12.15 15.28

**Catalogue values for unused stamps in this section, from this point to the end of the section, are for Never Hinged items.**

**Peace Issue**
Common Design Type

**1946, Nov. 1 Engr.** ***Perf. 13½x14***
104 CD303 1½p dp mag 10 8
105 CD303 3p brown 20 18

**Silver Wedding Issue**
Common Design Types

**1949, Jan. 3 Photo.** ***Perf. 14x14½***
106 CD304 2½p brt ultra 18 18

**Engraved; Name Typographed**
***Perf. 11½x11.***
107 CD305 5sh rose car 8.50 *12.50*

**UPU Issue**
Common Design Types

**Engr.; Name Typo. on 3p and 6p**
***Perf. 13½, 11x11½***

**1949, Oct. 10 Wmk. 4**
108 CD306 2½p ultra 45 45
109 CD307 3p chocolate 65 65
110 CD308 6p lilac 95 95
111 CD309 1sh rose vio 1.40 1.40

**University Issue**
Common Design Types

**1951, Feb. 16 Engr.** ***Perf. 14x14½***
112 CD310 3c rose lil & gray blk 30 30
113 CD311 12c vio & blk 90 90

Government House — A11

Designs (portrait at right on 12c, 24c and $2.40): 2c, $1.20, Cotton field. 3c, Map of Presidency. 4c, 24c, Picking tomatoes. 5c, 12c, St. Anthony's Church. 6c, $4.80, Badge of Presidency. 8c, 60c, Cotton ginning.

***Perf. 11½x11***

**1951, Sept. 17 Engr. Wmk. 4**
114 A11 1c gray 12 12
115 A11 2c green 20 20
116 A11 3c org brn 15 15
117 A11 4c rose car 15 15
118 A11 5c red vio 20 20
119 A11 6c dk brn 25 25
120 A11 8c dk bl 35 35
121 A11 12c red brn & bl 65 65
122 A11 24c emer & rose car 1.00 1.00
123 A11 60c rose car & gray blk 2.00 2.00
124 A11 $1.20 dp bl & emer 6.00 6.00
125 A11 $2.40 dp grn & gray blk 7.50 *9.00*
126 A11 $4.80 pur & gray blk 15.00 *20.00*
*Nos. 114-126 (13)* 33.57 40.07

**Coronation Issue.**
Common Design Type

**1953, June 2** ***Perf. 13½x13***
127 CD312 2c dk grn & blk 28 28

Type of 1951 with Portrait of Queen Elizabeth II

Designs: ½c, 3c, "Map of Presidency." 6c, $4.80, "Badge of Presidency." 48c, Cotton field.

**1953-57** ***Perf. 11½x11.***
128 A11 ½c vio ('56) 6 6
129 A11 1c gray blk 5 5
130 A11 2c green 5 5
131 A11 3c org brn 30 30
132 A11 4c rose car ('55) 8 8
133 A11 5c red vio ('55) 10 10
134 A11 6c dk brn ('55) 35 35
135 A11 8c dp ultra ('55) 15 15
136 A11 12c red brn & bl ('55) 18 18
137 A11 24c emer & rose car ('55) 35 35
138 A11 48c rose vio & ol ('57) 80 80
139 A11 60c rose car & blk ('55) 1.00 1.00
140 A11 $1.20 bl & emer ('55) 2.00 2.00
141 A11 $2.40 dp grn & blk ('55) 4.00 4.00
142 A11 $4.80 pur & gray blk ('55) 17.50 17.50
*Nos. 128-142 (15)* 26.97 26.97

See Nos. 146-149, 156.

**West Indies Federation**
Common Design Type
***Perf. 11½x11***

**1958, Apr. 22 Engr. Wmk. 314**
143 CD313 3c green 15 15
144 CD313 6c blue 28 28
145 CD313 12c car rose 48 48

Type of 1953-57

Designs as before, but inscribed: "Map of the Colony" (½c, 3c) "Badge of the Colony" (6c, $4.80).

**1958 Wmk. 4** ***Perf. 11½x11***
146 A11 ½c violet 5 5
147 A11 3c org brn 6 6
148 A11 6c dk brn 20 20
149 A11 $4.80 pur & gray blk 14.00 14.00

**Freedom from Hunger Issue**
Common Design Type
***Perf. 14x14½***

**1963, June 4 Photo. Wmk. 314**
150 CD314 12c lilac 1.10 1.00

**Red Cross Centenary Issue**
Common Design Type

**963, Sept. 2 Litho. *Perf. 13***
*51* CD315 4c blk & red 15 12
*52* CD315 12c ultra & red 1.00 75

**Shakespeare Issue**
Common Design Type

**964, Apr. 23 Photo. *Perf. 14x14½***
*53* CD316 12c sl bl 40 30

Type of 1953-57
***Perf. 11½x11***

**964, Oct. 30 Engr. Wmk. 314**
*56* A11 2c green 28 22

**ITU Issue**
Common Design Type
***Perf. 11x11½***

**965, May 17 Litho. Wmk. 314**
*57* CD317 4c ver & lil 20 18
*58* CD317 48c emer & rose red 1.40 1.25

Pineapple — A12

**Wmk. 314 Upright**

**1965, Aug. 16 Photo. *Perf. 15x14***

| No. | Type | Value | Description | Unused | Used |
|---|---|---|---|---|---|
| *159* | A12 | 1c | shown | 6 | 5 |
| *160* | A12 | 2c | Avacado | 6 | 5 |
| *161* | A12 | 3c | Soursop | 10 | 6 |
| *162* | A12 | 4c | Peppers | 10 | 7 |
| *163* | A12 | 5c | Mango | 12 | 8 |
| *164* | A12 | 6c | Tomatoes | 12 | 10 |
| *165* | A12 | 8c | Guava | 15 | 15 |
| *166* | A12 | 10c | Okra | 20 | 18 |
| *167* | A12 | 12c | Limes | 30 | 25 |
| *168* | A12 | 20c | Oranges | 40 | 35 |
| *169* | A12 | 24c | Bananas | 60 | 50 |
| *170* | A12 | 42c | Onion | 1.25 | 90 |
| *171* | A12 | 48c | Cabbage | 1.50 | 1.00 |
| *172* | A12 | 60c | Papayas | 1.75 | 1.25 |
| *173* | A12 | $1.20 | Pumpkin | 2.00 | 1.75 |
| *174* | A12 | $2.40 | Sweet potato | 5.00 | 4.00 |
| *175* | A12 | $4.80 | Eggplant | 10.00 | 8.00 |
| | | | *Nos. 159-175 (17)* | 23.71 | 18.74 |

**1969 Wmk. 314 Sideways**

| No. | Type | Value | Unused | Used |
|---|---|---|---|---|
| *159a* | A12 | 1c | 15 | 15 |
| *160a* | A12 | 2c | 30 | 30 |
| *161a* | A12 | 3c | 38 | 38 |
| *162a* | A12 | 4c | 52 | 52 |
| *163a* | A12 | 5c | 60 | 60 |
| *166a* | A12 | 10c | 1.15 | 1.15 |
| *168a* | A12 | 20c | 1.40 | 1.40 |
| | | *Nos. 159a-168a (7)* | 4.50 | 4.50 |

**Intl. Cooperation Year Issue**
Common Design Type

**1965, Oct. 25 Litho. *Perf. 14½***
*176* CD318 2c lt grn & cl 10 10
*177* CD318 12c lt vio & grn 42 42

**Churchill Memorial Issue**
Common Design Type

**1966, Jan. 24 Photo. *Perf. 14***
**Design in Black, Gold and Carmine Rose**
*178* CD319 1c brt bl 5 5
*179* CD319 2c green 6 6
*180* CD319 24c brown 60 60
*181* CD319 42c violet 1.10 1.10

**Royal Visit Issue**
Common Design Type
***Perf. 11x12***

**1966, Feb. 4 Litho. Wmk. 314**
*182* CD320 14c vio bl 38 38
*183* CD320 24c dk car rose 70 70

**WHO Headquarters Issue**
Common Design Type

**1966, Sept. 20 Litho. *Perf. 14***
*184* CD322 12c multi 20 20
*185* CD322 60c multi 90 90

**UNESCO Anniversary Issue**
Common Design Type

**1966, Dec. 1. Litho. *Perf. 14***
*186* CD323 4c "Education" 12 12
  **a** Orange omitted 50.00
*187* CD323 60c "Science" 65 65
*188* CD323 $1.80 "Culture" 2.75 2.75

On No. 186a, the squares of the lowercase letters appear in yellow.

Sailing and ITY Emblem A13

Design (ITY Emblem and): 15c, Waterfall, Chance Mountain (vert.). 16c, Beach scene. 24c, Golfers.

**1967, Dec. 29 Photo. Wmk. 314**
*189* A13 5c multi 7 7
*190* A13 15c multi 20 20
*191* A13 16c multi 25 25
*192* A13 24c multi 50 50

Issued for International Tourist Year 1967.

Nos. 167, 169, 171, 173-175 and Type Surcharged **15c**

**1968, May 6 *Perf. 15x14***

| No. | Type | Description | Unused | Used |
|---|---|---|---|---|
| *193* | A12 | 15c on 12c multi | 28 | 28 |
| **a** | | Wmkd. sideways ('69) | 1.00 | 1.00 |
| *194* | A12 | 25c on 24c multi | 42 | 42 |
| **a** | | Wmkd. sideways ('69) | 1.75 | 1.75 |
| *195* | A12 | 50c on 48c multi | 85 | 85 |
| **a** | | Wmkd. sideways ('69) | 3.50 | 3.50 |
| *196* | A12 | $1 on $1.20 multi | 1.35 | 1.35 |
| *197* | A12 | $2.50 on $2.40 multi | 3.00 | 3.00 |
| *198* | A12 | $5 on $4.80 multi | 5.75 | 5.75 |
| | | *Nos. 193-198 (6)* | 11.65 | 11.65 |

The surcharge bars are slightly thinner on the "Wmkd. sideways" varieties.

Woman Runner A14

Designs: 25c, Weight lifter. 50c, Athlete on rings. $1, Runner and Toltec sculptures (vert.).

***Perf. 14½x14, 14x14½***

**1968, July 31 Photo. Wmk. 314**
*199* A14 15c gold, brt grn & rose cl 14 14
*200* A14 25c gold, org & bl 22 22
*201* A14 50c gold, ver & grn 45 45
*202* A14 $1 multi 95 95

Issued to publicize the 19th Olympic Games, Mexico City, Oct. 12-27.

Albert T. Marryshow — A15

Portraits and Human Rights Flame: 5c, Alexander Hamilton. 25c, William Wilberforce. 50c, Dag Hammarskjold. $1, Rev. Martin Luther King, Jr.

***Perf. 14x14½***

**1968, Dec. 2 Photo. Wmk. 314**
*203* A15 5c multicolored 5 5
*204* A15 15c multicolored 12 12
*205* A15 25c multicolored 20 20
*206* A15 50c multicolored 40 40
*207* A15 $1 multicolored 80 80
  *Nos. 203-207 (5)* 1.57 1.57

International Human Rights Year.

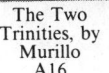

The Two Trinities, by Murillo A16

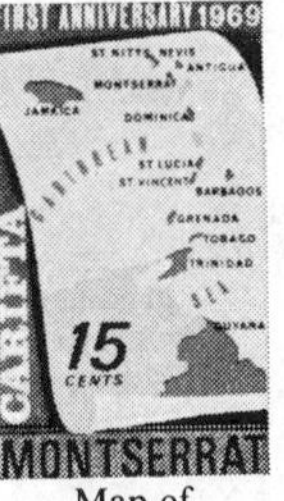

Map of Caribbean A17

Christmas: 15c, 50c, The Adoration of the Magi, by Botticelli.

**1968, Dec. 16 *Perf. 14½x14***
*208* A16 5c red & multi 6 6
*209* A16 15c dk grn & multi 18 18
*210* A16 25c pur & multi 28 28
*211* A16 50c brn & multi 55 55

**1969, May 27 Photo. *Perf. 14***

Design: 35c, 50c, "Strength in Unity" (horiz.).

*212* A17 15c grn & multi 16 16
*213* A17 20c brn & multi 24 24
*214* A17 35c dp car & multi 48 48
*215* A17 50c multi 65 65

First anniversary of CARIFTA (Caribbean Free Trade Area).

Telephone and Map — A18

Designs (Map and): 25c, Book and "New Schools." 50c, Planes (air transport service). $1, Pylon and power lines.

**Wmk. 314**

**1969, July 29 Litho. *Perf. 13½***
*216* A18 15c multi 12 12
*217* A18 25c multi 20 20
*218* A18 50c multi 42 42
*219* A18 $1 multi 90 90

Development projects.

Dolphin A19

Fish: 15c, Atlantic sailfish. 25c, Blackfin tuna and fishing boat. 40c, Spanish mackerel.

**1969, Nov. 1 Photo. *Perf. 13x14***
*220* A19 5c multi 9 9
*221* A19 15c multi 30 30
*222* A19 25c multi 60 60
*223* A19 40c multi 1.00 1.00

King Caspar, Virgin and Child (Stained-glass Window) — A20

Design: 50c, Nativity, by Leonard Limosin (horiz.).

***Perf. 12½x13, 13x12½***

**1969, Dec. 10 Litho. Wmk. 314**
*224* A20 15c vio & multi 16 16
*225* A20 25c red & multi 32 32
*226* A20 50c org & multi 65 65

Christmas 1969.

Red Cross and Distribution of Hearing Aids — A21

Designs (Red Cross and): 3c, Fund raising sale and invalid. 15c, Car bringing handicapped to work. 20c, Instruction for blind worker.

**1970, Apr. 13 Litho. *Perf. 14½***
*227* A21 3c multi 7 7
*228* A21 4c multi 10 10
*229* A21 15c multi 32 32
*230* A21 20c multi 50 50

Centenary of British Red Cross Society.

Red-footed Booby A22

Birds: 2c, Killy hawk (vert.). 3c, Frigate bird (vert.). 4c, White egret (vert.). 5c, Brown pelican (vert.). 10c, Bananaquit (vert.). 15c, Common ani. 20c, Tropic bird. 25c, Montserrat oriole. 50c, Greenthroated carib (vert.). $1, Antillean crested hummingbird. $2.50, Little blue heron (vert.). $5, Purple-throated carib. $10, Forest thrush.

**Wmk. 314 Upright on Horiz. Stamps, Sideways on Vert. Stamps**
***Perf. 14x14½, 14½x14***

**1970-74 Photo.**

| No. | Type | Value | Description | Unused | Used |
|---|---|---|---|---|---|
| *231* | A22 | 1c | yel org & multi | 5 | 5 |
| *232* | A22 | 2c | lt vio & multi | 6 | 6 |
| *233* | A22 | 3c | multi | 6 | 6 |
| *234* | A22 | 4c | lt grn & multi | 8 | 8 |
| *235* | A22 | 5c | bis & multi | 10 | 10 |
| *236* | A22 | 10c | gray & multi | 20 | 20 |
| *237* | A22 | 15c | multi | 30 | 30 |
| *238* | A22 | 20c | rose brn & multi | 40 | 40 |
| *239* | A22 | 25c | brn & multi | 50 | 50 |
| *240* | A22 | 50c | lt vio & multi | 1.00 | 1.00 |
| *241* | A22 | $1 | multi | 1.75 | 1.75 |
| *242* | A22 | $2.50 | dl bl & multi | 4.00 | 4.00 |
| *243* | A22 | $5 | multi | 8.00 | 8.00 |
| *243A* | A22 | $10 | bl & multi | 16.00 | 16.00 |
| | | | *Nos. 231-243A (14)* | 32.50 | 32.50 |

Issue dates: $10, Oct. 30, 1974; others July 2, 1970.

**Wmk. Sideways on Horiz. Stamps, Upright on Vert. Stamps**

**1972-74**

| No. | Type | Value | Description | Unused | Used |
|---|---|---|---|---|---|
| *231a* | A22 | 1c | multi | 16 | 12 |
| *232a* | A22 | 2c | multi | 25 | 20 |
| *233a* | A22 | 3c | multi | 25 | 20 |
| *234a* | A22 | 4c | multi | 35 | 25 |
| *235a* | A22 | 5c | multi | 45 | 28 |
| *237a* | A22 | 15c | multi | 1.20 | 75 |
| *238a* | A22 | 20c | multi | 1.75 | 1.20 |
| *239a* | A22 | 25c | multi | 2.50 | 1.50 |
| | | | *Nos. 231a-239a (8)* | 6.91 | 4.50 |

"Madonna and Child with Animals," after Dürer — A23

Christmas: 15c, $1, Adoration of the Shepherds, by Domenichino (Domenico Zampieri).

**1970, Sept. 21 Litho. *Perf. 14***
*244* A23 5c lt bl & multi 8 8
*245* A23 15c red org & multi 25 25
*246* A23 20c ol grn & multi 30 30
*247* A23 $1 multi 1.50 1.50

War Memorial, Plymouth — A24

Designs: 15c, Fort St. George and view of Plymouth. 25c, Beach at Carrs Bay. 50c, Golf Course.

**1970, Nov. 30 Litho. *Perf. 14***
*248* A24 5c multi 9 9
*249* A24 15c multi 30 30
*250* A24 25c multi 45 45
*251* A24 50c multi 90 90
*a* Souvenir sheet of 4 3.00 3.00

Tourist publicity. No. 251a contains one each of Nos. 248-251. Light blue border with black design and inscription. Size: 134x108mm.

Girl Guide — A25

"Noli me Tangere," by Orcagna (Andrea di Cione) — A26

Design: 15c, 25c, Brownie.

**1970, Dec. 31**
*252* A25 10c org & multi 14 14
*253* A25 15c lt bl & multi 25 25
*254* A25 25c lil & multi 42 42
*255* A25 40c multi 70 70

Girl Guides' 60th anniversary.

***Perf. 13½x13***
**1971, Mar. 22 Photo. Wmk. 314**

Easter: 5c, 20c, Descent from the Cross, by Jan van Hemessen.

*256* A26 5c org brn & multi 12 12
*257* A26 15c multi 35 35
*258* A26 20c grn & multi 45 45
*259* A26 40c bl grn & multi 90 90

Distinguished Flying Cross and Medal — A27

"Nativity with Saints" (detail), by Romanino A28

Highest Awards for Military Personnel: 20c, Military Cross and Medal. 40c, Distinguished Service Cross and Medal. $1, Victoria Cross.

***Perf. 14½x14***
**1971, July 8 Litho. Wmk. 314**
*260* A27 10c gray, vio & sil 12 12
*261* A27 20c grn & multi 24 24
*262* A27 40c lt bl, dk bl & sil 48 48
*263* A27 $1 red, dk brn & gold 1.25 1.25

50th anniversary of the British Commonwealth Ex-services League.

**1971, Sept. 16 *Perf. 14x13½***

Paintings: 15c, $1, Angels' Choir, by Simon Marmion.

*264* A28 5c brn & multi 12 12
*265* A28 15c emer & multi 35 35
*266* A28 20c ultra & multi 48 48
*267* A28 $1 red & multi 2.50 2.50

Christmas 1971.

Piper Apache, First Landing at Olveston Airfield — A29

Designs: 10c, Beech Twin Bonanza. 15c, De Havilland Heron. 20c, Britten Norman Islander. 40c, De Havilland Twin Otter. 75c, Hawker Siddeley 748 and stewardesses.

**1971, Dec. 16 *Perf. 13½x14***
*268* A29 5c multi 24 24
*269* A29 10c multi 50 50
*270* A29 15c multi 70 70
*271* A29 20c multi 1.00 1.00
*272* A29 40c multi 2.00 2.00
*273* A29 75c multi 3.50 3.50
*a* Souvenir sheet of 6 13.00 13.00
*Nos. 268-273 (6)* 7.94 7.94

14th anniversary of Leeward Islands Air Transport (LIAT). No. 273a contains one each of Nos. 268-273 with blue decorative margin and inscription. Size: 202x102mm.

Chapel of Christ in Gethsemane, Coventry Cathedral — A30

Designs: 10c, 75c, The Agony in the Garden, by Giovanni Bellini.

**1972, Mar. 9 Litho. *Perf. 13½x13***
*274* A30 5c red & multi 8 8
*275* A30 10c bl & multi 20 20
*276* A30 20c emer & multi 40 40
*277* A30 75c lil & multi 2.00 2.00

Easter 1972.

Iguana A31

Designs: 15c, Spotted ameiva (lizard) (vert.). 20c, Frog ("mountain chicken") (vert.). $1, Redfoot tortoises.

**1972, June 8 Litho. *Perf. 14½***
*278* A31 15c lil rose & multi 50 50
*279* A31 20c blk & multi 60 60
*280* A31 40c bl & multi 1.25 1.25
*281* A31 $1 grn & multi 2.50 2.50

Madonna of the Chair, by Raphael A32

Paintings: 35c, Virgin and Child with Cherubs, by Bernardino Fungai. 50c, Magnificat Madonna, by Botticelli. $1, Virgin and Child with St. John and Angel, by Botticelli.

**1972, Oct. 18 *Perf. 13½***
*282* A32 10c vio & multi 20 20
*283* A32 35c brt red & multi 60 60
*284* A32 50c red brn & multi 1.00 1.00
*285* A32 $1 ol & multi 2.00 2.00

Christmas 1972.

**Silver Wedding Issue, 1972**
**Common Design Type**

Design: Queen Elizabeth II, Prince Philip, tomatoes, papayas, limes.

***Perf. 14x14½***
**1972, Nov. 20 Photo. Wmk. 314**
*286* CD324 35c car rose & multi 35 35
*287* CD324 $1 ultra & multi 1.10 1.10

Passionflower A33

Designs: 35c, Passiflora vitifolia. 75c, Passiflora amabilis. $1, Passiflora alata caerulea.

**1973, Apr. 9 Litho. *Perf. 14x13½***
*288* A33 20c pur & multi 60 60
*289* A33 35c multi 95 95
*290* A33 75c brt bl & multi 1.50 1.50
*291* A33 $1 multi 2.50 2.50

Easter 1973. Black backprinting gives story of passionflower.

Montserrat Monastery, Spain — A34

Designs: 35c, Columbus aboard ship sight ing Montserrat. 60c, Columbus' ship of Montserrat. $1, Arms and map of Montserra and neighboring islands.

***Perf. 13½x14***
**1973, July 16 Litho. Wmk. 31**
*292* A34 10c multi 65 6
*293* A34 35c multi 1.65 1.6
*294* A34 60c multi 2.75 2.7
*295* A34 $1 multi 4.00 4.0
*a* Souvenir sheet of 4 25.00 25.0

480th anniversary of the discovery o Montserrat by Columbus. No. 295a contains one each of Nos. 292-295. Multicolored margin with ship and flags. Size: 127x130mm.

Virgin and Child, Studio of David A35

Masqueraders A36

Paintings: 35c, Holy Family with St. John, by Jacob Jordaens. 50c, Virgin and Child, by Bellini. 90c, Virgin and Child by Carlo Dolci.

**1973, Oct. 15 Litho. *Perf. 14x13½***
*296* A35 20c bl & multi 38 38
*297* A35 35c ol bis & multi 65 65
*298* A35 50c brt grn & multi 1.40 1.40
*299* A35 90c brt rose & multi 2.75 2.75

Christmas 1973.

**Princess Anne's Wedding Issue**
**Common Design Type**

**1973, Nov. 14 *Perf. 14***
*300* CD325 35c brt grn & multi 30 30
*301* CD325 $1 multi 90 90

**1974, Apr. 8**
*302* A36 20c *Steel band* (horiz.) 45 45
*303* A36 35c *shown* 90 90
*304* A36 60c *Girl weaving* 1.40 1.40
*305* A36 $1 *University Center* (horiz.) 2.25 2.25
*a* Souvenir sheet of 4 20.00 20.00

25th anniversary of the University of the West Indies. No. 305a contains one each of Nos. 302-305; dull blue border and inscription. Size: 130x90mm.

Hands Holding Letters, UPU Emblem A37

Designs: 2c, 5c, $1, Hands and figures from UPU Monument, Bern; UPU emblem. 3c, 50c, Like 1c.

**1974, July 3 Litho. *Perf. 14***
*306* A37 1c vio & multi 5 5
*307* A37 2c red & blk 6 6
*308* A37 3c ol & multi 8 8
*309* A37 5c org & blk 9 9
*310* A37 50c brn & multi 75 75
*311* A37 $1 grnsh bl & blk 1.50 1.50
*Nos. 306-311 (6)* 2.53 2.53

Centenary of Universal Postal Union.

Prices of premium quality never hinged stamps will be in excess of catalogue price.

Churchill, Parliament, Big Ben — A38

Churchill and Blenheim Palace — A39

*Perf. 13x13½*

**1974, Nov. 30** **Unwmk.**

| | | | |
|---|---|---|---|
| *312* A38 35c ocher & multi | 35 | 35 |
| *313* A39 70c brt grn & multi | 90 | 90 |
| *a* Souvenir sheet of 2 | 1.50 | 1.50 |

Sir Winston Churchill (1874-1965), birth centenary. No. 313a contains one each of Nos. 312-313, yellow and green margin. Size: 86x89mm.

### Nos. 241, 304, 310-311 Surcharged with New Value and Two Bars

*Perf. 14x14½, 14*

**Photo., Litho.**

**1974, Oct. 2** **Wmk. 314**

| | | |
|---|---|---|
| *314* A22 2c on $1 multi | 30 | 30 |
| *315* A37 5c on 50c multi | 1.50 | 1.50 |
| *316* A36 10c on 60c multi | 4.00 | 4.00 |
| *317* A22 20c on $1 multi | 1.30 | 1.30 |
| *a* One bar in surch. | 3.25 | 3.25 |
| *318* A37 35c on $1 multi | 3.25 | 3.25 |
| *Nos. 314-318 (5)* | 10.35 | 10.35 |

Carib Carbet (House) A40

Carib Artifacts: 20c, Necklace (caracoli). 35c, Club. 70c, Canoe.

**Wmk. 314**

**1975, Mar. 3** **Litho.** ***Perf. 14***

| | | |
|---|---|---|
| *319* A40 5c dk red, ocher & blk | 6 | 6 |
| *320* A40 20c blk, ocher & dk red | 24 | 24 |
| *321* A40 35c blk, dk red & ocher | 40 | 40 |
| *322* A40 70c ocher, dk red & blk | 75 | 75 |
| *a* Souvenir booklet | 3.25 | |

No. 322a contains 2 self-adhesive panes printed on peelable paper backing with bicolored advertising on back. One pane of 6 contains 3 each similar to Nos. 320-321; the other pane of 4 contains one each similar to Nos. 319-322. Stamps are imperf. x roulette. Panes have commemorative marginal inscription.

One Bitt A41

Old Local Coinage (1785-1801): 10c, Eighth of a dollar. 35c, Quarter dollars. $2, One dollar.

**Wmk. 314**

**1975, Sept. 1** **Litho.** ***Perf. 14***

| | | |
|---|---|---|
| *323* A41 5c ultra, sil & blk | 7 | 7 |
| *324* A41 10c brn org, sil & blk | 14 | 14 |
| *325* A41 35c grn, sil & blk | 55 | 55 |
| *326* A41 $2 brt rose, sil & blk | 2.50 | 2.50 |
| *a* Souvenir sheet of 4 | 4.25 | 4.25 |

No. 326a contains one each of Nos. 323-326; deep violet, silver and black margin with inscriptions shows special markings from coins. Explanation and description of coinage printed in black on back of souvenir sheet. Size: 141½x141½mm.

Montserrat Nos. 1 and 2 — A42

Designs: 10c, Post Office, Montserrat, and No. 1a (bisect) with AO8 cancel. 40c, Cover with Nos. 1a and 1b. 55c, G.B. No. 27 with AO8 cancel, and No. 2. 70c, 2 No. 1 and one No. 1a with AO8 cancels. $1.10, Packet "Antelope" and No. 2.

**1976, Jan. 5** ***Perf. 13½***

| | | |
|---|---|---|
| *327* A42 5c multi | 7 | 7 |
| *328* A42 10c multi | 14 | 14 |
| *329* A42 40c multi | 55 | 55 |
| *330* A42 55c multi | 70 | 70 |
| *331* A42 70c multi | 90 | 90 |
| *332* A42 $1.10 multi | 1.40 | 1.40 |
| *a* Souvenir sheet of 6 | 5.50 | 5.50 |
| *Nos. 327-332 (6)* | 3.76 | 3.76 |

Centenary of Montserrat's postage stamps. No. 332a contains one each of Nos. 327-332; blue and black margin showing early cancels and map of packet and mailboat routes. Size: 180x156mm.

Trinity, by Orcagna — A43

Paintings by Orcagna (Andrea di Cione): 40c, Resurrection. 55c, Ascension. $1.10, Pentecost.

*Perf. 14x13½*

**1976, Apr. 5** **Litho.** **Wmk. 373**

| | | |
|---|---|---|
| *333* A43 15c multi | 18 | 18 |
| *334* A43 40c multi | 42 | 42 |
| *335* A43 55c multi | 50 | 50 |
| *336* A43 $1.10 multi | 1.00 | 1.00 |
| *a* Souvenir sheet of 4 | 3.00 | 3.00 |

Easter 1976. Nos. 333-336 were prepared, but not issued in 1975. Stamps are surcharged with new values; date "1975" obliterated with heavy bar. No. 336a contains one each of Nos. 333-336; purple and yellow margin with white cross and lilac rose and black inscription. "1975" in margin obliterated with heavy bar. Size: 157x140mm.

Nos. 235-236, 233 Surcharged

2¢

*Perf. 14½x14*

**1976, Apr. 12** **Photo.** **Wmk. 314**

| | | |
|---|---|---|
| *337* A22 2c on 5c multi | 10 | 10 |
| *338* A22 30c on 10c multi | 95 | 95 |
| *339* A22 45c on 3c multi | 1.50 | 1.50 |

White Frangipani — A44

Designs: Flowering trees of Montserrat.

*Perf. 13½x14*

**1976, July 5** **Litho.** **Wmk. 373**

| | | |
|---|---|---|
| *340* A44 1c *shown* | 5 | 5 |
| *341* A44 2c *Cannonball tree* | 5 | 5 |
| *342* A44 3c *Lignum vitae* | 5 | 5 |
| *343* A44 5c *Malay apple* | 5 | 5 |
| *344* A44 10c *Jacaranda* | 7 | 7 |
| *345* A44 15c *Orchid tree* | 10 | 10 |
| *346* A44 20c *Manjak* | 14 | 14 |
| *347* A44 25c *Tamarind* | 18 | 18 |
| *348* A44 40c *Flame of the Forest* | 28 | 28 |
| *349* A44 55c *Pink cassia* | 40 | 40 |
| *350* A44 70c *Long John* | 50 | 50 |
| *351* A44 $1 *Saman* | 70 | 70 |
| *352* A44 $2.50 *Immortelle* | 1.75 | 1.75 |
| *353* A44 $5 *Yellow poui* | 3.50 | 3.50 |
| *354* A44 $10 *Flamboyant* | 7.00 | 7.00 |
| *Nos. 340-354 (15)* | 14.82 | 14.82 |

Mary and Joseph on Road to Bethlehem — A45

Designs (Map of Montserrat and): 20c, Shepherds. 55c, Virgin and Child. $1.10, Three Kings.

**1976, Oct. 4** ***Perf. 14½***

| | | |
|---|---|---|
| *355* A45 15c vio bl & multi | 24 | 24 |
| *356* A45 20c grn & multi | 28 | 28 |
| *357* A45 55c lil & multi | 65 | 65 |
| *358* A45 $1.10 multi | 1.35 | 1.35 |
| *a* Souvenir sheet of 4 | 4.25 | 4.25 |

Christmas 1976. No. 358a contains one each of Nos. 355-358; greenish blue margin with map of Montserrat, compass rose and violet blue inscription. Size: 118x165mm.

Hudson River Review of Opsail 76
A46 A47

Designs: 40c, Raleigh. 75c, HMS Druid (Raleigh attacking Druid, 1776).

**1976, Dec. 13** **Litho.** ***Perf. 13***

| | | |
|---|---|---|
| *359* A46 15c multi | 25 | 25 |
| *360* A46 40c multi | 60 | 60 |
| *361* A47 75c multi | 1.10 | 1.10 |
| *362* A47 $1.25 multi | 1.75 | 1.75 |
| *a* Souvenir sheet of 4 | 4.00 | 4.00 |

American Bicentennial. 15c and $1.25, 40c and 75c printed se-tenant in sheets of 50. No. 362a contains one each of Nos. 359-362, perf. 14x13½. Stars and stripes in margin. Size: 95x145mm.

Queen Arriving for 1966 Visit, Yacht Britannia — A48

Designs: 45c, Firing of cannons at Tower of London. $1, The crowning.

**1977, Feb. 7**

| | | |
|---|---|---|
| *363* A48 30c multi | 38 | 38 |
| *364* A48 45c multi | 55 | 55 |
| *365* A48 $1 multi | 1.40 | 1.40 |

25th anniversary of the reign of Queen Elizabeth II. Nos. 363-365 were issued also in booklet panes of 4.

Epiphyllum Hookeri — A49

Flowers of the Night: 15c, Ipomoea alba (vert.). 55c, Cereus hexagonus. $1.50, Cestrum nocturnum (vert.).

**1977, June 1** **Litho.** ***Perf. 14***

| | | |
|---|---|---|
| *366* A49 15c multi | 18 | 18 |
| *367* A49 40c multi | 50 | 50 |
| *368* A49 55c multi | 70 | 70 |
| *369* A49 $1.50 multi | 1.90 | 1.90 |
| *a* Souvenir sheet of 4 | 4.50 | 4.50 |

No. 369a contains one each of Nos. 366-369; blue and yellow margin with design descriptions. Size: 126x130mm.

Princess Anne at Ground-breaking Ceremony, Glendon Hospital — A50

Designs: 40c, New deep-water jetty, Plymouth. 55c, Glendon Hospital. $1.50, Freighter unloading at new jetty.

**Wmk. 373**

**1977, Oct. 3** **Litho.** ***Perf. 14½***

| | | |
|---|---|---|
| *370* A50 20c multi | 14 | 14 |
| *371* A50 40c multi | 30 | 30 |
| *372* A50 55c multi | 42 | 42 |
| *373* A50 $1.50 multi | 1.10 | 1.10 |
| *a* Souvenir sheet of 4 | 2.75 | 2.75 |

Development. No. 373a contains one each of Nos. 370-373, multicolored margin shows crane on jetty. Size: 146x105mm.

### Nos. 349-350, 352 Surcharged with New Value and Bars and Overprinted: "SILVER JUBILEE 1977 / ROYAL VISIT / TO THE CARIBBEAN"

**1977, Oct.** **Litho.** ***Perf. 13½x14***

| | | |
|---|---|---|
| *374* A44 $1 on 55c multi | 1.00 | 1.00 |
| *375* A44 $1 on 70c multi | 1.00 | 1.00 |
| *376* A44 $1 on $2.50 multi | 1.00 | 1.00 |

Caribbean visit of Queen Elizabeth II. Surcharge has bars of differing thickness and length. No. 374 has two settings.

"Silent Night, Holy Night" — A51

Christmas Carols and Map of Montserrat: 40c, "We Three Kings of Orient Are." 55c, "I Saw Three Ships Come Sailing In." $2, "Hark the Herald Angels Sing."

**1977, Nov. 14** **Litho.** ***Perf. 14½***

| | | |
|---|---|---|
| *377* A51 5c bl & multi | 5 | 5 |
| *378* A51 40c bis & multi | 25 | 25 |
| *379* A51 55c lt bl & multi | 35 | 35 |
| *380* A51 $2 rose & multi | 1.25 | 1.25 |
| *a* Souvenir sheet of 4 | 3.00 | 3.00 |

Christmas 1977. No. 380a contains one each of Nos. 377-380; dark blue margin shows Angels around crib. Size: 118x115mm.

Four-eye Butterflyfish — A52

Fish: 40c, French angelfish. 55c, Blue tang. $1.50, Queen triggerfish.

**Wmk. 373**

**1978, Feb. 27 Litho. *Perf. 14***

| | | | | |
|---|---|---|---|---|
| *381* | A52 | 30c multi | 30 | 30 |
| *382* | A52 | 40c multi | 40 | 40 |
| *383* | A52 | 55c multi | 55 | 55 |
| *384* | A52 | $1.50 multi | 1.50 | 1.50 |
| *a* | | Souvenir sheet of 4 | 3.75 | 3.75 |

No. 384a contains one each of Nos. 381-384; multicolored margin shows fish. Size: 152x102mm.

Elizabeth II and St. Paul's, London — A53

Designs: 55c, Chichester Cathedral. $1, Lincoln Cathedral. $2.50, Llandaff Cathedral, Cardiff.

**1978, June 2 *Perf. 13½***

| | | | | |
|---|---|---|---|---|
| *385* | A53 | 40c multi | 24 | 24 |
| *386* | A53 | 55c multi | 35 | 35 |
| *387* | A53 | $1 multi | 60 | 60 |
| *388* | A53 | $2.50 multi | 1.50 | 1.50 |
| *a* | | Souvenir sheet of 4 | 2.75 | 2.75 |

25th anniversary of coronation of Elizabeth II, Defender of the Faith. Nos. 385-388 printed in sheets of 10 stamps and 2 labels. No. 388a contains one each of Nos. 385-388; salmon and brown margin. Size: 131x102mm.

Nos. 385-388 were also issued in booklet panes of 2.

Alpinia — A54

Private, 1796 — A55

Flowering Plants: 55c, Allamanda cathartica. $1, Blue tree petrea. $2, Amaryllis.

**1978, Sept. 18 Litho. *Perf. 13½x13***

| | | | | |
|---|---|---|---|---|
| *389* | A54 | 40c multi | 40 | 40 |
| *390* | A54 | 55c multi | 55 | 55 |
| *391* | A54 | $1 multi | 1.00 | 1.00 |
| *392* | A54 | $2 multi | 2.00 | 2.00 |

**1978, Nov. 20 Litho. *Perf. 14½***

Uniforms: 40c, Corporal, 1831. 55c, Sergeant, 1837. $1.50, Officer, 1784.

| | | | | |
|---|---|---|---|---|
| *393* | A55 | 30c multi | 24 | 24 |
| *394* | A55 | 40c multi | 32 | 32 |
| *395* | A55 | 55c multi | 45 | 45 |
| *396* | A55 | $1.50 multi | 1.25 | 1.25 |
| *a* | | Souvenir sheet of 4 | 2.25 | 2.25 |

No. 396a contains Nos. 393-396; light blue margin with red lilac ornaments. Size: 140x89mm. See Nos. 401-404.

Cub Scouts A56

Boy Scouts: 55c, Signaling. $1.25, Cooking (vert.). $2, Flag folding ceremony (vert.).

**1979, Apr. 2 Litho. *Perf. 14***

| | | | | |
|---|---|---|---|---|
| *397* | A56 | 40c multi | 28 | 28 |
| *398* | A56 | 55c multi | 38 | 38 |
| *399* | A56 | $1.25 multi | 85 | 85 |
| *400* | A56 | $2 multi | 1.35 | 1.35 |
| *a* | | Souvenir sheet of 4 | 3.75 | 3.75 |

50th anniversary of Scouting in Montserrat. No. 400a contains Nos. 397-400; yellow and green margin. Size: 120x110mm.

Uniform Type of 1978

Uniforms: 30c, Private, 1783. 40c, Private, 1819. 55c, Officer, 1819. $2.50, Highlander officer, 1830.

**Wmk. 373**

**1979, July 4 Litho. *Perf. 14***

| | | | | |
|---|---|---|---|---|
| *401* | A55 | 30c multi | 24 | 24 |
| *402* | A55 | 40c multi | 32 | 32 |
| *403* | A55 | 55c multi | 42 | 42 |
| *404* | A55 | $2.50 multi | 2.00 | 2.00 |
| *a* | | Souvenir sheet of 4 | 3.00 | 3.00 |

No. 404a contains Nos. 401-404; rose and blue margin. Size: 138x89mm.

IYC Emblem, Learning to Walk — A56a

**1979, Sept. 17 Litho. *Perf. 13½x14***

| | | | | |
|---|---|---|---|---|
| *405* | A56a | $2 brn org & blk | 1.25 | 1.25 |
| *a* | | Souvenir sheet | 3.50 | 3.50 |

International Year of the Child. No. 405a has light green margin showing IYC emblem. Size: 85x99mm.

Hill, Penny Black, Montserrat No. 1 — A57

Designs: 55c, UPU Emblem, charter. $1, UPU Emblem, cover. $2, Hill, Post Office regulations.

**1979, Oct. 1 *Perf. 14***

| | | | | |
|---|---|---|---|---|
| *406* | A57 | 40c multi | 25 | 25 |
| *407* | A57 | 55c multi | 35 | 35 |
| *408* | A57 | $1 multi | 65 | 65 |
| *409* | A57 | $2 multi | 1.35 | 1.35 |
| *a* | | Souvenir sheet of 4 | 7.00 | 7.00 |

Sir Rowland Hill (1795-1879), originator of penny postage; Universal Postal Union membership, centenary. No. 409a contains Nos. 406-409; multicolored margin shows frame of Penny Black. Size: 137x154mm.

Tree Lizard A58

**1980, Feb. 4 Litho. *Perf. 14***

| | | | | |
|---|---|---|---|---|
| *410* | A58 | 40c *Tree frog* | 38 | 38 |
| *411* | A58 | 55c *shown* | 52 | 52 |
| *412* | A58 | $1 *Crapaud* | 95 | 95 |
| *413* | A58 | $2 *Wood slave* | 1.90 | 1.90 |

Marquis of Salisbury; 1817, Postmarks, 1838, London 1980 Emblem — A59

London 1980 Emblem, Ships or Planes, Stamps of Montserrat: 55c, H.S. 748, No. 349. No. 416, La Plata, 1901, type A4. No. 417, Lady Hawkins, 1929, No. 84. No. 418, Avon, 1843, Gt Britain No. 3. No. 419, Aeronca, No. 140.

**1980, Apr. 14 Litho. *Perf. 14½***

| | | | | |
|---|---|---|---|---|
| *414* | A59 | 40c multi | 32 | 32 |
| *415* | A59 | 55c multi | 45 | 45 |
| *416* | A59 | $1.20 multi | 95 | 95 |
| *417* | A59 | $1.20 multi | 95 | 95 |
| *418* | A59 | $1.20 multi | 95 | 95 |
| *419* | A59 | $1.20 multi | 95 | 95 |
| *a* | | Souvenir sheet of 6 | 5.25 | 5.25 |
| | | *Nos. 414-419 (6)* | 4.57 | 4.57 |

London 1980 International Stamp Exhibition, May 6-14. No. 419a contains Nos. 414-419; margin shows London 1980 emblem. Size: 115x109mm.

No. 352 Overprinted: 75th Anniversary of / Rotary International

**1980, July 7 Litho. *Perf. 13½x14***

| | | | | |
|---|---|---|---|---|
| *420* | A44 | $2.50 multi | 1.65 | 1.65 |

Discus Thrower, Stadium, Olympic Rings — A60

Olympic Rings and Flags of Host Countries: 40c, Greece, 1896; France, 1900; U.S.A., 1904. 55c, Great Britain, 1908; Sweden, 1912; Belgium, 1920. 70c, France, 1924; Netherlands, 1928; U.S.A., 1932. $1, Germany, 1936; Great Britain, 1948; Finland, 1952. $1.50, Australia, 1956; Italy, 1960; Japan, 1964. $2, Mexico, 1968,; Fed. Rep. of Germany, 1972; Canada, 1976.

**1980, July 7 Litho. *Perf. 14***

| | | | | |
|---|---|---|---|---|
| *421* | A60 | 40c multi | 22 | 22 |
| *422* | A60 | 55c multi | 32 | 32 |
| *423* | A60 | 70c multi | 40 | 40 |
| *424* | A60 | $1 multi | 60 | 60 |
| *425* | A60 | $1.50 multi | 90 | 90 |
| *426* | A60 | $2 multi | 1.25 | 1.25 |
| *427* | A60 | $2.50 multi | 1.50 | 1.50 |
| *a* | | Souvenir sheet of 7 | 5.25 | |
| | | *Nos. 421-427 (7)* | 5.19 | 5.19 |

22nd Summer Olympic Games, Moscow, July 19-Aug. 3. No. 427a contains Nos. 421-427; 2 multicolored labels show Olympic torch and rings. Size: 150x101mm.

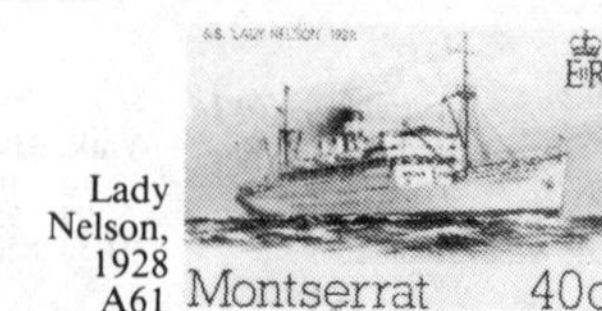
Lady Nelson, 1928 A61

**1980 Litho. *Perf. 14***

| | | | | |
|---|---|---|---|---|
| *428* | A61 | 40c *shown* | 22 | 22 |
| *429* | A61 | 55c *Chignecto, 1913* | 32 | 32 |
| *430* | A61 | $1 *Solent, 1878* | 60 | 60 |
| *431* | A61 | $2 *Dee, 1841* | 1.25 | 1.25 |



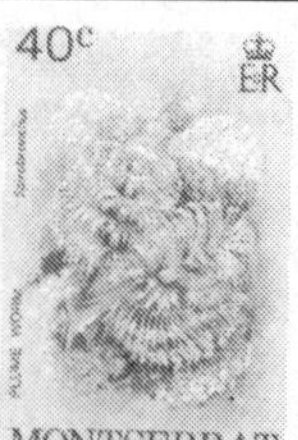
Plume Worm — A62

**1980 Litho. *Perf. 14***

| | | | | |
|---|---|---|---|---|
| *432* | A62 | 40c *shown* | 45 | 45 |
| *433* | A62 | 55c *Sea fans* | 60 | 60 |
| *434* | A62 | $2 *Coral, sponges* | 2.25 | 2.25 |

Nos. 340, 342, 345, 348 Surcharged.

**1980, Sept. 30 Litho. *Perf. 14***

| | | | | |
|---|---|---|---|---|
| *435* | A44 | 5c on 3c (#342) | 5 | 5 |
| *436* | A44 | 35c on 1c (#340) | 22 | 22 |
| *437* | A44 | 35c on 3c (#342) | 22 | 22 |
| *438* | A44 | 35c on 15c (#345) | 22 | 22 |
| *439* | A44 | 55c on 40c (#348) | 35 | 35 |
| *440* | A44 | $5 on 40c (#348) | 3.25 | 3.25 |
| | | *Nos. 435-440 (6)* | 4.31 | 4.31 |

Zebra Butterfly — A63

Spadefish — A64

**1981, Feb. 2 Wmk. 373**

| | | | | |
|---|---|---|---|---|
| *441* | A63 | 50c shown | 42 | 42 |
| *442* | A63 | 65c Tropical checkered skipper | 55 | 55 |
| *443* | A63 | $1.50 Large orange sulphur | 1.25 | 1.25 |
| *444* | A63 | $2.50 Monarch | 2.25 | 2.25 |

**Wmk. 373**

**1981, Mar. 20 Litho. *Perf. 13½***

| | | | | |
|---|---|---|---|---|
| *445* | A64 | 5c shown | 5 | 5 |
| *446* | A64 | 10c Hogfish | 6 | 5 |
| *447* | A64 | 15c Creole wrasse | 9 | 7 |
| *448* | A64 | 20c Yellow damselfish | 12 | 10 |
| *449* | A64 | 25c Sergeant major | 15 | 12 |
| *450* | A64 | 35c Clown wrasse | 22 | 18 |
| *451* | A64 | 45c Schoolmaster | 28 | 22 |
| *452* | A64 | 55c Striped parrotfish | 35 | 28 |
| *453* | A64 | 65c Bigeye | 40 | 32 |
| *454* | A64 | 75c French grunt | 45 | 38 |
| *455* | A64 | $1 Rock beauty | 60 | 50 |
| *456* | A64 | $2 Blue chromis | 1.25 | 1.00 |
| *457* | A64 | $3 Fairy basslet, blueheads | 1.90 | 1.50 |
| *458* | A64 | $5 Cherubfish | 3.00 | 2.50 |
| *459* | A64 | $7.50 Longspine squirrelfish | 4.50 | 3.75 |
| *460* | A64 | $10 Longsnout butterflyfish | 6.00 | 5.00 |
| | | *Nos. 445-460 (16)* | 19.42 | 16.02 |

Inscribed 1983

**1983 Wmk. 380**

| | | | | |
|---|---|---|---|---|
| *445a* | A64 | 5c | 5 | 5 |
| *446a* | A64 | 10c | 7 | 7 |
| *449a* | A64 | 25c | 16 | 16 |
| *450a* | A64 | 35c | 24 | 24 |
| *454a* | A64 | 75c | 50 | 50 |
| *455a* | A64 | $1 | 65 | 65 |
| *458a* | A64 | $5 | 3.25 | 3.25 |
| *460a* | A64 | $10 | 6.50 | 6.50 |
| | | *Nos. 445a-460a (8)* | 11.42 | 11.42 |

Fort St. George (National Trust) — A65

**Wmk. 373**

**1981, May 18 Litho. *Perf. 13½***

*461* A65 50c shown 32 32
*462* A65 65c Bird Sanctuary, Fox's Bay 42 42
*463* A65 $1.50 The Museum 1.00 1.00
*464* A65 $2.50 Bransby Point Battery 1.65 1.65

Prince Charles, Lady Diana, Royal Yacht Charlotte A66

Prince Charles and Lady Diana — A67

Illustration A67 is greatly reduced.

**Wmk. 380**

**1981, July 13 Litho. *Perf. 14***

*465* A66 90c shown 70 70
*a* Bklt pane of 4, perf. 12 3.00
*466* A67 90c shown 70 70
*467* A66 $3 Portsmouth 2.50 2.50
*468* A67 $3 like #466 2.50 2.50
*a* Bklt pane of 2, perf. 12 5.00
*469* A66 $4 Britannia 3.25 3.25
*470* A67 $4 like #466 3.25 3.25
*Nos. 465-470 (6)* 12.90 12.90

Royal wedding. Each denomination issued in sheets of 7 (6 type A66, 1 type A67).

**1981, Dec. Souvenir Sheet *Perf. 12***

*471* A67 $5 multi 3.25 3.25

No. 471 has light ultramarine decorative margin. Size: 120x109mm.

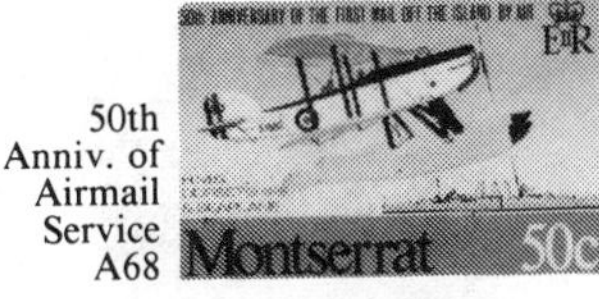


50th Anniv. of Airmail Service A68

**Wmk. 373**

**1981, Aug. 31 Litho. *Perf. 14***

*472* A68 50c Seaplane, Dorsetshire 35 35
*473* A68 65c Beechcraft Twin Bonanza 45 45
*474* A68 $1.50 DeHaviland Dragon Rapide 1.00 1.00
*475* A68 $2.50 Hawker Siddeley Avro 748 1.75 1.75

Methodist Church, Bethel — A69

Christmas 1981 (Churches): 65c, St. George's Anglican, Harris. $1.50, St. Peter's Anglican, St. Peter's. $2.50, St. Patrick's Roman Catholic, Plymouth.

**Wmk. 373**

**1981, Nov. 16 Litho. *Perf. 14***

*476* A69 50c multi 35 35
*477* A69 65c multi 45 45
*478* A69 $1.50 multi 1.00 1.00
*479* A69 $2.50 multi 1.75 1.75
*a* Souvenir sheet of 4 3.75 3.75

No. 479a contains Nos. 476-479; multicolored margin shows St. Anthony's Anglican Church, Plymouth. Size: 177x122mm.

Wild Flowers First Discovered on Montserrat — A70

**1982, Jan. 18 Litho. *Perf. 14½***

*480* A70 50c Rondeletia buxifolia, vert. 35 35
*481* A70 65c Heliotropium ternatum 45 45
*482* A70 $1.50 Picramnia pentandra, vert. 1.00 1.00
*483* A70 $2.50 Diospyros revoluta 1.75 1.75

300th Anniv. of Settlement of Montserrat by Sir Thomas Warner — A70a

Jubilee Type of 1932.

**Wmk. 373**

**1982, Apr. 17 Litho. *Perf. 14½***

*483A* A70a 40c green 30 30
*483B* A70a 55c red 42 42
*483C* A70a 65c brown 48 48
*483D* A70a 75c gray 55 55
*483E* A70a 85c ultra 65 65
*483F* A70a 95c orange 70 70
*483G* A70a $1 purple 75 75
*483H* A70a $1.50 olive 1.10 1.10
*483I* A70a $2 car rose 1.50 1.50
*483J* A70a $2.50 sepia 1.90 1.90
*Nos. 483A-483J (10)* 8.35 8.35

Princess Diana Type of Kiribati

**Wmk. 380**

**1982, June Litho. *Perf. 14***

*484* A64 75c Catherine of Aragon, 1501 60 60
*485* A64 $1 Aragon arms 80 80
*486* A64 $5 Diana 4.00 4.00

Scouting Year — A71

**1982, Sept. 13 Litho. *Perf. 14***

*487* A71 $1.50 Scout 1.10 1.10
*488* A71 $2.50 Baden-Powell 1.75 1.75

Christmas 1982 — A72

**Wmk. 373**

**1982, Nov. 18 Litho. *Perf. 14***

*489* A72 35c Annunciation 24 24
*490* A72 75c Shepherds' vision 50 50
*491* A72 $1.50 Virgin and Child 1.00 1.00
*492* A72 $2.50 Flight into Egypt 1.65 1.65

Dragonflies — A73

***Perf. 13½x14***

**1983, Jan. 19 Litho. Wmk. 373**

*493* A73 50c Lepthemis vesiculosa 35 35
*494* A73 65c Orthemis ferruginea 45 45
*495* A73 $1.50 Triacanthagyna trifida 1.10 1.10
*496* A73 $2.50 Erythrodiplax umbrata 1.75 1.75

Blue-headed Hummingbird A74

**Wmk. 373**

**1983, May 24 Litho. *Perf. 14***

*497* A74 35c shown 32 32
*498* A74 75c Green-throated carib 70 70
*499* A74 $2 Antillean crested hummingbird 1.90 1.90
*500* A74 $3 Purple-throated carib 2.75 2.75

Manned Flight Bicentenary — A76

**Wmk. 373**

**1983, Sept. 19 Litho. *Perf. 14***

*503* A76 35c Montgolfiere, 1783, vert. 24 24
*504* A76 75c De Havilland Twin Otter 310, 1981 52 52
*505* A76 $1.50 Lockheed Vega's around the world flight, 1933 1.00 1.00
*506* A76 $2 British R34 airship transatlantic flight, 1919 1.40 1.40
*a* Souvenir sheet 3.50 3.50

No. 506a contains Nos. 503-506. Size: 109x145mm.

Nos. 449, 446, 467-468, 453-454, 469-470, 456 Surcharged.

**Wmk. 373 (A64), 380**

**1983, Aug. 15 Litho. *Perf. 13½x14***

*507* A64 40c on 25c multi 45 45
*508* A64 70c on 10c multi 75 75
*509* A66 70c on $3 multi 75 75
*510* A67 70c on $3 multi 75 75
*511* A64 90c on 65c multi 1.00 1.00
*512* A64 $1.15 on 75c multi 1.25 1.25
*513* A66 $1.15 on $4 multi 1.25 1.25
*514* A67 $1.15 on $4 multi 1.25 1.25
*515* A64 $1.50 on $2 multi 1.75 1.75
*Nos. 507-515 (9)* 9.20 9.20

Christmas Carnival 1983 — A77

**Wmk. 380**

**1983, Nov. 18 Litho. *Perf. 14***

*516* A77 55c Clowns 40 40
*517* A77 90c Star Bursts 65 65
*518* A77 $1.15 Flower Girls 85 85
*519* A77 $2 Masqueraders 1.50 1.50

See Nos. 547-550.

1984 Summer Olympics — A78

**Wmk. 380**

**1984, Mar. 6 Litho. *Perf. 14***

*520* A78 90c Discobolus 60 60
*521* A78 $1 Torch 65 65
*522* A78 $1.15 Stadium 75 75
*523* A78 $2.50 Flags 1.65 1.65
*a* Souvenir sheet of 4 4.25 4.25

No. 523a contains Nos. 520-523.

Cattle Egret A79

**1984, May 11**

*524* A79 5c shown 5 5
*525* A79 10c Carib grackles 7 7
*526* A79 15c Common gallinule 8 8
*527* A79 20c Brown boobys 10 10
*528* A79 25c Black-whiskered vireos 14 14
*529* A79 40c Scaly-breasted thrashers 20 20
*530* A79 55c Laughing gulls 30 30
*531* A79 70c Glossy ibis 36 36
*532* A79 90c Green heron 52 52
*533* A79 $1 Belted kingfisher 55 55
*534* A79 $1.15 Bananaquits 65 65
*535* A79 $3 Sparrow hawks 1.75 1.75
*536* A79 $5 Forest thrush 2.75 2.75
*537* A79 $7.50 Black-crowned night heron 4.25 4.25
*538* A79 $10 Bridled quail doves 5.50 5.50
*Nos. 524-538 (15)* 17.27 17.27

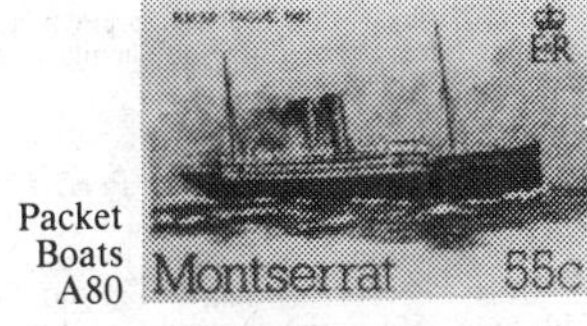


Packet Boats A80

**Wmk. 380**

**1984, July 9 Litho. *Perf. 14***

*539* A80 55c Tagus, 1907 45 45
*540* A80 90c Cobequid, 1913 80 80
*541* A80 $1.15 Lady Drake, 1942 1.00 1.00
*542* A80 $2 Factor, 1948 1.75 1.75
*a* Souvenir sheet of 4 4.00 4.00

No. 542a contains Nos. 539-542; multicolored margin shows early editions of Lloyd's List newspaper (250th anniv.); Lutine Bell. Size: 153x102mm.

Marine Life A81

The lack of a price for a listed item does not necessarily indicate rarity.

**Wmk. 380**

**1984, Sept. Litho.** ***Perf. 14***

*543* A81 90c Top shell & hermit crab 65 65
*544* A81 $1.15 Rough file shell 80 80
*545* A81 $1.50 True tulip snail 1.10 1.10
*546* A81 $2.50 West Indian fighting conch 2.00 2.00

Christmas Carnival Type of 1983

**1984, Nov. 12**

*547* A77 55c Bull Man 40 40
*548* A77 $1.15 Masquerader Captain 85 85
*549* A77 $1.50 Carnival Queen contestant 1.15 1.15
*550* A77 $2.30 Contestant, diff. 1.75 1.75

National Emblems — A82

**1985, Feb. 8 Litho.** ***Perf. 14***

*551* A82 $1.15 Mango 90 90
*552* A82 $1.50 Lobster Claw 1.20 1.20
*553* A82 $3 Montserrat Oriole 2.50 2.50

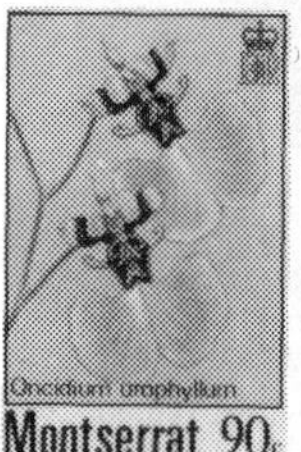


Indigenous Orchids — A83

Queen Mother, 85th Birthday — A84

**Wmk. 380**

**1985, May 9 Litho.** ***Perf. 14***

*554* A83 90c Oncidium urophyllum 70 70
*555* A83 $1.15 Epidendrum difforme 95 95
*556* A83 $1.50 Epidendrum ciliare 1.25 1.25
*557* A83 $2.50 Brassavola cucullata 2.00 2.00
*a* Souvenir sheet of 4, #554-557 5.00 5.00

No. 557a has multicolored margin picturing Epidendrum secundum and Sacoila lanceolata. Size: 121x140mm.

**1985, Aug. 7 Unwmk.** ***Perf. 12½***

Portraits.

*558* A84 55c Facing right 40 40
*559* A84 55c Facing forward 40 40
*560* A84 90c Facing right, diff. 65 65
*561* A84 90c Facing left 65 65
*562* A84 $1.15 Facing right, diff. 85 85
*563* A84 $1.15 Glancing right 85 85
*564* A84 $1.50 Facing right, diff. 1.10 1.10
*565* A84 $1.50 Facing left, diff. 1.10 1.10
*Nos. 558-565 (8)* 6.00 6.00

**Souvenir Sheets**

*566* Sheet of 2 3.25 3.25
*a* A84 $2.00 Facing right, diff. 1.50 1.50
*b* A84 $2.00 Facing forward, diff. 1.50 1.50

**1986, Jan. 10**

*567* Sheet of 2 5.50 5.50
*a* A84 $3.50 like #564 2.75 2.75
*b* A84 $3.50 like #565 2.75 2.75
*568* Sheet of 2 9.00 9.00
*a* A84 $6 like #558 4.50 4.50
*b* A84 $6 like #559 4.50 4.50

Stamps of the same denomination printed se-tenant. Nos. 566-568 have multicolored margins picturing Glamis Castle or the Concorde, flora and fauna. Sizes: 86x114mm, 141x109mm (#567-568).

Cotton Industry A85

**Unwmk.**

**1985, Sept. 23 Litho.** ***Perf. 15***

*569* A85 90c Cotton, lemon, magenta, Soufriere Hills 55 55
*570* A85 $1 Carding 65 65
*571* A85 $1.15 Automated loom 70 70
*572* A85 $2.50 Hand loom 1.60 1.60
*a* Souvenir sheet of 4, #569-572 3.50 3.50

No. 572a has multicolored decorative margin picturing plants in bloom. Size: 148x103mm.

Nos. 504, 484, 562-563, 505, 469-470 Ovptd. or Surcharged "CARIBBEAN ROYAL VISIT 1985" in 2 or 3 Lines.

***Perf. 14, 12½ ($1.15)***

**Wmk. as Before**

**1985, Nov. 14 Litho.**

*573* A76 75c multi 3.00 3.00
*574* A64 $1 multi 4.25 4.25
*575* A84 $1.15 multi 4.75 4.75
*576* A84 $1.15 multi 4.75 4.75
*577* A76 $1.50 multi 6.00 6.00
*578* A66 $1.60 on $4 multi 3.00 3.00
*579* A67 $1.60 on $4 multi 10.00 10.00
*Nos. 573-579 (7)* 35.75 35.75

Nos. 575-576 printed se-tenant. Nos. 578-579 issued in sheets of 7 (6 type A66, 1 type A67). No. 579 surcharged but not overprinted.

Audubon Birth Bicentenary A86

Illustrations of North American bird species by John J. Audubon.

**1985, Nov. 29 Unwmk.** ***Perf. 12½***

*580* A86 15c Black-throated blue warbler 12 12
*581* A86 15c Palm warbler 12 12
*582* A86 30c Bobolink 24 24
*583* A86 30c Lark sparrow 24 24
*584* A86 55c Chipping sparrow 40 40
*585* A86 55c Northern oriole 40 40
*586* A86 $2.50 American goldfinch 1.85 1.85
*587* A86 $2.50 Blue grosbeak 1.85 1.85
*Nos. 580-587 (8)* 5.22 5.22

Stamps of the same denomination printed se-tenant.

Christmas A87

**1985, Dec. 2 Wmk. 380** ***Perf. 15***

*588* A87 70c Angel of the Lord 52 52
*589* A87 $1.15 Three wise men 85 85
*590* A87 $1.50 Caroling, Plymouth War Memorial 1.10 1.10
*591* A87 $2.30 Our Lady of Montserrat 1.75 1.75

Girl Guides, 50th Anniv. — A88

**1986, Apr. 11**

*592* A88 20c Lord Baden-Powell 20 20
*593* A88 20c Guide saluting 20 20
*594* A88 75c Lady Baden-Powell 70 70
*595* A88 75c Guide cutting hair 70 70
*596* A88 90c Lord and Lady Baden-Powell 85 85
*597* A88 90c Guides in public service 85 85
*598* A88 $1.15 Troop inspection, 1936 1.10 1.10
*599* A88 $1.15 Guides saluting 1.10 1.10
*Nos. 592-599 (8)* 5.70 5.70

Stamps of same denomination printed se-tenant.

Queen Elizabeth II, 60th Birthday — A89

Various portraits.

**1986, Apr. 11 Unwmk.** ***Perf. 12½***

*600* A89 10c multi 9 9
*601* A89 $1.50 multi 1.25 1.25
*602* A89 $3 multi 2.50 2.50
*603* A89 $6 multi, vert. 5.00 5.00

**Souvenir Sheet**

*604* A89 $8 multi 7.00 7.00

No. 604 has multicolored margin picturing portrait enlargement. Size: 86x115mm.

Halley's Comet — A90

Designs: 35c, Bayeux Tapestry (detail), 1066 sighting. 50c, Adoration of the Magi, by Giotto. 70c, Edmond Halley, trajectory diagram, 1531 sighting. $1, Sightings, 1066 and 1910. $1.15, Sighting, 1910. $1.50, Giotto space probe, comet, diagram. $2.30, US Space Telescope, comet. $4, Computer picture of photograph, 1910.

**1986, May 9** ***Perf. 14***

*605* A90 35c multi 32 32
*606* A90 50c multi 48 48
*607* A90 70c multi 65 65
*608* A90 $1 multi 95 95
*609* A90 $1.15 multi 1.10 1.10
*610* A90 $1.50 multi 1.40 1.40
*611* A90 $2.30 multi 2.25 2.25
*612* A90 $4 multi 3.75 3.75
*Nos. 605-612 (8)* 10.90 10.90

See Nos. 625-626.

Wedding of Prince Andrew and Sarah Ferguson — A91

Design: No. 613, Andrew, vert. No. 614, Sarah, vert. No. 615, Andrew wearing cowboy hat. No. 616, Sarah wearing fur hat.

***Perf. 12½x13, 13x12½***

**1986, July 23 Litho.**

*613* A91 70c multi 52 52
*614* A91 70c multi 52 52
*615* A91 $2 multi 1.50 1.50
*616* A91 $2 multi 1.50 1.50

Stamps of the same denomination printed se-tenant.

Clipper Ships A92

**1986, Aug. 29** ***Perf. 14***

*617* A92 90c Antelope, 1793 68 68
*618* A92 $1.15 Montagu, 1840 85 85
*619* A92 $1.50 Little Catherine, 1813 1.10 1.10
*620* A92 $2.30 Hinchingbrook, 1813 1.70 1.70
*a* Souvenir sheet of 4, #617-620 4.35 4.35

No. 620a has multicolored margin picturing 19th century pistol, letters, map and dividers. Size: 163x124mm.

Communications — A93

Designs: 70c, Radio Montserrat, near Dagenham. $1.15, Radio Gem ZGM-FM 94, Plymouth. $1.50, Radio Antilles, O'Garro's. $2.30, Cable & Wireless telegraph office, Plymouth.

**Wmk. 380**

**1986, Sept. 29 Litho.** ***Perf. 14***

*621* A93 70c multi 52 52
*622* A93 $1.15 multi 85 85
*623* A93 $1.50 multi 1.10 1.10
*624* A93 $2.30 multi 1.70 1.70

Halley's Comet Type of 1986

**Unwmk.**

**1986, Oct. 10 Litho.** ***Perf. 14***

**Souvenir Sheets**

*625* Sheet of 4 5.35 5.35
*a* A90 40c like #605 30 30
*b* A90 $1.75 like #606 1.30 1.30
*c* A90 $2 like #607 1.50 1.50
*d* A90 $3 like #608 2.25 2.25
*626* Sheet of 4 5.25 5.25
*a* A90 55c like #609 40 40
*b* A90 60c like #610 45 45
*c* A90 80c like #611 60 60
*d* A90 $5 like #612 3.75 3.75

Nos. 625-626 have multicolored decorative margins. Sizes: 140x115mm.

Souvenir Sheet

Wedding of Prince Andrew and Sarah Ferguson — A94

**1986, Oct. 15** *Perf. 13x12½*
627 A94 $10 multi 7.50 7.50

No. 627 has multicolored margin continuing the photograph. Size: 115x85mm.

Nos. 613-616 Ovptd. in Silver: "Congratulations to T.R.H. The Duke & Duchess of York"

*Perf. 12½x13, 13x12½*
**1986, Nov. 14** **Litho.**
628 A91 70c No. 613 52 52
629 A91 70c No. 614 52 52
630 A91 $2 No. 615 1.50 1.50
631 A91 $2 No. 616 1.50 1.50

Stamps of the same denomination exist printed tete-beche and se-tenant.

Christmas — A95

**Unwmk.**
**1986, Dec. 12** **Litho.** *Perf. 14*
632 A95 70c Christmas rose 55 55
633 A95 $1.15 Candle flower 90 90
634 A95 $1.50 Christmas tree kalanchoe 1.20 1.20
635 A95 $2.30 Snow on the mountain 1.85 1.85
*a* Souv. sheet of 4, perf. 12x12½ 4.50 4.50

No. 635a has multicolored inscribed margin picturing jumbie table. Size: 149x109mm.

**Souvenir Sheets**

Statue of Liberty, Cent. — A96

**1986, Nov. 18** **Litho.** *Perf. 14*
636 A96 $3 Statue, pedestal 2.40 2.40
637 A96 $4.50 Head 3.60 3.60
638 A96 $5 Statue, New York City 4.00 4.00

Nos. 636-638 have multicolored margins picturing different views of statue and presidents George Washington, Andrew Jackson or Millard Fillmore. Sizes: 85x115mm.

Sailing A97

**1986, Dec. 10** *Perf. 15*
639 A97 70c shown 55 55
640 A97 $1.15 Golf 90 90
641 A97 $1.50 Plymouth Public Market 1.20 1.20
642 A97 $2.30 Air Studios 1.85 1.85

Sharks A98

**Wmk. 380**
**1987, Feb. 2** **Litho.** *Perf. 14*
643 A98 40c Tiger 32 32
644 A98 90c Lemon 72 72
645 A98 $1.15 White 90 90
646 A98 $3.50 Whale 2.75 2.75
*a* Souv. sheet of 4, #643-646, Perf. 12½x12 4.00 4.00

No. 646a has multicolored margin picturing marine habitat. Size: 150x102mm.

Butterflies — A99

**Wmk. 380**
**1987, Aug. 10** **Litho.** *Perf. 14*
647 A99 90c Straight-line sulpher 70 70
648 A99 $1.15 Red rim 90 90
649 A99 $1.50 Hammock skipper 1.20 1.20
650 A99 $2.50 Mimic 2.00 2.00

Nos. 521, 527, 525, 532 and 535 Surcharged

**1987, Apr. 6**
651 A79 5c on 70c multi 5 5
652 A79 $1 on 20c multi 80 80
653 A79 $1.15 on 10c multi 90 90
654 A79 $1.50 on 90c multi 1.20 1.20
655 A79 $2.50 on $3 multi 1.85 1.85
*Nos. 651-655 (5)* 4.80 4.80

Nos. 625-626 Ovptd. for CAPEX '87 in Red and Black

**Souvenir Sheets**

**1987, June 13** **Unwmk.**
656 Sheet of 4 5.35 5.35
*a* A90 40c on No. 625a 30 30
*b* A90 $1.75 on No. 625b 1.30 1.30
*c* A90 $2 on No. 625c 1.50 1.50
*d* A90 $3 on No. 625d 2.25 2.25
657 Sheet of 4 5.25 5.25
*a* A90 55c on No. 626a 40 40
*b* A90 60c on No. 626b 45 45
*c* A90 80c on No. 626c 60 60
*d* A90 $5 on No. 626d 3.75 3.75

Orchids — A100

**Unwmk.**
**1987, Nov. 13** **Litho.** *Perf. 14*
658 A100 90c Oncidium variegatum, vert. 68 68
659 A100 $1.15 Vanilla planifolia 85 85
660 A100 $1.50 Gongora quinquenervis, vert. 1.15 1.15
661 A100 $3.50 Brassavola nodosa 2.60 2.60

**Souvenir Sheet**
662 A100 $5 Oncidium lanceanum 3.75 3.75

Christmas. No. 662 has multicolored margin continuing the design. Size: 100x75mm.

Nos. 525, 528-529 and 532 Surcharged and Ovptd. "40th Wedding Anniversary / HM Queen Elizabeth II / HRH Duke of Edinburgh / November 1987."

**Wmk. 380**
**1987, Nov. 20** **Litho.** *Perf. 14*
663 A79 5c on 90c No. 532 68 68
664 A79 $1.15 on 10c No. 525 85 85
665 A79 $2.30 on 25c No. 528 1.85 1.85
666 A79 $5 on 40c No. 529 3.75 3.75

Exists spelled "Edingburgh."

Tropical Bats — A101

**Wmk. 380**
**1988, Feb. 8** **Litho.** *Perf. 14*
667 A101 55c Free-tailed bat 38 38
668 A101 90c Fruit bat 68 68
669 A101 $1.15 Fisherman bat 85 85
670 A101 $2.30 Fruit bat, diff. 1.70 1.70

**Souvenir Sheet**
671 A101 $2.50 Funnel-eared bat 1.90 1.90

No. 671 has multicolored decorative margin picturing bats in flight at dusk and informative text. Size: 133x110mm.

Marine Birds — A102

**1988, Apr. 2** **Unwmk.**
672 A102 90c Magnificent frigatebird 70 70
673 A102 $1.15 Caribbean elaenia 90 90
674 A102 $1.50 Glossy ibis 1.20 1.20
675 A102 $3.50 Purple-throated carib 2.75 2.75

**Souvenir Sheet**
676 A102 $5 Brown pelican 4.00 4.00

Easter 1988. No. 676 has multicolored inscribed margin picturing brown pelicans in flight. Size: 100x75mm.

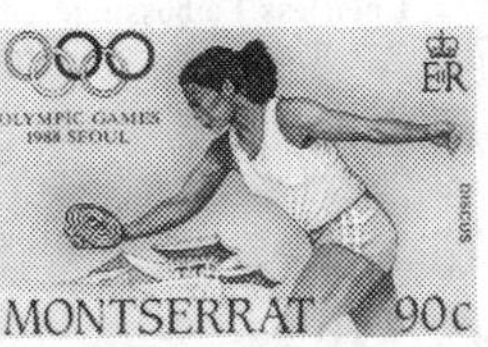

1988 Summer Olympics, Seoul — A103

Eastern architecture and events: 90c, Women's discus. $1.15, High jump. $3.50, Women's 200-meter and Seoul university building. $5, Single scull rowing, pagoda.

**Unwmk.**
**1988, July 29** **Litho.** *Perf. 14*
677 A103 90c multi 68 68
678 A103 $1.15 multi 88 88
679 A103 $3.50 multi 2.65 2.65

**Souvenir Sheet**
680 A103 $5 multi 3.75 3.75

No. 680 has multicolored background picturing double-sculls, spectators and flags. Size: 103x78mm.

Sea Shells A104

**1988, Aug. 30**
681 A104 5c Golden tulip 5 5
682 A104 10c Little knobby scallop 8 8
683 A104 15c Sozoni's cone 12 12
684 A104 20c Globular coral shell 15 15
685 A104 25c Sundial 18 18
686 A104 40c King helmet 30 30
687 A104 55c Channeled turban 42 42
688 A104 70c True tulip shell 52 52
689 A104 90c Music volute 68 68
690 A104 $1 Flame auger 75 75
691 A104 $1.15 Rooster-tail conch 88 88
692 A104 $1.50 Queen conch 1.15 1.15
693 A104 $3 Teramachi's slit shell 2.25 2.25
694 A104 $5 Florida crown conch 3.75 3.75
695 A104 $7.50 Beau's murex 5.60 5.60
696 A104 $10 Triton's trumpet 7.50 7.50
*Nos. 681-696 (16)* 24.38 24.38

University of the West Indies, 40th Anniv. — A105

**1988** **Litho.** *Perf. 14*
697 A105 $5 multi 3.75 3.75

**WAR TAX STAMPS**

No. 43 Overprinted in Red or Black **WAR STAMP**

**1917-18** **Wmk. 3** *Perf. 14*
MR1 A6 ½p green (R) 15 15
MR2 A6 ½p green ('18) 15 15

Type of Regular Issue of 1919 Overprinted **WAR STAMP**

**1918**
MR3 A6 1½p orange & black 25 25

Denomination on No. MR3 in black on white ground. Two dots under "d".

---

**OFFICIAL STAMPS**

Nos. 235-236, 338-339 Overprinted **O.H.M.S.**

*Perf. 12½x14*
**1976, Apr. 12** **Photo.** **Wmk. 314**
O1 A22 5c multi 2.85
O2 A22 10c multi 4.00
O3 A22 30c on 10c multi 8.00
O4 A22 45c on 3c multi 10.00

Used on Post Office and Philatelic Bureau mail. Not sold to public, used or unused.
Nos. 243-243A, also received this overprint.

Nos. 343-347, 349-351, 353 Overprinted

***O.H.M.S.***

**Perf. 13½x14**

**1976, Oct. 1 Litho. Wmk. 373**

*O10* A44 5c multi 5
*O11* A44 10c multi 7
*O12* A44 15c multi 10
*O13* A44 20c multi 14
*O14* A44 25c multi 18
*O15* A44 55c multi 40
*O16* A44 70c multi 50
*O17* A44 $1 multi 70
*O18* A44 $5 multi 3.50
*O19* A44 $10 multi 7.00
*Nos. O10-O19 (10)* 12.64

Nos. 343-347, 349-351, 353-354 Overprinted O.H.M.S.

**Wmk. 373**

**1980, Sept. 30 Litho. *Perf. 14***

*O20* A44 5c multi 5
*O21* A44 10c multi 6
*O22* A44 15c multi 9
*O23* A44 20c multi 12
*O24* A44 25c multi 15
*O25* A44 55c multi 35
*O26* A44 70c multi 45
*O27* A44 $1 multi 65
*O28* A44 $5 multi 3.25
*O29* A44 $10 multi 6.50
*Nos. O20-O29 (10)* 11.67

Available only canceled.

Nos. 341-351, 353-354 Overprinted or Surcharged O.H.M.S.

**1980, Sept. 30 Litho. *Perf. 14***

*O30* A44 5c multi 5
*O31* A44 5c on 3c multi 5
*O32* A44 10c multi 8
*O33* A44 15c multi 12
*O34* A44 20c multi 16
*O35* A44 25c multi 20
*O36* A44 30c on 15c multi 25
*O37* A44 35c on 2c multi 42
*O38* A44 40c multi 32
*O39* A44 55c multi 45
*O40* A44 70c multi 60
*O41* A44 $1 multi 80
*O42* A44 $2.50 on 40c multi 2.00
*O43* A44 $5 multi 4.00
*O44* A44 $10 multi 8.00
*Nos. O30-O44 (15)* 17.50

Available only canceled.

**Catalogue values for unused stamps in this section, from this point to the end of the section, are for Never Hinged items.**

Fish Type of 1981 Nos. 445-449, 451, 453, 455, 457-458, 460 Overprinted O.H.M.S.

**1981, Mar. 20 Litho. *Perf. 13½***

*O45* A64 5c multi 5 5
*O46* A64 10c multi 8 8
*O47* A64 15c multi 12 12
*O48* A64 20c multi 16 16
*O49* A64 25c multi 20 20
*O50* A64 45c multi 35 35
*O51* A64 65c multi 50 50
*O52* A64 $1 multi 75 75
*O53* A64 $3 multi 2.25 2.25
*O54* A64 $5 multi 3.75 3.75
*O55* A64 $10 multi 7.50 7.50
*Nos. O45-O55 (11)* 15.71 15.71

Nos. 465-470 Surcharged O.H.M.S. and New Value

**1982, Nov. 17 Litho. *Perf. 14***

*O56* A66 45c on 90c (#465) 30 30
*O57* A67 45c on 90c (#466) 30 30
*O58* A66 75c on $3 (#467) 50 50
*O59* A67 75c on $3 (#468) 50 50
*O60* A66 $1 On $4 (#469) 65 65
*O61* A67 $1 on $4 (#470) 65 65
*Nos. O56-O61 (6)* 2.90 2.90

Nos. 484-486 Overprinted or Surcharged O.H.M.S.

**1983, Oct. 19 Litho. *Perf. 14***

*O62* A64 70c on 75c (#484) 50 50
*O63* A64 $1 (#485) 70 70
*O64* A64 $1.50 on $5 (#486) 1.00 1.00

Nos. 524-536, 538 Ovptd. "OHMS"

**Wmk. 380**

**1985, Apr. 12 Litho. *Perf. 14***

*O65* A79 5c multi 5 5
*O66* A79 10c multi 7 7
*O67* A79 15c multi 10 10
*O68* A79 20c multi 14 14
*O69* A79 25c multi 18 18
*O70* A79 40c multi 28 28
*O71* A79 55c multi 35 35
*O72* A79 70c multi 48 48
*O73* A79 90c multi 60 60
*O74* A79 $1 multi 70 70
*O75* A79 $1.15 multi 75 75
*O76* A79 $3 multi 2.00 2.00
*O77* A79 $5 multi 3.50 3.50
*O78* A79 $10 multi 6.75 6.75
*Nos. O65-O78 (14)* 15.95 15.95

## NATAL

LOCATION — On the southern coast of Africa, bordering on the Indian Ocean.
GOVT. — Former British Crown Colony.
AREA — 35,284 sq. mi.
POP. — 1,206,386 (1908).
CAPITAL — Pietermaritzburg.

Natal united with Cape of Good Hope, Orange Free State and the Transvaal in 1910 to form the Union of South Africa.

12 Pence = 1 Shilling
20 Shillings = 1 Pound

Values for Nos. 1 to 7 are for copies cut into the embossing on one or more sides. Perfect specimens command far higher prices.

Crown and V R (Victoria Regina) A1 A2

Crown and Laurel — A3

A4

A5

**Colorless Embossing.**

**1857 Unwmk. *Imperf.***

*1* A1 3p *rose* 160.00
*a.* Tete beche pair *11,500.*
*2* A2 6p *green* 600.00
*a.* Diagonal half used as 3p on cover *5,000.*
*3* A3 9p *blue* *6,500.*
*4* A4 1sh *buff* *4,250.*

**1858**

*5* A5 1p *blue* 600.00
*6* A5 1p *rose* 700.00
*a.* No. 1 embossed over No. 6
*7* A5 1p *buff* 500.00

*Reprints: The paper is slightly glazed, the embossing sharper and the colors as follows: 1p pale blue, deep blue, carmine rose or yellow; 3p pale rose or carmine rose; 6p bright green or yellow green; 1sh pale buff or pale yellow. Bogus cancellations are found on the reprints.*

The stamps printed on surface-colored paper are revenue stamps with trimmed perforations.

Queen Victoria
A6 A7

**1860 Engr. *Perf. 14***

*8* A6 1p rose 135.00 55.00
*9* A6 3p blue 80.00 24.00

**1863 *Perf. 13***

*10* A6 1p car lake 20.00 12.50

**1861 *Clean-cut Perf. 14 to 16.***

*11* A6 3p blue 150.00 25.00

**1862 *Rough Perf. 14 to 16.***

*12* A6 3p blue 65.00 8.50
*a.* Imperf., pair *1,250.*
*b.* Imperf. horiz. or vert., pair *2,250.*
*13* A6 6p gray 135.00 15.00

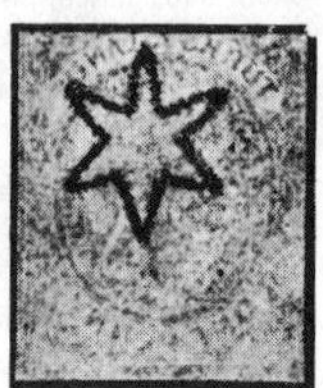

Wmk. 5

**1862 Wmk. Small Star. (5)**

*14* A6 1p rose 65.00 22.50

Imperforate copies of the 1p and 3p on paper watermarked small star are proofs.

**1864 Wmk. 1 *Perf. 12½***

*15* A6 1p car red 65.00 16.00
*a.* 1p brn red 65.00 18.00
*b.* Imperf.
*16* A6 6p violet 35.00 10.00
*a.* 6p dl vio 65.00 10.00

**1867 Typo. *Perf. 14***

*17* A7 1sh green 130.00 21.00

Stamps of 1860-67 Overprinted: **Postage.**

Overprint 12¾mm

**1869**

*18* A6 1p rose red (#15) 225.00 32.50
*a.* Double overprint 500.00
*19* A6 3p bl (#12) 360.00 82.50
*19A* A6 3p bl (#9) 475.00
*19B* A6 3p bl (#11) 600.00 275.00
*20* A6 6p violet (#16) 425.00 60.00
*21* A7 1sh green (#17) 450.00

**Same Overprint 13¾mm**

*22* A6 1p rose red (#15) 400.00 120.00
*23* A6 3p bl (#12) 1,350. 235.00
*a.* Inverted overprint
*23B* A6 3p bl (#9)
*23C* A6 3p bl (#11)
*24* A6 6p violet (#16) 900.00 120.00
*25* A7 1sh green (#17) *1,250.*

**Same Overprint 14½ to 15½mm**

*26* A6 1p rose red (#15) 625.00 165.00
*27* A6 3p bl (#12) 330.00
*27A* A6 3p bl (#11) 250.00
*27B* A6 3p bl (#9)
*28* A6 6p violet (#16) 950.00 75.00
*29* A7 1sh green (#17) *1,250.*

Overprinted **POSTAGE.**

*30* A6 1p rose red (#15) 50.00 14.00
*a.* 1p car red 97.50 14.00
*b.* Invtd. ovpt.
*31* A6 3p bl (#12) 125.00 17.50
*a.* Double overprint 550.00
*31B* A6 3p bl (#11) 75.00 27.50
*31C* A6 3p bl (#9) 225.00 40.00
*32* A6 6p violet (#16) 65.50 17.50
*33* A7 1sh green (#17) 82.00 32.50

Overprinted **POSTAGE**

*34* A6 1p rose red (#15) 165.00 32.50
*35* A6 3p bl (#12) 300.00 67.50
*35A* A6 3p bl (#11) 325.00 165.00
*35B* A6 3p bl (#9)
*36* A6 6p violet (#16) 195.00 25.00
*a.* Invtd. ovpt.
*37* A7 1sh green (#17) *1,000.*

Overprinted in Black or Red POSTAGE POSTAGE

**1870-73 Wmk. 1 *Perf. 12½***

*38* A6 1p red 35.00 5.50
*39* A6 3p ultra (R) ('72) 37.50 5.50
*40* A6 6p lil ('73) 100.00 24.00

Overprinted in Red, Black or Green g POSTAGE

**1870 *Perf. 14.***

*41* A7 1sh grn (R) *3,000.*
*42* A7 1sh grn (Bk) *1,500.* *800.00*
*a.* Double overprint *2,750.* *900.00*
*43* A7 1sh grn (G) 25.00 2.75

See No. 76.

Type of 1867 Overprinted POSTAGE

**1873**

*44* A7 1sh brn lil 60.00 9.00

No. 44 without overprint is a revenue.

Type of 1864 Overprinted POSTAGE POSTAGE

**1874 *Perf. 12½.***

*45* A6 1p rose red 90.00 12.00
*a.* Double overprint

Overprinted **POSTAGE**

**1875**

*46* A6 1p carmine 75.00 7.50
*a.* 1p rose red 75.00 27.50
*b.* Double overprint 400.00 360.00

Overprinted **POSTAGE**

(Overprint 14½mm)

**1875 *Perf. 12½***

*47* A6 1p yellow 32.50 32.50
*48* A6 1p rose red 32.50 30.00
*a.* Inverted overprint 750.00 360.00
*49* A6 6p violet 22.50 2.50
*a.* Inverted overprint 500.00 240.00
*b.* Double overprint 450.00

***Perf. 14***

*50* A7 1sh green 30.00 3.00
*a.* Double overprint 275.00

The 1p yellow without overprint is a revenue.

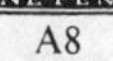

A8

A9

A10

A11

Queen Victoria — A12

**Wmk. Crown and C. C. (1)**

**874-78 Typo. *Perf. 14.***

*1* A8 1p rose 4.50 1.10
*2* A9 3p ultra 20.00 15.00
**a.** Perf. 14x12½ 1,250. 900.00
*3* A10 4p brn ('78) 20.00 4.75
*4* A11 6p violet 20.00 2.75

***Perf. 15½x15***

*5* A12 5sh claret 125.00 75.00

***Perf. 14***

*6* A12 5sh cl ('78) 70.00 11.50
*7* A12 5sh rose ('78) 32.50 8.25

***Perf. 12½.***

*8* A10 4p brn ('78) 325.00 40.00

Surcharged in Black:

HALF
½ n
½ No. 60
POSTAGE
o
Half-penny

**1877 *Perf. 14***

*59* A8 (n) ½p on 1p rose 15.00 20.00
**a.** Double surcharge "1/2"
*60* A8 (n) ½p on 1p rose 21.00 25.00

The "1/2" only of No. 60 is illustrated. Surcharge "n" exists in 3 or more types each of the large "1/2" (No. 59) and the small "1/2" (No. 60).

"HALF" and "½" were overprinted separately; "½" may be above, below or overlapping.

***Perf. 12½***

*61* A6 (o) ½p on 1p yel 5.50 6.00
**a.** Double surcharge 150.00 100.00
**b.** Inverted surcharge 150.00 100.00
**c.** Pair, one without surcharge 875.00 750.00
**d.** "POTAGE" 130.00 85.00
**e.** "POSAGE" 130.00 85.00
**f.** "POSTAGE" omitted 750.00
*62* A6 (o) 1p on 6p vio 18.00 2.25
**a.** "POSTAGE" omitted
**b.** "POTAGE" 200.00 150.00
*63* A6 (o) 1p on 6p rose 25.00 9.00
**a.** Inverted surcharge 100.00
**b.** Double surcharge 110.00
**c.** Double surcharge, one inverted 185.00 150.00
**d.** Triple surcharge, one inverted
**e.** Quadruple surcharge 300.00 120.00
**f.** "POTAGE" 225.00

No. 63 without overprint is a revenue.

A14

**1880 Typo. *Perf. 14***

*64* A14 ½p bl grn 1.75 1.50
**a.** Vertical pair, imperf. between

**1882-89 Wmk. Crown and C. A. (2)**

*65* A14 ½p bl grn ('84) 50.00 15.00
*66* A14 ½p gray grn ('84) 18 15
*67* A8 1p rose ('84) 12 9
*68* A9 3p ultra ('84) 32.50 8.75
*69* A9 3p gray ('89) 38 38
*70* A10 4p brown 75 35
*71* A11 6p violet 85 50
*Nos. 65-71 (7)* 84.78 25.22

Surcharged in Black:

ONE HALF·
PENNY.
p

TWO PENCE
q

**1885-86**

*72* A8 (p) ½p on 1p rose 13.00 8.00
*73* A9 (q) 2p on 3p gray ('86) 14.00 6.00

A17

**1887**

*74* A17 2p ol grn, die B 1.00 50
**a.** Die A 15.00 1.50

For explanation of dies A and B see back of this section of the Catalogue.

Type of 1867 Overprinted Type "g" in Red.

**1888**

*76* A7 1sh orange 1.25 50
**a.** Double overprint

Surcharged in Black

TWOPENCE
HALFPENNY

**1891**

*77* A10 2½p on 4p brn 5.25 5.00
**a.** "PENGE" 40.00 32.50
**b.** "PENN" 325.00 90.00
**c.** Double surcharge 175.00 100.00
**d.** Inverted surch. 185.00 110.00

A20

**1891, June**

*78* A20 2½p ultra 1.00 1.00

Surcharged in Red or Black:

POSTAGE.
Half-Penny
No. 79

HALF
No. 80

**Wmk. Crown and C. C. (1)**

**1895, Mar. *Perf. 12½***

*79* A6 ½p on 6p vio (R) 45 *2.50*
**a.** "Ealf" 12.50 *20.00*
**b.** "Penny" 10.00 *16.00*
**c.** Double surch., one vertical 325.00

Stamps with fancy "P," "T" or "A" in surcharge sell for twice as much.

**Wmk. Crown and C. A. (2)**

***Perf. 14***

*80* A8 ½p on 1p rose (Bk) 50 75
**a.** Pair, one without and the other with double surcharge

King Edward VII
A23 A24

**1902-03 Typo. *Perf. 14***

*81* A23 ½p bl grn 1.65 55
*82* A23 1p rose 22 6
*83* A23 1½p blk & bl grn 18 55
*84* A23 2p ol grn & scar 45 22
*85* A23 2½p ultra 50 55
*86* A23 3p gray & red vio 45 18
*87* A23 4p brn & scar 70 1.10
*88* A23 5p org & blk 90 95
*89* A23 6p mar & bl grn 90 32
*90* A23 1sh pale bl & dp rose 4.50 38
*91* A23 2sh vio & bl grn 9.75 6.75
*92* A23 2sh6p red vio 17.50 11.00
*93* A23 4sh yel & dp rose 19.00 15.00

**Wmk. Crown and C. C. (1)**

*94* A24 5sh car lake & dk bl 12.00 5.00
*95* A24 10sh brn & dp rose 32.50 8.75
*96* A24 £1 ultra & blk 120.00 30.00
*97* A24 £1 10sh vio & bl grn 180.00 67.50
Revenue cancel 1.65
*98* A24 £5 blk & vio *1,500.* *300.00*
Revenue cancel 11.00
*99* A24 £10 org & grn *7,500.*
Revenue cancel 82.50
*100* A24 £20 grn & car *11,500.*
Revenue cancel 140.00
*Nos. 81-96 (16)* 221.20 81.36

**1904-08 Wmk. 3**

*101* A23 ½p bl grn 10 6
*102* A23 1p rose 10 6
**a.** Booklet pane of 6
**b.** Booklet pane of 5 + 1 label
*103* A23 2p ol grn & scar 28 28
*104* A23 4p brn & scar 75 30
*105* A23 5p org & blk ('08) 1.25 1.25
*106* A23 1sh pale bl & dp rose 18.00 4.50
*107* A23 2sh vio & bl grn 24.00 15.00
*108* A23 2sh6p red vio 27.50 13.00
*109* A24 £1 10sh vio & org brn, chalky paper 1,200.
Revenue cancel 18.00
*Nos. 101-108 (8)* 71.98 34.45

No. 109 is on chalky paper.

A25 A26

**1908-09**

*110* A25 6p red vio 3.50 1.75
*111* A25 1sh blk, *green* 6.00 1.75
*112* A25 2sh bl & vio, *bl* 9.00 3.25
*113* A25 2sh6p red & blk, *bl* 15.00 2.50
*114* A26 5sh red & grn, *yel* 18.00 10.50
*115* A26 10sh red & grn, *grn* 45.00 35.00
*116* A26 £1 blk & vio, *red* 300.00 150.00
*Nos. 110-115 (6)* 96.50 54.75

**OFFICIAL STAMPS**

Nos. 101-103, 106 and Type A23 Overprinted NAURU

**1904 Wmk. 3 *Perf. 14***

*O1* A23 ½p bl grn 3.00 60
*O2* A23 1p rose 1.50 60
*O3* A23 2p ol grn & scar 21.00 18.00
*O4* A23 3p gray & red vio 6.00 *7.50*
*O5* A23 6p mar & bl grn 30.00 30.00
*O6* A23 1sh pale bl & dp rose 60.00 *90.00*
*Nos. O1-O6 (6)* 121.50 *146.70*

Stamps of Natal were replaced by those of the Union of South Africa.

## NAURU

LOCATION — An island on the Equator in the west central Pacific Ocean, midway between the Marshall and Solomon Islands.
GOVT. — Republic.
AREA — 8½ sq. mi.
POP. — 8,421 (est. 1983).
CAPITAL — Uaboe District.

The island, a German possession, was captured by Australian forces in 1914 and, following World War I, was mandated to the British Empire. It was administered jointly by Great Britain, Australia and New Zealand.

In 1947 Nauru was placed under United Nations trusteeship, administered by Australia. On January 31, 1968, Nauru became a republic.

See North West Pacific Islands.

12 Pence = 1 Shilling
100 Cents = 1 Dollar (1966)

**Catalogue values for unused stamps in this country are for Never Hinged items, beginning with Scott 39.**

Great Britain Stamps of 1912-13 Overprinted at Bottom of Stamp. NAURU

**1916-23 Wmk. 33 *Perf. 14½x14***

*1* A82 ½p green 32 *80*
**a.** Overprint centered ('23) 9.25 *30.00*
*2* A83 1p scarlet 45 *1.10*
**a.** Overprint centered ('23) 13.50 *26.00*
*3* A84 1½p red brn ('23) 67.50 *95.00*
**a.** Overprint centered ('23) 18.50 *40.00*
*4* A85 2p org (die I) 80 *1.65*
**a.** 2p dp org (die II) ('23) 55.00 *80.00*
**b.** As "a", overprint centered ('23) 40.00 *65.00*
*6* A86 2½p ultra 1.65 *3.50*
*7* A87 3p violet 2.25 *4.25*
*8* A88 4p sl grn 2.50 *5.25*
**a.** Double overprint
*9* A89 5p yel brn 3.75 *8.00*
*10* A89 6p dl vio 4.25 *9.50*
*11* A90 9p blk brn 8.00 *16.50*
*12* A90 1sh bister 9.50 *15.00*
*Nos. 1-12 (11)* 100.97 *160.55*

On Nos. 1-12 "NAURU" is usually 12¾mm wide and at the foot of the stamp. In 1923 four values were overprinted with the word 13½mm wide and across the middle of the stamp.

Overprinted OFFICIAL

**Wmk. 34 *Perf. 11x12***

*13* A91 2sh6p lt brn 70.00 100.00
**a.** 2sh6p blk brn 550.00 550.00
*14* A91 6sh carmine 175.00 185.00
**a.** 5sh rose car 2,500. 2,500.
*15* A91 10sh lt bl (R) 275.00 *375.00*
**a.** 10sh indigo blue *6,000.* *6,000.*

Same Ovpt. on Great Britain No. 179

**1920**

*16* A91 2sh6p gray brn 90.00 *150.00*

Freighter — A1

George VI — A2

**1924-47 Unwmk. Engr. *Perf. 11***

*17* A1 ½p org brn 1.40 1.75
**a.** Perf. 14 ('47) 1.10 1.40
*18* A1 1p green 1.40 1.75
*19* A1 1½p red 1.40 1.75
*20* A1 2p orange 1.65 1.75
*21* A1 2½p blue 90 1.00
**a.** Horiz. pair, imperf. between
*22* A1 3p grnsh gray ('37) 2.00 2.25
**a.** 3p pale bl 2.75 3.50
*23* A1 4p ol grn 2.75 3.00
*24* A1 5p dk brn 1.60 2.00
*25* A1 6p dk vio 2.00 2.00
*26* A1 9p brn ol 4.50 4.75
*27* A1 1sh brn red 3.75 4.00
*28* A1 2sh6p sl grn 14.00 17.50
*29* A1 5sh claret 35.00 *45.00*
*30* A1 10sh yellow 52.50 *62.50*
*Nos. 17-30 (14)* 124.85 *151.00*

In 1937 new printings of Nos. 17-30 were made on glazed-surface paper in slighly different shades.

Stamps of Type A1 Overprinted in Black

HIS MAJESTY'S JUBILEE.
1910-1935

**1935, July 12 Glazed Paper *Perf. 11***

| No. | Type | Description | Unused | Used |
|---|---|---|---|---|
| 31 | A1 | 1½p red | 80 | 1.00 |
| 32 | A1 | 2p orange | 1.85 | 2.25 |
| 33 | A1 | 2½p blue | 4.00 | 4.25 |
| 34 | A1 | 1sh brn red | 10.50 | *12.50* |

25th anniv. of the reign of George V.

**Coronation Issue**

**1937, May 10 Engr.**

| No. | Type | Description | Unused | Used |
|---|---|---|---|---|
| 35 | A2 | 1½p sal rose | 8 | 8 |
| 36 | A2 | 2p dl org | 12 | 12 |
| 37 | A2 | 2½p blue | 14 | 14 |
| 38 | A2 | 1sh brn vio | 42 | 42 |

Coronation of George VI & Queen Elizabeth.

**Catalogue values for unused stamps in this section, from this point to the end of the section, are for Never Hinged items.**

Casting Throw-net — A3

Anibare Bay — A4

Designs: 3½p, Loading phosphate. 4p, Frigate bird. 6p, Nauruan canoe. 9p, Meeting house (domaneab). 1sh, Palms. 2sh6p, Buada lagoon. 5sh, Map.

**1954, Feb. 6 *Perf. 14½x14, 14x14½***

| No. | Type | Description | Unused | Used |
|---|---|---|---|---|
| 39 | A3 | ½p purple | 16 | 9 |
| 40 | A4 | 1p green | 24 | 12 |
| 41 | A3 | 3½p red | 55 | 30 |
| 42 | A3 | 4p dp bl | 70 | 40 |
| 43 | A3 | 6p orange | 80 | 42 |
| 44 | A3 | 9p brn lake | 1.40 | 75 |
| 45 | A4 | 1sh dk rose vio | 1.60 | 1.00 |
| 46 | A3 | 2sh6p dk gray grn | 7.50 | 4.50 |
| 47 | A4 | 5sh lil rose | 15.00 | 8.25 |
| | | *Nos. 39-47 (9)* | 27.95 | 15.83 |

See Nos. 58-71.

Balsam — A5

Black Lizard — A6

Capparis — A7

Coral Pinnacles — A8

White Tern — A9

Designs: 2p, Micronesian pigeon (vert.). 3p, Poison nut flower. 3sh3p, Nightingale reed warbler.

Foreign postal stationery (stamped envelopes, postal cards and air letter sheets) lies beyond the scope of this Catalogue, which is limited to adhesive postage stamps.

***Perf. 13½, Perf. 14½x13½ (10p), Perf. 14½ (2sh3p)***

**Photo.; Engraved (10p, 2sh3p)**

**1963-65 Unwmk.**

| No. | Type | Description | Unused | Used |
|---|---|---|---|---|
| 49 | A9 | 2p multi ('65) | 25 | 18 |
| 50 | A6 | 3p red org, sl grn & yel | 38 | 30 |
| 51 | A5 | 5p gray, bl grn & yel | 95 | 65 |
| 52 | A6 | 8p grn & blk | 1.90 | 85 |
| 53 | A7 | 10p black | 2.50 | 1.40 |
| 54 | A9 | 1sh3p ap grn, blk & Prus bl ('65) | 3.75 | 2.50 |
| 55 | A8 | 2sh3p vio bl | 4.75 | 3.00 |
| 56 | A6 | 3sh3p lt yel, bl, brn & blk ('65) | 9.50 | 6.25 |
| | | *Nos. 49-56 (8)* | 23.98 | 15.13 |

**ANZAC Issue**

Type of Australia

***Perf. 13½x13***

**1965, Apr. 14 Photo. Unwmk.**

| No. | Type | Description | Unused | Used |
|---|---|---|---|---|
| 57 | A150 | 5p brt grn, sep & blk | 1.00 | 1.00 |

See note after Australia No. 387.

Types of 1954-65
Values in Cents and Dollars

Designs: 1c, Anibare Bay. 2c, Casting throw-net. 3c, Loading phosphate. 4c, Balsam. 5c, Palms. 7c, Black lizard. 8c, Capparis. 10c, Frigate bird. 15c, White tern. 25c, Coral pinnacles. 30c, Poison nut flower. 35c, Reed warbler. 50c, Micronesian pigeon (vert.). $1, Map.

**Engr.; Photo. (4c, 7c, 15c, 30c-50c)**

**1966 *Perf. 14½x14, 14x14½***

| No. | Type | Description | Unused | Used |
|---|---|---|---|---|
| 58 | A4 | 1c dk bl | 8 | 6 |
| 59 | A3 | 2c claret | 12 | 10 |
| 60 | A3 | 3c green | 20 | 10 |
| 61 | A5 | 4c lil, grn & yel | 24 | 20 |
| 62 | A4 | 5c vio bl | 35 | 28 |
| 63 | A6 | 7c fawn & blk | 40 | 35 |
| 64 | A7 | 8c ol grn | 48 | 40 |
| 65 | A3 | 10c dk red | 60 | 48 |
| 66 | A9 | 15c ap grn, blk & Prus bl | 75 | 65 |
| 67 | A3 | 25c sepia | 1.40 | 1.10 |
| 68 | A6 | 30c brick red, sl grn, & yel | 1.60 | 1.40 |
| 69 | A6 | 35c lt yel, bl, brn & blk | 2.75 | 2.25 |
| 70 | A9 | 50c yel, bluish blk & brn | 3.50 | 3.25 |
| 71 | A4 | $1 claret | 7.25 | 6.00 |
| | | *Nos. 58-71 (14)* | 19.72 | 16.62 |

The engraved stamps are luminescent.

**Republic**

Nos. 58-71 Overprinted in Red, Black or Orange
"REPUBLIC / OF / NAURU"

**1968**

| No. | Type | Description | Unused | Used |
|---|---|---|---|---|
| 72 | A4 | 1c dk bl (R) | 5 | 5 |
| 73 | A3 | 2c claret | 6 | 6 |
| 74 | A3 | 3c green | 8 | 8 |
| 75 | A5 | 4c lil, grn & yel | 12 | 12 |
| 76 | A4 | 5c vio bl (O) | 14 | 14 |
| 77 | A6 | 7c fawn & blk (R) | 24 | 24 |
| 78 | A7 | 8c ol grn (R) | 30 | 30 |
| 79 | A3 | 10c dk red | 38 | 38 |
| 80 | A9 | 15c ap grn, blk & Prus bl | 4.00 | 4.00 |
| 81 | A3 | 25c sep (R) | 1.10 | 1.10 |
| 82 | A6 | 30c brick red, sl grn & yel | 1.90 | 1.35 |
| 83 | A6 | 35c multi | 2.50 | 1.90 |
| 84 | A9 | 50c yel, bluish blk & brn | 3.00 | 3.00 |
| 85 | A4 | $1 claret | 5.50 | 5.50 |
| | | *Nos. 72-85 (14)* | 19.37 | 18.22 |

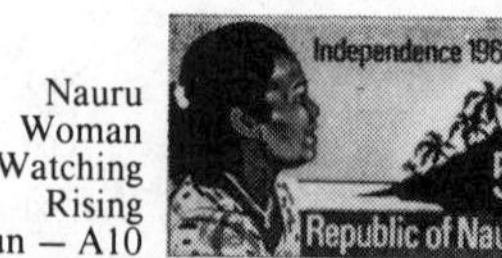

Nauru Woman Watching Rising Sun — A10

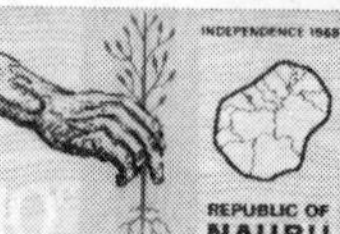

Planting Seedling and Map of Nauru — A11

***Perf. 13x13½***

**1968, Sept. 11 Photo. Unwmk.**

| No. | Type | Description | Unused | Used |
|---|---|---|---|---|
| 86 | A10 | 5c multi | 25 | 25 |
| 87 | A11 | 10c brt bl, blk & grn | 50 | 50 |

Independence of Nauru.

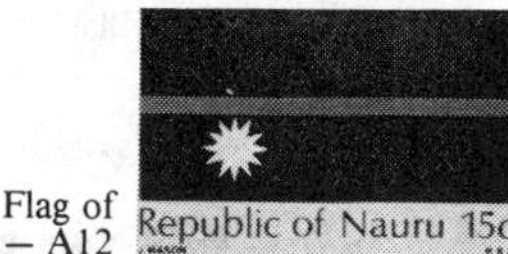

Flag of Nauru — A12

**1969, Jan. 31 Litho. *Perf. 13½***

| No. | Type | Description | Unused | Used |
|---|---|---|---|---|
| 88 | A12 | 15c dk vio bl, yel & org | 80 | 75 |

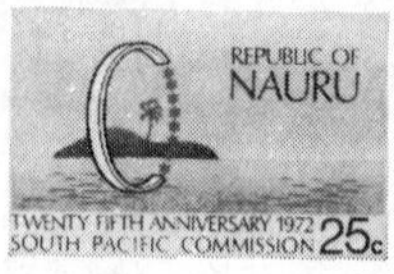

Commission Emblem and Nauru — A13

**1972, Feb. 7 Litho. *Perf. 14½x14***

| No. | Type | Description | Unused | Used |
|---|---|---|---|---|
| 89 | A13 | 25c bl, yel & blk | 85 | 85 |

South Pacific Commission, 25th anniversary.

No. 88 Overprinted in Gold:

**Independence 1968-1973**

**1973, Jan. 31 *Perf. 13½***

| No. | Type | Description | Unused | Used |
|---|---|---|---|---|
| 90 | A12 | 15c multi | 1.35 | 1.35 |

Fifth anniversary of independence.

Lotus (Ekwenababae) A14

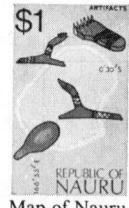

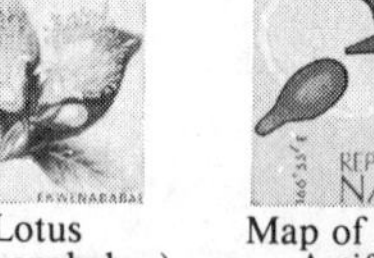

Map of Nauru, Artifacts A15

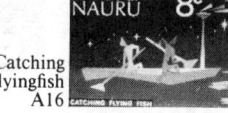

Catching Flyingfish A16

Designs: 2c, Kauwe iud. 3c, Rimone. 4c, Denea. 5c, Beach morning-glory. 7c, Golden butterflyfish. 10c, Nauruan ball game (itsibweb). 15c, Nauruan wrestling. 20c, Snaring frigate birds. 25c, Nauruan girl with flower garland. 30c, Men catching noddies. 50c, Frigate birds.

**1973 Litho. *Perf. 13½x14***

| No. | Type | Description | Unused | Used |
|---|---|---|---|---|
| 91 | A14 | 1c pale yel & multi | 5 | 5 |
| 92 | A14 | 2c pale ocher & multi | 7 | 7 |
| 93 | A14 | 3c pale vio & multi | 12 | 12 |
| 94 | A14 | 4c pale grn & multi | 15 | 15 |
| 95 | A14 | 5c pale bl & multi | 18 | 18 |

***Perf. 14½x14, 14x14½***

| No. | Type | Description | Unused | Used |
|---|---|---|---|---|
| 96 | A16 | 7c bl & multi | 25 | 25 |
| 97 | A16 | 8c blk & multi | 30 | 30 |
| 98 | A16 | 10c multi | 38 | 38 |
| 99 | A15 | 15c grn & multi | 40 | 40 |
| 100 | A15 | 20c bl & multi | 52 | 52 |
| 101 | A15 | 25c yel & multi | 60 | 60 |
| 102 | A16 | 30c multi | 80 | 80 |
| 103 | A16 | 50c multi | 1.50 | 1.50 |
| 104 | A15 | $1 bl & multi | 3.00 | 3.00 |
| | | *Nos. 91-104 (14)* | 8.32 | 8.32 |

Issue dates: Nos. 97-100, May 23; Nos. 96, 101-103, July 25; others Mar. 28, 1973.

Cooperative Store — A17

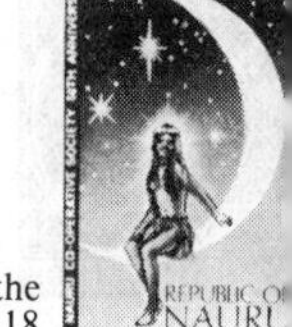

Eigigu, the Girl in the Moon — A18

Design: 25c, Timothy Detudamo and cooperative store emblem.

**1973, Dec. 20 Litho. *Perf. 14½x1…***

| No. | Type | Description | Unused | Used |
|---|---|---|---|---|
| 105 | A17 | 5c multi | 50 | 35 |
| 106 | A17 | 25c multi | 1.75 | 1.40 |
| 107 | A18 | 50c multi | 4.00 | 3.50 |

50th anniversary of Nauru Cooperative Society, founded by Timothy Detudamo.

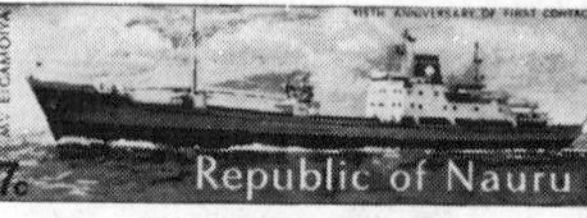

"Eigamoiya" — A19

Designs: 10c, Phosphate mining. 15c, "Nauru Chief" plane over Nauru. 25c, Nauru chieftain with frigate-bird headdress. 35c, Capt. J. Fearn, sailing ship "Hunter" and map of Nauru. 50c, "Hunter" off Nauru.

***Perf. 13x13½, 13½x13***

**1974, May 21 Litho.**

**Sizes: 70x22mm (7c, 35c, 50c); 33x20mm (10c, 15c, 25c)**

| No. | Type | Description | Unused | Used |
|---|---|---|---|---|
| 108 | A19 | 7c multi | 60 | 28 |
| 109 | A19 | 10c multi | 80 | 35 |
| 110 | A19 | 15c multi | 1.50 | 75 |
| 111 | A19 | 25c multi | 4.00 | 1.75 |
| 112 | A19 | 35c multi | 14.00 | 6.25 |
| 113 | A19 | 50c multi | 13.50 | 5.50 |
| | | *Nos. 108-113 (6)* | 34.40 | 14.88 |

175th anniversary of Nauru's first contact with the outside world.

Map of Nauru A20

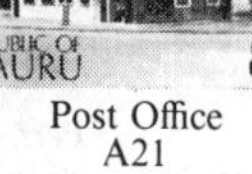

Post Office A21

Designs (UPU Emblem and): 20c, Mailman on motorcycle. $1, Flag of Nauru and UPU Building, Bern (vert.).

**1974, July 23 Litho. *Perf. 14***

| No. | Type | Description | Unused | Used |
|---|---|---|---|---|
| 114 | A20 | 5c multi | 16 | 22 |

***Perf. 13½x13, 13x13½***

| No. | Type | Description | Unused | Used |
|---|---|---|---|---|
| 115 | A21 | 8c multi | 24 | 28 |
| 116 | A21 | 20c multi | 95 | 70 |
| 117 | A21 | $1 multi | 5.50 | 5.00 |
| *a.* | | Souvenir sheet of 4 | 11.50 | 9.75 |

Centenary of Universal Postal Union. No. 117a contains 4 imperf. stamps similar to Nos. 114-117. Light blue margin with black and white inscription, arms of Nauru and UPU emblem. Size: 156x104mm.

Rev. P. A. Delaporte — A22

**974, Dec. 10 Litho. *Perf. 14½***

*18* A22 15c brt pink & multi 85 60
*19* A22 20c bl & multi 1.60 1.35

Christmas 1974. Delaporte, a German-orn American missionary, took Christianity › Nauru and translated the New Testament ıto Nauruan.

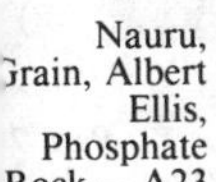

Nauru, ›rain, Albert Ellis, Phosphate Rock — A23

Designs: 7c, Phosphate mining and coolie arrying load. 15c, Electric freight train, tugs ınd ship. 25c, Excavator, cantilever and ruck.

**975, July 23 Litho. *Perf. 14½x14***

'20 A23 5c multi 16 16
'21 A23 7c multi 24 22
'22 A23 15c multi 1.10 85
'23 A23 25c multi 1.75 1.25

75th anniv. of discovery of phosphate (5c); '0th anniv. of Pacific Phosphate Co. Mining ›greement (7c); 50th anniv. of British 'hosphate Commissioners (15c); 5th anniv. ›f Nauru Phosphate Corp. (25c).

Melanesian Outrigger and Map of SPC's Area — A24

**1975, Sept. 1 Litho. *Perf. 14x14½***

'24 A24 20c *Micronesian outrigger* 1.10 80
'25 A24 20c *Polynesian double hull* 1.10 80
'26 A24 20c *shown* 1.10 80
'27 A24 20c *Polynesian outrigger* 1.10 80

South Pacific Commission Conference, Nauru, Sept. 29-Oct. 10. Nos. 124-127 printed se-tenant in sheets of 16 (4x4).

New Civic Center A25

Design: 50c, "Domaneab" (meeting house) and flags of participating nations.

**1975, Sept. 29 Litho. *Perf. 14½***

*128* A25 30c multi 95 95
*129* A25 50c multi 1.75 1.50

South Pacific Commission Conference, Nauru, Sept. 29-Oct. 10.

Virgin Mary, Stained-glass Window — A26

Designs: 7c, 15c, "Suffer little children to come unto me," stained-glass window, Orro Protestant Church. 25c, like 5c, Yaren Catholic Church.

**1975, Nov. 7 Litho. *Perf. 14½***

*130* A26 5c gray bl & multi 20 15
*131* A26 7c grn & multi 30 25
*132* A26 15c brn & multi 75 60
*133* A26 25c lil & multi 1.25 1.00

Christmas 1975.

Frangipani Forming Lei Around Nauru — A27

Designs: 14c, Hand crowning Nauru with lei. 25c, Reed warbler, birds flying from Truk to Nauru. 40c, Reunion of islanders in Boar Harbor.

**1976, Jan. 31 Litho. *Perf. 14½***

*134* A27 10c grn & multi 25 22
*135* A27 14c vio & multi 40 35
*136* A27 25c red & multi 75 60
*137* A27 40c bl & multi 1.40 1.10

30th anniversary of the return of the islanders from Japanese internment on Truk.

Nauru Nos. 7 and 11 A28

Designs: 15c, Nauru Nos. 10 and 12. 25c, Nauru No. 13. 50c, Nauru No. 14, "Specimen."

**1976, May 6 Litho. *Perf. 13½x14***

*138* A28 10c multi 30 24
*139* A28 15c multi 45 35
*140* A28 25c multi 70 60
*141* A28 50c multi 1.40 1.25

60th anniv. of Nauru's 1st postage stamps.

Nauru Shipping and Pandanus — A29

Designs: 20c, Air Nauru Boeing 737 and Fokker F28, and tournefortia argentea. 30c, Earth satellite station and thespesia populnea. 40c, Area produce and cordia subcordata.

**1976, July 26 Litho. *Perf. 13½x14***

*142* A29 10c multi 30 22
*143* A29 20c multi 55 45
*144* A29 30c multi 90 70
*145* A29 40c multi 1.25 90

7th South Pacific Forum, Nauru, July 1976.

Nauruan Children's Choir A30 A31

Designs: 20c, Angels. Designs after children's paintings.

**1976, Nov. Litho. *Perf. 14x13½***

*146* A30 15c multi 50 42
*147* A31 15c multi 50 42
*148* A30 20c multi 65 60
*149* A31 20c multi 65 60

Christmas 1976. Stamps of same denomination printed se-tenant in sheets of 30 (6x5).

Nauru House, Melbourne, and Coral Pinnacles — A32

Cable-laying Ship Anglia, 1902 — A33

Design: 30c, Nauru House and Melbourne skyline.

**1977, Apr. 14 Photo. *Perf. 14½***

*150* A32 15c multi 55 50
*151* A32 30c multi 1.10 1.00

Opening of Nauru House in Melbourne, Australia.

**1977, Sept. 7 Photo. *Perf. 14½***

Designs: 15c, Nauru radar station. 20c, Stern of Anglia. 25c, Radar antenna.

*152* A33 7c multi 18 15
*153* A33 15c multi 35 30
*154* A33 20c multi 50 40
*155* A33 25c multi 60 50

1st transpacific cable, 75th anniv., and 1st artificial earth satellite, 20th anniv.

Catholic Church, Yaren, and Father Kayser — A34

Coat of Arms of Nauru — A35

Designs: 25c, Congregational Church, Orro. 30c, Catholic Church, Arubo.

**1977, Oct. Photo. *Perf. 14½***

*156* A34 15c multi 32 32
*157* A34 25c multi 55 55
*158* A34 30c multi 65 65

Christmas 1977, and 55th anniversary of first Roman Catholic Church on Nauru.

**1978, Jan. 31 Litho. *Perf. 14½***

*159* A35 15c bl & multi 35 32
*160* A35 60c emer & multi 1.40 1.25

10th anniversary of independence.

### Nos. 150-151 Surcharged with New Value and Two Bars

**1978, Apr. Photo. *Perf. 14½***

*161* A32 4c on 15c multi 6.25 6.25
*162* A32 5c on 15c multi 6.25 6.25
*163* A32 8c on 30c multi 6.25 6.25
*164* A32 10c on 30c multi 6.25 6.25

Girls Catching Fish in Buada Lagoon A36

Designs: 1c, Fisherman and family collecting shellfish. 2c, Pigs foraging near coral reef. 3c, Gnarled tree and birds. 4c, Girl catching fish with hands. 5c, Bird catching fish. 10c, Ijuw Lagoon. 15c, Young girl and coral formation. 20c, Reef pinnacles, Anibare Bay. 25c, Pinnacles, Meneng shore. 30c, Frigate bird. 32c, Coconut palm and noddies. 40c, Iwiyi, wading bird. 50c, Frigate birds. $1, Pinnacles, Topside. $2, Newly uncovered pinnacles, Topside. $5, Old pinnacles, Topside.

**1978-79 Photo. *Perf. 14½***

*165* A36 1c multi 5 5
*166* A36 2c multi 5 5
*167* A36 3c multi 6 6
*168* A36 4c multi 8 8
*169* A36 5c multi 10 10
*170* A36 7c multi 15 15
*171* A36 10c multi 20 20
*172* A36 15c multi 30 30
*173* A36 20c multi 38 38
*174* A36 25c multi 48 48
*175* A36 30c multi 60 60
*176* A36 32c multi 65 65
*177* A36 40c multi 75 75
*178* A36 50c multi 95 95
*179* A36 $1 multi 1.90 1.90
*180* A36 $2 multi 3.75 3.75
*181* A36 $5 multi 9.50 9.50
*Nos. 165-181 (17)* 19.95 19.95

Issue dates: Nos. 166-169, June 6, 1979. Others, May 1978.

"APU" — A37

Mother and Child — A38

**1978, Aug. 28 Litho. *Perf. 13½***

*182* A37 15c multi 1.10 1.00
*183* A37 20c gold, blk & dk bl 1.40 1.20

14th General Assembly of Asian Parliamentary Union, Nauru, Aug. 28-Sept. 1. On sale during conf. only.

**1978, Nov. 1 Litho. *Perf. 14***

Designs: 15c, 20c, Angel over the Pacific (horiz.). 30c, like 7c.

*184* A38 7c multi 12 12
*185* A38 15c multi 25 25
*186* A38 20c multi 35 35
*187* A38 30c multi 52 52

Christmas 1978.

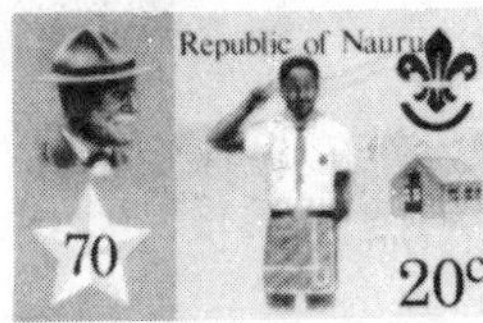


Lord Baden-Powell and Cub Scout — A39

Lord Baden-Powell and: 30c, Boy Scout. 50c, Explorer.

**1978, Dec. 1 Litho. *Perf. 14***

*188* A39 20c multi 35 35
*189* A39 30c multi 48 48
*190* A39 50c multi 80 80

70th anniversary of 1st Scout Troop.

Flyer A over Nauru Airfield A40

Designs: No. 192, "Southern Cross" and Boeing 727. No. 193, "Southern Cross" and Boeing 737. 30c, Wright Flyer over Nauru.

**1979, Jan. *Perf. 14½***

*191* A40 10c multi 20 20
*192* A40 15c multi 28 28
*193* A40 15c multi 28 28
*194* A40 30c multi 60 60

75th anniversary of 1st powered flight and 50th anniversary of Kingsford Smith's USA-Australia and Australia-New Zealand flights.

Nos. 192-193 printed se-tenant checkerwise in sheets of 25.

Rowland Hill, Marshall Islands No. 15 with Nauru Cancel
A41

**1979, Feb. 27 Litho. *Perf. 14½***

| | | | | | |
|---|---|---|---|---|---|
| *195* | A41 | 5c | shown | 8 | 8 |
| *196* | A41 | 15c | Nauru No. 15 | 22 | 22 |
| *197* | A41 | 60c | Nauru No. 160 | 90 | 90 |
| *a.* | | | Souvenir sheet of 3 | 1.25 | 1.25 |

Sir Rowland Hill (1795-1879), originator of penny postage. No. 197a contains Nos. 195-197; yellow and black margin with Nauru coat of arms and STAMPEX 1979 cancellation. Size: 160x101mm.

Dish Antenna, Earth Station, ITU Emblem — A42

Designs (ITU Emblem and): 32c, Woman operating Telex machine. 40c, Radio beacon operator.

**1979, Aug. Litho. *Perf. 14½***

| | | | | | |
|---|---|---|---|---|---|
| *198* | A42 | 7c | multi | 12 | 12 |
| *199* | A42 | 32c | multi | 52 | 52 |
| *200* | A42 | 40c | multi | 65 | 65 |

Intl. Radio Consultative Committee (CCIR) of the ITU, 50th anniv.

Nauruan Girl — A43

IYC Emblem, Nauruan Children: 15c, Boy. 25c, 32c, 50c, Girls (diff.).

**1979, Oct. 3 Litho. *Perf. 14½***

| | | | | | |
|---|---|---|---|---|---|
| *201* | A43 | 8c | multi | 12 | 12 |
| *202* | A43 | 15c | multi | 22 | 22 |
| *203* | A43 | 25c | multi | 38 | 38 |
| *204* | A43 | 32c | multi | 48 | 48 |
| *205* | A43 | 50c | multi | 75 | 75 |
| | | | *Nos. 201-205 (5)* | 1.95 | 1.95 |

International Year of the Child. Nos. 201-205 printed se-tenant in sheets of 25 (5x5).

Star, Scroll, Ekwenababa Flower — A44

Star and Flowers: 15c, Milos. 20c, Denea. 30c, Morning glories.

**1979, Nov. 14 Litho. *Perf. 14½***

| | | | | | |
|---|---|---|---|---|---|
| *206* | A44 | 7c | multi | 12 | 12 |
| *207* | A44 | 15c | multi | 25 | 25 |
| *208* | A44 | 20c | multi | 32 | 32 |
| *209* | A44 | 30c | multi | 50 | 50 |

Christmas 1979.

Nauruan Plane over Melbourne — A45

Air Nauru, 10th Anniversary (Plane Over): 20c, Tarawa. 25c, Hong Kong. 30c, Auckland.

**1980, Feb. 28 Litho. *Perf. 14½***

| | | | | | |
|---|---|---|---|---|---|
| *210* | A45 | 15c | multi | 24 | 24 |
| *211* | A45 | 20c | multi | 32 | 32 |
| *212* | A45 | 25c | multi | 40 | 40 |
| *213* | A45 | 30c | multi | 50 | 50 |

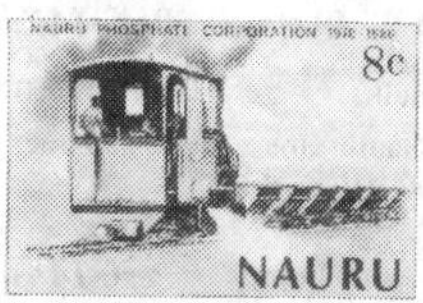


Early Steam Locomotive A46

**1980, May 6 Litho. *Perf. 15***

| | | | | | |
|---|---|---|---|---|---|
| *214* | A46 | 8c | *shown* | 14 | 14 |
| *215* | A46 | 32c | *Electric locomotive* | 52 | 52 |
| *216* | A46 | 60c | *Clyde diesel-hydraulic locomotive* | 1.00 | 1.00 |
| *a.* | | | Souvenir sheet of 3 | 1.75 | 1.75 |

Nauru Phosphate Corporation, 10th anniversary. No. 216a also for London 1980 International Stamp Exhibition, May 6-14; Penny Black, 140th anniversary. No. 216a contains Nos. 214-216; multicolored margin shows London 1980 emblem, Penny Black map of Nauru. Size: 168x117½mm.

Christmas 1980
A47 A48

Designs: 30c, "Glory to God in the Highest . . ." in English and Nauruan. Stamps of same denomination se-tenant.

**1980, Sept. 24 Litho. *Perf. 15***

| | | | | | |
|---|---|---|---|---|---|
| *217* | A47 | 20c | multi | 32 | 32 |
| *218* | A48 | 20c | multi | 32 | 32 |
| *219* | A47 | 30c | multi | 48 | 48 |
| *220* | A48 | 30c | multi | 48 | 48 |

Flags of Nauru, Australia, Gt. Britain and New Zealand U.N. Emblem — A49

**1980, Dec. 20 Litho. *Perf. 14½***

| | | | | | |
|---|---|---|---|---|---|
| *221* | A49 | 25c | shown | 60 | 60 |

**Size: 72x22mm**
***Perf. 14***

| | | | | | |
|---|---|---|---|---|---|
| *222* | A49 | 30c | UN Trusteeship Council | 70 | 70 |
| *223* | A49 | 50c | 1968 independence ceremony | 1.10 | 1.10 |

UN de-colonization declaration, 20th anniv.
No. 222 printed se-tenant with label showing flags of UN and Nauru, issued Feb. 11, 1981.

Timothy Detudamo (Former Head Chief), Domaneab (Meeting House) — A50

**1981, Feb. Litho. *Perf. 14½***

| | | | | | |
|---|---|---|---|---|---|
| *224* | A50 | 20c | shown | 35 | 35 |
| *225* | A50 | 30c | Raymond Gadabu | 50 | 50 |
| *226* | A50 | 50c | Hammer DeRoburt | 85 | 85 |

Legislative Council, 30th anniversary.

Casting Net by Hand A51

**1981 Litho. *Perf. 12***

| | | | | | |
|---|---|---|---|---|---|
| *227* | A51 | 8c | shown | 14 | 14 |
| *228* | A51 | 20c | Ancient canoe | 32 | 32 |
| *229* | A51 | 32c | Powered boat | 55 | 55 |
| *230* | A51 | 40c | Fishing vessel | 90 | 90 |
| *a.* | | | Souvenir sheet of 4 | 3.00 | 3.00 |

No. 230a contains 4 No. 230; multicolored margin shows fisherman and emblem of WIPA (International Philatelic Exhibition, Vienna, May 22-31). Size: 168x116mm.

Bank of Nauru, 5th Anniv. A52

**1981, July 21 Litho. *Perf. 14x14½***

| | | | | | |
|---|---|---|---|---|---|
| *231* | A52 | $1 | multi | 1.50 | 1.50 |

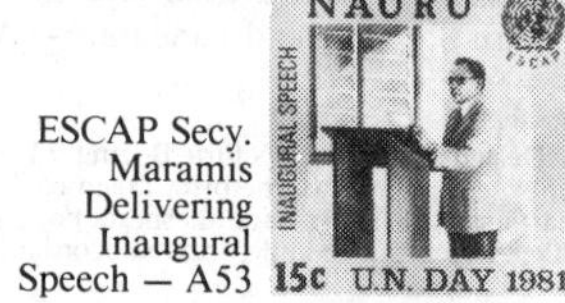


ESCAP Secy. Maramis Delivering Inaugural Speech — A53

**1981, Oct. 24 Litho. *Perf. 14½***

| | | | | | |
|---|---|---|---|---|---|
| *232* | A53 | 15c | shown | 25 | 25 |
| *233* | A53 | 20c | Maramis, Pres. de Robert | 35 | 35 |
| *234* | A53 | 25c | Plaque | 45 | 45 |
| *235* | A53 | 30c | Raising UN flag | 52 | 52 |

UN Day and first anniv. of Economic and Social Commission for Asia and Pacific (ESCAP) liason office in Nauru.

### Christmas Type of 1980

Christmas 1981 (Biblical Scriptures in English and Nauruan): 20c, His Name Shall Be Called Emmanuel. 30c, To You is Born This Day. . . . Stamps of same denomination se-tenant.

**1981, Nov. 14 Litho. *Perf. 14½***

| | | | | | |
|---|---|---|---|---|---|
| *236* | A47 | 20c | multi | 35 | 35 |
| *237* | A48 | 20c | multi | 35 | 35 |
| *238* | A47 | 30c | multi | 55 | 55 |
| *239* | A48 | 30c | multi | 55 | 55 |

10th Anniv. of South Pacific Forum A54

**1981, Dec. 9 Litho. *Perf. 13½x1***

| | | | | | |
|---|---|---|---|---|---|
| *240* | A54 | 10c | Globe, dish antenna | 20 | 2 |
| *241* | A54 | 20c | Ship | 40 | 4 |
| *242* | A54 | 30c | Jet | 60 | 6 |
| *243* | A54 | 40c | Produce | 80 | 8 |

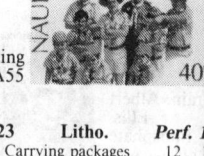

Scouting Year — A55

**1982, Feb. 23 Litho. *Perf. 1***

| | | | | | |
|---|---|---|---|---|---|
| *244* | A55 | 7c | Carrying packages | 12 | 1 |
| *245* | A55 | 8c | Scouts, life preserver, vert. | 14 | 1 |
| *246* | A55 | 15c | Pottery making, vert. | 25 | 2 |
| *247* | A55 | 20c | Inspection | 32 | 3 |
| *248* | A55 | 25c | Scout, cub | 40 | 4 |
| *249* | A55 | 40c | Troop | 65 | 6 |
| *a.* | | | Souvenir sheet of 6 | 2.00 | 2.0 |
| | | | *Nos. 244-249 (6)* | 1.88 | 1.8 |

No. 249a contains Nos. 244-249 (imperf.) tan and bark brown margin shows Brownse Isld. Camp, 1907. Size: 153x114mm.

A56

Ocean Thermal Energy Conversion — A57

Designs: No. 250, Plant under construction. No. 251, Completed plant.

**1982, June 10 Litho. *Perf. 13½***

| | | | | |
|---|---|---|---|---|
| *250* | | Pair | 90 | 90 |
| *a.* | A56 | 25c multi | 45 | 45 |
| *b.* | A57 | 25c multi | 45 | 45 |
| *251* | | Pair | 1.40 | 1.40 |
| *a.* | A56 | 40c multi | 70 | 70 |
| *b.* | A57 | 40c multi | 70 | 70 |

75th Anniv. of Phosphate Industry A58

**1982, Oct. 11 Litho. *Perf. 14***

| | | | | | |
|---|---|---|---|---|---|
| *252* | A58 | 5c | Freighter Fido, 1907 | 9 | 9 |
| *253* | A58 | 10c | Locomotive Nellie, 1907 | 18 | 18 |
| *254* | A58 | 30c | Modern Clyde diesel train, 1982 | 50 | 50 |
| *255* | A58 | 60c | Flagship Eigamoiya, 1969 | 1.00 | 1.00 |

**Souvenir Sheet**

| | | | | | |
|---|---|---|---|---|---|
| *256* | A58 | $1 | Freighters | 2.25 | 2.25 |

ANPEX '82 Natl. Stamp Exhibition, Brisbane, Australia, Nos. 252-255 se-tenant with labels describing stamp. No. 256 contains one stamp (68x27mm.); margin shows map of ports.

Visit of Queen Elizabeth II and Prince Philip — A59

**1982, Oct. 21** *Perf. 14½*

*257* A59 20c Elizabeth, vert. 35 35
*258* A59 50c Philip, vert. 85 85
*259* A59 $1 Couple 1.75 1.75

Christmas 1982 A60

Clergymen: 20c, Father Bernard Lahn, Catholic Mission Church. 30c, Rev. Itubwa Amram, Orro Central Church. 40c, Pastor James Aingimea, Tsiminita Memorial Church, Denigomodu. 50c, Bishop Paul Mea, Diocese of Tarawa-Nauru-Tuvalu.

**1982, Nov. 17**

*260* A60 20c multi 28 28
*261* A60 30c multi 42 42
*262* A60 40c multi 55 55
*263* A60 50c multi 70 70

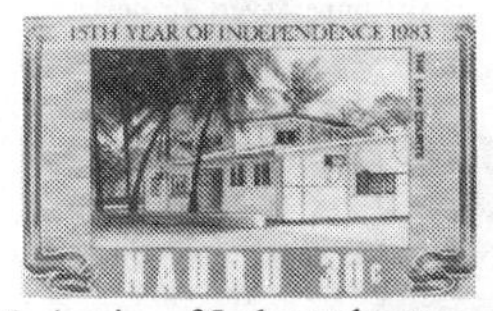


15th Anniv. of Independence — A61

**Wmk. 373**

**1983, Mar. 23** **Litho.** *Perf. 14½*

*264* A61 15c Speaker of Parliament, vert. 25 25
*265* A61 20c People's Court, vert. 35 35
*266* A61 30c Law Courts 50 50
*267* A61 50c Parliament 85 85

World Communications Year — A62

**1983, May. 11** **Litho.** *Perf. 14*

*268* A62 5c Earth Satellite Staion NZ 8 8
*269* A62 10c Omni-directional Range Installation 16 16
*270* A62 20c Fixed-station ambulance driver 32 32
*271* A62 25c Radio Nauru broadcaster 42 42
*272* A62 40c Air mail service 65 65
*Nos. 268-272 (5)* 1.63 1.63

Angam Day (Homecoming) — A63

*Perf. 14x13½*

**1983, Sept. 14** **Litho.** **Wmk. 373**

*273* A63 15c MV Trinza arriving 24 24

**Size: 25x40mm**

*Perf. 14*

*274* A63 20c Elsie Agio in exile 32 32
*275* A63 30c Baby on scale 48 48
*276* A63 40c Children 65 65

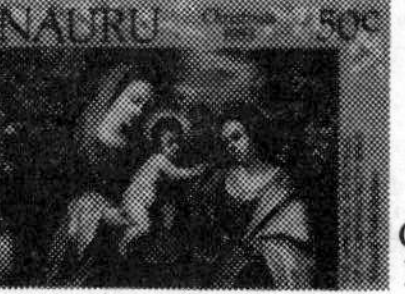


Christmas 1983 — A64

Designs: 5c, The Holy Virgin, the Holy Child and St. John, School of Raphael. 15c, The Mystical Betrothal of St. Cathrin with Jesus, School of Paolo Veronese. 50c, Madonna on the Throne Surrounded by Angels, School of Seville.

*Perf. 14½x14, 14x14½*

**1983, Nov. 16** **Litho.** **Wmk. 373**

*277* A64 5c multi, vert. 8 8
*278* A64 15c multi, vert. 25 25
*279* A64 50c multi 85 85

**Lloyd's List Issue**

Common Design Type

**1984, May 23** **Litho.** *Perf. 14½x14*

*280* CD335 20c Ocean Queen 38 38
*281* CD335 25c Enna G. 48 48
*282* CD335 30c Baron Minto loading phosphate 60 60
*283* CD335 40c Triadic, 1940 75 75

1984 UPU Congress — A65

**Wmk. 373**

**1984, June 4** **Litho.** *Perf. 14*

*284* A65 $1 No. 117 1.50 1.50

Coastal Scene A66

*Perf. 13½x14, 14x13½*

**1984, Sept. 21**

*285* A66 1c shown 5 5
*286* A66 3c Woman, vert. 6 6
*287* A66 5c Fishing vessel 9 9
*288* A66 10c Golfer 18 18
*289* A66 15c Phosphate excavation, vert. 25 25
*290* A66 20c Surveyor, vert. 35 35
*291* A66 25c Air Nauru jet 45 45
*292* A66 30c Elderly man, vert. 52 52
*293* A66 40c Social service 70 70
*294* A66 50c Fishing, vert. 85 85
*295* A66 $1 Tennis, vert. 1.75 1.75
*296* A66 $2 Lagoon Anabar 3.50 3.50
*Nos. 285-296 (12)* 8.75 8.75

Local Butterflies A67

**1984, July 24** *Perf. 14*

*297* A67 25c Common eggfly (female) 50 50
*298* A67 30c Common eggfly (male) 60 60
*299* A67 50c Wanderer (female) 1.00 1.00

Christmas 1984 A68

**1984, Nov. 14**

*300* A68 30c Buada Chapel, vert. 55 55
*301* A68 40c Detudamo Memorial Church, vert. 70 70
*302* A68 50c Candle-light service 90 90

Air Nauru, 15th Anniv. A69

**Wmk. 373**

**1985, Feb. 26** **Litho.** *Perf. 14*

*303* A69 20c Jet 35 35
*304* A69 30c Crew, vert. 55 55
*305* A69 40c Fokker F28 over Nauru 70 70
*306* A69 50c Cargo handling, vert. 90 90

Nauru Phosphate Corp., 15th Anniv. A70

**1985, July 31**

*307* A70 20c Open-cut mining 38 38
*308* A70 25c Rail transport 48 48
*309* A70 30c Phosphate drying plant 55 55
*310* A70 50c Early steam engine 90 90

Christmas 1985 — A71

**1985, Oct.**

*311* A71 50c Canoe 95 95
*312* A71 50c Mother and child 95 95

Se-tenant in continuous design.

Audubon Birth Bicentenary A72

Illustrations of the brown noddy by John J. Audubon.

**1985, Dec. 31**

*313* A72 10c Adult and young 18 18
*314* A72 20c Flying 35 35
*315* A72 30c Two adults 52 52
*316* A72 50c Adult 90 90

Early Transportation — A73

**1986, Mar. 5** **Wmk. 384**

*317* A73 15c Douglas motorcycle 28 28
*318* A73 20c Truck 35 35
*319* A73 30c German steam locomotive, 1910 55 55
*320* A73 40c Baby Austin 75 75

Bank of Nauru, 10th Anniv. A74

Design competition winning children's drawings.

**1986, July 21** **Litho.** *Perf. 14*

*321* A74 20c multi 38 38
*322* A74 25c multi 48 48
*323* A74 30c multi 55 55
*324* A74 40c multi 75 75

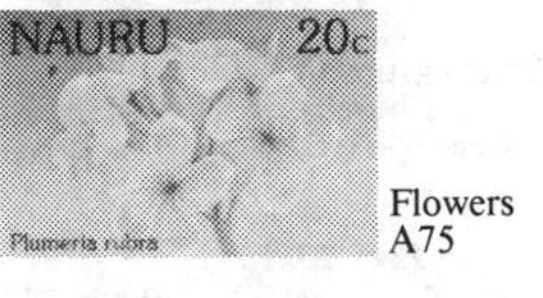


Flowers A75

**Wmk. 384**

**1986, Sept. 30** **Litho.** *Perf. 14*

*325* A75 20c Plumeria rubra 38 38
*326* A75 25c Tristellateia australis 48 48
*327* A75 30c Bougainvillea cultivar 55 55
*328* A75 40c Delonix regia 75 75

Christmas A76

**Wmk. 373**

**1986, Dec. 8** **Litho.** *Perf. 14*

*329* A76 20c Men caroling 35 35
*330* A76 $1 Carolers, invalid 1.75 1.75

Tribal Dances — A77

**1987, Jan. 31**

*331* A77 20c Girls 24 24
*332* A77 30c Men and women 35 35
*333* A77 50c Boy, vert. 60 60

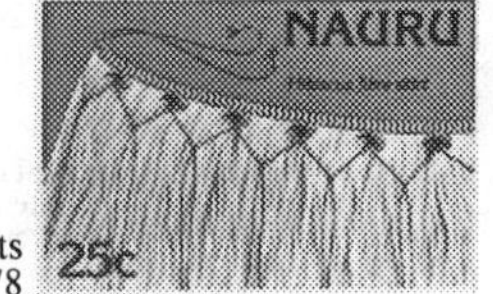


Artifacts A78

**1987, July 30** *Perf. 14*

*334* A78 25c Hibiscus-fiber skirt 28 28
*335* A78 30c Headband, necklaces 35 35
*336* A78 45c Necklaces 52 52
*337* A78 60c Pandanus-leaf fan 70 70

World Post Day — A79

*Perf. 14½x14*

**1987, Oct. 9** **Litho.** **Wmk. 384**

*338* A79 40c UPU emblem, airmail label 58 58

**Souvenir Sheet**

**1987, Oct. 20** *Imperf.*

*339* A79 $1 Emblem, vert. 1.55 1.55

No. 339 has multicolored margin picturing map of Nauru mail routes. Size: 123x83mm.

Common Design Types are pictured in section before Great Britain.

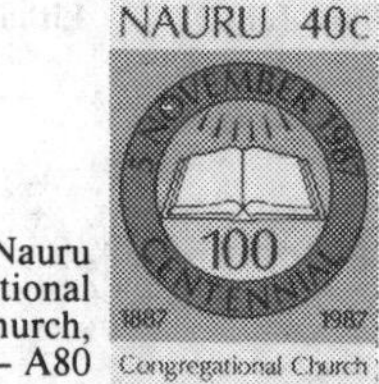


Nauru Congregational Church, Cent. — A80

*Perf. 13x13½*

**1987, Nov. 5 Wmk. 373**

340 A80 40c multi 55 55

Island Christmas Celebration — A81

**1987, Nov. 27 Wmk. 384 *Perf. 14***

341 A81 20c shown 28 28
342 A81 $1 Sign on building 1.40 1.40

A82

Natl. Independence, 20th Anniv. — A83

Heraldic elements independent of or as part of the natl. arms: 25c, Phosphate mining and shipping. 40c, Tomano flower, vert. 55c, Frigate bird, vert. $1, Natl. arms.

*Perf. 13½x14, 14x13½*

**1988, May 16 Unwmk.**

343 A82 25c multi 35 35
344 A82 40c multi 58 58
345 A82 55c multi 78 78

*Perf. 13*

346 A83 $1 multi 1.40 1.40

Nauru Post Office, 80th Anniv. A84

Designs: 30c, Nauru highlighted on German map of the Marshall Islands, and canceled Marshall Islands No. 25. 50c, Letter mailed from Nauru to Dresden and post office, 1908. 70c, Post office, 1988, and Nauru No. 348 canceled on airmail cover.

**1988, July 14 Wmk. 384 *Perf. 14***

347 A84 30c multi 50 50
348 A84 50c multi 82 82
349 A84 70c multi 1.15 1.15

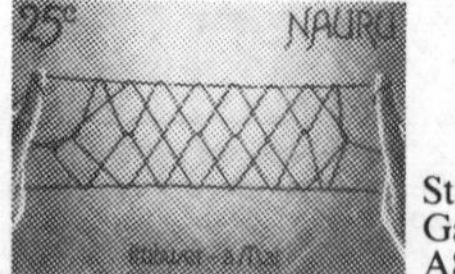


String Games A85

**1988, Aug. 1 Unwmk. *Perf. 13½x14***

350 A85 25c Mat 40 40
351 A85 40c The Pursuer 65 65
352 A85 55c Holding Up the Sky 90 90
353 A85 80c Manujie's Sword 1.30 1.30

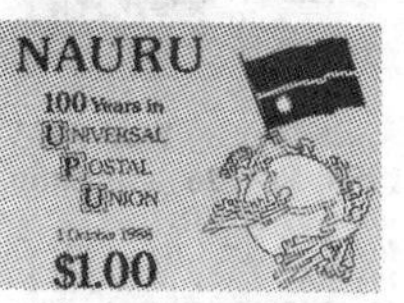


UPU, Cent. A86

*Perf. 13½x14*

**1988, Oct. 1 Litho. Unwmk.**

354 A86 $1 multi 1.70 1.70

## NEPAL

LOCATION — In the Himalaya Mountains between India and Tibet.
GOVT. — Kingdom.
AREA — 56,136 sq. mi.
POP. — 16,100,000 (est. 1982).
CAPITAL — Kathmandu.

Although an independent state, Nepal's close political and economic ties with India make it advisable to include its stamps in this section. The stamps were valid only in Nepal and India until April 1959, when they became valid to all parts of the world.

4 Pice = 1 Anna
64 Pice = 16 Annas = 1 Rupee
100 Paisa = 1 Rupee (1958)

**Catalogue values for unused stamps in this country are for Never Hinged items, beginning with Scott 103 in the regular postage section, Scott C1 in the air post section and Scott O1 in the officials section.**

Sripech and Crossed Khukris — A1

**1881 Typo. Unwmk. *Pin-perf.***
**European Wove Paper**

1 A1 1a ultra 165.00 135.00
2 A1 2a purple 225.00 200.00
a. Tete beche pair
3 A1 4a green 350.00 300.00

*Imperf.*

4 A1 1a blue 105.00 95.00
5 A1 2a purple 130.00 110.00
a. Tete beche pair
6 A1 4a green 130.00 85.00

**1886 Native Wove Paper *Imperf.***

7 A1 1a ultra 14.00 8.75
a. Tete beche pair 60.00 47.50
8 A1 2a violet 20.00 17.50
a. Tete beche pair 160.00 125.00
9 A1 4a green 27.50 21.00
a. Tete beche pair 150.00 125.00

Siva's Bow and Two Khukris — A2

**1899-1903 *Imperf.***
**Native Wove Paper**

10 A2 ½a black 11.50
a. Tete beche pair 55.00
11 A2 ½a red org ('03) 250.00
a. Tete beche pair 2,500.

*Pin-perf.*

12 A2 ½a black 5.00 4.00
a. Tete beche pair 25.00 20.00

Type of 1881

**1898-1904 *Imperf.***

13 A1 1a pale bl 4.75 3.00
a. 1a bluish grn
b. Tete beche pair 22.50 17.00
14 A1 2a gray vio 5.75 2.00
a. Tete beche pair 40.00 24.00
15 A1 2a claret 8.75 3.00
a. Tete beche pair 50.00 27.50
16 A1 2a brown 7.25 3.25
a. Tete beche pair 45.00 27.50
17 A1 4a dl grn 4.75 2.00
a. Tete beche pair 40.00 27.50
b. Cliche of 1a in plate of 4a ('04) 175.00

No. 17b has the recut frame of the 1904 issue.

*Pin-perf.*

18 A1 1a pale bl 5.00 4.25
a. Tete beche pair 22.50 22.50
19 A1 2a gray vio 8.75 6.00
a. Tete beche pair 40.00 32.50
20 A1 2a claret 8.75 6.00
a. Tete beche pair 45.00 32.50
21 A1 2a brown 7.50
a. Tete beche pair 45.00
22 A1 4a dl grn 7.50 4.50
a. Tete beche pair 50.00 42.50

Frame Recut on All Cliches, Fewer Lines

**1903-04 Native Wove Paper *Imperf.***

23 A1 1a bright blue 5.50
a. Tete beche pair 17.50

*Pin-perf.*

24 A1 1a bright blue 7.00
a. Tete beche pair 40.00

No. 23 exists on European wove paper.

Siva Mahadeva — A3

A4

**1907 Engr. *Perf. 13½***
**European Wove Paper.**

26 A3 2p brown 60 30
27 A3 4p green 1.00 50
28 A3 8p carmine 4.25 50
29 A3 16p violet 7.00 80

Type A3 has five characters in bottom panel, reading "Gurkha Sirkar." Date divided in lower corners is "1964." Outer side panels carry denomination (also on A5).

**1917-18 *Imperf.***

29A A4 1a indigo 5.50 1.50
b. 1a brt bl 8.75 6.25
c. Pin-perf.

**During 1917-18, due to a shortage of current stamps, remainder stocks and further printings of types A1 and A4 were used provisionally on official mail and to prepay telegrams. The usual telegraph cancellation is crescent-shaped.**

A5

Type of 1907 Redrawn.
**Nine characters in bottom panel reading "Nepal Sirkar"**

**1929 *Perf. 14, 14½***
**Size: 24¾x18¾mm**

30 A5 2p dk brn 50 20
31 A5 4p green 75 20
32 A5 8p dp red 85 25
33 A5 16p dk red vio 1.50 45
34 A5 24p org yel 2.25 85
35 A5 32p dk ultra 2.50 1.00

**Size: 26x19½mm**

36 A5 1r org red 3.75 2.50

**Size: 28x21mm**

37 A5 5r brn & blk 15.00 15.00
*Nos. 30-37 (8)* 27.10 20.45

On Nos. 30-37 the date divided in lower corners is "1986."

Type of 1929 Redrawn.
**Date characters in Lower Corners read "1992."**

**1935 Unwmk. Engr. *Perf. 14***

38 A5 2p dk brn 50 18
39 A5 4p green 75 15
40 A5 8p brt red 7.50 2.50
41 A5 16p dk red vio 1.50 38
42 A5 24p org yel 1.75 40
43 A5 32p dk ultra 3.75 1.25
*Nos. 38-43 (6)* 15.75 4.86

Redrawn Type of 1935.
***Perf. 11, 11x11½, 12x11½***

**1941-46 Typo.**

44 A5 2p blk brn 35 25
a. 2p grn (error) 7.50 7.50
45 A5 4p brt grn 35 30
46 A5 8p rose red 50 15
47 A5 16p choc ('42) 1.50 1.50
48 A5 24p org ('46) 1.75 1.75
49 A5 32p dp bl ('46) 4.00 4.00

**Size: 29x19½mm.**

50 A5 1r hn brn ('46) 8.00 8.00
*Nos. 44-50 (7)* 16.45 15.95

Exist imperf. vert. or horiz.

Swayambhunath Stupa — A6

Temple of Krishna — A7

View of Kathmandu — A8

Pashupati (Siva Mahadeva) A9

Designs: 4p, Temple of Pashupati. 6p, Tri-Chundra College. 8p, Mahabuddha Temple. 24p, Guheswori Temple, Patan. 32p, The 22 Fountains, Balaju.

***Perf. 13½x14, 13½, 14***

**1949, Oct. 1 Litho. Unwmk.**

51 A6 2p brown
52 A6 4p green
53 A6 6p rose pink
54 A6 8p vermilion
55 A7 16p rose lake
56 A8 20p blue
57 A8 24p carmine
58 A8 32p ultra
59 A9 1r red org
*Nos. 51-59 (9)* 30.00 10.00

King Tribhuvana Bir Bikram — A10

**1954, Apr. 15 Unwmk. *Perf. 14***
**Size: 18x22mm**

60 A10 2p chocolate 12 5
61 A10 4p green 15 6
62 A10 6p rose 18 8
63 A10 8p violet 20 8
64 A10 12p red org 32 14

**Size: 25½x29½mm**

65 A10 16p red brn 42 20
66 A10 20p car rose 50 25
67 A10 24p rose lake 80 40
68 A10 32p ultra 1.00 50
69 A10 50p rose pink 1.35 70

| No. | Type | Description | Unused | Used |
|---|---|---|---|---|
| *70* | A10 | 1r vermilion | 2.00 | 1.35 |
| *71* | A10 | 2r orange | 4.50 | 2.75 |
| | | *Nos. 60-71 (12)* | 11.54 | 6.56 |

Map of Nepal — A11

**1954, Apr. 15**

**Size: 29½x17½mm**

| No. | Type | Description | Unused | Used |
|---|---|---|---|---|
| *72* | A11 | 2p chocolate | 20 | 5 |
| *73* | A11 | 4p green | 22 | 5 |
| *74* | A11 | 6p rose | 38 | 5 |
| *75* | A11 | 8p violet | 45 | 8 |
| *76* | A11 | 12p red org | 75 | 12 |

**Size: 38x21½mm**

| No. | Type | Description | Unused | Used |
|---|---|---|---|---|
| *77* | A11 | 16p red brn | 1.00 | 22 |
| *78* | A11 | 20p car rose | 1.10 | 25 |
| *79* | A11 | 24p rose lake | 1.10 | 25 |
| *80* | A11 | 32p ultra | 1.50 | 35 |
| *81* | A11 | 50p rose pink | 2.25 | 50 |
| *82* | A11 | 1r vermilion | 4.50 | 1.75 |
| *83* | A11 | 2r orange | 9.00 | 5.00 |
| | | *Nos. 72-83 (12)* | 22.45 | 8.67 |

Planting Rice — A12

Throne — A13

Hanuman Gate — A14

King Mahendra Bir Bikram and Queen Ratna — A15

Design: 8p, Ceremonial arch and elephant.

***Perf. 13½x14, 11½, 13½, 14***

**Litho., Photo. (6p).**

**1956 Granite Paper Unwmk.**

| No. | Type | Description | Unused | Used |
|---|---|---|---|---|
| *84* | A12 | 4p green | 7 | 7 |
| *85* | A13 | 6p crim & org | 10 | 7 |
| *86* | A12 | 8p lt vio | 10 | 10 |
| *87* | A14 | 24p car rose | 22 | 25 |
| *88* | A15 | 1r brn red | 22.50 | 17.50 |
| | | *Nos. 84-88 (5)* | 22.99 | 17.99 |

Coronation of King Mahendra Bir Bikram and Queen Ratna Rajya Lakshmi.

Mountain Village and UN Emblem A16

**1956, Dec. 14 Litho. *Perf. 13½***

| No. | Type | Description | Unused | Used |
|---|---|---|---|---|
| *89* | A16 | 12p ultra & org | 1.00 | 70 |

1st anniv. of Nepal's admission to the UN.

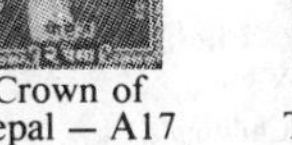

Crown of Nepal — A17

Lumbini Temple — A18

***Perf. 13½x14***

**1957, June 22 Unwmk.**

**Size: 18x22mm**

| No. | Type | Description | Unused | Used |
|---|---|---|---|---|
| *90* | A17 | 2p dl red brn | 18 | 18 |
| *91* | A17 | 4p lt grn | 18 | 18 |
| *92* | A17 | 6p pink | 20 | 20 |
| *93* | A17 | 8p lt vio | 28 | 28 |
| *94* | A17 | 12p org ver | 35 | 35 |

**Size: 25½x30mm**

| No. | Type | Description | Unused | Used |
|---|---|---|---|---|
| *95* | A17 | 16p red brn | 42 | 10 |
| *96* | A17 | 20p dp pink | 55 | 12 |
| *97* | A17 | 24p brt car rose | 70 | 15 |
| *98* | A17 | 32p ultra | 85 | 20 |
| *99* | A17 | 50p rose red | 1.40 | 38 |
| *100* | A17 | 1r brn org | 2.50 | 1.40 |
| *101* | A17 | 2r orange | 5.00 | 3.00 |
| | | *Nos. 90-101 (12)* | 12.61 | 6.54 |

**1958, Dec. 10 Typo. *Perf. 11***

**Without Gum.**

| No. | Type | Description | Unused | Used |
|---|---|---|---|---|
| *102* | A18 | 6pa yellow | 12 | 6 |

10th anniversary of Universal Declaration of Human Rights. Exists imperf.

**Catalogue values for unused stamps in this section, from this point to the end of the section, are for Never Hinged items.**

Map and Flag — A19

**1959, Feb. 18 Engr. *Perf. 14½***

| No. | Type | Description | Unused | Used |
|---|---|---|---|---|
| *103* | A19 | 6pa car & lt grn | 10 | 7 |

First general elections in Nepal.

Statue of Vishnu, Changu Narayan — A20

Krishna Conquering Black Serpent — A21

Designs: 4pa, Nepalese glacier. 6pa, Golden Gate, Bhaktapur. 8pa, Nepalese musk deer. 12pa, Rhinoceros. 16pa, 20pa, 24pa, 32pa and 50pa, Nyatapola Temple, Bhatgaon. 1r, 2r, Himalayan impeyan pheasant. 5r, Satyr tragopan.

***Perf. 13½x14, 14x13½***

**1959-60 Litho. Unwmk.**

**Size: 18x22mm**

| No. | Type | Description | Unused | Used |
|---|---|---|---|---|
| *104* | A20 | 1pa chocolate | 5 | 5 |
| *105* | A21 | 2pa gray vio | 6 | 5 |
| *106* | A20 | 4pa lt ultra | 5 | 5 |
| *107* | A20 | 6pa vermilion | 5 | 5 |
| *108* | A21 | 8pa sepia | 12 | 5 |
| *109* | A21 | 12pa grnsh gray | 12 | 5 |

**Size: 25½x30mm**

| No. | Type | Description | Unused | Used |
|---|---|---|---|---|
| *110* | A20 | 16pa brn & lt vio | 10 | 6 |
| *111* | A20 | 20pa bl & dl rose | 24 | 10 |
| *112* | A20 | 24pa grn & pink | 16 | 12 |
| *113* | A20 | 32pa brt vio & ultra | 24 | 16 |
| *114* | A20 | 50pa rose red & grn | 48 | 20 |
| *115* | A20 | 1r redsh brn & bl | 5.50 | 2.25 |
| *116* | A20 | 2r rose lil & ultra | 1.65 | 90 |
| *117* | A20 | 5r vio & rose red ('60) | 20.00 | 10.00 |
| | | *Nos. 104-117 (14)* | 28.82 | 14.09 |

Nepal's admission to the UPU.

Spinning Wheel — A22

King Mahendra — A23

**1959, Apr. 10 Typo. *Perf. 11***

| No. | Type | Description | Unused | Used |
|---|---|---|---|---|
| *118* | A22 | 2pa dk red brn | 6 | 5 |

Issued to promote development of cottage industries. Exists imperf.

**1959, Apr. 14**

| No. | Type | Description | Unused | Used |
|---|---|---|---|---|
| *119* | A23 | 12pa bluish blk | 8 | 8 |

Issued to commemorate Nepal's admission to UPU. Exists imperf. and ungummed.

King Mahendra Opening Parliament — A24

**1959, July 1 Unwmk. *Perf. 10½***

| No. | Type | Description | Unused | Used |
|---|---|---|---|---|
| *120* | A24 | 6pa dp car | 6 | 6 |

First session of Parliament. Exists imperf.

Sri Pashupati Nath A25

King Mahendra A26

**1959, Nov. 19 *Perf. 11***

**Size: 18x24½mm**

| No. | Type | Description | Unused | Used |
|---|---|---|---|---|
| *121* | A25 | 4pa dp yel grn | 8 | 5 |

**Size: 20½x28mm**

| No. | Type | Description | Unused | Used |
|---|---|---|---|---|
| *122* | A25 | 8pa carmine | 18 | 5 |

**Size: 24½x33mm**

| No. | Type | Description | Unused | Used |
|---|---|---|---|---|
| *123* | A25 | 1r light blue | 70 | 32 |

Issued to commemorate the renovation of Sri Pashupati Temple. The 4pa exists imperf.

**1960, June 11 Photo. *Perf. 14***

**Size: 25x30mm**

| No. | Type | Description | Unused | Used |
|---|---|---|---|---|
| *124* | A26 | 1r red lil | 70 | 28 |

King Mahendra's 40th birthday. See Nos. 147-151A, O15.

Children, Temple and Mt. Everest — A27

Mount Everest — A28

**1960 Typo. *Perf. 11***

| No. | Type | Description | Unused | Used |
|---|---|---|---|---|
| *125* | A27 | 6pa dk bl | 7.00 | 3.50 |

Issued for the first Children's Day, Mar. 1, 1960. Printed in sheets of four. Exists imperf.; value $25 unused.

**1960-61 Photo. *Perf. 14***

Himalaya mountain peaks: 5pa, Machha Puchhre. 40pa, Mansalu.

| No. | Type | Description | Unused | Used |
|---|---|---|---|---|
| *126* | A28 | 5pa cl & brn ('61) | 5 | 5 |
| *127* | A28 | 10pa ultra & rose lil | 10 | 7 |
| *128* | A28 | 40pa vio & red brn ('61) | 24 | 20 |

King Tribhuvana A29

King Mahendra A30

**1961, Feb. 18 *Perf. 13x13½***

| No. | Type | Description | Unused | Used |
|---|---|---|---|---|
| *129* | A29 | 10pa red brn & org | 6 | 6 |

Tenth Democracy Day.

**1961, June 11 *Perf. 14x14½***

| No. | Type | Description | Unused | Used |
|---|---|---|---|---|
| *130* | A30 | 6pa emerald | 5 | 5 |
| *131* | A30 | 12pa ultra | 7 | 6 |
| *132* | A30 | 50pa car rose | 18 | 14 |
| *133* | A30 | 1r brown | 42 | 35 |

King Mahendra's 41st birthday.

Prince Gyanendra Canceling Stamps — A31

Malaria Eradication Emblem and Temple — A32

**1961 Typo. *Perf. 11***

| No. | Type | Description | Unused | Used |
|---|---|---|---|---|
| *134* | A31 | 12pa orange | 20.00 | 8.75 |

Issued for Children's Day, March 1, 1961.

**1962, Apr. 7 Litho. *Perf. 13x13½***

Design: 1r, Emblem and Nepalese flag.

| No. | Type | Description | Unused | Used |
|---|---|---|---|---|
| *135* | A32 | 12pa bl & lt bl | 7 | 5 |
| *136* | A32 | 1r mag & org | 35 | 35 |

WHO drive to eradicate malaria.

King Mahendra A33

**1962, June 11 Unwmk. *Perf. 13***

| No. | Type | Description | Unused | Used |
|---|---|---|---|---|
| *137* | A33 | 10pa sl bl | 7 | 5 |
| *138* | A33 | 15pa brown | 10 | 7 |
| *139* | A33 | 45pa dl red brn | 28 | 18 |
| *140* | A33 | 1r ol gray | 55 | 38 |

King Mahendra's 42nd birthday.

Bhanu Bhakta Acharya A34

King Mahendra A35

Portraits: 10pa, Moti Ram Bhatta. 40pa, Shambu Prasad.

**1962 Photo. Perf. 14x14**

*141* A34 5pa org brn 5 5
*142* A34 10pa dp aqua 5 5
*143* A34 40pa ol bis 12 12

Issued to honor Nepalese poets.

Mahendra Type of 1960 and Type A35

**1962-66 Perf. 14½x14**

*144* A35 1pa car rose 6 6
*145* A35 2pa brt bl 10 6
*145A* A35 3pa gray ('66) 6 6
*146* A35 5pa gldn brn 6 6

***Perf. 14x14½***
**Size: 21½x38mm**

*147* A26 10pa rose cl 6 6
*148* A26 40pa brown 10 10
*149* A26 75pa bl grn 2.50 2.50

***Perf. 14***
**Size: 25x30mm**

*150* A26 2r red org 70 45
*151* A26 5r gray grn 2.00 1.00
*151A* A26 10r vio ('66) 3.75 3.50
*Nos. 144-151A (10)* 9.39 7.85

See Nos. 199, O12-O14.

Blackboard, Book and U.N. Emblem A36

**1963, Jan. 6 Perf. 14½x14**

*152* A36 10pa dk gray 7 6
*153* A36 15pa brown 8 7
*154* A36 50pa vio bl 28 20

UNESCO "Education for All" campaign.

Five-pointed Star and Hands Holding Lamps — A37

Man, Tractor and Wheat — A38

**Unwmk.**

**1963, Feb. 19 Photo. Perf. 13**

*155* A37 5pa blue 5 5
*156* A37 10pa redsh brn 7 5
*157* A37 50pa rose lil 18 10
*158* A37 1r bl grn 35 20

Panchayat System and National Day.

**1963, Mar. 21 Perf. 14x14½**

*159* A38 10pa orange 5 5
*160* A38 15pa dk ultra 5 5
*161* A38 50pa green 9 9
*162* A38 1r brown 18 18

"Freedom from Hunger" campaign of the FAO.

Map of Nepal and Hand — A39

**1963, Apr. 14 Unwmk. Perf. 13**

*163* A39 10pa green 5 5
*164* A39 15pa claret 6 5
*165* A39 50pa slate 18 9
*166* A39 1r vio bl 35 18

Rastriya Panchayat system.

King Mahendra — A40

**1963, June 11 Perf. 13**

*167* A40 5pa violet 5 5
*168* A40 10pa brn org 6 6
*169* A40 15pa dl grn 9 9

King Mahendra's 43rd birthday.

East-West Highway on Map of Nepal and King Mahendra A41

**1964, Feb. 19 Photo. Perf. 13**

*170* A41 10pa bl & dp org 5 5
*171* A41 15pa dk bl & dp org 6 6
*172* A41 50pa dk grn & redsh brn 18 18

Issued to publicize the East-West Highway as "The Prosperity of the Country."

King Mahendra Speaking Before Microphone A42

Crown Prince Birendra A43

**1964, June 11 Perf. 14**

*173* A42 1pa brn ol 6 6
*174* A42 2pa gray 6 6
*175* A42 2r gldn brn 75 55

King Mahendra's 44th birthday.

***Perf. 14x14½***

**1964, Dec. 28 Photo. Unwmk.**

*176* A43 10pa dk grn 15 7
*177* A43 15pa brown 24 10

19th birthday (coming of age) of Crown Prince Birendra Bir Bikram Shah Deva.

Nepalese Flag and Swords, Olympic Emblem A44

**1964, Dec. 31 Litho. Perf. 13x13½**

*178* A44 10pa red & ultra 15 9

18th Olympic Games, Tokyo, Oct. 10-25.

Farmer Plowing — A45

Family — A46

Designs: 5pa, Grain. 10pa, Chemical plant.

**1965 Photo. Perf. 13½**

*179* A45 2pa brt grn & blk 5 5
*180* A45 5pa pale yel grn & brn 5 5
*181* A45 10pa gray & pur 9 5
*182* A46 15pa yel & brn 15 9

Issued to publicize land reform.
The 2pa also exists on light green paper.
Issue dates: 15p, Feb. 10; others, Dec. 16.

Mail Circling Globe A47

**1965, Apr. 13 Perf. 14½x14**

*183* A47 15pa rose lil 9 6

Issued for Nepalese New Year.

King Mahendra — A48

Victims of Revolution, 1939-40 A49

***Perf. 14x14½***

**1965, June 11 Photo. Unwmk.**

*184* A48 50pa rose vio 30 12

King Mahendra's 45th birthday.

**1965, June 11 Perf. 13**

*185* A49 15pa brt grn 9 6

The men executed by the Rana Government 1939-40 were: Shukra Raj Shastri, Dasharath Chand, Dharma Bhakta and Ganga Lal Shresta.

ITU Emblem A50

Devkota A51

**1965, Sept. 15 Photo. Perf. 13**

*186* A50 15pa dp plum & blk 9 6

Cent. of the ITU.

**1965, Oct. 14 Perf. 14x14½**

*187* A51 15pa red brn 9 6

Lakshmi Prasad Devkota (1908-1959), poet.

ICY Emblem A52

**Engr. and Litho.**

**1965, Oct. 24 Perf. 11½x12**

*188* A52 1r multi 45 25

International Cooperation Year, 1965.

Nepalese Flag and King A53

**1966, Feb. 18 Photo. Perf. 14½x14**

*189* A53 15pa dp bl & red 12 6

Issued for Democracy Day.

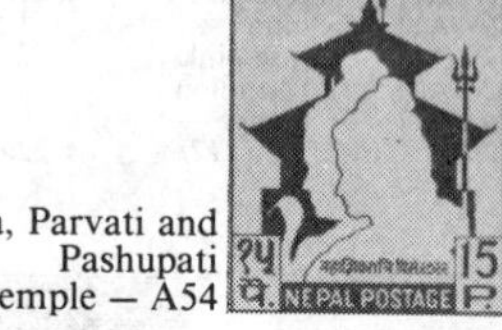

Siva, Parvati and Pashupati Temple — A54

**1966, Feb. 18 Perf. 14**

*190* A54 15pa violet 9 5

Hindu festival Maha Sivaratri.

Emblem — A55

***Perf. 14½x14***

**1966, June 10 Photo. Unwmk.**

*191* A55 15pa dk grn & org 9 6

National Philatelic Exhib., June 10-16.

King Mahendra A56

Kanti Rajya Lakshmi A57

**1966, June 11 Perf. 13x13½**

*192* A56 15pa yel & vio brn 9 5

Issued for King Mahendra's 46th birthday.

**1966, July 5 Photo. Perf. 14x14½**

*193* A57 15pa gldn brn 9 6

Issued to commemorate the 60th birthday of Queen Mother Kanti Rajya Lakshmi.

Queen Ratna Rajya Lakshmi Devi Shah — A58

**1966, Aug. 19 Photo. Perf. 13**

*194* A58 15pa yel & brn 9 6

Issued for Children's Day.

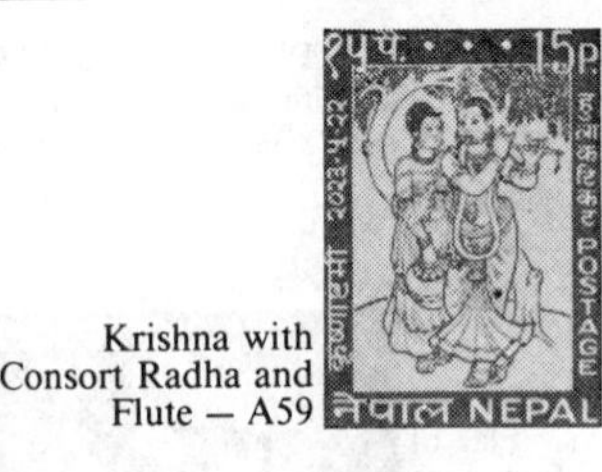
Krishna with Consort Radha and Flute — A59

**1966, Sept. 7**
*195* A59 15pa dk pur & yel 9 6

Krishnastami 2023, the birthday of Krishna.

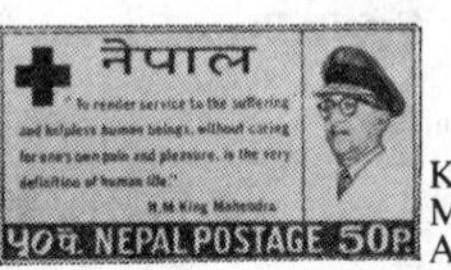
King Mahendra A60

**1966, Oct. 1 Photo. *Perf. 14½x14***
*196* A60 50pa sl grn & dp car 45 20

Issued to commemorate the official recognition of the Nepalese Red Cross.

WHO Headquarters Building, Geneva A61

Lekhnath Paudyal A62

**1966, Nov. 11 Photo. *Perf. 14***
*197* A61 1r purple 60 30

Opening of WHO Headquarters, Geneva.

**1966, Dec. 29 Photo. *Perf. 14***
*198* A62 15pa dl vio bl 9 6

Lekhnath Paudyal (1884-1966), poet.

King Type of 1962

**1967, Feb. 10 Photo. *Perf. 14½x14***
*199* A35 75pa bl grn 28 24

Rama and Sita — A63

**1967, Apr. 18 Litho. *Perf. 14***
*200* A63 15pa brn & yel 9 6

Rama Navami 2024, the birthday of Rama.

Buddha — A64

**1967, May 23 Photo. *Perf. 13½x13***
*201* A64 75pa org & pur 30 30

2,511th birthday of Buddha.

King Mahendra Addressing Crowd and Himalayas — A65

**1967, June 11 *Perf. 13***
*202* A65 15pa dk brn & lt bl 9 6

King Mahendra's 47th birthday.

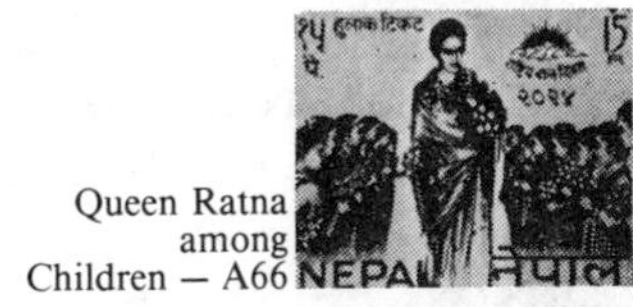
Queen Ratna among Children — A66

**1967, Aug. 20 Photo. *Perf. 13***
*203* A66 15pa pale yel & dp brn 9 6

Issued for Children's Day on the birthday of Queen Ratna Rajya Lakshmi Devi Shah.

Durbar Square, Bhaktapur A67

Design: 5p, Ama Dablam Mountain and ITY emblem.

**1967, Oct. 24 *Perf. 13½x14***
**Size: 29½x21mm**
*204* A67 5p violet 5 5

***Perf. 14½x14***
**Size: 37½x19½mm**
*205* A67 65p brown 30 30

Intl. Tourist Year, 1967. See No. C2.

Official Reading Proclamation — A68

**1967, Dec. 16 Litho. *Perf. 13***
*206* A68 15p multi 7 5

"Back to the Villages" campaign.

Crown Prince Birendra, Boy Scouts and Scout Emblem A69

**1967, Dec. 29 Photo. *Perf. 14½x14***
*207* A69 15p ultra 7 5

60th anniv. of Boy Scouts.

Prithvi Narayan A70

Arms of Nepal A71

**1968, Jan. 11 *Perf. 14x14½***
*208* A70 15p bl & rose 7 5

Rajah Prithvi Narayan (1779-1839), founder of modern Nepal.

**1968, Feb. 19 Photo. *Perf. 14x14½***
*209* A71 15p crini & dk bl 20 12

Issued for National Day.

WHO Emblem and Flag of Nepal A72

**1968, Mar. 25 *Perf. 13***
*210* A72 1.20r dl yel, red & ultra 60 32

World Health Day (UN WHO).

Goddess Sita and Shrine A73

**1968, May 6 Photo. *Perf. 14½x14***
*211* A73 15p vio & org brn 15 7

King Mahendra, Pheasant and Himalayas A74

**1968, June 11 Photo. *Perf. 13½***
*212* A74 15p multi 12 5

King Mahendra's 48th birthday.

Flag, Children and Queen Ratna — A75

**1968, Aug. 19 Litho. *Perf. 13x13½***
*213* A75 5p bl grn, yel & ver 10 5

Fourth National Children's Day.

Buddha and Human Rights Flame A76

**1968, Dec. 10 Photo. *Perf. 14½x14***
*214* A76 1r dk grn & red 45 20

International Human Rights Year.

Young People Dancing Around Flag — A77

**1968, Dec. 28 Photo. *Perf. 14½x14***
*215* A77 25p vio bl 12 6

23rd birthday of Crown Prince Birendra, which is celebrated as Youth Festival.

U.N. Building, Nepalese and U.N. Flags A78

Amsu Varma A79

**1969, Jan. 1 *Perf. 13½x13***
*216* A78 1r multi 45 20

Issued to commemorate Nepal's admission to the U.N. Security Council for 1969-1970.

**1969, Apr. 13 Photo. *Perf. 14x14½***

Portraits: 25p, Ram Shah. 50p, Bhimsen Thapa.

*217* A79 15p grn & pur 9 5
*218* A79 25p bl grn 15 9
*219* A79 50p org brn 30 18

Amsu Varma, 7th cent. ruler and reformer; Ram Shah, 17th cent. ruler and reformer, and Bhimsen Thapa, 18-19th cent. administrator and reformer.

ILO Emblem A80

**1969, May 1 Photo. *Perf. 14½x14***
*220* A80 1r car rose, blk & lt brt 60 35

50th anniv. of the ILO.

King Mahendra — A81

**1969, June 20 *Perf. 13½x13***
*221* A81 25p gold & multi 15 9

Issued to commemorate King Mahendra's 49th birthday (50th by Oriental count). Issuance delayed from June 11 to 20.

King Tribhuvana and Wives — A82

**1969, July 1 *Perf. 14½x14***
*222* A82 25p yel & ol gray 12 6

Issued to commemorate the 64th anniversary of the birth of King Tribhuvana.

Queen Ratna and Child Playing A83

Rhododendron and Himalayas A84

**1969, Aug. 20 Photo. *Perf. 14x14½***
*223* A83 25p gray & rose car 15 9

Issued for the 5th National Children's Day and to commemorate the 41st birthday of Queen Ratna Rajya Lakshmi Devi Shah.

**1969, Sept. 17 Photo. *Perf. 13½***

Flowers: No. 225, Narcissus. No. 226, Marigold. No. 227, Poinsettia.

*224* A84 25p lt bl & multi 28 24
*225* A84 25p brn red & multi 28 24
*226* A84 25p blk & multi 28 24
*227* A84 25p multi 28 24

Nos. 224-227 printed in se-tenant blocks of 4 in sheets of 16 (4x4).

Durga, Goddess of Victory A85

Crown Prince Birendra and Princess Aishwarya A86

**1969, Oct. 17 Photo. *Perf. 14x14½***
*228* A85 15p blk & org 9 5
*229* A85 50p blk, bis brn & vio 20 10

Issued to celebrate the Dasain Festival.

**1970, Feb. 27 Photo. *Perf. 13½***
*230* A86 25p multi 12 6

Issued to commemorate the wedding of Crown Prince Birendra Bir Bikram Shah Deva and Crown Princess Aishwarya Rajya Lakshmi Devi Rana, Feb. 27-28.

Agricultural Products, Cow, Fish — A87

**1970, Mar. 21 Litho. *Perf. 12½***
*231* A87 25p multi 12 6

Issued to publicize the Agricultural Year.

Bal Bhadra Kunwar A88

**1970, Apr. 13 Photo. *Perf. 14½x14***
*232* A88 1r ol bis & red lil 30 24

Bal Bhadra Kunwar, leader in the 1814 battle of Kalanga against British forces.

King Mahendra, Mountain Peak and Crown — A89

**1970, June 11 Litho. *Perf. 11½***
*233* A89 50p gold & multi 15 12

King Mahendra's 50th birthday.

Gosainkund A90

Lakes: 25p, Phewa Tal. 1r, Rara Daha.

**1970, June 11 Photo. *Perf. 13½***
*234* A90 5p dl yel & multi 5 5
*235* A90 25p gray & multi 9 7
*236* A90 1r pink & multi 30 28

A.P.Y. Emblem A91

**1970, July 1 *Perf. 14½x14***
*237* A91 1r dk bl & bl 30 24

Asian Productivity Year 1970.

Bal Mandir Building and Queen Ratna A92

**1970, Aug. 20 Photo. *Perf. 14½x14***
*238* A92 25p gray & bis brn 6 6

Issued for Children's Day. The Bal Mandir Building in Taulihawa is the headquarters of the National Children's Organization.

U.P.U. Headquarters, Bern — A93

**1970, Oct. 9 Photo. *Perf. 14½x14***
*239* A93 2.50r ocher & sep 60 60

Inauguration of new Universal Postal Union Headquarters in Bern.

U.N. Flag A94

**1970, Oct. 24 Photo. *Perf. 14½x14***
*240* A94 25p bl & brn 9 6

25th anniversary of the United Nations.

Royal Palace and Square, Patan A95

Designs: 25p, Bodhnath stupa, near Kathmandu (vert.). 1r, Gauri Shankar, holy mountain.

***Perf. 11x11½, 11½x11***

**1970, Dec. 28 Litho.**
*241* A95 15p multi 6 5
*242* A95 25p multi 9 7
*243* A95 1r multi 35 28

Crown Prince Birendra's 25th birthday.

Statue of Harihar (Vishnu-Siva) — A96

**1971, Jan. 26 Photo. *Perf. 14x14½***
*244* A96 25p bis brn & blk 9 6

Torch and Target — A97

**1971, Mar. 21 Photo. *Perf. 13½x13***
*245* A97 1r bluish gray & dp org 35 24

Intl. year against racial discrimination.

King Mahendra and Subjects A98

**1971, June 11 Photo. *Perf. 14½x14***
*246* A98 25p dl pur & bl 9 6

King Mahendra's 51st birthday.

Sweta Bhairab (Siva) — A99

Sculptures of Siva: 25p, Manhankal Bhairab. 50p, Kal Bhairab.

**1971, July 11 *Perf. 13x13½***
*247* A99 15p org brn & blk 7 5
*248* A99 25p lt grn & blk 12 7
*249* A99 50p bl & blk 24 15

Queen Ratna Receiving Garland A100

**1971, Aug. 20 Photo. *Perf. 11½***
**Granite Paper**
*250* A100 25p gray & multi 9 6

Children's Day, Queen Ratna's birthday.

Map and Flag of Iran, Flag of Nepal A101

**1971, Oct. 14**
**Granite Paper**
*251* A101 1r pink & multi 45 28

2500th anniversary of the founding of the Persian empire by Cyrus the Great.

UNICEF Emblem, Mother and Child A102

**1971, Dec. 11 *Perf. 14½x14***
*252* A102 1r gray bl 45 28

25th anniversary of UNICEF.

Everest A103

Himalayan Peaks: 1r, Kangchenjunga. 1.80r, Annapurna I.

**1971, Dec. 28 *Perf. 13½x13***
*253* A103 25p bl & brn 6 5
*254* A103 1r dp bl & brn 30 20
*255* A103 1.80r bl & yel brn 60 45

"Visit Nepal."

Royal Standard A104

Araniko and White Dagoba, Peking A105

**1972, Feb. 19 Photo. *Perf. 13***
*256* A104 25p dk red & blk 9 6

National Day.

**1972, Apr. 13 Litho. *Perf. 13***
*257* A105 15p lt bl & ol gray 6 5

Araniko, a 14th century Nepalese architect, who built the White Dagoba at the Miaoying Monastery, Peking, 1348.

Book Year Emblem, Ancient Book A106

**1972, Sept. 8 Photo. *Perf. 14½x14***
*258* A106 2p ocher & brn 5 5
*259* A106 5p tan & blk 5 5
*260* A106 1r bl & blk 30 24

International Book Year 1972.

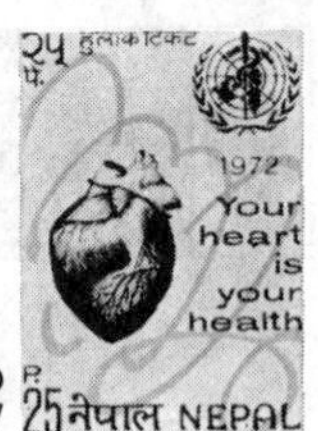


Heart and WHO Emblem — A107

**1972, Nov. 6 Photo. *Perf. 13x13½***
*261* A107 25p dl grn & cl 6 5

"Your heart is your health," World Health Month.

King Mahendra A108

**1972, Dec. 15 Photo. *Perf. 13½x13***
*262* A108 25p brn & blk 6 5

King Mahendra (1920-72).

King Birendra — A109

**1972, Dec. 28 Photo. *Perf. 13x13½***
*263* A109 50p ocher & pur 18 8

King Birendra's 27th birthday.

Northern Border Costume A110

Nepalese Costumes: 50p, Hill dwellers. 75p, Kathmandu Valley couple. 1r, Inner Terai couple.

**1973, Feb. 18 Photo. *Perf. 13***
*264* A110 25p dl lil & multi 6 5
*265* A110 50p lem & multi 12 9
*266* A110 75p multi 18 12
*267* A110 1r multi 24 18
Block of 4 65 60

National Day. Printed se-tenant in blocks of 4 with unifying dark green border.

Babu Ram Acharya — A111

**1973, Mar. 12 Photo. *Perf. 13***
*268* A111 25p ol gray & car 7 5

Babu Ram Acharya (1888-1972), historian.

Nepalese Family and Home A112

**1973, Apr. 7 Photo. *Perf. 14½x14***
*269* A112 1r Prus bl & ocher 50 30

25th anniv. of the WHO.

Lumbini Garden, Birthplace of Buddha — A113

**1973, May 17 Photo. *Perf. 13x13½***
*270* A113 25p *shown* 9 5
*271* A113 75p *Mt. Makalu* 20 15
*272* A113 1r *Gorkha Village* 30 20

FAO Emblem, Women Farmers A114

**1973, June 29 Photo. *Perf. 14½x14***
*273* A114 10p dk gray & vio 7 5

World food program, 10th anniversary.

INTERPOL Headquarters and Emblem — A115

**1973, Sept. 3**
*274* A115 25p bis & bl 7 5

50th anniversary of the International Criminal Police Organization (INTERPOL).

Shom Nath Sigdyal — A116

**1973, Oct. 5 Photo. *Perf. 13x13½***
*275* A116 1.25r vio bl 32 24

Shom Nath Sigdyal (1884-1972), scholar.

Cow — A117

Design: 3.25r, Yak.

**1973, Oct. 25 Photo. *Perf. 13½x13***
*276* A117 2p multi 5 5
*277* A117 3.25r multi 75 75

Festival of Lights (Tihar).

King Birendra — A118

***Perf. 13, 13½x14, 15x14½***

**1973-74 Photo.**
*278* A118 5p dk brn 5 5
*279* A118 15p ol brn & dk brn ('74) 12 9
*280* A118 1r redsh brn & dk brn ('74) 30 24

King Birendra's 28th birthday.

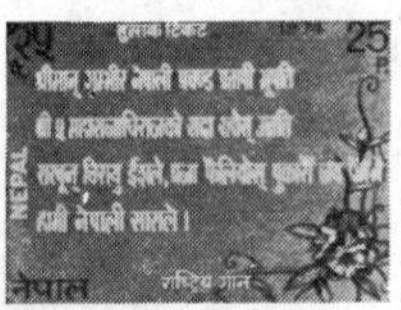


National Anthem A119

Design: 1r, Score of national anthem.

**1974, Feb. 18 Photo. *Perf. 13½x13***
*281* A119 25p rose car 5 5
*282* A119 1r dp grn 24 24

National Day.

King Janak on Throne — A120

**1974, Apr. 14 Litho. *Perf. 13½***
*283* A120 2.50r multi 75 60

Children's Village and SOS Emblem — A121

**1974, May 20 Litho. *Perf. 13½x13***
*284* A121 25p ultra & red 7 5

25th anniv. of SOS Children's Village Intl.

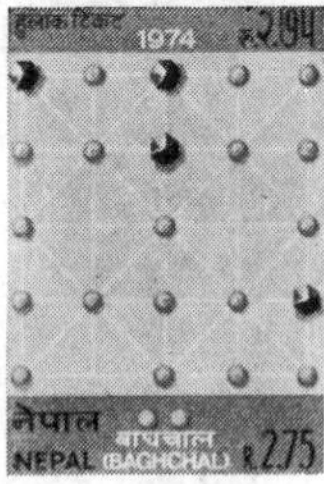


Baghchal — A122

Design: 2p, Soccer.

**1974, July 1 Litho. *Perf. 13***
*285* A122 2p multi 5 5
*286* A122 2.75r multi 75 60

Popular Nepalese games.

WPY Emblem A123

UPU Monument, Bern A124

**1974, Aug. 19 Litho. *Perf. 13***
*287* A123 5p ocher & bl 5 5

World Population Year, 1974.

**1974, Oct. 9 Litho. *Perf. 13***
*288* A124 1r ol & blk 24 18

Centenary of Universal Postal Union.

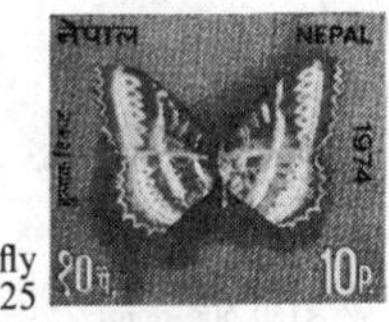


Butterfly A125

Designs: Nepalese butterflies.

**1974, Oct. 16**
*289* A125 10p lt brn & multi 5 5
*290* A125 15p lt bl & multi 5 5
*291* A125 1.25r multi 35 28
*292* A125 1.75r buff & multi 60 45

King Birendra A126

Muktinath A127

Peacock Window A128

**1974, Dec. 28 Litho. *Perf. 13½x13***
*293* A126 25p gray grn & blk 6 5

King Birendra's 29th birthday.

***Perf. 13x13½, 13½x13***

**1974, Dec. 31**
*294* A127 25p multi 6 5
*295* A128 1r multi 30 18

Tourist publicity.

Guheswari Temple — A129

Rara A130

Pashupati Temple — A131

Values quoted in this catalogue are for stamps graded at Fine-Very Fine and with no faults. An illustrated guide to grade is provided in introductory material, beginning on Page V.

King Birendra and Queen Aishwarya — A132

Designs: 1r, Throne. 1.25r, Royal Palace.

**1975, Feb. 24 Litho. *Perf. 13x13½***
*296* A129 25p multi 6 5

**Photo. *Perf. 14½x14***
*297* A130 50p multi 12 8

***Perf. 11½, 11 (A131)***
**Granite Paper**

| | | | | |
|---|---|---|---|---|
| *298* | A132 | 1r ol & multi | 24 | 18 |
| *299* | A132 | 1.25r multi | 30 | 22 |
| *300* | A131 | 1.75r multi | 35 | 30 |
| *301* | A132 | 2.75r gold & multi | 60 | 50 |
| *a* | | Souvenir sheet of 3 | 1.50 | 1.50 |
| | | *Nos. 296-301 (6)* | 1.67 | 1.33 |

Coronation of King Birendra, Feb. 24, 1975. No. 301a contains 3 imperf. stamps similar to Nos. 298-299, 301 and label with commemorative inscription. Gray margin with gold border. Size: 142x104mm.

Tourist Year Emblem A133

Swayambhunath Stupa, Kathmandu — A134

***Perf. 12½x13½, 13½x12½***
**1975, May 25 Litho.**
*302* A133 2p yel & multi 5 5
*303* A134 25p vio & blk 7 5

South Asia Tourism Year 1975.

Tiger A135

**1975, July 17 Litho. *Perf. 13***
*304* A135 2p *shown* 5 5
*305* A135 5p *Deer* (vert.) 5 5
*306* A135 1r *Panda* 28 18

Wildlife conservation.

Queen Aishwarya and IWY Emblem — A136

**1975, Nov. 8 Litho. *Perf. 13***
*307* A136 1r lt bl & multi 30 18

International Women's Year 1975.

Ganesh Peak — A137

Rupse Falls — A138

Kumari, Living Goddess of Nepal — A139

**1975, Dec. 16 Litho. *Perf. 13½***
*308* A137 2p multi 5 5
*309* A138 25p multi 12 7
*310* A139 50p multi 24 15

Tourist publicity.

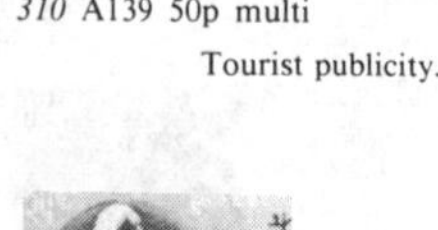


King Birendra — A140

**1975, Dec. 28 Photo. *Perf. 13***
*311* A140 25p rose lil & red lil 6 5

King Birendra's 30th birthday.

Flag and Map of Nepal A141

**1976, Feb. 19 Litho. *Perf. 13***
*312* A141 2.50r dk bl & red 45 45

National or Democracy Day.

Rice Cultivation — A142

**1976, Apr. 11 Litho. *Perf. 13***
*313* A142 25p multi 7 5

Agricultural development.

Flags of Nepal and Colombo Plan — A143

Runner — A144

**1976, July 1 Photo. *Perf. 13x13½***
*314* A143 1r multi 24 18

Colombo Plan, 25th anniversary.

**1976, July 31 Photo. *Perf. 13x13½***
*315* A144 3.25r blk & ultra 45 45

21st Olympic Games, Montreal, Canada, July 17-Aug. 1.

Dove and Map of South East Asia — A145

**1976, Aug. 17 Litho. *Perf. 13½***
*316* A145 5r bis, blk & ultra 75 75

5th Summit Conference of Non-aligned Countries, Colombo, Sri Lanka, Aug. 9-19.

Lakha Mask Dance A146

Folk Dances: 15p, Maruni. 30p, Jhangad. 1r, Sebru.

**1976, Sept. 27 Litho. *Perf. 13½x13***
*317* A146 10p multi 5 5
*318* A146 15p multi 5 5
*319* A146 30p multi 9 6
*320* A146 1r multi 30 20

Nepalese Lily A147

King Birendra A148

Flowers: No. 322, Meconopsis grandis. No. 323, Cardiocrinum giganteum (horiz.). No. 324, Megacodon stylophorus (horiz.).

**1976-77 Litho. *Perf. 13***
*321* A147 30p lt ultra & multi 6 5
*322* A147 30p brn & multi ('77) 6 5
*323* A147 30p vio & multi ('77) 6 5
*324* A147 30p grn & multi ('77) 6 5

**1976, Dec. 28 Photo. *Perf. 14***
*325* A148 5p green 5 5
*326* A148 30p multi 9 6

King Birendra's 31st birthday.

Bell and American Bicentennial Emblem A149

**1976, Dec. 31 Litho. *Perf. 13½***
*327* A149 10r multi 1.75 1.75

American Bicentennial.

Warrior Kazi Amar Singh Thapa, Natl. Hero — A150

**1977, Feb. 18 Photo. *Perf. 13x13½***
*328* A150 10p multi 5 5

Terracotta Figurine, Kapilavastu Excavations A151

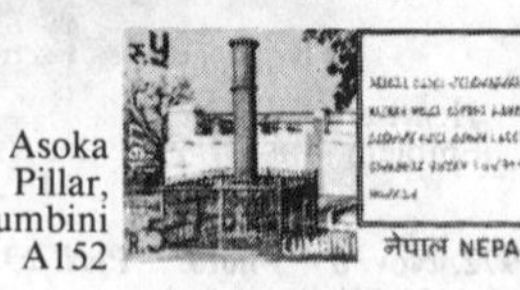


Asoka Pillar, Lumbini A152

**1977, May 3 Photo. *Perf. 14½x14***
*329* A151 30p dk vio 5 5
*330* A152 5r grn & brn 90 90

Tourist publicity.

Cheer Pheasant A153

Birds of Nepal: 5p, Great pied hornbill (vert.). 1r, Green magpie. 2.30r, Nepalese laughing thrush (vert.).

**1977, Sept. 17 Photo. *Perf. 13***
*331* A153 5p multi 5 5
*332* A153 15p multi 5 5
*333* A153 1r multi 18 18
*334* A153 2.30r multi 40 40

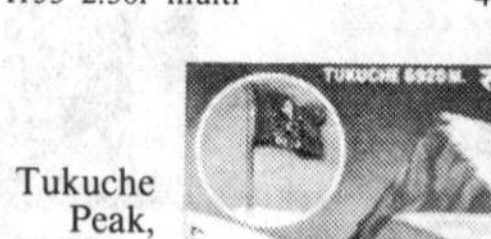


Tukuche Peak, Nepalese Police Flag — A154

**1977, Oct. 2**
*335* A154 1.25r multi 22 22

Ascent of Tukuche, Himalaya Mountains, by Nepalese police team, first anniversary.

Scout Emblem, Map of Nepal — A155

**1977, Nov. 7 Litho. *Perf. 13½***
*336* A155 3.50r multi 65 65

Boy Scouts of Nepal, 25th anniversary.

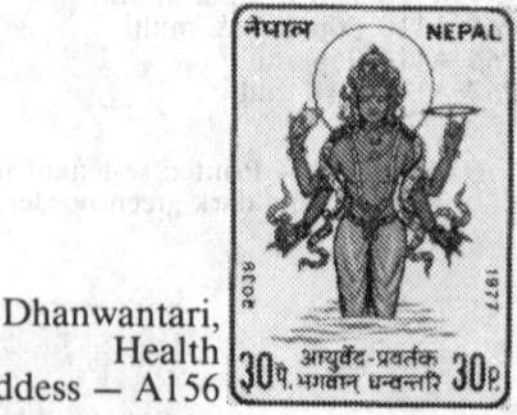


Dhanwantari, Health Goddess — A156

**1977, Nov. 9 Photo. *Perf. 13***
*337* A156 30p bluish grn 5 5

Health Day.

Flags, Map of Nepal A157

King Birendra A158

**1977, Dec. 5 Photo. *Perf. 13½***
*338* A157 1r multi 18 18

Colombo Plan, 26th Consultative Meeting, Kathmandu, Nov. 29-Dec. 7.

**1977, Dec. 28**
*339* A158 5p olive 5 5
*340* A158 1r red brn 18 18

King Birendra's 32nd birthday.

Post Office Seal, New Post Office A159

Design: 75p, Post Office date stamp and new Post Office.

**1978, Apr. 14 Photo. *Perf. 14½x14***
*341* A159 25p org brn & blk 5 5
*342* A159 75p bis & blk 14 14

Centenary of Nepalese postal service.

Mt. Everest A160

Design: 4r, Mt. Everest, different view.

**1978, May 29 Photo. *Perf. 13½x13***
*343* A160 2.30r red brn & sl 40 40
*344* A160 4r grn & vio bl 70 70

1st ascent of Mt. Everest, 25th anniv.

Mountains, Trees, Environmental Emblem — A161

**1978, June 5**
*345* A161 1r bl grn & org 18 18

World Environment Day, June 5.

Queen Mother Ratna — A162

**1978, Aug. 20 Photo. *Perf. 14***
*346* A162 2.30r ol gray 40 40

Queen Mother Ratna, 50th birthday.

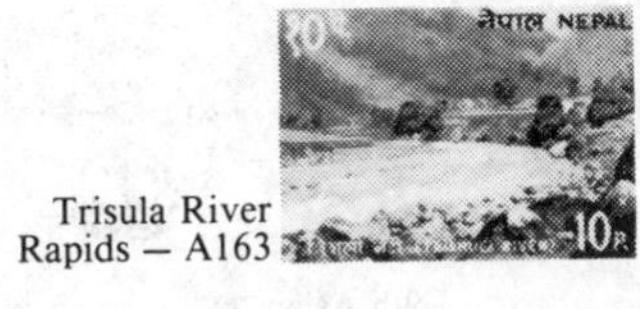

Trisula River Rapids — A163

Tourist Publicity: 50p, Nepalese window. 1r, Dancer, Mahakali dance (vert.).

**1978, Sept. 15 Litho. *Perf. 14***
*347* A163 10p multi 5 5
*348* A163 50p multi 9 9
*349* A163 1r multi 18 18

Human Rights Emblem — A164

**1978, Oct. 10 Litho. *Perf. 13½***
*350* A164 25p red brn & red 8 8
*351* A164 1r dk bl & red 18 18

Universal Declaration of Human Rights, 30th anniversary.

Choerospondias Axillaris — A165

Designs: 1r, Castanopsis indica (vert.). 1.25r, Elaeocarpus sphaericus.

**1978, Oct. 31 Photo. *Perf. 13***
*352* A165 5p multi 5 5
*353* A165 1r multi 18 18
*354* A165 1.25r multi 22 22

King Birendra — A166

**1978, Dec. 17 *Perf. 13½x14***
*355* A166 30p brn & ind 6 6
*356* A166 2r vio & blk 35 35

King Birendra's 33rd birthday.

Kamroop and Patan Temples and Deity A167

Red Machhindra Chariot — A168

***Perf. 14½x14, 13½***
**1979 Photo., Litho.**
*357* A167 75p cl & ol 15 15
*358* A168 1.25r multi 22 22

Red Machhindra Nath Festival, Lalitpur (Patan). Issue dates: 75p, Apr. 27; 1.25r, July 25.

Bas-relief A169

Tree Planting A170

**1979, May 12 Photo. *Perf. 13***
*359* A169 1r yel & brn 18 18

Lumbini Year.

**1979, June 29 Photo. *Perf. 13x13½***
*360* A170 2.30r multi 40 40

Afforestation campaign.

Children with Flag, IYC Emblem — A172

**1979, Aug. 20 *Perf. 13½***
*362* A172 1r lt brn 18 18

Intl. Year of the Child; Natl. Children's Day.

Mount Pabil — A173

Tourism: 50p, Swargadwari Temple. 1.25r, Altar with statues of Shiva and Parbati.

**1979, Sept. 26 Photo. *Perf. 13½x13***
*363* A173 30p dk bl grn 6 6
*364* A173 50p multi 9 9
*365* A173 1.25r multi 22 22

Northern Shrike — A174

***Perf. 14½x13½***
**1979, Nov. 22 Photo.**
*366* A174 10p *shown* 5 5
*367* A174 10r *Aethopyga ignicauda* 2.00 2.00

International World Pheasant Association Symposium, Kathmandu, Nov. 21-23. See No. C7.

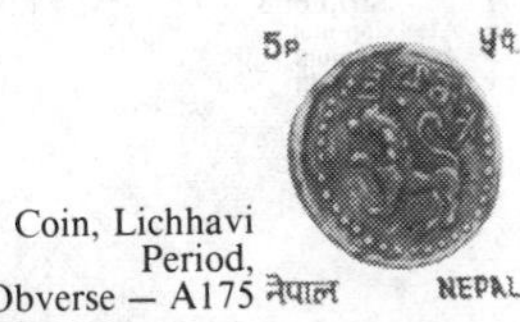


Coin, Lichhavi Period, Obverse — A175

Ancient Coins: No. 369, Lichhavi Period, reverse. No. 370, Malla Period, obverse. No. 371, Malla Period, reverse. No. 372, Shah Period, obverse. No. 373, Shah Period, reverse. Stamps of same denomination printed se-tenant.

**1979, Dec. 16 Photo. *Perf. 15***
*368* A175 5p brn, brn org 5 5
*369* A175 5p brn, brn org 5 5
*370* A175 15p dk bl 5 5
*371* A175 15p dk bl 5 5
*372* A175 1r sl bl 18 18
*373* A175 1r sl bl 18 18
*Nos. 368-373 (6)* 56 56

King Birendra A176

Ban-Ganga Dam A177

**1979, Dec. 28 Litho. *Perf. 14***
*374* A176 25p multi 5 5
*375* A177 2.30r multi 42 42

King Birendra's 35th birthday.

Samyak Pooja Festival A178

**1980, Jan. 15 *Perf. 13½***
*376* A178 30p vio brn & gray 6 6

Holy Basil — A179

**1980, Mar. 24 Photo. *Perf. 14x14½***
*377* A179 5p *shown* 5 5
*378* A179 30p *Himalayan valerian* 6 6
*379* A179 1r *Nepalese pepper* 18 18
*380* A179 2.30r *Himalayan rhubarb* 42 42

Gyandil Das A180

Nepalese Writers: 30p, Shddhi Das Amatya. 1r, Pahal Man Singh Snwar. 2.30r, Jay Prithibi Bahadur Singh.

**1980, Apr. 13 *Perf. 13½x13***
*381* A180 5p bis & rose lil 5 5
*382* A180 30p vio brn & lt red brn 6 6
*383* A180 1r bl & ol gray 18 18
*384* A180 2.30r ol grn & dk bl 42 42

The Catalogue editors cannot undertake to appraise, identify or judge the genuineness or condition of stamps.

Jwalaji Dailekh (Temple), Holy Flame A181

Temple Statue A182

**1980, Sept. 14 Litho. *Perf. 14½***

*385* A181 10p *shown* 5 5
*386* A181 1r *Godavari Pond* 18 18
*387* A181 5r *Mt. Dhaulagiri* 90 90

**1980, Oct. 29 *Perf. 14x13½***

*388* A182 25r multi 4.50 4.50

World Tourism Conf., Manila, Sept. 27.

King Birendra's 36th Birthday — A183

**1980, Dec. 28 Litho. *Perf. 14***

*389* A183 1r multi 18 18

International Year of the Disabled A184

**1981, Jan. 1**

*390* A184 5r multi 90 90

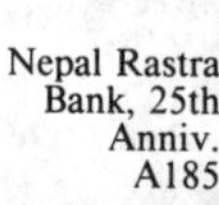

Nepal Rastra Bank, 25th Anniv. A185

**1981, Apr. 26 Litho. *Perf. 14***

*391* A185 1.75r multi 32 32

No. 1 — A186

**1981, July 16**

*392* A186 10p shown 5 5
*393* A186 40p No. 2 7 7
*394* A186 3.40r No. 3 60 60
*a* Souvenir sheet of 3 75 75

Nepalese stamp centenary. No. 394a contains Nos. 392-394; multicolored decorative margin. Size: 118x76mm.

Intl. Hotel Assoc., 70th Council Meeting, Kathmandu — A187

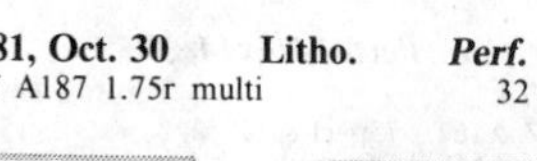

**1981, Oct. 30 Litho. *Perf. 14***

*395* A187 1.75r multi 32 32

Stamp Centenary A188

King Birendra's 37th Birthday A189

**1981, Dec. 27 Litho. *Perf. 14***

*396* A188 40p multi 7 7

Nepal '81 Stamp Exhibition, Kathmandu, Dec. 27-31.

**1981, Dec. 28**

*397* A189 1r multi 18 18

Hrishikesh, Buddhist Stone Carving, Ridi — A190

**1981, Dec. 30**

*398* A190 5p shown 5 5
*399* A190 25p Tripurasundari Pavilion, Baitadi 5 5
*400* A190 2r Mt. Langtang Lirung 35 35

Royal Nepal Academy, 25th Anniv. — A191

Balakrishna Sama — A192

**1982, June 23 Litho. *Perf. 14***

*401* A191 40p multi 7 7

**1982, July 21 *Perf. 13½***

*402* A192 1r multi 18 18

Dish Antenna, Satellite — A193

Mt. Nuptse — A194

**1982, Nov. 7 Litho. *Perf. 14***

*403* A193 5r multi 90 90

**1982, Nov. 18 *Perf. 13½***

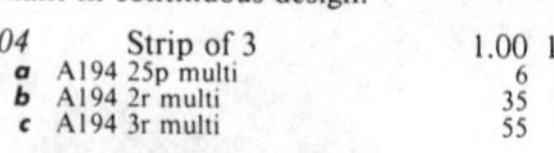

Intl. Union of Alpinists Assoc., 50th Anniv. (Himalaya Peaks): b. Mt. Lhotse (31x31mm). c. Mt. Everest (40x31mm). Se-tenant in continuous design.

*404* Strip of 3 1.00 1.00
*a* A194 25p multi 6 6
*b* A194 2r multi 35 35
*c* A194 3r multi 55 55

9th Asian Games — A195

Kulekhani Hydro-electric Plant — A196

**1982, Nov. 19 *Perf. 14***

*405* A195 3.40r multi 65 65

**1982, Dec. 2 *Perf. 13½***

*406* A196 2r Lake, dam 35 35

King Birendra's 38th Birthday — A197

**1982, Dec. 28 *Perf. 12½***

*407* A197 5p multi 5 5

25th Anniv. of Nepal Industrial Development Co. — A198

**1983, June 15 Litho. *Perf. 14***

*408* A198 50p multi 5 5

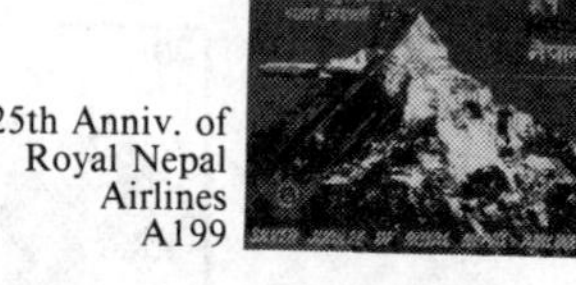
25th Anniv. of Royal Nepal Airlines A199

**1983, Aug. 1 *Perf. 13½***

*409* A199 1r multi 9 9

World Communications Year — A200

**1983, Oct. 30 Litho. *Perf. 12***

*410* A200 10p multi 5 5

Musical Instruments — A201

**1983, Nov. 3**

*411* A201 5p Sarangi 5 5
*412* A201 10p Kwota 5 5
*413* A201 50p Narashinga 5 5
*414* A201 1r Murchunga 8 8

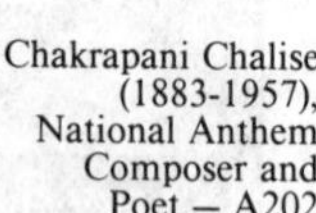
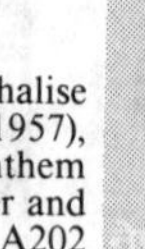
Chakrapani Chalise (1883-1957), National Anthem Composer and Poet — A202

**1983, Dec. 20**

*415* A202 4.50r multi 38 38

King Birendra's 39th Birthday A203

**1983, Dec. 28 *Perf. 14***

*416* A203 5r multi 42 42

Temple, Barahkshetra A204

**1983, Dec. 30 *Perf. 14***

*417* A204 1r shown 8 8
*418* A204 2.20r Triveni pilgrimage site 20 20
*419* A204 6r Mt. Cho-oyu 50 50

Auditor General, 25th Anniv. — A204a

**1984, June 28 Litho. *Perf. 14***

*419A* A204a 25p Open ledger 5 5

Asia-Pacific Broadcasting Union, 20th Anniv. — A205

**1984, July 1 Litho. *Perf. 14***

*420* A205 5r Transmission tower 42 42

Tribhuvan University, 25th Anniv. — A206

**1984, July 8**

*421* A206 50p University emblem 5 5

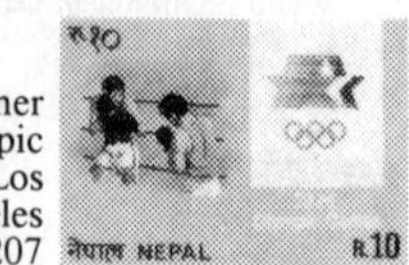
1984 Summer Olympic Games, Los Angeles A207

**1984, Aug. 5**

*422* A207 10r Boxing 85 85

Family Planning Assoc., 25th Anniv. — A208

**1984, Sept. 18**
*423* A208 1r multi 9 9

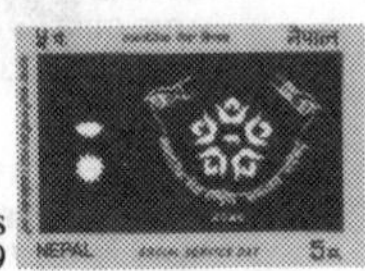

Social Services Day — A209

**1984, Sept. 24**
*424* A209 5p multi 5 5

Wildlife A210

**1984, Nov. 30**
*425* A210 10p Gavialis gangeticus 5 5
*426* A210 25p Panthera uncia 5 5
*427* A210 50p Antilope cervicapra 5 5

Chhinna Masta Bhagvati Temple and Goddess Sakhandeshwari Devi, Statue — A211

Designs: 10p, Lord Vishu the Giant, Yajna Ceremony on Bali, bas-relief, A. D. 467, vert. 5r, Mt. Api, Himalayas, vert.

**1984, Dec. 21**
*428* A211 10p multi 5 5
*429* A211 1r multi 9 9
*430* A211 5r multi 42 42

King Birendra, 40th Birthday A212

**1984, Dec. 28**
*431* A212 1r multi 9 9

Sagarmatha Natl. Park — A213

**1985, May 6**
*432* A213 10r Mt. Everest, wild-life 85 85

King Mahendra Trust Congress for Nature Conservation, May 6-11.

Illustration from Shiva Dharma Purana, 13th Cent. Book — A214

Design: Maheshware, Lord Shiva, with brahma and vishnu.

**1985, May 30**
*433* Strip of 5 24 24
*a.-e.* A214 50p. any single 5 5

Nos. 433a-433e printed se-tenant in a continuous design. No. 433 also exists imperf. between stamps. Size of Nos. 433a, 433e: 26x22mm. Size of Nos. 433b, 433d: 24x22mm. Size of No. 433c: 17x22mm.

UN, 40th Anniv. — A215

**1985, Oct. 24 Litho. *Perf. 13½x14***
*434* A215 5r multi 30 30

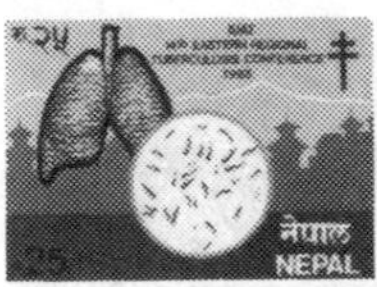

14th Eastern Regional Tuberculosis Conference A216

**1985, Nov. 25**
*435* A216 25r multi 1.50 1.50

First South Asian Regional Cooperation Summit — A217

**1985, Dec. 8 *Perf. 14***
*436* A217 5r Flags 30 30

Temple of Jaleshwar, Mohottary Underwater Project — A218

**1985, Dec. 15 Litho. *Perf. 14x13½***
*437* A218 10p shown 5 5
*438* A218 1r Temple of Shaileshwari, Doti 6 6
*439* A218 2r Lake Phoksundo, Dolpa 12 12

Intl. Youth Year — A219

**1985, Dec. 21 *Perf. 14***
*440* A219 1r multi 6 6

Devi Ghat Hydro-electric Dam Project A220

King Birendra, 41st Birthday A221

**1985, Dec. 28 Litho. *Perf. 14***
*441* A220 2r multi 12 12

**1985, Dec. 28**
*442* A221 50p Portrait 5 5

Panchayat System, 25th Anniv. — A222

**1986, Apr. 10 *Perf. 13½***
*443* A222 4r multi 24 24

Pharping Hydroelectric Station, 75th Anniv. — A223

**1986, Oct. 9 Litho. *Perf. 14x13½***
*444* A223 15p multi 5 5

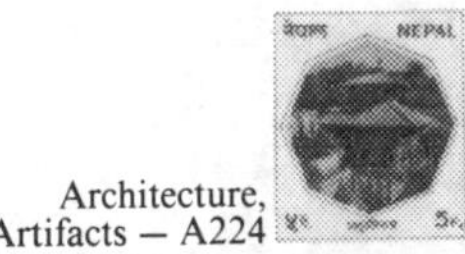

Architecture, Artifacts — A224

**1986, Oct. 9 Photo. *Perf. 13x13½***
*445* A224 5p Pashupati Temple 5 5
*446* A224 10p Lumbini Fort 5 5
*446A* A224 50p like 5p ('87) 5 5
*447* A224 1r Crown of Nepal 6 6

No. 446A issued Apr. 14.

Asian Productivity Org., 25th Anniv. A225

**1986, Oct. 26 Litho. *Perf. 13½x14***
*448* A225 1r multi 6 6

Reclining Buddha, Kathmandu Valley — A226

Mt. Pumori, Khumbu Range A227

***Perf. 14, 13½x13***
**1986, Oct. 26 Litho.**
*449* A226 60p multi 5 5
*450* A227 8r multi 48 48

King Birendra, 42nd Birthday A228

Intl. Peace Year A229

**1986, Dec. 28 Litho. *Perf. 13x13½***
*451* A228 1r multi 9 9

**1986, Dec. 28 *Perf. 14***
*452* A229 10r multi 75 75

Social Service Natl. Coordination Council, 10th Anniv. — A230

**1987, Sept. 22 Litho. *Perf. 13½***
*453* A230 1r Natl. flag, emblem 12 12

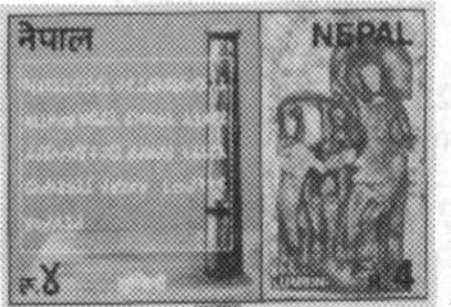

Birth of Buddha A231

Design: Asoka Pillar, enlargement of commemorative text and bas-relief of birth.

**1987, Oct. 28 *Perf. 14***
*454* A231 4r multi 45 45

First Natl. Boy Scout Jamboree, Kathmandu — A232

**1987, Oct. 28 Litho. *Perf. 14***
*455* A232 1r dark red brn, pale brn org & dark blue 12 12

3rd SAARC Summit Conference, Kathmandu A233

**1987, Nov. 2**
*456* A233 60p gold & lake 7 7

Southeast Asian Assoc. for Regional Cooperation.

Rastriya Samachar Samiti (Natl. News Agency), 25th Anniv. — A234

**1987, Nov. 10**
*457* A234 4r dark vio, lt ultra & dark red 45 45

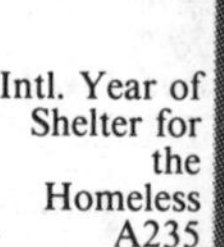

Intl. Year of Shelter for the Homeless A235

**1987, Dec. 21 Litho. *Perf. 14***
*458* A235 5r multi 85 85

Kashthamandap Temple, Kathmandu A236

Surya Bikram Gyawali (b. 1898), Historian A237

**1987, Dec. 21 Photo. *Perf. 13½x13***
*459* A236 25p multi 5 5

**1987, Dec. 21 *Perf. 13x13½***
*460* A237 60p multi 12 12

King Birendra, 43rd Birthday — A238

***Perf. 14½x13½***
**1987, Dec. 28 Litho.**
*461* A238 25p multi 5 5

Mount Kanjiroba A239

**1987, Dec. 30 *Perf. 14***
*462* A239 10r multi 1.70 1.70

The indexes in each volume of the Scott Catalogue contain many listings which help to identify stamps.

Crown Prince Dipendra's 18th Birthday — A240

Nepal Bank, Ltd., 50th Anniv. — A241

**1988, Mar. 28 Litho. *Perf. 14***
*463* A240 1r multi 20 20

**1988, Apr. 8**
*464* A241 2r multi 38 38

Kanti Childrens' Hospital, 25th Anniv. A242

**1988, Apr. 8**
*465* A242 60p multi 12 12

Royal Shuklaphanta Wildlife Reserve — A243

**1988, Apr. 8**
*466* A243 60p Swamp deer 12 12

Queen Mother Ratna Rajya Laxmi Devi Shah, 75th Birthday — A244

**1988, Aug. 20 Litho. *Perf. 14x13½***
*467* A244 5r mutli 95 95

Nepal Red Cross, 25th Anniv. — A245

**1988, Sept. 12 Litho. *Perf. 14x13½***
*468* A245 1r dull fawn & dark red 18 18

Bindhyabasini, Pokhara — A246

**1988 Litho. *Perf. 14½***
*469* A246 15p multi 10 10

## AIR POST STAMPS

**Catalogue values for unused stamps in this section, from this point to the end of the section, are for Never Hinged items.**

Bird over Kathmandu — AP1

***Rough Perf 11½***
**1958, Oct. 16 Typo. Unwmk.**
**Without Gum**
*C1* AP1 10p dark blue 15 15

Plane over Kathmandu AP2

**1967, Oct. 24 Photo. *Perf. 13½x13***
*C2* AP2 1.80r multi 75 60

International Tourist Year, 1967.

God Akash Bhairab and Nepal Airlines Emblem AP3

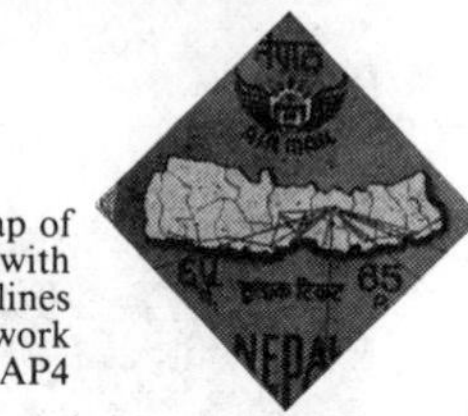

Map of Nepal with Airlines Network AP4

Design: 2.50r, Plane over Himalayas.

***Perf. 14½x14, 13 (65p)***
**1968, July 1 Photo.**
*C3* AP3 15p bl & bis brn 5 5
*C4* AP4 65p vio bl 18 15
*C5* AP3 2.50r dp bl & scar 60 45

10th anniv. of the Royal Nepal Airlines Corp.

Flyer and Jet — AP5

**1978, Dec. 12 Photo. *Perf. 13***
*C6* AP5 2.30r bl & ocher 42 42

75th anniversary of 1st powered flight.

Pheasant Type of 1979

**1979, Nov. 22 Photo. *Perf. 14½x14***
*C7* A174 3.50r *Impeyan pheasant,* horiz. 1.00 1.00

*Nevis stamps can be mounted in Scott's British Leeward Islands Album.*

## OFFICIAL STAMPS

**Catalogue values for unused stamps in this section, from this point to the end of the section, are for Never Hinged items.**

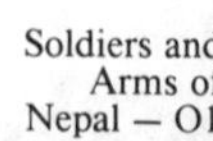

Soldiers and Arms of Nepal — O1

***Perf. 13½***
**1959, Nov. 1 Litho. Unwmk.**

**Size: 29x17½mm**

| | | | | |
|---|---|---|---|---|
| *O1* | O1 | 2p redsh brn | 6 | 5 |
| *O2* | O1 | 4p yel grn | 9 | 5 |
| *O3* | O1 | 6p sal pink | 12 | 5 |
| *O4* | O1 | 8p brt vio | 15 | 5 |
| *O5* | O1 | 12p red org | 18 | 5 |

**Size: 37½x21½mm**

| | | | | |
|---|---|---|---|---|
| *O6* | O1 | 16p red brn | 24 | 5 |
| *O7* | O1 | 24p carmine | 30 | 6 |
| *O8* | O1 | 32p rose car | 45 | 7 |
| *O9* | O1 | 50p ultra | 60 | 9 |
| *O10* | O1 | 1r rose red | 1.25 | 18 |
| *O11* | O1 | 2r orange | 2.75 | 30 |
| | | *Nos. O1-O11 (11)* | 6.19 | 1.00 |

Nos. 144-146 and 124 Overprinted in Black काज सरकारी

**1960-62 Photo. *Perf. 14½x14***
**Overprint 12½mm Long**
*O12* A35 1pa car rose ('62) 6 6
*O13* A35 2pa bright bl ('62) 9 9
*O14* A35 5pa golden brn ('62) 12 12

***Perf. 14***
**Overprint 14½mm Long**
*O15* A26 1r red lilac 18

The overprint, "Kaj Sarkari" in Devanagari characters means "Service." Five other denominations, 10p, 40p, 75p, 2r and 5r, were similarly overprinted but not issued.

In 1983 substantial quantities of the set of nine values were sold as remainders by the Post Office at face value (under $1 for the set).

# NEVIS

LOCATION — In the West Indies, southeast of Puerto Rico.
GOVT. — A former presidency of the Leeward Islands Colony (British).
AREA — 50 sq. mi.
POP. — 11,864 (1883).
CAPITAL — Charlestown.

See Leeward Islands and St. Kitts-Nevis.

12 Pence = 1 Shilling

Medicinal Spring
A1 A2

A3 A4

**1861 Unwmk. Engr. *Perf. 13***
**Bluish Paper**

| | | | | |
|---|---|---|---|---|
| *1* | A1 | 1p lake rose | 250.00 | 100.00 |
| *2* | A2 | 4p dl rose | 875.00 | 275.00 |
| *3* | A3 | 6p gray | 500.00 | 275.00 |
| *4* | A4 | 1sh green | 1,000. | 250.00 |

### Grayish Paper

*5* A1 1p lake rose 15.00 15.00
*6* A2 4p dl rose 67.50 55.00
*7* A3 6p lil gray 45.00 30.00
*8* A4 1sh green 125.00 32.50

**1867** **White Paper** ***Perf. 15***

*9* A1 1p red 11.50 11.50
*10* A2 4p orange 70.00 16.00
*11* A4 1sh yel grn 1,000. 100.00
*12* A4 1sh bl grn 145.00 27.50

### Laid Paper

*13* A4 1sh yel grn *16,500.* 5,750.
Ms. cancel 900.00

**1876** **Litho.**

### Wove Paper

*14* A1 1p rose 8.25 9.00
*14A* A1 1p red 8.25 9.00
**b.** 1p vermilion 8.25 9.00
**c.** Imperf., pair 360.00
**d.** Half used as ½p on cover 900.00
*15* A2 4p orange 165.00 20.00
**a.** Imperf.
**b.** Vert. pair, imperf. between *3,000.*
*16* A3 6p olive gray 175.00 175.00
*17* A4 1sh gray green 27.50 45.00
**a.** 1sh dark green 27.50 55.00
**b.** Horiz. strip of 3, perf. all around & imperf. btwn. *3,750.*

### *Perf. 11½*

*18* A1 1p vermilion 19.00 25.00
**a.** Horiz. pair, imperf. btwn.
**b.** Half used as ½p on cover 1,000.
**c.** Imperf., pair 195.00

Queen Victoria — A5

### Wmk. Crown and C. C. (1)

**1879-80** **Typo.** ***Perf. 14***

*19* A5 1p violet ('80) 20.00 15.00
**a.** Diagonal half used as ½p on cover 475.00
*20* A5 2½p red brown 82.50 65.00

**1882-90** **Wmk. Crown and C. A. (2)**

*21* A5 ½p green ('83) 2.00 2.50
*22* A5 1p violet 47.50 21.00
**a.** Half used as ½p on cover 400.00
*23* A5 1p rose ('84) 1.90 1.90
*24* A5 2½p red brown 75.00 35.00
*25* A5 2½p ultra ('84) 3.00 3.00
*26* A5 4p blue 200.00 35.00
*27* A5 4p gray ('84) 5.50 3.50
*28* A5 6p green ('83) 250.00 *350.00*
*29* A5 6p brn org ('86) 15.00 20.00
*30* A5 1sh violet ('90) 42.50 62.50

Half of No. 22 Surcharged in Black or Violet

**NEVIS. ½d**

**1883**

*31* A5 ½p on half of 1p vio *1,000.* 30.00
**a.** Double surcharge 450.00
*32* A5 ½p on half of 1p vio (V) *1,250.* 30.00
**a.** Double surcharge 450.00

Nevis stamps were discontinued in 1890 and replaced by those of the Leeward Islands.

## NEW BRITAIN

LOCATION — In the South Pacific Ocean, northeast of New Guinea.
GOVT. — Australian military government.
AREA — 13,000 sq. mi. (approx.).
POP. — 50,600 (approx.).
CAPITAL — Rabaul.

The island Neu-Pommern, a part of former German New Guinea, was captured during World War I by Australian troops and named New Britain. Following the war it was mandated to Australia and designated a part of the Mandated Territory of New Guinea. See German New Guinea, North West Pacific Islands and New Guinea.

12 Pence = 1 Shilling

Kaiser's Yacht "The Hohenzollern"
A3 A4

Stamps of German New Guinea, 1900, Surcharged

### First Setting

Surcharge lines spaced 6mm on 1p-8p, 4mm on 1sh-5sh.

### *Perf. 14, 14½*

**1914, Oct. 17** **Unwmk.**

*1* A3 1p on 3pf brn 82.50 82.50
*2* A3 1p on 5pf grn 16.00 16.00
*3* A3 2p on 10pf car *125.00* *135.00*
*4* A3 2p on 20pf ultra 20.00 20.00
**a.** "2d." dbl., "G.R.I." omitted 725.00
**b.** Inverted surcharge
*5* A3 2½p on 10pf car 37.50 37.50
*6* A3 2½p on 20pf ultra 67.50 67.50
**a.** Inverted surcharge
*7* A3 3p on 25pf org & blk, *yel* 115.00 115.00
*8* A3 3p on 30pf org & blk, *sal* 125.00 125.00
**a.** Double surcharge
**b.** Triple surcharge
*9* A3 4p on 40pf lake & blk 200.00 200.00
**a.** Double surcharge 850.00 850.00
**b.** Inverted surcharge 850.00
**c.** "4d." omitted
*10* A3 5p on 50pf pur & blk, *sal* 385.00 360.00
**a.** Double surcharge
*11* A3 8p on 80pf lake & blk, *rose* 425.00. 425.00.
**a.** No period after "8d"
*12* A4 1sh on 1m car 1,000. 1,000.
*13* A4 2sh on 2m bl 900.00 900.00
*14* A4 3sh on 3m blk vio 1,400. 1,400.
*15* A4 5sh on 5m sl & car 2,400. 2,400.
**a.** No period after "I"

"G.R.I." stands for Georgius Rex Imperator.

### Second Setting

Surcharge lines spaced 5mm on 1p-8p, 5½mm on 1sh-5sh.

**1914, Dec. 16**

*16* A3 1p on 3pf brn 27.50 27.50
**a.** Double surcharge 200.00
**b.** "1" omitted 315.00
**c.** Same as "b", double surcharge
**d.** Inverted surcharge 200.00
**e.** "4" for "1"
**f.** Small "1"
*17* A3 1p on 5pf grn 6.50 6.50
**a.** Double surcharge 315.00
**b.** "G. I. R." 1,500.
**c.** "d" inverted 500.00 500.00
**d.** No periods after "G R I" 110.00
**e.** Small "1" 14.00 14.00
**f.** "1d" double 175.00
**g.** No period after "1d"
**h.** Triple surcharge
*18* A3 2p on 10pf car 18.00 18.00
**a.** Double surcharge 410.00
**b.** Double surcharge, one inverted 775.00
**c.** Surcharged "G. I. R., 3d" *4,150.*
**d.** Surcharged "1d" 1,100. 1,100.
**e.** Period before "G" *1,500.*
**f.** No period after "2d"
**g.** Inverted surcharge
**h.** "2d" double, one inverted
**i.** "1d" on "2d"
**j.** In pair with "2½d" on 10pf
*19* A3 2p on 20pf ultra 20.00 20.00
**a.** Double surcharge 775.00 775.00
**b.** Double surcharge, one inverted 900.00 900.00
**c.** "R" inverted 1,000.
**d.** Surcharged "1d" 3,500. 3,150.
**f.** Inverted surcharge
**g.** "1d" on "2d" *8,750.*
**h.** Pair, one without surcharge
**i.** In pair with "2½d" on 20pf
*20* A3 2½p on 10pf car 55.00 55.00
*21* A3 2½p on 20pf ultra 900.00 900.00
**a.** Double surch., one invtd.
**b.** "2½" triple
**c.** Surcharged "3d"
*22* A3 3p on 25pf org & blk, *yel* 60.00 55.00
**a.** Double surcharge
**b.** Inverted surcharge
**c.** "G. R. I." only
**d.** "G. I. R." 1,100. 1,100.
**e.** Pair, one without surcharge
**f.** Surcharged "G. I. R., 5d"
*23* A3 3p on 30pf org & blk, *sal* 60.00 60.00
**a.** Double surcharge 725.00
**b.** Double surch., one invtd. 1,000.
**c.** "d" inverted 550.00
**d.** Surcharged "1d" 2,750.
**e.** Triple surcharge
**g.** Double inverted surcharge
**h.** Pair, one without surcharge
*24* A3 4p on 40pf lake & blk 55.00 55.00
**a.** Double surcharge 675.00 675.00
**b.** Double surch., one invtd. 900.00 900.00
**e.** Surcharged "1d"
**f.** "1" on "4"
*25* A3 5p on 50pf pur & blk, *sal* 145.00 145.00
**a.** Double surcharge 550.00
**b.** Double surch., one invtd. 575.00
**c.** "5" omitted 550.00
**d.** Inverted surcharge
**e.** Double inverted surcharge 675.00
**f.** "G. I. R."
*26* A3 8p on 80pf lake & blk, *rose* 380.00 325.00
**a.** Double surch. 1,400. 1,250.
**b.** Double surch., one invtd. 1,400. 1,250.
**c.** Triple surch. 1,400. 1,250.
**d.** No period after "8d"
**e.** Inverted surcharge
**f.** Surcharged "3d" 1,400.
*27* A4 1sh on 1m car 1,100. 900.00
*28* A4 2sh on 2m bl 1,400. 925.00
**a.** Surcharged "5s"
**b.** Double surcharge
*29* A4 3sh on 3m blk vio 2,000. 1,800.
**a.** No periods after "R I"
**b.** "G.R.I." double
*29C* A4 5sh on 5m sl & car 6,750. 6,000.
**d.** No periods after "R I"
**e.** Surcharged "1s"

Same Surcharge on Stamps of Marshall Islands

**1914**

*30* A3 1p on 3pf brn 25.00 25.00
**a.** Inverted surcharge 650.00
*31* A3 1p on 5pf grn 40.00 40.00
**a.** Double surcharge
**b.** No period after "d"
**c.** Inverted surcharge 900.00
*32* A3 2p on 10pf car 11.00 11.00
**a.** Double surcharge 600.00
**b.** Double surch., one invtd. 650.00
**c.** Surcharge sideways
**d.** No period after "2d"
**e.** No period after "G"
*33* A3 2p on 20 pf ultra 11.00 11.00
**a.** No period after "d" 35.00
**b.** Double surcharge 400.00
**c.** Double surch., one invtd. 825.00
**d.** Inverted surcharge
**e.** "I" omitted
*34* A3 3p on 25pf org & blk, *yel* 325.00 325.00
**a.** Double surcharge 975.00 825.00
**b.** Double surch., one invtd. 1,100.
**c.** No period after "d" 550.00 550.00
**d.** Inverted surcharge
*35* A3 3p on 30pf org & blk, *sal* 375.00 375.00
**a.** No period after "d" 550.00
**b.** Inverted surcharge
**c.** Double surcharge
**d.** Double surch., one invtd.
*36* A3 4p on 40pf lake & blk 67.50 67.50
**a.** No period after "d" 165.00 165.00
**b.** Double surcharge
**c.** "4d" omitted
**d.** "1d" on "4d"
**e.** No period after "R"
**f.** Inverted surcharge 825.00
**g.** Surcharged "1d" 975.00
*37* A3 5p on 50pf pur & blk, *sal* 82.50 82.50
**a.** "d" omitted 525.00
**b.** Double surcharge
**c.** "5d" double 475.00
*38* A3 8p on 80pf lake & blk, *rose* 375.00 375.00
**a.** Inverted surcharge
**b.** Double surcharge
**c.** Double surch., one invtd.
**d.** Triple surcharge
*39* A4 1sh on 1m car 900.00 750.00
**a.** Double surcharge
**b.** Double surcharge, one with "s1" for "1s"
**c.** No period after "I" 2,000.
*40* A4 2sh on 2m bl 675.00 675.00
**a.** Double surch., one invtd. 2,100.
**b.** Double surchage
**c.** Large "S"
**d.** No period after "I"
*41* A4 3sh on 3m blk vio 2,200. 2,200.
**a.** Double surcharge
**b.** No period after "I" 2,700.
**c.** No period after "R I" 2,700.
**d.** Inverted surcharge
*42* A4 5sh on 5m sl & car 5,000. 5,000.
**a.** Double surch., one invtd. 6,500.

A5

G.R.I. Rabaul
(Deutsch Neuguinea)
R 2d. № 510

Surcharged in Black on Registration Label

**1914** ***Perf. 12***

*43* A5 3p blk & red (Rabaul) 75.00 85.00
**a.** "Friedrich Wilhelmshaven" 150.00 165.00
**b.** "Herbertshohe" 165.00 175.00
**c.** "Kawieng" 125.00 140.00
**d.** "Kieta" 375.00 380.00
**e.** "Manus" 300.00 325.00
**f.** Double surch. (Rabaul) 500.00 425.00
**g.** As "c." double surcharge *625.00*
**h.** As "e." double surcharge *750.00*

Nos. 43a, 43c and 43e exist with town name in letters with serifs. The varieties Deutsch-Neuguinea, Deutsch Neu-Guinea, etc., are known.

Nos. 32 and 33 Surcharged with Large Figure "1"

**1915**

*44* A3 1p on 2p on 10pf car 175.00 100.00
**a.** "1" double
**b.** "1" inverted
*45* A3 1p on 2p on 20pf ultra 3,750. 2,400.
**a.** "1" inverted
**b.** No period after "d"

The stamps of Marshall Islands surcharged "G. R. I." and new values in British currency were all used in New Britain and are therefore listed here.

### OFFICIAL STAMPS

O1

German New Guinea Nos. 7-8 Surcharged

**1915** **Unwmk.** ***Perf. 14***

*O1* O1 1p on 3pf brn 8.25 9.75
**a.** Double surcharge 900.00
*O2* O1 1p on 5pf grn 67.50 97.50

## NEW BRUNSWICK

LOCATION — In eastern Canada, bordering on the Bay of Fundy and the Gulf of St. Lawrence.
GOVT. — Former British Province.
AREA — 27,985 sq. mi.
POP. — 285,594 (1871).
CAPITAL — Fredericton.

At one time a part of Nova Scotia, New Brunswick became a separate province in 1784. Upon joining the Canadian Confederation in 1867 its postage stamps were superseded by those of Canada.

12 Pence = 1 Shilling
100 Cents = 1 Dollar (1860)

Values of New Brunswick Nos. 1-4 vary according to condition. Quotations are for fine copies. Very fine to superb specimens sell at much higher prices, and inferior or poor copies sell at reduced prices, depending on the condition of the individual specimen.

Crown of Great Britain and Heraldic Flowers of the United Kingdom — A1

**1851** **Unwmk.** **Engr.** ***Imperf.***

### Blue Paper

*1* A1 3p red 1,350. 150.00
**a.** 3p dark red 1,500. 175.00
**b.** Half used as 1½p on cover *3,500.*
*2* A1 6p olive yel 3,000. 250.00
**a.** 6p orange yellow 3,000. 250.00
**b.** Half used as 3p on cover *3,000.*
**c.** Quarter used as 1½p on cover *17,500.*
*3* A1 1sh brt red vio 12,500. 2,500.
**a.** Half used as 6p on cover
**b.** Quarter used as 3p on cover
*4* A1 1sh dull violet 11,500. 3,750.
**a.** Half used as 6p on cover *20,000.*
**b.** Quarter used as 3p on cover *20,000.*

*The reprints are on stout white paper. The 3p is printed in orange and the 6p and 1sh in violet black. Value about $100 per set of 3.*

Charles Connell — A2

**1860** *Perf. 12*

| | | | | |
|---|---|---|---|---|
| *5* | A2 | 5c brown | 2,500. | |

No. 5 was prepared for use but not issued.

Locomotive A3

Victoria A4

A5

A6

Steam and Sailing Ship — A7

Edward VII as Prince of Wales — A8

**1860-63 White Paper** *Perf. 12*

| | | | | |
|---|---|---|---|---|
| *6* | A3 | 1c red lilac | 8.50 | 8.50 |
| **a.** | | 1c brown violet | 16.00 | 14.00 |
| **b.** | | Horiz. pair, imperf. vert. | 350.00 | |
| *7* | A4 | 2c orange ('63) | 4.00 | 4.00 |
| **a.** | | Vertical pair, imperf. horiz. | 350.00 | |
| *8* | A5 | 5c yellow grn | 3.50 | 3.50 |
| **a.** | | 5c blue green | 3.50 | 3.50 |
| **b.** | | 5c olive green | 50.00 | 11.00 |
| *9* | A6 | 10c vermilion | 17.50 | 15.00 |
| **a.** | | Half used as 5c on cover | | 600.00 |
| *10* | A7 | 12½c blue | 19.00 | 19.00 |
| *11* | A8 | 17c black | 18.00 | 18.00 |

The stamps of New Brunswick have been superseded by those of Canada.

## NEWFOUNDLAND

LOCATION — An island in the Atlantic Ocean off the coast of Canada, and Labrador, a part of the mainland.
GOVT. — Former British Dominion.
AREA — 42,734 sq. mi.
POP. — 321,177 (1945).
CAPITAL — St. John's.

Newfoundland was a self-governing Dominion of the British Empire from 1855 to 1933, when it became a Crown Colony. In 1949 it united with Canada.

Values of early Newfoundland stamps vary according to condition. Quotations for Nos. 1-23 are for fine copies. Very fine to superb specimens sell at much higher prices, and inferior or poor copies sell at reduced prices, depending on the condition of the individual specimen.

12 Pence = 1 Shilling
100 Cents = 1 Dollar (1866)

*New Brunswick stamps can be mounted in Scott's Canada Specialty and Master Canada Albums.*

Crown of Great Britain and Heraldic Flowers of the United Kingdom — A1

Rose, Thistle and Shamrock — A3

A2

A4

A5

A6

A7

A8

**1857 Unwmk. Engr.** ***Imperf.***
**Thick Porous Wove Paper with Mesh**

| | | | | |
|---|---|---|---|---|
| *1* | A1 | 1p brn vio | 42.50 | *75.00* |
| *2* | A2 | 2p scar ver | 9,000. | 3,250. |
| *3* | A3 | 3p green | 250.00 | 265.00 |
| *4* | A4 | 4p scar ver | 4,000. | 2,000. |
| **a.** | | Half used as 2p on cover | | *15,000.* |
| *5* | A1 | 5p brn vio | 200.00 | 250.00 |
| *6* | A5 | 6p scar ver | 8,500. | 2,250. |
| *7* | A6 | 6½pscar ver | 1,500. | *1,650.* |
| *8* | A7 | 8p scar ver | 175.00 | *225.00* |
| **a.** | | Half used as 4p on cover | | 3,750. |
| *9* | A8 | 1sh scar ver | 10,000. | 3,500. |
| **a.** | | Half used as 6p on cover | | *13,500.* |

**1860**
**Thin to Thick Wove Paper, No Mesh**

| | | | | |
|---|---|---|---|---|
| *11* | A2 | 2p orange | 135.00 | *100.00* |
| *11A* | A3 | 3p green | 37.50 | 80.00 |
| *12* | A4 | 4p orange | 1,500. | 600. |
| **b.** | | Half used as 2p on cover | | *10,750.* |
| *12A* | A1 | 5p vio brown | 42.50 | *100.00* |
| *13* | A5 | 6p orange | 1,350. | 350.00 |
| *15* | A8 | 1sh orange | 16,500. | 4,250. |
| **b.** | | Half used as 6p on cover | | *13,500.* |

A 6½p orange exists as a souvenir item.

**1861-62**

| | | | | |
|---|---|---|---|---|
| *15A* | A1 | 1p vio brown | 90.00 | *150.00* |
| *16* | A1 | 1p redsh brn | 2,750. | |
| *17* | A2 | 2p rose | 75.00 | 75.00 |
| *18* | A4 | 4p rose | 30.00 | *60.00* |
| **a.** | | Half used as 2p on cover | | |
| *19* | A1 | 5p redsh brn | 30.00 | 60.00 |
| **a.** | | 5p orange brown | 30.00 | *60.00* |
| *20* | A5 | 6p rose | 11.50 | *45.00* |
| **a.** | | Half used as 3p on cover | | *5,000.* |
| *21* | A6 | 6½p rose | 35.00 | *80.00* |
| *22* | A7 | 8p rose | 30.00 | *105.00* |
| *23* | A8 | 1sh rose | 17.50 | *105.00* |
| **a.** | | Half used as 6p on cover | | *12,000.* |

Some sheets of Nos. 11-23 are known with the papermaker's watermark "STACEY WISE 1858" in large capitals.
No. 16 was prepared but not issued.
False cancellations are found on Nos. 1, 3, 5, 8, 11, 11A, 12A and 17-23.

Codfish — A9

Harp Seal — A10

Prince Albert A11

Victoria A12

Fishing Ship A13

Victoria A14

**1865-94** *Perf. 12*
**Thin Yellowish Paper (Except No. 29)**

| | | | | |
|---|---|---|---|---|
| *24* | A9 | 2c green | 37.50 | 18.00 |
| **a.** | | White paper | 25.00 | 12.50 |
| **b.** | | Half used as 1c on cover | | *3,750.* |
| *25* | A10 | 5c brown | 275.00 | 175.00 |
| **a.** | | Half used as 2c on cover | | |
| *26* | A10 | 5c black ('68) | 110.00 | 65.00 |
| *27* | A11 | 10c black | 110.00 | 50.00 |
| **a.** | | White paper | 60.00 | 22.50 |
| **b.** | | Half used as 5c on cover | | *3,500.* |
| *28* | A12 | 12c pale red brn | 165.00 | 110.00 |
| **a.** | | White paper | 19.00 | 19.00 |
| **b.** | | Half used as 6c on cover | | *2,250.* |
| *29* | A12 | 12c brn, *white* ('94) | 17.50 | 15.00 |
| *30* | A13 | 13c orange | 45.00 | 37.50 |
| *31* | A14 | 24c blue | 15.00 | 13.00 |

Edward VII as Prince of Wales A15

Queen Victoria A16

**1868-94**

| | | | | |
|---|---|---|---|---|
| *32* | A15 | 1c violet | 17.50 | 17.50 |
| *32A* | A15 | 1c brn lil (re-engr. '71) | 24.00 | 24.00 |
| *33* | A16 | 3c ver ('70) | 110.00 | 75.00 |
| *34* | A16 | 3c blue ('73) | 150.00 | 12.00 |
| *35* | A16 | 6c dl rose ('70) | 5.25 | 5.25 |
| *36* | A16 | 6c car lake ('94) | 9.50 | 9.50 |

In the re-engraved 1c the top of the letters "N" and "F" are about ½mm from the ribbon with "ONE CENT". In No. 32 they are fully 1mm away. There are many small differences in the engraving.

**1876-79** ***Rouletted***

| | | | | |
|---|---|---|---|---|
| *37* | A15 | 1c brn lilac ('77) | 25.00 | 14.00 |
| *38* | A9 | 2c green ('79) | 47.50 | 22.50 |
| *39* | A16 | 3c blue ('77) | 125.00 | 5.50 |
| *40* | A10 | 5c blue | 100.00 | 5.50 |

A17

A19

A18

A20

**1880-96** *Perf. 12*

| | | | | |
|---|---|---|---|---|
| *41* | A17 | 1c violet brown | 6.50 | 5.75 |
| *42* | A17 | 1c gray brown | 6.50 | 5.75 |
| *43* | A17 | 1c brown ('96) | 20.00 | 20.00 |
| *44* | A17 | 1c deep grn ('87) | 4.50 | 2.00 |
| **a.** | | 1c gray green | 6.50 | 2.75 |
| *45* | A17 | 1c green ('97) | 4.50 | 2.00 |
| *46* | A19 | 2c yellow green | 10.00 | 8.00 |
| *47* | A19 | 2c green ('96) | 20.00 | 12.00 |
| *48* | A19 | 2c red org ('87) | 8.00 | 4.00 |
| **a.** | | Imperf., pair | 140.00 | |
| *49* | A18 | 3c blue | 13.00 | 3.00 |
| *51* | A18 | 3c umber brn ('87) | 9.00 | 2.75 |
| *52* | A18 | 3c vio brown ('96) | 22.50 | 22.50 |
| *53* | A20 | 5c pale blue | 150.00 | 6.50 |
| *54* | A20 | 5c dark bl ('87) | 65.00 | 4.50 |
| *55* | A20 | 5c bright bl ('94) | 10.00 | 3.00 |

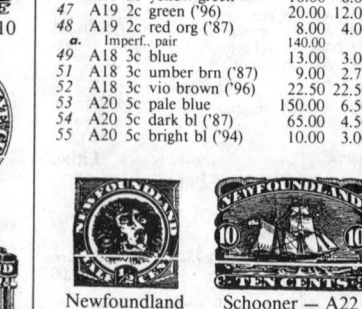

Newfoundland Dog — A21

Schooner — A22

**1887-96**

| | | | | |
|---|---|---|---|---|
| *56* | A21 | ½c rose red | 3.50 | 3.00 |
| *57* | A21 | ½c org red ('96) | 17.50 | 17.50 |
| *58* | A21 | ½c black ('94) | 3.50 | 3.00 |
| *59* | A22 | 10c black | 30.00 | 24.00 |

Queen Victoria — A23

**1890**

| | | | | |
|---|---|---|---|---|
| *60* | A23 | 3c slate | 4.75 | 50 |
| **a.** | | 3c gray lilac | 6.50 | 50 |
| **b.** | | 3c brown lilac | 10.00 | 50 |
| **c.** | | 3c lilac | 6.50 | 50 |
| **d.** | | 3c slate violet | 12.00 | 65 |
| **e.** | | Imperf. horizontally, pair | 400.00 | |

Victoria A24

Cabot (John?) A25

Cape Bonavista A26

Caribou Hunting A27

Mining — A28

Logging — A29

Fishing A30

Cabot's Ship "Matthew" A31

Willow Ptarmigan A32

Seals A33

Salmon Fishing — A34

Colony Seal — A35

Iceberg off St. John's A36

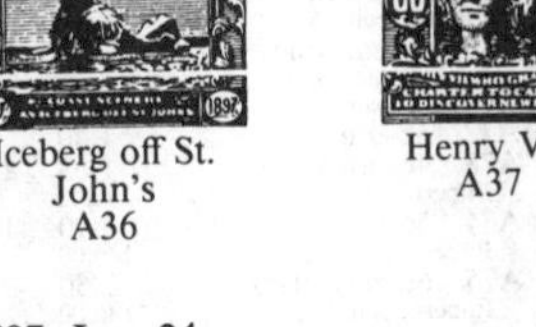

Henry VII A37

**1897, June 24**

| No. | Type | Description | Unused | Used |
|---|---|---|---|---|
| *61* | A24 | 1c deep green | 1.40 | 90 |
| *62* | A25 | 2c carmine lake | 1.75 | 90 |
| *63* | A26 | 3c ultramarine | 2.75 | 90 |
| *64* | A27 | 4c olive green | 3.50 | 1.75 |
| *65* | A28 | 5c violet | 4.00 | 1.75 |
| *66* | A29 | 6c red brown | 3.75 | 2.00 |
| *67* | A30 | 8c red orange | 6.25 | 3.00 |
| *68* | A31 | 10c black brown | 7.25 | 3.00 |
| *69* | A32 | 12c dark blue | 8.00 | 3.50 |
| *70* | A33 | 15c scarlet | 8.75 | 3.25 |
| *71* | A34 | 24c gray violet | 9.50 | 4.50 |
| *72* | A35 | 30c slate | 20.00 | 12.00 |
| *73* | A36 | 35c red | 40.00 | 24.00 |
| *74* | A37 | 60c black | 6.50 | 3.50 |
| | | *Nos. 61-74 (14)* | 123.40 | 64.95 |

400th anniv. of John Cabot's discovery of Newfoundland; 60th year of Victoria's reign. The ship on the 10c was previously used by the American Bank Note Co. as the "Flagship of Columbus" on U.S. No. 232. The portrait on the 2c, intended to be of John Cabot, is said to be a Holbein painting of his son, Sebastian.

No. 60a Surcharged with Bars and

**ONE CENT**
No. 75

ONE CENT
No. 76

**ONE CENT**
No. 77

**1897, Oct.**

| No. | Type | Description | Unused | Used |
|---|---|---|---|---|
| *75* | A23 | 1c on 3c gray lilac | 10.50 | 8.50 |
| *76* | A23 | 1c on 3c gray lilac | 70.00 | 62.50 |
| *77* | A23 | 1c on 3c gray lilac | 350.00 | 325.00 |

Nos. 75-77 exist with red surcharge and with double surcharge, one in red and one in black, but are not known to have been issued.

Edward VIII as a Child — A38

Victoria — A39

Edward VII as Prince of Wales — A40

Queen Alexandra as Princess of Wales — A41

Queen Mary as Duchess of York — A42

George V as Duke of York — A43

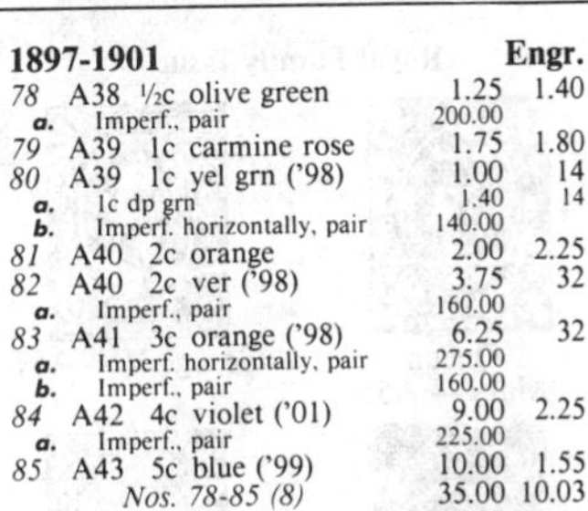

**1897-1901** **Engr.**

| No. | Type | Description | Unused | Used |
|---|---|---|---|---|
| *78* | A38 | ½c olive green | 1.25 | 1.40 |
| *a.* | | Imperf., pair | 200.00 | |
| *79* | A39 | 1c carmine rose | 1.75 | 1.80 |
| *80* | A39 | 1c yel grn ('98) | 1.00 | 14 |
| *a.* | | 1c dp grn | 1.40 | 14 |
| *b.* | | Imperf. horizontally, pair | 140.00 | |
| *81* | A40 | 2c orange | 2.00 | 2.25 |
| *82* | A40 | 2c ver ('98) | 3.75 | 32 |
| *a.* | | Imperf., pair | 160.00 | |
| *83* | A41 | 3c orange ('98) | 6.25 | 32 |
| *a.* | | Imperf. horizontally, pair | 275.00 | |
| *b.* | | Imperf., pair | 160.00 | |
| *84* | A42 | 4c violet ('01) | 9.00 | 2.25 |
| *a.* | | Imperf., pair | 225.00 | |
| *85* | A43 | 5c blue ('99) | 10.00 | 1.55 |
| | | *Nos. 78-85 (8)* | 35.00 | 10.03 |

Map of Newfoundland — A44

**1908, Sept.**

| No. | Type | Description | Unused | Used |
|---|---|---|---|---|
| *86* | A44 | 2c rose carmine | 10.50 | 90 |

**Guy Issue**

James I — A45

Arms of the London and Bristol Co. — A46

*Newfoundland stamps can be mounted in Scott's Canada Specialty Album.*

John Guy A47

Guy's Ship, the "Endeavour" A48

View of Cupids A49

Lord Bacon A50

View of Mosquito — A51

Logging Camp — A52

Paper Mills — A53

Edward VII — A54

George V — A55

SIX CENTS.
Type I- "Z" of "COLONIZATION" reversed.
Type II- "Z" of "COLONIZATION" normal.

**1910, Aug. 15** **Litho.** ***Perf. 12***

| | | | |
|---|---|---|---|
| *87* A45 | 1c deep green, perf. 12x11 | 65 | 45 |
| a. | Perf. 12 | 1.50 | 90 |
| b. | Perf. 12x14 | 1.10 | 65 |
| c. | Horizontal pair, imperf. between | 200.00 | |
| d. | "NFW" for "NEW" | 25.00 | 20.00 |
| e. | Vert. pair, imperf. btwn. | 240.00 | |
| f. | As "d", horiz. pair, imperf. between | | |
| *88* A46 | 2c carmine | 2.75 | 45 |
| a. | Perf. 12x14 | 3.25 | 35 |
| b. | Same as "a", horizontal pair, imperf. between | 275.00 | |
| c. | Perf. 12x11½ | 75.00 | 50.00 |
| *89* A47 | 3c brown ol | 4.50 | 4.50 |
| *90* A48 | 4c dl violet | 6.75 | 4.50 |
| *91* A49 | 5c ultramarine, perf. 14x12 | 5.00 | 1.50 |
| a. | Perf. 12 | 6.75 | 2.25 |
| *92* A50 | 6c cl, type I | 30.00 | 25.00 |
| *92A* A50 | 6c cl, type II | 10.50 | 10.50 |
| b. | Imperf., pair | 240.00 | |
| *93* A51 | 8c pale brown | 18.00 | 18.00 |
| *94* A52 | 9c olive green | 18.00 | 18.00 |
| *95* A53 | 10c vio black | 18.00 | 16.00 |
| *96* A54 | 12c lilac brn | 18.00 | 18.00 |
| a. | Imperf., pair | 360.00 | |
| *97* A55 | 15c gray black | 22.50 | 22.50 |
| | *Nos. 87-97 (12)* | 154.65 | 139.40 |

Tercentenary of colonization of Newfoundland.

**1911** **Engr.** ***Perf. 14***

| | | | |
|---|---|---|---|
| *98* A50 | 6c brown vio | 10.00 | 9.00 |
| a. | Imperf., pair | 275.00 | |
| *99* A51 | 8c bister brn | 25.00 | 22.50 |
| a. | Imperf., pair | 160.00 | |
| *100* A52 | 9c olive grn | 20.00 | 19.00 |
| a. | Imperf., pair | 275.00 | |
| *101* A53 | 10c violet blk | 35.00 | 35.00 |
| a. | Imperf., pair | 275.00 | |
| *102* A54 | 12c red brown | 30.00 | 30.00 |
| *103* A55 | 15c slate grn | 30.00 | 30.00 |
| a. | Imperf., pair | 275.00 | |
| b. | Horiz. pair, imperf. btwn. | | |
| | *Nos. 98-103 (6)* | 150.00 | 145.50 |

**Royal Family Issue**

Queen Mary — A56

George V — A57

Prince of Wales (Edward VIII) — A58

Prince Albert (George VI) — A59

Princess Mary — A60

Prince Henry — A61

Prince George — A62

Prince John — A63

Queen Alexandra A64

Duke of Connaught A65

Seal of Colony — A66

**1911, June 19** ***Perf. 13½x14, 14***

| | | | |
|---|---|---|---|
| *104* A56 | 1c yellow grn | 1.10 | 12 |
| a. | Imperf., pair | 275.00 | |
| *105* A57 | 2c carmine | 1.25 | 10 |
| a. | Imperf., pair | 275.00 | |
| *106* A58 | 3c red brown | 12.00 | 12.00 |
| *107* A59 | 4c violet | 10.50 | 7.75 |
| *108* A60 | 5c ultra | 4.50 | 85 |
| a. | Imperf., pair | 200.00 | |
| *109* A61 | 6c black | 10.00 | 10.00 |
| *110* A62 | 8c blue (paper colored through) | 30.00 | 30.00 |
| a. | 8c peacock blue | 32.50 | 32.50 |
| *111* A63 | 9c bl violet | 12.00 | 12.00 |
| *112* A64 | 10c dark green | 16.00 | 16.00 |
| *113* A65 | 12c plum | 16.00 | 16.00 |
| a. | Imperf., pair | 225.00 | |
| *114* A66 | 15c magenta | 16.00 | 16.00 |
| a. | Imperf., pair | 47.50 | |
| | *Nos. 104-114 (11)* | 129.35 | 120.82 |

Coronation of King George V.

**Trail of the Caribou Issue**

Caribou
A67 A68

**1919, Jan. 2** ***Perf. 14***

| | | | |
|---|---|---|---|
| *115* A67 | 1c green | 65 | 15 |
| *116* A68 | 2c scarlet | 85 | 28 |
| *117* A67 | 3c red brown | 1.00 | 12 |
| *118* A67 | 4c violet | 1.50 | 65 |
| *119* A68 | 5c ultra | 1.75 | 65 |
| *120* A67 | 6c gray | 9.00 | 7.75 |
| *121* A68 | 8c magenta | 6.50 | 5.75 |
| *122* A67 | 10c dark green | 4.25 | 1.75 |
| *123* A68 | 12c orange | 16.00 | 12.00 |
| *124* A67 | 15c dark blue | 13.00 | 13.00 |
| *125* A67 | 24c bister | 15.00 | 13.00 |
| *126* A67 | 36c olive green | 12.00 | 12.00 |
| | *Nos. 115-126 (12)* | 81.50 | 67.10 |

Services of the Newfoundland contingent in WWI.

Each denomination of type A67 is inscribed with the name of a different action in which Newfoundland troops took part.

Exist imperf., value per pair, $175.

No. 72 Surcharged in Black

**TWO CENTS**

**1920** ***Perf. 12***

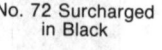

| | | | |
|---|---|---|---|
| *127* A35 | 2c on 30c slate | 3.50 | 3.50 |
| a. | Inverted surcharge | 275.00 | |

Nos. 70 and 73 Surcharged in Black

**THREE CENTS**

THREE CENTS
Type I- Bars 10½mm apart.
Type II- Bars 13½mm apart.

| | | | |
|---|---|---|---|
| *128* A33 | 3c on 15c scar (I) | 135.00 | 135.00 |
| a. | Inverted surcharge | *1,000.* | |
| *129* A33 | 3c on 15c scar (II) | 6.00 | 6.00 |
| *130* A36 | 3c on 35c red | 6.00 | 6.00 |
| a. | Lower bar omitted | 100.00 | 100.00 |
| b. | Inverted surcharge | | |
| c. | "THREE" omitted | *400.00* | |

Twin Hills, Tor's Cove — A70

South West Arm, Trinity — A71

War Memorial, St. John's — A72

Humber River — A73

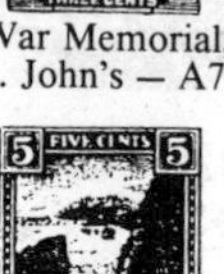

Coast of Trinity — A74

Upper Steadies, Humber River — A75

Quidi Vidi, near St. John's — A76

Caribou Crossing Lake — A77

Humber River Canyon — A78

Shell Bird Island — A79

Mt. Moriah, Bay of Islands — A80

Humber River near Little Rapids — A81

Placentia, from Mt. Pleasant — A82

Topsail Falls near St. John's — A83

**1923-24** **Engr.** ***Perf. 14, 13½ x 14***

| | | | |
|---|---|---|---|
| *131* A70 | 1c gray green | 90 | 15 |
| a. | Booklet pane of 8 | 240.00 | 240.00 |
| b. | Imperf., pair | 140.00 | |
| *132* A71 | 2c carmine | 90 | 12 |
| a. | Booklet pane of 8 | 100.00 | 100.00 |
| b. | Imperf., pair | 140.00 | |
| *133* A72 | 3c brown | 1.40 | 12 |
| *134* A73 | 4c brn violet | 1.65 | 1.10 |
| a. | Imperf., pair | 140.00 | |
| *135* A74 | 5c ultra | 1.90 | 1.25 |
| a. | Imperf., pair | 140.00 | |
| *136* A75 | 6c gray black | 2.50 | 2.50 |
| a. | Imperf., pair | 140.00 | |
| *137* A76 | 8c dl violet | 1.90 | 1.75 |
| a. | Imperf., pair | 140.00 | |
| *138* A77 | 9c slate grn | 12.00 | 12.00 |
| a. | Imperf., pair | 140.00 | |
| *139* A78 | 10c dk violet | 2.25 | 1.25 |
| a. | Imperf., pair | 140.00 | |
| *140* A79 | 11c olive grn | 4.00 | 4.00 |
| a. | Imperf., pair | 140.00 | |
| *141* A80 | 12c lake | 3.75 | 3.75 |
| a. | Imperf., pair | 140.00 | |
| *142* A81 | 15c deep blue | 4.50 | 4.25 |
| a. | Imperf., pair | 130.00 | |
| *143* A82 | 20c red brn ('24) | 4.25 | 3.50 |
| *144* A83 | 24c blk brn ('24) | 21.00 | 21.00 |
| | *Nos. 131-144 (14)* | 62.90 | 56.74 |

Map of Newfoundland A84

Steamship "Caribou" A85

Queen Mary, George V A86

Prince of Wales A87

Express Train — A88

Newfoundland Hotel, St. John's — A89

Heart's Content — A90

Cabot Tower, St. John's — A91

War Memorial, St. John's A92

GPO, St. John's A93

First Nonstop Transatlantic Flight, 1919 — A94

Colonial Building, St. John's — A95

Grand Falls, Labrador — A96

*Perf. 14, 13½x13, 13x13½*

**1928, Jan. 3**

| | | | | |
|---|---|---|---|---|
| *145* | A84 | 1c deep green | 75 | 40 |
| *146* | A85 | 2c deep carmine | 1.10 | 35 |
| ***a.*** | | Imperf., pair | 175.00 | |
| *147* | A86 | 3c brown | 1.25 | 28 |
| *148* | A87 | 4c lilac rose | 1.65 | 1.10 |
| *149* | A88 | 5c slate grn | 3.00 | 2.00 |
| *150* | A89 | 6c ultra | 2.00 | 1.90 |
| *151* | A90 | 8c lt red brown | 3.00 | 2.50 |
| *152* | A91 | 9c myrtle grn | 3.50 | 3.25 |
| *153* | A92 | 10c dark violet | 3.50 | 2.75 |
| *154* | A93 | 12c brn carmine | 2.50 | 2.00 |
| *155* | A91 | 14c red brown | 3.50 | 2.75 |
| *156* | A94 | 15c dark blue | 4.75 | 3.50 |
| *157* | A95 | 20c gray black | 4.75 | 2.50 |
| *158* | A93 | 28c gray green | 12.00 | 12.00 |
| *159* | A96 | 30c olive brown | 5.50 | 3.50 |
| | | *Nos. 145-159 (15)* | 52.75 | 40.78 |

See Nos. 163-182.

No. 136 Surcharged in Red or Black

**THREE CENTS**

Type I- Space of 5mm between "CENTS" and the bar.

Type II- Space of 3mm between "CENTS" and the bar.

**1929** *Perf. 14x13½*

| | | | | |
|---|---|---|---|---|
| *160* | A75 | 3c on 6c gray black (II) (R) | 1.90 | 1.90 |
| ***a.*** | | Inverted surcharge (II) | 500.00 | |
| ***b.*** | | Black surcharge (I) | 875.00 | |
| ***c.*** | | Black surcharge (II) | 875.00 | |

The stamps with black surcharge were first or trial printings, and were not issued. There were fifty copies of each type.

### Types of 1928 Issue Re-engraved

1c- On No. 145 the lines of the engraving are thinner and the impression is clearer than on No. 163. On the former "C. BAULD" is above "C. NORMAN". On the latter these words are transposed.

2c- On the 1928 stamp the "D" of "NEWFOUNDLAND" is 1mm from the scroll at the right; the flag at the stern is lower than the top of the boat davit. On the 1929 stamp the "D" is ½mm from the scroll and the flag rises above the davits.

3c- On the 1928 stamp the pearls at the top of the crown, the jewels of the tiara and the pillars flanking the portraits are all unshaded. On the reengraved stamp there are small curved lines inside the pearls, the jewels of the tiara are in solid color, and the pillars have vertical shading lines. On the 1928 stamps the tablets with "THREE" and "CENTS" have a background of crossed lines (vertical and horizontal). On the 1929 stamp the background is of horizontal lines only.

4c- On the 1928 stamp the figures "4" have shading of horizontal and diagonal crossed lines. There are six circles at each side of the portrait.

On the 1929 stamp the "4s" have shading of horizontal lines only. There are five roses at each side of the portrait.

5c- The crossbars of the telegraph pole touch the frame at the left on the 1929 stamp but just clear it on the 1928 stamp. In the 1928 issue the foliate ornaments beside and below the figures "5" end in small scrolls and a small spur. These spurs are omitted on the 1929 stamp.

6c- On the re-engraved stamp the columns at right and left of the picture have heavy wavy outlines on the inner sides. There is no period after "JOHNS". The numerals in the lower corners are 1½mm wide instead of 1¼mm.

8c- The impression of the 1928 stamp is clear, that of 1931 is slightly blurred. The 1928 stamp has three horizontal lines above "EIGHT CENTS" and four berries on the laurel branch at the right side. On the 1931 stamp there are two horizontal lines and three berries.

10c- On the re-engraved stamp there is no period after "ST. JOHN'S". The letters of "TEN CENTS" are slightly larger and the numerals "10" slightly smaller than in 1928. Inside the "0" of "10" at the right there are two vertical lines instead of three. The clouds are fainter in 1929 and the cross upheld by the figure on the monument is more distinct. On the 1928 stamp the torch at the left side terminates in a single tongue of flame. On the 1929-30 stamp it terminates in two tongues.

15c- On the 1928 stamp the "N" of "NEWFOUNDLAND" is 1½mm. from the left frame, the "L" of "LEAVING" is under the first "A" of "AIRPLANE" and the apostrophe in "JOHN'S" breaks the first line above it.

On the 1929 stamp the "N" of "NEWFOUNDLAND" is 1mm from the left frame, the "L" of "LEAVING" is below the "T" of "FIRST" and the apostrophe in "JOHN'S" does not touch the line above it.

20c- On the 1928 stamp the points of the "W" of "NEWFOUNDLAND" are truncated. The "O" is wide and nearly round. The columns that form the sides of the frame have a shading of evenly spaced horizontal lines at their inner sides.

On the 1929-31 stamp the points of the "W" form sharp angles. The "O" is narrow and has a small opening. Many lines have been added to the shading on the inner sides of the columns, making it almost solid.

30c- 1928 stamp. Size: 19¼x24½mm. At the outer side of the right column there are three strong and two faint vertical lines. Faint period after "FALLS".

1931 stamp. Size: 19x25mm. At the outer side of the right column there are two strong vertical lines and a fragment of the lower end of a faint one. Clear period after "FALLS". A great many of the small lines of the design have been deepened making the whole stamp appear darker.

**1929-31** **Unwmk.** ***Perf. 13½ to 14***

| | | | | |
|---|---|---|---|---|
| *163* | A84 | 1c green | 80 | 25 |
| ***a.*** | | Double impression | 300.00 | |
| ***b.*** | | Imperf. horiz., pair | 145.00 | |
| ***c.*** | | Imperf., pair | 110.00 | |
| *164* | A85 | 2c deep carmine | 80 | 12 |
| ***a.*** | | Imperf., pair | 100.00 | |
| *165* | A86 | 3c dp red brown | 95 | 10 |
| ***a.*** | | Imperf., pair | 100.00 | |
| *166* | A87 | 4c magenta | 1.40 | 60 |
| ***a.*** | | Imperf., pair | 100.00 | |
| *167* | A88 | 5c slate green | 2.00 | 60 |
| *168* | A89 | 6c ultramarine | 5.50 | 4.00 |
| *169* | A92 | 10c dark violet | 2.75 | 85 |
| *170* | A94 | 15c deep bl ('30) | 16.00 | 14.00 |
| *171* | A95 | 20c gray blk ('31) | 27.50 | 11.50 |
| | | *Nos. 163-171 (9)* | 57.70 | 32.02 |

Wmk. 224- Coat of Arms

As the watermark 224 does not show on every stamp in the sheet, pairs are found one with and one without watermark. This applies to all stamps with watermark 224.

### Types of 1928 Issue
***Perf. 13½ to 14***

**1931** **Re-engraved** **Wmk. 224**

| | | | | |
|---|---|---|---|---|
| *172* | A84 | 1c green | 1.00 | 50 |
| ***a.*** | | Horiz. pair, imperf. btwn. | 360.00 | |
| *173* | A85 | 2c red | 1.50 | 60 |
| *174* | A86 | 3c red brown | 1.50 | 50 |
| *175* | A87 | 4c rose | 2.00 | 75 |
| *176* | A88 | 5c grnsh gray | 5.00 | 3.50 |
| *177* | A89 | 6c ultramarine | 10.00 | 8.25 |
| *178* | A90 | 8c lt red brn | 10.00 | 8.25 |
| *179* | A92 | 10c dk violet | 6.25 | 3.75 |
| *180* | A94 | 15c deep blue | 20.00 | 15.00 |
| *181* | A95 | 20c gray black | 16.00 | 4.50 |
| *182* | A96 | 30c olive brown | 15.00 | 12.50 |
| | | *Nos. 172-182 (11)* | 88.25 | 58.10 |

Codfish A97

George V A98

Queen Mary A99

Prince of Wales A100

Caribou A101

Princess Elizabeth A102

Salmon Leaping Falls — A103

Newfoundland Dog — A104

Harp Seal Pup — A105

Cape Race — A106

Sealing Fleet — A107

Fishing Fleet Leaving for "The Banks" — A108

FIVE CENT

Dic I- Antlers even, or equal in height.

Die II- Antler under "T" higher.

**1932-37** **Engr.** ***Perf. 13½, 14***

| | | | | |
|---|---|---|---|---|
| *183* | A97 | 1c green | 75 | 18 |
| ***a.*** | | Booklet pane of 4, perf. 13 | 57.50 | |
| ***b.*** | | Imperf., pair | 72.50 | |
| *184* | A97 | 1c gray black | 12 | 6 |
| ***a.*** | | Bklt. pane of 4, perf. 13½ | 40.00 | |
| ***b.*** | | Booklet pane of 4, perf. 14 | 47.50 | |
| ***c.*** | | Imperf., pair | 32.50 | |
| *185* | A98 | 2c rose | 75 | 12 |
| ***a.*** | | Booklet pane of 4, perf. 13 | 32.50 | |
| *186* | A98 | 2c green | 60 | 6 |
| ***a.*** | | Bklt. pane of 4, perf. 13½ | 18.00 | |
| ***b.*** | | Booklet pane of 4, perf. 14 | 24.00 | |
| ***c.*** | | Imperf., pair | 32.50 | |
| ***d.*** | | Horiz. pair, imperf. btwn. | 160.00 | |
| *187* | A99 | 3c orange brn | 60 | 10 |
| ***a.*** | | Bklt. pane of 4, perf. 13½ | 40.00 | |
| ***b.*** | | Booklet pane of 4, perf. 14 | 47.50 | |
| ***c.*** | | Booklet pane of 4, perf. 13 | 57.50 | |
| ***d.*** | | Imperf., pair | 57.50 | |
| *188* | A100 | 4c dp violet | 2.50 | 85 |
| *189* | A100 | 4c rose lake | 30 | 8 |
| ***a.*** | | Imperf., pair | 47.50 | |
| *190* | A101 | 5c vio brn, perf. 13½ (Die I) | 3.75 | 50 |
| ***a.*** | | Imperf., pair | 100.00 | |
| *191* | A101 | 5c dp vio, perf. 13½ (Die II) | 50 | 10 |
| ***a.*** | | 5c dp vio, perf. 13½ (Die I) | 6.00 | 60 |
| ***b.*** | | Imperf., pair | 40.00 | |
| ***c.*** | | Horiz. pair, imperf. btwn., (I) | 160.00 | |
| *192* | A102 | 6c dull blue | 5.00 | 5.00 |
| ***a.*** | | Imperf., pair | 100.00 | |
| *193* | A103 | 10c olive blk | 60 | 40 |
| ***a.*** | | Imperf., pair | 65.00 | |
| *194* | A104 | 14c int black | 1.40 | 1.10 |
| *195* | A105 | 15c magenta | 1.40 | 1.10 |
| *196* | A106 | 20c gray green | 1.40 | 45 |
| ***a.*** | | Imperf., pair | 100.00 | |
| *197* | A107 | 25c gray | 1.50 | 1.00 |
| ***a.*** | | Imperf., pair | 100.00 | |
| ***b.*** | | Vert. pair, imperf. btwn. | 225.00 | |
| *198* | A108 | 30c ultra | 16.00 | 14.00 |
| ***a.*** | | Imperf., pair | 325.00 | |
| *199* | A108 | 48c red brn ('37) | 5.00 | 2.50 |
| ***a.*** | | Imperf., pair | 80.00 | |
| | | *Nos. 183-199 (17)* | 42.17 | 27.60 |

Two dies were used for 2c green, one for 2c rose.

See Nos. 253-266.

Queen Elizabeth when Duchess of York — A109

Corner Brook Paper Mills — A110

Loading Iron Ore at Bell Island — A111

**1932**

| | | | | |
|---|---|---|---|---|
| *208* | A109 | 7c red brown | 70 | 70 |
| ***a.*** | | Horiz. pair, imperf. between | 350.00 | |
| *209* | A110 | 8c orange red | 70 | 55 |
| ***a.*** | | Imperf., pair | 80.00 | |
| *210* | A111 | 24c light blue | 1.65 | 1.65 |
| ***a.*** | | Imperf., pair | 100.00 | |

See Nos. 259, 264.

No. C9 Overprinted Bars and **L. & S. Post.**

**1933, Feb. 9** **Wmk. 224** ***Perf. 14***

| | | | | |
|---|---|---|---|---|
| *211* | AP6 | 15c brown | 6.00 | 4.75 |
| ***a.*** | | Pair, one without overprint | 1,250. | |
| ***b.*** | | Ovpt. reading up | 800. | |

"L. & S." stands for "Land and Sea".

### Sir Humphrey Gilbert Issue

Sir Humphrey Gilbert A112

Compton Castle, Home of the Gilbert Family A113

Gilbert Coat of Arms — A114

Eton College — A115

Token from Queen Elizabeth I A116

Sir Humphrey Receiving Royal Patents for Colonization A117

Sir Humphrey's Ships Leaving Plymouth, 1583 — A118

The Ships Arriving at St. John's — A119

Annexation of Newfoundland, Aug. 5, 1583 — A120

Coat of Arms of England A121

Sir Humphrey on the Deck of the "Squirrel" A122

Capt. John Mason's Map of Newfoundland, 1626 — A123

Queen Elizabeth I A124

Gilbert Statue at Truro A125

*Perf. 13½, 14*

**1933, Aug. 3 Wmk. 224 Engr.**

| | | | |
|---|---|---|---|
| *212* A112 | 1c gray black | 50 | 38 |
| *a.* | Imperf., pair | 32.50 | |
| *213* A113 | 2c green | 60 | 38 |
| *a.* | Imperf., pair | 32.50 | |
| *214* A114 | 3c yellow brn | 85 | 60 |
| *a.* | Imperf., pair | 125.00 | |
| *215* A115 | 4c carmine | 85 | 25 |
| *a.* | Imperf., pair | 35.00 | |
| *216* A116 | 5c dull violet | 1.10 | 60 |
| *a.* | Imperf., pair | 100.00 | |
| *217* A117 | 7c blue | 6.00 | 6.00 |
| *218* A118 | 8c orange red | 3.50 | 3.50 |
| *219* A119 | 9c ultramarine | 4.00 | 4.00 |
| *a.* | Imperf., pair | 100.00 | |
| *220* A120 | 10c red brown | 4.00 | 3.00 |
| *a.* | Imperf., pair | 110.00 | |
| *221* A121 | 14c black | 8.25 | 8.00 |
| *222* A122 | 15c claret | 7.50 | 7.50 |
| *223* A123 | 20c deep green | 5.00 | 4.00 |
| *224* A124 | 24c vio brown | 9.00 | 9.00 |
| *a.* | Imperf., pair | 110.00 | |
| *225* A125 | 32c gray | 9.00 | 9.00 |
| | *Nos. 212-225 (14)* | 60.15 | 56.21 |

350th anniv. of annexation of Newfoundland to England, Aug. 5, 1583, by authority of Letters Patent issued by Queen Elizabeth I to Sir Humphrey Gilbert.

**Silver Jubilee Issue**

Common Design Type

**1935, May 6 Wmk. 4 *Perf. 11x12***

| | | | |
|---|---|---|---|
| *226* CD301 | 4c bright rose | 75 | 45 |
| *227* CD301 | 5c violet | 75 | 60 |
| *228* CD301 | 7c dark blue | 1.75 | 1.75 |
| *229* CD301 | 24c olive green | 4.50 | 4.50 |

**Coronation Issue**

Common Design Type

**1937, May 12 *Perf. 11x11½***

| | | | |
|---|---|---|---|
| *230* CD302 | 2c deep green | 35 | 35 |
| *231* CD302 | 4c carmine rose | 35 | 25 |
| *232* CD302 | 5c dark violet | 60 | 60 |

Codfish A126

Map of Newfoundland — A127

Caribou A128

Corner Brook Paper Mills A129

Salmon A130

Newfoundland Dog — A131

Harp Seal Pup A132

Cape Race A133

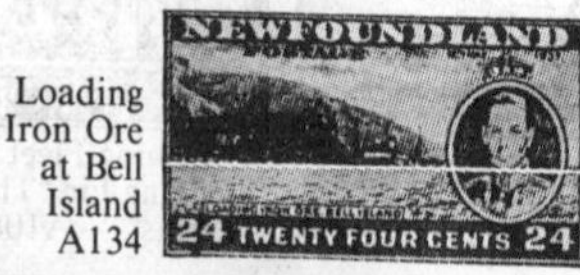

Loading Iron Ore at Bell Island A134

Sealing Fleet A135

Fishing Fleet Leaving for "The Banks" A136

Two dies of the 3c

Die I- Fine impression.

Die II- Coarse impression.

*Perf. 13, 13½, 14*

**1937, May 12 Wmk. 224**

| | | | |
|---|---|---|---|
| *233* A126 | 1c gray black | 25 | 12 |
| *234* A127 | 3c org brn, die I | 1.00 | 38 |
| *a.* | Die II | 75 | 25 |
| *b.* | Vert. or horiz. pair, imperf. btwn. (II) | 200.00 | |
| *235* A128 | 7c blue | 1.10 | 85 |
| *236* A129 | 8c orange red | 1.10 | 85 |
| *a.* | Imperf., pair | 140.00 | |
| *237* A130 | 10c olive gray | 2.00 | 1.65 |
| *a.* | Double impression | | |
| *238* A131 | 14c black | 1.50 | 1.50 |
| *239* A132 | 15c rose lake | 1.75 | 1.50 |
| *a.* | Vert. pair, imperf. between | 160.00 | |
| *240* A133 | 20c green | 1.40 | 1.10 |
| *241* A134 | 24c turq blue | 1.90 | 1.75 |
| *a.* | Vert. pair, imperf. between | 250.00 | |
| *242* A135 | 25c gray | 1.90 | 1.65 |
| *243* A136 | 48c dark violet | 2.00 | 1.90 |
| | *Nos. 233-243 (11)* | 15.90 | 13.25 |

Princess Elizabeth — A139

Designs: 2c, King George VI. 3c, Queen Elizabeth. 7c, Queen Mother Mary.

**1938, May 12 *Perf. 13½***

| | | | |
|---|---|---|---|
| *245* A139 | 2c green | 1.40 | 15 |
| *246* A139 | 3c dark carmine | 1.40 | 20 |
| *247* A139 | 4c light blue | 1.40 | 15 |
| *248* A139 | 7c dark ultra | 1.10 | 75 |

See Nos. 254-256, 258, 269.

George VI and Queen Elizabeth A141

**1939, June 17 Unwmk.**

| | | | |
|---|---|---|---|
| *249* A141 | 5c violet blue | 55 | 55 |

Visit of King George and Queen Elizabeth.

No. 249 Surcharged in Brown or Red

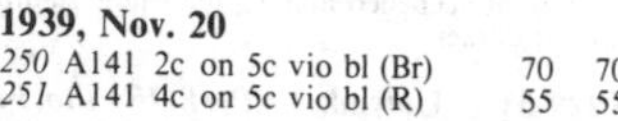

2

▲ CENTS ▲

**1939, Nov. 20**

| | | | |
|---|---|---|---|
| *250* A141 | 2c on 5c vio bl (Br) | 70 | 70 |
| *251* A141 | 4c on 5c vio bl (R) | 55 | 55 |

There are many varieties of broken letters and figures in the settings of the surcharges.

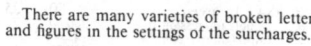

Sir Wilfred Grenfell and "Strathcona II" — A142

**1941, Dec. 1 Engr. *Perf. 12***

| | | | |
|---|---|---|---|
| *252* A142 | 5c dull blue | 22 | 20 |

Grenfell Mission, 50th anniv.

Types of 1931-38

**1941-44 Wmk. 224 *Perf. 12½***

| | | | |
|---|---|---|---|
| *253* A97 | 1c dark gray | 12 | 8 |
| *254* A139 | 2c deep green | 15 | 8 |
| *255* A139 | 3c rose car | 18 | 8 |
| *256* A139 | 4c blue | 35 | 8 |
| *257* A101 | 5c violet (Die I) | 35 | 8 |
| *258* A139 | 7c vio blue ('42) | 55 | 55 |
| *259* A110 | 8c red | 42 | 35 |
| *260* A103 | 10c brownish blk | 42 | 30 |
| *261* A104 | 14c black | 80 | 65 |
| *262* A105 | 15c pale rose vio | 85 | 75 |
| *263* A106 | 20c green | 75 | 60 |
| *264* A111 | 24c deep blue | 1.00 | 85 |
| *265* A107 | 25c slate | 1.00 | 85 |
| *266* A108 | 48c red brn ('44) | 1.50 | 1.00 |
| | *Nos. 253-266 (14)* | 8.44 | 6.30 |

Nos. 254 and 255 are re-engraved.

Memorial University College A143

**Unwmk.**

**1943, Jan. 2 Engr. *Perf. 12***

| | | | |
|---|---|---|---|
| *267* A143 | 30c carmine | 80 | 75 |

No. 267 Surcharged in Black

TWO

CENTS

**1946, Mar. 23**

| | | | |
|---|---|---|---|
| *268* A143 | 2c on 30c carmine | 18 | 18 |

Princess Elizabeth A144

Deck of the Matthew A145

**Wmk. 224**

**1947, Apr. 21 Engr. *Perf. 12½***

| | | | |
|---|---|---|---|
| *269* A144 | 4c light blue | 20 | 6 |

Princess Elizabeth's 21st birthday.

**1947, June 23**

| | | | |
|---|---|---|---|
| *270* A145 | 5c rose violet | 20 | 14 |
| *a.* | Horiz. pair, imperf. between | | |

Cabot's arrival off Cape Bonavista, 450th anniv.

---

## AIR POST STAMPS

No. 117 Overprinted in Black

FIRST TRANS-ATLANTIC AIR POST, April, 1919.

**1919, Apr. 12 Unwmk. *Perf. 14***

| | | | |
|---|---|---|---|
| *C1* A67 | 3c red brown | 15,000. | 11,000. |

No. 70 Surcharged in Black

Trans-Atlantic AIR POST, 1919. ONE DOLLAR.

**1919, June 9 *Perf. 12***

| | | | |
|---|---|---|---|
| *C2* A33 | $1 on 15c scar | 87.50 | 87.50 |
| *a.* | Without comma after "Post" | 125.00 | 125.00 |
| *b.* | As "a", without period after "1919" | 285.00 | 285.00 |

No. 73 Overprinted in Black

AIR MAIL to Halifax, N.S. 1921

**1921, Nov. 7**

| | | | |
|---|---|---|---|
| *C3* A36 | 35c red | 75.00 | 75.00 |
| *a.* | With period after "1921" | 95.00 | 95.00 |
| *b.* | Inverted overprint | 2,500. | |
| *c.* | As "a," inverted | 2,800. | |

No. C3 was printed in sheets of twenty-five, containing varieties of wide and narrow space between "AIR" and "MAIL", date shifted to right, and with and without period after date.

No. 74 Overprinted in Red

Air Mail DE PINEDO 1927

**1927, May 21**

| | | | |
|---|---|---|---|
| *C4* A37 | 60c black | 22,500. | 10,500. |

No. 126 Surcharged in Black

Trans-Atlantic AIR MAIL By B. M. "Columbia" September 1930 Fifty Cents

**1930, Sept. 25 *Perf. 14***

| | | | |
|---|---|---|---|
| *C5* A67 | 50c on 36c ol grn | 5,000. | 5,000. |

Dog Sled and Airplane — AP6

First Transatlantic Mail Airplane and Packet Ship — AP7

Routes of Historic Transatlantic Flights — AP8

**1931, Jan. 2 Engr. Unwmk.**

*C6* AP6 15c brown 5.50 5.50
a. Horiz. or vert. pair, imperf. between 450.00
*C7* AP7 50c green 9.50 9.50
a. Horiz. or vert. pair, imperf. between 625.00 625.00
*C8* AP8 $1 blue 32.50 32.50
a. Horiz. or vert. pair, imperf. between 450.00

**1931 Wmk. 224**

*C9* AP6 15c brown 4.50 4.50
a. Horiz. pair, imperf. btwn. 450.00
b. Vert. pair, imperf. btwn. 600.00
c. Imperf., pair
*C10* AP7 50c green 18.00 18.00
a. Horiz. or vert. pair, imperf. between 400.00
b. Imperf. vert., pair 400.00
*C11* AP8 $1 blue 52.50 47.50
a. Vert. pair, imperf. btwn. 450.00
b. Imperf. vert., pair
c. Horiz. pair, imperf. btwn. 450.00
d. Vert. pair, imperf. horiz. 325.00

As the watermark 224 does not show on every stamp in the sheet, pairs are found one with and one without watermark.

No. C11 Surcharged in Red

**TRANS-ATLANTIC**
**WEST TO EAST**
**Per Dornier DO-X**
**May, 1932.**
**One Dollar and Fifty Cents**

**1932, May 19**

*C12* AP8 $1.50 on $1 blue 190.00 190.00
a. Inverted surcharge *10,000.*

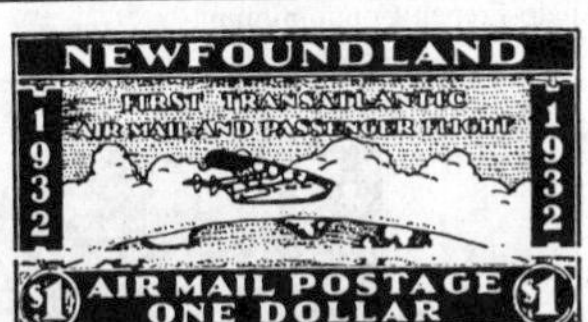

A stamp of this design was produced in the US in 1932 by a private company under contract with Newfoundland authorities. The government canceled the contract and the stamp was not valid for prepayment of postage.

"Put to Flight" — AP9

"Land of Heart's Delight" AP10

"Spotting the Herd" AP11

"News from Home" AP12

"Labrador, The Land of Gold" AP13

**1933, June 9 Engr. *Perf. 11½, 14***

*C13* AP9 5c lt brown 6.00 6.00
a. Imperf. pair 150.00
b. Horiz. pair, imperf. btwn.
*C14* AP10 10c yellow 7.50 7.50
a. Imperf. pair 100.00
*C15* AP11 30c blue 16.00 16.00
a. Imperf. pair 350.00
*C16* AP12 60c green 27.50 27.50
a. Imperf. pair 400.00
*C17* AP13 75c bister 27.50 27.50
a. Imperf. pair 275.00
*Nos. C13-C17 (5)* 84.50 84.50

No. C17 Surcharged in Black

**1933, July 24 *Perf. 14***

*C18* AP13 $4.50 on 75c bis 300.00 300.00

Return flight from Chicago to Rome of the squadron of Italian seaplanes under the command of Gen. Italo Balbo.

The inverted surcharge was not regularly issued. The $4.50 on No. C14, 10c yellow, is a proof.

View of St. John's AP14

**1943, June 1 Unwmk. *Perf. 12***

*C19* AP14 7c bright ultra 30 24

## POSTAGE DUE STAMPS

D1

***Perf. 10-10½, Compound***

**1939-49 Litho. Unwmk.**

*J1* D1 1c yellow green 1.40 1.40
a. Perf. 11 ('49) 2.75 2.75
*J2* D1 2c vermilion 1.60 1.60
a. Perf. 11x9 ('46) 2.75 2.75
*J3* D1 3c ultramarine 2.00 2.00
a. Perf. 11x9 ('49) 3.25 3.25
*J4* D1 4c yellow orange 2.25 2.25
a. Perf. 11x9 ('49) 4.50 4.50
*J5* D1 5c pale brown 1.75 1.75
*J6* D1 10c dark violet 1.75 1.75
*Nos. J1-J6 (6)* 10.75 10.75

**1949 Wmk. 224 *Perf. 11***

*J7* D1 10c dark violet 6.00 6.00
a. Vert. pair, imperf. btwn. 175.00

# NEW GUINEA

LOCATION — On an island of the same name in the South Pacific Ocean, north of Australia.

GOVT. — Mandate administered by Australia.

AREA — 93,000 sq. mi.

POP. — 675,369 (1940).

CAPITAL — Rabaul.

The territory occupies the northeastern part of the island and includes New Britain and other nearby islands. It was formerly a German possession and should not be confused with British New Guinea (Papua) which is in the southeastern part of the same island, nor Netherlands New Guinea (Vol. III). For previous issues see German New Guinea, New Britain, North West Pacific Islands. Issues for 1952 and later are listed under Papua.

12 Pence = 1 Shilling
20 Shillings = 1 Pound

Native Huts — A1

Bird of Paradise — A2

***Perf. 11, 11½***

**1925-28 Unwmk. Engr.**

*1* A1 ½p orange 80 *1.65*
*2* A1 1p yellow green 1.10 2.25
*3* A1 1½p ver ('26) 1.90 1.40
*4* A1 2p claret 2.75 1.65
*5* A1 3p deep blue 4.50 3.25
*6* A1 4p olive green 9.75 *14.00*
*7* A1 6p yel bis ('28) 5.50 *9.75*
a. 6p light brown 8.25 *14.00*
b. 6p olive bister ('27) 7.00 *11.00*
*8* A1 9p deep violet 11.00 20.00
*9* A1 1sh gray green 11.00 19.00
*10* A1 2sh red brown 19.00 25.00
*11* A1 5sh ol bister 27.50 37.50
*12* A1 10sh dull rose 67.50 90.00
*13* A1 £1 grnsh gray 200.00 250.00
*Nos. 1-13 (13)* 362.30 *475.45*

**1931, Aug. 2**

*18* A2 1p light green 65 65
*19* A2 1½p red 2.50 4.00
*20* A2 2p violet brown 1.40 1.40
*21* A2 3p deep blue 1.40 1.40
*22* A2 4p olive green 3.00 *3.75*
*23* A2 5p slate green 3.00 5.00
*24* A2 6p bister 3.00 6.25
*25* A2 9p dull violet 3.75 7.50
*26* A2 1sh bluish gray 4.00 *8.75*
*27* A2 2sh red brown 7.50 *12.50*
*28* A2 5sh olive brown 30.00 32.50
*29* A2 10sh rose red 72.50 80.00
*30* A2 £1 gray 110.00 125.00
*Nos. 18-30 (13)* 242.70 288.70

10th anniversary of Australian Mandate.

Type of 1931 without date scrolls

**1932-34 *Perf. 11***

*31* A2 1p light green 45 28
*32* A2 1½p violet brn 90 90
*33* A2 2p red 52 45
*34* A2 2½p dp grn ('34) 4.25 6.25
*35* A2 3p gray blue 90 75
*36* A2 3½p magenta ('34) 6.25 *10.50*
*37* A2 4p olive green 90 75
*38* A2 5p slate green 90 75
*39* A2 6p bister 1.00 1.00
*40* A2 9p dull violet 5.25 *7.00*
*41* A2 1sh bluish gray 4.25 4.25
*42* A2 2sh red brown 4.25 4.25
*43* A2 5sh olive brown 21.00 22.50
*44* A2 10sh rose red 70.00 70.00
*45* A2 £1 gray 87.50 77.50
*Nos. 31-45 (15)* 208.32 207.13

**Silver Jubilee Issue**

Stamps of 1932-34 Overprinted

**HIS MAJESTY'S**
**JUBILEE.**
**1910 — 1935**

**1935, June 27**

**Glazed Paper**

*46* A2 1p light green 75 75
*47* A2 2p red 1.10 1.10

King George VI — A3

**1937 May 18 Engr.**

*48* A3 2p salmon rose 20 20
*49* A3 3p blue 20 20
*50* A3 5p green 32 32
*51* A3 1sh brn violet 60 60

Coronation of George VI and Queen Elizabeth.

## AIR POST STAMPS

Regular Issues of 1925-28 Overprinted

**1931, June *Perf. 11, 11½***

*C1* A1 ½p orange 28 *75*
*C2* A1 1p yellow grn 38 *95*
*C3* A1 1½p vermilion 75 *1.90*
*C4* A1 2p claret 1.25 *2.75*
*C5* A1 3p deep blue 1.90 2.00
*C6* A1 4p olive green 2.75 2.75
*C7* A1 6p light brown 2.75 2.75
*C8* A1 9p deep violet 3.75 3.75
*C9* A1 1sh gray green 4.75 4.75
*C10* A1 2sh red brown 8.25 8.25
*C11* A1 5sh ol bister 19.00 24.50
*C12* A1 10sh light red 40.00 60.00
*C13* A1 £1 grnsh gray 97.00 125.00
*Nos. C1-C13 (13)* 182.81 240.10

Type of Regular Issue of 1931 and Nos. 18-30 Overprinted

**AIR**
**MAIL**

**1931, August**

*C14* A2 ½p orange 35 35
*C15* A2 1p light green 55 55
*C16* A2 1½p red 1.50 1.50
*C17* A2 2p violet brn 1.50 1.65
*C18* A2 3p deep blue 2.00 2.00
*C19* A2 4p olive green 2.50 2.50
*C20* A2 5p slate green 2.75 3.00
*C21* A2 6p bister 3.50 4.00
*C22* A2 9p dull violet 4.00 4.00
*C23* A2 1sh bluish gray 4.50 4.50
*C24* A2 2sh red brown 6.75 8.25
*C25* A2 5sh olive brown 22.50 15.00
*C26* A2 10sh rose red 57.50 75.00
*C27* A2 £1 gray 125.00 185.00
*Nos. C14-C27 (14)* 234.90 307.30

10th anniversary of Australian Mandate.

Same Overprint on Type of Regular Issue of 1932-34 and Nos. 31-45

**1932-34 *Perf. 11***

*C28* A2 ½p orange 22 22
*C29* A2 1p light green 22 22
*C30* A2 1½p violet brn 45 45
*C31* A2 2p red 90 90
*C32* A2 2½p dp grn ('34) 1.65 1.65
*C33* A2 3p gray blue 1.25 1.25
*C34* A2 3½p magenta ('34) 1.65 1.65
*C35* A2 4p olive green 1.75 1.75
*C36* A2 5p slate green 3.00 3.00
*C37* A2 6p bister 3.00 3.25
*C38* A2 9p dull violet 3.50 3.75
*C39* A2 1sh bluish gray 2.00 2.25
*C40* A2 2sh red brown 6.50 8.00
*C41* A2 5sh olive brown 16.00 16.00
*C42* A2 10sh rose red 55.00 60.00
*C43* A2 £1 gray 72.50 47.50
*Nos. C28-C43 (16)* 169.59 151.84

No. C28 exists without overprint, but is believed not to have been issued in this condition.

*New Guinea stamps can be mounted in Scott's Australia and Dependencies Album.*

Plane over Bulolo Goldfield AP1

**1935, May 1 Engr. Unwmk.**

| No. | Description | Unused | Used |
|---|---|---|---|
| C44 | AP1 £2 violet | 175.00 | 150.00 |
| C45 | AP1 £5 green | 675.00 | 425.00 |

AP2

**1939, Mar. 1**

| No. | Description | Unused | Used |
|---|---|---|---|
| C46 | AP2 ½p orange | 24 | 50 |
| C47 | AP2 1p green | 25 | 42 |
| C48 | AP2 1½p vio brown | 65 | 1.25 |
| C49 | AP2 2p red orange | 1.10 | 1.65 |
| C50 | AP2 3p dark blue | 2.00 | 4.00 |
| C51 | AP2 4p ol bister | 1.65 | 4.00 |
| C52 | AP2 5p slate grn | 1.50 | 1.75 |
| C53 | AP2 6p bister brn | 2.00 | 4.00 |
| C54 | AP2 9p dl violet | 2.75 | 5.00 |
| C55 | AP2 1sh sage green | 3.25 | 6.50 |
| C56 | AP2 2sh car lake | 16.00 | 20.00 |
| C57 | AP2 5sh ol brown | 32.50 | 40.00 |
| C58 | AP2 10sh rose red | 95.00 | 82.50 |
| C59 | AP2 £1 grnsh gray | 50.00 | 57.50 |
| | *Nos. C46-C59 (14)* | 208.89 | 229.07 |

## OFFICIAL STAMPS

Regular Issue of 1925 Overprinted

**1925-29 Unwmk. Perf. 11, 11½**

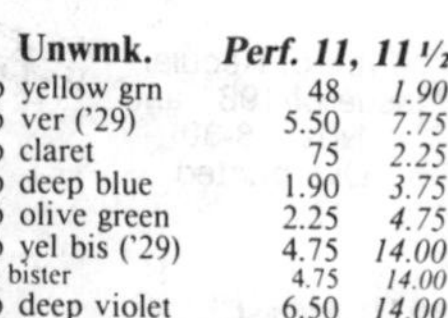

| No. | Description | Unused | Used |
|---|---|---|---|
| O1 | A1 1p yellow grn | 48 | 1.90 |
| O2 | A1 1½p ver ('29) | 5.50 | 7.75 |
| O3 | A1 2p claret | 75 | 2.25 |
| O4 | A1 3p deep blue | 1.90 | 3.75 |
| O5 | A1 4p olive green | 2.25 | 4.75 |
| O6 | A1 6p yel bis ('29) | 4.75 | 14.00 |
| a. | 6p olive bister | 4.75 | 14.00 |
| O7 | A1 9p deep violet | 6.50 | 14.00 |
| O8 | A1 1sh gray green | 9.50 | 19.00 |
| O9 | A1 2sh red brown | 19.00 | 37.50 |
| | *Nos. O1-O9 (9)* | 50.63 | 104.90 |

Nos. 18-28 Overprinted **O S**

**1931, Aug. 2**

| No. | Description | Unused | Used |
|---|---|---|---|
| O12 | A2 1p light green | 1.00 | 2.50 |
| O13 | A2 1½p red | 1.40 | 4.00 |
| O14 | A2 2p violet brn | 2.50 | 4.00 |
| O15 | A2 3p deep blue | 3.00 | 6.00 |
| O16 | A2 4p olive green | 4.00 | 7.75 |
| O17 | A2 5p slate green | 4.00 | 9.00 |
| O18 | A2 6p bister | 5.00 | 10.00 |
| O19 | A2 9p dull violet | 6.00 | 15.00 |
| O20 | A2 1sh bluish gray | 7.75 | 16.00 |
| O21 | A2 2sh red brown | 21.00 | 40.00 |
| O22 | A2 5sh olive brown | 90.00 | 135.00 |
| | *Nos. O12-O22 (11)* | 145.65 | 249.25 |

10th anniversary of Australian Mandate.

Same Overprint on Nos. 31-43

**1932-34**

| No. | Description | Unused | Used |
|---|---|---|---|
| O23 | A2 1p light green | 45 | 90 |
| O24 | A2 1½p violet brn | 75 | 1.75 |
| O25 | A2 2p red | 1.75 | 2.75 |
| O26 | A2 2½p dp grn ('34) | 3.00 | 5.00 |
| O27 | A2 3p gray blue | 3.50 | 6.50 |
| O28 | A2 3½p magenta ('34) | 3.50 | 7.75 |
| O29 | A2 4p olive green | 3.00 | 3.50 |
| O30 | A2 5p slate green | 3.50 | 4.50 |
| O31 | A2 6p bister | 4.50 | 7.25 |
| O32 | A2 9p dull violet | 7.75 | 14.00 |
| O33 | A2 1sh bluish gray | 11.00 | 17.50 |
| O34 | A2 2sh red brown | 27.50 | 52.50 |
| O35 | A2 5sh olive brown | 82.50 | 125.00 |
| | *Nos. O23-O35 (13)* | 152.70 | 248.90 |

# NEW HEBRIDES

LOCATION — A group of islands in the South Pacific Ocean northeast of New Caledonia.

GOVT. — Condominium under the joint administration of Great Britain and France.

AREA — 5,790 sq. mi.

POP. — 100,000 (est. 1976).

CAPITAL — Vila (Port-Vila).

Stamps were issued by both Great Britain and France. In 1911 a joint issue bore the coats of arms of both countries. The British stamps bore the arms of Great Britain and the value in British currency on the right and the French arms and value at the left. On the French stamps the positions were reversed. After World War II when the franc dropped in value, both series were sold for their value in francs.

New Hebrides became the independent state of Vanuatu in 1980.

12 Pence = 1 Shilling
100 Centimes = 1 Franc
100 Centimes = 1 Hebrides Franc (FNH) (1977)

**See Volume III for French Issues.**

**Catalogue values for unused stamps in this country are for Never Hinged items, beginning with Scott 62 in the regular postage section, Scott J11 in the postage due section.**

### British Issues

Stamps of Fiji, 1903-06, Overprinted

NEW HEBRIDES
CONDOMINIUM.

**1908-09 Wmk. 2 Perf. 14**
**Colored Bar Covers "FIJI" on Nos. 2-6, 9**

| No. | Description | Unused | Used |
|---|---|---|---|
| 1 | A22 ½p gray grn ('09) | 50.00 | 50.00 |
| 2 | A22 2p vio & org | 1.40 | 1.40 |
| 3 | A22 2½p vio & ultra, *bl* | 1.40 | 1.40 |
| 4 | A22 5p vio & grn | 3.50 | 3.50 |
| 5 | A22 6p vio & car rose | 3.50 | 3.50 |
| 6 | A22 1sh grn & car rose | 175.00 | 175.00 |
| | *Nos. 1-6 (6)* | 234.80 | 234.80 |

**Wmk. Multiple Crown and C. A. (3)**

| No. | Description | Unused | Used |
|---|---|---|---|
| 7 | A22 ½p gray green | 40 | 1.25 |
| 8 | A22 1p carmine | 50 | 1.00 |
| a. | Pair, one without overprint | 4,500. | |
| 9 | A22 1sh grn & car rose ('09) | 11.00 | 14.00 |

Nos. 2 to 6 and 9 are on chalk-surfaced paper.

Stamps of Fiji, 1904-11, Overprinted in Black or Red

NEW HEBRIDES
CONDOMINIUM

**1910, Dec. 15**

| No. | Description | Unused | Used |
|---|---|---|---|
| 10 | A22 ½p green | 2.75 | 6.50 |
| 11 | A22 1p carmine | 5.00 | 6.50 |
| 12 | A22 2p gray | 80 | 1.75 |
| 13 | A22 2½p ultra | 1.00 | 2.00 |
| 14 | A22 5p vio & ol grn | 1.40 | 3.50 |
| 15 | A22 6p violet | 2.00 | 5.00 |
| 16 | A22 1sh blk, *grn* (R) | 2.75 | 5.50 |
| | *Nos. 10-16 (7)* | 15.70 | 30.75 |

Nos. 14-16 are on chalk-surfaced paper.

Native Idols — A1

**1911, July 25 Engr. Wmk. 3**

| No. | Description | Unused | Used |
|---|---|---|---|
| 17 | A1 ½p pale grn | 40 | 1.00 |
| 18 | A1 1p red | 1.10 | 80 |
| 19 | A1 2p gray | 2.00 | 2.75 |
| 20 | A1 2½p ultra | 1.50 | 2.75 |
| 21 | A1 5p ol grn | 1.10 | 2.00 |
| 22 | A1 6p claret | 1.75 | 2.25 |
| 23 | A1 1sh *green* | 2.00 | 4.00 |
| 24 | A1 2sh vio, *bl* | 8.00 | 14.00 |
| 25 | A1 5sh grn, *yel* | 16.00 | 35.00 |
| | *Nos. 17-25 (9)* | 33.85 | 64.55 |

Surcharged **1d.**

**1920-21**

| No. | Description | Unused | Used |
|---|---|---|---|
| 26 | A1 1p on 5p ol grn ('21) | 14.00 | 27.50 |
| a. | Inverted surcharge | 1,400. | |
| 27 | A1 1p on 1sh *grn* | 4.00 | 6.50 |
| 28 | A1 1p on 2sh vio, *bl* | 2.50 | 6.50 |
| 29 | A1 1p on 5sh grn, *yel* | 2.50 | 7.50 |

**On French Issue No. 16**

| No. | Description | Unused | Used |
|---|---|---|---|
| 30 | A2 2p on 40c red, *yel* ('21) | 2.25 | 3.00 |
| | *Nos. 26-30 (5)* | 25.25 | 51.00 |

**On French Issue No. 27**
**Wmk. R F in Sheet**

| No. | Description | Unused | Used |
|---|---|---|---|
| 31 | A2 2p on 40c red, *yel* ('21) | 175.00 | 225.00 |

The letters "R.F." are the initials of "Republique Francaise." They are large double-lined Roman capitals, about 120mm high. About one-fourth of the stamps in each sheet show portions of the watermark, the other stamps are without watermark.

Type of 1910 Issue

**1921, Oct. Wmk. 4**

| No. | Description | Unused | Used |
|---|---|---|---|
| 33 | A1 1p rose red | 2.50 | 6.50 |
| 34 | A1 2p gray | 3.50 | 8.00 |
| 37 | A1 6p claret | 8.00 | 20.00 |

Stamps of 1910-21 Surcharged with New Values as in 1920-21

**1924 Wmk. 3**

| No. | Description | Unused | Used |
|---|---|---|---|
| 38 | A1 1p on ½p pale grn | 1.40 | 3.50 |
| 39 | A1 5p on 2½p ultra | 3.50 | 3.50 |
| a. | Inverted surch. | 1,200. | |

**Wmk. 4**

| No. | Description | Unused | Used |
|---|---|---|---|
| 40 | A1 3p on 1p rose red | 3.50 | 8.25 |

A3

The values at the lower right denote the currency and amount for which the stamps were to be sold. The English stamps could be bought at the French post office in French money.

**1925 Engr.**

| No. | Description | Unused | Used |
|---|---|---|---|
| 41 | A3 ½p (5c) blk | 50 | 1.00 |
| 42 | A3 1p (10c) grn | 60 | 1.40 |
| 43 | A3 2p (20c) grnsh gray | 65 | 1.40 |
| 44 | A3 2½p (25c) brn | 1.00 | 2.00 |
| 45 | A3 5p (50c) ultra | 2.00 | 3.00 |
| 46 | A3 6p (60c) cl | 2.50 | 6.50 |
| 47 | A3 1sh (1.25fr) blk, *grn* | 2.50 | 7.00 |
| 48 | A3 2sh (2.50fr) vio, *bl* | 6.50 | 10.00 |
| 49 | A3 5sh (6.25fr) grn, *yel* | 8.00 | 14.00 |
| | *Nos. 41-49 (9)* | 24.25 | 46.30 |

Beach Scene — A5

**1938, June 1 Wmk. 4 Perf. 12**

| No. | Description | Unused | Used |
|---|---|---|---|
| 50 | A5 5c green | 50 | 50 |
| 51 | A5 10c dk org | 65 | 65 |
| 52 | A5 15c violet | 65 | 65 |
| 53 | A5 20c rose red | 80 | 80 |
| 54 | A5 25c brown | 80 | 80 |
| 55 | A5 30c dk bl | 1.00 | 1.00 |
| 56 | A5 40c ol grn | 1.40 | 1.40 |
| 57 | A5 50c brn vio | 1.40 | 1.40 |
| 58 | A5 1fr car, *emer* | 3.00 | 3.00 |
| 59 | A5 2fr dk bl, *emer* | 6.50 | 6.50 |
| 60 | A5 5fr red, *yel* | 22.50 | 24.00 |
| 61 | A5 10fr vio, *bl* | 40.00 | 42.50 |
| | *Nos. 50-61 (12)* | 79.20 | 83.20 |

**Catalogue values for unused stamps in this section, from this point to the end of the section, are for Never Hinged items.**

### UPU Issue
Common Design Type

**1949, Oct. 10 Engr. Perf. 13½**

| No. | Description | Unused | Used |
|---|---|---|---|
| 62 | CD309 10c red org | 30 | 30 |
| 63 | CD309 15c violet | 50 | 40 |
| 64 | CD309 30c vio bl | 80 | 50 |
| 65 | CD309 50c rose vio | 1.40 | 1.00 |

Outrigger Canoes with Sails — A6

Designs: 25c, 30c, 40c and 50c, Native Carving. 1fr, 2fr and 5fr, Island couple.

**1953, Apr. 30 Perf. 12½**

| No. | Description | Unused | Used |
|---|---|---|---|
| 66 | A6 5c green | 15 | 14 |
| 67 | A6 10c red | 14 | 12 |
| 68 | A6 15c yellow | 22 | 18 |
| 69 | A6 20c ultra | 25 | 22 |
| 70 | A6 25c olive | 38 | 30 |
| 71 | A6 30c lt brn | 45 | 38 |
| 72 | A6 40c blk brn | 70 | 55 |
| 73 | A6 50c violet | 75 | 65 |
| 74 | A6 1fr dp org | 1.50 | 1.25 |
| 75 | A6 2fr red vio | 4.50 | 7.50 |
| 76 | A6 5fr scarlet | 11.00 | 16.00 |
| | *Nos. 66-76 (11)* | 20.04 | 27.29 |

### Coronation Issue.
Common Design Type

**1953, June 2 Perf. 13½x13**

| No. | Description | Unused | Used |
|---|---|---|---|
| 77 | CD312 10c car & blk | 1.10 | 1.10 |

Discovery of New Hebrides, 1606 — A7

Designs: 20c, 50c, Britannia, Marianne, Flags and Mask.

**Perf. 14½x14**
**1956, Oct. 20 Photo. Wmk. 4**

| No. | Description | Unused | Used |
|---|---|---|---|
| 78 | A7 5c emerald | 8 | 8 |
| 79 | A7 10c crimson | 15 | 15 |
| 80 | A7 20c ultra | 25 | 25 |
| 81 | A7 50c purple | 65 | 65 |

50th anniv. of the establishment of the Anglo-French Condominium.

Port Vila and Iririki Islet — A8

Designs: 25c, 30c, 40c, 50c, Tropical river and spear fisherman. 1fr, 2fr, 5fr, Woman drinking from coconut (inscribed: "Franco-British Alliance 4th March 1947").

**1957, Sept. 3 Engr. Perf. 13½x13**

| No. | Description | Unused | Used |
|---|---|---|---|
| 82 | A8 5c green | 8 | 8 |
| 83 | A8 10c red | 8 | 8 |
| 84 | A8 15c org yel | 14 | 14 |
| 85 | A8 20c ultra | 18 | 18 |
| 86 | A8 25c olive | 25 | 25 |
| 87 | A8 30c lt brn | 40 | 40 |
| 88 | A8 40c sepia | 50 | 50 |
| 89 | A8 50c violet | 65 | 65 |
| 90 | A8 1fr orange | 1.25 | 1.25 |
| 91 | A8 2fr rose lil | 3.50 | 2.50 |
| 92 | A8 5fr black | 8.00 | 5.50 |
| | *Nos. 82-92 (11)* | 15.03 | 11.53 |

**Freedom from Hunger Issue**
Common Design Type
*Perf. 14x14½*

**1963, Sept. 2 Photo. Wmk. 314**
*93* CD314 60c green 1.10 75

**Red Cross Centenary Issue**
Common Design Type with Royal Cipher and "RF" Replacing Queen's Portrait

**1963, Sept. 2 Litho. *Perf. 13***
*94* CD315 15c blk & red 40 25
*95* CD315 45c ultra & red 1.10 90

Copra Industry A9

Designs: 5c, Manganese loading, Forari Wharf. 10c, Cacao. 20c, Map of New Hebrides, tuna, marlin, ships. 25c, Striped triggerfish. 30c, Pearly nautilus (mollusk). 40c, 60c, Turkeyfish. 50c, Lined tang (fish). 1fr, Cardinal honey-eater and hibiscus. 2fr, Buff-bellied flycatcher. 3fr, Thicket warbler. 5fr, White-collared kingfisher.

**Wmk. 314 (10c, 20c, 40c, 60c, 3fr); Unwmk (others)**
***Perf. 12½ (10c, 20c, 40c, 60c); 14 (3fr); 13 (others)***
**Photo. (10c, 20c, 40c, 60c, 3fr); Engraved (others)**

**1963-67**
*96* A9 5c Prus bl & cl ('66) 15 12
*97* A9 10c brt grn, org brn & dk brn ('65) 12 12
*98* A9 15c dk pur, yel & brn 18 18
*99* A9 20c brt bl, gray & cit ('65) 22 22
*100* A9 25c vio, rose lil & org brn ('66) 40 40
*101* A9 30c lil, brn & cit 65 65
*102* A9 40c dk bl & ver ('65) 90 90
*103* A9 50c Prus bl, yel & grn 65 65
*103A* A9 60c dk bl & ver ('67) 1.10 1.10
*104* A9 1fr bl grn, blk & red ('66) 1.75 1.75
*105* A9 2fr ol, blk & brn 2.50 2.50
*106* A9 3fr org grn, brt grn & blk ('65) 5.50 4.50
*107* A9 5fr ind, dp bl & gray ('67) 12.50 9.00
*Nos. 96-107 (13)* 26.62 22.09

ITU Emblem CD317

*Perf. 11x11½*

**1965, May 17 Litho. Wmk. 314**
*108* CD317 15c ver & ol bis 25 20
*109* CD317 60c ultra & ver 1.00 75

Cent. of the ITU.

**Intl. Cooperation Year Issue**
Common Design Type with Royal Cipher and "RF" Replacing Queen's Portrait

**1965, Sept. 24 *Perf. 14½***
*110* CD318 5c bl grn & cl 6 6
*111* CD318 55c lt vio & grn 65 65

**Churchill Memorial Issue**
Common Design Type with Royal Cipher and "RF" Replacing Queen's Portrait

**1966, Jan. 24 Photo. *Perf. 14***
**Design in Black, Gold and Carmine Rose**
*112* CD319 5c brt bl 15 10
*113* CD319 15c green 35 22
*114* CD319 25c brown 75 40
*115* CD319 30c violet 1.10 75

**World Cup Soccer Issue**
Common Design Type with Royal Cipher and "RF" Replacing Queen's Portrait

**1966, July 1 Litho. *Perf. 14***
*116* CD321 20c multi 35 35
*117* CD321 40c multi 75 75

**WHO Headquarters Issue**
Common Design Type with Royal Cipher and "RF" Replacing Queen's Portrait

**1966, Sept. 20 Litho. *Perf. 14***
*118* CD322 25c multi 30 30
*119* CD322 60c multi 80 80

**UNESCO Anniversary Issue**
Common Design Type with Royal Cipher and "RF" Replacing Queen's Portrait

**1966, Dec. 1 Litho. *Perf. 14***
*120* CD323 15c "Education" 30 30
*121* CD323 30c "Science" 60 60
*122* CD323 45c "Culture" 1.00 1.00

Coast Watchers — A11

Designs: 25c, Map of South Pacific war zone, U.S. Marine and Australian soldier. 60c, Australian cruiser Canberra. 1fr, Flying fortress taking off from Bauer Field, and view of Vila.

*Perf. 14x13*

**1967, Sept. 26 Photo. Wmk. 314**
*123* A11 15c lt bl & multi 16 16
*124* A11 25c yel & multi 35 35
*125* A11 60c multi 80 80
*126* A11 1fr pale sal & multi 1.40 1.40

25th anniv. of the Allied Forces' campaign in the South Pacific War Zone.

Globe and World Map — A12

Designs: 25c, Ships La Boudeuse and L'Etoile and map of Bougainville Strait. 60c, Louis Antoine de Bougainville, ship's figure-head and bougainvillaea.

**1968, May 23 Engr. *Perf. 13***
*127* A12 15c ver, emer & dl vio 16 16
*128* A12 25c ultra, ol & brn 35 35
*129* A12 60c mag, grn & brn 65 65

Issued to commemorate the 200th anniversary of Louis Antoine de Bougainville's (1729-1811) voyage around the world.

Concorde Airliner A13

Design: 60c, Concorde, sideview.

**1968, Oct. 9 Litho. *Perf. 14x13½***
*130* A13 25c vio bl, red & lt bl 1.00 65
*131* A13 60c red, ultra & blk 1.75 1.10

Development of the Concorde supersonic airliner, a joint Anglo-French project to produce a high speed plane.

Kauri Pine — A14

*Perf. 14x14½*

**1969, June 30 Litho. Wmk. 314**
*132* A14 20c brn & multi 35 35

Issued to publicize the New Hebrides timber industry. Issued in sheets of 9 (3x3) on simulated wood grain background.

Relay Race, French and British Flags — A15

Design: 1fr, Runner at right.

***Perf. 12½x13***

**1969, Aug. 13 Photo. Unwmk.**
*133* A15 25c ultra, car, brn & gold 35 35
*134* A15 1fr brn, car, ultra & gold 1.40 1.40

3rd South Pacific Games, Port Moresby, Papua and New Guinea, Aug. 13-23.

Land Diver, Pentecost Island — A16

Designs: 15c, Diver in starting position on tower. 1fr, Diver nearing ground.

**Wmk. 314**

**1969, Oct. 15 Litho. *Perf. 12½***
*135* A16 15c yel & multi 16 16
*136* A16 25c pink & multi 30 30
*137* A16 1fr gray & multi 1.10 1.10

UPU Headquarters and Monument, Bern — A17

**Unwmk.**

**1970, May 20 Engr. *Perf. 13***
*138* A17 1.05fr org, lil & sl 1.10 1.10

Opening of the new UPU Headquarters, Bern.

Charles de Gaulle — A18

**1970, July 20 Photo. *Perf. 13***
*139* A18 65c brn & multi 65 65
*140* A18 1.10fr dp bl & multi 1.40 1.40

Issued to commemorate the 30th anniversary of the rallying to the Free French.

No. 99 Surcharged
35

**1970, Oct. 15 Wmk. 314 *Perf. 12½***
*141* A9 35c on 20c multi 75 75

Virgin and Child, by Giovanni Bellini — A19

Christmas: 50c, Virgin and Child, by Giovanni Cima.

***Perf. 14½x14***

**1970, Nov. 30 Litho. Wmk. 314**
*142* A19 15c tan & multi 22 22
*143* A19 50c lt grn & multi 65 65

Nos. 139-140 Overprinted with 2 Black Vertical Bars and Gold Inscription: "1890-1970 / IN MEMORIAM / 9-11-70"

**Unwmk.**

**1971, Jan. 19 Photo. *Perf. 13***
*144* A18 65c brn & multi 60 60
*145* A18 1.10fr dp bl & multi 1.10 1.10

In memory of Gen. Charles de Gaulle (1890-1970), President of France.

NEW HEBRIDES CONDOMINIUM
gold 20 centimes postage
4th SOUTH PACIFIC GAMES - FOOTBALL
Soccer A20

Design: 65c, Basketball (vert.).

**1971, July 13 Photo. *Perf. 12½***
*146* A20 20c multi 28 28
*147* A20 65c multi 80 80

4th South Pacific Games, Papeete, French Polynesia, Sept. 8-19.

A particular stamp may be scarce, but if few collectors want it, its market value may remain relatively low.

Kauri Pine, Cone and Arms of Royal Society — A21

*Perf. 14½x14*

**1971, Sept. 7 Litho. Wmk. 314**

| | | | | |
|---|---|---|---|---|
| *148* | A21 | 65c multi | 90 | 90 |

Royal Society of London for the Advancement of Science expedition to study vegetation and fauna, July 1-October.

Adoration of the Shepherds, by Louis Le Nain — A22

Design: 50c, Adoration of the Shepherds, by Jacopo Tintoretto.

**1971, Nov. 23** *Perf. 14x13½*

| | | | | |
|---|---|---|---|---|
| *149* | A22 | 25c lt grn & multi | 35 | 35 |
| *150* | A22 | 50c lt bl & multi | 80 | 80 |

Christmas 1971. See Nos. 167-168.

Drover Mk III A23

Airplanes: 25c, Sandringham seaplane. 30c, Dragon Rapide. 65c, Caravelle.

*Perf. 13½x13*

**1972, Feb. 29 Photo. Unwmk.**

| | | | | |
|---|---|---|---|---|
| *151* | A23 | 20c lt grn & multi | 35 | 35 |
| *152* | A23 | 25c ultra & multi | 40 | 40 |
| *153* | A23 | 30c org & multi | 60 | 60 |
| *154* | A23 | 65c dk bl & multi | 1.40 | 1.40 |

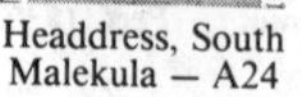


Headdress, South Malekula — A24

Baker's Pigeon — A25

Artifacts: 15c, Slit gong and carved figure, North Ambrym. 1fr, Carved figures, North Ambrym. 3fr, Ceremonial headdress, South Malekula.

Birds: 20c, Red-headed parrot-finch. 35c, Chestnut-bellied kingfisher. 2fr, Green palm lorikeet.

Sea shells: 25c, Cribraria fischeri. 30c, Oliva rubrolabiata. 65c, Strombus plicatus. 5fr, Turbo marmoratus.

**1972, July 24 Photo.** *Perf. 12½x13*

| | | | | |
|---|---|---|---|---|
| *155* | A24 | 5c plum & multi | 6 | 5 |
| *156* | A25 | 10c bl & multi | 10 | 8 |
| *157* | A24 | 15c red & multi | 14 | 12 |
| *158* | A25 | 20c org brn & multi | 20 | 16 |
| *159* | A24 | 25c dp bl & multi | 28 | 25 |
| *160* | A24 | 30c dk grn & multi | 35 | 28 |
| *161* | A25 | 35c gray bl & multi | 40 | 35 |
| *162* | A24 | 65c dk grn & multi | 65 | 1.10 |
| *163* | A24 | 1fr org & multi | 1.10 | 1.00 |
| *164* | A25 | 2fr multi | 2.00 | 1.40 |
| *165* | A24 | 3fr yel & multi | 3.00 | 2.00 |
| *166* | A24 | 5fr pink & multi | 5.00 | 4.00 |
| | | *Nos. 155-166 (12)* | 13.28 | 10.79 |

Christmas Type of 1971

Designs: 25c, Adoration of the Magi (detail), by Bartholomaeus Spranger. 70c, Virgin and Child, by Jan Provoost.

*Perf. 14x13½*

**1972, Sept. 25 Litho. Wmk. 314**

| | | | | |
|---|---|---|---|---|
| *167* | A22 | 25c lt grn & multi | 25 | 25 |
| *168* | A22 | 70c lt bl & multi | 75 | 75 |

**Silver Wedding Issue, 1972**

Common Design Type

Design: Elizabeth II and Prince Philip.

**1972, Nov. 20 Photo.** *Perf. 14x14½*

| | | | | |
|---|---|---|---|---|
| *169* | CD324 | 35c vio blk & multi | 25 | 25 |
| *170* | CD324 | 65c ol & multi | 50 | 50 |

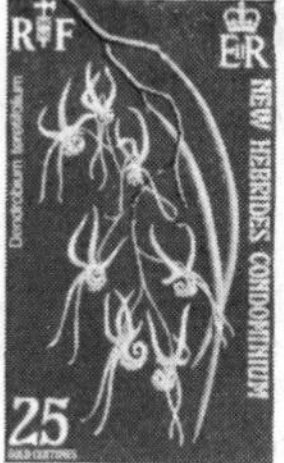
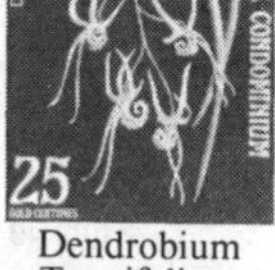


Dendrobium Teretifolium A26

New Wharf, Vila A27

Orchids: 30c, Ephemerantha comata. 35c, Spathoglottis petri. 65c, Dendrobium mohlianum.

**1973, Feb. 26 Litho.** *Perf. 14*

| | | | | |
|---|---|---|---|---|
| *171* | A26 | 25c bl vio & multi | 25 | 20 |
| *172* | A26 | 30c multi | 30 | 25 |
| *173* | A26 | 35c vio & multi | 35 | 30 |
| *174* | A26 | 65c dk grn & multi | 75 | 65 |

**1973, May 14 Wmk. 314**

Design: 70c, New wharf (horiz.).

| | | | | |
|---|---|---|---|---|
| *175* | A27 | 25c multi | 25 | 25 |
| *176* | A27 | 70c multi | 90 | 90 |

New wharf at Vila, finished Nov. 1972.

Wild Horses, Tanna Island — A28

*Perf. 13x12½*

**1973, Aug. 13 Photo. Unwmk.**

| | | | | |
|---|---|---|---|---|
| *177* | A28 | 35c *shown* | 35 | 35 |
| *178* | A28 | 70c *Yasur Volcano, Tanna* | 1.10 | 90 |

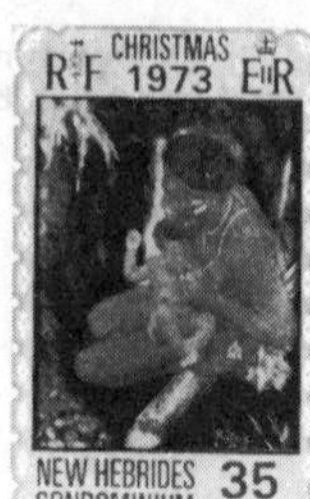


Mother and Child, by Marcel Moutouh — A29

Design: 70c, Star over Lagoon, by Tatin d'Avesnieres.

*Perf. 14x13½*

**1973, Nov. 19 Litho. Wmk. 314**

| | | | | |
|---|---|---|---|---|
| *179* | A29 | 35c tan & multi | 40 | 40 |
| *180* | A29 | 70c lil rose & multi | 1.00 | 1.00 |

Christmas 1973.

Nos. 161 and 164 Overprinted in Red or Black: "ROYAL VISIT / 1974"

*Perf. 12½x13*

**1974, Feb. 11 Photo. Unwmk.**

| | | | | |
|---|---|---|---|---|
| *181* | A25 | 35c multi (R) | 30 | 30 |
| *182* | A25 | 2fr multi (B) | 1.75 | 1.75 |

Visit of British Royal Family, Feb. 11-12.

Pacific Dove — A30

Designs: 35c, Night swallowtail. 70c, Green sea turtle. 1.15fr, Flying fox.

**1974, Feb. 11** *Perf. 13x12½*

| | | | | |
|---|---|---|---|---|
| *183* | A30 | 25c gray & multi | 55 | 40 |
| *184* | A30 | 35c gray & multi | 90 | 55 |
| *185* | A30 | 70c gray & multi | 1.50 | 1.10 |
| *186* | A30 | 1.15fr gray & multi | 1.75 | 1.50 |

Nature conservation.

Old Post Office, Vila — A31

Design: 70c, New Post Office.

**1974, May 6 Unwmk.** *Perf. 12*

| | | | | |
|---|---|---|---|---|
| *187* | A31 | 35c bl & multi | 40 | 40 |
| *188* | A31 | 70c red & multi | 80 | 80 |

Opening of New Post Office, May, 1974. Nos. 187-188 printed se-tenant at the base in sheets of 50.

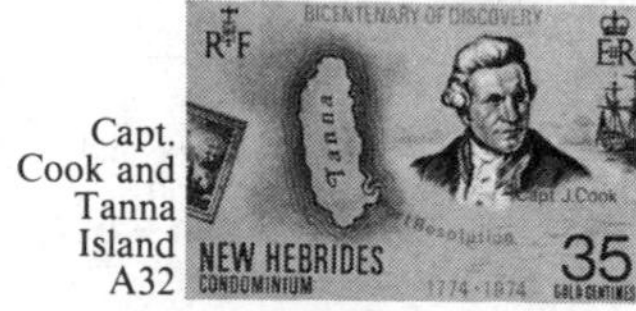


Capt. Cook and Tanna Island A32

Designs: No. 190, William Wales, and boat landing on island. No. 191, William Hodges painting islanders and landscape. 1.15fr, Capt. Cook, "Resolution" and map of New Hebrides.

**Wmk. 314**

**1974, Aug. 1 Litho.** *Perf. 13*

**Size: 40x25mm**

| | | | | |
|---|---|---|---|---|
| *189* | A32 | 35c multi | 1.10 | 50 |
| *190* | A32 | 35c multi | 1.10 | 50 |
| *191* | A32 | 35c multi | 1.10 | 50 |

*Perf. 11*

**Size: 58x34mm**

| | | | | |
|---|---|---|---|---|
| *192* | A32 | 1.15fr lil & multi | 2.25 | 2.00 |

Bicentenary of the discovery of the New Hebrides by Capt. Cook. Nos. 189-191 printed se-tenant in continuous design in sheets of 30 (6x5).

Exchange of Letters, UPU Emblem A33

*Perf. 13x12½*

**1974, Oct. 9 Photo. Unwmk.**

| | | | | |
|---|---|---|---|---|
| *193* | A33 | 70c multi | 55 | 55 |

Centenary of Universal Postal Union.

Nativity, by Gerard van Honthorst — A34

Christmas: 35c, Adoration of the Kings, by Velazquez (vert.).

**Wmk. 314**

**1974, Nov. 14 Litho.** *Perf. 13½*

| | | | | |
|---|---|---|---|---|
| *194* | A34 | 35c multi | 40 | 40 |
| *195* | A34 | 70c multi | 80 | 80 |

Charolais Bull — A35

**1975, Apr. 29 Engr.** *Perf. 13*

| | | | | |
|---|---|---|---|---|
| *196* | A35 | 10fr multi | 8.00 | 11.00 |

Kayak Race, Nordjamb Emblem — A36

**1975, Aug. 5 Litho.** *Perf. 14x13½*

| | | | | |
|---|---|---|---|---|
| *197* | A36 | 25c *shown* | 22 | 22 |
| *198* | A36 | 35c *Camp cooks* | 28 | 28 |
| *199* | A36 | 1fr *Map makers* | 75 | 75 |
| *200* | A36 | 5fr *Fishermen* | 6.00 | 5.00 |

Nordjamb 75, 14th Boy Scout Jamboree, Lillehammer, Norway, July 29-Aug. 7.

Pitti Madonna, by Michelangelo A37

Christmas (After Michelangelo): 70c, Bruges Madonna. 2.50fr, Taddei Madonna.

*Perf. 14½x14*

**1975, Nov. 11 Litho. Wmk. 373**

| | | | | |
|---|---|---|---|---|
| *201* | A37 | 35c ol grn & multi | 30 | 30 |
| *202* | A37 | 70c brn & multi | 60 | 60 |
| *203* | A37 | 2.50fr bl & multi | 2.00 | 2.00 |

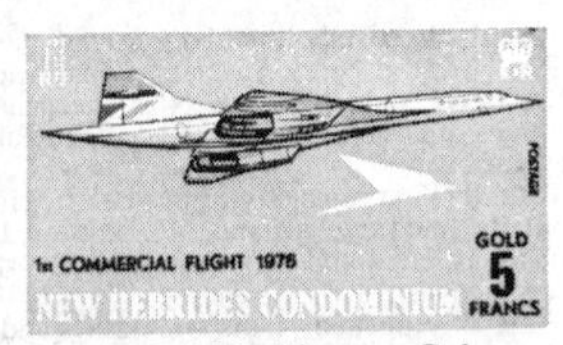


Concorde, British Airways Colors and Emblem — A38

**Unwmk.**

**1976, Jan. 30 Typo. *Perf. 13***

*204* A38 5fr bl & multi 10.00 7.50

First commercial flight of supersonic jet Concorde from London to Bahrain, Jan. 21.

Telephones, 1876 and 1976 — A39

Designs: 70c, Alexander Graham Bell. 1.15fr, Noumea earth station and satellite.

**1976, Mar. 31 Photo. *Perf. 13***

| | | | | |
|---|---|---|---|---|
| *205* | A39 | 25c blk, car & bl | 20 | 20 |
| *206* | A39 | 70c blk & multi | 50 | 50 |
| *207* | A39 | 1.15fr blk, org & vio bl | 90 | 90 |

Centenary of first telephone call by Alexander Graham Bell, Mar. 10, 1876.

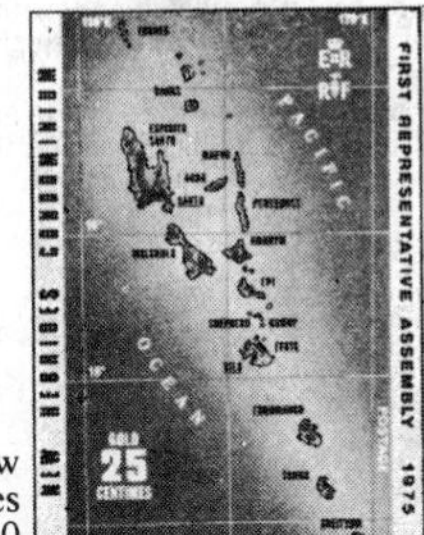


Map of New Hebrides A40

View of Santo — A41

Design: 2fr, View of Vila.

**1976, June 29 Photo. *Perf. 13***

| | | | | |
|---|---|---|---|---|
| *208* | A40 | 25c bl & multi | 20 | 20 |
| *209* | A41 | 1fr multi | 75 | 75 |
| *210* | A41 | 2fr multi | 1.75 | 1.75 |

Opening of First Representative Assembly, June 29 (25c); first Santo Municipal Council (1fr); first Vila Municipal Council (2fr).

Flight into Egypt, by Francisco Vieira Lusitano — A42

Christmas (Portuguese 16th Cent. Paintings): 70c, Adoration of the Shepherds. 2.50fr, Adoration of the Kings.

**Wmk. 373**

**1976, Nov. 8 Litho. *Perf. 14***

| | | | | |
|---|---|---|---|---|
| *211* | A42 | 35c pur & multi | 25 | 25 |
| *212* | A42 | 70c bl & multi | 50 | 50 |
| *213* | A42 | 2.50fr lt grn & multi | 1.75 | 1.75 |

Queen's Visit, 1974 — A43

Designs: 70c, Imperial state crown. 2fr, The blessing.

***Perf. 14x13½***

**1977, Feb. 7 Litho. Wmk. 373**

| | | | | |
|---|---|---|---|---|
| *214* | A43 | 35c lt grn & multi | 22 | 22 |
| *215* | A43 | 70c bl & multi | 45 | 45 |
| *216* | A43 | 2fr pink & multi | 1.25 | 1.25 |

25th anniv. of the reign of Elizabeth II.

Nos. 155-166, 196 Surcharged with New Value, "FNH" and Bars

***Perf. 12½x13***

**1977, July 1 Photo. Unwmk.**

| | | | | |
|---|---|---|---|---|
| *217* | A24 | 5fr on 5c multi | 14 | 14 |
| *218* | A25 | 10fr on 10c multi | 28 | 28 |
| *219* | A24 | 15fr on 15c multi | 40 | 40 |
| *220* | A25 | 20fr on 20c multi | 50 | 50 |
| *221* | A24 | 25fr on 25c multi | 65 | 65 |
| *222* | A24 | 30fr on 30c multi | 80 | 80 |
| *223* | A25 | 35fr on 35c multi | 1.00 | 1.00 |
| *224* | A24 | 40fr on 65c multi | 1.10 | 1.10 |
| *225* | A24 | 50fr on 1fr multi | 2.00 | 1.50 |
| *226* | A25 | 70fr on 2fr multi | 3.50 | 2.00 |
| *227* | A24 | 100fr on 3fr multi | 5.00 | 3.00 |
| *228* | A24 | 200fr on 5fr multi | 6.50 | 6.00 |

**Wmk. 314**

**Engr. *Perf. 13***

| | | | | |
|---|---|---|---|---|
| *229* | A35 | 500fr on 10fr multi | 14.00 | 11.00 |
| | | *Nos. 217-229 (13)* | 35.87 | 28.37 |

Nos. 217-229 were surcharged in Paris. Eleven denominations were surcharged later in Vila with slightly larger, different letters and different bars; nine were sold at post offices.

Erromango and Kaori Tree — A44

Tempi Madonna, by Raphael — A45

Designs: 10fr, Archipelago and man making copra. 15fr, Espiritu Santo Island and cattle. 20fr, Efate Island and Post Office, Vila. 25fr, Malakula Island and headdresses. 30fr, Aoba and Maewo Islands and pig tusks. 35fr, Pentecost Island and land diving. 40fr, Tanna Island and Prophet John Frum's Red Cross. 50fr, Shepherd Island and canoe with sail. 70fr, Banks Island and dancers. 100fr, Ambrym Island and carvings. 200fr, Aneityum Island and decorated baskets. 500fr, Torres Islands and fishing with bow and arrow.

**1977-78 Wmk. 373 Litho. *Perf. 14***

| | | | | |
|---|---|---|---|---|
| *238* | A44 | 5fr multi | 8 | 8 |
| *239* | A44 | 10fr multi | 16 | 16 |
| *240* | A44 | 15fr multi | 22 | 22 |
| *241* | A44 | 20fr multi | 32 | 32 |
| *242* | A44 | 25fr multi | 40 | 40 |
| *243* | A44 | 30fr multi | 50 | 50 |
| *244* | A44 | 35fr multi | 60 | 60 |
| *245* | A44 | 40fr multi | 65 | 65 |
| *246* | A44 | 50fr multi | 80 | 80 |
| *247* | A44 | 70fr multi | 1.10 | 1.10 |
| *248* | A44 | 100fr multi | 1.75 | 1.75 |
| *249* | A44 | 200fr multi | 3.50 | 3.50 |
| *250* | A44 | 500fr multi | 8.00 | 8.00 |
| | | *Nos. 238-250 (13)* | 18.08 | 18.08 |

Issue dates: 5fr, 20fr, 50fr, 100fr, 200fr, Sept. 7; 15fr, 25fr, 30fr, 40fr, Nov. 23, 1977; 10fr, 35fr, 70fr, 500fr, May 9, 1978.

**1977, Dec. 8 Litho. *Perf. 12***

Christmas: 15fr, Virgin and Child, by Gerard David. 30fr, Virgin and Child, by Pompeo Batoni.

| | | | | |
|---|---|---|---|---|
| *251* | A45 | 10fr multi | 20 | 20 |
| *252* | A45 | 15fr multi | 30 | 30 |
| *253* | A45 | 30fr multi | 65 | 65 |

British Airways Concorde over New York City — A46

Designs: 20fr, British Airways Concorde over London. 30fr, Air France Concorde over Washington. 40fr, Air France Concorde over Paris.

**Wmk. 373**

**1978, May 9 Litho. *Perf. 14***

| | | | | |
|---|---|---|---|---|
| *254* | A46 | 10fr multi | 40 | 20 |
| *255* | A46 | 20fr multi | 65 | 40 |
| *256* | A46 | 30fr multi | 1.00 | 60 |
| *257* | A46 | 40fr multi | 1.25 | 80 |

Concorde, first commercial flight, Paris to New York.

**Elizabeth II Coronation Anniversary Issue**

Common Design Types

Souvenir Sheet

**Unwmk.**

**1978, June 2 Litho. *Perf. 15***

| | | | | |
|---|---|---|---|---|
| *258* | | Sheet of 6 | 5.00 | 5.00 |
| *a.* | | CD326 40fr *White horse of Hanover* | 80 | 80 |
| *b.* | | CD327 40fr *Elizabeth II* | 80 | 80 |
| *c.* | | CD328 40fr *Gallic cock* | 80 | 80 |

No. 258 contains 2 se-tenant strips of Nos. 258a-258c, separated by horizontal gutter with commemorative and descriptive inscriptions and showing central part of coronation procession with coach. Size: 100x135mm.

Virgin and Child, by Dürer — A47

Dürer Paintings: 15fr, Virgin and Child with St. Anne. 30fr, Virgin and Child with Goldfinch. 40fr, Virgin and Child with Pear.

***Perf. 14x13½***

**1978, Dec. 1 Litho. Wmk. 373**

| | | | | |
|---|---|---|---|---|
| *259* | A47 | 10fr multi | 20 | 20 |
| *260* | A47 | 15fr multi | 30 | 30 |
| *261* | A47 | 30fr multi | 60 | 60 |
| *262* | A47 | 40fr multi | 90 | 90 |

Christmas and 450th death anniv. of Albrecht Dürer (1471-1528), German painter.

Type of 1976 Surcharged with New Value, Bars over Denomination and Inscription at Right. Longitude changed to "166E."

**1979, Jan. 11 Photo. *Perf. 13***

| | | | | |
|---|---|---|---|---|
| *263* | A40 | 10fr on 25c bl & multi | 20 | 20 |
| *264* | A40 | 40fr on 25c lt grn & multi | 80 | 80 |

1st anniv. of Internal Self-Government.

New Hebrides No. 50 — A48

Rowland Hill and New Hebrides Stamps: 20fr, No. 136. 40fr, No. 43.

**1979, Sept. 10 Litho. *Perf. 14***

| | | | | |
|---|---|---|---|---|
| *265* | A48 | 10fr multi | 20 | 20 |
| *266* | A48 | 20fr multi | 40 | 40 |
| *a.* | | Souvenir sheet of 2 | 80 | 80 |
| *267* | A48 | 40fr multi | 80 | 80 |

Sir Rowland Hill (1795-1879), originator of penny postage. No. 266a contains New Hebrides, British, No. 266, and French, No. 286; margin shows Mulready envelope. Size: 144x95mm.

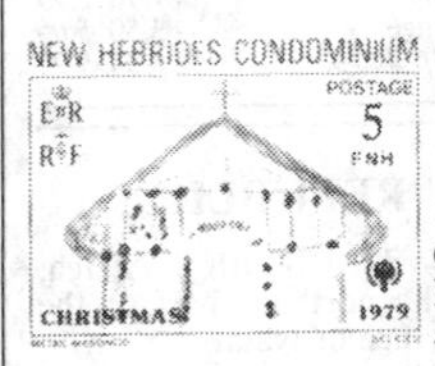


Arts Festival — A49

Designs: 10fr, Clubs and spears. 20fr, Ritual puppet. 40fr, Headdress.

**Wmk. 373**

**1979, Nov. 16 Litho. *Perf. 14***

| | | | | |
|---|---|---|---|---|
| *268* | A49 | 5fr multi | 10 | 10 |
| *269* | A49 | 10fr multi | 18 | 18 |
| *270* | A49 | 20fr multi | 40 | 40 |
| *271* | A49 | 40fr multi | 75 | 75 |

Church, IYC Emblem A50

IYC Emblem, Children's Drawings: 10fr, Father Christmas. 20fr, Cross and Bible (vert.). 40fr, Stars, candle and Santa Claus (vert.).

**1979, Dec. 4 *Perf. 13x13½***

| | | | | |
|---|---|---|---|---|
| *272* | A50 | 5fr multi | 10 | 10 |
| *273* | A50 | 10fr multi | 18 | 18 |
| *274* | A50 | 20fr multi | 40 | 40 |
| *275* | A50 | 40fr multi | 65 | 65 |

Christmas 1979; Intl. Year of the Child.



White-bellied Honeyeater — A51

**1980, Feb. 27 Litho. *Perf. 14***

| | | | | |
|---|---|---|---|---|
| *276* | A51 | 10fr *shown* | 35 | 18 |
| *277* | A51 | 20fr *Scarlet robins* | 50 | 40 |
| *278* | A51 | 30fr *Yellow white-eyes* | 80 | 55 |

| | | | | |
|---|---|---|---|---|
| 279 | A51 | 40fr *Fan-tailed brush cuckoo* | 1.00 | 75 |

New Hebrides stamps were replaced in 1980 by these of Vanuatu.

## POSTAGE DUE STAMPS

### British Issues

Type of 1925 Overprinted **POSTAGE DUE.**

**1925 Engr. Wmk. 4 *Perf. 14***

| No. | Type | Description | Unused | Used |
|---|---|---|---|---|
| J1 | A3 | 1p (10c) grn | 25.00 | 50 |
| J2 | A3 | 2p (10c) gray | 30.00 | 55 |
| J3 | A3 | 3p (30c) car | 32.50 | 55 |
| J4 | A3 | 5p (50c) ultra | 37.50 | 1.25 |
| J5 | A3 | 10p (1fr) car, *bl* | 45.00 | 1.25 |
| | | *Nos. J1-J5 (5)* | 170.00 | 4.10 |

Regular Stamps of 1938 Overprinted in Black **POSTAGE DUE**

**1938 *Perf. 12***

| No. | Type | Description | Unused | Used |
|---|---|---|---|---|
| J6 | A5 | 5c green | 6.25 | 6.25 |
| J7 | A5 | 10c dk org | 7.00 | 7.00 |
| J8 | A5 | 20c rose red | 7.50 | 6.25 |
| J9 | A5 | 40c ol grn | 10.00 | 7.50 |
| J10 | A5 | 1fr car, *emer* | 20.00 | 20.00 |
| | | *Nos. J6-J10 (5)* | 50.75 | 47.00 |

**Catalogue values for unused stamps in this section, from this point to the end of the section, are for Never Hinged items.**

Regular Stamps of 1953 Overprinted in Black **POSTAGE DUE**

**1953 *Perf. 12½***

| No. | Type | Description | Unused | Used |
|---|---|---|---|---|
| J11 | A6 | 5c green | 50 | *1.00* |
| J12 | A6 | 10c red | 60 | *1.40* |
| J13 | A6 | 20c ultra | 1.75 | *3.50* |
| J14 | A6 | 40c blk brn | 3.50 | *6.50* |
| J15 | A6 | 1fr dp org | 4.00 | *8.00* |
| | | *Nos. J11-J15 (5)* | 10.35 | *20.40* |

Same Overprint on Nos. 82-83, 85, 88 and 90

**1957 *Perf. 13½x13***

| No. | Type | Description | Unused | Used |
|---|---|---|---|---|
| J16 | A8 | 5c green | 16 | *35* |
| J17 | A8 | 10c red | 28 | *65* |
| J18 | A8 | 20c ultramarine | 65 | *1.00* |
| J19 | A8 | 40c sepia | 1.75 | *2.25* |
| J20 | A8 | 1fr orange | 3.50 | *5.00* |
| | | *Nos. J16-J20 (5)* | 6.34 | *9.25* |

# NEW REPUBLIC

LOCATION — In South Africa, located in the northern part of the present province of Natal.
GOVT. — A former Republic.
CAPITAL — Vryheid.

New Republic was created in 1884 by Boer adventurers from Transvaal who proclaimed Dinizulu king of Zululand and claimed as their reward a large tract of country as their own, which they called New Republic. This area was excepted when Great Britain annexed Zululand in 1887, but New Republic became a part of Transvaal in 1888 and was included in the Union of South Africa.

12 Pence = 1 Shilling
20 Shillings = 1 Pound

A1

A2

### Handstamped

**1886 Unwmk. *Perf. 11½***

| No. | Type | Description | Unused | Used |
|---|---|---|---|---|
| 1 | A1 | 1p vio, *yel* | 7.25 | 7.25 |
| 1A | A1 | 1p blk, *yel* | | 4,250. |
| 2 | A1 | 2p vio, *yel* | 6.75 | 6.75 |
| a. | | Without date | | |
| b. | | Tete beche pair | | |
| 3 | A1 | 3p vio, *yel* | 11.00 | 11.00 |
| a. | | Double impression | | |
| 4 | A1 | 4p vio, *yel* | 27.50 | |
| a. | | Without date | | |
| 5 | A1 | 6p vio, *yel* | 27.50 | 27.50 |
| a. | | Double impression | | |
| 6 | A1 | 9p vio, *yel* | 27.50 | |
| 7 | A1 | 1sh vio, *yel* | 90.00 | |
| 8 | A1 | 1sh6p vio, *yel* | 65.00 | |
| a. | | Without date | | |
| 9 | A1 | 2sh vio, *yel* | 30.00 | |
| a. | | Tete beche pair | 550.00 | |
| 10 | A1 | 2sh6p vio *yel* | 125.00 | |
| a. | | Without date | | |
| 11 | A1 | 4sh vio, *yel* | 360.00 | |
| 12 | A1 | 5sh vio, *yel* | 30.00 | 30.00 |
| a. | | Without date | | |
| 13 | A1 | 5sh6p vio, *yel* | 30.00 | 30.00 |
| 14 | A1 | 7sh6p vio, *yel* | 110.00 | |
| 15 | A1 | 10sh vio, *yel* | 90.00 | 90.00 |
| 16 | A1 | 10sh 6p vio, *yel* | 47.50 | |
| 16A | A1 | 13sh vio, *yel* | 330.00 | |
| 17 | A1 | £1 vio, *yel* | 125.00 | |
| 18 | A1 | 30sh vio, *yel* | 70.00 | |
| a. | | Tete beche pair | 675.00 | |

### Granite Paper

| No. | Type | Description | Unused | Used |
|---|---|---|---|---|
| 19 | A1 | 1p vio, *gray* | 10.00 | 10.00 |
| 20 | A1 | 2p vio, *gray* | 10.00 | 10.00 |
| a. | | Without "ZUID AFRIKA" | | |
| 21 | A1 | 3p vio, *gray* | 12.50 | 12.50 |
| a. | | Tete beche pair | 360.00 | |
| 22 | A1 | 4p vio, *gray* | 10.00 | 10.00 |
| 23 | A1 | 6p vio, *gray* | 22.50 | 22.50 |
| 24 | A1 | 9p vio, *gray* | 250.00 | |
| 25 | A1 | 1sh vio, *gray* | 26.00 | 26.00 |
| a. | | Tete beche pair | 850.00 | |
| 26 | A1 | 1sh6p vio, *gray* | 60.00 | |
| a. | | Tete beche pair | 700.00 | |
| 27 | A1 | 2sh vio, *gray* | 110.00 | |
| 28 | A1 | 2sh6p vio, *gray* | 135.00 | |
| 29 | A1 | 4sh vio, *gray* | 200.00 | |
| 30 | A1 | 5sh6p vio, *gray* | 200.00 | |
| 31 | A1 | 7sh6p vio, *gray* | 275.00 | |
| 32 | A1 | 10sh vio, *gray* | 250.00 | |
| a. | | Tete beche pair | 850.00 | |
| 32B | A1 | 10sh 6p vio, *gray* | 185.00 | |
| c. | | Without date | | |
| 33 | A1 | 12sh vio, *gray* | 275.00 | |
| 34 | A1 | 13sh vio, *gray* | 400.00 | |
| 35 | A1 | £1 vio, *gray* | 250.00 | |
| 36 | A1 | 30sh vio, *gray* | 250.00 | |

### Same with Embossed Arms

| No. | Type | Description | Unused | Used |
|---|---|---|---|---|
| 37 | A1 | 1p vio, *yel* | 11.00 | 11.00 |
| a. | | Arms inverted | 25.00 | 25.00 |
| b. | | Arms tete beche | 105.00 | 105.00 |
| 38 | A1 | 2p vio, *yel* | 12.00 | 12.00 |
| a. | | Arms inverted | 35.00 | 35.00 |
| 39 | A1 | 4p vio, *yel* | 18.00 | 18.00 |
| a. | | Arms inverted | 105.00 | 105.00 |
| b. | | Arms tete beche | 275.00 | |
| 40 | A1 | 6p vio, *yel* | 35.00 | 35.00 |

### Granite Paper

| No. | Type | Description | Unused | Used |
|---|---|---|---|---|
| 41 | A1 | 1p vio, *gray* | 11.00 | 11.00 |
| a. | | Imperf. vert., pair | | |
| b. | | Arms inverted | 30.00 | 30.00 |
| c. | | Arms tete beche | | |
| 42 | A1 | 2p vio, *gray* | 11.00 | 11.00 |
| a. | | Imperf. horiz., pair | | |
| b. | | Arms inverted | 45.00 | |
| c. | | Arms tete beche | | |

There were several printings of the above stamps and the date upon them varies from "9 JAN. 86" to "20 JAN. 87".

Nos. 7, 8, 10, 14, 26, 28 and 30 exist with the denomination expressed in two ways. Example: "1s 6d" or "1/6".

**1887 Arms Embossed**

| No. | Type | Description | Unused | Used |
|---|---|---|---|---|
| 43 | A2 | 3p vio, *yel* | 11.00 | 11.00 |
| a. | | Arms inverted | 24.00 | 24.00 |
| b. | | Tete beche pair | 360.00 | |
| c. | | Imperf. vert., pair | | |
| d. | | Arms omitted | | |
| e. | | Arms tete beche | | |
| 44 | A2 | 4p vio, *yel* | 11.00 | 11.00 |
| a. | | Arms inverted | 27.50 | 27.50 |
| 45 | A2 | 6p vio, *yel* | 11.00 | 11.00 |
| a. | | Arms inverted | 52.50 | 52.50 |
| b. | | Arms omitted | 200.00 | |
| c. | | Arms tete beche | 315.00 | |
| 46 | A2 | 9p vio, *yel* | 11.00 | 11.00 |
| 47 | A2 | 1sh vio, *yel* | 9.00 | 9.00 |
| a. | | Arms inverted | 45.00 | |
| b. | | Arms omitted | 55.00 | |
| 48 | A2 | 1sh6p vio, *yel* | 12.00 | 12.00 |
| 49 | A2 | 2sh vio, *yel* | 24.00 | 24.00 |
| a. | | Arms inverted | 75.00 | |
| b. | | Arms omitted | 35.00 | 35.00 |
| 50 | A2 | 2sh6p vio, *yel* | 21.00 | 21.00 |
| a. | | Arms inverted | 24.00 | 24.00 |
| 50B | A2 | 3sh vio, *yel* | 42.50 | 42.50 |
| c. | | Arms inverted | 47.50 | 47.50 |
| 51 | A2 | 4sh vio, *yel* | 12.00 | 12.00 |
| a. | | Arms omitted | | |
| 52 | A2 | 5sh vio, *yel* | 12.00 | 12.00 |
| a. | | Imperf. vert., pair | | |
| b. | | Arms inverted | 90.00 | |
| 53 | A2 | 5sh6p vio, *yel* | 12.00 | 12.00 |
| 54 | A2 | 7sh6p vio, *yel* | 18.00 | 18.00 |
| a. | | Arms inverted | 80.00 | |
| b. | | Arms tete beche | | |
| 55 | A2 | 10sh vio, *yel* | 12.00 | 12.00 |
| a. | | Arms inverted | 21.00 | 21.00 |
| b. | | Arms omitted | 75.00 | 75.00 |
| c. | | Imperf. vert., pair | | |
| d. | | Arms tete beche | 210.00 | |
| 56 | A2 | 10sh6p vio, *yel* | 20.00 | 20.00 |
| a. | | Imperf. vert., pair | | |
| b. | | Arms inverted | | |
| c. | | Arms omitted | | |
| 57 | A2 | £1 vio, *yel* | 47.50 | 47.50 |
| a. | | Arms inverted | 52.50 | |
| b. | | Tete beche pair | 475.00 | 475.00 |
| 58 | A2 | 30sh vio, *yel* | 100.00 | 100.00 |

### Granite Paper

| No. | Type | Description | Unused | Used |
|---|---|---|---|---|
| 59 | A2 | 1p vio, *gray* | 12.50 | 12.50 |
| a. | | Arms omitted | 110.00 | 110.00 |
| b. | | Arms inverted | 21.00 | 21.00 |
| c. | | Imperf. vert., pair | | |
| d. | | Tete beche pair | 225.00 | |
| 60 | A2 | 2p vio, *gray* | 8.00 | 8.00 |
| a. | | Arms omitted | 100.00 | 100.00 |
| b. | | Arms inverted | 22.50 | 22.50 |
| c. | | Tete beche pair | 500.00 | |
| 61 | A2 | 3p vio, *gray* | 12.00 | 12.00 |
| a. | | Arms inverted | 65.00 | 65.00 |
| b. | | Tete beche pair | 465.00 | |
| 62 | A2 | 4p vio, *gray* | 12.00 | 12.00 |
| a. | | Arms inverted | 92.50 | 92.50 |
| b. | | Tete beche pair | 330.00 | |
| 63 | A2 | 6p vio, *gray* | 12.00 | 12.00 |
| a. | | Arms inverted | 100.00 | 100.00 |
| 64 | A2 | 1sh6p vio, *gray* | 12.00 | 12.00 |
| a. | | Arms inverted | | |

All these stamps were valid for postage but bona-fide canceled specimens of any but the 1p and 2p stamps are quite rare.

# NEW SOUTH WALES

LOCATION — On the southeast coast of Australia in the South Pacific Ocean.
GOVT. — A former British Crown Colony.
AREA — 309,432 sq. mi.
POP. — 1,500,000 (estimated, 1900).
CAPITAL — Sydney.

In 1901 New South Wales united with five other British colonies to form the Commonwealth of Australia. Stamps of Australia are now used.

12 Pence = 1 Shilling
20 Shillings = 1 Pound

Values of early New South Wales stamps vary according to condition. Quotations for Nos. 1-34C are for fine copies. Very fine to superb specimens sell at much higher prices, and inferior or poor copies sell at reduced prices, depending on the condition of the individual specimen.

Seal of the Colony
A1 A2

A1 has no clouds. A2 has clouds added to the design, except in pos. 15.

**1850 Unwmk. Engr. *Imperf.***

| No. | Type | Description | Unused | Used |
|---|---|---|---|---|
| 1 | A1 | 1p red, *yelsh wove* | 4,750. | 325.00 |
| b. | | 1p red, *bluish wove* | 4,750. | 325.00 |
| 2 | A2 | 1p red, *yelsh wove* | 2,500. | 235.00 |
| b. | | 1p red, *yellowish laid* | 4,000. | 275.00 |
| c. | | 1p red, *bluish wove* | 2,500. | 235.00 |
| e. | | 1p red, *bluish laid* | 4,000. | 235.00 |
| f. | | Hill unshaded | 4,000. | 235.00 |
| g. | | No clouds | 4,000. | 235.00 |
| h. | | No trees | 4,000. | 235.00 |

Twenty-five varieties.

Stamps from early impressions of the plate sell at considerably higher prices.

No. 1 was reproduced by the collotype process in a souvenir sheet distributed at the London International Stamp Exhibition 1950. The paper is white.

Plate I Plate II
A3 A4

Plate I: Vertically lined background.

Plate I re-touched: Lines above and below "POSTAGE" and "TWO PENCE" deepened. Outlines of circular band around picture also deepened.

Plate II (First re-engraving of Plate I): Horizontally lined background; the bale on the left side is dated and there is a dot in the star in each corner.

Plate II retouched: Dots and dashes added in lower spandrels.

### Plate I

#### Late (worn plate) Impressions

| No. | Type | Description | Unused | Used |
|---|---|---|---|---|
| 3 | A3 | 2p bl, *yelsh wove* | 1,000. | 110.00 |

Twenty-four varieties.

#### Early Impressions

| No. | Type | Description | Unused | Used |
|---|---|---|---|---|
| 3a | A3 | 2p bl, *yelsh wove* | 4,500. | 450.00 |

#### Plate I, Retouched

| No. | Type | Description | Unused | Used |
|---|---|---|---|---|
| 4 | A3 | 2p bl, *yelsh wove* | 2,750. | 275.00 |

Twelve varieties.

### Plate II

#### Late (worn plate) Impressions

| No. | Type | Description | Unused | Used |
|---|---|---|---|---|
| 5 | A4 | 2p bl, *yelsh wove* | 1,150. | 175.00 |
| a. | | 2p blue, *bluish wove* | | 175.00 |
| b. | | 2p blue, *grysh wove* | | 175.00 |
| c. | | "CREVIT" omitted | 2,750. | 300.00 |
| d. | | Pick and shovel omitted | 2,750. | 300.00 |
| e. | | No whip | 1,800. | 250.00 |

#### Early Impressions

| No. | Type | Description | Unused | Used |
|---|---|---|---|---|
| 5h | A4 | 2p bl, *yelsh wove* | 4,000. | 300.00 |

#### Plate II, Retouched

| No. | Type | Description | Unused | Used |
|---|---|---|---|---|
| 5F | A4 | 2p bl, *bluish wove* | 1,800. | 200.00 |
| g. | | No whip | 3,250. | 275.00 |
| i. | | "CREVIT" omitted | | 275.00 |

Twelve varieties.

Plate III
A5

Plate IV
A6

Plate III (Second re-engraving of Plate I): The bale is not dated and, with the exception of Nos. 7, 10 and 12, it is single-lined. There are no dots in the stars.

Plate IV (Third re-engraving of Plate I): The bale is double-lined and there is a circle in the center of each star.

**1850-51**

| No. | Type | Description | Unused | Used |
|---|---|---|---|---|
| 6 | A5 | 2p bl, *grysh wove* | 1,650. | 210.00 |
| a. | | Fan with 6 segments | 2,500. | 300.00 |
| b. | | Double-lined bale | 2,300. | 250.00 |
| c. | | No whip | 2,500. | 250.00 |
| 7 | A6 | 2p bl, *bluish wove* ('51) | 1,650. | 170.00 |
| a. | | 2p blue, *white laid* | 2,150. | 170.00 |
| b. | | 2p blue, *grysh wove* | 1,650. | 170.00 |
| c. | | Fan with 6 segments | 2,500. | 200.00 |
| d. | | No clouds | 2,500. | 200.00 |

Twentyfour varieties.

Plate V — A7

A8

Plate V (Fourth re-engraving of Plate I): There is a pearl in the fan-shaped ornament below the central design.

**1850-51**

| No. | Type | Description | Unused | Used |
|---|---|---|---|---|
| 8 | A7 | 2p blue, *grayish wove* ('51) | 1,650. | 110.00 |
| a. | | 2p blue, *white laid* | 3,250. | 275.00 |
| b. | | Fan with 6 segments | 2,500. | 200.00 |
| c. | | Pick and shovel omitted | 2,500. | 200.00 |
| 9 | A8 | 3p grn, *bluish wove* | 2,150. | 110.00 |
| a. | | 3p grn, *yellowish wove* | 2,750. | 200.00 |
| b. | | 3p grn, *yellowish laid* | 4,250. | 275.00 |
| c. | | 3p grn, *bluish laid* | 4,250. | 275.00 |
| d. | | No whip | 2,500. | 240.00 |

Twentyfour varieties.

Queen Victoria
A9 A10

TWO PENCE
Plate I- Background of wavy lines.
Plate II- Stars in corners.
Plate III (Plate I re-engraved)- Background of crossed lines.

SIX PENCE
Plate I- Background of fine lines.
Plate II (Plate I re-engraved)- Background of coarse lines.

**1851 Yellowish Wove Paper**

10 A9 1p carmine 1,650. 250.00
b. No leaves to right of "SOUTH" *3,250.* 365.00
c. Two leaves to right of "SOUTH" *3,250.* 365.00
d. "WALE" *3,250.* 365.00
11 A9 2p ultra, Plate I 650.00 62.50

**1852 Bluish Laid Paper**

12 A9 1p carmine 3,000. 375.00
a. No leaves to right of "SOUTH" 500.00
b. Two leaves to right of "SOUTH" 500.00
c. "WALE" 500.00

**1852-55**
**Bluish or Grayish Wove Paper**

13 A9 1p red 750.00 85.00
a. 1p carmine 1,000. 140.00
b. No leaves to right of "SOUTH" 190.00
c. Two leaves to right of "SOUTH" 250.00
d. "WALE" 200.00
14 A9 2p blue, Plate I 300.00 25.00
a. 2p ultramarine 325.00 25.00
b. 2p slate 425.00 25.00
15 A10 2p bl, Plate II ('53) 900.00 87.50
a. "WAEES" *2,300.* 250.00
16 A9 2p blue, Plate III ('55) 425.00 35.00
17 A9 3p green 900.00 87.50
a. 3p emerald 1,300. 100.00
b. "WACES" 2,300. 325.00
18 A9 6p brown, Plate I 2,000. 190.00
a. 6p black brown 2,000. 225.00
b. "WALLS" 4,250. 425.00
19 A9 6p brn, Plate II 2,000. 225.00
a. 6p bister brown 2,000. 225.00
20 A9 8p yellow ('53) 3,600. 500.00
a. 8p orange 3,600. 500.00
b. No leaves to right of "SOUTH" 1,250.

The plates of the 1, 2, 3 and 8 pence each contained fifty varieties and those of the 6 pence twentyfive varieties.

*The 2 pence, Plate II, 6 pence, Plate II, and the 8 pence have been reprinted on grayish blue wove paper. The reprints of the 2 pence have the spandrels and background much worn. Most of the reprints of the 6 pence have no floreate ornaments to the right and left of "South". On all the values the wreath has been retouched.*

A11 Queen Victoria — A12

Wmk. 49- Double-lined Numerals Corresponding with the Value



**1854-55 Wmk. 49**

23 A9 1p orange 110.00 10.00
a. No leaves to right of "SOUTH" 165.00 32.50
b. Two leaves to right of "SOUTH" 365.00 65.00
c. "WALE" 365.00 65.00
24 A9 2p blue 100.00 6.50
a. 2p ultramarine 100.00 8.00
25 A9 3p green 130.00 18.00
a. "WACES" 50.00
b. Wmkd. "2" 4,000.
26 A11 5p green 1,000. 475.00
27 A12 6p sage green 415.00 20.00
28 A12 6p brown 450.00 18.00
a. Wmkd. "8" 1,650. 60.00
29 A12 6p gray 325.00 20.00
a. Wmkd. "8" 1,650. 80.00

A13 A14

30 A13 8p orange ('55) 4,750. 450.00
a. 8p yellow 4,750. 450.00
31 A14 1sh pale red 500.00 30.00
a. 1sh red 500.00 30.00
b. Wmkd. "8" 2,500. 110.00

See Nos. 38-42, 56, 58, 65, 67.

Nos. 38-42 exist with wide margins. Copies with perforations trimmed are often offered as Nos. 26, 30, and 30a.

A15

**1856**

32 A15 1p red 90.00 8.00
a. 1p orange 90.00 8.00
b. Printed on both sides *2,250.*
33 A15 2p blue 85.00 5.00
a. Wmkd. "1" 5,000.
b. Wmkd. "5" 550.00 25.00
c. Wmkd. "8"
34 A15 3p green 750.00 50.00
a. 3p yellow green 725.00 50.00
b. Wmkd. "2" *4,000.*

*The 1 penny has been reprinted in orange on paper watermarked Small Crown and N.S.W., and the 2 pence in deep blue on paper watermarked single lined "2." These reprints are usually overprinted "SPECIMEN".*

See Nos. 34C-37, 54, 63, 90.

**1859 Litho.**

34C A15 2p light blue 600.00

**1860-63 Engr. Wmk. 49 *Perf. 13***

35 A15 1p red 55.00 7.25
a. 1p orange 55.00 7.25
b. Perf. 12x13 2,000.
c. Perf. 12 90.00 10.50
36 A15 2p bl, perf. 12 100.00 9.00
a. Wmkd. "1" 3,500.
c. Perf. 12x13 2,600. 360.00
37 A15 3p blue green 45.00 7.25
a. 3p yellow green 50.00 7.50
b. 3p deep green 25.00 7.50
c. Wmkd. "6" 60.00 10.50
d. Perf. 12 600.00 45.00
38 A11 5p dark green 32.50 12.50
a. 5p yellow green 50.00 21.00
b. Perf. 12 135.00 42.50
39 A12 6p brn, perf. 12 275.00 30.00
a. 6p gray, perf. 12 275.00 30.00
40 A12 6p violet 55.00 3.00
a. 6p aniline lilac 950.00 150.00
b. Wmkd. "5" 360.00 30.00
c. Wmkd. "12" 240.00 21.00
e. Perf. 12 275.00 35.00
41 A13 8p yellow 150.00 24.00
a. 8p orange 150.00 24.00
b. Perf. 12 2,100. 400.00
42 A14 1sh rose 45.00 5.75
a. 1sh carmine 55.00 5.75
c. Perf. 12 400.00 50.00

Wmk. 50- Single-lined Numeral

**1864 Wmk. 50 *Perf. 13***

43 A15 1p red 30.00 25.00

Queen Victoria — A16

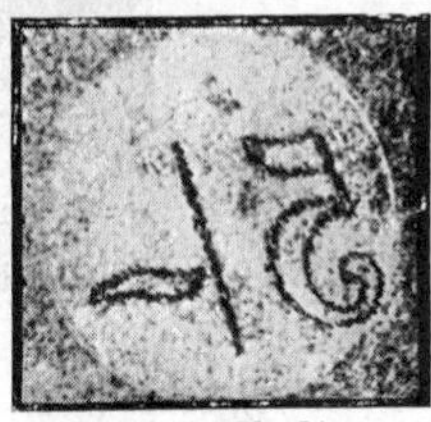

Wmk. 53- 5/-

**1861-80 Wmk. 53 *Perf. 13***

44 A16 5sh dull vio 275.00 30.00
a. 5sh purple 250.00 30.00
b. 5sh dull vio, perf. 12 1,650. 400.00
c. 5sh purple, perf. 12 250.00 50.00
d. 5sh purple, perf. 10 250.00 42.50
e. 5sh purple, perf. 12x10 450.00 65.00

See No. 101.

*Reprints are perf. 10 and overprinted "REPRINT" in black.*

A17 A18

***Perf. 12, 13, 14***

**1862-65 Typo. Unwmk.**

45 A17 1p red ('65) 72.50 55.00
46 A18 2p blue 60.00 18.00

**1863-64 Wmk. 50 *Perf. 12, 13***

47 A17 1p red, perf. 13 21.00 90
a. Wmkd. "2" 90.00 10.50
48 A18 2p blue 7.50 35
a. Wmkd. "1" 135.00 5.00

**1862 Wmk. 49 *Perf. 13***

49 A18 2p blue 50.00 9.50
a. Wmkd. "5" 135.00 18.00
b. Perf. 12x13 600.00
c. Perf. 12 165.00 16.00

See Nos. 52-53, 61-62, 70-76.

A19

Queen Victoria — A20

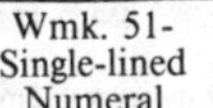

Wmk. 51- Single-lined Numeral Wmk. 52- Single-lined Numeral

**1867, Sept. Wmk. 51, 52 *Perf. 13***

50 A19 4p red brown 30.00 3.25
a. Imperf.
51 A20 10p lilac 9.00 3.50
a. Imperf.
b. Horiz. pair, imperf. between 600.00

See Nos. 55, 64, 91, 97, 117, 129.

A21 A22

A23 Wmk. 54- Small Crown and NSW

**Typo.; Engr. (3p, 5p, 8p)**

**1871-84 Wmk. 54 *Perf. 13***

52 A17 1p red 4.50 15
a. Perf. 10 400.00 13.00
b. Perf. 13x10 15.00 18
c. Horiz. pair imperf. between
53 A18 2p blue 4.50 18
a. Imperf.
b. Horiz. pair, imperf. vert. *800.00*
c. Perf. 10 400.00 20.00
d. Perf. 13x10 4.50 18
e. Perf. 12x13
f. Perf. 11x12 30.00
54 A15 3p green ('74) 21.00 1.75
a. Perf. 11 225.00 150.00
b. Perf. 12 *500.00* 250.00
c. Perf. 10x12 175.00 35.00
d. Perf. 12x11 135.00 50.00
e. Perf. 10 70.00 4.50
f. Perf. 10x13 135.00 13.00
55 A19 4p red brn ('77) 40.00 5.00
a. Perf. 10 300.00 50.00
b. Perf. 13x10 75.00 2.50
56 A11 5p dk grn, perf. 10 ('84) 15.00 7.50
a. Imperf.
b. Perf. 12 325.00 135.00
c. Perf. 10x12 24.00 9.00
d. Perf. 13x10

57 A21 6p lilac ('72) 35.00 45
- a. Imperf.
- b. Perf. 13x10 50.00 1.75
- c. Perf. 10 325.00 9.00

58 A13 8p yellow ('77) 90.00 9.00
- a. Imperf.
- b. Perf. 10 325.00 21.00
- c. Perf. 13x10 225.00 18.00

59 A22 9p on 10p red brown, perf. 12 (Bk) 12.00 3.00
- a. Double surcharge, blk & bl 195.00
- b. Perf. 10x12 375.00 300.00
- c. Perf. 10 12.00 3.25
- d. Perf. 12x11 18.00 5.75
- e. Perf. 11x12 18.00 5.75
- f. Perf. 13 24.00 2.75
- g. Perf. 11 40.00 7.25
- h. Perf. 10x11 50.00 12.00

60 A23 1sh black ('76) 75.00 1.10
- a. Imperf.
- b. Perf. 10x13 275.00 3.25
- c. Perf. 10 550.00 12.00
- d. Perf. 11

The surcharge on No. 59 measures 15mm. See Nos. 66, 68.

Wmk. 55- Large Crown and NSW

### Typo.; Engr. (3p, 5p, 8p)

**1882-91 Wmk. 55 *Perf. 11x12***

61 A17 1p red 1.75 10
- a. Perf. 10 9.00 15
- b. Perf. 10x13 120.00 5.00
- c. Perf. 10x12 325.00 85.00
- d. Perf. 12x11 150.00
- e. Perf. 10x11 600.00 150.00
- f. Perf. 11 195.00
- g. Perf. 13 135.00

62 A18 2p blue 3.00 15
- a. Perf. 10 12.00 10
- b. Perf. 13x10 90.00 2.50
- c. Perf. 13 600.00 135.00
- d. Perf. 12x10 325.00 70.00
- e. Perf. 11 135.00
- f. Perf. 12x11 135.00
- g. Perf. 10x11 600.00 135.00
- h. Perf. 12 275.00

63 A15 3p green 4.75 20
- a. Imperf., pair 200.00
- b. Vert. pair, imperf. btwn. 225.00
- c. Imperf. vert., pair
- d. Double impression
- e. Perf. 10 7.25 20
- f. Perf. 11 7.25 20
- g. Perf. 12 8.00 20
- h. Perf. 12x11 8.00 25
- i. Perf. 10x12 215.00 12.50
- m. Perf. 10x11 20.00 1.25
- n. Perf. 12x10 100.00 3.50

64 A19 4p red brown 27.50 1.40
- a. Perf. 10 27.50 1.65
- b. Perf. 10x12 150.00
- c. Perf. 12 40.00

65 A11 5p dk bl green 7.25 70
- a. Imperf., pair 225.00
- b. Perf. 11 13.00 75
- c. Perf. 10 13.00 80
- d. Perf. 12 13.00 80
- e. Perf. 10x12
- g. 5p grn, perf. 11x10 42.50 2.00
- h. 5p grn, perf. 12x10 75.00 3.25
- i. 5p grn, perf. 10x11 35.00 3.75
- j. 5p grn, perf. 11 3.75

66 A21 6p lilac, perf. 10 18.00 14
- a. Horiz. pair, imperf. between 825.00
- b. Perf. 10x12 30.00 75
- c. Perf. 11x12 32.50 1.25
- d. Perf. 12 95.00 2.75
- e. Perf. 10x11 60.00 65
- f. Perf. 11 95.00 6.00
- g. Perf. 10x13 325.00

67 A13 8p yellow, perf. 10 75.00 9.00
- a. Perf. 11 75.00 9.00
- b. Perf. 12 120.00 18.00
- c. Perf. 10x12 75.00 12.00

68 A23 1sh black 60.00 75
- a. Perf. 10x13 12.00
- b. Perf. 10 55.00 75
- c. Perf. 11 225.00 12.00
- d. Perf. 10x12

Nos. 63 and 65 exist with two types of watermark 55 - spacings of 1mm or 2mm between crown and NSW.

See No. 90.

*The 1, 2, 4, 6, 8p and 1sh have been reprinted on paper watermarked Large Crown and NSW. The 1, 2, 4p and 1sh are perforated 11x12, the 6p is perforated 10 and the 8p 11. All are overprinted "REPRINT", the 1sh in red and the others in black.*

Wmk. 56- NSW

***Perf. 11x12***

**1886-87 Typo. Wmk. 56**

**Bluish Revenue Stamp Paper**

70 A17 1p scarlet 9.00 2.50
- a. Perf. 10 18.00 4.50

71 A18 2p dark blue 15.00 4.50
- a. Perf. 10 65.00 9.00

A24

***Perf. 12 (#73-75), 12x10 (#72, 75A) and Compound***

**1885-86**

**"POSTAGE" in Black**

72 A24 5sh grn & vio 375.00 65.00
- a. Perf. 10

73 A24 10sh rose & vio 1,250. 240.00

74 A24 £1 rose & vio 2,750. 1,000.
- a. Perf. 13 2,100.

**"POSTAGE" in Blue**

**Bluish Paper**

75 A24 10sh rose & vio 175.00 35.00
- b. Perf. 10 750.00 165.00
- c. Perf. 12x11 375.00 *150.00*

**White Paper**

75A A24 £1 rose & vio 3,750. *1,750.*

*The 5sh with black overprint and the £1 with blue overprint have been reprinted on paper watermarked NSW. They are perforated 12x10 and are overprinted "REPRINT" in black.*

**1894 White Paper**

76 A24 10sh rose & vio 165.00 30.00
- a. Double overprint

See No. 108B.

View of Sydney — A25

Emu — A26

Captain Cook A27

Victoria and Coat of Arms A28

Lyrebird A29

Kangaroo A30

**1888-89 Wmk. 55 *Perf. 11x12***

77 A25 1p violet 2.75 5
- a. Perf. 12 4.50 6
- b. Perf. 12x11½ 14.00 9

78 A26 2p blue 2.25 6
- a. Imperf., pair 125.00
- b. Perf. 12 7.50 6
- c. Perf. 12x11½ 13.00 8

79 A27 4p brown 5.75 18
- a. Perf. 12x11½ 15.00 20
- b. Perf. 12 15.00 18
- c. Perf. 11 450.00 135.00
- d. Imperf.

80 A28 6p carmine rose 15.00 1.25
- a. Perf. 12 15.00 1.25
- b. Perf. 12x11½ 35.00 1.75

81 A29 8p red violet 10.00 75
- a. Perf. 12 9.00 1.50
- b. Perf. 12x11½ 12.00 1.50

82 A30 1sh vio brn ('89) 12.00 55
- a. Imperf., pair 725.00
- b. Perf. 12x11½ 14.00 55
- c. Perf. 12 24.00 55
- *Nos. 77-82 (6)* 47.75 2.84

First British settlement in Australia, cent.

**1888 Wmk. 56 *Perf. 11 x 12***

83 A25 1p violet 11.00 1.40

84 A26 2p blue 47.50 6.75

See Nos. 104B-106C, 113-115, 118, 125-127, 130.

Map of Australia — A31

Governors Capt. Arthur Phillip (above) and Lord Carrington — A32

**1888-89 Wmk. 53 *Perf. 10***

85 A31 5sh violet 265.00 55.00

86 A32 20sh ultra 375.00 220.00

See Nos. 88, 120.

Wmk. 57- 5/- NSW in Diamond

Wmk. 58- 20/- NSW in Circle

**1890 Wmk. 57 *Perf. 10***

87 A31 5sh violet 200.00 17.50
- a. Perf. 11 200.00 22.50
- b. Perf. 10x11 225.00 17.50
- c. Perf. 12 360.00 25.00

**Wmk. 58 *Perf. 11x12***

88 A32 20sh ultra 275.00 57.50
- a. Perf. 11 275.00 57.50
- b. Perf. 10 350.00 77.50
- c. Perf. 12 410.00 135.00

"Australia" A33

Victoria A37

**1890, Dec. 22 Wmk. 55 *Perf. 11x12***

89 A33 2½p ultra 1.10 14
- a. Perf. 12 11.50 14
- b. Perf. 12x11½ 67.50 *50.00*

Type of 1856

**1891 Engr. Wmk. 52 *Perf. 10***

90 A15 3p green 6.00 4.00
- a. Double impression

Type of 1867

**1893 Typo. *Perf. 11***

91 A20 10p lilac 15.00 6.00
- a. Perf. 10 16.00 7.50
- b. Perf. 11x10 or 10x11 24.00 12.00
- c. Perf. 12x11 175.00 24.00

Types of 1862-84 Surcharged in Black:

SEVEN-PENCE

Halfpenny — a

HALFPENNY — b

**1891, Jan. 5 Wmk. 55 *Perf. 11x12***

92 A17(a) ½p on 1p gray 1.25 75
- a. Imperf.
- b. Surcharge omitted
- c. Double surcharge

93 A21(b) 7½p on 6p brn 3.50 1.25
- a. Perf. 10 3.50 1.25
- b. Perf. 11 3.50 1.25
- c. Perf. 12 4.25 1.75
- d. Perf. 10x12 4.25 1.75

94 A23(b) 12½p on 1sh red 4.50 1.75
- a. Perf. 12x11½ 3.25 1.75
- b. Perf. 10 4.50 1.90
- c. Perf. 11 4.50 1.90
- d. Perf. 12 5.50 1.75

**1892**

95 A37 ½p slate 1.25 15
- a. Perf. 12x11½ 1.25 15
- b. Perf. 12 1.25 15
- c. Perf. 10 27.50 90
- d. Perf. 10x12 150.00 10.50
- e. Perf. 11 165.00 9.00

See Nos. 102, 109, 121.

Types of 1867-71

**1897 *Perf. 11x12***

96 A22 9p on 10p red brn (Bk) 5.75 3.25
- a. 9p on 10p org brn (Bk) 5.75 3.25
- b. Surch. omitted 125.00
- c. Double surch. 125.00 100.00
- d. Perf. 11 9.00 7.50
- e. Perf. 12 9.00 7.50

97 A20 10p violet 5.50 5.50
- a. Perf. 12x11½ 5.50 5.50
- b. Perf. 11 13.00 6.00
- c. Perf. 12 13.00 6.00

The surcharge on No. 96 measures 13½mm.

Seal A38

Victoria A39

A40

ONE PENNY:

Die I- The first pearl in the crown at the left is merged into the arch, the shading under the fleur-de-lis is indistinct, and the "s" of "WALES" is open.

Die II- The first pearl is circular, the vertical shading under the fleur-de-lis is clear, and the "s" of "WALES" not so open.

2½ PENCE:

Die I- There are 12 radiating lines in the star on the Queen's breast.

Die II- There are 16 radiating lines in the star. The eye is nearly full of color.

**1897 *Perf. 12***

98 A38 1p rose red (II) 2.50 6
- a. Die I, perf. 11x12 3.00 10
- b. Imperf., pair 75.00
- c. Imperf. horiz., pair 600.00
- d. Die I, perf. 12x11½ 4.50 10
- e. Die I, perf. 12 7.50 60
- f. Die II, perf. 12x11½ 2.00 6
- g. Die II, perf. 11x12 3.00 6

99 A39 2p deep blue 2.75 9
- a. Perf. 11x12 2.75 9
- b. Perf. 12x11½ 2.75 9

100 A40 2½p deep pur (II) 4.50 32
- a. Die I, perf. 12x11 6.50 75
- b. Die I, perf. 11 7.50 1.90
- c. Die I, perf. 11½x12 10.50 60
- d. Die II, perf. 11x12 4.50 32
- e. Die II, perf. 11½x12 8.50 75

Sixtieth year of Queen Victoria's reign.

See Nos. 103-104, 110-112, 122-124.

Type of 1861

**1897 Engr. Wmk. 53 *Perf. 11***

101 A16 5sh red vio 75.00 12.50
- a. Horiz. pair, imperf. btwn. *4,500.*
- b. Perf. 11x12 or 12x11 75.00 14.00
- c. Perf. 12 82.50 15.00

***Perf. 12x11½, 11½x12***

**1899, Oct. Typo. Wmk. 55**

HALF PENNY:
Die I- Narrow "H" in "HALF".

*102* A37 ½p blue grn (I) 1.00 12
a. Imperf., pair 60.00 45.00
*103* A39 2p ultra 1.25 12
a. Imperf., pair 55.00
*104* A40 2½p dk bl (II) 1.25 12
a. Imperf., pair 90.00
*104B* A27 4p org brn 5.00 50
c. Imperf. pair 300.00
*105* A28 6p emerald 32.50 2.50
a. Imperf., pair 235.00
*106* A28 6p orange 5.00 65
a. 6p yellow 5.00 65
b. Imperf., pair 195.00
*106C* A29 8p magenta 10.00 2.00
*Nos. 102-106C (7)* 56.00 6.01

Lyrebird — A41

**1903** ***Perf. 12x11½***

*107* A41 2sh6p blue green 42.50 5.00

See Nos. 119, 131.

"Australia" — A42

Wmk. 70- V and Crown

**1903 Wmk. 70** ***Perf. 12½***

*108* A42 9p org brn & ultra 10.00 2.75
a. Perf. 11 750.00 425.00

See No. 128.

Type of 1885-86

**1904 Wmk. 56** ***Perf. 11***

**Chalky Paper**

**"POSTAGE" in Blue**

*108B* A24 10sh brt rose & vio 165.00 25.00
c. Perf. 12x11 125.00 25.00
d. Perf. 12 125.00 25.00

The watermark (NSW) of No. 108B is 20x7mm, with rounded angles in "N" and "W." On No. 75, the watermark is 21x7mm, with sharp angles in the "N" and "W."

Wmk. 12- Crown and Single-lined A

Wmk. 13- Large Crown and Double-lined A

Wmk. 199- Crown and A in Circle

HALF PENNY:
Die II- Wide "H" in "HALF".

***Perf. 11, 11x12½, 12x11½ and Compound***

**1905-06 Wmk. 12**

*109* A37 ½p bl grn (II) 1.50 38
a. ½p blue green (I) 3.50 38
b. Booklet pane of 12
*110* A38 1p car rose (II) 1.50 8
a. Booklet pane of 6
b. Booklet pane of 12
*111* A39 2p deep ultra 1.50 10
*112* A40 2½p dk bl (II) 2.50 38
*113* A27 4p org brn 5.75 38
*114* A28 6p orange 3.75 55
a. 6p yellow 6.50 55
b. Perf. 11 250.00
*115* A29 8p magenta 9.25 1.50
*117* A20 10p violet 5.75 2.25
*118* A30 1sh vio brn 6.50 55
*119* A41 2sh6p blue grn 22.50 13.00

**Wmk. 199**

*120* A32 20sh ultra 265.00 75.00
*Nos. 109-115,117-120 (11)* 325.50 94.17

**1906 Wmk. 13**

*121* A37 ½p green (I) 4.00 50
*122* A38 1p rose (II) 3.00 32
*123* A39 2p ultra 3.00 32
*124* A40 2½p blue (II) 75.00
*125* A27 4p org brn 10.00 3.25
*126* A28 6p orange 22.50 8.25
*127* A29 8p red vio 27.50 9.25
*128* A42 9p orange brn & ultra, perf. 12x12½ 6.50 1.65
a. Perf. 11 65.00 55.00
*129* A20 10p violet 60.00
*130* A30 1sh vio brn 22.50 6.50
*131* A41 2sh6p blue grn 65.00 32.50
*Nos. 121-131 (11)* 299.00

Portions of some of the sheets on which the above are printed show the watermark "COMMONWEALTH OF AUSTRALIA". Stamps may also be found from portions of the sheet without watermark.

## SEMI-POSTAL STAMPS

Allegory of Charity — SP1

Allegory of Charity — SP2

**1897, June Wmk. 55** ***Perf. 11***

*B1* SP1 1p (1sh) grn & brn 14.00 16.00
*B2* SP2 2½p (2sh6p) rose, bl & gold 175.00 215.00

Diamond Jubilee of Queen Victoria.

The difference between the postal and face values of these stamps was donated to a fund for a home for consumptives.

## REGISTRATION STAMPS

Queen Victoria — R1

**1856, Jan. 1 Unwmk. Engr.** ***Imperf.***

*F1* R1 (6p) orange & bl 600.00 75.00
*F2* R1 (6p) red & bl 575.00 75.00
a. Frame printed on back *2,750. 1,350.*

**1860** ***Perf. 12, 13***

*F3* R1 (6p) orange & bl 280.00 30.00
*F4* R1 (6p) red & bl 265.00 30.00

Nos. F1 to F4 exist also on paper with papermaker's watermark in sheet.

**1863 Wmk. 49**

*F5* R1 (6p) red & bl 75.00 15.00

Fifty varieties.

*No. F1 and F2 have been reprinted on thin white wove unwatermarked paper and on thick yellowish wove unwatermarked paper; the former are usually overprinted "SPECIMEN". No. F4 has been reprinted on thin white wove unwatermarked paper; it is perforated 10 and overprinted "REPRINT" in black.*

## POSTAGE DUE STAMPS

D1

***Perf. 10, 11, 11½, 12 and Compound***

**1891-92 Typo. Wmk. 55**

*J1* D1 ½p green 3.25 50
*J2* D1 1p green 4.00 30
a. Perf. 12 20.00 3.75
*J3* D1 2p green 5.00 38
a. Perf. 10x12 20.00 4.00
*J4* D1 3p green 11.50 2.50
*J5* D1 4p green 10.00 75
*J6* D1 6p green 20.00 2.25
*J7* D1 8p green 70.00 1.85
*J8* D1 5sh green 200.00 17.50
a. Perf. 11 265.00 85.50
*J9* D1 10sh green 230.00 50.00
a. Perf. 10 365.00
*J10* D1 20sh green 300.00 75.00
a. Perf. 10 465.00 62.50
b. Perf. 12 465.00
*Nos. J1-J10 (10)* 853.75 151.03

Nos. J1 to J5 exist on both ordinary and chalky paper.

## OFFICIAL STAMPS

Regular Issues Overprinted in Black or Red **O S**

***Perf. 10, 11, 12, 13 and Compound***

**1879-80 Wmk. 54**

*O1* A17 1p red 9.25 1.25
a. Perf. 10 325.00 22.50
b. perf. 10x13 22.50 1.65
*O2* A18 2p blue 8.25 1.25
a. Perf. 11x12 265.00
b. Perf. 10 265.00 50.00
*O3* A15 3p green (R) 300.00
*O4* A15 3p green 225.00 65.00
a. Wmkd. "6" 500.00
b. Double ovpt.
*O5* A19 4p red brown 225.00 11.50
a. Perf. 10x13 300.00 14.00
*O6* A11 5p dark green 20.00 13.00
*O7* A21 6p lilac 300.00 10.00
a. Perf. 10 65.00
b. Perf. 10x13
*O8* A13 8p yellow (R) *1,000.* 200.00
*O9* A13 8p yellow 16.00
a. Perf. 10 375.00 115.00
*O10* A23 1sh black (R) 300.00 7.50
a. Perf. 10 16.00
b. Perf. 10x13 42.50

**1880 Wmk. 53**

*O11* A16 5sh lil, perf. 11 265.00 65.00
a. Double overprint
b. Perf. 10 375.00 130.00
c. Perf. 12x10 425.00 130.00
d. Perf. 13 465.00 82.50
e. Perf. 10x12

**1881 Wmk. 55**

*O12* A17 1p red 6.25 50
a. Perf. 10x13 225.00
*O13* A18 2p blue 6.50 1.00
a. Perf. 10x13 360.00 100.00
*O14* A15 3p green 6.25 1.65
a. Double overprint
b. Perf. 12 240.00 130.00
c. Perf. 11
*O15* A19 4p red brown 11.00 2.25
a. Perf. 10x12 82.50
b. Perf. 12 360.00 225.00
*O16* A11 5p dark green 12.00 5.00
a. Perf. 12 200.00
b. Perf. 10x12 400.00 130.00
*O17* A21 6p lilac 22.50 1.65
a. Perf. 12 60.00
b. Perf. 11x12 72.50 16.00
*O18* A13 8p yellow 20.00 2.00
a. Double overprint
b. Perf. 12 240.00 50.00
*O19* A23 1sh black (R) 20.00 *3.25*
a. Double overprint
b. Perf. 10x13 70.00
c. Perf. 11
*Nos. O12-O19 (8)* 104.50 17.30

**1881 Wmk. 56**

*O20* A17 1p red 32.50 5.00

**1887-90**

*O21* A24 10sh rose & vio (#75) *350.00*
*O22* A24 £1 rose & vio (#75A) *4,000. 4,000.*

Overprinted **O S**

**1889**

*O23* A24 10sh rose & vio (#75) *1,950. 700.00*
a. Perf. 10 *3,500. 2,250.*

Overprinted **O S**

**1888-89 Wmk. 55**

*O24* A25 1p violet 1.50 15
a. Overprinted "O" only
*O25* A26 2p blue 1.50 15
*O26* A27 4p red brown 3.50 50
*O27* A28 6p carmine 4.00 65
*O28* A29 8p red lilac 11.00 1.65
*O29* A30 1sh vio brown 14.00 1.10
a. Double overprint
*Nos. O24-O29 (6)* 35.50 4.20

**Wmk. 53**

*O30* A31 5sh violet (R) *800.00 450.00*
*O31* A32 20sh ultra *1,750.*

**1890 Wmk. 57**

*O32* A31 5sh violet *225.00* 40.00
a. Perf. 12 625.00

**Wmk. 58**

*O33* A32 20sh ultra *2,500.*

Centenary of the founding of the Colony (Nos. O24-O33).

**1891 Wmk. 55**

*O34* A17(a) ½p on 1p gray & black 27.50 14.00
a. Double overprint
*O35* A33 2½p ultra 3.25 3.25
*O36* A21(b) 7½p on 6p brn & black 27.50 12.00
*O37* A23(b) 12½p on 1sh red & black 18.00 12.00

**1892**

*O38* A37 ½p gray 1.25 1.25

**1894 Wmk. 54**

*O39* A22 9p on 10p red brn 300.00 300.00

**Wmk. 52**

*O40* A20 10p lil, perf. 10 225.00 200.00
a. Perf. 11x10 350.00 325.00

*The official stamps became obsolete on Dec. 31, 1894. In Aug., 1895, sets of 32 varieties of "O.S." stamps, together with some envelopes and postal cards, were placed on sale at the Sydney post office at £2 per set. These sets contained most of the varieties listed above and a few which are not known in the original issues. An obliteration consisting of the letters G.P.O. or N.S.W. in three concentric ovals was lightly applied to the center of each block of four stamps. It is understood that the earlier stamps and many of the overprints were reprinted to make up these sets.*

# NEW ZEALAND

LOCATION — A group of islands in the south Pacific Ocean, southeast of Australia.

GOVT. — Self-governing dominion of the British Commonwealth.

AREA — 107,241 sq. mi.

POP. — 3,230,000 (est. 1983)

CAPITAL — Wellington

12 Pence = 1 Shilling
20 Shillings = 1 Pound
100 Cents = 1 Dollar (1967)

Values of early New Zealand stamps vary according to condition. Quotations for Nos. 1-50 are for fine copies. Very fine to superb specimens sell at much higher prices, and inferior or poor copies sell at reduced prices, depending on the condition of the individual specimen.



**Catalogue values for unused stamps in this country are for Never Hinged items, beginning with Scott 246 in the regular postage section, Scott AR99 in the postal-fiscal section, Scott B9 in the semi-postal section, Scott J21 in the postage due section, Scott O92 in the officials section, Scott OY29 in the Life Insurance Department section, and Scott 1 in Ross Dependency.**

Victoria — A1

Wmk. 6- Large Star

**London Print**
**Wmk. 6**

**1855, July 18** **Engr.** ***Imperf.***

**White Paper**

*1* A1 1p dull car *22,500.* *9,000.*

**Blued Paper**

*2* A1 2p dp bl *7,500.* 550.00
*3* A1 1sh yel grn *18,000.* *4,000.*
**a** Half used as 6p on cover *18,000.*

The blueing was caused by chemical action in the printing process. "White" paper varieties are believed to be those where the blueing has later disappeared.

**Auckland Print**

**1855-58** **Blue Paper** **Unwmk.**

*4* A1 1p orange red 3,500. 550.00
*5* A1 2p blue ('56) 2,000. 175.00
*6* A1 1sh green ('58) *9,000.* 1,000.
**a** Half used as 6p on cover *12,500.*

Nos. 4-6 may be found with parts of the papermaker's name in double-lined letters.

**1858-61** **Unwmk.**

**Thin Hard or Thick Soft White Paper**

*7* A1 1p orange ('58) 450.00 165.00
**e** Wmk. 6 ('57) *16,000.*
*8* A1 2p blue ('58) 450.00 100.00
*9* A1 6p brown ('59) 450.00 165.00
**e** 6p bister brown ('59) 900.00 225.00
**f** 6p chestnut ('59) 1,250. 310.00
*10* A1 1sh blue green ('61) 5,500. 700.00
**e** 1sh emerald 5,500. 700.00

Color of No. 7e matches that of No. 7.

**1859** ***Pin Rouletted 9-10***

*7a* A1 1p dull orange 2,000.
*8a* A1 2p blue 1,500.
*9a* A1 6p brown 2,500.
*10a* A1 1sh greenish blue 8,000.

**1859** ***Serrate Rouletted 16, 18***

*7b* A1 1p dull orange 4,000.
*8b* A1 2p blue 2,000.
*9b* A1 6p brown 2,000.
**g** 6p chestnut 4,000.
*10b* A1 1sh greenish blue 6,000.

**1859** ***Rouletted 7***

*7c* A1 1p dull orange *5,500.* 2,500.
*8c* A1 2p blue *6,500.* 2,000.
*9c* A1 6p brown *4,250.* 2,000.
*10c* A1 1sh greensh blue *7,500.* 4,000.

**1862** ***Perf. 13***

*7d* A1 1p orange vermilion
*8d* A1 2p blue 5,000. 2,000.
*9d* A1 6p brown *6,000.*

**1862-63** **Wmk. 6** ***Imperf.***

*11* A1 1p org ver 250.00 85.00
**d** 1p carmine vermilion ('63) 250.00 85.00
**e** 1p vermilion 250.00 85.00
*12* A1 2p blue 250.00 50.00
**d** 2p slate blue 1,250. 215.00
*13* A1 3p brown lilac ('63) 325.00 70.00
*14* A1 6p red brown ('63) 275.00 60.00
**d** 6p black brown 550.00 85.00
**e** 6p brown ('63) 575.00 90.00
*15* A1 1sh yellow green 500.00 110.00
**d** 1sh deep green 550.00 150.00

**1862** ***Pin Rouletted 9-10***

*12a* A1 2p deep blue
*14a* A1 6p black brown 2,000.

**1862** ***Serrate Rouletted 16, 18***

*11b* A1 1p org vermilion 1,400.
*12b* A1 2p blue 1,400.
*13b* A1 3p lilac brown 2,000.
*14b* A1 6p black brown 2,250.
*15b* A1 1sh yellow green 2,500.

**1862** ***Rouletted 7***

*11c* A1 1p vermilion 2,000. 325.00
*12c* A1 2p blue 1,400. 300.00
*13c* A1 3p brown lilac 1,250. 250.00
*14c* A1 6p red brown 1,250. 200.00
*15c* A1 1sh yellow green 2,000. 375.00

The 1p, 2p, 6p and 1sh come in two or more shades.

**1863** ***Perf. 13***

*16* A1 1p car ver 500.00 97.50
*17* A1 2p blue 225.00 32.50
*18* A1 3p brown lilac 500.00 90.00
*19* A1 6p red brown 325.00 37.50
*20* A1 1sh yellow green 325.00 90.00

The 1p, 2p, 6p and 1sh come in two or more shades.

**1862** **Unwmk.** ***Imperf.***

**Pelure Paper**

*21* A1 1p vermilion 4,250. 1,100.
**b** Rouletted 7 2,750.
*22* A1 2p pale dull ultra 2,500. 400.00
**c** gray blue 2,500 400.00
*23* A1 3p brown lilac *37,500.*
*24* A1 6p black brown 1,000. 145.00
**b** Rouletted 7 2,000. 310.00
**c** Serrate perf. 16 3,250.
*25* A1 1sh deep yel grn 3,750. 400.00
**b** 1sh deep green 3,750. 400.00
**c** Rouletted 7 3,250. 1,000.

No. 23 was never placed in use.

**1863** ***Perf. 13***

*21a* A1 1p vermilion 7,500. 3,750.
*22a* A1 2p gray blue 3,500. 400.00
**b** 2p pale dull ultramarine 3,500. 400.00
*24a* A1 6p black brown 3,000. 225.00
*25a* A1 1sh deep green 4,500. 1,000.

**1863** **Unwmk.** ***Imperf.***

**Thick White Paper**

*26* A1 2p dull dark blue 1,500. 275.00
**a** Perf. 13 1,250. 275.00

Nos. 26 and 26a differ from 8 and 8d by a white patch of wear at right of head.

WSmk. 59- NZ

**1864** **Wmk. 59** ***Imperf.***

*27* A1 1p car ver 625.00 125.00
*28* A1 2p blue 700.00 125.00
*29* A1 6p red brown 2,250. 310.00
*30* A1 1sh green 750.00 165.00

**1864** ***Rouletted 7***

*27a* A1 1p car ver 4,000.
*28a* A1 2p blue 1,000
*29a* A1 6p deep red brown 3,000.
*30a* A1 1sh green 1,000.

**1864** ***Perf. 12½***

*27B* A1 1p car ver 2,750.
*28B* A1 2p blue 200.00 30.00
*29B* A1 6p red brown 225.00 17.50
*30B* A1 1sh deep yel grn 2,750.

**1864** ***Perf. 13***

*27C* A1 1p car ver 7,500. 4,250.
*28C* A1 2p blue 575.00 225.00
*30C* A1 1sh yel grn 1,500. 575.00
**d** Horiz. pair, imperf. btwn. 10,000.

**1864-71** **Wmk. 6** ***Perf. 12½***

*31* A1 1p vermilion 60.00 20.00
**a** 1p orange ('71) 125.00 40.00
*32* A1 2p blue 60.00 15.00
**a** 2p blue, worn plate 60.00 15.00
**b** Horiz. pair, imperf. btwn. (#32) *1,500.*
**c** Perf. 10x12½ 6,250.
**d** Imperf., pair (#32) 1,150. 1,150.
*33* A1 3p lilac 45.00 17.50
**a** 3p mauve 200.00 37.50
**b** Imperf., pair (#33) 1,500. 950.00
**c** As "a", imperf., pair 1,250. 1,000.
*34* A1 4p deep rose ('65) 1,250. 140.00
*35* A1 4p yellow ('65) 47.50 27.50
**a** 4p orange yellow 1,100. 1,000.
*36* A1 6p red brown 65.00 14.00
**a** 6p brown 75.00 14.00
**b** Horiz. pair, imperf. btwn.
*37* A1 1sh pale yel grn 65.00 40.00
**a** 1sh yellow green 65.00 40.00
**b** 1sh green 225.00 90.00

The 1p, 2p and 6p come in two or more shades.

*Imperforate examples of the 1p pale orange, worn plate; 2p dull blue and 6p dull chocolate brown are reprints. Value, each $100.*

**1871** **Wmk. 6** ***Perf. 10***

*38* A1 1p deep brown 300.00 60.00

**1871** ***Perf. 12½***

*39* A1 1p brown 60.00 22.50
**a** Imperf. 1,000.
*40* A1 2p orange 55.00 17.50
**a** 2p vermilion 70.00 20.00
**b** Imperf., pair 1,250.
*41* A1 6p blue 60.00 22.50

Shades exist.

**1871** ***Perf. 10x12½***

*42* A1 1p brown 60.00 22.50
*43* A1 2p orange 60.00 22.50
*44* A1 6p blue 500.00 200.00

The 6p often has only one side perf. 10, the 1p and 2p more rarely so.
Shades exist.

**1872** **Wmk. 59** ***Perf. 12½***

*45* A1 1p brown 3,250.
*46* A1 2p vermilion 200.00 67.50

**1872** **Unwmk.** ***Perf. 12½***

*47* A1 1p brown 200.00 37.50
*48* A1 2p vermilion 42.50 19.00
*49* A1 4p yellow orange 125.00 *285.00*

The watermark "T.H. SAUNDERS" in double-line capitals falls on 16 of the 240 stamps in a sheet. The 1p and 2p also are known with script "WT & CO" watermark.

Wmk. 60-Lozenges

This watermark includes the vertical word "INVICTA" once in each quarter of the sheet.

**1872** **Wmk. 60**

*50* A1 2p vermilion *4,000.* 825.00

A2 A3 A4

A5 A6 A7

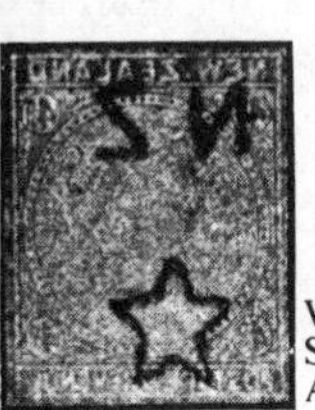

Wmk. 62- N Z and Small Star Wide Apart

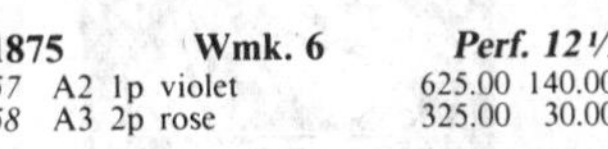

**Perf. 10 x 12½, 11½, 12, 12½**

**1874 Typo. Wmk. 62**

51 A2 1p violet 27.50 90
 a Bluish paper 75.00 21.00
 b Imperf. 475.00
52 A3 2p rose 27.50 90
 a Bluish paper 90.00 21.00
53 A4 3p brown 55.00 20.00
 a Bluish paper 150.00 50.00
54 A5 4p claret 75.00 20.00
 a Bluish paper 400.00 105.00
55 A6 6p blue 40.00 9.00
 a Bluish paper 300.00 75.00
56 A7 1sh green 75.00 17.50
 a Bluish paper 1,000. 275.00
 *Nos. 51-56 (6)* 300.00 68.30

**1875 Wmk. 6 Perf. 12½**

57 A2 1p violet 625.00 140.00
58 A3 2p rose 325.00 30.00

A8

**1878 Wmk. 62 Perf. 12x11½**

59 A8 2sh deep rose 300.00 230.00
60 A8 5sh gray 325.00 230.00

No. 60 has numeral "5" in each of the four spandrels.

A9 A10

A11 A12

A13 A14

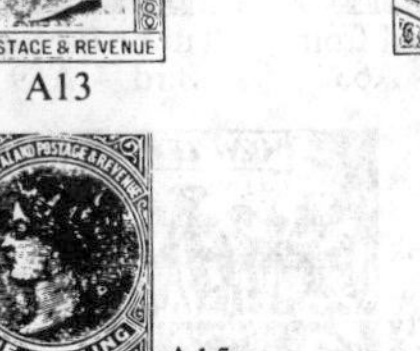

A15

**Perf. 10, 11, 11½, 12, 12½ and Compound**

**1882**

61 A9 1p rose 5.25 20
 a Vert. pair, imperf. horiz. 475.00
 b Perf. 12x11½ 30.00 7.00
 c Perf. 12½ 265.00 110.00
62 A10 2p violet 7.00 16
 a Vert. pair, imperf. btwn. 450.00
 b Perf. 12½ 200.00 110.00
63 A11 3p orange 25.00 2.00
 a 3p yellow 25.00 2.00
64 A12 4p blue green 25.00 2.50
 a Perf. 10x11 52.50 7.00
65 A13 6p brown 35.00 1.90
66 A14 8p blue 60.00 30.00
67 A15 1sh red brown 55.00 11.50
 *Nos. 61-67 (7)* 212.25 48.26

See No. 87.

A15a A16 A17

**1891-95**

67A A15a ½p black ('95) 1.40 12
 b Perf. 12x11½ 14.00 14.00
68 A16 2½p ultramarine 25.00 2.50
 a Perf. 12½ 275.00 110.00
69 A17 5p olive gray 35.00 7.00

In 1893 advertisements were printed on the backs of Nos. 61-67, 68-69. See No. 86C.

Mt. Cook A18

Lake Taupo A19

Pembroke Peak — A20

Mt. Earnslaw, Lake Wakatipu — A21

Mt. Earnslaw, Lake Wakatipu — A22

Huia, Sacred Birds — A23

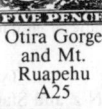

White Terrace, Rotomahana A24

Otira Gorge and Mt. Ruapehu A25

Kiwi — A26

Maori Canoe — A27

Pink Terrace, Rotomahana A28

Kea and Kaka (Hawk-billed Parrots) A29

Milford Sound — A30

Mt. Cook — A31

**Perf. 12 to 16**

**1898, Apr. 5 Engr. Unwmk.**

70 A18 ½p lilac gray 2.75 28
 a Horiz. or vert. pair, imperf. btwn. 650.00 600.00
71 A19 1p yel brn & bl 1.75 7
 a Horiz. pair, imperf. btwn. 550.00 550.00
72 A20 2p rose brown 14.00 12
 a Horiz. pair, imperf. vert. 550.00 550.00
73 A21 2½p bl *(Wakitipu)* 7.00 *17.50*
74 A22 2½p bl *(Wakatipu)* 10.50 2.00
 a Vert. pair, imperf. horiz.
75 A23 3p org brn 10.50 3.75
76 A24 4p rose 10.50 7.00
77 A25 5p red brown 21.00 4.50
 a 5p violet brown 42.50 *52.50*
78 A26 6p green 42.50 21.00
79 A27 8p dull blue 25.00 17.50
80 A28 9p lilac 21.00 10.50
81 A29 1sh dull red 37.50 10.50
82 A30 2sh blue green 77.50 62.50
 a Vert. pair, imperf. btwn. 1,000.
83 A31 5sh vermilion 225.00 210.00
 *Nos. 70-83 (14)* 506.50 367.22

See Nos. 84, 88-89, 91-98, 99B, 102, 104, 106-107, 111-112, 114-121, 126-128.

A32 A33 A34

Wmk. 63- Double-lined N Z and Star

**1900 Wmk. 63 Perf. 11**

**Thick Soft Wove Paper**

84 A18 ½p green 5.00 7
85 A32 1p carmine rose 2.75 10
 a 1p lake 10.00 2.50
86 A33 2p red violet 3.25 22
 a Vert. pair, imperf. horiz. 550.00 550.00
 b Horiz. pair, imperf. vert.

Nos. 84 and 86 are re-engravings of Nos. 70 and 72 and are slightly smaller.

**1899-1900 Wmk. 63**

86C A15a ½p black ('00) 7.50 4.00
87 A10 2p violet ('00) 9.00 5.50

**Unwmk.**

88 A22 2½p blue 9.00 2.00
 a Vert. pair, imperf. horiz. 550.00 550.00
89 A23 3p org brn 13.00 1.40
 a Horiz. pair, imperf. vert. 450.00 450.00
 b Horiz. pair, imperf. btwn. 450.00 450.00
90 A34 4p yel brn & bl ('00) 4.50 1.10
 a Imperf.
 b Dbl. impression of center
91 A25 5p red brown 13.00 2.25
 a 5p violet brown 16.00 1.75
92 A26 6p green 50.00 45.00
 a Imperf.
93 A26 6p rose ('00) 10.50 1.65
 a 6p carmine 21.00 4.00
 b Double impression 475.00 475.00
 c Imperf., pair 165.00 165.00
 d Horiz. pair, imperf. vert. 300.00 300.00
94 A27 8p dark blue 12.00 5.50
95 A28 9p red lilac 15.00 8.75
96 A29 1sh red 13.00 1.90
97 A30 2sh blue green 57.50 30.00
98 A31 5sh vermilion 200.00 140.00
 *Nos. 86C-98 (13)* 414.00 249.05

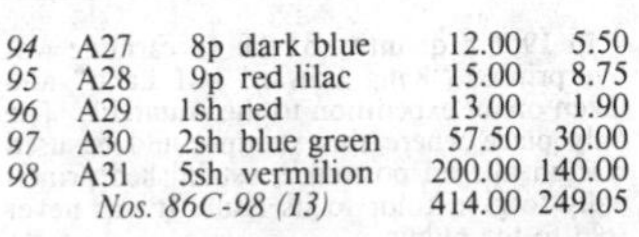

"Commerce" A35

Boer War Contingent A36

**1901, Jan. 1 Unwmk. Perf. 12 to 16**

99 A35 1p carmine 5.25 2.50

Universal Penny Postage.

**Perf. 14, 11x14, 14x11**

**1901 Wmk. 63**

**Thick Soft Paper**

99B A18 ½p green 6.00 1.50

**Perf. 11, 14 and Compound**

100 A35 1p carmine 3.00 20
 a Horiz. pair, imperf. vert. 300.00 300.00
101 A36 1½p brn org 4.00 3.50
 a Vert. pair, imperf. horiz. 525.00 525.00
 b Imperf., pair 650.00 650.00

No. 101 was issued to honor the New Zealand forces in the South African War.

**Thin Hard Paper**

102 A18 ½p green 25.00 16.00
103 A35 1p carmine 16.00 6.25
 a Horiz. pair, imperf. vert. 300.00

**1902 Unwmk.**

104 A18 ½p green 5.00 1.75
105 A35 1p carmine 14.00 1.65

**1902 Perf. 11**

**Thin White Wove Paper**

106 A26 6p rose red 20.00 8.25
 a Watermarked letters 55.00 42.50

The sheets of No. 106 are watermarked with the words "LISBON SUPERFINE" in two lines, covering ten stamps.

Wmk. 61- N Z and Star Close Together

The margins of the sheets are watermarked "NEW ZEALAND POSTAGE" and parts of the double-lined letters of these words are frequently found on the stamps. It occasionally happens that a stamp shows no watermark whatever.

**Perf. 11, 14, 11x14, 14x13, 14x14½**

**1902-07 Wmk. 61**

107 A18 ½p green 1.50 8
 a Horiz. pair, imperf. vert. 250.00 250.00
108 A35 1p carmine 1.50 10
 a 1p rose carmine 1.50 10
 b Imperf., pair 250.00 250.00
 c Imperf. x serrate perf. 175.00 175.00
 d Imperf. horiz. or vert. pair 250.00 250.00
 f Booklet pane of 6 165.00
109 A36 1½p brn org ('07) 5.25 4.75
110 A33 2p dl vio ('03) 2.75 18
 a Horiz. pair, imperf. vert. 315.00 315.00
 b Vert. pair, imperf. horiz. 315.00 315.00
111 A22 2½p blue 2.00 90
112 A23 3p org brn 5.25 60
113 A34 4p yel brn & bl 7.50 1.25
 a Horiz. pair, imperf. vert. 285.00 285.00
 b Center inverted
114 A25 5p red brown 11.50 2.25
 a 5p violet brown 14.00 3.00
115 A26 6p rose red 20.00 1.50
 a 6p rose 16.00 1.50
 b 6p pink 18.00 2.25
 c 6p brick red 16.00 1.65
 d Horiz. pair, imperf. vert. 315.00 315.00
116 A27 8p deep blue 8.00 3.25
117 A28 9p red violet 14.00 5.00
118 A29 1sh orange red 10.50 1.50
 a 1sh scarlet 10.50 1.50
 b 1sh brown red 13.00 1.50
119 A30 2sh blue green 45.00 20.00
120 A31 5sh vermilion 150.00 115.00
 *Nos. 107-120 (14)* 284.75 156.36

Wmk. 61 is normally sideways on 3p, 6p, 8p and 1sh.

In 1908 a quantity of the 1p carmine was overprinted "King Edward VII Land" and taken on an expedition to the Antarctic. The only place where this stamp could be used was an alleged postoffice, established principally to give color to its issue. It was never sold to the public.

Similar conditions prevailed for the 1909-12 ½p green and 1p carmine overprinted "Victoria Land".

See No. 129.

**1903 Unwmk. Perf. 11**
**Laid Paper**

*121* A30 2sh blue green 225.00 125.00

### Christchurch Exhibition Issue

Arrival of the Maoris A37

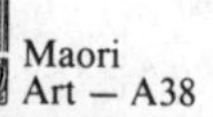

Maori Art — A38

Landing of Capt. Cook A39

Annexation of New Zealand A40

**1906, Nov. Wmk. 61 Typo. Perf. 14**

*122* A37 ½p emerald 7.50 6.25
*123* A38 1p vermilion 7.50 6.25
  *a* 1p claret *10,000. 12,500.*
*124* A39 3p blue & brown 42.50 50.00
*125* A40 6p gray grn & rose 87.50 100.00

Designs of 1902-07 Issue, but smaller
***Perf. 14, 14x13, 14x14½***

**1907-08 Engr.**

*126* A23 3p orange brown *35.00* 5.50
*127* A26 6p carmine rose *45.00* 1.75
*128* A29 1sh orange red *125.00* 9.00

The small stamps are about 21mm high, those of 1898-1902 about 23mm.

Type of 1902 Redrawn

**1908 Typo. Perf. 14x14½**

*129* A35 1p carmine 9.00 12

REDRAWN, 1p: The lines of the sky appear unbroken, instead of broken up into dots to simulate clouds, as in the original. The smoke-stack of the steamship is broad and touches the woman's dress, instead of narrow and separated from the dress, as in the original.

Edward VII A41

"Commerce" A42

**1909-12 Perf. 14x14½**

*130* A41 ½p yellow green 1.00 8
  *a* Booklet pane of 6 *225.00*
  *b* Booklet pane 5 + label *650.00*
  *c* Imperf., pair 225.00
*131* A42 1p carmine 25 6
  *a* Imperf., pair 250.00 250.00
  *b* Booklet pane of 6 100.00

***Perf. 14x14½, 14x13½, 14***
**Engr.**
**Various Frames**

*132* A41 2p mauve 8.00 85
*133* A41 3p orange brown 8.00 35
*134* A41 4p red orange 13.00 16.00
*135* A41 4p yellow ('12) 11.50 1.50
*136* A41 5p red brown 5.50 1.25
*137* A41 6p carmine rose 13.00 32
*138* A41 8p deep blue 6.50 40
*139* A41 1sh vermilion 26.00 1.65
  *Nos. 130-139 (10)* 92.75 22.46

See No. 177.

Stamps of 1909 Overprinted in Black: "AUCKLAND EXHIBITION, 1913," in Three Lines

**1913 Typo., Engr.**

*130d* A41 ½p yellow green 25.00 *27.50*
*131d* A42 1p carmine 15.00 *21.00*
*133d* A41 3p orange brown 125.00 *160.00*
*137d* A41 6p carmine rose 140.00 *210.00*

This issue was valid only within New Zealand and to Australia from Dec. 1, 1913, to Feb. 28, 1914. The Auckland Stamp Collectors Club inspired this issue.

King George V — A43

**1915 Typo. Perf. 14x15**

*144* A43 ½p yellow green 38 10
  *b* Booklet pane of 6 *140.00*

See Nos. 163-164, 176, 178.

A44

A45

***Perf. 14x14½, 14x13½***

**1915-22 Engr.**

*145* A44 1½p gray 65 40
*146* A45 2p purple 7.50 7.50
*147* A45 2p org yel ('16) 7.50 7.25
*148* A44 2½p dull blue 3.75 1.10
*149* A45 3p violet brown 5.75 25
*150* A45 4p orange yellow 3.75 4.50
*151* A45 4p purple ('16) 6.75 15
  *a* Imperf., pair *1,500.*
  *b* Horiz. pair, imperf. vert.
*152* A44 4½p dark green 10.50 5.75
*153* A45 5p light blue ('21) 9.75 55
  *a* Imperf., pair 150.00
*154* A45 6p carmine rose 3.75 25
  *a* Horiz. pair, imperf. vert.
*155* A44 7½p red brown 11.00 7.50
*156* A45 8p blue ('21) 11.00 11.00
*157* A45 8p red brown ('22) 13.00 75
*158* A45 9p olive green 15.00 75
  *a* Imperf., pair *1,250.*
*159* A45 1sh vermilion 15.00 75
  *a* Imperf., pair 425.00
  *Nos. 145-159 (15)* 124.65 48.45

A46

A47

**1916-19 Typo. Perf. 14x15, 14**

*160* A46 1½p gray black 3.50 10
*161* A47 1½p gray black 8.00 12
*162* A47 1½p brown orange ('18) 90 10
*163* A43 2p yellow 90 12
*164* A43 3p chocolate ('19) 3.00 20
  *Nos. 160-164 (5)* 16.30 64

The engr. stamps have a background of geometric lathe-work; the typo. stamps have a background of crossed dotted lines.

Type A43 has three diamonds at each side of the crown, type A46 has two, and type A47 has one.

In 1916 the 1½, 2, 3 and 6p of the 1915-16 issue and the 8p of the 1909 issue were printed on paper intended for the long rectangular stamps of the 1902-07 issue. In this paper the watermarks are set wide apart, so that the smaller stamps often show only a small part of the watermark or miss it altogether.

### Victory Issue

"Peace" and British Lion — A48

Peace and Lion — A49

Maori Chief — A50

British Lion A51

"Victory" A52

King George V, Lion and Maori Fern at sides — A53

**1920, Jan. 27 Perf. 14**

*165* A48 ½p yellow green 60 18
*166* A49 1p carmine 75 10
*167* A50 1½p brown orange 35 10
*168* A51 3p black brown 9.00 5.50
*169* A52 6p purple 6.00 5.50
*170* A53 1sh vermilion 20.00 20.00
  *Nos. 165-170 (6)* 36.70 31.38

No. 165 Surcharged in Red

**2d. 2d.**

**TWOPENCE**

**1922, Mar.**

*174* A48 2p on ½p yellow green 1.25 40

Map of New Zealand — A54

**1923 Typo. Perf. 14x15**

*175* A54 1p carmine rose 80 8

Restoration of Penny Postage. The paper varies from thin to thick.

Types of 1909-15
N Z and Star printed on back in blue

**1925 Unwmk. Perf. 14x14½**

*176* A43 ½p yellow green 1.40 40
*177* A42 1p carmine 2.25 30
*178* A43 2p yellow 12.50 *25.00*

### Dunedin Exhibition Issue

Exhibition Buildings A55

**1925, Nov. 17 Wmk. 61**
**Surface Tinted Paper**

*179* A55 ½p yel grn, *grnsh* 1.50 2.00
*180* A55 1p car rose, *pink* 1.50 2.00
*181* A55 4p red vio, *lil* 25.00 45.00

George V in Admiral's Uniform — A56

In Field Marshal's Uniform — A57

**1926 Perf. 14, 14½x14**

*182* A56 2sh blue 30.00 9.25
  *a* 2sh dark blue 37.50 9.25
*183* A56 3sh violet 50.00 75.00
  *a* 3sh deep violet 50.00 62.50

***Perf. 14, 14x14½***

*184* A57 1p rose red 20 6
  *a* Booklet pane of 6 75.00
  *b* Imperf., pair 75.00

Pied Fantail and Clematis — A58

Kiwi and Cabbage Palm — A59

Maori Woman Cooking in Boiling Spring — A60

Maori Council House (Whare) — A61

Mt. Cook and Mountain Lilies — A62

Maori Girl Wearing Tiki — A63

Mitre Peak — A64

Striped Marlin A65

Harvesting A66

Tuatara Lizard A67

Maori Panel from Door — A68

Tui or Parson Bird — A69

Capt. Cook Landing at Poverty Bay — A70

Mt. Egmont, North Island A71

***Perf. 14x14½, 14x13½, 13½x14, 13½***

| **1935, May 1** | | **Engr.** | **Wmk. 61** | |
|---|---|---|---|---|
| *185* | A58 | ½p bright green | 9 | 5 |
| *186* | A59 | 1p copper red | 10 | 5 |
| *186A* | A59 | 1p copper red, re-engraved | 2.25 | 1.25 |
| ***b*** | | Booklet pane of 6 | 25.00 | |
| *187* | A60 | 1½p red brown | 90 | 65 |
| *188* | A61 | 2p red orange | 45 | 8 |
| *189* | A62 | 2½p dk gray & dk brn | 90 | 90 |
| *190* | A63 | 3p chocolate | 5.00 | 22 |
| *191* | A64 | 4p blk brn & blk | 65 | 10 |
| *192* | A65 | 5p violet blue | 4.50 | 1.60 |
| *193* | A66 | 6p red | 1.40 | 10 |
| *194* | A67 | 8p dark brown | 1.40 | 35 |

**Litho.**

**Size: 18x21¼mm**

| | | | | |
|---|---|---|---|---|
| *195* | A68 | 9p blk & scar | 4.50 | 65 |

**Engr.**

| | | | | |
|---|---|---|---|---|
| *196* | A69 | 1sh dk sl grn | 4.50 | 45 |
| *197* | A70 | 2sh olive green | 10.50 | 1.60 |
| *198* | A71 | 3sh yel brn & brn blk | 9.00 | 4.50 |
| | | *Nos. 185-198 (15)* | 46.14 | 12.55 |

On No. 186A, the horizontal lines in the sky are much darker

The 2½p, 5p, 2sh and 3sh are perf. 13½ vertically; perf. 14 horizontally with alternate rows mixed perf. 14 and 13.

See Nos. 203-216, 244-245.

**Silver Jubilee Issue**

Queen Mary and King George V A72

| **1935, May 7** | | | ***Perf. 11x11½*** | |
|---|---|---|---|---|
| *199* | A72 | ½p blue green | 7 | 10 |
| *200* | A72 | 1p dk car rose | 9 | 14 |
| *201* | A72 | 6p vermilion | 13.00 | *20.00* |

25th anniv. of the reign of King George V.

Wmk. 253- Multiple N Z and Star

Types of 1935

***Perf. 12½ to 15 and Compound***

| **1936-41** | | | **Wmk. 253** | |
|---|---|---|---|---|
| *203* | A58 | ½p bright green | 14 | 6 |
| *204* | A59 | 1p copper red | 18 | 5 |
| *205* | A60 | 1½p red brown | 2.25 | 2.25 |
| *206* | A61 | 2p red orange | 9 | 5 |
| ***a*** | | Perf. 14 | 80 | 35 |
| ***b*** | | Perf. 14x15 | 1.10 | 35 |
| *207* | A62 | 2½p dk gray & dk brn | 32 | 16 |
| *208* | A63 | 3p chocolate | 5.50 | 14 |
| *209* | A64 | 4p blk brn & blk | 35 | 6 |
| *210* | A65 | 5p violet blue | 1.10 | 9 |
| *211* | A66 | 6p red | 40 | 5 |
| *212* | A67 | 8p dark brown | 55 | 9 |

**Litho.**

**Size: 18x21½mm**

| | | | | |
|---|---|---|---|---|
| *213* | A68 | 9p gray & scarlet | 4.00 | 10 |
| ***a*** | | 9p black & scarlet | 4.00 | 9 |

**Engr.**

| | | | | |
|---|---|---|---|---|
| *214* | A69 | 1sh dark slate grn | 65 | 6 |
| *215* | A70 | 2sh olive green | 4.00 | 20 |
| ***a*** | | Perf. 13½x14 | 27.50 | 80 |
| *216* | A71 | 3sh yel brn & blk brn | 5.75 | 80 |
| ***a*** | | Perf. 12½ ('41) | 9.00 | 2.25 |
| | | *Nos. 203-216 (14)* | 25.28 | 4.16 |

Wool Industry A73

Butter Industry A74

Sheep Farming A75

Apple Industry A76

Shipping A77

| **1936, Oct. 1** | | **Wmk. 61** | ***Perf. 11*** | |
|---|---|---|---|---|
| *218* | A73 | ½p deep green | 9 | 7 |
| *219* | A74 | 1p red | 10 | 7 |
| *220* | A75 | 2½p deep blue | 90 | 90 |
| *221* | A76 | 4p dark purple | 90 | 90 |
| *222* | A77 | 6p red brown | 90 | 90 |
| | | *Nos. 218-222 (5)* | 2.89 | 2.84 |

Congress of the Chambers of Commerce of the British Empire held in New Zealand.

Queen Elizabeth and King George VI A78

***Perf. 13½x13***

| **1937, May 13** | | | **Wmk. 253** | |
|---|---|---|---|---|
| *223* | A78 | 1p rose carmine | 15 | 6 |
| *224* | A78 | 2½p dark blue | 16 | 16 |
| *225* | A78 | 6p vermilion | 20 | 18 |

Coronation of George VI and Elizabeth.

A79

A80

| **1938-44** | | **Engr.** | ***Perf. 13½*** | |
|---|---|---|---|---|
| *226* | A79 | ½p emerald | 16 | 5 |
| *226B* | A79 | ½p brn org ('41) | 5 | 5 |
| *227* | A79 | 1p rose red | 32 | 5 |
| *227A* | A79 | 1p lt bl grn ('41) | 5 | 5 |
| *228* | A80 | 1½p violet brown | 2.25 | 28 |
| *228B* | A80 | 1½p red ('44) | 8 | 5 |
| *228C* | A80 | 3p blue ('41) | 8 | 5 |
| | | *Nos. 226-228C (7)* | 2.99 | 58 |

See Nos. 258-264.

Landing of the Maoris in 1350 — A81

Captain Cook, His Map of New Zealand, 1769, H.M.S. Endeavour A82

Victoria, Edward VII, George V, Edward VIII and George VI — A83

Abel Tasman, Ship, and Chart of West Coast of New Zealand A84

Treaty of Waitangi, 1840 — A85

Pioneer Settlers Landing on Petone Beach, 1840 — A86

The Progress of Transport A87

H. M. S. "Britomart" at Akaroa — A88

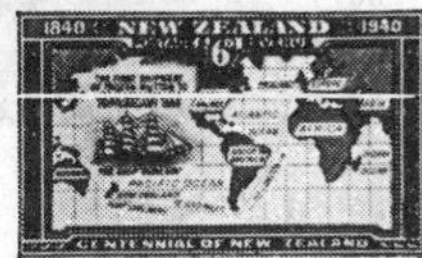
Route of Ship Carrying First Shipment of Frozen Mutton to England- A89

Maori Council A90

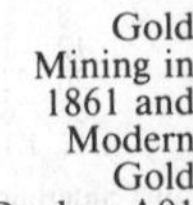

Gold Mining in 1861 and Modern Gold Dredge- A91

Giant Kauri — A92

***Perf. 13½x13, 13x13½, 14x13½***

| **1940, Jan. 2** | | **Engr.** | **Wmk. 253** | |
|---|---|---|---|---|
| *229* | A81 | ½p dark bl grn | 7 | 7 |
| *230* | A82 | 1p scar & sepia | 20 | 20 |
| *231* | A83 | 1½p brt vio & ultra | 28 | 28 |
| *232* | A84 | 2p black brown & Prussian green | 35 | 35 |
| *233* | A85 | 2½p dk bl & myr grn | 28 | 28 |
| *234* | A86 | 3p dp plum & dk vio | 1.25 | 1.25 |
| *235* | A87 | 4p dk red vio & vio brn | 1.90 | 1.90 |
| *236* | A88 | 5p brn & lt bl | 1.50 | 1.50 |
| *237* | A89 | 6p vio & brt grn | 1.75 | 1.75 |
| *238* | A90 | 7p org red & blk | 2.00 | 2.00 |
| *239* | A90 | 8p org red & blk | 3.50 | 3.50 |
| *240* | A91 | 9p dp org & olive | 4.25 | 4.25 |
| *241* | A92 | 1sh dk sl grn & ol | 5.25 | 5.25 |
| | | *Nos. 229-241 (13)* | 22.58 | 22.58 |

Centenary of British sovereignty established by the treaty of Waitangi.

Stamps of 1938 Surcharged with New Values in Black

| **1941** | | **Wmk. 253** | ***Perf. 13½*** | |
|---|---|---|---|---|
| *242* | A79 | 1p on ½p emerald | 15 | 5 |
| *243* | A80 | 2p on 1½p vio brn | 15 | 6 |

Type of 1935 Redrawn

**1941 Typo. Wmk. 61 *Perf. 14x15***

**Size 17¼x20¼mm**

| | | | | |
|---|---|---|---|---|
| *244* | A68 | 9p int blk & scar | 40.00 | 7.50 |

**Wmk. 253**

| | | | | |
|---|---|---|---|---|
| *245* | A68 | 9p int blk & scarlet | 2.50 | 30 |

**Catalogue values for unused stamps in this section, from this point to the end of the section, are for Never Hinged items.**

No 231 Surcharged in Black

**TENPENCE**

| **1944** | | | ***Perf. 13½x13*** | |
|---|---|---|---|---|
| *246* | A83 | 10p on 1½p brt vio & ultra | 35 | 35 |

**Peace Issue**

Lake Matheson A93

Parliament House, Wellington A94

St. Paul's Cathedral, London A95

The Royal Family — A96

Badge of Royal New Zealand Air Force A97

New Zealand Army Overseas Badge A98

Badge of Royal Navy A99

New Zealand Coat of Arms A100

Knight, Window of Wellington Boys' College — A101

Southern Alps and Chapel Altar A102

National Memorial Campanile, Wellington — A103

**Engr.; Photo. (1½p, 1sh)**
***Perf. 13x13½, 13½x13.***

| **1946, Apr. 1** | | | **Wmk. 253** | |
|---|---|---|---|---|
| *247* A93 | ½p | choc & dk bl grn | 6 | 6 |
| *248* A94 | 1p | emerald | 5 | 5 |
| *249* A95 | 1½p | scarlet | 8 | 8 |
| *250* A96 | 2p | rose violet | 8 | 5 |
| *251* A97 | 3p | dk grn & ultra | 8 | 8 |
| *252* A98 | 4p | brn org & ol grn | 10 | 10 |
| *253* A99 | 5p | ultra & bl grn | 14 | 10 |
| *254* A100 | 6p | org red & red brn | 14 | 8 |
| *255* A101 | 8p | brn lake & blk | 16 | 16 |
| *256* A102 | 9p | blk & brt bl | 28 | 28 |
| *257* A103 | 1sh | gray black | 30 | 30 |
| | | *Nos. 247-257 (11)* | 1.47 | 1.34 |

Return to peace at the close of WWII.

George VI Type of 1938 and

King George VI — A104

| **1947** | | **Engr.** | ***Perf. 13½*** | |
|---|---|---|---|---|
| *258* A80 | 2p | orange | 12 | 5 |
| *260* A80 | 4p | rose lilac | 40 | 5 |
| *261* A80 | 5p | gray | 1.10 | 6 |
| *262* A80 | 6p | rose carmine | 60 | 6 |
| *263* A80 | 8p | deep violet | 1.10 | 8 |
| *264* A80 | 9p | chocolate | 1.40 | 6 |
| | | ***Perf. 14*** | | |
| *265* A104 | 1sh | dk car rose & chnt | 1.10 | 8 |
| *266* A104 | 1sh3p | ultra & chnt | 1.40 | 10 |
| *267* A104 | 2sh | dk grn & brn org | 2.25 | 10 |
| *268* A104 | 3sh | gray blk & chnt | 5.75 | 35 |
| | | *Nos. 258-268 (10)* | 15.22 | 99 |

Nos. 265-267 have watermark either upright or sideways. On No. 268 watermark is always sideways.

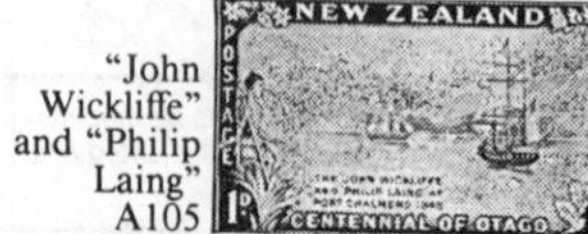

"John Wickliffe" and "Philip Laing" A105

Cromwell, Otago A106

First Church, Dunedin — A107

University of Otago A108

| **1948, Feb. 23** | | | ***Perf. 13½*** | |
|---|---|---|---|---|
| *269* A105 | 1p | green & blue | 5 | 5 |
| *270* A106 | 2p | brown & green | 5 | 5 |
| *271* A107 | 3p | violet | 10 | 10 |
| *272* A108 | 6p | lil rose & gray blk | 15 | 15 |

Otago Province settlement, cent.

A109

Cathedral at Christchurch A110

"They Passed this Way" A111

**Wmk. 253**

| **1950, July 28** | **Typo.** | | ***Perf. 14*** | |
|---|---|---|---|---|
| | **Black Surcharge** | | | |
| *273* A109 | 1½p | rose red | 15 | 5 |

See No. 367.

| **1950, Nov. 20** | **Engr.** | ***Perf. 13x13½*** | | |
|---|---|---|---|---|

Designs: 3p, John Robert Godley. 6p, Canterbury University College. 1sh, View of Timaru.

| | | | | |
|---|---|---|---|---|
| *274* A110 | 1p | bl grn & bl | 8 | 8 |
| *275* A111 | 2p | car & red org | 8 | 8 |
| *276* A110 | 3p | indigo & blue | 12 | 10 |
| *277* A111 | 6p | brown & blue | 20 | 20 |
| *278* A111 | 1sh | claret & blue | 65 | 65 |
| | | *Nos. 274-278 (5)* | 1.13 | 1.11 |

Centenary of the founding of Canterbury Provincial District.

No. 227A Surcharged in Black

| **1952, Dec.** | | ***Perf. 13½*** | |
|---|---|---|---|
| *279* A79 | 3p on 1p lt bl grn | 12 | 8 |

**Coronation Issue**

Buckingham Palace and Elizabeth II A112

Queen Elizabeth II A113

Westminster Abbey A114

Designs: 4p, Queen Elizabeth and state coach. 1sh6p, Crown and royal scepter.

***Perf. 13x12½, 14x14½ (3p, 8p)***
**Engr., Photo. (3p, 8p)**

| **1953, May 25** | | | | |
|---|---|---|---|---|
| *280* A112 | 2p | ultramarine | 12 | 8 |
| *281* A113 | 3p | brown | 16 | 5 |
| *282* A112 | 4p | carmine | 60 | 35 |
| *283* A114 | 8p | slate black | 80 | 70 |
| *284* A112 | 1sh6p | vio bl & pur | 1.50 | 1.50 |
| | | *Nos. 280-284 (5)* | 3.18 | 2.68 |

No. 226B Surcharged in Black

| **1953, Sept.** | | ***Perf. 13½*** | |
|---|---|---|---|
| *285* A79 | 1p on ½p brn org | 10 | 10 |

Queen Elizabeth II — A115

Queen Elizabeth II and Duke of Edinburgh A116

***Perf. 12½x13½, 13½x13***

| **1953, Dec. 9** | | | **Engr.** | |
|---|---|---|---|---|
| *286* A115 | 3p | lilac | 10 | 6 |
| *287* A116 | 4p | deep blue | 20 | 18 |

Visit of Queen Elizabeth II and the Duke of Edinburgh.

A117

A118

A119

| **1953-57** | | | ***Perf. 13½*** | |
|---|---|---|---|---|
| *288* A117 | ½p | gray | 9 | 5 |
| *289* A117 | 1p | orange | 9 | 5 |
| *290* A117 | 1½p | rose brown | 28 | 9 |
| *291* A117 | 2p | blue green | 18 | 5 |
| *292* A117 | 3p | red | 12 | 5 |
| *293* A117 | 4p | blue | 32 | 5 |
| *294* A117 | 6p | rose violet | 55 | 5 |
| *295* A117 | 8p | rose carmine | 45 | 12 |
| *296* A118 | 9p | emerald & orange brown | 50 | 9 |
| *297* A118 | 1sh | car & blk | 50 | 9 |
| *298* A118 | 1sh6p | bl & blk | 90 | 9 |
| *298A* A118 | 1sh9p | org & blk | 3.75 | 90 |
| *298B* A119 | 2sh6p | redsh brn | 32.50 | 6.75 |
| *299* A119 | 3sh | blue green | 9.00 | 90 |
| *300* A119 | 5sh | rose car | 27.50 | 1.65 |
| *301* A119 | 10sh | vio blue | 35.00 | 18.00 |
| | | *Nos. 288-301 (16)* | 111.73 | 28.98 |

The 1½p was issued in 1953; 1sh9p and 2sh6p in 1957; all others in 1954.

No. 298A exists on both ordinary and chalky paper.

Two dies of the 1sh differ in shading on the sleeve.

See Nos. 306-312.

Maori Mailman A120

Queen Elizabeth II A121

Douglas DC-3 A122

***Perf. 13½ (2p), 14 (3p), 13 (4p)***

| **1955, July 18** | | | **Wmk. 253** | |
|---|---|---|---|---|
| *302* A120 | 2p | dp grn & brn | 10 | 5 |
| *303* A121 | 3p | claret | 15 | 5 |
| *304* A122 | 4p | ultra & blk | 42 | 42 |

Cent. of New Zealand's 1st postage stamps.

Type of 1953-54 Redrawn

| **1955-59** | | **Wmk. 253** | ***Perf. 13½*** | |
|---|---|---|---|---|
| *306* A117 | 1p | orange ('56) | 6 | 5 |
| *307* A117 | 1½p | rose brown | 30 | 10 |
| *308* A117 | 2p | blue green ('56) | 12 | 5 |
| *309* A117 | 3p | vermilion ('56) | 60 | 5 |
| *310* A117 | 4p | blue ('58) | 1.50 | 8 |
| *311* A117 | 6p | violet | 1.50 | 8 |
| *312* A117 | 8p | brn red ('59) | 6.00 | 4.00 |
| | | *Nos. 306-312 (7)* | 10.08 | 4.41 |

The numeral has been enlarged and the ornament in the lower right corner omitted.

Nos. 306, 308-310 exist on both ordinary and chalky paper.

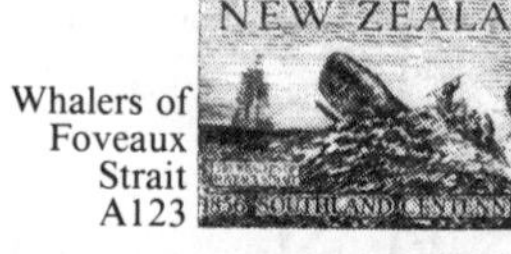

Whalers of Foveaux Strait A123

"Agriculture" with Cow and Sheep — A124

Notornis (Takahe) — A125

| **1956, Jan.** | | ***Perf. 13x12½, 13 (8p)*** | | |
|---|---|---|---|---|
| *313* A123 | 2p | deep green | 12 | 8 |
| *314* A124 | 3p | sepia | 15 | 8 |
| *315* A125 | 8p | car & bl vio | 1.50 | 1.50 |

Southland centennial.

Lamb and Map of New Zealand — A126

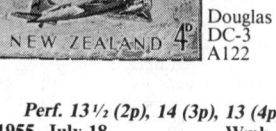

Lamb, S. S. "Dunedin" and Refrigeration Ship — A127

*Perf. 14x14½, 14½x14*

**1957, Feb. 15** **Photo.**

*316* A126 4p bright blue 1.00 70
*317* A127 8p brick red 1.75 1.40

75th anniv. of the New Zealand Meat Export Trade.

Sir Truby King — A128

Nelson Diocese Seal — A129

**1957, May 14** **Engr.** ***Perf. 13***

*318* A128 3p rose red 18 12

Plunket Society, 50th anniversary.

Nos. 307, 290 Surcharged **2d**

**1958, Jan. 15** ***Perf. 13½***

*319* A117 2p on 1½p (#307) 20 8
  *a* Small surcharge 20 8
*320* A117 2p on 1½p (#290) 175.00 *225.00*

Surcharge measures 9½mm vert. on Nos. 319-320; 9mm on No. 319a. Diameter of dot 4½mm on Nos. 319-320; 3¾mm on No. 319a.

Sir Charles Kingsford-Smith and "Southern Cross" — A129a

*Perf. 14x14½*

**1958, Aug. 27** **Engr.** **Wmk. 253**

*321* A129a 6p brt vio bl 32 32

30th anniv. of the 1st air crossing of the Tasman Sea.

See Australia No. 310.

**1958, Sept. 29** ***Perf. 13***

*322* A129 3p carmine rose 18 8

Centenary of Nelson City.

Statue of "Pania," Napier — A130

Gannet Sanctuary, Cape Kidnappers A131

Design: 8p, Maori shearing sheep.

*Perf. 13½x14½, 14½x14*

**1958, Nov. 3** **Photo.** **Wmk. 253**

*323* A130 2p yellow green 12 8
*324* A131 3p ultramarine 12 6
*325* A130 8p red brown 2.25 2.25

Centenary of Hawkes Bay province.

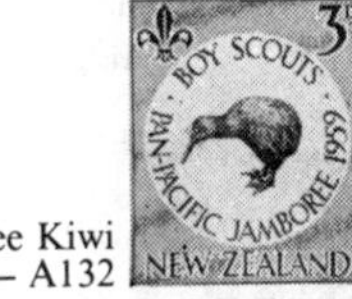


Jamboree Kiwi Badge — A132

**1959, Jan. 5** **Engr.** ***Perf. 13***

*326* A132 3p car rose & brown 22 10

Pan-Pacific Scout Jamboree, Auckland, Jan. 3-10.

"Endeavour" at Ship Cove — A133

Designs: 3p, Shipping wool at Wairau bar, 1857. 8p, Salt Industry, Grassmere.

**1959, Mar. 2** **Photo.** ***Perf. 14½x14***

*327* A133 2p green 12 8
*328* A133 3p dark blue 15 8
*329* A133 8p brown 2.75 2.75

Centenary of Marlborough Province.

The Explorer — A134

Designs: 3p, The Gold Digger. 8p, The Pioneer Woman.

**1960, May 16** ***Perf. 14x14½***

*330* A134 2p green 12 6
*331* A134 3p orange 15 6
*332* A134 8p gray 2.50 2.00

Westland centennial.

Kaka Beak Flower — A135

Timber Industry — A136

Tiki — A137

Maori Rock Drawing — A138

Butter Making A139

Designs: ½p, Manuka flower. 1p, Karaka flower. 2½p, Titoki flower. 3p, Kowhai flower. 4p, Hibiscus. 5p, Mountain daisy. 6p, Clematis. 7p, Koromiko flower. 8p, Rata flower. 9p, Flag. 1sh3p, Rainbow trout. 1sh9p, Plane spraying farmland. 3sh, Ngauruhoe Volcano, Tongariro National Park. 5sh, Sutherland Falls. 10sh, Tasman Glacier, Mount Cook. £1, Pohutu Geyser.

*Perf. 14½x14, 14x14½*

**1960-66** **Photo.** **Wmk. 253**

*333* A135 ½ dp car, grn & pale bl 8 5
  *b* Green omitted 70.00
  *c* Pale blue omitted 55.00
*334* A135 1p brn, org & green 12 5
  *b* Orange omitted 150.00
  *c* Perf. 14½x13, wmkd. sideways ('63) 1.75 1.75
*335* A135 2p grn, rose car, blk & yellow 12 5
  *b* Black omitted 200.00
  *c* Yellow omitted 225.00
*336* A135 2½p blk, grn, red & brn ('61) 16 5
  *a* Brown omitted 50.00
  *b* Green & red omitted 160.00
  *c* Green omitted 75.00
  *d* Red omitted 90.00
*337* A135 3p Prus bl, yel, brn & grn 14 5
  *b* Yellow omitted 55.00
  *c* Brown omitted 55.00
  *d* Green omitted 45.00
  *e* Perf. 14½x13, wmkd. sideways ('63) 2.00 2.00
*338* A135 4p bl, grn, yel & lilac 20 5
  *a* Yellow omitted 100.00
  *b* Lilac omitted 45.00
*339* A135 5p pur, blk, yel & grn ('62) 70 16
  *a* Yellow omitted 125.00
*340* A135 6p dp grn, lt grn & lil 35 8
  *a* Light green omitted 60.00
  *b* Lilac omitted 70.00
*340C* A135 7p pink, red, grn & yel ('66) 70 70
*341* A135 8p gray, grn, pink & yel 52 10
*342* A136 9p ultra & car 52 16
  *a* Carmine omitted 175.00
*343* A136 1sh grn & brn 60 8
*344* A137 1sh3p bl, brn & car 1.00 16
  *a* Carmine omitted 150.00
*345* A137 1sh6p org brn & olive grn 1.40 20
*346* A136 1sh9p pale brown 7.00 52
*347* A138 2sh buff & blk 1.90 14
*348* A139 2sh6p red brn & yellow 3.50 80
  *a* Yellow omitted 275.00
*349* A139 3sh gray brown 17.50 1.75
*350* A138 5sh dark green 8.75 70
*351* A139 10sh blue 7.00 4.25
*352* A138 £1 magenta 12.00 8.75
  *Nos. 333-352 (21)* 64.26 18.85

Nos. 334c and 337e were issued in coils.

Only on chalky paper: 2½p, 5p, 7p. On ordinary and chalky paper: 1p, 3p, 4p, 6p, 1sh9p, 2sh, 3sh, 5sh, 10sh. Others on ordinary paper only.

See Nos. 360-361, 382-404.

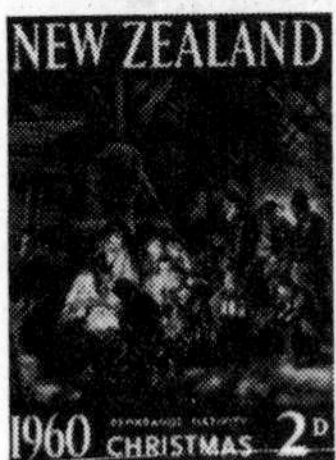


Adoration of the Shepherds, by Rembrandt A140

*Perf. 11½x12*

**1960, Nov. 1** **Wmk. 253**

**Size: 30x39½mm**

*353* A140 2p dp brn & red, *cream* 75 12
  *a* Red omitted *500.00 250.00*

Christmas 1960. See No. 355.

No. 309 Surcharged with New Value and Bars

Two types of surcharge:
I. "2½d" is 5½mm wide.
II. "2½d" is 5mm.

**1961, Sept. 1** **Engr.** ***Perf. 13½***

*354* A117 2½p on 3p vermilion, I 25 5
  *a* Type II 25 6

Type of 1960

Christmas: 2½p, Adoration of the Magi, by Dürer.

**1961, Oct. 16** **Photo.** ***Perf. 14½x14***

**Size: 30x34mm**

*355* A140 2½p multicolored 55 20

Morse Key and Port Hills, Lyttelton, 1862 A141

Design: 8p, Teleprinter and tape, 1962.

**1962, June 1** **Wmk. 253**

*356* A141 3p dk brn & grn 9 5
  *a* Green omitted
*357* A141 8p dk red & gray 1.90 1.90
  *a* Imperf. pair 900.00
  *b* Gray omitted 300.00

Centenary of the New Zealand telegraph.

Madonna in Prayer by Sassoferrato A142

**1962, Oct. 15** ***Perf. 14½x14***

*358* A142 2½p multicolored 40 6

Christmas 1962.

Holy Family by Titian A143

**1963, Oct. 14** **Photo.** ***Perf. 12½***

*359* A143 2½p multicolored 18 7
  *a* Imperf., pair *275.00*
  *b* Yellow omitted *400.00*

Christmas 1963.

Types of 1960-62

Designs: 1sh9p, Plane spraying farmland. 3sh, Ngauruhoe volcano, Tongariro National Park.

**1963-64** ***Perf. 14½x14***

*360* A136 1sh9p brt bl, grn & yel 1.65 85
*361* A139 3sh blue, green & bister ('64) 6.25 2.00

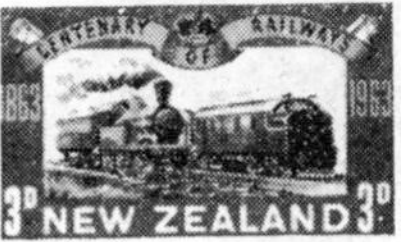


Old and New Engines A144

Design: 1sh9p, Express train and Mt. Ruapehu.

**1963, Nov. 25** ***Perf. 14***

*362* A144 3p multicolored 30 10
  *a* Blue (sky) omitted *300.00*
*363* A144 1sh9p bl, blk, yel & carmine 4.00 3.00
  *a* Carmine (value) omitted *750.00*

Centenary of New Zealand Railways.

Cable Around World and Under Sea — A144a

**1963, Dec. 3 Unwmk. *Perf. 13½***

*364* A147 8p yel, car, blk & bl 2.25 1.90

Opening of the Commonwealth Pacific (telephone) cable service (COMPAC).

See Australia No. 381.

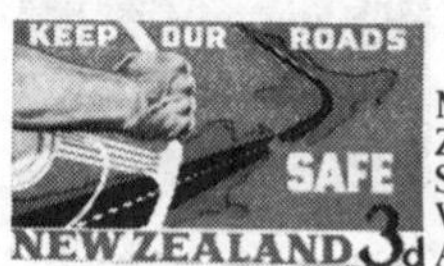


Map of New Zealand and Steering Wheel A145

***Perf. 14½x14***

**1964, May 1 Wmk. 253**

*365* A145 3p multicolored 18 8

National Road Safety Campaign.

Rev. Samuel Marsden Conducting First Christian Service, Rangihoua Bay, Christmas 1814 — A146

**1964, Oct. 12 *Perf. 14x13½***

*366* A146 2½p multicolored 22 7

Christmas 1964.

Postal-Fiscal Type of 1950

**1964, Dec. 14 Typo. *Perf. 14***

**Black Surcharge**

*367* A109 7p rose red 38 38

**ANZAC Issue**

Anzac Cove, Gallipoli A147

Design: 5p, Anzac Cove and poppy.

***Perf. 12½***

**1965, Apr. 14 Unwmk. Photo.**

*368* A147 4p light brown 12 6

*369* A147 5p green & red 35 35

50th anniv. of the landing of the Australian and New Zealand Army Corps, ANZAC, at Gallipoli, Turkey, Apr. 25, 1915.

ITU Emblem, Old and New Communication Equipment — A148

***Perf. 14½x14***

**1965, May 17 Photo. Wmk. 253**

*370* A148 9p lt brn & dk bl 60 60

Centenary of the ITU.

Sir Winston Spencer Churchill (1874-1965) — A148a

**1965, May 24 Unwmk. *Perf. 13½***

*371* A148a 7p lt bl, gray & blk 48 48

See Australia No. 389.

Provincial Council Building, Wellington A149

***Perf. 14½x14***

**1965, July 26 Photo. Wmk. 253**

*372* A149 4p multicolored 25 10

Centenary of the establishment of Wellington as seat of government. The design is from a water color by L. B. Temple, 1867.

ICY Emblem A150

**1965, Sept. 28 Litho. *Perf. 14***

*373* A150 4p ol bis & dk red 22 9

International Cooperation Year, 1965.

"The Two Trinities" by Murillo — A151

**1965, Oct. 11 Photo. *Perf. 13½x14***

*374* A151 3p multicolored 22 10

*a* Gold omitted 900.00

Christmas 1965.

Parliament House, Wellington and Commonwealth Parliamentary Association Emblem — A152

Designs: 4p, Arms of New Zealand and Queen Elizabeth II. 2sh, Wellington from Mt. Victoria.

**1965, Nov. 30 Unwmk. *Perf. 14***

*375* A152 4p multicolored 40 14

*a* Blue omitted 500.00

*376* A152 9p multicolored 1.40 95

*377* A152 2sh multicolored 5.00 4.50

11th Commonwealth Parliamentary Assoc. Conf.

Scout Emblem, Maori Pattern — A153

Virgin with Child, by Carlo Maratta — A154

***Perf. 14x14½***

**1966, Jan. 5 Photo. Wmk. 253**

*378* A153 4p green & gold 22 15

*a* Gold omitted 500.00

4th National Scout Jamboree, Trentham.

**1966, Oct. 3 Wmk. 253 *Perf. 14***

*379* A154 3p multicolored 25 15

Christmas 1966.

Queens Victoria and Elizabeth II — A155

Design: 9p, Reverse of half sovereign, 1867, and 1967 dollar.

***Perf. 14x14½***

**1967, Feb. 3 Photo. Wmk. 253**

*380* A155 4p plum, gold & blk 14 8

*381* A155 9p dk grn, bl, blk, sil & gold 45 45

New Zealand PO Savings Bank cent.

Types of 1960-62

Decimal Currency

Designs: ½c, Manuka flower. 1c, Karaka flower. 2c, Kaka beak flower. 2½c, Kowhai flower. 3c, Hibiscus. 4c, Mountain daisy. 5c, Clematis. 6c, Koromiko flower. 7c, Rata flower. 7½c, Brown trout. 8c, Flag. 10c, Timber industry. 15c, Tiki. 20c, Maori rock drawing. 25c, Butter making. 28c, Fox Glacier, Westland National Park. 30c, Ngauruhoe Volcano, Tongarino National Park. 50c, Sutherland Falls. $1, Tasman Glacier, Mount Cook. $2, Pohutu Geyser.

**Wmk. 253, Unwmkd. (#400)**

**1967-70 Photo. *Various Perfs.***

| | | | | | |
|---|---|---|---|---|---|
| *382* | A135 | ½c | multicolored | 10 | 5 |
| *383* | A135 | 1c | multicolored | 12 | 5 |
| *a* | | | Booklet pane of 5 + label | 2.25 | |
| *384* | A135 | 2c | multicolored | 12 | 5 |
| *385* | A135 | 2½c | multicolored | 15 | 5 |
| *386* | A135 | 3c | multicolored | 20 | 5 |
| *387* | A135 | 4c | multicolored | 30 | 8 |
| *388* | A135 | 5c | multicolored | 40 | 8 |
| *389* | A135 | 6c | multicolored | 75 | 25 |
| *390* | A135 | 7c | multicolored | 90 | 30 |
| *391* | A137 | 7½c | multicolored | 1.50 | 1.00 |
| *392* | A136 | 8c | ultra & car | 1.00 | 35 |
| *393* | A136 | 10c | grn & brn | 1.75 | 85 |
| *394* | A137 | 15c | org brn & slate green | 2.25 | 1.25 |
| *395* | A137 | 15c | grn, sl grn & red ('68) | 1.75 | 90 |
| *396* | A138 | 20c | buff & black | 2.50 | 35 |
| *397* | A139 | 25c | brn & yel | 2.75 | 2.00 |
| *398* | A138 | 28c | multi ('68) | 3.00 | 60 |
| *399* | A139 | 30c | multicolored | 7.50 | 2.50 |
| *400* | A139 | 30c | multi ('70) | 10.00 | 5.00 |
| *401* | A138 | 50c | dark green | 5.00 | 1.20 |
| *402* | A139 | $1 | blue | 12.50 | 5.00 |
| *403* | A138 | $2 | magenta | 15.00 | 12.50 |
| *404* | A138 | $2 | multi ('68) | 50.00 | 35.00 |
| | | | *Nos. 382-404 (23)* | 119.54 | 69.46 |

Perf. 13½x14: ½c to 3c, 5c, 7c. Perf. 14½x14: 4c, 6c, 8c, 10c, 25c, 30c, $1. Perf. 13½: 7½c. Perf. 14x14½: 15c, 20c, 28c, $2.

Issue dates: 7½c, Aug. 29, 1967. No. 395, Mar. 19, 1968. 28c, July 30, 1968. No. 404, Dec. 10, 1968. No. 400, 1970. Others, July 10, 1967.

The 7½c was issued to commemorate the centenary of the brown trout's introduction to New Zealand, and retained as part of the regular series.

No. 395 has been redrawn. The "c" on No. 395 lacks serif; No. 394 has serif.

An enhanced introduction to the Scott Catalogue begins on Page V. A thorough understanding of the material presented there will greatly aid your use of the catalogue itself.

Adoration of the Shepherds, by Poussin A156

Sir James Hector A157

***Perf. 13½x14***

**1967, Oct. 3 Photo. Wmk. 253**

*405* A156 2½c multicolored 18 10

Christmas 1967.

**1967, Oct. 10 Litho. *Perf. 14***

Design: 4c, Mt. Aspiring, aurora australis and Southern Cross.

*406* A157 4c multicolored 20 12

*407* A157 8c multicolored 50 48

Centenary of the Royal Society of New Zealand to Promote Science.

Maori Bible — A158

**1968, Apr. 23 Litho. *Perf. 13½***

*408* A158 3c multi 25 18

*a* gold omitted 100.00

Publication of the Bible in Maori, cent.

Soldiers of Two Eras and Tank A159

Designs: 10c, Airmen of two eras, insigne and plane. 28c, Sailors of two eras, insigne and battleships.

**1968, May 7 *Perf. 14x13½***

*409* A159 4c multi 30 15

*410* A159 10c multi 75 75

*411* A159 28c multi 2.75 2.75

Issued to honor the Armed Services.

"Universal Suffrage" — A160

Human Rights Flame — A161

***Perf. 13½***

**1968, Sept. 19 Photo. Unwmk.**

*412* A160 3c ol grn, lt bl & grn 15 12

*413* A161 10c dp grn, yel & red 60 60

75th anniv. of universal suffrage in New Zealand; Intl. Human Rights Year.

Adoration of the Holy Child, by Gerard van Honthorst A162

*Perf. 14x14½*

**968, Oct. 1 Wmk. 253**

*'14* A162 2½c multi 25 12

Christmas 1968.

Romney Marsh Sheep and Woolmark on Carpet A163

Designs: 7c, Trawler and catch. 8c, Apples nd orchard. 10c, Radiata pines and stacked umber. 20c, Cargo hoist and grazing cattle. 5c, Dairy farm in Taranaki, Mt. Egmont and rated dairy products.

**Wmk. 253 (10c, 18c, 25c); others Unwmkd.**

***Perf. 13½; 14½x14 (10c, 25c)***

**968-69 Litho.; Photo. (10c, 25c)**

*15* A163 7c multi ('69) 1.50 1.00
*16* A163 8c multi ('69) 1.50 1.00
*17* A163 10c multi 1.00 32
*18* A163 18c multi ('69) 1.50 80
*19* A163 20c multi ('69) 1.50 90
*20* A163 25c multi 4.75 2.50
*Nos. 415-420 (6)* 11.75 6.52

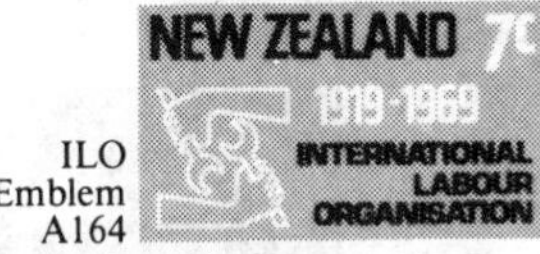

ILO Emblem A164

***Perf. 14½x14***

**1969, Feb. 11 Photo. Wmk. 253**

*421* A164 7c scar & blk 75 75

50th anniv. of the ILO.

Law Society Coat of Arms A165 Otago University A166

Designs: 3c, Supreme Court Building, Auckland (horiz.). 18c, "Justice" from memorial window of the University of Canterbury Hall, Christchurch.

**1969, Apr. 8 Litho. *Perf. 13½***

*422* A165 3c multi 15 8
*423* A165 10c multi 60 55
*424* A165 18c multi 2.50 2.00

Centenary of New Zealand Law Society.

**1969, June 3**

Design: 10c, Conferring degree and arms of the University (horiz.).

*425* A166 3c multi 14 9
*426* A166 10c multi 1.50 1.40

Centenary of the University of Otago.

Oldest House in New Zealand, Kerikeri A167

Design: 6c, Bay of Islands.

**1969, Aug. 18 Litho. Wmk. 253**

*427* A167 4c multi 70 70
*428* A167 6c multi 1.10 1.10

Early European settlements in New Zealand on the 150th anniv. of the founding of Kerikeri, the oldest existing European settlement.

Nativity, by Federico Fiori — A168

***Perf. 13½x14***

**1969, Oct. 1 Photo. Wmk. 253**

*429* A168 2½c multi 22 10

**Unwmk.**

*430* A168 2½c multi 22 16

Christmas 1969.

Capt. Cook, Transit of Venus and Octant A169

Designs: 6c, Joseph Banks and bark Endeavour. 18c, Dr. Daniel Solander and matata branch (rhabdothamnus solandri). 28c, Queen Elizabeth II and map showing Cook's chart of 1769.

**1969, Oct. 9 *Perf. 14½x14***

*431* A169 4c dk bl, blk & brt rose 50 50
*432* A169 6c sl grn & choc 1.00 1.00
*433* A169 18c choc, sl grn & blk 3.50 3.50
*434* A169 28c dk ultra, blk & brt rose 6.00 6.00
*a* Souv. sheet of 4 30.00 30.00

Bicentenary of Capt. Cook's landing in New Zealand.

No. 434a contains one each of Nos. 431-434; black marginal inscription. Size: 108x89mm.

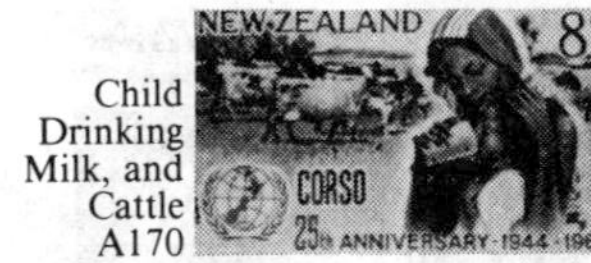

Child Drinking Milk, and Cattle A170

Design: 7c, Wheat and child with empty bowl.

**1969, Nov. 18 Photo. *Perf. 13***

*435* A170 7c multi 1.50 1.50
*436* A170 8c multi 1.70 1.70

25th anniv. of CORSO (Council of Organizations for Relief Services Overseas).

Cardigan Bay A171

**1970, Jan. 28 Unwmk. *Perf. 11½***

**Granite Paper**

*437* A171 10c multi 65 55

Return to New Zealand from the US of Cardigan Bay, 1st standard bred light-harness race horse to win a million dollars in stake money.

Glade Copper Butterfly A172 Scarlet Parrotfish A173

New Zealand Coat of Arms and Queen Elizabeth II — A174

Maori Fishhook A175

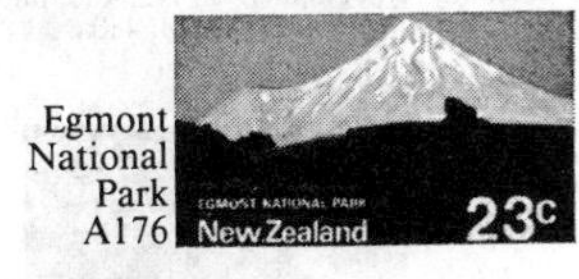

Egmont National Park A176

Hauraki Gulf Maritime Park — A177

Designs: 1c, Red admiral butterfly. 2c, Tussock butterfly. 2½c, Magpie moth. 3c, Lichen moth. 4c, Puriri moth. 6c, Sea horses. 7c, Leatherjackets (fish). 7½c, Garfish. 8c, John dory (fish). 18c, Maori club. 20c, Maori tattoo pattern. 30c, Mt. Cook National Park (chamois). 50c, Abel Tasman National Park. $1, Geothermal power plant. $2, Helicopter over field, molecule (agricultural technology).

**1970-71 Wmk. 253 *Perf. 13½x13***

*438* A172 ½c ultra & multi 20 16
*439* A172 1c dp bis & multi 14 10
*a* Bklt. pane of 3 + 3 labels ('71) 1.75
*440* A172 2c ol grn & multi 14 8
*441* A172 2½c yel & multi 40 15
*442* A172 3c brn & multi 16 8
*443* A172 4c dk brn & multi 16 12
*444* A173 5c dk grn & multi 30 14
*445* A173 6c dp car & multi 30 14
*446* A173 7c brn red & multi 45 20
*447* A173 7½c dk vio & multi 1.40 1.00
*448* A173 8c bl grn & multi 52 20

***Perf. 14½x14***

*449* A174 10c dk bl, sil, red & ultra 45 24

***Perf. 14x13, 13x14***

*450* A175 15c brick red, sal & blk ('71) 1.50 35
*451* A177 18c yel grn, blk & red brn ('71) 2.50 45
*452* A175 20c yel brn & blk ('71) 2.50 55

***Perf. 13½x12½***

**Unwmk.**

*453* A176 23c bl, grn & blk ('71) 60 30

**Litho. *Perf. 13½***

*454* A177 25c gray & multi ('71) 2.50 52
*a* Perf. 14 ('76) 90 30
*455* A177 30c tan & multi ('71) 1.50 50
*a* Perf. 14 ('76) 1.90 90

***Perf. 13½x12½***

**Photo.**

*456* A176 50c sl grn & multi ('71) 90 55

***Perf. 11½***

**Granite Paper**

*457* A175 $1 light ultra & multi ('71) 1.75 70
*458* A175 $2 ol & multi ('71) 3.25 1.50
*Nos. 438-458 (21)* 21.62 8.03

The 10c was issued Mar. 12, 1970, to commemorate the visit of Queen Elizabeth II, Prince Philip and Princess Anne.

See Nos. 533-546.

EXPO '70 Emblem, Geyser Restaurant — A178

Designs: 8c, EXPO '70 emblem and New Zealand Pavilion. 18c, EXPO '70 emblem and bush walk (part of N.Z. exhibit).

***Perf. 13x13½***

**1970, Apr. 8 Photo. Unwmk.**

*459* A178 7c multi 1.00 1.00
*460* A178 8c multi 1.00 1.00
*461* A178 18c multi 2.25 2.25

EXPO '70 Intl. Expo., Osaka, Japan.

UN Headquarters, New York — A179

UN, 25th anniv.: 10c, Plowing toward the sun and "25" with laurel.

**1970, June 24 Litho. *Perf. 13½***

*462* A179 3c multicolored 20 14
*463* A179 10c yellow & red 75 75

Adoration, by Correggio — A180

Tower, Catholic Church, Sockburn A181

Design: 3c, Holy Family, stained glass window, First Presbyterian Church, Invercargill.

**1970, Oct. 1 Unwmk. *Perf. 12½***

*464* A180 2½c multicolored 18 12
*465* A180 3c multicolored 22 22
*a* Green omitted 200.00
*466* A181 10c sil, org & blk 95 95

Christmas 1970.

Chatham Islands Mollymawk — A182

**1970, Dec. 2 Photo. *Perf. 13x13½***

*467* A182 1c Chatham Islands lily 15 15
*468* A182 2c shown 22 22

G Clef, Emblem and Spinning Wheel A183

Rotary Emblem and Map of New Zealand A184

**1971, Feb. 10 Photo.** ***Perf. 13x13½***

*469* A183 4c multicolored 22 22
*470* A184 10c lem, dk bl & gold 60 60

50th anniv. of Country Women's Inst. (4c) and Rotary Intl. in New Zealand (10c).

Ocean Racer A185

Design: 8c, One Ton Cup and blueprint of racing yacht.

**1971, Mar. 3 Litho.** ***Perf. 13½x13***

*471* A185 5c bl, blk & red 35 35
*472* A185 8c ultra & blk 85 85

First challenge in New Zealand waters for the One Ton Cup ocean race.

Coats of Arms A186

**1971, May 12 Photo.** ***Perf. 13x13½***

*473* A186 3c Palmerston North 15 8
*474* A186 4c Auckland 28 28
*475* A186 5c Invercargill 48 48

Centenary of New Zealand cities.

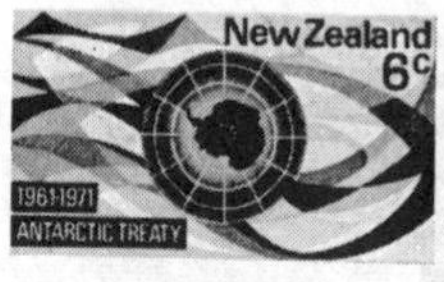

Map of Antarctica A187

**1971, June 9 Photo.** ***Perf. 13x13½***

*476* A187 6c dk bl, pur & grn 2.25 2.25

10th anniv. of the Antarctic Treaty pledging peaceful uses of and scientific cooperation in Antarctica.

Child on Swing — A188

**1971, June 9** ***Perf. 13½x13***

*477* 188 7c yellow & multi 1.10 1.10

25th anniv. of UNICEF.

Demand, as well as supply, determines a stamp's market value. One is as important as the other.

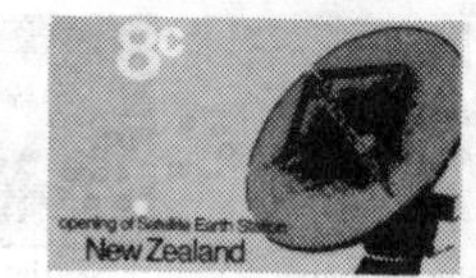

Opening of New Zealand's 1st satellite earth station near Warkworth — A189

**1971, July 14** ***Perf. 11½***

*478* A189 8c Radar Station 95 95
*479* A189 10c Satellite 1.25 1.25

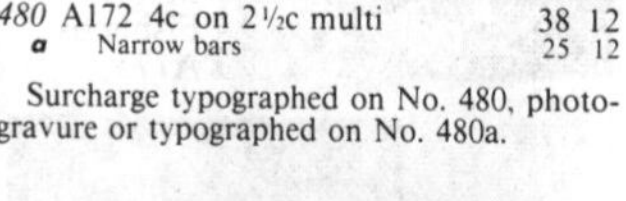

No. 441 Surcharged

**1971 Wmk. 253** ***Perf. 13½x13***

*480* A172 4c on 2½c multi 38 12
*a* Narrow bars 25 12

Surcharge typographed on No. 480, photogravure or typographed on No. 480a.

Holy Night, by Carlo Maratta — A190

The Three Kings A191

World Rose Convention A192

Christmas: 4c, Annunciation, stained glass window, St. Luke's Anglican Church, Havelock North.

***Perf. 13x13½***

**1971, Oct. 6 Photo. Unwmk.**

*481* A190 3c org & multi 18 12
*482* A191 4c multicolored 22 15
*483* A191 10c dk bl & multi 95 95

**1971, Nov. 3** ***Perf. 11½***

*484* A192 2c Tiffany rose 20 10
*485* A192 5c Peace rose 38 30
*486* A192 8c Chrysler Imperial rose 70 70

Rutherford and Alpha Particles Passing Atomic Nucleus A193

Design: 7c, Lord Rutherford, by Sir Oswald Birley, and formula of disintegration of nitrogen atom.

**1971, Dec. 1 Litho.** ***Perf. 13½x13***

*487* A193 1c gray & multi 12 12
*488* A193 7c multicolored 90 90

Centenary of the birth of Ernest Lord Rutherford (1871-1937), physicist.

Benz, 1895 A194

Vintage Cars: 4c, Oldsmobile, 1904. 5c, Model T Ford, 1914. 6c, Cadillac service car, 1915. 8c, Chrysler, 1924. 10c, Austin 7, 1923.

**1972, Feb. 2** ***Perf. 14x14½***

*489* A194 3c brn, car & multi 18 18
*490* A194 4c brt lil & multi 30 30
*491* A194 5c lil rose & multi 42 42
*492* A194 6c gray grn & multi 75 75
*493* A194 8c vio bl & multi 90 90
*494* A194 10c sepia & multi 1.90 1.90
*Nos. 489-494 (6)* 4.45 4.45

13th International Vintage Car Rally, New Zealand, Feb. 1972.

Asian-Oceanic Postal Union — A195

Designs: 3c, Wanganui City arms and Drurie Hill tower (vert). 5c, De Havilland DH89 and Boeing 737 planes (vert.). 8c, French frigate and Maori palisade at Motorua (vert.). 10c, Stone cairn at Kaeo (site of first Methodist mission).

**1972, Apr. 5** ***Perf. 13x14, 14x13***

*495* A195 3c vio & multi 10 8
*496* A195 4c brn org, blk & brn 15 12
*497* A195 5c blue & multi 25 25
*498* A195 8c green & multi 1.75 1.75
*499* A195 10c olive, yel & blk 2.10 2.10
*Nos. 495-499 (5)* 4.35 4.30

Cent. of Council government at Wanganui (3c); 10th anniv. of Asian-Oceanic Postal Union (4c); 25th anniv. of Nat. Airways Corp. (5c); bicent. of the landing by Marion du Fresne at the Bay of Islands (8c); 150th anniv. of the Methodist Church in New Zealand (10c).

Black Scree Cotula A196

Madonna and Child, by Murillo A197

Alpine Plants: 6c, North Is. edelweiss. 8c, Haast's buttercup. 10c, Brown mountain daisy.

**1972, June 7 Litho.** ***Perf. 13x14***

*500* A196 4c org & multi 32 22
*501* A196 6c dp bl & multi 65 65
*502* A196 8c rose lil & multi 1.10 1.10
*503* A196 10c yel grn & multi 3.25 3.25

**1972, Oct. 4 Photo.** ***Perf. 11½***

Christmas: 5c, Resurrection, stained-glass window, St. John's Methodist Church, Levin. 10c, Pohutukawa (New Zealand's Christmas flower).

*504* A197 3c gray & multi 10 9
*505* A197 5c gray & multi 20 20
*506* A197 10c gray & multi 1.10 1.10

New Zealand Lakes — A198

**1972, Dec. 6 Photo. Unwmk**

*507* A198 6c Waikaremoana 1.10 1.1
*508* A198 8c Hayes 1.50 1.5
*509* A198 18c Wakatipu 3.75 3.7
*510* A198 23c Rotomahana 4.00 4.0

Old Pollen Street A199

Coal Mining and Landscape A200

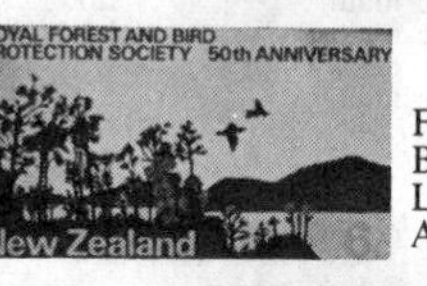

Cloister, University of Canterbury A201

Forest, Birds and Lake A202

Rowing and Olympic Emblems A203

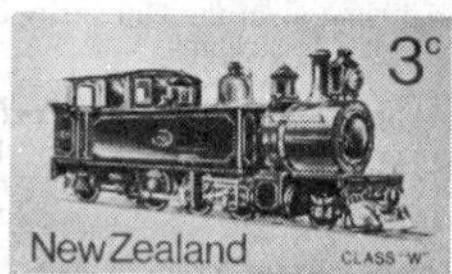

Progress Chart A204

**1973, Feb. 7 Litho.** ***Perf. 13½x1***

*511* A199 3c ocher & multi 15 1
*512* A200 4c blue & multi 18 1
*513* A201 5c multicolored 30 3
*514* A202 6c blue & multi 45 4
*515* A203 8c multicolored 90 9
*516* A204 10c blue & multi 1.50 1.5
*Nos. 511-516 (6)* 3.48 3.4

Centenaries of Thames and Westport Boroughs (3c, 4c); centenary of the Univ. of Canterbury, Christchurch (5c); 50th anniv. o Royal Forest and Bird Protection Soc. (6c) success of New Zealand rowing team at 20th Olympic Games (8c); 25th anniv. of the Economic Commission for Asia and the Far Eas (ECAFE, 10c).

Class W Locomotive, 1889 — A205

New Zealand Steam Locomotives: 4c, Class X, 1908. 5c, "Passchendale" Ab Class. 10c, Ja Class, last steam locomotive.

**1973, Apr. 4 Litho.** ***Perf. 14½***

*517* A205 3c lt grn & multi 45 30
*518* A205 4c lil rose & multi 60 42
*519* A205 5c lt bl & multi 90 60
*520* A205 10c cream & multi 2.50 1.75

Maori Woman and Child, by Hodgkins A206

Christmas in New Zealand A207

Paintings by Frances Hodgkins: 8c, The Hill Top. 10c, Barn in Picardy. 18c, Self-portrait, Still Life.

**1973, June 6 Photo. *Perf. 12x11½***

| | | | | | |
|---|---|---|---|---|---|
| *521* | A206 | 5c | multicolored | 35 | 35 |
| *522* | A206 | 8c | multicolored | 90 | 90 |
| *523* | A206 | 10c | multicolored | 1.40 | 1.40 |
| *524* | A206 | 18c | multicolored | 2.00 | 2.00 |

**1973, Oct. 3 Photo. *Perf. 12½x13½***

Christmas: 3c, Tempi Madonna, by Raphael. 5c, Three Kings, stained-glass window, St. Theresa's R.C. Church, Auckland.

| | | | | | |
|---|---|---|---|---|---|
| *525* | A207 | 3c | gold & multi | 14 | 11 |
| *526* | A207 | 5c | gold & multi | 25 | 25 |
| *527* | A207 | 10c | gold & multi | 95 | 95 |

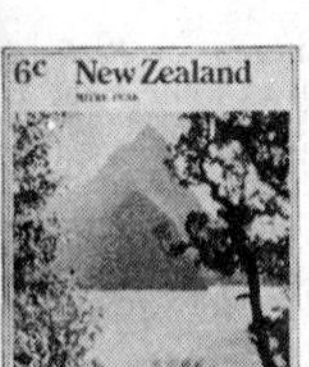


Mitre Peak — A208

Hurdles and Games' Emblem — A209

***Perf. 13x13½, 13½x13***

**1973, Dec. 5 Photo.**

| | | | | | |
|---|---|---|---|---|---|
| *528* | A208 | 6c | *shown* | 65 | 60 |
| *529* | A208 | 8c | *Mt. Ngauruhoe* | 1.10 | 1.10 |
| *530* | A208 | 18c | *Mt. Sefton* (horiz.) | 2.25 | 2.25 |
| *531* | A208 | 23c | *Burnett Range* (horiz.) | 2.75 | 2.75 |

Types of 1970-71

Designs as before.

***Perf. 13½x13***

**1973-76 Photo. Unwmk.**

| | | | | | |
|---|---|---|---|---|---|
| *533* | A172 | 1c | multi ('74) | 28 | 8 |
| *534* | A172 | 2c | multicolored | 35 | 14 |
| *536* | A172 | 3c | multi ('75) | 42 | 20 |
| *537* | A172 | 4c | multicolored | 50 | 14 |
| *538* | A173 | 5c | multi ('75) | 50 | 25 |
| *539* | A173 | 6c | multi ('74) | 50 | 25 |
| *540* | A173 | 7c | multi ('75) | 70 | 50 |
| *542* | A173 | 8c | multi ('75) | 1.75 | 70 |

***Perf. 14x13½***

| | | | | | |
|---|---|---|---|---|---|
| *543* | A174 | 10c | multicolored | 90 | 28 |

***Perf. 13x14, 14x13***

| | | | | | |
|---|---|---|---|---|---|
| *544* | A175 | 15c | multi ('76) | 1.00 | 42 |
| *545* | A177 | 18c | multi ('75) | 1.25 | 55 |
| *546* | A175 | 20c | yel brn & blk ('75) | 1.25 | 55 |
| | | | *Nos. 533-546 (12)* | 9.40 | 4.06 |

**1974, Jan. 9 Litho. *Perf. 13x13½***

Designs: 5c, Paraplegic ballplayer. 10c, Bicycling. 18c, Rifle shooting. 23c, Lawn bowling. 4c, 10c, 18c and 23c stamps also show Commonwealth Games' emblem.

| | | | | | |
|---|---|---|---|---|---|
| *547* | A109 | 4c | yel & multi | 14 | 14 |
| *548* | A109 | 5c | vio & blk | 18 | 18 |
| *549* | A109 | 10c | brt red & multi | 40 | 40 |
| *550* | A109 | 18c | brown & multi | 80 | 80 |
| *551* | A109 | 23c | yel grn & multi | 1.10 | 1.10 |
| | | | *Nos. 547-551 (5)* | 2.62 | 2.62 |

10th British Commonwealth Games, Christchurch, Jan. 24-Feb. 2. No. 548 publicizes the 4th Paraplegic Games, Dunedin, Jan. 10-20.

New Zealand Day — A210

Illustration reduced.

**1974, Feb. 6 Litho. *Perf. 13***

| | | | | |
|---|---|---|---|---|
| *552* | A210 | Souvenir sheet of 5 | 2.00 | 2.00 |
| *a* | | 4c *Treaty House, Waitangi* | 25 | 25 |
| *b* | | 4c *Parliament extension buildings* | 25 | 25 |
| *c* | | 4c *Signing Treaty of Waitangi* | 25 | 25 |
| *d* | | 4c *Queen Elizabeth II* | 25 | 25 |
| *e* | | 4c *Integrated school* | 25 | 25 |

New Zealand Day (Waitangi Day). No. 552 has marginal inscription and imprint in black. Size: 131x74mm.

"Spirit of Napier" Fountain — A211

Clock Tower, Bern — A212

Design: 8c, UPU emblem.

**1974, Apr. 3 Photo. *Perf. 11½***

| | | | | | |
|---|---|---|---|---|---|
| *553* | A211 | 4c | bl grn & multi | 15 | 15 |
| *554* | A212 | 5c | brown & multi | 18 | 18 |
| *555* | A212 | 8c | lemon & multi | 1.10 | 1.10 |

Centenaries of Napier (4c); UPU (5c, 8c).

Boeing Seaplane, 1919 A213

Designs: 4c, Lockheed Electra, 1937. 5c, Bristol freighter, 1958. 23c, Empire S40 flying boat, 1940.

**1974, June 5 Litho. *Perf. 14x13***

| | | | | | |
|---|---|---|---|---|---|
| *556* | A213 | 3c | multicolored | 25 | 20 |
| *557* | A213 | 4c | multicolored | 32 | 25 |
| *558* | A213 | 5c | multicolored | 42 | 32 |
| *559* | A213 | 23c | multicolored | 2.75 | 2.25 |

Development of New Zealand's air transport.

Adoration of the Kings, by Conrad Witz — A214

Christmas: 5c, Angels, stained glass window, St. Paul's Church, Wellington. 10c, Christmas lily (lilium candidum).

**1974, Oct. 2 Photo. *Perf. 11½***

**Granite Paper**

| | | | | | |
|---|---|---|---|---|---|
| *560* | A214 | 3c | olive & multi | 12 | 6 |
| *561* | A214 | 5c | lilac & multi | 22 | 22 |
| *562* | A214 | 10c | orange & multi | 1.00 | 60 |

Offshore Islands — A215

**1974, Dec. 4 Photo. *Perf. 13½x13***

| | | | | | |
|---|---|---|---|---|---|
| *563* | A215 | 6c | *Great Barrier* | 28 | 28 |
| *564* | A215 | 8c | *Stewart* | 75 | 75 |
| *565* | A215 | 18c | *White* | 1.25 | 1.25 |
| *566* | A215 | 23c | *The Brothers* | 1.90 | 1.90 |

Child Using Walker A216

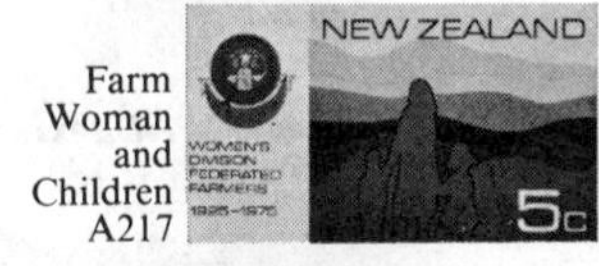


Farm Woman and Children A217

IWY Symbol A218

Otago Medical School A219

**1975, Feb. 5 Litho. *Perf. 13½x13***

| | | | | | |
|---|---|---|---|---|---|
| *567* | A216 | 3c | orange & multi | 10 | 10 |
| *568* | A217 | 5c | green & multi | 15 | 15 |
| *569* | A218 | 10c | blue & multi | 50 | 50 |
| *570* | A219 | 18c | multicolored | 1.00 | 1.00 |

New Zealand Crippled Children's Soc., 40th anniv. (3c); Women's Division Federated Farmers of N. Z., 50th anniv. (5c); IWY (10c); Otago Medical School cent. (18c).

Scow "Lake Erie," 1873 A220

Historic Sailing Ships: 5c, Schooner "Herald," 1826. 8c, Brigantine "New Zealander," 1828. 10c, Topsail schooner "Jessie Kelly," 1866. 18c, Barque "Tory," 1834. 23c, Clipper "Rangitiki," 1863.

**1975, Apr. 2 Litho. *Perf. 13½x13***

| | | | | | |
|---|---|---|---|---|---|
| *571* | A220 | 4c | vermilion & blk | 18 | 12 |
| *572* | A220 | 5c | grnsh bl & blk | 24 | 15 |
| *573* | A220 | 8c | yellow & black | 45 | 28 |
| *574* | A220 | 10c | yel grn & blk | 55 | 35 |
| *575* | A220 | 18c | brown & black | 1.40 | 1.10 |
| *576* | A220 | 23c | dull lil & blk | 1.75 | 1.40 |
| | | | *Nos. 571-576 (6)* | 4.57 | 3.40 |

State Forest Parks A221

**1975, June 4 Photo. *Perf. 13½x13***

| | | | | | |
|---|---|---|---|---|---|
| *577* | A221 | 6c | *Lake Sumner* | 40 | 30 |
| *578* | A221 | 8c | *North West Nelson* | 75 | 45 |
| *579* | A221 | 18c | *Kaweka* | 1.50 | 1.10 |
| *580* | A221 | 23c | *Coromandel* | 2.00 | 1.50 |

Virgin and Child, by Zanobi Machiavelli (1418-1479) — A222

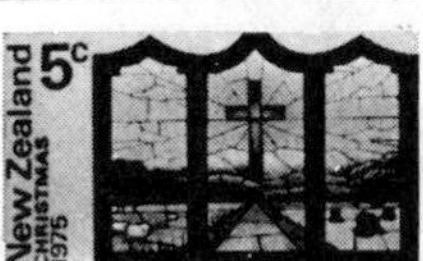


Stained Glass Window, Greendale Methodist/Presbyterian Church — A223

Christmas: 10c, Medieval ships and doves.

***Perf. 13½x14, 14x13½***

**1975, Oct. 1 Photo.**

| | | | | | |
|---|---|---|---|---|---|
| *581* | A222 | 3c | multicolored | 14 | 14 |
| *582* | A223 | 5c | multicolored | 22 | 22 |
| *583* | A223 | 10c | multicolored | 95 | 65 |

Sterling Silver — A224

Roses: 2c, Lilli Marlene. 3c, Queen Elizabeth. 4c, Super star. 5c, Diamond jubilee. 6c, Cresset. 7c, Michele Meilland. 8c, Josephine Bruce. 9c, Iceberg.

***Perf. 14½x14; 14½ (6c, 7c, 8c)***

**1975, Nov. 26 Photo.**

| | | | | | |
|---|---|---|---|---|---|
| *584* | A224 | 1c | multicolored | 5 | 5 |
| *585* | A224 | 2c | orange & multi | 5 | 5 |
| *586* | A224 | 3c | ultra & multi | 7 | 5 |
| *a* | | | Perf. 14½ ('79) | 12 | 5 |
| *587* | A224 | 4c | purple & multi | 9 | 6 |
| *588* | A224 | 5c | brown & multi | 11 | 8 |
| *589* | A224 | 6c | multicolored | 40 | 22 |
| *a* | | | Perf. 14½x14 ('76) | 14 | 10 |
| *590* | A224 | 7c | multicolored | 40 | 22 |
| *a* | | | Perf. 14½x 14 ('76) | 15 | 11 |
| *591* | A224 | 8c | yellow & multi | 40 | 22 |
| *a* | | | Perf. 14½x14 ('76) | 18 | 14 |
| *592* | A224 | 9c | blue & multi | 9 | 7 |
| | | | *Nos. 584-592 (9)* | 1.66 | 1.02 |

Family and Mothers' League Emblem A225

Designs: 7c, "Weight, measure, temperature and capacity." 8c, 1st emigrant ship "William Bryan" and Mt. Egmont. 10c, Maori and Caucasian women and YWCA emblem. 25c, Telecommunications network on Goode's equal area projection.

**1976, Feb. 4 Litho. *Perf. 14***

| | | | | | |
|---|---|---|---|---|---|
| *593* | A225 | 6c | olive & multi | 18 | 14 |
| *594* | A225 | 7c | lilac & multi | 20 | 18 |
| *595* | A225 | 8c | red & multi | 25 | 20 |
| *596* | A225 | 10c | yellow & multi | 32 | 30 |
| *597* | A225 | 25c | tan & multi | 80 | 70 |
| | | | *Nos. 593-597 (5)* | 1.75 | 1.52 |

League of Mothers of New Zealand, 50th anniv. (6c); Metric conversion, 1976 (7c); cent. of New Plymouth (8c); YWCA in New Zealand, 50th anniv. (10c); cent. of link into intl. telecommunications network (25c).

Gig A226

Farm Vehicles: 7c, Thornycroft truck. 8c, Scandi wagon. 9c, Traction engine. 10c, Wool wagon. 25c, One-horse cart.

**1976, Apr. 7 Litho. *Perf. 14x13½***

| | | | | | |
|---|---|---|---|---|---|
| *598* | A226 | 6c | dk ol & multi | 30 | 25 |
| *599* | A226 | 7c | gray & multi | 38 | 30 |
| *600* | A226 | 8c | dk bl & multi | 1.75 | 75 |
| *601* | A226 | 9c | maroon & multi | 60 | 50 |
| *602* | A226 | 10c | brown & multi | 85 | 50 |
| *603* | A226 | 25c | multicolored | 2.75 | 1.75 |
| | | | *Nos. 598-603 (6)* | 6.63 | 4.05 |

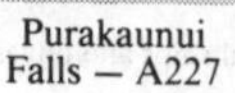

Purakaunui Falls — A227

Nativity, Carved Ivory, Spain, 16th Century — A228

Waterfalls: 14c, Marakopa Falls. 15c, Bridal Veil Falls. 16c, Papakorito Falls.

**1976, June 2 Photo. *Perf. 11½***

| | | | | |
|---|---|---|---|---|
| *604* | A227 10c blue & multi | 32 | 32 |
| *605* | A227 14c lilac & multi | 65 | 42 |
| *606* | A227 15c ocher & multi | 75 | 50 |
| *607* | A227 16c multicolored | 85 | 65 |

***Perf. 14x14½, 14½x14***

**1976, Oct. 6 Photo.**

Christmas: 11c, Risen Christ, St. Joseph's Church, Grey Lynn, Auckland (horiz.). 18c, "Hark the Herald Angels Sing" (horiz.).

| | | | |
|---|---|---|---|
| *608* | A228 7c ocher & multi | 15 | 15 |
| *609* | A228 11c ocher & multi | 60 | 50 |
| *610* | A228 18c ocher & multi | 1.25 | 90 |

Maripi (Carved Wooden Knife) — A229

Maori Artifacts: 12c, Putorino, carved flute. 13c, Wahaika, hardwood club. 14c, Kotiate, violin-shaped weapon.

**1976, Nov. 24 Photo. *Perf. 11½***
**Granite Paper**

| | | | |
|---|---|---|---|
| *611* | A229 11c multicolored | 20 | 9 |
| *612* | A229 12c multicolored | 20 | 10 |
| *613* | A229 13c multicolored | 22 | 12 |
| *614* | A229 14c multicolored | 24 | 14 |

Arms of Hamilton A230

Automobile Assoc. Emblem A231

Designs: No. 616, Arms of Gisborne. No. 617, Arms of Masterton. No. 619, Emblem of Royal Australasian College of Surgeons.

**1977, Jan. 19 Litho. *Perf. 13x13½***

| | | | |
|---|---|---|---|
| *615* | A230 8c multicolored | 32 | 20 |
| *616* | A230 8c multicolored | 32 | 20 |
| *617* | A230 8c multicolored | 32 | 20 |
| *618* | A231 10c multicolored | 42 | 32 |
| *619* | A230 10c multicolored | 42 | 32 |
| | *Nos. 615-619 (5)* | 1.80 | 1.24 |

Centenaries of Hamilton, Gisborne and Masterton (cities); 75th anniv. of the New Zealand Automobile Assoc. and 50th anniv. of the Royal Australasian College of Surgeons. Stamps of same denomination printed se-tenant in sheets of 100 (10x10).

Souvenir Sheet

Queen Elizabeth II, 1976 — A232

Designs: Various portraits.

**1977, Feb. Photo. *Perf. 14x14½***

| | | | |
|---|---|---|---|
| *620* | sheet of 5 | 1.40 | 1.40 |
| *a.-e.* | A232 8c, single stamp | 12 | 12 |
| *f* | Sheet imperf. | | |

25th anniv. of the reign of Elizabeth II. No. 620 has black marginal inscription and silver decoration. Size: 180x80mm.

Physical Education, Maori Culture — A233

Education Dept., Geography, Science — A234

Designs: No. 623, Special school for the deaf; kindergarten. No. 624, Language class. No. 625, Home economics, correspondence school, teacher training.

**1977, Apr. 6 Litho. *Perf. 13x13½***

| | | | |
|---|---|---|---|
| *621* | A233 8c multicolored | 65 | 65 |
| *622* | A234 8c multicolored | 65 | 65 |
| *623* | A233 8c multicolored | 65 | 65 |
| *624* | A234 8c multicolored | 65 | 65 |
| *625* | A233 8c multicolored | 65 | 65 |
| | *Nos. 621-625 (5)* | 3.25 | 3.25 |

Cent. of Education Act, establishing Dept. of Education. Nos. 621-625 printed se-tenant in sheets of 100.

Karitane Beach — A235

Seascapes and beach scenes: 16c, Ocean Beach, Mount Maunganui. 18c, Piha Beach. 30c, Kaikoura Coast.

**1977, June 1 Photo. *Perf. 14½***

| | | | |
|---|---|---|---|
| *626* | A235 10c multicolored | 22 | 22 |
| *627* | A235 16c multicolored | 32 | 32 |
| *628* | A235 18c multicolored | 40 | 40 |
| *629* | A235 30c multicolored | 65 | 65 |

Nos. 536-537 Surcharged with New Value and Heavy Bar

**1977 Unwmk. *Perf. 13½x13***

| | | | |
|---|---|---|---|
| *630* | A172 7c on 3c multicolored | 38 | 38 |
| *631* | A172 8c on 4c multicolored | 38 | 38 |

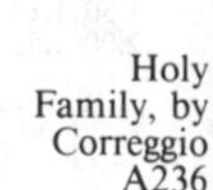

Holy Family, by Correggio A236

Window, St. Michael's and All Angels Church — A237

Partridge in a Pear Tree — A238

**1977, Oct. 5 Photo. *Perf. 11½***

| | | | |
|---|---|---|---|
| *632* | A236 7c multicolored | 16 | 16 |
| *633* | A237 16c multicolored | 45 | 35 |
| *634* | A238 23c multicolored | 70 | 52 |

Christmas 1977.

Merryweather Manual Pump, 1860 — A239

Fire Fighting Equipment: 11c, 2-wheel hose reel and ladder, 1880. 12c, Shand Mason Steam Fire Engine, 1873. 23c, Chemical fire engine, 1888.

**1977, Dec. 7 Litho. *Perf. 14x13½***

| | | | |
|---|---|---|---|
| *635* | A239 10c multicolored | 24 | 24 |
| *636* | A239 11c multicolored | 28 | 28 |
| *637* | A239 12c multicolored | 30 | 30 |
| *638* | A239 23c multicolored | 55 | 55 |

A240

A240a

Parliament Building, Wellington — A241

A242

**1977, Dec. 7 Photo. *Perf. 14½x14***

| | | | |
|---|---|---|---|
| *648* | A240 10c ultra & multi | 50 | 32 |
| *b* | Perf. 14½ ('79) | 12 | 10 |
| *649* | A240a 24c bl & lt grn ('83) | 30 | 30 |
| *a* | Perf. 13x12½ ('82) | 30 | 30 |
| *650* | A241 $5 multi | 6.50 | 6.50 |

Coil Stamps

**1978 Photo. *Perf. 13½x13***

| | | | |
|---|---|---|---|
| *651* | A242 1c red lilac | 5 | 5 |
| *652* | A242 2c orange | 5 | 5 |
| *653* | A242 5c brown | 10 | 10 |

***Perf. 14½x14***

| | | | |
|---|---|---|---|
| *654* | A242 10c ultramarine | 20 | 15 |

Ashburton A244

Stratford A245

Old Telephone — A246

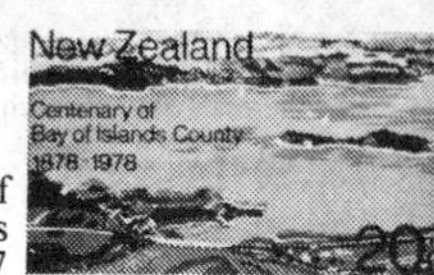


Bay of Islands A247

**1978, Feb. 1 Litho. *Perf. 14***

| | | | |
|---|---|---|---|
| *656* | A244 10c multicolored | 20 | 20 |
| *657* | A245 10c multicolored | 20 | 20 |
| *658* | A246 12c multicolored | 28 | 28 |
| *659* | A247 20c multicolored | 45 | 45 |

Cent. of the cities of Ashburton, Stratford, the NZ Telephone Co. and Bay of Islands County. Nos. 656-657 printed se-tenant in sheets of 100.

Students and Ivey Hall — A248

Maui Gas Drilling Platform — A249

Designs: 12c, Grazing sheep. 15c, Mechanical fertilization. 16c, Furrow, plow and tractor. 20c, Combine harvester. 30c, Grazing cattle.

**1978, Apr. 26 *Perf. 14½***

| | | | |
|---|---|---|---|
| *660* | A248 10c multicolored | 18 | 18 |
| *661* | A248 12c multicolored | 20 | 20 |
| *662* | A248 15c multicolored | 25 | 25 |
| *663* | A248 16c multicolored | 25 | 25 |
| *664* | A248 20c multicolored | 32 | 32 |
| *665* | A248 30c multicolored | 50 | 50 |
| | *Nos. 660-665 (6)* | 1.70 | 1.70 |

Cent. of Lincoln Univ. College of Agriculture.

**1978, June 7 Litho. *Perf. 13½x14***

The sea and its resources: 15c, Fishing boat. 20c, Map of New Zealand and 200-mile limit. 23c, Whale and bottle-nosed dolphins. 35c, Kingfish, snapper, grouper and squid.

| | | | |
|---|---|---|---|
| *666* | A249 12c multicolored | 24 | 18 |
| *667* | A249 15c multicolored | 28 | 24 |
| *668* | A249 20c multicolored | 32 | 28 |
| *669* | A249 23c multicolored | 40 | 32 |
| *670* | A249 35c multicolored | 70 | 50 |
| | *Nos. 666-670 (5)* | 1.94 | 1.52 |

All Saints Church, Howick A250

Christmas: 7c, Holy Family, by El Greco (vert.). 23c, Beach scene.

**1978, Oct. 4 Photo. Perf. 11½**
*671* A250 7c gold & multi 18 18
*672* A250 16c gold & multi 45 45
*673* A250 23c gold & multi 60 60

Paua (Haliotis Iris) — A251

Sea Shells: 30c, Toheroa (paphies ventricosa). 40c, Coarse dosinia (dosinia anus). 50c, Spiny murex (poirieria zelandica).

**1978, Nov. 29 Photo. Perf. 13x12½**
*674* A251 20c multicolored 28 20
*675* A251 30c multicolored 45 30
*676* A251 40c multicolored 55 45
*677* A251 50c multicolored 70 52

See Nos. 696-697.

Julius Vogel — A252

Portraits: No. 679, George Grey. No. 680, Richard John Seddon.

**1979, Feb. 7 Litho. Perf. 13x13½**
*678* A252 10c lt & dk brn 38 30
*679* A252 10c lt & dk brn 38 30
*680* A252 10c lt & dk brn 38 30

19th cent. NZ statesmen. Nos. 678-680 printed se-tenant horizontally in sheets of 100 (10x10), No. 678 appears in first and last rows.

Riverlands Cottage, Blenheim A253

Early NZ Architecture: 12c, Mission House, Waimate North, 1831-32. 15c, The Elms, Anglican Church Mission, Tauranga, 1847. 20c, Provincial Council Buildings, Christchurch, 1859.

**1979, Apr. 4 Perf. 13½x13**
*681* A253 10c multicolored 15 15
*682* A253 12c multicolored 20 20
*683* A253 15c black & gray 25 25
*684* A253 20c multicolored 32 32

Whangaroa Harbor — A254

Small Harbors: 20c, Kawau Island. 23c, Akaroa Harbor (vert.). 35c, Picton Harbor (vert.).

**Perf. 13x13½, 13½x13**
**1979, June 6 Photo.**
*685* A254 15c multicolored 22 22
*686* A254 20c multicolored 30 30
*687* A254 23c multicolored 32 32
*688* A254 35c multicolored 52 52

IYC A255

**1979, June 6 Litho. Perf. 14**
*689* A255 10c Children playing 25 20

Virgin and Child, by Lorenzo Ghiberti — A256

Christmas: 25c, Christ Church, Russell, 1835. 35c, Pohutakawa ("Christmas") tree.

**1979, Oct. 3 Photo. Perf. 11½**
*690* A256 10c multicolored 12 12
*691* A256 25c multicolored 35 30
*692* A256 35c multicolored 45 42

### Nos. 591, 648 and 589 Surcharged

**1979, Sept. Perf. 14½, 14½x14 (14c)**
*693* A224 4c on 8c multi 8 6
*694* A240 14c on 10c multi 20 15
*695* A224 17c on 6c multi 25 18

### Shell Type of 1978

Sea Shells: $1, Scallop (pecten novaezelandiae). $2, Circular saw (astraea heliotropium).

**1979, Nov. 26 Photo. Perf. 13x12½**
*696* A251 $1 multicolored 1.25 1.00
*697* A251 $2 multicolored 2.75 1.25

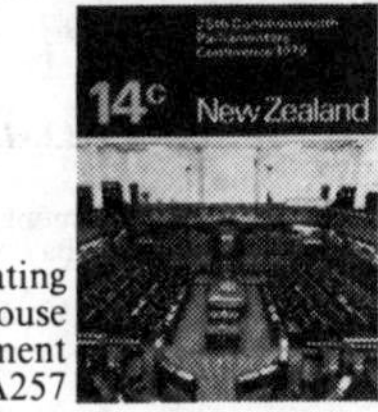


Debating Chamber, House of Parliament A257

**1979, Nov. 26 Litho. Perf. 14x13½**
*698* A257 14c *shown* 18 18
*699* A257 20c *Mace, black rod* 28 28
*700* A257 30c *Wall hanging* 45 45

25th Commonwealth Parliamentary Conference, Wellington, Nov. 26-Dec. 2.

NZ No. 1 A258

**1980, Feb. 7 Litho. Perf. 14x13½**
*701* A258 14c *shown* 35 35
*702* A258 14c *No. 2* 35 35
*703* A258 14c *No. 3* 35 35
*a* Souvenir sheet of 3 3.75 3.75

Nos. 701-703 printed se-tenant.
NZ postage stamps, 125th anniv. No. 703a publicizes Zeapex '80 Intl. Stamp Exhib., Auckland, Aug. 23-31; it contains Nos. 701-703; dark brown and dull yellow margin shows portrait of Queen Victoria. Size: 146x95mm. Sold for 52c, of which 10c went to exhib. fund.

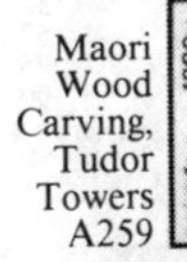
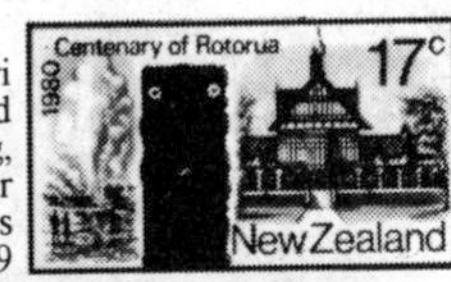


Maori Wood Carving, Tudor Towers A259

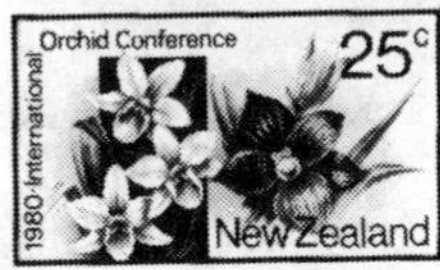


Earina Autumnalis and Thelymitra Venosa — A260

Tractor Plowing, Golden Plow Trophy A261

**1980, Feb. 7 Perf. 14½**
*704* A259 17c multicolored 24 24
*705* A260 25c multicolored 35 35
*706* A261 30c multicolored 45 45

Rotorua cent.; Intl. Orchid Conf., Auckland, Oct.; World Plowing Championship, Christchurch, May.

Ewelme Cottage, Parnell, 1864 A262

Early NZ Architecture: 17c, Broadgreen, Nelson, 1855. 25c, Courthouse, Oamaru, 1822. 30c, Government Buildings, Wellington, 1877.

**1980, Apr. 2 Litho. Perf. 13½x13**
*707* A262 14c multicolored 18 18
*708* A262 17c multicolored 22 22
*709* A262 25c multicolored 32 32
*710* A262 30c multicolored 40 40

Harbors — A263

**1980, June 4 Photo. Perf. 13x13½**
*711* A263 25c *Auckland* 32 32
*712* A263 30c *Wellington* 40 40
*713* A263 35c *Lyttelton* 45 45
*714* A263 50c *Port Chalmers* 65 65

Madonna and Child with Cherubim, by Andrea della Robbia — A264

**1980, Oct. 1 Photo. Perf. 12**
*715* A264 10c *shown* 12 12
*716* A264 25c *St. Mary's Church, New Plymouth* 32 32
*717* A264 35c *Picnic* 45 45

Christmas 1980.

### No. 590 Surcharged

**1980, Sept. 29 Photo. Perf. 14½x14**
*718* A224 20c on 7c multi 28 28

Te Heu Heu Tukino IV, Ngati Tuwharetoa Tribal Chief — A265

Maori Leaders: 25c, Te Hau-Takiri Wharepapa. 35c, Princess Te Puea Herangi. 45, Apirana Ngata. 60c, Hakopa Te Ata-o-tu.

**1980, Nov. 26 Perf. 13**
*719* A265 15c multicolored 20 20
*720* A265 25c multicolored 32 32
*721* A265 35c multicolored 45 45
*722* A265 45c multicolored 60 60
*723* A265 60c multicolored 85 85
*Nos. 719-723 (5)* 2.42 2.42

Henry A. Feilding, Borough Emblem A266

**1981, Feb. 4 Litho. Perf. 14½**
*724* A266 20c multicolored 28 28

Borough of Feilding centenary.

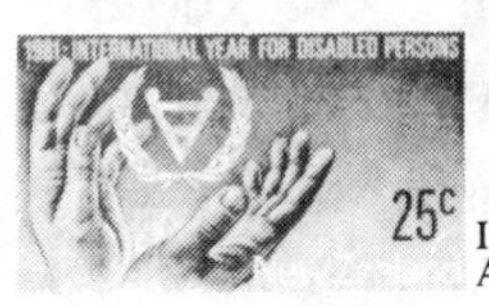


IYD A267

**1981, Feb. 4**
*725* A267 25c orange & black 35 35

Family and Dog — A268

**1981, Apr. 1 Litho. Perf. 13**
*726* A268 20c shown 25 25
*727* A268 25c Grandparents 32 32
*728* A268 30c Parents reading to children 40 40
*729* A268 35c Family outing 45 45

Shotover River — A269

**1981, June 3 Photo. Perf. 13½**
*730* A269 30c Kaiauai River, vert. 40 40
*731* A269 35c Mangahao River, vert. 45 45
*732* A269 40c shown 52 52
*733* A269 60c Cleddau River 85 85

Prince Charles and Lady Diana A270

**1981, July 29 Litho. Perf. 14½**
*734* A270 20c shown 40 40
*735* A270 20c St. Paul's Cathedral 40 40

Royal Wedding. Nos. 734-735 se-tenant.

Golden Tainui — A271

Christmas 1981: 14c, Madonna and Child, by Marco d'Oggiono, 15th cent. 30c, St. John's Church, Wakefield.

**1981, Oct. Photo. *Perf. 11½***
**Granite Paper**

*736* A271 14c multicolored 18 18
*737* A271 30c multicolored 40 40
*738* A271 40c multicolored 52 52

SPCA Centenary A272

Intl. Science Year A273

Centenaries: No. 739, Tauranga. No. 740, Hawera. 30c, Frozen meat exports. Nos. 739-740 se-tenant.

**1982, Feb. 3 Litho. *Perf. 14½***

*739* A272 20c multicolored 28 28
*740* A272 20c multicolored 28 28
*741* A272 25c multicolored 35 35
*742* A272 30c multicolored 45 45
*743* A273 35c multicolored 50 50
*Nos. 739-743 (5)* 1.86 1.86

Alberton Farmhouse, Auckland, 1867 — A274

**1982, Apr. 7 Litho.**

*744* A274 20c shown 24 24
*745* A274 25c Caccia Birch, Palmerston North, 1893 30 30
*746* A274 30c Dunedin Railway Station, 1904 35 35
*747* A274 35c PO, Ophir, 1886 42 42

Summer, Kaiteriteri A275

**1982, June 2 Photo. *Perf. 13½***

*748* A275 35c shown 50 50
*749* A275 40c Autumn, Queenstown 55 55
*750* A275 45c Winter, Mt. Ngauruhoe 60 60
*751* A275 70c Spring, Wairarapa 1.00 1.00

Madonna with Child and Two Angels, by Piero di Cosimo — A276

Christmas: 35c, Rangiatea Maori Church, Otaki. 45c, Surf life-saving patrol.

**1982, Oct. 6 Photo. *Perf. 14***

*752* A276 18c multicolored 20 20
*753* A276 35c multicolored 42 42
*754* A276 45c multicolored 55 55

Common Design Types are pictured in section before Great Britain.

Nephrite A277

Fruit Export A278

**1982-83**

*755* A277 1c shown 5 5
*756* A277 2c Agate 5 5
*757* A277 3c Iron pyrites 6 6
*758* A277 4c Amethyst 8 8
*759* A277 5c Carnelian 10 10
*760* A277 9c Native sulphur 18 18
*761* A278 10c Grapes 12 12
*762* A278 20c Citrus fruit 25 25
*763* A278 30c Nectarines 38 38
*764* A278 40c Apples 50 50
*765* A278 50c Kiwifruit 65 65
*Nos. 755-765 (11)* 2.42 2.42

Issue dates: A277, Dec. 1; A278, Dec. 7, 1983.

Native Birds — A279

**1985-86 *Perf. 14½***

*766* A279 30c Kakapo ('86) 35 35
*767* A279 45c Falcon ('86) 50 50
*768* A279 $1 Kokako 1.00 1.00
*769* A279 $2 Black Robin 2.00 2.00
*770* A279 $3 Stitchbird ('86) 3.50 3.50
*770A* A279 $4 Saddleback ('86) 4.50 4.50
*Nos. 766-770A (6)* 11.85 11.85

See Nos. 830-835, 919-926.

Salvation Army in NZ Cent. — A280

Univ. of Auckland Cent. — A281

NZ-Australia Closer Economic Relationship Agreement — A282

Introduction of Rainbow Trout Cent. — A283


WCY — A284

***Perf. 14, 14x13½ (35c)***
**1983, Feb. 2 Litho.**

*771* A280 24c multicolored 30 30
*772* A281 30c multicolored 35 35
*773* A282 35c multicolored 42 42
*774* A283 40c multicolored 48 48
*775* A284 45c multicolored 55 55
*Nos. 771-775 (5)* 2.10 2.10

**Commonwealth Day**
Common Design Type

**1983, Mar. 14 Litho. *Perf. 14***

*776* CD334 24c Queen Elizabeth II 30 30
*777* CD334 35c Maori rock painting 42 42
*778* CD334 40c Wool industry logos 48 48
*779* CD334 45c Arms 55 55

Island Bay, by Rita Angus (1908-1970) A286

Landscapes.

**1983, Apr. 6 Litho. *Perf. 14½***

*780* A286 24c shown 32 32
*781* A286 30c Central Otago 40 40
*782* A286 35c Wanaka 45 45
*783* A286 45c Tree, Greymouth 60 60

Lake Matheson A287

***Perf. 13½x13, 13x13½***
**1983, June 1 Photo.**

*784* A287 35c Mt. Egmont, vert. 45 45
*785* A287 40c Cooks Bay, vert. 52 52
*786* A287 45c shown 60 60
*787* A287 70c Lake Alexandrina 90 90

Christmas 1983 — A288

**1983, Oct. 5 Photo. *Perf. 12***

*788* A288 18c Holy Family of the Oak Tree, by Raphael 22 22
*789* A288 35c St. Patrick's Church, Greymouth 42 42
*790* A288 45c Star, poinsettias 55 55

Antarctic Research A289

**1984, Feb. 1 Litho. *Perf. 13½x13***

*791* A289 24c Geology 32 32
*792* A289 40c Biology 52 52
*793* A289 58c Glaciology 75 75
*794* A289 70c Meteorology 90 90
*a* Souvenir sheet of 4

Ferry Mountaineer, Lake Wakatipu, 1879 — A290

**1984, Apr. 4 Litho. *Perf. 13½***

*795* A290 24c shown 32 32
*796* A290 40c Waikana, Otago Harbor, 1909 52 52
*797* A290 58c Britannia, Waitemata Harbor, 1885 75 75
*798* A290 70c Wakatere, Firth of Thames, 1896 90 90

Skier, Mount Hutt — A291

**1984, June 6 Litho. *Perf. 13½x13***

*799* A291 35c shown 38 38
*800* A291 40c Coronet Peak 42 42
*801* A291 45c Turoa 50 50
*802* A291 70c Whakapapa 75 75


Hamilton's Frog — A292

**1984, July 11 *Perf. 13½***

*803* A292 24c shown 28 28
*804* A292 24c Great barrier skink 28 28
*805* A292 30c Harlequin gecko 35 35
*806* A292 58c Otago skink 60 60
*807* A292 70c Gold-striped gecko 75 75
*Nos. 803-807 (5)* 2.26 2.26

Nos. 803-804 se-tenant in continuous design.

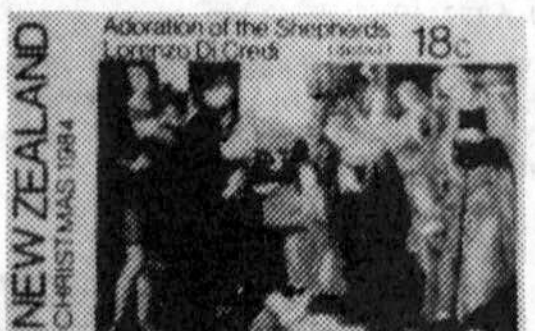

Christmas 1984 — A293

Designs: 18c, Adoration of the Shepherds, by Lorenzo Di Credi. 35c, Old St. Paul's Church, Wellington. 45c, Bell. 35c, 45c vert.

***Perf. 13½x14, 14x13½***
**1984, Sept. 26 Photo.**

*808* A293 18c multicolored 24 24
*809* A293 35c multicolored 46 46
*810* A293 45c multicolored 60 60

Military History A294

**1984, Nov. 7 Litho. *Perf. 15x14***

*811* A294 24c South Africa, 1901 32 32
*812* A294 40c France, 1917 52 52
*813* A294 58c North Africa, 1942 78 78
*814* A294 70c Korea & Southeast Asia, 1950-72 95 95
*a* Souv. sheet of 4, Nos. 811-814 2.75 2.75

St. John Ambulance Assoc. Cent. in NZ — A295

**1985, Jan. 16 Litho. *Perf. 14***

*815* A295 24c multicolored 32 32
*816* A295 30c multicolored 40 40
*817* A295 40c multicolored 52 52

Early Transportation — A296

**1985, Mar. 6 Litho. Perf. 13½**

| | | |
|---|---|---|
| 818 A296 24c Nelson Horse Tram, 1862 | 32 | 32 |
| 819 A296 30c Graham's Town-Steam, 1871 | 40 | 40 |
| 820 A296 35c Dunedin Cable Car, 1881 | 45 | 45 |
| 821 A296 40c Auckland Electric, 1902 | 52 | 52 |
| 822 A296 45c Wellington Electric, 1904 | 60 | 60 |
| 823 A296 58c Christchurch Electric, 1905 | 75 | 75 |
| *Nos. 818-823 (6)* | 3.04 | 3.04 |

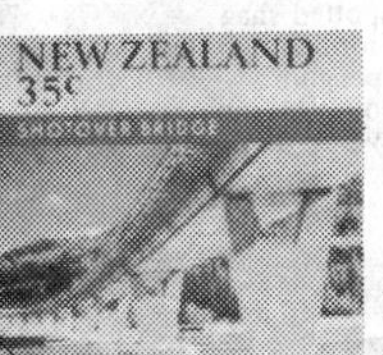
Bridges A297

**1985, June 12 Photo. Perf. 11½**

| | | |
|---|---|---|
| 824 A297 35c Shotover | 32 | 32 |
| 825 A297 40c Alexandra | 38 | 38 |
| 826 A297 45c So. Rangitikei | 42 | 42 |
| 827 A297 70c Twin Bridges | 66 | 66 |

Bird Type of 1985 and

Elizabeth II — A298

**1985-88 Litho. Perf. 14½x14**

| | | |
|---|---|---|
| 828 A298 25c multicolored | 25 | 25 |
| 829 A298 35c multicolored | 35 | 35 |
| ***Perf. 14½*** | | |
| 830 A279 40c Blue duck | 45 | 45 |
| 831 A279 60c Brown teal | 68 | 68 |
| 832 A279 70c Paradise shelduck | 1.00 | 1.00 |
| 835 A279 $5 Takahe | 6.75 | 6.75 |
| *Nos. 828-835 (6)* | 9.48 | 9.48 |

Issue dates: 25c, 35c, July 1. 40c, 60c, Feb. 2, 1987. 70c, June 7, 1988. $5, Apr. 20, 1988.

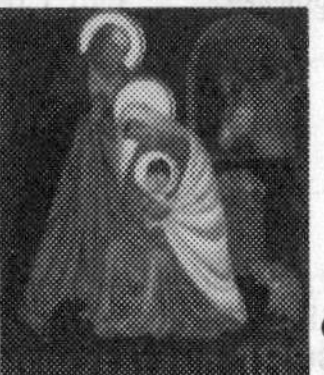
Christmas 1985 — A301

Carol "Silent Night, Holy Night," by Joseph Mohr (1792-1848), Austrian clergyman and poet.

***Perf. 13½x12½***

**1985, Sept. 18 Litho.**

| | | |
|---|---|---|
| 836 A301 18c The Stable | 18 | 18 |
| 837 A301 40c The Shepherds | 40 | 40 |
| 838 A301 50c The Angels | 50 | 50 |

Navy Ships A302

**1985, Nov. 6 Litho. Perf. 13½**

| | | |
|---|---|---|
| 839 A302 25c Philomel, 1914-1947 | 25 | 25 |
| 840 A302 45c Achilles, 1936-1946 | 45 | 45 |
| 841 A302 60c Rotoiti, 1949-1965 | 60 | 60 |
| 842 A302 75c Canterbury, 1971- | 75 | 75 |
| *a* Souvenir sheet of 4, #839-842 | 2.25 | 2.25 |

No. 842a has multicolored margin picturing map of Anzcan Cable and HMNZS Monowai, 1978. Size: 124x108mm.

Police Force Act, Cent. — A303

Designs: a. Radio operators, 1940-1985. b. Mounted policeman, 1890, forensic specialist in mobile lab, 1985. c. Police station, 1895, policewoman and badge, 1985. d. 1920 motorcycle, 1940s car, modern patrol cars and graphologist. e., Original Mt. Cook Training Center and modern Police College, Poriria.

**1986, Jan. 15 Perf. 14½x14**

| | | |
|---|---|---|
| 843 Strip of 5 | 1.40 | 1.40 |
| *a.-e.* A303 25c, any single | 28 | 28 |

Intl. Peace Year A304

**1986, Mar. 5 Perf. 13½x13**

| | | |
|---|---|---|
| 844 A304 25c Tree | 28 | 28 |
| 845 A304 25c Dove | 28 | 28 |

Nos. 844-845 printed se-tenant.

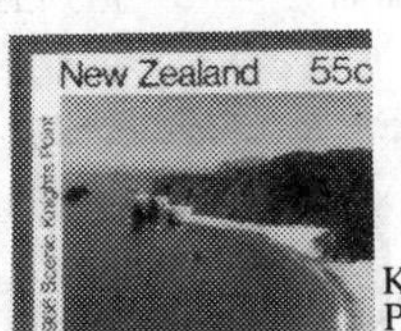
Motorcycles — A305

**1986, Mar. 5**

| | | |
|---|---|---|
| 846 A305 35c 1920 Indian Power Plus | 38 | 38 |
| 847 A305 45c 1927 Norton CS1 | 50 | 50 |
| 848 A305 60c 1930 BSA Sloper | 65 | 65 |
| 849 A305 75c 1915 Triumph Model H | 80 | 80 |

Knight's Point — A306

**1986, June 11 Litho. Perf. 14**

| | | |
|---|---|---|
| 850 A306 55c shown | 65 | 65 |
| 851 A306 60c Beck's Bay | 70 | 70 |
| 852 A306 65c Doubtless Bay | 75 | 75 |
| 853 A306 80c Wainui Bay | 90 | 90 |
| *a* Miniature sheet of one | 1.50 | 1.50 |

No. 853a sold for $1.20. Surtax benefited the "NZ 1990" executive committee. Multicolored margin continuing view of Wainui Bay. Size: 123x99mm.

The Twelve Days of Christmas — A307

**1986, Sept. 17 Photo. Perf. 14½**

| | | |
|---|---|---|
| 854 A307 25c First day | 30 | 30 |
| 855 A307 55c Second | 65 | 65 |
| 856 A307 65c Third | 80 | 80 |

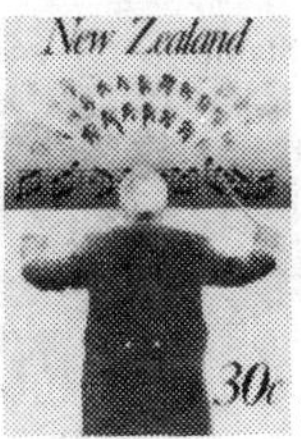
Music — A308

**1986, Nov. 5 Litho. Perf. 14½x14**

| | | |
|---|---|---|
| 857 A308 30c Conductor | 28 | 28 |
| 858 A308 60c Brass band | 55 | 55 |
| 859 A308 80c Highland pipe band | 75 | 75 |
| 860 A308 $1 Country music | 90 | 90 |

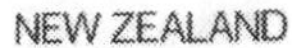

Tourism — A309

**1987, Jan. 14 Perf. 14½x14**

| | | |
|---|---|---|
| 861 A309 60c Boating | 55 | 55 |
| 862 A309 70c Aviation | 65 | 65 |
| 863 A309 80c Camping | 70 | 70 |
| 864 A309 85c Windsurfing | 75 | 75 |
| 865 A309 $1.05 Mountain climbing | 1.10 | 1.00 |
| 866 A309 $1.30 White water rafting | 1.25 | 1.25 |
| *Nos. 861-866 (6)* | 5.00 | 4.90 |

Blue Water Classics A310

**1987, Feb. 2 Perf. 14x14½**

| | | |
|---|---|---|
| 867 A310 40c Southern Cross Cup | 45 | 45 |
| 868 A310 80c Admiral's Cup | 90 | 90 |
| 869 A310 $1.05 Kenwood Cup | 1.20 | 1.20 |
| 870 A310 $1.30 America's Cup | 1.45 | 1.45 |

Vesting Day A311

Designs: No. 871a, Automotives, plane. No. 871b, Train, bicycle.

**1987, Apr. 1 Litho. Perf. 13½**

| | | |
|---|---|---|
| 871 Pair | 1.00 | 1.00 |
| *a.-b.* A311 40c, any single | 48 | 48 |

Establishment of NZ Post Ltd., Apr. 1, replacing the NZ PO.

Royal NZ Air Force, 50th Anniv. A312

Designs: 40c, Avro 626, Wigram Airfield, c. 1937. 70c, P-40 Kittyhawks. 80c, Sunderland seaplane. 85c, A4 Skyhawks.

**1987, Apr. 15 Perf. 14x14½**

| | | |
|---|---|---|
| 872 A312 40c multicolored | 48 | 48 |
| 873 A312 70c multicolored | 82 | 82 |
| 874 A312 80c multicolored | 95 | 95 |
| 875 A312 85c multicolored | 1.00 | 1.00 |
| *a* Souv. sheet of 4, Nos. 872-875 | 3.25 | 3.25 |

No. 875a has multicolored margin picturing Wigram Airfield, c. 1923. Size: 115x105mm.

Natl. Parks System, Cent. — A313

**1987, June 17 Litho. Perf. 14½**

| | | |
|---|---|---|
| 876 A313 70c Urewera | 85 | 85 |
| 877 A313 80c Mt. Cook | 95 | 95 |
| 878 A313 85c Fiordland | 1.00 | 1.00 |
| 879 A313 $1.30 Tongariro | 1.50 | 1.50 |
| *a* Souv. sheet of one | 2.00 | 2.00 |

No. 879a sold for $1.70 to benefit the NZ 1990 World Phil. Exhib., Auckland. Size: 124x99mm.

Christmas Carols — A314

**1987, Sept. 16 Litho. Perf. 14x14½**

| | | |
|---|---|---|
| 880 A314 35c Hark! The Herald Angels Sing | 45 | 45 |
| 881 A314 70c Away in a Manger | 85 | 85 |
| 882 A314 85c We Three Kings of Orient Are | 1.05 | 1.05 |

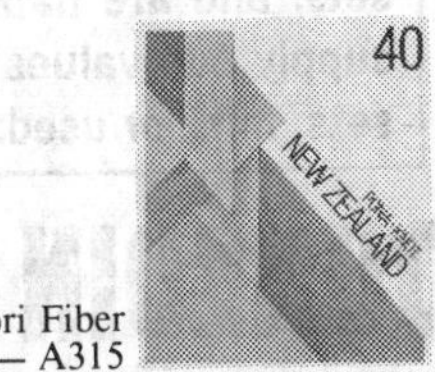
Maori Fiber Art — A315

**1987, Nov. 4 Litho. Perf. 12**

| | | |
|---|---|---|
| 883 A315 40c Knot | 55 | 55 |
| 884 A315 60c Binding | 80 | 80 |
| 885 A315 80c Plait | 1.10 | 1.10 |
| 886 A315 85c Flax fiber | 1.15 | 1.15 |

Royal Phil. Soc. of NZ, Cent. A316

Portrait of Queen Victoria by Chalon — A317

Queen Elizabeth II and: No. 887, No. 61 (blue background). No. 888, No. 62 (red background).

**1988, Jan. 13** ***Perf. 14x14½***

| | | | | | |
|---|---|---|---|---|---|
| *887* | A316 | 40c | multicolored | 55 | 55 |
| *888* | A316 | 40c | multicolored | 55 | 55 |

**Souvenir Sheet**

| | | | | | |
|---|---|---|---|---|---|
| *889* | A317 | $1 | multicolored | 1.35 | 1.35 |

Nos. 887-888 printed se-tenant. No. 889 has multicolored margin continuing the design and picturing 6p of Type A1 at LL. Size: 107x160mm.

NZ Electrification, Cent. — A318

**1988, Jan. 13** ***Perf. 14x14½***

| | | | | | |
|---|---|---|---|---|---|
| *890* | A318 | 40c | Geothermal | 55 | 55 |
| *891* | A318 | 60c | Thermal | 80 | 80 |
| *892* | A318 | 70c | Gas | 95 | 95 |
| *893* | A318 | 80c | Hydroelectric | 1.10 | 1.10 |

Maori Rafter Paintings A319

**1988, Mar. 2** **Litho.** ***Perf. 14½***

| | | | | | |
|---|---|---|---|---|---|
| *894* | A319 | 40c | Mangopare | 55 | 55 |
| *895* | A319 | 40c | Koru | 55 | 55 |
| *896* | A319 | 40c | Raupunga | 55 | 55 |
| *897* | A319 | 60c | Koiri | 80 | 80 |

Booklet Stamps

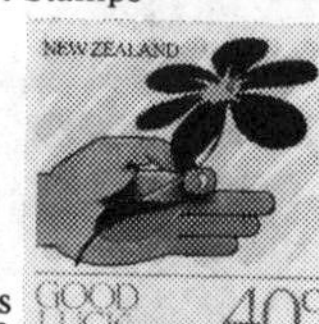


Greetings Messages — A320

**1988, May 18** **Litho.** ***Perf. 13½***

**Size of Nos. 901 and 902: 41x27mm**

| | | | | | |
|---|---|---|---|---|---|
| *902* | A320 | 40c | Get well soon | 58 | 58 |
| *898* | A320 | 40c | Good luck | 58 | 58 |
| *900* | A320 | 40c | Happy birthday | 58 | 58 |
| *899* | A320 | 40c | Keeping in touch | 58 | 58 |
| *901* | A320 | 40c | Congratulations | 58 | 58 |
| *a.* | | | Bklt. pane of 5, Nos. 898-902 | 2.90 | |

Landscapes A321

**1988, June 8** ***Perf. 14½***

| | | | | | |
|---|---|---|---|---|---|
| *903* | A321 | 70c | Milford Track | 1.00 | 1.00 |
| *904* | A321 | 80c | Heaphy Track | 1.15 | 1.15 |
| *905* | A321 | 85c | Copland Track | 1.25 | 1.25 |
| *906* | A321 | $1.30 | Routeburn Track | 1.85 | 1.85 |
| *a.* | | | Miniature sheet of one | 2.50 | 2.50 |

No. 906a has multicolored margin continuing the design, picturing the Mount Aspiring Natl. Park landscape, and New Zealand 1990 world philatelic exhibition emblem. Sold for $1.70 to benefit the exhibition. Size: 124x99mm.

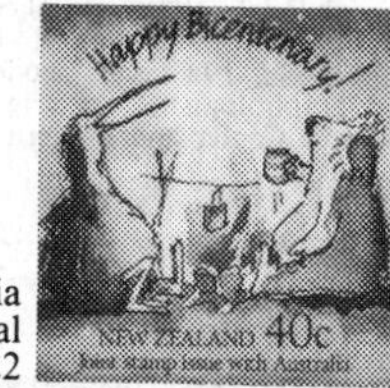


Australia Bicentennial A322

Caricature: Kiwi and koala around campfire.

**1988, June 21**

| | | | | | |
|---|---|---|---|---|---|
| *907* | A322 | 40c | multi | 58 | 58 |

See Australia No. 1086.

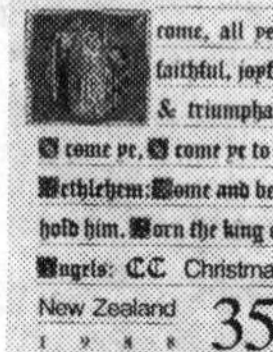


Christmas Carols — A323

Illuminated manuscripts: 35c, *O, Come All Ye Faithful,* by John Francis Wade, 1742. 70c, *Hark! the Herald Angels Sing.* 80c, *Ding Dong! Merrily on High.* 85c, *The First Noel,* first published in Davies & Gilbert's *Some Ancient Christmas Carols,* 1832.

**1988, Sept. 14** **Litho.** ***Perf. 14½***

| | | | | | |
|---|---|---|---|---|---|
| *908* | A323 | 35c | multi | 48 | 48 |
| *909* | A323 | 70c | multi | 95 | 95 |
| *910* | A323 | 80c | multi | 1.10 | 1.10 |
| *911* | A323 | 85c | multi | 1.15 | 1.15 |

New Zealand Heritage A324

The Land. Paintings by 19th cent. artists: 40c, *Lake Pukaki,* 1862, by John Gully. 60c, *On the Grass Plain Below Lake Arthur,* 1846, by William Fox. 70c, *View of Auckland,* 1873, by John Hoyte. 80c, *Mt. Egmont from the Southward,* 1840, by Charles Heaphy. $1.05, *Anakiwa, Queen Charlotte Sound,* 1871, by John Kinder. $1.30, *White Terraces, Lake Rotomahana,* 1880, by Charles Barraud.

**1988, Oct. 5** **Litho.** ***Perf. 14x14½***

| | | | | | |
|---|---|---|---|---|---|
| *912* | A324 | 40c | multi | 50 | 50 |
| *913* | A324 | 60c | multi | 75 | 75 |
| *914* | A324 | 70c | multi | 88 | 88 |
| *915* | A324 | 80c | multi | 1.00 | 1.00 |
| *916* | A324 | $1.05 | multi | 1.35 | 1.35 |
| *917* | A324 | $1.30 | multi | 1.65 | 1.65 |
| | | | *Nos. 912-917 (6)* | 6.13 | 6.13 |

Treaty of Waitangi, 150th anniv.

Kiwi — A325

**1988, Oct. 19** **Engr.** ***Perf. 14½***

**Booklet Stamp**

| | | | | | |
|---|---|---|---|---|---|
| *918* | A325 | $1 | | 1.25 | 1.25 |
| *a.* | | | Bklt. pane of 6 | 7.50 | |

No. 918 issued in booklets only.

Bird Type of 1985

**1988, Nov. 2** **Litho.** ***Perf. 14½x14***

| | | | | | |
|---|---|---|---|---|---|
| *919* | A279 | 10c | Banded dotterel | 14 | 14 |
| *920* | A279 | 20c | Yellowhead | 25 | 25 |
| *921* | A279 | 30c | Silvereye | 40 | 40 |
| *922* | A279 | 40c | Brown kiwi | 52 | 52 |
| *923* | A279 | 50c | Kingfisher | 65 | 65 |
| *924* | A279 | 60c | Spotted shag | 78 | 78 |
| *925* | A279 | 80c | Fiordland crested penguin | 1.05 | 1.05 |
| *926* | A279 | 90c | South Is. robin | 1.20 | 1.20 |
| | | | *Nos. 919-926 (8)* | 4.99 | 4.99 |

Whales of the Southern Oceans A326

**1988, Nov. 2** **Litho.** ***Perf. 13½***

| | | | | | |
|---|---|---|---|---|---|
| *936* | A326 | 60c | Humpback | 78 | 78 |
| *937* | A326 | 70c | Killer | 92 | 92 |
| *938* | A326 | 80c | Southern right | 1.05 | 1.05 |
| *939* | A326 | 85c | Blue | 1.10 | 1.10 |
| *940* | A326 | $1.05 | Southern bottle-nose | 1.40 | 1.40 |
| *941* | A326 | $1.30 | Sperm | 1.70 | 1.70 |
| | | | *Nos. 936-941 (6)* | 6.95 | 6.95 |

Wildflowers A327

**1989, Jan. 18** **Litho.** ***Perf. 14½***

| | | | | | |
|---|---|---|---|---|---|
| *942* | A327 | 40c | Clover | 55 | 55 |
| *943* | A327 | 60c | Lotus | 82 | 82 |
| *944* | A327 | 70c | Montbretia | 95 | 95 |
| *945* | A327 | 80c | Wild ginger | 1.10 | 1.10 |

## POSTAL-FISCAL

In 1881 fiscal stamps of New Zealand of denominations over one shilling were made acceptable for postal duty. Values for canceled stamps are for postal cancellations. Denominations above £5 appear to have been used primarily for fiscal purposes.

Queen Victoria
PF1 PF2

**Perf. 11, 12, 12½**

**1882 Typo. Wmk. 62**

AR1 PF1 2sh blue 60.00 3.50
AR2 PF1 2sh6p dk brn 65.00 3.25
AR3 PF1 3sh violet 90.00 3.50
AR4 PF1 4sh brn vio 165.00 8.00
AR5 PF1 4sh red brn 165.00 8.00
AR6 PF1 5sh green 90.00 2.50
AR7 PF1 6sh rose 165.00 12.50
AR8 PF1 7sh ultra 180.00 12.50
AR9 PF1 7sh6p ol gray 275.00 42.50
AR10 PF1 8sh dull bl 225.00 25.00
AR11 PF1 9sh org red 275.00 25.00
AR12 PF1 10sh red brn 275.00 6.25

**1882-90**

AR13 PF2 15sh dk grn 475.00 25.00
AR15 PF2 £1 rose 400.00 35.00
AR16 PF2 25sh blue 50.00
AR17 PF2 30sh brown 35.00
AR18 PF2 £1 15sh yellow 165.00
AR19 PF2 £2 purple 17.50

PF3

PF4

AR20 PF3 £2 10sh red brown 75.00
AR21 PF3 £3 yel green 50.00
AR22 PF3 £3 10sh rose 210.00
AR23 PF3 £4 ultramarine 150.00
AR24 PF3 £4 10sh olive brn 210.00
AR25 PF3 £5 dark blue 20.00
AR26 PF4 £6 org red 100.00
AR27 PF4 £7 brown red 100.00
AR28 PF4 £8 green 100.00
AR29 PF4 £9 rose 165.00
AR30 PF4 £10 blue 55.00

With "COUNTERPART" at Bottom

**1901**

AR31 PF1 2sh6p brown 210.00 175.00

**Perf. 11, 14, 14½x14**

**1903-15 Wmk. 61**

AR32 PF1 2sh blue ('07) 40.00 3.00
AR33 PF1 2sh6p brown 40.00 3.00
AR34 PF1 3sh violet 55.00 3.75
AR35 PF1 4sh brown red 75.00 4.50
AR36 PF1 5sh green ('06) 52.50 2.25
AR37 PF1 6sh rose 150.00 13.00
AR38 PF1 7sh dull blue 115.00 13.00
AR39 PF1 7sh6p ol gray ('06) 300.00 55.00
AR40 PF1 8sh dark blue 135.00 16.00
AR41 PF1 9sh dl org ('06) 185.00 18.00
AR42 PF1 10sh dp claret 215.00 3.50
AR43 PF2 15sh bl grn 300.00 32.50
AR44 PF2 £1 rose 500.00 35.00

**Perf. 14½**

AR45 PF2 £2 deep vio ('25) 350.00 57.50
*a.* Perf. 14 625.00 57.50
Nos. AR32-AR45 (14) 2,512. 260.00

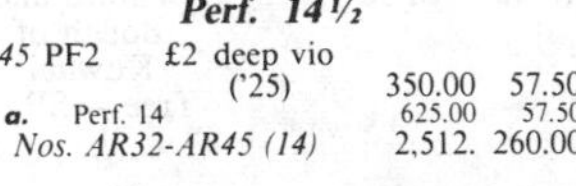
Coat of Arms — PF5

**1931-39 Perf. 14**

**Type PF5**

AR46 1sh3p lemon 11.00 8.25
AR47 1sh3p org ('32) 3.00 75
AR48 2sh6p brown 5.50 80
AR49 4sh dull red ('32) 7.50 95
AR50 5sh green 17.00 2.75
AR51 6sh brt rose ('32) 19.00 5.00
AR52 7sh gray bl 19.00 5.00
AR53 7sh6p olive gray ('32) 40.00 40.00
AR54 8sh dk bl 16.00 6.50
AR55 9sh brn org 22.50 9.50
AR56 10sh dk car 13.00 4.00
AR57 12sh6p brn vio ('35) 125.00 110.00
AR58 15sh ol grn ('32) 47.50 16.00
AR59 £1 pink ('32) 47.50 12.50
AR60 25sh turq bl ('38) 165.00 165.00
AR61 30sh dk brn ('36) 200.00 110.00
AR62 35sh yel ('37) 1,750. 1,750.
AR63 £2 vio ('33) 275.00 47.50
AR64 £2 10sh dark red ('36) 200.00 200.00
AR65 £3 light grn ('32) 250.00 80.00
AR66 £3 10sh rose ('39) 1,100. 750.00
AR67 £4 light bl 300.00 75.00
AR68 £4 10sh dk ol gray ('39) 875.00 750.00
AR69 £5 dk bl ('32) 375.00 105.00

No. AR62 Surcharged in Black **35/-**

**1939 Perf. 14**

AR70 PF5 35sh on 35sh yel 325.00 265.00

Type PF5 Surcharged in Black

**1940**

AR71 3sh6p on 3sh6p dl grn 7.50 3.00
AR72 5sh6p on 5sh6p rose lil 17.50 10.00
AR73 11sh on 11sh pale yel 45.00 32.50
AR74 22sh on 22sh scarlet 125.00 100.00

Type of 1931

**1940-58 Wmk. 253 Perf. 14**

AR75 PF5 1sh3p orange 1.90 35
AR76 PF5 2sh6p brown 5.50 20
AR77 PF5 4sh dull red 7.50 50
AR78 PF5 5sh green 8.50 75
AR79 PF5 6sh brt rose 13.00 1.65
AR80 PF5 7sh gray bl 16.00 2.75
AR81 PF5 7sh6p ol gray ('50) 42.50 65.00
AR82 PF5 8sh dk bl 20.00 6.00
AR83 PF5 9sh org ('46) 20.00 6.00
AR84 PF5 10sh dk car 12.50 1.25
AR85 PF5 15sh ol ('45) 22.50 10.50
AR86 PF5 £1 pink('45) 20.00 1.25
*a.* Perf. 14x13½ ('58) 27.50 9.00
AR87 PF5 25sh bl ('46) 200.00 200.00
AR88 PF5 30sh choc('46) 130.00 65.00
AR89 PF5 £2 vio ('46) 57.50 18.00
AR90 PF5 £2 10sh dk red ('51) 175.00 150.00
AR91 PF5 £3 lt grn ('46) 60.00 27.50
AR92 PF5 £3 10sh rose ('48) 1,250. 900.00
AR93 PF5 £4 lt bl ('52) 90.00 35.00
AR94 PF5 £5 dk bl ('40) 90.00 40.00

Type PF5 Surcharged in Black

**1942-45**

AR95 3sh6p on 3sh6p grn 5.25 4.25
AR96 5sh6p on 5sh6p rose lil ('44) 7.00 4.25
AR97 11sh on 11sh yel 30.00 30.00
AR98 22sh on 22sh car ('45) 135.00 125.00

**Catalogue values for unused stamps in this section, from this point to the end of the section, are for Never Hinged items.**

Type of 1931 Redrawn Surcharged in Black

**1953 Typo.**

AR99 PF5 3sh6p on 3sh6p grn 35.00 35.00

Denomination of basic stamp is in small, sans-serif capitals without period after "sixpence."

Type of 1931

**1955 Wmk. 253 Perf. 14**

**Denomination in Black**

AR100 PF5 1sh3p orange 2.25 40

**1956 Denomination in Blue**

AR101 PF5 1sh3p org yel 12.50 10.00

**1967, July 10 Perf. 14**

AR102 PF5 $4 purple 5.00 2.50
AR103 PF5 $6 green 7.50 5.00
*a.* Unwatermarked ('87) 7.25 7.25
AR104 PF5 $8 light blue 10.00 8.00
*a.* Unwatermarked ('87) 9.50 9.50
AR105 PF5 $10 dark blue 12.50 10.00
*a.* Unwatermarked ('87) 12.00 12.00

## SEMI-POSTAL STAMPS

Nurse
SP1 SP2

Inscribed: "Help Stamp out Tuberculosis, 1929"

**Wmk. 61**

**1929, Dec. 11 Typo. Perf. 14**

B1 SP1 1p + 1p scar 6.50 6.50

Inscribed: "Help Promote Health, 1930"

**1930, Oct. 29**

B2 SP2 1p + 1p scar 15.00 18.00

Boy — SP3

Hygeia, Goddess of Health — SP4

**1931, Oct. 31 Perf. 14½x14**

B3 SP3 1p + 1p scarlet 75.00 75.00
B4 SP3 2p + 1p dark bl 75.00 70.00

**1932, Nov. 18 Engr. Perf. 14**

B5 SP4 1p + 1p carmine 21.00 21.00

Road to Health SP5

Crusader SP6

**1933, Nov. 8**

B6 SP5 1p + 1p carmine 10.00 11.00

**1934, Oct. 25 Perf. 14x13½**

B7 SP6 1p + 1p dark car 6.25 7.00

Child at Bathing Beach — SP7

Anzac — SP8

**1935, Sept. 30 Perf. 11**

B8 SP7 1p + 1p scarlet 1.75 1.40

**Catalogue values for unused stamps in this section, from this point to the end of the section, are for Never Hinged items.**

**1936, Apr. 27**

B9 SP8 ½p + ½p green 50 50
B10 SP8 1p + 1p red 50 50

21st anniv. of Anzac landing at Gallipoli.

"Health" SP9

**1936, Nov. 2**

B11 SP9 1p + 1p red 2.00 1.50

Boy Hiker SP10

Children at Play SP11

**1937, Oct. 1**

B12 SP10 1p + 1p red 2.50 2.25

**Perf. 14x13½**

**1938, Oct. 1 Wmk. 253**

B13 SP11 1p + 1p red 1.65 1.50

Children at Play — SP12

Children in Swing — SP13

**1939, Oct. 16 Wmk. 61 Perf. 11½**

**Black Surcharge**

B14 SP12 1p on ½p + ½p grn 2.75 2.75
B15 SP12 2p on 1p + 1p scar 2.75 2.75

**1940, Oct. 1**

B16 SP12 1p + ½p green 3.50 3.50
B17 SP12 2p + 1p org brown 4.00 4.00

The surtax was used to help maintain children's health camps.

Semi-Postal Stamps of 1940, Overprinted in Black "1941"

**1941, Oct. 4 Perf. 11½**

B18 SP12 1p + ½p green 90 90
B19 SP12 2p + 1p org brown 1.20 1.20

**1942, Oct. 1 Engr.**

B20 SP13 1p + ½p green 50 50
B21 SP13 2p + 1p dp org brown 60 60

Princess Margaret Rose — SP14

Design: 2p + 1p, Princess Elizabeth.

**1943, Oct. 1 Wmk. 253 Perf. 12**

B22 SP14 1p + ½p dark green 15 15
*a.* Pair, imperf. between
B23 SP14 2p + 1p red brown 20 20
*a.* Pair, imperf. between

Princesses Margaret Rose and Elizabeth SP16

**1944, Oct. 9** *Perf. 13½*

*B24* SP16 1p + ½p blue green 10 10
*B25* SP16 2p + 1p chalky blue 18 18

Peter Pan Statue, London SP17

Statue of Eros, London SP19

Soldier Helping Child over Stile — SP18

**1945, Oct. 1**

*B26* SP17 1p + ½p gray green & bister brown 10 10
*B27* SP17 2p + 1p car & ol bis 15 15

**1946, Oct. 24** *Perf. 13½x13*

*B28* SP18 1p + ½p dk grn & org brn 10 10
*B29* SP18 2p + 1p dk brn & org brn 12 12

**1947, Oct. 1** **Engr.** *Perf. 13x13½*

*B30* SP19 1p + ½p deep green 10 10
*B31* SP19 2p + 1p deep carmine 12 12

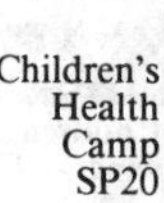

Children's Health Camp SP20

**1948, Oct. 1** *Perf. 13½x13*

*B32* SP20 1p + ½p bl grn & ultra 10 8
*B33* SP20 2p + 1p red & dk brn 12 12

Nurse and Child — SP21

**1949, Oct. 3** **Photo.** *Perf. 14x14½*

*B34* SP21 1p + ½p deep green 10 10
*B35* SP21 2p + 1p ultramarine 15 12

Princess Elizabeth and Prince Charles — SP22

**1950, Oct. 2**

*B36* SP22 1p + ½p green 10 10
*B37* SP22 2p + 1p violet brown 15 12

Racing Yachts SP23

*Perf. 13½x13*

**1951, Nov. 1** **Engr.** **Wmk. 253**

*B38* SP23 1½p + ½p red & yellow 12 12
*B39* SP23 2p + 1p dp grn & yel 12 12

Princess Anne SP24

Prince Charles SP25

*Perf. 14x14½*

**1952, Oct. 1** **Photo.** **Wmk. 253**

*B40* SP24 1½p + ½p crimson 15 15
*B41* SP25 2p + 1p brown 20 15

Girl Guides Marching SP26

Boy Scouts at Camp SP27

**1953, Oct. 7**

*B42* SP26 1½p + ½p bright blue 14 14
*B43* SP27 2p + 1p deep green 24 15

The border of No. B43 consists of Morse code reading "Health" at top and bottom and "New Zealand" on each side. On No. B42 the top border line is replaced by "Health" in Morse code.

Young Mountain Climber Studying Map — SP28

**1954, Oct. 4** **Engr.** *Perf. 13½*

*B44* SP28 1½p + ½p pur & brn 16 12
*B45* SP28 2p + 1p vio gray & brn 20 16

Child's Head — SP29

Children Picking Apples — SP30

**1955, Oct. 3** **Wmk. 253** *Perf. 13*

*B46* SP29 1½p + ½p brn org & sep 12 12
*B47* SP29 2p + 1p grn & org brn 18 9
*B48* SP29 3p + 1p car & sep 22 20

**1956, Sept. 24**

*B49* SP30 1½p + ½p chocolate 14 10
*B50* SP30 2p + 1p blue green 16 8
*B51* SP30 3p + 1p dark carmine 18 16

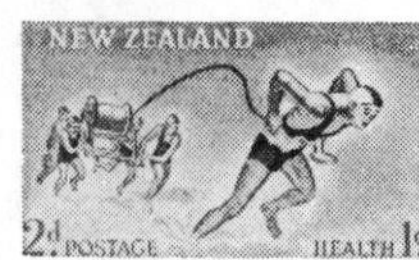
Life-Saving Team SP31

Design: 3p+1p, Children playing and boy in canoe.

**1957, Sept. 25** *Perf. 13½*

*B52* SP31 2p + 1p emer & blk 22 18
 *a.* Miniature sheet of 6 5.75 5.75
*B53* SP31 3p + 1p car & ultra 22 18
 *a.* Miniature sheet of 6 5.75 5.75

The watermark is sideways on Nos. B52a and B53a. In a second printing, the watermark is upright; values double.

Girls' Life Brigade Cadet — SP32

Design: 3p+1p, Bugler, Boys' Brigade.

**1958, Aug. 20** **Photo.** *Perf. 14x14½*

*B54* SP32 2p + 1p green 15 12
 *a.* Miniature sheet of 6 5.75 5.75
*B55* SP32 3p + 1p ultramarine 15 12
 *a.* Miniature sheet of 6 5.75 5.75

75th anniv. of the founding of the Boys' Brigade.

The surtax on this and other preceding semi-postals was for the maintenance of children's health camps.

Globes and Red Cross Flag SP33

**1959, June 3** *Perf. 14½x14*

*B56* SP33 3p + 1p ultra & car 25 15
 *a.* Red Cross omitted *1,200.*

The surtax was for the Red Cross.

Gray Teal (Tete) — SP34

Sacred Kingfisher (Kotare) — SP35

Design: 3p+1p, Pied stilt (Poaka).

**1959, Sept. 16** *Perf. 14x14½*

*B57* SP34 2p + 1p pink, black, yellow & gray 16 14
 *a.* Miniature sheet of 6 6.50 6.50
*B58* SP34 3p + 1p blue, black & pink 16 14
 *a.* Miniature sheet of 6 6.50 6.50
 *b.* Pink omitted *150.00* *50.00*

**1960, Aug. 10** **Engr.** *Perf. 13x13½*

Design: 3p+1p, NZ pigeon (Kereru).

*B59* SP35 2p + 1p grnsh bl & sepia 30 25
 *a.* Min. sheet of 6, perf. 11½x11 12.00 12.00
*B60* SP35 3p + 1p org & sepia 38 30
 *a.* Min. sheet of 6, perf. 11½x11 12.00 12.00

Type of 1959

Birds: 2p+1p, Great white egret (kotuku). 3p+1p, NZ falcon (karearea).

**1961, Aug. 2** **Wmk. 253**

*B61* SP34 2p + 1p pale lil & blk 24 20
 *a.* Miniature sheet of 6 8.00 8.00
*B62* SP34 3p + 1p yellow green & black brown 30 28
 *a.* Miniature sheet of 6 8.00 8.00

Type of 1959

Birds: 2½p+1p, Red-fronted parakeet (kakariki). 3p+1p, Saddleback (tieke).

**1962, Oct. 3** **Photo.** *Perf. 15x14*

*B63* SP34 2½p + 1p lt bl, blk, grn & org 22 20
 *a.* Miniature sheet of 6 10.00 10.00
*B64* SP34 3p + 1p salmon, blk, grn & org 25 22
 *a.* Miniature sheet of 6 10.00 10.00
 *b.* Orange omitted

Prince Andrew SP36

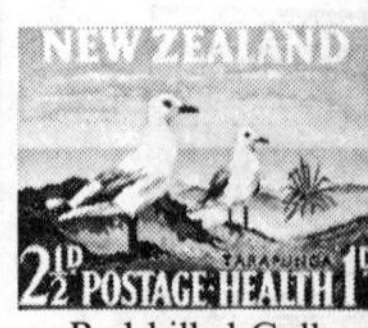
Red-billed Gull (Tarapunga) SP37

Design: 3p+1p, Prince without book.

**1963, Aug. 7** **Engr.** *Perf. 14*

*B65* SP36 2½p + 1p ultra 18 12
 *a.* Miniature sheet of 6 7.75 7.75
*B66* SP36 3p + 1p rose car 22 15
 *a.* Miniature sheet of 6 7.75 7.75

**1964, Aug. 5** **Photo.** *Perf. 14*

Design: 3p+1p, Blue penguin (korora).

*B67* SP37 2½p + 1p lt bl, pale yel, red & blk 28 18
 *a.* Miniature sheet of 8 15.00 15.00
 *b.* Red omitted
 *c.* Yellow omitted
*B68* SP37 3p + 1p blue, yellow & black 32 28
 *a.* Miniature sheet of 8 15.00 15.00

Kaka — SP38

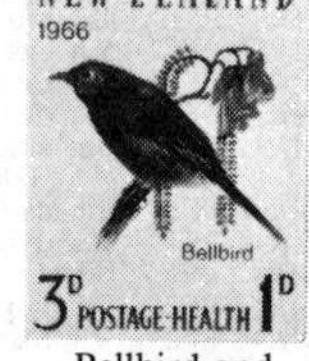
Bellbird and Bough of Kowhai Tree — SP39

Design: 4p+1p, Fantail (piwakawaka).

**1965, Aug. 4** *Perf. 14x14½*

*B69* SP38 3p + 1p gray, red, brn & yellow 22 18
 *a.* Miniature sheet of 6 13.00 13.00
*B70* SP38 4p + 1p yel, blk, emerald & brown 25 22
 *a.* Miniature sheet of 6 13.00 13.00

**1966, Aug. 3** **Photo.** **Wmk. 253**

Design: 4p+1p, Flightless rail (weka) and fern.

*B71* SP39 3p + 1p lt bl & multi 18 15
 *a.* Miniature sheet of 6 7.50 7.50
*B72* SP39 4p + 1p light green & multicolored 24 20
 *a.* Miniature sheet of 6 7.50 7.50
 *b.* Brown omitted

National Team Rugby Player and Boy — SP40

Design: 3c+1c, Man and boy placing ball or place kick (horiz.).

**967, Aug. 2 *Perf. 14½x14, 14x14½***

*373* SP40 2½c + 1c multi 18 15
*a.* Miniature sheet of 6 9.00 9.00
*374* SP40 3c + 1c multi 20 18
*a.* Miniature sheet of 6 9.00 9.00

Boy Running and Olympic Rings — SP41

Design: 3c+1c, Girl swimming and Olympic rings.

**1968, Aug. 7 *Perf. 14½x14***

*375* SP41 2½c + 1c multi 15 12
*a.* Miniature sheet of 6 8.25 8.25
*376* SP41 3c + 1c multi 18 15
*a.* Miniature sheet of 6 8.25 8.25

Boys Playing Cricket SP42

Dr. Elizabeth Gunn — SP43

Design: 3c+1c, playing cricket.

***Perf. 13½x13, 13x13½***

**1969, Aug. 6 Litho. Unwmk.**

*B77* SP42 2½c + 1c multi 15 10
*a.* Miniature sheet of 6 8.00 8.00
*B78* SP42 3c + 1c multi 18 15
*a.* Miniature sheet of 6 8.00 8.00
*B79* SP43 4c + 1c multi 2.00 2.00

50th anniv. of Children's Health Camps, founded by Dr. Elizabeth Gunn.

Boys Playing Soccer SP44

Design: 2½c+1c, Girls playing basketball (vert.).

**1970, Aug. 5 Unwmk. *Perf. 13½***

*B80* SP44 2½c + 1c multi 20 18
*a.* Miniature sheet of 6 7.75 7.75
*B81* SP44 3c + 1c multi 22 20
*a.* Miniature sheet of 6 7.75 7.75

Hygienist and Child SP45

Designs: 3c+1c, Girls playing hockey. 4c+1c, Boys playing hockey.

**1971, Aug. 4 Litho. *Perf. 13½***

*B82* SP45 3c + 1c multicolored 25 22
*a.* Miniature sheet of 6 8.00 8.00
*B83* SP45 4c + 1c multicolored 30 25
*a.* Miniature sheet of 6 8.00 8.00
*B84* SP45 5c + 1c multicolored 65 65

50th anniv. of School Dental Service (No. B84).

Boy Playing Tennis — SP46

Prince Edward — SP47

Design: 4c+1c, Girl playing tennis.

**1972, Aug. 2 Litho. *Perf. 13x13½***

*B85* SP46 3c + 1c gray & lt brn 24 20
*a.* Miniature sheet of 6 9.25 9.25
*B86* SP46 4c + 1c brown, yellow & gray 24 20
*a.* Miniature sheet of 6 9.25 9.25

**1973, Aug. 1 Photo.**

*B87* SP47 3c + 1c grn & brown 24 20
*a.* Miniature sheet of 6 8.25 8.25
*B88* SP47 4c + 1c dk red & blk 24 20
*a.* Miniature sheet of 6 8.25 8.25

Children with Cat and Dog — SP48

Designs: 4c+1c, Girl with dogs and cat. 5c+1c, Children and dogs.

**1974, Aug. 7 Litho. *Perf. 13½x14***

*B89* SP48 3c + 1c multicolored 20 16
*B90* SP48 4c + 1c multicolored 28 24
*a.* Miniature sheet of 10 25.00 25.00
*B91* SP48 5c + 1c multicolored 90 90

Girl Feeding Lamb SP49

Designs: 4c+1c, Boy with hen and chicks. 5c+1c, Boy with duck and duckling.

**1975, Aug. 6 Litho. *Perf. 14x13½***

*B92* SP49 3c + 1c multicolored 20 16
*B93* SP49 4c + 1c multicolored 24 20
*a.* Miniature sheet of 10 18.00 18.00
*B94* SP49 5c + 1c multicolored 60 60

Boy and Piebald Pony — SP50

Girl and Bluebird — SP51

Designs: 8c+1c, Farm girl and calf. 10c+1c, 2 girls watching nest-bound thrush.

**1976, Aug. 4 Litho. *Perf. 13½x14***

*B95* SP50 7c + 1c multicolored 25 25
*B96* SP50 8c + 1c multicolored 30 30
*B97* SP50 10c + 1c multicolored 52 52
*a.* Miniature sheet of 6 7.25 7.25

No. B97a contains 2 each of Nos. B95-B97.

**1977, Aug. 3 Litho. *Perf. 13½x14***

Designs: 8c+2c, Boy and frog. 10c+2c, Girl and butterfly.

*B98* SP51 7c + 2c multi 20 14
*B99* SP51 8c + 2c multi 24 20
*B100* SP51 10c + 2c multi 30 30
*a.* Miniature sheet of 6 4.25 4.25

No. B100a contains 2 each of Nos. B98-B100 in 2 strips of continuous design.

NZ No. B1 SP52

Heart Surgery SP53

**1978, Aug. 2 Litho. *Perf. 13½x14***

*B101* SP52 10c + 2c multi 32 32
*B102* SP53 12c + 2c multi 35 35
*a.* Miniature sheet of 6 4.50 4.50

50th Health Stamp issue (No. B101) and National Heart Foundation (No. B102). No. B102a contains 3 each of Nos. B101-B102.

Demoiselle Fish — SP54

Designs: No. B104, Sea urchin. 12c+2c, Underwater photographer and red mullet (vert.).

***Perf. 13½x13, 13x13½***

**1979, July 25**

*B103* SP54 10c + 2c multi 20 16
*B104* SP54 10c + 2c multi 20 16
*B105* SP54 12c + 2c multi 28 28
*a.* Miniature sheet of 6 3.50 3.50

Nos. B103-B104 printed se-tenant in sheets of 100. No. B105a contains 2 each of Nos. B103-B105.

Children Wharf Fishing SP55

**1980, Aug. 6 Litho. *Perf. 13½x13***

*B106* SP55 14c + 2c *shown* 22 22
*B107* SP55 14c + 2c *Surfcasting* 22 22
*B108* SP55 17c + 2c *Underwater fishing* 28 28
*a.* Miniature sheet of 6 2.10 2.10

Nos. B106-B107 se-tenant in sheets of 100. No. B108a contains 2 each Nos. B106-B108; blue and black margin shows bubbles. Size: 149x75mm.

Boy and Girl at Rock Pool — SP56

**1981, Aug. 5 Litho. *Perf. 14½***

*B109* SP56 20c + 2c Girl, starfish 35 35
*B110* SP56 20c + 2c Boy fishing 35 35
*B111* SP56 25c + 2c shown 40 40
*a.* Miniature sheet of 6 2.00 2.00

Nos. B109-B110 se-tenant in sheets of 100. No. B111a contains 2 each Nos. B109-B111; dark purple margin shows starfish. Size: 100x125mm.

Labrador SP57

Persian Cat SP58

**1982, Aug. 4 Litho. *Perf. 13x13½***

*B112* SP57 24c + 2c shown 35 35
*B113* SP57 24c + 2c Border collie 35 35
*B114* SP57 30c + 2c Cocker spaniel 45 45
*a.* Miniature sheet of 6 2.50 2.50

Nos. B112-B113 se-tenant in sheets of 100. No. B114a contains 2 each Nos. B112-B114, perf. 14x13½. Size: 99x127mm.

**1983, Aug. 3 Litho. *Perf. 14½***

*B115* SP58 24 + 2c Tabby 35 35
*B116* SP58 24 + 2c Siamese 35 35
*B117* SP58 30 + 2c shown 45 45
*a.* Miniature sheet of 6 2.50 2.50

Nos. B115-B116 se-tenant in sheets of 100. No. B117a contains 2 each Nos. B115-B117.

Clydesdales — SP59

**1984, Aug. 1 Litho. *Perf. 13½x13***

*B118* SP59 24c + 2c shown 34 34
*B119* SP59 24c + 2c Shetlands 34 34
*B120* SP59 30c + 2c Thoroughbreds 42 42
*a.* Miniature sheet of 6, 2 each #B118-B120 2.25 2.25

Nos. B118-B119 se-tenant in sheets of 100.

Health, 1985 — SP60

Princess Diana and: No. B121, Prince William. No. B122, Prince Henry. No. B123, Princes Charles, William and Henry.

**1985, July 31 Litho. *Perf. 13½***

*B121* SP60 25c + 2c multi 28 28
*B122* SP60 25c + 2c multi 28 28
*B123* SP60 35c + 2c multi 38 38
*a.* Miniature sheet of 6, 2 each #B121-B123 2.00 2.00

Nos. B121-B122 se-tenant in sheets of 100. Surtax for children's health camps.

No. B123a has decorative inscribed margin. Size: 118x84mm.

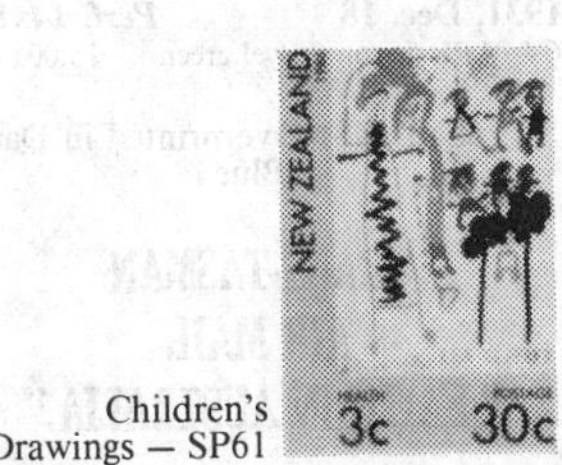


Children's Drawings — SP61

**1986, July 30 Litho. *Perf. 14½x14***

*B124* SP61 30c + 3c shown 38 38
*B125* SP61 30c + 3c Children playing 38 38

*B126* SP61 45c + 3c Skipping rope, horiz. 55 55
*a.* Miniature sheet of 6, 2 each #B124-B126 2.75 2.75

Nos. B124-B125 printed se-tenant in sheets of 100. Surtax benefited children's health camps.

Children's Drawings SP62

**1987, July 29 Litho. *Perf. 14½***
*B127* SP62 40c + 3c shown 52 52
*B128* SP62 40c + 3c Swimming 52 52
*B129* SP62 60c + 3c Riding horse, vert. 75 75
*a.* Miniature sheet of 6, 2 each Nos. B127-B129 3.75 3.75

Nos. B127-B128 printed se-tenant. Surtax benefited children's health camps. No. B129a has inscribed multicolored margin. Size: 100x118mm.

1988 Summer Olympics, Seoul — SP63

**1988, July 27 Litho. *Perf. 14½***
*B130* SP63 40c +3c Swimming 60 60
*B131* SP63 60c +3c Running 88 88
*B132* SP63 70c +3c Rowing 1.00 1.00
*B133* SP63 80c +3c Equestrian 1.15 1.15
*a.* Souv. sheet of 4, Nos. B130-B133 3.75 3.75

No. B133a has multicolored inscribed margin picturing torch-bearer and five-ring emblem. Size: 120x90mm.

## AIR POST STAMPS

Plane over Lake Manapouri AP1

***Perf. 14x14½***
**1931, Nov. 10 Typo. Wmk. 61**
*C1* AP1 3p chocolate 17.50 15.00
*a.* Perf. 14x15 200.00 425.00
*C2* AP1 4p dark violet 17.50 16.00
*C3* AP1 7p orange 22.50 20.00

Type of 1931 Surcharged in Red **FIVE PENCE**

**1931, Dec. 18 *Perf. 14x14½***
*C4* AP1 5p on 3p yel green 15.00 8.00

Type of 1931 Overprinted in Dark Blue

**TRANS-TASMAN AIR MAIL "FAITH IN AUSTRALIA."**

**1934, Feb. 17**
*C5* AP1 7p bright blue 27.50 30.00

1st official air mail flight between NZ and Australia.

Airplane over Landing Field AP2

**1935, May 4 Engr. *Perf. 14***
*C6* AP2 1p rose carmine 55 28
*C7* AP2 3p dark violet 1.40 1.25
*C8* AP2 6p gray blue 2.25 1.80

## SPECIAL DELIVERY STAMPS

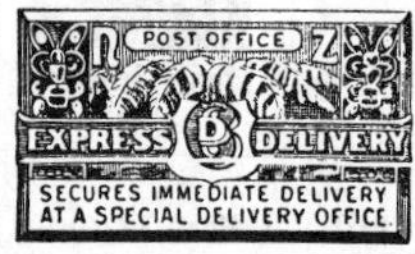

SD1

**1903 Typo. Wmk. 61 *Perf. 11***
*E1* SD1 6p violet & red 27.50 14.00
*a.* 6p purple & red, perf. 14x15 21.00 14.00

Mail Car — SD2

**1939, Aug. 16 Engr. *Perf. 14***
*E2* SD2 6p violet 1.65 2.25

## POSTAGE DUE STAMPS

D1

D2

**Wmk. 62**
**1899, Dec. 1 Typo. *Perf. 11***
*J1* D1 ½p green & red 1.10 1.10
*a.* No period after "D" 37.50 37.50
*J2* D1 1p green & red 6.25 1.25
*J3* D1 2p green & red 15.00 2.00
*J4* D1 3p green & red 8.75 2.50
*J5* D1 4p green & red 20.00 7.50
*J6* D1 5p green & red 17.50 17.50
*J7* D1 6p green & red 20.00 17.50
*J8* D1 8p green & red 62.50 70.00
*J9* D1 10p green & red 65.00 65.00
*J10* D1 1sh green & red 55.00 55.00
*J11* D1 2sh green & red 110.00 110.00
*Nos. J1-J11 (11)* 381.10 349.35

Nos. J1-J11 may be found with N. Z. and D. varying in size.

**1902, Feb. 28 Unwmk.**
*J12* D2 ½p gray green & red 95 1.10

**Wmk. 61**
*J13* D2 ½p gray grn & red 1.40 80
*J14* D2 1p gray grn & red 8.25 2.25
*J15* D2 2p gray grn & red 160.00 160.00

**1904-28 *Perf. 14, 14x14½***
*J16* D2 ½p green & car 2.25 90
*J17* D2 1p green & car 90 12
*J18* D2 2p green & car 4.50 24
*J19* D2 3p grn & rose ('28) 18.00 20.00

N Z and Star printed on the back in Blue

**1925 Unwmk. *Perf. 14x14½, 14x15***
*J20* D2 ½p green & rose 1.25 6.00
*J21* D2 2p green & rose 4.00 6.00

**Catalogue values for unused stamps in this section, from this point to the end of the section, are for Never Hinged items.**

D3

**1939 Wmk. 61 Typo. *Perf. 15x14***
*J22* D3 ½p turquoise green 60 60
*J23* D3 1p rose pink 60 60
*J24* D3 2p ultramarine 2.75 65
*J25* D3 3p brown orange 10.00 10.00

**1945-49 Wmk. 253**
*J27* D3 1p rose pink ('49) 1.90 1.90
*J28* D3 2p ultramarine ('47) 2.00 2.00
*J29* D3 3p brown orange 11.00 11.00

The use of postage due stamps was discontinued in September, 1951.

## WAR TAX STAMP

No. 144 Overprinted in Black

**WAR STAMP**

***Perf. 14x14½***
**1915, Sept. 24 Wmk. 61**
*MR1* A43 ½p green 50 10

## OFFICIAL STAMPS

Regular Issues Ovptd. "O. P. S. O." Handstamped on Stamps of 1882-92 Rose or Magenta Handstamp

**1892 Wmk. 62 *Perf. as before***
*O1* A9 1p rose *325.00*
*O2* A10 2p violet *475.00*
*O3* A16 2½p ultra *275.00*
*O4* A17 5p olive gray *475.00*
*O5* A13 6p brown *550.00*

**Violet Handstamp**
*O6* N1 ½p rose *625.00*
*O7* A9 1p rose *210.00*
*O8* A10 2p violet

Handstamped on No. 67A in Rose

**1899 *Perf. 10, 10x11, 11***
*O9* A15a ½p black *210.00*

Handstamped on No. 79 in Violet

**Unwmk. *Perf. 14, 15***
*O10* A27 8p dull blue *550.00*

Handstamped on Stamps of 1899-1900 in Violet

**1902 *Perf. 11***
*O11* A22 2½p blue *425.00*
*O12* A23 3p org brn *500.00*
*O13* A25 5p red brown *400.00*
*O14* A27 8p dark blue *385.00*

**Green Handstamp**
*O15* A25 5p red brown *385.00*

Handstamped on Stamp of 1901 in Violet

**Wmk. 63 *Perf. 11, 14***
*O16* A35 1p carmine *250.00*

Handstamped on Stamps of 1902-07 in Violet or Magenta

**1905-07 Wmk. 61**
*O17* A18 ½p green *250.00*
*O18* A35 1p carmine *250.00*
*O19* A22 2½p blue *300.00*
*O20* A25 5p red brown
*O21* A27 8p deep blue
*O22* A30 2sh blue green *1,000.*

The "O. P. S. O." handstamp is usually struck diagonally, reading up, but on No. O19 it also occurs horizontally. The letters stand for "On Public Service Only."

Overprinted in Black **OFFICIAL.**

On Stamps of 1902-07

**1907 *Perf. 14, 14x13, 14x14½***
*O23* A18 ½p green 4.50 6
*O24* A35 1p carmine 4.75 1
*a.* Booklet pane of 6 60.00
*O25* A33 2p violet 5.50 2
*O26* A23 3p org brn 21.00 2.50
*O27* A26 6p car rose 60.00 10.00
*a.* Horiz. pair, imperf. vert. *1,000.*
*O28* A29 1sh brown red 65.00 10.00
*O29* A30 2sh blue grn 60.00 25.00
*a.* Horiz. pair, imperf. vert. *1,500.*
*O30* A31 5sh vermilion 200.00 125.00
*Nos. O23-O30 (8)* 420.75 173.52

On No. 127

***Perf. 14x13, 14x14½***
*O31* A26 6p carmine rose 175.00 27.50

On No. 129

**1909 *Perf. 14x14½***
*O32* A35 1p car (redrawn) 42.50 60

On Nos. 130-131, 133, 137, 139

**1910 *Perf. 14, 14x13½, 14x14½***
*O33* A41 ½p yellow green 1.90 14
*O34* A42 1p carmine 1.10 8
*O35* A41 3p orange brown 12.50 55
*O36* A41 6p carmine rose 19.00 2.75
*O37* A41 1sh vermilion 32.50 8.25
*Nos. O33-O37 (5)* 67.00 11.77

On Postal-Fiscal Stamps No. AR32, AR36, AR44

**1911-14**
*O38* PF1 2sh blue ('14) 19.00 14.00
*O39* PF1 5sh green ('13) 67.50 67.50
*O40* PF2 £1 rose 700.00 450.00

On Stamps of 1909-19

***Perf. 14x13½, 14x14½***
**1915-19 Typo.**
*O41* A43 ½p green 28 8
*O42* A46 1½p gray black ('16) 1.10 1.40
*O43* A47 1½p gray black ('16) 4.50 10
*O44* A47 1½p brn org ('19) 1.10 6
*O45* A43 2p yellow ('17) 1.25 6
*O46* A43 3p chocolate ('19) 4.50 28

**Engr.**
*O47* A45 3p vio brn ('16) 1.80 40
*O48* A45 6p car rose ('16) 1.80 25
*O49* A41 8p dp bl (R) ('16) 3.75 3.25
*O50* A45 1sh vermilion ('16) 8.25 1.80
*a.* 1sh orange 8.25 1.80
*Nos. O41-O50 (10)* 28.33 7.68

On No. 157

**1922**
*O51* A45 8p red brown 100.00 65.00

On Nos. 151, 158

**1925**
*O52* A45 4p purple 11.00 1.10
*O53* A45 9p olive green 30.00 22.50

On No. 177

**1925 *Perf. 14x14½***
*O54* A42 1p carmine 3.25 3.25

On Nos. 184, 182

**1927-28 Wmk. 61 *Perf. 14, 14½x14***
*O55* A57 1p rose red 80 6
*O56* A56 2sh blue 60.00 50.00

On No. AR50

**1933 *Perf. 14***
*O57* PF5 5sh green 285.00 285.00

Nos. 186, 187, 196 Overprinted in Black ***Official***

**1936 *Perf. 14x13½, 13½x14, 14***
*O58* A59 1p copper red 55 8
*O59* A60 1½p red brown 7.50 7.50
*O60* A69 1sh dk slate grn 5.50 5.50

Same Overprint Horizontally in Black or Green on Stamps of 1936.

***Perf. 12½, 13½, 13x13½, 14x13½, 13½x14, 14***
**1936-42 Wmk. 253**
*O61* A58 ½p brt grn ('37) 80 80
*O62* A59 1p copper red 80 6
*O63* A60 1½p red brown 1.65 1.65
*O64* A61 2p red org ('38) 28 6
*a.* Perf. 12½ ('42) 27.50 11.00
*O65* A62 2½p dk gray & dk brown 2.75 2.75
*O66* A63 3p choc ('38) 9.75 1.10
*O67* A64 4p blk brn & blk 95 22
*O68* A66 6p red ('37) 80 32
*O68B* A67 8p dp brn ('42) 2.75 2.25

O69 A68 9p black & scar (G) ('38) 11.00 11.00
O70 A69 1sh dk slate grn 1.90 28

**Overprint Vertical**

O71 A70 2sh ol grn ('37) 14.00 2.75
*Nos. O61-O71 (12)* 47.43 23.24

Same Overprint Horizontally in Black on Nos. 226, 227, 228

**1938**
O72 A79 ½p emerald 75 20
O73 A79 1p rose red 90 6
O74 A80 1½p vio brn 15.00 9.00

Same Overprint on No. AR50

**1938 Wmk. 61 *Perf. 14***
O75 PF5 5sh green 16.00 13.00

Nos. 229-235, 237, 239-241 Overprinted in Red or Black — *Official*

***Perf. 13½x13, 13x13½, 14x13½***

**1940 Wmk. 253**
O76 A81 ½p dk bl grn (R) 20 8
a. "ff" joined 20.00 18.00
O77 A82 1p scar & sepia 50 8
a. "ff" joined 20.00 18.00
O78 A83 1½p brt vio & ultra 50 38
O79 A84 2p black brown & Prussian green 50 10
a. "ff" joined 20.00 18.00
O80 A85 2½p dk bl & myr grn 1.00 75
a. "ff" joined 20.00 18.00
O81 A86 3p deep plum & dark vio (R) 2.00 50
a. "ff" joined 20.00 18.00
O82 A87 4p dark red vio & violet brn 2.50 85
a. "ff" joined 24.00 24.00
O83 A89 6p vio & brt grn 7.50 1.00
a. "ff" joined 30.00 24.00
O84 A90 8p org red & blk 5.00 4.00
a. "ff" joined 30.00 24.00
O85 A91 9p dp org & olive 3.00 2.75
O86 A92 1sh dk sl grn & ol 17.50 4.00
*Nos. O76-O86 (11)* 40.20 14.49

Nos. 227A, 228C Overprinted in Black — *Official*

**1941 Wmk. 253 *Perf. 13½***
O88 A79 1p light blue green 15 8
O89 A80 3p blue 18 10

Same Overprint on No. 245

**1944 *Perf. 14x15***
**Size: 17¼x20¼mm**
O90 A68 9p int blk & scar 9.00 9.00

**Same Overprint on No. AR78**
***Perf. 14***
O91 PF5 5sh green 7.75 5.00

**Catalogue values for unused stamps in this section, from this point to the end of the section, are for Never Hinged items.**

Same Ovpt. on Stamps of 1941-47

**1946-51 *Perf. 13½, 14***
O92 A79 ½p brn org ('46) 1.10 12
O92B A80 1½p red 3.25 35
O93 A80 2p orange 45 5
O94 A80 4p rose lilac 2.25 42
O95 A80 6p rose carmine 4.50 30
O96 A80 8p deep violet 7.50 2.50
O97 A80 9p chocolate 12.00 3.50
O98 A104 1sh dk car rose & chestnut 11.00 75
O99 A104 2sh dark green & brn org 19.00 3.00
*Nos. O92-O99 (9)* 61.05 10.99

Queen Elizabeth II — O1

***Perf. 13½x13***

**1954, Mar. 1 Engr. Wmk. 253**
O100 O1 1p orange 35 20
O101 O1 1½p rose brown 1.40 1.10
O102 O1 2p green 1.00 22
O103 O1 3p red 38 6
O104 O1 4p blue 65 22
O105 O1 9p rose carmine 1.10 60
O106 O1 1sh rose violet 1.65 70
*Nos. O100-O106 (7)* 6.53 3.10

Nos. O102, O101 Surcharged with New Value and Dots

**1959-61**
O107 O1 2½p on 2p grn ('61) 1.00 1.00
O108 O1 6p on 1½p rose brn 1.00 1.00

**1963, Mar. 1**
O109 O1 2½p dark olive 2.50 1.25
O111 O1 3sh slate 32.50 32.50

## LIFE INSURANCE

Lighthouses
LI1 LI2

***Perf. 10, 11, 10x11, 12x11½***

**1891, Jan. 2 Typo. Wmk. 62**
OY1 LI1 ½p purple 60.00 1.40
OY2 LI1 1p blue 60.00 45
OY3 LI1 2p red brown 65.00 1.50
OY4 LI1 3p chocolate 275.00 22.50
OY5 LI1 6p green 375.00 55.00
OY6 LI1 1sh rose pink 725.00 115.00
*Nos. OY1-OY6 (6)* 1,560. 195.85

Stamps from outside rows of the sheets sometimes lack watermark.

***Perf. 11, 14x11, 14***

**1903-04 Wmk. 61**
OY7 LI1 ½p purple 42.50 2.25
OY8 LI1 1p blue 42.50 50
OY9 LI1 2p red brown 65.00 4.00

**1905-32 *Perf. 11, 14, 14x14½***
OY10 LI2 ½p yel grn ('13) 1.25 20
OY11 LI2 ½p green ('32) 1.25 38
OY12 LI2 1p blue 165.00 25.00
OY13 LI2 1p dp rose ('13) 11.00 25
OY14 LI2 1p scarlet ('31) 5.00 50
OY15 LI2 1½p gray ('17) 20.00 3.00
OY16 LI2 1½p brn org ('19) 1.00 1.00
OY17 LI2 2p red brown 1,800. 125.00
OY18 LI2 2p violet ('13) 25.00 10.00
OY19 LI2 2p yellow ('21) 2.75 2.00
OY20 LI2 3p ocher ('13) 22.50 17.50
OY21 LI2 3p choc ('31) 11.00 11.00
OY22 LI2 6p car rose ('13) 19.00 12.50
OY23 LI2 6p pink ('31) 15.00 15.00
*Nos. OY10-OY23 (14)* 2,099. 223.33

Nos. OY15 and OY16 have "POSTAGE" at each side.
Stamps from outside rows of the sheets sometimes lack watermark.

**1946-47 Wmk. 253 *Perf. 14x15***
OY24 LI2 ½p yel grn ('47) 1.90 1.90
OY25 LI2 1p scarlet 1.40 1.40
OY26 LI2 2p yellow 1.40 70
OY27 LI2 3p chocolate 9.75 9.75
OY28 LI2 6p pink ('47) 6.50 6.50
*Nos. OY24-OY28 (5)* 20.95 20.25

**Catalogue values for unused stamps in this section, from this point to the end of the section, are for Never Hinged items.**

**New Zealand Lighthouses**

Castlepoint LI3

Taiaroa — LI4

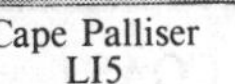

Cape Palliser LI5

Cape Campbell LI6

Eddystone (England) LI7

Stephens Island LI8

The Brothers LI9
Cape Brett LI10

***Perf. 13½x13, 13x13½***

**1947-65 Engr. Wmk. 253**
OY29 LI3 ½p dk grn & red orange 3.00 2.75
OY30 LI4 1p dk ol grn & bl 35 35
OY31 LI5 2p int bl & gray 42 42
OY32 LI6 2½p ultramarine & blk ('63) 8.50 8.50
OY33 LI7 3p red vio & bl 48 48
OY34 LI8 4p dk brn & org 1.50 1.25
a. Wmkd. sideways ('65) 15.00 15.00
OY35 LI9 6p dk brn & bl 1.50 1.50
OY36 LI10 1sh red brn & bl 1.75 1.75
*Nos. OY29-OY36 (8)* 17.50 17.00

Set first issued Aug. 1, 1947.

Nos. OY30, OY32-OY33, OY34a, OY35-OY36 and Types Surcharged

1c

2c

***Perf. 13½x13, 13x13½***

**1967-68 Engr. Wmk. 253**
OY37 LI4 1c on 1p dk ol grn & lt bl 1.40 1.40
a. Wmkd. upright ('68) 1.40 1.40
OY38 LI6 2c on 2½p ultra & blk 5.50 5.50
OY39 LI7 2½c on 3p, wmkd. sideways ('68) 2.75 2.75
a. Watermarked upright 3.25 3.25
OY40 LI8 3c on 4p dk brn & org 5.00 5.00
OY41 LI9 5c on 6p dk brn & bl 4.50 4.50
OY42 LI10 10c on 1sh red brn & bl, wmkd. sideways 2.75 2.75
a. Watermarked upright 9.00 9.00
*Nos. OY37-OY42 (6)* 21.90 21.90

The surcharge is different on each stamp and is adjusted to obliterate old denomination. One dot only on 2½.
Set first issued July 10, 1967.

Moeraki Point Lighthouse — LI11

Lighthouses: 2½c, Puysegur Point (horiz.). 3c, Baring Head. 4c, Cape Egmont (horiz.). 8c, East Cape. 10c, Farewell Spit. 15c, Dog Island.

***Perf. 13x13½, 13½x13, 14 (8c, 10c)***

**1969-76 Litho. Unwmk.**
OY43 LI11 ½c pur bl & yel 2.00 2.00
OY44 LI11 2½c yel ultra & grn 1.10 1.10
OY45 LI11 3c yel & brown 20 20
OY46 LI11 4c lt ultra & ocher 22 22
OY47 LI11 8c multicolored 30 30
OY48 LI11 10c multicolored 32 32
OY49 LI11 15c multi 1.25 1.25
a. Perf. 14 ('78) 40 40
*Nos. OY43-OY49 (7)* 5.39 5.39

Cent. of Government Life Insurance Office.
Nos. OY47-OY48 issued Nov. 17, 1976, others Mar. 27, 1969.

No. OY44 Surcharged with New Value and 4 Diagonal Bars

***Perf. 13½x13***

**1978, Mar. 8 Litho. Wmk. 253**
OY50 LI11 25c on 2½c multi 75 75

Lighthouse LI12

**1981, June 3 Litho. *Perf. 14½***
OY51 LI12 5c multicolored 6 6
OY52 LI12 10c multicolored 12 12
OY53 LI12 20c multicolored 25 25
OY54 LI12 30c multicolored 40 40
OY55 LI12 40c multicolored 52 52
OY56 LI12 50c multicolored 65 65
*Nos. OY51-OY56 (6)* 2.00 2.00

## NEWSPAPER STAMPS

Queen Victoria — N1
Wmk. 64- Large Star

**Wmk. 59**

**1873, Jan. 1 Typo. *Perf. 10***
P1 N1 ½p rose 40.00 12.50
a. Perf. 12½x10 125.00 62.50
b. Perf. 12½ 125.00 47.50

The "N Z" watermark (illustrated over No. 30) is widely spaced and intended for larger stamps. About a third of the stamps in each sheet are unwatermarked. They are worth a slight premium.

**1875, Jan. Wmk. 64 *Perf. 12½***
P3 N1 ½p rose 7.50 65
a. Pair, imperf. btwn 750.00 375.00
b. Perf. 12 50.00 4.50

**1892 Wmk. 62 *Perf. 12½***
P4 N1 ½p bright rose 2.00 25
a. Unwatermarked 10.00 4.50

The only foreign revenue stamps listed in this Catalogue are those authorized for prepayment of postage.

## ROSS DEPENDENCY

**Catalogue values for unused stamps in this section, from this point to the end of the section, are for Never Hinged items.**

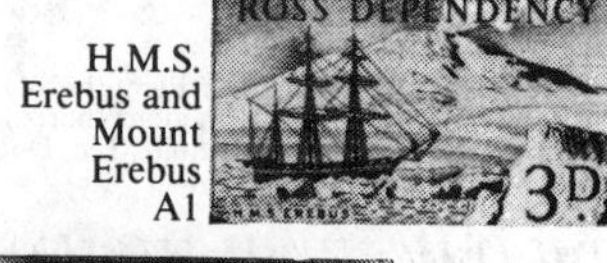

H.M.S. Erebus and Mount Erebus A1

Ernest H. Shackleton and Robert F. Scott — A2

Map Showing Location of Ross Dependency A3

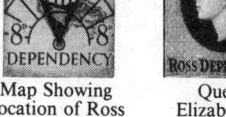

Queen Elizabeth II A4

*Perf. 14, 13 (A4)*

**1957, Jan. 11 Engr. Wmk. 253**

*L1* A1 3p dark blue 2.50 2.50
*L2* A2 4p dark carmine 2.75 2.75
*L3* A3 8p ultra & car rose 3.25 3.25
*L4* A4 1sh6p dull violet 6.00 6.00

**1967, July 10**

*L5* A1 2c dark blue 6.50 4.50
*L6* A2 3c dark carmine 6.50 4.50
*L7* A3 7c ultra & car rose 7.75 5.25
*L8* A4 15c dull violet 16.00 10.50

Skua — A5

Scott Base — A6

Designs: 4c, Hercules plane unloading at Williams Field. 5c, Shackleton's hut, Cape Royds. 8c, Naval supply ship Endeavour unloading. 18c, Tabular ice floe.

*Perf. 13x13½*

**1972, Jan. 18 Litho. Unwmk.**

*L9* A5 3c lt bl, blk & gray 55 50
*L10* A5 4c blk & violet 45 42
*L11* A5 5c rose lil, blk & gray 50 45
*L12* A5 8c blk, dk gray & brn 80 75

*Perf. 14x13½*

*L13* A6 10c slate grn, brt grn & blk ('79) 65 60
*a.* Perf. 14½x14 45 45
*L14* A6 18c pur & blk ('79) 1.25 1.10
*a.* Perf. 14½x14 1.10 1.10
*Nos. L9-L14 (6)* 4.20 3.82

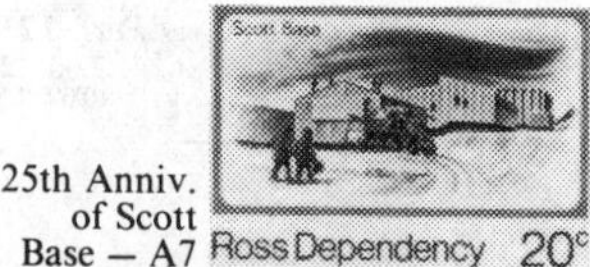

25th Anniv. of Scott Base — A7

*Ross Dependency stamps can be mounted in Scott's New Zealand Album.*

**1982, Jan. 20 Litho. *Perf. 15½***

*L15* A7 5c Adelie penguins 10 8
*L16* A7 10c Tracked vehicles 20 15
*L17* A7 20c shown 40 35
*L18* A7 30c Field party, Upper Taylor Valley 60 50
*L19* A7 40c Vanda Station 80 75
*L20* A7 50c Scott's hut, Cape Evans, 1911 1.00 85
*Nos. L15-L20 (6)* 3.10 2.68

## NIGER COAST PROTECTORATE

### (Oil Rivers Protectorate)

LOCATION — West coast of Africa on Gulf of Guinea.
GOVT. — British Protectorate.

This territory was originally known as the Oil Rivers Protectorate, and its affairs were conducted by the British Royal Niger Company. The Company surrendered its charter to the Crown in 1899. In 1900 all of the territories formerly controlled by the Royal Niger Company were incorporated into the two protectorates of Northern and Southern Nigeria, the latter absorbing the area formerly known as Niger Coast Protectorate. In 1914 Northern and Southern Nigeria joined to form the Crown Colony of Nigeria. (See Nigeria, Northern Nigeria, Southern Nigeria and Lagos.)

12 Pence = 1 Shilling

BRITISH PROTECTORATE

OIL RIVERS

Stamps of Great Britain, 1881-87, Overprinted in Black

**1892 Wmk. 30 *Perf. 14***

*1* A54 ½p vermilion 5.75 2.75
*2* A40 1p lilac 5.25 2.00
*a.* "OIL RIVERS" at top 5,250.
*b.* Half used as ½p on cover 3,000.
*3* A56 2p grn & car 5.75 2.75
*a.* Half used as 1p on cover
*4* A57 2½p vio, *bl* 2.75 1.65
*5* A61 5p lil & bl 4.00 3.25
*6* A65 1sh green 37.50 40.00
*Nos. 1-6 (6)* 61.00 52.40

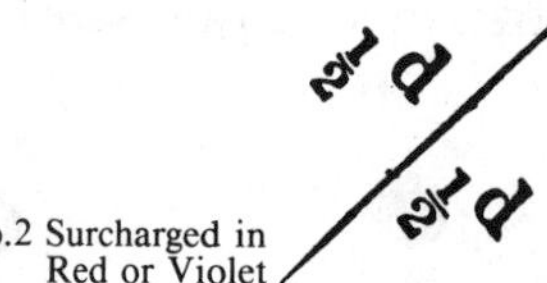

No.2 Surcharged in Red or Violet

**1893**

*7* A40 ½p on half of 1p lil (R) 150.00 125.00
*c.* Unsevered pair 550.00 550.00
*d.* "½" omitted
*7A* A40 ½p on half of 1p lil (V) 5,500. 4,750.
*b.* Overprint "a" double 9,000.

Nos. 3-6 Handstamp Surcharged in Violet, Red, Carmine, Bluish Black, Deep Blue, Green or Black

*Half Penny*

**1893 Wmk. 30 *Perf. 14***

*8* A56 ½p on 2p (V) 165.00 165.00
*9* A57 ½p on 2½p (V) 3,000.
*10* A57 ½p on 2½p (R) 165.00 130.00
*11* A57 ½p on 2½p (C) 7,250. 6,500.
*12* A57 ½p on 2½p (B) 7,250. 6,500.
*13* A57 ½p on 2½p (G) 375.00 375.00

HALF PENNY.

*14* A56 ½p on 2p (V) 175.00 150.00
*15* A56 ½p on 2p (Bl) 650.00 600.00
*16* A57 ½p on 2½p (V) 3,000.
*17* A57 ½p on 2½p (R) 225.00 185.00
*18* A57 ½p on 2½p (Bl) 300.00 300.00
*19* A57 ½p on 2½p (G) 300.00 300.00

HALF PENNY

*20* A56 ½p on 2p (V) 200.00 200.00
*21* A57 ½p on 2½p (R) 250.00 250.00
*22* A57 ½p on 2½p (C) 200.00 200.00
*23* A57 ½p on 2½p (Bl Bk) 2,500.
*24* A57 ½p on 2½p (Bl) 165.00 135.00
*25* A57 ½p on 2½p (G) 135.00 135.00
*26* A57 ½p on 2½p (Bk) 2,000.

*HALF PENNY*

*27* A57 ½p on 2½p (R) 4,000.
*28* A57 ½p on 2½p (G) 225.00 225.00

One Shilling

*29* A56 1sh on 2p (V) 225.00 225.00
*30* A56 1sh on 2p (R) 375.00 475.00
*31* A56 1sh on 2p (Bk) 6,750.

5/—

*32* A56 5sh on 2d (V) 6,000. 5,750
*33* A61 10sh on 5p (R) 5,000. 5,000.
*34* A65 20sh on 1sh (V) 62,500.
*35* A65 20sh on 1sh (R) 25,000.
*36* A65 20sh on 1sh (Bk) 85,000.

The handstamped 1893 surcharges are known inverted, vertical, etc.

Queen Victoria
A8 A9

A10

A11

A12

A13

**1893 Unwmk. *Perf. 12 to 15***

*37* A8 ½p vermilion 2.75 2.75
*38* A9 1p lt bl 3.00 3.00
*a.* Half used as ½p on cover 850.00
*39* A10 2p green 5.00 6.00
*a.* Half used as 1p on cover 1,650.
*b.* Horiz. pair, imperf. between 5,500.
*40* A11 2½p car lake 2.50 2.75
*41* A12 5p gray lil 2.75 3.00
*a.* 5p lil 4.25 4.50
*42* A13 1sh black 12.50 11.00
*Nos. 37-42 (6)* 28.50 28.50

A15

A16

A17 A18

A19

A20

**1894 Engr.**

*43* A15 ½p yel grn 90 90
*44* A16 1p vermilion 2.50 2.00
*a.* 1p org ver 2.75 2.75
*b.* Diagonal half, used as ½p on cover 850.00
*45* A17 2p car lake 1.90 1.90
*a.* Half used as 1p on cover
*46* A18 2½p blue 2.25 2.25
*47* A19 5p dp vio 1.75 1.75
*48* A20 1sh black 3.25 3.25
*Nos. 43-48 (6)* 12.55 12.05

See Nos. 55-59, 61.

Halves of Nos. 38, 3 and 44 Surcharged in Red, Blue, Violet or Black:

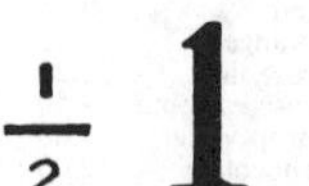

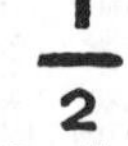

No. 49 No. 50 Nos. 51-53

**1894**

*49* A9 ½p on half of 1p (R) 1,075. 90.00
*a.* Inverted surcharge 5,250.

**Wmk. 30 *Perf. 14***

*50* A56 1p on half of 2p (R) 600.00 150.00
*a.* Double surcharge 1,250. 1,100.
*b.* Inverted surcharge 1,100.

***Perf. 12 to 15***
**Unwmk.**

*51* A16 ½p on half of 1p (Bl) 1,100. 125.00
*a.* Double surcharge
*52* A16 ½p on half of 1p (V) 1,100. 140.00
*53* A16 ½p on half of 1p (Bk) 1,750. 350.00

This surcharge is found on both vertical and diagonal halves of the 1p.

No. 46 Surcharged in Black

ONE
HALF PENNY

**1894**

*54* A18 ½p on 2½p bl 325.00 110.00
*a.* Double surcharge 2,250. 1,750.
*b.* Error "OIE" instead of ONE 1,750. 1,250.
*c.* As "b," double surch. 2,500.

The surcharge is found in eight types.

A27

A28

A29

**1897-98** **Wmk. 2**

*55* A15 ½p yel grn 55 52
*56* A16 1p vermilion 75 65
*57* A17 2p car lake 1.25 1.25
*58* A18 2½p blue 1.25 1.25
*a.* 2½p slate blue 1.65 1.65
*59* A19 5p deep vio 3.75 4.50
*60* A27 6p yel brn ('98) 4.50 3.75
*61* A20 1sh black 5.75 5.75
*62* A28 2sh6p olive bis 15.00 27.50
*63* A29 10sh dp pur ('98) 57.50 75.00
*a.* 10sh bright purple 67.50 95.00
*Nos. 55-63 (9)* 90.30 120.17

The stamps of Niger Coast Protectorate were superseded in January, 1900, by those of Northern and Southern Nigeria.

## NIGERIA

LOCATION — On the west coast of Africa, bordering on the Gulf of Guinea.
GOVT. — Republic.
AREA — 356,669 sq. mi.
POP. — 82,390,000 (est. 1983).
CAPITAL — Lagos.

The colony and protectorate were formed in 1914 by the union of Northern and Southern Nigeria. The mandated territory of Cameroons (British) was also attached for administrative purposes. The Federation of Nigeria was formed in 1960. It became a republic in 1963. See Niger Coast Protectorate, Lagos, Northern Nigeria and Southern Nigeria.

12 Pence = 1 Shilling
20 Shillings = 1 Pound
100 Kobo = 1 Naira (1973)

**Catalogue values for unused stamps in this country are for Never Hinged items, beginning with Scott 71 in the regular postage section, Scott B1 in the semi-postal section and Scott J1 in the postage due section.**

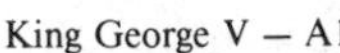
King George V — A1

Numerals of 3p, 4p, 6p, 5sh and £1 of type A1 are in color on plain tablet.
Dies I and II are described at back of this volume.

**Wmk. Multiple Crown and C. A. (3)**
**1914-27** **Typo.** ***Perf. 14***
**Die I**
**Ordinary Paper**

*1* A1 ½p green 14 10
*a* Booklet pane of 6
*2* A1 1p carmine 16 16
*a* Booklet pane of 6
*b* 1p scar 65 65
*3* A1 2p gray 1.10 22
*4* A1 2½p ultra 60 22

**Chalky Paper**

*5* A1 3p vio, *yel* 95 45
*6* A1 4p blk & red, *yel* 75 70
*7* A1 6p dl vio & red vio 1.35 65
*8* A1 1sh blk, *green* 1.85 65
*a* 1sh blk, *emer* 1.35 1.35
*b* 1sh blk, *bl grn*, ol back 1.60 95
*c* As "a," ol back 4.00 4.00
*9* A1 2sh6p blk & red, *bl* 3.25 1.50
*10* A1 5sh grn & red, *yel* 6.75 9.25
*11* A1 10sh grn & red, *grn* 20.00 26.00
*a* 10sh grn & red, *emer* 30.00 26.00
*b* 10sh grn & red, *bl grn*, ol back 675.00 *800.00*
*c* As "a," ol back 35.00 35.00
*12* A1 £1 vio & blk, *red* 110.00 *110.00*
*a* Die II ('27) 120.00 *160.00*
*Nos. 1-12 (12)* 146.90 149.90

**Surface-colored Paper**

*13* A1 3p vio, *yel* 48 48
*14* A1 4p blk & red, *yel* 80 80
*15* A1 1sh blk, *green* 80 80
*a* 1sh blk, *emer*
*16* A1 5sh grn & red, *yel* 12.00 *16.00*
*17* A1 10sh grn & red, *grn* 40.00 *60.00*
*Nos. 13-17 (5)* 54.08 78.08

**1921-33** **Wmk. 4**
**Die II**
**Ordinary Paper**

*18* A1 ½p green 48 10
*a* Die I 35 35
*19* A1 1p carmine 20 8
*a* Booklet pane of 6 22.50
*b* Die I 20 14
*c* Booklet pane of 6, Die I 22.50
*20* A1 1½p org ('31) 40 16
*21* A1 2p gray 2.25 16
*a* Die I 1.65 95
*b* Booklet pane of 6, Die I 45.00
*22* A1 2p red brn ('27) 1.35 55
*a* Booklet pane of 6 45.00
*23* A1 2p dk brn ('28) 48 16
*a* Booklet pane of 6 22.50
*b* Die I ('32) 2.50 35
*24* A1 2½p ultra (die I) 38 35
*25* A1 3p dp vio 2.75 1.65
*a* Die I ('24) 2.25 1.35
*26* A1 3p ultra ('31) 2.00 1.10

**Chalky Paper**

*27* A1 4p blk & red, *yel* 22 20
*a* Die I ('32) 11.50 11.50
*28* A1 6p dl vio & red vio 1.65 28
*a* Die I 2.25 1.85
*29* A1 1sh blk, *emerald* 48 28
*30* A1 2sh6p blk & red, *bl* 4.50 6.75
*a* Die I ('32) 13.50 16.00
*31* A1 5sh grn & red, *yel* ('26) 15.00 *22.50*
*a* Die I ('32) 32.50 *45.00*
*32* A1 10sh grn & red, *emer* 40.00 50.00
*a* Die I ('32) 67.50 *95.00*
*Nos. 18-32 (15)* 72.14 84.32

**Silver Jubilee Issue**
Common Design Type

**1935, May 6** **Engr.** ***Perf. 11x12***

*34* CD301 1½p blk & ultra 20 20
*35* CD301 2p ind & grn 24 24
*36* CD301 3p ultra & brn 45 45
*37* CD301 1sh brn vio & ind 1.50 1.50

Wharf at Apapa — A2

Picking Cacao Pods — A3

Dredging for Tin — A4

Timber — A5

Fishing Village — A6

Ginning Cotton — A7

Minaret at Habe — A8

Fulani Cattle — A9

Victoria-Buea Road — A10

Oil Palms — A11

View of Niger at Jebba — A12

Nigerian Canoe — A13

**1936, Feb. 1** ***Perf. 11½x13***

*38* A2 ½p green 16 15
*39* A3 1p rose car 18 7
*40* A4 1½p brown 28 15
*a* Perf. 12½x13½ 14.00 80
*41* A5 2p black 55 22
*42* A6 3p dk bl 80 65
*a* Perf. 12½x13½ 32.50 13.00
*43* A7 4p red brn 95 95
*44* A8 6p dl vio 80 65
*45* A9 1sh ol grn 2.75 19.00

***Perf. 14***

*46* A10 2sh6p ultra & blk 7.50 7.50
*47* A11 5sh ol grn & blk 13.50 *17.00*
*48* A12 10sh sl & blk 35.00 *40.00*
*49* A13 £1 org & blk 80.00 *95.00*
*Nos. 38-49 (12)* 142.47 181.34

**Coronation Issue**
Common Design Type

**1937, May 12** ***Perf. 11x11½***

*50* CD302 1p dk car 6 6
*51* CD302 1½p dk brn 9 9
*52* CD302 3p dp ultra 12 12

King George VI — A14

Victoria-Buea Road — A15

Niger at Jebba — A16

**1938-51** **Wmk. 4** ***Perf. 12***

*53* A14 ½p dp grn 6 5
*a* Perf. 11½ ('50) 6 5
*54* A14 1p dk car 9 5
*55* A14 1½p red brn 9 5
*a* Perf. 11½ ('50) 9 5
*56* A14 2p black 18 9
*57* A14 2½p org ('41) 12 18
*58* A14 3p dp bl 12 6
*59* A14 4p orange 14.00 4.25
*60* A14 6p brn vio 12 7
*a* Perf. 11½ ('51) 18 7
*61* A14 1sh ol grn 25 10
*a* Perf. 11½ ('50) 25 9
*62* A14 1sh3p turq bl ('40) 35 18
*a* Perf. 11½ ('50) 35 18
*63* A15 2sh6p ultra & blk ('51) 3.25 2.75
*a* Perf. 13½ ('42) 1.25 70
*b* Perf. 14 ('42) 1.25 70
*c* Perf. 13x11½ 5.75 2.00
*64* A16 5sh org & blk, perf. 13½ ('42) 2.25 1.10
*a* Perf. 12 ('49) 3.50 1.10
*b* Perf. 14 ('48) 2.25 1.10
*c* Perf. 13x11½ 22.50 3.50

**1944-50** ***Perf. 12***

*65* A14 1p red vio 5 5
*a* Perf. 11½ ('50) 5 5
*66* A14 2p dp red 6 5
*a* Perf. 11½ ('50) 6 5
*67* A14 3p black 9 6
*68* A14 4p dk bl 10 9
*Nos. 53-68 (16)* 21.18 9.18

**Catalogue values for unused stamps in this section, from this point to the end of the section, are for Never Hinged items.**

**Peace Issue**
Common Design Type

**1946, Oct. 21** **Engr.** ***Perf. 13½x14***

*71* CD303 1½p brown 12 12
*72* CD303 4p dp bl 20 20

**Silver Wedding Issue**
Common Design Types

**1948, Dec. 20** **Photo.** ***Perf. 14x14½***

*73* CD304 1p brt red vio 25 25

**Engraved; Name Typographed**
***Perf. 11½x11.***

*74* CD305 5sh brn org 10.00 *17.50*

**UPU Issue**
Common Design Types
**Engr.; Name Typo. on 3p, 6p**
***Perf. 13½, 11x11½***

**1949, Oct. 10** **Wmk. 4**

*75* CD306 1p red vio 20 12
*76* CD307 3p indigo 40 30
*77* CD308 6p rose vio 1.20 90
*78* CD309 1sh olive 2.00 1.50

**Coronation Issue**
Common Design Type

**1953, June 2** **Engr.** ***Perf. 13½x13***

*79* CD312 1½p brt grn & blk 28 14

Manilla (Bracelet) Currency A17

Olokun Head, Ife — A18

Designs: 1p, Bornu horsemen. 1½p, Peanuts, Kano City. 2p, Mining tin. 3p, Jebba Bridge over Niger River. 4p, Cocoa industry. 1sh, Logging. 2sh 6p, Victoria harbor. 5sh, Loading palm oil. 10sh, Goats and Fulani cattle. £1, Lagos waterfront, 19th and 20th centuries.

**1953, Sept. 1** ***Perf. 13½, 14***

**Size: 35½x22½mm**

| | | | | |
|---|---|---|---|---|
| *80* | A17 | ½p red org & blk | 10 | 5 |
| *a* | | Bklt. pane of 4 ('57) | 50 | |
| *81* | A17 | 1p ol gray & blk | 12 | 5 |
| *a* | | Bklt. pane of 4 ('57) | 50 | |
| *82* | A17 | 1½p bl grn | 20 | 7 |
| *83* | A17 | 2p bis & blk | 25 | 7 |
| *84* | A17 | 3p pur & blk | 25 | 5 |
| *a* | | Bklt. pane of 4 ('57) | 1.00 | |
| *85* | A17 | 4p ultra & blk | 30 | 14 |
| *86* | A18 | 6p blk & org brn | 38 | 7 |
| *87* | A17 | 1sh brn vio & blk | 65 | 9 |
| *a* | | Bklt. pane of 4 ('57) | 2.75 | |

**Size: 40½x24½mm**

| | | | | |
|---|---|---|---|---|
| *88* | A17 | 2sh6p grn & blk | 2.50 | 28 |
| *89* | A17 | 5sh ver & blk | 3.25 | 55 |
| *90* | A17 | 10sh red brn & blk | 4.00 | 1.10 |

**Size: 42x31½mm**

| | | | | |
|---|---|---|---|---|
| *91* | A17 | £1 vio & blk | 9.50 | 4.00 |
| | | *Nos. 80-91 (12)* | 21.50 | 6.52 |

See No. 93.

No. 83 Overprinted in Black **ROYAL VISIT 1956**

**1956, Jan. 28 Wmk. 4** ***Perf. 13½***

*92* A17 2p bis & blk 14 12

Issued to commemorate the visit of Queen Elizabeth II to Nigeria, Jan.-Feb., 1956.

Mining Tin Type of 1953.

Two types:
I. Broken row of dots between "G" and miner's head.
II. Complete row of dots.

**1956-57**

| | | | | |
|---|---|---|---|---|
| *93* | A17 | 2p bluish gray (shades) (I) | 10 | 5 |
| *a* | | Bklt pane of 4 (I) ('57) | 65 | |
| *b* | | 2p gray (shades) (II) | 6 | 5 |

Ambas Bay, Victoria Harbor A19

**Wmk. 314**

**1958, Dec. 1 Engr.** ***Perf. 13½***

*94* A19 3p pur & blk 12 12

Cent. of the founding of Victoria, Southern Cameroons.

**1959, Mar. 14**

Designs: 3p, Lugard Hall, Kaduna. 1sh, Kano Mosque.

| | | | | |
|---|---|---|---|---|
| *95* | A19 | 3p pur & blk | 12 | 9 |
| *96* | A19 | 1sh grn & blk | 35 | 30 |

Attainment of self-government by the Northern Region, Mar. 15, 1959.

**Federation of Nigeria**

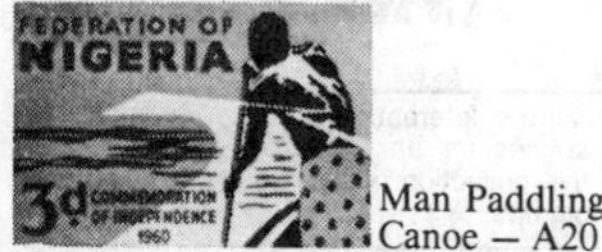

Man Paddling Canoe — A20

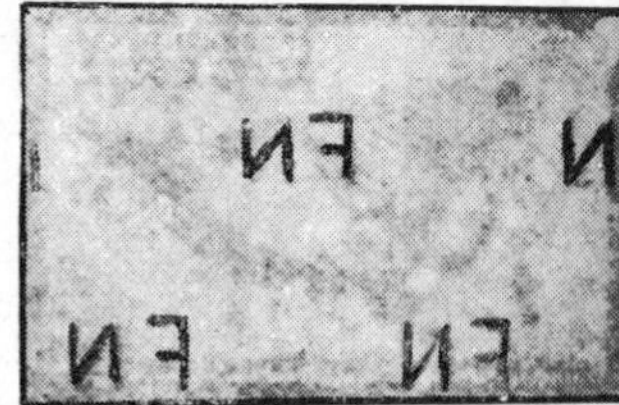

Wmk.335 — FN Multiple

Designs: 1p, Federal Legislature. 6p, Federal Supreme Court. 1sh3p, Map of Africa, dove and torch.

**Wmk. 335**

**1960, Oct. 1 Photo.** ***Perf. 13½***

**Size: 35x22mm**

| | | | | |
|---|---|---|---|---|
| *97* | A20 | 1p car & blk | 5 | 5 |
| *98* | A20 | 3p bl & blk | 5 | 5 |
| *99* | A20 | 6p dk red brn & emer | 14 | 12 |

**Size: 39½x23½mm**

*100* A20 1sh3p ultra & yel 30 25

Nigeria's independence, Oct. 1, 1960.

Peanuts — A21

Central Bank, Lagos A22

Designs: 1p, Coal miner. 1½p, Adult education. 2p, Potter. 3p, Oyo carver. 4p, Weaver. 6p, Benin mask. 1sh, Yellow-casqued hornbill. 1sh3p, Camel train and map. 5sh, Nigeria museum and sculpture. 10sh, Kano airport. £1, Lagos terminal.

***Perf. 14½x14***

**1961, Jan. 1** **Wmk. 335**

| | | | | |
|---|---|---|---|---|
| *101* | A21 | ½p emerald | 5 | 5 |
| *102* | A21 | 1p purple | 7 | 5 |
| *a* | | Bklt. pane of 6 | 42 | |
| *103* | A21 | 1½p rose red | 9 | 7 |
| *104* | A21 | 2p ultra | 7 | 5 |
| *105* | A21 | 3p dk grn | 10 | 5 |
| *a* | | Bklt. pane of 6 | 50 | |
| *106* | A21 | 4p blue | 14 | 7 |
| *107* | A21 | 6p blk & yel | 18 | 5 |
| *a* | | Bklt. pane of 6 | 1.10 | |
| *b* | | Yellow omitted | 375.00 | |
| *108* | A21 | 1sh yel grn | 32 | 5 |
| *109* | A21 | 1sh3p orange | 55 | 9 |
| *a* | | Bklt. pane of 6 | 3.50 | |
| *110* | A22 | 2sh6p yel & blk | 1.10 | 22 |
| *111* | A22 | 5sh emer & blk | 2.25 | 44 |
| *112* | A22 | 10sh dp ultra & blk | 3.50 | 1.10 |
| *113* | A22 | £1 dp car & blk | 5.50 | 3.25 |
| | | *Nos. 101-113 (13)* | 13.92 | 5.54 |

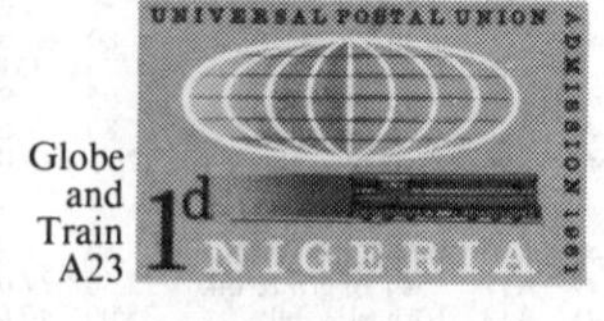

Globe and Train A23

**1961, July 25** **Wmk. 335**

| | | | | |
|---|---|---|---|---|
| *114* | A23 | 1p shown | 6 | 6 |
| *115* | A23 | 3p Truck | 8 | 6 |
| *116* | A23 | 1sh3p Plane | 32 | 28 |
| *117* | A23 | 2sh6p Ship | 65 | 65 |

Nigeria's admission to the UPU.

Coat of Arms — A24

Map and Natural Resources — A25

Designs: 6p, Eagle carrying banner. 1sh3p, Flying eagles forming flag. 2sh6p, Young couple looking at flag and government building.

***Perf. 14½x14, 14x14½***

**1961, Oct. 1 Photo. Wmk. 335**

| | | | | |
|---|---|---|---|---|
| *118* | A24 | 3p multi | 5 | 5 |
| *119* | A25 | 4p org, yel grn & dk red | 16 | 16 |
| *120* | A25 | 6p emerald | 16 | 9 |
| *121* | A25 | 1sh3p ultra, emer & gray | 25 | 22 |
| *122* | A25 | 2sh6p bl, emer & sep | 52 | 52 |
| | | *Nos. 118-122 (5)* | 1.14 | 1.04 |

First anniversary of independence.

Map of Africa and Staff of Aesculapius — A26

Designs (Map of Africa and): 3p, Lyre, book and scroll. 6p, Cogwheel. 1sh, Radio beacon. 1sh3p, Hands holding globe.

**1962, Jan. 25** ***Perf. 14x14½***

| | | | | |
|---|---|---|---|---|
| *123* | A26 | 1p bister | 6 | 6 |
| *124* | A26 | 3p dp mag | 7 | 6 |
| *125* | A26 | 6p bl grn | 18 | 14 |
| *126* | A26 | 1sh chestnut | 28 | 22 |
| *127* | A26 | 1sh3p brt bl | 42 | 35 |
| | | *Nos. 123-127 (5)* | 1.01 | 83 |

Issued to honor the conference of heads of state of African and Malagasy Governments.

Malaria Eradication Emblem and Larvae — A27

Designs (Emblem and): 6p, Man with spray gun. 1sh3p, Plane spraying insecticide. 2sh6p, Microscope, retort and patient.

**1962, Apr. 7** ***Perf. 14½***

| | | | | |
|---|---|---|---|---|
| *128* | A27 | 3p emer, brn & ver | 5 | 5 |
| *129* | A27 | 6p lil rose & dk bl | 16 | 12 |
| *130* | A27 | 1sh3p dk bl & lil rose | 26 | 22 |
| *131* | A27 | 2sh6p yel brn & bl | 52 | 52 |

WHO drive to eradicate malaria.

National Monument, Lagos A28

Ife Bronze Head and Flag — A29

***Perf. 14½x14, 14x14½***

**1962, Oct. 1 Wmk. 335 Photo.**

| | | | | |
|---|---|---|---|---|
| *132* | A28 | 3p lt ultra & emer | 8 | 6 |
| *a* | | Emerald omitted | | |
| *133* | A29 | 5sh vio, emer & org red | 1.75 | 1.75 |

Second anniversary of independence.

Fair Emblem — A30

Globe and Arrows — A31

Designs (horizontal): 6p, "Wheels of Industry." 1sh, Cornucopia, goods and trucks. 2sh6p, Oil derricks and tanker.

**1962, Oct. 27** **Wmk. 335**

| | | | | |
|---|---|---|---|---|
| *134* | A30 | 1p brn ol & org | 5 | 5 |
| *135* | A30 | 6p crim & blk | 12 | 9 |
| *136* | A30 | 1sh dp org & blk | 22 | 18 |
| *137* | A30 | 2sh6p dk ultra, yel & blk | 52 | 50 |

Lagos Intl. Trade Fair, Oct. 27-Nov. 8.

**1962, Nov. 5**

Designs: 4p, National Hall and Commonwealth emblem (horiz.). 1sh3p, Palm tree, emblem and doves.

| | | | | |
|---|---|---|---|---|
| *138* | A31 | 2½p sky bl | 9 | 9 |
| *139* | A31 | 4p dp rose & sl bl | 14 | 10 |
| *140* | A31 | 1sh3p gray & yel | 45 | 45 |

8th Commonwealth Parliamentary Conf., Lagos.

Herdsman with Cattle — A32

U. S. Mercury Capsule over Kano Tracking Station — A33

Design: 6p, Tractor and corn (horiz.)

**1963, Mar. 21 Photo.** ***Perf. 14½***

| | | | | |
|---|---|---|---|---|
| *141* | A32 | 3p ol grn | 10 | 8 |
| *142* | A32 | 6p brt lil rose | 32 | 25 |

"Freedom from Hunger" campaign of the FAO.

**1963, June 21** ***Perf. 14½***

Design: 1sh3p, Syncom II satellite and U. S. tracking ship "Kingsport," Lagos harbor.

| | | | | |
|---|---|---|---|---|
| *143* | A33 | 6p dk bl & yel grn | 18 | 15 |
| *144* | A33 | 1sh3p blk & dp grn | 38 | 38 |

Peaceful uses of outer space.
Printed in sheets of 12 (4x3) with ornamental borders and inscriptions.

Nigerian and Greek Scouts Shaking Hands and Jamboree Emblem — A34

Design: 1sh, Scouts dancing around campfire.

**1963, Aug. 1 Photo. *Perf. 14***
*145* A34 3p gray ol & red 14 10
*146* A34 1sh red & blk 42 42
*a* Souv. sheet of 2 1.10 1.10

Issued to commemorate the 11th Boy Scout Jamboree, Marathon, Greece, Aug. 1963. No. 146a contains one each of Nos. 145-146 with black marginal inscription. Size: 94x94mm.

**Republic**

First Aid — A35

Designs: 6p, Blood donors and ambulances. 1sh3p, Helping the needy.

**1963, Sept. 1 Wmk. 335 *Perf. 14½***
*147* A35 3p dk bl & red 10 8
*148* A35 6p dk grn & red 22 22
*149* A35 1sh3p blk & red 55 55
*a* Souv. sheet of 4 2.75 2.75

Cent. of the Intl. Red Cross. No. 149a contains four of No. 149. Red marginal inscription. Size: 101x101mm.

Pres. Nnamdi Azikiwe and State House A36

"Freedom of Worship" A37

Designs: 1sh3p, President and Federal Supreme Court. 2sh6p, President and Parliament Building.

**1963, Oct. 1 Unwmk. *Perf. 14x13***
*150* A36 3p dl grn & yel grn 6 5
*151* A36 1sh3p brn & bis 25 22
*a* Bister (head) omitted
*152* A36 2sh6p vio bl & brt grnsh bl 50 50

Independence Day, Oct. 1, 1963.

**1963, Dec. 10 Wmk. 335 *Perf. 13***

Designs: 3p, Charter and broken whip (horiz.). 1sh3p, "Freedom from Want." 2sh6p, "Freedom of Speech."

*153* A37 3p vermilion 5 5
*154* A37 6p green 7 7
*155* A37 1sh3p dp ultra 18 16
*156* A37 2sh6p red lil 35 35

15th anniv. of the Universal Declaration of Human Rights.

Queen Nefertari — A38

**1964, March 8 Photo. *Perf. 14***
*157* A38 6p shown 20 20
*158* A38 2sh6p Ramses II 90 90

UNESCO world campaign to save historic monuments in Nubia.

John F. Kennedy, U.S. and Nigerian Flags — A39

Designs: 1sh3p, Kennedy bust and laurel. 5sh, Kennedy coin (U.S.), flags of U.S. and Nigeria at half-mast.

**1964, Aug. 20 Unwmk. *Perf. 13x14***
*159* A39 1sh3p blk & lt vio 28 25
*160* A39 2sh6p multi 55 55
*161* A39 5sh multi 1.10 1.10
*a* Souv. sheet of 4 5.25 5.25

Issued in memory of President John F. Kennedy (1917-1963). No. 161a contains 4 imperf. stamps similar to No. 161 with simulated perforations. Buff border with black and green inscription; picture of Mrs. Kennedy with children and Nigerian flag in margin. Size: 154x135mm.

Pres. Nnamdi Azikiwe A40

Herbert Macaulay A41

Design: 2sh6p, King Jaja of Opobo.

***Perf. 14x13, 14***
**1964, Oct. 1 Photo. Unwmk.**
*162* A40 3p red brn 6 6
*163* A41 1sh3p green 25 25
*164* A41 2sh6p sl grn 55 55

First anniversary of the Republic.

Boxing Gloves and Torch A42

Hurdling — A43

Designs: 6p, High jump. 1sh3p, Woman runner (vert.).

**1964, Oct. *Perf. 14½***
*165* A42 3p ol grn & sep 7 7
*166* A42 6p dk bl & emer 14 14
*167* A42 1sh3p ol & brn 28 28

***Perf. 14***
*168* A43 2sh6p org red & brn 50 50
*a* Souv. sheet of 4 3.25 3.25

18th Olympic Games, Tokyo, Oct. 10-25.

No. 168a contains 4 imperf. stamps similar to No. 168 with simulated perforations. Brown margin with white inscription. Size: 102x102mm.

Mountain Climbing Scouts — A44

IQSY Emblem and Telstar, Map of Africa — A45

Designs: 3p, Golden Jubilee emblem. 6p, Nigeria's Scout emblem and merit badges. 1sh3p, Lord Baden-Powell and Nigerian Boy Scout.

**1965, Jan. Photo. *Perf. 14½***
*169* A44 1p brown 5 5
*170* A44 3p emer, blk & red 9 6
*171* A44 6p yel grn, red & blk 15 15
*172* A44 1sh3p sep, yel & dk grn 38 38
*a* Souv. sheet of 4 3.00 3.00

50th anniv. of the founding of the Nigerian Boy Scouts.

No. 172a contains four imperf. stamps similar to No. 172 with simulated perforation. Dark green border with white inscription. Size: 76x114mm.

**1965, Apr. 1 Unwmk. *Perf. 14x13***

Design: 1sh3p, Explorer XII over map of Africa.

*173* A45 6p grnsh bl & vio 18 18
*174* A45 1sh3p lil & grn 42 42

Issued for the International Quiet Sun Year, 1964-65. Printed in sheets of 12 (4x3) with ornamental borders and inscriptions.

ITU Emblem, Drummer, Man at Desk and Telephone A46

Designs: 1sh3p, ITU emblem and telecommunication tower (vert.). 5sh, ITU emblem, Relay satellite and map of Africa showing Nigeria.

***Perf. 11x11½, 11½x11***
**1965, Aug. 2 Photo. Unwmk.**
*175* A46 3p ocher, red & blk 10 10
*176* A46 1sh3p ultra, grn & blk 65 65
*177* A46 5sh multi 2.75 2.75

Cent. of the ITU.

ICY Emblem, Diesel Locomotive and Camel Caravan A47

Designs (ICY Emblem and): 1sh, Students and hospital, Lagos. 2sh6p, Kainji Dam, Niger River.

**1965, Sept. 1 Wmk. 335 *Perf. 14x15***
*178* A47 3p org, grn & car 22 8
*179* A47 1sh ultra, blk & yel 50 35
*180* A47 2sh6p ultra, yel & grn 2.50 1.10

Intl. Cooperation Year and the 20th anniv. of the UN.

Stone Images, Ikom — A48

Designs: 3p, Carved frieze (horiz.). 5sh, Seated man, Taba bronze.

***Perf. 14x15, 15x14***
**1965, Oct. 1 Photo. Unwmk.**
*181* A48 3p ocher, blk & red 6 6
*182* A48 1sh3p lt ultra, grn & redsh brn 40 40
*183* A48 5sh emer, dk brn & redsh brn 1.75 1.75

Second anniversary of the Republic.

Elephants A49

Designs: ½p, Lioness and cubs (vert.). 1½p, Splendid sunbird. 2p, Weaverbirds. 3p, Cheetah. 4p, Leopard and cubs. 6p, Saddle-billed storks (vert.). 9p, Gray parrots. 1sh, Kingfishers. 1sh3p, Crowned cranes. 2sh6p, Buffon's kobs (antelopes). 5sh, Giraffes. 10sh, Hippopotami (vert.). £1, Buffalos.

**"MAURICE FIEVET" below Design.***
***Perf. 12x12½, 12½x12, 14x13½ (1p, 2p, 3p, 4p, 9p)***

**1965-66 Photo.**
**Size: 23x38mm, 38x23mm**
*184* A49 ½p multi 6 5
*185* A49 1p red & multi 10 5
*186* A49 1½p lt bl & multi 12 10
*187* A49 2p brt red & multi 12 5
*a* White "2d" ('70) 7.00 2.00
*188* A49 3p brt grn, yel & dl brn 75 50
*189* A49 4p lil & multi 25 5
*a* Perf 12½x12 40 5
*b* "4" 5mm wide ('71) 3.75 1.00
*190* A49 6p vio & multi 30 6
*191* A49 9p bl & org 1.00 50

***Perf. 12½***
**Size: 45x26mm, 26x45mm**
*192* A49 1sh gray & multi 60 8
*a* Red omitted
*193* A49 1sh3p brt bl & multi 65 12
*194* A49 2sh6p dk brn, yel & ocher 1.25 25
*195* A49 5sh brn, yel & red brn 2.50 60
*196* A49 10sh grnsh bl & multi 3.50 2.50
*197* A49 £1 brt grn & multi 8.00 5.00
*Nos. 184-197 (14)* 19.20 9.91

* The designer's name, Maurice Fievet, appears at right or left, in small or large capitals. Nos. 187a and 189b have "MAURICE FIEVET" at right, 5mm wide. No. 187a has "2d" in white instead of yellow. No. 189b has "REPUBLIC" and "4d" larger, bolder.

Issue dates: ½p, 1p, 1965. Others, 1966.

Nine values were overprinted "F. G. N. / F. G. N." (Federal Government of Nigeria) in 1969. They were not issued, but some were irregularly sold. Later the Nigerian Philatelic Service sold copies, stating they were not postally valid.

See Nos. 258-267.

No. 110 Overprinted in Red: "COMMONWEALTH / P.M. MEETING / 11. Jan. 1966"

***Perf. 14½x14***
**1966, Jan. 11 Photo. Wmk. 335**
*198* A22 2sh6p yel & blk 52 52

Conf. of British Commonwealth Prime Ministers, Lagos.

Y.W.C.A. Building, Lagos
A50

**Unwmk.**

**1966, Sept. 1 Litho. *Perf. 14***

*199* A50 4p yel, grn & multi 12 12
*200* A50 9p brt grn & multi 32 32

60th anniv. of the Nigerian YWCA.

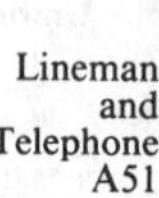

Lineman and Telephone
A51

Designs: 4p, Flag and letter carrying pigeon (vert.). 2sh6p, Niger Bridge.

***Perf. 14½x14, 14x14½***

**1966, Oct. 1 Photo. Wmk. 335**

*201* A51 4p green 10 10
*202* A51 1sh6p lil, blk & sep 60 60
*203* A51 2sh6p multi 1.00 1.00

Third anniversary of the Republic.

Book, Chemical Apparatus, Carved Head and UNESCO Emblem
A52

**1966, Nov. 4 *Perf. 14½x14***

*204* A52 4p dl org, mar & blk 40 9
*205* A52 1sh6p bl grn, plum & blk 1.25 80
*206* A52 2sh6p pink, plum & blk 2.50 2.50

20th anniv. of UNESCO.

Surveyors and Hydrological Decade Emblem — A53

Design: 2sh6p, Water depth gauge on dam and Hydrological Decade emblem (vert.).

***Perf. 14½x14, 14x14½***

**1967, Feb. 1 Photo. Wmk. 335**

*207* A53 4p multi 12 10
*208* A53 2sh6p multi 1.25 1.25

Hydrological Decade (UNESCO), 1965-74.

Weather Satellite Orbiting Earth
A54

Design: 1sh6p, Storm over land and sea and World Meteorological Organization emblem.

**1967, Mar. 23 Photo. *Perf. 14½x14***

*209* A54 4p dp ultra & brt rose 15 10
*210* A54 1sh6p ultra & yel 75 75

World Meteorological Day, March 23.

Eyo Masqueraders — A55

Designs: 1sh6p, Acrobat. 2sh6p, Stilt dancer (vert.).

***Perf. 11x11½, 11½x11***

**1967, Oct. 1 Photo. Unwmk.**

*211* A55 4p multi 9 8
*212* A55 1sh6p turq bl & multi 1.25 1.25
*213* A55 2sh6p pale grn & multi 2.00 1.50

4th anniversary of the Federal Republic.

Vaccination of Cattle
A56

***Perf. 14½x14***

**1967, Dec. 1 Photo. Unwmk.**

*214* A56 4p mar & multi 16 10
*215* A56 1sh6p ultra & multi 95 95

Campaign to eradicate cattle plague.

Anopheles Mosquito and Sick Man — A57

Design: 4p, World Health Organization emblem and vaccination.

**1968, Apr. 7 Litho. *Perf. 14***

*216* A57 4p dp lil rose & blk 14 10
*217* A57 1sh6p org yel & blk 80 80

20th anniv. of the WHO.

Shackled Hands, Map of Nigeria and Human Rights Flame
A58

Design: 1sh6p, Flag of Nigeria and human rights flame (vert.).

**1968, July 1 Photo. *Perf. 14***

*218* A58 4p dp bl, yel & blk 10 7
*219* A58 1sh6p grn, blk & red 55 55

International Human Rights Year, 1968.

Hand and Doves — A59

**1968, Oct. 1 Unwmk. *Perf. 14***

*220* A59 4p brt bl & multi 9 6
*221* A59 1sh6p blk & multi 50 50

5th anniversary of the Federal Republic.

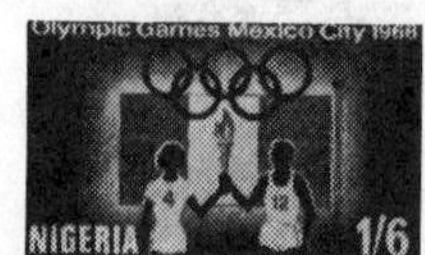


Olympic Rings, Nigerian Flag and Athletes
A60

Design: 4p, Map of Nigeria and Olympic rings.

**1968, Oct. 14 Photo. *Perf. 14***

*222* A60 4p red, blk & emer 9 6
*223* A60 1sh6p multi 50 50

Issued to commemorate the 19th Olympic Games, Mexico City, Oct. 12-27.

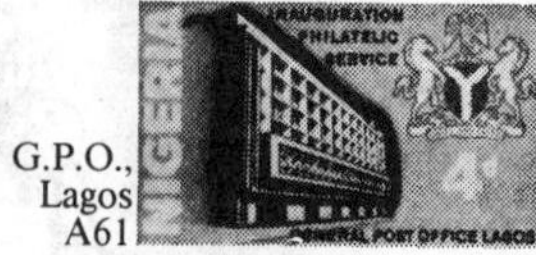


G.P.O., Lagos
A61

**1969, Apr. 11 Unwmk. *Perf. 14***

*224* A61 4p emer & blk 7 6
*225* A61 1sh6p dk bl & blk 48 48

Opening of the Nigerian Philatelic Service of the GPO, Lagos.

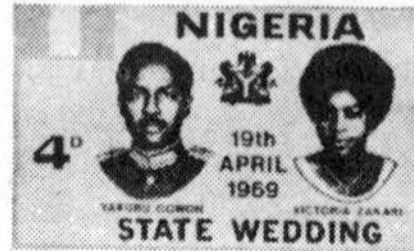


Gen. Yakubu Gowon and Victoria Zakari
A62

***Perf. 13x13½***

**1969, Sept. 20 Litho. Unwmk.**

*226* A62 4p emer & choc 7 6
*227* A62 1sh6p emer & blk 48 48

Issued to commemorate the wedding of Yakubu Gowon, head of state of Nigeria, and Miss Victoria Zakari, Apr. 19, 1969.

Development Bank Emblem and "5" — A63

Design: 1sh6p, Emblem and rays.

**1969, Oct. 18 Litho. *Perf. 14***

*228* A63 4p dk bl, blk & org 8 7
*229* A63 1sh6p dk pur, yel & blk 55 55

Issued to commemorate the 5th anniversary of the African Development Bank.

ILO Emblem
A64

Design: 1sh6p, ILO emblem and world map.

**1969, Nov. 15 Photo.**

*230* A64 4p pur & blk 8 7
*231* A64 1sh6p grn & blk 55 55

50th anniv. of the ILO.

Tourist Year Emblem and Musicians
A65

12-Spoke Wheel and Arms of Nigeria
A66

Designs: 4p, Olumo Rock and Tourist Year emblem (horiz.). 1sh6p, Assob Falls.

**1969, Dec. 30 Photo. *Perf. 14***

*232* A65 4p bl & multi 8 7
*233* A65 1sh emer & blk 36 36
*234* A65 1sh6p multi 55 55

International Year of African Tourism.

***Perf. 11½x11, 11x11½***

**1970, May 28 Photo. Unwmk.**

Designs: 4p, Map of Nigeria and tree with 12 fruits representing 12 tribes. 1sh6p, People bound by common destiny and map of Nigeria. 2sh, Torch with 12 flames and map of Africa (horiz.).

*235* A66 4p gold, bl & blk 7 6
*236* A66 1sh gold & multi 38 38
*237* A66 1sh6p grn & blk 55 55
*238* A66 2sh bl, org, gold & blk 75 75

Establishment of a 12-state administrative structure in Nigeria.

UPU Headquarters, Bern — A67

**1970, June 29 Unwmk. *Perf. 14***

*239* A67 4p pur & yel 8 7
*240* A67 1sh6p bl & vio bl 50 50

Opening of the new UPU Headquarters, Bern.

U.N. Emblem and Charter
A68

Student
A69

Design: 1sh6p, U.N. emblem and headquarters, New York.

**1970, Sept. 1 Photo. *Perf. 14***

*241* A68 4p brn org, buff & blk 8 6
*242* A68 1sh6p dk bl, gold & bis brn 48 48

25th anniversary of the United Nations.

**1970, Sept. 30 Litho. *Perf. 14x13½***

Designs: 2p, Oil drilling platform. 6p, Durbar horsemen. 9p, Soldier and sailors raising flag. 1sh, Soccer player. 1sh6p, Parliament Building. 2sh, Kainji Dam. 2sh6p, Export products: Timber, rubber, peanuts, cocoa and palm produce.

*243* A69 2p bl & multi 5 5
*244* A69 4p bl & multi 8 8
*245* A69 6p bl & multi 14 14
*246* A69 9p bl & multi 25 25
*247* A69 1sh bl & multi 35 35
*248* A69 1sh6p bl & multi 65 65
*249* A69 2sh bl & multi 85 85
*250* A69 2sh6p bl & multi 1.10 1.10
*Nos. 243-250 (8)* 3.47 3.47

Ten years of independence.

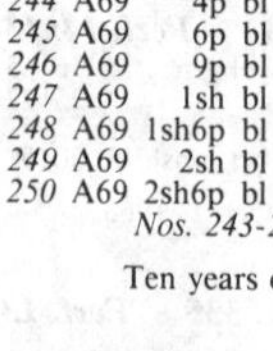

Black and White Men Uprooting Racism
A70

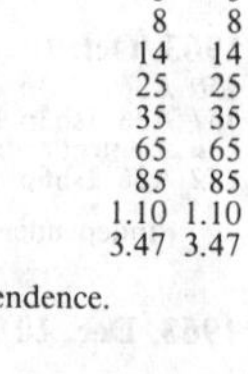

Ibibio Mask, c. 1900
A71

Designs: 4p, Black and white school children and globe (horiz.). 1sh6p, World map with black and white stripes. 2sh, Black and white men, shoulder to shoulder (horiz.).

*Perf. 13½x14, 14x13½*

**1971, March 22 Photo. Unwmk.**

*251* A70 4p multi 7 6
*252* A70 1sh yel & multi 20 20
*253* A70 1sh6p bl, yel & blk 38 38
*254* A70 2sh multi 60 60

Intl. year against racial discrimination.

**1971, Sept. 30** ***Perf. 13½x14***

Nigerian Antiquities: 1sh3p, Bronze mask of a King of Benin, c. 1700. 1sh9p, Bronze figure of a King of Ife.

*255* A71 4p lt bl & blk 75 6
*256* A71 1sh3p yel bis & blk 44 44
*257* A71 1sh9p ap grn, dp grn & blk 60 60

Type of 1965-66 Redrawn
Imprint: "N.S.P. & M. Co. Ltd."
Added to "MAURICE FIEVET"

*Perf. 13x13½; 14x13½ (6p)*

**1969-72 Photo.**

**Size: 38x23mm**

*258* A49 1p red & multi 10 5
*259* A49 2p brt red & multi 20 5
*260* A49 3p multi ('71) 20 5
*261* A49 4p lil & multi 32 5
*262* A49 6p brt vio & multi ('71) 80 24
*263* A49 9p dl bl & dp org ('70) 80 32

**Size: 45x26mm**

*264* A49 1sh multi ('71) 90 40
*265* A49 1sh3p multi ('71) 1.25 48
*266* A49 2sh6p multi ('72) 4.75 2.00
*267* A49 5sh multi ('72) 6.50 3.25
*Nos. 258-267 (10)* 15.82 6.89

UNICEF Emblem and Children A72

Satellite Earth Station A73

**1971, Dec. 11** ***Perf. 14***

UNICEF 25th anniv.: 1sh3p, Mother and child. 1sh9p, African mother carrying child on back.

*270* A72 4p pur & yel 8 6
*271* A72 1sh3p org, pur & plum 45 45
*272* A72 1sh9p bl & dk bl 65 65

**1971, Dec. 30 Photo.** ***Perf. 14***

Designs: Various views of satellite communications earth station, Lanlate, Nigeria. All horizontal.

*273* A73 4p multi 10 9
*274* A73 1sh3p bl, blk & grn 65 65
*275* A73 1sh9p org & blk 95 95
*276* A73 3sh brt pink & blk 1.50 1.50

Satellite communications earth station, Lanlate, Nigeria.

Fair Emblem — A74

Designs (Fair Emblem and): 1sh3p, Map of Africa (horiz.). 1sh9p, Globe with map of Africa.

*Perf. 13½x13, 13x13½*

**1972, Feb. 23 Litho.**

*277* A74 4p multi 8 7
*278* A74 1sh3p dl pur, yel & gold 48 48
*279* A74 1sh9p org, yel & blk 70 70

First All-Africa Trade Fair, Nairobi, Kenya, Feb. 23-Mar. 5.

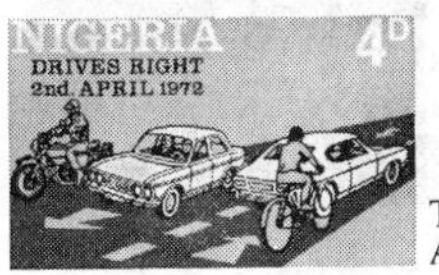

Traffic A75

Designs: 1sh3p, Traffic flow at circle. 1sh9p, Car and truck on road. 3sh, Intersection with lights and pedestrians.

**1972, June 23 Photo.** ***Perf. 13x13½***

*280* A75 4p org & blk 14 12
*281* A75 1sh3p lt bl & multi 90 90
*282* A75 1sh9p emer & multi 1.35 1.35
*283* A75 3sh yel & multi 2.00 2.00

Introduction of right-hand driving in Nigeria, Apr. 2, 1972.

Nok Style Terra-cotta Head, Katsina Ala — A76

Designs: 1sh3p, Roped bronze vessel, Igbo Ukwu. 1sh9p, Bone harpoon, Daima (horiz.).

*Perf. 13½x13, 13x13½*

**1972, Sept. 1 Litho.**

*284* A76 4p dk bl & multi 14 10
*285* A76 1sh3p gold & multi 65 65
*286* A76 1sh9p dp bl & multi 85 85

All-Nigeria Festival of the Arts, Kaduna, Dec. 9.

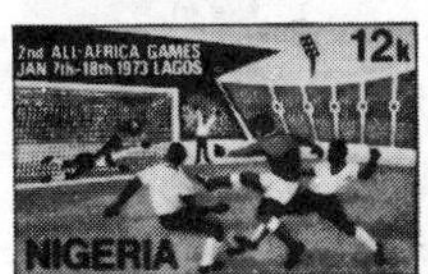

Games Emblem and Soccer A77

Designs: 5k, Running. 18k, Table tennis. 25k, Stadium (vert.).

**1973, Jan. 8 Litho.** ***Perf. 13x13½***

*287* A77 5k lil, bl & blk 20 20
*288* A77 12k multi 45 45
*289* A77 18k yel & multi 70 70
*290* A77 25k brn & multi 1.00 1.00

2nd All-Africa Games, Lagos, Jan. 7-18.

Hides and Skins — A78

Wmk. 379- NIGERIA in Continuous Wavy Lines

Designs: 2k, Natural gas tanks. 3k, Cement works. 5k, Cattle ranching. 7k, Lumbermill. 8k, Oil refinery. 10k, Leopards, Yankari Game Reserve. 12k, New civic building. 15k, Sugar cane harvesting. 18k, Palm oil production (vert.). 20k, Vaccine production. 25k, Modern docks. 30k, Argungu Fishing Festival (vert.). 35k, Textile industry. 50k, Pottery (vert.). 1n, Eko Bridge. 2n, Teaching Hospital, Lagos.

Imprint at left: "N S P & M Co Ltd"
6mm on Litho. Stamps, 5¼ mm on Photo. Stamps

**Litho.; Photo. (50k)**

**1973-74** ***Perf. 14***

*291* A78 1k multi, buff imprint 22 22
*292* A78 2k multi ('74) 35 32
*293* A78 3k multi ('74) 10 5
*294* A78 5k grn & multi ('74) 45 32
*295* A78 7k multi 22 16
*296* A78 8k multi 25 18
*297* A78 10k multi 55 35
*298* A78 12k multi 40 25
*299* A78 15k multi 45 35
*300* A78 18k multi 60 40
*301* A78 20k multi 65 45
*302* A78 25k multi 75 55
*303* A78 30k multi 85 65
*304* A78 35k multi 1.00 70
*305* A78 50k blk background 4.50 2.75
*306* A78 1n multi 3.00 2.25
*307* A78 2n multi 4.50 5.25
*Nos. 291-307 (17)* 18.84 15.20

Imprint at left: "N. S. P. & M. Co. Ltd."

**1973 Photo., Imprint 5¼mm**

*291a* A78 1k multi, dk grn foliage 10 9
*291b* A78 1k multi, brt grn foliage 10 9
*292a* A78 2k multi 9 5
*294a* A78 5k multi, emer fields 65 45
*294b* A78 5k multi, yel grn fields 35 22
*297a* A78 10k multi 45 25
*298a* A78 12k multi 1.10 1.00
*300a* A78 18k multi 1.50 1.25
*301a* A78 20k multi 2.75 2.50
*303a* A78 30k multi 3.00 2.50
*305a* A78 50k dk brn background 2.25 1.75
*306a* A78 1n multi 9.00 8.00
*Nos. 291a-306a (12)* 21.34 18.15

**1975-79 Wmk. 379**

*291c* A78 1k multi, dk grn foliage 9 9
*292b* A78 2k multi ('75) 9 9
*293a* A78 3k multi ('75) 10 7
*294c* A78 5k emer fields ('76) 18 10
*296a* A78 8k multi ('76) 22 14
*297b* A78 10k multi ('76) 35 18
*299a* A78 15k multi 45 35
*301b* A78 20k multi, pale pink table, door, windows ('79) 65 45
*302a* A78 25k multi, pur barges 70 70
*302b* A78 25k multi, brn barges 70 70
*305b* A78 50k dk brn background, grn imprint 1.50 1.25
*307a* A78 2n multi 5.50 5.25
*Nos. 291c-307a (12)* 10.53 9.37

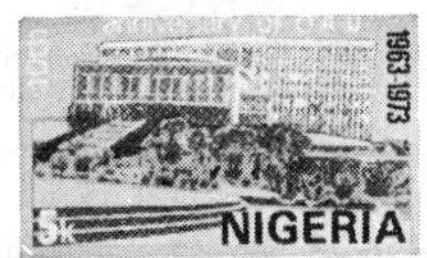

OAU Headquarters — A79

Designs: 18k, OAU flag (vert.). 30k, Stairs leading to OAU emblem (vert.).

**1973, May 25 Litho.** ***Perf. 14***

*308* A79 5k bl & multi 16 16
*309* A79 18k ol grn & multi 65 65
*310* A79 30k lil & multi 1.10 1.10

Org. for African Unity, 10th anniv.

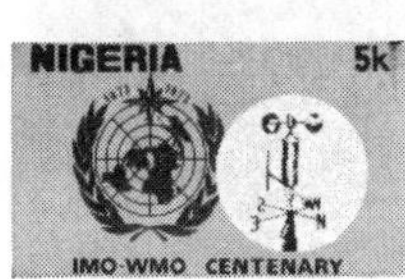

WMO Emblem, Weather Vane — A80

**1973, Sept. 4 Litho.** ***Perf. 13***

*311* A80 5k multi 18 18
*312* A80 30k multi 1.40 1.40

Cent. of intl. meteorological cooperation.

View of Ibadan University A81

Designs: 12k, Campus, crest and graph showing growth (vert.). 18k, Campus, students and crest. 30k, Teaching hospital.

**1973, Nov. 17** ***Perf. 14***

*313* A81 5k lt bl & multi 20 20
*314* A81 12k lil & multi 50 50
*315* A81 18k org & multi 75 75
*316* A81 30k bl, org & blk 1.25 1.25

University of Ibadan, 25th anniversary.

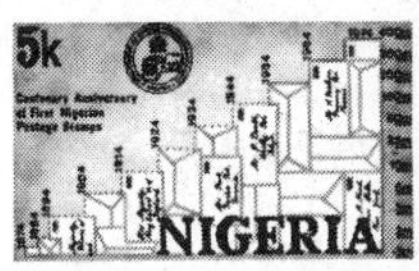

Growth of Mail, 1874-1974 A82

Designs: 12k, Nigerian Post emblem and Northern Nigeria No. 18A. 18k, Postal emblem and Lagos No. 1. 30k, Map of Nigeria and means of transportation.

**1974, June 10 Litho.** ***Perf. 14***

*317* A82 5k grn, blk & org 20 20
*318* A82 12k grn & multi 48 48
*319* A82 18k grn, lil & blk 1.25 1.25
*320* A82 30k blk & multi 1.65 1.65

Centenary of first Nigerian postage stamps.

Globe and UPU Emblem A83

UPU cent.: 18k, World map and means of transportation. 30k, Letters.

**1974, Oct. 9**

*321* A83 5k bl & multi 28 28
*322* A83 18k org & multi 1.00 1.00
*323* A83 30k brn & multi 1.65 1.65

Hungry and Well-fed Children — A84

Designs: 12k, Chicken farm (horiz.). 30k, Irrigation project.

**1974, Nov. 25 Litho.** ***Perf. 14***

*324* A84 5k org, blk & grn 24 24
*325* A84 12k multi 55 55
*326* A84 30k multi 1.40 1.40

Freedom from Hunger.

A85

Map of Nigeria with Telex Network, Teleprinter — A86

**1975, July 3 Litho.** ***Perf. 14***

*327* A85 5k multi 20 20
*328* A85 12k multi 50 50
*329* A86 18k multi 75 75
*330* A86 30k multi 1.25 1.25

Inauguration of Nigeria Telex Network.

A little time given to the study of the arrangement of the Scott Catalogue can make it easier to use effectively.

Queen Amina of Zaria (1536-1566) A87

Alexander Graham Bell A88

**1975, Aug. 18 Litho. Perf. 14**

| | | |
|---|---|---|
| *331* A87 5k multi | 25 | 25 |
| *332* A87 18k multi | 90 | 90 |
| *333* A87 30k multi | 1.50 | 1.50 |

International Women's Year 1975.

**1976, Mar. 10 Wmk. 379**

Designs: 18k, Hands beating gong, modern telephone operator (horiz.). 25k, Telephones, 1876, 1976.

| | | |
|---|---|---|
| *334* A88 5k pink, blk & ocher | 22 | 22 |
| *335* A88 18k dp lil & multi | 80 | 80 |
| *336* A88 25k lt bl, vio bl & blk | 1.10 | 1.10 |

Centenary of first telephone call by Alexander Graham Bell, Mar. 10, 1876.

Children Going to School — A89

Designs: 5k, Child learning to write (horiz.). 25k, Classroom.

**1976, Sept. 20 Litho. Perf. 14**

| | | |
|---|---|---|
| *337* A89 5k multi | 22 | 22 |
| *338* A89 18k multi | 80 | 80 |
| *339* A89 25k multi | 1.10 | 1.10 |

Launching of universal primary education in 1976.

Traditional Musical Instruments A90

Designs: 5k, Carved mask (festival emblem). 10k, National Arts Theater, Lagos. 12k, Nigerian and African women's hair styles. 30k, Nigerian carvings.

**1976-77 Wmk. 379**

| | | |
|---|---|---|
| *340* A90 5k blk, gold & grn | 18 | 18 |
| *341* A90 10k multi | 35 | 35 |
| *342* A90 12k multi | 45 | 45 |
| *343* A90 18k brn, ocher & blk | 65 | 65 |
| *344* A90 30k multi | 1.10 | 1.10 |
| *Nos. 340-344 (5)* | 2.73 | 2.73 |

2nd World Black and African Festival of Arts and Culture, Lagos, Jan. 15-Feb. 12, 1977. Issue dates: 5k, 18k, Nov. 1, 1976; others Jan. 15, 1977.

Gen. Muhammed Broadcasting and Map of Nigeria A91

Designs: 18k, Gen. Muhammed as Commander in Chief (vert.). 30k, in battle dress (vert.).

**1977, Feb. 13 Litho. Perf. 14**

| | | |
|---|---|---|
| *345* A91 5k multi | 16 | 16 |
| *346* A91 18k multi | 60 | 60 |
| *347* A91 30k multi | 1.00 | 1.00 |

Gen. Murtala Ramat Muhammed, Head of State and Commander in Chief, 1st death anniversary.

Scouts Clearing Street A92

Designs: 5k, Senior and Junior Boy Scouts saluting (vert.). 25k, Scouts working on farm. 30k, African Scout Jamboree emblem, map of Africa.

**1977, Apr. 1 Wmk. 379**

| | | |
|---|---|---|
| *348* A92 5k multi | 22 | 22 |
| *349* A92 18k multi | 65 | 65 |
| *350* A92 25k multi | 95 | 95 |
| *351* A92 30k multi | 1.30 | 1.30 |

First All-Africa Boy Scout Jamboree, Sherehills, Jos, Nigeria, Apr. 2-8, 1977.

Trade Fair Emblem A93

Designs (Emblem and): 5k, View of Fair grounds. 30k, Weaver and potter.

**1977, Nov. 27 Litho. Perf. 13**

| | | |
|---|---|---|
| *352* A93 5k multi | 16 | 16 |
| *353* A93 18k multi | 55 | 55 |
| *354* A93 30k multi | 95 | 95 |

1st Lagos Intl. Trade Fair, Nov. 27-Dec. 11.

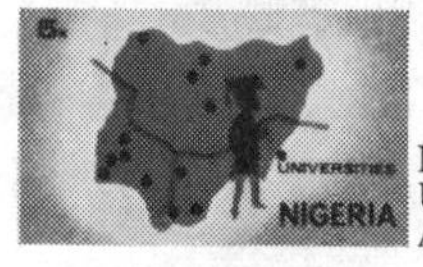

Nigeria's 13 Universities A94

Designs: 12k, Map of West African highways and telecommunications network. 18k, Training of technicians, and cogwheel. 30k, World map and map of Argentina with Buenos Aires.

**1978, Apr. 28 Wmk. 379**

| | | |
|---|---|---|
| *355* A94 5k multi | 12 | 12 |
| *356* A94 12k multi | 32 | 32 |
| *357* A94 18k multi | 48 | 48 |
| *358* A94 30k multi | 80 | 80 |

Global Conf. on Technical Cooperation among Developing Countries, Buenos Aires.

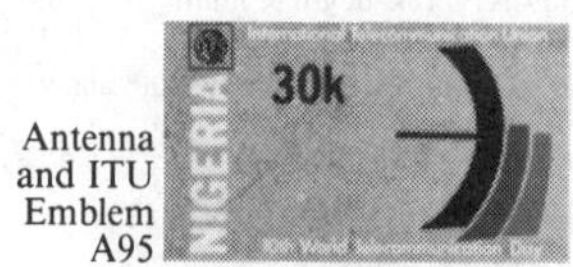

Antenna and ITU Emblem A95

**1978, May 17 Litho. Perf. 14**

| | | |
|---|---|---|
| *359* A95 30k multi | 1.00 | 1.00 |

10th World Telecommunications Day.

Students on Cassava Plantation A96

Designs: 18k, Woman working in backyard vegetable garden. 30k, Plantain harvest (vert.).

**1978, July 7 Litho. Perf. 14**

| | | |
|---|---|---|
| *360* A96 5k multi | 14 | 14 |
| *361* A96 18k multi | 42 | 42 |
| *362* A96 30k multi | 65 | 65 |

"Operation Feed the Nation."

Mother Holding Sick Child A97

Designs: 12k, Sick boy at health station. 18k, Vaccination of children. 30k, Syringe and WHO emblem (vert.).

**1978, Aug. 31 Wmk. 379**

| | | |
|---|---|---|
| *363* A97 5k multi | 15 | 15 |
| *364* A97 12k multi | 34 | 34 |
| *365* A97 18k multi | 48 | 48 |
| *366* A97 30k multi | 75 | 75 |

Global eradication of smallpox.

Bronze Horseman from Benin — A98

Nigerian antiquities: 5k, Nok terracotta figure from Bwari. 12k, Bronze snail and animal from Igbo-Ukwu (horiz.). 18k, Bronze statue of a king of Ife.

**1978, Oct. 27 Litho. Perf. 14**

| | | |
|---|---|---|
| *367* A98 5k multi | 12 | 12 |
| *368* A98 12k multi | 32 | 32 |
| *369* A98 18k multi | 48 | 48 |
| *370* A98 30k multi | 70 | 70 |

Anti-Apartheid Emblem — A99

**1978, Dec. 10 Perf. 14**

| | | |
|---|---|---|
| *371* A99 18k red, yel & blk | 45 | 45 |

Anti-Apartheid Year.

Wright Brothers, Flyer A — A100

Design: 18k, Nigerian Air Force fighters flying in formation.

**1978, Dec. 28**

| | | |
|---|---|---|
| *372* A100 5k multi | 10 | 10 |
| *373* A100 18k multi | 48 | 48 |

75th anniversary of powered flight.

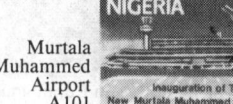

Murtala Muhammed Airport A101

**1979, Mar. 15 Litho. Perf. 14**

| | | |
|---|---|---|
| *374* A101 5k brt bl & blk | 15 | 15 |

Inauguration of Murtala Muhammed Airport.

Young Stamp Collector A102

**1979, Apr. 11**

| | | |
|---|---|---|
| *375* A102 5k multi | 15 | 15 |

Philatelic Week and 10th anniversary of National Philatelic Service.

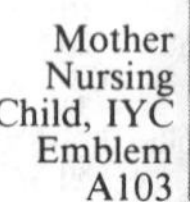

Mother Nursing Child, IYC Emblem A103

Designs: 18k, Children at study. 25k, Children at play (vert.).

**1979, June 28 Wmk. 379 Perf. 14**

| | | |
|---|---|---|
| *376* A103 5k multi | 9 | 9 |
| *377* A103 18k multi | 38 | 38 |
| *378* A103 25k multi | 48 | 48 |

International Year of the Child.

Preparation of Audio-visual Material — A104

Design: 30k, Adult education class.

**1979, July 25 Photo. & Engr.**

| | | |
|---|---|---|
| *379* A104 10k multi | 18 | 18 |
| *380* A104 30k multi | 55 | 55 |

Intl. Bureau of Education, Geneva, 50th anniv.

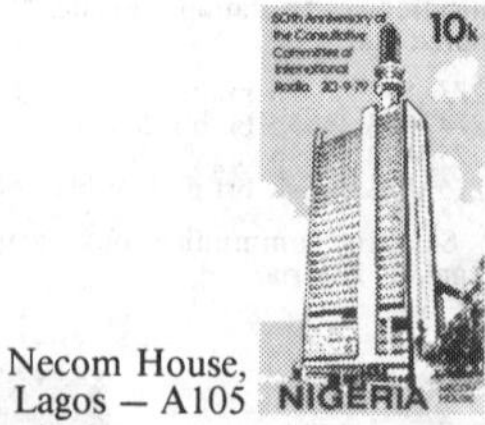

Necom House, Lagos — A105

**1979, Sept. 20 Litho. Perf. 13½x14**

| | | |
|---|---|---|
| *381* A105 10k multi | 30 | 30 |

Intl. Radio Consultative Committee (CCIR) of the ITU, 50th anniv.

Trainees and Survey Equipment A106

**1979, Dec. 12 Photo. Perf. 14**

| | | |
|---|---|---|
| *382* A106 10k multi | 30 | 30 |

Economic Commission for Africa, 21st anniversary.

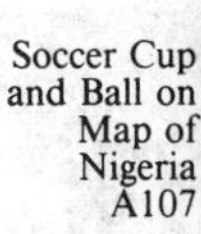

Soccer Cup and Ball on Map of Nigeria
A107

**1980, Mar. 8**

*383* A107 10k *shown* 14 14
*384* A107 30k *Player,* vert. 45 45

12th African Cup of Nations Soccer Championship, Lagos and Ibadan, Mar.

Swimming, Moscow '80 Emblem
A108

**Litho. &. Engr.**

**1980, July 19** ***Perf. 14***

*385* A108 10k *Wrestling,* vert. 22 22
*386* A108 20k *Long jump, vert.* 42 42
*387* A108 30k *shown* 65 65
*388* A108 45k *Women's basketball,* vert. 1.00 1.00

22nd Summer Olympic Games, Moscow, July 19-Aug. 3.

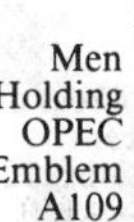

Men Holding OPEC Emblem
A109

**1980, Sept. 15** **Litho. & Engr.**

*389* A109 10k *shown* 18 18
*390* A109 45k *Anniversary emblem,* vert. 80 80

OPEC, 20th anniversary.

First Steam Locomotive in Nigeria
A110

**1980, Oct. 2** **Wmk. 379** ***Perf. 14***

*391* A110 10k *shown* 22 22
*392* A110 20k *Unloading freight car* 42 42
*393* A110 30k *Freight train* 65 65

Nigerian Railway Corp., 75th anniv.

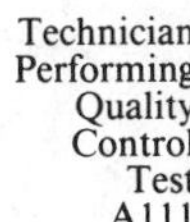

Technician Performing Quality Control Test
A111

**1980, Oct. 14**

*394* A111 10k *Scale, ruler,* vert. 18 18
*395* A111 30k *shown* 55 55

World Standards Day.

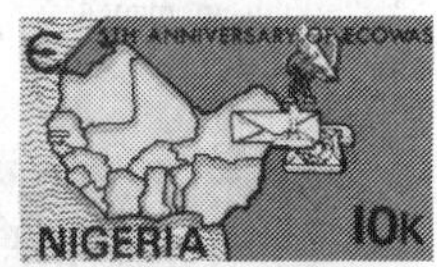
Map of West Africa showing ECOWAS Members, Modes of Communication — A112

**1980, Nov. 5** **Litho. & Engr.**

*396* A112 10k shown 20 20
*396A* A112 25k Transportation 48 48
*397* A112 30k Map, cow, cocoa 60 60
*398* A112 45k Map, industrial symbols 85 85

Woman with Cane Sweeping — A113

**Wmk. 379**

**1981, June 25** **Litho.** ***Perf. 14***

*399* A113 10k shown 16 16
*400* A113 30k Amputee photographer 50 50

Intl. Year of the Disabled.

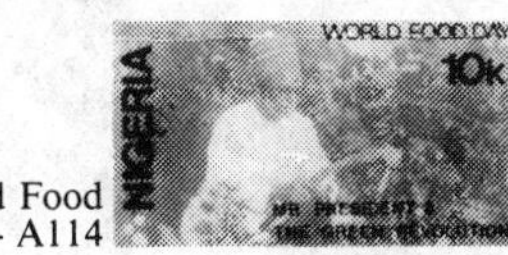
World Food Day — A114

**1981, Oct. 16** **Litho. & Engr.**

*401* A114 10k Pres. Shenu Shagari 20 20
*402* A114 25k Produce, vert. 50 50
*403* A114 30k Tomato crop, vert. 60 60
*404* A114 45k Pig farm 90 90

Anti-apartheid Year — A115

**1981, Dec. 10** **Litho.**

*405* A115 30k Soweto riot 55 55
*406* A115 45k Police hitting man, vert. 80 80

Scouting Year
A116

**1982, Feb. 22** **Litho.** ***Perf. 14***

*407* A116 30k Animal first aid 50 50
*408* A116 45k Baden-Powell, scouts 75 75

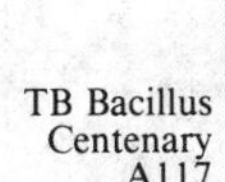
TB Bacillus Centenary
A117

**1982, Mar. 24** **Litho.** ***Perf. 14***

*409* A117 10k Inoculation 16 16
*410* A117 30k Research 48 48
*411* A117 45k Patient being x-rayed, vert. 70 70

10th Anniv. of UN Conference on Human Environment — A118

**1982, June 10** **Litho.**

*412* A118 10k Keep your environment clean 15 15
*413* A118 20k Check air pollution 30 30
*414* A118 30k Preserve natural environment 48 48
*415* A118 45k Reafforestation concerns all 70 70

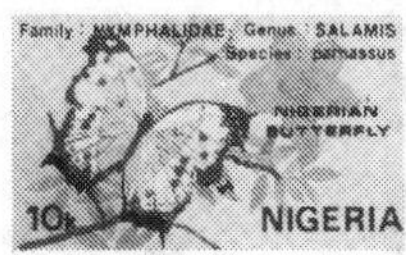
Salamis Parnassus
A119

**1982, Sept. 15** **Litho.**

*416* A119 10k shown 20 20
*417* A119 20k Papilio zalmoxis 38 38
*418* A119 30k Pachylophus beckeri 60 60
*419* A119 45k Papilio hesperus 85 85

25th Anniv. of Natl. Museum
A120

**1982, Nov. 18** **Wmk. 379**

*420* A120 10k Statuettes, vert. 16 16
*421* A120 20k Bronze leopard 30 30
*422* A120 30k Soapstone seated figure, vert. 48 48
*423* A120 45k Wooden helmet mask 70 70

Family Day — A121

Commonwealth Day — A122

**1983, Mar. 8** **Litho.** ***Perf. 14***

*424* A121 10k Extended family, house, horiz. 25 25
*425* A121 30k Family 75 75

**1983, Mar. 14**

*426* A122 10k Satellite view, horiz. 22 22
*427* A122 25k Natl. Assembly buildings, horiz. 55 55
*428* A122 30k Oil exploration 70 70
*429* A122 45k Runners 1.00 1.00

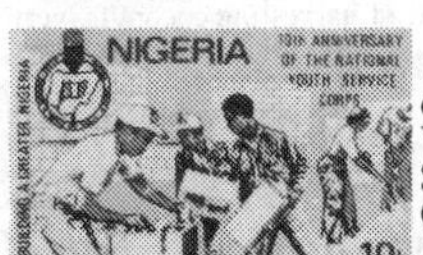
10th Anniv. of Natl. Youth Service Corps
A123

**1983, May 25** **Litho.** ***Perf. 14***

*430* A123 10k Construction 25 25
*431* A123 25k Climbing wall, vert. 55 55
*432* A123 30k Marching, vert. 75 75

World Communications Year — A124

**Wmk. 380**

**1983, July 22** **Litho.** ***Perf. 14***

*433* A124 10k Mailman, vert. 20 20
*434* A124 25k Newspaper stand 52 52
*435* A124 30k Traditional horn messenger 65 65
*436* A124 45k TV news broadcast 95 95

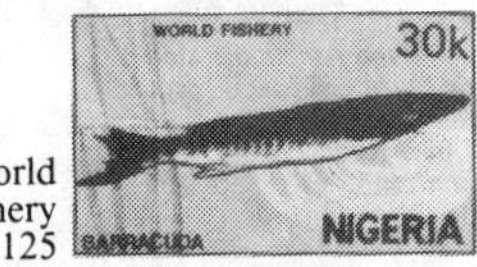
World Fishery
A125

**1983, Sept. 22** **Litho.** **Wmk. 373**

*437* A125 10k Pink shrimp 20 20
*438* A125 25k Long neck groaker 50 50
*439* A125 30k Barracuda 60 60
*440* A125 45k Fishing technique 90 90

Boys' Brigade, 75th Anniv.
A126

**1983, Oct. 14** ***Perf. 14***

*441* A126 10k Boys, emblem, vert. 22 22
*442* A126 30k Food production 55 55
*443* A126 45k Skill training 1.00 1.00

Fight Against Polio Campaign
A127

**1984, Feb. 29** **Litho.** ***Perf. 14***

*444* A127 10k Crippled boy, vert. 20 20
*445* A127 25k Vaccination 50 50
*446* A127 30k Healthy child, vert. 65 65

Hartebeests
A128

**Wmk. 380**

**1984, May 25** **Litho.** ***Perf. 14***

*447* A128 10k Waterbuck, vert. 20 20
*448* A128 25k shown 50 50
*449* A128 30k Buffalo 65 65
*450* A128 45k African golden monkey, vert. 95 95

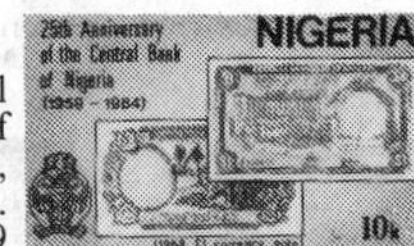
Central Bank of Nigeria, 25th Anniv.
A129

**1984, July 2** **Wmk. 380**

*451* A129 10k £1 note, 1968 22 22
*452* A129 25k Bank 55 55
*453* A129 30k £5 note, 1959 70 70

1984 Summer Olympics, Los Angeles
A130

African Development Bank, 20th Anniv.
A131

**Wmk. 379**

**1984, Aug. 9** **Litho.** ***Perf. 14***

*454* A130 10k Boxing 18 18
*455* A130 25k Discus 42 42
*456* A130 30k Weight lifting 50 50
*457* A130 45k Bicycling 75 75

**1984, Sept. 10**

Designs: 10k, Irrigation project, Lesotho. 25k, Bomi Hills roadway, Liberia. 30k, Education development, Seychelles. 45k, Coal mining and transportation, Niger. Nos. 459-461 horiz.

*458* A131 10k multi 18 18
*459* A131 25k multi 45 45
*460* A131 30k multi 52 52
*461* A131 45k multi 80 80

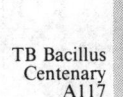

Rare Bird Species — A132

**1984, Oct. 24**

| | | | | | |
|---|---|---|---|---|---|
| *462* | A132 | 10k | Pin-tailed whydah | 20 | 20 |
| *463* | A132 | 25k | Spur-winged plover | 50 | 50 |
| *464* | A132 | 30k | Red bishop | 60 | 60 |
| *465* | A132 | 45k | Francolin | 90 | 90 |

Inscriptions, including country name, denomination and descriptions vary widely in size and style.

Intl. Civil Aviation Organization, 40th Anniv. — A132a

**1984, Dec. 7 Litho. *Perf. 14***

| | | | | | |
|---|---|---|---|---|---|
| *465A* | A132a | 10k | shown | 28 | 28 |
| *465B* | A132a | 45k | Jet circling Earth | 1.25 | 1.25 |

Fight Against Indiscipline A133

**1985, Feb. 27**

| | | | | | |
|---|---|---|---|---|---|
| *466* | A133 | 20k | Encourage punctuality | 38 | 38 |
| *467* | A133 | 50k | Discourage bribery | 95 | 95 |

Intl. Youth Year A134

OPEC, 25th Anniv. A135

**1985, June 5**

| | | | | | |
|---|---|---|---|---|---|
| *468* | A134 | 20k | Sports, horiz. | 25 | 25 |
| *469* | A134 | 50k | Nationalism | 65 | 65 |
| *470* | A134 | 55k | Service organizations | 75 | 75 |

**1985, Sept. 15**

| | | | | | |
|---|---|---|---|---|---|
| *471* | A135 | 20k | shown | 38 | 38 |
| *472* | A135 | 50k | World map, horiz. | 95 | 95 |

Natl. Independence, 25th Anniv. — A136

**1985, Sept. 25**

| | | | | | |
|---|---|---|---|---|---|
| *473* | A136 | 20k | Oil refinery | 35 | 35 |
| *474* | A136 | 50k | Map of states | 85 | 85 |
| *475* | A136 | 55k | Monument | 90 | 90 |
| *476* | A136 | 60k | Eleme Oil Refinery | 1.00 | 1.00 |
| *a* | | | Souv. sheet of 4, Nos. 473-476 | 10.00 | |

No. 476a has multicolored inscribed margin. Size: 101x100mm.

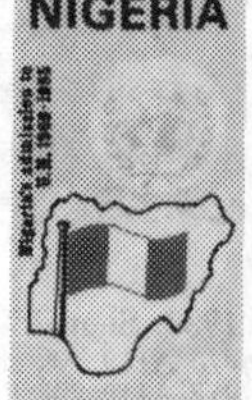


World Tourism Day A137

UN, 40th Anniv. A138

**1985, Sept. 27**

| | | | | | |
|---|---|---|---|---|---|
| *477* | A137 | 20k | Waterfalls | 24 | 24 |
| *478* | A137 | 50k | Crafts | 60 | 60 |
| *479* | A137 | 55k | Carved calabashes, flag | 65 | 65 |
| *480* | A137 | 60k | Leather goods, rug | 75 | 75 |

**1985, Oct. 7**

| | | | | | |
|---|---|---|---|---|---|
| *481* | A138 | 20k | Emblem, map, flag | 40 | 40 |
| *482* | A138 | 50k | UN building, horiz. | 1.00 | 1.00 |
| *483* | A138 | 55k | Emblem, horiz. | 1.10 | 1.10 |

Admission of Nigeria to UN, 25th anniv.

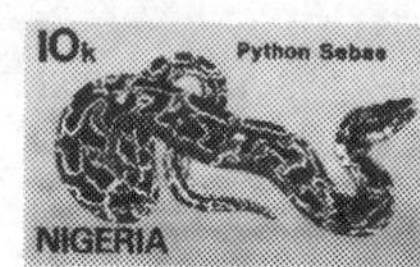


African Reptiles A139

**1986, Apr. 15 Wmk. 379 *Perf. 14***

| | | | | | |
|---|---|---|---|---|---|
| *484* | A139 | 10k | Python | 20 | 20 |
| *485* | A139 | 20k | Crocodile | 40 | 40 |
| *486* | A139 | 25k | Gopher tortoise | 50 | 50 |
| *487* | A139 | 30k | Chameleon | 60 | 60 |

Volkswagen Automobile Assembly Factory — A140

Designs: 1k, Social worker with children, vert. 5k, Modern housing development. 10k, Modern method of harvesting coconuts, vert. 15k, Port activities. 20k, Tecoma stans, flower, vert. 25k, Medical care. 35k, Telephone operators. 40k, Nkpokiti dancers, vert. 45k, Hibiscus. 50k, Modern p.o. 1n, Stone quarry. 2n, Technical education.

**1986, June 16 Wmk. 379 *Perf. 14***

| | | | | | |
|---|---|---|---|---|---|
| *488* | A140 | 1k | multi | 5 | 5 |
| *489* | A140 | 2k | multi | 5 | 5 |
| *490* | A140 | 5k | multi | 5 | 5 |
| *491* | A140 | 10k | multi | 5 | 5 |
| *492* | A140 | 15k | multi | 8 | 8 |
| *493* | A140 | 20k | multi | 10 | 10 |
| *494* | A140 | 25k | multi | 12 | 12 |
| *495* | A140 | 35k | multi | 18 | 18 |
| *496* | A140 | 40k | multi | 20 | 20 |
| *497* | A140 | 45k | multi | 22 | 22 |
| *498* | A140 | 50k | multi | 25 | 25 |
| *499* | A140 | 1n | multi | 50 | 50 |
| *500* | A140 | 2n | multi | 1.00 | 1.00 |
| | | | *Nos. 488-500 (13)* | 2.85 | 2.85 |

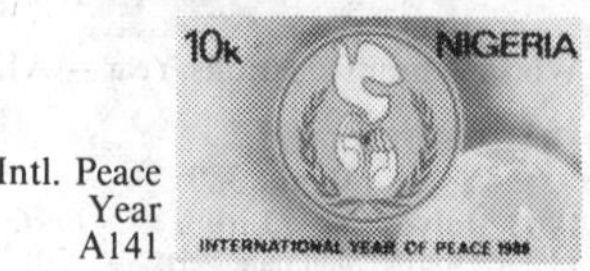


Intl. Peace Year A141

**Wmk. 379**

**1986, June 20 Litho. *Perf. 14***

| | | | | | |
|---|---|---|---|---|---|
| *501* | A141 | 10k | Emblem | 16 | 16 |
| *502* | A141 | 20k | Hands touching globe | 34 | 34 |

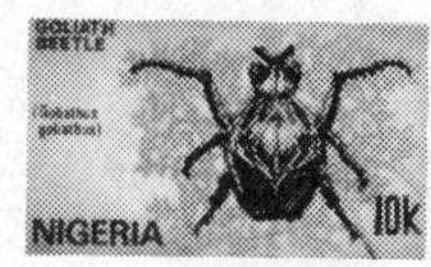


Insects A142

**1986, July 14**

| | | | | | |
|---|---|---|---|---|---|
| *503* | A142 | 10k | Goliath beetle | 20 | 20 |
| *504* | A142 | 20k | Wasp | 40 | 40 |
| *505* | A142 | 25k | Cricket | 50 | 50 |
| *506* | A142 | 30k | Carpet beetle | 60 | 60 |
| *a* | | | Souv. sheet of 4, Nos. 503-506 | 1.75 | 1.75 |

No. 506a has multicolored margin picturing habitat. Size: 120x101mm.

UNICEF, 40th Anniv. A143

Institute of Intl. Affairs, 25th Anniv. A144

**1986, Nov. 11**

| | | | | | |
|---|---|---|---|---|---|
| *507* | A143 | 10k | Oral rehydration | 10 | 10 |
| *508* | A143 | 20k | Immunization | 22 | 22 |
| *509* | A143 | 25k | Breast-feeding | 28 | 28 |
| *510* | A143 | 30k | Mother playing with child | 34 | 34 |

UN Child Survival Campaign.

**1986, Dec. 13**

| | | | | | |
|---|---|---|---|---|---|
| *511* | A144 | 20k | Intl. understanding, horiz. | 14 | 14 |
| *512* | A144 | 30k | shown | 22 | 22 |

Seashells A145

**1987, Mar. 31**

| | | | | | |
|---|---|---|---|---|---|
| *513* | A145 | 10k | Freshwater clam | 6 | 6 |
| *514* | A145 | 20k | Periwinkle | 12 | 12 |
| *515* | A145 | 25k | Bloddy cockle | 16 | 16 |
| *516* | A145 | 30k | Mangrove oyster | 20 | 20 |

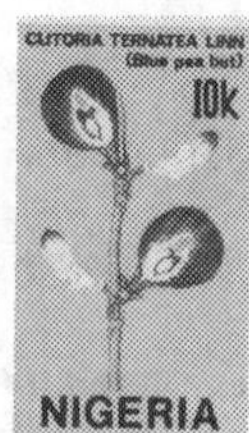

A146 A147

**1987, May 28**

| | | | | | |
|---|---|---|---|---|---|
| *517* | A146 | 10k | Blue pea but | 7 | 7 |
| *518* | A146 | 20k | Hibiscus | 15 | 15 |
| *519* | A147 | 25k | Acanthus montanus | 18 | 18 |
| *520* | A147 | 30k | Combretum racemosum | 20 | 20 |

Hair Styles A148

Intl. Year of Shelter for the Homeless A149

**Wmk. 379**

**1987, Sept. 15 Litho. *Perf. 14***

| | | | | | |
|---|---|---|---|---|---|
| *521* | A148 | 10k | Doka | 5 | 5 |
| *522* | A148 | 20k | Eting | 10 | 10 |
| *523* | A148 | 25k | Agogo | 12 | 12 |
| *524* | A148 | 30k | Goto | 15 | 15 |

**1987, Dec. 10**

| | | | | | |
|---|---|---|---|---|---|
| *525* | A149 | 20k | Homeless family | 10 | 10 |
| *526* | A149 | 30k | Moving to new home | 15 | 15 |

Intl. Red Cross and Red Crescent Organizations, 125th Annivs. — A150

**Wmk. 379**

**1988, Feb. 17 Litho. *Perf. 14***

| | | | | | |
|---|---|---|---|---|---|
| *527* | A150 | 20k | Help the Needy | 10 | 10 |
| *528* | A150 | 30k | Care for the sick | 15 | 15 |

WHO, 40th Anniv. A151

**Wmk. 379**

**1988, Apr. 7 *Perf. 14***

| | | | | | |
|---|---|---|---|---|---|
| *529* | A151 | 10k | Immunization | 5 | 5 |
| *530* | A151 | 20k | Map, globe, emblem | 10 | 10 |
| *531* | A151 | 30k | Mobile hospital | 15 | 15 |

Organization of African Unity, 25th Anniv. — A152

**1988, May 25**

| | | | | | |
|---|---|---|---|---|---|
| *532* | A152 | 10k | shown | 10 | 10 |
| *533* | A152 | 20k | Emblem, map, 4 men | 15 | 15 |

Shrimp A153

**1988, June 2**

| | | | | | |
|---|---|---|---|---|---|
| *534* | A153 | 10k | Pink shrimp | 5 | 5 |
| *535* | A153 | 20k | Tiger shrimp | 10 | 10 |
| *536* | A153 | 25k | Deepwater roseshrimp | 12 | 12 |

537 A153 30k Estuarine prawn 15 15
a. Miniature sheet of 4, Nos. 534-537 65 65

No. 537a has multicolored margin picturing habitat. Size: 121x101mm.

1988 Summer Olympics, Seoul A154

**Wmk. 379**

**1988, Sept. 6 Litho. *Perf. 14***

538 A154 10k Weight lifting 5 5
539 A154 20k Boxing 10 10
540 A154 30k Running, vert. 14 14

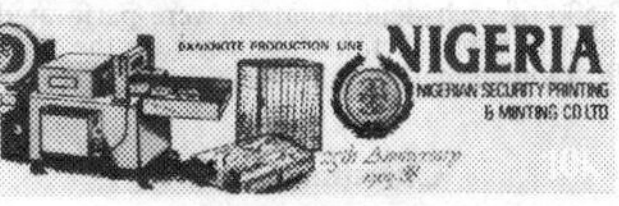

A155

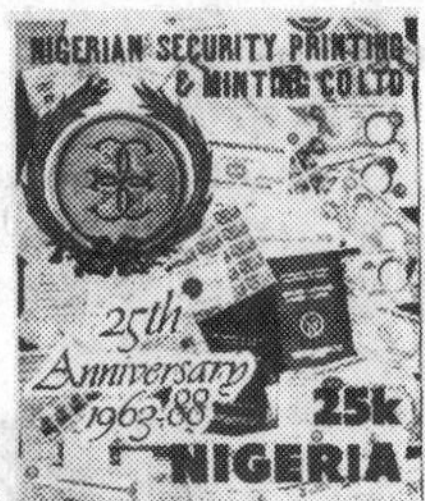

A156

Nigerian Security Printing and Minting Co., Ltd., 25th Anniv. A157

**1988, Oct. 28**

541 A155 10k Bank note production 5 5
542 A155 20k Coin production 10 10
543 A156 25k Products 12 12
544 A157 30k Anniv. emblem 15 15

## SEMI-POSTAL STAMPS

**Catalogue values for unused stamps in this section, from this point to the end of the section, are for Never Hinged items.**

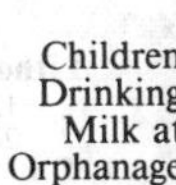

Children Drinking Milk at Orphanage SP1

Designs: 1sh6p+3p, Civilian first aid (vert.). 2sh6p+3p, Military first aid.

**1966, Dec. 1 Photo. *Perf. 14½x14***

B1 SP1 4p + 1p pur, blk & red 28 28
B2 SP1 1sh6p + 3p multi 1.00 1.00
B3 SP1 2sh6p + 3p multi 1.75 1.75

The surtax was for the Nigerian Red Cross.

Dr. Armauer G. Hansen — SP2

**1973, July 30 Litho. *Perf. 14***

B4 SP2 5k + 2k blk, brn & buff 40 40

Centenary of the discovery of the Hansen bacillus, the cause of leprosy. The surtax was for the Nigerian Anti-Leprosy Association.

## POSTAGE DUE STAMPS

**Catalogue values for unused stamps in this section, from this point to the end of the section, are for Never Hinged items.**

D1 D2

***Perf. 14½x14***

**1959, Jan. 4 Wmk. 4 Litho.**

J1 D1 1p orange 8 8
J2 D1 2p orange 10 10
J3 D1 3p orange 18 18
J4 D1 6p orange 1.40 *1.40*
J5 D1 1sh black 3.25 *3.25*
*Nos. J1-J5 (5)* 5.01 5.01

**1961, Aug. 1 Wmk. 335**

J6 D1 1p red 5 5
J7 D1 2p blue 12 12
J8 D1 3p emerald 18 18
J9 D1 6p yellow 40 40
J10 D1 1sh dark blue 1.25 *1.25*
*Nos. J6-J10 (5)* 2.00 2.00

***Perf. 12½x13½***

**1973, May 3 Litho. Unwmk.**

J11 D2 2k red 8 8
J12 D2 3k blue 12 12
J13 D2 5k orange 20 20
J14 D2 10k yellow green 35 35

# NIUE

LOCATION — An island in the south Pacific Ocean, northeast of New Zealand.
GOVT. — Self-government, in free association with New Zealand.
AREA — 100 sq. mi.
POP. — 3,019 (est. 1984).
CAPITAL — Alofi.

Niue, also known as Savage Island, was annexed to New Zealand in 1901 with the Cook Islands. Niue achieved internal self-government in 1974.

12 Pence = 1 Shilling
20 Shillings = 1 Pound
100 Cents = 1 Dollar (1967)

**Catalogue values for unused stamps in this country are for Never Hinged items, beginning with Scott 90 in the regular postage section, Scott B1 in the semi-postal section, Scott C1 in the air post section, and Scott O1 in the officials section.**

New Zealand No. 100 Handstamped in Green

NIUE

**1902 Wmk. 63 *Perf. 11***
**Thick Soft Paper**

1 A35 1p carmine 250.00 250.00

Stamps of New Zealand Surcharged in Carmine, Vermilion or Blue:

NIUE. ½ PENI. — 1/2p
NIUE. TAHA PENI. — 1p
NIUE. 2½ PENI — 2 1/2p

Wmk. 61- Single-lined NZ and Star Close Together

***Perf. 14***
***Thin Hard Paper***

3 A18 ½p grn (C) 1.50 *3.00*
a. Inverted surcharge 350.00 *400.00*
4 A35 1p car (Bl) 8.00 10.00
a. No period after "PENI" 85.00 110.00
b. Perf. 11x14 1.00 1.10
c. As "a." perf. 11x14 8.50 10.00

***Perf. 14***

**Wmk. Single-lined N. Z. and Star Close Together. (61)**

6 A18 ½p grn (V) 60 85
7 A35 1p car (Bl) 85 1.10
a. No period after "PENI" 9.00 *16.00*
b. Double surcharge *650.00*

***Perf. 11***
**Unwmk.**

8 A22 2½p bl (C) 4.00 4.50
a. No period after "PENI" 45.00 47.50
9 A22 2½p bl (V) 1.75 2.00
a. No period after "PENI" 20.00 25.00

The surcharge on the ½ and 1p stamps is printed in blocks of sixty. Two stamps in each block have a space between the "U" and "E" of "NIUE" and one of the 1p stamps has a broken "E" like an "F".

Blue Surcharge on Stamps of New Zealand, Types of 1898:

NIUE. Tolu e Pene. — e
NIUE Ono e Pene. — f
NIUE. Taha e Sileni. — g
NIUE. Tahae Sileni. — h

**1903 Wmk. 61 *Perf. 11.***

10 A23(e) 3p yel brn 3.50 4.00
11 A26(f) 6p rose 4.00 8.00
13 A29(g) 1sh org red 7.50 11.00
a. 1sh scar 9.00 12.00
b. 1sh brn red 15.00 17.50
c. As "b" surcharge "h" (error) 1,000. *1,400.*

Surcharged in Carmine or Blue on Stamps of New Zealand

NIUE. ½ PENI. — j

**1911-12 *Perf. 14, 14x14½***

14 A41 (j) ½p yel grn (C) 60 70
15 A41 (f) 6p car rose (Bl) 2.50 *5.00*
16 A41 (g) 1sh ver (Bl) 8.00 *16.00*

**1915 *Perf. 14***

18 A22 (d) 2½p dk bl (C) 2.50 3.25

Surcharged in Brown or Dark Blue on Stamps of New Zealand

**1917 *Perf. 14x13½, 14x14½***

19 A42 1p car (Br) 1.25 1.50
a. No period after "PENI" 140.00 150.00
20 A45(e) 3p vio brn (Bl) 60.00 85.00
a. No period after "Pene" 650.00 700.00

New Zealand Stamps of 1909-19 Overprinted in Dark Blue or Red

NIUE. — k

**1917-20 Typo.**

21 A43 ½p yel grn (R) 40 50
22 A42 1p car (Bl) 65 85
23 A47 1½p gray blk (R) 16 60
24 A47 1½p brn org (R) 1.00 2.00
25 A43 3p choc (Bl) 1.60 3.50

**Engr.**

26 A44 2½p dl bl (R) 1.00 2.00
27 A45 3p vio brn (Bl) 1.40 1.50
28 A45 6p car rose (Bl) 3.00 3.25
29 A45 1sh ver (Bl) 3.50 3.75
*Nos. 21-29 (9)* 12.71 17.95

Same Overprint On Postal-Fiscal Stamps of New Zealand, 1906-15

***Perf. 14, 14½ and Compound***

**1918-23**

30 PF1 2sh bl (R) 14.00 20.00
31 PF1 2sh6p brn (Bl) ('23) 14.00 20.00
32 PF1 5sh grn (R) 15.00 *27.50*
33 PF1 10sh red brn (Bl) ('23) 65.00 80.00
34 PF2 £1 rose (Bl) ('23) 100.00 110.00

Landing of Captain Cook A16

Avarua Waterfront A17

Capt. James Cook — A18

Coconut Palm — A19

Arorangi Village — A20

Avarua Harbor — A21

**Unwmk.**

**1920, Aug. 23 Engr. *Perf. 14***

35 A16 ½p yel grn & blk 65 *1.25*
36 A17 1p car & blk 45 65
37 A18 1½p red & blk 85 1.50
38 A9 3p pale bl & blk 1.00 *2.50*
39 A20 6p dp grn & red brn 1.25 *3.50*
a. Center inverted *500.00*
40 A21 1sh blk brn & blk 2.50 *5.00*
*Nos. 35-40 (6)* 6.70 14.40

See Nos. 41-42.

Types of 1920 Issue and

Rarotongan Chief (Te Po) — A22

Avarua Harbor — A23

**1925-27 Wmk. 61**

41 A16 ½p yel grn & blk ('26) 15 20
42 A17 1p car & blk 15 20
43 A22 2½p dk bl & blk ('27) 1.50 2.75
44 A23 4p dl vio & blk ('27) 1.50 3.00

New Zealand No. 182 Overprinted Type "k" in Red.

**1927**
*47* A56 2sh blue 10.00 20.00
*a.* 2sh dk bl 16.00 20.00

No. 37 Surcharged **TWO PENCE**

**1931** **Unwmk.** ***Perf. 14.***
*48* A18 2p on 1½p red & blk 1.10 1.10

New Zealand Postal-Fiscal Stamps of 1931-32 Overprinted Type "k" in Blue or Red.

**1931-32** **Wmk. 61**
*49* PF5 2sh6p dp brn 9.00 15.00
*50* PF5 5sh grn (R) 19.00 22.50
*51* PF5 10sh dk car 26.00 37.50
*52* PF5 £1 pink ('32) 55.00 67.50

See Nos. 86-89D, 116-119.

Landing of Captain Cook – A24

Capt. James Cook – A25

Polynesian Migratory Canoe – A26

Islanders Unloading Ship – A27

View of Avarua Harbor A28

R. M. S. Monowai A29

King George V – A30

***Perf. 13, 14 (4p, 1sh)***
**1932** **Engr.** **Unwmk.**
*53* A24 ½p yel grn & blk 50 55
*a.* Perf. 14x13 85.00 *100.00*
*54* A25 1p dp red & blk 35 38
*55* A26 2p org brn & blk 35 65
*56* A27 2½p ind & blk 1.50 2.75
*57* A28 4p Prus bl & blk 2.00 3.50
*a.* Perf. 13 2.00 3.50
*58* A29 6p dp org & blk 1.00 1.50
*59* A30 1sh dl vio & blk 3.50 4.25
*Nos. 53-59 (7)* 9.20 13.58

**1933-36** **Wmk. 61** ***Perf. 14***
*60* A24 ½p yel grn & blk 14 16
*61* A25 1p dp red & blk 16 20
*62* A26 2p brn & blk ('36) 28 30
*63* A27 2½p ind & blk 40 42
*64* A28 4p Prus bl & blk 45 50
*65* A29 6p org & blk ('36) 55 55
*66* A30 1sh dk vio & blk ('36) 4.00 5.50
*Nos. 60-66 (7)* 5.98 7.63

See Nos. 77-82.

**Silver Jubilee Issue**

Types of 1932 Overprinted in Black or Red **SILVER JUBILEE OF KING GEORGE V. 1910-1935.**

*Niue stamps can be mounted in Scott's annual New Zealand Dependencies Album.*

**1935, May 7** ***Perf. 14***
*67* A25 1p car & brn red 45 45
*68* A27 2½p ind & bl (R) 1.00 1.00
*a.* Vert. pair, imperf. horiz. 650.00
*69* A29 6p dl org & grn 2.75 2.75

The vertical spacing of the overprint is wider on No. 69.

**Coronation Issue**

New Zealand Stamps of 1937 Overprinted in Black **NIUE**

Wmk. 253

***Perf. 13½x13***
**1937, May 13** **Wmk. 253**
*70* A78 1p rose car 14 14
*71* A78 2½p dk bl 14 14
*72* A78 6p vermilion 28 28

George VI – A31

Village Scene – A32

Coastal Scene with Canoe – A33

Mt. Ikurangi behind Avarua – A34

**1938, May 2** **Wmk. 61** ***Perf. 14***
*73* A31 1sh dp vio & blk 65 65
*74* A32 2sh dk red brn & blk 1.40 1.40
*75* A33 3sh yel grn & bl 2.25 2.25

See Nos. 83-85.

***Perf. 13½x14***
**1940, Sept. 2** **Engr.** **Wmk. 253**
*76* A34 3p on 1½p rose vio & blk 14 14

Types of 1932-38.

**1944-46** **Wmk. 253** ***Perf. 14.***
*77* A24 ½p yel grn & blk 25 25
*78* A25 1p dp red & blk ('45) 18 18
*79* A26 2p org brn & blk ('46) 16 16
*80* A27 2½p dk bl & blk ('45) 1.40 1.75
*81* A28 4p Prus bl & blk 50 50
*82* A29 6p dp org & blk 45 45
*83* A31 1sh dp vio & blk 1.00 2.00
*84* A32 2sh brn car & blk ('45) 1.60 2.50
*85* A33 3sh yel grn & bl ('45) 2.50 4.25
*Nos. 77-85 (9)* 8.04 12.04

New Zealand Postal-Fiscal Stamps Overprinted Type "k" (narrow "E") in Blue or Red

**1941-45** **Wmk. 61** ***Perf. 14***
*86* PF5 2sh6p brown 14.00 16.00
*87* PF5 5sh grn (R) 90.00 100.00
*88* PF5 10sh rose 75.00 *100.00*
*89* PF5 £1 pink 100.00 110.00

**Wmk. 253**
*89A* PF5 2sh6p brown 2.25 2.50
*89B* PF5 5sh grn (R) 4.00 4.00
*e.* 5sh lt yel grn, wmkd. sideways ('67) 35.00 37.50
*89C* PF5 10sh rose 14.00 15.00
*89D* PF5 £1 pink 18.00 20.00

No. 89e exists in both line and comb perf.

**Catalogue values for unused stamps in this section, from this point to the end of the section, are for Never Hinged items.**

**Peace Issue**

New Zealand Nos. 248, 250, 254 and 255 Overprinted in Black or Blue:

NIUE p     NIUE     q     NIUE

**1946, June 4** ***Perf. 13x13½, 13½x13***
*90* A94 (p) 1p emerald 10 10
*91* A96 (q) 2p rose vio (Bl) 12 12
*92* A100 (p) 6p org red & red brn 20 20
*93* A101 (p) 8p brn lake & blk (Bl) 25 25

Map of Niue A35

H. M. S. Resolution A36

Designs: 2p, Alofi landing. 3p, Thatched Dwelling. 4p, Arch at Hikutavake. 6p, Alofi bay. 9p, Fisherman. 1sh, Cave at Makefu. 2sh, Gathering bananas. 3sh, Matapa Chasm.

***Perf. 14x13½, 13½x14.***
**1950, July 3** **Engr.** **Wmk. 253**
*94* A35 ½p red org & bl 10 8
*95* A36 1p grn & brn 10 8
*96* A36 2p rose car & blk 12 10
*97* A36 3p bl vio & bl 18 15
*98* A36 4p brn vio & ol grn 30 25
*99* A36 6p brn org & bl grn 42 35
*100* A35 9p dk brn & brn org 65 55
*101* A36 1sh blk & pur 80 65
*102* A35 2sh dp grn & brn org 1.00 90
*103* A35 3sh blk & dp bl 2.00 1.50
*Nos. 94-103 (10)* 5.67 4.61

**Coronation Issue.**
Types of New Zealand.

**1953, May 24** **Photo.** ***Perf. 14x14½***
*104* A113 3p brown 32 32
*105* A114 6p sl blk 65 65

Nos. 94-103 Surcharged

***Perf. 14x13½, 13½x14***
**1967, July 10** **Engr.** **Wmk. 253**
*106* A35 ½c on ½p red org & bl 6 5
*107* A36 1c on 1p grn & brn 35 7
*108* A36 2c on 2p rose car & blk 10 10
*109* A36 2½c on 3p bl vio & bl 14 14
*110* A36 3c on 4p brn vio & ol grn 16 16
*111* A36 5c on 6p brn org & grn 28 28
*112* A35 8c on 9p dk brn & brn org 40 40
*113* A36 10c on 1sh blk & pur 1.00 1.00
*114* A35 20c on 2sh dp grn & brn org 1.40 1.40
*115* A35 30c on 3sh blk & dp bl 1.60 1.60
*Nos. 106-115 (10)* 5.49 5.20

The position of the numeral varies on each denomination. The surcharge on the ½c, 2½c, 8c, 10c and 20c contains one dot only.

New Zealand Arms – A37

**Wmk. 253**
**1967, July 10** **Typo.** ***Perf. 14***
**Black Surcharge**
*116* A37 25c yel brn 90 90
*a.* Perf. 11 11.00 14.00
*117* A37 50c green 1.75 1.75
*a.* Perf. 11 12.00 15.00
*118* A37 $1 cerise 3.75 3.75
*a.* Perf. 11 16.00 18.00
*119* A37 $2 pale pink 6.00 6.00
*a.* Perf. 11 27.50 30.00

The perf. 11 stamps were produced when a normal perforating machine broke down and 2,500 of each denomination were perforated on a treadle machine first used by the N.Z. Post Office in 1899.

**Christmas Issue**
Type of New Zealand
***Perf. 13½x14***
**1967, Oct. 3** **Photo.** **Wmk. 253**
*120* A156 2½c multi 25 25

**Christmas Issue**
Type of New Zealand
**1969, Oct. 1** **Photo.** **Wmk. 253**
*121* A168 2½c multi 25 25

Pua – A38

Flowers (except 20c): 1c, Golden shower. 2c, Flamboyant. 2½c, Frangipani. 3c, Niue crocus. 5c, Hibiscus. 8c, Passion fruit. 10c, Kamapui. 20c, Queen Elizabeth II. 30c, Tapeu orchid.

***Perf. 12½x13***
**1969, Nov. 27** **Litho.** **Unwmk.**
*122* A38 ½c grn & multi 5 5
*123* A38 1c org & multi 8 5
*124* A38 2c gray & multi 14 9
*125* A38 2½c bis & multi 15 12
*126* A38 3c bl & multi 18 14
*127* A38 5c ver & multi 30 22
*128* A38 8c vio & multi 50 38
*129* A38 10c yel & multi 60 45
*130* A38 20c dk bl & multi 1.10 90
*131* A38 30c ol grn & multi 1.75 1.40
*Nos. 122-131 (10)* 4.85 3.80

Edible Crab A39

***Perf. 13½x12½***
**1969, Aug. 19** **Litho.**
*132* A39 3c Kalahimu 12 12
*133* A39 5c Kalavi 22 22
*134* A39 30c Unga 1.25 1.25

**Christmas Issue**
Type of New Zealand
**1970, Oct. 1** **Litho.** ***Perf. 12½***
*135* A180 2½c multi 22 22

Plane over Outrigger Canoe A40

Designs: 5c, Plane over ships in harbor. 8c, Civair plane over island.

**1970, Dec. 9 Litho. *Perf. 13½***

| | | | |
|---|---|---|---|
| *136* A40 3c multi | 15 | 15 |
| *137* A40 5c multi | 25 | 25 |
| *138* A40 8c multi | 40 | 40 |

Opening of Niue Airport.

Polynesian Triller (Heahea) A41

Birds: 10c, Crimson-crowned fruit pigeon (kulukulu). 20c, Blue-crowned lory (henga).

**1971, June 23 Litho. *Perf. 13½x13***

| | | |
|---|---|---|
| *139* A41 5c multi | 25 | 25 |
| *140* A41 10c multi | 50 | 50 |
| *141* A41 20c multi | 1.00 | 1.00 |

**Christmas Issue**
Type of New Zealand

**1971, Oct. 6 Photo. *Perf. 13x13½***

| | | |
|---|---|---|
| *142* A190 3c org & multi | 22 | 22 |

People of Niue A42

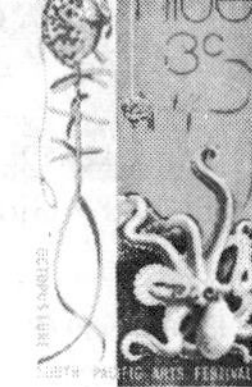


Octopus Lure and Octopus A43

**1971, Nov. 17**

| | | |
|---|---|---|
| *143* A42 4c Boy | 16 | 16 |
| *144* A42 6c Girl | 28 | 28 |
| *145* A42 9c Man | 40 | 40 |
| *146* A42 14c Woman | 65 | 65 |

**1972, May 3 Litho. *Perf. 13x13½***

Designs: 5c, Warrior and weapons. 10c, Sika (spear) throwing (horiz.). 25c, Vivi dance (horiz.).

| | | |
|---|---|---|
| *147* A43 3c bl & multi | 8 | 8 |
| *148* A43 5c rose & multi | 15 | 15 |
| *149* A43 10c bl & multi | 25 | 25 |
| *150* A43 25c yel & multi | 65 | 65 |

So. Pacific Festival of Arts, Fiji, May 6-20.

Alofi Wharf A44

Designs (South Pacific Commission Emblem and): 5c, Health service. 6c, School children. 18c, Cattle and dwarf palms.

**1972, Sept. 6 Litho. *Perf. 13½x14***

| | | |
|---|---|---|
| *151* A44 4c bl & multi | 12 | 12 |
| *152* A44 5c bl & multi | 15 | 15 |
| *153* A44 6c bl & multi | 18 | 18 |
| *154* A44 18c bl & multi | 55 | 55 |

So. Pacific Commission, 25th anniv.

**Christmas Issue, 1972**
Type of New Zealand

Design: Madonna and Child, by Murillo.

**1972, Oct. 4 Photo. *Perf. 11½***

| | | |
|---|---|---|
| *155* A197 3c gray & multi | 15 | 15 |

Pempheris Oualensis A45

Designs: Various fish.

***Perf. 13½x13***

**1973, June 27 Litho. Unwmk.**

| | | |
|---|---|---|
| *156* A45 8c *shown* | 30 | 30 |
| *157* A45 10c *Cephalopholis* | 40 | 40 |
| *158* A45 15c *Variola louti* | 60 | 60 |
| *159* A45 20c *Etelis carbunculus* | 80 | 80 |

Flowers, by Jan Breughel — A46

Paintings of Flowers: 5c, by Hans Bollongier. 10c, by Rachel Ruysch.

**1973, Nov. 21 Litho. *Perf. 13½x13***

| | | |
|---|---|---|
| *160* A46 4c bis & multi | 12 | 12 |
| *161* A46 5c org brn & multi | 15 | 15 |
| *162* A46 10c emer & multi | 40 | 40 |

Christmas 1973.

Capt. Cook and "Resolution" — A47

Designs (Capt. Cook and): 3c, Cook's landing place and ship. 8c, Map of Niue. 20c, Administration Building and flag of 1774.

**1974, June 20 Litho. *Perf. 13½x14***

| | | |
|---|---|---|
| *163* A47 2c multi | 10 | 10 |
| *164* A47 3c multi | 16 | 16 |
| *165* A47 8c multi | 40 | 40 |
| *166* A47 20c multi | 1.00 | 1.00 |

Bicentenary of . Cook's landing on Niue.

King Fataaiki A48

Annexation Day, Oct. 19, 1900 A49

Village Meeting A50

Design: 10c, Legislative Assembly Building.

***Perf. 14x13½, 13½x14***

**1974, Oct. 19 Litho.**

| | | |
|---|---|---|
| *167* A48 4c multi | 14 | 14 |
| *168* A49 8c multi | 30 | 30 |
| *169* A50 10c multi | 40 | 40 |
| *170* A50 20c multi | 75 | 75 |

Referendum for Self-government, Sept. 3, 1974.

Decorated Bicycle — A51

Christmas: 10c, Decorated motorcycle. 20c, Going to church by truck.

**1974, Nov. 13 Litho. *Perf. 12½***

| | | |
|---|---|---|
| *171* A51 3c grn & multi | 8 | 8 |
| *172* A51 10c dl bl & multi | 30 | 30 |
| *173* A51 20c brn & multi | 65 | 65 |

Children Going to Church A52

Children's Drawings: 5c, Child on bicycle trailing balloons. 10c, Balloons and gifts hanging from tree.

**1975, Oct. 29 Litho. *Perf. 14½***

| | | |
|---|---|---|
| *174* A52 4c multi | 12 | 12 |
| *175* A52 5c multi | 20 | 20 |
| *176* A52 10c multi | 40 | 40 |

Christmas 1975.

Tourist Hotel A53

Design: 20c, Hotel, building and floor plan.

**1975, Nov. 19 Litho. *Perf. 14x13½***

| | | |
|---|---|---|
| *177* A53 8c multi | 20 | 20 |
| *178* A53 20c multi | 50 | 50 |

Opening of Tourist Hotel.

Preparing Ground for Taro — A54

Designs: 2c, Planting taro (root vegetable). 3c, Banana harvest. 4c, Bush plantation. 5c, Shellfish gathering. 10c, Reef fishing. 20c, Luku (fern) harvest. 50c, Canoe fishing. $1, Husking coconuts. $2, Hunting uga (land crab).

**1976, Mar. 3 Litho. *Perf. 13½x14***

| | | |
|---|---|---|
| *179* A54 1c multi | 5 | 5 |
| *180* A54 2c bl & multi | 5 | 5 |
| *181* A54 3c lil & multi | 6 | 6 |
| *182* A54 4c red & multi | 8 | 8 |
| *183* A54 5c grn & multi | 10 | 10 |
| *184* A54 10c ocher & multi | 20 | 20 |
| *185* A54 20c multi | 45 | 45 |
| *186* A54 50c yel & multi | 90 | 90 |
| *187* A54 $1 multi | 1.60 | 1.60 |
| *188* A54 $2 multi | 3.50 | 3.50 |
| *Nos. 179-188 (10)* | 6.99 | 6.99 |

See Nos. 222-231.

Water Tower, Girl Drawing Water — A55

Designs: 15c, Teleprinter and Niue radio station. 20c, Instrument panel, generator and power station.

**1976, July 7 Litho. *Perf. 14x14½***

| | | |
|---|---|---|
| *189* A55 10c multi | 20 | 20 |
| *190* A55 15c multi | 30 | 30 |
| *191* A55 20c multi | 40 | 40 |

Technical achievements.

Christmas Tree (Flamboyant) and Administration Building — A56

Christmas: 15c, Avatele Church, interior.

**1976, Sept. 15 Litho. *Perf. 14½***

| | | |
|---|---|---|
| *192* A56 9c org & multi | 20 | 20 |
| *193* A56 15c org & multi | 35 | 35 |

Elizabeth II, Coronation Portrait, and Westminster Abbey — A57

Design: $2, Coronation regalia.

**1977, June 7 Photo. *Perf. 13½***

| | | |
|---|---|---|
| *194* A57 $1 multi | 1.50 | 1.40 |
| *195* A57 $2 multi | 4.50 | 4.00 |
| *a.* Souvenir sheet of 2 | 7.00 | 7.00 |

25th anniv. of reign of Elizabeth II. Nos. 194-195 each printed in sheets of 5 stamps and label showing Niue flag and Union Jack. No. 195a contains one each of Nos. 194-195, silver and multicolored margin. Size: 72x105mm.

Mothers and Infants A58

Designs: 15c, Mobile school dental clinic. 20c, Elderly couple and home.

**1977, June 29 Litho. *Perf. 14½***

| | | |
|---|---|---|
| *196* A58 10c multi | 20 | 20 |
| *197* A58 15c multi | 25 | 25 |
| *198* A58 20c multi | 35 | 35 |

Personal (social) services.

Annunciation, by Rubens — A59

Rubens Paintings (details, Virgin and Child): 12c, Adoration of the Kings. 20c, Virgin with Garland. 35c, Holy Family.

**1977, Nov. 15 Photo. *Perf. 13x13½***

| | | |
|---|---|---|
| *199* A59 10c multi | 10 | 10 |
| *200* A59 12c multi | 15 | 15 |
| *201* A59 20c multi | 25 | 25 |
| *202* A59 35c multi | 45 | 45 |
| *a.* Souvenir sheet of 4 | 1.25 | 1.25 |

Christmas 1977 and 400th birth anniversary of Peter Paul Rubens (1577-1640). Nos. 199-202 each printed in sheets of 6 stamps.

No. 202a contains one each of Nos. 199-202; gold and brown margin shows Angels. Size: 82x128mm.

### Stamps of 1976-77 Surcharged with New Value and 4 Bars in Black or Gold

### Printing and Perforations as Before

**1977, Nov. 15**

| | | | | |
|---|---|---|---|---|
| *203* | A54 | 12c on 1c (#179) | 22 | 22 |
| *204* | A54 | 16c on 2c (#180) | 28 | 28 |
| *205* | A54 | 30c on 3c (#181) | 50 | 50 |
| *206* | A54 | 35c on 4c (#182) | 60 | 60 |
| *207* | A54 | 40c on 5c (#183) | 75 | 75 |
| *208* | A54 | 60c on 20c (#185) | 1.00 | 1.00 |
| *209* | A54 | 70c on $1 (#187) | 1.10 | 1.10 |
| *210* | A54 | 85c on $2 (#188) | 1.50 | 1.50 |
| *211* | A54 | $1.10 on 10c (#196) | 1.75 | 1.75 |
| *212* | A54 | $2.60 on 20c (#198) | 4.00 | 4.00 |
| *213* | A54 | $3.20 on $2 (#195, G) | 10.00 | 10.00 |
| | | *Nos. 203-213 (11)* | 21.70 | 21.70 |

"An Inland View in Atooi," by John Webber — A60

Scenes in Hawaii, by John Webber: 16c, A View of Karakooa in Owyhee. 20c, An Offering Before Capt. Cook in the Sandwich Islands. 30c, Tereoboo, King of Owyhee, bringing presents (boats). 35c, Masked rowers in boat.

**1978, Jan. 18 Photo. *Perf. 13½***

| | | | | |
|---|---|---|---|---|
| *214* | A60 | 12c gold & multi | 25 | 20 |
| *215* | A60 | 16c gold & multi | 32 | 28 |
| *216* | A60 | 20c gold & multi | 40 | 35 |
| *217* | A60 | 30c gold & multi | 65 | 55 |
| *218* | A60 | 35c gold & multi | 75 | 65 |
| ***a.*** | | Souvenir sheet of 5 | 2.75 | 2.25 |
| | | *Nos. 214-218 (5)* | 2.37 | 2.03 |

Bicentenary of Capt. Cook's arrival in Hawaii. Nos. 214-218 printed in sheets of 5 stamps and one label showing flags of Hawaii and Niue. No. 218a contains one each of Nos. 214-218 and label with portraits of Capt. Cook and John Webber. Green and gold margin. Size: 122x122mm.

Descent from the Cross, by Caravaggio — A61

Design: 20c, Burial of Christ, by Bellini.

**1978, Mar. 15 Photo. *Perf. 13x13½***

| | | | | |
|---|---|---|---|---|
| *219* | A61 | 10c multi | 18 | 18 |
| *220* | A61 | 20c multi | 38 | 38 |
| ***a.*** | | Souvenir sheet of 2 | 75 | 75 |

Easter 1978. Nos. 219-220 issued in sheets of 8. No. 220a contains one each of Nos. 219-220, perf. 13½; margin in silver and slate green shows St. Peter's, Rome. Size: 102x88mm.

### Souvenir Sheet

Elizabeth II — A62

**1978, June 26 Photo. *Perf. 13***

| | | | | |
|---|---|---|---|---|
| *221* | | Sheet of 6 | 10.00 | 10.00 |
| ***a.*** | | A62 $1.10 *Niue and UK flags* | 1.50 | 1.50 |
| ***b.*** | | A62 $1.10 *shown* | 1.50 | 1.50 |
| ***c.*** | | A62 $1.10 *Queen's New Zealand flag* | 1.50 | 1.50 |
| ***d.*** | | Souvenir sheet of 3 | 6.00 | 6.00 |

25th anniversary of coronation of Queen Elizabeth II. No. 221 contains 2 horizontal se-tenant strips of Nos. 221a-221c, separated by horizontal gutter showing coronation coach. Size: 123x117mm. No. 221d contains a vertical se-tenant strip of Nos. 221a-221c; multicolored margin shows Westminster Abbey. Size: 86½x98mm.

### Type of 1977

Designs: 12c, Preparing ground for taro. 16c, Planting taro. 30c, Banana harvest. 35c, Bush plantation. 40c, Shellfish gathering. 60c, Reef fishing. 75c, Luku (fern) harvest. $1.10, Canoe fishing. $3.20, Husking coconuts. $4.20, Hunting uga (land crab).

**1978, Oct. 27 Litho. *Perf. 14***

| | | | | |
|---|---|---|---|---|
| *222* | A54 | 12c sil & multi | 25 | 25 |
| *223* | A54 | 16c sil & multi | 30 | 30 |
| *224* | A54 | 30c sil & multi | 60 | 60 |
| *225* | A54 | 35c sil & multi | 65 | 65 |
| *226* | A54 | 40c sil & multi | 70 | 70 |
| *227* | A54 | 60c sil & multi | 1.10 | 1.10 |
| *228* | A54 | 75c sil & multi | 1.50 | 1.50 |
| *229* | A54 | $1.10 sil & multi | 2.25 | 2.25 |
| *230* | A54 | $3.20 sil & multi | 5.00 | 5.00 |
| *231* | A54 | $4.20 sil & multi | 6.00 | 6.00 |
| | | *Nos. 222-231 (10)* | 18.35 | 18.35 |

Celebration of the Rosary, by Dürer — A63

Designs: 30c, Nativity, by Dürer. 35c, Adoration of the Kings, by Dürer.

**1978, Nov. 30 Photo. *Perf. 13***

| | | | | |
|---|---|---|---|---|
| *232* | A63 | 20c multi | 28 | 28 |
| *233* | A63 | 30c multi | 45 | 45 |
| *234* | A63 | 35c multi | 50 | 50 |
| ***a.*** | | Souvenir sheet of 3 | 1.50 | 1.50 |

Christmas 1978 and 450th death anniversary of Albrecht Dürer (1471-1528). Nos. 232-234 each printed in sheets of 5 stamps and descriptive label. No. 234a contains Nos. 232-234 and label. Gray and gold margin shows lute-playing angel. Size: 143x82mm.

Pietà, by Gregorio Fernandez — A64

Design: 35c, Burial of Christ, by Pedro Roldan.

**1979, Apr. 2**

| | | | | |
|---|---|---|---|---|
| *235* | A64 | 30c multi | 42 | 42 |
| *236* | A64 | 35c multi | 50 | 50 |
| ***a.*** | | Souvenir sheet of 2 | 1.10 | 1.10 |

Easter 1979. No. 236a contains Nos. 235-236. Green & gold margin shows Jesus with crown of thorns. Size: 82x82mm.

Child, by Franz Hals — A65

IYC Emblem and Details from Paintings: 16c, (shown) Nurse and Child. 20c, Child of the Duke of Osuna, by Goya. 30c, Daughter of Robert Strozzi, by Titian. 35c, Children Eating Fruit, by Murillo.

**1979, May 31 Photo. *Perf. 14***

| | | | | |
|---|---|---|---|---|
| *237* | A65 | 16c multi | 22 | 22 |
| *238* | A65 | 20c multi | 28 | 28 |
| *239* | A65 | 30c multi | 42 | 42 |
| *240* | A65 | 35c multi | 50 | 50 |
| ***a.*** | | Souvenir sheet of 4 | 1.75 | 1.75 |

International Year of the Child. Nos. 237-240 issued in sheets of 6. No. 240a contains Nos. 237-240; lilac and gold decorative frame. Size: 80x115mm.

Penny Black, Bath Mail Coach, Rowland Hill

A66 A67

Designs: 30c, Basel No. 3L1 and Alpine village coach. 35c, U.S. No. 1 and 1st U.S. transatlantic mail ship. 50c, France No. 3 and French railroad mail car, 1849. 60c, Bavaria No. 1 and Bavarian mail coach.

**1979, July 3 Photo. *Perf. 14***

| | | | | |
|---|---|---|---|---|
| *241* | A66 | 20c multi | 25 | 25 |
| *242* | A67 | 20c multi | 25 | 25 |
| *243* | A66 | 30c multi | 38 | 38 |
| *244* | A67 | 30c multi | 38 | 38 |
| *245* | A66 | 35c multi | 45 | 45 |
| *246* | A67 | 35c multi | 45 | 45 |
| *247* | A66 | 50c multi | 65 | 65 |
| *248* | A67 | 50c multi | 65 | 65 |
| *249* | A66 | 60c multi | 75 | 75 |
| *250* | A67 | 60c multi | 75 | 75 |
| ***a.*** | | Souvenir sheet of 10 | 6.00 | 6.00 |
| | | *Nos. 241-250 (10)* | 4.96 | 4.96 |

Sir Rowland Hill (1795-1879), originator of penny postage. Stamps of same denomination printed se-tenant in sheets of 20. No. 250a contains Nos. 241-250 and 2 labels showing flags of Niue and Great Britain. Size: 145x150mm.

Cook's Landing at Botany Bay A68

18th Century Paintings: 30c, Cook's Men during a Landing on Erromanga. 35c, Resolution and Discovery in Queen Charlotte's Sound. 75c, Death of Capt. Cook on Hawaii, by Johann Zoffany.

**1979, July 30 Photo. *Perf. 14***

| | | | | |
|---|---|---|---|---|
| *251* | A68 | 20c multi | 28 | 28 |
| *252* | A68 | 30c multi | 42 | 42 |
| *253* | A68 | 35c multi | 50 | 50 |
| *254* | A68 | 75c multi | 1.10 | 1.10 |
| ***a.*** | | Souvenir sheet of 4 | 2.75 | 2.75 |

200th death anniversary of Capt. James Cook (1728-1779). No. 254a contains Nos. 251-254, perf. 13½; silver and dark blue decorative margin. Size: 104x80mm.

Apollo 11 Lift-off — A69

**1979, Sept. 27 Photo. *Perf. 13½***

| | | | | |
|---|---|---|---|---|
| *255* | A69 | 30c *shown* | 42 | 42 |
| *256* | A69 | 35c *Lunar module* | 50 | 50 |
| *257* | A69 | 60c *Splashdown* | 90 | 90 |
| ***a.*** | | Souvenir sheet of 3 | 2.25 | 2.25 |

Apollo 11 moon landing, 10th anniversary. No. 257a contains Nos. 255-257 in changed colors. Multicolored margin shows Apollo 11 astronauts and lunar globe. Size: 120x81½mm.

Virgin and Child, by P. Serra — A70

Virgin and Child by: 25c, R. di Mur. 30c, S. diG. Sasseta, 50c, J. Huguet.

**1979, Nov. 29 Photo. *Perf. 13***

| | | | | |
|---|---|---|---|---|
| *258* | A70 | 20c multi | 28 | 28 |
| *259* | A70 | 25c multi | 35 | 35 |
| *260* | A70 | 30c multi | 42 | 42 |
| *261* | A70 | 50c multi | 70 | 70 |
| ***a.*** | | Souvenir sheet of 4 | 2.25 | 2.25 |

Christmas 1979. No. 261a contains Nos. 258-261; multicolored margin shows angels. Size: 95x113mm. See Nos. B12-B15.

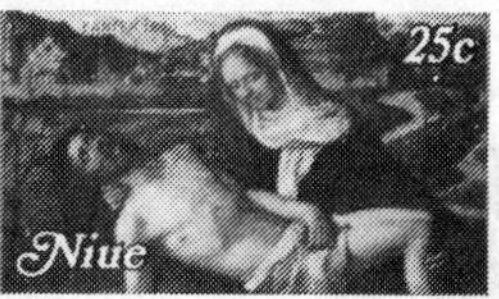


Pietà, by Giovanni Bellini — A71

Easter 1980 (Pietà, Paintings by): 30c, Botticelli. 35c, Anthony Van Dyck.

**1980, Apr. 2 Photo. *Perf. 13***

| | | | | |
|---|---|---|---|---|
| *262* | A71 | 25c multi | 25 | 25 |
| *263* | A71 | 30c multi | 30 | 30 |
| *264* | A71 | 35c multi | 35 | 35 |

Ceremonial Stool, New Guinea — A72

**1980, July 30 Photo. *Perf. 13***

| | | | | |
|---|---|---|---|---|
| *265* | A72 | 20c *shown* | 20 | 20 |
| *266* | A72 | 20c *Kutagwa plaque* | 20 | 20 |
| *267* | A72 | 20c *Suspension hook* | 20 | 20 |
| *268* | A72 | 20c *Ancestral board* | 20 | 20 |
| *269* | A72 | 25c *Platform post* | 25 | 25 |
| *270* | A72 | 25c *Canoe ornament* | 25 | 25 |
| *271* | A72 | 25c *Carved figure* | 25 | 25 |
| *272* | A72 | 25c *Woman and child* | 25 | 25 |
| *273* | A72 | 30c *God A'a, statue* | 30 | 30 |
| *274* | A72 | 30c *Tangaroa, statue* | 30 | 30 |
| *275* | A72 | 30c *Ivory pendant* | 30 | 30 |
| *276* | A72 | 30c *Tapa cloth* | 30 | 30 |
| *277* | A72 | 35c *Maori feather box* | 35 | 35 |
| *278* | A72 | 35c *Hei-tiki* | 35 | 35 |
| *279* | A72 | 35c *House post* | 35 | 35 |
| *280* | A72 | 35c *Go Ku, feather image* | 35 | 35 |
| ***a.*** | | Sheet of 4 (#265, 269, 273, 277) | 1.50 | 1.50 |
| ***b.*** | | Sheet of 4 (#266, 270, 274, 278) | 1.50 | 1.50 |
| ***c.*** | | Sheet of 4 (#267, 271, 275, 279) | 1.50 | 1.50 |
| ***d.*** | | Sheet of 4 (#268, 272, 276, 280) | 1.50 | 1.50 |
| | | *Nos. 265-280 (16)* | 4.40 | 4.40 |

3rd South Pacific Festival of Arts, Port Moresby, Papua New Guinea, June 30-July 12. Stamps of same denomination se-tenant horizontally in sheets of 24. Souvenir sheet stamps have 2c surcharge.

Nos. 241-250, Overprinted in Black on Silver

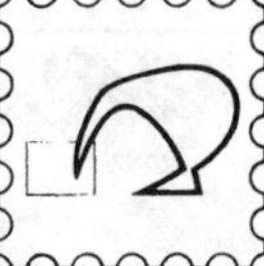

**1980, Aug. 22** *Perf. 14*

| | | | | |
|---|---|---|---|---|
| *281* | A66 20c multi | | 28 | 28 |
| *282* | A67 20c multi | | 28 | 28 |
| *283* | A66 30c multi | | 40 | 40 |
| *284* | A67 30c multi | | 40 | 40 |
| *285* | A66 35c multi | | 45 | 45 |
| *286* | A67 35c multi | | 45 | 45 |
| *287* | A66 50c multi | | 65 | 65 |
| *288* | A67 50c multi | | 65 | 65 |
| *289* | A66 60c multi | | 80 | 80 |
| *290* | A67 60c multi | | 80 | 80 |
| | *Nos. 281-290 (10)* | | 5.16 | 5.16 |

ZEAPEX '80, New Zealand International Stamp Exhibition, Auckland, Aug. 23-31.

Queen Mother Elizabeth, 80th Birthday — A73

**1980, Sept. 15 Photo.** *Perf. 13x13½*

| | | | |
|---|---|---|---|
| *291* | A73 $1.10 multi | 1.75 | 1.75 |

**Souvenir Sheet**

| | | | |
|---|---|---|---|
| *292* | A73 $3 multi | 4.50 | 4.50 |

No. 291 issued in sheets of 5 and label showing coad of arms. No. 292 has multicolored margin in continuous design. Size: 55x81mm.

100-Meter Dash — A74

Allen Wells — A75

Designs: Nos. 295-296, 400-Meter freestyle. Nos. 297-298, Soling class yachting. Nos. 299-300, Soccer. Stamps of same denomination se-tenant in sheets of 32.

**1980, Oct. 30 Photo.** *Perf. 14*

| | | | |
|---|---|---|---|
| *293* | A74 20c multi | 28 | 28 |
| *294* | A75 20c multi | 28 | 28 |
| *295* | A74 25c multi | 35 | 35 |
| *296* | A75 25c multi | 35 | 35 |
| *297* | A74 30c multi | 40 | 40 |
| *298* | A75 30c multi | 40 | 40 |
| *299* | A74 35c multi | 45 | 45 |
| *300* | A75 35c multi | 45 | 45 |
| | *Nos. 293-300 (8)* | 2.96 | 2.96 |

22nd Summer Olympic Games, Moscow, July 19-Aug. 3.

Virgin and Child, by del Sarto — A76

Designs: Paintings of Virgin and Child, by Andrea del Sarto.

**1980, Nov. 28 Photo.** *Perf. 13x13½*

| | | | |
|---|---|---|---|
| *301* | A76 20c multi | 28 | 28 |
| *302* | A76 25c multi | 35 | 35 |
| *303* | A76 30c multi | 40 | 40 |
| *304* | A76 35c multi | 50 | 50 |
| *a.* | Souvenir sheet of 4 | 1.75 | 1.75 |

Christmas 1980 and 450th death anniversary of Andrea del Sarto. No. 304a contains Nos. 301-304; multicolored decorative margin. Size: 87x113mm.

Moth Orchid — A77

Golden Shower Tree — A77a

**1981 Photo.** *Perf. 13x13½*

| | | | |
|---|---|---|---|
| *305* | A77 2c Phalaenopsis sp. | 5 | 5 |
| *306* | A77 2c shown | 5 | 5 |
| *307* | A77 5c Euphorbia pulcherrima | 7 | 7 |
| *308* | A77 5c Poinsettia | 7 | 7 |
| *309* | A77 10c Thunbergia alata | 14 | 14 |
| *310* | A77 10c Black-eyed Susan | 14 | 14 |
| *311* | A77 15c Cochlospermum hibiscoides | 20 | 20 |
| *312* | A77 15c Buttercup tree | 20 | 20 |
| *313* | A77 20c Begonia sp. | 28 | 28 |
| *314* | A77 20c Begonia | 28 | 28 |
| *315* | A77 25c Plumeria sp. | 35 | 35 |
| *316* | A77 25c Frangipani | 35 | 35 |
| *317* | A77 30c Sterlitzia reginae | 40 | 40 |
| *318* | A77 30c Bird of paradise | 40 | 40 |
| *319* | A77 35c Hibiscus syriacus | 45 | 45 |
| *320* | A77 35c Rose of Sharon | 45 | 45 |
| *321* | A77 40c Nymphaea sp. | 50 | 50 |
| *322* | A77 40c Water lily | 50 | 50 |
| *323* | A77 50c Tibouchina sp. | 65 | 65 |
| *324* | A77 50c Princess flower | 65 | 65 |
| *325* | A77 60c Nelumbo sp. | 80 | 80 |
| *326* | A77 60c Lotus | 80 | 80 |
| *327* | A77 80c Hybrid hibiscus | 1.10 | 1.10 |
| *328* | A77 80c Yellow hibiscus | 1.10 | 1.10 |

Issue dates: 2c, 5c, 10c, 15c, 20c, 25c, Apr. 2, others, May 26. Stamps of same denomination se-tenant.

**1981-82 Photo.** *Perf. 13½*

| | | | |
|---|---|---|---|
| *329* | A77a $1 shown | 1.40 | 1.40 |
| *330* | A77a $2 Orchid var. | 2.75 | 2.75 |
| *331* | A77a $3 Orchid sp. | 4.00 | 4.00 |
| *332* | A77a $4 Poinsettia | 5.50 | 5.50 |
| *333* | A77a $6 Hybrid hibiscus | 8.00 | 8.00 |
| *334* | A77a $10 Hibiscus rosasinensis | 14.00 | 14.00 |
| | *Nos. 305-334 (30)* | 45.63 | 45.63 |

Issue dates: $1, $2, $3, Dec. 9, 1981; others, Jan. 15, 1982.

Jesus Defiled, by El Greco A78

Easter 1981 (Paintings): 50c, Pieta, by Fernando Gallego. 60c, The Supper of Emaus, by Jacopo da Pontormo.

**1981, Apr. 10** *Perf. 14*

| | | | |
|---|---|---|---|
| *337* | A78 35c multi | 55 | 55 |
| *338* | A78 50c multi | 75 | 75 |
| *339* | A78 60c multi | 90 | 90 |

Prince Charles and Lady Diana — A79

**1981, June 26 Photo.** *Perf. 14*

| | | | |
|---|---|---|---|
| *340* | A79 75c Charles | 90 | 90 |
| *341* | A79 95c Lady Diana | 1.10 | 1.10 |
| *342* | A79 $1.20 shown | 1.50 | 1.50 |
| *a.* | Souvenir sheet of 3 | 4.50 | 4.50 |

Royal Wedding. Nos. 340-342 each printed in sheets of 5 plus label showing St. Paul's Cathedral. No. 342a contains Nos. 340-342; multicolored margin shows St. Paul's Cathedral. Size: 79x85mm.

1982 World Cup Soccer A80

**1981, Oct. 16 Photo.** *Perf. 13*

| | | | |
|---|---|---|---|
| *343* | Strip of 3 | 1.20 | 1.20 |
| *a.* | A80 30c, any single | 40 | 40 |
| *344* | Strip of 3 | 1.50 | 1.50 |
| *a.* | A80 35c, any single | 50 | 50 |
| *345* | Strip of 3 | 1.60 | 1.60 |
| *a.* | A80 40c, any single | 52 | 52 |

Christmas 1981 — A81

Rembrandt Paintings: 20c, Holy Family with Angels, 1645. 35c, Presentation in the Temple, 1631. 50c, Virgin and Child in Temple, 1629. 60c, Holy Family, 1640.

**1981-82 Photo.** *Perf. 14x13*

| | | | |
|---|---|---|---|
| *346* | A81 20c multi | 30 | 30 |
| *347* | A81 35c multi | 55 | 55 |
| *348* | A81 50c multi | 75 | 75 |
| *349* | A81 60c multi | 90 | 90 |
| *a.* | Souvenir sheet of 4 | 2.75 | 2.75 |

**Souvenir Sheets**

| | | | |
|---|---|---|---|
| *350* | A81 80c + 5c like #346 | 1.10 | 1.10 |
| *351* | A81 80c + 5c like #347 | 1.10 | 1.10 |
| *352* | A81 80c + 5c like #348 | 1.10 | 1.10 |
| *353* | A81 80c + 5c like #349 | 1.10 | 1.10 |

No. 349a contains Nos. 346-349; lilac and gold decorative margin. Size: 80x112mm. Nos. 350-353 have multicolored margins showing entire painting. Size: 66x81mm. Surtax was for school children. Issue dates: Nos. 346-349a, Dec. 11, 1981; others, Jan. 22, 1982.

21st Birthday of Princess Diana — A82

**1982, July 1** *Perf. 14*

| | | | |
|---|---|---|---|
| *354* | A82 50c Charles | 50 | 50 |
| *355* | A82 $1.25 Wedding | 1.25 | 1.25 |
| *356* | A82 $2.50 Diana | 2.50 | 2.50 |
| *a.* | Souvenir sheet of 3 | 5.25 | 5.25 |

Nos. 354-356 each printed in sheets of 5 plus label showing wedding day picture. No. 356a contains Nos. 354-356; multicolored decorative margin. Size: 82x102mm.

Nos. 340-342a Overprinted: "COMMEMORATING THE ROYAL BIRTH 21 JUNE 1982" or "BIRTH OF PRINCE WILLIAM OF WALES 21 JUNE 1982"

**1982, July 23** *Perf. 14*

| | | | |
|---|---|---|---|
| *357* | A79 75c multi | 1.25 | 1.25 |
| *358* | A79 95c multi | 1.50 | 1.50 |
| *359* | A79 $1.20 multi | 2.00 | 2.00 |
| *a.* | Souvenir sheet of 3 | 5.00 | 5.00 |

Birthday Stamps of 1982 Inscribed "COMMEMORATING THE BIRTH OF PRINCE WILLIAM OF WALES—21 JUNE 1982."

**1982 Photo.** *Perf. 14*

| | | | |
|---|---|---|---|
| *359B* | A82 50c like #354 | 45 | 45 |
| *359C* | A82 $1.25 like #355 | 1.10 | 1.10 |
| *359D* | A82 $2.50 like #356 | 2.25 | 2.25 |
| *e.* | Souvenir sheet of 3 | 4.00 | 4.00 |

Christmas 1982 — A83

Princess Diana Holding Prince William and Paintings of Infants by: 40c, Bronzino (1502-1572). 52c, Murillo (1617-1682). 83c, Boucher (1703-1770). Singles in No. 363a: 34x30mm., showing paintings only.

**1982, Dec. 3 Photo.** *Perf. 13½x14½*

| | | | |
|---|---|---|---|
| *360* | A83 40c multi | 55 | 55 |
| *361* | A83 52c multi | 65 | 65 |
| *362* | A83 83c multi | 1.10 | 1.10 |
| *363* | A83 $1.05 multi | 1.40 | 1.40 |
| *a.* | Souvenir sheet of 4 | 4.00 | 4.00 |

**Souvenir Sheets**

| | | | |
|---|---|---|---|
| *364* | A83 80c + 5c like #360 | 1.25 | 1.25 |
| *365* | A83 80c + 5c like #361 | 1.25 | 1.25 |
| *366* | A83 80c + 5c like #362 | 1.25 | 1.25 |
| *367* | A83 80c + 5c like #363 | 1.25 | 1.25 |

Nos. 364-367 each contain one stamp (30x42mm.) showing Royal family; margins show entire paintings. Size: 73x58mm. Surtax was for children's funds.

Commonwealth Day — A84

**1983, Mar. 14 Photo.** *Perf. 13*

| | | | |
|---|---|---|---|
| *368* | A84 70c Flag, Premier Robert R. Rex | 90 | 90 |
| *369* | A84 70c Resolution, Adventurer | 90 | 90 |
| *370* | A84 70c Passion flower | 90 | 90 |
| *371* | A84 70c Lime branch | 90 | 90 |

Scouting Year — A85

**1983, Apr. 28 Photo.** *Perf. 13*

| | | | |
|---|---|---|---|
| *372* | A85 40c Flag signals | 55 | 55 |
| *373* | A85 50c Tree planting | 65 | 65 |
| *374* | A85 83c Map reading | 1.20 | 1.20 |

**Souvenir Sheet**

| | | | |
|---|---|---|---|
| *375* | Sheet of 3 | 2.50 | 2.50 |
| *a.* | A85 40c + 3c like 40c | 60 | 60 |
| *b.* | A85 50c + 3c like 50c | 65 | 65 |
| *c.* | A85 83c + 3c like 83c | 1.10 | 1.10 |

Nos. 372-375 Overprinted in Black on Silver: "XV WORLD JAMBOREE CANADA"

**1983, July 14** **Photo.**

| | | | |
|---|---|---|---|
| *376* | A85 40c multi | 55 | 55 |
| *377* | A85 50c multi | 65 | 65 |
| *378* | A85 83c multi | 1.10 | 1.10 |

**Souvenir Sheet**

| | | | |
|---|---|---|---|
| *379* | Sheet of 3 | 2.50 | 2.50 |
| *a.* | A85 40c + 3c multi | 60 | 60 |
| *b.* | A85 50c + 3c multi | 65 | 65 |
| *c.* | A85 83c + 3c multi | 1.25 | 1.25 |

Save the Whales Campaign — A86

**1983, Aug. 15** *Perf. 13x14*

380 A86 12c Right whale 16 16
381 A86 25c Fin whale 35 35
382 A86 35c Sei whale 45 45
383 A86 40c Blue whale 55 55
384 A86 58c Bowhead whale 80 80
385 A86 70c Sperm whale 1.00 1.00
386 A86 83c Humpback whale 1.20 1.20
387 A86 $1.05 Lesser rorqual 1.40 1.40
388 A86 $2.50 Gray whale 3.50 5.50
*Nos. 380-388 (9)* 9.41 11.41

Manned Flight Bicentenary — A87

**1983, Oct. 14** **Photo.** *Perf. 14*

389 A87 25c Montgolfier, 1783 35 35
390 A87 40c Wright Bros. Flyer, 1903 55 55
391 A87 58c Graf Zeppelin, 1928 75 75
392 A87 70c Boeing 247, 1933 1.00 1.00
393 A87 83c Apollo VIII, 1968 1.10 1.10
394 A87 $1.05 Columbia space shuttle 1.40 1.40
*a.* Souvenir sheet of 6 5.50 5.50
*Nos. 389-394 (6)* 5.15 5.15

No. 394a contains Nos. 389-394 inscribed "AIRMAIL". Size: 109x130mm.

Christmas 1983 — A87a

Paintings by Raphael (1483-1520): 30c, Garvagh Madonna, National Gallery, London. 40c, Granduca Madonna, Pitti Gallery, Florence. 58c, Goldfinch Madonna, Uffizi Gallery, Florence. 70c, Holy Family of Francis I, Louvre, Paris. 83c, Holy Family with Saints, Alte Pinakothek, Munich.

**1983, Nov. 25** **Photo.** *Perf. 14*

395 A87a 30c multi 28 28
396 A87a 40c multi 35 35
397 A87a 58c multi 50 50
398 A87a 70c multi 60 60
399 A87a 83c multi 75 75
*Nos. 395-399 (5)* 2.48 2.48

**Souvenir Sheets**

*Perf. 13½*

400 Sheet of 5 2.75 2.75
*a.* A87a 30c + 3c like #395 30 30
*b.* A87a 40c + 3c like #396 40 40
*c.* A87a 58c + 3c like #397 55 55
*d.* A87a 70c + 3c like #398 65 65
*e.* A87a 83c + 3c like #399 75 75

**1983, Dec. 29**

401 A87a 85c + 5c like #395 80 80
402 A87a 85c + 5c like #396 80 80
403 A87a 85c + 5c like #397 80 80
404 A87a 85c + 5c like #398 80 80
405 A87a 85c + 5c like #399 80 80

500th birth anniv. of Raphael. No. 400 has multicolored decorative margin. Size: 120x114mm. Nos. 401-405 have multicolored margins continuing each painting. Size: 65x80mm.

**Nos. 317-318, 323-328, 341, 355, 342, 356 and 331 Surcharged in Black or Gold with One or Two Bars.**

**1983, Nov. 30** **Photo.**

406 A77 52c on 30c #317 35 35
407 A77 52c on 30c #318 35 35
408 A77 58c on 50c #323 40 40
409 A77 58c on 50c #324 40 40
410 A77 70c on 60c #325 50 50
411 A77 70c on 60c #326 50 50
412 A77 83c on 80c #327 60 60
413 A77 83c on 80c #328 60 60
413A A79 $1.10 on 95c #341 75 75
413B A82 $1.10 on $1.25 #355 (G) 75 75
413C A79 $2.60 on $1.20 #342 1.90 1.90

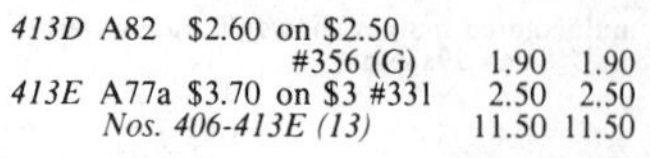

413D A82 $2.60 on $2.50 #356 (G) 1.90 1.90
413E A77a $3.70 on $3 #331 2.50 2.50
*Nos. 406-413E (13)* 11.50 11.50

World Communications Year — A88

**1984, Jan. 23** **Photo.** *Perf. 13x13½*

414 A88 40c Telegraph sender 45 45
415 A88 52c Early telephone 55 55
416 A88 83c Satellite 90 90
*a.* Souvenir sheet of 3 2.00 2.00

No. 416a contains Nos. 414-416. Size: 115x91mm.

Moth Orchid — A89

Golden Shower Tree A90

**1984** *Perf. 13x13½*

417 A89 12c shown 18 18
418 A89 25c Poinsettia 38 38
419 A89 30c Buttercup tree 45 45
420 A89 35c Begonia 52 52
421 A89 40c Frangipani 60 60
422 A89 52c Bird of paradise 75 75
423 A89 58c Rose of Sharon 80 80
424 A89 70c Princess flower 1.00 1.00
425 A89 83c Lotus 1.25 1.25
426 A89 $1.05 Yellow hibiscus 1.60 1.60
427 A90 $1.75 shown 1.65 1.65
428 A90 $2.30 Orchid var. 2.50 2.50
429 A90 $3.90 Orchid sp. 3.75 3.75
430 A90 $5 Poinsettia, diff. 4.75 4.75
431 A90 $6.60 Hybrid hibiscus 6.00 6.00
431A A90 $8.30 Hibiscus rosasinensis 8.00 8.00
*Nos. 417-431A (16)* 34.18 34.18

Issue dates: Nos. 417-426, Feb. 20; Nos. 427-429, May 10; others June 18.

1984 Summer Olympics A91

Designs: Greek pottery designs, 3rd cent. BC. 30c, 70c vert.

**1984, Mar. 15** **Photo.** *Perf. 14*

432 A91 30c Discus 40 40
433 A91 35c Running 45 45
434 A91 40c Equestrian 52 52
435 A91 58c Boxing 75 75
436 A91 70c Javelin 90 90
*Nos. 432-436 (5)* 3.02 3.02

AUSIPEX '84, Australian Animals — A92

**1984** **Photo.** *Perf. 14*

437 A92 25c Koala 28 28
438 A92 35c Koala, diff. 35 35
439 A92 40c Koala, diff. 42 42
440 A92 58c Koala, diff. 60 60
441 A92 70c Koala, diff. 75 75
442 A92 83c Kangaroo with joey 90 90
443 A92 $1.05 Kangaroo with joey, diff. 1.10 1.10
444 A92 $2.50 Kangaroo, diff. 2.50 2.50
*Nos. 437-444 (8)* 6.90 6.90

**Souvenir Sheets**

445 Sheet of 2 + label 3.00 3.00
*a.* A92 $1.75 Wallaby 1.50 1.50
*b.* A92 $1.75 Koala, diff. 1.50 1.50
*c.* Sheet of 6 (1 each, #437-441, 445b), perf. 13½ 3.50 3.50
*d.* Sheet of 4 (1 each, #442-444, 445a), perf. 13½ 5.00 5.00

Nos. 442-444 airmail.

Sizes: No. 445c, 110x107mm. No. 445d, 80x106mm. Issue date: Sept. 20, 1984.

**Nos. 432-436 Ovptd. with Event, Names of Gold Medalists, Country in Gold or Red.**

**1984, Sept. 7** *Perf. 14*

446 A91 30c Danneberg 30 30
447 A91 35c Coe (R) 35 35
448 A91 40c Todd 40 40
449 A91 58c Biggs 58 58
450 A91 70c Haerkoenen 70 70
*Nos. 446-450 (5)* 2.33 2.33

10th Anniv. of Self Government — A93

**1984, Oct. 19** **Photo.** *Perf. 13*

451 A93 40c Niue flag 40 40
452 A93 58c Niue map 58 58
453 A93 70c Ceremony 70 70
*a.* Souvenir sheet of 3 1.75 1.75

**Souvenir Sheet**

454 A93 $2.50 like 70c 2.50 2.50

No. 453a contains Nos. 451-453, plus label. Size: 110x84mm. No. 454 contains flags in margin. Size: 100x75mm.

**Nos. 340, 354 Surcharged: "Prince Henry / 15.9.84" and Bars and New Values in Red or Silver**

**1984, Oct. 22** **Photo.** *Perf. 14*

455 A79 $2 on 75c multi (R) 2.00 2.00
456 A79 $2 on 50c multi (S) 2.00 2.00

Nos. 455-456 issued in sheets of five plus label.

Christmas 1984 — A94

Paintings: 40c, The Nativity, by A. Vaccaro. 58c, Virgin with Fly, anonymous. 70c, Adoration of the Shepherds, by B. Murillo. 83c, Flight into Egypt, by B. Murillo.

**1984, Oct. 19** **Photo.** *Perf. 13x13½*

457 A94 40c multi 55 55
458 A94 58c multi 80 80
459 A94 70c multi 90 90
460 A94 83c multi 1.10 1.10

**Souvenir Sheets**

461 Sheet of 4 2.70 2.70
*a.* A94 40c + 5c Like 40c 45 45
*b.* A94 58c + 5c Like 58c 58 58
*c.* A94 70c + 5c Like 70c 75 75
*d.* A94 83c + 5c Like 83c 82 82

*Perf. 13½*

462 A94 95c + 10c Like 40c 1.05 1.05
463 A94 95c + 10c Like 58c 1.05 1.05
464 A94 95c + 10c Like 70c 1.05 1.05
465 A94 95c + 10c Like 83c 1.05 1.05

No. 461 has flowered margin. Size: 116x111mm. Nos. 462-465 have design extending into margin. Size: 66x99mm.

Audubon Birth Bicentenary A95

Illustrations of North American bird species by artist/naturalist John J. Audubon.

**1985, Apr. 15** **Photo.** *Perf. 14½*

466 A95 40c House wren 32 32
467 A95 70c Veery 55 55
468 A95 83c Grasshopper sparrow 70 70
469 A95 $1.05 Henslow's sparrow 85 85
470 A95 $2.50 Vesper sparrow 2.00 2.00
*Nos. 466-470 (5)* 4.42 4.42

**Souvenir Sheets**

*Perf. 14*

471 A95 $1.75 like #466 1.50 1.50
472 A95 $1.75 like #467 1.50 1.50
473 A95 $1.75 like #468 1.50 1.50
474 A95 $1.75 like #469 1.50 1.50
475 A95 $1.75 like #470 1.50 1.50

Nos. 471-475 have multicolored margins continuing designs. Size: 55x60mm.

Queen Mother, 85th Birthday A96

Designs: 70c, Wearing mantle of the Order of the Garter. $1.15, With Queen Elizabeth II. $1.50, With Prince Charles. $3, Writing letter.

**1985, June 14** *Perf. 13½x13*

476 A96 70c multi 70 70
477 A96 $1.15 multi 1.15 1.15
478 A96 $1.50 multi 1.50 1.50
*a.* Souvenir sheet of 3 + label, #476-478 3.35 3.35

**Souvenir Sheet**

*Perf. 13½*

479 A96 $3 multi 3.00 3.00

Nos. 476-478 issued in sheets of 5 plus label. No. 479 contains one stamp (size: 39x36mm); multicolored margin continues portrait of the Queen Mother seated at a desk. Size: 71x70mm.

No. 478a issued on Aug. 4, 1986, for 86th birthday; multicolored decorative margin. Size: 109x84mm.

**Nos. 432-433, 435-436 Overprinted: "Mini South Pacific Games, Rarotonga" and Surcharged with Gold Bar and New Value in Black**

**1985, July 26** *Perf. 14*

480 A91 52c on 95c multi 52 52
481 A91 83c on 58c multi 85 85
482 A91 95c on 35c multi 95 95
483 A91 $2 on 30c multi 2.00 2.00

Nos. 368-371 Overprinted with Conference Emblem and: "Pacific Islands Conference, Rarotonga."

**1985, July 26** *Perf. 13½x13*

| | | | | |
|---|---|---|---|---|
| *484* | A84 | 70c on #368 | 70 | 70 |
| *485* | A84 | 70c on #369 | 70 | 70 |
| *486* | A84 | 70c on #370 | 70 | 70 |
| *487* | A84 | 70c on #371 | 70 | 70 |

Nos. 484-487 printed se-tenant.

Portrait of R. Strozzi's Daughter, by Titian — A97

Paintings of children: 70c, The Fifer, by Manet. $1.15, Portrait of a Young Girl, by Renoir. $1.50, Portrait of M. Berard, by Renoir.

**1985, Oct. 11** *Perf. 13*

| | | | | |
|---|---|---|---|---|
| *488* | A97 | 58c multi | 58 | 58 |
| *489* | A97 | 70c multi | 70 | 70 |
| *490* | A97 | $1.15 multi | 1.15 | 1.15 |
| *491* | A97 | $1.50 multi | 1.50 | 1.50 |

**Souvenir Sheets**

***Perf. 13x13½***

| | | | | |
|---|---|---|---|---|
| *492* | A97 | $1.75 + 10c like #488 | 2.00 | 2.00 |
| *493* | A97 | $1.75 + 10c like #489 | 2.00 | 2.00 |
| *494* | A97 | $1.75 + 10c like #490 | 2.00 | 2.00 |
| *495* | A97 | $1.75 + 10c like #491 | 2.00 | 2.00 |

Intl. Youth Year. Nos. 492-495 have multicolored margins continuing each portrait. Size: 64x80mm.

Christmas — A98

Paintings (details) by Correggio: 58c, No. 500a, Virgin and Child. 85c, No. 500b, Adoration of the Magi. $1.05, No. 500c, Virgin and Child, diff. $1.45, No. 500d, Virgin and Child with St. Catherine.

**1985, Nov. 29** **Photo.** *Perf. 13x13½*

| | | | | |
|---|---|---|---|---|
| *496* | A98 | 58c multi | 70 | 70 |
| *497* | A98 | 85c multi | 1.05 | 1.05 |
| *498* | A98 | $1.05 multi | 1.25 | 1.25 |
| *499* | A98 | $1.45 multi | 1.75 | 1.75 |

**Souvenir Sheets**

| | | | | |
|---|---|---|---|---|
| *500* | | Sheet of 4 | 3.50 | 3.50 |
| ***a.-d.*** | | A98 60c + 10c, any single | 85 | 85 |

***Imperf***

| | | | | |
|---|---|---|---|---|
| *501* | A98 | 65c like #496 | 78 | 78 |
| *502* | A98 | 95c like #497 | 1.15 | 1.15 |
| *503* | A98 | $1.20 like #498 | 1.50 | 1.50 |
| *504* | A98 | $1.75 like #499 | 2.25 | 2.25 |

No. 500 has multicolored decorative margin. Size: 83x123mm. Nos. 501-504 contain one stamp each (size 61x71mm); multicolored decorative margin. Sizes: 80x91mm.

Halley's Comet — A99

The Constellations, fresco by Giovanni De Vecchi, Farnesio Palace, Caprarola, Italy.

**1986, Jan. 24** *Perf. 13½*

| | | | | |
|---|---|---|---|---|
| *505* | A99 | 60c multi | 68 | 68 |
| *506* | A99 | 75c multi | 85 | 85 |
| *507* | A99 | $1.10 multi | 1.25 | 1.25 |
| *508* | A99 | $1.50 multi | 1.75 | 1.75 |

**Souvenir Sheet**

| | | | | |
|---|---|---|---|---|
| *509* | | Sheet of 4 | 4.50 | 4.50 |
| ***a.*** | | A99 95c like #505 | 1.10 | 1.10 |
| ***b.*** | | A99 95c like #506 | 1.10 | 1.10 |
| ***c.*** | | A99 95c like #507 | 1.10 | 1.10 |
| ***d.*** | | A99 95c like #508 | 1.10 | 1.10 |

No. 509 has Prussian blue and gold margin. Size: 126x91mm.

Elizabeth II, 60th Birthday — A100

Designs: $1.10, No. 513a, Elizabeth and Prince Philip at Windsor Castle. $1.50, No. 513b, At Balmoral. $2, No. 513c, Elizabeth at Buckingham Palace. $3, Elizabeth seated and Prince Philip.

**1986, Apr. 28** *Perf. 14½x13½*

| | | | | |
|---|---|---|---|---|
| *510* | A100 | $1.10 multi | 1.30 | 1.30 |
| *511* | A100 | $1.50 multi | 1.75 | 1.75 |
| *512* | A100 | $2 multi | 2.40 | 2.40 |

**Souvenir Sheets**

| | | | | |
|---|---|---|---|---|
| *513* | | Sheet of 3 | 2.75 | 2.75 |
| ***a.-c.*** | | A100 75c, any single | 90 | 90 |
| *514* | A100 | $3 multi | 3.50 | 3.50 |

No. 513 has multicolored decorative margin. Size: 111x71mm. No. 514 has multicolored margin continuing design. Size:

Mt. Rushmore — A101

Statue of Liberty, Cent. — A102

**1986, May 22** **Photo.** *Perf. 14*

| | | | | |
|---|---|---|---|---|
| *515* | A101 | $1 Washington, US #1 | 1.15 | 1.15 |
| *516* | A101 | $1 Jefferson, Roosevelt, Lincoln | 1.15 | 1.15 |

AMERIPEX '86. Nos. 515-516 printed setenant in a continuous design.

**1986, July 4** *Perf. 13x13½*

Paintings: $1, Statue under construction, 1883, by Victor Dargaud. $2.50, Unveiling the Statue of Liberty, 1886, by Edmund Morand (1829-1901).

| | | | | |
|---|---|---|---|---|
| *517* | A102 | $1 multi | 1.15 | 1.15 |
| *518* | A102 | $2.50 multi | 2.75 | 2.75 |

**Souvenir Sheet**

| | | | | |
|---|---|---|---|---|
| *519* | | Sheet of 2 | 2.90 | 2.90 |
| ***a.*** | | A102 $1.25 like #517 | 1.45 | 1.45 |
| ***b.*** | | A102 $1.25 like #518 | 1.45 | 1.45 |

No. 519 has multicolored decorative margin picturing portrait of Bartholdi. Size: 107x74mm.

Wedding of Prince Andrew and Sarah Ferguson — A103

Designs: $2.50, Portraits, Westminster Abbey. $5, Portraits.

**1986, July 23** *Perf. 13½x13*

| | | | | |
|---|---|---|---|---|
| *520* | A103 | $2.50 multi | 2.75 | 2.75 |

**Souvenir Sheet**

| | | | | |
|---|---|---|---|---|
| *521* | A103 | $5 Portraits | 5.50 | 5.50 |

No. 520 printed in sheets of 4. No. 521 contains one stamp (size: 45x32mm); multicolored margin pictures abbey facade. Size: 106x68mm.

STAMPEX '86, Adelaide, Aug. 4-10 — A104

Birds.

***Perf. 13x13½, 13½x13***

**1986, Aug. 4** **Photo.**

| | | | | |
|---|---|---|---|---|
| *522* | A104 | 40c Egretta alba, vert. | 45 | 45 |
| *523* | A104 | 60c Emblema picta | 65 | 65 |
| *524* | A104 | 75c Aprosmictus scapularis, vert. | 80 | 80 |
| *525* | A104 | 80c Malurus lamberti | 88 | 88 |
| *526* | A104 | $1 Falco peregrinus, vert. | 1.10 | 1.10 |
| *527* | A104 | $1.65 Halcyon azurea | 1.80 | 1.80 |
| *528* | A104 | $2.20 Melopsittacus undulatus, vert. | 2.40 | 2.40 |
| *529* | A104 | $4.25 Dromaius novaehollandiae | 4.60 | 4.60 |
| | | *Nos. 522-529 (8)* | 12.68 | 12.68 |

Christmas — A105

Paintings in the Vatican Museum: 80c, No. 534a, Virgin and Child, by Perugino (1446-1523). $1.15, No. 534b, Virgin of St. N. dei Frari, by Titian. $1.80, No. 534c, Virgin with Milk, by Lorenzo di Credi (1459-1537). $2.60, $7.50, No. 534d, Foligno Madonna, by Raphael.

**1986, Nov. 14** **Litho.** *Perf. 14*

| | | | | |
|---|---|---|---|---|
| *530* | A105 | 80c multi | 85 | 85 |
| *531* | A105 | $1.15 multi | 1.25 | 1.25 |
| *532* | A105 | $1.80 multi | 1.90 | 1.90 |
| *533* | A105 | $2.60 multi | 2.75 | 2.75 |

**Souvenir Sheets**

***Perf. 13½***

| | | | | |
|---|---|---|---|---|
| *534* | | Sheet of 4 | 6.40 | 6.40 |
| ***a.-d.*** | | A105 $1.50, any single | 1.60 | 1.60 |

***Perf. 14½x13½***

| | | | | |
|---|---|---|---|---|
| *535* | A105 | $7.50 multi | 8.00 | 8.00 |

No. 534 has multicolored decorative margin. Size: 89x110mm. No. 535 has multicolored inscribed margin continuing the painting. Size: 70x100mm.

**Souvenir Sheets**

Statue of Liberty, Cent. — A106

Photographs: No. 536a, Tall ship, bridge. NO. 536b, Workmen, flame from torch. No. 536c, Workman, flame, diff. No. 536d, Ships, New York City. No. 536e, Tall ship, sailboat, bridge. No. 537a, Statue, front. No. 537b, Statue, left side. No. 537c,

**1987, May 20**

| | | | | |
|---|---|---|---|---|
| *536* | | Sheet of 5+label | 5.25 | 5.25 |
| ***a.-e.*** | | A106 75c any single | 1.05 | 1.05 |
| *537* | | Sheet of 5+label | 5.25 | 5.25 |
| ***a.-e.*** | | A106 75c any single | 1.05 | 1.05 |

Sizes of Nos. 536-537: 123x122mm, 121x123mm.

Tennis Champions — A107

Olympic emblem, coin and: 80c, $1.15, $1.40, $1.80, Boris Becker. 85c, $1.05, $1.30, $1.75, Steffi Graf. Various action scenes.

**1987**

| | | | | |
|---|---|---|---|---|
| *538* | A107 | 80c multi | 1.10 | 1.10 |
| *539* | A107 | 85c multi | 1.20 | 1.20 |
| *540* | A107 | $1.05 multi | 1.45 | 1.45 |
| *541* | A107 | $1.15 multi | 1.60 | 1.60 |
| *542* | A107 | $1.30 multi | 1.80 | 1.80 |
| *543* | A107 | $1.40 multi | 1.95 | 1.95 |
| *544* | A107 | $1.75 multi | 2.40 | 2.40 |
| *545* | A107 | $1.80 multi | 2.50 | 2.50 |
| | | *Nos. 522-529 (8)* | 12.68 | 12.68 |

Issue dates: 80c, $1.15, $1.40, $1.80, Sept. 25. Others, Oct. 20.

Nos. 511-512 Surcharged "40th /WEDDING / ANNIV." with Denomination in Black on Gold

***Perf. 14½x13½***

**1987, Nov. 20** **Photo.**

| | | | | |
|---|---|---|---|---|
| *546* | A100 | $4.85 on No. 511 | 6.00 | 6.00 |
| *547* | A100 | $4.85 on No. 512 | 6.00 | 6.00 |

40th Wedding anniv. of Queen Elizabeth II and Prince Philip, Duke of Edinburgh.

Christmas — A108

Paintings (details) by Albrecht Durer (Angel with Lute on 80c, $1.05, $2.80): 80c, No. 551a, The Nativity. $1.05, No. 551b, Adoration of the Magi. $2.80, No. 551c, $7.50, Celebration of the Rosary.

**1987, Dec. 4** **Photo.** *Perf. 13½*

| | | | | |
|---|---|---|---|---|
| *548* | A108 | 80c multi | 1.00 | 1.00 |
| *549* | A108 | $1.05 multi | 1.35 | 1.35 |
| *550* | A108 | $2.80 multi | 3.55 | 3.55 |

**Souvenir Sheets**

| | | | | |
|---|---|---|---|---|
| *551* | | Sheet of 3 | 4.95 | 4.95 |
| ***a.-c.*** | | A108 $1.30 any single | 1.65 | 1.65 |
| *552* | A108 | $7.50 multi | 9.50 | 9.50 |

No. 551 has gold and brown violet inscribed margin; size of Nos. 551a-551c: 49½x38½mm. No. 552 contains one stamp (size: 51x33mm); multicolored decorative margin continues the painting. Sizes: 100x140mm (No. 551); 90x80mm (No. 552).

For unused stamps, more recent issues are valued as never hinged, with the beginning point determined on a country-by-country basis. Notes to show the beginning points are prominently placed in the text.

European Soccer Championships — A109

Highlights from Franz Beckenbauer's career: 20c, Match scene. 40c, German all-star team. 60c, Brussels, 1974. 80c, England, 1966. $1.05, Mexico, 1970. $1.30, Munich, 1974. $1.80, FC Bayern Munchen vs. Athletico Madrid.

**1988, June 20 Litho. *Perf. 14***

| | | | | |
|---|---|---|---|---|
| *553* A109 | 20c multi | | 28 | 28 |
| *554* A109 | 40c multi | | 55 | 55 |
| *555* A109 | 60c multi | | 85 | 85 |
| *556* A109 | 80c multi | | 1.10 | 1.10 |
| *557* A109 | $1.05 multi | | 1.45 | 1.45 |
| *558* A109 | $1.30 multi | | 1.80 | 1.80 |
| *559* A109 | $1.80 multi | | 2.50 | 2.50 |
| | *Nos. 553-559 (7)* | | 8.53 | 8.53 |

Nos. 539-540, 542 and 543 Ovptd.

*a.* "Australia 24 Jan 88 / French Open 4 June 88"

*b.* "Wimbledon 2 July 88 / U S Open 10 Sept. 88"

*c.* "Women's Tennis Grand / Slam: 10 September 88"

*d.* "Seoul Olympic Games / Gold Medal Winner"

**1988, Oct. 14 Litho. *Perf. 13½x14***

| | | | |
|---|---|---|---|
| *560* A107(a) | 85c on No. 539 | 1.20 | 1.20 |
| *561* A107(b) | $1.05 on No. 540 | 1.45 | 1.45 |
| *562* A107(c) | $1.30 on No. 542 | 1.80 | 1.80 |
| *563* A107(d) | $1.75 on No. 543 | 2.40 | 2.40 |

Steffi Graf, 1988 Olympic gold medalist; opportunities for youth in sports.

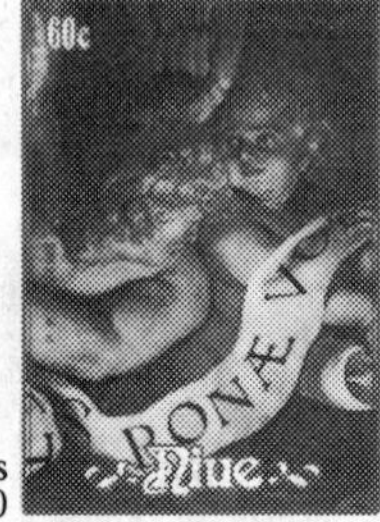


Christmas A110

*Adoration of the Shepherds,* by Rubens: 60c, Angels. 80c, Joseph and witness. $1.05, Madonna. $1.30, Christ child. $7.20, Entire painting.

**1988, Oct. 28 Photo. *Perf. 13½***

| | | | |
|---|---|---|---|
| *564* A110 | 60c multi | 75 | 75 |
| *565* A110 | 80c multi | 1.05 | 1.05 |
| *566* A110 | $1.05 multi | 1.35 | 1.35 |
| *567* A110 | $1.30 multi | 1.65 | 1.65 |

**Souvenir Sheet**

| | | | |
|---|---|---|---|
| *568* A110 | $7.20 multi | 9.25 | 9.25 |

No. 568 contains one stamp (size: 40x50mm); multicolored inscribed margin continues the painting. Size: 83x103mm.

## SEMI-POSTAL STAMPS

**Catalogue values for unused stamps in this section, from this point to the end of the section, are for Never Hinged items.**

Easter Type of 1978

Souvenir Sheets

Designs: No. B1, Descent from the Cross, by Caravaggio. No. B2, Burial of Christ, by Bellini. Sheets show paintings from which stamp designs were taken.

**1978, Mar. 15 Photo. *Perf. 13½***

| | | | |
|---|---|---|---|
| *B1* A61 | 70c + 5c multi | 1.75 | 1.75 |
| *B2* A61 | 70c + 5c multi | 1.75 | 1.75 |

Easter 1978. Surtax was for school children in Niue. Silver margin. Size: 102x88mm.

Christmas Type of 1978

Souvenir Sheets

Designs: No. B3, like No. 232. No. B4, like No. 233. No. B5, like No. 234.

**1978, Nov. 30 Photo. *Perf. 13***

| | | | |
|---|---|---|---|
| *B3* A63 | 60c + 5c multi | 1.40 | 1.40 |
| *B4* A63 | 60c + 5c multi | 1.40 | 1.40 |
| *B5* A63 | 60c + 5c multi | 1.40 | 1.40 |

Christmas 1978. Surtax was for school children of Niue. The sheets show paintings from which designs of stamps were taken. Size: 75x65½mm.

Easter Type of 1979

Souvenir Sheets

Designs: No. B6, like No. 235. No. B7, like No. 236.

**1979, Apr. 2**

| | | | |
|---|---|---|---|
| *B6* A64 | 70c + 5c multi | 1.50 | 1.50 |
| *B7* A64 | 70c + 5c multi | 1.50 | 1.50 |

Easter 1979. Surtax was for school children of Niue. The sheets show altarpiece from which designs of stamps were taken. Sizes: 70x86mm. (No. B6); 86x70mm. (No. B7).

IYC Type of 1979

Souvenir Sheets

Designs: No. B8, like No. 237. No. B9, like No. 238. No. B10, like No. 239. No. B11, like No. 240.

**1979, May 31 Photo. *Perf. 13***

| | | | |
|---|---|---|---|
| *B8* A65 | 70c + 5c multi | 1.50 | 1.50 |
| *B9* A65 | 70c + 5c multi | 1.50 | 1.50 |
| *B10* A65 | 70c + 5c multi | 1.50 | 1.50 |
| *B11* A65 | 70c + 5c multi | 1.50 | 1.50 |

International Year of the Child. Sheets show paintings from which designs of stamps were taken. Size: 100x120mm.

Christmas Type of 1979

Souvenir Sheets

**1979, Nov. 29 Photo. *Perf. 13***

| | | | |
|---|---|---|---|
| *B12* A70 | 85c + 5c *like #258* | 1.40 | 1.40 |
| *B13* A70 | 85c + 5c *like #259* | 1.40 | 1.40 |
| *B14* A70 | 85c + 5c *like #260* | 1.40 | 1.40 |
| *B15* A70 | 85c + 5c *like #261* | 1.40 | 1.40 |

Christmas 1979. Multicolored margins show entire paintings. Size: 48½x85mm.

Nos. 241-250, 251-254, 255-257, 258-261 Surcharged in Black (2 lines) or Silver (3 lines): Hurricane Relief Plus 2c.

**1980, Jan. 25 Photo. *Perf. 14, 13½***

| | | | |
|---|---|---|---|
| *B16* A66 | 20c + 2c multi | 40 | 40 |
| *B17* A67 | 20c + 2c multi | 40 | 40 |
| *B18* A68 | 20c + 2c multi (S) | 40 | 40 |
| *B19* A70 | 20c + 2c multi (S) | 40 | 40 |
| *B20* A70 | 25c + 2c multi (S) | 52 | 52 |
| *B21* A66 | 30c + 2c multi | 60 | 60 |
| *B22* A67 | 30c + 2c multi | 60 | 60 |
| *B23* A68 | 30c + 2c multi (S) | 60 | 60 |
| *B24* A69 | 30c + 2c multi (S) | 60 | 60 |
| *B25* A70 | 30c + 2c multi (S) | 60 | 60 |
| *B26* A66 | 35c + 2c multi | 75 | 75 |
| *B27* A67 | 35c + 2c multi | 75 | 75 |
| *B28* A68 | 35c + 2c multi (S) | 75 | 75 |
| *B29* A69 | 35c + 2c multi (S) | 75 | 75 |
| *B30* A66 | 50c + 2c multi | 90 | 90 |
| *B31* A67 | 50c + 2c multi | 90 | 90 |
| *B32* A70 | 50c + 2c multi (S) | 90 | 90 |
| *B33* A66 | 60c + 2c multi | 1.25 | 1.25 |
| *B34* A67 | 60c + 2c multi | 1.25 | 1.25 |
| *B35* A69 | 60c + 2c multi (S) | 1.25 | 1.25 |
| *B36* A68 | 75c + 2c multi (S) | 1.50 | 1.50 |
| | *Nos. B16-B36 (21)* | 16.07 | 16.07 |

Easter Type of 1980

Souvenir Sheets

**1980, Apr. 2 Photo. *Perf. 13***

| | | | |
|---|---|---|---|
| *B37* | Sheet of 3 | 1.00 | 1.00 |
| **a.** | A71 25c + 2c *like #262* | 28 | 28 |
| **b.** | A71 30c + 2c *like #263* | 32 | 32 |
| **c.** | A71 35c + 2c *like #264* | 38 | 38 |

**1980, Apr. 2**

| | | | |
|---|---|---|---|
| *B38* A71 | 85c + 5c *like #262* | 1.20 | 1.20 |
| *B39* A71 | 85c + 5c *like #263* | 1.20 | 1.20 |
| *B40* A71 | 85c + 5c *like #264* | 1.20 | 1.20 |

Surtax was for hurricane relief. Nos. B37-B40 have dark blue and gold decorative margins. Sizes: No. B37, 75x114mm; B38-B40, 75½x52mm.

Souvenir Sheet

No. 250a Overprinted Like Nos. 281-290 and Surcharged

**1980, Aug. 22 Photo. *Perf. 14***

| | | | |
|---|---|---|---|
| *B41* | Souvenir sheet of 10 | 5.00 | 5.00 |
| **a.** | A66 20c + 2c | 25 | 25 |
| **b.** | A67 20c + 2c | 25 | 25 |
| **c.** | A66 30c + 2c | 35 | 35 |
| **d.** | A67 30c + 2c | 35 | 35 |
| **e.** | A66 35c + 2c | 45 | 45 |
| **f.** | A67 35c + 2c | 45 | 45 |
| **g.** | A66 50c + 2c | 65 | 65 |
| **h.** | A67 50c + 2c | 65 | 65 |
| **i.** | A66 60c + 2c | 80 | 80 |
| **j.** | A67 60c + 2c | 80 | 80 |

ZEAPEX '80, New Zealand Intl. Stamp Exhib., Auckland, Aug. 23-31. Each stamp and one label overprinted with exhibition seal in black on silver, other label overprinted with design of New Zealand No. 1.

Souvenir Sheet

**1980, Oct. 30 Photo. *Perf. 14***

| | | | |
|---|---|---|---|
| *B42* | Sheet of 8 | 4.00 | 4.00 |
| **a.** | A74 20c + 2c *like #293* | 35 | 35 |
| **b.** | A75 20c + 2c *like #294* | 35 | 35 |
| **c.** | A74 25c + 2c *like #295* | 45 | 45 |
| **d.** | A75 25c + 2c *like #296* | 45 | 45 |
| **e.** | A74 30c + 2c *like #297* | 52 | 52 |
| **f.** | A75 30c + 2c *like #298* | 52 | 52 |
| **g.** | A74 35c + 2c *like #299* | 60 | 60 |
| **h.** | A75 35c + 2c *like #300* | 60 | 60 |

22nd Summer Olympic Games, Moscow, July 19-Aug. 3. No. B42 has multicolored margin showing flags of New Zealand and Niue, Moscow '80 emblem. Size: 120x129mm.

Christmas Type of 1980

Souvenir Sheets

**1980, Nov. 28 Photo. *Perf. 13½x13***

| | | | |
|---|---|---|---|
| *B43* A76 | 80c + 5c *like #301* | 1.10 | 1.10 |
| *B44* A76 | 80c + 5c *like #302* | 1.10 | 1.10 |
| *B45* A76 | 80c + 5c *like #303* | 1.10 | 1.10 |
| *B46* A76 | 80c + 5c *like #304* | 1.10 | 1.10 |

Nos. B43-B46 each contain one stamp (31x39mm.); multicolored margins show entire paintings. Size: 63x84½mm.

Easter Type of 1981

Souvenir Sheets

**1981, Apr. 10 Photo. *Perf. 13½***

| | | | |
|---|---|---|---|
| *B47* | Sheet of 3 | 2.50 | 2.50 |
| **a.** | A78 35c + 2c like #337 | 60 | 60 |
| **b.** | A78 50c + 2c like #338 | 75 | 75 |
| **c.** | A78 60c + 2c like #339 | 90 | 90 |

Dark blue and gold decorative margin. Size: 69x112mm.

**1981, Apr. 10 *Perf. 13½***

| | | | |
|---|---|---|---|
| *B48* A78 | 80c + 5c like #337 | 1.40 | 1.40 |
| *B49* A78 | 80c + 5c like #338 | 1.40 | 1.40 |
| *B50* A78 | 80c + 5c like #339 | 1.40 | 1.40 |

Multicolored margins show entire paintings. Size: 78½x86mm.

Soccer Type of 1981

**1981, Oct. 16 Photo. *Perf. 13***

| | | | |
|---|---|---|---|
| *B51* A80 | Sheet of 9 | 5.00 | 5.00 |

No. B51 contains Nos. 343-345 each with 3J surtax; light green and gold margin. Size: 162x122mm.

Royal Wedding Type of 1981

Nos. 340-342a Surcharged.

**1981, Nov. 3 Photo. *Perf. 14***

| | | | |
|---|---|---|---|
| *B52* A79 | 75 + 5c like #340 | 1.60 | 1.60 |
| *B53* A79 | 95 + 5c like #341 | 2.00 | 2.00 |
| *B54* A79 | $1.20 + 5c like #342 | 2.50 | 2.50 |

**Souvenir Sheet**

| | | | |
|---|---|---|---|
| *B55* | Sheet of 3 | 6.50 | 6.50 |
| **a.** | A79 75 + 10c like #340 | 1.70 | 1.70 |
| **b.** | A79 95 + 10c like #341 | 2.10 | 2.10 |
| **c.** | A79 $1.20 + 10c like #342 | 2.60 | 2.60 |

Intl. Year of the Disabled. Surtax was for disabled.

Nos. 530-535 Surcharged "CHRISTMAS VISIT TO SOUTH PACIFIC OF / POPE JOHN PAUL II, NOVEMBER 21-24 1986" in Black on Silver.

**1986, Nov. 21 Litho. *Perf. 14***

| | | | |
|---|---|---|---|
| *B56* A105 | 80c + 10c multi | 95 | 95 |
| *B57* A105 | $1.15 + 10c multi | 1.35 | 1.35 |
| *B58* A105 | $1.80 + 10c multi | 2.00 | 2.00 |
| *B59* A105 | $2.60 + 10c multi | 2.90 | 2.90 |

**Souvenir Sheets**

***Perf. 13½***

| | | | |
|---|---|---|---|
| *B60* | Sheet of 4 | 6.80 | 6.80 |
| **a.-d.** | A105 $1.50 + 10c on Nos. 534a-534d | 1.70 | 1.70 |

***Perf. 14½x13½***

| | | | |
|---|---|---|---|
| *B61* A105 | $7.50 + 50c multi | 8.50 | 8.50 |

No. B60 ovptd. "FIRST VISIT OF A POPE TO SOUTH PACIFIC" and "HIS HOLINESS POPE JOHN PAUL II" on margin. No. B61 ovptd. on margin only "Visit of Pope John Paul II, Nov 21-24 1986 / First Papal Visit to the South Pacific."

## AIR POST STAMPS

**Catalogue values for unused stamps in this section, from this point to the end of the section, are for Never Hinged items.**

Type of 1977

Designs: 15c, Preparing ground for taro. 20c, Banana harvest. 23c, Bush plantation. 50c, Canoe fishing. 90c, Reef fishing. $1.35, Preparing ground for taro. $2.10, Shellfish gathering. $2.60, Luku harvest.

**1979 Litho. *Perf. 14***

| | | | |
|---|---|---|---|
| *C1* A54 | 15c gold & multi | 18 | 18 |
| *C2* A54 | 20c gold & multi | 25 | 25 |
| *C3* A54 | 23c gold & multi | 30 | 30 |
| *C4* A54 | 50c gold & multi | 65 | 65 |
| *C5* A54 | 90c gold & multi | 1.00 | 1.00 |
| *C6* A54 | $1.35 gold & multi | 1.50 | 1.50 |
| *C7* A54 | $2.10 gold & multi | 2.50 | 2.50 |
| *C8* A54 | $2.60 gold & multi | 3.00 | 3.00 |
| *C9* A54 | $5.10 like #187 | 6.00 | 6.00 |
| *C10* A54 | $6.35 like #188 | 7.50 | 7.50 |
| | *Nos. C1-C10 (10)* | 22.88 | 22.88 |

Issue dates: Nos. C1-C5, Feb. 26. Nos. C6-C8, Mar. 30. C9-C10, May 28.

## OFFICIAL STAMPS

**Catalogue values for unused stamps in this section, from this point to the end of the section, are for Never Hinged items.**

Nos. 334 417-430, 332-333, 431-431A and 334 Overprinted "O.H.M.S." in Metallic Blue or Gold.

***Perf. 13½, 13½x13, 13x13½, 13***

**1985-87 Photo.**

| | | | |
|---|---|---|---|
| *O1* A89 | 12c multi | 12 | 12 |
| *O2* A89 | 25c multi | 25 | 25 |
| *O3* A89 | 30c multi | 30 | 30 |
| *O4* A89 | 35c multi | 35 | 35 |
| *O5* A89 | 40c multi | 40 | 40 |
| *O6* A89 | 52c multi | 52 | 52 |
| *O7* A89 | 58c multi | 58 | 58 |
| *O8* A89 | 70c multi | 70 | 70 |
| *O9* A89 | 83c multi | 85 | 85 |
| *O10* A89 | $1.05 multi | 1.05 | 1.05 |
| *O11* A90 | $1.75 multi | 1.75 | 1.75 |
| *O12* A90 | $2.30 multi | 2.75 | 2.75 |
| *O13* A90 | $3.90 multi | 4.75 | 4.75 |
| *O14* A77a | $4 multi (G) | 4.50 | 4.50 |
| *O15* A90 | $5 multi | 5.50 | 5.50 |
| *O16* A77a | $6 multi ('87) (G) | 12.00 | 12.00 |
| *O17* A89 | $6.60 multi ('86) | 7.25 | 7.25 |
| *O18* A89 | $8.30 multi ('86) | 9.00 | 9.00 |
| *O19* A77a | $10 multi ('87) (G) | 20.00 | 20.00 |
| | *Nos. O1-O19 (19)* | 72.62 | 72.62 |

# NORFOLK ISLAND

LOCATION — An island in the south Pacific Ocean, 800 miles east of Australia.

GOVT. — Territory of Australia.

AREA — 13½ sq. mi.

POP. — 1,800 (est. 1982).

12 Pence = 1 Shilling

100 Cents = 1 Dollar (1966)

**Catalogue values for all unused stamps in this country are for Never Hinged items.**

View of Ball Bay — A1

Unwmk.

**1947, June 10 Engr. Perf. 14**

1 A1 ½p dp org 25 30
2 A1 1p violet 35 40
3 A1 1½p brt grn 60 70
4 A1 2p red vio 75 85
5 A1 2½p red 90 1.00
6 A1 3p brn org 1.00 1.10
7 A1 4p rose lake 1.25 1.25
8 A1 5½p slate 1.50 1.40
9 A1 6p sepia 1.75 1.75
10 A1 9p lil rose 2.25 2.50
11 A1 1sh gray grn 2.25 2.50
12 A1 2sh ol bis 6.00 5.50
*Nos. 1-12 (12)* 18.85 19.25

See Nos. 23-24.

Warder's Tower — A2

Airfield — A3

Designs: 7½p, First Governor's Residence. 8½p, Barracks entrance. 10p, Salt House. 5sh, Bloody Bridge.

**1953, June 10 Perf. 14½**

13 A2 3½p rose brn 2.50 1.65
14 A3 6½p dk grn 2.75 2.50
15 A3 7½p dp ultra 4.25 3.75
16 A2 8½p chocolate 6.25 6.00
17 A2 10p rose lil 5.00 4.75
18 A3 5sh dk brn 47.50 45.00
*Nos. 13-18 (6)* 68.25 63.65

See Nos. 35 and 40.

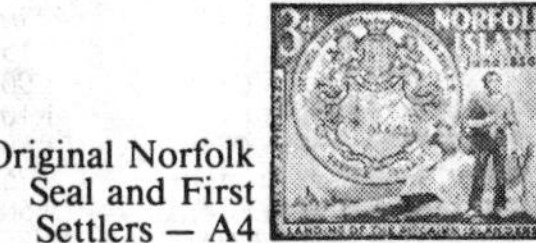

Original Norfolk Seal and First Settlers — A4

**1956, June 8**

19 A4 3p bluish grn 1.25 1.10
20 A4 2sh violet 5.50 *8.25*

Cent. of the landing of the Pitcairn Islanders on Norfolk Island.

Nos. 15 and 16 Surcharged with New Value and Bars

**1958, July 1**

21 A3 7p on 7½p dp ultra 2.50 *3.75*
22 A2 8p on 8½p choc 3.25 *5.00*

Ball Bay Type of 1947.

**1959, July 6 Engr. Perf. 14**

23 A1 3p green 13.00 13.50
24 A1 2sh dk bl 32.50 34.00

A5

Australia #332 Surcharged in Red

**1959, Dec. 7**

25 A5 5p on 4p dk gray bl 2.00 2.00

No. 14 and Types of 1953 Surcharged with New Values and Bars

**1960, Sept. 26 Perf. 14½**

26 A2 1sh1p on 3½p dk bl 7.50 *12.00*
27 A3 2sh5p on 6½p dk grn 9.00 *16.00*
28 A3 2sh8p on 7½p dk brn 15.00 *22.50*

Types of 1953 and

Island Hibiscus A6

Fairy Tern A7

Red-Tailed Tropic Bird — A8

Designs: 2p, Lagunaria patersonii (flowers). 5p, Lantana. 8p, Red hibiscus. 9p, Cereus and Queen Elizabeth II. 10p, Salt House. 1sh1p, Fringed hibiscus. 2sh, Providence petrel (vert.). 2sh5p, Passion flower. 2sh8p, Rose apple. 5sh, Bloody Bridge.

**1960-62 Unwmk. Engr. Perf. 14½**

29 A6 1p bl grn 15 14
30 A6 2p gray grn & brt pink 20 15
31 A7 3p brt grn ('61) 35 30
32 A6 5p lilac 1.10 90
33 A6 8p vermilion 2.00 1.90
34 A6 9p ultra 2.00 1.90
35 A2 10p pale pur & brn ('61) 3.50 2.50
36 A6 1sh1p dk red ('61) 2.75 2.25
37 A6 2sh sep ('61) 2.75 2.50
38 A6 2sh5p dk pur ('62) 2.75 2.50
39 A6 2sh8p grn & sal ('62) 4.25 3.00
40 A3 5sh grn & gray ('61) 6.75 5.00

***Perf. 14½x14***

41 A8 10sh grn ('61) 42.50 42.50
*Nos. 29-41 (13)* 71.05 65.54

Map of Norfolk Island — A9

**1960, Oct. 24 Engr. Perf. 14**

42 A9 2sh8p rose vio 35.00 *50.00*

Issued to commemorate the introduction of local government for Norfolk Island.

Christmas Stamp, 1960
Bible Type of Australia

**1960, Nov. 21 Perf. 14½**

43 A122 5p brt lil rose 5.75 *9.25*

Christmas Stamp, 1961
Bible Type of Australia.

**1961, Nov. 20 Perf. 14½x14**

44 A125 5p sl bl 1.90 *3.75*

Nos. 43-44 were issued to mark the beginning and the end of the 350th anniversary year of the publication of the King James translation of the Bible.

Christmas Stamp, 1962
Type of Australia

**1962, Nov. 19 Perf. 14½**

45 A129 5p blue 1.90 2.10

Overlooking Kingston A10

Dreamfish A11

Designs: 6p, Tweed trousers (fish). 8p, Kingston scene. 9p, "The Arches." 10p, Slaughter Bay. 11p, Trumpeter fish. 1sh, Po'ov (wrasse). 1sh6p, Queensland grouper. 2sh3p, Ophie (carangidae).

***Perf. 14½x14***

**1962-64 Unwmk. Photo.**

49 A10 5p multi ('64) 75 65
50 A11 6p multi 90 90
51 A10 8p multi ('64) 1.25 1.00
52 A10 9p multi ('64) 1.75 1.50
53 A10 10p multi ('64) 2.25 2.00
54 A11 11p multi ('63) 3.00 2.00
55 A11 1sh ol, bl & pink 3.50 3.00
57 A11 1sh3p bl, mar & grn ('63) 4.00 3.50
58 A11 1sh6p bl, brn & lil ('63) 4.50 4.50
60 A11 2sh3p dl bl, yel & red ('63) 5.25 5.00
*Nos. 49-60 (10)* 27.15 24.05

Christmas Stamp, 1963
Type of Australia

**1963, Nov. 11 Engr. Perf. 14½**

65 A146 5p vermilion 1.75 2.50

Symbolic Pine Tree — A12

**1964, July 1 Photo. Perf. 13½x13**

66 A12 5p org, blk & red 1.00 65
67 A12 8p gray grn, blk & red 1.60 1.60

50th anniv. of Norfolk Island as an Australian Territory.

Christmas Issue
Type of Australia

**1964, Nov. 9 Perf. 13½**

68 A149 5p multi 1.25 *1.90*

ANZAC Issue
Type of Australia, 1965

**1965, Apr. 14 Photo. Perf. 13½x13**

69 A150 5p brt grn, sep & blk 85 90

See note after Australia No. 387.

Christmas Issue
Type of Australia

**1965, Oct. 25 Unwmk. Perf. 13½**

70 A156 5p gold, blk, ultra & redsh brn 50 *80*

No. 70 is luminescent. See note after Australia No. 331.

Nos. 29-33 and 35-41 Surcharged in Black on Overprinted Metallic Rectangles

Two types of 1c on 1p:
I. Silver rectangle 4x5½mm.
II. Silver rectangle 5½x5¼mm.
Two types of $1 on 10sh:
I. Silver rectangle 7x6½mm.
II. Silver rectangle 6x4mm.

***Perf. 14½, 14½x14***

**1966, Feb. 14 Engr.**

71 A6 1c on 1p bl grn (I) 18 25
a. Type II 35 60
72 A6 2c on 2p gray grn & brt pink 18 28
73 A7 3c on 3p brt grn 22 40
74 A6 4c on 5p lil 28 45
75 A6 5c on 8p ver 35 65
76 A2 10c on 10p pale pur & brn 70 1.40
77 A6 15c on 1sh1p dk red 1.10 1.60
78 A6 20c on 2sh sep 1.40 *2.75*
79 A6 25c on 2sh5p dk pur 2.00 *4.00*
80 A6 30c on 2sh8p grn & sal 2.75 *5.00*
81 A3 50c on 5sh grn & gray 5.25 *10.00*
82 A8 $1 on 10sh grn (I) 7.00 *13.00*
a. Type II 7.00 13.00
*Nos. 71-82 (12)* 21.41 39.78

Headstone Bridge — A13

**1966, June 27 Photo. Perf. 14½**

88 A13 7c shown 35 50
89 A13 9c Cemetary road 50 75

St. Barnabas Chapel — A14

Design: 4c, Interior of St. Barnabas Chapel.

***Perf. 14x14½***

**1966, Aug. 23 Photo. Unwmk.**

97 A14 4c multi 14 25
98 A14 25c multi 75 *1.50*

Centenary of the Melanesian Mission.

Star over Philip Island — A15

**1966, Oct. 24 Photo. Perf. 14½**

99 A15 4c vio, grn, bl & sil 40 40

Christmas, 1966.

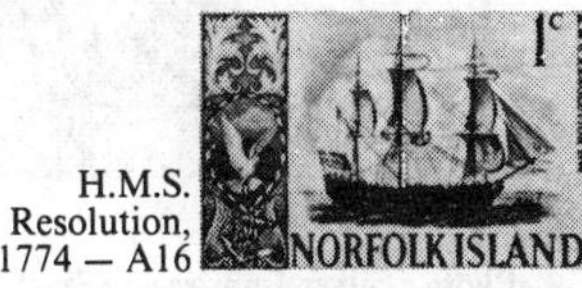

H.M.S. Resolution, 1774 — A16

Ships: 2c, La Boussole and Astrolabe, 1788. 3c, Brig Supply, 1788. 4c, Sirius, 1790. 5c, The Norfolk, 1798. 7c, Survey cutter Mermaid, 1825. 9c, The Lady Franklin, 1853. 10c The Morayshire, 1856. 15c, Southern Cross, 1866. 20c, The Pitcairn, 1891. 25c, Norfolk Island whaleboat, 1895. 30c, Cable ship Iris, 1907. 50c, The Resolution, 1926. $1, S.S. Morinda, 1931.

**1967-68 Photo. Perf. 14x14½**

100 A16 1c multi 6 5
101 A16 2c multi 10 9
102 A16 3c multi 14 14
103 A16 4c multi 20 18
104 A16 5c multi 30 24
105 A16 7c multi 35 32
106 A16 9c multi 45 42
107 A16 10c multi 60 55
108 A16 15c multi ('68) 90 85
109 A16 20c multi ('68) 1.30 1.25
110 A16 25c multi ('68) 2.25 1.75
111 A16 30c multi ('68) 2.75 2.50
112 A16 50c multi ('68) 3.25 3.00
113 A16 $1 multi ('68) 5.25 5.00
*Nos. 100-113 (14)* 17.90 16.34

Issue Dates: Nos. 100-103, Apr. 17, 1967; Nos. 104-107, Aug. 19, 1967; Nos. 108-110, Mar. 18, 1968. Nos. 111-113, June 18, 1968.

Lions Issue
Type of Australia

**1967, June 7 Photo. Perf. 13½**

114 A164 4c cit, blk & bl grn 40 90

50th anniversary of Lions International.
Printed on luminescent paper; see note after Australia No. 331.

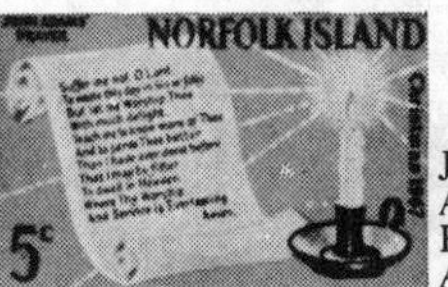

John Adams' Prayer A17

**1967, Oct. 16 Photo. Perf. 14x14½**

115 A17 5c brick red, blk & buff 40 45

Christmas 1967.

Queen Elizabeth II Type of Australia, 1966-67

Coil Stamps

*Perf. 15 Horizontally*

**1968-71 Photo. Unwmk.**

| | | | | |
|---|---|---|---|---|
| *116* | A157 | 3c brn org, blk & buff | 8 | 10 |
| *117* | A157 | 4c bl grn, blk & buff | 12 | 15 |
| *118* | A157 | 5c brt pur, blk & buff | 20 | 25 |
| *118A* | A157 | 6c dk red, brn, blk & buff ('71) | 40 | 50 |

DC-4 Skymaster and Lancastrian Plane — A18

**1968, Sept. 25** ***Perf. 14½x14***

| | | | | |
|---|---|---|---|---|
| *119* | A18 | 5c dk car, sky bl & ind | 20 | 30 |
| *120* | A18 | 7c dk car, bl grn & sep | 30 | 50 |

21st anniv. of the Sydney to Norfolk Island air service by Qantas Airways.

Star and Hibiscus Wreath — A19

**Photo.; Silver Impressed (Star)**

**1968, Oct. 24** ***Perf. 14½x14***

| | | | | |
|---|---|---|---|---|
| *121* | A19 | 5c sky bl & multi | 30 | 40 |

Christmas 1968.

Map of Pacific, Transit of Venus before Sun, Capt. Cook and Quadrant A20

**1969, June 3 Photo.** ***Perf. 14x14½***

| | | | | |
|---|---|---|---|---|
| *122* | A20 | 10c brn, ol, pale brn & yel | 35 | *75* |

Bicent. of the observation at Tahiti by Capt. James Cook of the transit of the planet Venus across the sun.

Map of Van Diemen's Land and Norfolk Island — A21

**1969, Sept. 29** ***Perf. 14x14½***

| | | | | |
|---|---|---|---|---|
| *123* | A21 | 5c multi | 15 | *30* |
| *124* | A21 | 30c multi | 90 | *1.75* |

125th anniv. of the annexation of Norfolk Island by Van Diemen's Land (Tasmania).

Nativity (Mother-of-Pearl carving) — A22

**1969, Oct. 27 Photo.** ***Perf. 14½x14***

| | | | | |
|---|---|---|---|---|
| *125* | A22 | 5c brn & multi | 30 | *45* |

Christmas 1969.

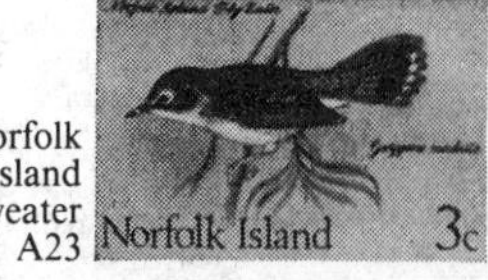


Norfolk Island Flyeater A23

Birds of Norfolk Island from Book by Gregory Mathews: 1c, Robins (vert.). 2c, Norfolk Island whistlers (thickheads) (vert.). 4c, Long-tailed cuckoos. 5c, Red-fronted parakeet (vert.). 7c, Long-tailed trillers (vert.). 9c, Island thrush. 10c, Owl (vert.). 15c, Norfolk Island pigeon (extinct; vert.). 20c, White-breasted white-eye. 25c, Norfolk Island parrots (vert.). 30c, Gray fantail. 45c, Norfolk Island starlings. 50c, Crimson rosella (vert.). $1, Sacred kingfisher.

***Perf. 14x14½, 14½x14***

**1970-71 Photo. Unwmk.**

| | | | | |
|---|---|---|---|---|
| *126* | A23 | 1c multi | 14 | 8 |
| *127* | A23 | 2c multi ('71) | 25 | 18 |
| *128* | A23 | 3c multi | 30 | 25 |
| *129* | A23 | 4c multi | 40 | 30 |
| *130* | A23 | 5c multi ('71) | 45 | 35 |
| *131* | A23 | 7c multi | 60 | 45 |
| *132* | A23 | 9c multi | 85 | 60 |
| *133* | A23 | 10c multi | 1.00 | 85 |
| *134* | A23 | 15c multi ('71) | 1.25 | 85 |
| *135* | A23 | 20c multi ('71) | 2.50 | 1.25 |
| *136* | A23 | 25c multi | 2.50 | 1.50 |
| *137* | A23 | 30c multi ('71) | 6.00 | 3.50 |
| *138* | A23 | 45c multi | 6.50 | 5.00 |
| *139* | A23 | 50c multi ('71) | 8.00 | 5.75 |
| *140* | A23 | $1 multi ('71) | 10.00 | 8.25 |
| | | *Nos. 126-140 (15)* | 40.74 | 29.16 |

Map of Australia, James Cook and Southern Cross A24

Design: 10c, "Endeavour" entering Botany Bay, Apr. 29, 1770, and aborigine with spear. The 1776 portrait of James Cook on the 5c is by John Webber.

**1970, Apr. 29 Photo.** ***Perf. 14x14½***

| | | | | |
|---|---|---|---|---|
| *141* | A24 | 5c multi | 30 | 28 |
| *142* | A24 | 10c multi | 60 | 55 |

200th anniv. of Cook's discovery and exploration of the eastern coast of Australia.

First Christmas, Sydney Bay, 1788 — A25

**1970, Oct. 15 Photo.** ***Perf. 14x14½***

| | | | | |
|---|---|---|---|---|
| *143* | A25 | 5c multi | 32 | 34 |

Christmas 1970.

Bishop Patteson, Open Bible — A26

Designs: No. 145, Bible opened to Acts Chap. 7, martyrdom of St. Stephen, and knotted palm fronds. No. 146, Bishop Patteson, rose window of Melanesian Mission Chapel on Norfolk Island. No. 147, Cross erected at Nukapu where Patteson died and his arms.

**1971, Sept. 20**

| | | | | |
|---|---|---|---|---|
| *144* | A26 | 6c brn & multi | 25 | 35 |
| *145* | A26 | 6c brn & multi | 25 | 35 |
| *146* | A26 | 10c pur & multi | 45 | 50 |
| *147* | A26 | 10c pur & multi | 45 | 50 |

Centenary of the death of Bishop John Coleridge Patteson (1827-1871), head of the Melanesian mission. Stamps of same denomination printed se-tenant in sheets of 60.

Rose Window, St. Barnabas Chapel, Norfolk Island — A27

**1971, Oct. 25** ***Perf. 14x13½***

| | | | | |
|---|---|---|---|---|
| *148* | A27 | 6c dk vio bl & multi | 30 | *45* |

Christmas 1971.

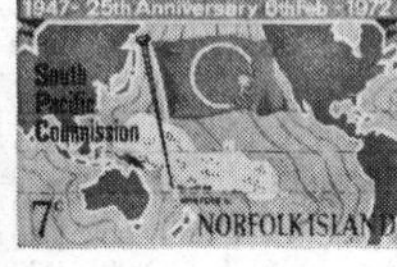


Map of South Pacific and Commission Flag — A28

**1972, Feb. 6** ***Perf. 14x14½***

| | | | | |
|---|---|---|---|---|
| *149* | A28 | 7c multi | 80 | 1.00 |

So. Pacific Commission, 25th anniv.

Stained-glass Window — A29

Cross, Church, Pines — A30

**1972, Oct. 16 Photo.** ***Perf. 14x14½***

| | | | | |
|---|---|---|---|---|
| *150* | A29 | 7c dk ol & multi | 30 | 55 |

Christmas 1972. The stained-glass window by Edward Coley Burne-Jones is in All Saints Church, Norfolk Island.

**1972, Nov. 20**

| | | | | |
|---|---|---|---|---|
| *151* | A30 | 12c multi | 50 | 95 |

Centenary of All Saints Church, first built by Pitcairners on Norfolk Island.

"Resolution" in Antarctica — A31

**1973, Jan. 17 Photo.** ***Perf. 14½x14***

| | | | | |
|---|---|---|---|---|
| *152* | A31 | 35c multi | 3.75 | *4.50* |

200th anniv. of the 1st crossing of the Antarctic Circle by Cook, Jan. 17, 1773.

*Norfolk Island stamps can be mounted in Scott's annually supplemented Australia and Dependencies Album.*

Sleeping Child, and Christmas Tree — A32

Christmas: 12c, like 7c. 35c, Star ove lagoon.

**1973, Oct. 22 Photo.** ***Perf. 14x14½***

| | | | | |
|---|---|---|---|---|
| *153* | A32 | 7c blk & multi | 35 | 50 |
| *154* | A32 | 12c blk & multi | 60 | 90 |
| *155* | A32 | 35c blk & multi | 2.00 | 3.00 |

Protestant Clergyman's House — A33

Designs: 2c, Royal Engineer Office. 3c Double quarters for free overseers. 4c, Guard House. 5c, Pentagonal Gaol entrance. 7c Pentagonal Gaol, aerial view. 8c, Convict barracks. 10c, Officers' quarters, New Military Barracks. 12c, New Military Barracks 14c, Beach stores. 15c, Magazine. 20c, Old Military Barracks, entrance. 25c, Old Military Barracks. 30c, Old stores, Crankmill 50c, Commissariat stores. $1, Government House.

**1973-75 Photo.** ***Perf. 14x14½***

| | | | | |
|---|---|---|---|---|
| *156* | A33 | 1c pur & multi | 6 | 6 |
| *157* | A33 | 2c multi ('74) | 12 | 15 |
| *158* | A33 | 3c multi ('75) | 18 | 25 |
| *159* | A33 | 4c multi ('74) | 22 | 30 |
| *160* | A33 | 5c gray & multi | 25 | 35 |
| *161* | A33 | 7c multi ('74) | 35 | 45 |
| *162* | A33 | 8c multi ('75) | 42 | 50 |
| *163* | A33 | 10c red & multi | 50 | 70 |
| *164* | A33 | 12c multi ('74) | 55 | 75 |
| *165* | A33 | 14c multi ('74) | 70 | 90 |
| *166* | A33 | 15c multi ('75) | 75 | *1.00* |
| *167* | A33 | 20c multi ('74) | 90 | *1.25* |
| *168* | A33 | 25c multi ('75) | 1.10 | *1.50* |
| *169* | A33 | 30c multi ('74) | 1.50 | *2.00* |
| *170* | A33 | 50c grn & multi | 2.75 | *3.50* |
| *171* | A33 | $1 multi ('74) | 4.50 | *5.00* |
| | | *Nos. 156-171 (16)* | 14.85 | 18.66 |

Map of Norfolk Island — A34

**1974, Feb. 8 Photo.** ***Perf. 14x14½***

| | | | | |
|---|---|---|---|---|
| *172* | A34 | 7c red lil & multi | 40 | 55 |
| *173* | A34 | 25c dl bl & multi | 1.75 | *2.50* |

Visit of Queen Elizabeth II and the Duke of Edinburgh, Feb. 11-12.

Gipsy Moth over Norfolk Island A35

**1974, Mar. 28 Litho.** ***Perf. 14x14½***

| | | | | |
|---|---|---|---|---|
| *174* | A35 | 14c multi | 2.50 | 2.75 |

1st aircraft to visit Norfolk, Sir Francis Chichester's "Mme. Elijah," Mar. 28, 1931.

Capt. Cook — A36

Nativity — A37

Designs: 10c, "Resolution," by Henry Roberts. 14c, Norfolk Island pine, cone and seedling. 25c, Norfolk Island flax, by George Raper, 1790. Portrait of Cook on 7c by William Hodges, 1770.

**1974, Oct. 8 Litho. *Perf. 14***

*175* A36 7c multi 60 60
*176* A36 10c multi 75 90
*177* A36 14c multi 1.50 1.75
*178* A36 25c multi 4.50 5.25

Bicentenary of the discovery of Norfolk Island by Capt. James Cook.

**1974, Oct. 18 Photo. *Perf. 14***

*179* A37 7c rose & multi 40 50
*180* A37 30c vio & multi 2.00 2.50

Christmas 1974.

Norfolk Island Pine — A38

Designs: 15c, Off-shore islands. 35c, Crimson rosella and sacred kingfisher. 40c, Map showing Norfolk's location. Stamps in shape of Norfolk Island.

**1974, Dec. 16 Litho. *Imperf.***
**Self-adhesive**

*181* A38 10c brn & multi 60 *1.15*
*182* A38 15c dk bl & multi 90 *1.75*
*183* A38 35c dk pur & multi 2.25 *4.00*
*184* A38 40c dk bl grn & multi 2.75 *5.00*
*a.* Souvenir sheet of 4 36.00 35.00

Centenary of Universal Postal Union. Stamps printed on peelable paper backing with green and black design and inscription. No. 184a contains 4 imperf. stamps similar to Nos. 181-184 in reduced size on a background of map of Norfolk Island. Peelable paper backing shows beach scene on Norfolk Island. Size (approx.): 105x115mm.

Survey Cutter "Mermaid," 1825 — A39

Design: 35c, Kingston, 1835, after painting by Thomas Seller. Stamps outlined in shape of Norfolk Island map.

**1975, Aug. 18 Litho. *Imperf.***
**Self-adhesive**

*185* A39 10c multi 25 *50*
*186* A39 35c multi 1.00 *2.00*

Sesquicentennial of 2nd settlement of Norfolk Island. Printed on peelable paper backing with green and black design and inscription.

Star over Norfolk Island Pine and Map — A40

Brass Memorial Cross — A41

**1975, Oct. 6 Photo. *Perf. 14½x14***

*187* A40 10c lt bl & multi 35 50
*188* A40 15c lt brn & multi 50 75
*189* A40 35c lil & multi 1.40 2.00

Christmas 1975.

***Perf. 14½x14, 14x14½***
**1975, Nov. 24 Photo.**

Design: 60c, Laying foundation stone, 1875, and chapel, 1975 (horiz.).

*190* A41 30c multi 65 75
*191* A41 60c multi 1.50 1.75

St. Barnabas Chapel, centenary.

Launching "Resolution" A42

Design: 45c, "Resolution" under sail.

**1975, Dec. 1 *Perf. 14x14½***

*192* A42 25c multi 80 *1.50*
*193* A42 45c multi 1.40 *2.25*

50th anniversary of launching of schooner "Resolution."

Bedford Flag, Charles W. Morgan Whaler A43

Designs: 25c, Grand Union Flag, church interior. 40c, 15-stari flag, 1795, and plane over island, WWII. 45c, 13-star flag and California quail.

**1976, July 5 Photo. *Perf. 14***

*194* A43 18c multi 40 *75*
*195* A43 25c multi 60 *1.10*
*196* A43 40c multi 80 *1.50*
*197* A43 45c multi 90 *1.75*

American Bicentennial.

Bird in Flight, Brilliant Sun — A44

**1976, Oct. 4 Photo. *Perf. 14***

*198* A44 18c bl grn & multi 60 75
*199* A44 25c dp bl & multi 90 1.10
*200* A44 45c vio & multi 1.60 2.00

Christmas 1976.

Bassaris Itea — A45

Butterflies and Moths: 2c, Utetheisa pulchelloides vaga. 3c, Agathia asterias jowettorum. 4c, Cynthia kershawi. 5c, Leucania loreyimima. 10c, Hypolimnas bolina nerina. 15c, Pyrrhorachis pyrrhogona. 16c, Austrocarea iocephala millsi. 17c, Pseudocoremia christiani. 18c, Cleora idiocrossa. 19c, Simplicia caeneusalis buffetti. 20c, Austrocidaria ralstonae. 30c, Hippotion scrofa. 40c, Papilio ilioneus. 50c, Tiracola plagiata. $1, Precis villida. $2, Cepora perimale.

**1976-77 Photo. *Perf. 14***

*201* A45 1c multi 5 5
*202* A45 2c multi 7 5
*203* A45 3c multi 8 10
*204* A45 4c multi 9 12
*205* A45 5c multi 12 14
*206* A45 10c multi 18 25
*207* A45 15c multi 25 38
*208* A45 16c multi 30 42
*209* A45 17c multi 35 45
*210* A45 18c multi 40 48
*211* A45 19c multi 40 48
*212* A45 20c multi 42 55
*213* A45 30c multi 65 90
*214* A45 40c multi 75 1.00
*215* A45 50c multi 1.10 1.40
*216* A45 $1 multi 1.50 2.00
*217* A45 $2 multi 3.00 3.50
*Nos. 201-217 (17)* 9.71 12.27

Issue dates: 1c, 5c, 10c, 16c, 18c and $1, Nov. 17, 1976. Others, 1977.

View of Kingston A46

**1977, June 10**

*218* A46 25c multi 90 1.10

25th anniv. of reign of Elizabeth II.

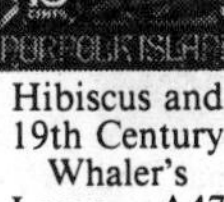

Hibiscus and 19th Century Whaler's Lamp — A47

Capt. Cook, by Nathaniel Dance — A48

**1977, Oct. 4 Photo. *Perf. 14½***

*219* A47 18c multi 40 *70*
*220* A47 25c multi 60 *1.00*
*221* A47 45c multi 90 *1.50*

Christmas 1977.

**1978, Jan. 18 Photo. *Perf. 14½***

Designs: 25c, Discovery of Northern Hawaiian Islands (Cook aboard ship; horiz.). 80c, British flag and Island (horiz.).

*222* A48 18c multi 40 *75*
*223* A48 25c multi 75 *1.25*
*224* A48 80c multi 1.75 *3.25*

Bicentenary of Capt. Cook's arrival in Hawaiian Islands.

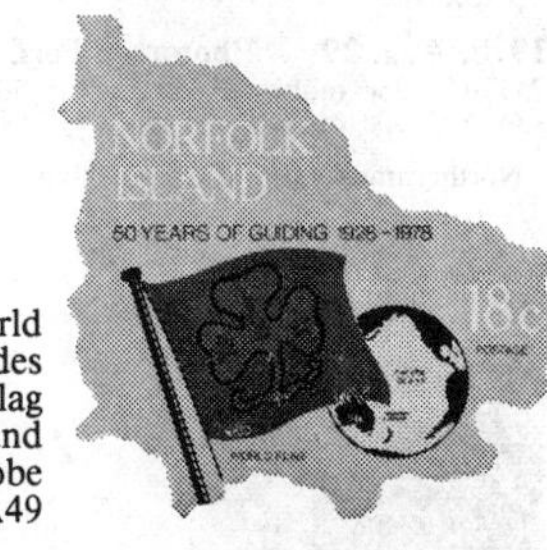

World Guides Flag and Globe A49

Designs: 25c, Norfolk Guides' scarf badge and trefoil. 35c, Elizabeth II and trefoil. 45c, FAO Ceres medal with portrait of Lady Olive Baden-Powell, and trefoil. Stamps outlined in shape of Norfolk Island map.

**1978, Feb. 22 Litho. *Imperf.***
**Self-adhesive**

*225* A49 18c lt ultra & multi 30 *50*
*226* A49 25c yel & multi 40 *75*
*227* A49 35c lt grn & multi 65 *1.25*
*228* A49 45c yel grn & multi 90 *1.75*

50th anniversary of Norfolk Island Girl Guides. Printed on peelable paper backing with green multiple pines and tourist publicity inscription.

St. Edward's Crown — A50

Design: 70c, Coronation regalia.

**1978, June 29 Photo. *Perf. 14½***

*229* A50 25c multi 50 70
*230* A50 70c multi 1.50 2.00

25th anniv. of coronation of Elizabeth II.

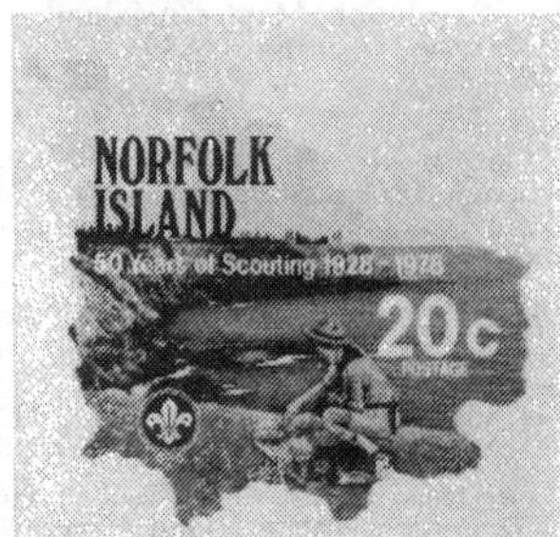

Cliffs, Duncombe Bay, Scout Making Fire — A51

Designs: 25c, Emily Bay, Philip and Nepean Islands from Kingston. 35c, Anson Bay, Cub and Boy Scouts. 45c, Sunset and Lord Baden-Powell. Stamps outlined in shape of Norfolk Island map.

**1978, Aug. 22 Litho. *Imperf.***
**Self-adhesive**

*231* A51 20c multi 40 60
*232* A51 25c multi 55 80
*233* A51 35c multi 80 *1.20*
*234* A51 45c multi 1.00 *1.50*

Norfolk Island Boy Scouts, 50th anniversary. Printed on peelable paper backing with green multiple pines and tourist publicity inscription and picture.

Map of Bering Sea and Pacific Ocean, Routes of Discovery and Resolution A52

Design: 90c, Discovery and Resolution trapped in ice, by John Webber.

**1978, Aug. 29 Photo. *Perf. 14½***

*235* A52 25c multi 50 *80*
*236* A52 90c multi 2.00 *3.00*

Northernmost point of . Cook's voyages.

Poinsettia and Bible — A53

Christmas: 30c, Native oak (flowers) and Bible. 55c, Hibiscus and Bible.

**1978, Oct. 3 Photo. *Perf. 14½***

*237* A53 20c multi 40 50
*238* A53 30c multi 60 75
*239* A53 55c multi 1.10 *1.65*

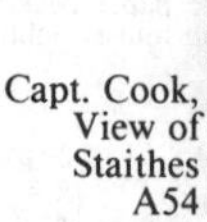

Capt. Cook, View of Staithes A54

Design: 80c, Capt. Cook and view of Whitby harbor.

**1978, Oct. 27**

*240* A54 20c multi 50 65
*241* A54 80c multi 2.00 2.50

Resolution, Map of Asia and Australia — A55

Designs: No. 243, Map of Hawaii and Americas, Cook's route and statue. No. 244, Capt. Cook's death. No. 245, Ships off Hawaii.

**1979, Feb. 14 Photo. *Perf. 14½***

*242* A55 20c multi 48 60
*243* A55 20c multi 48 60
*244* A55 40c multi 1.00 1.20
*245* A55 40c multi 1.00 1.20

Bicentenary of Capt. Cook's death. Stamps of same denomination printed se-tenant in continuous design in sheets of 60.

Rowland Hill and Tasmania No. 1 — A56

Rowland Hill and: 30c, Great Britain No. 8. 55c, Norfolk Island No. 2.

**1979, Aug. 27 *Perf. 14x14½***

*246* A56 20c multi 25 42
*247* A56 30c multi 35 60
*248* A56 55c multi 70 1.10
*a.* Souvenir sheet 1.25 1.50

Sir Rowland Hill (1795-1879), originator of penny postage. No. 248a contains No. 248; buff and black margin shows Mulready envelope. Size: 140x91mm.

Legislative Assembly — A57

**1979, Aug. Photo. *Perf. 14½x14***

*249* A57 $1 multi 1.75 2.00

First session of Legislative Assembly.

Map of Pacific Ocean, IYC Emblem A58

**1979, Sept. 25 Litho. *Perf. 15***

*250* A58 80c multi 1.25 1.75

International Year of the Child.

Emily Bay Beach — A59

**1979, Oct. 2 Photo. *Perf. 12½x13***

*251* A59 15c *shown* 32 35
*252* A59 20c *Emily Bay* 40 45
*253* A59 30c *Salt House* 65 70
*a.* Souvenir sheet of 3 2.25 2.25

Christmas 1979. Nos. 251-253 printed se-tenant in continuous design. No. 253a contains Nos. 251-253, perf. 14x14½; light blue and black margin. Size: 152½x83mm.

Lions District Convention 1980 — A60

**1980, Jan. 25 Litho. *Perf. 15***

*254* A60 50c multi 90 1.10

Rotary International, 75th Anniversary — A61

**1980, Feb. 21**

*255* A61 50c multi 90 1.10

DH-60 "Gypsy Moth" A62

**1980-81 Litho. *Perf. 14½***

*256* A62 1c Hawker Siddeley HS-748 5 5
*257* A62 2c shown 5 5
*258* A62 3c Curtiss P-40 Kittyhawk 6 9
*259* A62 4c Chance Vought Corsair 8 12
*260* A62 5c Grumman Avenger 9 14
*261* A62 15c Douglas Dauntless 28 40
*262* A62 20c Cessna 172 35 50
*262A* A62 25c Lockheed Hudson 45 70
*263* A62 30c Lockheed PV-1 Ventura 55 80
*264* A62 40c Avro York 70 1.00
*265* A62 50c DC-3 90 1.25
*266* A62 60c Avro 691 Lancastrian 1.00 1.50
*267* A62 80c DC-4 1.50 2.25
*268* A62 $1 Beechcraft Super King Air 1.75 2.50
*269* A62 $2 Fokker Friendship 2.25 3.25
*270* A62 $5 Lockheed C-130 Hercules 5.75 8.75
*Nos. 256-270 (16)* 15.81 23.35

Queen Mother Elizabeth, 80th Birthday A63

**1980, Aug. 4 Litho. *Perf. 14½***

*271* A63 22c multi 35 40
*272* A63 60c multi 85 1.20

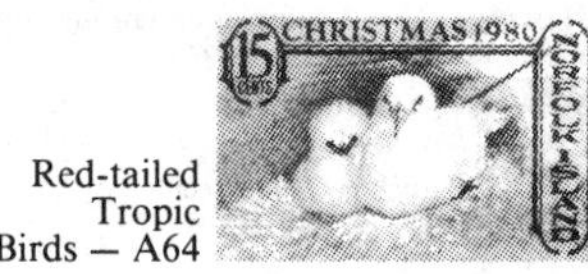


Red-tailed Tropic Birds — A64

**1980, Oct. 28 Litho. *Perf. 14x14½***

*273* A64 15c *shown* 25 36
*274* A64 22c *Fairy terns* 35 50
*275* A64 35c *White-capped noddys* 60 80
*276* A64 60c *Fairy terns*, diff. 1.00 *1.40*

Christmas 1980. Nos. 273-275 se-tenant in continuous design.

Citizens Arriving at Norfolk Island A65

**1981, June 5 Litho. *Perf. 14½***

*277* A65 5c Departure 9 9
*278* A65 35c shown 60 60
*279* A65 60c Settlement 1.00 1.00
*a.* Souvenir sheet of 3 1.75 1.75

Pitcairn migration to Norfolk Island, 125th anniv. No. 279a contains Nos. 277-279; multicolored margin shows historical vignettes. Size: 184x128mm.

### Royal Wedding Issue

Common Design Type

**1981, July 22 Litho. *Perf. 14***

*280* CD331 35c Bouquet 50 65
*281* CD331 55c Charles 80 1.10
*282* CD331 60c Couple 90 1.25

Nos. 280-282 each se-tenant with decorative label.

Uniting Church of Australia A66

**1981, Sept. 15 Litho. *Perf. 14½***

*283* A66 18c shown 30 40
*284* A66 24c Seventh Day Adventist Church 40 50
*285* A66 30c Church of the Sacred Heart 50 65
*286* A66 $1 St. Barnabas Church 1.60 2.25

Christmas 1981.

White-breasted Silvereye — A67

**1981, Nov. 10 Litho. *Perf. 14½***

*287* Strip of 5 3.00 3.75
*a.-e.* A67 35c, any single 60 75

Philip Island A68

Views, Flora and Fauna: No. 288, Philip Isld. No. 289, Nepean Isld.

**1982, Jan. 12 Litho. *Perf. 14***

*288* Strip of 5 1.75 2.50
*a.-e.* A68 24c multi 35 50
*289* Strip of 5 2.75 3.75
*a.-e.* A68 35c multi 55 75

Sperm Whale A69

**1982, Feb. 23 Litho. *Perf. 14½***

*290* A69 24c shown 40 50
*291* A69 55c Southern right whale 90 1.10
*292* A69 80c Humpback whale 1.50 1.75

Shipwrecks — A70

**1982 Litho. *Perf. 14½***

*293* A70 24c Sirius, 1790 40 50
*294* A70 27c Diocet, 1873 45 60
*295* A70 35c Friendship, 1835 55 75
*296* A70 40c Mary Hamilton, 1873 65 90
*297* A70 55c Fairlie, 1840 80 1.10
*298* A70 65c Warrigal, 1918 1.00 1.40
*Nos. 293-298 (6)* 3.85 5.25

Christmas 1982 and 40th Anniv. of Aircraft Landing — A71

**1982, Sept. 7 *Perf. 14***

*299* A71 27c Supplies drop 40 60
*300* A71 40c Landing 65 90
*301* A71 75c Sharing supplies 1.25 1.75

Battalion Company Officer, 50th Regiment, 1835-1842 — A72

British Army Uniforms, Second Settlement, 1839-1848: 40c, Light Company Officer, 58th Reg., 1845. 55c, Private, 80th Bat., 1838. 65c, Bat. Company Officer, 11th Reg., 1847.

**1982, Nov. 9** ***Perf. 14½***

| No. | Type | Description | Unused | Used |
|---|---|---|---|---|
| *302* | A72 | 27c multi | 40 | 65 |
| *303* | A72 | 40c multi | 65 | 1.00 |
| *304* | A72 | 55c multi | 80 | 1.20 |
| *305* | A72 | 65c multi | 1.00 | 1.50 |

Local Mushrooms — A73

**1983, Mar. 29** **Litho.** ***Perf. 14x13½***

| No. | Type | Description | Unused | Used |
|---|---|---|---|---|
| *306* | A73 | 27c Panaeolus papilonaceus | 40 | 65 |
| *307* | A73 | 40c Coprinus domesticus | 65 | 1.00 |
| *308* | A73 | 55c Marasmius niveus | 80 | 1.20 |
| *309* | A73 | 65c Cymatoderma elegans | 1.00 | 1.50 |

Manned Flight Bicentenary — A74

**1983, July 12** **Litho.** ***Perf. 14½x14***

| No. | Type | Description | Unused | Used |
|---|---|---|---|---|
| *310* | A74 | 10c Beech 18, aerial mapping | 18 | 25 |
| *311* | A74 | 27c Fokker F-28 | 40 | 65 |
| *312* | A74 | 45c DC4 | 80 | 1.15 |
| *313* | A74 | 75c Sikorsky helicopter | 1.25 | 1.75 |
| ***a.*** | | Souvenir sheet of 4 | 2.75 | 4.24 |

No. 313a contains Nos. 310-313. Size: 105x100mm.

Christmas 1983 — A75

Stained-glass Windows by Edward Burne-Jones (1833-1898), St. Barnabas Chapel.

**1983, Oct. 4** **Litho.** ***Perf. 14***

| No. | Type | Description | Unused | Used |
|---|---|---|---|---|
| *314* | A75 | 5c multi | 10 | 12 |
| *315* | A75 | 24c multi | 40 | 60 |
| *316* | A75 | 30c multi | 45 | 75 |
| *317* | A75 | 45c multi | 65 | *1.15* |
| *318* | A75 | 85c multi | 1.25 | *2.15* |
| | | *Nos. 314-318 (5)* | 2.85 | 4.77 |

World Communications Year — A76

ANZCAN Cable Station: 30c, Chantik, Cable laying Ship. 45c, Shore end. 75c, Cable Ship Mercury. 85c, Map of cable route.

**1983, Nov. 15** **Litho.** ***Perf. 14½x14***

| No. | Type | Description | Unused | Used |
|---|---|---|---|---|
| *319* | A76 | 30c multi | 40 | 70 |
| *320* | A76 | 45c multi | 60 | *1.00* |
| *321* | A76 | 75c multi | 1.00 | *1.75* |
| *322* | A76 | 85c multi | 1.10 | *1.90* |

Local Flowers — A77

**1984** **Litho.** ***Perf. 14***

| No. | Type | Description | Unused | Used |
|---|---|---|---|---|
| *323* | A77 | 1c Myoporum obsurum | 5 | 5 |
| *324* | A77 | 2c Ipomoea pes-caprae | 5 | 5 |
| *325* | A77 | 3c Phreatia crassiuscula | 6 | 6 |
| *326* | A77 | 4c Streblorrhiza speciosa | 7 | 8 |
| *327* | A77 | 5c Rhopalostylis baueri | 8 | 12 |
| *328* | A77 | 10c Alyxia gynopogon | 15 | 22 |
| *329* | A77 | 15c Ungeria floribunda | 22 | 32 |
| *330* | A77 | 20c Capparis nobilis | 28 | 42 |
| *331* | A77 | 25c Lagunaria patersonia | 35 | 52 |
| *332* | A77 | 30c Cordyline obtecta | 45 | 65 |
| *333* | A77 | 35c Hibiscus insularis | 50 | 75 |
| *334* | A77 | 40c Millettia australis | 55 | 85 |
| *335* | A77 | 50c Jasminum volubile | 65 | *1.05* |
| *336* | A77 | $1 Passiflora aurantia | 1.40 | *2.10* |
| *337* | A77 | $3 Oberonia titania | 4.25 | *6.25* |
| *338* | A77 | $5 Araucaria heterophylla | 7.00 | *10.50* |
| | | *Nos. 323-338 (16)* | 16.11 | 23.99 |

Issue dates: Jan. 10: 2c, 3c, 10c, 20c, 25c, 40c, 50c. $5; others Mar. 27.

Reef Fish — A78

***Perf. 13½x14***

**1984, Apr. 17** **Litho.** **Wmk. 373**

| No. | Type | Description | Unused | Used |
|---|---|---|---|---|
| *339* | A78 | 30c Painted morwong | 65 | 65 |
| *340* | A78 | 45c Black-spot goatfish | 95 | 95 |
| *341* | A78 | 75c Ring-tailed surgeon fish | 1.60 | 1.60 |
| *342* | A78 | 85c Three-striped butterfly fish | 1.70 | 1.70 |

Boobook Owl — A79

Designs: a. Laying eggs. b. Standing at treehole. c. Sitting on branch looking sideways. d. Looking head on. e. Flying.

**Wmk. 373**

**1984, July 17** **Litho.** ***Perf. 14***

| No. | Type | Description | Unused | Used |
|---|---|---|---|---|
| *343* | | Strip of 5 | 3.25 | 3.25 |
| ***a.-e.*** | | A79 30c, any single | 65 | 65 |

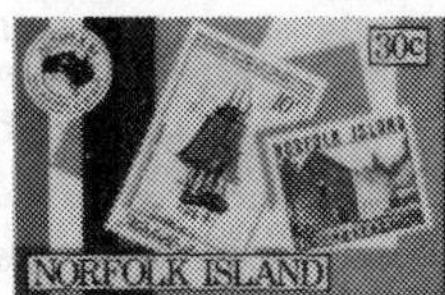


AUSIPEX '84 — A80

**1984, Sept. 18** **Litho.** ***Perf. 14½***

| No. | Type | Description | Unused | Used |
|---|---|---|---|---|
| *344* | A80 | 30c Nos. 15 and 176 | 65 | 65 |
| *345* | A80 | 45c First day cover | 98 | 98 |
| *346* | A80 | 75c Presentation pack | 1.65 | 1.65 |
| ***a.*** | | Souvenir sheet of 3, #344-346 | 3.00 | 3.00 |

No. 346a has multicolored inscribed margin picturing various philatelic items. Size: 157x93mm.

Christmas 1984 — A81

**1984, Oct. 9** **Litho.** ***Perf. 13½***

| No. | Type | Description | Unused | Used |
|---|---|---|---|---|
| *347* | A81 | 5c The Font | 12 | 12 |
| *348* | A81 | 24c Church at Kingston, interior | 52 | 52 |
| *349* | A81 | 30c Pastor and Mrs. Phelps | 65 | 65 |
| *350* | A81 | 45c Phelps, Church of Chester | 98 | 98 |
| *351* | A81 | 85c Phelps, Methodist Church, modern interior | 1.90 | 1.90 |
| | | *Nos. 347-351 (5)* | 4.17 | 4.17 |

Rev. George Hunn Nobbs, Death Centenary — A82

**1984, Nov. 6** **Litho.** ***Perf. 14x15***

| No. | Type | Description | Unused | Used |
|---|---|---|---|---|
| *352* | A82 | 30c As teacher | 65 | 65 |
| *353* | A82 | 45c As minister | 1.00 | 1.00 |
| *354* | A82 | 75c As chaplain | 1.60 | 1.60 |
| *355* | A82 | 85c As community leader | 2.00 | 2.00 |

Whaling Ships — A83

**1985** **Litho.** ***Perf. 13½x14***

| No. | Type | Description | Unused | Used |
|---|---|---|---|---|
| *356* | A83 | 5c Fanny Fisher | 10 | 10 |
| *357* | A83 | 15c Waterwitch | 30 | 30 |
| *358* | A83 | 20c Canton | 38 | 38 |
| *359* | A83 | 33c Costa Rica Packet | 62 | 62 |
| *360* | A83 | 50c Splendid | 90 | 90 |
| *361* | A83 | 60c Aladin | 1.10 | 1.10 |
| *362* | A83 | 80c California | 1.50 | 1.50 |
| *363* | A83 | 90c Onward | 1.70 | 1.70 |
| | | *Nos. 356-363 (8)* | 6.60 | 6.60 |

Issue dates: Feb. 19: 5c, 33c, 50c, 90c; others Apr. 30.

**Queen Mother 85th Birthday**

Common Design Type

***Perf. 14½x14***

**1985, June 6** **Litho.** **Wmk. 384**

| No. | Type | Description | Unused | Used |
|---|---|---|---|---|
| *364* | CD336 | 5c Portrait, 1926 | 12 | 12 |
| *365* | CD336 | 33c With Princess Anne | 65 | 65 |
| *366* | CD336 | 50c Photograph by N. Parkinson | 1.00 | 1.00 |
| *367* | CD336 | 90c Holding Prince Henry | 1.90 | 1.90 |

**Souvenir Sheet**

| No. | Type | Description | Unused | Used |
|---|---|---|---|---|
| *368* | CD336 | $1 With Princess Anne, Ascot Races | 2.75 | 2.75 |

No. 368 has multicolored margin continuing design. Size: 92x74mm.

Intl. Youth Year — A84

Children's drawings.

**1985, July 9** **Litho.** ***Perf. 13½x14***

| No. | Type | Description | Unused | Used |
|---|---|---|---|---|
| *369* | A84 | 33c Swimming | 75 | 75 |
| *370* | A84 | 50c Nature walk | 1.25 | 1.25 |

Girl, Prize-winning Cow — A85

Designs: 90c, Embroidery, jam-making, baking, animal husbandry.

**1985, Sept. 10** **Litho.** ***Perf. 13½x14***

| No. | Type | Description | Unused | Used |
|---|---|---|---|---|
| *371* | A85 | 80c multi | 1.15 | 1.15 |
| *372* | A85 | 90c multi | 1.25 | 1.25 |
| ***a.*** | | Souvenir sheet of 2, #371-372 | 3.25 | 3.25 |

Royal Norfolk Island Agricultural & Horticultural Show, 125th anniv. No. 372a has multicolored inscribed margin picturing various scenes from show. Size: 132x85mm.

Christmas — A86

**1985, Oct. 3** ***Perf. 13½***

| No. | Type | Description | Unused | Used |
|---|---|---|---|---|
| *373* | A86 | 27c Three Shepherds | 50 | 50 |
| *374* | A86 | 33c Journey to Bethlehem | 65 | 65 |
| *375* | A86 | 50c Three Wise Men | 90 | 90 |
| *376* | A86 | 90c Nativity | 1.75 | 1.75 |

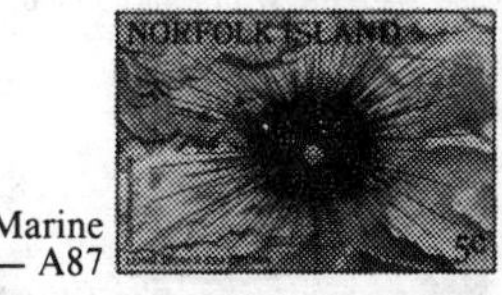


Marine Life — A87

**1986, Jan. 14** ***Perf. 13½x14***

| No. | Type | Description | Unused | Used |
|---|---|---|---|---|
| *377* | A87 | 5c Long-spined sea urchin | 14 | 14 |
| *378* | A87 | 33c Blue starfish | 75 | 75 |
| *379* | A87 | 55c Eagle ray | 1.25 | 1.25 |
| *380* | A87 | 75c Moray eel | 1.75 | 1.75 |
| ***a.*** | | Souvenir sheet of 4, #377-380 | 4.00 | 4.00 |

No. 380a has multicolored margin picturing shore. Size: 100x96mm.

The first price column gives the catalogue value of an unused stamp, the second that of a used stamp.

Norfolk Island $1.00 Halley's Comet — A88

Designs: No. 381a, Giotto space probe. No. 381b, Comet.

**1986, Mar. 11** *Perf. 15*

| | | | |
|---|---|---|---|
| *381* | Pair | 4.00 | 4.00 |
| *a.-b.* | A88 $1, any single | 2.00 | 2.00 |

Se-tenant in continuous design.

AMERIPEX '86 — A89

Designs: 33c, Isaac Robinson, US consul in Norfolk, 1887-1908, vert. 50c, Ford Model-T. 80c, Statue of Liberty.

**1986, May 22 Litho.** *Perf. 13½*

| | | | | |
|---|---|---|---|---|
| *382* | A89 | 33c multi | 60 | 60 |
| *383* | A89 | 50c multi | 90 | 90 |
| *384* | A89 | 80c multi | 1.50 | 1.50 |
| *a.* | | Souv. sheet of #382-384 | 3.25 | 3.25 |

No. 384a has multicolored margin picturing Chicago. Size: 126x101mm.

Queen Elizabeth II, 60th Birthday — A90

Various portraits.

**1986, June 12**

| | | | | |
|---|---|---|---|---|
| *385* | A90 | 5c As Princess | 12 | 12 |
| *386* | A90 | 33c Contemporary photograph | 75 | 75 |
| *387* | A90 | 80c Opening N.I. Golf Club | 1.60 | 1.60 |
| *388* | A90 | 90c With Prince Philip | 2.00 | 2.00 |

Christmas A91

**1986, Sept. 23 Litho.** *Perf. 13½x14*

| | | | | |
|---|---|---|---|---|
| *389* | A91 | 30c multi | 50 | 50 |
| *390* | A91 | 40c multi | 65 | 65 |
| *391* | A91 | $1 multi | 1.60 | 1.60 |

Commission of Gov. Phillip, Bicent. — A92

**1986, Oct. 14 Litho.** *Perf. 14x13½*

| | | | | |
|---|---|---|---|---|
| *392* | A92 | 36c British prison, 1787 | 65 | 65 |
| *393* | A92 | 55c Transportation, Court of Assize | 1.00 | 1.00 |
| *394* | A92 | 90c Gov. meeting Home Society | 1.60 | 1.60 |
| *395* | A92 | 90c Gov. meeting Home Secretary | 1.60 | 1.60 |
| *396* | A92 | $1 Gov. Phillip, 1738-1814 | 1.75 | 1.75 |
| | | *Nos. 392-396 (5)* | 6.60 | 6.60 |

No. 395 was issued because No. 394 is incorrectly inscribed.

Commission of Gov. Phillip, Bicent. — A93

**1986, Dec. 16** *Perf. 13½*

| | | | | |
|---|---|---|---|---|
| *397* | A93 | 36c Maori chief | 50 | 50 |
| *398* | A93 | 36c Bananas, taro | 50 | 50 |
| *399* | A93 | 36c Stone tools | 50 | 50 |
| *400* | A93 | 36c Polynesian outrigger | 50 | 50 |

Pre-European occupation of the Island.

Island Scenery — A94

**1987-88 Litho.** *Perf. 13½*

| | | | | |
|---|---|---|---|---|
| *401* | A94 | 1c Cockpit Creek Bridge | 5 | 5 |
| *402* | A94 | 2c Cemetery Bay Beach | 5 | 5 |
| *403* | A94 | 3c Guesthouse | 5 | 5 |
| *404* | A94 | 5c Philip Island from Point Ross | 6 | 6 |
| *405* | A94 | 15c Cattle grazing | 15 | 15 |
| *406* | A94 | 30c Rock fishing | 25 | 25 |
| *407* | A94 | 37c Old home | 40 | 40 |
| *408* | A94 | 40c Shopping center | 40 | 40 |
| *409* | A94 | 50c Emily Bay | 50 | 50 |
| *410* | A94 | 60c Bloody Bridge | 60 | 60 |
| *411* | A94 | 80c Pitcairner-style shop | 80 | 80 |
| *412* | A94 | 90c Government House | 90 | 90 |
| *413* | A94 | $1 Melanesian Memorial Chapel | 1.00 | 1.00 |
| *414* | A94 | $2 Kingston convict settlement | 1.50 | 1.50 |
| *415* | A94 | $3 Ball Bay | 3.00 | 3.00 |
| *416* | A94 | $5 Northerly cliffs | 7.25 | 7.25 |
| | | *Nos. 401-416 (16)* | 16.96 | 16.96 |

Issue dates: 5c, 50c, 90c, $1, Feb. 17. 30c, 40c, 80c, $2, Apr. 17. 15c, 37c, 60c, $3, July 27. 1c, 2c, 3c, $5, May 17, 1988.

Norfolk Is. Bicentennial — A95

Designs: 5c, Loading supplies at Deptford, England, 1787. No. 418, First Fleet sailing from Spithead (buoy in water). No. 419, Sailing from Spithead (ship flying British merchant flag). $1, Convicts below deck.

**1987, May 13 Litho.** *Perf. 14x13½*

| | | | | |
|---|---|---|---|---|
| *417* | A95 | 5c multi | 6 | 6 |
| *418* | A95 | 55c multi | 50 | 50 |
| *419* | A95 | 55c multi | 50 | 50 |
| *420* | A95 | $1 multi | 1.00 | 1.00 |

Nos. 418-419 printed se-tenant in a continuous design.

See Nos. 426-436.

World Wildlife Fund — A96

Green parrot.

**1987, Sept. 16** **Unwmk.**

| | | | |
|---|---|---|---|
| *421* | Strip of 4 | 1.25 | 1.25 |
| *a.* | A96 5c Parrot facing right | 7 | 7 |
| *b.* | A96 15c Parrot, chick, egg | 18 | 18 |
| *c.* | A96 36c Parrots | 40 | 40 |
| *d.* | A96 55c Parrot facing left | 60 | 60 |

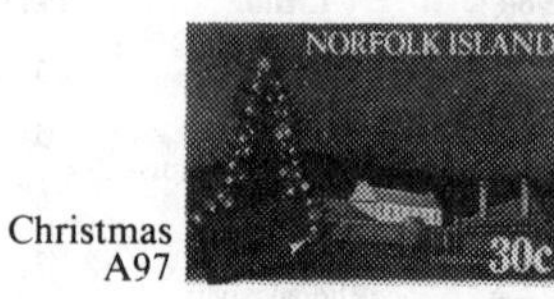

Christmas A97

Children's party: 30c, Norfolk Island pine tree, restored convicts' settlement. 42c, Santa Claus, children opening packages. 58c, Santa, children, gifts in fire engine. 63c, Meal.

***Perf. 13½x14***

**1987, Oct. 13 Litho. Wmk. 384**

| | | | | |
|---|---|---|---|---|
| *422* | A97 | 30c multi | 45 | 45 |
| *423* | A97 | 42c multi | 65 | 65 |
| *424* | A97 | 58c multi | 85 | 85 |
| *425* | A97 | 63c multi | 95 | 95 |

Bicentennial Type of 1987

Designs: 5c, Lt. Philip Gidley King. No. 427, La Perouse and Louis XVI of France. No. 428, Gov. Phillip sailing in ship's cutter from Botany Bay to Port Jackson. No. 429, Flag raising on Norfolk Is. 55c, Lt. King and search party exploring the island. 70c, Landfall, Sydney Bay. No. 432, L'Astrolabe and La Boussole off coast of Norfolk. No. 433, HMS Supply. No. 434, Wrecking of L'Astrolabe off the Solomon Isls. No. 435, First Fleet landing at Sydney Cove. No. 436, First settlement, Sydney Bay, 1788.

**1987-88 Litho.** *Perf. 14x13½*

| | | | | |
|---|---|---|---|---|
| *426* | A95 | 5c multi | 5 | 5 |
| *427* | A95 | 37c multi | 30 | 30 |
| *428* | A95 | 37c multi | 30 | 30 |
| *429* | A95 | 37c multi | 30 | 30 |
| *430* | A95 | 55c multi | 40 | 40 |
| *431* | A95 | 70c multi | 55 | 55 |
| *432* | A95 | 90c multi | 70 | 70 |
| *433* | A95 | 90c multi | 70 | 70 |
| *434* | A95 | $1 multi | 75 | 75 |
| *435* | A95 | $1 multi | 75 | 75 |
| *436* | A95 | $1 multi | 75 | 75 |
| | | *Nos. 426-436 (11)* | 5.55 | 5.55 |

Visit of Jean La Perouse (1741-88), French navigator, to Norfolk Is. (Nos. 427, 432, 434); arrival of the First Fleet at Sydney Cove (Nos. 428, 435); founding of Norfolk Is. (Nos. 426, 429-431, 433, 436).

Issue dates: Dec. 8, 1987 (Nos. 427, 432, 434); Jan. 25, 1988 (Nos. 428, 435); others, Mar. 4, 1988.

SYDPEX '88, July 30-Aug. 7 A98

Sydney-Norfolk transportation and communication links.

***Perf. 14x13½, 13½x14***

**1988, July 30** **Litho.**

| | | | | |
|---|---|---|---|---|
| *437* | A98 | 37c Air and sea transports, vert. | 62 | 62 |
| *438* | A98 | 37c shown | 62 | 62 |
| *439* | A98 | 37c Telecommunications, vert. | 62 | 62 |
| *a.* | | Souv. sheet of 3, Nos. 437-439 | 1.90 | 1.90 |

No. 438 exists perf. 13½ within No. 439a. No. 439a has multicolored margin picturing map linking Sydney and Norfolk Is. Size: 118x86mm.

Christmas — A99

**1988, Sept. 27 Litho.** *Perf. 14x13½*

| | | | | |
|---|---|---|---|---|
| *440* | A99 | 30c shown | 48 | 48 |
| *441* | A99 | 42c Flowers, diff. | 68 | 68 |
| *442* | A99 | 58c Trees, fish | 95 | 95 |
| *443* | A99 | 63c Trees, sailboats | 1.00 | 1.00 |

Convict Era Georgian Architecture, c. 1825-1850 A100

Designs: 39c, Waterfront shop and boat shed. 55c, Royal Engineers' Building. 90c, Old military barracks. $1, Commissary and new barracks.

**1988, Dec. 6 Litho.** *Perf. 13½x14*

| | | | | |
|---|---|---|---|---|
| *444* | A100 | 39c multi | 62 | 62 |
| *445* | A100 | 55c multi | 88 | 88 |
| *446* | A100 | 90c multi | 1.40 | 1.40 |
| *447* | A100 | $1 multi | 1.60 | 1.60 |

## NORTH BORNEO

LOCATION — Northeast part of island of Borneo, Malay archipelago.
GOVT. — Former British colony.
AREA — 29,388 sq. mi.
POP. — 470,000 (est. 1962)
CAPITAL — Jesselton

The British North Borneo Company administered North Borneo, under a royal charter granted in 1881, until 1946 when it became a British colony. Labuan (q.v.) became part of the new colony. As "Sabah," North Borneo joined with Singapore, Sarawak and Malaya to form the Federation of Malaysia on Sept. 16, 1963. (See Sabah.)

100 Cents = 1 Dollar

Quantities of most North Borneo stamps have been canceled "to order" with an oval of bars. Values given for used stamps are for those with this form of cancellation. Stamps that do not exist cto have used values in italics. Stamps with dated town cancellations sell for much higher prices.

**Catalogue values for unused stamps in this country are for Never Hinged items, beginning with Scott 238.**

**North Borneo**

Coat of Arms — A1

**1883-84 Unwmk. Litho.** *Perf. 12*

| | | | | |
|---|---|---|---|---|
| *1* | A1 | 2c brown | 12.00 | 12.00 |
| *a.* | | Horiz. pair, imperf. btwn. | | |
| *2* | A1 | 4c rose ('84) | 9.00 | *18.00* |
| *3* | A1 | 8c green ('84) | 18.00 | *21.00* |

No. 1 Surcharged in Black **EIGHT CENTS**

4 A1 8c on 2c brown 225.00 90.00
a. Double surcharge 4,250.

Coat of Arms with Supporters
A4 A5

*Perf. 14*

6 A4 50c violet 50.00 10.00
7 A5 $1 red 45.00 7.75

**1886**

8 A1 ½c magenta 35.00 70.00
9 A1 1c orange 140.00
a. Imperf., pair 275.00
10 A1 2c brown 7.00 7.00
a. Horiz. pair, imperf. between 425.00
11 A1 4c rose 9.50 21.00
12 A1 8c green 9.50 21.00
a. Horiz. pair, imperf. between
13 A1 10c blue 8.75 21.00
a. Imperf., pair 275.00

Nos. 8, 11, 12 and 13 Surcharged or Overprinted in Black:

**and Revenue**
b

**3 CENTS** c  **3 CENTS** d

**1886**

14 A1 (b) ½c magenta 70.00 100.00
15 A1 (c) 3c on 4c rose 27.50 70.00
16 A1 (d) 3c on 4c rose 1,300.
17 A1 (c) 5c on 8c grn 32.50 70.00
a. Inverted surcharge 2,250.
18 A1 (b) 10c blue 100.00 175.00

**On Nos. 2 and 3**

*Perf. 12*

19 A1 (c) 3c on 4c rose 110.00 200.00
20 A1 (d) 3c on 4c rose 4,500.
a. Double surcharge, both types of "3"
21 A1 (c) 5c on 8c grn 175.00 175.00

Common Design Types pictured in section before Great Britain.

**British North Borneo**

A9

**1886 Unwmk. Litho. *Perf. 12***

22 A9 ½c lil rose 100.00 250.00
23 A9 1c orange 82.50 110.00

*Perf. 14*

25 A9 ½c rose 1.65 1.75
a. ½c lil rose 1.80
b. Imperf., pair 12.00 4.00
26 A9 1c orange 75 1.00
a. Imperf., pair 10.50 3.00
27 A9 2c brown 1.00 1.25
a. Imperf., pair 5.50 3.00
b. Horiz. pair, imperf. between 52.50
28 A9 4c rose 75 90
a. Cliche of 1c in plate of 4c 125.00 250.00
b. Imperf., pair 6.00 3.00
c. As "a," imperf. in pair with #28 2,750.
29 A9 8c green 1.75 3.50
a. Imperf., pair 9.50 3.75
30 A9 10c blue 4.25 7.50
a. Imperf., pair 9.50 5.75
*Nos. 25-30 (6)* 10.15 15.90

A10

A11

A12

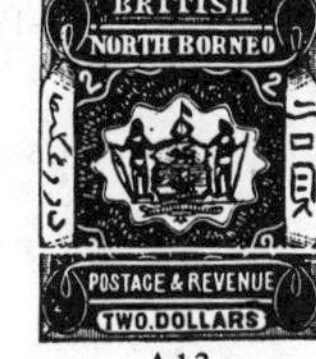
A13

31 A10 25c slate bl 60.00 7.75
a. Imperf., pair 72.50 12.00
32 A11 50c violet 60.00 6.00
a. Imperf., pair 52.50 8.50
33 A12 $1 red 125.00 7.25
a. Imperf., pair 60.00 8.50
34 A12 $2 sage grn 165.00 16.00
a. Imperf., pair 82.50 15.00

A14

**1887-92 *Perf. 14***

35 A14 ½c rose 22 22
a. ½c magenta 3.00 3.00
36 A14 1c orange 22 22
37 A14 2c red brn 42 22
a. Horiz. pair imperf. between 200.00
38 A14 3c violet 90 22
39 A14 4c rose 90 22
a. Horiz. pair, imperf. vert.
40 A14 5c slate 90 22
41 A14 6c lake ('92) 1.40 22
42 A14 8c green 2.00 32
a. Horiz. pair, imperf. between
43 A14 10c blue 2.00 35
*Nos. 35-43 (9)* 8.96 2.21

Exist imperf. Value $1.50 each, unused or used. Forgeries exist, perf. 11½.

**1888**

**Redrawn**

25c. The letters of "BRITISH NORTH BORNEO" are 2mm high instead of 1½mm.

50c. The club of the native at left does not touch the frame. The 0's of "50" are flat at top and bottom instead of being oval.

$1.00. The spear of the native at right does not touch the frame. There are 14 pearls at each side of the frame instead of 13.

$2.00. "BRITISH" is 11mm long instead of 12mm. There are only six oars at the side of the dhow.

44 A10 25c slate bl 9.00 42
b. Horiz. pair, imperf. between
c. Imperf., pair 65.00 2.75
45 A11 50c violet 18.00 42
a. Imperf., pair 90.00 3.50
46 A12 $1 red 18.00 42
a. Imperf., pair 90.00 3.50
47 A13 $2 sage green 35.00 1.25
a. Imperf., pair 95.00 4.25

A15

A16

**1889**

48 A15 $5 red violet 75.00 6.00
a. Imperf., pair 52.50 12.00
49 A16 $10 brown 60.00 6.00
a. "DOLLAPS" 1,100. 425.00
b. Imperf., pair 125.00 21.00
c. As "a", imperf., in pair with #49 1,800. 850.00

**Two Cents.** e  **6 cents.** f

No. 44 Surcharged Type "e" in Red

**1890**

50 A10 2c on 25c sl bl 35.00 45.00
a. Inverted surcharge 250.00 275.00
b. With additional surcharge "2 cents" in black
51 A10 8c on 25c sl bl 47.50 60.00

Surcharged Type "f" in Black On Nos. 42-43

**1891-92**

52 A14 6c on 8c grn 4.75 9.00
a. "c" of "cents" inverted 300.00 325.00
b. "cetns" 325.00 400.00
c. Inverted surcharge 200.00 275.00
53 A14 6c on 10c blue 27.50 9.50

**On Nos. 29 and 30**

54 A9 6c on 8c green 5,250. 4,500.
55 A9 6c on 10c blue 25.00 9.00
a. Invtd. surch 140.00 140.00
b. Double surch. 900.00
c. Triple surch. 300.00

Nos. 39, 40 and 44 Surcharged in Red:

**1 cent.**  **8 Cents.**

**1892**

56 A14 1c on 4c rose 9.00 12.00
a. Dbl. surch. 325.00
b. Surcharged on face and on back 400.00
57 A14 1c on 5c sl 6.00 4.75
58 A10 8c on 25c bl 90.00 125.00

**North Borneo**

Dyak Chief
A21

Malayan Sambar
A22

Sago Palm
A23

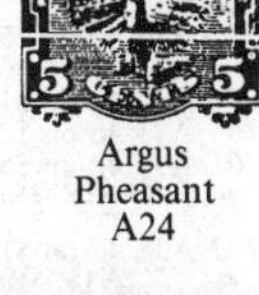
Argus Pheasant
A24

Coat of Arms – A25

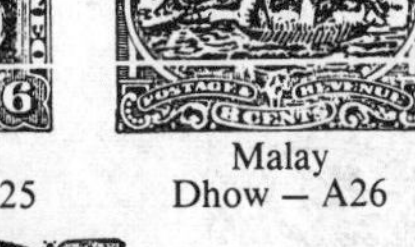
Malay Dhow – A26

Saltwater Crocodile – A27

Mt. Kinabalu – A28

Coat of Arms with Supporters – A29

A30

A31 A32

A33

A34

A35

***Perf. 12 to 15 and Compound***

**1894 Engr. Unwmk.**

*59* A21 1c bis brn & blk 1.40 40
**a.** Vert. pair, imperf. btwn.
*60* A22 2c rose & blk 4.00 75
*61* A23 3c vio & ol grn 4.00 55
**a.** Horiz. pair, imperf. btwn. 325.00
*62* A24 5c org red & blk 3.25 75
**a.** Horiz. pair, imperf. btwn. 325.00
*63* A25 6c brn ol & blk 3.00 55
*64* A26 8c lil & blk 2.50 75
**a.** Vert. pair, imperf. btwn. 325.00 *350.00*
**b.** Horiz. pair, imperf. btwn. *325.00*
*65* A27 12c ultra & blk 21.00 1.25
**a.** 12c bl & blk 27.50 1.75
*66* A28 18c grn & blk 15.00 1.75
*67* A29 24c cl & bl 17.00 1.75

**Litho.** ***Perf. 14***

*68* A30 25c slate bl 15.00 55
**a.** Imperf., pair 3.00
*69* A31 50c violet 21.00 60
**a.** Imperf., pair 3.00
*70* A32 $1 red 9.50 75
**a.** Perf. 14x11 175.00
**b.** Imperf., pair 6.00
*71* A33 $2 gray grn 18.00 75
**a.** Imperf., pair 4.50
*72* A34 $5 red vio 140.00 4.75
**a.** Imperf., pair 15.00
*73* A35 $10 brown 150.00 6.00
**a.** Imperf., pair 15.00
*Nos. 59-73 (15)* 424.65 21.90

For Nos. 68 to 70 in other colors see Labuan, Nos. 63a to 65a.

No. 70 Surcharged in Black

**4**
**CENTS**

**1895**

*74* A32 4c on $1 red 3.00 1.25
**a.** Dbl. surch. 325.00
*75* A32 10c on $1 red 6.00 60
*76* A32 20c on $1 red 7.25 60
*77* A32 30c on $1 red 9.00 75
*78* A32 40c on $1 red 12.00 75
*Nos. 74-78 (5)* 37.25 3.95

See No. 99.

A37 A38

A39 A40

A41 A42

A43

"Postal Revenue" – A44

A45

***Perf. 13 to 16 and Compound***

**1897-1900 Engr.**

*79* A37 1c bis brn & blk 3.25 55
**a.** Horiz. pair, imperf. btwn.
*80* A38 2c dp rose & blk 4.75 55
*81* A38 2c grn & blk ('00) 8.75 55
*82* A39 3c lil & ol grn 3.25 55
*83* A40 5c org & blk 8.25 50
*84* A41 6c ol brn & blk 7.50 35
*85* A42 8c brn lil & blk 5.50 50
*86* A43 12c bl & blk 42.50 85
*87* A44 18c grn & blk 9.50 55
**a.** Vert. pair, imperf. btwn. *100.00*
*88* A45 24c cl & bl 9.50 85
*Nos. 79-88 (10)* 102.75 5.80

"Postage & Revenue"
A46 A47

**1897**

*89* A46 18c grn & blk 32.50 75
*90* A47 24c cl & bl 37.50 75

Stamps of 1893-97 Surcharged in Black

**4**
**CENTS**

**1899**

*91* A40 4c on 5c org & blk 10.00 *14.00*
*92* A41 4c on 6c ol brn & blk 7.75 *18.00*
*93* A42 4c on 8c brn lil & blk 11.00 *13.00*
*94* A43 4c on 12c bl & blk 11.00 *18.00*
**a.** Horiz. or vert. pair, imperf. btwn. 425.00 *500.00*
*95* A46 4c on 18c grn & blk 11.00 *18.00*
*96* A47 4c on 24c cl & bl 11.00 *18.00*
**a.** Perf. 16 42.50 *50.00*
*97* A30 4c on 25c sl bl 7.75 *14.00*
*98* A31 4c on 50c vio 11.00 *18.00*
*99* A32 4c on $1 red 7.75 *14.00*
*100* A33 4c on $2 gray grn 9.00 *19.00*
*101* A34 4c on $5 red vio 32.50 *40.00*
**a.** "CENTS" 8½mm below "4" 14.00 *18.00*
*102* A35 4c on $10 brn 32.50 *40.00*
**a.** "CENTS" 8½mm below "4" 14.00 *18.00*
*Nos. 91-102 (12)* 162.25 244.00

No. 99 differs from No. 74 in the distance between "4" and "cents" which is 4¾mm. on No. 99 and 3¾mm. on No. 74.

Orangutan – A48

**1899-1900 Engr.**

*103* A48 4c grn & blk 5.00 3.25
*104* A48 4c dp rose & blk ('00) 5.50 55

Stamps of 1893-1900 Overprinted in Red, Black, Green or Blue

**BRITISH**

m

**PROTECTORATE.**

**1901-05**

*105* A37 1c bis brn & blk (R) 1.90 22
*106* A38 2c grn & blk (R) 1.65 22
*107* A39 3c lil & ol grn (Bk) 1.10 32
*108* A48 4c dp rose & blk (G) 2.25 32
*109* A40 5c org & blk (G) 2.25 32
*110* A41 6c ol brn & blk (R) 2.75 32
*111* A42 8c brn & blk (Bl) 3.50 35
**a.** Vertical pair, imperf. between
*112* A43 12c bl & blk (R) 27.50 65
*113* A46 18c grn & blk (R) 8.50 65
*114* A47 24c red & bl (Bk) 15.00 65
*115* A30 25c sl bl (R) 3.00 45
**a.** Invtd. ovpt. 425.00
*116* A31 50c vio (R) 7.50 50
*117* A32 $1 red (R) 20.00 3.75
*118* A32 $1 red (Bk) 10.00 2.75
**a.** Double overprint 325.00
*119* A33 $2 gray grn (R) 32.50 3.25
**a.** Dbl. overprint 950.00
*Nos. 105-119 (15)* 139.40 14.72

Nos. 110, 111 and 122 are known without period after "PROTECTORATE".
See Nos. 150-151.

Bruang (Sun Bear) – A49

Railroad Train – A50

**1902 Engr.**

*120* A49 10c sl & dk brn 27.50 2.50
**a.** Vertical pair, imperf. between
*121* A50 16c yel brn & grn 27.50 90

Overprinted type "m" in Red or Black.

*122* A49 10c sl & dk brn (R) 13.00 32
**a.** Dbl. overprint 350.00 275.00
*123* A50 16c yel brn & grn (Bk) 21.00 45

Stamps of 1893-97 Surcharged in Black

**4.**
**cents**

**1904**

*124* A40 4c on 5c org & blk 14.00 *22.50*
*125* A41 4c on 6c ol brn & blk 4.25 *8.75*
**a.** Inverted surcharge 325.00 *325.00*
*126* A42 4c on 8c brn lil & blk 9.50 *11.00*
**a.** Inverted surcharge 350.00 *350.00*
*127* A43 4c on 12c bl & blk 14.00 *26.00*
*128* A46 4c on 18c grn & blk 15.00 *27.50*
*129* A47 4c on 24c cl & bl 14.00 *14.00*
*130* A30 4c on 25c sl bl 4.50 *4.50*
*131* A31 4c on 50c vio 4.50 *5.25*
*132* A32 4c on $1 red 5.75 *6.25*
*133* A33 4c on $2 gray grn 10.50 *8.75*
*134* A34 4c on $5 red vio 11.00 *10.50*
*135* A35 4c on $10 brn 11.00 *10.50*
**a.** Invtd. surch. 1,700.
*Nos. 124-135 (12)* 118.00 155.50

Malayan Tapir – A51

Traveler's Palm – A52

Railroad Station – A53

Meeting of the Assembly – A54

Elephant and Mahout A55

Sumatran Rhinoceros A56

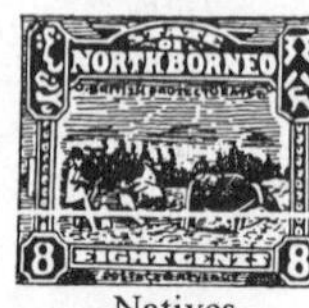
Natives Plowing – A57

Wild Boar – A58

Palm Cockatoo A59

Rhinoceros Hornbill A60

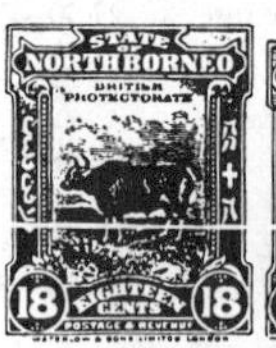

Banteng (Wild Ox)
A61 A62

Cassowary – A63

**1909-22 Unwmk. Engr. *Perf. 14***
**Center in Black**

*136* A51 1c chocolate 3.75 15
**b.** Perf. 13½
**c.** Perf. 15 6.50 *4.25*
*137* A52 2c green 1.10 15
**b.** Perf. 15 3.00 *1.50*
*138* A53 3c dp rose 1.25 30
**b.** Perf. 15 75
*139* A53 3c grn ('22) 11.00 *40*
*140* A54 4c dull red 1.90 15
**b.** Perf. 13½ *11.00* *10.50*
**c.** Perf. 15 7.50 *1.00*
*141* A55 5c yel brn 5.25 30
**b.** Perf. 15
*142* A56 6c ol grn 7.50 30
**b.** Perf. 15 19.00 1.00
*143* A57 8c rose 4.50 30
*144* A58 10c blue 15.00 30
**b.** Perf. 13½ *2.50*
**c.** Perf. 15 16.00 *6.50*
*145* A59 12c dp bl 19.00 75
**c.** Perf. 15
*146* A60 16c red brn 20.00 1.25
**b.** Perf. 13½ 20.00 6.50
*147* A61 18c bl grn 57.50 1.25
*148* A62 20c on 18c bl grn (R) 4.50 55
**b.** Perf. 15 190.00 *75.00*
*149* A63 24c violet 22.50 1.50
*Nos. 136-149 (14)* 174.75 7.65

See Nos. 167-178. Nos. 136a-149a follow No. 162.

Nos. 72-73 Overprinted type "m" in Red

**1910**

| | | | | |
|---|---|---|---|---|
| *150* | A34 | $5 red vio | 87.50 | 4.50 |
| *151* | A35 | $10 brown | 92.50 | 6.75 |
| **a.** | | Double ovpt. | | |
| **b.** | | Inverted ovpt. | | |

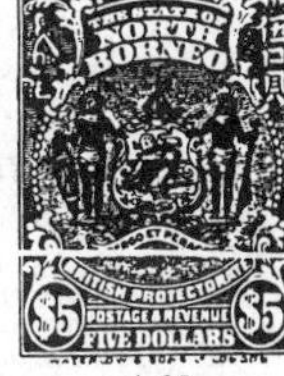

A64 A65

**1911** **Engr.** ***Perf. 14***

**Center in Black**

| | | | | |
|---|---|---|---|---|
| *152* | A64 | 25c yel grn | 4.75 | *85* |
| **a.** | | Perf. 15 | 10.00 | |
| **b.** | | Imperf. pair | 50.00 | |
| *153* | A64 | 50c sl bl | 8.50 | *1.40* |
| **a.** | | Perf. 15 | 24.00 | *8.50* |
| **b.** | | Imperf. pair | 67.50 | |
| *154* | A64 | $1 brown | 17.00 | *1.40* |
| **a.** | | Perf. 15 | 32.50 | *6.75* |
| **c.** | | Imperf. pair | 67.50 | |
| *155* | A64 | $2 dk vio | 32.50 | *6.75* |
| *156* | A65 | $5 claret | 67.50 | *32.50* |
| **a.** | | Perf. 13½ | *82.50* | |
| **b.** | | Imperf. pair | 100.00 | |
| *157* | A65 | $10 vermilion | 150.00 | *67.50* |
| **a.** | | Imperf. pair | 100.00 | |
| | | *Nos. 152-157 (6)* | 280.25 | *110.40* |

See Nos. 179-184. Nos. 152c-153c follow No. 162.

BRITISH

Nos. 72-73 Overprinted in Red

PROTECTORATE

**1912**

| | | | | |
|---|---|---|---|---|
| *158* | A34 | $5 red vio | 700.00 | 9.25 |
| *159* | A35 | $10 brown | 950.00 | 9.25 |

Nos. 158 and 159 were prepared for use but not regularly issued.

Nos. 138, 142 and 145 Surcharged in Black or Red

2 cents

**1916** **Center in Black** ***Perf. 14***

| | | | | |
|---|---|---|---|---|
| *160* | A53 | 2c on 3c dp rose | 5.75 | *6.50* |
| **a.** | | Inverted "S" | 87.50 | *87.50* |
| *161* | A56 | 4c on 6c ol grn (R) | 5.75 | *6.50* |
| **a.** | | Inverted "S" | 100.00 | *100.00* |
| *162* | A59 | 10c on 12c bl (R) | 9.25 | *16.00* |
| **a.** | | Inverted "S" | 110.00 | *110.00* |

Stamps and Types of 1909-11 Overprinted in Red or Blue in Three Lines: "MALAYA-BORNEO EXHIBITION 1922."

**1922**

**Center in Black**

| | | | | |
|---|---|---|---|---|
| *136a* | A51 | 1c brown | 5.50 | *22.50* |
| *137a* | A52 | 2c green | 1.90 | *13.00* |
| *138a* | A53 | 3c dp rose (B) | 4.75 | *18.00* |
| *140a* | A54 | 4c dl red (B) | 2.50 | *13.00* |
| *141a* | A55 | 5c yel brn (B) | 5.50 | *22.50* |
| *142a* | A56 | 6c ol grn | 4.75 | *27.50* |
| *143a* | A57 | 8c rose (B) | 4.75 | *27.50* |
| *144a* | A58 | 10c gray bl | 5.25 | *35.00* |
| *145a* | A59 | 12c dp bl | 7.50 | *45.00* |
| *146a* | A60 | 16c red brn (B) | 7.50 | *50.00* |
| *148a* | A62 | 20c on 18c bl grn | 13.00 | *57.50* |
| *149a* | A63 | 24c violet | 11.00 | *55.00* |
| *152c* | A64 | 25c yel grn | 11.00 | *40.00* |
| *153c* | A64 | 50c sl bl | 9.50 | *45.00* |
| | | *Nos. 136a-153c (14)* | 94.40 | *471.50* |

Industrial fair, Singapore, Mar. 31-Apr. 15, 1922.

THREE

No. 140 Surcharged in Black

CENTS

**1923**

| | | | | |
|---|---|---|---|---|
| *166* | A54 | 3c on 4c dl red & blk | 1.50 | 1.65 |
| **a.** | | Double surcharge | | |

Types of 1909-22 Issues

**1926-28** **Engr.** ***Perf. 12½***

**Center in Black**

| | | | | |
|---|---|---|---|---|
| *167* | A51 | 1c chocolate | 40 | 30 |
| *168* | A52 | 2c lake | 40 | 25 |
| *169* | A53 | 3c green | 40 | 30 |
| *170* | A54 | 4c dl red | 40 | 25 |
| *171* | A55 | 5c yel brn | 2.75 | 3.50 |
| *172* | A56 | 6c yel grn | 2.50 | 45 |
| *173* | A57 | 8c rose | 1.90 | 30 |
| *174* | A58 | 10c brt bl | 1.90 | 35 |
| *175* | A59 | 12c dp bl | 1.90 | 65 |
| *176* | A60 | 16c org brn | 3.50 | 4.00 |
| *177* | A62 | 20c on 18c bl grn (R) | 3.50 | 4.00 |
| *178* | A63 | 24c dl vio | 17.00 | *32.50* |
| *179* | A64 | 25c yel grn | 5.50 | 5.50 |
| *180* | A64 | 50c sl bl | 8.50 | *12.50* |
| *181* | A64 | $1 brown | 30.00 | *40.00* |
| *182* | A64 | $2 dk vio | 50.00 | *70.00* |
| *183* | A65 | $5 dp rose | 70.00 | 92.50 |
| *184* | A65 | $10 dl ver | 150.00 | 225.00 |
| | | *Nos. 167-184 (18)* | 350.55 | 492.35 |

Murut A66

Orangutan A67

Dyak — A68

Mt. Kinabalu A69

Clouded Leopard A70

Coat of Arms — A71

Arms with Supporters and Motto A72

Arms with Supporters — A73

**1931, Jan. 1** **Engr.** ***Perf. 12½***

**Center in Black**

| | | | | |
|---|---|---|---|---|
| *185* | A66 | 3c bl grn | 2.00 | 1.50 |
| *186* | A67 | 6c org red | 11.00 | 4.75 |
| *187* | A68 | 10c carmine | 4.75 | 6.25 |
| *188* | A69 | 12c ultra | 3.25 | 4.00 |
| *189* | A70 | 25c dp vio | 20.00 | 22.50 |
| *190* | A71 | $1 yel grn | 24.00 | 30.00 |
| *191* | A72 | $2 red brn | 30.00 | 37.50 |
| *192* | A73 | $5 red vio | 65.00 | *110.00* |
| | | *Nos. 185-192 (8)* | 160.00 | *216.50* |

50th anniv. of the North Borneo Co.

Buffalo Transport A74

Palm Cockatoo A75

Murut — A76

Proboscis Monkey — A77

Bajaus — A78

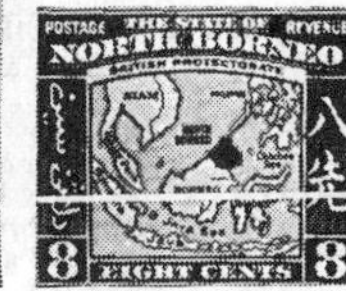

Map of North Borneo and Surrounding Lands — A79

Orangutan A80

Murut with Blowgun A81

Dyak — A82

River Scene — A83

Proa — A84

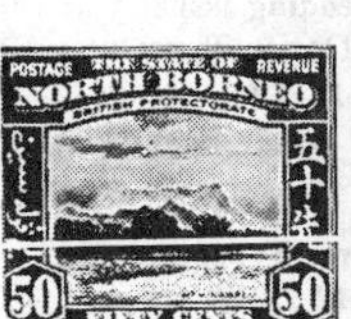

Mt. Kinabalu — A85

Coat of Arms — A86

Arms with Supporters A87

**1939, Jan. 1** ***Perf. 12½***

| | | | | |
|---|---|---|---|---|
| *193* | A74 | 1c red brn & dk grn | 22 | 15 |
| *194* | A75 | 2c Prus bl & red vio | 24 | 20 |
| *195* | A76 | 3c dk grn & sl bl | 28 | 24 |
| *196* | A77 | 4c rose vio & ol grn | 48 | 28 |
| *197* | A78 | 6c dp cl & dk bl | 45 | 28 |
| *198* | A79 | 8c red | 60 | 35 |
| *199* | A80 | 10c ol grn & vio | 7.00 | 2.75 |
| *200* | A81 | 12c ultra & grn | 60 | 48 |
| *201* | A82 | 15c bis brn & brt bl grn | 1.25 | 80 |
| *202* | A83 | 20c ind & rose vio | 1.75 | 1.25 |
| *203* | A84 | 25c dk brn & bl grn | 2.75 | 2.50 |
| *204* | A85 | 50c pur & brn | 2.75 | 2.50 |
| *205* | A86 | $1 car & brn | 14.00 | 12.50 |
| *206* | A86 | $2 ol grn & pur | 52.50 | 47.50 |
| *207* | A87 | $5 bl & ind | 125.00 | 100.00 |
| | | *Nos. 193-207 (15)* | 209.87 | 171.78 |

Nos. 193 to 207 Overprinted in Black BMA

**1945, Dec. 17** **Unwmk.** ***Perf. 12½***

| | | | | |
|---|---|---|---|---|
| *208* | A74 | 1c red brn & dk grn | 20 | 20 |
| *209* | A75 | 2c Prus bl & red vio | 22 | 20 |
| *210* | A76 | 3c dk grn & sl bl | 20 | 20 |
| *211* | A77 | 4c rose vio & ol grn | 7.25 | 5.00 |
| *212* | A78 | 6c dp cl & dk bl | 22 | 22 |
| *213* | A79 | 8c red | 35 | 35 |
| *214* | A80 | 10c ol grn & vio | 90 | 60 |
| *215* | A81 | 12c ultra & grn | 45 | 42 |
| *216* | A82 | 15c bis brn & brt bl grn | 2.50 | 2.50 |
| *217* | A83 | 20c ind & rose vio | 75 | 75 |
| *218* | A84 | 25c dk brn & bl grn | 75 | 75 |
| *219* | A85 | 50c pur & brn | 1.50 | 1.50 |
| *220* | A86 | $1 car & brn | 8.75 | 10.00 |
| *221* | A86 | $2 ol grn & pur | 8.75 | 10.00 |
| **a.** | | Double overprint | | |
| *222* | A87 | $5 bl & ind | 8.75 | 8.75 |
| | | *Nos. 208-222 (15)* | 41.54 | 41.44 |

"BMA" stands for British Military Administration.

Nos. 193 to 207 Overprinted in Black or Carmine With Bars

**1947**

| | | | | |
|---|---|---|---|---|
| *223* | A74 | 1c red brn & dk grn | 7 | 7 |
| *224* | A75 | 2c Prus bl & red vio | 15 | 9 |
| *225* | A76 | 3c dk grn & sl bl (C) | 15 | 9 |
| *226* | A77 | 4c rose vio & ol grn | 15 | 9 |
| *227* | A78 | 6c dp cl & dk bl (C) | 15 | 15 |
| *228* | A79 | 8c red | 9 | 9 |
| *229* | A80 | 10c ol grn & vio | 28 | 12 |
| *230* | A81 | 12c ultra & grn | 18 | 18 |
| *231* | A82 | 15c bis brn & brt bl grn | 18 | 18 |
| *232* | A83 | 20c ind & rose vio | 22 | 22 |
| *233* | A84 | 25c dk brn & bl grn | 30 | 30 |
| *234* | A85 | 50c pur & brn | 35 | 35 |
| *235* | A86 | $1 car & brn | 42 | 42 |
| *236* | A86 | $2 ol grn & pur | 2.25 | 2.25 |
| *237* | A87 | $5 bl & ind (C) | 3.75 | 3.75 |
| | | *Nos. 223-237 (15)* | 8.69 | 8.35 |

The bars obliterate "The State of" and "British Protectorate."

**Catalogue values for unused stamps in this section, from this point to the end of the section, are for Never Hinged items.**

**Silver Wedding Issue**
Common Design Types
*Perf. 14x14½*

**1948, Nov. 1 — Wmk. 4 — Photo.**

| | | | | |
|---|---|---|---|---|
| *238* | CD304 | 8c scarlet | 32 | 20 |

**Engraved; Name Typographed**
*Perf. 11½x11*

| | | | | |
|---|---|---|---|---|
| *239* | CD305 | $10 purple | 14.00 | 8.75 |

**UPU Issue**
Common Design Types
**Engr.; Name Typo. on 10c and 30c**

**1949, Oct. 10 — *Perf. 13½, 11x11½***

| | | | | |
|---|---|---|---|---|
| *240* | CD306 | 8c rose car | 26 | 20 |
| *241* | CD307 | 10c chocolate | 35 | 28 |
| *242* | CD308 | 30c dp org | 1.10 | 85 |
| *243* | CD309 | 55c blue | 1.75 | 1.40 |

Mount Kinabalu — A88

Coconut Grove — A89

Designs: 2c, Musician. 4c, Hemp drying. 5c, Cattle at Kota Belud. 8c, Map. 10c, Logging. 15c, Proa at Sandakan. 20c Bajau Chief. 30c, Suluk Craft. 50c, Clock tower. $1, Bajau horsemen. $2, Murut with blowgun. $5, Net fishing. $10, Arms.

*Perf. 13½x14½, 14½x13½*

**1950, July 1 — Photo.**

| | | | | |
|---|---|---|---|---|
| *244* | A88 | 1c red brn | 15 | 8 |
| *245* | A88 | 2c blue | 15 | 8 |
| *246* | A89 | 3c green | 24 | 8 |
| *247* | A89 | 4c red vio | 30 | 15 |
| *248* | A89 | 5c purple | 1.65 | 15 |
| *249* | A88 | 8c red | 75 | 18 |
| *250* | A88 | 10c vio brn | 40 | 12 |
| *251* | A88 | 15c brt ultra | 48 | 20 |
| *252* | A88 | 20c dk brn | 60 | 24 |
| *253* | A89 | 30c brown | 1.00 | 20 |
| *254* | A89 | 50c cer *(Jessleton)* | 1.00 | 50 |
| *255* | A89 | $1 red org | 1.65 | 85 |
| *256* | A88 | $2 dk grn | 4.00 | 2.00 |
| *257* | A88 | $5 emerald | 11.00 | 5.50 |
| *258* | A88 | $10 gray bl | 20.00 | 10.00 |
| | | *Nos. 244-258 (15)* | 43.37 | 20.33 |

Redrawn

**1952, May 1 — *Perf. 14½x13½***

| | | | | |
|---|---|---|---|---|
| *259* | A89 | 50c cerise *(Jesselton)* | 50 | 50 |

**Coronation Issue**
Common Design Type

**1953, June 3 — Engr. — *Perf. 13½x13***

| | | | | |
|---|---|---|---|---|
| *260* | CD312 | 10c car & blk | 35 | 35 |

Types of 1950 with Portrait of Queen Elizabeth II

*Perf. 13½x14½, 14½x13½.*

**1954-57 — Photo.**

| | | | | |
|---|---|---|---|---|
| *261* | A88 | 1c red brn | 6 | 5 |
| *262* | A88 | 2c brt bl ('56) | 30 | 18 |
| *263* | A89 | 3c grn ('57) | 30 | 18 |
| *264* | A89 | 4c red vio ('55) | 12 | 8 |
| *265* | A89 | 5c purple | 20 | 8 |
| *266* | A88 | 8c red | 14 | 12 |
| *267* | A88 | 10c vio brn | 16 | 8 |
| *268* | A88 | 15c brt ultra ('55) | 30 | 12 |
| *269* | A88 | 20c dk brn | 45 | 12 |
| *270* | A89 | 30c brown | 45 | 18 |
| *271* | A89 | 50c cer ('56) | 65 | 26 |
| *272* | A89 | $1 red org ('55) | 1.65 | 62 |
| *273* | A88 | $2 dk grn ('55) | 3.25 | 1.65 |
| *274* | A88 | $5 emer ('57) | 10.00 | 6.25 |
| *275* | A88 | $10 gray bl ('57) | 20.00 | 11.00 |
| | | *Nos. 261-275 (15)* | 38.03 | 20.97 |

In 1960, the 30c plate was remade, using a finer, smaller-dot (250) screen instead of the 200 screen. The background appears smoother. Value $2.75 unused.

Canceled-to-order stamps are often from remainders. Most collectors of canceled stamps prefer postally used specimens.

Borneo Railway, 1902 A90

Arms of Chartered Company A91

Designs: 15c, Proa (sailboat). 35c, Mount Kinabalu.

*Perf. 13x13½, 13½x13*

**1956, Nov. 1 — Engr. — Wmk. 4**

| | | | | |
|---|---|---|---|---|
| *276* | A90 | 10c rose car & blk | 16 | 16 |
| *277* | A90 | 15c red brn & blk | 26 | 26 |
| *278* | A90 | 35c grn & blk | 50 | 50 |
| *279* | A91 | $1 sl & blk | 1.25 | 1.25 |

75th anniv. of the founding of the Chartered Company of North Borneo.

Malayan Sambar A92

Orangutan A93

Designs: 4c, Honey bear. 5c, Clouded leopard. 6c, Dusun woman with gong. 10c, Map of Borneo. 12c, Banteng (wild ox). 20c, Butterfly orchid. 25c, Rhinoceros. 30c, Murut with blowgun. 35c, Mount Kinabalu. 50c, Dusun with buffalo transport. 75c, Bajau horsemen. $2, Rhinoceros hornbill. $5, Crested wood partridge. $10, Coat of arms.

*Perf. 13x12½, 12½x13*

**1961, Feb. 1 — Wmk. 314 — Engr.**

| | | | | |
|---|---|---|---|---|
| *280* | A92 | 1c lt red brn & grn | 10 | 9 |
| *281* | A92 | 4c org & ol | 18 | 16 |
| *282* | A92 | 5c vio & sep | 22 | 12 |
| *283* | A92 | 6c bluish grn & sl | 20 | 16 |
| *284* | A92 | 10c rose red & lt grn | 20 | 12 |
| *285* | A92 | 12c dl grn & brn | 30 | 28 |
| *286* | A92 | 20c ultra & bl grn | 42 | 28 |
| *287* | A92 | 25c rose red & gray | 60 | 55 |
| *288* | A92 | 30c gray ol & sep | 60 | 38 |
| *289* | A92 | 35c redsh brn & stl bl | 70 | 50 |
| *290* | A92 | 50c brn org & bl grn | 85 | 55 |
| *291* | A92 | 75c red vio & sl bl | 1.10 | 85 |
| *292* | A93 | $1 yel grn & brn | 2.25 | 1.10 |
| *293* | A93 | $2 sl & brn | 4.50 | 2.25 |
| *294* | A93 | $5 brn vio & grn | 14.00 | 6.00 |
| *295* | A93 | $10 bl & car | 27.50 | 16.00 |
| | | *Nos. 280-295 (16)* | 53.72 | 29.39 |

**Freedom from Hunger Issue**
Common Design Type

**1963, June 4 — Photo. — *Perf. 14x14½***

| | | | | |
|---|---|---|---|---|
| *296* | CD314 | 12c ultra | 90 | 40 |

Sabah stamps replaced those of North Borneo in 1964.

---

## SEMI-POSTAL STAMPS

Nos. 136-138, 140-146, 148-149, 152 Overprinted in Carmine or Vermilion

**1916 — Unwmk. — *Perf. 14.***
**Center in Black**

| | | | | |
|---|---|---|---|---|
| *B1* | A51 | 1c chocolate | 4.00 | *12.00* |
| *B2* | A52 | 2c green | 16.00 | *27.50* |
| **a.** | | Perf. 15 | 22.50 | *32.50* |
| *B3* | A53 | 3c deep rose | 12.00 | *20.00* |
| *B4* | A54 | 4c dull red | 6.00 | *12.00* |
| **a.** | | Perf. 15 | | *72.50* |
| *B5* | A55 | 5c yel brn | 24.00 | *24.00* |
| *B6* | A56 | 6c ol grn | 18.00 | *30.00* |
| **a.** | | Perf. 15 | | |
| *B7* | A57 | 8c rose | 12.00 | *24.00* |
| *B8* | A58 | 10c brt bl | 24.00 | *35.00* |
| *B9* | A59 | 12c deep bl | 24.00 | *37.50* |
| *B10* | A60 | 16c red brn | 26.00 | *37.50* |
| *B11* | A62 | 20c on 18c bl grn | 26.00 | *40.00* |
| *B12* | A63 | 24c violet | 40.00 | *45.00* |

***Perf. 15***

| | | | | |
|---|---|---|---|---|
| *B13* | A64 | 25c yel grn | 180.00 | *225.00* |
| | | *Nos. B1-B13 (13)* | 412.00 | *569.50* |

All values exist with the vermilion overprint and all but the 4c with the carmine.

Of the total overprinting, a third was given to the National Philatelic War Fund Committee in London to be auctioned for the benefit of the wounded and veterans' survivors. The balance was lost en route from London to Sandakan when a submarine sank the ship. Very few were postally used.

Nos. 136-138, 140-146, 149, 152-157 Surcharged

**RED CROSS**

**TWO CENTS**

**1918 — *Perf. 14***
**Center in Black**

| | | | | |
|---|---|---|---|---|
| *B14* | A51 | 1c + 2c choc | 1.25 | *5.50* |
| *B15* | A52 | 2c + 2c green | 30 | *3.25* |
| *B16* | A53 | 3c + 2c dp rose | 1.65 | *7.00* |
| **a.** | | Perf. 15 | 19.00 | *40.00* |
| *B17* | A54 | 4c + 2c dl red | 32 | *2.25* |
| **a.** | | Inverted surcharge | 275.00 | |
| *B18* | A55 | 5c + 2c yel brn | 2.75 | *9.50* |
| *B19* | A56 | 6c + 2c ol grn | 2.75 | *17.00* |
| **a.** | | Perf. 15 | 125.00 | |
| *B20* | A57 | 8c + 2c rose | 2.25 | *5.50* |
| *B21* | A58 | 10c + 2c brt bl | 2.75 | *11.00* |
| *B22* | A59 | 12c + 2c deep bl | 2.50 | *11.00* |
| **a.** | | Inverted surcharge | 500.00 | |
| *B23* | A60 | 16c + 2c red brn | 4.50 | *16.00* |
| *B24* | A63 | 24c + 2c violet | 4.50 | *16.00* |
| *B25* | A64 | 25c + 2c yel grn | 11.00 | *40.00* |
| *B26* | A64 | 50c + 2c sl bl | 13.00 | *35.00* |
| *B27* | A64 | $1 + 2c brn | 30.00 | *52.50* |
| *B28* | A64 | $2 + 2c dk vio | 45.00 | *85.00* |
| *B29* | A65 | $5 + 2c claret | 225.00 | *400.00* |
| *B30* | A65 | $10 + 2c ver | 225.00 | *400.00* |
| | | *Nos. B14-B30 (17)* | 574.52 | *1,116.* |

On Nos. B14-B24 the surcharge is 15mm high, on Nos. B25-B30 it is 19mm high.

Nos. 136-138, 140-146, 149, 152-157 Surcharged in Red

**FOUR CENTS**

**1918**
**Center in Black**

| | | | | |
|---|---|---|---|---|
| *B31* | A51 | 1c + 4c choc | 32 | *2.50* |
| *B32* | A52 | 2c + 4c grn | 40 | *3.00* |
| *B33* | A53 | 3c + 4c dp rose | 32 | *3.00* |
| *B34* | A54 | 4c + 4c dl red | 40 | *3.25* |
| *B35* | A55 | 5c + 4c yel brn | 55 | *4.25* |
| *B36* | A56 | 6c + 4c ol grn | 65 | *5.50* |
| **a.** | | Vert. pair, imperf. btwn. | 900.00 | |
| *B37* | A57 | 8c + 4c rose | 65 | *5.25* |
| *B38* | A58 | 10c + 4c brt bl | 3.25 | *9.50* |
| *B39* | A59 | 12c + 4c dp bl | 3.25 | *9.50* |
| *B40* | A60 | 16c + 4c red brn | 3.25 | *13.00* |
| *B41* | A63 | 24c + 4c vio | 4.25 | *16.00* |
| *B42* | A64 | 25c + 4c yel grn | 8.50 | *21.00* |
| *B43* | A64 | 50c + 4c sl bl | 12.00 | *27.50* |
| **a.** | | Perf. 15 | 40.00 | |
| *B44* | A64 | $1 + 4c brn | 15.00 | *32.50* |
| **a.** | | Perf. 15 | *40.00* | |
| *B45* | A64 | $2 + 4c dk vio | 27.50 | *47.50* |
| *B46* | A65 | $5 + 4c claret | 200.00 | *275.00* |
| *B47* | A65 | $10 + 4c ver | 200.00 | *275.00* |
| | | *Nos. B31-B47 (17)* | 480.29 | 753.25 |

---

## POSTAGE DUE STAMPS

Regular Issues Overprinted

**POSTAGE DUE**

Vertically reading up (V), or Horizontally (H).

**1895 — Unwmk. — *Perf. 14, 15***
**On Nos. 60 to 67**

| | | | | |
|---|---|---|---|---|
| *J1* | A22 | 2c rose & blk (V) | 9.00 | 95 |
| *J2* | A23 | 3c vio & ol grn (V) | 7.50 | 80 |
| *J3* | A24 | 5c org red & blk (V) | 12.00 | 1.00 |
| **a.** | | Period after "DUE" (V) | 45.00 | |
| *J4* | A25 | 6c ol brn & blk (V) | 12.00 | 1.50 |
| *J5* | A26 | 8c lil & blk (H) | 22.50 | 2.00 |
| **a.** | | Double ovpt. (H) | | |
| *J6* | A27 | 12c bl & blk (H) | 12.00 | 1.50 |
| **a.** | | Double oveprint (H) | | *325.00* |
| *J7* | A28 | 18c grn & blk (V) | 30.00 | 3.00 |
| **a.** | | Ovpt. reading down | 400.00 | *275.00* |
| **b.** | | Overprinted horizontally | 20.00 | 2.75 |
| **c.** | | Same as "b" inverted | 300.00 | *275.00* |
| *J8* | A29 | 24c cl & bl (H) | 20.00 | 1.65 |
| | | *Nos. J1-J8 (8)* | 125.00 | 12.40 |

On Nos. 80 and 85

**1897**

| | | | | |
|---|---|---|---|---|
| *J9* | A38 | 2c dp rose & blk (V) | 4.50 | 45 |
| **a.** | | Overprinted horizontally | 12.00 | *15.00* |
| *J10* | A42 | 8c brn lil & blk (H) | 15.00 | *15.00* |
| **a.** | | Period after "DUE" | 22.50 | *22.50* |

On Nos. 81-88 and 104
Vertically reading up

**1901**

| | | | | |
|---|---|---|---|---|
| *J11* | A38 | 2c grn & blk | 21.00 | 55 |
| **a.** | | Overprinted horizontally | 27.50 | |
| *J12* | A39 | 3c lil & ol grn | 4.50 | 36 |
| **a.** | | Period after "DUE" | 18.00 | *30.00* |
| *J13* | A48 | 4c dp rose & blk | 4.50 | 45 |
| *J14* | A40 | 5c org & blk | 7.50 | 55 |
| **a.** | | Period after "DUE" | 30.00 | |
| *J15* | A41 | 6c ol brn & blk | 2.25 | 45 |
| *J16* | A42 | 8c brn & blk | 4.50 | 45 |
| **a.** | | Overprinted horizontally | 30.00 | |
| **b.** | | Period after "DUE" (H) | 60.00 | |
| *J17* | A43 | 12c bl & blk | 18.00 | 90 |
| *J18* | A46 | 18c grn & blk | 12.00 | 90 |
| *J19* | A47 | 24c red & bl | 12.50 | 90 |
| | | *Nos. J11-J19 (9)* | 86.75 | 5.51 |

On Nos. 105-114, 122-123
Horizontally

**1903-11 — *Perf. 14***

| | | | | |
|---|---|---|---|---|
| *J20* | A37 | 1c bis brn & blk, period after "DUE" | 13.00 | 13.00 |
| **a.** | | Period omitted | | |
| *J21* | A38 | 2c grn & blk | 3.50 | 25 |
| **a.** | | Ovpt. vert., perf. 16 | | *150.00* |
| **b.** | | Perf 15 (ovpt. horiz.) | 55.00 | *55.00* |
| *J22* | A39 | 3c lil & ol grn | 5.00 | 38 |
| **a.** | | Ovpt. vert. | 110.00 | *110.00* |
| **b.** | | Perf. 15 (ovpt. horiz.) | 95.00 | *17.00* |
| *J23* | A48 | 4c dp rose & blk, perf. 15 | 1.65 | 45 |
| **a.** | | "Postage Due" double | 110.00 | |
| **b.** | | Perf. 14 | 4.75 | 1.00 |
| *J24* | A40 | 5c org & blk | 5.25 | 45 |
| **a.** | | Ovpt. vert., perf. 15 | 165.00 | *110.00* |
| **b.** | | Perf. 13½ (ovpt. horiz.) | | |
| **c.** | | Perf. 15 (ovpt. horiz.) | 13.00 | *10.00* |
| *J25* | A41 | 6c ol brn & blk | 7.25 | 38 |
| **a.** | | "Postage Due" double | | |
| **b.** | | "Postage Due" inverted | | *150.00* |
| **c.** | | Perf. 16 | 25.00 | *25.00* |
| *J26* | A42 | 8c brn & blk | 9.25 | 52 |
| **a.** | | Ovpt. vert. | 150.00 | *125.00* |
| *J27* | A49 | 10c sl & brn | 19.00 | 75 |
| *J28* | A43 | 12c bl & blk | 10.50 | 75 |
| *J29* | A50 | 16c yel brn & grn | 10.50 | 65 |
| *J30* | A46 | 18c grn & blk | 7.00 | 60 |
| **a.** | | "Postage Due" double | | *80.00* |
| *J31* | A47 | 24c cl & bl | 12.50 | 1.25 |
| **a.** | | "Postage Due" double | | *125.00* |
| **b.** | | Ovpt. vert. | | *85.00* |
| | | *Nos. J20-J31 (12)* | 104.40 | 19.43 |

On Nos. 137 and 139-146

**1921-31 — *Perf. 14, 15***

| | | | | |
|---|---|---|---|---|
| *J32* | A52 | 2c grn & blk | 5.50 | 12.00 |
| **a.** | | Perf. 13½ | 12.00 | 12.00 |
| *J33* | A53 | 3c grn & blk | 2.50 | 2.75 |
| *J34* | A54 | 4c dl red & blk | 1.75 | 1.75 |
| *J35* | A55 | 5c yel brn & blk | 2.50 | 2.50 |
| *J36* | A56 | 6c ol grn & blk | 6.50 | 6.50 |
| *J37* | A57 | 8c rose & blk | 2.50 | 2.50 |
| *J38* | A58 | 10c bl & blk | 3.25 | 2.75 |
| **a.** | | Perf. 15 | 60.00 | 60.00 |
| *J39* | A59 | 12c dp vio & blk | 4.50 | 5.25 |
| *J40* | A60 | 16c red brn & blk | 12.00 | 12.00 |
| | | *Nos. J32-J40 (9)* | 41.00 | 48.00 |

On Nos. 168 to 176

**1926-28 — *Perf. 12½***

| | | | | |
|---|---|---|---|---|
| *J41* | A52 | 2c lake & blk | 40 | *2.50* |
| *J42* | A53 | 3c grn & blk | 1.25 | *4.00* |
| *J43* | A54 | 4c dl red & blk | 2.25 | *2.75* |
| *J44* | A55 | 5c yel brn & blk | 3.75 | *10.50* |
| *J45* | A56 | 6c yel grn & blk | 5.25 | *3.00* |
| *J46* | A57 | 8c rose & blk | 4.75 | *5.50* |
| *J47* | A58 | 10c brt bl & blk | 6.00 | *16.00* |
| *J48* | A59 | 12c dp bl & blk | 11.00 | *24.00* |
| *J49* | A60 | 16c org brn & blk | 22.50 | *52.50* |
| | | *Nos. J41-J49 (9)* | 57.15 | *120.75* |

Crest of British North Borneo Company — D1

**1939, Jan. 1 — Engr. — *Perf. 12½***

| | | | | |
|---|---|---|---|---|
| *J50* | D1 | 2c brown | 3.25 | *25.00* |
| *J51* | D1 | 4c carmine | 4.25 | *32.50* |
| *J52* | D1 | 6c dp rose vio | 7.00 | *42.50* |
| *J53* | D1 | 8c dk bl grn | 10.00 | *52.50* |
| *J54* | D1 | 10c dp ultra | 16.00 | *70.00* |
| | | *Nos. J50-J54 (5)* | 40.50 | *222.50* |

### WAR TAX STAMPS

Nos. 193-194 Overprinted

WAR TAX
No. MR1

WAR
TAX
No. MR2

**1941, Feb. 24 Unwmk. *Perf. 12½***

| | | | | |
|---|---|---|---|---|
| *MR1* | A74 | 1c red brn & dk grn | 30 | 30 |
| *MR2* | A75 | 2c Prus bl & red vio | 50 | 55 |

### OCCUPATION STAMPS

**Issued under Japanese Occupation**

Nos. 193-207 Handstamped in Violet or Black 府政国帝本日大

**1942 Unwmk. *Perf. 12½***

| | | | | |
|---|---|---|---|---|
| *N1* | A74 | 1c red brn & dk grn | 60.00 | 70.00 |
| *N2* | A75 | 2c Prus bl & red vio | 55.00 | 62.50 |
| *N3* | A76 | 3c dk grn & sl bl | 55.00 | 62.50 |
| *N4* | A77 | 4c rose vio & ol grn | 30.00 | 55.00 |
| *N5* | A78 | 6c dp cl & dk bl | 55.00 | 62.50 |
| *N6* | A79 | 8c red | 55.00 | 62.50 |
| *N7* | A80 | 10c ol grn & vio | 55.00 | 62.50 |
| *N8* | A81 | 12c ultra & grn | 70.00 | 110.00 |
| *N9* | A82 | 15c bis brn & brt bl grn | 70.00 | 110.00 |
| *N10* | A83 | 20c ind & rose vio | 100.00 | *150.00* |
| *N11* | A84 | 25c dk brn & bl grn | 100.00 | *150.00* |
| *N12* | A85 | 50c pur & brn | 125.00 | *175.00* |
| *N13* | A86 | $1 car & brn | 125.00 | *225.00* |
| *N14* | A86 | $2 ol grn & pur | 165.00 | *325.00* |
| *N15* | A87 | $5 bl & ind | 250.00 | *450.00* |
| | | *Nos. N1-N15 (15)* | 1,370. | *2,132.* |

Same Overprint on Nos. MR1-MR2 in Black or Violet.

**1942**

| | | | | |
|---|---|---|---|---|
| *N15A* | A74 | 1c red brn & dk grn | 100.00 | *87.50* |
| *N15B* | A75 | 2c Prus bl & red vio | 125.00 | *87.50* |

On Nos. N1-N15B, the violet overprint is attributed to Jesselton, the black to Sandakan. Nos. N1-N15 are generally found with violet overprint, Nos. N15A-N15B with black.

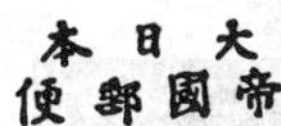

Nos. 193 to 207 Overprinted in Black

オネルボ北

**1944, Sept. 30 Unwmk. *Perf. 12½***

| | | | | |
|---|---|---|---|---|
| *N16* | A74 | 1c red brn & dk grn | 1.00 | 1.75 |
| *N17* | A75 | 2c Prus bl & red vio | 1.00 | 1.75 |
| *N18* | A76 | 3c dk grn & sl bl | 1.00 | 1.75 |
| *N19* | A77 | 4c rose vio & ol grn | 1.00 | 1.75 |
| *N20* | A78 | 6c dp cl & dk bl | 1.25 | 1.25 |
| *N21* | A79 | 8c red | 1.75 | 2.50 |
| *N22* | A80 | 10c ol grn & vio | 1.50 | 1.75 |
| *a.* | | On #N7 | 150.00 | |
| *N23* | A81 | 12c ultra & grn | 1.50 | 2.50 |
| *N24* | A82 | 15c bis brn & brt bl grn | 1.50 | 2.50 |
| *N25* | A83 | 20c ind & rose vio | 5.50 | 7.50 |
| *N26* | A84 | 25c dk brn & bl grn | 6.25 | *17.50* |
| *N27* | A85 | 50c pur & brn | 17.50 | *37.50* |
| *N28* | A86 | $1 car & brn | 30.00 | *50.00* |
| | | *Nos. N16-N28 (13)* | 70.75 | *130.00* |

Nos. 193 and 205 Surcharged in Black

本日大

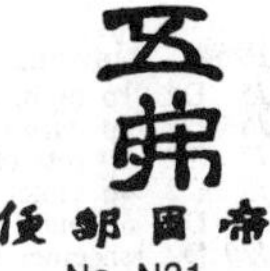

No. N30 No. N31

**1944, May**

| | | | | |
|---|---|---|---|---|
| *N30* | A74 | $2 on 1c red brn & dk grn | *1,900.* | *1,900.* |
| *N31* | A86 | $5 on $1 car & brn | 1,500. | 1,500. |
| *a.* | | on No. N13 | 1,250. | 1,250. |

Mt. Kinabalu — OS1

Boat and Traveler's Palm — OS2

**1943, Apr. 29 Litho.**

| | | | | |
|---|---|---|---|---|
| *N32* | OS1 | 4c dl rose red | 10.50 | 12.50 |
| *N33* | OS2 | 8c dark blue | 10.50 | 12.50 |

Aviator Saluting and Japanese Flag — A150

Miyajima Torii, Itsukushima Shrine — A96

Stamps of Japan, 1938-43, Overprinted in Black オネルボ北

Designs: 1s, War factory girl. 2s, Gen. Maresuke Nogi. 3s, Power plant. 4s, Hyuga Monument and Mt. Fuji. 5s, Adm. Heihachiro Togo. 6s, Garambi Lighthouse, Formosa. 8s, Meiji Shrine, Tokyo. 10s, Palms and map of "Greater East Asia." 20s, Mt. Fuji and cherry blossoms. 25s, Horyu Temple, Nara. 50s, Golden Pavilion, Kyoto. 1y, Great Buddha, Kamakura. (See Burma for illustrations of 2s, 3s, 5s, 8s, 20s and watermark. For others, see Japan, Vol. III.)

**Wmk. Curved Wavy Lines. (257)**
**1944, Sept. 30 *Perf. 13***

| | | | | |
|---|---|---|---|---|
| *N34* | A144 | 1s org brn | 1.00 | 1.25 |
| *N35* | A84 | 2s vermilion | 1.00 | 1.25 |
| *N36* | A85 | 3s green | 1.25 | 1.50 |
| *N37* | A146 | 4s emerald | 1.25 | 1.50 |
| *N38* | A86 | 5s brn lake | 1.50 | 2.50 |
| *N39* | A88 | 6s orange | 1.75 | 3.00 |
| *N40* | A90 | 8s dk pur & pale vio | 2.00 | 3.00 |
| *N41* | A148 | 10s crim & dl rose | 2.00 | 4.00 |
| *N42* | A150 | 15s dl bl | 2.50 | 4.00 |
| *N43* | A94 | 20s ultra | 100.00 | 125.00 |
| *N44* | A95 | 25s brown | 32.50 | 35.00 |
| *N45* | A96 | 30s pck bl | 150.00 | 110.00 |
| *N46* | A97 | 50s olive | 30.00 | 35.00 |
| *N47* | A98 | 1y lt brn | 50.00 | 62.50 |
| | | *Nos. N34-N47 (14)* | 376.75 | 389.50 |

The overprint translates "North Borneo."

## NORTHERN NIGERIA

LOCATION — Western Africa.
GOVT. — A former British Protectorate.
AREA — 281,703 sq. mi.
POP. — 11,866,250.
CAPITAL — Zungeru.

In 1914 Northern Nigeria united with Southern Nigeria to form the Colony and Protectorate of Nigeria.

12 Pence = 1 Shilling
20 Shillings = 1 Pound

Victoria A1

Edward VII A2

Numerals of 5p and 6p, types A1 and A2, are in color on plain tablet.

**Wmk. Crown and C. A. (2)**
**1900, Mar. Typo. *Perf. 14***

| | | | | |
|---|---|---|---|---|
| *1* | A1 | ½p lil & grn | 45 | 1.00 |
| *2* | A1 | 1p lil & rose | 2.25 | 1.00 |
| *3* | A1 | 2p lil & yel | 1.65 | *6.00* |
| *4* | A1 | 2½p lil & bl | 1.65 | *7.50* |
| *5* | A1 | 5p lil & brn | 5.50 | *15.00* |
| *6* | A1 | 6p lil & vio | 6.75 | *13.00* |
| *7* | A1 | 1sh grn & blk | 8.25 | *17.50* |
| *8* | A1 | 2sh6p grn & bl | 35.00 | *100.00* |
| *9* | A1 | 10sh grn & brn | 145.00 | *350.00* |
| | | *Nos. 1-9 (9)* | 206.50 | 511.00 |

**1902, July 1**

| | | | | |
|---|---|---|---|---|
| *10* | A2 | ½p vio & grn | 18 | 24 |
| *11* | A2 | 1p vio & car ros | 75 | 20 |
| *12* | A2 | 2p vio & org | 1.75 | 1.25 |
| *13* | A2 | 2½p vio & ultra | 35 | 35 |
| *14* | A2 | 5p vio & org brn | 1.40 | 2.50 |
| *15* | A2 | 6p vio & pur | 4.50 | 2.75 |
| *16* | A2 | 1sh grn & blk | 1.90 | 1.90 |
| *17* | A2 | 2sh6p grn & ultra | 7.50 | *12.00* |
| *18* | A2 | 10sh grn & brn | 30.00 | *40.00* |
| | | *Nos. 10-18 (9)* | 48.33 | *61.19* |

**1904, Apr. Wmk. 3**

| | | | | |
|---|---|---|---|---|
| *18A* | A2 | £25 grn & car | *40,000.* | |

No. 18A was available for postage but probably was used only for fiscal purposes.

**1905**

| | | | | |
|---|---|---|---|---|
| *19* | A2 | ½p vio & grn | 635 | 20 |
| *20* | A2 | 1p vio & car rose | 30 | 15 |
| *21* | A2 | 2p vio & org | 75 | 75 |
| *22* | A2 | 2½p vio & ultra | 2.00 | 2.75 |
| *23* | A2 | 5p vio & org brn | 3.00 | 2.75 |
| *24* | A2 | 6p vio & pur | 2.50 | 2.50 |
| *25* | A2 | 1sh grn & blk | 6.00 | *7.50* |
| *26* | A2 | 2sh6p grn & ultra | 13.00 | *16.00* |
| | | *Nos. 19-26 (8)* | 33.90 | 32.60 |

All values exist on ordinary paper and all but the ½p on chalky paper.

**1910-11 Ordinary Paper**

| | | | | |
|---|---|---|---|---|
| *28* | A2 | ½p green | 60 | 30 |
| *29* | A2 | 1p carmine | 1.25 | 30 |
| *30* | A2 | 2p gray | 80 | 1.50 |
| *31* | A2 | 2½p ultra | 65 | 1.10 |
| | | **Chalky Paper** | | |
| *32* | A2 | 3p vio, *yel* | 75 | 48 |
| *33* | A2 | 5p vio & ol grn | 1.75 | 2.00 |
| *34* | A2 | 6p vio & red vio ('11) | 1.10 | 75 |
| *a.* | | 6p vio & dp vio | 1.25 | 1.50 |
| *35* | A2 | 1sh *green* | 1.50 | 90 |
| *36* | A2 | 2sh6p blk & red, *bl* | 4.75 | 3.50 |
| *37* | A2 | 5sh grn & red, *yel* | 15.00 | 18.00 |
| *38* | A2 | 10sh grn & red, *grn* | 27.50 | 32.50 |
| | | *Nos. 28-38 (11)* | 55.65 | 61.33 |

King George V — A3

For description of dies I and II see back of this section of the Catalogue.

Die I.

**1912 Ordinary Paper**

| | | | | |
|---|---|---|---|---|
| *40* | A3 | ½p green | 55 | 55 |
| *41* | A3 | 1p carmine | 45 | 8 |
| *42* | A3 | 2p gray | 70 | 1.25 |
| | | **Chalky Paper** | | |
| *43* | A3 | 3p vio, *yel* | 35 | 35 |
| *44* | A3 | 4p blk & red, *yel* | 45 | 45 |
| *45* | A3 | 5p vio & ol grn | 70 | 1.40 |
| *46* | A3 | 6p vio & red vio | 70 | 70 |
| *47* | A3 | 9p vio & scar | 90 | *2.50* |
| *48* | A3 | 1sh *green* | 1.75 | 1.00 |
| *49* | A3 | 2sh6p blk & red, *bl* | 5.25 | *7.00* |
| *50* | A3 | 5sh grn & red, *yel* | 17.50 | *27.50* |
| *51* | A3 | 10sh grn & red, *grn* | 37.50 | *45.00* |
| *52* | A3 | £1 vio & blk, *red* | 100.00 | 70.00 |
| | | *Nos. 40-52 (13)* | 166.80 | 157.78 |

Numerals of 3p, 4p, 5p and 6p, type A3, are in color on plain tablet.

Stamps of Northern Nigeria were replaced in 1914 by those of Nigeria.

## NORTHERN RHODESIA

LOCATION — In southern Africa, east of Angola and separated from Southern Rhodesia by the Zambezi River.
GOVT. — Former British Protectorate.
AREA — 287,640 sq. mi.
POP. — 2,550,000 (est. 1962).
CAPITAL — Lusaka.

Prior to April 1, 1924, Northern Rhodesia was administered by the British South Africa Company. It joined the Federation of Rhodesia and Nyasaland in 1953 and used its stamps in 1954-63. It resumed issuing its own stamps in December, 1963, after the Federation was dissolved. On Oct. 24, 1964, Northern Rhodesia became the independent republic of Zambia. See Rhodesia, Southern Rhodesia, Rhodesia and Nyasaland, Zambia.

12 Pence = 1 Shilling
20 Shillings = 1 Pound

**Catalogue values for unused stamps in this country are for Never Hinged items, beginning with Scott 46 in the regular postage section and Scott J5 in the postage due section.**

King George V
A1 A2

**1925-29 Engr. Wmk. 4 *Perf. 12½***

| | | | | |
|---|---|---|---|---|
| *1* | A1 | ½p dk grn | 10 | 6 |
| *2* | A1 | 1p dk brn | 12 | 6 |
| *3* | A1 | 1½p carmine | 25 | 22 |
| *4* | A1 | 2p brn org | 45 | 15 |
| *5* | A1 | 3p ultra | 65 | 35 |
| *6* | A1 | 4p dk vio | 1.00 | 52 |
| *7* | A1 | 6p gray | 1.00 | 35 |
| *8* | A1 | 8p rose lil | 5.00 | 11.50 |
| *9* | A1 | 10p ol grn | 5.00 | 11.50 |
| *10* | A2 | 1sh blk & org | 2.00 | 1.10 |
| *11* | A2 | 2sh ultra & brn | 11.50 | 10.00 |
| *12* | A2 | 2sh grn & blk 6p | 5.00 | 3.75 |
| *13* | A2 | 3sh ind & vio ('29) | 14.00 | 8.25 |
| *14* | A2 | 5sh dk vio & gray | 13.00 | 8.25 |
| *15* | A2 | 7sh6p blk & lil rose | 100.00 | *115.00* |
| *16* | A2 | 10sh blk & grn | 37.50 | 27.50 |
| *17* | A2 | 20sh rose lil & red | 180.00 | 150.00 |
| | | *Nos. 1-17 (17)* | 376.57 | 348.56 |

High values with revenue cancellations are inexpensive.

**Silver Jubilee Issue**
Common Design Type

**1935, May 6 *Perf. 13½x14***

| | | | | |
|---|---|---|---|---|
| *18* | CD301 | 1p ol grn & ultra | 55 | 50 |
| *19* | CD301 | 2p ind & grn | 95 | 90 |
| *20* | CD301 | 3p bl & brn | 1.00 | 1.00 |
| *21* | CD301 | 6p brt vio & ind | 3.75 | 3.75 |

**Coronation Issue**
Common Design Type

**1937, May 12 *Perf. 11x11½***

| | | | | |
|---|---|---|---|---|
| *22* | CD302 | 1½p dark car | 15 | 15 |
| *23* | CD302 | 2p yel brn | 30 | 30 |
| *24* | CD302 | 3p deep ultra | 50 | 50 |

King George VI — A3

**1938-52 Wmk. 4 Perf. 12½**

**Size: 19x24mm**

| No. | Design | Description | Unused | Used |
|---|---|---|---|---|
| 25 | A3 | ½p green | 12 | 12 |
| 26 | A3 | ½p dk brn ('51) | 15 | 15 |
| a. | | Perf. 12½x14 | 18 | 15 |
| 27 | A3 | 1p dk brn | 6 | 6 |
| 28 | A3 | 1p grn ('51) | 70 | 70 |
| 29 | A3 | 1½p carmine | 2.50 | 10 |
| a. | | Horiz. pair, imperf. between | 12,500. | |
| 30 | A3 | 1½p brn org ('41) | 6 | 5 |
| 31 | A3 | 2p brn org | 12.50 | 1.25 |
| 32 | A3 | 2p car ('41) | 8 | 6 |
| 33 | A3 | 2p rose lil ('51) | 6 | 6 |
| 34 | A3 | 3p ultra | 10 | 10 |
| 35 | A3 | 3p red ('51) | 22 | 12 |
| 36 | A3 | 4p dk vio | 22 | 10 |
| 37 | A3 | 4½p dp bl ('52) | 1.50 | 1.40 |
| 38 | A3 | 6p dk gray | 22 | 12 |
| 39 | A3 | 9p vio ('52) | 1.50 | 1.50 |

**Size: 21½x26¾mm**

| No. | Design | Description | Unused | Used |
|---|---|---|---|---|
| 40 | A3 | 1sh blk & brn org | 30 | 20 |
| 41 | A3 | 2sh6p grn & blk | 1.25 | 70 |
| 42 | A3 | 3sh ind & dk vio | 1.40 | 1.10 |
| 43 | A3 | 5sh vio & gray | 1.90 | 1.65 |
| 44 | A3 | 10sh blk & grn | 2.25 | 5.50 |
| 45 | A3 | 20sh rose lil & red | 11.00 | 14.00 |
| | | *Nos. 25-45 (21)* | 38.09 | 29.04 |

Common Design Types pictured in section before Great Britain.

**Catalogue values for unused stamps in this section, from this point to the end of the section, are for Never Hinged items.**

**Peace Issue**

Common Design Type

**1946, Nov. 26 Engr. Perf. 13½x14**

| No. | Design | Description | Unused | Used |
|---|---|---|---|---|
| 46 | CD303 | 1½p dp org | 18 | 18 |
| a. | | Perf. 13½ | 30 | 30 |
| 47 | CD303 | 2p carmine | 24 | 24 |

**Silver Wedding Issue**

Common Design Types

**1948, Dec. 1 Photo. Perf. 14x14½**

| No. | Design | Description | Unused | Used |
|---|---|---|---|---|
| 48 | CD304 | 1½p orange | 12 | 12 |

**Engr. Perf. 11½x11**

| No. | Design | Description | Unused | Used |
|---|---|---|---|---|
| 49 | CD305 | 20sh rose brn | 45.00 | 80.00 |

**UPU Issue**

Common Design Types

**Engr.; Name Typo. on 3p, 6p.**

**Perf. 13½, 11x11½**

**1949, Oct. 10 Wmk. 4**

| No. | Design | Description | Unused | Used |
|---|---|---|---|---|
| 50 | CD306 | 2p rose car | 28 | 28 |
| 51 | CD307 | 3p indigo | 48 | 48 |
| 52 | CD308 | 6p gray | 1.00 | 1.00 |
| 53 | CD309 | 1sh red org | 2.00 | 2.00 |

Victoria Falls and Railway Bridge, Cecil Rhodes and Elizabeth II — A4

**1953, May 30 Engr. Perf. 12x11**

| No. | Design | Description | Unused | Used |
|---|---|---|---|---|
| 54 | A4 | ½p brown | 14 | 10 |
| 55 | A4 | 1p green | 18 | 15 |
| 56 | A4 | 2p dp claret | 22 | 18 |
| 57 | A4 | 4½p deep blue | 75 | 75 |
| 58 | A4 | 1sh gray & org | 95 | 95 |
| | | *Nos. 54-58 (5)* | 2.24 | 2.13 |

Cecil Rhodes (1853-1902).

Type of Nyasaland Protectorate

**1953, May 30 Perf. 14x13½**

| No. | Design | Description | Unused | Used |
|---|---|---|---|---|
| 59 | A17 | 6p purple | 48 | 48 |

Central African Rhodes Centenary Exhib.

**Coronation Issue**

Common Design Type

**1953, June 2 Perf. 13½x13**

| No. | Design | Description | Unused | Used |
|---|---|---|---|---|
| 60 | CD312 | 1½p org & blk | 35 | 35 |

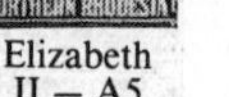

Elizabeth II — A5

Coat of Arms — A6

**Perf. 12½x13½**

**1953, Sept. 15 Engr.**

**Size: 19x23mm**

| No. | Design | Description | Unused | Used |
|---|---|---|---|---|
| 61 | A5 | ½p dk brn | 7 | 7 |
| 62 | A5 | 1p green | 9 | 9 |
| 63 | A5 | 1½p brn org | 12 | 12 |
| 64 | A5 | 2p rose lil | 12 | 12 |
| 65 | A5 | 3p red | 20 | 20 |
| 66 | A5 | 4p dk vio | 32 | 32 |
| 67 | A5 | 4½p dp bl | 40 | 40 |
| 68 | A5 | 6p dk gray | 45 | 45 |
| 69 | A5 | 9p violet | 80 | 80 |

**Size: 21x27mm**

| No. | Design | Description | Unused | Used |
|---|---|---|---|---|
| 70 | A5 | 1sh blk & brn org | 90 | 90 |
| 71 | A5 | 2sh6p grn & blk | 2.50 | 2.50 |
| 72 | A5 | 5sh vio & gray | 4.50 | 4.50 |
| 73 | A5 | 10sh blk & grn | 7.25 | 7.25 |
| 74 | A5 | 20sh rose lil & red | 18.00 | 18.00 |
| | | *Nos. 61-74 (14)* | 35.72 | 35.72 |

**Perf. 14½**

**1963, Dec. 1 Unwmk. Photo.**

**Size: 23x19mm**

**Arms in Black, Blue and Orange**

| No. | Design | Description | Unused | Used |
|---|---|---|---|---|
| 75 | A6 | ½p vio & blk | 10 | 8 |
| a. | | Value omitted | 300.00 | |
| 76 | A6 | 1p bl & blk | 15 | 10 |
| a. | | Value omitted | 11.50 | |
| 77 | A6 | 2p brn & blk | 15 | 10 |
| 78 | A6 | 3p org & blk | 18 | 12 |
| a. | | Bklt. pane of 4 | 1.00 | |
| b. | | Value omitted | 90.00 | |
| 79 | A6 | 4p grn & blk | 22 | 18 |
| a. | | Value omitted | 100.00 | |
| 80 | A6 | 6p yel grn & blk | 25 | 22 |
| a. | | Value omitted | 175.00 | |
| 81 | A6 | 9p ocher & blk | 45 | 35 |
| a. | | Value omitted | 150.00 | |
| 82 | A6 | 1sh dk gray & blk | 40 | 40 |
| a. | | Value omitted | | |
| 83 | A6 | 1sh3p brt red lil & blk | 1.00 | 90 |

**Perf. 13**

**Size: 27x23mm**

| No. | Design | Description | Unused | Used |
|---|---|---|---|---|
| 84 | A6 | 2sh dp org & blk | 1.10 | 1.00 |
| 85 | A6 | 2sh6p mar & blk | 1.50 | 1.50 |
| 86 | A6 | 5sh dk car rose & blk | 3.00 | 2.75 |
| 87 | A6 | 10sh brt pink & blk | 6.00 | 5.00 |
| 88 | A6 | 20sh dk bl & blk | 14.00 | 12.50 |
| a. | | Value omitted | 1,000. | |
| | | *Nos. 75-88 (14)* | 28.50 | 25.20 |

Stamps of Northern Rhodesia were replaced by those of Zambia, starting Oct. 24, 1964.

---

**POSTAGE DUE STAMPS**

D1

**1929 Typo. Wmk. 4 Perf. 14**

| No. | Design | Description | Unused | Used |
|---|---|---|---|---|
| J1 | D1 | 1p black | 2.25 | 3.75 |
| a. | | Wmk. 4a (error) | 110.00 | |
| J2 | D1 | 2p black | 3.25 | 6.50 |
| J3 | D1 | 3p black | 8.25 | 22.50 |
| a. | | Wmk. 4a (error) | 150.00 | |
| J4 | D1 | 4p black | 9.00 | 25.00 |

**Catalogue values for unused stamps in this section, from this point to the end of the section, are for Never Hinged items.**

*North West Pacific Islands stamps can be mounted in Scott's Australia and Dependencies Album.*

D2

**1964 Unwmk. Litho. Perf. 12½**

| No. | Design | Description | Unused | Used |
|---|---|---|---|---|
| J5 | D2 | 1p orange | 40 | 1.00 |
| J6 | D2 | 2p dark blue | 80 | 2.00 |
| J7 | D2 | 3p rose claret | 1.25 | 2.50 |
| J8 | D2 | 4p violet blue | 2.00 | 4.00 |
| J9 | D2 | 6p purple | 3.00 | 6.00 |
| J10 | D2 | 1sh emerald | 4.00 | 8.00 |
| | | *Nos. J5-J10 (#)* | * | * |

## NORTH WEST PACIFIC ISLANDS

LOCATION — A group of islands in the West Pacific Ocean including a part of New Guinea and adjacent islands of the Bismarck Archipelago.

GOVT. — Australian military government.

AREA — 96,160 sq. mi.

POP. — 636,563.

Stamps of Australia were overprinted for use in the former German possessions of Nauru and German New Guinea which Australian troops had captured. Following the League of Nations' decision which placed these territories under mandate to Australia, these provisional issues were discontinued. See German New Guinea, New Britain, Nauru and New Guinea.

12 Pence = 1 Shilling
20 Shillings = 1 Pound

Stamps of Australia Overprinted **N. W. PACIFIC ISLANDS**

There are two varieties of the letter "S" in the overprint: variety a, normal "S"; variety b, "S" with small head and long bottom stroke. Three combinations of these letters are found in the word "Islands": I, both are variety a; II, varieties b and a; III, both are variety b.

**1915-16 Wmk. 8 Perf. 12**

| No. | Design | Description | Unused | Used |
|---|---|---|---|---|
| 1 | A1 | 2p gray | 7.00 | 11.00 |
| 2 | A1 | 2½p dk bl | 1.65 | 1.90 |
| 3 | A1 | 3p ol bis | 5.50 | 6.00 |
| 4 | A1 | 6p ultra | 22.50 | 25.00 |
| 5 | A1 | 9p violet | 11.50 | 12.00 |
| 6 | A1 | 1sh bl grn | 22.50 | 25.00 |
| 8 | A1 | 5sh yel & gray | 650.00 | 650.00 |
| 9 | A1 | 10sh pink & gray | 90.00 | 130.00 |
| | | Revenue cancel | | 27.50 |
| 10 | A1 | £1 ultra & brn | 600.00 | 650.00 |
| | | *Nos. 1-6,8-10 (9)* | 1,410. | 1,510. |

**Wmk. Wide Crown and Narrow A. (9)**

**Perf. 12, 14**

| No. | Design | Description | Unused | Used |
|---|---|---|---|---|
| 11 | A4 | ½p emerald | 90 | 1.10 |
| a. | | Double overprint | | |
| 12 | A4 | 1p car (Die I) | 90 | 1.10 |
| a. | | 1p car rose (Die I) | 1.40 | 1.40 |
| b. | | 1p car (Die Ia) | 125.00 | 125.00 |
| 13 | A1 | 2p gray | 11.00 | 15.00 |
| 14 | A1 | 2½p dk bl | 7,000. | 7,000. |
| 16 | A4 | 4p orange | 3.25 | 3.75 |
| 17 | A4 | 5p org brn | 3.00 | 3.50 |
| 18 | A1 | 6p ultra | 6.50 | 6.75 |
| 19 | A1 | 9p violet | 4.50 | 4.75 |
| 20 | A1 | 1sh bl grn | 6.50 | 6.75 |
| 21 | A1 | 2sh brown | 80.00 | 85.00 |
| 22 | A1 | 5sh yel & gray | 80.00 | 85.00 |
| | | *Nos. 11-13,16-22 (10)* | 196.55 | 212.70 |

For description of the dies of No. 12 see Australia.

**1915-19 Wmk. 10**

| No. | Design | Description | Unused | Used |
|---|---|---|---|---|
| 27 | A1 | 2p gray | 2.50 | 2.75 |
| 28 | A1 | 2½p dk bl | 4.00 | 4.00 |
| a. | | "1" of fraction omitted | 7,000. | 8,000. |
| 29 | A1 | 3p ol bis | 4.00 | 4.00 |
| 32 | A1 | 6p ultra | 4.75 | 5.00 |
| 33 | A1 | 9p violet | 9.50 | 10.50 |
| 34 | A1 | 1sh bl grn | 4.25 | 4.50 |
| 35 | A1 | 2sh brown | 21.00 | 24.00 |
| 36 | A1 | 5sh yel & gray | 47.50 | 47.50 |
| 37 | A1 | 10sh pink & gray | 150.00 | 175.00 |
| 38 | A1 | £1 ultra & brn | 250.00 | 275.00 |
| | | *Nos. 27-29,32-38 (10)* | 497.50 | 552.25 |

Nos. 6 and 17 Surcharged **One Penny**

**1918 Wmk. 8 Perf. 12**

| No. | Design | Description | Unused | Used |
|---|---|---|---|---|
| 39 | A1 | 1p on 1sh bl grn | 100.00 | 80.00 |

**Wmk. Wide Crown and Narrow A. (9)**

**Perf. 14**

| No. | Design | Description | Unused | Used |
|---|---|---|---|---|
| 40 | A4 | 1p on 5p org brn | 100.00 | 80.00 |

**1919 Wmk. 11**

| No. | Design | Description | Unused | Used |
|---|---|---|---|---|
| 41 | A4 | ½p emerald | 50 | 50 |

**1921-22 Wmk. 9**

| No. | Design | Description | Unused | Used |
|---|---|---|---|---|
| 42 | A4 | 1p violet | 2.50 | 2.75 |
| 43 | A4 | 2p orange | 5.25 | 5.50 |
| 44 | A4 | 2p red | 3.50 | 3.75 |
| 45 | A4 | 4p violet | 25.00 | 30.00 |
| 46 | A4 | 4p lt ultra | 14.00 | 21.00 |
| | | *Nos. 42-46 (5)* | 50.25 | 63.00 |

North West Pacific Islands stamps were largely used in New Britain. Some were used in Nauru. They were intended to serve the Bismarck Archipelago and other places.

## NOVA SCOTIA

LOCATION — On the eastern coast of Canada between the Gulf of St. Lawrence and the Atlantic Ocean.

GOVT. — A former British Crown Colony.

AREA — 21,428 sq. mi.

POP. — 386,500 (1871)

CAPITAL — Halifax.

Nova Scotia joined the Canadian Confederation in 1867 and is now a province of the Dominion. Postage stamps of Canada are used.

12 Pence = 1 Shilling
100 Cents = 1 Dollar (1860)

Values of Nova Scotia stamps vary according to condition. Quotations for Nos. 1-7 are for fine copies. Very fine to superb specimens sell at much higher prices, and inferior or poor copies sell at reduced prices, depending on the condition of the individual specimen.

Queen Victoria — A1

Crown of Great Britain and Heraldic Flowers of the Empire — A2

**1851-53 Unwmk. Engr. Imperf.**

**Blue Paper**

| No. | Design | Description | Unused | Used |
|---|---|---|---|---|
| 1 | A1 | 1p red brn ('53) | 1,150. | 125.00 |
| a. | | Half used as ½p on cover | | |
| 2 | A2 | 3p blue | 400.00 | 75.00 |
| a. | | Half used as 1½p on cover | | 2,500. |
| 3 | A2 | 3p dark blue | 600.00 | 50.00 |
| a. | | Half used as 1½p on cover | | 2,500. |
| 4 | A2 | 6p yellow green | 2,500. | 175.00 |
| a. | | Half used as 3p on cover | | 3,500. |
| 5 | A2 | 6p dark green | 4,500. | 300.00 |
| a. | | Half used as 3p on cover | | 5,000. |
| 6 | A2 | 1sh reddish vio | 15,500. | 1,500. |
| a. | | Half used as 6p on cover | | 30,000. |
| 7 | A2 | 1sh dull violet | 14,000. | 1,500. |

*Reprints are on thin hard white paper. 1p in brown, 3p in blue, 6p dark green, 1sh violet black. Value about $300 per set.*

*No. 6 was reproduced by the collotype process in a souvenir sheet distributed at the London International Stamp Exhibition 1950.*

*Nova Scotia stamps can be mounted in Scott's Canada Specialty and Master Canada Albums.*

Queen Victoria — A3

A5 A6

**1860-63** *Perf. 12*

**White or Yellowish Paper**

| No. | Type | Description | Unused | Used |
|---|---|---|---|---|
| 8 | A3 | 1c black | 2.75 | 2.75 |
| a. | | White paper | 2.75 | 2.75 |
| b. | | Half used as ½c on cover | | 5,000. |
| c. | | Imperf. vertically (pair) | 125.00 | |
| 9 | A3 | 2c lilac | 3.25 | 2.75 |
| a. | | Yellowish paper | 3.25 | 3.00 |
| b. | | Half used as 1c on cover | | 2,500. |
| 10 | A3 | 5c blue | 175.00 | 2.75 |
| a. | | Yellowish paper | 225.00 | 3.50 |
| b. | | Half used as 2½c on cover | | |
| 11 | A5 | 8½c green | 2.75 | 6.00 |
| a. | | White paper | 2.75 | 6.00 |
| 12 | A5 | 10c vermilion | 3.50 | 3.50 |
| a. | | Yellowish paper | 3.25 | 3.25 |
| b. | | Half used as 5c on cover | | 1,000. |
| 13 | A6 | 12½c black | 11.75 | 11.50 |
| a. | | White paper | 11.75 | 11.50 |
| | | *Nos. 8-13 (6)* | 199.00 | 29.25 |

The stamps of Nova Scotia were replaced by those of Canada.

## NYASALAND PROTECTORATE

LOCATION — In southern Africa, bordering on Lake Nyasa.
GOVT. — British Protectorate
AREA — 49,000 sq. mi.
POP. — 2,950,000 (est. 1962)
CAPITAL — Zomba

For previous issues, see British Central Africa.

Nyasaland joined the Federation of Rhodesia and Nyasaland in 1953, using its stamps until 1963. As the Federation began to dissolve in 1963, Nyasaland withdrew its postal services and issued provisional stamps. On July 6, 1964, Nyasaland became the independent state of Malawi.

12 Pence = 1 Shilling
20 Shillings = 1 Pound

**Catalogue values for unused stamps in this country are for Never Hinged items, beginning with Scott 68 in the regular postage section and Scott J1 in the postage due section.**

King Edward VII
A1 A2

**Wmk. Crown and C. A. (2)**

**1908, July 22** **Typo.** *Perf. 14*

**Chalky Paper**

| No. | Type | Description | Unused | Used |
|---|---|---|---|---|
| 1 | A1 | 1sh blk, *green* | 2.00 | 4.50 |

**Wmk. Multiple Crown and C. A. (3)**

**Ordinary Paper**

| No. | Type | Description | Unused | Used |
|---|---|---|---|---|
| 2 | A1 | ½p green | 30 | 28 |
| 3 | A1 | 1p carmine | 60 | 15 |

**Chalky Paper**

| No. | Type | Description | Unused | Used |
|---|---|---|---|---|
| 4 | A1 | 3p vio, *yel* | 1.25 | 2.00 |
| 5 | A1 | 4p scar & blk, *yel* | 1.50 | 2.00 |
| 6 | A1 | 6p red vio & vio | 3.00 | 4.75 |
| 7 | A2 | 2sh 6p car & blk, *bl* | 21.00 | 24.00 |
| 8 | A2 | 4sh blk & car | 27.50 | 35.00 |
| 9 | A2 | 10sh red & grn, *grn* | 45.00 | 65.00 |
| 10 | A2 | £1 blk & vio, *red* | 250.00 | 275.00 |
| 11 | A2 | £10 ultra & lil | 10,000. | 12,500. |
| | | *Nos. 1-10 (10)* | 352.15 | 412.68 |

King George V
A3 A4

**1913-18**

**Ordinary Paper**

| No. | Type | Description | Unused | Used |
|---|---|---|---|---|
| 12 | A3 | ½p green | 35 | 30 |
| 13 | A3 | 1p scarlet | 40 | 18 |
| a. | | 1p car | 65 | 18 |
| 14 | A3 | 2p gray | 1.25 | 24 |
| 15 | A3 | 2½p ultra | 50 | 60 |

**Chalky Paper**

| No. | Type | Description | Unused | Used |
|---|---|---|---|---|
| 16 | A3 | 3p vio, *yel* | 1.50 | 1.50 |
| 17 | A3 | 4p scar & blk, *yel* | 1.25 | 1.50 |
| 18 | A3 | 6p red vio & dl vio | 1.50 | 1.75 |
| 19 | A3 | 1sh *green* | 1.65 | 1.50 |
| a. | | 1sh *emer* | 1.10 | 1.10 |
| b. | | 1sh *bl grn*, ol back | 1.25 | 1.25 |
| 20 | A4 | 2sh6p red & blk, *bl* ('18) | 10.50 | 13.00 |
| 21 | A4 | 4sh blk & red ('18) | 16.00 | 18.00 |
| 22 | A4 | 10sh red & grn, *grn* | 65.00 | 65.00 |
| 23 | A4 | £1 blk & vio, *red* ('18) | 92.50 | 95.00 |
| 24 | A4 | £10 ultra & dl vio ('14) | 5,250. | 4,500. |
| | | Revenue cancel | | 250.00 |
| | | *Nos. 12-23 (12)* | 192.40 | 198.57 |

Stamps of Nyasaland Protectorate overprinted "N. F." are listed under German East Africa.

**1921-30** **Wmk. 4**

**Ordinary Paper**

| No. | Type | Description | Unused | Used |
|---|---|---|---|---|
| 25 | A3 | ½p green | 30 | 12 |
| 26 | A3 | 1p rose red | 32 | 12 |
| 27 | A3 | 1½p orange | 6.50 | 10.00 |
| 28 | A3 | 2p gray | 65 | 30 |

**Chalky Paper**

| No. | Type | Description | Unused | Used |
|---|---|---|---|---|
| 29 | A3 | 3p vio, *yel* | 2.00 | 65 |
| 30 | A3 | 4p scar & blk, *yel* | 1.65 | 1.65 |
| 31 | A3 | 6p red vio & dl vio | 2.50 | 2.75 |
| 32 | A3 | 1sh blk, *grn* ('30) | 5.00 | 4.00 |
| 33 | A4 | 2sh ultra & dl vio, *bl* | 6.50 | 10.00 |
| 34 | A4 | 2sh6p red & blk, *bl* ('24) | 10.00 | 11.50 |
| 35 | A4 | 4sh blk & car | 6.50 | 8.25 |
| 36 | A4 | 5sh red & grn, *yel* ('29) | 20.00 | 27.50 |
| 37 | A4 | 10sh red & grn, *emer* | 82.50 | 100.00 |
| | | *Nos. 25-37 (13)* | 144.42 | 176.84 |

George V and Leopard — A5

**1934-35** **Engr.** *Perf. 12½.*

| No. | Type | Description | Unused | Used |
|---|---|---|---|---|
| 38 | A5 | ½p green | 18 | 18 |
| 39 | A5 | 1p dk brn | 18 | 18 |
| 40 | A5 | 1½p rose | 55 | 55 |
| 41 | A5 | 2p gray | 75 | 55 |
| 42 | A5 | 3p dk bl | 1.50 | 1.50 |
| 43 | A5 | 4p rose lil ('35) | 2.50 | 2.50 |
| 44 | A5 | 6p dk vio | 3.00 | 3.00 |
| 45 | A5 | 9p ol bis ('35) | 3.75 | 5.75 |
| 46 | A5 | 1sh org & blk | 3.75 | 3.75 |
| | | *Nos. 38-46 (9)* | 16.16 | 17.96 |

**Silver Jubilee Issue**

Common Design Type

**1935, May 6** *Perf. 11x12*

| No. | Type | Description | Unused | Used |
|---|---|---|---|---|
| 47 | CD301 | 1p gray blk & ultra | 35 | 35 |
| 48 | CD301 | 2p ind & grn | 1.90 | 1.10 |
| 49 | CD301 | 3p ultra & brn | 2.50 | 4.25 |
| 50 | CD301 | 1sh brn vio & ind | 7.75 | 8.50 |

**Coronation Issue**

Common Design Type

**1937, May 12** *Perf. 11x11½*

| No. | Type | Description | Unused | Used |
|---|---|---|---|---|
| 51 | CD302 | ½p dp grn | 12 | 12 |
| 52 | CD302 | 1p dk brn | 16 | 16 |
| 53 | CD302 | 2p gray blk | 32 | 32 |

A6

King George VI — A7

**1938-44** **Engr.** *Perf. 12½*

| No. | Type | Description | Unused | Used |
|---|---|---|---|---|
| 54 | A6 | ½p green | 9 | 7 |
| 54A | A6 | ½p dk brn ('42) | 9 | 9 |
| 55 | A6 | 1p dk brn | 12 | 9 |
| 55A | A6 | 1p grn ('42) | 14 | 7 |
| 56 | A6 | 1½p dk car | 45 | 75 |
| 56A | A6 | 1½p gray ('42) | 12 | 12 |
| 57 | A6 | 2p gray | 55 | 22 |
| 57A | A6 | 2p dk car ('42) | 12 | 12 |
| 58 | A6 | 3p blue | 18 | 15 |
| 59 | A6 | 4p rose lil | 18 | 18 |
| 60 | A6 | 6p dk vio | 22 | 22 |
| 61 | A6 | 9p ol bis | 38 | 75 |
| 62 | A6 | 1sh org & blk | 52 | 45 |

**Typo.**

*Perf. 14*

**Chalky Paper**

| No. | Type | Description | Unused | Used |
|---|---|---|---|---|
| 63 | A7 | 2sh ultra & dl vio, *bl* | 75 | 75 |
| 64 | A7 | 2sh6pred & blk, *bl* | 95 | 95 |
| 65 | A7 | 5sh red & grn, *yel* | 16.00 | 15.00 |
| a. | | 5sh dk red & dp grn, *yel* ('44) | 37.50 | 20.00 |
| 66 | A7 | 10sh red & grn, *grn* | 13.00 | 11.00 |

**Wmk. 3**

| No. | Type | Description | Unused | Used |
|---|---|---|---|---|
| 67 | A7 | £1 blk & vio, *red* | 16.00 | 15.00 |
| | | *Nos. 54-67 (18)* | 49.86 | 45.98 |

**Catalogue values for unused stamps in this section, from this point to the end of the section, are for Never Hinged items.**

Canoe on Lake Nyasa — A8

Soldier of King's African Rifles — A9

Tea Estate, Mlanje Mountain A10

Map and Coat of Arms — A11

Fishing Village, Lake Nyasa — A12

Tobacco Estate — A13

Arms of Nyasaland and George VI A14

**1945, Sept. 1** **Engr.** *Perf. 12*

| No. | Type | Description | Unused | Used |
|---|---|---|---|---|
| 68 | A8 | ½p brn vio & blk | 10 | 8 |
| 69 | A9 | 1p dp grn & blk | 15 | 12 |
| 70 | A10 | 1½p gray grn & blk | 18 | 12 |
| 71 | A11 | 2p scar & blk | 15 | 12 |
| 72 | A12 | 3p bl & blk | 25 | 15 |
| 73 | A13 | 4p rose vio & blk | 50 | 40 |
| 74 | A10 | 6p vio & blk | 50 | 35 |
| 75 | A8 | 9p ol grn & blk | 75 | 1.40 |
| 76 | A11 | 1sh myr grn & ind | 55 | 40 |
| 77 | A12 | 2sh dl red brn & grn | 1.75 | 1.40 |
| 78 | A13 | 2sh6p ultra & grn | 2.00 | 1.65 |
| 79 | A14 | 5sh ultra & lt vio | 3.00 | 3.50 |
| 80 | A11 | 10sh grn & lake | 5.50 | 5.00 |
| 81 | A14 | 20sh blk & scar | 12.50 | 20.00 |
| | | *Nos. 68-81 (14)* | 27.88 | 34.69 |

**Peace Issue**

Common Design Type

*Perf. 13½x14*

**1946, Dec. 16** **Wmk. 4**

| No. | Type | Description | Unused | Used |
|---|---|---|---|---|
| 82 | CD303 | 1p brt grn | 20 | 20 |
| 83 | CD303 | 2p red org | 25 | 25 |

A15

**1947, Oct. 20** *Perf. 12*

| No. | Type | Description | Unused | Used |
|---|---|---|---|---|
| 84 | A15 | 1p emer & org brn | 25 | 10 |

**Silver Wedding Issue**

Common Design Types

**1948, Dec. 15** **Photo.** *Perf. 14x14½*

| No. | Type | Description | Unused | Used |
|---|---|---|---|---|
| 85 | CD304 | 1p dk grn | 15 | 10 |

**Engr.; Name Typo.**

*Perf. 11½x11.*

| No. | Type | Description | Unused | Used |
|---|---|---|---|---|
| 86 | CD305 | 10sh purple | 11.50 | 10.50 |

**UPU Issue**

Common Design Types

**Engr.; Name Typo. on 3p, 6p**

*Perf. 13½, 11x11½*

**1949, Nov. 21** **Wmk. 4**

| No. | Type | Description | Unused | Used |
|---|---|---|---|---|
| 87 | CD306 | 1p bl grn | 14 | 14 |
| 88 | CD307 | 3p Prus bl | 45 | 45 |
| 89 | CD308 | 6p rose vio | 1.40 | 90 |
| 90 | CD309 | 1sh vio bl | 2.25 | 2.75 |

Arms of British Central Africa and Nyasaland Protectorate — A16

**1951, May 15** **Engr.** *Perf. 11x12*

**Arms in Black**

| No. | Type | Description | Unused | Used |
|---|---|---|---|---|
| 91 | A16 | 2p rose | 16 | 16 |
| 92 | A16 | 3p blue | 24 | 24 |
| 93 | A16 | 6p purple | 40 | 80 |
| 94 | A16 | 5sh dp bl | 2.50 | 3.50 |

60th anniv. of the Protectorate, established in 1891 under the name British Central Africa.

Exhibition Seal — A17

**1953, May 30** *Perf. 14x13½*
95 A17 6p purple 42 40

Central African Rhodes Cent. Exhib.

### Coronation Issue
Common Design Type

**1953, June 2** *Perf. 13½x13*
96 CD312 2p org & blk 22 22

Types of 1945-47 with Portrait of Queen Elizabeth II and

Grading Cotton A18

**1953-54** *Perf. 12*
97 A8 ½p red brn & blk 9 9
a. Booklet pane of 4 60
b. Perf. 12x12½ ('54) 8 8
98 A15 1p emer & org brn 10 10
a. Booklet pane of 4 70
99 A10 1½p gray grn & blk 18 18
100 A11 2p org & blk 15 15
a. Booklet pane of 4 1.00
b. Perf. 12x12½ ('54) 15 15
101 A18 2½p blk & brt grn 15 18
102 A13 3p scar & blk 24 24
103 A12 4½p bl & blk 42 42
104 A10 6p vio & blk 45 45
a. Booklet pane of 4 3.00
b. Perf. 12x12½ ('54) 45 45
105 A8 9p ol & blk 70 1.65
106 A11 1sh myr grn & ind 85 85
107 A12 2sh rose brn & grn 1.50 1.50
108 A13 2sh6p ultra & grn 2.00 2.00
109 A14 5sh Prus bl & rose lil 3.00 3.00
110 A11 10sh grn & lake 6.75 7.75
111 A14 20sh blk & scar 10.50 12.50
*Nos. 97-111 (15)* 27.08 31.06

Revenue Stamps Overprinted "POSTAGE" and Bars in Black

Arms of Nyasaland A19

*Perf. 11½x12*
**1963, Nov. 1** **Engr.** **Unwmk.**
112 A19 ½p on 1p bl 8 8
113 A19 1p green 8 8
114 A19 2p rose red 12 12
115 A19 3p dk bl 24 20
116 A19 6p rose lake 38 38
117 A19 9p on 1sh car rose 50 50
118 A19 1sh purple 52 52
119 A19 2sh6p black 1.00 1.00
120 A19 5sh brown 1.40 1.40
121 A19 10sh gray ol 3.50 3.50
122 A19 £1 violet 6.25 6.25
*Nos. 112-122 (11)* 14.07 14.03

Nos. 112, 117 have 3 bars over old value.

Mother and Child — A20

Designs: 1p, Chambo fish. 2p, Zebu bull. 3p, Peanuts. 4p, Fishermen in boat. 6p, Harvesting tea. 1sh, Lumber and tropical pine branch. 1sh3p, Tobacco industry. 2sh6p, Cotton industry. 5sh, Monkey Bay, Lake Nyasa. 10sh, Afzelia tree (pod mahogany). £1, Nyala antelope (vert.).

*Perf. 14½*
**1964, Jan. 1** **Unwmk.** **Photo.**
**Size: 23x19mm**
123 A20 ½p lilac 9 9
124 A20 1p grn & blk 14 10
125 A20 2p red brn 18 15
126 A20 3p pale brn, brn red & grn 22 14
127 A20 4p org yel & ind 28 28
**Size: 41½x25mm, 25x41½mm**
128 A20 6p bl pur & brt yel grn 35 32
129 A20 1sh yel brn & dk grn 70 70
130 A20 1sh3p red brn & ol 75 70
131 A20 2sh6p bl & brn 1.40 1.40
132 A20 5sh grn, bl, sep & yel 2.00 2.00
133 A20 10sh org brn grn & gray 3.50 3.50
134 A20 £1 yel & dk brn 6.75 6.75
*Nos. 123-134 (12)* 16.36 16.13

Stamps of Malawi replaced those of Nyasaland Protectorate starting July 6, 1964.

### POSTAGE DUE STAMPS.

**Catalogue values for unused stamps in this section, from this point to the end of the section, are for Never Hinged items.**

D1

**Wmk. 4**
**1950, July 1** **Typo.** *Perf. 14*
J1 D1 1p rose red 2.75 *5.50*
J2 D1 2p ultramarine 6.50 *12.00*
J3 D1 3p green 10.00 *12.00*
J4 D1 4p claret 18.00 *40.00*
J5 D1 6p ocher 27.50 *52.50*
*Nos. J1-J5 (5)* 64.75 122.00

# OMAN
## (Muscat and Oman)

LOCATION — In the southeastern corner of the Arabian Peninsula.
GOVT. — Sultanate.
AREA — 105,000 sq. mi.
POP. — 1,500,000 (est. 1982).
CAPITAL — Muscat.

Nos. 16-93, the stamps with "value only" surcharges, were used not only in Muscat, but also in Dubai (April 1, 1948, to January 6, 1961), Qatar (August 1950 to March 31, 1957), Abu Dhabi (March 30, 1963, to March 29, 1964). Occasionally they also were used in Bahrain and Kuwait.

The Sultanate of Muscat and Oman changed its name to Oman in 1970.

12 Pies = 1 Anna
16 Annas = 1 Rupee
100 Naye Paise = 1 Rupee (1957)
64 Baizas = 1 Rupee (1966)
1000 Baizas = 1 Rial Saidi (1970)

**Catalogue values for all unused stamps in this country are for Never Hinged items.**

### Muscat

Stamps of India 1937-43 Overprinted in Black

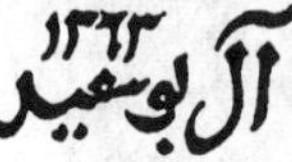

**Wmk. Multiple Stars (196)**
**1944, Nov. 20** *Perf. 13½x14*
1 A83 3p slate 5 5
2 A83 ½a rose vio 10 10
3 A83 9p lt grn 10 10
4 A83 1a car rose 10 10
5 A84 1½a dk pur 16 16
a. Double ovpt. 400.00
6 A84 2a scarlet 30 30
7 A84 3a violet 38 38
8 A84 3½a ultra 38 38
9 A85 4a chocolate 45 45
10 A85 6a pck bl 60 60
11 A85 8a bl vio 90 90
12 A85 12a car lake 1.25 1.25
13 A81 14a rose vio 1.25 1.25
14 A82 1r brn & sl 2.50 2.50
15 A82 2r dk brn & dk vio 4.00 4.00
*Nos. 1-15 (15)* 12.52 12.52

200th anniv. of Al Busaid Dynasty. On Nos. 1-13 the overprint is smaller—13x6mm.

Great Britain, Nos. 258 to 263, 243, 248, 249A Surcharged

*Perf. 14½x14*
**1948, Apr. 1** **Wmk. 251**
16 A101 ½a on ½p grn 10 10
17 A101 1a on 1p ver 20 20
18 A101 1½a on 1½p lt red brn 40 40
19 A101 2a on 2p lt org 52 52
20 A101 2½a on 2½p ultra 60 60
21 A101 3a on 3p vio 20 20
22 A102 6a on 6p rose lil 48 28
23 A103 1r on 1sh brn 1.90 1.60

**Wmk. 259** *Perf. 14*
24 A104 2r on 2sh6p yel grn 17.50 17.50
*Nos. 16-24 (9)* 21.90 21.40

### Silver Wedding Issue
Great Britain, Nos. 267 and 268, Surcharged with New Value in Black,
*Perf. 14½x14, 14x14½.*
**1948, Apr. 26** **Wmk. 251**
25 A109 2½a on 2½p brt ultra 15 15
26 A110 15r on £1 dp chlky bl 35.00 45.00

Three bars obliterate the original denomination on No. 26.

### Olympic Games Issue
Great Britain, Nos. 271 to 274, Surcharged with New Value in Black
**1948, July 29** *Perf. 14½x14*
27 A113 2½a on 2½p brt ultra 25 18
28 A114 3a on 3p dp vio 30 22
29 A115 6a on 6p red vio 45 38
30 A116 1r on 1sh dk brn 1.10 75
a. Double surcharge 300.00

A square of dots obliterates the original denomination on Nos. 28 to 30.

### UPU Issue
Great Britain Nos. 276 to 279 Surcharged with New Value and Square of Dots in Black
**1949, Oct. 10** **Photo.**
31 A117 2½a on 2½p brt ultra 30 30
32 A118 3a on 3p brt vio 50 50
33 A119 6a on 6p red vio 85 85
34 A120 1r on 1sh brn 1.50 1.50

Great Britain Nos. 280-286 Surcharged with New Value in Black
**1951**
35 A101 ½a on ½p lt org 30 30
36 A101 1a on 1p ultra 45 45
37 A101 1½a on 1½p grn 1.75 1.75
38 A101 2a on 2p lt red brn 90 90
39 A101 2½a on 2½p ver 1.75 1.75
40 A102 4a on 4p ultra 1.50 1.50

*Perf. 11x12*
**Wmk. 259**
41 A121 2r on 2sh 6p grn 17.50 17.50
*Nos. 35-41 (7)* 24.15 24.15

Stamps of Great Britain, 1952-54, Surcharged with New Value in Black and Dark Blue
**1952-54** **Wmk. 298** *Perf. 14½x14*
42 A126 ½a on ½p red org ('53) 8 8
43 A126 1a on 1p ultra ('53) 10 10
44 A126 1½a on 1½p grn ('52) 12 12
45 A126 2a on 2p red brn ('53) 20 20
46 A127 2½a on 2½p scar ('52) 25 25
47 A127 3a on 3p dk pur (Dk Bl) 28 28
48 A128 4a on 4p ultra ('53) 45 45
49 A129 6a on 6p lil rose 60 45
50 A132 12a on 1sh 3p dk grn ('53) 1.60 1.40
51 A131 1r on 1sh 6p dk bl ('53) 2.00 1.60
*Nos. 42-51 (10)* 5.68 4.93

### Coronation Issue
Great Britain Nos. 313-316 Surcharged with New Value in Black
**1953, June 10**
52 A134 2½a on 2½p scar 30 30
53 A135 4a on 4p brt ultra 50 50
54 A136 12a on 1sh 3p dk grn 1.50 1.50
55 A137 1r on 1sh 6p dk bl 1.75 1.75

Squares of dots obliterate the original denominations on Nos. 54 and 55.

Great Britain Stamps of 1955-56 Surcharged with New Value in Black
*Perf. 14½x14*
**1955-57** **Wmk. 308** **Photo.**
56 A126 1a on 1p ultra ('57) 35 35
56A A126 1½a on 1½p grn ('56) *800.00*
57 A126 2a on 2p red brn ('56) 55 55
58 A127 2½a on 2½p scar 85 85
59 A127 3a on 3p dk pur ('57) 1.25 1.25
60 A128 4a on 4p ultra ('56) 1.75 1.75
61 A129 6a on 6p lil rose ('57) 1.00 1.00
62 A131 1r on 1sh 6p dk bl ('56) 1.40 1.40

**Engr.** *Perf. 11x12*
63 A133 2r on 2sh 6p dk brn 8.50 8.50
64 A133 5r on 5sh crim ('57) 15.00 15.00
*Nos. 56,57-64 (9)* 30.65 30.65

Surcharge on No. 63 exists in three types, on No. 64 in two types.

Great Britain Nos. 317-325, 328, 332 Surcharged with New Value in Black
**1957, Apr. 1** *Perf. 14½x14*
65 A129 1np on 5p lt brn 5 5
66 A126 3np on ½p red org 15 15
67 A126 6np on 1p ultra 35 35
68 A126 9np on 1½p grn 70 70
69 A126 12np on 2p red brn 50 50
70 A127 15np on 2½p scar, type I 80 80
a. Type II 60 60
71 A127 20np on 3p dk pur 30 30
72 A128 25np on 4p ultra 60 60
73 A129 40np on 6p lil rose 80 80
74 A130 50np on 9p dp ol grn 80 80
75 A132 75np on 1sh 3p dk grn 1.25 1.25
*Nos. 65-75 (11)* 6.30 6.30

The arrangement of the surcharge varies on different values; there are three bars through value on No. 74.

### Jubilee Jamboree Issue
Great Britain Nos. 334-336 Surcharged with New Value and Square of Dots in Black
*Perf. 14½x14*
**1957, Aug. 1** **Wmk. 308**
76 A138 15np on 2½p scar 50 50
77 A138 25np on 4p ultra 75 75
78 A138 75np on 1sh3p dk grn 90 90

50th anniv. of the Boy Scout movement and the World Scout Jubilee Jamboree, Aug. 1-12.

Great Britain Stamps of 1958-60 Surcharged with New Value in Black
*Perf. 14½x14*
**1960-61** **Wmk. 322** **Photo.**
79 A129 1np on 5p lt brn 5 5
80 A126 3np on ½p red org 90 90
81 A126 5np on 1p ultra ('61) 15 10
82 A126 6np on 1p ultra 1.60 1.60
83 A126 10np on 1½p grn ('61) 40 25
84 A126 12np on 2p red brn 2.75 2.75
85 A127 15np on 2½p scar 28 28
86 A127 20np on 3p dk pur 28 28
87 A128 30np on 4½p hn brn ('61) 65 60
88 A129 40np on 6p lil rose 55 55
89 A130 50np on 9p dp ol grn ('61) 80 65
90 A132 75np on 1sh3p dk grn ('61) 1.40 1.10
91 A131 1r on 1sh6p dk bl ('61) 1.65 1.40
92 A133 2r on 2sh6p dk brn ('61) 6.00 5.00
93 A133 5r on 5sh crim ('61) 14.00 12.00
*Nos. 79-93 (15)* 31.46 27.51

## Muscat and Oman

Crest — A1

View of Harbor — A2

Nakhal Fort — A3

Designs (Crest and): 50b, Samail Fort. 1r, Sohar Fort. 2r, Nizwa Fort. 5r, Matrah Fort. 10r, Mirani Fort.

***Perf. 14½x14 (A1), 14x14½ (A2), 14x13½ (A3)***

**1966, Apr. 29 — Photo. — Unwmk.**

| No. | Type | Description | Unused | Used |
|---|---|---|---|---|
| *94* | A1 | 3b plum | 5 | 5 |
| *95* | A1 | 5b brown | 5 | 5 |
| *96* | A1 | 10b red brn | 15 | 12 |
| *97* | A2 | 15b blk & vio | 28 | 20 |
| *98* | A2 | 20b blk & ultra | 40 | 25 |
| *99* | A2 | 25b blk & org | 48 | 32 |
| *100* | A3 | 30b dk bl & lil rose | 65 | 45 |
| *101* | A3 | 50b red brn & brt grn | 1.00 | 60 |
| *a.* | | Value in "baizas" in Arabic | 18.00 | 9.50 |
| *102* | A3 | 1r org & dk bl | 2.00 | 1.10 |
| *103* | A3 | 2r grn & brn org | 4.00 | 2.25 |
| *104* | A3 | 5r dp car & vio | 10.00 | 6.50 |
| *105* | A3 | 10r dk vio & car rose | 16.00 | 14.00 |
| | | *Nos. 94-105 (12)* | 35.06 | 25.89 |

No. 101 has value in rupees in Arabic.

Mina al Fahal Harbor A4

Designs: 25b, Oil tanks. 40b, Oil installation in the desert. 1r, View of Arabian Peninsula from Gemini IV.

***Perf. 13½x13***

**1969, Jan. 1 — Litho. — Unwmk.**

| No. | Type | Description | Unused | Used |
|---|---|---|---|---|
| *106* | A4 | 20b multi | 80 | 60 |
| *107* | A4 | 25b multi | 1.00 | 75 |
| *108* | A4 | 40b multi | 1.60 | 1.25 |
| *109* | A4 | 1r multi | 4.00 | 3.00 |

Issued to commemorate the first oil shipment from Muscat and Oman, July, 1967.

### Types of 1966

Designs: 50b, Nakhal Fort. 75b, Samail Fort. 100b, Sohar Fort. ¼r, Nizwa Fort. ½r, Matrah Fort. 1r, Mirani Fort.

***Perf. 14½x14 (A1), 14x14½ (A2), 14x13½ (A3)***

**1970, June 27 — Photo. — Unwmk.**

| No. | Type | Description | Unused | Used |
|---|---|---|---|---|
| *110* | A1 | 5b plum | 5 | 5 |
| *111* | A1 | 10b brown | 12 | 8 |
| *112* | A1 | 20b red brn | 28 | 15 |
| *113* | A2 | 25b blk & vio | 35 | 20 |
| *114* | A2 | 30b blk & ultra | 40 | 28 |
| *115* | A2 | 40b blk & org | 55 | 38 |
| *116* | A3 | 50b dk bl & lil rose | 75 | 45 |
| *117* | A3 | 75b red brn & brt grn | 1.00 | 65 |
| *118* | A3 | 100b org & dk bl | 1.40 | 95 |
| *119* | A3 | ¼r grn & brn org | 4.00 | 2.75 |
| *120* | A3 | ½r brn car & vio | 8.50 | 5.50 |
| *121* | A3 | 1r dk vio & car rose | 16.50 | 11.00 |
| | | *Nos. 110-121 (12)* | 33.90 | 22.44 |

## Sultanate of Oman

Nos. 110-121 Overprinted

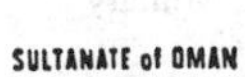

a

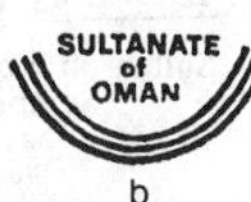

b

c

***Perf. 14½x14, 14x14½, 14x13½***

**1971, Jan. 16 — Photo. — Unwmk.**

| No. | Type | Description | Unused | Used |
|---|---|---|---|---|
| *122* | A1 (a) | 5b plum | 5 | 5 |
| *123* | A1 (a) | 10b brown | 16 | 10 |
| *124* | A1 (a) | 20b red brn | 32 | 20 |
| *125* | A2 (b) | 25b blk & vio | 40 | 25 |
| *126* | A2 (b) | 30b blk & ultra | 50 | 32 |
| *127* | A2 (b) | 40b blk & org | 65 | 50 |
| *128* | A3 (c) | 50b dk bl & lil rose | 85 | 55 |
| *129* | A3 (c) | 75b red brn & brt grn | 1.20 | 80 |
| *130* | A3 (c) | 100b org & dk bl | 1.60 | 1.10 |
| *131* | A3 (c) | ¼r grn & brn org | 5.00 | 3.25 |
| *132* | A3 (c) | ½r brn car & vio | 10.00 | 6.50 |
| *133* | A3 (c) | 1r dk vio & car rose | 20.00 | 14.00 |
| | | *Nos. 122-133 (12)* | 40.73 | 27.62 |

Two types of overprint on 5b, 10b and 20b: 1. Lower bars 15¼mm. long; letter "A" has low, thick crossbar. 2. Lower bars 14¾mm.; "A" crossbar high, thin.

No. 94 Surcharged Type "a", Nos. 127, 102 Surcharged

***Perf. 14½x14, 14x14½, 14½x13½***

**1971-72**

| No. | Type | Description | Unused | Used |
|---|---|---|---|---|
| *133A* | A1 | 5b on 3b plum | 7.00 | 4.00 |
| *133B* | A2 | 25b on 40b blk & org ('72) | 9.00 | 5.00 |
| *133C* | A3 | 25b on 1r org & dk bl ('72) | 11.00 | 6.00 |

No. 133C surcharge resembles type "c" with "Sultanate of Oman" omitted and bars of crisscross lines.

Sultan Qaboos bin Said and New Buildings — A5

National Day: 40b, Sultan Qaboos and freedom symbols. 50b, Crest of Oman and health clinic. 100b, Crest of Oman, classrooms and school.

**1971, July 23 — Litho. — *Perf. 13½x14***

| No. | Type | Description | Unused | Used |
|---|---|---|---|---|
| *134* | A5 | 10b multi | 1.40 | 20 |
| *135* | A5 | 40b multi | 1.40 | 50 |
| *136* | A5 | 50b multi | 1.75 | 75 |
| *137* | A5 | 100b multi | 3.25 | 1.25 |

Open Book A6

**1972, Jan. 3 — *Perf. 14x14½***

| No. | Type | Description | Unused | Used |
|---|---|---|---|---|
| *138* | A6 | 25b ap grn, dk bl & dk red | 3.50 | 2.00 |

International Book Year, 1972.

View of Muscat, 1809 A7

Designs: 5, 10, 20, 25b, View of Matrah, 1809. 30, 40, 50, 75b, View of Shinas, 1809.

**Wmk. 314 Sideways**

**1972, July 23 — Litho. — *Perf. 14x14½***

**Size: 21x17mm**

| No. | Type | Description | Unused | Used |
|---|---|---|---|---|
| *139* | A7 | 5b tan & multi | 5 | 5 |
| *140* | A7 | 10b bl & multi | 14 | 8 |
| *141* | A7 | 20b gray grn & multi | 30 | 18 |
| *142* | A7 | 25b vio & multi | 40 | 22 |

***Perf. 14½x14***

**Size: 25x21mm**

| No. | Type | Description | Unused | Used |
|---|---|---|---|---|
| *143* | A7 | 30b tan & multi | 50 | 30 |
| *144* | A7 | 40b gray bl & multi | 65 | 35 |
| *145* | A7 | 50b rose brn & multi | 90 | 48 |
| *146* | A7 | 75b ol & multi | 1.40 | 75 |

***Perf. 14***

**Size: 46x25mm**

| No. | Type | Description | Unused | Used |
|---|---|---|---|---|
| *147* | A7 | 100b lil & multi | 1.50 | 80 |
| *148* | A7 | ¼r grn & multi | 3.00 | 1.65 |
| *149* | A7 | ½r bis & multi | 5.75 | 3.25 |
| *150* | A7 | 1r dl bl grn & multi | 12.00 | 6.25 |
| | | *Nos. 139-150 (12)* | 26.59 | 14.36 |

***Perf. 14x14½, 14½x14***

**1972-75 — Wmk. 314 Upright**

| No. | Type | Description | Unused | Used |
|---|---|---|---|---|
| *139a* | A7 | 5b tan & multi ('75) | 5 | 5 |
| *140a* | A7 | 10b bl & multi ('75) | 60 | 35 |
| *141a* | A7 | 20b gray grn & multi ('75) | 1.10 | 65 |
| *142a* | A7 | 25b vio & multi ('75) | 1.50 | 90 |
| *143a* | A7 | 30b tan & multi | 2.00 | 1.20 |
| *144a* | A7 | 40b bl & multi | 2.50 | 1.50 |
| *145a* | A7 | 50b rose brn & multi | 3.00 | 1.75 |
| *146a* | A7 | 75b ol & multi | 5.00 | 3.00 |
| | | *Nos. 139a-146a (8)* | 15.75 | 9.40 |

***Perf. 14x14½, 14½x14, 14***

**1975-82 — Wmk. 373**

| No. | Type | Description | Unused | Used |
|---|---|---|---|---|
| *139b* | A7 | 5b tan & multi | 5 | 5 |
| *140b* | A7 | 10b bl & multi | 25 | 25 |
| *141b* | A7 | 20b gray grn & multi ('82) | 35 | 25 |
| *142b* | A7 | 25b vio & multi | 40 | 25 |
| *143b* | A7 | 30b tan & multi | 45 | 30 |
| *144b* | A7 | 40b bl & multi | 65 | 45 |
| *145b* | A7 | 50b rose brn & multi | 75 | 50 |
| *146b* | A7 | 75b ol & multi | 1.20 | 75 |
| *147b* | A7 | 100b lil & multi | 1.65 | 1.10 |
| *148a* | A7 | ¼r grn & multi | 4.00 | 2.50 |
| *149a* | A7 | ½r bis & multi | 7.50 | 5.00 |
| *150a* | A7 | 1r dl bl grn & multi | 15.00 | 10.00 |
| | | *Nos. 139b-150a (12)* | 32.25 | 21.40 |

Ministerial Complex — A8

**Litho.; Date Typo.**

**1973, Sept. 20 — Unwmk. — *Perf. 13***

| No. | Type | Description | Unused | Used |
|---|---|---|---|---|
| *151* | A8 | 25b emer & multi | 1.00 | 50 |
| *152* | A8 | 100b brn org & multi | 3.50 | 1.75 |

Opening of ministerial complex.

Nos. 151-152 exist with date omitted and hyphen omitted.

Dhows — A9

***Perf. 12½x12***

**1973, Nov. 18 — Litho. — Wmk. 314**

| No. | Type | Description | Unused | Used |
|---|---|---|---|---|
| *153* | A9 | 15b *shown* | 55 | 35 |
| *154* | A9 | 50b *Seeb Airport* | 2.00 | 1.40 |
| *155* | A9 | 65b *Dhow and tanker* | 2.75 | 1.75 |
| *156* | A9 | 100b *Camel rider* | 3.75 | 2.50 |

National Day.

Port Qaboos — A10

**1974, July 30 — Litho. — *Perf. 13***

| No. | Type | Description | Unused | Used |
|---|---|---|---|---|
| *157* | A10 | 100b multi | 4.00 | 3.00 |

Opening of Port Qaboos.

Open Book, Map of Arab World A11

Design: 100b, Hands reaching for book (vert.).

**1974, Sept. 8 — Wmk. 314 — *Perf. 14½***

| No. | Type | Description | Unused | Used |
|---|---|---|---|---|
| *158* | A11 | 25b multi | 75 | 50 |
| *159* | A11 | 100b multi | 2.50 | 1.75 |

International Literacy Day, Sept. 8.

Sultan Qaboos, UPU and Arab Postal Union Emblems — A12

**1974, Oct. 29 — Litho. — *Perf. 13½***

| No. | Type | Description | Unused | Used |
|---|---|---|---|---|
| *160* | A12 | 100b multi | 2.00 | 1.25 |

Centenary of Universal Postal Union.

Old Man Learning to Write A13

**1975, May 8 — Photo. — *Perf. 13x14***

| No. | Type | Description | Unused | Used |
|---|---|---|---|---|
| *161* | A13 | 15b multi | 4.00 | 3.00 |

Eradication of illiteracy.

New Harbor at Mina Raysoot — A14

Designs: 50b, Stadium and map of Oman. 75b, Water desalination plant. 100b, Oman color television station. 150b, Satellite earth station and map. 250b, Telephone, radar, cable and map.

***Perf. 14x13½***

**1975, Nov. 18 — Litho. — Wmk. 373**

| No. | Type | Description | Unused | Used |
|---|---|---|---|---|
| *162* | A14 | 30b multi | 30 | 16 |
| *163* | A14 | 50b multi | 55 | 30 |
| *164* | A14 | 75b multi | 85 | 45 |
| *165* | A14 | 100b multi | 1.10 | 60 |
| *166* | A14 | 150b multi | 1.90 | 95 |
| *167* | A14 | 250b multi | 3.00 | 1.60 |
| | | *Nos. 162-167 (6)* | 7.70 | 4.06 |

National Day 1975.

Mother with Child, Nurse, Globe, Red Crescent, IWY Emblem — A15

Design: 150b, Hand shielding mother and children, Omani flag, IWY emblem (vert.).

*Perf. 13½x14, 14x13½*

**1975, Dec. 27** **Litho.**

*168* A15 75b cit & multi 1.00 75
*169* A15 150b ultra & multi 2.00 1.40

International Women's Year 1975.

Sultan Presenting Colors and Opening Seeb-Nizwa Road — A16

National Day: 40b, Paratroopers bailing out from plane and mechanized harvester. 75b, Helicopter squadron and Victory Day procession. 150b, Army building road and Salalah television station.

**1976, Nov. 15** **Litho.** ***Perf. 14½***

*173* A16 25b multi 50 25
*174* A16 40b multi 70 45
*175* A16 75b multi 1.20 80
*176* A16 150b multi 2.00 1.75

Great Bath at Mohenjo-Daro — A17

**1977, Jan. 6** **Wmk. 373** ***Perf. 13½***

*177* A17 125b multi 3.00 2.00

UNESCO campaign to save Mohenjo-Daro excavations in Pakistan.

APU Emblem, Members' Flags A18

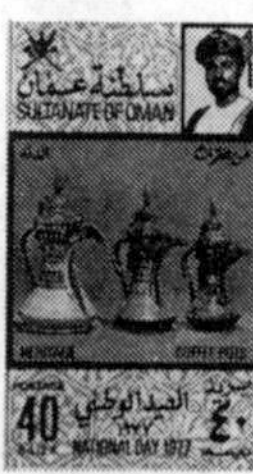


Coffeepots A19

**1977, Apr. 4** **Litho.** ***Perf. 12***

*178* A18 30b emer & multi 1.00 60
*179* A18 75b bl & multi 2.75 1.60

Arab Postal Union, 25th anniversary.

**1977, Nov. 18** **Litho.** ***Perf. 13½***

Designs: 75b, Earthenware. 100b, Stone tablet, Khor Rori, 100 B.C. 150b, Jewelry.

*180* A19 40b multi 45 32
*181* A19 75b multi 85 65
*182* A19 100b multi 1.10 80
*183* A19 150b multi 1.75 1.25

National Day 1977.

Forts A20

**Wmk. 373**

**1978, Nov. 18** **Litho.** ***Perf. 14***

*184* A20 20b Jalali 25 16
*185* A20 25b Nizwa 35 25
*186* A20 40b Rostaq 55 40
*187* A20 50b Sohar 70 45
*188* A20 75b Bahla 1.00 70
*189* A20 100b Jibrin 1.40 90
*Nos. 184-189 (6)* 4.25 2.86

National Day 1978.

Pilgrims, Mt. Arafat, Holy Kaaba A21

**1978, Nov. 1** **Litho.** ***Perf. 13½***

*190* A21 40b multi 2.00 1.50

Pilgrimage to Mecca.

Nos. 166, 169 and 167 Surcharged.

***Perf. 14x13½***

**1978** **Litho.** **Wmk. 373**

*190A* A14 40b on 150b #166 15.00 15.00
*190B* A15 50b on 150b #169 17.50 17.50
*190C* A14 75b on 250b #167 27.50 27.50

World Map, Book, Symbols of Learning A22

**1979, Mar. 22** **Litho.** ***Perf. 14x13½***

*191* A22 40b multi 65 45
*192* A22 100b multi 1.60 1.10

Cultural achievements of the Arabs.

Girl on Swing, IYC Emblem A23

**1979, Oct. 28** **Litho.** ***Perf. 14***

*193* A23 40b multi 2.75 1.75

International Year of the Child.

Gas Plant A24

National Day: 75b, Fisheries.

**1979, Nov. 18** **Photo.** ***Perf. 11½***

*194* A24 25b multi 1.25 55
*195* A24 75b multi 1.75 1.60

Sultan on Horseback, Military Symbols — A25

Design: 100b, Soldier, parachutes, tank.

**1979, Dec. 11**

*196* A25 40b multi 2.25 1.10
*197* A25 100b multi 3.75 2.75

Armed Forces Day.

Hegira (Pilgrimage Year) — A26

**1980, Nov. 9** **Photo.** ***Perf. 11½***

*198* A26 50b *shown* 75 55
*199* A26 150b *Hegira emblem* 2.50 1.75

Omani Women — A27

**1980, Nov. 18**

**Granite Paper**

*200* A27 75b *Bab Alkabir* 55 42
*201* A27 100b *Corniche Highway* 75 55
*202* A27 250b *Polo match* 1.90 1.40
*203* A27 500b *shown* 3.50 2.75

10th National Day.

Sultan and Patrol Boat — A28

**1980, Dec. 11**

**Granite Paper**

*204* A28 150b *shown* 2.00 1.50
*205* A28 750b *Sultan, mounted troops* 10.00 6.50

Armed Forces Day.

Policewoman and Children Crossing Street — A29

**1981, Feb. 7** **Litho.** ***Perf. 13½x14***

*206* A29 50b *shown* 45 28
*207* A29 100b *Marching band* 80 55
*208* A29 150b *Mounted police on beach* 1.25 85
*209* A29 ½r *Headquarters* 4.25 2.80

First National Police Day.

Nos. 204-205, 200, 203 Surcharged in Black on Silver.

**1981, Apr. 8** **Photo.** ***Perf. 11½***

*210* A28 20b on 150b multi 70 40
*211* A28 30b on 750b multi 1.00 60
*212* A27 50b on 75b multi 1.75 90
*213* A27 100b on 500b multi 3.00 1.75

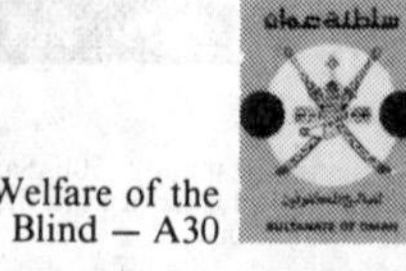


Welfare of the Blind — A30

**1981, Oct. 14** **Photo.** ***Perf. 11½***

*214* A30 10b multi 60 10

World Food Day — A31

**1981, Oct. 16** **Photo.** ***Perf. 12***

*215* A31 50b multi 1.75 75

Hegira (Pilgrimage Year) — A32

**1981, Oct. 25** **Litho.** ***Perf. 14½***

*216* A32 50b multi 1.75 75

11th Natl. Day — A32a

**1981, Nov. 18** **Photo.** ***Perf. 12***

*216A* A32a 160b Al-Razha match (sword vs. stick) 1.40 1.00
*216B* A32a 300b Sultan, map, vert. 2.50 1.90

Voyage of Sinbad — A33

**1981, Nov. 23** **Litho.** ***Perf. 14½x14***

*217* A33 50b Muscat Port, 1981 55 35
*218* A33 100b Dhow Shohar 1.10 75
*219* A33 130b Map 1.40 1.00
*220* A33 200b Muscat Harbor, 1650 2.25 1.50
*a* Souvenir sheet of 4 7.00 4.50

No. 220a contains Nos. 217-220; multicolored margin shows map of voyage. Size: 173x130mm.

Armed Forces Day — A34

**1981, Dec. 11 Photo. *Perf. 11½***
*221* A34 100b Sultan, planes 1.50 80
*222* A34 400b Patrol boats 6.00 3.50

Natl. Police Day A35

**1982, Jan. 5 Litho. *Perf. 14½***
*223* A35 50b Patrol launch 80 55
*224* A35 100b Band, vert. 1.60 1.10

Nerium Mascatense A36

Red-legged Partridge A37

**1982, July 7 Photo. *Perf. 12½***
**Granite Paper**
*225* A36 5b shown 5 5
*226* A36 10b Dionysia mira 5 5
*227* A36 20b Teucrium mascatense 12 12
*228* A36 25b Geranium mascatense 14 14
*229* A36 30b Cymatium boschi, horiz. 18 18
*230* A36 40b Acteon eloiseae, horiz. 24 24
*231* A36 50b Cypraea teulerei, horiz. 28 28
*232* A36 75b Cypraea pulchra, horiz. 42 42
*233* A37 100b shown 55 55
*234* A37 ¼r Hoopoe 1.40 1.40
**Size: 25x38mm**
*235* A37 ½r Tahr 2.80 2.80
*236* A37 1r Arabian oryx 5.50 5.50
*Nos. 225-236 (12)* 11.73 11.73

2nd Municipalities Week (1981) — A38

***Perf. 13½x14½***
**1982, Oct. 28 Litho.**
*237* A38 40b multi 1.25 65

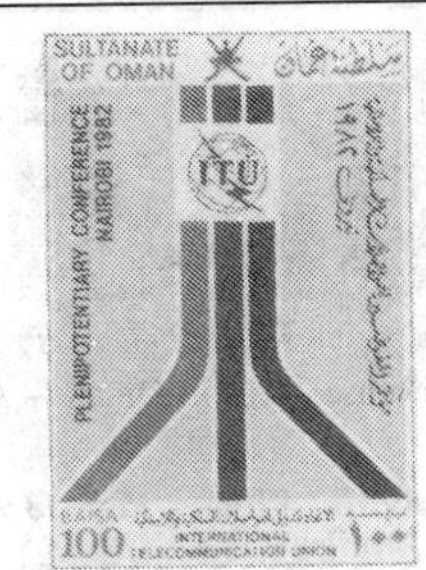


ITU Plenipotentiaries Conference, Nairobi, Sept. — A39

**1982, Nov. 6 *Perf. 14½x13½***
*238* A39 100b multi 1.50 75

12th Natl. Day A40

**1982, Nov. 18 *Perf. 12***
*239* A40 40 State Consultative Council inaugural session 55 38
*240* A40 100b Oil refinery 1.25 80

Armed Forces Day A41

**1982, Dec. 11 *Perf. 13½x14***
*241* A41 50b Soldiers 75 45
*242* A41 100b Mounted band 1.50 90

Arab Palm Tree Day — A42

***Perf. 13½x14½***
**1982, Sept. 19 Litho.**
*243* A42 40b Picking coconuts 75 38
*244* A42 100b Dates 1.75 90

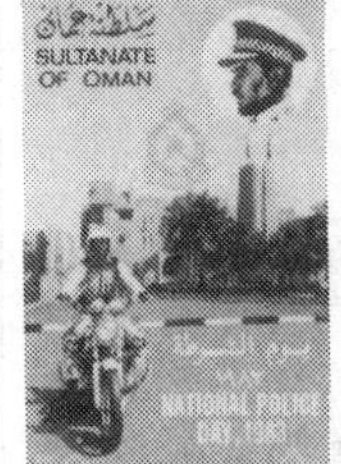


Natl. Police Day — A43

**1983, Jan. 5 Litho. *Perf. 14x13½***
*245* A43 50b multi 1.50 75

World Communications Year — A44

**1983, May 17 *Perf. 13½x14***
*246* A44 50b multi 1.50 75

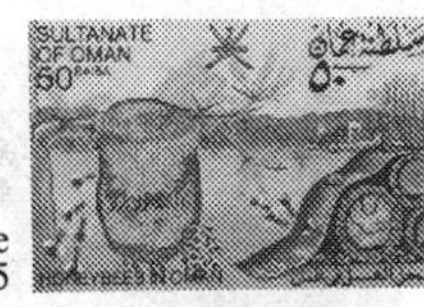


Beehive A45

**1983, Aug. 15 Litho. *Perf. 13½***
*247* Strip of 2 1.50 1.00
*a.-b.* A45 50b. any single 75 50

Hegira (Pilgrimage Year) — A46

**1983, Sept. 14 Photo. *Perf. 13½***
*248* A46 40b multi 1.50 75

Youth Year — A47

***Perf. 12½x13½***
**1983, Nov. 15 Litho.**
*249* A47 50b multi 1.25 65

National Day 1983 — A48

**1983, Nov. 18 Litho. *Perf. 13½x14***
*250* A48 50b Sohar Copper Factory 90 40
*251* A48 100b Sultan Qaboos University 1.60 80

Armed Forces Day A49

**1983, Dec. 11 Litho. *Perf. 13½x14***
*252* A49 100b multi 1.25 65

Police Day A50

**1984, Jan. 5 Litho. *Perf. 13½x14***
*253* A50 100b multi 1.25 65

7th Arabian Gulf Soccer Tournament, Muscat, Mar. 9-26 — A51

**1984, Mar. 9 Litho. *Perf. 13½***
*254* A51 40b Players, cup, vert. 50 22
*255* A51 50b Emblem 65 38

Pilgrims at Stone-Throwing Ceremony — A52

**1984, Sept. 5 Litho. *Perf. 13½x14***
*256* A52 50b multi 75 50

Pilgrimage to Mecca.

National Day 1984 — A53

***Perf. 13½x14, 14x13½***
**1984, Nov. 18 Litho.**
*257* A53 130b Mail sorting, new p.o. 1.40 70
*258* A53 160b Map, vert. 1.60 80

Inauguration of the new Central P.O., development of telecommunications.

16th Arab Scout Conference, Muscat — A54

**1984, Dec. 5 Litho. *Perf. 14½***
*259* A54 50b Setting-up camp 50 50
*260* A54 50b Map reading 50 50
*261* A54 130b Saluting natl. flag 1.25 1.25
*262* A54 130b Scouts and girl guides 1.25 1.25

Stamps of the same denomination printed se-tenant.

Armed Forces Day A55

**1984, Dec. 11** *Perf. 13½x14*
263 A55 100b multi 1.00 60

Police Day — A56

**1985, Jan. 5** *Perf. 14x13½*
264 A56 100b multi 1.25 60

Hegira (Pilgrimage Year) — A57

**1985, Aug. 20 Litho.** *Perf. 13½x14*
265 A57 50b Al-Khaif Mosque, Mina 75 50

Intl. Youth Year A58

**1985, Sept. 22 Litho.** *Perf. 13½x14*
266 A58 50b Emblems 55 28
267 A58 100b Emblem, youth activities 1.00 52

Jabrin Palace Restoration — A59

**1985, Sept. 22 Litho.** *Perf. 13½x14*
268 A59 100b Interior 75 75
269 A59 250b Restored ceiling 2.25 2.00

Intl. Symposium on Traditional Music — A60

**1985, Oct. 6 Litho.** *Perf. 13½x14*
270 A60 50b multi 75 50

UN Child Survival Campaign — A61

**1985, Oct. 25 Litho.** *Perf. 13½x14*
271 A61 50b multi 75 50

Flags, Map and Sultan Qaboos — A62

**1985, Nov. 3 Litho.** *Perf. 12½*
272 A62 40b shown 50 30
273 A62 50b Supreme Council, vert. 60 35

6th Session of Arab Gulf States Supreme Council, Muscat.

Natl. Day 1985 — A63

Progress and development. 20b, Sultan Qaboos University. 50b, Date picking, plowing field. 100b, Port Qaboos Cement Factory. 200b, Post, transportation and communications. 250b, Sultan Qaboos, vert.

**1985, Nov. 18**

| | | | | |
|---|---|---|---|---|
| 274 | A63 | 20b multi | 15 | 12 |
| 275 | A63 | 50b multi | 40 | 30 |
| 276 | A63 | 100b multi | 80 | 58 |
| 277 | A63 | 200b multi | 1.50 | 1.15 |
| 278 | A63 | 250b multi | 1.90 | 1.40 |
| | | *Nos. 274-278 (5)* | 4.75 | 3.55 |

Armed Forces Day A64

**1985, Dec. 11** *Perf. 13½x14*
279 A64 100b multi 1.00 65

Fish and Crustaceans — A65

*Perf. 11½x12, 12x11½*

**1985, Dec. 15** **Photo.**

| | | | | |
|---|---|---|---|---|
| 280 | A65 | 20b Chaetodon collaris | 15 | 15 |
| 281 | A65 | 50b Chaetodon melapterus | 45 | 40 |
| 282 | A65 | 100b Chaetodon gardineri | 85 | 75 |
| 283 | A65 | 150b Scomberomorus commerson | 1.25 | 1.10 |
| 284 | A65 | 200b Panulirus homarus | 1.65 | 1.50 |
| | | *Nos. 280-284 (5)* | 4.35 | 3.90 |

Nos. 280-282, vert.

Frankincense Trees in Oman — A66

**1985, Dec. 15 Litho.** *Perf. 13½x14*
285 A66 100b multi 65 52
286 A66 3r multi 20.00 15.60

Police Day A67

**1986, Jan. 5 Litho.** *Perf. 13½x14*
287 A67 50b Camel Corps, Muscat 50 30

Statue of Liberty, Cent. A68

Maps and: 50b, Sultanah, voyage from Muscat to US 1840. 100b, Statue, Shabab Oman voyage from Oman to US, 1986, and fortress.

**1986, July 4** *Perf. 14½*
288 A68 50b multi 40 30
289 A68 100b multi 80 60
a Souv. sheet of 2, #288-289 2.00 1.50

No. 289a has multicolored decorative margin picturing portraits of Sultans Qaboos of Oman and Said Bin, maps, eastern and western architecture, tea posts and navigational instruments. Sold for 250b. Size: 162x127mm.

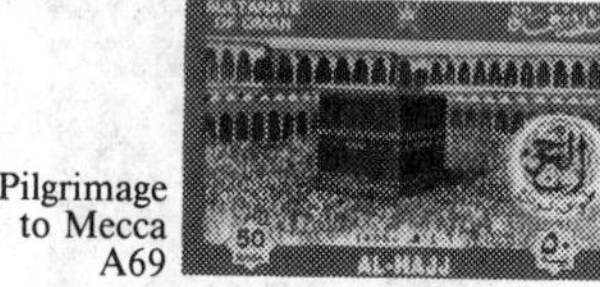

Pilgrimage to Mecca A69

**1986, Aug. 9**
290 A69 50b Holy Kaaba 50 30

17th Arab Scout Camp — A70

**1986, Aug. 20**
291 A70 50b Erecting tent 40 30
292 A70 100b Surveying 80 60

Sultan Qaboos Sports Complex Inauguration — A71

**1986, Oct. 18 Litho.** *Perf. 14½*
293 A71 100b multi 90 60

Intl. Peace Year A72

**1986, Oct. 24** *Perf. 13½x13*
294 A72 130b multi 1.10 80

A73

A74

Natl. Day 1986 — A75

**1986, Nov. 18** *Perf. 14½*
295 A73 50b mutli 30 30
296 A74 100b multi 60 60

*Perf. 13½x13*

297 A75 130b multi 2.00 80

Police Day A76

**1987, Jan. 5** *Perf. 13½x14*
298 A76 50b multi 40 30

Second Arab Gulf Week for Social Work, Bahrain — A77

**1987, Mar. 21 Litho.** *Perf. 13½x13*
299 A77 50b multi 40 25

Intl. Environment Day — A78

**Perf. 13½x13, 13x13½**

**1987, June 5** **Litho.**

| | | | | |
|---|---|---|---|---|
| 300 | A78 | 50b Flamingos in flight | 35 | 28 |
| 301 | A78 | 130b Irrigation canal, vert. | 85 | 68 |

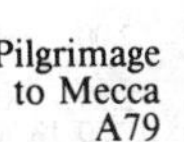

Pilgrimage to Mecca A79

Stages of Pilgrimage (not in consecutive order): a, Pilgrims walking the tawaf, circling the Holy Kaaba 7 times. b, Tent City, Mina. c, Symbolic stoning of Satan. d, Pilgrims in Muzdalifah at dusk, picking up stones. e, Veneration of the prophet (pilgrims praying), Medina. f, Pilgrims wearing ihram, Pilgrim's Village, Jeddah.

**1987, July 29** **Litho.** **Perf. 13½**

| | | | |
|---|---|---|---|
| 302 | Strip of 6 | 2.40 | 1.80 |
| a.-f. | A79 50b any single | 40 | 30 |

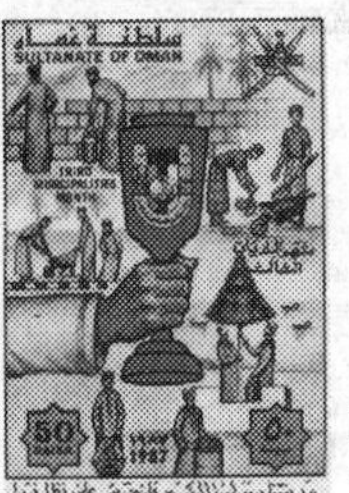
Third Municipalities Month — A80

**1987, Oct. 1** **Perf. 13x13½**

| | | | | |
|---|---|---|---|---|
| 303 | A80 | 50b multi | 40 | 30 |

Natl. Day A81

Designs: 50b, Marine Biology and Fisheries Center. 130b, Royal Hospital.

**1987, Nov. 18** **Litho.** **Perf. 13½x13**

| | | | | |
|---|---|---|---|---|
| 304 | A81 | 50b multi | 26 | 26 |
| 305 | A81 | 130b multi | 68 | 68 |

Royal Omani Amateur Radio Soc., 15th Anniv. — A82

**1987, Dec. 23** **Litho.** **Perf. 13½x13**

| | | | | |
|---|---|---|---|---|
| 306 | A82 | 130b multi | 78 | 78 |

Traditional Handicrafts — A83

**1988, June 1** **Photo.** **Perf. 12x11½**
**Granite Paper**

| | | | | |
|---|---|---|---|---|
| 307 | A83 | 50b Weaver | 25 | 25 |
| 308 | A83 | 100b Potter | 52 | 52 |
| 309 | A83 | 150b Halwa maker | 78 | 78 |
| 310 | A83 | 200b Silversmith | 1.05 | 1.05 |
| a. | | Souv. Sheet of 4, Nos 307-310 | 3.25 | 3.25 |

No. 310a has multicolored decorative margin picturing craftsmen. Sold for 600b.

1988 Summer Olympics, Seoul — A84

**1988, Sept. 17** **Litho.** **Perf. 14½**

| | | | | |
|---|---|---|---|---|
| 311 | A84 | 100b Equestrian | 52 | 52 |
| 312 | A84 | 100b Field hockey | 52 | 52 |
| 313 | A84 | 100b Soccer | 52 | 52 |
| 314 | A84 | 100b Running | 52 | 52 |
| 315 | A84 | 100b Swimming | 52 | 52 |
| 316 | A84 | 100b Shooting | 52 | 52 |
| a. | | Block of 6, Nos. 311-316 | 3.15 | 3.15 |
| b. | | Souv. sheet of 6, Nos. 311-316 | 3.75 | 3.75 |
| | | *Nos. 311-316 (6)* | 3.12 | 3.12 |

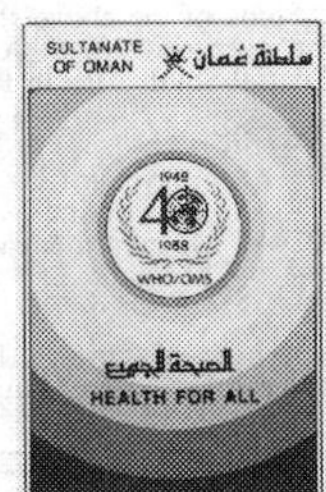
WHO, 40th Anniv. — A85

**1988, Nov. 1** **Litho.** **Perf. 13½**

| | | | | |
|---|---|---|---|---|
| 317 | A85 | 100b multi | 52 | 52 |

Natl. Day, Agriculture Year — A86

**Perf. 14½x13½**

**1988, Nov. 18** **Litho.**

| | | | | |
|---|---|---|---|---|
| 318 | A86 | 100b Tending crops | 52 | 52 |
| 319 | A86 | 100b Animal husbandry | 52 | 52 |

Printed se-tenent in a continuous design.

Prices of premium quality never hinged stamps will be in excess of catalogue price.

## SEMI-POSTAL STAMP

UNICEF Emblem, Girl with Book — SP1

**Wmk. 314**

**1971, Dec. 25** **Litho.** **Perf. 14**

| | | | | |
|---|---|---|---|---|
| B1 | SP1 | 50b + 25b multi | 5.75 | 3.50 |

25th anniv. of UNICEF.

## OFFICIAL STAMPS

Official Stamps of India 1938-43 Overprinted in Black

**Perf. 13½x14**

**1944, Nov. 20** **Wmk. 196**

| | | | | |
|---|---|---|---|---|
| O1 | O8 | 3p slate | 5 | 5 |
| O2 | O8 | ½a dk rose vio | 5 | 5 |
| O3 | O8 | 9p green | 12 | 8 |
| O4 | O8 | 1a car rose | 15 | 10 |
| O5 | O8 | 1½a dl pur | 25 | 16 |
| O6 | O8 | 2a scarlet | 30 | 20 |
| O7 | O8 | 2½a purple | 35 | 25 |
| O8 | O8 | 4a dk brn | 40 | 28 |
| O9 | O8 | 8a bl vio | 70 | 48 |
| O10 | A82 | 1r brn & sl | 1.60 | 1.10 |
| | | *Nos. O1-O10 (10)* | 3.97 | 2.75 |

Issued to commemorate the 200th anniversary of the Al Busaid Dynasty. On Nos. O1-O9 the overprint is smaller—13x6mm.

# ORANGE RIVER COLONY

## (Orange Free State)

LOCATION — In South Africa, north of the Cape of Good Hope between the Orange and Vaal Rivers.
GOVT. — A former British Crown Colony.
AREA — 49,647 sq. mi.
POP. — 528,174 (1911).
CAPITAL — Bloemfontein.

Orange Free State was an independent republic, 1854-1900. Orange River Colony existed from May, 1900, to June, 1910, when it united with Cape of Good Hope, Natal and the Transvaal to form the Union of South Africa.

12 Pence = 1 Shilling

### Issues of the Republic.

Orange Tree — A1

**1868-1900** **Unwmk.** **Typo.** **Perf. 14**

| | | | | |
|---|---|---|---|---|
| 1 | A1 | ½p red brn ('83) | 52 | 35 |
| 2 | A1 | ½p org ('97) | 45 | 35 |
| 3 | A1 | 1p brown | 1.25 | 12 |
| 4 | A1 | 1p vio ('94) | 30 | 10 |
| 5 | A1 | 2p vio ('83) | 1.40 | 28 |
| 6 | A1 | 3p ultra ('83) | 2.25 | 1.25 |
| 7 | A1 | 4p ultra ('78) | 6.75 | 1.25 |
| 8 | A1 | 6p car rose ('90) | 1.50 | 85 |
| a. | | 6p rose ('68) | 7.00 | 3.00 |
| b. | | 6p ultramarine ('00) | 75.00 | |
| 10 | A1 | 1sh orange | 3.50 | 90 |
| a. | | 1sh orange buff | 7.75 | 4.00 |
| 11 | A1 | 1sh brn ('97) | 2.75 | 2.00 |
| 12 | A1 | 5sh grn ('78) | 9.00 | 6.50 |
| | | *Nos. 1-8,10-12 (11)* | 29.67 | 13.95 |

No. 8b was not placed in use without surcharge.

No. 8a Surcharged in Black:

**4** *a* **4** *b* **4** *c* **4** *d*

**1877**

| | | | |
|---|---|---|---|
| 13 | (a) 4p on 6p rose | 70.00 | 21.00 |
| a. | Invtd. surcharge | *1,000.* | 500.00 |
| b. | Double surcharge, one inverted ("a" and "c") | | 1,000. |
| 14 | (b) 4p on 6p rose | 1,000. | 125.00 |
| a. | Invtd. surcharge | *1,400.* | 600.00 |
| b. | Double surcharge, one inverted ("b" and "d") | *1,500.* | 750.00 |
| 15 | (c) 4p on 6p rose | 42.50 | 15.00 |
| a. | Invtd. surcharge | *500.00* | 225.00 |
| 16 | (d) 4p on 6p rose | 52.50 | 24.00 |
| a. | Invtd. surcharge | *750.00* | 375.00 |

No. 12 Surcharged in Black with Bar and:

**1d.** *f* **1d.** *g* **1d.** *h* **1d.** *i* **1d.** *k*

**1881**

| | | | |
|---|---|---|---|
| 17 | (f) 1p on 5sh grn | 20.00 | 6.00 |
| 18 | (g) 1p on 5sh grn | 13.00 | 8.50 |
| a. | Invtd. surcharge | 425.00 | 350.00 |
| b. | Double surcharge | | 350.00 |
| 19 | (h) 1p on 5sh grn | 9.00 | 9.00 |
| a. | Inverted surch. | 350.00 | 325.00 |
| b. | Double surcharge | 350.00 | 325.00 |
| 20 | (i) 1p on 5sh grn | 12.00 | 4.75 |
| a. | Double surcharge | *725.00* | 350.00 |
| b. | Inverted surch. | 450.00 | 380.00 |
| 21 | (k) 1p on 5sh grn | 75.00 | 75.00 |
| a. | Inverted surcharge | 650.00 | 500.00 |
| b. | Double surcharge | | |

No. 12 Surcharged in Black: **½d**

**1882**

| | | | |
|---|---|---|---|
| 22 | A1 ½p on 5sh grn | 1.40 | 1.40 |
| a. | Double surcharge | 350.00 | 325.00 |
| b. | Inverted surcharge | *800.00* | *800.00* |

No. 7 Surcharged in Black with Thin Line and:

**3d** *m* **3d** *n* **3d** *o* **3d** *p* **3d** *q*

**1882**

| | | | |
|---|---|---|---|
| 23 | (m) 3p on 4p ultra | 22.50 | 20.00 |
| a. | Double surcharge | | 450.00 |
| 24 | (n) 3p on 4p ultra | 20.00 | 15.00 |
| a. | Double surcharge | | 475.00 |
| 25 | (o) 3p on 4p ultra | 20.00 | 18.00 |
| a. | Double surcharge | | 475.00 |
| 26 | (p) 3p on 4p ultra | 125.00 | 60.00 |
| a. | Double surcharge | | 500.00 |
| 27 | (q) 3p on 4p ultra | 30.00 | 20.00 |
| a. | Double surcharge | | 475.00 |

No. 6 Surcharged in Black **2d**

**1888**

| | | | |
|---|---|---|---|
| 28 | A1 2p on 3p ultra | 4.00 | 1.75 |
| a. | Wide "2" | 15.00 | 6.00 |
| b. | Inverted surcharge | | 350.00 |

Nos. 6 and 7 Surcharged in Black:

**1d** *r* **1d** *s* **Id** *t*

**1890-91**

| | | | |
|---|---|---|---|
| 29 | (r) 1p on 3p ultra ('91) | 1.00 | 60 |
| a. | Double surcharge | 65.00 | 65.00 |
| 30 | (r) 1p on 4p ultra | 10.00 | 3.00 |
| a. | Double surcharge | 105.00 | 90.00 |
| 31 | (s) 1p on 3p ultra ('91) | 3.25 | 1.75 |
| a. | Double surcharge | 80.00 | 80.00 |
| 32 | (s) 1p on 4p ultra | 35.00 | 30.00 |
| a. | Double surcharge | 125.00 | 125.00 |
| 33 | (t) 1p on 4p ultra | *600.00* | *500.00* |

No. 6 Surcharged in Black **2½d.**

**1892**

| | | | |
|---|---|---|---|
| 34 | A1 2½p on 3p ultra | 1.00 | 60 |
| a. | Without period | 30.00 | 30.00 |

No. 6 Surcharged in Black:

½d ½d ½d ½d ½d
v w x y z

**1896**

| | | | | |
|---|---|---|---|---|
| 35 | (v) | ½p on 3p ultra | 90 | 90 |
| a. | | Double surcharge "v" and "y" | 10.00 | 10.00 |
| 36 | (w) | ½p on 3p ultra | 3.00 | 3.00 |
| a. | | Double surcharge "w" and "y" | 11.00 | 11.00 |
| 37 | (x) | ½p on 3p ultra | 3.00 | 3.00 |
| 38 | (y) | ½p on 3p ultra | 2.00 | 2.00 |
| a. | | Double surcharge | 11.00 | 11.00 |
| 39 | (z) | ½p on 3p ultra | 2.75 | 2.75 |

**Surcharged as "v" but "1" with Straight Serif.**

| | | | | |
|---|---|---|---|---|
| 40 | A1 | ½p on 3p ultra | 2.75 | 2.75 |
| a. | | Double sur., one type "y" | 13.00 | 13.00 |

**Surcharged as "z" but "1" with Straight Serif.**

| | | | | |
|---|---|---|---|---|
| 41 | A1 | ½p on 3p ultra | 2.75 | 2.75 |
| a. | | Double sur., one type "y" | 11.00 | 11.00 |

No. 6 Surcharged in Black

Halve Penny.

**1896**

| | | | | |
|---|---|---|---|---|
| 42 | A1 | ½p on 3p ultra | 25 | 25 |
| a. | | No period after "Penny" | 9.00 | 9.00 |
| b. | | "Peuny" | 8.50 | 8.50 |
| c. | | Inverted surcharge | 60.00 | 60.00 |
| d. | | Double surcharge, one inverted | 210.00 | 210.00 |
| e. | | Without bar | 4.50 | 4.50 |
| f. | | With additional surcharge as on Nos. 35 to 41 | 75.00 | 75.00 |

No. 6 Surcharged in Black 2½

**1897**

| | | | | |
|---|---|---|---|---|
| 43 | A1 | 2½p on 3p ultra | 65 | 65 |
| a. | | Roman "I" instead of "1" in "½" | 135.00 | 90.00 |

**Issued under British Occupation.**

A4

Black Surcharge or Overprint

**1900, Mar.-Apr. Unwmk. *Perf. 14***

**Periods in "V.R.I." Level with Bottoms of Letters**

| | | | | |
|---|---|---|---|---|
| 44 | A4 | ½p on ½p org | 28 | 20 |
| a. | | No period after "V" | 12.00 | 12.00 |
| b. | | No period after "I" | 135.00 | 135.00 |
| c. | | "I" and period after "R" omitted | | |
| d. | | "V.R.I." omitted | 175.00 | *175.00* |
| e. | | "½d" omitted | 175.00 | 175.00 |
| f. | | "½" omitted | *300.00* | *300.00* |
| g. | | Small "½" | 45.00 | 45.00 |
| h. | | Double surcharge | 125.00 | *125.00* |
| i. | | As "g," double surcharge | 300.00 | |
| 45 | A4 | 1p on 1p vio | 20 | 15 |
| a. | | No period after "V" | 10.50 | 10.50 |
| b. | | "I" and period after "R" omitted | 90.00 | 90.00 |
| c. | | "V.R.I." omitted | 165.00 | *165.00* |
| d. | | "1" of "1d" omitted | 165.00 | 165.00 |
| e. | | "d" omitted | 300.00 | 300.00 |
| f. | | "1d" omitted, "V.R.I." at top | 375.00 | |
| g. | | Pair, one without surcharge | 450.00 | |
| 45O | A4 | 1p on 1p brn | *300.00* | *300.00* |
| y. | | No period after "V" | *2,250.* | |
| 46 | A4 | 2p on 2p vio | 25 | 18 |
| a. | | No period after "V" | 7.25 | 7.25 |
| b. | | No period after "R" | 300.00 | |
| c. | | No period after "I" | 300.00 | |
| d. | | "V.R.I." omitted | 240.00 | 240.00 |
| 47 | A4 | '2½'on 3p ultra | 4.50 | 4.00 |
| a. | | No period after "V" | 55.00 | 55.00 |
| b. | | Roman "I" in "½" | 165.00 | 275.00 |
| 48 | A4 | 3p on 3p ultra | 28 | 20 |
| a. | | No period after "V" | 13.00 | 13.00 |
| b. | | Dbl. surch. one diagonal | 425.00 | |
| c. | | Pair, one without surcharge | 300.00 | 300.00 |
| 49 | A4 | 4p on 4p ultra | 1.75 | 1.50 |
| a. | | No period after "V" | 35.00 | 35.00 |
| 50 | A4 | 6p on 6p car rose | 35.00 | 35.00 |
| a. | | No period after "V" | 225.00 | 225.00 |
| b. | | "6" omitted | 325.00 | 325.00 |
| 51 | A4 | 6p on 6p ultra | 75 | 65 |
| a. | | No period after "V" | 21.00 | 21.00 |
| b. | | "V.R.I." omitted | *210.00* | |
| c. | | "6" omitted | 105.00 | 105.00 |
| 52 | A4 | 1sh on 1sh brn | 90 | 90 |
| a. | | No period after "V" | 18.00 | 18.00 |
| b. | | "V.R.I." omitted | 175.00 | 125.00 |
| c. | | "1" of "1s" omitted | 90.00 | 90.00 |
| d. | | "1s" omitted | | 175.00 |
| 52G | A4 | 1sh on 1sh org | *2,250.* | *1,800.* |
| 53 | A4 | 5sh on 5sh grn | 15.00 | 15.00 |
| a. | | No period after "V" | 175.00 | 175.00 |
| b. | | "5" omitted | 750.00 | 750.00 |

Nos. 47, 47c overprinted "V.R.I." on No. 43.

No. 45f ("1d" omitted) with "V.R.I." at bottom is a shift which sells for a fifth of the value of the listed item.

**1900-01**

**Periods in "V.R.I." Raised Above Bottoms of Letters**

| | | | | |
|---|---|---|---|---|
| 44j | A4 | ½p on ½p org | 18 | 15 |
| k. | | Mixed periods | 1.10 | 1.10 |
| l. | | Pair, one with level periods | 5.50 | 5.50 |
| m. | | No period after "V" | 5.50 | 5.50 |
| n. | | No period after "I" | 18.00 | 18.00 |
| o. | | "V" omitted | 350.00 | 350.00 |
| p. | | Small "½" | 10.00 | 10.00 |
| q. | | "1" for "I" in "V.R.I." | 9.00 | 9.00 |
| r. | | Thick "V" | 28 | 45 |
| 45i | A4 | 1p on 1p vio | 15 | 8 |
| j. | | Mixed periods | 1.10 | 1.10 |
| k. | | Pair, one with level periods | 15.00 | 15.00 |
| l. | | No period after "V" | 6.00 | 6.00 |
| m. | | No period after "R" | 12.00 | 12.00 |
| n. | | No period after "I" | 12.00 | 12.00 |
| p. | | Double surcharge | 90.00 | 90.00 |
| q. | | Inverted surcharge | 325.00 | |
| r. | | Pair, one without surch. | 300.00 | |
| s. | | Small "1" in "1d" | 105.00 | 105.00 |
| t. | | "1" for "I" in "V.R.I." | 13.00 | 13.00 |
| u. | | Thick "V" | 28 | 25 |
| v. | | As "u," invtd. "1" for "I" in "V.R.I." | 7.25 | 7.25 |
| w. | | As "u," double surcharge | 325.00 | 325.00 |
| z. | | As "u," no period after "R" | 30.00 | 30.00 |
| 46e | A4 | 2p on 2p vio | 20 | 9 |
| f. | | Mixed periods | 3.25 | 3.25 |
| g. | | Pair, one with level periods | 7.25 | 7.25 |
| h. | | Inverted surcharge | 350.00 | 350.00 |
| i. | | Thick "V" | 35 | 28 |
| j. | | As "i," invtd. "1" for "I" in "V.R.I." | 15.00 | 15.00 |
| 47c | A4 | '2½' on 3p ultra | 225.00 | 225.00 |
| d. | | Thick "V" | 600.00 | 600.00 |
| f. | | As "d," Roman "I" on "½" | | |
| 48d | A4 | 3p on 3p ultra | 28 | 20 |
| e. | | Mixed periods | 3.50 | 3.50 |
| f. | | Pair, one with level periods | 8.00 | 8.00 |
| g. | | Double surcharge | 425.00 | |
| h. | | Thick "V" | 90 | 90 |
| i. | | As "h," invtd. "1" for "I" in "V.R.I." | 65.00 | 65.00 |
| 49b | A4 | 4p on 4p ultra | 1.10 | 85 |
| c. | | Mixed periods | 4.00 | 4.00 |
| d. | | Pair, one with level periods | 12.00 | 12.00 |
| 50c | A4 | 6p on 6p car rose | 35.00 | 35.00 |
| d. | | Mixed periods | 175.00 | 175.00 |
| e. | | Pair, one with level periods | 225.00 | |
| f. | | Thick "V" | *600.00* | *600.00* |
| 51d | A4 | 6p on 6p ultra | 48 | 30 |
| e. | | Mixed periods | 4.50 | 4.50 |
| f. | | Pair, one with level periods | 12.00 | 12.00 |
| g. | | Thick "V" | 3.00 | 3.00 |
| 52e | A4 | 1sh on 1sh brn | 55 | 48 |
| f. | | Mixed periods | 6.00 | 6.00 |
| h. | | Pair, one with level periods | 15.00 | 15.00 |
| i. | | Thick "V" | 1.75 | 1.50 |
| 52j | A4 | 1sh on 1sh org | *1,200.* | *1,200.* |
| 53c | A4 | 5sh on 5sh grn | 4.75 | 3.50 |
| d. | | Mixed periods | 275.00 | 275.00 |
| e. | | Pair, one with level periods | 1,150. | 1,150. |
| f. | | "5" with short flag | 60.00 | 60.00 |
| g. | | Thick "V" | 18.00 | 18.00 |

Stamps with mixed periods have one or two periods level with the bottoms of the letters. One stamp in each pane had all periods level. Later settings had several stamps with thick "V." Excellent forgeries of the scarcer varieties exist.

"V.R.I." stands for Victoria Regina Imperatrix. On No. 59, "E.R.I." stands for Edward Rex Imperator.

Cape of Good Hope Stamps of 1893-98 Overprinted in Black

ORANGE RIVER COLONY.

**1900 Wmk. 16**

| | | | | |
|---|---|---|---|---|
| 54 | A15 | ½p green | 18 | 12 |
| a. | | No period after "COLONY" | 7.50 | 6.00 |
| b. | | Double ovpt. | 600.00 | 600.00 |
| 55 | A13 | 2½p ultra | 30 | 30 |
| a. | | No period after "COLONY" | 21.00 | 21.00 |

Overprinted as in 1900

**1902**

| | | | | |
|---|---|---|---|---|
| 56 | A15 | 1p car rose | 30 | 30 |
| a. | | No period after "COLONY" | 10.00 | 10.00 |

A5

A6

A7

Carmine or Vermilion and Black Surcharges

**1902 Unwmk.**

| | | | | |
|---|---|---|---|---|
| 57 | A5 | 4p on 6p on 6p ultra | 20 | 20 |
| a. | | Thick "V" | 1.75 | 1.25 |
| b. | | As "a," inverted "1" instead of "I" | 4.50 | 4.50 |
| c. | | No period after "R" | 30.00 | 30.00 |

**Black Surcharge**

| | | | | |
|---|---|---|---|---|
| 59 | A6 | 6p on 6p ultra | 1.25 | 1.10 |
| a. | | Double surcharge, one inverted | *600.00* | *600.00* |

**Orange Surcharge**

| | | | | |
|---|---|---|---|---|
| 60 | A7 | 1sh on 5sh grn | 2.50 | 2.50 |
| a. | | Thick "V" | 6.00 | 6.00 |
| b. | | "5" with short flag | 60.00 | 60.00 |

"E.R.I." stands for Edward Rex Imperator.

King Edward VII — A8

**1903-04 Wmk. 2 Typo.**

| | | | | |
|---|---|---|---|---|
| 61 | A8 | ½p yel grn | 45 | 38 |
| 62 | A8 | 1p carmine | 45 | 22 |
| 63 | A8 | 2p chocolate | 1.50 | 1.90 |
| 64 | A8 | 2½p ultra | 95 | 1.25 |
| 65 | A8 | 3p violet | 1.25 | 1.50 |
| 66 | A8 | 4p ol grn & car | 3.50 | 3.50 |
| a. | | "IOSTAGE" | 1,100. | 825.00 |
| 67 | A8 | 6p vio & car | 1.25 | 1.25 |
| 68 | A8 | 1sh bis & car | 7.50 | 2.53 |
| 69 | A8 | 5sh red brn & bl ('04) | 45.00 | 32.50 |
| | | *Nos. 61-69 (9)* | 61.85 | 45.03 |

Some of the above stamps are found with the overprint "C. S. A. R." for use by the Central South African Railway.

**1907-08 Wmk. 3**

| | | | | |
|---|---|---|---|---|
| 70 | A8 | ½p yel grn | 32 | 45 |
| 71 | A8 | 1p carmine | 12 | 18 |
| 72 | A8 | 4p ol grn & car | 1.75 | 1.90 |
| a. | | "IOSTAGE" | 225.00 | 195.00 |
| 73 | A8 | 1sh bis & car | 21.00 | 3.75 |

Stamps of Orange River Colony were replaced by those of Union of South Africa.

# PAKISTAN

LOCATION — In southern, central Asia.
GOVT. — Republic.
AREA — 307,293 sq. mi.
POP. — 88,000,000 (est. 1983).
CAPITAL — Islamabad.

Pakistan was formed August 15, 1947, when India was divided into the Dominions of the Union of India and Pakistan, with some princely states remaining independent. Pakistan became a republic on March 23, 1956.

Pakistan had two areas made up of all or part of several predominantly Moslem provinces in the northwest and northeast corners of pre-1947 India. Western Pakistan consists of the entire provinces of Baluchistan, Sind (Scinde) and "Northwest Frontier," and 15 districts of the Punjab. Eastern, consisting of the Sylhet district in Assam and 14 districts in Bengal Province, became independent as Bangladesh in December 1971.

The state of Las Bela was incorporated into Pakistan.

12 Pies = 1 Anna
16 Annas = 1 Rupee
100 Paisa = 1 Rupee (1961)

**Catalogue values for all unused stamps in this country are for Never Hinged items.**

Stamps of India, 1937-43, Overprinted in Black:

PAKISTAN Nos. 1-12 PAKISTAN Nos. 13-19

**1947-49 Wmk. 196 *Perf. 13½x14***

| | | | | |
|---|---|---|---|---|
| 1 | A83 | 3p slate | 5 | 5 |
| 2 | A83 | ½a rose vio | 5 | 5 |
| 3 | A83 | 9p lt grn | 5 | 5 |
| 4 | A83 | 1a car rose | 5 | 5 |
| 4A | A84 | 1a3p bis ('49) | 2.00 | 2.00 |
| 5 | A84 | 1½a dk pur | 5 | 5 |
| 6 | A84 | 2a scarlet | 7 | 5 |
| 7 | A84 | 3a violet | 10 | 5 |
| 8 | A84 | 3½a ultra | 35 | 35 |
| 9 | A85 | 4a chocolate | 10 | 7 |
| 10 | A85 | 6a pck bl | 18 | 10 |
| 11 | A85 | 8a bl vio | 20 | 20 |
| 12 | A85 | 12a car lake | 35 | 35 |
| 13 | A81 | 14a rose vio | 50 | 50 |
| 14 | A82 | 1r brn & sl | 55 | 55 |
| a | | Inverted overprint | 110.00 | |
| b | | Pair, one without ovpt. | 425.00 | |
| 15 | A82 | 2r dk brn & dk vio | 75 | 65 |
| 16 | A82 | 5r dp ultra & dk grn | 2.00 | 85 |
| 17 | A82 | 10r rose car & dk vio | 2.25 | 85 |
| 18 | A82 | 15r dk grn & dk brn | 17.50 | 13.50 |
| 19 | A82 | 25r dk vio & bl vio | 20.00 | 17.50 |
| | | *Nos. 1-19 (20)* | 47.15 | 37.82 |

The overprint on Nos. 14 to 19 is slightly smaller than the illustration.

Provisional use of stamps of India handstamped "PAKISTAN" was authorized in 1947-48.

Constituent Assembly Building, Karachi — A1

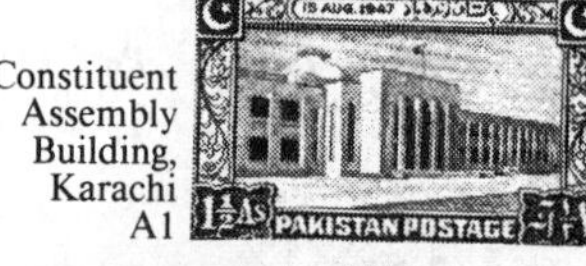

Crescent and Urdu Inscription — A2

Designs: 2½a, Karachi Airport entrance. 3a, Lahore Fort gateway.

**Unwmk.**

**1948, July 9 Engr. *Perf. 14***

| | | | | |
|---|---|---|---|---|
| 20 | A1 | 1½a brt ultra | 5 | 5 |
| 21 | A1 | 2½a green | 8 | 8 |
| 22 | A1 | 3a chocolate | 10 | 10 |

***Perf. 12***

| | | | | |
|---|---|---|---|---|
| 23 | A2 | 1r red | 38 | 35 |
| a | | Perf. 14 | 4.00 | 4.00 |

Pakistan's independence, Aug. 15, 1947.

Scales, Star and Crescent — A3

Star and Crescent — A4

Karachi Airport Building — A5

Karachi Port Authority Building — A6

Khyber Pass — A7

Designs: 2½a, 3½a, 4a, Ghulan Muhammed Dam, Indus River, Sind. 1r, 2r, 5r, Salimullah Hostel.

**Perf. 12½, 13½x14, 14x13½.**

**1948-57** **Unwmk.**

| No. | Type | Description | Unused | Used |
|---|---|---|---|---|
| 24 | A3 | 3p org red, perf. 13 ('54) | 5 | 5 |
| a | | Perf. 12½ | 5 | 5 |
| 25 | A3 | 6p pur, perf. 13 ('54) | 18 | 5 |
| a | | Perf. 12½ | 5 | 5 |
| 26 | A3 | 9p dk grn, perf. 12½ | 5 | 5 |
| a | | Perf. 13 ('54) | 5 | 5 |
| 27 | A4 | 1a dk bl | 5 | 5 |
| 28 | A4 | 1½a gray grn | 5 | 5 |
| 29 | A4 | 2a org red | 6 | 5 |
| 30 | A6 | 2½a green | 8 | 5 |
| 31 | A5 | 3a ol grn | 8 | 5 |
| 32 | A6 | 3½a vio bl | 12 | 6 |
| 33 | A6 | 4a chocolate | 10 | 5 |
| 34 | A6 | 6a dp bl | 12 | 6 |
| 35 | A6 | 8a black | 20 | 7 |
| 36 | A5 | 10a red | 22 | 10 |
| 37 | A6 | 12a red | 28 | 7 |
| 38 | A5 | 1r ultra, perf. 13 ('54) | 50 | 8 |
| a | | Perf. 13½x14 | 32 | 8 |
| 39 | A5 | 2r dk brn, perf. 13 ('54) | 1.00 | 18 |
| a | | Perf. 13½x14 | 60 | 18 |
| 40 | A5 | 5r car, perf. 13½x14 | 1.40 | 10 |
| a | | Perf. 13 ('54) | 3.50 | 65 |

**Perf. 13½x13**

| No. | Type | Description | Unused | Used |
|---|---|---|---|---|
| 41 | A7 | 10r rose lil ('51) | 5.00 | 20 |
| a | | Perf. 14x13½ | 3.50 | 2.75 |
| b | | Perf. 12 | 5.25 | 85 |
| 42 | A7 | 15r bl grn ('57) | 6.00 | 2.25 |
| a | | Perf. 14x13½ | 7.50 | 6.00 |
| b | | Perf. 12 | 3.50 | 1.00 |
| 43 | A7 | 25r pur ('54) | 11.00 | 5.00 |
| a | | Perf. 14x13½ | 11.00 | 5.25 |
| b | | Perf. 12 | 11.00 | 5.25 |
| | | *Nos. 24-43 (20)* | 26.54 | 8.62 |

See No. 259.

"Quaid-i-Azam" (Great Leader), "Mohammed Ali Jinnah" — A8

**1949, Sept. 11** **Engr.** ***Perf. 13½x14***

| No. | Type | Description | Unused | Used |
|---|---|---|---|---|
| 44 | A8 | 1½a brown | 38 | 14 |
| 45 | A8 | 3a dk grn | 50 | 18 |
| 46 | A8 | 10a blk *(English inscriptions)* | 2.25 | 1.00 |

1st anniv. of the death of Mohammed Ali Jinnah (1876-1948), Moslem lawyer, pres. of All-India Moslem League.

Re-engraved (Crescents Reversed)

A9 A10

A11

***Perf. 12½, 13½x14, 14x13½***

**1949-53**

| No. | Type | Description | Unused | Used |
|---|---|---|---|---|
| 47 | A10 | 1a dk bl, perf. 12½ ('50) | 5 | 5 |
| a | | Perf. 13 ('52) | 8 | 5 |
| 48 | A10 | 1½a gray grn, perf. 13 ('53) | 6 | 5 |
| a | | Perf. 12½ | 6 | 5 |
| 49 | A10 | 2a org red, perf. 13 ('52) | 6 | 5 |
| a | | Perf. 12½ | 6 | 5 |
| 50 | A9 | 3a ol grn | 20 | 5 |
| 51 | A11 | 6a dp bl ('50) | 22 | 5 |
| 52 | A11 | 8a blk ('50) | 22 | 5 |
| 53 | A9 | 10a red | 50 | 7 |
| 54 | A11 | 12a red ('50) | 85 | 10 |
| | | *Nos. 47-54 (8)* | 2.16 | 47 |

Vase and Plate — A12

Star and Crescent, Plane and Hour Glass — A13

Moslem Leaf Pattern — A14

Arch and Lamp of Learning — A15

**1951-56** **Engr.** ***Perf. 13.***

| No. | Type | Description | Unused | Used |
|---|---|---|---|---|
| 55 | A12 | 2½a dk red | 6 | 6 |
| 56 | A13 | 3a dk rose lake | 8 | 5 |
| 57 | A12 | 3½a dp ultra (Urdu "½3") | 35 | 22 |
| 57A | A12 | 3½a dp ultra (Urdu "3½") ('56) | 65 | 50 |
| 58 | A14 | 4a dp grn | 12 | 5 |
| 59 | A14 | 6a red org | 18 | 5 |
| 60 | A15 | 8a brown | 22 | 6 |
| 61 | A15 | 10a purple | 40 | 18 |
| 62 | A13 | 12a dk sl bl | 50 | 18 |
| | | *Nos. 55-62 (9)* | 2.56 | 1.35 |

Fourth anniversary of independence.

On No. 57, the characters of the Urdu denomination at right appears as "½3." On the reengraved No. 57A, they read "3½."
See No. 88.

Scinde District Stamp and Camel Train A16

**1952, Aug. 14**

| No. | Type | Description | Unused | Used |
|---|---|---|---|---|
| 63 | A16 | 3a ol grn, *cit* | 40 | 22 |
| 64 | A16 | 12a dk brn, *sal* | 1.10 | 65 |

5th anniv. of Pakistan's Independence and the cent. of the 1st postage stamps in the Indo-Pakistan sub-continent.

Peak K-2, Karakoram Mountains A17

**1954, Dec. 25**

| No. | Type | Description | Unused | Used |
|---|---|---|---|---|
| 65 | A17 | 2a violet | 20 | 10 |

Conquest of K-2, world's 2nd highest mountain peak, in July 1954.

Kaghan Valley — A18

Gilgit Mountains A19

Tea Garden, East Pakistan A20

Designs: 1a, Badshahi Mosque, Lahore. 1½a, Emperor Jahangir's Mausoleum, Lahore. 1r, Cotton field. 2r, River craft and jute field.

**1954, Aug. 14** **Engr.**

| No. | Type | Description | Unused | Used |
|---|---|---|---|---|
| 66 | A18 | 6p rose vio | 5 | 5 |
| a | | Booklet pane of 4 | 20 | |
| 67 | A19 | 9p blue | 6 | 5 |
| 68 | A19 | 1a car rose | 5 | 5 |
| 69 | A18 | 1½a red | 6 | 5 |
| a | | Booklet pane of 4 | 22 | |
| 70 | A20 | 14a dk grn | 60 | 7 |
| 71 | A20 | 1r yel grn | 85 | 6 |
| 72 | A20 | 2r orange | 1.75 | 8 |
| | | *Nos. 66-72 (7)* | 3.42 | 41 |

Seventh anniversary of independence.

Karnaphuli Paper Mill, East Pakistan (Urdu "½2") — A21

Designs: 6a, Textile mill. 8a, Jute mill. 12a, Sui gas plant.

**1955-56** **Unwmk.** ***Perf. 13***

| No. | Type | Description | Unused | Used |
|---|---|---|---|---|
| 73 | A21 | 2½a dk car (Urdu "½2") | 20 | 5 |
| 73A | A21 | 2½a dk car (Urdu "2½") ('56) | 22 | 10 |
| 74 | A21 | 6a dk bl | 25 | 5 |
| 75 | A21 | 8a violet | 35 | 6 |
| 76 | A21 | 12a car lake & org | 60 | 7 |
| | | *Nos. 73-76 (5)* | 1.62 | 33 |

Eighth anniversary of independence.

On No. 73, the characters of the Urdu denomination at right appear as "½2." On the reengraved No. 73A, they read "2½."
See No. 87.

Nos. 69 and 76 Overprinted in Ultramarine

TENTH ANNIVERSARY UNITED NATIONS

24.10.55.

**1955, Oct. 24**

| No. | Type | Description | Unused | Used |
|---|---|---|---|---|
| 77 | A18 | 1½a red | 1.75 | 1.75 |
| 78 | A21 | 12a car lake & org | 1.75 | 1.75 |

UN, 10th anniv.

Map of West Pakistan — A22

**1955, Dec. 7** **Unwmk.** ***Perf. 13½x13***

| No. | Type | Description | Unused | Used |
|---|---|---|---|---|
| 79 | A22 | 1½a dark green | 12 | 8 |
| 80 | A22 | 2a dark brown | 18 | 10 |
| 81 | A22 | 12a deep carmine | 75 | 50 |

West Pakistan unification, Nov. 14, 1955.

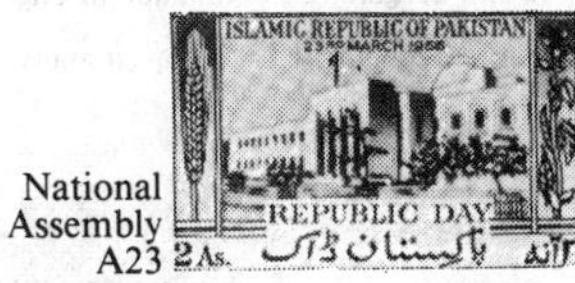

National Assembly A23

**1956, Mar. 23** **Litho.** ***Perf. 13x12½***

| No. | Type | Description | Unused | Used |
|---|---|---|---|---|
| 82 | A23 | 2a green | 10 | 5 |

Issued to commemorate the proclamation of the Republic of Pakistan, March 23, 1956.

Crescent and Star — A24

Map of East Pakistan — A25

**1956, Aug. 14** **Engr.** ***Perf. 13***

| No. | Type | Description | Unused | Used |
|---|---|---|---|---|
| 83 | A24 | 2a red | 7 | 5 |

Ninth anniversary of independence.

**1956, Oct. 15** ***Perf. 13½x13***

| No. | Type | Description | Unused | Used |
|---|---|---|---|---|
| 84 | A25 | 1½a dk grn | 20 | 14 |
| 85 | A25 | 2a dk brn | 20 | 8 |
| 86 | A25 | 12a dp red | 85 | 50 |

1st Session at Dacca (East Pakistan) of the National Assembly of Pakistan.

Redrawn Types of 1951, 1955 and

Orange Tree — A26

***Perf. 13x13½, 13½x13***

**1957, Mar. 23 Engr.**

*87* A21 2½a dk car 8 5
*88* A12 3½a brt bl 12 7
*89* A26 10r dk grn & org 3.50 1.40

Nos. 87-89 inscribed "Pakistan" in English, Urdu and Bengali. Denomination in English only.

Islamic Republic of Pakistan, 1st anniv.

See Nos. 95, 258, 475A.

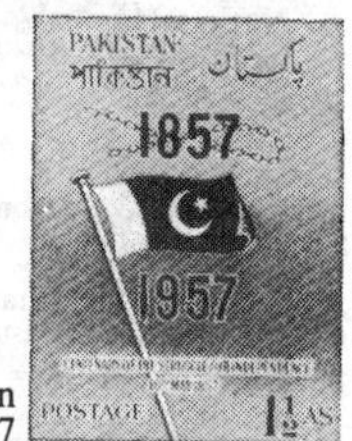

Flag and Broken Chain — A27

**1957, May 10 Litho. *Perf. 13***

*90* A27 1½a green 18 14
*91* A27 12a blue 40 35

Cent. of the struggle for Independence (Indian Mutiny).

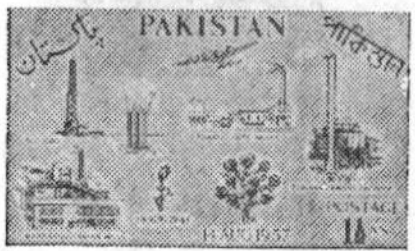

Industrial Plants and Roses as Symbols of Progress A28

**1957, Aug. 14 Unwmk. *Perf. 13½***

*92* A28 1½a lt ultra 8 7
*93* A28 4a org ver 18 10
*94* A28 12a red lil 35 35

Tenth anniversary of independence.

Type of 1957.

Design: 15r, Coconut Tree.

**1958, Mar. 23 Engr. *Perf. 13½x13***

*95* A26 15r rose lil & red 4.00 3.50

Issued to commemorate the second anniversary of the Islamic Republic of Pakistan.

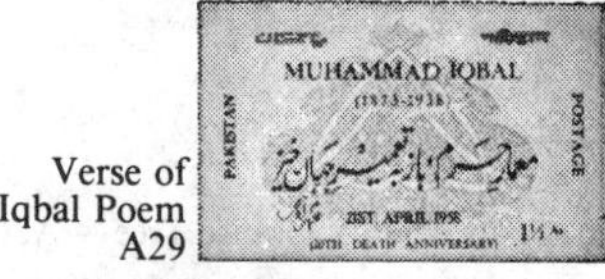

Verse of Iqbal Poem A29

**1958, Apr. 21 Photo. *Perf. 14½x14***

**Black Inscriptions.**

*96* A29 1½a citron 7 7
*97* A29 2a org brn 14 7
*98* A29 14a aqua 40 30

20th anniv. of the death of Mohammad Iqbal (1877-1938), Moslem poet and philosopher.

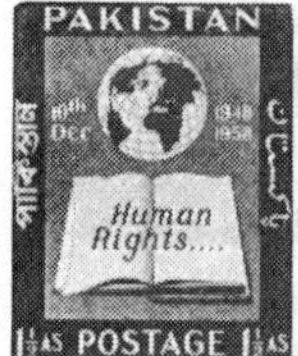

Globe and Book — A30

**1958, Dec. 10 Litho. *Perf. 13***

*99* A30 1½a Prus bl 7 6
*100* A30 14a dk brn 40 35

10th anniv. of the signing of the Universal Declaration of Human Rights.



Nos. 66 and 75 Overprinted: "Pakistan Boy Scout 2nd National Jamboree Chittagong Dec. 58-Jan. 59"

**1958, Dec. 28 Engr. *Perf. 13***

*101* A18 6p rose vio 8 8
*102* A21 8a violet 40 40

2nd National Boy Scout Jamboree held at Chittagong, Dec. 28-Jan. 4.

No. 74 Overprinted in Red: "Revolution Day, Oct. 27, 1959."

**1959, Oct. 27**

*103* A21 6a dk bl 18 10

First anniversary of the 1958 Revolution.

Red Cross — A31

**Engr.; Cross Typo.**

**1959, Nov. 19 Unwmk. *Perf. 13***

*104* A31 2a grn & red 18 10
*105* A31 10a dk bl & red 85 18

Armed Forces Emblem — A32

**1960, Jan. 10 Litho. *Perf. 13***

*106* A32 2a bl grn, red & ultra 6 5
*107* A32 14a ultra & red 35 22

Issued for Armed Forces Day.

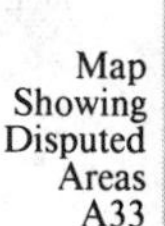

Map Showing Disputed Areas A33

**1960, Mar. 23 Engr. Unwmk.**

*108* A33 6p purple 5 5
*109* A33 2a cop red 6 5
*110* A33 8a green 18 10
*111* A33 1r blue 38 28

Issued to publicize the border dispute with India over Jammu and Kashmir, Junagarh and Manavadar.

Uprooted Oak Emblem — A34

**1960, Apr. 7**

*112* A34 2a car rose 6 5
*113* A34 10a green 28 22

Issued to publicize World Refugee Year, July 1, 1959-June 30, 1960.

House, Field and Column (Allegory of Democratic Development) A35

**1960, Oct. 27 Photo. *Perf. 13***

*114* A35 2a brn, pink & grn 6 5
*a* Green & pink omitted 13.50
*115* A35 14a multi 35 28

Revolution Day, Oct. 27, 1960.

Punjab Agricultural College, Lyallpur A36

Design: 8a, College shield.

**1960, Oct. Engr. *Perf. 12½x14***

*116* A36 2a rose red & gray bl 6 5
*117* A36 8a lil & grn 35 28

50th anniv. of the Punjab Agricultural College, Lyallpur.

Caduceus, College Emblem — A37

**1960, Nov. 16 Photo. *Perf. 13½x13***

*118* A37 2a bl, yel & blk 7 7
*119* A37 14a car rose, blk & emer 35 30

Issued to commemorate the centenary of the King Edward Medical College, Lahore.

Map of South-East Asia and Commission Emblem — A38

**1960, Dec. 5 Engr. *Perf. 13***

*120* A38 14a red org 30 22

Conf. of the Commission on Asian and Far Eastern Affairs of the Intl. Chamber of Commerce, Karachi, Dec. 5-9.

"Kim's Gun" and Scout Badge A39

***Perf. 12½x14***

**1960, Dec. 24 Unwmk.**

*121* A39 2a dk grn, car & yel 18 7

Issued to commemorate the Third National Boy Scout Jamboree, Lahore, Dec. 24-31.

No. 110 Overprinted in Red

LAHORE STAMP EXHIBITION 1961

**1961, Fed. 12**

*122* A33 8a green 35 22

10th Lahore Stamp Exhibition, Feb. 12.

Nos. 24, 68-69, 83, 108-109 Surcharged with New Value in Paisa.

**1961 *Perf. 13***

*123* A18 1pa on 1½a red 5 5
*124* A3 2pa on 3p org red 5 5
*125* A33 3pa on 6p pur 7 5
*126* A19 7pa on 1a car rose 14 8
*127* A24 13pa on 2a red 20 10
*128* A33 13pa on 2a cop red 28 12
*Nos. 123-128 (6)* 79 45

Various violet handstamped surcharges were applied to a variety of regular-issue stamps. Most of these repeat the denomination of the basic stamp and add the new value. Example: "8 Annas (50 Paisa)" on No. 75. Many errors exist.

Khyber Pass — A40

Chota Sona Masjid Gate — A41

Design: 10pa, 13pa, 25pa, 40pa, 50pa, 75pa, 90pa, Shalimar Gardens, Lahore.

Type I Type II

Two types of 1pa, 2pa and 5pa:
I. First Bengali character beside "N" lacks appendage at left side of loop.
II. This character has a downward-pointing appendage at left side of loop.

**1961-63 Engr. *Perf. 13½x14***

*129* A40 1pa vio (II) 14 14
*a* Type I 5 5
*130* A40 2pa rose red (II) 18 14
*a* Type I 5 5
*131* A40 3pa magenta 5 5
*132* A40 5pa ultra (II) 14 14
*a* Type I 7 5
*133* A40 7pa emerald 10 5
*134* A40 10pa brown 10 5
*135* A40 13pa bl vio 12 5
*136* A40 25pa dk bl ('62) 12 5
*137* A40 40pa dl pur ('62) 22 6
*138* A40 50pa dl grn ('62) 35 6
*139* A40 75pa dk car ('62) 50 8
*140* A40 90pa lt ol grn ('62) 50 7

***Perf. 13½x13***

*141* A41 1r ver ('63) 55 7
*142* A41 1.25r purple 65 35
*143* A41 2r org ('63) 1.10 10
*144* A41 5r grn ('63) 3.50 1.40
*Nos. 129-144 (16)* 8.32 2.86

See Nos. 200-203.

Designs Redrawn

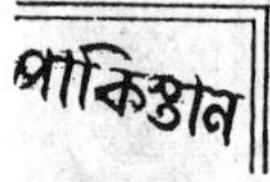

1961-62 Bengali Inscription

Redrawn Bengali Inscription

Bengali inscription redrawn with straight connecting line across top of characters. Shading of scenery differs, especially in Shalimar Gardens design where reflection is strengthened and trees at right are composed of horizontal lines instead of vertical lines and dots.

Designs as before; 15pa, 20pa, Shalimar Gardens.

**1963-70 *Perf. 13½x14***

*129b* A40 1pa violet 5 5
*130b* A40 2pa rose red ('64) 5 5
*131a* A40 3pa mag ('70) 5 5
*132b* A40 5pa ultra 5 5
*133a* A40 7pa emer ('64) 5 5
*134a* A40 10pa brown 5 5
*135a* A40 13pa bl vio 5 5
*135B* A40 15pa rose lil ('64) 5 5
*135C* A40 20pa dl grn ('70) 7 7
*136a* A40 25pa dk bl 7 6
*137a* A40 40pa dl pur ('64) 10 6
*138a* A40 50pa dl grn ('64) 18 6
*139a* A40 75pa dk car ('64) 22 6
*140a* A40 90pa lt ol grn ('64) 50 7
*Nos. 129b-140a (14)* 1.54 78

Warsak Dam, Kabul River A42

**961, July 1 Engr.** ***Perf. 12½x13½***
50 A42 40pa blk & lt ultra 20 10

)edication of hydrolelectric Warsak Project.

Symbolic Flower — A43

**961, Oct. 2 Unwmk.** ***Perf. 14***
51 A43 13pa grnsh bl 8 6
52 A43 90pa red lil 42 28

Issued for Children's Day.

Roses — A44

**1961, Nov. 4** ***Perf. 13½x13***
153 A44 13pa dp grn & ver 10 5
154 A44 90pa bl & ver 50 18

Cooperative Day.

Police Crest and Traffic Policeman's Hand — A45

**1961, Nov. 30 Photo.** ***Perf. 13x12½***
155 A45 13pa dk bl, sil & blk 7 5
156 A45 40pa red, sil & blk 28 20

Centenary of the police force.

"Eagle Locomotive, 1861" — A46

Design: 50pa, Diesel Engine, 1961.

**1961, Dec. 31** ***Perf. 13½x14***
157 A46 13pa yel, grn & blk 20 7
158 A46 50pa grn, blk & yel 60 28

Centenary of Pakistan railroads.

No. 87 Surcharged in Red with New Value, Boeing 720-B Jetliner and: "FIRST JET FLIGHT KARACHI-DACCA"

**1962, Feb. 6 Engr.** ***Perf. 13***
159 A21 13pa on 2½a dk car 28 18

Issued to commemorate the first jet flight from Karachi to Dacca, Feb. 6, 1962.

Mosquito and Malaria Eradication Emblem A47

Design: 13pa, Dagger pointing at mosquito, and emblem.

**1962, Apr. 7 Photo.** ***Perf. 13½x14***
160 A47 10pa multi 18 7
161 A47 13pa multi 18 7

WHO drive to eradicate malaria.

Map of Pakistan and Jasmine — A48

**1962, June 8 Unwmk.** ***Perf. 12***
162 A48 40pa grn, yel grn & gray 28 18

Introduction of new Pakistan Constitution.

Soccer A49

Designs: 13pa, Hockey and Olympic gold medal. 25pa, Squash rackets and British squash rackets championship cup. 40pa, Cricket and Ayub challenge cup.

***Perf. 12½x13½***
**1962, Aug. 14 Engr.**
163 A49 7pa bl & blk 10 5
164 A49 13pa grn & blk 18 5
165 A49 25pa lil & blk 30 8
166 A49 40pa brn org & blk 1.10 18

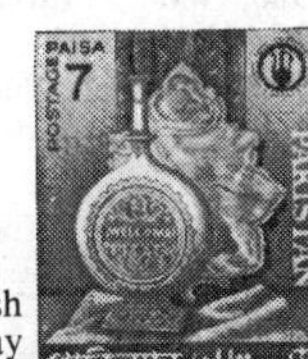

Marble Fruit Dish and Clay Flask — A50

Designs: 13pa, Sporting goods. 25pa, Camel skin lamp and brass jug. 40pa, Wooden powder bowl and cane basket. 50pa, Inlaid box and brassware.

**1962, Nov. 10** ***Perf. 13½x13***
167 A50 7pa dk red 7 5
168 A50 13pa dk grn 8 5
169 A50 25pa brt pur 12 7
170 A50 40pa yel grn 35 12
171 A50 50pa dl red 38 20
*Nos. 167-171 (5)* 1.00 49

Issued in connection with the Pakistan International Industries Fair, Oct. 12-Nov. 20, to publicize Pakistan's small industries.

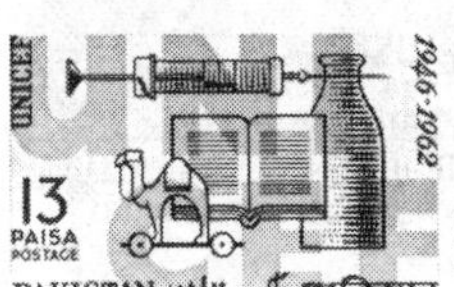

Children's Needs A51

**1962, Dec. 11 Photo.** ***Perf. 13½x14***
172 A51 13pa bl, plum & blk 6 5
173 A51 40pa multi 20 18

16th anniv. of UNICEF.

No. 135a Overprinted in Red: "U.N. FORCE W. IRIAN"

**1963, Feb. 15 Engr. Unwmk.**
174 A40 13pa bl vio 10 8

Issued to commemorate the despatch of Pakistani troops to West New Guinea.

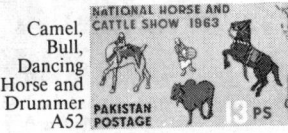

Camel, Bull, Dancing Horse and Drummer A52

**1963, Mar. 13 Photo.** ***Perf. 12***
175 A52 13pa multi 10 7

National Horse and Cattle Show, 1963.

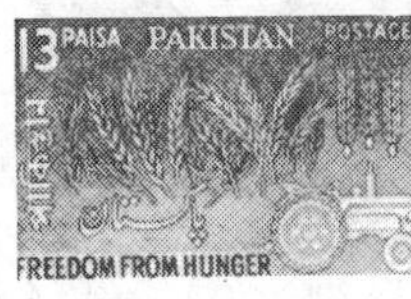

Wheat and Tractor A53

Design: 50pa, Hands and heap of rice.

***Perf. 12½x13½***
**1963, Mar. 21 Engr.**
176 A53 13pa brn org 22 6
177 A53 50pa brown 85 18

"Freedom from Hunger" campaign of the FAO.

No. 109 Surcharged with New Value and: "INTERNATIONAL/DACCA STAMP/EXHIBITION/1963"

**1963, Mar. 23** ***Perf. 13***
178 A33 13pa on 2a cop red 20 18

International Stamp Exhibition at Dacca.

Centenary Emblem — A54

**Engr. and Typo.**
**1963, June 25** ***Perf. 13½x12½***
179 A54 40pa dk gray & red 40 10

International Red Cross, cent.

Paharpur Stupa A55

Designs: 13pa, Cistern, Mohenjo-Daro (vert.). 40pa, Stupas, Taxila. 50pa, Stupas, Mainamati.

***Perf. 12½x13½, 13½x12½***
**1963, Sept. 16 Engr. Unwmk.**
180 A55 7pa ultra 6 5
181 A55 13pa brown 8 5
182 A55 40pa car rose 22 18
183 A55 50pa dk vio 35 20

No. 131 Surcharged and Overprinted: "100 YEARS OF P.W.D. OCTOBER, 1963"

**1963, Oct. 7** ***Perf. 13½x14***
184 A40 13pa on 3pa mag 10 7

Centenary of Public Works Department.

Atatürk Mausoleum, Ankara A56

**1963, Nov. 10** ***Perf. 13x13½***
185 A56 50pa red 22 18

25th anniv. of the death of Kemal Atatürk, pres. of Turkey.

Globe and UNESCO Emblem A57

**1963, Dec. 10 Photo.** ***Perf. 13½x14***
186 A57 50pa dk brn, vio bl & red 22 18

15th anniv. of the Universal Declaration of Human Rights.

Multan Thermal Power Station A58

***Perf. 12½x13½***
**1963, Dec. 25 Engr.**
187 A58 13pa ultra 8 6

Issued to mark the opening of the Multan Thermal Power Station.

Type of 1961-63

Wmk. 351-Crescent and Star Multiple

***Perf. 13½x13***
**1963-65 Engr. Wmk. 351**
200 A41 1r vermilion 35 7
201 A41 1.25r pur ('64) 40 18
202 A41 2r orange 65 10
203 A41 5r grn ('65) 1.75 50

Temple of Thot, Dakka, and Queen Nefertari with Goddesses Hathor and Isis — A59

Design: 50pa, Ramses II, Abu Simbel, and View of Nile.

***Perf. 13x13½***
**1964, March 30 Unwmk.**
204 A59 13pa brick red & turq bl 10 6
205 A59 50pa blk & rose lil 38 28

UNESCO world campaign to save historic monuments in Nubia.

Pakistan Pavilion and Unisphere A60

Design: 1.25r, Pakistan pavilion and Unisphere (vert.).

***Perf. 12½x14, 14x12½***
**1964, Apr. 22 Engr. Unwmk.**
206 A60 13pa ultra 7 6
207 A60 1.25r dp org & ultra 60 40

New York World's Fair, 1964-65.

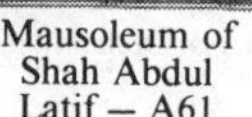

Mausoleum of Shah Abdul Latif – A61

Mausoleum of Jinnah – A62

**1964, June 25** ***Perf. 13½x13***
*208* A61 50pa mag & ultra 22 10

Bicentenary (?) of the death of Shah Abdul Latif of Bhit (1689-1752).

**1964, Sept. 11 Unwmk.** ***Perf. 13***

Design: 15pa, Mausoleum (horiz.).

*209* A62 15pa green 8 6
*210* A62 50pa grnsh gray 22 20

Issued to commemorate the 16th anniversary of the death of Mohammed Ali Jinnah (1876-1948), the Quaid-i-Azam (Great Leader), founder and president of Pakistan.

Bengali Alphabet on Slate and Slab with Urdu Alphabet – A63

**1964, Oct. 5** **Engr.**
*211* A63 15pa brown 7 6

Issued for Universal Children's Day.

West Pakistan University of Engineering and Technology A64

**1964, Dec. 21** ***Perf. 12½x14***
*212* A64 15pa hn brn 7 6

1st convocation of the West Pakistan University of Engineering and Technology, Lahore, Dec., 1964.

Eyeglasses and Book – A65

***Perf. 13x13½***
**1965, Feb. 28 Litho. Unwmk.**
*213* A65 15pa yel & ultra 7 6

Issued to publicize aid for the blind.

ITU Emblem, Telegraph Pole and Transmission Tower A66

**1965, May 17 Engr.** ***Perf. 12½x14***
*214* A66 15pa deep claret 42 6

Cent. of the ITU.

ICY Emblem A67

**1965, June 26 Litho.** ***Perf. 13½***
*215* A67 15pa bl & blk 30 6
*216* A67 50pa yel & grn 60 8

International Cooperation Year, 1965.

Hands Holding Book – A68

Design: 50pa, Map and flags of Turkey, Iran and Pakistan.

***Perf. 13½x13, 13x12½***
**1965, July 21 Litho. Unwmk.**
**Size: 46x35mm**
*217* A68 15pa org brn, dk brn & buff 10 6
**Size: 54x30½mm**
*218* A68 50pa multi 22 20

1st anniv. of the signing of the Regional Cooperation for Development Pact by Turkey, Iran and Pakistan.

Tanks, Army Emblem and Soldier – A69

Designs: 15pa, Navy emblem, corvette No. O204 and officer. 50pa, Air Force emblem, two F-104 Starfighters and pilot.

**1965, Dec. 25 Litho.** ***Perf. 13½x13***
*219* A69 7pa multi 10 5
*220* A69 15pa multi 18 6
*221* A69 50pa multi 60 18

Issued to honor the Pakistani armed forces.

Emblems of Pakistan Armed Forces – A70

**1966, Feb. 13 Litho.** ***Perf. 13½x13***
*222* A70 15pa buff, grn & dk bl 10 6

Issued for Armed Forces Day.

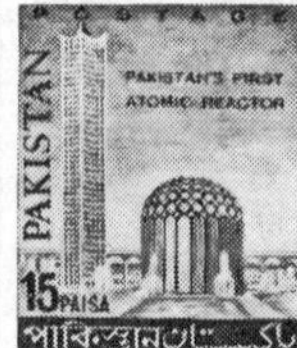


Atomic Reactor, Islamabad – A71

**Unwmk.**
**1966, Apr. 30 Engr.** ***Perf. 13***
*223* A71 15pa black 7 6

Pakistan's first atomic reactor.

Habib Bank Emblem A72

***Perf. 12½x13½***
**1966, Aug. 25 Litho. Unwmk.**
*224* A72 15pa brn, org & dk grn 7 6

25th anniversary of the Habib Bank.

Boy and Girl – A73

**1966, Oct. 3 Litho.** ***Perf. 13x13½***
*225* A73 15pa multi 7 6

Issued for Children's Day.

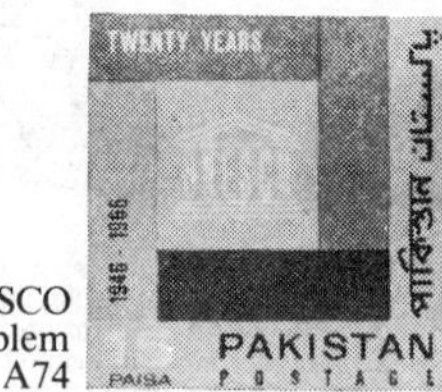


UNESCO Emblem A74

**1966, Nov. 24 Unwmk.** ***Perf. 14***
*226* A74 15pa multi 18 7

20th anniv. of UNESCO.

Secretariat Buildings, Islamabad, Flag and Pres. Mohammed Ayub Khan – A75

**1966, Nov. 29 Litho.** ***Perf. 13***
*227* A75 15pa multi 7 6
*228* A75 50pa multi 18 12

Issued to publicize the new capital, Islamabad.

Avicenna – A76

Mohammed Ali Jinnah – A77

**1966, Dec. 3** ***Perf. 13½***
*229* A76 15pa sal pink & sl grn 7 6

Issued to publicize the Health Institute.

**Lithographed and Engraved**
**1966, Dec. 25 Unwmk.** ***Perf. 13***

Design: 50pa, Different frame.

*230* A77 15pa org, blk & bl 7 6
*231* A77 50pa lil, blk & vio bl 18 12

90th anniv. of the birth of Mohammed Ali Jinnah (1876-1948), 1st Governor General of Pakistan.

ITY Emblem – A78

**1967, Jan. 1** **Litho.**
*232* A78 15pa bis brn, bl & blk 7 6

International Tourist Year, 1967.

Red Crescent Emblem – A79

**1967, Jan. 10 Litho.** ***Perf. 13½***
*233* A79 15pa brn, brn org & red 7 6

Tuberculosis eradication campaign.

Scout Sign and Emblem A80

***Perf. 12½x13½***
**1967, Jan. 29** **Photo.**
*234* A80 15pa dp plum & brn org 18 7

4th National Pakistan Jamboree.

Justice Holding Scales – A81

**Unwmk.**
**1967, Feb. 17 Litho.** ***Perf. 13***
*235* A81 15pa multi 7 6

Centenary of High Court of West Pakistan.

Mohammad Iqbal – A82

**1967, Apr. 21** **Litho.** ***Perf. 13***
*236* A82 15pa red & brn 8 6
*237* A82 1r dk grn & brn 35 28

90th anniv. of the birth of Mohammad Iqbal (1877-1938), poet and philosopher.

Holy War Flag — A83

**1967, May 15** **Litho.** ***Perf. 13***
*238* A83 15pa multi 7 6

Holy War Flag awarded for valor to the cities of Lahore, Sialkot and Sargodha.

Star and "20" — A84

**1967, Aug. 14** **Photo.** **Unwmk.**
*239* A84 15pa red & sl grn 7 6

20th anniversary of independence.

Rice Plant and Globe A85

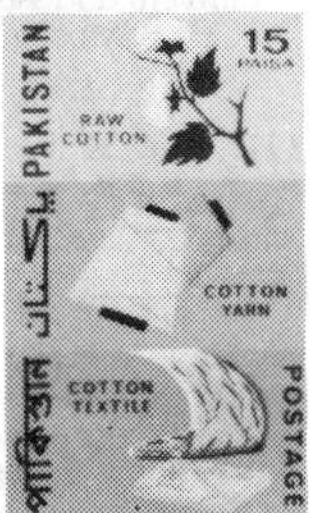

Cotton Plant, Bale and Cloth — A86

Design: 50pa, Raw jute, bale and cloth.

**1967, Sept. 26** **Photo.** ***Perf. 13x13½***
*240* A85 10pa dk bl & yel 5 5

***Perf. 13***
*241* A86 15pa org, bl grn & yel 7 6
*242* A86 50pa bl grn, brn & tan 18 12

Issued to publicize major export products.

Toys A87

**1967, Oct. 2** **Litho.** ***Perf. 13***
*243* A87 15pa multi 10 6

Issued for International Children's Day.

Shah and Empress Farah of Iran — A88

**Lithographed and Engraved**

**1967, Oct. 26** ***Perf. 13***
*244* A88 50pa yel, bl & lil 20 18

Coronation of Shah Mohammed Riza Pahlavi and Empress Farah of Iran.

"Each for all, . . ." — A89

**1967, Nov. 4** **Litho.** ***Perf. 13***
*245* A89 15pa multi 7 6

Cooperative Day, 1967.

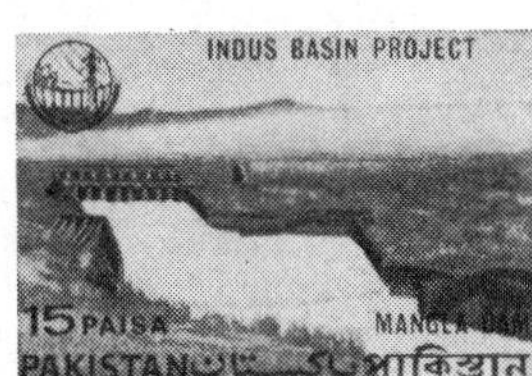

Mangla Dam — A90

**1967, Nov. 23** **Litho.** ***Perf. 13***
*246* A90 15pa multi 10 6

Issued to publicize the Indus Basin Project, to harness the Indus River for flood control and irrigation.

"Fight Against Cancer" — A91

Human Rights Flame — A92

**1967, Dec. 26**
*247* A91 15pa red & dk brn 10 6

Issued to publicize the fight against cancer.

**1968, Jan. 31** **Photo.** ***Perf. 14x12½***
*248* A92 15pa Prus grn & red 8 6
*249* A92 50pa yel, sil & red 28 14

International Human Rights Year 1968.

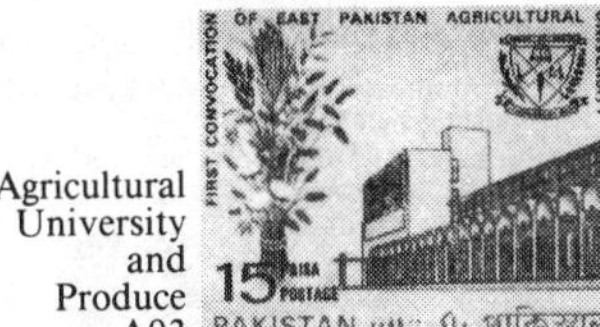

Agricultural University and Produce A93

**1968, Mar. 28** **Litho.** ***Perf. 13½***
*250* A93 15pa multi 7 6

Issued to publicize the first convocation of the East Pakistan Agricultural University.

WHO Emblem — A94

**1968, Apr. 7** **Photo.** ***Perf. 13½x12½***
*251* A94 15pa emer & org 8 6
*252* A94 50pa org & dk bl 28 12

20th anniv. of WHO.

Kazi Nazrul Islam A95

**Lithographed and Engraved**

**1968, June 25** **Unwmk.** ***Perf. 13***
*253* A95 15pa dl yel & brn 8 6
*254* A95 50pa rose & brn 22 14

Issued to honor Kazi Nazrul Islam, poet and composer.

Nos. 56, 61 and 74 Surcharged with New Value and Bars in Black or Red.

**1968, Sept.** **Engr.** ***Perf. 13***
*255* A13 4pa on 3a dk rose lake 5 5
*256* A21 4pa on 6a dk bl (R) 5 5
*257* A15 60pa on 10a pur (R) 28 18
*a* Black surcharge 35 24

Types of 1948-57

**1968** **Wmk. 351** **Engr.** ***Perf. 13***
*258* A26 10r dk grn & org 3.50 1.40
*259* A7 25r purple 6.50 5.00

Children with Hoops A96

**Unwmk.**

**1968, Oct. 7** **Litho.** ***Perf. 13***
*260* A96 15pa buff & multi 7 6

Issued for International Children's Day.

Symbolic of Political Reforms — A97

Designs: 15pa, Agricultural and industrial development. 50pa, Defense. 60pa, Scientific and cultural advancement.

**1968, Oct. 27** **Litho.** ***Perf. 13***
*261* A97 10pa multi 5 5
*262* A97 15pa multi 7 6
*263* A97 50pa multi 20 14
*264* A97 60pa multi 28 18

Development Decade, 1958-1968.

Chittagong Steel Mill — A98

**1969, Jan. 7** **Unwmk.** ***Perf. 13***
*265* A98 15pa lt gray grn, lt bl & blk 7 6

Opening of Pakistan's first steel mill.

Family of Four — A99

**1969, Jan. 14** **Litho.** ***Perf. 13½***
*266* A99 15pa lt bl & plum 7 6

Issued to publicize family planning.

Hockey Player and Medal — A100

**1969, Jan. 30** **Photo.** ***Perf. 13½***
*267* A100 15pa grn, lt bl, blk & gold 8 6
*268* A100 1r grn, sal pink, blk & gold 50 22

Pakistan's hockey victory at the 19th Olympic Games in Mexico.

Mirza Ghalib — A101

**1969, Feb. 15** **Litho.** ***Perf. 13***
*269* A101 15pa bl & multi 7 6
*270* A101 50pa multi 18 14

Mirza Ghalib (Asad Ullab Beg Khan, 1797-1869), poet who modernized the Urdu language.

Dacca Railroad Station A102

**1969, Apr. 27** **Litho.** ***Perf. 13***
*271* A102 15pa yel, grn, blk & dl bl 20 7

Opening of the new railroad station in Kamalpur area of Dacca.

ILO Emblem and Ornamental Border A103

**1969, May 15** **Litho.** ***Perf. 13½***
*272* A103 15pa brt grn & ocher 7 6
*273* A103 50pa car rose & ocher 28 18

50th anniv. of the ILO.

Common Design Types are pictured in section before Great Britain.

Lady on Balcony, Mogul Miniature, Pakistan A104

Designs: 50pa, Lady Serving Wine, Safavi miniature, Iran. 1r, Sultan Suleiman Receiving Sheik Abdul Latif, 16th century miniature, Turkey.

**1969, July 21 Litho. *Perf. 13***
*274* A104 20pa multi 7 6
*275* A104 50pa multi 18 14
*276* A104 1r multi 35 28

5th anniv. of the signing of the Regional Cooperation for Development Pact by Turkey, Iran and Pakistan.

Eastern Refinery, Chittagong A105

**1969, Sept. 14 Photo. *Perf. 13½***
*277* A105 20pa yel, blk & vio bl 10 7

Issued to commemorate the opening of the first oil refinery in East Pakistan.

Children Playing — A106

**1969, Oct. 6 *Perf. 13***
*278* A106 20pa bl & multi 10 7

Issued for Universal Children's Day.

Japanese Doll, Map of Dacca-Tokyo Pearl Route — A107

**1969, Nov. 1 Litho. *Perf. 13½x13***
*279* A107 20pa multi 8 6
*280* A107 50pa ultra & multi 20 14

Inauguration of the Pakistan International Airways' Dacca-Tokyo "Pearl Route."

Reflection of Light Diagram — A108

**1969, Nov. 4 *Perf. 13***
*281* A108 20pa multi 8 6

Alhazen (abu-Ali al Hasan ibn-al-Haytham, 965-1039), astronomer and optician.

Vickers Vimy and London-Darwin Route over Karachi — A109

**1969, Dec. 2 Photo. *Perf. 13½x13***
*282* A109 50pa multi 35 18

Issued to commemorate the 50th anniversary of the first England to Australia flight.

View of EXPO '70, Sun Tower, Flags of Pakistan, Iran and Turkey — A110

**1970, Feb. 15 Litho. *Perf. 13***
*283* A110 50pa multi 18 14

Issued to publicize EXPO '70 International Exhibition, Osaka, Japan, Mar. 15-Sept. 13.

UPU Headquarters, Bern — A111

**1970, May 20 Litho. *Perf. 13½x13***
*284* A111 20pa multi 8 6
*285* A111 50pa multi 30 14

Opening of new UPU headquarters in Bern.

A souvenir sheet of 2 exists, inscribed "U.P.U. Day 9th Oct. 1971". It contains stamps similar to Nos. 284-285, imperf.

U.N. Headquarters, New York — A112

Design: 50pa, U.N. emblem.

**1970, June 26**
*286* A112 20pa grn & multi 8 6
*287* A112 50pa vio & multi 28 14

25th anniversary of the United Nations.

Education Year Emblem and Open Book — A113

**1970, July 6 Litho. *Perf. 13***
*288* A113 20pa bl & multi 8 5
*289* A113 50pa org & multi 22 10

International Education Year, 1970.

Saiful Malook Lake, Pakistan A114

Designs: 50pa, Seeyo-Se-Pol Bridge, Esfahan, Iran. 1r, View, Fethiye, Turkey.

**1970, July 21**
*290* A114 20pa yel & multi 7 5
*291* A114 50pa yel & multi 18 8
*292* A114 1r yel & multi 35 18

6th anniv. of the signing of the Regional Cooperation for Development Pact by Pakistan, Iran and Turkey.

Asian Productivity Year Emblem — A115

**1970, Aug. 18 Photo. *Perf. 12½x14***
*293* A115 50pa blk, yel & grn 18 10

Asian Productivity Year, 1970.

Dr. Maria Montessori A116

**1970, Aug. 31 Litho. *Perf. 13***
*294* A116 20pa red & multi 7 5
*295* A116 50pa multi 18 10

Maria Montessori (1870-1952) Italian educator and physician.

Tractor and Fertilizer Factory — A117

**1970, Sept. 12**
*296* A117 20pa yel grn & brn org 7 5

10th Regional Food and Agricultural Organization Conf. for the Near East in Islamabad.

Boy, Girl, Open Book A118

Flag and Inscription A119

**1970, Oct. 5 Photo. *Perf. 13***
*297* A118 20pa multi 7 5

Issued for Children's Day.

**1970, Dec. 7 Litho. *Perf. 13½x13***
*298* A119 20pa vio & grn 7 5
*299* A119 20pa brt pink & grn 7 5

No. 298 inscribed "Elections for National Assembly 7th Dec. 1970," No. 299 inscribed "Elections for Provincial Assemblies 17th Dec. 1970."

Emblem and Burning of Al Aqsa Mosque — A120

**1970, Dec. 26 *Perf. 13½x12½***
*300* A120 20pa multi 65 35

Islamic Conference of Foreign Ministers, Karachi, Dec. 26-28.

Coastal Embankment — A121

**1971, Feb. 25 Litho. *Perf. 13***
*301* A121 20pa multi 7 5

Development of coastal embankments in East Pakistan.

Men of Different Races — A122

**1971, March 21 Litho. *Perf. 13***
*302* A122 20pa multi 7 5
*303* A122 50pa lil & multi 18 10

Intl. Year against Racial Discrimination.

Cement Factory, Daudkhel — A123

**1971, July 1** **Litho.** ***Perf. 13***
*304* A123 20pa pur, blk & brn 7 5

20th anniversary of Colombo Plan.

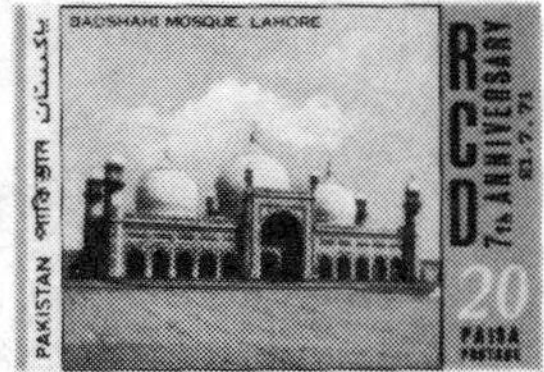

Badshahi Mosque, Lahore — A124

Designs: 10pa, Mosque of Selim, Edirne, Turkey. 50pa, Religious School, of Chaharbagh, Isfahan, Iran (vert.).

**1971, July 21** **Litho.** ***Perf. 13***
*305* A124 10pa red & multi 7 5
*306* A124 20pa grn & multi 10 5
*307* A124 50pa bl & multi 28 18

7th anniversary of Regional Cooperation among Pakistan, Iran and Turkey.

Electric Train and Boy with Toy Locomotive — A125

**1971, Oct. 4** **Litho.** ***Perf. 13***
*308* A125 20pa sl & multi 35 18

Children's Day.

Messenger and Statue of Cyrus the Great — A126

**1971, Oct. 15**
*309* A126 10pa grn & multi 5 5
*310* A126 20pa bl & multi 10 5
*311* A126 50pa red & multi 30 18

2500th anniversary of the founding of the Persian Empire by Cyrus the Great.
A souvenir sheet of 3 contains stamps similar to Nos. 309-311, imperf.

Hockey Player and Cup — A127

**1971, Oct. 24**
*312* A127 20pa red & multi 18 5

First World Hockey Cup, Barcelona, Spain, Oct. 15-24.

Great Bath at Mohenjo-Daro — A128

**1971, Nov. 4**
*313* A128 20pa dp org, dk brn & blk 10 5

25th anniv. of UNESCO.

UNICEF Emblem A129

**1971, Dec. 11** **Litho.** ***Perf. 13***
*314* A129 50pa dl bl, org & grn 22 8

25th anniv. of UNICEF.

King Hussein and Jordan Flag A130

**1971, Dec. 25**
*315* A130 20pa bl & multi 7 5

50th anniversary of the Hashemite Kingdom of Jordan.

Pakistan Hockey Federation Emblem, and Cup — A131

**1971, Dec. 31**
*316* A131 20pa yel & multi 18 5

Pakistan, world hockey champions, Barcelona, Oct. 1971.

Arab Scholars — A132

**1972, Jan. 15** **Litho.** ***Perf. 13½***
*317* A132 20pa brn, blk & bl 7 5

International Book Year 1972.

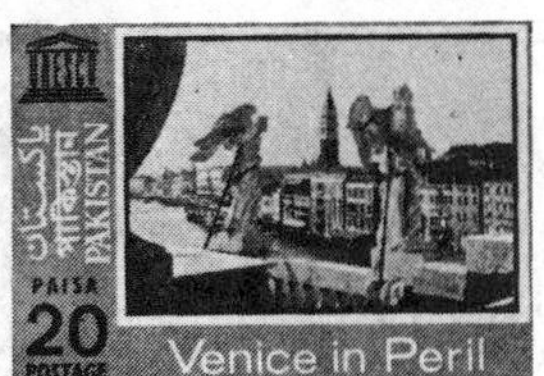

Angels and Grand Canal, Venice — A133

**1972, Feb. 5** ***Perf. 13***
*318* A133 20pa bl & multi 14 5

UNESCO campaign to save Venice.

ECAFE Emblem A134

**1972, Mar. 28** **Litho.** ***Perf. 13***
*319* A134 20pa bl & multi 10 5

Economic Commission for Asia and the Far East (ECAFE), 25th anniversary.

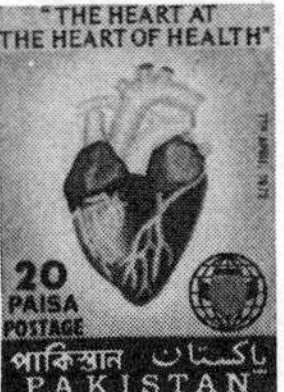

"Your Heart is your Health" — A135

**1972, Apr. 7** ***Perf. 13x13½***
*320* A135 20pa vio bl & multi 14 5

World Health Day 1972.

"Only One Earth" — A136

**1972, June 5** **Litho.** ***Perf. 12½x14***
*321* A136 20pa ultra & multi 18 5

U.N. Conference on Human Environment, Stockholm, June 5-16.

Young Man, by Abdur Rehman Chughtai A137

Paintings: 10pa, Fisherman, by Cevat Dereli (Turkey). 20pa, Persian Woman, by Behzad.

**1972, July 21** **Litho.** ***Perf. 13***
*322* A137 10pa multi 5 5
*323* A137 20pa multi 7 5
*324* A137 50pa multi 18 10

Regional Cooperation for Development Pact among Pakistan, Turkey and Iran, 8th anniversary.

Jinnah and Independence Memorial — A138

"Land Reforms" — A139

Designs: Nos. 326-329, Principal reforms. 60pa, State Bank, Islamabad, meeting-place of National Assembly (horiz.).

***Perf. 13 (A138), 13½x12½ (A139)***

**1972, Aug. 14**
*325* A138 10pa *shown* 5 5
*326* A139 20pa *shown* 10 5
*327* A139 20pa *Labor reforms* 10 5
*328* A139 20pa *Education* 10 5
*329* A139 20pa *Health care* 10 5
*330* A138 60pa rose lil & car 22 10
*Nos. 325-330 (6)* 67 35

25th anniversary of independence. Nos. 326-329 printed se-tenant in vertical rows, decorative labels adjoining.

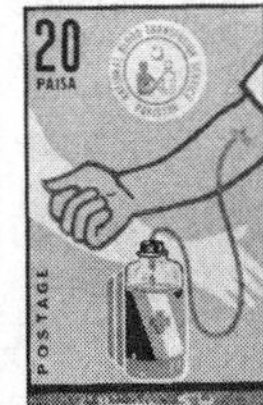

Blood Donor, Society Emblem — A140

**1972, Sept. 6** **Litho.** ***Perf. 14x12½***
*331* A140 20pa multi 14 5

Pakistan National Blood Transfusion Service.

Census Chart A141

**1972, Sept. 16 Litho. *Perf. 13½***
*332* A141 20pa multi 14 5

Centenary of population census.

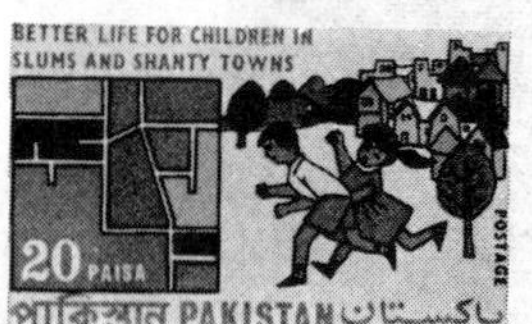


Children Leaving Slum for Modern City — A142

**1972, Oct. 2 Litho. *Perf. 13***
*333* A142 20pa multi 14 5

Children's Day.

Giant Book and Children A143

**1972, Oct. 23**
*334* A143 20pa pur & multi 14 5

Education Week.

Nuclear Power Plant, Karachi A144

**1972, Nov. 28 Litho. *Perf. 13***
*335* A144 20pa multi 14 5

Pakistan's first nuclear power plant.

Copernicus in Observatory, by Jan Matejko — A145

**1973, Feb. 19 Litho. *Perf. 13***
*336* A145 20pa multi 7 5

500th anniversary of the birth of Nicolaus Copernicus (1473-1543), Polish astronomer.

Dancing Girl, Public Baths, Mohenjo-Daro — A146

**1973, Feb. 23 *Perf. 13½x13***
*337* A146 20pa multi 7 5

50th anniv. of the Mohenjo-Daro excavations.

Foreign postal stationery (stamped envelopes, postal cards and air letter sheets) lies beyond the scope of this Catalogue, which is limited to adhesive postage stamps.

Radar, Lightning, WMO Emblem — A147

**1973, Mar. 23 Litho. *Perf. 13***
*338* A147 20p multi 14 5

Cent. of intl. meteorological cooperation.

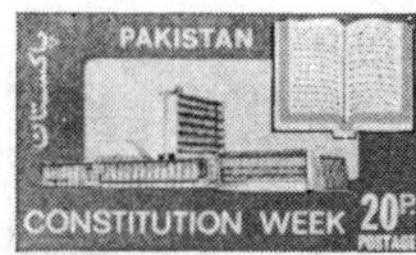


Prisoners of War A148

**1973, Apr. 18**
*339* A148 1.25r blk & multi 38 28

A plea for Pakistani prisoners of war in India.

National Assembly, Islamabad A149

**1973, Apr. 21 *Perf. 12½x13½***
*340* A149 20p grn & multi 7 5

Constitution Week.

State Bank and Emblem — A150

**1973, July 1 Litho. *Perf. 13***
*341* A150 20p multi 7 5
*342* A150 1r multi 28 20

State Bank of Pakistan, 25th anniversary.

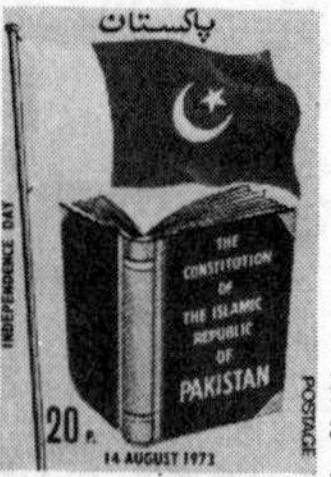


Street, Mohenjo-Daro, Pakistan — A151

Designs: 20p, Statue of man, Shahdad, Kerman, Persia, 4000 B.C. 1.25r, Head from mausoleum of King Antiochus I (69-34 B.C.), Turkey.

**1973, July 21 *Perf. 13x13½***
*343* A151 20p bl & multi 6 5
*344* A151 60p emer & multi 16 10
*345* A151 1.25r red & multi 35 25

Regional Cooperation for Development Pact among Pakistan, Turkey and Iran, 9th anniversary.

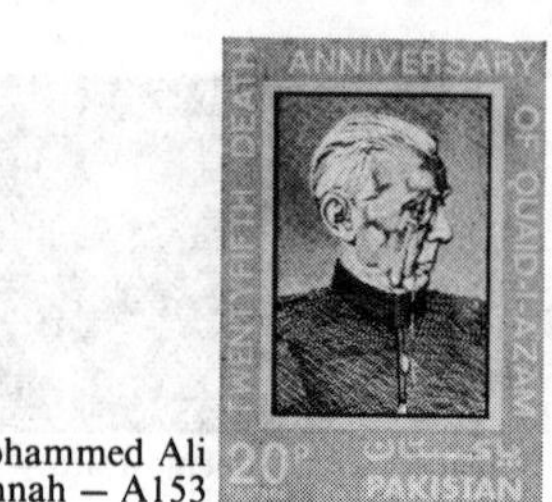


Pakistani Flag and Constitution A152

**1973, Aug. 14 Litho. *Perf. 13***
*346* A152 20p bl & multi 14 5

Independence Day.

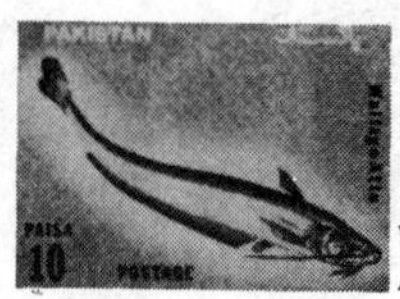


Mohammed Ali Jinnah — A153

**1973, Sept. 11 Litho. *Perf. 13***
*347* A153 20p emer, yel & blk 7 5

25th anniversary of the death of Mohammed Ali Jinnah (1876-1948), president of All-India Moslem League.

Wallago Attu — A154

Fish: 20p, Labeo rohita. 60p, Tilapia mossambica. 1r, Catla catla.

**1973, Sept. 24 Litho. *Perf. 13½***
*348* A154 10p multi 20 5
*349* A154 20p multi 25 5
*350* A154 60p multi 50 20
*351* A154 1r ultra & multi 85 35

Nos. 348-351 printed se-tenant horizontally.

Book, Torch, Child and School — A155

**1973, Oct. 1**
*352* A155 20p multi 7 5

Universal Children's Day.

Sindhi Farmer and FAO Emblem A156

**1973, Oct. 15 Litho. *Perf. 13***
*353* A156 20p multi 14 5

World Food Organization, 10th anniv.

Kemal Ataturk and Ankara — A157

**1973, Oct. 29**
*354* A157 50p multi 14 1

50th anniversary of Turkish Republic.

Scout Pointing to Planet and Stars — A158

Human Rights Flame, Sheltered Home — A159

***Perf. 13½x12½***

**1973, Nov. 11 Litho**
*355* A158 20p dl bl & multi 35 18

25th anniversary of Pakistani Boy Scouts and Silver Jubilee Jamboree.

**1973, Nov. 16**
*356* A159 20p multi 10 5

25th anniversary of the Universal Declaration of Human Rights.

al-Biruni and Jhelum Observatory — A160

**1973, Nov. 26 Litho. *Perf. 13***
*357* A160 20p multi 14 5
*358* A160 1.25r multi 50 35

International Congress on Millenary of abu-al-Rayhan al-Biruni, Nov. 26-Dec. 12.



Dr. A. G. Hansen — A161

**1973, Dec. 29**
*359* A161 20p ultra & multi 14 5

Centenary of the discovery by Dr. Armauer Gerhard Hansen of the Hansen bacillus, the cause of leprosy.

Family and WPY Emblem A162

**1974, Jan. 1 Litho. *Perf. 13***
*360* A162 20p yel & multi 6 5
*361* A162 1.25r sal & multi 35 25

World Population Year 1974.

Summit Emblem and Ornament — A163

Emblem, Crescent and Rays A164

**1974, Feb. 22** *Perf. 14x12½, 13*
*362* A163 20p multi 6 5
*363* A164 65p multi 18 14
*a* Souvenir sheet of 2 1.75 1.75

Islamic Summit Meeting. No. 363a contains two stamps similar to Nos. 362-363 with simulated perforations. Salmon and multicolored margin with Arabic inscription. Size: 102½x102½mm.

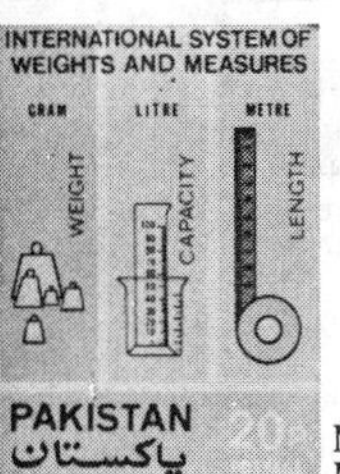


Metric Measures — A165

**1974, July 1** **Litho.** *Perf. 13*
*364* A165 20p multi 10 5

Introduction of metric system.

Kashan Rug, Lahore A166

Designs: 60p, Persian rug, late 16th century. 1.25r, Anatolian rug, 15th century.

**1974, July 21**
*365* A166 20p multi 6 5
*366* A166 60p multi 16 10
*367* A166 1.25r multi 35 25

10th anniversary of the Regional Cooperation for Development Pact among Pakistan, Iran and Turkey.

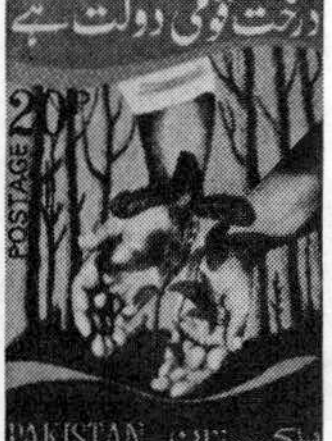


Hands Protecting Sapling — A167

**1974, Aug. 9** **Litho.** *Perf. 13*
*368* A167 20p multi 6 5

Arbor Day.

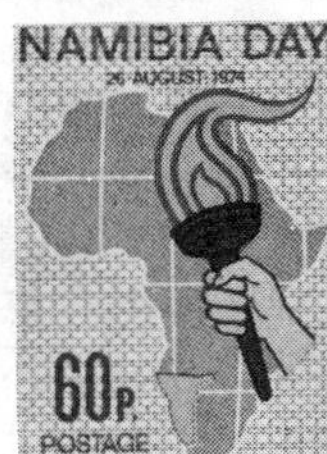


Torch over Map of Africa with Namibia A168

**1974, Aug. 26**
*369* A168 60p grn & multi 20 10

Namibia (South-West Africa) Day. See note after United Nations No. 241.

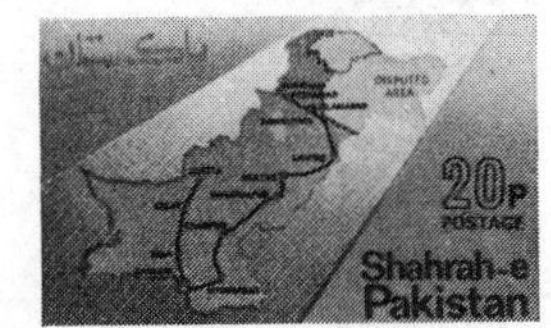


Map of Pakistan with Highways and Disputed Area — A169

**1974, Sept. 23**
*370* A169 20p multi 6 5

Highway system under construction.

Child and Students A170

**1974, Oct. 7** **Litho.** *Perf. 13*
*371* A170 20p multi 6 5

Universal Children's Day.

UPU Emblem A171

Liaqat Ali Khan A172

Design: 2.25r, Jet, UPU emblem, mail coach.

**1974, Oct. 9**
**Size: 24x36mm**
*372* A171 20p multi 6 5
**Size: 29x41mm**
*373* A171 2.25r multi 60 50
*a* Souvenir sheet of 2 1.75 1.75

Centenary of Universal Postal Union. No. 373a contains 2 imperf. stamps similar to Nos. 372-373, yellow margin with UPU emblem and inscription. Size: 103x102mm.

**1974, Oct. 16** **Litho.** *Perf. 13x13½*
*374* A172 20p blk & red 6 5

Liaqat Ali Khan, Prime Minister 1947-1951.

Mohammad Allama Iqbal — A173

**1974, Nov. 9** **Litho.** *Perf. 13*
*375* A173 20p multi 6 5

Mohammad Allama Iqbal (1877-1938), poet and philosopher.

Dr. Schweitzer on Ogowe River, 1915 — A174

**1975, Jan. 14** **Litho.** *Perf. 13*
*376* A174 2.25r multi 1.00 65

Dr. Albert Schweitzer (1875-1965), medical missionary, birth centenary.

Tourism Year 75 Emblem A175

**1975, Jan. 15**
*377* A175 2.25r multi 60 50

South Asia Tourism Year, 1975.

Flags of Participants, Memorial and Pres. Bhutto — A176

**1975, Feb. 22** **Litho.** *Perf. 13*
*378* A176 20p lt bl & multi 6 5
*379* A176 1r brt pink & multi 28 28

1st anniversary of 2nd Lahore Islamic Summit, Feb. 22.

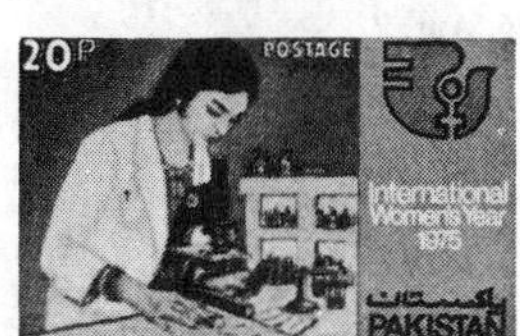


IWY Emblem and Woman Scientist — A177

Design: 2.25r, Old woman and girl learning to read and write.

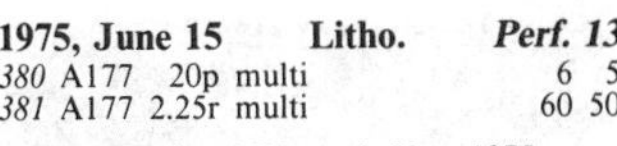
**1975, June 15** **Litho.** *Perf. 13*
*380* A177 20p multi 6 5
*381* A177 2.25r multi 60 50

International Women's Year 1975.

Globe with Dates, Arabic "X" — A178

Camel Leather Vase, Pakistan — A179

**1975, July 14** **Litho.** *Perf. 13*
*382* A178 20p multi 6 5

International Congress of Mathematical Sciences, Karachi, July 14-20.

**1975, July 21**

Designs: 60p, Ceramic plate and RCD emblem, Iran (horiz.). 1.25r, Porcelain vase, Turkey.

*383* A179 20p lil & multi 6 5
*384* A179 60p vio blk & multi 16 10
*385* A179 1.25r bl & multi 30 18

Regional Cooperation for Development Pact among Turkey, Iran and Pakistan.

Sapling, Trees and Ant — A180

Black Partridge — A181

**1975, Aug. 9** **Litho.** *Perf. 13x13½*
*386* A180 20p multi 6 5

Tree Planting Day.

**1975, Sept. 30** **Litho.** *Perf. 13*
*387* A181 20p bl & multi 35 18
*388* A181 2.25r yel & multi 1.75 65

Wildlife Protection.

Girls — A182

**1975, Oct. 6**
*389* A182 20p multi 6 5

Universal Children's Day.

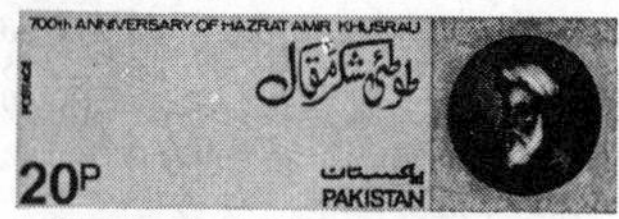


Hazrat Amir Khusrau, Sitar and Tabla — A183

**1975, Oct. 24** **Litho.** ***Perf. 14x12½***
*390* A183 20p lt bl & multi 10 5
*391* A183 2.25r pink & multi 60 50

700th anniversary of Hazrat Amir Khusrau (1253-1325), musician who invented the sitar and tabla instruments.

Mohammad Iqbal — A184

**1975, Nov. 9** ***Perf. 13***
*392* A184 20p multi 6 5

Mohammad Allama Iqbal (1877-1938), poet and philosopher, birth centenary.

Wild Sheep of the Punjab — A185

**1975, Dec. 31** **Litho.** ***Perf. 13***
*393* A185 20p multi 35 18
*394* A185 3r multi 2.00 65

Wildlife Protection. See Nos. 410-411.

Mohenjo-Daro and UNESCO Emblem — A186

Designs: View of Mohenjo-Daro excavations.

**1976, Feb. 29** **Litho.** ***Perf. 13***
*395* A186 10p multi 5 5
*396* A186 20p multi 6 5
*397* A186 65p multi 10 8
*398* A186 3r multi 50 40
*399* A186 4r multi 65 60
Strip of 5, #395-399 1.40 1.40

UNESCO campaign to save Mohenjo-Daro excavations. Printed se-tenant.

The Scott Catalogue value is a retail price, what you could expect to pay for the stamp in a grade of Fine-Very Fine. The value listed is a reference which reflects recent actual dealer selling price.

Dome and Minaret of Rauza-e-Mubarak Mausoleum A187

**1976, Mar. 3** **Photo.** ***Perf. 13½x14***
*400* A187 20p bl & multi 5 5
*401* A187 3r gray & multi 50 40

International Congress on Seerat, the teachings of Mohammed, Mar. 3-15.

Alexander Graham Bell, 1876 Telephone and Dial — A188

**1976, Mar. 10** ***Perf. 13***
*402* A188 3r bl & multi 85 85

Centenary of first telephone call by Alexander Graham Bell, Mar. 10, 1876.

College Emblem — A189

**1976, Mar. 15** **Litho.** ***Perf. 13***
*403* A189 20p multi 5 5

Cent. of Natl. College of Arts, Lahore.

Peacock A190

**1976, Mar. 31** **Litho.** ***Perf. 13***
*404* A190 20p lt bl & multi 35 18
*405* A190 3r pink & multi 2.00 65

Wildlife protection.

Eye and WHO Emblem — A191

**1976, Apr. 7**
*406* A191 20p multi 5 5

World Health Day: "Foresight prevents blindness."

Mohenjo-Daro, UNESCO Emblem, Bull (from Seal) — A192

**1976, May 31** **Litho.** ***Perf. 13***
*407* A192 20p multi 5 5

UNESCO campaign to save Mohenjo-Daro excavations.

Jefferson Memorial, U.S. Bicentennial Emblem — A193

Declaration of Independence, by John Trumbull — A194

**1976, July 4** ***Perf. 13***
*408* A193 90p multi 15 10
***Perf. 13½x13***
*409* A194 4r multi 1.40 1.40

American Bicentennial.

Wildlife Type of 1975

Wildlife protection: 20p, 3r, Ibex.

**1976, July 12**
*410* A185 20p multi 35 18
*411* A185 3r multi 2.00 65

Mohammed Ali Jinnah — A195

Designs: 65p, Riza Shah Pahlavi. 90p, Kemal Ataturk.

**1976, July 21** **Litho.** ***Perf. 14***
*412* A195 20p multi 5 5
*413* A195 65p multi 12 10
*414* A195 90p multi 18 14

Regional Cooperation for Development Pact among Pakistan, Turkey and Iran, 12th anniversary. Nos. 412-414 printed se-tenant.

Ornament A196

Jinnah and Wazir Mansion A197

Designs (Jinnah and): 40p, Sind Madressah (building). 50p, Minar Qarardad (minaret). 3r, Mausoleum.

**1976, Aug. 14** **Litho.** ***Perf. 13½***
*415* A196 5p multi 7 5
*416* A196 10p multi 10 5
*417* A196 15p multi 14 5
*418* A197 20p multi 18 5
*419* A197 40p multi 20 8
*420* A197 50p multi 28 10
*421* A196 1r multi 35 14
*422* A197 3r multi 65 50
Block of 8, #415-422 2.25 2.00

Mohammed Ali Jinnah (1876-1948), first Governor General of Pakistan, birth centenary. Horizontal rows of types A196 and A197 alternate in sheet.

Mohenjo-Daro and UNESCO Emblem — A198

**1976, Aug. 31** ***Perf. 14***
*423* A198 65p multi 12 10

UNESCO campaign to save Mohenjo-Daro excavations.

Racial Discrimination Emblem — A199

***Perf. 12½x13½***
**1976, Sept. 15** **Litho.**
*424* A199 65p multi 22 18

Fight against racial discrimination.

Child's Head, Symbols of Health, Education and Food — A200

**1976, Oct. 4** ***Perf. 13***
*425* A200 20p bl & multi 5 5

Universal Children's Day.

Verse by Allama Iqbal A201

**1976, Nov. 9** **Litho.** ***Perf. 13***
*426* A201 20p multi 5 5

Mohammed Allama Iqbal (1877-1938), poet and philosopher, birth centenary.

Scout Emblem, Jinnah Giving Salute — A202

Children Reading — A203

**1976, Nov. 20**
*427* A202 20p multi 8 5

Quaid-I-Azam Centenary Jamboree, Nov. 1976.

**1976, Dec. 15 Litho. *Perf. 13***
*428* A203 20p multi 5 5

Books for children.

Mohammed Ali Jinnah A204

**Lithographed and Embossed**

**1976, Dec. 25 *Perf. 12½***
*429* A204 10r gold & grn 1.50 1.50

Mohammed Ali Jinnah (1876-1948), 1st Governor General of Pakistan.

Farm Family and Village, Tractor, Ambulance A205

**1977, Apr. 14 Litho. *Perf. 13***
*430* A205 20p multi 5 5

Social Welfare and Rural Development Year, 1976-77.

Terracotta Bullock Cart, Pakistan — A206

Designs: 20p, Terra-cotta jug, Turkey. 90p, Decorated jug, Iran.

**1977, July 21 Litho. *Perf. 13***
*431* A206 20p ultra & multi 8 5
*432* A206 65p bl grn & multi 20 10
*433* A206 90p lil & multi 35 18

Regional Cooperation for Development Pact among Pakistan, Turkey and Iran, 13th anniversary.

Trees — A207

**1977, Aug. 9 Litho. *Perf. 13***
*434* A207 20p multi 5 5

Tree planting program.

Desert A208

**1977, Sept. 5 Litho. *Perf. 13***
*435* A208 65p multi 12 10

U.N. Conference on Desertification, Nairobi, Kenya, Aug. 29-Sept. 9.

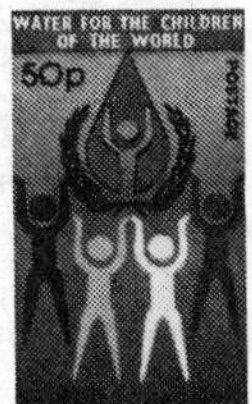


"Water for the Children" — A209

**1977, Oct. 3 Litho. *Perf. 14x12½***
*436* A209 50p multi 10 8

Universal Children's Day.

Aga Khan III — A210

**1977, Nov. 2 Litho. *Perf. 13***
*437* A210 2r multi 35 35

Aga Khan III (1877-1957), spiritual ruler of Ismaeli sect, statesman, birth centenary.

Mohammad Iqbal — A211

Designs: 20p, Spirit appearing to Iqbal, painting by Behzad. 65p, Iqbal looking at Jamaluddin Afghani and Saeed Halim offering prayers, by Behzad. 1.25r, Verse in Urdu. 2.25r, Verse in Persian.

**1977, Nov. 9**
*438* A211 20p multi 5 5
*439* A211 65p multi 14 12
*440* A211 1.25r multi 20 18
*441* A211 2.25r multi 40 35
*442* A211 3r multi 85 65
*Nos. 438-442 (5)* 1.64 1.35

Mohammad Allama Iqbal (1877-1938), poet and philosopher, birth centenary. Nos. 438-442 printed se-tenant in sheets of 50.

Holy Kaaba, Mecca — A212

**1977, Nov. 21 *Perf. 14***
*443* A212 65p grn & multi 12 10

1977 pilgrimage to Mecca.

Healthy and Sick Bodies A213

Woman from Rawalpindi-Islamabad A214

**1977, Dec. 19 Litho. *Perf. 13***
*444* A213 65p bl grn & multi 12 10

World Rheumatism Year.

**1978, Feb. 5 Litho. *Perf. 12½x13½***
*445* A214 75p multi 20 14

Indonesia-Pakistan Economic and Cultural Cooperation Organization.

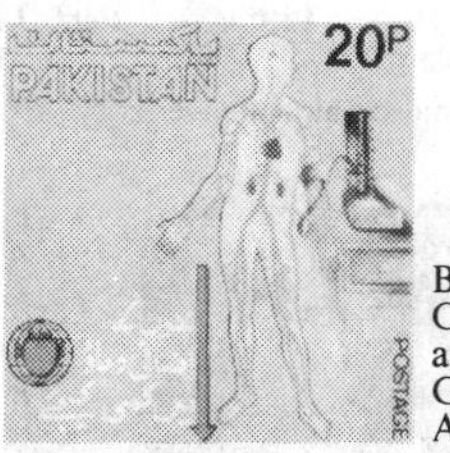


Blood Circulation and Pressure Gauge A215

**1978, Apr. 20 Litho. *Perf. 13***
*446* A215 20p bl & multi 5 5
*447* A215 2r yel & multi 35 35

Campaign against hypertension.

Henri Dunant, Red Cross, Red Crescent A216

**1978, May 8 *Perf. 14***
*448* A216 1r multi 18 18

Henri Dunant (1828-1910), founder of Red Cross, 150th birth anniversary.

Red Roses, Pakistan — A217

Designs: 90p, Pink roses, Iran. 2r, Yellow rose, Turkey.

**1978, July 21 Litho. *Perf. 13½***
*449* A217 20p multi 5 5
*450* A217 90p multi 15 14
*451* A217 2r multi 35 35

Regional Cooperation for Development Pact among Turkey, Iran and Pakistan. Nos. 449-451 printed se-tenant.

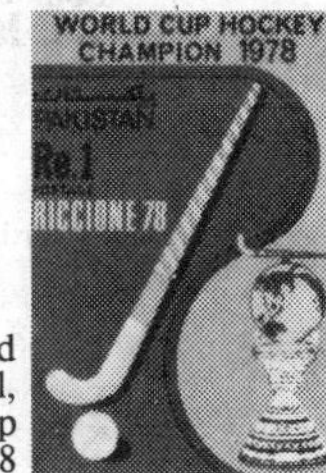


Hockey Stick and Ball, Championship Cup — A218

Fair Building, Fountain, Piazza Tourismo A219

**1978, Aug. 26 Litho. *Perf. 13***
*452* A218 1r multi 18 18
*453* A219 2r multi 35 35

Riccione '78, 30th International Stamp Fair, Riccione, Italy, Aug. 26-28. No. 452 also commemorates Pakistan as World Hockey Cup Champion.

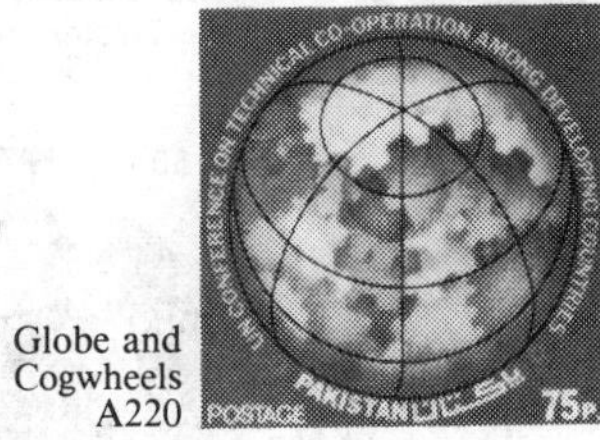


Globe and Cogwheels A220

**1978, Sept. 3**
*454* A220 75p multi 12 10

U.N. Conference on Technical Cooperation among Developing Countries, Buenos Aires, Argentina, Sept. 1978.

St. Patrick's Cathedral, Karachi A221

Design: 2r, Stained-glass window.

**1978, Sept. 29 Litho. *Perf. 13***
*455* A221 1r multi 22 18
*456* A221 2r multi 50 35

St. Patrick's Cathedral, Karachi, centenary.

The lack of a price for a listed item does not necessarily indicate rarity.

"Four Races" – A222

**1978, Nov. 20 Litho. *Perf. 13***

*457* A222 1r multi 18 14

Anti-Apartheid Year.

Maulana Jauhar – A223

**1978, Dec. 10 Litho. *Perf. 13***

*458* A223 50p multi 7 5

Maulana Muhammad Ali Jauhar, writer, journalist and patriot, birth centenary.

Qarardad Monument A224

Tractor A225

Tomb of Ibrahim Khan Makli – A225a

**Engr.; Litho. (10p, 25p, 40p, 50p, 90p)**
**1978-81 *Perf. 14***

*459* A224 2p dk grn 5 5
*460* A224 3p black 5 5
*461* A224 5p vio bl 5 5
*462* A225 10p lt bl & bl ('79) 5 5
*463* A225 20p yel grn ('79) 5 5
*464* A225 25p rose car & grn ('79) 5 5
*465* A225 40p car & bl 10 5
*466* A225 50p bl grn & vio ('79) 14 5
*467* A225 60p black 18 5
*468* A225 75p dl red 20 6
*469* A225 90p bl & car 25 7

***Perf. 13½x13***
**Engr. Wmk. 351**

*470* A225a 1r ol ('80) 28 7
*471* A225a 1.50r dp org ('79) 40 12
*472* A225a 2r car rose ('79) 55 16
*473* A225a 3r ind ('80) 85 22
*474* A225a 4r blk ('81) 1.10 35
*475* A225a 5r dk brn ('81) 1.40 40
*475A* A26 15r rose lil & red ('79) 5.00 4.00
*Nos. 459-475A (18)* 10.75 5.90

Lithographed stamps, type A225, have bottom panel in solid color with colorless lettering and numerals 2mm. high instead of 3mm.

Tornado Jet Fighter, de Havilland Rapide and Flyer A – A226

Designs (Wright Flyer A and): 1r, Phantom F4F jet fighter and Tristar airliner. 2r, Bell X15 fighter and TU-104 airliner. 2.25r, MiG fighter and Concorde.

**1978, Dec. 24 Litho. *Perf. 13***

*476* A226 65p multi 14 6
*477* A226 1r multi 20 8
*478* A226 2r multi 35 18
*479* A226 2.25r multi 40 20

75th anniv. of 1st powered flight. Nos. 476-479 printed se-tenant in sheets of 40.

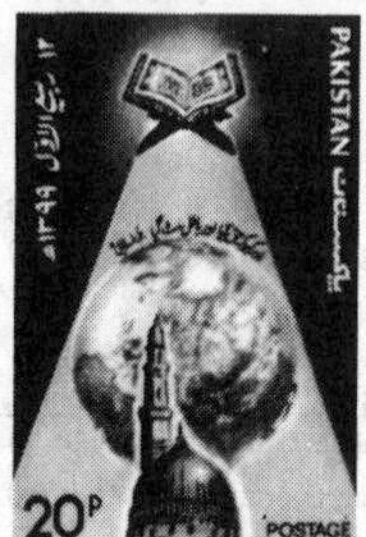


Koran Lighting the World and Mohammed's Tomb – A227

**1979, Feb. 10 Litho. *Perf. 13***

*480* A227 20p multi 5 5

Mohammed's birth anniversary.

Mother and Children A228

**1979, Feb. 25**

*481* A228 50p multi 14 5

APWA Services, 30th anniversary.

Lophophorus Impejanus – A229

Pheasants: 25p, Lophura leucomelana. 40p, Puccrasia macrolopha. 1r, Catreus walichii.

**1979, June 17 Litho. *Perf. 13***

*482* A229 20p multi 5 5
*483* A229 25p multi 5 5
*484* A229 40p multi 10 5
*485* A229 1r multi 35 8

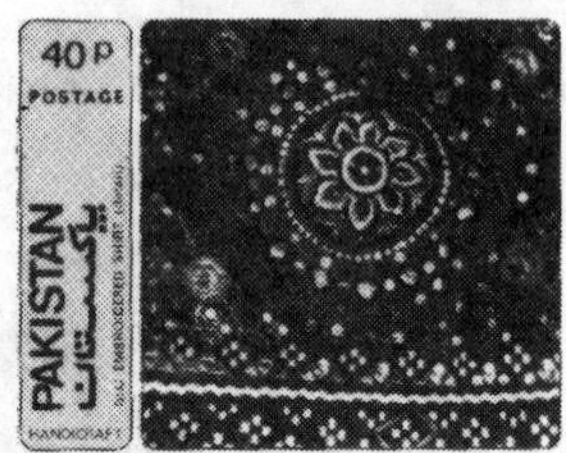


At the Well, by Allah Baksh – A230

Paintings: 75p, Potters, by Kamalel Molk, Iran. 1.60r, Plowing, by Namik Ismail, Turkey.

**1979, July 21 Litho. *Perf. 14x13***

*486* A230 40p multi 6 5
*487* A230 75p multi 10 6
*488* A230 1.60r multi 22 12

Regional Cooperation for Development Pact among Pakistan, Iran and Turkey, 15th anniversary. Nos. 486-488 printed se-tenant.

Guj Embroidery – A231

Handicrafts: 1r, Enamel inlay brass plate. 1.50r, Baskets. 2r, Peacock, embroidered rug.

**1979, Aug. 23 Litho. *Perf. 14x13***

*489* A231 40p multi 6 5
*490* A231 1r multi 14 8
*491* A231 1.50r multi 20 12
*492* A231 2r multi 28 16

Nos. 489-492 printed se-tenant.



Children, IYC and SOS Emblems A232

**1979, Sept. 10 Litho. *Perf. 13***

*493* A232 50p multi 14 5

SOS Children's Village, Lahore, opening.

Playground, IYC Emblem – A233

IYC Emblem and: Children's drawings.

**1979, Oct. 22 *Perf. 14x12½***

*494* A233 40p multi 6 5
*495* A233 75p multi 10 6
*496* A233 1r multi 14 70
*497* A233 1.50r multi 20 10

**Souvenir Sheet**

***Imperf***

*498* A233 2r multi, vert. 1.75 1.40

International Year of the Child. Nos. 494-497 se-tenant. No. 498 has multicolored margin with IYC emblems. Size: 81x65mm.

Fight Against Cancer A234

**Unwmk.**
**1979, Nov. 12 Litho. *Perf. 14***

*499* A234 40p multi 6 5

Pakistan Customs Service Centenary – A235

**1979, Dec. 10 *Perf. 13x13½***

*500* A235 1r multi 14 8

Tippu Sultan Shaheed – A236

**Wmk. 351**
**1979, Mar. 23 Litho. *Perf. 14***

*501* A236 10r shown 1.50 1.00
*502* A236 15r Syed Ahmad Khan 2.25 1.75
*503* A236 25r Altaf Hussain Hali 4.00 2.75

Nos. 501-503 se-tenant.

A237

A238

Ornament – A239

**1980, *Perf. 12***

*506* A237 10p dk grn & yel org 5 5
*507* A237 15p dk grn & ap grn 6 5
*508* A237 25p multi 7 5
*509* A237 35p multi 10 5
*510* A238 40p red & lt brn 12 5
*511* A239 50p ol & vio bl 14 5
*512* A239 80p blk & yel grn 22 6
*Nos. 506-512 (7)* 76 36

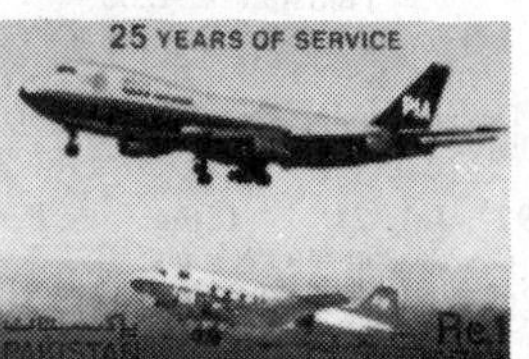


Pakistan International Airline, 25th Anniversary – A240

**1980, Jan. 10 Litho. *Perf. 13***
*516* A240 1r multi 14 7

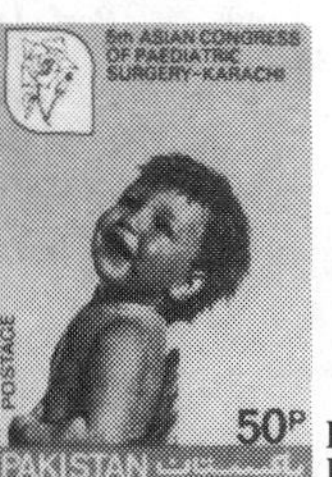

Infant, Rose — A241

**1980, Feb. 16 *Perf. 13***
*517* A241 50p multi 7 5

5th Asian Congress of Pediatric Surgery, Karachi, Feb. 16-19.

Conference Emblem A242

**1980, May 17 Litho. *Perf. 13***
*518* A242 1r multi 20 7

11th Islamic Conference of Foreign Ministers, Islamabad, May 17-21.

Lighthouse, Oil Terminal, Map Showing Karachi Harbor — A243

**1980, July 15 *Perf. 13½***
*519* A243 1r multi 20 7

Karachi Port, centenary of independent management.

Nos. 494-497 Overprinted in Red: RICCIONE 80

**1980, Aug. 30 Litho. *Perf. 14x12½***
*520* A233 40p multi 7 5
*521* A233 75p multi 18 6
*522* A233 1r multi 35 7
*523* A233 1.50r multi 65 10

RICCIONE 80 International Stamp Exhibition, Riccione, Italy, Aug. 30-Sept. 2.

Quetta Command and Staff College, 75th Anniversary A244

**1980, Sept. 18 Litho. *Perf. 13***
*524* A244 1r multi 14 7

No. 485 Overprinted: "World Tourism Conference/Manila 80"

**1980, Sept. 27**
*525* A229 1r multi 14 7

World Tourism Conf., Manila, Sept. 27.

Birth Centenary of Mohammed Shairani — A245

**1980, Oct. 5 Litho. *Perf. 13***
*526* A245 40p multi 6 5

Aga Khan Architecture Award — A246

**1980, Oct. 23 Litho. *Perf. 13½***
*527* A246 2r multi 28 14

Rising Sun A247

**1981, Mar. 7 Litho. *Perf. 13***
**Size: 30x41mm.**
*528* A247 40p Hegira emblem 10 5

**1980, Nov. 6 Litho. *Perf. 13***
*529* A247 40p *shown* 6 5

***Perf. 14***
**Size: 33x33mm.**
*530* A247 2r *Moslem symbols* 28 14

***Perf. 13x13½***
**Size: 31x54mm.**
*531* A247 3r *Globe, hands holding Koran* 40 20

**Souvenir Sheet**
***Imperf***
*532* A247 4r *Candles* 1.75 65

Hegira (Pilgrimage Year). Size of No. 532, 103x85mm.

Airmail Service, 50th Anniversary — A248

Postal History: No. 533, Postal card centenary. No. 534, Money order service centenary.

**1980-81 *Perf. 13***
*533* A248 40p multi 6 5
*534* A248 40p multi 6 5
*535* A248 1r multi 14 7

Issue dates: No. 533, Dec. 20; No. 534, Dec. 27; No. 535, Feb. 15, 1981

Heinrich von Stephan, UPU Emblem A249

**1981, Jan. 7 *Perf. 13½***
*536* A249 1r multi 14 7

Von Stephan (1831-97), founder of UPU.

Conference Emblem, Afghan Refugee A250

Conference Emblem, Flags of Participants, Men — A251

Conference Emblem, Map of Afghanistan — A252

**1981, Mar. 29 Litho. *Perf. 13***
*537* A250 40p multi 7 5
*538* A251 40p multi 7 5
*539* A250 1r multi 28 10
*540* A251 1r multi 28 10
*541* A252 2r multi 50 35
*Nos. 537-541 (5)* 1.20 65

3rd Islamic Summit Conference, Makkah al-Mukarramah, Jan. 25-28.

Conference Emblem in Ornament A253

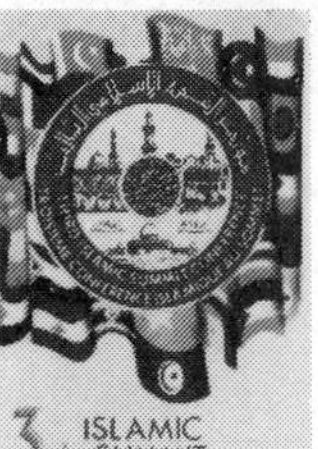

Conference Emblem, Flags of Participants A254

**1981, Mar. 29 Litho. *Perf. 13½***
*542* A253 40p multi 7 5
*543* A254 40p multi 7 5
*544* A253 85p multi 22 10
*545* A254 85p multi 22 10

3rd Islamic Summit Conference, Makkah al-Mukarramah, Jan. 25-28.

Kemal Ataturk (1881-1938), First President of Turkey — A255

**1981, May 19 Litho. *Perf. 13x13½***
*546* A255 1r multi 20 7

Green Turtle — A256

**1981, June 20 Litho. *Perf. 12x11½***
*547* A256 40p multi 30 5

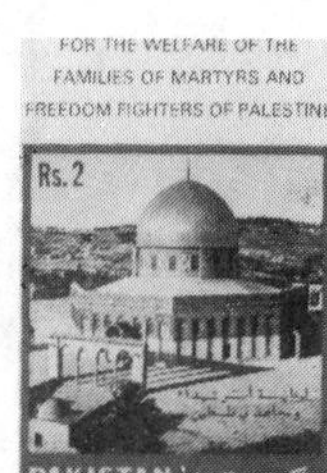

Palestinian Cooperation A257

**1981, July 25 Litho. *Perf. 13***
*548* A257 2r multi 65 35

Mt. Haramosh
A258 A259

Designs: Mountain ranges and peaks. Stamps of same denomination se-tenant.

**1981, Aug. 20 *Perf. 14x13½***
*549* A258 40p Malubiting West, range 6 5
*550* A259 40p Peak 6 5
*551* A258 1r shown 18 7
*552* A259 1r shown 18 7
*553* A258 1.50r K6, range 28 10
*554* A259 1.50r Peak 28 10
*555* A258 2r K2, range 35 14
*556* A259 2r Peak 35 14
*Nos. 549-556 (8)* 1.74 72

Inauguration of Pakistan Steel Furnace No. 1, Karachi — A260

**1981, Aug. 31** *Perf. 13*

*557* A260 40p multi 6 5
*558* A260 2r multi 28 14

Western Tragopan in Summer A261

**1981, Sept. 15 Litho.** *Perf. 14*

*559* A261 40p shown 10 6
*560* A261 2r Winter 55 28

Intl. Year of the Disabled A262

**1981, Dec. 12 Litho.** *Perf. 13*

*561* A262 40p multi 6 5
*562* A262 2r multi 28 14

World Cup Championship A263

**1982, Jan. 31 Litho.** *Perf. 13½x13*

*563* A263 1r Cup, flags in arc 14 7
*564* A263 1r Cup, flags, diff 14 7

Nos. 563-564 se-tenant.

Camel Skin Lampshade A264

**1982, Feb. 20 Litho.** *Perf. 14*

*565* A264 1r shown 14 7
*566* A264 1r Hala pottery 14 7

See Nos. 582-583.

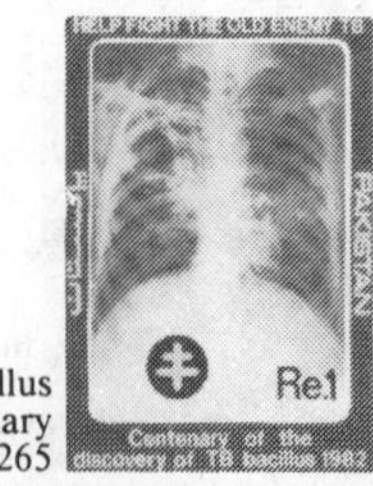


TB Bacillus Centenary A265

**1982, Mar. 24**

*567* A265 1r multi 20 18

Blind Indus Dolphin A266

**1982, Apr. 24 Litho.** *Perf. 12x11½*

*568* A266 40p Dolphin 10 6
*569* A266 1r Dolphin, diff. 28 14

Peaceful Uses of Outer Space — A267

**1982, June 7 Litho.** *Perf. 13*

*570* A267 1r multi 20 7

50th Anniv. of Sukkur Barrage — A268

**1982, July 17 Litho.** *Perf. 13*

*571* A268 1r multi 14 7

Independence Day — A269

**1982, Aug. 14**

*572* A269 40p Flag 6 5
*573* A269 85p Map 12 7

No. 571 Overprinted: "RICCIONE-82/1932-1982"

**1982, Aug. 28**

*574* A268 1r multi 35 18

RICCIONE '82 Intl. Stamp Exhibition, Riccione, Italy, Aug. 28-30.

University of the Punjab Centenary — A270

**1982, Oct. 14 Litho.** *Perf. 13½*

*575* A270 40p multi 6 5

Scouting Year — A271

**1982, Dec. 23 Litho.** *Perf. 13*

*576* A271 2r Emblem 50 20

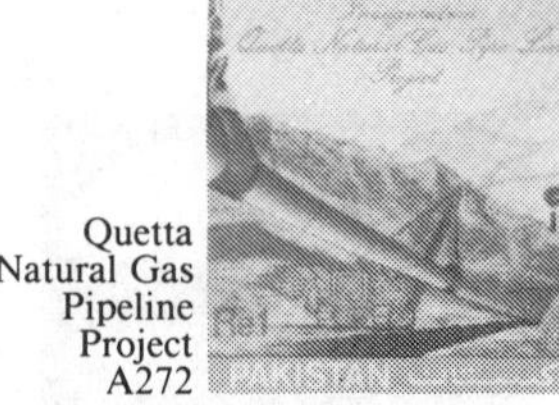


Quetta Natural Gas Pipeline Project A272

**1983, Jan. 6 Litho.** *Perf. 13*

*577* A272 1r multi 20 7

Common Peacock A273

**1983, Feb. 15 Litho.** *Perf. 14*

*578* A273 40p shown 6 5
*579* A273 50p Common rose 7 5
*580* A273 60p Plain tiger 8 5
*581* A273 1.50r Lemon butterfly 28 14

Handicraft Type of 1982

**1983, Mar. 9**

*582* A264 1r Straw mats 14 7
*583* A264 1r Five-flower cloth design 14 7

Opening of Aga Khan University — A274

**1983, Mar. 16** *Perf. 13½*

*584* A274 2r multi 28 14

Yak Caravan, Zindiharam-Darkot Pass, Hindu Kush Mountains — A275

**1983, Apr. 28 Litho.** *Perf. 13*

*585* A275 1r multi 20 7

Marsh Crocodile A276

**1983, May 19** *Perf. 13½x14*

*586* A276 3r multi 55 28

**1983, June 20 Litho.** *Perf. 14*

**Size: 50x40mm**

*587* A276 1r Gazelle 28 14

36th Anniv. of Independence A277

**1983, Aug. 14** *Perf. 13*

*588* A277 60p Star 8 5
*589* A277 4r Torch 55 28

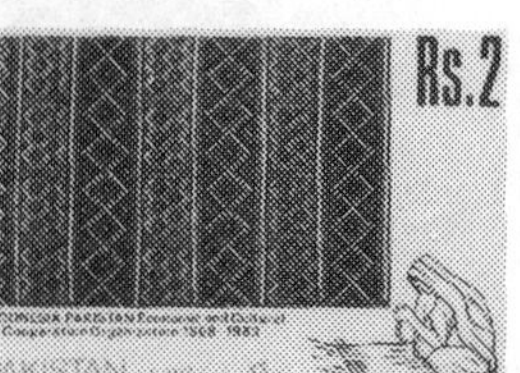


25th Anniv. of Indonesia-Pakistan Economic and Cultural Cooperation Org. — A278

Weavings.

**1983, Aug. 19 Litho.** *Perf. 13*

*590* A278 2r Pakistani (geometric) 28 14
*591* A278 2r Indonesian (figures) 28 14

Siberian Cranes — A279

**1983, Sept. 8** *Perf. 13½*

*592* A279 3r multi 50 20

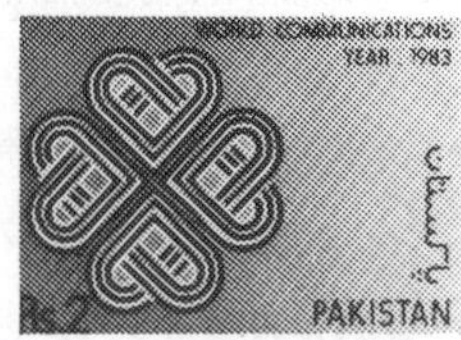


World Communications Year — A280

**1983, Oct. 9 Litho.** *Perf. 13*

*593* A280 2r multi 28 14

**Size: 33x33mm**

*594* A280 3r Symbol, diff. 40 20

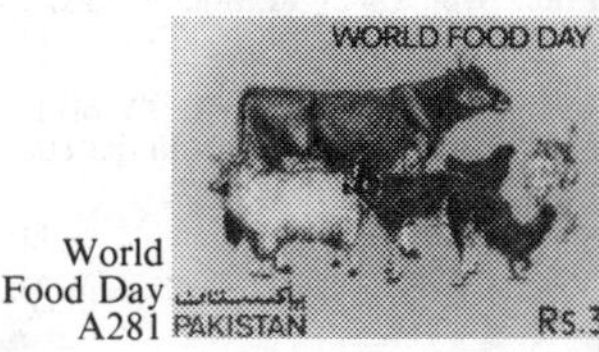


World Food Day A281

**1983, Oct. 24 Litho.** *Perf. 13*

*595* A281 3r Livestock 42 20
*596* A281 3r Fruit 42 20
*597* A281 3r Grain 42 20
*598* A281 3r Seafood 42 20

National Fertilizer Corp. — A282

**1983, Oct. 24** **Litho.** ***Perf. 13½***

| | | | |
|---|---|---|---|
| *599* A282 60p multi | | 14 | 5 |

PAKPHILEX '83 Natl. Stamp Exhibition A283

**1983, Nov. 13** **Litho.** ***Perf. 13***

| | | | |
|---|---|---|---|
| *600* | Strip of 6, View of Lahore City, 1852 | 85 | 28 |
| *a.-f* | A283 60p any single | 10 | 5 |

Yachting Victory in 9th Asian Games, 1982 — A284

**1983, Dec. 31** **Litho.** ***Perf. 13***

| | | |
|---|---|---|
| *601* A284 60p OK Dinghy | 14 | 5 |
| *602* A284 60p Enterprise | 14 | 5 |


Snow Leopard — A285

**1984, Jan. 21** ***Perf. 14***

| | | |
|---|---|---|
| *603* A285 40p lt grn & multi | 10 | 5 |
| *604* A285 1.60r bl & multi | 40 | 10 |

Jehangir Khan (b. 1963), World Squash Champion A286

**1984, Mar. 17** **Litho.** ***Perf. 13***

| | | |
|---|---|---|
| *605* A286 3r multi | 30 | 15 |

Pakistan Intl. Airway China Service, 20th Anniv. — A287

**1984, Apr. 29** **Litho.** ***Perf. 13***

| | | |
|---|---|---|
| *606* A287 3r Jet | 30 | 15 |

Glass Work, Lahore Fort A288

Various glass panels.

**1984, May 31** **Litho.** ***Perf. 13***

| | | |
|---|---|---|
| *607* A288 1r grn & multi | 10 | 6 |
| *608* A288 1r pur & multi | 10 | 6 |
| *609* A288 1r ver & multi | 10 | 6 |
| *610* A288 1r brt bl & multi | 10 | 6 |

Forts — A289

**1984-86** **Litho.** ***Perf. 11***

| | | | |
|---|---|---|---|
| *612* | A289 5p Kot Diji | 5 | 5 |
| *613* | A289 10p Rohtas | 5 | 5 |
| *613A* | A289 15p Bala Hissar ('86) | 5 | 5 |
| *614* | A289 20p Attock | 5 | 5 |
| *617* | A289 50p Hyderabad ('86) | 10 | 5 |
| *618* | A289 60p Lahore | 14 | 5 |

Issue dates: 5p, Nov. 1. 10p, Sept. 25.


Shah Rukn-i-Alam Tomb, Multan — A290

**1984, June 26** **Litho.** ***Perf. 13***

| | | |
|---|---|---|
| *624* A290 60p multi | 10 | 6 |

Aga Khan Award for Architecture.

Asia-Pacific Broadcasting Union, 20th Anniv. — A290a

**1984, July 1** **Litho.** ***Perf. 13***

| | | |
|---|---|---|
| *625* A290a 3r multi | 28 | 14 |

1984 Summer Olympics, Los Angeles — A291

**1984, July 31**

| | | |
|---|---|---|
| *626* A291 3r Athletics | 50 | 14 |
| *627* A291 3r Boxing | 50 | 14 |
| *628* A291 3r Hockey | 50 | 14 |
| *629* A291 3r Yachting | 50 | 14 |
| *630* A291 3r Wrestling | 50 | 14 |
| *Nos. 626-630 (5)* | 2.50 | 70 |

Issued in sheets of 10.

Independence, 37th Anniv. — A292

**1984, Aug. 14**

| | | |
|---|---|---|
| *631* A292 60p Jasmine | 10 | 6 |
| *632* A292 4r Lighted torch | 65 | 35 |

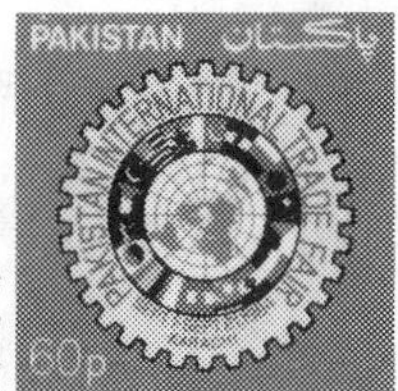

Intl. Trade Fair, Sept. 1-21, Karachi A293

**1984, Sept. 1**

| | | |
|---|---|---|
| *633* A293 60p multi | 10 | 6 |

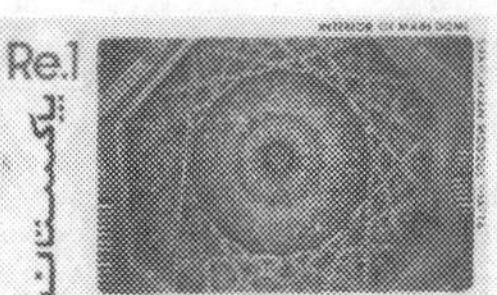

1984 Natl. Tourism Convention, Karachi, Nov. 5-8 — A293a

Shah Jahan Mosque: No. 634a, Main dome interior. No. 634b, Tile work. No. 634c, Entrance. No. 634d, Archways. No. 634e, Dome interior, diff.

**1984, Nov. 5** **Litho.** ***Perf. 13½***

| | | | |
|---|---|---|---|
| *634* | Strip of 5 | 50 | 28 |
| *a.-e* | A293a 1r, any single | 10 | 6 |

United Bank Limited, 25th Anniv. A294

**1984, Nov. 7**

| | | |
|---|---|---|
| *635* A294 60p multi | 7 | 5 |

UNCTAD, UN Conference on Trade and Development, 20th Anniv. — A294a

**1984, Dec. 24** ***Perf. 14½x14***

| | | |
|---|---|---|
| *636* A294a 60p multi | 7 | 5 |

Postal Life Insurance, Cent. — A295

**1984, Dec. 29** ***Perf. 13½x14***

| | | |
|---|---|---|
| *637* A295 60p multi | 6 | 5 |
| *638* A295 1r multi | 10 | 6 |

UNESCO World Heritage Campaign A296

**1984, Dec. 31**

| | | |
|---|---|---|
| *639* A296 2r Unicorn, rock painting | 20 | 10 |
| *640* A296 2r Unicorn seal, round | 20 | 10 |

Restoration of Mohenjo-Daro. Nos. 639-640 printed se-tenant.

IYY, Girl Guides 75th Anniv. A297

**1985, Jan. 5** ***Perf. 13½***

| | | |
|---|---|---|
| *641* A297 60p Emblems | 10 | 5 |

Smelting A298

Pouring Steel — A299

**1985, Jan. 15** *Perf. 13*
642 A298 60p multi 6 5
643 A299 1r multi 10 6

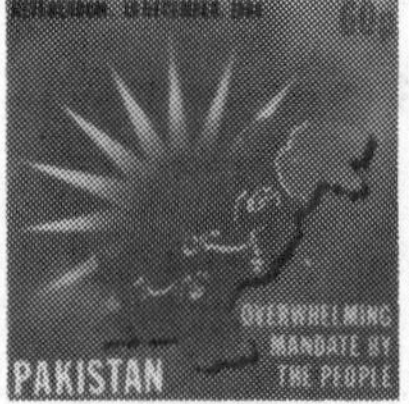

Referendum Reinstating Pres. Zia — A300

**1985, Mar. 20** Litho. *Perf. 13*
644 A300 60p Map, sunburst 6 5

Minar-e-Qarardad-e-Pakistan Tower — A301

Ballot Box — A302

1985 Elections.

**1985, Mar. 23**
645 A301 1r multi 10 6
646 A302 1r multi 10 6

Mountaineering — A303

**1985, May 27** Litho. *Perf. 14*
647 A303 40p Mt. Rakaposhi, Karakoram 5 5
648 A303 2r Mt. Nangaparbat, Western Himalayas 20 10

Championship Pakistani Men's Field Hockey Team — A304

Design: 1984 Olympic gold medal, 1985 Dhaka Asia Cup, 1982 Bombay World Cup.

**1985, June 5** Litho. *Perf. 13*
649 A304 1r multi 10 6

King Edward Medical College, Lahore, 125th Anniv. — A305

**1985, July 28** Litho. *Perf. 13*
650 A305 3r multi 40 20

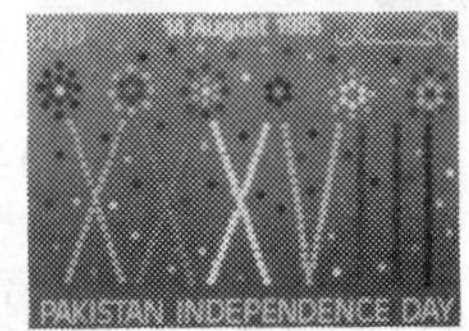

Natl. Independence Day — A306

Designs: No. 651a, 37th Independence Day written in English. No. 651b, In Arabic.

**1985, Aug. 14**
651 Pair 20 10
*a.-b.* A306 60p, any single 10 6

Sind Madressah-Tul-Islam, Karachi, Education Cent. — A307

**1985, Sept. 1**
652 A307 2r multi 35 18

Mosque, Jinnah Avenue, Karachi — A308

**1985, Sept. 14**
653 A308 1r Mosque by day 18 8
654 A308 1r At night 18 8

35th anniv. of the Jamia Masjid Pakistan Security Printing Corporation's miniature replica of the Badshahi Mosque, Lahore.

Lawrence College, Murree, 125th Anniv. — A309

**1985, Sept. 21**
655 A309 3r multi 50 25

UN, 40th Anniv. — A310

**1985, Oct. 24** Litho. *Perf. 14x14½*
656 A310 1r UN building, sun 10 6
657 A310 2r Building emblem 20 10

10th Natl. Scouting Jamboree, Lahore, Nov. 8-15 — A311

**1985, Nov. 8** *Perf. 13*
658 A311 60p multi 10 5

Islamabad and Capital Development Authority Emblem — A312

**1985, Nov. 30** *Perf. 14½*
659 A312 3r multi 50 25

Islamabad, capital of Pakistan, 25th anniv.

Flags and Map of SAARC Nations A313

Flags as Flower Petals A314

**1985, Dec. 8** *Perf. 13½, 13*
660 A313 1r multi *10 6*
661 A314 2r multi *20 10*

SAARC, South Asian Assoc. for Regional Cooperation.

Dove and World Map A315

**1985, Dec. 14** *Perf. 13*
662 A315 60p multi 6 5

UN Declaration on the Granting of Independence to Colonial Countries and Peoples, 25th Anniv.

Shaheen Falcon — A316

**1986, Jan. 20** *Perf. 13½x14*
663 A316 1.50r multi 35 18

Agricultural Development Bank, 25th Anniv. — A317

**1986, Feb. 18** Litho. *Perf. 13*
664 A317 60p multi 7 5

Sadiq Egerton College, Bahawalpur, Cent. — A318

**1986, Apr. 25**
665 A318 1r multi 10 6

Asian Productivity Organization, 25th Anniv. — A319

**1986, May 11** *Perf. 13½*
666 A319 1r multi 10 6

Independence Day, 39th Anniv. — A320

**1986, Aug. 14** Litho. *Perf. 14½x14*
667 A320 80p "1947-1986" 10 5
668 A320 1r Urdu text, fireworks 10 6

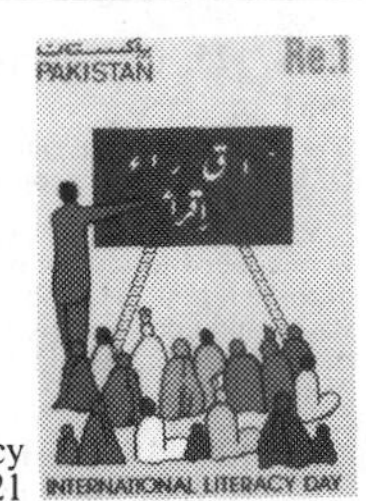


Intl. Literacy Day — A321

**1986, Sept. 8** ***Perf. 13***
*669* A321 1r Teacher, students 10 6

UN Child Survival Campaign — A322

**1986, Oct. 28** **Litho.** ***Perf. 13½x13***
*670* A322 80p multi 10 5

Aitchison College, Lahore, Cent. — A323

**1986, Nov. 3** ***Perf. 13½***
*671* A323 2.50r multi 28 14

Intl. Peace Year — A324

**1986, Nov. 20** ***Perf. 13***
*672* A324 4r multi 42 22

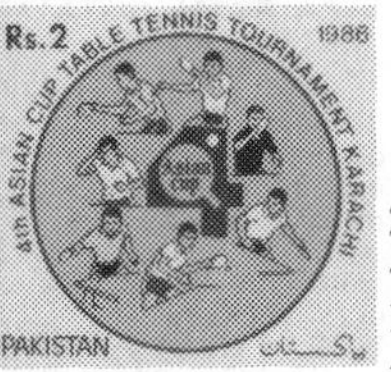


4th Asian Cup Table Tennis Tournament, Karachi A325

**1986, Nov. 25** ***Perf. 14½***
*673* A325 2r multi 22 10

Marcopolo Sheep — A326

**1986, Dec. 4** **Litho.** ***Perf. 14***
*674* A326 2r multi 22 10

See No. 698.

Eco Philex '86 — A327

Mosques: No. 675a, Selimiye, Turkey. No. 675b, Gawhar Shad, Iran. No. 675c, Grand Mosque, Pakistan.

**1986, Dec. 20** ***Perf. 13***
*675* Strip of 3 1.00 48
***a.-c*** A327 3r, any single 32 16

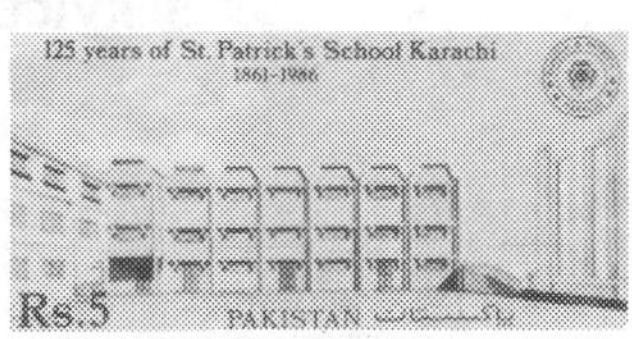


St. Patrick's School, Karachi, 125th Anniv. — A328

**1987, Jan. 29** **Litho.** ***Perf. 13***
*676* A328 5r multi 55 28

Savings Bank Week — A329

Birds, berries and: a, National defense. b, Education. c, Agriculture. d, Industry.

**1987, Feb. 21** **Litho.** ***Perf. 13***
*677* Block of 4 + 2 labels 2.25 1.10
***a.-d*** A329 5r any single 55 28

No. 677 printed se-tenant with 2 labels picturing posthorn and bank emblem.

Parliament House Opening, Islamabad — A330

**1987, Mar. 23**
*678* A330 3r multi 32 16

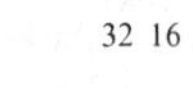

Fight Against Drug Abuse A331

**1987, June 30** **Litho.** ***Perf. 13***
*679* A331 1r multi 14 7

Natl. Independence, 40th Anniv. — A332

Natl. flag and: 80p, Natl. anthem, written in Urdu. 3r, Quaid-i-Azam's first natl. address, the Minar-e-Qarardad-e-Pakistan and natl. coat of arms.

**1987, Aug. 14** **Litho.** ***Perf. 13***
*680* A332 80p multi 10 6
*681* A332 3r multi 40 20

**Miniature Sheet**

Air Force, 40th Anniv. — A333

Aircraft: a. Tempest II. b. Hawker Fury. c. Super Marine Attacker. d. F86 Sabre. e. F104 Star Fighter. f. C130 Hercules. g. F6. h. Mirage III. i. A5. j. F16 Fighting Falcon.

**1987, Sept. 7** **Litho.** ***Perf. 13½***
*682* Sheet of 10 4.00 2.00
***a.-j*** A333 3r any single 40 20

Size of No. 682: 139x189mm.

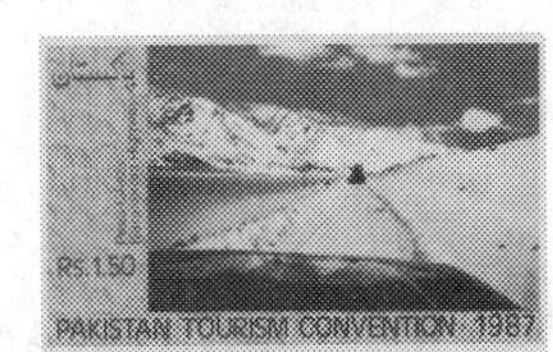


Tourism Convention 1987 — A334

Views along Karakoram Highway: a. Pasu Glacier. b. Apricot trees. c. Highway winding through hills. d. Khunjerab peak.

**1987, Oct. 1** ***Perf. 13***
*683* Block of 4 80 40
***a.-d*** A334 1.50r any single 20 10

Shah Abdul Latif Bhitai Mausoleum — A335

**1987, Oct. 8** ***Perf. 13***
*684* A335 80p multi 10 6

D.J. Sind Government Science College, Karachi, Cent. — A336

**1987, Nov. 7**
*685* A336 80p multi 10 6

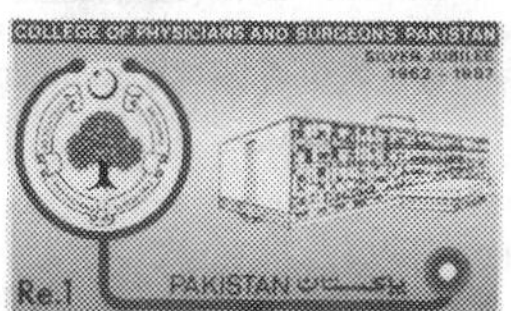


College of Physicians and Surgeons, 25th Anniv. — A337

**1987, Dec. 9** **Litho.** ***Perf. 13***
*686* A337 1r multi 15 8

Intl. Year of Shelter for the Homeless — A338

**1987, Dec. 15**
*687* A338 3r multi 45 22

Cathedral Church of the Resurrection, Lahore, Cent. — A339

**1987, Dec. 20**
*688* A339 3r multi 45 22

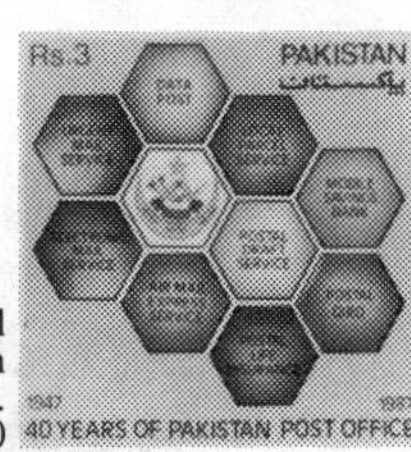


Natl. Postal Service, 40th Anniv. A340

**1987, Dec. 28**
*689* A340 3r multi 45 22

Radio Pakistan A341

**1987, Dec. 31**
*690* A341 80p multi 12 6

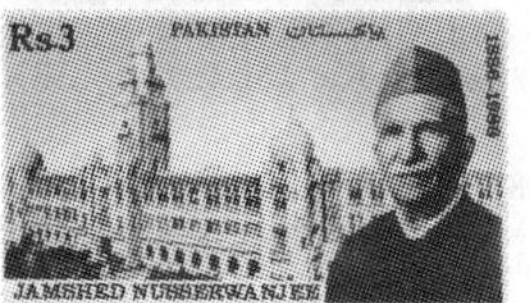


Jamshed Nusserwanjee Mehta (1886-1952), Mayor of Karachi, Member of the Sind Legislative Assembly — A342

**1988, Jan. 7**
*691* A342 3r multi 45 22

World Leprosy Day — A343

**1988, Jan. 31**
*692* A343 3r multi 45 22

World Health Organization, 40th Anniv. — A344

**1988, Apr. 7 Litho. *Perf. 13***
*693* A344 4r multi 50 25

Intl. Red Cross and Red Crescent Organizations, 125th Annivs. — A345

**1988, May 8**
*694* A345 3r red brn, grn & turq blue 45 22

Independence Day, 41st Anniv. — A346

**1988, Aug. 14 Litho. *Perf. 13½***
*695* A346 80p multi 12 6
*696* A346 4r multi 50 25

Miniature Sheet

1988 Summer Olympics, Seoul — A347

Events: a, Discus, shot put, hammer throw, javelin. b, Relay, hurdles, running, walking. c, High jump, long jump, triple jump, pole vault. d, Gymnastic floor exercises, rings, parallel bars. e, Table tennis, tennis, field hockey, baseball. f, Volleyball, soccer, basketball, team handball. g, Wrestling, judo, boxing, weight lifting. h, Sport pistol, fencing, rifle shooting, archery. i, Swimming, diving, yachting, quadruple-sculling, kayaking. j, Equestrian jumping, cycling, steeplechase.

**1988, Sept. 17 Litho. *Perf. 13½x13***
*697* Sheet of 10+32 labels 12.50 6.25
*a.-j.* A347 10r any single 1.25 62

Labels contained in No. 697 picture the Seoul Games character trademark or emblem. Size of No. 697: 251x214mm.

Fauna Type of 1986

**1988, Oct. 29 Litho. *Perf. 14***
*698* A326 2r Suleman markhor, vert. 25 12

## OFFICIAL STAMPS

Official Stamps of India, 1939-43, Overprinted in Black **PAKISTAN**

**1947-49 Wmk. 196 *Perf. 13½x14***
*O1* O8 3p slate 5 5
*O2* O8 ½a dk rose vio 5 5
*O3* O8 9p green 5 5
*O4* O8 1a car rose 5 5
*O4A* O8 1a3p bis ('49) 1.75 1.75
*O5* O8 1½a dl pur 5 5
*O6* O8 2a scarlet 6 5
*O7* O8 2½a purple 10 10
*O8* O8 4a dk brn 10 7
*O9* O8 8a bl vio 35 35

India Nos. O100-O103 Overprinted in Black **PAKISTAN**

*O10* A82 1r brn & sl 65 35
*O11* A82 2r dk brn & dk vio 1.40 18
*O12* A82 5r dp ultra & dk grn 5.00 5.00
*O13* A82 10r rose car & dk vio 13.50 13.50
*Nos. O1-O13 (14)* 23.16 21.60

Regular Issue of 1948 Overprinted in Black or Carmine — a **SERVICE**

***Perf. 12½, 13, 13½x14, 14x13½.***
**1948 Unwmk.**
*O14* A3 3p org red 5 5
*O15* A3 6p pur (C) 5 5
*O16* A3 9p dk grn (C) 5 5
*O17* A4 1a dk bl (C) 6 5
*O18* A4 1½a gray grn (C) 6 5
*O19* A4 2a org red 7 5
*O20* A5 3a ol grn 8 5
*O21* A6 4a chocolate 8 6
*O22* A6 8a blk (C) 14 10
*O23* A5 1r ultra 28 8
*O24* A5 2r dk brn 55 18
*O25* A5 5r carmine 1.10 65
*O26* A7 10r rose lil, perf. 14x13½ 3.00 1.40
*a.* Perf. 12 5.00 1.40
*b.* Perf. 13 4.00 85
*Nos. O14-O26 (13)* 5.57 2.82

Nos. 47-50 and 52 Overprinted Type "a" in Black or Carmine.

**1949-50 *Perf. 12½, 13½x14***
*O27* A10 1a dk bl (C) 5 5
*O28* A10 1½a gray grn (C) 5 5
*a.* Inverted ovpt. 35.00
*O29* A10 2a org red 5 5
*O30* A9 3a ol grn ('49) 6 6
*O31* A11 8a blk (C) 14 7
*Nos. O27-O31 (5)* 35 28

Types of Regular Issue of 1951, "Pakistan" or "Pakistan Postage" Replaced by "SERVICE"

**1951 Unwmk. Engr. *Perf. 13.***
*O32* A13 3a dk rose lake 6 5
*O33* A14 4a dp grn 7 5
*O34* A15 8a brown 18 6

Nos. 24-26, 47-49, 38-41 Overprinted in Black or Carmine

b **SERVICE**

**1954**
*O35* A3 3p org red 5 5
*O36* A3 6p pur (C) 5 5
*O37* A3 9p dk grn (C) 5 5
*O38* A10 1a dk bl (C) 5 5
*O39* A10 1½a gray grn (C) 5 5
*O40* A10 2a org red 6 5
*O41* A5 1r ultra 30 14
*O42* A5 2r dk brn 50 22
*O43* A5 5r carmine 1.10 30
*O43A* A7 10r rose lil 3.50 1.40
*Nos. O35-O43A (10)* 5.71 2.36

Nos. 66-72 Overprinted Type "b" in Carmine or Black

**1954**
*O44* A18 6p rose vio (C) 5 5
*O45* A19 9p bl (C) 5 5
*O46* A19 1a car rose 5 5
*O47* A18 1½a red 5 5
*O48* A20 14a dk grn (C) 22 20
*O49* A20 1r yel grn (C) 30 28
*O50* A20 2r orange 60 35
*Nos. O44-O50 (7)* 1.32 1.03

No. 75 Overprinted in Carmine Type "b" Overprint: 13x2½mm

**1955 Unwmk. *Perf. 13***
*O51* A21 8a violet 18 6

Nos. 24, 40, 66-72, 74-75, 83, 89 Overprinted in Black or Carmine

c **SERVICE**

**1957-61**
*O52* A3 3p org red ('58) 5 5
*O53* A18 6p rose vio (C) 5 5
*O54* A19 9p bl (C) ('58) 6 6
*O55* A19 1a car rose 5 5
*O56* A18 1½a red 5 5
*O57* A24 2a red ('58) 5 5
*O58* A21 6a dk bl (C) ('60) 10 6
*O59* A21 8a vio (C) ('58) 14 7
*O60* A20 14a dk grn (C) ('58) 25 25
*O61* A20 1r yel grn (C) ('58) 30 7
*O62* A20 2r org ('58) 60 7
*O63* A5 5r car ('58) 1.40 20
*O64* A26 10r dk grn & org (C) ('61) 2.75 1.00
*Nos. O52-O64 (13)* 5.85 2.03

Nos. 110-111 Overprinted Type "c"

**1961**
*O65* A33 8a green 18 6
*O66* A33 1r blue 25 6
*a.* Inverted overprint 8.25

Nos. O52, O55-O57 Surcharged with New Value in Paisa.

**1961**
*O67* A18 1p on 1½a red 5 5
*a.* Overprinted type "b" 85 85
*O68* A3 2p on 3p org red 5 5
*a.* Overprinted type "b" 1.75 1.75
*O69* A19 6p on 1a car rose 50 14
*O70* A19 7p on 1a car rose 5 5
*a.* Overprinted type "b" 2.25 2.25
*O71* A18 9p on 1½a red 50 35
*O72* A24 13p on 2a red ("PAISA") 5 5
*O73* A24 13p on 2a red ("Paisa") 6 6
*Nos. O67-O73 (7)* 1.26 75

Nos. 125, 128 Overprinted Type "c"

**1961**
*O74* A33 3p on 6p pur 5 5
*O75* A33 13p on 2a cop red 5 5

Various violet handstamped surcharges were applied to several official stamps. Most of these repeat the denomination of the basic stamp and add the new value. Example: "4 ANNAS (25 Paisa)" on No. O33.

Nos. 129-135, 135B, 135C, 137-140a Overprinted in Carmine

d **SERVICE**

**1961-79 *Perf. 13½x14***
*O76* A40 1p vio (II) 5 5
*a.* Type I 5 5
*b.* Redrawn (#129b) ('63) 5 5
*O77* A40 2p rose red (II) 5 5
*a.* Type I 5 5
*b.* Redrawn (#130b) ('64) 5 5
*O78* A40 3p magenta 5 5
*a.* Redrawn ('66) (#131a) 5 5
*O79* A40 5p ultra (II) 5 5
*a.* Type I 5 5
*b.* Redrawn (#132b) ('63) 5 5
*O80* A40 7p emerald 5 5
*O81* A40 10p brown 5 5
*a.* Redrawn (#134a) ('64) 5 5
*O82* A40 13p bl vio 5 5
*a.* Redrawn (#135a) ('63) 5 5
*O83* A40 15p rose lil (#135B) ('64) 5 5
*O84* A40 20p dl grn (#135C) ('70) 8 8
*O85* A40 40p dl pur ('62) 14 5
*O86* A40 50p dl grn ('62) 18 5
*a.* Redrawn (#138a) ('64) 18 5
*O87* A40 75p dk car ('62) 22 5
*O88* A40 90p lt ol grn ('78) 30 5
*Nos. O76-O88 (13)* 1.32 68

Nos. 141, 143-144 Overprinted Type "c" in Black or Carmine

**1963 Unwmk. *Perf. 13½x13***
*O89* A41 1r vermilion 28 7
*O90* A41 2r orange 55 12
*O91* A41 5r grn (C) 1.40 65

Nos. 200, 202 Overprinted Type "c"

**1968-? Wmk. 351 *Perf. 13½x13***
*O92* A41 1r vermilion 28 28
*O93* A41 2r orange 28 28

Nos. 459-468, 470-475 Overprinted Type "d" in Carmine or Black

**1980-81**
*O94* A224 2p dark grn 5 5
*O95* A224 3p black 5 5
*O96* A224 5p vio bl 5 5
*O97* A225 10p grnsh bl 5 5
*O98* A225 20p yel grn ('81) 5 5
*O99* A225 25p rose car & grn ('81) 5 5
*O100* A225 40p car & bl ('81) 6 5
*O101* A225 50p bl grn & vio 7 5
*O102* A225 60p black 8 5
*O103* A225 75p dp org 10 10
*O105* A225a 1r ol ('81) 14 7
*O106* A225a 1.50r dp org 20 18
*O107* A225a 2r car rose (B) 28 14
*O108* A225a 3r ind ('81) 40 35
*O109* A225a 4r blk('84) 65 50
*O110* A225a 5r dk brn ('84) 85 65
*Nos. O94-O110 (16)* 3.13 2.44

Types A237-A239 Inscribed "SERVICE POSTAGE"

***Perf. 12, 11½x12 (A238), 12x11½ (A239)***
**1980 Litho.**
*O111* A237 10p dk grn & yel org 5 5
*O112* A237 15p dk grn & ap grn 5 5
*O113* A237 25p dp vio & rose car 5 5
*O114* A237 35p rose pink & brt yel grn 6 5
*O115* A238 40p red & lt brn 7 5
*O116* A239 50p ol & vio bl 8 5
*O117* A239 80p blk & yel grn 14 7
*Nos. O111-O117 (7)* 50 37

No. 614, 618 Ovptd. "SERVICE" in Red

**1984-86 Litho. *Perf. 11***
*O120* A289 20p Attock Fort 5 5
*O122* A289 60p Lahore ('86) 7 5

## BAHAWALPUR

LOCATION — A State of Pakistan.
AREA — 17,494 sq. mi.
POP. — 1,341,209 (1941).
CAPITAL — Bahawalpur.

Bahawalpur was a State of India until 1947. These stamps had franking power solely within Bahawalpur.

Amir Muhammad Bahawal Khan I Abbasi — A1

Wmk. 274

*Perf. 12½x12*

**1947, Dec. Wmk. 274 Engr.**

| | | | | |
|---|---|---|---|---|
| *1* | A1 | ½a brt car rose & blk | 10 | 10 |

Bicentenary of the ruling family.

Nawab Sadiq Muhammad Khan V Abbasi Bahadur — A2

Tombs of the Amirs — A3

Mosque, Sadiq Garh — A4

Fort Dirawar A5

Nur-Mahal Palace — A6

Palace, Sadiq Garh — A7

Nawab Sadiq Muhammad Khan V Abbasi Bahadur — A8

A9

***Perf. 12½ (A2), 12x12½ (A3, A5, A6, A7), 12½x12 (A4, A8), 13x13½ (A9)***

**1948, Apr. 1 Engr. Wmk. 274**

| | | | | |
|---|---|---|---|---|
| *2* | A2 | 3p dp bl & blk | 5 | 5 |
| *3* | A2 | ½a lake & blk | 5 | 5 |
| *4* | A2 | 9p dk grn & blk | 5 | 5 |
| *5* | A2 | 1a dp car & blk | 5 | 5 |
| *6* | A2 | 1½a vio & blk | 6 | 6 |
| *7* | A3 | 2a car & dp grn | 7 | 7 |
| *8* | A4 | 4a brn & org red | 12 | 12 |
| *9* | A5 | 6a dp bl & vio brn | 14 | 14 |
| *10* | A6 | 8a brt pur & car | 18 | 18 |
| *11* | A7 | 12a dp car & dk bl grn | 28 | 28 |
| *12* | A8 | 1r choc & vio | 35 | 35 |
| *13* | A8 | 2r dp mag & dk grn | 40 | 40 |
| *14* | A8 | 5r pur & blk | 1.40 | 1.40 |
| *15* | A9 | 10r blk & car | 4.00 | 2.75 |
| | | *Nos. 2-15 (14)* | 7.20 | 5.95 |

See Nos. 18-21.

Soldiers of 1848 and 1948 — A10

**1948, Oct. 15 Engr. *Perf. 11½***

| | | | | |
|---|---|---|---|---|
| *16* | A10 | 1½a dp car & blk | 7 | 7 |

Centenary of the Multan Campaign.

Amir Khan V and Mohammed Ali Jinnah — A11

**1948, Oct. 3 *Perf. 13x12½***

| | | | | |
|---|---|---|---|---|
| *17* | A11 | 1½a grn & car rose | 7 | 5 |

1st anniv. of the union of Bahawalpur with Pakistan.

Types of 1948.

**1948 *Perf. 12x11½***

| | | | | |
|---|---|---|---|---|
| *18* | A8 | 1r org & dp grn | 7 | 7 |
| *19* | A8 | 2r car & blk | 10 | 10 |
| *20* | A8 | 5r ultra & red brn | 28 | 28 |

***Perf. 13½***

| | | | | |
|---|---|---|---|---|
| *21* | A9 | 10r grn & red brn | 55 | 55 |

Panjnad Weir — A12

**1949, Mar. 3 *Perf. 14***

**Center in Black.**

| | | | | |
|---|---|---|---|---|
| *22* | A12 | 3p ultra | 5 | 5 |
| *23* | A12 | ½a org*(Wheat)* | 5 | 5 |
| *24* | A12 | 9p grn *(Cotton)* | 5 | 5 |
| *25* | A12 | 1a car rose*(Sahiwal Bull)* | 5 | 5 |

25th anniv. of the acquisition of full ruling powers by Amir Khan V.

UPU Monument, Bern — A13

**1949, Oct. 10 *Perf. 13, 18***

**Center in Black.**

| | | | | |
|---|---|---|---|---|
| *26* | A13 | 9p green | 6 | 5 |
| *27* | A13 | 1a red vio | 6 | 5 |
| *28* | A13 | 1½a brn org | 6 | 5 |
| *29* | A13 | 2½a blue | 14 | 7 |

75th anniv. of the UPU.
Nos. 26 to 29 exist imperforate.

## OFFICIAL STAMPS

Panjnad Weir — O1

Camel and Colt — O2

Antelopes O3

Pelicans — O4

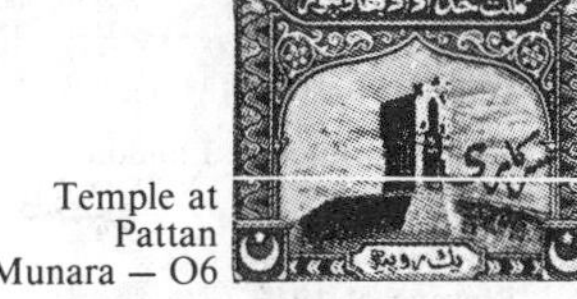

Juma Masjid Palace, Fort Derawar — O5

Temple at Pattan Munara — O6

Red Overprint

**1945 Wmk. 274 Engr. *Perf. 14***

| | | | | |
|---|---|---|---|---|
| *O1* | O1 | ½a brt grn & blk | 5 | 5 |
| *O2* | O2 | 1a car & blk | 6 | 6 |
| *O3* | O3 | 2a vio & blk | 8 | 8 |
| *O4* | O4 | 4a ol & blk | 12 | 12 |
| *O5* | O5 | 8a brn & blk | 20 | 20 |
| *O6* | O6 | 1r org & blk | 40 | 40 |
| | | *Nos. O1-O6 (6)* | 91 | 91 |

Types of 1945, Without Red Overprint, Surcharged in Black

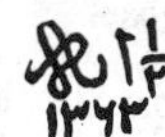

**1945 Unwmk.**

| | | | | |
|---|---|---|---|---|
| *O7* | O5 | ½a on 8a lake & blk | 4.00 | *4.00* |
| *O8* | O6 | 1½a on 1r org & blk | 10.00 | *10.00* |
| *O9* | O1 | 1½a on 2r ultra & blk | 20.00 | *20.00* |

Camels — O7

**1945 Red Overprint**

| | | | | |
|---|---|---|---|---|
| *O10* | O7 | 1a brn & blk | 27.50 | *35.00* |

Types of 1945, Without Red Overprint Overprinted in Black

SERVICE

**1945**

| | | | | |
|---|---|---|---|---|
| *O11* | O1 | ½a car & blk | 5 | 5 |
| *O12* | O2 | 1a car & blk | 7 | 7 |
| *O13* | O3 | 2a org & blk | 14 | 14 |

Nawab Sadiq Muhammad Khan V Abbasi Bahadur — O8

**1945**

| | | | | |
|---|---|---|---|---|
| *O14* | O8 | 3p deep blue | 6 | 6 |
| *O15* | O8 | 1½a deep violet | 7 | 7 |

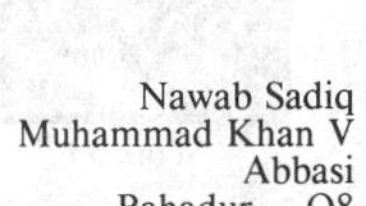

Flags of Allied Nations — O9

**1946, May**

| | | | | |
|---|---|---|---|---|
| *O16* | O9 | 1½a emer & gray | 28 | 28 |

Victory of Allied Nations in World War II.

Stamps of 1948 Overprinted in Carmine or Black

***Perf. 12½, 12½x12, 12x11½, 13½.***

**1948 Wmk. 274**

| | | | | |
|---|---|---|---|---|
| *O17* | A2 | 3p dp bl & blk (C) | 5 | 5 |
| *O18* | A2 | 1a dp car & blk | 5 | 5 |
| *O19* | A3 | 2a car & dp grn | 5 | 5 |
| *O20* | A4 | 4a brn & org red | 5 | 5 |
| *O21* | A8 | 1r org & dp grn (C) | 6 | 6 |
| *O22* | A8 | 2r car & blk (C) | 10 | 10 |
| *O23* | A8 | 5r ultra & red brn (C) | 18 | 18 |
| *O24* | A9 | 10r grn & red brn (C) | 28 | 28 |
| | | *Nos. O17-O24 (8)* | 82 | 82 |

Same Overprint in Carmine on Nos. 26 to 29

**1949** *Perf. 13, 18*

**Center in Black**

| No. | Type | Description | Unused | Used |
|---|---|---|---|---|
| *O25* | A13 | 9p green | 5 | 5 |
| *O26* | A13 | 1a red vio | 5 | 5 |
| *O27* | A13 | 1½a brn org | 5 | 5 |
| *O28* | A13 | 2½a blue | 5 | 5 |

75th anniv. of the UPU.

Nos. O25 to O28 exist imperforate.

---

## PALESTINE

LOCATION — In western Asia bordering on the Mediterranean Sea.
GOVT. — Former British Mandate.
AREA — 10,429 sq. mi.
POP. — 1,605,816 (estimated).
CAPITAL — Jerusalem.

Formerly a part of Turkey, Palestine was occupied by the Egyptian Expeditionary Forces of the British Army in World War I and was mandated to Great Britain in 1923. Mandate ended May 14, 1948.

10 Milliemes = 1 Piastre
1000 Milliemes = 1 Egyptian Pound
1000 Mils = 1 Palestine Pound (1928)

**Issued under British Military Occupation**

For use in Palestine, Trans-Jordan, Lebanon, Syria and in parts of Cilicia and northeastern Egypt.

A1

Wmk.33

**Wmk. Crown and "GvR" (33)**

**1918** **Litho.** ***Rouletted 20***

| No. | Type | Description | Unused | Used |
|---|---|---|---|---|
| *1* | A1 | 1pi dp bl | 250.00 | 165.00 |
| *2* | A1 | 1pi ultra | 1.75 | 1.40 |

No. 2 Surcharged in Black

5 MILLIEMES

| No. | Type | Description | Unused | Used |
|---|---|---|---|---|
| *3* | A1 | 5m on 1pi ultra | 7.50 | 6.25 |
| *a.* | | 5m on 1pi gray bl | 175.00 | |
| *b.* | | "MILLILMES" | 4,000. | |

Nos. 1 and 3a were issued without gum. No. 3a is on paper with a surface sheen.

**1918** **Typo.** ***Perf. 15x14***

| No. | Type | Description | Unused | Used |
|---|---|---|---|---|
| *4* | A1 | 1m dk brn | 15 | 15 |
| *5* | A1 | 2m bl grn | 18 | 15 |
| *6* | A1 | 3m lt brn | 38 | 38 |
| *7* | A1 | 4m scarlet | 30 | 25 |
| *8* | A1 | 5m orange | 38 | 22 |
| *9* | A1 | 1pi indigo | 35 | 22 |
| *10* | A1 | 2pi ol grn | 45 | 45 |
| *11* | A1 | 5pi plum | 1.50 | 1.25 |
| *12* | A1 | 9pi bister | 3.25 | 3.25 |
| *13* | A1 | 10pi ultra | 3.50 | 4.50 |
| *14* | A1 | 20pi gray | 11.50 | 15.00 |
| | | *Nos. 4-14 (11)* | 21.94 | 25.82 |

Many shades exist.

Nos. 4-11 exist with rough perforation.

Nos. 4-11 with overprint "O. P. D. A." (Ottoman Public Debt Administration) or "H.J.Z." (Hejaz-Jemen Railway) are revenue stamps; they exist postally used.

**Issued under British Administration**

Overprinted at Jerusalem

فلسطين

Stamps and Type of 1918 Overprinted in Black or Silver

PALESTINE

פלשתינה א״י

**1920** **Wmk. 33** ***Perf. 15x14***

**Arabic Overprint 8mm long**

| No. | Type | Description | Unused | Used |
|---|---|---|---|---|
| *15* | A1 | 1m dk brn | 1.25 | 1.25 |
| *d.* | | Hebrew overprint only | | |
| *16* | A1 | 2m bl grn, perf. 14 | 95 | 85 |
| *d.* | | Perf. 15x14 | 4.75 | 3.00 |
| *e.* | | "PALESTINE" omitted | | |
| *17* | A1 | 3m lt brn, perf. 15x14 | 2.75 | 2.50 |
| *d.* | | Perf. 14 | 40.00 | *55.00* |
| *e.* | | Inverted overprint | 500.00 | 600.00 |
| *18* | A1 | 4m scarlet | 1.40 | 1.40 |
| *19* | A1 | 5m org, perf. 14 | 1.40 | 95 |
| *e.* | | Perf. 15x14 | 3.75 | 2.00 |
| *20* | A1 | 1pi indigo (S) | 1.00 | 40 |
| *21* | A1 | 2pi ol grn | 1.25 | 90 |
| *22* | A1 | 5pi plum | 4.50 | 6.50 |
| *23* | A1 | 9pi bister | 4.50 | 9.00 |
| *24* | A1 | 10pi ultra | 6.50 | 8.00 |
| *25* | A1 | 20pi gray | 11.25 | 15.00 |
| | | *Nos. 15-25 (11)* | 36.75 | 46.75 |

Similar Overprint, with Arabic Line 10mm Long, Arabic "S" and "T" Joined

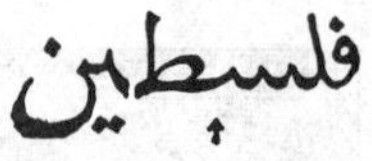

**1920-21** ***Perf. 14, 15x14***

| No. | Type | Description | Unused | Used |
|---|---|---|---|---|
| *15a* | A1 | 1m dk brn, perf. 15x14 | 50 | 45 |
| *15e* | A1 | 1m dk brn, perf. 14 | 800.00 | 850.00 |
| *16a* | A1 | 2m bl grn | 2.50 | 2.50 |
| *17a* | A1 | 3m lt brn | 50 | 45 |
| *18a* | A1 | 4m scar, perf. 15x14 | 1.40 | 1.10 |
| *18b* | A1 | 4m scar, perf. 14 | 55.00 | 57.50 |
| *19a* | A1 | 5m yel org, perf. 15x14 | 2.25 | 70 |
| *19f* | A1 | 5m yel org, perf. 14 | 2.00 | 1.00 |
| *20a* | A1 | 1pi ind, perf. 14 (S) | 21.00 | 1.75 |
| *20d* | A1 | 1pi ind, perf. 15x14 (S) | 800.00 | 12.00 |
| *21a* | A1 | 2pi ol grn | 55.00 | 21.00 |
| *22a* | A1 | 5pi plum, perf. 15x14 | 21.00 | 6.50 |
| *22d* | A1 | 5pi plum, perf. 14 | 225.00 | 425.00 |

This overprint often looks grayish to grayish black. In the English line the letters are frequently uneven and damaged.

Similar Overprint, with Arabic Line 10mm. Long, Arabic "S" and "T" Separated and 6mm Between English and Hebrew Lines

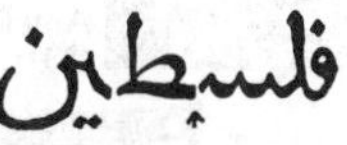

**1920**

| No. | Type | Description | Unused | Used |
|---|---|---|---|---|
| *15b* | A1 | 1m dk brn, perf. 14 | 24.00 | 27.50 |
| *17b* | A1 | 3m lt brn, perf. 15x14 | 37.50 | 40.00 |
| *19b* | A1 | 5m org, perf. 14 | 625.00 | 37.50 |
| *19d* | A1 | 5m org, perf. 15x14 | *15,000.* | *11,000.* |

Overprinted as Before, 7½mm Between English and Hebrew Lines

**1921** ***Perf. 15x14***

| No. | Type | Description | Unused | Used |
|---|---|---|---|---|
| *15c* | A1 | 1m dk brn | 3.75 | 2.50 |
| *15f* | A1 | 1m dl brn, perf. 14 | | *3,750.* |
| *16c* | A1 | 2m bl grn | 6.50 | 4.25 |
| *17c* | A1 | 3m lt brn | 20.00 | 3.00 |
| *f.* | | "PALESTINE" omitted | 2,500. | |
| *18c* | A1 | 4m scarlet | 14.00 | 3.25 |
| *19c* | A1 | 5m yel org | 17.50 | 2.00 |
| *20c* | A1 | 1pi indigo (S) | 17.50 | 1.40 |
| *21c* | A1 | 2pi ol grn | 22.50 | 8.00 |
| *22c* | A1 | 5pi plum | 27.50 | 11.00 |
| *23c* | A1 | 9pi bister | 32.50 | *100.00* |
| *24c* | A1 | 10pi ultra | 32.50 | 15.00 |
| *25c* | A1 | 20pi pale gray | 75.00 | 55.00 |
| *25d* | A1 | 20pi pale gray, perf. 14 | *12,000.* | *3,750.* |

Overprinted at London

فلسطين

Stamps of 1918 Overprinted

PALESTINE

פלשתינה א״י

**1921** ***Perf. 15x14***

| No. | Type | Description | Unused | Used |
|---|---|---|---|---|
| *37* | A1 | 1m dk brn | 50 | 22 |
| *38* | A1 | 2m bl grn | 55 | 22 |
| *39* | A1 | 3m lt brn | 55 | 22 |
| *40* | A1 | 4m scarlet | 55 | 35 |
| *41* | A1 | 5m orange | 60 | 20 |
| *42* | A1 | 1pi brt bl | 75 | 20 |
| *43* | A1 | 2pi ol grn | 1.10 | 40 |
| *44* | A1 | 5pi plum | 3.25 | 3.00 |
| *45* | A1 | 9pi bister | 10.00 | 10.00 |
| *46* | A1 | 10pi ultra | 15.00 | *500.00* |
| *47* | A1 | 20pi gray | 37.50 | *800.00* |
| | | *Nos. 37-47 (11)* | 70.35 | |

Deformed or damaged letters exist in all three lines of the overprint.

Similar Overprint on Type of 1921 Issue

**1922** **Wmk. 4** ***Perf. 14***

| No. | Type | Description | Unused | Used |
|---|---|---|---|---|
| *48* | A1 | 1m dark brown | 30 | 14 |
| *a.* | | Inverted overprint | | *15,000.* |
| *b.* | | Double overprint | 350.00 | 425.00 |
| *c.* | | 1m light brown | 35 | 10 |
| *49* | A1 | 2m yellow | 40 | 14 |
| *50* | A1 | 3m Prus bl | 35 | 10 |
| *51* | A1 | 4m rose | 35 | 16 |
| *52* | A1 | 5m orange | 40 | 10 |
| *53* | A1 | 6m bl grn | 70 | 22 |
| *54* | A1 | 7m yel brn | 90 | 20 |
| *55* | A1 | 8m red | 70 | 20 |
| *56* | A1 | 1pi gray | 90 | 16 |
| *57* | A1 | 13m ultra | 90 | 14 |
| *58* | A1 | 2pi ol grn | 1.40 | 30 |
| *a.* | | Inverted overprint | 500.00 | 500.00 |
| *59* | A1 | 5pi plum | 3.50 | 80 |
| *a.* | | Perf. 15 x 14 | 25.00 | 3.00 |

***Perf. 15x14***

| No. | Type | Description | Unused | Used |
|---|---|---|---|---|
| *60* | A1 | 9pi bister | 11.00 | 8.50 |
| *a.* | | Perf. 14 | 1,250. | 350.00 |
| *61* | A1 | 10pi lt bl | 10.00 | 1.25 |
| *a.* | | Perf. 14 | 22.50 | 3.50 |
| *b.* | | "E. F. F." for "E. E. F." in lower panel | 800.00 | 650.00 |
| *62* | A1 | 20pi violet | 15.00 | 6.50 |
| *a.* | | Perf. 14 | 140.00 | 100.00 |
| | | *Nos. 48-62 (15)* | 46.80 | 18.91 |

Rachel's Tomb — A3

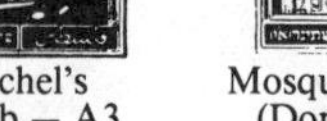

Mosque of Omar (Dome of the Rock) — A4

Citadel at Jerusalem A5

Tiberias and Sea of Galilee A6

**1927-45** **Typo.** ***Perf. 13½x14½***

| No. | Type | Description | Unused | Used |
|---|---|---|---|---|
| *63* | A3 | 2m Prus bl | 5 | 5 |
| *a.* | | Booklet pane of 6 | | |
| *64* | A3 | 3m yel grn | 5 | 5 |
| *a.* | | Booklet pane of 6 | | |
| *65* | A4 | 4m rose red | 2.00 | 65 |
| *66* | A4 | 4m vio brn ('32) | 10 | 6 |
| *67* | A5 | 5m brn org | 7 | 5 |
| *a.* | | Booklet pane of 6 | | |
| *b.* | | 5m org ('45) | 14 | 14 |
| *c.* | | Perf. 14½x14 (coil stamp) ('36) | 6.00 | 5.00 |
| *68* | A4 | 6m dp grn | 16 | 7 |
| *69* | A5 | 7m dp red | 2.25 | 28 |
| *70* | A5 | 7m dk vio ('32) | 10 | 5 |
| *71* | A4 | 8m yel brn | 4.75 | 2.25 |
| *72* | A4 | 8m scar ('32) | 35 | 6 |
| *73* | A3 | 10m dp gray | 10 | 5 |
| *a.* | | Perf. 14½x14 (coil stamp) ('38) | 7.00 | 7.00 |
| *b.* | | Booklet pane of 6 | | |
| *74* | A4 | 13m ultra | 3.25 | 16 |
| *75* | A4 | 13m ol bis ('32) | 40 | 7 |
| *76* | A4 | 15m ultra ('32) | 50 | 5 |
| *a.* | | Booklet pane of 6 | | |
| *77* | A5 | 20m ol grn | 16 | 6 |

***Perf. 14***

| No. | Type | Description | Unused | Used |
|---|---|---|---|---|
| *78* | A6 | 50m vio brn | 65 | 8 |
| *79* | A6 | 90m bister | 22.50 | 16.00 |
| *80* | A6 | 100m brt bl | 85 | 14 |
| *81* | A6 | 200m dk vio | 1.50 | 28 |
| *82* | A6 | 250m dp brn ('41) | 65 | 60 |
| *83* | A6 | 500m red ('41) | 1.40 | 1.40 |
| *84* | A6 | £1 gray blk ('41) | 2.00 | 2.00 |
| | | *Nos. 63-84 (22)* | 43.84 | 24.46 |

### POSTAGE DUE STAMPS

D1

**1923** **Unwmk.** **Typo.** ***Perf. 11***

| No. | Type | Description | Unused | Used |
|---|---|---|---|---|
| *J1* | D1 | 1m bis brn | 35.00 | 45.00 |
| *a.* | | Imperf., pair | 450.00 | |
| *b.* | | Horiz. pair, imperf. btwn. | 1,300. | |
| *J2* | D1 | 2m green | 15.00 | 15.00 |
| *a.* | | Imperf., pair | 750.00 | |
| *J3* | D1 | 4m red | 19.00 | 22.50 |
| *J4* | D1 | 8m violet | 9.00 | 9.00 |
| *a.* | | Imperf., pair | 175.00 | |
| *b.* | | Horiz. pair, imperf. btwn. | | *2,750.* |
| *J5* | D1 | 13m dark blue | 10.00 | 10.00 |
| *a.* | | Horiz. pair, imperf. btwn. | 1,150. | |
| | | *Nos. J1-J5 (5)* | 88.00 | 101.50 |

D2

D3

**Wmk. 4**

| No. | Type | Description | Unused | Used |
|---|---|---|---|---|
| *J6* | D2 | 1m brown | 60 | 60 |
| *J7* | D2 | 2m yellow | 75 | 60 |
| *J8* | D2 | 4m green | 75 | 65 |
| *J9* | D2 | 8m red | 1.50 | 65 |
| *J10* | D2 | 13m ultra | 2.00 | 1.75 |
| *J11* | D2 | 5pi violet | 3.75 | 2.00 |
| | | *Nos. J6-J11 (6)* | 9.35 | 6.25 |

**1928-45** ***Perf. 14***

| No. | Type | Description | Unused | Used |
|---|---|---|---|---|
| *J12* | D3 | 1m lt brn | 12 | 12 |
| *a.* | | Perf. 15x14 ('45) | 8.75 | 12.50 |
| *J13* | D3 | 2m yellow | 12 | 12 |
| *J14* | D3 | 4m green | 18 | 15 |
| *a.* | | 4m bluish grn, perf. 15x14 ('45) | 8.00 | 11.25 |
| *J15* | D3 | 6m brn org ('33) | 2.25 | 2.25 |
| *J16* | D3 | 8m red | 35 | 35 |
| *J17* | D3 | 10m lt gray | 50 | 50 |
| *J18* | D3 | 13m ultra | 75 | 75 |
| *J19* | D3 | 20m ol grn | 75 | 65 |
| *J20* | D3 | 50m violet | 75 | 70 |
| | | *Nos. J12-J20 (9)* | 5.77 | 5.59 |

The Hebrew word for "mil" appears below the numeral on all values but the 1m.

---

## PAPUA NEW GUINEA

LOCATION — Eastern half of island of New Guinea, north of Australia.
GOVT. — Independent state in British Commonwealth.
AREA — 185,136 sq. mi.
POP. — 3,260,000 (est. 1984).
CAPITAL — Port Moresby.

In 1884 a British Protectorate was proclaimed over this part of the island, called "British New Guinea." In 1905 the administration was transferred to Australia and in 1906 the name was changed to Territory of Papua.

In 1949 the administration of Papua and New Guinea was unified, as the 1952 issue indicates. In 1972 the name was changed to Papua New Guinea. In 1974 came self-government, followed by independence on September 16, 1975.

Issues of 1925-39 for the mandated Territory of New Guinea are listed under New Guinea.

12 Pence = 1 Shilling
20 Shillings = 1 Pound
100 Cents = 1 Dollar (1966)
100 Toea = 1 Kina (1975)

**Catalogue values for unused stamps in this country are for Never Hinged items, beginning with Scott 122 in the regular postage section and Scott J1 in the postage due section.**

**British New Guinea**

Lakatoi — A1

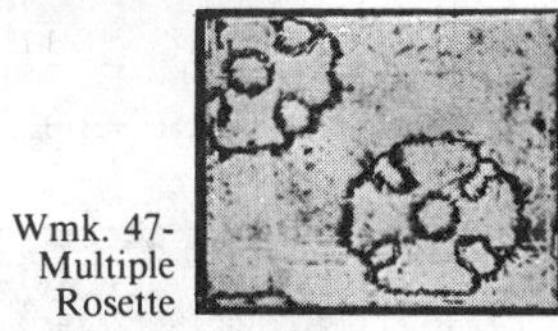

Wmk. 47- Multiple Rosette

**1901-05 Engr. Wmk. 47 *Perf. 14***

**Center in Black**

| | | | | |
|---|---|---|---|---|
| *1* | A1 | ½p yel grn | 2.50 | 2.50 |
| *2* | A1 | 1p carmine | 2.50 | 2.00 |
| *3* | A1 | 2p violet | 2.75 | 2.50 |
| *4* | A1 | 2½p ultra | 6.00 | 6.50 |
| *5* | A1 | 4p blk brn | 25.00 | 25.00 |
| *6* | A1 | 6p dk grn | 20.00 | 22.50 |
| *7* | A1 | 1sh orange | 32.50 | 40.00 |
| *8* | A1 | 2sh6p brown | 475.00 | 475.00 |
| | | *Nos. 1-8 (8)* | 566.25 | 576.00 |

The paper varies in thickness and the watermark is found in two positions, with the greater width of the rosette either horizontal or vertical.

**Papua**

Stamps of British New Guinea, Overprinted **Papua.**

**1907 Wmk. 47 *Perf. 14***

**Center in Black**

| | | | | |
|---|---|---|---|---|
| *11* | A1 | ½p yel grn | 5.00 | 6.00 |
| *12* | A1 | 1p carmine | 8.50 | 9.50 |
| *13* | A1 | 2p violet | 4.50 | 4.50 |
| *14* | A1 | 2½p ultra | 5.00 | 5.00 |
| *15* | A1 | 4p blk brn | 175.00 | 175.00 |
| *16* | A1 | 6p dk grn | 20.00 | 22.50 |
| *17* | A1 | 1sh orange | 20.00 | 22.50 |
| *18* | A1 | 2sh6p brown | 140.00 | 150.00 |
| | | *Nos. 11-18 (8)* | 378.00 | 395.00 |

Overprinted **Papua.**

**Center in Black**

| | | | | |
|---|---|---|---|---|
| *19* | A1 | ½p yel grn | 3.50 | 3.75 |
| **a** | | Double overprint | 1,750. | |
| *20* | A1 | 1p carmine | 3.00 | 3.00 |
| **a** | | Vertical overprint, up | 500.00 | 500.00 |
| *21* | A1 | 2p violet | 2.50 | 2.75 |
| *22* | A1 | 2½p ultra | 4.50 | 4.75 |
| **a** | | Double overprint | | |
| *23* | A1 | 4p blk brn | 22.50 | 25.00 |
| *24* | A1 | 6p dk grn | 22.50 | 25.00 |
| **a** | | Double ovpt. | 1,650. | 1,650. |
| *25* | A1 | 1sh orange | 30.00 | 35.00 |
| **a** | | Double overprint | | |
| *26* | A1 | 2sh6p brown | 30.00 | 32.50 |
| **b** | | Vert. ovpt., down | *1,350.* | |
| **d** | | Dbl. horiz. ovpt. | | 1,350. |
| | | *Nos. 19-26 (8)* | 118.50 | 131.75 |

A2

Small "PAPUA"

Wmk. 13- Crown and Double-Lined A

***Perf. 11, 12½***

**1907-08 Litho. Wmk. 13**

**Center in Black**

| | | | | |
|---|---|---|---|---|
| *28* | A2 | 1p car ('08) | 4.00 | 4.00 |
| *29* | A2 | 2p vio ('08) | 4.00 | 4.00 |
| *30* | A2 | 2½p ultra ('08) | 5.25 | 5.25 |
| **a** | | Perf. 12½ | 37.50 | 45.00 |
| *31* | A2 | 4p blk brn | 3.25 | 3.25 |
| **a** | | Perf 12½ | 6.75 | 7.50 |
| *32* | A2 | 6p dk grn ('08) | 11.00 | 11.00 |
| *33* | A2 | 1sh org ('08) | 13.50 | 13.50 |
| **a** | | Perf. 12½ | 52.50 | 75.00 |
| | | *Nos. 28-33 (6)* | 41.00 | 41.00 |

**1909-10 Wmk. Sideways**

**Center in Black**

| | | | | |
|---|---|---|---|---|
| *34* | A2 | ½p yel grn | 1.40 | 1.75 |
| **a** | | Perf. 11x12½ | *2,000.* | *2,000.* |
| **b** | | Perf. 11 | 1.40 | 1.75 |
| *35* | A2 | 1p carmine | 6.25 | 6.00 |
| **a** | | Perf. 11 | 10.00 | 10.00 |
| *36* | A2 | 2p vio ('10) | 3.00 | 1.75 |
| **a** | | Perf. 11x12½ | 750.00 | |
| **b** | | Perf. 11 | 4.00 | 3.00 |
| *37* | A2 | 2½p ultra ('10) | 4.00 | 5.00 |
| **a** | | Perf. 12½ | 6.50 | 7.00 |
| *38* | A2 | 4p blk brn ('10) | 4.75 | 5.00 |
| **a** | | Perf. 11x12½ | *3,500.* | |
| *39* | A2 | 6p dk grn | 16.00 | 15.00 |
| **a** | | Perf. 12½ | 1,125. | 1,000. |
| *40* | A2 | 1sh org ('10) | 12.00 | *20.00* |
| **a** | | Perf. 11 | 50.00 | *65.00* |
| | | *Nos. 34-40 (7)* | 47.40 | 54.50 |

One stamp in each sheet has a white line across the upper part of the picture which is termed the "rift in the clouds."

Large "PAPUA"

Two Types of 2sh6p:
Type I. The numerals are thin and irregular. The body of the "6" encloses a large spot of color. The dividing stroke is thick and uneven.
Type II. The numerals are thick and well formed. The "6" encloses a narrow oval of color. The dividing stroke is thin and sharp.

**1910 Wmk. 13**

**Center in Black**

| | | | | |
|---|---|---|---|---|
| *41* | A2 | ½p yel grn | 1.50 | 1.75 |
| *42* | A2 | 1p carmine | 5.00 | 3.50 |
| *43* | A2 | 2p violet | 4.25 | 4.00 |
| *44* | A2 | 2½p bl vio | 3.75 | 4.00 |
| *45* | A2 | 4p blk brn | 5.00 | 8.25 |
| *46* | A2 | 6p dk grn | 6.50 | *10.00* |
| *47* | A2 | 1sh orange | 8.25 | *12.50* |
| *48* | A2 | 2sh6p brn, type II | 55.00 | *70.00* |
| **a** | | 2sh6p brn, type I | 55.00 | *70.00* |
| | | *Nos. 41-48 (8)* | 89.25 | 114.00 |

**Wmk. Sideways**

| | | | | |
|---|---|---|---|---|
| *49* | A2 | 2sh6p choc, type I | 80.00 | *100.00* |

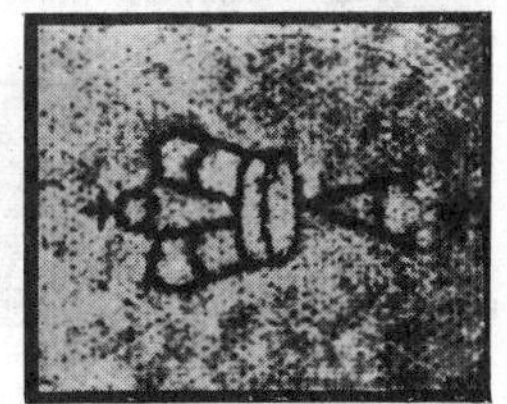

Wmk. 74- Crown and Single-Lined A Sideways

**1911-12 Typo. Wmk. 74 *Perf. 12½***

| | | | | |
|---|---|---|---|---|
| *50* | A2 | ½p yel grn | 65 | 65 |
| *51* | A2 | 1p lt red | 1.10 | 1.10 |
| *52* | A2 | 2p lt vio | 1.00 | 1.00 |
| *53* | A2 | 2½p ultra | 3.50 | 3.50 |
| *54* | A2 | 4p ol grn | 4.00 | 5.00 |
| *55* | A2 | 6p org brn | 3.75 | 3.75 |
| *56* | A2 | 1sh yellow | 7.00 | 10.00 |
| *57* | A2 | 2sh6p rose | 22.50 | *35.00* |
| | | *Nos. 50-57 (8)* | 43.50 | 60.00 |

**1915 *Perf. 14***

| | | | | |
|---|---|---|---|---|
| *59* | A2 | 1p lt red | 6.50 | 5.00 |

A3

**1916-31**

| | | | | |
|---|---|---|---|---|
| *60* | A3 | ½p pale yel grn & myr grn ('19) | 22 | 22 |
| *61* | A3 | 1p rose red & blk | 90 | 90 |
| *62* | A3 | 1½p yel brn & gray bl ('25) | 60 | 60 |
| *63* | A3 | 2p red vio & vio brn ('19) | 2.50 | 1.00 |
| *64* | A3 | 2p red brn & vio brn ('31) | 3.25 | 2.25 |
| **a** | | 2p cop red & vio brn ('31) | 35.00 | 7.50 |
| *65* | A3 | 2½p ultra & dk grn ('19) | 2.25 | 2.50 |
| *66* | A3 | 3p emer & blk | 1.00 | 1.00 |
| **a** | | 3p dp bl grn & blk | 2.00 | 2.00 |
| *67* | A3 | 4p org & lt brn ('19) | 3.75 | 3.75 |
| *68* | A3 | 5p ol brn & sl ('31) | 5.25 | 6.00 |
| *69* | A3 | 6p vio & dl vio ('23) | 2.25 | 2.50 |
| *70* | A3 | 1sh ol grn & dk brn ('19) | 3.00 | 3.25 |
| *71* | A3 | 2sh6p rose & red brn ('19) | 11.25 | 13.50 |
| *72* | A3 | 5sh dp grn & blk | 17.50 | 17.50 |
| *73* | A3 | 10sh gray bl & grn ('25) | 175.00 | 190.00 |
| | | *Nos. 60-73 (14)* | 228.72 | 244.97 |

Type A3 is a redrawing of type A2.
The lines of the picture have been strengthened, making it much darker, especially the sky and water.

Stamps of 1911-12 Surcharged **ONE PENNY**

**1917 *Perf. 12½***

| | | | | |
|---|---|---|---|---|
| *74* | A2 | 1p on ½p yel grn | 70 | 80 |
| *75* | A2 | 1p on 2p lt vio | 7.00 | 8.25 |
| *76* | A2 | 1p on 2½p ultra | 2.00 | 3.50 |
| *77* | A2 | 1p on 4p ol grn | 2.00 | 3.50 |
| *78* | A2 | 1p on 6p org brn | 7.00 | *10.00* |
| *79* | A2 | 1p on 2sh6p rose | 1.75 | *3.50* |
| | | *Nos. 74-79 (6)* | 20.45 | 29.55 |

No. 62 Surcharged **TWO PENCE**

**1931, Jan. 1 *Perf. 14***

| | | | | |
|---|---|---|---|---|
| *88* | A3 | 2p on 1½p yel brn & gray blue | 1.75 | 1.75 |

**5d.**

Nos. 70, 71 and 72 Surcharged in Black

**FIVE PENCE**

**1931**

| | | | | |
|---|---|---|---|---|
| *89* | A3 | 5p on 1sh #70 | 1.10 | 1.75 |
| *90* | A3 | 9p on 2sh6p #71 | 2.00 | 2.50 |
| *91* | A3 | 1sh3p on 5sh #72 | 2.75 | 3.50 |

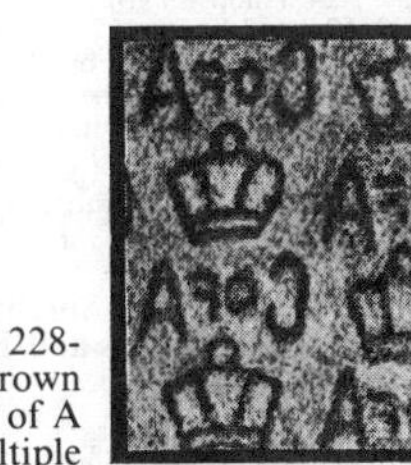

Wmk. 228- Small Crown and C of A Multiple

Type of 1916 Issue

**1932 Wmk. 228 *Perf. 11***

| | | | | |
|---|---|---|---|---|
| *92* | A3 | 9p dp vio & gray | 15.00 | *27.50* |
| *93* | A3 | 1sh3p pale bl & gray blk | 20.00 | *35.00* |

Motuan Girl — A5

Bird of Paradise and Boar's Tusk — A6

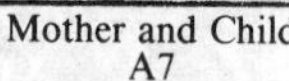


Mother and Child A7

Papuan Motherhood A8

Dubu (Ceremonial Platform) — A9

Fire Maker — A10

Designs: 1p, Steve, son of Oala. 1½p, Tree houses. 3p, Papuan dandy. 5p, Masked dancer. 9p, Shooting fish. 1sh3p, Lakatoi. 2sh, Delta art. 2sh6p, Pottery making. 5sh, Sgt.-Major Simoi. £1, Delta house.

**Unwmk.**

**1932, Nov. 14 Engr. *Perf. 11***

| No. | Type | Denom. | Color | Unused | Used |
|---|---|---|---|---|---|
| *94* | A5 | ½p | org & blk | 25 | 25 |
| *95* | A5 | 1p | yel grn & blk | 16 | 16 |
| *96* | A5 | 1½p | red brn & blk | 1.10 | 1.10 |
| *97* | A6 | 2p | lt red | 2.25 | 50 |
| *98* | A5 | 3p | bl & blk | 2.75 | 2.50 |
| *99* | A7 | 4p | ol grn | 2.25 | 2.25 |
| *100* | A5 | 5p | grnsh sl & blk | 2.50 | 2.50 |
| *101* | A8 | 6p | bis brn | 4.25 | 4.25 |
| *102* | A5 | 9p | lil & blk | 8.25 | *10.00* |
| *103* | A9 | 1sh | bluish gray | 3.50 | 3.25 |
| *104* | A5 | 1sh3p | brn & blk | 14.00 | *16.00* |
| *105* | A5 | 2sh | bluish sl & blk | 16.00 | *22.50* |
| *106* | A5 | 2sh6p | rose lil & blk | 22.50 | *35.00* |
| *107* | A5 | 5sh | ol & blk | 50.00 | 50.00 |
| *108* | A10 | 10sh | gray lil | 90.00 | 90.00 |
| *109* | A5 | £1 | lt gray & blk | 175.00 | 150.00 |
| | | | *Nos. 94-109 (16)* | 394.76 | 390.26 |

Hoisting Union Jack at Port Moresby A21

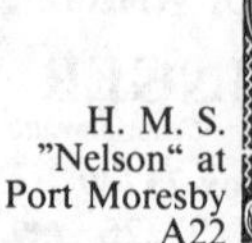

H. M. S. "Nelson" at Port Moresby A22

**1934, Nov. 6**

| No. | Type | Denom. | Color | Unused | Used |
|---|---|---|---|---|---|
| *110* | A21 | 1p | dl grn | 90 | 90 |
| *111* | A22 | 2p | red brn | 1.10 | 1.10 |
| *112* | A21 | 3p | blue | 2.75 | 2.75 |
| *113* | A22 | 5p | vio brn | 6.25 | 6.25 |

50th anniv. of the Declaration of British Protection.

**Silver Jubilee Issue**

Stamps of 1932 Issue Overprinted in Black:

HIS MAJESTY'S JUBILEE.
1910 1935
a

HIS MAJESTY'S
JUBILEE.
1910 — 1935
b

**1935, July 9**

**Glazed Paper**

| No. | Type | Denom. | Color | Unused | Used |
|---|---|---|---|---|---|
| *114* | A5 (a) | 1p | yel grn & blk | 25 | 25 |
| *115* | A6 (b) | 2p | lt red | 65 | 65 |
| *116* | A5 (a) | 3p | lt bl & blk | 2.50 | 2.50 |
| *117* | A5 (a) | 5p | grnsh sl & blk | 5.00 | 5.00 |

25th anniv. of the reign of George V.

**Coronation Issue**

Type of New Guinea, 1937

**Unwmk.**

**1937, May 14 Engr. *Perf. 11***

| No. | Type | Denom. | Color | Unused | Used |
|---|---|---|---|---|---|
| *118* | A3 | 1p | green | 7 | 7 |
| *119* | A3 | 2p | sal rose | 14 | 14 |
| *120* | A3 | 3p | blue | 20 | 20 |
| *121* | A3 | 5p | brn vio | 30 | 30 |

**Catalogue values for unused stamps in this section, from this point to the end of the section, are for Never Hinged items.**

**Papua and New Guinea**

Tree-climbing Kangaroo A23

Kiriwina Chief's House A24

Copra Making A25

Designs: 1p, Buka head-dress. 2p, Youth. 2½p, Bird of paradise. 3p, Policeman. 3½p, Chimbu headdress. 7½p, Kiriwina yam house. 1sh, Trading canoe. 1sh 6p, Rubber tapping. 2sh, Shields and spears. 2sh 6p, Plumed shepherd. 10sh, Map. £1, Spearing fish.

**Unwmk.**

**1952, Oct. 30 Engr. *Perf. 14***

| No. | Type | Denom. | Color | Unused | Used |
|---|---|---|---|---|---|
| *122* | A23 | ½p | bl grn | 25 | 20 |
| *123* | A23 | 1p | chocolate | 25 | 20 |
| *124* | A23 | 2p | dp ultra | 65 | 20 |
| *125* | A23 | 2½p | orange | 2.75 | 1.00 |
| *126* | A23 | 3p | dk grn | 1.00 | 28 |
| *127* | A23 | 3½p | dk car | 1.20 | 40 |
| *128* | A24 | 6½p | vio brn | 2.00 | 55 |
| *129* | A24 | 7½p | dp ultra | 14.00 | 11.00 |
| *130* | A25 | 9p | chocolate | 4.25 | 1.40 |
| *131* | A25 | 1sh | yel grn | 2.75 | 85 |
| *132* | A24 | 1sh6p | dk grn | 8.00 | 2.00 |
| *133* | A24 | 2sh | dp bl | 8.50 | 1.65 |
| *134* | A25 | 2sh6p | dk red brn | 9.50 | 2.75 |
| *135* | A25 | 10sh | gray blk | 80.00 | 27.50 |
| *136* | A24 | £1 | chocolate | 85.00 | 40.00 |
| | | | *Nos. 122-136 (15)* | 220.10 | 89.98 |

See Nos. 139-141.

Nos. 125 and 131 Surcharged with New Values and Bars

**1957, Jan. 29 *Perf. 14***

| No. | Type | Surcharge | Unused | Used |
|---|---|---|---|---|
| *137* | A23 | 4p on 2½p org | 50 | 30 |
| *138* | A25 | 7p on 1sh yel grn | 1.00 | 80 |

Type of 1952 and

Klinki Plymill A26

Designs: 3½p, Chimbu headdress. 4p, 5p, Cacao. 8p, Klinki Plymill. 1sh7p, Cattle. 2sh5p, Cattle. 5sh, Coffee (vert.).

**1958-60 Engr. *Perf. 14***

| No. | Type | Denom. | Color | Unused | Used |
|---|---|---|---|---|---|
| *139* | A23 | 3½p | black | 9.00 | 5.00 |
| *140* | A23 | 4p | vermilion | 75 | 15 |
| *141* | A23 | 5p | grn ('60) | 75 | 10 |
| *142* | A26 | 7p | gray grn | 5.00 | 1.00 |
| *143* | A26 | 8p | dk ultra ('60) | 3.50 | 2.25 |
| *144* | A26 | 1sh7p | red brn | 50.00 | 35.00 |
| *145* | A26 | 2sh5p | ver ('60) | 8.00 | 7.00 |
| *146* | A26 | 5sh | gray ol & brn red | 10.00 | 3.50 |
| | | | *Nos. 139-146 (8)* | 87.00 | 54.00 |

No. 122 Surcharged with New Value

**1959, Dec. 1**

| No. | Type | Surcharge | Unused | Used |
|---|---|---|---|---|
| *147* | A23 | 5p on ½p bl grn | 1.00 | 30 |

Council Chamber and Frangipani Flowers A27

**1961, Apr. 10 Photo. *Perf. 14½x14***

| No. | Type | Denom. | Color | Unused | Used |
|---|---|---|---|---|---|
| *148* | A27 | 5p | grn & yel | 3.00 | 1.75 |
| *149* | A27 | 2sh3p | grn & sal | 22.50 | 20.00 |

Reconstitution of the Legislative Council.

Woman's Head — A28

Red-plumed Bird of Paradise — A29

Port Moresby Harbor A30

Woman Dancer A31

Elizabeth II A34

Constable Ragas Amis Matia, Port Moresby A32

View of Rabaul, by Samuel Terarup Cham — A33

Designs: 3p, Man's head. 6p, Golden opossum. 2sh, Male dancer with drum. 2sh3p, Piaggio transport plane landing at Tapini.

***Perf. 14 (A28, A31, A32), 11½ (A29, A33), 14x13½ (A30), 14 ½ (A34)***

**1961-63 Engr. Unwmk.**

| No. | Type | Denom. | Color | Unused | Used |
|---|---|---|---|---|---|
| *153* | A28 | 1p | dk car | 18 | 8 |
| *154* | A28 | 3p | bluish blk | 22 | 12 |
| | | | **Photo.** | | |
| *155* | A29 | 5p | lt brn, red brn, blk & yel ('63) | 25 | 12 |
| *156* | A29 | 6p | gray, ocher & slate ('63) | 90 | 90 |
| | | | **Engr.** | | |
| *157* | A30 | 8p | grn ('63) | 45 | 35 |
| *158* | A31 | 1sh | gray grn | 6.00 | 75 |
| *159* | A31 | 2sh | rose lake | 1.40 | 70 |
| *160* | A30 | 2sh3p | dk bl ('63) | 1.20 | 75 |
| *161* | A32 | 3sh | grn ('62) | 1.50 | 1.20 |
| | | | **Photo.** | | |
| *162* | A33 | 10sh | multi ('63) | 30.00 | 22.50 |
| *163* | A34 | £1 | brt grn, blk & gold ('63) | 20.00 | 12.50 |
| | | | *Nos. 153-163 (11)* | 62.10 | 39.97 |

The 5p and 6p are on granite paper.

Malaria Eradication Emblem — A35

**1962, Apr. 7 Litho. *Perf. 14***

| No. | Type | Denom. | Color | Unused | Used |
|---|---|---|---|---|---|
| *164* | A35 | 5p | lt bl & mar | 75 | 22 |
| *165* | A35 | 1sh | lt brn & red | 3.75 | 1.50 |
| *166* | A35 | 2sh | yel grn & blk | 7.50 | 4.50 |

WHO drive to eradicate malaria.

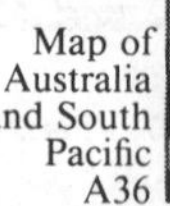

Map of Australia and South Pacific A36

**1962, July 9 Engr. Unwmk.**

| No. | Type | Denom. | Color | Unused | Used |
|---|---|---|---|---|---|
| *167* | A36 | 5p | dk red & lt grn | 55 | 25 |
| *168* | A36 | 1sh6p | dk vio & yel | 3.00 | 2.25 |
| *169* | A36 | 2sh6p | grn & lt bl | 9.00 | 6.00 |

5th So. Pacific Conf., Pago Pago, July 1962.

High Jump — A37

Games Emblem — A38

**1962, Oct. 24 Photo. *Perf. 11½***

**Size: 26x21mm**

**Granite Paper**

| No. | Type | Denom. | Description | Unused | Used |
|---|---|---|---|---|---|
| *171* | A37 | 5p | shown | 55 | 25 |
| *172* | A37 | 5p | Javelin | 55 | 25 |
| | | | **Size: 32½x22½mm** | | |
| *173* | A37 | 2sh3p | runners | 5.00 | 3.75 |

British Empire and Commonwealth Games, Perth, Australia, Nov. 22-Dec. 1.

Nos. 171 and 172 printed in alternating horizontal rows in sheet.

Red Cross Type of Australia, 1963

**1963, May 1 *Perf. 13½***

| No. | Type | Denom. | Color | Unused | Used |
|---|---|---|---|---|---|
| *174* | A135 | 5p | bl grn, gray & red | 75 | 40 |

Centenary of the International Red Cross.

**1963, Aug. 14 Engr. *Perf. 13½x14***

| No. | Type | Denom. | Color | Unused | Used |
|---|---|---|---|---|---|
| *176* | A38 | 5p | ol bis | 35 | 16 |
| *177* | A38 | 1sh | green | 1.40 | 1.25 |

So. Pacific Games, Suva, Aug. 29-Sept. 7.

Top of Wooden Shield — A39

Casting Ballot — A40

Various Carved Heads.

***Perf. 11½***

**1964, Feb. 5 Unwmk. Photo.**

**Granite Paper**

| No. | Type | Denom. | Color | Unused | Used |
|---|---|---|---|---|---|
| *178* | A39 | 11p | multi | 40 | 28 |
| *179* | A39 | 2sh5p | multi | 1.25 | 85 |
| *180* | A39 | 2sh6p | multi | 1.00 | 65 |
| *181* | A39 | 5sh | multi | 2.75 | 1.75 |

**1964, March 4 Unwmk. Perf. 11½**
**Granite Paper**

| | | | | |
|---|---|---|---|---|
| 182 | A40 | 5p dk brn & pale brn | 16 | 16 |
| 183 | A40 | 2sh3p dk brn & lt bl | 1.25 | 1.25 |

First Common Roll elections.

Patients at Health Center Clinic — A41

Designs: 8p, Dentist and school child patient. 1sh, Nurse holding infant. 1sh2p, Medical student using microscope.

**1964, Aug. 5 Engr. Perf. 14**

| | | | | |
|---|---|---|---|---|
| 184 | A41 | 5p violet | 16 | 10 |
| 185 | A41 | 8p green | 35 | 35 |
| 186 | A41 | 1sh dp ultra | 50 | 50 |
| 187 | A41 | 1sh2p rose brn | 65 | 65 |

Territorial health services.

Lawes Six-wired Birds of Paradise — A42

Designs: 1p, Striped gardener bower birds. 3p, New Guinea regent bower birds. 5p, Blue birds of paradise. 8p, Sickle-billed birds of paradise. 1sh, Emperor birds of paradise. 2sh, Brown sickle-billed bird of paradise. 2sh3p, Lesser bird of paradise. 3sh, Magnificent bird of paradise. 5sh, Twelve-wired bird of paradise. 10sh, Magnificent rifle birds.

**1964-65 Unwmk. Photo. Perf. 11½**
**Birds in Natural Colors**
**Size: 21x26mm**

| | | | | |
|---|---|---|---|---|
| 188 | A42 | 1p brt cit & dk brn ('65) | 16 | 7 |
| 189 | A42 | 3p gray & dk brn ('65) | 25 | 10 |
| 190 | A42 | 5p sal pink & blk ('65) | 25 | 10 |
| 191 | A42 | 6p pale grn & sep | 35 | 20 |
| 192 | A42 | 8p pale lil & dk brn | 50 | 28 |

**Size: 25x36mm.**

| | | | | |
|---|---|---|---|---|
| 193 | A42 | 1sh sal & blk | 65 | 50 |
| 194 | A42 | 2sh bl & dk brn | 2.25 | 1.40 |
| 195 | A42 | 2sh3p lt grn & dk brn ('65) | 3.25 | 2.00 |
| 196 | A42 | 3sh yel & dk brn ('65) | 3.50 | 2.50 |
| 197 | A42 | 5sh lt ultra & dk brn ('65) | 10.00 | 5.50 |
| 198 | A42 | 10sh gray & dk bl | 8.50 | 6.50 |
| | | *Nos. 188-198 (11)* | 29.66 | 19.15 |

Carved Crocodile's Head — A43

Designs: Wood carvings from Sepik River Region used as ship's prows and as objects of religious veneration.

**1965, Mar. 24 Photo. Perf. 11½**

| | | | | |
|---|---|---|---|---|
| 199 | A43 | 4p multi | 50 | 20 |
| 200 | A43 | 1sh2p gray brn, bis & dk brn | 2.00 | 1.50 |
| 201 | A43 | 1sh6p lil, dk brn & buff | 85 | 65 |
| 202 | A43 | 4sh bl, dk vio & mar | 2.50 | 2.00 |

**ANZAC Issue**
Type of Australia, 1965

**1965, Apr. 14 Perf. 13½x13**

| | | | | |
|---|---|---|---|---|
| 203 | A150 | 2sh3p brt grn, sep & blk | 1.00 | 1.00 |

See note after Australia No. 387.

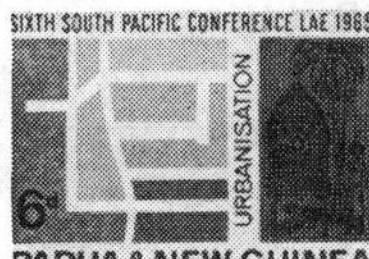

Urbanized Community and Stilt House — A44

Design: 1sh, Stilt house at left.

**1965, July 7 Photo. Perf. 11½**

| | | | | |
|---|---|---|---|---|
| 204 | A44 | 6p multi | 25 | 16 |
| 205 | A44 | 1sh multi | 50 | 50 |

Sixth South Pacific Conference, Lae, New Guinea, July, 1965.

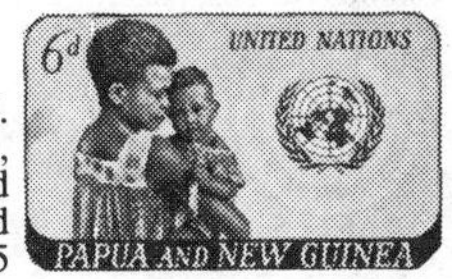

U.N. Emblem, Mother and Child A45

Designs (U.N. Emblem and): 1sh, Globe and orbit (vert.). 2sh, Four globes in orbit (vert.).

**1965, Oct. 13 Unwmk. Perf. 11½**

| | | | | |
|---|---|---|---|---|
| 206 | A45 | 6p brn, grnsh bl & dp bl | 25 | 20 |
| 207 | A45 | 1sh dl pur, bl & org | 50 | 50 |
| 208 | A45 | 2sh dp bl, pale grn & grn | 65 | 65 |

20th anniversary of the United Nations.

New Guinea Birdwing A46

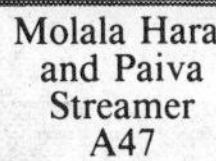

Molala Harai and Paiva Streamer A47

Discus A48

Butterflies: 1c, Blue emperor (vert.). 3c, White-banded map butterfly (vert.). 4c, Mountain swallowtail (vert.). 5c, Port Moresby terinos (vert.). 12c, Blue crow. 15c, Euchenor butterfly. 20c, White-spotted parthenos. 25c, Orange Jezebel. 50c, New Guinea emperor. $1, Blue-spotted leaf-wing. $2, Paradise birdwing.

Myths of Elema People: 7c, Marai, the fisherman. 30c, Meavea Kivovia and the Black Cockatoo. 60c, Toivita Tapaivita (symbolic face decorations).

**1966 Photo. Perf. 11½**
**Granite Paper**

| | | | | |
|---|---|---|---|---|
| 209 | A46 | 1c sal, blk & aqua | 10 | 10 |
| 210 | A47 | 2c blk & car | 16 | 16 |
| 211 | A46 | 3c gray grn, brn & org | 14 | 10 |
| 212 | A46 | 4c multi | 16 | 14 |
| 213 | A46 | 5c multi | 20 | 10 |
| 214 | A47 | 7c bl, blk & yel | 50 | 50 |
| 215 | A46 | 10c multi | 45 | 40 |
| 216 | A46 | 12c sal & multi | 1.25 | 1.25 |
| 217 | A46 | 15c pale vio, dk brn & buff | 1.25 | 90 |
| 218 | A46 | 20c yel bis, dk brn & yel org | 1.75 | 1.25 |
| 219 | A46 | 25c gray, blk & yel | 3.25 | 2.25 |
| 220 | A47 | 30c blk, yel grn & car | 1.75 | 1.00 |
| 221 | A46 | 50c multi | 5.00 | 3.50 |
| 222 | A47 | 60c blk, org & car | 3.50 | 2.75 |
| 223 | A46 | $1 pale bl, dk brn & dp org | 6.50 | 6.00 |
| 224 | A46 | $2 multi | 11.00 | 10.00 |
| | | *Nos. 209-224 (16)* | 36.96 | 30.40 |

In 1967 Courvoisier made new plates for the $1 and $2. Stamps from these plates show many minor differences and slight variations in shade.

**1966, Aug. 31 Perf. 11½**
**Granite Paper**

| | | | | |
|---|---|---|---|---|
| 225 | A48 | 5c shown | 14 | 10 |
| 226 | A48 | 10c Soccer | 65 | 65 |
| 227 | A48 | 20c Tennis | 85 | 85 |

Second South Pacific Games, Noumea, New Caledonia, Dec. 8-18.

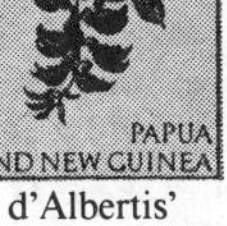

d'Albertis' Creeper — A49

Book and Pen ("Fine Arts") — A50

Flowers: 10c, Tecomanthe dendrophila. 20c, Rhododendron macgregoriae. 60c, Rhododendron konori.

**1966, Dec. 7 Photo. Perf. 11½**

| | | | | |
|---|---|---|---|---|
| 228 | A49 | 5c multi | 16 | 14 |
| 229 | A49 | 10c multi | 40 | 40 |
| 230 | A49 | 20c multi | 70 | 70 |
| 231 | A49 | 60c multi | 2.00 | 2.00 |

**1967, Feb. 8 Photo. Perf. 12½x12**

Designs: 3c, "Surveying," transit, view finder and pencil. 4c, "Civil Engineering," buildings and compass. 5c, "Science," test tubes and chemical formula. 20c, "Justice," Justitia and scales.

| | | | | |
|---|---|---|---|---|
| 232 | A50 | 1c org & multi | 5 | 5 |
| 233 | A50 | 3c bl & multi | 14 | 14 |
| 234 | A50 | 4c brn & multi | 16 | 16 |
| 235 | A50 | 5c grn & multi | 20 | 20 |
| 236 | A50 | 20c pink & multi | 85 | 85 |
| | | *Nos. 232-236 (5)* | 1.40 | 1.40 |

Issued to publicize the development of the University of Papua and New Guinea and the Institute of Higher Technical Education.

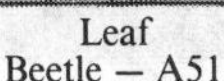

Leaf Beetle — A51

Hydroelectric Power — A52

Beetles: 10c, Eupholus schoenherri. 20c, Sphingnotus albertisi. 25c, Cyphogastra albertisi.

**1967, Apr. 12 Unwmk. Perf. 11½**

| | | | | |
|---|---|---|---|---|
| 237 | A51 | 5c bl & multi | 16 | 16 |
| 238 | A51 | 10c lt grn & multi | 40 | 40 |
| 239 | A51 | 20c rose & multi | 65 | 65 |
| 240 | A51 | 25c yel & multi | 85 | 85 |

**1967, June 28 Photo. Perf. 12x12½**

Designs: 10c, Pyrethrum (Chrysanthemum cinerariaefolium). 20c, Tea. 25c, like 5c.

| | | | | |
|---|---|---|---|---|
| 241 | A52 | 5c multi | 16 | 16 |
| 242 | A52 | 10c multi | 40 | 40 |
| 243 | A52 | 20c multi | 65 | 65 |
| 244 | A52 | 25c multi | 85 | 85 |

Issued to commemorate the completion of part of the Laloki River Hydroelectric Works near Port Moresby, and to commemorate the Hydrological Decade (UNESCO), 1965-74.

Battle of Milne Bay — A53

Designs: 5c, Soldiers on Kokoda Trail (vert.). 20c, The coast watchers. 50c, Battle of the Coral Sea.

**1967, Aug. 30 Unwmk. Perf. 11½**

| | | | | |
|---|---|---|---|---|
| 245 | A53 | 2c multi | 6 | 6 |
| 246 | A53 | 5c multi | 12 | 12 |
| 247 | A53 | 20c multi | 50 | 50 |
| 248 | A53 | 50c multi | 1.25 | 1.25 |

25th anniv. of the battles in the Pacific, which stopped the Japanese from occupying Papua and New Guinea.

Pesquet's Parrot — A54

Parrots: 5c, Fairy lory. 20c, Dusk-orange lory. 25c, Edward's fig parrot.

**1967, Nov. 29 Photo. Perf. 12**

| | | | | |
|---|---|---|---|---|
| 249 | A54 | 5c multi | 15 | 15 |
| 250 | A54 | 7c multi | 25 | 25 |
| 251 | A54 | 20c multi | 70 | 70 |
| 252 | A54 | 25c multi | 90 | 90 |

Chimbu District Headdress — A55

Headdress from: 10c, Southern Highlands District (horiz.). 20c, Western Highlands District (horiz.). 60c, Chimbu District (different from 5c).

**Perf. 12x12½, 12½x12**
**1968, Feb. 21 Photo. Unwmk.**

| | | | | |
|---|---|---|---|---|
| 253 | A55 | 5c multi | 12 | 8 |
| 254 | A55 | 10c multi | 25 | 18 |
| 255 | A55 | 20c multi | 50 | 40 |
| 256 | A55 | 60c multi | 1.65 | 1.25 |

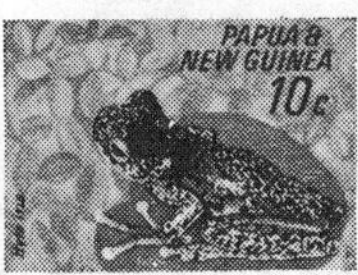

Frogs — A56

**1968, Apr. 24 Photo. Perf. 11½**

| | | | | |
|---|---|---|---|---|
| 257 | A56 | 5c Tree | 20 | 20 |
| 258 | A56 | 10c Tree, diff. | 45 | 45 |
| 259 | A56 | 15c Swamp | 65 | 65 |
| 260 | A56 | 20c Tree, diff. | 90 | 85 |

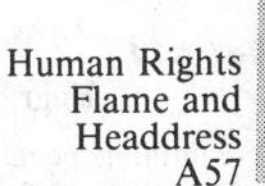

Human Rights Flame and Headdress A57

Symbolic Designs: 10c, Human Rights Flame surrounded by the world. 20c, 25c, "Universal Suffrage" in 2 abstract designs.

**1968, June 26** **Litho.** ***Perf. 14x13***

| | | | | |
|---|---|---|---|---|
| *261* | A57 | 5c blk & multi | 16 | 16 |
| *262* | A57 | 10c blk & multi | 35 | 35 |
| *263* | A57 | 20c blk & multi | 85 | 65 |
| *264* | A57 | 25c blk & multi | 1.00 | 85 |

Issued for Human Rights Year, 1968, and to publicize free elections.

Frilled Clam — A58

Sea Shells: 1c, Egg cowry. 3c, Crested stromb. 4c, Lithograph bone. 5c, Marble cone. 7c, Orange-spotted miter. 10c, Red volute. 12c, Checkerboard helmet shell. 15c, Scorpion shell. 25c, Chocolate-flamed Venus shell. 30c, Giant murex. 40c, Chambered nautilus. 60c, Triton's trumpet. $1, Emerald snails. $2, Glory of the sea (vert.).

***Perf. 12½x12, 12x12½***

**1968-69** **Photo.**

**Granite Paper**

| | | | | |
|---|---|---|---|---|
| *265* | A58 | 1c multi ('69) | 7 | 5 |
| *266* | A58 | 3c multi | 14 | 6 |
| *267* | A58 | 4c multi ('69) | 20 | 10 |
| *268* | A58 | 5c multi | 30 | 10 |
| *269* | A58 | 7c multi ('69) | 40 | 20 |
| *270* | A58 | 10c multi | 50 | 35 |
| *271* | A58 | 12c multi ('69) | 75 | 50 |
| *272* | A58 | 15c multi | 85 | 60 |
| *273* | A58 | 20c multi | 1.00 | 65 |
| *274* | A58 | 25c multi | 1.50 | 1.00 |
| *275* | A58 | 30c multi | 1.75 | 1.25 |
| *276* | A58 | 40c multi | 3.00 | 1.75 |
| *277* | A58 | 60c multi | 3.50 | 2.50 |
| *278* | A58 | $1 multi | 6.00 | 5.00 |
| *279* | A58 | $2 multi ('69) | 15.00 | 10.00 |
| | | *Nos. 265-279 (15)* | 34.96 | 24.11 |

Issue dates: 5c, 20c, 25c, 30c, 60c, Aug. 28, 1968; 3c, 10c, 15c, 40c, $1, Oct. 30, 1968. Others, Jan. 29, 1969.

Legend of Tito-Iko A59

Fireball Class Sailboat, Port Moresby Harbor A60

Myths of Elema People: No. 281, 5c inscribed "Iko." No. 282, 10c inscribed "Luvuapo." No. 283, 10c inscribed "Miro."

***#280 & 282: Perf. 12½ x 13½ x Roul. 9 x Perf. 13½. #281 & 283: Roul. 9 x Perf. 13½ x 12½ x 13½***

**1969, Apr. 9** **Litho.** **Unwmk.**

| | | | | |
|---|---|---|---|---|
| *280* | A59 | 5c blk, yel & red | 16 | 14 |
| *281* | A59 | 5c blk, yel & red | 16 | 14 |
| *282* | A59 | 10c blk, gray & red | 40 | 35 |
| *283* | A59 | 10c blk, gray & red | 40 | 35 |

The two 5c and the two 10c stamps are printed se-tenant in vertical pairs with continuous designs, rouletted between.

***Perf. 14x14½, 14½x14***

**1969, June 25** **Engr.**

Designs: 10c, Games' swimming pool, Boroko (horiz.). 20c, Main Games area, Konedobu (horiz.).

| | | | | |
|---|---|---|---|---|
| *284* | A60 | 5c black | 16 | 16 |
| *285* | A60 | 10c brt vio | 35 | 35 |
| *286* | A60 | 20c green | 65 | 65 |

Issued to publicize the 3rd South Pacific Games, Port Moresby, Aug. 13-23.

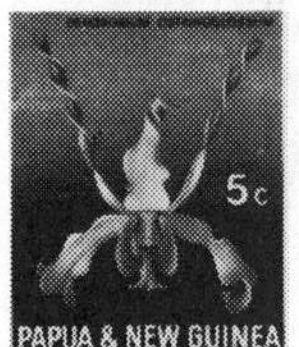

Dendrobium Ostrinoglossum A61

Potter A62

Orchids: 10c, Dendrobium lawesii. 20c, Dendrobium pseudofrigidum. 30c, Dendrobium conanthum.

**1969, Aug. 27** **Photo.** ***Perf. 11½***

**Granite Paper**

| | | | | |
|---|---|---|---|---|
| *287* | A61 | 5c multi | 20 | 20 |
| *288* | A61 | 10c multi | 50 | 40 |
| *289* | A61 | 20c multi | 85 | 85 |
| *290* | A61 | 30c multi | 1.50 | 1.40 |

Issued to publicize the 6th World Orchid Conference, Sydney, Australia, Sept. 1969.

**1969, Sept. 24** **Photo.** ***Perf. 11½***

**Granite Paper**

| | | | | |
|---|---|---|---|---|
| *291* | A62 | 5c multi | 28 | 20 |

50th anniv. of the ILO.

Bird of Paradise A63

Seed Pod Rattle (Tareko) A64

Coil Stamps

**1969-71** ***Perf. 14½ Horiz.***

| | | | | |
|---|---|---|---|---|
| *291A* | A63 | 2c red, dp bl & blk | 7 | 6 |
| *292* | A63 | 5c org & emer | 16 | 14 |

**1969, Oct. 29** **Photo.** ***Perf. 12½***

Musical Instruments: 10c, Hand drum (garamut). 25c, Pan pipes (iviliko). 30c, Hourglass drum (kundu).

| | | | | |
|---|---|---|---|---|
| *293* | A64 | 5c multi | 16 | 14 |
| *294* | A64 | 10c multi | 45 | 35 |
| *295* | A64 | 25c multi | 1.10 | 85 |
| *296* | A64 | 30c multi | 1.40 | 1.00 |

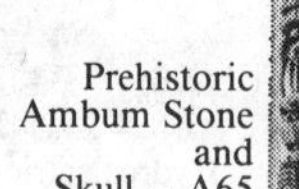

Prehistoric Ambum Stone and Skull — A65

Designs: 10c, Masawa canoe of the Kula Circuit. 25c, Map of Papua and New Guinea made by Luis Valez de Torres, 1606. 30c, H.M.S. Basilisk, 1873.

**1970, Feb. 11** **Photo.** ***Perf. 12½***

| | | | | |
|---|---|---|---|---|
| *297* | A65 | 5c vio brn & multi | 20 | 16 |
| *298* | A65 | 10c ocher & multi | 45 | 35 |
| *299* | A65 | 25c org brn & multi | 1.10 | 90 |
| *300* | A65 | 20c ol grn & multi | 1.40 | 1.10 |

King of Saxony Bird of Paradise — A66

Birds of Paradise: 10c, King. 15c, Augusta Victoria. 25c, Multi-crested.

**1970, May 13** **Photo.** ***Perf. 11½***

| | | | | |
|---|---|---|---|---|
| *301* | A66 | 5c tan & multi | 50 | 20 |
| *302* | A66 | 10c multi | 1.00 | 45 |
| *303* | A66 | 15c lt bl & multi | 2.00 | 1.40 |
| *304* | A66 | 25c multi | 3.50 | 2.00 |

Canceled to Order
Starting in 1970 or earlier, the Philatelic Bureau at Port Moresby began to sell new issues canceled to order at face value.

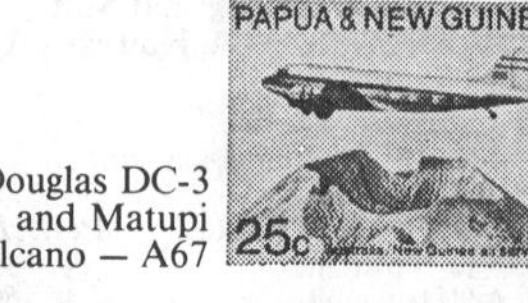

Douglas DC-3 and Matupi Volcano — A67

Aircraft: No. 305, DC-6B and Mt. Wilhelm. No. 306, Lockheed Mark II Electra and Mt. Yule. No. 307, Boeing 727 and Mt. Giluwe. No. 308, Fokker F27 Friendship and Manam Island Volcano. 30c, Boeing 707 and Hombom's Bluff.

**1970, July 8** **Photo.** ***Perf. 14½x14***

| | | | | |
|---|---|---|---|---|
| *305* | A67 | 5c *"TAA" on tail* | 16 | 16 |
| *306* | A67 | 5c *striped tail* | 16 | 16 |
| *307* | A67 | 5c *"T" on tail* | 16 | 16 |
| *308* | A67 | 5c *Red tail* | 16 | 16 |
| *309* | A67 | 25c multi | 1.10 | 1.00 |
| *310* | A67 | 30c multi | 1.40 | 1.10 |
| | | *Nos. 305-310 (6)* | 3.14 | 2.74 |

Issued to commemorate the development of air service during the last 25 years between Australia and New Guinea. Nos. 305-308 printed se-tenant in sheets of 100.

Nicolaus N. de Miklouho-Maclay, Explorer, and Mask — A68

Designs: 10c, Bronislaw Kaspar Malinowski, anthropologist, and hut. 15c, Count Tommaso Salvadori, ornithologist, and cassowary. 20c, Friedrich R. Schlechter, botanist, and orchid.

**1970, Aug. 19** **Photo.** ***Perf. 11½***

| | | | | |
|---|---|---|---|---|
| *311* | A68 | 5c brn, blk & lil | 20 | 20 |
| *312* | A68 | 10c multi | 50 | 40 |
| *313* | A68 | 15c dl lil & multi | 85 | 65 |
| *314* | A68 | 20c sl & multi | 1.40 | 1.00 |

42nd Cong. of the Australian and New Zealand Assoc. for the Advancement of Science, Port Moresby, Aug. 17-21.

Wogeo Island Food Bowl — A69

Eastern Highlands Round House — A70

National Handicraft: 10c, Lime pot. 15c, Aibom sago storage pot. 30c, Manus Island bowl (horiz.).

**1970, Oct. 28** **Photo.** ***Perf. 12½***

| | | | | |
|---|---|---|---|---|
| *315* | A69 | 5c multi | 20 | 20 |
| *316* | A69 | 10c multi | 50 | 50 |
| *317* | A69 | 15c multi | 70 | 70 |
| *318* | A69 | 30c multi | 1.50 | 1.40 |

**1971, Jan. 27** **Photo.** ***Perf. 11½***

Local Architecture: 7c, Milne Bay house. 10c, Purari Delta house. 40c, Sepik or Men's Spirit House.

| | | | | |
|---|---|---|---|---|
| *319* | A70 | 5c dk ol & multi | 25 | 20 |
| *320* | A70 | 7c Prus bl & multi | 40 | 35 |
| *321* | A70 | 10c dp org & multi | 60 | 50 |
| *322* | A70 | 40c brn & multi | 1.75 | 1.50 |

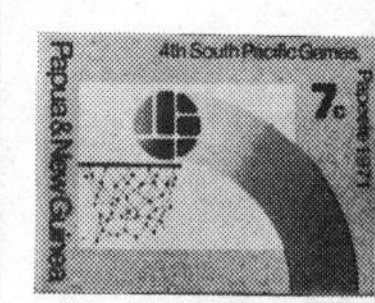

Spotted Cuscus — A71

Basketball — A72

Animals: 10c, Brown and white striped possum. 15c, Feather-tailed possum. 25c, Spiny anteater (horiz.). 30c, Good-fellow's tree-climbing kangaroo (horiz.).

**1971, Mar. 31** **Photo.** ***Perf. 11½***

| | | | | |
|---|---|---|---|---|
| *323* | A71 | 5c bl grn & multi | 22 | 20 |
| *324* | A71 | 10c multi | 60 | 50 |
| *325* | A71 | 15c multi | 1.00 | 85 |
| *326* | A71 | 25c dl yel & multi | 1.50 | 1.10 |
| *327* | A71 | 30c ol & multi | 2.00 | 1.50 |
| | | *Nos. 323-327 (5)* | 5.32 | 4.15 |

**1971, June 9** **Litho.** ***Perf. 14***

Designs: 14c, Yachting. 21c, Boxing. 28c, Stop watch; field events.

| | | | | |
|---|---|---|---|---|
| *328* | A72 | 7c org & multi | 28 | 28 |
| *329* | A72 | 14c red org & multi | 55 | 50 |
| *330* | A72 | 21c ol & multi | 1.00 | 75 |
| *331* | A72 | 28c dl bl & multi | 1.25 | 1.00 |

Fourth South Pacific Games, Papeete, French Polynesia, Sept. 8-19.

Bartering Fish for Coconuts and Taro — A73

Siaa Dancer — A74

Designs: 9c, Man stacking yams and taro. 14c, Market scene. 30c, Farm couple tending yams.

**1971, Aug. 18** **Photo.** ***Perf. 11½***

| | | | | |
|---|---|---|---|---|
| *332* | A73 | 7c multi | 28 | 25 |
| *333* | A73 | 9c multi | 50 | 40 |
| *334* | A73 | 14c multi | 75 | 60 |
| *335* | A73 | 30c multi | 1.50 | 1.40 |

Primary industries.

**1971, Oct. 27** **Photo.** ***Perf. 11½***

Designs: 9c, Urasena masked dancer. 20c, Two Siassi masked dancers (horiz.). 28c, Three Siaa dancers (horiz.).

| | | | | |
|---|---|---|---|---|
| *336* | A74 | 7c org & multi | 20 | 20 |
| *337* | A74 | 9c yel grn & multi | 40 | 38 |
| *338* | A74 | 20c bis & multi | 1.10 | 1.00 |
| *339* | A74 | 28c multi | 1.75 | 1.50 |

Papua New Guinea and Australia Arms — A75

Design: No. 341, Papua New Guinea and Australia flags.

**1972, Jan. 26** ***Perf. 12½x12***

| | | | | |
|---|---|---|---|---|
| *340* | A75 | 7c gray bl, org & blk | 50 | 35 |
| *341* | A75 | 7c gray bl, blk, red & yel | 50 | 35 |

Constitutional development for the 1972 House of Assembly elections. Nos. 340-341 printed se-tenant in sheets of 50.

Papua New Guinea Map, South Pacific Commission Emblem — A76

Design: No. 343, Man's head and South Pacific Commission flag.

**1972, Jan. 26**

| | | | | |
|---|---|---|---|---|
| *342* | A76 | 15c brt grn & multi | 1.10 | 65 |
| *343* | A76 | 15c brt grn & multi | 1.10 | 65 |

25th anniversary of the South Pacific Commission. Nos. 342-343 printed se-tenant in sheets of 50.

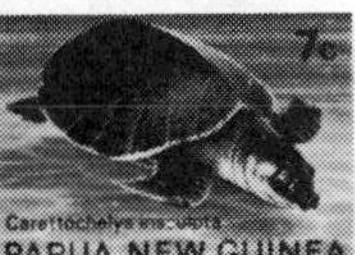


Pitted-shelled Turtle — A77

Designs: 14c, Angle-headed agamid. 21c, Green python. 30c, Water monitor.

**1972, Mar. 15 Photo. *Perf. 11½***

| | | | | |
|---|---|---|---|---|
| *344* | A77 | 7c multi | 40 | 20 |
| *345* | A77 | 14c car rose & multi | 1.40 | 60 |
| *346* | A77 | 21c yel & multi | 1.75 | 90 |
| *347* | A77 | 30c yel grn & multi | 2.25 | 1.40 |

Curtiss Seagull MF 6 and Ship A78

Designs: 14c, De Havilland 37 and porters from gold fields. 20c, Junkers G 31 and heavy machinery. 25c, Junkers F 13 and Lutheran mission church.

**1972, June 7**

**Granite Paper**

| | | | | |
|---|---|---|---|---|
| *348* | A78 | 7c dp yel & multi | 35 | 28 |
| *349* | A78 | 14c dp org & multi | 1.00 | 65 |
| *350* | A78 | 20c ol & multi | 1.75 | 1.00 |
| *351* | A78 | 25c multi | 2.00 | 1.10 |

50th anniversary of aviation in Papua New Guinea.

National Day Unity Emblem — A79

Designs: 10c, Unity emblem and kundu (drum). 30c, United emblem and conch.

**1972, Aug. 16 *Perf. 12x12½***

| | | | | |
|---|---|---|---|---|
| *352* | A79 | 7c vio bl & multi | 20 | 22 |
| *353* | A79 | 10c org & multi | 80 | 50 |
| *354* | A79 | 30c ver & multi | 1.75 | 1.10 |

National Day, Sept. 15, 1972.

Rev. Copland King — A80

Pioneering Missionaries: No. 356, Pastor Ruatoka. No. 357, Bishop Stanislaus Henry Verjus. No. 358, Rev. Dr. Johannes Flierl.

**1972, Oct. 25 Photo. *Perf. 11½***

| | | | | |
|---|---|---|---|---|
| *355* | A80 | 7c dk bl & multi | 65 | 50 |
| *356* | A80 | 7c dk red & multi | 65 | 50 |
| *357* | A80 | 7c dk grn & multi | 65 | 50 |
| *358* | A80 | 7c dk ol bis & multi | 65 | 50 |

Christmas 1972.

Relay Station on Mt. Tomavatur A81

**1973, Jan. 24 Photo. *Perf. 12½***

| | | | | |
|---|---|---|---|---|
| *359* | A81 | 7c *shown* | 55 | 28 |
| *360* | A81 | 7c *Mt. Kerigomna* | 55 | 28 |
| *361* | A81 | 7c *Sattelburg* | 55 | 28 |
| *362* | A81 | 7c *Wideru* | 55 | 28 |
| *363* | A81 | 9c *Teleprinter* | 85 | 35 |
| *364* | A81 | 30c *Map of telecommunications network* | 2.75 | 1.40 |
| | | *Nos. 359-364 (6)* | 5.80 | 2.87 |

Telecommunications development 1968-1972. The 7c stamps are printed se-tenant in blocks of 4 with unifying frame.

Queen Carol's Bird of Paradise — A82

Birds of Paradise: 14c, Goldie's. 21c, Ribbon-tailed astrapia. 28c, Princess Stephanie's.

**1973, Mar. 30 Photo. *Perf. 11½***

**Size: 22½x38mm**

| | | | | |
|---|---|---|---|---|
| *365* | A82 | 7c cit & multi | 65 | 40 |
| *366* | A82 | 14c dl grn & multi | 1.40 | 75 |

**Size: 17x48mm**

| | | | | |
|---|---|---|---|---|
| *367* | A82 | 21c lem & multi | 1.75 | 1.10 |
| *368* | A82 | 28c lt bl & multi | 2.75 | 1.65 |

Wood Carver, Milne Bay — A83

Designs: 3c, Wig makers, Southern Highlands. 5c, Bagana Volcano, Bougainville. 6c, Pig Exchange, Western Highlands. 7c, Coastal village, Central District. 8c, Arawe mother, West New Britain. 9c, Fire dancers, East New Britain. 10c, Tifalmin hunter, West Sepik District. 14c, Crocodile hunters, Western District. 15c, Mt. Elimbari, Chimbu. 20c, Canoe racing, Manus District. 21c, Making sago, Gulf District. 25c, Council House, East Sepik. 28c, Menyamya bowmen, Morobe. 30c, Shark snaring, New Ireland. 40c, Fishing canoes, Madang. 60c, Women making tapa cloth, Northern District. $1, Asaro mudmen, Eastern Highlands. $2, Sing festival, Enga District.

**1973-74 Photo. *Perf. 11½***

**Granite Paper**

| | | | | |
|---|---|---|---|---|
| *369* | A83 | 1c multi | 5 | 5 |
| *370* | A83 | 3c multi ('74) | 8 | 7 |
| *371* | A83 | 5c multi | 15 | 12 |
| *372* | A83 | 6c multi ('74) | 18 | 14 |
| *373* | A83 | 7c multi | 22 | 15 |
| *374* | A83 | 8c multi ('74) | 22 | 16 |
| *375* | A83 | 9c multi | 28 | 18 |
| *376* | A83 | 10c multi ('74) | 28 | 20 |
| *377* | A83 | 14c multi | 40 | 20 |
| *378* | A83 | 15c multi | 45 | 30 |
| *379* | A83 | 20c multi ('74) | 60 | 40 |
| *380* | A83 | 21c multi | 60 | 40 |
| *381* | A83 | 25c multi | 75 | 50 |
| *382* | A83 | 28c multi | 85 | 55 |
| *383* | A83 | 30c multi | 85 | 60 |
| *385* | A83 | 40c multi | 1.10 | 85 |
| *386* | A83 | 60c multi ('74) | 1.75 | 1.10 |
| *387* | A83 | $1 multi ('74) | 6.50 | 3.75 |
| *388* | A83 | $2 multi ('74) | 11.00 | 6.50 |
| | | *Nos. 369-383,385-388 (19)* | 26.31 | 16.22 |

Papua New Guinea No. 7 — A84

Designs: 1c, German New Guinea Nos. 1-2. 6c, German New Guinea No. 17. 7c, New Britain No. 43. 25c, New Guinea No. 1. 30c, Papua New Guinea No. 108.

**Litho. (1c, 7c); Litho. & Engr. (others)**

**1973, Oct. 24 *Perf. 13½x14***

**Size: 54x31mm**

| | | | | |
|---|---|---|---|---|
| *389* | A84 | 1c gold, brn, grn & blk | 7 | 7 |
| *390* | A84 | 6c sil, bl & ind | 38 | 38 |
| *391* | A84 | 7c gold, red, blk & buff | 50 | 50 |

***Perf. 14x14½***

**Size: 45x38mm**

| | | | | |
|---|---|---|---|---|
| *392* | A84 | 9c gold, org, blk & brn | 60 | 60 |
| *393* | A84 | 25c gold & org | 1.75 | 1.75 |
| *394* | A84 | 30c sil & dp lil | 2.00 | 2.00 |
| | | *Nos. 389-394 (6)* | 5.30 | 5.30 |

75th anniv. of stamps in Papua New Guinea.

Masks — A85

**1973, Dec. 5 Photo. *Perf. 12½***

**Granite Paper**

| | | | | |
|---|---|---|---|---|
| *395* | A85 | 7c multi | 40 | 35 |
| *396* | A85 | 10c vio bl & multi | 75 | 65 |

Self-government.

Queen Elizabeth II — A86

**1974, Feb. 22 Photo. *Perf. 14x14½***

| | | | | |
|---|---|---|---|---|
| *397* | A86 | 7c dp car & multi | 35 | 35 |
| *398* | A86 | 30c vio bl & multi | 2.00 | 1.75 |

Visit of Queen Elizabeth II and the Royal Family, Feb. 22-27.

Wreathed Hornbill A87

Size of No. 400, 32½x48mm.

***Perf. 12, 11½ (10c)***

**1974, June 12 Photo.**

**Granite Paper**

| | | | | |
|---|---|---|---|---|
| *399* | A87 | 7c *shown* | 1.10 | 1.00 |
| *400* | A87 | 10c *Great cassowary* | 1.75 | 1.50 |
| *401* | A87 | 30c *Kapul eagle* | 4.00 | 3.75 |

Dendrobium Bracteosum — A88

Orchids: 10c, Dendrobium anosmum. 20c, Dendrobium smillieae. 30c, Dendrobium insigne.

**1974, Nov. 20 Photo. *Perf. 11½***

**Granite Paper**

| | | | | |
|---|---|---|---|---|
| *402* | A88 | 7c dk grn & multi | 35 | 20 |
| *403* | A88 | 10c dk bl & multi | 50 | 28 |
| *404* | A88 | 20c bis & multi | 1.00 | 55 |
| *405* | A88 | 30c grn & multi | 1.75 | 80 |

Motu Lakatoi A89

Traditional Canoes: 10c, Tami two-master morobe. 25c, Aramia racing canoe. 30c, Buka Island canoe.

**1975, Feb. 26 Photo. *Perf. 11½***

**Granite Paper**

| | | | | |
|---|---|---|---|---|
| *406* | A89 | 7c multi | 20 | 20 |
| *407* | A89 | 10c org & multi | 35 | 30 |
| *408* | A89 | 25c ap grn & multi | 1.00 | 85 |
| *409* | A89 | 30c cit & multi | 1.20 | 1.00 |

Paradise Birdwing Butterfly, 1t Coin — A90

Ornate Butterfly Cod on 2t and Plateless Turtle on 5t — A91

New coinage: 10t, Cuscus on 10t. 20t, Cassowary on 20t. 1k, River crocodiles on 1k coin with center hole; obverse and reverse of 1k.

***Perf. 11, 11½ (A91)***

**1975, Apr. 21 Photo.**

**Granite Paper**

| | | | | |
|---|---|---|---|---|
| *410* | A90 | 1t grn & multi | 6 | 5 |
| *411* | A91 | 7t brn & multi | 35 | 20 |
| *412* | A90 | 10t vio bl & multi | 50 | 28 |
| *413* | A90 | 20t car & multi | 65 | 55 |
| *414* | A91 | 1k dl bl & multi | 5.00 | 3.00 |
| | | *Nos. 410-414 (5)* | 6.56 | 4.08 |

Ornithoptera Alexandrae A92

Boxing and Games' Emblem A93

Birdwing Butterflies: 10t, O. victoriae regis. 30t, O. allottei. 40t, O. chimaera.

**1975, June 11 Photo. Perf. 11½**
**Granite Paper**

| | | | | |
|---|---|---|---|---|
| *415* A92 | 7t multi | | 28 | 20 |
| *416* A92 | 10t multi | | 40 | 30 |
| *417* A92 | 30t multi | | 1.40 | 90 |
| *418* A92 | 40t multi | | 2.00 | 1.20 |

**1975, Aug. 2 Photo. Perf. 11½**
**Granite Paper**

| | | | | |
|---|---|---|---|---|
| *419* A93 | 7t *shown* | | 25 | 22 |
| *420* A93 | 20t *Track and field* | | 70 | 60 |
| *421* A93 | 25t *Basketball* | | 90 | 75 |
| *422* A93 | 30t *Swimming* | | 1.25 | 90 |

5th South Pacific Games, Guam, Aug. 1-10.

Map of South East Asia and Flag of PNG
A94

Design: 30t, Map of South East Asia and Papua New Guinea coat of arms.

**1975, Sept. 10 Photo. Perf. 11½**
**Granite Paper**

| | | | | |
|---|---|---|---|---|
| *423* A94 | 7t red & multi | | 35 | 35 |
| *424* A94 | 30t bl & multi | | 1.50 | 1.50 |
| a | Souvenir sheet of 2 | | 2.00 | 2.00 |

Papua New Guinea independence, Sept. 16, 1975. No. 424a contains one each of Nos. 423-424; gray marginal inscription and coat of arms. Size: 115x58mm.

M. V. Bulolo
A95

Ships of the 1930's: 15t, M.V. Macdhui. 25t, M.V. Malaita. 60t, S.S. Montoro.

**1976, Jan. 21 Photo. Perf. 11½**
**Granite Paper**

| | | | | |
|---|---|---|---|---|
| *425* A95 | 7t multi | | 28 | 16 |
| *426* A95 | 15t multi | | 50 | 35 |
| *427* A95 | 25t multi | | 85 | 55 |
| *428* A95 | 60t multi | | 2.00 | 1.50 |

Rorovana Carvings — A96

Bougainville Art: 20t, Upe hats. 25t, Kapkaps (tortoise shell ornaments). 30t, Carved canoe paddles.

**1976, Mar. 17 Photo. Perf. 11½**
**Granite Paper**

| | | | | |
|---|---|---|---|---|
| *429* A96 | 7t multi | | 25 | 22 |
| *430* A96 | 20t bl & multi | | 75 | 60 |
| *431* A96 | 25t dp org & multi | | 90 | 75 |
| *432* A96 | 30t multi | | 1.10 | 90 |

Houses
A97

**1976, June 9 Photo. Perf. 11½**
**Granite Paper**

| | | | | |
|---|---|---|---|---|
| *433* A97 | 7t Rabaul | | 28 | 16 |
| *434* A97 | 15t Aramia | | 55 | 40 |
| *435* A97 | 30t Telefomin | | 1.00 | 85 |
| *436* A97 | 40t Tapini | | 1.50 | 1.00 |

Boy Scouts and Scout Emblem
A98

De Havilland Sea Plane, Map of Pacific — A99

Designs: 15t, Sea Scouts on outrigger canoe, Scout emblem. 60t, Plane on water.

**1976, Aug. 18 Photo. Perf. 11½**
**Granite Paper**

| | | | | |
|---|---|---|---|---|
| *437* A98 | 7t multi | | 25 | 20 |
| *438* A99 | 10t lil & multi | | 35 | 28 |
| *439* A98 | 15t multi | | 65 | 40 |
| *440* A99 | 60t multi | | 2.00 | 1.75 |

50th anniversaries: Papua New Guinea Boy Scouts; 1st flight from Australia.

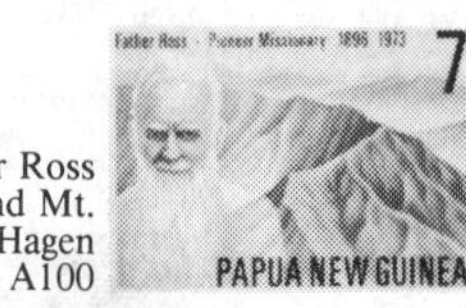


Father Ross and Mt. Hagen
A100

**1976, Oct. 28 Photo. Perf. 11½**
**Granite Paper**

| | | | |
|---|---|---|---|
| *441* A100 | 7t multi | 40 | 28 |

Rev. Father William Ross (1896-1973), American missionary in New Guinea.

Clouded Rainbow Fish — A101

Tropical Fish: 15t, Imperial angelfish. 30t, Freckled rock cod. 40t, Threadfin butterflyfish.

**1976, Oct. 28**
**Granite Paper**

| | | | | |
|---|---|---|---|---|
| *442* A101 | 5t multi | | 25 | 18 |
| *443* A101 | 15t multi | | 75 | 50 |
| *444* A101 | 30t multi | | 1.50 | 90 |
| *445* A101 | 40t multi | | 1.75 | 1.20 |

Kundiawa Man — A102

Mekeo Headdress
A103

Headdresses: 5t, Masked dancer, East Sepik Province. 10t, Dancer, Koiari area. 15t, Hanuabada woman. 20t, Young woman, Orokaiva. 25t, Haus Tambaran dancer, East Sepik Province. 30t, Asaro Valley man. 35t, Garaina man, Morobe. 40t, Waghi Valley man. 50t, Trobriand dancer, Milne Bay. 1k, Wasara.

**Perf. 11½ (1, 5, 10, 20, 35, 40, 50t), Perf. 12 (15, 25, 30t), Perf 14½x14 (1k), 14½x15 (2k)**

**1977-78 Photo.**

**Size: 25x30mm (1, 5, 20t), 26x26mm (10, 15, 25, 30, 50t), 23x38mm (35, 40t), 28x35½mm. (1k), 33x23mm (2k)**

| | | | | |
|---|---|---|---|---|
| *446* A102 | 1t multi | | 5 | 5 |
| *447* A102 | 5t multi | | 14 | 14 |
| *448* A102 | 10t multi | | 28 | 28 |
| *449* A102 | 15t multi | | 40 | 40 |
| *450* A102 | 20t multi | | 56 | 56 |
| *451* A102 | 25t multi | | 70 | 70 |
| *452* A102 | 30t multi | | 80 | 80 |
| *453* A102 | 35t multi | | 95 | 95 |
| *454* A102 | 40t multi | | 1.10 | 1.10 |
| *455* A102 | 50t multi | | 1.40 | 1.40 |

**Litho.**

| | | | | |
|---|---|---|---|---|
| *456* A102 | 1k multi | | 2.80 | 2.80 |
| *457* A103 | 2k multi | | 5.60 | 5.60 |
| | *Nos. 446-457 (12)* | | 14.78 | 14.78 |

Issue dates: Nos. 456-457, Jan. 12, 1977. Nos. 448, 450, 453, 455, June 7, 1978. Others, Mar. 29, 1978.

Elizabeth II and P.N.G. Arms
A104

Designs: 7t, Queen and P.N.G. flag. 35t, Queen and map of P.N.G.

**1977, Mar. 16 Photo. Perf. 15x14**

| | | | | |
|---|---|---|---|---|
| *462* A104 | 7t multi | | 25 | 16 |
| *463* A104 | 15t multi | | 50 | 40 |
| *464* A104 | 35t multi | | 1.10 | 1.00 |

25th anniv. of the reign of Elizabeth II.

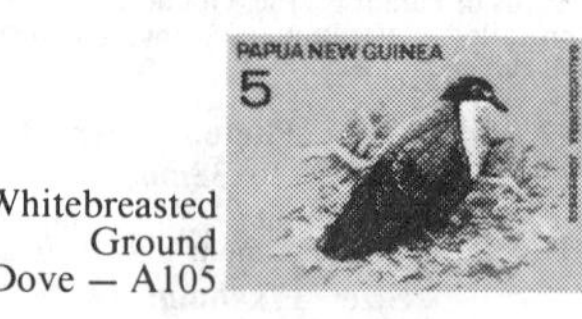


Whitebreasted Ground Dove — A105

Protected Birds: 7t, Victoria crowned pigeon. 15t, Pheasant pigeon. 30t, Orange-fronted fruit dove. 50t, Banded imperial pigeon.

**1977, June 8 Photo. Perf. 11½**
**Granite Paper**

| | | | | |
|---|---|---|---|---|
| *465* A105 | 5t multi | | 15 | 14 |
| *466* A105 | 7t multi | | 25 | 16 |
| *467* A105 | 15t multi | | 50 | 35 |
| *468* A105 | 30t multi | | 1.00 | 65 |
| *469* A105 | 50t multi | | 1.75 | 1.10 |
| | *Nos. 465-469 (5)* | | 3.65 | 2.40 |

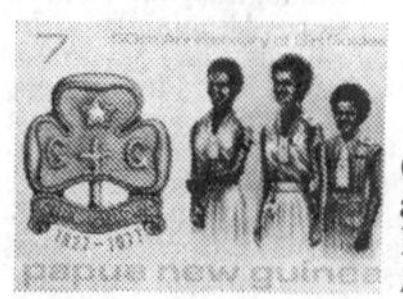


Girl Guides and Gold Badge
A106

Designs (Girl Guides): 15t, Mapping and blue badge. 30t, Doing laundry in brook and red badge. 35t, Wearing grass skirts, cooking and green badge.

**1977, Aug. 10 Litho. Perf. 14½**

| | | | | |
|---|---|---|---|---|
| *470* A106 | 7t multi | | 20 | 16 |
| *471* A106 | 15t multi | | 40 | 35 |
| *472* A106 | 30t multi | | 80 | 65 |
| *473* A106 | 35t multi | | 1.00 | 85 |

50th anniversary of Girl Guides of Papua New Guinea.

Legend of Kari Marupi — A107

Myths of Elema People: 20t, Savoripi Clan. 30t, Oa-Laea. 35t, Oa-Iriarapo.

**1977, Oct. 19 Litho. Perf. 13½**

| | | | | |
|---|---|---|---|---|
| *474* A107 | 7t blk & multi | | 20 | 16 |
| *475* A107 | 20t blk & multi | | 55 | 45 |
| *476* A107 | 30t blk & multi | | 80 | 65 |
| *477* A107 | 35t blk & multi | | 1.00 | 85 |

Blue-tailed Skink
A108

Lizards: 15t, Green tree skink. 35t, Crocodile skink. 40t, New Guinea blue-tongued skink.

**1978, Jan. 25 Photo. Perf. 11½**
**Granite Paper**

| | | | | |
|---|---|---|---|---|
| *478* A108 | 10t bl & multi | | 28 | 25 |
| *479* A108 | 15t lil & multi | | 40 | 38 |
| *480* A108 | 35t ol & multi | | 80 | 75 |
| *481* A108 | 40t org & multi | | 1.00 | 85 |

Roboastra Arika — A109

Sea Slugs: 15t, Chromodoris fidelis. 35t, Flabellina macassarana. 40t, Chromodoris trimarginata.

**1978, Aug. 29 Photo. Perf. 11½**

| | | | | |
|---|---|---|---|---|
| *482* A109 | 10t multi | | 25 | 20 |
| *483* A109 | 15t multi | | 35 | 28 |
| *484* A109 | 35t multi | | 85 | 65 |
| *485* A109 | 40t multi | | 1.00 | 85 |

Mandated New Guinea Constabulary
A110

Constabulary and Badge: 10t, Royal Papua New Guinea. 20t, Armed British New Guinea. 25t, German New Guinea police. 30t, Royal Papua and New Guinea.

**1978, Oct. 26 Photo. Perf. 14½x14**

| | | | | |
|---|---|---|---|---|
| *486* A110 | 10t multi | | 20 | 18 |
| *487* A110 | 15t multi | | 30 | 28 |
| *488* A110 | 20t multi | | 40 | 38 |
| *489* A110 | 25t multi | | 50 | 45 |
| *490* A110 | 30t multi | | 60 | 55 |
| | *Nos. 486-490 (5)* | | 2.00 | 1.84 |

Ocarina, Chimbu Province — A111

Prow and Paddle, East New Britain — A112

Musical Instruments: 20t, Musical bow, New Britain (horiz.). 28t, Launut, New Ireland. 35t, Nose flute, New Hanover (horiz.).

***Perf. 14½x14, 14x14½***

**1979, Jan. 24** **Litho.**

*491* A111 7t multi 14 14
*492* A111 20t multi 40 38
*493* A111 28t multi 55 50
*494* A111 35t multi 75 65

**1979, Mar. 28** **Litho.** ***Perf. 14½***

Canoe Prows and Paddles: 21t, Sepik war canoe. 25t, Trobriand Islands. 40t, Milne Bay.

*495* A112 14t multi 35 30
*496* A112 21t multi 50 45
*497* A112 25t multi 60 55
*498* A112 40t multi 1.00 90

Belt of Shell Disks — A113

Traditional Currency: 15t, Tusk chest ornament. 25t, Shell armband. 35t, Shell necklace.

**1979, June 6** **Litho.** ***Perf. 12½x12***

*499* A113 7t multi 14 14
*500* A113 15t multi 40 40
*501* A113 25t multi 65 60
*502* A113 35t multi 1.00 90

Oenetus A114

Moths: 15t, Celerina vulgaris. 20t, Alcidis aurora (vert.). 25t, Phyllodes conspicillator. 30t, Nyctalemon patroclus (vert.).

**1979, Aug. 29** **Photo.** ***Perf. 11½***

*503* A114 7t multi 16 16
*504* A114 15t multi 35 35
*505* A114 20t multi 40 40
*506* A114 25t multi 50 50
*507* A114 30t multi 65 65
*Nos. 503-507 (5)* 2.06 2.06

Baby in String Bag Scale — A115

IYC Emblem and: 7t, Mother nursing baby. 30t, Boy playing with dog and ball. 60t, Girl in classroom.

**1979, Oct. 24** **Litho.** ***Perf. 14x13½***

*508* A115 7t multi 16 16
*509* A115 15t multi 35 35
*510* A115 30t multi 65 65
*511* A115 60t multi 1.40 1.40

International Year of the Child.

Mail Sorting, Mail Truck A116

UPU Membership: 25t, Wartime mail delivery. 35t, UPU monument, airport and city. 40t, Hand canceling, letter carrier.

**1980, Jan. 23** **Litho.** ***Perf. 13½x14***

*512* A116 7t multi 15 15
*513* A116 25t multi 50 50
*514* A116 35t multi 75 75
*515* A116 40t multi 90 90

Male Dancer, Betrothal Ceremony — A117

Third South Pacific Arts Festival, Port Moresby (Minj Betrothal Ceremony Mural): No. 516 se-tenant in continuous design.

**1980, Mar. 26** **Photo.** ***Perf. 11½***

**Granite Paper**

*516* Strip of 5 2.00 2.00
*a* A117 20t, single stamp 40 40

National Census — A118

**1980, June 4** **Litho.** ***Perf. 14***

*517* A118 7t *shown* 14 14
*518* A118 15t *Population symbol* 30 30
*519* A118 40t *P. N. G. map* 75 75
*520* A118 50t *Faces* 1.00 1.00

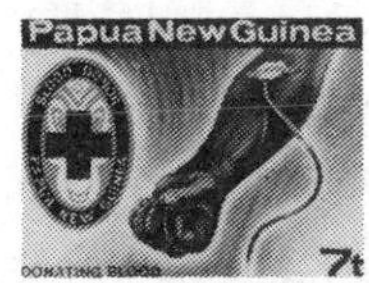


Blood Transfusion, Donor's Badge — A119

**1980, Aug. 27** **Litho.** ***Perf. 14½***

*521* A119 7t *shown* 14 14
*522* A119 15t *Donating blood* 30 30
*523* A119 30t *Map of donation centers* 60 60
*524* A119 60t *Blood components and types* 1.10 1.10

Dugong — A120

**1980, Oct. 29** **Photo.** ***Perf. 11½***

*525* A120 7t *shown* 15 15
*526* A120 30t *Native spotted cat, vert.* 65 65
*527* A120 35t *Tube-nosed bat, vert.* 75 75
*528* A120 45t *Raffray's bandicoot* 1.00 1.00

Beach Kingfisher — A121

**1981, Jan. 21** **Photo.** ***Perf. 12***

**Granite Paper**

*529* A121 3t *shown* 6 6
*530* A121 7t *Forest kingfisher* 15 15
*531* A121 20t *Sacred kingfisher* 45 45

**Size: 26x45½mm**

*532* A121 25t *White-tailed paradise kingfisher* 50 50

**Size: 26x36mm**

*533* A121 60t *Blue-winged kookaburra* 1.40 1.40
*Nos. 529-533 (5)* 2.56 2.56

Mask — A122

Coil Stamps

***Perf. 14½ Horiz.***

**1981, Jan. 21** **Photo.**

*534* A122 2t *shown* 5 5
*535* A122 5t *Hibiscus* 10 10

Defense Force Soldiers Firing Mortar A123

**1981, Mar. 25** **Photo.** ***Perf. 13½x14***

*536* A123 7t shown 14 14
*537* A123 15t DC-3 military plane 32 32
*538* A123 40t Patrol boat Eitape 85 85
*539* A123 50t Medics treating civilians 1.00 1.00

Missionary Aviation Fellowship Plane — A124

Planes of Missionary Organizations: 15t, Holy Ghost Society. 20t, Summer Institute of Linguistics. 30t, Lutheran Mission. 35t, Seventh Day Adventist.

**1981, June 17** **Litho.** ***Perf. 14***

*540* A124 10t multi 25 25
*541* A124 15t multi 35 35
*542* A124 20t multi 45 45
*543* A124 30t multi 70 70
*544* A124 35t multi 80 80
*Nos. 540-544 (5)* 2.55 2.55

Scoop Net Fishing A125

**1981, Aug. 26**

*545* A125 10t shown 20 20
*546* A125 15t Kite fishing 30 30
*547* A125 30t Rod fishing 60 60
*548* A125 60t Scissor net fishing 1.20 1.20

Forcartia Buhleri A126

**1981, Oct. 28** **Photo.** ***Perf. 12***

**Granite Paper**

*549* A126 5t shown 12 12
*550* A126 15t Naninia citrina 35 35
*551* A126 20t Papuina adonis, papuina hermione 45 45
*552* A126 30t Papustyla hindei, papustyla novaepommeraniae 70 70
*553* A126 40t Rhynchotrochus strabo 90 90
*Nos. 549-553 (5)* 2.52 2.52

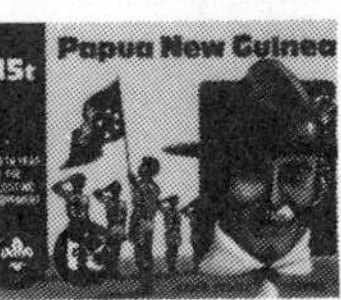


75th Anniv. of Boy Scouts — A127

**1982, Jan. 20** **Photo.** ***Perf. 11½***

**Granite Paper**

*554* A127 15t Lord Baden-Powell, flag raising 30 30
*555* A127 25t Leader, campfire 50 50
*556* A127 35t Scout, hut building 65 65
*557* A127 50t Percy Chatterton, first aid 1.00 1.00

Wanigela Pottery A128

**1982, Mar. 24** **Litho.** ***Perf. 14***

**Size: 29x29mm**

*558* A128 10t Boiken, East Sepik 25 25
*559* A128 20t Gumalu, Madang 48 48

***Perf. 14½***

**Size: 36x23mm**

*560* A128 40t shown 1.00 1.00
*561* A128 50t Ramu Valley, Madang 1.25 1.25

Nutrition A129

**1982, May 5** **Litho.** ***Perf. 14½x14***

*562* A129 10t Mother, child 30 30
*563* A129 15t Protein 45 45
*564* A129 30t Fruits, vegetables 90 90
*565* A129 40t Carbohydrates 1.20 1.20

Coral — A130

**1982, July 21** **Photo.** ***Perf. 11½***

**Granite Paper**

*566* A130 1t Stylophora sp. 5 5
*567* A130 5t Acropora humilis 10 10
*568* A130 15t Distichopora sp. 30 30
*569* A130 1k Xenia sp. 2.00 2.00

See Nos. 575-579, 588-591, 614.

Centenary of Catholic Church in Papua New Guinea — A131

**1982, Sept. 15** **Photo.** ***Perf. 11½***

*570* Strip of 3 1.00 1.00
*a* A131 10t, any single 30 30

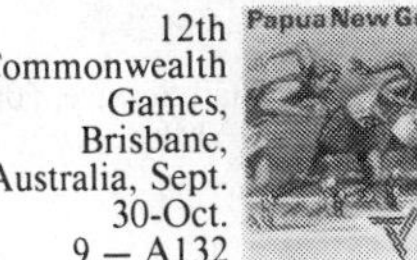

12th Commonwealth Games, Brisbane, Australia, Sept. 30-Oct. 9 — A132

**1982, Oct. 6 Litho. *Perf. 14½***

*571* A132 10t Running 20 20
*572* A132 15t Boxing 30 30
*573* A132 45t Shooting 90 90
*574* A132 50t Lawn bowling 1.00 1.00

Coral Type of 1982

**1983, Jan. 12 Photo. *Perf. 11½***

**Granite Paper**

*575* A130 3t Dendrophyllia 7 7
*576* A130 10t Dendronephthya 20 20
*577* A130 30t Dendronephthya, diff. 60 60
*578* A130 40t Antipathes 80 80
*579* A130 3k Distichopora 6.00 6.00
*Nos. 575-579 (5)* 7.67 7.67

Nos. 575-579 vert.

Commonwealth Day — A133

**1983, Mar. 9 Litho. *Perf. 14***

*580* A133 10t Flag, arms 20 20
*581* A133 15t Youth, recreation 30 30
*582* A133 20t Technical assistance 40 40
*583* A133 50t Export assistance 1.00 1.00

World Communications Year — A134

**1983, Sept. 7 Litho. *Perf. 14***

*584* A134 10t Mail transport 20 20
*585* A134 25t Writing & receiving letter 50 50
*586* A134 30t Telephone calls 60 60
*587* A134 60t Family reunion 1.20 1.20

Coral Type of 1982

**1983, Nov. 9 Photo. *Perf. 11½***

*588* A130 20t Isis sp. 40 40
*589* A130 25t Acropora sp. 65 65
*590* A130 35t Stylaster elegans 1.00 1.00
*591* A130 45t Turbinarea sp. 1.20 1.20

Nos. 588-591 vert.

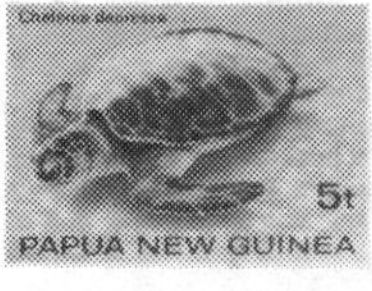


Turtles A135

**1984, Feb. 8 Photo.**

**Granite Paper**

*592* A135 5t Chelonia depressa 15 15
*593* A135 10t Chelonia mydas 30 30
*594* A135 15t Eretkmochelys imbricata 45 45
*595* A135 20t Lepidochelys olivacea 60 60
*596* A135 25t Caretta caretta 75 75
*597* A135 40t Dermochelys coriacea 1.20 1.20
*Nos. 592-597 (6)* 3.45 3.45

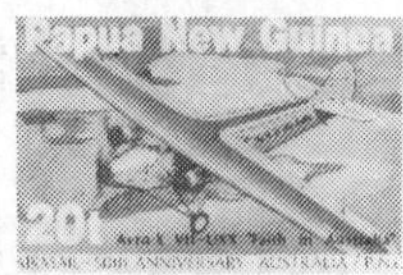


Papua-Australia Airmail Service, 50th Anniv. — A136

Mail planes.

**1984, May 9 Litho. *Perf. 14½x14***

*598* A136 20t Avro X VH-UXX 65 65
*599* A136 25t DH86B VH-UYU Carmania 80 80
*600* A136 40t Westland Widgeon 1.40 1.40
*601* A136 60t Consolidated Catalina NC777 2.00 2.00

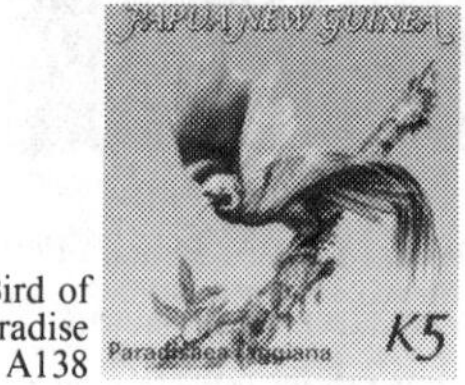

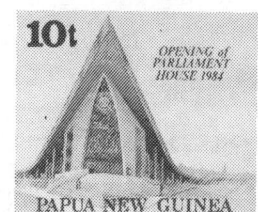


Parliament House Opening — A137

**1984, Aug. 7 Litho. *Perf. 13½x14***

*602* A137 10t multi 40 40

Bird of Paradise A138

**1984, Aug. 7 Photo. *Perf. 11½***

**Granite Paper**

*603* A138 5k multi 10.00 10.00

Ceremonial Shield — A139

**1984, Sept. 21**

*604* A139 10t Central Province 40 40
*605* A139 20t West New Britain 90 90
*606* A139 30t Madang 1.40 1.40
*607* A139 50t East Sepik 2.25 2.25

A140

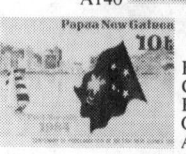

British New Guinea Proclamation Centenary A141

**1984, Nov. 6 Litho. *Perf. 14½x14***

*608* Pair 65 65
*a* A140 10t Nelson, Port Moresby, 1884 32 32
*b* A141 10t Port Moresby, 1984 32 32
*609* Pair 3.00 3.00
*a* A140 45t Rabaul, 1984 1.50 1.50
*b* A141 45t Elizabeth, Rabaul, 1884 1.50 1.50

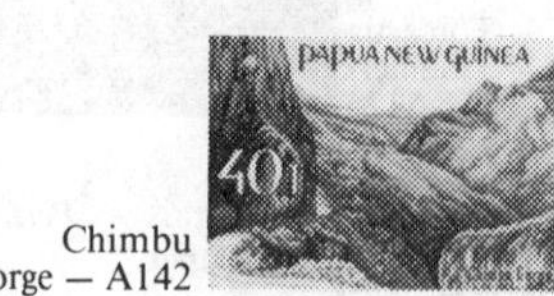


Chimbu Gorge — A142

**1985, Feb. 6 Photo. *Perf. 11½***

*610* A142 10t Fergusson Island, vert. 30 30
*611* A142 25t Sepik River, vert. 80 80
*612* A142 40t shown 1.25 1.25
*613* A142 60t Dali Beach, Vanimo 2.00 2.00

Coral Type of 1982

**1985, May 29 Photo. *Perf. 11½***

*614* A130 12t Dendronephthya sp. 50 50

No. 536 Surcharged.

**1985, Apr. 1 Litho. *Perf. 13½x14***

*615* A123 12t on 7t multi 50 50

Ritual Structures A143

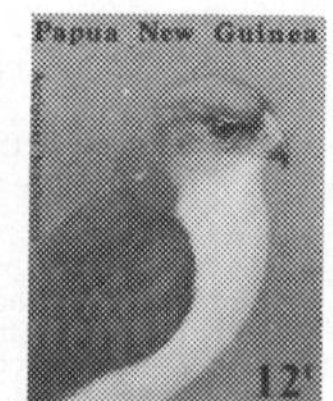


Indigenous Birds of Prey A144

Designs: 15t, Dubu platform, Central Province. 20t, Tamuniai house, West New Britain. 30t, Yam tower, Trobriand Island. 60t, Huli grave, Tari.

**1985, May 1 *Perf. 13x13½***

*616* A143 15t multi 55 55
*617* A143 20t multi 75 75
*618* A143 30t multi 1.10 1.10
*619* A143 60t multi 2.00 2.00

**1985, Aug. 26 *Perf. 14x14½***

*620* A144 12t Accipiter brachyurus 35 35
*621* A144 12t In flight 35 35
*622* A144 30t Megatriorchis doriae 80 80
*623* A144 30t In Flight 80 80
*624* A144 60t Henicopernis longicauda 1.65 1.65
*625* A144 60t In flight 1.65 1.65
*Nos. 620-625 (6)* 5.60 5.60

Stamps of the same denomination printed se-tenant.

Flag and Gable of Parliament House, Port Moresby — A145

**1985, Sept. 11 *Perf. 14½x15***

*626* A145 12t multi 40 40

Post Office Centenary A146

Designs: 12t, No. 631a, 1901 Postal card, aerogramme, spectacles and inkwell. 30t, No. 631b, Queensland Type A15, No. 628. 40t, No. 631c, Plane and news clipping, 1885. 60t, No. 631d, 1892 German canceler, 1985 first day cancel.

**1985, Oct. 9 *Perf. 14½x14***

*627* A146 12t multi 32 32
*628* A146 30t multi 80 80
*629* A146 40t multi 1.10 1.10
*630* A146 60t multi 1.65 1.65

**Souvenir Sheet**

*631* Sheet of 4 4.50 4.50
*a* A146 12t multi 38 38
*b* A146 30t multi 90 90
*c* A146 40t multi 1.25 1.25
*d* A146 60t multi 1.90 1.90

No. 631 has multicolored decorative margin continuing the designs. Size: 90x80mm.

Nombowai Cave Carved Funerary Totems — A147

**1985, Nov. 13 *Perf. 11½***

*632* A147 12t Bird Rulowlaw, headman 30 30
*633* A147 30t Barn owl Raus, headman 75 75
*634* A147 60t Melerawuk 1.50 1.50
*635* A147 80t Cockerel, woman 2.00 2.00

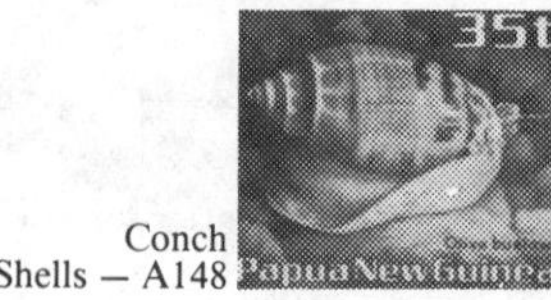


Conch Shells — A148

**1986, Feb. 12 *Perf. 11½***

*636* A148 15t Cypraea valentia 32 32
*637* A148 35t Oliva buelowi 75 75
*638* A148 45t Oliva parkinsoni 95 95
*639* A148 70t Cypraea aurantium 1.50 1.50

**Queen Elizabeth II 60th Birthday**

Common Design Type

Designs: 15t, In ATS officer's uniform, 1945. 35t, Silver wedding anniv. portrait by Patrick Lichfield, Balmoral, 1972. 50t, Inspecting troops, Port Moresby, 1982. 60t, Banquet aboard Britannia, state tour, 1982. 70t, Visiting Crown Agents' offices, 1983.

***Perf. 14½***

**1986, Apr. 21 Litho. Unwmk.**

*640* CD337 15t scar, blk & sil 30 30
*641* CD337 35t ultra & multi 70 70
*642* CD337 50t grn & multi 1.00 1.00
*643* CD337 60t vio & multi 1.20 1.20
*644* CD337 70t rose vio & multi 1.40 1.40
*Nos. 640-644 (5)* 4.60 4.60

AMERIPEX '86 A149

Small birds.

**1986, May 22 Photo. *Perf. 12½***

**Granite Paper**

*645* A149 15t Pitta erythrogaster 30 30
*646* A149 35t Melanocharis striativentris 70 70
*647* A149 45t Rhipidura rufifrons 90 90
*648* A149 70t Poecilodryas placens, vert. 1.40 1.40

Lutheran Church, Cent. — A150

**1986, July 7 Litho. *Perf. 14x15***

*649* A150 15t Monk, minister 30 30
*650* A150 70t Churches from 1886, 1986 1.40 1.40

Indigenous Orchids — A151

**1986, Aug. 4 Litho. *Perf. 14***

*651* A151 15t Dendrobium vexillarius 30 30
*652* A151 35t Dendrobium lineale 70 70
*653* A151 45t Dendrobium johnsoniae 90 90
*654* A151 70t Dendrobium cuthbertsonii 1.40 1.40

Folk Dancers — A152

**1986, Nov. 12 Litho. *Perf. 14***

*655* A152 15t Maprik 30 30
*656* A152 35t Kiriwina 70 70
*657* A152 45t Kundiawa 90 90
*658* A152 70t Fasu 1.40 1.40

Fish A153

**Unwmk.**

**1987, Apr. 15 Litho. *Perf. 15***

*659* A153 17t White-cap anemonefish 35 35
*660* A153 30t Black anemonefish 60 60
*661* A153 35t Tomato clownfish 70 70
*662* A153 70t Spine-cheek anemonefish 1.40 1.40

Ships A154

**1987-88 Litho. Unwmk. *Perf. 11½***
**Granite Paper**

*663* A154 1t La Boudeuse, 1768 5 5
*664* A154 5t Roebuck, 1700 10 10
*665* A154 10t Swallow, 1767 24 24
*666* A154 15t Fly, 1845 32 32
*667* A154 17t like 15t 40 40
*668* A154 20t Rattlesnake, 1849 45 45
*669* A154 30t Vitiaz, 1871 70 70
*670* A154 35t San Pedrico, Zabre, 1606 70 70
*671* A154 40t L'Astrolabe, 1827 90 90
*672* A154 45t Neva, 1876 90 90
*673* A154 60t Caravel of Jorge De Meneses, 1526 1.35 1.35
*674* A154 70t Eendracht, 1616 1.40 1.40
*675* A154 1k Blanche, 1872 2.35 2.35
*676* A154 2k Merrie England, 1889 4.00 4.00
*676A* A154 3k Samoa, 1884 7.00 7.00
*Nos. 663-676A (15)* 20.86 20.86

Issue dates: 5, 35, 45, 70t, 2k, June 15. 15, 20, 40, 60t, Feb. 17, 1988. 17t, 1k, Mar. 16, 1988. 1, 10, 30t, 3k, Nov. 16, 1988.

War Shields — A155

***Perf. 11½x12***

**1987, Aug. 19 Photo. Unwmk.**

*677* A155 15t Elema shield, Gulf Province, c. 1880 32 32
*678* A155 35t East Sepik Province 75 75
*679* A155 45t Simbai region, Madang Province 95 95
*680* A155 70t Telefomin region, West Sepik 1.45 1.45

Starfish A156

**1987, Sept. 30 Litho. *Perf. 14***

*682* A156 17t Protoreaster nodosus 35 35
*683* A156 35t Gomophia egeriae 75 75
*684* A156 45t Choriaster granulatus 95 95
*685* A156 70t Neoferdina ocellata 1.45 1.45

No. 614 Surcharged 15t

**1987, Sept. 23 Photo. *Perf. 11½***
**Granite Paper**

*686* A130 15t on 12t multi 35 35

Aircraft A157

Designs: 15t, Cessna Stationair 6, Rabaraba Airstrip. 35t, Britten-Norman Islander over Hombrum Bluff. 45t, DHC Twin Otter over the Highlands. 70t, Fokker F28 over Madang.

**Unwmk.**

**1987, Nov. 11 Litho. *Perf. 14***

*687* A157 15t multi 35 35
*688* A157 35t multi 85 85
*689* A157 45t multi 1.05 1.05
*690* A157 70t multi 1.65 1.65

Royal Papua New Guinea Police Force, Cent. — A158

Historic and modern aspects of the force: 17t, Motorcycle constable and pre-independence officer wearing a lap-lap. 35t, Sir William McGregor, Armed Native Constabulary founder, 1890, and recruit. 45t, Badges. 70t, Albert Hahl, German official credited with founding the island's police movement in 1888, and badge, early officer.

***Perf. 14x15***

**1988, June 15 Litho. Unwmk.**

*691* A158 17t multi 40 40
*692* A158 35t multi 80 80
*693* A158 45t multi 1.05 1.05
*694* A158 70t multi 1.60 1.60

Sydney Opera House and a Lakatoi (ship) — A159

Fireworks and Globes — A160

**1988, July 30 Litho. *Perf. 13½***

*695* A159 35t multi 80 80
*696* A160 Pair 1.60 1.60
*a.-b.* 35t any single 80 80
*c.* Souv. sheet of 2, Nos. 696a-696b 1.60 1.60

SYDPEX '88, Australia (No. 695); Australia bicentennial (No. 696). Nos. 696a-696b printed se-tenant in a continuous design.

World Wildlife Fund A161

Metamorphosis of a Queen Alexandra's birdwing butterfly.

**1988, Sept. 19 *Perf. 14½***

*697* A161 5t Courtship 12 12
*698* A161 17t Ovipositioning and larvae, vert. 40 40
*699* A161 25t Emergence from pupa, vert. 60 60
*700* A161 35t Adult male on leaf 80 80

1988 Summer Olympics, Seoul — A162

**1988, Sept. 19 Litho. *Perf. 13½***

*701* A162 17t Running 40 40
*702* A162 45t Weight lifting 1.05 1.05

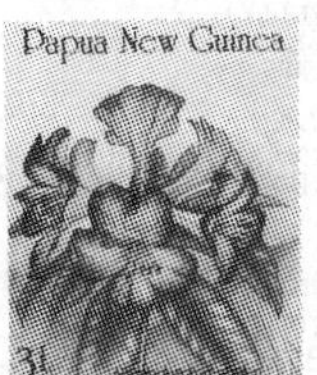


Rhododendrons A163

The indexes in each volume of the Scott Catalogue contain many listings which help to identify stamps.

**Wmk. 387**

**1989, Jan. 25 Litho. *Perf. 14***

*703* A163 3t *R. zoelleri* 8 8
*704* A163 20t *R. cruttwellii* 50 50
*705* A163 60t *R. superbum* 1.50 1.50
*706* A163 70t *R. christianae* 1.75 1.75

## AIR POST STAMPS

Regular Issue of 1916 Overprinted **AIR MAIL**

**1929 Wmk. 74 *Perf. 14***

*C1* A3 3p bl grn & dk gray 1.25 1.40
*b.* Vert. pair, one without ovpt. *2,100.*
*c.* Horiz.l pair, one without ovpt. *3,000.*
*d.* 3p bl grn & sep blk (Harrison printing) 50.00 62.50
*e.* Ovpt. on back, vert. *2,500.*

No. C1 exists on white and on yellowish paper, C1d on yellowish paper only.

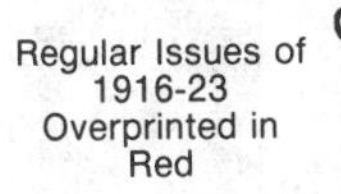

Regular Issues of 1916-23 Overprinted in Red

**1930, Sept. 15 Wmk. 74**

*C2* A3 3p bl grn & blk 1.00 1.20
*a.* Yellowish paper (Harrison printing) 500.00
*b.* Double overprint 1,400.
*C3* A3 6p vio & dl vio 3.50 3.75
*a.* Yellowish paper (Harrison printing) 6.50 7.00
*C4* A3 1sh ol grn & ol brn 4.25 5.00
*a.* Inverted overprint *2,250.*
*b.* Yellowish paper (Harrison printing) 17.50 35.00

Port Moresby AP1

**Unwmk.**

**1938, Sept. 6 Engr. *Perf. 11***

*C5* AP1 2p carmine 1.25 1.40
*C6* AP1 3p ultra 1.50 1.65
*C7* AP1 5p dk grn 2.00 2.25
*C8* AP1 8p red brn 3.00 3.25
*C9* AP1 1sh violet 12.50 7.50
*Nos. C5-C9 (5)* 20.25 16.05

50th anniv. of Papua as a British possession.

Papuans Poling Rafts — AP2

**1939-41**

*C10* AP2 2p carmine 2.00 1.10
*C11* AP2 3p ultra 1.25 1.40
*C12* AP2 5p dk grn 3.00 3.25
*C13* AP2 8p red brn 2.75 3.00
*C14* AP2 1sh violet 3.25 3.50
*C15* AP2 1sh6p lt ol ('41) 27.50 32.50
*Nos. C10-C15 (6)* 39.75 44.75

## POSTAGE DUE STAMPS

**Catalogue values for unused stamps in this section, from this point to the end of the section, are for Never Hinged items.**

Nos. 128, 122, 129, 139 and 125 Surcharged in Black, Blue, Red or Orange

**POSTAL CHARGES 6d.**

**1960 Unwmk. Engr. *Perf. 14***

*J1* A24 1p on 6½p vio brn 8.00 6.00
*J2* A23 3p on ½p bl grn (Bl) 12.00 8.00
*a.* Double surcharge 525.00
*J3* A24 6p on 7½p dp ultra (R) 20.00 12.00
*a.* Double surcharge 525.00
*J4* A23 1sh3p on 3½p blk (O) 27.50 20.00
*J5* A23 3sh on 2½p org 35.00 32.50
*Nos. J1-J5 (5)* 102.50 78.50

No. 129 Surcharged with New Value in Red

POSTAL CHARGES

6d.

IXIXIXIXIX

*J6* A24 6p on 7½p dp ultra 500.00 300.00
*a.* Double surcharge 2,000. 1,600.

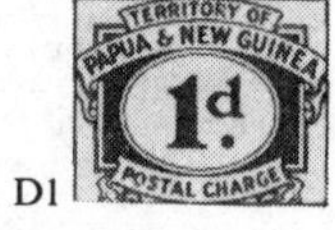


D1

***Perf. 13½x14***

**1960, June 2 Litho. Wmk. 228**

*J7* D1 1p orange 20 10
*J8* D1 3p ocher 50 28
*J9* D1 6p lt ultra 85 40
*J10* D1 9p vermilion 1.40 65
*J11* D1 1sh emerald 2.00 1.00
*J12* D1 1sh3p brt vio 3.50 1.75
*J13* D1 1sh6p light blue 4.00 3.75
*J14* D1 3sh yellow 5.00 3.50
*Nos. J7-J14 (8)* 17.45 11.43

## OFFICIAL STAMPS

Regular Issues of 1916-25 Overprinted

O S

**1931 Wmk. 74 *Perf. 14½***

*O1* A3 ½p pale yel grn & myr grn 65 2.25
*O2* A3 1p rose red & blk 65 2.75
*O3* A3 1½p yel brn & gray bl 2.25 6.50
*O4* A3 2p red vio & vio brn 2.75 8.25
*O5* A3 3p emer & gray blk 3.00 10.00
*O6* A3 4p org & lt brn 3.00 10.00
*O7* A3 5p ol brn & sl 4.50 14.00
*O8* A3 6p vio & dl vio 5.00 10.00
*O9* A3 1sh ol grn & dk brn 6.50 14.00
*O10* A3 2sh6p rose & red brn 27.50 52.50
*Nos. O1-O10 (10)* 55.80 130.25

Same Overprint on Stamps of 1931

**1932 Wmk. 228 *Perf. 11½***

*O11* A3 9p dp vio & gray 20.00 50.00
*O12* A3 1sh3p pale bl & gray blk 27.50 52.50

# PENRHYN ISLAND

## (Tongareva)

AREA — 3 sq. mi.
POP. — 395 (1926)

*Penrhyn Island stamps can be mounted in Scott's annual New Zealand Dependencies Supplement.*

Stamps of Cook Islands were used in Penrhyn from 1932 until 1973.

12 Pence = 1 Shilling

**Catalogue values for unused stamps in this country are for Never Hinged items, beginning with Scott 35 in the regular postage section, Scott B1 in the semi-postal section and Scott O1 in the officials section.**

Stamps of New Zealand Surcharged in Carmine, Vermilion, Brown or Blue:

PENRHYN ISLAND.
½ PENI.
a

PENRHYN ISLAND.
TAI PENI.
b

**1902 Wmk. 63 *Perf. 14***

*1* A18 ½p grn (C) (a) 90 1.75
*a* No period after "ISLAND" 90.00 100.00
*2* A35 1p car (Br) (b) 1.00 2.00
*a* Perf. 11 *1,500. 1,750.*
*b* Perf. 11x14 *2,000. 2,250.*

**Wmk. 61 *Perf. 14***

*5* A18 (a) ½p grn (V) 1.00 2.50
*a* No period after "ISLAND" 60.00 65.00
*6* A35 (b) 1p car (Bl) 1.00 2.00
*a* No period after "ISLAND" 32.50 40.00
*b* Perf. 11x14 *8,000. 8,500.*

PENRHYN ISLAND.
2½ PENI.

**1902 Unwmk. *Perf. 11***

*8* A22 2½p blue (C) 2.25 3.50
*a* "½" and "PENI" 2mm apart 11.50 *15.00*
*9* A22 2½p blue (V) 1.50 *2.25*
*a* "½" and "PENI" 2mm apart 9.25 *15.00*

PENRHYN ISLAND.
Toru Pene.
d

PENRHYN ISLAND.
Ono Pene.
e

PENRHYN ISLAND.
Tahi Silingi.
f

**1903 Wmk. 61**

*10* A23 (d) 3p yel brn (Bl) 8.50 10.00
*11* A26 (e) 6p rose (Bl) 12.00 *22.50*
*12* A29 (f) 1sh org red (Bl) 30.00 *57.50*
*a* 1sh bright red (Bl) 30.00 *57.50*
*b* 1sh brown red (Bl) 30.00 *57.50*

**1914-15 *Perf. 14, 14x14½***

*13* A41 (a) ½p yel grn (C) 1.50 3.00
*a* No period after "ISLAND" 27.50 *40.00*
*b* No period after "PENI" 75.00 *90.00*
*14* A41 (a) ½p yel grn (V) ('15) 1.00 1.75
*a* No period after "ISLAND" 16.00 17.50
*b* No period after "PENI" 37.50 *50.00*
*15* A41 (e) 6p car rose (Bl) 22.50 25.00
*16* A41 (f) 1sh ver (Bl) 35.00 *50.00*

New Zealand Stamps of 1915-19 Overprinted in Red or Dark Blue

PENRHYN ISLAND.

***Perf. 14x13½, 14x14½***

**1917-20 Typo.**

*17* A43 ½p yel grn (R) ('20) 55 1.25
*18* A47 1½p gray blk (R) 2.50 3.00
*19* A47 1½p brn org (R) ('19) 1.25 *3.00*
*20* A43 3p choc (Bl) ('19) 2.00 3.50

**Engr.**

*21* A44 2½p dl bl (R) ('20) 1.50 2.00
*22* A45 3p vio brn (Bl) ('18) 6.00 *12.50*
*23* A45 6p car rose (Bl) ('18) 4.50 *9.00*
*24* A45 1sh ver (Bl) 9.00 *17.50*
*Nos. 17-24 (8)* 27.30 *51.75*

Landing of Capt. Cook
A10

Avarua Waterfront
A11

Capt. James Cook — A12

Coconut Palm — A13

Arorangi Village, Rarotonga
A14

Avarua Harbor
A15

**1920 Unwmk. *Perf. 14***

*25* A10 ½p emer & blk 75 *2.00*
*a* Center inverted 625.00
*26* A11 1p red & blk 1.00 1.75
*a* Center inverted 850.00
*27* A12 1½p vio & blk 1.75 *3.50*
*28* A13 3p red org & blk 3.00 4.00
*29* A14 6p dk brn & red brn 3.50 4.50
*30* A15 1sh dl bl & blk 6.50 *12.50*
*Nos. 25-30 (6)* 16.50 *28.25*

Rarotongan Chief (Te Po) — A16

**1927 Engr. Wmk. 61**

*31* A16 2½p bl & red brn 1.50 3.00

Types of 1920 Issue

**1928-29**

*33* A10 ½p yel grn & blk 75 2.00
*34* A11 1p car rose & blk 1.25 2.60

# PENRHYN

## Northern Cook Islands

POP. — 2,030 (1976).

The Northern Cook Islands include six besides Penrhyn that are inhabited: Nassau, Palmerston (Avarua), Manihiki (Humphrey), Rakahanga (Reirson), Pukapuka (Danger) and Suwarrow (Anchorage).

100 Cents = 1 Dollar

**Catalogue values for unused stamps in this section, from this point to the end of the section, are for Never Hinged items.**

Cook Islands Nos. 200-201, 203, 205-208, 211-212, 215-217 Overprinted

PENRHYN
NORTHERN

**1973 Photo. Unwmk. *Perf. 14x13½***

*35* A34 1c gold & multi 5 5
*36* A34 2c gold & multi 8 8
*37* A34 3c gold & multi 12 12
*38* A34 4c gold & multi 18 18
*a.* Ovptd. on #204
*39* A34 5c gold & multi 22 22
*40* A34 6c gold & multi 28 28
*41* A34 8c gold & multi 40 40
*42* A34 15c gold & multi 70 70
*43* A34 20c gold & multi 90 90
*44* A34 50c gold & multi 2.75 2.75
*45* A35 $1 gold & multi 3.00 3.00
*46* A35 $2 gold & multi 6.75 6.75
*Nos. 35-46 (12)* 15.43 15.43

Nos. 45-46 are overprinted "Penrhyn" only. The overprint exists with broken "E" or "O".

Issue dates: Nos. 35-45, Oct. 24; No. 46, Nov. 14.

Cook Islands Nos. 369-371 Overprinted in Silver: "PENRHYN / NORTHERN"

**1973, Nov. 14 Photo. *Perf. 14***

*47* A60 25c *Princess Anne* 1.75 1.75
*48* A60 30c *Mark Phillips* 2.25 2.25
*49* A60 50c *Princess and Mark Phillips* 3.00 3.00

Wedding of Princess Anne and Capt. Mark Phillips.

Fluorescence

Starting with No. 50, stamps carry a "fluorescent security underprinting" in a multiple pattern combining a sailing ship, "Penrhyn Northern Cook Islands" and stars.

Ostracion
A17

Aerial View of Penrhyn Atoll — A18

Designs: ½c-$1, Various fish of Penrhyn. $5, Map showing Penrhyn's location.

**1974-75 Photo. *Perf. 13½x14***

*50* A17 ½c multi 5 5
*51* A17 1c multi 5 5
*52* A17 2c multi 5 5
*53* A17 3c multi 6 6
*54* A17 4c multi 9 9
*55* A17 5c multi 10 10
*56* A17 8c multi 15 15
*57* A17 10c multi 20 20
*58* A17 20c multi 45 45
*59* A17 25c multi 48 48
*60* A17 60c multi 1.20 1.20
*61* A17 $1 multi 2.00 2.00
*62* A18 $2 multi 4.00 4.00
*63* A18 $5 multi 9.50 9.50
*Nos. 50-63 (14)* 18.38 18.38

Issue dates: $2, Feb. 12, 1975; $5, Mar. 12, 1975; others Aug. 15, 1974.

Map of Penrhyn and Nos. 1-2 — A19

UPU, cent.: 50c, UPU emblem, map of Penrhyn and Nos. 27-28.

**1974, Sept. 27** *Perf. 13*
*64* A19 25c vio & multi 65 65
*65* A19 50c sl grn & multi 1.40 1.40

Adoration of the Kings, by Memling — A20

Christmas: 10c, Adoration of the Shepherds, by Hugo van der Goes. 25c, Adoration of the Kings, by Rubens. 30c, Holy Family, by Orazio Borgianni.

**1974, Oct. 30**
*66* A20 5c multi 15 15
*67* A20 10c multi 28 28
*68* A20 25c multi 65 65
*69* A20 30c multi 75 75

Churchill Giving "V" Sign — A21

Design: 50c, Churchill portrait.

**1974, Nov. 30** **Photo.**
*70* A21 30c multi 1.00 1.00
*71* A21 50c multi 1.50 1.50

Winston Churchill (1874-1965).

No. 63 Overprinted 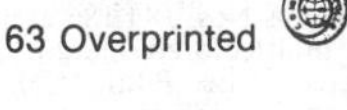


**1975, July 24** *Perf. 13½x13*
*72* A18 $5 multi 10.00 10.00

Safe splashdown of Apollo space capsule.

Madonna, by Dirk Bouts A22

Pieta, by Michelangelo A23

Madonna Paintings: 15c, by Leonardo da Vinci. 35c, by Raphael.

**1975, Nov. 21** **Photo.** *Perf. 14½x13*
*73* A22 7c gold & multi 18 18
*74* A22 15c gold & multi 42 42
*75* A22 35c gold & multi 90 90

Christmas 1975.

**1976, Mar. 19** **Photo.** *Perf. 14x13*
*76* A23 15c gold & dk brn 40 40
*77* A23 20c gold & dp pur 50 50
*78* A23 35c gold & dk grn 75 75
*a.* Souvenir sheet of 3 2.00 2.00

Easter 1976 and for the 500th birth anniversary of Michelangelo Buonarroti (1475-1564), Italian sculptor, painter and architect. No. 78a contains one each of Nos. 76-78; lilac and gold decorative margin. Size: 112x72mm.

The Spirit of '76, by Archibald M. Willard — A24

Design: No. 79, Washington Crossing the Delaware, by Emmanuel Leutze.

**1976, May 20** **Photo.** *Perf. 13½*
*79* A24 Strip of 3 2.00 2.00
*a.* 30c *Boatsman* 60 60
*b.* 30c *Washington* 60 60
*c.* 30c *Men in boat* 60 60
*80* A24 Strip of 3 3.50 3.50
*a.* 50c *Drummer boy* 1.00 1.00
*b.* 50c *Old drummer* 1.00 1.00
*c.* 50c *Fifer* 1.00 1.00
*d.* Souvenir sheet 5.25 5.25

American Bicentennial. Nos. 79-80 printed in sheets of 15, 5 strips of 3 and 3-part corner labels showing Queen Elizabeth II, Independence Hall and Liberty Bell. No. 80d contains Nos. 79-80, multicolored margin with Queen Elizabeth II, Bicentennial emblem, dates and inscription. Size: 102x102mm.

Running A25

Designs (Montreal Olympic Games Emblem and): 30c, Long jump. 75c, Javelin.

**1976, July 9** **Photo.** *Perf. 13½*
*81* A25 25c multi 45 45
*82* A25 30c multi 50 50
*83* A25 75c multi 1.50 1.50
*a.* Souvenir sheet of 3 3.25 3.25

21st Olympic Games, Montreal, Canada, July 17-Aug. 1. Nos. 81-83 printed in sheets of 6 (2x3). No. 83a contains one each of Nos. 81-83, perf. 14½x13½; light blue and gold margin. Size: 86x128mm.

Flight into Egypt, by Dürer A26

Etchings by Albrecht Durer: 15c, Adoration of the Shepherds. 35c, Adoration of the Kings.

**1976, Oct. 20** **Photo.** *Perf. 13x13½*
*84* A26 7c sil & dk brn 18 18
*85* A26 15c sil & sl grn 35 35
*86* A26 35c sil & pur 75 75

Christmas 1976. Nos. 84-86 printed in sheets of 8 (2x4) with decorative border.

Elizabeth II and Westminster Abbey — A27

Designs: $1, Elizabeth II and Prince Philip. $2, Elizabeth II.

**1977, Mar. 24** **Photo.** *Perf. 13½x13*
*87* A27 50c sil & multi 1.10 1.00
*88* A27 $1 sil & multi 2.75 2.50
*89* A27 $2 sil & multi 5.50 4.75
*a.* Souvenir sheet of 3 10.50 10.50

25th anniversary of reign of Queen Elizabeth II. Nos. 87-89 issued in sheets of 4. No. 89a contains one each of Nos. 87-89; beige and silver decorative margin. Size: 127x86mm.

Annunciation A28

Designs: 15c, Announcement to Shepherds. 35c, Nativity. Designs from "The Bible in Images," by Julius Schnorr von Carolsfeld (1794-1872).

**1977, Sept. 23** **Photo.** *Perf. 13½*
*90* A28 7c multi 15 15
*91* A28 15c multi 30 30
*92* A28 35c multi 75 75

Christmas 1977. Issued in sheets of 6.

Red Sickle-bill (I'wii) — A29

Chief's Feather Cloak — A30

Designs: No. 95, Crimson creeper (apapane). No. 96, Feathered head of Hawaiian god. No. 97, Hawaiian gallinule (alae). No. 98, Chief's regalia: feather cape, staff (kahili) and helmet. No. 99, Yellow-tufted bee-eater (o'o). No. 100, Scarlet feathered image (head). Birds are extinct; their feathers were used for artifacts shown.

**1978, Jan. 19** **Photo.** *Perf. 12½x13*
*93* A29 20c sil & multi 38 38
*94* A30 20c sil & multi 38 38
*95* A29 30c sil & multi 60 60
*96* A30 30c sil & multi 60 60
*97* A29 35c sil & multi 65 65
*98* A30 35c sil & multi 65 65
*99* A29 75c sil & multi 1.40 1.40
*a.* Souvenir sheet of 4 3.75 3.75
*100* A30 75c sil & multi 1.40 1.40
*a.* Souvenir sheet of 4 3.75 3.75
*Nos. 93-100 (8)* 6.06 6.06

Bicentenary of Capt. Cook's arrival in Hawaii. Stamps of same denomination printed se-tenant in sheets of 8 (4x2). No. 99a contains one each of Nos. 93, 95, 97, 99; No. 100a, Nos. 94, 96, 98, 100. No. 99a has silver and dark purple margin; No. 100a, silver and dark blue green margin. Size: 89x119mm.

Values quoted in this catalogue are for stamps graded at Fine-Very Fine and with no faults. An illustrated guide to grade is provided in introductory material, beginning on Page V.

St. Veronica by Rubens — A31

Rubens' Paintings: 15c, Crucifixion. 35c, Descent from the Cross.

**1978, Mar. 10** **Photo.** *Perf. 13½x13*
**Size: 25x36mm.**
*101* A31 10c multi 25 25
*102* A31 15c multi 40 40
*103* A31 35c multi 90 90
*a.* Souvenir sheet of 3 1.25 1.25

Easter 1978 and 400th birth anniversary of Peter Paul Rubens (1577-1640). Nos. 101-103 issued in sheets of 6. No. 103a contains one each of Nos. 101-103 (27x36mm). Multicolored margin shows Rubens' self-portrait. Size: 87x138mm.

Miniature Sheet

Queen Elizabeth II — A32

**1978, May 24** **Photo.** *Perf. 13*
*104* Sheet of 6 10.00 10.00
*a.* A32 90c *Arms of United Kingdom* 1.50 1.25
*b.* A32 90c *shown* 1.50 1.25
*c.* A32 90c *Arms of New Zealand* 1.50 1.25
*d.* Souvenir sheet of 3 5.25 4.00

25th anniv. of coronation of Elizabeth II.
No. 104 contains 2 horizontal se-tenant strips of Nos. 104a-104c, separated by horizontal gutter showing coronation. Size: 95x114mm.
No. 104d contains a vertical se-tenant strip of Nos. 104a-104c; multicolored margin shows Westminster Abbey. Size 75x122mm.

Virgin and Child, by Dürer — A33

Design: 35c, Virgin and Child with St. Anne, by Dürer.

**1978, Nov. 29** **Photo.** *Perf. 14x13½*
*105* A33 30c multi 50 50
*106* A33 35c multi 60 60
*a.* Souvenir sheet of 2 1.25 1.25

Christmas 1978 and 450th death anniversary of Albrecht Dürer (1471-1528), German painter. Nos. 105-106 issued in sheets of 6. No. 106a contains Nos. 105-106; lilac, black and gold margin showing Dürer's self-portrait as a boy. Size: 101x60mm.

Rowland Hill, Penny Black — A34

Designs: No. 107, Penrhyn Nos. 64-65. No. 109, Penrhyn No. 104b. No. 110, Hill portrait.

**1979, Sept. 26 Photo. *Perf. 14***

*107* A34 75c multi 1.00 1.00
*108* A34 75c multi 1.00 1.00
*109* A34 90c multi 1.25 1.25
*110* A34 90c multi 1.25 1.25
**a.** Souvenir sheet of 4 5.00 5.00

Sir Rowland Hill (1795-1879), originator of penny postage. Nos. 107-108 and 109-110 issued se-tenant in sheets of 8. No. 110a contains Nos. 107-110; multicolored margin. Size: 116x58mm.

Max and Moritz, IYC Emblem — A35

Designs: Scenes from Max and Moritz, by Wilhelm Busch (1832-1908).

**1979, Nov. 20 Photo. *Perf. 13x12½***

*111* Sheet of 4 75
**a.** A35 12c *shown* 18
**b.** A35 12c *Looking down chimney* 18
**c.** A35 12c *With stolen chickens* 18
**d.** A35 12c *Woman and dog, empty pan* 18
*112* Sheet of 4 90
**a.** A35 15c *Sawing bridge* 20
**b.** A35 15c *Man falling into water* 20
**c.** A35 15c *Broken bridge* 20
**d.** A35 15c *Running away* 20
*113* Sheet of 4 1.25
**a.** A35 20c *Baker* 30
**b.** A35 20c *Sneaking into bakery* 30
**c.** A35 20c *Falling into dough* 30
**d.** A35 20c *Baked into breads* 30

International Year of the Child. Gold and black margins show text in English and German. Size: 72x97mm.

Jesus Carrying the Cross — A36

Easter 1980 (15th Century Prayerbook Illustrations): 20c, Crucifixion, by William Vreland. 35c, Descent from the Cross.

**1980, Mar. 28 Photo. *Perf. 13x13½***

*114* A36 12c multi 20 20
*115* A36 20c multi 35 35
*116* A36 35c multi 60 60
**a.** Souvenir sheet of 3 1.10 1.10

No. 116a contains Nos. 114-116; multicolored decorative margin. Size: 111x65½mm.

Queen Mother Elizabeth, 80th Birthday — A37

**1980, Sept. 17 Photo. *Perf. 13***

*117* A37 $1 multi 2.25 2.25

**Souvenir Sheet**

*118* A37 $2.50 multi 5.50 5.50

No. 118 shows full coronation portrait of Queen Elizabeth. Size: 55x85mm.

Falk Hoffman, DDR, Platform Diving — A38

Designs: Nos. 119-120, Platform diving. Nos. 121-122, Archery. Nos. 123-124, Soccer. Nos. 125-126, Running. Stamps of same denomination se-tenant in continuous design.

**1980, Nov. 14 Photo. *Perf. 13½***

*119* A38 10c *shown* 15 15
*120* A38 10c *Martina Jaschke* 15 15
*121* A38 20c *Tomi Polkolainen* 30 30
*122* A38 20c *Kete Losaberidse* 30 30
*123* A38 30c *Czechoslovakia, gold* 40 40
*124* A38 30c *DDR, silver* 40 40
*125* A38 50c *Barbel Wockel* 75 75
*126* A38 50c *Pietro Mennea* 75 75
**a.** Souvenir sheet of 8 3.75 3.75
*Nos. 119-126 (8)* 3.20 3.20

22nd Summer Olympic Games, Moscow, July 19-Aug. 3. No. 126a contains Nos. 119-126 with gold border; blue and black margin shows Moscow '80 emblem. Size: 150x106mm.

Virgin and Child, by Luis Dalmau — A39

Christmas 1980 (15th Century Virgin and Child Paintings by): 35c, Serra brothers. 50c, Master of the Porciuncula.

**1980, Dec. 5 Photo. *Perf. 13***

*127* A39 20c multi 35 35
*128* A39 35c multi 50 50
*129* A39 50c multi 65 65
**a.** Souvenir sheet of 3 2.00 2.00

No. 129a contains Nos. 127-129; multicolored margin shows angels. Size: 135x75mm.

Amatasi — A40

A41

Cutty Sark, 1869 A42

**1981, Feb. 16 Photo. *Perf. 14***

*130* A40 1c shown 5 5
*131* A40 1c Ndrua 5 5
*132* A40 1c Waka 5 5
*133* A40 1c Tongiaki 5 5
*134* A40 3c Va'a teu'ua 7 7
*135* A40 3c Victoria, 1500 7 7
*136* A40 3c Golden Hinde, 1560 7 7
*137* A40 3c Boudeuse, 1760 7 7
*138* A40 4c Bounty, 1787 8 8
*139* A40 4c Astrolabe, 1811 8 8
*140* A40 4c Star of India, 1861 8 8
*141* A40 4c Great Rep., 1853 8 8
*142* A40 6c Balcutha, 1886 12 12
*143* A40 6c Coonatto, 1863 12 12
*144* A40 6c Antiope, 1866 12 12
*145* A40 6c Teaping, 1863 12 12
*146* A40 10c Preussen, 1902 20 20
*147* A40 10c Pamir, 1921 20 20
*148* A40 10c Cap Hornier, 1910 20 20
*149* A40 10c Patriarch, 1869 20 20

***Perf. 13½x14½***

**1981, Mar. 16 Photo.**

*150* A41 15c shown 28 28
*151* A41 15c Ndrua 28 28
*152* A41 15c Waka 28 28
*153* A41 15c Tongiaki 28 28
*154* A41 20c Va'a Teu'ua 40 40
*155* A41 20c Victoria, 1500 40 40
*156* A41 20c Golden Hind, 1560 40 40
*157* A41 20c Boudeuse, 1760 40 40
*158* A41 30c Bounty, 1787 60 60
*159* A41 30c Astrolabe, 1811 60 60
*160* A41 30c Star of India, 1861 60 60
*161* A41 30c Great Rep., 1853 60 60
*162* A41 50c Balcutha, 1886 1.00 1.00
*163* A41 50c Coonatto, 1863 1.00 1.00
*164* A41 50c Antiope, 1866 1.00 1.00
*165* A41 50c Teaping, 1863 1.00 1.00

**1981 Photo. *Perf. 13½x14½***

*166* A41 $1 Preussen, 1902 2.00 2.00
*167* A41 $1 Pamir, 1921 2.00 2.00
*168* A41 $1 Cap Hornier, 1910 2.00 2.00
*169* A41 $1 Patriarch, 1869 2.00 2.00
*170* A42 $2 shown 4.00 4.00
*171* A42 $4 Mermerus, 1872 8.00 8.00

**1981, Sept. 21 Photo. *Perf. 13½***

*172* A42 $6 Resolution, Discovery, 1776 12.00 12.00
*Nos. 130-172 (43)* 43.20 43.20

Stamps of same denomination se-tenant. Issue dates: $1, May 15; $2, $4, June 26.

Christ with Crown of Thorns, by Titan — A44

Easter 1981: 30c, Jesus at the Grove, by Paolo Veronese. 50c, Pieta, by Van Dyck.

**1981, Apr. 5 *Perf. 14***

*173* A44 30c multi 50 50
*174* A44 40c multi 65 65
*175* A44 50c multi 80 80
**a.** Souvenir sheet of 3 2.25 2.25

No. 175a contains Nos. 173-175 (perf. 13½); dark blue and gold decorative margin. Size: 109x68mm.

Prince Charles — A45

Designs: Portraits of Prince Charles.

**1981, July 10 Photo. *Perf. 14***

*176* A45 40c multi 65 65
*177* A45 50c multi 80 80
*178* A45 60c multi 1.00 1.00
*179* A45 70c multi 1.25 1.25
*180* A45 80c multi 1.40 1.40
**a.** Souvenir sheet of 5 5.00 5.00
*Nos. 176-180 (5)* 5.10 5.10

Royal wedding. Nos. 176-180 each issued in sheets of 5 plus label showing couple. No. 180a contains Nos. 176-180 plus label; pink and gold decorative margin. Size: 100x89mm.

1982 World Cup Soccer — A46

**1981, Dec. 7 Photo. *Perf. 13***

*181* Strip of 3 60 60
**a.** A46 15c, any single 20 20
*182* Strip of 3 1.50 1.50
**a.** A46 35c, any single 50 50
*183* Strip of 3 2.00 2.00
**a.** A46 50c, any single 65 65

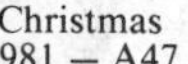

Christmas 1981 — A47

21st Birthday of Princess Diana — A48

Dürer Engravings: 30c, Virgin on a Crescent, 1508. 40c, Virgin at the Fence, 1503. 50c, Holy Virgin and Child, 1505.

**1981, Dec. 15 Photo. *Perf. 13x13½***

*184* A47 30c multi 50 50
*185* A47 40c multi 65 65
*186* A47 50c multi 80 80
**a.** Souvenir sheet of 3 2.00 2.00

**Souvenir Sheets**

*187* A47 70c + 5c like #184 1.50 1.50
*188* A47 70c + 5c like #185 1.50 1.50
*189* A47 70c + 5c like #186 1.50 1.50

No. 186a contains Nos. 184-186 each with 2c surcharge; multicolored margin shows scene from Dürer's Three Putti, 1500. Size: 135x76mm., Nos. 187-189 each contain one stamp (25x40mm., perf. 14x13½); multicolored margins show entire engraving. Size: 58x85mm. Surtaxes were for childrens' charities.

**1982, July 1 Photo. *Perf. 14***

Designs: Portraits of Diana.

*190* A48 30c multi 50 50
*191* A48 50c multi 90 90
*192* A48 70c multi 1.25 1.25
*193* A48 80c multi 1.50 1.50
*194* A48 $1.40 multi 2.50 2.50
**a.** Souvenir sheet of 5 6.50 6.50
*Nos. 190-194 (5)* 6.65 6.65

No. 194a contains Nos. 190-194 plus label; gold and light green margin. Size: 89x110mm.

Nos. 176-180a Overprinted: "BIRTH OF PRINCE WILLIAM OF WALES 21 JUNE 1982"

**1982, July 30**

*195* A45 40c multi 80 80
*196* A45 50c multi 1.00 1.00
*197* A45 60c multi 1.25 1.25
*198* A45 70c multi 1.40 1.40
*199* A45 80c multi 1.60 1.60
**a.** Souvenir sheet of 5 6.00 6.00
*Nos. 195-199 (5)* 6.05 6.05

Nos. 190-194a Overprinted in Silver: 21 JUNE 1982 BIRTH OF/PRINCE WILLIAM OF WALES or COMMEMORATING THE BIRTH OF/PRINCE WILLIAM OF WALES

**1982 Photo. *Perf. 14***

*200* A48 30c multi 50 50
*201* A48 50c multi 80 80
*202* A48 70c multi 1.25 1.25
*203* A48 80c multi 1.40 1.40
*204* A48 $1.40 multi 2.50 2.50
**a.** Souvenir sheet of 5 6.00 6.00
*Nos. 200-204 (5)* 6.45 6.45

Christmas 1982 — A49

Virgin and Child Paintings.

**1982, Dec. 10 Photo. *Perf. 14***

*205* A49 35c Joos Van Cleve (1485-1540) 60 60
*206* A49 48c Filippino Lippi (1457-1504) 80 80
*207* A49 60c Cima Da Conegliano (1459-1517) 1.00 1.00
*a.* Souvenir sheet of 3 2.75 2.75

**Souvenir Sheets**

*208* A49 70c + 5c like 35c 1.50 1.50
*209* A49 70c + 5c like 48c 1.50 1.50
*210* A49 70c + 5c like 60c 1.50 1.50

No. 207a contains Nos. 205-207 each with 2c surcharge. Size: 135x73mm. Nos. 208-210 each contain one stamp (perf. 13½); multicolored margins show entire painting. Size: 60x85mm. Surtaxes were for childrens' charities.

Commonwealth Day — A50

**1983, Mar. 14 *Perf. 13½x13***

*211* A50 60c Red coral 1.00 1.00
*212* A50 60c Aerial view 1.00 1.00
*213* A50 60c Eleanor Roosevelt, grass skirt 1.00 1.00
*214* A50 60c Map 1.00 1.00

Nos. 211-214 se-tenant.

Scouting Year A51

Emblem and various tropical flowers.

**1983, Apr. 5 *Perf. 13½x14½***

*215* A51 36c multi 60 60
*216* A51 48c multi 80 80
*217* A51 60c multi 1.00 1.00

**Souvenir Sheet**

*218* A51 $2 multi, 86x46mm. 3.25 3.25

Nos. 215-218 Overprinted: "XV / WORLD JAMBOREE / CANADA / 1983"

**1983, July 8 Photo. *Perf. 13½x14½***

*219* A51 36c multi 60 60
*220* A51 48c multi 1.00 1.00
*221* A51 60c multi 1.00 1.00

**Souvenir Sheet**

*222* A51 $2 multi 3.25 3.25

15th World Boy Scout Jamboree.

Save the Whales Campaign A52

Various whale hunting scenes.

**1983, July 29 Photo. *Perf. 13***

*223* A52 8c multi 15 15
*224* A52 15c multi 25 25
*225* A52 35c multi 60 60
*226* A52 60c multi 1.00 1.00
*227* A52 $1 multi 1.75 1.75
*Nos. 223-227 (5)* 3.75 3.75

World Communications Year — A53

Designs: Cable laying Vessels.

**1983, Sept. Photo. *Perf. 13***

*228* A53 36c multi 60 60
*229* A53 48c multi 80 80
*230* A53 60c multi 1.00 1.00

**Souvenir Sheet**

*231* Sheet of 3 2.50 2.50
*a.* A53 36c + 3c like No. 228 65 65
*b.* A53 48c + 3c like No. 229 85 85
*c.* A53 60c + 3c like No. 230 95 95

Surtax was for local charities. Size: 113x147mm.

Nos. 146-149, 154-161, 170, 172, 178-180, 192-194, 202-204 Surcharged.

***Perf. 14, 13½x14½, 13½***

**1983 Photo.**

*232* A40 18c on 10c #146 35 35
*233* A40 18c on 10c #147 35 35
*234* A40 18c on 10c #148 35 35
*235* A40 18c on 10c #149 35 35
*236* A41 36c on 20c #154 70 70
*237* A41 36c on 20c #155 70 70
*238* A41 36c on 20c #156 70 70
*239* A41 36c on 20c #157 70 70
*240* A41 36c on 30c #158 70 70
*241* A41 36c on 30c #159 70 70
*242* A41 36c on 30c #160 70 70
*243* A41 36c on 30c #161 70 70
*244* A45 48c on 60c multi 90 90
*245* A45 72c on 70c multi 1.50 1.50
*246* A48 72c on 70c #192 1.50 1.50
*247* A48 72c on 70c #202 1.50 1.50
*248* A45 96c on 80c multi 1.75 1.75
*249* A48 96c on 80c #193 1.75 1.75
*250* A48 96c on 80c #203 1.75 1.75
*251* A42 $1.20 on $2 multi 2.25 2.25
*252* A48 $1.20 on $1.40 #194 2.25 2.25
*253* A48 $1.20 on $1.40 #204 2.25 2.25
*254* A42 $5.60 on $6 multi 10.50 10.50
*Nos. 232-254 (23)* 34.90 34.90

Issue dates: Nos. 232-243, 245, 251, Sept. 26; Nos. 244, 246, 249, 252, 254, Oct. 28; others Dec. 1.

First Manned Balloon Flight, 200th Anniv. — A54

Designs: 36c, Airship, Sir George Cayley (1773-1857). 48c, Man-powered airship, Dupuy de Lome (1818-1885). 60c, Brazilian Aviation Pioneer, Alberto Santos Dumont (1873-1932). 96c, Practical Airship, Paul Lebaudy (1858-1937). $1.32, L-Z 127 Graf Zeppelin.

**1983, Oct. 31 Litho. *Perf. 13***

*255* A54 36c multi 70 70
*256* A54 48c multi 90 90
*257* A54 60c multi 1.10 1.10
*258* A54 96c multi 1.75 1.75
*259* A54 $1.32 multi 2.50 2.50
*a.* Souvenir sheet of 5 6.50 6.50
*Nos. 255-259 (5)* 6.95 6.95

Nos. 255-259 se-tenant with labels. Sheets of 5 for each value exist. No. 259a has multicolored margin showing Montgolfier balloon. Size: 113x132mm.

See Nos. 287-291.

Christmas 1983 — A55

Raphael Paintings: 36c, Madonna in the Meadow. 42c, Tempi Madonna. 48c, Small Cowper Madonna. 60c, Madonna Della Tenda.

**1983, Nov. 30 Photo. *Perf. 13x13½***

*260* A55 36c multi 60 60
*261* A55 42c multi 70 70
*262* A55 48c multi 80 80
*263* A55 60c multi 1.00 1.00
*a.* Souvenir sheet of 4 3.50 3.50

**Souvenir Sheets**

*264* A55 75c + 5c like #260 1.50 1.50
*265* A55 75c + 5c like #261 1.50 1.50
*266* A55 75c + 5c like #262 1.50 1.50
*267* A55 75c + 5c like #263 1.50 1.50

No. 263a contains Nos. 260-263 each with 3c surcharge. Size: 87x115mm. Nos. 264-267 each contain one stamp (29x41mm., perf. 13½); multicolored margins show entire painting. Size: 65x84mm. Issued Dec. 28. Surtaxes were for children's charities.

Waka Canoe — A56

**1984 Photo. *Perf. 14½***

*268* A56 2c shown 5 5
*269* A56 4c Amatasi fishing boat 6 6
*270* A56 5c Ndrua canoe 8 8
*271* A56 8c Tongiaki canoe 10 10
*272* A56 10c Victoria, 1500 12 12
*273* A56 18c Golden Hind, 1560 25 25
*274* A56 20c Boudeuse, 1760 28 28
*275* A56 30c Bounty, 1787 40 40
*276* A56 36c Astrolabe, 1811 50 50
*277* A56 48c Great Republic, 1853 65 65
*278* A56 50c Star of India, 1861 68 68
*279* A56 60c Coonatto, 1863 80 80
*280* A56 72c Antiope, 1866 1.00 1.00
*281* A56 80c Balcutha, 1886 1.10 1.10
*282* A56 96c Cap Hornier, 1910 1.40 1.40
*283* A56 $1.20 Pamir, 1921 1.60 1.60

***Perf. 13***

**Size: 42x34mm**

*284* A56 $3 Mermerus, 1872 3.00 3.00
*285* A56 $5 Cutty Sark, 1869 4.75 4.75
*286* A56 $9.60 Resolution, Discovery 9.00 9.00
*Nos. 268-286 (19)* 25.82 25.82

Issue dates: Nos. 268-277, Feb. 8. Nos. 278-283, Mar. 23. Nos. 284-286 June 15.

Nos. 255-259 Ovptd. with Silver Bar and "NORTHERN COOK ISLANDS" in Black.

**1984 Litho. *Perf. 13***

*287* A54 36c multi 90 90
*288* A54 48c multi 1.20 1.20
*289* A54 60c multi 1.50 1.50
*290* A54 96c multi 2.40 2.40
*291* A54 $1.32 multi 3.25 3.25
*Nos. 287-291 (5)* 9.25 9.25

1984 Los Angeles Summer Olympic Games — A57

**1984, July 20 Photo. *Perf. 13½x13***

*292* A57 35c Olympic flag 38 38
*293* A57 60c Torch, flags 60 60
*294* A57 $1.80 Classic runners, Memorial Coliseum 1.90 1.90

**Souvenir Sheet**

*295* Sheet of 3 + label 2.75 2.75
*a.* A57 35c + 5c like #292 30 30
*b.* A57 50c + 5c like #293 55 55
*c.* A57 $1.80 + 5c like #294 1.90 1.90

No. 295 contains label picturing 1984 Summer Games emblem and torch. Size: 104x86mm. Surtax for amateur sports.

AUSIPEX '84 — A57a

**1984, Sept. 20**

*296* A57a 60c Nos. 136, 108, 180, 104b 60 60
*297* A57a $1.20 Map of South Pacific 1.25 1.25

**Souvenir Sheet**

*298* Sheet of 2 2.00 2.00
*a.* A57a 96c like #296 1.00 1.00
*b.* A57a 96c like #297 1.00 1.00

No. 298 has aquamarine, gold and black inscribed margin picturing the AUSIPEX '84 emblem. Size: 90x90mm.

Nos. 176-177, 190-191 Ovptd. "Birth of/Prince Henry/15 Sept. 1984" and Surcharged in Black or Gold.

**1984, Oct. 18 *Perf. 14***

*299* A45 $2 on 40c 2.25 2.25
*300* A45 $2 on 50c 2.25 2.25
*301* A48 $2 on 30c 2.25 2.25
*302* A48 $2 on 50c 2.25 2.25

Nos. 209-302 printed in sheets of 5 plus one label each picturing a portrait of the royal couple or an heraldic griffin.

Christmas 1984 — A58

Paintings: 36c, Virgin and Child, by Giovanni Bellini. 48c, Virgin and Child, by Lorenzo di Credi. 60c, Virgin and Child, by Palma, the Older. 96c, Virgin and Child, by Raphael.

**1984, Nov. 15 Photo. *Perf. 13x13½***

*303* A58 36c multi 35 35
*304* A58 48c multi 50 50
*305* A58 60c multi 60 60

A particular stamp may be scarce, but if few collectors want it, its market value may remain relatively low.

*306* A58 96c multi 1.00 1.00
*a.* Souvenir sheet of 4 3.00 3.00

**Souvenir Sheets**

*307* A58 96c + 10c like #303 1.20 1.20
*308* A58 96c + 10c like #304 1.20 1.20
*309* A58 96c + 10c like #305 1.20 1.20
*310* A58 96c + 10c like #306 1.20 1.20

No. 306a contains Nos. 303-306, each with 5c surcharge. Nos. 307-310 contain one stamp; multicolored margins show entire painting. Issued Dec. 10. Surtax for children's charities.

Audubon Bicentenary — A59

**1985, Apr. 9 Photo. *Perf. 13***

*311* A59 20c Harlequin duck 20 20
*312* A59 55c Sage grouse 54 54
*313* A59 65c Solitary sandpiper 64 64
*314* A59 75c Red-backed sandpiper 75 75

***Perf. 13½x13***

**Souvenir Sheets**

*315* A59 95c Like #311 85 85
*316* A59 95c Like #312 85 85
*317* A59 95c Like #313 85 85
*318* A59 95c Like #314 85 85

Nos. 315-318 have design continuing into margin.

Queen Mother, 85th Birthday — A60

**1985, June 24 Photo. *Perf. 13x13½***

*319* A60 75c Photograph, 1921 75 75
*320* A60 95c New mother, 1926 90 90
*321* A60 $1.20 Coronation day, 1937 1.10 1.10
*322* A60 $2.80 70th birthday 2.75 2.75
*a.* Souvenir sheet of 4, #319-322 3.50 3.50

**Souvenir Sheet**

*323* A60 $5 Portrait, c. 1980 4.75 4.75

No. 323 has ocher and silver decorative margin. Size: 66x91mm.

No. 322a issued on Aug. 4, 1986, for 86th birthday; silver and ocher decorative margin. Size: 91x120mm.

Intl. Youth Year — A61

Grimm Brothers' fairy tales.

**1985, Sept. 10 *Perf. 13x13½***

*324* A61 75c House in the Wood 90 90
*325* A61 95c Snow White and Rose Red 1.15 1.15
*326* A61 $1.15 Goose Girl 1.40 1.40

Christmas 1985 A62

Paintings (details) by Murillo: 75c, No. 330a, The Annunciation. $1.15, No. 330b, Adoration of the Shepherds. $1.80, No. 330c, The Holy Family.

**1985, Nov. 25 Photo. *Perf. 14***

*327* A62 75c multi 90 90
*328* A62 $1.15 multi 1.40 1.40
*329* A62 $1.80 multi 2.25 2.25

***Perf. 13½***

**Souvenir Sheets**

*330* Sheet of 3 3.50 3.50
*a.-c.* A62 95c, any single 1.15 1.15
*331* A62 $1.20 like #327 1.50 1.50
*332* A62 $1.45 like #328 1.75 1.75
*333* A62 $2.75 like #329 3.25 3.25

Nos. 330-333 have multicolored margins picturing The Annunciation. Sizes: 66x131mm (#330), 66x72mm.

Halley's Comet — A63

Fire and Ice, by Camille Rendal. Nos. 334-335 se-tenant in continuous design.

**1986, Feb. 4 *Perf. 13½x13***

*334* A63 $1.50 Comet head 1.75 1.75
*335* A63 $1.50 Comet tail 1.75 1.75

**Size: 109x43mm**

***Imperf***

*336* A63 $3 multicolored 3.50 3.50

No. 336 has silver and dark violet blue margin. Size: 109x43mm.

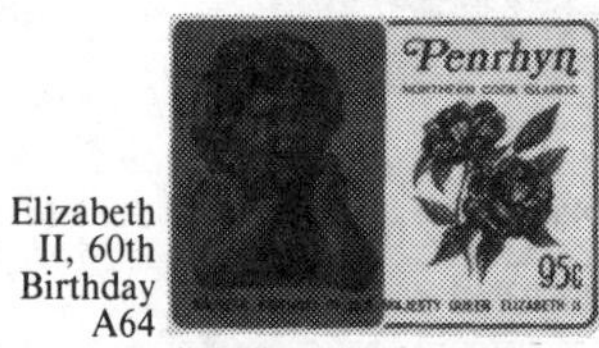

Elizabeth II, 60th Birthday A64

**1986, Apr. 21 *Perf. 14***

*337* A64 95c Age 3 1.15 1.15
*338* A64 $1.45 Wearing crown 1.75 1.75

**Size: 60x34mm.**

***Perf. 13½x13***

*339* A64 $2.50 Both portraits 3.00 3.00

Statue of Liberty, Cent. — A65

Designs: 95c, Statue, scaffolding. $1.75 Removing copper facade. $3, Restored statue on Liberty Island.

**1986, June 27 Photo. *Perf. 13½***

*340* A65 95c gold, pale grn & sep 1.05 1.05
*341* A65 $1.75 gold, pale grn & sep 1.95 1.95
*342* A65 $3 gold, pale grn & sep 3.30 3.30

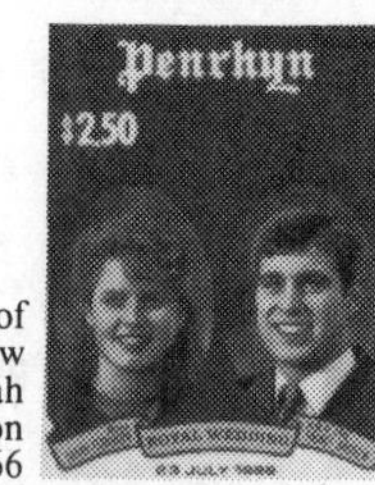

Wedding of Prince Andrew and Sarah Ferguson A66

**1986, July 23 *Perf. 13x13½***

*343* A66 $2.50 Portraits 2.75 2.75
*344* A66 $3.50 Profiles 4.00 4.00

Nos. 343-344 each printed in sheets of 4 plus 2 center decorative labels.

No. 298 Surcharged with Gold Cirle, Bar, New Value in Black and Exhibition Emblem in Gold and Black.

**1986, Aug. 4**

*345* Sheet of 2 4.50 4.50
*a.* A57a $2 on 96c #298a 2.25 2.25
*b.* A57a $2 on 96c #298b 2.25 2.25

STAMPEX '86, Adelaide, Aug. 4-10.

Christmas A67

Engravings by Rembrandt: 65c, No. 349a, Adoration of the Shepherds. $1.75, No. 349b, Virgin and Child. $2.50, No. 349c, The Holy Family.

**1986, Nov. 20 Litho. *Perf. 13x13½***

*346* A67 65c gold, hn brn & buff 70 70
*347* A67 $1.75 gold, hn brn & buff 1.85 1.85
*348* A67 $2.50 gold, hn brn & buff 2.65 2.65

**Souvenir Sheet**

***Perf. 13½x13***

*349* Sheet of 3 4.80 4.80
*a.-c.* A67 $1.50, any single 1.60 1.60

No. 349 has multicolored inscribed margin picturing Self-portrait (detail), by Rembrandt. Corrected inscription is black on silver. Size: 120x88mm.

**Souvenir Sheets**

Statue of Liberty, Cent. — A68

Photographs: No. 350a, Workmen, crown. No. 350b, Ellis Is., aerial view. No. 350c, Immigration building, Ellis Is. No. 350d, Buildings, opposite side of Ellis Is. No. 350e, Workmen inside torch structure. No. 351a, Liberty's head and torch. No. 351b, Torch. No. 351c, Workmen on scaffold. No. 351d, Statue, full figure. No. 351e, Workmen beside statue. Nos. 351a-351e vert.

**1987, Apr. 15 Litho. *Perf. 14***

*350* Sheet of 5 + label 3.50 3.50
*a.-e.* A68 65c any single 70 70
*351* Sheet of 5 + label 3.50 3.50
*a.-e.* A68 65c any single 70 70

Sizes of Nos. 350-351: 123x122mm, 122x123mm.

Nos. 62-63 Ovptd. "Fortieth Royal Wedding / Anniversary 1947-87" in Lilac Rose.

**1987, Nov. 20 Photo. *Perf. 13½x14***

*352* A18 $2 multi 2.60 2.60
*353* A18 $5 multi 6.50 6.50

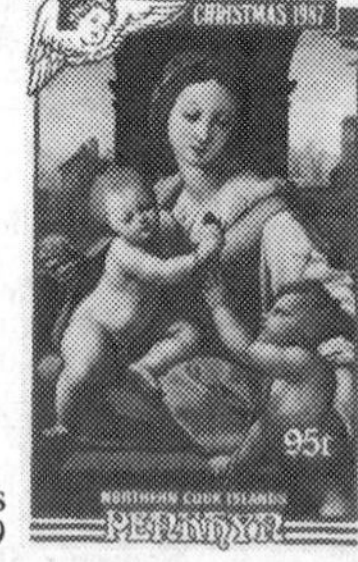

Christmas A69

Paintings (details) by Raphael: 95c, No. 357a, The Garvagh Madonna, the National Gallery, London. $1.60, No. 357b, The Alba Madonna, the National Gallery of Art, Washington. $2.25, No. 357c, $4.80, The Madonna of the Fish, Prado Museum, Madrid.

**1987, Dec. 11 Photo. *Perf. 13½***

*354* A69 95c multi 1.25 1.25
*355* A69 $1.60 multi 2.05 2.05
*356* A69 $2.25 multi 2.90 2.90

**Souvenir Sheets**

*357* Sheet of 3 + label 4.35 4.35
*a.-c.* A69 $1.15 any single 1.45 1.45
*358* A69 $4.80 multi 6.25 6.25

No. 357 has multicolored inscribed margin; label pictures detail of Raphael's Madonna of the Chair, the Pitti Gallery, Florence. Size: 91x126mm. No. 358 contains one stamp (size: 31x39mm); gold inscribed decorative margin continues the painting. Size: 70x86mm.

1988 Summer Olympics, Seoul — A70

Events and: 55c, $1.25, Seoul Games emblem. 95c, Obverse of a $50 silver coin issued in 1987 to commemorate the participation of Cook Islands atheletes in the Olympics for the 1st time. $1.50, Coin reverse.

***Perf. 13½x13, 13x13½***

**1988, July 29 Photo.**

*359* A70 55c Running 75 75
*360* A70 95c High jump, vert. 1.30 1.30
*361* A70 $1.25 Shot put 1.70 1.70
*362* A70 $1.50 Tennis, vert. 2.00 2.00

**Souvenir Sheet**

*363* Sheet of 2 6.75 6.75
*a.* A70 $2.50 like 95c 3.35 3.35
*b.* A70 $2.50 like $1.50 3.35 3.35

No. 363 has multicolored inscribed margin picturing the Seoul Games emblem. Size: 110x70mm.

Nos. 359-363 Ovptd. for Olympic Gold Medalists

*a.* "CARL LEWIS / UNITED STATES / 100 METERS"

*b.* "LOUISE RITTER / UNITED STATES / HIGH JUMP"

*c.* "ULF TIMMERMANN / EAST GERMANY / SHOT-PUT"

*d.* "STEFFI GRAF / WEST GERMANY / WOMEN'S TENNIS"

*e.* "JACKIE / JOYNER-KERSEE / United States / Heptathlon"

*f.* "STEFFI GRAF / West Germany / Women's Tennis / MILOSLAV MECIR / Czechoslovakia / Men's Tennis"

***Perf. 13½x13, 13x13½***

**1988, Oct. 14** **Photo.**

| | | | | |
|---|---|---|---|---|
| *364* | A70(a) | 55c on No. 359 | 75 | 75 |
| *365* | A70(b) | 95c on No. 360 | 1.30 | 1.30 |
| *366* | A70(c) | $1.25 on No. 361 | 1.70 | 1.70 |
| *367* | A70(d) | $1.50 on No. 362 | 2.00 | 2.00 |

**Souvenir Sheet**

| | | | |
|---|---|---|---|
| *368* | Sheet of 2 | 6.75 | 6.75 |
| ***a.*** | A70(e) $2.50 on No. 363a | 3.35 | 3.35 |
| ***b.*** | A70(f) $2.50 on No. 363b | 3.35 | 3.35 |

Christmas A71

*Virgin and Child* paintings by Titian.

**1988, Nov. 9** ***Perf. 13x13½***

| | | | | |
|---|---|---|---|---|
| *369* | A71 | 70c multi | 90 | 90 |
| *370* | A71 | 85c multi, diff. | 1.10 | 1.10 |
| *371* | A71 | 95c multi, diff. | 1.20 | 1.20 |
| *372* | A71 | $1.25 multi, diff. | 1.60 | 1.60 |

**Souvenir Sheet**

***Perf. 13***

| | | | | |
|---|---|---|---|---|
| *373* | A71 | $6.40 multi, diff. | 8.25 | 8.25 |

No. 373 contains one diamond-shaped stamp (size: 55x55mm); multicolored inscribed margin continues the painting. Size: 100x80mm.

## SEMI-POSTAL STAMPS

**Catalogue values for unused stamps in this section, from this point to the end of the section, are for Never Hinged items.**

Easter Type of 1978

Souvenir Sheets

Rubens Paintings: No. B1, like No. 101. No. B2, like No. 102. No. B3, like No. 103.

**1978, Apr. 17** **Photo.** ***Perf. 13½x13***

| | | | | |
|---|---|---|---|---|
| *B1* | A31 | 60c + 5c multi | 1.40 | 1.40 |
| *B2* | A31 | 60c + 5c multi | 1.40 | 1.40 |
| *B3* | A31 | 60c + 5c multi | 1.40 | 1.40 |

Surtax was for school children. Nos. B1-B3 contain one stamp each; multicolored margin shows entire painting. Size: 50x68mm.

Easter Type of 1980

Souvenir Sheets

**1980, Mar. 28** **Photo.** ***Perf. 13x13½***

| | | | | |
|---|---|---|---|---|
| *B4* | A36 | 70c + 5c *like #114* | 1.25 | 1.25 |
| *B5* | A36 | 70c + 5c *like #115* | 1.25 | 1.25 |
| *B6* | A36 | 70c + 5c *like #116* | 1.25 | 1.25 |

Surtax was for local charities. Nos. B4-B6 have multicolored margins showing entire illustrations. Size of stamps: 30x42mm; size of sheet: 53x86mm.

**Christmas Type of 1980**

Souvenir Sheets

**1980, Dec. 5** **Photo.** ***Perf. 13***

| | | | | |
|---|---|---|---|---|
| *B7* | A39 | 70c + 5c like #127 | 1.50 | 1.50 |
| *B8* | A39 | 70c + 5c like #128 | 1.50 | 1.50 |
| *B9* | A39 | 70c + 5c like #129 | 1.50 | 1.50 |

Surtax was for local charities. Multicolored margins show entire paintings. Size: 54x77mm.

Easter Type of 1981

Souvenir Sheets

**1981, Apr. 5** **Photo.** ***Perf. 13½***

| | | | | |
|---|---|---|---|---|
| *B10* | A44 | 70c + 5c like #173 | 1.90 | 1.90 |
| *B11* | A44 | 70c + 5c like #174 | 1.90 | 1.90 |
| *B12* | A44 | 70c + 5c like #175 | 1.90 | 1.90 |

Surtax was for local charities. Multicolored margins show entire paintings. Size: 70x86mm.

Royal Wedding Type of 1981

Nos. 176-180a Surcharged

**1981, Nov. 30** **Photo.** ***Perf. 14***

| | | | | |
|---|---|---|---|---|
| *B13* | A45 | 40c + 5c like #176 | 1.15 | 1.15 |
| *B14* | A45 | 50c + 5c like #177 | 1.40 | 1.40 |
| *B15* | A45 | 60c + 5c like #178 | 1.65 | 1.65 |
| *B16* | A45 | 70c + 5c like #179 | 1.90 | 1.90 |
| *B17* | A45 | 80c + 5c like #180 | 2.15 | 2.15 |
| | | *Nos. B13-B17 (5)* | 8.25 | 8.25 |

**Souvenir Sheet**

| | | | |
|---|---|---|---|
| *B18* | Sheet of 5 | 7.75 | 7.75 |
| ***a.*** | A45 40c + 10c like #176 | 1.10 | 1.10 |
| ***b.*** | A45 50c + 10c like #177 | 1.25 | 1.25 |
| ***c.*** | A45 60c + 10c like #178 | 50 | 50 |
| ***d.*** | A45 70c + 10c like #179 | 1.90 | 1.90 |
| ***e.*** | A45 80c + 10c like #180 | 2.00 | 2.00 |

Intl. Year of the Disabled. Surtax was for the disabled.

Soccer Type of 1981

**1981, Dec. 7** ***Perf. 13***

| | | | | |
|---|---|---|---|---|
| *B19* | A46 | Sheet of 9 | 5.50 | 5.50 |

No. B19 contains Nos. 181-183; black and light green margin. Size: 113x151mm. Surtax was for local sports.

Nos. 346-349 Surcharged ".SOUTH PACIFIC PAPAL VISIT . 21 TO 24 NOVEMBER 1986" in Metallic Blue.

**1986, Nov. 24** **Litho.** ***Perf. 13x13½***

| | | | | |
|---|---|---|---|---|
| *B20* | A67 | 65c + 10c multi | 80 | 80 |
| *B21* | A67 | $1.75 + 10c multi | 1.95 | 1.95 |
| *B22* | A67 | $2.50 + 10c multi | 2.75 | 2.75 |

**Souvenir Sheet**

***Perf. 13½x13***

| | | | |
|---|---|---|---|
| *B23* | Sheet of 3 | 5.10 | 5.10 |
| ***a.-c.*** | A67 $1.50 + 10c on Nos. 349a-349c | 1.70 | 1.70 |

No. B23 inscribed "COMMEMORATING FIRST PAPAL VISIT TO SOUTH PACIFIC / VISIT OF POPE JOHN PAUL II . NOVEMBER 1986."

## OFFICIAL STAMPS

**Catalogue values for unused stamps in this section, from this point to the end of the section, are for Never Hinged items.**

Nos. 51-60, 80, 88-89 Overprinted or Surcharged in Black, Silver or Gold

**O.H.M.S**

***Perf. 13½x14, 13½, 13½x13***

**1978, Nov. 14** **Photo.**

| | | | | |
|---|---|---|---|---|
| *O1* | A17 | 1c multi | 5 | 5 |
| *O2* | A17 | 2c multi | 5 | 5 |
| *O3* | A17 | 3c multi | 6 | 6 |
| *O4* | A17 | 4c multi | 8 | 8 |
| *O5* | A17 | 5c multi | 10 | 10 |
| *O6* | A17 | 8c multi | 15 | 15 |
| *O7* | A17 | 10c multi | 18 | 18 |
| *O8* | A17 | 15c on 60c multi | 25 | 25 |
| *O9* | A17 | 18c on 60c multi | 35 | 35 |
| *O10* | A17 | 20c multi | 38 | 38 |
| *O11* | A17 | 25c multi (S) | 40 | 40 |
| *O12* | A17 | 30c on 60c multi | 60 | 60 |
| *O13* | A24 | Strip of 3, multi | 2.75 | 2.75 |
| ***a.*** | | 50c, No. 80a (G) | 80 | 80 |
| ***b.*** | | 50c, No. 80b (G) | 80 | 80 |
| ***c.*** | | 50c, No. 80c (G) | 80 | 80 |
| *O14* | A27 | $1 multi (S) | 2.00 | 2.00 |
| *O15* | A27 | $2 multi (G) | 4.00 | 4.00 |
| | | *Nos. O1-O15 (15)* | 11.40 | 11.40 |

Overprint on No. O14 diagonal.

Nos. 268-276, 278, 277, 211-214, 280, 282, 281, 283, 170, 284, 171, 285, 172, 286 Surcharged with Bar and New Value or Ovptd. "O.H.M.S." in Silver or Metallic Red.

**1985-87** **Photo.** ***Perfs. as before***

| | | | | |
|---|---|---|---|---|
| *O16* | A56 | 2c multi | 5 | 5 |
| *O17* | A56 | 4c multi | 5 | 5 |
| *O18* | A56 | 5c multi | 6 | 6 |
| *O19* | A56 | 8c multi | 10 | 10 |
| *O20* | A56 | 10c multi | 12 | 12 |
| *O21* | A56 | 18c multi | 20 | 20 |
| *O22* | A56 | 20c multi | 22 | 22 |
| *O23* | A56 | 30c multi | 35 | 35 |
| *O24* | A56 | 40c on 36c | 45 | 45 |
| *O25* | A56 | 50c multi | 55 | 55 |
| *O26* | A56 | 55c on 48c | 62 | 62 |
| *O27* | A50 | 65c on 60c #211 | 72 | 72 |
| *O28* | A50 | 65c on 60c #212 | 72 | 72 |
| *O29* | A50 | 65c on 60c #213 | 72 | 72 |
| *O30* | A50 | 65c on 60c #214 | 72 | 72 |
| *O31* | A56 | 75c on 72c | 85 | 85 |
| *O32* | A56 | 75c on 96c | 85 | 85 |
| *O33* | A56 | 80c multi | 90 | 90 |
| *O34* | A56 | $1.20 multi | 1.35 | 1.35 |
| *O35* | A42 | $2 multi (R) | 2.25 | 2.25 |
| *O36* | A56 | $3 multi | 3.35 | 3.35 |
| *O37* | A42 | $4 multi (R) | 4.50 | 4.50 |
| *O38* | A56 | $5 multi | 6.00 | 6.00 |
| *O39* | A42 | $6 multi (R) | 7.25 | 7.25 |
| *O40* | A56 | $9.60 multi | 11.75 | 11.75 |
| | | *Nos. O16-O40 (25)* | 44.70 | 44.70 |

Issue dates: Nos. O16-O30, Aug. 15. Nos. O31-O37, Apr. 29, 1986. Nos. O38-O40, Nov. 2, 1987.

# PITCAIRN ISLANDS

LOCATION — In the south Pacific Ocean, nearly equidistant from Australia and South America.

GOVT. — British colony under the British High Commissioner in New Zealand.

AREA — 1.75 sq. mi.

POP. — 57 (1984).

The district of Pitcairn also includes the uninhabited islands of Ducie, Henderson and Oeno.

Postal affairs are administered by Fiji.

12 Pence = 1 Shilling

100 Cents = 1 Dollar (1967)

**Catalogue values for all unused stamps in this country are for Never Hinged items.**

Cluster of Oranges A1

Fletcher Christian with Crew and View of Pitcairn Island — A2

John Adams and His House — A3

William Bligh and H. M. Armed Vessel "Bounty" A4

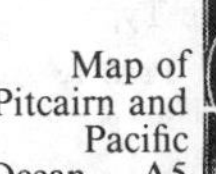

Map of Pitcairn and Pacific Ocean — A5

Bounty Bible — A6

H. M. Armed Vessel "Bounty" A7

Pitcairn School, 1949 — A8

Fletcher Christian and View of Pitcairn Island — A9

Fletcher Christian with Crew and Coast of Pitcairn A10

***Perf. 12½, 11½x11***

**1940-51** **Engr.** **Wmk. 4**

| | | | | |
|---|---|---|---|---|
| *1* | A1 | ½p bl grn & org | 40 | 25 |
| *2* | A2 | 1p red lil & rose vio | 60 | 40 |
| *3* | A3 | 1½p rose car & blk | 1.00 | 65 |
| *4* | A4 | 2p dk brn & brt grn | 1.50 | 1.00 |
| *5* | A5 | 3p dk bl & yel grn | 2.00 | 1.25 |
| *5A* | A6 | 4p dk bl grn & blk ('51) | 10.00 | 6.50 |
| *6* | A7 | 6p sl grn & dp brn | 2.75 | 1.75 |
| *6A* | A8 | 8p lil rose & grn ('51) | 10.00 | 6.50 |
| *7* | A9 | 1sh sl & vio | 3.50 | 2.25 |
| *8* | A10 | 2sh6p dk brn & brt grn | 7.50 | 5.00 |
| | | *Nos. 1-8 (10)* | 39.25 | 25.55 |

Nos. 1-5, 6 and 7-8 exist in a booklet of eight panes of one.

**Peace Issue**

Common Design Type

**1946, Dec. 2** ***Perf. 13½x14***

| | | | | |
|---|---|---|---|---|
| *9* | CD303 | 2p brown | 50 | 50 |
| *10* | CD303 | 3p dp bl | 95 | 95 |

Common Design Types pictured in section before Great Britain.

**Silver Wedding Issue**

Common Design Types

**1949, Aug. 1** **Photo.** ***Perf. 14x14½***

| | | | | |
|---|---|---|---|---|
| *11* | CD304 | 1½p scarlet | 1.00 | 45 |

**Engraved; Name Typographed**

***Perf. 11½x11***

| | | | | |
|---|---|---|---|---|
| *12* | CD305 | 10sh purple | 85.00 | *60.00* |

25th anniv. of the marriage of King George VI and Queen Elizabeth.

**UPU Issue**

Common Design Types

**Engr.; Name Typo. on 3p & 6p**

**1949, Oct. 10** ***Perf. 13½, 11x11½***

| | | | | |
|---|---|---|---|---|
| *13* | CD306 | 2½p red brn | 6.00 | 2.75 |
| *14* | CD307 | 3p indigo | 6.00 | 2.75 |
| *15* | CD308 | 6p green | 11.00 | 5.00 |
| *16* | CD309 | 1sh rose vio | 22.50 | 10.00 |

**Coronation Issue**
Common Design Type

**1953, June 2** *Perf. 13½x13*
*19* CD312 4p dk grn & blk 4.00 1.50

Ti Plant — A11

Map — A12

Designs: 2p, John Adams and Bounty Bible. 2½p, Handicraft (Carving). 3p, Bounty Bay. 4p, School (actually School-teacher's House). 6p, Fiji-Pitcairn connection (Map). 8p, Inland scene. 1sh, Handicraft (Ship model). 2sh, Wheelbarrow. 2sh6p, Whaleboat.

*Perf. 13x12½, 12½x13.*
**1957, July 2 Engr. Wmk. 4**
*20* A11 ½p lil & grn 38 16
*21* A12 1p ol grn & blk 52 20
*22* A12 2p bl & brn 65 28
*23* A11 2½p org & brn 90 32
*24* A11 3p ultra & emer 1.00 40
*25* A11 4p ultra & rose red *("Pitcairn School")* 3.75 1.25
*26* A11 6p ind & buff 2.25 75
*27* A11 8p mag & grn 2.50 85
*28* A11 1sh brn & blk 3.00 1.10
*29* A12 2sh dp org & grn 22.50 7.50
*30* A11 2sh6p mag & ultra 15.00 6.25
*Nos. 20-30 (11)* 52.45 19.06

See No. 38.

Type of 1957 Redrawn

**1958, Nov. 5** *Perf. 13x12½*
*31* A11 4p ultra & rose red *(School-teacher's House)* 75 50

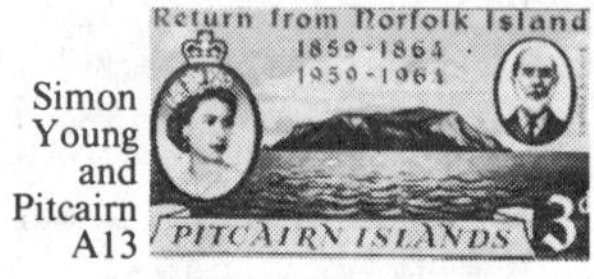
Simon Young and Pitcairn A13

Designs: 6p, Maps of Norfolk and Pitcairn Islands. 1sh, Schooner Mary Ann.

*Perf. 14½x13½*
**1961, Nov. 15 Photo. Wmk. 314**
*32* A13 3p yel & blk 1.00 70
*33* A13 6p bl & red brn 1.75 1.25
*34* A13 1sh brt grn & dp org 4.25 3.00

Issued to commemorate the return of the Pitcairn Islanders from Norfolk Island.

**Freedom from Hunger Issue**
Common Design Type

**1963, June 4** *Perf. 14x14½*
*35* CD314 2sh6p ultra 30.00 21.00

**Red Cross Centenary Issue**
Common Design Type

**1963, Dec. 9 Litho.** *Perf. 13*
*36* CD315 2p blk & red 48 32
*37* CD315 2sh6p ultra & red 16.00 9.75

Type of 1957

*Perf. 13x12½*
**1963, Dec. 4 Engr. Wmk. 314**
*38* A11 ½p lil & grn 1.25 1.25

Pitcairn Longboat A14

Queen Elizabeth II — A15

Designs: 1p, H.M. Armed Vessel Bounty. 2p, Oarsmen rowing longboat. 3p, Great frigate bird. 4p, Fairy tern 6p, Pitcairn reed warbler. 8p, Red-footed booby. 10p, Red-tailed tropic birds. 1sh, Henderson Island flightless rail. 1sh6p, Henderson Island lory. 2sh6p, Murphy's petrel. 4sh, Henderson Island fruit pigeon.

**1964-65 Photo.** *Perf. 14x14½*
*39* A14 ½p multi 10 6
*40* A14 1p vio bl, blk & tan 10 6
*41* A14 2p multi 14 8
*42* A14 3p ocher & multi 20 12
*43* A14 4p multi 30 20
*44* A14 6p multi 52 30
*45* A14 8p multi 70 38
*a.* Gray (beak) omitted 100.00
*46* A14 10p bl, blk & org 90 50
*47* A14 1sh multi 1.00 65
*48* A14 1sh6p multi 1.50 1.00
*49* A14 2sh6p multi 3.50 2.25
*50* A14 4sh brn & multi 5.25 3.75
*51* A15 8sh multi ('65) 14.00 10.00
*Nos. 39-51 (13)* 28.21 19.35

Issue dates: Aug. 5, 1964, Nos. 39-50; Apr. 5, 1965, No. 51.

**ITU Issue**
Common Design Type

**1965, May 17 Litho.** *Perf. 11x11½*
*52* CD317 1p red lil & org brn 42 22
*53* CD317 2sh6p grnsh bl & ultra 21.00 11.00

**Intl. Cooperation Year Issue**
Common Design Type

**1965, Oct. 25** *Perf. 14½*
*54* CD318 1p bl grn & cl 35 22
*55* CD318 1sh6p lt vio & grn 17.50 11.00

**Churchill Memorial Issue**
Common Design Type

**1966, Jan. 24 Photo.** *Perf. 14*
**Design in Black, Gold and Carmine Rose**
*56* CD319 2p brt bl 1.25 50
*57* CD319 3p green 2.50 1.00
*58* CD319 6p brown 6.00 4.00
*59* CD319 1sh violet 18.00 10.00

**World Cup Soccer Issue**
Common Design Type

**1966, Aug. 1 Litho.** *Perf. 14*
*60* CD321 4p multi 1.65 1.10
*61* CD321 2sh6p multi 8.50 6.75

**WHO Headquarters Issue**
Common Design Type

**1966, Sept. 20 Litho.** *Perf. 14*
*62* CD322 8p multi 2.75 2.00
*63* CD322 1sh6p multi 12.00 7.50

**UNESCO Anniversary Issue**
Common Design Type

**1966, Dec. 1 Litho.** *Perf. 14*
*64* CD323 ½p "Education" 22 16
*65* CD323 10p "Science" 2.50 2.00
*66* CD323 2sh "Culture" 12.50 8.50

Mangarevan Canoe, c. 1325, and Pitcairn Island — A16

Designs: 1p, Pedro Fernandez de Quiros and galleon, 1606. 8p, "San Pedro," 17th century Spanish brigantine, 1606. 1sh, Capt. Philip Carteret and H.M.S. Swallow. 1sh6p, "Hercules," 1819.

**Wmk. 314**
**1967, Mar. 1 Photo.** *Perf. 14½*
*67* A16 ½p multi 6 6
*68* A16 1p multi 7 7
*69* A16 8p multi 40 40
*70* A16 1sh multi 75 60
*71* A16 1sh6p multi 1.10 1.00
*Nos. 67-71 (5)* 2.38 2.13

Bicentenary of the discovery of Pitcairn Islands by Capt. Philip Carteret.

Nos. 39-51 Surcharged in Gold

20c

**1967, July 10** *Perf. 14x14½*
*72* A14 ½c on ½p multi 8 8
*a.* Brown omitted 400.00
*73* A14 1c on 1p multi 9 9
*74* A14 2c on 2p multi 20 15
*75* A14 2½c on 3p multi 25 22
*76* A14 3c on 4p multi 38 32
*77* A14 5c on 6p multi 60 60
*78* A14 10c on 8p multi 1.10 1.00
*a.* "10c" omitted 240.00
*79* A14 15c on 10p multi 1.75 1.50
*80* A14 20c on 1sh multi 2.50 2.25
*81* A14 25c on 1sh6p multi 3.25 3.25
*82* A14 30c on 2sh6p multi 4.50 4.00
*83* A14 40c on 4sh multi 6.25 6.25
*84* A15 45c on 8sh multi 10.00 10.00
*Nos. 72-84 (13)* 30.95 29.71

Size of gold rectangle and anchor varies. The anchor symbol is designed after the anchor of H.M.S. Bounty.

Admiral Bligh and Bounty's Launch A17

Designs: 8c, Bligh and his followers adrift in a boat. 20c, Bligh's tomb, St. Mary's Cemetery, Lambeth, London.

**Unwmk.**
**1967, Dec. 7 Litho.** *Perf. 13*
*85* A17 1c ultra, lt bl & blk 10 10
*86* A17 8c brt rose, yel & blk 50 50
*87* A17 20c brn, yel & blk 1.65 1.50

150th anniv. of the death of Admiral William Bligh (1754-1817), capt. of the Bounty.

Human Rights Flame A18

*Perf. 13½x13*
**1968, Mar. 4 Litho. Wmk. 314**
*88* A18 1c rose & multi 6 6
*89* A18 2c ocher & multi 8 8
*90* A18 25c multi 1.65 1.25

International Human Rights Year.

Flower and Wood of Miro Tree A19

Pitcairn Handicraft: 10c, Carved flying fish. 15c, Two "hand" vases (vert.). 20c, Old and new woven baskets (vert.).

*Perf. 14½x14, 14x14½*
**1968, Aug. 19 Photo. Wmk. 314**
*91* A19 5c choc & multi 50 32
*92* A19 10c dp grn & multi 1.00 65
*93* A19 15c brt vio & multi 1.50 1.10
*94* A19 20c blk & multi 2.00 1.65

See Nos. 194-197.

Microscope, Cell, Germs and WHO Emblem — A20

Design: 20c, Hypodermic and jars containing pills.

**1968, Nov. 25 Litho.** *Perf. 14*
*95* A20 2c vio bl, grnsh bl & blk 15 12
*96* A20 20c blk, mag & org 1.90 1.50

20th anniv. of WHO.

Capt. Bligh and his Larcum-Kendall Chronometer — A21

Designs: 1c, Pitcairn Island. 3c, Bounty's anchor (vert.). 4c, Plan of the Bounty, drawn 1787. 5c, Breadfruit and method of transporting young plants. 6c, Bounty Bay. 8c, Pitcairn longboat. 10c, Ship Landing Point and palms. 15c, Fletcher Christian's Cave. 20c, Thursday October Christian's house. 25c, "Flying Fox" cable system (for hauling cargo; vert.). 30c, Radio Station at Taro Ground. 40c, Bounty Bible.

*Perf. 13x12½, 12½x13*
**1969, Sept. 17 Litho. Wmk. 314**
*97* A21 1c brn, yel & gold 15 6
*98* A21 2c brn, blk & gold 18 8
*99* A21 3c red, blk & gold 24 15
*100* A21 4c buff, brn & gold 30 18
*101* A21 5c gold & multi 35 25
*102* A21 6c gold & multi 45 32
*103* A21 8c gold & multi 65 45
*104* A21 10c gold & multi 1.25 85
*105* A21 15c gold & multi 1.50 1.10
*a.* Gold (Queen's head) omitted 500.00
*106* A21 20c gold & multi 1.90 1.50
*107* A21 25c gold & multi 3.50 2.50
*108* A21 30c gold & multi 4.50 3.50
*109* A21 40c red lil, blk & gold 6.00 4.00
*Nos. 97-109 (13)* 20.97 14.94

Lantana — A22

Pitcairn Islands Flowers: 2c, Indian shot (canna indica). 5c, Pulau (hibiscus tiliaceus). 25c, Wild gladioli.

**1970, Mar. 23 Litho.** *Perf. 14*
*110* A22 1c blk & multi 15 10
*111* A22 2c blk & multi 50 25
*112* A22 5c blk & multi 1.25 65
*113* A22 25c blk & multi 10.00 5.00

Rudderfish (Dream Fish) — A23

Fish: 5c, Groupers (Auntie and Ann). 15c, Wrasse (Elwyn's trousers). 20c, Wrasse (Whistling daughter).

*Perf. 14½x14*

**1970, Oct. 12 Photo. Wmk. 314**

| | | | | |
|---|---|---|---|---|
| *114* | A23 | 5c blk & multi | 1.25 | 1.10 |
| *115* | A23 | 10c grnsh bl & blk | 2.50 | 2.25 |
| *116* | A23 | 15c multi | 3.50 | 3.25 |
| *117* | A23 | 20c multi | 4.75 | 4.00 |

No. 104 Overprinted in Silver: "ROYAL VISIT 1971"

**1971, Feb. 22 Litho. *Perf. 13x12½***

| | | | | |
|---|---|---|---|---|
| *118* | A21 | 10c gold & multi | 14.00 | 7.00 |

Polynesian Artifacts — A24

Polynesian Art on Pitcairn: 5c, Rock carvings (vert.). 15c, Making of stone fishhook. 20c, Seated deity (vert.).

**1971, May 3 Litho. *Perf. 13½***
**Queen's Head in Gold.**

| | | | | |
|---|---|---|---|---|
| *119* | A24 | 5c dk brn & bis | 1.00 | 1.00 |
| *120* | A24 | 10c ol grn & blk | 2.00 | 2.00 |
| *121* | A24 | 15c blk & lt vio | 3.25 | 2.50 |
| *122* | A24 | 20c blk & rose red | 4.00 | 3.25 |

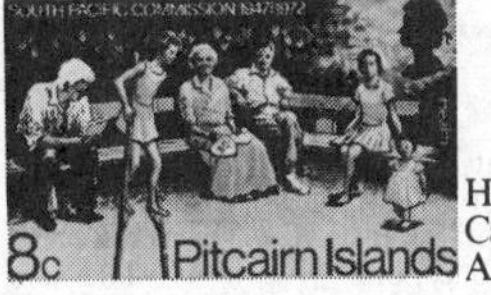


Health Care A25

Designs: 4c, South Pacific Commission flag and Southern Cross (vert.). 18c, Education (elementary school). 20c, Economy (country store).

**1972, Apr. 4 Litho. *Perf. 14x14½***

| | | | | |
|---|---|---|---|---|
| *123* | A25 | 4c vio bl, yel & ultra | 1.25 | 65 |
| *124* | A25 | 8c brn & multi | 2.25 | 1.65 |
| *125* | A25 | 18c yel grn & multi | 3.00 | 2.25 |
| *126* | A25 | 20c org & multi | 3.75 | 3.00 |

So. Pacific Commission, 25th anniv.

**Silver Wedding Issue, 1972**
Common Design Type

Design: Queen Elizabeth II, Prince Philip, skuas and longboat.

**1972, Nov. 20 Photo. Wmk. 314**

| | | | | |
|---|---|---|---|---|
| *127* | CD324 | 4c sl grn & multi | 38 | 25 |
| *128* | CD324 | 20c ultra & multi | 1.65 | 1.00 |

Pitcairn Coat of Arms A26

**1973, Jan. 2 Litho. *Perf. 14½x14***

| | | | | |
|---|---|---|---|---|
| *129* | A26 | 50c multi | 4.25 | 4.25 |

Rose Apple — A27

**1973, June 25 *Perf. 14***

| | | | | |
|---|---|---|---|---|
| *130* | A27 | 4c *shown* | 90 | 40 |
| *131* | A27 | 8c *Mountain apple* | 1.50 | 75 |
| *132* | A27 | 15c *Lata (myrtle)* | 2.25 | 1.40 |
| *133* | A27 | 20c *Cassia* | 2.50 | 1.75 |
| *134* | A27 | 35c *Guava* | 5.00 | 3.50 |
| | | *Nos. 130-134 (5)* | 12.15 | 7.80 |

**Princess Anne's Wedding Issue**
Common Design Type

**1973, Nov. 14 Litho. *Perf. 14***

| | | | | |
|---|---|---|---|---|
| *135* | CD325 | 10c lil & multi | 60 | 48 |
| *136* | CD325 | 25c gray grn & multi | 1.40 | 1.25 |

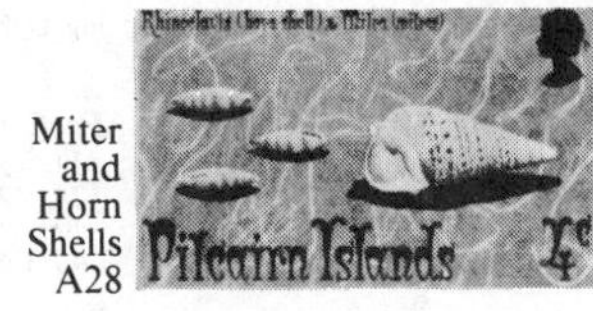


Miter and Horn Shells A28

**1974, Apr. 15**

| | | | | |
|---|---|---|---|---|
| *137* | A28 | 4c *shown* | 60 | 48 |
| *138* | A28 | 10c *Dove shells* | 1.50 | 1.40 |
| *139* | A28 | 18c *Limpets and false limpet* | 2.50 | 2.25 |
| *140* | A28 | 50c *Lucine shells* | 6.50 | 6.25 |
| *a.* | | Souvenir sheet of 4 | 15.00 | 9.25 |

No. 140a contains one each of Nos. 137-140. Yellow margin with shell border and black inscription. Size: 130x121mm.

Pitcairn Post Office, UPU Emblem A29

UPU, cent.: 20c, Stampless cover, "Posted at Pitcairn Island No Stamps Available." 35c, Longboat leaving Bounty Bay for ship offshore.

**1974, July 22 Wmk. 314 *Perf. 14½***

| | | | | |
|---|---|---|---|---|
| *141* | A29 | 4c multi | 22 | 20 |
| *142* | A29 | 20c multi | 90 | 85 |
| *143* | A29 | 35c multi | 2.00 | 1.90 |

Centenary of Universal Postal Union.

Churchill: "Lift up your hearts . . ." — A30

Design: 35c, Churchill and "Give us the tools and we will finish the job."

**1974, Nov. 30 Litho. Wmk. 373**

| | | | | |
|---|---|---|---|---|
| *144* | A30 | 20c blk & cit | 1.10 | 1.00 |
| *145* | A30 | 35c blk & yel | 1.75 | 1.50 |

Sir Winston Churchill (1874-1965).

Queen Elizabeth II — A31

**1975, Apr. 21 Wmk. 314 *Perf. 14½***

| | | | | |
|---|---|---|---|---|
| *146* | A31 | $1 multi | 10.00 | 10.00 |

Mailboats — A32

**1975, July 22 Litho. *Perf. 14½***

| | | | | |
|---|---|---|---|---|
| *147* | A32 | 4c *Seringapatam, 1830* | 35 | 30 |
| *148* | A32 | 10c *Pitcairn, 1890* | 95 | 85 |
| *149* | A32 | 18c *Athenic, 1901* | 1.65 | 1.50 |
| *150* | A32 | 50c *Gothic, 1948* | 4.75 | 4.25 |
| *a.* | | Souvenir sheet of 4 | 15.00 | 13.00 |

No. 150a contains one each of Nos. 147-150, perf. 14. Pale blue margin with white description of ships. Size: 145x110mm.

Pitcairn Wasp A33

Insects: 6c, Grasshopper. 10c, Pitcairn moths. 15c, Dragonfly. 20c, Banana moth.

**Wmk. 314**

**1975, Nov. 9 Litho. *Perf. 14½***

| | | | | |
|---|---|---|---|---|
| *151* | A33 | 4c bl grn & multi | 70 | 35 |
| *152* | A33 | 6c car & multi | 1.00 | 52 |
| *153* | A33 | 10c pur & multi | 1.75 | 1.25 |
| *154* | A33 | 15c blk & multi | 2.50 | 1.50 |
| *155* | A33 | 20c multi | 2.75 | 2.00 |
| | | *Nos. 151-155 (5)* | 8.70 | 5.62 |

Fletcher Christian — A34

H.M.S. Bounty — A35

Designs: 30c, George Washington. 50c, Mayflower.

**1976, July 4 Wmk. 373 *Perf. 13½***

| | | | | |
|---|---|---|---|---|
| *156* | A34 | 5c multi | 30 | 28 |
| *157* | A35 | 10c multi | 60 | 55 |
| *158* | A34 | 30c multi | 1.50 | 1.40 |
| *159* | A35 | 50c multi | 2.00 | 1.75 |

American Bicentennial.

Nos. 156, 158 and 157, 159, respectively, are printed se-tenant in sheets of 30 (6x5).

Common Design Types are pictured in section before Great Britain.

Prince Philip's Arrival, 1971 Visit — A36

Designs: 20c, Chair of homage. 50c, The enthronement.

**1977, Feb. 6 *Perf. 13***

| | | | | |
|---|---|---|---|---|
| *160* | A36 | 8c sil & multi | 30 | 28 |
| *161* | A36 | 20c sil & multi | 75 | 65 |
| *162* | A36 | 50c sil & multi | 1.75 | 1.65 |

25th anniv. of the reign of Elizabeth II.

Building Longboat A37

Designs: 1c, Man ringing Island Bell (vert.). 5c, Landing cargo. 6c, Sorting supplies. 9c, Cleaning wahoo (fish; vert.). 10c, Farming. 15c, Sugar mill. 20c, Women grating coconuts and bananas. 35c, Island church. 50c, Gathering miro logs, Henderson Island. 70c, Burning obsolete stamps (vert.). $1, Prince Philip and "Britannia." $2, Elizabeth II (vert.).

**1977, Sept. 12 Litho. *Perf. 14½***

| | | | | |
|---|---|---|---|---|
| *163* | A37 | 1c multi | 5 | 5 |
| *164* | A37 | 2c multi | 5 | 5 |
| *165* | A37 | 5c multi | 6 | 6 |
| *166* | A37 | 6c multi | 8 | 8 |
| *167* | A37 | 9c multi | 12 | 12 |
| *168* | A37 | 10c multi | 14 | 14 |
| *168A* | A37 | 15c multi ('81) | 22 | 22 |
| *169* | A37 | 20c multi | 28 | 28 |
| *170* | A37 | 35c multi | 50 | 50 |
| *171* | A37 | 50c multi | 70 | 70 |
| *171A* | A37 | 70c multi ('81) | 95 | 95 |
| *172* | A37 | $1 multi | 1.40 | 1.40 |
| *173* | A37 | $2 multi | 2.75 | 2.75 |
| | | *Nos. 163-173 (13)* | 7.30 | 7.30 |

Nos. 168A, 171A issued Oct. 1, 1981.

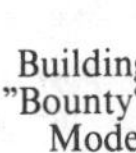

Building "Bounty" Model A38

Designs: 20c, Bounty model afloat. 35c, Burning Bounty.

**1978, Jan. 9 *Perf. 14½***

| | | | | |
|---|---|---|---|---|
| *174* | A38 | 6c yel & multi | 28 | 24 |
| *175* | A38 | 20c yel & multi | 1.25 | 1.00 |
| *176* | A38 | 35c yel & multi | 2.00 | 1.90 |
| *a.* | | Souvenir sheet of 3 | 11.00 | 10.00 |

Bounty Day. No. 176a contains one each of Nos. 174-176; yellow and multicolored margin shows Bounty and design description. Size: 167x121mm.

Souvenir Sheet

Elizabeth II in Coronation Regalia — A39

**Wmk. 373**

**1978, Sept. Litho. *Perf. 12***
*177* A39 $1.20 sil & multi 6.50 5.00

25th anniversary of coronation of Queen Elizabeth II. No. 177 has multicolored margin showing Queen with Bishops and Prince Philip. Size: 94x79mm.

Unloading "Sir Geraint" A40

Designs: 15c, Harbor before development. 30c, Work on the jetty. 35c, Harbor after development.

**Wmk. 373**

**1978, Dec. 18 Litho. *Perf. 13½***
*178* A40 15c multi 32 32
*179* A40 20c multi 50 50
*180* A40 30c multi 85 85
*181* A40 35c multi 1.00 1.00

Development of new harbor on Pitcairn.

John Adams A41

Design: 70c, John Adams' grave.

**1979, Mar. 5 Litho. *Perf. 14½***
*182* A41 35c multi 90 90
*183* A41 70c multi 1.75 1.75

John Adams (1760-1829), founder of Pitcairn Colony, 150th death anniversary.

Pitcairn Island Seen from "Amphitrite" – A42

Engravings (c. 1850): 9c, Bounty Bay and Pitcairn Village. 20c, Lookout Ridge. 70c, Church and schoolhouse.

**1979, Sept. 12 Litho. *Perf. 14***
*184* A42 6c multi 16 16
*185* A42 9c multi 24 24
*186* A42 20c multi 48 48
*187* A42 70c multi 1.65 1.65

Taking Presents to the Square, IYC Emblem – A43

IYC Emblem and Children's Drawings: 9c, Decorating trees with presents. 20c, Distributing presents. 35c, Carrying the presents home.

**Wmk. 373**

**1979, Nov. 28 Litho. *Perf. 13½***
*188* A43 6c multi 16 16
*189* A43 9c multi 24 24
*190* A43 20c multi 55 55
*191* A43 35c multi 1.00 1.00
*a.* Souvenir sheet of 4 3.75 3.75

Christmas 1979 and International Year of the Child. No. 191a contains Nos. 188-191; multicolored margin shows presents and story of local Christmas tradition. Size: 198x73mm.

Souvenir Sheet

Mail Transport by Longboat – A44

**Wmk. 373**

**1980, May 6 Litho. *Perf. 14½***
*192* Sheet of 4 2.25 2.25
*a.* A44 35c *shown* 55 55
*b.* A44 35c *Mail crane lift* 55 55
*c.* A44 35c *Tractor transport* 55 55
*d.* A44 35c *Arrival at post office* 55 55

London 80 Intl. Phil. Exhib., May 6-14. Margin inscribed with mail handling steps, London 80 emblem. Size: 121x135mm.

**Queen Mother Elizabeth Birthday Issue**

Common Design Type

**Wmk. 373**

**1980, Aug. 4 Litho. *Perf. 14***
*193* CD330 50c multi 1.25 1.25

Handicraft Type of 1968

***Perf. 14½x14, 14x14½***

**1980, Sept. 29 Litho. Wmk. 373**
*194* A19 9c *Turtles* 16 16
*195* A19 20c *Wheelbarrow* 38 38
*196* A19 35c *Gannet*, vert. 65 65
*197* A19 40c *Bonnet and fan*, vert. 75 75

Big George A45

**Wmk. 373**

**1981, Jan. 22 Litho. *Perf. 14***
*198* A45 6c *View of Adamstown* 10 10
*199* A45 9c *shown* 15 15
*200* A45 20c *Christian's Cave, Gannet's Ridge* 35 35
*201* A45 35c *Pawala Valley Ridge* 60 60
*202* A45 70c *Tatrimoa* 1.25 1.25
*Nos. 198-202 (5)* 2.45 2.45

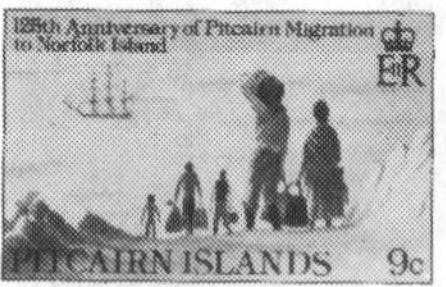


Citizens Departing for Norfolk Island A46

**1981, May 3 Photo. *Perf. 13x14½***
*203* A46 9c shown 18 18
*204* A46 35c Norfolk Isld. from Morayshire 75 75
*205* A46 70c Morayshire 1.50 1.50

Migration to Norfolk Island, 125th anniversary.

**Royal Wedding Issue**

Common Design Type

**Wmk. 373**

**1981, July 22 Litho. *Perf. 14***
*206* CD331 20c Bouquet 28 28
*207* CD331 35c Charles 50 50
*208* CD331 $1.20 Couple 1.65 1.65

Lemon A47

**1982, Feb. 23 Litho. *Perf. 14½***
*209* A47 9c shown 22 22
*210* A47 20c Pomegranate 50 50
*211* A47 35c Avocado 90 90
*212* A47 70c Pawpaw 1.80 1.80

**Princess Diana Issue**

Common Design Type

**1982, July 1 Litho. *Perf. 14½x14***
*213* CD333 6c Arms 9 9
*214* CD333 9c Diana 14 14
*215* CD333 70c Wedding 1.10 1.10
*216* CD333 $1.20 Portrait 1.75 1.75

Christmas 1982 – A48

Designs: Various paintings of angels by Raphael. 50c, $1 vert.

**1982, Oct. 19 Litho. *Perf. 14***
*217* A48 15c multi 22 22
*218* A48 20c multi 28 28
*219* A48 50c multi 70 70
*220* A48 $1 multi 1.40 1.40

**Commonwealth Day**

Common Design Type

**1983, Mar. 14**
*221* CD334 6c Radio operator 8 8
*222* CD334 9c Postal clerk 12 12
*223* CD334 70c Fisherman 85 85
*224* CD334 $1.20 Artist 1.50 1.50

175th Anniv. of Capt. Folger's Discovery of the Settlers A49

**Wmk. 373**

**1983, June 14 Litho. *Perf. 14***
*225* A49 6c Topaz off Pitcairn Isld. 9 9
*226* A49 20c Topaz, islanders 30 30
*227* A49 70c John Adams welcoming Folger 1.10 1.10
*228* A49 $1.20 Presentation of Chronometer 1.75 1.75

Local Trees A50

**1983, Oct. 6 Litho. *Perf. 13½***
*229* Pair 1.25 1.25
*a.* A50 35c Hattie 60 60
*b.* A50 35c Branch, wood painting 60 60
*230* Pair 2.25 2.25
*a.* A50 70c Pandanus 1.10 1.10
*b.* A50 70c Branch, basket weaving 1.10 1.10

See Nos. 289-290.

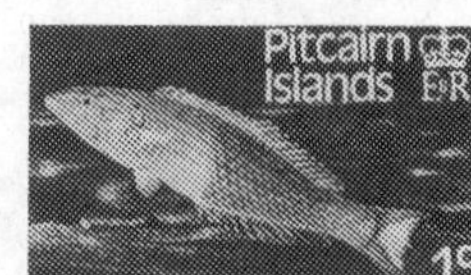


Pseudojuloides Atavai – A51

**Wmk. 373**

**1984, Jan. 11 Litho. *Perf. 14½***
*231* A51 1c shown 5 5
*232* A51 4c Halichoeres melasmapomus 6 6
*233* A51 6c Scarus longipinis 8 8
*234* A51 9c Variola louti 12 12
*235* A51 10c Centropyge hotumatua 14 14
*236* A51 15c Stegastes emeryi 22 22
*237* A51 20c Chaetodon smithi 28 28
*238* A51 35c Xanthichthys mento 50 50
*239* A51 50c Chrysiptera galba 70 70
*240* A51 70c Genicanthus spinus 95 95
*241* A51 $1 Myripristis tiki 1.10 1.10
*242* A51 $1.20 Anthias ventralis 1.10 1.10
*243* A51 $2 Pseudocaranx dentex 2.25 2.25
*Nos. 231-243 (13)* 7.55 7.55

See Nos. 295-296.

Constellations – A52

**Wmk. 373**

**1984, May 14 Litho. *Perf. 14***
*244* A52 15c Crux Australis 25 25
*245* A52 20c Piscis Australis 35 35
*246* A52 70c Canis Minor 1.25 1.25
*247* A52 $1 Virgo 1.75 1.75

Souvenir Sheet

AUSIPEX '84 – A53

Longboats.

**1984, Sept. 21 Litho. Wmk. 373**
*248* Sheet of 2 4.00 4.00
*a.* A53 50c multi 75 75
*b.* A53 $2 multi 3.25 3.25

Multicolored margin shows emblem, shipbuilding. Size:

HMS Portland off Bounty Bay, by J. Linton Palmer, 1853 – A54

Paintings by J. Linton Palmer, 1853, and William Smyth, 1825: 9c, Christian's Look Out at Pitcairn Island. 35c, The Golden Age. $2, View of Village, by Smyth.

**Wmk. 373**

**1985, Jan. 16 Litho. *Perf. 14***
*249* A54 6c multi 6 6
*250* A54 9c multi 8 8
*251* A54 35c multi 48 48

**Size: 48x32mm.**

*252* A54 $2 multi 2.75 2.75

See Nos. 291-294.

**Queen Mother 85th Birthday**

Common Design Type

***Perf. 14½x14***

**1985, June 7 Litho. Wmk. 384**
*253* CD336 6c In Dundee, 1964 6 6
*254* CD336 35c At 80th birthday celebration 28 28
*255* CD336 70c Queen Mother 55 55
*256* CD336 $1.20 Holding Prince Henry 1.00 1.00

**Souvenir Sheet**

257 CD336 $2 In coach at the Races, Ascot 1.65 1.65

No. 257 has multicolored margin continuing design. Size: 92x74mm.

Act 6 — A55

Essi Gina A56

**1985, Aug. 28** ***Perf. 14½x14***

258 A55 50c shown 80 80
259 A55 50c Columbus Louisiana 80 80

***Perf. 14***

260 A56 50c shown 80 80
261 A56 50c Stolt Spirit 80 80

See Nos. 281-284.

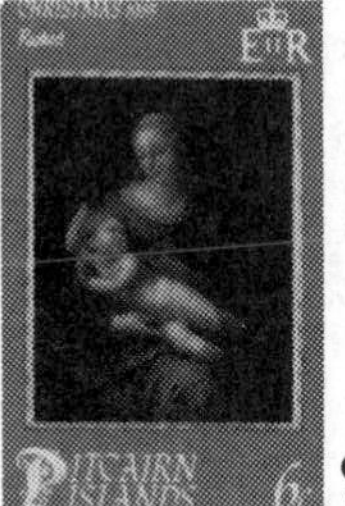
Christmas 1985 — A57

Madonna & child paintings: 6c, By Raphael. 9c, By Krause. 35c, By Andreas Mayer. $2, By an unknown Austrian master.

**1985, Nov. 26** ***Perf. 14***

262 A57 6c multi 8 8
263 A57 9c multi 10 10
264 A57 35c multi 45 45
265 A57 $2 multi 2.50 2.50

Turtles A58

Designs: 9c, 20c, Chelonia mydas. 70c, $1.20, Eretmochelys imbricata.

**Wmk. 384**

**1986, Feb. 12** **Litho.** ***Perf. 14½***

266 A58 9c multi 10 10
267 A58 20c multi, diff. 28 28
268 A58 70c multi 1.00 1.00
269 A58 $1.20 multi, diff. 1.90 1.90

**Queen Elizabeth II 60th Birthday**
Common Design Type

Designs: 6c, In Royal Lodge garden, Windsor, 1946. 9c, Wedding of Princess Anne and Capt. Mark Philips, 1973. 20c, Wearing mantle and robes of Order of St. Paul's Cathedral, 1961. $1.20, Concert, Royal Festival Hall, London, 1971. $2, Visting Crown Agents' offices, 1983.

**1986, Apr. 21** **Litho.** ***Perf. 14½***

270 CD337 6c scar, blk & sil 8 8
271 CD337 9c ultra & multi 12 12
272 CD337 20c grn & multi 24 24
273 CD337 $1.20 vio & multi 1.45 1.45
274 CD337 $2 rose vio & multi 2.40 2.40
Nos. 270-274 (5) 4.29 4.29

**Royal Wedding Issue, 1986**
Common Design Type

Designs: 20c, Informal portrait. $1.20, Andrew aboard royal navy vessel.

**Wmk. 384**

**1986, July 23** **Litho.** ***Perf. 14***

275 CD338 20c multi 32 32
276 CD338 $1.20 multi 2.00 2.00

7th Day Adventist Church, Cent. — A59

Designs: 6c, First church, 1886, and John I. Tay, missionary. 20c, Second church, 1907, and mission ship Pitcairn, 1890. 35c, Third church, 1945, baptism and Down Isaac. $2, Church, 1954, and sailing ship.

**Wmk. 384**

**1986, Oct. 18** **Litho.** ***Perf. 14***

277 A59 6c multi 6 6
278 A59 20c multi 22 22
279 A59 35c multi 38 38
280 A59 $2 multi 2.15 2.15

Ship Type of 1985

***Perf. 14x14½***

**1987, Jan. 20** **Litho.** **Wmk. 384**

281 A55 50c Brussel 70 70
282 A55 50c Samoan Reefer 70 70

***Perf. 14***

283 A56 50c Australian Exporter 70 70
284 A56 50c Taupo 70 70

Island Houses — A60

**1987, May 21** **Wmk. 373** ***Perf. 14***

285 A60 70c lt greenish blue, bluish grn & blk 70 70
286 A60 70c cream, yel bister & blk 70 70
287 A60 70c lt blue, brt blue & blk 70 70
288 A60 70c lt lil, brt vio & blk 70 70

Tree Type of 1983

**1987, Aug. 10** **Wmk. 384** ***Perf. 14½***

289 Pair 80 80
a. A50 40c Leaves, blossoms 40 40
b. A50 40c Monkey puzzle tree 40 40
290 Pair 3.50 3.50
a. A50 $1.80 Leaves, blossoms, nuts 1.75 1.75
b. A50 $1.80 Duduinut tree 1.75 1.75

Art Type of 1985

Paintings by Lt. Conway Shipley, 1848: 20c, House and Tomb of John Adams. 40c, Bounty Bay, with H.M.S. Calypso. 90c, School House and Chapel. $1.80, Pitcairn Island with H.M.S. Calypso.

**1987, Dec. 7** **Litho.** ***Perf. 14***

291 A54 20c multi 20 20
292 A54 40c multi 40 40
293 A54 90c multi 95 95

**Size: 48x32mm**

294 A54 $1.80 multi 1.75 1.75

Fish Type of 1984

**Wmk. 384**

**1988, Jan. 14** **Litho.** ***Perf. 14½***

295 A51 90c Variola louti 1.15 1.15
296 A51 $3 Gymnothorax eurostus 3.75 3.75

Souvenir Sheet

Australia Bicentennial — A61

**1988, May 9** **Wmk. 384** ***Perf. 14***

297 A61 $3 HMS *Bounty* replica under sail 4.00 4.00

No. 297 has inscribed multicolored margin picturing Pacific map of Australia and the Pitcairn Islands. Size: 112x75mm.

Visiting Ships — A62

**Wmk. 373**

**1988, Aug. 14** **Litho.** ***Perf. 13½***

298 A62 5c HMS *Swallow*, 1767 6 6
299 A62 10c HMS *Pandora*, 1791 14 14
300 A62 15c HMS *Briton* and HMS *Tagus*, 1814 20 20
301 A62 20c HMS *Blossom*, 1825 28 28
302 A62 30c S.V. *Lucy Anne*, 1831 40 40
303 A62 35c S.V. *Charles Doggett*, 1831 48 48
304 A62 40c HMS *Fly*, 1838 55 55
305 A62 60c LMS *Camden*, 1840 82 82
306 A62 90c HMS *Virago*, 1853 1.25 1.25
307 A62 $1.20 S.S. *Rakaia*, 1867 1.65 1.65
308 A62 $1.80 HMS *Sappho*, 1882 2.45 2.45
309 A62 $5 HMS *Champion*, 1893 6.75 6.75
Nos. 298-309 (12) 15.03 15.03

Constitution, 150th Anniv. — A63

Text and: 20c, Raising the Union Jack. 40c, Signing of the constitution aboard the H.M.S. "Fly," 1838. $1.05, Suffrage. $1.80, Equal education.

**Wmk. 373**

**1988, Nov. 30** **Litho.** ***Perf. 14***

315 A63 20c multi 25 25
316 A63 40c multi 50 50
317 A63 $1.05 multi 1.35 1.35
318 A63 $1.80 multi 2.30 2.30

Christmas A64

Designs: a, Angel, animals in stable. b, Holy Family. c, Two Magi. d, Magus and shepherd boy.

**1988, Nov. 30** **Wmk. 384** ***Perf. 14***

319 Strip of 4 4.60 4.60
a.-d. A64 90c any single 1.15 1.15

## PRINCE EDWARD ISLAND

LOCATION — In the Gulf of St. Lawrence, opposite the provinces of New Brunswick and Nova Scotia.
GOVT. — A former British Crown Colony.
AREA — 2,184 sq. mi.
POP. — 92,000 (estimated).
CAPITAL — Charlottetown.

Originally annexed to Nova Scotia, Prince Edward Island was a separate colony from 1769 to 1873, when it became a part of the Canadian Confederation. Postage stamps of Canada are now used.

12 Pence = 1 Shilling
100 Cents = 1 Dollar (1872)

A1

A2

Queen Victoria — A3

**1861, Jan. 1** **Unwmk.** **Typo.** ***Perf. 9***

1 A1 2p dull rose 350.00 175.00
a. 2p deep rose 350.00 175.00
b. Rouletted *2,000.*
c. Horiz. pair, imperf. between *7,500.*
d. Diagonal half used as 1p on cover *1,500.*
2 A2 3p blue 400.00 225.00
a. Diagonal half used as 1½p on cover
b. Double impression 1,500.
3 A3 6p yel green 600.00 300.00

A4

A5

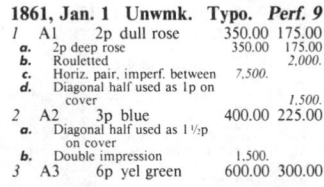

***Perf. 11, 11½, 12 and Compound***

**1862-65**

**White or Yellowish Paper**

4 A4 1p yellow org 12.00 12.00
a. 1p brown orange 12.00 12.00
b. Imperf., pair 150.00
c. Half used as ½p on cover *750.00*
5 A1 2p rose 3.50 3.50
a. Yellowish paper 3.50 3.50
b. Imperf., pair 75.00
c. Horiz. pair, imperf. vert. 125.00
d. Vert. pair, imperf. horiz. 125.00
e. Diagonal half used as 1p on cover *1,500.*
f. "TWC" for "TWO" 24.00 15.00

| | | | | |
|---|---|---|---|---|
| 6 | A2 | 3p blue | 4.75 | 4.75 |
| a. | | Yellowish paper | 6.50 | 4.75 |
| b. | | Imperf., pair | 90.00 | |
| c. | | Vert. pair, imperf. horiz. | 150.00 | |
| d. | | Diagonal half used as 1½p on cover | | 200.00 |
| 7 | A3 | 6p yel green | 30.00 | 30.00 |
| a. | | 6p blue green | 30.00 | 30.00 |
| b. | | Imperf. | | |
| c. | | Diagonal half used as 3p on cover | | |
| 8 | A5 | 9p violet | 21.00 | 21.00 |
| a. | | Imperf., pair | 200.00 | 200.00 |
| b. | | Horiz. pair, imperf. vert. | 200.00 | |
| c. | | Diagonal half used as 4½p on cover | | 1,500. |

Queen Victoria
A6 A7

**1868**

| | | | | |
|---|---|---|---|---|
| 9 | A6 | 4p black | 4.75 | 9.50 |
| a. | | Yellowish paper | 7.50 | 10.50 |
| b. | | Horiz. pair, imperf. vert. | 75.00 | |
| c. | | Diagonal half used as 2p on cover | | 1,000. |
| d. | | Imperf., pair | 60.00 | |
| e. | | Horiz. pair, imperf. between | 75.00 | |

**1870, June 1 Engr. *Perf. 12***

| | | | | |
|---|---|---|---|---|
| 10 | A7 | 4½p brown | 18.00 | 22.50 |

A8

A9

THREE CENTS
A10

FOUR CENTS
A11

POSTAGE
SIX CENTS
A12

A13

**1872, Jan. 1 Typo. *Perf. 12, 12½***

| | | | | |
|---|---|---|---|---|
| 11 | A8 | 1c brn orange | 2.50 | 3.00 |
| a. | | Imperf., pair | 75.00 | |
| 12 | A9 | 2c ultra | 6.00 | 12.00 |
| a. | | Imperf., pair | 125.00 | |
| b. | | Diagonal half used as 1c on cover | | |
| 13 | A10 | 3c rose | 12.00 | 7.75 |
| a. | | Imperf., pair | 125.00 | |
| b. | | Diagonal half used as 1½c on cover | | |
| c. | | Horiz. or vert. pair, imperf. between | 175.00 | |
| 14 | A11 | 4c green | 2.50 | 9.00 |
| a. | | Imperf., pair | 100.00 | |
| 15 | A12 | 6c black | 2.50 | 9.00 |
| a. | | Horiz. pair, imperf. btwn. | 100.00 | |
| b. | | Half used as 3c on cover | | 600.00 |
| 16 | A13 | 12c violet | 2.50 | 12.00 |
| a. | | Imperf., pair | 100.00 | |
| b. | | Half used as 6c on cover | | |
| | | *Nos. 11-16 (6)* | 28.00 | 52.75 |

The stamps of Prince Edward Island have been superseded by those of Canada.

---

# QATAR

LOCATION — A peninsula in eastern Arabia.
GOVT. — Independent state.
AREA — 4,575 sq. mi.
POP. — 260,000 (est. 1982).
CAPITAL — Doha.

Qatar was a British protected sheikdom until September 1, 1971, when it declared its independence.

Stamps of Muscat were used until 1957.

100 Naye Paise = 1 Rupee
100 Dirhams = 1 Riyal (1967)

**Catalogue values for all unused stamps in this country are for Never Hinged items.**

Great Britain Nos. 317-325, 328, 332-333 and 309-311 Surcharged "QATAR" and New Value in Black.

***Perf. 14½x14***

**1957, Apr. 1 Photo. Wmk. 308**

| | | | | |
|---|---|---|---|---|
| 1 | A129 | 1np on 5p lt brn | 5 | 5 |
| 2 | A126 | 3np on ½p red org | 10 | 8 |
| 3 | A126 | 6np on 1p ultra | 12 | 10 |
| 4 | A126 | 9np on 1½p grn | 12 | 10 |
| 5 | A126 | 12np on 2p red brn | 20 | 10 |
| 6 | A127 | 15np on 2½p scar | 24 | 20 |
| 7 | A127 | 20np on 3p dk pur | 25 | 20 |
| 8 | A128 | 25np on 4p ultra | 50 | 45 |
| 9 | A129 | 40np on 6p lil rose | 50 | 45 |
| 10 | A130 | 50np on 9p dp ol grn | 1.00 | 50 |
| 11 | A132 | 75np on 1sh3p dk grn | 2.75 | 1.00 |
| 12 | A131 | 1r on 1sh6p dk bl | 3.50 | 1.00 |

**Engr. *Perf. 11x12.***

| | | | | |
|---|---|---|---|---|
| 13 | A133 | 2r on 2sh6p dk brn | 7.00 | 2.25 |
| 14 | A133 | 5r on 5sh crim | 16.00 | 6.50 |
| 15 | A133 | 10r on 10sh brt ultra | 35.00 | 13.50 |
| | | *Nos. 1-15 (15)* | 67.33 | 26.48 |

Both typeset and stereotyped overprints were used on Nos. 13-15. The typeset have bars close together and thick, bold letters. The stereotyped have bars wider apart and thinner letters.

**Scout Jamboree Issue**

Great Britain Nos. 334-336 Surcharged "QATAR," New Value and Square of Dots in Black

***Perf. 14½x14***

**1957, Aug. 1 Photo. Wmk. 308**

| | | | | |
|---|---|---|---|---|
| 16 | A138 | 15np on 2½p scar | 50 | 35 |
| 17 | A138 | 25np on 4p ultra | 1.00 | 75 |
| 18 | A138 | 75np on 1sh3p dk grn | 1.50 | 1.25 |

50th anniv. of the Boy Scout movement and the World Scout Jubilee Jamboree, Aug. 1-12.

Great Britain Nos. 353-358, 362 Surcharged "QATAR" and New Value.

**1960 Wmk. 322 *Perf. 14½x14***

| | | | | |
|---|---|---|---|---|
| 19 | A126 | 3np on ½p red org | 90 | 2.00 |
| 20 | A126 | 6np on 1p ultra | 1.50 | 3.00 |
| 21 | A126 | 9np on 1½p grn | 1.25 | 1.25 |
| 22 | A126 | 12np on 2p red brn | 6.00 | 10.00 |
| 23 | A127 | 15np on 2½p scar | 40 | 35 |
| 24 | A127 | 20np on 3p dk pur | 40 | 35 |
| 25 | A129 | 40np on 6p lil rose | 1.00 | 60 |
| | | *Nos. 19-25 (7)* | 11.45 | 17.55 |

Sheik Ahmad bin Ali al Thani — A1

Peregrine Falcon — A2

Oil Derrick — A3

Designs: 75np, Dhow. 5r, 10r, Mosque.

***Perf. 14½***

**1961, Sept. 2 Unwmk. Photo.**

| | | | | |
|---|---|---|---|---|
| 26 | A1 | 5np rose car | 5 | 5 |
| 27 | A1 | 15np brn blk | 10 | 8 |
| 28 | A1 | 20np claret | 14 | 10 |
| 29 | A1 | 30np dp grn | 20 | 15 |
| 30 | A2 | 40np red | 30 | 12 |
| 31 | A2 | 50np sepia | 40 | 30 |
| 32 | A2 | 75np ultra | 60 | 40 |

**Engr. *Perf. 13***

| | | | | |
|---|---|---|---|---|
| 33 | A3 | 1r rose red | 70 | 40 |
| 34 | A3 | 2r blue | 1.40 | 1.00 |
| 35 | A3 | 5r green | 3.50 | 2.50 |
| 36 | A3 | 10r black | 7.50 | 4.50 |
| | | *Nos. 26-36 (11)* | 14.89 | 9.60 |

Nos. 31-32, 34-36 Overprinted or Surcharged

**1964, Oct. 25 Photo. *Perf. 14½***

| | | | | |
|---|---|---|---|---|
| 37 | A2 | 50np sepia | 75 | 1.00 |
| 38 | A2 | 75np ultra | 1.00 | 1.50 |

**Engr. *Perf. 13***

| | | | | |
|---|---|---|---|---|
| 39 | A3 | 1r on 10r black | 2.00 | 1.50 |
| 40 | A3 | 2r blue | 4.75 | 3.00 |
| 41 | A3 | 5r green | 11.00 | 7.00 |
| | | *Nos. 37-41 (5)* | 19.50 | 14.00 |

18th Olympic Games, Tokyo, Oct. 10-25.

Nos. 31-32, 34-36 with Typographed Overprint or Surcharge

John F. Kennedy
1917 - 1963

**1964, Nov. 22 Photo. *Perf. 14½***

| | | | | |
|---|---|---|---|---|
| 42 | A2 | 50np sepia | 70 | 50 |
| 43 | A2 | 75np ultra | 90 | 75 |

**Engr. *Perf. 13***

| | | | | |
|---|---|---|---|---|
| 44 | A3 | 1r on 10r blk | 1.75 | 1.50 |
| 45 | A3 | 2r blue | 4.25 | 4.00 |
| 46 | A3 | 5r green | 10.00 | 8.25 |
| | | *Nos. 42-46 (5)* | 17.60 | 15.00 |

Pres. John F. Kennedy (1917-63).

Column — A4

Designs: 2np, 1.50r, Isis Temple and Colonnade, Philae. 3np, 1r, Trajan's kiosk, Philae.

***Perf. 14½x14***

**1965, Jan. 17 Photo. Unwmk.**

| | | | | |
|---|---|---|---|---|
| 47 | A4 | 1np multi | 50 | 5 |
| 48 | A4 | 2np multi | 50 | 5 |
| 49 | A4 | 3np multi | 50 | 5 |
| 50 | A4 | 1r multi | 75 | 40 |
| 51 | A4 | 1.50r multi | 1.40 | 60 |
| 52 | A4 | 2r multi | 50 | 50 |
| | | *Nos. 47-52 (6)* | 4.15 | 1.65 |

UNESCO world campaign to save historic monuments in Nubia.

Qatar Scout Emblem, Tents and Sheik Ahmad — A5

Scouts Saluting and Sheik Ahmad — A6

Designs: 1np, 4np, Qatar scout emblem.

***Perf. 14 (A5), 14½x14 (A6)***

**1965, May 22 Photo. Unwmk.**

| | | | | |
|---|---|---|---|---|
| 53 | A5 | 1np ol grn & dk red brn | 20 | 5 |
| 54 | A5 | 2np sal & dk vio bl | 20 | 5 |
| 55 | A5 | 3np dk vio bl & grn | 20 | 5 |
| 56 | A5 | 4np bl & dk red brn | 20 | 5 |
| 57 | A5 | 5np dk vio bl & grnsh bl | 20 | 5 |
| 58 | A6 | 30np multi | 65 | 45 |
| 59 | A6 | 40np multi | 80 | 60 |
| 60 | A6 | 1r multi | 2.00 | 1.25 |
| | | *Nos. 53-60 (8)* | 4.45 | 2.55 |

Issued to honor the Qatar Boy Scouts. Perf. and imperf. souvenir sheets contain one each of Nos. 58-60 with red brown marginal inscription. Size: 108x76mm.

Eiffel Tower, Telstar, ITU Emblem and "Qatar" in Morse Code — A7

Designs: 2np, 1r, Tokyo Olympic Games emblem and Syncom III. 3np, 40np, Radar tracking station and Relay satellite. 4np, 50np, Post Office Tower, London, and Echo II, Syncom III, Telstar and Relay satellites around globe.

***Perf. 13½x14***

**1965, Oct. 16 Photo. Unwmk.**

| | | | | |
|---|---|---|---|---|
| 61 | A7 | 1np dk bl & red brn | 20 | 5 |
| 62 | A7 | 2np bl & dk red brn | 20 | 5 |
| 63 | A7 | 3np dp yel grn & brt pur | 20 | 5 |
| 64 | A7 | 4np org brn & brt bl | 20 | 5 |
| 65 | A7 | 5np dl vio & dk ol bis | 20 | 5 |
| 66 | A7 | 40np dk car rose & blk | 60 | 40 |
| 67 | A7 | 50np sl grn & bis | 75 | 50 |
| 68 | A7 | 1r emer & car | 1.50 | 1.00 |
| a | | Souv. sheet of 2 | 5.00 | 3.50 |
| | | *Nos. 61-68 (8)* | 3.85 | 2.15 |

Cent. of the ITU. No. 68a contains one each of Nos. 67-68. Black marginal inscription. Size: 88½x88½mm. Sheet also exists imperf.

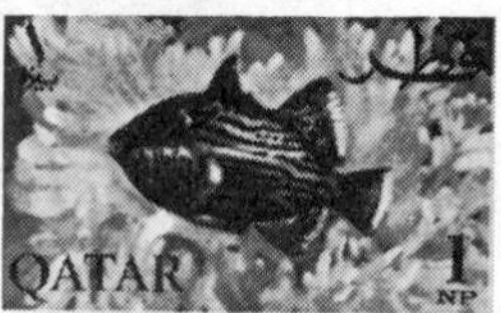


Triggerfish — A8

Various Fish, including: 2np, 50np, Clown grunt. 2np, 10r, Saddleback butterflyfish. 4np, 5r, Butterflyfish. 15np, 3r, Paradisefish. 20np, 1r, Rio Grande perch. 75np, Triggerfish.

**1965, Oct. 18 *Perf. 14x14½***

| | | | | |
|---|---|---|---|---|
| 69 | A8 | 1np multi & blk | 6 | 5 |
| 70 | A8 | 2np multi & blk | 6 | 5 |
| 71 | A8 | 3np multi & blk | 6 | 5 |
| 72 | A8 | 4np multi & blk | 8 | 5 |
| 73 | A8 | 5np multi & blk | 8 | 5 |
| 74 | A8 | 15np multi & blk | 20 | 9 |
| 75 | A8 | 20np multi & blk | 25 | 15 |
| 76 | A8 | 30np multi & blk | 30 | 22 |
| 77 | A8 | 40np multi & blk | 40 | 25 |
| 78 | A8 | 50np multi & gold | 50 | 35 |
| 79 | A8 | 75np multi & gold | 80 | 50 |
| 80 | A8 | 1r multi & gold | 1.00 | 65 |
| 81 | A8 | 2r multi & gold | 2.25 | 1.25 |
| 82 | A8 | 3r multi & gold | 3.25 | 1.90 |
| 83 | A8 | 4r multi & gold | 4.00 | 2.50 |

| | | | | |
|---|---|---|---|---|
| *84* | A8 | 5r multi & gold | 6.00 | 3.50 |
| *85* | A8 | 10r multi & gold | 12.50 | 6.50 |
| | | *Nos. 69-85 (17)* | 31.79 | 18.11 |

Basketball — A9

Sports: No. 87, Horse jumping. No. 88, Running. No. 89, Soccer. No. 90, Weight lifting.

**1966, Jan. 10 Photo. *Perf. 11½***

**Granite Paper**

| | | | | |
|---|---|---|---|---|
| *86* | A9 | 1r gray, blk & dk red | 1.00 | 60 |
| *87* | A9 | 1r brn & ol grn | 1.00 | 60 |
| *88* | A9 | 1r dl rose & bl | 1.00 | 60 |
| *89* | A9 | 1r grn & blk | 1.00 | 60 |
| *90* | A9 | 1r bl & brn | 1.00 | 60 |
| | | *Nos. 86-90 (5)* | 5.00 | 3.00 |

4th Pan Arab Games, Cairo, Sept. 2-11. Nos. 86-90 are printed in one sheet of 25 in horizontal rows of five.

Nos. 61-68 Overprinted

**1966, Feb. 9 Photo. *Perf. 13½x14***

| | | | | |
|---|---|---|---|---|
| *91* | A7 | 1np dk bl & red brn | 12 | 5 |
| *92* | A7 | 2np bl & dk red brn | 12 | 5 |
| *93* | A7 | 3np dp yel grn & brt pur | 12 | 5 |
| *94* | A7 | 4np org brn & brt bl | 12 | 5 |
| *95* | A7 | 5np dl vio & dk ol bis | 12 | 5 |
| *96* | A7 | 40np dk car rose & blk | 45 | 25 |
| *97* | A7 | 50np sl grn & bis | 50 | 30 |
| *98* | A7 | 1r emer & car | 1.00 | 60 |
| | | *Nos. 91-98 (8)* | 2.55 | 1.40 |

Issued to commemorate the rendezvous in space of Gemini 6 and 7, Dec. 15, 1965.

John F. Kennedy, U.N. Headquarters, N.Y., and ICY Emblem — A10

Designs (ICY emblem and): No. 99, U.N. emblem. No. 101, Dag Hammarskjold and U.N. General Assembly. No. 102, Jawaharlal Nehru and dove.

**1966, Mar. 8 *Perf. 11½***

**Granite Paper**

| | | | | |
|---|---|---|---|---|
| *99* | A10 | 40np brt bl, vio bl & red brn | 1.50 | 1.00 |
| *100* | A10 | 40np brt grn, vio & brn | 1.50 | 1.00 |
| *101* | A10 | 40np red brn, brt bl & blk | 1.50 | 1.00 |
| *102* | A10 | 40np dk vio & brt grn | 1.50 | 1.00 |

Issued to commemorate the United Nations International Cooperation Year, 1965. Nos. 99-102 are printed se-tenant in blocks of four in sheets of 16 with wide gutters between the blocks. Nos. 99-100 se-tenant in one horizontal row and Nos. 101-102 se-tenant in next horizontal row.

An imperf. souvenir sheet of 4 contains one each of Nos. 99-102.

Arab Postal Union Emblem A11

Traffic Light and Intersection A12

**1967, Apr. 15 Photo. *Perf. 11x11½***

| | | | | |
|---|---|---|---|---|
| *103* | A11 | 70d mag & sep | 90 | 28 |
| *104* | A11 | 80d dl bl & sep | 1.10 | 32 |

Qatar's joining the Arab Postal Union.

**1967, May 24 Litho. *Perf. 13½***

| | | | | |
|---|---|---|---|---|
| *105* | A12 | 20d vio & multi | 30 | 8 |
| *106* | A12 | 30d multi | 50 | 12 |
| *107* | A12 | 50d multi | 80 | 20 |
| *108* | A12 | 1r ultra & multi | 1.65 | 40 |

Issued for Traffic Day.

Boy Scouts and Sheik Ahmad A13

Designs: 1d, First Boy Scout camp, Brownsea Island, 1907, and tents, Idaho, U.S.A., 1967. 2d, Lord Baden-Powell. 5d, Boy Scout canoeing. 15d, Swimming. 75d, Mountain climbing. 2r, Boy Scout saluting flag and emblem of 12th World Jamboree. 1d and 2d lack head of Sheik Ahmad.

**1967, Sept. 15 Litho. *Perf. 11½x11***

| | | | | |
|---|---|---|---|---|
| *109* | A13 | 1d multi | 35 | 5 |
| *110* | A13 | 2d buff & multi | 35 | 5 |

**Litho. and Engr.**

| | | | | |
|---|---|---|---|---|
| *111* | A13 | 3d rose & multi | 35 | 5 |
| *112* | A13 | 5d lil & multi | 35 | 5 |
| *113* | A13 | 15d multi | 55 | 25 |
| *114* | A13 | 75d grn & multi | 1.10 | 80 |
| *115* | A13 | 2r sep & multi | 5.00 | 3.25 |
| | | *Nos. 109-115 (7)* | 8.05 | 4.50 |

Nos. 109-110 commemorate the 60th anniversary of the Boy Scouts, Nos. 111-115 commemorate the 12th Boy Scout World Jamboree, Farragut State Park, Idaho, Aug. 1-9.

Viking Ship (from Bayeux Tapestry) A14

Famous Ships: 2d, Santa Maria (Columbus). 3d, San Gabriel (Vasco da Gama). 75d, Victoria (Ferdinand Magellan). 1r, Golden Hind (Sir Francis Drake). 2r, Gipsy Moth IV (Sir Francis Chichester).

**1967, Nov. 27 Litho. *Perf. 13½***

| | | | | |
|---|---|---|---|---|
| *116* | A14 | 1d org & multi | 25 | 5 |
| *117* | A14 | 2d lt bl, tan & blk | 25 | 5 |
| *118* | A14 | 3d lt bl & multi | 25 | 5 |
| *119* | A14 | 75d fawn & multi | 80 | 60 |
| *120* | A14 | 1r gray, yel grn & red | 1.50 | 1.25 |
| *121* | A14 | 2r multi | 3.50 | 2.50 |
| | | *Nos. 116-121 (6)* | 6.55 | 4.50 |

Professional Letter Writer — A15

Designs: 2d, Carrier pigeon and man releasing pigeon (vert.). 3d, Postrider. 60d, Mail transport by rowboat (vert.). 1.25r, Mailman riding camel, jet plane and modern buildings. 2r, Qatar No. 1, hand holding pen, paper, envelopes and inkwell.

**1968, Feb. 14**

| | | | | |
|---|---|---|---|---|
| *122* | A15 | 1d multi | 22 | 5 |
| *123* | A15 | 2d multi | 22 | 5 |
| *124* | A15 | 3d multi | 22 | 5 |
| *125* | A15 | 60d multi | 1.10 | 70 |
| *126* | A15 | 1.25r multi | 2.25 | 1.40 |
| *127* | A15 | 2r multi | 3.75 | 2.25 |
| | | *Nos. 122-127 (6)* | 7.76 | 4.50 |

Ten years of Qatar postal service.

Human Rights Flame and Barbed Wire A16

Designs (Human Rights Flame and): 2d, Arab refugee family leaving concentration camp. 3d, Scales of Justice. 60d, Hands opening gates to the sun. 1.25r, Family and sun (vert.). 2r, Stylized family groups.

**1968, Apr. 10**

| | | | | |
|---|---|---|---|---|
| *128* | A16 | 1d gray & multi | 20 | 5 |
| *129* | A16 | 2d multi | 20 | 5 |
| *130* | A16 | 3d brt grn, org & blk | 20 | 5 |
| *131* | A16 | 60d org, brn & blk | 1.00 | 70 |
| *132* | A16 | 1.25r brt grn, blk & yel | 1.75 | 1.40 |
| *133* | A16 | 2r multi | 3.00 | 2.25 |
| | | *Nos. 128-133 (6)* | 6.35 | 4.50 |

International Human Rights Year.

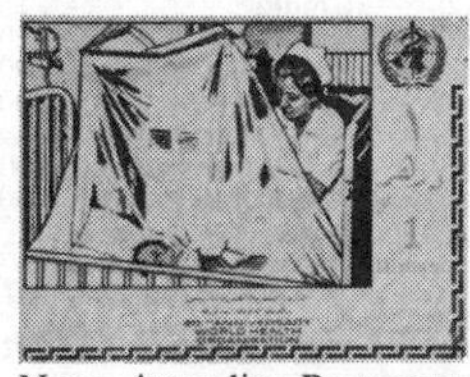

Nurse Attending Premature Baby — A17

Designs (WHO Emblem and): 2d, Operating room. 3d, Dentist. 60d, X-ray examination. 1.25r, Medical laboratory. 2r, State Hospital.

**1968, June 20**

| | | | | |
|---|---|---|---|---|
| *134* | A17 | 1d multi | 20 | 5 |
| *135* | A17 | 2d multi | 20 | 5 |
| *136* | A17 | 3d multi | 20 | 5 |
| *137* | A17 | 60d multi | 1.00 | 70 |
| *138* | A17 | 1.25r multi | 2.00 | 1.40 |
| *139* | A17 | 2r multi | 3.50 | 2.25 |
| | | *Nos. 134-139 (6)* | 7.10 | 4.50 |

Issued to commemorate the 20th anniversary of the World Health Organization.

Olympic Rings and Gymnast A18

Designs (Olympic Rings and): 1d, Discobolus and view of Mexico City. 2d, Runner and flaming torch. 60d, Weight lifting and torch. 1.25r, Olympic flame as a mosaic (vert.). 2r, Mythological bird.

**1968, Aug. 24**

| | | | | |
|---|---|---|---|---|
| *140* | A18 | 1d multi | 18 | 5 |
| *141* | A18 | 2d red yel & dk grn | 18 | 5 |
| *142* | A18 | 3d dk brn gray grn & ocher | 18 | 5 |
| *143* | A18 | 60d org brn pink & bl grn | 90 | 65 |
| *144* | A18 | 1.25r multi | 1.75 | 1.25 |
| *145* | A18 | 2r yel & multi | 3.00 | 2.00 |
| | | *Nos. 140-145 (6)* | 6.19 | 4.05 |

Issued to publicize the 19th Olympic Games, Mexico City, Oct. 12-27.

Sheik Ahmad bin Ali al Thani A19 A21

Dhow A20

Designs: 40d, Desalination plant. 60d, Loading platform and oil tanker. 70d, Qatar Mosque. 1r, Clock Tower, Market Place, Doha. 1.25r, Doha Fort. 1.50r, Falcon.

**1968 Litho. *Perf. 13½***

| | | | | |
|---|---|---|---|---|
| *146* | A19 | 5d bl & grn | 6 | 5 |
| *147* | A19 | 10d brt bl & red brn | 18 | 5 |
| *148* | A19 | 20d blk & ver | 25 | 8 |
| *149* | A19 | 25d brt mag & brt grn | 35 | 12 |

**Lithographed and Engraved**

***Perf. 13***

| | | | | |
|---|---|---|---|---|
| *150* | A20 | 35d grn & brt pink | 55 | 30 |
| *151* | A20 | 40d pur, lt bl & org | 55 | 35 |
| *152* | A20 | 60d lt bl, brn & lil | 80 | 50 |
| *153* | A20 | 70d blk, lt bl & brt grn | 1.00 | 60 |
| *154* | A20 | 1r vio bl, yel & brt grn | 1.40 | 90 |
| *155* | A20 | 1.25r ind, brt bl & ocher | 1.90 | 1.10 |
| *156* | A20 | 1.50r lt bl, dk grn & rose lil | 2.00 | 1.25 |

***Perf. 11½***

| | | | | |
|---|---|---|---|---|
| *157* | A21 | 2r brn, ocher & bl gray | 2.25 | 1.75 |
| *158* | A21 | 5r grn, lt grn & pur | 6.50 | 4.50 |
| *159* | A21 | 10r ultra, lt bl & sep | 19.00 | 9.00 |
| | | *Nos. 146-159 (14)* | 36.79 | 20.55 |

UN Headquarters, NY, and Flags — A22

Designs (UN Emblem and): 1d, Flags. 4d, World map and dove. 60d, Classroom. 1.50r, Farmers, wheat and tractor. 2r, Sec. Gen. U Thant and General Assembly Hall.

**1968, Oct. 24 Litho. *Perf. 13½x13***

| | | | | |
|---|---|---|---|---|
| *160* | A22 | 1d multi | 15 | 5 |
| *161* | A22 | 4d multi | 15 | 5 |
| *162* | A22 | 5d multi | 15 | 5 |
| *163* | A22 | 60d multi | 90 | 55 |
| *164* | A22 | 1.50r multi | 2.00 | 1.25 |
| *165* | A22 | 2r multi | 2.50 | 1.75 |
| | | *Nos. 160-165 (6)* | 5.85 | 3.70 |

United Nations Day, Oct. 24, 1968.

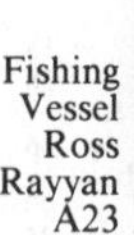

Fishing Vessel Ross Rayyan A23

Progress in Qatar: 4d, Elementary School and children playing. 5d, Doha Intl. Airport. 60d, Cement factory and road building. 1.50r, Power station. 2r, Housing development.

**1969, Jan. 13**

| No. | Type | Description | Unused | Used |
|---|---|---|---|---|
| *166* | A23 | 1d brt bl & multi | 15 | 8 |
| *167* | A23 | 4d grn & multi | 15 | 8 |
| *168* | A23 | 5d dl org & multi | 18 | 10 |
| *169* | A23 | 60d lt brn & multi | 90 | 50 |
| *170* | A23 | 1.50r brt lil & multi | 2.25 | 1.25 |
| *171* | A23 | 2r buff & multi | 2.75 | 1.50 |
| | | *Nos. 166-171 (6)* | 6.38 | 3.51 |

Armored Cars A24

Designs: 2d, Traffic police. 3d, Military helicopter. 60d, Military band. 1.25r, Field gun. 2r, Mounted police.

**1969, May 6 Litho. *Perf. 13½***

| No. | Type | Description | Unused | Used |
|---|---|---|---|---|
| *172* | A24 | 1d multi | 18 | 12 |
| *173* | A24 | 2d lt bl & multi | 18 | 12 |
| *174* | A24 | 3d gray & multi | 18 | 12 |
| *175* | A24 | 60d multi | 75 | 50 |
| *176* | A24 | 1.25r multi | 2.25 | 1.50 |
| *177* | A24 | 2r bl & multi | 3.25 | 2.25 |
| | | *Nos. 172-177 (6)* | 6.79 | 4.61 |

Issued to honor the public security forces.

Oil Tanker A25

Designs: 2d, Research laboratory. 3d, Offshore oil rig and helicopter. 60d, Oil rig and storage tanks. 1.50r, Oil refinery. 2r, Oil tankers, 1890-1968.

**1969, July 4**

| No. | Type | Description | Unused | Used |
|---|---|---|---|---|
| *178* | A25 | 1d gray & multi | 5 | 5 |
| *179* | A25 | 2d ol & multi | 5 | 5 |
| *180* | A25 | 3d ultra & multi | 5 | 5 |
| *181* | A25 | 60d lil & multi | 90 | 60 |
| *182* | A25 | 1.50r red brn & multi | 2.25 | 1.50 |
| *183* | A25 | 2r brn & multi | 3.00 | 2.00 |
| | | *Nos. 178-183 (6)* | 6.30 | 4.25 |

Qatar oil industry.

Boy Scouts Building Boats A26

Designs: 2d, Scouts at work and 10 symbolic candles. 3d, Parade. 60d, Gate to camp interior. 1.25r, Main camp gate. 2r, Hoisting Qatar flag, and Sheik Ahmad.

**1969, Sept. 18 Litho. *Perf. 13½x13***

| No. | Type | Description | Unused | Used |
|---|---|---|---|---|
| *184* | A26 | 1d multi | 5 | 5 |
| *185* | A26 | 2d multi | 5 | 5 |
| *186* | A26 | 3d multi | 5 | 5 |
| *187* | A26 | 60d multi | 1.00 | 65 |
| *a* | | Souv. sheet of 4 | 4.00 | 3.00 |
| *188* | A26 | 1.25r multi | 2.00 | 1.25 |
| *189* | A26 | 2r multi | 3.25 | 2.00 |
| | | *Nos. 184-189 (6)* | 6.40 | 4.05 |

10th Qatar Boy Scout Jamboree. No. 187a contains one each of Nos. 184-187. Multicolored ornamental border. Size: 127x111mm. Sold for 1r.

Neil A. Armstrong A27

Designs: 2d, Col. Edwin E. Aldrin, Jr. 3d, Lt. Col. Michael Collins. 60d, Astronaut walking on moon. 1.25r, Blast-off from moon. 2r, Capsule and raft in Pacific (horiz.).

**1969, Dec. 6 *Perf. 13x13½, 13½x13***

| No. | Type | Description | Unused | Used |
|---|---|---|---|---|
| *190* | A27 | 1d bl & multi | 15 | 9 |
| *191* | A27 | 2d multi | 15 | 9 |
| *192* | A27 | 3d grn & multi | 20 | 12 |
| *193* | A27 | 60d multi | 85 | 50 |
| *194* | A27 | 1.25r pur & multi | 1.90 | 1.10 |
| *195* | A27 | 2r multi | 2.75 | 1.60 |
| | | *Nos. 190-195 (6)* | 6.00 | 3.50 |

See note after U.S. No. C76.

UPU Emblem, Boeing Jet Loading in Qatar A28

Designs (UPU Emblem and): 2d, Transatlantic ocean liner. 3d, Mail truck and mail bags. 60d, Qatar Post Office. 1.25r, UPU Headquarters, Bern. 2r, UPU emblem.

**1970, Jan. 31 Litho. *Perf. 13½x13***

| No. | Type | Description | Unused | Used |
|---|---|---|---|---|
| *196* | A28 | 1d multi | 15 | 9 |
| *197* | A28 | 2d multi | 15 | 9 |
| *198* | A28 | 3d multi | 20 | 12 |
| *199* | A28 | 60d multi | 90 | 50 |
| *200* | A28 | 1.25r multi | 1.90 | 1.10 |
| *201* | A28 | 2r brt yel grn, blk & lt brn | 3.00 | 1.90 |
| | | *Nos. 196-201 (6)* | 6.30 | 3.80 |

Qatar's admission to the UPU.

Arab League Type of Kuwait

**1970, Mar. *Perf. 13x13½***

| No. | Type | Description | Unused | Used |
|---|---|---|---|---|
| *202* | A104a | 35d yel & multi | 50 | 38 |
| *203* | A104a | 60d bl & multi | 70 | 50 |
| *204* | A104a | 1.25r multi | 1.50 | 1.10 |
| *205* | A104a | 1.50r vio & multi | 2.00 | 1.50 |

25th anniversary of the Arab League.

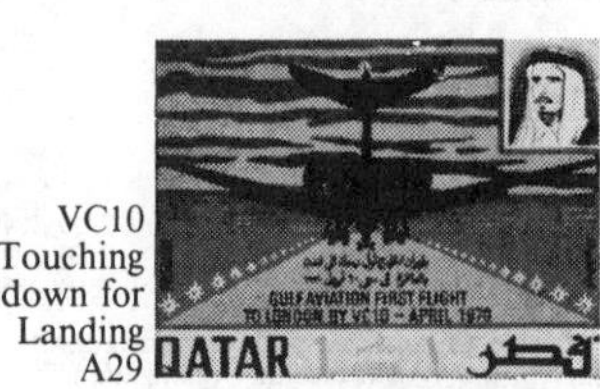


VC10 Touching down for Landing A29

Designs: 2d, Hawk, and VC10 in flight. 3d, VC10 and airport. 60d, Map showing route Doha to London. 1.25r, VC10 over Gulftown. 2r, Tail of VC10 with emblem of Gulf Aviation.

**1970, Apr. 5 *Perf. 13½x13***

| No. | Type | Description | Unused | Used |
|---|---|---|---|---|
| *206* | A29 | 1d multi | 12 | 9 |
| *207* | A29 | 2d multi | 12 | 9 |
| *208* | A29 | 3d multi | 16 | 12 |
| *209* | A29 | 60d multi | 80 | 50 |
| *210* | A29 | 1.25r multi | 1.50 | 1.00 |
| *211* | A29 | 2r multi | 2.50 | 1.50 |
| | | *Nos. 206-211 (6)* | 5.20 | 3.30 |

Issued to publicize the first flight to London from Doha by Gulf Aviation Company.

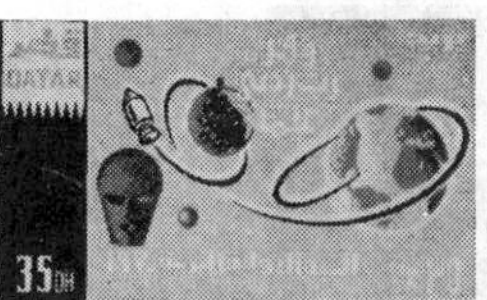

Education Year Emblem, Spaceship Trajectory, Koran Quotation — A30

**1970, May 24 *Perf. 13x12½***

| No. | Type | Description | Unused | Used |
|---|---|---|---|---|
| *212* | A30 | 35d bl & multi | 70 | 35 |
| *213* | A30 | 60d bl & multi | 1.50 | 75 |

Issued for International Education Year, 1970. Translation of Koran quotation: "And say, O God, give me more knowledge."

Azalea — A31

Flowers: 1d, Freesia. 3d, Ixia. 60d, Amaryllis. 1.25r, Cineraria. 2r, Rose.

**1970, July 2 *Perf. 13x13½***

| No. | Type | Description | Unused | Used |
|---|---|---|---|---|
| *214* | A31 | 1d ultra & multi | 18 | 15 |
| *215* | A31 | 2d lil & multi | 18 | 15 |
| *216* | A31 | 3d lt ultra & multi | 22 | 18 |
| *217* | A31 | 60d lem & multi | 75 | 60 |
| *218* | A31 | 1.25r bis & multi | 1.60 | 1.25 |
| *219* | A31 | 1.25r bis & multi | 2.75 | 1.75 |
| | | *Nos. 214-219 (6)* | 5.68 | 4.08 |

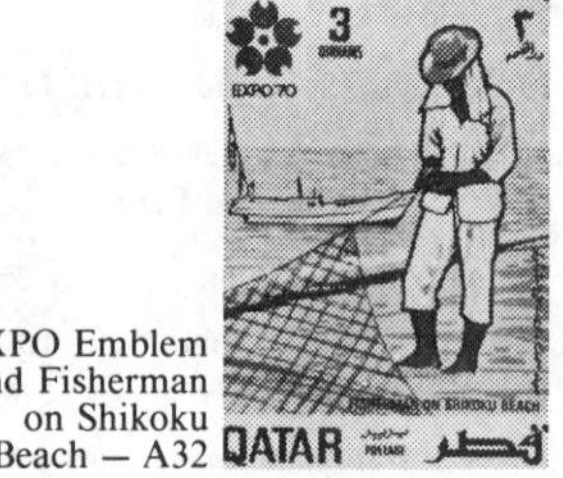


EXPO Emblem and Fisherman on Shikoku Beach — A32

Designs (EXPO Emblem and): 1d, Toyahama fishermen honoring ocean gods (horiz.). 2d, Map of Japan (horiz.). 60d, Mt. Fuji. 1.50r, Camphorwood torii (horiz.). 2r, Tower of Motherhood, EXPO Tower and Mt. Fuji.

***Perf. 13½x13, 13x13½***

**1970, Sept. 29**

| No. | Type | Description | Unused | Used |
|---|---|---|---|---|
| *220* | A32 | 1d multi | 12 | 9 |
| *221* | A32 | 2d multi | 12 | 9 |
| *222* | A32 | 3d multi | 16 | 12 |
| *223* | A32 | 60d multi | 70 | 50 |
| *a* | | Souvenir sheet of 4 | 4.00 | 3.00 |
| *224* | A32 | 1.50r multi | 2.00 | 1.50 |
| *225* | A32 | 2r multi | 2.50 | 2.00 |
| | | *Nos. 220-225 (6)* | 5.60 | 4.30 |

EXPO '70 Intl. Exhib., Osaka, Japan, Mar. 15-Sept. 13. No. 223a contains 4 imperf. stamps similar to Nos. 220-223 with simulated perforations. Sun tower design and inscription in margin. Size: 127x111mm. Sold for 1r.

Globe and UN Emblem — A33

UN, 25th anniv.: 2d, Cannon used as flower vase. 3d, Birthday cake and dove. 35d, Emblems of UN agencies forming wall. 1.50r, Trumpet and emblems of UN agencies. 2r, Two men, black and white, embracing, and globe.

**1970, Dec. 7 Litho. *Perf. 14x13½***

| No. | Type | Description | Unused | Used |
|---|---|---|---|---|
| *226* | A33 | 1d bl & multi | 9 | 6 |
| *227* | A33 | 2d multi | 9 | 6 |
| *228* | A33 | 3d brt pur & multi | 12 | 8 |
| *229* | A33 | 35d grn & multi | 30 | 20 |
| *230* | A33 | 1.50r multi | 1.50 | 1.00 |
| *231* | A33 | 2r brn red & multi | 1.90 | 1.25 |
| | | *Nos. 226-231 (6)* | 4.00 | 2.65 |

Al Jahiz and Old World Map — A34

Designs: 2d, Sultan Saladin and palace. 3d, Al Farabi, sailboat and musical instruments. 35d, Iben al Haithum and palace. 1.50r, Al Motanabbi and camels. 2r, Avicenna and old world map.

**1971, Feb. 20 *Perf. 13½x14***

| No. | Type | Description | Unused | Used |
|---|---|---|---|---|
| *232* | A34 | 1d brt pink & multi | 12 | 8 |
| *233* | A34 | 2d pale bl & multi | 12 | 8 |
| *234* | A34 | 3d dl yel & multi | 16 | 10 |
| *235* | A34 | 35d lt bl & multi | 50 | 32 |
| *236* | A34 | 1.50r yel grn & multi | 2.00 | 1.40 |
| *237* | A34 | 2r pale grn & multi | 3.00 | 2.00 |
| | | *Nos. 232-237 (6)* | 5.90 | 3.98 |

Famous men of Islam.

Cormorant — A35

Designs: 2d, Lizard and prickly pear. 3d, Flamingos and palms. 60d, Oryx and yucca. 1.25r, Gazelle and desert dandelion. 2r, Camel, palm and bronzed chenopod.

**1971, Apr. 14 Litho. *Perf. 11x12***

| No. | Type | Description | Unused | Used |
|---|---|---|---|---|
| *238* | A35 | 1d multi | 18 | 5 |
| *239* | A35 | 2d multi | 18 | 5 |
| *240* | A35 | 3d multi | 18 | 5 |
| *241* | A35 | 60d multi | 90 | 60 |
| *242* | A35 | 1.25r multi | 1.75 | 1.10 |
| *243* | A35 | 2r multi | 3.00 | 1.75 |
| | | *Nos. 238-243 (6)* | 6.19 | 3.60 |

Goonhilly Satellite Tracking Station — A36

Designs: 2d, Cable ship, and section of submarine cable. 3d, 35d, London Post Office Tower, and television control room. 4d, Various telephones. 5d, 75d, Video telephone. 3r, Telex machine and tape.

**1971, May 17 *Perf. 13½x13***

| No. | Type | Description | Unused | Used |
|---|---|---|---|---|
| *244* | A36 | 1d vio bl & multi | 10 | 6 |
| *245* | A36 | 2d multi | 10 | 6 |
| *246* | A36 | 3d rose red & multi | 10 | 6 |
| *247* | A36 | 4d mag & multi | 10 | 6 |
| *248* | A36 | 5d rose red & multi | 10 | 6 |
| *249* | A36 | 35d multi | 30 | 16 |
| *250* | A36 | 75d mag & multi | 60 | 35 |
| *251* | A36 | 3r ocher & multi | 2.75 | 1.50 |
| | | *Nos. 244-251 (8)* | 4.15 | 2.31 |

3rd World Telecommunications Day.

## State of Qatar

Arab Postal Union Emblem — A37

**1971, Sept. 4** ***Perf. 13***

*252* A37 35d red & multi 40 25
*253* A37 55d bl & multi 50 40
*254* A37 75d brn & multi 80 55
*255* A37 1.25r vio & multi 1.40 90

25th anniv. of the Conf. of Sofar, Lebanon, establishing the Arab Postal Union.

Boy Reading — A38

**1971, Aug. 10** ***Perf. 13x13½***

*256* A38 35d brn & multi 45 25
*257* A38 55d ultra & multi 75 40
*258* A38 75d grn & multi 90 50

International Literacy Day, Sept. 8.

Men Splitting Racism A39

Designs: 2d, 3r, People fighting racism. 3d, Soldier helping war victim. 4d, Men of 4 races rebuilding (vert.). 5d, Children on swing (vert.). 35d, Wave of racism engulfing people. 75d, like 1d.

***Perf. 13½x13, 13x13½***

**1971, Oct. 12** **Litho.**

*259* A39 1d multi 6 6
*260* A39 2d multi 6 6
*261* A39 3d multi 6 6
*262* A39 4d multi 8 8
*263* A39 5d multi 8 8
*264* A39 35d multi 20 20
*265* A39 75d multi 50 50
*266* A39 3r multi 2.25 2.25
*Nos. 259-266 (8)* 3.29 3.29

International Year Against Racial Discrimination.

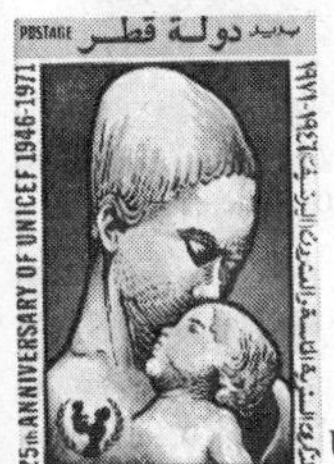

UNICEF Emblem, Mother and Child — A40

UNICEF, 25th anniv.: 2d, Child's head (horiz.). 3d, 75d, Child with book. 4d, Nurse and child (horiz.). 5d, Mother and child (horiz.). 35d, Woman and daffodil. 3r, like 1d.

**1971, Dec. 6** ***Perf. 14x13½, 13½x14***

*267* A40 1d bl & multi 6 6
*268* A40 2d lil rose & multi 6 6
*269* A40 3d bl & multi 6 6
*270* A40 4d yel & multi 8 8
*271* A40 5d bl & multi 8 8
*272* A40 35d lil rose & multi 25 25
*273* A40 75d yel & multi 40 40
*274* A40 3r multi 2.00 1.40
*Nos. 267-274 (8)* 2.99 2.39

Sheik Ahmad, Flags of Arab League and Qatar A41

"International Cooperation" A42

Designs: 75d, Sheik Ahmad, flags of United Nations and Qatar. 1.25r, Sheik Ahmad bin Ali al Thani.

***Perf. 13½x13, 13x13½***

**1972, Jan. 17**

*275* A41 35d blk & multi 35 20
*276* A41 75d blk & multi 75 45
*277* A42 1.25r lt brn & blk 1.00 65
*278* A42 3r multi 3.00 1.75
*a* Souvenir sheet 4.00 3.00

Independence 1971. No. 278a contains one stamp with simulated perforations. Multicolored margin with portrait of ruler and black inscription. Size: 100x127mm.

European Roller — A43

Birds: 2d, European kingfisher. 3d, Rock thrush. 4d, Caspian tern. 5d, Hoopoe. 35d, European bee-eater. 75d, European golden oriole. 3r, Peregrine falcon.

**1972, Mar. 1** **Litho.** ***Perf. 12x11***

*279* A43 1d sep & multi 10 5
*280* A43 2d emer & multi 10 5
*281* A43 3d bis & multi 10 5
*282* A43 4d lt bl & multi 10 5
*283* A43 5d yel & multi 10 5
*284* A43 35d vio bl & multi 40 20
*285* A43 75d pink & multi 1.00 50
*286* A43 3r bl & multi 4.00 2.00
*Nos. 279-286 (8)* 5.90 2.95

Nos. 217-219 Surcharged

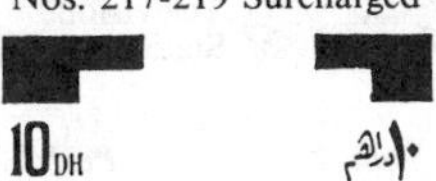


**1972, Mar. 7** ***Perf. 13x13½***

*287* A31 10d on 60d multi 9 6
*288* A31 1r on 1.25r multi 90 60
*289* A31 5r on 2r multi 4.00 2.75

Sheik Khalifa bin Hamad al Thani — A44

**1972, Mar. 7** ***Perf. 14***

**Size: 23x27mm.**

*290* A44 5d pur & ultra 6 5
*291* A44 10d brn & rose red 10 5
*292* A44 35d org & dl grn 30 24
*293* A44 55d brt grn & lil 45 38
*294* A44 75d vio & lil rose 60 50

**Size: 26½x32mm.**

*295* A44 1r bis & blk 90 75
*296* A44 1.25r ol & blk 1.00 80
*297* A44 5r bl & blk 4.25 3.50
*298* A44 10r red & blk 8.50 7.00
*Nos. 290-298 (9)* 16.16 13.27

Book Year Emblem A45

**1972, Apr. 23** ***Perf. 13½x13***

*299* A45 35d lt ultra & blk 30 30
*300* A45 55d lt brn & blk 50 50
*301* A45 75d grn & blk 70 70
*302* A45 1.25r vio & blk 1.00 1.00

International Book Year 1972.

Olympic Rings, Soccer A46

Designs (Olympic Rings and): 2d, 3r, Running. 3d, Bicycling. 4d, Gymnastics. 5d, Basketball. 35d, Discus. 75d, Like 1d.

**1972, June 12** ***Perf. 13½x13***

*303* A46 1d grn & multi 5 5
*304* A46 2d yel grn & multi 5 5
*305* A46 3d bl & multi 5 5
*306* A46 4d lil & multi 5 5
*307* A46 5d bl & multi 5 5
*308* A46 35d gray & multi 28 16
*a* Souvenir sheet of 6 2.50 1.50
*309* A46 75d grn & multi 60 35
*310* A46 3r multi 2.50 1.40
*Nos. 303-310 (8)* 3.63 2.16

20th Olympic Games, Munich, Aug. 26-Sept. 10. No. 308a contains stamps with simulated perforations similar to Nos. 303-308. Black marginal inscription, Olympic rings and multicolored torch. Size: 148½x107mm.

Installation of Underwater Pipe Line — A47

**1972, Aug. 8** **Litho.** ***Perf. 13x13½***

*311* A47 1d *Drilling for oil (vert.)* 12 9
*312* A47 4d *shown* 12 9
*313* A47 5d *Drilling platform* 16 12
*314* A47 35d *Ship searching for oil* 40 30
*315* A47 75d *like 1d* (vert.) 90 68
*316* A47 3r *like 5d* 3.50 2.50
*Nos. 311-316 (6)* 5.20 3.78

Oil from the sea.

Government Palace — A48

Designs: 35d, Clasped hands, Qatar flag. 75d, Clasped hands, U.N. flag. 1.25r, Sheik Khalifa bin Hamad al-Thani (vert.).

**1972, Sept. 3** ***Perf. 13½x13, 13x13½***

*317* A48 10d yel & multi 10 6
*318* A48 35d blk & multi 40 25
*319* A48 75d blk & multi 85 50
*320* A48 1.25r gold & multi 1.25 75
*a* Souvenir sheet of 1 4.00 3.00

Independence Day, 1st anniversary of independence.

No. 320a contains one stamp with simulated perforations similar to No. 320. Multicolored margin with flag, and Qatar and UN emblems. Size: 128x103mm.

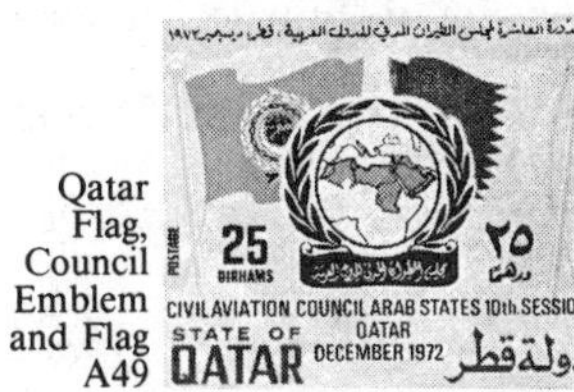

Qatar Flag, Council Emblem and Flag A49

**1972, Dec. 4** **Litho.** ***Perf. 14x13½***

*321* A49 25d bl & multi 60 45
*322* A49 30d vio bl & multi 80 60

Civil Aviation Council of Arab States, 10th session.

Tracking Station, Satellite, Telephone, ITU and UN Emblems A50

Designs (Agency and UN Emblems): 2d, Surveyor, artist; UNESCO. 3d, Tractor, helicopter, fish, grain and fruit; FAO. 4d, Reading children, teacher; UNICEF. 5d, Weather satellite and map; WMO. 25d, Workers and crane; ILO. 55d, Health clinic; WHO. 1r, Mail plane and post office; UPU.

**1972, Oct. 24** ***Perf. 13½x14***

*323* A50 1d multi 10 6
*324* A50 2d multi 10 6
*325* A50 3d multi 10 6
*326* A50 4d multi 15 8
*327* A50 5d multi 15 8
*328* A50 25d multi 38 20
*329* A50 55d multi 85 45
*330* A50 1r multi 1.40 75
*Nos. 323-330 (8)* 3.23 1.74

United Nations Day, Oct. 24, 1972. Each stamp dedicated to a different U.N. agency.

Road Building — A51

**1973, Feb. 22** **Litho.** ***Perf. 13x13½***

*331* A51 2d *shown* 10 5
*332* A51 3d *Housing development* 10 5
*333* A51 4d *Operating room* 10 5
*334* A51 5d *Telephone operators* 10 5
*335* A51 15d *School, classroom* 15 10
*336* A51 20d *Television studio* 25 15
*337* A51 35d *Sheik Khalifa* 35 28
*338* A51 55d *New Gulf Hotel* 60 40
*339* A51 1r *Fertilizer plant* 90 80
*340* A51 1.35r *Flour mill* 1.65 1.10
*Nos. 331-340 (10)* 4.30 3.03

1st anniv. of the accession of Sheik Khalifa bin Hamad al Thani as Emir of Qatar.

Aerial Pest Control — A52

WHO, 25th anniv.: 3d, Medicines. 4d, Poliomyelitis prevention. 5d, Malaria control. 55d, Mental health. 1r, Pollution control.

**1973, May 14 Litho. *Perf. 14***

| | | | | |
|---|---|---|---|---|
| *341* | A52 | 2d bl & multi | 10 | 8 |
| *342* | A52 | 3d bl & multi | 10 | 8 |
| *343* | A52 | 4d bl & multi | 10 | 8 |
| *344* | A52 | 5d bl & multi | 10 | 8 |
| *345* | A52 | 55d bl & multi | 1.00 | 65 |
| *346* | A52 | 1r bl & multi | 1.50 | 1.50 |
| | | *Nos. 341-346 (6)* | 2.90 | 2.47 |

Weather Ship A53

Designs (WMO Emblem and): 3d, Launching of radiosonde balloon. 4d, Plane and meteorological data checking. 5d, Cup anemometers and meteorological station. 10d, Weather plane in flight. 1r, Nimbus I weather satellite. 1.55r, Launching of rocket carrying weather satellite.

**1973, July Litho. *Perf. 14x13***

| | | | | |
|---|---|---|---|---|
| *347* | A53 | 2d multi | 10 | 8 |
| *348* | A53 | 3d multi | 10 | 8 |
| *349* | A53 | 4d multi | 10 | 8 |
| *350* | A53 | 5d multi | 10 | 8 |
| *351* | A53 | 10d multi | 10 | 8 |
| *352* | A53 | 1r multi | 1.00 | 65 |
| *353* | A53 | 1.55r multi | 1.50 | 1.00 |
| | | *Nos. 347-353 (7)* | 3.00 | 2.05 |

Cent. of intl. meteorological cooperation.

Sheik Khalifa — A54

Clock Tower, Doha — A55

**1973-74 Litho. *Perf. 14***

**Size: 18x27mm**

| | | | | |
|---|---|---|---|---|
| *354* | A54 | 5d grn & multi | 6 | 5 |
| *355* | A54 | 10d lt bl & multi | 8 | 5 |
| *356* | A54 | 20d ver & multi | 15 | 10 |
| *357* | A54 | 25d org & multi | 20 | 15 |
| *358* | A54 | 35d pur & multi | 30 | 20 |
| *359* | A54 | 55d dk gray & multi | 45 | 30 |

**Engr.**

***Perf. 13½***

| | | | | |
|---|---|---|---|---|
| *360* | A55 | 75d lil, bl & yel grn | 65 | 45 |

**Photo.**

***Perf. 13***

**Size: 27x32mm**

| | | | | |
|---|---|---|---|---|
| *360A* | A54 | 1r multi ('74) | 90 | 60 |
| *360B* | A54 | 5r multi ('74) | 4.50 | 3.00 |
| *360C* | A54 | 10r multi ('74) | 9.00 | 6.00 |
| | | *Nos. 354-360C (10)* | 16.29 | 10.90 |

Issue dates: 20d, 75d, July 3, 1973. 1r-10r, July 1974. Others, Jan. 27, 1973.

Flag of Qatar, Handclasp, Sheik Khalifa — A56

Designs (Flag, Sheik and): 35d, Harvest. 55d, Government Building. 1.35r, Market and Clock Tower, Doha. 1.55r, Illuminated fountain.

**1973, Oct. 4 Litho. *Perf. 13***

| | | | | |
|---|---|---|---|---|
| *361* | A56 | 15d red & multi | 10 | 8 |
| *362* | A56 | 35d buff & multi | 20 | 16 |
| *363* | A56 | 55d multi | 38 | 30 |
| *364* | A56 | 1.35r vio & multi | 1.00 | 80 |
| *365* | A56 | 1.55r multi | 1.25 | 1.00 |
| | | *Nos. 361-365 (5)* | 2.93 | 2.34 |

2nd anniversary of independence.

Planting Tree, Qatar and UN Flags, UNESCO Emblem — A57

Designs (Qatar and UN Flags and): 4d, UN Headquarters and flags. 5d, Pipe laying, cement mixer, helicopter and ILO emblem. 35d, Nurse, patient and UNICEF emblem. 1.35r, Telecommunications and ITU emblem. 3r, Cattle, wheat disease analysis and FAO emblem.

**1973, Oct. 24**

| | | | | |
|---|---|---|---|---|
| *366* | A57 | 2d multi | 8 | 5 |
| *367* | A57 | 4d multi | 8 | 5 |
| *368* | A57 | 5d multi | 10 | 7 |
| *369* | A57 | 35d multi | 25 | 16 |
| *370* | A57 | 1.35r multi | 1.00 | 60 |
| *371* | A57 | 3r multi | 2.50 | 1.40 |
| | | *Nos. 366-371 (6)* | 4.01 | 2.33 |

United Nations Day.

Prison Gates Opening — A58

Designs (Human Rights Flame and): 4d, Marchers with flags. 5d, Scales of Justice. 35d, Teacher and pupils. 1.35r, U.N. General Assembly. 3r, Human Rights flame (vert.).

**1973, Dec. Litho. *Perf. 13x13½***

| | | | | |
|---|---|---|---|---|
| *372* | A58 | 2d yel & multi | 12 | 10 |
| *373* | A58 | 4d pale lil & multi | 12 | 10 |
| *374* | A58 | 5d rose & multi | 12 | 10 |
| *375* | A58 | 35d ocher & multi | 32 | 25 |
| *376* | A58 | 1.35r lt bl & multi | 1.40 | 1.00 |
| *377* | A58 | 3r cit & multi | 2.50 | 2.00 |
| | | *Nos. 372-377 (6)* | 4.58 | 3.55 |

25th anniversary of the Universal Declaration of Human Rights.

Highway Overpass — A59

**1974, Feb. 22 *Perf. 14x13½***

| | | | | |
|---|---|---|---|---|
| *378* | A59 | 2s *shown* | 8 | 6 |
| *379* | A59 | 3d *Symbol of learning* | 8 | 6 |
| *380* | A59 | 5d *Oil field* | 10 | 8 |
| *381* | A59 | 35d *Gulf Hotel, Doha* | 25 | 20 |
| *382* | A59 | 1.55r *Radar station* | 1.40 | 1.00 |
| *383* | A59 | 2.25r *Sheik Khalifa* | 2.00 | 1.50 |
| | | *Nos. 378-383 (6)* | 3.91 | 2.90 |

2nd anniversary of the accession of Sheik Khalifa as Emir.

Mail Truck, Camel Caravan and UPU Emblem — A60

UPU cent.: 3d, Old and new trains, Arab Postal Union emblem. 10d, Old and new ships and Qatar coat of arms. 35d, Old and new planes. 75d, Mail sorting by hand and computer, and Arab Postal Union emblem. 1.25r, Old and new post offices, and Qatar coat of arms.

**1974, May 22 Litho. *Perf. 13½***

| | | | | |
|---|---|---|---|---|
| *384* | A60 | 2d brt yel & multi | 8 | 6 |
| *385* | A60 | 3d lt bl & multi | 8 | 6 |
| *386* | A60 | 10d dp org & multi | 8 | 8 |
| *387* | A60 | 35d sl & multi | 40 | 30 |
| *388* | A60 | 75d yel & multi | 80 | 60 |
| *389* | A60 | 1.25r lt bl & multi | 1.40 | 1.00 |
| | | *Nos. 384-389 (6)* | 2.84 | 2.10 |

Doha Hospital — A61

**1974, July 13 Litho. *Perf. 13½***

| | | | | |
|---|---|---|---|---|
| *390* | A61 | 5d *shown* | 6 | 6 |
| *391* | A61 | 10d *WPY emblem and people* | 6 | 6 |
| *392* | A61 | 15d *WPY emblem* | 9 | 8 |
| *393* | A61 | 35d *World map* | 22 | 20 |
| *394* | A61 | 1.75r *Clock and infants* | 1.10 | 1.00 |
| *395* | A61 | 2.25r *Family* | 1.40 | 1.25 |
| | | *Nos. 390-395 (6)* | 2.93 | 2.65 |

World Population Year 1974.

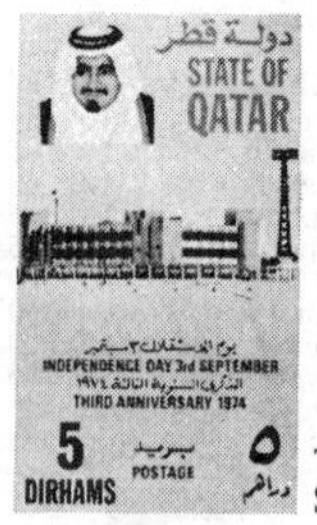


Television Station — A62

**1974, Sept. 2 *Perf. 13½x13***

| | | | | |
|---|---|---|---|---|
| *399* | A62 | 5d *shown* | 8 | 6 |
| *400* | A62 | 10d *Palace of Doha* | 8 | 6 |
| *401* | A62 | 15d *Teachers' College* | 10 | 8 |
| *402* | A62 | 75d *Clock Tower and Mosque* | 65 | 50 |
| *403* | A62 | 1.55r *Traffic circle, Doha* | 1.00 | 75 |
| *404* | A62 | 2.25r *Sheik Khalifa* | 1.60 | 1.25 |
| | | *Nos. 399-404 (6)* | 3.51 | 2.70 |

3rd anniversary of independence.

Operating Room and WHO Emblem — A63

United Nations Day: 10d, Satellite earth station and ITU emblem. 20d, Tractor, UN and FAO emblems. 25d, School children, UN and UNESCO emblems. 1.75r, Open air court, UN Headquarters, emblems. 2r, UPU and UN emblems.

**1974, Oct. 24 Litho. *Perf. 13x13½***

| | | | | |
|---|---|---|---|---|
| *405* | A63 | 5d multi | 6 | 6 |
| *406* | A63 | 10d multi | 9 | 8 |
| *407* | A63 | 20d multi | 12 | 10 |
| *408* | A63 | 25d multi | 16 | 15 |
| *409* | A63 | 1.75r multi | 1.10 | 1.00 |
| *410* | A63 | 2r multi | 1.40 | 1.25 |
| | | *Nos. 405-410 (6)* | 2.93 | 2.64 |

VC-10, Gulf Aviation Airliner — A64

Arab League and Qatar Flags, Civil Aviation Emblem — A65

Design: 25d, Doha Airport.

**1974, Dec. 1 Litho. *Perf. 13½***

| | | | | |
|---|---|---|---|---|
| *411* | A64 | 20d multi | 25 | 20 |
| *412* | A64 | 25d yel & dk bl | 32 | 25 |
| *413* | A65 | 30d multi | 40 | 30 |
| *414* | A65 | 50d multi | 65 | 50 |

Arab Civil Aviation Day.

Caspian Terns, Hoopoes and Shara'o Island — A66

Dhow by Moonlight — A67

Designs: 5d, Clock Tower, Doha (vert.). 15d, Zubara Fort. 35d, Gulf Hotel and sailboats. 75d, Arabian oryx. 1.25r, Khor Al-Udein. 1.75r, Ruins, Wakrah.

**1974, Dec. 21 Litho. *Perf. 13½***

| | | | | |
|---|---|---|---|---|
| *415* | A66 | 5d multi | 10 | 8 |
| *416* | A66 | 10d multi | 10 | 8 |
| *417* | A66 | 15d multi | 12 | 10 |
| *418* | A66 | 35d multi | 25 | 18 |
| *419* | A67 | 55d multi | 45 | 35 |
| *420* | A66 | 75d multi | 65 | 50 |
| *421* | A67 | 1.25r multi | 1.20 | 90 |
| *422* | A66 | 1.75r multi | 1.75 | 1.25 |
| | | *Nos. 415-422 (8)* | 4.62 | 3.44 |

Traffic Circle, Doha A68

Sheik Khalifa – A69

Designs: 35d, Pipe line from offshore platform. 55d, Laying underwater pipe line. 1r, Refinery.

**1975, Feb. 22 Litho. *Perf. 13½***

*423* A68 10d multi 15 12
*424* A68 35d multi 55 40
*425* A68 55d multi 80 60
*426* A68 1r multi 1.75 1.20
*427* A69 1.35r sil & multi 2.00 1.50
*428* A69 1.55r gold & multi 2.50 1.75
*Nos. 423-428 (6)* 7.75 5.57

3rd anniversary of the accession of Sheik Khalifa.

Qatar Flag and Arab Labor Charter Emblem – A70

**1975, May 28 Litho. *Perf. 13***

*429* A70 10d bl red brn & blk 12 10
*430* A70 35d multi 42 35
*431* A70 1r grn & multi 1.20 1.00

Arab Labor Charter and Constitution, 10th anniversary.

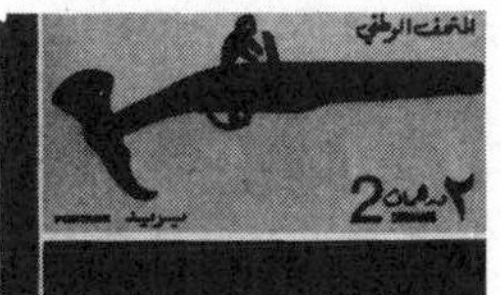

Flintlock Pistol with Ornamental Grip – A71

Designs: 3d, Ornamental mosaic. 35d, View of museum. 75d, Arch and museum (vert.). 1.25r, Flint arrowheads and tool. 3r, Gold necklace (vert.).

**1975, June 23 *Perf. 13***

*432* A71 2d multi 12 7
*433* A71 3d ver blk & gold 16 9
*434* A71 35d bis & multi 40 25
*435* A71 75d ver & multi 90 55
*436* A71 1.25r vio & multi 1.50 90
*437* A71 3r fawn & multi 3.50 2.00
*Nos. 432-437 (6)* 6.58 3.86

Opening of Qatar National Museum.

Traffic Signs, Policeman, Doha – A72

Designs: 15d, 55d, Cars, arrows, traffic lights, Doha Clock Tower. 35d, Like 5d.

**1975, June 24**

*438* A72 5d lt grn & multi 6 5
*439* A72 15d lt bl & multi 30 18
*440* A72 35d lem & multi 70 45
*441* A72 55d lt vio & multi 1.10 75

Traffic Week.

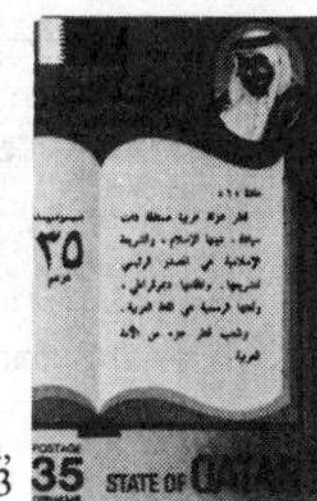


Constitution, Arabic Text – A73

Designs: 5d, Government buildings (horiz.). 15d, Museum and Clock Tower (horiz.). 55d, 1.25r, Sheik Khalifa and Qatar flag. 75d, Constitution, English text.

**1975, Sept. 2**

*442* A73 5d multi 12 10
*443* A73 15d multi 28 25
*444* A73 35d multi 32 30
*445* A73 55d multi 50 45
*446* A73 75d multi 65 60
*447* A73 1.25r multi 1.10 1.00
*Nos. 442-447 (6)* 2.97 2.70

4th anniversary of independence.

Satellite over Globe, ITU Emblem – A74

UN, 30th anniv.: 15d, UN Headquarters, NY and UN emblem. 35d, UPU emblem over Eastern Arabia, UN emblem. 1r, Nurses and infant, WHO emblem. 1.25r, Road building equipment, ILO emblem. 2r, Students, UNESCO emblem.

**1975, Oct. 25 Litho. *Perf. 13x13½***

*448* A74 5d multi 8 6
*449* A74 15d multi 20 15
*450* A74 35d multi 25 18
*451* A74 1r multi 65 50
*452* A74 1.25r multi 80 60
*453* A74 2r multi 1.40 1.00
*Nos. 448-453 (6)* 3.38 2.49

Fertilizer Plant – A75

Designs: 10d, Flour mill (vert.). 35d, Natural gas plant. 75d, Oil refinery. 1.25r, Cement works. 1.55r, Steel mill.

**1975, Dec. 6**

*454* A75 5d sal & multi 12 8
*455* A75 10d yel & multi 18 10
*456* A75 35d multi 42 25
*457* A75 75d multi 90 60
*458* A75 1.25r mag & multi 1.60 1.00
*459* A75 1.55r multi 2.25 1.40
*Nos. 454-459 (6)* 5.47 3.43

Modern Building, Doha – A76

Designs: 10d, 35d, 1.55r, Various modern buildings. 55d, 75d, Sheik Khalifa and Qatar flag (diff. designs).

**1976, Feb. 22 Litho. *Perf. 13***

*460* A76 5d multi 7 6
*461* A76 10d multi 10 8
*462* A76 35d multi 25 20
*463* A76 55d multi 38 30
*464* A76 75d multi 55 45
*465* A76 1.55r multi 1.10 90
*Nos. 460-465 (6)* 2.45 1.99

4th anniversary of accession of Sheik Khalifa.

Satellite Earth Station – A77

Designs: 55d, 1r, Satellite. 75d, Like 35d.

**1976, Mar. 1**

*466* A77 35d multi 40 22
*467* A77 55d dp bis & multi 55 30
*468* A77 75d ver & multi 80 45
*469* A77 1r vio & multi 1.00 60

Inauguration of satellite earth station in Qatar.

Telephones, 1876 and 1976 – A78

Arabian Soccer League Emblem – A79

**1976, Mar. 10**

*470* A78 1r rose & multi 1.00 75
*471* A78 1.35r lt bl & multi 1.40 1.00

Centenary of first telephone call by Alexander Graham Bell, Mar. 10, 1876.

**1976, Mar. 25 Litho. *Perf. 13½x13***

Designs: 10d, 1.25r, Stadium, Doha. 35d, Like 5d. 55d, Players. 75d, One player.

*472* A79 5d lil & multi 12 10
*473* A79 10d pink & multi 12 10
*474* A79 35d bl grn & multi 30 25
*475* A79 55d multi 48 40
*476* A79 75d multi 72 60
*477* A79 1.25r multi 1.25 1.00
*Nos. 472-477 (6)* 2.99 2.45

4th Arabian Gulf Soccer Cup Tournament, Doha, Mar. 22-Apr.

Dhow A80

Designs: Various dhows.

**1976, Apr. 19 *Perf. 13½x14***

*478* A80 10d bl & multi 8 6
*479* A80 35d bl & multi 28 20
*480* A80 80d bl & multi 60 45
*481* A80 1.25r bl & multi 1.00 75
*482* A80 1.50r bl & multi 1.20 90
*483* A80 2r bl & multi 2.00 1.40
*Nos. 478-483 (6)* 5.16 3.76

Soccer – A81

Designs (Olympic Rings and): 10d, Yachting. 35d, Steeplechase. 80d, Boxing. 1.25r, Weight lifting. 1.50r, Basketball.

**1976, May 15 Litho. *Perf. 14x13½***

*484* A81 5d multi 6 6
*485* A81 10d bl & multi 8 8
*486* A81 35d org & multi 22 20
*487* A81 80d bis & multi 45 40
*488* A81 1.25r lil & multi 85 75
*489* A81 1.50r rose & multi 1.10 1.00
*Nos. 484-489 (6)* 2.76 2.49

21st Olympic Games, Montreal, Canada, July 17-Aug. 1.

Village and Emblems – A82

Designs (UN and Habitat Emblems): 35d, Emblems. 80d, Village. 1.25r, Sheik Khalifa.

**1976, May 31 *Perf. 13½x14***

*490* A82 10d org & multi 8 5
*491* A82 35d yel & multi 28 20
*492* A82 80d cit & multi 60 45
*493* A82 1.25r dp bl & multi 1.00 75

Habitat, UN Conf. on Human Settlements, Vancouver, Canada, May 31-June 11.

Snowy Plover A83

Birds: 10d, Great cormorant. 35d, Osprey. 80d, Flamingo. 1.25r, Rock thrush. 2r, Saker falcon. 35d, 80d, 1.25r, 2r, vertical.

***Perf. 13½x14, 14x13½***

**1976, July 19 Litho.**

*494* A83 5d multi 15 8
*495* A83 10d multi 22 10
*496* A83 35d multi 60 28
*497* A83 80d multi 1.10 65
*498* A83 1.25r multi 1.90 1.10
*499* A83 2r multi 2.25 1.60
*Nos. 494-499 (6)* 6.22 3.81

Sheik Khalifa and Qatar Flag – A84

Demand, as well as supply, determines a stamp's market value. One is as important as the other.

Government Building — A85

Designs: 10d, like 5d. 80d, Government building. 1.25r, Offshore oil platform. 1.50r, U.N. emblem and Qatar coat of arms.

**1976, Sept. 2** ***Perf. 14x13½, 13½x14***

*500* A84 5d gold & multi 8 6
*501* A84 10d sil & multi 10 8
*502* A85 40d multi 32 25
*503* A85 80d multi 65 50
*504* A85 1.25r multi 1.00 75
*505* A85 1.50r multi 1.25 90
*Nos. 500-505 (6)* 3.40 2.54

5th anniversary of independence.

Qatar Flag and U.N. Emblem — A86

**1976, Oct. 24 Litho.** ***Perf. 13½x14***

*506* A86 2r multi 2.50 1.25
*507* A86 3r multi 3.50 1.75

United Nations Day 1976.

Sheik Khalifa — A87

Sheik Khalifa — A88

**1977, Feb. 22 Litho.** ***Perf. 14x13½***

*508* A87 20d sil & multi 20 15
*509* A87 1.80r gold & multi 1.90 1.40

5th anniversary of the accession of Sheik Khalifa.

**1977, Mar. 1 Litho.** ***Perf. 14x14½***

**Size: 22x27mm.**

*510* A88 5d multi 10 5
*511* A88 10d aqua & multi 10 5
*512* A88 35d org & multi 30 14
*513* A88 80d multi 65 32

***Perf. 13½***

**Size: 25x30mm.**

*514* A88 1r vio bl & multi 1.10 45
*515* A88 5r yel & multi 4.00 2.25
*516* A88 10r multi 10.00 4.50
*Nos. 510-516 (7)* 16.25 7.76

Letter, APU Emblem, Flag — A89

**1977, Apr. 12** ***Perf. 14x13½***

*517* A89 35d bl & multi 25 25
*518* A89 1.35r bl & multi 1.00 1.00

Arab Postal Union, 25th anniversary.

Waves and Sheik Khalifa A90

**1977, May 17 Litho.** ***Perf. 13½x14***

*519* A90 35d multi 25 25
*520* A90 1.80r multi 1.50 1.50

World Telecommunications Day.

Sheik Khalifa — A90a

***Perf. 13½x13***

**1977, June 29 Litho. Wmk. 368**

*520A* A90a 5d multi 5 5
*520B* A90a 10d multi 5 5
*520C* A90a 35d multi 20 20
*520D* A90a 80d multi 45 45
*e.* Bklt. pane of 10 (4 5d, 3 10d, 2 35d, 80d) 6.00 6.00

Issued in booklets only.

Parliament, Clock Tower, Minaret — A91

Designs: No. 522, Main business district, Doha. No. 523, Highway crossings, Doha.

**1977, Sept. 1 Litho.** ***Perf. 13x13½***

*521* A91 80d multi 80 65
*522* A91 80d multi 80 65
*523* A91 80d multi 80 65

6th anniversary of independence.

U.N. Emblem, Flag — A92

**1977, Oct. 24 Litho.** ***Perf. 13½x14***

*524* A92 20d grn & multi 15 15
*525* A92 1r bl & multi 75 75

United Nations Day.

Surgery A93

Designs: 20d, Steel mill. 1r, Classroom. 5r, Sheik Khalifa.

**1978, Feb. 22 Litho.** ***Perf. 13½x14***

*526* A93 20d multi 10 10
*527* A93 80d multi 40 40
*528* A93 1r multi 50 50
*529* A93 5r multi 2.50 2.50

6th anniversary of the accession of Sheik Khalifa.

Oil Refinery — A94

Designs: 80d, Office buildings, Doha. 1.35r, Traffic Circle, Doha. 1.80r, Sheik Khalifa and flag.

**1978, Aug. 31 Litho.** ***Perf. 13½x14***

*530* A94 35d multi 24 20
*531* A94 80d multi 60 50
*532* A94 1.35r multi 90 75
*533* A94 1.80r multi 1.25 1.00

7th anniversary of independence.

Man Learning to Read — A95

**1978, Sept. 8 Litho.** ***Perf. 13½x14***

*534* A95 35d multi 24 20
*535* A95 80d multi 75 65

International Literacy Day.

Flag and U.N. Emblem — A96

**1978, Oct. 14** ***Perf. 13x13½***

*536* A96 35d multi 24 20
*537* A96 80d multi 75 65

United Nations Day.

Human Rights Emblem — A97

IYC Emblem — A98

Designs: 80d, like 35d. 1.25r, 1.80r, Scales and Human Rights emblem.

**1978, Dec. 10 Litho.** ***Perf. 14x13½***

*538* A97 35d multi 22 22
*539* A97 80d multi 60 60
*540* A97 1.25r multi 80 80
*541* A97 1.80r multi 1.25 1.25

30th anniversary of Universal Declaration of Human Rights.

**Wmk. JEZ Multiple (368)**

**1979, Jan. 1 Litho.** ***Perf. 13½x13***

*542* A98 35d multi 25 25
*543* A98 1.80r multi 1.25 1.25

International Year of the Child.

Sheik Khalifa — A99

**1979, Jan. 15 Unwmk.** ***Perf. 14***

*544* A99 5d multi 5 5
*545* A99 10d multi 5 5
*546* A99 20d multi 12 10
*547* A99 25d multi 16 10
*548* A99 35d multi 20 16
*549* A99 60d multi 40 30
*550* A99 80d multi 55 40

**Size: 27x32mm.**

*551* A99 1r multi 65 50
*552* A99 1.25r multi 80 60
*553* A99 1.35r multi 1.00 75
*554* A99 1.80r multi 1.20 90
*555* A99 5r multi 3.25 2.50
*556* A99 10r multi 6.50 5.00
*Nos. 544-556 (13)* 14.93 11.41

Sheik Khalifa — A100

**1979, Feb. 22 Wmk. 368**

*557* A100 35d multi 20 20
*558* A100 80d multi 50 50
*559* A100 1r multi 60 60
*560* A100 1.25r multi 75 75

7th anniversary of accession of Sheik Khalifa.

Cables and People — A101

**1979, May 17 Litho.** ***Perf. 14x13½***

*561* A101 2r multi 1.10 1.10
*562* A101 2.80r multi 1.40 1.40

World Telecommunications Day.

Children Holding Globe, UNESCO Emblem — A102

***Perf. 13x13½***

**1979, July 15 Litho. Unwmk.**

*563* A102 35d multi 24 20
*564* A102 80d multi 75 60

International Bureau of Education, Geneva, 50th anniversary.

Rolling Mill — A103

**Wmk. 368**

**1979, Sept. 2 Litho. *Perf. 13½***

| | | | | |
|---|---|---|---|---|
| *565* A103 | 5d | *shown* | 5 | 5 |
| *566* A103 | 10d | *Doha, aerial view* | 5 | 5 |
| *567* A103 | 1.25r | *Qatar flag* | 75 | 75 |
| *568* A103 | 2r | *Sheik Khalifa* | 1.00 | 1.00 |

Independence, 8th anniversary.

United Nations Day — A104

**1979, Oct. 24 Litho. *Perf. 13½x13***

| | | | | |
|---|---|---|---|---|
| *569* A104 | 1.25r | multi | 75 | 75 |
| *570* A104 | 2r | multi | 1.25 | 1.25 |

Conference Emblem — A105

**1979, Nov. 24 *Perf. 13x13½***

| | | | | |
|---|---|---|---|---|
| *571* A105 | 35d | multi | 32 | 25 |
| *572* A105 | 1.80r | multi | 1.60 | 1.25 |

Hegira (Pilgrimage Year); 3rd World Conference on Prophets.

Sheik Khalifa, 8th Anniversary of Accession — A106

**1980, Feb. 22 Litho. *Perf. 13x13½***

| | | | | |
|---|---|---|---|---|
| *573* A106 | 20d | multi | 10 | 10 |
| *574* A106 | 60d | multi | 35 | 35 |
| *575* A106 | 1.25r | multi | 65 | 65 |
| *576* A106 | 2r | multi | 1.25 | 1.25 |

Map of Arab Countries — A107

**1980, Mar. 1 Litho. *Perf. 13½x14***

| | | | | |
|---|---|---|---|---|
| *577* A107 | 2.35r | multi | 1.50 | 95 |
| *578* A107 | 2.80r | multi | 1.75 | 1.15 |

6th Congress of Arab Town Organization, Doha, Mar. 1-4.

Oil Refinery A108

**1980, Sept. 2 Litho. *Perf. 14½***

| | | | | |
|---|---|---|---|---|
| *579* A108 | 10d | *shown* | 10 | 8 |
| *580* A108 | 35d | *View of Doha* | 32 | 25 |
| *581* A108 | 2r | *Oil rig* | 1.50 | 1.10 |
| *582* A108 | 2.35r | *Hospital* | 1.75 | 1.65 |

9th anniversary of independence.

Men Holding OPEC Emblem — A109

United Nations Day 1980 — A110

**1980, Sept. 15 *Perf. 14x13½***

| | | | | |
|---|---|---|---|---|
| *583* A109 | 1.35r | multi | 90 | 60 |
| *584* A109 | 2r | multi | 1.40 | 90 |

OPEC, 20th anniversary.

**1980, Oct. 24**

| | | | | |
|---|---|---|---|---|
| *585* A110 | 1.35r | multi | 90 | 60 |
| *586* A110 | 1.80r | multi | 1.10 | 80 |

Hegira (Pilgrimage Year) — A111

**1980, Nov. 8 Litho. *Perf. 14½***

| | | | | |
|---|---|---|---|---|
| *587* A111 | 10d | multi | 6 | 6 |
| *588* A111 | 35d | multi | 24 | 24 |
| *589* A111 | 1.25r | multi | 80 | 80 |
| *590* A111 | 2.80r | multi | 1.90 | 1.90 |

International Year of the Disabled — A112

**1981, Jan. 5 Photo. *Perf. 11½***

**Granite Paper**

| | | | | |
|---|---|---|---|---|
| *591* A112 | 2r | multi | 1.40 | 1.00 |
| *592* A112 | 3r | multi | 2.00 | 1.50 |

Education Day A113

Sheik Khalifa, 9th Anniversary of Accession A114

***Perf. 14x13½***

**1981, Feb. 22 Litho. Wmk. 368**

| | | | | |
|---|---|---|---|---|
| *593* A113 | 2r | multi | 1.20 | 80 |
| *594* A113 | 3r | multi | 1.90 | 1.25 |

**1981, Feb. 22**

| | | | | |
|---|---|---|---|---|
| *595* A114 | 10d | multi | 5 | 5 |
| *596* A114 | 35d | multi | 20 | 14 |
| *597* A114 | 80d | multi | 50 | 35 |
| *598* A114 | 5r | multi | 3.50 | 2.25 |

13th World Telecommunications Day — A115

**1981, May 17 Litho. *Perf. 13½x13***

| | | | | |
|---|---|---|---|---|
| *599* A115 | 2r | multi | 1.50 | 95 |
| *600* A115 | 2.80r | multi | 1.90 | 1.25 |

Championship Emblem — A116

**1981, June 11 Litho. *Perf. 14x13½***

| | | | | |
|---|---|---|---|---|
| *601* A116 | 1.25r | multi | 1.10 | 55 |
| *602* A116 | 2.80r | multi | 2.50 | 1.25 |

30th Intl. Military Soccer Championship, Doha.

10th Anniv. of Independence — A117

***Perf. 13½x14***

**1981, Sept. 2 Litho. Wmk. 368**

| | | | | |
|---|---|---|---|---|
| *603* A117 | 5d | multi | 5 | 5 |
| *604* A117 | 60d | multi | 50 | 32 |
| *605* A117 | 80d | multi | 65 | 40 |
| *606* A117 | 5r | multi | 4.00 | 2.75 |

The only foreign revenue stamps listed in this Catalogue are those authorized for prepayment of postage.

World Food Day A118

**1981, Oct. 16 Litho. *Perf. 13***

| | | | | |
|---|---|---|---|---|
| *607* A118 | 2r | multi | 1.25 | 80 |
| *608* A118 | 2.80r | multi | 1.75 | 1.15 |

Red Crescent Society — A119

**1982, Jan. 16 Litho. *Perf. 14x13½***

| | | | | |
|---|---|---|---|---|
| *609* A119 | 20d | multi | 20 | 12 |
| *610* A119 | 2.80r | multi | 2.75 | 2.00 |

10th Anniv. of Sheik Khalifa's Accession — A120

***Perf. 13½x14***

**1982, Feb. 22 Litho. Wmk. 368**

| | | | | |
|---|---|---|---|---|
| *611* A120 | 10d | multi | 5 | 5 |
| *612* A120 | 20d | multi | 15 | 10 |
| *613* A120 | 1.25r | multi | 1.00 | 65 |
| *614* A120 | 2.80r | multi | 2.00 | 1.40 |

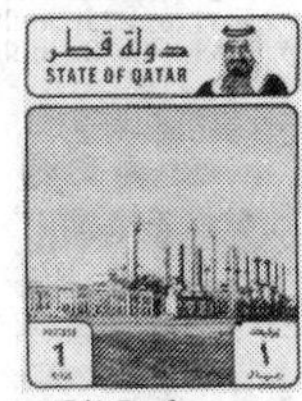


Sheik Khalifa A121

Oil Refinery A122

Designs: 5r, 10r, 15r, Hoda Clock Tower.

**1982, Mar. 1 Photo. *Perf. 11½x12***

**Granite Paper**

| | | | | |
|---|---|---|---|---|
| *615* A121 | 5d | multi | 5 | 5 |
| *616* A121 | 10d | multi | 5 | 5 |
| *617* A121 | 15d | multi | 8 | 6 |
| *618* A121 | 20d | multi | 10 | 8 |
| *619* A121 | 25d | multi | 12 | 10 |
| *620* A121 | 35d | multi | 20 | 15 |
| *621* A121 | 60d | multi | 32 | 25 |
| *622* A121 | 80d | multi | 45 | 35 |
| *623* A122 | 1r | multi | 60 | 45 |
| *624* A122 | 1.25r | multi | 75 | 55 |
| *625* A122 | 2r | multi | 1.20 | 90 |
| *626* A122 | 5r | multi | 3.00 | 2.25 |
| *627* A122 | 10r | multi | 6.00 | 4.50 |
| *628* A122 | 15r | multi | 8.50 | 6.50 |
| | | *Nos. 615-628 (14)* | 21.42 | 16.24 |

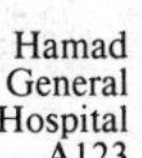

Hamad General Hospital A123

**1982, Mar. Litho. *Perf. 13x13½***

| | | | | |
|---|---|---|---|---|
| *629* A123 | 10d | multi | 5 | 5 |
| *630* A123 | 2.35r | multi | 1.90 | 1.40 |

6th Anniv. of United Arab Shipping Co. — A124

**1982, Mar. 6 Litho.** ***Perf. 13x13½***

*631* A124 20d multi 12 10
*632* A124 2.35r multi 1.90 1.40

30th Anniv. of Arab Postal Union — A125

**1982, Apr. 12 Litho.** ***Perf. 13½x13***

*633* A125 35d yel & multi 25 18
*634* A125 2.80r bl & multi 2.00 1.40

11th Anniv. of Independence A126

**1982, Sept. 2 Litho.** ***Perf. 13½x13***

*635* A126 10d multi 5 5
*636* A126 80d multi 55 40
*637* A126 1.25r multi 90 65
*638* A126 2.80r multi 2.00 1.40

World Communications Year — A127

**1983, Jan. 10 Litho.** ***Perf. 13½x13***

*639* A127 35d multi 30 14
*640* A127 2.80r multi 2.25 1.15

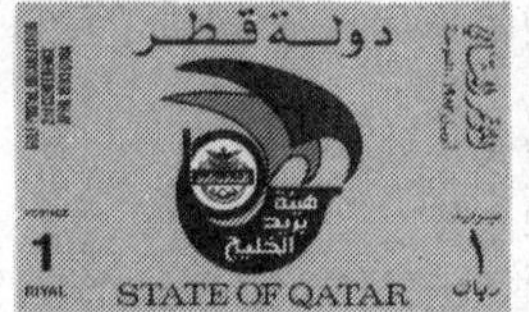

Gulf Postal Org., 2nd Conference, Doha, Apr. — A128

**1983, Apr. 9 Litho.** ***Perf. 13½x14***

*641* A128 1r multi 75 40
*642* A128 1.35r multi 1.00 55

12th Anniv. of Independence A129

**1983, Sept. 2 Litho.** ***Perf. 14***

*643* A129 10d multi 5 5
*644* A129 35d multi 25 14
*645* A129 80d multi 60 32
*646* A129 2.80r multi 2.25 1.15

GCC Supreme Council, 4th Regular Session — A130

**1983, Nov. 7 Litho.** ***Perf. 13½x14***

*647* A130 35d multi 30 14
*648* A130 2.80r multi 2.25 1.10

35th Anniv. of UN Declaration of Human Rights — A131

**1983, Dec. 10 Litho.** ***Perf. 13½x14***

*649* A131 1.25r Globe, emblem 1.40 68
*650* A131 2.80r Scale 2.50 1.50

A132

A133

**1984, Mar. 1 Litho.** ***Perf. 13x13½***

*651* A132 15d multi 8 8
*652* A132 40d multi 28 25
*653* A132 50d multi 35 32

***Perf. 14½x13½***

*654* A133 1r multi 65 60
*655* A133 1.50r multi 1.00 90
*656* A133 2.50r multi 1.65 1.50
*657* A133 3r multi 1.90 1.75
*658* A133 5r multi 3.25 3.00
*659* A133 10r multi 6.50 6.00
*Nos. 651-659 (9)* 15.66 14.40

13th Anniv. of Independence — A134

**1984, Sept. 2 Photo.** ***Perf. 12***

*660* A134 15d multi 12 10
*661* A134 1r multi 80 54
*662* A134 2.50r multi 1.75 1.35
*663* A134 3.50r multi 2.50 1.90

Literacy Day, 1984 — A135

40th Anniv., ICAO — A136

**1984, Sept. 8 Litho.** ***Perf. 14x13½***

*664* A135 1r lil & multi 75 54
*665* A135 1r org & multi 75 54

**1984, Dec. 7 Litho.** ***Perf. 13½x13***

*666* A136 20d multi 22 12
*667* A136 3.50r multi 3.50 1.90

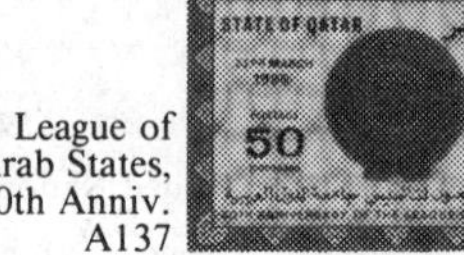

League of Arab States, 40th Anniv. A137

**1985, Mar. 22 Photo.** ***Perf. 11½***

*668* A137 50d multi 38 25
*669* A137 4r multi 3.00 2.00

Intl. Youth Year — A138

Traffic Crossing — A139

**1985, Mar. 4** ***Perf. 11½x12***

**Granite Paper**

*670* A138 50d multi 75 25
*671* A138 1r multi 1.60 50

**1985, Mar. 9** ***Perf. 14x13½***

*672* A139 1r lt bl & multi 90 50
*673* A139 1r pink & multi 90 50

Gulf Cooperation Council Traffic Safety Week, Mar. 16-22.

Natl. Independence, 14th Anniv. — A140

**1985, Sept. 2** ***Perf. 11½x12***

**Granite Paper**

*674* A140 40d Doha 28 20
*675* A140 50d Earth satellite station 32 25
*676* A140 1.50r Oil refinery 1.00 75
*677* A140 4r Storage facility 2.75 2.00

Org. of Petroleum Exporting Countries, 25th Anniv. — A141

**1985, Sept. 14** ***Perf. 13½x14***

*678* A141 1r brt yel grn & multi 75 50
*679* A141 1r sal rose & multi 75 50

UN, 40th Anniv. A142

**1985, Oct. 24 Litho.** ***Perf. 13½x14***

*680* A142 1r multi 65 50
*681* A142 3r multi 2.00 1.50

Population and Housing Census — A143

**1986, Mar. 1 Photo.** ***Perf. 11½x12***

*682* A143 1r multi 80 55
*683* A143 3r multi 2.25 1.65

United Arab Shipping Co., 10th Anniv. — A144

**1986, May 30 Litho.** ***Perf. 13½x14***

*684* A144 1.50r Qatari ibn al Fuja'a 1.00 85
*685* A144 4r Al Wajba 2.75 2.25

Natl. Independence, 15th Anniv. — A145

***Perf. 13x13½***

**1986, Sept. 2 Litho. Unwmk.**

*686* A145 40d multi 28 22
*687* A145 50d multi 40 30
*688* A145 1r multi 80 58
*689* A145 4r multi 3.00 2.25

Sheik Khalifa — A146

**1987, Jan. 1 Photo.** ***Perf. 11½x12***

**Granite Paper**

*690* A146 15r multi 8.50 8.50
*691* A146 20r multi 11.00 11.00
*692* A146 30r multi 17.00 17.00

15th Anniv. of Sheik Khalifa's Accession A147

**1987, Feb. 22** *Perf. 12x11½*

**Granite Paper**

| | | | | |
|---|---|---|---|---|
| *693* | A147 | 50d multi | 35 | 30 |
| *694* | A147 | 1r multi | 65 | 58 |
| *695* | A147 | 1.50r multi | 1.00 | 85 |
| *696* | A147 | 4r multi | 2.75 | 2.25 |

Arab Postal Union, 35th Anniv. — A148

*Perf. 14x13½*

**1987, Apr. 12** **Litho.** **Unwmk.**

| | | | | |
|---|---|---|---|---|
| *697* | A148 | 1r multi | 58 | 58 |
| *698* | A148 | 1.50r multi | 85 | 85 |

Natl. Independence, 16th Anniv. — A149

**1987, Sept. 2** **Litho.** *Perf. 13x13½*

| | | | | |
|---|---|---|---|---|
| *699* | A149 | 25d Housing complex | 14 | 14 |
| *700* | A149 | 75d Water tower, city | 42 | 42 |
| *701* | A149 | 2r Modern office building | 1.15 | 1.15 |
| *702* | A149 | 4r Oil refinery | 2.25 | 2.25 |

Intl. Literacy Day — A150

*Perf. 13½x13*

**1987, Sept. 8** **Litho.** **Unwmk.**

| | | | | |
|---|---|---|---|---|
| *703* | A150 | 1.50r multi | 85 | 85 |
| *704* | A150 | 4r multi | 2.25 | 2.25 |

## QUEENSLAND

LOCATION — In the northeastern part of Australia.

GOVT. — A former British Crown Colony.

AREA — 670,500 sq. mi.

POP. — 498,129 (1901).

CAPITAL — Brisbane.

Originally a part of New South Wales, Queensland was constituted a separate colony in 1859. It was one of the six British Colonies that united in 1901 to form the Commonwealth of Australia.

12 Pence = 1 Shilling
20 Shillings = 1 Pound

> Values of early Queensland stamps vary according to condition. Quotations for Nos. 1-3 are for fine copies. Very fine to superb specimens sell at much higher prices, and inferior or poor copies sell at reduced prices, depending on the condition of the individual specimen.

Queen Victoria — A1

Wmk. 5- Small Star

Wmk. 6- Large Star

**1860, Nov. 1** **Engr.** **Wmk. 6** ***Imperf.***

| | | | | |
|---|---|---|---|---|
| *1* | A1 | 1p deep rose | 3,000. | 400.00 |
| *2* | A1 | 2p deep blue | 6,750. | 2,250. |
| *3* | A1 | 6p deep green | 6,000. | 300.00 |
| | | ***Clean-Cut Perf. 14 to 16*** | | |
| *4* | A1 | 1p deep rose | 1,500. | 135.00 |
| *5* | A1 | 2p deep blue | 475.00 | 67.50 |
| *6* | A1 | 6p deep green | 475.00 | 35.00 |

***Clean-Cut Perf. 14 to 16***

**1860-61** **Wmk. 5**

| | | | | |
|---|---|---|---|---|
| *6A* | A1 | 2p blue | 425.00 | 80.00 |
| **b.** | | Horiz. pair, imperf. vert | | 675.00 |
| *6D* | A1 | 3p brown ('61) | 225.00 | 45.00 |
| *6E* | A1 | 6p deep green | 550.00 | 45.00 |
| *6F* | A1 | 1sh gray vio | 475.00 | 47.50 |
| | | ***Regular Perf. 14*** | | |
| *6H* | A1 | 1p rose | 125.00 | 25.00 |
| *6I* | A1 | 2p deep blue | 325.00 | 37.50 |
| | | ***Rough Perf. 14 to 16*** | | |
| *7* | A1 | 1p deep rose | 60.00 | 25.00 |
| *8* | A1 | 2p blue | 90.00 | 17.50 |
| *9* | A1 | 3p brown ('61) | 37.50 | 17.50 |
| **a.** | | Horiz. pair, imperf. vert. | 2,000. | |
| *10* | A1 | 6p deep grn | 175.00 | 20.00 |
| *11* | A1 | 1sh dull vio | 400.00 | 50.00 |

Thick Yellowish Paper

***Square Perf. 12½ to 13***

**1862-67** **Unwmk.**

| | | | | |
|---|---|---|---|---|
| *12* | A1 | 1p indian red | 325.00 | 50.00 |
| *13* | A1 | 1p orange ('63) | 60.00 | 15.00 |
| **a.** | | Perf. 13, round holes ('67) | 45.00 | 15.00 |
| **b.** | | Horiz. pair, imperf. between | | |
| **c.** | | Imperf., pair | 200.00 | |
| *14* | A1 | 2p deep blue | 40.00 | 14.00 |
| **a.** | | 2p pale blue | 90.00 | 26.00 |
| **b.** | | Perf. 13, round holes ('67) | 60.00 | 14.00 |
| **c.** | | Imperf., pair | | 175.00 |
| **e.** | | Horiz. pair, imperf. between | | *900.00* |
| *15* | A1 | 3p brown ('63) | 55.00 | 16.00 |
| **a.** | | Imperf. | | |
| **b.** | | Perf. 13, round holes ('67) | | 300.00 |
| *16* | A1 | 6p yel grn ('63) | 75.00 | 8.50 |
| **a.** | | 6p grn | 85.00 | 10.00 |
| **b.** | | Perf. 13, round holes ('67) | 75.00 | 9.25 |
| **c.** | | Imperf., pair | | 275.00 |
| *17* | A1 | 1sh gray ('63) | 125.00 | 10.00 |
| **b.** | | Imperf. horizontally | | |
| **c.** | | Horiz. pair, imperf. between | | 900.00 |
| **d.** | | Perf. 13, round holes ('67) | | |

White Wove Paper

**1865** **Wmk. 5** ***Rough Perf. 13***

| | | | | |
|---|---|---|---|---|
| *18* | A1 | 1p orange | 50.00 | 8.75 |
| **a.** | | Horiz. pair, imperf. vert. | 425.00 | |
| *19* | A1 | 2p light bl | 50.00 | 10.00 |
| **a.** | | Vert. pair, imperf. horiz. | 900.00 | |
| **b.** | | Half used as 1p on cover | | 2,000. |
| *20* | A1 | 6p yel green | 135.00 | 12.50 |

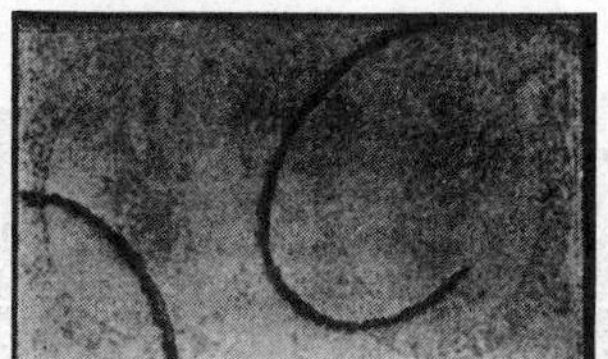

Wmk. 65- "Queensland Postage Stamps" in Sheet in Script Capitals

***Perf. 13, Round Holes***

**1866** **Wmk. 65**

| | | | | |
|---|---|---|---|---|
| *21* | A1 | 1p org ver | 165.00 | 15.00 |
| *22* | A1 | 2p blue | 45.00 | 9.25 |
| **b.** | | Diagonal half used as 1p on cover | | |

**1866** **Unwmk.** **Litho.** ***Perf. 13***

| | | | | |
|---|---|---|---|---|
| *23* | A1 | 4p lilac | 60.00 | 8.00 |
| **a.** | | 4p slate | 135.00 | 16.00 |
| *24* | A1 | 5sh pink | 225.00 | 32.50 |
| **b.** | | Vert. pair, imperf between | | 725.00 |

Wmks. 66 & 67- "Queensland" in Large Single-lined Roman Capitals in the Sheet and Short-pointed Star to Each Stamp (Stars Vary Slightly in Size and Shape)

**Wmk. 66, 67**

**1868-74** **Engr.** ***Perf. 13***

| | | | | |
|---|---|---|---|---|
| *25* | A1 | 1p orange ('71) | 45.00 | 2.75 |
| *26* | A1 | 2p blue | 30.00 | 1.00 |
| *27* | A1 | 3p grnsh brn ('71) | 85.00 | 1.75 |
| **a.** | | 3p brown | 87.50 | 3.50 |
| **b.** | | 3p olive brown | 87.50 | 3.50 |
| *28* | A1 | 6p yel green ('71) | 150.00 | 5.75 |
| **a.** | | 6p deep green | 175.00 | 11.00 |
| *29* | A1 | 1sh dull cl ('72) | 375.00 | 30.00 |
| *30* | A1 | 1sh grnsh gray ('72) | 375.00 | 27.50 |
| *31* | A1 | 1sh violet ('74) | 210.00 | 20.00 |
| | | ***Perf. 12*** | | |
| *32* | A1 | 1p orange | 275.00 | 25.00 |
| *33* | A1 | 2p blue | | 30.00 |
| *34* | A1 | 3p brown | 275.00 | 110.00 |
| *35* | A1 | 6p deep green | 900.00 | 35.00 |
| *36* | A1 | 1sh violet | | 37.50 |
| | | ***Perf. 13x12*** | | |
| *36A* | A1 | 1p orange | | 250.00 |
| *37* | A1 | 2p blue | *1,500.* | 75.00 |
| *37A* | A1 | 3p brown | | *1,250.* |

*The reprints are perforated 13 and the colors differ slightly from those of the originals.*

Wmk. 68- Crown and Q

**1868-75** **Wmk. 68** ***Perf. 13.***

| | | | | |
|---|---|---|---|---|
| *38* | A1 | 1p orange | 50.00 | 3.50 |
| *39* | A1 | 1p rose ('74) | 50.00 | 7.00 |
| *40* | A1 | 2p blue | 35.00 | 1.50 |
| **b.** | | Imperf., pair | 315.00 | |
| *41* | A1 | 3p brown ('75) | 65.00 | 11.00 |
| *42* | A1 | 6p yel green ('69) | 90.00 | 5.00 |
| **a.** | | 6p apple green | 135.00 | 8.00 |
| **b.** | | 6p deep green | 125.00 | 6.75 |
| *43* | A1 | 1sh violet ('75) | *150.00* | 26.00 |

No. 40 exists in vert. pair, imperf. btwn.

**1876-78** ***Perf. 12***

| | | | | |
|---|---|---|---|---|
| *44* | A1 | 1p orange | 37.50 | 1.50 |
| **a.** | | Imperf. | 300.00 | |
| *45* | A1 | 1p rose | 45.00 | 5.50 |
| *46* | A1 | 2p blue | 16.00 | 60 |
| **a.** | | Imperf. | | |
| *47* | A1 | 3p brown | 60.00 | 8.75 |
| *48* | A1 | 6p yellow grn | 100.00 | 4.00 |
| **a.** | | 6p apple green | 135.00 | 4.75 |
| **b.** | | 6p deep green | 135.00 | 4.75 |
| *49* | A1 | 1sh violet | 45.00 | 4.25 |

Nos. 44, 49 exist in vertical pairs, imperf. between.

***Perf. 13x12***

| | | | | |
|---|---|---|---|---|
| *49B* | A1 | 1p orange | | 165.00 |
| *49C* | A1 | 2p blue | *1,800.* | 200.00 |
| *49D* | A1 | 4p yellow | | |
| *49E* | A1 | 6p deep green | | 200.00 |

*The reprints are perforated 12 and are in paler colors than the originals.*

**1879** **Unwmk.** ***Perf. 12***

| | | | | |
|---|---|---|---|---|
| *50* | A1 | 6p pale emerald | 200.00 | 22.50 |
| **a.** | | Horiz. pair, imperf. vert. | | 650.00 |

A2

A3

**1875-81** **Litho.** **Wmk. 68** ***Perf. 13***

| | | | | |
|---|---|---|---|---|
| *50B* | A1 | 4p yellow ('75) | 800.00 | 42.50 |
| | | ***Perf. 12*** | | |
| *51* | A1 | 4p buff ('76) | 600.00 | 21.00 |
| **a.** | | 4p yellow | 600.00 | 21.00 |
| *52* | A1 | 2sh pale bl ('81) | 60.00 | 12.00 |
| **a.** | | 2sh deep blue | 75.00 | 12.00 |
| **b.** | | Imperf. | | |
| *53* | A2 | 2sh6p lt red ('81) | 90.00 | 30.00 |
| *54* | A1 | 5sh org brn ('81) | 82.50 | 27.50 |
| **a.** | | 5sh fawn | 100.00 | 27.50 |
| *55* | A1 | 10sh brown ('81) | 350.00 | 110.00 |
| **a.** | | Imperf. pair | 550.00 | |
| *56* | A1 | 20sh rose ('81) | 650.00 | 90.00 |

Nos. 53-56, 62-64, 74-83 with pen (revenue) cancellations removed are often offered as unused.

**1879-81** **Typo.** **Wmk. 68** ***Perf. 12***

| | | | | |
|---|---|---|---|---|
| *57* | A3 | 1p rose red | 7.50 | 1.40 |
| **a.** | | 1p red orange | 7.50 | 1.40 |
| **b.** | | 1p brown orange | 30.00 | 5.50 |
| **c.** | | "QOEENSLAND" | 110.00 | 32.50 |
| **d.** | | Imperf. | | |
| **e.** | | Vert. pair, imperf. horiz. | | 90.00 |
| *58* | A3 | 2p gray blue | 18.00 | 70 |
| **a.** | | 2p deep ultra | 24.00 | 80 |
| **b.** | | Imperf. | | |
| **c.** | | "PENGE" | | 70.00 |
| **d.** | | "TW" joined | 20.00 | 1.10 |
| **e.** | | Vert. pair, imperf. horiz. | 450.00 | |
| *59* | A3 | 4p org yellow | 47.50 | 2.50 |
| **a.** | | Imperf. | | |
| *60* | A3 | 6p yellow grn | 40.00 | 2.75 |
| **a.** | | Imperf. | | |
| *61* | A3 | 1sh pale vio ('81) | 35.00 | 3.25 |
| **a.** | | 1sh deep violet | 45.00 | 3.75 |
| | | *Nos. 57-61 (5)* | 148.00 | 10.60 |

The stamps of type A3 were electrotyped from plates made up of groups of four types, differing in minor details. Two dies were used for the 1p and 2p, giving eight varieties for each of those values.

There are two varieties of the watermark, differing slightly in the position and shape of the crown and the tongue of the "Q."

Nos. 59-60 exist imperf. vertically.

**Moire on Back**

**1878-79** **Unwmk.**

| | | | | |
|---|---|---|---|---|
| *62* | A3 | 1p brn org ('79) | 450.00 | 60.00 |
| **a.** | | "QOEENSLAND" | | 2,000. |
| *63* | A3 | 2p dp ultra ('79) | 600.00 | 30.00 |
| **a.** | | "PENGE" | 4,750. | 725.00 |
| *64* | A1 | 1sh red violet | 100.00 | 47.50 |

No. 57b Surcharged Vertically in Black **Half-penny**

**1881** **Wmk. 68**

| | | | | |
|---|---|---|---|---|
| *65* | A3 | ½p on 1p brn org | 175.00 | 95.00 |
| **a.** | | "QOEENSLAND" | 1,000. | 825.00 |

A4

A5

**1882-83 Typo. *Perf. 12***

*66* A4 1p pale red 6.00 18
*a.* 1p rose 6.00 18
*b.* Imperf. pair 30.00 30.00
*67* A4 2p gray blue 9.00 15
*a.* 2p deep ultra 9.00 15
*b.* Imperf.
*68* A4 4p yellow ('83) 20.00 1.00
*a.* "PENGE" 125.00 45.00
*b.* Imperf., pair 150.00
*69* A4 6p yellow grn 8.50 60
*70* A4 1sh violet ('83) 8.50 1.00

There are eight minor varieties of the 1p, twelve of the 2p and four each of the other values. On the 1p there is a period after "PENNY". On all values the lines of shading on the neck extend from side to side.

**1883 *Perf. 9½x12***

*71* A4 1p rose 160.00 25.00
*72* A4 2p gray blue 350.00 55.00
*73* A4 1sh pale violet 225.00 30.00

See Nos. 94, 95, 100.

**Wmk. 68 Twice Sideways**
**1882-85 Engr. *Perf. 12***
**Thin Paper**

*74* A5 2sh ultra 65.00 15.00
*75* A5 2sh6p vermilion 50.00 15.00
*76* A5 5sh car rose ('85) 50.00 17.50
*77* A5 10sh brown 95.00 32.50
*78* A5 £1 dark grn ('83) 180.00 55.00
*Nos. 74-78 (5)* 440.00 135.00

The 2sh, 5sh and £1 exist imperf.
There are two varieties of the watermark on Nos. 74-78, as in the 1879-81 issue.

Wmk. 69- Large Crown and Q

**1886 Wmk. 69 *Perf. 12***
**Thick Paper**

*79* A5 2sh ultra 75.00 25.00
*80* A5 2sh6p vermilion 32.50 16.00
*81* A5 5sh car rose 32.50 25.00
*82* A5 10sh dark brn 75.00 40.00
*83* A5 £1 dk green 175.00 40.00
*Nos. 79-83 (5)* 390.00 146.00

High value stamps with cancellations removed are offered as unused.
See Nos. 126-127, 141-144.

A6

Redrawn

**1887-89 Typo. Wmk. 68 *Perf. 12***

*84* A6 1p orange 4.50 20
*a.* Imperf., pair 40.00 60.00
*85* A6 2p gray blue 9.00 18
*a.* 2p deep ultra 11.50 24
*86* A6 2sh red brn ('89) 55.00 20.00

***Perf. 9½x12***

*88* A6 2p deep ultra *250.00* 35.00

The 1p has no period after the value.
In the redrawn stamps the shading lines on the neck are not completed at the left, leaving an irregular white line along that side.
Variety "LA" joined exists on Nos. 84-86, 88, 90, 91, 93, 97, 98, 102.

A7

A8

**1890-92 *Perf. 12½, 13***

*89* A7 ½p green 4.50 32
*90* A6 1p orange red 3.00 10
*91* A6 2p gray blue 4.00 8
*92* A8 2½p rose car 9.25 22
*93* A6 3p brown ('92) 6.50 2.00
*94* A4 4p orange 14.00 1.25
*a.* 4p yellow 16.00 1.25
*b.* "PENGE" 65.00 27.50
*95* A4 6p green 9.25 2.00
*96* A6 2sh red brown 32.50 8.25
*Nos. 89-96 (8)* 83.00 14.22

The ½p and 3p exist imperf.

**1895 Wmk. 69 *Perf. 12½, 13***
**Thick Paper**

*98* A6 1p orange 4.00 50
*99* A6 2p gray blue 3.25 50

***Perf. 12***

*100* A4 1sh pale violet 13.00 3.75

A9

A10

**Moiré on Back**

**1895 Unwmk. *Perf. 12½, 13***

*101* A9 ½p green 1.65 1.90
*a.* Without moire 55.00
*102* A6 1p orange 2.25 2.25
*a.* "PE" missing

**Wmk. 68**

*103* A9 ½p green 1.65 28
*a.* ½p deep green 1.65 28
*b.* Printed on both sides 60.00
*104* A10 1p orange 2.25 12
*105* A10 2p gray blue 2.25 25

**Wmk. 69**
**Thick Paper**

*106* A9 ½p green 1.65 1.90

**1895-96 Unwmk. Thin Paper**
**Crown and Q Faintly Impressed**

*107* A9 ½p green 2.25 80
*108* A10 1p orange 3.25 1.10
*108A* A6 2p gray blue 9.00

A11

A12

A13

**1895-96 Wmk. 68**

*109* A11 1p red 2.50 10
*110* A12 2½p rose 7.50 1.50
*111* A13 5p violet brn 7.50 1.50
*111A* A11 6p yellow grn

A14

A15

A16

A17

A18

A19

TWO PENCE:
Type I - Point of bust does not touch frame.
Type II - First redrawing. The top of the crown, the chignon and the point of the bust touch the frame. The forehead is completely shaded.
Type III - Second redrawing. The top of crown does not touch the frame, though the chignon and the point of the bust do. The forehead and the bridge of the nose are not shaded.

**1897-1900 *Perf. 12, 12½, 13***

*112* A14 ½p deep green 1.25 75
*a.* Perf. 12 150.00
*113* A15 1p red 1.50 5
*114* A16 2p gray blue (I) 2.00 8
*115* A17 2½p rose 12.50 6.25
*116* A17 2½p vio, *blue* 4.00 30
*117* A15 3p brown 4.00 60
*118* A15 4p bright yel 5.00 60
*119* A18 5p violet brn 6.75 1.25
*120* A15 6p yellow grn 6.75 35
*121* A19 1sh lilac 10.50 1.65
*a.* 1sh light violet 14.00 1.65
*122* A19 2sh turq blue 25.00 4.75
*Nos. 112-122 (11)* 79.25 16.63

**1898 *Serrated Roulette 13***

*123* A15 1p scarlet 2.75 2.00
*a.* Serrated and perf. 13 5.00 3.00
*b.* Serrated in black 10.00 10.00
*c.* Serrated without color and in black 9.00 9.00
*d.* Same as "b", and perf. 13 75.00
*e.* Same as "c", and perf. 13 100.00

Queen Victoria — A20

**1899 Typo. *Perf. 12½, 13***

*124* A20 ½p blue green 1.00 25

Unwatermarked stamps are proofs.

"Australia" — A21

Wmk. 70- V and Crown

NINE PENCE:
Type I- "QUEENSLAND" measures 18x1½mm.
Type II- "QUEENSLAND" measures 17½x1¼mm.

**1903 Wmk. 70 *Perf. 12½***

*125* A21 9p org brn & ultra, type I 12.00 3.00
*a.* 9p org brn & ultra, type II 12.00 3.00

See No. 128.

Type of 1882

***Perf. 12, 12½, 13***
**1906 Litho. Wmk. 68**

*126* A5 5sh rose 100.00 82.50
*127* A5 £1 dark green 400.00 150.00

Wmk. 12- Crown and Single-lined A

Wmk. 13- Crown and Double-lined A

**1907 Typo. Wmk. 13 *Perf. 12½***

*128* A21 9p yel brn & ultra, type I 12.00 3.00
*a.* 9p yel brn & ultra, type II 27.50 4.25
*b.* Perf. 11, type II 240.00

**1907 Wmk. 68 *Perf. 12½, 13***

*129* A16 2p ultra, type II 9.00 1.25
*129A* A18 5p dark brown 9.00 1.90
*b.* 5p olive brown 9.00 1.90

**1907-09 Wmk. 12**

*130* A20 ½p deep green 75 30
*131* A15 1p red 1.25 8
*a.* Imperf., pair 200.00
*132* A16 2p ultra, type II 4.25 15
*133* A16 2p ultra, type III 2.25 12
*134* A15 3p pale brown 9.00 1.00
*135* A15 4p bright yellow 10.50 2.75
*136* A15 4p gray blk ('09) 8.25 1.65
*137* A18 5p brown 8.50 1.65
*a.* 5p olive brown 10.50 3.25
*138* A15 6p yellow green 10.50 2.50
*139* A19 1sh violet 15.00 3.75
*140* A19 2sh turquoise bl 27.50 9.00

**Wmk. 12 Sideways**
**Litho.**

*141* A5 2sh6p dp orange 60.00 37.50
*142* A5 5sh rose 60.00 37.50
*143* A5 10sh dark brn 77.50 55.00
*144* A5 £1 bl green 235.00 210.00
*Nos. 130-144 (15)* 530.25 362.95

## SEMI-POSTAL STAMPS

Queen Victoria, Colors and Bearers — SP1

SP2

**1900 Wmk. 68 *Perf. 12, 12½***

*B1* SP1 1p red lilac 60.00 75.00
*B2* SP2 2p dp violet 150.00 165.00

These stamps were sold at 1 shilling and 2 shillings respectively. The difference between their face value and selling price was applied to a patriotic fund in connection with the Boer War.

## REGISTRATION STAMPS

R1

*Clean-Cut Perf. 14 to 16*

**1861 Wmk. 5 Engr.**

| No. | Type | Description | Unused | Used |
|---|---|---|---|---|
| F1 | R1 | (6p) olive yel | 400.00 | 75.00 |
| a. | | Horiz. pair, imperf. vert. | 4,500. | |

*Rough Perf. 14 to 16*

| No. | Type | Description | Unused | Used |
|---|---|---|---|---|
| F2 | R1 | (6p) dl yellow | 50.00 | 35.00 |

**1864 Perf. 12½ to 13**

| No. | Type | Description | Unused | Used |
|---|---|---|---|---|
| F3 | R1 | (6p) golden yel | 70.00 | 40.00 |
| a. | | Imperf. | | |
| b. | | Double impression | 900.00 | |

*The reprints are watermarked with a small truncated star and perforated 12.*

## RAS AL KHAIMA

LOCATION — Oman Peninsula, Arabia, on Persian Gulf.
GOVT. — Sheikdom under British protection.

Ras al Khaima is one of six Persian Gulf sheikdoms to join the United Arab Emirates which proclaimed independence Dec. 2, 1971.

See United Arab Emirates.

100 Naye Paise = 1 Rupee

**Catalogue values for all unused stamps in this country are for Never Hinged items.**

Sheik Saqr bin Mohammed al Qasimi
A1

Seven Palm Trees
A2

Dhow — A3

*Perf. 14½x14*

**1964, Dec. 21 Photo. Unwmk.**

| No. | Type | Description | Unused | Used |
|---|---|---|---|---|
| 1 | A1 | 5np brown & black | 6 | 5 |
| 2 | A1 | 15np deep bl & blk | 15 | 6 |
| 3 | A2 | 30np ocher & black | 35 | 10 |
| 4 | A2 | 40np blue & black | 42 | 18 |
| 5 | A2 | 75np brn red & blk | 85 | 30 |
| 6 | A3 | 1r lt grn & sepia | 1.10 | 35 |
| 7 | A3 | 2r brt vio & sepia | 1.75 | 90 |
| 8 | A3 | 5r bl gray & sepia | 5.50 | 2.25 |
| | | *Nos. 1-8 (8)* | 10.18 | 4.19 |

## RHODESIA

(British South Africa.)

LOCATION — Southeastern Africa.
GOVT. — Formerly administered by the British South Africa Company.
AREA — 440,653 sq. mi.
POP. — 1,738,000 (estimated 1921).
CAPITAL — Salisbury.

In 1923 the area was divided and the portion south of the Zambezi River became the British Crown Colony of Southern Rhodesia. In the following year the remaining territory was formed into the Protectorate of Northern Rhodesia. The Federation of Rhodesia and Nyasaland (comprising Southern Rhodesia, Northern Rhodesia and Nyasaland) was established Sept. 3, 1953.

12 Pence = 1 Shilling
20 Shillings = 1 Pound

A1

A2

Coat of Arms — A3

Thin Paper

**Engr. (A1, A3); Engr., Typo. (A2)**

**1890-94 Unwmk. Perf. 14, 14½**

| No. | Type | Description | Unused | Used |
|---|---|---|---|---|
| 1 | A2 | ½p bl & ver ('91) | 1.65 | 1.25 |
| 2 | A1 | 1p black | 3.50 | 1.50 |
| 3 | A2 | 2p gray grn & ver ('91) | 2.75 | 1.10 |
| 4 | A2 | 3p gray & grn ('91) | 4.50 | 1.10 |
| 5 | A2 | 4p red brn & blk ('91) | 4.25 | 1.50 |
| 6 | A1 | 6p ultra | 47.50 | 18.00 |
| 7 | A1 | 6p dp bl | 12.00 | 3.75 |
| 8 | A2 | 8p rose & bl ('91) | 4.00 | 2.75 |
| 9 | A1 | 1sh gray brn | 15.00 | 10.00 |
| 10 | A1 | 2sh vermilion | 22.50 | 11.50 |
| 11 | A1 | 2sh6p dl lil | 13.00 | 13.00 |
| 12 | A2 | 3sh brn & grn ('94) | 50.00 | 65.00 |
| 13 | A2 | 4sh gray & ver ('93) | 16.00 | 18.00 |
| 14 | A1 | 5sh yellow | 27.50 | 22.50 |
| | | Revenue cancellation | | 75 |
| 15 | A1 | 10sh dp grn | 65.00 | 65.00 |
| | | Revenue cancellation | | 1.85 |
| 16 | A3 | £1 dk bl | 125.00 | 120.00 |
| | | Revenue cancellation | | 1.50 |
| 17 | A3 | £2 rose | 400.00 | 115.00 |
| | | Revenue cancellation | | 2.00 |
| 18 | | £5 yel grn | 2,750. | *600.00* |
| | | Revenue cancellation | | 1.50 |
| 19 | | £10 org brn | 5,000. | *1,200.* |
| | | Revenue cancellation | | 2.00 |
| | | *Nos. 1-16 (16)* | 414.15 | 355.95 |

The paper of the 1891 issue has the trademark and initials of the makers in a monogram watermarked in each sheet. Some of the lower values were also printed on a slightly thicker paper without watermark.

Copies of Nos. 16 to 19 with cancellations removed are frequently offered as unused specimens.

See Nos. 24-25, 58.

Nos. 6 and 9 Surcharged in Black

½d.

**1891, Mar.**

| No. | Type | Description | Unused | Used |
|---|---|---|---|---|
| 20 | A1 | ½p on 6p ultra | 67.50 | *105.00* |
| 21 | A1 | 2p on 6p ultra | 65.00 | *125.00* |
| 22 | A1 | 4p on 6p ultra | 75.00 | *175.00* |
| 23 | A1 | 8p on 1sh brn | 90.00 | *300.00* |

Thick Soft Paper

**1895 Perf. 12½**

| No. | Type | Description | Unused | Used |
|---|---|---|---|---|
| 24 | A2 | 2p green & red | 17.50 | 3.50 |
| 25 | A2 | 4p ocher & black | 17.50 | *6.25* |
| a. | | Imperf., pair | 1,750. | |

A4

**1896 Engraved, Typo. Perf. 14**

| No. | Type | Description | Unused | Used |
|---|---|---|---|---|
| 26 | A4 | ½p sl & vio | 65 | 38 |
| 27 | A4 | 1p scar & emer | 65 | 32 |
| 28 | A4 | 2p brn & rose lil | 1.75 | 75 |
| 29 | A4 | 3p red brn & ultra | 90 | 38 |
| 30 | A4 | 4p bl & red lil | 90 | 28 |
| a. | | ultra & red lil | 3.00 | 2.25 |
| b. | | Horizontal pair, imperf. between | | |
| 31 | A4 | 6p vio & pale rose | 1.75 | 45 |
| a. | | 6p vio & pink | 8.25 | 2.75 |
| 32 | A4 | 8p dp grn & vio, *buff* | 1.25 | 85 |
| a. | | Imperf. pair | 3,000. | |
| b. | | Horizontal pair, imperf. between | | |
| 33 | A4 | 1sh brt grn & ultra | 6.00 | 3.25 |
| 34 | A4 | 2sh dk bl & grn, *buff* | 17.50 | 5.00 |
| 35 | A4 | 2sh6p brn & vio, *yel* | 25.00 | 22.50 |
| 36 | A4 | 3sh grn & red vio, *bl* | 35.00 | 20.00 |
| a. | | Imperf. pair | 3,500. | |
| 37 | A4 | 4sh red & bl, *grn* | 30.00 | 17.50 |
| 38 | A4 | 5sh org red & grn | 25.00 | 20.00 |
| 39 | A4 | 10sh sl & car, *rose* | 100.00 | 90.00 |
| | | *Nos. 26-39 (14)* | 246.35 | 181.66 |

The plates for this issue were made from two dies. Stamps of die I have a small dot at the right of the tail of the supporter at the right of the shield, and the body of the lion is not fully shaded. Stamps of die II have not the dot and the lion is heavily shaded.

Stamps of 1890-94 Surcharged

Surcharged in Black

One Penny

**1896, Apr. Perf. 14**

| No. | Type | Description | Unused | Used |
|---|---|---|---|---|
| 40 | A2 | 1p on 3p gray & grn | 500.00 | 500.00 |
| a. | | "P" of "Penny" inverted | 10,000. | |
| 41 | A2 | 1p on 4sh gray & ver | 400.00 | 400.00 |
| a. | | "P" of "Penny" inverted | 10,000. | |
| b. | | Single bar in surch. | 2,000. | 2,500. |
| c. | | "y" of "Penny" inverted | 10,000. | |

Surcharged in Black

THREE
PENCE.

| No. | Type | Description | Unused | Used |
|---|---|---|---|---|
| 42 | A1 | 3p on 5s yel | 200.00 | *300.00* |
| a. | | "T" of "THREE" inverted | 10,000. | |
| b. | | "R" of "THREE" inverted | 10,000. | |

Cape of Good Hope Stamps Overprinted in Black

BRITISH
SOUTH AFRICA
COMPANY.

**1896, May 22 Wmk. Anchor. (16)**

| No. | Type | Description | Unused | Used |
|---|---|---|---|---|
| 43 | A6 | ½p slate | 7.00 | 8.75 |
| 44 | A15 | 1p carmine | 7.00 | 8.75 |
| 45 | A6 | 2p bis brn | 8.75 | 10.50 |
| 46 | A6 | 4p dp bl | 10.50 | 14.00 |
| a. | | "COMPANY" omitted | 10,750 | |
| 47 | A6 | 6p violet | 27.50 | 35.00 |
| 48 | A6 | 1sh yel buff | 60.00 | 70.00 |

**Wmk. Crown and C. A. (2)**

| No. | Type | Description | Unused | Used |
|---|---|---|---|---|
| 49 | A6 | 3p claret | 27.50 | 42.50 |
| | | *Nos. 43-49 (7)* | 148.25 | 189.50 |

A7

Type A7 differs from type A4 in having the ends of the scroll which is below the shield curved between the hind legs of the supporters instead of passing behind one leg of each. There are other minor differences.

*Perf. 13½ to 16*

**1897 Unwmk. Engr.**

| No. | Type | Description | Unused | Used |
|---|---|---|---|---|
| 50 | A7 | ½p sl & vio | 1.25 | 1.25 |
| 51 | A7 | 1p ver & gray grn | 2.25 | 2.00 |
| 52 | A7 | 2p brn & lil rose | 1.65 | 50 |
| 53 | A7 | 3p red brn & gray bl | 1.65 | 50 |
| a. | | Vertical pair, imperf. between | *1,750.* | |
| 54 | A7 | 4p ultra & red lil | 2.25 | 32 |
| a. | | Horizontal pair, imperf. between | *5,000.* | *5,000.* |
| 55 | A7 | 6p vio & sal | 2.25 | 1.00 |
| 56 | A7 | 8p dk grn & vio, *buff* | 8.25 | 1.25 |
| 57 | A7 | £1 blk & red, *grn* | 400.00 | 130.00 |
| | | Revenue cancellation | | 10.00 |
| | | *Nos. 50-56 (7)* | 19.55 | 6.82 |

**Thick Paper**

*Perf. 15*

| No. | Type | Description | Unused | Used |
|---|---|---|---|---|
| 58 | A3 | £2 bright red | *2,000.* | 550.00 |
| | | Revenue cancellation | | *50.00* |

A8

A9

A10

**1898-1908 Perf. 13½ to 16**

| No. | Type | Description | Unused | Used |
|---|---|---|---|---|
| 59 | A8 | ½p yel grn | 18 | 7 |
| a. | | Imperf. pair | 900.00 | |
| b. | | Horiz. pair, imperf. vert. | 900.00 | |
| 60 | A8 | 1p rose | 22 | 6 |
| a. | | 1p red | 75 | 6 |
| b. | | Horiz. or vert. pair, imperf. between | 550.00 | |
| d. | | Imperf. pair | *650.00* | *650.00* |
| 61 | A8 | 2p brown | 55 | 9 |
| 62 | A8 | 2½p cob bl ('03) | 2.25 | 10 |
| a. | | Horiz. pair, imperf. between | *750.00* | *750.00* |
| 63 | A8 | 3p cl ('08) | 1.65 | 65 |
| a. | | Vert. pair, imperf. between | 900.00 | |
| 64 | A8 | 4p ol grn | 1.25 | 22 |
| a. | | Vertical pair, imperf. between | *1,200.* | |
| 65 | A8 | 6p lilac | 1.50 | 35 |
| a. | | Vertical pair, imperf. between | | |
| 66 | A9 | 1sh ol bis | 1.90 | 38 |
| a. | | Imperf., pair | *3,500.* | |
| b. | | Horiz. or vert. pair, imperf. between | *3,500.* | |
| 67 | A9 | 2sh6p bluish gray ('06) | 6.25 | 65 |
| a. | | Vertical pair, imperf. between | *1,350.* | *750.00* |
| 68 | A9 | 3sh pur ('08) | 4.75 | 1.00 |
| 69 | A9 | 5sh org ('01) | 11.50 | 2.75 |
| 70 | A9 | 7sh6p blk ('01) | 24.00 | 22.50 |
| 71 | A9 | 10sh bluish grn ('08) | 7.00 | 2.00 |

72 A10 £1 gray vio ('01) 100.00 25.00
Revenue cancellation 1.00
73 A10 £2 red brn ('08) 30.00 8.75
74 A10 £5 dk bl ('01) 5,000.
Revenue cancellation 6.00
75 A10 £10 bl lil ('01) 6,750.
Revenue cancellation 5.50
*Nos. 59-73 (15)* 193.00 64.57

Victoria Falls — A11

**1905, July 13** ***Perf. 13½ to 15***

76 A11 1p rose red 1.65 2.00
77 A11 2½p ultra 5.75 5.75
78 A11 5p magenta 11.00 11.00
79 A11 1sh bl grn 13.00 15.00
a. Pair, imperf. between 10,750.
b. Imperf., pair 12,500.
80 A11 2sh6p black 65.00 75.00
81 A11 5sh violet 55.00 45.00
*Nos. 76-81 (6)* 151.40 153.75

Opening of the Victoria Falls bridge across the Zambezi River.

Stamps of 1898-1908 Overprinted or Surcharged:

RHODESIA. RHODESIA. 5d

**1909** ***Perf. 14, 15***

82 A8 ½p yel grn 12 12
83 A8 1p red 15 8
a. Horiz. pair, imperf. vert. 450.00
84 A8 2p brown 90 90
85 A8 2½p cob bl 30 10
86 A8 3p claret 60 18
b. Double ovpt.
87 A8 4p ol grn 1.75 45
88 A8 5p on 6p lil 1.10 1.65
89 A8 6p lilac 4.25 60
90 A9 7½p on 2sh 6p bluish gray 75 60
91 A9 10p on 3sh pur 1.25 1.25
92 A9 1sh ol bis 3.00 35
93 A9 2sh on 5sh org 2.50 1.65
94 A9 2sh6p bluish gray 9.00 3.50
95 A9 3sh purple 9.00 6.00
96 A9 5sh orange 18.00 5.50
97 A9 7sh6p black 40.00 22.50
98 A9 10sh bluish grn 22.50 6.00
99 A10 £1 gray vio 90.00 40.00
a. Pair, one without overprint 15,000.
b. Violet ovpt. 250.00 180.00
100 A10 £2 red brn 2,250. 325.00
*Nos. 82-99 (18)* 205.17 91.43

Rhodesian authorities made available remainders in large quantities of all stamps in this group, CTO, including inverted overprints of the 3p ($25), 4p ($15) and 2s6p ($27.50).

Nos. 82-87, 89, 92, 94, 96 and 98 exist without period after "Rhodesia."

Queen Mary and King George V
A12 A13

**1910** **Engr.** ***Perf. 14, 15x14, 14x15***

101 A12 ½p green 2.50 25
a. ½p ol grn 14.00 1.25
b. Perf. 15 225.00 13.00
c. Imperf., pair 6,000. 6,750.
d. Perf. 13½ 300.00 37.50
102 A12 1p rose car 2.75 25
a. Vertical pair, imperf. btwn. 18,500.
b. Perf. 15 400.00 7.00
c. Perf. 13½ 2,250. 55.00
103 A12 2p gray & blk 13.00 5.00
a. Horiz. pair, imperf. between 
b. Perf. 15 575.00 27.50
104 A12 2½p lt bl 11.00 6.00
a. 2½p ultra 9.00 6.00
b. Perf. 15 125.00 60.00
c. Perf. 13½ 35.00 37.50
105 A12 3p ol yel & vio 12.50 7.00
a. Perf. 15 1,600. 55.00
106 A12 4p org & blk 16.00 15.00
a. 4p org & vio blk 52.50 35.00
b. Perf. 15x14 575.00
c. Perf. 15 35.00 67.50
107 A12 5p ol grn & brn 25.00 27.50
a. 5p ol yel & brn (error) 400.00 115.00
b. Perf. 15 450.00 115.00
108 A12 6p cl & brn 13.00 7.25
a. Perf. 15 1,000. 55.00
109 A12 8p brn vio & gray blk 75.00 32.50
a. Perf. 13½ 50.00 50.00
110 A12 10p plum & rose red 25.00 27.50
111 A12 1sh turq grn & blk 13.00 4.00
a. Horiz. pair, imperf. between 
b. Perf. 15 475.00 35.00
112 A12 2sh gray bl & blk 42.50 25.00
a. Perf. 15 575.00 325.00
113 A12 2sh6p car rose & blk 225.00 225.00
114 A12 3sh vio & bl grn 80.00 87.50
115 A12 5sh yel grn & brn red 150.00 145.00
116 A12 7sh6p brt bl & car 600.00 600.00
117 A12 10sh red org & myr grn 450.00 250.00
a. 10sh red org & bl grn 350.00 250.00
118 A12 £1 bluish sl & car 650.00 250.00
a. £1 blk & red 700.00 250.00
c. Perf. 15 13,500. 5,500.
*Nos. 101-118 (18)* 2,406. 1,714.

The £1 exists in plum and red, an unissued variety of which 100 were found in the remainders sold in London in 1924

**1913-19** ***Perf. 14***

119 A13 ½p green 85 15
a. Imperf. vert., pair 600.00 600.00
b. Perf. 15 4.00 2.50
c. Perf. 14x15 2,000. 200.00
d. Perf. 15x14 2,000. 225.00
120 A13 1p brt rose 85 12
a. 1p brn rose 1.50 12
b. Horizontal pair, imperf. between 600.00 600.00
c. Perf. 15 1.50 1.50
121 A13 1½p bister 1.25 20
a. Perf. 15 5.25 2.75
b. Perf. 15x14
c. Vert. pair, imperf. between 750.00 750.00
d. Horiz. pair, imperf. between 750.00 750.00
122 A13 2p gray & blk 2.00 60
a. 2p vio blk & blk 2.25 1.10
b. Perf. 15 2.25 2.25
c. Horiz. pair, imperf. between 5,000. 5,500.
123 A13 2½p ultra 3.50 3.50
a. Perf. 15 8.25 8.25
124 A13 3p yel & blk 3.50 1.50
a. 3p org yel & blk 3.50 1.25
b. Perf. 15 6.00 5.25
125 A13 4p org red & blk 3.25 3.00
a. Perf. 15 30.00 13.00
126 A13 5p yel grn & blk 3.75 4.00
127 A13 6p lil & blk 2.75 1.50
a. Perf. 15 4.00 4.00
128 A13 8p gray grn & vio 10.00 9.25
a. Perf. 15 30.00 30.00
129 A13 10p car rose & bl, perf. 15 6.50 6.50
a. Perf. 14 6.50 7.25
130 A13 1sh turq bl & blk 3.00 1.25
a. Perf. 15 6.50 1.75
131 A13 1sh lt grn & blk ('19) 27.50 2.00
132 A13 2sh brn & blk, perf. 15 10.00 9.25
a. Perf. 14 10.00 5.25
133 A13 2sh6p gray & bl 20.00 8.50
a. 2sh6p ol gray & vio bl 20.00 8.50
b. Perf. 15 20.00 20.00
134 A13 3sh brt bl & red brn 25.00 13.00
a. Perf. 15 130.00 130.00
135 A13 5sh grn & bl 32.50 20.00
a. Perf. 15 52.50 35.00
136 A13 7sh6p blk & vio, perf. 15 82.50 90.00
a. Perf. 14 130.00 130.00
137 A13 10sh yel grn & car 115.00 100.00
a. Perf. 15 225.00 275.00
138 A13 £1 vio & blk 430.00 500.00
a. £1 mag & blk 430.00 500.00
b. Perf. 15 725.00 725.00
*Nos. 119-138 (20)* 783.70 774.32

Three dies were used for the stamps of this issue. They differ in the shading of the King's left ear and the outline of the top of the cap.

No. 120 Surcharged in Dark Violet:

Half Penny — No. 139
Half. Penny. — No. 140

**1917**

139 A13 ½p on 1p bright rose 1.00 1.00
a. Inverted surcharge 1,200. 1,200.
140 A13 ½p on 1p bright rose 65 65

Nos. 141-190 are accorded to Rhodesia and Nyasaland.

## RHODESIA

### Self-Governing State (formerly Southern Rhodesia)

LOCATION — Southeastern Africa, bordered by Zambia, Mozambique, South Africa and Botswana.
GOVT. — Self-governing member of British Commonwealth.
AREA — 150,333 sq. mi.
POP. — 4,670,000 (est. 1968).
CAPITAL — Salisbury.

In 1965, Southern Rhodesia assumed the name Rhodesia. On Nov. 11, 1965, the white minority government declared Rhodesia independent. Rhodesia became Zimbabwe on Dec. 31, 1978. For earlier issues, see Southern Rhodesia and Rhodesia and Nyasaland.

12 Pence = 1 Shilling
20 Shillings = 1 Pound
100 Cents = 1 Dollar (1967)

**Catalogue values for all unused stamps in this country are for Never Hinged items.**

ITU Emblem, Old and New Communication Equipment — A27

**Unwmk.**

**1965, May 17** **Photo.** ***Perf. 14***

200 A27 6p ap grn & brt vio 1.40 55
201 A27 1sh3p brt vio & dk vio 2.00 1.40
202 A27 2sh6p org brn & dk vio 6.75 5.75

Cent. of the ITU.

Bangala Dam — A28

Designs: 4p, Irrigation canal through sugar plantation. 2sh6p, Worker cutting sugar cane.

**1965, July 19** **Photo.** ***Perf. 14***

203 A28 3p dl bl, grn & ocher 32 15
204 A28 4p bl, grn & brn 1.00 80
205 A28 2sh6p multi 5.25 4.50

Issued to publicize Conservation Week of the Natural Resources Board.

Churchill, Parliament, Quill and Sword
A29

**1965, Aug. 16**

206 A29 1sh3p ultra & blk 1.50 1.10

Sir Winston Spencer Churchill (1874-1965), statesman and WW II leader.

### Issues of Smith Government

Arms of Rhodesia
A30

**1965, Dec. 8** **Photo.** ***Perf. 11***

207 A30 2sh6p vio & multi 70 60
a. Imperf., pair 500.00

Declaration of independence by the government of Prime Minister Ian Smith.

Southern Rhodesia Nos. 95-108 Overprinted

**INDEPENDENCE 11th November 1965**

***Perf. 14½***

**1966, Jan. 17** **Unwmk.** **Photo.**

**Size: 23x19mm**

208 A30 ½p lt bl, yel & grn 5 5
209 A30 1p ocher & pur 6 6
210 A30 2p vio & org yel 9 8
211 A30 3p lt bl & choc 18 15
212 A30 4p sl grn & org 20 18

***Perf. 13½x13***

**Size: 27x23mm**

213 A30 6p dl grn, red & yel 22 20
a. Pair, one without ovpt.
214 A30 9p ol grn, yel & brn 35 30
a. Double ovpt. 125.00
b. Inverted ovpt.
215 A30 1sh ocher & brt grn 38 35
a. Double ovpt. 150.00
216 A30 1sh3p grn, vio & dk red 50 45
217 A30 2sh dl bl & yel 1.40 1.25
218 A30 2sh6p ultra & red 85 75
a. Red omitted

***Perf. 14½x14***

**Size: 32x27mm**

**Overprint 26mm Wide**

219 A30 5sh bl, grn, ocher & lt brn 19.00 13.00
220 A30 10sh ocher, blk, red & bl 4.50 4.00
221 A30 £1 rose, sep, ocher & grn 8.25 7.50
*Nos. 208-221 (14)* 36.03 28.32

No. 206 Surcharged in Red

**INDEPENDENCE 11th November 1965 = 5/-**

***Perf. 14***

222 A29 5sh on 1sh3p 57.50 75.00

Ansellia Orchid — A31

Designs: 1p, Cape Buffalo. 2p, Oranges. 3p, Kudu. 4p, Emeralds. 6p, Flame lily. 9p, Tobacco. 1sh, Corn. 1sh3p, Lake Kyle. 2sh, Aloe. 2sh6p, Tigerfish. 5sh, Cattle. 10sh, Gray-breasted helmet guinea fowl. £1, Arms of Rhodesia.

Printed by Harrison & Sons, London.

**1966, Feb. 9** **Photo.** ***Perf. 14½***

**Size: 23x19mm.**

223 A31 1p ocher & pur 5 5
224 A31 2p sl grn & org 6 5
225 A31 3p lt bl & choc 8 5
b. Queen's head omitted
c. Bklt. pane of 4 1.00
226 A31 4p gray & brt grn 12 10

***Perf. 13½x13***

**Size: 27x23mm.**

*227* A31 6p dl grn, red & yel 18 8
*228* A31 9p pur & ocher 30 30
*229* A31 1sh lt bl, yel & grn 35 18
*230* A31 1sh3p dl bl & yel 55 35
*231* A31 1sh6p ol grn, yel & brn 75 45
*232* A31 2sh lt ol grn, vio & dk red 85 55
*233* A31 2sh6p brt grnsh bl, ultra & ver 1.00 70

***Perf. 14½x14***

**Size: 32x27mm.**

*234* A31 5sh bl, grn, ocher & lt brn 3.25 2.25
*235* A31 10sh dl yel, blk, red & bl 8.50 7.50
*236* A31 £1 sal pink, sep, ocher & grn 20.00 17.50
*Nos. 223-236 (14)* 36.04 30.11

Printed by Mardon Printers, Salisbury

**1966-68 Litho. *Perf. 14½***

*223a* A31 1p ocher & pur 14 12
*224a* A31 2p sl grn & org ('68) 28 18
*225a* A31 3p lt bl & choc ('68) 40 28
*226a* A31 4p sep & brt grn 55 45
*227a* A31 6p gray grn, red & yel 85 65
*228a* A31 9p pur & ocher ('68) 1.10 85
*230a* A31 1sh3p dl bl & yel 1.40 1.10
*232a* A31 2sh lt ol grn, vio & dk red 5.50 4.50

***Perf. 14***

*234a* A31 5sh brt bl, grn, ocher & brn 15.00 11.00
*235a* A31 10sh ocher, blk, red & bl 45.00 37.50
*236a* A31 £1 sal pink, sep, ocher & grn 67.50 55.00
*Nos. 223a-236a (11)* 137.72 111.63

Zeederberg Coach A32

Designs: 9p, Sir Rowland Hill. 1sh6p, Penny Black. 2sh6p, Rhodesia No. 18, £5.

***Perf. 14½***

**1966, May 2 Litho. Unwmk.**

*237* A32 3p bl, org & blk 55 45
*238* A32 9p beige & brn 75 65
*239* A32 1sh6p bl & blk 1.90 1.50
*240* A32 2sh6p rose, yel grn & blk 3.50 3.25
**a.** Souv. sheet of 4 27.50 27.50

28th Cong. of the Southern Africa Phil. Fed. and the RHOPEX Exhib., Bulawayo, May 2-7. No. 240a contains one each of Nos. 237-240. Black marginal inscription. Size: 124x84mm.

De Havilland Dragon Rapide A33

Planes: 1sh3p, Douglas DC-3. 2sh6p, Vickers Viscount. 5sh, Jet.

**1966, June 1**

*241* A33 6p multi 1.40 1.25
*242* A33 1sh3p multi 2.25 1.50
*243* A33 2sh6p multi 6.25 5.50
*244* A33 5sh bl & blk 10.50 8.75

20th anniversary of Central African Airways.

**Dual Currency Issue**

Type of 1966 with Denominations in Cents and Pence-Shillings

**1967-68 Litho. *Perf. 14½***

*245* A31 3p/2½c lt bl & choc 50 40
*246* A31 1sh/10c bl, yel & grn 2.00 1.50
*247* A31 1sh6p/15c grn, yel & brn 15.00 7.50
*248* A31 2sh/20c ol, vio & dk red 22.50 15.00
*248A* A31 2sh6p/25c multi 60.00 70.00
*Nos. 245-248A (5)* 100.00 94.40

These locally printed stamps were issued to acquaint Rhodesians with the decimal currency to be introduced in 1969-1970.

Issue dates: 3p, Mar. 15, 1967. 1sh, Nov. 1, 1967. 1sh6p, 2sh, Mar. 11, 1968. 2sh6p, Dec. 9, 1968.

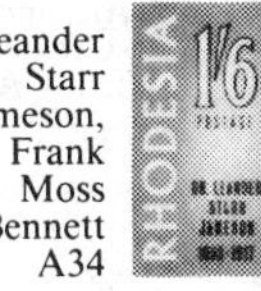

Leander Starr Jameson, by Frank Moss Bennett A34

**1967, May 17**

*249* A34 1sh6p emer & multi 1.65 1.50

Dr. Leander Starr Jameson (1853-1917), pioneer with Cecil Rhodes and Prime Minister of Cape Colony. See No. 262.

Soapstone Sculpture, by Joram Mariga A35

Designs: 9p, Head of Burgher of Calais, by Auguste Rodin. 1sh3p, "Totem," by Roberto Crippa. 2sh6p, St. John the Baptist, by Michele Tosini.

**1967, July 12 Litho. *Perf. 14***

*250* A35 3p brn, blk & ol grn 32 30
*251* A35 9p brt bl, blk & ol grn 1.00 90
*252* A35 1sh3p multi 1.50 1.40
*253* A35 2sh6p multi 3.00 2.75

10th anniv. of the Rhodes Natl. Gallery, Salisbury.

White Rhinoceros A36

Designs: No. 255, Parrot's beak gladioli (vert.). No. 256, Baobab tree. No. 257, Elephants.

**1967, Sept. 6 Unwmk. *Perf. 14½***

*254* A36 4p ol & blk 65 65
*255* A36 4p dp org & blk 65 65
*256* A36 4p brn & blk 65 65
*257* A36 4p gray & blk 65 65

Issued to publicize nature conservation.

Wooden Hand Plow, c. 1820 A37

Designs: 9p, Ox-drawn plow, c. 1860. 1sh6p, Steam tractor and plows, c. 1905. 2sh6p, Tractor and moldboard plow, 1968.

**1968, Apr. 26 Litho. *Perf. 14½***

*258* A37 3p multi 20 20
*259* A37 9p multi 45 45
*260* A37 1sh6p multi 1.00 1.00
*261* A37 2sh6p multi 2.75 2.75

Issued to commemorate the 15th world plowing contest, Kent Estate, Norton.

Portrait Type of 1967

Design: 1sh6p, Alfred Beit (portrait at left).

**1968, July 15 Unwmk. *Perf. 14½***

*262* A34 1sh6p org, blk & red 1.75 1.75

Alfred Beit (1853-1906), philanthropist and friend of Cecil Rhodes.

Allan Wilson, Matopos Hills — A38

Matabeleland, 75th Anniversary: 3p, Flag raising, Bulawayo, 1893. 9p, Bulawayo arms, view of Bulawayo.

**1968, Nov. 4 Litho. *Perf. 14½***

*263* A38 3p multi 35 35
*264* A38 9p multi 1.25 1.25
*265* A38 1sh6p multi 2.50 2.50

William Henry Milton (1854-1930), Adminstrator — A39

**1969, Jan. 15**

*266* A39 1sh6p multi 1.75 1.75

See Nos. 298-303.

Locomotive, 1890's — A40

Beira-Salisbury Railroad, 70th Anniversary: 9p, Steam locomotive, 1901. 1sh6p, Garratt articulated locomotive, 1950. 2sh6p, Diesel, 1955.

**1969, May 22**

*267* A40 3p multi 55 25
*268* A40 9p multi 1.65 95
*269* A40 1sh6p multi 6.75 5.00
*270* A40 2sh6p multi 10.50 8.50

Low Level Bridge A41

Bridges: 9p, Mpudzi River. 1sh6p, Umniati River. 2sh6p, Birchenough over Sabi River.

**1969, Sept. 18**

*271* A41 3p multi 38 28
*272* A41 9p multi 1.40 75
*273* A41 1sh6p multi 4.75 3.50
*274* A41 2sh6p multi 6.25 4.25

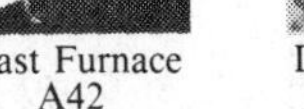

Blast Furnace A42

Devil's Cataract, Victoria Falls A43

Designs: 1c, Wheat harvest. 2½c, Ruins, Zimbabwe. 3c, Trailer truck. 3½c, 4c, Cecil Rhodes statue. 5c, Mining. 6c, Hydrofoil, "Seaflight." 7½c, like 8c. 10c, Yachting, Lake McIlwaine. 12½c, Hippopotamus. 14c, 15c, Kariba Dam. 20c, Irrigation canal. 25c, Bateleur eagles. 50c, Radar antenna and Viscount plane. $1, "Air Rescue." $2, Rhodesian flag.

**1970-73 Litho. *Perf. 14½***

**Size: 22x18mm**

*275* A42 1c multi 12 10
*276* A42 2c multi 12 10
*277* A42 2½c multi 12 10
*278* A42 3c multi ('73) 2.00 28
*279* A42 3½c multi 18 10
*280* A42 4c multi ('73) 2.00 28
*281* A42 5c multi 25 15

**Size: 27x23mm**

*282* A43 6c multi ('73) 3.25 1.25
*283* A43 7½c multi ('73) 6.25 4.00
*284* A43 8c multi 2.75 1.00
*285* A43 10c multi 55 32
*286* A43 12½c multi 65 32
*287* A43 14c multi ('73) 9.25 3.25
*288* A43 15c multi ('71) 2.75 50
*289* A43 20c multi 3.25 55

**Size: 30x25mm**

*290* A43 25c multi 3.50 1.25
*291* A43 50c multi 6.25 5.00
*292* A43 $1 multi 12.00 10.50
*293* A43 $2 multi 32.50 30.00
*Nos. 275-293 (19)* 87.74 59.05

In 1972 Nos. 275, 277, and 279 were issued in sheets of four to commemorate Rhophil '72 Philatelic Exhibition.

Despatch Rider, c. 1890 — A44

Posts and Telecommunications Corporation, Inauguration: 3½c, Loading mail, Salisbury Airport. 15c, Telegraph line construction, c.1890. 25c, Telephone and telecommunications equipment.

**1970, July 1**

*294* A44 2½c multi 30 30
*295* A44 3½c multi 70 70
*296* A44 15c multi 2.25 2.25
*297* A44 25c multi 4.00 4.00

Famous Rhodesians Type of 1969

Portraits: 13c Dr. Robert Moffat (1795-1883), missionary. No. 299, Dr. David Livingstone (1813-73), explorer. No. 300, George Pauling (1854-1919), engineer No. 301, Thomas Baines (1820-75), self-portrait. No. 302, Mother Patrick (1863-1900), Dominican nurse and teacher. No. 303, Frederick Courteney Selous (1851-1917), explorer, big game hunter.

**1970-75 Litho. *Perf. 14½***

*298* A39 13c multi ('72) 2.25 2.25
*299* A39 14c multi ('73) 2.25 2.25
*300* A39 14c multi ('74) 2.50 2.50
*301* A39 14c multi ('75) 2.50 2.50
*302* A39 15c multi 2.50 2.50
*303* A39 15c multi ('71) 2.50 2.50
*Nos. 298-303 (6)* 14.50 14.50

African Hoopoe — A45

Porphyritic Granite — A46

Birds: 2½c, Half-collared kingfisher (horiz.). 5c, Golden-breasted bunting. 7½c, Carmine bee-eater. 8c, Red-eyed bulbul. 25c, Wattled plover (horiz.).

**1971, June 1**

*304* A45 2c multi 1.00 45
*305* A45 2½c multi 1.25 50
*306* A45 5c multi 2.75 1.10
*307* A45 7½c multi 3.50 1.75

308 A45 8c multi 3.50 1.75
309 A45 25c multi 10.00 4.25
*Nos. 304-309 (6)* 22.00 9.80

**1971, Aug. 30**

Granite '71, Geological Symposium, Aug. 30-Sept. 19: 7½c, Muscovite mica, seen through microscope. 15c, Granite, seen through microscope. 25c, Geological map of Rhodesia.

310 A46 2½c multi 45 40
311 A46 7½c multi 2.00 1.50
312 A46 15c multi 3.00 2.50
313 A46 25c multi 4.50 4.00

"Be Airwise" A47

Prevent Pollution: 3½c, Antelope (Be Country-wise). 7c, Fish (Be Waterwise). 13c, City (Be Citywise).

**1972, July 17**

314 A47 2½c multi 30 30
315 A47 3½c multi 60 60
316 A47 7c multi 1.40 1.40
317 A47 13c multi 2.00 2.00

The Three Kings A48

W.M.O. Emblem A49

**1972, Oct. 18**

318 A48 2c multi 14 14
319 A48 5c multi 55 55
320 A48 13c multi 1.50 1.50

Christmas 1972.

**1973, July 2**

321 A49 3c multi 12 12
322 A49 14c multi 1.40 1.40
323 A49 25c multi 2.50 2.50

Intl. Meteorological Cooperation, cent.

Arms of Rhodesia A50

**1973, Oct. 10**

324 A50 2½c multi 35 35
325 A50 4c multi 65 65
326 A50 7½c multi 1.50 1.50
327 A50 14c multi 2.75 2.75

Responsible Government, 50th Anniversary.

Kudu A51

Thunbergia A52

Pearl Charaxes — A53

**1974-76 Litho. *Perf. 14½***

328 A51 1c *shown* 18 9
329 A51 2½c *Eland* 55 15
330 A51 3c *Roan antelope* 18 8
331 A51 4c *Reedbuck* 18 8
332 A51 5c *Bushbuck* 22 9
333 A52 6c *shown* 32 15
334 A52 7½c *Flame lily* 3.75 2.00
335 A52 8c *like 7½c ('76)* 28 10
336 A52 10c *Devil thorn* 28 12
337 A52 12c *Hibiscus ('76)* 45 20
338 A52 12½c *Pink sabi star* 3.75 2.00
339 A52 14c *Wild pimpernel* 5.50 3.00
340 A52 15c *like 12½c ('76)* 55 30
341 A52 16c *like 14c ('76)* 55 30
342 A53 20c *shown* 55 30
343 A53 24c *Yellow pansy ('76)* 1.10 60
344 A53 25c *like 24c* 5.50 3.00
345 A53 50c *Queen purple tip* 1.40 75
346 A53 $1 *Striped sword-tail* 2.75 1.50
347 A53 $2 *Guinea fowl butterfly* 5.50 3.00
*Nos. 328-347 (20)* 33.54 17.81

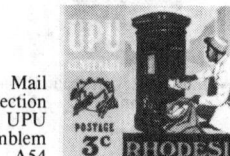

Mail Collection and UPU Emblem A54

**1974, Nov. 20 *Perf. 14½***

348 A54 3c *shown* 42 42
349 A54 4c *Mail sorting* 60 60
350 A54 7½c *Mail delivery* 1.10 1.10
351 A54 14c *Parcel post* 2.00 2.00

Universal Postal Union Centenary.

Euphorbia Confinalis — A55

**1975, July 16**

352 A55 2½c *shown* 16 16
353 A55 3c *Aloe excelsa* 18 18
354 A55 4c *Hoodia lugardii* 35 25
355 A55 7½c *Aloe ortholopha* 65 48
356 A55 14c *Aloe musapana* 1.50 1.25
357 A55 25c *Aloe Saponaria* 2.00 1.90
*Nos. 352-357 (6)* 4.84 4.22

International Succulent Congress, Salisbury, July 1975.

Head Injury and Safety Helmet — A56

Occupational Safety: 4c, Bandaged hand and safety glove. 7½c, Injured eye and safety eyeglass. 14c, Blind man and protective shield.

**1975, Oct. 15**

358 A56 2½c multi 18 18
359 A56 4c multi 65 65
360 A56 7½c multi 1.00 1.00
361 A56 14c multi 1.75 1.75

Telephones, 1876 and 1976 — A57

Alexander Graham Bell — A58

**1976, Mar. 10**

362 A57 3c lt bl & blk 15 10
363 A58 14c buff & blk 65 65

Centenary of first telephone call, by Alexander Graham Bell, Mar. 10, 1876.

Nos. 334, 339 and 344 Surcharged with New Value and Two Bars

**1976, July 1**

364 A52 8c on 7½c multi 30 30
365 A52 16c on 14c multi 60 60
366 A53 24c on 25c multi 1.90 1.90

Wildlife Protection A59

**1976, July 21**

367 A59 4c *Roan Antelope* 24 24
368 A59 6c *Brown hyena* 35 35
369 A59 8c *Wild dog* 48 48
370 A59 16c *Cheetah* 1.10 1.10

Brachystegia Spiciformis A60

Black-eyed Bulbul A61

**1976, Nov. 17**

371 A60 4c *shown* 16 16
372 A60 6c *Red mahogany* 20 20
373 A60 8c *Pterocarpus angolensis* 50 50
374 A60 16c *Rhodesian teak* 1.00 1.00

Flowering trees.

**1977, Mar. 16**

Birds: 4c, Yellow-mantled whydah. 6c, Orange-throated longclaw. 8c, Long-tailed shrike. 16c, Lesser blue-eared starling. 24c, Red-billed wood hoopoe.

375 A61 3c multi 15 15
376 A61 4c multi 20 20
377 A61 6c multi 30 30
378 A61 8c multi 45 45
379 A61 16c multi 90 90
380 A61 24c multi 1.10 1.10
*Nos. 375-380 (6)* 3.10 3.10

Lake Kyle, by Joan Evans A62

Landscape Paintings: 4c, Chimanimani Mountains, by Evans. 6c, Rocks near Bonsor Reef, by Alice Balfour. 8c, Dwala (rock) near Devil's Pass, by Balfour. 16c, Zimbabwe, by Balfour. 24c, Victoria Falls, by Thomas Baines.

**1977, July 20 Litho. *Perf. 14½***

381 A62 3c multi 12 12
382 A62 4c multi 16 16
383 A62 6c multi 25 25
384 A62 8c multi 35 35
385 A62 16c multi 65 65
386 A62 24c multi 1.00 1.00
*Nos. 381-386 (6)* 2.53 2.53

Virgin and Child A63

Fair Spire and Fairgrounds A64

**1977, Nov. 16**

387 A63 3c multi 10 10
388 A63 6c multi 20 20
389 A63 8c multi 32 32
390 A63 16c multi 60 60

Christmas 1977.

**1978, Mar. 15**

19th Rhodesian Trade Fair, Bulawayo: 8c, Fair spire.

391 A64 4c multi 15 15
392 A64 8c multi 35 35

Morganite A65

Black Rhinoceros A66

Odzani Falls — A67

**1978, Aug. 16 Litho. *Perf. 14½***

393 A65 1c *shown* 5 5
394 A65 3c *Amethyst* 8 5
395 A65 4c *Garnet* 10 5
396 A65 5c *Citrine* 10 5
397 A65 7c *Blue topaz* 12 10
398 A66 9c *shown* 12 10
399 A66 11c *Lion* 15 12
400 A66 13c *Warthog* 15 12
401 A66 15c *Giraffe* 15 15
402 A66 17c *Zebra* 20 15
403 A67 21c *shown* 24 24
404 A67 25c *Goba Falls* 28 28
405 A67 30c *Inyangombe Falls* 40 40
406 A67 $1 *Bridal Veil Falls* 1.75 1.75
407 A67 $2 *Victoria Falls* 2.75 1.75
*Nos. 393-407 (15)* 6.64 5.36

Wright's Flyer A — A68

**1978, Oct. 18**

408 A68 4c *shown* 6 6
409 A68 5c *Bleriot XI* 12 12
410 A68 7c *Vickers Vimy* 18 18
411 A68 9c *A.W. 15 Atalanta* 30 30
412 A68 17c *Vickers Viking 1B* 60 60
413 A68 25c *Boeing 720* 85 85
*Nos. 408-413 (6)* 2.11 2.11

75th anniversary of powered flight.

Rhodesia stamps were replaced in 1978 by stamps of Zimbabwe.

### POSTAGE DUE STAMPS

Type of Rhodesia and Nyasaland, 1961, Inscribed "RHODESIA"

***Hyphen Hole Perf. 5***

**1965, June 17 Typo. Unwmk.**

*J5* D1 1p vermilion 90 90
**a.** Rouletted 9½ 45 45

***Rouletted 9½***

*J6* D1 2p dk bl 45 45
*J7* D1 4p emerald 70 70
*J8* D1 6p purple 1.50 1.50

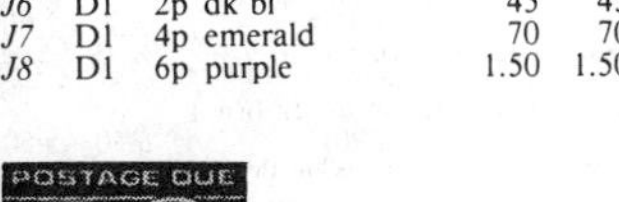

Soapstone Zimbabwe Bird — D2

**1967 Litho. *Perf. 14½***

*J9* D2 1p crimson 60 60
*J10* D2 2p vio bl 75 75
*J11* D2 4p emerald 1.25 1.25
*J12* D2 6p lilac 1.50 1.50
*J13* D2 1sh dl red brn 2.00 2.00
*J14* D2 2sh black 3.00 3.00
*Nos. J9-J14 (6)* 9.10 9.10

**1970-73 Litho. *Perf. 14½***

**Size: 26x22½mm.**

*J15* D2 1c brt grn 10 10
*J16* D2 2c ultra 20 20
*J17* D2 5c red vio 30 30
*J18* D2 6c lem ('73) 1.00 1.00
*J19* D2 10c rose red 70 70
*Nos. J15-J19 (5)* 2.30 2.30

## RHODESIA AND NYASALAND

LOCATION — Southern Africa.
GOVT. — Former Federal State in British Commonwealth.
AREA — 486,973 sq. mi.
POP. — 8,510,000 (est. 1961).
CAPITAL — Salisbury, Southern Rhodesia.

The Federation of Southern Rhodesia, Northern Rhodesia and Nyasaland was created in 1953, dissolved at end of 1963.

12 Pence = 1 Shilling
20 Shillings = 1 Pound

**Catalogue values for all unused stamps in this country are for Never Hinged items.**

A14

A15

Queen Elizabeth II A16

***Perf. 13½ (A14), 13½x13 (A15), 14x13 (A16)***

**1954-56 Engr. Unwmk.**

*141* A14 ½p vermilion 9 5
**a.** Booklet pane of 6 1.40
**b.** Perf. 12½x13½ 65 40
*142* A14 1p ultra 9 5
**a.** Booklet pane of 6 1.40
**b.** Perf. 12½x13½ 80 50
*143* A14 2p emerald 18 5
**a.** Booklet pane of 6 1.75
*143B* A14 2½p ocher ('56) 70 5
*144* A14 3p carmine 22 5
*145* A14 4p red brn 55 6
*146* A14 4½p bl grn 60 18
*147* A14 6p red lil 80 8
*148* A14 9p purple 1.10 40
*149* A14 1sh gray 90 10
*150* A15 1sh3p ultra & ver 1.10 14
*151* A15 2sh brn & dp bl 4.00 75
*152* A15 2sh6p car & blk 4.50 60
*153* A15 5sh ol & pur 9.00 1.50
*154* A16 10sh red org & aqua 22.50 7.75
*155* A16 £1 brn car & ol 37.50 14.00
*Nos. 141-155 (16)* 83.83 25.81

Plane and Victoria Falls — A17

David Livingstone and Victoria Falls — A18

**1955, June 15 *Perf. 13½***

*156* A17 3p dk grn & ultra 32 18
*157* A18 1sh gray bl & rose lil 85 60

Centenary of discovery of Victoria Falls.

Tea Picking A19

Rhodes' Grave, Matopos A20

Designs: 1p, V. H. F. Mast. 2p, Copper mining. 2½p, Kingsley Fairbridge Memorial. 4p, Boat on Lake Bangweulu. 6p, Victoria Falls. 9p, Railroad trains. 1sh, Tobacco. 1sh3p, Ship on Lake Nyasa. 2sh, Chirundu Bridge, Zambezi River. 2sh6p, Salisbury Airport. 5sh, Cecil Rhodes statue, Salisbury. 10sh, Mlanje mountain. £1, Coat of arms.

***Perf. 13½x14, 14x13½***

**1959-63 Engr. Unwmk.**

**Size: 18½x22½mm, 22½x18½mm**

*158* A19 ½p emer & blk 10 10
**a.** Perf. 12½x13½ 60 60
*159* A19 1p blk & rose red 6 6
**a.** Perf. 12½x13½ 65 65
*160* A19 2p ocher & vio 12 12
*161* A19 2½p sl & lil, perf. 14½ 35 35
*162* A20 3p bl & blk 18 6
**a.** Bklt. pane of 4 ('63) 1.50
**b.** Black omitted

***Perf. 14½***

**Size: 24x27mm, 27x24mm**

*163* A19 4p ol & mag 25 10
*164* A19 6p grn & ultra 28 15
*164A* A20 9p pur & ocher ('62) 2.75 2.75
*165* A20 1sh ultra & yel grn 65 18
*166* A20 1sh3p sep & brt grn, perf. 14 1.50 18
*167* A20 2sh lake & grn 4.00 1.10
*168* A20 2sh6p ocher & bl 4.75 1.10

***Perf. 11½***

**Size: 32x27mm**

*169* A20 5sh yel grn & choc 8.00 1.75
*170* A20 10sh brt rose & ol 24.00 10.00
*171* A20 £1 vio & blk 32.50 20.00
*Nos. 158-171 (15)* 79.49 38.00

Nos. 158a and 159a are coils.

Kariba Gorge, 1955 — A21

Designs: 6p, Power lines. 1sh, View of dam. 1sh3p, View of dam and lake. 2sh6p, Power station. 5sh, Dam and Queen Mother Elizabeth.

**1960, May 17 Photo. *Perf. 14½x14***

*172* A21 3p org & sl grn 65 12
*173* A21 6p yel brn & brn 90 60
*174* A21 1sh dl bl & emer 1.75 1.00
*175* A21 1sh3p grnsh bl & ocher 2.75 1.25
*176* A21 2sh6p org ver & blk 6.75 4.00
*177* A21 5sh grnsh bl & lil 13.00 7.00
*Nos. 172-177 (6)* 25.80 13.97

Issued to commemorate the opening of the Kariba hydroelectric scheme, Zambezi River.

Miner with Drill — A22

Design: 1sh3p, Mining surface installations.

**1961, May 8 Unwmk.**

*178* A22 6p chnt brn & ol grn 1.10 75
*179* A22 1sh3p lt bl & blk 1.90 1.75

7th Commonwealth Mining and Metallurgical Cong., Apr. 10-May 20.

DH Hercules Biplane A23

Designs: 1sh3p, Flying boat over Zambezi River. 2sh6p, DH Comet, Salisbury Airport.

**1962, Feb. 6**

*180* A23 6p ver & ol grn 50 50
*181* A23 1sh3p bl, blk, grn & yel 1.25 1.25
*182* A23 2sh6p dk pur & car rose 8.00 8.00

30th anniv. of the inauguration of the Rhodesia-London airmail service.

Tobacco Plant — A24

Designs: 6p, Tobacco field. 1sh3p, Auction floor. 2sh6p, Cured tobacco.

**1963, Feb. 18 Photo. *Perf. 14x14½***

*184* A24 3p gray brn & grn 20 10
*185* A24 6p bl, grn & brn 40 35
*186* A24 1sh3p sl & red brn 1.25 90
*187* A24 2sh6p brn & org yel 4.75 4.00

3rd World Tobacco Scientific Cong., Salisbury, Feb. 18-26 and the 1st Intl. Tobacco Trade Cong., Salisbury, March 6-16.

Red Cross A25

**1963, Aug. 6 *Perf. 14½x14***

*188* A25 3p red 45 25

Centenary of the International Red Cross.

"Round Table" Emblem A26

**1963, Sept. 11 Unwmk.**

*189* A26 6p brt yel grn, blk & gold 65 65
*190* A26 1sh3p lil, blk, gold & brt yel grn 1.10 1.10

World Council of Young Men's Service Clubs at University College of Rhodesia and Nyasaland, Sept. 8-15.

### POSTAGE DUE STAMPS

D1

***Perf. 12½***

**1961, Apr. 19 Unwmk. Typo.**

*J1* D1 1p vermilion 85 *2.25*
**a.** Horiz. pair, imperf. btwn. *350.00*
*J2* D1 2p dark blue 1.65 *3.50*
*J3* D1 4p emerald 2.50 *5.00*
*J4* D1 6p dark purple 3.50 *8.75*

## SABAH

LOCATION — Northeast part of Borneo, Malay archipelago.
GOVT. — A state in the Federation of Malaysia.
AREA — 29,388 sq. mi.
POP. — 655,295 (1970).
CAPITAL — Kota Kinabalu (Jesselton).

Sabah was the British colony of North Borneo until it took this name and joined with Malaya, Sarawak and Singapore to form the Federation of Malaysia in 1963.

100 Cents = 1 Dollar

**Catalogue values for all unused stamps in this country are for Never Hinged items.**

North Borneo Nos. 280-295 Overprinted:

**SABAH** On 1c-75c
**SABAH** On $1-$10

***Perf. 13x12½, 12½x13***

**1964, July 1 Engr. Wmk. 314**

*1* A92 1c lt red brn & grn 5 5
*2* A92 4c org & ol 5 5
*3* A92 5c vio & sep 5 5
*4* A92 6c bluish grn & sl 6 6
*5* A92 10c rose red & lt grn 7 7
*6* A92 12c dl grn & brn 10 10
*7* A92 20c ultra & bl grn 15 12
*8* A92 25c rose red & gray 32 25
*9* A92 30c gray ol & sep 40 32
*10* A92 35c redsh brn & stl bl 50 40
*11* A92 50c brn org & bl grn 65 50
*12* A92 75c red vio & sl bl 1.00 70
*13* A93 $1 yel grn & brn 1.50 1.00
*14* A93 $2 sl & brn 3.00 2.75
*15* A93 $5 brn vio & grn 8.00 6.50
*16* A93 $10 bl & car 16.00 13.00
*Nos. 1-16 (16)* 31.90 25.92

Orchid Type of Johore (Malaysia), 1965, with State Crest

**Wmk. 338**

**1965, Nov. 15 Photo. *Perf. 14½***

**Flowers in Natural Colors**

*17* A14 1c blk & lt grnsh bl 6 5
*18* A14 2c blk, red & gray 6 5
*19* A14 5c blk & Prus bl 10 6
*20* A14 6c blk & lt lil 15 10
*21* A14 10c blk & lt ultra 25 18
**a.** Watermark sideways ('70) 50 50
*22* A14 15c blk, lil rose & grn 40 20
*23* A14 20c blk & brn 60 45
*Nos. 17-23 (7)* 1.62 1.09

Butterfly Type of Johore (Malaysia), 1971, with State Crest

***Perf. 13½x13***

**1971, Feb. 1 Litho. Unwmk.**

*24* A15 1c multi 5 5
**a.** Photo. ('77) 10 10

25 A15 2c multi 5 5
a. Photo. ('77) 10 10
26 A15 5c multi 5 5
a. Booklet pane of 4 ('73) 25
b. Photo. ('77) 10 10
27 A15 6c multi 8 6
28 A15 10c multi 15 10
a. Booklet pane of 4 ('73) 65
b. Photo. ('77) 15 15
29 A15 15c multi 20 18
a. Booklet pane of 4 ('73) 1.00
b. Photo. ('77) 30 30
30 A15 20c multi 35 25
*Nos. 24-30 (7)* 93 74

Flower Type of Johore (Malaysia) 1979, with State Crest

**Wmk. 378**

**1979, Apr. 30 Litho. *Perf. 14½***

32 A16 1c multi 5 5
33 A16 2c multi 5 5
34 A16 5c multi 5 5
35 A16 10c multi 8 5
a. Unwmkd. ('85) 2.15
36 A16 15c multi 12 6
a. Unwmkd. ('83) 3.25
37 A16 20c multi 16 8
38 A16 25c multi 20 10
*Nos. 32-38 (7)* 71 44

Agriculture and State Arms Type of Johore (Malaysia)

**Wmk. 388**

**1986, Oct. 25 Litho. *Perf. 12***

39 A19 1c multi 5 5
40 A19 2c multi 5 5
41 A19 5c multi 5 5
42 A19 10c multi 8 5
43 A19 15c multi 12 6
44 A19 20c multi 24 12
45 A19 30c multi 24 12
*Nos. 39-45 (7)* 75 46

## ST. CHRISTOPHER

LOCATION — An island in the West Indies, southeast of Puerto Rico.
GOVT. — A Presidency of the former Leeward Islands Colony.
AREA — 68 sq. mi.
POP. — 18,578 (estimated).
CAPITAL — Basseterre.

Stamps of St. Christopher were discontinued in 1890 and replaced by those of Leeward Islands. For later issues, inscribed "St. Kitts-Nevis" or "St. Christopher-Nevis-Anguilla," see St. Kitts-Nevis.

12 Pence = 1 Shilling

Queen Victoria — A1

**Wmk. Crown and C. C. (1)**

**1870 Typo. *Perf. 12½***

1 A1 1p dull rose 47.50 35.00
2 A1 1p lilac rose 16.00 16.00
3 A1 6p green 82.50 13.00

**1875-79 *Perf. 14.***

4 A1 1p lil rose 55.00 12.00
b. Diagonal half used as ½ p on cover 1,050.
5 A1 2½p red brn ('79) 130.00 130.00
6 A1 4p bl ('79) 125.00 15.00
7 A1 6p green 22.50 6.75
a. Horiz. pair, imperf. vert.

**1882-90 Wmk. Crown and C. A. (2)**

8 A1 ½p green 50 50
9 A1 1p rose 38 50
a. Half used as ½p on cover
10 A1 1p lil rose 650.00 70.00
a. Diagonal half used as ½ p on cover
11 A1 2½p red brn 260.00 65.00
12 A1 2½p ultra ('84) 2.00 2.50
13 A1 4p blue 325.00 37.50
14 A1 4p gray ('84) 1.00 1.25
15 A1 6p ol brn ('90) 65.00 *325.00*
16 A1 1sh vio ('87) 65.00 65.00

*St. Christopher stamps can be mounted in Scott's British Leeward Album.*

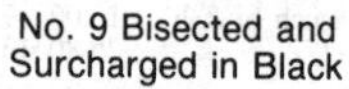
No. 9 Bisected and Surcharged in Black

**1885**

17 A1 ½p on half of 1p rose 16.00 22.50
a. Surch. vertically
b. Invtd. surcharge 400.00 250.00
c. Unsevered pair 100.00 110.00
d. Double surch.

No. 7 Surcharged in Black:

ONE PENNY.
Nos. 18, 21

FOUR PENCE
No. 19

4d.
No. 20

**1885-86 Wmk. Crown and C. C. (1)**

18 A1 1p on 6p grn ('86) 14.00 25.00
a. Invtd. surcharge 6,250.
b. Double surcharge 1,500.
19 A1 4p on 6p grn 37.50 *47.50*
a. Period after "PENCE" 57.50 75.00
b. Double surcharge 1,750.
20 A1 4p on 6p grn ('86) 45.00 60.00
a. Without period after "d" 210.00 250.00
b. Double surcharge 1,400. 1,500.

No. 18b used is known only with revenue cancellation.

Nos. 8 and 12 Surcharged in Black Like No. 18 or:

ONE PENNY.
No. 22

ONE PENNY.
No. 23

**1887-88 Wmk. Crown and C. A. (2)**

21 A1 1p on ½p grn 19.00 27.50
22 A1 1p on 2½p ('88) 35.00 50.00
a. Inverted surcharge *7,000. 4,500.*
23 A1 1p on 2½p ('88) *8,500. 8,500.*

## ST. HELENA

LOCATION — An island in the Atlantic Ocean, 1,200 miles west of Angola (Africa).
GOVT. — British Crown Colony.
AREA — 47 sq. mi.
POP. — 5,499 (1982).
CAPITAL — Jamestown.

12 Pence = 1 Shilling
20 Shillings = 1 Pound
100 Pence = 1 Pound (1971)

**Catalogue values for unused stamps in this country are for Never Hinged items, beginning with Scott 128 in the regular postage section, Scott B1*** in the semi-postal section and Scott J1 in the postage due section..**

Queen Victoria — A1

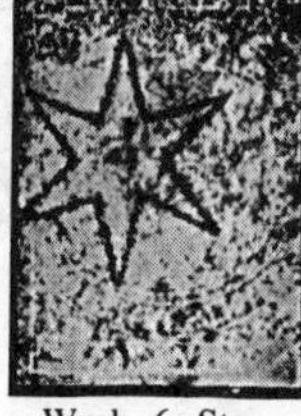
Wmk. 6- Star

**1856, Jan. Wmk. 6 Engr. *Imperf.***

1 A1 6p blue 425.00 115.00

**1861 *Clean-Cut Perf. 14 to 15½***

2 A1 6p blue 2,000. 160.00

**1863 *Rough Perf. 14 to 15½***

2B A1 6p blue 350.00 75.00

**1873-74 Wmk. 1 *Perf. 12½***

3 A1 6p dl bl 550.00 65.00
4 A1 6p ultra ('74) 275.00 47.50

**1879 *Perf. 14x12½***

5 A1 6p gray bl 275.00 14.00

**1889 *Perf. 14***

6 A1 6p gray bl 250.00 19.00

**1889 Wmk. Crown and C. A. (2)**

7 A1 6p gray 7.50 5.50

Type of 1856 Surcharged

ONE PENNY
a

ONE PENNY
b

**1863 Wmk. 1 *Imperf.***

**Long Bar, 16, 17, 18 or 19mm**

8 A1 (a) 1p on 6p brn red (surch. 17mm) 95.00 95.00
a. Double surcharge 5,500. 2,750.
9 A1 (a) 1p on 6p brn red (surch. 19mm) 95.00 95.00
10 A1 (b) 4p on 6p car 325.00 165.00
a. Surcharge omitted
b. Dbl. surch. *9,000. 9,000.*

**1864-73 *Perf. 12½***

11 A1 (a) 1p on 6p brn red 15.00 15.00
12 A1 (b) 1p on 6p brn red ('71) 12.00 12.00
a. Blue blk surch. 1,300. 875.
13 A1 (b) 2p on 6p yel ('73) 55.00 15.00
a. Blue blk surch. 6,750. 4,000.
14 A1 (b) 3p on 6p dk vio ('73) 42.50 25.00
15 A1 (b) 4p on 6p car 45.00 19.00
a. Double surcharge *9,000. 6,250.*
16 A1 (b) 1sh on 6p grn (bar 16 to 17mm) 35.00 18.00
17 A1 (b) 1sh on 6p dp grn (bar 18mm) ('73) 165.00 9.50
a. Blue blk surcharge

**1868**

**Short Bar, 14 or 15mm**

18 A1 (a) 1p on 6p brn red ('68) 57.50 45.00
a. Imperf., pair 7,500.
b. Dbl. surch.
19 A1 (b) 2p on 6p yel ('68) 67.50 45.00
a. Imperf., pair 17,000.
20 A1 (b) 3p on 6p dk vio ('68) 50.00 25.00
a. Dbl. surch. 6,750.
b. Imperf., pair 2,250.
21 A1 (b) 4p on 6p car (words 18mm) ('68) 40.00 30.00
a. Double surcharge *5,500.* 5,500.
b. Imperf., pair 19,000.
22 A1 (b) 4p on 6p car (words 19mm) ('68) 140.00 85.00
a. Words double, 18 and 19mm *12,500. 12,500.*
b. Imperf.
23 A1 (a) 1sh on 6p yel grn ('68) 300.00 165.00
a. Double surcharge 7,750.
b. Pair, one without surcharge 7,750.
24 A1 (a) 5sh on 6p org ('68) 25.00 25.00

No. 21 exists with surcharge omitted.

**1882 *Perf. 14x12½***

25 A1 (a) 1p on 6p brn red 20.00 12.00
26 A1 (b) 2p on 6p yel 32.50 16.00
27 A1 (b) 3p on 6p vio 165.00 37.50
28 A1 (b) 4p on 6p car (words 16mm) 50.00 20.00

**1883 *Perf. 14***

29 A1 (a) 1p on 6p brn red 19.00 11.00
30 A1 (b) 2p on 6p yellow 30.00 22.50
31 A1 (a) 1sh on 6p yel grn 17.50 11.00

**1882 *Perf. 14x12½***

**Long Bar, 18mm**

32 A1 (b) 1sh on 6p dp grn 300.00 15.00

**1884-94 Wmk. 2 *Perf. 14***

**Short Bar, 14 or 14½mm**

33 A1 (b) ½p on 6p grn (words 17mm) 85 85
a. ½p on 6p emer, blurred print (words 17mm) ('84) 2.50 2.50
b. Dbl. surch. 1,600.
34 A1 (b) ½p on 6p grn (words 15mm) ('94) 1.50 1.65
35 A1 (a) 1p on 6p red ('87) 1.40 1.40
36 A1 (b) 2p on 6p yel ('94) 1.40 1.90
37 A1 (b) 3p on 6p dp vio ('87) 2.50 2.00
a. 3p on 6p red vio 1.75 2.00
b. Dbl. surcharge *6,750. 6,750.*
38 A1 (b) 4p on 6p dk brn ('90) 5.50 5.50
a. With thin bar below thick one

**1894**

**Long Bar, 18mm.**

39 A1 (b) 1sh on 6p yel grn 13.00 11.00
a. Dbl. surch. *6,750.*

See note after No. 47.

Queen Victoria — A3

**1890-97 Typo. *Perf. 14***

40 A3 ½p grn ('97) 3.00 4.00
41 A3 1p rose ('96) 3.00 3.50
42 A3 1½p red brn & grn 3.00 3.50
43 A3 2p yel ('96) 3.75 4.00
44 A3 2½p ultra ('96) 6.25 5.50
45 A3 5p vio ('96) 6.75 8.25
46 A3 10p brn ('96) 14.00 *24.00*
*Nos. 40-46 (7)* 39.75 52.75

Type of 1856 Surcharged

2½d

**1893 Engr. Wmk. 2**

47 A1 2½p on 6p blue 1.10 1.10
a. Double surcharge *16,500.*
b. Double impression 7,500.

**In 1905 remainders Nos. 34 to 47 were sold by the postal officials. They are canceled with bars, arranged in the shape of diamonds, in purple ink. No such cancellation was ever used in the Island and the stamps so canceled are of slight value. With this cancellation removed, these remainders are sometimes offered as unused. Some have been recanceled with a false dated postmark.**

King Edward VII — A5

**1902 Typo. Wmk. 2**

48 A5 ½p green 38 *1.10*
49 A5 1p car rose 95 85

Government House — A6

"The Wharf" — A7

**1903, June Wmk. 1**

50 A6 ½p gray grn & brn 1.25 1.50
a. Bluish paper 95.00 65.00
51 A7 1p car & blk 3.75 1.25
a. Bluish paper 95.00 65.00
52 A6 2p ol grn & blk 6.00 6.00
a. Bluish paper 95.00 65.00
53 A7 8p brn & blk 11.00 *22.50*
54 A6 1sh org buff & brn 14.00 *18.00*
55 A7 2sh vio & blk 24.00 *37.50*
*Nos. 50-55 (6)* 60.00 86.75

A8

**1908, May** **Wmk. 3**

56 A8 2½p ultra 1.40 2.75
57 A8 4p blk & red, *yel* 1.40 4.25
58 A8 6p dl vio 2.75 8.25

**Wmk. 2**

60 A8 10sh grn & red, *grn* 185.00 225.00

Nos. 57 and 58 exist on both ordinary and chalky paper; No. 56 on ordinary and No. 60 on chalky paper.

Government House — A9

"The Wharf" — A10

**1912-16** **Ordinary Paper** **Wmk. 3**

61 A9 ½p grn & blk 38 55
62 A10 1p car & blk 1.65 1.90
a 1p scar & blk ('16) 22.50 27.00
63 A10 1½p org & blk 1.65 1.90
64 A9 2p gray & blk 1.50 1.75
65 A10 2½p ultra & blk 2.75 3.25
66 A9 3p vio & blk, *yel* 3.25 6.50
67 A10 8p dl vio & blk 6.75 13.00
68 A9 1sh blk, *green* 10.00 12.50
69 A10 2sh ultra & blk, *bl* 27.50 35.00
70 A10 3sh vio & blk 35.00 52.50
*Nos. 61-70 (10)* 90.43 128.85

See Nos. 75-77.

A11

A12

Die I

For description of dies I and II see back of this section of the Catalogue.

**1912**

**Chalky Paper**

71 A11 4p blk & red, *yel* 4.25 17.00
72 A11 6p dl vio & red vio 2.50 10.00

**1913**

**Ordinary Paper**

73 A12 4p blk & red, *yel* 1.75 1.75
74 A12 6p dl vio & red vio 7.50 22.50

**1922** **Wmk. 4**

75 A10 1p green 1.25 7.50
76 A10 1½p rose red 6.00 17.50
77 A9 3p ultra 10.50 24.00

Badge of the Colony — A13

**1922-27** **Wmk. 4**

**Chalky Paper**

79 A13 ½p blk & gray 22 40
80 A13 1p grn & blk 35 45
81 A13 1½p rose red 1.10 2.75
82 A13 2p pale gray & gray 1.10 1.10
83 A13 3p ultra 1.10 2.75
84 A13 5p red & grn, *emer* ('27) 1.90 3.75
85 A13 6p red vio & blk 1.50 4.25
86 A13 8p vio & blk 2.75 5.75
87 A13 1sh dk brn & blk 2.75 5.75
88 A13 1sh6p grn & blk, *emer* ('27) 7.50 15.00
89 A13 2sh ultra & vio, *bl* ('27) 10.50 19.00
90 A13 2sh6p car & blk, *yel* ('27) 11.00 20.00
91 A13 5sh grn & blk, *yel* ('27) 24.00 45.00
92 A13 7sh6p org & blk 67.50 110.00
93 A13 10sh ol grn & blk 90.00 125.00
94 A13 15sh vio & blk, *bl* 800. 1,100.
*Nos. 79-93 (15)* 223.27 360.95

Nos. 88, 90, and 91 are on ordinary paper.

**Wmk. 3**

**Chalky Paper**

95 A13 4p blk, *yellow* 2.50 5.00
96 A13 1sh6p bl grn & blk, *grn* 14.00 27.50
97 A13 2sh6p car & blk, *yel* 24.00 47.50
98 A13 5sh grn & blk, *yel* 30.00 57.50
99 A13 £1 red vio & blk, *red* 350.00 375.00
*Nos. 95-99 (5)* 420.50 512.50

**Centenary Issue**

Lot and Lot's Wife — A14

Plantation; Queen Victoria and Kings William IV, Edward VII, George V
A15

Map of the Colony — A16

Quay, Jamestown A17

View of James Valley — A18

View of Jamestown A19

View of Mundens A20

St. Helena A21

View of High Knoll — A22

Badge of the Colony — A23

**Wmk. 4**

**1934, Apr. 23** **Engr.** **Perf. 12**

101 A14 ½p dk vio & blk 52 60
102 A15 1p grn & blk 70 85
103 A16 1½p red & blk 1.40 1.50
104 A17 2p org & blk 1.75 1.90
105 A18 3p bl & blk 2.75 3.75
106 A19 6p lt bl & blk 5.50 8.75
107 A20 1sh dk brn & blk 10.50 14.00
108 A21 2sh 6p car & blk 22.50 40.00
109 A22 5sh choc & blk 42.50 57.50
110 A23 10sh red vio & blk 175.00 190.00
*Nos. 101-110 (10)* 263.12 318.85

**Silver Jubilee Issue**

Common Design Type

**1935, May 6** ***Perf. 13½x14***

111 CD301 1½p car & dk bl 55 55
112 CD301 2p gray blk & ultra 1.25 1.25
113 CD301 6p ind & grn 4.25 4.50
114 CD301 1sh brt vio & ind 8.50 9.25

**Coronation Issue**

Common Design Type

**1937, May 19**

115 CD302 1p dp grn 9 9
116 CD302 2p dp org 20 20
117 CD302 3p brt ultra 28 28

Badge of the Colony — A24

**1938-40** ***Perf. 12½***

118 A24 ½p purple 6 6
119 A24 1p dp grn 9.25 9.00
119A A24 1p org yel ('40) 18 18
120 A24 1½p carmine 18 18
121 A24 2p orange 18 18
122 A24 3p ultra 35.00 27.50
122A A24 3p gray ('40) 28 28
122B A24 4p ultra ('40) 28 28
123 A24 6p gray bl 42 42
123A A24 8p ol ('40) 1.10 1.10
124 A24 1sh sepia 55 55
125 A24 2sh 6p dp claret 3.00 3.00
126 A24 5sh brown 5.00 7.00
127 A24 10sh violet 11.00 14.00
*Nos. 118-127 (14)* 66.48 63.73

See Nos. 136-138.

**Catalogue values for unused stamps in this section, from this point to the end of the section, are for Never Hinged items.**

**Peace Issue**

Common Design Type

***Perf. 13½x14***

**1946, Oct. 21** **Wmk. 4** **Engr.**

128 CD303 2p dp org 18 18
129 CD303 4p dp bl 25 25

**Silver Wedding Issue**

Common Design Types

**1948, Oct. 20** **Photo.** ***Perf. 14x14½***

130 CD304 3p black 25 25

**Engr.; Name Typo.**

***Perf. 11½x11***

131 CD305 10sh bl vio 20.00 30.00

**UPU Issue**

Common Design Types

**Engr.; Name Typo. on 4p, 6p**

**1949, Oct. 10** ***Perf. 13½, 11x11½***

132 CD306 3p rose car 32 32
133 CD307 4p indigo 90 90
134 CD308 6p olive 1.90 1.90
135 CD309 1sh slate 3.00 3.00

George VI Type of 1938

**1949, Nov. 1** **Engr.** ***Perf. 12½***

**Center in Black**

136 A24 1p bl grn 60 60
137 A24 1½p car rose 80 80
138 A24 2p carmine 80 80

**Coronation Issue**

Common Design Type

**1953, June 2** ***Perf. 13½x13***

139 CD312 3p pur & blk 1.10 1.10

Badge of the Colony A25

Heart-Shaped Waterfall A26

Queen Elizabeth II and First Postage Stamp — A27

Designs: 1p, Flax plantation. 2p, Lace making. 2½p, Drying flax. 3p, Wire bird. 4p, Flagstaff and barn. 6p, Donkeys carrying flax. 7p, Map. 1sh, Entrance, government offices. 2sh 6p, Cutting flax. 5sh, Jamestown. 10sh, Longwood house.

**1953, Aug. 4** ***Perf. 13½x14, 14x13½***

**Center and Denomination in Black**

| | | | | |
|---|---|---|---|---|
| *140* | A25 | ½p emerald | 12 | 8 |
| *141* | A25 | 1p dk grn | 16 | 12 |
| *142* | A26 | 1½p red vio | 24 | 16 |
| *143* | A25 | 2p rose lake | 28 | 20 |
| *144* | A25 | 2½p red | 32 | 24 |
| *145* | A25 | 3p brown | 40 | 28 |
| *146* | A25 | 4p dp bl | 55 | 40 |
| *147* | A25 | 6p purple | 80 | 55 |
| *148* | A25 | 7p gray | 1.00 | 65 |
| *149* | A25 | 1sh dk car rose | 1.40 | 1.00 |
| *150* | A25 | 2sh 6p violet | 8.00 | 4.75 |
| *151* | A25 | 5sh chocolate | 16.00 | 10.00 |
| *152* | A25 | 10sh orange | 42.50 | 24.00 |
| | | *Nos. 140-152 (13)* | 71.77 | 42.43 |

***Perf. 11½***

**1956, Jan.** **Wmk. 4** **Engr.**

| | | | | |
|---|---|---|---|---|
| *153* | A27 | 3p dk car rose & bl | 18 | 18 |
| *154* | A27 | 4p redsh brn & bl | 40 | 40 |
| *155* | A27 | 6p pur & bl | 65 | 65 |

Cent. of the 1st St. Helena postage stamp.

Arms of East India Company A28

Designs: 6p, Dutton's ship "London" off James Bay. 1sh, Memorial stone from fort built by Governor Dutton.

***Perf. 12½x13***

**1959, May 5** **Wmk. 314**

| | | | | |
|---|---|---|---|---|
| *156* | A28 | 3p rose & blk | 22 | 22 |
| *157* | A28 | 6p gray & yel grn | 55 | 55 |
| *158* | A28 | 1sh org & blk | 80 | 80 |

300th anniv. of the landing of Capt. John Dutton on St. Helena and of the 1st settlement.

Cape Canary A29

Queen Elizabeth II A30

Queen and Prince Andrew A31

Designs: 1p, Cunning fish (horiz.). 2p, Brittle starfish (horiz.). 4½p, Redwood flower. 6p, Red fody (Madagascar weaver). 7p, Trumpetfish (horiz.). 10p, Keeled feather starfish (horiz.). 1sh, Gumwood flowers. 1sh6p, Fairy tern. 2sh6p, Orange starfish (horiz.). 5sh, Night-blooming cereus. 10sh, Deepwater bull's-eye (horiz.).

***Perf. 11½x12, 12x11½***

**1961, Dec. 12** **Photo.** **Wmk. 314**

| | | | | |
|---|---|---|---|---|
| *159* | A29 | 1p multi | 15 | 15 |
| *a* | | Booklet pane of 4 ('62) | 65 | |
| *160* | A29 | 1½p multi | 12 | 10 |
| *a* | | Booklet pane of 4 ('62) | 50 | |
| *161* | A29 | 2p gray & red | 18 | 18 |
| *a* | | Booklet pane of 4 ('62) | 75 | |
| *162* | A30 | 3p dk bl, rose & grnsh bl | 35 | 35 |
| *a* | | Booklet pane of 4 ('62) | 1.50 | |
| *163* | A29 | 4½p sl, brn & grn | 35 | 35 |
| *164* | A29 | 6p cit, brn & dp car | 42 | 42 |
| *a* | | Booklet pane of 4 ('62) | 1.75 | |
| *165* | A29 | 7p vio, blk & red brn | 42 | 42 |
| *166* | A29 | 10p bl & dp cl | 65 | 65 |
| *167* | A29 | 1sh red brn, grn & yel | 65 | 65 |
| *168* | A29 | 1sh6p gray bl & blk | 2.50 | 1.75 |
| *169* | A29 | 2sh6p grnsh bl, yel & red | 3.75 | 2.75 |
| *170* | A29 | 5sh grn, brn & yel | 5.00 | 4.25 |
| *171* | A29 | 10sh gray bl, blk & sal | 10.50 | 9.50 |

***Perf. 14x14½***

| | | | | |
|---|---|---|---|---|
| *172* | A31 | £1 turq bl & choc | 19.00 | 22.50 |
| | | *Nos. 159-172 (14)* | 44.04 | 44.02 |

**Freedom from Hunger Issue**

Common Design Type

**1963, June 4** ***Perf. 14x14½***

| | | | | |
|---|---|---|---|---|
| *173* | CD314 | 1sh6p ultra | 4.50 | 3.25 |

**Red Cross Centenary Issue**

Common Design Type

**Wmk. 314**

**1963, Sept. 2** **Litho.** ***Perf. 13***

| | | | | |
|---|---|---|---|---|
| *174* | CD315 | 3p blk & red | 35 | 35 |
| *175* | CD315 | 1sh6p ultra & red | 5.00 | 3.75 |

Nos. 159, 162, 164 and 168 Overprinted: "FIRST LOCAL POST / 4th JANUARY 1965"

***Perf. 11½x12, 12x11½***

**1965, Jan. 4** **Photo.** **Wmk. 314**

| | | | | |
|---|---|---|---|---|
| *176* | A29 | 1p multi | 8 | 8 |
| *177* | A30 | 3p dk bl, rose & grnsh bl | 16 | 16 |
| *178* | A29 | 6p cit, brn & dp car | 35 | 35 |
| *179* | A29 | 1sh6p gray bl & blk | 70 | 70 |

Establishment of the 1st internal postal service on the island.

**ITU Issue**

Common Design Type

***Perf. 11x11½***

**1965, May 17** **Litho.** **Wmk. 314**

| | | | | |
|---|---|---|---|---|
| *180* | CD317 | 3p ultra & gray | 42 | 42 |
| *181* | CD317 | 6p red lil & bl grn | 1.00 | 1.00 |

**Intl. Cooperation Year Issue**

Common Design Type

**1965, Oct. 25** **Litho.** ***Perf. 14½***

| | | | | |
|---|---|---|---|---|
| *182* | CD318 | 1p bl grn & cl | 9 | 9 |
| *183* | CD318 | 6p lt vio & grn | 1.90 | 1.90 |

**Churchill Memorial Issue**

Common Design Type

**1966, Jan. 24** **Photo.** ***Perf. 14***

**Design in Black, Gold and Carmine Rose**

| | | | | |
|---|---|---|---|---|
| *184* | CD319 | 1p brt bl | 7 | 7 |
| *185* | CD319 | 3p green | 28 | 28 |
| *186* | CD319 | 6p brown | 85 | 85 |
| *187* | CD319 | 1sh6p violet | 3.00 | 3.00 |

**World Cup Soccer Issue**

Common Design Type

**1966, July 1** **Litho.** ***Perf. 14***

| | | | | |
|---|---|---|---|---|
| *188* | CD321 | 3p multi | 55 | 55 |
| *189* | CD321 | 6p multi | 1.65 | 1.32 |

**WHO Headquarters Issue**

Common Design Type

**1966, Sept. 20** **Litho.** ***Perf. 14***

| | | | | |
|---|---|---|---|---|
| *190* | CD322 | 3p multi | 45 | 45 |
| *191* | CD322 | 1sh6p multi | 2.75 | 2.25 |

**UNESCO Anniversary Issue**

Common Design Type

**1966, Dec. 1** **Litho.** ***Perf. 14***

| | | | | |
|---|---|---|---|---|
| *192* | CD323 | 3p "Education" | 90 | 65 |
| *193* | CD323 | 6p "Science" | 1.40 | 1.10 |
| *194* | CD323 | 1sh6p "Culture" | 4.50 | 4.00 |

Badge of St. Helena — A32

***Perf. 14½x14***

**1967, May 5** **Photo.** **Wmk. 314**

| | | | | |
|---|---|---|---|---|
| *195* | A32 | 1sh dk grn & multi | 30 | 30 |
| *196* | A32 | 2sh6p bl & multi | 70 | 70 |
| *a* | | Carmine omitted | 450.00 | |

St. Helena's New Constitution.

The Great Fire of London A33

Designs: 3p, Three-master Charles. 6p, Boats bringing new settlers to shore. 1sh6p, Settlers at work.

***Perf. 13½x13***

**1967, Sept. 4** **Engr.** **Wmk. 314**

| | | | | |
|---|---|---|---|---|
| *197* | A33 | 1p blk & car | 6 | 6 |
| *198* | A33 | 3p blk & vio bl | 18 | 18 |
| *199* | A33 | 6p blk & dl vio | 35 | 35 |
| *200* | A33 | 1sh6p blk & ol grn | 90 | 90 |

Tercentenary of the arrival of settlers from London after the Great Fire of Sept. 2-4, 1666.

Maps of Tristan da Cunha and St. Helena A34

Designs: 8p, 2sh3p, Maps of St. Helena and Tristan da Cunha.

***Perf. 14x14½***

**1968, June 4** **Photo.** **Wmk. 314**

**Maps in Sepia**

| | | | | |
|---|---|---|---|---|
| *201* | A34 | 4p dp red lil | 8 | 8 |
| *202* | A34 | 8p olive | 22 | 22 |
| *203* | A34 | 1sh9p dp ultra | 52 | 52 |
| *204* | A34 | 2sh3p Prus bl | 80 | 80 |

30th anniv. of Tristan da Cunha as a Dependency of St. Helena.

Sir Hudson Lowe A35

Designs: 1sh6p, 2sh6p, Sir George Bingham.

***Perf. 13½x13***

**1968, Sept. 4** **Litho.** **Wmk. 314**

| | | | | |
|---|---|---|---|---|
| *205* | A35 | 3p multi | 10 | 10 |
| *206* | A35 | 9p multi | 30 | 30 |
| *207* | A35 | 1sh6p multi | 60 | 60 |
| *208* | A35 | 2sh6p multi | 95 | 95 |

Issued to commemorate the 150th anniversary of the abolition of slavery in St. Helena.

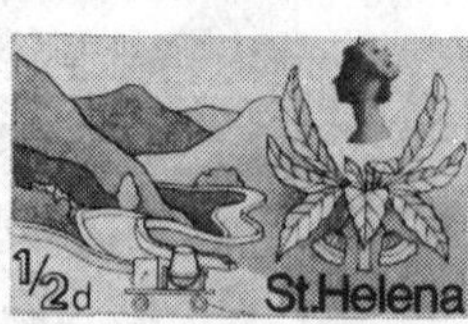

Road Construction — A36

Designs: 1p, Electricity development. 1½p, Dentist. 2p, Pest control. 3p, Apartment houses in Jamestown. 4p, Pasture and livestock improvement. 6p, School children listening to broadcast. 8p, Country cottages. 10p, New school buildings. 1sh, Reforestation. 1sh6p, Heavy lift crane. 2sh6p, Playing children in Lady Field Children's Home. 5sh, Agricultural training. 10sh, Ward in New General Hospital. £1, Lifeboat "John Dutton."

**Wmk. 314**

**1968, Nov. 4** **Litho.** ***Perf. 13½***

| | | | | |
|---|---|---|---|---|
| *209* | A36 | ½p multi | 8 | 8 |
| *210* | A36 | 1p multi | 8 | 8 |
| *a* | | Booklet pane of 4 | 32 | |
| *211* | A36 | 1½p multi | 10 | 10 |
| *212* | A36 | 2p multi | 12 | 12 |
| *a* | | Booklet pane of 4 | 48 | |
| *213* | A36 | 3p multi | 20 | 20 |
| *a* | | Booklet pane of 4 | 80 | |
| *214* | A36 | 4p multi | 28 | 28 |
| *a* | | Booklet pane of 4 | 1.15 | |
| *215* | A36 | 6p multi | 32 | 32 |
| *a* | | Booklet pane of 4 | 1.30 | |
| *216* | A36 | 8p multi | 40 | 40 |
| *217* | A36 | 10p multi | 48 | 48 |
| *218* | A36 | 1sh multi | 60 | 60 |
| *219* | A36 | 1sh6p multi | 80 | 80 |
| *220* | A36 | 2sh6p multi | 1.40 | 1.40 |
| *221* | A36 | 5sh multi | 2.75 | 2.75 |
| *222* | A36 | 10sh multi | 5.50 | 5.50 |
| *223* | A36 | £1 multi | 14.00 | 14.00 |
| | | *Nos. 209-223 (15)* | 27.11 | 27.11 |

See Nos. 244-256.

Brig Perseverance, 1819 — A37

Ships: 8p, M.S. Dane, 1857. 1sh9p, S.S. Llandovery Castle, 1925. 2sh3p, M.S. Good Hope Castle, 1969.

**1969, Apr. 19** **Litho.** ***Perf. 13½***

| | | | | |
|---|---|---|---|---|
| *224* | A37 | 4p vio & multi | 18 | 18 |
| *225* | A37 | 8p ocher & multi | 55 | 55 |
| *226* | A37 | 1sh9p ver & multi | 1.40 | 1.40 |
| *227* | A37 | 2sh3p dk bl & multi | 1.65 | 1.65 |

Issued in recognition of St. Helena's dependence on sea mail.

Surgeon and Officer (Light Company) 20th Foot, 1816 — A38

British Uniforms: 6p, Warrant Officer and Drummer, 53rd Foot, 1815. 1sh8p, Drum Major, 66th Foot, 1816, and Royal Artillery Officer, 1820. 2sh6p, Private 91st Foot and 2nd Corporal, Royal Sappers and Miners, 1832.

***Perf. 14x14½***

**1969, Sept. 3** **Litho.** **Wmk. 314**

| | | | | |
|---|---|---|---|---|
| *228* | A38 | 6p red & multi | 42 | 32 |
| *229* | A38 | 8p bl & multi | 65 | 48 |
| *230* | A38 | 1sh8p grn & multi | 1.90 | 1.60 |
| *231* | A38 | 2sh6p gray & multi | 3.25 | 3.00 |

Charles Dickens, "The Pickwick Papers" A39

Designs (Dickens and): 8p, "Oliver Twist." 1sh6p, "Martin Chuzzlewit." 2sh6p, "Bleak House."

***Perf. 13½x13***

**1970, June 9** **Litho.** **Wmk. 314**

| | | | | |
|---|---|---|---|---|
| *232* | A39 | 4p dk brn & multi | 35 | 30 |
| *233* | A39 | 8p sl & multi | 80 | 65 |
| *234* | A39 | 1sh6p multi | 1.75 | 1.50 |
| *235* | A39 | 2sh6p multi | 3.00 | 2.50 |

Charles Dickens (1812-70), English novelist.

Mouth to Mouth Resuscitation — A40

Designs: 9p, Girl in wheelchair and nurse. 1sh9p, First aid. 2sh3p, British Red Cross Society emblem.

**1970, Sept. 15** *Perf. 14½*
*236* A40 6p bis, red & blk 16 16
*237* A40 9p lt bl grn, red & blk 28 28
*238* A40 1sh9p gray, red & blk 70 70
*239* A40 2sh3p pale vio, red & blk 85 85

Centenary of British Red Cross Society.

Officer's Shako Plate, 20th Foot, 1812-16 — A41

Designs (Regimental Emblems): 9p, Officer's breast plate, 66th Foot, before 1818. 1sh3p, Officer's full dress shako, 91st Foot, 1816. 2sh11p, Ensign's shako, 53rd Foot, 1815.

**Wmk. 314**
**1970, Nov. 2 Litho.** *Perf. 14½*
*240* A41 4p multi 35 28
*241* A41 9p red & multi 1.00 85
*242* A41 1sh3p dk gray & multi 1.75 1.40
*243* A41 2sh11p dk gray grn & multi 3.75 3.25

See Nos. 263-270, 273-276.

Type of 1968
"P" instead of "d"

**1971, Feb. 15 Litho.** *Perf. 13½*
*244* A36 ½p like #210 6 6
*245* A36 1p like #211 15 15
*246* A36 1½p like #212 20 20
*247* A36 2p like #213 30 30
*a* Perf. 14½ ('75) 55 55
*248* A36 2½p like #214 35 35
*249* A36 3½p like #215 45 45
*250* A36 4½p like #216 55 55
*251* A36 5p like #217 70 70
*252* A36 7½p like #218 95 95
*253* A36 10p like #219 1.10 1.10
*254* A36 12½p like #220 1.50 1.50
*255* A36 25p like #221 3.00 3.00
*256* A36 50p like #222 13.00 13.00
*Nos. 244-256 (13)* 22.31 22.31

The paper of Nos. 244-256 is thinner than the paper of Nos. 209-223 and No. 223 (£1) has been reprinted in slightly different colors.

St. Helena, from Italian Miniature, 1460 — A42

*Perf. 14x14½*
**1971, Apr. 5 Litho. Wmk. 314**
*257* A42 2p vio bl & multi 14 14
*258* A42 5p multi 35 35
*259* A42 7½p multi 60 60
*260* A42 12½p ol & multi 90 90

Easter 1971.

Napoleon, after J. L. David, and Tomb in St. Helena A43

Design: 34p, Napoleon, by Hippolyte Paul Delaroche.

**1971, May 5** *Perf. 13½*
*261* A43 2p multi 45 35
*262* A43 34p multi 6.00 4.50

Sesquicentennial of the death of Napoleon Bonaparte (1769-1821).

Military Type of 1970

Designs: 1½p, Sword Hilt, Artillery Private, 1815. 4p, Baker rifle and socket bayonet, c. 1816. 6p, Infantry officer's sword hilt, 1822. 22½p, Baker rifle and light sword bayonet, c. 1823.

**1971, Nov. 10** *Perf. 14½*
*263* A41 1½p grn & multi 30 30
*264* A41 4p gray & multi 90 90
*265* A41 6p pur & multi 1.40 1.40
*266* A41 22½p multi 4.50 4.50

**1972, June 19**

Designs: 2p, Royal Sappers and Miners breastplate, 1823. 5p, Infantry sergeant's pike, 1830. 7½p, Royal Artillery officer's breastplate, 1830. 12½p, English military pistol, 1800.

*267* A41 2p multi 30 30
*268* A41 5p plum & blk 90 90
*269* A41 7½p dp bl & multi 1.50 1.50
*270* A41 12½p ol & multi 3.00 3.00

**Silver Wedding Issue, 1972**
Common Design Type

Design: Queen Elizabeth II, Prince Philip, St. Helena plover and white fairy tern.

**1972, Nov. 20 Photo.** *Perf. 14x14½*
*271* CD324 2p sl grn & multi 14 14
*272* CD324 16p rose brn & multi 1.00 1.00

Military Type of 1971

Designs: 2p, Shako, 53rd Foot, 1815. 5p, Band and Drums sword hilt, 1830. 7½p, Royal Sappers and Miners officers' hat, 1830. 12½p, General's sword hilt, 1831.

**1973, Sept. 20 Litho.** *Perf. 14½*
*273* A44 2p dl brn & multi 70 35
*274* A44 5p multi 1.00 1.00
*275* A44 7½p ol grn & multi 4.25 2.25
*276* A44 12½p lil & multi 5.50 4.50

**Princess Anne's Wedding Issue**
Common Design Type

**1973, Nov. 14 Wmk. 314** *Perf. 14*
*277* CD325 2p multi 9 9
*278* CD325 18p multi 60 60

Westminster and Claudine Beached During Storm, 1849 — A45

Designs: 4p, East Indiaman True Briton, 1790. 6p, General Goddard in action off St. Helena, 1795. 22½p, East Indiaman Kent burning in Bay of Biscay, 1825.

*Perf. 14½x14*
**1973, Dec. 17 Litho. Wmk. 314**
*279* A45 1½p multi 42 20
*280* A45 4p multi 85 65
*281* A45 6p multi 1.25 85
*282* A45 22½p multi 3.75 3.25

Tercentenary of the East India Company Charter.

UPU Emblem, Ships A46

Design: 25p, UPU emblem and letters.

**1974, Oct. 15** *Perf. 14½x14*
*283* A46 5p bl & multi 32 32
*284* A46 25p red & multi 1.25 1.25
*a* Souvenir sheet of 2 1.65 1.10

Centenary of Universal Postal Union. No. 284a contains one each of Nos. 283-284. Blue and red decorative margin. Size: 89x84mm.

Churchill and Blenheim Palace A47

Design: 25p, Churchill, Tower Bridge and Thames.

**1974, Nov. 30 Wmk. 373** *Perf. 14½*
*285* A47 5p blk & multi 28 28
*286* A47 25p blk & multi 1.10 1.10
*a* Souvenir sheet of 2 2.75 1.90

Sir Winston Churchill (1874-1965), birth centenary. No. 286a contains one each of Nos. 285-286, brown and gold margin with quotation in white. Size: 106x91mm.

Capt. Cook and Jamestown — A48

Design: 5p, Capt. Cook and "Resolution" (vert.).

*Perf. 14x13½, 13½x14*
**1975, July 14 Litho.**
*287* A48 5p multi 70 70
*288* A48 25p multi 3.75 3.75

Bicentenary of the return of Capt. James Cook to St. Helena.

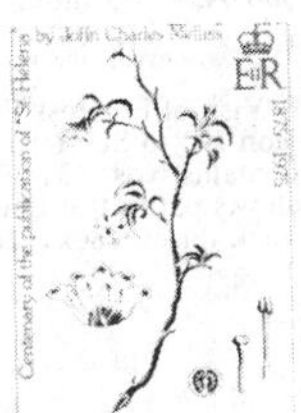

Mellissia Begonifolia — A49

Designs: 5p, Mellissius adumbratus (insect). 12p, Aegialitis St. Helena (bird; horiz.). 25p, Scorpaenia mellissii (fish; horiz.).

**1975, Oct. 20 Wmk. 373** *Perf. 13*
*289* A49 2p gray & multi 18 18
*290* A49 5p gray & multi 42 42
*291* A49 12p gray & multi 85 85
*292* A49 25p gray & multi 1.75 1.75

Centenary of the publication of "St. Helena," by John Charles Melliss.

Pound Note A50

Design: 33p, 5-pound note.

**1976, Apr. 15 Wmk. 314** *Perf. 13½*
*293* A50 8p cl & multi 65 50
*294* A50 33p multi 2.00 1.65

First issue of St. Helena bank notes.

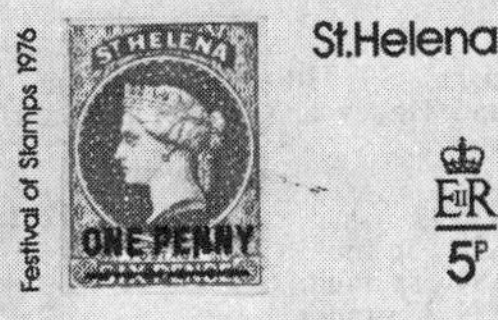

St. Helena No. 8 — A51

Designs: 8p, St. Helena No. 80 (vert.). 25p, Freighter Good Hope Castle.

*Perf. 13½x14, 14x13½*
**1976, May 4 Litho. Wmk. 373**
*295* A51 5p buff, brn & blk 25 25
*296* A51 8p lt grn, grn & blk 40 40
*297* A51 25p multi 1.25 1.25

Festival of stamps 1976. For souvenir sheet containing No. 297 see Ascension No. 214a.

High Knoll, by Capt. Barnett A52

Views on St. Helena, lithographs: 3p, Friar Rock, by G. H. Bellasis, 1815. 5p, Column Lot, by Bellasis. 6p, Sandy Bay Valley, by H. Salt, 1809. 8p, View from Castle terrace, by Bellasis. 9p, The Briars, 1815. 10p, Plantation House, by J. Wathen, 1821. 15p, Longwood House, by Wathen, 1821. 18p, St. Paul's Church, by Vincent Brooks. 26p, St. James's Valley, by Capt. Hastings, 1815. 40p, St. Matthew's Church, Longwood, by Brooks. £1, St. Helena and sailing ship, by Bellasis. £2, Sugar Loaf Hill, by Wathen, 1821.

**Wmk. 373**
**1976, Nov. 28 Litho.** *Perf. 14*
**Size: 38½x25mm**
*298* A52 1p multi 5 5
*299* A52 3p multi 9 9
*300* A52 5p multi 14 14
*301* A52 6p multi 18 18
*302* A52 8p multi 22 22
*303* A52 9p multi 25 25
*304* A52 10p multi 28 28
*305* A52 15p multi 42 42
*306* A52 18p multi 52 52
*307* A52 26p multi 75 75
*308* A52 40p multi 1.10 1.10

**Size: 47½x35mm**
*Perf. 13½*
*309* A52 £1 multi 2.75 2.75
*310* A52 £2 multi 5.75 5.75
*Nos. 298-310 (13)* 12.50 12.50

Issue dates: 1p, 3p, 5p, 8p, 10p, 18p, 26p, 40p, £1, Sept. 28; others Nov. 23.
1p, 10p and £2 reissued inscribed 1982.

Royal Party Leaving St. Helena, 1947 — A53

Designs: 15p, Queen's scepter and dove. 26p, Prince Philip paying homage to the Queen.

**1977, Feb. 7 Wmk. 373** *Perf. 13*
*311* A53 8p multi 26 26
*312* A53 15p multi 45 45
*313* A53 26p multi 90 90

25th anniv. of the reign of Elizabeth II.

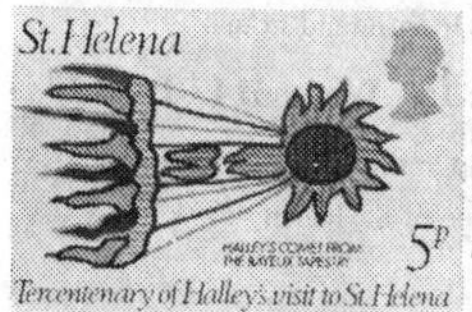
Halley's Comet, from Bayeux Tapestry A54

Designs: 8p, 17th century sextant. 27p, Edmund Halley and Halley's Mount, St. Helena.

**1977, Aug. 23 Litho. Perf. 14**

| | | | |
|---|---|---|---|
| 314 A54 5p multi | 65 | 65 |
| 315 A54 8p multi | 95 | 95 |
| 316 A54 27p multi | 2.75 | 2.75 |

300th anniversary of Edmund Halley's visit to St. Helena.

**Elizabeth II Coronation Anniversary Issue**

Common Design Types

**Souvenir Sheet**

**Unwmk.**

**1978, June 2 Litho. Perf. 15**

| | | |
|---|---|---|
| 317 Sheet of 6 | 4.25 | 4.25 |
| a CD326 25p *Black dragon of Ulster* | 65 | 65 |
| b CD327 25p *Elizabeth II* | 65 | 65 |
| c CD328 25p *Sea Lion* | 65 | 65 |

No. 317 contains 2 se-tenant strips of Nos. 317a-317c, separated by horizontal gutter with commemorative and descriptive inscriptions and showing central part of coronation procession with coach. Size: 100x135mm.

St. Helena, 17th Century Engraving — A55

Designs: 5p, 9p, 15p, Various Chinese porcelain and other utensils salvaged from wreck. 8p, Bronze cannon. 20p, Dutch East Indiaman.

**Wmk. 373**

**1978, Aug. 14 Litho. Perf. 14½**

| | | |
|---|---|---|
| 318 A55 3p multi | 15 | 15 |
| 319 A55 5p multi | 25 | 25 |
| 320 A55 8p multi | 42 | 42 |
| 321 A55 9p multi | 50 | 50 |
| 322 A55 15p multi | 75 | 75 |
| 323 A55 20p multi | 1.00 | 1.00 |
| *Nos. 318-323 (6)* | 3.07 | 3.07 |

Wreck of the Witte Leeuw, 1613.

"Discovery" A56

Designs: 8p, Cook's portable observatory. 12p, Pharnaceum acidum (plant), after sketch by Joseph Banks. 25p, Capt. Cook, after Flaxman/Wedgwood medallion.

**1979, Feb. 19 Litho. Perf. 11**

| | | |
|---|---|---|
| 324 A56 3p multi | 18 | 14 |
| 325 A56 8p multi | 52 | 40 |
| 326 A56 12p multi | 75 | 65 |

**Litho.; Embossed**

| | | |
|---|---|---|
| 327 A56 25p multi | 1.50 | 1.25 |

Capt. Cook's voyages.

A little time given to the study of the arrangement of the Scott Catalogue can make it easier to use effectively.

St. Helena No. 176 A57

Designs: 5p, Rowland Hill and his signature (vert.). 20p, St. Helena No. 8. 32p, St. Helena No. 49.

**Wmk. 373**

**1979, Aug. 20 Litho. Perf. 14**

| | | |
|---|---|---|
| 328 A57 5p multi | 15 | 15 |
| 329 A57 8p multi | 22 | 22 |
| 330 A57 20p multi | 60 | 60 |
| 331 A57 32p multi | 90 | 90 |

Sir Rowland Hill (1795-1879), originator of penny postage.

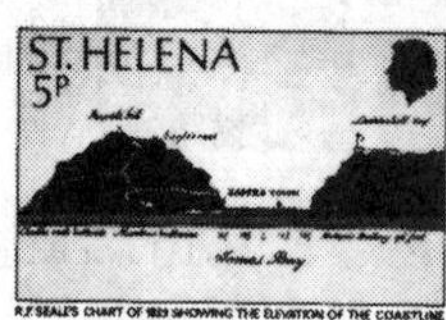
Seale's Chart, 1823 — A58

Designs: 8p, Jamestown and Inclined Plane, 1829. 50p, Inclined Plane (stairs), 1979 (vert.).

**Wmk. 373**

**1979, Dec. 10 Litho. Perf. 14**

| | | |
|---|---|---|
| 332 A58 5p multi | 14 | 14 |
| 333 A58 8p multi | 22 | 22 |
| 334 A58 50p multi | 1.40 | 1.40 |

Inclined Plane, 150th anniversary.

Tomb of Napoleon I, 1848 — A59

Empress Eugenie: 8p, Landing at St. Helena. 62p, Visiting Napoleon's tomb.

**1980, Feb. 23 Litho. Perf. 14½**

| | | |
|---|---|---|
| 335 A59 5p multi | 14 | 14 |
| 336 A59 8p multi | 22 | 22 |
| 337 A59 62p multi | 1.75 | 1.75 |
| a Souvenir sheet of 3 | 2.25 | 2.25 |

Visit of Empress Eugenie (widow of Napoleon III) to St. Helena, centenary. No. 337a contains Nos. 335-337; multicolored margin shows portrait of Empress and history of her visit. Size: 180x112mm.

East Indiaman, London 1980 Emblem — A60

**1980, May 6 Litho. Perf. 14½**

| | | |
|---|---|---|
| 338 A60 5p *shown* | 14 | 14 |
| 339 A60 8p *"Dolphin" postal stone* | 22 | 22 |
| 340 A60 47p *Jamestown castle postal stone* | 1.25 | 1.25 |
| a Souvenir sheet of 3 | 1.90 | 1.90 |

London 1980 International Stamp Exhibition, May 6-14. No. 340a contains Nos. 338-340; marginal inscription gives history of postal stones, London 1980 emblem. Size: 111x121mm.

**Queen Mother Elizabeth Birthday Issue**

Common Design Type

**1980, Aug. 18 Litho. Perf. 14**

| | | |
|---|---|---|
| 341 CD330 24p multi | 85 | 85 |

The Briars, 1815 A61

**1980, Nov. 17 Litho. Perf. 14**

| | | |
|---|---|---|
| 342 A61 9p *shown* | 30 | 30 |
| 343 A61 30p *Wellington, by Goya*, vert. | 95 | 95 |

Duke of Wellington's visit to St. Helena, 175th anniversary. Nos. 342-343 issued in sheets of 10 with gutter giving historical background. Size: 154x168½mm.

Redwood Flower A62

**1981, Jan. 5 Perf. 13½**

| | | |
|---|---|---|
| 344 A62 5p *shown* | 15 | 15 |
| 345 A62 8p *Old father-live-forever* | 24 | 24 |
| 346 A62 15p *Gumwood* | 45 | 45 |
| 347 A62 27p *Black cabbage* | 80 | 80 |

John Thornton's Map of St. Helena, 1700 — A63

**1981, May 22 Litho. Perf. 14½**

| | | |
|---|---|---|
| 348 A63 5p Reinel Portolan Chart, 1530 | 12 | 12 |
| 349 A63 8p shown | 20 | 20 |
| 350 A63 20p St. Helena, 1815 | 48 | 48 |
| 351 A63 30p St. Helena, 1817 | 75 | 75 |

**Souvenir Sheet**

| | | |
|---|---|---|
| 352 A63 24p Gastaldi's map of Africa, 16th cent. | 85 | 85 |

No. 352 has black margin showing entire map. Size: 114x82mm.

**Royal Wedding Issue**

Common Design Type

**Wmk. 373**

**1981, July 22 Litho. Perf. 14**

| | | |
|---|---|---|
| 353 CD331 14p Bouquet | 38 | 38 |
| 354 CD331 29p Charles | 80 | 80 |
| 355 CD331 32p Couple | 90 | 90 |

Charonia Variegata — A64

**1981, Sept. 10 Litho. Perf. 14**

| | | |
|---|---|---|
| 356 A64 7p shown | 20 | 20 |
| 357 A64 10p Cypraea spurca sanctahelenae | 30 | 30 |
| 358 A64 25p Janthina janthina | 75 | 75 |
| 359 A64 53p Pinna rudis | 1.65 | 1.65 |

Traffic Guards Taking Oath — A65

**1981, Nov. 5**

| | | |
|---|---|---|
| 360 A65 7p shown | 22 | 22 |
| 361 A65 11p Posting signs | 35 | 35 |
| 362 A65 25p Animal care | 75 | 75 |
| 363 A65 50p Duke of Edinburgh | 1.50 | 1.50 |

Duke of Edinburgh's Awards, 25th anniv.

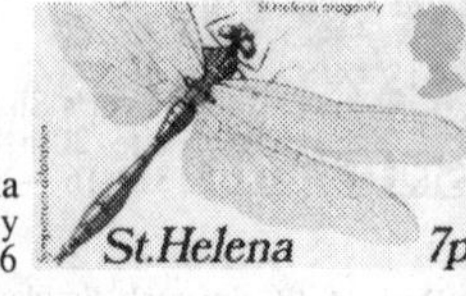
St. Helena Dragonfly A66

**1982, Jan. 4 Litho. Perf. 14½**

| | | |
|---|---|---|
| 364 A66 7p shown | 16 | 16 |
| 365 A66 10p Burchell's beetle | 32 | 32 |
| 366 A66 25p Cockroach wasp | 85 | 85 |
| 367 A66 32p Earwig | 1.10 | 1.10 |

See Nos. 386-389.

Sesquicentennial of Charles Darwin's Visit — A67

**1982, Apr. 19 Litho. Perf. 14**

| | | |
|---|---|---|
| 368 A67 7p Portrait | 20 | 20 |
| 369 A67 14p Flagstaff Hill, hammer | 45 | 45 |
| 370 A67 25p Ring-necked pheasants | 75 | 75 |
| 371 A67 29p Beagle | 90 | 90 |

**Princess Diana Issue**

Common Design Type

**1982, July 1 Litho. Perf. 14**

| | | |
|---|---|---|
| 372 CD333 7p Arms | 20 | 20 |
| 373 CD333 11p Honeymoon | 32 | 32 |
| 374 CD333 29p Diana | 85 | 85 |
| 375 CD333 55p Portrait | 1.65 | 1.65 |

Nos. 305, 307 Overprinted: "1st PARTICIPATION / COMMONWEALTH GAMES 1982"

**1982, Oct. 25 Litho. Perf. 14**

| | | |
|---|---|---|
| 376 A52 15p multi | 48 | 48 |
| 377 A52 26p multi | 80 | 80 |

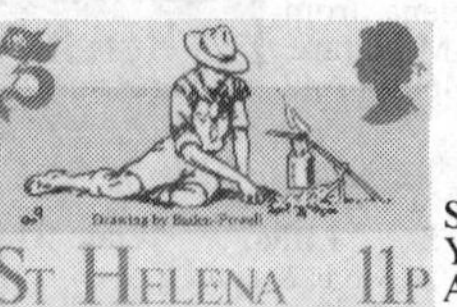
Scouting Year A68

**1982, Nov. 29**

| | | |
|---|---|---|
| 378 A68 3p Baden-Powell, vert. | 8 | 8 |
| 379 A68 11p Campfire | 32 | 32 |
| 380 A68 29p Canon Walcott, vert. | 90 | 90 |
| 381 A68 59p Thompsons Wood camp | 1.75 | 1.75 |

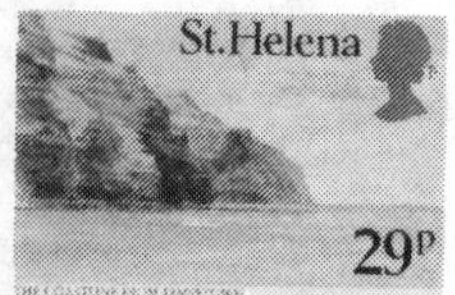
Coastline from Jamestown — A69

**1983, Jan.**
*382* A69 7p King and Queen Rocks, vert. 20 20
*383* A69 11p Turk's Cap, vert. 32 32
*384* A69 29p shown 90 90
*385* A69 55p Munden's Point 1.75 1.75

Insect Type of 1982

**1983, Apr. 22 Litho. *Perf. 14½***
*386* A66 11p Death's-head hawk-moth 32 32
*387* A66 15p Saldid-shore bug 42 42
*388* A66 29p Click beetle 85 85
*389* A66 59p Weevil 1.65 1.65

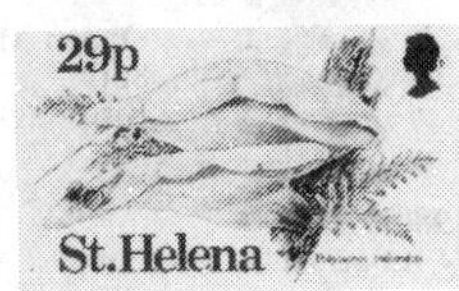

Local Fungi A70

**Wmk. 373**

**1983, June 16 Litho. *Perf. 14***
*390* A70 11p Coriolus versicolor, vert. 32 32
*391* A70 15p Pluteus brunneisucus, vert. 42 42
*392* A70 29p Polyporus induratus 85 85
*393* A70 59p Coprinus angulatus, vert. 1.65 1.65

Local Birds — A71 Christmas 1983 — A72

**1983, Sept. 12 Litho. *Perf. 14x14½***
*394* A71 7p Padda oryzivora 20 20
*395* A71 15p Foudia madagascariensis 40 40
*396* A71 33p Estrilda astrild 90 90
*397* A71 59p Serinus flaviventris 1.65 1.65

**Souvenir Sheet**

**1983, Oct. 17 Litho. *Perf. 14x13½***

Stained Glass, Parish Church of St. Michael.

*398* Sheet of 10 2.75 2.75
*a.* A72 10p multi 22 22
*b.* A72 15p multi 32 32

Sheet contains strips of 10p and 15p with center margin telling St. Helena story. Size: 184x171mm.

150th Anniv. of the Colony — A73

**1984, Jan. 3 Litho. *Perf. 14***
*399* A73 1p No. 101 5 5
*400* A73 3p No. 102 9 9
*401* A73 6p No. 103 16 16
*402* A73 7p No. 104 18 18
*403* A73 11p No. 105 30 30
*404* A73 15p No. 106 42 42
*405* A73 29p No. 107 85 85
*406* A73 33p No. 109 95 95
*407* A73 59p No. 110 1.65 1.65
*408* A73 £1 No. 108 2.75 2.75
*409* A73 £2 New coat of arms 5.75 5.75
*Nos. 399-409 (11)* 13.15 13.15

Visit of Prince Andrew A74

**1984, Apr. 4 Litho. *Perf. 14***
*410* A74 11p Andrew, Invincible 30 30
*411* A74 60p Andrew, Herald 1.65 1.65

**Lloyd's List Issue**

Common Design Type

**1984, May *Perf. 14½x14***
*412* CD335 10p St. Helena, 1814 28 28
*413* CD335 18p Solomon's facade 50 50
*414* CD335 25p Lloyd's Coffee House 70 70
*415* CD335 50p Papanui, 1898 1.40 1.40

New Coin Issue A75

**1984, July *Perf. 14***
*416* A75 10p 2p, Donkey 30 30
*417* A75 15p 5p, Wire bird 45 45
*418* A75 29p 1p, Yellowfin tuna 90 90
*419* A75 50p 10p, Arum lily 1.50 1.50

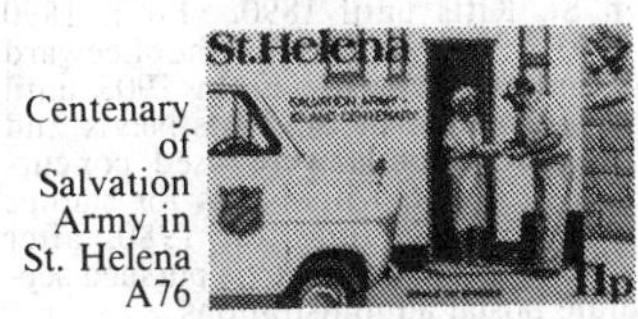

Centenary of Salvation Army in St. Helena A76

**1984, Sept. Litho. Wmk. 373**
*420* A76 7p Secretary Rebecca Fuller, vert. 20 20
*421* A76 11p Meals on Wheels service 30 30
*422* A76 25p Jamestown SA Hall 65 65
*423* A76 60p Hymn playing, clock tower 1.65 1.65

Christmas 1984 — A77

Stained-glass windows.

**1984, Nov. 9**
*424* A77 6p St. Helena visits prisoners 16 16
*425* A77 10p Betrothal of St. Helena 28 28
*426* A77 15p Marriage of St. Helena & Constantius 40 40
*427* A77 33p Birth of Constantine 90 90

See Nos. 442-445.

**Queen Mother 85th Birthday Issue**

Common Design Type

***Perf. 14½x14***

**1985, June 7 Litho. Wmk. 384**
*428* CD336 11p Portrait, age 2 32 32
*429* CD336 15p Queen Mother, Elizabeth II 45 45
*430* CD336 29p Attending ballet, Covent Garden 85 85
*431* CD336 55p Holding Prince Henry 1.75 1.75

**Souvenir Sheet**

*432* CD336 70p Queen Mother and Ford V8 Pilot 3.00 3.00

No. 432 has multicolored margin continuing design showing Sandringham House. Size: 92x74mm.

Marine Life — A78

***Perf. 13x13½***

**1985, July 12 Litho. Wmk. 373**
*433* A78 7p Rock bullseye 18 18
*434* A78 11p Mackerel 30 30
*435* A78 15p Skipjack tuna 42 42
*436* A78 33p Yellowfin tuna 1.00 1.00
*437* A78 50p Stump 1.40 1.40
*Nos. 433-437 (5)* 3.30 3.30

Audubon Birth Bicent. A79

Portrait of naturalist and his illustrations of American bird species.

**1985, Sept. 2 *Perf. 14***
*438* A79 11p John Audubon, vert. 30 30
*439* A79 15p Common gallinule 42 42
*440* A79 25p Tropic bird 70 70
*441* A79 60p Noddy tern 1.75 1.75

Stained Glass Windows Type of 1984

Christmas: 7p, St. Helena journeys to the Holy Land. 10p, Zambres slays the bull. 15p, The bull restored to life, conversion of St. Helena. 60p, Resurrection of the corpse, the true cross identified.

**1985, Oct. 14**
*442* A77 7p multi 22 22
*443* A77 10p multi 30 30
*444* A77 15p multi 50 50
*445* A77 60p multi 1.90 1.90

Society Banners A80

Designs: 10p, Church Provident Society for Women. 11p, Working Men's Christian Assoc. 25p, Church Benefit Society for Children. 29p, Mechanics & Friendly Benefit Society. 33p, Ancient Order of Foresters.

***Perf. 13x13½***

**1986, Jan. 7 Wmk. 384**
*446* A80 10p multi 30 30
*447* A80 11p multi 32 32
*448* A80 25p multi 75 75
*449* A80 29p multi 85 85
*450* A80 33p multi 1.00 1.00
*Nos. 446-450 (5)* 3.22 3.22

**Queen Elizabeth II 60th Birthday**

Common Design Type

Designs: 10p, Making 21st birthday broadcast, royal tour of South Africa, 1947. 15p, In robes of state, Throne Room, Buckingham Palace, Silver Jubilee, 1977. 20p, Onboard HMS Implacable, en route to South Africa, 1947. 50p, State visit to U.S., 1976. 65p, Visiting Crown Agents' offices, 1983.

**1986, Apr. 21 *Perf. 14½***
*451* CD337 10p scar, blk & sil 32 32
*452* CD337 15p ultra & multi 48 48
*453* CD337 20p grn, blk & sil 62 62
*454* CD337 50p vio & multi 1.55 1.55
*455* CD337 65p rose vio & multi 2.00 2.00
*Nos. 451-455 (5)* 4.97 4.97

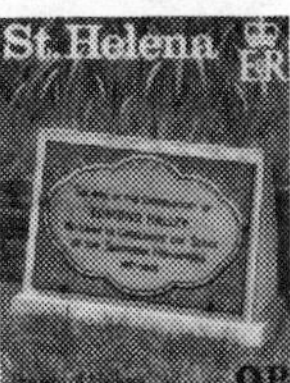

Halley's Comet — A81

Designs: 9p, Site of Halley's observatory on St. Helena. 12p, Edmond Halley, astronomer. 20p, Halley's planisphere of the southern stars. 65p, Voyage to St. Helena on the Unity.

**1986, May 15 Wmk. 373 *Perf. 14½***
*456* A81 9p multi 28 28
*457* A81 12p multi 38 38
*458* A81 20p multi 48 48
*459* A81 65p multi 1.40 1.40

**Royal Wedding Issue, 1986**

Common Design Type

Designs: 10p, Informal portrait. 40p, Andrew in dress uniform at parade.

**Wmk. 384**

**1986, July 23 Litho. *Perf. 14***
*460* CD338 10p multi 32 32
*461* CD338 40p multi 1.25 1.25

Explorers and Ships A82

Designs: 1p, James Ross (1800-62), Erebus. 3p, Robert FitzRoy (1805-65), Beagle. 5p, Adam Johann von Krusenstern (1770-1846), Nadezhda, Russia. 9p, William Bligh (1754-1817), Resolution. 10p, Otto von Kotzebue (1786-1846), Rurik, Germany. 12p, Philip Carteret (1639-82), Swallow. 15p, Thomas Cavendish (c.1560-92), Desire. 20p, Louis-Antoine de Bougainville (1729-1811), La Boudeuse, France. 25p, Fyodor Petrovitch Litke (1797-1882), Seniavin, Russia. 40p, Louis Isidore Duperrey (1786-1865), La Coquille, France. 60p, John Byron (1723-86), Dolphin. £1, James Cook, Endeavour. £2, Jules Dumont d'Urville (1790-1842), L'Astrolabe, France.

**Wmk. 384**

**1986, Sept. 22 Litho. *Perf. 14½***
*462* A82 1p red brn 5 5
*463* A82 3p brt ultra 10 10
*464* A82 5p ol grn 15 15
*465* A82 9p dp cl 28 28
*466* A82 10p sepia 30 30
*467* A82 12p brt bl grn 36 36
*468* A82 15p brn lake 45 45
*469* A82 20p sapphire 60 60
*470* A82 25p red brn 75 75
*471* A82 40p myr grn 1.20 1.20
*472* A82 60p brown 1.80 1.80
*473* A82 £1 Prus bl 3.00 3.00
*474* A82 £2 brt vio 6.00 6.00
*Nos. 462-474 (13)* 15.04 15.04

Ships of Royal Visitors A83

Portraits and vessels: 9p, Prince Edward, HMS Repulse, 1925. 13p, King George VI, HMS Vanguard, 1947. 38p, Prince Philip, HMY Britannia, 1957. 45p, Prince Andrew, HMS Herald, 1984.

**1987, Feb. 16 Wmk. 373 *Perf. 14***
*475* A83 9p multi 28 28
*476* A83 13p multi 40 40
*477* A83 38p multi 1.20 1.20
*478* A83 45p multi 1.40 1.40

Rare Plants — A84

**1987, Aug. 3** *Perf. 14½x14*

| | | | | |
|---|---|---|---|---|
| *479* A84 | 9p St. Helena tea plant | 28 | 28 |
| *480* A84 | 13p Baby's toes | 40 | 40 |
| *481* A84 | 38p Salad plant | 1.20 | 1.20 |
| *482* A84 | 45p Scrubwood | 1.40 | 1.40 |

Marine Mammals A85

**Wmk. 384**

**1987, Oct. 24** **Litho.** *Perf. 14*

| | | | |
|---|---|---|---|
| *483* A85 | 9p Lesser rorqual | 28 | 28 |
| *484* A85 | 13p Risso's dolphin | 42 | 42 |
| *485* A85 | 45p Sperm whale | 1.45 | 1.45 |
| *486* A85 | 60p Euphrosyne dolphin | 1.90 | 1.90 |

**Souvenir Sheet**

| | | | |
|---|---|---|---|
| *487* A85 | 75p Humpback whale | 2.50 | 2.50 |

No. 487 has multicolored margin continuing the design. Size: 102x71mm.

Nos. 451-455 Ovptd. "40TH WEDDING ANNIVERSARY" in Silver.

**Wmk. 384**

**1987, Dec. 9** **Litho.** *Perf. 14½*

| | | | |
|---|---|---|---|
| *488* CD337 | 10p scar, blk & sil | 35 | 35 |
| *489* CD337 | 15p ultra & multi | 50 | 50 |
| *490* CD337 | 20p grn, blk & sil | 68 | 68 |
| *491* CD337 | 50p vio & multi | 1.70 | 1.70 |
| *492* CD337 | 65p rose vio & multi | 2.20 | 2.20 |
| | *Nos. 488-492 (5)* | 5.43 | 5.43 |

Australia Bicentennial A86

Ships and signatures: 9p, HMS *Defence*, 1691, and William Dampier. 13p, HMS *Resolution*, 1775, and James Cook. 45p, HMS *Providence*, 1792, and William Bligh. 60p, HMS *Beagle*, 1836, and Charles Darwin.

**Wmk. 384**

**1988, Mar. 1** **Litho.** *Perf. 14½*

| | | | |
|---|---|---|---|
| *493* A86 | 9p multi | 35 | 35 |
| *494* A86 | 13p multi | 48 | 48 |
| *495* A86 | 45p multi | 1.65 | 1.65 |
| *496* A86 | 60p multi | 2.20 | 2.20 |

Christmas — A87

Religious paintings by unknown artists: 5p, *The Holy Family with Child*. 20p, *Madonna*. 38p, *The Holy Family with St. John*. 60p, *The Holy Virgin with the Child*.

**Wmk. 373**

**1988, Oct. 11** **Litho.** *Perf. 14*

| | | | |
|---|---|---|---|
| *497* A87 | 5p multi | 18 | 18 |
| *498* A87 | 20p multi | 68 | 68 |
| *499* A87 | 38p multi | 1.30 | 1.30 |
| *500* A87 | 60p multi | 2.05 | 2.05 |

**Lloyds of London, 300th Anniv.**

Common Design Type

Designs: 9p, Underwriting room, 1886. 20p, *Edinburgh Castle*, horiz. 45p, *Bosun Bird*, horiz. 60p, *Spangereid* on fire off St. Helena, 1920.

**Wmk. 384**

**1988, Nov. 1** **Litho.** *Perf. 14*

| | | | |
|---|---|---|---|
| *501* CD341 | 9p multi | 30 | 30 |
| *502* CD341 | 20p multi | 68 | 68 |
| *503* CD341 | 45p multi | 1.50 | 1.50 |
| *504* CD341 | 60p multi | 2.00 | 2.00 |

Rare Plants — A88

**1989, Jan. 6** **Wmk.** *Perf.*

| | | | |
|---|---|---|---|
| *505* A88 | 9p Ebony | 30 | 30 |
| *506* A88 | 20p St. Helena lobelia | 68 | 68 |
| *507* A88 | 45p Large bellflower | 1.55 | 1.55 |
| *508* A88 | 60p She cabbage tree | 2.05 | 2.05 |

## SEMI-POSTAL STAMPS

**Catalogue values for unused stamps in this section are for Never Hinged items.**

Tristan da Cunha Nos. 46, 49-51 Overprinted "ST. HELENA / Tristan Relief" and Surcharged with New Value and "+".

*Perf. 12½x13*

**1961, Oct. 12** **Wmk. 314** **Engr.**

| | | | |
|---|---|---|---|
| *B1* A3 | 2½c + 3p rose red & blk | | *500.00* |
| *B2* A3 | 5c + 6p bl & blk | | *500.00* |
| *B3* A3 | 7½c + 9p rose car & blk | | *575.00* |
| *B4* A3 | 10c + 1sh brn org & blk | | *700.00* |
| | *Nos. B1-B4 (4)* | 6000. | 2750. |

Withdrawn from sale Oct. 19.

## POSTAGE DUE STAMPS

**Catalogue values for unused stamps in this section are for Never Hinged items.**

Map — D1

*Perf. 15x14*

**1986, June 9** **Litho.** **Wmk. 384**

**Background Color**

| | | | |
|---|---|---|---|
| *J1* D1 | 1p tan | 5 | 5 |
| *J2* D1 | 2p orange | 6 | 6 |
| *J3* D1 | 5p vermilion | 15 | 15 |
| *J4* D1 | 7p violet | 22 | 22 |
| *J5* D1 | 10p chlky bl | 30 | 30 |
| *J6* D1 | 25p dull yel grn | 78 | 78 |
| | *Nos. J1-J6 (6)* | 1.56 | 1.56 |

## WAR TAX STAMPS

No. 62a Surcharged

**WAR TAX**

**ONE PENNY**

**1916** **Wmk. 3** *Perf. 14*

| | | | |
|---|---|---|---|
| *MR1* A10 | 1p + 1p scar & blk | 60 | 60 |
| *a.* | Double surcharge | | *9,500.* |

No. 62 Surcharged

**WAR TAX**

**1d**

**1919**

| | | | |
|---|---|---|---|
| *MR2* A10 | 1p + 1p car & blk | 40 | 40 |

# ST. KITTS

LOCATION — In the West Indies southeast of Puerto Rico.
GOVT. — With Nevis, Associated State in British Commonwealth.
AREA — 65 sq. mi.
POP. — 35,104 (1980).
CAPITAL — Basseterre

See St. Christopher for stamps used in St. Kitts until 1890. From 1890 until 1903, stamps of the Leeward Islands were used. From 1903 until 1956, stamps of St. Kitts-Nevis and Leeward Islands were used concurrently. See St. Kitts-Nevis for stamps used through June 22, 1980, after which St. Kitts and Nevis pursued separate postal administrations.

100 Cents = 1 Dollar

**Catalogue values for all unused stamps in this country are for Never Hinged items.**

St. Kitts-Nevis Nos. 357-369 Ovptd.

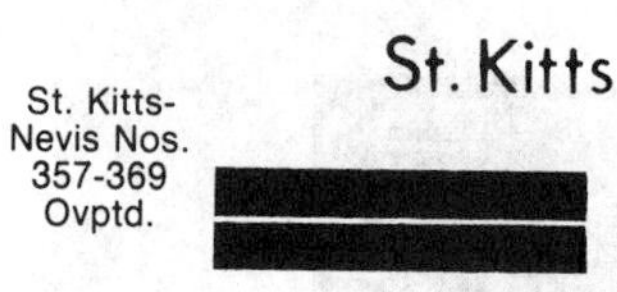


*Perf. 14½x14*

**1980, June 23** **Litho.** **Wmk. 373**

| | | | |
|---|---|---|---|
| *25* A61 | 5c multi | 5 | 5 |
| *26* A61 | 10c multi | 8 | 8 |
| *27* A61 | 12c multi | 10 | 10 |
| *28* A61 | 15c multi | 12 | 12 |
| *29* A61 | 25c multi | 20 | 20 |
| *30* A61 | 30c multi | 22 | 22 |
| *31* A61 | 40c multi | 30 | 30 |
| *32* A61 | 45c multi | 35 | 35 |
| *33* A61 | 50c multi | 38 | 38 |
| *34* A61 | 55c multi | 42 | 42 |
| *35* A61 | $1 multi | 75 | 75 |
| *36* A61 | $5 multi | 3.75 | 3.75 |
| *37* A61 | $10 multi | 7.50 | 7.50 |
| | *Nos. 25-37 (13)* | 14.22 | 14.22 |

Ships — A2

**1980, Aug. 8** *Perf. 13½*

| | | | |
|---|---|---|---|
| *38* A2 | 4c HMS *Vanguard*, 1762 | 5 | 5 |
| *39* A2 | 10c HMS *Boreas*, 1787 | 6 | 6 |
| *40* A2 | 30c HMS *Druid*, 1827 | 18 | 18 |
| *41* A2 | 55c HMS *Winchester*, 1831 | 35 | 35 |
| *42* A2 | $1.50 *Philosopher*, 1857 | 95 | 95 |
| *43* A2 | $2 S.S. *Contractor*, 1930 | 1.25 | 1.25 |
| | *Nos. 38-43 (6)* | 2.84 | 2.84 |

Nos. 38-43 not issued without overprint.

Queen Mother, 80th Birthday — A3

**1980, Sept. 4** *Perf. 14*

| | | | |
|---|---|---|---|
| *44* A3 | $2 multi | 1.00 | 1.00 |

Christmas — A4

**1980, Nov. 10** *Perf. 14½*

| | | | |
|---|---|---|---|
| *45* A4 | 5c Magi following star | 5 | 5 |
| *46* A4 | 15c Shepherds, star | 9 | 9 |
| *47* A4 | 30c Bethlehem, star | 16 | 16 |
| *48* A4 | $4 Adoration of the Magi | 2.25 | 2.25 |

Birds — A5

Military Uniforms — A6

**1981** **Wmk. 373** *Perf. 13½x14*

| | | | |
|---|---|---|---|
| *49* A5 | 1c Frigatebird | 5 | 5 |
| *50* A5 | 4c Rusty-tailed fly-catcher | 5 | 5 |
| *51* A5 | 5c Purple-throated carib | 5 | 5 |
| *52* A5 | 6c Burrowing owl | 5 | 5 |
| *53* A5 | 8c Purple martin | 5 | 5 |
| *54* A5 | 10c Yellow-crowned night heron | 6 | 6 |

*Perf. 14*

**Size: 38x25mm**

| | | | |
|---|---|---|---|
| *55* A5 | 15c Bananaquit | 10 | 10 |
| *56* A5 | 20c Scaly-breasted thrasher | 12 | 12 |
| *57* A5 | 25c Grey kingbird | 16 | 16 |
| *58* A5 | 30c Green-throated carib | 18 | 18 |
| *59* A5 | 40c Ruddy turnstone | 24 | 24 |
| *60* A5 | 45c Black-faced grass-quit | 28 | 28 |
| *61* A5 | 50c Cattle egret | 30 | 30 |
| *62* A5 | 55c Brown pelican | 32 | 32 |
| *63* A5 | $1 Lesser Antillean bullfinch | 60 | 60 |
| *64* A5 | $2.50 Zenaida dove | 1.50 | 1.50 |
| *65* A5 | $5 Sparrow hawk | 3.00 | 3.00 |
| *66* A5 | $10 Antillean crested hummingbird | 6.00 | 6.00 |
| | *Nos. 49-66 (18)* | 13.11 | 13.11 |

Issue dates: Nos. 51, 54-66, Feb. 5. Others, May 30. Also exist with "1982" imprint.

**1981-83** *Perf. 14½*

Foot Regiments: 5c, Battalion Company sergeant, 3rd Regiment, c. 1801. 15c, Light Company private, 15th Regiment, c. 1814. No. 69, Battalion Company officer, 45th Regiment, 1796-7. No. 70, Officer, 15th Regiment, c. 1780. No. 71, Officer, 9th Regiment, 1790. No. 72, Light Company officer, 5th Regiment, c. 1822. No. 73, Grenadier, 38th Regiment, 1751. No. 74, Battalion Company officer, 11th Regiment, c. 1804.

| | | | |
|---|---|---|---|
| *67* A6 | 5c multi | 5 | 5 |
| *68* A6 | 15c multi ('83) | 10 | 10 |
| *69* A6 | 30c multi | 18 | 18 |

70 A6 30c multi ('83) 18 18
71 A6 55c multi 35 35
72 A6 55c multi ('83) 35 35
73 A6 $2.50 multi 1.50 1.50
74 A6 $2.50 multi ('83) 1.50 1.50
*Nos. 67-74 (8)* 4.21 4.21

Issue dates: 5c, Nos. 69, 71 and 73, Mar. 5, 1981. Others, May 25, 1983.

### Royal Wedding Types of Montserrat

**1981, June 23** ***Perf. 14***

75 A66 55c *Saudadoes* 38 38
76 A67 55c Couple 38 38
*a.* Bklt. pane of 4, perf. 12½x12, unwmkd. 1.65
77 A66 $2.50 *The Royal George* 1.65 1.65
78 A67 $2.50 like 55c 1.65 1.65
*a.* Bklt. pane of 2, perf. 12½x12, unwmkd. 3.50
79 A66 $4 HMY *Britannia* 2.75 2.75
80 A67 $4 like 55c 2.75 2.75
*Nos. 75-80 (6)* 9.56 9.56

**Souvenir Sheet**

**1981, Dec. 14** ***Perf. 12½x12***

81 A67 $5 like 55c 6.00 6.00

Wedding of Prince Charles and Lady Diana Spencer. Nos. 76a and 78a issued Nov. 19, 1981. No. 81 has orange and white decorative margin. Size: 121x108mm.

Natl. Girl Guide Movement, 50th Anniv. — A7

Christmas — A8

Designs: 5c, Miriam Pickard, 1st Guide commissioner. 30c, Lady Baden-Powell's visit, 1964. 55c, Visit of Princess Alice, 1960. $2, Thinking-Day Parade, 1980s.

**1981, Sept. 21**

82 A7 5c multi 5 5
83 A7 30c multi 18 18
84 A7 55c multi 35 35
85 A7 $2 multi 1.25 1.25

**1981, Nov. 30**

Stained-glass windows.

86 A8 5c Annunciation 5 5
87 A8 30c Nativity, baptism 18 18
88 A8 55c Last supper, crucifixion 35 35
89 A8 $3 Appearance before Apostles, ascension to heaven 1.90 1.90

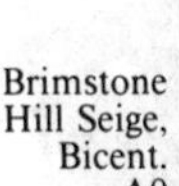
Brimstone Hill Seige, Bicent. A9

**1982, Mar. 15**

90 A9 15c Adm. Samuel Hood 14 14
91 A9 55c Marquis de Bouille 48 48

**Souvenir Sheet**

92 A9 $5 Battle scene 3.25 3.25

No. 92 has multicolored margin picturing battle scene. Size: 96x71mm.

For unused stamps, more recent issues are valued as never hinged, with the beginning point determined on a country-by-country basis. Notes to show the beginning points are prominently placed in the text.

21st Birthday of Princess Diana, July 1 — A10

Designs: 15c, Alexandra of Denmark, Princess of Wales, 1863. 55c, Paternal arms of Alexandra. $6, Diana.

**1982, June 22** ***Perf. 13½x14***

93 A10 15c multi 9 9
94 A10 55c multi 32 32
95 A10 $6 multi 3.50 3.50

Nos. 93-95 Ovptd. ROYAL BABY

**1982, July 12**

96 A10 15c multi 10 10
97 A10 55c multi 32 32
98 A10 $6 multi 3.50 3.50

Birth of Prince William of Wales.

Scouting, 75th Anniv. — A11

Merit badges.

**1982, Aug. 18** ***Perf. 14x13½***

99 A11 5c Nature 5 5
100 A11 55c Rescue 35 35
101 A11 $2 First aid 1.25 1.25

Christmas — A12

Children's drawings.

**1982, Oct. 20**

102 A12 5c shown 5 5
103 A12 55c Nativity 32 32
104 A12 $1.10 Three Kings 65 65
105 A12 $3 Annunciation 1.75 1.75

**Commonwealth Day**
Common Design Type

Designs: 55c, Cruise ship *Stella Oceanis* docked. $2, RMS *Queen Elizabeth 2* anchored in harbor off St. Kitts.

**1983, Mar. 14** ***Perf. 14***

106 CD334 55c multi 35 35
107 CC334 $2 multi 1.25 1.25

Boys' Brigade, Cent. — A14

Designs: 10c, Sir William Smith, founder. 45c, Brigade members outside Sandy Point Methodist Church. 50c, Drummers. $3, Badge.

**1983, July 27**

108 A14 10c multi 8 8
109 A14 45c multi 30 30
110 A14 50c multi 32 32
111 A14 $3 multi 1.90 1.90

Nos. 51, 55-59 and 62-66 Ovptd.

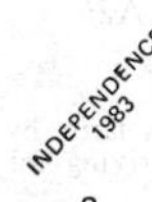


a

INDEPENDENCE
1983

b

**1983, Sept. 19**

112 A5 (a) 5c multi 5 5
*a.* Local overprint 8.25 4.25
113 A5 (b) 15c multi 10 10
114 A5 (b) 20c multi 12 12
115 A5 (b) 25c multi 16 16
116 A5 (b) 30c multi 18 18
117 A5 (b) 40c multi 25 25
118 A5 (b) 55c multi 35 35
119 A5 (b) $1 multi 60 60
120 A5 (b) $2.50 multi 1.65 1.65
121 A5 (b) $5 multi 3.00 3.00
122 A5 (b) $10 multi 6.25 6.25
*Nos. 112-122 (11)* 12.71 12.71

Nos. 113-122 have "1982" imprint. Nos. 113, 116, 118-122 exist without imprint. No. 112 is without imprint. No. 112 with imprint is twice the value.

No. 112a has serifed letters and reads down on imprinted stamp. Exists reading up and without imprint.

Manned Flight Bicent. A15

Designs: 10c, *Montgolfiere*, 1783, vert. 45c, Sikorsky *Russian Knight*, 1913. 50c, Lockheed TriStar. $2.50, Bell XS-1, 1947.

**1983, Sept. 28** **Wmk. 380**

123 A15 10c multi 7 7
124 A15 45c multi 30 30
125 A15 50c multi 32 32
126 A15 $2.50 multi 1.65 1.65
*a.* Souv. sheet of 4, Nos. 123-126 2.40 2.40

1st Flight of a 4-engine aircraft, May 1913 (45c); 1st manned supersonic aircraft, 1947 ($2.50).

No. 126a has multicolored decorative margin picturing aircraft. Size: 108x145mm.

Christmas A16

**1983, Nov. 7**

127 A16 15c shown 12 12
128 A16 30c Shepherds 22 22
129 A16 55c Mary, Joseph 42 42
130 A16 $2 Nativity 1.50 1.50
*a.* Souv. sheet of 4, Nos. 127-130 2.30 2.30

No. 130a has multicolored decorative margin picturing score of *Mary's Boy Child*, by Jester Hairston. Size: 130x130mm.

Batik Art A17

**1984-85**

131 A17 15c Country bus 8 8
132 A17 40c Donkey cart 20 20
133 A17 45c Parrot, vert. 24 24
134 A17 50c Man under palm tree, vert. 25 25
135 A17 60c Rum shop, cyclist 30 30
136 A17 $1.50 Fruit seller, vert. 80 80
137 A17 $3 Butterflies, vert. 1.50 1.50
138 A17 $3 S.V. *Polynesia* 1.50 1.50
*Nos. 131-138 (8)* 4.87 4.87

Issue dates: 15c, 40c, 60c, No. 138, Feb. 6, 1985. Others, Jan. 30, 1984.

Marine Life A18

**1984, July 4**

139 A18 5c Cushion star 5 5
140 A18 10c Rough file shell 6 6
*a.* Wmk. 384 ('86) 6 6
141 A18 15c Red-lined cleaning shrimp 9 9
142 A18 20c Bristleworm 12 12
143 A18 25c Flamingo tongue 14 14
144 A18 30c Christmas tree worm 16 16
145 A18 40c Pink-tipped anemone 22 22
146 A18 50c Smallmouth grunt 28 28
147 A18 60c Glasseye snapper 35 35
*a.* Wmk. 384 ('88) 35 35
148 A18 75c Reef squirrelfish 42 42
149 A18 $1 Sea fans, flamefish 55 55
150 A18 $2.50 Reef butterflyfish 1.40 1.40
151 A18 $5 Black soldierfish 2.75 2.75
*a.* Wmk. 384 ('88) 2.75 2.75
152 A18 $10 Cocoa damselfish 5.75 5.75
*a.* Wmk. 384 ('88) 5.75 5.75
*Nos. 139-152 (14)* 12.34 12.34

Nos. 149-152 vert.

No. 140a has "1986" imprint; also exists with "1988" imprint. Nos. 147a, 151a and 152a have "1988" imprint.

4-H in St. Kitts, 25th Anniv. A19

**1984, Aug. 15**

153 A19 30c Agriculture 20 20
154 A19 55c Animal husbandry 38 38
155 A19 $1.10 Pledge, flag, youths 75 75
156 A19 $3 Parade 2.00 2.00

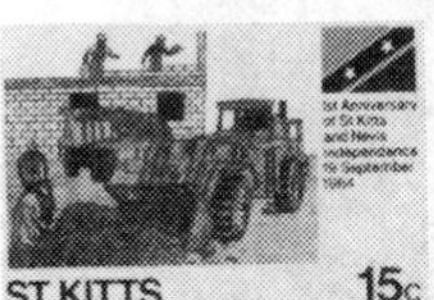


1st Anniv. of Independence — A20

Designs: 15c, Construction of Royal St. Kitts Hotel. 30c, Folk dancers. $1.10, *O Land of Beauty*, vert. $3, Sea, palm trees, map, vert.

**1984, Sept. 18**

*157* A20 15c multi 12 12
*158* A20 30c multi 20 20
*159* A20 $1.10 multi 80 80
*160* A20 $3 multi 2.25 2.25

Christmas A21

**1984, Nov. 1**

*161* A21 15c Opening gifts 12 12
*162* A21 60c Caroling 42 42
*163* A21 $1 Nativity 70 70
*164* A21 $2 Leaving church 1.40 1.40

Ships A22

**1985, Mar. 27** ***Perf. 13½x14***

*165* A22 40c *Tropic Jade* 28 28
*166* A22 $1.20 *Atlantic Clipper* 85 85
*167* A22 $2 M.V. *Cunard Countess* 1.40 1.40
*168* A22 $2 *Mandalay* 1.40 1.40

Mt. Olive Masonic Lodge, 150th Anniv. — A23

Christmas — A24

Designs: 15c, James Derrick Cardin (1871-1954). 75c, Lodge banner. $1.20, Compass, Bible, square, horiz. $3, Charter, 1835.

**1985, Nov. 9** ***Perf. 15***

*169* A23 15c multi 12 12
*170* A23 75c multi 55 55
*171* A23 $1.20 multi 90 90
*172* A23 $3 multi 2.25 2.25

**1985, Nov. 27** **Unwmk.**

*173* A24 10c Map of St. Kitts 8 8
*174* A24 40c *Golden Hind* 30 30
*175* A24 60c Sir Francis Drake 45 45
*176* A24 $3 Drake's shield of arms 2.25 2.25

Visit of Sir Francis Drake to St. Kitts, 400th anniv.

Queen Elizabeth II, 60th Birthday — A25

Designs: 10c, With Prince Philip. 20c, Walking with government officials. 40c, Riding horse in parade. $3, Portrait.

**1986, July 9** ***Perf. 14***

*177* A25 10c multi 8 8
*178* A25 20c multi 15 15
*179* A25 40c multi 30 30
*180* A25 $3 multi 2.25 2.25

**Royal Wedding Issue, 1986**
Common Design Type

Designs: 15c, Prince Andrew and Sarah Ferguson, formal engagement announcement. $2.50, Prince Andrew in military dress uniform.

***Perf. 14½x14***

**1986, July 23** **Wmk. 384**

*181* CD338 15c multi 12 12
*182* CD338 $2.50 multi 1.85 1.85

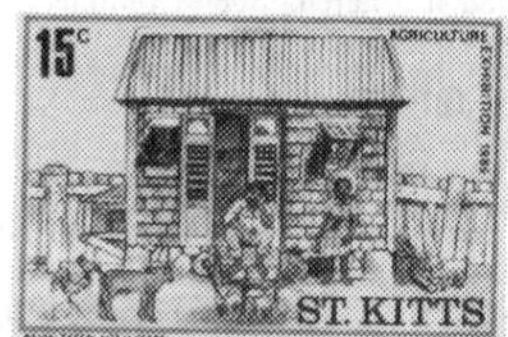

Agriculture Exhibition — A26

Children's drawings: 15c, Family farm, by Kevin Tatem, age 14. $1.20, Striving for growth, by Alister Williams, age 19.

**1986, Sept. 18** ***Perf. 13½x14***

*183* A26 15c multi 12 12
*184* A26 $1.20 multi 90 90

Nos. 177-180 Ovptd. "40th ANNIVERSARY / U.N. WEEK 19-26 OCT." in Gold.

**1986, Oct. 22** **Unwmk.** ***Perf. 14***

*185* A25 10c multi 8 8
*186* A25 20c multi 15 15
*187* A25 40c multi 30 30
*188* A25 $3 multi 2.25 2.25

World Wildlife Fund — A27

Various green monkeys, *Cercopithecus aethiops sabaeus.*

**1986, Dec. 1**

*189* A27 15c multi 12 12
*190* A27 20c multi, diff. 16 16
*191* A27 60c multi, diff. 48 48
*192* A27 $1 multi, diff. 80 80

Auguste Bartholdi — A28

Statue of Liberty, Cent. — A29

***Perf. 14x14½, 14½x14***

**1986, Dec. 17**

*193* A28 40c shown 32 32
*194* A28 60c Torch, head, 1876-78 48 48
*195* A28 $1.50 Warship *Isere*, France 1.20 1.20
*196* A28 $3 Delivering statue, 1884 2.40 2.40

**Souvenir Sheet**

*197* A29 $3.50 Head 2.75 2.75

Nos. 194-195 horiz. No. 197 has inscribed multicolored margin continuing the design. Size: 70x85mm.

British and French Uniforms — A30

Designs: No. 198, Officer, East Norfolk Regiment, 1792. No. 199, Officer, De Neustrie Regiment, 1779. No. 200, Sergeant, Third Foot the Buffs, 1801. No. 201, Artillery officer, 1812. No. 202, Private, Light Company, 5th Foot Regiment, 1778. No. 203, Grenadier, Line Infantry, 1796.

**1987, Feb. 25** ***Perf. 14½***

*198* A30 15c multi 12 12
*199* A30 15c multi 12 12
*200* A30 40c multi 30 30
*201* A30 40c multi 30 30
*202* A30 $2 multi 1.50 1.50
*203* A30 $2 multi 1.50 1.50
*a.* Souv. sheet of 6, Nos. 198-203 4.00 4.00
*Nos. 198-203 (6)* 3.84 3.84

No. 203a has multicolored margin picturing weapons and accessories. Size: 121x145mm.

Sugar Cane Industry — A31

Designs: No. 204a, Warehouse. No. 204b, Barns. No. 204c, Steam emitted by processing plant. No. 204d, Processing plant. No. 204e, Field hands. No. 205a, Locomotive. No. 205b, Locomotive and tender. No. 205c, Open cars. No. 205d, Empty and loaded cars, tractor. No. 205e, Loading sugar cane.

**1987, Apr. 15** ***Perf. 14***

*204* Strip of 5 60 60
*a.-e.* A31 15c any single 12 12
*205* Strip of 5 3.00 3.00
*a.-e.* A31 75c any single 60 60

Visiting Aircraft A32

***Perf. 14x14½***

**1987, June 24** **Wmk. 373**

*206* A32 40c L-1011-500 Tri-Star 30 30
*207* A32 60c BAe Super 748 45 45
*208* A32 $1.20 DHC-6 Twin Otter 90 90
*209* A32 $3 Aerospatiale ATR-42 2.25 2.25

Fungi — A33

**1987, Aug. 26** **Wmk. 384** ***Perf. 14***

*210* A33 15c *Hygrocybe occidentalis* 12 12
*211* A33 40c *Marasmius haematocephalus* 30 30
*212* A33 $1.20 *Psilocybe cubensis* 90 90
*213* A33 $2 *Hygrocybe acutoconica* 1.50 1.50
*214* A33 $3 *Boletellus cubensis* 2.25 2.25
*Nos. 210-214 (5)* 5.07 5.07

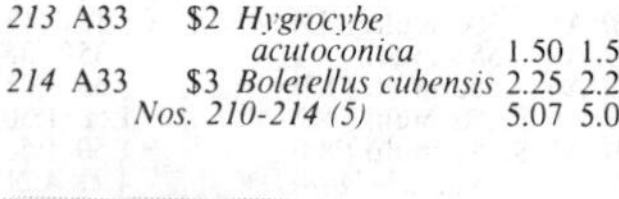

Carnival Clowns — A34

**1987, Oct. 28** ***Perf. 14½***

*215* A34 15c multi 12 12
*216* A34 40c multi, diff. 30 30
*217* A34 $1 multi, diff. 75 75
*218* A34 $3 multi, diff. 2.25 2.25

Christmas 1987. See Nos. 235-238.

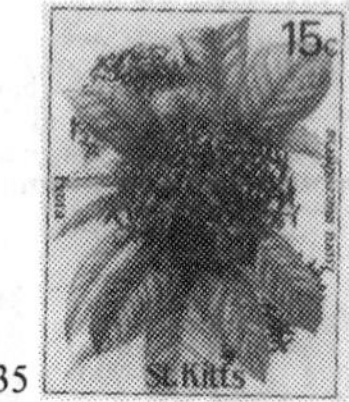

Flowers — A35

**1988, Jan. 20**

*219* A35 15c Ixora 12 12
*220* A35 40c Shrimp plant 30 30
*221* A35 $1 Poinsettia 75 75
*222* A35 $3 Honolulu rose 2.25 2.25

Tourism A36

**1988, Apr. 20** **Wmk. 373**

*223* A36 60c Ft. Thomas Hotel 45 45
*224* A36 60c Fairview Inn 45 45
*225* A36 60c Frigate Bay Beach Hotel 45 45
*226* A36 60c Ocean Terrace Inn 45 45
*227* A36 $3 The Golden Lemon 2.25 2.25
*228* A36 $3 Royal St. Kitts Casino and Jack Tar Village 2.25 2.25
*229* A36 $3 Rawlins Plantation Hotel and Restaurant 2.25 2.25
*Nos. 223-229 (7)* 8.55 8.55

See Nos. 239-245.

Leeward Islands Cricket Tournament, 75th Anniv. — A37

Independence, 5th Anniv. — A38

Designs: 40c, Leeward Islands Cricket Assoc. emblem, ball and wicket. $3, Cricket match at Warner Park.

**1988, July 13** ***Perf. 13x13½***

*230* A37 40c multi 30 30
*231* A37 $3 multi 2.25 2.25

**1988, Sept. 19** **Wmk. 384** ***Perf. 14½***

Designs: 15c, Natl. flag. 60c, Natl. coat of arms. $5, Princess Margaret presenting the Nevis Constitution Order to Prime Minister Simmonds, Sept. 19, 1983.

232 A38 15c shown 12 12
233 A38 60c multi 45 45

**Souvenir Sheet**

234 A38 $5 multi 3.75 3.75

No. 234 has multicolored margin continuing the design. Size: 60x52mm.

Christmas Type of 1987

Carnival clowns.

**1988, Nov. 2 Wmk. 373**

235 A34 15c multi 12 12
236 A34 40c multi, diff. 30 30
237 A34 80c multi, diff. 60 60
238 A34 $3 multi, diff. 2.25 2.25

Tourism Type of 1988

**Wmk. 384**

**1989, Jan. 25 Litho. *Perf. 14***

239 A36 20c Old Colonial House 15 15
240 A36 20c Georgian House 15 15
241 A36 $1 Romney Manor 75 75
242 A36 $1 Lavington Great House 75 75
243 A36 $2 Treasury Building 1.50 1.50
244 A36 $2 Government House 1.50 1.50
*Nos. 239-244 (6)* 4.80 4.80

## OFFICIAL STAMPS

Nos. 28-37 Ovptd. "OFFICIAL."

***Perf. 14½x14***

**1980, June 23 Litho. Wmk. 373**

O1 A61 15c multi 9 9
O2 A61 25c multi 15 15
O3 A61 30c multi 16 16
O4 A61 40c multi 24 24
O5 A61 45c multi 26 26
O6 A61 50c multi 30 30
O7 A61 55c multi 32 32
O8 A61 $1 multi 60 60
O9 A61 $5 multi 3.00 3.00
O10 A61 $10 multi 5.75 5.75
*Nos. O1-O10 (10)* 10.87 10.87

Nos. O2-O4 and O7-O10 exist with "1982" imprint.

Nos. 55-66 Ovptd. "OFFICIAL."

**1981, Feb. 5 *Perf. 14***

O11 A5 15c multi 10 10
O12 A5 20c multi 12 12
O13 A5 25c multi 18 18
O14 A5 30c multi 18 18
O15 A5 40c multi 26 26
O16 A5 45c multi 30 30
O17 A5 50c multi 32 32
O18 A5 55c multi 35 35
O19 A5 $1 multi 65 65
O20 A5 $2.50 multi 1.65 1.65
O21 A5 $5 multi 3.25 3.25
O22 A5 $10 multi 6.50 6.50
*Nos. O11-O22 (12)* 13.86 13.86

Nos. 75-80 Ovptd. or Surcharged "OFFICIAL" in Ultra or Black

**1983, Feb. 2**

O23 A66 45c on $2.50 No. 77 42 42
O24 A67 45c on $2.50 No. 78 42 42
O25 A66 55c No. 75 50 50
O26 A67 55c No. 76 50 50
O27 A66 $1.10 on $4 No. 79 (B) 1.00 1.00
O28 A67 $1.10 on $4 No. 80 (B) 1.00 1.00
*Nos. O23-O28 (6)* 3.84 3.84

Nos. 141-152 Ovptd. "OFFICIAL."

**1984, July 4 Wmk. 380**

O29 A18 15c multi 9 9
O30 A18 20c multi 12 12
O31 A18 25c multi 14 14
O32 A18 30c multi 16 16
O33 A18 40c multi 22 22
O34 A18 50c multi 28 28
O35 A18 60c multi 35 35
O36 A18 75c multi 42 42
O37 A18 $1 multi 60 60
O38 A18 $2.50 multi 1.50 1.50
O39 A18 $5 multi 3.00 3.00
O40 A18 $10 multi 5.75 5.75
*Nos. O29-O40 (12)* 12.63 12.63

# ST. KITTS-NEVIS

## (St. Christopher-Nevis-Anguilla)

LOCATION — In the West Indies southeast of Puerto Rico.
GOVT. — Associated State in British Commonwealth.
AREA — 153 sq. mi.
POP. — 48,000, excluding Anguilla (est. 1976).
CAPITAL — Basseterre, St. Kitts.

St. Kitts-Nevis was one of the presidencies of the former Leeward Islands colony until it became a colony itself in 1956. In 1967 Britain granted internal self-government.

See "St. Christopher" for stamps used in St. Kitts before 1890. From 1890 until 1903, stamps of the Leeward Islands were used. From 1903 until 1956, stamps of St. Kitts-Nevis and Leeward Islands were used concurrently.

Starting in 1967, issues of Anguilla are listed under that heading.

12 Pence = 1 Shilling
20 Shillings = 1 Pound
100 Cents = 1 Dollar (1951)

**Catalogue values for unused stamps in this country are for Never Hinged items, beginning with Scott 91 in the regular postage section and Scott O1 in the officials section.**

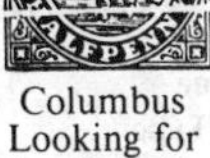

Columbus Looking for Land — A1

Medicinal Spring — A2

**Wmk. Crown and C. A. (2)**

**1903 Typo. *Perf. 14***

1 A1 ½p grn & vio 2.75 2.00
2 A2 1p car & blk 3.25 40
3 A1 2p brn & vio 5.00 12.00
4 A1 2½p ultra & blk 10.00 3.25
5 A2 3p org & grn 6.00 8.25
6 A1 6p red vio & blk 4.00 4.00
7 A1 1sh org & grn 6.50 10.00
8 A2 2sh blk & grn 8.25 10.00
9 A1 2sh 6p vio & blk 13.00 22.50
10 A2 5sh ol grn & gray vio 26.00 42.50
*Nos. 1-10 (10)* 84.75 114.90

**1905-18 Wmk. 3**

11 A1 ½p grn & vio 5.50 4.25
12 A1 ½p green 32 28
13 A2 1p car & blk 3.25 1.10
14 A2 1p carmine 32 28
15 A1 2p brn & vio 90 1.25
16 A1 2½p ultra & blk 16.00 7.00
17 A1 2½p ultra 52 52
18 A2 3p org & grn 1.40 2.50
19 A1 6p red vio & gray blk ('08) 2.00 7.75
a. 6p pur & gray ('08) 4.25 7.75
20 A1 1sh org & grn ('09) 4.25 14.00
21 A2 5sh ol grn & gray vio ('18) 24.00 52.50
*Nos. 11-21 (11)* 58.46 91.43

Nos. 13, 19a and 21 are on chalky paper only and Nos. 15, 18 and 20 are on both ordinary and chalky paper.

King George V — A3

A4

**1920-22**

**Ordinary Paper**

24 A3 ½p green 90 1.10
25 A4 1p carmine 1.10 55
26 A3 1½p orange 70 70
27 A4 2p gray 3.00 4.25
28 A3 2½p ultra 1.40 3.00

**Chalky Paper**

29 A4 3p vio & dl vio, *yel* 1.65 4.25
30 A3 6p red vio & dl vio 2.00 5.25
31 A4 1sh blk, *gray grn* 2.25 6.00
32 A3 2sh ultra & dl vio, *bl* 9.00 18.00
33 A4 2sh 6p red & blk, *bl* 9.00 20.00
34 A3 5sh red & grn, *yel* 10.00 32.50
35 A4 10sh red & grn, *grn* 27.50 55.00
36 A3 £1 blk & vio, *red* ('22) 180.00 350.00
*Nos. 24-36 (13)* 248.50 500.60

**1921-29 Wmk. 4**

**Ordinary Paper**

37 A3 ½p green 22 30
38 A4 1p rose red 28 30
39 A4 1p dp vio ('22) 90 90
40 A3 1½p rose red ('25) 1.75 3.00
41 A3 1½p fawn ('28) 35 75
42 A4 2p gray 1.40 1.75
43 A3 2½p ultra ('22) 45 60
44 A3 2½p brn ('22) 90 3.00

**Chalky Paper**

45 A4 3p ultra ('22) 1.50 3.25
46 A4 3p vio & dl vio, *yel* 60 1.75
47 A3 6p red vio & dl vio ('24) 1.75 3.00
48 A4 1sh blk, *grn* ('29) 3.00 5.50
49 A3 2sh ultra & vio, *bl* ('22) 4.25 11.00
50 A4 2sh 6p red & blk, *bl* ('27) 9.00 18.00
51 A3 5sh red & grn, *yel* ('29) 17.00 35.00
*Nos. 37-51 (15)* 43.35 88.10

No. 43 exists on ordinary and chalky paper.

Caravel in Old Road Bay — A5

**1923 Wmk. 4**

52 A5 ½p grn & blk 1.25 2.50
53 A5 1p vio & blk 1.40 1.90
54 A5 1½p car & blk 2.50 3.75
55 A5 2p dk gray & blk 2.50 2.75
56 A5 2½p brn & blk 3.75 5.75
57 A5 3p ultra & blk 3.75 5.75
58 A5 6p red vio & blk 5.00 10.00
59 A5 1sh ol grn & blk 8.00 16.00
60 A5 2sh ultra & blk, *bl* 22.50 45.00
61 A5 2sh 6p red & blk, *bl* 40.00 62.50
62 A5 10sh red & blk, *emer* 190.00 325.00
*Nos. 52-62 (11)* 280.65 480.90

**Wmk. Multiple Crown and C. A. (3)**

63 A5 5sh red & blk, *yel* 87.50 175.00
64 A5 £1 vio & blk, *red* 1,300. 1,700.

Tercentenary of the founding of the colony of St. Kitts (or St. Christopher).

**Silver Jubilee Issue**

Common Design Type

Inscribed "St. Christopher and Nevis"

***Perf. 11x12***

**1935, May 6 Engr. Wmk. 4**

72 CD301 1p car & dk bl 35 35
73 CD301 1½p gray blk & ultra 50 50
74 CD301 2½p ultra & brn 1.25 1.25
75 CD301 1sh brn vio & ind 4.00 4.00

**Coronation Issue**

Common Design Type

Inscribed "St. Christopher and Nevis"

**1937, May 12 *Perf. 13½x14***

76 CD302 1p carmine 18 18
77 CD302 1½p brown 18 18
78 CD302 2½p brt ultra 38 38

George VI — A6

Medicinal Spring — A7

Columbus Looking for Land — A8

Map Showing Anguilla — A9

***Perf. 13½x14 (A6, A9), 14 (A7, A8)***

**1938-48 Typo.**

79 A6 ½p green 5 5
80 A6 1p carmine 7 7
81 A6 1½p orange 9 9
82 A7 2p gray & car ('41) 16 16
a. Perf. 13x11½ 7.25 3.50
83 A6 2½p ultra 28 28
84 A7 3p car & pale lil ('42) 35 35
a. Perf. 13x11½ 1.40 1.40
85 A8 6p rose lil & dl grn ('42) 1.40 1.10
a. Perf. 13x11½ 1.40 1.40
86 A7 1sh grn & gray blk ('43) 90 90
a. Perf. 13x11½ 2.75 2.25
87 A7 2sh 6p car & gray blk ('42) 3.00 2.50
a. Perf. 13x11½ 9.25 9.25
88 A8 5sh car & dl grn ('42) 3.00 3.00
a. Perf. 13x11½ 35.00 22.50

**Typo., Center Litho.**

**Chalky Paper**

89 A9 10sh brt ultra & blk ('48) 13.00 21.00
90 A9 £1 brn & blk ('48) 18.00 22.50
*Nos. 79-90 (12)* 40.30 52.00

**Catalogue values for unused stamps in this section, from this point to the end of the section, are for Never Hinged items.**

**Peace Issue**

Common Design Type

Inscribed "St. Kitts-Nevis"

**1946, Nov. 1 Engr. *Perf. 13½x14***

91 CD303 1½p dp org 10 10
92 CD303 3p carmine 15 15

**Silver Wedding Issue**

Common Design Types

Inscribed: "St. Kitts-Nevis"

**1949, Jan. 3 Photo. *Perf. 14x14½***

93 CD304 2½p brt ultra 16 16

**Engraved; Name Typographed**

***Perf. 11½x11***

94 CD305 5sh rose car 4.50 6.00

**UPU Issue**

Common Design Types

Inscribed: "St. Kitt's-Nevis"

**Engr.; Name Typo. on 3p, 6p.**

**1949, Oct. 10 *Perf. 13½, 11x11½***

95 CD306 2½p ultra 18 18
96 CD307 3p dp car 35 35
97 CD308 6p red lil 90 90
98 CD309 1sh bl grn 1.50 1.50

Types of 1938 Overprinted in Black or Carmine:

ANGUILLA ANGUILLA

TERCENTENARY 1650-1950
a

TERCENTENARY 1650—1950
b

***Perf. 13½x14, 13x12½***

**1950, Nov. 10 Wmk. 4**

99 A6 (a) 1p carmine 8 8
100 A6 (a) 1½p orange 10 10
a. Wmk. 4a (error) 600.00
101 A6 (a) 2½p ultra 14 14
102 A7 (b) 3p car & pale lil 12 12
103 A8 (b) 6p rose lil & dl grn 25 25

*104* A7 (b) 1sh grn & gray blk (C) 42 42
*Nos. 99-104 (6)* 1.11 1.11

300th anniv. of the settlement of Anguilla.

**University Issue**
Common Design Types
Inscribed: "St. Kitts-Nevis"
***Perf. 14x14½***

**1951, Feb. 16 Engr. Wmk. 4**
*105* CD310 3c org yel & gray blk 18 18
*106* CD311 12c red vio & aqua 52 52

**St. Christopher-Nevis-Anguilla**

Bath House and Spa, Nevis — A10

Map — A11

Designs: 2c, Warner Park, St. Kitts. 4c, Brimstone Hill, St. Kitts. 5c, Nevis. 6c, Pinney's Beach, Nevis. 12c, Sir Thomas Warner's Tomb. 24c, Old Road Bay, St. Kitts. 48c, Picking Cotton. 60c, Treasury, St. Kitts. $1.20, Salt Pond, Anguilla. $4.80, Sugar Mill, St. Kitts.

**1952, June 14** ***Perf. 12½***
*107* A10 1c ocher & dp grn 8 8
*108* A10 2c emerald 16 16
*109* A11 3c pur & red 20 20
*110* A10 4c red 25 25
*111* A10 5c gray & ultra 35 35
*112* A10 6c dp ultra 42 42
*113* A11 12c redsh brn & dp bl 65 65
*114* A10 24c car & gray blk 1.00 75
*115* A10 48c vio brn & ol bis 2.75 2.75
*116* A10 60c dp grn & ocher 2.75 2.75
*117* A10 $1.20 dp ultra & dp grn 6.75 6.75
*118* A10 $4.80 car & emer 15.00 15.00
*Nos. 107-118 (12)* 30.36 30.11

**Coronation Issue**
Common Design Type

**1953, June 2** ***Perf. 13½x13***
*119* CD312 2c brt grn & blk 18 14

Types of 1952 with Portrait of Queen Elizabeth II.

Design: ½c, Salt Pond, Anguilla. 8c, Sombrero Lighthouse. $2.40, Map of Anguilla and Dependencies.

**1954-57 Engr.** ***Perf. 12½.***
*120* A10 ½c gray ol ('56) 12 10
*121* A10 1c ocher & dp grn 8 6
*a.* Horiz. pair, imperf. vert.
*122* A10 2c emerald 10 8
*123* A11 3c pur & red 10 8
*124* A10 4c red 12 10
*125* A10 5c gray & ultra 18 15
*126* A10 6c dp ultra 30 25
*127* A11 8c dk gray ('57) 50 25
*128* A11 12c redsh brn & dp bl 30 25
*129* A10 24c car & blk 60 50
*130* A10 48c brn & ol bis 1.50 1.40
*131* A10 60c dp grn & ocher 2.00 1.75
*132* A10 $1.20 dp ultra & dp grn 4.25 3.00
*133* A10 $2.40 red org & blk ('57) 7.50 4.75
*134* A10 $4.80 car & emer 15.00 12.50
*Nos. 120-134 (15)* 32.65 25.22

Alexander Hamilton and Nevis Scene A12

**1957, Jan. 11** ***Perf. 12½***
*135* A12 24c dp ultra & yel grn 38 38

Issued to commemorate the bicentenary of the birth of Alexander Hamilton.

**West Indies Federation**
Common Design Type
***Perf. 11½x11***

**1958, Apr. 22 Engr. Wmk. 314**
*136* CD313 3c green 14 14
*137* CD313 6c blue 25 25
*138* CD313 12c car rose 50 50

Issued to commemorate the federation of the West Indies, April 22, 1958.

Stamp of Nevis, 1861 — A13

Designs (Stamps of Nevis, 1861 issue): 8c, 4p stamp. 12c, 6p stamp. 24c, 1sh stamp.

**1961, July 15** ***Perf. 14***
*139* A13 2c grn & brn 12 12
*140* A13 8c bl & pale brn 22 22
*141* A13 12c car & gray 32 32
*142* A13 24c org & grn 70 70

Centenary of the first stamps of Nevis.

**Red Cross Centenary Issue**
Common Design Type

**1963, Sept. 2 Litho.** ***Perf. 13***
*143* CD315 3c blk & red 18 18
*144* CD315 12c ultra & red 1.40 1.40

New Lighthouse, Sombrero — A14

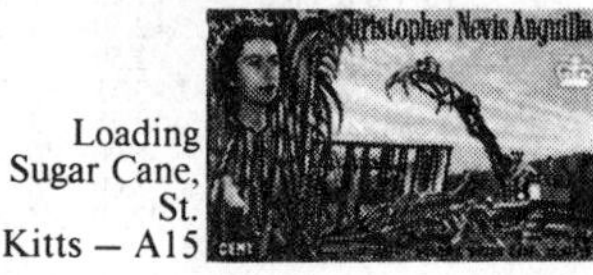


Loading Sugar Cane, St. Kitts — A15

Designs: 2c, Pall Mall Square, Basseterre. 3c, Gateway, Brimstone Hill Fort, St. Kitts. 4c, Nelson's Spring, Nevis. 5c, Grammar School, St. Kitts. 6c, Mt. Misery Crater, St. Kitts. 10c, Hibiscus. 15c, Sea Island cotton, Nevis. 20c, Boat building, Anguilla. 25c, White-crowned pigeon. 50c, St. George's Church tower, Basseterre. 60c, Alexander Hamilton. $1, Map of St. Kitts-Nevis. $2.50, Map of Anguilla. $5, Arms of St. Christopher-Nevis-Anguilla.

**1963, Nov. 20 Photo.** ***Perf. 14***
*145* A14 ½c bl & dk brn 5 5
*146* A15 1c grn, bl, blk & bis 5 5
*147* A14 2c bl, blk, grn & yel 5 5
*a.* Yellow omitted *150.00*
*148* A14 3c bl, blk, brn & grn 7 7
*149* A15 4c bl, brn, grn & yel 9 9
*150* A15 5c bl, blk, grn & brn 10 10
*151* A15 6c vio bl, grn & yel 14 14
*152* A15 10c grn, blk, yel & red 22 22
*153* A14 15c gray, sl, yel, brn & grn 30 30
*154* A15 20c grn, bl, brn & yel 40 40
*155* A14 25c lt bl, sl, yel & red 52 52
*156* A15 50c bl, blk, grn & red 1.10 1.10
*157* A14 60c dl bl, dk bl, blk & sep 1.25 1.25
*158* A14 $1 ultra & brt yel 2.25 2.25
*159* A15 $2.50 grnsh bl, sl & buff 4.00 4.00
*160* A14 $5 org, grn, bl & pink 7.00 7.00
*Nos. 145-160 (16)* 17.59 17.59

**1967-69 Wmk. 314 Sideways**
**Colors as in 1963 Issue.**
*145a* A14 ½c ('69) 6 6
*147b* A14 2c 10 10
*148a* A14 3c ('68) 18 18
*153a* A14 15c ('68) 42 42
*155a* A14 25c ('68) 1.50 75
*158a* A14 $1 ('68) 4.50 4.50
*Nos. 145a-158a (6)* 6.76 6.01

Nos. 148 and 155 Overprinted: "ARTS/FESTIVAL/ST. KITTS/1964"

**1964, Sept. 14**
*161* A14 3c bl, blk, brn & grn 8 8
*162* A14 25c lt bl, sl, yel & red 30 30

**ITU Issue**
Common Design Type
***Perf. 11x11½***

**1965, May 17 Litho. Wmk. 314**
*163* CD317 2c bis & rose red 8 8
*164* CD317 50c grnsh bl & ol 95 95

**Intl. Cooperation Year Issue**
Common Design Type

**1965, Oct. 25** ***Perf. 14½***
*165* CD318 2c bl grn & cl 12 12
*166* CD318 25c lt vio & grn 70 70

**Churchill Memorial Issue**
Common Design Type

**1966, Jan. 24 Photo.** ***Perf. 14***
**Design in Black, Gold and Carmine Rose**
*167* CD319 ½c brt bl 5 5
*168* CD319 3c green 8 8
*169* CD319 15c brown 55 55
*170* CD319 25c violet 1.00 1.00

**Royal Visit Issue**
Common Design Type

**1966, Feb. 14 Litho.** ***Perf. 11x12***
*171* CD320 3c vio bl 7 7
*172* CD320 25c dk car rose 70 70

**World Cup Soccer Issue**
Common Design Type

**1966, July 1 Litho.** ***Perf. 14***
*173* CD321 6c multi 9 9
*174* CD321 25c multi 50 50

Festival Emblem With Dolphins — A16

**Unwmk.**

**1966, Aug. 15 Photo.** ***Perf. 14***
*175* A16 3c gold, grn, yel & blk 6 6
*176* A16 25c sil, grn, yel & blk 42 42

Arts Festival of 1966.

**WHO Headquarters Issue**
Common Design Type

**1966, Sept. 20 Litho.** ***Perf. 14***
*177* CD322 3c multi 6 6
*178* CD322 40c multi 70 70

**UNESCO Anniversary Issue**
Common Design Type

**1966, Dec. 1 Litho.** ***Perf. 14***
*179* CD323 3c "Education" 9 9
*180* CD323 6c "Science" 18 18
*181* CD323 40c "Culture" 1.10 1.10

**Independent State**

Government Headquarters, Basseterre — A17

Designs: 10c, Flag and map of Anguilla, St. Christopher and Nevis. 25c, Coat of Arms.

**Wmk. 314**

**1967, July 1 Photo.** ***Perf. 14½***
*182* A17 3c multi 5 5
*183* A17 10c multi 15 15
*184* A17 25c multi 38 38

Issued to commemorate the achievement of independence, Feb. 27, 1967.

Charles Wesley, Cross and Palm — A18

Designs: 3c, John Wesley. 40c, Thomas Coke.

**1967, Dec. 1 Litho.** ***Perf. 13x13½***
*185* A18 3c dp lil, dp car & blk 6 6
*186* A18 25c ultra, grnsh bl & blk 28 28
*187* A18 40c ocher, yel & blk 55 55

Issued to commemorate the attainment of autonomy by the Methodist Church in the Caribbean and the Americas, and to commemorate the opening of headquarters near St. John's, Antigua, May 1967.

Cargo Ship and Plane A19

***Perf. 13½x13***

**1968, July 30 Litho. Wmk. 314**
*188* A19 25c multi 26 26
*189* A19 50c brt bl & multi 55 55

Issued to publicize the organization of the Caribbean Free Trade Area, CARIFTA.

Martin Luther King, Jr. — A20

Mystical Nativity, by Botticelli — A21

***Perf. 12x12½***

**1968, Sept. 30 Litho. Wmk. 314**
*190* A20 50c multi 48 48

Dr. Martin Luther King, Jr. (1929-68), American civil rights leader.

***Perf. 14½x14***

**1968, Nov. 27 Photo. Wmk. 314**

Paintings: 25c, 50c, The Adoration of the Magi, by Rubens.

*191* A21 12c brt vio & multi 12 12
*192* A21 25c multi 25 25
*193* A21 40c gray & multi 45 45
*194* A21 50c crim & multi 55 55

Christmas 1968.

Snook A22

Fish: 12c, Needlefish (gar). 40c, Horse-eye jack. 50c, Red snapper. The 6c is misinscribed "tarpon."

*Perf. 14x14½*

**1969, Feb. 25 Photo. Wmk. 314**

| | | | | |
|---|---|---|---|---|
| *195* | A22 | 6c brt grn & multi | 9 | 9 |
| *196* | A22 | 12c bl & multi | 18 | 18 |
| *197* | A22 | 40c gray bl & multi | 60 | 60 |
| *198* | A22 | 50c multi | 75 | 75 |

Arms of Sir Thomas Warner and Map of Islands — A23

Designs: 25c, Warner's tomb in St. Kitts. 40c, Warner's commission from Charles I.

**1969, Sept. 1 Litho. *Perf. 13½***

| | | | | |
|---|---|---|---|---|
| *199* | A23 | 20c multi | 24 | 24 |
| *200* | A23 | 25c multi | 30 | 30 |
| *201* | A23 | 40c multi | 60 | 60 |

Issued in memory of Sir Thomas Warner, first Governor of St. Kitts-Nevis, Barbados and Montserrat.

Adoration of the Kings, by Jan Mostaert — A24

Painting: 40c, 50c, Adoration of the Kings, by Geertgen tot Sint Jans.

**1969, Nov. 17 *Perf. 13½***

| | | | | |
|---|---|---|---|---|
| *202* | A24 | 10c ol & multi | 9 | 9 |
| *203* | A24 | 25c vio & multi | 28 | 28 |
| *204* | A24 | 40c yel grn & multi | 52 | 52 |
| *205* | A24 | 50c mar & multi | 65 | 65 |

Christmas 1969.

Pirates Burying Treasure, Frigate Bay — A25

Caravels, 16th Century A26

Designs: 1c, English two-decker, 1650. 2c, Flags of England, Spain, France, Holland and Portugal. 3c, Hilt of 17th cent. rapier. 5c, Henry Morgan and fire boats. 6c, The pirate L'Ollonois and a carrack (pirate vessel). 10c, Smugglers' ship. 15c, Spanish 17th cent. piece of eight and map of Caribbean. 20c, Garrison and ship cannon and map of Spanish Main. 25c, Humphrey Cole's astrolabe, 1574. 50c, Flintlock pistol and map of Spanish Main. 60c, Dutch Flute (ship). $1, Capt. Bartholomew Roberts and document with death sentence for his crew. $2.50, Railing piece (small cannon), 17th cent. and map of Spanish Main. $5, Francis Drake, John Hawkins and ships. $10, Edward Teach (Blackbeard) and his capture.

**Wmk. 314 Upright (A25), Sideways (A26)**

**1970, Feb. 1 Litho. *Perf. 14***

| | | | | |
|---|---|---|---|---|
| *206* | A25 | ½c multi | 7 | 7 |
| *207* | A25 | 1c multi | 5 | 5 |
| *208* | A25 | 2c multi | 7 | 7 |
| *209* | A25 | 3c multi | 7 | 7 |
| *210* | A26 | 4c multi | 10 | 10 |
| *211* | A26 | 5c multi | 10 | 10 |
| *212* | A26 | 6c multi | 12 | 12 |
| *213* | A26 | 10c multi | 22 | 22 |
| *214* | A25 | 15c *Hispanianum* | 50 | 50 |
| *215* | A25 | 15c *Hispaniarum* | 38 | 38 |
| *216* | A26 | 20c multi | 38 | 38 |
| *217* | A25 | 25c multi | 42 | 42 |
| *218* | A26 | 50c multi | 85 | 85 |
| *219* | A25 | 60c multi | 2.00 | 1.00 |
| *220* | A25 | $1 multi | 2.50 | 1.65 |
| *221* | A26 | $2.50 multi | 3.75 | 3.25 |
| *222* | A26 | $5 multi | 7.50 | 6.75 |
| | | *Nos. 206-222 (17)* | 19.08 | 15.98 |

Coin inscription was misspelled on No. 214, corrected on No. 215 (issued Sept. 8).

**Wmk. 314 Sideways (A25), Upright (A26)**

**1973-74**

| | | | | |
|---|---|---|---|---|
| *206a* | A25 | ½c multi | 5 | 5 |
| *208a* | A25 | 2c multi | 7 | 7 |
| *209a* | A25 | 3c multi | 10 | 10 |
| *211a* | A26 | 5c multi | 12 | 12 |
| *212a* | A26 | 6c multi | 16 | 16 |
| *213a* | A26 | 10c multi | 25 | 25 |
| *215a* | A25 | 15c multi | 30 | 30 |
| *216a* | A26 | 20c multi | 50 | 50 |
| *217a* | A25 | 25c multi | 35 | 35 |
| *218a* | A26 | 50c multi | 85 | 85 |
| *220a* | A25 | $1 multi | 1.40 | 1.40 |
| *222A* | A26 | $10 multi ('74) | 12.50 | 12.50 |
| | | *Nos. 206a-220a,222A (12)* | 16.65 | 16.65 |

**1975-77 Wmk. 373**

| | | | | |
|---|---|---|---|---|
| *207b* | A25 | 1c multi ('77) | 5 | 5 |
| *209b* | A25 | 3c multi ('76) | 6 | 5 |
| *210b* | A26 | 4c multi ('76) | 7 | 5 |
| *211b* | A26 | 5c multi | 8 | 7 |
| *212b* | A26 | 6c multi | 10 | 8 |
| *213b* | A26 | 10c multi ('76) | 16 | 15 |
| *215b* | A25 | 15c multi ('76) | 25 | 22 |
| *216b* | A26 | 20c multi | 22 | 16 |
| *219b* | A25 | 60c multi ('76) | 1.00 | 1.00 |
| *220b* | A25 | $1 multi ('77) | 2.00 | 1.50 |
| | | *Nos. 207b-220b (10)* | 3.99 | 3.33 |

Pip Meeting Convict, from "Great Expectations" — A27

Designs: 20c, Miss Havisham from "Great Expectations." 25c, Dickens' birthplace, Portsmouth (vert.). 40c, Charles Dickens (vert.).

***Perf. 13x13½, 13½x13***

**1970, May 1 Litho. Wmk. 314**

| | | | | |
|---|---|---|---|---|
| *223* | A27 | 4c gold, Prus bl & brn | 7 | 7 |
| *224* | A27 | 20c gold, cl & brn | 32 | 32 |
| *225* | A27 | 25c gold, ol & brn | 42 | 42 |
| *226* | A27 | 40c dk bl, gold & brn | 75 | 75 |

Charles Dickens (1812-70), English novelist.

Local Steel Band A28

Designs: 25c, Local string band. 40c, "A Midsummer Night's Dream," 1963 performance.

**1970, Aug. 1 *Perf. 13½***

| | | | | |
|---|---|---|---|---|
| *227* | A28 | 20c multi | 28 | 28 |
| *228* | A28 | 25c multi | 38 | 38 |
| *229* | A28 | 40c multi | 60 | 60 |

Issued to publicize the 1970 Arts Festival.

St. Christopher No. 1 and St. Kitts Post Office, 1970 — A29

Designs: 20c, 25c, St. Christopher Nos. 1 and 3. 50c, St. Christopher No. 3 and St. Kitts postmark, Sept. 2, 1871.

**Wmk. 314**

**1970, Sept. 14 Litho. *Perf. 14½***

| | | | | |
|---|---|---|---|---|
| *230* | A29 | ½c grn & rose | 5 | 5 |
| *231* | A29 | 20c vio bl, rose & grn | 40 | 40 |
| *232* | A29 | 25c brn, rose & grn | 55 | 55 |
| *233* | A29 | 50c blk, grn & dk red | 1.90 | 1.90 |

Centenary of stamps of St. Christopher.

Holy Family, by Anthony van Dyck — A30

Christmas: 3c, 40c, Adoration of the Shepherds, by Frans Floris.

**1970, Nov. 16 *Perf. 14***

| | | | | |
|---|---|---|---|---|
| *234* | A30 | 3c multi | 5 | 5 |
| *235* | A30 | 20c ocher & multi | 30 | 30 |
| *236* | A30 | 25c dl red & multi | 40 | 40 |
| *237* | A30 | 40c grn & multi | 60 | 60 |

Monkey Fiddle A31

Flowers: 20c, Mountain violets. 30c, Morning glory. 50c, Fringed epidendrum.

**1971, Mar. 1 Litho. *Perf. 14***

| | | | | |
|---|---|---|---|---|
| *238* | A31 | ½c multi | 5 | 5 |
| *239* | A31 | 20c multi | 30 | 30 |
| *240* | A31 | 30c multi | 48 | 48 |
| *241* | A31 | 50c multi | 85 | 85 |

Chateau de Poincy, St. Kitts — A32

Designs: 20c, Royal poinciana. 50c, De Poincy's coat of arms (vert.).

**1971, June 1 Litho. Wmk. 314**

| | | | | |
|---|---|---|---|---|
| *242* | A32 | 20c grn & multi | 30 | 30 |
| *243* | A32 | 30c dl yel & multi | 45 | 45 |
| *244* | A32 | 50c brn & multi | 90 | 90 |

Philippe de Longvilliers de Poincy became first governor of French possessions in the Antilles in 1639.

East Yorks A33

Designs: 20c, Royal Artillery. 30c, French Infantry. 50c, Royal Scots.

**1971, Sept. 1 *Perf. 14***

| | | | | |
|---|---|---|---|---|
| *245* | A33 | ½c blk & multi | 5 | 5 |
| *246* | A33 | 20c blk & multi | 48 | 42 |
| *247* | A33 | 30c blk & multi | 80 | 65 |
| *248* | A33 | 50c blk & multi | 1.25 | 1.10 |

Siege of Brimstone Hill, 1782.

Common Design Types pictured in section before Great Britain.

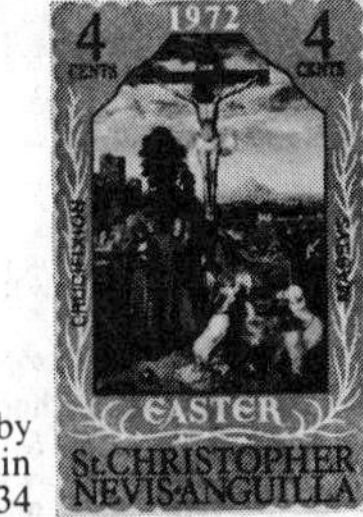


Crucifixion, by Quentin Massys — A34

*Perf. 14x13½*

**1972, Apr. 1 Litho. Wmk. 314**

| | | | | |
|---|---|---|---|---|
| *249* | A34 | 4c brick red & multi | 9 | 9 |
| *250* | A34 | 20c gray grn & multi | 48 | 48 |
| *251* | A34 | 30c dl bl & multi | 70 | 70 |
| *252* | A34 | 40c lt brn & multi | 95 | 95 |

Easter 1972.

Madonna and Child, by Bergognone A35

Paintings: 20c, Adoration of the Kings, by Jacopo da Bassano (horiz.). 25c, Adoration of the Shepherds, by Il Domenichino. 40c, Madonna and Child, by Fiorenzo di Lorenzo.

**1972, Oct. 2 *Perf. 13½x14, 14x13½***

| | | | | |
|---|---|---|---|---|
| *253* | A35 | 3c gray grn & multi | 6 | 6 |
| *254* | A35 | 20c dp plum & multi | 38 | 38 |
| *255* | A35 | 25c sep & multi | 45 | 45 |
| *256* | A35 | 40c red & multi | 70 | 70 |

Christmas 1972.

**Silver Wedding Issue, 1972**

Common Design Type

Design: Queen Elizabeth II, Prince Philip and pelicans.

**1972, Nov. 20 Photo. *Perf. 14x14½***

| | | | | |
|---|---|---|---|---|
| *257* | CD324 | 20c car rose & multi | 35 | 35 |
| *258* | CD324 | 25c ultra & multi | 48 | 48 |

Warner Landing at St. Kitts — A36

Designs: 25c, Settlers growing tobacco. 40c, Building fort at "Old Road." $2.50, Warner's ship off St. Kitts, Jan. 28, 1623.

*St. Kitts-Nevis stamps can be mounted in Scott's British Leeward Album.*

**1973, Jan. 28 Litho. *Perf. 14x13½***

| | | | | |
|---|---|---|---|---|
| *259* | A36 | 4c pink & multi | 9 | 9 |
| *260* | A36 | 25c brn & multi | 55 | 55 |
| *261* | A36 | 40c bl & multi | 90 | 90 |
| *262* | A36 | $2.50 multi | 3.75 | 3.75 |

350th anniversary of the landing of Sir Thomas Warner at St. Kitts.

The Last Supper, by Juan de Juanes — A37

Designs (The Last Supper, by): 4c, Titian (vert.). 25c, ascribed to Roberti (vert.).

***Perf. 14x13½, 13½x14***

**1973, Apr. 16 Photo. Wmk. 314**

| | | | | |
|---|---|---|---|---|
| *263* | A37 | 4c bl blk & multi | 9 | 9 |
| *264* | A37 | 25c multi | 52 | 52 |
| *265* | A37 | $2.50 pur & multi | 3.25 | 3.25 |

Easter 1973.

Nos. 259-262 Overprinted:

VISIT OF
H. R. H. THE PRINCE OF WALES 1973

**1973, May 31 Litho. *Perf. 14x13½***

| | | | | |
|---|---|---|---|---|
| *266* | A36 | 4c pink & multi | 5 | 5 |
| *267* | A36 | 25c brn & multi | 24 | 24 |
| *268* | A36 | 40c bl & multi | 38 | 38 |
| *269* | A36 | $2.50 multi | 2.75 | 2.75 |

Visit of Prince Charles, May 1973.

Harbor Scene and St. Kitts-Nevis No. 3 — A38

Designs: 25c, Sugar mill and No. 2. 40c, Unloading of boat and No. 1. $2.50, Rock carvings and No. 5.

**1973, Oct. 1 Litho. *Perf. 13½x14***

| | | | | |
|---|---|---|---|---|
| *270* | A38 | 4c sal & multi | 8 | 8 |
| *271* | A38 | 25c lt bl & multi | 60 | 60 |
| *272* | A38 | 40c multi | 1.10 | 1.10 |
| *273* | A38 | $2.50 multi | 3.75 | 3.75 |
| *a.* | | Souvenir sheet of 4 | 8.75 | 8.75 |

70th anniversary of first St. Kitts-Nevis stamps. No. 273a contains one each of Nos. 270-273. Multicolored margin with black inscription. Size: 143x94mm.

**Princess Anne's Wedding Issue**

Common Design Type

**1973, Nov. 14 *Perf. 14***

| | | | | |
|---|---|---|---|---|
| *274* | CD325 | 25c brt grn & multi | 22 | 22 |
| *275* | CD325 | 40c cit & multi | 40 | 40 |

Virgin and Child, by Murillo — A39

Christ Carrying Cross, by Sebastiano del Piombo — A40

Paintings: 40c, Holy Family, by Anton Raphael Mengs. 60c, Holy Family, by Sassoferrato. $1, Holy Family, by Filippino Lippi (horiz.).

**1973, Dec. 1 Litho. *Perf. 14x13½***

| | | | | |
|---|---|---|---|---|
| *276* | A39 | 4c brt bl & multi | 6 | 6 |
| *277* | A39 | 40c org & multi | 5 | 50 |
| *278* | A39 | 60c multi | 80 | 80 |
| *279* | A39 | $1 multi | 1.40 | 1.40 |

Christmas 1973.

**1974, Apr. 8 *Perf. 13***

Easter: 25c, Crucifixion, by Goya. 40c, Trinity, by Diego Ribera. $2.50, Burial of Christ, by Fra Bartolomeo (horiz.).

| | | | | |
|---|---|---|---|---|
| *280* | A40 | 4c ol & multi | 7 | 7 |
| *281* | A40 | 25c lt bl & multi | 30 | 30 |
| *282* | A40 | 40c pur & multi | 48 | 48 |
| *283* | A40 | $2.50 gray & multi | 3.00 | 3.00 |

University Center, St. Kitts, Chancellor Hugh Wooding — A41

**1974, June 1 *Perf. 13½***

| | | | | |
|---|---|---|---|---|
| *284* | A41 | 10c bl & multi | 15 | 15 |
| *285* | A41 | $1 pink & multi | 1.25 | 1.25 |
| *a.* | | Souvenir sheet of 2 | 1.90 | 1.90 |

25th anniversary of the University of the West Indies. No. 285a contains one each of Nos. 284-285, multicolored margin with coat of arms and inscription. Size: 99x95mm.

Nurse Explaining Family Planning — A42

Designs: 4c, Globe and hands reaching up (vert.). 40c, Family (vert.). $2.50, WPY emblem and scale balancing embryo and world.

**Wmk. 314**

**1974, Aug. 5 Litho. *Perf. 14***

| | | | | |
|---|---|---|---|---|
| *286* | A42 | 4c blk, bl & brn | 5 | 5 |
| *287* | A42 | 25c multi | 26 | 26 |
| *288* | A42 | 40c multi | 42 | 42 |
| *289* | A42 | $2.50 lil & multi | 2.50 | 2.50 |

Family planning and World Population Week, Aug. 4-10.

Churchill as Lieutenant, 21st Lancers — A43

Knight of the Garter — A44

Designs: 25c, Churchill as Prime Minister. 60c, Churchill Statue, Parliament Square, London.

**1974, Nov. 30**

| | | | | |
|---|---|---|---|---|
| *290* | A43 | 4c dl vio & multi | 7 | 7 |
| *291* | A43 | 25c yel & multi | 30 | 30 |
| *292* | A44 | 40c lt bl & multi | 42 | 42 |
| *293* | A44 | 60c lt bl & multi | 65 | 65 |
| *a.* | | Souvenir sheet of 4 | 1.50 | 1.50 |

Sir Winston Churchill (1874-1965), birth centenary. No. 293a contains one each of Nos. 290-293, brown margin, showing Churchill and members of his family. Size: 98x147mm.

Souvenir Sheets

Boeing 747 over St. Kitts-Nevis — A45

**1974, Dec. 16 *Perf. 14x13½***

| | | | | |
|---|---|---|---|---|
| *294* | A45 | 40c multi | 60 | 60 |
| *295* | A45 | 45c multi | 70 | 70 |

Opening of Golden Rock International Airport. Nos. 294-295 each contain one stamp. Multicolored margins show air routes to New York and Europe and description of airport. Sheet size: 98x148mm.

The Last Supper, by Dore — A46

Easter: 25c, Jesus mocked. 40c, Jesus falling beneath the Cross. $1, Raising the Cross. Designs based on Bible illustrations by Paul Gustave Dore (1833-1883).

**1975, Mar. 24 *Perf. 14½***

| | | | | |
|---|---|---|---|---|
| *296* | A46 | 4c ultra & multi | 5 | 5 |
| *297* | A46 | 25c lt bl & multi | 30 | 30 |
| *298* | A46 | 40c bis & multi | 45 | 45 |
| *299* | A46 | $1 sal pink & multi | 1.10 | 1.10 |

ECCA Headquarters, Basseterre, and Map of St. Kitts — A47

Designs: 25c, Specimen of $1 note, issued by ECCA. 40c, St. Kitts half dollar, 1801, and $4 coin, 1875. 45c, Nevis "9 dogs" coin, 1801, and 2c, 5c, coins, 1975.

***Perf. 13½x14***

**1975, June 2 Wmk. 373**

| | | | | |
|---|---|---|---|---|
| *300* | A47 | 12c org & multi | 16 | 16 |
| *301* | A47 | 25c ol & multi | 32 | 32 |
| *302* | A47 | 40c ver & multi | 50 | 50 |
| *303* | A47 | 45c brt bl & multi | 55 | 55 |

East Caribbean Currency Authority Headquarters, Basseterre, opening.

Evangeline Booth, Salvation Army — A48

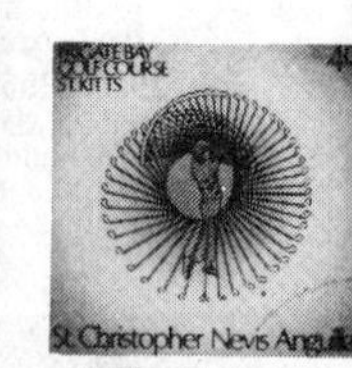


Colfer Swinging Club — A49

Designs (IWY Emblem and): 25c, Sylvia Pankhurst, suffragette. 40c, Marie Curie, scientist. $2.50, Lady Annie Allen, teacher.

***Perf. 14x14½***

**1975, Sept. 15 Litho. Wmk. 314**

| | | | | |
|---|---|---|---|---|
| *304* | A48 | 4c org brn & blk | 5 | 5 |
| *305* | A48 | 25c lil pur & blk | 32 | 32 |
| *306* | A48 | 40c bl vio bl & blk | 52 | 52 |
| *307* | A48 | $2.50 yel brn & blk | 3.25 | 3.25 |

International Women's Year 1975.

**1975, Nov. 1 *Perf. 14***

| | | | | |
|---|---|---|---|---|
| *308* | A49 | 4c rose red & blk | 5 | 5 |
| *309* | A49 | 25c yel & blk | 30 | 30 |
| *310* | A49 | 40c emer & blk | 45 | 45 |
| *311* | A49 | $1 bl & blk | 1.10 | 1.10 |

Opening of Frigate Bay Golf Course.

St. Paul, by Sacchi Pier Francesco — A50

Christmas (Paintings, details): 40c, St. James, by Bonifazio di Pitati. 45c, St. John, by Pier Francesco Mola. $1, Virgin Mary, by Raphael.

**Wmk. 373**

**1975, Dec. 1 Litho. *Perf. 14***

| | | | | |
|---|---|---|---|---|
| *312* | A50 | 25c ultra & multi | 25 | 25 |
| *313* | A50 | 40c multi | 45 | 45 |
| *314* | A50 | 45c red brn & multi | 52 | 52 |
| *315* | A50 | $1 gold & multi | 1.10 | 1.10 |

Virgin Mary — A51

The Last Supper — A52

Stained Glass Windows: No. 317, Christ on the Cross. No. 318, St. John. 40c, The

Last Supper (different). $1, Baptism of Christ.

*Perf. 14x13½*

**1976, Apr. 14 Litho. Wmk. 373**

*316* A51 4c blk & multi 5 5
*317* A51 4c blk & multi 5 5
*318* A51 4c blk & multi 5 5
*a.* Triptych #316-318 16 16

*Perf. 14½*

*319* A52 25c blk & multi 26 26
*320* A52 40c blk & multi 40 40
*321* A52 $1 blk & multi 1.00 1.00
*Nos. 316-321 (6)* 1.81 1.81

Easter 1976. Nos. 316-318 printed se-tenant in sheets of 60 (30x2) showing continuous design.

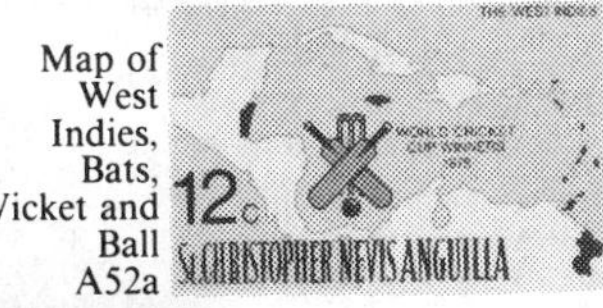


Map of West Indies, Bats, Wicket and Ball A52a

Prudential Cup — A52b

**Unwmk.**

**1976, July 8 Litho. *Perf. 14***

*322* A52a 12c lt bl & multi 52 45
*323* A52b 40c lil rose & blk 1.65 1.25
*a.* Souvenir sheet of 2 4.00 4.00

World Cricket Cup, won by West Indies Team, 1975. No. 323a contains one each of Nos. 322-323; violet blue and black margin showing cricket players. Size: 93x80mm.

Crispus Attucks and Boston Massacre — A53

Designs: 40c, Alexander Hamilton and Battle of Yorktown. 45c, Thomas Jefferson and Declaration of Independence. $1, George Washington and Crossing of the Delaware.

**1976, July 26 Litho. Wmk. 373**

*324* A53 20c gray & multi 18 18
*325* A53 40c gray & multi 32 32
*326* A53 45c gray & multi 35 35
*327* A53 $1 gray & multi 1.00 75

American Bicentennial.

Nativity, Sforza Book of Hours — A54

Queen Planting Tree, 1966 Visit — A55

Paintings: 40c, Virgin and Child, by Bernardino Pintoricchio. 45c, Our Lady of Good Children, by Ford Maddox Brown. $1, Christ Child, by Margaret W. Tarrant.

**1976, Nov. 1 *Perf. 14***

*328* A54 20c pur & multi 18 18
*329* A54 40c dk bl & multi 40 40
*330* A54 45c multi 42 42
*331* A54 $1 multi 90 90

Christmas 1976.

**1977, Feb. 7 Litho. *Perf. 14x13½***

Designs: 55c, The scepter. $1.50, Bishops paying homage to the Queen.

*332* A55 50c multi 35 35
*333* A55 55c multi 40 40
*334* A55 $1.50 multi 1.10 1.10

25th anniv. of the reign of Elizabeth II.

Christ on the Cross, by Niccolo di Liberatore — A56

Easter: 30c, Resurrection (Imitator of Mantegna). 50c, Resurrection, by Ugolino (horiz.). $1, Christ Rising from Tomb, by Gaudenzio.

**Wmk. 373**

**1977, Apr. 1 Litho. *Perf. 14***

*335* A56 25c yel & multi 20 20
*336* A56 30c dp bl & multi 24 24
*337* A56 50c ol grn & multi 40 40
*338* A56 $1 red & multi 80 80

Estridge Mission A57

Designs: 20c, Mission emblem. 40c, Basseterre Mission.

**1977, June 27 Litho. *Perf. 12½***

*339* A57 4c bl & blk 5 5
*340* A57 20c multi 22 22
*341* A57 40c org yel & blk 42 42

Bicentenary of Moravian Mission.

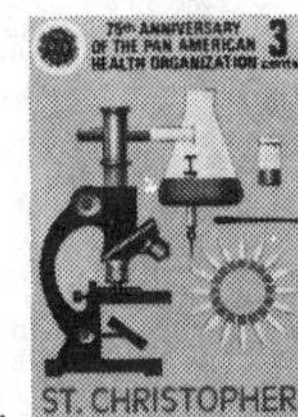


Microscope, Flask, Syringe — A58

Designs: 12c, Blood, fat and nerve cells. 20c, Symbol of community participation. $1, Inoculation.

**1977, Oct. 11 Litho. *Perf. 14***

*342* A58 3c multi 5 5
*343* A58 12c multi 10 10
*344* A58 20c multi 16 16
*345* A58 $1 multi 85 85

Pan American Health Organization, 75th anniversary (PAHO).

Three Kings — A59

Green Monkey and Young — A60

Christmas, Stained-glass Windows, Chartres Cathedral: 4c, Nativity, West Window. 40c, Virgin and Child. $1, Virgin and Child, Rose Window.

**1977, Nov. 15 Wmk. 373**

*346* A59 4c multi 5 5
*347* A59 6c multi 5 5
*348* A59 40c multi 30 30
*349* A59 $1 multi 75 75

**Wmk. 373**

**1978, Apr. 15 Litho. *Perf. 14½***

Green Monkeys: 5c, $1.50, Mother and young sitting on branch. 55c, like 4c.

*350* A60 4c multi 5 5
*351* A60 5c multi 5 5
*352* A60 55c multi 45 38
*353* A60 $1.50 multi 1.25 1.00

**Elizabeth II Coronation Anniversary Issue**

Souvenir Sheet

Common Design Types

**Unwmk.**

**1978, Apr. 21 Litho. *Perf. 15***

*354* Sheet of 6 5.00 5.00
*a.* CD326 $1 *Falcon of Edward III* 75 75
*b.* CD327 $1 *Elizabeth II* 75 75
*c.* CD328 $1 *Pelican* 75 75

No. 354 contains 2 se-tenant strips of Nos. 354a-354c, separated by horizontal gutter with commemorative and descriptive inscriptions and showing central part of coronation procession with coach. Size: 100x135mm.

Tomatoes A61

Designs: 2c, Defense Force band. 5c, Radio and TV station. 10c, Technical College. 12c, TV assembly plant. 15c, Sugar cane harvest. 25c, Craft Center. 30c, Cruise ship. 40c, Sea crab and lobster. 45c, Royal St. Kitts Hotel and golf course. 50c, Pinneys Beach, Nevis. 55c, New Runway at Golden Rock. $1, Cotton pickers. $5, Brewery. $10, Pineapples and peanuts.

*Perf. 14½x14*

**1978, Sept. 8 Wmk. 373**

*355* A61 1c multi 5 5
*356* A61 2c multi 5 5
*357* A61 5c multi 5 5
*358* A61 10c multi 6 6
*359* A61 12c multi 7 7
*360* A61 15c multi 9 9
*361* A61 25c multi 14 14
*362* A61 30c multi 18 18
*363* A61 40c multi 22 22
*364* A61 45c multi 25 25
*365* A61 50c multi 28 28
*366* A61 55c multi 32 32
*367* A61 $1 multi 55 55
*368* A61 $5 multi 2.75 2.75
*369* A61 $10 multi 5.75 5.75
*Nos. 355-369 (15)* 10.81 10.81

Investiture A62

King Bringing Gift A63

Designs: 10c, Map reading. 25c, Pitching tent. 40c, Cooking. 50c, First aid. 55c, Rev. W. A. Beckett, founder of Scouting in St. Kitts.

**Wmk. 373**

**1978, Oct. 9 Litho. *Perf. 13½***

*370* A62 5c multi 5 5
*371* A62 10c multi 10 10
*372* A62 25c multi 25 25
*373* A62 40c multi 45 45
*374* A62 50c multi 52 52
*375* A62 55c multi 55 55
*Nos. 370-375 (6)* 1.92 1.92

50th anniversary of St. Kitts-Nevis Scouting.

**1978, Dec. 1 *Perf. 14x13½***

Christmas: 15c, 30c, King bringing gift (diff.). $2.25, Three Kings paying homage to Infant Jesus.

*376* A63 5c multi 5 5
*377* A63 15c multi 15 15
*378* A63 30c multi 28 28
*379* A63 $2.25 multi 2.00 2.00

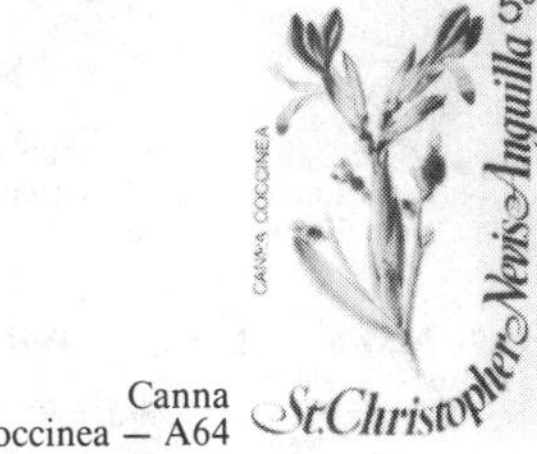


Canna Coccinea — A64

Flowers: 30c, Heliconia bihai. 55c, Ruellia tuberosa. $1.50, Gesneria ventricosa.

**1979, Mar. 19 *Perf. 14***

*380* A64 5c multi 5 5
*381* A64 30c multi 28 25
*382* A64 55c multi 52 42
*383* A64 $1.50 multi 1.40 1.10

See Nos. 393-396.

Rowland Hill and St. Christopher No. 1 — A65

Rowland Hill and: 15c, St. Kitts-Nevis No. 233. 50c, Great Britain No. 4. $2.50, St. Kitts-Nevis No. 64.

**Wmk. 373**

**1979, July 2 Litho. *Perf. 14½***

*384* A65 5c multi 5 5
*385* A65 15c multi 9 9
*386* A65 50c multi 32 32
*387* A65 $2.50 multi 1.50 1.50

Sir Rowland Hill (1795-1879), originator of penny postage.

The first price column gives the catalogue value of an unused stamp, the second that of a used stamp.

The Woodman's Daughter, by Millais — A66

Paintings by John Everett Millais and IYC Emblem: 25c, Cherry Ripe. 30c, The Rescue (horiz.). 55c, Bubbles. $1, Christ in the House of His Parents.

**1979, Nov. 12 Litho. *Perf. 14***
*388* A66 5c multi 6 6
*389* A66 25c multi 28 28
*390* A66 30c multi 32 32
*391* A66 55c multi 60 60

**Souvenir Sheet**

*392* A66 $1 multi 1.10 1.10

Christmas 1979; International Year of the Child. No. 392 has multicolored margin showing entire painting. Size: 101x68mm.

Flower Type of 1979

Flowers: 4c, Clerodendrum aculeatum. 55c, Inga laurina. $1.50, Epidendrum difforme. $2, Sage.

**1980, Feb. Litho. *Perf. 14***
*393* A64 4c multi 5 5
*394* A64 55c multi 40 40
*395* A64 $1.50 multi 1.10 1.10
*396* A64 $2 multi 1.50 1.50

Nevis Lagoon, London 1980 Emblem — A67

**1980, May 6 Litho. *Perf. 13½***
*397* A67 5c *shown* 5 5
*398* A67 30c *Fig Tree Church, vert.* 20 20
*399* A67 55c *Nisbet Plantation* 35 35
*400* A67 $3 *Lord Nelson, by Fuger, vert.* 1.90 1.90

**Souvenir Sheet**

*401* A67 75c *Nelson Falling, by D. Dighton* 90 65

London 80 Intl. Phil. Exhib., May 6-14; Lord Nelson, (1758-1805), 175th death anniv. No. 401 has multicolored margin showing entire painting. Size: 107½x77½mm.

Separate issues for Nevis are recorded in the *Scott Chronicle of New Issues* beginning with Vol. 1, No. 1. Issues for St. Kitts are found immediately before St. Kitts-Nevis.

## WAR TAX STAMPS

No. 12 Overprinted **WAR TAX**

**1916 Wmk. 3 *Perf. 14***
*MR1* A1 ½p green 10 10

Type of 1905-18 Issue Overprinted **WAR STAMP**

**1918**
*MR2* A1 1½p orange 15 15

## OFFICIAL STAMPS

**Catalogue values for unused stamps in this section, from this point to the end of the section, are for Never Hinged items.**

Nos. 359, 361, 363-369 Overprinted: OFFICIAL

***Perf. 14½x14***

**1980 Litho. Wmk. 373**
*O1* A61 12c multi 8 8
*O2* A61 25c multi 16 16
*O3* A61 40c multi 26 26
*O4* A61 45c multi 30 30
*O5* A61 50c multi 32 32
*O6* A61 55c multi 35 35
*O7* A61 $1 multi 65 65
*O8* A61 $5 multi 3.25 3.25
*O9* A61 $10 multi 6.75 6.75
*Nos. O1-O9 (9)* 12.12 12.12

# ST. LUCIA

LOCATION — An island in the West Indies, one of the Windward group.
GOVT. — Independent state in British Commonwealth.
AREA — 240 sq. mi.
POP. — 126,800 (est. 1984).
CAPITAL — Castries.

The British colony of St. Lucia became an associated state March 1, 1967, and independent in 1979.

12 Pence = 1 Shilling
100 Cents = 1 Dollar (1949)

**Values for Nos. 1-26 are for fine copies.**

**Catalogue values for unused stamps in this country are for Never Hinged items, beginning with Scott 127 in the regular postage section, Scott C1 in the air post section, Scott J3 in the postage due section, and Scott O1 in the officials section.**

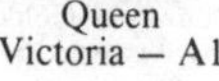
Queen Victoria — A1

Wmk. 5- Small Star

***Perf. 14 to 16***

**1860, Dec. 18 Engr. Wmk. 5**
*1* A1 (1p) rose red 90.00 75.00
  *a* Double impression
*2* A1 (4p) dp bl 325.00 250.00
*3* A1 (6p) green 450.00 300.00

**1863 Wmk. 1 *Perf. 12½***
*4* A1 (1p) lake 35.00 40.00
  *a* Imperf., pair 4,250.
*5* A1 (4p) slate blue 120.00 100.00
  *a* Imperf., pair 4,500.
*6* A1 (6p) emerald 210.00 150.00

**1864**
*7* A1 (1p) dp blk 9.75 9.75
  *b* Imperf., pair 1,000.
*8* A1 (4p) yellow 100.00 50.00
  *a* (4p) ol yel 250.00 65.00
*9* A1 (6p) violet 50.00 30.00
  *a* (6p) lil 175.00 42.50
  *b* Imperf., pair 2,000.
*10* A1 (1sh) red org 175.00 42.50
  *a* (1sh) org 250.00 42.50
  *b* Imperf., pair 2,250.

***Perf. 14***
*11* A1 (1p) dp blk 14.00 14.00
*12* A1 (4p) yellow 52.50 25.00
*13* A1 (6p) pale lil 52.50 25.00
  *a* (6p) dp lil 55.00 32.50
*14* A1 (1sh) orange 190.00 32.50

Type of 1860 Surcharged in Black or Red:

**HALFPENNY** a  **2½ PENCE** b

**1881**
*15* A1 (a) ½p green 25.00 30.00
*17* A1 (b) 2½p scarlet 17.50 15.00

**1883-84 Wmk. Crown and C. A. (2)**
*19* A1 (a) ½p green 12.50 14.00
*20* A1 (a) 1p blk (R) 15.00 14.00
  *a* Half used as ½p on cover *2,000.*
*21* A1 (a) 4p yellow 200.00 27.50
*22* A1 (a) 6p violet 27.50 27.50
  *a* Without surcharge
*23* A1 (a) 1sh orange 200.00 95.00

**1884 *Perf. 12***
*24* A1 (a) 4p yellow 650.00 32.50

**Half penny**

**1885 Wmk. 1 *Perf. 12½***
*25* A1 ½p emerald 60.00
*26* A1 6p slate blue 1,750.

Nos. 25 and 26 were prepared for use but not issued.

A5

Die B

For explanation of dies A and B see back of this section of the Catalogue.

**1883-98 Typo. Wmk. 2 *Perf. 14***
*27* A5 ½p grn ('91) 28 28
  *a* Die A ('83) 2.75 2.25
*28* A5 1p rose (die A) ('83) 18.00 16.00
*29* A5 1p lil ('91) 60 40
  *a* Die A ('86) 2.75 2.75
  *b* Die A, imperf., pair 700.00
*30* A5 2p ultra & brn org ('98) 1.50 1.50
*31* A5 2½p ultra ('91) 1.50 60
  *a* Die A ('83) 11.50 2.25
*32* A5 3p lil & grn ('91) 2.75 2.75
  *a* Die A ('86) 24.00 16.00
*33* A5 4p brn ('93) 2.50 2.50
  *a* Die A ('85) 11.50 3.50
  *b* Die A, imperf., pair 1,050.
*34* A5 6p vio (die A) ('85) 275.00 275.00
  *a* Imperf., pair 1,800.
*35* A5 6p lil & bl ('86) 7.50 10.50
  *a* Die A ('91) 3.00 3.00
*36* A5 1sh brn org (die A) ('85) 350.00 135.00
*37* A5 1sh lil & red ('91) 2.50 *4.50*
  *a* Die A ('86) 35.00 30.00
*38* A5 5sh lil & org ('91) 16.00 *35.00*
*39* A5 10sh lil & blk ('91) 35.00 *55.00*
*Nos. 27-39 (13)* 713.13 539.03

Nos. 32, 32a, 35a and 33a Surcharged in Black:

**ONE HALF PENNY**
No. 40

**½d.**
No. 41

No. 42
**ONE PENNY**

**1892**
*40* A5 ½p on 3p lil & grn 27.50 22.50
  *a* Die A 50.00 50.00
  *b* Dbl. surch., die B 900.00 850.00
  *c* Invtd. surch., die B 2,000. 750.00
  *d* Triple surcharge, one on the back *1,800.* *1,650.*
*41* A5 ½p on half of 6p lil & bl 12.00 10.50
  *a* Slanting serif 180.00 180.00
  *c* Without the bar of "½" 180.00 160.00
  *d* "2" of "½" omitted 400.00 400.00
  *e* Surcharged sideways 425.00
  *f* Double surch. 500.00 500.00
*42* A5 1p on 4p brn 4.50 5.50
  *b* Dbl. surch. 200.00
  *c* Inverted surcharge 1,050. 475.00

No. 40 is found with wide or narrow "O" in "ONE".

Edward VII
A9

The Pitons
A10

Numerals of 3p, 6p, 1sh and 5sh of type A9 are in color on plain tablet.

**1902-03 Typo.**
*43* A9 ½p vio & grn 60 40
*44* A9 1p vio & car rose 1.60 65
*46* A9 2½p vio & ultra 4.50 4.50
*47* A9 3p vio & yel 4.50 5.00
*48* A9 1sh grn & blk 6.50 7.00
*Nos. 43-48 (5)* 17.70 17.55

**Wmk. 1 sideways**

**1902, Dec. 16 Engr.**
*49* A10 2p brn & grn 3.25 3.25

Commemorative of the fourth centenary of the discovery of the island by Columbus.

**1904-05 Typo. Wmk. 3**
*50* A9 ½p vio & grn 60 40
*51* A9 1p vio & car rose 1.00 25
*52* A9 2½p vio & ultra 3.00 1.50
*53* A9 3p vio & yel 5.00 2.75
*54* A9 6p vio & dp vio ('05) 3.25 3.25
*55* A9 1sh grn & blk ('05) 13.00 15.00
*56* A9 5sh grn & car ('05) 25.00 32.50
*Nos. 50-56 (7)* 50.85 55.65

Nos. 50, 51, 52 and 54 are on both ordinary and chalky paper. No. 55 is on chalky paper only.

**1907-10**
*57* A9 ½p green 75 24
*58* A9 1p carmine 2.00 24
*59* A9 2½p ultra 1.50 1.25

**Chalky Paper**

*60* A9 3p vio, *yel* ('09) 3.25 3.25
*61* A9 6p vio & red vio 4.25 4.50
  *a* 6p vio & dl vio ('10) 7.50 *10.50*
*62* A9 1sh blk, *grn* ('09) 6.50 7.25
*63* A9 5sh grn & red, *yel* 30.00 *40.00*
*Nos. 57-63 (7)* 48.25 56.73

King George V
A11 A12

Numerals of 3p, 6p, 1sh and 5sh of type A11 are in color on plain tablet.
For description of dies I and II see back of this section of the Catalogue.

Die I

**1912-19**

**Ordinary Paper**

*64* A11 ½p dp grn 32 25
*65* A11 1p scarlet 55 32
  *a* 1p car 55 18
*66* A12 2p gray ('13) 2.00 3.50
*67* A11 2½p ultra 1.25 70

**Chalky Paper**

**Numeral on White Tablet**

*68* A11 3p vio, *yel* 70 85
  *a* Die II 3.75 5.75
*69* A11 6p vio & red vio 2.25 *4.75*
*70* A11 1sh blk, *green* 4.25 5.25
  *a* 1sh blk, *bl grn*, ol back 3.50 4.00
*71* A11 1sh fawn 3.00 4.75
*72* A11 5sh grn & red, *yel* 25.00 *40.00*
*Nos. 64-72 (9)* 39.32 60.37

A13

A14

**1913-14**

**Chalky Paper**

| | | | | |
|---|---|---|---|---|
| 73 | A13 | 4p scar & blk, *yel* | 2.50 | *4.50* |
| 74 | A14 | 2sh6p blk & red, *bl* | 9.50 | *18.00* |

**Surface-colored Paper**

| | | | | |
|---|---|---|---|---|
| 75 | A13 | 4p scar & blk, *yel* | 90 | *1.75* |

Die II

**1921-24** **Wmk. 4**

**Ordinary Paper**

| | | | | |
|---|---|---|---|---|
| 76 | A11 | ½p green | 38 | 16 |
| 77 | A11 | 1p carmine | 2.25 | *4.75* |
| 78 | A11 | 1p dk brn ('22) | 40 | 35 |
| 79 | A13 | 1½p rose red ('22) | 1.25 | 85 |
| 80 | A12 | 2p gray | 35 | 35 |
| 81 | A11 | 2½p ultra | 65 | *1.25* |
| 82 | A11 | 2½p org ('24) | 4.75 | *7.50* |
| 83 | A11 | 3p ultra ('22) | 1.10 | *2.00* |

**Chalky Paper**

| | | | | |
|---|---|---|---|---|
| 84 | A11 | 3p vio, *yel* | 65 | *1.75* |
| 85 | A13 | 4p scar & blk, *yel* ('24) | 65 | *1.25* |
| 86 | A11 | 6p vio & red vio | 1.10 | *3.50* |
| 87 | A11 | 1sh fawn | 1.50 | *4.00* |
| 88 | A14 | 2sh6p blk & red, *bl* ('24) | 9.50 | *15.00* |
| 89 | A11 | 5sh grn & red, *yel* | 18.50 | *32.50* |
| | | *Nos. 76-89 (14)* | 43.03 | 75.21 |

**Silver Jubilee Issue**

Common Design Type

**1935, May 6** **Engr.** ***Perf. 13½x14***

| | | | | |
|---|---|---|---|---|
| 91 | CD301 | ½p grn & blk | 22 | 22 |
| 92 | CD301 | 2p gray blk & ultra | 65 | 65 |
| 93 | CD301 | 2½p bl & brn | 1.50 | 1.50 |
| 94 | CD301 | 1sh brt vio & ind | 4.25 | 4.25 |

Port Castries
A15

Columbus Square, Castries
A16

Ventine Falls
A17

Soldiers' Monument
A19

Fort Rodney, Pigeon Island — A18

Government House — A20

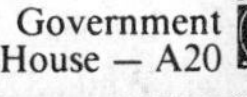

Seal of the Colony
A21

**1936** ***Perf. 14***

**Center in Black**

| | | | | |
|---|---|---|---|---|
| 95 | A15 | ½p lt grn | 14 | 14 |
| *a* | | Perf. 13x12 | 38 | 38 |
| 96 | A16 | 1p dk brn | 18 | 18 |
| *a* | | Perf. 13x12 | 1.90 | 1.90 |
| 97 | A17 | 1½p carmine | 25 | 25 |
| *a* | | Perf. 12x13 | 10.50 | 3.75 |
| 98 | A15 | 2p gray | 52 | 60 |
| 99 | A16 | 2½p blue | 52 | 52 |
| 100 | A17 | 3p dl grn | 65 | 85 |
| 101 | A15 | 4p brown | 65 | 85 |
| 102 | A16 | 6p orange | 95 | 1.10 |
| 103 | A18 | 1sh lt bl, perf. 13x12 | 1.50 | 1.65 |
| 104 | A19 | 2sh6p ultra | 9.25 | 11.00 |
| 105 | A20 | 5sh violet | 14.00 | *22.50* |
| 106 | A21 | 10sh car rose, perf. 13x12 | 55.00 | 62.50 |
| | | *Nos. 95-106 (12)* | 83.61 | 102.14 |

Nos. 95a, 96a and 97a are coils.

**Coronation Issue**

Common Design Type

**1937, May 12** ***Perf. 11x11½***

| | | | | |
|---|---|---|---|---|
| 107 | CD302 | 1p dk pur | 12 | 12 |
| 108 | CD302 | 1½p dk car | 18 | 18 |
| 109 | CD302 | 2½p dp ultra | 18 | 18 |

King George VI
A22

Columbus Square, Castries
A23

Government House
A24

The Pitons
A25

Loading Bananas
A26

Arms of the Colony — A27

***Perf. 12½ (#111, 1½, 2½, 3, 3½, 8p, 3sh, 5sh, £1), 12 (2sh, 10sh)***

**1938-48**

| | | | | |
|---|---|---|---|---|
| 110 | A22 | ½p grn, perf. 14½x14 | 5 | 5 |
| *a* | | Perf. 12½ ('43) | 5 | 5 |
| 111 | A22 | 1p dp vio | 82 | 5 |
| *a* | | Perf. 14½x14 | 1.00 | 40 |
| 112 | A22 | 1p red, Perf. 14½x14 ('47) | 32 | 24 |
| *a* | | Perf. 12½ | 24 | 20 |
| 113 | A22 | 1½p car ('43) | 12 | 12 |
| *a* | | Perf. 14½x14 | 20 | 16 |
| 114 | A22 | 2p gray, Perf. 14½x14 | 12 | 12 |
| *a* | | Perf. 12½ ('43) | 16 | 16 |
| 115 | A22 | 2½p ultra ('43) | 12 | 10 |
| *a* | | Perf. 14½x14 | 16 | 12 |
| 116 | A22 | 2½p vio ('47) | 10 | 10 |
| 117 | A22 | 3p red org ('43) | 32 | 24 |
| *a* | | Perf. 14½x14 | 20 | 20 |
| 118 | A22 | 3½p brt ultra ('47) | 20 | 20 |
| 119 | A23 | 6p mag, perf. 13½ | 50 | 50 |
| *a* | | Perf. 12 ('48) | 1.50 | 1.10 |
| 120 | A22 | 8p choc ('46) | 42 | 42 |
| 121 | A24 | 1sh lt brn, perf. 13½ | 50 | 50 |
| *a* | | Perf. 12 ('48) | 1.50 | 1.10 |
| 122 | A25 | 2sh red vio & sl bl | 1.30 | 1.30 |
| 123 | A22 | 3sh brt red vio ('46) | 3.25 | 3.25 |
| 124 | A26 | 5sh rose vio & blk | 2.25 | 2.25 |
| 125 | A27 | 10sh blk, *yel* | 3.75 | 3.75 |
| 126 | A22 | £1 sep ('46) | 8.50 | 8.50 |
| | | *Nos. 110-126 (17)* | 22.64 | 21.69 |

See Nos. 135-148.

**Catalogue values for unused stamps in this section, from this point to the end of the section, are for Never Hinged items.**

**Peace Issue**

Common Design Type

***Perf. 13½x14***

**1946, Oct. 8** **Wmk. 4** **Engr.**

| | | | | |
|---|---|---|---|---|
| 127 | CD303 | 1p lilac | 10 | 10 |
| 128 | CD303 | 3½p dp bl | 45 | 45 |

**Silver Wedding Issue**

Common Design Types

**1948, Nov. 26** **Photo.** ***Perf. 14x14½***

| | | | | |
|---|---|---|---|---|
| 129 | CD304 | 1p scarlet | 14 | 14 |

**Engraved; Name Typographed**

***Perf. 11½x11***

| | | | | |
|---|---|---|---|---|
| 130 | CD305 | £1 vio brn | 22.50 | 32.50 |

**UPU Issue**

Common Design Types

**Engr.; Name Typo. on 6c, 12c.**

***Perf. 13½, 11x11½***

**1949, Oct. 10** **Wmk. 4**

| | | | | |
|---|---|---|---|---|
| 131 | CD306 | 5c violet | 20 | 20 |
| 132 | CD307 | 6c dp org | 28 | 28 |
| 133 | CD308 | 12c red lil | 60 | 60 |
| 134 | CD309 | 24c bl grn | 1.00 | 1.00 |

Types of 1938

Values in Cents and Dollars

**1949-52** **Engr.** ***Perf. 12½***

| | | | | |
|---|---|---|---|---|
| 135 | A22 | 1c green | 22 | 12 |
| *a* | | Perf. 14 | 95 | 85 |
| 136 | A22 | 2c rose lil | 28 | 12 |
| *a* | | Perf. 14½x14 | 2.35 | 2.35 |
| 137 | A22 | 3c red | 38 | 22 |
| 138 | A22 | 4c gray | 38 | 28 |
| *a* | | Perf. 14½x14 | | *2,500.* |
| 139 | A22 | 5c violet | 48 | 28 |
| 140 | A22 | 6c red org | 48 | 28 |
| 141 | A22 | 7c ultra | 55 | 35 |
| 142 | A22 | 12c rose lake | 1.00 | 85 |
| *a* | | Perf. 14½x14 | 400.00 | 275.00 |
| 143 | A22 | 16c brown | 85 | 75 |

***Perf. 11½***

| | | | | |
|---|---|---|---|---|
| 144 | A27 | 24c Prus bl | 1.10 | 95 |
| 145 | A27 | 48c ol grn | 2.75 | 2.75 |
| 146 | A27 | $1.20 purple | 3.75 | 3.75 |
| 147 | A27 | $2.40 bl grn | 9.00 | 9.00 |
| 148 | A27 | $4.80 dk car rose | 19.00 | 19.00 |
| | | *Nos. 135-148 (14)* | 40.22 | 38.70 |

Nos. 144 to 148 are of a type similar to A27, but with the denomination in the top corners and "St. Lucia" at the bottom.

**University Issue**

Common Design Types

***Perf. 14x14½***

**1951, Feb. 16** **Wmk. 4**

| | | | | |
|---|---|---|---|---|
| 149 | CD310 | 3c red & gray blk | 16 | 16 |
| 150 | CD311 | 12c brn car & blk | 45 | 45 |

Phoenix Rising from Burning Buildings — A28

**Engr. and Typo.**

**1951, June 19** ***Perf. 13½x13***

| | | | | |
|---|---|---|---|---|
| 151 | A28 | 12c dp bl & car | 42 | 42 |

Reconstruction of Castries.

Nos. 136, 138, 139 and 142 Overprinted in Black

**NEW CONSTITUTION 1951**

**1951, Sept. 25** ***Perf. 12½***

| | | | | |
|---|---|---|---|---|
| 152 | A22 | 2c rose lil | 12 | 12 |
| 153 | A22 | 4c gray | 20 | 20 |
| 154 | A22 | 5c violet | 24 | 24 |
| 155 | A22 | 12c rose lil | 40 | 40 |

Adoption of a new constitution for the Windward Islands, 1951.

**Coronation Issue**

Common Design Type

**1953, June 2** **Engr.** ***Perf. 13½x13***

| | | | | |
|---|---|---|---|---|
| 156 | CD312 | 3c car & blk | 18 | 18 |

Queen Elizabeth II
A29

Arms of St. Lucia
A30

**1953-54** **Engr.** ***Perf. 14½x14***

| | | | | |
|---|---|---|---|---|
| 157 | A29 | 1c green | 6 | 5 |
| 158 | A29 | 2c rose lil ('53) | 6 | 5 |
| 159 | A29 | 3c red | 10 | 8 |
| 160 | A29 | 4c gray | 12 | 10 |
| 161 | A29 | 5c violet | 12 | 12 |
| 162 | A29 | 6c orange | 15 | 15 |
| 163 | A29 | 8c rose lake | 20 | 20 |
| 164 | A29 | 10c ultra | 25 | 25 |
| 165 | A29 | 15c brown | 35 | 30 |

***Perf. 11x11½***

| | | | | |
|---|---|---|---|---|
| 166 | A30 | 25c Prus bl | 65 | 60 |
| 167 | A30 | 50c brn ol | 1.50 | 1.25 |
| 168 | A30 | $1 bl grn | 3.50 | 3.25 |
| 169 | A30 | $2.50 dk car rose | 11.00 | 8.75 |
| | | *Nos. 157-169 (13)* | 18.06 | 15.15 |

**West Indies Federation**

Common Design Type

***Perf. 11½x11***

**1958, Apr. 22** **Wmk. 314**

| | | | | |
|---|---|---|---|---|
| 170 | CD313 | 3c green | 12 | 12 |
| 171 | CD313 | 6c blue | 20 | 20 |
| 172 | CD313 | 12c car rose | 40 | 40 |

16th Century Ship and Pitons — A31

St. Lucia Stamp of 1860 — A32

**1960, Jan. 1** ***Perf. 12½x13***

| | | | | |
|---|---|---|---|---|
| 173 | A31 | 8c car rose | 24 | 24 |
| 174 | A31 | 10c orange | 32 | 32 |
| 175 | A31 | 25c dk bl | 70 | 70 |

Granting of new constitution.

**1960, Dec. 18** **Engr.** ***Perf. 13½***

| | | | | |
|---|---|---|---|---|
| 176 | A32 | 5c ultra & red brn | 32 | 32 |
| 177 | A32 | 16c yel grn & bl blk | 65 | 65 |
| 178 | A32 | 25c car & grn | 90 | 90 |

Centenary of St. Lucia's first postage stamps.

**Freedom from Hunger Issue**

Common Design Type

**1963, June 4** **Photo.** ***Perf. 14x14½***

| | | | | |
|---|---|---|---|---|
| 179 | CD314 | 25c green | 70 | 70 |

**Red Cross Centenary Issue**

Common Design Type

**Wmk. 314**

**1963, Sept. 2** **Litho.** ***Perf. 13***

| | | | | |
|---|---|---|---|---|
| 180 | CD315 | 4c blk & red | 14 | 14 |
| 181 | CD315 | 25c ultra & red | 1.00 | 1.00 |

A33

A34

Fishing Boats, Soufriere Bay — A35

Designs: 15c, Pigeon Island. 25c, Reduit Beach. 35c, Castries Harbor. 50c, The Pitons. $1, Vigie Beach (vert.). $2.50, Queen Elizabeth II, close-up.

**Wmk. 314**

**1964, Mar. 1 Photo. *Perf. 14½***

*182* A33 1c dk car rose 5 5
*183* A33 2c violet 5 5
*184* A33 4c brt bl grn 5 5
*185* A33 5c sl bl 6 6
*186* A33 6c brown 8 8
*187* A34 8c lt bl & multi 12 12
*188* A34 10c multi 16 16
*189* A35 12c multi 20 20
*190* A35 15c bl & ocher 28 28
a. Wmkd. sideways ('68) 24 24
*191* A35 25c multi 48 48
*192* A35 35c dk bl & buff 80 60
*193* A35 50c brt bl, blk & yel 1.10 1.00
*194* A35 $1 multi 2.50 2.00
*195* A34 $2.50 multi 4.75 4.25
*Nos. 182-195 (14)* 10.68 9.38

**Shakespeare Issue**
Common Design Type

**1964, Apr. 23 *Perf. 14x14½***
*196* CD316 10c brt grn 38 38

**ITU Issue**
Common Design Type

***Perf. 11x11½***
**1965, May 17 Litho. Wmk. 314**
*197* CD317 2c red lil & brt pink 10 10
*198* CD317 50c lil & yel grn 1.75 1.75

**Intl. Cooperation Year Issue**
Common Design Type

**1965, Oct. 25 Wmk. 314 *Perf. 14½***
*199* CD318 1c bl grn & cl 6 6
*200* CD318 25c lt vio & grn 50 50

**Churchill Memorial Issue**
Common Design Type

**1966, Jan. 24 Photo. *Perf. 14***
**Design in Black, Gold and Carmine Rose**
*201* CD319 4c brt bl 5 5
*202* CD319 6c green 9 9
*203* CD319 25c brown 40 40
*204* CD319 35c violet 60 60

**Royal Visit Issue**
Common Design Type

**1966, Feb. 4 Litho. *Perf. 11x12***
*205* CD320 4c vio bl 12 12
*206* CD320 25c dk car rose 75 75

**World Cup Soccer Issue**
Common Design Type

**1966, July 1 Litho. *Perf. 14***
*207* CD321 4c multi 7 7
*208* CD321 25c multi 45 45

**WHO Headquarters Issue**
Common Design Type

**1966, Sept. 20 Litho. *Perf. 14***
*209* CD322 4c multi 5 5
*210* CD322 25c multi 45 45

Common Design Types pictured in section before Great Britain.

**UNESCO Anniversary Issue**
Common Design Type

**1966, Dec. 1 Litho. *Perf. 14***
*211* CD323 4c "Education" 7 7
*212* CD323 12c "Science" 30 30
*213* CD323 25c "Culture" 70 70

**Associated State**

Nos. 183, 185-194 Overprinted in Red: "STATEHOOD / 1st MARCH 1967"

**Wmk. 314**

**1967, Mar. 1 Photo. *Perf. 14½***
*215* A33 2c violet 20 16
*216* A33 5c sl bl 30 24
*217* A33 6c brown 35 30
*218* A34 8c lt bl & multi 50 40
*219* A34 10c multi 60 50
*220* A35 12c multi 80 70
*221* A35 15c bl & ocher 1.65 90
*222* A35 25c multi 2.00 1.25
*223* A35 35c dk bl & buff 3.00 1.65
*224* A35 50c multi 3.00 2.00
*225* A35 $1 multi 7.00 5.00
*Nos. 215-225 (11)* 19.40 13.10

The 1c and $2.50, similarly overprinted, were not sold to the public at the post office but were acknowledged belatedly (May 10) by the government and declared valid. The 1c, 6c and $2.50 overprints exist in black as well as red. No. 213 also exists with this overprint in blue and in black.

Madonna and Child with St. John, by Raphael — A36

Cricket Batsman and Gov. Frederick Clarke — A37

**1967, Oct. 16 Wmk. 314 *Perf. 14½***
*227* A36 4c blk, gold & multi 9 9
*228* A36 25c multi 35 35

Christmas 1967.

***Perf. 14½x14***
**1968, Mar. 8 Photo. Wmk. 314**
*229* A37 10c multi 14 14
*230* A37 35c multi 55 55

Visit of the Marylebone Cricket Club to the West Indies, Jan.-Feb. 1968.

"Noli me Tangere," by Titian — A38

Martin Luther King, Jr. — A39

Designs: 10c, 25c, The Crucifixion, by Raphael.

**1968, Mar. 25 *Perf. 14½***
*231* A38 10c multi 8 8
*232* A38 15c multi 12 12
*233* A38 25c multi 20 20
*234* A38 35c multi 28 28

Easter 1968.

***Perf. 13½x14***
**1968, July 4 Photo. Wmk. 314**
*235* A39 25c dp bl, blk & brn 25 25
*236* A39 35c vio, blk & brn 35 35

Dr. Martin Luther King, Jr. (1929-68), American civil rights leader.

Virgin and Child in Glory, by Murillo — A40

Christmas: 10c, 35c, Virgin and Child, by Bartolomé E. Murillo.

***Perf. 14½x14***
**1968, Oct. 17 Photo. Wmk. 314**
*237* A40 5c dk bl & multi 7 7
*238* A40 10c multi 18 18
*239* A40 25c red brn & multi 35 35
*240* A40 35c dp bl & multi 52 52

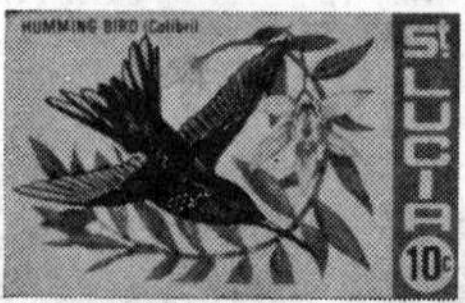

Purple-throated Carib — A41

Birds: 15c, 35c, St. Lucia parrot.

**1969, Jan. 10 Litho. *Perf. 14½***
*241* A41 10c multi 34 34
*242* A41 15c multi 38 38
*243* A41 25c multi 75 75
*244* A41 35c multi 1.10 1.10

Ecce Homo, by Guido Reni — A42

Painting: 15c, 35c, The Resurrection, by Il Sodoma (Giovanni Antonio de Bazzi).

***Perf. 14½x14***
**1969, Mar. 20 Photo. Wmk. 314**
*245* A42 10c pur & multi 10 10
*246* A42 15c grn & multi 16 16
*247* A42 25c blk & multi 28 28
*248* A42 35c ocher & multi 48 48

Easter 1969.

Map of Caribbean — A43

Design: 25c, 35c, Clasped hands and arrows with names of CARIFTA members.

**1969, May 29 Wmk. 314 *Perf. 14***
*249* A43 5c vio bl & multi 6 6
*250* A43 10c dp plum & multi 8 8
*251* A43 25c ultra & multi 28 28
*252* A43 35c grn & multi 38 38

First anniversary of CARIFTA (Caribbean Free Trade Area).

Silhouettes of Napoleon and Josephine A44

***Perf. 14½x13***
**1969, Sept. 22 Photo. Unwmk.**
**Gold Inscription; Gray and Brown Medallions**
*253* A44 15c dull blue 12 12
*254* A44 25c deep claret 25 25
*255* A44 35c deep green 38 38
*256* A44 50c yellow brown 60 60

Issued to commemorate the 200th anniversary of the birth of Napoleon Bonaparte.

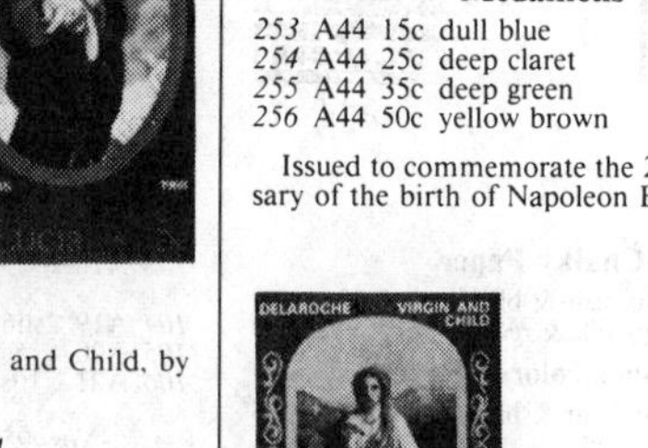

Madonna and Child, by Paul Delaroche — A45

Christmas: 10c, 35c, Holy Family, by Rubens.

***Perf. 14½x14***
**1969, Oct. 27 Photo. Wmk. 314**
**Center Multicolored**
*257* A45 5c dp rose lil & gold 5 5
*258* A45 10c Prus bl & gold 8 8
*259* A45 25c mar & gold 28 28
*260* A45 35c dp yel grn & gold 45 45

House of Assembly — A46

Queen Elizabeth II, by A. C. Davidson-Houston A47

Designs: 2c, Roman Catholic Cathedral. 4c, Castries Boulevard. 5c, Castries Harbor. 6c, Sulphur springs. 10c, Vigie Airport. 12c, Reduit beach. 15c, Pigeon Island. 25c, The Pitons and sailboat. 35c, Marigot Bay. 50c, Diamond Waterfall. $1, St. Lucia flag and motto. $2.50, Coat of arms. $10, Map of St. Lucia.

**Wmk. 314 Sideways, Upright (#271-274)**

**1970-73 Litho. *Perf. 14½***
*261* A46 1c lil & multi 5 5
*262* A46 2c brn & multi 12 12
a. Wmk. upright 55 55
*263* A46 4c dk vio & multi 12 12
a. Wmk. upright 1.10 1.10
*264* A46 5c brt bl & multi 9 9
*265* A46 6c ver & multi 12 12
*266* A46 10c bl & multi 20 20
*267* A46 12c multi 20 20
*268* A46 15c multi 24 24
*269* A46 25c ultra & multi 32 32
*270* A46 35c pur & multi 40 40
*271* A47 50c grn & multi 58 58
*272* A47 $1 bis & multi 1.10 1.00
*273* A47 $2.50 multi 2.50 2.25
*274* A47 $5 gray & multi 5.25 4.25
*274A* A47 $10 multi ('73) 10.00 10.00
*Nos. 261-274A (15)* 21.29 19.94

Issue dates: Nos. 261-274, Feb. 1, 1970; No. 274A, Dec. 3, 1973.

**1975 Wmk. 373**
*263b* A46 4c dk vio & multi 38 38
*264a* A46 5c brt bl & multi 48 48
*266a* A46 10c bl & multi 95 95
*268a* A46 15c multi 1.50 1.50

The Three Marys at the Tomb, by Hogarth — A48

Designs: 25c, The Sealing of the Tomb. $1, The Ascension. The designs are from the altarpiece painted by William Hogarth for the Church of St. Mary Redcliffe in Bristol, 1755-56.

***Roulette 8½xPerf. 12½***

**1970, Mar. 7 Litho. Wmk. 314**

**Size: 27x54mm**

*275* A48 25c dk brn & multi 48 48
*276* A48 35c dk brn & multi 65 65

**Size: 38x54mm**

*277* A48 $1 dk brn & multi 1.90 1.90
Triptych (Nos. 275-277) 3.25 3.25

Easter 1970.

Nos. 275-277 printed se-tenant in sheets of 30 (10 triptychs) with the center $1 stamp 10mm. raised compared to the flanking 25c and 35c stamps.

Charles Dickens and Characters from his Works — A49

**1970, June 8 Wmk. 314 *Perf. 14***

*278* A49 1c brn & multi 5 5
*279* A49 25c Prus bl & multi 32 32
*280* A49 35c brn red & multi 40 40
*281* A49 50c red lil & multi 60 60

Charles Dickens (1812-70), English novelist.

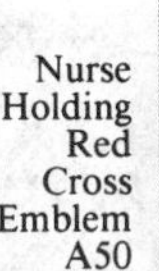
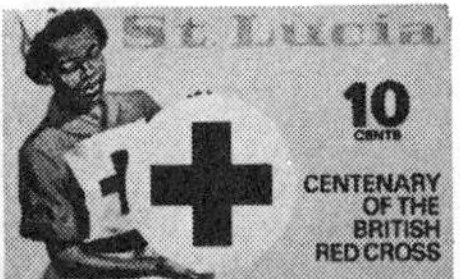


Nurse Holding Red Cross Emblem A50

Design: 15c, 35c, British, St. Lucia and Red Cross flags.

***Perf. 14½x14***

**1970, Aug. 18 Litho. Wmk. 314**

*282* A50 10c multi 8 8
*283* A50 15c multi 18 18
*284* A50 25c buff & multi 28 28
*285* A50 35c multi 42 42

Centenary of British Red Cross Society.

Madonna with the Lilies, by Luca della Robbia A51

**Lithographed and Embossed**

**1970, Nov. 16 Unwmk. *Perf. 11***

*286* A51 5c dk bl & multi 8 8
*287* A51 10c vio bl & multi 16 16
*288* A51 35c car lake & multi 55 55
*289* A51 40c dp grn & multi 70 70

Christmas 1970.

Christ on the Cross, by Rubens — A52

Easter: 15c, 40c, Descent from the Cross, by Peter Paul Rubens.

***Perf. 14x13½***

**1971, Mar. 29 Litho. Wmk. 314**

*290* A52 10c dl grn & multi 8 8
*291* A52 15c dl red & multi 14 14
*292* A52 35c brt bl & multi 36 36
*293* A52 40c multi 48 48

Moule à Chique Lighthouse — A53

Design: 25c, Beane Field Airport.

**1971, Apr. 30 *Perf. 14½x14***

*294* A53 5c ol & multi 8 8
*295* A53 25c bis & multi 50 50

Opening of Beane Field Airport.

View of Morne Fortune (Old Days) — A54

Designs show for each denomination an old print and a contemporary photograph of the same view. 10c, Castries City. 25c, Pigeon Island. 50c, View from Government House. Plain frame around contemporary views.

***Perf. 13½x14***

**1971, Aug. 10 Litho. Wmk. 314**

*296* A54 5c yel & multi 9 9
*297* A54 5c lt bl & multi 9 9
*298* A54 10c yel & multi 18 18
*299* A54 10c lt bl & multi 18 18
*300* A54 25c yel & multi 45 45
*301* A54 25c lt bl & multi 45 45
*302* A54 50c yel & multi 90 90
*303* A54 50c lt bl & multi 90 90
*Nos. 296-303 (8)* 3.24 3.24

Stamps of the same denomination are printed se-tenant in sheets of 30.

Virgin and Child, by Verrocchio — A55

Virgin and Child painted by: 10c, Paolo Moranda. 35c, Giovanni Battista Cima. 40c, Andrea del Verrocchio.

**1971, Oct. 15 *Perf. 14***

*304* A55 5c grn & multi 7 7
*305* A55 10c brn & multi 14 14
*306* A55 35c ultra & multi 50 50
*307* A55 40c red & multi 65 65

Christmas 1971.

St. Lucia, School of Dolci, and Arms A56

**1971, Dec. 13 *Perf. 14x14½***

*308* A56 5c gray & multi 12 12
*309* A56 10c lt grn & multi 18 18
*310* A56 25c tan & multi 45 45
*311* A56 50c lt bl & multi 90 90

National Day.

Lamentation, by Carracci — A57

Easter: 25c, 50c, Angels Weeping over Body of Jesus, by Guercino.

**1972, Feb. 15 Wmk. 314**

*312* A57 10c lt vio & multi 14 14
*313* A57 25c ocher & multi 42 42
*314* A57 35c ultra & multi 50 50
*315* A57 50c lt grn & multi 85 85

Teachers' College and Science Building A58

Designs: 15c, University Center and coat of arms. 25c, Secondary School. 35c, Technical College.

**1972, Apr. 18 Litho. *Perf. 14***

*316* A58 5c multi 5 5
*317* A58 15c multi 16 16
*318* A58 25c multi 28 28
*319* A58 35c multi 40 40

Opening of Morne Educational Complex.

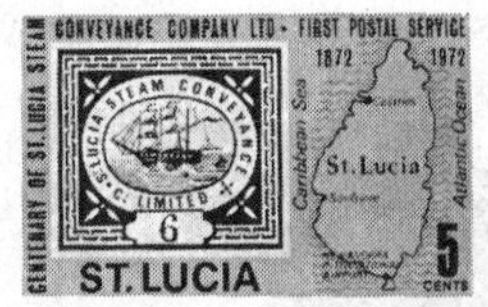


Steam Conveyance Co. Stamp and Map of St. Lucia — A59

Designs: 10c, Castries Harbor and 3c stamp. 35c, Soufriere Volcano and 1c stamp. 50c, One cent, 3c, 6c stamps.

**1972, June 22 *Perf. 14½***

*320* A59 5c yel & multi 7 7
*321* A59 10c vio bl & multi 15 15
*322* A59 35c car rose & multi 44 44
*323* A59 50c emer & multi 1.00 90

Centenary of St. Lucia Steam Conveyance Co. Ltd. postal service.

*St. Lucia stamps can be mounted in Scott's annually supplemented British Windward Islands Album.*

Holy Family, by Sebastiano Ricci — A60

**1972, Oct. 18 *Perf. 14½x14***

*324* A60 5c dk brn & multi 8 8
*325* A60 10c grn & multi 16 16
*326* A60 35c car & multi 60 60
*327* A60 40c dk bl & multi 80 80

Christmas 1972.

**Silver Wedding Issue, 1972**

Common Design Type

Design: Queen Elizabeth II, Prince Philip, St. Lucia coat of arms and St. Lucia parrot.

**1972, Nov. Photo. *Perf. 14x14½***

*328* CD324 15c car rose & multi 20 20
*329* CD324 35c ol & multi 42 42

Weekday Headdress A61

Arms of St. Lucia A62

Women's Headdresses: 10c, For church wear. 25c, Unmarried girl. 50c, Formal occasions.

**1973, Feb. 1 Wmk. 314 *Perf. 13***

*330* A61 5c multi 9 9
*331* A61 10c dk gray & multi 18 18
*332* A61 25c multi 45 45
*333* A61 50c sl bl & multi 90 90

Coil Stamps

**1973, Apr. 19 Litho. *Perf. 14½x14***

*334* A62 5c gray ol 30 30
*a* Watermark sideways ('76) 6 6
*335* A62 10c blue 45 45
*a* Watermark sideways ('76) 14 14
*336* A62 25c claret 45 45

H.M.S. St. Lucia A63

Designs: Old Sailing ships.

**1973, May 24 Litho. *Perf. 13½x14***

*337* A63 15c *shown* 20 20
*338* A63 35c *"Prince of Wales"* 52 52
*339* A63 50c *"Oliph Blossom"* 70 70
*340* A63 $1 *"Rose"* 1.40 1.40
*a* Souvenir sheet of 4 4.25 4.25

No. 340a contains one each of Nos. 337-340, perf. 15. Short description of the ships' histories in margin.

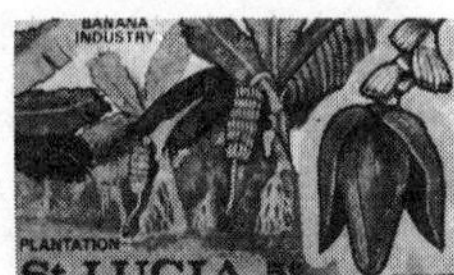


Banana Plantation and Flower — A64

Designs: 15c, Aerial spraying. 35c, Washing and packing bananas. 50c, Loading.

**1973, July 26 Litho. *Perf. 14***

| | | | | |
|---|---|---|---|---|
| *341* | A64 | 5c multi | 15 | 12 |
| *342* | A64 | 15c multi | 50 | 35 |
| *343* | A64 | 35c multi | 1.10 | 90 |
| *344* | A64 | 50c multi | 1.75 | 1.50 |

Banana industry.

Madonna and Child, by Carlo Maratta — A65

Paintings: 15c, Virgin in the Meadow, by Raphael. 35c, Holy Family, by Angelo Bronzino. 50c, Madonna of the Pear, by Durer.

**1973, Oct. 17 Litho. *Perf. 14x13½***

| | | | | |
|---|---|---|---|---|
| *345* | A65 | 5c cit & multi | 6 | 6 |
| *346* | A65 | 15c ultra & multi | 18 | 18 |
| *347* | A65 | 35c dp grn & multi | 48 | 48 |
| *348* | A65 | 50c red & multi | 80 | 80 |

Christmas 1973.

**Princess Anne's Wedding Issue**
Common Design Type

**1973, Nov. 14 Wmk. 314 *Perf. 14***

| | | | | |
|---|---|---|---|---|
| *349* | CD325 | 40c gray grn & multi | 28 | 28 |
| *350* | CD325 | 50c lil & multi | 38 | 38 |

The Betrayal of Christ, by Ugolino — A66

Paintings by Ugolino (14th Century): 35c, The Way to Calvary. 80c, Descent from the Cross. $1, Resurrection.

**1974, Apr. 1 *Perf. 13½x13***

| | | | | |
|---|---|---|---|---|
| *351* | A66 | 5c ocher & multi | 5 | 5 |
| *352* | A66 | 35c ocher & multi | 30 | 30 |
| *353* | A66 | 80c ocher & multi | 70 | 70 |
| *354* | A66 | $1 ocher & multi | 80 | 80 |
| *a* | | Souvenir sheet of 4 | 2.75 | 2.75 |

Easter 1974. No. 354a contains one each of Nos. 351-354; gray margin with black design and ocher border and crucifix. Size: 182x145mm.

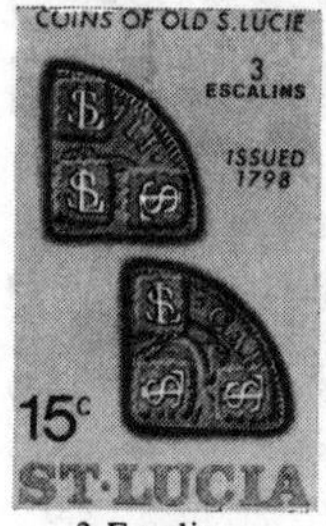

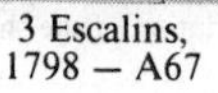


3 Escalins, 1798 — A67

Baron de Laborie, 1784 — A68

Pieces of Eight: 35c, 6 escalins, 1798. 40c, 2 livres 5 sols, 1813. $1, 6 livres 15 sols, 1813.

**1974, May 20 *Perf. 13½***

| | | | | |
|---|---|---|---|---|
| *355* | A67 | 15c lt ol & multi | 16 | 16 |
| *356* | A67 | 35c multi | 35 | 35 |
| *357* | A67 | 40c grn & multi | 40 | 40 |
| *358* | A67 | $1 brn & multi | 95 | 95 |
| *a* | | Souvenir sheet of 4 | 2.50 | 2.50 |

Coins of Old St. Lucia. No. 358a contains one each of Nos. 355-358. Multicolored margin with coins and inscription. Size: 150x115mm.

**Wmk. 314**

**1974, Aug. 29 Litho. *Perf. 14½***

Portraits: 35c, Sir John Moore, Lieutenant Governor, 1796-97. 80c, Major General Sir Dudley St. Leger Hill, 1834-37. $1, Sir Frederick Joseph Clarke, 1967-71.

| | | | | |
|---|---|---|---|---|
| *359* | A68 | 5c ocher & multi | 6 | 6 |
| *360* | A68 | 35c brt bl & multi | 38 | 38 |
| *361* | A68 | 80c vio & multi | 85 | 85 |
| *362* | A68 | $1 multi | 1.00 | 1.00 |
| *a* | | Souvenir sheet of 4 | 2.75 | 2.75 |

Past Governors of St. Lucia. No. 362a contains one each of Nos. 359-362. Brown and black margin with St. Lucia coat of arms. Size: 152x116mm.

Virgin and Child, by Verrocchio — A69

Virgin and Child: 35c, by Andrea della Robbia. 80c, by Luca della Robbia. $1, by Antonio Rossellino.

**1974, Nov. 13 Wmk. 314 *Perf. 13½***

| | | | | |
|---|---|---|---|---|
| *363* | A69 | 5c gray & multi | 5 | 5 |
| *364* | A69 | 35c pink & multi | 28 | 28 |
| *365* | A69 | 80c brn & multi | 60 | 60 |
| *366* | A69 | $1 ol & multi | 75 | 75 |
| *a* | | Souvenir sheet of 4 | 2.25 | 2.25 |

Christmas 1974. No. 366a contains one each of Nos. 363-366, blue margin showing angels. Size: 91x140mm.

Churchill and Gen. Montgomery — A70

Design: $1, Churchill and Pres. Truman.

**1974, Nov. 30 *Perf. 14***

| | | | | |
|---|---|---|---|---|
| *367* | A70 | 5c multi | 5 | 5 |
| *368* | A70 | $1 multi | 75 | 75 |

Sir Winston Churchill (1874-1965).

Crucifixion, by Van der Weyden — A71

Easter: 35c, "Noli me Tangere," by Julio Romano. 80c, Crucifixion, by Fernando Gallego. $1, "Noli me Tangere," by Correggio.

***Perf. 14x13½***

**1975, Mar. 27 Wmk. 314**

| | | | | |
|---|---|---|---|---|
| *369* | A71 | 5c brn & multi | 6 | 6 |
| *370* | A71 | 35c ultra & multi | 32 | 32 |
| *371* | A71 | 80c red brn & multi | 70 | 70 |
| *372* | A71 | $1 grn & multi | 80 | 80 |

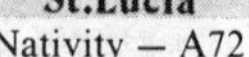


Nativity — A72

Adoration of the Kings — A73

Designs: No. 375, Virgin and Child. No. 376, Adoration of the Shepherds. 40c, Nativity. $1, Virgin and Child with Sts. Catherine of Alexandria and Siena.

**Wmk. 314**

**1975, Dec. Litho. *Perf. 14½***

| | | | | |
|---|---|---|---|---|
| *373* | A72 | 5c lil rose & multi | 6 | 6 |
| *374* | A73 | 10c yel & multi | 10 | 10 |
| *375* | A73 | 10c yel & multi | 10 | 10 |
| *376* | A73 | 10c yel & multi | 10 | 10 |
| | | Strip of 3 | 40 | 40 |
| *377* | A72 | 40c yel & multi | 40 | 40 |
| *378* | A72 | $1 bl & multi | 1.00 | 1.00 |
| *a* | | Souvenir sheet of 3 | 1.75 | 1.75 |
| | | *Nos. 373-378 (6)* | 1.76 | 1.76 |

Christmas 1975. Nos. 374-376 printed setenant in sheets of 30. No. 378a contains one each of Nos. 373, 377-378; blue and multicolored margin. Size: 105x108mm.

"Hanna," First U.S. Warship — A74

Revolutionary Era Ships: 1c, "Prince of Orange," British packet. 2c, "Edward," British sloop. 5c, "Millern," British merchantman. 15c, "Surprise," Continental Navy lugger. 35c, "Serapis," British warship. 50c, "Randolph," first Continental Navy frigate. $1, Frigate "Alliance."

***Perf. 14½***

**1976, Jan. 26 Litho. Unwmk.**

| | | | | |
|---|---|---|---|---|
| *379* | A74 | ½c multi | 7 | 5 |
| *380* | A74 | 1c multi | 7 | 5 |
| *381* | A74 | 2c multi | 7 | 5 |
| *382* | A74 | 5c multi | 10 | 5 |
| *383* | A74 | 15c multi | 32 | 16 |
| *384* | A74 | 35c multi | 85 | 40 |
| *385* | A74 | 50c multi | 1.10 | 60 |
| *386* | A74 | $1 multi | 2.75 | 1.25 |
| *a* | | Souvenir sheet of 4 | 5.50 | 3.75 |
| | | *Nos. 379-386 (8)* | 5.33 | 2.61 |

American Bicentennial. No. 386a contains one each of Nos. 383-386, perf. 13; multicolored margin showing ships' tools. Size: 142x116mm.

Laughing Gull — A75

Arms of H.M.S. Ceres — A76

Map of West Indies, Bats, Wicket and Ball A75a

Prudential Cup — A75b

Birds: 2c, Little blue heron. 4c, Belted kingfisher. 5c, St. Lucia parrot. 6c, St. Lucia oriole. 8c, Brown trembler. 10c, American kestrel. 12c, Red-billed tropic bird. 15c, Common gallinule. 25c, Brown noddy. 35c, Sooty tern. 50c, Osprey. $1, White-breasted thrasher. $2.50, St. Lucia black finch. $5 Rednecked pigeon. $10, Caribbean elaenia.

**Wmk. 314 (1c); 373 (others)**

**1976, May 7 Litho. *Perf. 14½***

| | | | | |
|---|---|---|---|---|
| *387* | A75 | 1c gray & multi | 5 | 5 |
| *388* | A75 | 2c gray & multi | 5 | 5 |
| *389* | A75 | 4c gray & multi | 5 | 5 |
| *390* | A75 | 5c gray & multi | 6 | 5 |
| *391* | A75 | 6c gray & multi | 7 | 6 |
| *392* | A75 | 8c gray & multi | 9 | 7 |
| *393* | A75 | 10c gray & multi | 10 | 9 |
| *394* | A75 | 12c gray & multi | 12 | 10 |
| *395* | A75 | 15c gray & multi | 16 | 12 |
| *396* | A75 | 25c gray & multi | 25 | 22 |
| *397* | A75 | 35c gray & multi | 32 | 28 |
| *398* | A75 | 50c gray & multi | 48 | 42 |
| *399* | A75 | $1 gray & multi | 1.00 | 85 |
| *400* | A75 | $2.50 gray & multi | 2.50 | 2.25 |
| *401* | A75 | $5 gray & multi | 5.00 | 4.25 |
| *402* | A75 | $10 gray & multi | 10.00 | 8.50 |
| | | *Nos. 387-402 (16)* | 20.30 | 17.41 |

**1976, July 19 Unwmk. *Perf. 14***

| | | | | |
|---|---|---|---|---|
| *403* | A75a | 50c lt bl & multi | 1.00 | 1.00 |
| *404* | A75b | $1 lil rose & blk | 2.00 | 2.00 |
| *a* | | Souvenir sheet of 2 | 3.25 | 3.25 |

World Cricket Cup, won by West Indies Team, 1975. No. 404a contains one each of Nos. 403-404; light ultramarine and black margin showing cricket players. Size: 93x80mm.

**1976, Sept. 6 Wmk. 373 *Perf. 14½***

Coats of Arms of Royal Naval Ships: 20c, Pelican. 40c, Ganges. $2, Ariadne.

| | | | | |
|---|---|---|---|---|
| *405* | A76 | 10c gold & multi | 10 | 10 |
| *406* | A76 | 20c gold & multi | 20 | 20 |
| *407* | A76 | 40c gold & multi | 40 | 40 |
| *408* | A76 | $2 gold & multi | 1.75 | 1.75 |

Madonna and Child, by Murillo — A77

Paintings: 20c, Virgin and Child, by Lorenzo Costa. 50c, Madonna and Child, by Adriaea Isenbrandt. $2, Madonna and Child with St. John, by Murillo. $2.50, Like 10c.

**1976, Nov. 15 Litho. *Perf. 14½***

| | | | | |
|---|---|---|---|---|
| *409* | A77 | 10c multi | 14 | 14 |
| *410* | A77 | 20c multi | 28 | 28 |
| *411* | A77 | 50c multi | 60 | 60 |
| *412* | A77 | $2 multi | 2.25 | 2.25 |

**Souvenir Sheet**

| | | | | |
|---|---|---|---|---|
| *413* | A77 | $2.50 multi | 3.00 | 3.00 |

Christmas 1976. No. 413 has gold and multicolored margin showing poinsettias. Size: 106x93mm.

Elizabeth II, "Palms and Water" — A78

**Wmk. 373**

**1977, Feb. 7 Litho. *Perf. 14½***

| | | | | |
|---|---|---|---|---|
| *414* | A78 | 10c multi | 7 | 7 |
| *415* | A78 | 20c multi | 15 | 15 |
| *416* | A78 | 40c multi | 30 | 30 |
| *417* | A78 | $2 multi | 1.40 | 1.40 |

**Souvenir Sheet**

| | | | | |
|---|---|---|---|---|
| *418* | A78 | $2.50 multi | 1.75 | 1.75 |

25th anniversary of the reign of Queen Elizabeth II. No. 418 has multicolored margin. Size: 127x96mm.

Scouts of Tapion School — A79

Nativity, by Giotto — A80

Designs: 1c, Sea Scouts, St. Mary's College. 2c, Scout giving oath. 10c, Tapion School Cub Scouts. 20c, Venture Scout, Soufriere. 50c, Scout from Gros Islet Division. $1, $2.50, Boat drill, St. Mary's College.

**1977, Oct. 17 Unwmk. *Perf. 15***

| | | | | |
|---|---|---|---|---|
| *419* | A79 | ½c multi | 5 | 5 |
| *420* | A79 | 1c multi | 5 | 5 |
| *421* | A79 | 2c multi | 5 | 5 |
| *422* | A79 | 10c multi | 10 | 10 |
| *423* | A79 | 20c multi | 20 | 20 |
| *424* | A79 | 50c multi | 50 | 50 |
| *425* | A79 | $1 multi | 1.00 | 1.00 |
| | | *Nos. 419-425 (7)* | 1.95 | 1.95 |

**Souvenir Sheet**

| | | | | |
|---|---|---|---|---|
| *426* | A79 | $2.50 multi | 2.00 | 2.00 |

6th Caribbean Boy Scout Jamboree, Kingston, Jamaica, Aug. 5-14. No. 426 has multicolored margin with Scout emblems. Size: 75x85mm.

**1977, Oct. 31 Litho. *Perf. 14***

Virgin and Child by: 1c, Fra Angelico. 2c, El Greco. 20c, Caravaggio. 50c, Velazquez. $1, Tiepolo. $2.50, Adoration of the Kings, by Tiepolo.

| | | | | |
|---|---|---|---|---|
| *427* | A80 | ½c multi | 5 | 5 |
| *428* | A80 | 1c multi | 5 | 5 |
| *429* | A80 | 2c multi | 5 | 5 |
| *430* | A80 | 20c multi | 14 | 14 |
| *431* | A80 | 50c multi | 35 | 35 |
| *432* | A80 | $1 multi | 70 | 70 |
| *433* | A80 | $2.50 multi | 1.75 | 1.75 |
| | | *Nos. 427-433 (7)* | 3.09 | 3.09 |

Christmas 1977.

Suzanne Fourment in Velvet Hat, by Rubens — A81

Rubens Paintings: 35c, Rape of the Sabine Women (detail). 50c, Ludovicus Nonnius, portrait. $2.50, Minerva Protecting Pax from Mars (detail).

***Perf. 14x14½***

**1977, Nov. 28 Litho. Wmk. 373**

| | | | | |
|---|---|---|---|---|
| *434* | A81 | 10c multi | 9 | 9 |
| *435* | A81 | 35c multi | 14 | 14 |
| *436* | A81 | 50c multi | 48 | 48 |
| *437* | A81 | $2.50 multi | 2.25 | 2.25 |
| *a.* | | Souvenir sheet of 4 | 3.25 | 3.25 |

Peter Paul Rubens (1577-1640).

No. 437a contains one each of Nos. 434-437, perf. 15; black and brown margin with Rubens portrait and short biography. Size: 146x120mm.

Yeoman of the Guard and Life Guard A82

Dress Uniforms: 20c, Groom and postilion. 50c, Footman and coachman. $3, State trumpeter and herald. $5, Master of the Queen's House and Gentleman at Arms.

**Unwmk.**

**1978, June 2 Litho. *Perf. 14***

| | | | | |
|---|---|---|---|---|
| *438* | A82 | 15c multi | 10 | 10 |
| *439* | A82 | 20c multi | 14 | 14 |
| *440* | A82 | 50c multi | 32 | 32 |
| *441* | A82 | $3 multi | 2.00 | 2.00 |

**Souvenir Sheet**

| | | | | |
|---|---|---|---|---|
| *442* | A82 | $5 multi | 3.00 | 3.00 |

25th anniversary of coronation of Queen Elizabeth II. No. 442 has multicolored margin showing royal lions, crown and "25" multiple. Size: 114x88mm.

Nos. 438-441 exist in miniature sheets of 3 plus label, perf. 12. Size: 128x128mm.

Queen Angelfish A83

Tropical Fish: 20c, Four-eyed butterflyfish. 50c, French angelfish. $2, Yellowtail damselfish. $2.50, Rock beauty.

**1978, June 19 Litho. *Perf. 14½***

| | | | | |
|---|---|---|---|---|
| *443* | A83 | 10c multi | 9 | 9 |
| *444* | A83 | 20c multi | 8 | 8 |
| *445* | A83 | 50c multi | 45 | 45 |
| *446* | A83 | $2 multi | 1.75 | 1.75 |

**Souvenir Sheet**

| | | | | |
|---|---|---|---|---|
| *447* | A83 | $2.50 multi | 2.50 | 2.50 |

No. 447 has multicolored margin showing underwater scene. Size: 116x89mm.

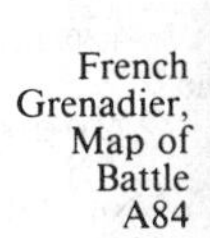

French Grenadier, Map of Battle A84

Designs: 30c, British Grenadier and Bellin map of St. Lucia, 1762. 50c, British fleet opposing French landing and map of coast from Gros Islet to Cul-de-Sac. $2.50, Light infantrymen and Gen. James Grant.

**1978, Nov. 15 Litho. *Perf. 14***

| | | | | |
|---|---|---|---|---|
| *448* | A84 | 10c multi | 8 | 8 |
| *449* | A84 | 30c multi | 24 | 24 |
| *450* | A84 | 50c multi | 40 | 40 |
| *451* | A84 | $2.50 multi | 2.00 | 2.00 |

Bicent. of Battle of St. Lucia (Cul-de-Sac).

Annunciation — A85

Christmas: 55c, 80c, Adoration of the Kings.

***Perf. 14x14½***

**1978, Dec. 4 Wmk. 373**

| | | | | |
|---|---|---|---|---|
| *452* | A85 | 30c multi | 22 | 22 |
| *453* | A85 | 50c multi | 35 | 35 |
| *454* | A85 | 55c multi | 40 | 40 |
| *455* | A85 | 80c multi | 55 | 55 |

**Independent State**

Hewanorra Airport A86

Designs: 30c, New coat of arms. 50c, Government house and Allen Lewis, first Governor General. $2, Map of St. Lucia, French, St. Lucia and British flags.

**1979, Feb. 22 Litho. *Perf. 14***

| | | | | |
|---|---|---|---|---|
| *456* | A86 | 10c multi | 6 | 6 |
| *457* | A86 | 30c multi | 20 | 20 |
| *458* | A86 | 50c multi | 32 | 32 |
| *459* | A86 | $2 multi | 1.25 | 1.25 |
| *a.* | | Souvenir sheet of 4 | 2.00 | 2.00 |

Independence. No. 459a contains Nos. 456-459; multicolored margin with national anthem. Size: 125x79mm.

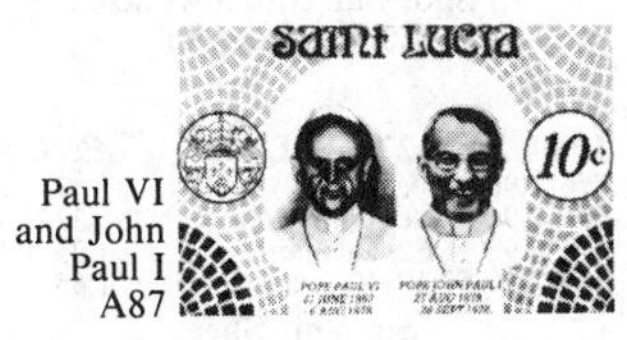


Paul VI and John Paul I A87

Pope Paul VI and: 30c, Pres. Anwar Sadat of Egypt. 50c, Secretary General U Thant and U.N. emblem. 55c, Prime Minister Golda Meir of Israel. $2, Martin Luther King, Jr.

**1979, May 7 Litho. *Perf. 14***

| | | | | |
|---|---|---|---|---|
| *460* | A87 | 10c multi | 8 | 8 |
| *461* | A87 | 30c multi | 25 | 25 |
| *462* | A87 | 50c multi | 42 | 42 |
| *463* | A87 | 55c multi | 45 | 45 |
| *464* | A87 | $2 multi | 1.75 | 1.75 |
| | | *Nos. 460-464 (5)* | 2.95 | 2.95 |

In memory of Popes Paul VI and John Paul I.

Jersey Cows A88

Agricultural Diversification: 35c, Fruits and vegetables. 50c, Waterfall (water conservation). $3, Coconuts, copra industry.

**1979, July 2 Litho. *Perf. 14***

| | | | | |
|---|---|---|---|---|
| *465* | A88 | 10c multi | 8 | 8 |
| *466* | A88 | 35c multi | 30 | 30 |
| *467* | A88 | 50c multi | 42 | 42 |
| *468* | A88 | $3 multi | 2.50 | 2.50 |

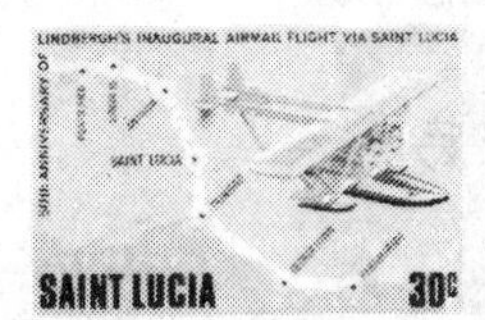


Lindbergh's Route over St. Lucia, Puerto Rico-Paramaribo — A89

**1979, Nov. Litho. *Perf. 14***

| | | | | |
|---|---|---|---|---|
| *469* | A89 | 10c Lindbergh, hydroplane | 8 | 8 |
| *470* | A89 | 30c shown | 24 | 24 |
| *471* | A89 | 50c Landing at La Toc | 40 | 40 |
| *472* | A89 | $2 Flight covers | 1.65 | 1.65 |

Lindbergh's inaugural airmail flight (U.S.-Guyana) via St. Lucia, 50th anniversary.

Canceled-to-order stamps are often from remainders. Most collectors of canceled stamps prefer postally used specimens.

Prince of Saxony, by Cranach the Elder — A90

IYC Emblem and: 50c, Infanta Margarita, by Velazquez. $2, Girl Playing Badminton, by Jean Baptiste Chardin. $2.50, Mary and Francis Wilcox, by Stock. $5, Two Children, by Pablo Picasso.

**1979, Dec. 6 Litho. *Perf. 14***

| | | | | |
|---|---|---|---|---|
| *473* | A90 | 10c multi | 8 | 8 |
| *474* | A90 | 50c multi | 40 | 40 |
| *475* | A90 | $2 multi | 1.65 | 1.65 |
| *476* | A90 | $2.50 multi | 2.00 | 2.00 |

**Souvenir Sheet**

| | | | | |
|---|---|---|---|---|
| *477* | A90 | $5 multi | 3.50 | 3.50 |

International Year of the Child. No. 477 has multicolored margin showing "Two Women Teaching a Child to Walk," by Rembrandt. Size: 113x94mm.

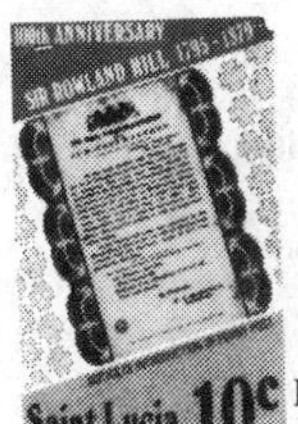


Penny Post Notice, 1839 — A91

Maltese Cross Cancels and: 50c, Hill's original stamp design. $2, St. Lucia No. 1. $2.50, Penny Black. $5, Hill portrait.

**1979, Dec. 10**

| | | | | |
|---|---|---|---|---|
| *478* | A91 | 10c multi | 6 | 6 |
| *479* | A91 | 50c multi | 32 | 32 |
| *480* | A91 | $2 multi | 1.25 | 1.25 |
| *481* | A91 | $2.50 multi | 1.50 | 1.50 |

**Souvenir Sheet**

| | | | | |
|---|---|---|---|---|
| *482* | A91 | $5 multi | 3.00 | 3.00 |

Sir Rowland Hill (1793-1879), originator of penny postage. No. 482 has multicolored margin showing mail coach and Penny Black silhouette. Size: 111½x84½mm.

Nos. 478-481 also issued in sheets of 5 plus label, perf. 12x12½.

Virgin and Child, by Bernardino Fungi, IYC Emblem — A92

IYC Emblem, Virgin and Child Paintings by: 50c, Carlo Dolci. $2, Titian. $2.50, Giovanni Bellini.

**1980, Jan. 14**

| | | | | |
|---|---|---|---|---|
| *483* | A92 | 10c multi | 8 | 8 |
| *484* | A92 | 50c multi | 40 | 40 |
| *485* | A92 | $2 multi | 1.65 | 1.65 |
| *486* | A92 | $2.50 multi | 2.00 | 2.00 |
| *a.* | | Souvenir sheet of 4 | 4.50 | 4.50 |

Christmas 1979; International Year of the Child. No. 486a contains Nos. 483-486. Gold and black margin shows IYC emblem. Size: 95x119½mm.

St. Lucia Conveyance Co. Ltd. Stamp, 1873 — A93

London 1980 Emblem and Covers: 30c, "Assistance" 1p postmark, 1879. 50c, Postage due handstamp, 1929. $2, Postmarks on 1844 cover.

**Wmk. 373**

**1980, May 6 Litho. *Perf. 14***

| | | |
|---|---|---|
| *487* A93 10c multi | 7 | 7 |
| *488* A93 30c multi | 20 | 20 |
| *489* A93 50c multi | 35 | 35 |
| *490* A93 $2 multi | 1.40 | 1.40 |
| *a* Souvenir sheet of 4 | 2.50 | 2.50 |

London 1980 International Stamp Exhibition, May 6-14. No. 490a contains Nos. 487-490; margin shows London 1980 emblem in black. Size: 85x77mm.

Intl. Year of the Child A93a

Designs: Space scenes.

**1980, May 29 Litho. *Perf. 11***

| | | |
|---|---|---|
| *491* A93a ½c *Mickey on rocket* | 5 | 5 |
| *492* A93a 1c *Donald Duck spacewalking, horiz.* | 5 | 5 |
| *493* A93a 2c *Minnie Mouse on moon* | 5 | 5 |
| *494* A93a 3c *Goofy hitch hiking* | 5 | 5 |
| *495* A93a 4c *Goofy on moon, horiz.* | 5 | 5 |
| *496* A93a 5c *Pluto digging on moon, horiz.* | 5 | 5 |
| *497* A93a 10c *Donald Duck, space creature, horiz.* | 10 | 10 |
| *498* A93a $2 *Donald Duck paddling satellite horiz.* | 2.00 | 2.00 |
| *499* A93a $2.50 *Mickey Mouse in lunar rover, horiz.* | 2.50 | 2.50 |
| *Nos. 491-499 (9)* | 4.90 | 4.90 |

**Souvenir Sheet**

| | | |
|---|---|---|
| *500* A93a $5 *Goofy on moon* | 4.00 | 4.00 |

No. 500 has multicolored margin showing Mickey Mouse in space craft. Size: 102x127mm.

Queen Mother Elizabeth, 80th Birthday A94

**1980, Aug. 4 Litho. *Perf. 14***

| | | |
|---|---|---|
| *501* A94 10c multi | 7 | 7 |
| *502* A94 $2.50 multi | 1.75 | 1.75 |

**Souvenir Sheet**

***Perf. 12½x12***

| | | |
|---|---|---|
| *503* A94 $3 multi | 2.00 | 2.00 |

No. 503 has multicolored margin with flowers. Size: 85x65mm.

HS-748 on Runway, St. Lucia Airport, Hewanorra — A95

**Wmk. 373**

**1980, Aug. 11 Litho. *Perf. 14½***

| | | |
|---|---|---|
| *504* A95 5c *shown* | 5 | 5 |
| *505* A95 10c *DC-10, St. Lucia Airport* | 7 | 7 |
| *506* A95 15c *Bus, Castries* | 10 | 10 |
| *507* A95 20c *Refrigerator ship* | 15 | 15 |
| *a* Wmk. 380 ('84) | 15 | 15 |
| *508* A95 25c *Islander plane* | 18 | 18 |
| *a* Wmk. 380 ('84) | 18 | 18 |
| *509* A95 30c *Pilot boat* | 22 | 22 |
| *a* Wmk. 380 ('84) | 22 | 22 |
| *510* A95 50c *Boeing 727* | 38 | 38 |
| *511* A95 75c *Cruise ship* | 55 | 55 |
| *512* A95 $1 *Lockheed Tristar, Piton Mountains* | 75 | 75 |
| *a* Wmk. 380 ('84) | 75 | 75 |
| *513* A95 $2 *Cargo ship* | 1.50 | 1.50 |
| *a* Wmk. 380 ('84) | 1.50 | 1.50 |
| *514* A95 $5 *Boeing 707* | 3.75 | 3.75 |
| *515* A95 $10 *Queen Elizabeth 2* | 7.25 | 7.25 |
| *a* Wmk. 380 ('84) | 7.25 | 7.25 |
| *Nos. 504-515 (12)* | 14.95 | 14.95 |

Shot Put, Moscow '80 Emblem — A96

**1980, Sept. 22 Litho. *Perf. 14***

| | | |
|---|---|---|
| *516* A96 10c *shown* | 7 | 7 |
| *517* A96 50c *Swimming* | 32 | 32 |
| *518* A96 $2 *Gymnastics* | 1.25 | 1.25 |
| *519* A96 $2.50 *Weight lifting* | 1.65 | 1.65 |

**Souvenir Sheet**

| | | |
|---|---|---|
| *520* A96 $5 *Passing the torch* | 3.25 | 3.25 |

22nd Summer Olympic Games, Moscow, July 19-Aug. 3. No. 520 has multicolored margin showing stadium and Moscow '80 emblem. Size: 108x82mm.

Palms and Coast at Dusk — A97

**1980, Sept. 30 *Perf. 14***

| | | |
|---|---|---|
| *521* A97 10c *shown* | 7 | 7 |
| *522* A97 50c *Rocky shore* | 32 | 32 |
| *523* A97 $2 *Sand beach* | 1.25 | 1.25 |
| *524* A97 $2.50 *Pitons at sunset* | 1.65 | 1.65 |

**Souvenir Sheet**

| | | |
|---|---|---|
| *525* A97 $5 *Two-master* | 3.25 | 3.25 |

Rotary International, 75th Anniversary. No. 525 has multicolored margin with Rotary emblem and Paul P. Harris portrait. Size: 103x106mm.

Sir Arthur Lewis, Economics — A98

Nobel Prize Winners: 50c, Martin Luther King, Jr., peace, 1964. $2, Ralph Bunche, peace, 1950. $2.50, Albert Schweitzer, peace, 1952. $5, Albert Einstein, physics, 1921.

**1980, Oct. 23 Litho. *Perf. 14***

| | | |
|---|---|---|
| *526* A98 10c multi | 7 | 7 |
| *527* A98 50c multi | 32 | 32 |
| *528* A98 $2 multi | 1.25 | 1.25 |
| *529* A98 $2.50 multi | 1.65 | 1.65 |

**Souvenir Sheet**

| | | |
|---|---|---|
| *530* A98 $5 multi | 3.25 | 3.25 |

No. 530 has multicolored margin showing Nobel medal. Size: 115x91mm.

Nos. 506-507, 510 Overprinted:

**$1.50 RELIEF**

**1980, Nov. 3 Litho. *Perf. 14½***

| | | |
|---|---|---|
| *531* A95 $1.50 on 15c multi | 1.50 | 1.50 |
| *532* A95 $1.50 on 20c multi | 1.50 | 1.50 |
| *533* A95 $1.50 on 50c multi | 1.50 | 1.50 |

Nativity, by Battista — A99

Angel and Citizens of St. Lucia — A100

**1980, Dec. 1 *Perf. 14***

Designs: 30c, Adoration of the Kings, by Bruegel the Elder. $2, Adoration of the Shepherds, by Murillo.

| | | |
|---|---|---|
| *534* A99 10c multi | 8 | 8 |
| *535* A99 30c multi | 22 | 22 |
| *536* A99 $2 multi | 1.50 | 1.50 |

**Souvenir Sheet**

| | | |
|---|---|---|
| *537* Sheet of 3 | 2.00 | 2.00 |
| *a* A100 $1, any single | 65 | 65 |

Christmas 1980. Size of No. 537: 102x88mm.

Agouti — A101

**1981, Jan. 19 Litho. *Perf. 14***

| | | |
|---|---|---|
| *538* A101 10c *shown* | 8 | 8 |
| *539* A101 50c *St. Lucia parrot* | 38 | 38 |
| *540* A101 $2 *Purple-throated carib* | 1.50 | 1.50 |
| *541* A101 $2.50 *Fiddler crab* | 1.90 | 1.90 |

**Souvenir Sheet**

| | | |
|---|---|---|
| *542* A101 $4 *Monarch butterfly* | 4.00 | 4.00 |

No. 542 has multicolored margin showing flora and fauna. Size: 104½x87mm.

**Royal Wedding Issue**

Common Design Type

**1981, June 16 Litho. *Perf. 14***

| | | |
|---|---|---|
| *543* CD331 25c Couple | 16 | 16 |
| *544* CD331 50c Clarence House | 32 | 32 |
| *545* CD331 $4 Charles | 2.50 | 2.50 |

**Souvenir Sheet**

| | | |
|---|---|---|
| *546* CD331 $5 Glass coach | 4.50 | 4.50 |

No. 546 has lemon and black margin showing heraldic designs. Size: 96x82mm.

Nos. 543-545 also printed in sheets of 5 plus label, perf. 12, in changed colors.

| | | |
|---|---|---|
| *549* CD331 Booklet | 8.75 | 8.75 |
| *a* Pane of 1, $5, Couple | 3.50 | 3.50 |
| *b* Pane of 6 (3x50c, Diana, 3x$2, Charles) | 5.25 | 5.25 |

The Cock by Picasso — A102

Picasso Birth Centenary: 50c, Man with Ice Cream. 55c, Woman Dressing her Hair. $3, Seated Woman. $5, Night Fishing at Antibes.

**1981, May Litho. *Perf. 14***

| | | |
|---|---|---|
| *550* A102 30c multi | 20 | 20 |
| *551* A102 50c multi | 35 | 35 |
| *552* A102 55c multi | 38 | 38 |
| *553* A102 $3 multi | 2.00 | 2.00 |

**Souvenir Sheet**

| | | |
|---|---|---|
| *554* A102 $5 multi | 4.00 | 4.00 |

No. 554 has multicolored margin showing entire painting. Size: 128x103mm.

Duke of Edinburgh's Awards, 25th Anniv. — A103

**Wmk. 373**

**1981, Sept. 28 Litho. *Perf. 14½***

| | | |
|---|---|---|
| *555* A103 10c Industry | 10 | 10 |
| *556* A103 35c Community service | 35 | 35 |
| *557* A103 50c Hikers | 50 | 50 |
| *558* A103 $2.50 Duke of Edinburgh | 2.50 | 2.50 |

Intl. Year of the Disabled A104

**1981, Oct. 30 Litho. *Perf. 14***

| | | |
|---|---|---|
| *559* A104 10c Louis Braille | 6 | 6 |
| *560* A104 50c Sarah Bernhardt | 32 | 32 |
| *561* A104 $2 Joseph Pulitzer | 1.25 | 1.25 |
| *562* A104 $2.50 Henri de Toulouse-Lautrec | 1.65 | 1.65 |

**Souvenir Sheet**

| | | |
|---|---|---|
| *563* A104 $5 Franklin D. Roosevelt | 3.50 | 3.50 |

No. 563 has multicolored margin showing IYD emblems. Size: 116x91mm.

Christmas 1981 — A105

Adoration of the King Paintings.

**1981, Dec. 15**
*564* A105 10c Sfoza 7 7
*565* A105 30c Orcanga 22 22
*566* A105 $1.50 Gerard 1.10 1.10
*567* A105 $2.50 Foppa 1.90 1.90

First Anniv. of UPU Membership — A106

**1981, Dec. 29** **Unwmk.**
*568* A106 10c No. 1 12 12
*569* A106 30c No. 251 34 34
*570* A106 50c No. 459 55 55
*571* A106 $2 UPU, St. Lucia flags 2.25 2.25

**Souvenir Sheets**

*572* A106 $5 GPO, Castries 5.50 5.50

No. 572 has tan and black margin. Size: 129x110mm.

Fanny Travis Cochran, by Cecilia Beaux — A107

1980s Decade for Women (Paintings of Women by Women): 50c, Women with Dove, by Marie Laurencin. $2, Portrait of a Young Pupil of David. $2.50, Self-portrait, by Rosalba Carriera. $5, Self-portrait, by Elisabeth Vigee-Le Brun.

**Unwmk.**

**1981, Dec. 11** **Litho.** ***Perf. 14***
*573* A107 10c multi 7 7
*574* A107 50c multi 35 35
*575* A107 $2 multi 1.50 1.50
*576* A107 $2.50 multi 1.75 1.75

**Souvenir Sheet**

*577* A107 $5 multi 3.50 3.50

No. 577 has multicolored margin showing palette. Size: 103x78mm.

1982 World Cup Soccer A108

Designs: Various soccer players.

**1982, Feb. 15** **Litho.** ***Perf. 14½***
*578* A108 10c multi 8 8
*579* A108 50c multi 38 38
*580* A108 $2 multi 1.50 1.50
*581* A108 $2.50 multi 1.90 1.90

**Souvenir Sheet**

*582* A108 $5 multi 2.75 3.75

No. 582 has multicolored margin continuing design. Size: 104x84mm.

Battle of the Saints Bicentenary — A109

**Wmk. 373**

**1982, Apr. 13** **Litho.** ***Perf. 14***
*583* A109 10c Pigeon Isld. 8 8
*584* A109 35c Battle 28 28
*585* A109 50c Admirals Rodney, DeGrasse 38 38
*586* A109 $2.50 Map 1.90 1.90
*a* Souvenir sheet of 4 3.00 3.00

No. 586a contains Nos. 583-586; light blue and black margin shows arms, scroll. Size: 126x76mm.

Scouting Year — A110

**1982, Aug. 4** **Litho.** ***Perf. 14***
*587* A110 10c Map reading 8 8
*588* A110 50c First aid 40 40
*589* A110 $1.50 Camping 1.25 1.25
*590* A110 $2.50 Campfire sing 2.00 2.00

**Princess Diana Issue**
Common Design Type
***Perf. 14½x14***

**1982, Sept. 1** **Unwmk.**
*591* CD332 50c Leeds Castle 35 35
*592* CD332 $2 Diana 1.40 1.40
*593* CD332 $4 Wedding 2.75 2.75

**Souvenir Sheet**

*594* CD332 $5 Diana, diff. 3.50 3.50

No. 594 has multicolored margin showing family tree, Bertrand Russell. Size: 103x76mm.

Christmas 1982 — A111

Paintings: 10c, Adoration of the Kings, by Brueghel the Elder. 30c, Nativity, by Lorenzo Costa. 50c, Virgin and Child, Fra Filippo Lippi. 80c, Adoration of the Shepherds, by Nicolas Poussin.

**Wmk. 373**

**1982, Nov. 10** **Litho.** ***Perf. 14***
*595* A111 10c multi 8 8
*596* A111 30c multi 22 22
*597* A111 50c multi 38 38
*598* A111 80c multi 60 60

**Commonwealth Day**
Common Design Type

**1983, Mar. 14** **Litho.**
*599* CD334 10c Twin Peaks 9 9
*600* CD334 30c Beach 28 28
*601* CD334 50c Banana harvester 45 45
*602* CD334 $2 Flag 1.75 1.75

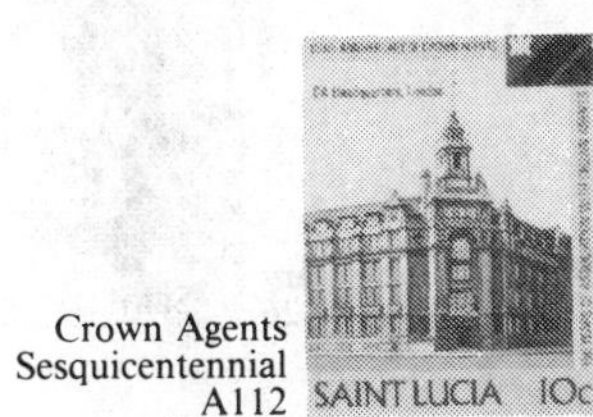


Crown Agents Sesquicentennial A112

**Wmk. 373**

**1983, Apr. 1** **Litho.** ***Perf. 14½***
*603* A112 10c Headquarters, London 8 8
*604* A112 15c Road construction 12 12
*605* A112 50c Map 42 42
*606* A112 $2 First stamp 1.65 1.65

World Communications Year — A113

**Unwmk.**

**1983, July 12** **Litho.** ***Perf. 15***
*607* A113 10c Shipboard intercommunication 9 9
*608* A113 50c Air-to-air 45 45
*609* A113 $1.50 Satellite 1.40 1.40
*610* A113 $2.50 Computer communications 2.25 2.25

**Souvenir Sheet**

*611* A113 $5 Weather satellite 4.25 4.25

No. 611 has multicolored margin showing modes of communication. Size: 108x89mm.

Coral Reef Fish A114

**1983, Aug. 23**
*612* A114 10c Longspine squirrelfish 9 9
*613* A114 50c Banded butterflyfish 48 48
*614* A114 $1.50 Blackbar soldierfish 1.40 1.40
*615* A114 $2.50 Yellowtail snappers 2.25 2.25

**Souvenir Sheet**

*616* A114 $5 Red hind 4.50 4.50

No. 616 has multicolored margin showing underwater scene. Size: 123x98mm.

Locomotives — A115

***Perf. 12½***

**1983, Oct. 13** **Litho.** **Unwmk.**
*617* A115 35c Princess Coronation 22 22
*618* A115 35c Princess Coronation, diff. 22 22
*619* A115 35c Duke of Sutherland 22 22
*620* A115 35c Duke of Sutherland, diff. 22 22
*621* A115 50c Leeds United 30 30
*622* A115 50c Leeds United, diff. 30 30
*623* A115 50c Lord Nelson 30 30
*624* A115 50c Lord Nelson, diff. 30 30
*625* A115 $1 Bodmin 60 60
*626* A115 $1 Bodmin, diff. 60 60
*627* A115 $1 Eton 60 60
*628* A115 $1 Eton, diff. 60 60
*629* A115 $2 Flying Scotsman 1.25 1.25
*630* A115 $2 Flying Scotsman, diff. 1.25 1.25
*631* A115 $2 Stephenson's Rocket 1.25 1.25
*632* A115 $2 Stephenson's Rocket, diff. 1.25 1.25
*Nos. 617-632 (16)* 9.48 9.48

Stamps of same denominations printed in se-tenant pairs.

See Nos. 653-660, 674-701, 711-726, 739-746, 774-781, 851-861.

Virgin and Child Paintings by Raphael — A115a

**Wmk. 373**

**1983, Oct. 24** **Litho.** ***Perf. 14***
*632A* A115a 10c Niccolini-Cowper Madonna 7 7
*632B* A115a 30c Holy Family with a Palm Tree 18 18
*632C* A115a 50c Sistine Madonna 32 32
*632D* A115a $5 Alba Madonna 3.00 3.00

Christmas 1983.

Battle of Waterloo, King George III
A116 A117

***Perf. 12½***

**1984, Mar. 13** **Litho.** **Unwmk.**
*633* A116 5c shown 5 5
*634* A117 5c shown 5 5
*635* A116 10c George III, diff. 5 5
*636* A117 10c Kew Palace 5 5
*637* A116 35c Arms of Elizabeth I 18 18
*638* A117 35c Elizabeth I 18 18
*639* A116 60c Arms of George III 30 30
*640* A117 60c George III, diff. 30 30
*641* A116 $1 Elizabeth I, diff. 50 50
*642* A117 $1 Hatfield Palace 50 50
*643* A116 $2.50 Spanish Armada 1.25 1.25
*644* A117 $2.50 Elizabeth, I, diff. 1.25 1.25
*Nos. 633-644 (12)* 4.66 4.66

Stamps of same denomination se-tenant in continuous design.

Colonial Building, Late 19th Cent. — A118

Local Architecture. 10c vert.

***Perf. 14x13½, 13½x14***

**1984, Apr. 6** **Wmk. 380**
*645* A118 10c Buildings, mid-19th cent. 8 8
*646* A118 45c shown 35 35
*647* A118 65c Wooden chattel, early 20th cent. 50 50
*648* A118 $2.50 Treasury, 1906 1.90 1.90

Logwood Tree and Blossom — A119

Prices of premium quality never hinged stamps will be in excess of catalogue price.

*Perf. 13½x14, 14x13½*

**1984, June 12 Wmk. 380**

*649* A119 10c shown 8 8
*650* A119 45c Calabash 35 35
*651* A119 65c Gommier, vert. 50 50
*652* A119 $2.50 Rain tree 1.90 1.90

Locomotive Type of 1983

Cars (side and front views). Stamps of same denomination se-tenant.

*Perf. 12½*

**1984, June 25 Litho. Unwmk.**

*653* A115 5c Bugatti 57SC, 1939 5 5
*654* A115 5c Side 5 5
*655* A115 10c Chevrolet Bel Air, 1957 7 7
*656* A115 10c Side 7 7
*657* A115 $1 Alfa Romeo, 1930 65 65
*658* A115 $1 Side 65 65
*659* A115 $2.50 Duesenberg, 1932 1.50 1.50
*660* A115 $2.50 Side 1.50 1.50
*Nos. 653-660 (8)* 4.54 4.54

Endangered Reptiles — A120

**Wmk. 380**

**1984, Aug. 8 Litho. *Perf. 14***

*661* A120 10c Pygmy gecko 8 8
*662* A120 45c Maria Isld. ground lizard 35 35
*663* A120 65c Green iguana 50 50
*664* A120 $2.50 Couresse snake 1.90 1.90

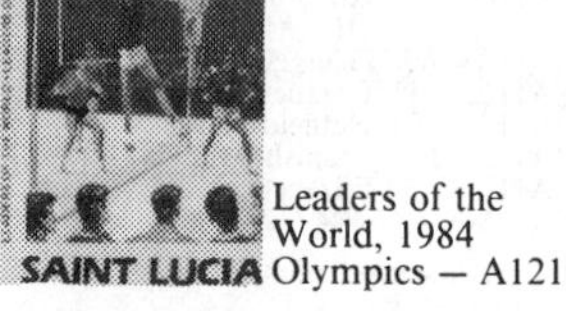


Leaders of the World, 1984 Olympics — A121

*Perf. 12½*

**1984, Sept. 21 Litho. Unwmk.**

*665* A121 5c Volleyball 5 5
*666* A121 5c Volleyball, diff. 5 5
*667* A121 10c Women's hurdles 8 8
*668* A121 10c Men's hurdles 8 8
*669* A121 65c Showjumping 52 52
*670* A121 65c Dressage 52 52
*671* A121 $2.50 Women's gymnastics 2.00 2.00
*672* A121 $2.50 Men's gymnastics 2.00 2.00
*Nos. 665-672 (8)* 5.30 5.30

Stamps of same denomination se-tenant horiz.

Locomotive Type of 1983

**1984, Sept. 21 Litho. *Perf. 12½***

*674* A115 1c TAW 2-6-2T, 1897 5 5
*675* A115 1c Side view only 5 5
*676* A115 15c Crocodile 1-C.C.-1, 1920 12 12
*677* A115 15c Side view only 12 12
*678* A115 50c The Countess 0.6.0T, 1903 38 38
*679* A115 50c Side view only 38 38
*680* A115 75c Class GE6/6C.C., 1921 55 55
*681* A115 75c Side view only 55 55
*682* A115 $1 Class P8, 4.6.0, 1906 75 75
*683* A115 $1 Side view only 75 75
*684* A115 $2 Der Alder 2.2.2., 1835 1.50 1.50
*685* A115 $2 Side view only 1.50 1.50
*Nos. 674-685 (12)* 6.70 6.70

Stamps of same denomination printed se-tenant vert.

Locomotive Type of 1983

Designs: Automobiles

**1984, Dec. 19 Litho. *Perf. 12½***

*686* A115 10c Panhard and Levassor, 1889 7 7
*687* A115 10c Side view only 7 7
*688* A115 30c N.S.U. R0-80 Saloon, 1968 22 22
*689* A115 30c Side view only 22 22
*690* A115 55c Abarth, Balbero, 1958 42 42
*691* A115 55c Side view only 42 42
*692* A115 65c TRV Vixen 2500M, 1972 48 48
*693* A115 65c Side view only 48 48
*694* A115 75c Ford Mustang Convertible, 1965 55 55
*695* A115 75c Side view only 55 55
*696* A115 $1 Ford Model T, 1914 75 75
*697* A115 $1 Side view only 75 75
*698* A115 $2 Aston Martin DB3S, 1954 1.50 1.50
*699* A115 $2 Side view only 1.50 1.50
*700* A115 $3 Chrysler Imperial CG, 1931 2.25 2.25
*701* A115 $3 Side view only 2.25 2.25
*Nos. 686-701 (16)* 12.48 12.48

Stamps of same denomination printed se-tenant vert.

Christmas 1984 — A122

**Wmk. 380**

**1984, Oct. 31 Litho. *Perf. 14***

*702* A122 10c Wine glass 7 7
*703* A122 35c Altar 28 28
*704* A122 65c Creche 55 55
*705* A122 $3 Holy family, abstract 2.50 2.50
*a* Souv. sheet of 4, #702-705 3.50 3.50

No. 705a has multicolored decorative margin. Size: 148x78mm.

Abolition of Slavery, 150th Anniv. — A123

Engraving details, Natl. Archives, Castries: 10c, Preparing manioc. 35c, Working with cassava flour. 55c, Cooking, twisting and drying tobacco. $5, Tobacco production, diff.

**1984, Dec. 12 Litho. *Perf. 14***

*706* A123 10c brt buff & blk 8 8
*707* A123 35c brt buff & blk 25 25
*708* A123 55c brt buff & blk 40 40
*709* A123 $5 brt buff & blk 3.50 3.50

**Souvenir Sheet**

*710* Sheet of 4 5.00 5.00
*a* A123 10c like No. 706 8 8
*b* A123 35c like No. 707 25 25
*c* A123 55c like No. 708 40 40
*d* A123 $5 like No. 709 3.50 3.50

Nos. 710a-710d printed se-tenant in continuous design. Size: 154x110mm.

Locomotives Type of 1983

**1985, Feb. 4 Unwmk. *Perf. 12½***

*711* A115 5c J.N.R. Class C-53, 1928, Japan 6 6
*712* A115 5c C-53, diff. 6 6
*713* A115 15c Heavy L, 1885, India 12 12
*714* A115 15c Heavy L, diff. 12 12
*715* A115 35c QGR Class B18¼, 1926, Australia 30 30
*716* A115 35c QGR, diff. 30 30
*717* A115 60c Owain Glyndwr, 1923, U.K. 50 50
*718* A115 60c Glyndwr, diff. 50 50
*719* A115 75c Lion, 1838, U.K. 65 65
*720* A115 75c Lion, diff. 65 65
*721* A115 $1 Coal Engine, 1873, U.K. 85 85
*722* A115 $1 Coal Engine, diff. 85 85
*723* A115 $2 No. 2238 Class Q6, 1921, U.K. 1.65 1.65
*724* A115 $2 Q6, diff. 1.65 1.65
*725* A115 $2.50 Class H, 1920, U.K. 2.00 2.00
*726* A115 $2.50 Class H, diff. 2.00 2.00
*Nos. 711-726 (16)* 12.26 12.26

Stamps of same denomination printed se-tenant.

Girl Guides, 75th Anniv. — A124

Butterflies — A125

**1985, Feb. 21 Wmk. 380 *Perf. 14***

*727* A124 10c multi 10 10
*728* A124 35c multi 30 30
*729* A124 65c multi 60 60
*730* A124 $3 multi 2.75 2.75

**1985, Feb. 28 Unwmk. *Perf. 12½***

*731* A125 15c Clossiana selene 10 10
*732* A125 15c Inachis io 10 10
*733* A125 40c Philaethria werneckei 35 35
*734* A125 40c Catagramma sorana 35 35
*735* A125 60c Kallima inachus 48 48
*736* A125 60c Hypanartia paullus 48 48
*737* A125 $2.25 Morpho rhetenor helena 1.75 1.75
*738* A125 $2.25 Ornithoptera meridionalis 1.75 1.75
*Nos. 731-738 (8)* 5.36 5.36

Stamps of same denomination printed se-tenant.

Locomotive Type of 1983

Designs: Automobiles

**1985, Mar. 29**

*739* A115 15c 1940 Hudson Eight, USA 12 12
*740* A115 15c Hudson, diff. 12 12
*741* A115 50c 1937 KdF, Germany 45 45
*742* A115 50c KdF, diff. 45 45
*743* A115 $1 1925 Kissel Goldbug, USA 90 90
*744* A115 $1 Goldbug, diff. 90 90
*745* A115 $1.50 1973 Ferrari 246GTS, Italy 1.25 1.25
*746* A115 $1.50 Ferrari, diff. 1.25 1.25
*Nos. 739-746 (8)* 5.44 5.44

Stamps of same denomination printed se-tenant.

Military Uniforms — A126

Designs: 5c, Grenadier, 70th Foot Regiment, c. 1775. 10c, Grenadier Company Officer, 14th Foot Regiment, 1780. 20c, Battalion Company Officer, 46th Foot Regiment, 1781. 25c, Officer, Royal Artillery Regiment, c. 1782. 30c, Officer, Royal Engineers Corps., 1782. 35c, Battalion Company Officer, 54th Foot Regiment, 1782. 45c, Grenadier Company Private, 14th Foot Regiment, 1782. 50c, Gunner, Royal Artillery Regiment, 1796. 65c, Battalion Company Private, 85th Foot Regiment, c. 1796. 75c, Battalion Company Private, 76th Foot Regiment, 1796. 90c, Battalion Company Private, 81st Foot Regiment, c. 1796. $1, Sergeant, 74th (Highland) Foot Regiment, 1796. $2.50, Private, Light Company, 93rd Foot Regiment, 1803. $5, Battalion Company Private, 1st West India Regiment, 1803. $15, Officer, Royal Artillery Regiment, 1850.

**1985, May 7 Wmk. 380 *Perf. 15***

*747* A126 5c multi 5 5
*a.* Unwmkd. ('87) 5 5
*748* A126 10c multi 9 9
*a.* Unwmkd. ('87) 9 9
*749* A126 20c multi 18 18
*750* A126 25c multi 20 20
*a.* Wmk. 384 ('88) 25 25
*751* A126 30c multi 25 25
*a.* Unwmkd. ('87) 25 25
*752* A126 35c multi 28 28
*753* A126 45c multi 35 35
*a.* Unwmkd. ('87) 35 35
*754* A126 50c multi 40 40
*a.* Unwmkd. ('87) 40 40
*755* A126 65c multi 55 55
*756* A126 75c multi 65 65
*757* A126 90c multi 75 75
*758* A126 $1 multi 80 80
*759* A126 $2.50 multi 2.00 2.00
*a.* Unwmkd. ('87) 2.00 2.00
*760* A126 $5 multi 4.00 4.00
*a.* Unwmkd. ('87) 4.00 4.00
*761* A126 $15 multi 10.50 10.50
*Nos. 747-761 (15)* 21.05 21.05

Nos. 749-750 reissued inscribed 1986. Issue dates: Nos. 747a-748a, Feb. 24. Nos. 751a-760a, Mar. 16. Dated 1986.

See Nos. 876-879.

World War II Aircraft A127

**1985, May 30 Unwmk. *Perf. 12½***

*762* A127 5c Messerschmitt 109-E 5 5
*763* A127 5c 109-E, diff. 5 5
*764* A127 55c Avro 683 Lancaster Mark I Bomber 40 40
*765* A127 55c Mark I, diff. 40 40
*766* A127 60c North American P.51-D Mustang 42 42
*767* A127 60c Mustang, diff. 42 42
*768* A127 $2 Supermarine Spitfire Mark II 1.40 1.40
*769* A127 $2 Mark II, diff. 1.40 1.40
*Nos. 762-769 (8)* 4.54 4.54

Stamps of the same denomination printed se-tenant.

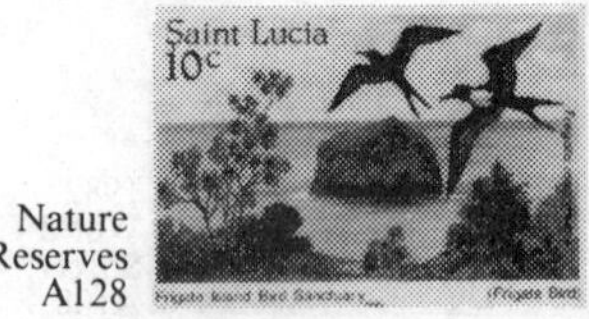


Nature Reserves A128

Birds in habitats: 10c, Frigate bird, Frigate Island Sanctuary. 35c, Mangrove cuckoo, Savannes Bay, Scorpion Island. 65c, Yellow sandpiper, Maria Island. $3, Audubon's shearwater, Lapins Island.

**1985, June 20 Wmk. 380 *Perf. 15***

*770* A128 10c multi 10 10
*771* A128 35c multi 30 30
*772* A128 65c multi 55 55
*773* A128 $3 multi 2.75 2.75

Locomotives Type of 1983

**1985, June 26 Unwmk. *Perf. 12½***

*774* A115 10c No. 28 Tender engine, 1897, U.K. 8 8
*775* A115 10c No. 28, diff. 8 8
*776* A115 30c No. 1621 Class M, 1893, U.K. 22 22
*777* A115 30c No. 1621, diff. 22 22
*778* A115 75c Class Dunalastair, 1896, U.K. 55 55
*779* A115 75c Dunalastair, diff. 55 55

*780* A115 $2.50 Big Bertha No. 2290, 1919, U.K. 1.75 1.75
*781* A115 $2.50 Bertha, diff. 1.75 1.75
*Nos. 774-781 (8)* 5.20 5.20

Stamps of same denomination printed se-tenant.

Queen Mother, 85th Birthday — A129

Intl. Youth Year — A130

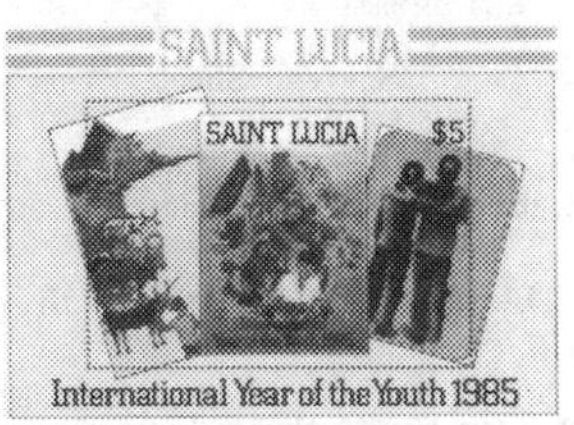


Abstracts, by Lyndon Samuel — A131

**1985, Aug. 16**

*782* A129 40c Facing right 30 30
*783* A129 40c Facing left 30 30
*784* A129 75c Facing right, diff. 55 55
*785* A129 75c Facing left, diff. 55 55
*786* A129 $1.10 Facing right, diff. 80 80
*787* A129 $1.10 Facing front 80 80
*788* A129 $1.75 Facing front, diff. 1.10 1.10
*789* A129 $1.75 Facing left, diff. 1.10 1.10
*Nos. 782-789 (8)* 5.50 5.50

**Souvenir Sheets**

*790* Sheet of 2 2.50 2.50
***a.-b*** A129 $2, any single 1.25 1.25
*790C* Sheet of 2 4.50 4.50
***e*** A129 $3 like No. 782 2.25 2.25
***f*** A129 $3 like No. 783 2.25 2.25
*790D* Sheet of 2 9.00 9.00
***g*** A129 $6 like No. 786 4.50 4.50
***h*** A129 $6 like No. 787 4.50 4.50

Stamps of same denomination printed se-tenant. No. 790 has multicolored margin picturing Broadlands House. Size: 86x115mm. Nos. 790C-790D have multicolored margins picturing Concorde jet, fauna and flora. Sizes: 142x110mm (No. 790C), 141x109mm (No. 790D).

**1985, Sept. 5 Wmk. 380 *Perf. 15***

Illustrations by local artists: 10c, Youth playing banjo, by Wayne Whitfield. 45c, Riding tricycle, by Mark D. Maragh. 75c, Youth against landscape, by Bartholemew Eugene. $3.50, Abstract, by Lyndon Samuel.

*791* A130 10c multi 10 10
*792* A130 45c multi 42 42
*793* A130 75c multi 75 75
*794* A130 $3.50 multi 3.00 3.00

**Souvenir Sheet**

*794A* A131 $5 multi 4.00 4.00

Intl. Youth Year. No. 794A has multicolored inscribed margin continuing the design. Size: 124x78mm.

Stamps of 1983-5 Ovptd. "CARIBBEAN ROYAL VISIT 1985" in Two or Three Lines.

**Wmk. as before**

**1985, Nov. *Perfs. as before***

*795* A124 35c No. 728 90 90
*796* A118 65c No. 647 1.75 1.75
*797* A120 65c No. 663 1.75 1.75
*798* A129 $1.10 No. 786 3.00 3.00
*799* A129 $1.10 No. 787 3.00 3.00
*800* A114 $2.50 No. 615 6.50 6.50
*801* A118 $2.50 No. 648 6.50 6.50
*802* A119 $2.50 No. 652 6.50 6.50
*Nos. 795-802 (8)* 29.90 29.90

Masquerade Figures — A132

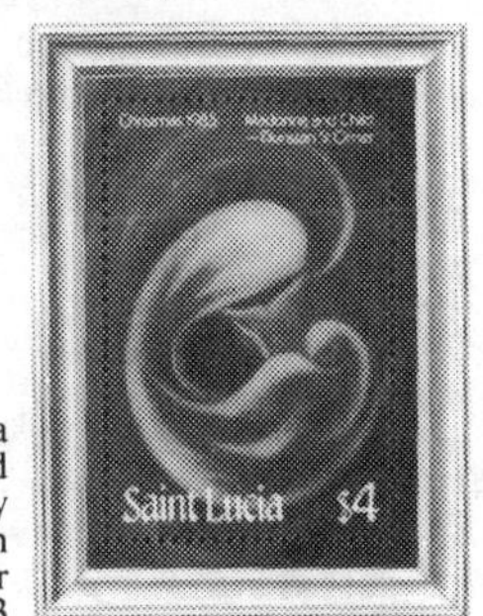


Madonna and Child, by Dunstan St. Omer A133

**Unwmk.**

**1985, Dec. 23 Litho. *Perf. 15***

*803* A132 10c Papa Jab 8 8
*804* A132 45c Paille Bananne 35 35
*805* A132 65c Cheval Bois 48 48

**Miniature Sheet**

*806* A133 $4 multi 3.00 3.00

Christmas 1985. No. 806 has multicolored margin continuing the design. Size: 70x83mm.

Locomotives Type of 1983

Designs: Nos. 807-808, 1983 MWCR Rack Loco Tip Top, US. Nos. 809-810, 1975 BR Class 87 Stephenson Bo-Bo, UK. Nos. 811-812, 1901 Class D No. 737, UK. Nos. 813-814, 1922 No. 13 2-Co-2, UK. Nos. 815-816, 1954 BR Class EM2 Electra Co-Co, UK. Nos. 817-818, 1922 City of Newcastle, UK. Nos. 819-820, 1930 DRG Von Kruckenberg, Propeller-driven Rail Car, Germany. Nos. 821-822, 1893 JNR No. 860, Japan.

**1986, Jan. 17 *Perf. 12½x13***

*807* A115 5c multi 5 5
*808* A115 5c multi, diff. 5 5
*809* A115 15c multi 10 10
*810* A115 15c multi, diff. 10 10
*811* A115 30c multi 20 20
*812* A115 30c multi, diff. 20 20
*813* A115 60c multi 40 40
*814* A115 60c multi, diff. 40 40
*815* A115 75c multi 48 48
*816* A115 75c multi, diff. 48 48
*817* A115 $1 multi 65 65
*818* A115 $1 multi, diff. 65 65
*819* A115 $2.25 multi 1.50 1.50
*820* A115 $2.25 multi, diff. 1.50 1.50
*821* A115 $3 multi 2.00 2.00
*822* A115 $3 multi, diff. 2.00 2.00
*Nos. 807-822 (16)* 10.76 10.76

Stamps of the same denomination printed se-tenant.

Miniature Sheets

Cook-out — A134

Designs: No. 823b, Scout sign. No. 824a, Wicker basket, weavings. No. 824b, Lady Olave Baden-Powell, Girl Guides founder.

**1986, Mar. 3 Litho. *Perf. 13x12½***

*823* Sheet of 2 5.50 5.50
***a.-b*** A134 $4, any single 2.75 2.75
*824* Sheet of 2 8.00 8.00
***a.-b*** A134 $6, any single 4.00 4.00

Scouting anniv., Girl Guides 75th anniv. Nos. 823-824 have buff or light ultramarine margins picturing scouting trefoil or Girl Guides emblem. Sizes: 85x113mm.

A135

Queen Elizabeth II, 60th Birthday — A136

Various photographs.

***Perf. 13x12½, 14x15 (A136), 12½x13 (#832)***

**1986**

*825* A135 5c Pink hat 5 5
*826* A136 10c Visiting Marian Home 7 7
*827* A136 45c Mindoo Phillip Park speech 30 30
*828* A136 50c Opening Leon Hess School 34 34
*829* A135 $1 Princess Elizabeth 65 65
*830* A135 $3.50 Blue hat 2.25 2.25
*831* A136 $5 Government House 3.25 3.25
*832* A135 $6 Canberra, 1982, vert. 3.75 3.75
*Nos. 825-832 (8)* 10.66 10.66

**Souvenir Sheets**

*833* A136 $7 HMY Britannia, Castries Harbor 4.50 4.50
*834* A135 $8 Straw hat 5.25 5.25

Issue dates: Nos. 825, 829-830, 832, Apr. 21. Nos. 826-828, 831, 833, June 14. No. 834 has multicolored margin picturing enlargement of stamp design. No. 833 shows another view of yacht. Sizes: 121x85mm, 85x115mm (#833).

State Visit of Pope John Paul II — A137

**1986, July 7 *Perf. 14x15, 15x14***

*835* A137 55c Kissing the ground 42 42
*836* A137 60c St. Joseph's Convent 45 45
*837* A137 80c Cathedral, Castries 60 60

**Souvenir Sheet**

*838* A137 $6 Pope 4.45 4.45

Nos. 837-838 vert. No. 838 has multicolored margin continuing the design. Size: 86x124mm.

Wedding of Prince Andrew and Sarah Ferguson — A138

**1986, July 23 *Perf. 12½***

*839* A138 80c Sarah, vert. 60 60
*840* A138 80c Andrew, vert. 60 60
*841* A138 $2 Couple 1.50 1.50
*842* A138 $2 Andrew, Nancy Reagan 1.50 1.50

Stamps of the same denomination printed se-tenant. Nos. 841-842 show Westminster Abbey in LR.

US Peace Corps in St. Lucia, 25th Anniv. A139

**1986, Sept. 25 Litho. *Perf. 14***

*843* A139 80c Technical instruction 60 60
*844* A139 $2 Pres. Kennedy, vert. 1.50 1.50
*845* A139 $3.50 Natl. crests, corps emblem 2.60 2.60

Wedding of Prince Andrew and Sarah Ferguson — A140

**1986, Oct. 15 *Perf. 15***

*846* A140 50c Andrew 38 38
*847* A140 80c Sarah 60 60
*848* A140 $1 At altar 75 75
*849* A140 $3 In open carriage 2.25 2.25

**Souvenir Sheet**

*849A* A140 $7 Andrew, Sarah 5.25 5.25

No. 849A has multicolored margin continuing the design, picturing royal family on Buckingham Palace balcony. Size: 115x85mm.

Locomotives Type of 1983

Designs: Automobiles

**1986, Oct. 23 Litho. *Perf. 12½x13***

*850* A115 20c 1969 AMC AMX, US 12 12
*851* A115 20c AMX, diff. 12 12
*852* A115 50c 1912 Russo-Baltique, Russia 30 30
*853* A115 50c Russo-Baltique, diff. 30 30
*854* A115 60c 1932 Lincoln KB, US 35 35
*855* A115 60c KB, diff. 35 35
*856* A115 $1 1933 Rolls Royce Phantom II Continental, UK 60 60
*857* A115 $1 Phantom II, diff. 60 60
*858* A115 $1.50 1939 Buick Century, US 90 90
*859* A115 $1.50 Century, diff. 90 90
*860* A115 $3 1957 Chrysler 300 C, US 1.75 1.75
*861* A115 $3 300 C, diff. 1.75 1.75
*Nos. 850-861 (12)* 8.04 8.04

Stamps of the same denomination printed se-tenant.

Chak-Chak Band A141

**1986, Nov. 7 *Perf. 15***

*862* A141 15c shown 12 12
*863* A141 45c Folk dancing 35 35
*864* A141 80c Steel band 60 60
*865* A141 $5 Limbo dancer 3.75 3.75

**Souvenir Sheet**

*866* A141 $10 Gros Islet 7.50 7.50

No. 866 has multicolored margin continuing the design picturing the local Friday night gathering. Size: 157x110mm.

Christmas A142

Churches: 10c, St. Ann Catholic, Mon Repos. 40c, St. Joseph the Worker Catholic, Gros Islet. 80c, Holy Trinity Anglican, Castries. $4, Our Lady of the Assumption Catholic, Soufriere, vert. $7, St. Lucy Catholic, Micoud.

**1986, Nov.**

*867* A142 10c multi 8 8
*868* A142 40c multi 30 30
*869* A142 80c multi 60 60
*870* A142 $4 multi 3.00 3.00

**Souvenir Sheet**

*871* A142 $7 multi 5.25 5.25

No. 871 has multicolored margin picturing church interior. Size: 120x101mm.

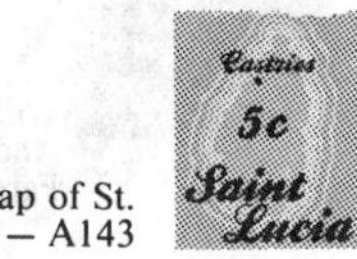


Map of St. Lucia — A143

***Perf. 14x14½***

**1987, Feb. 24 Litho. Wmk. 373**

*872* A143 5c beige & blk 5 5
*873* A143 10c pale yel grn & blk 8 8
*874* A143 45c org & blk 34 34
*875* A143 50c pale vio & blk 38 38

Nos. 872-873 exist inscribed "1988."

Uniforms Type of 1985

Designs: 15c, Battalion company private, 2nd West India Regiment, 1803. 60c, Battalion company officer, 5th Regiment of Foot, 1778. 80c, Battalion company officer, 27th (or Inniskilling) Regiment of Foot, c. 1780. $20, Grenadier company private, 46th Regiment of Foot, 1778.

**1987, Mar. 16 Wmk. 380 *Perf. 15***

*876* A126 15c multi 12 12
*a.* Wmk. 384 ('88) 12 12
*877* A126 60c multi 42 42
*a.* Wmk. 384 ('88) 42 42
*878* A126 80c multi 55 55
*a.* Wmk. 384 ('88) 55 55
*879* A126 $20 multi 13.75 13.75

Dated 1986.

A144

Statue of Liberty, Cent. — A145

**1987, Apr. 29 Wmk. 373 *Perf. 14½***

*880* A144 15c Statue, flags 12 12
*881* A144 80c Statue, ship 60 60
*882* A144 $1 Statue, Concorde jet 75 75
*883* A144 $5 Statue, flying boat 3.75 3.75

**Souvenir Sheet**

*884* A145 $6 Statue, New York City 4.50 4.50

No. 884 has inscribed multicolored margin continuing the design. Size: 107x88mm.

Maps, Surveying Instruments A147

**Wmk. 384**

**1987, Aug. 31 Litho. *Perf. 14***

*888* A147 15c 1775 12 12
*889* A147 60c 1814 45 45
*890* A147 $1 1888 75 75
*891* A147 $2.50 1987 1.90 1.90

First cadastral survey of St. Lucia.

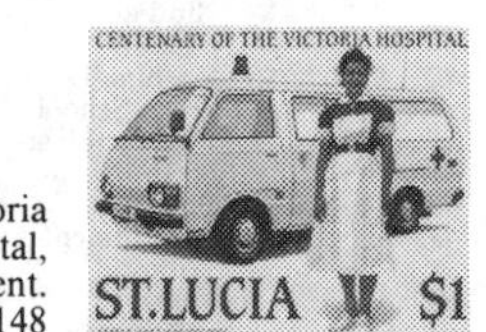


Victoria Hospital, Cent. A148

**Wmk. 384**

**1987, Nov. 4 Litho. *Perf. 14½***

*892* A148 $1 Ambulance, nurse, 1987 75 75
*893* A148 $1 Nurse, hammock, 1913 75 75
*894* A148 $2 Hospital, 1987 1.50 1.50
*895* A148 $2 Hospital, 1887 1.50 1.50

**Souvenir Sheet**

*896* A148 $4.50 Main gate, 1987 3.35 3.35

Stamps of the same denomination printed se-tenant. No. 896 has multicolored margin continuing the design. Size: 86x68mm.

Christmas A149

Paintings (details) by unidentified artists.

**1987, Nov. 30**

*897* A149 15c The Holy Family 12 12
*898* A149 50c Adoration of the Shepherds 38 38
*899* A149 60c Adoration of the Magi 45 45
*900* A149 90c Madonna and Child 68 68

**Souvenir Sheet**

*901* A149 $6 Holy Family 4.50 4.50

No. 901 has multicolored margin continuing the painting. Size: 82x67mm.

An enhanced introduction to the Scott Catalogue begins on Page V. A thorough understanding of the material presented there will greatly aid your use of the catalogue itself.

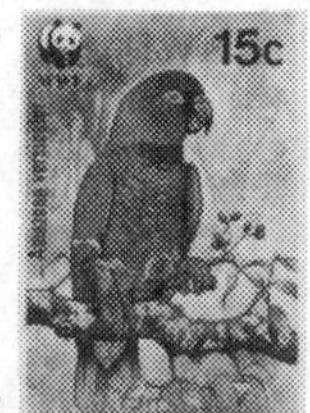


World Wildlife Fund — A150

Amazonian parrots, *Amazona versicolor.*

**Wmk. 384**

**1987, Dec. 18 Litho. *Perf. 14***

*902* A150 15c multi 12 12
*903* A150 35c multi, diff. 25 25
*904* A150 50c multi, diff. 38 38
*905* A150 $1 multi, diff. 75 75

American Indian Artifacts — A151

**Wmk. 384**

**1988, Feb. 12 Litho. *Perf. 14½***

*906* A151 25c Carib clay zemi 18 18
*907* A151 30c Troumassee cylinder 22 22
*908* A151 80c Three-pointer stone 60 60
*909* A151 $3.50 Dauphine petroglyph 2.60 2.60

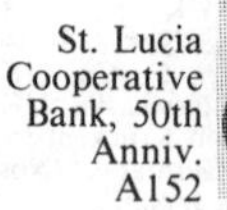

St. Lucia Cooperative Bank, 50th Anniv. A152

***Perf. 15x14***

**1988, Apr. 29 Litho. Wmk. 373**

*910* A152 10c Coins, banknotes 8 8
*911* A152 45c Branch in Castries 35 35
*912* A152 60c like 45c 45 45
*913* A152 80c Branch in Vieux Fort 60 60

Cable and Wireless in St. Lucia, 50th Anniv. A153

Designs: 15c, Rural telephone exchange. 25c, Antique and modern telephones. 80c, St. Lucia Teleport (satellite dish). $2.50, Map of Eastern Caribbean microwave communications system.

**Wmk. 384**

**1988, June 10 Litho. *Perf. 14***

*914* A153 15c multi 12 12
*915* A153 25c multi 18 18
*916* A153 80c multi 60 60
*917* A153 $2.50 multi 1.90 1.90

Cent. of the Methodist Church in St. Lucia — A154

**Wmk. 384**

**1988, Aug. 15 Litho. *Perf. 14½***

*918* A154 15c Altar, window 12 12
*919* A154 80c Chancel 60 60
*920* A154 $3.50 Exterior 2.60 2.60

Tourism — A155

Lagoon and: 10c, Tourists, gourmet meal. 30c, Beverage, tourists. 80c, Tropical fruit. $2.50, Fish and chef. $5.50, Market.

***Perf. 14x13½***

**1988, Sept. 15 Litho. Wmk. 384**

*921* A155 Strip of 4 2.75 2.75
*a.* 10c multi 8 8
*b.* 30c multi 22 22
*c.* 80c multi 60 60
*d.* $2.50 multi 1.85 1.85

**Souvenir Sheet**

*922* A155 $5.50 multi 4.00 4.00

No. 922 has multicolored margin continuing the design. Size: 88x104mm.

**Lloyds of London, 300th Anniv.**
Common Design Type

Designs: 10c, San Francisco earthquake, 1906. 60c, Castries Harbor, horiz. 80c, *Lady Nelson*, sunk off Castries Harbor, 1942, horiz. $2.50, Castries on fire, 1948.

**Wmk. 373**

**1988, Oct. 17 Litho. *Perf. 14***

*923* CD341 10c multi 8 8
*924* CD341 60c multi 45 45
*925* CD341 80c multi 60 60
*926* CD341 $2.50 multi 1.85 1.85

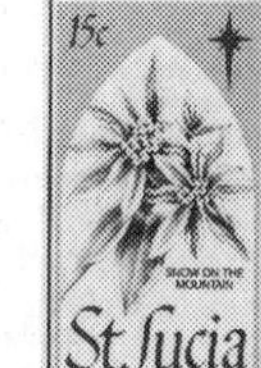


Christmas — A156

Flowers.

***Perf. 14½x14***

**1988, Nov. 22 Litho. Wmk. 384**

*927* A156 15c Snow on the mountain 12 12
*928* A156 45c Christmas candle 35 35
*929* A156 60c Balisier 45 45
*930* A156 80c Poinsettia 60 60

**Souvenir Sheet**

*931* A156 $5.50 Flower arrangement 4.00 4.00

No. 931 has multicolored inscribed margin continuing the design.

---

**AIR POST STAMP**

**Catalogue values for unused stamps in this section, from this point to the end of the section, are for Never Hinged items.**

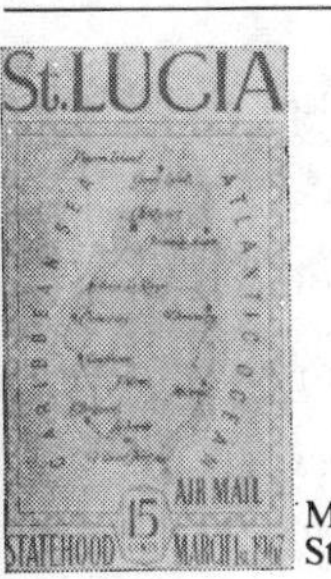

Map of St. Lucia – AP1

*Perf. 14½x14*

**1967, Mar. 1 Photo. Unwmk.**
*C1* AP1 15c blue 30 30

St. Lucia's independence.
Exists imperf. and also in souvenir sheet.

## POSTAGE DUE STAMPS

D1

D2

Type I. "No." 3mm wide (shown).
Type II. "No." 4mm wide.

*Rough Perf. 12*

**1931 Unwmk. Typeset**
*J1* D1 1p blk, *gray bl*, type I 3.00 3.50
*a.* Type II 7.50 8.00
*J2* D1 2p blk, *yel*, type I 4.00 6.00
*a.* Type II 15.00 16.00
*b.* Vertical pair, imperf. btwn. *4,000.*

The serial numbers are handstamped. Type II has round "o" and period. Type I has tall "o" and square period.

**Catalogue values for unused stamps in this section, from this point to the end of the section, are for Never Hinged items.**

**1933-47 Typo. Wmk. 4 *Perf. 14***
*J3* D2 1p black 1.50 *3.00*
*J4* D2 2p black 3.00 *5.00*
*J5* D2 4p black ('47) 2.50 *6.25*
*J6* D2 8p black ('47) 3.00 *7.50*

Values in Cents

**1950**
*J7* D2 2c black 25 25
*a.* Wmk. 4a (error) 30.00
*J8* D2 4c black 50 50
*a.* Wmk. 4a (error) 35.00
*J9* D2 8c black 1.00 1.00
*a.* Wmk. 4a (error) 67.50
*J10* D2 16c black 1.75 1.75
*a.* Wmk. 4a (error) 82.50

**1965 Wmk. 314 Typo. *Perf. 14***
*J11* D2 2c black 1.00 *3.00*
*J12* D2 4c black 1.25 *5.00*

In the 2c center the "c" is heavier and the period bigger.
Nos. J9-J12 exist with overprint "Statehood/1st Mar. '67" in red.

Arms of St. Lucia – D3

**1981, Aug. 4 Litho. Wmk. 373**
*J13* D3 5c red brown 5 5
*J14* D3 15c green 8 8
*J15* D3 25c deep orange 14 14
*J16* D3 $1 dark blue 55 55

## WAR TAX STAMPS

No. 65 Overprinted WAR TAX

**1916 Wmk. 3 *Perf. 14***
*MR1* A11 1p scarlet 3.50 5.00
*a.* Double overprint 400.00 *450.00*
*b.* 1p carmine 27.50 30.00

Overprinted WAR TAX

*MR2* A11 1p scarlet 20 20

## OFFICIAL STAMPS

**Catalogue values for unused stamps in this section, from this point to the end of the section, are for Never Hinged items.**

Nos. 504-515 Overprinted "OFFICIAL"
**Wmk. 373**

**1983, Oct. 13 Litho. *Perf. 14½***
*O1* A95 5c multi 5 5
*O2* A95 10c multi 8 8
*O3* A95 15c multi 12 12
*O4* A95 20c multi 15 15
*O5* A95 25c multi 20 20
*O6* A95 30c multi 25 25
*O7* A95 50c multi 40 40
*O8* A95 75c multi 60 60
*O9* A95 $1 multi 75 75
*O10* A95 $2 multi 1.50 1.50
*O11* A95 $5 multi 3.75 3.75
*O12* A95 $10 multi 7.50 7.50
*Nos. O1-O12 (12)* 15.35 15.35

Nos. 747-761 Ovptd. "OFFICIAL."

**1985, May 7 Litho. *Perf. 15***
*O13* A126 5c multi 5 5
*O14* A126 10c multi 7 7
*O15* A126 20c multi 12 12
*O16* A126 25c multi 15 15
*O17* A126 30c multi 18 18
*O18* A126 35c multi 20 20
*O19* A126 45c multi 28 28
*O20* A126 50c multi 30 30
*O21* A126 65c multi 40 40
*O22* A126 75c multi 45 45
*O23* A126 90c multi 55 55
*O24* A126 $1 multi 60 60
*O25* A126 $2.50 multi 1.50 1.50
*O26* A126 $5 multi 3.00 3.00
*O27* A126 $15 multi 7.50 7.50
*Nos. O13-O27 (15)* 15.35 15.35

# ST. VINCENT

LOCATION – An island in the West Indies.
GOVT. – Independent state in the British Commonwealth.
AREA – 150 sq. mi.
POP. – 123,000 (est. 1984).
CAPITAL – Kingstown.

The British colony of St. Vincent became an associated state in 1969 and independent in 1979.

12 Pence = 1 Shilling
20 Shillings = 1 Pound
100 Cents = 1 Dollar (1949)

**Catalogue values for unused stamps in this country are for Never Hinged items, beginning with Scott 152 in the regular postage section, Scott B1 in the semi-postal section, and Scott O1 in the officials section.**

Queen Victoria – A1

Wmk. 5- Small Star

*Clean-Cut Perf. 14 to 16*

**1861 Engr. Unwmk.**
*1* A1 1p rose *7,500.* 500.00
*a* Imperf., (pair) 375.00
*1B* A1 6p yel grn *9,000.* 300.00

**1862-66 *Rough Perf. 14 to 16***
*2* A1 1p rose 22.50 10.00
*a* Horiz. pair, imperf. vert. 500.00
*3* A1 6p dk grn 60.00 14.00
*a* Imperf., (pair) 600.00
*b* Horiz. pair, imperf. between 1,500.
*4* A1 1sh slate ('66) 250.00 100.00

**1863-69 *Perf. 11 to 13.***
*5* A1 1p rose 22.50 14.00
*6* A1 4p bl ('66) 250.00 100.00
*a* Imperf. vert., pair
*7* A1 4p org ('69) 250.00 100.00
*8* A1 6p dp grn 200.00 50.00
*8A* A1 1sh sl ('66) *3,000.* 1,500.
*9* A1 1sh ind ('69) 275.00 80.00
*10* A1 1sh brn ('69) 425.00 150.00

***Perf. 11 to 13x14 to 16***
*11* A1 1p rose *4,000.* 1,500.
*12* A1 1sh sl ('66) 200.00 90.00

**Wmk. Small Star. (5)**

**1871-78 *Rough Perf. 14 to 16.***
*13* A1 1p black 20.00 11.00
*a* Vert. pair, imperf. between *6,000.*
*14* A1 6p dk bl grn 300.00 85.00

***Clean-Cut Perf. 14 to 16***
*14A* A1 1p black 27.50 11.00
*14B* A1 6p bl grn 550.00 37.50
*c* 6p dl bl grn 550.00 37.50
*15* A1 6p pale yel grn ('78) 400.00 37.50
*15A* A1 1sh ver ('77) *15,000.*

***Perf. 11 to 13.***
*16* A1 4p dk bl ('77) 300.00 90.00
*17* A1 1sh dp rose ('72) 750.00 110.00
*18* A1 1sh cl ('75) 750.00 200.00

***Perf. 11 to 13x14 to 16***
*20* A1 1p black 40.00 9.00
*a* Horizontal pair, imperf. between *4,000.*
*21* A1 6p pale yel grn ('77) 400.00 50.00
*22* A1 1sh lil rose ('72) 6,000. 400.00
*23* A1 1sh ver ('77) 400.00 110.00
*a* Imperf. vertically (pair)

Victoria A2

Seal of Colony A3

**1880-81 *Perf. 11 to 13***
*24* A2 ½p org ('81) 5.00 3.50
*25* A1 1p gray grn 95.00 6.50
*26* A1 1p db ('81) 750.00 14.00
*27* A1 4p ultra ('81) 1,000. 70.00
*a* Horizontal pair, imperf. between
*28* A1 6p yel grn 450.00 45.00
*28A* A1 1sh vermilion 650.00 50.00
*29* A3 5sh rose 900.00 900.00

See No. 598.

No. 14B Bisected and Surcharged in Red d. 1

**1880 *Perf. 14 to 16.***
*30* A1 1p on half of 6p bl grn 500.00 300.00
*a* Unsevered pair 1,750. 1,000.

No. 28 Bisected and Surcharged in Red d ½

**1881**
*31* A1 ½p on half of 6p yel grn ('81) 100.00 100.00
*a* Unsevered pair 225.00 225.00
*b* "1" with straight top 900.00
*c* Without fraction bar, pair, #31, 31c 5,000. *6,000.*
*d* Pair, one without surcharge

Nos. 28 and 28A Surcharged in Black:

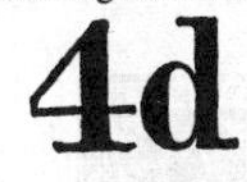

c d

**1881 *Perf. 11 to 13.***
*32* A1 (c) 1p on 6p yel grn 400.00 300.00
*33* A1 (d) 4p on 1sh ver 1,000. 800.00

**1883-84 Wmk. 2 *Perf. 12***
*35* A2 ½p grn ('84) 25.00 20.00
*36* A1 4p ultra 350.00 10.00
*37* A1 4p dl bl ('84) 1,250. 300.00
*38* A1 6p yel grn 300.00 250.00
*39* A1 1sh org ver 37.50 30.00
*a* Imperf., pair

The ½p orange, 1p rose red, 1p milky blue and 5sh carmine lake were never placed in use. Some authorities believe them to be color trials. Values: ½p orange, $2500; 1p rose red, $2500; 1p milky blue, $3750; 5sh $5000.

Nos. 35-60 may be found watermarked with single straight line. This is from the frame which encloses each group of 60 watermark designs.

Type of A1 Surcharged in Black
2½ PENCE
e

**1883 *Perf. 14.***
*40* A1 2½p on 1p lake 6.25 1.75

**1883-97**
*41* A2 ½p grn ('85) 50 50
*42* A1 1p db 17.50 2.75
*43* A1 1p rose red ('85) 75 35
*44* A1 1p pink ('86) 14.00 4.00
*45* A1 2½p brt bl ('97) 1.25 1.75
*46* A1 4p ultra 350.00 20.00
*47* A1 4p red brn ('85) 900.00 20.00
*48* A1 4p lake brn ('86) 15.00 2.50
*a* 4p pur brn 15.00 2.50
*49* A1 4p yel ('93) 1.00 2.50
*a* 4p ol yel 350.00 350.00
*50* A1 5p gray brn ('97) 5.00 *10.00*
*a* 5p blk brn 5.00 *10.00*
*51* A1 6p vio ('88) 100.00 *200.00*
*52* A1 6p red vio ('91) 1.25 2.50
*53* A1 1sh org ver ('91) 5.00 7.50
*54* A3 5sh car lake ('88) 15.00 *22.50*
*a* 5sh brn lake 20.00 25.00

No. 40 Resurcharged in Black 1d

**1885**
*55* A1 1p on 2½p on 1p lake 5.00 5.00

Stamps of Type A1 Surcharged in Black or Violet:

2½d. 5 PENCE
g h
j FIVE PENCE

**1890-91**
56 A1 (e) 2½p on 1p brt bl 50 35
a 2½p on 1p mlky bl 7.00 2.50
b 2½p on 1p gray bl 7.00 1.75
57 A1 (g) 2½p on 4p vio brn ('90) 80.00 80.00
a Without fraction bar 200.00 225.00

**1892-93**
58 A1 (h) 5p on 4p lake brn (V) 9.00 10.00
59 A1 (j) 5p on 6p dp lake ('93) 1.00 1.40
a 5p on 6p car lake 6.50 7.00
b Dbl. surcharge 5,000.

**1897**
60 A1 (j) 3p on 1p lil 2.75 3.75

Victoria A13 — Edward VII A14

Numerals of 1sh and 5sh, type A13, and of 2p, 1sh, 5sh and £1, type A14, are in color on plain tablet.

**1898** **Typo.** ***Perf. 14***
62 A13 ½p lil & grn 85 45
63 A13 1p lil & car rose 2.25 30
64 A13 2½p lil & ultra 3.50 1.40
65 A13 3p lil & ol grn 2.25 3.50
66 A13 4p lil & org 2.25 4.25
67 A13 5p lil & blk 4.25 6.50
68 A13 6p lil & brn 11.00 14.00
69 A13 1sh grn & car rose 14.00 21.00
70 A13 5sh grn & ultra 50.00 65.00
*Nos. 62-70 (9)* 90.35 116.40

**1902**
71 A14 ½p vio & grn 55 50
72 A14 1p vio & car rose 1.10 16
73 A14 2p vio & blk 1.75 2.25
74 A14 2½p vio & ultra 4.25 2.75
75 A14 3p vio & ol grn 4.25 2.25
76 A14 6p vio & brn 7.50 12.00
77 A14 1sh grn & car rose 11.00 17.50
78 A14 2sh grn & vio 20.00 27.50
79 A14 5sh grn & ultra 35.00 42.50
*Nos. 71-79 (9)* 85.40 107.41

**1904-11** **Wmk. 3**
**Chalky Paper**
82 A14 ½p vio & grn ('05) 1.00 40
83 A14 1p vio & car rose 4.00 35
84 A14 2½p vio & ultra ('06) 6.25 12.00
85 A14 6p vio & brn ('05) 10.00 15.00
86 A14 1sh grn & car rose ('08) 7.50 12.00
87 A14 2sh vio & bl, *bl* ('09) 21.00 32.50
88 A14 5sh grn & red, *yel* ('09) 21.00 40.00
89 A14 £1 vio & blk, *red* ('11) 275.00 250.00
*Nos. 82-88 (7)* 70.75 112.25

Nos. 82, 83 and 86 also exist on ordinary paper.

"Peace and Justice"
A15 A16

**1907** **Engr.**
**Ordinary Paper.**
90 A15 ½p yel grn 60 60
91 A15 1p carmine 1.50 50
92 A15 2p orange 1.25 2.50
93 A15 2½p ultra 4.25 6.00
94 A15 3p dk vio 4.25 9.00
*Nos. 90-94 (5)* 11.85 18.60

**1909**
**Without Dot under "d"**
95 A16 1p carmine 1.25 35
96 A16 6p red vio 7.00 14.00
97 A16 1sh blk, *green* 3.50 4.75

**1909-11**
**With Dot under "d"**
98 A16 ½p yel grn ('10) 20 20
99 A16 1p carmine 40 12
100 A16 2p gray ('11) 1.50 2.25
101 A16 2½p ultra 1.25 1.40
102 A16 3p vio, *yel* 65 1.40
103 A16 6p red vio 2.25 4.50
*Nos. 98-103 (6)* 6.25 9.87

King George V — A17

**1913-14** ***Perf. 14***
104 A17 ½p gray grn 20 20
105 A17 1p carmine 20 14
106 A17 2p gray 1.25 1.50
107 A17 2½p ultra 50 50
108 A17 3p vio, *yel* 1.00 2.50
109 A17 4p red, *yel* 65 1.50
110 A17 5p ol grn 2.00 6.50
111 A17 6p claret 1.25 2.50
112 A17 1sh *green* 1.50 2.50
113 A17 1sh bis ('14) 2.50 5.00
114 A16 2sh vio & ultra 7.00 15.00
115 A16 5sh dk grn & car 15.00 25.00
116 A16 £1 blk & vio 80.00 125.00
*Nos. 104-116 (13)* 113.05 187.84

No. 112 Surcharged in Carmine

**ONE**
**PENNY.**

**1915**
117 A17 1p on 1sh blk, *grn* 2.00 2.75
a "PENNY" & bar double 900.00
b Without period 14.00
c "ONE" omitted 900.00
d "ONE" double 900.00

Space between surcharge lines varies from 8 to 10mm.

**1921-32** **Wmk. 4**
118 A17 ½p green 8 8
119 A17 1p rose red 12 8
120 A17 1½p yel brn ('32) 80 18
121 A17 2p gray 22 18
122 A17 2½p ultra ('26) 55 45
123 A17 3p ultra 2.25 4.50
124 A17 3p vio, *yel* ('27) 45 1.40
125 A17 4p red, *yel* ('30) 1.50 4.50
126 A17 5p ol grn 45 2.25
127 A17 6p cl ('27) 55 2.25
128 A17 1sh bister 1.00 2.75
129 A16 2sh brn vio & ultra 4.50 7.50
130 A16 5sh dk grn & car 11.25 22.50
131 A16 £1 blk & vio ('28) 90.00 150.00
*Nos. 118-131 (14)* 113.72 198.62

**Silver Jubilee Issue**
Common Design Type
**1935, May 6** ***Perf. 11x12***
134 CD301 1p car & dk bl 25 25
135 CD301 1½p gray blk & ultra 25 25
136 CD301 2½p ultra & brn 75 75
137 CD301 1sh brn vio & ind 2.25 2.25

**Coronation Issue**
Common Design Type
**1937, May 12** ***Perf. 11x11½***
138 CD302 1p dk pur 10 10
139 CD302 1½p dk car 16 16
140 CD302 2½p dp ultra 40 40

Seal of the Colony — A18

Young's Island and Fort Duvernette — A19

*St. Vincent stamps can be mounted in Scott's annually supplemented British Windward Islands Album.*

Kingstown and Fort Charlotte — A20

Villa Beach — A21

Victoria Park, Kingstown — A22

**1938-47** **Wmk. 4** ***Perf. 12***
141 A18 ½p grn & brt bl 5 5
142 A19 1p cl & bl 7 7
143 A20 1½p scar & lt grn 10 10
144 A18 2p blk & grn 12 12
145 A21 2½p pck bl & ind 12 12
145A A22 2½p choc & grn ('47) 20 20
146 A18 3p dk vio & org 12 12
146A A21 3½p dp bl grn & ind ('47) 60 50
147 A18 6p cl & blk 25 25
148 A22 1sh grn & vio 45 45
149 A18 2sh dk vio & brt bl 85 85
149A A18 2sh6p dp bl & org brn ('47) 1.75 1.75
150 A18 5sh dk grn & car 4.00 2.50
150A A18 10sh choc & dp vio ('47) 5.00 9.00
151 A18 £1 blk & vio 10.00 12.00
*Nos. 141-151 (15)* 23.68 28.08

See Nos. 156-169, 180-184.

**Catalogue values for unused stamps in this section, from this point to the end of the section, are for Never Hinged items.**

**Peace Issue**
Common Design Type
**1946, Oct. 15** **Engr.** ***Perf. 13½x14***
152 CD303 1½p carmine 20 20
153 CD303 3½p dp bl 30 30

**Silver Wedding Issue**
Common Design Types
**1948, Nov. 30** **Photo.** ***Perf. 14x14½***
154 CD304 1½p scarlet 15 15

**Engraved; Name Typographed**
***Perf. 11½x11.***
155 CD305 £1 red vio 25.00 35.00

Types of 1938
**1949, Mar. 26** **Engr.** ***Perf. 12***
156 A18 1c grn & brt bl 7 5
157 A19 2c cl & bl 10 8
158 A20 3c scar & lt grn 32 24
159 A18 4c gray blk & grn 15 12
160 A22 5c choc & grn 16 15
161 A18 6c dk vio & org 16 15
162 A21 7c pck bl & ind 52 35
163 A18 12c cl & blk 48 32
164 A22 24c grn & vio 80 80
165 A18 48c dk vio & brt bl 1.60 1.60
166 A18 60c dp bl & org brn 1.75 1.75
167 A18 $1.20 dk grn & car 4.75 4.75
168 A18 $2.40 choc & dp vio 6.00 6.00
169 A18 $4.80 gray blk & vio 10.00 10.00
*Nos. 156-169 (14)* 26.86 26.36

**UPU Issue**
Common Design Types
**Engr.; Name Typo. on 6c, 12c**
***Perf. 13½, 11x11½***
**1949, Oct. 10** **Wmk. 4**
170 CD306 5c blue 25 25
171 CD307 6c dp rose vio 28 28
172 CD308 12c red lil 65 65
173 CD309 24c bl grn 1.40 1.40

**University Issue**
Common Design Types
**1951, Feb. 16** **Engr.** ***Perf. 14x14½***
174 CD310 3c red & bl grn 25 25
175 CD311 12c rose lil & blk 75 75

Nos. 158-160 and 163 Overprinted in Black

**NEW**
**CONSTITUTION**
**1951**

**1951, Sept. 21** ***Perf. 12***
176 A20 3c scar & lt grn 20 20
177 A18 4c gray blk & grn 20 20
178 A22 5c choc & grn 20 20
179 A18 12c cl & blk 35 35

Adoption of a new constitution for the Windward Islands, 1951.

Type of 1938-47
**1952**
180 A18 1c gray blk & grn 5 5
181 A18 3c dk vio & org 14 14
182 A18 4c grn & brt bl 14 14
183 A20 6c scar & dp grn 16 16
184 A21 10c pck bl & ind 28 28
*Nos. 180-184 (5)* 77 77

**Coronation Issue**
Common Design Type
**1953, June 2** ***Perf. 13½x13***
185 CD312 4c dk grn & blk 1.00 1.00

Elizabeth II — A23

Seal of Colony — A24

***Perf. 13x14***
**1955, Sept. 16** **Wmk. 4** **Engr.**
186 A23 1c orange 7 6
187 A23 2c vio bl 14 12
188 A23 3c gray 14 12
189 A23 4c dk red brn 18 16
190 A23 5c scarlet 25 20
191 A23 10c purple 38 35
192 A23 15c dp bl 38 35
193 A23 20c green 65 60
194 A23 25c brn blk 1.25 1.00

***Perf. 14***
195 A24 50c chocolate 2.25 2.00
196 A24 $1 dl grn 6.50 6.00
197 A24 $2.50 dp bl 22.50 15.00
*Nos. 186-197 (12)* 34.69 25.96

**West Indies Federation**
Common Design Type
***Perf. 11½x11***
**1958, Apr. 22** **Wmk. 314**
198 CD313 3c green 30 28
199 CD313 6c blue 50 50
200 CD313 12c car rose 1.00 1.00

**Freedom from Hunger Issue**
Common Design Type
**1963, June 4** **Photo.** ***Perf. 14x14½***
201 CD314 8c lilac 2.50 1.75

**Red Cross Centenary Issue**
Common Design Type
**1963, Sept. 2** **Litho.** ***Perf. 13***
202 CD315 4c blk & red 1.00 50
203 CD315 8c ultra & red 2.00 1.50

**Types of 1955**
***Perf. 13x14***
**1964-65** **Wmk. 314** **Engr.**
205 A23 1c orange 10 10
206 A23 2c vio bl 20 20
207 A23 3c gray 65 50
208 A23 5c scarlet 40 38
209 A23 10c purple 55 42
a Perf. 12½ 42 35
210 A23 15c dp bl 1.00 75
a Perf. 12½ 95 75
211 A23 20c green 85 65
a Perf. 12½ 21.00 8.75
212 A23 25c brn blk 1.50 1.25
a Perf. 12½ 2.25 2.25

***Perf. 14***
213 A24 50c choc ('65) 6.25 5.25
a Perf. 12½ 4.25 4.25
*Nos. 205-213 (9)* 11.50 9.50
*Nos. 209a-213a (5)* 28.87 16.35

Scout Emblem and Merit Badges — A25

**1964, Nov. 23 Litho. *Perf. 14***

*216* A25 1c dk brn & brt yel grn 5 5
*217* A25 4c dk red brn & brt bl 18 10
*218* A25 20c dk vio & org 50 30
*219* A25 50c grn & red 1.25 60

Issued to commemorate the 50th anniversary of the Boy Scouts of St. Vincent.

Breadfruit and Capt. Bligh's Ship "Providence" A26

Designs: 1c, Tropical fruit. 25c, Doric temple and pond (vert.). 40c, Blooming talipot palm and Doric temple (vert.).

***Perf. 14½x13½, 13½x14½***

**1965, Mar. 23 Photo. Wmk. 314**

*220* A26 1c dk grn & multi 5 5
*221* A26 4c lt & dk brn grn & yel 18 10
*222* A26 25c bl, grn & bis 60 40
*223* A26 40c dk bl & multi 1.00 60

Bicentenary of the Botanic Gardens.

**ITU Issue**
Common Design Type

**1965, May 17 Litho. *Perf. 11x11½***

*224* CD317 4c bl & yel grn 30 15
*225* CD317 48c yel & org 3.50 2.50

Boat Building, Bequia A27

Woman Carrying Bananas — A28

Designs: 2c, Friendship Beach, Bequia. 3c, Terminal building. 5c, Crater Lake. 6c, Rock carvings, Carib Stone. 8c, Arrowroot. 10c, Owia saltpond. 12c, Ship at deep water wharf. 20c, Sea Island cotton. 25c, Map of St. Vincent and neighboring islands. 50c, Breadfruit. $1, Baleine Falls. $2.50, St. Vincent parrot. $5, Coat of arms.

***Perf. 14x13½, 13½x14***

**1965-67 Photo. Wmk. 314**

*226* A27 1c multi (BEOUIA) 8 6
*226A* A27 1c multi (BEQUIA) ('67) 18 18
*227* A27 2c lt ultra, grn, yel & red 6 5
*228* A27 3c red, yel & brn 9 6
*229* A28 4c brn, ultra & yel 75 55
a. Wmkd. sideways 55 38
*230* A27 5c pur, bl, yel & grn 15 12
*231* A28 6c sl grn, yel & gray 18 15
*232* A28 8c pur, yel & grn 25 22
*233* A27 10c org brn, yel & bluish grn 30 25
*234* A27 12c grnsh bl, yel & pink 35 35
*235* A28 20c brt yel, grn, pur & brn 45 38
*236* A28 25c ultra, grn & vio bl 55 48
*237* A28 50c grn, yel & bl 1.10 85
*238* A28 $1 vio bl, lt grn & dk sl grn 3.00 2.25
*239* A28 $2.50 pale lil & multi 7.50 6.00
*240* A28 $5 dl vio bl & multi 15.00 11.00
*Nos. 226-240 (16)* 29.99 22.95

Issue date for original set: Aug. 16, 1965. No. 226A, Aug. 8, 1967.

**Churchill Memorial Issue**
Common Design Type

**1966, Jan. 24 *Perf. 14***
**Design in Black, Gold and Carmine Rose**

*241* CD319 1c brt bl 7 7
*242* CD319 4c green 35 35
*243* CD319 20c brown 2.00 1.40
*244* CD319 40c violet 4.50 3.00

**Royal Visit Issue**
Common Design Type

**1966, Feb. 4 Litho. *Perf. 11x12***
**Portrait in Black**

*245* CD320 4c vio bl 55 38
*246* CD320 25c dk car rose 6.00 3.75

**WHO Headquarters Issue**
Common Design Type

**1966, Sept. 20 Litho. *Perf. 14***

*247* CD322 4c multi 35 25
*248* CD322 25c multi 2.75 1.75

**UNESCO Anniversary Issue**
Common Design Type

**1966, Dec. 1 Litho. *Perf. 14***

*249* CD323 4c "Education" 25 18
*250* CD323 8c "Science" 50 40
*251* CD323 25c "Culture" 3.00 2.00

View of Mt. Coke Area A29

Designs: 8c, Kingstown Methodist Church. 25c, First license to perform marriage, May 15, 1867. 35c, Arms of Conference of the Methodist Church in the Caribbean and the Americas.

***Perf. 14x14½***

**1967, Dec. 1 Photo. Wmk. 314**

*252* A29 2c multi 5 5
*253* A29 8c multi 15 10
*254* A29 25c multi 50 30
*255* A29 35c multi 60 40

Issued to commemorate the attainment of autonomy by the Methodist Church in the Caribbean and the Americas, and to commemorate the opening of headquarters near St. John's, Antigua, May 1967.

Caribbean Meteorological Institute, Barbados — A30

***Perf. 14x14½***

**1968, June 28 Photo. Wmk. 314**

*256* A30 4c cer & multi 10 6
*257* A30 25c ver & multi 35 25
*258* A30 35c vio bl & multi 50 35

Issued for World Meteorological Day.

Martin Luther King, Jr. and Cotton Pickers A31

***Perf. 13½x13***

**1968, Aug. 28 Litho. Wmk. 314**

*259* A31 5c vio & multi 8 8
*260* A31 25c gray & multi 40 35
*261* A31 35c brn red & multi 50 40

Dr. Martin Luther King, Jr. (1929-68), American civil rights leader.

Scales of Justice and Human Rights Flame — A32

Carnival Costume — A33

Design: 3c, Speaker addressing demonstrators (horiz.).

***Perf. 13x14, 14x13***

**1968, Nov. 1 Photo. Unwmk.**

*262* A32 3c org & multi 6 5
*263* A32 35c grnsh bl & vio bl 50 35

International Human Rights Year.

**1969, Feb. 17 Litho. *Perf. 14½***

Designs: 5c, Sketch of a steel bandsman. 8c, Revelers (horiz.). 25c, Queen of Bands and attendants.

*264* A33 1c multi 6 5
*265* A33 5c red & dk brn 15 10
*266* A33 8c multi 25 18
*267* A33 25c multi 75 50

St. Vincent Carnival celebration, Feb. 17.

Nos. 252-253, 236 and 255 Overprinted: "METHODIST / CONFERENCE / MAY / 1969"

***Perf. 14x14½, 13½x14***

**1969, May 14 Photo. Wmk. 314**

*268* A29 2c multi 12 10
*269* A29 8c multi 28 16
*270* A28 25c ultra, grn & vio bl 50 40
*271* A29 35c multi 10.00 10.00

Issued to commemorate the 1st Caribbean Methodist Conference held outside Antigua.

"Strength in Unity" — A34

Designs: 5c, 25c, Map of the Caribbean (vert.).

***Perf. 13½x13, 13x13½***

**1969, July 1 Litho.**

*272* A34 2c org, yel & blk 6 6
*273* A34 5c lil & multi 10 8
*274* A34 8c emer, yel & blk 22 18
*275* A34 25c bl & multi 90 50

1st anniv. of CARIFTA (Caribbean Free Trade Area.)

Flag and Arms of St. Vincent — A35

Designs: 10c, Uprising of 1795. 50c, Government House.

***Perf. 14x14½***

**1969, Oct. 27 Photo. Wmk. 314**

*276* A35 4c dp ultra & multi 10 7
*277* A35 10c ol & multi 20 18
*278* A35 50c org, gray & blk 75 60

Green Heron A36

Birds: ½c, House wren (vert.). 2c, Bullfinches. 3c, St. Vincent parrots. 4c, St. Vincent solitaire (vert.). 5c, Scalynecked pigeon (vert.). 6c, Bananaquits. 8c, Purple-throated Carib. 10c, Mangrove cuckoo (vert.). 12c, Black hawk (vert.). 20c, Bare-eyed thrush. 25c, Hooded tanager. 50c, Blue-hooded euphonia. $1, Barn owl (vert.). $2.50, Yellow-bellied elaenia (vert.). $5, Ruddy quail-dove.

**Wmk. 314 Upright on ½c, 4c, 5c, 10c, 12c, 50c, $5, Sideways on Others**

**1970, Jan. 12 Photo. *Perf. 14***

*279* A36 ½c multi 8 5
*280* A36 1c multi 12 8
*281* A36 2c multi 15 9
*282* A36 3c multi 16 12
*283* A36 4c multi 20 16
*284* A36 5c multi 1.20 60
*285* A36 6c multi 40 40
*286* A36 8c multi 40 28
*287* A36 10c multi 48 35
*288* A36 12c multi 55 40
*289* A36 20c multi 80 48
*290* A36 25c multi 80 48
*291* A36 50c multi 1.20 80
*292* A36 $1 multi 3.25 1.65
*293* A36 $2.50 multi 6.50 4.00
*294* A36 $5 multi 16.00 10.00
*Nos. 279-294 (16)* 32.29 19.94

See Nos. 379-381.

**Wmk. 314 Upright on 2c, 3c, 6c, 20c, Sideways on Others**

**1973**

*281a* A36 2c multi 25 15
*282a* A36 3c multi 40 20
*283a* A36 4c multi 52 28
*284a* A36 5c multi 80 40
*285a* A36 6c multi 80 45
*287a* A36 10c multi 80 45
*288a* A36 12c multi 1.40 65
*289a* A36 20c multi 2.00 1.00
*Nos. 281a-289a (8)* 6.97 3.58

Booklet Panes

**1974**

*280a* 1c pane of 4 48
*280b* 1c pane of 5 60
*281b* 2c pane of 4 60
*281c* 2c pane of 5 75
*282b* 3c pane of 4 65
*282c* 3c pane of 5 80
*283b* 4c pane of 4 80
*283c* 4c pane of 5 1.00
*284b* 5c pane of 4 4.80
*284c* 5c pane of 5 6.00

DHC6 Twin Otter A37

20th anniv. of regular air services: 8c, Grumman Goose amphibian. 10c, Hawker Siddeley 748. 25c, Douglas DC-3.

***Perf. 14x13***

**1970, Mar. 13 Litho. Wmk. 314**

*295* A37 5c lt bl & multi 18 15
*296* A37 8c lt grn & multi 38 30
*297* A37 10c pink & multi 65 40
*298* A37 25c yel & multi 1.75 1.25

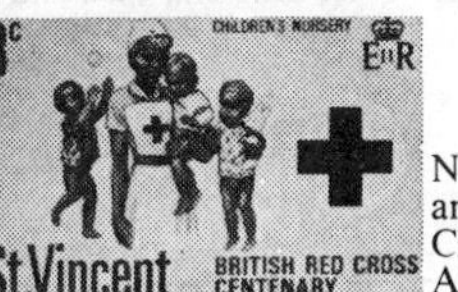


Nurse and Children A38

Designs (Red Cross and): 5c, First aid. 12c, Volunteers. 25c, Blood transfusion.

**1970, June 1 Photo. *Perf. 14***

| | | | | | |
|---|---|---|---|---|---|
| *299* | A38 | 3c bl & multi | 6 | 6 |
| *300* | A38 | 5c yel & multi | 15 | 8 |
| *301* | A38 | 12c lt grn & multi | 30 | 22 |
| *302* | A38 | 25c pale sal & multi | 60 | 55 |

Centenary of British Red Cross Society.

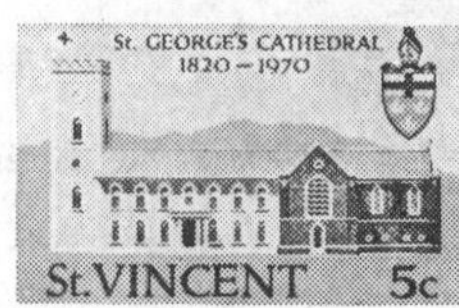


St. George's Cathedral – A39

Designs: ½c, 50c, Angel and Two Marys at the Tomb, stained glass window (vert.). 25c, St. George's Cathedral, front view (vert.). 35c, Interior with altar.

***Perf. 14x14½, 14½x14***

**1970, Sept. 7 Litho. Wmk. 314**

| | | | | |
|---|---|---|---|---|
| *303* | A39 ½c multi | 5 | 5 |
| *304* | A39 5c multi | 10 | 8 |
| *305* | A39 25c multi | 35 | 25 |
| *306* | A39 35c multi | 50 | 35 |
| *307* | A39 50c multi | 65 | 50 |
| | *Nos. 303-307 (5)* | 1.65 | 1.23 |

Issued to commemorate the 150th anniversary of St. George's Anglican Cathedral.

Virgin and Child, by Giovanni Bellini – A40

Christmas: 25c, 50c, Adoration of the Shepherds, by Louis Le Nain (horiz.).

**1970, Nov. 23 Litho. Wmk. 314**

| | | | |
|---|---|---|---|
| *308* A40 8c brt vio & multi | 18 | 15 |
| *309* A40 25c crim & multi | 40 | 35 |
| *310* A40 35c yel grn & multi | 65 | 40 |
| *311* A40 50c saph & multi | 1.10 | 80 |

Post Office and St. Vincent No. 1B A41

Designs (New Post Office and): 4c, $1, St. Vincent No. 1. 25c, as 2c.

**1971, Mar. 29 *Perf. 14½x14***

| | | | |
|---|---|---|---|
| *312* A41 2c vio & multi | 7 | 5 |
| *313* A41 4c ol & multi | 18 | 10 |
| *314* A41 25c brn org & multi | 60 | 40 |
| *315* A41 $1 lt grn & multi | 2.25 | 1.75 |

110th anniv. of 1st stamps of St. Vincent.

National Trust Emblem, Fish and Birds – A42

Designs: 30c, 45c, Cannon at Ft. Charlotte.

Common Design Types are pictured in section before Great Britain.

***Perf. 13½x14***

**1971, Aug. 4 Litho. Wmk. 314**

| | | | |
|---|---|---|---|
| *316* A42 12c emer & multi | 25 | 18 |
| *317* A42 30c lt bl & multi | 55 | 50 |
| *318* A42 40c brt pink & multi | 90 | 60 |
| *319* A42 45c blk & multi | 1.10 | 80 |

Publicity for the National Trust (for conservation of wild life and historic buildings).

Holy Family with Angels (detail), by Pietro da Cortona A43

Paintings: 5c, 25c, Madonna Appearing to St. Anthony, by Domenico Tiepolo (vert.).

**1971, Oct. 6 *Perf. 14x14½, 14½x14***

| | | | |
|---|---|---|---|
| *320* A43 5c rose & multi | 15 | 8 |
| *321* A43 10c lt grn & multi | 25 | 20 |
| *322* A43 25c lt bl & multi | 60 | 40 |
| *323* A43 $1 yel & multi | 2.25 | 1.75 |

Christmas 1971.

Careening – A44

Designs: 5c, 20c, Seine fishermen. 6c, 50c, Map of Grenadines. 15c, as 1c.

**1971, Nov. 25 *Perf. 14x13½***

| | | | |
|---|---|---|---|
| *324* A44 1c dp ver & multi | 5 | 5 |
| *325* A44 5c bl & multi | 15 | 12 |
| *326* A44 6c yel grn & multi | 25 | 18 |
| *327* A44 15c org brn & multi | 60 | 45 |
| *328* A44 20c yel & multi | 70 | 55 |
| *329* A44 50c bl, blk & plum | 1.75 | 1.50 |
| *a* Souvenir sheet of 6 | 12.50 | 10.00 |
| *Nos. 324-329 (6)* | 3.50 | 2.85 |

The Grenadines of St. Vincent tourist issue. No. 329a contains one each of Nos. 324-329; violet margin with decorative inscription and sailboat design. Size: 177x139mm.

Grenadier Company Private, 1764 – A45

Designs: 30c, Battalion Company officer, 1772. 50c, Grenadier Company private, 1772.

**1972, Feb. 14 *Perf. 14x13½***

| | | | |
|---|---|---|---|
| *330* A45 12c gray vio & multi | 1.00 | 80 |
| *331* A45 30c gray bl & multi | 2.50 | 2.00 |
| *332* A45 50c dk gray & multi | 4.50 | 3.50 |

Breadnut – A46

**1972, May 16 Litho. *Perf. 14x13½***

| | | | |
|---|---|---|---|
| *333* A46 3c *shown* | 16 | 14 |
| *334* A46 5c *Papaya* | 35 | 28 |
| *335* A46 12c *Rose apples* | 1.40 | 85 |
| *336* A46 25c *Mangoes* | 3.50 | 2.50 |

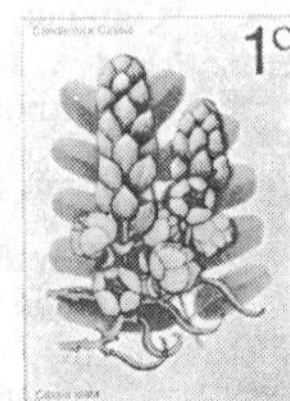


Flowers of St. Vincent – A47

**1972, July 31 Litho. *Perf. 13½x13***

| | | | |
|---|---|---|---|
| *337* A47 1c *Candlestick Cassia* | 8 | 8 |
| *338* A47 30c *Lobster claw* | 1.00 | 85 |
| *339* A47 40c *White trumpet* | 1.10 | 1.00 |
| *340* A47 $1 *Flowers, Soufriere tree* | 3.00 | 2.25 |

Sir Charles Brisbane, Arms of St. Vincent – A48

Designs: 30c, Sailing ship "Arethusa." $1, Sailing ship "Blake."

**1972, Sept. 29 Wmk. 314 *Perf. 13½***

| | | | |
|---|---|---|---|
| *341* A48 20c yel, brn & gold | 75 | 60 |
| *342* A48 30c lil & multi | 90 | 75 |
| *343* A48 $1 multi | 3.25 | 2.50 |
| *a* Souvenir sheet of 3 | 11.00 | 5.00 |

Bicentenary of the birth of Sir Charles Brisbane, naval hero, governor of St. Vincent. No. 343a contains one each of Nos. 341-343. Light ultramarine margin with white inscription. Size: 170x111mm.

**Silver Wedding Issue, 1972**

Common Design Type

Design: Queen Elizabeth II, Prince Philip, arrowroot plant, breadfruit foliage and fruit.

**1972, Nov. 20 Photo. *Perf. 14x14½***

| | | | |
|---|---|---|---|
| *344* CD324 30c rose brn & multi | 45 | 30 |
| *345* CD324 $1 multi | 1.25 | 75 |

Columbus Sighting St. Vincent – A49

Designs: 12c, Caribs watching Columbus' ships. 30c, Christopher Columbus. 50c, Santa Maria.

**1973, Jan. 18 Litho. *Perf. 13***

| | | | |
|---|---|---|---|
| *346* A49 5c multi | 25 | 20 |
| *347* A49 12c multi | 50 | 40 |
| *348* A49 30c multi | 1.75 | 1.00 |
| *349* A49 50c multi | 3.50 | 2.25 |

475th anniversary of Columbus's Third Voyage to the West Indies.

The Last Supper – A50

***Perf. 14x13½***

**1973, Apr. 19 Litho. Wmk. 314**

| | | | |
|---|---|---|---|
| *350* A50 15c red & multi | 15 | 14 |
| *351* A50 60c red & multi | 60 | 50 |
| *352* A50 $1 red & multi | 1.25 | 1.00 |
| Strip of 3 | 2.25 | 2.00 |

Easter 1973. Nos. 350-352 printed se-tenant.

William Wilberforce and Slave Auction Poster – A51

Designs: 40c, Slaves working on sugar plantation. 50c, Wilberforce and medal commemorating first anniversary of abolition of slavery.

**1973, July 11 *Perf. 14x13½***

| | | | |
|---|---|---|---|
| *353* A51 30c multi | 50 | 40 |
| *354* A51 40c multi | 60 | 55 |
| *355* A51 50c multi | 1.00 | 65 |

140th anniversary of the death of William Wilberforce (1759-1833), member of British Parliament who fought for abolition of slavery.

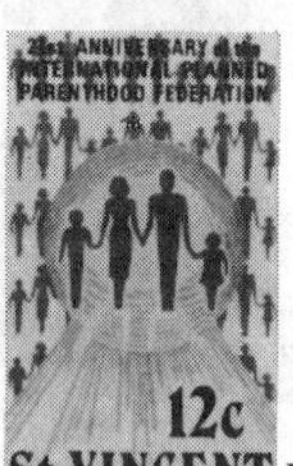


Families – A52

Design: 40c, Families and "IPPF."

**1973, Oct. 3 *Perf. 14½***

| | | | |
|---|---|---|---|
| *356* A52 12c multi | 30 | 20 |
| *357* A52 40c multi | 1.00 | 75 |

International Planned Parenthood Association, 21st anniversary.

**Princess Anne's Wedding Issue**

Common Design Type

**1973, Nov. 14 *Perf. 14***

| | | | |
|---|---|---|---|
| *358* CD325 50c sl & multi | 75 | 50 |
| *359* CD325 70c gray grn & multi | 1.00 | 70 |

Administration Buildings, Mona University – A53

Designs: 10c, University Center, Kingstown. 30c, Mona University, aerial view. $1, Coat of arms of University of West Indies.

*Perf. 14½x14, 14x14½*

**1973, Dec. 13**

| No. | Type | Description | Unused | Used |
|---|---|---|---|---|
| *360* | A53 | 5c multi | 12 | 7 |
| *361* | A53 | 10c multi | 22 | 12 |
| *362* | A53 | 30c multi | 55 | 45 |
| *363* | A53 | $1 multi | 1.40 | 90 |

25th anniversary of the University of the West Indies.

Nos. 291, 286 and 292 Surcharged

**1973, Dec. 15 Photo. *Perf. 14***

| No. | Type | Description | Unused | Used |
|---|---|---|---|---|
| *364* | A36 | 30c on 50c multi | 50 | 50 |
| *365* | A36 | 40c on 8c multi | 65 | 65 |
| *366* | A36 | $10 on $1 multi | 20.00 | 15.00 |

The position of the surcharge and shape of obliterating bars differs on each denomination.

Descent from the Cross — A54

Easter: 30c, Descent from the Cross. 40c, Pieta. $1, Resurrection. Designs are from sculptures in Victoria and Albert Museum, London, and Provincial Museum, Valladolid (40c).

**1974, Apr. 10 Litho. *Perf. 13½x13***

| No. | Type | Description | Unused | Used |
|---|---|---|---|---|
| *367* | A54 | 5c multi | 6 | 6 |
| *368* | A54 | 30c multi | 35 | 25 |
| *369* | A54 | 40c multi | 40 | 30 |
| *370* | A54 | $1 multi | 90 | 60 |

"Istra" A55

**1974, June 28 *Perf. 14½***

| No. | Type | Description | Unused | Used |
|---|---|---|---|---|
| *371* | A55 | 15c *shown* | 28 | 18 |
| *372* | A55 | 20c *"Oceanic"* | 38 | 30 |
| *373* | A55 | 30c *"Alexander Pushkin"* | 60 | 45 |
| *374* | A55 | $1 *"Europa"* | 1.75 | 1.10 |
| *a* | | Souvenir sheet of 4 | 4.00 | 3.25 |

Cruise ships visiting Kingstown. No. 374a contains one each of Nos. 371-374. Orange and black margin. Size: 133x82mm.

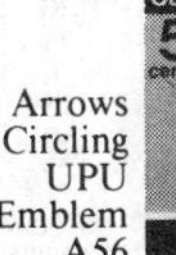

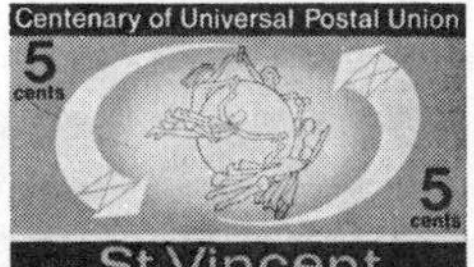

Arrows Circling UPU Emblem A56

UPU, cent.: 12c, Post horn and globe. 60c, Target over map of islands, hand canceler. 90c, Goode's map projection.

**1974, July 25 *Perf. 14½***

| No. | Type | Description | Unused | Used |
|---|---|---|---|---|
| *375* | A56 | 5c vio & multi | 6 | 6 |
| *376* | A56 | 12c ocher, grn & bl | 14 | 10 |
| *377* | A56 | 60c bl grn & multi | 50 | 40 |
| *378* | A56 | 90c red & multi | 75 | 15 |

Bird Type of 1970

Birds: 30c, Royal tern. 40c, Brown pelican (vert.). $10, Magnificent frigate bird (vert.).

**Wmk. 314 Sideways on 40c, $10, Upright on 30c.**

**1974, Aug. 29 Litho. *Perf. 14½***

| No. | Type | Description | Unused | Used |
|---|---|---|---|---|
| *379* | A36 | 30c multi | 80 | 60 |
| *380* | A36 | 40c multi | 1.25 | 90 |
| *381* | A36 | $10 multi | 24.00 | 16.00 |

Scout Emblem and Badges — A57

Churchill as Prime Minister — A58

*Perf. 13½x14*

**1974, Oct. 9 Wmk. 314**

| No. | Type | Description | Unused | Used |
|---|---|---|---|---|
| *385* | A57 | 10c lil & multi | 16 | 14 |
| *386* | A57 | 25c bis & multi | 40 | 35 |
| *387* | A57 | 45c gray & multi | 65 | 50 |
| *388* | A57 | $1 multi | 1.40 | 1.00 |

St. Vincent Boy Scouts, 60th anniversary.

**1974, Nov. 28 *Perf. 14½x14***

Designs (Churchill as): 35c, Lord Warden of the Cinque Ports. 45c, First Lord of the Admiralty. $1, Royal Air Force officer.

| No. | Type | Description | Unused | Used |
|---|---|---|---|---|
| *389* | A58 | 25c multi | 30 | 20 |
| *390* | A58 | 35c multi | 40 | 25 |
| *391* | A58 | 45c multi | 50 | 30 |
| *392* | A58 | $1 multi | 1.00 | 70 |

Sir Winston Churchill (1874-1965), birth centenary. Sheets of 30 in 2 panes of 15 with inscribed gutter between.

Shepherds A59

St. Joseph, Ass and Ox A60

**1974, Dec. 5 *Perf. 12x12½***

| No. | Type | Description | Unused | Used |
|---|---|---|---|---|
| *393* | A59 | 3c *like 8c* | 6 | 5 |
| *394* | A59 | 3c *Virgin, Child and Star* | 6 | 5 |
| *395* | A60 | 3c *like 45c* | 6 | 5 |
| *396* | A60 | 3c *Three Kings* | 6 | 5 |
| *397* | A59 | 8c *shown* | 20 | 15 |
| *398* | A59 | 35c *like No. 394* | 42 | 32 |
| *399* | A60 | 45c *shown* | 55 | 42 |
| *400* | A60 | $1 *like No. 396* | 1.40 | 90 |
| | | *Nos. 393-400 (8)* | 2.81 | 1.99 |

Christmas 1974. Nos. 393-396 printed se-tenant in a continuous picture.

Giant Mask and Dancers — A61

Designs: 15c, Pineapple dancers. 25c, Giant bouquet. 35c, Girl dancers. 45c, Butterfly dancers. $1.25, Sun and moon dancers and float.

**Wmk. 314**

**1975, Feb. 7 Litho. *Perf. 14***

| No. | Type | Description | Unused | Used |
|---|---|---|---|---|
| *401* | A61 | 1c multi | 5 | 5 |
| *a* | | Bklt. pane of 2 + label | 50 | |
| *b* | | Bklt. pane of 3 (#401, 403, 405) | 1.25 | |
| *402* | A61 | 15c multi | 20 | 15 |
| *a* | | Bklt. pane of 3 (#402, 404, 406) | 3.00 | |
| *403* | A61 | 25c multi | 30 | 20 |
| *404* | A61 | 35c multi | 40 | 25 |
| *405* | A61 | 45c multi | 50 | 30 |
| *406* | A61 | $1.25 multi | 1.40 | 90 |
| *a* | | Souvenir sheet of 6 | 3.00 | 2.00 |
| | | *Nos. 401-406 (6)* | 2.85 | 1.85 |

Kingstown carnival 1975. No. 406a contains one each of Nos. 401-406; multicolored margin. Size: 146x127mm.

French Angelfish A62

Designs: Fish and whales.

Two types of $2.50:
I. Line to fish's mouth.
II. Line removed (1976).

**Wmk. 373**

**1975, Apr. 10 Litho. *Perf. 14***

| No. | Type | Description | Unused | Used |
|---|---|---|---|---|
| *407* | A62 | 1c *shown* | 6 | 5 |
| *408* | A62 | 2c *Spotfin butterflyfish* | 6 | 5 |
| *409* | A62 | 3c *Horse-eyed jack* | 6 | 5 |
| *410* | A62 | 4c *Mackerel* | 10 | 5 |
| *411* | A62 | 5c *French grunts* | 10 | 6 |
| *412* | A62 | 6c *Spotted goatfish* | 12 | 8 |
| *413* | A62 | 8c *Ballyhoos* | 15 | 10 |
| *414* | A62 | 10c *Sperm whale* | 18 | 12 |
| *415* | A62 | 12c *Humpback whale* | 20 | 15 |
| *416* | A62 | 15c *Cowfish* | 40 | 30 |
| *417* | A62 | 20c *Queen angelfish* | 35 | 25 |
| *418* | A62 | 25c *Princess parrotfish* | 40 | 30 |
| *419* | A62 | 35c *Red hind* | 60 | 40 |
| *420* | A62 | 45c *Atlantic flying fish* | 65 | 50 |
| *421* | A62 | 50c *Porkfish* | 80 | 60 |
| *422* | A62 | $1 *Queen triggerfish* | 1.75 | 1.25 |
| *423* | A62 | $2.50 *Sailfish*, type I | 3.50 | 2.50 |
| *a* | | Type II | 6.25 | 3.50 |
| *424* | A62 | $5 *Dolphinfish* | 8.00 | 5.00 |
| *425* | A62 | $10 *Blue marlin* | 15.00 | 10.00 |
| | | *Nos. 407-425 (19)* | 32.48 | 21.81 |

The 4c, 10c, 20c, $1, were reissued with "1976" below design; 1c, 2c, 3c, 5c, 6c, 8c, 12c, 50c, $10, with "1977" below design; 10c with "1978" below design.

See Nos. 472-474.

Cutting Bananas — A63

Banana industry: 35c, La Croix packing station. 45c, Women cleaning and packing bananas. 70c, Freighter loading bananas.

**1975, June 26 Wmk. 314 *Perf. 14***

| No. | Type | Description | Unused | Used |
|---|---|---|---|---|
| *426* | A63 | 25c bl & multi | 35 | 28 |
| *427* | A63 | 35c bl & multi | 50 | 40 |
| *428* | A63 | 45c car & multi | 65 | 50 |
| *429* | A63 | 70c car & multi | 1.00 | 85 |

Snorkel Diving — A64

Designs: 20c, Aquaduct Golf Course. 35c, Steel band at Mariner's Inn. 45c, Sunbathing at Young Island. $1.25, Yachting marina.

**Wmk. 373**

**1975, July 31 Litho. *Perf. 13½***

| No. | Type | Description | Unused | Used |
|---|---|---|---|---|
| *430* | A64 | 15c multi | 15 | 10 |
| *431* | A64 | 20c multi | 25 | 15 |
| *432* | A64 | 35c multi | 40 | 25 |
| *433* | A64 | 45c multi | 50 | 30 |
| *434* | A64 | $1.25 multi | 1.25 | 70 |
| | | *Nos. 430-434 (5)* | 2.55 | 1.50 |

Tourist publicity.

Presidents Washington, John Adams, Jefferson and Madison — A65

U.S. Presidents: 1c, Monroe, John Quincy Adams, Jackson, Van Buren. 1½c, Wm. Harrison, Tyler, Polk, Taylor. 5c, Fillmore, Pierce, Buchanan, Lincoln. 10c, Johnson, Grant, Hayes, Garfield. 25c, Arthur, Cleveland, Benjamin Harrison, McKinley. 35c, Theodore Roosevelt, Taft, Wilson, Harding. 45c, Coolidge, Hoover, Franklin D. Roosevelt, Truman. $1, Eisenhower, Kennedy, Lyndon B. Johnson, Nixon. $2, Ford and White House.

**1975, Sept. 11 Unwmk. *Perf. 14½***

| No. | Type | Description | Unused | Used |
|---|---|---|---|---|
| *435* | A65 | ½c vio & blk | 5 | 5 |
| *436* | A65 | 1c grn & blk | 5 | 5 |
| *437* | A65 | 1½c rose lil & blk | 5 | 5 |
| *438* | A65 | 5c yel grn & blk | 6 | 5 |
| *439* | A65 | 10c ultra & blk | 10 | 8 |
| *440* | A65 | 25c ocher & blk | 25 | 18 |
| *441* | A65 | 35c brt bl & blk | 35 | 28 |
| *442* | A65 | 45c car & blk | 38 | 32 |
| *443* | A65 | $1 org & blk | 80 | 65 |
| *444* | A65 | $2 lt ol & blk | 1.75 | 1.40 |
| *a* | | Souvenir sheet of 10 | 7.50 | 6.00 |
| | | *Nos. 435-444 (10)* | 3.84 | 3.11 |

Bicentenary of American Independence. Issued in sheets of 10 stamps and 2 labels picturing the White House, Capitol, Mt. Vernon, etc.

No. 444a contains one each of Nos. 435-444 and 2 labels, one with inscription, the other showing Washington and George III; blue margin with lilac ornaments and black and lilac inscriptions. Size: 177x154mm.

Nativity-A66

A67

Designs: No. 445, 8c, Star of Bethlehem. No. 446, 45c, Shepherds. No. 447, $1, Kings. No. 448, 35c, Nativity.

**Wmk. 314**

**1975, Dec. 4 Litho. *Perf. 14***

| No. | Type | Description | Unused | Used |
|---|---|---|---|---|
| *445* | A66 | 3c dp rose & blk | 5 | 5 |
| *446* | A66 | 3c dp rose & blk | 5 | 5 |
| *447* | A66 | 3c dp rose & blk | 5 | 5 |
| *448* | A67 | 3c dp rose & blk | 5 | 5 |
| *449* | A66 | 8c bl & blk | 8 | 8 |
| *450* | A67 | 8c bl & blk | 8 | 8 |
| *451* | A66 | 35c yel & blk | 25 | 22 |
| *452* | A67 | 35c yel & blk | 25 | 22 |
| *453* | A66 | 45c yel grn & blk | 38 | 28 |
| *454* | A67 | 45c yel grn & blk | 38 | 28 |
| *455* | A66 | $1 vio & blk | 75 | 65 |
| *456* | A67 | $1 vio & blk | 75 | 65 |
| | | *Nos. 445-456 (12)* | 3.12 | 2.66 |

Christmas 1975. Stamps of same denomination printed se-tenant.

Carnival Costumes — A68

Designs: 2c, Humpty-Dumpty people. 5c, Smiling faces (masks). 35c, Dragon worshippers. 45c, Duck costume. $1.25, Bumble bee dance.

*Perf. 13x13½*

**1976, Feb. 19 Litho. Wmk. 373**

| | | | | |
|---|---|---|---|---|
| *457* | A68 | 1c car & multi | 5 | 5 |
| *a* | | Booklet pane of 2 | 20 | |
| *458* | A68 | 2c blk & multi | 5 | 5 |
| *a* | | Booklet pane of 3 | 60 | |
| *459* | A68 | 5c lt bl & multi | 7 | 5 |
| *460* | A68 | 35c lt bl & multi | 40 | 30 |
| *a* | | Booklet pane of 3 | 2.25 | |
| *461* | A68 | 45c blk & multi | 50 | 40 |
| *462* | A68 | $1.25 car & multi | 1.25 | 1.00 |
| | | *Nos. 457-462 (6)* | 2.32 | 1.85 |

Kingstown carnival 1976. No. 457a contains one each of Nos. 457-458 with inscribed gutter between; No. 458a contains one each of Nos. 458-460; No. 460a contains one each of Nos. 460-462.

Nos. 409 and 421 Surcharged with New Value and Bar

**1976, Apr. 8 Wmk. 314 *Perf. 14***

| | | | | |
|---|---|---|---|---|
| *463* | A62 | 70c on 3c multi | 75 | 75 |
| *464* | A62 | 90c on 50c multi | 1.00 | 1.00 |

Yellow Hibiscus and Blue-headed Hummingbird A69

Designs: 10c, Single pink hibiscus and crested hummingbird. 35c, Single white hibiscus and purple-throated carib. 45c, Common red hibiscus and blue-headed hummingbird. $1.25, Single peach hibiscus and green-throated carib.

**1976, May 20 Litho. Wmk. 373**

| | | | | |
|---|---|---|---|---|
| *465* | A69 | 5c multi | 25 | 18 |
| *466* | A69 | 10c multi | 50 | 35 |
| *467* | A69 | 35c multi | 1.50 | 1.10 |
| *468* | A69 | 45c multi | 2.50 | 1.75 |
| *469* | A69 | $1.25 multi | 7.50 | 4.50 |
| | | *Nos. 465-469 (5)* | 12.25 | 7.88 |

Map of West Indies, Bats, Wicket and Ball A69a

Prudential Cup — A69b

**1976, Sept. 16 Unwmk. *Perf. 14***

| | | | | |
|---|---|---|---|---|
| *470* | A63 | 15c lt bl & multi | 60 | 38 |
| *471* | A64 | 45c lil rose & blk | 1.75 | 1.10 |

World Cricket Cup, won by West Indies Team, 1975.

Fish Type of 1975

**1976, Oct. 14 Wmk. 373 *Perf. 14***

| | | | | |
|---|---|---|---|---|
| *472* | A62 | 15c *Skipjack* | 10 | 10 |
| *473* | A62 | 70c *Albacore* | 65 | 65 |
| *474* | A62 | 90c *Pompano* | 75 | 75 |

The 15c was reissued with "1977" below design.

St. Mary's R.C. Church, Kingstown — A70

Christmas: 45c, Anglican Church, Georgetown. 50c, Methodist Church, Georgetown. $1.25, St. George's Anglican Cathedral, Kingstown.

**1976, Nov. 18 Litho. *Perf. 14***

| | | | | |
|---|---|---|---|---|
| *475* | A70 | 35c multi | 35 | 35 |
| *476* | A70 | 45c multi | 45 | 45 |
| *477* | A70 | 50c multi | 55 | 55 |
| *478* | A70 | $1.25 multi | 1.40 | 1.40 |

Barrancoid Pot-stand, c. 450 A.D. — A71

Designs (National Trust Emblem and): 45c, National Museum. 70c, Carib stone head, c. 1510. $1, Ciboney petroglyph, c. 4000 B.C.

**1976, Dec. 16 *Perf. 13½***

| | | | | |
|---|---|---|---|---|
| *479* | A71 | 5c multi | 6 | 6 |
| *480* | A71 | 45c multi | 40 | 40 |
| *481* | A71 | 70c multi | 60 | 60 |
| *482* | A71 | $1 multi | 90 | 90 |

Carib Indian art and establishment of National Museum in Botanical Gardens, Kingstown.

Kings William I, William II, Henry I, Stephen A72

Kings and Queens of England: 1c, Henry II, Richard I, John, Henry III. 1½c, Edward I, II, III, Richard II. 2c, Henry IV, V, VI, Edward IV. 5c, Edward V, Richard III, Henry VII, VIII. 10c, Edward VI, Lady Jane Grey, Mary I, Elizabeth I. 25c, James I, Charles I, II, James II. 35c, William III, Mary II, Anne, George I. 45c, George II, III, IV. 75c, William IV, Victoria, Edward VII. $1, George V, Edward VIII, George VI. $2, Elizabeth II, coronation.

**Wmk. 373**

**1977, Feb. 7 Litho. *Perf. 13½***

| | | | | |
|---|---|---|---|---|
| *483* | A72 | ½c multi | 5 | 5 |
| *a* | | Bklt. pane of 4, #483-486 | 15.00 | |
| *484* | A72 | 1c multi | 5 | 5 |
| *485* | A72 | 1½c multi | 5 | 5 |
| *486* | A72 | 2c multi | 5 | 5 |
| *487* | A72 | 5c multi | 6 | 6 |
| *a* | | Bklt. pane of 4, #487-490 | 15.00 | |
| *488* | A72 | 10c multi | 8 | 8 |
| *489* | A72 | 25c multi | 20 | 18 |
| *490* | A72 | 35c multi | 28 | 22 |
| *491* | A72 | 45c multi | 38 | 30 |
| *a* | | Bklt. pane of 4, #491-494 | 17.50 | |
| *492* | A72 | 75c multi | 50 | 40 |
| *493* | A72 | $1 multi | 65 | 50 |
| *494* | A72 | $2 multi | 1.25 | 1.00 |
| *a* | | Souvenir sheet of 12 | 4.00 | 4.00 |
| | | *Nos. 483-494 (12)* | 3.60 | 2.94 |

25th anniv. of the reign of Elizabeth II. No. 494a contains one each of Nos. 483-494, perf. 14½x14; multicolored margin. Size: 170x146mm.

Nos. 483a, 487a and 491a are unwkd.

Bishop Alfred P. Berkeley, Bishop's Miters — A73

Designs: 15c, Grant of Arms to Bishopric, 1951, and names of former Bishops. 45c, Coat of arms and map of Diocese. $1.25, Interior of St. George's Anglican Cathedral and Bishop G. C. M. Woodroffe.

**Wmk. 373**

**1977, May 12 Litho. *Perf. 13½***

| | | | | |
|---|---|---|---|---|
| *495* | A73 | 15c multi | 12 | 10 |
| *496* | A73 | 35c multi | 30 | 25 |
| *497* | A73 | 45c multi | 40 | 35 |
| *498* | A73 | $1.25 multi | 1.10 | 90 |

Diocese of the Windward Islands, centenary.

Nos. 411, 414, 472, 417, 422 Overprinted in Black or Red: "CARNIVAL 1977/ JUNE 25TH - JULY 5TH"

**1977, June 2 Litho. *Perf. 14***

| | | | | |
|---|---|---|---|---|
| *499* | A62 | 5c multi | 7 | 6 |
| *500* | A62 | 10c multi (R) | 14 | 10 |
| *501* | A62 | 15c multi (R) | 30 | 20 |
| *502* | A62 | 20c multi (R) | 50 | 35 |
| *503* | A62 | $1 multi (R) | 2.25 | 2.00 |
| | | *Nos. 499-503 (5)* | 3.26 | 2.71 |

St. Vincent Carnival, June 25-July 5.

5c, 15c dated "1977", 10c, 20c, $1 dated "1976".

Girl Guide and Emblem — A74

Designs: 15c, Early Guide's uniform, Ranger, Brownie and Guide. 20c, Guide uniforms, 1917 and 1977. $2, Lady Baden-Powell, World Chief Guide, 1930-1977.

**Wmk. 373**

**1977, Sept. 1 Litho. *Perf. 13½***

| | | | | |
|---|---|---|---|---|
| *504* | A74 | 5c multi | 6 | 5 |
| *505* | A74 | 15c multi | 12 | 8 |
| *506* | A74 | 20c multi | 18 | 12 |
| *507* | A74 | $2 multi | 1.50 | 1.25 |

St. Vincent Girl Guides, 50th anniversary.

No. 494 with Additional Inscription: "CARIBBEAN / VISIT 1977"

**1977, Oct. 27**

| | | | | |
|---|---|---|---|---|
| *508* | A72 | $2 multi | 1.50 | 1.50 |

Caribbean visit of Queen Elizabeth II.

"While Shepherds Watched" — A75

Designs: 10c, "Fear not" said He. 15c, David's Town. 25c, The Heavenly Babe. 50c, Thus Spake and Seraph. $1.25, All Glory be to God.

**1977, Nov. Litho. *Perf. 13x11***

| | | | | |
|---|---|---|---|---|
| *509* | A75 | 5c buff & multi | 5 | 5 |
| *510* | A75 | 10c buff & multi | 8 | 6 |
| *511* | A75 | 15c buff & multi | 12 | 9 |
| *512* | A75 | 25c buff & multi | 18 | 15 |
| *513* | A75 | 50c buff & multi | 38 | 30 |
| *514* | A75 | $1.25 buff & multi | 90 | 75 |
| *a* | | Souvenir sheet of 6 | 1.75 | 1.60 |
| | | *Nos. 509-514 (6)* | 1.71 | 1.40 |

Christmas 1977. No. 514a contains one each of Nos. 509-514, perf. 13½; multicolored decorative margin shows opening bars of carol "While Shepherds watched their flocks by night." Size: 150x170mm.

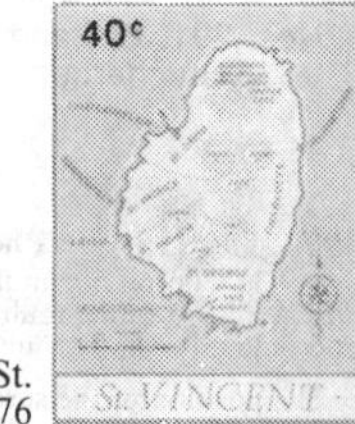


Map of St. Vincent — A76

*Perf. 14½x14*

**1977-78 Litho. Wmk. 373**

| | | | | |
|---|---|---|---|---|
| *515* | A76 | 20c dk bl & lt bl ('78) | 20 | 15 |
| *516* | A76 | 40c sal & blk | 40 | 30 |
| *517* | A76 | 40c car, sal & ocher ('78) | 40 | 30 |

No. 516 issued Nov. 30, Nos. 515, 517, Jan. 31.

Painted Lady and Bougainvillea — A77

Butterflies and Bougainvillea: 25c, Silver spot. 40c, Red anartia. 50c, Mimic. $1.25, Giant hairstreak.

**1978, Apr. 6 Litho. *Perf. 14***

| | | | | |
|---|---|---|---|---|
| *523* | A77 | 5c multi | 5 | 5 |
| *524* | A77 | 25c multi | 20 | 18 |
| *525* | A77 | 40c multi | 30 | 28 |
| *526* | A77 | 50c multi | 40 | 35 |
| *527* | A77 | $1.25 multi | 1.00 | 90 |
| | | *Nos. 523-527 (5)* | 1.95 | 1.76 |

Westminster Abbey — A78

Cathedral: 50c, Gloucester. $1.25, Durham. $2.50, Exeter.

*Perf. 13x13½*

**1978, June 2 Litho. Wmk. 373**

| | | | | |
|---|---|---|---|---|
| *528* | A78 | 40c multi | 25 | 20 |
| *529* | A78 | 50c multi | 30 | 25 |
| *530* | A78 | $1.25 multi | 75 | 65 |
| *531* | A78 | $2.50 multi | 1.50 | 1.25 |
| *a* | | Souvenir sheet of 4 | 2.50 | 2.50 |

25th anniversary of coronation of Queen Elizabeth II. Nos. 528-531 issued in sheets of 10. No. 531a contains Nos. 528-531, perf. 13½x14; yellow green margin with brown inscription. Size: 131x103mm.

Nos. 528-531 also exist in booklet panes of two.

Rotary Emblem A79

Designs: 50c, Lions International emblem. $1, Jaycees emblem.

**Wmk. 373**

**1978, July 13 Litho. *Perf. 14½***

| | | | | |
|---|---|---|---|---|
| *532* | A79 | 40c brn & multi | 25 | 25 |
| *533* | A79 | 50c dk grn & multi | 30 | 30 |
| *534* | A79 | $1 crim & multi | 60 | 60 |

Service clubs aiding in development of St. Vincent.

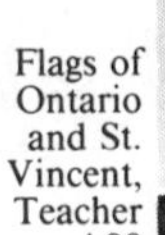

Flags of Ontario and St. Vincent, Teacher A80

Design: 40c, Flags of St. Vincent and Ontario, teacher pointing to board (vert.).

**1978, Sept. 7 Litho. *Perf. 14***

| | | | | |
|---|---|---|---|---|
| *535* | A80 | 40c multi | 25 | 20 |
| *536* | A80 | $2 multi | 1.10 | 1.00 |

School to School Project between children of Ontario, Canada, and St. Vincent, 10th anniversary.

Arnos Vale Airport A81

Designs: 40c, Wilbur Wright landing Flyer I. 50c, Flyer I airborne. $1.25, Orville Wright and Flyer I.

**1978, Oct. 19 *Perf. 14½***

| | | | | |
|---|---|---|---|---|
| *537* | A81 | 10c multi | 6 | 6 |
| *538* | A81 | 40c multi | 25 | 25 |
| *539* | A81 | 50c multi | 30 | 30 |
| *540* | A81 | $1.25 multi | 75 | 75 |

75th anniversary of 1st powered flight.

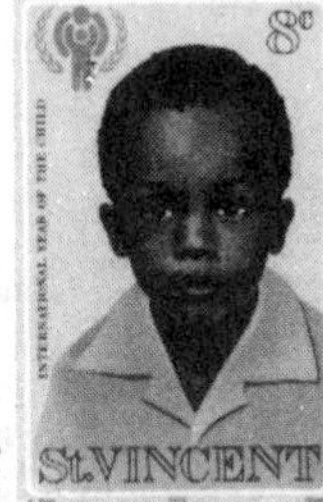


Vincentian Boy, IYC Emblem — A82

Children and IYC Emblem: 20c, Girl. 50c, Boy. $2, Girl and boy.

**1979, Feb. 14 Litho. *Perf. 14x13½***

| | | | | |
|---|---|---|---|---|
| *541* | A82 | 8c multi | 6 | 5 |
| *542* | A82 | 20c multi | 20 | 10 |
| *543* | A82 | 50c multi | 50 | 28 |
| *544* | A82 | $2 multi | 2.00 | 1.00 |

International Year of the Child.

Rowland Hill A83

Designs: 50c, Great Britain Nos. 1-2. $3, St. Vincent Nos. 1-1B.

**1979, May 31 Litho. *Perf. 14***

| | | | | |
|---|---|---|---|---|
| *545* | A83 | 40c multi | 20 | 20 |
| *546* | A83 | 50c multi | 25 | 25 |
| *547* | A83 | $3 multi | 1.50 | 1.50 |
| *a.* | | Souvenir sheet of 6 | 4.00 | 4.00 |

Sir Rowland Hill (1795-1879), originator of penny postage.

No. 547a contains Nos. 545-547 and Nos. 560, 561 and 565. Ocher margin shows synopsis of postage stamp history. Size: 170x122mm.

Buccament Cancellations, Map of St. Vincent — A84

Designs: Cancellations and location of village.

**1979, Sept. 1 Litho. *Perf. 14***

| | | | | |
|---|---|---|---|---|
| *548* | A84 | 1c *shown* | 5 | 5 |
| *549* | A84 | 2c *Sion Hill* | 5 | 5 |
| *550* | A84 | 3c *Cumberland* | 5 | 5 |
| *551* | A84 | 4c *Questelles* | 5 | 5 |
| *552* | A84 | 5c *Layou* | 5 | 5 |
| *553* | A84 | 6c *New Ground* | 5 | 5 |
| *554* | A84 | 8c *Mesopotamia* | 5 | 5 |
| *555* | A84 | 10c *Troumaca* | 5 | 5 |
| *556* | A84 | 12c *Arnos Vale* | 6 | 6 |
| *557* | A84 | 15c *Stubbs* | 8 | 8 |
| *558* | A84 | 20c *Orange Hill* | 10 | 10 |
| *559* | A84 | 25c *Calliaqua* | 12 | 12 |
| *560* | A84 | 40c *Edinboro* | 20 | 20 |
| *561* | A84 | 50c *Colonarie* | 25 | 25 |
| *562* | A84 | 80c *Babou St. Vincent* | 40 | 40 |
| *563* | A84 | $1 *Chateaubelair* | 50 | 50 |
| *564* | A84 | $2 *Kingstown* | 1.00 | 1.00 |
| *565* | A84 | $3 *Barrouallie* | 1.50 | 1.50 |
| *566* | A84 | $5 *Georgetown* | 2.50 | 2.50 |
| *567* | A84 | $10 *Kingstown* | 5.00 | 5.00 |
| | | *Nos. 548-567 (20)* | 12.11 | 12.11 |

See No. 547a. The 5c, 10c, 25c reissued inscribed 1982.

No. 537 Overprinted in Red: "ST. VINCENT AND THE GRENADINES AIR SERVICE 1979"

**1979, Aug. 6 Litho. *Perf. 14½***

| | | | | |
|---|---|---|---|---|
| *568* | A81 | 10c multi | 10 | 10 |

St. Vincent and Grenadines air service inauguration.

**Independent State**

St. Vincent Flag, Ixora Coccinea A85

Designs: 50c, House of Assembly, ixora stricta. 80c, Prime Minister R. Milton Cato.

**1979, Oct. 27 *Perf. 12½x12***

| | | | | |
|---|---|---|---|---|
| *569* | A85 | 20c multi | 10 | 10 |
| *570* | A85 | 50c multi | 25 | 25 |
| *571* | A85 | 80c multi | 40 | 40 |

Independence of St. Vincent Nos. 569-571 each printed se-tenant with label inscribed "Peace and Justice."

Nos. 407, 410-416, 418, 421, 473-474, 422-423, 425 Overprinted in Black: "INDEPENDENCE 1979"

**1979, Oct. 27 Litho. *Perf. 14½***

| | | | | |
|---|---|---|---|---|
| *572* | A62 | 1c multi | 5 | 5 |
| *573* | A62 | 4c multi | 5 | 5 |
| *574* | A62 | 5c multi | 5 | 5 |
| *575* | A62 | 6c multi | 5 | 5 |
| *576* | A62 | 8c multi | 5 | 5 |
| *577* | A62 | 10c multi | 7 | 7 |
| *578* | A62 | 12c multi | 8 | 8 |
| *579* | A62 | 15c multi | 10 | 10 |
| *580* | A62 | 25c multi | 16 | 16 |
| *581* | A62 | 50c multi | 35 | 35 |
| *582* | A62 | 70c multi | 50 | 50 |
| *583* | A62 | 90c multi | 60 | 60 |
| *584* | A62 | $1 multi | 65 | 65 |
| *585* | A62 | $2.50 multi | 1.75 | 1.75 |
| *586* | A62 | $10 multi | 6.50 | 6.50 |
| | | *Nos. 572-586 (15)* | 11.01 | 11.01 |

Silent Night Text, Virgin and Child A86

Silent Night Text and: 20c, Infant Jesus and angels. 25c, Shepherds. 40c, Angel. 50c, Angels holding Jesus. $2, Nativity.

**1979, Nov. 1 *Perf. 13½x14***

| | | | | |
|---|---|---|---|---|
| *587* | A86 | 10c multi | 7 | 7 |
| *588* | A86 | 20c multi | 14 | 14 |
| *589* | A86 | 25c multi | 16 | 16 |
| *590* | A86 | 40c multi | 28 | 28 |
| *591* | A86 | 50c multi | 35 | 35 |
| *592* | A86 | $2 multi | 1.40 | 1.40 |
| *a.* | | Souvenir sheet of 6 | 2.50 | 2.50 |
| | | *Nos. 587-592 (6)* | 2.40 | 2.40 |

Christmas 1979. No. 592a contains Nos. 587-592. Multicolored margin shows score, author and composer of Silent Night; silver inscription. Size: 151½x170½mm.

Oleander and Wasp — A87

Oleander and Insects: 10c, Beetle. 25c, Praying mantis. 50c, Green guava beetle. $2, Citrus weevil.

**1979, Dec. 13 Litho. *Perf. 14***

| | | | | |
|---|---|---|---|---|
| *593* | A87 | 5c multi | 5 | 5 |
| *594* | A87 | 10c multi | 7 | 7 |
| *595* | A87 | 25c multi | 16 | 16 |
| *596* | A87 | 50c multi | 35 | 35 |
| *597* | A87 | $2 multi | 1.40 | 1.40 |
| | | *Nos. 593-597 (5)* | 2.03 | 2.03 |

Souvenir Sheet
Type of 1880

**1980, Feb. 28 Litho. *Perf. 14x13½***

| | | | | |
|---|---|---|---|---|
| *598* | | Sheet of 3 | 2.50 | 2.50 |
| *a.* | A3 | 50c brown | 35 | 35 |
| *b.* | A3 | $1 dark green | 65 | 65 |
| *c.* | A3 | $2 dark blue | 1.40 | 1.40 |

Coat of arms stamps centenary; London 1980 International Stamp Exhibition, May 6-14. Silver decorative margin. Size: 116x72mm.

London '80 Intl. Stamp Exhibition, May 6-14 A88

**Wmk. 373**

**1980, Apr. 24 Litho. *Perf. 14***

| | | | | |
|---|---|---|---|---|
| *599* | A88 | 80c Queen Elizabeth II | 55 | 55 |
| *600* | A88 | $1 GB #297, SV #190 | 65 | 65 |
| *601* | A88 | $2 Unissued stamp, 1971 | 1.40 | 1.40 |

Steel Band A89

**1980, June 12 Litho. *Perf. 14***

| | | | | |
|---|---|---|---|---|
| *602* | A89 | 20c *shown* | 14 | 14 |
| *603* | A89 | 20c *Drummers, dancers* | 14 | 14 |

Kingstown Carnival, July 7-8. Nos. 602-603 se-tenant.

Soccer, Olympic Rings — A90

**1980, Aug. 7 *Perf. 13½***

| | | | | |
|---|---|---|---|---|
| *604* | A90 | 10c *shown* | 7 | 7 |
| *605* | A90 | 60c *Bicycling* | 40 | 40 |
| *606* | A90 | 80c *Women's basketball* | 55 | 55 |
| *607* | A90 | $2.50 *Boxing* | 1.75 | 1.75 |

Sport for all.

Agouti — A91

**1980, Oct. 2 Litho. *Perf. 14x14½***

| | | | | |
|---|---|---|---|---|
| *608* | A91 | 25c *shown* | 16 | 16 |
| *609* | A91 | 50c *Giant toad* | 35 | 35 |
| *610* | A91 | $2 *Mongoose* | 1.40 | 1.40 |

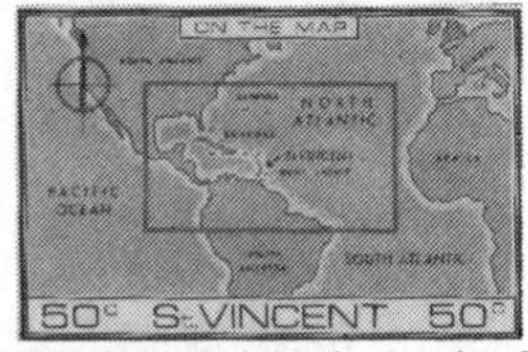


Map of North Atlantic showing St. Vincent — A92

Maps showing St. Vincent: 10c, World. $1, Caribbean. $2, St. Vincent, sail boats, plane.

**1980, Dec. 4 Litho. *Perf. 13½x14***

| | | | | |
|---|---|---|---|---|
| *611* | A92 | 10c multi | 7 | 7 |
| *612* | A92 | 50c multi | 35 | 35 |
| *613* | A92 | $1 multi | 65 | 65 |
| *614* | A92 | $2 multi | 1.40 | 1.40 |
| *a.* | | Souvenir sheet | 1.40 | 1.40 |

No. 614a contains No. 614 (perf. 12); multicolored margin shows map of Caribbean. Size: 143x95mm.

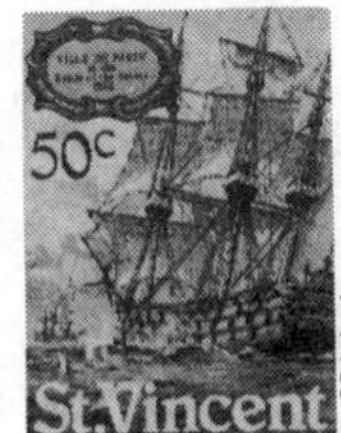


Ville de Paris in Battle of the Saints, 1782 — A93

**Wmk. 373**

**1981, Feb. 19 Litho. *Perf. 14***

| | | | | |
|---|---|---|---|---|
| *615* | A93 | 50c shown | 35 | 35 |
| *616* | A93 | 60c Ramillies lost in storm, 1782 | 40 | 40 |
| *617* | A93 | $1.50 Providence, 1793 | 1.00 | 1.00 |
| *618* | A93 | $2 Mail Packet Dee, 1840 | 1.40 | 1.40 |

Arrowroot Cultivation A94

**Wmk. 373**

**1981, May 21 Litho. *Perf. 14***

*619* A94 25c Arrowroot processing 12 12
*620* A94 25c shown 12 12
*621* A94 50c Banana packing plant 25 25
*622* A94 50c Banana cultivation 25 25
*623* A94 60c Copra drying frames 30 30
*624* A94 60c Coconut plantation 30 30
*625* A94 $1 Cocoa beans 50 50
*626* A94 $1 Cocoa cultivation 50 50
*Nos. 619-626 (8)* 2.34 2.34

Stamps of same denomination se-tenant.

Royal Wedding Types of Montserrat

**Wmk. 380**

**1981, July 13 Litho. *Perf. 14***

*627* A66 60c Couple, Isabella 40 40
*a* Bklt pane of 4, perf. 12 1.60
*628* A67 60c Couple 40 40
*629* A66 $2.50 Alberta 1.60 1.60
*630* A67 $2.50 like #628 1.60 1.60
*a* Bklt pane of 4, perf. 12 6.50
*631* A66 $4 Britannia 2.75 2.75
*632* A67 $4 like #628 2.75 2.75
*Nos. 627-632 (6)* 9.50 9.50

Each denomination issued in sheets of 7 (6 type A66, 1 type A67).

Souvenir Sheet

**1981 Litho. *Perf. 12***

*632A* A67 $5 Couple 3.50 3.50

No. 632A has orange yellow decorative margin. Size: 120x109mm.

Kingstown General Post Office
A95 A96

**Wmk. 373**

**1981, Sept. 1 Litho. *Perf. 14***

*633* A95 $2 multi 1.40 1.40
*634* A96 $2 multi 1.40 1.40

UPU membership centenary.

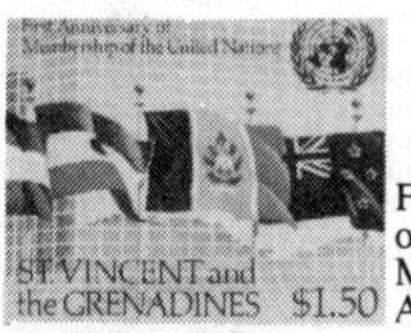


First Anniv. of UN Membership A96a

**Wmk. 373**

**1981, Sept. 1 Litho. *Perf. 14***

*634A* A96a $1.50 Flags 75 75
*634B* A96a $2.50 Prime Minister Cato 1.25 1.25

"The People that Walked in Darkness . . ." – A97

**1981, Nov. 19 Litho. *Perf. 12***

*635* A97 50c shown 25 25
*636* A97 60c Angel 30 30
*637* A97 $1 "My soul . . ." 50 50
*638* A97 $2 Flight into Egypt 1.00 1.00
*a* Souvenir sheet of 4 2.00 2.00

Christmas 1981. No. 638a contains Nos. 635-638; lilac and gold margin shows score from Bach's Christmas Oratorio. Size: 130x127mm.

Re-introduction of Sugar Industry, First Anniv. – A98

**1982, Apr. 5 Litho. *Perf. 14***

*639* A98 50c Boilers 35 35
*640* A98 60c Drying plant 40 40
*641* A98 $1.50 Gearwheels 1.00 1.00
*642* A98 $2 Loading sugar cane 1.40 1.40

50th Anniv. of Airmail Service A99

**1982, July 29 Litho. *Perf. 14***

*643* A99 50c DH Moth, 1932 35 35
*644* A99 60c Grumman Goose, 1952 40 40
*645* A99 $1.50 Hawker-Siddeley 748, 1968 1.00 1.00
*646* A99 $2 Britten-Norman Islander, 1982 1.40 1.40

Princess Diana Type of Kiribati

**Wmk. 380**

**1982, June Litho. *Perf. 14***

*647* A64 50c Augusta of Saxe, 1736 35 35
*648* A64 60c Saxe arms 40 40
*649* A64 $6 Diana 4.00 4.00

Scouting Year – A100

**1982, July 15 Wmk. 373**

*650* A100 $1.50 Emblem 1.00 1.00
*651* A100 $2.50 "75" 1.75 1.75

Nos. 647-649 Overprinted: "ROYAL BABY"

**1982, July Wmk. 380**

*652* A64 50c multi 35 35
*653* A64 60c multi 40 40
*654* A64 $6 multi 4.00 4.00

Birth of Prince William of Wales, June 21.

Carnival 1982 A101

**1982, June 10 Litho. *Perf. 13½***

*655* A101 50c Butterfly float 35 35
*656* A101 60c Angel dancer, vert. 40 40
*657* A101 $1.50 Winged dancer, vert. 1.00 1.00
*658* A101 $2 Eagle float 1.40 1.40

Cruise ships A103

**Wmk. 373**

**1982, Dec. 29 Litho. *Perf. 14***

*662* A103 45c Geestport 30 30
*663* A103 60c Stella Oceanis 40 40
*664* A103 $1.50 Victoria 1.00 1.00
*665* A103 $2 QE 2 1.40 1.40

Pseudocorynactis Caribbeorum – A104

Sea Horses and Anemones. 60c, $1.50, $2 vert.

**1983, Jan. 12 Wmk. 373 *Perf. 12***

*666* A104 50c shown 35 35
*667* A104 60c Actinoporus elegans 40 40
*668* A104 $1.50 Arachnanthus nocturnus 1.00 1.00
*669* A104 $2 Hippocampus reidi 1.40 1.40

Commonwealth Day – CD334

**Wmk. 373**

**1983, Mar. 14 Litho. *Perf. 14***

*670* CD334 45c Map 30 30
*671* CD334 60c Flag 40 40
*672* CD334 $1.50 Prime Minister Cato 1.00 1.00
*673* CD334 $2 Banana industry 1.40 1.40

No. 635 Surcharged.

**Wmk. 373**

**1983, Apr. 26 Litho. *Perf. 12***

*674* A97 45c on 50c multi 45 45

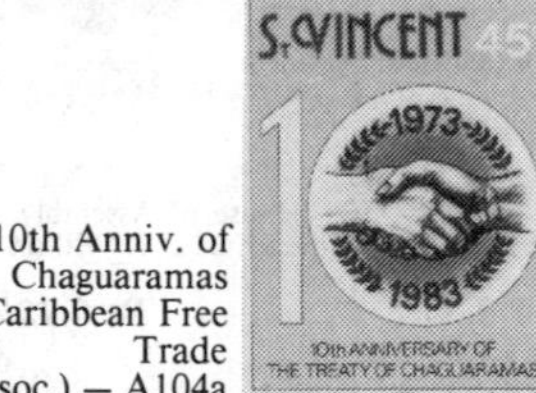


10th Anniv. of Chaguaramas (Caribbean Free Trade Assoc.) – A104a

**Wmk. 373**

**1983, July 6 Litho. *Perf. 12***

*675* A104a 45c Handshake 35 35
*676* A104a 60c Emblem 48 48
*677* A104a $1 Map 80 80
*678* A104a $2 Flags 1.60 1.60

Boys' Brigade Centenary – A105

***Perf. 12x11½***

**1983, Oct. 6 Litho. Wmk. 373**

*679* A105 45c Founder William A. Smith 30 30
*680* A105 60c Boy, officer 40 40
*681* A105 $1.50 Emblem 1.00 1.00
*682* A105 $2 Community service 1.40 1.40

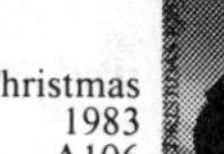

Christmas 1983 A106

**1983, Nov. 15 Litho. *Perf. 12***

*683* A106 10c Shepherds at Watch 8 8
*684* A106 50c The Angel of the Lord 40 40
*685* A106 $1.50 A Glorious Light 1.15 1.15
*686* A106 $2.40 At the Manger 2.00 2.00
*a* Souvenir sheet of 4 (#683-686) 3.75 3.75

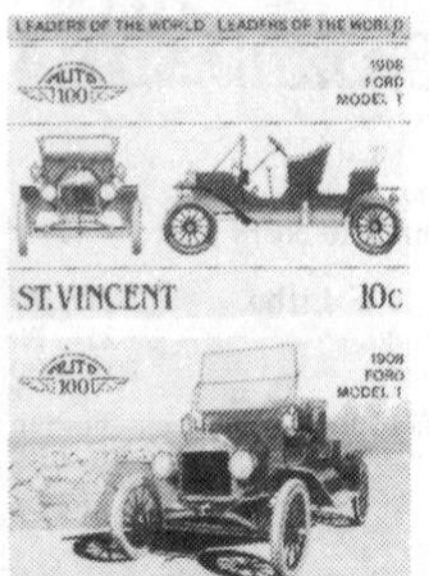


Classic Cars A107

**1983, Nov. 9 Litho. *Perf. 12½***

*687* A107 10c Ford Model T 8 8
*688* A107 10c Ford Model T, diff. 8 8
*689* A107 60c Supercharged Cord 45 45
*690* A107 60c Supercharged Cord, diff. 45 45
*691* A107 $1.50 Mercedes-Benz 1.15 1.15
*692* A107 $1.50 Mercedes-Benz, diff. 1.15 1.15
*693* A107 $1.50 Citroen Open Tourer 1.15 1.15
*694* A107 $1.50 Citroen Open Tourer, diff. 1.15 1.15
*695* A107 $2 Ferrari Boxer 1.50 1.50
*696* A107 $2 Ferrari Boxer, diff. 1.50 1.50
*697* A107 $2 Rolls-Royce Phantom 1.50 1.50
*698* A107 $2 Rolls-Royce Phantom, diff. 1.50 1.50
*Nos. 687-698 (12)* 11.66 11.66

Stamps of same denomination printed in se-tenant pairs.

**1983, Dec. 8 Litho. *Perf. 12½x13***

Locomotives. Stamps of same denomination se-tenant.

*699* A107 10c King Henry VIII 6 6
*700* A107 10c King Henry VIII, diff. 6 6
*701* A107 10c Royal Scots Greys 6 6
*702* A107 10c Royal Scots Greys, diff. 6 6
*703* A107 25c Hagley Hall 12 12
*704* A107 25c Hagley Hall, diff. 12 12
*705* A107 50c Sir Lancelot 25 25
*706* A107 50c Sir Lancelot, diff. 25 25
*707* A107 60c B12 Class 30 30
*708* A107 60c B12 Class, diff. 30 30
*709* A107 75c No. 1000 Deeley Compound 40 40
*710* A107 75c No. 1000, diff. 40 40
*711* A107 $2.50 Cheshire 1.25 1.25
*712* A107 $2.50 Cheshire, diff. 1.25 1.25
*713* A107 $3 Bulleid Austerity 1.50 1.50
*714* A107 $3 Austerity, diff. 1.50 1.50
*Nos. 699-714 (16)* 7.88 7.88

See Nos. 747-760A, 773-782, 815-828A, 906-917.

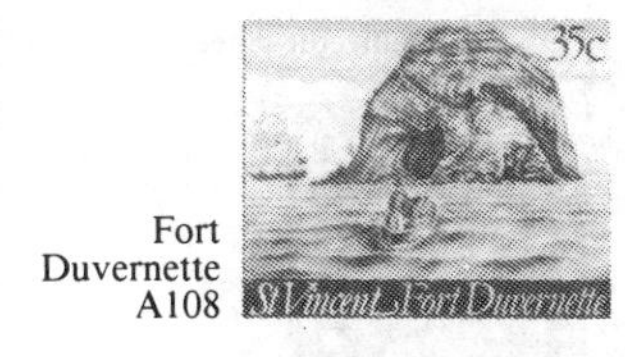


Fort Duvernette
A108

*Perf. 14x14½*

**1984, Feb. 13 Litho. Wmk. 380**

*715* A108 35c View 26 26
*716* A108 45c Wall, flag 34 34
*717* A108 $1 Canon 72 72
*718* A108 $3 Map 2.30 2.30

Flowering Trees — A109

*Perf. 13½x14*

**1984, Apr. 2 Litho. Wmk. 373**

*719* A109 5c White frangipani 5 5
*720* A109 10c Genip 8 8
*721* A109 15c Immortelle 12 12
*722* A109 20c Pink poui 15 15
*723* A109 25c Buttercup 18 18
*724* A109 35c Sandbox 26 26
*725* A109 45c Locust 34 34
*726* A109 60c Colville's glory 45 45
*727* A109 75c Lignum vitae 55 55
*728* A109 $1 Golden shower 72 72
*729* A109 $5 Angelin 3.60 3.60
*730* A109 $10 Roucou 7.25 7.25
*Nos. 719-730 (12)* 13.75 13.75

World War I Battle Scene, King George V
A110 A111

**1984, Apr. 25 Litho. *Perf. 13x12½***

*731* A110 1c shown 5 5
*732* A111 1c shown 5 5
*733* A110 5c Battle of Bannockburn 5 5
*734* A111 5c Edward II 5 5
*735* A110 60c George V, diff. 55 55
*736* A111 60c York Cottage, Sandringham 55 55
*737* A110 75c Edward II, diff. 70 70
*738* A111 75c Berkeley Castle 70 70
*739* A110 $1 Arms of Edward II 90 90
*740* A111 $1 Edward II, diff. 90 90
*741* A110 $4 Arms of George V 3.50 3.50
*742* A111 $4 George V, diff. 3.50 3.50
*Nos. 731-742 (12)* 11.50 11.50

Stamps of same denomination se-tenant in continuous design.

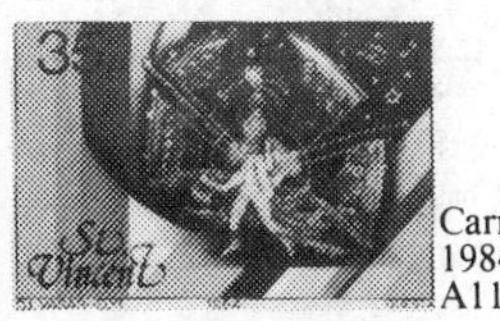


Carnival 1984
A112

**Wmk. 380**

**1984, June 25 Litho. *Perf. 14***

*743* A112 35c Musical fantasy 26 26
*744* A112 45c African woman 34 34
*745* A112 $1 Market woman 75 75
*746* A112 $3 Carib hieroglyph 2.25 2.25

Car Type of 1983

Locomotives (front and side views). Stamps of same denomination se-tenant.

**1984, July 27 Litho. *Perf. 12½***

*747* A107 1c Liberation Class 141R, 1945 5 5
*748* A107 1c Side 5 5
*749* A107 2c Dreadnought Class 50, 1967 5 5
*750* A107 2c Side 5 5
*751* A107 3c No. 242A1, 1946 5 5
*752* A107 3c Side 5 5
*753* A107 50c Dean Goods, 1883 30 30
*754* A107 50c Side 30 30
*755* A107 75c Hetton Colliery, 1822 40 40
*756* A107 75c Side 40 40
*757* A107 $1 Penydarren, 1804 60 60
*758* A107 $1 Side 60 60
*759* A107 $2 Novelty, 1829 1.10 1.10
*759A* A107 $2 Side 1.10 1.10
*760* A107 $3 Class 44, 1925 1.75 1.75
*760A* A107 $3 Side 1.75 1.75
*Nos. 747-760A (16)* 8.60 8.60

Slavery Abolition Sesquicentennial — A113

**1984, Aug. 1 Litho. *Perf. 14***

*761* A113 35c Hoeing 26 26
*762* A113 45c Gathering sugar cane 34 34
*763* A113 $1 Cutting sugar cane 75 75
*764* A113 $3 Abolitionist William Wilberforce 2.25 2.25

1984 Summer Olympics — A114

**1984, Aug. 30 Unwmk. *Perf. 12½***

*765* A114 1c Judo 5 5
*766* A114 1c Weight lifting 5 5
*767* A114 3c Bicycling (facing left) 5 5
*768* A114 3c Bicycling (facing right) 5 5
*769* A114 60c Swimming (back stroke) 35 35
*770* A114 60c Breast stroke 35 35
*771* A114 $3 Running (start) 1.75 1.75
*772* A114 $3 Running (finish) 1.75 1.75
*Nos. 765-772 (8)* 4.40 4.40

Stamps of same denomination se-tenant.

Car Type of 1983

**1984, Oct. 22 Litho. *Perf. 12½***

*773* A107 5c Austin-Healey Sprite, 1958 5 5
*774* A107 5c Side 5 5
*775* A107 20c Maserati, 1971 10 10
*776* A107 20c Side 10 10
*777* A107 55c Pontiac GTO, 1964 28 28
*778* A107 55c Side 28 28
*779* A107 $1.50 Jaguar, 1957 75 75
*780* A107 $1.50 Side 75 75
*781* A107 $2.50 Ferrari, 1970 1.25 1.25
*782* A107 $2.50 Side 1.75 1.75
*Nos. 773-782 (10)* 5.36 5.36

Stamps of same denomination se-tenant.

Military Uniforms — A115

**1984, Nov. 12 Wmk. 380 *Perf. 14***

*783* A115 45c Grenadier, 1773 34 34
*784* A115 60c Grenadier, 1775 45 45
*785* A115 $1.50 Grenadier, 1768 1.15 1.15
*786* A115 $2 Battalion Co. Officer, 1780 1.50 1.50

Locomotives Type of 1985

**1984, Nov. 21 Litho. *Perf. 12½x13***

*787* A120 5c 1954 R.R. Class 20, Zimbabwe 5 5
*788* A120 5c Class 20, diff. 5 5
*789* A120 40c 1928 Southern Maid, U.K. 25 25
*790* A120 40c Southern Maid, diff. 25 25
*791* A120 75c 1911 Prince of Wales, U.K. 48 48
*792* A120 75c Prince of Wales, diff. 48 48
*793* A120 $2.50 1935 D.R.G. Class 05, Germany 1.50 1.50
*794* A120 $2.50 Class 05, diff. 1.50 1.50
*Nos. 787-794 (8)* 4.56 4.56

Stamps of the same denomination printed se-tenant.

Cricket Players — A116

**1985, Jan. 7 Litho. *Perf. 12½***

*795* A116 5c N.S. Taylor, portrait 5 5
*796* A116 5c Taylor at wicket 5 5
*797* A116 35c T.W. Graveney with bat 20 20
*798* A116 35c Graveney, portrait 20 20
*799* A116 50c R.G.D. Willis at wicket 30 30
*800* A116 50c Willis, portrait 30 30
*801* A116 $3 S.D. Fletcher at wicket 1.75 1.75
*802* A116 $3 Fletcher, portrait 1.75 1.75
*Nos. 795-802 (8)* 4.60 4.60

Orchids — A117

**1985, Jan. 31 Litho. *Perf. 14***

*803* A117 35c Epidendrum ciliare 26 26
*804* A117 45c Ionopsis utricularioides 34 34
*805* A117 $1 Epidendrum secundum 75 75
*806* A117 $3 Oncidium altissimum 2.25 2.25

Audubon Birth Bicentenary
A118

Illustrations of North American bird species by artist/naturalist John J. Audubon.

**1985, Feb. 7 Litho. *Perf. 12½***

*807* A118 15c Brown pelican 8 8
*808* A118 15c Green heron 8 8
*809* A118 40c Pileated woodpecker 25 25
*810* A118 40c Common flicker 25 25
*811* A118 60c Painted bunting 35 35
*812* A118 60c White-winged crossbill 35 35
*813* A118 $2.25 Red-shouldered hawk 1.40 1.40
*814* A118 $2.25 Crested caracara 1.40 1.40
*Nos. 807-814 (8)* 4.16 4.16

Stamps of the same denomination printed se-tenant.

Car Type of 1983

**1985**

*815* A107 1c 1937 Lancia Aprilia, Italy 5 5
*816* A107 1c Aprilia, diff. 5 5
*817* A107 25c 1922 Essex Coach, USA 15 15
*818* A107 25c Essex, diff. 15 15
*819* A107 55c 1973 Pontiac Firebird Trans Am, USA 30 30
*820* A107 55c Trans Am, diff. 30 30
*821* A107 60c 1950 Nash Rambler, USA 35 35
*822* A107 60c Nash, diff. 35 35
*823* A107 $1 1961 Ferrari Tipo 156, Italy 60 60
*824* A107 $1 Ferrari, diff. 60 60
*825* A107 $1.50 1967 Eagle-Weslake Type 58, USA 90 90
*826* A107 $1.50 Eagle, diff. 90 90
*827* A107 $2 1953 Cunningham C-5R, USA 1.25 1.25
*828* A107 $2 C-5R, diff. 1.25 1.25
*Nos. 815-828 (14)* 7.20 7.20

**Souvenir Sheet**

*828A* Sheet of 4 11.00 11.00
*b* A107 $4 1967 Eagle-Weslake Type 58, US 2.50 2.50
*c* A107 $4 Eagle-Weslake, diff. 2.50 2.50
*d* A107 $5 1961 Ferrari Tipo 156, Italy 3.00 3.00
*e* A107 $5 Tipo, diff. 3.00 3.00

Stamps of the same denomination printed se-tenant. Issue dates: 1c, 55c, $2, Mar. 11. 25c, 60c, $1, $1.50, June 7.

No. 828A has multicolored margin picturing Dan Gurney and Phil Hill, champion drivers, and racetrack. Size: 180x126mm.

Herbs and Spices — A119

**1985, Apr. 22 *Perf. 14***

*829* A119 25c Pepper 20 20
*830* A119 35c Sweet marjoram 28 28
*831* A119 $1 Nutmeg 75 75
*832* A119 $3 Ginger 2.25 2.25

Locomotives of the United Kingdom — A120

**1985, Apr. 26 *Perf. 12½***

*833* A120 1c 1913 Glen Douglas 5 5
*834* A120 1c Front 5 5
*835* A120 10c 1872 Fenchurch Terrier 6 6
*836* A120 10c Rear 6 6
*837* A120 40c 1870 No. 1 Stirling Single 20 20
*838* A120 40c Front 20 20
*839* A120 60c 1866 No. 158A 30 30
*840* A120 60c Front 30 30
*841* A120 $1 1893 No. 103 Class Jones Goods 50 50
*842* A120 $1 Front 50 50

*843* A120 $2.50 1908 Great Bear 1.40 1.40
*844* A120 $2.50 Front 1.40 1.40
*Nos. 833-844 (12)* 5.02 5.02

Stamps of the same denomination printed se-tenant. See Nos. 787-794, 849-860, 960-967.

Traditional Instruments — A121

**1985, May 16** ***Perf. 15***
*845* A121 25c Bamboo flute 20 20
*846* A121 35c Quatro 28 28
*847* A121 $1 Bamboo base, vert. 75 75
*848* A121 $2 Goat-skin drum, vert. 1.50 1.50
*a* Sheet of 4, #845-848 2.75 2.75

No. 848a has multicolored margin picturing bamboo drums; Nos. 845-846 printed se-tenant. Size: 142x100mm.

Locomotives Type of 1985

**1985, June 27** ***Perf. 12½***
*849* A120 5c 1874 Loch, U.K. 5 5
*850* A120 5c Front 5 5
*851* A120 30c 1919 Class 47XX, U.K. 18 18
*852* A120 30c Front 18 18
*853* A120 60c 1876 P.L.M. Class 121, France 35 35
*854* A120 60c Front 35 35
*855* A120 75c 1927 D.R.G. Class 24, Germany 40 40
*856* A120 75c Front 40 40
*857* A120 $1 1889 No. 1008, U.K. 60 60
*858* A120 $1 Front 60 60
*859* A120 $2.50 1926 S.R. Class PS-4, USA 1.50 1.50
*860* A120 $2.50 Front 1.50 1.50
*Nos. 849-860 (12)* 6.16 6.16

Stamps of the same denomination printed se-tenant.

Queen Mother, 85th Birthday — A122

Photographs.

**1985, Aug. 9**
*861* A122 35c Facing right 25 25
*862* A122 35c Facing left 25 25
*863* A122 85c Facing right, diff. 60 60
*864* A122 85c Facing left, diff. 60 60
*865* A122 $1.20 Facing right, diff. 85 85
*866* A122 $1.20 Facing left, diff. 85 85
*867* A122 $1.60 Facing front 1.20 1.20
*868* A122 $1.60 Facing left, diff. 1.20 1.20
*Nos. 861-868 (8)* 5.80 5.80

**Souvenir Sheet**

*869* Sheet of 2 3.00 3.00
*a* A122 $2.10 Facing right, diff. 1.50 1.50
*b* A122 $2.10 Facing front, diff. 1.50 1.50

Stamps of the same denomination printed se-tenant.

**1985, Dec. 19** **Litho.** ***Perf. 12½***
*869C* Sheet of 2 5.25 5.25
*e* A122 $3.50 like #863 2.60 2.60
*f* A122 $3.50 like #864 2.60 2.60
*869D* Sheet of 2 9.00 9.00
*g* A122 $6 like #861 4.50 4.50
*h* A122 $6 like #862 4.50 4.50

Nos. 869C-869D have multicolored margins picturing the Concorde jet, flora and fauna. Sizes: 141x109mm.

Elvis Presley (1935-1977), American Entertainer A123

Photographs.

**1985, Aug. 16**
*870* A123 10c In concert 6 6
*871* A123 10c Facing front 6 6
*872* A123 60c In concert, diff. 35 35
*873* A123 60c Facing left 35 35
*874* A123 $1 In concert, diff. 60 60
*875* A123 $1 Facing front, diff. 60 60
*876* A123 $5 Wearing leather jacket 3.00 3.00
*877* A123 $5 Facing left, diff. 3.00 3.00
*Nos. 870-877 (8)* 8.02 8.02

**Souvenir Sheets**

*878* Sheet of 4 72 72
*a* A123 30c like #870 18 18
*b* A123 30c like #871 18 18
*879* Sheet of 4 1.20 1.20
*a* A123 50c like #872 30 30
*b* A123 50c like #873 30 30
*880* Sheet of 4 3.50 3.50
*a* A123 $1.50 like #874 85 85
*b* A123 $1.50 like #875 85 85
*881* Sheet of 4 10.00 10.00
*a* A123 $4.50 like #876 2.50 2.50
*b* A123 $4.50 like #877 2.50 2.50

Nos. 878-881 contain two of each stamp and have multicolored margins picturing various photographs of Elvis Presley playing the guitar, in uniform, as a youth idol, and in concert. Size: 145x107mm.

Stamps of the same denomination printed se-tenant.

Flour Milling A124

**1985, Oct. 17** **Wmk. 373** ***Perf. 15***
*882* A124 20c Conveyor from elevators 15 15
*883* A124 30c Roller mills 22 22
*884* A124 75c Office 55 55
*885* A124 $3 Bran finishers 2.25 2.25

**Nos. 667, 680, 863-864, 650, 631-632, 651 Ovptd. "CARIBBEAN / ROYAL VISIT / -1985-" or Surcharged with 3 Black Bars and New Value in Black.**

**1985, Oct. 27** ***Perfs. as before***
*886* A104 60c multi 45 45
*887* A105 60c multi 45 45
*888* A122 85c multi 65 65
*889* A122 85c multi 65 65
*890* A100 $1.50 multi 1.15 1.15
*891* A66 $1.60 on $4 1.20 1.20
*892* A67 $1.60 on $4 1.20 1.20
*893* A100 $2.50 multi 1.90 1.90
*Nos. 886-893 (8)* 7.65 7.65

Michael Jackson (b. 1960), American Entertainer A125

Photographs.

**1985, Dec. 2** ***Perf. 12½***
*894* A125 60c Portrait 35 35
*895* A125 60c On stage 35 35
*896* A125 $1 Singing 60 60
*897* A125 $1 Portrait, diff. 60 60
*898* A125 $2 Black jacket 1.25 1.25
*899* A125 $2 Red jacket 1.25 1.25
*900* A125 $5 Portrait, diff. 3.00 3.00
*901* A125 $5 Wearing white glove 3.00 3.00
*Nos. 894-901 (8)* 10.40 10.40

Stamps of same denomination printed se-tenant.

***Perf. 13x12½***
**Souvenir Sheets**

*902* Sheet of 4, 2 each 1.10 1.10
*d.-e* A125 45c, like #894-895 25 25
*902A* Sheet of 4, 2 each 2.25 2.25
*f.-g* A125 90c, like #896-897 55 55
*902B* Sheet of 4, 2 each 3.50 3.50
*h.-i* A125 $1.50, like #898-899 85 85
*902C* Sheet of 4, 2 each 10.00 10.00
*j.-k* A125 $4, like #900-901 2.50 2.50

Nos. 902-902C have multicolored margins picturing Jackson in concert. Sizes: 144x109mm.

Christmas A126

Children's drawings: 25c, Serenade. 75c, Poinsettia. $2.50, Jesus, Our Master.

**1985, Dec. 9** **Wmk. 373** ***Perf. 14***
*903* A126 25c multi 18 18
*904* A126 75c multi 55 55
*905* A126 $2.50 multi 1.90 1.90

Car Type of 1983

**1986, Jan. 27** ***Perf. 12½***
*906* A107 30c 1916 Cadillac Type 53, US 22 22
*907* A107 30c Cadillac, diff. 22 22
*908* A107 45c 1939 Triumph Dolomite, UK 35 35
*909* A107 45c Dolomite, diff. 35 35
*910* A107 60c 1972 Panther J-72, UK 45 45
*911* A107 60c Panther, diff. 45 45
*912* A107 90c 1967 Ferrari 275 GTB/4, Italy 70 70
*913* A107 90c Ferrari, diff. 70 70
*914* A107 $1.50 1953 Packard Caribbean, US 1.15 1.15
*915* A107 $1.50 Packard, diff. 1.15 1.15
*916* A107 $2.50 1931 Bugatti Type 41 Royale, France 1.90 1.90
*917* A107 $2.50 Royale, diff. 1.90 1.90
*Nos. 906-917 (12)* 9.54 9.54

Stamps of same denomination printed se-tenant.

Halley's Comet A127

**Wmk. 380**

**1986, Apr. 14** **Litho.** ***Perf. 15***
*918* A127 45c shown 35 35
*919* A127 60c Edmond Halley 45 45
*920* A127 75c Newton's reflector telescope 55 55
*921* A127 $3 Local astronomer 2.25 2.25
*a* Souvenir sheet of 4, #918-921 3.60 3.60

No. 921a has multicolored margin picturing observatories. Size: 156x104mm.

**Souvenir Sheets**

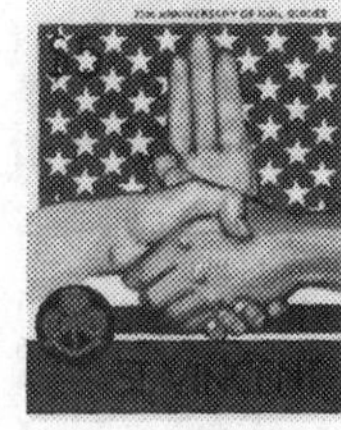

Scouting Movement, 75th Anniv. — A127a

American flag and Girl Guides or Boy Scouts emblem and: No. 922b, Scout sign, handshake. No. 922c, Paintbrushes and pallet. No. 922d, Knots. No. 922e, Lord Baden-Powell.

**1986, Feb. 25** **Litho.** ***Perf. 13x12½***
*922* Sheet of 2 5.00 5.00
*b.-c* A127a $5 any single 2.50 2.50
*922A* Sheet of 2 6.50 6.50
*d.-e* A127a $6 any single 3.25 3.25

Nos. 922-922A have pale green or tan margins picturing the Girl Guides or Boy Scouts emblem. Sizes: 86x114mm.

Elizabeth II Wearing Crown Jewels — A128

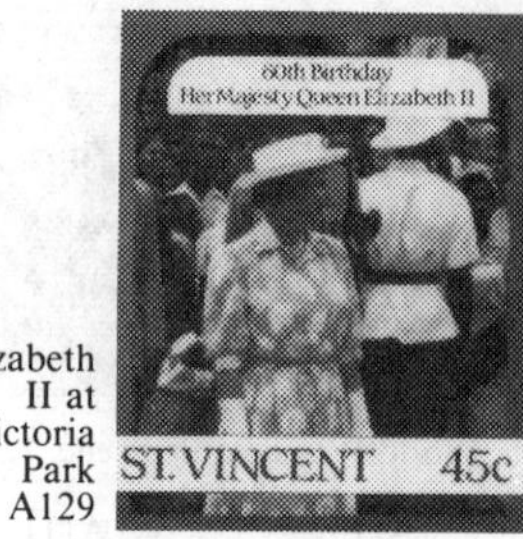


Elizabeth II at Victoria Park A129

Various portraits.

**1986, Apr. 21** **Wmk. 373** ***Perf. 12½***
*923* A128 10c multi 8 8
*924* A128 90c multi 68 68
*925* A128 $2.50 multi 1.90 1.90
*926* A128 $8 multi, vert. 6.00 6.00

**Souvenir Sheet**

*927* A128 $10 multi 7.50 7.50

No. 927 has multicolored margin.

***Perf. 15x14***

**1986, June 14** **Wmk. 373**

Designs: No. 928, with Prime Minister Mitchell. No. 929, Arriving at Port Elizabeth. No. 930, at Independence Day Parade.

*928* A129 45c multi 35 35
*929* A129 60c multi 45 45
*930* A129 75c multi 55 55
*931* A129 $2.50 multi 1.90 1.90

**Souvenir Sheet**

*932* A129 $3 multi 2.25 2.25

No. 932 has multicolored margin. Size: 121x85.

Queen Elizabeth II, 60th birthday.

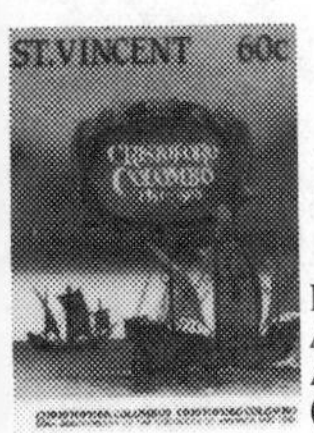


Discovery of America, 500th Anniv. (1992) — A130

**1986, Jan. 23 Litho. *Perf. 12½***

| | | | | | |
|---|---|---|---|---|---|
| *933* | A130 | 60c | Fleet | 45 | 45 |
| *934* | A130 | 60c | Columbus | 45 | 45 |
| *935* | A130 | $1.50 | At Spanish Court | 1.10 | 1.10 |
| *936* | A130 | $1.50 | Ferdinand, Isabella | 1.10 | 1.10 |
| *937* | A130 | $2.75 | Fruit, Santa Maria | 2.05 | 2.05 |
| *938* | A130 | $2.75 | Fruit | 2.05 | 2.05 |

**Souvenir Sheet**

| | | | | | |
|---|---|---|---|---|---|
| *939* | A130 | $6 | Columbus, diff. | 4.50 | 4.50 |

Stamps of same denomination printed se-tenant in continuous designs. No. 939 has multicolored margin picturing Columbus's fleet. Size: 95x85mm.

1986 World Cup Soccer Championships, Mexico — A131

***Perf. 15, 13½ (#948-955)***

**1986, May 7 Litho.**

| | | | | | |
|---|---|---|---|---|---|
| *940* | A131 | 1c | Emblem | 5 | 5 |
| *941* | A131 | 2c | Mexico | 5 | 5 |
| *942* | A131 | 5c | Mexico, diff. | 5 | 5 |
| *943* | A131 | 5c | Hungary vs. Scotland | 5 | 5 |
| *944* | A131 | 10c | Spain vs. Scotland | 8 | 8 |
| *945* | A131 | 30c | England vs. USSR | 22 | 22 |
| *946* | A131 | 45c | Spain vs. France | 35 | 35 |
| *947* | A131 | $1 | England vs. Italy | 75 | 75 |

**Size: 56x36mm**

| | | | | | |
|---|---|---|---|---|---|
| *948* | A131 | 75c | Mexico | 55 | 55 |
| *949* | A131 | $2 | Scotland | 1.50 | 1.50 |
| *950* | A131 | $4 | Spain | 3.00 | 3.00 |
| *951* | A131 | $5 | England | 3.75 | 3.75 |
| | | | *Nos. 940-951 (12)* | 10.40 | 10.40 |

**Souvenir Sheets**

| | | | | | |
|---|---|---|---|---|---|
| *952* | A131 | $1.50 | like #950 | 1.10 | 1.10 |
| *953* | A131 | $2.25 | like #949 | 1.65 | 1.65 |
| *954* | A131 | $2.50 | like #948 | 1.85 | 1.85 |
| *954A* | A131 | $3 | like #946 | 2.00 | 2.00 |
| *955* | A131 | $5.50 | like #951 | 4.10 | 4.10 |

Nos. 941-944, 946, 947, vert. Nos. 952-955 have multicolored decorative margins picturing the soccer cup, Mexico '86 character trademark, emblem or Azteca Stadium interior. Sizes: 85x115mm.

Wedding of Prince Andrew and Sarah Ferguson A132

A132a

***Perf. 12½x13, 13x12½***

**1986, July 23 Litho.**

| | | | | | |
|---|---|---|---|---|---|
| *956* | A132 | 60c | Andrew | 45 | 45 |
| *957* | A132 | 60c | Sarah | 45 | 45 |
| *958* | A132 | $2 | Andrew, vert. | 1.50 | 1.50 |
| *959* | A132 | $2 | Andrew, Nancy Reagan, vert. | 1.50 | 1.50 |

Stamps of the same denomination printed se-tenant. No. 958 pictures Westminster Abbey in LR.

**1986, Nov. Litho. *Perf. 13x12½***

| | | | | | |
|---|---|---|---|---|---|
| *959A* | A132a | $10 | In coach | 7.50 | 7.50 |

No. 959A has inscribed multicolored margin continuing the design. Size: 115x85mm.

Locomotives Type of 1985

Designs: Nos. 960-961, 1926 JNR ABT Rack & Adhesion Class ED41 BZZB, Japan. Nos. 962-963, 1883 Chicago RR Exposition, The Judge, 1A Type, US. Nos. 964-965, 1973 BM & LPRR E60C Co-Co, US. Nos. 966-967, 1972 GM (EMD) SD40-2 Co-Co, US.

**1986, July *Perf. 12½x13***

| | | | | | |
|---|---|---|---|---|---|
| *960* | A120 | 30c | multi | 22 | 22 |
| *961* | A120 | 30c | multi, diff. | 22 | 22 |
| *962* | A120 | 50c | multi | 38 | 38 |
| *963* | A120 | 50c | multi, diff. | 38 | 38 |
| *964* | A120 | $1 | multi | 75 | 75 |
| *965* | A120 | $1 | multi, diff. | 75 | 75 |
| *966* | A120 | $3 | multi | 2.25 | 2.25 |
| *967* | A120 | $3 | multi, diff. | 2.25 | 2.25 |
| | | | *Nos. 960-967 (8)* | 7.20 | 7.20 |

Stamps of the same denomination printed se-tenant.

Trees — A133

**1986, Sept. *Perf. 14***

| | | | | | |
|---|---|---|---|---|---|
| *968* | A133 | 10c | Acrocomia aculeata | 8 | 8 |
| *969* | A133 | 60c | Pithecellobium saman | 45 | 45 |
| *970* | A133 | 75c | Tabebuia pallida | 55 | 55 |
| *971* | A133 | $3 | Andira inermis | 2.25 | 2.25 |

Anniversaries — A134

**1986, Sept. 30**

| | | | | | |
|---|---|---|---|---|---|
| *972* | A134 | 45c | Cadet Force emblem, vert. | 35 | 35 |
| *973* | A134 | 60c | Grimble Building, GHS | 45 | 45 |
| *974* | A134 | $1.50 | GHS class | 1.10 | 1.10 |
| *975* | A134 | $2 | Cadets in formation | 1.50 | 1.50 |

St. Vincent Cadet Force, 50th anniv., and Girls' High School, 75th anniv.

The lack of a price for a listed item does not necessarily indicate rarity.

Nos. 956-959 Ovptd. "Congratulations to T.R.H. The Duke & Duchess of York" in Silver.

***Perf. 12½x13, 13x12½***

**1986, Oct. Litho.**

| | | | | | |
|---|---|---|---|---|---|
| *976* | A132 | 60c | No. 956 | 45 | 45 |
| *977* | A132 | 60c | No. 957 | 45 | 45 |
| *978* | A132 | $2 | No. 958 | 1.50 | 1.50 |
| *979* | A132 | $2 | No. 959 | 1.50 | 1.50 |

Stamps of the same denomination exist printed tete-beche and se-tenant.

The Legend of King Arthur — A134a

**1986, Nov. 3 *Perf. 14***

| | | | | | |
|---|---|---|---|---|---|
| *980* | A134a | 30c | King Arthur | 18 | 18 |
| *980A* | A134a | 45c | Merlin raises Arthur | 28 | 28 |
| *980B* | A134a | 60c | Arthur pulls Excalibur from stone | 38 | 38 |
| *980C* | A134a | 75c | Camelot | 45 | 45 |
| *980D* | A134a | $1 | Lady of the Lake | 60 | 60 |
| *980E* | A134a | $1.50 | Knights of the Round Table | 90 | 90 |
| *980F* | A134a | $2 | Holy Grail | 1.20 | 1.20 |
| *980G* | A134a | $5 | Sir Lancelot | 3.00 | 3.00 |
| | | | *Nos. 980-980G (8)* | 6.99 | 6.99 |

Statue of Liberty, Cent. — A134b

**1986, Nov. 26 Litho. *Perf. 14***

| | | | | | |
|---|---|---|---|---|---|
| *980H* | A134b | 15c | Statue at night | 12 | 12 |
| *980I* | A134b | 25c | Torch, men on scaffold | 18 | 18 |
| *980J* | A134b | 40c | Torch, fireworks | 30 | 30 |
| *980K* | A134b | 55c | Torch | 42 | 42 |
| *980L* | A134b | 75c | Statue in profile | 58 | 58 |
| *980M* | A134b | 90c | Statue, diff. | 68 | 68 |
| *980N* | A134b | $1.75 | Torch observatory | 1.30 | 1.30 |
| *980O* | A134b | $2 | Statue at night, close-up | 1.50 | 1.50 |
| *980P* | A134b | $2.50 | Face, crown observatory | 1.90 | 1.90 |
| *980Q* | A134b | $3 | Statue at night, front | 2.25 | 2.25 |
| | | | *Nos. 980H-980Q (10)* | 9.23 | 9.23 |

Souvenir Sheets

Statue of Liberty, Cent. — A135

Various views of the statue.

**1986, Nov. 26 Litho. *Perf. 14***

| | | | | | |
|---|---|---|---|---|---|
| *981* | A135 | $3.50 | multi | 2.65 | 2.65 |
| *982* | A135 | $4 | multi | 3.00 | 3.00 |
| *983* | A135 | $5 | multi | 3.75 | 3.75 |

Nos. 981-983 have multicolored margins picturing views of the statue and American presidents John Adams, Martin Van Buren and Franklin Pierce. Sizes: 85x115mm.

Fresh-water Fishing — A136

**1986, Dec. 10 *Perf. 15***

| | | | | | |
|---|---|---|---|---|---|
| *984* | A136 | 75c | Tri tri fishing | 58 | 58 |
| *985* | A136 | 75c | Tri tri | 58 | 58 |
| *986* | A136 | $1.50 | Crayfishing | 1.10 | 1.10 |
| *987* | A136 | $1.50 | Crayfish | 1.10 | 1.10 |

Stamps of the same denomination printed se-tenant.

1987 Wimbledon Tennis Championships A137

Natl. Child Survival Campaign A138

**1987, June 22 *Perf. 13x12½***

| | | | | | |
|---|---|---|---|---|---|
| *988* | A137 | 40c | Hana Mandlikova | 30 | 30 |
| *989* | A137 | 60c | Yannick Noah | 45 | 45 |
| *990* | A137 | 80c | Ivan Lendl | 60 | 60 |
| *991* | A137 | $1 | Chris Evert Lloyd | 75 | 75 |
| *992* | A137 | $1.25 | Steffi Graf | 95 | 95 |
| *993* | A137 | $1.50 | John McEnroe | 1.15 | 1.15 |
| *994* | A137 | $1.75 | Martina Navratilova | 1.35 | 1.35 |
| *995* | A137 | $2 | Boris Becker | 1.50 | 1.50 |
| | | | *Nos. 988-995 (8)* | 7.05 | 7.05 |

**Souvenir Sheet**

| | | | | | |
|---|---|---|---|---|---|
| *996* | | | Sheet of 2 | 3.50 | 3.50 |
| *a.* | A137 | $2.25 | like $2 | 1.75 | 1.75 |
| *b.* | A137 | $2.25 | like $1.75 | 1.75 | 1.75 |

No. 996 has multicolored margin picturing match. Size: 115x85mm.

**1987, June 10 *Perf. 14x14½***

| | | | | | |
|---|---|---|---|---|---|
| *997* | A138 | 10c | Growth monitoring | 8 | 8 |
| *998* | A138 | 50c | Oral rehydration therapy | 38 | 38 |
| *999* | A138 | 75c | Breast-feeding | 58 | 58 |
| *1000* | A138 | $1 | Universal immunization | 75 | 75 |

Carnival, 10th Anniv. A139

Designs: 20c, Queen of the Bands, Miss Prima Donna 1986. 45c, Donna Young, Miss Carival 1985. 55c, M. Haydock, Miss. St. Vincent and the Grenadines 1986.

**1987, June 29** ***Perf. 12½x13***

*1001* A139 20c multi 15 15
*1002* A139 45c multi 35 35
*1003* A139 55c multi 42 42
*1004* A139 $3.70 multi 2.75 2.75

Nos. 870-881 Overprinted "THE KING OF ROCK AND ROLL LIVES FOREVER • AUGUST 16TH" and "1977-1987" (Nos. 1005-1012) or "TENTH ANNIVERSARY" (Nos. 1013-1016).

**1987, Aug. 26** **Litho.** ***Perf. 12½***

*1005* A123 10c like No. 870 8 8
*1006* A123 10c like No. 871 8 8
*1007* A123 60c like No. 872 45 45
*1008* A123 60c like No. 873 45 45
*1009* A123 $1 like No. 874 75 75
*1010* A123 $1 like No. 875 75 75
*1011* A123 $5 like No. 876 3.75 3.75
*1012* A123 $5 like No. 877 3.75 3.75
*Nos. 1005-1012 (8)* 10.06 10.06

**Souvenir Sheets**

*1013* Sheet of 4 90 90
**a.** A123 30c like No. 870 22 22
**b.** A123 30c like No. 871 22 22
*1014* Sheet of 4 1.50 1.50
**a.** A123 50c like No. 872 35 35
**b.** A123 50c like No. 873 35 35
*1015* Sheet of 4 4.50 4.50
**a.** A123 $1.50 like No. 874 1.10 1.10
**b.** A123 $1.50 like No. 875 1.10 1.10
*1016* Sheet of 4 13.00 13.00
**a.** A123 $4.50 like No. 876 3.25 3.25
**b.** A123 $4.50 like No. 877 3.25 3.25

Stamps of the same denomination printed se-tenant. Nos. 1013-1016 contain two of each stamp.

Portrait of Queen Victoria, 1841, by R. Thorburn A140

Portraits and photographs: 75c, Elizabeth and Charles, 1948. $1, Coronation, 1953. $2.50, Duke of Edinburgh, 1948. $5, Elizabeth, c. 1980. $6, Elizabeth and Charles, 1948, diff.

**1987, Nov. 20** **Litho.** ***Perf. 12½x13***

*1017* A140 15c multi 12 12
*1018* A140 75c multi 58 58
*1019* A140 $1 multi 75 75
*1020* A140 $2.50 multi 1.90 1.90
*1021* A140 $5 multi 3.75 3.75
*Nos. 1017-1021 (5)* 7.10 7.10

**Souvenir Sheet**

*1022* A140 $6 multi 4.50 4.50

Sesquicentennial of Queen Victoria's accession to the throne, wedding of Queen Elizabeth II and Prince Philip, 40th anniv. No. 1022 has multicolored inscribed margin showing the royal family. Size: 86x116mm.

Nos. 997-1000 Ovptd. "WORLD POPULATION / 5 BILLION / 11TH JULY 1987."

**1987, July 11** **Litho.** ***Perf. 14x14½***

*1040* A138 10c on No. 997 8 8
*1041* A138 50c on No. 998 38 38
*1042* A138 75c on No. 999 58 58
*1043* A138 $1 on No. 1000 75 75

Automobile Centenary — A143

Automotive pioneers and vehicles: $1, $3, Carl Benz (1844-1929) and the Velocipede, patented 1886. $2, No. 1049, Enzo Ferrari (b. 1898) and 1966 Ferrari Dino 206SP. $4, $6, Charles Rolls (1877-1910), Sir Henry Royce (1863-1933) and 1907 Rolls Royce Silver Ghost. No. 1047, $8, Henry Ford (1863-1947) and Model T Ford.

**1987, Dec. 4** ***Perf. 13x12½***

*1044* A143 $1 multi 75 75
*1045* A143 $2 multi 1.50 1.50
*1046* A143 $4 multi 3.00 3.00
*1047* A143 $5 multi 3.75 3.75

**Souvenir Sheets**

*1048* A143 $3 like No. 1044 2.25 2.25
*1049* A143 $5 like No. 1045 3.75 3.75
*1050* A143 $6 like No. 1046 4.50 4.50
*1051* A143 $8 like No. 1047 6.00 6.00

Nos. 1048-1051 have multicolored margins picturing various mass models, race cars, military vehicles, famous people, manufacturers' emblems and engine parts. Sizes: 145x75mm.

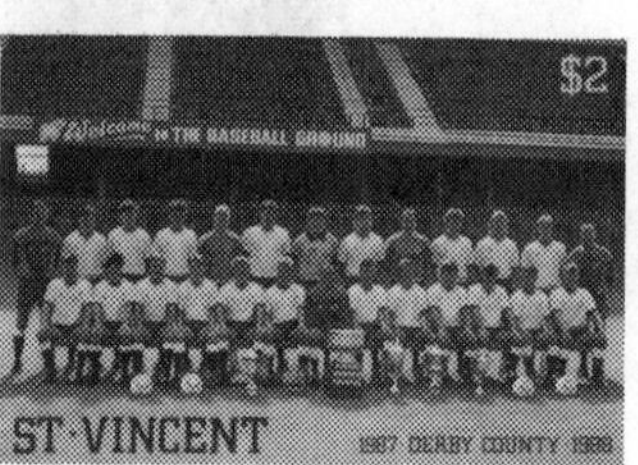


Soccer Teams — A144

**1987, Dec. 4**

*1052* A144 $2 Derby County 1.50 1.50
*1053* A144 $2 Leeds United 1.50 1.50
*1054* A144 $2 Tottenham Hotspur 1.50 1.50
*1055* A144 $2 Manchester United 1.50 1.50
*1056* A144 $2 Everton 1.50 1.50
*1057* A144 $2 Liverpool 1.50 1.50
*1058* A144 $2 Portsmouth 1.50 1.50
*1059* A144 $2 Arsenal 1.50 1.50
*Nos. 1052-1059 (8)* 12.00 12.00

A145 A146

A Christmas Carol, by Charles Dickens (1812-1870) — A147

Portrait of Dickens as left page of book and various scenes from novels as right page of book.

**1987, Dec. 17** ***Perf. 14x14½***

*1060* A145 6c multi 5 5
*1061* A146 6c Mr. Fezziwig's Ball 5 5
*1062* A145 25c multi 20 20
*1063* A146 25c Ghost of Christmases to Come 20 20
*1064* A145 50c multi 38 38
*1065* A146 50c The Cratchits 38 38
*1066* A145 75c multi 55 55
*1067* A146 75c Carolers 55 55
*Nos. 1060-1067 (8)* 2.36 2.36

**Souvenir Sheet**

*1068* A147 $5 Reading book to children 3.75 3.75

Stamps of the same denomination printed se-tenant in continuous designs. No. 1068 has multicolored margin continuing the design and picturing children, Christmas tree, snowflakes and creche. Size: 142x102mm.

Eastern Caribbean Currency — A148

Various Eastern Caribbean coins (Nos. 1069-1081) and banknotes (Nos. 1082-1086) in denominations equaling that of the stamp on which they are pictured.

**1987, Dec. 11** **Litho.** ***Perf. 15***

*1069* A148 5c multi 5 5
*1070* A148 6c multi 5 5
*1071* A148 10c multi 8 8
*1072* A148 12c multi 9 9
*1073* A148 15c multi 12 12
*1074* A148 20c multi 15 15
*1075* A148 25c multi 20 20
*1076* A148 30c multi 24 24
*1077* A148 35c multi 28 28
*1078* A148 45c multi 35 35
*1079* A148 50c multi 38 38
*1080* A148 65c multi 50 50
*1081* A148 75c multi 58 58
*1082* A148 $1 multi, horiz. 75 75
*1083* A148 $2 multi, horiz. 1.50 1.50
*1084* A148 $3 multi, horiz. 2.25 2.25
*1085* A148 $5 multi, horiz. 3.75 3.75
*1086* A148 $10 multi, horiz. 7.50 7.50
*Nos. 1069-1086 (18)* 18.82 18.82

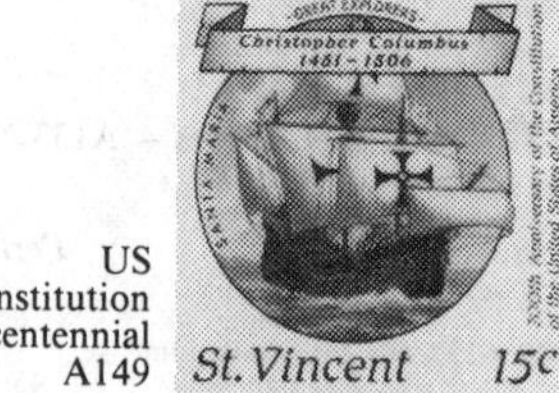


US Constitution Bicentennial A149

Christopher Columbus's fleet: 15c, Santa Maria. 75c, Nina and Pinta. $1, Hour glass, compass. $1.50, Columbus planting flag of Spain on American soil. $3, Arawak natives. $4, Parrot, hummingbird, corn, pineapple, eggs. $5, Columbus, Spanish royal coat of arms and caravel.

**1988, Jan. 11** ***Perf. 14½x14***

*1087* A149 15c multi 12 12
*1088* A149 75c multi 58 58
*1089* A149 $1 multi 75 75
*1090* A149 $1.50 multi 1.15 1.15
*1091* A149 $3 multi 2.25 2.25
*1092* A149 $4 multi 3.00 3.00
*Nos. 1087-1092 (6)* 7.85 7.85

**Souvenir Sheet**

***Perf. 14x14½***

*1093* A149 $5 multi 3.75 3.75

No. 1093 has multicolored inscribed margin picturing map of first voyage. Size: 115x86mm.

Brown Pelican — A150

**1988, Feb. 15** ***Perf. 14***

*1094* A150 45c multi 35 35

A151

Tourism — A152

**1988, Feb. 22** **Litho.** ***Perf. 15***

*1095* A151 10c Windsurfing, diff., vert. 8 8
*1096* A151 45c Scuba diving, vert. 35 35
*1097* A151 65c shown 50 50
*1098* A151 $5 Chartered ship 3.75 3.75

**Souvenir Sheet**

***Perf. 13x12½***

*1099* A152 $10 shown 7.50 7.50

No. 1099 has multicolored margin continuing the design. Size: 115x85mm.

A153

Destruction of the Spanish Armada by the English, 400th Anniv. — A154

16th cent. ships and artifacts: 15c, *Nuestra Senora del Rosario,* Spanish Chivalric Cross. 75c, *Ark Royal,* Armada medal. $1.50, English fleet, 16th cent. navigational instrument. $2, Dismasted galleon, cannon balls. $3.50, English fireships among the Armada, firebomb. $5, *Revenge,* Drake's drum. $8, Shoreline sentries awaiting the outcome of the battle.

**1988, July 29** **Litho.** ***Perf. 12½***

*1100* A153 15c multi 12 12
*1101* A153 75c multi 58 58
*1102* A153 $1.50 multi 1.15 1.15
*1103* A153 $2 multi 1.50 1.50
*1104* A153 $3.50 multi 2.60 2.60
*1105* A153 $5 multi 3.75 3.75
*Nos. 1100-1105 (6)* 9.70 9.70

**Souvenir Sheet**

*1106* A154 $8 multi 6.00 6.00

No. 1106 has multicolored margin continuing the design and picturing signal fire ready to be lit. Size: 124x92mm.

Cricket Players A156

**1988, July 29 Litho.** ***Perf. 14½x14***
*1108* A156 15c D.K. Lillee 12 12
*1109* A156 50c G.A. Gooch 38 38
*1110* A156 75c R.N. Kapil Dev 58 58
*1111* A156 $1 S.M. Gavaskar 75 75
*1112* A156 $1.50 M.W. Gatting 1.15 1.15
*1113* A156 $2.50 Imran Khan 1.90 1.90
*1114* A156 $3 I.T. Botham 2.25 2.25
*1115* A156 $4 I.V.A. Richards 3.00 3.00
*Nos. 1108-1115 (8)* 10.13 10.13

**Souvenir Sheet**

***Perf. 14x14½***

*1116* Sheet of 2 4.10 4.10
**a.** A156 $2 like $4 1.50 1.50
**b.** A156 $3.50 like $3 2.60 2.60

No. 1116 has multicolored decorative margin picturing match scene. Size: 130x80mm.

Christmas – A159

Walt Disney characters: 1c, Minnie Mouse in freight car. 2c, Morty and Ferdy in open rail car. 3c, Chip'n'Dale in open boxcar. 4c, Huey, Dewey, Louie and reindeer. 5c, Donald and Daisy Duck aboard dining car. 10c, Gramma Duck conducting chorus including Scrooge McDuck, Goofy and Clarabelle Cow. No. 1127, Mickey Mouse in locomotive. $6, Santa Claus in caboose. No. 1129, Mickey, Minnie Mouse and nephews in train station, vert. No. 1130, Characters riding carousel, vert.

***Perf. 14x13½, 13½x14***

**1988, Dec. 23 Litho.**
*1121* A159 1c multi 5 5
*1122* A159 2c multi 5 5
*1123* A159 3c multi 5 5
*1124* A159 4c multi 5 5
*1125* A159 5c multi 5 5
*1126* A159 10c multi 8 8
*1127* A159 $5 multi 3.75 3.75
*1128* A159 $6 multi 4.50 4.50
*Nos. 1121-1128 (8)* 8.58 8.58

**Souvenir Sheets**

*1129* A159 $5 multi 3.75 3.75
*1130* A159 $5 multi 3.75 3.75

Nos. 1129-1130 have multicolored decorative margins continuing the designs. Size: 127x101mm.

Babe Ruth (1895-1948), American Baseball Star – A160

**1988, Dec. 7 Litho.** ***Perf. 14***
*1131* A160 $2 multi 1.50 1.50

## SEMI-POSTAL STAMPS

**Catalogue values for unused stamps in this section, from this point to the end of the section, are for Never Hinged items.**

Map Type of 1977-78 Overprinted: "SOUFRIERE / RELIEF / FUND 1979"

**Litho. and Typo.**

**1979 Wmk. 373** ***Perf. 14½x14***
*B1* A76 10c + 5c multi 10 10
*B2* A76 50c + 25c multi 50 50
*B3* A76 $1 + 50c multi 1.00 1.00
*B4* A76 $2 + $1 multi 2.00 2.00

The surtax was for victims of the eruption of Mt. Soufrière.

Nos. 604-607 Surcharged: "HURRICANE / RELIEF / 50c"

**1980, Aug. 7 Litho.** ***Perf. 13½***
*B5* A90 10c + 50c multi 35 35
*B6* A90 60c + 50c multi 60 60
*B7* A90 80c + 50c multi 75 75
*B8* A90 $2.50 + 50c multi 1.75 1.75

Surtax was for victims of Hurricane Allen.

## WAR TAX STAMPS

No. 105 Overprinted **WAR STAMP.**

Type I. Words 2 to 2½mm apart.
Type II. Words 1½mm apart.
Type III. Words 3½mm apart.

**1916 Wmk. 3** ***Perf. 14***
*MR1* A17 1p car, type III 1.50 1.50
**a.** Double ovpt., type III 225.00 225.00
**b.** 1p carmine, type I 1.75 1.75
**c.** Comma after "STAMP", type I 7.50 10.00
**d.** Double ovpt., type I 150.00 150.00
**e.** 1p carmine, type II 80.00 80.00

Overprinted **WAR STAMP**

*MR2* A17 1p carmine 25 25

## OFFICIAL STAMPS

**Catalogue values for unused stamps in this section, from this point to the end of the section, are for Never Hinged items.**

Nos. 627-632 Overprinted OFFICIAL

**1982, Nov. Litho.** ***Perf. 14***
*O1* A66 60c Couple, Isabella 30 30
*O2* A67 60c Couple 30 30
*O3* A66 $2.50 Couple, Alberta 1.25 1.25
*O4* A67 $2.50 Couple 1.25 1.25
*O5* A66 $4 Couple, Britannia 2.00 2.00
*O6* A67 $4 Couple 2.00 2.00
*Nos. O1-O6 (6)* 7.10 7.10

# SAMOA

## (Western Samoa)

LOCATION – An archipelago in the south Pacific Ocean, east of Fiji.
GOVT. – Independent state; former territory mandated by New Zealand.
AREA – 1,093 sq. mi.
POP. – 156,349 (1981).
CAPITAL – Apia.

In 1861-99, Samoa was an independent kingdom under the influence of the United States, to which the harbor of Pago Pago had been ceded, and that of Great Britain and Germany. In 1898 a disturbance arose, resulting in the withdrawal of Great Britain, and the partitioning of the islands between Germany and the United States. Early in World War I the islands under German domination were occupied by New Zealand troops and in 1920 the League of Nations declared them a mandate to New Zealand. Western Samoa became independent January 1, 1962. See Vol. 4 for German issues.

12 Pence = 1 Shilling
20 Shillings = 1 Pound
100 Sene (Cents) = 1 Tala (Dollar) (1967).

**Catalogue values for unused stamps in this country are for Never Hinged items, beginning with Scott 191 in the regular postage section, Scott B1 in the semi-postal section and Scott C1 in the air post section.**

### Issues of the Kingdom.

A1

Type I. Line above "X" is usually unbroken. Dots over "SAMOA" are uniform and evenly spaced. Upper right serif of "M" is horizontal.

Type II. Line above "X" is usually broken. Small dot near upper right serif of "M".

Type III. Line above "X" roughly retouched. Upper right serif of "M" bends down.

Type IV. Speck of color on curved line below center of "M".

***Perf. 12, 12½***

**1877-82 Litho. Unwmk.**
*1* A1 1p bl (III) ('79) 17.50 22.50
**a.** 1p ultra (III) ('79) 19.00 27.50
**b.** 1p ultra (II) ('78) 67.50 65.00
**c.** 1p ultra (I) ('77) 200.00 82.50
*2* A1 2p lil rose (IV) ('82) 17.50
*3* A1 3p ver (III) ('79) 20.00 22.50
**a.** 3p brt scar (III) 20.00 22.50
**b.** 3p scar (I) ('77) 210.00 72.50
**c.** 3p dp scar (I) ('77) 90.00 72.50
*4* A1 6p vio (III) ('79) 20.00 22.50
**a.** 6p vio (II) ('78) 150.00 85.00
**b.** 6p vio (I) ('77) 210.00 90.00
*5* A1 9p yel brn (IV) ('80) 32.50 82.50
**a.** 9p org brn (IV) ('80) 32.50 82.50
*6* A1 1sh org yel (II) ('78) 60.00 60.00
**a.** 1sh dl yel (I) ('77) 35.00 32.50
*7* A1 2sh dp brn (III) ('79) 77.50 82.50
**a.** 2sh red brn (II) ('78) 200.00 175.00
**b.** 2sh brn (II) ('78) 200.00 175.00
*8* A1 5sh yel grn (III) ('79) 425.00 500.00
**a.** 5sh dp grn (III) ('79) 425.00 500.00
**b.** 5sh gray grn (II) ('78) 1.000. 1.250.

The 1p often has a period after "PENNY." The 2p was never placed in use.

Imperforates of this issue are proofs.

Sheets of the first issue were not perforated around the outer sides. All values except the 2p were printed in sheets of 10 (2x5). The 1p, 3p and 6p type I and the 1p type III were also printed in sheets of 20 (4x5), and six stamps on each of these sheets were perforated all around. The 2p was printed in sheets of 21 (3x7) and five stamps in the second row were perforated all around. These are the only varieties of the original stamps which have not one or two imperforate edges.

*Reprints are of type IV and nearly always perforated on all sides. They have a spot of color at the edge of the panel below the "M". This spot is not on any originals except the 2p, which may be distinguished by its color, and the 9p which may be distinguished by having a rough blind perf. 12.*

Palms A2

King Malietoa Laupera A3

Wmk. 62- N Z and Star Wide Apart

**1895-99 Typo. Wmk. 62** ***Perf. 11***
*9* A2 ½p brn vio ('95) 60 1.25
*10* A2 ½p grn ('99) 42 55
*11* A2 1p grn ('95) 90 1.25
*12* A2 1p red brn ('99) 40 50
*13* A2 2p brt yel ('95) 90 90
*14* A3 2½p rose ('92) 75 75
*15* A3 2½p blk, perf. 10x11 ('96) 1.10 1.10
**a.** Perf. 11 ('95) 75.00 65.00
*16* A2 4p bl ('95) 1.00 1.25
*17* A2 6p mar ('95) 1.10 3.00
*18* A2 1sh rose ('95) 1.40 4.50
*19* A2 2sh6p red vio ('95) 4.50 9.00
**c.** Vert. pair, imperf. between 500.00
*Nos. 9-19 (11)* 13.07 24.05

**1886-92** ***Perf. 12½***
*9a* A2 ½p brn vio 10.00 15.00
*11a* A2 1p green 5.50 11.00
*13a* A2 2p orange 5.50 5.50
*14a* A3 2½p rose ('92) 95 1.90
*16a* A2 4p blue 5.00 5.00
*17a* A2 6p maroon 650.00
*18a* A2 1sh rose 20.00 7.75
**c.** Diagonal half used as 6p on cover 350.00
*19a* A2 2sh6p purple 30.00 22.50
*Nos. 9a-16a,18a-19a (7)* 76.95 68.65

**1887-92** ***Perf. 12x11½***
*9b* A2 ½p brn vio 18 18
*11b* A2 1p green 4.50 1.10
*13b* A2 2p brn org 5.50 1.65
*14b* A3 2½p rose ('92) 165.00 2.75
*16b* A2 4p blue 82.50 3.25
*17b* A2 6p maroon 11.00 5.50
*18b* A2 1sh rose 8.25 2.75
*19b* A2 2sh6p red vio 8.75 1.40
*Nos. 9b-19b (8)* 285.68 18.58

Three forms of watermark 62 are found on stamps of type A2: 1. Wide "N Z" and wide star, 6mm. apart (used 1886-87). 2. Wide "N Z" and narrow star, 4mm. apart (1890). 3. Narrow "NZ" and narrow star, 7mm. apart (1890-1900). The 2½p has only the last form.

No. 16b Handstamp Surcharged in Black or Red:

FIVE PENCE (a) FIVE PENCE (b) 5d (c)

**1893** ***Perf. 12x11½***
*20* A2(a) 5p on 4p bl 37.50 37.50
*21* A2(b) 5p on 4p bl 45.00 50.00
*22* A2(c) 5p on 4p bl (R) 10.00 10.00

As the surcharges on Nos. 20-21 were handstamped in two steps and on No. 22 in three steps, various varieties exist.

Flag Design – A7

**1894-95 Typo.** ***Perf. 11½x12***
*23* A7 5p vermilion 5.00 2.50
**a.** Perf. 11 ('95) 1.50 7.00

Foreign postal stationery (stamped envelopes, postal cards and air letter sheets) lies beyond the scope of this Catalogue, which is limited to adhesive postage stamps.

Types of 1887-1895 Surcharged in Blue, Black, Red or Green:

Surcharged
1½d.
1 1/2p, 2 1/2p

R
3d.
3p

**1895** *Perf. 11*

*24* A2 1½p on 2p org (Bl) 1.50 1.50
*a.* 1½p on 2p brn org, perf. 12x11½ (bl) 2.00 2.00
*b.* 1½p on 2p yel, "2" ends with vertical stroke 1.00 1.00
*25* A2 3p on 2p org (Bk) 2.00 2.00
*a.* 3p on 2p brn org, perf. 12x11½ (Bk) 3.00 3.00
*b.* 3p on 2p yel, perf. 11 (Bk) 30.00 30.00
*c.* Vert. pair, imperf. btwn 425.00

**1898-1900** *Perf. 11*

*26* A2 2½p on 1sh rose (Bk) 95 95
*a.* Double surcharge 425.00
*27* A2 2½p on 2sh6p vio (Bk) 3.75 5.50
*28* A2 2½p on 1p bl grn (R) 40 80
*a.* Inverted surcharge 425.00
*29* A2 2½p on 1sh rose (R) 5.50 6.00
*30* A2 3p on 2p org (G) 60

No. 30 was a reissue, available for postage.

Stamps of 1886-99 Overprinted in Red or Blue

PROVISIONAL
GOVT.

**1899**

*31* A2 ½p grn (R) 20 22
*32* A2 1p red brn (bl) 20 22
*33* A2 2p org (R) 32 40
*a.* 2p yel 40 50
*34* A2 4p bl (R) 32 40
*35* A7 5p scar (bl) 38 38
*36* A2 6p mar (bl)52 52 70
*37* A2 1sh rose (bl) 1.25 1.40
*38* A2 2sh6p vio (R) 2.25 2.50
*Nos. 31-38 (8)* 5.44 6.22

In 1900 the Samoan islands were partitioned between the United States and Germany. The part which became American has since used U.S. stamps.

**Issued under British Dominion.**

Kaiser's Yacht "Hohenzollern"
A12 A13

Stamps of German Samoa Surcharged:

G.R.I.
2½ d.
On A12

G.R.I.
1 Shillings.
On A13

**1914** **Unwmk.** *Perf. 14*

*101* A12 ½p on 3pf brn 8.25 7.25
*a.* Double surcharge 500.00 400.00
*b.* Fraction bar omitted 45.00 30.00
*c.* Comma after "I" 435.00 360.00
*102* A12 ½p on 5pf grn 19.00 6.75
*a.* Double surcharge 450.00 325.00
*b.* Fraction bar omitted 45.00 35.00
*c.* Two fraction bars
*d.* Comma after "I" 360.00 300.00
*103* A12 1p on 10pf car 97.50 35.00
*a.* Double surcharge 435.00 425.00
*104* A12 2½p on 20pf ultra 22.50 8.25
*a.* Fraction bar omitted 40.00 32.50
*b.* Inverted surcharge 725.00 650.00
*c.* Double surcharge 650.00 600.00
*d.* Commas after "I" 350.00 310.00
*105* A12 3p on 25pf org & blk, *yel* 55.00 22.50
*a.* Double surcharge 425.00 360.00
*b.* Comma after "I" 4,500. 800.00
*106* A12 4p on 30pf org & blk, *sal* 97.50 62.50
*a.* Surch. "3d" 4,250. 3,750.
*107* A12 5p on 40pf lake & blk 100.00 62.50
*a.* Surch. "4d" 4,000. 3,600.
*108* A12 6p on 50pf pur & blk, *sal* 55.00 22.50
*a.* Inverted "9" for "6" 135.00 100.00
*b.* Double surcharge 500.00 500.00
*109* A12 9p on 80pf lake & blk, *rose* 200.00 82.50

*Perf. 14½x14*

*110* A13 1sh on 1m car ("1 Shillings.") 2,500. 2,000.
*a.* "1 Shilling." *12,500.* *7,000.*
*111* A13 2sh on 2m bl 3,500. 3,500.
*112* A13 3sh on 3m blk vio 1,150. 600.00
*a.* Double surcharge *7,500.* *7,500.*
*113* A13 5sh on 5m sl & car 900.00 800.00
*a.* Double surcharge 11,000. 11,000.

G.R.I. stands for Georgius Rex Imperator.

Stamps of New Zealand Overprinted in Red or Blue:

SAMOA.
k

S A M O A.
m

*Perf. 14, 14x13½, 14x14½*

**1914, Sept. 29** **Wmk. 61**

*114* A41 (k) ½p yel grn (R) 25 28
*115* A42 (k) 1p car (Bl) 25 20
*116* A41 (k) 2p mv (R) 75 85
*117* A22 (m) 2½p Bl (R) 2.25 1.25
*118* A41 (k) 6p car rose, perf. 14x14½ (Bl) 1.50 1.75
*a.* Perf. 14x13½ 11.00 11.00
*119* A41 (k) 1sh ver (Bl) 3.75 6.25
*Nos. 114-119 (6)* 8.75 10.58

Overprinted Type "m"

**1914-25** *Perf. 14, 14½x14*

*120* PF1 2sh bl (R) 4.50 5.00
*121* PF1 2sh6p brn (Bl) 5.00 6.25
*122* PF1 3sh vio (R) ('22) 8.75 *25.00*
*123* PF1 5sh grn (R) 6.00 *8.75*
*124* PF1 10sh red brn (Bl) 20.00 24.00
*125* PF2 £1 rose (Bl) 50.00 55.00
*126* PF2 £2 vio (R) ('25) 325.00 350.00

Overprinted Type "k"

*Perf. 14x13½, 14x14½.*

**1916-19** **Typo.**

*127* A43 ½p yel grn (R) 15 18
*128* A47 1½p gray blk (R) ('17) 22 25
*129* A47 1½p brn org (R) ('19) 18 25
*130* A43 2p yel (R) ('18) 38 30
*131* A43 3p choc (Bl) 1.25 3.00

**Engr.**

*132* A44 2½p dl bl (R) 50 55
*133* A45 3p vio brn (Bl) 50 65
*134* A45 6p car rose (Bl) 1.40 1.50
*135* A45 1sh ver (Bl) 1.75 1.75
*Nos. 127-135 (9)* 6.33 8.43

Overprinted Type "k" On New Zealand Victory Issue of 1919

**1920, June** *Perf. 14*

*136* A48 ½p yel grn (R) 25 35
*137* A49 1p car (Bl) 35 45
*138* A50 1½p brn org (R) 75 95
*139* A51 3p blk brn (Bl) 3.25 3.75
*140* A52 6p pur (R) 3.00 3.50
*141* A53 1sh ver (Bl) 3.50 4.00
*Nos. 136-141 (6)* 11.10 13.00

British Flag and Samoan House — A22

**1921, Dec. 23** **Engr.** *Perf. 14x13½*

*142* A22 ½p green 32 32
*a.* Perf. 14x14½ 50 60
*143* A22 1p lake 32 20
*a.* Perf. 14x14½ 32 42
*144* A22 1½p org brn, perf. 14x14½ 48 55
*a.* Perf. 14x13½ 3.00 3.25
*145* A22 2p yel, perf. 14x14½ 48 48
*a.* Perf. 14x13½ 1.90 1.50
*146* A22 2½p dl bl 75 75
*147* A22 3p dk brn 1.65 1.75
*148* A22 4p violet 1.50 1.75
*149* A22 5p brt bl 1.50 1.75
*150* A22 6p car rose 2.25 2.50
*151* A22 8p red brn 3.00 3.50
*152* A22 9p ol grn 3.00 3.50
*153* A22 1sh vermilion 4.00 4.25
*Nos. 142-153 (12)* 19.25 21.30

New Zealand Nos. 182-183 Overprinted Type "m" in Red

**1926-28** *Perf. 14½x14*

*154* A56 2sh dark blue 4.50 *8.75*
*a.* 2sh blue ('28) 10.00 *20.00*
*155* A56 3sh deep violet 10.00 *20.00*
*a.* 3sh violet ('28) 42.50 *55.00*

New Zealand Postal-Fiscal Stamps, Overprinted Type "m" in Blue or Red.

**1932** *Perf. 14.*

*156* PF5 2sh6p brown 11.00 *15.00*
*157* PF5 5sh grn (R) 12.00 *19.00*
*158* PF5 10sh lake 40.00 45.00
*159* PF5 £1 pink 55.00 *65.00*
*160* PF5 £2 vio (R) *725.00*
*161* PF5 £5 dk bl (R) *1,500.*

See Nos. 175-180, 195-202, 216-219.

**Silver Jubilee Issue.**

Stamps of 1921 Overprinted in Black

SILVER JUBILEE
OF
KING GEORGE V
1910 - 1935.

**1935, May 7** *Perf. 14x13½*

*163* A22 1p lake 28 30
*a.* Perf. 14x14½ *75.00* *82.50*
*164* A22 2½p dl bl 80 95
*165* A22 6p car rose 4.50 5.00

25th anniv. of the reign of George V.

**Western Samoa.**

Samoan Girl and Kava Bowl — A23

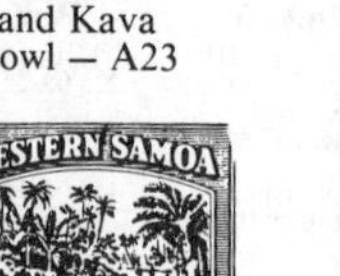


View of Apia — A24

River Scene — A25

Samoan Chief and Wife — A26

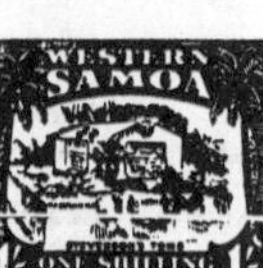


Samoan Canoe and House — A27

"Vailima," Stevenson's Home — A28

Stevenson's Tomb A29

Lake Lanuto'o A30

Falefa Falls — A31

*Perf. 14x13½, 13½x14*

**1935, Aug. 7** **Engr.** **Wmk. 61**

*166* A23 ½p yel grn 6 6
*167* A24 1p car lake & blk 14 14
*168* A25 2p red org & blk, perf. 14 40 40
*a.* Perf. 13½x14 1.40 2.75
*169* A26 2½p dp bl & blk 22 22
*170* A27 4p blk brn & dk gray 50 50
*171* A28 6p plum 50 50
*172* A29 1sh brn & vio 80 80
*173* A30 2sh red brn & yel grn 1.25 1.25
*174* A31 3sh org brn & brt bl 2.00 2.00
*Nos. 166-174 (9)* 5.87 5.87

See Nos. 186-188.

Postal-Fiscal Stamps of New Zealand Overprinted in Blue or Carmine

WESTERN
SAMOA.

**1935** *Perf. 14*

*175* PF5 2sh6p brown 3.25 4.00
*176* PF5 5sh green 5.00 5.75
*177* PF5 10sh dp car 16.00 25.00
*178* PF5 £1 pink 32.50 42.50
*179* PF5 £2 vio (C) 100.00 125.00
*180* PF5 £5 dk bl (C) 290.00 300.00

See Nos. 195-202, 216-219.

Samoan Coastal Village — A32

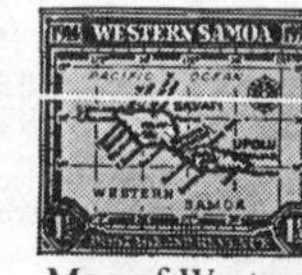


Map of Western Samoa — A33

Samoan Dancing Party A34

Robert Louis Stevenson A35

Wmk. 253- Multiple N Z and Star

*Perf. 13½x14*

**1939, Aug. 29** **Engr.** **Wmk. 253**

*181* A32 1p scar & ol 25 25
*182* A33 1½p cop brn & bl 50 50
*183* A34 2½p dk bl & brn 1.00 1.00

*Perf. 14x13½*

*184* A35 7p dp sl grn & vio 2.50 2.50

25th anniv. of New Zealand's control of the mandated territory of Western Samoa.

Samoan Chief — A36

Apia Post Office — A37

**1940, Sept. 2** *Perf. 14x13½*

*185* A36 3p on 1½p brn 15 15

Types of 1935 and A37

**1944-49** **Wmk. 253** *Perf. 14*

*186* A23 ½p yel grn 38 38
*187* A25 2p red org & blk 50 50
*188* A26 2½p dp bl & blk ('49) 1.25 1.25

*Perf. 13½x14*

*189* A37 5p dp ultra & ol brn ('49) 25 25

**Catalogue values for unused stamps in this section, from this point to the end of the section, are for Never Hinged items.**

**Peace Issue**

New Zealand Nos. 248, 250, 254, and 255 Overprinted in Black or Blue

WESTERN SAMOA
p

WESTERN SAMOA
q

**1946, June 1** ***Perf. 13x13½, 13½x13***

| | | | | |
|---|---|---|---|---|
| *191* | A94 (p) | 1p emerald | 12 | 12 |
| *192* | A96 (q) | 2p rose vio (Bl) | 15 | 15 |
| *193* | A100 (p) | 6p org red & red brn | 25 | 25 |
| *194* | A101 (p) | 8p brn lake & blk (Bl) | 30 | 30 |

Stamps and Type of New Zealand, 1931-50 Overprinted Like Nos. 175-180 in Blue or Carmine

**1945-50** **Wmk. 253** ***Perf. 14***

| | | | | |
|---|---|---|---|---|
| *195* | PF5 | 2sh6p brown | 1.25 | 2.50 |
| *196* | PF5 | 5sh green | 5.00 | 6.25 |
| *197* | PF5 | 10sh car ('48) | 15.00 | 15.00 |
| *198* | PF5 | £1 pink ('48) | 50.00 | 55.00 |
| *199* | PF5 | 30sh choc ('48) | 110.00 | 140.00 |
| *200* | PF5 | £2 vio (C) | 125.00 | 150.00 |
| *201* | PF5 | £3 lt grn ('50) | 175.00 | 225.00 |
| *202* | PF5 | £5 dk bl (C) ('50) | 325.00 | 375.00 |

Making Siapo Cloth — A38

Thatching Hut — A40

Western Samoa and New Zealand Flags, Village A39

Samoan Chieftainess — A41

Designs: 2p, Western Samoa seal. 3p, Aleisa Falls (actually Malifa Falls). 5p, Manumea (tooth-billed pigeon). 6p, Fishing canoe. 8p, Harvesting cacao. 2sh, Preparing copra.

***Perf. 13, 13½x13***

**1952, Mar. 10** **Engr.** **Wmk. 253**

| | | | | |
|---|---|---|---|---|
| *203* | A38 | ½p org brn & cl | 8 | 6 |
| *204* | A39 | 1p grn & ol | 18 | 14 |
| *205* | A38 | 2p dp car | 24 | 20 |
| *206* | A39 | 3p ind & bl | 38 | 32 |
| *207* | A38 | 5p dk grn & org brn | 55 | 45 |
| *208* | A39 | 6p dp rose pink & bl | 60 | 50 |
| *209* | A39 | 8p rose car | 90 | 70 |
| *210* | A40 | 1sh bl & brn | 1.10 | 90 |
| *211* | A39 | 2sh yel brn | 2.75 | 2.25 |
| *212* | A41 | 3sh ol gray & vio brn | 4.75 | 3.75 |
| | | *Nos. 203-212 (10)* | 11.53 | 9.27 |

**Coronation Issue**

Types of New Zealand 1953

**1953, May 25** **Photo.** ***Perf. 14x14½***

| | | | | |
|---|---|---|---|---|
| *214* | A113 | 2p brown | 38 | 38 |
| *215* | A114 | 6p sl blk | 1.10 | 1.10 |

Type of New Zealand 1944-52 Overprinted in Blue or Carmine

WESTERN

SAMOA

**Wmk. 253**

**1955, Nov. 14** **Typo.** ***Perf. 14***

| | | | | |
|---|---|---|---|---|
| *216* | PF5 | 5sh yel grn | 11.00 | 14.00 |
| *217* | PF5 | 10sh car rose | 14.00 | 19.00 |
| *218* | PF5 | £1 dl rose | 30.00 | 35.00 |
| *219* | PF5 | £2 vio (C) | 72.50 | 115.00 |

Redrawn Types of 1952 and

Map of Western Samoa and Mace A42

Designs: 4p, as 1p. 6p, as 2p.

Inscribed: "Fono Fou 1958" and "Samoal Sisifo"

***Perf. 13½x13, 13***

**1958, Mar. 21** **Engr.** **Wmk. 253**

| | | | | |
|---|---|---|---|---|
| *220* | A39 | 4p rose car | 25 | 25 |
| *221* | A38 | 6p dl pur | 25 | 25 |
| *222* | A42 | 1sh lt vio bl | 45 | 45 |

**INDEPENDENT STATE**

Samoa College A43

Designs: 1p, Woman holding ceremonial mat (vert.). 3p, Public Library. 4p, Fono House (Parliament). 6p, Map of Western Samoa, ship and plane. 8p, Faleolo airport. 1sh, Talking chief with fly whisk (vert.). 1sh3p, Government House, Vailima. 2sh6p, Flag of Western Samoa. 5sh, State Seal.

**Wmk. 253**

**1962, July 2** **Litho.** ***Perf. 13½***

| | | | | |
|---|---|---|---|---|
| *223* | A43 | 1p car & brn | 6 | 6 |
| *224* | A43 | 2p org, lt grn, red & brn | 12 | 12 |
| *225* | A43 | 3p bl, grn & brn | 25 | 25 |
| *226* | A43 | 4p dk grn, bl & car | 40 | 40 |
| *227* | A43 | 6p yel, grn & ultra | 50 | 50 |
| *228* | A43 | 8p bl & emer | 65 | 65 |
| *229* | A43 | 1sh brt grn & brn | 1.00 | 1.00 |
| *230* | A43 | 1sh3p bl & emer | 1.25 | 1.25 |
| *231* | A43 | 2sh6p vio bl & red | 1.90 | 1.90 |
| *232* | A43 | 5sh ol gray, red & dk bl | 4.75 | 4.75 |
| | | *Nos. 223-232 (10)* | 10.88 | 10.88 |

Issued to commemorate Western Samoa's independence. See also Nos. 242-247.

Tupua Tamasese Mea'ole, Malietoa Tanumafili II and Seal — A44

**1963, Oct. 1** **Photo.** ***Perf. 14***

| | | | | |
|---|---|---|---|---|
| *233* | A44 | 1p grn & blk | 6 | 6 |
| *234* | A44 | 4p dl bl & blk | 10 | 10 |
| *235* | A44 | 8p car rose & blk | 20 | 20 |
| *236* | A44 | 2sh org & blk | 55 | 55 |

First anniversary of independence.

Signing of Western Samoa-New Zealand Friendship Treaty — A45

**1964, Sept. 1** **Unwmk.** ***Perf. 13½***

| | | | | |
|---|---|---|---|---|
| *237* | A45 | 1p multi | 8 | 8 |
| *238* | A45 | 8p multi | 18 | 18 |
| *239* | A45 | 2sh multi | 40 | 40 |
| *240* | A45 | 3sh multi | 55 | 55 |

Issued to commemorate the 2nd anniversary of the signing of the Treaty of Friendship between Western Samoa and New Zealand. Signers: J. B. Wright, N. Z. High Commissioner for Western Pacific, and Fiame Mata'afa, Prime Minister of Western Samoa.

Type of 1962

Wmk. 355- Kava Bowl and WS, Multiple

**Wmk. 355**

**1965, Oct. 4** **Litho.** ***Perf. 13½***

| | | | | |
|---|---|---|---|---|
| *242* | A43 | 1p car & brn | 35 | 35 |
| *243* | A43 | 3p bl, grn & brn | 30.00 | 12.00 |
| *244* | A43 | 4p dk grn, bl & car | 35 | 35 |
| *245* | A43 | 6p yel, grn & ultra | 38 | 38 |
| *246* | A43 | 8p bl & emer | 45 | 45 |
| *247* | A43 | 1sh brt grn & brn | 60 | 60 |
| | | *Nos. 242-247 (6)* | 32.13 | 14.13 |

Aerial View of Deep-Sea Wharf A46

Design: 8p, 2sh, View of Apia harbor and deep-sea wharf.

**1966, Mar. 2** **Photo.** ***Perf. 13½***

| | | | | |
|---|---|---|---|---|
| *251* | A46 | 1p multi | 6 | 6 |
| *252* | A46 | 8p multi | 18 | 18 |
| *253* | A46 | 2sh multi | 38 | 38 |
| *254* | A46 | 3sh multi | 60 | 60 |

Opening of Western Samoa's first deep-sea wharf at Apia.

WHO Headquarters, Geneva — A47

Design: 4p, 1sh, WHO building and flag.

**1966, July 4** **Photo.** **Wmk. 355**

| | | | | |
|---|---|---|---|---|
| *255* | A47 | 3p gray, ultra & bis | 8 | 8 |
| *256* | A47 | 4p multi | 12 | 12 |
| *257* | A47 | 6p lt ol grn, pur & grn | 25 | 25 |
| *258* | A47 | 1sh multi | 50 | 50 |

Inauguration of the WHO Headquarters, Geneva.

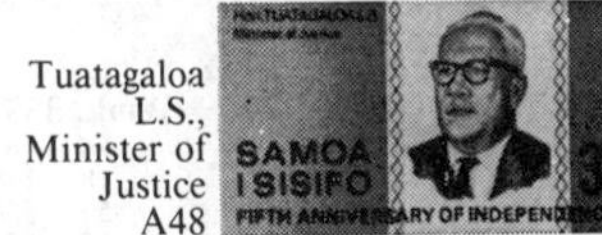

Tuatagaloa L.S., Minister of Justice A48

Designs: 8p, F.C.F. Nelson, Minister of Works, Marine and Civil Aviation. 2sh, To'omata T. L., Minister of Lands. 3sh, Fa'alava'au Galu, Minister of Post Office, Radio and Broadcasting.

***Perf. 14½x14***

**1967, Jan. 16** **Photo.** **Wmk. 355**

| | | | | |
|---|---|---|---|---|
| *259* | A48 | 3p vio & sep | 6 | 6 |
| *260* | A48 | 8p bl & sep | 18 | 18 |
| *261* | A48 | 2sh lt ol grn & sep | 35 | 35 |
| *262* | A48 | 3sh lil rose & sep | 55 | 55 |

Fifth anniversary of Independence.

Samoan Fales, 1900, and Fly Whisk A49

Design: 1sh, Fono House (Parliament) and mace.

**1967, May 16** ***Perf. 14½***

| | | | | |
|---|---|---|---|---|
| *263* | A49 | 8p multi | 30 | 30 |
| *264* | A49 | 1sh multi | 45 | 45 |

Centenary of Mulinu'u as Government Seat.

Wattled Honey-Eater — A50

Birds of Western Samoa: 2s, Pacific pigeon. 3s, Samoan starling. 5s, Samoan broadbill. 7s, Red-headed parrot finch. 10s, Purple swamp hen. 20s, Barn owl. 25s, Tooth-billed pigeon. 50s, Island thrush. $1, Samoan fantail. $2, Mao (gymnomyza samoensis). $4, Samoan white-eye (zosterops samoensis).

***Perf. 14x14½***

**1967, July 10** **Photo.** **Wmk. 355**

**Birds in Natural Colors**

**Size: 37x24mm**

| | | | | |
|---|---|---|---|---|
| *265* | A50 | 1s blk & lt brn | 6 | 5 |
| *266* | A50 | 2s lt ultra, blk & brn org | 9 | 8 |
| *267* | A50 | 3s blk, lt brn & emer | 14 | 12 |
| *268* | A50 | 5s lil, blk & vio bl | 22 | 18 |
| *269* | A50 | 7s blk, vio bl & gray | 30 | 25 |
| *270* | A50 | 10s Prus bl & blk | 45 | 38 |
| *271* | A50 | 20s dk gray & bl | 95 | 75 |
| *272* | A50 | 25s pink, blk & dk grn | 1.10 | 95 |
| *273* | A50 | 50s brn, blk & lt ol grn | 2.25 | 1.90 |
| *274* | A50 | $1 yel & blk | 4.50 | 3.75 |

**1969** **Size: 43x28mm** ***Perf. 13½***

| | | | | |
|---|---|---|---|---|
| *274A* | A50 | $2 blk & lt grnsh bl | 11.00 | 9.25 |
| *274B* | A50 | $4 dp org & blk | 37.50 | 40.00 |
| | | *Nos. 265-274B (12)* | 58.56 | 57.66 |

Child Care A51

Designs: 7s, Leprosarium. 20s, Mobile X-ray unit. 25s, Apia Hospital.

**1967, Dec. 1** **Litho.** ***Perf. 14***

| | | | | |
|---|---|---|---|---|
| *275* | A51 | 3s multi | 6 | 6 |
| *276* | A51 | 7s multi | 12 | 12 |
| *277* | A51 | 20s multi | 38 | 38 |
| *278* | A51 | 25s multi | 50 | 50 |

South Pacific Health Service.

Thomas Trood A52

Portraits: 7s, Dr. Wilhelm Solf. 20s, John C. Williams. 25s, Fritz Marquardt.

**1968, Jan. 1** **Unwmk.** ***Perf. 13½***

| | | | | |
|---|---|---|---|---|
| *279* | A52 | 2s multi | 5 | 5 |
| *280* | A52 | 7s multi | 16 | 16 |
| *281* | A52 | 20s multi | 45 | 45 |
| *282* | A52 | 25s multi | 55 | 55 |

Sixth anniversary of independence.

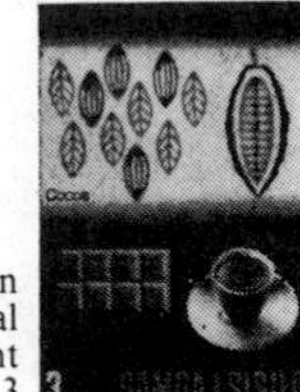

Samoan Agricultural Development A53

*Perf. 13x12½*

**1968, Feb. 15 Photo. Wmk. 355**

| No. | Type | Description | Unused | Used |
|---|---|---|---|---|
| *283* | A53 | 3s Cocoa | 8 | 8 |
| *284* | A53 | 5s Breadfruit | 14 | 14 |
| *285* | A53 | 10s Copra | 28 | 28 |
| *286* | A53 | 20s Bananas | 55 | 55 |

Curio Vendors, Pago Pago A54

Designs: 20s, Palm trees at the shore. 25s, A'Umi Beach.

*Perf. 14½x14*

**1968, Apr. 22 Photo. Wmk. 355**

| No. | Type | Description | Unused | Used |
|---|---|---|---|---|
| *287* | A54 | 7s multi | 18 | 18 |
| *288* | A54 | 20s multi | 50 | 50 |
| *289* | A54 | 25s multi | 65 | 65 |

Issued to commemorate the 21st anniversary of the South Pacific Commission.

Bougainville and Compass Rose — A55

Designs: 3s, Map showing Western Samoa Archipelago and Bougainville's route. 20s, Bougainvillea. 25s, Bougainville's ships La Boudeuse and L'Etoile.

**1968, June 10 Litho. *Perf. 14***

| No. | Type | Description | Unused | Used |
|---|---|---|---|---|
| *290* | A55 | 3s brt bl & blk | 6 | 6 |
| *291* | A55 | 7s ocher & blk | 15 | 15 |
| *292* | A55 | 20s grnsh blk, brt rose & grn | 50 | 50 |
| *293* | A55 | 25s brt lil, vio, blk & org | 65 | 65 |

200th anniv. of the visit of Louis Antoine de Bougainville (1729-1811) to Samoa.

**No. 270 Surcharged with New Value, Three Bars and: "1928-1968 / KINGSFORD-SMITH / TRANSPACIFIC FLIGHT"**

**1968, June 13 Photo. *Perf. 14x14½***

| No. | Type | Description | Unused | Used |
|---|---|---|---|---|
| *294* | A50 | 20s on 10s multi | 55 | 55 |

40th anniv. of the 1st Transpacific flight under Capt. Charles Kingsford-Smith (Oakland, CA to Brisbane, Australia, via Honolulu and Fiji).

Human Rights Flame and Globe A56

*Perf. 14½x14*

**1968, Aug. 26 Photo. Wmk. 355**

| No. | Type | Description | Unused | Used |
|---|---|---|---|---|
| *295* | A56 | 7s gold, Prus bl & emer | 14 | 14 |
| *296* | A56 | 20s gold, org & emer | 42 | 42 |
| *297* | A56 | 25s gold, brt pur & emer | 55 | 55 |

International Human Rights Year, 1968.

Martin Luther King, Jr. — A57

Polynesian Madonna — A58

**1968, Sept. 23 Litho. *Perf. 14***

| No. | Type | Description | Unused | Used |
|---|---|---|---|---|
| *298* | A57 | 7s grn & blk | 12 | 12 |
| *299* | A57 | 20s brt rose lil & blk | 40 | 40 |

Rev. Dr. Martin Luther King, Jr. (1929-68), American civil rights leader.

**1968, Oct. 12 Wmk. 355**

| No. | Type | Description | Unused | Used |
|---|---|---|---|---|
| *300* | A58 | 1s ol & multi | 5 | 5 |
| *301* | A58 | 3s multi | 6 | 6 |
| *302* | A58 | 20s crim & multi | 45 | 45 |
| *303* | A58 | 30s dp org & multi | 55 | 55 |

Christmas 1968.

Frangipani — A59

Flowers: 7s, Chinese hibiscus (vert.). 20s, Red ginger (vert.). 30s, Canangium odoratum.

**1969, Jan. 20 Unwmk. *Perf. 14***

| No. | Type | Description | Unused | Used |
|---|---|---|---|---|
| *304* | A59 | 2s brt bl & multi | 8 | 8 |
| *305* | A59 | 7s multi | 28 | 28 |
| *306* | A59 | 20s yel & multi | 90 | 90 |
| *307* | A59 | 30s multi | 1.25 | 1.25 |

Seventh anniversary of independence.

R. L. Stevenson and Silver from "Treasure Island" A60

Designs (Robert Louis Stevenson and): 7s, Stewart and Balfour on the moor from "Kidnapped." 20s, "Doctor Jekyll and Mr. Hyde." 22s, Archie Weir and Christiana Elliot from "Weir of Hermiston."

*Perf. 14x13½*

**1969, Apr. 21 Litho. Wmk. 355**

| No. | Type | Description | Unused | Used |
|---|---|---|---|---|
| *308* | A60 | 3s gray & multi | 6 | 6 |
| *309* | A60 | 7s gray & multi | 18 | 18 |
| *310* | A60 | 20s gray & multi | 55 | 55 |
| *311* | A60 | 22s gray & multi | 65 | 65 |

75th anniv. of the death of Robert Louis Stevenson, who is buried in Samoa.

Weight Lifting — A61

*Perf. 13½x13*

**1969, July 21 Photo. Unwmk.**

| No. | Type | Description | Unused | Used |
|---|---|---|---|---|
| *312* | A61 | 3s shown | 7 | 7 |
| *313* | A61 | 20s Sailing | 50 | 50 |
| *314* | A61 | 22s Boxing | 55 | 55 |

3rd Pacific Games, Port Moresby, Papua and New Guinea, Aug. 13-23.

American Astronaut on Moon, Splashdown and Map of Samoan Islands — A62

**1969, July 24 Photo.**

| No. | Type | Description | Unused | Used |
|---|---|---|---|---|
| *315* | A62 | 7s red, blk, sil & grn | 20 | 20 |
| *316* | A62 | 20s car, blk, sil & ultra | 55 | 55 |

US astronauts. See note after US No. C76.

Holy Family by El Greco — A63

Paintings: 1s, Virgin and Child, by Murillo. 20s, Nativity, by El Greco. 30s, Virgin and Child (from Adoration of the Kings), by Velazquez.

**1969, Oct. 13 Unwmk. *Perf. 14***

| No. | Type | Description | Unused | Used |
|---|---|---|---|---|
| *317* | A63 | 1s gold, red & multi | 5 | 5 |
| *318* | A63 | 3s gold, red & multi | 6 | 6 |
| *319* | A63 | 20s gold, red & multi | 55 | 55 |
| *320* | A63 | 30s gold, red & multi | 85 | 85 |
| *a.* | | Souvenir sheet of 4 | 1.60 | 1.60 |

Christmas 1969. No. 320a contains one each of Nos. 317-320. Size: 115x126mm.

Seventh Day Adventists' Sanatorium, Apia — A64

Designs: 7s, Father Louis Violette and R. C. Cathedral, Apia. 20s, Church of Latter Day Saints (Mormon), Tuasivi, Safotulafai (vert.). 22s, John Williams and London Missionary Society Church, Sapapali'i.

**1970, Jan. 19 Litho. Wmk. 355**

| No. | Type | Description | Unused | Used |
|---|---|---|---|---|
| *321* | A64 | 2s brn, blk & gray | 6 | 6 |
| *322* | A64 | 7s vio, blk & bis | 18 | 18 |
| *323* | A64 | 20s rose, blk & lt vio | 45 | 45 |
| *324* | A64 | 22s ol, blk & bis | 50 | 50 |

Eighth anniversary of independence.

U.S.S. Nipsic A65

Designs: 5s, Wreck of German ship Adler. 10s, British ship Calliope in storm. 20s, Apia after hurricane.

**1970, Apr. 27 *Perf. 13½x14***

| No. | Type | Description | Unused | Used |
|---|---|---|---|---|
| *325* | A65 | 5s multi | 40 | 40 |
| *326* | A65 | 7s multi | 55 | 55 |
| *327* | A65 | 10s multi | 90 | 90 |
| *328* | A65 | 20s multi | 1.75 | 1.75 |

The great Apia hurricane of 1889.

Cook Statue, Whitby, England — A66

Designs: 1s, Kendal's chronometer and Cook's sextant. 20s, Capt. Cook bust, in profile. 30s, Capt. Cook, island scene and "Endeavour" (horiz.).

*Perf. 14x14½*

**1970, Sept. 14 Litho. Wmk. 355**

**Size: 25x41mm**

| No. | Type | Description | Unused | Used |
|---|---|---|---|---|
| *329* | A66 | 1s sil, dp car & blk | 12 | 9 |
| *330* | A66 | 2s multi | 28 | 18 |
| *331* | A66 | 20s gold, blk & ultra | 2.75 | 1.75 |

*Perf. 14½x14*

**Size: 83x25mm**

| No. | Type | Description | Unused | Used |
|---|---|---|---|---|
| *332* | A66 | 30s multi | 4.00 | 2.75 |

Bicentenary of Capt. James Cook's exploration of South Pacific.

"Peace for the World" by Frances B. Eccles — A67

Pope Paul VI — A68

Christmas: 3s, Samoan coat of arms and Holy Family, by Werner Erich Jahnke. 20s, Samoan Mother and Child, by F. B. Eccles. 30s, Prince of Peace, by Sister Melane Fe'ao.

*Perf. 13½*

**1970, Oct. 26 Photo. Unwmk.**

| No. | Type | Description | Unused | Used |
|---|---|---|---|---|
| *333* | A67 | 2s gold & multi | 6 | 6 |
| *334* | A67 | 3s gold & multi | 8 | 8 |
| *335* | A67 | 20s gold & multi | 55 | 55 |
| *336* | A67 | 30s gold & multi | 85 | 85 |
| *a.* | | Souvenir sheet of 4 | 2.50 | 2.50 |

No. 336a contains one each of Nos. 333-336 and a label inscribed "Christmas 1970." Light blue and gold margin. Size: 110x155mm.

**Wmk. 355**

**1970, Nov. 29 Litho. *Perf. 14***

| No. | Type | Description | Unused | Used |
|---|---|---|---|---|
| *337* | A68 | 8s Prus bl & blk | 22 | 22 |
| *338* | A68 | 20s dp plum & blk | 55 | 55 |

Visit of Pope Paul VI, Nov. 29, 1970.

Lumberjack A69

Designs: 8s, Woman and tractor in clearing (horiz.). 20s, Log and saw carrier (horiz.). 22s, Logging and ship.

*Perf. 14x13½, 13½x14*

**1971, Feb. 1 Litho. Unwmk.**

| | | | | |
|---|---|---|---|---|
| *339* | A69 | 3s multi | 16 | 6 |
| *340* | A69 | 8s multi | 18 | 18 |
| *341* | A69 | 20s multi | 50 | 50 |
| *342* | A69 | 22s multi | 60 | 60 |

Development of the timber industry on Savaii Island by the American Timber Company of Potlatch.

Souvenir Sheet

Longboat in Apia Harbor; Samoa No. 3 and US No. 3 — A70

**1971, Mar. 12 Photo. *Perf. 11½***
**Granite Paper**

| | | | | |
|---|---|---|---|---|
| *343* | A70 | 70s bl & multi | 3.00 | 3.00 |

INTERPEX, 13th Intl. Stamp Exhib., NYC, Mar. 12-14. No. 343 contains one stamp; ocher and brown margin showing New York skyline. Size: 138x80mm.

Siva Dance A71

Tourist Publicity: 7s, Samoan cricket game. 8s, Hideaway Resort Hotel. 10s, Aggie Grey and Aggie's Hotel.

**Wmk. 355**

**1971, Aug. 9 Litho. *Perf. 14***

| | | | | |
|---|---|---|---|---|
| *344* | A71 | 5s org brn & multi | 45 | 45 |
| *345* | A71 | 7s org brn & multi | 60 | 60 |
| *346* | A71 | 8s org brn & multi | 75 | 75 |
| *347* | A71 | 10s org brn & multi | 90 | 90 |

Queen Salamasina — A72

Samoan Legends, carved by Sven Ortquist: 8s, Lu and his sacred hens (Samoa). 10s, God Tagaloa fishing Samoan islands of Upolu and Savaii from the sea. 22s, Mt. Vaea and Pool of Tears.

**1971, Sept. 20**

| | | | | |
|---|---|---|---|---|
| *348* | A72 | 3s dk vio & multi | 10 | 10 |
| *349* | A72 | 8s multi | 28 | 28 |
| *350* | A72 | 10s dk bl & multi | 32 | 32 |
| *351* | A72 | 22s dk bl & multi | 75 | 75 |

See Nos. 399-402.

Virgin and Child, by Giovanni Bellini — A73

Christmas: 20c, 30c, Virgin and Child with St. Anne and St. John the Baptist, by Leonardo da Vinci.

**1971, Oct. 4 *Perf. 14x13½***

| | | | | |
|---|---|---|---|---|
| *352* | A73 | 2s bl & multi | 6 | 6 |
| *353* | A73 | 3s blk & multi | 9 | 9 |
| *354* | A73 | 20s yel & multi | 60 | 60 |
| *355* | A73 | 30s dk red & multi | 90 | 90 |

Samoan Islands, Scales of Justice A74

**1972, Jan. 10 Photo. *Perf. 11½x12***

| | | | | |
|---|---|---|---|---|
| *356* | A74 | 10s lt bl & multi | 48 | 48 |

First South Pacific Judicial Conference, Samoa, Jan. 1972.

Asau Wharf, Savaii A75

Designs: 8s, Parliament Building. 10s, Mothers' Center. 22s, Portraits of Tupua Tamasese Mea'ole and Malietoa Tanumafili II, and view of Vailima.

*Perf. 13x13½*

**1972, Jan. 10 Litho. Wmk. 355**

| | | | | |
|---|---|---|---|---|
| *357* | A75 | 1s brt pink & multi | 5 | 5 |
| *358* | A75 | 8s lil & multi | 25 | 25 |
| *359* | A75 | 10s grn & multi | 32 | 32 |
| *360* | A75 | 22s multi | 70 | 70 |

10th anniversary of independence.

Commission Members' Flags — A76

Designs: 7s, Afoafouvale Misimoa, Secretary-General, 1970-71 and Commission flag. 8s, Headquarters Building, Noumea, New Caledonia (horiz.). 10s, Flag of Samoa, flag and map of South Pacific Commission area (horiz.).

*Perf. 14x13½, 13½x14*

**1972, Mar. 17**

| | | | | |
|---|---|---|---|---|
| *361* | A76 | 3s ultra & multi | 8 | 8 |
| *362* | A76 | 7s yel, blk & ultra | 25 | 25 |
| *363* | A76 | 8s multi | 28 | 28 |
| *364* | A76 | 10s lt grn & multi | 35 | 35 |

South Pacific Commission, 25th anniv.

Sunset and Ships — A77

Designs: 8s, Sailing ships Arend, Thienhoven and Africaansche Galey in storm. 10s, Outrigger canoe and Roggeveen's ships. 30s, Hemispheres with exploration route and map of Samoan Islands. All horiz.

**1972, June 14 *Perf. 14½***
**Size: 24½x41, 41x24½mm.**

| | | | | |
|---|---|---|---|---|
| *365* | A77 | 2s car rose & multi | 12 | 10 |
| *366* | A77 | 8s vio bl & multi | 42 | 35 |
| *367* | A77 | 10s ultra multi | 50 | 42 |

**Size: 85x25mm.**

| | | | | |
|---|---|---|---|---|
| *368* | A77 | 30s ocher & multi | 2.25 | 1.25 |

250th anniversary of Jacob Roggeveen's Pacific voyage and of his discovery of Samoa in June 1722.

Bull Conch A78

**1972-75 Litho. *Perf. 14½***
**Size: 41x24mm**

| | | | | |
|---|---|---|---|---|
| *369* | A78 | 1s *shown* | 5 | 5 |
| *370* | A78 | 2s *Rhinoceros beetle* | 6 | 6 |
| *371* | A78 | 3s *Skipjack (fish)* | 9 | 9 |
| *372* | A78 | 4s *Painted crab* | 12 | 12 |
| *373* | A78 | 5s *Butterflyfish* | 15 | 15 |
| *374* | A78 | 7s *Samoan monarch* | 22 | 22 |
| *375* | A78 | 10s *Triton shell* | 30 | 30 |
| *376* | A78 | 20s *Jewel beetle* | 60 | 60 |
| *377* | A78 | 50s *Spiny lobster* | 1.50 | 1.50 |

***Perf. 14x13½***
**Size: 29x45mm**

| | | | | |
|---|---|---|---|---|
| *378* | A78 | $1 *Hawk moth* | 3.00 | 3.00 |
| *378A* | A78 | $2 *Green turtle* | 6.00 | 6.00 |
| *378B* | A78 | $4 *Black marlin* | 12.00 | 12.00 |
| *378C* | A78 | $5 *Green tree lizard* | 15.00 | 15.00 |
| | | *Nos. 369-378C (13)* | 39.09 | 39.09 |

Issue dates: Nos. 369-378, Oct. 18, 1972; No. 378A, June 18, 1973; No. 378B, Mar. 27, 1974; No. 378C, June 30, 1975.

Ascension, Stained Glass Window — A79

Stained Glass Windows in Apia Churches: 4s, Virgin and Child. 10s, St. Andrew blessing Samoan canoe. 30s, The Good Shepherd.

*Perf. 14x14½*

**1972, Nov. 1 Wmk. 355**

| | | | | |
|---|---|---|---|---|
| *379* | A79 | 1s ocher & multi | 8 | 8 |
| *380* | A79 | 4s gray & multi | 15 | 15 |
| *381* | A79 | 10s dl grn & multi | 40 | 40 |
| *382* | A79 | 30s bl & multi | 1.10 | 1.10 |
| *a.* | | Souvenir sheet of 4 | 2.00 | 2.00 |

Christmas 1972. No. 382a contains one each of Nos. 379-382. Violet margin with black inscription. Size: 70x158mm.

Scouts Saluting Flag, Emblems A80

**1973, Jan. 29 *Perf. 14***

| | | | | |
|---|---|---|---|---|
| *383* | A80 | 2s *shown* | 12 | 12 |
| *384* | A80 | 3s *First aid* | 20 | 20 |
| *385* | A80 | 8s *Pitching tent* | 48 | 48 |
| *386* | A80 | 20s *Action song* | 1.25 | 1.25 |

Boy Scouts of Samoa.

Apia General Hospital — A81

"A Prince is Born," by Jahnke — A82

Designs: 8s, Baby clinic. 20s, Filariasis research. 22s, Family welfare.

**1973, Aug. 20 Wmk. 355**

| | | | | |
|---|---|---|---|---|
| *387* | A81 | 2s grn & multi | 8 | 8 |
| *388* | A81 | 8s multi | 28 | 28 |
| *389* | A81 | 20s brn & multi | 65 | 65 |
| *390* | A81 | 22s ver & multi | 75 | 75 |

WHO, 25th anniv.

**1973, Oct. 15 Litho. *Perf. 14***

Designs: 4s, "Star of Hope," by Fiasili Keil. 10s, "Mother and Child," by Ernesto Coter. 30s, "The Light of the World," by Coter.

| | | | | |
|---|---|---|---|---|
| *391* | A82 | 3s bl & multi | 15 | 15 |
| *392* | A82 | 4s pur & multi | 18 | 18 |
| *393* | A82 | 10s red & multi | 42 | 42 |
| *394* | A82 | 30s bl & multi | 1.25 | 1.25 |
| *a.* | | Souvenir sheet of 4 | 2.25 | 2.25 |

Christmas 1973. No. 394a contains one each of Nos. 391-394. Dark blue and gold margin. Size: 144x102mm.

Boxing and Games' Emblem A83

**1974, Jan. 24**

| | | | | |
|---|---|---|---|---|
| *395* | A83 | 8s *shown* | 45 | 45 |
| *396* | A83 | 10s *Weight lifting* | 60 | 60 |
| *397* | A83 | 20s *Lawn bowling* | 1.20 | 1.20 |
| *398* | A83 | 30s *Stadium* | 1.80 | 1.80 |

10th British Commonwealth Games, Christchurch, New Zealand, Jan. 24-Feb. 2.

Legends Type of 1971

Samoan Legends, Wood Carvings by Sven Ortquist: 2s, Tigilau and dove. 8s, Pili with his sons and famous fish net. 20s, The girl Sina and the eel which became the coconut tree. 30s, Nafanua who returned from the spirit world to free her village.

**1974, Aug. 13 Wmk. 355 *Perf. 14***

| | | | | |
|---|---|---|---|---|
| *399* | A72 | 2s lem & multi | 7 | 7 |
| *400* | A72 | 8s rose red & multi | 30 | 30 |
| *401* | A72 | 20s yel grn & multi | 85 | 85 |
| *402* | A72 | 30s lt vio & multi | 1.25 | 1.25 |

A particular stamp may be scarce, but if few collectors want it, its market value may remain relatively low.

Faleolo Airport — A84

Designs: 20s, Apia Wharf. 22s, Early post office, Apia. 50s, William Willis, raft "Age Unlimited" and route from Callao, Peru, to Tully, Western Samoa.

**1974, Sept. 4 Unwmk. *Perf. 13½***

**Size: 47x29mm**

| | | | | |
|---|---|---|---|---|
| *403* | A84 | 8s multi | 22 | 22 |
| *404* | A84 | 20s multi | 55 | 55 |
| *405* | A84 | 22s multi | 70 | 70 |

**Size: 86x29mm**

| | | | | |
|---|---|---|---|---|
| *406* | A84 | 50s multi | 1.50 | 1.50 |
| *a.* | | Souvenir sheet | 1.75 | 1.75 |

Cent. of UPU. The 8s is inscribed "Air Mail"; 20s, "Sea Mail"; 22s, "Raft Mail."

No. 406a contains one No. 406, perf. 13; blue margin with multicolored world map, UPU emblem and black inscription. Size: 137x80mm.

Holy Family, by Sebastiano A85

Designs: 4s, Virgin and Child with Saints, by Lotto. 10s, Virgin and Child with St. John, by Titian. 30s, Adoration of the Shepherds, by Rubens.

**1974, Nov. 18 Litho. *Perf. 13x13½***

| | | | | |
|---|---|---|---|---|
| *407* | A85 | 3s ocher & multi | 9 | 9 |
| *408* | A85 | 4s fawn & multi | 12 | 12 |
| *409* | A85 | 10s dl grn & multi | 30 | 30 |
| *410* | A85 | 30s bl & multi | 90 | 90 |
| *a.* | | Souvenir sheet of 4 | 1.50 | 1.50 |

Christmas 1974. No. 410a contains one each of Nos. 407-410, olive green decorative margin. Size: 128x87mm.

Winged Passion Flower A86

Flowers: 20s, Gardenias (vert.). 22s, Lecythidaceae (vert.). 30s, Malay apple.

**Wmk. 355**

**1975, Jan. 17 Litho. *Perf. 14½***

| | | | | |
|---|---|---|---|---|
| *411* | A86 | 8s dl yel & multi | 25 | 25 |
| *412* | A86 | 20s pale pink & multi | 65 | 65 |
| *413* | A86 | 22s pink & multi | 70 | 70 |
| *414* | A86 | 30s lt grn & multi | 1.00 | 1.00 |

Joyita Loading at Apia A87

Designs: 8s, Joyita, Samoa and Tokelau Islands. 20s, Joyita sinking. 22s, Rafts in storm. 50s, Plane discovering wreck.

**1975, Mar. 14 Photo. *Perf. 13***

| | | | | |
|---|---|---|---|---|
| *415* | A87 | 1s multi | 5 | 5 |
| *416* | A87 | 8s multi | 20 | 20 |
| *417* | A87 | 20s multi | 50 | 50 |
| *418* | A87 | 22s multi | 55 | 55 |
| *419* | A87 | 50s multi | 1.25 | 1.25 |
| *a.* | | Souvenir sheet of 5 | 2.75 | 2.75 |
| | | *Nos. 415-419 (5)* | 2.55 | 2.55 |

17th INTERPEX Phil. Exhib., NYC, Mar. 14-16. No. 419a contains 5 imperf. stamps similar to Nos. 415-419. Black design descriptions about the mystery of the Joyita, an inter-island boat shipwrecked in Oct. 1955. Size: 150x100mm.

Pate Drum — A88

**1975, Sept. 30 Litho. *Perf. 14½x14***

| | | | | |
|---|---|---|---|---|
| *420* | A88 | 8s shown | 24 | 24 |
| *421* | A88 | 20s Lali drum | 60 | 60 |
| *422* | A88 | 22s Logo drum | 65 | 65 |
| *423* | A88 | 30s Pu shell horn | 90 | 90 |

Mother and Child, by Meleane Fe'ao — A89

Paintings: 4s, Christ Child and Samoan flag, by Polataia Tuigamala. 10s, "A Star is Born," by Iosua Toafa. 30s, Mother and Child, by Ernesto Coter.

**1975, Nov. 25 Litho. Wmk. 355**

| | | | | |
|---|---|---|---|---|
| *424* | A89 | 3s multi | 8 | 8 |
| *425* | A89 | 4s multi | 12 | 12 |
| *426* | A89 | 10s multi | 30 | 30 |
| *427* | A89 | 30s multi | 90 | 90 |
| *a.* | | Souvenir sheet of 4 | 1.40 | 1.40 |

Christmas 1975. No. 427a contains one each of Nos. 424-427; multicolored margin with stars. Size: 100x132mm.

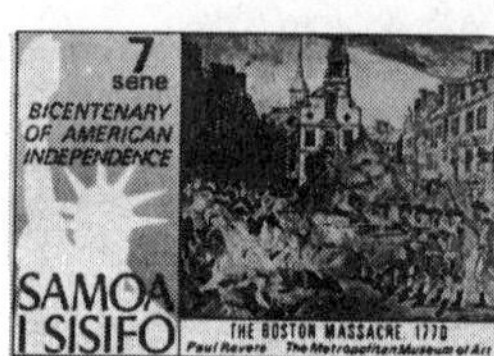


Boston Massacre, by Paul Revere — A90

Designs (Statue of Liberty and): 8s, Declaration of Independence, by John Trumbull. 20s, The Sinking of the Bonhomme Richard, by J. L. G. Ferris. 22s, Wm. Pitt Addressing House of Commons, by R. A. Hickel. 50s, Battle of Princeton, by William Mercer.

***Perf. 13½x14***

**1976 Jan. 20 Litho. Wmk. 355**

| | | | | |
|---|---|---|---|---|
| *428* | A90 | 7s sal & multi | 25 | 25 |
| *429* | A90 | 8s grn & multi | 30 | 30 |
| *430* | A90 | 20s lil & multi | 75 | 75 |
| *431* | A90 | 22s bl & multi | 80 | 80 |
| *432* | A90 | 50s yel & multi | 1.90 | 1.90 |
| *a.* | | Souvenir sheet of 5 | 4.75 | 4.75 |
| | | *Nos. 428-432 (5)* | 4.00 | 4.00 |

Bicentenary of American Independence. No. 432a contains one each of Nos. 428-432 and decorative label; multicolored margin with Statue of Liberty. Size: 160x126mm.

Mullet Fishing A91

**1976, Apr. 27 Litho. *Perf. 14½***

| | | | | |
|---|---|---|---|---|
| *433* | A91 | 10s *shown* | 28 | 28 |
| *434* | A91 | 12s *Fish traps* | 32 | 32 |
| *435* | A91 | 22s *Fishermen* | 60 | 60 |
| *436* | A91 | 50s *Net fishing* | 1.40 | 1.40 |

Souvenir Sheet

Samoan $100 Gold Coin with Paul Revere and US Map — A92

**Unwmk.**

**1976, May 29 Photo. *Perf. 13***

| | | | | |
|---|---|---|---|---|
| *437* | A92 | $1 grn & gold | 3.75 | 3.75 |

American Bicentennial and Interphil 76 International Philatelic Exhibition, Philadelphia, Pa., May 29-June 6. No. 437 has gold, black & brown margin showing Liberty Bell. Size: 120x80mm.

Boxing A93

Designs (Olympic Rings and): 12s, Wrestling. 22s, Javelin. 50s, Weight lifting.

***Perf. 14½x14***

**1976, June 21 Litho. Wmk. 355**

| | | | | |
|---|---|---|---|---|
| *438* | A93 | 10s blk & multi | 28 | 28 |
| *439* | A93 | 12s dk brn & multi | 32 | 32 |
| *440* | A93 | 22s dk pur & multi | 60 | 60 |
| *441* | A93 | 50s dk bl & multi | 1.40 | 1.40 |

21st Olympic Games, Montreal, Canada, July 17-Aug. 1.

Mary and Joseph on Road to Bethlehem A94

Designs: 5s, Adoration of the Shepherds. 22s, Nativity. 50s, Adoration of the Kings.

**1976, Oct. 18 Litho. *Perf. 14x13½***

| | | | | |
|---|---|---|---|---|
| *442* | A94 | 3s multi | 10 | 10 |
| *443* | A94 | 5s multi | 15 | 15 |
| *444* | A94 | 22s multi | 70 | 70 |
| *445* | A94 | 50s multi | 1.65 | 1.65 |
| *a.* | | Souvenir sheet of 4 | 2.75 | 2.75 |

Christmas 1976. No. 445a contains one each of Nos. 442-445; multicolored decorative margin. Size: 148x115mm.

Presentation of the Spurs of Chivalry — A95

Designs: 12s, Queen and view of Apia. 32s, Royal Yacht Britannia and Queen. 50s, Queen leaving Westminster Abbey.

***Perf. 13½x14***

**1977, Feb. 11 Wmk. 355**

| | | | | |
|---|---|---|---|---|
| *446* | A95 | 12s multi | 22 | 22 |
| *447* | A95 | 26s multi | 45 | 45 |
| *448* | A95 | 32s multi | 70 | 70 |
| *449* | A95 | 50s multi | 1.10 | 1.10 |

25th anniv. of the reign of Elizabeth II.

Lindbergh and Spirit of St. Louis A96

Designs: 22s, Map of transatlantic route and plane. 24s, Spirit of St. Louis in flight. 26s, Spirit of St. Louis taking off.

**1977, May 20 Litho. *Perf. 14***

| | | | | |
|---|---|---|---|---|
| *450* | A96 | 22s multi | 42 | 42 |
| *451* | A96 | 24s multi | 48 | 48 |
| *452* | A96 | 26s multi | 50 | 50 |
| *453* | A96 | 50s multi | 1.00 | 1.00 |
| *a.* | | Souvenir sheet of 4 | 2.75 | 2.75 |

Charles A. Lindbergh's solo transatlantic flight from New York to Paris, 50th anniversary. No. 453a contains one each of Nos. 450-453; dark blue and red margin shows map of transatlantic route. Size: 192x92mm.

Apia Automatic Telephone Exchange — A97

Designs: 13s, Mulinuu radio terminal. 26s, Old wall and new dial telephones. 50s, Global communications (2 telephones and globe).

**1977, July 11 Litho. *Perf. 14***

| | | | | |
|---|---|---|---|---|
| *454* | A97 | 12s multi | 22 | 22 |
| *455* | A97 | 13s multi | 25 | 25 |
| *456* | A97 | 26s multi | 55 | 55 |
| *457* | A97 | 50s multi | 95 | 95 |

Telecommunications.

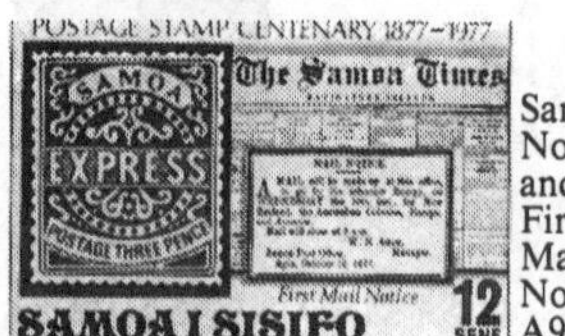


Samoa No. 3 and First Mail Notice A98

Designs: 13s, Samoa No. 4 and 1881 cover. 26s, Samoa No. 1 and Chief Post Office, Apia. 50s, Samoa No. 4 and schooner "Energy," which carried first mail.

**1977, Aug. 29 Wmk. 355 *Perf. 13½***

| | | | | |
|---|---|---|---|---|
| *458* | A98 | 12s multi | 24 | 24 |
| *459* | A98 | 13s multi | 28 | 28 |
| *460* | A98 | 26s multi | 55 | 55 |
| *461* | A98 | 50s multi | 1.10 | 1.10 |

Samoan postage stamp centenary.

Nativity — A99

Designs: 6s, People bringing gifts to Holy Family in Samoan hut. 26s, Virgin and Child. 50s, Stars over Christ Child.

**1977, Oct. 11 Litho. *Perf. 14***
*462* A99 4s multi 8 8
*463* A99 6s multi 10 10
*464* A99 26s multi 50 50
*465* A99 50s multi 1.65 1.65
*a.* Souvenir sheet of 4 2.50 2.50

Christmas 1977. No. 465a contains one each of Nos. 462-465; multicolored margin shows star and palms. Size: 117x159mm.

Polynesian Airlines' Boeing 737 A100

Aviation Progress: 24s, Kitty Hawk. 26s, Kingsford-Smith Fokker. 50s, Concorde.

**Unwmk.**
**1978, Mar. 21 Litho. *Perf. 14***
*466* A100 12s multi 24 24
*467* A100 24s multi 50 50
*468* A100 26s multi 55 55
*469* A100 50s multi 1.10 1.10
*a.* Souvenir sheet of 4 2.50 2.50

No. 469a contains one each of Nos. 466-469, perf. 13½; multicolored margin shows various aircraft. Size: 145x107mm.


Turtle Hatchery, Aleipata A101

Design: $1, Hawksbill turtle and Wildlife Fund emblem.

**1978, Apr. 14 Wmk. 355 *Perf. 14½***
*470* A101 24s multi 55 55
*471* A101 $1 multi 2.25 2.25

Project to replenish endangered hawksbill turtles.

**Elizabeth II Coronation Anniversary Issue**
Souvenir Sheet
Common Design Types

**1978, Apr. 21 Unwmk. *Perf. 15***
*472* Sheet of 6 3.25 3.25
*a.* CD326 26s *King's lion* 50 50
*b.* CD327 26s *Elizabeth II* 50 50
*c.* CD328 26s *Pacific pigeon* 50 50

No. 472 contains 2 se-tenant strips of Nos. 472a-472c, separated by horizontal gutter with commemorative and descriptive inscriptions and showing central part of coronation procession with coach. Size: 100x135mm.

Souvenir Sheet

Canadian and Samoan Flags A102

**Wmk. 355**
**1978, June 9 Litho. *Perf. 14½***
*473* A102 $1 multi 3.00 3.00

CAPEX Canadian Intl. Phil. Exhib., Toronto, June 9-18. No. 473 contains one stamp; red and black margin. Size: 118x79mm.

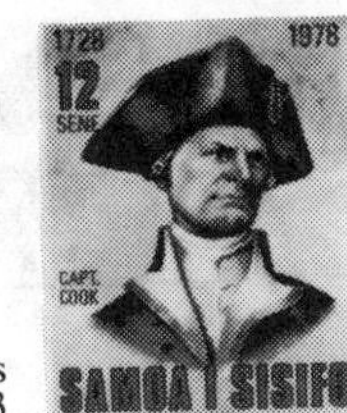

Capt. James Cook — A103

Designs: 24s, Cook's cottage, now in Melbourne, Australia. 26s, Old drawbridge over River Esk, Whitby, 1766-1833. 50s, Resolution and map of Hawaiian Islands.

**1978, Aug. 28 Litho. *Perf. 14½x14***
*474* A103 12s multi 32 32
*475* A103 24s multi 65 65
*476* A103 26s multi 85 85
*477* A103 50s multi 1.65 1.65

Thick-edged Cowrie — A104

Cowrie Shells: 2s, Isabella cowrie. 3s, Money cowrie. 4s, Eroded cowrie. 6s, Honey cowrie. 7s, Banded cowrie. 10s, Globe cowrie. 11s, Mole cowrie. 12s, Children's cowrie. 13s, Flag cone. 14s, Soldier cone. 24s, Cloth-of-gold cone. 26s, Lettered cone. 50s, Tiled cone. $1, Black marble cone. $2, Marlinspike auger. $3, Scorpion spider conch. $5, Common harp.

**1978-80 Photo. Unwmk. *Perf. 12½***
**Size: 31x24mm.**
**Granite Paper**
*478* A104 1s multi 5 5
*479* A104 2s multi 5 5
*480* A104 3s multi 6 6
*481* A104 4s multi 8 8
*482* A104 6s multi 8 8
*483* A104 7s multi 10 10
*484* A104 10s multi 12 12
*485* A104 11s multi 14 14
*486* A104 12s multi 15 15
*487* A104 13s multi 15 15
*488* A104 14s multi 20 20
*489* A104 24s multi 32 32
*490* A104 26s multi 32 32
*491* A104 50s multi 65 65
*492* A104 $1 multi 1.25 1.25

***Perf. 11½***
**Size: 36x26mm.**
*493* A104 $2 multi ('79) 2.50 2.50
*494* A104 $3 multi ('79) 4.00 4.00
*494A* A104 $5 multi ('80) 10.50 10.50
*Nos. 478-494A (18)* 20.72 20.72

The Virgin in Glory, by Dürer — A105

Works by Dürer: 6s, Nativity. 26s, Adoration of the Kings. 50s, Annunciation.

**Wmk. 355**
**1978, Nov. 6 Litho. *Perf. 14***
*495* A105 4s lt brn & blk 7 7
*496* A105 6s grnsh bl & blk 12 12
*497* A105 26s vio bl & blk 55 55
*498* A105 50s pur & blk 1.10 1.10
*a.* Souvenir sheet of 4 1.90 1.90

Christmas 1978 and for 450th death anniv. of Albrecht Dürer. No. 498a contains Nos. 495-498; light brown and black margin. Size: 102x154mm.

Boy Carrying Coconuts A106

Designs: 24s, Children leaving church on White Sunday. 26s, Children pumping water. 50s, Girl playing ukulele.

**1979, Apr. 10 Litho. *Perf. 14***
*499* A106 12s multi 24 24
*500* A106 24s multi 50 50
*501* A106 26s multi 55 55
*502* A106 50s multi 1.10 1.10

International Year of the Child.

Charles W. Morgan A107

**1979, May 29 Litho. *Perf. 13½***
*503* A107 12s multi 25 25
*504* A107 14s Lagoda 32 32
*505* A107 24s James T. Arnold 52 52
*506* A107 50s Splendid 1.10 1.10

See Nos. 521-524, 543-546.

Saturn V Launch — A108

Designs: 14s, Landing module and astronaut on moon (horiz.). 24s, Earth seen from moon. 26s, Astronaut on moon (horiz.). 50s, Lunar and command modules. $1, Command module after splashdown (horiz.).

***Perf. 14½x14, 14x14½***
**1979, June 20 Litho. Wmk. 355**
*507* A108 12s multi 18 18
*508* A108 14s multi 20 20
*509* A108 24s multi 35 35
*510* A108 26s multi 38 38
*511* A108 50s multi 75 75
*512* A108 $1 multi 1.50 1.50
*a.* Souvenir sheet 1.75 1.75
*Nos. 507-512 (6)* 3.36 3.36

1st moon landing, 10th anniv. No. 512a contains No. 512; pale and dark green margin shows Navy helicopter. Size: 90x132mm.

Penny Black, Hill Statue — A109

Designs: 24s, Great Britain No. 2 with Maltese Cross postmark. 26s, Penny Black and Rowland Hill. $1, Great Britain No. 2 and Hill statue.

**1979, Aug. 27 *Perf. 14***
*513* A109 12s multi 18 18
*514* A109 24s multi 35 35
*515* A109 26s multi 38 38
*516* A109 $1 multi 1.50 1.50
*a.* Souvenir sheet of 4 2.50 2.50

Sir Rowland Hill (1795-1879), originator of penny postage. No. 516a contains Nos. 513-516; multicolored margin shows Penny Black and Rowland Hill. Size: 129x95mm.

Anglican Church, Apia A110

Samoan Churches: 6s, Congregational Christian Church, Leulumoega. 26s, Methodist Church, Piula. 50s, Protestant Church, Apia.

**1979, Oct. 22 Photo. *Perf. 12x11½***
*517* A110 4s lt bl & blk 7 7
*518* A110 6s lt yel grn & blk 10 10
*519* A110 26s dl yel & blk 48 48
*520* A110 50s lt lil & blk 90 90
*a.* Souvenir sheet of 4 1.65 1.65

Christmas 1979. No. 520a contains Nos. 517-520. Gray margin shows various churches. Size: 149½x125mm.

Ship Type of 1979
**Wmk. 355**
**1980, Jan. 22 Litho. *Perf. 14***
*521* A107 12s William Hamilton 20 20
*522* A107 14s California 25 25
*523* A107 24s Liverpool II 42 42
*524* A107 50s Two Brothers 90 90

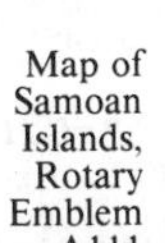

Map of Samoan Islands, Rotary Emblem A111

Missionary Flag, John Williams, Plaque A112

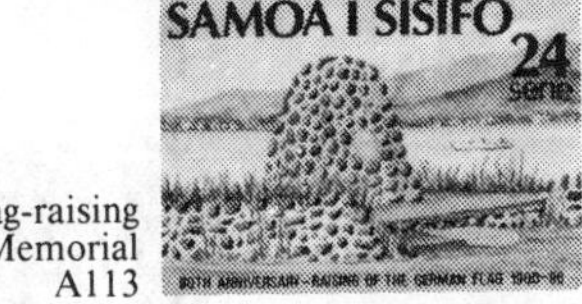

Flag-raising Memorial A113

**1980, Mar. 26 Photo. *Perf. 14***
*525* A111 12s *shown* 20 20
*526* A112 13s *shown* 24 24
*527* A112 14s *German flag, Dr. Wilhelm Solf, plaque* 25 25
*528* A113 24s *shown* 45 45
*529* A113 26s *Williams Memorial, Savai'i* 48 48
*530* A111 50s *Emblem, Paul P. Harris, founder* 90 90
*Nos. 525-530 (6)* 2.52 2.52

Rotary Intl., 75th anniv. (A111); arrival of John Williams, Missionary in Samoa, 150th anniv. (13s, 26s); raising of the German flag, 80th anniv. (14s, 24s).

Souvenir Sheet

Village and Long Boat — A114

**Wmk. 355**
**1980, May 6 Litho. *Perf. 14***
*531* A114 $1 multi 2.25 2.25

London 80 Intl. Phil. Exhib., May 6-14. Multicolored margin shows London Tower, Tower Bridge, Beefeater, Samoan warrior, London 80 emblem; Size: 139x81mm.

**Queen Mother Elizabeth Birthday Issue**
Common Design Type

**1980, Aug. 4 Litho.**
*532* CD330 50s multi 80 80

Souvenir Sheet

Samoa No. 239, ZEAPEX Emblem — A115

**Unwmk.**

**1980, Aug. 23 Litho. *Perf. 14***

*533* A115 $1 multi 2.50 2.50

ZEAPEX '80, New Zealand International Stamp Exhibition, Auckland, Aug. 23-31. No. 533 has multicolored margin showing Samoan and New Zealand flags and New Zealand No. 3. Size: 130x80mm.

Afiamalu Satellite Earth Station A116

Designs: 14s, Station (diff.). 24s, Station, map of Samoa. 50s, Satellite sending waves to earth. $2, Samoa No. 536, Sydpex '80 emblem.

**1980, Sept. 17 Litho. *Perf. 11½***

**Granite Paper**

*534* A116 12s multi 20 20
*535* A116 14s multi 25 25
*536* A116 24s multi 42 42
*537* A116 50s multi 90 90

Souvenir Sheet

**1980, Sept. 29 *Imperf.***

*538* A116 $2 multi 3.50 3.50

Sydpex '80 Natl. Phil. Exhib., Sydney. Multicolored margin shows flags of Samoa and Australia, Sydney Harbor Bridge. Size: 130x80mm.

The Savior, by John Poynton — A117

Christmas 1980 (Paintings by Local Artists): 14s, Madonna and Child, by Lealofi F. Siaopo. 27s, Nativity, by Pasila Feata. 50s, Yuletide, by R.P. Aiono.

**Wmk. 355**

**1980, Oct. 28 Litho. *Perf. 14***

*539* A117 8s multi 10 10
*540* A117 14s multi 18 18
*541* A117 27s multi 35 35
*542* A117 50s multi 65 65
***a.*** Souvenir Sheet of 4 1.50 1.50

No. 542a contains Nos. 539-542; light brown decorative margin. Size: 90½x105½mm.

Ship Type of 1979

**1981, Jan. 26 Litho. *Perf. 13½***

*543* A107 12s *Ocean* 24 24
*544* A107 18s *Horatio* 38 38
*545* A107 27s *Calliope* 55 55
*546* A107 32s *Calypso* 65 65

Pres. Franklin Roosevelt and Hyde Park Home A118

International Year of the Disabled: Scenes of Franklin D. Roosevelt.

**Wmk. 355**

**1981, Apr. 29 Litho. *Perf. 14***

*547* A118 12s shown 12 12
*548* A118 18c Inauguration 20 20
*549* A118 27s Pres. & Mrs. Roosevelt 28 28
*550* A118 32s Atlantic convoy (Lend Lease Bill) 32 32
*551* A118 38s With stamp collection 38 38
*552* A118 $1 Campobello House 1.00 1.00
*Nos. 547-552 (6)* 2.30 2.30

Hotel Tusitala — A119

***Perf. 14½x14***

**1981, June 29 Litho. Wmk. 355**

*553* A119 12s shown 14 14
*554* A119 18s Apia Harbor 20 20
*555* A119 27s Aggie Grey's Hotel 30 30
*556* A119 32s Ceremonial kava preparation 35 35
*557* A119 54s Piula Pool 60 60
*Nos. 553-557 (5)* 1.59 1.59

**Royal Wedding Issue**

Common Design Type

**Wmk. 355**

**1981, July 22 Litho. *Perf. 14***

*558* CD331 18s Bouquet 18 18
*559* CD331 32s Charles 30 30
*560* CD331 $1 Couple 95 95

Tattooing Instruments A120

**1981, Sept. 29 Litho. *Perf. 13½x14***

*561* Strip of 4 1.75 1.75
***a.*** A120 12s shown 14 14
***b.*** A120 18s 1st stage 20 20
***c.*** A120 27s Later stage 30 30
***d.*** A120 $1 Tattooed man 1.10 1.10

Christmas 1981 — A121

**1981, Nov. 30 Litho. *Perf. 13½***

*562* A121 11s Milo tree blossom 12 12
*563* A121 15s Copper leaf 18 18
*564* A121 23s Yellow allamanda 30 30
*565* A121 $1 Mango blossom 1.10 1.10
***a.*** Souv. sheet of 4, #562-565 2.00 2.00

Souvenir Sheet

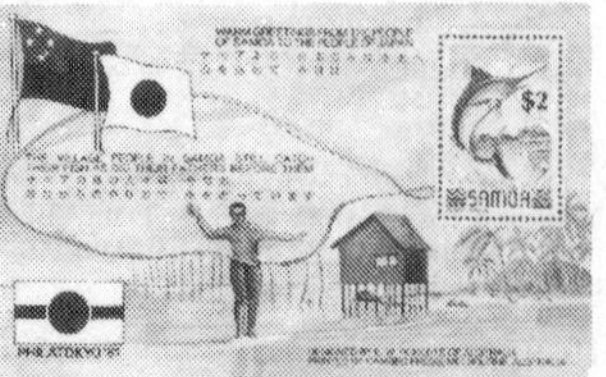


Philatokyo '81 Intl. Stamp Exhibition — A122

**1981, Oct. 9 Litho. *Perf. 14x13½***

*566* A122 $2 multi 2.25 2.25

Size: 130x80mm.

250th Birth Anniv. of George Washington A123

**1982, Feb. 26 Litho. *Perf. 14***

*567* A123 23s Pistol 45 45
*568* A123 25s Mt. Vernon 50 59
*569* A123 34s Portrait 70 70

**Souvenir Sheet**

*570* A123 $1 Taking oath 2.00 2.00

No. 570 contains one stamp; tan and black margin shows Federal Building, New York. Size: 104x103mm.

20th Anniv. of Independence — A124

**1982, May 24 Litho. *Perf. 13½x14***

*571* A124 18s Freighter Forum Samoa 20 20
*572* A124 23s Jet, routes 28 28
*573* A124 25s Natl. Provident Fund building 30 30
*574* A124 $1 Intl. subscriber dialing system 1.10 1.10

Scouting Year — A125

**1982, July 20 Wmk. 355 *Perf. 14½***

*575* A125 5s Map reading 7 7
*576* A125 38s Salute 50 50
*577* A125 44s Rope bridge 60 60
*578* A125 $1 Troop 1.10 1.10
***a.*** Souvenir sheet 1.25 1.25

No. 578a contains one stamp similar to No. 578 (48x36mm.; perf. 11); green and black margin shows symbols, emblem. Size: 94x81mm.

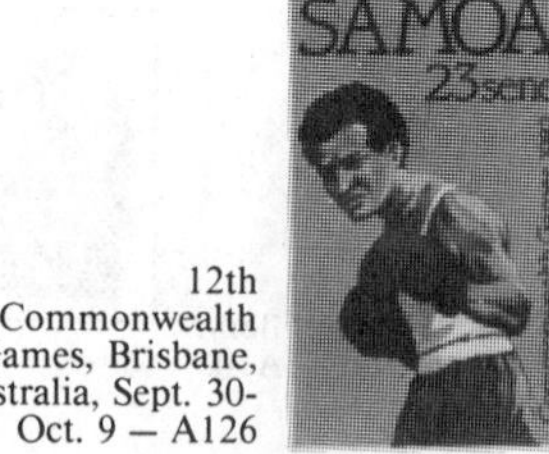


12th Commonwealth Games, Brisbane, Australia, Sept. 30-Oct. 9 — A126

***Perf. 14x14½***

**1982, Sept. 20 Wmk. 373**

*579* A126 23s Boxing 28 28
*580* A126 25s Hurdles 30 30
*581* A126 34s Weightlifting 42 42
*582* A126 $1 Lawn bowling 1.10 1.10

Christmas 1982 — A127

Children's Drawings: 11s, 15s, Flight into Egypt (diff.). 38s, $1, Virgin and Child (diff.).

**1982, Nov. 15 Litho. Wmk. 355**

*583* A127 11s multi 12 12
*584* A127 15s multi 20 20
*585* A127 38s multi 50 50
*586* A127 $1 multi 1.10 1.10
***a.*** Souv. sheet of 4, #583-586 2.00 2.00

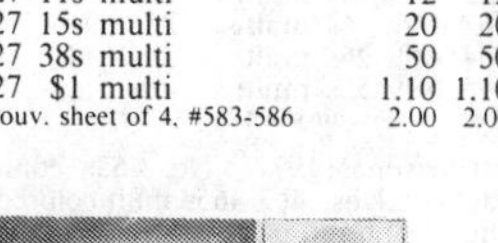

Commonwealth Day — A128

***Perf. 13½x14***

**1983, Feb. 23 Litho. Wmk. 373**

*587* A128 14s Map 16 16
*588* A128 29s Flag 35 35
*589* A128 43s Harvesting copra 50 50
*590* A128 $1 Malietoa Tanumafili II 1.10 1.10

Manned Flight Bicentenary and 50th Anniv. of Douglas Aircraft A129

Designs: a. DC-1. b. DC-2. c. DC-3. d. DC-4. e. DC-5. f. DC-6. g. DC-7. h. DC-8. i. DC-9. j. DC-10. Size: 215x113mm.

**Wmk. 373**

**1983, June 7 Litho. *Perf. 14***

*591* Sheet of 10 3.50 3.50
***a.-j.*** A129 32s multi 35 35

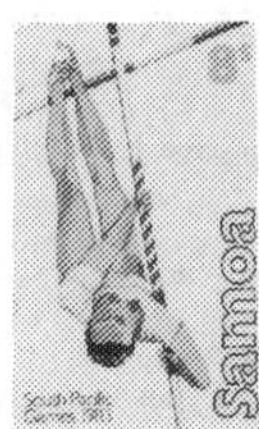


7th South Pacific Games, Apia — A130

**1983, Aug. 29 Litho. *Perf. 14x14½***

*592* A130 8s Pole vault 7 7
*593* A130 15s Basketball 14 14
*594* A130 25c Tennis 22 22
*595* A130 32s Weightlifting 28 28
*596* A130 35s Boxing 30 30
*597* A130 46s Soccer 40 40
*598* A130 48s Golf 45 45
*599* A130 56s Rugby 50 50
*Nos. 592-599 (8)* 2.36 2.36

Local Fruit — A131

***Perf. 14 x 13½***

**1983-84 Litho. Wmk. 373**

*600* A131 1s Limes 5 5
*601* A131 2s Star fruit 5 5
*602* A131 3s Mangosteen 5 5
*603* A131 4s Lychee 5 5
*604* A131 7s Passion fruit 8 8
*605* A131 8s Mangoes 10 10
*606* A131 11s Papaya 14 14
*607* A131 13s Pineapple 16 16
*608* A131 14s Breadfruit 18 18
*609* A131 15s Bananas 20 20
*610* A131 21s Cashew nut 28 28
*611* A131 25s Guava 32 32
*612* A131 32s Water Melon 40 40
*613* A131 48s Sasalapa 62 62
*614* A131 56s Avocado 72 72
*615* A131 $1 Coconut 1.25 1.25

*Perf. 13½*

*616* A131 $2 Apples ('84) 2.50 2.50
*617* A131 $4 Grapefruit ('84) 5.00 5.00
*618* A131 $5 Oranges ('84) 6.25 6.25
*Nos. 600-618 (19)* 18.40 18.40

Miniature Sheet

Boys' Brigade Centenary — A132

**1983, Oct. 10** ***Perf. 14½***
*619* A132 $1 multi 1.00 1.00

Togitogiga Falls, Upolu A133

**Wmk. 373**
**1984, Feb. 15 Litho.** ***Perf. 14***
*620* A133 25s shown 24 24
*621* A133 32s Lano Beach, Savai'i 30 30
*622* A133 48s Mulinu'u Point, Upolu 45 45
*623* A133 56s Nu'utele Isld. 52 52

**Lloyd's List Issue**
Common Design Type
***Perf. 14½x14***
**1984, May 24 Litho. Wmk. 373**
*624* CD335 32s Apia Harbor 28 28
*625* CD335 48s Apia hurricane, 1889 45 45
*626* CD335 60s Forum Samoa 55 55
*627* CD335 $1 Matua 90 90

No. 615 Overprinted: "19th U.P.U. CONGRESS / HAMBURG 1984"
**1984, June 7** ***Perf. 14x13½***
*628* A131 $1 multi 1.00 1.00

Los Angeles Coliseum — A134

**1984, June 26 Litho.** ***Perf. 14½***
*629* A134 25s shown 25 25
*630* A134 32s Weightlifting 35 35
*631* A134 48s Boxing 52 52
*632* A134 $1 Running 1.10 1.10
*a.* Souvenir sheet of 4 2.25 2.25

1984 Summer Olympics and Samoa's first Olympic participation. No. 632a contains Nos. 629-632. Size: 171x121mm.

Souvenir Sheet

Ausipex '84 A135

**1984, Sept. 21 Litho.** ***Perf. 14***
*633* A135 $2.50 Nomad N24 2.50 2.50

Multicolored margin continues design. Size: 132x91mm.

Christmas 1984 — A136

The Three Virtues, by Raphael.

**1984, Nov. 7** ***Perf. 14½x14***
*634* A136 25s Faith 24 24
*635* A136 35s Hope 30 30
*636* A136 $1 Charity 95 95
*a.* Souv. sheet of 3, #634-636 1.50 1.50

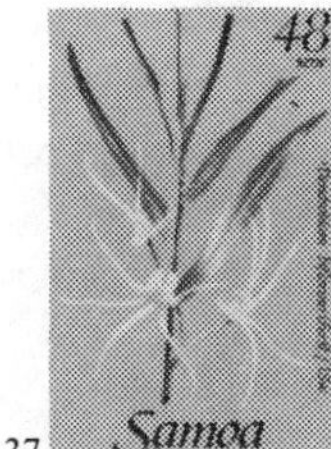


Orchids — A137

**Unwmk.**
**1985, Jan. 23 Litho.** ***Perf. 14***
*637* A137 48s Dendrobium biflorum 42 42
*638* A137 56s Dendrobium vaupelianum kraenzl 50 50
*639* A137 67s Glomera montana 60 60
*640* A137 $1 Spathoglottis plicata 90 90

Vintage Automobiles — A138

**Wmk. 373**
**1985, Mar. 26 Litho.** ***Perf. 14***
*641* A138 48s Ford Model A, 1903 45 45
*642* A138 56s Chevrolet Tourer, 1912 52 52
*643* A138 67s Morris Oxford, 1913 60 60
*644* A138 $1 Austin Seven, 1923 95 95

Fungi — A139

**1985, Apr. 17 Litho.** ***Perf. 14½***
*645* A139 48s Dictyophora indusiata 45 45
*646* A139 56s Ganoderma tornatum 52 52
*647* A139 67s Mycena chlorophos 60 60
*648* A139 $1 Mycobonia flava 95 95

**Queen Mother 85th Birthday**
Common Design Type
***Perf. 14½x14***
**1985, June 7 Litho. Wmk. 384**
*649* CD336 32s Photograph, age 9 32 32
*650* CD336 48s With Prince William at christening of Prince Henry 50 50
*651* CD336 56s At Liverpool street station 60 60
*652* CD336 $1 Holding Prince Henry 1.00 1.00

**Souvenir Sheet**
*653* CD336 $2 Arriving at Tattenham corner station 2.00 2.00

No. 653 has multicolored margin continuing design and depicting Elizabeth II and Margaret. Size: 92x74mm.

Souvenir Sheet

EXPO '85, Tsukuba, Japan — A140

**Unwmk.**
**1985, Aug. 26 Litho.** ***Perf. 14***
*654* A140 $2 Emblem, elevation map 1.75 1.75

Intl. Youth Year — A141

Christmas 1985 — A142

Portions of world map and: a, Emblem, map of No. America, Europe and Africa. b, Hands reaching high. c, Arms reaching, hands limp. d, Hands clenched. e, Emblem and map of Africa, Asia and Europe.

**1985, Sept. 18 Wmk. 373**
*655* Strip of 5 2.60 2.60
*a.-e.* A141 60s, any single 52 52

**1985, Nov. 5 Unwmk.** ***Perf. 14x14½***

Illustrations by Millicent Sowerby from A Child's Garden of Verses, by Robert Louis Stevenson.

*656* A142 32s System 28 28
*657* A142 48s Time to Rise 42 42
*658* A142 56s Auntie's skirts 50 50
*659* A142 $1 Good Children 90 90
*a.* Souvenir sheet of 4, #656-659 2.10 2.10

No. 659a has decorative violet margin. Size: 87x109mm.

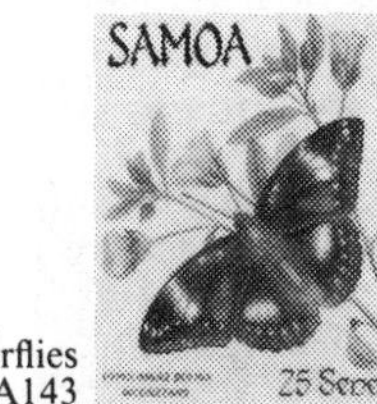


Butterflies A143

**1986, Feb. 13 Wmk. 384** ***Perf. 14½***
*660* A143 25s Hypolimnas bolina inconstans 20 20
*661* A143 32s Anapheis java sparrman 25 25
*662* A143 48s Deudorix epijarbas doris 38 38
*663* A143 56s Badamia exclamationis 45 45
*664* A143 60s Tirumala hamata mellitula 48 48
*665* A143 $1 Catochrysops taitensis 80 80
*Nos. 660-665 (6)* 2.56 2.56

Halley's Comet A144

Designs: 32s, Comet over Apia. 48s, Edmond Halley, astronomer. 60s, Comet orbiting the Earth. $2, Giotto space probe under construction at British Aerospace.

**1986, Mar. 24**
*666* A144 32s multi 28 28
*667* A144 48s multi 42 42
*668* A144 60s multi 52 52
*669* A144 $2 multi 1.75 1.75

**Queen Elizabeth II 60th Birthday**
Common Design Type

Designs: 32s, Engagement to the Duke of Edinburgh, 1947. 48s, State visit to US, 1976. 56s, Attending outdoor ceremony, Apia, 1977. 67s, At Badminton Horse Trials, 1978. $2, Visiting Crown Agents' offices, 1983.

**1986, Apr. 21**
*670* CD337 32s scar, blk & sil 28 28
*671* CD337 48s ultra & multi 42 42
*672* CD337 56s grn & multi 50 50
*673* CD337 67s vio & multi 60 60
*674* CD337 $2 rose vio & multi 1.75 1.75
*Nos. 670-674 (5)* 3.55 3.55

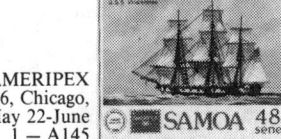


AMERIPEX '86, Chicago, May 22-June 1 — A145

**1986, May 22 Unwmk.**
*675* A145 48s USS Vincennes 42 42
*676* A145 56s Sikorsky S-42 50 50
*677* A145 60s USS Swan 52 52
*678* A145 $2 Apollo 10 splashdown 1.75 1.75

Souvenir Sheet

Vailima, Estate of Novelist Robert Louis Stevenson, Upolu Is. — A146

**1986, Aug. 4 Litho.** ***Perf. 13½***
*679* A146 $3 multi 2.75 2.75

STAMPEX '86, Adelaide, Aug. 4-10. No. 679 has inscribed multicolored margin picturing Parliament House, Apia, natl. and Australian flags. Size: 158x97mm.

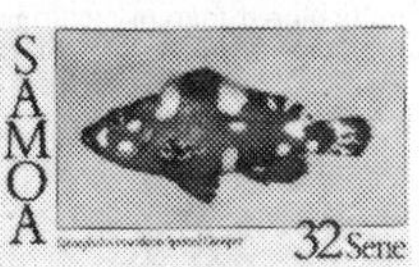


Fish A147

**Unwmk.**
**1986, Aug. 13 Litho.** ***Perf. 14***
*680* A147 32s Spotted grouper 28 28
*681* A147 48s Sabel squirrelfish 42 42
*682* A147 60s Lunartail grouper 52 52
*683* A147 67s Longtail snapper 60 60
*684* A147 $1 Berndt's soldierfish 90 90
*Nos. 680-684 (5)* 2.72 2.72

US Peace Corps in Samoa, 25th Anniv. A148

Statesmen: Vaai Kolone of Samoa, Ronald Reagan of US and: 45s, Fiame Mata'afa, John F. Kennedy (1961) and Parliament House. 60s, Jules Grevy, Grover Cleveland (1886) and the Statue of Liberty.

**1986, Dec. 1** *Perf. 14½*

*685* A148 45s multi 40 40
*686* A148 60s multi 55 55
*a.* Souv. sheet of 2, #685-686 95 95

Christmas, Statue of Liberty, cent. No. 686a has inscribed multicolored margin picturing natl. flags. Size: 131x73.

Natl. Independence, 25th Anniv. — A149

*Perf. 14x14½*

**1987, Feb. 16** **Litho.** **Unwmk.**

*687* A149 15s Map, hibiscus 12 12
*688* A149 45s Parliament 40 40
*689* A149 60s Rowing race, 1987 55 55
*690* A149 70s Dove 62 62
*691* A149 $2 Prime minister, flag 1.75 1.75
*Nos. 687-691 (5)* 3.44 3.44

Nos. 687-690 vert.

Marine Life A150

**1987, Mar. 31**

*692* A150 45s Gulper 40 40
*693* A150 60s Hatchet-fish 55 55
*694* A150 70s Angler 62 62
*695* A150 $2 Gulper, diff. 1.75 1.75

**Souvenir Sheet**

CAPEX '87 — A151

**1987, June 13** *Perf. 14½*

*696* A151 $3 Logger, construction workers 2.75 2.75

No. 696 has multicolored margin picturing trees and a completed Samoan fale. Size: 122x66mm.

Landscapes — A152

**1987, July 29** *Perf. 14*

*697* A152 45s Lefaga Beach, Upolu 42 42
*698* A152 60s Vaisala Beach, Savaii 55 55
*699* A152 70s Solosolo Beach, Upolu 65 65
*700* A152 $2 Neiafu Beach, Savaii 1.90 1.90

Australia Bicentennial A153

Explorers of the Pacific: 40s, Abel Tasman (c. 1603-1659), Dutch navigator, discovered Tasmania, 1642. 45s, James Cook. 80s, Count Louis-Antoine de Bougainville (1729-1811), French navigator, discovered Bougainvelle Is., largest of the Solomon Isls., 1768. $2, Comte de La Perouse (1741-1788), French navigator, discovered La Perouse Strait.

**1987, Sept. 30** **Litho.** *Perf. 14½*

*701* A153 40s multi 38 38
*702* A153 45s multi 42 42
*703* A153 80s multi 78 78
*704* A153 $2 multi 1.90 1.90
*a.* Souv. sheet of one 1.95 1.95

No. 704a has multicolored margin picturing map of South Pacific. Size: 90x73mm.

No. 704a Ovptd. with HAFNIA '87 Emblem in Scarlet

**1987, Oct. 16**

*705* A153 $2 multi 1.95 1.95

Christmas 1987 — A154

**1987, Nov. 30** *Perf. 14*

*706* A154 40s Christmas tree 38 38
*707* A154 45s Going to church 42 42
*708* A154 50s Bamboo fire-gun 48 48
*709* A154 80s Going home 78 78

Australia Bicentennial A155

Designs: a. Samoan natl. crest, Australia Post emblem. b. Two jets, postal van. c. Loading airmail. d. Jet, van, postman. e. Congratulatory aerogramme.

**1988, Jan. 27** *Perf. 14½*

*710* Strip of 5 2.15 2.15
*a.-e.* A155 45s any single 42 42

Faleolo Intl. Airport A156

*Perf. 13x13½*

**1988, Mar. 24** **Litho.** **Unwmk.**

*711* A156 40s Terminal, Boeing 727 40 40
*712* A156 45s Boeing 727, Fuatino 45 45
*713* A156 60s So. Pacific Is. N43SP, terminal 60 60
*714* A156 70s Air New Zealand Boeing 737 68 68
*715* A156 80s Tower, jet 78 78
*716* A156 $1 Hawaiian Air DC-9, VIP house 98 98
*Nos. 711-716 (6)* 3.89 3.89

EXPO '88, Brisbane, Australia A157

**1988, Apr. 27** *Perf. 14½*

*717* A157 45s Island village display 45 45
*718* A157 70s EXPO complex, monorail and flags 70 70
*719* A157 $2 Map 2.00 2.00

**Souvenir Sheet**

Arrival of the Latter Day Saints in Samoa, Cent. — A158

**1988, June 9** **Litho.** *Perf. 13½*

*720* A158 $3 The Temple, Apia 3.00 3.00

No. 720 has violet inscribed margin picturing map of Savai'i, Upolu and Tutuila plus quote from 2 Nephi 10:21, "Great are the promises of the Lord unto them who are upon the isles of the sea." Size: 86x76mm.

1988 Summer Olympics, Seoul — A159

**1988, Aug. 10** **Litho.** *Perf. 14*

*721* A159 15s Running 15 15
*722* A159 60s Weight lifting 60 60
*723* A159 80s Boxing 80 80
*724* A159 $2 Olympic Stadium 2.00 2.00
*a.* Souv. sheet of 4, Nos. 721-724 3.55 3.55

Birds — A160

**1988, Aug. 17** **Unwmk.** *Perf. 13½*

*725* A160 10s Polynesian triller 10 10
*726* A160 15s Samoan wood rail 15 15
*727* A160 20s Flat-billed kingfisher 20 20
*728* A160 25s Samoan fantail 25 25
*729* A160 35s Scarlet robin 35 35
*730* A160 40s Mao 38 38
*731* A160 50s Cardinal honey-eater 48 48
*732* A160 65s Samoan whistler 62 62
*733* A160 75s Many-colored fruit dove 72 72
*734* A160 85s White-throated pigeon 80 80

**1989** **Litho.** **Unwmk.** **Size:** *Perf.*

*735* A160 75s Silver gull 72 72
*736* A160 85s Great frigatebird 80 80
*737* A160 90s Eastern reef heron 86 86
*738* A160 $3 Short-tailed albatross 2.90 2.90
*739* A160 $10 Common fairy tern 9.25 9.25
*740* A160 $20 Shy albatross 18.50 18.50
*Nos. 725-740 (16)* 37.08 37.08

Issue dates: Nos. 735-738, Feb. 28; others, July 31.

Conservation — A161

**1988, Oct. 25** *Perf. 14*

*741* A161 15s Forests, vert. 15 15
*742* A161 40s Culture, vert. 38 38
*743* A161 45s Wildlife, vert. 45 45
*744* A161 50s Water 48 48
*745* A161 60s Marine resources 58 58
*746* A161 $1 Land and soil 95 95
*Nos. 741-746 (6)* 2.99 2.99

Christmas A162

Designs: 15s, 40s, Congregational Church of Jesus, Apia. 40s, Roman Catholic Church, Leauvaa. 45s, Congregational Christian Church, Moataa. $2, Baha'i Temple, Vailima.

*Perf. 14x14½*

**1988, Nov. 14** **Litho.** **Unwmk.**

*747* A162 15s multi 15 15
*748* A162 40s multi 38 38
*749* A162 45s multi 45 45
*750* A162 $2 multi 1.95 1.95
*a.* Souv. sheet of 4, Nos. 747-750 3.00 3.00

## SEMI-POSTAL STAMP

**Catalogue values for unused stamps in this section, from this point to the end of the section, are for Never Hinged items.**

No. 246 Surcharged: "HURRICANE RELIEF / 6d"

**Wmk. 355**

**1966, Sept. 1** **Litho.** *Perf. 13½*

*B1* A43 8p + 6p bl & emer 20 20

Surtax for aid to plantations destroyed by the hurricane of Jan. 29, 1966.

## AIR POST STAMPS

**Catalogue values for unused stamps in this section, from this point to the end of the section, are for Never Hinged items.**

Red-tailed Tropic Bird — AP1

**Wmk. 355**

**1965, Dec. 29 Photo. *Perf. 14½***

| | | | | |
|---|---|---|---|---|
| *C1* | AP1 | 8p shown | 35 | 35 |
| *C2* | AP1 | 2sh Flying fish | 85 | 85 |

Sir Gordon Taylor's Bermuda Flying Boat "Frigate Bird III" — AP2

Designs: 7s, Polynesian Airlines DC-3. 20s, Pan American Airways "Samoan Clipper." 30s, Air Samoa Britten-Norman "Islander."

***Perf. 13½x13***

**1970, July 27 Photo. Unwmk.**

| | | | | |
|---|---|---|---|---|
| *C3* | AP2 | 3s multi | 14 | 14 |
| *C4* | AP2 | 7s multi | 30 | 30 |
| *C5* | AP2 | 20s multi | 90 | 90 |
| *C6* | AP2 | 30s multi | 1.40 | 1.40 |

Hawker Siddeley 748 — AP3

Planes at Faleolo Airport: 10s, Hawker Siddeley 748 in the air. 12s, Hawker Siddeley 748 on ground. 22s, BAC 1-11 planes on ground.

**1973, Mar. 9 *Perf. 11½***

**Granite Paper**

| | | | | |
|---|---|---|---|---|
| *C7* | AP3 | 8s multi | 30 | 30 |
| *C8* | AP3 | 10s multi | 38 | 38 |
| *C9* | AP3 | 12s multi | 45 | 45 |
| *C10* | AP3 | 22s multi | 85 | 85 |

## SARAWAK

LOCATION — In the northwestern part of the island of Borneo, bordering on the South China Sea.
GOVT. — Former British Crown Colony.
AREA — 48,250 sq. mi. (approx.).
POP. — 975,918 (1970)
CAPITAL — Kuching.

The last ruling Raja, who retired in 1946 when he ceded Sarawak to the British Crown, was Sir Charles Vyner Brooke, an Englishman. He inherited the title from his father, Sir Charles Johnson Brooke, who in turn received it from his uncle, Sir James Brooke. The title of Raja was conferred on Sir James by Raja Muda Hassim after Sir James had aided him in subduing a rebellion. The title and right of succession were duly recognized by the Sultan of Brunei and by Great Britain.

Sarawak joined the Federation of Malaysia in 1963.

100 Cents = 1 Dollar

**Catalogue values for unused stamps in this country are for Never Hinged items, beginning with Scott 155.**

Sir James Brooke
A1

Sir Charles Johnson Brooke
A2

**Unwmk.**

**1869, Mar. 1 Litho. *Perf. 11***

| | | | | |
|---|---|---|---|---|
| *1* | A1 | 3c brn, *yel* | 80.00 | *310.00* |
| *a.* | | Imperf. | | |

**1871, Jan.**

| | | | | |
|---|---|---|---|---|
| *2* | A2 | 3c brn, *yel* | 2.50 | *3.25* |
| *a.* | | Imperf. | | |
| *b.* | | Period after "THREE" | 32.50 | *45.00* |

No. 2 surcharged "TWO CENTS" is believed to be bogus.

**1875, Jan. 1 *Perf. 12***

| | | | | |
|---|---|---|---|---|
| *3* | A2 | 2c gray lil, *lil* | 3.25 | *4.75* |
| *a.* | | Imperf. pair | | |
| *4* | A2 | 4c brn, *yel* | 4.50 | *4.25* |
| *a.* | | Imperf. pair | | |
| *b.* | | Vertical pair, imperf between | *575.00* | |
| *5* | A2 | 6c grn, *grn* | 4.00 | *4.75* |
| *a.* | | Imperf. pair | | |
| *6* | A2 | 8c bl, *bl* | 3.00 | *3.50* |
| *a.* | | Imperf. pair | | |
| *c.* | | Laid paper | | |
| *7* | A2 | 12c red, *rose* | 9.50 | *9.00* |
| *a.* | | Imperf. pair | | |
| | | *Nos. 3-7 (5)* | 24.25 | 26.25 |

Nos. 3 to 7 have each five varieties of the words of value.

Sir Charles Johnson Brooke — A4

**1888-97 Typo. *Perf. 14.***

| | | | | |
|---|---|---|---|---|
| *8* | A4 | 1c lil & blk ('92) | 60 | 48 |
| *9* | A4 | 2c lil & rose | 1.25 | 48 |
| *10* | A4 | 3c lil & bl | 1.10 | 75 |
| *11* | A4 | 4c lil & yel | 9.00 | *12.00* |
| *12* | A4 | 5c lil & grn ('91) | 4.00 | 1.10 |
| *13* | A4 | 6c lil & brn | 4.75 | *9.00* |
| *14* | A4 | 8c grn & rose | 3.00 | 1.65 |
| *a.* | | 8c grn & car | 9.00 | 4.25 |
| *15* | A4 | 10c grn & vio ('93) | 21.00 | 10.50 |
| *16* | A4 | 12c grn & bl | 3.00 | *6.00* |
| *17* | A4 | 16c gray grn & org ('97) | 18.00 | *24.00* |
| *18* | A4 | 25c grn & brn | 20.00 | *22.50* |
| *19* | A4 | 32c gray grn & blk ('97) | 18.00 | *30.00* |
| *20* | A4 | 50c gray grn ('97) | 22.50 | *40.00* |
| *21* | A4 | $1 gray grn & blk ('97) | 35.00 | *60.00* |
| | | *Nos. 8-21 (14)* | 161.20 | 218.46 |

No. 21 shows the numeral on white tablet.

Three higher values—$2, $5, $10—were prepared but not issued. Value $250 each.

Nos. 14 and 16 Surcharged in Black:

**2c.** a **5c.** No. 23 **5c.** No. 24

**1889-91**

| | | | | |
|---|---|---|---|---|
| *22* | A4 | 2c on 8c grn & rose | 2.25 | 4.50 |
| *a.* | | Dbl. surch. | 300.00 | |
| *b.* | | Pair, one without surch. | 2,000. | |
| *c.* | | Inverted surcharge | 2,000. | |
| *23* | A4 | 5c on 12c grn & bl ('91) | 11.00 | 15.00 |
| *a.* | | Double surcharge | 1,100. | *1,100.* |
| *b.* | | Pair, one without surch. | | |
| *c.* | | No period after "C" | 18.00 | 21.00 |
| *d.* | | Without "C" | 250.00 | |
| *e.* | | Dbl. surch., one vert. | 1,750. | |
| *24* | A4 | 5c on 12c grn & bl ('91) | 90.00 | *105.00* |
| *a.* | | No period after "C" | 90.00 | *105.00* |
| *b.* | | Dbl. surch. | 600.00 | |
| *c.* | | "C" omitted | 375.00 | 300.00 |

No. 2 Surcharged in Black

**ONE CENT**

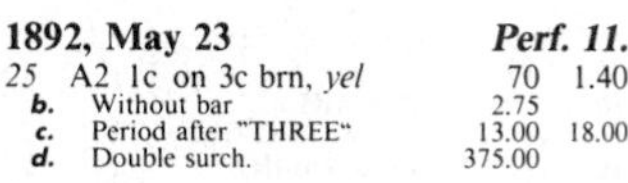

**1892, May 23 *Perf. 11.***

| | | | | |
|---|---|---|---|---|
| *25* | A2 | 1c on 3c brn, *yel* | 70 | 1.40 |
| *b.* | | Without bar | 2.75 | |
| *c.* | | Period after "THREE" | 13.00 | 18.00 |
| *d.* | | Double surch. | 375.00 | |

No. 10 Surcharged in Black:

**one cent.** e **One Cent.** f

***Perf. 14.***

| | | | | |
|---|---|---|---|---|
| *26* | A4 (e) | 1c on 3c lil & bl | 2.75 | 5.50 |
| *a.* | | No period after "cent" | 67.50 | 67.50 |
| *27* | A4 (f) | 1c on 3c lil & bl | 32.50 | 32.50 |
| *a.* | | "Cent" | | |
| *b.* | | Double surch. | 360.00 | 240.00 |

Sir Charles Johnson Brooke
A11 A12

A13 A14

**1895, Jan. 1 Engr. *Perf. 11½, 12***

| | | | | |
|---|---|---|---|---|
| *28* | A11 | 2c red brn, perf. 12½ | 2.00 | 3.00 |
| *a.* | | Perf. 11½ | 4.00 | 4.25 |
| *29* | A12 | 4c black | 6.00 | 1.75 |
| *30* | A13 | 6c violet | 4.00 | 6.00 |
| *31* | A14 | 8c dp grn | 9.00 | 10.50 |

The 2c and 8c exist imperf., but were not regularly issued.

Stamps of 1871-75 Surcharged in Black or Red

**2 CENTS.**

**1899 *Perf. 11***

| | | | | |
|---|---|---|---|---|
| *32* | A2 | 2c on 3c brn, *yel* | 1.65 | 2.00 |
| *a.* | | Period after "THREE" | 50.00 | |

***Perf. 12***

| | | | | |
|---|---|---|---|---|
| *33* | A2 | 2c on 12c red, *rose* | 1.25 | *2.00* |
| *a.* | | Inverted surcharge | 900.00 | *1,050.* |
| *34* | A2 | 4c on 6c grn, *grn* (R) | 20.00 | *40.00* |
| *a.* | | Inverted surcharge | | |
| *35* | A2 | 4c on 8c bl, *bl* (R) | 6.50 | 7.25 |

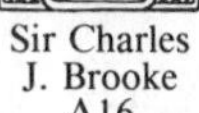

Sir Charles J. Brooke
A16

Sir Charles Vyner Brooke
A17

**1899-1908 Typo. *Perf. 14***

| | | | | |
|---|---|---|---|---|
| *36* | A16 | 1c bl & car ('01) | 40 | 55 |
| *37* | A16 | 2c gray grn | 32 | 20 |
| *38* | A16 | 3c dl vio ('08) | 2.00 | 35 |
| *39* | A16 | 4c rose | 2.00 | 38 |
| *40* | A16 | 8c yel & blk | 1.40 | 1.00 |
| *41* | A16 | 10c ultra | 2.25 | 50 |
| *42* | A16 | 12c lt vio | 1.65 | 1.00 |
| *43* | A16 | 16c org brn & grn | 3.00 | 1.75 |
| *44* | A16 | 20c brn ol & vio ('00) | 2.50 | 2.25 |
| *45* | A16 | 25c brn & ultra | 2.25 | 4.00 |
| *46* | A16 | 50c ol grn & rose | 6.25 | *12.50* |
| *47* | A16 | $1 rose & grn | 17.50 | *25.00* |
| | | *Nos. 36-47 (12)* | 41.52 | 49.48 |

A 5c, type A16, was prepared but not issued. Value $25.

The Catalogue editors cannot undertake to appraise, identify or judge the genuineness or condition of stamps.

Wmk.71

**1901 Wmk. Rosette. (71)**

| | | | | |
|---|---|---|---|---|
| *48* | A16 | 2c gray grn | 15.00 | 5.00 |

**1918-23 Unwmk.**

| | | | | |
|---|---|---|---|---|
| *50* | A17 | 1c sl bl & rose | 12 | 12 |
| *51* | A17 | 2c dp grn | 90 | 20 |
| *52* | A17 | 2c vio ('23) | 30 | 30 |
| *53* | A17 | 3c vio brn | 1.00 | 1.00 |
| *54* | A17 | 3c dp grn ('22) | 35 | 30 |
| *55* | A17 | 4c car rose | 90 | 40 |
| *56* | A17 | 4c pur brn ('23) | 42 | 12 |
| *57* | A17 | 5c org ('23) | 1.10 | 20 |
| *58* | A17 | 6c lake brn ('22) | 1.10 | 40 |
| *59* | A17 | 8c yel & blk | 2.25 | *7.50* |
| *60* | A17 | 8c car rose ('22) | 65 | 65 |
| *61* | A17 | 10c ultra | 1.00 | 75 |
| *a.* | | 10c bl | 1.00 | 75 |
| *62* | A17 | 10c blk ('23) | 65 | 65 |
| *63* | A17 | 12c violet | 1.40 | 1.50 |
| *64* | A17 | 12c ultra ('22) | 1.90 | 2.00 |
| *65* | A17 | 16c brn & bl grn | 2.00 | 1.50 |
| *66* | A17 | 20c ol bis & vio | 1.40 | 1.40 |
| *a.* | | 20c ol grn & vio | 1.40 | 1.40 |
| *67* | A17 | 25c brn & bl | 2.25 | *3.50* |
| *68* | A17 | 30c bis & gray ('22) | 1.65 | *2.50* |
| *69* | A17 | 50c ol grn & rose | 5.50 | 2.50 |
| *70* | A17 | $1 car rose & grn | 5.50 | *7.50* |
| | | *Nos. 50-70 (21)* | 32.34 | 34.99 |

In 1918 a supply of the 1c (No. 50) had the value tablet printed, by error, in slate blue instead of rose. It is officially stated that this stamp was never issued and had no franking power. Value $50.

The $1 denomination shows numeral of value in color on white tablet.

Nos. 61 and 63 Surcharged

**ONE cent**

First Printing, Bars 1¼ mm apart.
Second Printing, Bars ¾ mm apart.

**1923**

| | | | | |
|---|---|---|---|---|
| *77* | A17 | 1c on 10c ultra | 25.00 | *50.00* |
| *a.* | | "cnet" | 300.00 | *600.00* |
| *b.* | | Bars ¾ mm apart | 75.00 | |
| *78* | A17 | 2c on 12c vio | 3.50 | *10.00* |
| *a.* | | Bars ¾ mm apart | 50.00 | |

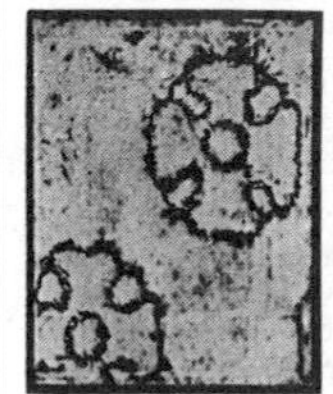

Wmk. 47- Multiple Rosettes

Wmk. 231- Oriental Crown

Type of 1918 Issue.

**1928-29 Typo. Wmk. 47**

| | | | | |
|---|---|---|---|---|
| *79* | A17 | 1c sl bl & rose | 22 | 22 |
| *80* | A17 | 2c dl vio | 75 | 25 |
| *81* | A17 | 3c dp grn | 22 | *1.00* |
| *82* | A17 | 4c pur brn | 50 | 20 |
| *83* | A17 | 5c org ('29) | 4.00 | *5.00* |
| *84* | A17 | 6c brn lake | 35 | 40 |
| *85* | A17 | 8c carmine | 1.50 | *6.00* |
| *86* | A17 | 10c black | 65 | 1.00 |
| *87* | A17 | 12c ultra | 2.00 | 2.25 |
| *88* | A17 | 16c dp brn & bl grn | 1.50 | *2.00* |
| *89* | A17 | 20c dp ol & vio | 85 | 1.40 |
| *90* | A17 | 25c dk brn & ultra | 1.00 | *3.00* |
| *91* | A17 | 30c ol bis & gray | 2.50 | 2.50 |
| *92* | A17 | 50c ol grn & rose | 2.25 | *3.00* |
| *93* | A17 | $1 car rose & grn | 12.50 | *20.00* |

Sir Charles Vyner Brooke
A18 A19

Wmk. 231

**1932, Jan. 1 Engr. *Perf. 12½***

| No. | Type | Description | Unused | Used |
|---|---|---|---|---|
| *94* | A18 | 1c indigo | 32 | 28 |
| *95* | A18 | 2c dk grn | 32 | 32 |
| *96* | A18 | 3c dp vio | 65 | 40 |
| *97* | A18 | 4c dp org | 50 | 25 |
| *98* | A18 | 5c brn lake | 90 | 18 |
| *99* | A18 | 6c dp red | 1.75 | *4.00* |
| *100* | A18 | 8c org yel | 2.50 | *3.75* |
| *101* | A18 | 10c black | 2.50 | *5.00* |
| *102* | A18 | 12c vio bl | 2.00 | *3.00* |
| *103* | A18 | 15c org brn | 2.00 | *3.75* |
| *104* | A18 | 20c vio & org | 2.50 | *3.75* |
| *105* | A18 | 25c org brn & yel | 3.00 | *5.00* |
| *106* | A18 | 30c org red & ol brn | 3.75 | *6.25* |
| *107* | A18 | 50c ol grn & red | 6.25 | *8.75* |
| *108* | A18 | $1 car & grn | 11.00 | *17.50* |
| | | *Nos. 94-108 (15)* | 39.94 | 62.18 |

**1934-41 Unwmk. *Perf. 12.***

| No. | Type | Description | Unused | Used |
|---|---|---|---|---|
| *109* | A19 | 1c brn vio | 14 | 10 |
| *110* | A19 | 2c bl grn | 14 | 10 |
| *111* | A19 | 2c blk ('41) | 70 | *1.40* |
| *112* | A19 | 3c black | 20 | 14 |
| *113* | A19 | 3c bl grn ('41) | 14 | 45 |
| *114* | A19 | 4c magenta | 45 | 14 |
| *115* | A19 | 5c violet | 16 | 10 |
| *116* | A19 | 6c dp rose | 20 | 24 |
| *117* | A19 | 6c red brn ('41) | 70 | *2.00* |
| *118* | A19 | 8c red brn | 24 | 24 |
| *119* | A19 | 8c dp rose ('41) | 28 | 48 |
| *120* | A19 | 10c red | 52 | 45 |
| *121* | A19 | 12c dp ultra | 45 | 50 |
| *122* | A19 | 12c org ('41) | 70 | *5.25* |
| *123* | A19 | 15c orange | 1.00 | *5.00* |
| *124* | A19 | 15c dp bl ('41) | 45 | *5.25* |
| *125* | A19 | 20c dp rose & ol | 70 | 60 |
| *126* | A19 | 25c org & vio | 35 | *70* |
| *127* | A19 | 30c vio & red brn | 1.40 | 1.90 |
| *128* | A19 | 50c red & vio | 1.90 | 1.90 |
| *129* | A19 | $1 dk brn & red | 2.50 | 2.75 |
| *130* | A19 | $2 vio & mag | 2.75 | *5.50* |
| *131* | A19 | $3 bl grn & rose | 5.25 | *6.25* |
| *132* | A19 | $4 red & ultra | 7.00 | *9.00* |
| *133* | A19 | $5 red brn & red | 14.00 | *27.50* |
| *134* | A19 | $10 org & blk | 27.50 | *42.50* |
| | | *Nos. 109-134 (26)* | 69.82 | 120.44 |

Stamps of 1934-41 Overprinted in Black or Red **B M A**

**1945, Dec. 17**

| No. | Type | Description | Unused | Used |
|---|---|---|---|---|
| *135* | A19 | 1c brn vio | 8 | 8 |
| *136* | A19 | 2c blk (R) | 5 | 5 |
| *137* | A19 | 3c bl grn | 6 | 5 |
| *138* | A19 | 4c magenta | 6 | 5 |
| *139* | A19 | 5c vio (R) | 18 | 8 |
| *140* | A19 | 6c red brn | 18 | 8 |
| *141* | A19 | 8c dp rose | 6.00 | 6.00 |
| *142* | A19 | 10c red | 25 | 10 |
| *143* | A19 | 12c orange | 32 | *2.00* |
| *144* | A19 | 15c dp bl | 32 | 12 |
| *145* | A19 | 20c dp rose & ol | 55 | 45 |
| *146* | A19 | 25c org & vio (R) | 42 | *85* |
| *147* | A19 | 30c vio & red brn | 55 | *1.25* |
| *148* | A19 | 50c red & vio | 85 | 25 |
| *149* | A19 | $1 dk brn & red | 2.00 | 95 |
| *150* | A19 | $2 vio & mag | 5.00 | 2.50 |
| *151* | A19 | $3 bl grn & rose | 10.50 | 17.00 |
| *152* | A19 | $4 red & ultra | 15.00 | 17.00 |
| *153* | A19 | $5 red brn & red | 30.00 | 42.50 |
| *154* | A19 | $10 org & blk (R) | 50.00 | 55.00 |
| | | *Nos. 134-154 (21)* | 149.87 | 188.86 |

**Catalogue values for unused stamps in this section, from this point to the end of the section, are for Never Hinged items.**

Sir James Brooke, Sir Charles V. Brooke and Sir Charles J. Brooke A20

**1946, May 18**

| No. | Type | Description | Unused | Used |
|---|---|---|---|---|
| *155* | A20 | 8c dk car | 12 | 12 |
| *156* | A20 | 15c dk bl | 32 | 32 |
| *157* | A20 | 50c red & blk | 60 | 60 |
| *158* | A20 | $1 sep & blk | 3.25 | *5.50* |

Type of 1934-41 Overprinted in Blue or Red 

**1947, Apr. 16 Wmk. 4 *Perf. 12***

| No. | Type | Description | Unused | Used |
|---|---|---|---|---|
| *159* | A19 | 1c brn vio | 5 | 5 |
| *160* | A19 | 2c blk (R) | 5 | 5 |
| *161* | A19 | 3c bl grn (R) | 6 | 6 |
| *162* | A19 | 4c magenta | 8 | 8 |
| *163* | A19 | 6c red brn | 8 | 8 |
| *164* | A19 | 8c dp rose | 8 | 8 |
| *165* | A19 | 10c red | 12 | 12 |
| *166* | A19 | 12c orange | 15 | 15 |
| *167* | A19 | 15c dp bl (R) | 20 | 20 |
| *168* | A19 | 20c dp rose & ol (R) | 24 | 24 |
| *169* | A19 | 25c org & vio (R) | 24 | 24 |
| *170* | A19 | 50c red & vio (R) | 40 | 40 |
| *171* | A19 | $1 dk brn & red | 1.10 | 1.10 |
| *172* | A19 | $2 vio & mag | 2.75 | 2.75 |
| *173* | A19 | $5 red brn & red | 5.75 | 5.75 |
| | | *Nos. 159-173 (15)* | 11.35 | 11.35 |

**Silver Wedding Issue**

Common Design Types

**1948, Oct. 25 Photo. *Perf. 14x14½***

| No. | Type | Description | Unused | Used |
|---|---|---|---|---|
| *174* | CD304 | 8c scarlet | 15 | 15 |

**Engraved; Name Typographed**
***Perf. 11½x11.***

| No. | Type | Description | Unused | Used |
|---|---|---|---|---|
| *175* | CD305 | $5 lt brn | 21.00 | 25.00 |

**UPU Issue**

Common Design Types

**Engr.; Name Typo. on 15c, 25c.**
***Perf. 13½, 11x11½***

**1949, Oct. 10 Wmk. 4**

| No. | Type | Description | Unused | Used |
|---|---|---|---|---|
| *176* | CD306 | 8c rose car | 75 | 75 |
| *177* | CD307 | 15c indigo | 1.00 | 1.00 |
| *178* | CD308 | 25c green | 1.90 | 1.90 |
| *179* | CD309 | 50c violet | 4.50 | 4.50 |

Troides Brookiana A21

Western Tarsier — A22

Designs: 3c, Kayan tomb. 4c, Kayan girl and boy. 6c, Bead work. 8c, Dyak dancer. 10c, Scaly anteater. 12c, Kenyah boys. 15c, Fire making. 20c, Kelemantan rice barn. 25c, Pepper vines. 50c, Iban woman. $1, Kelabit smithy. $2, Map of Sarawak. $5, Arms of Sarawak.

***Perf. 11½x11, 11x11½***

**1950, Jan. 3 Engr.**

| No. | Type | Description | Unused | Used |
|---|---|---|---|---|
| *180* | A21 | 1c black | 20 | 15 |
| *181* | A22 | 2c org red | 20 | 15 |
| *182* | A22 | 3c green | 24 | 20 |
| *183* | A22 | 4c brown | 24 | 20 |
| *184* | A22 | 6c aqua | 30 | 20 |
| *185* | A21 | 8c red | 45 | 30 |
| *186* | A21 | 10c orange | 2.25 | 2.25 |
| *187* | A21 | 12c purple | 45 | 30 |
| *188* | A21 | 15c dp bl | 50 | 24 |
| *189* | A21 | 20c red org & brn | 75 | 50 |
| *190* | A21 | 25c car & grn | 85 | 60 |
| *191* | A22 | 50c pur & brn | 1.25 | 1.00 |
| *192* | A21 | $1 dk brn & bl grn | 2.25 | 2.25 |
| *193* | A21 | $2 rose car & bl | 16.00 | 15.00 |

**Engr. and Typo.**

| No. | Type | Description | Unused | Used |
|---|---|---|---|---|
| *194* | A21 | $5 dp vio, blk, red & yel | 16.00 | 10.00 |
| | | *Nos. 180-194 (15)* | 41.93 | 33.34 |

**1952, Feb. 1**

| No. | Type | Description | Unused | Used |
|---|---|---|---|---|
| *195* | A21 | 10c org *(Map)* | 70 | 35 |

**Coronation Issue.**

Common Design Type

**1953, June 3 Engr. *Perf. 13½x13***

| No. | Type | Description | Unused | Used |
|---|---|---|---|---|
| *196* | CD312 | 10c ultra & blk | 60 | 60 |

Logging — A23

Hornbill — A24

Elizabeth II — A25

Designs: 2c, Young Orangutan. 4c, Kayan Dancing. 8c, Shield with spears. 10c, Kenyah ceremonial carving. 12c, Barong Panau (sailboat). 15c, Turtles. 20c, Melanau basket making. 25c, Astana, Kuching (Governor's Residence). $1, $2, Queen Elizabeth II (Portrait like Fiji A39). $5, Arms.

***Perf. 11x11½, 11½x11, 12x12½ (A25)***

**1955-57 Wmk. 4 Engr.**

| No. | Type | Description | Unused | Used |
|---|---|---|---|---|
| *197* | A23 | 1c green | 8 | 6 |
| *198* | A23 | 2c red org | 8 | 6 |
| *199* | A23 | 4c brn car | 8 | 6 |
| *200* | A24 | 6c grnsh bl | 20 | 18 |
| *201* | A24 | 8c rose red | 12 | 8 |
| *202* | A24 | 10c dk grn | 20 | 10 |
| *203* | A24 | 12c purple | 24 | 15 |
| *204* | A24 | 15c ultra | 30 | 15 |
| *205* | A24 | 20c brn & ol | 35 | 20 |
| *206* | A24 | 25c brt grn & brn | 50 | 20 |
| *207* | A25 | 30c vio & red brn ('55) | 75 | 15 |
| *208* | A25 | 50c car rose & blk | 70 | 35 |
| *209* | A25 | $1 org brn & grn | 2.25 | 65 |
| *210* | A25 | $2 grn & vio | 5.00 | 1.75 |

**Engr. and Typo.**

| No. | Type | Description | Unused | Used |
|---|---|---|---|---|
| *211* | A24 | $5 dp vio, blk, red & yel | 15.00 | 4.50 |
| | | *Nos. 197-211 (15)* | 25.85 | 8.64 |

See Nos. 215-222.

**Freedom from Hunger Issue**

Common Design Type

***Perf. 14x14½***

**1963, June 4 Photo. Wmk. 314**

| No. | Type | Description | Unused | Used |
|---|---|---|---|---|
| *212* | CD314 | 12c sepia | 1.25 | 1.25 |

Types of 1955-57

***Perf. 11x11½, 11½x11***

**1964-65 Engr. Wmk. 314**

| No. | Type | Description | Unused | Used |
|---|---|---|---|---|
| *215* | A23 | 1c green | 5 | 5 |
| *216* | A23 | 2c red org ('65) | 50 | *2.00* |
| *217* | A24 | 6c grn bl | 30 | *1.00* |
| *218* | A24 | 10c dk grn | 60 | 60 |
| *219* | A24 | 12c purple | 75 | *1.50* |
| *220* | A24 | 15c ultra ('65) | 2.50 | *5.00* |
| *221* | A24 | 20c brn & ol | 1.25 | 1.25 |
| *222* | A24 | 25c brt grn & brn | 2.25 | 2.25 |
| | | *Nos. 215-222 (8)* | 8.20 | 13.65 |

**STATE OF MALAYSIA**

Orchid Type of Johore (Malaysia), 1965, with State Crest

**Wmk. 338**

**1965, Nov. 15 Photo. *Perf. 14½***

**Flowers in Natural Colors**

| No. | Type | Description | Unused | Used |
|---|---|---|---|---|
| *228* | A14 | 1c blk & lt grnsh bl | 6 | 5 |
| *229* | A14 | 2c blk, red & gray | 6 | 5 |
| *230* | A14 | 5c blk & Prus bl | 24 | 6 |
| *231* | A14 | 6c blk & lt lil | 35 | 20 |
| *232* | A14 | 10c blk & lt ultra | 80 | 30 |
| *233* | A14 | 15c blk, lil rose & grn | 1.00 | 30 |
| *234* | A14 | 20c blk & brn | 1.25 | 50 |
| | | *Nos. 228-234 (7)* | 3.76 | 1.46 |

Clipper and State Crest — A26

***Perf. 13½x13***

**1971, Feb. 1 Litho. Unwmk.**

| No. | Type | Description | Unused | Used |
|---|---|---|---|---|
| *235* | A26 | 1c *Malayan Jezebel* | 6 | 5 |
| *236* | A26 | 2c *Black-veined tiger* | 6 | 5 |
| *237* | A26 | 5c *shown* | 15 | 5 |
| *a.* | | Booklet pane of 4 ('73) | 75 | |
| *238* | A26 | 6c *Lime Butterfly* | 18 | 6 |
| *239* | A26 | 10c *Great orange tip* | 38 | 15 |
| *a.* | | Booklet pane of 4 ('73) | 1.90 | |
| *240* | A26 | 15c *Blue pansy* | 45 | 22 |
| *a.* | | Booklet pane of 4 ('73) | 2.25 | |
| *241* | A26 | 20c *Wanderer* | 90 | 38 |
| | | *Nos. 235-241 (7)* | 2.18 | 96 |

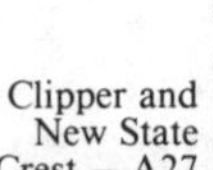

Clipper and New State Crest — A27

Changed Colors, Designs as Before.

**1977-78 Photo. Unwmk.**

| No. | Type | Description | Unused | Used |
|---|---|---|---|---|
| *242* | A27 | 1c multi ('78) | 1.00 | 75 |
| *243* | A27 | 2c multi ('78) | 10 | 5 |
| *244* | A27 | 5c multi | 20 | 10 |
| *245* | A27 | 10c multi | 35 | 20 |
| *246* | A27 | 15c multi | 50 | 30 |
| *247* | A27 | 20c multi ('78) | 75 | 40 |
| | | *Nos. 242-247 (6)* | 2.90 | 1.80 |

Flower Type of Johore, 1979, with State Crest

**1979, Apr. 30 Wmk. 378 *Perf. 14½***

| No. | Type | Description | Unused | Used |
|---|---|---|---|---|
| *248* | A16 | 1c multi | 5 | 5 |
| *249* | A16 | 2c multi | 5 | 5 |
| *250* | A16 | 5c multi | 5 | 5 |
| *a.* | | Unwmkd. ('86) | 1.05 | |
| *251* | A16 | 10c multi | 8 | 5 |
| *a.* | | Unwmkd. ('85) | 2.15 | |
| *252* | A16 | 15c multi | 12 | 6 |
| *253* | A16 | 20c multi | 16 | 8 |
| *a.* | | Unwmkd. ('84) | 4.25 | |
| *254* | A16 | 25c multi | 20 | 10 |
| | | *Nos. 248-254 (7)* | 71 | 44 |

Agriculture and State Arms Type of Johore

**Wmk. 388**

**1986, Oct. 25 Litho. *Perf. 12***

| No. | Type | Description | Unused | Used |
|---|---|---|---|---|
| *255* | A19 | 1c multi | 5 | 5 |
| *256* | A19 | 2c multi | 5 | 5 |
| *257* | A19 | 5c multi | 5 | 5 |
| *258* | A19 | 10c multi | 8 | 5 |
| *259* | A19 | 15c multi | 12 | 6 |
| *260* | A19 | 20c multi | 16 | 8 |
| *261* | A19 | 30c multi | 24 | 12 |
| | | *Nos. 255-261 (7)* | 75 | 46 |

---

**OCCUPATION STAMPS**

**Issued under Japanese Occupation.**

Stamps of 1934-41 Handstamped in Violet 府政国帝本日大

**1942 Unwmk. *Perf. 12***

| No. | Type | Description | Unused | Used |
|---|---|---|---|---|
| *N1* | A19 | 1c brn vio | 12.50 | 15.00 |
| *N2* | A19 | 2c bl grn | 20.00 | 25.00 |
| *N3* | A19 | 2c black | 25.00 | 32.50 |
| *N3A* | A19 | 3c black | *75.00* | *87.50* |
| *N4* | A19 | 3c bl grn | 25.00 | 32.50 |
| *N5* | A19 | 4c magenta | 17.50 | 17.50 |
| *N6* | A19 | 5c violet | 12.50 | 15.00 |
| *N7* | A19 | 6c dp rose | 25.00 | 25.00 |
| *N8* | A19 | 6c red brn | 25.00 | 30.00 |
| *N8A* | A19 | 8c red brn | *75.00* | *87.50* |
| *N9* | A19 | 8c dp rose | 50.00 | 100.00 |
| *N10* | A19 | 10c red | 15.00 | 17.50 |
| *N11* | A19 | 12c dp ultra | 20.00 | 22.50 |
| *N12* | A19 | 12c orange | 50.00 | 60.00 |
| *N12A* | A19 | 15c orange | *75.00* | *87.50* |
| *N13* | A19 | 15c dp bl | 17.50 | 25.00 |
| *N14* | A19 | 20c dp rose & ol | 15.00 | 25.00 |
| *N15* | A19 | 25c org & vio | 15.00 | 25.00 |
| *N16* | A19 | 30c vio & red brn | 20.00 | 30.00 |
| *N17* | A19 | 50c red & vio | 20.00 | 25.00 |
| *N18* | A19 | $1 dk brn & red | 25.00 | 35.00 |
| *N19* | A19 | $2 vio & mag | 50.00 | 60.00 |
| *N19A* | A19 | $3 bl grn & rose | *325.00* | *375.00* |
| *N20* | A19 | $4 red & ultra | 50.00 | 75.00 |
| *N21* | A19 | $5 red brn & red | 50.00 | 75.00 |
| *N22* | A19 | $10 org & blk | 75.00 | 100.00 |
| | | *Nos. N1-N22 (26)* | 1,185. | 1,505. |

Stamps overprinted with Japanese characters in oval frame or between 2 vertical black lines were not for paying postage.

---

# SEYCHELLES

LOCATION — A group of islands in the Indian Ocean, off the coast of Africa north of Madagascar.
GOVT. — Republic.
AREA — 156 sq. mi.
POP. — 64,718 (est. 1984).
CAPITAL — Victoria.

The islands were attached to the British colony of Mauritius from 1810 to 1903, when they became a separate colony. Seychelles achieved internal self-government in October 1975 and independence on June 29, 1976.

100 Cents = 1 Rupee

**Catalogue values for unused stamps in this country are for Never Hinged items, beginning with Scott 149 in the regular postage section and Scott J1 in the postage due section.**

Queen Victoria — A1

Two dies of 2c, 4c, 8c, 10c, 13c, 16c:

Die I. Shading lines at right of diamond in tiara band.
Die II. No shading lines in this rectangle.

**Wmk. Crown and C. A. (2)**

**1890-1900 Typo. *Perf. 14.***

1 A1 2c grn & rose (II) 42 42
a Die I 85 *3.25*
2 A1 2c org brn & grn ('00) 32 32
3 A1 3c dk vio & org ('93) 26 26
4 A1 4c car rose & grn (II) 45 45
a Die I 4.50 *6.00*
5 A1 6c car rose ('00) 1.40 *85*
6 A1 8c brn vio & ultra (II) 85 85
a 8c brn vio & bl (I) 2.50 *5.00*
7 A1 10c ultra & brn (II) 1.00 1.00
a 10c bl & brn (I) 3.00 *5.00*
8 A1 12c ol gray & grn ('93) 55 55
9 A1 13c sl & blk (II) 85 85
a Die I 3.75 *6.00*
10 A1 15c ol grn & vio ('93) 2.50 1.75
11 A1 15c ultra ('00) 3.25 2.75
12 A1 16c org brn & bl (I) 1.40 1.40
a 16c org brn & ultra (II) 10.00 10.00
13 A1 18c ultra ('97) 1.40 1.75
14 A1 36c brn & rose ('97) 10.50 5.50
15 A1 45c brn & rose ('93) 13.00 15.00
16 A1 48c ocher & grn 8.50 10.50
17 A1 75c yel & pur ('00) 21.00 21.00
18 A1 96c vio & car 22.50 *32.50*
19 A1 1r vio & red ('97) 8.50 5.75
20 A1 1.50r blk & rose ('00) 32.50 40.00
21 A1 2.25r vio & grn ('00) 45.00 *47.50*
*Nos. 1-21 (21)* 176.15 190.95

Numerals of 75c, 1r, 1.50r and 2.25r of type A1 are in color on plain tablet.

Surcharged in Black **3 cents**

**1893**

22 A1 3c on 4c car rose & grn (II) 48 60
a Inverted surch. 350.00 *400.00*
b Double surcharge 575.00
d Pair, one without surcharge *4,750.*
23 A1 12c on 16c org brn & ultra (II) 90 1.65
a 12c on 16c org brn & bl (I) 90 90
b Invtd. surch. (I) 550.00 550.00
d Dbl. surch. (I) *4,250.* *5,000.*
e Dbl. surch. (II)
24 A1 15c on 16c org brn & ultra (II) 2.25 2.25
a 15c on 16c org brn & bl (I) 5.00 6.50
b Invtd. surch. (I) 400.00 400.00
c Inverted surcharge (II) 650.00 650.00
d Dbl. surch. (I) 650.00 650.00
e Dbl. surch. (II) 1,000. 1,000.
f Triple surch. (II) *3,250.*
25 A1 45c on 48c ocher & grn 4.00 3.50
26 A1 90c on 96c vio & car 14.00 14.00
*Nos. 22-26 (5)* 21.63 22.00

No. 15 Surcharged in Black **18 CENTS**

**1896**

27 A1 18c on 45c brn & rose 4.75 3.25
a Double surcharge 1,100. 1,100.
b Triple surcharge *1,600.*
28 A1 36c on 45c brn & rose 7.00 *14.00*
a Double surcharge 1,250.

Surcharged in Black:

**3 cents** **6 cents**

**1901**

29 A1 3c on 10c bl & brn (II) 60 70
a Double surcharge 825.00
30 A1 3c on 16c org brn & ultra (II) 60 *1.75*
a "3 cents" omitted (II) 725.00 725.00
b Inverted surcharge (II) 825.00 825.00
c Double surcharge (II) 700.00
31 A1 3c on 36c brn & rose 60 95
a Without bars
b Double surcharge 1,000. *1,300.*
c "3 cents" omitted 775.00 825.00
32 A1 6c on 8c brn vio & ultra (II) 60 *1.40*
a Inverted surcharge 850.00 925.00

Stamps of 1890-1900 Surcharged **2 cents**

**1902**

33 A1 2c on 4c car rose & grn (II) 2.50 2.50
34 A1 30c on 75c yel & pur 2.50 *7.75*
a Narrow "0" in "30" 15.00 *32.50*
35 A1 30c on 1r vio & red 5.25 *13.00*
a Narrow "0" in "30" 25.00 *87.50*
b Double surcharge *850.00*
36 A1 45c on 1r vio & red 5.25 *13.00*
37 A1 45c on 2.25r vio & grn 12.00 *24.00*
a Narrow "5" in "45" 92.50 110.00
*Nos. 33-37 (5)* 27.50 60.25

King Edward VII — A6

Numerals of 75c, 1.50r and 2.25r of type A6 are in color on plain tablet.

**1903 Typo. Wmk. 2**

38 A6 2c red brn & grn 20 20
39 A6 3c green 35 35
40 A6 6c car rose 42 30
41 A6 12c ol gray & grn 1.25 1.25
42 A6 15c ultra 2.25 1.75
43 A6 18c pale yel grn & rose 2.25 *4.25*
44 A6 30c pur & grn 2.75 *6.50*
45 A6 45c brn & rose 5.50 *8.75*
46 A6 75c yel & pur 6.50 *16.00*
47 A6 1.50r blk & rose 22.50 *42.50*
48 A6 2.25r red vio & grn 30.00 *57.50*
*Nos. 38-48 (11)* 73.97 *139.35*

Nos. 42-43, 45 Surcharged **3 cents**

**1903**

49 A6 3c on 15c ultra 1.50 *2.75*
50 A6 3c on 18c pale yel grn & rose 4.25 *18.00*
51 A6 3c on 45c brn & rose 1.90 *5.25*

Type of 1903

**1906 Wmk. 3**

52 A6 2c red brn & grn 26 *1.00*
53 A6 3c green 35 26
54 A6 6c car rose 60 24
55 A6 12c ol gray & grn 2.00 60
56 A6 15c ultra 1.75 *2.75*
57 A6 18c pale yel grn & rose 2.25 *4.25*
58 A6 30c pur & grn 4.25 *6.75*
59 A6 45c brn & rose 2.75 *5.25*
60 A6 75c yel & pur 10.50 *18.00*
61 A6 1.50r blk & rose 21.00 *30.00*
62 A6 2.25r red vio & grn 26.00 *42.50*
*Nos. 52-62 (11)* 71.71 *111.60*

King George V
A7 A8

Numerals of 75c, 1.50r and 2.25r of type A7 are in color on plain tablet.

**1912 *Perf. 14***

63 A7 2c org brn & grn 24 24
64 A7 3c green 28 24
65 A7 6c car rose 2.25 38
66 A7 12c ol gray & grn 40 45
67 A7 15c ultra 85 95
68 A7 18c pale yel grn & rose 60 95
69 A7 30c pur & grn 2.75 1.25
70 A7 45c brn & rose 1.10 1.50
71 A7 75c yel & pur 2.50 3.50
72 A7 1.50r blk & rose 14.00 1.25
73 A7 2.25r red vio & grn 40.00 14.00
*Nos. 63-73 (11)* 64.97 24.71

Die I

For description of dies I and II see back of this section of the Catalogue.

The 5c of type A8 has a colorless numeral on solid-color tablet. Numerals of 9c, 20c, 25c, 50c, 75c, and 1r to 5r of type A8 are in color on plain tablet.

**1917-20**

74 A8 2c org brn & grn 16 32
75 A8 3c green 20 32
76 A8 5c brn ('20) 20 *1.10*
77 A8 6c car rose 32 20
78 A8 12c gray 35 *1.50*
79 A8 15c ultra 40 *1.10*
80 A8 18c vio, *yel* 65 *3.75*
a Die II ('20) 1.90 *5.50*
81 A8 25c blk & red, *yel* ('20) 1.50 *4.25*
a Die II ('20) 1.50 *4.25*
82 A8 30c dl vio & ol grn 1.50 *5.50*
83 A8 45c dl vio & org 1.90 *6.75*
84 A8 50c dl vio & blk ('20) 2.00 *6.75*
85 A8 75c blk, *bl grn*, ol back 2.25 *6.75*
a 75c blk, *emer* (Die II) ('20) 3.75 *9.50*
86 A8 1r dl vio & red ('20) 10.50 *15.00*
87 A8 1.50r vio & bl, *bl* 13.00 *26.00*
a Die II ('20) 7.50 *18.00*
88 A8 2.25r gray grn & dp vio 21.00 *42.50*
89 A8 5r gray grn & ultra ('20) 52.50 *100.00*
*Nos. 74-89 (16)* 108.43 *221.79*

Die II

**1921-32 Wmk. 4**

**Ordinary Paper**

91 A8 2c org brn & grn 14 20
92 A8 3c green 15 20
93 A8 3c blk ('22) 28 28
94 A8 4c grn ('22) 24 24
95 A8 4c ol grn & rose red ('28) 2.50 *7.75*
96 A8 5c dk brn 1.25 *2.50*
97 A8 6c car rose 50 *1.75*
98 A8 6c vio ('22) 24 20
99 A8 9c rose red ('27) 42 65
100 A8 12c gray 28 28
a Die I ('32) 65 65
101 A8 12c car ('22) 32 32
102 A8 15c ultra 5.00 *17.50*
103 A8 15c yel ('22) 80 95
104 A8 18c vio, *yel* 1.50 1.50
105 A8 20c ultra ('22) 65 65

**Chalky Paper**

106 A8 25c blk & red, *yel* ('22) 85 *5.00*
107 A8 30c dl vio & ol grn 1.25 *5.00*
108 A8 45c dl vio & org 95 *6.25*
109 A8 50c dl vio & blk 95 *3.75*
110 A8 75c blk, *emerald* 7.75 *14.00*
111 A8 1r dl vio & red 10.00 *21.00*
a Die I ('32) 14.00 *27.50*
112 A8 1.50r vio & bl, *bl* 10.00 *16.00*
113 A8 2.25r grn & vio 12.50 *25.00*
114 A8 5r grn & ultra 65.00 *90.00*
*Nos. 91-114 (24)* 123.52 *220.97*

**Silver Jubilee Issue**

Common Design Type

**1935, May 6 Engr. *Perf. 11x12***

118 CD301 6c blk & ultra 20 20
119 CD301 12c ind & grn 45 45
120 CD301 20c ultra & brn 75 75
121 CD301 1r brn vio & ind 2.75 *5.25*

**Coronation Issue**

Common Design Type

**1937, May 12 *Perf. 11x11½***

122 CD302 6c ol grn 10 10
123 CD302 12c dp org 14 14
124 CD302 20c dp ultra 20 20

Coco-de-mer Palm — A9

Seychelles Giant Tortoise — A10

Fishing Canoe — A11

***Perf. 13½x14½, 14½x13½***

**1938-41 Photo. Wmk. 4**

125 A9 2c vio brn 5 5
126 A10 3c green 42 30
127 A10 3c org ('41) 6 6
128 A11 6c orange 42 30
129 A11 6c grn ('41) 7 7
130 A9 9c rose red 1.25 *1.65*
131 A9 9c pck bl ('41) 10 10
132 A10 12c violet 2.50 2.50
133 A10 15c cop red ('41) 12 12
134 A9 18c rose lake ('41) 12 12
135 A11 20c brt bl 3.25 2.00
136 A11 20c ocher ('41) 12 12
137 A9 25c ocher 12.50 8.50
138 A10 30c rose lake 12.50 8.50
139 A9 30c brt bl ('41) 15 15
140 A11 45c vio brn 22 22
141 A9 50c dl vio 28 28
142 A10 75c gray bl 25.00 25.00
143 A10 75c dl vio ('41) 30 30
144 A11 1r yel grn 42.50 32.50
145 A11 1r gray ('41) 30 30
146 A9 1.50r ultra 55 55
147 A10 2.25r ol bis 85 85
148 A11 5r cop red 2.00 2.25
*Nos. 125-148 (24)* 105.63 86.79

See Nos. 158-169, 174-188.

**Catalogue values for unused stamps in this section, from this point to the end of the section, are for Never Hinged items.**

**Peace Issue**

Common Design Type

***Perf. 13½x14***

**1946, Sept. 23 Engr. Wmk. 4**

149 CD303 9c lt bl 9 9
150 CD303 30c dk bl 18 18

**Silver Wedding Issue**

Common Design Types

**1948, Nov. 11 Photo. *Perf. 14x14½***

151 CD304 9c brt ultra 20 20

**Engraved; Name Typographed**

***Perf. 11½x11***

152 CD305 5r rose car 9.50 8.00

**UPU Issue**

Common Design Types

***Perf. 13½, 11x11½***

**1949, Oct. 10 Engr.**

153 CD306 18c red vio 18 18
154 CD307 50c dp rose vio 45 45
155 CD308 1r gray 75 75
156 CD309 2.25r olive 1.65 1.65

The indexes in each volume of the Scott Catalogue contain many listings which help to identify stamps.

Types of 1938-41 Redrawn and

Sailfish — A12

Map — A13

***Perf. 14½x13½, 13½x14½.***

**1952, Mar. 3 Photo. Wmk. 4**

*157* A12 2c violet 15 12
*158* A10 3c orange 24 18
*159* A9 9c pck bl 45 35
*160* A11 15c yel grn 45 35
*161* A13 18c rose lake 45 35
*162* A11 20c ocher 45 35
*163* A10 25c brt red 52 40
*164* A12 40c ultra 1.25 1.00
*165* A11 45c vio brn 1.00 75
*166* A9 50c brt vio 1.00 75
*167* A13 1r gray 1.25 1.00
*168* A9 1.50r brt bl 2.25 1.75
*169* A10 2.25r ol bis 3.25 2.50
*170* A13 5r cop red 6.75 5.00
*171* A12 10r green 10.50 8.00
*Nos. 157-171 (15)* 29.96 22.85

The redrawn design shows a new portrait of King George VI surmounted by crown, as on type A12.

Nos. 157-170 exist with watermark 4a.

**Coronation Issue**
Common Design Type

**1953, June 2 Engr. *Perf. 13½x13***

*172* CD312 9c dk bl & blk 32 32

Types of 1938-52 with Portrait of Queen Elizabeth II

***Perf. 14½x13½, 13½x14½***

**1954-56 Photo.**

*173* A12 2c violet 22 18
*174* A10 3c orange 26 22
*175* A9 9c pck bl 26 22
*176* A9 10c bl ('56) 35 32
*177* A11 15c yel grn 14 8
*178* A13 18c rose lake 45 42
*179* A11 20c ocher 18 14
*180* A10 25c brt red 22 18
*181* A13 35c mag ('56) 55 42
*182* A12 40c ultra 42 38
*183* A11 45c vio brn 75 75
*184* A9 50c brt vio 35 28
*185* A11 70c vio brn ('56) 1.00 85
*186* A13 1r gray 70 60
*187* A9 1.50r brt bl 1.50 1.40
*188* A10 2.25r ol bis 3.50 2.00
*189* A13 5r cop red 10.00 3.50
*190* A12 10r green 19.00 7.75
*Nos. 173-190 (18)* 39.85 19.69

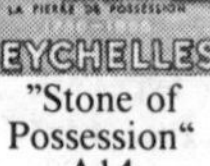
"Stone of Possession" A14

Flying Fox A15

***Perf. 14½x14***

**1956, Nov. 15 Wmk. 4**

*191* A14 40c ultra 38 38
*192* A14 1r gray blk 65 65

Bicentenary of French colonization.

No. 183 Surcharged "5 cents" and Bars.

**1957, Sept. 16 *Perf. 13½x14½***

*193* A11 5c on 45c vio brn 32 32
*a.* Double surcharge 200.00
*b.* Thick bars omitted 450.00

The "c," "e" or "s" of surcharge may be found in italic.

**1957, Oct. 25 *Perf. 14½x13½***

*194* A15 5c lt vio 10 10

Mauritius Stamp of 1859 with Seychelles "B64" Cancellation A16

**Engr. & Typo.**
***Perf. 11½x11***

**1961, Dec. 11 Wmk. 314**
**Stamp in Dull Blue & Black**

*195* A16 10c lilac 12 12
*196* A16 35c dl grn 30 30
*197* A16 2.25r org brn 1.10 1.10

Issued to commemorate the centenary of the first post office in Victoria, Seychelles.

Black Parrot — A17

Anse Royal Bay — A18

Designs: 10c, Vanilla. 15c, Fisherman. 20c, Denis Island Lighthouse. 25c, Clock Tower, Victoria. 30c, 35c, Anse Royal Bay. 40c, Government House. 45c, Fishing boat. 50c, Cascade Church. 60c, Flying fox. 70c, 85c, Sailfish. 75c, Coco-de-mer palm. 1r, Cinnamon. 1.50r, Copra. 2.25r, Map of Indian Ocean. 3.50r, Settlers' homes. 5r, Regina Mundi Convent. 10r, Badge of Seychelles.

***Perf. 14½x13½, 13½x14½***

**1962-69 Photo. Wmk. 314**
**Size: 24x31mm, 31x24mm**

*198* A17 5c yel grn, brn & crim 6 6
*a.* Wmkd. sideways ('67) 18 12
*199* A17 10c ocher, grn & dk bl 6 6
*a.* Wmkd. sideways ('68) 22 18
*200* A17 15c multi 6 6
*201* A17 20c brt bl, blk & grn 7 7
*202* A17 25c Prus bl, org brn & grn 12 12
*202A* A18 30c multi ('68) 90 90
*203* A18 35c bl, grn & dk brn 1.10 1.10
*204* A18 40c bl, dk grn & yel grn 26 26
*204A* A18 45c brt bl & yel ('66) 1.10 75
*205* A17 50c multi 38 38
*b.* Wmkd. sideways ('69) 90 90
*205A* A17 60c bl, rose & blk ('68) 90 90
*206* A17 70c grnsh bl & vio bl 2.50 2.50
*206A* A17 75c multi ('66) 1.10 1.10
*206B* A17 85c grnsh bl & vio bl ('68) 1.10 1.10
*207* A18 1r yel brn, emer & yel 75 75
*208* A18 1.50r dk grn, choc & yel 1.50 1.50
*209* A18 2.25r ocher, bl grn & crimson 2.50 2.50
*210* A18 3.50r multi 3.75 3.75
*211* A18 5r multi 5.25 5.25

***Perf. 13x14***
**Size: 22½x39mm**

*212* A17 10r multi 15.00 15.00
*Nos. 198-212 (20)* 38.46 38.11

Issue dates: 45c and 75c, Aug. 1, 1966. No. 198a, Feb. 7, 1967. The 30c, 60c, 85c, July 15, 1968. Others, Feb. 21, 1962.

The 60c and 85c have watermark sideways.

**Freedom from Hunger Issue**
Common Design Type

**1963, June 4 *Perf. 14x14½***

*213* CD314 70c lilac 1.00 80

**Red Cross Centenary Issue**
Common Design Type

**1963, Sept. 2 Litho. *Perf. 13***

*214* CD315 10c blk & red 22 15
*215* CD315 75c ultra & red 1.25 90

Nos. 203 and 206 Surcharged with New Value and Bars

***Perf. 14x14½, 14½x14***

**1965, Apr. Photo. Wmk. 314**

*216* A18 45c on 35c bl, grn & dk brn 32 32
*217* A17 75c on 70c grnsh bl & vio bl 48 48

**ITU Issue**
Common Design Type
***Perf. 11x11½***

**1965, June 1 Litho. Wmk. 314**

*218* CD317 5c org & vio bl 12 9
*219* CD317 1.50r red lil & ap grn 1.25 1.10

**Intl. Cooperation Year Issue**
Common Design Type

**1965, Oct. 25 *Perf. 14½***

*220* CD318 5c bl grn & cl 7 7
*221* CD318 40c lt vio & grn 48 48

**Churchill Memorial Issue**
Common Design Type

**1966, Jan. 24 Photo. *Perf. 14***
**Design in Black, Gold and Carmine Rose**

*222* CD319 5c brt bl 5 5
*223* CD319 15c green 16 10
*224* CD319 75c brown 80 55
*225* CD319 1.50r violet 1.50 1.10

**World Cup Soccer Issue**
Common Design Type

**1966, July 1 Litho. *Perf. 14***

*226* CD321 15c multi 8 8
*227* CD321 1r multi 55 55

**WHO Headquarters Issue**
Common Design Type

**1966, Sept. 20 Litho. *Perf. 14***

*228* CD322 20c multi 10 10
*229* CD322 50c multi 55 55

**UNESCO Anniversary Issue**
Common Design Type

**1966, Dec. 1 Litho. *Perf. 14***

*230* CD323 15c "Education" 12 12
*231* CD323 1r "Science" 60 60
*232* CD323 5r "Culture" 3.50 3.50

Nos. 200, 204A, 206A and 210 Overprinted: "UNIVERSAL / ADULT / SUFFRAGE / 1967"

***Perf. 14½x14, 14x14½***

**1967, Sept. 18 Photo. Wmk. 314**

*233* A17 15c multi 6 6
*234* A18 45c brt bl & yel 18 18
*235* A17 75c multi 30 30
*236* A18 3.50r multi 1.10 1.10

Cowries: Tiger, Mole, Money A19

Sea Shells (ITY Emblem and): 40c, Textile, betulinus and virgin cones. 1r, Arthritic spider conch. 2.25r, Triton and subulate auger.

***Perf. 14x13½***

**1967, Dec. 4 Photo. Wmk. 314**

*237* A19 15c multi 9 9
*238* A19 40c multi 26 26
*239* A19 1r multi 60 60
*240* A19 2.25r multi 1.25 1.25

Issued for International Tourist Year, 1967.

Nos. 204, 204A and 206A Surcharged

***Perf. 14x14½, 14½x14***

**1968 Photo. Wmk. 314**

*241* A18 30c on 40c multi 10 10
*242* A18 60c on 45c bl & yel 22 22
*243* A17 85c on 75c multi 35 35

The surcharge on No. 241 includes 2 bars; on Nos. 242-243 it includes 3 bars and "CENTS."

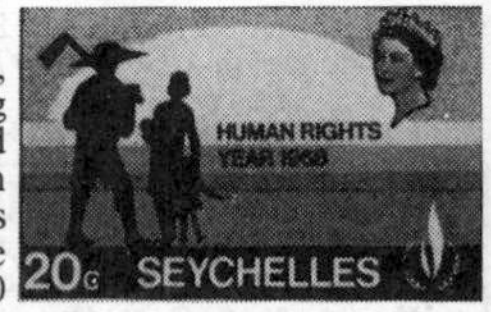
Family, Rising Sun and Human Rights Flame A20

***Perf. 14½x14***

**1968, Sept. 2 Litho. Wmk. 314**

*244* A20 20c choc & multi 5 5
*245* A20 50c vio bl & multi 12 12
*246* A20 85c blk & multi 22 22
*247* A20 2.25r brn & multi 65 65

International Human Rights Year.

First Landing on Praslin Island — A21

Designs: 50c, La Digue and La Curieuse at anchor (vert.). 85c, Coco-de-mer and black parrot (vert.). 2.25r, La Digue and La Curieuse under sail.

**Litho.; Head Embossed in Gold**
***Perf. 14x14½***

**1968, Dec. 30 Wmk. 314**

*248* A21 20c multi 10 10
*249* A21 50c dk bl, blk & red 24 24
*250* A21 85c rose red & multi 40 40
*251* A21 2.25r ultra & multi 1.90 1.90

Issued to commemorate the 200th anniversary of the landing on Praslin Island of the Chevalier Marion Dufresne expedition.

Separation of Rocket and Spacecraft — A22

Designs: 5c, Launching of Apollo XI (vert.). 50c, Landing module and men on the moon. 85c, Seychelles tracking station. 2.25r, Moonscape and earth.

**1969, Sept. 9 Litho. *Perf. 13½***

*252* A22 5c multi 5 5
*253* A22 20c multi 10 10
*254* A22 50c multi 28 28
*255* A22 85c multi 45 45
*256* A22 2.25r multi 1.40 1.40
*Nos. 252-256 (5)* 2.28 2.28

See note after U.S. No. C76.

Lazare Picault Landing in 1741 — A23

History of Seychelles: 10c, U.S. satellite tracking station. 15c, German cruiser Königsberg at Aldabra, 1915. 20c, British fleet refueling, St. Anne, 1939-45. 25c, Ashanti King Prempeh in exile, 1896. 30c, 40c, Stone of Possession placed, 1756. 50c, 65c, Pirates. 60c, Corsairs. 85c, 95c, Jet and airport. 1r, First capitulation of the French to the British, 1794. 1.50r, Battle between the sailing vessels Sybille and Chiffone, 1801. 3.50r, Visit of Duke of Edinburgh, 1956. 5r, Chevalier Queau de Quincy. 10r, Map of Indian Ocean, 1574. 15r, Seychelles coat of arms.

***Perf. 13x12½***

**1969, Nov. 3 Litho. Wmk. 314**

*257* A23 5c multi 5 5
*258* A23 10c multi 5 5
*259* A23 15c multi 8 8
*260* A23 20c multi 10 10

*261* A23 25c multi 14 14
*262* A23 30c multi 65 65
*262A* A23 40c multi ('72) 32 32
*263* A23 50c multi 22 22
*264* A23 60c multi 95 95
*264A* A23 65c multi ('72) 48 48
*265* A23 85c multi 1.00 1.00
*265A* A23 95c multi ('72) 48 48
*266* A23 1r multi 42 42
*267* A23 1.50r multi 65 65
*268* A23 3.50r multi 1.65 1.65
*269* A23 5r multi 2.25 2.25
*270* A23 10r multi 4.50 4.50
*271* A23 15r multi 7.25 7.25
*Nos. 257-271 (18)* 21.24 21.24

Issue dates: 40, 65, 95c, Dec. 11, 1972.

St. Anne Island, Ship and Gulls A24

Designs: 50c, Flying fish, island and ship. 85c, Map of Seychelles and compass rose. 3.50r, Anchor, chain on sea bottom.

**1970, Apr. 27** ***Perf. 14***
*272* A24 20c multi 14 14
*273* A24 50c multi 40 40
*274* A24 85c multi 65 65
*275* A24 3.50r multi 2.00 2.00

Bicentenary of first settlement on St. Anne.

Girl and Eye Chart A25

Designs: 50c, Infant on scales and milk bottles. 85c, Mother and child (vert.). 3.50r, Red Cross branch headquarters.

**1970, Aug. 4 Litho. Wmk. 314**
*276* A25 20c lt bl & multi 12 12
*277* A25 50c multi 32 32
*278* A25 85c multi 52 52
*279* A25 3.50r multi 1.50 1.50

Centenary of British Red Cross Society.

Pitcher Plant — A26

Flowers: 50c, Wild vanilla. 85c, Tropic-bird flower. 3.50r, Vare hibiscus.

**1970, Dec. 29** ***Perf. 14½***
*280* A26 20c multi 26 26
*281* A26 50c multi 65 65
*282* A26 85c multi 1.25 1.25
*283* A26 3.50r multi 6.50 6.50
*a* Souvenir sheet of 4 20.00 16.00

No. 283a contains one each of Nos. 280-283; red brown decorative margin with inscription. Size: 86x134mm.

Souvenir Sheet

Map Showing Location of Seychelles — A27

***Perf. 13½x14***
**1971, Apr. 20 Litho. Wmk. 314**
*284* A27 5r yel grn & multi 16.00 16.00

Issued to publicize Seychelles' location. Size of stamp: 47x31mm., sheet: 152x101mm.

Consolidated Catalina Amphibian — A28

Designs: 5c, Piper Navajo (vert.). 20c, Westland Wessex (vert.). 60c, Grumman Albatross amphibian (vert.). 85c, "G" class Short Brothers flying boat. 3.50r, Vickers supermarine "Walrus" amphibian.

***Perf. 14x14½, 14½x14***
**1971, June 28 Litho. Wmk. 314**
*285* A28 5c org & multi 12 7
*286* A28 20c pur & multi 22 14
*287* A28 50c ol & multi 42 22
*288* A28 60c sep & multi 55 28
*289* A28 85c brn & multi 70 42
*290* A28 3.50r bl & multi 5.75 2.25
*Nos. 285-290 (6)* 7.76 3.38

Completion of Seychelles Airport.

Santa Claus, by Jean-Claude Waye Hive — A29

Children's Drawings: 15c, Santa Claus riding a tortoise, by Edison Theresine. 3.50r, Santa Claus on the seashore, by Isabelle Tirant.

**1971, Oct. 12** ***Perf. 13½***
*291* A29 10c dk bl & multi 7 7
*292* A29 15c dk grn & multi 12 12
*293* A29 3.50r vio & multi 1.65 1.65

Christmas 1971.

Nos. 262, 264-265 Surcharged with New Value and 5 Bars.

**1971, Dec. 21** ***Perf. 13x12½***
*294* A23 40c on 30c multi 35 35
*295* A23 65c on 60c multi 55 55
*296* A23 95c on 85c multi 75 75

Nos. 260, 269 Overprinted in Black or Gold: "ROYAL VISIT 1972"

**1972, Mar. 21 Litho. Wmk. 314**
*297* A23 20c multi 15 15
*298* A23 5r multi (G) 2.75 2.75

Visit of Queen Elizabeth II and Prince Philip.

Brush Warbler A30

Fireworks A31

**1972, July 15** ***Perf. 14x13½***
*299* A30 5c *shown* 9 6
*300* A30 20c *Scops owl* 35 24
*301* A30 50c *Blue pigeons* 1.00 52
*302* A30 65c *Magpie robin* 1.40 80
*303* A30 95c *Paradise fly-catchers* 2.50 1.40
*304* A30 3.50r *Kestrel* 10.00 5.00
*a* Souvenir sheet of 6 24.00 19.00
*Nos. 299-304 (6)* 15.34 8.02

Nos. 299-304 contains one each of Nos. 299-304. Bright blue margin with bird design and black inscription. Size: 143x163mm.

**1972, Sept. 18 Litho.** ***Perf. 14***
*305* A31 10c *shown* 6 6
*306* A31 15c *Canoe race (horiz.)* 8 8
*307* A31 25c *Women in local costumes* 14 14
*308* A31 5r *Water-skiing (horiz.)* 2.00 2.00

Seychelles Festival 1972.

**Silver Wedding Issue, 1972**
Common Design Type

Design: Queen Elizabeth II, Prince Philip, giant tortoise and leaping sailfish.

**1972, Nov. 20 Photo.** ***Perf. 14x14½***
*309* CD324 95c multi 38 38
*310* CD324 1.50r multi 60 60

**Princess Anne's Wedding Issue**
Common Design Type

**1973, Nov. 14 Litho.** ***Perf. 14***
*311* CD325 95c ocher & multi 32 32
*312* CD325 1.50r sl & multi 52 52

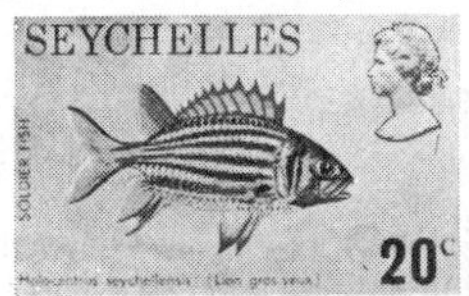


Soldierfish — A32

**Wmk. 314**
**1974, Mar. 5 Litho.** ***Perf. 14***
*313* A32 20c *shown* 20 20
*314* A32 50c *Filefish* 42 42
*315* A32 95c *Butterflyfish* 80 80
*316* A32 1.50r *Gaterin* 1.75 1.75

Envelope and Globe A33

UPU, cent.: 50c, Globe with location of Seychelles and radio tower. 95c, Cancellation and globe. 1.50r, "UPU" with emblems.

***Perf. 12½x12***
**1974, Oct. 9 Wmk. 314**
*317* A33 20c multi 12 12
*318* A33 50c multi 28 28
*319* A33 95c multi 52 52
*320* A33 1.50r multi 80 80

Common Design Types are pictured in section before Great Britain.

Winston Churchill A34

Design: 1.50r, Churchill, different portrait.

**1974, Nov. 30 Litho.** ***Perf. 14½***
*321* A34 95c lt bl & multi 42 42
*322* A34 1.50r lt grn & multi 65 65
*a* Souvenir sheet of 2 1.40 1.40

Sir Winston Churchill (1874-1965), birth centenary. No. 322a contains one each of Nos. 321-322, light blue margin. Size: 80x109mm.

Nos. 260, 263, 265A and 267 Overprinted in Black or Silver

***Perf. 13x12½***
**1975, Feb. 8 Wmk. 314**
*323* A23 20c multi (B) 9 9
*324* A23 50c multi (B) 28 28
*325* A23 95c multi (S) 45 45
*326* A23 1.50r multi (B) 75 75

Visit of cruise ship Queen Elizabeth II, Mahe, Seychelles.

Nos. 260, 264A, 266, 268 Overprinted in Gold

INTERNAL
SELF-GOVERNMENT
OCTOBER
1975

**1975, Oct. 1 Litho. Wmk. 314**
*327* A23 20c multi 10 10
*328* A23 65c multi 32 32
*329* A23 1r multi 42 42
*330* A23 3.50r multi 1.40 1.40

Queen Elizabeth I — A35

Portraits: 15c, Gladys Aylward. 20c, Elizabeth Fry. 25c, Emmeline Pankhurst. 65c, Florence Nightingale. 1r, Amy Johnson. 1.50r, Joan of Arc. 3.50r, Eleanor Roosevelt.

**Wmk. 314**
**1975, Dec. 15 Litho.** ***Perf. 13½***
*331* A35 10c dp brn & multi 7 7
*332* A35 15c dk brn & multi 9 9
*333* A35 20c dk grn & multi 10 10
*334* A35 25c pur & multi 14 14
*335* A35 65c dk bl & multi 35 35
*336* A35 1r Prus bl & multi 50 50
*337* A35 1.50r dp vio & multi 75 75
*338* A35 3.50r dk ol & multi 2.00 2.00
*Nos. 331-338 (8)* 4.00 4.00

International Women's Year 1975.

Praslin Map and Grand Anse Postmark, 1907 — A36

First Landing, 1609, and James Mancham — A37

Designs: 65c, La Digue map and postmark, 1916. 1r, Partial map of Maheand Victoria postmark, 1917. 1.50r, Southern part of Mahe and Anse Royale postmark, 1938.

**1976, Mar. 30 Wmk. 373 *Perf. 14***

| | | | | |
|---|---|---|---|---|
| *339* | A36 | 20c lt bl & multi | 12 | 12 |
| *340* | A36 | 65c lt bl & multi | 40 | 40 |
| *341* | A36 | 1r lt bl & multi | 65 | 65 |
| *342* | A36 | 1.50r lt bl & multi | 95 | 95 |
| *a* | | Souvenir sheet of 4 | 2.50 | 2.50 |

Rural posts of Seychelles. No. 342a contains one each of Nos. 339-342; multicolored margin with historic postmarks. Size: 165x127mm.

**1976, June 29 *Perf. 14***

Designs: 25c, Stone of Possession. 40c, Arrival of 1st settlers, 1770 (ship). 75c, Le Chevalier Queau de Quincy. 1r, Sir Bickham Sweet-Escott. 1.25r, Government House. 1.50r, Coat of arms of Internal Self-government. 3.50r, Seychelles flag.

| | | | | |
|---|---|---|---|---|
| *343* | A37 | 20c rose & multi | 7 | 7 |
| *344* | A37 | 25c yel & multi | 9 | 9 |
| *345* | A37 | 40c lil & multi | 16 | 16 |
| *346* | A37 | 75c grn & multi | 28 | 28 |
| *347* | A37 | 1r sal & multi | 38 | 38 |
| *348* | A37 | 1.25r multi | 45 | 45 |
| *349* | A37 | 1.50r ocher & multi | 55 | 55 |
| *350* | A37 | 3.50r bl & multi | 1.25 | 1.25 |
| | | *Nos. 343-350 (8)* | 3.23 | 3.23 |

Seychelles' independence, June 29, 1976.

Flags of Seychelles and US — A38

US bicent.: 10r, State House, Seychelles, and Independence Hall, Philadelphia.

**1976, July 12 Litho.**

| | | | | |
|---|---|---|---|---|
| *351* | A38 | 1r bl & multi | 35 | 35 |
| *352* | A38 | 10r red & multi | 3.50 | 3.50 |

Swimming — A39

Designs (Olympic Rings and): 65c, Hockey. 1r, Basketball. 3.50r, Soccer.

**1976, July 26 *Perf. 14½***

| | | | | |
|---|---|---|---|---|
| *353* | A39 | 20c vio bl & blk | 7 | 7 |
| *354* | A39 | 65c dk grn, yel grn & blk | 24 | 24 |
| *355* | A39 | 1r brn, grn & blk | 35 | 35 |
| *356* | A39 | 3.50r car rose & blk | 1.25 | 1.25 |

21st Olympic Games, Montreal, Canada, July 17-Aug. 1.

Seychelles Sunbird — A40

Seychelles Birds (James R. Mancham, Congress Emblem and): 20c, Paradise flycatcher (vert.). 1.50r, Gray white-eye. 5r, Black parrot (vert.).

**Wmk. 373**

**1976, Nov. 8 Litho. *Perf. 14½***

| | | | | |
|---|---|---|---|---|
| *357* | A40 | 20c multi | 12 | 10 |
| *358* | A40 | 1.25r multi | 70 | 60 |
| *359* | A40 | 1.50r multi | 85 | 75 |
| *360* | A40 | 5r multi | 2.50 | 2.25 |
| *a* | | Souvenir sheet of 4 | 5.50 | 5.50 |

4th Pan-African Ornithological Congress, Mahe Beach Hotel, Nov. 6-13. No. 360a contains one each of Nos. 357-360; olive margin with black and orange inscription giving description of birds. Size: 174x119mm.

### Nos. 260, 263, 265A-266, 268-271, 264A Overprinted or Surcharged: "Independence / 1976"

***Perf. 13x12½***

**1976, Nov. 22 Litho. Wmk. 314**

| | | | | |
|---|---|---|---|---|
| *361* | A23 | 20c multi | 14 | 10 |
| *362* | A23 | 50c multi | 28 | 24 |
| *363* | A23 | 95c multi | 48 | 40 |
| *364* | A23 | 1r multi | 48 | 40 |
| *365* | A23 | 3.50r multi | 2.00 | 1.75 |
| *366* | A23 | 5r multi | 2.50 | 2.00 |
| *367* | A23 | 10r multi | 4.75 | 4.00 |
| *368* | A23 | 15r multi | 6.75 | 6.00 |
| *369* | A23 | 25r on 65c multi | 12.00 | 10.00 |
| | | *Nos. 361-369 (9)* | 29.38 | 24.89 |

Washington's Inauguration — A41

Designs: 2c, Jefferson and map of Louisiana Purchase. 3c, William H. Seward and map of Alaska Purchase. 4c, Pony Express, 1860. 5c, Lincoln's Emancipation Proclamation, 1863. 1.50r, Completion of Transcontinental Railroad, 1869. 3.50r, Wright Brothers' first flight, 1903. 5r, Ford assembly line, 1913. 10r, John F. Kennedy and Apollo 11 moon landing, 1969. 25r, Declaration of Independence, 1776.

***Perf. 14x13½***

**1976, Dec. 21 Wmk. 373**

| | | | | |
|---|---|---|---|---|
| *370* | A41 | 1c rose & plum | 5 | 5 |
| *371* | A41 | 2c lil & vio | 5 | 5 |
| *372* | A41 | 3c bl & vio bl | 5 | 5 |
| *373* | A41 | 4c yel & brn | 5 | 5 |
| *374* | A41 | 5c brt yel & grn | 5 | 5 |
| *375* | A41 | 1.50r yel brn & brn | 40 | 40 |
| *376* | A41 | 3.50r brt grn & bl grn | 95 | 95 |
| *377* | A41 | 5r yel & brn | 1.40 | 1.40 |
| *378* | A41 | 10r dl bl & dk bl | 2.75 | 2.75 |
| | | *Nos. 370-378 (9)* | 5.75 | 5.75 |

**Souvenir Sheet**

| | | | | |
|---|---|---|---|---|
| *379* | A41 | 25r lil rose & pur | 10.00 | 10.00 |

American Bicentennial. No. 379 has tan and sepia margin showing facsimile of Declaration of Independence. Size: 141x142mm.

Seychelles Islands and Arms A42

The Orb — A43

Designs: 40c, 5r, 10r, similar to 20c. 1r, St. Edward's Crown. 1.25r, Ampulla and Spoon. 1.50r, Scepter with Cross.

**1977, Sept. 5 Litho. *Perf. 14***

| | | | | |
|---|---|---|---|---|
| *380* | A42 | 20c multi | 5 | 5 |
| *381* | A42 | 40c multi | 10 | 10 |
| *382* | A43 | 50c multi | 12 | 12 |
| *383* | A43 | 1r multi | 25 | 25 |
| *384* | A43 | 1.25r multi | 32 | 32 |
| *385* | A43 | 1.50r multi | 38 | 38 |
| *386* | A42 | 5r multi | 1.25 | 1.25 |
| *387* | A42 | 10r multi | 2.50 | 2.50 |
| *a* | | Souvenir sheet of 4 | 3.50 | 3.50 |
| | | *Nos. 380-387 (8)* | 4.97 | 4.97 |

25th anniversary of reign of Queen Elizabeth II. No. 387a contains one each of Nos. 380, 382, 383, 387; carmine and yellow margin. Size: 133x136mm.

Coral Reef — A44

***Perf. 14x14½***

**1977-78 Litho. Wmk. 373**

| | | | | |
|---|---|---|---|---|
| *388* | A44 | 5c Reef fish | 5 | 5 |
| *389* | A44 | 10c Hawksbill turtle | 5 | 5 |
| *390* | A44 | 15c Coco de mer | 5 | 5 |
| *391* | A44 | 20c Wild vanilla | 5 | 5 |
| *392* | A44 | 25c Butterfly | 6 | 6 |
| *393* | A44 | 40c Coral reef | 9 | 9 |
| *394* | A44 | 50c Giant tortoise | 10 | 10 |
| *395* | A44 | 75c Crayfish | 16 | 16 |
| *396* | A44 | 1r Madagascar cardinal | 22 | 22 |
| *397* | A44 | 1.25r Fairy tern | 28 | 28 |
| *398* | A44 | 1.50r Flying fox | 32 | 32 |
| *399* | A44 | 3.50r Green gecko | 75 | 75 |

***Perf. 13***

**Size: 27x35mm**

| | | | | |
|---|---|---|---|---|
| *400* | A44 | 5r Octopus, vert. | 1.10 | 1.10 |
| *401* | A44 | 10r Tiger cowrie, vert. | 2.25 | 2.25 |
| *402* | A44 | 15r Pitcher plant, vert. | 3.25 | 3.25 |
| *403* | A44 | 20r Arms, vert. | 4.50 | 4.50 |
| | | *Nos. 388-403 (16)* | 13.28 | 13.28 |

Issue dates: 40c, 1r, 1.25r, 1.50r, Oct. 31, 1977. Others, 1978.

Reissued dated "1979" below design: 10, 15, 25, 40, 50, 75c, 1r, 1.50r. Dated "1981": 40c. Dated "1982": 40c.

See No. 446.

### Denomination "R" Instead of "Re." or "Rs."

**1981, Jan. 6 Litho. *Perf. 14x14½***

| | | | | |
|---|---|---|---|---|
| *403A* | A44 | 1r like No. 396 | 30 | 30 |
| *403B* | A44 | 1.10r Green gecko | 35 | 35 |
| *403C* | A44 | 1.25r like No. 397 | 38 | 38 |
| *403D* | A44 | 1.50r like No. 398 | 45 | 45 |

***Perf. 13***

| | | | | |
|---|---|---|---|---|
| *403E* | A44 | 5r like No. 400 | 1.50 | 1.50 |
| *403F* | A44 | 10r like No. 401 | 3.00 | 3.00 |
| *403G* | A44 | 15r like No. 402 | 4.50 | 4.50 |
| *403H* | A44 | 20r like No. 403 | 6.00 | 6.00 |
| | | *Nos. 403A-403H (8)* | 16.48 | 16.48 |

Reissued dated "1981" below design: 1.50r. Dated "1982": 1r, 1.50r. Dated "1985": 5r. Dated "1986": 1r.

Cruiser Aurora, Star and Flag — A45

**1977, Nov. 7 Unwmk. *Perf. 12***

| | | | | |
|---|---|---|---|---|
| *404* | A45 | 1.50r red, blk & gold | 45 | 45 |
| *a* | | Souvenir sheet | 55 | 55 |

60th anniversary of Russian October Revolution. No. 404a contains one stamp; gray decorative margin with hammer and sickle emblem and inscription. Size: 101x129mm.

St. Roch Roman Catholic Church, Bel Ombre — A46

Christmas: 1r, Anglican Cathedral, Victoria. 1.50r, R. C. Cathedral, Victoria. 5r, St. Mark's Anglican Church, Praslin.

***Perf. 13½x14***

**1977, Dec. 5 Wmk. 373**

| | | | | |
|---|---|---|---|---|
| *405* | A46 | 20c multi | 5 | 5 |
| *406* | A46 | 1r multi | 25 | 25 |
| *407* | A46 | 1.50r multi | 38 | 38 |
| *408* | A46 | 5r multi | 1.25 | 1.25 |

Calendar Page, June 5, 1977 A47

Edward VII, George V, George VI A48

Designs: 1.25r, Hands holding rifle, torch and Seychelles flag. 1.50r, Fisherman and farmer holding hands. 5r, Soldiers and waving children.

***Perf. 14x13½***

**1978, June 5 Litho. Wmk. 373**

| | | | | |
|---|---|---|---|---|
| *409* | A47 | 40c multi | 10 | 10 |
| *410* | A47 | 1.25r multi | 28 | 28 |
| *411* | A47 | 1.50r multi | 40 | 40 |
| *412* | A47 | 5r multi | 1.40 | 1.40 |

First anniversary of Liberation Day.

**1978, Aug. 21 Litho. *Perf. 14***

Designs: 1.50r, Queens Victoria and Elizabeth II. 3r, Queen Victoria Monument, Seychelles. 5r, Queen's Building, Victoria, Seychelles.

| | | | | |
|---|---|---|---|---|
| *413* | A48 | 40c multi | 10 | 10 |
| *414* | A48 | 1.50r multi | 35 | 35 |
| *415* | A48 | 3r multi | 75 | 75 |
| *416* | A48 | 5r multi | 1.25 | 1.25 |
| *a* | | Souvenir sheet of 4 | 3.00 | 3.00 |

25th anniversary of coronation of Queen Elizabeth II. No. 416a contains Nos. 413-416; multicolored margin. Size: 87x127mm.

Gardenia from Aride Island — A49

Designs (Coat of Arms and): 1.25r, Magpie robin of Fregate Island. 1.50r, Seychelles paradise flycatchers. 5r, Green turtle.

***Perf. 13½x14***

**1978, Oct. 16 Litho. Wmk. 373**

| | | | | |
|---|---|---|---|---|
| *417* | A49 | 40c multi | 22 | 22 |
| *418* | A49 | 1.25r multi | 60 | 60 |
| *419* | A49 | 1.50r multi | 70 | 70 |
| *420* | A49 | 5r multi | 2.50 | 2.50 |

"Stone of Possession" — A50

**1978, Dec. 15 Litho. *Perf. 13½***

| | | | | |
|---|---|---|---|---|
| *421* | A50 | 20c shown | 5 | 5 |
| *422* | A50 | 1.25r Map, 1782 | 32 | 32 |
| *423* | A50 | 1.50r Clock tower | 40 | 40 |
| *424* | A50 | 5r Pierre Poivre | 1.25 | 1.25 |

Bicentennary of the founding of Victoria.

Seychelles Fody
A51

Patrice Lumumba
A52

Birds: No. 426, Green-backed heron. No. 427, Seychelles bulbul. No. 428, Seychelles cave swiftlets. No. 429, Grayheaded lovebirds.

**1979, Feb. 27 Litho. Perf. 14**

*425* A51 2r multi 70 70
*426* A51 2r multi 70 70
*427* A51 2r multi 70 70
*428* A51 2r multi 70 70
*429* A51 2r multi 70 70
*Nos. 425-429 (5)* 3.50 3.50

Nos. 425-429 printed se-tenant in sheets of 10.

**1979, June 5 Litho. Perf. 14½**

African Liberation Heroes: 2r, Kwame Nkrumah. 2.25r, Dr. Eduardo Mondlane. 5r, Amilcar Cabral.

*430* A52 40c vio & blk 8 8
*431* A52 2r dk bl & blk 45 45
*432* A52 2.25r org brn & blk 50 50
*433* A52 5r ol grn & blk 1.10 1.10

Coat of Arms, Rowland Hill, Seychelles No. 412 — A53

Coat of Arms, Hill, Seychelles stamps: 2.25r, No. 301. 3r, No. 205. 5r, No. 4.

**1979, Aug. Litho. Perf. 14x14½**

*434* A53 40c multi 9 9
*435* A53 2.25r multi 55 55
*436* A53 3r multi 75 75

**Souvenir Sheet**

*437* A53 5r multi 1.40 1.40

Sir Rowland Hill (1795-1879), originator of penny postage. No. 437 has gray and blue gray margin showing Seychelles stamp and Rowland Hill. Size: 112x89mm.

Schoolboy, IYC Emblem — A54

IYC Emblem and: 2.25r, Children. 3r, Boy with ball (vert.). 5r, Girl with puppet (vert.).

***Perf. 14½x14, 14x14½***

**1979, Oct. 25 Litho.**

*438* A54 40c multi 8 8
*439* A54 2.25r multi 45 45
*440* A54 3r multi 60 60
*441* A54 5r multi 1.00 1.00

International Year of the Child.

Three Kings Bearing Gifts
A55

Stained Glass Windows: 20c, Angel (vert.). 2.25r, Virgin and Child (vert.). 5r, Flight into Egypt.

**1979, Dec. 3 Litho. Perf. 14½**

*442* A55 20c multi 5 5
*443* A55 2.25r multi 60 60
*444* A55 3r multi 80 80

**Souvenir Sheet**

*445* A55 5r multi 1.40 1.40

Christmas 1979. No. 445 has multicolored margin showing gold star and rays. Size: 87x74½mm.

No. 399 Surcharged
**Wmk. 373**

**1979, Dec. 7 Litho. Perf. 14**

*446* A44 1.10r on 3.50r multi 42 42

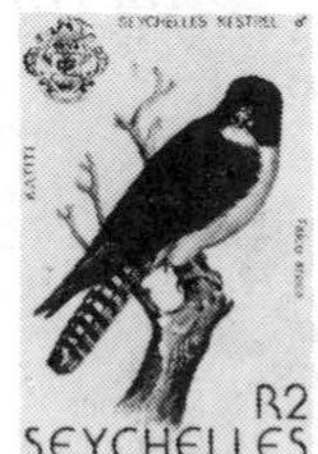

Seychelles Kestrel — A56

Seychelles Kestrel: a. shown. b. Pair. c. Female, eggs. d. Mother and chick. e. Chicks nesting.

**1980, Feb. 29 Litho. Perf. 14**

*447* Strip of 5 3.00 3.00
*a.-e.* A56 2r, any single 60 60

See Nos. 468, 483.

50-Rupee Bank Note, London 1980 Emblem — A57

Sprinting, Moscow '80 Emblem — A58

New Currency: 40c, 1.50r, horiz.

**1980, Apr. 18 Litho. Perf. 14**

*448* A57 40c multi 8 8
*449* A57 1.50r multi 32 32
*450* A57 2.25r multi 48 48
*451* A57 5r multi 1.00 1.00
*a* Souvenir sheet of 4 2.25 2.25

London 1980 International Stamp Exhibition, May 6-14. No. 451a contains Nos. 448-451; margin shows London 1980 emblem, arms of Seychelles. Size: 119x103mm.

**1980, June 13 Perf. 14½**

*452* A58 40c *shown* 7 7
*453* A58 2.25r *Weight lifting* 40 40
*454* A58 3r *Boxing* 52 52
*455* A58 5r *Yachting* 1.90 1.90
*a* Souvenir sheet of 4 3.00 3.00

22nd Summer Olympic Games, Moscow, July 19-Aug. 3. No. 455a contains Nos. 452-455; blue and lilac rose margin shows Olympic rings. Size: 90x121mm.

Boeing 747 — A59

**1980, Aug. 22 Litho. Perf. 14**

*456* A59 40c *shown* 10 10
*457* A59 2.25r *Tour bus* 55 55
*458* A59 3r *Ocean liner, pirogue* 75 75
*459* A59 5r *Tour motor boat* 1.25 1.25

World Tourism Conf., Manila, Sept. 27.

Female Coco-de-Mer Palm Tree — A60

**1980, Oct. 31 Litho. Perf. 14**

*460* A60 40c *shown* 10 10
*461* A60 2.25r *Male tree* 55 55
*462* A60 3r *Bowls* 75 75
*463* A60 5r *Gourds, canoes* 1.25 1.25
*a* Souvenir sheet of 4 2.75 2.75

No. 463a contains Nos. 460-463; orange and black margin. Size: 83x140mm.

Vasco da Gama's San Gabriel, 1497
A61

**Wmk. 373**

**1981, Feb. Litho. Perf. 14½**

*464* A61 40c shown 8 8
*465* A61 2.25r Mascarenhas' Caravel, 1505 52 52
*466* A61 3.50r Darwin's Beagle, 1831 80 80
*467* A61 5r Queen Elizabeth 2, 1968 1.10 1.10
*a* Souvenir sheet of 4 2.50 2.50

No. 467a contains Nos. 464-467; light blue and black margin shows ships' rope. Size: 141x92mm.

Bird Type of 1980

**1981, Apr. 10 Litho. Perf. 14**

*468* Strip of 5, multi 4.00 4.00
*a* A56 2r Male fairy tern 80 80
*b* A56 2r Pair 80 80
*c* A56 2r Female 80 80
*d* A56 2r Female, diff. 80 80
*e* A56 2r Adult bird, chick 80 80

Royal Wedding Types of Montserrat
**Wmk. 380**

**1981, June 23 Litho. Perf. 14**

*469* A66 1.50r Couple, Victoria and Albert I 55 55
*a* Bklt pane of 4, perf. 12 1.75
*470* A67 1.50r Couple 55 55
*471* A66 5r Cleveland 1.75 1.75
*472* A67 5r like #470 1.75 1.75
*a* Bklt pane of 2, perf. 12 2.75
*473* A66 10r Britannia 3.75 3.75
*474* A67 10r like #470 3.75 3.75
*Nos. 469-474 (6)* 12.10 12.10

Each denomination issued in sheets of 7 (6 type A66, 1 type A67).

Souvenir Sheet

**1981 Litho. Perf. 12**

*474A* A67 7.50r Couple 2.50 2.50

No. 474A has rose carmine decorative margin. Size: 120x109mm.

Seychelles Intl. Airport, 10th Anniv. — A62

**Wmk. 373**

**1981, July 27 Litho. Perf. 14½**

*475* A62 40c Britten-Norman Islander 10 10
*476* A62 2.25r Britten-Norman Trislander 60 60
*477* A62 3.50r Vickers VC-10 90 90
*478* A62 5r Boeing 747 1.25 1.25

Flying Foxes — A63

Designs: Various flying foxes.

**1981, Oct. 9 Litho. Perf. 14**

*479* A63 40c multi 12 12
*480* A63 2.25r multi 75 75
*481* A63 3r multi 95 95
*482* A63 5r multi 1.65 1.65
*a* Souv. sheet, #479-482 5.25 5.25

Bird Type of 1980

Designs: a. Male Chinese bittern. b. Female. c. Hen on nest. d. Nest, eggs. e. Hen, chicks.

**Wmk. 373**

**1982, Feb. 4 Litho. Perf. 14**

*483* Strip of 5, multi 5.25 5.25
*a.-e.* A56 3r, any single 1.00 1.00

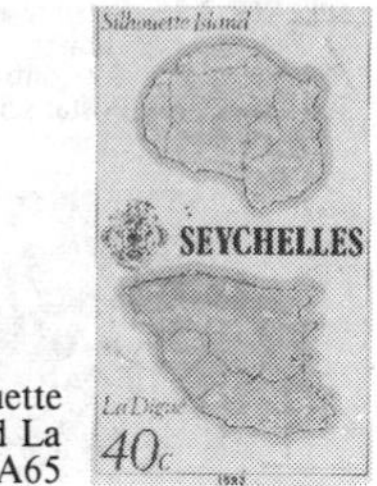

Map of Silhouette Island and La Digue — A65

**1982, Apr. 22 Litho. Perf. 14½**

*487* A65 40c shown 10 10
*488* A65 1.50r Denis & Bird Islds. 40 40
*489* A65 2.75r Curieuse Isld., Praslin 75 75
*490* A65 7r Mahe 1.90 1.90
*a* Souvenir sheet of 4 3.25 3.25

No. 490a contains Nos. 487-490. Size: 93x128mm.

5th Anniv. of Liberation A66

**1982, June 5 Perf. 14**

*491* A66 40c Bookmobile 10 10
*492* A66 1.75r Mobile dental clinic 48 48
*493* A66 2.75r Farming 75 75
*494* A66 7r Construction site 1.90 1.90
*a* Souv. sheet of 4, Nos. 491-494 3.25 3.25

Tourist Board Emblem A67

Tourism: Hotels.

**1982, Sept. 1**

*495* A67 1.75r Northolme 48 48
*496* A67 1.75r Reef 48 48
*497* A67 1.75r Barbarons Beach 48 48
*498* A67 1.75r Coral Strand 48 48
*499* A67 1.75r Beau Vallon Bay 48 48
*500* A67 1.75r Fisherman's Cove 48 48
*501* A67 1.75r Mahe Beach, shown 48 48
*502* A67 1.75r Island scene 48 48
*Nos. 495-502 (8)* 3.84 3.84

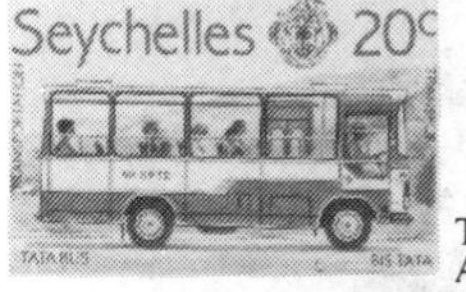

Tata Bus A68

**Wmk. 373**

**1982, Nov. 18 Litho. *Perf. 14***

*503* A68 20c shown 5 5
*504* A68 1.75r Mini moke 35 35
*505* A68 2.75r Ox cart 55 55
*506* A68 7r Truck 1.40 1.40

World Communications Year — A69

**1983, Feb. 25**

*507* A69 40c Radio control room 9 9
*508* A69 2.75r Satellite earth station 65 65
*509* A69 3.50r TV control room 85 85
*510* A69 5r Postal services 1.25 1.25

Commonwealth Day — A70

**1983, Mar. 14**

*511* A70 40c Agricultural research 9 9
*512* A70 2.75r Food processing plant 60 60
*513* A70 3.50r Fishing industry 80 80
*514* A70 7r Flag 1.65 1.65

Denis Isld. Lighthouse, 1910 — A71

**1983, July 14 *Perf. 14x13½***

*515* A71 40c shown 12 12
*516* A71 2.75r Seychelles Hospital, 1924 85 85
*517* A71 3.50r Supreme Court, 1894 1.10 1.10
*518* A71 7r State House, 1911 2.25 2.25
*a* Souvenir sheet of 4 4.50 4.50

No. 518a contains Nos. 515-518.

Manned Flight Bicentenary — A72

**1983, Sept. 15 *Perf. 14***

*519* A72 40c Royal Vauxhall balloon, 1836 12 12
*520* A72 1.75r DeHavilland D.H.-50j 55 55
*521* A72 2.75r Grumman Albatross 85 85
*522* A72 7r Sweavingen Merlin 2.25 2.25

First Intl. Air Seychelles Flight A73

**1983, Oct. 26 Litho.**

*523* A73 2r DC10 aircraft 65 65

Paintings, Marianne North — A74

**1983, Nov. 17 Litho. *Perf. 14***

*524* A74 40c Swamp Plant and Moorhen 12 12
*525* A74 1.75r Wormia flagellaria 55 55
*526* A74 2.75r Asiatic Pancratium 85 85
*527* A74 7r Pitcher Plant 2.25 2.25
*a* Souvenir sheet of 4 3.75 3.75

No. 527a contains Nos. 524-527, margin depicts flora.

Nos. 469-474 Surcharged

**Wmk. 380**

**1983, Dec. 28 Litho. *Perf. 14***

*528* A66 50c on 1.50r multi 15 15
*529* A67 50c on 1.50r multi 15 15
*530* A66 2.25r on 5r multi 68 68
*531* A67 2.25r on 5r multi 68 68
*532* A66 3.75r on 10r multi 1.15 1.15
*533* A67 3.75r on 10r multi 1.15 1.15
*Nos. 528-533 (6)* 3.96 3.96

Handicrafts — A75

**Wmk. 373**

**1984, Feb. 29 Litho. *Perf. 14***

*534* A75 50c Coconut kettle 15 15
*535* A75 2r Scarf, doll 60 60
*536* A75 3r Coconut-fiber roses 90 90
*537* A75 10r Carved fishing boat, doll 3.00 3.00

**Lloyd's List Issue**

Common Design Type

**1984, May 21 Litho. *Perf. 14½x14***

*538* CD335 50c Port Victoria 15 15
*539* CD335 2r Steamship, 1930s 60 60
*540* CD335 3r Cruise liner 90 90
*541* CD335 10r Ennerdale 3.00 3.00

People's United Party, 20th Anniv. A76

**1984, June 2 Litho. *Perf. 14***

*542* A76 50c Original headquarters 15 15
*543* A76 2r Liberation statue, vert. 60 60
*544* A76 3r New headquarters 90 90
*545* A76 10r Pres. Rene, vert. 3.00 3.00

Souvenir Sheet

UPU Congress A77

**1984, June 18 *Perf. 14½***

*546* A77 5r No. 156 1.50 1.50

Size: 70x85mm.

1984 Summer Olympics A78

**1984, July 28 *Perf. 14***

*547* A78 50c Long jump 15 15
*548* A78 2r Boxing 60 60
*549* A78 3r Diving 90 90
*550* A78 10r Weight lifting 3.00 3.00
*a* Souvenir sheet of 4 4.75 4.75

No. 550a contains Nos. 547-550. Size: 100x100mm.

Scuba Diving A79

**1984, Sept. 24**

*551* A79 50c shown 15 15
*552* A79 2r Paragliding 60 60
*553* A79 3r Sailing 90 90
*554* A79 10r Water skiing 3.00 3.00

Whale Conservation — A80

**1984, Nov. Litho.**

*555* A80 50c Humpback whale 15 15
*556* A80 2r Sperm whale 60 60
*557* A80 3r Right whale 90 90
*558* A80 10r Blue whale 3.00 3.00

Audubon Birth Bicentenary — A81

Bare-legged scops owls.

**1985, Mar. 11 Litho. *Perf. 1***

*559* A81 50c multi 15 1
*560* A81 2r multi 60 6
*561* A81 3r multi 90 9
*562* A81 10r multi 3.00 3.0

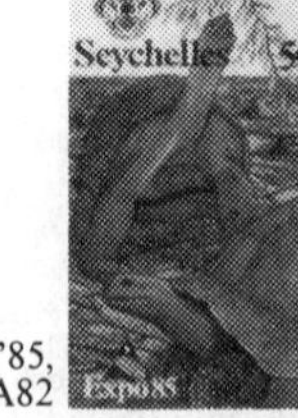

EXPO '85, Tsukuba — A82

**Wmk. 373**

**1985, Mar. 15 Litho. *Perf. 1***

*563* A82 50c Giant tortoise 14 1
*564* A82 2r Fairy tern 55 5
*565* A82 3r Wind surfing 80 8
*566* A82 5r Coco de mer 1.40 1.4
*a* Souvenir sheet of 4, #563-566 3.00 3.0

No. 566a has multicolored margin pictur ing exposition emblem and map of Japan and the Seychelles. Size: 130x82mm.

See No. 604.

**Queen Mother 85th Birthday**

Common Design Type

***Perf. 14½x14***

**1985, June 7 Litho. Wmk. 38**

*567* CD336 50c Queen Elizabeth, 1930 15 1
*568* CD336 2r With grandchildren, 1970 60 6
*569* CD336 3r 75th birthday celebration 90 9
*570* CD336 5r Holding Prince Henry 1.50 1.5

**Souvenir Sheet**

*571* CD336 10r Deplaning from helicopter 3.00 3.0

No. 571 has multicolored margin continu ing design. Size: 92x74mm.

2nd Indian Ocean Islands Games A83

**1985, Aug. 24**

*572* A83 50c Boxing 14 1
*573* A83 2r Soccer 55 5
*574* A83 3r Swimming 80 8
*575* A83 10r Wind surfing 2.75 2.7

Air Seychelles First Airbus — A83a

**1985, Nov. 1 Litho. *Perf. 14½x1***

*576* A83a 1.25r Fairy tern 35 3

Intl. Youth Year — A84

**1985, Nov. 28**

*577* A84 50c Agriculture 14 1
*578* A84 2r Construction 55 5
*579* A84 3r Carpentry 80 8
*580* A84 10r Science education 2.75 2.7

Vintage Cars
A85

**1985, Dec. 18**

*581* A85 50c 1919 Ford Model T 14 14
*582* A85 2r 1922 Austin Seven 55 55
*583* A85 3r 1924 Morris Bull-nose Oxford 80 80
*584* A85 10r 1929 Humber Coupe 2.75 2.75

Halley's Comet — A86

**1986, Feb. Wmk. 384 *Perf. 14x14½***

*585* A86 50c Transit instrument 14 14
*586* A86 2r Quadrant 55 55
*587* A86 3r Trajectory diagram 80 80
*588* A86 10r Edmond Halley 2.75 2.75

Giselle, Performed by the Ballet Louvre, Apr. 4-8 — A87

**Wmk. 384**

**1986, Apr. 4 Litho. *Perf. 14***

*589* A87 2r Heroine 60 60
*590* A87 3r Hero 90 90

**Souvenir Sheet**

*591* A87 10r United 3.00 3.00

First ballet performed in the Seychelles. No. 591 has tan and brown decorative margin. Size: 81x90mm.

**Queen Elizabeth II 60th Birthday**
Common Design Type

Designs: 50c, Marrying the Duke of Edinburgh, 1947. 1.25r, Silver Jubilee celebration. 2r, Greeting child aboard the Britannia, Qatar Harbor. 3r, State opening of Parliament, 1982. 5r, Visiting Crown Agents' offices, 1983.

**1986, Apr. 21 *Perf. 14½***

*592* CD337 50c scar, blk & sil 15 15
*593* CD337 1.25r ultra & multi 38 38
*594* CD337 2r grn & multi 60 60
*595* CD337 3r vio & multi 90 90
*596* CD337 5r rose vio & multi 1.50 1.50
*Nos. 592-596 (5)* 3.53 3.53

AMERIPEX '86, Inter-island Communications — A88

**Wmk. 384**

**1986, May 22 Litho. *Perf. 14***

*597* A88 50c La Digue Ferry 16 16
*598* A88 2r Phone booth, vert. 62 62
*599* A88 3r Victoria P.O., vert. 90 90
*600* A88 7r Air Seychelles trislander 2.25 2.25

Coptic Catholic Knights of Malta Celebration Day — A89

***Perf. 14½x14***

**1986, June 7 Litho. Wmk. 384**

*601* A89 5r Natl. arms, assoc. emblem 1.65 1.65
*a* Souv. sheet 1.65 1.65

No. 601a has tan and sepia margin picturing scenes from history of the Knights of Malta. Size: 101x81mm.

**Royal Wedding Issue, 1986**
Common Design Type

Designs: 2r, Informal portrait. 10r, Andrew, helicopter.

**1986, July 23 Litho. *Perf. 14***

*602* CD338 2r multi 62 62
*603* CD338 10r multi 3.25 3.25

Tsukuba Expo Type of 1985

**Wmk. 384**

**1986, July 12 Litho. *Perf. 14***

**Souvenir Sheet**

*604* Sheet of 4 3.00 3.00
*a* A82 50c multi 14 14
*b* A82 2r multi 55 55
*c* A82 3r multi 80 80
*d* A82 5r multi 1.40 1.40

No. 604 inscribed "Seychelles Philatelic Exhibition-Tokyo-1986" and printed without EXPO '85 emblem on margin or on individual stamps. Nos. 604a-604d inscribed "1986."

No. 396 Ovptd. "Lazournen Enternasyonal Kreol" and "1986."

***Perf. 14½x14***

**1986, Oct. 28 Wmk. 373**

*605* A44 1r multi 30 30

Intl. Creole Day.

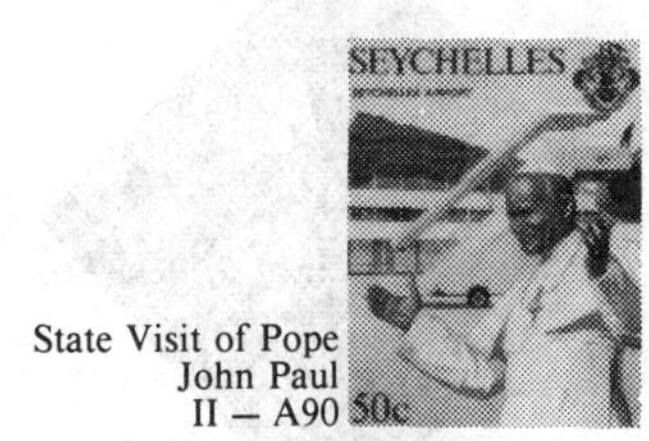

State Visit of Pope John Paul II — A90

Pope and: 50c, Seychelles Airport. 2r, Cathedral. 3r, Baie Lazare parish church. 10r, People's Stadium.

**1986, Dec. 1 Wmk. 384 *Perf. 14½***

*606* A90 50c multi 16 16
*607* A90 2r multi 62 62
*608* A90 3r multi 92 92
*609* A90 10r multi 3.00 3.00
*a* Souv. sheet of 4, #606-609 4.75 4.75

No. 609a has inscribed multicolored margin picturing arms of Pope John Paul II, the papacy, the Holy See and the Seychelles. Size: 95x105mm.

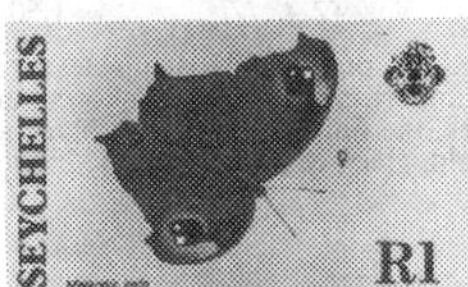

Butterflies — A91

**Wmk. 384**

**1987, Feb. 18 Litho. *Perf. 14½***

*610* A91 1r Melanitis leda 32 32
*611* A91 2r Phalanta philiberti 62 62
*612* A91 3r Danaus chrysippus 92 92
*613* A91 10r Euploea mitra 3.00 3.00

Seashells — A92 Liberation, 10th Anniv. — A93

**1987, May 7 Wmk. 373**

*614* A92 1r Gloripallium pallium 32 32
*615* A92 2r Spondylus aurantius 62 62
*616* A92 3r Harpa ventricosa, Lioconcha ornata 92 92
*617* A92 10r Strombus lentiginosus 3.00 3.00

***Perf. 14x14½, 14½x14***

**1987, June 5 Wmk. 384**

*618* A93 1r Liberation monument 32 32
*619* A93 2r Hospital, horiz. 62 62
*620* A93 3r Orphanage, horiz. 92 92
*621* A93 10r Fish monument 3.00 3.00

Natl. Banking Cent. — A94

**1987, June 25 *Perf. 14½x14***

*622* A94 1r Savings Bank, Praslin 35 35
*623* A94 2r Development Bank 65 65
*624* A94 10r Central Bank 3.15 3.15

Nos. 592-596 Ovptd. "40TH WEDDING ANNIVERSARY" in Silver

**Wmk. 384**

**1987, Dec. 9 Litho. *Perf. 14½***

*625* CD337 50c scar, blk & sil 18 18
*626* CD337 1.25r ultra & multi 45 45
*627* CD337 2r grn & multi 75 75
*628* CD337 3r vio & multi 1.10 1.10
*629* CD337 5r rose vio & multi 1.85 1.85
*Nos. 625-629 (5)* 4.33 4.33

Fishing Industry
A95

**Wmk. 384**

**1987, Dec. 11 Litho. *Perf. 14***

*630* A95 50c Tuna cannery 18 18
*631* A95 2r Fishing trawler 75 75
*632* A95 3r Weighing fish 1.10 1.10
*633* A95 10r Hauling catch from net 3.65 3.65

Beach Scenes A96

**Wmk. 384**

**1988, Feb. 9 Litho. *Perf. 14½***

*634* A96 1r Para-sailing, windsurfing, kayaks 38 38
*635* A96 2r Boating 78 78
*636* A96 3r Yacht at anchor 1.15 1.15
*637* A96 10r Hotel, cabanas 3.75 3.75

Green Turtles — A97

No. 638, Newly hatched turtles headed toward ocean. No. 639, Offspring hatching. No. 640, Female emerging from ocean. No. 641, Female laying eggs in sand. Stamps of same denomination printed se-tenant in a continuous design.

**1988, Apr. 22 Wmk. 373**

*638* A97 2r multi 75 75
*639* A97 2r multi 75 75
*640* A97 3r multi 1.15 1.15
*641* A97 3r multi 1.15 1.15

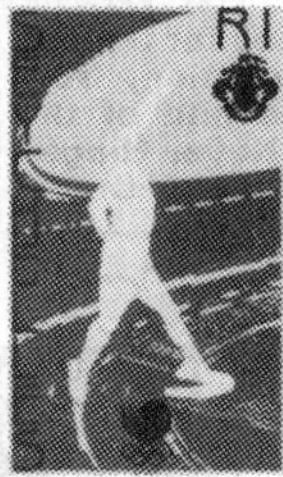

1988 Summer Olympics, Seoul — A98

Designs: 1r, No. 647a, Shot put. Nos. 643, 647b, High jump. 3r, No. 647c, Medal winner, grandstand and flags. 4r, No. 647d, Running. 5r, No. 647e, Javelin. 10r, Tennis.

**1988, July 29 Wmk. 384 *Perf. 14½***

*642* A98 1r multi 38 38
*643* A98 2r multi 75 75
*644* A98 3r multi 1.10 1.10
*645* A98 4r multi 1.50 1.50
*646* A98 5r multi 1.85 1.85
*647* Strip of 5 3.75 3.75
*a.-e.* A98 2r any single 75 75
*Nos. 642-647 (6)* 9.33 9.33

**Souvenir Sheet**

**Wmk. 373**

*648* A98 10r multi 3.75 3.75

Nos. 647a-647e printed se-tenant in a continuous design.

International Tennis Federation, 75th anniv. (10r). No. 648 contains one stamp (size: 28x39mm); multicolored margin pictures stadium and Olympic rings.

**Lloyds of London, 300th Anniv.**
Common Design Type

Designs: 1r, Leadenhall Street, London, 1928. 2r, *Cinq Juin,* horiz. 3r, *Queen Elizabeth II,* horiz. 10r, Explosion of the *Hindenburg,* Lakehurst, New Jersey, 1937.

**Wmk. 384**

**1988, Sept. 30 Litho. *Perf. 14***

*649* CD341 1r multi 38 38
*650* CD341 2r multi 72 72
*651* CD341 3r multi 1.05 1.05
*652* CD341 10r multi 3.50 3.50

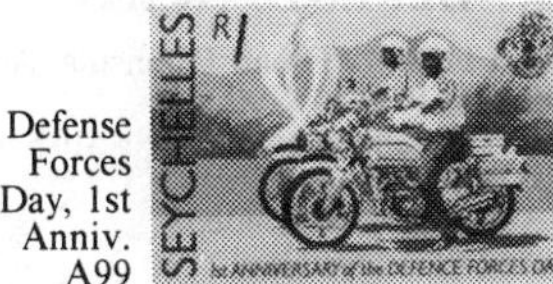

Defense Forces Day, 1st Anniv. A99

**1988, Nov. 25 Litho. Wmk. 373**

*653* A99 1r Motorcycle police 38 38
*654* A99 2r Air force helicopter 72 72
*655* A99 3r Navy patrol boat 1.05 1.05
*656* A99 10r Tank 3.50 3.50

Demand, as well as supply, determines a stamp's market value. One is as important as the other.

Christmas — A100

Illustrations by local artists.

**1988, Dec. 1 Litho. Wmk. 373**

| No. | Type | Description | Unused | Used |
|---|---|---|---|---|
| *657* | A100 | 50c Selwyn Hoareau | 10 | 10 |
| *658* | A100 | 2r Robin Leste | 72 | 72 |
| *659* | A100 | 3r France Anacoura | 1.10 | 1.10 |
| *660* | A100 | 10r Andre McGaw | 3.65 | 3.65 |

## POSTAGE DUE STAMPS

**Catalogue values for unused stamps in this section, from this point to the end of the section, are for Never Hinged items.**

D1

**Engr.; Denomination Typo. in Carmine**

**1951, Mar. 1 Wmk. 4 *Perf. 11½***

| No. | Type | Description | Unused | Used |
|---|---|---|---|---|
| *J1* | D1 | 2c carmine | 1.25 | *3.25* |
| *J2* | D1 | 3c bl grn | 1.25 | *3.25* |
| *J3* | D1 | 6c ocher | 85 | *1.65* |
| *J4* | D1 | 9c brn org | 1.00 | *5.00* |
| *J5* | D1 | 15c purple | 1.25 | *6.25* |
| *J6* | D1 | 18c deep blue | 1.50 | *7.00* |
| *J7* | D1 | 20c blk brn | 1.65 | *8.25* |
| *J8* | D1 | 30c red brn | 2.00 | *10.50* |
| | | *Nos. J1-J8 (8)* | 10.75 | *45.15* |

**Engr.; Denomination Typo.**

**1964-65 Wmk. 314**

| No. | Type | Description | Unused | Used |
|---|---|---|---|---|
| *J9* | D1 | 2c carmine | 50 | 50 |
| *J10* | D1 | 3c grn & red ('65) | 1.50 | 1.50 |

Dated "1980"

**1980 Litho. *Perf. 14***

| No. | Type | Description | Unused | Used |
|---|---|---|---|---|
| *J11* | D1 | 5c lil rose & red | 5 | 5 |
| *J12* | D1 | 10c dk grn & red | 5 | 5 |
| *J13* | D1 | 15c bis & red | 5 | 5 |
| *J14* | D1 | 20c brn org & red | 6 | 6 |
| *J15* | D1 | 25c vio & red | 8 | 8 |
| *J16* | D1 | 75c dk red brn & red | 25 | 25 |
| *J17* | D1 | 80c dk bl & red | 28 | 28 |
| *J18* | D1 | 1r cl & red | 30 | 30 |
| | | *Nos. J11-J18 (8)* | 1.12 | 1.12 |

# SHARJAH & DEPENDENCIES

LOCATION — Oman Peninsula, Arabia, on Persian Gulf.

GOVT. — Sheikdom under British protection

POP. — 5,000 (estimated)

CAPITAL — Sharjah

The dependencies on the Gulf of Oman are Dhiba, Khor Fakkan, and Kalba.

Sharjah is one of six Persian Gulf sheikdoms to join the United Arab Emirates which proclaimed independence Dec. 2, 1971. See United Arab Emirates.

100 Naye Paise = 1 Rupee

**Catalogue values for all unused stamps in this country are for Never Hinged items.**

Sheik Saqr bin Sultan al Qasimi, Flag and Map — A1

Malaria Eradication Emblem — A2

***Perf. 14½x14***

**1963, July 10 Photo. Unwmk.**

**Black Portrait and Inscriptions; Lilac Rose Flag**

| No. | Type | Description | Unused | Used |
|---|---|---|---|---|
| *1* | A1 | 1np lt bl grn & pink | 5 | 5 |
| *2* | A1 | 2np grnsh bl & sal | 5 | 5 |
| *3* | A1 | 3np vio & yel | 5 | 5 |
| *4* | A1 | 4np emer & gray | 5 | 5 |
| *5* | A1 | 5np aqua & lt grn | 6 | 6 |
| *6* | A1 | 6np dl grn & brt yel | 6 | 6 |
| *7* | A1 | 8np Prus bl & bis | 6 | 6 |
| *8* | A1 | 10np aqua & tan | 6 | 6 |
| *9* | A1 | 16np ultra & bis | 8 | 8 |
| *10* | A1 | 20np lt vio & lem | 10 | 10 |
| *11* | A1 | 30np rose lil & brt yel grn | 16 | 16 |
| *12* | A1 | 40np dk bl & yel grn | 20 | 20 |
| *13* | A1 | 50np grn & fawn | 28 | 28 |
| *14* | A1 | 75np ultra & fawn | 40 | 40 |
| *15* | A1 | 100np ol bis & rose | 50 | 50 |
| | | *Nos. 1-15 (15)* | 2.16 | 2.16 |

**1963, Aug. 8**

| No. | Type | Description | Unused | Used |
|---|---|---|---|---|
| *16* | A2 | 1np grnsh bl | 5 | 5 |
| *17* | A2 | 2np dl bl | 6 | 5 |
| *18* | A2 | 3np vio bl | 8 | 5 |
| *19* | A2 | 4np emerald | 10 | 5 |
| *20* | A2 | 90np yel brn | 50 | 50 |
| | | *Nos. 16-20 (5)* | 79 | 70 |

**Miniature Sheet**

***Imperf***

| No. | Type | Description | Unused | Used |
|---|---|---|---|---|
| *21* | A2 | 100np brt bl | 80 | 80 |

WHO drive to eradicate malaria. No. 21 contains one stamp; bright blue marginal inscription. Size of stamp: 39x67mm, size of sheet: 64x90mm.

Red Crescent and Sheik — A3

**1963, Aug. 25 *Perf. 14x14½***

| No. | Type | Description | Unused | Used |
|---|---|---|---|---|
| *22* | A3 | 1np pur & red | 5 | 5 |
| *23* | A3 | 2np brt grn & red | 5 | 5 |
| *24* | A3 | 3np dk bl & red | 5 | 5 |
| *25* | A3 | 4np dk grn & red | 5 | 5 |
| *26* | A3 | 5np dk brn & red | 5 | 5 |
| *27* | A3 | 85np grn & red | 40 | 40 |
| | | *Nos. 22-27 (6)* | 65 | 65 |

**Miniature Sheet**

***Imperf***

| No. | Type | Description | Unused | Used |
|---|---|---|---|---|
| *28* | A3 | 100np plum & red | 1.00 | 1.00 |

Cent. of the Intl. Red Cross. Imperfs. exist. No. 28 contains one stamp, plum marginal inscription. Size of stamp: 67x39mm, size of sheet: 90x63mm.

Nos. 36-40 and No. 20 Surcharged

Nos. 29-34

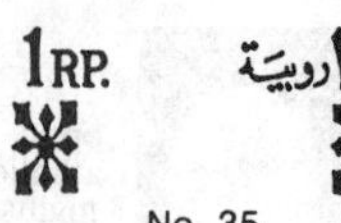

No. 35

**1963, Oct. 6 Photo. *Perf. 14½x14***

| No. | Type | Description | Unused | Used |
|---|---|---|---|---|
| *29* | A4 | 10np on 1np brt grn | 10 | 10 |
| *30* | A4 | 20np on 2np red brn | 20 | 20 |
| *31* | A4 | 30np on 3np ol grn | 30 | 30 |
| *32* | A4 | 40np on 4np dp ultra | 40 | 40 |
| *33* | A4 | 75np on 90np car | 65 | 65 |
| *34* | A4 | 80np on 90np car | 80 | 80 |
| *35* | A2 | 1r on 90np yel brn | 1.10 | 1.10 |
| | | *Nos. 29-35 (7)* | 3.55 | 3.55 |

Due to a stamp shortage the surcharged set appeared before the commemorative issue.

Wheat Emblem and Hands with Broken Chains — A4

**1963, Oct. 15 *Perf. 14½x14***

| No. | Type | Description | Unused | Used |
|---|---|---|---|---|
| *36* | A4 | 1np brt grn | 5 | 5 |
| *37* | A4 | 2np red brn | 5 | 5 |
| *38* | A4 | 3np ol grn | 5 | 5 |
| *39* | A4 | 4np dp ultra | 5 | 5 |
| *40* | A4 | 90np carmine | 40 | 40 |
| | | *Nos. 36-40 (5)* | 60 | 60 |

**Miniature Sheet**

***Imperf***

| No. | Type | Description | Unused | Used |
|---|---|---|---|---|
| *41* | A4 | 100np purple | 50 | 50 |

"Freedom from Hunger" campaign of the FAO. Imperfs. exist. No. 41 contains one stamp; purple marginal inscription. Size of stamp: 39x67mm, size of sheet: 63x89mm.

Orbiting Astronomical Observatory — A5

Satellites: 2np, Nimbus weather satellite. 3np, Pioneer V space probe. 4np, Explorer XIII. 5np, Explorer XII. 35np, Relay satellite. 50np, Orbiting Solar Observatory.

**1964, Feb. 5 Photo. *Perf. 14***

| No. | Type | Description | Unused | Used |
|---|---|---|---|---|
| *42* | A5 | 1np blue | 6 | 6 |
| *43* | A5 | 2np red brn & yel grn | 6 | 6 |
| *44* | A5 | 3np blk & grnsh bl | 6 | 6 |
| *45* | A5 | 4np lem & blk | 6 | 6 |
| *46* | A5 | 5np brt pur & lem | 6 | 6 |
| *47* | A5 | 35np grnsh bl & pur | 50 | 50 |
| *48* | A5 | 50np ol grn & redsh brn | 70 | 70 |
| | | *Nos. 42-48 (7)* | 1.50 | 1.50 |

Issued to publicize space research. A 100np imperf. souvenir sheet shows various satellites, the Earth and stars. Colors: dark blus, gold, green & pink. Size: 112x80mm.

Runner — A6

**1964, March 3 Unwmk.**

| No. | Type | Description | Unused | Used |
|---|---|---|---|---|
| *49* | A6 | 1np shown | 5 | 5 |
| *50* | A6 | 2np Discus | 5 | 5 |
| *51* | A6 | 3np Hurdler | 5 | 5 |
| *52* | A6 | 4np Shot put | 5 | 5 |
| *53* | A6 | 20np High jump | 14 | 14 |
| *54* | A6 | 30np Weight lifting | 20 | 20 |
| *55* | A6 | 40np Javelin | 28 | 28 |
| *56* | A6 | 1r Diving | 65 | 65 |
| | | *Nos. 49-56 (8)* | 1.47 | 1.47 |

18th Olympic Games, Tokyo, Oct. 10-25, 1964. An imperf. souvenir sheet contains one 1r stamp similar to No. 56. Size of stamp: 67x67mm, size of sheet: 102x102mm.

Girl Scouts A7

**1964, June 30 *Perf. 14x14½***

| No. | Type | Description | Unused | Used |
|---|---|---|---|---|
| *57* | A7 | 1np grnsh gray | 5 | 5 |
| *58* | A7 | 2np emerald | 5 | 5 |
| *59* | A7 | 3np brt bl | 5 | 5 |
| *60* | A7 | 4np brt vio | 5 | 5 |
| *61* | A7 | 5np car rose | 5 | 5 |
| *62* | A7 | 2r dk red brn | 1.00 | 1.00 |
| | | *Nos. 57-62 (6)* | 1.25 | 1.25 |

Issued to honor the Girl Scouts. An imperf. souvenir sheet contains one 2r bright red stamp. Size of stamp: 67x40mm. Size of sheet: 102½x76mm.

Sharjah Boy Scout — A8

Marching Scouts With Drummers — A9

Designs: 3np, 2r, Boy Scout portrait.

***Perf. 14½x14, 14x14½***

**1964, June 30 Photo. Unwmk.**

| No. | Type | Description | Unused | Used |
|---|---|---|---|---|
| *63* | A8 | 1np gray grn | 7 | 7 |
| *64* | A9 | 2np emerald | 7 | 7 |
| *65* | A8 | 3np brt bl | 7 | 7 |
| *66* | A8 | 4np brt vio | 7 | 7 |
| *67* | A9 | 5np brt car rose | 7 | 7 |
| *68* | A8 | 2r dk red brn | 1.00 | 1.00 |
| | | *Nos. 63-68 (6)* | 1.35 | 1.35 |

Issued to honor the Sharjah Boy Scouts. An imperf. souvenir sheet exists with one 2r bright red stamp in design of No. 68. Size of stamp: 39½x67mm. Size of sheet: 77x103mm.

Olympic Torch and Rings — A10

**1964, Oct. 15 Litho. *Perf. 14***

*69* A10 1np ol grn 5 5
*70* A10 2np ultra 5 5
*71* A10 3np org brn 5 5
*72* A10 4np bl grn 5 5
*73* A10 5np dk vio 5 5
*74* A10 40np brt bl 35 35
*75* A10 50np dk red brn 40 40
*76* A10 2r bister 1.60 1.60
*Nos. 69-76 (8)* 2.60 2.60

18th Olympic Games, Tokyo, Oct. 10-25. An imperf. souvenir sheet exists with one 2r yellow green stamp. Size of stamp: 82mm. at base. Size of sheet: 107x76mm.

Early Telephone — A11

Designs: No. 78, Modern telewriter. No. 79, 1895 car. No. 80, American automobile, 1964. No. 81, Early X-ray. No. 82, Modern X-ray. No. 83, Mail coach. No. 84, Telstar and Delta rocket. No. 85, Sailing vessel. No. 86, Nuclear ship "Savannah." No. 87, Early astronomers. No. 88, Jodrell Bank telescope. No. 89, Greek messengers. No. 90, Relay satellite, Delta rocket and globe. No. 91, Early flying machine. No. 92, Caravelle plane. No. 93, Persian water wheel. No. 94, Hydroelectric dam. No. 95, Old steam locomotive. No. 96, Diesel locomotive.

**Unwmk.**

**1965, Apr. 23 Litho. *Perf. 14***

*77* A11 1np rose red & blk 7 6
*78* A11 1np rose red & blk 17 6
*79* A11 2np org & ind 7 6
*80* A11 2np org & ind 7 6
*81* A11 3np dk brn & emer 7 6
*82* A11 3np emer & dk brn 7 6
*83* A11 4np yel grn & dk vio 7 6
*84* A11 4np dk vio & yel grn 7 6
*85* A11 5np bl grn & brn 7 6
*86* A11 5np bl grn & brn 7 6
*87* A11 30np gray & bl 14 8
*88* A11 30np bl & gray 14 8
*89* A11 40np vio bl & yel 20 10
*90* A11 40np vio bl & yel 20 10
*91* A11 50np bl & sep 28 14
*92* A11 50np bl & sep 28 14
*93* A11 75np brt grn & dk brn 40 20
*94* A11 75np brt grn & dk brn 40 20
*95* A11 1r yel & vio bl 50 25
*96* A11 1r yel & vio bl 50 25
*Nos. 77-96 (20)* 3.84 2.14

Issued to show progress in science, transport and communications. Each two stamps of same denomination are printed se tenant. Two imperf. souvenir sheets exist. One contains one each of Nos. 89-90 and the other, of Nos. 95-96. Size: 102x75mm.

Stamps of Sharjah & Dependencies were replaced in 1972 by those of United Arab Emirates.

## AIR POST STAMPS

Type of Regular Issue, 1963 with Flying Hawk and "Air Mail" in English and Arabic Added.

***Perf. 14½x14***

**1963, July 10 Photo. Unwmk.**

**Black Portrait and Inscriptions; Lilac Rose Flag**

*C1* A1 1r ultra & fawn 40 40
*C2* A1 2r lt vio & lem 70 70
*C3* A1 3r dl grn & brt yel 1.00 1.00
*C4* A1 4r grnsh bl & sal 1.40 1.40
*C5* A1 5r emer & gray 1.60 1.60
*C6* A1 10r ol bis & rose 3.50 3.50
*Nos. C1-C6 (6)* 8.60 8.60

ذكرى جون ف. كنيدي ١٩١٧-١٩٦٣

Nos. C1-C6 Overprinted

John F Kennedy 1917-1963

**1964, Apr. 7**

**Black Portrait and Inscriptions; Lilac Rose Flag**

*C7* A1 1r ultra & fawn
*C8* A1 2r lt vio & lem
*C9* A1 3r dl grn & brt yel
*C10* A1 4r grnsh bl & sal
*C11* A1 5r emer & gray
*C12* A1 10r ol bis & rose
*Nos. C7-C12* 40.00 27.50

Pres. John F. Kennedy (1917-63).

World Map and Flame AP1

**1964, Apr. 15 *Perf. 14x14½***

*C13* AP1 50np red brn 20 20
*C14* AP1 1r purple 40 40
*C15* AP1 150np Prus grn 60 60

Issued for Human Rights Day. An imperf. souvenir sheet contains one 3r carmine rose stamp. Size of stamp: 67x40mm. Size of sheet: 89x64mm.

View of Khor Fakkan — AP2

Designs: 20np, Beni Qatab Bedouin camp near Dhaid. 30np, Oasis of Dhaid. 40np, Kalba Castle. 75np, Sharjah street with wind tower. 100np, Sharjah Fortress.

**1964, Aug. 13 Photo. Unwmk.**

*C16* AP2 10np multi 5 5
*C17* AP2 20np multi 8 6
*C18* AP2 30np multi 10 7
*C19* AP2 40np multi 15 10
*C20* AP2 75np multi 28 18
*C21* AP2 100np multi 40 22
*Nos. C16-C21 (6)* 1.06 68

Unisphere and Sheik Saqr — AP3

J. F. Kennedy, Statue of Liberty — AP4

Designs: 20np, Offshore oil rig. 1r, New York skyline (horiz.).

***Perf. 14½x14***

**1964, Sept. 5 Photo. Unwmk.**

**Size: 26x45mm**

*C22* AP3 20np yel, blk & brt bl 8 8
*C23* AP3 40np blk, bl & yel 15 15

**Size: 86x45mm**

*C24* AP3 1r brt bl & multi 40 40
Strip of 3, Nos. C22-C24 60 60

Issued for the New York World's Fair, 1964-65. Nos. C22-C24 were printed setenant in the same sheet.

An imperf. souvenir sheet exists with one 40np stamp in AP3 design. Size of stamp: 40x68mm. Size of sheet: 76x108mm.

**1964, Nov. 22 *Perf. 14x13½***

*C25* AP4 40np ol grn, gold, ultra & ocher 50 50
*C26* AP4 60np ultra, gold, ol grn & ocher 80 80
*C27* AP4 100np ocher, gold, ol grn & ultra 1.40 1.40

Pres. John F. Kennedy. A souvenir sheet contains one each of Nos. C25-C27, imperf. Size: 107x76mm.

Rock Dove AP5

Birds: 40np, 2r, Red jungle fowl. 75np, 3r, Hoopoe.

***Perf. 14x14½***

**1965, Feb. 20 Photo. Unwmk.**

*C28* AP5 30np gray & multi 10 6
*C29* AP5 40np multi 15 7
*C30* AP5 75np brt bl & multi 28 10
*C31* AP5 150np bl & multi 60 20
*C32* AP5 2r multi 65 28
*C33* AP5 3r red & multi 1.00 40
*Nos. C28-C33 (6)* 2.78 1.11

## OFFICIAL STAMPS

Nos. 7-15 Overprinted

ON STATE SERVICE

***Perf. 14½x14***

**1965, Jan. 13 Photo. Unwmk.**

*O1* A1 8np multi 7 7
*O2* A1 10np multi 7 7
*O3* A1 16np multi 10 10
*O4* A1 20np multi 10 10
*O5* A1 30np multi 16 16
*O6* A1 40np multi 20 20
*O7* A1 50np multi 22 22
*O8* A1 75np multi 35 35
*O9* A1 100np multi 50 50
*Nos. O1-O9 (9)* 1.77 1.77

# SIERRA LEONE

LOCATION — West coast of Africa, between Guinea and Liberia.
GOVT. — Republic in British Commonwealth.
AREA — 27,925 sq. mi.
POP. — 3,354,000 (est. 1982).
CAPITAL — Freetown.

Sierra Leone was a British colony and protectorate. In 1961 it became fully independent, remaining within the Commonwealth. It became a republic April 19, 1971.

12 Pence = 1 Shilling
20 Shillings = 1 Pound
100 Cents = 1 Leone (1964)

**Catalogue values for unused stamps in this country are for Never Hinged items, beginning with Scott 186 in the regular postage section and Scott C1 in the air post section.**

Queen Victoria
A1 A2

**1859 Unwmk. Typo. *Perf. 14***

*3* A1 6p dl vio 37.50 16.00
**a** 6p bright violet 125.00 20.00

**1872 *Perf. 12½.***

*5* A1 6p violet 200.00 35.00

**Wmk. 1 Sideways**

**1872-73 *Perf. 12½***

*6* A2 1p rose 27.50 12.00
**a** Wmk. upright ('73) 35.00 15.00
*7* A2 2p mag, wmk. upright ('73) 60.00 25.00
*8* A2 3p yel buff 45.00 19.00
**a** Wmk. upright ('73) 650.00 67.50
*9* A2 4p blue 125.00 20.00
**a** Wmk. upright ('73) 265.00 20.00
*10* A2 1sh yel grn 165.00 20.00
**a** Wmk. upright ('73) 325.00 80.00
*Nos. 6-10 (5)* 422.50 96.00

**1876-96 Wmk. 1 Upright *Perf. 14***

*11* A2 ½p bister 1.90 2.50
*12* A2 1p rose 15.00 6.25
*13* A2 1½p vio ('77) 12.00 6.25
*14* A2 2p magenta 24.00 3.50
*15* A2 3p yel buff 21.00 3.25
*16* A2 4p blue 105.00 2.75
*17* A1 6p brt vio ('85) 42.50 17.50
**a** Half used as 3p on cover 3,000.
*18* A1 6p vio brn ('90) 8.25 6.25
*19* A1 6p brn vio ('96) 2.00 4.25
*20* A2 1sh green 37.50 5.00
*Nos. 11-20 (10)* 269.15 57.50

**1883-93 Wmk. Crown and C. A. (2)**

*21* A2 ½p bister 21.00 15.00
*22* A2 ½p dl grn ('84) 18 18
*23* A2 1p car ('84) 38 20
**a** 1p rose car 20.00 4.00
**b** 1p rose 190.00 27.50
*24* A2 1½p vio ('93) 38 65
*25* A2 2p magenta 25.00 2.25
*26* A2 2p sl ('84) 2.50 1.00
*27* A2 2½p ultra ('91) 2.50 30
*28* A2 3p org yel ('92) 80 1.25
*29* A2 4p blue 700.00 17.50
*30* A2 4p bis ('84) 80 75
*31* A2 1sh org brn ('88) 5.50 2.25
*Nos. 21-28,30-31 (10)* 59.04 23.83

HALF
PENNY

Nos. 13 and 24 Surcharged in Black

**1893 Wmk. Crown and C. C. (1)**

*32* A2 ½p on 1½p vio 400.00 *425.00*
**a** "PFNNY" 2,500. *3,250.*

**Wmk. Crown and C. A. (2)**

*33* A2 ½p on 1½p vio 2.00 2.25
**a** "PFNNY" 50.00 *60.00*
**b** Inverted surch. 110.00 110.00
**c** Same as "a" inverted 1,750.
**d** Double surch *900.00*

A4

**1896-97**

*34* A4 ½p lil & grn ('97) 35 35
*35* A4 1p lil & car 45 12
*36* A4 1½p lil & blk ('97) 90 1.40
*37* A4 2p lil & org 90 1.40
*38* A4 2½p lil & ultra 90 28
*39* A4 3p lil & sl ('97) 2.50 2.75
*40* A4 4p lil & car ('97) 2.50 4.50
*41* A4 5p lil & blk 4.50 5.50
*42* A4 6p lil ('97) 4.50 5.50
*43* A4 1sh grn & blk 5.50 6.50
*44* A4 2sh grn & ultra 22.50 27.50
*45* A4 5sh grn & car 35.00 45.00
*46* A4 £1 vio, *red* 125.00 150.00
*Nos. 34-46 (13)* 205.50 250.80

Numerals of Nos. 39-46 of type A4 are in color on plain tablet.

A5

A6

2½d. 2½d. 2½d.
a b c

2½d. 2½d. 2½d.
d e f

**1897 Wmk. C. A. over Crown. (46)**

| | | | | |
|---|---|---|---|---|
| *47* | A5 | 1p lil & grn | 1.40 | 1.40 |
| *a* | | Double surch. | 1,300. | 1,750. |
| *48* | A6 (a) | 2½p on 3p lil & grn | 15.00 | 18.00 |
| *49* | A6 (b) | 2½p on 3p | 60.00 | 67.50 |
| *50* | A6 (c) | 2½p on 3p | 125.00 | 140.00 |
| *51* | A6 (d) | 2½p on 3p | 250.00 | 265.00 |
| *52* | A6 (a) | 2½p on 6p lil & grn | 10.00 | 12.50 |
| *53* | A6 (b) | 2½p on 6p | 42.50 | 47.50 |
| *54* | A6 (c) | 2½p on 6p | 140.00 | 160.00 |
| *55* | A6 (d) | 2½p on 6p | 165.00 | 185.00 |
| *56* | A6 (a) | 2½p on 1sh lil | 85.00 | 65.00 |
| *57* | A6 (b) | 2½p on 1sh lil | 500.00 | 550.00 |
| *58* | A6 (c) | 2½p on 1sh lil | 300.00 | 315.00 |
| *59* | A6 (e) | 2½p on 1sh lil | 1,750. | 2,000. |
| *59A* | A6 (f) | 2½p on 1sh lil | 1,750. | 2,000. |
| *60* | A6 (a) | 2½p on 2sh lil | 1,000. | 1,150. |
| *61* | A6 (b) | 2½p on 2sh lil | *9,000.* | |
| *62* | A6 (c) | 2½p on 2sh lil | 5,000. | |
| *63* | A6 (e) | 2½p on 2sh lil | *27,500.* | |
| *63A* | A6 (f) | 2½p on 2sh lil | *27,500.* | |

The words "POSTAGE AND REVENUE" on Nos. 56-63A are set in two lines and overprinted below instead of above "2½d."

The "d" in type "f" is 3½mm. wide; that in type "a" is 3mm.

Nos. 56-59A are often found discolored. Such copies sell for half the values quoted.

King Edward VII — A7

Numerals of 3p to £1 of type A7 are in color on plain tablet.

**1903 Wmk. Crown and C. A. (2)**

| | | | | |
|---|---|---|---|---|
| *64* | A7 | ½p vio & grn | 65 | 75 |
| *65* | A7 | 1p vio & car | 48 | 20 |
| *66* | A7 | 1½p vio & blk | 65 | 1.25 |
| *67* | A7 | 2p vio & brn org | 2.00 | 3.00 |
| *68* | A7 | 2½p vio & ultra | 2.50 | 2.50 |
| *69* | A7 | 3p vio & gray | 2.50 | 2.75 |
| *70* | A7 | 4p vio & car | 2.25 | 2.75 |
| *71* | A7 | 5p vio & blk | 1.75 | 1.90 |
| *72* | A7 | 6p vio & dl vio | 4.75 | 2.75 |
| *73* | A7 | 1sh grn & blk | 6.50 | 8.00 |
| *74* | A7 | 2sh grn & ultra | 14.00 | 12.00 |
| *75* | A7 | 5sh grn & car | 24.00 | 27.50 |
| *76* | A7 | £1 vio, *red* | 110.00 | 140.00 |
| | | *Nos. 64-76 (13)* | 172.03 | 205.35 |

**1904-05 Wmk. 3**

**Chalky Paper**

| | | | | |
|---|---|---|---|---|
| *77* | A7 | ½p vio & grn | 3.00 | 50 |
| *78* | A7 | 1p vio & car | 55 | 20 |
| *79* | A7 | 1½p vio & blk | 1.50 | *5.75* |
| *80* | A7 | 2p vio & brn org | 2.25 | 2.25 |
| *81* | A7 | 2½p vio & ultra | 2.50 | 1.25 |
| *82* | A7 | 3p vio & gray | 6.00 | 3.00 |
| *83* | A7 | 4p vio & car | 70 | 1.25 |
| *84* | A7 | 5p vio & blk | 3.75 | *5.00* |
| *85* | A7 | 6p vio & dl vio | 1.50 | *2.00* |
| *86* | A7 | 1sh grn & blk | 5.00 | *6.00* |
| *87* | A7 | 2sh grn & ultra | 10.00 | 12.00 |
| *88* | A7 | 5sh grn & car | 30.00 | 35.00 |
| *89* | A7 | £1 vio, *red* | 135.00 | 150.00 |
| | | *Nos. 77-89 (13)* | 201.75 | 224.20 |

The 1p also exists on ordinary paper.

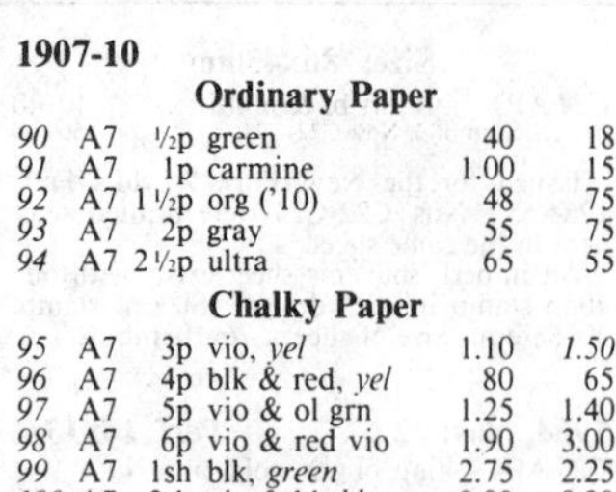

**1907-10**

**Ordinary Paper**

| | | | | |
|---|---|---|---|---|
| *90* | A7 | ½p green | 40 | 18 |
| *91* | A7 | 1p carmine | 1.00 | 15 |
| *92* | A7 | 1½p org ('10) | 48 | 75 |
| *93* | A7 | 2p gray | 55 | 75 |
| *94* | A7 | 2½p ultra | 65 | 55 |

**Chalky Paper**

| | | | | |
|---|---|---|---|---|
| *95* | A7 | 3p vio, *yel* | 1.10 | *1.50* |
| *96* | A7 | 4p blk & red, *yel* | 80 | 65 |
| *97* | A7 | 5p vio & ol grn | 1.25 | 1.40 |
| *98* | A7 | 6p vio & red vio | 1.90 | 3.00 |
| *99* | A7 | 1sh blk, *green* | 2.75 | 2.25 |
| *100* | A7 | 2sh vio & bl, *bl* | 9.00 | 8.00 |
| *101* | A7 | 5sh grn & red, *yel* | 19.00 | 22.50 |
| *102* | A7 | £1 vio & blk, *red* | 100.00 | 140.00 |
| | | *Nos. 90-102 (13)* | 138.88 | 181.68 |

The 3p also exists on ordinary paper.

King George V and Seal of the Colony
A8 A9

Die I

For description of dies I and II see back of this volume.

Numerals of 3p, 4p, 5p, 6p and 10p of type A8 are in color on plain tablet. Numerals of 7p and 9p are on solid-color tablet.

**1912-24 Ordinary Paper Wmk. 3**

| | | | | |
|---|---|---|---|---|
| *103* | A8 | ½p green | 45 | 15 |
| *104* | A8 | 1p scarlet | 24 | 7 |
| *a* | | 1p car | 24 | 6 |
| *105* | A8 | 1½p orange | 1.00 | 75 |
| *106* | A8 | 2p gray | 90 | 18 |
| *107* | A8 | 2½p ultra | 45 | 45 |

**Chalky Paper**

| | | | | |
|---|---|---|---|---|
| *108* | A9 | 3p vio, *yel* | 1.40 | 1.75 |
| *109* | A8 | 4p blk & red, *yel* | 45 | 48 |
| *a* | | Die II ('24) | 45 | *3.00* |
| *110* | A8 | 5p vio & ol grn | 1.40 | 2.00 |
| *111* | A8 | 6p vio & red vio | 1.10 | 1.40 |
| *112* | A8 | 7p vio & org | 75 | 1.65 |
| *113* | A8 | 9p vio & blk | 3.50 | *5.50* |
| *114* | A8 | 10p vio & red | 1.65 | *3.50* |
| *115* | A9 | 1sh blk, *green* | 75 | 65 |
| *a* | | 1sh blk, *emer* | | *165.00* |
| *116* | A9 | 2sh vio & ultra, *bl* | 4.25 | 3.75 |
| *117* | A9 | 5sh grn & red, *yel* | 7.75 | *13.00* |
| *118* | A9 | 10sh grn & red, *grn* | 22.50 | 27.50 |
| *119* | A9 | £1 vio & blk, *red* | 85.00 | 125.00 |
| *120* | A9 | £2 vio & ultra | 275.00 | *425.00* |
| *121* | A9 | £5 gray grn & org | *700.00* | |
| | | *Nos. 103-119 (17)* | 133.54 | 187.78 |

Die II

**1921-27 Wmk. 4**

**Ordinary Paper.**

| | | | | |
|---|---|---|---|---|
| *122* | A8 | ½p green | 35 | 15 |
| *123* | A8 | 1p vio ('26) | 45 | 6 |
| *a* | | Die I ('24) | 45 | 6 |
| *124* | A8 | 1½p scarlet | 1.00 | 55 |
| *125* | A8 | 2p gray ('22) | 32 | 15 |
| *126* | A8 | 2½p ultra | 30 | 65 |
| *127* | A8 | 3p ultra ('22) | 55 | 28 |
| *128* | A8 | 4p blk & red, *yel* | 1.75 | 2.00 |
| *129* | A8 | 5p vio & ol grn | 48 | 75 |

**Chalky Paper**

| | | | | |
|---|---|---|---|---|
| *130* | A8 | 6p dp vio & red vio | 55 | 60 |
| *131* | A8 | 7p vio & org ('27) | 1.25 | 4.00 |
| *132* | A8 | 9p dl vio & blk ('22) | 2.00 | 3.50 |
| *133* | A8 | 10p vio & red | 1.65 | 4.00 |
| *134* | A9 | 1sh blk, *emerald* | 1.75 | 2.00 |
| *135* | A9 | 2sh vio & ultra, *bl* | 4.50 | 4.50 |
| *136* | A9 | 5sh grn & red, *yel* | 9.00 | 15.00 |
| *137* | A9 | 10sh grn & red, *grn* | 32.50 | 45.00 |
| *138* | A9 | £2 vio & ultra | 350.00 | *525.00* |
| *139* | A9 | £5 gray grn & org | *800.00* | *2,500.* |
| | | *Nos. 122-137 (16)* | 58.40 | 83.19 |

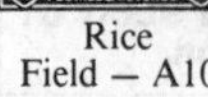
Rice Field — A10

Palms and Kola Tree — A11

**1932, Mar. Engr. *Perf. 12½***

| | | | | |
|---|---|---|---|---|
| *140* | A10 | ½p green | 14 | 12 |
| *141* | A10 | 1p dk vio | 14 | 12 |
| *142* | A10 | 1½p rose car | 28 | 28 |
| *143* | A10 | 2p yel brn | 30 | 12 |
| *144* | A10 | 3p ultra | 35 | 30 |
| *145* | A10 | 4p orange | 40 | 40 |
| *146* | A10 | 5p ol grn | 52 | 70 |
| *147* | A10 | 6p lt bl | 70 | *80* |
| *148* | A10 | 1sh red brn | 1.40 | *2.50* |

***Perf. 12.***

| | | | | |
|---|---|---|---|---|
| *149* | A11 | 2sh dk brn | 6.00 | *8.25* |
| *150* | A11 | 5sh indigo | 10.00 | *14.00* |
| *151* | A11 | 10sh dp grn | 30.00 | 40.00 |
| *152* | A11 | £1 dp vio | 60.00 | 110.00 |
| | | *Nos. 140-152 (13)* | 110.23 | 177.59 |

**Wilberforce Issue.**

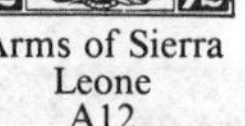
Arms of Sierra Leone
A12

Slave Throwing Off Shackles
A13

Map of Sierra Leone — A14

Old Slave Market, Freetown — A15

Fruit Seller
A16

Government Sanatorium
A17

Bullom Canoe — A18

Punting near Banana Islands — A19

Government Buildings, Freetown — A20

Old Slavers' Resort, Bunce Island — A21

African Elephant — A22

George V — A23

Freetown Harbor — A24

**1933, Oct. 2**

| | | | | |
|---|---|---|---|---|
| *153* | A12 | ½p dp grn | 50 | 50 |
| *154* | A13 | 1p brn & blk | 50 | 45 |
| *155* | A14 | 1½p org brn | 1.40 | 1.65 |
| *156* | A15 | 2p violet | 1.10 | 1.10 |
| *157* | A16 | 3p ultra | 1.25 | 1.25 |
| *158* | A17 | 4p dk brn | 3.25 | *6.50* |
| *159* | A18 | 5p red brn & sl grn | 4.00 | *8.50* |
| *160* | A19 | 6p dp org & blk | 6.00 | *7.25* |
| *161* | A20 | 1sh dk vio | 6.50 | *8.50* |
| *162* | A21 | 2sh bl & dk brn | 22.50 | *32.50* |
| *163* | A22 | 5sh red vio & blk | 105.00 | *200.00* |
| *164* | A23 | 10sh grn & blk | 115.00 | *250.00* |
| *165* | A24 | £1 yel & dk vio | 325.00 | *400.00* |
| | | *Nos. 153-164 (12)* | 267.00 | 518.20 |

Issued in commemoration of the abolition of slavery in the British colonies and of the centenary of the death of William Wilberforce, English philanthropist and agitator against the slave trade.

**Silver Jubilee Issue**

Common Design Type

**1935, May 6 *Perf. 11x12***

| | | | | |
|---|---|---|---|---|
| *166* | CD301 | 1p blk & ultra | 20 | 20 |
| *167* | CD301 | 3p ultra & brn | 1.00 | 1.00 |
| *168* | CD301 | 5p ind & grn | 1.50 | *2.50* |
| *169* | CD301 | 1sh brn vio & ind | 3.25 | 3.25 |

**Coronation Issue**

Common Design Type

**1937, May 12 *Perf. 11x11½***

| | | | | |
|---|---|---|---|---|
| *170* | CD302 | 1p dp org | 25 | 25 |
| *171* | CD302 | 2p dk vio | 30 | 30 |
| *172* | CD302 | 3p dp ultra | 40 | 40 |

Freetown Harbor
A25

Rice Harvesting
A26

**1938-44 *Perf. 12½***

| | | | | |
|---|---|---|---|---|
| *173* | A25 | ½p grn & blk | 6 | 6 |
| *174* | A25 | 1p dp cl & blk | 8 | 8 |
| *175* | A26 | 1½p rose red | 3.25 | 24 |
| *175A* | A26 | 1½p red vio ('41) | 8 | 6 |
| *176* | A26 | 2p red vio | 7.00 | 1.25 |
| *176A* | A26 | 2p dk red ('41) | 8 | 6 |
| *177* | A25 | 3p ultra & blk | 10 | 8 |
| *178* | A25 | 4p red brn & blk | 24 | 20 |
| *179* | A26 | 5p ol grn | 45 | 70 |
| *180* | A26 | 6p gray | 20 | 7 |
| *181* | A25 | 1sh ol grn & blk | 38 | 16 |
| *181A* | A26 | 1sh 3p org yel ('44) | 38 | 24 |
| *182* | A25 | 2sh sep & blk | 55 | 35 |
| *183* | A26 | 5sh red brn | 1.00 | 60 |
| *184* | A26 | 10sh emerald | 1.50 | 1.50 |
| *185* | A25 | £1 dk bl | 3.25 | 2.75 |
| | | *Nos. 173-185 (16)* | 18.60 | 8.40 |

**Catalogue values for unused stamps in this section, from this point to the end of the section, are for Never Hinged items.**

**Peace Issue**

Common Design Type

***Perf. 13½x14***

**1946, Oct. 1 Engr. Wmk. 4**

| | | | | |
|---|---|---|---|---|
| *186* | CD303 | 1½p lilac | 10 | 10 |
| *187* | CD303 | 3p brt ultra | 15 | 15 |

**Silver Wedding Issue**

Common Design Types

**1948, Dec. 1 Photo. *Perf. 14x14½***

| | | | | |
|---|---|---|---|---|
| *188* | CD304 | 1½p brt red vio | 15 | 18 |

**Engraved; Name Typographed**
***Perf. 11½x11***

| | | | | |
|---|---|---|---|---|
| *189* | CD305 | £1 dk bl | 17.50 | 19.00 |

### UPU Issue
Common Design Types

**Engr.; Name Typo. on 3p, 6p.**
**1949, Oct. 10** ***Perf. 13½, 11x11½***

| | | | | |
|---|---|---|---|---|
| *190* | CD306 | 1½p rose vio | 35 | 35 |
| *191* | CD307 | 3p indigo | 45 | 45 |
| *192* | CD308 | 6p gray | 80 | 80 |
| *193* | CD309 | 1sh olive | 1.65 | 1.65 |

### Coronation Issue
Common Design Type

**1953, June 2 Engr.** ***Perf. 13½x13***

| | | | | |
|---|---|---|---|---|
| *194* | CD312 | 1½p pur & blk | 15 | 12 |

Cape Lighthouse A27

Cotton Tree, Freetown — A28

Designs: 1p, Queen Elizabeth II Quay. 1½d, Piassava workers. 3p, Rice harvesting. 4p, Iron ore production, Marampa. 6p, Whale Bay, York Village. 1sh, Bullom boat. 1sh3p, Map of Sierra Leone and plane. 2sh6p, Orugu Bridge. 5sh, Kuranko chief. 10sh, Law Courts, Freetown. £1, Government House.

***Perf. 13 (A27), 13½ (A28)***
**1956, Jan. 2 Engr. Wmk. 4**
**Center in Black.**

| | | | | |
|---|---|---|---|---|
| *195* | A27 | ½p lt vio | 8 | 5 |
| *196* | A27 | 1p reseda | 8 | 5 |
| *197* | A27 | 1½p ultra | 12 | 8 |
| *198* | A28 | 2p lt brn | 10 | 5 |
| *199* | A28 | 3p ultra | 12 | 8 |
| **a** | | Perf 13x13½ | 3.50 | 2.25 |
| *200* | A27 | 4p gray bl | 16 | 8 |
| *201* | A27 | 6p violet | 20 | 8 |
| *202* | A28 | 1sh carmine | 25 | 20 |
| *203* | A27 | 1sh 3p gray brn | 48 | 16 |
| *204* | A28 | 2sh 6p brn org | 90 | 52 |
| *205* | A28 | 5sh green | 2.00 | 1.25 |
| *206* | A27 | 10sh red vio | 6.50 | 2.75 |
| *207* | A27 | £1 orange | 11.00 | 5.75 |
| | | *Nos. 195-207 (13)* | 21.99 | 11.10 |

### Independent State

Carrying Oil Palm Fruit — A29

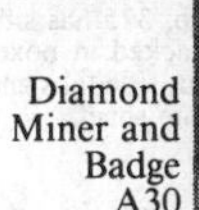

Diamond Miner and Badge A30

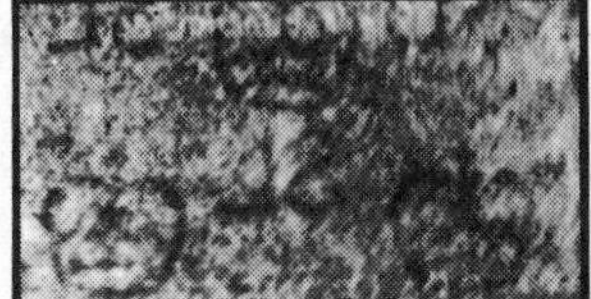
Wmk. 336- St. Edwards Crown & SL, Multiple

Designs (Badge and): 1½p, 5sh, Bundu mask. 2p, 10sh, Bishop Crowther and Old Fourah Bay College. 3p, 6p, Sir Milton Margai. 4p, 1sh3p, Lumley Beach, Freetown. £1, Bugler.

***Perf. 13x13½, 13½x13***
**1961, Apr. 27 Engr. Wmk. 336**

| | | | | |
|---|---|---|---|---|
| *208* | A29 | ½p bl grn & dk brn | 5 | 5 |
| *209* | A30 | 1p gray grn & brn org | 6 | 5 |
| *210* | A29 | 1½p grn & blk | 8 | 8 |
| *211* | A29 | 2p vio bl & blk | 8 | 6 |
| *212* | A30 | 3p brn org & ultra | 8 | 8 |
| *213* | A30 | 4p rose red & grnsh bl | 12 | 12 |
| *214* | A30 | 6p lil & gray | 16 | 12 |
| *215* | A29 | 1sh org & dk brn | 32 | 32 |
| *216* | A30 | 1sh3p vio & grnsh bl | 32 | 24 |
| *217* | A30 | 2sh6p blk & grn | 70 | 65 |
| *218* | A29 | 5sh rose red & blk | 1.40 | 1.25 |
| *219* | A29 | 10sh emer & blk | 2.75 | 2.75 |
| *220* | A29 | £1 car & yel | 4.75 | 4.75 |
| | | *Nos. 208-220 (13)* | 10.87 | 10.52 |

Sierra Leone's Independence.

Royal Charter, 1799 — A31

House of Representatives, Freetown, 1924 — A32

Designs: 4p, King's Yard Gate, Freetown, 1817. 1sh3p, Yacht "Britannia."

**1961, Nov. 25 Engr. Wmk. 336**

| | | | | |
|---|---|---|---|---|
| *221* | A31 | 3p ver & blk | 12 | 12 |
| *222* | A31 | 4p vio & blk | 22 | 22 |
| *223* | A32 | 6p org & blk | 30 | 30 |
| *224* | A32 | 1sh3p bl & blk | 60 | 60 |

Visit of Elizabeth II to Sierra Leone, Nov., 1961.

Malaria Eradication Emblem — A33

**1962, Apr. 7** ***Perf. 11x11½***

| | | | | |
|---|---|---|---|---|
| *225* | A33 | 3p crimson | 12 | 12 |
| *226* | A33 | 1sh3p green | 60 | 60 |

WHO drive to eradicate malaria.

Fireball Lily — A34

Jina Gbo — A35

Plants: 1½p, Stereospermum. 2p, Black-eyed Susan. 3p, Beniseed. 4p, Blushing hibiscus. 6p, Climbing lily. 1sh, Beautiful crinum. 1sh3p, Bluebells. 2sh6p, Broken hearts. 5sh, Ra-ponthi. 12sh, Blue plumbago. £1, African tulip tree.

**1963, Jan. 1 Photo.** ***Perf. 14***
**Flowers in Natural Colors**

| | | | | |
|---|---|---|---|---|
| *227* | A34 | ½p ol brn | 6 | 5 |
| *228* | A35 | 1p org ver & dk red | 8 | 5 |
| *229* | A34 | 1½p green | 8 | 6 |
| *230* | A35 | 2p lemon | 8 | 5 |
| *231* | A34 | 3p dk grn | 10 | 6 |
| *232* | A34 | 4p lt vio bl | 12 | 10 |
| *233* | A35 | 6p indigo | 16 | 12 |
| *234* | A34 | 1sh brt yel grn & red | 40 | 24 |
| *235* | A35 | 1sh3p dk yel grn | 48 | 24 |
| *236* | A34 | 2sh6p dk gray | 1.00 | 70 |
| *237* | A34 | 5sh dp vio | 1.50 | 1.25 |
| *238* | A34 | 10sh red lil | 3.25 | 2.75 |
| *239* | A35 | £1 brt bl | 8.50 | 6.75 |
| | | *Nos. 227-239 (13)* | 15.81 | 12.42 |

Wheat Emblem, Grain Bin and Threshing Machine A36

Design: 1sh3p, Bullom woman examining onion crop.

***Perf. 11½x11***
**1963, Mar. 21 Engr. Wmk. 336**

| | | | | |
|---|---|---|---|---|
| *240* | A36 | 3p org yel & blk | 15 | 15 |
| *241* | A36 | 1sh3p grn & brn | 65 | 65 |

"Freedom from Hunger" campaign of the FAO.

Nos. 195, 197 and 199 Surcharged in Red, Brown, Orange, Violet or Blue:

| | |
|---|---|
| 2ND YEAR OF INDEPENDENCE 19 PROGRESS 63 DEVELOPMENT **3d.** on A27 | **2nd Year Independence Progress Development 1963** **10d.** on A28 |

***Perf. 13, 13½***
**1963, Apr. 27 Wmk. 4**
**Center in Black**

| | | | | |
|---|---|---|---|---|
| *242* | A27 | 3p on ½p lt vio (R) | 9 | 9 |
| *243* | A27 | 4p on 1½p ultra (Br) | 10 | 10 |
| *244* | A27 | 6p on ½p lt vio (O) | 10 | 10 |
| *245* | A28 | 10p on 3p ultra (R) | 30 | 30 |
| *246* | A28 | 1sh6p on 3p ultra (V) | 40 | 40 |
| *247* | A28 | 3sh6p on 3p ultra (Bl) | 90 | 90 |
| | | *Nos. 242-247 (6)* | 1.89 | 1.89 |

Type "a" exists in two settings, varying in the width of the line "19 Progress 63". In each sheet of 60, this line measures 19½-21mm. on 55 stamps, and 17½-18mm. on 5 stamps. See Nos. C1-C7.

Centenary Emblem — A37

Design: 6p, Red Cross. 1sh3p, Centenary Emblem with curved-lines background.

***Perf. 11x11½***
**1963, Nov. 1 Engr. Wmk. 336**

| | | | | |
|---|---|---|---|---|
| *248* | A37 | 3p pur & red | 9 | 9 |
| *249* | A37 | 6p blk & red | 15 | 15 |
| *250* | A37 | 1sh3p dk grn & red | 32 | 32 |

Centenary of International Red Cross.

Nos. 199, 197, 216 and 195 Overprinted or Surcharged in Pink, Red, Violet or Brown

**1853–1859–1963**
**Oldest Postal Service**
**Newest G.P.O.**
**in West Africa**

**4d.**

***Perf. 13, 13½, 13½x13***
**1963, Nov. 4 Engr. Wmk. 4**
**Center in Black except No. 254**

| | | | | |
|---|---|---|---|---|
| *251* | A28 | 3p ultra (P) | 6 | 6 |
| *252* | A27 | 4p on 1½p ultra (R) | 9 | 9 |
| *253* | A27 | 9p on 1½p ultra (V) | 22 | 22 |
| *254* | A30 | 1sh on 1sh3p vio & grnsh bl (R) | 25 | 25 |
| *255* | A27 | 1sh6p on ½p lt vio (P) | 35 | 35 |
| *256* | A28 | 2sh on 3p ultra (Br) | 45 | 45 |
| | | *Nos. 251-256,C8-C13(69 (12)* | 15.32 | 15.32 |

Oldest postal service (1st stamps in 1859) and the newest GPO in West Africa. Overprint in 5 lines on Nos. 251 and 256. A number of surcharge varieties and errors exist.

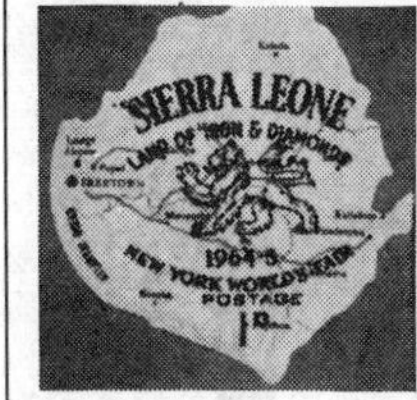

Map and Lion of Sierra Leone — A38

**Engraved and Lithographed**
**1964, Feb. 10 Unwmk.** ***Imperf.***
**Self-adhesive**

| | | | | |
|---|---|---|---|---|
| *257* | A38 | 1p multi | 5 | 5 |
| *258* | A38 | 3p multi | 6 | 6 |
| *259* | A38 | 4p multi | 8 | 8 |
| *260* | A38 | 6p multi | 10 | 10 |
| *261* | A38 | 1sh multi | 22 | 22 |
| *262* | A38 | 2sh multi | 42 | 42 |
| *263* | A38 | 5sh multi | 1.10 | 1.10 |
| | | *Nos. 257-263,C14-C20 (14)* | 7.01 | 7.01 |

New York World's Fair, 1964-65.

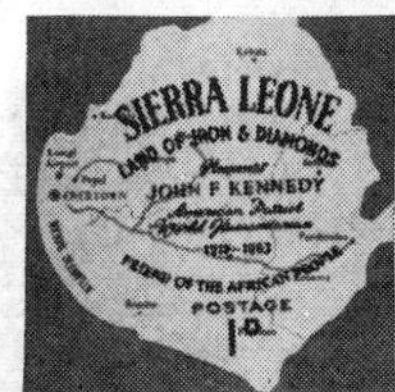

"John F. Kennedy, American Patriot, World Humanitarian" — A39

**1964, May 11**
**Self-adhesive**

| | | | | |
|---|---|---|---|---|
| *264* | A39 | 1p multi | 5 | 5 |
| *265* | A39 | 3p multi | 6 | 6 |
| *266* | A39 | 4p multi | 8 | 8 |
| *267* | A39 | 6p multi | 10 | 10 |
| *268* | A39 | 1sh multi | 22 | 22 |
| *269* | A39 | 2sh multi | 42 | 42 |
| *270* | A39 | 5sh multi | 1.10 | 1.10 |
| | | *Nos. 264-270,C21-C27 (14)* | 7.01 | 7.01 |

Issues of 1961-63 Surcharged in Red, Black, Dark Blue, Violet or Orange.

**1964, Aug. 4**

| | | | | |
|---|---|---|---|---|
| *271* | A35 | 1c on 6p (#233) (R) | 5 | 5 |
| *272* | A31 | 2c on 3p (#221) | 6 | 6 |
| *273* | A34 | 3c on 3p (#231) | 8 | 8 |
| *274* | A29 | 5c on ½p (#208) (DB) | 15 | 15 |
| *275* | A36 | 8c on 3p (#240) (R) | 20 | 20 |
| *276* | A35 | 10c on 1sh3p (#235) (R) | 28 | 25 |
| *277* | A34 | 15c on 1sh (#234) | 40 | 40 |
| *278* | A32 | 25c on 6p (#223) (V) | 60 | 60 |
| *279* | A30 | 50c on 2sh6p (#217) (O) | 1.20 | 1.20 |
| | | *Nos. 271-279 (9)* | 3.02 | 2.99 |

Issues of 1961-64 Surcharged in Black or Gold

**1965, Jan. 20**

| | | | | |
|---|---|---|---|---|
| *280* | A30 | 1c on 3p (#212) | 5 | 5 |
| *281* | A39 | 2c on 1p (#264) | 6 | 6 |
| *282* | A39 | 4c on 3p (#265) | 8 | 8 |

*283* A35 5c on 2p (#230) 10 10
*284* A34 1 le on 5sh (G) (#237) 2.50 2.50
*285* A29 2 le on £1 (#220) 5.25 5.25
*Nos. 280-285 (6)* 8.04 8.04

The surcharges on Nos. 284-285 are given in numerals and spelled out in two lines; numeral on Nos. 280-283.

### Issues of 1961-64 Surcharged in Red, Black, Orange, Blue or Pink

**1965, Apr.**

*286* A29 1c on 1½p (R) (#210) 5 5
*287* A39 2c on 3p (#265) 12 12
*288* A38 2c on 4p (#259) 12 12
*289* A35 3c on 1p (#228) 12 12
*290* A29 3c on 2p (O) (#211) 10 10
*291* A30 5c on 1sh3p (O) (#216) 12 12
*292* A39 15c on 6p (#267) 1.00 1.00
*293* A39 15c on 1sh (O) (#268) 1.75 1.75
*294* A30 20c on 6p (O) (#214) 40 40
*295* A35 25c on 6p (R) (#233) 55 55
*296* A30 50c on 3p (R) (#212) 1.25 1.25
*297* A38 60c on 5sh (Bl) (#263) 2.75 2.75
*298* A39 1 le on 4p (P) (#266) 3.50 3.50
*299* A29 2 le on £1 (Bl) (#220) 6.25 6.25
*Nos. 286-299 (14)* 18.08 18.08

Additional surcharges exist: "1c" on Nos. 260, 262, 269-270. See note after No. C41 for airmails. Value $4 each.

### Nos. 228, 231, 234, 235, 232, 237 Surcharged

Designs of Surcharge: Nos. 301, 304, Sir Milton Margai. Nos. 302, 305, Sir Winston Churchill.

**Wmk. 336**

**1965, May 19 Photo. *Perf. 14***

*300* A35 2c on 1p multi 6 6
*301* A34 3c on 3p multi 8 8
*302* A34 10c on 1sh multi 30 30
*303* A35 20c on 1sh3p multi 55 55
*304* A34 50c on 4p multi 1.25 1.25
*305* A34 75c on 5sh multi 2.25 2.25
*Nos. 300-305,C37-C41 (11)* 13.72 13.72

Cola Nut and Plant — A40

Coat of Arms — A41

**Typographed; Embossed on Silver Foil**

**1965 Unwmk. *Imperf.***

**Self-adhesive**

*310* A40 1c multi 15 15
*311* A40 2c multi 20 20
*312* A40 3c multi 20 20
*313* A40 4c multi 30 30
*314* A40 5c multi 30 30

**Engr.; Embossed on Paper**

*315* A41 20c multi, *cream* 75 60
*316* A41 50c multi, *cream* 2.00 1.75
*Nos. 310-316,C53-C557 (10)* 6.75 6.75

Various advertisements printed on peelable paper backing. Nos. 310-316 have side tabs for handling and come packed in boxes of 100. Nos. 310-312 and 314 were released during November due to a stamp shortage; official release date for set, Dec. 17, 1965. See Nos. 338-356, C97.

### Nos. 197-198, and 232-234, 236 Surcharged with New Value in Black or Ultramarine and Overprinted: "FIVE YEARS / INDEPENDENCE / 1961-1966"

**1966, Apr. 27 Wmk. 4, 336**

*317* A35 1c on 6p multi 5 5
*318* A34 2c on 4p multi 6 6
*319* A27 3c on 1½p ultra & blk (U) 10 10
*320* A34 8c on 1sh multi (U) 18 18
*321* A34 10c on 2sh6p multi (U) 22 22
*322* A28 20c on 2p lt brn (U) 45 45
*Nos. 317-322,C56-C60 (11)* 5.71 5.71

5th anniv. of independence. The surcharge on No. 317 includes an "X" over old denomination.

Lion's Head Coin — A42

Designs: 2c, 3c, ¼ Golde coin. 5c, 8c, ½ Golde coin. 25c, 1 le, 1 Golde coin. (3c, 8c, 1 le, Map of Sierra Leone.)

**Litho.; Embossed on Gilt Foil**

**1966, Nov. 12 Unwmk. *Imperf.***

**Self-adhesive**

Diameter: 2c, 3c, 38mm.; 5c, 8c, 54mm.; 25c, 1 le, 82mm.

*323* A42 2c org & dp plum 5 5
*324* A42 3c red lil & emer 6 6
*325* A42 5c vio bl & red org 8 8
*326* A42 8c blk & Prus bl 12 12
*327* A42 25c emer & vio 38 38
*328* A42 1 le red & org 1.75 1.75
*Nos. 323-328,C61-C66 (12)* 7.79 7.79

1st gold coinage of Sierra Leone. Advertising printed on paper backing.

### Nos. 297-298, 303-305 and 316 Surcharged in Red, Silver, Violet, Green, Blue or Black:

**12½** on A34, A35 **17½** on A38, A39

**=17½** on A41

**1967, Dec. 2**

*329* A34 6½c on 75c on 5sh (R) 30 30
*330* A34 7½c on 75c on 5sh (S) 30 30
*331* A34 9½c on 50c on 4p (G) 40 40
*332* A35 12½c on 20c on 1sh3p (V) 50 50
*333* A39 17½c on 1 le on 4p (Bl) 3.50 3.50
*334* A41 17½c on 50c (Bk) 3.50 3.50
*335* A38 18½c on 60c on 5sh (Bk) 10.00 10.00
*336* A39 18½c on 1 le on 4p (Bk) 3.50 3.50
*337* A41 25c on 50c (Bk) 1.00 1.00
*Nos. 329-337,C67-C69 (12)* 24.90 24.90

Self-adhesive & Imperf.

Nos. 338-421 are self-adhesive and imperforate.

### Cola Nut Type of 1965

**Typographed; Embossed on White Paper**

**1967-68 Unwmk.**

**White Numeral Tablet**

*338* A40 ½c brt car, grn & yel 15 15
*339* A40 1c brt car, grn & yel 8 8
*340* A40 1½c org, grn & yel 12 12
*341* A40 2c brt car, grn & yel 25 25
*342* A40 2½c emer, bl grn & yel 40 40
*343* A40 3c brt car, grn & yel 25 25
*344* A40 3½c ol, rose & ultra 25 25
*345* A40 4½c gray ol, grn & yel 40 40
*346* A40 5c brt car, grn & yel 40 40
*347* A40 5½c red brn, grn & yel 40 40
*Nos. 338-347 (10)* 2.70 2.70

Advertisements printed on peelable backing except on the 2c, 3c, 3½c and 5c.

**Colored Numeral Tablet**

*348* A40 ½c brt car, grn & yel 8 8
*349* A40 1c brt car, grn & yel 8 8
*350* A40 2c pink, brn & car 20 20
*351* A40 2c brt car, grn & yel 75 60
*352* A40 2½c bl grn, vio & org 1.00 75
*353* A40 2½c emer, bl grn & yel 30 20
*354* A40 3c brt car, grn & yel 20 20
*355* A40 3½c lil rose, grn & yel 30 30
*356* A40 4c brt car, grn & yel 25 25
*Nos. 348-356 (9)* 3.16 2.66

Nos. 344, 348-354 issued in 1968.

Advertisements printed on peelable backing on the 3½c and 4c.

Map of Africa Showing Rhodesia A43

Designs: Each denomination shows map of Africa with map of one of the following countries—Portuguese Guinea, South Africa, Mozambique, Rhodesia, South West Africa or Angola.

**1968, Sept. 25 Unwmk. Litho.**

*357* A43 ½c multi 5 5
*358* A43 2c multi 10 10
*359* A43 2½c multi 10 10
*360* A43 3½c multi 20 20
*361* A43 10c multi 40 40
*362* A43 11½c multi 45 45
*363* A43 15c multi 60 60
*Nos. 357-363 (7)* 1.90 1.90
7 Strips of 6 (one of each design) (42) 11.40

International Human Rights Year. Sheets of 30 (6x5) have 5 horizontal rows containing one stamp of each design. Advertisements printed on peelable backing. See Nos. C72-C78.

### No. 316 Surcharged

MEXICO 1968 OLYMPIC PARTICIPATION

*6½

**Engraved; Embossed on Paper**

**1968, Nov. 30**

*364* A41 6½c on 50c multi 15 15
*365* A41 17½c on 50c multi 35 35
*366* A41 22½c on 50c multi 50 50
*367* A41 28½c on 50c multi 65 65
*368* A41 50c on 50c multi 1.10 1.10
*Nos. 364-368,C79-C83 (10)* 5.70 5.70

19th Olympic Games, Mexico City, Oct. 12-27.

Sierra Leone Type A1, 1859 A44

Designs: 2c, Type A40, 2c, 1965. 3½c, No. 220. 5c, No. 315. 12½c, No. 189. 1 le. Type A9, #2, 1912.

**1969, Mar. 1 Litho.**

*369* A44 1c multi 5 5
*370* A44 2c multi 5 5
*371* A44 3½c multi 10 10
*372* A44 5c multi 15 15
*373* A44 12½c multi 40 40
*374* A44 1 le multi 5.00 5.00
*Nos. 369-374,C84-C89 (12)* 27.95 27.95

5th anniv. of free-form self-adhesive postage stamps. Various advertisements printed on peelable paper backing. No. 369 has side tab for handling and comes packed in boxes of 50. Nos. 370-374 are without side tabs and come 20 stamps attached to one sheet.

Globe, Freighter, Flags of Sierra Leone and Japan — A45

Map of Europe and Africa, Freighter, Flags of Sierra Leone and Netherlands — A46

Anvil Shape with Flags of Sierra Leone and: 3½c, Union Jack. 10c, 50c, West Germany. 18½c, Netherlands.

**1969, July 10**

*375* A45 1c multi 5 5
*376* A46 2c multi 5 5
*377* A46 3½c multi 8 8
*378* A46 10c multi 22 22
*379* A46 18½c multi 40 40
*380* A46 50c multi 1.10 1.10
*Nos. 375-380,C90-C95 (12)* 9.95 9.95

Completion of the Pepel Port iron ore carrier terminal. Various advertisements printed on peelable paper backing. No. 375 has side tab for handling and comes packed in boxes of 50. Nos. 376-380 are without side tabs and come 20 stamps attached to one sheet.

African Development Bank Emblem — A47

**Lithographed; Gold Impressed**

**1969, Sept. 10**

*381* A47 3½c lt bl, grn & gold 30 30

5th anniv. of the African Development Bank. Advertising printed on peelable paper backing, 20 imperf. stamps to a sheet of backing, roulette 10. See No. C96.

Diamond and Boy Scout Emblem A48

**1969, Dec. 6** **Litho.**

*382* A48 1c multi 8 5
*383* A48 2c multi 12 8
*384* A48 3½c multi 20 16
*385* A48 4½c multi 24 20
*386* A48 5c multi 32 28
*387* A48 75c multi 10.00 8.00
*Nos. 382-387,C100-C105 (12)* 123.29 90.85

60th anniv. of the Sierra Leone Boy Scouts. Various advertising printed on peelable paper backing. No. 382 has side tab for handling and comes packed in boxes of 100. Nos. 383-387 are without side tabs and come 20 stamps attached to one sheet.

EXPO '70 Emblems, Torii, Maps of Sierra Leone and Japan — A49

**1970, June 22**

*388* A49 2c blk, org & car 5 5
*389* A49 3½c car, yel grn & blk 7 7
*390* A49 10c bl, red & blk 20 20
*391* A49 12½c multi 28 28
*392* A49 20c multi 45 45
*393* A49 45c multi 1.00 1.00
*Nos. 388-393,C112-C117 (12)* 12.71 12.71

EXPO '70 Intl. Exhib., Osaka, Japan, Mar. 15-Sept. 13. Various advertising printed on peelable paper backing.

Diamond — A50

Palm Kernel — A51

**Lithographed and Embossed**

**1970, Oct. 3** **Unwmk.**

**Light Blue Background**

*394* A50 1c car & blk 8 8
*395* A50 1½c brt grn & car 10 10
*396* A50 2c lil & yel grn 12 12
*397* A50 2½c ocher & dk bl 15 15
*398* A50 3c vio bl & org red 20 20
*399* A50 3½c dk bl & grn 25 25
*400* A50 4c ol & ultra 25 25
*401* A50 5c blk & lil 30 30

**Orange Brown Background**

*402* A51 6c brt grn 30 30
*403* A51 7c rose lil 40 40
*404* A51 8½c orange 45 45
*405* A51 9c lilac 45 45
*406* A51 10c dk bl 50 50
*407* A51 11½c blue 65 65
*408* A51 18½c yel grn 1.00 1.00
*Nos. 394-408,C118-C124 (22)* 25.60 22.40

Advertisements printed on peelable paper backing. Packed in boxes of 500.

Sewa Diadem in Jewelry Box — A52

**1970, Dec. 30**

*409* A52 2c multi 8 8
*410* A52 3½c multi 12 12
*411* A52 10c multi 35 35
*412* A52 12½c multi 45 45
*413* A52 40c multi 1.50 1.35
*414* A52 1 le multi 7.50 5.00
*Nos. 409-414,C125-C130 (12)* 39.05 30.40

Diamond industry. Advertisement printed on peelable paper backing. Sheets of 20.

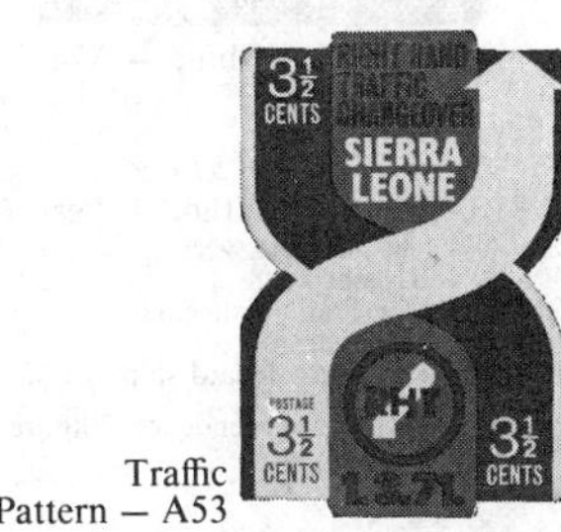


Traffic Pattern — A53

**1971, Mar. 1** **Litho.**

*415* A53 3½c org & vio bl 25 25

Right hand traffic change-over. See No. C131. Advertisements printed on peelable paper backing.

Flag and Lion's Head A54

**Lithographed; Embossed in Silver**

**1971, Apr. 27**

*416* A54 2c pale grn & multi 5 5
*417* A54 3½c multi 7 7
*418* A54 10c multi 20 20
*419* A54 12½c yel & multi 24 24
*420* A54 40c multi 90 90
*421* A54 1 le multi 2.00 2.00
*Nos. 416-421,C137-C142 (12)* 13.64 13.64

10th anniversary of independence. Advertisements printed on peelable paper backing. Stamps are in shape of Sierra Leone map.

Pres. Siaka Stevens — A55

**1972** **Litho.** ***Perf. 13***

*422* A55 1c pink & multi 5 5
*423* A55 2c vio & multi 5 5
*424* A55 4c lt ultra & multi 8 8
*425* A55 5c buff & multi 9 9
*426* A55 7c rose & multi 15 15
*427* A55 10c ol & multi 18 18
*428* A55 15c emer & multi 25 25
*429* A55 18c yel & multi 32 32
*430* A55 20c lt bl & multi 38 38
*431* A55 25c org & multi 45 45
*432* A55 50c brt grn & multi 95 95
*433* A55 1 le multi 1.75 1.75
*434* A55 2 le red org & multi 3.50 3.50
*435* A55 5 le multi 9.00 9.00
*Nos. 422-435 (14)* 17.20 17.20

Shades from later printings are found on several denominations including 1c, 2c, 7c, 10c, 1 le, 2 le.

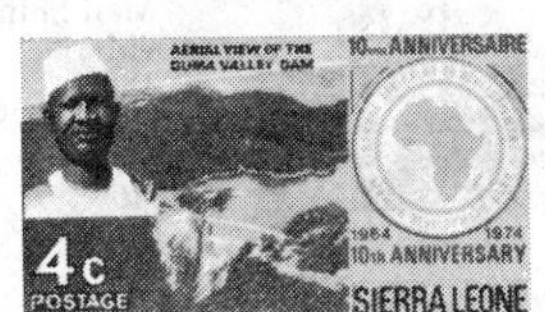


Guma Valley Dam and Bank Emblem — A56

**1975, Jan. 14** **Litho.** ***Perf. 13½***

*436* A56 4c multi *135.00 90.00*

African Development Bank, 10th anniversary. See No. C143.

Pres. Siaka Stevens and Opening of Congo Bridge — A57

**1975, Aug. 24** **Litho.** ***Perf. 13x13½***

*437* A57 5c multi *11.00 11.00*

Congo Bridge opening and Pres. Siaka Stevens' 70th birthday. See No. C144.

Pres. Tolbert and Stevens, Hands across Mano River — A58

**1975, Oct. 3** **Litho.** ***Perf. 13x13½***

*438* A58 4c multi 1.50 1.50

Mano River Union Agreement between Liberia and Sierra Leone, signed Oct. 3, 1973. See No. C145.

Mohammed Ali Jinnah, Flags of Sierra Leone and Pakistan A59

Elizabeth II A60

**1977, Jan. 28** **Litho.** ***Perf. 13 rough***

*439* A59 30c multi 90 90

Mohammed Ali Jinnah (1876-1948), First Governor General of Pakistan.

**1977, Nov. 28** **Litho.** ***Perf. 12½x12***

*440* A60 5c multi 9 9
*441* A60 1 le multi 1.75 1.75

25th anniv. of the reign of Elizabeth II.

Fourah Bay College — A61

Design: 20c, Old College (vert.).

***Perf. 12x12½, 12½x12***

**1977, Dec. 19** **Litho.**

*442* A61 5c multi 10 10
*443* A61 20c multi 35 35

Fourah Bay College, Mt. Aureol, Freetown, founded 1827.

St. Edward's Crown and Scepters — A62

Designs: 50c, Elizabeth II in coronation coach. 1 le, Elizabeth II and Prince Philip on coronation day.

**1978, Sept. 14** **Litho.** ***Perf. 14½x14***

*444* A62 5c multi 6 6
*445* A62 50c multi 60 60
*446* A62 1 le multi 1.25 1.25

25th anniv. of coronation of Elizabeth II.

Fig Tree Blue A63

Butterflies: 15c, Narrow blue-banded swallowtail. 25c, Pirate. 1 le, African giant swallowtail.

**1979, Apr. 9** **Litho.** ***Perf. 14½***

*447* A63 5c multi 14 14
*448* A63 15c multi 38 38
*449* A63 25c multi 65 65
*450* A63 1 le multi 2.75 2.75

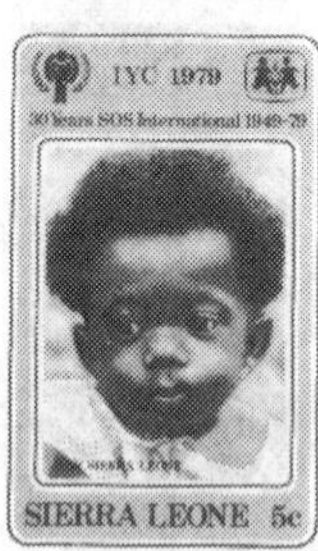


Child, IYC and SOS Emblems — A64

Designs (Emblems and): 27c, Girl and infant. 1 l, Mother and infant.

*Perf. 14x13½*

**1979, Aug. 13 Litho. Wmk. 373**

*451* A64 5c multi 10 10
*452* A64 27c multi 55 55
*453* A64 1 le multi 2.25 2.25
*a* Souvenir sheet 2.50 2.50

International Year of the Child and 30th anniversary of SOS villages (villages for homeless children). No. 453a contains No. 453; multicolored margin shows houses, children and women. Size: 115x84mm.

Presidents Stevens and Tolbert, Pigeon Post, Mano River — A65

**1979, Oct. 3 *Perf. 13½***

*454* A65 5c multi 8 8
*455* A65 22c multi 35 35
*456* A65 27c multi 45 45
*457* A65 35c multi 55 55
*458* A65 1 le multi 1.65 1.65
*a* Souvenir sheet 1.75 1.75
*Nos. 454-458 (5)* 3.08 3.08

Mano River Union, 5th anniversary; Postal Union, 1st anniversary. No. 458a contains No. 458. Multicolored margin shows flags of Sierra Leone and Liberia.

Sierra Leone No. 9, Hill — A66

**1979, Dec. 19 Litho. *Perf. 14½x14***

*459* A66 10c *Gt. Britain #6* 20 20
*460* A66 15c *shown* 28 28
*461* A66 50c *Sierra Leone #220* 1.00 1.00

**Souvenir Sheet**

*462* A66 1 le *Sierra Leone #119* 2.00 2.00

Sir Rowland Hill (1795-1879), originator of penny postage. No. 462 has black & red margin showing Penny Black. Size: 90x99½mm.

Touraco A67

**1980, Jan. 29 *Perf. 14***

*463* A67 1c *shown* 5 5
*464* A67 2c *Olive-bellied sunbird* 5 5
*465* A67 3c *Black-headed oriole* 8 8
*466* A67 5c *Spur-winged goose* 8 8
*467* A67 7c *White-bellied didric cuckoo* 10 10
*468* A67 10c *Gray parrot, vert.* 16 16
*469* A67 15c *African blue quail, vert.* 25 25
*470* A67 20c *West African wood owl, vert.* 32 32
*471* A67 30c *Blue plantain eater, vert.* 50 50
*472* A67 40c *Nigerian blue-breasted kingfisher, vert.* 65 65
*473* A67 50c *Black crake, vert.* 90 90
*474* A67 1 le *Hartlaub's duck* 1.65 1.65
*475* A67 2 le *Black bee-eater* 3.25 3.25
*476* A67 5 le *Denham's bustard* 8.50 8.50
*Nos. 463-476 (14)* 16.54 16.54

Reissues: Nos. 464-476 inscribed 1982. Nos. 463-464, 466, 468-473, 475-476 inscribed 1983.

Rotary Intl., 75th Anniv. A68

**1980, Feb. 23 *Perf. 14***

*477* A68 5c org & multi 8 8
*478* A68 27c red & multi 42 42
*479* A68 50c grn & multi 85 85
*480* A68 1 le bl & multi 1.65 1.65

Mail Ship "Maria," 1884, London '80 Emblem A69

**1980, May 6 Litho. *Perf. 14***

*481* A69 6c *shown* 9 9
*482* A69 31c *"Tarquah," 1902* 45 45
*483* A69 50c *"Aureol," 1951* 75 75
*484* A69 1 le *"Africa Palm," 1974* 1.50 1.50

London 80 Intl. Phil. Exhib., May 6-14.

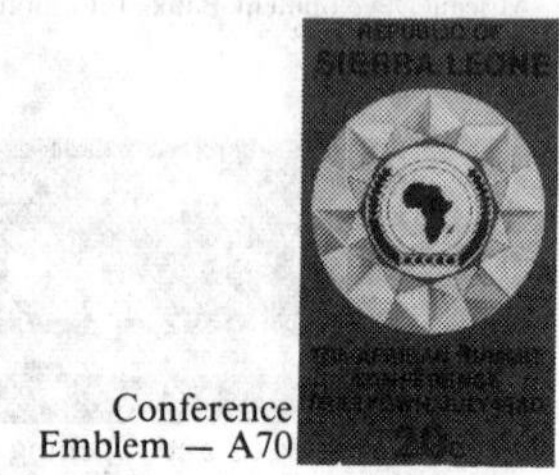


Conference Emblem — A70

**1980, July 1 Litho. *Perf. 14½***

*485* A70 20c multi 25 25
*486* A70 1 le multi 1.25 1.25

17th African Summit Conference, Freetown, July 1-4.

Small Striped Swordtail — A71

**1980, Oct. 6 Litho. *Perf. 14***

*487* A71 5c *shown* 8 8
*488* A71 27c *Pearl charaxes* 45 45
*489* A71 35c *White barred charaxes* 55 55
*490* A71 1 le *Zaddach's forester* 1.65 1.65

Freetown Airport — A72

**1980, Dec. 5 Litho. *Perf. 13½***

*491* A72 6c *shown* 8 8
*492* A72 26c *Mammy Yoko Hotel* 30 30
*493* A72 31c *Freetown Cotton Tree* 35 35
*494* A72 40c *Beindomgo Falls* 50 50
*495* A72 50c *Water skiing* 60 60
*496* A72 1 le *Elephant* 1.25 1.25
*Nos. 491-496 (6)* 3.08 3.08

Servals A73

Cats and Kittens: No. 498, Serval kittens. Nos. 499-500, African golden cats. Nos. 501-502, Leopards. Nos. 503-504, Lions. Stamps of same denomination se-tenant in continuous design.

**1981, Feb. 23 Litho. *Perf. 14***

*497* A73 6c multi 10 10
*498* A73 6c multi 10 10
*499* A73 31c multi 50 50
*500* A73 31c multi 50 50
*501* A73 50c multi 85 85
*502* A73 50c multi 85 85
*503* A73 1 le multi 1.65 1.65
*504* A73 1 le multi 1.65 1.65
*Nos. 497-504 (8)* 6.20 6.20

Ambulance Clinic — A74

**Wmk. 373**

**1981, April 18 Litho. *Perf. 14½***

*505* A74 6c Soldiers, vert. 10 10
*506* A74 31c shown 50 50
*507* A74 40c Traffic policeman, vert. 65 65
*508* A74 1 le Coast Guard ship 1.65 1.65

Anniversaries: independence, 20th; republic, 10th.

**Royal Wedding Issue**
Common Design Type

**1981 Litho. *Perf. 12, 14***

*509* CD331 31c Bouquet 60 60
*510* CD331 35c Sandringham 70 70
*511* CD331 45c Charles 95 95
*512* CD331 60c Charles 1.25 1.25
*513* CD331 70c like 35c 1.50 1.50
*514* CD331 1 le Couple 2.00 2.00
*515* CD331 1.30 le Charles 2.50 2.50
*516* CD331 1.50 le Couple 3.00 3.00
*517* CD331 2 le Couple 4.00 4.00
*Nos. 509-517 (9)* 16.50 16.50

**Souvenir Sheet**

*518* CD331 3 le Royal landau 6.25 6.25

31c, 45c, 1 le, 3 le issued July 22, perf. 14. 35c, 60c, 1.50 le issued in sheets of 5 plus label; perf. 12, Sept. 9. 70c, 1.30 le, 2 le issued in booklets only, perf. 14.

Soccer Player — A75

**Wmk. 373**

**1981, Sept. 30 Litho. *Perf. 14***

*519* A75 6c shown 9 9
*520* A75 31c Boys planting trees 45 45
*521* A75 1 le Duke of Edinburgh 1.50 1.50
*522* A75 1 le Pres. Stevens 1.50 1.50

Duke of Edinburgh's Awards and Pres. Steven's Awards, 25th anniv.

Pineapples — A76

Woman Tending Rice Plants A77

***Perf. 14, 14½ (A77)***

**1981 Litho. Wmk. 373**

*523* A76 6c shown 10 10
*524* A77 6c Peanuts for export 10 10
*525* A76 31c Peanuts 50 50
*526* A77 31c Crushing, eating cassava 50 50
*527* A76 50c Cassava fruits 85 85
*528* A77 50c shown 85 85
*529* A76 1 le Rice plants 1.65 1.65
*530* A77 1 le Men tending pineapple plants 1.65 1.65
*Nos. 523-530 (8)* 6.20 6.20

World Food Day. Issue dates: Nos. 523, 525, 527, 529, Oct. 16; others, Nov. 2.

**Princess Diana Issue**
Common Design Type

**1982, July Litho. *Perf. 14½***

*531* CD332 31c Caernarvon Castle 50 50
*532* CD332 50c Honeymoon 85 85
*533* CD332 2 le Wedding 3.00 3.00

**Souvenir Sheet**

*534* CD332 3 le Diana 4.75 4.75

No. 534 has multicolored margin showing family tree, Charles II. Size: 102x72mm.
Also issued in sheetlets of 5 + label.

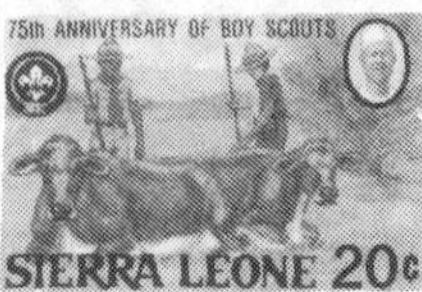


Scouting Year A78

**1982, Aug. 23 *Perf. 14***

*535* A78 20c Studying animal husbandry 32 32
*536* A78 50c Botanical study 85 85
*537* A78 1 le Baden-Powell 1.65 1.65
*538* A78 2 le Fishing at campsite 3.00 3.00

**Souvenir Sheet**

*539* A78 3 le Raising flag 4.75 4.75

No. 539 has multicolored margin continuing design. Size: 101x71mm.

Nos. 509-512, 514, 516, 518 Surcharged

**1982, Aug. 30** **Wmk. 373**

*540* CD331 50c on 31c 90 90
*541* CD331 50c on 35c 90 90
*542* CD331 50c on 45c 90 90
*543* CD331 50c on 60c 90 90
*544* CD331 90c on 1 le 1.40 1.40
*545* CD331 2 le on 1.50 le 3.25 3.25
*Nos. 540-545 (6)* 8.25 8.25

**Souvenir Sheet**

*546* CD331 3.50 le on 3 le 6.00 6.00

1982 World Cup — A79

Designs: Various soccer players.

**1982, Sept. 7**

*547* A79 20c multi 32 32
*548* A79 30c multi 45 45
*549* A79 1 le multi 1.65 1.65
*550* A79 2 le multi 3.00 3.00

**Souvenir Sheet**

*551* A79 3 le multi 4.75 4.75

No. 551 has green and black margin showing soccer balls. Size: 92x75mm.

Nos. 531-534 Overprinted: "ROYAL BABY/ 21.6.82"

**1982, Oct. 15** **Litho.** ***Perf. 14½***

*552* CD332 31c multi 50 50
*553* CD332 50c multi 85 85
*554* CD332 2 le multi 3.00 3.00

**Souvenir Sheet**

*555* CD332 3 le multi 4.75 4.75

Birth of Prince William of Wales, June 21. Also issued in sheetlets of 5 + label.

George Washington — A80

Designs: Various paintings of Washington. 31c, 1 le vert.

**1982, Oct. 30** **Litho.** ***Perf. 14***

*556* A80 6c multi 9 9
*557* A80 31c multi 45 45
*558* A80 50c multi 75 75
*559* A80 1 le multi 1.50 1.50

**Souvenir Sheet**

*560* A80 2 le multi 3.00 3.00

Size of No. 560: 104x71mm.

Nos. 547-551 Overprinted with Finalists and Score.

**1982, Nov. 9** ***Perf. 14***

*561* A79 20c multi 30 30
*562* A79 30c multi 42 42
*563* A79 1 le multi 1.50 1.50
*564* A79 2 le multi 2.75 2.75

**Souvenir Sheet**

*565* A79 3 le multi 4.25 4.25

Itlay's victory in 1982 World Cup.

Christmas 1982 Christmas 1982 — A81

Stained-glass Windows, St. George's Cathedral, Freetown.

**1982, Nov. 18** ***Perf. 14***

*566* A81 6c Temptation of Christ 10 10
*567* A81 31c Baptism of Christ 50 50
*568* A81 50c Annunciation 85 85
*569* A81 1 le Nativity 1.65 1.65

**Souvenir Sheet**

*570* A81 2 le Mary and Joseph 3.25 3.25

No. 570 has multicolored margin showing entire East Window. Size: 75x105mm.

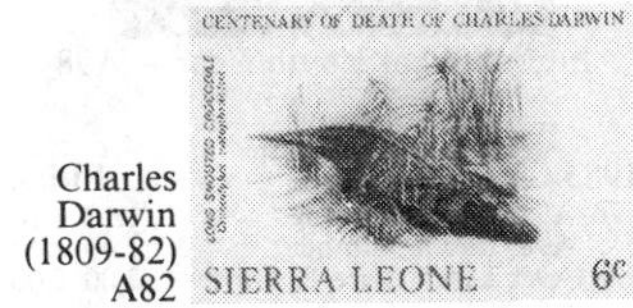


Charles Darwin (1809-82) A82

**1982, Dec. 10**

*571* A82 6c Long-snouted crocodile 8 8
*572* A82 31c Rainbow lizard 40 40
*573* A82 50c River turtle 70 70
*574* A82 1 le Chameleon 1.40 1.40

**Souvenir Sheet**

*575* A82 2 le Royal python, vert. 2.75 2.75

500th Birth Anniv. of Raphael — A83

School of Athens, Fresco, Vatican. Nos. 576-579 show details.

**1983, Jan. 28** **Litho.** ***Perf. 14***

*576* A83 6c Diogenes 9 9
*577* A83 31c Euclid, Ptolemy 45 45
*578* A83 50c Euclid and his Students 75 75
*579* A83 2 le Pythagoras, Heraclitus 3.00 3.00

**Souvenir Sheet**

*580* A83 3 le Entire painting 4.50 4.50

Size of No. 580: 127x102mm.

**Commonwealth Day**
Common Design Type

**1983, Mar. 14** **Litho.** ***Perf. 14***

*581* CD334 6c Agricultural training 9 9
*582* CD334 10c Tourism development 15 15
*583* CD334 50c Broadcast training 75 75
*584* CD334 1 le Airport services 1.50 1.50

25th Anniv. of Economic Commission for Africa — A84

**1983, Apr. 29** **Litho.** ***Perf. 13½x13***

*585* A84 1 le multi 1.40 1.40

Endangered Chimpanzees, World Wildlife Fund Emblem — A85

Various chimpanzees from Outamba-Kilimi Natl. Park. 10c, 31c vert.

**1983, May** **Litho.** ***Perf. 14***

*586* A85 6c multi 8 8
*587* A85 10c multi 10 10
*588* A85 31c multi 40 40
*589* A85 60c multi 80 80

**Souvenir Sheet**

*590* A85 3 le Elephants 4.00 4.00

No. 590 has multicolored margin continuing design. Size: 115x80mm.

World Communications Year — A86

**1983, July 14** ***Perf. 14***

*591* A86 6c Traditional communications 9 9
*592* A86 10c Mano River mail 15 15
*593* A86 20c Satellite ground station 30 30
*594* A86 1 le English packet, 1805 1.50 1.50

**Souvenir Sheet**

*595* A86 2 le Map, phone, envelope 3.00 3.00

No. 595 has multicolored margin showing maps, flags. Size: 115x85mm.

Manned Flight Bicentenary — A87

**1983, Aug. 31** **Litho.** ***Perf. 14***

*596* A87 6c Montgolfiere, 1783, vert. 8 8
*597* A87 20c Deutschland blimp, 1897 28 28
*598* A87 50c Norge I blimp, North Pole, 1926 70 70
*599* A87 1 le Cape Sierra sport balloon, Freetown, 1983, vert. 1.40 1.40

**Souvenir Sheet**

*600* A87 2 le Futuristic airship 2.75 2.75

No. 600 has multicolored margin continuing design. Size: 105x76mm.

Walt Disney, Space Ark Fantasy — A88

**1983, Nov.**

*601* A88 1c Hippopotamus, Huey, Dewey and Louie 5 5
*602* A88 1c Mickey Mouse and Snake 5 5
*603* A88 3c Elephant and Donald Duck 5 5
*604* A88 3c Zebra and Goofy 5 5
*605* A88 10c Lion and Ludwig von Drake 8 8
*606* A88 10c Rhinoceros and Goofy 8 8
*607* A88 2 le Giraffe and Mickey Mouse 1.75 1.75
*608* A88 3 le Monkey and Donald Duck 2.50 2.50
*Nos. 601-608 (8)* 4.61 4.61

**Souvenir Sheet**

*609* A88 5 le Mickey Mouse and animals 4.25 4.25

Multicolored margin continues design.

10th Anniv. of Mano River Union A89

**1984, Feb. 8** **Litho.** ***Perf. 15***

*610* A89 6c Teaching Program graduates 5 5
*611* A89 25c Emblem 20 20
*612* A89 31c Map, presidents 25 25
*613* A89 41c Guinea Accession signing 35 35
*a* Souvenir sheet of 1 50 50

23rd Olympic Games, Los Angeles, July 28-Aug. 12 — A90

**1984, Mar. 15** ***Perf. 14***

*614* A90 90c Gymnastics 65 65
*615* A90 11c Hurdles 70 70
*616* A90 3 le Javelin 2.25 2.25

**Souvenir Sheet**

*617* A90 7 le Boxing 5.25 5.25

No. 617 has multicolored margin showing maps in Olympic rings.

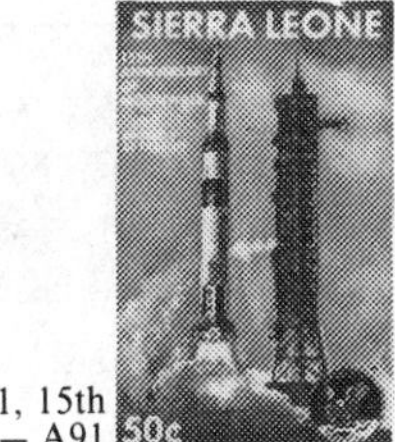


Apollo 11, 15th Anniv. — A91

**1984, May 14** **Litho.** ***Perf. 14***

*618* A91 50c Lift off 40 40
*619* A91 75c Lunar landing 60 60
*620* A91 1.25 le 1st step on moon 1.00 1.00
*621* A91 2.50 le Walking on moon 2.00 2.00

**Souvenir Sheet**

*622* A91 5 le TV transmission, horiz. 4.00 4.00

No. 622 has multicolored margin showing satellite, earth. Size: 99x69mm.

UPU Congress A92

**1984, June 19**

*623* A92 4 le Concorde 2.75 2.75

**Souvenir Sheet**

*624* A92 4 le UPU emblem, von Stephan 2.75 2.75

No. 624 has multicolored margin showing maps. UPU headquarters. Size: 100x70mm.

U.N. Decade for African Transportation — A93

Various cars.

**1984, July 16** ***Perf. 14½x15***

*625* A93 12c Citroen 9 9
*626* A93 60c Locomobile 42 42
*627* A93 90c AC Ace 60 60
*628* A93 1 le Vauxhall Prince Henry 70 70
*629* A93 1.50 le Delahaye-185 1.10 1.10
*630* A93 2 le Mazda 1.40 1.40
*Nos. 625-630 (6)* 4.31 4.31

**Souvenir Sheet**

***Perf. 15***

*631* A93 6 le Volkswagon Beetle 4.00 4.00

No. 631 has multicolored margin showing map, family. Size: 108x76mm.

Nos. 466, 468, 475 Surcharged.

**Wmk. 373**

**1984, Aug. 3 Litho.** ***Perf. 14***

*632* A67 25c on 10c multi 20 20
*633* A67 40c on 10c multi 32 32
*634* A67 50c on 2 le multi 50 50
*635* A67 70c on 5c multi 56 56
*636* A67 10 le on 5c multi 8.00 8.00
*Nos. 632-636 (5)* 9.58 9.58

Nos. 473, 476 Overprinted: "AUSIPEX 84"

**Wmk. 373**

**1984, Aug. 22 Litho.** ***Perf. 14***

*637* A67 50c multi 40 40
*638* A67 5 le multi 4.00 4.00

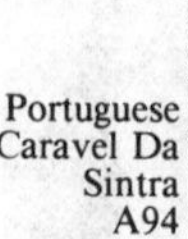

Portuguese Caravel Da Sintra A94

**1984**

*639* A94 2c shown 5 5
*a* Perf. 12½x12 ('85) 5 5
*640* A94 5c Merlin of Bristol 5 5
*a* Perf. 12½x12 ('85) 5 5
*641* A94 10c Golden Hind 8 8
*a* Perf. 12½x12 ('85) 5 5
*642* A94 15c Interloper Morduant 10 10
*643* A94 20c Navy Board Transport Atlantic 12 12
*a* Perf. 12½x12 ('85) 5 5
*644* A94 25c Navy Vessel Lapwing 16 16
*a* Perf. 12½x12 ('85) 6 6
*645* A94 30c Brig Traveller 20 20
*a* Perf. 12½x12 ('85) 8 8

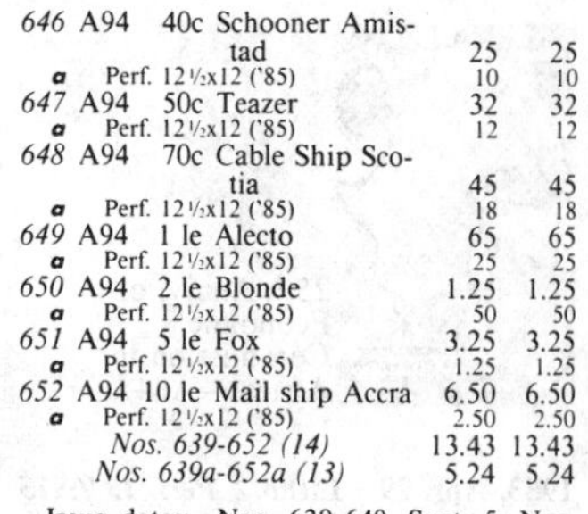

*646* A94 40c Schooner Amistad 25 25
*a* Perf. 12½x12 ('85) 10 10
*647* A94 50c Teazer 32 32
*a* Perf. 12½x12 ('85) 12 12
*648* A94 70c Cable Ship Scotia 45 45
*a* Perf. 12½x12 ('85) 18 18
*649* A94 1 le Alecto 65 65
*a* Perf. 12½x12 ('85) 25 25
*650* A94 2 le Blonde 1.25 1.25
*a* Perf. 12½x12 ('85) 50 50
*651* A94 5 le Fox 3.25 3.25
*a* Perf. 12½x12 ('85) 1.25 1.25
*652* A94 10 le Mail ship Accra 6.50 6.50
*a* Perf. 12½x12 ('85) 2.50 2.50
*Nos. 639-652 (14)* 13.43 13.43
*Nos. 639a-652a (13)* 5.24 5.24

Issue dates: Nos. 639-649, Sept. 5; Nos. 650-651, Oct. 9; 10 le Nov. 7.
See Nos. 739-740.

125th Anniv. of Sierra Leone Postage Stamps A95

**1984, Oct. 9**

*653* A95 50c Mail messenger, No. 2 32 32
*654* A95 2 le Post Master receiving letters, No. 2 1.25 1.25
*655* A95 3 le Cover 2.00 2.00

**Souvenir Sheet**

*656* A95 5 le Penny Black, No. 2 3.25 3.25

No. 656 has multicolored margin continuing design.

50th Anniv. of Donald Duck — A95a

**1984, Nov. Litho.** ***Perf. 14x13½***

*657* A95a 1c Wise Little Hen 5 5
*658* A95a 2c Boat Builders 5 5
*659* A95a 3c Three Caballeros 5 5
*660* A95a 4c Mathematic Land 5 5
*661* A95a 5c Mickey Mouse Club 5 5
*662* A95a 10c On Parade 8 8
*663* A95a 1 le Don Donald 80 80
*663A* A95a 2 le Donald gets drafted, p. 12½x12 1.60 1.60
*664* A95a 4 le Tokyo Disneyland 3.25 3.25
*Nos. 657-664 (9)* 5.98 5.98

**Souvenir Sheet**

*665* A95a 5 le Sketches 4.00 4.00

No. 665 has multicolored margin showing poses and sketches.

Christmas 1984 — A96

Mother and Child paintings.

**1984, Nov. 28** ***Perf. 14***

*666* A96 20c Pisanello 12 12
*667* A96 1 le Memling 70 70
*668* A96 2 le Raphael 1.40 1.40
*669* A96 3 le van der Werff 2.00 2.00

**Souvenir Sheet**

*670* A96 6 le Picasso 4.25 4.25

Songbirds A97

**1985, Jan. 31 Litho.**

*671* A97 40c Straw-tailed whydah 40 40
*672* A97 90c Spotted flycatcher 95 95
*673* A97 1.30 le Garden warbler 1.40 1.40
*674* A97 3 le Speke's weaver 3.00 3.00

**Souvenir Sheet**

*675* A97 5 le Great gray shrike 5.00 5.00

No. 675 has songbirds in margin.

International Youth Year — A98

**1985, Feb. 14 Litho.**

*676* A98 1.15 le Fishing 1.10 1.10
*677* A98 1.50 le Timber 1.40 1.40
*678* A98 2.15 le Rice farming 2.00 2.00

**Souvenir Sheet**

*679* A98 5 le Diamond polishing 4.50 4.50

No. 679 has IYY emblem in margin.

Intl. Civil Aviation Org., 40th Anniv. A100

Early aviators and their aircraft: 70c, Eddie Rickenbacker, Spad XIII (1918). 1.25 le, Samuel P. Langley, Aerodrome No. 5. 1.30 le, Orville and Wilbur Wright, Flyer 1. 2 le, Charles Lindbergh, Spirit of St. Louis.

**1985, Feb. 28 Litho.** ***Perf. 14***

*680* A100 70c multi 60 60
*681* A100 1.25 le multi 1.10 1.10
*682* A100 1.30 le multi 1.10 1.10
*683* A100 2 le multi 1.90 1.90

**Souvenir Sheet**

*684* A100 5 le Jet over Freetown 4.50 4.50

No. 684 has multicolored margin continuing design. Size: 100x70mm.

Easter 1985 A101

Religious paintings: Nos. 685, 687 689 by Botticelli (1445-1510). Nos. 686, 688 by Velazquez (1599-1660).

**1985, Apr. 29**

*685* A101 45c The Temptation of Christ 15 15
*686* A101 70c Christ at the Column 25 25
*687* A101 1.55 le Pieta 55 55
*688* A101 10 le Christ on the Cross 4.00 4.00

**Souvenir Sheet**

*689* A101 12 le Man of Sorrows 4.75 4.75

No. 689 has a multicolored margin continuing the painting and picturing angels. Size: 107x77mm.

Queen Mother, 85th Birthday — A102

Designs: 1 le, Queen Mother at St. Peter's Cathedral, London, vert. 1.70 le, With Double Star at Sandown Racetrack. 10 le, Attending the gala ballet at Covent Garden, 1971, vert. 12 le, With Princess Anne at Ascot, vert.

**1985, July 8 Litho.** ***Perf. 14***

*690* A102 1 le multi 32 32
*691* A102 1.70 le multi 60 60
*692* A102 10 le multi 3.25 3.25

**Souvenir Sheet**

*693* A102 12 le multi 4.00 4.00

No. 693 has multicolored inscribed margin that pictures orchids. Size: 57x85mm.

Nos. 535-539 Surcharged "75th Anniversary / of Girl Guides," Black Bar and New Value

**1985, July 25**

*694* A78 70c on 20c multi 35 35
*695* A78 1.30 le on 50c multi 65 65
*696* A78 5 le on 1 le multi 50 50
*697* A78 7 le on 2 le multi 1.00 1.00

**Souvenir Sheet**

*698* A78 15 le on 3 le multi 7.50 7.50

Nos. 614-617 Surcharged with Winners Names, Country, "Gold Medal," Black Bar and New Value

**1985, July 25**

*699* A90 2 le on 90c Ma Yanhonjg, China 65 65
*700* A90 4 le on 1 le E. Moses, USA 1.25 1.25
*701* A90 8 le on 3 le A. Haerkoenen, Finland 2.50 2.50

**Souvenir Sheet**

*702* A90 15 le on 7 le M. Taylor, USA 4.75 4.75

1905 Chater-Lea, Hill Station House — A103

Designs: 2 le, Honda XR 350 R, QE II Quay. 4 le, Kawasaki Vulcan, Bo Clock Tower. 5 le, Harley-Davidson Electra-Glide, Makeni. 12 le, 1893 Millet.

**1985, Aug. 15**

*703* A103 1.40 le multi 45 45
*704* A103 2 le multi 65 65
*705* A103 4 le multi 1.25 1.25
*706* A103 5 le multi 1.65 1.65

**Souvenir Sheet**

*707* A103 12 le multi 4.00 4.00

Motorcycle cent., Decade for African Transport. No. 707 has multicolored decorative margin picturing Gottlieb Daimler (1834-1900) and 1885 Einstur. Size: 104x70mm.

Johann Sebastian Bach (1685-1750), Composer — A104

**1985, Sept. 3**

*708* A104 70c Viola pomposa 24 24
*709* A104 3 le Spinet 1.00 1.00
*710* A104 4 le Lute 1.25 1.25
*711* A104 5 le Oboe 1.65 1.65

**Souvenir Sheet**

*712* A104 12 le Portrait 4.00 4.00

Nos. 708-712 bear the same portrait of Bach, his signature and music from "Clavier Ubang." No. 712 has decorative margin continuing portrait of Bach and family by Toby E. Rosenthal. Size: 103x77mm.

Nos. 510, 512, 516, 531-534, 552-555 Surcharged

***Perfs. as before***

**1985, Sept. 30** **Litho.**

*713* CD332 70c on 31c #531 48 48
*714* CD331 1.30 le on 60c #512 90 90
*715* CD332 1.30 le on 31c #552 90 90
*716* CD331 2 le on 35c #510 1.25 1.25
*717* CD332 4 le on 50c #532 2.75 2.75
*718* CD332 5 le on 2 le #533 3.25 3.25
*719* CD332 5 le on 50c #553 3.25 3.25
*720* CD332 7 le on 2 le #554 4.50 4.50
*721* CD331 8 le on 1.50 le #516 5.50 5.50
*Nos. 713-721 (9)* 22.78 22.78

**Souvenir Sheets**

*722* CD332 15 le on 3 le #534 10.00 10.00
*723* CD332 15 le on 3 le #555 10.00 10.00

Christmas — A105

Madonna and child paintings by: 70c, Carlo Crivelli (c. 1430-1494). 3 le, Dirk Bouts (c. 1400-1475). 4 le, Antonello de Messina (c. 1430-1479). 5 le, Stefan Lochner (c. 1400-1451). 12 le, Miniature from the Book of Kells, 9th cent., Ireland.

**1985, Oct. 18** **Litho.** ***Perf. 14***

*724* A105 70c multi 24 24
*725* A105 3 le multi 1.00 1.00
*726* A105 4 le multi 1.35 1.35
*727* A105 5 le multi 1.65 1.65

**Miniature Sheet**

*728* A105 12 le multi 4.00 4.00

No. 728 has multicolored decorative margin. Size: 114x85mm.

Jacob and Wilhelm Grimm, Fabulists — A106

Mark Twain, American Humorist A107

Walt Disney characters acting out Twain quotes or in Rumpelstiltskin.

**1985, Oct. 30** **Litho.** ***Perf. 14***

*729* A106 70c multi 22 22
*730* A106 1.30 le multi 38 38
*731* A107 1.50 le multi 42 42
*732* A106 2 le multi 55 55
*733* A107 3 le multi 85 85
*734* A107 4 le multi 1.25 1.25
*735* A107 5 le multi 1.40 1.40
*736* A106 10 le multi 2.75 2.75
*Nos. 729-736 (8)* 7.82 7.82

**Souvenir Sheets**

*737* A106 15 le multi 4.25 4.25
*738* A107 15 le multi 4.25 4.25

Nos. 731, 733-735 bear the Intl. Youth Year emblem. Nos. 737-738 have multicolored margins continuing the designs. Sizes: 126x101mm.

Ship Type of 1984

**1985, Nov. 15**

*739* A94 15 le Favourite 4.50 4.50
*740* A94 25 le Euryalus 7.50 7.50

UN, 40th Anniv. A108

Stamps of UN and famous men: 2 le, No. 30, John F. Kennedy. 4 le, No. 59, Albert Einstein. 7 le, No. 44, Maimonides (1135-1204), medieval Judaic scholar. 12 le, Dr. Martin Luther King, Jr. (1929-1968), civil rights leader, vert.

**1985, Nov. 28** **Litho.** ***Perf. 14½***

*741* A108 2 le multi 65 65
*742* A108 4 le multi 1.35 1.35
*743* A108 7 le multi 2.30 2.30

**Souvenir Sheet**

*744* A108 12 le multi 4.00 4.00

No. 744 has tan margin picturing UN No. 212, anniversary emblem and King's signature. Size: 111x86mm.

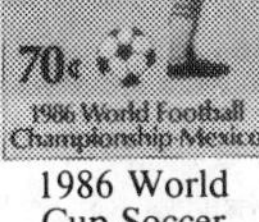


1986 World Cup Soccer Championships A109

Statue of Liberty, Cent. A110

Various soccer plays.

**1986, Mar. 3** ***Perf. 14***

*745* A109 70c multi 28 28
*746* A109 3 le multi 1.10 1.10
*747* A109 4 le multi 1.50 1.50
*748* A109 5 le multi 1.90 1.90

**Souvenir Sheet**

*749* A109 12 le multi 4.50 4.50

No. 749 has multicolored inscribed margin picturing goalie catching ball. Size: 104x72mm.

**1986, Mar. 11**

New York City: 40c, Times Square, 1905. 70c, Times Square, 1986. 1 le, Tally Ho Coach, c. 1880, horiz. 10 le, Liberty Lines express bus, 1986. 12 le, Statue of Liberty.

*750* A110 40c multi 16 16
*751* A110 70c multi 28 28
*752* A110 1 le multi 42 42
*753* A110 10 le multi 4.00 4.00

**Souvenir Sheet**

*754* A110 12 le multi 4.75 4.75

No. 754 has multicolored margin picturing New York City skyline and: Thomas Mann (1875-1955), writer; Enrico Caruso (1873-1921), opera singer; Charles P. Steinmetz (1865-1923), electrical engineer and inventor; and Walt Whitman (1819-1892), poet. Size: 105x76mm.

A111

Halley's Comet A112

Designs: 15c, Johannes Kepler (1571-1630), German astronomer, and Paris Observatory. 50c, US space shuttle landing, 1985. 70c, Bayeux Tapestry (detail), 1066 sighting. 10 le, Arthurian magician, Merlin, sights comet, 530. 12 le, Comet over Sierra Leone.

**1986, Apr. 1**

*755* A111 15c multi 5 5
*756* A111 50c multi 16 16
*757* A111 70c multi 24 24
*758* A111 10 le multi 3.35 3.35

**Souvenir Sheet**

*759* A112 12 le multi 4.00 4.00

No. 759 has multicolored margin picturing communications satellite station, Wilberforce. Size: 102x70mm.

**Queen Elizabeth II, 60th Birthday**

Common Design Type

**1986, Apr. 21**

*760* CD339 10c Cranwell, 1951 5 5
*761* CD339 1.70 le Garter Ceremony 55 55
*762* CD339 10 le Braemar Games, 1970 3.35 3.35

**Souvenir Sheet**

*763* CD339 12 le Windsor Castle, 1943 4.00 4.00

No. 763 has beige and gray inscribed margin. Size: 120x85mm.

AMERIPEX '86 — A113

Locomotives.

**1986, May 22**

*764* A113 50c Hiawatha, Milwaukee 16 16
*765* A113 2 le The Rocket, Rock Is. 65 65
*766* A113 4 le Prospector, Rio Grande 1.35 1.35
*767* A113 7 le Daylight, So. Pacific 2.35 2.35

**Souvenir Sheet**

*768* A113 12 le Broadway, Pennsylvania 4.00 4.00

No. 768 has multicolored margin picturing Pennsylvania countryside. Size: 104x85mm.

**Royal Wedding Issue, 1986**

Common Design Type

Designs: 10c, Prince Andrew and Sarah Ferguson. 1.70 le, Andrew with shotgun. 10 le, Andrew saluting. 12 le, Couple, diff.

**1986, July 23**

*769* CD340 10c multi 5 5
*770* CD340 1.70 le multi 55 55
*771* CD340 10 le multi 3.35 3.35

**Souvenir Sheet**

*772* CD340 12 le multi 4.00 4.00

No. 772 has multicolored margin picturing Andrew wearing tophat. Size: 88x88mm.

Indigenous Flowers — A114

**1986, Aug. 25** **Litho.** ***Perf. 15***

*773* A114 70c Monodora myristica 6 6
*774* A114 1.50 le Gloriosa simplex 14 14
*775* A114 4 le Mussaenda erythrophylla 35 35
*776* A114 6 le Crinum ornatum 52 52
*777* A114 8 le Bauhinia purpurea 75 75
*778* A114 10 le Bombax costatum 90 90
*779* A114 20 le Hibiscus rosa-sinensis 1.75 1.75
*780* A114 30 le Cassia fistula 2.75 2.75
*Nos. 773-780 (8)* 7.22 7.22

**Souvenir Sheets**

*781* A114 40 le Clitoria ternatea 3.50 3.50
*782* A114 40 le Plumbago auriculata 3.50 3.50

Nos. 781-782 have multicolored margins picturing flowers shown in stamp designs. Sizes: 101x92mm.

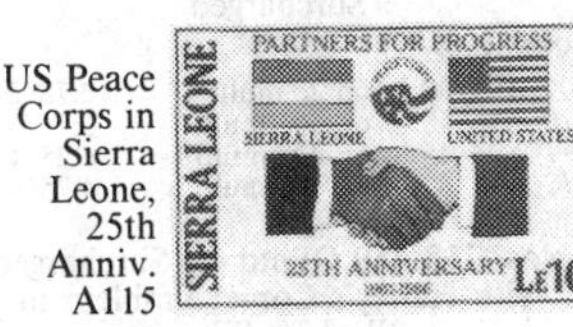


US Peace Corps in Sierra Leone, 25th Anniv. A115

**1986, Aug. 26** **Litho.** ***Perf. 14***

*783* A115 10 le multi 1.25 1.25

Intl. Peace Year A116

**1986, Sept. 1**

*784* A116 1 le Transportation 12 12
*785* A116 2 le Education 24 24
*786* A116 5 le Communications 60 60
*787* A116 10 le Fishing 1.25 1.25

Nos. 745-749 Ovptd. or Surcharged "WINNERS / Argentina 3 / West Germany 2" in Gold.

**1986, Sept. 15** ***Perf. 14***

*788* A109 70c multi 6 6
*789* A109 3 le multi 24 24
*790* A109 4 le multi 32 32
*791* A109 40 le on 5 le multi 3.20 3.20

**Souvenir Sheet**

*792* A109 40 le on 12 le multi 3.20 3.20

Nos. 760, 762-763 Surcharged in Silver or Black.

**1986, Sept. 15**

*793* CD339 70c on 10c multi 6 6
*794* CD339 45 le on 10 le multi 3.60 3.60

**Souvenir Sheet**

*795* CD339 50 le on 12 le (B) 4.00 4.00

Nos. 769, 771-772 Surcharged in Silver.

**1986, Sept. 15**

*796* CD340 70c on 10c multi 6 6
*797* CD340 45 le on 10 le multi 3.60 3.60

**Souvenir Sheet**

*798* CD340 50 le on 12 le multi 4.00 4.00

STOCKHOLMIA '86 — A117

Disney characters in Mother Goose fairy tales.

**1986, Sept. 22** *Perf. 11*

*799* A117 70c Jack and Jill 6 6
*800* A117 1 le Wee Willie Winkie 8 8
*801* A117 2 le Little Miss Muffet 16 16
*802* A117 4 le Old King Cole 32 32
*803* A117 5 le Mary Quite Contrary 40 40
*804* A117 10 le Little Bo Peep 80 80
*805* A117 25 le Polly Put the Kettle On 2.00 2.00
*806* A117 35 le Rub-a-Dub-Dub 2.80 2.80
*Nos. 799-806 (8)* 6.62 6.62

**Souvenir Sheets**

*807* A117 40 le Old Woman in the Shoe 3.20 3.20
*808* A117 40 le Simple Simon 3.20 3.20

Nos. 808-809 have multicolored margins continuing the designs.

### Nos. 639, 645-646 and 648 Surcharged

**1986, Oct. 15**

*809* A94 30 le on 2c multi 2.75 2.75
*810* A94 40 le on 30c multi 3.75 3.75
*811* A94 45 le on 40c multi 4.25 4.25
*812* A94 50 le on 70c multi 4.75 4.75

### Nos. 755-759 Ovptd. or Surcharged with Halley's Comet Emblem in Black or Silver

**1986, Oct. 15**

*813* A111 50c multi 5 5
*814* A111 70c multi 6 6
*815* A111 1.50 le on 15c multi 12 12
*816* A111 45 le on 10 le multi 4.25 4.25

**Souvenir Sheet**

*817* A112 50 le on 12 le multi (S) 4.75 4.75

Christmas A118

Paintings by Titian: 70c, Virgin and Child with St. Dorothy. $1.50 le, The Gypsy Madonna, vert. 20 le, The Holy Family. 30 le, Virgin and Child in an Evening Landscape, vert. 40 le, Madonna with the Pesaro Family.

**1986, Nov. 17** **Litho.** *Perf. 14*

*818* A118 70c multi 6 6
*819* A118 1.50 le multi 12 12
*820* A118 20 le multi 1.60 1.60
*821* A118 30 le multi 2.40 2.40

**Souvenir Sheet**

*822* A118 40 le multi 3.25 3.25

No. 822 has multicolored inscribed margin continuing the design. Size: 76x103mm.

Statue of Liberty, Cent. A119

Pictures of the statue by Peter B. Kaplan before and after renovation. Nos. 823, 825-826, 828-829, 831, vert.

**1987, Jan. 2** *Perf. 14*

*823* A119 70c Torch assembly 6 6
*824* A119 1.50 le Liberty holding torch 12 12
*825* A119 2 le Torch assembly, diff. 16 16
*826* A119 3 le Man, torch 24 24
*827* A119 4 le Crown 32 32
*828* A119 5 le Lighting of the statue 40 40
*829* A119 10 le Lighting, diff. 80 80
*830* A119 25 le Liberty Is. 2.00 2.00
*831* A119 30 le Face 2.40 2.40
*Nos. 823-831 (9)* 6.50 6.50

UNICEF, 40th Anniv. A120

**1987, Mar. 18** **Litho.** *Perf. 14*

*832* A120 10 le multi 80 80

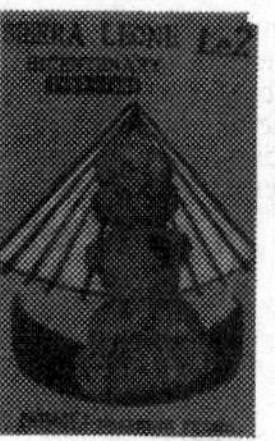

Nomoli Soapstone Sculpture A121

Tall Ship in Harbor, Freetown A122

**1987, Jan. 2** *Perf. 15*

*833* A121 2 le shown 14 14
*834* A121 5 le King's Yard Gate, 1817 35 35

**Souvenir Sheet**

*835* A122 60 le shown 4.00 4.00

First settlement of liberated slaves returned to the African continent by the British, Freetown, bicent. No. 835 has multicolored margin continuing the design, picturing an early view of Freetown. Size: 100x70mm.

America's Cup — A123

Constellation, 1964 — A124

**1987, June 15** **Litho.** *Perf. 14*

*836* A123 1 le USA, 1987 5 5
*837* A123 1.50 le New Zealand, 1987 6 6
*838* A123 2.50 le French Kiss, 1987 10 10
*839* A123 10 le Stars & Stripes, 1987 60 60
*840* A123 15 le Australia II, 1983 90 90
*841* A123 25 le Freedom, 1980 1.50 1.50
*842* A123 30 le Kookaburra III, 1987 1.75 1.75
*Nos. 836-842 (7)* 4.96 4.96

**Souvenir Sheet**

*843* A124 50 le shown 3.00 3.00

Nos. 837, 839 and 842 horiz. No. 843 has multicolored decorative margin continuing the design. Size: 100x70mm.

The Scott Catalogue value is a retail price, what you could expect to pay for the stamp in a grade of Fine-Very Fine. The value listed is a reference which reflects recent actual dealer selling price.

CAPEX '87 — A125

Disney characters, Canadian sights.

**1987, June 15** *Perf. 11*

*849* A125 2 le Parliament 8 8
*850* A125 5 le Totem poles 25 25
*851* A125 10 le Perce Rock 52 52
*852* A125 20 le Canadian Rockies 1.00 1.00
*853* A125 25 le Old Quebec City 1.40 1.40
*854* A125 45 le Aurora Borealis 2.25 2.25
*855* A125 50 le Yukon P.O. 2.75 2.75
*856* A125 75 le Niagara Falls 4.00 4.00
*Nos. 849-856 (8)* 12.25 12.25

**Souvenir Sheets**

*857* A125 100 le Exploring Newfoundland 5.25 5.25
*858* A125 100 le Calgary Exhibition and Stampede 5.25 5.25

Nos. 857-858 have multicolored margins continuing the designs. Sizes: 128x102mm.

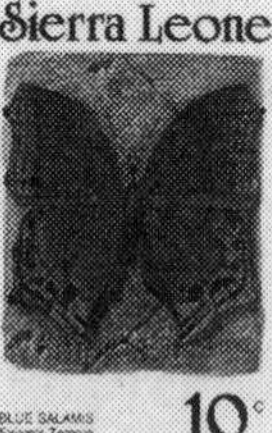

Butterflies A126

1988 Summer Olympics, Seoul A127

**1987, Aug. 4** *Perf. 14*

*859* A126 10c Blue salamis 5 5
*a.* Perf. 12x12½ 5 5
*860* A126 20c Pale-tailed blue 5 5
*a.* Perf. 12x12½ 5 5
*861* A126 40c Acraea swallowtail 5 5
*a.* Perf. 12x12½ 5 5
*862* A126 1 le Broad blue-banded swallowtail 5 5
*a.* Perf. 12x12½ 5 5
*863* A126 2 le Giant blue swallowtail 8 8
*a.* Perf. 12x12½ 8 8
*864* A126 3 le Blood-red cymothoe 12 12
*a.* Perf. 12x12½ 12 12
*865* A126 5 le Green-spotted swallowtail 20 20
*a.* Perf. 12x12½ 20 20
*866* A126 10 le Small-striped swordtail 40 40
*a.* Perf. 12x12½ 40 40
*867* A126 20 le Congo long-tailed blue 80 80
*a.* Perf. 12x12½ 80 80
*868* A126 25 le Blue monarch 1.00 1.00
*a.* Perf. 12x12½ 1.00 1.00
*869* A126 30 le Black and yellow swallowtail 1.20 1.20
*a.* Perf. 12x12½ 1.20 1.20
*870* A126 45 le Western blue charaxes 1.75 1.75
*a.* Perf. 12x12½ 1.75 1.75
*871* A126 60 le Violet-washed charaxes 2.40 2.40
*872* A126 75 le Orange admiral 3.00 3.00
*873* A126 100 le Blue-patched judy 4.00 4.00
*Nos. 859-873 (15)* 15.15 15.15
*Nos. 859a-868a (12)* 5.75 5.75

Perf. 12x12½ stamps issued in 1988.

**1987, Aug. 10**

*874* A127 5 le Cycling 20 20
*875* A127 10 le Equestrian 40 40
*876* A127 45 le Running 1.75 1.75
*877* A127 50 le Tennis 2.00 2.00

**Souvenir Sheet**

*878* A127 100 le Gold medal, map 4.00 4.00

No. 878 has inscribed multicolored margin continuing the design. Size: 73x85mm.

Works of Art by Marc Chagall, (1887-1985) A128

**1987, Aug. 17** *Perf. 14*

*879* A128 3 le The Quarrel, 1911-1912 12 12
*880* A128 5 le Rebecca Giving Abraham's Servant a Drink 20 20
*881* A128 10 le The Village 40 40
*882* A128 20 le Ida at the Window, 1924 40 40
*883* A128 25 le Promenade, 1913 1.00 1.00
*884* A128 45 le Peasants 1.80 1.80
*885* A128 50 le Turquoise Plate 2.00 2.00
*886* A128 75 le Cemetery Gate, 1917 3.00 3.00
*Nos. 879-886 (8)* 8.92 8.92

**Size: 111x95mm**

***Imperf***

*887* A128 100 le Wedding Feast, Stravinsky's Ballet, 1945 4.00 4.00
*888* A128 100 le The Falling Angel 4.00 4.00

Nos. 879-886 printed in sheets of 10 (5x2). Stamp selvage inscribed with name of painting.

Transportation Innovations — A129

**1987, Aug. 28** *Perf. 15*

*889* A129 3 le Apollo 8, 1968, vert. 12 12
*890* A129 5 le Blanchard's Balloon, 1793 20 20
*891* A129 10 le Lockheed Vega, 1932 40 40
*892* A129 15 le Vicker's Vimy, 1919 60 60
*893* A129 20 le Tank Mk1, c. 1918 80 80
*894* A129 25 le Sikorsky VS-300, 1939 1.00 1.00
*895* A129 30 le Flyer 1, 1903 1.20 1.20
*896* A129 35 le Bleriot XI, 1909 1.40 1.40
*897* A129 40 le Paraplane, 1983, vert. 1.60 1.60
*898* A129 50 le Daimler's motorcycle, 1885 2.00 2.00
*Nos. 889-898 (10)* 9.32 9.32

Rhinegold Express, Ireland (1st Electric Railroad, 1884) — A129a

**1987, Aug. 28 Litho. *Perf. 15***
*898A* A129a 100 le multi 4.00 4.00

No. 898A has multicolored margin continuing the design and picturing castle in Ireland. Size: 104x82mm.

Wimbledon Tennis Champions — A130

**1987, Sept. 4 *Perf. 14***
*899* A130 2 le Evonne Goolagong, Australia 8 8
*900* A130 5 le Martina Navratilova, U.S.-Czechoslovakia 20 20
*901* A130 10 le Jimmy Connors, U.S. 40 40
*902* A130 15 le Bjorn Borg, Sweden 60 60
*903* A130 30 le Boris Becker, West Germany 1.20 1.20
*904* A130 40 le John McEnroe, U.S. 1.60 1.60
*905* A130 50 le Chris Evert Lloyd, U.S. 2.00 2.00
*906* A130 75 le Virgina Wade, Great Britain 3.00 3.00
*Nos. 899-906 (8)* 9.08 9.08

**Souvenir Sheets**

*907* A130 100 le Steffi Graf, German Open 1986 4.00 4.00
*908* A130 100 le Boris Becker 4.00 4.00

Nos. 907-908 have multicolored decorative margins continuing the designs. Sizes: 105x75mm.

Discovery of America, 500th Anniv. (in 1992) A131

Designs: 5 le, Ducats, Santa Maria, Issac Abravanel (1437-1508), fundraiser. 10 le, Astrolabe, Pinta, Abraham Zacuto (1452-1515), astronomer. 45 le, Maravedis (coins), Nina, Luis de Santangel (1448-1498), fund raiser. 50 le, Tobacco leaves, plant, Luis de Torres (1453-1522), translator.

**1987, Sept. 11**
*909* A131 5 le multi 20 20
*910* A131 10 le multi 40 40
*911* A131 45 le multi 1.80 1.80
*912* A131 50 le multi 2.00 2.00

**Souvenir Sheet**

*913* A131 100 le Columbus, map 4.00 4.00

No. 913 has multicolored margin continuing the design and picturing a map, astrolabe, ships and coins. Size: 101x70mm.

Fauna and Flora A132

**1987, Sept. 15**
*914* A132 3 le Cotton tree 12 12
*915* A132 5 le Dwarf crocodile 20 20
*916* A132 10 le Kudu 40 40
*917* A132 20 le Yellowbells 80 80
*918* A132 25 le Hippopotamus 1.00 1.00
*919* A132 45 le Comet orchid 1.80 1.80
*920* A132 50 le Baobab tree 2.00 2.00
*921* A132 75 le Elephant 3.00 3.00
*Nos. 914-921 (8)* 9.32 9.32

**Souvenir Sheets**

*922* A132 100 le Banana, papaya, coconut, pineapple 4.00 4.00
*923* A132 100 le Leopard 4.00 4.00

Nos. 922-923 have multicolored margins continuing the designs. Sizes: 101x70mm.

16th World Scout Jamboree, Australia, 1987-88 A133

Scouts, jamboree emblem, map of Australia and: 5 le, Ayers Rock. 15le, Sailing. 40 le, Sydney skyline. 50 le, Sydney harbor bridge, opera house. 100 le, Flags of Sierra Leone, Australia and Scouts.

**1987, Oct. 5 Litho. *Perf. 15***
*924* A133 5 le multi 45 45
*925* A133 15 le multi 1.35 1.35
*926* A133 40 le multi 3.60 3.60
*927* A133 50 le multi 4.50 4.50

**Souvenir Sheet**

*928* A133 100 le multi 9.00 9.00

No. 928 has multicolored margin picturing maps and emblems. Size: 103x77mm.

U.S. Constitution Bicentennial — A134

Designs: 5 le, White House. 10 le, George Washington. 30 le, Patrick Henry. 65 le, New Hampshire state flag. 100 le, John Jay.

**1987, Nov. 9 *Perf. 14***
*929* A134 5 le multi 45 45
*930* A134 10 le multi, vert. 90 90
*931* A134 30 le multi, vert. 2.70 2.70
*932* A134 65 le multi 5.85 5.85

**Souvenir Sheet**

*933* A134 100 le multi, vert. 9.00 9.00

No. 933 has multicolored inscribed margin continuing the design and picturing colonial buildings and frontispiece of *The Federalist Papers.* Size: 105x75mm.

Tokyo Disneyland, 5th Anniv. — A135

Disney animated characters and attractions at Tokyo Disneyland.

**1987, Dec. 9 Litho. *Perf. 14***
*934* A135 20c Space Mountain 5 5
*935* A135 40c Country Bear Jamboree 5 5
*936* A135 80c Mickey Mouse Review 8 8
*937* A135 1 le Mark Twain's River Boat 10 10
*938* A135 2 le Western River Railroad 18 18
*939* A135 3 le Pirates of the Caribbean 28 28
*940* A135 10 le Big Thunder Mountain train 90 90
*941* A135 20 le It's a Small World 1.80 1.80
*942* A135 30 le Park entrance 2.70 2.70
*Nos. 934-942 (9)* 6.14 6.14

**Souvenir Sheet**

*943* A135 65 le Cinderella's Castle 5.85 5.85

Mickey Mouse, 60th anniv. No. 943 has multicolored margin continuing the design and picturing Space Mountain. Size: 127x102mm.

Christmas A136

Paintings by Titian: 2 le, The Annunciation. 10 le, Madonna and Child with Saints. 20 le, Madonna and Child with Saints Ulfus and Brigid. 35 le, Madonna of the Cherries. 65 le, Pesaro Altarpiece, vert.

**1987, Dec. 21**
*944* A136 2 le multi 18 18
*945* A136 10 le multi 90 90
*946* A136 20 le multi 1.80 1.80
*947* A136 35 le multi 3.20 3.20

**Souvenir Sheet**

*948* A136 65 le multi 5.85 5.85

No. 948 has multicolored inscribed margin continuing the painting. Size: 70x100mm.

40th Wedding Anniv. of Queen Elizabeth II and Prince Philip A137

Mushrooms A138

**1988, Feb. 15 Litho. *Perf. 14***
*949* A137 2 le Ceremony, 1947 18 18
*950* A137 3 le Elizabeth, Charles, 1948 28 28
*951* A137 10 le Elizabeth, Anne, Charles, c. 1950 90 90
*952* A137 50 le Elizabeth, c. 1970 4.50 4.50

**Souvenir Sheet**

*953* A137 65 le Wedding portrait 5.85 5.85

No. 953 has multicolored margin continuing the photograph. Size: 76x100mm.

**1988, Feb. 29**
*954* A138 3 le Russula cyanoxantha 18 18
*955* A138 10 le Lycoperdon perlatum 90 90
*956* A138 20 le Lactarius deliciosus 1.80 1.80
*957* A138 30 le Boletus edulis 2.70 2.70

**Miniature Sheet**

*958* A138 65 le Amanita muscaria 5.80 5.80

No. 958 has multicolored margin picturing Amanita muscaria. Size: 100x70mm.

Fish A139

**1988, Apr. 13 *Perf. 15***
*959* A139 3 le Golden pheasant 28 28
*960* A139 10 le Banded toothcarp 90 90
*961* A139 20 le Jewel fish 1.80 1.80
*962* A139 35 le Butterfly fish 3.20 3.20

**Miniature Sheet**

*963* A139 65 le African longfin 5.90 5.90

No. 963 has multicolored margin continuing the design. Size: 99x69mm.

Nos. 841, 903 and 911 Ovptd. for Philatelic Exhibitions in Black

a INDEPENDENCE 40

b

c

**1988, Apr. 19 Litho. *Perf. 14***
*964* A123 (a) 25 le multi 2.00 2.00
*965* A130 (b) 30 le multi 2.40 2.40
*966* A131 (c) 45 le multi 3.60 3.60

INDEPENDENCE 40 (25 le); PRAGA '88 (45 le); OLYMPHILEX '88 (30 le).

Intl. Fund for Agricultural Development (IFAD), 10th Anniv. — A140

**1988, May 3 Litho. *Perf. 14***
*967* A140 3 le Cocoa, coffee 28 28
*968* A140 15 le Tropical fruit 1.35 1.35
*969* A140 25 le Rice harvest 2.25 2.25

1988 Summer Olympics, Seoul — A141

Birds — A142

**1988, June 15**
*970* A141 3 le Basketball 24 24
*971* A141 10 le Judo 80 80
*972* A141 15 le Gymnastics 1.20 1.20
*973* A141 40 le Synchronized swimming 3.20 3.20

**Souvenir Sheet**

*974* A141 65 le Torch-bearer 5.25 5.25

No. 974 has multicolored margin picturing national colors and athelete accepting torch as part of Olympic Torch Relay. Size: 73x102mm.

**1988, June 25**
*975* A142 3 le Swallow-tailed bee-eater 24 24
*976* A142 5 le Tooth-billed barbet 40 40
*977* A142 8 le African golden oriole 65 65
*978* A142 10 le Red bishop 80 80
*979* A142 12 le Red-billed shrike 95 95
*980* A142 20 le European bee-eater 1.60 1.60
*981* A142 35 le Barbary shrike 2.80 2.80
*982* A142 40 le Black-headed oriole 3.20 3.20
*Nos. 975-982 (8)* 10.64 10.64

**Souvenir Sheets**

*983* A142 65 le Saddlebill stork 5.25 5.25
*984* A142 65 le Purple heron 5.25 5.25

Nos. 983-984 have multicolored margins continuing the designs. Sizes: 111x82mm.

Merchant Marine A143

**1988, July 1**

*985* A143 3 le *Aureol* 24 24
*986* A143 10 le *Dunkwa* 80 80
*987* A143 15 le *Melampus* 1.20 1.20
*988* A143 30 le *Dumbaia* 2.40 2.40

**Souvenir Sheet**

*989* A143 65 le Loading containers 5.25 5.25

No. 989 has multicolored inscribed margin picturing shipping company flags and outline map of Africa highlighting Sierra Leone. Size: 95x95mm.

Paintings by Titian A144

Designs: 1 le, *The Concert*, 1512. 2 le, *Philip II of Spain*, c. 1550-51. 3 le, *St. Sebastian*, c. 1520-22. 5 le, *Martyrdom of St. Peter Martyr*, c. 1528-30. 15 le, *St. Jerome*, 1560. 20 le, *St. Mark Enthroned with Saints Cosmas and Damian, Roch and Sebastian*, c. 1508-09. 25 le, *Portrait of a Young Man*, 1506. 30 le, *St. Jerome in Penitence*, 1555. No. 998, *Self-portrait*, 1567. No. 999, *Orpheus and Eurydice*, 1508.

**1988, Aug. 22 Litho. *Perf. 13½x14***

*990* A144 1 le multi 8 8
*991* A144 2 le multi 16 16
*992* A144 3 le multi 24 24
*993* A144 5 le multi 40 40
*994* A144 15 le multi 1.20 1.20
*995* A144 20 le multi 1.60 1.60
*996* A144 25 le multi 2.00 2.00
*997* A144 30 le multi 2.40 2.40
*Nos. 990-997 (8)* 8.08 8.08

**Souvenir Sheets**

*998* A144 50 le multi 4.00 4.00
*999* A144 50 le multi 4.00 4.00

Nos. 998-999 have multicolored inscribed margins continuing the designs. Sizes: 110x95mm.

John F. Kennedy — A145

Kennedy half-dollar and space achievements: 3 le, Recovery of a Mercury capsule by the U.S. Navy. 5 le, Splashdown and recovery of *Liberty Bell 7*, July 21, 1961, piloted by Virgil "Gus" Grissom, vert. 15 le, Launch of *Freedom 7*, piloted by Alan B. Shepherd, May 5, 1961, vert. 40 le, *Friendship 7* in orbit, piloted by John Glenn, Feb. 20, 1962. 65 le, Kennedy, speech excerpt.

**1988, Sept. 26 Litho. *Perf. 14***

*1000* A145 3 le multi 25 25
*1001* A145 5 le multi 40 40
*1002* A145 15 le multi 1.20 1.20
*1003* A145 40 le multi 1.60 1.60

**Souvenir Sheet**

*1004* A145 65 le multi 5.25 5.25

Nos. 1004 has multicolored decorative margin continuing the design and picturing astronaut walking on the Moon. Size: 99x69mm.

Intl. Red Cross and Red Crescent Organizations, 125th Annivs. — A146

**1988, Nov. 1**

*1005* A146 3 le Africa food relief 25 25
*1006* A146 10 le Battle of Solferino 80 80
*1007* A146 20 le WWII Pacific 1.60 1.60
*1008* A146 40 le WWI Europe 3.20 3.20

**Souvenir Sheet**

**Size: 41x28mm**

*1009* A146 65 le Alfred Nobel, Dunant, horiz. 5.25 5.25

No. 1009 has multicolored inscribed margin continuing the design.

Miniature Sheet

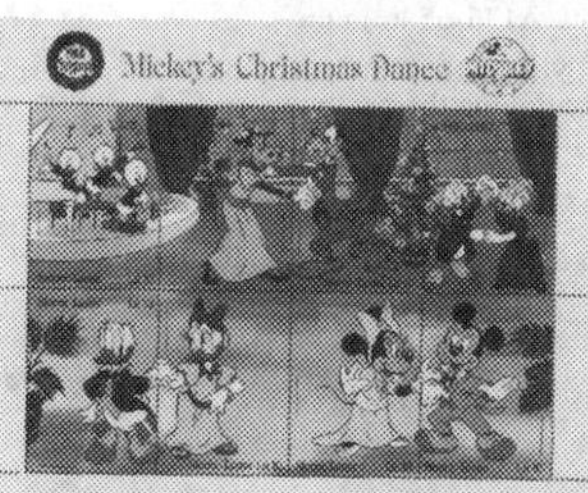


Christmas, Mickey Mouse 60th Anniv. — A147

Walt Disney characters dancing: No. 1010a, Huey, Dewey and Louie. No. 1010b, Clarabelle Cow. No. 1010c, Goofy. No. 1010d, Scrooge McDuck and Grandma Duck. No. 1010e, Donald Duck. No. 1010f, Daisy Duck. No. 1010g, Minnie Mouse. No. 1010h, Mickey Mouse. No. 1011, Dance, c. 1920. No. 1012, Dance, c. 1950.

**1988, Dec. 15 *Perf. 13½x14***

*1010* A147 Sheet of 8 6.50 6.50
*a.-h.* 10 le any single 80 80

**Souvenir Sheets**

*1011* A147 70 le multi 5.50 5.50
*1012* A147 70 le multi 5.50 5.50

Nos. 1011-1012 have multicolored decorative margins continuing the designs. Sizes: 127x102mm.

---

## AIR POST STAMPS

**Catalogue values for unused stamps in this section, from this point to the end of the section, are for Never Hinged items.**

**Independence—Progress Issue**

Nos. 197, 199, 204 and 206 Surcharged Like Nos. 242-247 plus "AIRMAIL" in Carmine, Red, Violet, Blue or Orange.

***Perf. 13, 13½***

**1963, Apr. 27 Wmk. 4 Engr.**

**Center in Black**

*C1* A27 7p on 1½p ultra (C) 10 10
*C2* A27 1sh3p on 1½p ultra (R) 20 20
*C3* A28 2sh6p brn org (V) 40 40
*C4* A28 3sh on 3p ultra (Bl) 45 45
*C5* A28 6sh on 3p ultra (O) 55 55
*C6* A27 11sh on 10sh red vio (C) 1.75 1.75
*C7* A27 11sh on £1 org (C) 525.00 90.00
*Nos. C1-C6 (6)* 3.45 3.45

Nos. 221, 224, 213, 223 and 207 Surcharged or Overprinted in Brown, Red, Black, Violet, Ultramarine or Orange

**1853–1859–1963**
**Oldest Postage Stamp**
**Newest G.P.O.**
**in West Africa**
**AIRMAIL 2/6**

***Perf. 13x13½, 13½x13, 13***

**1963, Nov. 4 Wmk. 4, 336**

*C8* A31 7p on 3p ver & blk (Br) 25 25
*C9* A32 1sh3p bl & blk (R) 30 30
*C10* A30 2sh6p on 4p rose red & grnsh bl (Bk) 60 60
*C11* A31 3sh on 3p ver & blk (V) 75 75
*C12* A32 6sh on 6p org & blk (U) 1.50 1.50
*C13* A27 £1 org & blk (O) 10.50 10.50
*Nos. C8-C13 (6)* 13.90 13.90

Overprint is in 6 lines on Nos. C8, C11 and C12. A number of surcharge varieties and errors exist.

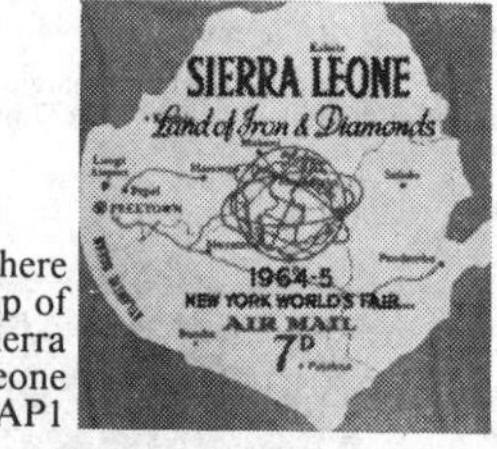


Unisphere and Map of Sierra Leone AP1

**Engraved and Lithographed**

**1964, Feb. 10 Unwmk. *Imperf.***

**Self-adhesive**

*C14* AP1 7p multi 12 12
*C15* AP1 9p multi 16 16
*C16* AP1 1sh3p multi 25 25
*C17* AP1 2sh6p multi 50 50
*C18* AP1 3sh6p multi 70 70
*C19* AP1 6sh multi 1.25 1.25
*C20* AP1 11sh multi 2.00 2.00
*Nos. C14-C20 (7)* 4.98 4.98

New York World's Fair, 1964-65.

John F. Kennedy AP2

Self-adhesive

**1964, May 11**

*C21* AP2 7p multi 12 12
*C22* AP2 9p multi 16 16
*C23* AP2 1sh3p multi 25 25
*C24* AP2 2sh6p multi 50 50
*C25* AP2 3sh6p multi 70 70
*C26* AP2 6sh multi 1.25 1.25
*C27* AP2 11sh multi 2.00 2.00
*Nos. C21-C27 (7)* 4.98 4.98

Nos. 241, 213, 219 and 218 Surcharged in Dark Blue, Black, Red or Violet Blue

***Perf. 11½x11, 13½x13, 13x13½***

**1964, Aug. 4 Engr. Wmk. 336**

*C28* A36 7c on 1sh3p (#241) (DB) 22 22
*C29* A30 20c on 4p (#213) 42 42
*C30* A29 30c on 10sh (#219) (R) 70 70
*C31* A29 40c on 5sh (#218) (VB) 85 85

Map-shaped Issues of 1964 Surcharged in Red or Black

**Engraved and Lithographed**

**1964-65 Unwmk. *Imperf.***

*C32* AP2 7c on 7p (#C21) (R) 12 12
*C33* AP1 7c on 9p (#C15) 85 85
*C34* AP2 60c on 9p (#C22) 1.25 1.25
*C35* AP2 1 le on 1sh3p (#C23) (R) 2.00 2.00
*C36* AP2 2 le on 11sh (#C27) 4.25 4.25
*Nos. C32-C36 (5)* 8.47 8.47

Issue dates: Aug. 4, 1964, Nos. C35-C36. Jan. 20, 1965, Nos. C32, C34. April, 1965, No. C33.

Regular Issue of 1963 Surcharged like Nos. 300-305 with "AIRMAIL" added

**Wmk. 336**

**1965, May 19 Photo. *Perf. 14***

Designs of Surcharge: No. C37, C39-C40, Sir Milton Margai and Sir Winston Churchill. No. C38, Margai. No. C41, Churchill.

*C37* A35 7c on 2p multi (#230) 15 15
*C38* A34 15c on ½p multi (#227) 40 40
*C39* A35 30c on 6p multi (#233) 75 75
*C40* A35 1 le on £1 multi (#239) 2.75 2.75
*C41* A34 2 le on 10sh multi (#238) 5.50 5.50
*Nos. C37-C41 (5)* 9.55 9.55

The portraits and inscription on No. C39 are white, the denomination and "AIRMAIL" are orange.

Ten more surcharges were issued Nov. 9, 1965: "2c" on Nos. C16, C23 and C25. "3c" on Nos. C14 and C22. "5c" on Nos. C17-C19, C24, and C26. Value $4 each.

One further surcharge was issued Jan. 28, 1966: "TWO/Leones" on No. C39. Value $10.

Type of Regular Issue and

Diamond Necklace — AP3

**Litho.; Reversed Embossing**

**1965, Dec. 17 Unwmk. *Imperf.***

**Self-adhesive**

*C53* AP3 7c blk, grn, gold & bl 35 35
*C54* AP3 15c blk, brnz, car & bl 75 75

**Engr. and Embossed on Paper**

*C55* A41 40c multi, *cream* 1.75 1.75

Various advertisements printed on peelable paper backing. Nos. C54-C55 have side tabs for handling and come packed in boxes of 100. No. C53 is without side tab and comes 25 stamps attached to one sheet.

Nos. 248, 229, 232, 234 and 236 Surcharged and Overprinted: "AIRMAIL/FIVE YEARS/INDEPENDENCE/1961-1966"

**1966, Apr. 27 Wmk. 336**

*C56* A37 7c on 3p pur & red 15 15
*C57* A34 15c on 1sh multi 35 35
*C58* A34 25c on 2sh6p multi 55 55
*C59* A34 50c on 1½p multi 1.10 1.10
*C60* A34 1 le on 4p multi 2.50 2.50
*Nos. C56-C60 (5)* 4.65 4.65

The denomination on No. C60 is spelled out "One Leone."

---

Self-adhesive & Imperf.
Nos. C61-C131, C135-C142 are self-adhesive and imperforate.

---

Gold Coin Type of Regular Issue

Designs: 7c, 10c, ¼ Golde coin. 15c, 30c, ½ Golde coin. 50c, 2 le, 1 Golde coin. (7c, 15c, 50c, Map of Sierra Leone. 10c, 30c, 2 le, Lion's head.)

Diameter: 7c, 10c, 38mm.; 15c, 30c, 54mm.; 50c, 2 le, 82mm.

**Lithographed; Embossed on Gilt Foil**

**1966, Nov. 12 Unwmk.**

*C61* A42 7c red & org 10 10
*C62* A42 10c dl bl & red 15 15
*C63* A42 15c red & org 20 20

*C64* A42 30c blk & rose lil 40 40
*C65* A42 50c rose lil & emer 75 75
*C66* A42 2 le grn & blk 3.75 3.75
*Nos. C61-C66 (6)* 5.35 5.35

Advertising printed on paper backing.

Type of Regular Issue, 1965 and No. C55 Surcharged

=11½

**1967, Dec. 2 Engr. & Embossed**
*C67* A41 10c multi (red frame), *cream* 50 50
*a.* Black frame 50 50
*C68* A41 11½c on 40c multi, *cr* 40 40
*C69* A41 25c on 40c multi, *cr* 1.00 1.00

Eagle — AP4

**Embossed Foil on Black Paper**

**1967, Dec. 2 Unwmk.**
*C70* AP4 9½c blk, gold & red 75 75
*C71* AP4 15c blk, gold & grn 90 90

Various advertisements printed on peelable paper backing. See Nos. C98-C99, C118-C124.

Map Type of Regular Issue

Designs: Each denomination shows map of Africa with map of one of the following countries—Portuguese Guinea, South Africa, Mozambique, Rhodesia, South West Africa or Angola. Sheets of 30 (6x5) have 5 horizontal rows containing one stamp of each design.

**1968, Sept. 25 Litho.**
*C72* A43 7½c multi 30 30
*C73* A43 9½c multi 45 45
*C74* A43 14½c multi 65 65
*C75* A43 18½c multi 75 75
*C76* A43 25c multi 1.25 1.25
*C77* A43 1 le multi 7.50 7.50
*C78* A43 2 le multi 17.50 17.50
*Nos. C72-C78 (7)* 28.40 28.40
7 Strips of 6 (one of each design) (42) 170.40

No. C55 Overprinted and Surcharged in Red Similarly to Nos. 364-368.

**Engraved and Embossed on Paper**

**1968, Nov. 30**
*C79* A41 6½c on 40c multi 15 15
*C80* A41 17½c on 40c multi 50 50
*C81* A41 22½c on 40c multi 50 50
*C82* A41 28½c on 40c multi 70 70
*C83* A41 40c multi 1.10 1.10
*Nos. C79-C83 (5)* 2.95 2.95

Scroll Type of Regular Issue.

Designs: 7½c, No. C54. 9½c, No. C70. 20c, No. C16. 30c, No. C26. 50c, No. 165. 2 le, No. 207 with "2nd Year of Independence" overprint. All are horizontal.

**1969, Mar. 1 Litho.**
*C84* A44 7½c multi 25 25
*C85* A44 9½c multi 30 30
*C86* A44 20c multi 65 65
*C87* A44 30c multi 1.00 1.00
*C88* A44 50c multi 2.50 2.50
*C89* A44 2 le multi 17.50 17.50
*Nos. C84-C89 (6)* 22.20 22.20

Various advertisements printed on peelable paper backing. No. C84 has side tab for handling and comes packed in boxes of 50. Nos. C85-C89 are without side tabs and come 20 stamps attached to one sheet.

Pepel Port Types of Regular Issue

Designs: 7½c, 15c, Globe, tanker, flags of Sierra Leone and Japan. Anvil Shape with Flags of Sierra Leone and: 9½c, 2 le, Union Jack. 25c, Netherlands. 1 le, West Germany.

**1969, July 10**
*C90* A45 7½c multi 18 18
*C91* A46 9½c multi 22 22
*C92* A45 15c multi 35 35
*C93* A46 25c multi 55 55
*C94* A46 1 le multi 2.25 2.25
*C95* A46 2 le multi 4.50 4.50
*Nos. C90-C95 (6)* 8.05 8.05

Various advertisements printed on peelable paper backing. No. C90 has side tab for handling and comes packed in boxes of 50. Nos. C91-C95 are without side tabs and come 20 stamps attached to one sheet.

Bank Type of Regular Issue

**Lithographed; Gold Impressed**

**1969, Sept. 10**
*C96* A47 9½c yel grn, vio & gold 90 90

Advertising printed on peelable paper backing; 20 imperf. stamps to a sheet of backing, roulette 10.

Cola Nut Type of Regular Issue and Type of 1967.

**Typo.; Embossed on White Paper**

**1969, Sept. 10**
*C97* A40 7c yel, mar & car 40 40

**Embossed Foil on Black Paper**
*C98* AP4 9½c blk, gold & bl 50 50
*C99* AP4 15c blk, gold & red 75 75

No. C97 has side tab for handling and comes packed in boxes of 100. Nos. C98-C99 have advertisements printed on peelable paper backing, side tabs and come packed in boxes of 50.

Boy Scout, Lord Baden-Powell and Scout Emblem — AP5

**1969, Dec. 6 Litho.**
*C100* AP5 7½c multi 48 40
*C101* AP5 9½c multi 60 48
*C102* AP5 15c multi 1.25 80
*C103* AP5 22c multi 2.00 1.40
*C104* AP5 55c multi 8.00 6.50
*C105* AP5 3 le multi 100.00 72.50
*Nos. C100-C105 (6)* 112.33 82.08

60th anniv. of the Sierra Leone Boy Scouts. Various advertising printed on peelable paper backing. No. C100 has side tab for handling and comes packed in boxes of 100. Nos. C101-C105 are without side tabs and come 20 stamps attached to one sheet.

No. 357 Surcharged "AIRMAIL" and New Denomination in Metallic Emerald, Lilac, Blue, Green, Bronze or Silver

**1970, Mar 28**
*C106* A43 7½c on ½c (E) 30 30
*C107* A43 9½c on ½c (L) 40 40
*C108* A43 15c on ½c (Bl) 50 50
*C109* A43 28c on ½c (G) 1.00 1.00
*C110* A43 40c on ½c (Br) 1.75 1.75
*C111* A43 2 le on ½c (S) 9.00 9.00
*Nos. C106-C111 (6)* 12.95 12.95

See design paragraph over No. 357.

EXPO Type of Regular Issue

Design: EXPO '70 emblem, maps of Sierra Leone and Japan.

**1970, June 22 Litho.**
*C112* A49 7½c multi 16 16
*C113* A49 9½c multi 20 20
*C114* A49 15c multi 35 35
*C115* A49 25c multi 70 70
*C116* A49 50c multi 1.50 1.50
*C117* A49 3 le multi 7.75 7.75
*Nos. C112-C117 (6)* 10.66 10.66

Various advertising printed on peelable paper backing.

Eagle Type of 1967

**1970, Oct. 3 Embossed Foil**
*C118* AP4 7½c crim & gold 40 40
*C119* AP4 9½c emer & cop 50 45
*C120* AP4 15½c grnsh bl & sil 75 60
*C121* AP4 25c brt red lil & gold 1.25 1.00
*C122* AP4 50c gold & emer 2.50 2.00
*C123* AP4 1 le sil & dk bl 5.00 4.25
*C124* AP4 2 le gold & brt bl 10.00 8.50
*Nos. C118-C124 (7)* 20.40 17.20

Advertisements printed on peelable paper backing. Issued in sheets of 10.

"Treasure of Sierra Leone" Diamond — AP6

**Lithographed and Embossed**

**1970, Dec. 30**
*C125* AP6 7½c dk car & multi 25 25
*C126* AP6 9½c dk car & multi 30 30
*C127* AP6 15c dk car & multi 50 50
*C128* AP6 25c dk car & multi 50 50
*C129* AP6 75c dk car & multi 5.00 4.00
*C130* AP6 2 le dk car & multi 22.50 17.50
*Nos. C125-C130 (6)* 29.05 23.05

Diamond industry. Advertisement printed on peelable paper backing. Sheets of 20.

Traffic Type of Regular Issue

**1971, Mar. 1 Litho.**
*C131* A53 9½c vio bl & org 75 75

Advertisements printed on peelable paper backing.

Nos. 211, 215, 228 and C87 Surcharged in Dark Red, Dark Blue or Black

**1971, Mar. 1 Engr. Wmk. 336**
*C132* A29 (a) 10c on 2p (DR) 35 32
*C133* A29 (a) 20c on 1sh (DB) 70 65

**Photo. Perf. 14**
*C134* A35 (a) 50c on 1p (Bk) 1.75 1.50

**Unwmk.**

**Litho. Imperf.**
*C135* A44 (b) 70c on 30c (DB) 2.75 2.50
*C136* A44 (b) 1 le on 30c (Bk) 4.00 3.25
*Nos. C132-C136 (5)* 9.55 8.22

Lion's Head and Bugles AP7

**Lithographed and Embossed (Gold)**

**1971, Apr. 27**
*C137* AP7 7½c multi 16 16
*C138* AP7 9½c multi 20 20
*C139* AP7 15c multi 30 30
*C140* AP7 25c multi 52 52
*C141* AP7 75c multi 2.00 2.00
*C142* AP7 2 le multi 7.00 7.00
*Nos. C137-C142 (6)* 10.18 10.18

10th anniversary of independence. Advertisements printed on peelable paper backing. Stamps are in shape of Sierra Leone map and in flag colors.

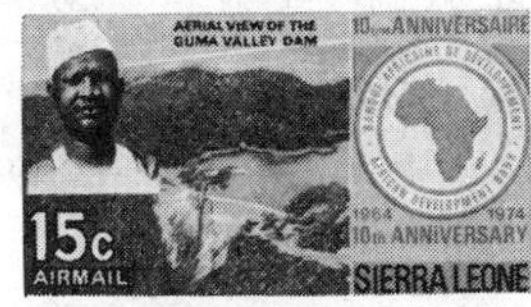


Guma Valley Dam and Bank Emblem — AP8

**1975, Jan. 14 Litho. Perf. 13½**
*C143* AP8 15c multi 1.10 1.10

African Development Bank, 10th anniv.

Congo River Type of 1975

**1975, Aug. 24 Litho. Perf. 13x13½**
*C144* A57 20c multi 75 75

Mano River Type of 1975

**1975, Oct. 3 Perf. 13x13½**
*C145* A58 15c multi 60 60

## SINGAPORE

LOCATION — An island just off the southern tip of the Malay Peninsula, south of Johore.
GOVT. — Republic in British Commonwealth.
AREA — 239 sq. mi.
POP. — 2,529,100 (est. 1984).
CAPITAL — Singapore.

Singapore, Malacca and Penang were the British settlements which, together with the Federated Malay States, composed the former colony of Straits Settlements. On April 1, 1946, Singapore became a separate colony when the Straits Settlements colony was dissolved. Malacca and Penang joined the Malayan Union, which was renamed the Federation of Malaya in 1948. In 1959 Singapore became a state with internal self-government.

Singapore joined the Federation of Malaysia in 1963 and withdrew in 1965.

100 Cents = 1 Dollar

**Catalogue values for all unused stamps in this country are for Never Hinged items.**

King George VI — A1

**1948 Wmk. 4 Typo. Perf. 14**
*1* A1 1c black 5 5
*2* A1 2c orange 6 6
*3* A1 3c green 8 6
*4* A1 4c chocolate 6 5
*6* A1 6c gray 25 6
*7* A1 8c rose red 38 30
*9* A1 10c plum 30 5
*11* A1 15c ultra 75 8
*12* A1 20c dk grn & blk 1.25 38
*14* A1 25c org & rose lil 1.40 8
*16* A1 40c dk vio & rose red 6.25 17.50
*17* A1 50c ultra & blk 7.50 25
*18* A1 $1 vio brn & ultra 11.00 38
*19* A1 $2 rose red & emer 62.50 3.00
*20* A1 $5 choc & emer 135.00 3.75
*Nos. 1-20 (15)* 226.83 26.05

**1949-52 Perf. 18**
*1a* A1 1c blk ('52) 50 5
*2a* A1 2c orange 50 5
*4a* A1 4c chocolate 50 5
*5* A1 5c rose vio ('52) 2.50 6
*6a* A1 6c gray ('52) 1.25 6
*8* A1 8c grn ('52) 5.00 2.50

9a A1 10c plum ('50) 75 5
10 A1 12c rose red ('52) 5.00 2.50
11a A1 15c ultra ('50) 2.50 30
12a A1 20c dk grn & blk 5.00 1.25
13 A1 20c ultra ('52) 4.25 75
14a A1 25c org & rose lil ('50) 2.50 6
15 A1 35c dk vio & rose red ('52) 7.50 3.00
16a A1 40c dk vio & rose red ('51) 20.00 15.00
17a A1 50c ultra & blk ('50) 7.50 8
18a A1 $1 vio brn & ultra 15.00 75
b Wmk. 4a (error) *1,000.*
19a A1 $2 rose red & emer ('51) 125.00 3.00
b Wmk. 4a (error) *1,000.*
20a A1 $5 choc & emer ('51) 200.00 3.75
*Nos. 1a-20a (18)* 405.25 33.26

**Silver Wedding Issue**
Common Design Types
Inscribed: "Singapore"

**1948, Oct. 25 Photo. *Perf. 14x14½***
21 CD304 10c purple 85 15

**Engraved; Name Typographed**
***Perf. 11½x11.***
22 CD305 $5 lt brn 110.00 22.50

**UPU Issue**
Common Design Types
Inscribed: "Malaya-Singapore"
**Engr.; Name Typo. on 15c, 25c**
***Perf. 13½, 11x11½***

**1949, Oct. 10 Wmk. 4**
23 CD306 10c rose vio 1.25 25
24 CD307 15c indigo 2.50 55
25 CD308 25c orange 4.00 95
26 CD309 50c slate 8.75 3.25

**Coronation Issue**
Common Design Type

**1953, June 2 Engr. *Perf. 13½x13***
27 CD312 10c mag & blk 1.75 15

Chinese Sampans — A2

Sir Stamford Raffles Statue — A3

Singapore River — A4

Designs: 2c, Malay kolek. 4c, Twa-kow. 5c, Lombok sloop. 6c, Trengganu pinas. 8c, Palari. 10c, Timber tongkong. 12c, Hylam trader. 20c, Cocos-Keeling schooner. 25c, Argonaut plane. 30c, Oil tanker. 50c, Liner (M.S. Chusan). $5, Arms of Singapore.

***Perf. 13½x14½***

**1955, Sept. 4 Photo. Wmk. 4**
28 A2 1c sepia 8 5
29 A2 2c org yel 10 5
30 A2 4c org brn 22 5
31 A2 5c magenta 22 5
32 A2 6c gray bl 22 6
33 A2 8c aqua 65 32
34 A2 10c dk pur 32 5
35 A2 12c rose red 1.40 65
36 A2 20c vio bl 1.40 8
37 A2 25c org & pur 75 8
38 A2 30c pur & plum 1.10 6
39 A2 50c brt bl 2.25 10

***Perf. 13½x14, 14x13½***
**Engr.**
40 A3 $1 bl & pur 6.50 18
41 A4 $2 bl grn & red 22.50 50

**Engr.; Arms Typo.**
42 A3 $5 multi 45.00 2.25
*Nos. 28-42 (15)* 82.71 4.53

For a later printing of the 10c and 50c, plates with finer screen (250) than normal (200) were used.

Singapore Lion and Administrative Center — A5

***Perf. 11½x12***
**1959, June 1 Photo. Wmk. 314**
**Lion in Gold**
43 A5 4c dp rose red 24 10
44 A5 10c magenta 48 6
45 A5 20c ultra 1.25 60
46 A5 25c yel grn 1.50 70
47 A5 30c brt vio 1.75 1.25
48 A5 50c bluish gray 4.00 2.50
*Nos. 43-48 (6)* 9.22 5.21

New Constitution of Singapore.

State Flag of Singapore A6

**1960, June 3 Litho. *Perf. 13½***
49 A6 4c bl, red & yel 50 25
50 A6 10c gray, red & yel 1.00 42

Issued for National Day, June 3, 1960.

Hands and Map of Singapore A7

**1961, June 3 Photo.**
51 A7 4c brn, yel & gray 60 30
52 A7 10c grn, yel & gray 90 38

Issued for National Day, June 3, 1961.

Sea Horse — A8

Malayan Fish: 4c, Tiger barb (horiz.). 5c, Anemone fish (horiz.). 6c, Archerfish. 10c, Harlequin fish (horiz.). 20c, Butterflyfish. 25c, Two-spot gournami (horiz.).

***Perf. 14½x13½, 13½x14½***
**1962, Mar. 31 Wmk. 314**
53 A8 2c lt grn & red brn 6 5
54 A8 4c red org & blk 10 5
a Black omitted 135.00
55 A8 5c gray & red org 14 5
a Red orange omitted 135.00
b Wmkd. sideways ('67) 22 5
56 A8 6c yel & blk 18 5
57 A8 10c dk gray & red org 28 5
a Red orange omitted 100.00
b Wmkd. sideways ('67) 42 5
58 A8 20c bl & org 80 8
a Orange omitted 150.00
59 A8 25c org & blk 80 10
a Black omitted 125.00
b Wmkd. sideways ('67) 85 24
*Nos. 53-59 (7)* 2.36 43

Symbolic of Labor's Role in Building the Nation — A9

**1962, June 3 Unwmk. *Perf. 11½***
60 A9 4c brt rose, blk & yel 35 12
61 A9 10c brt bl, blk & yel 55 22

Issued for National Day, June 3, 1962.

Vanda Tan Chay Yan — A10

Yellow-Breasted Sunbird — A11

Designs: 1c, Arachnis Maggie Oei (horiz.). 12c, Grammatophyllum speciosum. 30c, Vanda Miss Joaquim. 50c, Shama (horiz.). $1, White-breasted kingfisher (horiz.). $5, White-tailed sea eagle.

***Perf. 12½, 13½x13 (50c, $1), 13x13½ ($2, $5).***
**1963, Mar. 10 Photo. Wmk. 314**
**Flowers and Birds in Natural Colors**
**Size: 37x26mm, 26x37mm**
62 A10 1c brt pink & ultra 6 5
a Wmkd. sideways ('67) 6 5
63 A10 8c lt bl & mag 55 55
64 A10 12c sal & brn 1.10 28
65 A10 30c tan & ol grn 1.65 6
a tan omitted 50.00

**Size: 35½x25½mm, 25½x35½mm**
66 A11 50c yel grn & blk 1.90 10
a Wmkd. sideways ('66) 3.00 85
67 A11 $1 yel & blk 5.75 18
a Wmkd. sideways ('67) 6.25 3.25
68 A11 $2 dl bl & blk 11.00 1.10
69 A11 $5 pale bl & blk 32.50 2.75
*Nos. 62-69 (8)* 54.51 5.07

See No. 76.

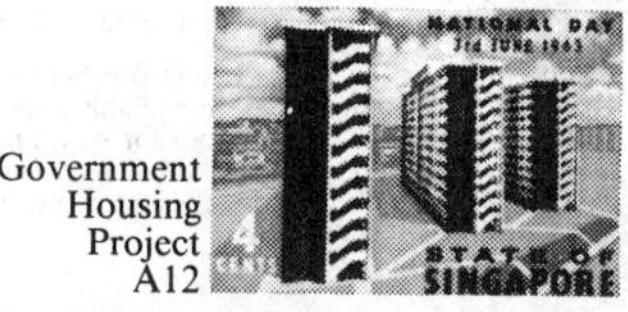

Government Housing Project A12

**1963, June 3 *Perf. 12½***
70 A12 4c multi 40 15
71 A12 10c multi 60 25

Issued for National Day, June 3, 1963.

Folk Dancers — A13

**1963, Aug. 8 Photo. *Perf. 14x14½***
72 A13 5c multi 20 10

Southeast Asia Cultural Festival.

The only foreign revenue stamps listed in this Catalogue are those authorized for prepayment of postage.

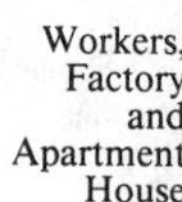

Workers, Factory and Apartment House A14

**Wmk. 314 (30c), Unwmd. (15, 20c)**
**1966, Aug. 9 Photo. *Perf. 12½x13***
73 A14 15c ultra & multi 40 20
74 A14 20c red & multi 60 40
75 A14 30c yel & multi 1.00 65

First anniversary of the Republic.

Bird Type of 1963

Design: 15c, Black-naped tern (sterna).

**1966, Nov. 9 Wmk. 314 *Perf. 12½***
**Bird in Natural Colors**
**Size: 26x37mm.**
76 A11 15c bl & blk 35 6
a Orange (eye) omitted 12.50

Marching Women, Chinese Inscription — A15

Designs: 15c, Malay inscription. 50c, Tamil inscription.

***Perf. 14x14½***
**1967, Aug. 9 Photo. Unwmk.**
77 A15 6c lt brn, gray & red 16 12
78 A15 15c multi 38 25
79 A15 50c multi 1.50 1.25

"Build a Vigorous Singapore" campaign.

Buildings and Map of Africa and Southeast Asia — A16

**1967, Oct. 7 *Perf. 14x13½***
**Black Overprint**
80 A16 10c multi 20 12
81 A16 25c multi 65 55
82 A16 50c multi 1.40 1.10

2nd Afro-Asian Housing Cong., Oct. 7-15.
No. 80 exists without overprint.

Map of Singapore and Symbolic Worker A17

Sword Dance A18

Stamps are inscribed "Work for Prosperity" in English and: 6c, Chinese. 15c, Malay. 50c, Tamil.

***Perf. 13½x14½***
**1968, Aug. 9 Photo. Unwmk.**
83 A17 6c red, blk & gold 20 18
84 A17 15c brt yel grn, blk & gold 45 32
85 A17 50c brt bl, blk & gold 1.40 1.25

Issued for National Day, 1968.

**Wmk. Rectangles (334)**

**1968 Photo. *Perf. 14***

Designs: 6c, Lion dance. 10c, Bharatha Natyam, Indian dance. 15c, Tari Payong, Sumatran dance. 20c, Kathak Kali, Indian dance mask. 25c, Lu Chih Shen and Lin Chung, Chinese opera masks. 30c, Dragon dance (horiz.). 50c, Tari Lilin, Malayan candle dance. 75c, Tarian Kuda Kepang, Javanese dance. $1, Yao Chi, Chinese opera mask.

*86* A18 5c yel & multi 20 5
*87* A18 6c org & multi 24 5
*88* A18 10c bl grn & multi 38 5
*89* A18 15c lt brn & multi 52 22
*a* Booklet pane of 4 ('69) 1.90
*90* A18 20c brn & multi 65 22
*91* A18 25c dp car & multi 1.00 38
*92* A18 30c pink & multi 1.40 38
*93* A18 50c brn org & multi 1.50 75
*94* A18 75c brt rose & multi 2.75 1.20
*95* A18 $1 ol grn & multi 3.50 1.50
*Nos. 86-95 (10)* 12.14 4.80

Issue dates: 6c, 20c, 30c, 50c, 75c, Dec. 1; 5c, 10c, 15c, 25c, $1, Dec. 29.

**1973 *Perf. 13***

*86a* A18 5c yel & multi 60 42
*88a* A18 10c bl grn & multi 85 50
*90a* A18 20c brn & multi 1.50 85
*91a* A18 25c dp car & multi 2.50 1.40
*92a* A18 30c pink & multi 3.50 1.75
*93a* A18 50c brn org & multi 5.00 3.00
*95a* A18 $1 ol grn & multi 12.00 6.00
*Nos. 86a-95a (7)* 25.95 13.92

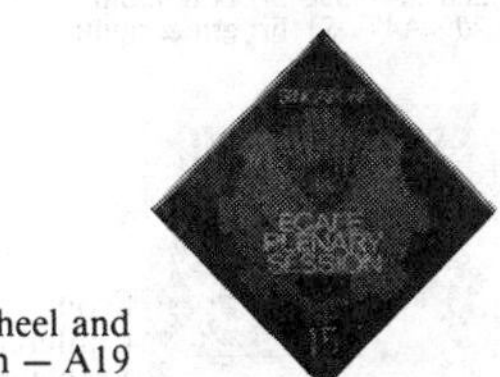


Cogwheel and Emblem — A19

**1969, Apr. 15 Unwmk. *Perf. 13***

*96* A19 15c bl blk & sil 50 30
*97* A19 30c red blk & sil 1.00 80
*98* A19 75c vio, blk & sil 2.50 2.00

25th Plenary Session of the Economic Commission for Asia and the Far East (ECAFE), Singapore, Apr. 15-28.

"Homes for the People" A20

Plane over Docks of Singapore A21

***Perf. 13x13½***

**1969, July 20 Litho. Unwmk.**

*99* A20 25c emer & blk 1.25 90
*100* A20 50c dk bl & blk 2.00 1.50

1960-69 building program of the Housing and Development Board.

**1969, Aug. 9 *Perf. 14x14½***

Designs: 30c, U.N. emblem and map of Singapore. 75c, Flags and map of Malaya and Borneo. $1, Uplifted hands and Singapore flag. $5, Tail of Japanese plane and searchlights. $10, Statue of Sir Thomas Stamford Raffles.

*101* A21 15c yel, blk & org *28* 24
*102* A21 30c brt bl & blk *60* 52
*103* A21 75c org & multi *1.90* 1.25
*104* A21 $1 red & blk *4.25* 2.25
*105* A21 $5 gray, blk & red *27.50* 17.50
*106* A21 $10 emer & blk *52.50* 35.00
*a* Souv. sheet of 6 *375.00* 325.00
*Nos. 101-106 (6)* *87.03* 56.76

Sesquicentennial of the founding of Singapore. No. 106a contains one each of Nos. 101-106; black marginal inscription. Size: 120x120mm.

Mirudhangam, South Indian Drum – A22

Wmk. 366- S multiple

Musical Instruments: 4c, Pi Pa, Chinese, 4 strings (vert.). $2, Rebab, Malay violin, 3 strings (vert.). $5, Vina, Indian, 7 strings. $10, Ta Ku, Chinese drum.

**1969 Photo. Wmk. 366 *Perf. 13***

*107* A22 1c multi 10 5
*108* A22 4c multi 12 5
*109* A22 $2 multi 5.00 2.75
*110* A22 $5 multi 11.00 6.75
*111* A22 $10 multi 27.50 15.00
*Nos. 107-111 (5)* 43.72 24.60

Issue dates: 1c, 4c, $2, $5, Nov. 10; $10, Dec. 6.

Sea Shells — A23

Designs: 30c, Tropical fish. 75c, Greater flamingo and helmeted hornbill. $1, Orchids.

***Perf. 13½***

**1970, Mar. 15 Unwmk. Litho.**

*112* A23 15c pale vio & multi 48 20
*113* A23 30c lt bl & multi 1.50 65
*114* A23 75c yel & multi 4.75 3.00
*115* A23 $1 lt grn & multi 5.25 3.25
*a* Souvenir sheet of 4 17.00 9.00

Issued to commemorate EXPO '70 International Exposition, Osaka, Japan, Mar. 15-Sept. 13. No. 115a contains one each of Nos. 112-115 with marginal inscription and decoration. Size: 93x153mm.

Common Design Types pictured in section before Great Britain.

Child Playing (Kindergarten) — A24

Designs: 50c, Sports activities. 75c, Cultural activities.

**1970, July Unwmk. *Perf. 13½***

*116* A24 15c dp org & blk 70 30
*117* A24 50c org, blk & vio bl 2.50 1.50
*118* A24 75c blk & dp lil rose 3.75 2.50

People's Association, 10th anniversary.

Soldier and Map of Singapore — A25

Designs: Map and soldiers in various positions.

**1970, Aug. 9 Litho. Unwmk.**

*119* A25 15c emer, blk & org 60 25
*120* A25 50c org, blk & brt mag 3.00 2.00
*121* A25 $1 brt mag, blk & emer 4.50 4.00

National military service.

Runners A26

Designs: 15c, Swimmers. 25c, Badminton. 50c, Automobile race.

**1970, Aug. 23 Photo. *Perf. 13***

*122* A26 10c blk, dp car & ultra 45 20
*123* A26 15c blk, ultra & brn org 80 40
*124* A26 25c blk, brn org & emer 1.40 1.40
*125* A26 50c blk, dp car & emer 2.50 2.50

Issued to publicize the 1970 Festival of Sports. Nos. 122-125 printed se-tenant in sheets of 40.

Ship and Emblem of National Line (Neptune Oriental Lines) — A27

Designs: 30c, Ship in first container berth. 75c, Ship repairing and ship building.

**1970, Nov. 1 Litho. *Perf. 12***

*126* A27 15c vio bl, lem & red 1.25 35
*127* A27 30c dp ultra & lem 3.00 1.25
*128* A27 75c red & lem 7.75 3.75

Singapore shipping industry.

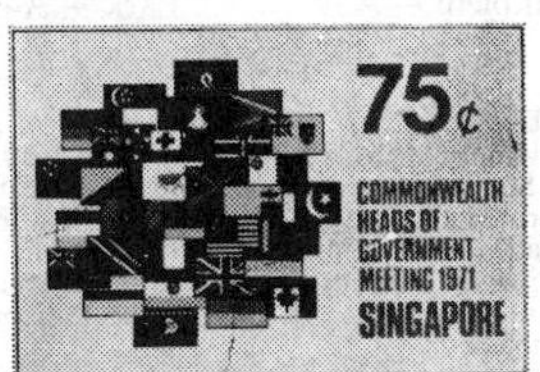


Flags of Commonwealth Nations — A28

Designs: 15c, Circular arrangement of names of Commonwealth members. 30c, Flags arranged in circle. $1, Flags (different arrangement).

**1971, Jan. 14 *Perf. 15x14½***

**Size: 46½x31mm**

*129* A28 15c gold & multi 45 22
*130* A28 30c gold & multi 1.10 65
*131* A28 75c gold & multi 1.75 1.65

**Size: 67x31mm**

***Perf. 14***

*132* A28 $1 gold & multi 4.00 2.50

Commonwealth Heads of Government Meeting, Singapore, Jan. 12-14.

Cycle Rickshaws A29

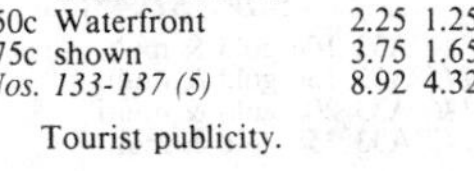


Houses of Worship in Singapore — A30

***Perf. 11½***

**1971, Apr. 4 Unwmk. Litho.**

*133* A29 15c shown 42 22
*134* A29 20c Sampans 60 45
*135* A29 30c Market place 1.90 75

***Perf. 13x13½***

*136* A30 50c Waterfront 2.25 1.25
*137* A30 75c shown 3.75 1.65
*Nos. 133-137 (5)* 8.92 4.32

Tourist publicity.

Chinese New Year — A31

Singapore Festivals: 30c, Hari Raya Puasa (Moslem). 50c, Deepavali (Hindu). 75c, Christmas.

**1971, Aug. 9 Litho. *Perf. 14***

*138* A31 15c multi 70 35
*139* A31 30c multi 1.50 1.10
*140* A31 50c multi 2.75 2.00
*141* A31 75c multi 4.25 3.00
*a* Souvenir sheet of 4 45.00 45.00

No. 141a contains one each of Nos. 138-141. Multicolored marginal inscription. Size: 149½x125mm.

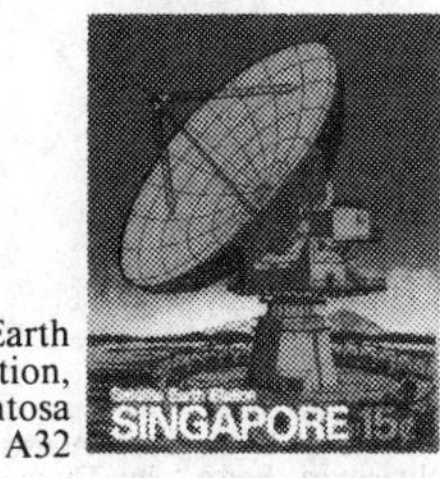


Satellite Earth Station, Sentosa Island — A32

Design: No. 143 as 15c, enlarged to cover 4 stamps. Sheets of 100.

**1971, Oct. 23 Unwmk. *Perf. 13½***

*142* A32 15c red & multi 3.75 1.10
*143* A32 Block of 4 37.50 35.00
*a* 30c (yel numeral) 9.00 8.00
*b* 30c (grn numeral) 9.00 8.00
*c* 30c (rose numeral) 9.00 8.00
*d* 30c (org numeral) 9.00 8.00

Establishment of Singapore's satellite earth station, Sentosa Island.

Singapore River and Fort Canning, 1843-1847 — A33

Views of Singapore, from 19th century art works: 15c, The Padang, 1851. 20c, Waterfront, 1848-1849. 35c, View from Fort Canning, 1846. 50c, View from Mount Wallich, 1857. $1, Waterfront with ships, from the sea, 1861.

**1971, Dec. 5 Unwmk. *Perf. 13x12½***
**Size: 52x45mm**

*144* A33 10c gold & multi 70 35
*145* A33 15c gold & multi 1.00 50
*146* A33 20c gold & multi 1.75 85
*147* A33 35c gold & multi 4.00 2.25

***Perf. 12½x13***
**Size: 68x47mm**

*148* A33 50c gold & multi 7.00 4.00
*149* A33 $1 gold & multi 17.00 8.75
*Nos. 144-149 (6)* 31.45 16.70

George V 1c Copper Coin, 1920 — A34

Singapore Coins: 35c, Silver dollar, 1969. $1, Gold $150, 1969 commemorative coin for sesquicentennial of founding of Singapore.

**1972, June 4 Litho. *Perf. 13½***

*150* A34 15c dk grn, dp org & blk 1.00 24
*151* A34 35c red & blk 2.50 90
*152* A34 $1 ultra, yel & blk 3.50 3.50

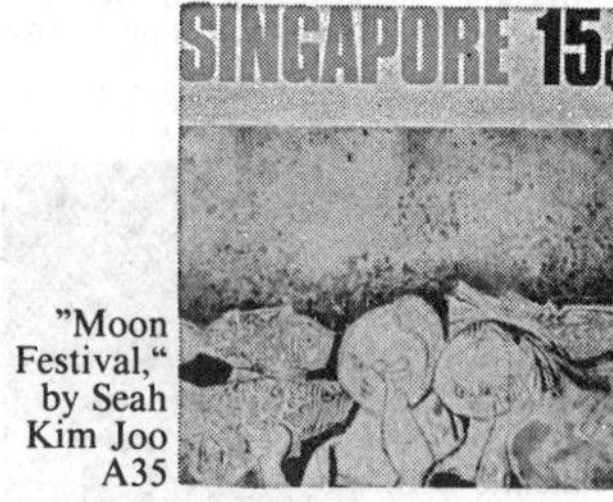


"Moon Festival," by Seah Kim Joo A35

Paintings by Singapore Artists: 35c, "Complimentary Force," by Thomas Yeo. 50c, "Rhythm in Blue," by Yusman Aman. $1, "Gibbons," by Chen Wen Hsi.

**1972, July 9 Litho. *Perf. 12½***
**Size: 40x43½mm**

*153* A35 15c brn org & multi 45 20

**Size: 35½x53½mm**

*154* A35 35c bl grn & multi 1.25 70
*155* A35 50c dl vio & multi 1.90 1.00

**Size: 40x43½mm**

*156* A35 $1 bis & multi 4.25 2.25

Chinese New Year — A36

Festivals: 35c, Hari Raya Puasa (candles and ornament). 50c, Deepavali (incense and teapot). 75c, Christmas (candle and stained glass window).

**1972, Aug. 9 Litho. *Perf. 13x12½***

*157* A36 15c dp rose & multi 50 25
*158* A36 35c vio & multi 1.50 1.00
*159* A36 50c grn & multi 2.00 1.35
*160* A36 75c bl & multi 3.00 2.00

Technical and Scientific Training A37

Designs: 35c, Sport. $1, Art and culture.

**1972, Oct. 1 Photo. *Perf. 12***

*161* A37 15c org & multi 50 30
*162* A37 35c bl & multi 1.25 1.00
*163* A37 $1 org & multi 3.50 3.00

Youth of Singapore.

Neptune Ruby A38

**1972, Dec. 17 Litho. *Perf. 14x14½***
**Size: 42x28½mm**

*164* A38 15c *shown* 38 25

**Size: 29½x28½mm**

*165* A38 75c *Maria Rickmers* 3.00 3.00
*166* A38 $1 *Chinese junk* 8.50 8.50
*a* Souvenir sheet of 3 15.00 11.00

Singapore shipping industry. No. 166a contains one each of Nos. 164-166. Gray and multicolored margin. Size: 151x83mm.

Quality and Reliability Emblem — A39

Birds, Jurong Bird Park — A40

Designs: 15c, Emblem and initials of participating organizations: Singapore Institute of Standards and Industrial Research, Singapore Manufacturers' Association, National Trades Union Congress. 75c, Emblem and "Prosperity through Quality and Reliability" in multiple rows. $1, Quality and Reliability emblem.

**1973, Feb. 25 Litho. *Perf. 14½x14***

*167* A39 15c gold & multi 32 28
*168* A39 35c gold & multi 85 75
*169* A39 75c gold & multi 1.90 1.75
*170* A39 $1 gold & multi 2.75 2.50

Prosperity through Quality and Reliability campaign.

**1973, Apr. 29 *Perf. 12½***

Landmarks: 35c, Dancers, National Theater. 50c, City Hall and ballplayers. $1, Singapore River with boats and buildings.

*171* A40 15c ver & blk 52 25
*172* A40 35c dl grn & blk 1.65 1.00
*173* A40 50c brn & blk 2.75 1.50
*174* A40 $1 dk vio & blk 5.25 3.00

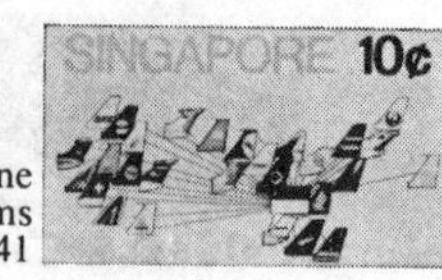


Airline Emblems A41

Designs: 35c, Emblem of Singapore Airlines and international destinations. 75c, SIA emblem on stylized tail of Boeing jet. $1, SIA emblems circling globe.

**1973, June 24 Litho. *Perf. 13½***

*175* A41 10c multi 40 20
*176* A41 35c multi 1.10 1.10
*177* A41 75c multi 2.75 2.25
*178* A41 $1 multi 4.00 3.75

Singapore Intl. Airport at Paya Lebar.

Entertainers — A42

Running, Judo, Boxing — A43

Design: Composite of various forms of entertainment.

**1973, Aug. 9 Litho. *Perf. 13½x14***

*179* A42 10c blk & org red 52 28
*180* A42 35c blk & org red 1.50 1.25
*181* A42 50c blk & org red 2.25 2.00
*182* A42 75c blk & org red 3.75 3.00

National Day 1973. Nos. 179-182 printed se-tenant in blocks of 4 in sheets of 100.

**1973, Sept. 1 Photo. *Perf. 14***

Designs: 15c, Bicycling, weight lifting, pistol shoot, yachting. 25c, Various balls. 35c, Tennis racket, ball, hockey stick. 50c, Swimming. $1, Singapore National Stadium.

**Size: 25x25mm**

*183* A43 10c gold, sil & ind 52 24
*184* A43 15c gold & dk brn 60 28
*185* A43 25c sil, gold & blk 1.00 70
*186* A43 35c gold, sil & dk pur 1.40 1.10

***Perf. 13x14***
**Size: 40½x25mm.**

*187* A43 50c gold & multi 1.75 1.40
*188* A43 $1 sil, vio bl & emer 4.75 4.00
*a* Souvenir sheet of 6 15.00 5.00
*Nos. 183-188 (6)* 10.02 7.72

7th South East Asia (SEAP) Games, Singapore. No. 188a contains one each of Nos. 183-188. Silver marginal inscription. Size: 129x110mm.

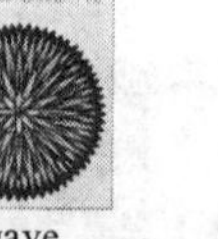

Agave A44

Mangosteen A45

Designs: Stylized flowers and fruit.

**1973 Photo. *Perf. 13***

*189* A44 1c *shown* 5 5
*190* A44 5c *Coleus blumei* 10 5
*a* Booklet pane of 10 (4 #190, 4 #191 + 2 #193) 2.25
*191* A44 10c *Madagascar periwinkle* 20 5
*192* A44 15c *Sunflower* 22 5
*193* A44 20c *Dwarf palm* 35 7
*194* A44 25c *Yellow daisy* 38 15
*195* A44 35c *Chrysanthemum* 65 35
*196* A44 50c *Costus* 90 45
*197* A44 75c *Transvaal daisy* 1.25 70
*198* A45 $1 *shown* 1.75 1.00
*199* A45 $2 *Jackfruit* 3.50 2.25
*200* A45 $5 *Coconuts* 9.00 5.50
*201* A45 $10 *Pineapple* 18.00 11.00
*Nos. 189-201 (13)* 36.35 21.67

Nos. 189-201 have fluorescent underprint "Singapore" in multiple rows.

Tiger and Orangutans A46

Tropical Fish A47

**1973, Dec. 16 Litho. *Perf. 13***

*202* A46 5c *shown* 50 10
*203* A46 10c *Leopard and deer* 1.00 32
*204* A46 35c *Panther and stag* 3.00 1.25
*205* A46 75c *White horse and lion* 5.75 3.00

Opening of Singapore Zoo.

**1974, Apr. 21 *Perf. 13½x14***

Designs: Various poecilia reticulata fish.

*206* A47 5c ap grn & multi 45 8
*207* A47 10c pink & multi 70 35
*208* A47 35c brt bl & multi 1.75 1.50
*209* A47 $1 brt grn & multi 6.00 4.50

Scout Conference Emblem — A48

**1974, June 9 *Perf. 13½x14½***

*210* A48 10c multi 50 30
*211* A48 75c multi 3.00 3.00

9th Asia-Pacific Boy Scout Conf., Singapore.

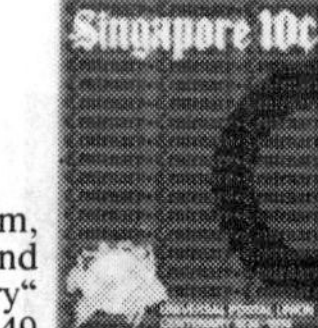


UPU Emblem, Circle and "Centenary" Multiple — A49

UPU, cent.: 35c, Circle and UN emblems, multiple. 75c, Circle and pigeons, multiple.

**1974, July 7 Litho. *Perf. 14½x13½***

*212* A49 10c org brn & multi 30 15
*213* A49 35c bl & multi 1.00 70
*214* A49 75c emer & multi 2.50 1.75

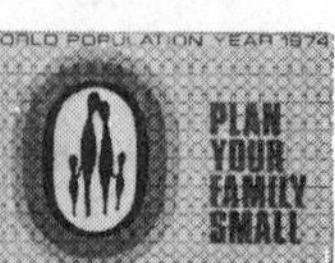


Family — A50

**1974, Aug. 9 Litho. *Perf. 13x13½***

*215* A50 10c *shown* 30 18
*216* A50 35c *Symbols for male & female* 1.10 90
*217* A50 75c *World map and WPY emblem* 2.75 2.50

Natl. Day and World Population Year 1974.

"Sun and Tree" – A51

Children's Drawings: 10c, "My Daddy and Mommy." 35c, "A Dump Truck." 50c, "My Aunt."

**1974, Oct. 1 Photo. *Perf. 14x13½***

218 A51 5c multi 38 8
219 A51 10c multi 90 60
220 A51 35c multi 2.50 2.00
221 A51 50c multi 3.75 3.00
a Souvenir sheet of 4 12.00 3.25

Children's drawings for Children's Day (UNICEF). No. 221a contains one each of Nos. 218-221, perf. 13; marginal inscription and decoration in silver. Size: 138x100mm.

Alfresco Dining A52

Tourist publicity: 20c, Singapore River. $1, "Kelong" fish traps.

**1975, Jan. 26 Litho. *Perf. 14***

222 A52 15c multi 50 30
223 A52 20c multi 60 50
224 A52 $1 multi 5.00 3.75

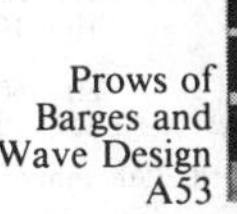

Prows of Barges and Wave Design A53

Designs: 25c, Cargo ships and ship's wheel. 50c, Tanker and signal flags. $1, Container ship and propellers.

**1975, Mar. 10 Litho. *Perf. 13½***

225 A53 5c multi 25 5
226 A53 25c multi 1.00 90
227 A53 50c multi 2.00 1.75
228 A53 $1 multi 3.50 3.50

9th Biennial Conf. of the Intl. Assoc. of Ports and Harbours, Singapore, Mar. 8-15.

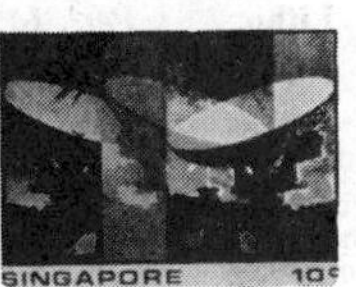
Satellite Earth Stations, Sentosa Island A54

Oil Refinery A55

Design: 75c, Brain surgery, Medical Center, Jurong.

**1975, June 29 Photo. *Perf. 13½***

229 A54 10c multi 25 15
230 A55 35c multi 75 55
231 A54 75c multi 2.50 1.50

Science and industry.

"10" and "Homes and Gardens for the People" – A56

Crowned Cranes – A57

Designs ("10" and): 35c, "Shipping and ship building." 75c, "Communications and technology." $1, "Trade, commerce and industry."

**1975, Aug. 9 Litho. *Perf. 13½***

232 A56 10c multi 30 12
233 A56 35c multi 1.00 70
234 A56 75c multi 2.50 1.50
235 A56 $1 multi 3.00 2.00

Tenth National Day.

**1975, Oct. 5 Litho. *Perf. 14½x13½***

Birds: 10c, Great hornbill. 35c, White-breasted and white-collared kingfishers. $1, Sulphur-crested cockatoo and blue and yellow macaw.

236 A57 5c emer & multi 45 8
237 A57 10c emer & multi 70 22
238 A57 35c emer & multi 3.75 1.50
239 A57 $1 emer & multi 9.00 4.75

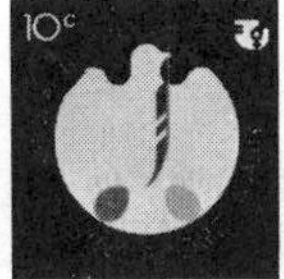
IWY Emblem, Peace Dove as "Equality" – A58

Designs (IWY Emblem): 35c, Peace dove with eggs in basket, symbolizing "Development." 75c, Peace dove and young, symbolizing "Peace."

**1975, Dec. 7 Litho. *Perf. 13½***

240 A58 10c blk, bl & pink 52 25
241 A58 35c org & multi 1.75 1.25
242 A58 75c dp vio & multi 3.50 2.75
a Souvenir sheet of 3 16.00 16.00

International Women's Year 1975.

No. 242a contains one each of Nos. 240-242, multicolored margin. Size: 127x100mm.

Yellow Flame – A59

Aranda Hybrid – A60

Wayside Trees: 35c, Cabbage tree. 50c, Rose of India. 75c, Variegated coral tree.

**1976, Apr. 18 Litho. *Perf. 14***

243 A59 10c multi 28 18
244 A59 35c multi 1.00 85
245 A59 50c multi 1.50 1.25
246 A59 75c multi 3.00 1.90

**1976, June 20 Litho. *Perf. 14***

Designs: Varieties of aranda orchids.

247 A60 10c blk & multi 40 15
248 A60 35c blk & multi 1.50 75
249 A60 50c blk & multi 3.00 1.10
250 A60 75c blk & multi 4.50 1.60

"10" and Children's Band A61

Designs ("10" and): 35c, Running boys. 75c, Dancing children.

**1976, Aug. 9 Litho. *Perf. 12½***

251 A61 10c multi 28 16
252 A61 35c multi 1.00 70
253 A61 75c multi 3.00 1.65

Singapore Youth Festival, 10th anniversary.

Queen Elizabeth Walk – A62

Paintings of Old Singapore, c. 1905-10: 50c, The Padang. $1, Raffles Place.

**1976, Nov. 14 Litho. *Perf. 14***

254 A62 10c multi 40 15
255 A62 50c multi 2.00 1.25
256 A62 $1 multi 4.50 2.50
a Souvenir sheet of 3 10.00 10.00

No. 256a contains one each of Nos. 254-256, perf. 13½; gold marginal inscription and border. Size: 164x92mm.

Chinese Bridal Costume A63

Radar, Surface to Air Missile, Soldiers A64

Designs: 35c, Indian bridal costume. 75c, Malay bridal costume.

**1976, Dec. 19 Litho. *Perf. 14½***

257 A63 10c lt grn & multi 36 14
258 A63 35c lil & multi 1.40 70
259 A63 75c yel & multi 3.00 1.75

**1977, Mar. 12 Litho. *Perf. 14½***

Designs: 50c, Infantry soldiers and tank. 75c, Jet fighter, pilot, telecommunications center.

260 A64 10c multi 30 16
261 A64 50c multi 1.50 95
262 A64 75c multi 2.75 1.50

National Service, 10th anniversary.

Lyrate Cockle A65

Spotted Hermit Crab A66

Sea Shells: 5c, Folded scallop. 10c, Marble cone. 15c, Scorpion conch. 20c, Amplustre bubble. 25c, Spiral Babylon. 35c, Regal thorny oyster. 50c, Winged frog shell. 75c, Troschel's murex. Marine Life: $2, Stingray. $5, Cuttlefish. $10, Lionfish.

**1977 *Perf. 13½***

263 A65 1c org & multi 5 5
264 A65 5c org & multi 8 5
a Bklt. pane of 12 (4 #264, 8 #265) 1.25
265 A65 10c org & multi 12 8
266 A65 15c org & multi 18 12
267 A65 20c org & multi 24 15
268 A65 25c org & multi 28 20
269 A65 35c org & multi 40 25
270 A65 50c org & multi 60 50
271 A65 75c org & multi 90 75

***Perf. 14***

272 A66 $1 multi 1.25 1.00
273 A66 $2 multi 2.50 2.00
274 A66 $5 multi 6.00 5.00
275 A66 $10 multi 12.00 10.00
*Nos. 263-275 (13)* 24.60 20.15

No. 264a has a large inscribed selvage, the size of 6 stamps.

Issue dates: Nos. 263-271, Apr. 9. Others, June 4.

Singapore Harbor Improvements A67

Designs: 50c, Construction workers. 75c, Road workers.

**1977, May 1 Litho. *Perf. 13x12½***

276 A67 10c multi 22 14
277 A67 50c multi 1.10 75
278 A67 75c multi 1.90 1.25

Labor Day.

"Key to Savings" A68

Grain and Cattle A69

Designs: 35c, "On-line Banking Service." 75c, "GIRO Service."

**1977, July 16 Litho. *Perf. 13***

279 A68 10c multi 20 10
280 A68 35c multi 75 50
281 A68 75c multi 2.25 1.50

Centenary of Post Office Savings Bank.

**1977, Aug. 8 Litho. *Perf. 14***

Designs: 10c, Flags of founding members: Thailand, Indonesia, Singapore, Malaysia and Philippines. 75c, Steel, oil and chemical industries.

282 A69 10c multi 20 10
283 A69 35c multi 75 45
284 A69 75c multi 2.25 1.00

Association of South East Asian Nations (ASEAN), 10th anniversary.

Bus Stop – A70

Children's Drawings: 10c, Chingay procession (vert.). 75c, Playground.

**1977, Oct. 1 *Perf. 12½***

285 A70 10c multi 35 10
286 A70 35c multi 1.00 65
287 A70 75c multi 3.25 1.50
a Souvenir sheet of 3 6.00 6.00

No. 287a contains one each of Nos. 285-287; multicolored margin. Size: 160x98mm.

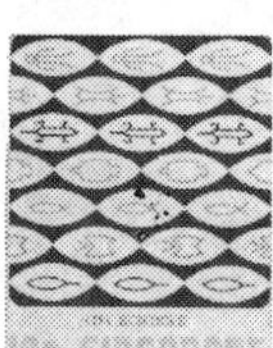

Symbols of Life Sciences — A71

Botanical Gardens — A72

Singapore Science Center: 35c, "Physical sciences." 75c, "Science and technology." $1, Science Center.

**1977, Dec. 10 Litho. *Perf. 14½x14***

| | | | | |
|---|---|---|---|---|
| *288* | A71 | 10c multi | 15 | 10 |
| *289* | A71 | 35c multi | 60 | 35 |
| *290* | A71 | 75c multi | 1.25 | 80 |
| *291* | A71 | $1 multi | 2.00 | 1.20 |

**1978, Apr. 22 Litho. *Perf. 14½***

Singapore Parks and Gardens: 10c, Jurong Bird Park (horiz.). 35c, East Coast Lagoon and Park.

| | | | | |
|---|---|---|---|---|
| *292* | A72 | 10c multi | 20 | 10 |
| *293* | A72 | 35c multi | 70 | 55 |
| *294* | A72 | 75c multi | 1.75 | 1.25 |

Red-whiskered Bulbul — A73

Songbirds: 35c, White eyes. 50c, White-rumped shama. 75c, White-crested laughing thrush.

**1978, July 1 Litho. *Perf. 13½***

| | | | | |
|---|---|---|---|---|
| *295* | A73 | 10c multi | 28 | 10 |
| *296* | A73 | 35c multi | 80 | 52 |
| *297* | A73 | 50c multi | 1.40 | 80 |
| *298* | A73 | 75c multi | 2.00 | 1.25 |

Thian Hock Keng Temple — A74

National Monuments: No. 303a, like No. 299. Nos. 300, 303b, Hajjah Fatimah Mosque. Nos. 301, 303c, Armenian Church. Nos. 302, 303d, Sri Mariamman Temple.

**1978, Aug. 9**

| | | | | |
|---|---|---|---|---|
| *299* | A74 | 10c tan & multi | 40 | 10 |
| *300* | A74 | 10c grn & multi | 40 | 10 |
| *301* | A74 | 10c bl & multi | 40 | 10 |
| *302* | A74 | 10c lil & multi | 40 | 10 |

**Souvenir Sheet**

| | | | |
|---|---|---|---|
| *303* | Sheet of 4 | 3.50 | 3.50 |
| *a* | A74 35c tan & multi | 50 | |
| *b* | A74 35c grn & multi | 50 | |
| *c* | A74 35c bl & multi | 50 | |
| *d* | A74 35c lil & multi | 50 | |

No. 303 has pale gray margin with blue inscription. Size: 174x87mm.

Map of Proposed Cable Network A75

**1978, Oct. 30 Litho. *Perf. 14***

| | | | | |
|---|---|---|---|---|
| *304* | A75 | 10c multi | 18 | 12 |
| *305* | A75 | 35c multi | 60 | 50 |
| *306* | A75 | 50c multi | 90 | 75 |
| *307* | A75 | 75c multi | 1.25 | 1.10 |

ASEAN Submarine Cable Network. Nos. 304-307 printed in sheets of 100. Stamps have perforations around design and around edges.

Neptune Spinel — A76

Ships: 35c, Neptune Aries. 50c, Arno Temasek. 75c, Neptune Pearl.

**1978, Nov. 18 Litho. *Perf. 13½x14***

| | | | | |
|---|---|---|---|---|
| *308* | A76 | 10c multi | 16 | 10 |
| *309* | A76 | 35c multi | 52 | 52 |
| *310* | A76 | 50c multi | 80 | 80 |
| *311* | A76 | 75c multi | 1.25 | 1.25 |

Neptune Oriental Shipping Lines, 10th anniversary.

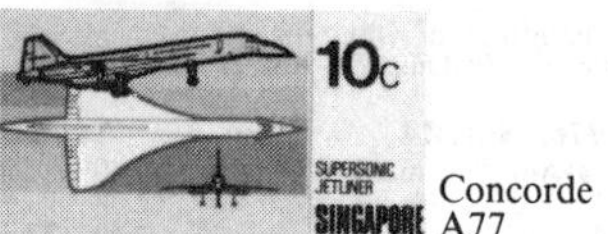


Concorde A77

Aviation Development: 35c, Vickers-Vimy, 1st aircraft to land in Singapore. 50c, Boeing 747B. 75c, Wright Brothers' Flyer I.

**1978, Dec. 16 *Perf. 13½***

| | | | | |
|---|---|---|---|---|
| *312* | A77 | 10c yel grn & blk | 16 | 10 |
| *313* | A77 | 35c bl & blk | 52 | 52 |
| *314* | A77 | 50c car & blk | 80 | 80 |
| *315* | A77 | 75c brn & blk | 1.25 | 1.25 |

75th anniversary of 1st powered flight.

Distance Marker in Kilometers A78

Vanda Orchids A79

Designs: 35c, Tape measure in centimeters. 75c, Scales in grams and kilograms.

**1979, Jan. 24 Litho. *Perf. 13x13½***

| | | | | |
|---|---|---|---|---|
| *316* | A78 | 10c multi | 15 | 10 |
| *317* | A78 | 35c multi | 50 | 35 |
| *318* | A78 | 75c multi | 1.00 | 75 |

Introduction of metric system.

***Perf. 14½x14, 14x14½***
**1979, Apr. 14 Litho.**

Designs: Varieties of vanda hybrids. 10c, 35c, horiz.

| | | | | |
|---|---|---|---|---|
| *319* | A79 | 10c multi | 15 | 15 |
| *320* | A79 | 35c multi | 52 | 52 |
| *321* | A79 | 50c multi | 75 | 75 |
| *322* | A79 | 75c multi | 1.10 | 1.10 |

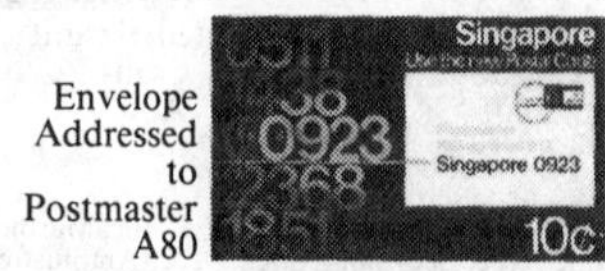


Envelope Addressed to Postmaster A80

Design: 50c, Envelope addressed to Philatelic Bureau.

**1979, July 1 Litho. *Perf. 12½x13***

| | | | | |
|---|---|---|---|---|
| *323* | A80 | 10c org & multi | 20 | 10 |
| *324* | A80 | 50c dk bl & multi | 80 | 50 |

Singapore's postal code system.

Old Phone, Telephone Lines — A81

Designs: 35c, Dial, world map. 50c, Push-button phone, skyline. 75c, Line network.

**1979, Oct. 5 Litho. *Perf. 13½***

| | | | | |
|---|---|---|---|---|
| *325* | A81 | 10c multi | 20 | 10 |
| *326* | A81 | 35c multi | 45 | 35 |
| *327* | A81 | 50c multi | 75 | 50 |
| *328* | A81 | 75c multi | 1.00 | 75 |

Telephone service centenary.

IYC Emblem, Lanterns Festival A82

IYC Emblem, Children's Drawings: 35c, Singapore Harbor. 50c, "Use Your Hands." 75c, Soccer.

**1979, Nov. 10 Litho. *Perf. 13***

| | | | | |
|---|---|---|---|---|
| *329* | A82 | 10c multi | 10 | 10 |
| *330* | A82 | 35c multi | 42 | 42 |
| *331* | A82 | 50c multi | 60 | 60 |
| *332* | A82 | 75c multi | 90 | 90 |
| *a* | | Souvenir sheet of 4 | 3.00 | 3.00 |

International Year of the Child. No. 332a contains Nos. 329-332. Ultramarine and purple margin shows IYC emblem. Size: 155x98mm.

Botanic Gardens, 120th Anniversary A83

**1979, Dec. 15 *Perf. 13½***

| | | | | |
|---|---|---|---|---|
| *333* | A83 | 10c *shown* | 18 | 10 |
| *334* | A83 | 50c *Gazebo* | 70 | 55 |
| *335* | A83 | $1 *Greenhouse* | 1.40 | 1.10 |

Hainan Junk — A84

**1980 Litho. *Perf. 14***

| | | | | |
|---|---|---|---|---|
| *336* | A84 | 1c *shown* | 5 | 5 |
| *337* | A84 | 5c *Clipper* | 5 | 5 |
| *338* | A84 | 10c *Fujian junk* | 10 | 10 |
| *a* | | Bklt. pane of 10 | 1.00 | |
| *339* | A84 | 15c *Golekkan* | 15 | 15 |
| *340* | A84 | 20c *Palari* | 20 | 20 |
| *341* | A84 | 25c *East Indiaman* | 25 | 25 |
| *342* | A84 | 35c *Galleon* | 35 | 35 |
| *343* | A84 | 50c *Caravel* | 50 | 50 |
| *344* | A84 | 75c *Jiangsu trader* | 75 | 75 |

**Size: 41½x24½mm**

***Perf. 13½***

**1980 Litho *Perf. 14***

| | | | | |
|---|---|---|---|---|
| *345* | A84 | $1 *Coaster* | 1.00 | 1.00 |
| *346* | A84 | $2 *Oil tanker* | 2.00 | 2.00 |
| *347* | A84 | $5 *Screw steamer* | 5.00 | 5.00 |
| *348* | A84 | $10 *Paddle wheel steamer* | 10.00 | 10.00 |
| | | *Nos. 336-348 (13)* | 20.40 | 20.40 |

Issue dates: Nos. 336-344, Apr. 26; others, Apr. 5.

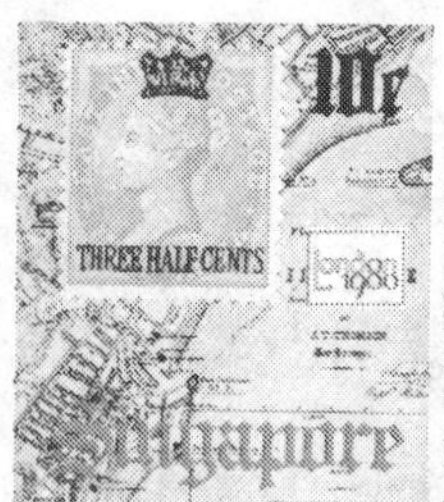


Straits Settlements No. 1, Old Singapore Map, London 1980 Emblem A85

London 1980 Emblem and: 35c, Straits Settlements No. 146, letter. $1, Singapore No. 19, map of Straits. $2, Singapore No. 106, letter, 1819.

**1980, May 6 Litho. *Perf. 13***

| | | | | |
|---|---|---|---|---|
| *349* | A85 | 10c multi | 16 | 10 |
| *350* | A85 | 35c multi | 30 | 30 |
| *351* | A85 | $1 multi | 85 | 85 |
| *352* | A85 | $2 multi | 1.65 | 1.65 |
| *a* | | Souvenir sheet of 4 | 4.25 | 4.25 |

London 1980 International Stamp Exhibition, May 6-14. No. 352a contains Nos. 349-352; multicolored margin shows London 1980 emblem. Size: 148½x114mm.

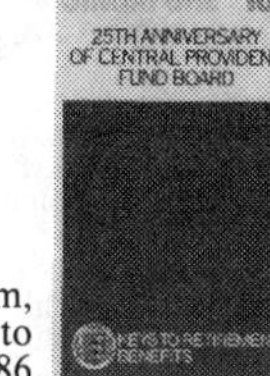

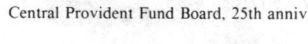

Fund Board Emblem, Keys to Retirement — A86

**1980, July 1 Litho. *Perf. 13***

| | | | | |
|---|---|---|---|---|
| *353* | A86 | 10c *shown* | 10 | 10 |
| *354* | A86 | 50c *Home ownership savings* | 60 | 60 |
| *355* | A86 | $1 *Old age savings* | 1.25 | 1.25 |

Central Provident Fund Board, 25th anniv.

Map Showing Singapore-Indonesia Cable Route — A87

**1980, Aug. 8 Litho. *Perf. 14***

| | | | | |
|---|---|---|---|---|
| *356* | A87 | 10c multi | 10 | 10 |
| *357* | A87 | 35c multi | 40 | 40 |
| *358* | A87 | 50c multi | 55 | 55 |
| *359* | A87 | 75c multi | 85 | 85 |

ASEAN Submarine Cable Network extension. Stamps perforated around design and around edges. See No. 429a.

Fair Emblem A88

**1980, Oct. 3 Litho. *Perf. 13***

| | | | | |
|---|---|---|---|---|
| *360* | A88 | 10c multi | 10 | 10 |
| *361* | A88 | 35c multi | 52 | 52 |
| *362* | A88 | 75c multi | 1.10 | 1.10 |

Asean Trade Fair, Oct. 3-12.

Flame of the Wood — A89

**1980, Nov. 2 Litho. *Perf. 13½***

| | | |
|---|---|---|
| *363* A89 10c *shown* | 10 | 10 |
| *364* A89 35c *Golden trumpet* | 45 | 45 |
| *365* A89 50c *Sky vine* | 60 | 60 |
| *366* A89 75c *Bougainvillea* | 95 | 95 |

Monetary Authority of Singapore, 10th Anniversary — A90

**1981, Jan. 24 Litho. *Perf. 14x14½***

| | | |
|---|---|---|
| *367* A90 10c multi | 10 | 10 |
| *368* A90 35c multi | 35 | 35 |
| *369* A90 75c multi | 75 | 75 |

No. 54 Surcharged

***Perf. 13½x14½***

**1981, Mar. 5 Photo. Wmk. 314**

| | | |
|---|---|---|
| *370* A8 10c on 4c red org & blk | 10 | 10 |

Technical Training (Woodworking) A91

**Unwmk.**

**1981, Apr. 11 Litho. *Perf. 13***

| | | |
|---|---|---|
| *371* A91 10c shown | 10 | 10 |
| *372* A91 35c Building construction | 35 | 35 |
| *373* A91 50c Electronics | 50 | 50 |
| *374* A91 75c Precision machinery | 75 | 75 |

Sports For All — A92

Designs: Various sports.

**1981, Aug. 25 Litho. *Perf. 14***

| | | |
|---|---|---|
| *375* A92 10c multi | 10 | 10 |
| *376* A92 75c multi | 90 | 90 |
| *377* A92 $1 multi | 1.25 | 1.25 |

Intl. Year of the Disabled — A93

**1981, Nov. 24 Litho. *Perf. 14½***

| | | |
|---|---|---|
| *378* A93 10c Man in wheelchair | 10 | 10 |
| *379* A93 35c Group | 35 | 35 |
| *380* A93 50c Teacher, student | 50 | 50 |
| *381* A93 75c Blind communications worker | 75 | 75 |

Changi Airport Opening — A94

**1981, Dec. 29 Litho. *Perf. 14x13½***

| | | |
|---|---|---|
| *382* A94 10c multi | 10 | 10 |
| *383* A94 35c multi | 30 | 30 |
| *384* A94 50c multi | 45 | 45 |
| *385* A94 75c multi | 65 | 65 |
| *386* A94 $1 multi | 90 | 90 |
| *a* Souvenir sheet of 5 | 3.00 | 3.00 |
| *Nos. 382-386 (5)* | 2.40 | 2.40 |

No. 386a contains Nos. 382-386; multicolored margin shows control tower. Size: 155x106mm.

Clipper — A95

**1982, Mar. 3 Litho. *Perf. 14x14½***

| | | |
|---|---|---|
| *387* A95 10c shown | 16 | 16 |
| *388* A95 50c Blue grassy tiger | 85 | 85 |
| *389* A95 $1 Raja Brooke's birdwing | 1.65 | 1.65 |

15th ASEAN Ministerial Meeting — A96

**1982, June 14 Litho. *Perf. 14***

| | | |
|---|---|---|
| *390* A96 10c multi | 10 | 10 |
| *391* A96 35c multi | 38 | 38 |
| *392* A96 50c multi | 55 | 55 |
| *393* A96 75c multi | 85 | 85 |

1982 World Cup — A97

**1982, July 9 Litho. *Perf. 12***

| | | |
|---|---|---|
| *394* A97 10c multi | 10 | 10 |
| *395* A97 75c multi | 90 | 90 |
| *396* A97 $1 multi | 1.25 | 1.25 |

Sultan Shoal Lighthouse, 1896 — A98

**1982, Aug. 7**

| | | |
|---|---|---|
| *397* A98 10c shown | 10 | 10 |
| *398* A98 75c Horsburgh, 1851 | 90 | 90 |
| *399* A98 $1 Raffles, 1855 | 1.25 | 1.25 |
| *a* Souvenir sheet of 3 | 2.75 | 2.75 |

No. 399a contains Nos. 397-399; multicolored margin shows photo of Horsburgh lighthouse. Size: 149x105mm.

10th Anniv. of PSA Container Terminal A99

**1982, Sept. 15 Litho. *Perf. 13½***

| | | |
|---|---|---|
| *400* A99 10c Yard gantry cranes | 10 | 10 |
| *401* A99 35c Computer | 38 | 38 |
| *402* A99 50c Freightlifter | 55 | 55 |
| *403* A99 75c Straddle carrier | 85 | 85 |

Scouting Year — A100

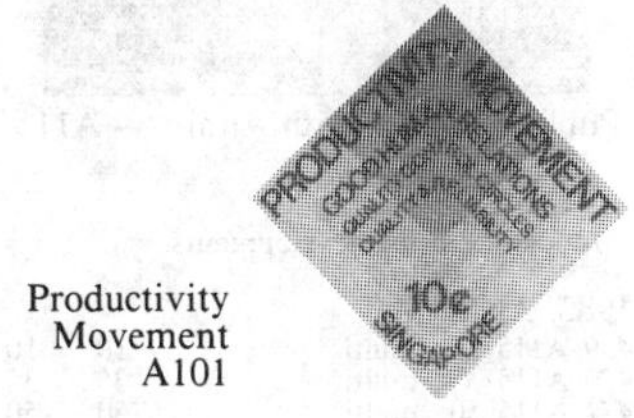


Productivity Movement A101

**1982, Oct. 15 Litho. *Perf. 14x13½***

| | | |
|---|---|---|
| *404* A100 10c Color guard | 10 | 10 |
| *405* A100 35c Hiking | 40 | 40 |
| *406* A100 50c Building tower | 55 | 55 |
| *407* A100 75c Kayaking | 85 | 85 |

**1982, Nov. 17 *Perf. 13½***

| | | |
|---|---|---|
| *408* A101 10c Text | 10 | 10 |
| *409* A101 35c Housing | 38 | 38 |
| *410* A101 50c Quality control meeting | 55 | 55 |
| *411* A101 75c Participation | 85 | 85 |

Commonwealth Day — A102

**1983, May 14 Litho. *Perf. 13½x13***

| | | |
|---|---|---|
| *412* A102 10c multi | 10 | 10 |
| *413* A102 35c multi | 35 | 35 |
| *414* A102 75c multi | 75 | 75 |
| *415* A102 $1 multi | 1.00 | 1.00 |

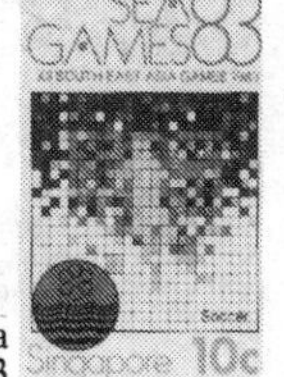


12th Southeast Asia Games — A103

**1983, May 28 Litho. *Perf. 14x13½***

| | | |
|---|---|---|
| *416* A103 10c Soccer | 10 | 10 |
| *417* A103 35c Racket games | 35 | 35 |
| *418* A103 75c Athletics | 75 | 75 |
| *419* A103 $1 Swimming | 1.00 | 1.00 |

Neighborhood Watch Safety Campaign A104

**1983, June 24 Litho. *Perf. 14***

| | | |
|---|---|---|
| *420* A104 10c Family | 10 | 10 |
| *421* A104 35c Children | 35 | 35 |
| *422* A104 75c Community | 75 | 75 |

BANGKOK '83 Intl. Stamp Show, Aug. 4-13 — A105

Designs: 10c, Nos. 282-284, statue of King Chulalongkorn (1868-1910). 35c, Nos. 304-307, map of southeast Asia. $1, Nos. 390-393, Declaration of ASEAN (Assoc. of South East Asian Nations) signatures, 1976.

**1983, Aug. 4 Litho. *Perf. 14x14½***

| | | |
|---|---|---|
| *423* A105 10c multi | 12 | 12 |
| *424* A105 35c multi | 42 | 42 |
| *425* A105 $1 multi | 1.25 | 1.25 |
| *a* Souvenir sheet of 3 | 1.90 | 1.90 |

No. 425a contains Nos. 423-425. Size: 148x104mm.

ASEAN Submarine Cable Network — A106

**1983, Sept. 27 Litho. *Perf. 14***

| | | |
|---|---|---|
| *426* A106 10c multi | 12 | 12 |
| *427* A106 35c multi | 42 | 42 |
| *428* A106 50c multi | 60 | 60 |
| *429* A106 75c multi | 90 | 90 |
| *a* Souvenir sheet of 6 | 2.55 | 2.55 |

No. 429a contains Nos. 304, 359, 426-429. Size: 147x100mm.

World Communications Year — A107

**1983, Nov. 10 Litho. *Perf. 13***

| | | |
|---|---|---|
| *430* A107 10c Telex service | 10 | 10 |
| *431* A107 35c Telephone numbering plan | 40 | 40 |
| *432* A107 75c Satellite transmission | 85 | 85 |
| *433* A107 $1 Sea communications | 1.10 | 1.10 |

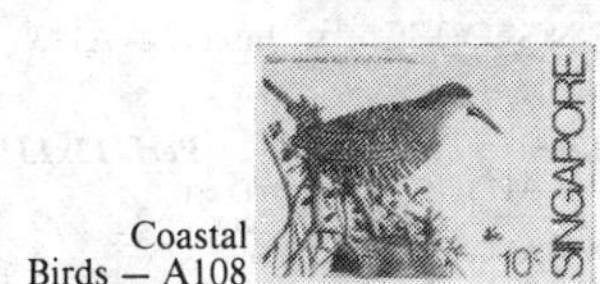


Coastal Birds — A108

***Perf. 14½x13½***

**1984, Mar. 15 Litho.**

| | | |
|---|---|---|
| *434* A108 10c Slaty-breasted rail | 10 | 10 |
| *435* A108 35c Black bittern | 42 | 42 |
| *436* A108 50c Brahminy kite | 60 | 60 |
| *437* A108 75c Common moorhens | 90 | 90 |

Natl. Monuments A109

Designs: 10c, House of Tan Yeok Nee (merchant), 1885. 35c, Thong Chai Building (former hospital), 1892. 50c, Telok Ayer Market, 1894. $1, Nagore Durgha Muslim Shrine, 1828.

**1984, June 7 Litho. *Perf. 12***

| | | | | |
|---|---|---|---|---|
| *438* | A109 | 10c multi | 10 | 10 |
| *439* | A109 | 35c multi | 40 | 40 |
| *440* | A109 | 50c multi | 55 | 55 |
| *441* | A109 | $1 multi | 1.10 | 1.10 |

25th Anniv. of Self-Government A110

**1984, Aug. 9 Litho. *Perf. 14***

| | | | | |
|---|---|---|---|---|
| *442* | A110 | 10c No. 121 | 10 | 10 |
| *443* | A110 | 35c No. 377 | 35 | 35 |
| *444* | A110 | 50c No. 99 | 50 | 50 |
| *445* | A110 | 75c No. 243 | 75 | 75 |
| *446* | A110 | $1 No. 386 | 1.00 | 1.00 |
| *447* | A110 | $2 No. 367 | 2.00 | 2.00 |
| *a* | | Souvenir sheet of 6, #442-447 | 4.75 | 4.75 |
| | | *Nos. 442-447 (6)* | 4.70 | 4.70 |

Defense — A111

Total Defense: a. This is our country. b. We are one. c. We work together. d. We are prepared. e. We are ready.

**1984, Oct. 26 Litho. *Perf. 12***

| | | | | |
|---|---|---|---|---|
| *448* | | Strip of 5 | 50 | 50 |
| *a.-e.* | A111 | 10c Any single | 10 | 10 |

Bridges A112

**1985, Mar. 15 Engr. *Perf. 14½x14***

| | | | | |
|---|---|---|---|---|
| *449* | A112 | 10c Coleman | 8 | 8 |
| *450* | A112 | 35c Cavenagh | 32 | 32 |
| *451* | A112 | 75c Elgin | 75 | 75 |
| *452* | A112 | $1 Benjamin Sheares | 1.00 | 1.00 |

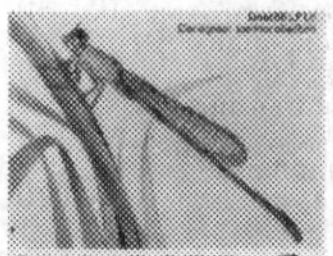

Insects — A113

**1985 Litho. *Perf. 13x13½***

| | | | | |
|---|---|---|---|---|
| *453* | A113 | 5c Ceriagrion cerinorubellum | 5 | 5 |
| *454* | A113 | 10c Apis javana | 8 | 8 |
| *455* | A113 | 15c Delta arcuata | 12 | 12 |
| *456* | A113 | 20c Xylocopa caerulea | 15 | 15 |
| *457* | A113 | 25c Donacia javana | 20 | 20 |
| *458* | A113 | 35c Heteroneda reticulata | 28 | 28 |
| *459* | A113 | 50c Catacanthus nigripes | 40 | 40 |
| *460* | A113 | 75c Chremistica pontianaka | 60 | 60 |

**Litho. & Engr.**
**Size: 35x30mm**

| | | | | |
|---|---|---|---|---|
| *461* | A113 | $1 Homoeoxipha lycoides | 80 | 80 |
| *462* | A113 | $2 Traulia azureipennis | 1.65 | 1.65 |
| *463* | A113 | $5 Trithemis aurora | 3.75 | 3.75 |
| *464* | A113 | $10 Scambophyllum sangiunolentum | 7.50 | 7.50 |
| | | *Nos. 453-464 (12)* | 15.58 | 15.58 |

Issue dates Nos. 453-460, Apr. 24. Nos. 461-464, June 5.

People's Assoc., 25th Anniv. — A114

Montage of public services.

**1985, July 1 *Perf. 13½x14***

| | | | | |
|---|---|---|---|---|
| *465* | A114 | 10c multi | 8 | 8 |
| *466* | A114 | 35c multi | 30 | 30 |
| *467* | A114 | 50c multi | 45 | 45 |
| *468* | A114 | 75c multi | 65 | 65 |

Public Housing, 25th Anniv. — A115

Modern housing developments.

**1985, Aug. 9**

| | | | | |
|---|---|---|---|---|
| *469* | A115 | 10c multi | 10 | 10 |
| *470* | A115 | 35c multi | 35 | 35 |
| *471* | A115 | 50c multi | 50 | 50 |
| *472* | A115 | 75c multi | 80 | 80 |
| *a* | | Souvenir sheet of 4 | 1.90 | 1.90 |

No. 472a contains Nos. 469-472, gray and vermilion margin pictures anniv. emblem. Size: 127x105mm.

Girl Guides, 75th Anniv. — A116

Activities.

**1985, Nov 6 *Perf. 14½x14***

| | | | | |
|---|---|---|---|---|
| *473* | A116 | 10c Brownies | 10 | 10 |
| *474* | A116 | 35c Guides | 38 | 38 |
| *475* | A116 | 50c Seniors | 55 | 55 |
| *476* | A116 | 75c Guide leaders | 85 | 85 |

Intl. Youth Year — A117

**1985, Dec. 18 *Perf. 13***

| | | | | |
|---|---|---|---|---|
| *477* | A117 | 10c Youth assoc. emblems | 10 | 10 |
| *478* | A117 | 75c Hand, sapling | 75 | 75 |
| *479* | A117 | $1 Dove, stick figures | 1.00 | 1.00 |

Indigenous Fruit — A118

Natl. Trade Unions Cong., 25th Anniv. — A119

**1986, Feb. 26 Litho. *Perf. 14½x14***

| | | | | |
|---|---|---|---|---|
| *480* | A118 | 10c Psidium guajava | 10 | 10 |
| *481* | A118 | 35c Eugenia aquea | 38 | 38 |
| *482* | A118 | 50c Nephelium lappaceum | 55 | 55 |
| *483* | A118 | 75c Manilkara zapota | 85 | 85 |

**1986, May 1 *Perf. 13½***

Progress: Nos. 484a, 485a, Science and technology. Nos. 484b, 485b, Communications. Nos. 484c, 485c, Industry. Nos. 484d, 485d, Education.

| | | | | |
|---|---|---|---|---|
| *484* | | Strip of 4 | 40 | 40 |
| *a.-d.* | A119 | 10c any single | 20 | 20 |

**Souvenir Sheet**

| | | | | |
|---|---|---|---|---|
| *485* | | Sheet of 4 | 1.40 | 1.40 |
| *a.-d.* | A119 | 35c any single | 35 | 35 |

No. 485 has silver and blue inscribed margin, NTUC emblem in black. Size: 148x100mm.

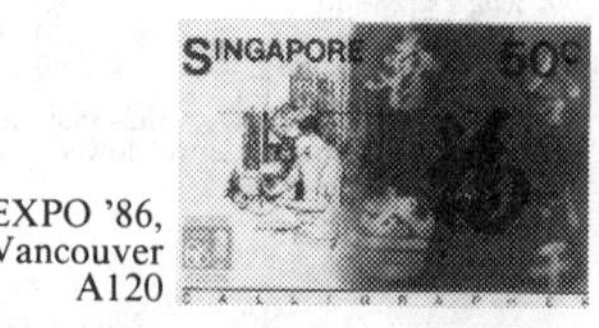

EXPO '86, Vancouver A120

**1986, May 2 *Perf. 14½x14***

| | | | | |
|---|---|---|---|---|
| *486* | | Strip of 3 | 2.25 | 2.25 |
| *a* | A120 | 50c Calligraphy | 50 | 50 |
| *b* | A120 | 75c Garland making | 75 | 75 |
| *c* | A120 | $1 Batik printing | 1.00 | 1.00 |

Economic Development Board, 25th Anniv. — A121

**1986, Aug. 1 *Perf. 15***

| | | | | |
|---|---|---|---|---|
| *487* | A121 | 10c Automation | 10 | 10 |
| *488* | A121 | 35c Precision engineering | 35 | 35 |
| *489* | A121 | 50c Electronics | 50 | 50 |
| *490* | A121 | 75c Biotechnology | 75 | 75 |

Submarine Cable — A122

**1986, Sept. 8 *Perf. 13½***

| | | | | |
|---|---|---|---|---|
| *491* | A122 | 10c multi | 10 | 10 |
| *492* | A122 | 35c multi | 35 | 35 |
| *493* | A122 | 50c multi | 50 | 50 |
| *494* | A122 | 75c multi | 75 | 75 |

Citizens' Consultative Committees, 21st Anniv. — A123

**1986, Oct 15 *Perf. 12***

| | | | | |
|---|---|---|---|---|
| *495* | A123 | Block of 4 | 1.70 | 1.70 |
| *a* | | 10c multi | 10 | 10 |
| *b* | | 35c multi | 35 | 35 |
| *c* | | 50c multi | 50 | 50 |
| *d* | | 75c multi | 75 | 75 |

Printed se-tenant in a continuous design.

Intl. Peace Year — A124

**1986, Dec. 17 Litho. *Perf. 14x13½***

| | | | | |
|---|---|---|---|---|
| *496* | A124 | 10c People | 10 | 10 |
| *497* | A124 | 35c Southeast Asia map | 35 | 35 |
| *498* | A124 | $1 Globe | 1.00 | 1.00 |

Views of Singapore A125

**1986, Feb. 25 *Perf. 12x12½***

| | | | | |
|---|---|---|---|---|
| *499* | A125 | 10c Orchard Road | 10 | 10 |
| *500* | A125 | 50c Central business district | 50 | 50 |
| *501* | A125 | 75c Marina Center, Raffles City | 75 | 75 |

Assoc. of Southeast Asian Nations (ASEAN), 20th Anniv. A126

National Service, 20th Anniv. A127

**1987, June 15 *Perf. 12***

| | | | | |
|---|---|---|---|---|
| *502* | A126 | 10c multi | 10 | 10 |
| *503* | A126 | 35c multi | 35 | 35 |
| *504* | A126 | 50c multi | 50 | 50 |
| *505* | A126 | 75c multi | 75 | 75 |

**1987, July 1 *Perf. 15x14***

Designs: a, Army. b, Navy. c, Air Force. d, Pledge of Allegiance. e, Singapore Lion.

| | | | | |
|---|---|---|---|---|
| *506* | | Strip of 4 | 40 | 40 |
| *a.-d.* | A127 | 10c any single | 10 | 10 |
| *507* | | Sheet of 5 | 1.75 | 1.75 |
| *a.-e.* | A127 | 35c any single | 35 | 35 |

No. 507 has multicolored inscribed margin picturing military exercises. Size: 148x100mm.

River Life — A128

**1987, Sept. 2 *Perf. 14***

| | | | | |
|---|---|---|---|---|
| *508* | A128 | 10c Singapore River | 10 | 10 |
| *509* | A128 | 50c Kallang Basin | 50 | 50 |
| *510* | A128 | $1 Kranji Reservoir | 1.00 | 1.00 |

Natl. Museum Cent. A129

Views of the museum and artifacts: 10c, Majapahis gold bracelet, 14th-15th cent. 75c, Ming fluted kendi (water jar). $1, Seventeen-wave kris (sword with silver hilt, sheath), property of Sultan Abdul Jalil Sabat, 1699.

**1987, Oct. 12 Litho. *Perf. 13½x14***

511 A129 10c multi 10 10
512 A129 75c multi 72 72
513 A129 $1 multi 95 95

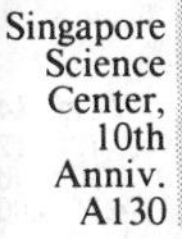

Singapore Science Center, 10th Anniv. A130

Attractions.

**1987, Dec. 10 *Perf. 14½***

514 A130 10c Omni Theater 10 10
515 A130 35c Omni Planetarium 35 35
516 A130 75c Cellular model 72 72
517 A130 $1 Science exhibits 95 95

Artillery, Cent. A131

Designs: 10c, 155-Gun Howitzer and Khaib Camp, headquarters of the Singapore Gunners. 35c, 25-Pound gun salute and Singapore City Hall. 50c, 4.5-inch Howitzer and Singapore Cricket Club, c. 1928. $1, Ft. Fullerton Drill Hall, c. 1893, and .405 Maxim gun.

**1988, Feb. 22 Litho. *Perf. 13½x14***

518 A131 10c multi 10 10
519 A131 35c multi 35 35
520 A131 50c multi 50 50
521 A131 $1 multi 1.00 1.00

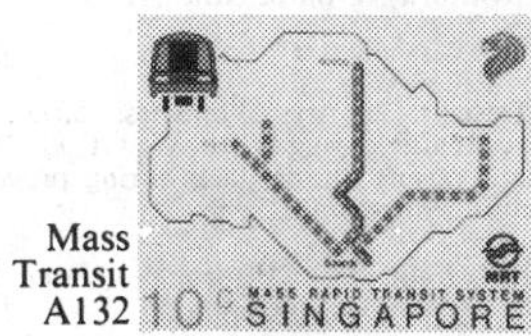

Mass Transit A132

**1988, Mar. 12 *Perf. 14***

522 A132 10c Rail car, map 10 10
523 A132 50c Elevated train 48 48
524 A132 $1 Urban subway 95 95

Natl. Television Broadcast System, 25th Anniv. A133

**1988, Apr. 4 Litho. *Perf. 13½x14***

525 A133 10c shown 10 10
526 A133 35c Studio 35 35
527 A133 75c Television, transmission tower 75 75
528 A133 $1 Screen, satellite dish 1.00 1.00

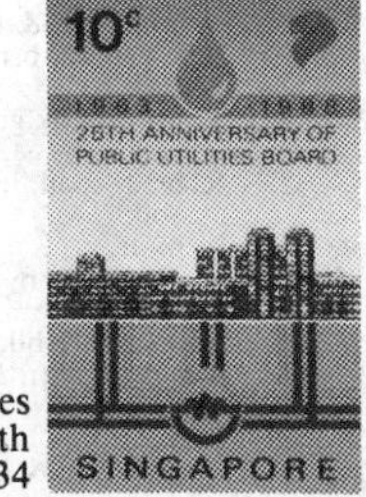

Public Utilities Board, 25th Anniv. — A134

**1988, May 4 Litho. *Perf. 13½***

529 A134 10c Water works 10 10
530 A134 50c Electric company 50 50
531 A134 $1 Fossil fuels 1.00 1.00
a. Souv. sheet of 3, Nos. 529-531 1.60 1.60

No. 531 has multicolored decorative margin continuing the design. Size: 116x75mm.

Courtesy Campaign, 10th Anniv. A135

Singa the lion (character trademark) and: 10c, Neighbors. 30c, Store service counter. $1, Helping the elderly.

**1988, July 6 Litho. *Perf. 14½***

532 A135 10c multi 10 10
533 A135 30c multi 30 30
534 A135 $1 multi 1.00 1.00

Fire Service, Cent. — A136

**1988, Nov. 1 Litho. *Perf. 13½***

535 A136 10c Turntable ladder truck 10 10
536 A136 $1 1890s Steam pump 1.00 1.00

## POSTAGE DUE STAMPS

D1

D2

**Wmk. 314**

**1968, Feb. 1 Litho. *Perf. 9***

J1 D1 1c emerald 6 6
J2 D1 2c red org 30 30
J3 D1 4c yel org 60 60
J4 D1 8c brown 70 70
J5 D1 10c rose mag 1.75 1.75
a. Perf. 13x13½ ('73) 90 90
J6 D1 12c dl vio 90 90
J7 D1 20c brt bl 2.00 2.00
J8 D1 50c gray grn 5.00 5.00
a. Perf. 13x13½ ('73) 5.00 5.00
*Nos. J1-J8 (8)* 11.31 11.31

1c, 4c, 10c, 25c, 50c issued perf. 12½x13 in 1977, unwmkd.

**1979, Mar. Unwmk. *Perf. 13x13½***

J9 D2 1c emerald 5 5
J10 D2 4c orange 5 5
J11 D2 10c carmine 12 12
J12 D2 20c light blue 22 22
J13 D2 50c light yel grn 55 55
*Nos. J9-J13 (5)* 99 99

Issued perf. 12x11½ in 1981. Values are for 1981 set.

# SOLOMON ISLANDS

## British Solomon Islands

LOCATION — In the west Pacific Ocean east of Papua.
GOVT. — Independent state in British Commonwealth.
AREA — 11,500 sq. mi.
POP. — 258,193 (1984).
CAPITAL — Honiara.

The Solomons include 10 large islands and four groups of small islands extending over an area of 375,000 square miles.

The British protectorate of British Solomon Islands changed its name to Solomon Islands in 1975 and achieved independence July 7, 1978.

12 Pence = 1 Shilling
20 Shillings = 1 Pound
100 Cents = 1 Dollar (1966)

**Catalogue values for unused stamps in this country are for Never Hinged items, beginning with Scott 80 in the regular postage section and Scott B1 in the semi-postal section.**

War Canoe — A1

**Unwmk.**

**1907, Feb. 14 Litho. *Perf. 11***

1 A1 ½p ultra 8.00 13.00
2 A1 1p red 18.00 22.50
3 A1 2p dl bl 18.00 25.00
a. Horiz. pair, imperf. btwn. 9,000.
4 A1 2½p orange 25.00 27.50
a. Vert. pair, imperf. btwn. 4,500.
b. Horiz. pair, imperf. btwn. 4,500. 4,500.
5 A1 5p yel grn 37.50 45.00
6 A1 6p chocolate 45.00 45.00
a. Vertical pair, imperf. btwn. 3,500.
b. Horiz. pair, imperf. btwn.
7 A1 1sh violet 70.00 70.00
*Nos. 1-7 (7)* 221.50 248.00

Excellent counterfeits are plentiful.

War Canoe A2

George V A3

**Wmk. Multiple Crown and C. A. (3)**

**1908-11 Engr. *Perf. 14.***

8 A2 ½p green 60 65
9 A2 1p carmine 1.10 1.20
10 A2 2p gray 3.50 3.75
11 A2 2½p ultra 2.50 3.00
12 A2 4p red, *yel* ('11) 3.00 4.75
13 A2 5p ol grn 5.75 6.00
14 A2 6p claret 7.00 7.25
15 A2 1sh *green* 9.75 12.00
16 A2 2sh vio, *bl* ('10) 25.00 30.00
17 A2 2sh6p red, *bl* ('10) 47.50 65.00
18 A2 5sh bl, *yel* ('10) 70.00 87.50
*Nos. 8-18 (11)* 175.70 221.10

Inscribed "POSTAGE - POSTAGE"

**1913-24 Typo.**

19 A3 ½p green 85 1.75
20 A3 1p carmine 2.00 8.75
21 A3 3p vio, *yel* 2.00 5.75
22 A3 11p dl vio & red 6.50 11.50

**Wmk. 4**

23 A3 1½p scar ('24) 1.50 3.75

Inscribed "POSTAGE - REVENUE"

**1914-23 Wmk. 3**

28 A3 ½p green 55 1.40
29 A3 1p carmine 55 90
a. scarlet ('17) 3.00 6.00
30 A3 2p gray 90 5.50
31 A3 2½p ultra 1.40 2.75

**Chalky Paper**

32 A3 3p vio, *yel* ('23) 22.50 45.00
33 A3 4p blk & red, *yel* 4.25 4.50
34 A3 5p dl vio & ol grn 6.50 13.50
35 A3 6p dl vio & red vio 3.50 11.00
36 A3 1sh blk, *green* 4.50 7.75
a. 1sh blk, *bl grn*, ol back 5.50 11.00
37 A3 2sh dl vio & ultra, *bl* 7.25 12.00
38 A3 2sh 6p blk & red, *bl* 9.00 18.00
39 A3 5sh grn & red, *yel* 27.50 37.50
40 A3 10sh grn & red, *grn* 75.00 85.00
41 A3 £1 vio & blk, *red* 200.00 110.00
*Nos. 28-41 (14)* 363.40 354.80

Inscribed "POSTAGE - REVENUE"

**1922-31 Wmk. 4**

43 A3 ½p green 45 1.40
44 A3 1p car ('23) 5.75 6.75
45 A3 1p vio ('27) 70 1.40
46 A3 2p gray ('23) 1.40 3.50
47 A3 3p ultra ('23) 90 2.25

**Chalky Paper**

48 A3 4p blk & red, *yel* ('27) 2.25 5.75
49 A3 4½p red brn ('31) 4.50 9.25
50 A3 5p dl vio & ol grn 2.25 7.75
51 A3 6p dl vio & red vio 2.75 5.75
52 A3 1sh blk, *emerald* 2.75 5.75
53 A3 2sh dl vio & ultra, *bl* ('27) 7.75 20.00
54 A3 2sh6p blk & red, *bl* 11.50 21.00
55 A3 5sh grn & red, *yel* 16.00 32.50
56 A3 10sh grn & red, *emer* ('25) 100.00 160.00
*Nos. 43-56 (14)* 158.95 283.05

No. 49 is on ordinary paper.

**Silver Jubilee Issue**
Common Design Type

**1935, May 6 Engr. *Perf. 13½x14***

60 CD301 1½p car & dk bl 1.20 1.25
61 CD301 3p bl & brn 4.50 5.25
62 CD301 6p ol grn & lt bl 4.75 5.75
63 CD301 1sh brt vio & ind 7.00 8.50

**Coronation Issue**
Common Design Type

**1937, May 13 *Perf. 11x11½***

64 CD302 1p dk pur 20 20
65 CD302 1½p dk car 25 25
66 CD302 3p dp ultra 38 38

Spears and Shield — A4

Policeman and Chief — A5

Artificial Island, Malaita — A6

Canoe House, New Georgia A7

Roviana War Canoe — A8

View of Munda Point — A9

Meeting House, Reef Islands A10

Coconut Plantation A11

Breadfruit A12

Tinakula Volcano, Santa Cruz Islands A13

Scrub Fowl — A14

Malaita Canoe — A15

***Perf. 12½, 13½ (A7, A13, A14)***

**1939-51** **Wmk. 4**

67 A4 ½p dp grn & ultra 5 5
68 A5 1p dk pur & choc 7 7
69 A6 1½p car & sl grn 18 18
70 A7 2p blk & org brn 28 28
a 2p blk & red brn ('43) 22 22
b Perf. 12 ('51) 22 22
71 A8 2½p ol grn & rose vio 38 38
a Imperf. horizontally, pair 10,000.
72 A9 3p ultra & blk, perf. 12 ('51) 55 55
a Perf. 13½ 85 85
73 A10 4½p dk brn & yel grn 6.75 8.50
74 A11 6p rose lil & dk pur 42 42
75 A12 1sh blk & grn 60 60
76 A13 2sh dp org & blk 2.00 2.00
a 2sh dp org & vio blk ('43) 2.00 2.00
77 A14 2sh6p dl vio & blk 7.50 6.00
78 A15 5sh red & brt bl grn 7.50 6.00
79 A10 10sh red lil & ol ('42) 6.75 6.75
*Nos. 67-79 (13)* 33.03 31.78

**Catalogue values for unused stamps in this section, from this point to the end of the section, are for Never Hinged items.**

**Peace Issue**
Common Design Type
***Perf. 13½x14***

**1946, Oct. 15** **Wmk. 4** **Engr.**
80 CD303 1½p carmine 20 30
81 CD303 3p deep blue 20 30

**Silver Wedding Issue**
Common Design Types

**1949, Mar. 14** **Photo.** ***Perf. 14x14½***
82 CD304 2p black 25 25

***Perf. 11½x11***
**Engr.; Name Typo.**
83 CD305 10sh red vio 30.00 35.00

**UPU Issue**
Common Design Types
**Engr.; Name Typo. on 3p and 5p**
***Perf. 13½, 11x11½***

**1949, Oct. 10** **Wmk. 4**
84 CD306 2p red brn 1.00 1.00
85 CD307 3p indigo 1.50 1.50
86 CD308 5p green 2.50 2.50
87 CD309 1sh slate 4.00 4.00

**Coronation Issue**
Common Design Type

**1953, June 2** **Engr.** ***Perf. 13½x13***
88 CD312 2p gray & blk 70 70

Ysabel Canoe — A16

Prow of Roviana Canoe — A17

Designs: 1p, Roviana canoe. 1½p, Artificial Island, Malaita. 2p, Canoe house. 3p, Malaita canoe. 5p, 1sh3p, Map. 6p, Trading schooner. 8p, 9p, Henderson Field, Guadalcanal. 1sh, Chart of Solomons and H.M.S. Swallow, recalling Capt. Philip Carteret's voyage of 1767. 2sh, Tinakula Volcano. 2sh6p, Meeting house, Reef Islands. 5sh, Alvaro de Mendana de Neyra and Caravel. 10sh, Constable and Chief. £1, Coat of Arms.

***Perf. 11½x11, 11x11½, 12, 13***

**1956-60** **Engr.** **Wmk. 4**
89 A16 ½p lil & org 5 5
90 A16 1p red brn & ol grn 6 6
91 A16 1½p dk car & sl bl 12 10
92 A16 2p gray grn & choc 16 15
93 A17 2½p gray bl & blk 15 12
94 A16 3p dl red & grn 28 22
95 A16 5p bl & blk 85 85
96 A16 6p bluish grn & blk 35 28
97 A16 8p blk & ultra 85 58
98 A16 9p blk & brt grn ('60) 4.75 1.40
99 A16 1sh brn org & sl bl 85 58
100 A16 1sh3p bl & blk ('60) 2.75 1.50
101 A16 2sh car rose & blk 2.75 1.40
102 A17 2sh6p rose lil & emer 3.25 1.75
103 A16 5sh red brn 6.50 4.25
104 A17 10sh blk brn 13.00 9.00
105 A16 £1 lt bl & blk ('58) 35.00 27.50
*Nos. 89-105 (17)* 71.72 49.79

Great Frigate Bird — A18

***Perf. 13x12½***

**1961, Jan. 19** **Litho.** **Wmk. 314**
106 A18 2p bl grn & blk 16 18
107 A18 3p rose red & blk 22 22
108 A18 9p lil & blk 60 60

New constitution, brought into operation Oct. 18, 1960. The watermark is sideways and may be found facing both left and right.

**Freedom from Hunger Issue**
Common Design Type

**1963, June 4** **Photo.** ***Perf. 14x14½***
109 CD314 1sh3p ultra 4.25 2.50

**Red Cross Centenary Issue**
Common Design Type

**1963, Sept. 2** **Litho.** ***Perf. 13***
110 CD315 2p blk & red 40 35
111 CD315 9p ultra & red 3.75 3.25

Types of 1956-60
***Perf. 12, 13, 11½x11***

**1963-64** **Engr.** **Wmk. 314**
113 A16 1p red brn & ol grn 32 20
114 A16 1½p dk car & sl bl 32 24
115 A16 2p gray grn & choc 32 32
117 A16 3p dl red & grn ('63) 70 50
119 A16 6p bluish grn & blk 1.25 1.25
121 A16 9p blk & brt grn 1.25 1.25
123 A16 1sh3p bl & blk 1.65 1.65
124 A16 2sh car rose & blk 4.00 5.00
125 A17 2sh6p rose lil & emer 14.00 14.00
*Nos. 113-125 (9)* 23.81 24.41

**ITU Issue**
Common Design Type
***Perf. 11x11½***

**1965, June 28** **Litho.** **Wmk. 314**
126 CD317 2p ver & grnsh bl 42 42
127 CD317 3p grnsh bl & ol bis 65 65

Makira Food Bowl — A19

Designs: 1p, 1sh, 1sh3p, Various orchids. 1½p, Scorpion shell. 2p, Papuan hornbill. 2½p, Ysabel shield. 3p, Rennellese club. 6p, Moorish idol (fish). 9p, Great frigate bird. 2sh, Sanford's sea eagle. 2sh6p, Malaita belt. 5sh, Ornithoptera Victoreae (butterfly). 10sh, White cockatoo. £1, Figurehead, western canoe.

***Perf. 13x12½***

**1965, May 24** **Litho.** **Wmk. 314**
**Design Subject in Black.**
128 A19 ½p sl bl & lt bl 5 5
129 A19 1p org & yel 6 6
130 A19 1½p bl & yel grn 7 7
131 A19 2p vio bl & lt bl 7 7
132 A19 2½p red brn & buff 9 9
133 A19 3p grn & lt grn 12 12
134 A19 6p brt car rose & org 22 22
135 A19 9p sl grn & buff 32 32
136 A19 1sh dp cl & rose 48 48
137 A19 1sh3p ver & buff 2.25 75
138 A19 2sh dp mag & lil 3.75 1.50
139 A19 2sh6p ol brn & buff 2.50 2.25
140 A19 5sh dk vio bl & lil 5.50 4.50
141 A19 10sh ol grn & yel 9.50 8.75
142 A19 £1 pur & red 15.00 15.00
*Nos. 128-142 (15)* 39.98 34.23

**Intl. Cooperation Year Issue**
Common Design Type

**1965, Oct. 25** **Litho.** ***Perf. 14½***
143 CD318 1p bl grn & cl 8 8
144 CD318 2sh6p lt vio & grn 1.40 1.40

**Churchill Memorial Issue**
Common Design Type

**1966, Jan. 24** **Photo.** ***Perf. 14***
145 CD319 2p multi 16 10
146 CD319 9p multi 48 40
147 CD319 1sh6p multi 1.00 80
148 CD319 2sh6p multi 1.65 1.50

Nos. 128-142 Surcharged with New Value and Three Bars in Black or Red
***Perf. 13x12½***

**1966-67** **Litho.** **Wmk. 314**
149 A19 1c on ½p multi 6 6
150 A19 2c on 1p multi 9 9
151 A19 3c on 1½p multi 15 15
152 A19 4c on 2p multi 15 15
153 A19 5c on 6p multi 18 18
154 A19 6c on 2½p multi 20 20
155 A19 7c on 3p multi 30 30
156 A19 8c on 9p multi 32 32
b "8" inverted 13.00 13.00
157 A19 10c on 1sh 45 45
158 A19 12c on 1sh3p multi ('67) 45 45
159 A19 13c on 1sh3p multi 50 50
160 A19 14c on 3p multi ('67) 50 50
161 A19 20c on 2sh multi 85 85
162 A19 25c on 2sh6p multi 1.10 1.10
163 A19 35c on 2p multi ('67) 2.00 1.65
164 A19 50c on 5sh multi (R) 2.50 2.25
165 A19 $1 on 10sh multi 4.25 4.25
166 A19 $2 on £1 multi 8.75 8.75
*Nos. 149-166 (18)* 22.80 22.20

Nos. 158, 160 and 163 have watermark sideways.

**1966** **Wmk. 314 Sideways**
149a A19 1c on ½p 5 5
150a A19 2c on 1p 8 8
151a A19 3c on 1½p 14 14
152a A19 4c on 2p 20 20
153a A19 5c on 6p 24 24
154a A19 6c on 2½p 30 30
155a A19 7c on 3p 35 35
156a A19 8c on 9p 40 40
157a A19 10c on 1sh 50 50
159a A19 13c on 1sh3p 60 60
161a A19 20c on 2sh 1.00 1.00
162a A19 25c on 2sh6p 1.25 1.25
164a A19 50c on 5sh (R) 2.50 2.50
165a A19 $1 on 10sh 5.00 5.00
166a A19 $2 on £1 8.50 8.50
*Nos. 149a-166a (15)* 21.11 21.11

**World Cup Soccer Issue**
Common Design Type

**1966, July 1** **Litho.** ***Perf. 14***
167 CD321 8c multi 30 30
168 CD321 35c multi 1.10 1.10

**WHO Headquarters Issue**
Common Design Type

**1966, Sept. 20** **Litho.** ***Perf. 14***
169 CD322 3c multi 14 14
170 CD322 50c multi 1.65 1.65

**UNESCO Anniversary Issue**
Common Design Type

**1966, Dec. 1** **Litho.** ***Perf. 14***
171 CD323 3c "Education" 18 12
172 CD323 25c "Science" 90 90
173 CD323 $1 "Culture" 4.75 4.00

Henderson Field, Guadalcanal — A20

Design: 35c, U.S. Marines landing, Red Beach, Guadalcanal, 1942.

***Perf. 14x14½***

**1967, Aug. 28** **Photo.** **Wmk. 314**
174 A20 8c multi & sil 20 20
175 A20 35c multi & gold 75 75

25th anniv. of the Guadalcanal campaign in WW II.

Mendaña's Ship Off Puerta de la Cruz (Honiara), Guadalcanal, 1568 — A21

Designs: 8c, Arrival of Missionaries. 35c, Naval battle during World War II. $1, Honor guard raising Union Jack during proclamation of Protectorate.

**1968, Feb. 2** **Photo.** ***Perf. 14½***
176 A21 3c pink & multi 7 7
177 A21 8c emer & multi 24 24
178 A21 35c multi 85 85
179 A21 $1 bl & multi 2.50 2.50

400th anniv. of the discovery of the British Solomon Islands by the Spanish navigator Alvaro de Mendaña de Neyra.

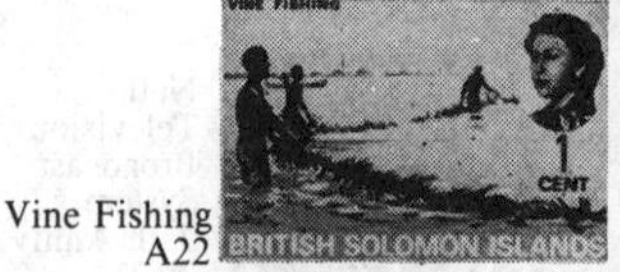
Vine Fishing A22

Designs: 2c, Kite fishing. 3c, Platform fishing. 4c, Net fishing. 6c, Gold lip shell diving. 8c, Night fishing. 12c, Boat building. 14c, Cocoa harvest. 15c, Road building. 20c, Geological survey by plane. 24c, Hauling timber. 35c, Copra. 45c, Harvesting rice. $1, Honiara Port. $2, Map of the Islands, plane and route of Internal Air Service.

**Wmk. 314**

**1968, May 20** **Photo.** ***Perf. 14½***
180 A22 1c aqua, brn & blk 5 5
181 A22 2c lt yel grn, brn & blk 8 8
182 A22 3c brt grn, dk grn & blk 12 12
183 A22 4c brt rose lil, brn & blk 15 15
184 A22 6c multi 22 22
185 A22 8c dp ultra, org & blk 30 30
186 A22 12c bis red & blk 45 45
187 A22 14c red org, brn & blk 55 55
188 A22 15c multi 60 60
189 A22 20c ultra, red & blk 85 85

*190* A22 24c scar, yel & blk 95 95
*191* A22 35c multi 1.90 1.90
*192* A22 45c yel, red & blk 2.75 2.75
*193* A22 $1 vio bl, emer & blk 4.75 4.75
*194* A22 $2 multi 9.50 9.50
*Nos. 180-194 (15)* 23.22 23.22

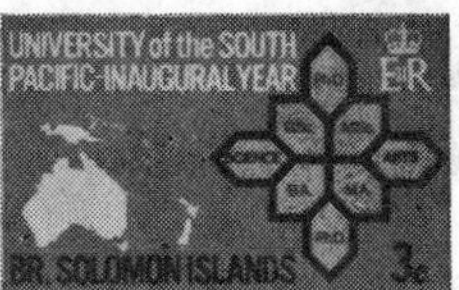


Map of South Pacific and University Degrees — A23

***Perf. 12½x12***

**1969, Feb. 10 Litho. Unwmk.**

*195* A23 3c multi 6 6
*196* A23 12c multi 24 24
*197* A23 35c multi 60 60

Issued to publicize the inauguration of the University of the South Pacific in 1969, at the Royal New Zealand Air Force Seaplane Station, Laucala Bay, Fiji.

Field Ball and Games' Emblem — A24

Stained Glass Window with Melanesian Peace Symbol — A25

Games' Emblem and: 8c, Soccer. 14c, Running. 45c, Rugby.

***Perf. 14½x14***

**1969, Aug. 13 Photo. Wmk. 314**

*198* A24 3c lt ultra & multi 8 8
*199* A24 8c brt pink & multi 16 16
*200* A24 14c yel & multi 30 30
*201* A24 45c multi 95 95
*a* Souv. sheet of 4 7.25 5.75

Issued to publicize the 3rd South Pacific Games, Port Moresby, Aug. 13-23. No. 201a contains one each of Nos. 198-201. Size: 127x120mm. In No. 201a, shading was added below athlete's foot on 14c, and strengthened on 8c and 45c.

**1969, Nov. 21 Photo. Wmk. 314**

Christmas: 8c, South Sea Islands scene with palms and Star of Bethlehem.

*202* A25 8c vio, grnsh bl & blk 25 25
*203* A25 35c blk & multi 1.00 1.00

C. M. Woodford and Stamp of 1907 — A26

Designs: 7c, British Solomon Islands 1906 handstamp and cancellation, and New South Wales No. 99. 18c, British Solomon Islands No. 18 and 1913 Tulagi cancellation. 23c, New General Post Office, Honiara.

**1970, Apr. 15 Litho. *Perf. 13***

*204* A26 7c lil rose & blk 16 16
*205* A26 14c lt ol & blk 40 40
*206* A26 18c org, yel & blk 55 55
*207* A26 23c multi 75 75

Issued to publicize the opening of the new General Post Office in Honiara.

Map of Solomon Islands A27

Design: 18c, British Solomon Islands coat of arms (vert.).

***Perf. 14½x14, 14x14½***

**1970, June 15 Litho. Wmk. 314**

*208* A27 18c multi 65 65
*209* A27 35c dk bl, lt grn & ocher 1.15 1.15

Adoption of the new 1970 Constitution.

Red Cross Headquarters, Honiara — A28

Design: 35c, Map of British Solomon Islands showing Red Cross stations, and wheelchair.

**1970, Aug. 17 *Perf. 14½x14***

*210* A28 3c multi 14 14
*211* A28 35c multi 1.10 1.10

Centenary of British Red Cross Society.

Carved Angel and Southern Cross — A29

Reredos: Symbols of Trinity and Light at St. Luke's Church, Kia — A30

***Perf. 14x13½, 13½x14***

**1970, Oct. 19 Litho. Wmk. 314**

*212* A29 8c vio & bis brn 35 35
*213* A30 45c org brn, ocher & blk 1.25 1.25

Christmas 1970.

Count de La Pérouse and "La Boussole" — A31

Designs: 4c, Astrolabe and Polynesian reed map. 12c, Abel Tasman and sailing ship Heemskerk, 1643. 35c, Te Puki canoe, Santa Cruz.

**1971, Jan. 28 *Perf. 14½x14***

*214* A31 3c multi 38 20
*215* A31 4c multi 45 30
*216* A31 12c multi 1.40 75
*217* A31 35c multi 3.50 2.75

In honor of famous explorers and ships. See Nos. 228-231, 250-253.

Bishop Patteson, J. Atkin and S. Taroniara — A32

Designs: 4c, Last landing of the "Southern Cross" at Nukapu. 14c, Memorial for Bishop Patteson and map of Nukapu (vert.). 45c, Ceremonial leaf tag (had been attached to Bishop's body; vert.).

***Perf. 14½x14, 14x14½***

**1971, Apr. 5 Litho. Wmk. 314**

*218* A32 2c lt grn & multi 8 8
*219* A32 4c bl grn & multi 16 16
*220* A32 14c brt pink & multi 45 45
*221* A32 45c brn & multi 1.50 1.50

Bishop John Coleridge Patteson (1827-71), head of the Melanesian mission.

Boxing, Games Emblem A33

Designs (Games Emblem and): 8c, Soccer. 12c, Running. 35c, Spear fishing.

**1971, Aug. 9 *Perf. 14½x14***

*222* A33 3c org & multi 12 12
*223* A33 8c emer & multi 24 24
*224* A33 12c yel & multi 35 35
*225* A33 35c bl & multi 1.25 1.25

4th South Pacific Games, Papeete, French Polynesia, Sept. 8-19.

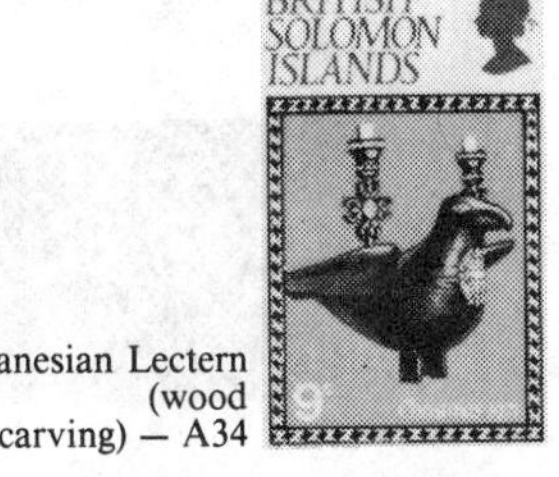


Melanesian Lectern (wood carving) — A34

Christmas: 45c, Stylized birds, painted by school girl Margarita Bara.

**1971, Nov. 15 Litho. Wmk. 314**

*226* A34 9c org & multi 25 25
*227* A34 45c bl & multi 1.25 1.25

### Explorer Type of 1971

Designs: 4c, Louis Antoine de Bougainville and La Boudeuse, 1776. 9c, Horizontal planisphere, 1574, and ivory backstaff, 1695. 15c, Philip Carteret and H.M.S. Swallow, 1707. 45c, Small canoe of Malaita.

**1972, Feb. 1 *Perf. 14½***

*228* A31 4c brn & multi 25 25
*229* A31 9c grn & multi 60 60
*230* A31 15c lt bl & multi 1.10 1.10
*231* A31 45c bl & multi 3.75 3.75

Cupha Woodfordi A35

Designs: 1c, 2c, 3c, 4c, $2, Butterflies. 5c, 8c, 9c, 15c, $1. Fishes. 12c, 20c, 25c, 35c, 45c, Orchids. $5, Birds.

**1972, July 2 *Perf. 14***

*232* A35 1c *shown* 5 5
*233* A35 2c *Ornithoptera priamus* 8 8
*234* A35 3c *Vindula sapor* 12 12
*235* A35 4c *Papilio orssippus* 16 16
*236* A35 5c *Great trevally* 20 20
*237* A35 8c *Little bonito* 32 32
*238* A35 9c *Sapphire demoiselle* 35 35
*239* A35 12c *Costus speciosus* 55 48
*240* A35 15c *Orange anemone* 80 65
*241* A35 20c *Spathoglottis plicata* 1.10 85
*242* A35 25c *Ephemerantha comata* 1.25 1.10
*243* A35 35c *Dendrobium cuthbertsonii* 2.00 1.50
*244* A35 45c *Heliconia salomonica* 2.25 2.00
*245* A35 $1 *Blue-finned triggerfish* 5.50 4.00
*246* A35 $2 *Ornithoptera allotti* 12.00 8.00
*247* A35 $5 *Great frigate bird* ('73) 20.00 20.00
*Nos. 232-247 (16)* 46.73 39.86

Issue date: No. 247, July 2, 1973.

### Silver Wedding Issue, 1972
Common Design Type

Design: Queen Elizabeth II, Prince Philip, scroll and message drum on woven mat.

**1972, Nov. 20 Photo. *Perf. 14x14½***

*248* CD324 8c car rose & multi 12 12
*249* CD324 45c ol & multi 65 65

### Explorer Type of 1971

Designs: 4c, Antoine R. J. d'Entrecasteaux and "The Recherche," 1791. 9c, Ship's hourglass, 17th century, and chronometer, 1761. 15c, Lieutenant Shortland and "The Alexander," 1788. 35c, Tomoko (war canoe).

**Wmk. 314**

**1973, Mar. 9 Litho. *Perf. 14½***

*250* A31 4c bl & multi 20 20
*251* A31 9c bl & multi 60 60
*252* A31 15c bl & multi 1.00 1.00
*253* A31 35c bl & multi 3.25 3.25

Pan Pipes A36

Musical Instruments: 9c, Castanets. 15c, Bamboo flute. 35c, Bauro gongs. 45c, Bamboo band.

**1973, Oct. 1 *Perf. 13½x14***

*254* A36 4c brick red & multi 15 15
*255* A36 9c yel bis & multi 30 30
*256* A36 15c pink & multi 50 50
*257* A36 35c bl grn & multi 1.25 1.25
*258* A36 45c multi 1.50 1.50
*Nos. 254-258 (5)* 3.70 3.70

### Princess Anne's Wedding Issue
Common Design Type

**1973, Nov. 14 *Perf. 14***

*259* CD325 4c sl & multi 9 9
*260* CD325 35c multi 60 60

Adoration of the Kings, by Jan Brueghel A37

Adoration of the Kings by: 22c, Peter Brueghel (vert.). 45c, Botticelli.

**1973, Nov. 26 Litho. *Perf. 14***
**Size: 39x25mm, 25x39mm**

*261* A37 8c pink & multi 45 45
*262* A37 22c lil & multi 1.10 1.10

**Perf. 13½**
**Size: 47x35mm**

| | | | | |
|---|---|---|---|---|
| *263* | A37 | 45c gray & multi | 2.50 | 2.50 |

Christmas 1973.

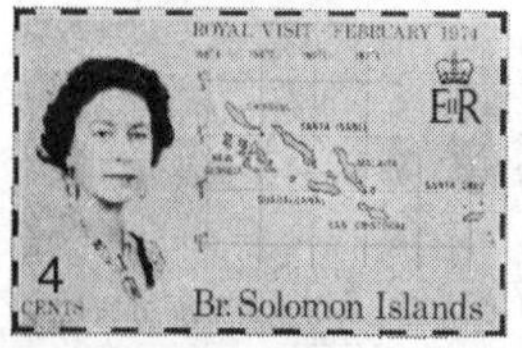


Map of Solomon Islands — A38

**1974, Feb. 18 Litho. *Perf. 13½***

| | | | | |
|---|---|---|---|---|
| *264* | A38 | 4c bl & multi | 12 | 12 |
| *265* | A38 | 9c cit & multi | 28 | 28 |
| *266* | A38 | 15c vio gray & multi | 48 | 48 |
| *267* | A38 | 35c emer & multi | 1.50 | 1.25 |

Visit of British Royal Family.

First Resident Commissioner Landing at Tulagi — A39

Designs: 9c, Marine radar and scanner unit, map of Islands. 15c, Islanders taken to "Blackbirder" ship. 45c, John F. Kennedy's P.T. 109 off Lumbari Island, 1943.

**1974, May 15 Litho. *Perf. 14½***

| | | | | |
|---|---|---|---|---|
| *268* | A39 | 4c multi | 24 | 24 |
| *269* | A39 | 9c multi | 55 | 55 |
| *270* | A39 | 15c multi | 80 | 80 |
| *271* | A39 | 45c multi | 3.25 | 3.25 |

Ships and navigators.

Mailman, Map of Islands — A40

Designs (UPU Emblem, map of Solomon Islands and): 9c, Carrier pigeon (horiz.). 15c, Angel Gabriel. 45c, Pegasus (horiz.). Designs based on origami (folded paper) figures.

**1974, Aug. 29 Wmk. 314 *Perf. 14***

| | | | | |
|---|---|---|---|---|
| *272* | A40 | 4c brt grn & multi | 14 | 14 |
| *273* | A40 | 9c lem & multi | 35 | 25 |
| *274* | A40 | 15c multi | 52 | 42 |
| *275* | A40 | 45c bl & multi | 1.50 | 1.25 |

Centenary of Universal Postal Union.

Solomon Islands No. 208 A41

**1974, Dec. 16 Litho. *Perf. 14½***

| | | | | |
|---|---|---|---|---|
| *276* | A41 | 4c *shown* | 14 | 14 |
| *277* | A41 | 9c *No. 107* | 32 | 32 |
| *278* | A41 | 15c *same* | 55 | 55 |
| *279* | A41 | 35c *like 4c* | 1.25 | 1.25 |
| *a.* | | Souvenir sheet of 4 | 4.50 | 4.00 |

New Constitution, inaugurated Oct. 18, 1960. No. 279a contains one each of Nos. 276-279, ocher and multicolored margin. Size: 133x84mm.

Golden Whistler A42

Birds: 2c, River kingfisher. 3c, Red-throated fruit dove. 4c, Button quail. $2, Duchess lorikeet.

**1975, Apr. 7 Wmk. 314 *Perf. 14***

| | | | | |
|---|---|---|---|---|
| *280* | A42 | 1c yel grn & multi | 10 | 5 |
| *281* | A42 | 2c lt bl & multi | 18 | 8 |
| *282* | A42 | 3c brt pink & multi | 28 | 14 |
| *283* | A42 | 4c org & multi | 42 | 20 |
| *284* | A42 | $2 dp org & multi | 16.00 | 7.00 |
| | | *Nos. 280-284 (5)* | 16.98 | 7.47 |

See Nos. 316-331.

Motor Vessel Walande A43

**1975, May 29 *Perf. 13½***

| | | | | |
|---|---|---|---|---|
| *285* | A43 | 4c *shown* | 22 | 18 |
| *286* | A43 | 9c *M. V. Melanesian* | 55 | 40 |
| *287* | A43 | 15c *Ship Marsina, house flag* | 90 | 75 |
| *288* | A43 | 45c *S. S. Himalaya* | 2.75 | 2.25 |

Runner, 800-meters — A44

**1975, Aug. 4 Litho. *Perf. 13½***

| | | | | |
|---|---|---|---|---|
| *289* | A44 | 4c shown | 10 | 10 |
| *290* | A44 | 9c Long jump | 24 | 24 |
| *291* | A44 | 15c Javelin | 35 | 35 |
| *292* | A44 | 45c Soccer | 1.00 | 1.00 |
| *a.* | | Souvenir sheet of 4 | 4.75 | 2.75 |

5th South Pacific Games, Guam, Aug. 1-10. No. 292a contains one each of Nos. 289-292; blue and Prussian blue margin. Size: 130x95mm.

Nativity and Candles A45

Designs: 35c, Angels, shepherds and candles. 45c, Three Kings approaching Bethlehem, and candles.

**1975, Oct. 13 Wmk. 373 *Perf. 14***

| | | | | |
|---|---|---|---|---|
| *293* | A45 | 15c multi | 42 | 42 |
| *294* | A45 | 35c multi | 1.00 | 1.00 |
| *295* | A45 | 45c multi | 1.40 | 1.40 |
| *a.* | | Souvenir sheet of 3 | 4.25 | 3.75 |

Christmas 1975. No. 295a contains one each of Nos. 293-295. Multicolored margin shows star over tropical lagoon.
Size: 140x129mm.

Nos. 236-245, 247, 280-284 Overprinted with Bar Obliterating "British" in Black or Silver

**1975, Nov. 12 Litho. Wmk. 314**

| | | | | |
|---|---|---|---|---|
| *296* | A42 | 1c multi | 5 | 5 |
| *297* | A42 | 2c multi | 9 | 9 |
| *298* | A42 | 3c multi | 14 | 14 |
| *299* | A42 | 4c multi | 18 | 18 |
| *300* | A35 | 5c multi | 26 | 26 |
| *301* | A35 | 8c multi | 48 | 48 |
| *302* | A35 | 9c multi | 48 | 48 |
| *303* | A35 | 12c multi | 65 | 65 |
| *304* | A35 | 15c multi | 90 | 90 |
| *305* | A35 | 20c multi | 1.10 | 1.10 |
| *306* | A35 | 25c multi | 1.25 | 1.25 |
| *307* | A35 | 35c multi | 2.00 | 2.00 |
| *308* | A35 | 45c multi | 2.25 | 2.25 |
| *309* | A35 | $1 multi | 4.50 | 4.50 |
| *310* | A42 | $2 multi | 8.75 | 8.75 |
| *311* | A35 | $5 multi (S) | 22.50 | 22.50 |
| | | *Nos. 296-311 (16)* | 45.58 | 45.58 |

Ceremonial Food Bowl — A46

Artifacts: 15c, Barava, chief's money. 35c, Nguzu-nguzu, canoe protector spirit (vert.). 45c, Nguzu-nguzu on canoe prow.

**Wmk. 314**

**1976, Jan. 12 Litho. *Perf. 14***

| | | | | |
|---|---|---|---|---|
| *312* | A46 | 4c scar & blk | 12 | 12 |
| *313* | A46 | 15c lt vio & multi | 38 | 38 |
| *314* | A46 | 35c multi | 1.00 | 1.00 |
| *315* | A46 | 45c multi | 1.10 | 1.10 |

Type of 1975 Inscribed "Solomon Islands" and

Golden Cowries A47

Designs: 1c, Golden whistler. 2c, River kingfisher. 3c, Red-throated fruit dove. 4c, Button quail. 5c, Willie wagtail. 10c, Glory-of-the-sea cones. 12c, Rainbow lory. 15c, Pearly nautilus. 20c, Venus comb murex. 25c, Commercial trochus. 35c, Melon or baler shell. 45c, Orange spider conch. $1, Pacific triton. $2, Duchess lorikeet. $5, Great frigate bird.

**1976 Wmk. 373 *Perf. 14***

| | | | | |
|---|---|---|---|---|
| *316* | A42 | 1c yel grn & multi | 5 | 5 |
| *317* | A42 | 2c lt bl & multi | 5 | 5 |
| *318* | A42 | 3c pink & multi | 8 | 8 |
| *319* | A42 | 4c org & multi | 10 | 10 |
| *320* | A42 | 5c red brn & multi | 14 | 14 |
| *321* | A47 | 6c rose & multi | 16 | 16 |
| *322* | A47 | 10c multi | 28 | 28 |
| *323* | A42 | 12c yel grn & multi | 32 | 32 |
| *324* | A47 | 15c lil & multi | 40 | 40 |
| *325* | A47 | 20c ultra & multi | 55 | 55 |
| *326* | A47 | 25c dl grn & multi | 65 | 65 |
| *327* | A47 | 35c bis & multi | 95 | 95 |
| *328* | A47 | 45c fawn & multi | 1.25 | 1.25 |
| *329* | A47 | $1 ol & multi | 2.75 | 2.75 |
| *330* | A42 | $2 multi | 5.25 | 5.25 |
| *331* | A42 | $5 multi | 13.00 | 13.00 |
| | | *Nos. 316-331 (16)* | 25.98 | 25.98 |

Issue dates: $5, Dec. 6; others Mar. 8.

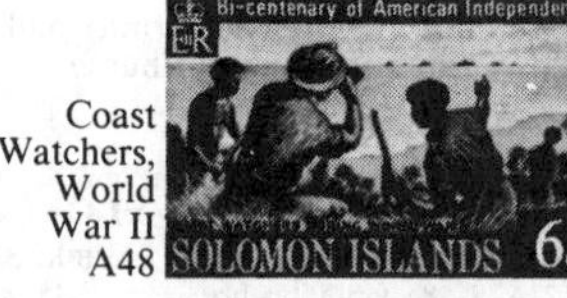


Coast Watchers, World War II A48

Designs: 20c, "Amagiri" ramming "P.T.109" and Lt. John F. Kennedy. 35c, Plane on Henderson Airfield. 45c, Map showing landing of U.S. forces on Guadalcanal.

**1976, May 24 *Perf. 14***

| | | | | |
|---|---|---|---|---|
| *333* | A48 | 6c blk & multi | 22 | 18 |
| *334* | A48 | 20c blk & multi | 85 | 70 |
| *335* | A48 | 35c blk & multi | 1.40 | 1.10 |
| *336* | A48 | 45c blk & multi | 1.75 | 1.40 |
| *a.* | | Souvenir sheet of 4 | 6.00 | 5.25 |

American Bicentennial. No. 336a contains one each of Nos. 333-336; multicolored margin shows map of Guadalcanal and Bicentennial emblem. Size: 96x116mm.

Alexander Graham Bell — A49

Designs: 20c, Radio-telephone and satellite. 35c, Ericsson's magneto telephone. 45c, Telephone, 1876, and stick telephone.

**1976, July 26 Litho. *Perf. 14½x14***

| | | | | |
|---|---|---|---|---|
| *337* | A49 | 6c lt ultra & multi | 18 | 18 |
| *338* | A49 | 20c multi | 60 | 60 |
| *339* | A49 | 35c org & multi | 90 | 90 |
| *340* | A49 | 45c bis & multi | 1.25 | 1.25 |

Centenary of first telephone call by Alexander Graham Bell, Mar. 10, 1876.

One-Eleven BAC — A50

Planes: 20c, Solair Britten Norman Islander. 35c, DC-3 Dakota. 45c, De Havilland DH50A.

**1976, Sept. 13 Wmk. 373 *Perf. 14***

| | | | | |
|---|---|---|---|---|
| *341* | A50 | 6c blk & multi | 18 | 18 |
| *342* | A50 | 20c blk & multi | 65 | 65 |
| *343* | A50 | 35c blk & multi | 1.10 | 1.10 |
| *344* | A50 | 45c blk & multi | 1.40 | 1.40 |

1st flight to Solomon Islands, 50th anniv.

Queen Receiving Lei, 1974 Visit — A51

Carved Wooden Figure — A52

Designs: 35c, Communion plate and cup. 45c, Communion.

**1977, Feb. 7 Litho. *Perf. 14x13½***

| | | | | |
|---|---|---|---|---|
| *345* | A51 | 6c multi | 14 | 14 |
| *346* | A51 | 35c multi | 65 | 65 |
| *347* | A51 | 45c multi | 85 | 85 |

25th anniv. of the reign of Elizabeth II.

**1977, May 9 *Perf. 14***

Artifacts: 20c, Sea adaro or spirit. 35c, Shark-headed man. 45c, Seated man.

| | | | | |
|---|---|---|---|---|
| *348* | A52 | 6c yel & multi | 18 | 18 |
| *349* | A52 | 20c bl & multi | 58 | 58 |
| *350* | A52 | 35c rose & multi | 95 | 95 |
| *351* | A52 | 45c multi | 1.25 | 1.25 |

Man Spraying House, Anopheles Mosquito A53

Designs: 20c, Taking blood samples. 35c, Microscope, map of Solomon Islands, Malaria Eradication Program emblem. 45c, Messenger delivering medicine to malaria patient.

**1977, July 27 Litho. Wmk. 373**

*352* A53 6c multi 18 18
*353* A53 20c multi 52 52
*354* A53 35c multi 90 90
*355* A53 45c multi 1.25 1.25

Malaria eradication.

Adoration of the Shepherds — A54

Christmas: 20c, Nativity. 35c, Adoration of the Kings. 45c, Flight into Egypt.

**Wmk. 373**

**1977, Sept. 12 Litho. *Perf. 14***

*356* A54 6c multi 16 16
*357* A54 20c multi 50 50
*358* A54 35c multi 90 90
*359* A54 45c multi 1.10 1.10

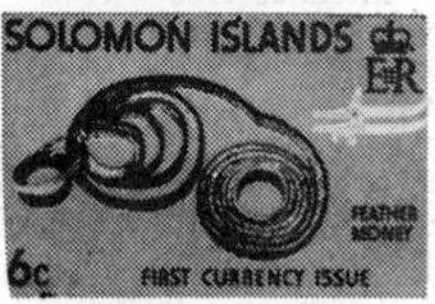


Traditional Feather Money — A55

Designs: No. 361, New coins. No. 362, Banknotes. No. 363, Traditional shell money.

**1977, Oct. 24 Litho. *Perf. 14x14½***

*360* A55 6c brt grn & multi 16 16
*361* A55 6c brt grn & multi 16 16
*362* A55 45c buff & multi 1.00 1.00
*363* A55 45c buff & multi 1.00 1.00

New coinage. Stamps of same denomination printed se-tenant in sheets of 60.

Shortland Islands Figure — A56

Artifacts: 20c, Ceremonial shield. 35c, Santa Cruz ritual figure. 45c, Decorative combs.

**1978, Jan. 11 *Perf. 14***

*364* A56 6c multi 16 16
*365* A56 20c multi 50 50
*366* A56 35c multi 90 90
*367* A56 45c multi 1.10 1.10

**Elizabeth II Coronation Anniversary Issue**

Common Design Types

**Souvenir Sheet**

**Unwmk.**

**1978, Apr. 21 Litho. *Perf. 15***

*368* Sheet of 6 3.75 3.75
**a** CD326 45c *King's dragon* 55 55
**b** CD327 45c *Elizabeth II* 55 55
**c** CD328 45c *Sandford eagle* 55 55

No. 368 contains 2 se-tenant strips of Nos. 368a-368c, separated by horizontal gutter with commemorative and descriptive inscriptions and showing central part of coronation procession with coach. Size: 100x135mm.

National Flag — A57

Apostles by Dürer — A58

Independence: 15c, Governor General's flag. 35c, Cenotaph, Honiara, flags of U.S., Great Britain, New Zealand and Australia. 45c, Coat of Arms.

**Wmk. 373**

**1978, July 7 Litho. *Perf. 14***

*369* A57 6c multi 15 15
*370* A57 15c multi 35 35
*371* A57 35c multi 85 85
*372* A57 45c multi 1.10 1.10

**1978, Oct. 4 Litho. *Perf. 14***

*373* A58 6c John 12 12
*374* A58 20c Peter 45 45
*375* A58 35c Paul 75 75
*376* A58 45c Mark 95 95

Albrecht Dürer (1471-1528), German painter, 450th death anniversary.

Scouts Making Fire — A59

Designs: 20c, Camping. 35c, Solomon Islands Scouts. 45c, Canoeing.

**1978, Nov. 15 Litho. *Perf. 14***

*377* A59 6c multi 15 15
*378* A59 20c multi 48 48
*379* A59 35c multi 85 85
*380* A59 45c multi 1.10 1.10

50 years of Scouting in Solomon Islands.

Discovery A60

Designs: 18c, Capt. Cook, 1776, painting by Nathaniel Dance. 35c, Sextant. 45c, Capt. Cook after Flaxman / Wedgwood medallion.

**Wmk. 373**

**1979, Jan. 16 Litho. *Perf. 11***

*381* A60 8c multi 20 20
*382* A60 18c multi 42 42
*383* A60 35c multi 80 80

**Litho.; Embossed**

*384* A60 45c multi 1.00 1.00

Capt. Cook's voyages.

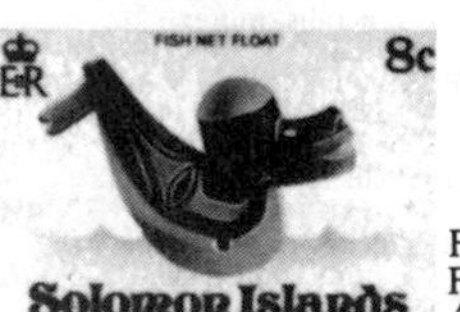


Fish Net Float A61

Artifacts: 20c, Armband made of shell money (vert.). 35c, Ceremonial food bowl. 45c, Forehead ornament (vert.).

**1979, Mar. 21 *Perf. 14***

*385* A61 8c multi 18 18
*386* A61 20c multi 40 40
*387* A61 35c multi 70 70
*388* A61 45c multi 85 85

6th South Pacific Games — A62

**1979, June 4 Litho. Wmk. 373**

*389* A62 8c Running 15 15
*390* A62 20c Hurdles 38 38
*391* A62 35c Soccer 65 65
*392* A62 45c Swimming 80 80

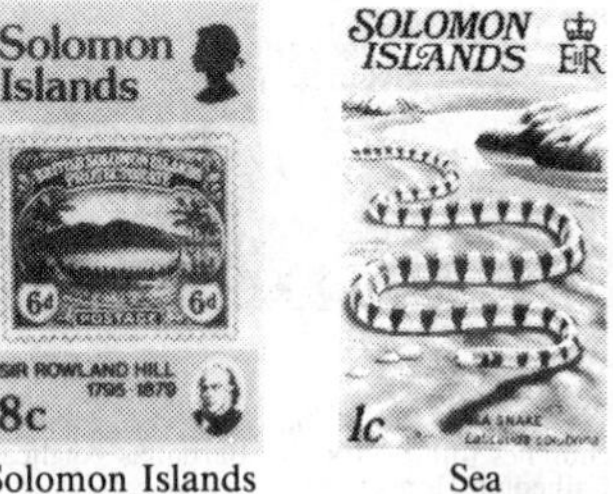


Solomon Islands No. 14 — A63

Sea Snake — A64

Designs (Rowland Hill and): 20c, Great Britain No. 27. 35c, Solomon Islands No. 372. 45c, Solomon Islands No. 40.

**1979, Aug. 16 Litho. *Perf. 14***

*393* A63 8c multi 15 15
*394* A63 20c multi 35 35
*395* A63 35c multi 60 60

**Souvenir Sheet**

*396* A63 45c multi 90 90

Sir Rowland Hill (1795-1879), originator of penny postage. No. 396 has multicolored margin showing Mulready envelope with Penny Black. Size: 122x82mm.

***Perf. 13½x13***

**1979-83 Litho. Wmk. 373**

*397* A64 1c Sea snake 5 5
*398* A64 3c Red-banded tree snake 6 6
*399* A64 4c Whip snake 8 8
*400* A64 6c Pacific boa 12 12
*401* A64 8c Skink 16 16
*402* A64 10c Gecko 20 20
*403* A64 12c Monitor 24 24
*404* A64 15c Angelhead 30 30
*405* A64 20c Giant toad 40 40
*406* A64 25c Marsh frog 50 50
*407* A64 30c Horned frog 60 60
*408* A64 35c Tree frog 70 70
*408A* A64 40c Burrowing snake ('83) 65 65
*409* A64 45c Guppy's snake 90 90
*409A* A64 50c Tree gecko ('83) 85 85
*410* A64 $1 Large skink 2.00 2.00
*411* A64 $2 Guppy's frog 4.00 4.00
*412* A64 $5 Estuarine crocodile 10.00 10.00
*412A* A64 $10 Hawksbill turtle ('82) 21.00 21.00
*Nos. 397-412A (19)* 42.81 42.81

Madonna and Child, by Morando — A65

IYC Emblem and Madonna and Child: 20c, Bernardino Luini. 35c, Bellini. 50c, Raphael.

**1979, Nov. 15 *Perf. 14½***

*413* A65 4c multi 6 6
*414* A65 20c multi 32 32
*415* A65 35c multi 55 55
*416* A65 50c multi 80 80
**a** Souvenir sheet of 4 1.90 1.90

Christmas 1979, International Year of the Child. No. 416a contains Nos. 413-416; yellow margin shows Christmas stars. Size: 92x134mm.

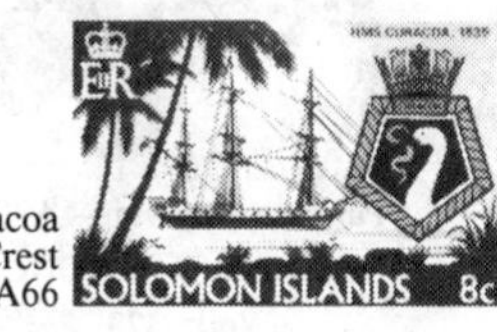


Curacoa and Crest A66

Ships and Crests: 20c, Herald, 1854. 35c, Royalist, 1889. 45c, Beagle, 1878.

**Wmk. 373**

**1980, Jan. 23 Litho. *Perf. 14***

*417* A66 8c multi 16 16
*418* A66 20c multi 40 40
*419* A66 35c multi 70 70
*420* A66 45c multi 90 90

See Nos. 435-438.

Steel Fishery Training Ship — A67

**1980, Mar. 27 Litho. *Perf. 13½***

*421* A67 8c *shown* 14 14
*422* A67 20c *Fishery training ship* 32 32
*423* A67 45c *Refrigerated carrier* 75 75
*424* A67 80c *Research ship* 1.25 1.25

"Comliebank," Tulag Cancel — A68

**1980, May 6 Litho. *Perf. 14½***

*425* Sheet of 4 multi 2.50 2.50
**a** A68 45c *shown* 60 60
**b** A68 45c *Douglas C-47* 60 60
**c** A68 45c *BAC 1-11, Honiara cancel* 60 60
**d** A68 45c *"Corabank," Auki cancel* 60 60

London 1980 International Stamp Exhibition, May 6-14. No. 425 has blue and black decorative margin. Size: 115x85mm.

**Queen Mother Elizabeth Birthday Issue**

Common Design Type

**Wmk. 373**

**1980, Aug. 4 Litho. *Perf. 14***

*426* CD330 45c multi 80 80

Angel with Trumpet — A69

Christmas: 20c, Angel with violin. 45c, Angel with trumpet. 80c, Angel with lute.

**Wmk. 373**

**1980, Sept. 2 Litho. *Perf. 14½***

*427* A69 8c multi 12 12
*428* A69 20c multi 30 30
*429* A69 45c multi 65 65
*430* A69 80c multi 1.10 1.10

Parthenos Sylvia — A70

**Wmk. 373**

**1980, Nov. 12 Litho. *Perf. 13½***

*431* A70 8c *shown* 12 12
*432* A70 20c *Delias schoenbergi* 30 30
*433* A70 45c *Jamides cephion* 70 70
*434* A70 80c *Ornithoptera victoriae* 1.25 1.25

See Nos. 461-464.

## Ship Crest Type of 1980

Ships and Crests: 8c, Mounts Bay, 1959. 20c, Charybdis, 1970. 45c, Hydra, 1972-1973. $1, Britannia, 1974.

**1981, Jan. 14**

*435* A66 8c multi 12 12
*436* A66 20c multi 30 30
*437* A66 45c multi 65 65
*438* A66 $1 multi 1.50 1.50

Maurelle's Map, 1742 — A71

**Wmk. 373**

**1981, Mar. 23 Litho. *Perf. 14***

*439* A71 8c Francisco Maurelle, vert. 12 12
*440* A71 10c shown 16 16
*441* A71 45c La Princesa 70 70
*442* A71 $1 Compass cards, vert. 1.65 1.65

**Souvenir Sheet**

*443* Sheet of 4 1.75 1.75
*a* A71 25c, any single 40 40

Bicentenary of arrival of Francisco Antonio Maurelle and of charts of mapmaker Jean Nicholas Buache (1741-1825). No. 443 contains 4 stamps (44x28mm, perf. 14½); multicolored margin shows map and description. Size: 126½x91mm.

Women's Basketball — A72

**Wmk. 373**

**1981, July 7 Litho. *Perf. 12***

*444* A72 8c shown 14 14
*445* A72 10c Tennis 18 18
*446* A72 25c Women's running 42 42
*447* A72 30c Soccer 52 52
*448* A72 45c Boxing 80 80
*Nos. 444-448 (5)* 2.06 2.06

**Souvenir Sheet**

*449* A72 $1 Emblem 1.75 1.75

Mini South Pacific Games, July. No. 449 has multicolored margin showing flags of participating countries. Size: 102x67mm.

## Royal Wedding Issue
Common Design Type

**1981, July 22 *Perf. 13½x13***

*450* CD331 8c Bouquet 14 14
*451* CD331 45c Charles 80 80
*452* CD331 $1 Couple 1.75 1.75

Duke of Edinburgh's Awards, 25th Anniv. — A73

**Wmk. 373**

**1981, Sept. 28 Litho. *Perf. 14***

*453* A73 8c Music 12 12
*454* A73 25c Handicrafts 38 38
*455* A73 45c Canoeing 70 70
*456* A73 $1 Duke of Edinburgh 1.50 1.50

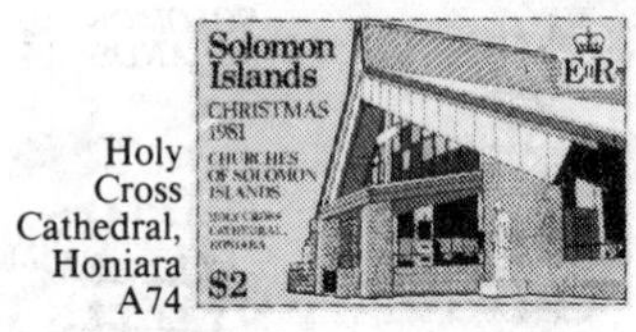


Holy Cross Cathedral, Honiara A74

Christmas 1981 (Churches): 8c, 25c, Old churches (diff.). 10c, St. Barnabas Anglican Cathedral, Honiara.

**1981, Oct. 12**

*457* A74 8c multi 12 12
*458* A74 10c multi 15 15
*459* A74 25c multi 35 35
*460* A74 $2 multi 3.00 3.00

## Butterfly Type of 1980

**Wmk. 373**

**1982, Jan. 5 Litho. *Perf. 13½***

*461* A70 10c Doleschallia bisaltide 16 16
*462* A70 25c Papilio bridgei hecataeus 42 42
*463* A70 35c Taenaris phorcas 60 60
*464* A70 $1 Graphium sarpedon 1.65 1.65

Sanford's Eagle — A75

**1982, May 15 Litho. *Perf. 14***

*465* A75 12c Pair facing left 26 26
*466* A75 12c Chick 26 26
*467* A75 12c Mother feeding chicks 26 26
*468* A75 12c Pair facing right 26 26
*469* A75 12c Male flying 26 26
*470* A75 12c Pair flying 26 26
*Nos. 465-470 (6)* 1.56 1.56

Se-tenant in sheets of 24.

## Princess Diana Issue
Common Design Type

***Perf. 14½x14***

**1982, July 1 Litho. Wmk. 373**

*471* CD333 12c Arms 18 18
*472* CD333 40c Diana 60 60
*473* CD333 50c Wedding 75 75
*474* CD333 $1 Portrait 1.50 1.50

12th Commonwealth Games, Brisbane, Australia, Sept. 30-Oct. 9 — A76

**1982, Oct. 11 Litho. *Perf. 14***

*475* A76 25c Running 50 50
*476* A76 25c Boxing 50 50

**Souvenir Sheet**

*477* Sheet of 3 3.00 3.00
*a* A76 $1 Britannia facing left 2.00 2.00

No. 477 contains Nos. 475-476, 477a; multicolored margin shows map. Size: 125x125mm.

Visit of Queen Elizabeth II and Prince Philip — A77

**1982, Oct. 11**

*478* A77 12c Royal couple 25 25
*479* A77 12c Flags 25 25

**Souvenir Sheet**

*480* Sheet of 3 2.50 2.50
*a* A77 $1 Britannia facing right 2.00 2.00

No. 480 contains Nos. 478-479; $1; multicolored margin shows map. Size: 125x125mm.

Scouting Year A78

Designs: Nos. 481, 485, Scout patroller. Nos. 482, 486, Brigade bugler. Nos. 483, 487, Baden-Powell. Nos. 484-488, William Smith.

**1982, Nov. 30**

*481* A78 12c dk bl & multi 18 18
*482* A78 12c brn & multi 18 18
*483* A78 25c dk bl & multi 35 35
*484* A78 25c brn & multi 35 35
*485* A78 35c grn & multi 50 50
*486* A78 35c red & multi 50 50
*487* A78 50c grn & multi 70 70
*488* A78 50c red & multi 70 70
*Nos. 481-488 (8)* 3.46 3.46

Turtles A79

**1983, Jan. 5 *Perf. 14***

*489* A79 18c Leatherback 26 26
*490* A79 35c Loggerhead 52 52
*491* A79 45c Pacific Ridley 65 65
*492* A79 50c Green 75 75

Commonwealth Day — A80

**1983, Mar. 14**

*493* A80 12c Oliva vidum, conus generalis, murex tribulus 18 18
*494* A80 35c Romu, kurila, kakadu, money belt 55 55
*495* A80 45c Shells, bride necklaces 70 70
*496* A80 50c Trochus niloticus, natural, polished 75 75

Manned Flight Bicentenary — A81

**Wmk. 373**

**1983, June 30 Litho. *Perf. 14***

*497* A81 30c Montgolfiere, 1783 38 38
*498* A81 35c Lockheed Hercules 45 45
*499* A81 40c Wright Brothers' Flyer III, 1905 50 50
*500* A81 45c Columbia space shuttle 55 55
*501* A81 50c Beechcraft Baron-Solair 65 65
*Nos. 497-501 (5)* 2.53 2.53

Christmas 1983 — A82

**1983, Aug. 25**

*502* A82 12c Weto dance 18 18
*503* A82 15c Custom wrestling 22 22
*504* A82 18c Girl dancers 26 26
*505* A82 20c Devil dancers 30 30
*506* A82 25c Bamboo band 38 38
*507* A82 35c Gilbertese dancers 52 52
*508* A82 40c Pan pipers 60 60
*509* A82 45c Afufu girl dancers 65 65
*510* A82 50c Cross, flowers 75 75
*a* Souvenir sheet of 9 3.75 3.75
*Nos. 502-510 (9)* 3.86 3.86

No. 510a contains Nos. 502-510. Size: 153x111mm.

World Communications Year — A83

**Wmk. 373**

**1983, Dec. 19 Litho. *Perf. 14***

*511* A83 12c Telephone Exchange building 15 15
*512* A83 18c Ham radio operator 22 22
*513* A83 25c No. 11 32 32
*514* A83 $1 No. 14 1.25 1.25
*a* Souvenir sheet of 1 1.50 1.50

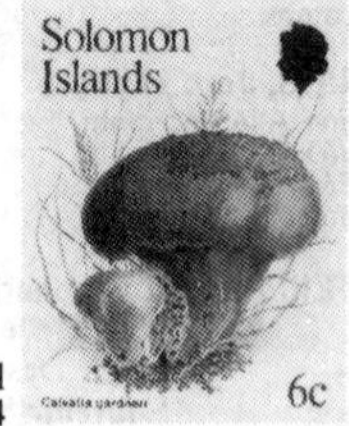


Local Fungi — A84

**1984, Jan. 30 *Perf. 13½***

*515* A84 6c Calvatia gardneri 8 8
*516* A84 18c Marasmiellus inoderma 25 25
*517* A84 35c Pycnoporus sanguineus 50 50
*518* A84 $2 Filoboletus manipularis 2.75 2.75

No. 510 and Type of 1983 overprinted "VISIT OF POPE JOHN PAUL II May 9th, 1984"

**Wmk. 373**

**1984, Apr. 16 Litho. *Perf. 14***

*519* A82 12c multi 18 18
*520* A82 50c multi 70 70

**Lloyd's List Issue**
Common Design Type

**1984, Apr. 21 Litho. *Perf. 14½x14***
*521* CD335 12c Olivebank, 1892 18 18
*522* CD335 15c Tinhow, 1906 22 22
*523* CD335 18c Oriana, Point Cruz 25 25
*524* CD335 $1 Point Cruz view 1.40 1.40

**Souvenir Sheet**

No. 14 — A85

**Wmk. 373**
**1984, June 18 Litho. *Perf. 14***
*525* A85 $1 multi 1.40 1.40

UPU Congress. Multicolored margin shows UPU emblem, text. Size: 133x105mm.

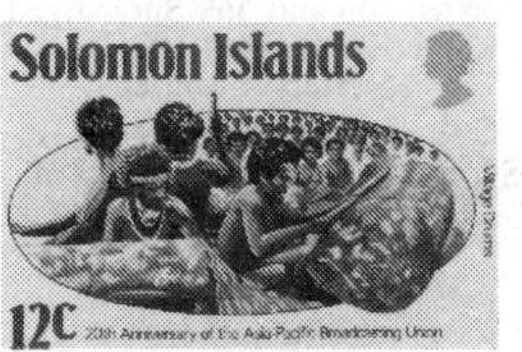


Asia-Pacific Broadcasting Union, 20th Anniv. — A86

**1984, July 2 *Perf. 13½***
*526* A86 12c Village drums 16 16
*527* A86 45c Radio City Guadalcanal 55 55
*528* A86 60c Broadcasting studio 75 75
*529* A86 $1 Broadcasting station 1.25 1.25

1984 Summer Olympics — A87

***Perf. 13½x14***
**1984, Aug. 4 Litho. Wmk. 373**
*530* A87 12c Flag, vert. 22 22
*531* A87 25c Lawson Tama Stadium, Honiara 45 45
*532* A87 50c Honiara Community Center 85 85
*533* A87 $1 Olympic Stadium 1.75 1.75

**Souvenir Sheet**
*534* A87 95c Bronte Baths 4.50 4.50

Solomon Islds. first olympic participation. No. 534 available in booklet only. Margin shows swimmer A. Wickham (1886-1976).

Little Pied Cormorant (Ausipex '84) — A88

**Wmk. 373**
**1984, Sept. 21 Litho. *Perf. 14½***
*535* A88 12c shown 22 22
*536* A88 18c Australian grey duck 30 30
*537* A88 35c Nankeen night-heron 60 60
*538* A88 $1 Dollarbird 1.65 1.65
*a* Souvenir sheet of 4, Nos. 535-538 3.00 3.00

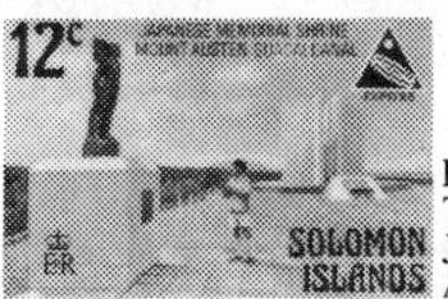


EXPO '85, Tsukuba, Japan A89

Designs: 12c, Japanese Memorial Shrine, Mt. Austen, Guadalcanal. 25c, Digital telephone exchange equipment. 45c, Soltai No. 7 fishing vessel. 85c, Coastal village.

**Wmk. 373**
**1985, June 28 Litho. *Perf. 14***
*539* A89 12c multi 18 18
*540* A89 25c multi 35 35
*541* A89 45c multi 60 60
*542* A89 85c multi 1.10 1.10

**Queen Mother 85th Birthday**
Common Design Type
***Perf. 14½x14***
**1985, June 7 Litho. Wmk. 384**
*543* CD336 12c VE Day, 1945 16 16
*544* CD336 25c With Margaret 35 35
*545* CD336 35c St. Patrick's Day celebration 48 48
*546* CD336 $1 Holding Prince Henry 1.40 1.40

**Souvenir Sheet**
*547* CD336 $1.50 In a gondola, Venice 2.00 2.00

No. 547 has multicolored margin continuing design. Size: 92x74mm.

Christmas — A90

**1985, Aug. 30 Wmk. 373 *Perf. 14½***
*548* A90 12c Titiana Village 18 18
*549* A90 25c Sigana, Santa Isabel 38 38
*550* A90 35c Artificial Island, Langa Lagoon 52 52

Intl. Youth Year — A91

Audubon Birth Bicent. — A92

Designs: 12c, Girl Guide activities. 15c, Stop Polio Campaign. 25c, Relay runners, views of the islands. 35c, Relay runners, views of Australia. 45c, Saluting natl. flag, badges.

**1985, Sept. 30 *Perf. 14***
*551* A91 12c multi 18 18
*552* A91 15c multi 22 22
*553* A91 25c multi 38 38
*554* A91 35c multi 52 52
*a* Souvenir sheet of 2, #553-554 90 90
*555* A91 45c multi 70 70
*Nos. 551-555 (5)* 2.00 2.00

Girl Guides 75th anniv., 12c, 45c; IYY, 15c, 25c, 35c. No. 554a has pale green margin containing historical data. Size: 100x75mm.

**Souvenir Sheet**

Bird illustration by Audubon.

**1985, Nov. 25 Wmk. 384**
*556* Sheet of 3 (1 45c, 2 50c) 2.00 2.00
*a* A92 45c Portrait 60 60
*b* A92 50c Osprey 65 65

No. 556 has multicolored decorative margin containing trees and historical data. Size: 121x108mm.

**Souvenir Sheet**

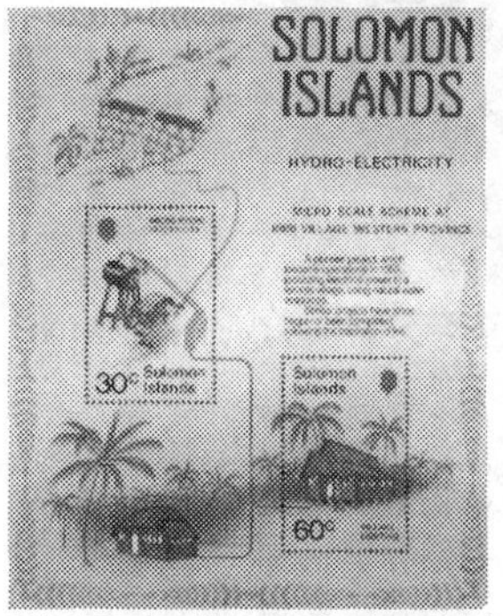


Mini Hydro-Electric Project, Iriri Village — A93

Designs: 30c, Water-driven generator. 60c, Illuminated village house.

**1986, Jan. 24 *Perf. 14***
*557* Sheet of 2 1.10 1.10
*a* A93 30c multi 35 35
*b* A93 60c multi 65 65

No. 557 has multicolored margin continuing design, picturing water supplying generator power to remote village. Size: 110x134mm.

Halley's Comet A94

Operation Raleigh, 1986: 18c, Construction of Red Cross Center, Gizo. 30c, Exploring rain forest. 60c, Observing Halley's Comet. $1, Ships Sir Walter Raleigh and Zebu.

***Perf. 14½x14***
**1986, Mar. 27 Wmk. 373**
*558* A94 18c multi 22 22
*559* A94 30c multi 38 38
*560* A94 60c multi 75 75
*561* A94 $1 multi 1.25 1.25

**Queen Elizabeth II 60th Birthday**
Common Design Type

Designs: 5c, Visiting Clydebank Town Hall with Prince Philip, 1947. 18c, At Queen Mother's 80th birthday, St. Paul's Cathedral, 1980. 22c, Walking among children of the islands, Pacific tour, 1982. 55c, 50th birthday, Windsor Castle, 1976. $2, Visiting Crown Agents' offices, 1983.

**1986, Apr. 21 Wmk. 384 *Perf. 14½***
*562* CD337 5c scar, blk & sil 6 6
*563* CD337 18c ultra & multi 20 20
*564* CD337 22c grn & multi 25 25
*565* CD337 55c vio & multi 65 65
*566* CD337 $2 rose vio & multi 2.25 2.25
*Nos. 562-566 (5)* 3.41 3.41

**Royal Wedding Issue, 1986**
Common Design Type

Designs: 55c, Informal portrait. 60c, Andrew aboard royal navy vessel.

**Wmk. 384**
**1986, July 23 Litho. *Perf. 14***
*567* CD338 55c multi 70 70
*568* CD338 60c multi 80 80

**Souvenir Sheet**

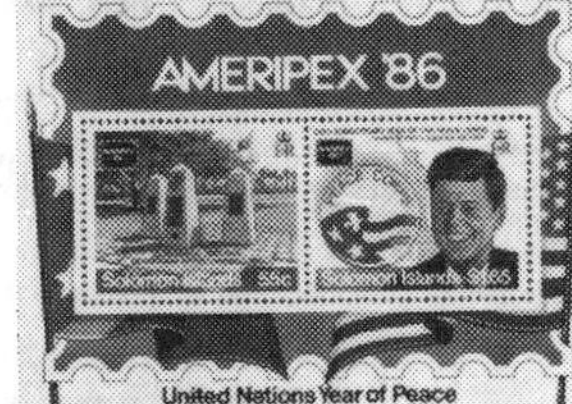


AMERIPEX '86 — A95

Designs: 55c, US Memorial, Henderson Field, Guadalcanal. $1.65, Peace Corps emblem, Statue of Liberty, Pres. John F. Kennedy.

**1986, May 22 Litho. *Perf. 13½***
*569* Sheet of 2 2.75 2.75
*a* A95 55c multi 65 65
*b* A95 $1.65 multi 2.00 2.00

Intl. Peace Year, Peace Corps 25th anniv. No. 569 has multicolored margin picturing natl. flags and exhibition emblem. Size: 100x75mm.

1987 America's Cup — A96

Previous winners, challengers, maps and club emblems: No. 570a, America, USA, 1851. b, Magic, USA, 1870. c, Madeleine, USA, 1876. d, Mischief, USA, 1881. e, Columbia, USA, 1871. f, British Cup course, 1851. g, America II, USA, 1987. h, America's Cup. i, Heart of America, USA, 1987. j, French Kiss, France, 1987.

No. 571a, Puritan, USA, 1885. b, Mayflower, USA, 1886. c, Defender, USA, 1895. d, Vigilant, USA, 1893. e, Volunteer, USA, 1887. f, America Cup course, Newport, 1930-1962. g, South Australia, Australia, 1987. h, KA14, Australia, 1987. i, New Zealand II, New Zealand, 1987. j, St. Francis IX, USA, 1987.

No. 572a, Columbia, USA, 1899. b, Columbia, USA, 1901. c, Enterprise, USA, 1930. d, Resolute, USA, 1920. e, Reliance, USA, 1903. f, America Cup course, 1964-1983. g, Kookaburra, Australia, 1987. h, Eagle, USA, 1987. i, True North, Canada, 1987. j, Italia, Italy, 1987.

No. 573a, Rainbow, USA, 1934. b, Ranger, USA, 1937. c, Constellation, USA, 1964. d, Weatherly, USA, 1962. e, Columbia, USA, 1958. f, Western Australia Cup course, 1987. g, Secret Cove, syndicate, 1987. h, Courageous III, USA, 1987. i, France, France, 1987. j, Azzurra, Italy, 1987.

No. 574a, Intrepid, USA, 1967. b, Intrepid, USA, 1970. c, Freedom, USA, 1980. d, Courageous, USA, 1977. e, Courageous, USA, 1974. f, Australia II, Australia, 1983. g, Crusader, Great Britain, 1987. h, Sail America, USA, 1987. i, Australia III, Australia, 1987. j, Royal Perth Yacht Club/America's Cup '87 emblem, 1987.

**1986, Aug. 22 Litho. *Perf. 14½***
*570* Strip of 10 + label 5.50 5.50
*a.-d* A96 18c, any single 18 18
*e.-f* A96 30c, any single 30 30
*g.-j* A96 $1, any single 1.00 1.00
*571* Strip of 10 + label 5.50 5.50
*a.-d* A96 18c, any single 18 18
*e.-f* A96 30c, any single 30 30
*g.-j* A96 $1, any single 1.00 1.00
*572* Strip of 10 + label 5.50 5.50
*a.-d* A96 18c, any single 18 18
*e.-f* A96 30c, any single 30 30
*g.-j* A96 $1, any single 1.00 1.00
*573* Strip of 10 + label 5.50 5.50
*a.-d* A96 18c, any single 18 18
*e.-f* A96 30c, any single 30 30
*g.-j* A96 $1, any single 1.00 1.00
*574* Strip of 10 + label 5.50 5.50
*a.-d* A96 18c, any single 18 18
*e.-f* A96 30c, any single 30 30
*g.-j* A96 $1, any single 1.00 1.00
*Nos. 570-574 (5)* 27.50 27.50

Nos. 570-574 printed se-tenant with center labels picturing natl. arms, 1987 America's Cup emblem and trophy in sheets of 50.

Souvenir Sheet

**1987, Feb. 4 Litho. *Perf. 14½***
*575* A96 $5 Stars and Stripes, US, victor 5.75 5.75

No. 575 has inscribed multicolored margin continuing the design and picturing trophy, diagram of race and flags. Size: 111x75mm.

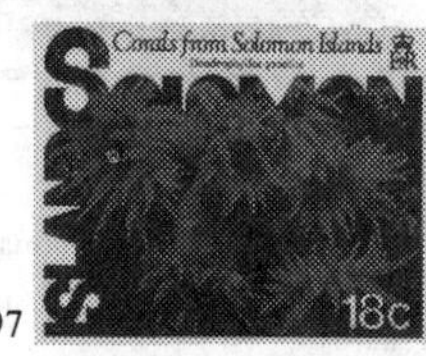


Coral — A97

***Perf. 14½x14***

**1987, Feb. 11 Litho. Wmk. 384**
*576* A97 18c Dendrophyllia gracilis 18 18
*577* A97 45c Dendronephthya 42 42
*578* A97 60c Clavularia 55 55
*579* A97 $1.50 Melithaea squamata 1.40 1.40

Flowering Plants — A98

**1987, May 12**
*580* A98 1c Cassia fistula 5 5
*581* A98 5c Allamanda cathartica 6 6
*582* A98 10c Catharanthus roseus 10 10
*583* A98 18c Mimosa pudica 20 20
*584* A98 20c Hibiscus rosa-sinensis 22 22
*585* A98 22c Clerodendrum thomsonae 24 24
*586* A98 25c Bauhinia variegata 28 28
*587* A98 28c Gloriosa rothschildiana 30 30
*588* A98 30c Heliconia solomonensis 32 32
*589* A98 40c Episcia hybrid 44 44
*590* A98 45c Bougainvillea hybrid 48 48
*591* A98 50c Alpinia purpurata 55 55
*592* A98 55c Plumeria rubra 60 60
*593* A98 60c Acacia farnesiana 65 65
*594* A98 $1 Ipomea purpurea 1.10 1.10
*595* A98 $2 Dianella ensifolia 2.25 2.25
*596* A98 $5 Passiflora foetida 5.50 5.50
*596A* A98 $10 Hemigraphis specie ('88) 10.25 10.25
*Nos. 580-596A (18)* 23.59 23.59

Issue date: $10, Mar. 1, 1988.

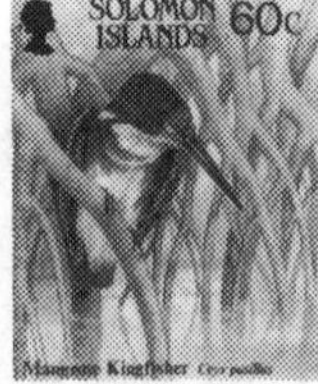


Mangrove Kingfisher A99

Designs: No. 597a, Perched on root. No. 597b, Diving. No. 597c, Landing in water. No. 597d, Emerging with fish.

***Perf. 14x14½***

**1987, July 15 Wmk. 373**
*597* Strip of 4 2.25 2.25
*a.-d.* A99 60c any single 55 55

Nos. 597a-597d printed in a continuous design.

Orchids — A100

***Perf. 13½x13***

**1987, Sept. 23 Wmk. 384**
*598* A100 18c Dendrobium conanthum 18 18
*599* A100 30c Spathoglottis plicata 30 30
*600* A100 55c Dendrobium gouldii 55 55
*601* A100 $1.50 Dendrobium goldfinchii 1.50 1.50

Christmas 1987.

Transportation and Communications Decade — A101

Designs: 18c, Telecommunications link. 30c, Express mail service. 60c, Guadalcanal Road Improvement Project. $2, Beechcraft Queen Air, Henderson Airfield control tower.

***Perf. 14x13½***

**1987, Oct. 31 Litho. Unwmk.**
*602* A101 18c multi 20 20
*603* A101 30c multi 32 32
*604* A101 60c multi 65 65
*605* A101 $2 multi 2.15 2.15

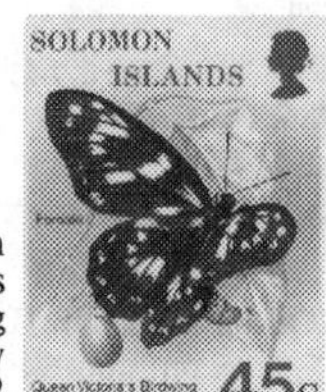


Queen Victoria's Birdwing Butterfly A102

Designs: No. 606a, Male. No. 606b, Larva. No. 606c, Pupa. No. 606d, Female.

**1987, Nov. 25 Wmk. 384 *Perf. 14½***
*606* Strip of 4 1.75 1.75
*a.-d.* A102 45c any single 42 42

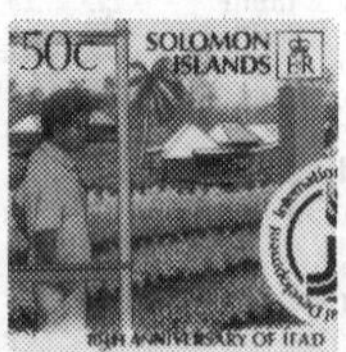


Intl. Fund for Agricultural Development (IFAD), 10th Anniv. — A103

Natl. colors and: No. 607, Student, Natl. Agricultural Training Institute (NATI) farm and emblem (left stamp). No. 608, Students in working in NATI field and emblem (right stamp). No. 609, Flatbed truck transporting produce and emblem (left stamp). No. 610, Canoes, seagulls and emblem (right stamp).

**Wmk. 384**

**1988, Feb. 12 Litho. *Perf. 14½***
*607* A103 50c multi 50 50
*608* A103 50c multi 50 50
*609* A103 $1 multi 1.00 1.00
*610* A103 $1 multi 1.00 1.00

Stamps of the same denomination printed se-tenant in continuous designs.

EXPO '88, Brisbane, Apr. 30-Oct. 30 — A104

Designs: 22c, Yacht in dry dock. 80c, Canoe. $1.50, Huts.

***Perf. 13½x14***

**1988, Apr. 30 Unwmk.**
*611* A104 22c multi 20 20
*612* A104 80c multi 80 80
*613* A104 $1.50 multi 1.50 1.50
*a.* Souv. sheet of 3, Nos. 611-613 2.50 2.50

No. 613a has multicolored margin continuing the design. Size: 130x53mm.

National Independence, 10th Anniv. — A105

***Perf. 13x13½***

**1988, July 7 Litho. Wmk. 373**
*614* A105 22c *Capitana* in Estrella Bay 20 20
*615* A105 55c Flag raising, 1893 55 55
*616* A105 80c Supreme Court 80 80
*617* A105 $1 Traditional celebration 1.00 1.00

Australia Bicentennial A106

Ships: 35c, M.V. *Papuan Chief.* 60c, M.V. *Nimos.* 70c, S.S. *Malaita.* $1.30, S.S. *Makambo.*

**1988, July 30 Wmk. 384 *Perf. 14***
*618* A106 35c multi 35 35
*619* A106 60c multi 60 60
*620* A106 70c multi 70 70
*621* A106 $1.30 multi 1.30 1.30
*a.* Souv. sheet of 4, Nos. 618-621 3.00 3.00

No. 621a has decorative inscribed margin picturing ocean and urban scenery. Size: 140x77mm.

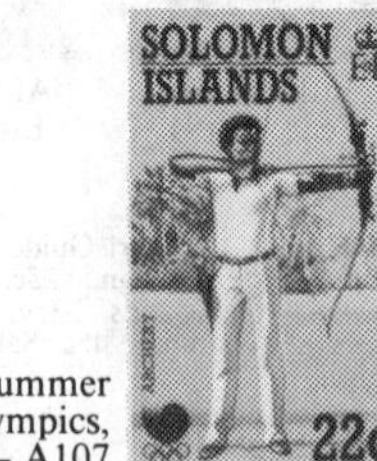


1988 Summer Olympics, Seoul — A107

**Wmk. 384**

**1988, Aug. 5 Litho. *Perf. 14½***
*622* A107 22c Archery 22 22
*623* A107 55c Weight lifting 55 55
*624* A107 70c Running 70 70
*625* A107 80c Boxing 80 80

**Souvenir Sheet**

**Wmk. 373**

*626* A107 $2 Olympic Stadium, horiz. 2.00 2.00

No. 626 has multicolored inscribed margin picturing grandstand and game emblems. Size: 100x80mm.

**Lloyds of London, 300th Anniv.**

Common Design Type

Designs: 22c, King George V and Queen Mary at Lloyd's ground-breaking ceremony, 1925. 50c, *Forthbank,* horiz. 65c, Soltel Satellite Ground Station, horiz. $2, *Empress of China.*

**1988, Oct. 31 *Perf. 14***
*627* CD341 22c multi 20 20
*628* CD341 50c multi 48 48
*629* CD341 65c multi 60 60
*630* CD341 $2 multi 1.85 1.85

## SEMI-POSTAL STAMPS

**Catalogue values for unused stamps in this section, from this point to the end of the section, are for Never Hinged items.**

No. 452 Overprinted in Red: "+ 50c SURCHARGE / CYCLONE RELIEF FUND / 1982"

***Perf. 13½x13***

**1982, May 3 Litho. Wmk. 373**
*B1* CD331 $1 + 50c multi 3.50 3.50

Nos. 546 and 569 Surcharged "Cyclone Relief Fund 1986" and New Value in Scarlet.

***Perf. 14½x14***

**1986, Sept. 23 Litho. Wmk. 384**
*B2* CD336 $1 + 50c multi 1.50 1.50

**Souvenir Sheet**

***Perf. 13½***

*B3* Sheet of 2 3.25 3.25
*a.* A95 55c + 25c multi 75 75
*b.* A95 $1.65 + 75c multi 2.50 2.50

## POSTAGE DUE STAMPS

D1

**Wmk. 4**

**1940, Sept. 1 Typo. *Perf. 12***
*J1* D1 1p emerald 3.00 *5.50*
*J2* D1 2p dk red 3.25 *5.75*
*J3* D1 3p chocolate 4.25 *6.25*
*J4* D1 4p dk bl 4.50 *7.75*
*J5* D1 5p dp grn 5.50 *11.50*
*J6* D1 6p brt red vio 6.75 *16.50*
*J7* D1 1sh dl vio 11.00 *22.00*
*J8* D1 1sh6p turq grn 24.00 *45.00*
*Nos. J1-J8 (8)* 62.25 *120.25*

# SOMALILAND PROTECTORATE

LOCATION — In eastern Africa, bordering on the Gulf of Aden.
GOVT. — Former British Protectorate.
AREA — 68,000 sq. mi.
POP. — 640,000 (estimated).
CAPITAL — Hargeisa.

Formerly administered by the Indian Government, the territory was taken over by the British Foreign Office in 1898 and transferred to the Colonial Office in 1905.

Somaliland Protectorate became part of independent Somalia in 1960.

16 Annas = 1 Rupee
100 Cents = 1 Shilling (1951)

**Catalogue values for unused stamps in this country are for Never Hinged items, beginning with Scott 108.**

Stamps of India, 1882-1900, Overprinted at Top of Stamp

BRITISH SOMALILAND

**1903 Wmk. 39 Perf. 14**

| No. | Type | Description | Unused | Used |
|---|---|---|---|---|
| 1 | A17 | ½a lt grn | 45 | 1.50 |
| 2 | A19 | 1a car rose | 45 | 1.50 |
| 3 | A21 | 2a violet | 48 | 75 |
| a. | | Double overprint | 750.00 | |
| 4 | A28 | 2½a ultra | 1.40 | 3.75 |
| 5 | A22 | 3a brn org | 90 | 2.50 |
| 6 | A23 | 4a ol grn | 1.10 | 3.75 |
| 7 | A25 | 8a red vio | 2.25 | 4.75 |
| 8 | A26 | 12a brn, *red* | 2.75 | 6.25 |
| a. | | Inverted overprint | | 1.200. |
| 9 | A29 | 1r car rose & grn | 4.50 | 10.00 |
| 10 | A30 | 2r yel brn & car rose | 12.00 | 21.00 |
| 11 | A30 | 3r grn & brn | 13.00 | 25.00 |
| 12 | A30 | 5r vio & bl | 20.00 | 37.50 |

### Wmk. Elephant's Head (38)

| No. | Type | Description | Unused | Used |
|---|---|---|---|---|
| 13 | A14 | 6a bister | 1.75 | 4.00 |
| | | *Nos. 1-13 (13)* | 61.03 | 122.25 |

Nos. 1 to 5 exist without the second "I" of "British".

### Same, but Overprinted at Bottom of Stamp

**1903 Wmk. 39**

| No. | Type | Description | Unused | Used |
|---|---|---|---|---|
| 14 | A28 | 2½a ultra | 1.75 | 4.00 |
| 15 | A26 | 12a vio, *red* | 5.00 | 10.00 |
| 16 | A29 | 1r car rose & grn | 5.00 | 10.00 |
| 17 | A30 | 2r yel brn & car rose | 50.00 | 55.00 |
| 18 | A30 | 3r grn & brn | 32.50 | 55.00 |
| a. | | Invtd. ovpt. | 1.250. | |
| 19 | A30 | 5r vio & bl | 45.00 | 67.50 |

### Wmk. 38

| No. | Type | Description | Unused | Used |
|---|---|---|---|---|
| 20 | A14 | 6a bister | 1.50 | 3.75 |
| | | *Nos. 14-20 (7)* | 140.75 | 205.25 |

### Stamps of India, 1902-03, Overprinted

**1903 Wmk. 39**

| No. | Type | Description | Unused | Used |
|---|---|---|---|---|
| 21 | A33 | ½a lt grn | 48 | 48 |
| 22 | A34 | 1a car rose | 55 | 50 |
| 23 | A35 | 2a violet | 1.50 | 2.75 |
| 24 | A37 | 3a brn org | 2.00 | 3.25 |
| 25 | A38 | 4a ol grn | 2.25 | 4.00 |
| 26 | A40 | 8a red vio | 2.75 | 5.50 |
| | | *Nos. 21-26 (6)* | 9.53 | 16.48 |

The above overprints vary in length, also in the relative positions of the letters. Nos. 21 to 23 exist without the second "I" of "British."

King Edward VII
A1 A2

**1904 Wmk. 2 Typo.**

| No. | Type | Description | Unused | Used |
|---|---|---|---|---|
| 27 | A1 | ½a gray grn | 55 | 50 |
| 28 | A1 | 1a car & blk | 1.25 | 1.40 |
| 29 | A1 | 2a red vio & dl vio | 80 | 95 |
| 30 | A1 | 2½a ultra | 1.10 | 1.25 |
| 31 | A1 | 3a gray grn & vio brn | 1.60 | 3.00 |
| 32 | A1 | 4a blk & gray grn | 1.75 | 3.50 |
| 33 | A1 | 6a vio & gray grn | 3.50 | 4.50 |
| 34 | A1 | 8a pale bl & blk | 4.50 | 7.25 |
| 35 | A1 | 12a ocher & blk | 6.75 | 8.00 |

### Wmk. Crown and C. C. (1)

| No. | Type | Description | Unused | Used |
|---|---|---|---|---|
| 36 | A2 | 1r gray grn | 9.00 | 12.50 |
| 37 | A2 | 2r red vio & dl vio | 20.00 | 27.50 |
| 38 | A2 | 3r blk & gray grn | 30.00 | 37.50 |
| 39 | A2 | 5r car & blk | 32.50 | 45.00 |
| | | *Nos. 27-39 (13)* | 113.30 | 152.85 |

**1905 Wmk. 3**

| No. | Type | Description | Unused | Used |
|---|---|---|---|---|
| 40 | A1 | ½a gray grn | 22 | 22 |
| 41 | A1 | 1a car & blk | 1.75 | 40 |
| 42 | A1 | 2a red vio & dl vio | 95 | 95 |
| 43 | A1 | 2½a ultra | 2.75 | 3.75 |
| 44 | A1 | 3a gray grn & vio brn | 2.75 | 4.50 |
| 45 | A1 | 4a blk & gray grn | 2.75 | 5.75 |
| 46 | A1 | 6a vio & gray grn | 3.25 | 5.75 |
| 47 | A1 | 8a pale bl & blk | 3.75 | 6.75 |
| 48 | A1 | 12a ocher & blk | 3.00 | 7.75 |
| | | *Nos. 40-48 (9)* | 21.17 | 35.82 |

Nos. 41, 42 and 44 to 48 inclusive are on both ordinary and chalky paper.

**1909**

| No. | Type | Description | Unused | Used |
|---|---|---|---|---|
| 50 | A1 | 1a carmine | 1.50 | 1.10 |

King George V
A3 A4

The ½, 1 and 2½a of type A3 are on ordinary paper, the other values of types A3 and A4 are on chalky paper.

**1912-19**

| No. | Type | Description | Unused | Used |
|---|---|---|---|---|
| 51 | A3 | ½a green | 16 | 16 |
| 52 | A3 | 1a carmine | 50 | 45 |
| 53 | A3 | 2a red vio & dl vio | 4.00 | 6.75 |
| 54 | A3 | 2½a ultra | 75 | 1.75 |
| 55 | A3 | 3a gray grn & vio brn | 75 | 2.50 |
| 56 | A3 | 4a blk & grn ('13) | 1.25 | 2.75 |
| 57 | A3 | 6a vio & grn | 90 | 2.00 |
| 58 | A3 | 8a lt bl & blk | 1.75 | 2.75 |
| 59 | A3 | 12a ocher & blk | 1.50 | 3.25 |
| 60 | A4 | 1r dl grn & grn | 2.50 | 4.50 |
| 61 | A4 | 2r red vio & dl vio ('19) | 10.50 | 22.50 |
| 62 | A4 | 3r blk & gray grn ('19) | 21.00 | 32.50 |
| 63 | A4 | 5r car & blk ('19) | 40.00 | 67.50 |
| | | *Nos. 51-63 (13)* | 85.56 | 149.36 |

**1921 Wmk. 4**

| No. | Type | Description | Unused | Used |
|---|---|---|---|---|
| 64 | A3 | ½a bl grn | 10 | 1.25 |
| 65 | A3 | 1a scarlet | 10 | 10 |
| 66 | A3 | 2a vio & dl vio | 32 | 65 |
| 67 | A3 | 2½a ultra | 45 | 1.40 |
| 68 | A3 | 3a gray grn & vio brn | 75 | 1.50 |
| 69 | A3 | 4a blk & grn | 75 | 2.75 |
| 70 | A3 | 6a vio & grn | 65 | 2.00 |
| 71 | A3 | 8a lt bl & blk | 1.10 | 3.50 |
| 72 | A3 | 12a ocher & blk | 1.40 | 4.00 |
| 73 | A4 | 1r dl grn & grn | 4.00 | 6.50 |
| 74 | A4 | 2r vio & dl vio | 11.00 | 18.00 |
| 75 | A4 | 3r blk & gray grn | 16.00 | 30.00 |
| 76 | A4 | 5r scar & blk | 40.00 | 65.00 |
| | | *Nos. 64-76 (13)* | 76.62 | 136.65 |

### Silver Jubilee Issue
Common Design Type

**1935, May 6 Engr. Perf. 11x12**

| No. | Type | Description | Unused | Used |
|---|---|---|---|---|
| 77 | CD301 | 1a car & dk bl | 75 | 925 |
| 78 | CD301 | 2a blk & ultra | 1.25 | 1.65 |
| 79 | CD301 | 3a ultra & brn | 1.90 | 2.25 |
| 80 | CD301 | 1r brn vio & ind | 5.75 | 6.75 |

### Coronation Issue
Common Design Type

**1937, May 13 Perf. 13½x14**

| No. | Type | Description | Unused | Used |
|---|---|---|---|---|
| 81 | CD302 | 1a carmine | 5 | 5 |
| 82 | CD302 | 2a black | 16 | 6 |
| 83 | CD302 | 3a brt ultra | 15 | 15 |

Blackhead Sheep
A5

Screwhorn Antelope
A6

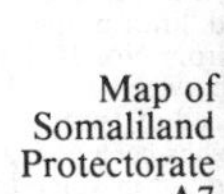

Map of Somaliland Protectorate
A7

**1938, May 10 Wmk. 4 Perf. 12½**

| No. | Type | Description | Unused | Used |
|---|---|---|---|---|
| 84 | A5 | ½a green | 25 | 35 |
| 85 | A5 | 1a carmine | 22 | 25 |
| 86 | A5 | 2a dp cl | 42 | 42 |
| 87 | A5 | 3a ultra | 85 | 1.65 |
| 88 | A6 | 4a dk brn | 85 | 1.65 |
| 89 | A6 | 6a purple | 75 | 1.50 |
| 90 | A6 | 8a gray blk | 1.25 | 3.75 |
| 91 | A6 | 12a orange | 1.50 | 3.00 |
| 92 | A7 | 1r green | 6.00 | 12.00 |
| 93 | A7 | 2r rose vio | 4.00 | 8.00 |
| 94 | A7 | 3r ultra | 4.50 | 9.25 |
| 95 | A7 | 5r black | 6.00 | 12.00 |
| a. | | Horiz. pair, imperf. btwn. | 4.000. | |
| | | *Nos. 85-95 (11)* | 26.34 | 53.47 |

Blackhead Sheep
A8

Screwhorn Antelope
A9

Map of Somaliland Protectorate
A10

**1942, Apr. 22**

| No. | Type | Description | Unused | Used |
|---|---|---|---|---|
| 96 | A8 | ½a green | 8 | 8 |
| 97 | A8 | 1a carmine | 10 | 10 |
| 98 | A8 | 2a dp cl | 12 | 12 |
| 99 | A8 | 3a ultra | 22 | 15 |
| 100 | A9 | 4a dk brn | 16 | 16 |
| 101 | A9 | 6a purple | 30 | 30 |
| 102 | A9 | 8a gray | 42 | 85 |
| 103 | A9 | 12a orange | 42 | 85 |
| 104 | A10 | 1r green | 70 | 1.25 |
| 105 | A10 | 2r rose vio | 1.10 | 2.00 |
| 106 | A10 | 3r ultra | 1.65 | 3.00 |
| 107 | A10 | 5r black | 2.75 | 4.25 |
| | | *Nos. 96-107 (12)* | 8.02 | 13.11 |

See Nos. 116-126.

**Catalogue values for unused stamps in this section, from this point to the end of the section, are for Never Hinged items.**

### Peace Issue
Common Design Type
*Perf. 13½x14*

**1946, Oct. 15 Engr. Wmk. 4**

| No. | Type | Description | Unused | Used |
|---|---|---|---|---|
| 108 | CD303 | 1a carmine | 10 | 10 |
| a. | | Perf. 13½ | 5.00 | 20.00 |
| 109 | CD303 | 3a dp bl | 15 | 15 |

### Silver Wedding Issue
Common Design Types

**1949, Jan. 28 Photo. Perf. 14x14½**

| No. | Type | Description | Unused | Used |
|---|---|---|---|---|
| 110 | CD304 | 1a scarlet | 15 | 15 |

**Engraved; Name Typographed**
*Perf. 11½x11*

| No. | Type | Description | Unused | Used |
|---|---|---|---|---|
| 111 | CD305 | 5r gray blk | 6.25 | 8.50 |

### UPU Issue
Common Design Types
Surcharged in Black or Carmine with New Values in Annas

**Engr.; Name Typo. on 3a, 6a**

**1949, Oct. 10 Perf. 13½, 11x11½**

| No. | Type | Description | Unused | Used |
|---|---|---|---|---|
| 112 | CD306 | 1a on 10c rose car | 25 | 12 |
| 113 | CD307 | 3a on 30c ind (C) | 50 | 25 |
| 114 | CD308 | 6a on 50c rose vio | 1.00 | 50 |
| 115 | CD309 | 12a on 1sh red org | 2.00 | 1.00 |

Nos. 96 and 98 to 107 Surcharged with New Value in Black or Carmine.

**1951, Apr. 2 Wmk. 4 Perf. 12½**

| No. | Type | Description | Unused | Used |
|---|---|---|---|---|
| 116 | A8 | 5c on ½a grn | 15 | 8 |
| 117 | A8 | 10c on 2a dp cl | 30 | 15 |
| 118 | A8 | 15c on 3a ultra | 35 | 18 |
| 119 | A9 | 20c on 4a dk brn | 40 | 20 |
| 120 | A9 | 30c on 6a pur | 45 | 22 |
| 121 | A9 | 50c on 8a gray | 50 | 25 |
| 122 | A9 | 70c on 12a red | 65 | 32 |
| 123 | A10 | 1sh on 1r grn | 85 | 42 |
| 124 | A10 | 2sh on 2r rose vio | 1.25 | 65 |
| 125 | A10 | 2sh on 3r ultra | 2.00 | 1.00 |
| 126 | A10 | 5sh on 5r blk (C) | 5.00 | 2.50 |
| | | *Nos. 116-126 (11)* | 11.90 | 5.97 |

### Coronation Issue
Common Design Type

**1953, June 2 Engr. Perf. 13½x13**

| No. | Type | Description | Unused | Used |
|---|---|---|---|---|
| 127 | CD312 | 15c dk grn & blk | 25 | 25 |

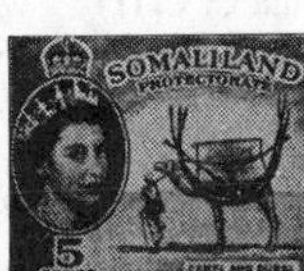


Camel Carrying Somali House
A11

Askari Militiaman
A12

Designs: 35c, 2sh, Rock Pigeon. 50c, 5sh, Martial eagle. 1sh, Blackhead sheep. 1sh30c, Tomb of Sheik Isaaq, Mait. 10sh, Taleh Fort.

**1953-58 Engr. Perf. 12½**

| No. | Type | Description | Unused | Used |
|---|---|---|---|---|
| 128 | A11 | 5c gray | 12 | 5 |
| 129 | A12 | 10c red org | 16 | 5 |
| 130 | A11 | 15c bl grn | 28 | 9 |
| 131 | A11 | 20c rose red | 35 | 12 |
| 132 | A12 | 30c lt choc | 40 | 18 |
| 133 | A11 | 35c blue | 50 | 22 |
| 134 | A11 | 50c lil rose & brn | 65 | 30 |
| 135 | A11 | 1sh grnsh bl | 80 | 35 |
| 136 | A11 | 1sh30c dk gray & ultra ('58) | 1.50 | 65 |
| 137 | A11 | 2sh vio & brn | 2.00 | 90 |
| 138 | A11 | 5sh emer & brn | 5.00 | 2.25 |
| 139 | A11 | 10sh rose lil & brn | 9.00 | 4.00 |
| | | *Nos. 128-139 (12)* | 20.76 | 9.16 |

Nos. 131 and 135 Overprinted: "Opening of the Legislative Council 1957."

**1957, May 21**

| No. | Type | Description | Unused | Used |
|---|---|---|---|---|
| 140 | A11 | 20c rose red | 25 | 25 |
| 141 | A11 | 1sh grnsh bl | 50 | 50 |

Nos. 131 and 136 Overprinted: "Legislative Council Unofficial Majority, 1960"

**1960, Apr. 5**

| No. | Type | Description | Unused | Used |
|---|---|---|---|---|
| 142 | A11 | 20c rose red | 25 | 25 |
| 143 | A11 | 1sh30c dk gray & ultra | 48 | 48 |

Issued to commemorate changes in the Legislative Council.

Three stamps of Somalia were overprinted "Somaliland Independence 26 June 1960" and issued in Hargeisa on that day. Somaliland Protectorate became part of Somalia on July 1, 1960. These three stamps are listed in Vol. IV as Somalia Nos. 242, C68-C69.

Stamps of Somaliland Protectorate were replaced by those of Somalia in 1960.

## OFFICIAL STAMPS

Official Stamps of India, 1883-1900, Overprinted **BRITISH SOMALILAND**

**1903, June 1 Wmk. 39 Perf. 14**

| No. | Type | Description | Unused | Used |
|---|---|---|---|---|
| O1 | A17 | ½a light grn | 4.00 | 35.00 |
| O2 | A19 | 1a car rose | 6.00 | 9.00 |
| O3 | A21 | 2a violet | 7.75 | 42.50 |
| O4 | A25 | 8a red vio | 22.50 | 450.00 |
| O5 | A29 | 1r car rose & grn | 22.50 | 300.00 |
| | | *Nos. O1-O5 (5)* | 62.75 | |

India Nos. 61-63, 68, 49 Overprinted **SERVICE BRITISH SOMALILAND**

**1903**

| No. | Type | Description | Unused | Used |
|---|---|---|---|---|
| O6 | A33 | ½a green | 75 | |
| O7 | A34 | 1a car rose | 75 | |
| O8 | A35 | 2a violet | 75 | |
| O9 | A40 | 8a red violet | 16.00 | |
| O10 | A29 | 1r car rose & grn | 27.50 | |
| | | *Nos. O6-O10 (5)* | 45.75 | |

Nos. O6-O10 were not regularly issued.

Regular Issue of 1904 Overprinted **O. H. M. S.**

**1904 Wmk. Crown and C. A. (2)**

| No. | Type | Description | Unused | Used |
|---|---|---|---|---|
| O11 | A1 | ½a gray green | 5.00 | 18.00 |
| O12 | A1 | 1a car & blk | 7.75 | 9.00 |
| O13 | A1 | 2a red vio & dl vio | 110.00 | 50.00 |
| O14 | A1 | 8a pale bl & blk | 55.00 | 100.00 |

**Wmk. Crown and C. C. (1)**

| | | | |
|---|---|---|---|
| *O15* A2 | 1r gray green | 175.00 | *500.00* |

Same Overprint on No. 42

**1905 Wmk. 3**

| | | | |
|---|---|---|---|
| *O16* A1 | 2a red vio & dl vio | 65.00 | *400.00* |

The period after "M" may be found missing on Nos. O11-O14 and O16.

## SOUTH AFRICA

LOCATION — Southern Africa.
GOVT. — Republic.
AREA — 433,678 sq. mi.
POP. — 26,749,000 (est. 1984).
CAPITAL — Pretoria (administrative); Cape Town (legislative).

The union was formed on May 31, 1910, comprising the former British colonies of Cape of Good Hope, Natal, Transvaal and the Orange Free State, which became provinces. The union became a republic in 1961.

For previous listings, see individual headings.

12 Pence = 1 Shilling
20 Shillings = 1 Pound
100 Cents = 1 Rand (1961)

**Catalogue values for unused stamps in this country are for Never Hinged items, beginning with Scott 74 in the regular postage section, Scott B1 in the semi-postal section, Scott J22 in the postage due section, and Scott O21 in the officials section.**

George V — A1

Wmk. 47- Multiple Rosette

**1910 Engr. Wmk. 47 *Perf. 14***

| | | | | |
|---|---|---|---|---|
| *1* | A1 | 2½p deep blue | 5.00 | 1.90 |

Union Parliament opening, Nov. 4, 1910.

George V — A2

Wmk. 177- Springbok's Head

**1913-22 Typo. Wmk. 177**

| | | | | |
|---|---|---|---|---|
| *2* | A2 | ½p green | 15 | 5 |
| *a.* | | Double impression | *16,500.* | |
| *3* | A2 | 1p scarlet | 30 | 5 |
| *4* | A2 | 1½p org brn ('20) | 48 | 5 |
| *a.* | | Tete beche pair | 5.00 | *10.00* |
| *5* | A2 | 2p dl vio | 90 | 5 |
| *6* | A2 | 2½p ultra | 1.40 | 24 |
| *7* | A2 | 3p brn org & blk | 1.75 | 15 |
| *8* | A2 | 3p ultra ('22) | 2.00 | 70 |
| *9* | A2 | 4p ol grn & org | 4.25 | 20 |
| *10* | A2 | 6p vio & blk | 3.25 | 10 |
| *11* | A2 | 1sh orange | 10.00 | 20 |
| *12* | A2 | 1sh3p vio ('20) | 17.50 | 10.00 |
| *13* | A2 | 2sh6p grn & cl | 55.00 | 2.00 |
| *14* | A2 | 5sh bl & cl | 125.00 | 11.00 |
| *15* | A2 | 10sh ol grn & bl | 250.00 | 16.00 |
| *16* | A2 | £1 red & dp grn ('16) | 900.00 | 275.00 |
| *a.* | | £1 lt red & gray grn ('24) | 1,000. | *1,750.* |
| | | *Nos. 2-16 (15)* | 1,371. | 315.79 |

The ½p, 1p and 1½p have the words "Revenue" and "Inkomst" on the stamps. On other stamps of this type these words are replaced by short vertical lines.

All values exist in many shades. No. 4a exists with and without gutter between.

Unwatermarked copies of the 1p are thre result of misplaced watermarks.

Coil Stamps

***Perf. 14 Horizontally***

| | | | | |
|---|---|---|---|---|
| *17* | A2 | ½p green | 3.50 | 85 |
| *18* | A2 | 1p scar ('14) | 4.00 | 1.65 |
| *19* | A2 | 1½p org brn ('20) | 5.00 | 3.00 |
| *20* | A2 | 2p dl vio ('21) | 5.00 | 2.75 |

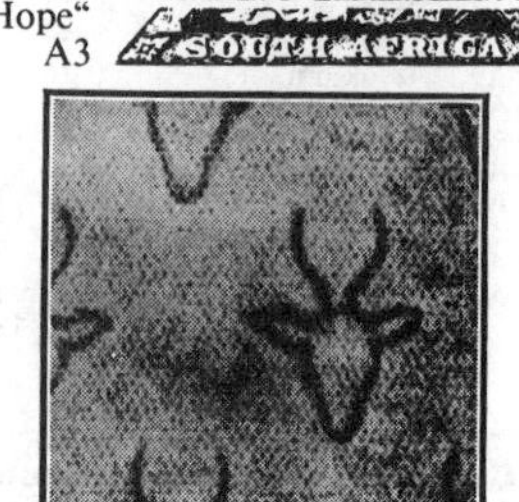

"Hope" A3

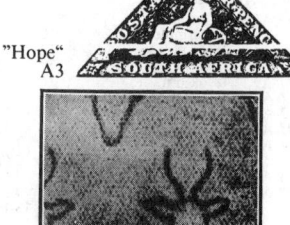

Wmk. 201- Multiple Springbok's Head

Design: No. 22, inscribed SUIDAFRIKA.

**1926 Engr. Wmk. 201 *Imperf.***

| | | | | |
|---|---|---|---|---|
| *21* | A3 | 4p blue gray | 75 | 65 |
| *22* | A3 | 4p blue gray | 75 | 65 |

Nos. 21 and 22 were privately rouletted and perforated, but such varieties were not officially made.

No. 21 (English inscription) was printed in a separate sheet from No. 22 (Afrikaans inscription).

**English-Afrikaans Se-Tenant**

Stamps with English inscriptions and with Afrikaans inscriptions were printed alternately in the same sheets, starting with No. 23. Major-number listings and values are for single stamps of either inscription. Pairs (horizontal or vertical) of such stamps consist of one English and one Afrikaans-inscribed stamp, unless otherwise described.

Springbok — A5

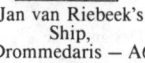

Jan van Riebeek's Ship, Drommedaris — A6

Orange Tree — A7

**1926 Typo. *Perf. 14½x14***

| | | | | |
|---|---|---|---|---|
| *23* | A5 | ½p dk grn & blk | 25 | 5 |
| *a.* | | Pair | 1.50 | 1.25 |
| *b.* | | Booklet pane of 6 | 50.00 | |
| *c.* | | Tete beche pair | 1,750. | |
| *d.* | | Center omitted | 275.00 | |
| *e.* | | As "b," perf. 14 | 725.00 | |
| *24* | A6 | 1p car & blk | 25 | 5 |
| *a.* | | Pair | 1.50 | 1.10 |
| *b.* | | Booklet pane of 6 | 40.00 | |
| *c.* | | Imperf., pair | 650.00 | |
| *d.* | | Tete beche pair | 1,750. | |
| *e.* | | Center omitted | 275.00 | |
| *f.* | | As "b," perf. 14 | 550.00 | |
| *25* | A7 | 6p org & grn | 1.65 | 8 |
| *a.* | | Pair | 18.00 | 8.25 |

Nos. 23c and 24d are from uncut sheets printed for the perf. 14 booklet panes of 1928, Nos. 23e and 24f.

Government Buildings, Pretoria — A8

"Groote Schuur," Rhodes's Home — A9

Kaffir Kraal — A10

Gnu — A11

Trekking — A12

Ox Wagon — A13

Cape Town and Table Mountain — A14

***Perf. 14, 14x13½***

**1927-28 Engr. Wmk. 201**

| | | | | |
|---|---|---|---|---|
| *26* | A8 | 2p vio brn & gray | 2.00 | 8 |
| *a.* | | Pair | 13.00 | 13.00 |
| *27* | A9 | 3p red & blk | 3.50 | 25 |
| *a.* | | Pair | 18.00 | 15.00 |
| *b.* | | Perf. 14x13½ | 11.00 | 3.25 |
| *c.* | | As "b," pair | 100.00 | 100.00 |
| *28* | A10 | 4p brn ('28) | 3.00 | 32 |
| *a.* | | Pair | 21.00 | 21.00 |
| *29* | A11 | 1sh dp bl & bis brn | 4.50 | 90 |
| *a.* | | Pair | 27.50 | 25.00 |
| *30* | A12 | 2sh6p brn & bl grn | 14.00 | 6.50 |
| *a.* | | Pair | 82.50 | *115.00* |
| *b.* | | Perf. 14x13½ | 60.00 | 22.50 |
| *c.* | | As "b," pair | 300.00 | 150.00 |
| *31* | A13 | 5sh dp grn & blk | 32.50 | 32.50 |
| *a.* | | Pair | 150.00 | *210.00* |
| *b.* | | Perf. 14x13½ | 90.00 | 90.00 |
| *c.* | | As "b," pair | 425.00 | 425.00 |
| *32* | A14 | 10sh ol brn & bl | 32.50 | 12.50 |
| *a.* | | Pair | 150.00 | 72.50 |
| *b.* | | Perf. 14x13½ | 75.00 | 32.50 |
| *c.* | | As "b," pair | 275.00 | 250.00 |
| | | *Nos. 26-32 (7)* | 92.00 | 53.05 |

Types of 1926-28 Redrawn "SUIDAFRIKA" (No Hyphen) on Afrikaans Stamps

The photogravure, unhyphenated stamps of 1930-45 are distinguished from the 1926-28 typographed or engraved stamps (also unhyphenated) by the following characteristics:

½p, 1p, 6p. Leg of "R" in AFRICA or AFRIKA ends in a straight line in the photogravure set; in a curved line in the typographed. No. 35 differs from No. 34, having 2mm space between POSSEEL—INKOMSTE instead of 1mm.

2p. A memorial statue has been added just above and leftward of the "2" in value tablet on Nos. 36-37 (photogravure).

3p. Top frame on No. 38 consists of 3 heavy lines. On No. 27 it has 3 heavy and 2 very thin lines.

4p. On Nos. 40-41 the background in upper corners is solid. On No. 28 it consists of horizontal and vertical lines. No. 41 has pretzel-shaped scroll endings at bottom. On No. 40 these scroll endings enclose a solid mass of color.

1sh. No. 43 has no fine shading lines projecting from the curved top of the left inner frame, as No. 29 has. On No. 43 the shading of the last "A" of the country name partly covers the flower below it.

2sh6p. On No. 44 the shading below the country name is solid or shows signs of wear. On No. 30 it is composed of fine lines.

The engraved pictorials are much more finely executed and show details more clearly than the photogravure.

***Perf. 15x14 (½p, 1p, 6p), 14***

**1930-45 Photo. Wmk. 201**

| | | | | |
|---|---|---|---|---|
| *33* | A5 | ½p bl grn & blk | 25 | 5 |
| *a.* | | Pair, bilingual | 1.00 | 90 |
| *b.* | | Vert. pair, monolingual | 60.00 | 65.00 |
| *c.* | | Tete-beche pair | 1,250. | |
| *d.* | | As "c," gutter between | 950.00 | |
| *e.* | | Booklet pane of 6 | 30.00 | 30.00 |
| *34* | A6 | 1p car & blk | 45 | 5 |
| *a.* | | Pair | 1.50 | 70 |
| *b.* | | Booklet pane of 6 | 30.00 | 30.00 |
| *c.* | | Center omitted | 850.00 | |
| *d.* | | Frame omitted | 650.00 | |
| *e.* | | Tete-beche pair | 1,250. | |
| *f.* | | As "e," gutter between | 750.00 | |
| *35* | A6 | 1p rose & blk ('32) | 1.50 | 8 |
| *a.* | | Pair | 7.75 | 3.25 |
| *b.* | | Center omitted | 750.00 | |
| *36* | A8 | 2p vio & gray ('31) | 1.10 | 40 |
| *a.* | | Pair | 6.00 | 2.25 |
| *b.* | | Booklet pane of 4 | 50.00 | 50.00 |
| *c.* | | Frame omitted | 800.00 | |
| *d.* | | Tete beche pair | 2,750. | |
| *37* | A8 | 2p vio & ind ('38) | 8.25 | 2.00 |
| *a.* | | Pair | 110.00 | 40.00 |
| *38* | A9 | 3p red & blk ('31) | 4.25 | 1.50 |
| *a.* | | Pair | 35.00 | 22.50 |
| *39* | A9 | 3p ultra & bl ('33) | 85 | 28 |
| *a.* | | Pair | 4.75 | 2.25 |
| *b.* | | Center omitted | 1,000. | |
| *40* | A10 | 4p redsh brn ('32) | 2.50 | 60 |
| *a.* | | Pair | 35.00 | 18.00 |
| *41* | A10 | 4p brn ('36) | 60 | 7 |
| *a.* | | Pair | 4.00 | 1.75 |
| *42* | A7 | 6p org & grn ('31) | 2.00 | 30 |
| *a.* | | Pair | 16.00 | 3.00 |
| *43* | A11 | 1sh dp bl & brn ('32) | 5.25 | 42 |
| *a.* | | Pair | 37.50 | 12.50 |
| *b.* | | 1sh dl bl & yel brn | 4.50 | 35 |
| *c.* | | As "b," pair | 32.50 | 10.00 |
| *44* | A12 | 2sh 6p red brn & grn ('32) | 8.75 | 3.00 |
| *a.* | | Pair | 90.00 | 67.50 |
| *b.* | | 2sh6p brn & sl grn ('36) | 7.25 | 3.00 |
| *c.* | | As "b," pair | 70.00 | 37.50 |
| *d.* | | 2sh6p choc & dp grn ('37) | 6.50 | 3.00 |
| *e.* | | As "d," pair | 57.50 | 30.00 |
| *f.* | | 2sh6p brn & bl ('45) | 1.65 | 32 |
| *g.* | | As "f," pair | 13.00 | 8.25 |

No. 34 unwatermarked, or watermarked multiple clover leaf, is a proof.

Types of 1926-28 with "SUID-AFRIKA" Hyphenated on Afrikaans Stamps, and

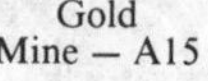

Gold Mine — A15

Government Buildings, Pretoria — A16

Groote Schuur — A17

Groot Constantia — A18

½p. No. 45 shading in leaves and ornaments strengthened; 40 lines in center background. Size: 18½x22½mm.

No. 46 has 28 heavy horizontal shading lines in center background and similar thicker lines in frame. Top and bottom green bars are scored by a white horizontal line. Size: 18½x22½mm.

No. 47 is smaller, 18x22mm.

1p. No. 48, size 18½x22½mm.

No. 49, size 18x22mm.

No. 50. Size: 17½x21½mm.

2p. On Nos. 53-54, S's in SOUTH and POSTAGE are narrower than on Nos. 36-37.

6p. Die I, "SUID-AFRIKA" 16½mm. Shading in leaves framing oval very faint and broken. Size: 18½x22½mm.

Die II, "SUID-AFRIKA" 17mm. Leaves strongly shaded. Heavy lines of shading in background of tree. Size: 18½x22½mm.

Die III, "question mark" scrolls below top panel are cleanly defined without intrusion of background shading. Size: 18x22mm.

Nos. 45-67 were printed in many shades. Some denominations in some printings were partly or wholly screened.

5sh. No. 65. Type I, letters "U" and "A" in SOUTH AFRICA have projections. Size: 27x21½mm.

No. 66. Type II, letters "U" and "A" redrawn to eliminate projections. Size: 26½x21½mm.

***Perf. 15x14 (½p, 1p, 6p), 14***

**1933-54 Photo. Wmk. 201**

*45* A5 ½p grn & gray ('36) 22 7
a. Pair 1.50 80
b. Bklt. pane of 6, marginal ads 30.00 30.00
c. Perf. 13½x14 (coil) 1.80 80
d. As "c," pair 11.00 9.75
*46* A5 ½p grn & gray, redrawn ('37) 7 5
a. Pair 55 18
b. Booklet pane of 6 37.50 30.00
c. Booklet pane of 2 2.10 1.00
d. As "b," 4 blank margins 35.00 35.00
e. Perf. 14½x14 (coil) 2.25 80
f. As "e," pair 12.50 7.25
*47* A5 ½p grn & gray ('47) 7 5
a. Pair 32 18
b. Bklt. pane of 6, marginal ads 5.00 3.50
c. As "b," no horiz. margins 5.00 3.00
*48* A6 1p car & gray ('34) 12 5
a. Pair 55 22
b. Booklet pane of 6 37.50 37.50
c. Booklet pane of 2 3.00 1.25
d. Perf. 13½x14 (coil) 1.40 1.00
e. As "d," pair 14.00 14.00
f. Center omitted, pair 310.00
g. Bklt. pane of 6, marginal ads 27.50 27.50
h. As "g," 4 blank margins 30.00 30.00
i. Perf. 14½x14 (coil) 1.40 1.40
j. As "i," pair 11.00 11.00
*49* A6 1p rose car & gray blk ('40) 8 5
a. Pair 35 28
b. Unwmk., pair 325.00 325.00
c. Booklet pane of 6 3.75 2.75
d. Perf. 14½x14 (coil) 1.40 90
e. As "d," pair 14.00 11.50
f. As "c," marginal ads 5.00 4.25
*50* A6 1p car & blk ('51) 10 5
a. Pair 30 14
*51* A15 1½p dk grn & gold, 27x21½mm ('36) 35 6
a. Pair 2.00 60
b. Center omitted, pair 1,000.
c. Booklet pane of 4 9.00 8.00
*52* A15 1½p sl grn & ocher, 22x18mm ('41) 14 5
a. Pair 80 22
b. Booklet pane of 6 5.75 4.50
c. Center omitted, pair 900.00
*53* A8 2p bl vio & dl bl ('38) 3.00 60
a. Pair 32.50 19.00
*54* A8 2p dl vio & gray ('41) 90 5
a. Pair 6.00 80
*55* A16 2p pur & sl bl, 27x21½mm ('45) 10 5
a. Pair 75 8
*56* A16 2p pur & sl bl, 21½x17¼mm ('50) 8 5
a. Pair 22 14
b. Booklet pane of 6 ('51) 3.75 2.75
*57* A17 3p ultra ('40) 20 5
a. Pair 2.00 55
b. 3p bl ('49) 8 5
c. As "b," pair 55 28
*58* A10 4p choc brn ('52) 18 5
a. Pair 70 55
*59* A7 6p org & bl grn, I ('37) 3.75 1.10
a. Pair 32.50 11.00
*60* A7 6p org & grn, II ('38) 90 22
a. Pair 4.50 2.75
*61* A7 6p org & grn, III ('46) 80 10
a. Pair 4.00 1.90
b. 6p red org & bl grn, III ('50) 12 5
c. As "b," pair 95 40
*62* A11 1sh lt bl & ol brn ('39) 75 14
a. Pair 5.50 2.00
b. 1sh chlky bl & lt brn ('50) 55 7
c. As "b," pair 3.50 55
d. 1sh vio bl & brnsh blk 35 6
e. As "d," pair 5.50 1.10
*63* A12 2sh6p brn & brt grn ('49) 90 25
a. Pair 6.50 4.50
*64* A13 5sh grn & blk 2.50 45
a. Pair 19.00 8.25
*65* A13 5sh bl grn & blk, I ('49) 2.50 60
a. Pair 16.00 11.00
*66* A13 5sh grn & blk, II ('54) 1.65 32
a. Pair 22.50 14.00
*67* A18 10sh ol blk & bl ('39) 3.00 38
a. Pair 27.50 5.50
*Nos. 45-67 (23)* 22.36 4.84

See Nos. 98-99.

George V and Springboks A19

**1935, May 1 Wmk. 201 *Perf. 15x14***

*68* A19 ½p Prus grn & blk 20 8
a. Pair 1.65 1.90
*69* A19 1p car rose & blk 28 6
a. Pair 1.75 1.25
*70* A19 3p bl & dk bl 3.00 2.50
a. Pair 27.50 37.50
*71* A19 6p org & grn 3.00 2.00
a. Pair 40.00 50.00

25th anniv. of the reign of George V.

English and Afrikaans inscriptions are transposed on alternate stamps. On the ½p, 3p and 6p with "SOUTH AFRICA" at top, "SILWER JUBILEUM" is at left of medallion, but on 1p with English at top, it is at the right.

**Johannesburg International Philatelic Exhibition Issue**

Souvenir Sheets

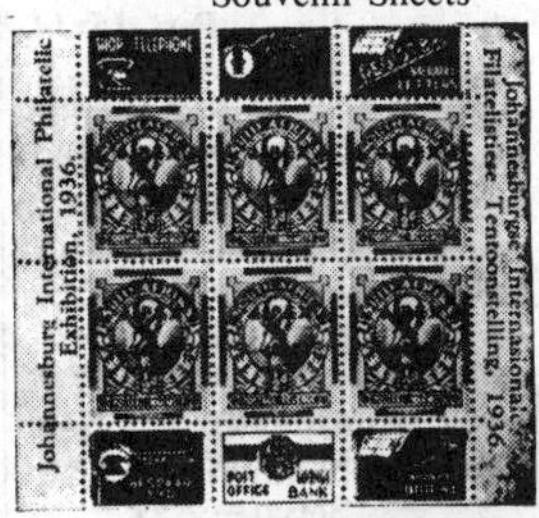
A20

A21

Black Overprint, "JIPEX 1936"

**1936, Nov. 2 *Perf. 15x14***

*72* A20 Sheet of 6 (½p grn & gray) 5.00 7.50
*73* A21 Sheet of 6 (1p car & gray) 4.25 6.00

Sheets made by overprinting booklet panes Nos. 45b and 48g. Sheets exist with and without horizontal perforations through right margin. Sheet size: 81x72½mm.

**Catalogue values for unused stamps in this section, from this point to the end of the section, are for Never Hinged items.**

George VI — A22

"KRONING SUID-AFRIKA" on alternate stamps.

**1937, May 12 *Perf. 14***

*74* A22 ½p grn & ol blk 6 6
a. Pair 35 35
*75* A22 1p car & ol blk 8 6
a. Pair 50 50
*76* A22 1½p Prus grn & org 8 8
a. Pair 50 50
*77* A22 3p bl & ultra 18 18
a. Pair 1.10 1.10
*78* A22 1sh Prus bl & org brn 50 50
a. Pair 3.00 3.00
*Nos. 74-78 (5)* 90 88
*Nos. 74a-78a (5)* 5.45 5.45

Coronation of George VI and Queen Elizabeth.

Wagon Wheel A23

Voortrekker Family — A24

Alternate stamps inscribed "SOUTH AFRICA", "SUID-AFRIKA".

**1938, Dec. 14 *Perf. 15x14***

*79* A23 1p rose & sl 30 25
a. Pair 5.50 5.50
*80* A24 1½p red brn & Prus bl 40 30
a. Pair 6.50 6.50

Issued to commemorate the Voortrekkers.

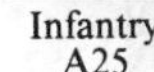
Infantry A25

Nurse and Ambulance A26

Airman and Spitfires (Flight Lt. Robert Kershaw) — A27

Sailor — A28

Women's Services A29

Artillery A30

Welder A31

Tank Corps A32

Signal Corps A33

Bilingual inscriptions on 2p and 1sh. Others have English and Afrikaans on alternate stamps.

***Perf. 14 (2p, 4p, 6p), 15x14***

**1941-43 Photo. Wmk. 201**

*81* A25 ½p dp bl grn 8 5
a. Pair 1.00 50
*82* A26 1p brt rose 10 5
a. Pair 1.00 50
*83* A27 1½p Prus grn ('42) 15 5
a. Pair 1.65 80
*84* A28 2p dk vio 60 10
*85* A29 3p dp bl 20 15
a. Pair 2.50 2.00
*86* A30 4p org brn 45 20
a. Pair 6.00 3.50
b. 4p red brn 60 15
c. As "b," pair 32.00 10.00
*87* A31 6p brt red org 50 30
a. Pair 6.00 5.00
*88* A32 1sh dk brn 3.00 1.00
*89* A33 1sh3p dk ol brn ('43) 40 18
a. Pair 5.00 2.50
b. 1sh3p dk brn 40 18
c. As "b," pair 5.00 2.50
*Nos. 81-89 (9)* 5.48 2.08

Infantry-Nurse-Airman-Sailor
A34 A35 A36 A37

Women's Services A38

Artillery A39

Welder A40

Tank Corps A41

Bilingual inscriptions on 4p and 1sh. Others have English and Afrikaans on alternate stamps.

***Pairs: Perf. 14, Roul. 6½ btwn.***
***Strips of 3: Perf. 15x14, Roul. 6½ btwn.***

**1942-43 Photo. Wmk. 201**

*90* A34 ½p dp bl grn 5 5
a. Horiz. strip of 3 80 40
b. As "a," imperf. between 350.00
*91* A35 1p brt car ('43) 5 5
a. Horiz. strip of 3 95 24
b. Horiz. strip of 3, imperf. between 350.00
*92* A36 1½p cop brn 6 5
a. Horiz. pair 95 48
b. Horiz. pair, imperf. btwn. 350.00
c. Horiz. pair, roul. 13 4.50 4.50
*93* A37 2p dk vio ('43) 6 5
a. Horiz pair 1.25 48
b. Horiz. pair, imperf. btwn. 350.00
*94* A38 3p dp bl 13 5
a. Vert. strip of 3 3.25 1.25
*95* A39 4p sl grn 16 6
a. Vert. strip of 3 4.00 1.65
*96* A40 6p brt red org 16 6
a. Horiz. pair 4.00 1.65
*97* A41 1sh dk brn 25 8
a. Vert pair 5.50 1.10
*Nos. 90-97 (8)* 92 45

Types of 1926, Redrawn
"SUID-AFRIKA" Hyphenated
Coil Stamps

**1943 Photo. *Perf. 15x14***

*98* A5 ½p myrtle grn 20 5
a. Pair 1.10 30
*99* A6 1p rose pink 20 5
a. Pair 1.40 38

"Victory" — A42

"Peace" — A43

Design: 3p, Profiles of couple ("Hope").

**1945, Dec. 3 Photo. *Perf. 14***

Inscribed alternately in English and Afrikaans.

*100* A42 1p rose pink & choc 8 6
a. Pair 18 14
*101* A43 2p vio & sl bl 10 6
a. Pair 22 14
*102* A43 3p ultra & dp ultra 15 12
a. Pair 32 28

World War II victory of the Allies.

George VI
A44

King George VI and Queen Elizabeth
A45

Princesses Margaret Rose and Elizabeth
A46

Inscribed alternately in English and Afrikaans.

*Perf. 15x14*

**1947, Feb. 17 Wmk. 201**

| | | | |
|---|---|---|---|
| *103* A44 1p cer & gray | | 6 | 5 |
| *a.* Pair | | 12 | 10 |
| *104* A45 2p purple | | 8 | 6 |
| *a.* Pair | | 16 | 12 |
| *105* A46 3p dk bl | | 15 | 12 |
| *a.* Pair | | 30 | 24 |

Issued to commemorate the visit of the British Royal Family, March-April, 1947.

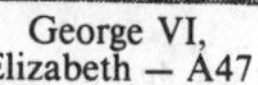

George VI, Elizabeth – A47

Gold Mine – A48

Inscribed alternately in English and Afrikaans.

**1948, Apr. 26 Photo. *Perf. 14***

| | | |
|---|---|---|
| *106* A47 3p dp chlky bl & sil | 15 | 8 |
| *a.* Pair | 50 | 30 |

25th anniv. of the marriage of George VI and Queen Elizabeth.

***Vertical Pairs Perf. 14 all around, Rouletted 6½ between.***

**1948, Apr.**

Inscribed alternately in English and Afrikaans.

| | | |
|---|---|---|
| *107* A48 1½p sl & ocher | 7 | 5 |
| *a.* Vertical pair | 16 | 10 |

"Wanderer" in Port Natal – A49

Inscribed alternately in English and Afrikaans.

**1949, May 2 Photo. *Perf. 15x14***

| | | |
|---|---|---|
| *108* A49 1½p red brn | 10 | 6 |
| *a.* Pair | 25 | 15 |

Mercury and Globe – A50

Inscribed alternately in English and Afrikaans.

**1949, Oct. 1 *Perf. 14x15***

| | | |
|---|---|---|
| *109* A50 ½p dk grn | 7 | 6 |
| *a.* Pair | 60 | 24 |
| *110* A50 1½p dk red | 10 | 6 |
| *a.* Pair | 1.00 | 24 |
| *111* A50 3p ultra | 15 | 15 |
| *a.* Pair | 1.50 | 60 |

75th anniv. of the UPU.

Voortrekkers en Route to Natal – A51

Voortrekker Monument, Pretoria – A52

Voortrekkers Looking Toward Natal, and Open Bible – A53

**1949, Dec. 1 *Perf. 15x14***

| | | |
|---|---|---|
| *112* A51 1p magenta | 6 | 5 |
| *113* A52 1½p dl grn | 10 | 6 |
| *114* A53 3p dk bl | 18 | 12 |

Issued to commemorate the inauguration of the Voortrekker Monument at Pretoria.

Riebeeck's Seal and Dutch East India Company Monogram
A54

Maria de la Quellerie – A55

Designs: 2p, van Riebeeck's Ships. 4½p, Jan van Riebeeck. 1sh, Landing of van Riebeeck.

***Perf. 15x14, 14x15***

**1952, Mar. 14 Wmk. 201**

| | | |
|---|---|---|
| *115* A54 ½p dk brn & red vio | 10 | 8 |
| *116* A55 1p dk grn | 10 | 5 |
| *117* A54 2p dk pur | 12 | 5 |
| *118* A55 4½p dk bl | 25 | 18 |
| *119* A54 1sh brown | 75 | 50 |
| *Nos. 115-119 (5)* | 1.32 | 86 |

300th anniv. of the landing of Jan van Riebeeck at the Cape of Good Hope.

Nos. 116-117 Overprinted "SATISE" (1p) and "SADIPU" (2p)

**1952, Mar. 26**

| | | |
|---|---|---|
| *120* A55 1p dk grn | 20 | 15 |
| *121* A54 2p dk pur | 25 | 18 |

Issued to publicize the South African Tercentenary International Stamp Exhibition, Cape Town, Mar. 26-Apr. 5, 1952.

A little time given to the study of the arrangement of the Scott Catalogue can make it easier to use effectively.

**Coronation Issue**

Queen Elizabeth II – A97

**1953, June 3 *Perf. 14x15***

| | | |
|---|---|---|
| *192* A97 2p violet blue | 20 | 6 |

Cape Triangle of 1853 – A98

**1953, Sept. 1 *Perf. 15x14***

| | | |
|---|---|---|
| *193* A98 1p red & dk brn | 8 | 6 |
| *194* A98 4p bl & ind | 25 | 20 |

Cent. of the introduction of postage stamps in South Africa.

Merino Ram and Sheep – A99

**1953, Oct. 1 *Perf. 14***

| | | |
|---|---|---|
| *195* A99 4½p shown | 90 | 40 |
| *196* A99 1sh3p Springbok | 3.00 | 20 |
| *197* A99 1sh6p Aloes | 2.50 | 50 |

Arms of Orange Free State, Pen and Scroll
A100

**1954, Feb. 23 *Perf. 15x14***

| | | |
|---|---|---|
| *198* A100 2p red org & dk brn | 15 | 8 |
| *199* A100 4½p gray & rose vio | 35 | 25 |

Orange Free State centenary.

Wart Hog
A101

White Rhinoceros
A102

Lion – A103

Animals: 1p, Gnu. 1½p, Leopard. 2p, Zebra. 4p, Elephant. 4½p, Hippopotamus. 1sh, Kudu. 1sh3p, Springbok. 1sh6p, Gemsbok. 2sh6p, Nyala. 5sh, Giraffe. 10sh, Sable antelope.

**1954, Oct. *Perf. 15x14, 14***

| | | | |
|---|---|---|---|
| *200* A101 | ½p dk bluish grn | 8 | 7 |
| *201* A101 | 1p rose brn | 8 | 5 |
| *202* A101 | 1½p sepia | 12 | 10 |
| *203* A101 | 2p purple | 16 | 5 |
| *204* A102 | 3p bl & dk brn | 16 | 5 |
| *205* A102 | 4p grn & bl gray | 25 | 6 |
| *206* A102 | 4½p lil & lil gray | 1.65 | 75 |
| *207* A103 | 6p org & dk brn | 50 | 6 |
| *208* A102 | 1sh rose brn & dk brn | 1.10 | 8 |
| *209* A103 | 1sh3p dl grn & dk brn | 1.65 | 8 |
| *210* A102 | 1sh6p pink & dk brn | 2.00 | 38 |
| *211* A102 | 2sh6p cit & blk brn | 2.50 | 22 |
| *212* A102 | 5sh org yel & blk brn | 15.00 | 85 |
| *213* A102 | 10sh lil & blk | 22.50 | 2.50 |
| | *Nos. 200-213 (14)* | 47.75 | 5.30 |

See also Nos. 221-228, 241-253.

Paul Kruger – A104

Portrait: 6p, Martinus Wessels Pretorius.

*Perf. 14x15*

**1955, Oct. 21 Photo. Wmk. 201**

| | | |
|---|---|---|
| *214* A104 3p sl grn | 25 | 10 |
| *215* A104 6p brn vio | 50 | 25 |

Centenary of Pretoria.

Andries Pretorius, Church of the Vow and Flag of Natalia – A105

German Wagon and House – A106

**1955, Dec. 1 *Perf. 14***

Inscribed alternately in English and Afrikaans.

| | | |
|---|---|---|
| *216* A105 2p ultra & cer | 10 | 6 |
| *a.* Pair | 90 | 45 |

Union Covenant Celebrations, Pietermaritzburg, Dec. 13-18, 1955.

**1958, July 1 *Perf. 14***

| | | |
|---|---|---|
| *218* A106 2p pale lil & brn | 15 | 7 |

Cent. of the arrival of German settlers.

Seal of Academy
A107

*Perf. 15x14*

**1959, May 1 Photo. Wmk. 201**

| | | |
|---|---|---|
| *219* A107 3p brt bl & dk bl | 18 | 8 |
| *a.* dk bl omitted | 800.00 | |

50th anniv. of the South African Academy of Science and Art, Pretoria.

Globe Showing Antarctica and South Africa – A108

Wmk. 330-Coat of Arms, Multiple

*Perf. 14x15*

**1959, Nov. 16 Wmk. 330**

*220* A108 3p bl grn, brn & org 20 10

South African Natl. Antarctic Expedition.

Animal Types of 1954.

**1959-60 Wmk. 330 *Perf. 15x14***

*221* A101 ½p dk bluish grn ('60) 35 *65*
*222* A101 1p rose brn 15 5
*a.* Redrawn 42 22

***Perf. 14***

*223* A102 3p bl & dk brn 42 7
*224* A102 4p grn & bl gray 1.10 35
*225* A103 6p org & dk brn 2.25 8
*226* A102 1sh rose brn & dk brn 3.25 15
*227* A102 2sh6p cit & blk brn 10.00 6.50
*228* A102 5sh org yel & blk brn ('60) 22.50 20.00
*Nos. 221-228 (8)* 40.02 27.85

On No. 222a, the numeral "1" is centered above "S." On No. 222, "1" is slightly to right of "S."

Prime Ministers Botha, Smuts, Hertzog, Malan, Strydom and Verwoerd
A109

Flag and Notes from National Anthem — A110

Pushing Wheel Uphill
A111

Designs: 6p, Arms of the Union and of four provinces. 1sh6p, Official Union festival emblem.

***Perf. 14x15, 15x14***

**1960 Photo. Wmk. 330**

*235* A109 3p chocolate 20 5
*236* A110 4p lt bl & red org 30 10
*237* A110 6p yel grn, red & brn 45 20
*238* A111 1sh yel, dk bl & blk 75 20
*239* A111 1sh6p lt bl & blk 3.00 1.75
*Nos. 235-239 (5)* 4.70 2.30

50th anniv. of the founding of the Union.
See Nos. 245-246, 248-249.

Map, Old and New Locomotives — A112

**1960, May 2 *Perf. 15x14***

*240* A112 1sh3p dk bl 3.75 90

Centenary of railways in South Africa.

Types of 1954 and 1960.

Designs: ½c, Wart hog. 1c, Gnu. 1½c, Leopard. 2c, Zebra. 2½c, Prime Ministers. 3½c, Flag and music notes. 5c, Lion. 7½c, Arms of Union and four provinces. 10c, Pushing wheel uphill. 12½c, Springbok. 20c, Gemsbok. 50c, Giraffe. 1r, Sable antelope.

***Perf. 15x14, 14x15, 14 (A102, A103)***

**1961, Feb. 14 Photo. Wmk. 330**

*241* A101 ½c dk bluish grn 10 5
*242* A101 1c rose brn 10 5
*243* A101 1½c sepia 12 5
*244* A101 2c purple 16 8
*245* A109 2½c chocolate 30 5
*246* A110 3½c lt bl & red org 50 10
*247* A103 5c org & dk brn 60 8
*248* A110 7½c yel grn, red & brn 75 12
*249* A111 10c yel, dk bl & blk 85 8
*250* A103 12½c dl grn & dk brn 1.25 12
*251* A102 20c pink & dk brn 2.25 42
*252* A102 50c org yel & blk brn 9.25 2.00
*253* A102 1r bl & blk 21.00 8.50
*Nos. 241-253 (13)* 37.23 11.70

**Republic**

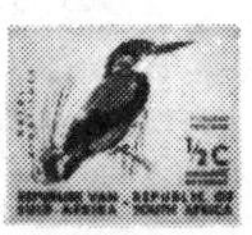


Natal Pigmy Kingfisher
A112a

Kaffir Boom Flower
A112b

Pouring Gold
A113

Groot Constantia
A114

Designs: 1½c, Afrikander bull. 3c, Crimson-breasted shrike. 5c, Baobab tree. 7½c, Corn. 10c, Castle entrance, Cape Town. 12½c, Protea flower. 20c, Secretary bird. 50c, Cape Town, harbor. 1r, Bird of Paradise flower.

Two types of 2½c.
Type I: Lines of building faint.
Type II: Lines of building very strong; strong line between bottom of building and top of name panel.

***Perf. 14x15, 15x14***

**1961, May 31 Photo. Wmk. 330**

*254* A112a ½c bl, mag & brn 6 5
*a.* Perf. 14x13½ ('63) 7 7
*255* A112b 1c gray & red 7 5
*256* A112a 1½c brn car 7 5

***Perf. 14***

*257* A113 2c ultra & org 8 5
*258* A114 2½c vio & grn (I) 32 5
*a.* Type II 40 6
*259* A113 3c pink, dk bl & red 28 5
*260* A114 5c grnsh bl & yel 35 5
*261* A114 7½c emer & brn 55 6
*a.* brn omitted
*262* A114 10c emer & dk brn 70 6
*263* A114 12½c dk grn, red & yel 1.65 7
*a.* yel omitted
*264* A114 20c sal, sl bl & pink 4.00 28
*265* A113 50c ultra & blk 32.50 1.65
*266* A113 1r bl, org & grn 22.50 1.90
*Nos. 254-266 (13)* 63.13 4.37

**1961-63 Unwmk. *Perf. 15x14***

*269* A112b 1c gray & red 25 6

***Perf. 14***

*270* A113 2c ultra & org ('63) 25 5
*271* A114 2½c vio & grn (II) 28 5
*272* A113 3c pink, dk bl & red 28 5
*273* A114 5c grnsh bl & yel 48 5
*274* A114 7½c emer & brn ('62) 70 10
*275* A114 10c grn & dk brn 95 15
*276* A114 20c sal, sl bl & pink ('63) 11.00 32
*277* A113 50c ultra & blk ('62) 16.00 2.75
*Nos. 269-277 (9)* 30.19 3.58

See Nos. 289-298, 317-324, 326-342, 376-377, 379-385.

Boeing 707 and Bleriot Monoplane
A115

Folk Dancers
A116

***Perf. 14x15***

**1961, Dec. 1 Photo. Wmk. 330**

*280* A115 3c bl & red 50 15

50th anniv. of South Africa's 1st air mail.

**1962, March 1**

*281* A116 2½c lt brn, choc & red org 25 5

Issued to commemorate the 50th anniversary of folk dancing in South Africa.

"Chapman" Arriving in 1820
A117

***Perf. 15x14***

**1962, Aug. 20 Photo. Wmk. 330**

*282* A117 2½c dp plum & bl grn 40 6
*283* A117 12½c choc & bl 3.50 1.50

Unveiling of the precinct stone of the British Settlers Monument at Grahamstown.

Red Disa Orchid, Castle Rock, Kirstenbosch Botanic Gardens — A118

**1963, Mar. 14 *Perf. 14***

*284* A118 2½c multi 35 10

50th anniv. of the Kirstenbosch Botanic Gardens, Cape Town.

Centenary Emblem and Nurse — A119

Wmk. 348- RSA in Triangle, Multiple

Design: 12½c, Centenary emblem and globe (horiz.).

**1963, Aug. 30 Wmk. 348 *Perf. 14***

*285* A119 2½c rose cl, blk & red 35 6

***Perf. 15x14***

*286* A119 12½c dk bl gray & red 3.50 1.60
*a.* Red Cross omitted *1,000.*

Centenary of the International Red Cross.

Assembly Seat, Bunga Building, Umtata
A120

***Perf. 14½x14***

**1963, Dec. 11 Wmk. 348**

*287* A120 2½c dk brn & lt grn 35 10
*a.* Light grn omitted *850.00*

Transkei Legislative Assembly, 1st meeting.

Types of 1961

***Perf. 15x14(1c), 14x15(1½c), 14***

**1963-67 Photo. Wmk. 348**

*289* A112b 1c gray & red 12 5
*290* A112a 1½c brn car ('67) 1.25 32
*291* A113 2c ultra & org ('64) 12 5
*292* A114 2½c vio & grn (II) ('64) 15 5
*293* A114 5c grnsh bl & yel ('66) 1.00 5
*294* A114 7½c emer & brn ('66) 6.50 5
*295* A114 10c emer & dk brn ('64) 52 5
*296* A114 20c sal, sl bl & pink ('64) 1.10 25
*297* A113 50c ultra & blk ('66) 32.50 3.25
*298* A113 1r bl, org & grn ('64) 55.00 20.00
*Nos. 289-298 (10)* 98.26 24.12

Rugby Board Emblem, Springbok and Ball
A121

John Calvin
A122

Design: 12½c, Rugby player diving over goal line (horiz.).

***Perf. 14x15, 15x14***

**1964, May 8 Photo. Wmk. 348**

*301* A121 2½c dk grn & brn 25 5
*302* A121 12½c yel grn & blk 3.75 2.50

Issued to commemorate the 75th anniversary of the South African Rugby Board.

**1964, July 10 *Perf. 14***

*303* A122 2½c choc, brt car & vio 40 10

John Calvin (1509-64), French theologian and leader of the Reformation.

Nurse's Lamp — A123

Design: 12½c, Nurse holding lamp (horiz.).

***Perf. 14x15, 15x14***

**1964, Oct. 12 Photo. Wmk. 348**

*304* A123 2½c gold & ultra 35 8
*305* A123 12½c ultra & gold 4.00 3.00
*a.* Gold omitted *800.00*

50th anniv. of the South African Nursing Association.

The first price column gives the catalogue value of an unused stamp, the second that of a used stamp.

ITU Emblem and Satellites A124

Design: 12½c, ITU emblem, old and new communication equipment.

**1965, May 17** *Perf. 15x14*

*306* A124 2½c brt bl & org 35 8
*307* A124 12½c grn & cl 3.75 2.50

Cent. of the ITU.

Pulpit, Groote Kerk, Cape Town A125

Diamond A126

Design: 12½c, Emblem of Dutch Reformed Church of South Africa (horiz.).

*Perf. 14x15, 15x14*

**1965, Oct. 21 Photo. Wmk. 348**

*308* A125 2½c dp brn & yel 28 5
*309* A125 12½c lt ultra, ocher & blk 3.25 2.75

Issued to commemorate the tercentenary of the Dutch Reformed Church in South Africa.

*Perf. 14, 14x15 (3c), 15x14 (7½c)*

**1966, May 31 Wmk. 348**

Designs: 2½c, Flying bird, symbol of freedom and the future (horiz.). 3c, Corn. 7½c, Table Mountain (horiz.). Inscribed alternately in English and Afrikaans.

*310* A126 1c blk, yel, dk & lt grn 5 5
*a.* Pair 30 30
*311* A126 2½c dk bl, ultra & yel grn 10 10
*a.* Pair 75 75
*312* A126 3c red brn, red & yel 10 8
*a.* Pair 1.50 1.50
*313* A126 7½c ultra, vio bl, ocher & blk 50 40
*a.* Pair 4.00 4.00

5th anniversary of the Republic.

Hendrik F. Verwoerd and Union Buildings, Pretoria A127

Designs: 3c, Verwoerd's portrait (vert.). 12½c, Verwoerd and map of South Africa.

*Perf. 15x14, 14x15*

**1966, Dec. 6 Photo. Wmk. 348**

*314* A127 2½c grnsh bl & blk 20 5
*315* A127 3c yel grn & blk 28 15
*316* A127 12½c dl bl & blk 1.75 1.40

Issued in memory of Dr. Hendrik F. Verwoerd (1901-1966), Prime Minister.

Types of 1961 Redrawn and

Industry — A128

(Inscriptions in larger, bolder type)

½c, 1½c and 1r

On the 1r, the "N" of "VAN" is over the final "A" of "AFRIKA." On Nos. 266 and 298, the "N" is over "KA."

1c, 7½c and 12½c

2½c, 5c, 10c and 20c

2c, 3c and 50c (similar)

*Perf. 14x15 (½c), 15x14 (1c), 14*

**1964-68 Photo. Wmk. 348**

*317* A112a ½c bl, mag & brn 15 5
*a.* Imperf., pair 400.00
*318* A112b 1c gray & red 20 5
*319* A113 2c ultra & org ('68) 25 5
*320* A114 2½c vio & grn 30 5
*321* A113 3c rose red & bluish blk 50 5
*322* A113 12½c dk bl grn, red & yel 2.00 10
*323* A128 15c org, yel & blk ('67) 4.50 15
*324* A113 1r bl, org & grn 15.00 2.50
*Nos. 317-324 (8)* 22.90 3.00

Redrawn Types of 1964-68

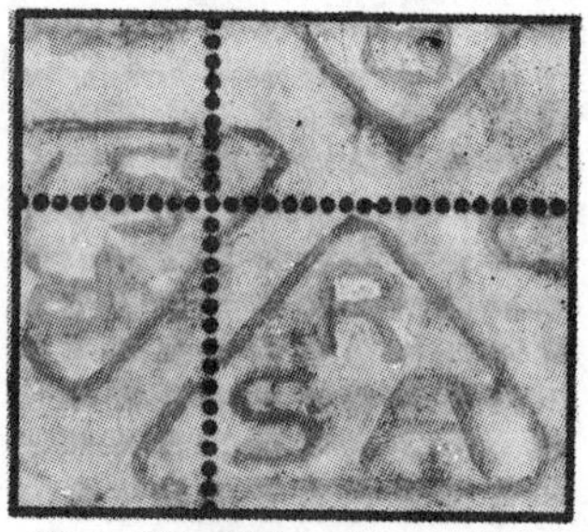
Wmk. 359- RSA in Triangle, Tete Beche

Designs: 4c, Groot Constantia (like 2½c). 6c, Corn (like 7½c). 9c, Protea flower (like 12½c).

**1967-71 Photo. Wmk. 359**

*326* A112a ½c bl, mag & brn 15 5
*327* A112b 1c gray & red 20 5
*328* A112a 1½c brn car 25 5
*329* A113 2c ultra & org ('68) 25 5
*330* A114 2½c vio & grn 30 5
*331* A113 3c rose red & bluish blk 30 5
*332* A114 4c vio & grn ('71) 40 5
*333* A114 5c grnsh bl & yel ('68) 60 5
*334* A114 6c emer & brn ('71) 75 5
*335* A114 7½c emer & brn 1.25 5
*336* A114 9c dk grn, red & yel ('71) 1.25 5
*337* A114 10c emer & dk brn ('68) 1.50 5
*338* A114 12½c dk bl grn, car & yel ('70) 2.50 6
*339* A128 15c org, yel & blk ('69) 2.50 6
*340* A114 20c sal, sl bl & pink ('68) 2.50 25
*341* A113 50c ultra & blk ('68) 6.00 60
*342* A113 1r bl, org & grn ('68) 12.00 1.50
*Nos. 326-342 (17)* 32.70 3.07

---

Luminescence

Starting in 1969, South Africa began to add phosphorescent "frames" to its definitive stamps.

In 1971, stamps began to appear with the phosphorescent element throughout the paper.

Phosphorescent commemoratives include Nos. 357, 359 et cetera.

---

Martin Luther A129

Door of Wittenberg Church A130

*Perf. 14x15*

**1967, Oct. 31 Litho. Wmk. 348**

*343* A129 2½c pink & blk 25 5

**Wmk. 359**

*344* A130 12½c blk & org 2.50 2.00

450th anniversary of the Reformation.

Pres. J. J. Fouche A133

James B. M. Hertzog Statue A134

Design: 12½c, Full-face portrait.

*Perf. 14x15*

**1968, Apr. 10 Photo. Wmk. 348**

*345* A133 2½c lt rose brn & dk brn 35 5
*346* A133 12½c grysh bl & vio bl 2.75 2.25

**Wmk. 359**

*347* A133 12½c grysh bl & vio bl 2.75 2.25

Pres. Jacobus Johannes Fouché, inauguration.

*Perf. 13½x14, 14x13½*

**1968, Sept. 21 Photo. Wmk. 359**

Designs: 2½c, Hertzog in 1902, with hat (horiz.). 3c, Hertzog in 1924 (horiz.).

*348* A134 2½c dk brn, lem & blk 25 6

**Wmk. 348**

*349* A134 3c multi 40 10
*350* A134 12½c org brn, org & blk 2.50 1.75

Unveiling of a monument in Bloemfontein honoring James Barry Munnik Hertzog (1866-1942), Boer general, prime minister of South Africa (1924-39).

Natal Pigmy Kingfisher A135

Kaffir Boom Flower A136

**1969 Wmk. 359 Photo.** *Perf. 14*

*351* A135 ½c bl & multi 20 8
*a.* Perf. 14x14½ (coil) 50 20
*352* A136 1c grysh brn & multi 20 8

See Nos. 374-375.

Springbok, Torch and Rings — A137

**1969, Mar. 15** *Perf. 14x13½*

*353* A137 2½c ol ind & red 25 5
*354* A137 12½c bis, ind & red 2.50 1.75

South African Natl. Games, Bloemfontein, Mar. 15-Apr. 19.

Groote Schuur Hospital and Dr. Barnard A138

Hands Holding Heart A139

*Perf. 13½x14*

**1969, July 7 Photo. Wmk. 348**

*355* A138 2½c dp rose, pink & plum 35 5

*Perf. 15x14*

**Wmk. 359**

*356* A139 12½c dp bl & dp car 3.50 2.50

1st heart transplant operation (by Dr. Christiaan Barnard) and opening of the 47th South African Medical Cong., Pretoria.

Stagecoach of 1869 A140

Transvaal No. 1 A141

Water Drop and Flower A142

*Perf. 13½x14, 14x13½*

**1969, Oct. 6 Photo. Wmk. 359**

*357* A140 2½c ocher, Prus bl & yel 35 5
*358* A141 12½c sal, grn & gold 3.00 2.25

Centenary of South African postage stamps.

**1970, Feb. 14** *Perf. 14*

Design: 3c, Waves (horiz.).

*359* A142 2½c brn, brt bl & grn 25 5
*360* A142 3c pale gray, bl & ind 50 22

Issued to publicize the Water 70 campaign of the Department of Water Affairs.

Sower — A143

"BIBLIA" A144

**1970, Aug. 24 Photo. *Perf. 14***
*361* A143 2½c multi 30 5

**Photo; Gold Impressed**
*362* A144 12½c ultra, blk & gold 3.25 2.50

150th anniv. of the South African Bible Soc.

Strijdom Tower, Johannes G. Strijdom — A145

Map of Antarctica A146

***Perf. 14x13½, 13½x14***
**1971, May 22 Photo. Wmk. 359**
*363* A145 5c bl, yel & blk 60 20
*364* A146 12½c grnsh bl, vio bl & red 8.00 7.00

**Wmk. 330**
*365* A145 5c bl, yel & blk 1.25 90

International Stamp Exhibition (INTERSTEX), Cape Town, May 22-31. No. 364 also for the 10th anniversary of the Antarctic Treaty pledging peaceful uses of and scientific cooperation in Antarctica.

Landing of British Settlers, 1820, by Thomas Baines A147

Martinus Steyn, Paul Kruger, Unification Monument — A148

**1971, May 31 Wmk. 359**
*366* A147 2c mag & rose red 18 6
*367* A148 4c bl grn & blk 35 12

10th anniv. of the Republic of South Africa.

Hendrik Verwoerd Dam A149

**1972, Mar. 4 Photo. *Perf. 14***
**Size: 37x22mm.**
*368* A149 4c *shown* 30 10
*369* A149 5c *Aerial view of dam* 50 15

**Size: 57x22mm.**
*370* A149 10c *Dam, reservoir and Verwoerd* 1.75 90

Inauguration of the Hendrik F. Verwoerd Dam of the Orange River Project.

Ram's Head and Wool Mark — A150

Lamb and Wool Mark — A151

**1972, May 15 Wmk. 359 *Perf. 14***
*371* A150 4c bl & multi 24 10
*a.* 4c brn & multi (unwmkd) 42 5
*372* A151 15c dl bl & dk bl 1.10 40

South African wool industry. Issued in sheets of 100 with advertisements in margin. See Nos. 378, 382A.

Cats — A152

**1972, Sept. 19 Wmk. 359**
*373* A152 5c multi 1.25 25

Centenary of the Society for the Prevention of Cruelty to Animals.

Redrawn Types of 1964-69 and Types of 1972

***Perf. 14x15 (½c), 14 (1c), 12½***
**1972-74 Photo. Unwmk.**
*374* A135 ½c bl & multi ('73) 75 15
*375* A136 1c grysh brn & red ('73) 14 5
*376* A113 2c brt bl & org 35 5
*377* A113 3c rose red & bluish blk ('73) 40 5
*378* A150 4c bl & multi ('73) 60 5
*379* A114 5c grnsh bl & yel ('73) 70 10
*380* A114 6c emer & brn ('74) 1.00 5
*381* A114 9c dk grn, red & yel ('73) 1.50 25
*382* A114 10c emer & dk brn ('73) 1.75 15
*382A* A151 15c dl bl & dk bl ('74) 2.00 60
*383* A114 20c sal, sl bl & pink ('73) 2.00 40
*384* A113 50c ultra & blk ('73) 5.00 1.50
*385* A113 1r bl, org & grn ('73) 12.50 3.50
*Nos. 374-385 (13)* 28.69 6.90

Pylon — A153

Designs: 4c, Electrical usage, pylon, power plant (horiz.). 15c, Smokestacks.

**1973, Feb. 1 Photo. *Perf. 12x12½***
**Size: 37½x20mm**
*386* A153 4c bl & multi 25 12

***Perf. 12½***
***Size: 20x27mm***
*387* A153 5c bl & blk 35 15
*388* A153 15c ocher & multi 3.75 1.50

Electricity Supply Commission, 50th anniv..

Arms of University — A154

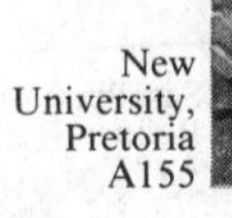

New University, Pretoria A155

Old University, Cape Town — A156

**1973, Apr. 2 Unwmk. *Perf. 12½***
*389* A154 4c bl & multi 28 14

***Perf. 12x12½***
**Wmk. 359**
*390* A155 5c gold & multi 38 18

**Unwmk. *Perf. 12½***
*391* A156 15c gold & blk 3.25 1.65

Cent. of the Univ. of South Africa (UNISA).

Woltemade, Sailor and Horse A157

Designs: 5c, Sinking ship in storm. 15c, "De Jonge Thomas" sinking.

**1973, June 2 Photo. *Perf. 12x12½***
*392* A157 4c brn red, ol & blk 32 18
*393* A157 5c ol, blk & cit 55 20
*394* A157 15c brn, blk & ocher 6.75 4.50

Bicentenary of Wolraad Woltemade's heroism in saving 14 people from the ship "De Jonge Thomas" in Table Bay.

C. J. Langenhoven and Anthem — A158

Designs: 4c, 5c (vert.), Portrait and signature.

**1973, Aug. 1 *Perf. 12½***
**Size: 27x20mm**
*395* A158 4c org, blk & ultra 40 12

***Perf. 12½x12, 12x12½***
**Size: 21x38mm, 37x21mm**
**1973, Aug. *Perf. 12½***
*396* A158 5c org, blk & ultra 50 15
*397* A158 15c org, blk & ultra 2.50 1.00

Cornelis Jacob Langenhoven (1873-1932), lawyer, writer, who worked for recognition of Africaans language.

World Map and Communications Network — A159

***Perf. 12½***
**1973, Oct. 1 Photo. Unwmk.**
*398* A159 15c ultra & multi 2.75 1.65
*a.* Wmk. 359 3.25 2.25

International Telecommunications Day.

Restored Houses, Tulbagh — A160

Design: 5c, Church Street, Tulbagh.

**1974, Mar. 14 Unwmk. *Perf. 12½***
**Size: 27x21mm.**
*400* A160 4c Prus grn & multi 24 8

**Size: 57x20mm.**
*401* A160 5c ocher & multi 45 14

Restoration of historic Church Street in Tulbagh after 1969 earthquake.

Burgerspond A161 Prime Minister D. F. Malan A162

**1974, Apr. 7 Photo. *Perf. 12½x12***
*402* A161 9c multi 1.00 52

Centenary of the first official coin struck in South Africa, 1874. The £1 gold coin shows portrait of Pres. Thomas Francois Burger.

**1974, May 22 Photo. Unwmk.**
*403* A162 4c lt ultra & dk bl 40 15

Centenary of the birth of Daniel F. Malan (1874-1959), prime minister of South Africa.

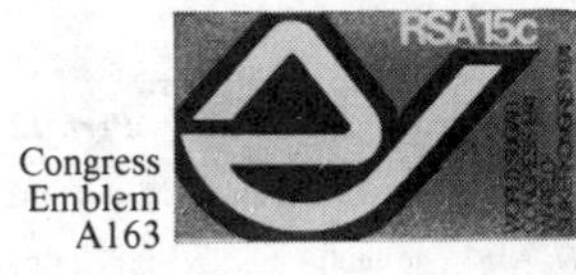

Congress Emblem A163

**1974, June 13 *Perf. 12x12½***
*404* A163 15c sil & dk bl 1.75 50

15th World Sugar Cong., Durban, June 13-30.

"50" A164

**1974, July 13 Photo. Unwmk.**
*405* A164 4c red & blk 45 15

50th anniversary of radio in South Africa.

Prices of premium quality never hinged stamps will be in excess of catalogue price.

Cultural Center, Grahamstown — A165

**1974, July 13** *Perf. 12x12½*

*406* A165 5c red & blk 50 15

Natl. Monument to British settlers of 1820.

Natal No. 78, Transvaal No. 145, Cape of Good Hope No. 28 and Orange River Colony No. 4 — A166

**1974, Oct. 9** **Photo.** *Perf. 12½*

*407* A166 15c multi 1.75 90

Centenary of Universal Postal Union.

Wild Iris — A167

Cape Gannet — A168

Galjoen — A169

Bokmakierie (Shrike) — A170

Designs: 2c, Heather. 3c, Geranium. 4c, Calla lily. 7c, Zebrafish. 9c, Angelfish. 10c, Moorish idol. 14c, Roman fish. 15c, Greater double-collared sunbird. 20c, Yellow-billed hornbill. 25c, Barberton daisy. 50c, Blue cranes. 1r, Bateleur eagles.

**Photo. and Engr.**

**1974, Nov. 11** **Unwmk.** *Perf. 12½*

*408* A167 1c pink & multi 5 5
*409* A167 2c yel & multi 10 6
*410* A167 3c multi 12 8
*411* A167 4c multi 15 10
*412* A168 5c dl bl & multi 20 12
*413* A169 6c multi 25 12
*414* A169 7c lil & multi 30 15
*415* A169 9c buff & multi 35 15
*416* A169 10c lt bl & multi 40 20
*417* A169 14c sal & multi 60 20
*418* A168 15c gray & multi 60 20
*419* A168 20c yel & multi 80 30
*420* A167 25c dk brn & multi 1.10 35

*Perf. 12x12½*

*421* A170 30c gray & multi 4.50 75
*422* A170 50c cit & multi 4.00 1.00
*423* A170 1r multi 7.50 2.00
*Nos. 408-423 (16)* 21.02 5.83

The coils that follow are two colors while the above sheet stamps are multicolored.

**1974-76** **Photo.** *Perf. 12½*

**Coil Stamps**

*430* A167 1c pink & vio 25 6
*a.* Perf. 14 ('75) 15 6
*431* A167 2c yel & grn 25 6
*a.* Perf. 14 ('76) 15 6
*432* A168 5c dl bl & blk 35 18
*433* A169 10c lt bl & ind 85 70
*a.* Perf. 14 ('76) 75 70

No. 430a has black control number on back of every fifth stamp.

Voortrekker Monument and Encampment — A171

**1974, Dec. 6** **Unwmk.** *Perf. 12½*

*438* A171 4c multi 45 18

Voortrekker Monument, 25th anniversary.

Sasolburg Refinery A172

*Perf. 12x12½, 12½*

**1975, Feb. 26** **Litho.**

*439* A172 15c red & multi 1.50 90

25th anniversary of South Africa Coal, Oil and Gas Corp., Ltd. (SASOL).

Pres. Nicolaes Diederichs A173

Jan C. Smuts A174

**Litho. and Engr.**

**1975, Apr. 19** *Perf. 12½x12*

*440* A173 4c brn & gold 25 12

**Litho.**

*441* A173 15c ultra & gold 1.50 1.10

Installation of Dr. Nicolaes Diederichs as third State President.

**1975, May 24** **Litho. and Engraved**

*442* A174 4c black 30 12

Smuts (1870-1950), lawyer, gen., statesman.

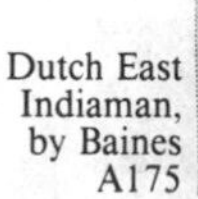

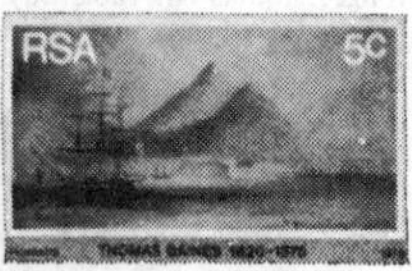


Dutch East Indiaman, by Baines A175

Designs: Paintings by John Thomas Baines.

**1975, June 18** **Photo.** *Perf. 12x12½*

*443* A175 5c gold & multi 28 15
*444* A175 9c gold & multi 55 48
*445* A175 15c gold & multi 95 80
*446* A175 30c gold & multi 1.90 1.90
*a.* Souvenir sheet of 4 6.00 6.00

John Thomas Baines (1820-1875), painter, death centenary. No. 446a contains 4 lithographed stamps similar to Nos. 443-446; gold margin and black inscription with Baines' signature. Size: 119x96mm.

Gideon Malherbe House, Paarl — A176

**Photo. and Engr.**

**1975, Aug. 14** *Perf. 12½*

*447* A176 4c multi 30 8

Centenary of founding of the Society of Real Afrikanders (Genootskap of Regte Afrikaaners).

Automatic Letter Sorting — A177

**1975, Sept. 11** **Photo.** *Perf. 12½x12*

*448* A177 4c brt bl & multi 30 8

Postal automation.

Title Page, First Afrikaans Paper — A178

Afrikaans Monument, Paarl — A179

**1975, Oct. 10** **Litho.** *Perf. 12½x12*

*449* A178 4c blk & org 20 8
*450* A179 5c multi 28 10

Inauguration of Afrikaans Language Monument.

Table Mountain — A180

**1975, Nov. 13** **Litho.** *Perf. 12½*

*451* A180 15c *shown* 1.75 1.50
*452* A180 15c *Johannesburg* 1.75 1.50
*453* A180 15c *Cape vineyards* 1.75 1.50
*454* A180 15c *Lions, Kruger Natl. Park* 1.75 1.50

Tourist publicity. Nos. 451-454 printed se-tenant.

Satellites, Radar and Africa on Globe — A181

**1975, Dec. 3** **Litho.** *Perf. 12½*

*455* A181 15c dk vio bl & multi 90 60

Satellite communications.

Lawn Bowler — A182

Designs: No. 457, Cricket batsman. No. 458, Polo player. No. 459, Golfer (Gary Player).

**1976** **Photo.** *Perf. 12½x12*

*456* A182 15c grn & blk 90 55
*457* A182 15c yel grn & blk 90 55
*458* A182 15c ol & blk 90 55
*459* A182 15c brt grn & blk 90 55
*a.* Miniature sheet of 4 4.50 3.25

No. 456 commemorates 3rd World Bowling Championships, Zoo Lake Club, Johannesburg, Feb. 1976; No. 457, centenary of cricket in South Africa; No. 458, international polo; No. 459, Gary Player, South African golf champion.

No. 459a contains one each of Nos. 456-459, green margin with olive border. Size: 96x122mm.

Issue dates: No. 456, Feb. 18. No. 457, Mar. 12. No. 458, Aug. 16. Nos. 459, 459a, Dec. 2.

No. 456 Overprinted in Gold

WÊRELDKAMPIOENE
WORLD CHAMPIONS

**1976, Apr. 6** **Photo.** *Perf. 12½x12*

*460* A182 15c grn & blk 65 75

Victory of South Africa in 3rd World Bowling championships.

Picnic under Baobab Tree A183

Paintings by Erich Mayer: 10c, Wagons at Foot of Blauberg, Transvaal. 15c, Hartbeesspoort Dam, near Pretorial. 20c, Street in Doornfontein.

**1976, Apr. 20** **Photo.** *Perf. 12x12½*

*461* A183 4c ocher & multi 30 12
*462* A183 10c dk grn & multi 60 50
*463* A183 15c multi 90 75
*464* A183 20c multi 1.50 1.10
*a.* Souvenir sheet of 4 6.00 6.00

Erich Mayer (1876-1960), painter, birth centenary. No. 464a contains one each of Nos. 461-464. Artist's signature in horizontal gutter between 2 se-tenant pairs. Size: 121x96mm.

Wildlife Protection A184

**1976, June 5** **Litho.** *Perf. 12x12½*

*465* A184 3c Cheetah 30 12
*466* A184 10c Black rhinoceros 60 45
*467* A184 15c Blesbok 1.20 90
*468* A184 20c Zebra 1.60 1.20

Emily Hobhouse, by Johan Hoekstra — A185

**1976, June 8** **Photo.** *Perf. 12½x12*

*469* A185 4c multi 25 15

Emily Hobhouse (1860-1926), the "Angel of Mercy" during Anglo-Boer War.

S.S. Dunrobin Castle, 1876
A186

**1976, Oct. 5 Litho. *Perf. 12x12½***
*470* A186 10c multi 1.00 40

Ocean Mail Service contract, centenary.

Family with Globe — A187

**1976, Nov. 6 Photo. *Perf. 12½x12***
*471* A187 4c sal & dl red 25 12

Family planning.

Wine Glasses
A188

Jacob Daniel du Toit
A189

**1977, Feb. 14 Litho. *Perf. 12½x12***
*472* A188 15c multi 80 38

Quality of the Vintage Symposium, Cape Town, Feb. 14-21.

**1977, Feb. 21 Photo.**
*473* A189 4c multi 14 8

Dr. Jacob Daniel du Toit (Totius; 1877-1953), theologian, educator, poet, birth centenary.

Transvaal Supreme Court
A190

**1977, May 18 Photo. *Perf. 12x12½***
*474* A190 4c red brn 14 8

Transvaal Supreme Court, centenary.

Sugarbush — A191

**Photo. (1-5, 8, 10, 15, 20c); Litho. (others).**

**1977, May 27 *Perf. 12½***

| | | | | | |
|---|---|---|---|---|---|
| *475* | A191 | 1c | shown | 5 | 5 |
| *476* | A191 | 2c | Protea punctata | 5 | 5 |
| *477* | A191 | 3c | P. neriifolia | 7 | 5 |
| *a.* | | | Perf. 14 | 7 | 5 |
| *478* | A191 | 4c | P. longifolia | 10 | 5 |
| *479* | A191 | 5c | King protea | 12 | 5 |
| *a.* | | | Perf. 14 | 12 | 5 |
| *480* | A191 | 6c | Mountain rose | 14 | 5 |
| *a.* | | | Perf. 14 | 14 | 5 |
| *481* | A191 | 7c | P. lovea | 18 | 5 |
| *a.* | | | Perf. 14 | 18 | 5 |
| *482* | A191 | 8c | P. mundii | 18 | 5 |
| *a.* | | | Perf. 14 | 18 | 5 |
| *483* | A191 | 9c | P. roupelliae | 20 | 5 |
| *a.* | | | Perf. 14 | 20 | 5 |
| *484* | A191 | 10c | P. aristata | 24 | 5 |
| *485* | A191 | 15c | P. eximia | 35 | 6 |
| *486* | A191 | 20c | Queen protea | 48 | 16 |
| *a.* | | | Perf. 14 | 2.50 | 2.50 |
| *487* | A191 | 25c | Red sugar basin | 60 | 22 |
| *a.* | | | Perf. 14 | 60 | 22 |
| *488* | A191 | 30c | P. amplexicaulis | 70 | 24 |
| *a.* | | | Perf. 14 | 70 | 24 |
| *489* | A191 | 50c | Pincushion | 1.25 | 40 |
| *a.* | | | Perf. 14 | 1.25 | 40 |
| *490* | A191 | 1r | Paranomus reflexus | 2.50 | 80 |
| *a.* | | | Perf. 14 | 2.50 | 80 |
| *491* | A191 | 2r | Marsh rose | 4.75 | 1.50 |
| *a.* | | | Perf. 14 | 4.75 | 1.50 |
| | | | *Nos. 475-491 (17)* | 11.96 | 3.88 |
| | | | *Nos. 477a-491a (12)* | 13.19 | 5.96 |

***Perf. 14 Vertically***
**Photo. Coil Stamps**

| | | | | | |
|---|---|---|---|---|---|
| *492* | A191 | 1c | Silver tree | 5 | 5 |
| *493* | A191 | 2c | Bottle brush | 5 | 5 |
| *494* | A191 | 5c | Blushing bride | 12 | 5 |
| *495* | A191 | 10c | Leucadendrom sessile | 23 | 5 |

Some printings of No. 495 have black control number on back of every fifth stamp.

Gymnastics — A192

**1977, Aug. 15 Litho. *Perf. 12½x12***
*496* A192 15c multi 50 40

8th International Congress of Physical Education and Sports for Girls and Women, Cape Town, Aug. 14-20.

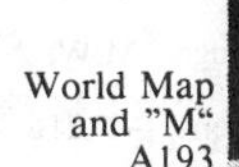

World Map and "M"
A193

**1977, Sept. 15 Litho. *Perf. 12x12½***
*497* A193 15c multi 50 40

Introduction of international metric system.

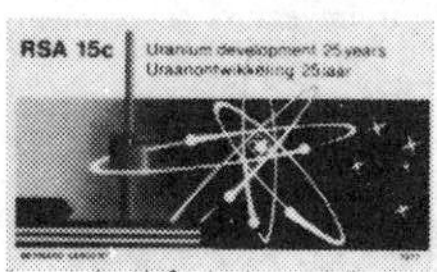

Nuclear Power Plant and Uranium Atom
A194

**1977, Oct. 8**
*498* A194 15c multi 50 40

Uranium development.

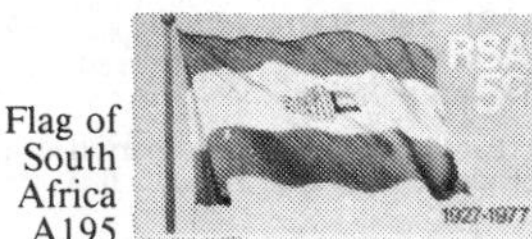

Flag of South Africa
A195

**1977, Nov. 11**
*499* A195 5c multi 25 10

50th anniversary of national flag.

Walvis Bay, 1878 — A196

**1978, Mar. 10 Litho. *Perf. 12½***
*500* A196 15c multi 65 45

Centenary of Walvis Bay annexation.

Dr. Andrew Murray — A197

**1978, May 9 *Perf. 12½x12***
*501* A197 4c multi 12 7

Dr. Andrew Murray, pioneer theologian, 150th birth anniversary.

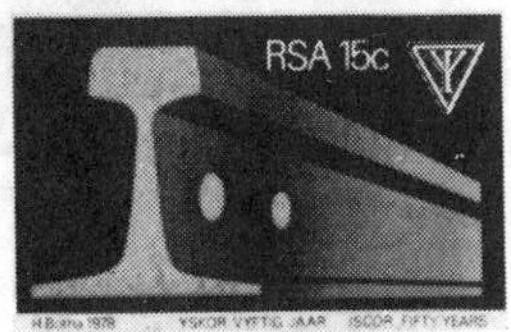

Steel Beam and ISCOR Emblem — A198

**1978, June 5 Litho. *Perf. 12***
*502* A198 15c multi 52 45

50th anniversary of ISCOR (Iron and Steel Industrial Corporation).

Saldanha Bay — A199

Design: No. 504, Richard's Bay.

**1978, July 21 Litho. *Perf. 12½***
*503* A199 15c multi 52 52
*504* A199 15c multi 52 52

Opening of new harbors on east and west coasts of South Africa. Nos. 503-504 printed se-tenant.

Landscape by Volschenk — A200

Designs: Landscapes by J. E. A. Volschenk.

**1978, Aug. 21**

| | | | | | |
|---|---|---|---|---|---|
| *505* | A200 | 10c | multi | 35 | 35 |
| *506* | A200 | 15c | multi | 50 | 50 |
| *507* | A200 | 20c | multi | 70 | 70 |
| *508* | A200 | 25c | multi | 90 | 90 |
| *a.* | | | Souvenir sheet of 4 | 3.00 | 3.00 |

Jan Ernst Abraham Volschenk (1853-1936), first South African professional artist. No. 508a contains Nos. 505-508; buff and gold margin with white inscription. Size: 124x90mm.

Canceled-to-order stamps are often from remainders. Most collectors of canceled stamps prefer postally used specimens.

B. J. Vorster — A201

**1978, Oct. 10 Litho. *Perf. 14½x14***
*509* A201 4c mar & gold 8 5
*510* A201 15c vio & gold 40 32

Inauguration of Balthazar John Vorster as president of South Africa.

Golden Gate Highlands National Park — A202

Designs: 15c, Blyde River Canyon, Transvaal. 20c, Amphitheater, Natal National Park. 25c, Cango Caves, Cape Province.

**1978, Nov. 13 *Perf. 12½***

| | | | | | |
|---|---|---|---|---|---|
| *511* | A202 | 10c | multi | 35 | 35 |
| *512* | A202 | 15c | multi | 50 | 50 |
| *513* | A202 | 20c | multi | 70 | 70 |
| *514* | A202 | 25c | multi | 1.10 | 1.00 |

Tourist publicity.

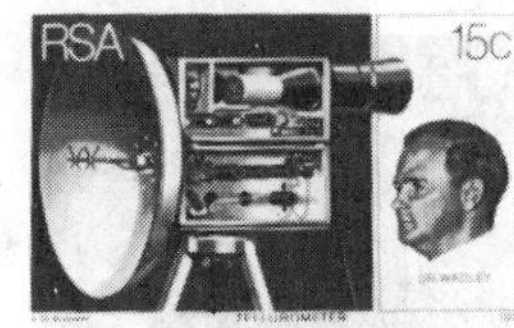

Tellurometer and Dr. I. R. Wadley — A203

**1979, Feb. 12 Litho. *Perf. 12½***
*515* A203 15c multi 48 40

15th anniversary of the invention of the tellurometer (to measure radio distances).

South Africa No. C5
A204

**1979, Mar. 30 Litho. *Perf. 14½x14***
*516* A204 15c multi 48 48

First stamp printed by South African Government Printer, 50th anniversary.

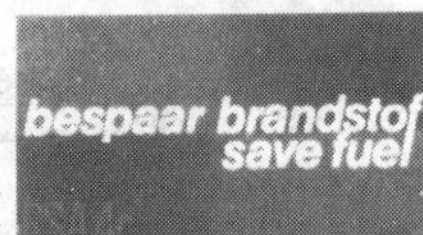

"Save Fuel"
A205

Design: No. 518, Language inscriptions reversed.

**1979, Apr. 2 Photo. *Perf. 12x12½***
*517* A205 4c red & blk 12 5
*518* A205 4c red & blk 12 5

Fuel economy.
Nos. 517-518 printed se-tenant.

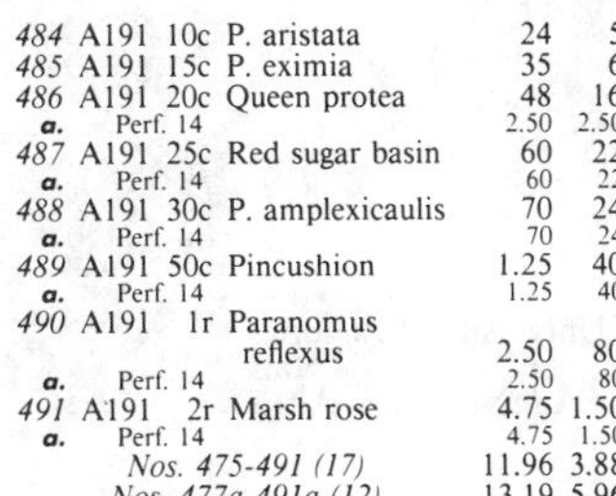

Battle of Isandlwana, by Melton Prior — A206

Designs: 15c, Battle of Ulundi, by Louis Creswicke. 20c, Battle of Rorke's Drift, by Lt. Col. Crealock.

**1979, May 25 Litho. *Perf. 14x13½***

*519* A206 4c red & blk 12 8
*520* A206 15c red & blk 45 40
*521* A206 20c red & blk 60 50
*a.* Souvenir sheet of 3 3.00 3.00

Centenary of Zulu War. No. 521a contains Nos. 519-521 and label showing medals. Gray decorative border. Size: 125x90mm.

"Health Care and Service" — A207

**1979, June 19 Litho. *Perf. 12½x12***

*522* A207 4c multi 12 8

Health Year.

Boy and Girl Watching Candle — A208

**1979, Sept. 13 Litho. *Perf. 14***

*523* A208 4c multi 10 8

South African Christmas Stamp Fund, 50th anniversary.

Cape Town University, 150th Anniversary A209

**1979, Oct. 1 Litho. *Perf. 14***

*524* A209 4c multi 10 8

Southern Sun Rose — A210

Designs: Roses.

**1979, Oct. 4 Litho. *Perf. 14***

*525* A210 4c multi 10 8
*526* A210 15c multi 38 30
*527* A210 20c multi 48 40
*528* A210 25c multi 65 55
*a.* Souvenir sheet of 4 2.25 2.25

Rosafari 1979, 4th World Rose Convention, Pretoria, October. No. 528a contains Nos. 525-528. Deep rose margin shows roses. Size: 100x125mm.

Stellenbosch University — A211

**1979, Nov. 8**

*529* A211 4c shown 10 8
*530* A211 15c Rhenish Church 35 30

Stellenbosch (oldest town in South Africa), 300th anniversary.

Federation of Afrikaans Cultural Societies, 50th Anniversary — A212

**1979, Dec. 18 Photo. *Perf. 12½x12***

*531* A212 4c multi 10 8

Still Life with Sweet Peas, by Pieter Wenning — A213

Paintings by Pieter Wenning (1873-1921): 25c, House in the Suburbs, Cape Town.

**1980, May 6 Litho. *Perf. 14***

*532* A213 5c multi 14 10

**Size: 45x37mm**

*533* A213 25c multi 70 50
*a.* Souvenir sheet of 2 2.00 1.00

No. 533a contains Nos. 532-533; multicolored margin shows portrait of Wenning. Size: 95x122mm.

Great Star of Africa Diamond — A214

**1980, May 12 Litho. *Perf. 14***

*534* A214 15c *shown* 50 35
*535* A214 20c *Cullinan II diamond* 65 50

World Diamond Congress.

Christian Louis Leipoldt (1880-1947). Writer and Physician — A215

**1980, Sept. 3 Litho. *Perf. 14***

*536* A215 5c multi 12 10

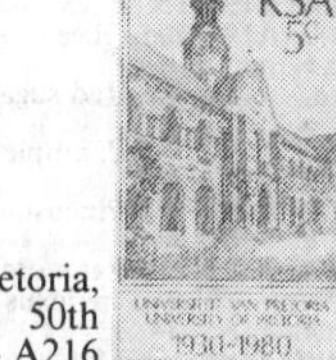

University of Pretoria, 50th Anniversary — A216

**1980, Oct. 9 Litho. *Perf. 14***

*537* A216 5c multi 12 10

Marine With Ships, by Willem van de Velde — A217

Paintings: 10c, Firetail and Trainer, by George Stubbs. 15c, Lavinia, by Thomas Gainsborough (vert.). 20c, Landscape, by Pieter Post.

**1980, Nov. 3 *Perf. 14½x14***

*538* A217 5c multi 10 8
*539* A217 10c multi 22 16
*540* A217 15c multi 32 24
*541* A217 20c multi 40 32
*a.* Souvenir sheet of 4 1.90 1.25

Natl. Gallery, 50th anniv. No. 541a contains Nos. 538-541; gold margin. Size: 126x90mm.

P.J. Joubert, Paul Kruger, M.W. Pretorius (First Leaders of Triumvirate Government) — A218

Design: 10c, Monument, flag of South African Republic, 1880 (vert.).

**1980, Dec. 15 *Perf. 14x14½ 14½x14***

*542* A218 5c multi 12 10
*543* A218 10c multi 25 20

Paardekraal Monument (built on site of founding of triumverate government) centennial.

British Troops in Battle of Amajuba — A219

**1981, Feb. 27 Litho. *Perf. 14***

*544* A219 5c Boer snipers, vert. 12 10
*545* A219 15c shown 36 30

Battle of Amajuba centenary (led to independence of Orange Free State).

Scene from Verdi's Aida A220

**1981, May 23 Litho. *Perf. 14½x14***

*546* A220 20c Raka ballet scene 40 32
*547* A220 25c shown 48 40
*a.* Souvenir sheet of 2 1.25 1.00

Opening of State Theater, Pretoria. No. 547a contains Nos. 546-547; multicolored margin shows musician. Size: 112x90mm.

Pres. Marais Viljoen A221

Deaf Girl Learning to Speak A222

**1981, May 30 *Perf. 14x14½***

**Size: 57x21mm**

*548* A221 5c Former presidents 12 10
*549* A221 15c shown 36 30

**1981, June 12 *Perf. 14***

*550* A222 5c shown 12 10
*551* A222 15c Man reading braille 36 30

Institute for the Deaf and Blind, Worcester, centenary.

Natl. Cancer Assn. 50th Anniv. — A223

**1981, July 10**

*552* A223 5c multi 12 10

Calanthe Natalensis A224

Voortrekker Movement, 50th Anniv. A225

**1981, Sept. 11 Litho. *Perf. 14***

*553* A224 5c shown 12 10
*554* A224 15c Eulophia speciosa 36 30
*555* A224 20c Disperis fanniniae 50 40
*556* A224 25c Disa uniflora 62 50
*a.* Souvenir sheet of 4 1.75 1.50

10th World Orchid Conference, Durban, Sept. 11-17. No. 556a contains Nos. 553-556; multicolored margin shows orchids. Size: 120x91mm.

**1981, Sept. 30 *Perf. 14x14½***

*557* A225 5c multi 12 10

Scouting Year
A226

TB Bacillus Centenary
A227

**1982, Feb. 22 Litho. *Perf. 14½x14***
*558* A226 15c Baden-Powell 36 30

**1982, Mar. 24 Litho. *Perf. 14***
*559* A227 20c multi 50 40

Return of Simonstown Naval Base, 25th Anniv. — A228

**1982, Apr. 2 *Perf. 14½x14***
*560* A228 8c Submarine 16 12
*561* A228 15c Strike craft 28 24
*562* A228 20c Mine sweeper 40 32
*563* A228 25c Harbor patrol boats 50 40
*a.* Souvenir sheet of 4 1.40 1.25

No. 563a contains Nos. 560-563; multicolored decorative margin. Size: 125x91mm.

Old Provost, Grahamstown
A229

Design: 2c, Tuynhuys, Kaapstad. 3c, Appelhof, Bloemfontein. 4c, Raadsaal, Pretoria. 5c, Die Kasteel, Kaapstad. 6c, Goewermentsgebou, Bloemfontein. 7c, Drostdy, Graaf-Reinet. 8c, Leeuwenhof, Cape Town. 9c, Libertas, Pretoria. 10c, City Hall, Pietermaritzburg. 11c, City Hall, Kimberley. 12c, City Hall, Port Elizabeth. 14c, Johannesburg City Hall. 15c, Hotel Milner, Matjesfontein. 20c, Post Office, Durban. 25c, Melrose House, Pretoria. 30c, Old Legislative Assembly Building, Pietermaritzburg. 50c, Raadsaal, Bloemfontein. 1r, Houses of Parliament, Cape Town. 2r, Uniegebou, Pretoria.
Coils have different designs.

**1982-86 Litho. *Perf. 14x14½***
*564* A229 1c engr. 5 5
*564A* A229 1c litho. ('84) 5 5
*565* A229 2c apple grn 5 5
*565A* A229 2c grn ('83) 5 5
*565B* A229 2c slate grn, engr. ('83) 5 5
*566* A229 3c engr. 8 6
*567* A229 4c engr. 6 6
*567A* A229 4c litho. ('85) 10 8
*568* A229 5c carmine 8 6
*568A* A229 5c dark lake, engr. ('83) 14 10
*569* A229 6c brt grn 9 7
*569A* A229 6c grn blk, engr. ('84) 15 12
*570* A229 7c gray grn 10 8
*571* A229 8c blue 12 9
*571A* A229 8c intense bl ('83) 12 9
*572* A229 9c brt rose lilac 15 10
*573* A229 10c lt red brn 15 12
*573A* A229 10c vio brn ('83) 15 12
*573B* A229 11c cerise ('84) 20 14
*573C* A229 12c dp ultra ('85) 7 6
*573D* A229 14c rose brn ('86) 7 6
*574* A229 15c engr. 22 20
*575* A229 20c ver 30 24
*575A* A229 20c blk, engr. ('83) 50 40
*576* A229 25c bister 38 30

**Size: 45x27mm**
***Perf. 14½x14***
*577* A229 30c engr. 45 35
*578* A229 50c engr. 70 60
*578A* A229 50c litho. ('86) 1.25 1.00
*579* A229 1r engr. 1.50 1.25
*580* A229 2r engr. 3.00 2.50
*Nos. 564-580 (30)* 10.38 8.50

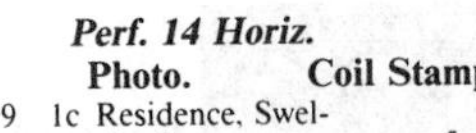

***Perf. 14 Horiz.***
**Photo. Coil Stamps**
*581* A229 1c Residence, Swellendam 5 5
*582* A229 2c City Hall, East London 5 5
*583* A229 5c Rissik St. PO, Johannesburg 14 10
*584* A229 10c Morgenster, Somerset West 25 20

Bradysaurus
A230

Prehistoric Animals (Karoo Fossils).

**1982, Dec. 1 Litho. *Perf. 14***
*585* A230 8c shown 12 10
*586* A230 15c Lystrosaurus 24 20
*587* A230 20c Euparkeria 32 25
*588* A230 25c Thrinaxodon 40 32
*a.* Souv. sheet of 4, #585-588 1.10

Weather Station, Gough Island
A231

**1983, Jan. 19 Litho. *Perf. 14x14½***
*589* A231 8c shown 12 10
*590* A231 20c Marion Isld. station 32 25
*591* A231 25c Reading instruments 40 32
*592* A231 40c Weather balloon, Antarctica 65 52

Steam Locomotives — A232

**1983, Apr. 27 Litho. *Perf. 14***
*593* A232 10c Class 82, 1952 18 14
*594* A232 20c Class 16E, 1935 38 30
*595* A232 25c Class 6H, 1901 45 38
*596* A232 40c Class 15F, 1939 75 60

Soccer — A233

**1983, July 20 Litho.**
*597* A233 10c Handball, vert. 16 12
*598* A233 20c shown 35 28
*599* A233 25c Sailing, vert. 45 35
*600* A233 40c Equestrian 70 55

Plettenberg Bay — A234

**1983, Oct. 12 Litho.**
*601* A234 10c shown 16 12
*602* A234 20c Durban Beach 35 24
*603* A234 25c West Coast beach 45 28
*604* A234 40c Clifton beach scene 70 52
*a.* Souv. sheet of 4, Nos. 601-604 1.75 1.25

No. 604a has decorative margin in the design of a picture frame. Size: 129x91mm.

English Writers of South Africa — A235

Designs: 10c, Thomas Pringle (1789-1834). 20c, Pauline Smith (1882-1959). 25c, Olive Schreiner (1855-1920). 40c, Percy FitzPatrick (1862-1931).

**1984, Feb. 24 Litho. *Perf. 14½x14***
*605* A235 10c multi 16 10
*606* A235 20c multi 32 20
*607* A235 25c multi 40 28
*608* A235 40c multi 65 40

Manganese
A236

**1984, June 8 Litho. *Perf. 14x14½***
*609* A236 11c shown 20 14
*610* A236 20c Chromium 38 24
*611* A236 25c Vanadium 48 32
*612* A236 30c Titanium 55 35

Bloukrans River Bridge
A237

**1984, Aug. 24**
*613* A237 11c shown 18 12
*614* A237 25c Durban 4-level Bridge Interchange 40 25
*615* A237 30c Mfolozi Railroad Bridge 48 30
*616* A237 45c Gouritz River Bridge 72 45

New Constitution
A238

Military Medals
A239

**1984, Sept. 3 Litho. *Perf. 14x14½***
*617* A238 11c Preamble (English) 20 14
*618* A238 11c Preamble (Africaans) 20 14
*619* A238 25c Symbolic pillars, anthem 48 30
*620* A238 30c Arms 55 35

Nos. 617-618 se-tenant.

**1984, Nov. 9 *Perf. 14½x14***
*621* A239 11c Pro Patria 18 12
*622* A239 25c De Wet 40 25
*623* A239 30c John Chard Decoration 48 30
*624* A239 45c Honoris Crux 72 45
*a.* Miniature sheet of 4 2.00 1.25

No. 624a contains Nos. 621-624. Size: 72x117mm.

Pres. Pieter Willem Botha (b. 1916) — A240

**1984, Nov. 2 Litho. *Perf. 14***
*625* A240 11c multi 18 12
*626* A240 25c multi 40 25

Frans David Oerder, Painter (1867-1944)
A241

**1985, Feb. 22 Litho. *Perf. 14***
*627* A241 11c Reflections 15 12
*628* A241 25c Ladies in a Garden 32 22
*629* A241 30c Still-Life with Lobster 42 28
*630* A241 50c Still-Life with Marigolds 65 45
*a.* Souvenir sheet of 4 2.00

No. 630a contains Nos. 627-630, multicolored margin showing self-portrait. Size: 130x74mm.

Cape Parliament Cent. — A242

**1985, May 15 Litho.**
*631* A242 12c Parliament 14 10
*632* A242 25c Speaker's chair 28 20
*633* A242 30c The National Convention, by Edward Roworth 32 22
*634* A242 50c South African arms 55 38

Indigenous Flowers
A243

Cape Silver
A244

**1985, Aug. 23 Litho. *Perf. 14½x14***
*635* A243 12c Freesia 10 8
*636* A243 25c Nerine 20 14
*637* A243 30c Ixia 24 16
*638* A243 50c Gladiolus 40 28

**1985, Nov. 5 *Perf. 14½x14, 14x14½***
*639* A244 12c Sugar bowl, horiz. 10 8
*640* A244 25c Tea pot, horiz. 22 15
*641* A244 30c Goblet 28 20
*642* A244 50c Coffee pot 45 30

Blood Transfusion Services
A245

**1986, Feb. 20 *Perf. 14½x14***
*643* A245 12c Blood donation 12 8
*644* A245 20c Transfusion 22 15
*645* A245 25c Surgery 28 20
*646* A245 30c Emergency aid 32 22

Republic of South Africa, 25th Anniv.
A246

**1986, May 30 Litho. *Perf. 14x14½***
*647* A246 14c Text in Afrikaans 12 10
*648* A246 14c Text in English 12 10

Nos. 647-648 printed se-tenant.

Cultural Heritage — A247

Restoration projects: 14c, Drostdyhof, Free Street, Graaff-Reinet, 19th cent. 20c, Pilgrim's Rest, Eastern Transvaal, 1873. 25c, J.T. Strapp and Son importers, c. 1893, Bethlehem. 30c, Palmdene, c. 1897, Pietermaritzburg.

**1986, Aug. 14** ***Perf. 14½x14***

| | | | | |
|---|---|---|---|---|
| *649* | A247 | 14c multi | 10 | 8 |
| *650* | A247 | 20c multi | 14 | 10 |
| *651* | A247 | 25c multi | 16 | 12 |
| *652* | A247 | 30c multi | 20 | 15 |

Johannesburg, Cent. — A248

Discovery of Gold in Roodepoort, Cent. — A249

**1986, Sept. 25** ***Perf. 14x14½***

| | | | | |
|---|---|---|---|---|
| *653* | A248 | 14c Johannesburg, 1886 | 10 | 8 |
| *654* | A249 | 20c Gold mine | 15 | 12 |
| *655* | A248 | 25c Johannesburg, 1986 | 18 | 14 |
| *656* | A249 | 30c Gold | 22 | 16 |
| *a.* | | Souvenir sheet | 45 | 45 |

No. 656a has multicolored margin picturing design of No. 654 and Johannesburg stamp exhibition emblem. Sold for 50c. Size: 105x70mm.

Pearl Mountain — A250

**1986, Nov. 20 Litho.** ***Perf. 14x14½***

| | | | | |
|---|---|---|---|---|
| *657* | A250 | 14c shown | 12 | 12 |
| *658* | A250 | 20c The Column, Drakensburg | 18 | 18 |
| *659* | A250 | 25c Maltese Cross, Cedarberg | 22 | 22 |
| *660* | A250 | 30c Bourke's Luck Potholes | 28 | 28 |

Importation Prohibited

Importation of stamps was prohibited effective November 24, 1986.

## SEMI-POSTAL STAMP

**Catalogue values for unused stamps in this section, from this point to the end of the section, are for Never Hinged items.**

English-Afrikaans Se-Tenant

Stamps with English inscriptions and with Afrikaans inscriptions of Nos. B1-B11 were printed alternately in the same sheets. Major-number listings and values are for single stamps of either inscription. Pairs (horizontal or vertical) consist of one English and one Afrikaans-inscribed stamp.

Church of the Vow — SP1

Cradock's Pass — SP2

Voortrekker SP3

Voortrekker Woman SP4

**1933-36 Photo. Wmk. 201** ***Perf. 14.***

| | | | | |
|---|---|---|---|---|
| *B1* | SP1 | ½p + ½p grn & blk ('36) | 30 | 35 |
| *a.* | | Pair | 3.25 | 3.75 |
| *B2* | SP2 | 1p + ½p rose & blk | 40 | 45 |
| *a.* | | Pair | 3.75 | 4.00 |
| *B3* | SP3 | 2p + 1p dl vio & gray | 1.50 | 1.50 |
| *a.* | | Pair | 7.50 | 7.50 |
| *B4* | SP4 | 3p + 1½p dp bl & gray | 2.25 | 2.25 |
| *a.* | | Pair | 15.00 | 15.00 |

Issued to commemorate the Voortrekkers. Surtax went to the National Memorial Fund for a national Voortrekker monument.

Voortrekker Plowing SP5

Crossing the Drakensberg SP6

Signing Dingaan-Retief Treaty — SP7

Proposed Monument — SP8

**1938, Dec. 14** ***Perf. 14***

| | | | | |
|---|---|---|---|---|
| *B5* | SP5 | ½p + ½p dl grn & ind | 35 | 40 |
| *a.* | | Pair | 4.50 | 4.75 |
| *B6* | SP6 | 1p + 1p rose & sl | 45 | 50 |
| *a.* | | Pair | 6.00 | 6.75 |

***Perf. 15x14***

| | | | | |
|---|---|---|---|---|
| *B7* | SP7 | 1½p + ½p Prus grn & choc | 1.10 | 1.10 |
| *a.* | | Pair | 11.00 | 13.50 |
| *B8* | SP8 | 3p + 3p chlky bl | 2.25 | 2.50 |
| *a.* | | Pair | 15.00 | 16.00 |

Issued to commemorate the Voortrekker centenary. Surtax went to the National Memorial Fund for a Voortrekker monument.

"The Old Vicarage," Huguenot Museum — SP9

Rising Sun and Cross — SP10

Huguenot Dwelling, Drakenstein Mountain Valley SP11

**1939, July 17 Photo.** ***Perf. 14***

| | | | | |
|---|---|---|---|---|
| *B9* | SP9 | ½p + ½p Prus grn & gray brn | 60 | 60 |
| *a.* | | Pair | 6.00 | 6.75 |
| *B10* | SP10 | 1p + 1p rose car & Prus grn | 90 | 90 |
| *a.* | | Pair | 6.75 | 7.00 |

***Perf. 15x14***

| | | | | |
|---|---|---|---|---|
| *B11* | SP11 | 1½p + 1½p multi | 1.50 | 1.50 |
| *a.* | | Pair | 9.00 | 11.00 |

250th anniv. of the landing of the Huguenots in South Africa. Surtax went to a fund to build a Huguenot memorial at Paarl.

## AIR POST STAMPS

Mail Plane — AP1

Biplane in Flight — AP2

**Unwmk.**

**1925, Feb. 26 Litho.** ***Perf. 12***

| | | | | |
|---|---|---|---|---|
| *C1* | AP1 | 1p red | 6.00 | 9.00 |
| *C2* | AP1 | 3p ultra | 9.00 | *10.50* |
| *C3* | AP1 | 6p violet | 10.50 | *15.00* |
| *C4* | AP1 | 9p gray grn | 24.00 | *40.00* |

**1929, Aug. 16 Typo.** ***Perf. 14x13½.***

| | | | | |
|---|---|---|---|---|
| *C5* | AP2 | 4p bl grn | 1.40 | 1.25 |
| *C6* | AP2 | 1sh orange | 13.00 | 12.00 |

## POSTAGE DUE STAMPS

D1

D2

**Wmk. Springbok's Head. (177)**

**1915 Typo.** ***Perf. 14.***

| | | | | |
|---|---|---|---|---|
| *J1* | D1 | ½p grn & blk | 1.10 | 1.25 |
| *J2* | D1 | 1p red & blk | 90 | 35 |
| *J3* | D1 | 2p vio & blk | 2.00 | 15 |
| *J4* | D1 | 3p ultra & blk | 1.10 | 18 |
| *J5* | D1 | 5p brn & blk | 4.50 | 4.50 |
| *J6* | D1 | 6p gray & blk | 7.50 | 9.00 |
| *J7* | D1 | 1sh blk & red | 80.00 | 100.00 |
| | | *Nos. J1-J7 (7)* | 97.10 | 115.43 |

**1922 Unwmk. Litho.** ***Rouletted 7-8***

| | | | | |
|---|---|---|---|---|
| *J8* | D1 | ½p bl grn & blk | 40 | 50 |
| *J9* | D1 | 1p dl red & blk | 60 | 70 |
| *J10* | D1 | 1½p yel brn & blk | 90 | 1.00 |

**1922-26** ***Perf. 14.***

| | | | | |
|---|---|---|---|---|
| *J11* | D1 | ½p bl grn & blk | 20 | 20 |
| *J12* | D1 | 1p rose & blk ('23) | 35 | 12 |
| *J13* | D1 | 1½p yel brn & blk ('24) | 1.00 | 80 |
| *J14* | D1 | 2p vio & blk ('23) | 85 | 38 |
| *a.* | | Imperf. pair | 250.00 | |
| *J15* | D1 | 3p bl & blk ('26) | 5.00 | 2.25 |
| *J16* | D1 | 6p gray & bl ('23) | 5.50 | 3.25 |
| | | *Nos. J11-J16 (6)* | 12.90 | 7.00 |

**1927-28** **Typo.**

| | | | | |
|---|---|---|---|---|
| *J17* | D2 | ½p bl grn & blk | 20 | 28 |
| *J18* | D2 | 1p rose & blk | 20 | 20 |
| *J19* | D2 | 2p vio & blk | 35 | 22 |
| *J20* | D2 | 3p ultra & blk | 3.25 | 3.25 |
| *J21* | D2 | 6p gray & blk | 5.00 | 5.25 |
| | | *Nos. J17-J21 (5)* | 9.00 | 9.20 |

**Catalogue values for unused stamps in this section, from this point to the end of the section, are for Never Hinged items.**

Type of 1927-28 Redrawn

***Perf. 15x14***

**1932-40 Photo. Wmk. 201**

| | | | | |
|---|---|---|---|---|
| *J22* | D2 | ½p bl grn & blk ('34) | 20 | 8 |
| *J23* | D2 | 1p rose car & blk ('34) | 24 | 5 |
| *J24* | D2 | 2p dk pur & blk ('40) | 60 | 20 |
| *a.* | | 2p blk vio & blk | 2.00 | 30 |
| *J25* | D2 | 3p dp bl & blk ('33) | 10.00 | 5.00 |
| *J26* | D2 | 3p ultra & dk bl ('35) | 4.00 | 2.50 |
| *J27* | D2 | 3p blk & dk bl ('40) | 7.00 | 5.00 |
| *J28* | D2 | 6p brn org & grn ('33) | 10.00 | 6.00 |
| *J29* | D2 | 6p red org & grn ('38) | 5.00 | 4.00 |
| | | *Nos. J22-J29 (8)* | 37.04 | 22.83 |

The ½p No. J22 photogravure has larger but thinner numeral and the "d" is taller and thinner than on No. J17.

The 1p No. J23 photogravure has numeral with parallel sides. The "d" is taller and thicker than on No. J18.

On Nos. J25 and J27 the numeral is followed by a large "d" with thick lines and a large round period below it.

Nos. J22, J24a and J25 have frame in photogravure, value typographed.

D3

***Strips of Three Perf. 15x14 All Around, Rouletted 6½ Between.***

**1943-44 Photo. Wmk. 201**

| | | | | |
|---|---|---|---|---|
| *J30* | D3 | ½p Prus grn ('44) | 8 | 6 |
| *a.* | | Horiz. strip of three | 3.00 | 3.50 |
| *J31* | D3 | 1p brt car | 6 | 5 |
| *a.* | | Horiz. strip of three | 2.00 | 2.00 |
| *J32* | D3 | 2p dk pur | 12 | 10 |
| *a.* | | Horiz. strip of three | 3.50 | 3.00 |
| *J33* | D3 | 3p dk bl | 16 | 18 |
| *a.* | | Horiz. strip of three | 10.00 | 10.00 |

Type of 1932-38, Redrawn.

Thick Numerals, Capital "D".

**1948-49** ***Perf. 15x14***

| | | | | |
|---|---|---|---|---|
| *J34* | D2 | ½p bl grn & blk | 60 | 30 |
| *J35* | D2 | 1p dp rose & blk | 75 | 30 |
| *J36* | D2 | 2p dk pur & blk ('49) | 1.00 | 60 |
| *J37* | D2 | 3p ultra & dk bl | 3.00 | 1.90 |
| *J38* | D2 | 6p dp org & grn ('49) | 5.25 | 3.00 |
| | | *Nos. J34-J38 (5)* | 10.60 | 6.10 |

Redrawn Type of 1948-49.

Hyphen between Suid-Afrika.

**1950-58** ***Perf. 15x14***

| | | | | |
|---|---|---|---|---|
| *J40* | D2 | 1p car rose & blk | 25 | 22 |
| *J41* | D2 | 2p dk pur & blk ('51) | 30 | 16 |
| *J42* | D2 | 3p ultra & dk bl | 1.25 | 75 |
| *J43* | D2 | 4p emer & dk grn ('58) | 70 | 75 |
| *J44* | D2 | 6p dp org & grn ('52) | 2.50 | 1.25 |
| *J45* | D2 | 1sh brn red & dk brn ('58) | 6.00 | 6.00 |
| | | *Nos. J40-J45 (6)* | 11.00 | 9.13 |

D4

D5

*Perf. 15x14*

**1961, Feb. 14 Photo. Wmk. 330**

| | | |
|---|---|---|
| *J46* D4 1c cer & blk | 15 | 20 |
| *J47* D4 2c pur & blk | 15 | 20 |
| *J48* D4 4c brt & dk grn | 1.00 | *2.25* |
| *J49* D4 5c chlky bl & sl | 2.00 | *2.75* |
| *J50* D4 6c ver & dk grn | 2.75 | *4.00* |
| *J51* D4 10c mar & dk brn | 6.50 | *8.25* |
| *Nos. J46-J51 (6)* | 12.55 | 17.65 |

### Republic

**1961-69** *Perf. 15x14*

**Afrikaans Inscription on Top and Left Side**

| | | |
|---|---|---|
| *J52* D5 1c cer & blk | 40 | 40 |
| *J53* D5 4c brt & dk grn | 45 | 45 |
| *J54* D5 6c ver & dk grn | 1.50 | 1.75 |

**English Inscription on Top and Left Side**

| | | |
|---|---|---|
| *J55* D5 1c cer & blk ('62) | 25 | 25 |
| *J56* D5 2c pur & blk | 35 | 35 |
| *J57* D5 4c brt & dk grn ('69) | 3.25 | 2.00 |
| *J58* D5 5c chlky bl & dk bl | 2.00 | 2.00 |
| *J59* D5 5c chlky bl & blk ('62) | 1.50 | 1.50 |
| *J60* D5 10c mar & dk brn | 5.00 | 3.50 |
| *Nos. J52-J60 (9)* | 14.70 | 12.20 |

**1967-70 Photo. Wmk. 359**

**Afrikaans Inscription on Top and Left Side**

| | | |
|---|---|---|
| *J61* D5 1c car rose & blk | 15 | 15 |
| *J62* D5 2c brt pur & blk | 16 | 16 |
| *J63* D5 4c lt grn & blk ('71) | 60 | 60 |
| a. 4c brt & dk grn ('70) | *75.00* | *75.00* |
| *J64* D5 5c dk bl & blk | 60 | 60 |
| *J65* D5 6c org & dk grn | 1.00 | 1.00 |
| *J66* D5 10c dk rose brn & blk | 1.50 | 1.50 |

**English Inscription on Top and Left Side**

| | | |
|---|---|---|
| *J67* D5 1c car rose & blk | 15 | 15 |
| *J68* D5 2c brt pur & blk | 30 | 30 |
| *J69* D5 4c lt grn & blk ('71) | 60 | 60 |
| a. brt & dk grn ('70) | *25.00* | *25.00* |
| *J70* D5 5c dk bl & blk | 60 | 60 |
| *J71* D5 6c org & dk grn | 1.00 | 1.00 |
| *J72* D5 10c dk rose brn & blk | 1.50 | 1.50 |
| *Nos. J61-J72 (12)* | 8.16 | 8.16 |

RSA TE BETAAL TO PAY 1c

D6

**1972, Mar. 22** *Perf. 14x13½*

| | | |
|---|---|---|
| *J73* D6 1c brt yel grn | 20 | 20 |
| *J74* D6 2c orange | 30 | 30 |
| *J75* D6 4c dl pur | 70 | 70 |
| *J76* D6 6c yellow | 1.00 | 1.00 |
| *J77* D6 8c brt bl | 1.50 | 1.50 |
| *J78* D6 10c rose red | 2.00 | 2.00 |
| *Nos. J73-J78 (6)* | 5.70 | 5.70 |

On the 2c, 6c and 10c "TO PAY" in first row at left.

---

## OFFICIAL STAMPS

Regular Issues Overprinted in Black

OFFICIAL. OFFISIEEL.

Periods in Overprint

On No. 5

**1926 Wmk. 177** *Perf. 14*

| | | |
|---|---|---|
| *O1* A2 2p dl vio | 10.00 | 2.00 |

See "English-Afrikaans Se-Tenant" note preceding No. 23.

---

On Nos. 23-25

*Perf. 14½x14*

**Wmk. 201**

| | | |
|---|---|---|
| *O2* A5 ½p dk grn & blk | 75 | 30 |
| a. Pair | 4.25 | 4.25 |
| *O3* A6 1p car & blk | 25 | 20 |
| a. Pair | 1.75 | 1.75 |
| *O4* A7 6p org & grn | 25.00 | 7.50 |
| a. Pair | *650.00* | *100.00* |

Nos. 26 and 25 Overprinted (Reading Up)

b OFFICIAL OFFISIEEL

No Periods in Overprint

**1928-29** *Perf. 14, 14½x14*

**Space between words 19mm**

| | | |
|---|---|---|
| *O5* A8 2p vio brn & gray ('29) | 40 | 30 |
| a. Pair | 2.50 | 2.50 |
| b. Space 17½mm | 25 | 20 |
| c. As "b." pair | 2.50 | 2.50 |

**Space between words 11½mm**

| | | |
|---|---|---|
| *O6* A7 6p org & grn | 1.00 | 70 |
| a. Pair | 5.00 | 5.00 |

Nos. 23-25 Overprinted type "b" Reading Down.

Space between words 13½-14mm

**1929** *Perf. 14½x14*

| | | |
|---|---|---|
| *O7* A5 ½p grn & blk | 10 | 10 |
| a. Pair | 50 | 50 |
| b. Period after "OFFISIEEL" on English stamp | 2.75 | 2.75 |
| c. Pair, "b" + normal ½p | 7.00 | 7.00 |
| d. Period after "OFFISIEEL." on Afrikaans stamp | 3.25 | 3.25 |
| e. Pair, "d" + normal ½p | 8.50 | 7.25 |
| *O8* A6 1p car & blk | 10 | 10 |
| a. Pair | 65 | 45 |
| *O9* A7 6p org & grn | 50 | 40 |
| a. Pair | 2.75 | 1.80 |
| b. Period after "OFFISIEEL." on English stamp | 8.00 | 8.00 |
| c. Pair, "b" + normal 6p | 18.00 | 18.00 |
| d. Period after "OFFISIEEL." on Afrikaans stamp | 8.00 | 8.00 |
| e. Pair, "d" + normal 6p | 18.00 | 18.00 |

Nos. 29-30 Overprinted type "b" Reading Down.

Space between words 17½-19mm

**1931 Engr.** *Perf. 14, 14x13½*

| | | |
|---|---|---|
| *O10* A11 1sh dp bl & bis brn | 2.25 | 2.25 |
| a. Pair | 12.00 | 12.00 |
| b. Period after "OFFICIAL." on Afrikaans stamp | 50.00 | 50.00 |
| c. Pair, "b" + normal 1sh | 75.00 | 75.00 |
| *O11* A12 2sh6p brn & bl grn | 2.50 | 2.50 |
| a. Pair | 15.00 | 15.00 |
| b. Period after "OFFICIAL." on Afrikaans stamp | 72.50 | 72.50 |
| c. Pair, "b" + normal 2sh6p | 300.00 | 300.00 |

Regular Issues of 1930-45 Overprinted type "b" Reading Down ("SUIDAFRIKA" on Afrikaans stamps)

***Perf. 15x14 (½p, 1p, 6p), 14***

**1930-47 Photo. Wmk. 201**

**Space between words 9½-12mm**

**(Various spacings occur in same setting.)**

| | | |
|---|---|---|
| *O12* A5 ½p bl grn & blk (#33) ('31) | 8 | 6 |
| a. Pair | 30 | 25 |
| b. Period after "OFFISIEEL." on English stamp | 4.50 | 4.50 |
| c. Pair, "b" + normal ½p | 7.50 | 7.50 |
| d. Period after "OFFISIEEL." on Afrikaans stamp | 5.00 | 5.00 |
| e. Pair, "d" + normal ½p | 9.00 | 9.00 |

**Space between words 12½-13½mm**

| | | |
|---|---|---|
| *O13* A5 ½p bl grn & blk (#33) | 8 | 8 |
| a. Pair | 75 | 75 |
| *O14* A6 1p car & blk (#34) | 12 | 8 |
| a. Pair | 45 | 35 |
| b. Period after "OFFISIEEL." on English stamp | 4.75 | 4.75 |
| c. Pair, "b" + normal 1p | 6.00 | 6.00 |
| d. Period after "OFFISIEEL." on Afrikaans stamp | 5.75 | 5.75 |
| e. Pair, "d" + normal 1p | 10.00 | 10.00 |
| *O15* A6 1p rose & blk (#35) ('33) | 25 | 20 |
| a. Pair | 90 | 75 |
| b. Double ovpt. | 57.50 | |
| c. As "b" pair | 400.00 | |

**Space between words 20½-22mm**

| | | |
|---|---|---|
| *O16* A8 2p vio & gray (#36) ('31) | 25 | 15 |
| a. Pair | 1.25 | 85 |
| *O17* A8 2p vio & ind (#37) | 1.25 | 50 |
| a. Pair | 16.00 | 10.00 |

**Space between words 12½-13½mm**

| | | |
|---|---|---|
| *O18* A7 6p org & grn (#42) | 55 | 35 |
| a. Pair | 9.50 | 3.00 |
| b. Period after "OFFISIEEL." on English stamp | 11.00 | 11.00 |
| c. Pair, "b" + normal 6p | 18.00 | 18.00 |
| d. Period after "OFFISIEEL." on Afrikaans stamp | 13.50 | 13.50 |
| e. Pair, "d" + normal 6p | 22.50 | 22.50 |

**Space between words 21mm**

| | | |
|---|---|---|
| *O19* A11 1sh dp bl & brn (#43) ('32) | 1.00 | 30 |
| a. Pair | 8.00 | 6.25 |
| b. 1sh dk bl & yel brn (#43b), 19mm | 70 | 25 |
| c. As "b," pair | 6.50 | 4.25 |
| d. As "b," spaced 21mm | 9.00 | 4.50 |
| e. As "d," pair | 30.00 | 35.00 |

**Space between words 17½-18½mm**

| | | |
|---|---|---|
| *O20* A12 2sh6p red brn & grn (#44) ('33) | 3.25 | 1.75 |
| a. Pair | 22.50 | 15.00 |
| b. Spaced 21 mm | 2.75 | 1.75 |
| c. As "b." pair | 50.00 | 50.00 |
| d. 2sh6p brn & sl grn (#44b) ('37) | 3.50 | 2.75 |
| e. As "d." pair | 22.50 | 22.50 |
| f. 2sh6p brn & bl, 19-20mm ('47) | 2.25 | 1.40 |
| g. As "f." pair | 50.00 | 40.00 |
| *Nos. O12-O20 (9)* | 6.83 | 3.47 |

**Catalogue values for unused stamps in this section, from this point to the end of the section, are for Never Hinged items.**

Regular Issue of 1933-54 Overprinted type "b" Reading Down ("SUID-AFRIKA" Hyphenated)

**1935-50 Photo.** *Perf. 15x14, 14*

**Space between words given with each listing.**

| | | |
|---|---|---|
| *O21* A5 ½p grn & gray (#45), 12½-13mm ('36) | 15 | 7 |
| a. Pair | 90 | 75 |
| *O22* A5 ½p grn & gray, (#46), 11½-13mm ('38) | 8 | 5 |
| a. Pair | 70 | 30 |
| *O23* A5 ½p grn & gray (#47), 11½mm ('48) | 7 | 5 |
| a. Pair | 55 | 35 |
| *O24* A6 1p car & gray (#48), 11-13mm | 8 | 5 |
| a. Pair | 40 | 40 |
| *O25* A6 1p rose car & gray blk (#49), 11½-12 mm ('41) | 8 | 5 |
| a. Pair | 75 | 50 |
| *O26* A15 1½p dk grn & gold (#51), 19-21mm ('37) | 25 | 15 |
| a. Pair | 1.50 | 1.00 |
| *O27* A15 1½p sl grn & ocher (#52), 14-14½mm ('44) | 8 | 7 |
| a. Pair | 50 | 30 |
| b. Ovpt. spaced 16mm | 30 | 25 |
| c. As "b." pair | 1.50 | 1.50 |
| *O28* A8 2p bl vio & dl bl (#53), 20-21mm ('39) | 60 | 30 |
| a. Pair | 4.50 | 3.00 |
| *O29* A16 2p pur & sl (#55), 19-21mm ('48) | 8 | 5 |
| a. Pair | 40 | 35 |
| *O30* A7 6p org & bl grn, I (#59), 12-13 mm ('38) | 5.25 | 3.50 |
| a. Pair | 27.50 | 21.00 |
| *O31* A7 6p org & grn, II (#60), 12-13mm ('39) | 30 | 25 |
| a. Pair | 3.00 | 3.00 |
| *O32* A7 6p org & grn III (#61), 11½-12 mm ('47) | 25 | 20 |
| a. Pair | 2.25 | 1.80 |
| *O33* A11 1sh lt bl & ol brn (#62), 19-21mm ('40) | 30 | 10 |
| a. Pair | 2.75 | 1.50 |
| b. "OFFICIAL" on both sides | 90.00 | |
| c. "OFFISIEEL" on both sides | 90.00 | |
| d. 1sh chlky bl & lt brn (#62b) | 60 | 15 |
| e. As "d." pair | 3.00 | 1.80 |
| f. 1sh vio bl & brnsh blk (#62d), 18-19 mm ('50) | 60 | 15 |
| g. As "f." pair | 3.00 | 1.80 |
| *O34* A13 5sh grn & blk (#64) 19-20 mm | 3.00 | 1.80 |
| a. Pair | 18.00 | 12.00 |
| *O35* A13 5sh bl grn & blk (#65), 20mm | 2.00 | 1.10 |
| a. Pair | 18.00 | 12.00 |
| *O36* A18 10sh ol blk & bl (#67), 19½-20mm ('48) | 4.50 | 2.00 |
| a. Pair | 30.00 | 25.00 |
| *Nos. O21-O36 (16)* | 17.07 | 9.79 |

Nos. 52 and 56 Overprinted type "b" Reading Up

Space between words 16mm

**1949-50 Size: 22x18mm** *Perf. 14*

| | | |
|---|---|---|
| *O37* A15 1½p sl grn & ocher | 15 | 10 |
| a. Pair | 2.00 | 75 |

**Size: 21½x17½mm**

| | | |
|---|---|---|
| *O38* A16 2p pur & sl bl ('50) | 100.00 | 50.00 |
| a. Pair | 650.00 | *1,250.* |

Nos. 64, 67 Overprinted

c OFFICIAL OFFISIEEL

Space between words 18-19mm

**1940** *Perf. 14*

| | | |
|---|---|---|
| *O39* A13 5sh grn & blk | 2.50 | 1.10 |
| a. Pair | 15.00 | 9.00 |
| *O40* A18 10sh ol brn & bl | 4.50 | 2.50 |
| a. Pair | 30.00 | 25.00 |

No. 54 Overprinted type "c" Reading Up

Space between words 19mm

**1945** *Perf. 14*

| | | |
|---|---|---|
| *O41* A8 2p dl vio & gray | 10 | 5 |
| a. Pair | 75 | 50 |

No. 47 Overprinted OFFICIAL OFFISIEEL

**1947** *Perf. 15x14*

| | | |
|---|---|---|
| *O42* A5 ½p grn & gray | 10 | 7 |
| a. Pair | 75 | 50 |

Stamps of 1937-54 Ovptd. OFFISIEEL OFFICIAL

**1950-54** *Perf. 15x14, 14*

**Space between words 10mm.**

| | | |
|---|---|---|
| *O43* A5 ½p grn & gray (#47) | 7 | 5 |
| a. Pair | 30 | 20 |
| *O44* A6 1p rose car & gray blk (#49) | 8 | 6 |
| a. Pair | 70 | 70 |
| *O45* A6 1p car & blk (#50) | 5 | 5 |
| a. Pair | 25 | 15 |

**Space between words 14½mm**

| | | |
|---|---|---|
| *O46* A15 1½p sl grn & ocher (#52) | 7 | 5 |
| a. Pair | 50 | 45 |
| *O47* A16 2p pur & sl bl (#56) | 8 | 5 |
| a. Pair | 50 | 45 |
| b. Ovpt. reading up, pair | | |

**Space between words 10mm**

| | | |
|---|---|---|
| *O48* A7 6p red org & bl grn, III (#61b) | 15 | 7 |
| a. Pair | 85 | 45 |

**Space between words 19mm**

| | | |
|---|---|---|
| *O49* A11 1sh chlky bl & lt brn (#62b) | 30 | 15 |
| a. Pair | 2.50 | 2.10 |
| b. 1sh vio bl & brnsh blk (#62d) | 6.00 | 2.50 |
| c. As "b." pair | 80.00 | 32.50 |
| *O50* A12 2sh6p brn & brt grn (#63) | 80 | 60 |
| a. Pair | 7.25 | 6.50 |
| *O51* A13 5sh grn & blk (#64) | 1.75 | 90 |
| a. Pair | 13.00 | 8.50 |
| *O52* A13 5sh bl grn & blk I (#65) | 2.00 | 70 |
| a. Pair | 12.00 | 6.50 |
| *O53* A13 5sh grn & blk II (#66) | 1.75 | 1.50 |
| a. Pair | 10.00 | 10.00 |
| *O54* A18 10sh ol blk & bl (#67) | 4.50 | 2.50 |
| a. Pair | 25.00 | 16.00 |

## SOUTH ARABIA

LOCATION — Southern Arabia.
GOVT. — Federation; British dependency.
AREA — 61,890 sq. mi.
POP. — 771,000 (est. 1966).
CAPITAL — Al Ittihad.

The Federation of South Arabia was established in 1959 and consists of 14 states including Aden colony and part of Aden protectorate. When the Federation became independent, Nov. 30, 1967, it became the People's Republic of Southern Yemen. See People's Democratic Republic of Yemen, Vol. IV.

100 Cents = 1 Shilling
1000 Fils = 1 Dinar (1965)

**Catalogue values for all unused stamps in this country are for Never Hinged items.**

**Red Cross Centenary Issue**
Common Design Type
**Wmk. 314**

**1963, Nov. 25 Litho. *Perf. 13***
*1* CD315 15c blk & red 15 12
*2* CD315 1sh 25c ultra & red 50 38

Arms of Federation of South Arabia — A1

Flag of Federation — A2

***Perf. 14½x14***
**1965, Apr. 1 Photo. Unwmk.**
*3* A1 5f blue 5 5
*4* A1 10f light vio bl 5 5
*5* A1 15f blue green 6 5
*6* A1 20f green 7 6
*7* A1 25f orange brn 10 7
*8* A1 30f lemon 12 7
*9* A1 35f red brown 14 10
*10* A1 50f rose red 18 12
*11* A1 65f light yel grn 22 14
*12* A1 75f rose carmine 28 16

***Perf. 14½***
**Flag in Black, Yellow, Green and Blue**
*13* A2 100f redsh brn 35 28
*14* A2 250f dark bl 90 55
*15* A2 500f dark red 1.90 90
*16* A2 1d violet 3.00 2.25
*Nos. 3-16 (14)* 7.42 4.85

**Intl. Cooperation Year Issue**
Common Design Type with Coat of Arms Replacing Queen's Portrait
**Wmk. 314**
**1965, Oct. 24 Litho. *Perf. 14½***
*17* CD318 5f bl grn & cl 5 5
*18* CD318 65f lt vio & grn 40 35

**Churchill Memorial Issue**
Common Design Type with Coat of Arms Replacing Queen's Portrait
**Unwmk.**
**1966, Jan. 24 Photo. *Perf. 14***
**Design in Black, Gold and Carmine Rose**
*19* CD319 5f brt bl 6 5
*20* CD319 10f green 10 8
*21* CD319 65f brown 50 40
*22* CD319 125f violet 1.00 75

**World Cup Soccer Issue**
Common Design Type with Coat of Arms Replacing Queen's Portrait
**1966, July 1 Litho. *Perf. 14***
*23* CD321 10f multi 10 7
*24* CD321 50f multi 35 28

**WHO Headquarters Issue**
Common Design Type with Coat of Arms Replacing Queen's Portrait
**1966, Sept. 20 Litho. Unwmk.**
*25* CD322 10f multi 8 6
*26* CD322 75f multi 50 40

**UNESCO Anniversary Issue**
Common Design Type with Coat of Arms Replacing Queen's Portrait
**1966, Dec. 15 Litho. *Perf. 14***
*27* CD323 10f "Education" 6 5
*28* CD323 65f "Science" 35 28
*29* CD323 125f "Culture" 65 50

## SOUTH AUSTRALIA

LOCATION — In the central part of southern Australia.
GOVT. — A former British Colony.
AREA — 380,070 sq. mi.
POP. — 358,346 (1901).
CAPITAL — Adelaide.

South Australia was one of the six British colonies that united in 1901 to form the Commonwealth of Australia.

12 Pence = 1 Shilling
20 Shillings = 1 Pound

Values of early South Australia stamps vary according to condition. Quotations for Nos. 1-9 are for fine copies. Very fine to superb specimens sell at much higher prices, and inferior or poor copies sell at reduced prices, depending on the condition of the individual specimen.

Queen Victoria — A1

Wmk. 6- Star with Long Narrow Points

**1855-56 Engr. Wmk. 6 *Imperf.***
**London Print**
*1* A1 1p dark green 2,750. 375.00
*2* A1 2p dl carmine 600.00 60.00
*3* A1 6p deep blue 2,500. 115.00
*4* A1 1sh vio ('56) *5,250.*

No. 4 was never put in use. Nos. 1 and 3 without watermark are proofs.

**1856-59 Local Print**
*5* A1 1p yel grn ('58) *6,000.* 375.00
*6* A1 2p blood red 1,500. 55.00
*a.* Printed on both sides
*7* A1 2p pale red ('57) 700. 45.00
*a.* Printed on both sides *1,000.*
*8* A1 6p slate bl ('57) 2,500. 175.00
*9* A1 1sh orange ('57) 4,750. 250.00
*a.* Printed on both sides

**1858-59 *Rouletted***
*10* A1 1p yel grn ('59) 475.00 40.00
*a.* Horiz. pair, imperf. between
*11* A1 2p pale red ('59) 125.00 9.75
*a.* Printed on both sides
*12* A1 6p slate blue 350.00 22.50
*13* A1 1sh orange ('59) 1,250. 35.00
*c.* Printed on both sides *1,750.*

A2

A3

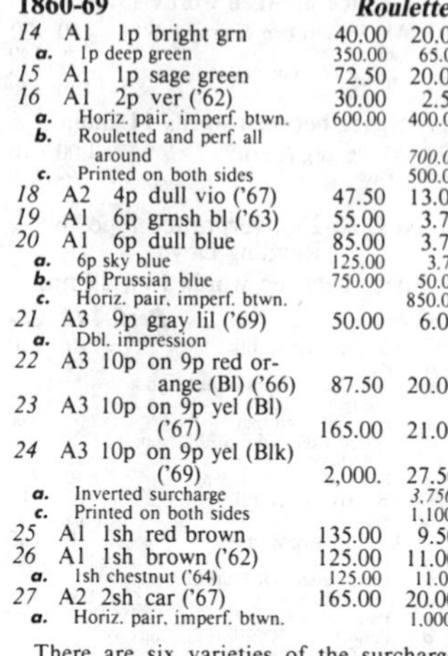

Surch. on Nos. 22-24, 34, 49-50

**1860-69 *Rouletted***
*14* A1 1p bright grn 40.00 20.00
*a.* 1p deep green 350.00 65.00
*15* A1 1p sage green 72.50 20.00
*16* A1 2p ver ('62) 30.00 2.50
*a.* Horiz. pair, imperf. btwn. 600.00 400.00
*b.* Rouletted and perf. all around 700.00
*c.* Printed on both sides 500.00
*18* A2 4p dull vio ('67) 47.50 13.00
*19* A1 6p grnsh bl ('63) 55.00 3.75
*20* A1 6p dull blue 85.00 3.75
*a.* 6p sky blue 125.00 3.75
*b.* 6p Prussian blue 750.00 50.00
*c.* Horiz. pair, imperf. btwn. 850.00
*21* A3 9p gray lil ('69) 50.00 6.00
*a.* Dbl. impression
*22* A3 10p on 9p red orange (Bl) ('66) 87.50 20.00
*23* A3 10p on 9p yel (Bl) ('67) 165.00 21.00
*24* A3 10p on 9p yel (Blk) ('69) 2,000. 27.50
*a.* Inverted surcharge 3,750.
*c.* Printed on both sides 1,100.
*25* A1 1sh red brown 135.00 9.50
*26* A1 1sh brown ('62) 125.00 11.00
*a.* 1sh chestnut ('64) 125.00 11.00
*27* A2 2sh car ('67) 165.00 20.00
*a.* Horiz. pair, imperf. btwn. 1,000.

There are six varieties of the surcharge "TEN PENCE" in this and subsequent issues.

Nos. 16b, 28a, 32c, 33a are rouletted remainders that were later perforated.

**1867-72 *Perf. 11½ to 12½xRoulette***
*28* A1 1p blue grn 225.00 21.50
*a.* Rouletted and perf. all around 650.00
*29* A1 1p yellow grn 135.00 12.00
*31* A2 4p dl violet 1,500. 125.00
*32* A1 6p Prus blue 450.00 16.00
*a.* 6p sky blue 700.00 17.50
*b.* Printed on both sides
*c.* Rouletted and perf. all around 300.00
*33* A3 9p gray lil ('72) 275.00
*a.* Rouletted and perf. all around 1,800. 275.00
*34* A3 10p on 9p yel (Bl) ('68) 1,000. 35.00
*a.* Printed on both sides 900.00
*35* A1 1sh brown ('68) 275.00 25.00
*36* A1 1sh red brn ('69) 275.00 25.00

A5

***Perf. 10, 11½, 12½ and Compound***
**1867-74**
*41* A1 1p yel green 45.00 17.50
*42* A1 1p bl green 60.00 12.50
*a.* Printed on both sides
*43* A1 2p vermilion 1,500.
*44* A5 3p on 4p dp bl (Blk) ('70) 60.00 5.50
*a.* 3p on 4p ultra, blk surcharge 125.00 5.50
*b.* Surcharge omitted *20,000.* *5,000.*
*c.* Double surch. 4,500.
*d.* Surcharged on both sides 3,250.
*45* A5 3p on 4p sl bl (Red) ('70) 425.00 32.50
*46* A2 4p dull vio 60.00 5.50
*47* A1 6p dark bl 75.00 4.25
*a.* 6p sky blue 350.00 9.25
*b.* Imperf. vert., pair
*48* A3 9p red lil ('72) 47.50 5.00
*a.* 9p violet 115.00 5.50
*b.* 9p red violet 115.00 5.50
*c.* Printed on both sides 350.00
*49* A3 10p on 9p yel (Bl) ('68) 1,500. 26.00
*50* A3 10p on 9p yel (Blk) ('69) 150.00 21.00
*51* A1 1sh deep brn 150.00 12.00
*52* A1 1sh red brn 100.00 10.50
*a.* 1sh chestnut 125.00 12.50
*53* A2 2sh carmine 60.00 7.50
*a.* Printed on both sides 400.00
*b.* Horiz. pair, imperf. vert.

See Nos. 59, 63, 68-70, 72-74, 112-113B, 118-120.

A6

A6a

Wmk. 72- Crown and S A

**1868 Typo. Wmk. 72 *Rouletted***
*54* A6a 2p orange red 60.00 3.00
*a.* Imperf.
*b.* Printed on both sides 275.00
*c.* Horiz. pair, imperf. btwn. 275.00

**1869 *Perf. 11½ to 12½xRoulette***
*55* A6a 2p orange red 150.00

**1870 *Perf. 10xRoulette***
*56* A6a 2p orange red 350.00 30.00

***Perf. 10, 11½, 12½ and Compound***
**1868-75**
*57* A6 1p bl grn ('75) 24.00 4.50
*58* A6a 2p org red 11.50 1.00
*a.* Printed on both sides 200.00
*b.* Horiz. pair, imperf. vert.

**Engr.**
*59* A3 10p on 9p yel (Bl) *2,250.*

**1869 Typo. Wmk. 6 *Rouletted***
*60* A6a 2p org red 65.00 11.50
*a.* Imperf.
*b.* Printed on both sides

***Perf. 11½ to 12½xRoulette***
*61* A6a 2p org red 125.00

***Perf. 11½ to 12½***
*61B* A6a 2p org red

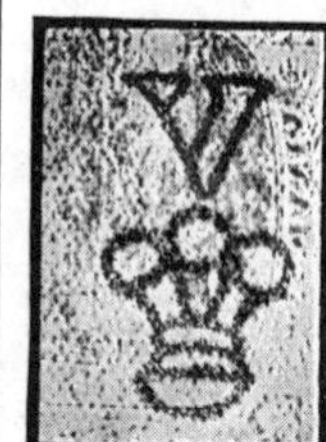
Wmk. 70- Crown and V

Wmk. 73- Crown and SA, Letters Close

**1871 Wmk. 70 *Perf. 10***
*62* A6a 2p org red 75.00 16.00

**Engr.**
*63* A2 4p dl vio 2,250. 340.00
*a.* Printed on both sides

Copies of the 4p from edge of sheet sometimes lack watermark.

***Perf. 10, 11½, 12½ and Compound***
**1876-80 Typo. Wmk. 73**
*64* A6 1p green 4.25 50
*65* A6a 2p orange 4.25 50
*66* A6a 2p blood red ('80) 225.00 7.50

See Nos. 97-98, 105-106, 115-116, 133-134, 145-146.

A7

Wmk. 7- Star with Short Broad Points

**1876-84 Engr. Wmk. 7**

*67* A5 3p on 4p ultra (Blk) 57.50 15.00
**a.** 3p on 4p deep blue 15.00
**b.** Double surcharge *1,500.*
*68* A2 4p reddish vio 40.00 3.00
**a.** 4p dull violet 60.00 9.00
*69* A1 6p deep blue 65.00 2.50
**a.** Horiz. pair, imperf. vert.
**b.** Imperf.
*70* A1 6p pale ultra ('84) 40.00 1.65
*71* A7 8p on 9p bis brn 57.50 2.50
**a.** 8p on 9p yellow brn 57.50 2.50
**b.** 8p on 9p gray brn ('80) 52.50 3.00
**d.** Double surcharge 380.00
*72* A3 9p rose lilac 9.25 3.00
**a.** Printed on both sides 300.00
*73* A1 1sh red brown 35.00 2.10
**a.** 1sh brown 40.00 2.50
**b.** Horiz. pair, imperf. betw. 300.00
*74* A2 2sh carmine 21.00 2.75
**a.** Horiz. pair, imperf. vert. *400.00*
**b.** Imperf., pair

A8

**1882 Wmk. 73 *Perf. 10***

**Black Surcharge**

*75* A8 ½p on 1p green 4.00 4.00

A9

A10

A11

A12

***Perf. 10, 11½, 12½ and Compound***

**1883-90 Typo.**

*76* A9 ½p choc brown 1.90 25
**a.** ½p red brown ('89) 1.90 25
**b.** ½p bister brown 3.50 25
*78* A10 3p deep grn ('86) 6.50 75
**a.** 3p olive green ('90) 11.00 1.50
*79* A11 4p violet ('90) 7.75 1.75
*80* A12 6p blue ('87) 7.75 1.00

See Nos. 96, 100-101, 104, 108-109, 111.

A13

**1886-96 *Perf. 10, 11½ to 12½***

*81* A13 2sh6p violet 20.00 5.00
*82* A13 5sh rose 37.50 16.00
*83* A13 10sh green 75.00 25.00
*84* A13 15sh buff 185.00 100.00
*85* A13 £1 blue 165.00 60.00
*86* A13 £2 red brn 475.00 150.00
*87* A13 50sh rose red 600.00 200.00
*88* A13 £3 ol grn 825.00
*89* A13 £4 lemon 900.00
*90* A13 £5 gray *2,700.*
*90A* A13 £5 brn ('96) *2,600.*
*91* A13 £10 bronze *3,000. 900.00*
*92* A13 £15 silver *6,500.*
*93* A13 £20 lilac *8,250.*

A14

A15

***Perf. 10, 11½x12½ and Compound***

**1891**

**Brown Surcharge**

*94* A14 2½p on 4p green 3.50 75
**a.** "½" nearer the "2" 22.50 20.00
**b.** Pair, imperf. between 375.00
**c.** Fraction bar omitted 90.00 80.00

**Carmine Surcharge**

*95* A15 5p on 6p red brn 9.00 6.00
**a.** No period after "D" 165.00

*Many stamps of the issues of 1855-91 have been reprinted; they are all on paper watermarked Crown and SA, letters wide apart, and are overprinted "REPRINT".*

**1893 Typo. *Perf. 15***

*96* A9 ½p brown 2.75 18
**a.** Horiz. pair, imperf. betw. 125.00
**b.** Pair, perf. 12 between and perf. 15 around 195.00 50.00
*97* A6 1p green 3.00 20
*98* A6a 2p orange 6.00 15
**a.** Vert. pair, imperf. between 225.00
*99* A14 2½p on 4p green 6.00 1.65
**a.** "½" nearer the "2" 32.50 32.50
**b.** Fraction bar omitted
*100* A11 4p gray vio 12.00 2.00
*101* A12 6p blue 30.00 4.25
*Nos. 96-101 (6)* 59.75 8.43

Kangaroo, Palm — A16

Coat of Arms — A17

**1894, Mar. 1**

*102* A16 2½p blue violet 9.75 1.50
*103* A17 5p dull violet 12.50 2.50

See Nos. 107, 110, 117, 135-136, 147, 151.

**1895-97 *Perf. 13***

*104* A9 ½p pale brown 1.65 25
*105* A6 1p green 4.00 50
**a.** Vert. pair, imperf. between
*106* A6a 2p orange 3.25 12
*107* A16 2½p blue violet 5.75 30
*108* A10 3p ol grn ('97) 3.75 30
*109* A11 4p bright vio 4.00 25
*110* A17 5p dull violet 3.25 30
*111* A12 6p blue 4.25 38
*Nos. 104-111 (8)* 29.90 2.40

Some authorities regard the so-called redrawn 1p stamps with thicker lettering (said to have been issued in 1897) as impressions from a new or cleaned plate.

***Perf. 11½, 12½, Clean-Cut, Compound***

**1896 Engr. Wmk. 7**

*112* A3 9p lilac rose 12.00 6.50
*113* A1 1sh dark brown 24.00 3.75
**a.** Horiz. pair, imperf. vert.
**c.** Vert. pair, imperf. btwn. 180.00
*113B* A2 2sh carmine 32.50 8.00

Adelaide Post Office — A18

**1899 Typo. Wmk. 73 *Perf. 13***

*114* A18 ½p yellow grn 1.10 25
*115* A6 1p carmine 1.65 20
**a.** 1p scarlet 2.75 50
*116* A6a 2p purple 1.10 25
*117* A16 2½p dark blue 6.00 75

See Nos. 132, 144.

***Perf. 11½, 12½***

**1901 Engr. Wmk. 72**

*118* A1 1sh dark brown 24.00 10.00
**a.** 1sh red brown 24.00 10.00
**b.** Horiz. pair, imperf. vert.
*119* A2 2sh carmine 22.50 15.00

**1902**

*120* A3 9p magenta 15.00 15.00

A19

A20

***Perf. 11½, 12½ and Compound***

**1902-03 Typo. Wmk. 73**

*121* A19 3p ol grn 4.75 75
*122* A19 4p red org 7.50 1.50
*123* A19 6p bl grn 6.00 1.50
*124* A19 8p ultra (value 19mm long) 7.50 2.25
*124A* A19 8p ultra (value 16½mm long) ('03) 12.00 3.00
**b.** "EIGNT" 1,400. *3,000.*
*125* A19 9p claret 7.50 2.25
**a.** Pair, imperf. between 300.00
*126* A19 10p org buff 7.50 3.50
*127* A19 1sh brn ('03) 9.00 3.00
**a.** Horiz. or vert. pair, imperf. btwn. 700.00
*128* A19 2sh6p purple 30.00 9.00
*129* A19 5sh rose 60.00 52.50
*130* A19 10sh grn ('03) 90.00 65.00
*131* A19 £1 blue 275.00 150.00
*Nos. 121-131 (12)* 516.75 294.25

**1904 *Perf. 12x11½***

*132* A18 ½p yellow green 2.50 60
*133* A6 1p rose 5.50 60
*134* A6a 2p purple 5.50 60
*135* A16 2½p dark blue 13.00 1.50
*136* A17 5p dull violet 9.00 1.75
*Nos. 132-136 (5)* 35.50 5.05

**1904-08 *Perf. 12 and 12x11½***

*137* A20 6p bl green 8.25 1.75
*138* A20 8p ultra ('06) 11.50 2.25
*139* A20 9p claret 8.00 1.65
*139A* A20 10p orange buff ('07) 20.00 5.25
**b.** Pair, imperf. between 325.00 225.00
*140* A20 1sh brown 10.00 2.00
**a.** Pair, imperf. between 250.00
*141* A20 2sh6p pur ('05) 50.00 8.25
*142* A20 5sh scarlet 50.00 32.50
*142B* A20 10sh grn ('08) 165.00 165.00
*143* A20 £1 deep bl 165.00 165.00
*Nos. 137-143 (9)* 487.75 383.65

Wmk. 74- Crown and Single-lined A

**1906-12 Wmk. 74**

*144* A18 ½p green 1.50 15
*145* A6 1p carmine 1.50 15
*146* A6a 2p purple 2.50 15
**a.** Horiz. pair, imperf. between
*147* A16 2½p dk bl ('11) 10.50 1.50
*148* A20 3p ol grn (value 19mm long) 6.50 1.25
**a.** Horiz. pair, imperf. between
*149* A20 3p ol grn (value 17mm long) ('09) 8.50 1.50
*150* A20 4p red orange 9.75 1.75
*151* A17 5p dl vio ('08) 8.50 2.00
*152* A20 6p bl grn ('07) 5.50 1.10
**a.** Vert. pair, imperf. btwn. 240.00
*153* A20 8p ultra ('09) 15.00 5.50
*154* A20 9p claret 15.00 3.00
**a.** Vert. pair, imperf. between 195.00
**b.** Horiz. pair, imperf. between 225.00
*155* A20 1sh brown 10.50 3.00
**a.** Pair, imperf. between 175.00
*156* A20 2sh6p purple ('09) 27.50 10.50
*157* A20 5sh lt red ('12) 67.50
*Nos. 144-157 (14)* 190.25 31.55



## OFFICIAL STAMPS

### For Departments

**Regular Issues Overprinted in Red, Black or Blue:**

A. (Architect), A. G. (Attorney General), A. O. (Audit Office), B. D. (Barracks Department), B. G. (Botanical Gardens), B. M. (Bench of Magistrates), C. (Customs), C. D. (Convict Department), C. L. (Crown Lands), C. O. (Commissariat Officer), C. S. (Chief Secretary), C. Sgn. (Colonial Surgeon), C. P. (Commissioner of Police), C. T. (Commissioner of Titles), D. B. (Destitute Board), D. R. (Deed Registry), E. (Engineer), E. B. (Education Board),

G. P. (Government Printer), G. S. (Government Storekeeper), G. T. (Goolwa Tramway), G. F. (Gold Fields), H. (Hospital), H. A. (House of Assembly), I. A. (Immigration Agent), I. E. (Intestate Estates), I. S. (Inspector of Sheep), L. A. (Lunatic Asylum), L. C. (Legislative Council), L. L. (Legislative Library), L. T. (Land Titles), M. (Military), M. B. (Marine Board), M. R. (Manager of Railways), M. R. G. (Main Roads Gambierton), N. T. (Northern Territory),

O. A. (Official Assignee), P. (Police), P. A. (Protector of Aborigines), P. O. (Post Office), P. S. (Private Secretary), P. W. (Public Works), R. B. (Road Board), R. G. (Registrar General of Births, &c.), S. (Sheriff), S. C. (Supreme Court), S.G. (Surveyor General), S. M. (Stipendiary Magistrate), S. T. (Superintendent of Telegraph), T. (Treasurer), T. R. (Titles Registry), V. (Volunteers), V. A. (Valuator), V. N. (Vaccination), W. (Waterworks).

**1868-74 Wmk. 6 *Rouletted***

*O1* A1 1p green
*O2* A1 2p pale red
*O3* A6a 2p vermilion
*O4* A2 4p dull violet
*O5* A1 6p slate blue
*O6* A3 9p gray lilac
*O7* A1 1sh brown
*O8* A2 2sh carmine

***Perf. 11½ to 12½xRoulette***

*O9* A1 1p green
*O10* A2 4p dull violet
*O11* A1 6p blue
*O12* A1 1sh brown

***Perf. 10, 11½, 12½ and Compound.***

*O13* A1 1p green
*O14* A5 3p on 4p slate blue (Red)
*O16* A2 4p dull violet
*O17* A1 6p deep blue
*O18* A3 9p violet
*O19* A3 10p on 9p yellow (Blk)
*O20* A1 1sh brown
*O21* A2 2sh carmine

***Rouletted***

**Wmk. 72**

*O22* A6a 2p orange

***Perf. 10 x Roulette***

*O23* A6a 2p orange

***Perf. 10, 11½, 12½ and Compound***

*O24* A6a 2p orange

**Wmk. 70**

***Perf. 10***

*O25* A6a 2p orange
*O26* A2 4p dull violet

### For General Use

Overprinted in Black **O.S.**

***Perf. 10, 11½, 12½ and Compound***

**1874 Wmk. 6**

*O27* A1 1p green 25.00
**a.** Printed on both sides
*O28* A5 3p on 4p ultra 150.00
**a.** No period after "S" 375.00
*O29* A2 4p dull vio 27.50 8.25
**a.** Inverted overprint
**b.** No period after "S" 25.00
**c.** Perf. 10 1,650. 400.00
*O30* A1 6p deep blue 55.00 8.25
**a.** No period after "S" 22.50
*O31* A3 9p violet 250.00 60.00
**a.** No period after "S" 300.00
*O32* A1 1sh red brown 55.00 14.00
**a.** Double overprint 27.50
**b.** No period after "S" 110.00 40.00
*O33* A2 2sh carmine 67.50 14.00
**a.** Double overprint
**b.** No period after "S" 32.50

**1874-75 Wmk. 72**

*O34* A6 1p blue grn 100.00 27.50
**a.** Inverted overprint
*O35* A6a 2p orange 14.00 1.40

**1876-86** **Wmk. 7**

*O36* A5 3p on 4p ultra
*O37* A2 4p dull violet 100.00 30.00
*O38* A2 4p reddish vio 17.50 1.25
- *a.* Double overprint
- *b.* Inverted overprint
- *c.* Dbl. ovpt., one inverted

*O39* A1 6p dark blue 30.00 2.25
- *a.* Double overprint 37.50
- *b.* Inverted overprint

*O40* A1 6p ultramarine 35.00 2.25
- *a.* Double overprint
- *b.* Inverted overprint

*O41* A7 8p on 9p yel brn 425.00 125.00
- *a.* Double overprint 750.00

*O41B* A3 9p violet 900.00
*O42* A1 1sh red brown 25.00 2.75
- *a.* Inverted overprint 150.00 75.00
- *b.* Double overprint

*O43* A2 2sh carmine 87.50 5.50
- *a.* Double overprint 70.00
- *b.* Inverted overprint 75.00

**1880-91** **Wmk. 73**

*O44* A6 1p blue green 5.25 50
- *a.* Inverted overprint 22.50
- *b.* Double overprint 35.00 20.00
- *c.* Dbl. ovpt., one inverted

*O45* A6 1p yellow grn 9.75 50
*O46* A6a 2p orange 5.25 25
- *a.* Inverted overprint 10.00
- *b.* Double overprint 70.00 25.00
- *c.* Overprinted sideways
- *d.* Dbl. ovpt., one inverted
- *e.* Dbl. ovpt., both inverted 57.50

*O47* A6a 2p blood red 52.50 3.75
*O48* A14 2½p on 4p green 35.00 7.50
- *a.* "½" nearer the "2" 75.00
- *b.* Double overprint
- *c.* Pair, one without ovpt.

**1882-90** ***Perf. 10***

*O49* A8 ½p on 1p green 25.00 2.50
- *a.* Inverted overprint

*O50* A11 4p violet 21.00 1.90
*O51* A12 6p blue 12.00 1.25
- *a.* Double overprint

Overprinted in Black **O.S.**

***Perf. 10, 11½, 12½ and Compound***

**1891** **Wmk. 7**

*O52* A1 1sh red brown 30.00 3.50
*O53* A2 2sh carmine 55.00 4.50
- *a.* Double overprint

**1891-95** **Wmk. 73**

*O54* A9 ½p brown 12.00 2.50
*O55* A6 1p blue green 12.00 30
- *a.* Double overprint 50.00

*O56* A6a 2p orange 8.75 30
*O57* A14 2½p on 4p green 19.00 1.75
- *a.* "½" nearer the "2" 52.50 18.00
- *b.* Inverted overprint 100.00

*O58* A11 4p violet 17.50 1.25
- *a.* Double overprint

*O59* A15 5p on 6p red brn 42.50 2.50
*O60* A12 6p blue 9.75 75
- *a.* Double overprint

*Nos. O54-O60 (7)* 121.50 9.35

**1893** ***Perf. 15***

*O61* A9 ½p brown 10.50 1.25
*O62* A6 1p green 3.75 30
*O63* A6a 2p orange 9.75 15
- *a.* Inverted overprint 18.00
- *b.* Double overprint 24.00

*O64* A11 4p gray violet 52.50 1.25
- *a.* Double overprint 21.00

*O65* A17 5p dull violet 30.00 4.50
*O66* A12 6p blue 7.50 45
*Nos. O61-O66 (6)* 114.00 7.90

**1896** ***Perf. 13***

*O67* A9 ½p brown 10.50 1.25
- *a.* Triple overprint

*O68* A6 1p green 9.25 15
*O69* A6a 2p orange 5.75 15
*O70* A16 2½p blue violet 17.50 90
*O71* A11 4p bright vio 11.00 60
- *a.* Double overprint 30.00 40.00

*O72* A17 5p dull violet 15.00 4.25
*O73* A12 6p blue 13.00 90
*Nos. O67-O73 (7)* 82.00 8.20

On No. O67a, one overprint is upright, two sideways.

Same Overprint in Dark Blue

**1891-95** ***Perf. 10***

*O74* A6 1p green 150.00 15.00
*O75* A12 6p blue

Black Overprint

***Perf. 11½, 12½, Clean-Cut***

**1897** **Wmk. 7**

*O76* A1 1sh brown 27.50 4.50
- *a.* Double overprint

Overprinted in Black **O. S.**

**1900** **Wmk. 73** ***Perf. 13***

*O77* A18 ½p yellow grn 4.00 90
*O78* A6 1p carmine rose 4.00 15
- *a.* Inverted overprint
- *b.* Double overprint

*O79* A6a 2p purple 4.00 15
- *a.* Inverted ovpt. 40.00

*O80* A16 2½p dark blue 12.00 1.25
- *a.* Inverted overprint 30.00

*O81* A11 4p violet 6.50 45
- *a.* Inverted ovpt. 125.00

*O82* A12 6p blue 8.00 60
*Nos. O77-O82 (6)* 38.50 3.50

**1901** ***Perf. 10***

*O83* A13 2sh6p violet 3,000. 2,250.
*O84* A13 5sh rose 3,000. 2,250.

On Nos. O77 to O82 the letters "O.S." are 11½mm apart; on Nos. O83 and O84 they are 14½mm apart.

Overprinted in Black **O.S.**

**1903** **Wmk. 72** ***Perf. 11½, 12½***

*O85* A1 1sh red brown 25.00 25.00

Many of the official stamps are found with one or both the periods after "O.S." missing. This occurs more often in the later than in the earlier issues.

## SOUTHERN NIGERIA

LOCATION — In western Africa bordering on the Gulf of Guinea.
GOVT. — A former British Crown Colony and Protectorate.
AREA — 90,896 sq. mi.
POP. — 8,590,545.
CAPITAL — Lagos.

The Protectorate of Southern Nigeria, formed in 1900, absorbed in that year the Niger Coast Protectorate. In 1906 it united with Lagos and became the Colony and Protectorate of Southern Nigeria. An amalgamation was effected in 1914 between Northern and Southern Nigeria to form the Colony and Protectorate of Nigeria. See Nigeria, Northern Nigeria, Niger Coast Protectorate and Lagos.

12 Pence = 1 Shilling
20 Shillings = 1 Pound

Victoria — A1

Edward VII — A2

**Wmk. Crown and C. A. (2)**

**1901** **Typo.** ***Perf. 14***

*1* A1 ½p yel grn & blk 20 22
*2* A1 1p car rose & blk 22 22
*3* A1 2p org brn & blk 55 80
*4* A1 4p ol grn & blk 1.10 1.40
*5* A1 6p red vio & blk 1.50 1.80
*6* A1 1sh blk & gray grn 2.50 2.50
*7* A1 2sh 6p brn & blk 11.00 *15.00*
*8* A1 5sh yel & blk 22.50 *32.50*
*9* A1 10sh vio & blk, *yel* 67.50 *105.00*
*Nos. 1-9 (9)* 107.07 *159.44*

**1903-04**

*10* A2 ½p yel grn & blk 40 20
*11* A2 1p car rose & blk 48 25
*12* A2 2p org brn & blk 1.75 95
*13* A2 2½p ultra & blk ('04) 3.50 70
*14* A2 4p ol grn & blk 80 90
*15* A2 6p red vio & blk 3.75 3.00
*16* A2 1sh blk & gray grn 4.75 4.25
*17* A2 2sh6p brn & blk 5.75 6.00
*18* A2 5sh yel & blk 24.00 30.00
*19* A2 10sh vio & blk, *yel* 24.00 30.00
*20* A2 £1 pur & gray grn 225.00 275.00
*Nos. 10-20 (11)* 294.18 351.25

**1904-07** **Wmk. 3**

**Chalky Paper**

*21* A2 ½p yel grn & blk 12 10
*22* A2 1p car & blk 24 18
*23* A2 2p org brn & blk 40 35
*24* A2 2½p ultra & blk 55 55
*24A* A2 3p vio & org brn ('07) 3.50 1.25
*25* A2 4p ol grn & blk ('05) 1.75 1.40
*26* A2 6p red vio & blk 1.25 1.10
*27* A2 1sh blk & gray grn 1.40 55
*28* A2 2sh6p brn & blk ('05) 3.25 3.25
*29* A2 5sh yel & blk 16.00 20.00
*30* A2 10sh vio & blk, *yel* ('08) 65.00 *90.00*
*31* A2 £1 pur & gray grn ('05) 85.00 *105.00*
*Nos. 21-31 (12)* 178.46 *223.73*

Nos. 23 and 24 are on ordinary paper, Nos. 24A and 25 on chalky, and the other values on both papers.

**1907-10**

**Ordinary Paper**

*32* A2 ½p grn ('08) 20 10
*33* A2 1p carmine 1.25 12
*34* A2 2p gray 50 65
*35* A2 2½p ultra 90 90

**Chalky Paper**

*36* A2 3p vio, *yel* 65 32
*37* A2 4p scar & blk, *yel* 60 60
*38* A2 6p red vio & dl vio 1.50 90
*39* A2 1sh blk, *green* 3.25 60
*40* A2 2sh6p car & blk, *bl* 4.00 1.10
*41* A2 5sh scar & grn, *yel* 14.00 18.00
*42* A2 10sh red & grn, *grn* 40.00 47.50
*43* A2 £1 blk & vio, *red* 82.50 100.00
*Nos. 32-43 (12)* 149.35 170.79

**1910** **Redrawn**

**Ordinary Paper**

*44* A2 1p carmine 14 10

In the redrawn stamp the "1" of "1d" is not as thick as in No. 33 but the "d" is taller and broader.

King George V — A3

**1912**

*45* A3 ½p green 35 14
*46* A3 1p carmine 22 6
*47* A3 2p gray 52 52
*48* A3 2½p ultra 52 60
*49* A3 3p vio, *yel* 35 25
*50* A3 4p scar & blk, *yel* 70 80
*51* A3 6p red vio & dl vio 1.10 60
*52* A3 1sh blk, *green* 80 60
*53* A3 2sh6p red & blk, *bl* 6.00 6.50
*54* A3 5sh red & grn, *yel* 10.00 14.00
*55* A3 10sh red & grn, *grn* 32.50 37.50
*56* A3 £1 blk & vio, *red* 80.00 97.50
*Nos. 45-56 (12)* 133.06 159.07

Stamps of Southern Nigeria were replaced in 1914 by those of Nigeria.

## SOUTHERN RHODESIA

LOCATION — In southeastern Africa between Northern Rhodesia and Mozambique.
GOVT. — British Colony.
AREA — 150,333 sq. mi.
POP. — 4,010,000 (est. 1963).
CAPITAL — Salisbury.

Prior to 1923 this territory was administered by the British South Africa Company. The colony was created in that year by the British Government at the request of the inhabitants. In 1953, Southern Rhodesia joined Northern Rhodesia and Nyasaland to form the Federation of Rhodesia and Nyasaland. When the Federation dissolved at the end of 1963, Southern Rhodesia again became an internally self-governing colony. See Rhodesia and Northern Rhodesia.

12 Pence = 1 Shilling
20 Shillings = 1 Pound

**Catalogue values for unused stamps in this country are for Never Hinged items, beginning with Scott 56 in the regular postage section and Scott J1 in the postage due section.**

King George V — A1

**1924-30** **Unwmk.** **Engr.** ***Perf. 14***

*1* A1 ½p dk grn 18 10
- *a.* Vertical pair, imperf. between 750.00
- *b.* Horizontal pair, imperf. between 750.00

*2* A1 1p scarlet 15 5
- *a.* Horiz. pair, imperf. between 950.00
- *b.* Perf. 12½ (coil) ('30) 11.00 *95.00*

*3* A1 1½p bis brn 55 12
- *a.* Horiz. pair, imperf. btwn. *10,000.*
- *b.* Vertical pair, imperf. between *3,000.*

*4* A1 2p vio blk & blk 90 25
- *a.* Horizontal pair, imperf. between *6,000.*

*5* A1 3p dp bl 2.00 1.50
*6* A1 4p org red & blk 2.50 1.50
- *a.* Horizontal pair, imperf. between

*7* A1 6p lil & blk 2.25 1.50
- *a.* Horiz. pair, imperf. btwn. *7,500.*

*8* A1 8p gray grn & vio 11.00 16.00
*9* A1 10p rose red & bl 11.00 16.00
*10* A1 1sh turq bl & blk 2.00 1.50
*11* A1 1sh6p yel & blk 14.00 16.00
- *a.* Horiz. pair, imperf. between *3,500.*

*12* A1 2sh brn & blk 16.00 16.00
*13* A1 2sh6p blk brn & bl 35.00 37.50
- *a.* Horiz. pair, imperf. between *5,000.*

*14* A1 5sh bl grn & bl 65.00 65.00
*Nos. 1-14 (14)* 162.53 173.02

George V A2

Victoria Falls A3

**1931-37** ***Perf. 11½, 12(1p)***

*16* A2 ½p dp grn ('33) 16 10
- *a.* Bklt. pane of 6 ('32) *150.00*
- *b.* Perf. 12 25 15
- *c.* Perf. 14 ('35) 25 10

*17* A2 1p scarlet 12 6
- *a.* Bklt. pane of 6 ('32) *150.00*
- *b.* Perf. 11½ ('33) 50 6
- *c.* Perf. 14 ('35) 25 6

*18* A2 1½p dp brn ('32) 55 20
- *a.* Bklt. pane of 6 ('32) *600.00*
- *b.* Perf. 12 ('33) 30.00 *50.00*

**Typo.** ***Perf. 14½x14***

*19* A3 2p blk brn & blk 2.25 1.65
*20* A3 3p dark blue 9.75 9.25

***Perf. 12, 11½ (10p)***

**Engr.**

*21* A2 4p org red & blk 1.75 42
- *a.* Perf. 14 ('37) 27.50 27.50
- *b.* Perf. 11½ ('35) 6.00 3.25

*22* A2 6p rose lil & blk 2.50 40
- *a.* Perf. 14 ('36) 14.00 65
- *b.* Perf. 11½ ('33) 9.00 65

*23* A2 8p grn & vio 2.50 2.00
- *a.* Perf. 11½ ('34) 19.00 *27.50*

*24* A2 9p gray grn & ver ('34) 9.00 9.25
*25* A2 10p car & ultra ('33) 4.50 2.75
- *a.* Perf. 12 4.75 3.50

*26* A2 1sh turq bl & blk 3.50 1.25
- *a.* Perf. 11½ ('36) 25.00 12.00
- *b.* Perf. 14 ('37) 165.00 75.00

*27* A2 1sh6p ocher & blk 12.00 9.25
- *a.* Perf. 11½ ('36) 40.00 40.00

*28* A2 2sh dk brn & blk 15.00 6.75
- *a.* Perf. 11½ ('33) 47.50 25.00

*29* A2 2sh6p ol brn & ultra 27.50 27.50
*a.* Perf. 11½ ('33) 40.00 27.50
*30* A2 5sh bl grn & ultra 50.00 47.50
*Nos. 16-30 (15)* 141.08 118.33

Victoria Falls — A4

**1932, May** ***Perf. 12½***
*31* A4 2p dk brn & grn 70 15
*32* A4 3p dk bl 3.00 55
*a.* Vert. pair, imperf. horiz. *9,000. 10,000.*

See Nos. 37-37A.

**Silver Jubilee Issue**

Victoria Falls and George V A5

**1935, May 6** ***Perf. 11x12***
*33* A5 1p car rose & ol 40 35
*34* A5 2p blk brn & lt grn 1.10 1.00
*35* A5 3p bl & vio 6.25 *8.00*
*36* A5 6p dp vio & blk 7.75 *9.00*

25th anniv. of the reign of George V.

"Postage and Revenue" A6

**1935-41** ***Perf. 14***
*37* A6 2p dk brn & grn ('41) 25 6
*b.* Perf. 12½ 1.50 1.50
*37A* A6 3p dp bl ('38) 75 20

Queen Elizabeth, George VI — A7

**1937, May 12** ***Perf. 12½***
*38* A7 1p car rose & gray grn 18 18
*39* A7 2p brn & grn 25 25
*40* A7 3p lt bl & vio 1.40 1.40
*41* A7 6p red vio & blk 95 95

Issued in commemoration of the coronation of King George VI and Queen Elizabeth.

King George VI — A8

**1937, Nov. 25** ***Perf. 14***
*42* A8 ½p yel grn 6 5
*43* A8 1p red 8 5
*44* A8 1½p red brn 10 6
*45* A8 4p org red 15 8
*46* A8 6p dk gray 25 8
*47* A8 8p bl grn 85 35
*48* A8 9p blue 42 32
*49* A8 10p violet 45 40
*50* A8 1sh grn & blk 55 12
*51* A8 1sh6p ocher & blk 2.00 35
*52* A8 2sh brn & blk 2.25 30
*53* A8 2sh6p vio & bl 2.75 45
*54* A8 5sh grn & bl 7.25 65
*Nos. 42-54 (13)* 17.16 3.26

**Catalogue values for unused stamps in this section, from this point to the end of the section, are for Never Hinged items.**

Seal of British South Africa Co. — A9

Fort Salisbury, 1890 — A10

Cecil John Rhodes — A11

Pioneer Fort and Mail Coach A12

Rhodes Makes Peace, 1896 — A13

Victoria Falls Bridge — A14

Sir Charles Coghlan — A15

Queen Victoria, George VI, Lobengula's Kraal and Government House A16

**Unwmk.**

**1940, June 3** **Engr.** ***Perf. 14***
*56* A9 ½p dp grn & dl vio 20 18
*57* A10 1p red & vio bl 20 18
*58* A11 1½p cop brn & blk 25 25
*59* A12 2p pur & brt grn 25 25
*60* A13 3p dk bl & blk 42 30
*61* A14 4p brn & brt grn 1.00 70
*62* A15 6p sep & dl grn 1.40 70
*63* A16 1sh dk bl & brt grn 2.25 1.10
*Nos. 56-63 (8)* 5.97 3.66

50th anniv. of the founding of Southern Rhodesia by Cecil John Rhodes.

Scott's editorial staff cannot undertake to identify, authenticate or appraise stamps and postal markings.

Pioneer — A17

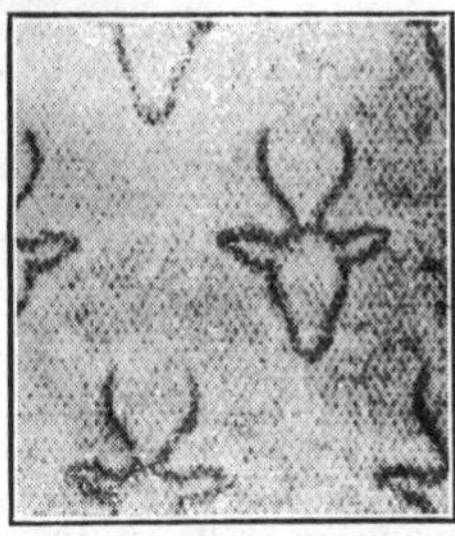

Wmk. 201- Multiple Springbok's Head

**1943, Nov. 1** **Photo.** **Wmk. 201**
*64* A17 2p Prus grn & choc 15 15

Issued to commemorate the 50th anniversary of Matabeleland under British control.

Princess Elizabeth and Princess Margaret Rose A18

King George VI and Queen Elizabeth A19

**Unwmk.**

**1947, Apr. 1** **Engr.** ***Perf. 14***
*65* A18 ½p dk grn & blk 9 9
*66* A19 1p car & blk 12 12

Issued to commemorate the visit of the British Royal Family, April, 1947.

**Victory Issue**

Queen Elizabeth — A20

George VI — A21

Princess Elizabeth A22

Princess Margaret Rose A23

**1947, May 8**
*67* A20 1p dp car 10 9
*68* A21 2p sl blk 18 18
*69* A22 3p dp bl 22 22
*70* A23 6p red org 38 38

Victory of the Allied Nations in WW II.

**UPU Issue**

Common Design Types

**Engr.; Name Typo.**

***Perf. 11x11½***

**1949, Oct. 10** **Wmk. 4**
*71* CD307 2p slate black 55 45
*72* CD308 3p slate blue 1.40 1.40

75th anniv. of the UPU.

Queen Victoria and King George VI A24

**Unwmk.**

**1950, Sept. 12** **Engr.** ***Perf. 14***
*73* A24 2p choc & bl grn 14 10

60th anniversary of Rhodesia.

Hospital, Doctor and Natives A25

Designs: 1p, African Scene. 2p, Native Houses, Modern City and Cecil Rhodes. 4½p, Dam and Natives. 1sh, Transportation.

**1953, Apr. 15**
*74* A25 ½p dk brn & bl 22 12
*75* A25 1p bl grn & fawn 22 10
*76* A25 2p vio & dk bl grn 35 22
*77* A25 4½p dk bl & bl grn 1.65 85
*78* A25 1sh chnt & blk 2.50 95
*Nos. 74-78 (5)* 4.94 2.24

No. 77 is inscribed Matabeleland Diamond Jubilee.

Type of Nyasaland Prot., 1953

**1953, May 30** ***Perf. 14x13½***
*79* A17 6p purple 60 60

Nos. 74-79 were issued to commemorate the Central African Cecil Rhodes Centenary Exhibition.

**Coronation Issue**

Elizabeth II — A26

**1953, June 1** ***Perf. 12x12½***
*80* A26 2sh6p cerise 5.00 5.00

Sable Antelope — A27

Rhodes' Grave — A28

Farm Worker — A29

Designs: 1p, Tobacco planter. 4p, Flame lily. 4½p, Victoria Falls. 6p, Baobab tree. 9p, Lion. 1sh, Zimbabwe ruins. 2sh, Birchenough Bridge. 2sh 6p, Kariba Gorge. 5sh, Basket maker. 10sh, Balancing rocks. £1, Arms.

***Perf. 14x13½, 13½x14***

**1953, Aug. 31**

**Portrait in Various Positions**
*81* A27 ½p rose lake & dk ol grn 10 8
*82* A27 1p choc & grn 10 6
*83* A28 2p rose vio & org brn 18 8

**Size: 28x22½mm**

| No. | Type | Denom. | Color | Unused | Used |
|---|---|---|---|---|---|
| 84 | A29 | 3p | car & sep | 30 | 22 |
| 85 | A29 | 4p | gray, brn, car & grn | 35 | 22 |
| 86 | A29 | 4½p | ultra & blk | 45 | 38 |
| 87 | A28 | 6p | aqua & ol | 45 | 25 |
| 88 | A29 | 9p | org brn & dp bl | 95 | 55 |
| 89 | A29 | 1sh | grnsh bl & rose vio | 75 | 45 |
| 90 | A29 | 2sh | red & rose vio | 3.50 | 1.65 |
| 91 | A29 | 2sh6p | org brn & ol grn | 4.75 | 2.00 |
| 92 | A28 | 5s | dk grn & org brn | 13.00 | 7.50 |

**Size: 37x27mm**

| No. | Type | Denom. | Color | Unused | Used |
|---|---|---|---|---|---|
| 93 | A29 | 10sh | ol grn & red brn | 22.50 | 22.50 |
| 94 | A29 | £1 | dk gray & car | 40.00 | 40.00 |
| | | | *Nos. 81-94 (14)* | 87.38 | 75.94 |

Ansellia Orchid — A30

Designs: ½p, Corn. 1p, Cape buffalo. 2p, Tobacco. 3p, Kudu. 4p, Oranges. 6p, Flame lily. 1sh, Emeralds. 1sh3p, Aloe. 2sh, Lake Kyle. 2sh6p, Tiger fish. 5sh, Cattle. 10sh, Guinea fowl. £1, Arms of Southern Rhodesia.

**1964, Feb. 19 Photo. *Perf. 14½***

**Size: 23x19mm**

| No. | Type | Denom. | Color | Unused | Used |
|---|---|---|---|---|---|
| 95 | A30 | ½p | lt bl, yel & grn | 6 | 6 |
| 96 | A30 | 1p | pur & ocher | 6 | 5 |
| a. | | | pur omitted | 650.00 | |
| 97 | A30 | 2p | vio & org yel | 8 | 5 |
| 98 | A30 | 3p | lt bl & choc | 9 | 5 |
| 99 | A30 | 4p | sl grn & org | 14 | 8 |

***Perf. 13½x13***

**Size: 27x23mm**

| No. | Type | Denom. | Color | Unused | Used |
|---|---|---|---|---|---|
| 100 | A30 | 6p | dl grn, red & yel | 18 | 12 |
| 101 | A30 | 9p | ol grn, yel & brn | 45 | 25 |
| 102 | A30 | 1sh | ocher & brt grn | 45 | 15 |
| a. | | | grn omitted | 1,250. | |
| 103 | A30 | 1sh3p | grn, vio & dk red | 1.10 | 22 |
| 104 | A30 | 2sh | dl bl & yel | 1.90 | 60 |
| 105 | A30 | 2sh6p | ultra & red | 2.00 | 80 |
| a. | | | red omitted | 375.00 | |

***Perf. 14½x14***

**Size: 32x27mm**

| No. | Type | Denom. | Color | Unused | Used |
|---|---|---|---|---|---|
| 106 | A30 | 5sh | bl, grn, ocher lt brn | 4.50 | 2.50 |
| 107 | A30 | 10sh | ocher, blk, red & bl | 13.00 | 6.75 |
| 108 | A30 | £1 | rose, sep, ocher & grn | 25.00 | 15.00 |
| | | | *Nos. 95-108 (14)* | 49.01 | 26.68 |

Nos. 95-108 with overprint "Independence 11th November 1965" are listed as Rhodesia Nos. 208-221.

Stamps of Southern Rhodesia were replaced in 1965 by those of Rhodesia (formerly Southern Rhodesia).

---

## POSTAGE DUE STAMPS

**Catalogue values for unused stamps in this section, from this point to the end of the section, are for Never Hinged items.**

Great Britain Postage Due Stamps of 1938-51 Overprinted in Black

SOUTHERN RHODESIA

**1951 Wmk. 251 *Perf. 14x14½.***

| No. | Type | Denom. | Color | Unused | Used |
|---|---|---|---|---|---|
| J1 | D1 | ½p | emerald | 3.00 | 4.50 |
| J2 | D1 | 1p | vio bl | 1.90 | 75 |
| J3 | D1 | 2p | blk brn | 3.75 | 1.90 |
| J4 | D1 | 3p | violet | 3.75 | 1.90 |
| J5 | D1 | 4p | brt bl | 1.90 | 3.50 |
| a. | | | 4p slate green | 175.00 | 225.00 |
| J6 | D1 | 1sh | blue | 3.75 | 1.90 |
| | | | *Nos. J1-J6 (6)* | 18.05 | 14.45 |

# SOUTH GEORGIA

LOCATION — Island in South Atlantic Ocean, 1,100 mi. east of Tierra del Fuego.

GOVT. — Dependency of Falkland Islands.

AREA — 1,450 sq. mi.

POP. — 22 (1975).

CAPITAL — Grytviken Harbor (chief town)

South Georgia remained a dependency of the Falkland Islands in 1962 when three other dependencies became Antarctic Territory, a separate colony. See Falkland Islands Dependencies stamps starting with No. 1L106, as well as Nos. 3L1-3L8.

12 Pence = 1 Shilling
20 Shillings = 1 Pound
100 Pence = 1 Pound (1971)

**Catalogue values for all unused stamps in this country are for Never Hinged items.**

Reindeer — A1

Sperm Whale — A2

Designs: 1p, South Sandwich Islands map. 2½p, Penguins. 3p, Fur seals. 4p, Finback whale and ship. 5½p, Elephant seals. 6p, Sooty albatross. 9p, Whaling ship. 1sh, Leopard seal. 2sh, Shackleton's cross. 2sh6p, Wandering albatross. 5sh, Elephant and fur seals. 10sh, Plankton and kril! (shrimp). £1, Blue whale.

**Wmk. 314 Upright**

**1963, July 10 Engr. *Perf. 15***

| No. | Type | Denom. | Color | Unused | Used |
|---|---|---|---|---|---|
| 1 | A1 | ½p | dl red | 30 | 30 |
| a. | | | Perf. 14x15 ('67) | 1.40 | 2.00 |
| b. | | | Watermark sideways ('70) | 1.40 | 3.75 |
| 2 | A2 | 1p | vio bl | 25 | 22 |
| 3 | A2 | 2p | bl grn | 35 | 25 |
| 4 | A1 | 2½p | black | 50 | 42 |
| 5 | A2 | 3p | olive | 60 | 42 |
| 6 | A1 | 4p | green | 70 | 50 |
| 7 | A1 | 5½p | dl vio | 75 | 75 |
| 8 | A2 | 6p | orange | 75 | 60 |
| 9 | A1 | 9p | blue | 1.40 | 1.10 |
| 10 | A1 | 1sh | lilac | 1.65 | 1.50 |
| 11 | A1 | 2sh | cit & lt bl | 7.25 | 5.75 |
| 12 | A1 | 2sh6p | blue | 7.25 | 7.25 |
| 13 | A1 | 5sh | ocher | 15.00 | 15.00 |
| 14 | A2 | 10sh | rose cl | 37.50 | 32.50 |
| 15 | A1 | £1 | ultra | 105.00 | 85.00 |

**1969, Dec. 1**

Design: £1, King penguins.

| No. | Type | Denom. | Color | Unused | Used |
|---|---|---|---|---|---|
| 16 | A2 | £1 | sl grn ('69) | 21.00 | 30.00 |
| | | | *Nos. 1-16 (16)* | 200.25 | 181.56 |

Stamps and Type of 1963 Surcharged with New Value (Decimal Currency) and 3 Bars

**Wmk. 314 Upright; Sideways on ½p**

**1971, Feb. 15 *Perf. 15***

| No. | Type | Description | Unused | Used |
|---|---|---|---|---|
| 17 | A1 | ½p on ½p dl red | 65 | 80 |
| a. | | Wmk. upright ('73) | 50 | 60 |
| 18 | A2 | 1p on 1p vio bl | 75 | 95 |
| a. | | Wmk. sideways ('76) | 2.50 | 3.00 |
| 19 | A1 | 1½p on 5½p dl vio | 60 | 75 |
| 20 | A2 | 2p on 2p bl grn | 50 | 60 |
| 21 | A1 | 2½p on 2½p blk | 60 | 75 |
| 22 | A2 | 3p on 3p ol | 65 | 80 |
| 23 | A1 | 4p on 4p grn | 75 | 95 |
| 24 | A2 | 5p on 6p org | 1.10 | 1.40 |
| 25 | A1 | 6p on 9p bl | 45 | 55 |
| 26 | A1 | 7½p on 1sh lil | 1.90 | 2.25 |
| 27 | A1 | 10p on 2sh cit & lt bl | 11.00 | 11.00 |
| 28 | A1 | 15p on 2sh6p bl | 15.00 | 19.00 |
| 29 | A1 | 25p on 5sh ocher | 11.00 | 11.00 |
| 30 | A2 | 50p on 10sh rose cl | 37.50 | 40.00 |
| a. | | Wmk. sideways ('76) | 37.50 | 37.50 |
| | | *Nos. 17-30 (14)* | 82.45 | 90.80 |

Two types of surcharge are found on ½p, 1p, 1½p and 50p.

**1977 Wmk. 373**

| No. | Type | Description | Unused | Used |
|---|---|---|---|---|
| 17b | A1 | ½p on ½p dl red | 30 | 30 |
| 18b | A2 | 1p on 1p vio bl | 80 | 80 |
| 19b | A1 | 1½p on 5½p dl vio | 1.25 | 1.25 |
| 21b | A1 | 2½p on 2½p blk | 1.40 | 1.40 |
| 22b | A2 | 3p on 3p ol | 1.50 | 1.50 |
| 23b | A1 | 4p on 4p grn | 4.00 | 4.00 |
| 24b | A2 | 5p on 6p org | 2.50 | 2.50 |
| 26b | A1 | 7½p on 1sh lil | 8.00 | 8.00 |
| 27b | A1 | 10p on 2sh cit & lt bl | 8.00 | 8.00 |
| 28b | A1 | 15p on 2sh6p bl | 8.00 | 8.00 |
| 29b | A1 | 25p on 5sh ocher | 8.00 | 8.00 |
| 30b | A2 | 50p on 10sh lil rose ('79) | 16.00 | 16.00 |
| | | *Nos. 17b-30b (12)* | 59.75 | 59.75 |

Ernest Shackleton and "Quest" — A3

Designs: 1½p, "Endurance" in ice of Weddell Sea. 5p, Launching of sailboat "James Caird." 10p, Route of "James Caird" to South Georgia.

**1972, Jan. 5 Litho. *Perf. 13½***

| No. | Type | Description | Unused | Used |
|---|---|---|---|---|
| 31 | A3 | 1½p vio bl, blk & yel | 65 | 65 |
| 32 | A3 | 5p bl grn, blk & yel | 1.10 | 1.10 |
| 33 | A3 | 10p lt bl & blk | 2.25 | 2.25 |
| 34 | A3 | 20p multi | 4.50 | 4.50 |

Sir Ernest Shackleton (1874-1922), explorer of Antarctica.

**Silver Wedding Issue, 1972**

Common Design Type

Design: Queen Elizabeth II, Prince Philip, elephant seal and king penguins.

**1972, Nov. 20 Photo. *Perf. 14x14½***

| No. | Type | Description | Unused | Used |
|---|---|---|---|---|
| 35 | CD324 | 5p sl grn & multi | 95 | 95 |
| 36 | CD324 | 10p vio & multi | 1.90 | 1.90 |

**Princess Anne's Wedding Issue**

Common Design Type

**1973, Dec. 1 Litho. *Perf. 14***

| No. | Type | Description | Unused | Used |
|---|---|---|---|---|
| 37 | CD325 | 5p cit & multi | 38 | 38 |
| 38 | CD325 | 15p sl & multi | 1.10 | 1.10 |

Churchill, Parliament and Big Ben — A4

Design: 25p, Churchill and battleship.

**1974, Dec. 14 Litho. *Perf. 14½***

| No. | Type | Description | Unused | Used |
|---|---|---|---|---|
| 39 | A4 | 15p vio bl & multi | 1.50 | 1.50 |
| 40 | A4 | 25p org & multi | 2.25 | 2.25 |
| a. | | Souvenir sheet of 2 | 6.75 | 6.75 |

Sir Winston Churchill (1874-1965), birth centenary. No. 40a contains one each of Nos. 39-40, black and gold margin showing Churchill walking. Size: 120x97mm.

Capt. James Cook — A5

Cook's "Possession" — A6

Design: 16p, Possession Bay.

**1975, Apr. 26 Wmk. 314**

| No. | Type | Description | Unused | Used |
|---|---|---|---|---|
| 41 | A5 | 2p multi | 1.50 | 1.00 |
| 42 | A6 | 8p multi | 2.50 | 2.00 |
| 43 | A6 | 16p multi | 4.00 | 3.75 |

Bicentenary of Capt. Cook's discovery of South Georgia.

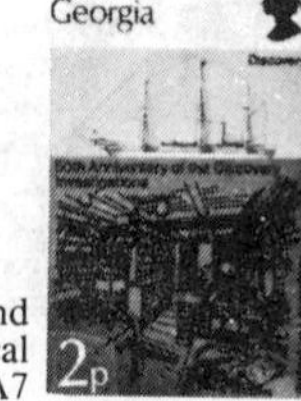


"Discovery" and Biological Laboratory — A7

Designs: 8p, "William Scoresby" and Nansen-Pettersson water sampling bottles. 11p, "Discovery II" and plankton net. 25p, Biological station and krill (shrimp).

**Wmk. 373**

**1976, Dec. 21 Litho. *Perf. 14***

| No. | Type | Description | Unused | Used |
|---|---|---|---|---|
| 44 | A7 | 2p multi | 55 | 45 |
| 45 | A7 | 8p multi | 1.40 | 1.10 |
| 46 | A7 | 11p multi | 1.65 | 1.65 |
| 47 | A7 | 25p multi | 3.75 | 3.75 |

25th anniversary of the biological investigations of the "Discovery."

Queen with Regalia and Westminster Abbey — A8

Designs: 6p, Prince Philip visiting Shackleton Memorial, 1957. 33p, Queen in procession after coronation.

**1977, Feb. 7 *Perf. 13½x14***

| No. | Type | Description | Unused | Used |
|---|---|---|---|---|
| 48 | A8 | 6p multi | 35 | 35 |
| 49 | A8 | 11p multi | 60 | 60 |
| 50 | A8 | 33p multi | 1.75 | 1.75 |

25th anniv. of the reign of Elizabeth II.

**Elizabeth II Coronation Anniversary Issue**

Common Design Types

**Souvenir Sheet**

**Unwmk.**

**1978, June 2 Litho. *Perf. 15***

| No. | Description | Unused | Used |
|---|---|---|---|
| 51 | Sheet of 6 | 4.50 | 6.50 |
| a. | CD326 25p *Panther of Henry VI* | 75 | 75 |
| b. | CD327 25p *Elizabeth II* | 75 | 75 |
| c. | CD328 25p *Fur seal* | 75 | 75 |

No. 51 contains 2 se-tenant strips of Nos. 51a-51c, separated by horizontal gutter with commemorative and descriptive inscriptions and showing central part of coronation procession with coach. Size: 100x135mm.

*South Georgia stamps can be mounted in Scott's British South Atlantic Album.*

Resolution
A9

Cook's voyages: 6p, Map of South Georgia and South Sandwich Islands with . Cook's route. 11p, King penguin, drawing by Forster. 25p, . Cook after Flaxman/Wedgwood medallion.

**1979, Feb. 14 — Litho. — *Perf. 11***

| | | | | |
|---|---|---|---|---|
| 52 | A9 | 3p multi | 60 | 60 |
| 53 | A9 | 6p multi | 80 | 80 |
| 54 | A9 | 11p multi | 1.50 | 1.25 |

**Lithographed; Embossed**

| | | | | |
|---|---|---|---|---|
| 55 | A9 | 25p multi | 1.90 | 1.50 |

Common Design Types pictured in section before Great Britain.

## SOUTH-WEST AFRICA

### (Namibia)

LOCATION — In southwestern Africa between Angola and Cape of Good Hope, bordering on the Atlantic Ocean.

GOVT. — Administered by the Republic of South Africa under a mandate of the League of Nations.

AREA — 318,261 sq. mi.

POP. — 1,039,800 (1982).

CAPITAL — Windhoek.

Formerly a German possession, South-West Africa was occupied by South African forces in 1915 and by the Treaty of Versailles was mandated to the Union of South Africa.

12 Pence = 1 Shilling
20 Shillings = 1 Pound
100 Cents = 1 Rand (1961)

**Catalogue values for unused stamps in this country are for Never Hinged items, beginning with Scott 125 in the regular postage section, Scott B1 in the semi-postal section, Scott J86 in the postage due section, and Scott O13 in the officials section.**

Stamps of South Africa, Nos. 2-3, 5 and 9-16, Overprinted in English or Afrikaans alternately throughout the sheets.

**Major-number listings and values of Nos. 1-40 and 85-93 are for singles with either overprint.**

Setting I

**South West** — **Zuid-West**

**Africa.** a — **Afrika.** b

"South West" 14½mm wide.
"Zuid-West" 13mm wide.
Overprint Spaced 14mm

**1923, Jan. 2 — Wmk. 177 — *Perf. 14***

| | | | | |
|---|---|---|---|---|
| 1 | A2 | ½p green | 8 | 6 |
| a. | | Pair | 45 | 65 |
| 2 | A2 | 1p red | 8 | 6 |
| a. | | Pair | 55 | 65 |
| b. | | Inverted overprint | 140.00 | |
| c. | | As "b." pair | 900.00 | |
| d. | | "Af.rica" | 315.00 | |
| e. | | Double overprint | 1,000. | |
| f. | | As "c." pair | | |
| 3 | A2 | 2p dl vio | 8 | 6 |
| a. | | Pair | 75 | 1.40 |
| b. | | Inverted overprint | 110.00 | |
| c. | | As "b." pair | 1,000. | |
| 4 | A2 | 3p ultra | 18 | 18 |
| a. | | Pair | 3.50 | 5.00 |
| 5 | A2 | 4p ol grn & org | 30 | 22 |
| a. | | Pair | 4.25 | 5.00 |
| 6 | A2 | 6p vio & blk | 35 | 35 |
| a. | | Pair | 5.00 | 5.75 |
| 7 | A2 | 1sh orange | 80 | 80 |
| a. | | Pair | 10.50 | 12.50 |
| 8 | A2 | 1sh3p violet | 1.00 | 1.00 |
| a. | | Pair | 15.00 | 19.00 |
| b. | | Inverted overprint | 40.00 | |
| c. | | As "b." pair | 300.00 | |
| 9 | A2 | 2sh6p grn & cl | 3.50 | 3.50 |
| a. | | Pair | 55.00 | 80.00 |
| 10 | A2 | 5sh bl & cl | 12.50 | 13.00 |
| a. | | Pair | 150.00 | 175.00 |
| 11 | A2 | 10sh ol grn & bl | 100.00 | 55.00 |
| a. | | Pair | 2,250. | 2,500. |
| 12 | A2 | £1 red & dp grn | 55.00 | 45.00 |
| a. | | Pair | 1,350. | 1,500. |
| | | *Nos. 1-12 (12)* | 173.87 | 119.23 |

Most values exist with "t" of "West" partly or totally missing. Vertical displacement in overprinting accounts for the copies with only one line of overprint.

See note after No. 27.

Setting II

**South West** — **Zuid-West**

**Africa.** c — **Afrika.** d

Words Same Width as Setting I
Overprint Spaced 9½-10mm

**1923, Apr.**

| | | | | |
|---|---|---|---|---|
| 13 | A2 | 5sh bl & cl | 13.00 | 15.00 |
| a. | | Pair | 125.00 | 200.00 |
| b. | | As "a." without period after "Afrika" | 3,250. | |
| 14 | A2 | 10sh ol grn & bl | 37.50 | 27.50 |
| a. | | Pair | 1,150. | 1,250. |
| b. | | As "a" without period after "Afrika" | 4,000. | 4,000. |
| 15 | A2 | £1 red & grn | 55.00 | 55.00 |
| a. | | Pair | 1,600. | 1,900. |
| b. | | As "a." without period after "Afrika" | 8,000. | |

Setting III

**South West** — **Zuidwest**

**Africa.** a — **Afrika.** f

English as in Setting I
"Zuidwest" 11mm wide, No Hyphen
Overprint Spaced 14mm

**1923-24**

| | | | | |
|---|---|---|---|---|
| 16 | A2 (f) | ½p grn ('24) | 6 | 6 |
| a. | | Pair | 85 | 1.00 |
| 17 | A2 (f) | 1p red | 6 | 6 |
| a. | | Pair | 1.00 | 1.10 |
| 18 | A2 (f) | 2p dl vio | 6 | 6 |
| a. | | Pair | 1.10 | 1.10 |
| b. | | Dbl. ovpt. (f or a) | 90.00 | |
| c. | | As "b." pair | 1,000. | |
| 19 | A2 (f) | 3p ultra | 10 | 16 |
| a. | | Pair | 1.50 | 2.00 |
| 20 | A2 (f) | 4p ol grn & org | 14 | 18 |
| a. | | Pair | 2.00 | 3.75 |
| 21 | A2 (f) | 6p vio & blk | 28 | 28 |
| a. | | Pair | 4.75 | 6.00 |
| 22 | A2 (f) | 1sh orange | 45 | 55 |
| a. | | Pair | 6.00 | 9.00 |
| 23 | A2 (f) | 1sh3p violet | 55 | 55 |
| a. | | Pair | 11.00 | 15.00 |
| 24 | A2 (f) | 2sh6p grn & cl | 2.75 | 3.00 |
| a. | | Pair | 30.00 | 40.00 |
| 25 | A2 (f) | 5sh bl & cl | 5.50 | 5.50 |
| a. | | Pair | 55.00 | 67.50 |
| 26 | A2 (f) | 10sh ol grn & bl | 7.75 | 8.50 |
| a. | | Pair | 165.00 | 240.00 |
| 27 | A2 (f) | £1 red & grn | 22.50 | 25.00 |
| a. | | Pair | 315.00 | 425.00 |
| | | *Nos. 16-27 (12)* | 40.20 | 43.90 |

The English overprint of Setting III is the same as that of Setting I. The value of an English single from either setting is the lower of the two values given for the major-number listings.

Setting IV

**South West** — **Zuidwest**

**Africa.** g — **Afrika.** h

"South West" 16mm wide
"Zuidwest" 12mm wide
Overprint Spaced 14mm

**1924, July**

| | | | | |
|---|---|---|---|---|
| 28 | A2 | 2sh6p grn & cl | 13.00 | 13.00 |
| a. | | Pair | 165.00 | 225.00 |

Setting VI

**South West** — **Zuidwest**

**Africa.** k — **Afrika.** l

"South West" 16, 16½mm wide
"Zuidwest" 12½mm wide
Overprint Spaced 9½mm

**1924, Dec.**

| | | | | |
|---|---|---|---|---|
| 29 | A2 | ½p green | 8 | 10 |
| a. | | Pair | 1.00 | 2.50 |
| 30 | A2 | 1p red | 10 | 10 |
| a. | | Pair | 70 | 1.50 |
| 31 | A2 | 2p dl vio | 12 | 10 |
| a. | | Pair | 1.00 | 2.00 |
| 32 | A2 | 3p ultra | 15 | 20 |
| a. | | Pair | 2.50 | 5.00 |
| 33 | A2 | 4p ol grn & org | 15 | 15 |
| a. | | Pair | 2.50 | 6.00 |
| 34 | A2 | 6p vio & blk | 32 | 40 |
| a. | | Pair | 3.50 | 7.25 |
| 35 | A2 | 1sh orange | 50 | 52 |
| a. | | Pair | 7.25 | 11.50 |
| 36 | A2 | 1sh3p violet | 85 | 85 |
| a. | | Pair | 11.50 | 16.00 |
| 37 | A2 | 2sh6p grn & cl | 2.25 | 2.50 |
| a. | | Pair | 35.00 | 40.00 |
| 38 | A2 | 5sh bl & cl | 4.50 | 4.00 |
| a. | | Pair | 65.00 | 100.00 |
| 39 | A2 | 10sh ol grn & bl | 8.00 | 8.25 |
| a. | | Pair | 100.00 | 115.00 |
| 40 | A2 | £1 red & grn | 27.50 | 30.00 |
| a. | | Pair | 450.00 | 600.00 |
| | | *Nos. 29-40 (12)* | 44.52 | 47.17 |
| | | *Nos. 29a-40a (12)* | 679.95 | 906.75 |

Setting VII
South Africa Nos. 21-22 Overprinted:

**SOUTH WEST AFRICA** m — **SUIDWES-AFRIKA** n

**SOUTH WEST AFRICA** o

**1926-27 — Wmk. 201 — *Imperf.***

| | | | | |
|---|---|---|---|---|
| 81 | A3 (m) | 4p bl gray | 65 | 90 |
| 82 | A3 (n) | 4p bl gray | 65 | 90 |
| 83 | A3 (o) | 4p bl gray ('27) | 5.25 | 5.50 |

Nos. 81-83 were not officially perforated, but firms and individuals applied various forms of perforation and rouletting for their own convenience. Perf. 11 examples of Nos. 81-82 were made by John Meinert, Ltd., Windhoek, same values.

Setting VIII
South Africa Nos. 23-25 Overprinted Alternately with type "p" on English-inscribed Stamps and type "q" on Afrikaans-inscribed Stamps

**South West** **Africa.** p — **Suidwes** **Afrika.** q

"South West" 16½mm wide
"Suidwes" 11mm wide
Overprint Spaced 11½mm

**1926 — Typo. — *Perf. 14½x14***

| | | | | |
|---|---|---|---|---|
| 85 | A5 | ½p dk grn & blk | 10 | 7 |
| a. | | Pair | 90 | 65 |
| b. | | Ovpt. *q* on English stamp | 10 | 7 |
| c. | | Ovpt. *p* on Afrikaans stamp | 12 | 10 |
| d. | | Pair, "b" + "c" | 90 | 65 |
| e. | | As "d", without period after "Africa" | 200.00 | |
| 86 | A6 | 1p car & blk | 15 | 10 |
| a. | | Pair | 85 | 85 |
| b. | | Ovpt. *q* on English stamp | 12 | 10 |
| c. | | Ovpt. *p* on Afrikaans stamp | 12 | 10 |
| d. | | Pair, "b" + "c" | 90 | 90 |
| e. | | As "d", without period after "Africa" | 275.00 | |
| 87 | A7 | 6p org & grn | 1.10 | 1.10 |
| a. | | Pair | 14.00 | 14.00 |
| b. | | Ovpt. *q* on English stamp | 65 | 65 |
| c. | | Ovpt. *p* on Afrikaans stamp | 65 | 65 |
| d. | | Pair, "b" + "c" | 8.25 | 9.25 |
| e. | | As "d", without period after "Africa" | 200.00 | |

Setting IX
South Africa Nos. 26-27, 29-32 Overprinted in Blue with types "p" and "q" Spaced 16mm

**1927 — Engr. — *Perf. 14***

| | | | | |
|---|---|---|---|---|
| 88 | A8 | 2p vio brn & gray | 8 | 8 |
| a. | | Pair | 2.75 | 2.75 |
| 89 | A9 | 3p red & blk | 10 | 10 |
| a. | | Pair | 1.90 | 3.25 |
| 90 | A11 | 1sh dp bl & bis brn | 50 | 50 |
| a. | | Pair | 11.00 | 16.00 |
| 91 | A12 | 2sh6p brn & bl grn | 3.00 | 3.00 |
| a. | | Pair | 37.50 | 55.00 |
| 92 | A13 | 5sh dp grn & blk | 7.25 | 7.25 |
| a. | | Pair | 55.00 | 75.00 |
| 93 | A14 | 10sh ol brn & bl | 7.50 | 7.50 |
| a. | | Pair | 87.50 | 110.00 |
| | | *Nos. 88-93 (6)* | 18.43 | 18.43 |
| | | *Nos. 88a-93a (6)* | 195.65 | 262.00 |

South Africa Nos. 12 and 16a Overprinted at Foot

**S.W.A.**
r

**1927 — Typo. — Wmk. 177**

| | | | | |
|---|---|---|---|---|
| 94 | A2 | 1sh3p violet | 2.75 | 4.00 |
| a. | | Without period after "A" | 250.00 | |
| 95 | A2 | £1 lt red & gray grn | 225.00 | 250.00 |
| a. | | Without period after "A" | 2,500. | 2,500. |

South Africa Nos. 23-25 Overprinted type "r" at Foot

**1927 — Wmk. 201 — *Perf. 14½x14***

| | | | | |
|---|---|---|---|---|
| 96 | A5 | ½p grn & blk | 8 | 8 |
| a. | | Pair | 85 | 85 |
| b. | | As "a." without period after "A" | 75.00 | |
| 97 | A6 | 1p car & blk | 10 | 8 |
| a. | | Pair | 1.00 | 1.00 |
| b. | | As "a." without period after "A" | 75.00 | |
| c. | | Ovpt. at top ('30) | 20 | 20 |
| d. | | As "c." pair | 3.25 | 3.25 |
| 98 | A7 | 6p org & grn | 65 | 65 |
| a. | | Pair | 10.00 | 14.00 |
| b. | | As "a." without period after "A" | 175.00 | |

South Africa Nos. 26-32 Overprinted type "r" at Top

**1927-28 — Engr. — *Perf. 14***

| | | | | |
|---|---|---|---|---|
| 99 | A8 | 2p vio brn & gray | 15 | 15 |
| a. | | Pair | 4.25 | 5.75 |
| b. | | Double ovpt. one inverted | 1,000. | 1,250. |
| c. | | As "a" without period after "A" | 150.00 | |
| 100 | A9 | 3p red & blk | 22 | 22 |
| a. | | Pair | 5.75 | 7.25 |
| b. | | As "a." without period after "A" | 165.00 | |
| 101 | A10 | 4p brn ('28) | 35 | 35 |
| a. | | Pair | 11.00 | 16.00 |
| b. | | As "a." without period after "A" | 165.00 | |
| 102 | A11 | 1sh dp bl & bis brn | 75 | 75 |
| a. | | Pair | 20.00 | 24.00 |
| b. | | As "a." without period after "A" | 1,900. | |
| 103 | A12 | 2sh6p brn & bl grn | 2.00 | 2.00 |
| a. | | Pair | 45.00 | 62.50 |
| b. | | As "a." without period after "A" | 300.00 | |
| 104 | A13 | 5sh dp grn & blk | 3.75 | 3.75 |
| a. | | Pair | 82.50 | 105.00 |
| b. | | As "a." without period after "A" | 450.00 | |
| 105 | A14 | 10sh ol brn & bl | 11.00 | 11.00 |
| a. | | Pair | 225.00 | 265.00 |
| b. | | As "a." without period after "A" | 750.00 | |
| | | *Nos. 99-105 (7)* | 18.22 | 18.22 |

South Africa Nos. 33-34 Overprinted type "r" at Foot

**1930 — Photo. — *Perf. 15x14***

| | | | | |
|---|---|---|---|---|
| 106 | A5 | ½p bl grn & blk | 20 | 20 |
| a. | | Pair | 2.25 | 2.50 |
| 107 | A6 | 1p car rose & blk | 20 | 20 |
| a. | | Pair | 2.25 | 2.50 |

Kori Bustard — A15

Cape Cross — A16

Mail Transport — A17

Bogenfels — A18

Windhoek — A19

Waterberg — A20

Lüderitz Bay — A21

Bush Scene — A22

Elands — A23

Zebras and Brindled Gnus — A24

Herero Houses — A25

Welwitschia Plant — A26

Okuwahakan Falls — A27

Inscribed alternately in English and Afrikaans.

*Perf. 14x13½*

**1931-37 Wmk. 201 Engr.**

| | | | | | |
|---|---|---|---|---|---|
| *108* | A15 | ½p | grn & blk | 10 | 5 |
| a. | Pair | | | 65 | 40 |
| *109* | A16 | 1p | red & ind | 6 | 5 |
| a. | Pair | | | 32 | 28 |
| *110* | A17 | 1½p | vio brn ('37) | 10 | 6 |
| a. | Pair | | | 65 | 55 |
| *111* | A18 | 2p | dk brn & dk bl | 8 | 6 |
| a. | Pair | | | 50 | 28 |
| *112* | A19 | 3p | dp bl & gray blk | 10 | 8 |
| a. | Pair | | | 65 | 55 |
| *113* | A20 | 4p | brn vio & grn | 15 | 12 |
| a. | Pair | | | 90 | 75 |
| *114* | A21 | 6p | ol brn & bl | 15 | 10 |
| a. | Pair | | | 90 | 52 |
| *115* | A22 | 1sh | bl & vio brn | 18 | 14 |
| a. | Pair | | | 1.50 | 1.80 |
| *116* | A23 | 1sh3p | ocher & pur | 45 | 20 |
| a. | Pair | | | 6.00 | 6.00 |
| *117* | A24 | 2sh6p | dk gray & rose | 45 | 28 |
| a. | Pair | | | 6.50 | 7.25 |
| *118* | A25 | 5sh | vio brn & ol grn | 90 | 50 |
| a. | Pair | | | 17.00 | 17.50 |
| *119* | A26 | 10sh | grn & brn | 3.00 | 1.40 |
| a. | Pair | | | 50.00 | 50.00 |
| *120* | A27 | 20sh | bl grn & mar | 4.50 | 2.75 |
| a. | Pair | | | 125.00 | 125.00 |
| | | | *Nos. 108-120 (13)* | 10.22 | 5.79 |
| | | | *Nos. 108a-120a (13)* | 210.57 | 210.88 |

George V A28

George VI A29

**1935, May 6** *Perf. 14x13½*

| | | | | | |
|---|---|---|---|---|---|
| *121* | A28 | 1p | car & blk | 32 | 40 |
| *122* | A28 | 2p | dk brn & blk | 40 | 60 |
| *123* | A28 | 3p | bl & blk | 7.00 | *11.00* |
| *124* | A28 | 6p | vio & blk | 4.25 | 6.50 |

25th anniv. of the reign of George V.

**Catalogue values for unused stamps in this section, from this point to the end of the section, are for Never Hinged items.**

### Coronation Issue

Inscribed alternately in English and Afrikaans

**1937, May 12 Engr.** *Perf. 13½x14*

| | | | | | |
|---|---|---|---|---|---|
| *125* | A29 | ½p | emer & blk | 6 | 5 |
| a. | Pair | | | 8 | 8 |
| *126* | A29 | 1p | car & blk | 8 | 6 |
| a. | Pair | | | 14 | 14 |
| *127* | A29 | 1½p | org & blk | 8 | 7 |
| a. | Pair | | | 14 | 14 |
| *128* | A29 | 2p | dk brn & blk | 8 | 8 |
| a. | Pair | | | 14 | 14 |
| *129* | A29 | 3p | brt bl & blk | 10 | 10 |
| a. | Pair | | | 18 | 18 |
| *130* | A29 | 4p | dk vio & blk | 12 | 10 |
| a. | Pair | | | 20 | 20 |
| *131* | A29 | 6p | yel & blk | 12 | 12 |
| a. | Pair | | | 30 | 30 |
| *132* | A29 | 1sh | gray & blk | 20 | 20 |
| a. | Pair | | | 55 | 55 |
| | | | *Nos. 125-132 (8)* | 84 | 78 |
| | | | *Nos. 125a-132a (8)* | 1.73 | 1.73 |

Coronation of George VI and Queen Elizabeth.

### Voortrekker Issue.

South Africa Nos. 79-80 Overprinted type "r"

**1938, Dec. 14 Photo.** *Perf. 15x14*

| | | | | | |
|---|---|---|---|---|---|
| *133* | A23 | 1p | rose & sl | 20 | 18 |
| a. | Pair | | | 90 | 90 |
| *134* | A24 | 1½p | red brn & Prus bl | 60 | 50 |
| a. | Pair | | | 1.65 | 1.65 |

Issued to commemorate the Voortrekkers.

South Africa Nos. 81-89 Overprinted

**SWA**

s

*Perf. 14 (2p, 4p, 6p); 15x14*

**1941-43 Wmk. 201**

| | | | | | |
|---|---|---|---|---|---|
| *135* | A25 | ½p | dp bl grn | 10 | 8 |
| a. | Pair | | | 50 | 50 |
| *136* | A26 | 1p | brt rose | 12 | 10 |
| a. | Pair | | | 60 | 60 |
| *137* | A27 | 1½p | Prus grn ('42) | 20 | 15 |
| a. | Pair | | | 1.00 | 1.00 |
| *138* | A28 | 2p | dk vio | 20 | 20 |
| *139* | A29 | 3p | dp bl | 20 | 18 |
| a. | Pair | | | 1.00 | 1.00 |
| *140* | A30 | 4p | brown | 25 | 20 |
| a. | Pair | | | 1.25 | 1.25 |
| *141* | A31 | 6p | brt red org | 35 | 30 |
| a. | Pair | | | 1.40 | 1.40 |
| *142* | A32 | 1sh | dk brn | 65 | 65 |
| *143* | A33 | 1sh3p | dk ol brn ('43) | 75 | 25 |
| a. | Pair | | | 4.00 | 3.50 |
| | | | *Nos. 135-143 (9)* | 2.82 | 2.11 |
| | | | *Nos. 135a-143a (7)* | 9.75 | 9.25 |

South Africa Nos. 90-97 Overprinted

**SWA** t  **SWA** u

***Pairs or Strips of Three Perf. 14 or 15x14 all around, Rouletted 6½ or 13 between.***

**1942-45 Wmk. 201**

| | | | | | |
|---|---|---|---|---|---|
| *144* | A34 (t) | ½p | dp grn ('43) | 6 | 6 |
| a. | | ½p | dp bl grn ('45) | 6 | 5 |
| b. | | | Horiz. strip of 3 | 60 | 50 |
| *145* | A35 (t) | 1p | brt car ('43) | 8 | 6 |
| a. | | 1p | rose car ('45) | 8 | 6 |
| b. | | | Horiz. strip of 3 | 70 | 50 |
| *146* | A36 (u) | 1½p | cop brn | 8 | 6 |
| a. | | | Horiz.. pair | 60 | 50 |
| *147* | A37 (t) | 2p | dk vio ('43) | 15 | 5 |
| a. | | | Horiz. pair | 1.00 | 80 |
| *148* | A38 (t) | 3p | dp bl ('43) | 20 | 10 |
| a. | | | Vert. strip of 3 | 1.75 | 1.40 |
| *149* | A39 (t) | 4p | sl grn ('43) | 25 | 15 |
| a. | | | Vert. strip of 3 | 2.25 | 1.75 |
| b. | | | Invtd. ovpt. | 25.00 | |
| c. | | | As "b." strip of 3 | 500.00 | |
| *150* | A40 (t) | 6p | brt red org ('43) | 30 | 18 |
| a. | | | Horiz. pair | 1.75 | 1.40 |
| b. | | | Inverted overprint | 50.00 | 35.00 |
| c. | | | As "b." pair | 650.00 | |
| *151* | A41 (u) | 1sh | dk brn ('43) | 60 | 30 |
| a. | | | Vert. pair | 3.50 | 2.75 |
| b. | | | Inverted ovpt. | 75.00 | |
| c. | | | As "b." pair | 500.00 | |
| *152* | A41 (t) | 1sh | dk brn ('44) | 60 | 30 |
| a. | | | Vert. pair | 3.50 | 2.75 |
| b. | | | Inverted ovpt. | 75.00 | 45.00 |
| c. | | | As "b." vert. pair | 500.00 | |
| | | | *Nos. 144-152 (9)* | 2.32 | 1.26 |

### Peace Issue

South Africa Nos. 100-102 Overprinted Type "w"

**1945 Wmk. 201** *Perf. 14*

| | | | | | |
|---|---|---|---|---|---|
| *153* | A42 | 1p | rose pink & choc | 12 | 12 |
| a. | Pair | | | 38 | 38 |
| b. | Inverted overprint | | | 42.50 | |
| c. | As "b." pair | | | 300.00 | |
| *154* | A43 | 2p | vio & sl bl | 15 | 15 |
| a. | Pair | | | 45 | 45 |
| *155* | A43 | 3p | ultra & dp ultra | 18 | 18 |
| a. | Pair | | | 60 | 60 |

WW II victory of the Allies.

### Royal Visit Issue

South Africa Nos. 103-105 Overprinted **S W A**

**1947, Feb. 17** *Perf. 15x14*

| | | | | | |
|---|---|---|---|---|---|
| *156* | A44 | 1p | cer & gray | 8 | 8 |
| a. | Pair | | | 20 | 20 |
| *157* | A45 | 2p | purple | 10 | 10 |
| a. | Pair | | | 25 | 25 |
| *158* | A46 | 3p | dk bl | 12 | 12 |
| a. | Pair | | | 30 | 30 |

Issued to commemorate the visit of the British Royal Family, Mar.-Apr., 1947.

South Africa No. 106 Overprinted **SWA**

**1948, Apr. 26** *Perf. 14.*

| | | | | | |
|---|---|---|---|---|---|
| *159* | A47 | 3p | dp chlky bl & sil | 15 | 8 |
| a. | Pair | | | 50 | 25 |

25th anniv. of the marriage of George VI and Queen Elizabeth.

### UPU Issue

South Africa Nos. 109-111 Overprinted type "w" 13mm wide

**1949, Oct. 1** *Perf. 14x15*

| | | | | | |
|---|---|---|---|---|---|
| *160* | A50 | ½p | dk grn | 6 | 6 |
| a. | Pair | | | 50 | 50 |
| *161* | A50 | 1½p | dk red | 8 | 8 |
| a. | Pair | | | 60 | 60 |
| *162* | A50 | 3p | ultra | 15 | 12 |
| a. | Pair | | | 90 | 90 |

75th anniv. of the UPU.

### Voortrekker Monument Issue.

South Africa Nos. 112-114 Overprinted **S W A**

**1949, Dec. 1** *Perf. 15x14.*

| | | | | | |
|---|---|---|---|---|---|
| *163* | A51 | 1p | magenta | 10 | 10 |
| *164* | A52 | 1½p | dl grn | 15 | 15 |
| *165* | A53 | 3p | dk bl | 25 | 25 |

Issued to commemorate the inauguration of the Voortrekker Monument at Pretoria.

South Africa Nos. 115-119 Overprinted

**SWA** w  **SWA** x

**1952, Mar. 14** *Perf. 15x14, 14x15*

| | | | | | |
|---|---|---|---|---|---|
| *166* | A54 (w) | ½p | dk brn & red vio | 6 | 6 |
| *167* | A55 (x) | 1p | dk grn | 6 | 5 |
| *168* | A54 (w) | 2p | dk pur | 10 | 6 |
| *169* | A55 (x) | 4½p | dk bl | 50 | 50 |
| *170* | A54 (w) | 1sh | brown | 1.00 | 1.00 |
| | | | *Nos. 166-170 (5)* | 1.72 | 1.67 |

300th anniv. of the landing of Jan van Riebeeck at the Cape of Good Hope.

### Coronation Issue

Queen Elizabeth II and Flowers — A54

**1953, June 2 Photo.** *Perf. 14*

**Various Flowers**

| | | | | | |
|---|---|---|---|---|---|
| *244* | A54 | 1p | car rose | 45 | 30 |
| *245* | A54 | 2p | dk grn | 60 | 45 |
| *246* | A54 | 4p | dp mag | 1.50 | 1.25 |
| *247* | A54 | 6p | dp bl | 1.75 | 1.50 |
| *248* | A54 | 1sh | chnt brn | 2.50 | 1.90 |
| | | | *Nos. 244-248 (5)* | 6.80 | 5.40 |

Rock Painting of Two Bucks — A55

Rhinoceros Hunt — A56

Designs: 2p, "White Lady" (rock painting). 4p, Elephant and giraffe (rock painting). 4½p, Karakul lamb. 6p, Orambo blowing Kudu horn. 1sh, Ukuanjama woman. 1sh3p, Herero woman. 1sh6p, Ukuanjama girl. 2sh6p, Lioness. 5sh, Cape Oryx. 10sh, Elephant.

**1954, Nov. 15 Wmk. 201** *Perf. 14*

| | | | | | |
|---|---|---|---|---|---|
| *249* | A55 | 1p | rose brn | 18 | 6 |
| *250* | A55 | 2p | dk brn | 28 | 8 |
| *251* | A56 | 3p | brn vio | 55 | 14 |
| *252* | A56 | 4p | ol gray | 80 | 40 |
| *253* | A55 | 4½ | bl vio | 1.10 | 75 |
| *254* | A55 | 6p | gray grn | 1.10 | 55 |
| *255* | A55 | 1sh | magenta | 2.00 | 90 |
| *256* | A55 | 1sh3p | rose pink | 4.00 | 2.00 |
| *257* | A55 | 1sh6p | dl pur | 4.50 | 2.50 |
| *258* | A55 | 2sh6p | yel brn | 9.00 | 3.75 |
| *259* | A55 | 5sh | blue | 18.00 | 7.50 |
| *260* | A55 | 10sh | dk grn | 55.00 | 37.50 |
| | | | *Nos. 249-260 (12)* | 96.51 | 56.13 |

**1960 Wmk. 330** *Perf. 14*

| | | | | | |
|---|---|---|---|---|---|
| *261* | A55 | 1p | rose brn | 45 | 14 |
| *262* | A55 | 2p | dk brn | 65 | 28 |
| *263* | A56 | 3p | brn vio | 1.40 | 75 |
| *264* | A56 | 4p | ol gray | 5.50 | 5.00 |
| *265* | A55 | 1sh6p | dl pur | 27.50 | 22.50 |
| | | | *Nos. 261-265 (5)* | 35.50 | 28.67 |

General Post Office, Windhoek A57

Fishing Industry A58

Designs: 1c, Finger Rock, Asab. 1½c, Monument, Mounted Soldier. 2c, Quivertree (aloe dichotoma masson). 2½c, Administrator's residence. 3p, Swakopmund Lighthouse and flamingoes. 5c, Flamingo. 7½c, Christchurch. 10c, Diamonds. 12½c, Fort Namutoni. 15c, Hardap Dam. 20c, Topaz. 50c, Tourmaline. 1r, Heliodor.

**1961-62 Wmk. 330 Photo.** *Perf. 14*

| | | | | | |
|---|---|---|---|---|---|
| *266* | A57 | ½c | bl & brn | 18 | 12 |
| *267* | A58 | 1c | pale lil & brn | 22 | 5 |
| *268* | A58 | 1½c | sal & dk pur | 30 | 16 |
| *269* | A58 | 2c | yel & grn | 38 | 12 |
| *270* | A57 | 2½c | lt bl & red brn | 50 | 16 |
| *271* | A58 | 3c | dp rose & vio bl ('62) | 60 | 18 |
| *272* | A58 | 3½c | bl grn & ind | 1.00 | 42 |
| *273* | A58 | 5c | bluish gray & red | 1.00 | 22 |
| *274* | A58 | 7½c | yel & brn | 1.25 | 95 |
| *275* | A58 | 10c | brt bl & yel | 2.50 | 75 |
| *276* | A57 | 12½c | yel & ind | 3.50 | 95 |
| *277* | A57 | 15c | dp brn & bl | 3.75 | 1.25 |
| *278* | A58 | 20c | sal, brn & blk | 5.25 | 1.50 |
| *279* | A58 | 50c | org yel & Prus grn | 9.25 | 5.00 |
| *280* | A58 | 1r | brt bl, mar & yel | 24.00 | 12.50 |
| | | | *Nos. 266-280 (15)* | 53.68 | 24.33 |

**1962-73** **Unwmk.**

281 A57 ½c bl & brn 55 25
282 A58 1½c sal & dk pur ('63) 75 25
283 A58 2c yel & grn 75 18
284 A57 2½c lt bl & red brn ('64) 1.25 25
285 A58 3c dp rose & vio bl ('73) 1.50 1.50
286 A58 3½c bl grn & ind ('66) 6.25 4.25
287 A58 5c bluish gray & red 2.50 60
*Nos. 281-287 (7)* 13.55 7.28

See Nos. 304-308, 314-328.

Hardap Dam and Development
A59

Centenary Emblem and S.W.A. Map
A60

**1963, Mar. 16** **Wmk. 330**

294 A59 3c sep & grn 90 90

Opening of Hardap Dam near Mariental.

**1963, Aug. 30** **Unwmk.** ***Perf. 14***

Design: 15c, Emblem and globe.

295 A60 7½c bl, blk & red 5.50 3.75
296 A60 15c brn org, blk & red 10.00 8.00

Centenary of the International Red Cross.

Assembly Hall
A61

John Calvin
A62

**1964, May 14** **Photo.** **Wmk. 330**

297 A61 3c sal pink & vio bl 90 75

Issued to commemorate the opening of the new hall of the Legislative Assembly.

**1964, Oct. 1** **Unwmk.** ***Perf. 14***

298 A62 2½c mag & gold 85 55
299 A62 15c grn & gold 4.50 3.50

John Calvin (1509-64), French theologian and leader of the Reformation.

Mail Runner, 1890
A63

Kurt von François
A64

**Wmk. 348**

**1965, Oct. 18** **Photo.** ***Perf. 14***

300 A63 3c red & dp brn 55 38
301 A64 15c grn & dp brn 3.50 2.50

75th anniversary of Windhoek.

H. H. Vedder — A65

**1966, July 4** ***Perf. 14***

302 A65 3c blk & sal 52 35
303 A65 15c blk & lt bl 3.25 2.75

Issued to honor on his 90th birthday Dr. H. H. Vedder, missionary, educator and senator.

Types of 1961-62

**1966-67** **Wmk. 348** **Photo.** ***Perf. 14***
**Chalky Paper**

304 A57 ½c lt bl & brn ('67) 28 14
304A A58 1c pale lil & brn ('67) 32 16
305 A58 2c brt yel & dp grn 32 16
306 A57 2½c gray bl & red brn 40 20
307 A58 3½c pale grn & vio bl ('67) 3.25 2.00
308 A58 7½c brt yel & brn ('67) 1.65 80
*Nos. 304-308 (6)* 6.22 3.46

The watermark on Nos. 304, 305-308 is very faint, and these stamps can be distinguished by the shades and by the thick chalky paper. The watermark on No. 304A is clear.

Camelthorn Tree — A66

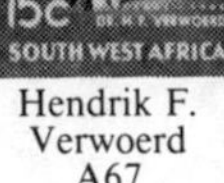

Hendrik F. Verwoerd
A67

Pres. Charles Robberts Swart
A68

Design: 3c, Waves breaking against rock.

***Perf. 14, 14x15 (15c)***

**1967, Jan. 6** **Litho.** **Wmk. 348**

309 A66 2½c grn & blk 38 22
310 A67 3c brt bl & brn 55 25
311 A67 15c rose lil & blk 3.75 3.50

Dr. Hendrik F. Verwoerd (1901-1966), Prime Minister of South Africa.

***Perf. 14x15***

**1968, Jan. 2** **Photo.** **Wmk. 359**

Design: 15c, President and Mrs. C. R. Swart.

312 A68 3c dl bl & multi 60 35
*a.* Strip of 3 4.50 4.50
313 A68 15c dl grn & multi 3.50 3.00
*a.* Strip of 3 12.50 12.50

Issued to honor Charles Robberts Swart, first president of South Africa, (1961-67). The stamps are alternately inscribed in English, Afrikaans and German. Strips of 3 contain one stamp in each language.

Types of 1961-62

Designs: 4c, like 2½c. 6c, Christchurch. 9c, Fort Namutoni.

**1968-72** **Wmk. 359** **Photo.** ***Perf. 14***

314 A57 ½c bl & brn 38 11
315 A57 ½c bl & brn, redrawn ('70) 95 60
316 A58 1c pale lil & brn ('70) 35 15
317 A58 1½c sal & dk pur 48 22
318 A58 1½c sal & dk pur, redrawn ('71) 5.25 4.00
319 A58 2c yel & grn, redrawn ('70) 55 22
320 A57 2½c lt bl & red brn ('70) 48 15
321 A58 3c dp rose & vio bl ('70) 75 18
322 A57 4c lt bl & red brn ('71) 1.25 52
323 A58 5c bluish gray & red 75 25
324 A58 6c yel & brn ('71) 3.75 2.25
325 A57 9c yel & ind ('71) 4.75 2.75
326 A57 10c brt bl & yel ('70) 2.25 95
327 A57 15c dp brn & bl ('72) 3.75 2.25
328 A57 20c org, brn & blk 3.50 1.25
*Nos. 314-328 (15)* 29.19 15.85

Nos. 315, 318-319 are without inscription "Posgeld Incomste Postage Revenue" and the numerals have been enlarged. The ½c (#315), 2c and 10c were also issued as coils.

Water Type of South Africa, 1970

Designs: 2½c, Water drop and flower (vert.). 3c, Waves (horiz.).

**1970, Feb. 14** ***Perf. 14***

329 A142 2½c brn, brt bl & grn 90 65
330 A142 3c pale gray, bl & ind 1.10 80

Water '70 campaign of the South African Department of Water Affairs.

Bible Society Types of South Africa

Designs: 2½c, Sower, stained glass window. 12½c, "BIBLIA" and open book.

**1970, Aug. 24** **Photo.** ***Perf. 14***

331 A143 2½c multi 1.10 55

**Photo.; Gold Impressed**

332 A144 12½c ultra, blk & gold 11.00 10.00

Issued to commemorate the 150th anniversary of the South African Bible Society.

Stamp Exhibition Types of South Africa

***Perf. 14x13½, 13½x14***

**1971, May 31** **Photo.** **Wmk. 359**

333 A145 5c bl, yel & blk 5.50 3.75
334 A146 12½c grnsh bl, vio bl & red 65.00 32.50

International Stamp Exhibition (INTERSTEX), Cape Town, May 22-31. No. 334 also for the 10th anniversary of the Antarctic Treaty pledging peaceful uses of and scientific cooperation in Antarctica.

Republic Anniversary Types of South Africa

**1971, May 31** ***Perf. 14***

335 A147 2c mag, rose red & buff 3.25 1.10
336 A148 4c bl grn & blk 5.50 1.40

10th anniv. of the Republic of South Africa.

Cat Type of South Africa

**1972, Sept. 19** ***Perf. 14***

337 A152 5c multi 1.75 1.25

Cent. of the SPCA.

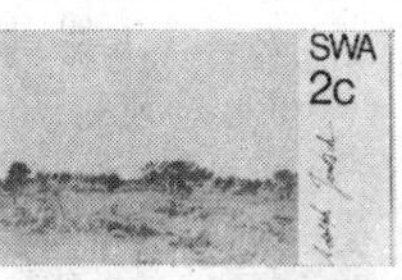

Landscape, by Adolph Jentsch
A69

Designs: Various landscapes by Adolph Jentsch (1888- ). 10c, 15c, vertical.

***Perf. 11½x12½***

**1973, Apr. 28** **Litho.**

338 A69 2c multi 1.00 1.00
339 A69 4c multi 2.25 2.25
340 A69 5c multi 3.25 3.25
341 A69 10c multi 6.50 6.50
342 A69 15c multi 10.00 10.00
*Nos. 338-342 (5)* 23.00 23.00

Sarcocaulon Rigidum
A70

Pachypodium Namaquanum
A71

Designs: 1c-50c, Various succulent plants. 1r, Welwitschia. (30c, 1r, horiz.)

**1973, Sept. 1** **Litho.** ***Perf. 12½***
**Plants in Natural Colors**

343 A70 1c lt bl 6 5
344 A70 2c yellow 10 6
*a.* Perf. 14 12 12
345 A70 3c sal pink 16 8
*a.* Perf. 14 18 16
346 A70 4c gray 20 12
347 A70 5c blue 22 16
*a.* Perf. 14 42 42
348 A70 6c grnsh gray 30 16
349 A70 7c brt yel 35 18
350 A70 9c dl yel 38 18
351 A70 10c bl grn 42 20
*a.* Perf. 14 60 60
352 A70 14c yel grn 60 35
353 A70 15c lt brn 75 35
354 A70 20c lt ol 85 42
355 A70 25c orange 1.10 50

***Perf. 12x12½, 12½x12***

356 A71 30c dl yel 1.50 55
*a.* Perf. 14 3.00 3.00
357 A71 50c lt grn 2.50 1.00
*a.* Perf. 14 2.75 2.75
358 A71 1r bl grn 5.00 2.00
*Nos. 343-358 (16)* 14.49 6.36

Coil Stamps

**1973, Sept. 1** **Photo.** ***Perf. 14***

359 A70 1c brt pink & bl 5 5
360 A70 2c yel & blk 15 15
361 A70 5c red & blk 30 30

**1978** ***Perf. 14 Vertically***

362 A70 2c yel & blk 6 5
362A A70 5c red & blk 13 10

Chat-shrike — A72

Designs: Rare birds.

***Perf. 12½x11½***

**1974, Feb. 13** **Litho.**

363 A72 4c *shown* 2.00 1.50
364 A72 5c *Rosy-faced lovebirds* 2.75 2.00
365 A72 10c *Damara rockjumper* 6.50 6.00
366 A72 15c *Rüppell's parrot* 12.00 9.00

Rock Carvings, Twyfelfontein
A73

Mining
A74

**1974, Apr. 10** **Litho.** ***Perf. 12½***

367 A73 4c *Giraffe & horse* 1.90 90
368 A73 5c *Elephant* 2.50 1.25

***Perf. 12x12½***
**Size: 37x21½mm**

369 A73 15c *Deer* (horiz.) 11.50 5.50

**1974, Sept. 30** ***Perf. 12½x11½***

370 A74 10c *Diamonds* 3.00 2.00
371 A74 15c *Diamond washing diagram* 4.25 3.00
*Nos. 367-371 (5)* 23.15 12.65

Map Showing Route, Covered Wagons
A75

*Perf. 11½x12*

**1974, Nov. 13** **Unwmk.**
*372* A75 4c yel & multi 1.25 85

Centenary of "Thirstland Trek" from Transvaal through Kalahari Desert to Angola.

Peregrine Falcon — A76

Designs: Protected Birds of Prey.

*Perf. 12½x11½*

**1975, Mar. 19** **Litho.**
*373* A76 4c *shown* 1.90 1.00
*374* A76 5c *blk eagle* 2.50 1.25
*375* A76 10c *Martial eagle* 5.50 2.75
*376* A76 15c *Egyptian vulture* 7.50 4.25

Kolmanskop, Ghost Diamond Mining Town — A77

Designs: 9c, German steam traction engine, 1896. 15c, Old Fort, Windhoek and statue of Colonial German trooper on horseback.

**1975, July 23** **Litho.** ***Perf. 12x12½***
*377* A77 5c vio & multi 42 35
*378* A77 9c ocher & multi 85 85
*379* A77 15c yel & multi 1.50 1.50

Historic monuments.

Swakopmund, by Otto Schröder — A78

Paintings by Otto Schröder (1913-75).

**1975, Oct. 15** **Litho.** ***Perf. 12x12½***
*380* A78 15c *shown* 1.50 1.40
*381* A78 15c *Luderitz* 1.50 1.40
*382* A78 15c *Unloading freighters* 1.50 1.40
*383* A78 15c *Ships at anchor, Walvis Bay* 1.50 1.40
*a.* Souvenir sheet of 4 8.75 8.75

Nos. 380-383 printed se-tenant. No. 383a contains one each of Nos. 380-383 with horizontal gutter with black inscription on silver panel; gray and silver border. Size: 121x95mm.

Elephants A79

Pre-historic Rock Paintings: 10c, Rhinoceros. 15c, Deer and hunter. 20c, Hunter with bow and arrow.

**1976, Mar. 12** **Litho.** ***Perf. 12x12½***
*384* A79 4c red brn & multi 27 22
*385* A79 10c red brn & multi 65 65
*386* A79 15c red brn & multi 1.00 1.00
*387* A79 20c red brn & multi 1.65 1.65
*a.* Souvenir sheet of 4 6.25 6.25

No. 387a contains one each of Nos. 384-387; multicolored margin. Size: 121x96mm.

Schloss Duwisib A80

Castles Built by German Settlers: 10c, Schwerinsburg. 20c, Heynitzburg.

**1976, May 14** **Litho.** ***Perf. 12x12½***
*388* A80 10c multi 60 60
*389* A80 15c multi 90 90
*390* A80 20c multi 1.25 1.25

Nature Protection A81

*Perf. 11½x12½*

**1976, July 16** **Litho.**
*391* A81 4c Daman 35 22
*392* A81 10c Dik-doks 90 70
*393* A81 15c Tree squirrel 1.40 1.10

Augustineum Training Institute, Windhoek — A82

Design: 20c, Katutura State Hospital, Windhoek.

**1976, Sept. 17** **Litho.** ***Perf. 12x12½***
*394* A82 15c ocher & blk 60 60
*395* A82 20c cit & blk 80 80

Owambo Canal System A83

Design: 20c, Ruacana Dam and hydroelectric station.

**1976, Nov. 19** **Litho.** ***Perf. 12x12½***
*396* A83 15c multi 60 60
*397* A83 20c multi 80 80

Water and electricity supply.

Sinking Ship off Namib Shore — A84

Designs: Namib Desert, various views.

**1977, Mar. 29** **Litho.** ***Perf. 12½***
*398* A84 4c multi 25 16
*399* A84 10c multi 60 50
*400* A84 15c multi 85 75
*401* A84 20c multi 1.25 1.10

Owambo Kraal A85

Designs: 10c, Giant grain baskets. 15c, Women pounding corn. 20c, Body painting.

The lack of a price for a listed item does not necessarily indicate rarity.

**1977, July 15** **Litho.** ***Perf. 12x12½***
*402* A85 4c multi 16 12
*403* A85 10c multi 42 42
*404* A85 15c multi 60 60
*405* A85 20c multi 85 85

Traditions of the Wambo people.

J. G. Strijdom Airport, Windhoek — A86

**1977, Aug. 22** ***Perf. 12½***
*406* A86 20c multi 65 65

Drostdy, Lüderitz, 1910 — A87

Historic Houses: 10c, Woermannhaus, Swakopmund, 1895. 15c, Neu-Heusis, Windhoek. 20c, Schmelenhaus, Bethanie, 1814.

**1977, Nov. 4** **Litho.** ***Perf. 12x12½***
*407* A87 5c multi 20 16
*408* A87 10c multi 40 40
*409* A87 15c multi 60 60
*410* A87 20c multi 80 80
*a.* Souvenir sheet of 4 2.50 2.50

No. 410a contains one each of Nos. 407-410; light brown decorative margin with inscription and arms. Size: 12x96mm.

Side-winding Adder — A88

Small Animals of the Namib Desert: 10c, Golden sand mole. 15c, Palmato gecko. 20c, Namaqua chameleon.

**1978, Feb. 6** **Litho.** ***Perf. 12½***
*411* A88 4c multi 18 14
*412* A88 10c multi 45 45
*413* A88 15c multi 65 65
*414* A88 20c multi 90 90

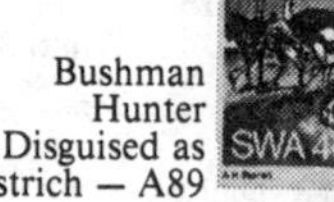

Bushman Hunter Disguised as Ostrich — A89

Bushmen: 10c, Woman carrying melons on back. 15c, Making fire. 20c, Family sitting in front of hut.

**1978, Apr. 14** **Litho.** ***Perf. 12x12½***
*415* A89 4c brn, buff & blk 14 10
*416* A89 10c brn, buff & blk 35 35
*417* A89 15c brn, buff & blk 55 55
*418* A89 20c brn, buff & blk 70 70

Lutheran Church, Windhoek — A90

Designs: 10c, Lutheran Church, Swakopmund. 15c, Rhenish Mission Church, Otjimbingwe. 20c, Rhenish Mission Church, Keetmanshoop.

**1978, June 16** **Litho.** ***Perf. 12½***
*419* A90 4c ol bis & blk 15 12
*420* A90 10c bis & blk 40 40
*421* A90 15c pale red brn & blk 60 60
*422* A90 20c bl gray & blk 80 80
*a.* Souvenir sheet of 4 2.50 2.50

No. 422a contains Nos. 419-422; lilac and blue decorative margin. Size: 125x91mm.

Type of 1973 Inscribed in English, German or Afrikaans:
a. UNIVERSAL / SUFFRAGE
b. ALLGEMEINES / WAHLRECHT
c. ALGEMENE / STEMREG

**1978, Nov. 1** **Litho.** ***Perf. 12½***
*423* Strip of 3 30 30
*a.-c.* A70 4c any single 10 10
*424* Strip of 3 38 38
*a.-c.* A70 5c any single 12 12
*425* Strip of 3 75 75
*a.-c.* A70 10c any single 25 25
*426* Strip of 3 1.10 1.10
*a.-c.* A70 15c any single 35 35
*427* Strip of 3 1.50 1.50
*a.-c.* A70 20c any single 50 50
*428* Strip of 3 1.90 1.90
*a.-c.* A70 25c any single 60 60
*Nos. 423-428 (6)* 5.93 5.93

General suffrage. Printed se-tenant with inscriptions alternating horisontally and vertically in sheets of 30 (3x10).

Greater Flamingoes — A91

Water Birds: 15c, White-breasted cormorants. 20c, Chestnut-banded plovers. 25c, White pelicans.

**1979, Apr. 5** **Litho.** ***Perf. 14x14½***
*429* A91 4c multi 12 12
*430* A91 15c multi 45 45
*431* A91 20c multi 60 60
*432* A91 25c multi 75 75

Silver Topaz A92

**1979, Nov. 26** **Litho.** ***Perf. 14***
*433* A92 4c *shown* 15 15
*434* A92 15c *Aquamarine* 40 40
*435* A92 20c *Malachite* 60 60
*436* A92 25c *Amethyst* 70 70

Killer Whale — A93

**1980, Mar. 25** **Litho.** ***Perf. 14x14½***
*437* A93 4c *shown* 22 15

**Size: 37½x21mm**

*438* A93 5c *Humpback whale* 22 18
*439* A93 10c *Southern right whale* 45 38

**Size: 57½x21mm**

*440* A93 15c *Sperm whale, octopus* 75 52
*441* A93 20c *Fin whale* 1.00 75

**Size: 87½x21mm**

*442* A93 25c *Blue whale, diver* 1.10 90
*a.* Souvenir sheet of 6 3.75 3.75
*Nos. 437-442 (6)* 3.74 2.88

No. 442a contains Nos. 437-442; silver and black margin. Size 203½x95½mm.

Sable Antelope — A94

**1980, June 25 Litho. Perf. 14½x14**

443 A94 5c *shown* 16 16
444 A94 10c *Roan antelope* 30 30
445 A94 15c *Tsessebe* 45 45
446 A94 20c *Black-nosed impala* 60 60

Cape Hunting Dog — A95

**1980-85 Litho. Perf. 14**

447 A95 1c *Black backed jackal* 5 5
448 A95 2c *shown* 5 5
449 A95 3c *Hyena* 8 8
450 A95 4c *Dorcas antelope* 8 8
451 A95 5c *Oryx* 8 8
452 A95 6c *Harnessed antelope* 12 12
453 A95 7c *Zebra, horiz.* 14 14
454 A95 8c *Porcupine, horiz.* 15 15
455 A95 9c *Honey badger, horiz.* 16 16
456 A95 10c *Leopard, horiz.* 18 18
456A A95 11c *Blue wildebeest ('84)* 14 14
456B A95 12c *Syncerus caffer, horiz.* 8 8
*c.* Bklt. pane of 10 80
457 A95 15c *Hippopotamus, horiz.* 25 25
458 A95 20c *Taurotagus oryx, horiz.* 38 38
459 A95 25c *Rhinoceros, horiz.* 45 45
460 A95 30c *Lion, horiz.* 55 55
461 A95 50c *Giraffe* 95 95
462 A95 1r *Tiger* 1.75 1.75
463 A95 2r *Elephant* 3.50 3.50
*Nos. 447-463 (19)* 9.14 9.14

Coil Stamps

**1980, Oct. 1 Litho. Perf. 14 Vert.**

464 A95 1c *Suricate* 5 5
465 A95 2c *Guenon* 5 5
466 A95 5c *South African chacma* 18 18

See No. 556.

Von Bach Dam, Swakop River — A96

**1980, Nov. 25 Litho. Perf. 14**

467 A96 5c *shown* 12 12
468 A96 10c *Swakoppoort Dam* 25 25
469 A96 15c *Naute Dam* 35 35
470 A96 20c *Hardap Dam* 50 50

Water conservation in the desert.

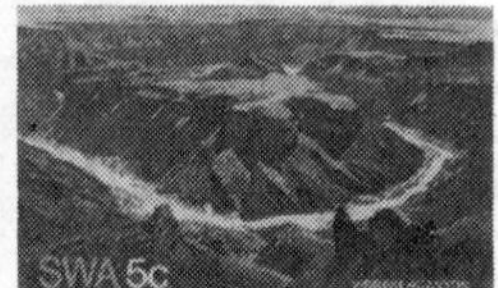

Fish River Canyon A97

Designs: Views of Fish River Canyon.

**1981, Mar. 20 Litho. Perf. 14**

471 A97 5c multi 10 10
472 A97 15c multi 28 28
473 A97 20c multi 40 40
474 A97 25c multi 50 50

Aloe Erinacea — A98

**1981, Aug. 14 Litho. Perf. 14**

475 A98 5c shown 10 10
476 A98 15c Aloe viridiflora 28 28
477 A98 20c Aloe pearsonii 40 40
478 A98 25c Aloe littoralis 50 50

Paul Weiss-Haus Building, 1909, Luderitz — A99

Designs: Historic buildings in Luderitz.

**1981, Oct. 16 Litho. Perf. 14**

479 A99 5c shown 10 10
480 A99 15c Deutsche Afrika Bank, 1906 28 28
481 A99 20c Schroederhaus, 1911 40 40
482 A99 25c Imperial P.O., 1908 50 50
*a.* Souvenir sheet of 4 1.40 1.40

No. 482a contains Nos. 479-482, tan and black decorative margin. Size: 125x91mm.

Salt Making A100

**1981, Dec. 4 Litho. Perf. 14x14½**

483 A100 5c Salt pan 10 10
484 A100 15c Dumping and washing 28 28
485 A100 20c Stockpiling 40 40
486 A100 25c Loading 50 50

Kalahari Starred Tortoise A101

**1982, Mar. 12 Litho. Perf. 14**

487 A101 5c shown 10 10
488 A101 15c Leopard tortoise 28 28
489 A101 20c Angulated tortoise 40 40
490 A101 25c Speckled padloper 50 50

Discoverers of South-West Africa — A102

**1982, May 28 Litho. Perf. 14½x14**

491 A102 15c Archbishop Olaus Magnus, sea monster 25 25
492 A102 20c Bartolomeu Dias, ships, map 38 38
493 A102 25c Caravel 45 45
494 A102 30c Dias erecting cross, Angra das Voltas 55 55

The Needle, Upper Brandberg A103

Designs: Mountain peaks.

**1982, Aug. 3 Litho. Perf. 14x14½**

495 A103 6c Brandberg 12 12
496 A103 15c Omatako twin peaks 28 28
497 A103 20c shown 38 38
498 A103 25c Spitzkuppe, Karakul sheep 45 45

Traditional Headdress, Herero Tribe — A104

**1982, Oct. 15 Litho. Perf. 14x14½**

499 A104 6c shown 12 12
500 A104 15c Himba 28 28
501 A104 20c Ngandjera 38 38
502 A104 25c Kwanyama 45 45

See Nos. 524-527.

Fort Vogelsang A105

Bethany Chief Joseph Fredericks — A106

**1983, Mar. 16 Perf. 14, 14½x14**

503 A105 6c shown 12 12
504 A106 20c shown 38 38
505 A105 25c Angra Pequena Bay 45 45
506 A106 30c Explorer Heinrich Vogelsang 55 55
507 A106 40c Adolf Luderitz (1834-1886) 75 75
*Nos. 503-507 (5)* 2.25 2.25

City of Luderitz centenary (1982).

Diamond Field, 1908 A107

Ernest Oppenheimer (1880-1957), Diamond Industry Leader — A108

**1983, June 8 Litho. Perf. 14**

508 A107 10c shown 20 20
509 A107 20c Field, diff. 40 40
510 A108 25c shown 50 50
511 A108 40c August Stauch, prospector 80 80

75th anniv. of discovery of diamonds at Luderitz.

Zebras Drinking, by J.J. van Ellinckhuijzen (b. 1940) — A109

Paintings: 20c, Rossing Mountain, by Herman H.-J. Henckert (b. 1906). 25c, Stampeding Buffalo, by Fritz Krampe (1913-1966). 40c, Erongo Mountains, by Johann Blatt (1905-1973).

**1983, Sept. 1**

512 A109 10c multi 20 20
513 A109 20c multi 40 40
514 A109 25c multi 52 52
515 A109 40c multi 80 80

Lobster Industry A110

**1983, Nov. 23 Perf. 13½x14**

516 A110 10c Lobsters 20 20
517 A110 20c Dinghies 40 40
518 A110 25c Raising trap 50 50
519 A110 40c Packaging 80 80

Historic Buildings, Swakopmund — A111

**1984, Mar. 8 Litho. Perf. 14x13½**

520 A111 10c Hohenzollern House 20 20
521 A111 20c Railway Station 40 40
522 A111 25c Imperial District Bureau 50 50
523 A111 30c Ritterburg 60 60

Headdress Type of 1982

**1984, May 25 Litho.**

524 A104 11c Kwambi 22 22
525 A104 20c Bushman 40 40
526 A104 25c Kwaludhi 50 50
527 A104 30c Mbukushu 60 60

German Colonization Centenary A112

**1984, Aug. 7 Litho. Perf. 13½x14**

528 A112 11c Map, flag 20 20
529 A112 25c Flag raising 48 48
530 A112 30c Land marker 55 55
531 A112 45c Corvettes Elisabeth & Leipzig 85 85

Spring Flowers — A113

**1984, Nov. 22 Litho. Perf. 14**

532 A113 11c Sweet thorn 20 20
533 A113 25c Camel thorn 48 48
534 A113 30c Hook thorn 55 55
535 A113 45c Candle-pod acacia 85 85

Ostrich A114

**1985, Mar. 15 Litho. Perf. 14½x14**

536 A114 11c Head of bird 14 14
537 A114 25c Female nesting 30 30
538 A114 30c Chick, eggs 35 35
539 A114 50c Male mating dance 60 60

Historic Buildings, 1900-1912, Windhoek — A115

**1985, June 6**

*540* A115 12c Erkrath, Gathemann Buildings, Kaiser Street 14 14
*541* A115 25c Gymnasium 30 30
*542* A115 30c Supreme Court 35 35
*543* A115 50c Railway Station 60 60

600mm Narrow-gauge Locomotives — A116

**1985, Aug. 2**

*544* A116 12c Zwilling Schmalspur, 1898 14 14
*545* A116 25c Feldspur Side-Tank 30 30
*546* A116 30c 0-6-2 Side-Tank, 1904 35 35
*547* A116 50c Henschel hd Smalspoor, 1912 60 60

Swakopmund-Tsumeb Railway line, 79th anniv.

Endemic Musical Instruments A117

**1985, Oct. 17**

*548* A117 12c Lidumu-dumu 14 14
*549* A117 25c Ngoma 30 30
*550* A117 30c Okambulum bumbwa 35 35
*551* A117 50c Gwashi 60 60

Diogo Cao, Portuguese Explorer, 1486 Visit to SWA A118

**1986, Jan. 24** ***Perf. 14½x14***

*552* A118 12c Erecting padroes on shore 14 14
*553* A118 20c Cao coat of arms 25 25
*554* A118 25c Caravel 30 30
*555* A118 30c Portrait 35 35

Wildlife Type of 1980

**1986, Apr. 1 Litho.** ***Perf. 14x14½***

*556* A95 14c Felis caracal 16 16

Rock Formations A119

Designs: 14c, Granite bornhardt, Erongo. 20c, Vingerklip, Outjo. 25c, Aeolian sandstone, Kuiseb River. 30c, Columnar dolerite, Twifelfontein.

**1986, Apr. 24** ***Perf. 14***

*566* A119 14c multi 16 16
*567* A119 20c multi 25 25
*568* A119 25c multi 30 30
*569* A119 30c multi 40 40

Karakul Wool (Swakara) Industry — A120

**1986, July 10**

*570* A120 14c Model 14 14
*571* A120 20c Hand loom 20 20
*572* A120 25c Sheep 25 25
*573* A120 30c Rams 30 30
*a.* Souvenir sheet 60 60

No. 573a has multicolored margin picturing design of No. 570 and Johannesburg stamp exhibition emblem. Sold for 50c to benefit stamp exhibition. Size: 102x67mm.

Caprivi Strip — A121

**1986, Nov. 6 Litho.** ***Perf. 14½x14***

*574* A121 14c Lake Liambezi 16 16
*575* A121 20c Stock and crop farming 25 25
*576* A121 25c Settlement 30 30
*577* A121 30c Map 40 40

Importation of stamps was prohibited effective November 24, 1986.

## SEMI-POSTAL STAMPS

**Catalogue values for unused stamps in this section, from this point to the end of the section, are for Never Hinged items.**

**Voortrekker Monument Issue.**

South Africa Nos. B1-B4 Overprinted **S.W.A.**

**1935-36 Wmk. 201** ***Perf. 14.***

*B1* SP1 ½p + ½p grn & blk 25 25
*a.* Pair 1.90 2.50
*B2* SP2 1p + ½p rose & blk 30 30
*a.* Pair 2.75 3.25
*B3* SP3 2p + 1p dl vio & gray 75 75
*a.* Pair 8.50 9.00
*B4* SP4 3p + 1½p dp bl & gray 1.50 1.50
*a.* Pair 15.00 17.50

**Voortrekker Centenary Issue.**

South Africa Nos. B5-B8 Overprinted **S.W.A.**

***Perf. 14 (No. B5), 15x14***

**1938, Dec. 14 Wmk. 201**

*B5* SP5 ½p + ½p dl grn & ind 25 25
*a.* Pair 1.10 1.25
*B6* SP6 1p + 1p rose & sl 35 35
*a.* Pair 1.50 1.75
*B7* SP7 1½p + 1½p Prus grn & choc 80 80
*a.* Pair 4.00 4.50
*B8* SP8 3p + 3p chlky bl 1.75 1.75
*a.* Pair 10.00 11.50

Same Overprint on South Africa Nos. B9-B11.

***Perf. 14, 15x14 (No. B11)***

**1939, July 17**

*B9* SP9 ½p + ½p Prus grn & gray brn 40 40
*a.* Pair 1.50 1.65
*B10* SP10 1p + 1p rose car & Prus grn 75 75
*a.* Pair 2.50 3.00
*B11* SP11 1½p+ 1½p rose vio, dk vio & Prus grn 1.25 1.25
*a.* Pair 4.50 5.25

250th anniv. of the landing of the Huguenots in South Africa. Surtax went to a fund to build a Huguenot memorial at Paarl.

## AIR POST STAMPS

South Africa Nos. C5-C6 Overprinted **S.W.A.**

**1930 Unwmk.** ***Perf. 14x13½***

*C1* AP2 4p bl grn 5.00 6.00
*a.* Without period after "A" 80.00 110.00
*C2* AP2 1sh orange 15.00 16.00
*a.* Without period after "A" 425.00 *500.00*

Overprinted **S.W.A.**

*C3* AP2 4p bl grn 2.25 3.00
*a.* Double overprint 150.00
*b.* Inverted overprint 125.00
*c.* Small "I" in "AIR" 6.00
*C4* AP2 1sh orange 4.00 5.75
*a.* Double overprint

Monoplane over Windhoek — AP3

Biplane over Windhoek — AP4

Inscribed alternately in English and Afrikaans.

**Wmk. 201**

**1931, Mar. 5 Engr.** ***Perf. 14.***

*C5* AP3 3p bl & dk brn 1.00 1.10
*a.* Pair 25.00 27.50
*C6* AP4 10p brn vio & blk 2.00 2.25
*a.* Pair 40.00 55.00

## POSTAGE DUE STAMPS

Postage Due Stamps of South Africa and Transvaal Overprinted like Regular Issues.

Setting I. On South Africa Nos. J11, J14

**1923 Unwmk.** ***Perf. 14***

*J1* D1 ½p bl grn & blk 12 15
*a.* Pair 50 50
*b.* As "a." without period after "Afrika" 55.00
*c.* Inverted ovpt. pair 325.00
*J2* D1 2p vio & blk 20 20
*a.* Pair 2.00 2.00
*b.* As "a." without period after "Afrika" 70.00 70.00

**On South Africa Nos. J9-J10**

***Rouletted 7-8***

*J3* D1 1p dl red & blk 12 14
*a.* Pair 2.00 2.00
*b.* As "a." without period after "Afrika" 70.00 70.00
*c.* Pair, imperf. between 825.00
*J4* D1 1½pyel brn & blk 12 12
*a.* Pair 1.50 1.75
*b.* As "a." without period after "Afrika" 42.50 42.50

**On South Africa Nos. J3-J4, J6.**

***Perf. 14***

**Wmk. 177**

*J5* D1 2p vio & blk 1.50 1.30
*a.* Pair 6.75 7.75
*b.* As "a." without period after "Afrika" 130.00
*J6* D1 3p ultra & blk 50 1.00
*a.* Pair 3.50 7.00
*J7* D1 6p gray & blk 1.00 1.00
*a.* Pair 10.00 12.00
*Nos. J1-J7 (7)* 3.56 3.91
*Nos. J1a-J2a-J3a-J4a-J5a-J6a-J7a (7)* 26.25 33.00

**On Transvaal Nos. J5-J6**

**Wmk. Multiple Crown and C. A. (3)**

*J8* D1 5p vio & blk 50 60
*a.* Pair 3.75 3.75
*b.* As "a." without period after "Africa" 60.00 60.00
*J9* D1 6p red brn & blk 1.00 1.50
*a.* Pair 7.50 10.00
*b.* As "a." without period after "Africa" 82.50

The "t" of "West" may be found partly or entirely missing on Nos. J1, J3-J6, J8-J9.

**Setting II. On South Africa No. J9**

***Rouletted***

**Unwmk.**

*J10* D1 1p dl red & blk 750.00
*a.* Pair *3,500.*

**On South Africa Nos. J3-J4**

***Perf. 14***

**Wmk. 177**

*J11* D1 2p vio & blk 30 40
*a.* Pair 5.00 6.00
*b.* AS "a." without period after "Afrika" 82.50 87.50
*J12* D1 3p ultra & blk 35 70
*a.* Pair 3.50 5.00
*b.* As "a." without period after "Afrika" 60.00 70.00

**On Transvaal No. J5**

**Wmk. Multiple Crown and C. A. (3)**

*J13* D1 5p vio & blk 15.00
*a.* Pair 75.00

**Setting III. On South Africa Nos. J11, J12, J9**

**Unwmk.**

*J14* D1 ½p bl grn & blk 25 25
*a.* Pair 1.50 2.00
*J15* D1 1p rose & blk 35 35
*a.* Pair 2.00 2.50

***Rouletted 7***

*J16* D1 1p dl red & blk 15 15
*a.* Pair 2.00 2.25

**On Transvaal No. J6**

***Perf. 14***

**Wmk. 3**

*J17* D1 6p red brn & blk 60 70
*a.* Pair 15.00 17.50

See note below No. 27.

Setting IV. On South Africa Nos. J11-J12, J16

**1924 Unwmk.**

*J18* D1 ½p bl grn & blk 12 12
*a.* Pair 80 1.00
*J19* D1 1p rose & blk 50 50
*a.* Pair 3.00 3.25
*J20* D1 6p gray & blk 30 30
*a.* Pair 2.00 2.25

**On Transvaal No. J5**

**Wmk. Multiple Crown and C. A. (3)**

*J21* D1 5p vio & blk 52.50
*a.* Pair 350.00

Setting V

| **South West** | **Zuidwest** |
|---|---|
| **Africa.** | **Afrika.** |
| i | j |

"South West" 16mm wide
"Zuidwest" 12mm wide
Overprint Spaced 12mm

On South Africa Nos. J4, J11, J13

**1924 Unwmk.**

*J22* D1 ½p grn & blk 12 12
*a.* Pair 1.00 1.25
*J23* D1 1½p yel brn & blk 12 12
*a.* Pair 1.00 1.25

**Wmk. Springbok's Head. (177)**

*J24* D1 3p ultra & blk 75 75
*a.* Pair 5.00 6.00

On Transvaal No. J5

**Wmk. Multiple Crown and C. A. (3)**

*J25* D1 5p vio & blk 75 75
*a.* Pair 5.00 6.00

Setting VI. On South Africa Nos. J4, J11-J16

**1924, Dec. Unwmk.**

*J26* D1 ½p bl grn & blk 35 35
*a.* Paid 1.00 1.10
*J27* D1 1p rose & blk 12 12
*a.* Pair 35 35
*b.* As "a." without period after "Africa" 87.50
*J28* D1 1½p yel brn & blk 12 12
*a.* Pair 50 60
*b.* As "a." without period after "Africa" 55.00

*J29* D1 2p vio & blk 15 15
a. Pair 70 75
b. As "a." without period after "Africa" 55.00
*J30* D1 3p bl & blk 20 20
a. Pair 75 85
b. As "a." without period after "Africa" 55.00
*J31* D1 6p gray & blk 75 75
a. Pair 3.50 4.00
b. As "a." without period after "Africa" 100.00
*Nos. J26-J31 (6)* 1.69 1.69

**Wmk. Springbok's Head. (177)**

*J32* D1 3p ultra & blk 70 70
a. Pair 4.00 5.00

On Transvaal No. J5

**Wmk. 3**

*J33* D1 5p vio & blk 25 25
a. Pair 1.50 1.75
b. As "a." without period after "Africa" 55.00 55.00

Setting VIII. On South Africa Nos. J18, J13-J16

**1927** **Unwmk.**

*J34* D2 1p rose & blk 12 12
a. Pair 75 75
b. As "a." without period after "Africa" 10.50 10.50
*J35* D1 1½p yel brn & blk 12 12
a. Pair 60 60
b. As "a." without period after "Africa" 50.00 50.00
*J36* D1 2p vio & blk 15 15
a. Pair 75 85
b. As "a." without period after "Africa" 50.00 50.00
*J37* D1 3p bl & blk 75 75
a. Pair 3.00 3.00
b. As "a." without period after "Africa" 70.00 70.00
*J38* D1 6p gray & blk 1.00 1.00
a. Pair 5.00 6.00
b. As "a." without period after "Africa" 100.00 115.00
*Nos. J34-J38 (5)* 2.14 2.14

On Transvaal No. J5

**Wmk. Multiple Crown and C. A. (3)**

*J39* D1 5p vio & blk 1.10 1.20
a. Pair 7.00 8.00

South Africa Nos. J15-J16 Overprinted **S.W.A.**

**1928** **Unwmk.**

*J79* D1 3p bl & blk 70 80
a. Without period after "A" 30.00 35.00
*J80* D1 6p gray & blk 2.50 2.75

**Same Overprint on South Africa Nos. J17-J21**

*J81* D2 ½p bl grn & blk 30 30
*J82* D2 1p rose & blk 60 40
a. Without period after "A" 40.00 40.00
*J83* D2 2p vio & blk 50 50
*J84* D2 3p ultra & blk 75 75
*J85* D2 6p gray & blk 2.00 3.00
a. Without period after "A" 30.00 45.00
*Nos. J81-J85 (5)* 4.15 4.95

**Catalogue values for unused stamps in this section, from this point to the end of the section, are for Never Hinged items.**

D3

D4

**Wmk. 201**

**1931, Feb. 23** **Litho.** ***Perf. 12***

**Size: 19x22mm**

*J86* D3 ½p yel grn & blk 30 35
*J87* D3 1p rose & blk 42 52
*J88* D3 2p vio & blk 42 52
*J89* D3 3p bl & blk 1.40 1.75
*J90* D3 6p gray & blk 3.75 4.25
*Nos. J86-J90 (5)* 6.29 7.39

**Photo. (Frame) & Typo. (Center)**

**1959** ***Perf. 14½x14***

**Size: 17x21mm**

*J91* D3 1p rose & blk 45 45
*J92* D3 2p vio & blk 90 90
*J93* D3 3p bl & blk 2.25 2.25

**1960** **Wmk. 330**

**Size: 17x21mm**

*J94* D3 1p rose & blk 2.50 2.50
*J95* D3 3p bl & blk 2.50 2.50

**1961, Feb.** **Photo.** ***Perf. 14½x14***

*J96* D4 1c grn & blk 10 15
*J97* D4 2c red & blk 10 15
*J98* D4 4c lil & blk 20 30
*J99* D4 5c bl & blk 25 30
*J100* D4 6c emer & blk 35 40
*J101* D4 10c yel & blk 75 85
*Nos. J96-J101 (6)* 1.75 2.15

Type of South Africa, 1972

**1972** **Wmk. 359** ***Perf. 14x13½***

*J102* D6 1c brt grn 30 40
*J106* D6 8c vio bl 2.00 2.50

## OFFICIAL STAMPS

Nos. 85-87 (Setting VIII) Overprinted at top with type "c" on English-inscribed Stamps and type "d" on Afrikaans-inscribed Stamps

**OFFICIAL** c  **OFFISIEEL** d

Without Periods after Words

**1927** **Wmk. 201** ***Perf. 14½x14***

*O1* A5 ½p dk grn & blk 8.50 4.00
a. Pair 62.50 75.00
*O2* A6 1p car & blk 8.50 4.00
a. Pair 62.50 75.00
*O3* A7 6p org & grn 8.50 4.00
a. Pair 75.00 75.00

**South Africa No. 5 Overprinted As Nos. 85-87 plus "c" and "d"**

***Perf. 14.***

**Wmk. 177**

*O4* A2 2p dl vio 22.50 7.50
a. Pair 125.00 125.00

Nos. 96-98 Overprinted like Nos. J79-J85 at foot, Overprinted Types "c" and "d" at Top

**1929** ***Perf. 14½x14***

*O5* A5 ½p grn & blk 15 15
a. Pair 75 75
*O6* A6 1p car & blk 20 20
a. Pair 1.00 1.00
*O7* A7 6p org & grn 75 75
a. Pair 3.75 3.75

No. 99 Overprinted like Nos. J79-J85 at foot, Overprinted at top

**OFFICIAL.**  **OFFISIEEL.**

With Periods after Words

***Perf. 14.***

*O8* A8 2p vio brn & gray 30 30
a. Pair 1.50 1.50
b. Without period after "OFFICIAL" 2.00 2.00
c. Pair, "b" + normal 2p 9.00 9.00
d. Without period after "OFFISIEEL" 2.00 2.00
e. Pair, "d" + normal 2p 9.50 9.50
f. Pair, "b" + "d" 9.00 9.00

In each sheet of 120 stamps there were 12 No. O8b and 10 No. O8d.

South Africa Nos. 23-25 Overprinted

**OFFICIAL** **S.W.A.** **OFFISIEEL** **S.W.A.**

Without Periods after Words

**1929** **Wmk. 201** ***Perf. 14½x14***

*O9* A5 ½p grn & blk 8 8
a. Pair 45 45
*O10* A6 1p car & blk 12 12
a. Pair 70 70
*O11* A7 6p org & grn 30 30
a. Pair 1.50 1.50

South Africa No. 26 Overprinted

**OFFICIAL. S.W.A.**  **OFFISIEEL. S.W.A.**

With Periods after Words

***Perf. 14***

*O12* A8 2p vio brn & gray 15 15
a. Pair 1.00 1.00
b. Without period after "OFFICIAL" 1.25 1.25
c. Pair, "b" + normal 2p 7.50 7.50
d. Without period after "OFFISIEEL" 1.25 1.25
e. Pair, "d" + normal 2p 7.50 7.50
f. Pair, "b" + "d" 11.00 11.00

**Catalogue values for unused stamps in this section, from this point to the end of the section, are for Never Hinged items.**

Nos. 108-109, 111 and 114 Overprinted in Red

**OFFICIAL**  **OFFISIEEL**

**1931**

*O13* A15 ½p grn & blk 6 6
a. Pair 25 25
*O14* A16 1p red & ind 10 8
a. Pair 40 30
*O15* A18 2p dk brn & dk bl 10 10
a. Pair 40 40
*O16* A21 6p ol brn & bl 24 24
a. Pair 1.25 1.25

No. 110 Overprinted in Red

**OFFICIAL**  **OFFISIEEL**

**1938, July 1** **Wmk. 201**

*O17* A17 1½p vio brn 75 50
a. Pair 4.50 4.00

Nos. 108-111, 114 Overprinted in Red

**OFFICIAL**  **OFFISIEEL**

**1945-50** **Wmk. 201** ***Perf. 14x13½.***

*O18* A15 ½p grn & blk 20 10
a. Pair 75 75
*O19* A16 1p red & ind ('50) 12 12
a. Pair 45 45
*O20* A17 1½p vio brn 15 15
a. Pair 60 60
*O21* A18 2p dk brn & dk bl ('47) 75.00 75.00
a. Pair *525.00* *800.00*
*O22* A21 6p ol brn & bl 40 40
a. Pair 1.50 1.50
*Nos. O18-O22 (5)* 75.87 75.77

Nos. 108-111, 114 Overprinted in Red

**OFFICIAL**  **OFFISIEEL**

**1951-52**

*O23* A15 ½p grn & blk ('52) 5 5
a. Pair 75 75
*O24* A16 1p red & ind 6 5
a. Pair 1.50 1.50
b. Ovpt. transposed 2.50
c. As "b," pair 12.50 12.50
*O25* A17 1½p vio brn 8 5
a. Pair 1.90 1.90
b. Ovpt. transposed 2.50
c. As "b," pair 12.50 12.50
*O26* A18 2p dk brn & dk bl 12 8
a. Pair 1.50 1.50
b. Ovpt. transposed 2.50
c. As "b," pair 12.50 12.50
*O27* A21 6p ol brn & bl 25 18
a. Pair 4.50 4.50
b. Ovpt. transposed 4.00
c. As "b," pair 18.00 18.00
*Nos. O23-O27 (5)* 56 41

"Overprint transposed" means English inscription on Afrikaans stamp, or vice versa. Use of official stamps ceased in Jan. 1955.

# SRI LANKA

LOCATION — Indian Ocean south of India.
GOVT. — Democratic Socialist Republic.
AREA — 26,244 sq. mi.
POP. — 14,850,001 (1981).
CAPITAL — Colombo.

Sri Lanka was named Ceylon until May 22, 1972. Issues inscribed "Ceylon" are listed under that name in this volume.

100 Cents = 1 Rupee

**Catalogue values for all unused stamps in this country are for Never Hinged items.**

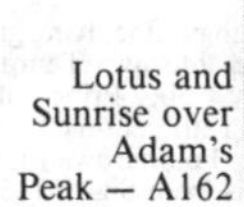
Lotus and Sunrise over Adam's Peak — A162

**1972, May 22** **Litho.** ***Perf. 13½x13***

*470* A162 15c bl & multi 12 12

Inauguration of Ceylon as Republic of Sri Lanka.

Ceylon No. 454 Overprinted "1972" in Red

**1972, May 26** ***Perf. 14x13½***

*471* A155 5c org brn & multi 8 8

World Fellowship of Buddhists, Ceylon, May 22-28.

Book Year Emblem, Oil Lamp — A163

**1972, Sept. 8** **Photo.** ***Perf. 13***

*472* A163 20c yel & dk brn 15 12

International Book Year 1972.

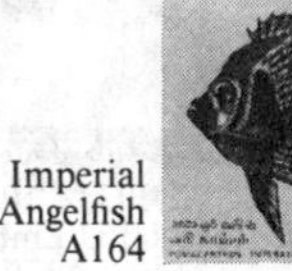
Imperial Angelfish A164

Tropical Fish: 3c, Green chromide. 30c, Skipjack bonito. 2r, Black ruby barbs.

***Perf. 14x13½***

**1972, Oct. 12** **Litho.** **Unwmk.**

*473* A164 2c ultra & multi 5 5
*474* A164 3c dp org & multi 5 5
*475* A164 30c brt grn & multi 12 8
*476* A164 2r dp grn & multi 80 40

3rd Session of Indian Ocean Fisheries Commission, Colombo, Oct. 9-14.

Bandaranaike Memorial Hall — A165

**1973, May 17** **Litho.** ***Perf. 14***

*477* A165 15c lt ultra & vio bl 8 8

Opening of Bandaranaike Memorial International Conference Hall.

Values quoted in this catalogue are for stamps graded at Fine-Very Fine and with no faults. An illustrated guide to grade is provided in introductory material, beginning on Page V.

Women Holding Lotus A166

Rock and Temple Paintings: 35c, King giving away his children, Degaldoruwa Temple, near Kandy, 18th century. 50c, Prince and gravedigger, Polonaruwa, 12th century. 90c, Holy man holding lotus, Polonaruwa, 12th century. Design of 1.55r is from Sigiriya, 5th century.

**1973, Sept. 3** *Perf. 13½x14*

| | | | | |
|---|---|---|---|---|
| *478* A166 | 35c lt gray & multi | 14 | 8 |
| *479* A166 | 50c gray & multi | 20 | 10 |
| *480* A166 | 90c sl & multi | 36 | 18 |
| *481* A166 | 1.55r brn & multi | 55 | 27 |
| *a* | Souvenir sheet of 4 | 1.50 | 1.50 |

No. 481a contains one each of Nos. 478-481; dark gray marginal inscription. Size: 115x140mm.

Bandaranaike Conference Hall — A167

**1974, Sept. 6** **Litho.** *Perf. 14*

*482* A167 85c multi 25 25

20th Commonwealth Parliamentary Conference, Sri Lanka, Sept. 1-15.

S.W.R.D. Bandaranaike A168

"UPU," "100" and UPU Emblem A170

**1974, Sept. 25** **Photo.** *Perf. 14½*

*486* A168 15c ultra & multi 8 8

**1974, Oct. 9** **Litho.** *Perf. 13*

*490* A170 50c multi 50 50

Parliament, Colombo A171

**1975, Apr. 1** **Litho.** *Perf. 13½*

*491* A171 1r multi 30 30

Interparliamentary Union, Spring Meeting at Bandaranaike Memorial International Conference Hall, Sri Lanka, Mar. 31-Apr. 5.

Ponnambalam Ramanathan A172

D. J. Wimalasurendra A173

**1975, Sept. 4** **Litho.** *Perf. 13½*

*492* A172 75c multi 25 25

Sir Ponnambalam Ramanathan (1851-1930), lawyer and educator.

**1975, Sept. 17**

*493* A173 75c ultra & bl blk 40 40

Devapura Jayasena Wimalasurendra (1874-1953), engineer and irrigation specialist.

Map, Mrs. Bandaranaike, Dove — A174

Rhododendron Zeylanicum A175

**1975, Dec. 22** **Litho.** *Perf. 13½*

*494* A174 1.15r bl & multi 35 35

International Women's Year 1975.

**1976, Jan. 1** **Litho.** *Perf. 13*

Flowers: 50c, Exacum trinerve. 75c, Daffodil orchid. 10r, Wormia triquetra.

| | | | |
|---|---|---|---|
| *495* A175 | 25c bl & multi | 10 | 10 |
| *496* A175 | 50c ocher & multi | 20 | 20 |
| *497* A175 | 75c blk & multi | 40 | 40 |
| *498* A175 | 10r blk & multi | 2.00 | 2.00 |
| *a* | Souvenir sheet of 4 | 3.50 | 3.50 |

No. 498a contains one each of Nos. 495-498; bright blue and multicolored margin showing flowers. Size: 152x152mm.

Mahaveli-ganga Sluice — A176

**1976, Jan. 8** **Litho.** *Perf. 13x12½*

*499* A176 85c lt bl, lt grn & lil 45 45

Mahaveli-ganga River diversion.

Radar Station — A177

**1976, May 6** **Litho.** *Perf. 14*

*500* A177 1r bl & multi 30 30

Opening of Satellite Earth Station, Padukka.

Prince Siddhartha as White Elephant and Sleeping Queen — A178

Designs: 10c, King consulting astrologers. 1.50r, King entertaining astrologers at banquet. 2r, Queen taken in procession to her parents. 2.25r, Flag bearers, musicians in procession. 5r, Queen giving birth to Prince Siddhartha, the Buddha. Designs taken from 18th century wall paintings in Dambawa Vihara Temple.

**1976, May 7** **Litho.** *Perf. 13½*

| | | | |
|---|---|---|---|
| *501* A178 | 5c bl & multi | 5 | 5 |
| *502* A178 | 10c bl & multi | 5 | 5 |
| *503* A178 | 1.50r bl & multi | 25 | 25 |
| *504* A178 | 2r bl & multi | 30 | 30 |
| *505* A178 | 2.25r bl & multi | 35 | 35 |
| *506* A178 | 5r bl & multi | 75 | 75 |
| *a* | Souvenir sheet of 6 | 3.50 | 3.50 |
| | *Nos. 501-506 (6)* | 1.75 | 1.75 |

Birth of Buddha. No. 506a contains one each of Nos. 501-506; brown marginal inscription. Size: 160x95mm.

Blue Sapphire A179

Gems of Sri Lanka: 1.15r, Cat's-eye. 2r, Star sapphire. 5r, Ruby.

**1976, June 16** *Perf. 12x12½*

| | | | |
|---|---|---|---|
| *507* A179 | 60c multi | 30 | 30 |
| *508* A179 | 1.15r multi | 40 | 40 |
| *509* A179 | 2r multi | 60 | 60 |
| *510* A179 | 5r multi | 1.50 | 1.50 |
| *a* | Souvenir sheet of 4 | 3.75 | 3.75 |

No. 510a contains one each of Nos. 507-510; multicolored margin showing gems and panners. Size: 152x152mm.

Prime Minister Sirimavo Bandaranaike A180

Statue of Liberty A181

**1976, Aug. 3** **Photo.** *Perf. 14x14½*

| | | | |
|---|---|---|---|
| *511* A180 | 1.15r pink & multi | 35 | 35 |
| *512* A180 | 2r pink & multi | 40 | 40 |

5th Summit Conference of Non-aligned Countries, Colombo, Aug. 9-19.

**1976, Nov. 29** **Litho.** *Perf. 14*

*513* A181 2.25r lt bl & ind 80 80

American Bicentennial.

A. G. Bell, Telephone and Telegraph Line A182

Maitreya Bodhisattva A183

**1976, Dec. 21** **Litho.** *Perf. 13x13½*

*514* A182 1r org & multi 30 30

Centenary of first telephone call by Alexander Graham Bell, Mar. 10, 1876.

**1977, Jan. 1** **Litho.** *Perf. 12½x13*

Bronze Statues: 1r, Sundara Murti Swami, 11th century. 5r, Goddess Tara.

| | | | |
|---|---|---|---|
| *515* A183 | 50c multi | 15 | 15 |
| *516* A183 | 1r multi | 20 | 20 |
| *517* A183 | 5r multi | 75 | 75 |

Colombo Museum, centenary.

Kandyan Crown, 1737-1815 A184

Design: 2r, Kandyan throne and footstool, 1693-1815.

**1977, Jan. 18**

| | | | |
|---|---|---|---|
| *518* A184 | 1r multi | 60 | 60 |
| *519* A184 | 2r multi | 80 | 80 |

Rahula Thero — A185

Brass Lamps — A186

Portrait: No. 521, Ponnambalam Arunachalam.

**1977** **Litho.** *Perf. 13½*

| | | | |
|---|---|---|---|
| *520* A185 | 1r multi | 30 | 30 |
| *521* A185 | 1r multi | 30 | 30 |

Sri Rahula Thero, 15th century poet and scholar, and Sir Ponnambalam Arunachalam (1851-1930), first president of Ceylon University Association, member of Congress.

Issue dates: No. 520, Feb. 23; No. 521, Mar. 10.

**1977, Apr. 7** *Perf. 13*

Handicrafts: 25c, Jewelry box and jewelry. 50c, Caparisoned ivory elephant. 5r, Sinhala wooden mask.

| | | | |
|---|---|---|---|
| *522* A186 | 20c multi | 8 | 8 |
| *523* A186 | 25c multi | 12 | 12 |
| *524* A186 | 50c multi | 22 | 22 |
| *525* A186 | 5r multi | 1.10 | 1.10 |
| *a* | Souvenir sheet of 4 | 3.00 | 3.00 |

No. 525a contains one each of Nos. 522-525. Blue and black design in margin shows artisans at work. Size: 205x89mm.

Mohammed Cassim Siddi Lebbe — A187

**1977, June 11** **Litho.** *Perf. 13*

*526* A187 1r multi 60 60

Mohammed Cassim Siddi Lebbe (1838-1898), lawyer, educator and Moslem journalist.

Girl Guide A188

**1977, Dec. 13** **Litho.** *Perf. 15*

*527* A188 75c multi 40 40

60th anniversary of Sri Lanka Girl Guides.

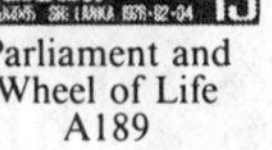
Parliament and Wheel of Life
A189

Runners
A190

**978, Feb. 4 Photo. *Perf. 12x12½***
*28* A189 15c grn & gold 8 8

J.R. Jayewardene, first elected president, ssumption of office.
See Nos. 559, 611, 611A, 847.

**978, Apr. 27 Litho. *Perf. 15***
*29* A190 15c multi 8 8

National Youth Service Council.

Bodhisattva in Royal Attire in Lotus Position
A191

Design: 50c, Bodhisattva without royal ttire cutting off his hair with sword. Both lesigns from rock carvings in Borobudur Temple, Java.

**1978, May 16 *Perf. 13***
*530* A191 15c multi 8 8
*531* A191 50c multi 30 30

Vesak festival.

Veera Puran Appu and his Flag
A192

Birdwing Butterfly
A193

**1978, Aug. 8 Litho. *Perf. 13***
*532* A192 15c multi 8 8

Veera Puran Appu (1848-1908), revolutionist, 130th birth anniversary.

**1978, Nov. 28 Litho. *Perf. 14x13½***

Butterflies: 50c, Tamil lacewing. 5r, Blue oakleaf. 10r, Blue mormon.

*534* A193 25c multi 6 5
*535* A193 50c multi 10 8
*536* A193 5r multi 80 60
*537* A193 10r multi 1.75 1.25
*a* Souvenir sheet of 4 3.50 3.50

No. 537a contains Nos. 534-537; multicolored margin shows butterflies and plants. Size: 122½x147mm.

Nos. 478, 480-481 Surcharged with New Value and Bar

**1978 Litho. *Perf. 13½x14***
*538* A166 5c on 90c multi 8 8
*539* A166 10c on 35c multi 8 8
*540* A166 1r on 1.55r multi 35 35

Nos. 486, 528 Surcharged with New Value and 2 Bars; No. 529 with New Value on Pink Panel

***Perf. 14½, 12x12½, 15***

**1979, Jan. Litho.; Engr.**
*541* A168 25c on 15c multi 75 75
*542* A189 25c on 15c multi 75 75
*543* A190 25c on 15c multi 75 75

Ceylon No. 390 Overprinted Vertically "SRI LANKA" in Green and Surcharged in Black

**1979, Mar. 22 Photo. *Perf. 11½***
**Granite Paper**
*544* A118 15c on 10c brt grn 15 15

Arrival of Sacred Tooth
A194

Wrestlers
A195

Wall Paintings from Kelaniya Temple: 25c, Prince Danta and Princess Hema Mala bringing Sacred Tooth from Kalinga, 4th century A.D. 1r, Princess Theri Sanghamitta bringing, by ship, the bodhi tree branch, 3rd century B.C. 10r, King Kirti offering fan of authority to supreme patriarch, 18th century.

**1979, May 3 Litho. *Perf. 13½***
*546* A194 25c multi 5 5
*547* A194 1r multi 15 15
*548* A194 10r multi 1.50 1.50
*a* Souvenir sheet of 3 1.75 1.75

2523rd Vesak Festival, May 11. No. 548a contains Nos. 546-548; gray and black margin. Size: 120x80mm.

**1979, May 18 Litho. *Perf. 14***

Design: 50r, Dancer. Woodcarvings from Embekke Temple.

*549* A195 20r multi 2.00 2.00
*550* A195 50r multi 6.00 6.00

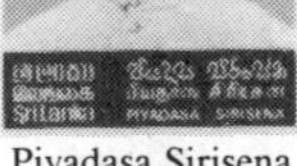
Piyadasa Sirisena
A196

Dudley S. Senanayake
A197

**1979, May 22 *Perf. 13x13½***
*551* A196 1.25r dp grn 20 20

Piyadasa Sirisena (1875-1946), patriot, journalist, novelist and poet.

**1979, June 19 Photo.**
*552* A197 1.25r dp grn 20 20

27th death anniversary of Prime Minister Dudley S. Senanayake.

Mother Feeding Child, IYC Emblem
A198

Designs: 3r, Faces and IYC emblem. 5r, Children with rope and ball, IYC emblem.

**1979, July 31 Litho. *Perf. 12½***
*553* A198 5r multi 5 5
*554* A198 3r multi 30 30
*555* A198 5r multi 50 50

International Year of the Child.

Ceylon No. 2, Rowland Hill
A199

Airlanka Emblem
A200

**1979, Aug. 27 Litho. *Perf. 13½***
*556* A199 3r multi 35 35

Sir Rowland Hill (1795-1879), originator of penny postage.

**1979, Sept. 1 Litho. *Perf. 12½***
*557* A200 3r red, dk grn & blk 35 35

Airlanka National Airline, inaugural flight, Colombo-Bangkok.

Coconut Palm — A201

**1979, Oct. 9 Litho. *Perf. 13½***
*558* A201 2r multi 25 25

Asian and Pacific Coconut Community, 10th anniversary.

No. 528 Redrawn Without Date

**1979, Oct. 9 Photo. *Perf. 13***
**Size: 20x24 mm.**
*559* A189 25c grn & gold 5 5

Family in Cogwheel, Parliament
A202

**1979, Oct. Litho. *Perf. 13½***
*560* A202 2r multi 30 30

International Conference of Parliamentarians on Population and Development, Colombo, Aug. 28-Sept. 1.

Swami Vipulananda — A203

**1979, Nov. 18 *Perf. 12½***
*561* A203 1.25r multi 20 20

Swami Vipulananda (1892-1947), philosopher and theologian.

Text and Crescent
A204

**1979, Nov. 22**
*562* A204 3.75r multi 60 60

Hegira (pilgrimage year).

Institute Emblem
A205

Blue Magpie
A206

**1979, Nov. 29 *Perf. 13***
*563* A205 15c multi 5 5

Ayurveda Medical Institute, 50th anniversary.

**1979, Dec. 13 Litho. *Perf. 14***
*564* A206 10c *shown* 5 5
*565* A206 15c *Lorikeet* 5 5
*566* A206 75c *Arrenga* 10 8
*567* A206 1r *Spurfowl* 18 12
*568* A206 5r *Yellow-fronted barbet* 75 60
*569* A206 10r *Yellow-eared bulbul* 1.50 60
*a* Souvenir sheet of 6 1.50 1.50
*Nos. 564-569 (6)* 2.63 1.50

No. 569a contains Nos. 564-569; multicolored margin shows birds in trees Size: 151½x151½mm.

Rotary Emblem, Map of Sri Lanka
A207

**1979, Dec. 27 Litho. *Perf. 14½***
*570* A207 1.50r multi 35 35

Rotary International, 75th anniversary.

A. Ratnayake — A208

**1980, Jan. 7 Photo. *Perf. 14x13½***
*571* A208 1.25r sl grn 20 20

A. Ratnayake, educator and president of Senate.

No. 559 Surcharged

**1980, Mar. 17 Photo. *Perf. 13***
*572* A189 35c on 25c multi 15 15

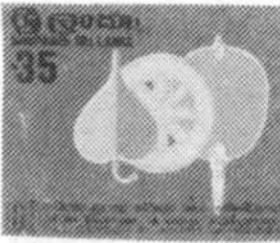
Leaf, Wheel, Fan (Buddhist Symbols) — A209

**1980, Mar. 25 Photo. *Perf. 13½x14***
*573* A209 10c *Steeple* 6 6
*574* A209 35c *shown* 8 8

All Ceylon Buddhist Congress, 60th anniversary.

Col. Henry Olcott, Buddhist Emblem — A210

Journey of Patachara, Temple Painting — A211

**1980, May 17 Litho. *Perf. 14***
*575* A210 2r multi 28 28

Col. Henry S. Olcott (1832-1907), American theosophist and Buddhist lecturer, centenary of arrival in Sri Lanka.

**1980, May 23 *Perf. 13½x14***

Vesak Festival (Paintings, life of Buddha): 1.60r, Patachara crossing river.

*576* A211 35c multi 5 5
*577* A211 1.60r multi 25 25

George E. De Silva — A212

**1980, June 8 *Perf. 13x13½***
*578* A212 1.60r multi 25 25

George E. de Silva (1879-1950), politician.

Siva Temples, Polonnaruwa — A213

**1980, Aug. 25 Litho. *Perf. 13½***
*579* A213 35c *shown* 5 5
*580* A213 35c *Cave Temples, Dambulla* 5 5
*581* A213 35c *Sacred Tooth Temple, Kandy* 5 5
*582* A213 1.60r *Abhayagiri Hill* 20 20
*583* A213 1.60r *Jetavanarama Hill* 20 20
*584* A213 1.60r *Sigiri* 20 20
*a* Souvenir sheet of 6 90 90
*Nos. 579-584 (6)* 75 75

UNESCO "Cultural Triangle" Project. No. 584a contains Nos. 579-584; multicolored margin with UNESCO emblem. Size: 216x116mm.

Department of Cooperative Development, 50th Anniversary A214

**1980, Oct. 1 Litho. *Perf. 13½***
*585* A214 20c multi 5 5

Women's Movement Emblem A215

**1980, Oct. 16 Photo. *Perf. 14x13½***
*586* A215 35c multi 5 5

Mahila Samiti (Rural Women's Movement), 50th anniversary.

Nativity — A216

**1980, Nov. 20 Litho. *Perf. 13½***
*587* A216 35c *shown* 5 5
*588* A216 3.75r *Three kings* 50 50
*a* Souvenir sheet of 2 65 65

Christmas 1980/Year of the family. No. 588a contains Nos. 587-588; multicolored margin continues design. Size: 125x75mm.

Colombo Public Library Opening A217

**1980, Dec. 17 *Perf. 12x12½***
*589* A217 35c multi 5 5

Peacock Banner A218

Designs: Ancient flags.

**1980, Dec. 18 *Perf. 13***
*590* A218 10c *shown* 5 5
*591* A218 25c *Elephant banner* 5 5
*592* A218 1.60r *Kings Civil Standard* 20 20
*593* A218 20r *Sinhalese royal flag* 2.25 2.25
*a* Souvenir sheet of 4 2.75 2.75

No. 593a contains Nos. 590-593; multicolored margin shows royal procession. Size: 216x139½mm.

Fishing Cat — A219

**1981, Feb. 10 Litho. *Perf. 14***
*594* A219 2.50r on 1.60r, shown 40 30
*595* A219 3r on 1.50r, Golden palm cat 45 30
*596* A219 4r on 2r, Mouse deer 60 45
*597* A219 5r on 3.75r, Rusty-spotted cat 75 60
*a* Souvenir sheet of 4, #594-597 2.25 2.25

See Nos. 728-730.

Population and Housing Census — A220

**1981, Mar. 2 Litho. *Perf. 12½x12***
*598* A220 50c multi 8 8

Ceylon Light Infantry Centenary A221

The Death of Buddha, Carved Panel, 1st Cent. A222

**1981, Apr. 1 Litho. *Perf. 12***
*599* A221 2r multi 30 30

**1981, May 5 *Perf. 13x13½***
*600* A222 35c shown 5 5
*601* A222 50c Silk banner 6 6
*602* A222 7r Statuette 90 90
*a* Souvenir sheet of 3 1.00 1.00

Vesak Festival. No. 602a contains Nos. 600-602; multicolored margin shows leaves. Size: 149x109mm.

St. John Baptist de la Salle A223

**1981, May 15 Litho. *Perf. 12½x12***
*603* A223 2r multi 30 30

De la Salle Brothers Order, 300th anniv.

Polwatte Sri Buddadatta A224

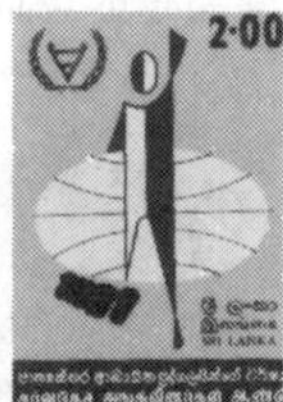

Intl. Year of the Disabled A225

Famous Men: No. 605, Mohottiwatte Gunananda, Buddhist leader. No. 606, Gnanapra Kasar, Catholic missionary. No. 607, Al-Haj T.B. Jayah, Muslim teacher. No. 608, James Peiris. No. 609, N.M. Perera, founded first Marxist Party in Sri Lanka, 1935.

**1981 Photo. *Perf. 12***
*604* A224 50c ol bis 8 8
*605* A224 50c dl red brn 8 8
*606* A224 50c lilac 8 8
*607* A224 50c gray grn 8 8
*608* A224 50c brown 8 8
*609* A224 50c crim rose 8 8
*Nos. 604-609 (6)* 48 48

Issue dates: Nos. 604-606 May 22; No. 607, May 31; No. 609, June 6.
See Nos. 623-624, 640-642, 646.

**1981, June 19 Litho. *Perf. 12x12½***
*610* A225 2r multi 25 25

No. 528 Redrawn with Denomination in Upper Right Corner.

**1981-83 Photo. *Perf. 13***
**Size: 20x24mm.**
*611* A189 50c grn & gold 15 15
*611A* A189 60c grn & gold 15 15

Issue dates: 50c, June 6. 60c, Dec. 30, 1983.

Hand Putting Ballot in Box A226

***Perf. 12½x12, 12x12½***
**1981, July 7 Litho.**
*612* A226 50c shown 6 6
*613* A226 7r Ballot box on map, vert. 90 90

Universal Franchise, 50th anniv.

Rhys Davids (Society Founder) A227

**1981, July 14 *Perf. 12½x12***
*614* A227 35c multi 10 10

All Ceylon Buddhist Students' Federation, 25th Anniv. A228

**1981, July 21 Litho. *Perf. 13½***
*615* A228 2r multi 25 25

Family Planning — A229

**1981, Sept. 25**
*616* A229 50c multi 10 10

7th World Acupuncture Congress — A230

**1981, Oct. 20 Litho. *Perf. 12x12½***
*617* A230 2r multi 30 30

Visit of Queen Elizabeth II, Oct. — A231

Designs: Flags of Gt. Britain and Sri Lanka.

**1981, Oct. 21 *Perf. 14***
*618* A231 50c multi 8 8
*619* A231 5r multi 75 75
*a* Souvenir sheet of 2 80 80

No. 619a contains Nos. 618-619; multicolored margin shows map of Sri Lanka. Size: 165x90mm.

Forest Conservation A232

**1981, Nov. 27** *Perf. 13½x13*
*620* A232 35c Forest 5 5
*621* A232 50c Tree planting 8 8
*622* A232 5r Jack tree 70 70
*a* Souvenir sheet of 3 80 80

No. 622a contains Nos. 620-622 (perf. 14x13); multicolored margin shows forest. Size: 180x90mm.

Famous Men Type of 1981

Designs: No. 623, F.R. Senanayaka (1882-1926), lawyer and politician. No. 624, Philip Gunawardhane, politician, 10th death anniv.

**1982** **Litho.** *Perf. 14*
*623* A224 50c brown 10 10
*624* A224 50c brt rose 10 10

Issue dates: No. 623, Jan. 1; No. 624, Jan. 11.

Dept. of Inland Revenue, 50th Anniv. A233

Natl. Television Inauguration A234

**1982, Feb. 9** **Litho.** *Perf. 14*
*625* A233 50c multi 8 8

**1982, Feb. 15**
*626* A234 2.50r multi 38 38

Sesquicentennial of Cricket Introduction and Centenary of Sri Lanka vs. England Match — A235

**1982, Feb. 17**
*627* A235 2.50r multi 38 38

Osbeckia Wightiana A236

**1982, Apr. 1** *Perf. 12*
*628* A236 35c shown 5 5
*629* A236 2r Mesua nagassarium 25 25
*630* A236 7r Rhodomyrtus tomentosa 80 80
*631* A236 20r Phaius tancarvilleae 2.25 2.25
*a* Souvenir sheet of 4 3.75 3.75

No. 631a contains Nos. 628-631; rose and tan margin. Size: 181x111mm.

Food and Nutrition Planning A237

World Hindu Conference A238

**1982, Apr. 6** **Litho.** *Perf. 13*
*632* A237 50c multi 8 8

**1982, Apr. 21** *Perf. 14x14½*
*633* A238 50c multi 10 10

Vesak Festival 1982 A239

Scenes from Jataka Story (Pre-incarnation of Buddha), Cloth Painting, 3rd cent. B.C., Hanguranketa Temple (King Vessantara and): 35c, Giving away white elephant. 50c, Royal Family in Vankagiri Forest. 2.50r, Giving away his children to a Brahmin. 5r, Royal family in chariot.

**1982, Apr. 23** *Perf. 14*
*634* A239 35c multi 5 5
*635* A239 50c multi 8 8
*636* A239 2.50r multi 38 38
*637* A239 5r multi 75 75
*a* Souvenir sheet of 4 1.25 1.25

No. 637a contains Nos. 634-637; multicolored margin. Size: 161x115mm.

New Parliament Building Opening A240

**1982, Apr. 29**
*638* A240 50c multi 10 10

Scouting Year A241

**1982, May 24** **Litho.** *Perf. 12½x12*
*639* A241 50c multi 10 10

Famous Men Type of 1981

**1982** *Perf. 12x12½*
*640* A224 50c C.W.W. Kannangara 10 10
*641* A224 50c G.P. Malalasekara 10 10
*642* A224 50c John Kotelawala 10 10

Issue dates: No. 640, May 22; No. 641, May 26, No. 642, June 8.

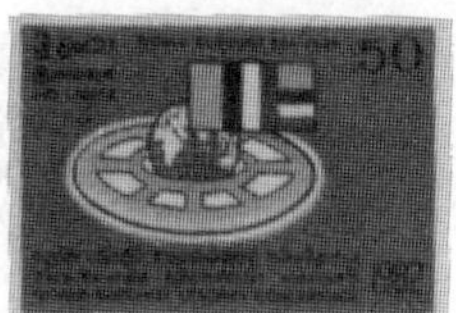


World Buddhist Leaders Conference — A242

**1982, June 10** *Perf. 12½x12*
*643* A242 50c multi 10 10

World Environment Day — A243

**1982, June 5**
*644* A243 50c multi 10 10

YMCA Centenary — A244

**1982, June 24** **Photo.** *Perf. 11½*
*645* A244 2.50r multi 50 50

Famous Men Type of 1981

**1982, June 14** **Litho.** *Perf. 12x12½*
*646* A224 50c Waitialingam Duraiswamy 10 10

Weliwita Saranankara Sangharaja — A245

**1982, July 5**
*647* A245 50c org & blk 10 10

25th Anniv. of Sasana Sevaka Samithiya A246

**1982, Aug. 8**
*648* A246 50c multi 10 10

TB Bacillus Centenary A247

**1982, Sept. 21**
*649* A247 50c Koch, microscope, bacillus 10 10

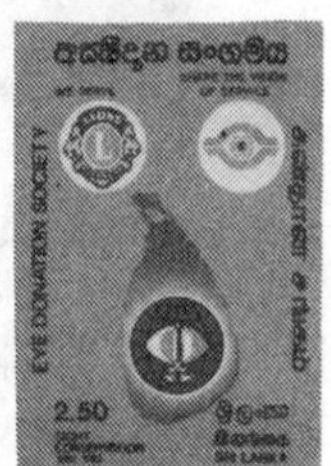


Eye Donation Society — A248

**1982, Nov. 16** **Litho.** *Perf. 12x12½*
*650* A248 2.50r Emblems, map 40 40

125th Anniv. of Ceylon Postage Stamps A249

**1982, Dec. 1** **Litho.** *Perf. 13½*
*651* A249 50c Ceylon Nos. 5, 302 8 8
*652* A249 2.50r Ceylon #12, #611 40 40
*a* Souvenir sheet of 2 50 50

Natl. Stamp Exhibition. No. 652a contains Nos. 651-652 (perf. 12). Size: 160x85mm.

Sir Oliver Goonetilleke A250

**1982, Dec. 17** **Litho.** *Perf. 12x12½*
*653* A250 50c blk & brn 6 6

25th Anniv. of Sarvodaya Social Movement A251

**1983, Jan. 1** *Perf. 13½*
*654* A251 50c multi 6 6

55th Anniv. of Amateur Radio Society A252

**1983, Jan. 17**
*655* A252 2.50r multi 30 30

Customs Cooperation Council and First Intl. Customs Day — A253

**1983, Jan. 26** **Litho.** *Perf. 12*
*656* A253 50c org & multi 6 6
*657* A253 5r grn & multi 30 30

Bottlenose Dolphin A254

**1983, Feb. 22** *Perf. 14½x14*
*658* A254 50c shown 6 6
*659* A254 2r Dugongs 25 25
*660* A254 2.50r Humpback whale 30 30
*661* A254 10r Great sperm whale 1.25 1.25

Ceylon Shipping Corp. A255

**1983, Mar. 1** *Perf. 12x12½*
*662* A255 50c Container ship 7 7
*663* A255 2.50r Liner services map 28 28

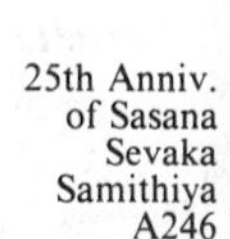

*664* A255 5r Conventional ship 60 60
*665* A255 20r Oil tanker 2.50 2.50

Intl. Women's Day — A256

**1983, Mar. 8** *Perf. 13½*
*666* A256 50c Woman, flag 6 6
*667* A256 5r Woman, map 60 60

Commonwealth Day — A257

**1983, Mar. 14**
*668* A257 50c Waterfall 6 6
*669* A257 2.50r Tea picking 20 20
*670* A257 5r Harvesting 50 50
*671* A257 20r Cultural pageant 1.75 1.75

Famous Men Type of 1981

**1983, May 22 Litho.** *Perf. 12*
*672* A224 50c Henry W. Amarasuriya 7 7

**Size: 29x40mm.**
*673* A224 50c Charles A. Lorenz 7 7
*674* A224 50c Simon G. Perera 7 7
*675* A224 50c Nordeen H.M. Abdul Cader 7 7
*676* A224 50c C.W. Tamotherampillai 7 7
*Nos. 672-676 (5)* 35 35

25th Anniv. of Lions Club A258

**1983, May 7 Litho.** *Perf. 14*
*677* A258 2.50r multi 35 35

Vesak Festival 1983 — A259

Various Colombo murals.

**1983, May 13** *Perf. 12½x12*
*678* A259 35c multi 5 5
*679* A259 50c multi 6 6
*680* A259 5r multi 40 40
*681* A259 10r multi 80 80
*a* Souvenir sheet of 4 1.75 1.75

No. 681a contains Nos. 678-681. Size: 150x92mm.

125th Anniv. of Telecommunication Service — A260

**1983, May 17** *Perf. 12x12½*
*682* A260 2r shown 20 20
*683* A260 10r World Communications Year 1.00 1.00

Gam Udawa Village Re-awakening Movement — A261

**1983, June 23 Litho.** *Perf. 12x12½*
*684* A261 50c Family 6 6
*685* A261 5r Village 50 50

Cattle Transport A262

**1983, Aug. 1 Litho.** *Perf. 12*
*686* A262 35c shown 5 5
*687* A262 2r Train 20 20
*688* A262 2.50r Cattle cart 25 25
*689* A262 5r Model T Ford 50 50

Sir Tikiri Banda Panabokke, 20th Death Anniv. — A263

**1983, Sept. 2 Litho.** *Perf. 13½x14*
*690* A263 50c dk red 10 10

Ceylon Wood Pigeon A264

**1983, Dec. 1 Litho.** *Perf. 14½*
*691* A264 25c shown 5 5
*692* A264 35c Ceylon White-Eye 5 5
*693* A264 2r Dusky-Blue Flycatcher 20 20
*694* A264 20r Ceylon Coucal 2.00 2.00
*a* Souvenir sheet of 4 2.25

No. 694a contains Nos. 691-694. Size: 183x93mm.
See No. 877.

Christmas, Stone Carvings — A265

**1983, Dec. 5 Litho.** *Perf. 12½x13*
*695* A265 50c multi 5 5
*696* A265 5r ultra & bis 50 50
*a* Souvenir sheet of 2 plus label 60

No. 696a contains Nos. 695-696. Size: 85x147mm.

Rev. Pelene Thero (1878-1955), Buddhist Leader — A266

**1983, Nov. 25 Litho.** *Perf. 14x15*
*697* A266 50c brown 10 10

Ahamed Orabi Al-Misri — A267

**1983 Litho.** *Perf. 13½*
*698* A267 50c green 10 10

No. 611 Surcharged with Four Bars and New Denomination

**1983, Dec. 1 Photo.** *Perf. 13*
*698A* A189 60c on 50c No. 611 12 12

Ovpt. also exists with two bars.

No. 611A Surcharged in Green

**1985, Dec. 1 Photo.** *Perf. 13*
**Size: 20x24 mm.**
*698B* A189 75c on 60c grn & gold 14 14

World Food Day (Oct. 16) — A268

**1984, Jan. 2** *Perf. 12½x12*
*699* A268 3r Rice paddy 24 24

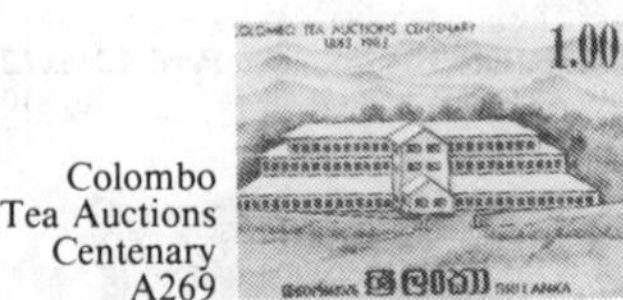

Colombo Tea Auctions Centenary A269

**1984, Jan. 31**
*700* A269 1r Auction House 8 8
*701* A269 2r Emblem 16 16
*702* A269 5r Tea picker 40 40
*703* A269 10r Auction 80 80

Mahapola Anniversary (Educational System) — A270

**1984, Feb. 10** *Perf. 12*
*704* A270 60c Students 5 5
*705* A270 1r Classroom 10 10
*706* A270 5.50r Student in library, lab 50 50
*707* A270 6r Emblem 60 60

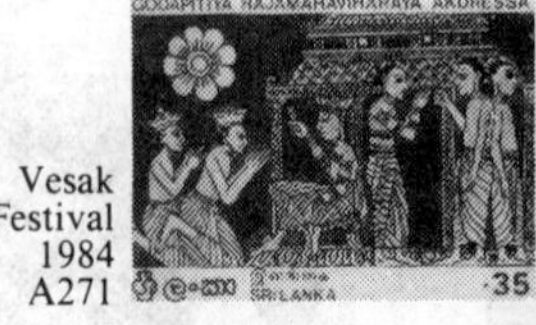

Vesak Festival 1984 A271

Wooden Casket Paintings, Temple Godapitiya Rajamaha Vihara, Akuressa: Scenes from Daham Sonda Jathaka legend.

**1984, Apr. 27 Litho.** *Perf. 14*
*708* A271 35c multi 5 5
*709* A271 60c multi 6 6
*710* A271 5r multi 55 55
*711* A271 10r multi 1.25 1.25
*a* Souvenir sheet of 4 1.75 1.75

No. 711a contains Nos. 708-711 (perf. 13x13 ½); multicolored margin shows flowers. Size: 155x110mm.

Lions Club Intl., District 306A — A272

**1984, May 5 Litho.** *Perf. 14x14½*
*712* A272 60c multi 8 8

Famous Men Type of 1981

Designs: No. 713, K. Balasingham, lawyer. No. 714, Mohamed Macan Markar (1879-1952), Muslim politician. No. 715, W. Arthur de Silva (d. 1942), industrialist. No. 716, Tissa Mahanayake Thero (1826-1907), Buddhist educator. No. 717, G.P. Wickremarachchi, medical pioneer.

**1984, May 22 Litho.** *Perf. 12x12½*
*713* A224 60c brown 8 8
*714* A224 60c green 8 8
*715* A224 60c org red 8 8
*716* A224 60c bister 8 8
*717* A224 60c yel grn 8 8
*Nos. 713-717 (5)* 40 40

Public Service Mutual Provident Assoc. Centenary A273

**1984, June 16** *Perf. 13x13½*
*718* A273 4.60r Emblem 35 35

Village Re-awakening Movement — A274

**1984, June 23** *Perf. 12x12½*
719 A274 60c "One Million Houses" 8 8

Asia-Pacific Broadcasting Union, 20th Anniv. — A275

**1984, June 30** *Perf. 12½x12*
720 A275 7r Map 65 65

Cultural Pageant A276

Procession: a. Drummers, elephant. b. Torch bearers, three elephants (green or red masks). c. Torch bearers, three elephants (orange or yellow masks). d. Dancers. Continuous design.

**1984, Aug. 11 Litho.** *Perf. 12½x12*
721 Strip of 4 1.65 1.65
a.-d. A276 4.60r, any single 40 40
e. Souvenir sheet of 4 1.65 1.65

Size of No. 721e: 222x106mm.

Orchid Circle of Sri Lanka, 50th Anniversary A277

**1984, Aug. 31** *Perf. 14*
722 A277 60c Vanda memoria 6 6
723 A277 4.60r Acanthephippium bicolor 45 45
724 A277 5r Vanda Tessellata 50 50
725 A277 10r Anoectochillus setaceus 1.10 1.10
a. Souvenir sheet of 4 1.75 1.75

No. 725a contains Nos. 722-725.

Natl. Coat of Arms — A278

*Perf. 14½x14*
**1984, Aug. 15 Engr. Wmk.**
726 A278 50r vermilion 5.00 5.00
727 A278 100r dp cl 10.00 10.00

Wildlife Type of 1981

**1984 Litho.** *Perf. 14*
728 A219 2.50r Felis viverrina 18 18
729 A219 3r Paradoxurus zeylonensis 22 22
730 A219 4r Tragulus meminna 30 30

No. 728 Surcharged in Brown.

**1985, Dec. 1 Litho.** *Perf. 14*
731 A219 5.75r on 2.50r multi 40 40

The Observer Newspaper, 150th Anniv. A280

**1984, Aug. 31 Litho.** *Perf. 13x13½*
732 A280 4.60r Publisher, Colombo 32 32

Natl. School Games — A281

**1984, Oct. 5** *Perf. 13½x13*
733 A281 60c bl, gray & blk 8 8

D. S. Senanayake (1884-1952), Prime Minister — A282

**1984, Oct. 20** *Perf. 14½x14*
734 A282 35c Irrigated field 5 5
735 A282 60c Statue 5 5
736 A282 4.60r Reservoir 32 32
737 A282 6r Parliament House, Colombo 42 42

World Food Program — A284

Baari Arabic College, Weligama, Cent. — A285

**1984, Dec. 10 Litho.** *Perf. 13x13½*
738 A284 7r Globe, Sri Lankans working field 60 60

**1984, Dec. 24** *Perf. 13x12½*
739 A285 4.60r dl bl grn & blk 35 35

Intl. Youth Year — A286

World Religion Day — A287

**1985, Jan. 1** *Perf. 12½x13*
740 A286 4.60r multi 35 35
741 A286 20r multi 1.50 1.50

**1985, Jan. 20** *Perf. 12*

Design: Emblems of World religions.

742 A287 4.60r multi 35 35

Royal College, Colombo, 150th Anniv. A288

Mahapola Scholarship Program for Development & Education, 5th Anniv. A289

**1985, Jan. 29** *Perf. 13x12½*
743 A288 60c College crest 10 10
744 A288 7r Campus 60 60

**1985, Feb. 7** *Perf. 14*
745 A289 60c Diplomas, freighter, office buildings 8 8

Wariyapola Sri Sumangala Thero, Leader of the 1818 Great Uva Rebellion — A290

**1985, Mar. 2** *Perf. 13x13½*
746 A290 60c brn & yel 8 8

Victoria Project A291

*Perf. 12½x12, 12x12½*
**1985, Apr. 12 Litho.**
747 A291 60c Victoria Dam 5 5
748 A291 7r Dam, map, vert. 50 50

Vesak Festival 1985 A292

Natl. Heroes A293

Designs: 35c, Frontispiece of the Buddhist Annual golden jubilee issue. 60c, Women worshiping at temple, Vesak Poya Holiday cent. 6r, Bauddha Mandiraya, Colombo. 9r, Buddhist flag cent.

**1985, Apr. 26** *Perf. 13x12½*
749 A292 35c multi 5 5
750 A292 60c multi 5 5
751 A292 6r multi 45 45
752 A292 9r multi 70 70
a. Souvenir sheet of 4, #749-752 1.40 1.40

No. 752a has gold and multicolored decorative margin. Size: 180x110mm.

**1985, May 22** *Perf. 13x12½*

Portraits: No. 753, Waskaduwe Sri Subhuthi Thero (1835-1917), Pali scholar, philologist responsible for the Sinhala dictionary. No. 754, Rev. Fr. Peter A. Pillai (1904-1964), educational and social reformer. No. 755, Dr. Senarath Paranavitane (c. 1900-1972), epigraphist. No. 756, A.M. Wapche Marikar (1829-1925), educational reformer, architect.

753 A293 60c pale yel org & tan 5 5
754 A293 60c pale yel org & brt rose lil 5 5
755 A293 60c pale yel org & brn 5 5
756 A293 60c pale yel org & emer 5 5

Gam Udawa--Yovur Udanaya Village Reformation Movement — A294

**1985, June 23** *Perf. 13½x13*
757 A294 60c multi 10 10

Colombo Young Poets Assoc., 50th Anniv. — A295

**1985, June 25** *Perf. 14*
758 A295 60c Emblem 10 10

Kothmale Project Commission — A296

**1985, Aug. 24**
759 A296 60c Dam, lake 5 5
760 A296 6r Hydro-electric power station 45 45

Child Survival — A297

Designs: 35c, Mother breastfeeding. 60c, Infant, oral inoculant. 6r, Weighing toddler. 9r, Infant, intravenous inoculant.

**1985, Sept. 1** *Perf. 13½*
761 A297 35c multi 5 5
762 A297 60c multi 5 5
763 A297 6r multi 45 45
764 A297 9r multi 70 70
a. Souvenir sheet of 4, #761-764 1.25 1.25

No. 764a has multicolored decorative margin. Size: 99x180mm.

10th Asian & Oceanic Congress of Obstetrics & Gynecology A298

**1985, Sept. 2** *Perf. 14*
765 A298 7r Womb, infant 52 52

World Tourism Org., 10th Anniv. A299

**1985, Sept. 27 Litho. *Perf. 14***

| | | | | |
|---|---|---|---|---|
| *766* | A299 | 1r Conch shell horn | 8 | 8 |
| *767* | A299 | 6r Parliament complex | 42 | 42 |
| *768* | A299 | 7r Tea plantation | 50 | 50 |
| *769* | A299 | 10r Buddhist monastery, Ruwanveliseya | 72 | 72 |
| *a* | | Souvenir sheet of 4, #766-769, perf. 13½ | 1.75 | 1.75 |

No. 769a has multicolored inscribed margin picturing enlargement of No. 768 design. Size: 180x90mm.

Land Development Ordinance, 50th Anniv. — A300

Sinhal Translation, Koran — A301

**1985, Oct. 15 *Perf. 14x15***

*770* A300 4.60r Deeds presentation 40 40

**1985, Oct. 17 Wmk. 385 *Perf. 13½***

*771* A301 60c vio & gold 10 10

Christmas — A302

**1985, Nov. 5 *Perf. 12***

| | | | | |
|---|---|---|---|---|
| *772* | A302 | 60c Our Lady of Matara | 5 | 5 |
| *773* | A302 | 9r Our Lady of Madhu | 65 | 65 |
| *a* | | Souv. sheet of 2, #772-773 | 70 | 70 |

No. 773a has inscribed multicolored margin picturing the three magi following the North Star.

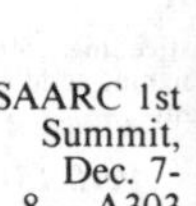

SAARC 1st Summit, Dec. 7-8 — A303

**1985, Dec. 8 *Perf. 14½x14***

| | | | | |
|---|---|---|---|---|
| *774* | A303 | 60c shown | 8 | 8 |
| *775* | A303 | 5.50r Flags on UN emblem | 50 | 50 |

No. 720 Surcharged in Intense Blue

**1986, Jan. 20 *Perf. 12½x12***

*776* A275 1r on 7r Map 8 8

Viceroy Special Train A304

**1986, Feb. 2 *Perf. 12½x13***

*777* A304 1r multi 10 10

Colombo-Kandy line inauguration.

Students A305

**1986, Feb. 14 *Perf. 14***

*778* A305 75c multi 8 8

Mahapola Scholarship Program for development and education, 6th anniv.

Don Richard Wijewardene (1886-1950), Newspaper Publisher A306

Welitara Gnanatillake Mahanayake Thero (1858-1941), Scientist A307

**1986, Feb. 23 *Perf. 14x15***

*779* A303 75c sage grn & brn 8 8

**1986, Feb. 26 Wmk. 385 *Perf. 13½***

*780* A307 75c multi 7 7

No. 692 Surcharged

**1986, Mar. 10 Litho. *Perf. 14½***

*780A* A264 7r on 35c Ceylon white-eye 1.00 1.00

Natl. Red Cross Society, 50th Anniv. A308

**1986, Mar. 31 *Perf. 12½x13***

*781* A308 75c multi 7 7

Halley's Comet A309

**1986, Apr. 5 *Perf. 12½***

| | | | | |
|---|---|---|---|---|
| *782* | A309 | 50c Comet is not an omen | 5 | 5 |
| *783* | A309 | 75c Constellations | 6 | 6 |
| *784* | A309 | 6.50r Trajectory diagrams | 48 | 48 |
| *785* | A309 | 8.50r Edmond Halley | 62 | 62 |
| *a* | | Souvenir sheet of 4, #782-785, perf. 12½x13 | 1.25 | 1.25 |

No. 785a has multicolored margin picturing comet. Size: 180x115mm.

Sinhalese and Tamil New Year — A310

Designs: 50c, Woman lighting lamp. 75c, Woman, holiday foods. 6.50r, Women celebrating around table. 8.50r, Food preparation, feast, anointment ritual.

**1986, Apr. 10**

| | | | | |
|---|---|---|---|---|
| *786* | A310 | 50c multi | 5 | 5 |
| *787* | A310 | 75c multi | 6 | 6 |
| *788* | A310 | 6.50r multi | 48 | 48 |
| *789* | A310 | 8.50r multi | 62 | 62 |
| *a* | | Souvenir sheet of 4, #786-789, perf. 13x12½ | 1.25 | 1.25 |

No. 789a has multicolored decorative margin. Size: 178x108mm.

No. 740 Surcharged

**1986, Apr. 29 *Perf. 12½x13***

*790* A286 1r on 4.60r multi 20 20

Vesak Festival A311

Jathaka Story frescoes from the house Samudragiri Vihara, Mirissa, recounting the life of Siddhartha (583-463 B.C.): 50c, King Kurudhamma Jathakaya gives elephant to the brahman. 75c, Vasavarthi heaven. 5r, Sujatha's milk rice offering. 10d, Thapassu and Bhalluka's parched corn and honey offering.

**1986, May 16**

| | | | | |
|---|---|---|---|---|
| *791* | A311 | 50c multi | 5 | 5 |
| *792* | A311 | 75c multi | 6 | 6 |
| *793* | A311 | 5d multi | 35 | 35 |
| *794* | A311 | 10d multi | 72 | 72 |

Natl. Heroes — A312

Natl. Cooperative Movement, 75th Anniv. — A313

Designs: No. 795, Kalukondayave Sri Prajnasekhara Mahanayaka Thero (1895-1977), theologian. No. 796, Brahmachari Walisinghe Harischandra (1876-1913), historian, social reformer. No. 797, Martin Wickramasinghe (1890-1970), author. No. 798, Ganapathipillai Gangaser Ponnambalam (1901-1972), diplomat. No. 799, Aboobucker Mohammed Abdul Azeez (1911-1973), scholar.

**1986, May 22 *Perf. 13x12½***

| | | | | |
|---|---|---|---|---|
| *795* | A312 | 75c multi | 6 | 6 |
| *796* | A312 | 75c multi | 6 | 6 |
| *797* | A312 | 75c multi | 6 | 6 |
| *798* | A312 | 75c multi | 6 | 6 |
| *799* | A312 | 75c multi | 6 | 6 |
| | | *Nos. 795-799 (5)* | 30 | 30 |

**1986, June 23**

*800* A313 1r multi 12 12

Gam Udawa, Intl. Year of Housing A314

**1986, June 23 *Perf. 13½x13***

*801* A314 75c multi 12 12

Arthur V. Dias — A315

**1986, July 31 *Perf. 14x15***

*802* A315 1r multi 12 12

World Wildlife Fund A316

Elephants: No. 803a, Adult with tusks. No. 803b, Adult, calf. No. 803c, Adult. No. 803d, Family in river.

**1986, Aug. 5 *Perf. 15x14***

| | | | | |
|---|---|---|---|---|
| *803* | | Strip of 4 | 1.40 | 1.40 |
| *a.-d.* | | A316 5r, any single | 35 | 35 |

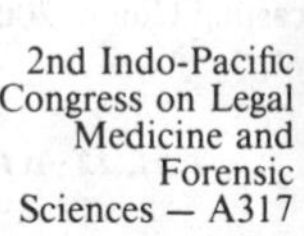

2nd Indo-Pacific Congress on Legal Medicine and Forensic Sciences — A317

**1986, Aug. 14 *Perf. 13½x13***

*804* A317 8.50r multi 62 62

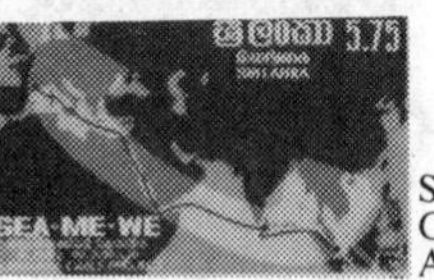

Submarine Cable A318

**1986, Sept. 8 *Perf. 13½x14***

*805* A318 5.75r Handset, map 40 40

South-East Asia, Middle East, Western Europe Submarine Cable System.

Randenigala Dam and Hydro-electric Project — A319

**1986, Aug. 29 Litho. *Perf. 12***

| | | | | |
|---|---|---|---|---|
| *806* | A319 | 75c shown | 6 | 6 |
| *807* | A319 | 5.75r Dam | 40 | 40 |

Dag Hammarskjold Award — A320

Second Natl. School Games, Sept. 22-27 — A321

**1986, Sept. 20 Litho. *Perf. 13x12½***

*808* A320 2r multi 16 16

**1986, Sept. 22 *Perf. 12***

*809* A321 1r multi 10 10

Natl. Surveyor's Institute, 60th Anniv. — A322

**1986, Sept. 27** ***Perf. 13½x13***
*810* A322 75c multi 10 10

Ananda College, Cent. — A323

College crest and: 75c, College. 5r, Athletic field. 5.75r, Founders Migettuwatte Gunananda, Hikkaduwe Sumangala and Col. H.S. Olcott, Buddhist flag and College, 1886, 1986. 6r, Crest on flag.

**1986, Nov. 1** ***Perf. 12***
*811* A323 75c multi 6 6
*812* A323 5r multi 40 40
*813* A323 5.75r multi 45 45
*814* A323 6r multi 48 48

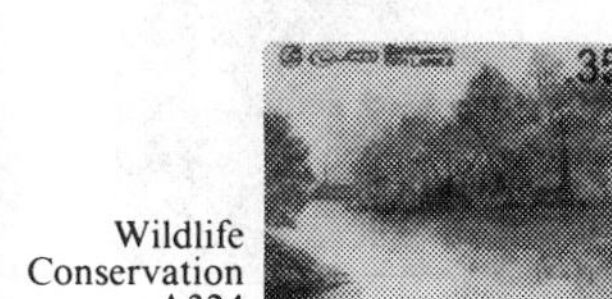


Wildlife Conservation A324

**1986, Nov. 11**
*815* A324 35c Mangrove habitat 5 5
*816* A324 50c Rhizophora apiculata 5 5
*817* A324 75c Germinating flower 6 6
*818* A324 6r Fiddler crab 48 48

Preservation of mangrove habitats.

Intl. Year of Shelter for the Homeless A325

**1987, Jan. 1 Litho.** ***Perf. 13x13½***
*819* A325 75c multi 10 10

A.I. Thero, 19th Cent. Theologian A326

Proctor John De Silva (b. 1854), Lawyer and Playwright A327

**1987, Jan. 29** ***Perf. 12***
*820* A326 5.75r multi 45 45

**1987, Jan. 31**
*821* A327 5.75r multi 45 45

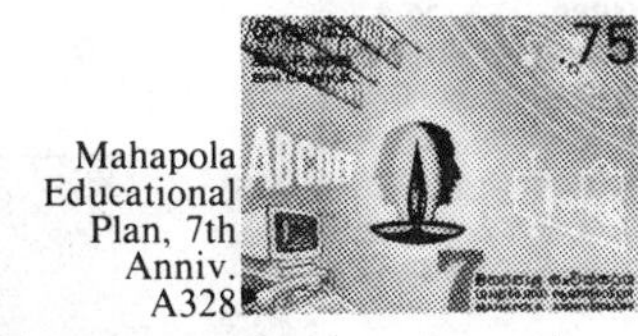


Mahapola Educational Plan, 7th Anniv. A328

**1987, Feb. 6**
*822* A328 75c multi 10 10

Dr. R.L. Brohier, Historian — A329

**1987, Feb. 14**
*823* A329 5.75r multi 45 45

Sri Lanka Tire Corp., 25th Anniv. A330

**1987, Mar. 23** ***Perf. 14***
*824* A330 5.75r multi 45 45

Sri Lanka Medical Assoc., Cent. A331

**1987, Mar. 24** ***Perf. 13x13½***
*825* A331 5.75r multi 45 45

Farmers' Pension and Social Security Plan A332

AGRO MAHAWELI '87 Agricultural Exposition A333

**1987, Mar. 29** ***Perf. 14***
*826* A332 75c multi 10 10

**1987, Apr. 2** ***Perf. 12***
*827* A333 75c multi 10 10

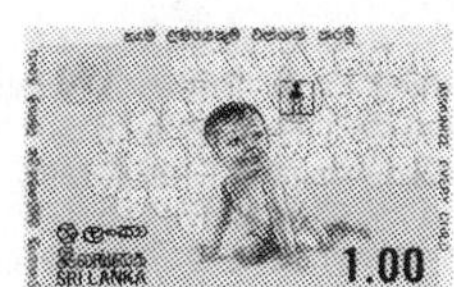


Child Immunization Program — A334

**1987, Apr. 7** ***Perf. 13½***
*828* A334 1r multi 10 10

World Health Day.

Sinhalese and Tamil New Year — A335

**1987, Apr. 9** ***Perf. 12***
*829* A335 75c Three girls, swing 6 6
*830* A335 5r Lamp, women 40 40

Vesak Festival Lanterns A336

**1987, May 4** ***Perf. 12***
*831* A336 50c Lotus 5 5
*832* A336 75c Octagonal 6 6
*833* A336 5r Star 40 40
*834* A336 10r Gok 80 80
*a* Souv. sheet of 4, Nos. 831-834 1.40 1.40

Size of No. 834a: 150x90mm.

Natl. Olympic Committee, 50th Anniv. — A337

**1987, May 8** ***Perf. 13½***
*835* A337 10r multi 80 80

Birds A338

**1987, May 18** ***Perf. 14***
*836* A338 50c Layard's parakeet 5 5
*837* A338 1r Legge's flowerpecker 8 8
*838* A338 5r Sri Lanka white-headed starling 40 40
*839* A338 10r Sri Lanka rufous babbler 80 80
*a* Souv. sheet of 4, Nos. 836-839 1.35 1.35

No. 839 has multicolored margin picturing bird. Size: 140x81mm.

Natl. Heroes — A339

Designs: No. 840, Heenatiyana Sri Dhammaloka Thero, 20th cent. theologian. No. 841, P. de S. Kularatne, educator. No. 842, M.C. Abdul Rahuman, politician.

**1987, May 22** ***Perf. 12***
*840* A339 75c multi 6 6
*841* A339 75c multi 6 6
*842* A339 75c multi 6 6

Gam Udawa A340

**1987, June 23**
*843* A340 75c multi 6 6

Village reformation movement.

Natl. Forestry Agency, Cent. A341

**1987, June 25**
*844* A341 75c Mesua nagassarium 6 6
*845* A341 5r Elephants in forest 40 40

Founder H.S. Olcott and College A342

**1987, June 30**
*846* A342 75c multi 6 6

Dharmaraja College, cent.

No. 528 Redrawn with Denomination in Upper Right Corner

**1987, July 1 Photo.** ***Perf. 13x13½***
**Size: 20x24mm.**
*847* A189 75c grn & gold 6 6

Youth Services Emblem A343

**1987, July 15 Litho.** ***Perf. 12***
*848* A343 75c multi 6 6

Natl. Youth Services Act, 20th anniv.

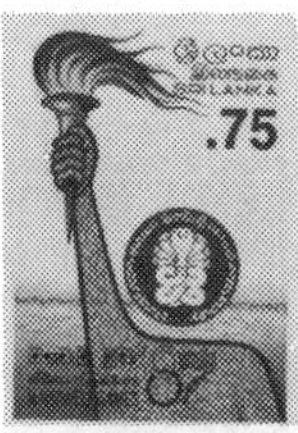

Mahaweli Games — A344

Ceylon Bible Society, 175th Anniv. — A345

**1987, Sept. 5 Litho.** ***Perf. 12***
*849* A344 75c multi 6 6

**1987, Oct. 2**
*850* A345 5.75r multi 48 48

Common Design Types are pictured in section before Great Britain.

Kandy Friend-in-Need Society, 150th Anniv. — A346

**1987, Nov. 4** ***Perf. 13½x13***
*851* A346 75c multi 6 6

Christmas 1987 A347

Sir Ernest de Silva (1887-1957), Banker, Philatelist A348

**1987, Nov. 25** **Litho.** ***Perf. 12***
*852* A347 75c Mother and Child 6 6
*853* A347 10r Infant, star, dove 80 80
*a* Souv. sheet of 2, Nos. 852-853 90 90

No. 853a has multicolored margin picturing angels heralding the birth of Christ, Star of Bethlehem and child. Size: 145x82mm.

**1987, Nov. 25** ***Perf. 13x13½***
*854* A348 75c multi 6 6

1st Convocation Ceremony at Buddhist and Pali University A349

Missionary Work of Fr. Joseph Vaz (1651-1711), 300th Anniv. A350

**1987, Dec. 14** ***Perf. 12***
*855* A349 75c yel, lake & org yel 6 6

**1987, Dec. 15**
*856* A350 75c multi 6 6

Buddhist Publication Soc., Kandy, 30th Anniv. — A351

Design: Wheel of Life, dagaba (temple cupola) and Bo (Tree of Life) leaf.

**1988, Jan. 1** **Litho.** ***Perf. 12***
*857* A351 75c multi 6 6

Mahapola Dharmayatra, 5th Anniv. — A352

**1988, Jan. 4** ***Perf. 13½x13***
*858* A352 75c multi 6 6

Ceylon Arts Soc., Cent. — A353

**1988, Jan. 8** ***Perf. 12***
*859* A353 75c multi 6 6

Opening of the Natl. Youth Center, Maharagama A354

**1988, Jan. 31** ***Perf. 13½x13***
*860* A354 1r multi 8 8

Natl. Independence, 40th Anniv. — A355

Mahapola Movement, 8th Anniv. — A356

**1988, Feb. 4** ***Perf. 12***
*861* A355 75c shown 6 6
*862* A355 8.50r Heraldic lion, "40" 68 68

**1988, Feb. 11**
*863* A356 75c Youth Education Services 6 6

Transportation Board, 30th Anniv. — A357

**1988, Feb. 19**
*864* A357 5.75r multi 48 48

Weligama Sri Sumangala Maha Nayake Thero (1825-1905), Buddhist Monk, Sanskrit Scholar — A358

**1988, Mar. 13**
*865* A358 75c multi 6 6

Artillery Regiment, Cent. — A359

**1988, Apr. 20**
*866* A359 5.75multi 48 48

Chevalier I.X. Pereira (1888-1951), Politician — A360

**1988, Apr. 26** **Litho.** ***Perf. 12***
*867* A360 5.75r multi 48 48

Vesak Festival A361

Paintings in Suriyagoda Sri Narendraramaya Viharaya temple, Kandy District: 50c, Buddha inviting deities and brahmas to be born into the world as Buddhists. 75c, Buddha walking seven steps on seven lotus flowers, followers paying homage.

**1988, May 13** ***Perf. 12½x12***
*868* A361 50c multi 5 5
*869* A361 75c multi 6 6
*a.* Souv. sheet of 2, Nos. 868-869 12 12

No. 869a has multicolored inscribed margin picturing Buddha and worshiper. Size: 151x92mm.

Natl. Heroes — A362

Designs: No. 870, Rev.-Father Ferdinand Bonnel (1873-1945), Jesuit priest who founded St. Michael's College, Batticaloa. No. 871, Sir Razik Fareed (1893-1984), political and social reformer. No. 872, W.F. Gunawardhana (b. 1861), founder of the Oriental Studies Soc. No. 873, Edward Alexander Nugawela (1898-1972), politician. No. 874, Sir Edwin Arthur Lewis Wijeyewardene (b. 1887), first Ceylonese chief justice, attorney general.

**1988, May 22** ***Perf. 12x12½***
*870* A362 75c multi 6 6
*871* A362 75c multi 6 6
*872* A362 75c multi 6 6
*873* A362 75c multi 6 6
*874* A362 75c multi 6 6
*Nos. 870-874 (5)* 30 30

Gam Udawa, 10th Anniv. A363

**1988, June 23** **Litho.** ***Perf. 12***
*875* A363 75c multi 6 6

Village reformation movement.

Maliyadeva College, Cent. — A364

**1988, June 30** ***Perf. 13½x13***
*876* A364 75c multi 6 6

Bird Type of 1983

**1988, Sept. 28** **Litho.** ***Perf. 14½***
*877* A264 7r like No. 692 42 42

Mohamed J.M. Lafir (1929-1980), World Amateur Billiards Champion — A365

**1988, July 5** **Litho.** ***Perf. 12½x12***
*878* A365 5.75r multi 45 45

Australia Bicentennial — A366

**1988, July 19** **Litho.** ***Perf. 12***
*879* A366 8.50r multi 52 52

Gunaratna Maha Nayake Thero (1752-1832), Buddhist and Sinhalese Language Scholar — A367

Mahaweli Games — A368

**1988, Aug. 11** ***Perf. 12x12½***
*880* A367 75c multi 6 6

**1988, Sept. 3** ***Perf. 12***
*881* A368 75c multi 6 6

1988 Summer Olympics, Seoul — A369

WHO, 40th Anniv. — A370

**1988, Sept. 6** ***Perf. 12x12½***
*882* A369 75c Running 6 6
*883* A369 1r Swimming 8 8
*884* A369 5.75r Boxing 45 45

885 A369 8.50r Handshake, map, embems 68 68
a. Souv. sheet of 4, Nos. 882-885 1.30 1.30

No. 885a has multicolored inscribed margin picturing Seoul '88 and five-ring emblems. Size: 181x101mm.

**1988, Sept. 12** *Perf. 12*
886 A370 75c multi 6 6

3rd Natl. School Games, Sept. 20-25 A371

**1988, Sept. 20**
887 A371 1r multi 8 8

Mahatma Gandhi — A372

**1988, Oct. 2** *Perf. 12*
888 A372 75c multi 6 6

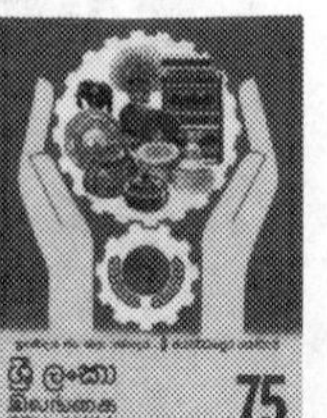

Opening of Gramodaya Folk Art Center — A375

**1988, Nov. 17 Litho.** *Perf. 13½*
893 A375 75c multi 6 6

Christmas — A376

**1988, Nov. 25** *Perf. 12x12½*
894 A376 75c shown 6 6
895 A376 8.50r Shepherds see star 68 68

## STELLALAND

LOCATION — South Africa.
GOVT. — Former Republic.
AREA — 5,000 sq. mi. (approx.).
CAPITAL — Vryburg.

This short-lived republic was set up by the Boers in an effort to annex territory ruled by the Bechuana chiefs. Great Britain refused to recognize it and in 1885 sent an expeditionary force which ended the political career of the country.

Stellaland was annexed by Great Britain in 1885 and became a part of British Bechuanaland.

12 Pence = 1 Shilling

Coat of Arms
A1 A2

**Unwmk.**

**1884, Feb. 1 Typo.** *Perf. 12*
1 A1 1p red 165.00
a. Horiz. pair, imperf. vert. 2,000.
b. Vert. pair, imperf. horiz. 2,000.
2 A1 3p orange 12.50
a. Horiz. pair, imperf. vert. 500.00
b. Vert. pair, imperf. horiz. 500.00
3 A1 4p gray 12.50
a. Horiz. pair, imperf. vert. 500.00
4 A1 6p lilac 12.50
a. Horiz. pair, imperf. vert. 1,000.
b. Vert. pair, imperf. horiz. 1,000.
5 A1 1sh green 12.50

Imperf. varieties are believed to be proofs.

Nos. 3 Handstamped "Twee" in Blackish Violet

**1885**
6 A2 2p on 4p gray 3,750.

## STRAITS SETTLEMENTS

LOCATION — Malay Peninsula in southeastern Asia.
GOVT. — Former British Colony
AREA — 1,356 sq. mi.
POP. — 1,435,895 (estimated).
CAPITAL — Singapore.

The colony comprised the settlements of Malacca, Singapore and Penang, which were incorporated under one government in 1826 and the administration transferred from India to the Secretary of State for the Colonies in 1867.

The colony was dissolved in 1946 when Singapore became a separate crown colony. Malacca and Penang were incorporated into the Malayan Union, which became the Federation of Malaya in 1948.

Stamps of India were used in Malacca, Penang and Singapore, 1854-67.

See Malaya for stamps of the Federated Malay States, the Federation of Malaya, Johore, Kedah, Kelantan, Malacca, Negri Sembilan, Pahang, Penang, Perak, Perlis, Selangor, Sungei Ujong and Trengganu.

100 Cents = 1 Dollar

Stamps of India Surcharged in Red, Blue, Black Violet or Green:

THREE HALF CENTS
Nos. 1-7

24 CENTS
Nos. 8-9

**1867, Sept. 1 Wmk. 38** *Perf. 14*
1 A7 1½c on ½a bl (R) 47.50 165.00
2 A7 2c on 1a brn (R) 42.50 30.00
3 A7 3c on 1a brn (Bl) 45.00 40.00
4 A7 4c on 1a brn (Bk) 82.50 125.00
5 A7 6c on 2a yel (V) 200.00 110.00
6 A7 8c on 2a yel (G) 65.00 26.00
7 A9 12c on 4a grn (R) 180.00 110.00
a. Double surcharge 825.00
8 A7 24c on 8a rose (Bl) 150.00 52.50
9 A7 32c on 2a yel (Bk) 100.00 47.50

**Manuscript Surcharge, Pen bar across "THREE HALF"**
9A A7 2(c) on 1½c on ½a bl 5,250. 4,000.

A2

A3

A4

A5

**Wmk. Crown and C. C. (1)**

**1867-72 Typo.** *Perf. 14*
10 A2 2c bis brn 3.50 2.00
11 A2 4c rose 4.25 2.25
12 A2 6c violet 17.00 7.50
13 A3 8c yellow 27.50 7.00
14 A3 12c ultra 22.50 5.25
a. 12c blue 22.50 4.50
15 A3 24c green 22.50 4.50
16 A4 30c cl ('72) 35.00 6.00
17 A5 32c pale red 75.00 22.50
18 A5 96c ol gray 57.50 17.50
Nos. 10-18 (9) 264.75 74.50

Corner ornaments of types A2, A3 and A5 differ for each value.

See Nos. 40-44, 48-50, 52-57.

Stamps of Straits Settlements, 1867-82, overprinted "B" are listed under Bangkok.

**1871** *Perf. 12½*
19 A5 96c ol gray 1,500. 150.00

Stamps of 1867-72 Surcharged:

Five Cents.

Seven Cents.

**1879, May** *Perf. 14*
20 A3 5c on 8c yel 40.00 40.00
a. No period after "CENTS" 325.00 400.00
21 A5 7c on 32c pale red 45.00 45.00
a. No period after "CENTS" 300.00 300.00

No. 16 Surcharged:

10 e — 10 f — 10 g — 10 h

10 j — 10 k — 10 m

**1880**
22 A4 (e) 10c on 30c 72.50 50.00
23 A4 (f) 10c on 30c 225.00 150.00
24 A4 (g) 10c on 30c 60.00 37.50
25 A4 (h) 10c on 30c 675.00
25A A4 (j) 10c on 30c 1,250. 325.00
25B A4 (k) 10c on 30c 1,300. 575.00
25C A4 (m) 10c on 30c 1,100. 450.00

With Additional Surcharge cents.

26 A4 (e) 10c on 30c 100.00 50.00
27 A4 (f) 10c on 30c
27A A4 (g) 10c on 30c 225.00 82.50
28 A4 (h) 10c on 30c 1,100. 600.00
28A A4 (j) 10c on 30c 325.00
28B A4 (k) 10c on 30c 325.00
28C A4 (m) 10c on 30c 1,100. 600.00

No. 13 Surcharged:

5 cents. n — 5 cents. o — 5 cents. p

**1880**
29 A3 (n) 5c on 8c yel 40.00 40.00
30 A3 (o) 5c on 8c yel 165.00 180.00
31 A3 (p) 5c on 8c yel 45.00 40.00

No. 11 Surcharged 5 cents.

**1882, Jan.**
32 A2 5c on 4c rose 250.00 325.00

Nos. 12, 14a, 16 Surcharged 10 cents.

**1880-81**
33 A2 10c on 6c vio 17.50 8.50
34 A3 10c on 12c bl ('81) 17.50 12.50
35 A4 10c on 30c claret 85.00 37.50

A6

A7

**1882, Jan. Typo.** *Perf. 14*
38 A6 5c vio brn 42.50 27.50
39 A7 10c slate 140.00 35.00

**1882-99 Wmk. Crown and C. A. (2)**
40 A2 2c bis brn 125.00 12.00
41 A2 2c car rose ('83) 25 15
a. 2c rose 5.00 1.00
42 A2 4c rose 60.00 10.50
43 A2 4c car rose ('99) 65 30
44 A2 4c bis brn ('83) 1.65 60
45 A6 5c ultra ('83) 60 32
46 A6 5c brn ('94) 85 85
47 A6 5c mag ('99) 85 85
48 A2 6c violet 90 60
49 A3 8c orange 1.65 42
50 A3 8c ultra ('94) 75 10
51 A7 10c slate 95 32
52 A3 12c vio brn ('83) 6.00 4.50
53 A3 12c cl ('94) 1.65 1.50
54 A3 24c bl grn ('83) 1.90 1.25
a. 24c yel grn ('84) 15.00 1.25
55 A4 30c cl ('91) 3.25 2.00
56 A5 32c red org ('87) 2.00 2.00
57 A5 96c ol gray ('88) 37.50 15.00
Nos. 40-57 (18) 246.40 53.26

Preceding Issues Surcharged

Surcharged Vertically TWO CENTS

**1883-84** **Wmk. 2, 1**
58 A3 2c on 8c org 32.50 32.50
a. Double surch. 1,500. 825.00
59 A5 2c on 32c pale red 275.00 72.50
a. Double surch.
60 A6 2c on 5c ultra ('84) 32.50 32.50
a. Pair, one without surcharge
b. Double surch.

Five types of surcharge on No. 58, two types on No. 59 and three types on No. 60.

Surcharged in Black 2 Cents.

**1883** **Wmk. 2**
61 A2 2c on 4c rose 20.00 20.00
b. "s" of "Cents." inverted 1,000. 1,200.

**Wmk. 1**
62 A3 2c on 12c bl 90.00 65.00
a. "s" of "Cents" inverted 2,000. 1,600.

Surcharged in Black or Blue 8 Cents

**1884**
63 A3 8c on 12c bl 100.00 60.00

**Wmk. 2**
64 A3 8c on 12c vio brn 125.00 100.00

With Additional Surcharge Handstamped in Red 8

65 A3 8c on 8c on 12c vio brn 100.00 110.00
66 A3 8c on 8c on 12c vio brn (Bl) 4,250.

Surcharged in Black or Red **4 Cents**

**1884**

67 A6 4c on 5c ultra (Bk) 1,900. 1,700.
68 A6 4c on 5c ultra (R) 32.50 40.00

No. 68 Surcharged in Red **4**

69 A6 4c on 4c on 5c ultra 10,000.

Surcharged in Black **3 CENTS**

**1885-87**

70 A6 3c on 5c ultra 40.00 *110.00*
  a. Double surch. 1,500.

Surcharged in Black **3 cents**

71 A6 3c on 5c vio brn ('86) 82.50 92.50

Surcharged **2 Cents.**

72 A6 2c on 5c ultra ('87) 8.75 13.00
  a. Double surcharge 475.00 375.00
  b. "C" omitted 1,700.

In the surcharged issues of 1883 to 1887, Nos. 59, 62, 63 and 71 are on stamps watermarked Crown and C. C., the others are watermarked Crown and C. A.

Surcharged **THREE CENTS**

**1885-94 Wmk. Crown and C. A. (2)**

73 A5 3c on 32c mag 85 85
74 A5 3c on 32c rose ('94) 48 48
  a. Without surch. 5,250.

Surcharged **10 CENTS**

**1891**

75 A3 10c on 24c grn 1.10 60
  a. Narrow "0" in "10" 20.00 30.00

Surcharged **THIRTY CENTS**

76 A5 30c on 32c red org 3.25 3.25

Surcharged **ONE CENT**

**1892**

77 A2 1c on 2c rose 42 42
78 A2 1c on 4c bis brn 65 65
  a. Double surcharge 750.00
79 A2 1c on 6c vio 60 60
  a. Dbl. surch., one invtd. 550.00 375.00
80 A3 1c on 8c org 42 42
81 A3 1c on 12c vio brn 2.50 4.75

Surcharged **ONE CENT**

82 A3 1c on 8c gray grn 20 20

Queen Victoria — A13

**1892-99 Typo.**

83 A13 1c gray grn 15 15
84 A13 3c car rose ('95) 1.25 55
85 A13 3c brn ('99) 52 18
86 A13 25c dk vio & grn 3.75 1.90
87 A13 50c ol grn & car 14.00 2.50
88 A13 $5 org & car ('98) 260.00 225.00
  *Nos. 83-88 (6)* 279.67 230.28

Denomination of $5, type A13, is in color on plain tablet.

Stamps of 1883-94 Surcharged **4 cents.**

**1899**

89 A6 4c on 5c ultra 42 42
90 A6 4c on 5c brn 42 42
91 A3 4c on 8c ultra 45 45
  a. Double surcharge *575.00 575.00*

Type of 1882 Issue Surcharged **FOUR CENTS**

92 A6 4c on 5c rose 15 9
  a. Without surch. *7,500.*

King Edward VII — A14

Numerals of 5c, 8c, 10c, 30c, $1 and $5, type A14, are in color on plain tablet.

**1902 Wmk. 2 Typo.**

93 A14 1c green 18 12
94 A14 3c vio & org 22 12
95 A14 4c vio, *red* 2.25 25
96 A14 5c violet 1.75 35
97 A14 8c vio, *bl* 2.50 42
98 A14 10c vio & blk, *yel* 4.25 70
99 A14 25c vio & grn 5.75 2.25
100 A14 30c gray & car rose 7.25 5.75
101 A14 50c grn & car rose 5.50 4.25
102 A14 $1 grn & blk 14.00 16.00
103 A14 $2 vio & blk 35.00 27.50
104 A14 $5 grn & brn org 72.50 57.50
104A A14 $100 dl vio & grn, *yel* *4,500.*
  *Nos. 93-104 (12)* 151.15 115.21

High values of the 1902 and 1904 issues with revenue cancellations are of minimal value. No. 104A is inscribed "Postage & Revenue" but the limit of weight probably precluded its use postally.

A15

A16

A17

A18

**1903-04**

105 A15 1c gray grn 28 35
106 A16 3c dl vio 3.00 90
107 A17 4c vio, *red* 1.65 22
108 A18 8c vio, *bl* 7.25 1.40

**1904-11 Wmk. 3**

**Chalky Paper**

109 A15 1c gray grn 22 7
110 A16 3c dl vio 28 18
111 A17 4c vio, *red* 50 10
112 A17 4c dl vio ('08) 14 14
113 A14 5c vio ('06) 2.00 1.40
114 A18 8c vio, *bl* 2.75 28
115 A14 10c vio & blk, *yel* 2.25 25
116 A14 10c vio, *yel* ('08) 55 25
117 A14 25c vio & grn 4.25 3.50
118 A14 25c vio ('09) 3.25 2.75
119 A14 30c gray & car rose 5.75 2.75
120 A14 30c vio & org ('09) 2.75 70
121 A14 50c grn & car rose 5.75 3.50
122 A14 50c blk, *grn* ('10) 1.75 1.10
123 A14 $1 grn & blk 10.50 5.75
124 A14 $1 blk & red, *bl* ('11) 4.25 1.75
125 A14 $2 vio & blk 57.50 42.50
126 A14 $2 grn & red, *yel* ('09) 14.00 12.50
127 A14 $5 grn & brn org 57.50 50.00
128 A14 $5 grn & red, *grn* ('10) 35.00 27.50
128A A14 $25 grn & blk 1,050.
128B A14 $100 dl vio & grn, *yel* *6,000.*
  Revenue cancel 225.00
  *Nos. 109-128 (20)* 210.94 156.97

Nos. 125, 128A and 128B are on chalky paper, the other values are on both ordinary and chalky. The note about No. 104A will apply to No. 128B.

**1906-11**

**Ordinary Paper.**

129 A15 1c bl grn ('10) 1.25 50
130 A16 3c car ('08) 22 22
131 A17 4c car ('07) 1.25 28
132 A17 4c lake ('11) 65 65
133 A14 5c org ('09) 1.75 35
134 A18 8c ultra ('06) 35 28
  *Nos. 129-134 (6)* 5.47 2.28

Stamps of Labuan 1902-03, Overprinted or Surcharged in Red or Black

**STRAITS SETTLEMENTS.** a

**Straits Settlements.** b

**FOUR CENTS.** c

***Perf. 12½ to 16 and Compound***

**1907 Unwmk.**

134A A38 (a) 1c vio & blk 32.50 40.00
135 A38 (a) 2c grn & blk 82.50 85.00
136 A38 (a) 3c brn & blk 15.00 16.00
137 A38 (c) 4c on 12c yel & blk 1.10 *2.00*
  a. No period after "CENTS" 110.00 110.00
138 A38 (c) 4c on 16c org brn & grn (Bk) 65 *2.00*
  a. With additional name in red 525.00 500.00
139 A38 (c) '4c on 18c bis & blk 1.00 *2.00*
  a. No period after "CENTS" 100.00 100.00
  b. "FOUR CENTS." & bar double 4,000.
140 A38 (a) 8c org & blk 1.00 *4.00*
141 A38 (b) 10c sl bl & brn 2.25 *3.25*
  a. No period after "Settlements" 110.00
142 A38 (a) 25c grnsh bl & grn 1.65 *5.25*
143 A38 (a) 50c gray lil & vio 5.25 6.50
144 A38 (a) $1 org & red brn 22.50 26.00
  *Nos. 134A-144 (11)* 165.40 192.00

A19

A20

**1908-11 Typo. Wmk. 3 *Perf. 14***

**Chalky Paper.**

145 A19 $25 bl & vio, *bl* ('11) 825.00 400.00
146 A19 $500 vio & org *35,000.*
  Revenue cancel 275.00

No. 146 is inscribed "Postage-Revenue" but was probably used only for revenue.

Excellent forgeries of No. 146 exist.

**1910**

**Chalky Paper**

147 A20 21c mar & vio 3.25 *8.00*
148 A20 45c black, *green* 3.25 2.65

King George V
A21 A22

A23

A24

A25

A26

Die I (Type A24).

For description of dies I and II see back of this section of the Catalogue.

The 25c, 50c and $2 denominations of type A24 show the numeral on horizontally-lined tablet.

**1912-18 Chalky Paper Wmk. 3**

149 A21 1c green 24 10
150 A21 1c blk ('18) 30 10
151 A25 2c dp grn ('18) 18 6
152 A22 3c scarlet 9 5
  a. 3c car 12 5
153 A23 4c gray vio 40 5
154 A23 4c scar ('18) 18 5
  a. Booklet pane of 1
  b. Booklet pane of 12
  c. 4c car ('18) 18 5
155 A24 5c orange 30 5
156 A25 6c cl ('18) 48 48
157 A25 8c ultra 52 10
158 A24 10c vio, *yel* 2.50 36
159 A24 10c ultra ('18) 3.00 18
160 A26 21c mar & vio 2.50 *3.50*
161 A24 25c vio & red vio 2.75 1.75
162 A24 30c vio & org ('14) 2.50 1.10
163 A26 45c blk, *bl grn,* ol back ('14) 1.40 *3.50*
  a. 45c blk, *emer* ('17) 1.25 *6.00*
164 A24 50c blk, *grn* ('14) 4.25 2.00
  a. 50c blk, *bl grn,* ol back 4.25 2.00
  b. 50c blk, *emer* 2.50 1.00
  c. Die II 2.25 1.00
165 A24 $1 blk & red, *bl* ('14) 4.75 3.50
166 A24 $2 grn & red, *yel* ('15) 7.50 6.00
167 A24 $5 grn & red, *grn* ('15) 35.00 12.00
  a. $5 grn & red, *bl grn,* ol back 35.00 12.00
  b. $5 grn & red, *emer* ('15) 45.00 16.00
  c. Die II 35.00 18.00
  *Nos. 149-167 (19)* 68.84 34.93

The 1c, 3c, 5c and 8c are on ordinary paper.

**Surface-colored Paper**

168 A24 10c vio, *yel* 30 18
169 A26 45c blk, *grn* ('14) 3.00 *6.00*
170 A24 $2 grn & red, *yel* ('14) 6.00 *9.00*
171 A24 $5 grn & red, *grn* 57.50 30.00

A27

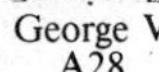
George V
A28

George VI
A29

**915**

72 A27 $25 bl & vio, *bl* 750.00 225.00
Revenue cancel 5.75
73 A27 $100 red & blk, *bl* 3,250.
Revenue cancel 37.50
74 A27 $500 org & dl vio 20,000.
Revenue cancel 150.00

Although Nos. 173 and 174 were available or postage, it is probable that they were used nly for fiscal purposes.

Die II (Type A24)

**921-32** **Wmk. 4**

**Ordinary Paper**

79 A21 1c black 7 7
80 A25 2c green 10 7
81 A25 2c brown 2.00 1.65
82 A22 3c green 50 20
83 A23 4c scarlet 1.10 65
84 A23 4c dp vio ('25) 20 5
85 A23 4c org ('29) 14 5
86 A24 5c org ('23) 32 5
*a.* Die I 85 5
87 A24 5c dk brn (II) ('32) 85 5
*a.* Die I ('32) 50 5
88 A25 6c claret 50 50
89 A25 6c rose red ('25) 6.50 3.25
*a.* 6c scar ('27) 32 14
90 A24 10c ultra (I) 1.00 16

**Chalky Paper**

91 A24 10c vio, *yel* ('27) 85 7
*a.* Die I ('25) 1.25 1.25
92 A25 12c ultra 65 7
93 A26 21c mar & vio 5.25 13.00
94 A24 25c vio & red vio 2.75 1.25
*a.* Die I 16.00 13.00
95 A24 30c vio & org 2.00 16
*a.* Die I 16.00 16.00
96 A26 35c org & vio 5.25 4.00
97 A26 35c vio & car ('31) 8.50 6.50
98 A24 50c blk, *emerald* 1.65 32
99 A24 $1 blk & red, *bl* 3.25 32
200 A24 $2 grn & red, *yel* 5.25 4.25
201 A24 $5 grn & red, *grn* 32.50 16.00
202 A27 $25 bl & vio, *bl* 375.00 82.50
203 A27 $100 red & blk, *bl* 1,900.
204 A27 $500 org & dl vio *13,000.*
*Nos. 179-201 (23)* 81.18 52.69

No. 192 is on ordinary paper.
Nos. 203 and 204 were probably used only for fiscal purposes.

Stamps of 1912-21 Overprinted in Black: "MALAYA-BORNEO EXHIBITION," in Three Lines

**1922** **Wmk. 3**

*151d* A25 2c dp grn 14.00 *27.50*
*154d* A23 4c scarlet 4.50 *10.50*
*155d* A24 5c orange 4.50 *9.00*
*157d* A25 8c ultra 2.00 *4.25*
*161d* A24 25c vio & red vio 5.25 *10.50*
*163d* A26 45c blk, *bl grn*, ol back 5.25 *10.50*
*165d* A24 $1 blk & red, *bl* 140.00 *275.00*
*166d* A24 $2 grn & red, *yel* 42.50 *77.50*
*167d* A24 $5 grn & red, *grn* 275.00 *525.00*

**Wmk. 4**

*179d* A21 1c black 35 *2.00*
*180d* A25 2c green 2.50 *7.00*
*183d* A23 4c scarlet 2.00 *8.75*
*186d* A24 5c org (II) 3.50 *10.50*
*190d* A24 10c ultra 3.50 *12.50*
*199d* A24 $1 blk & red, *bl* 27.50 *70.00*
*Nos. 151d-199d (15)* 532.35 1,060.

Industrial fair at Singapore, Mar. 31-Apr. 15, 1922.

**Silver Jubilee Issue**

Common Design Type

**1935, May 6** **Engr.** ***Perf. 11x12***

*213* CD301 5c blk & ultra 28 15
*214* CD301 8c ind & grn 80 70
*215* CD301 12c ultra & brn 1.00 80
*216* CD301 25c brn vio & ind 2.75 2.00

**1936-37** **Typo.** ***Perf. 14***

**Chalky Paper**

*217* A28 1c blk ('37) 8 5
*218* A28 2c green 16 5
*220* A28 4c org brn 20 5
*221* A28 5c brown 26 5
*222* A28 6c rose red 40 12
*223* A28 8c gray 45 12
*224* A28 10c dl vio 65 6
*225* A28 12c ultra 2.50 1.25
*226* A28 25c rose red & vio 1.65 12
*227* A28 30c org & dk vio 1.75 65
*229* A28 40c dk vio & car 2.00 1.50
*230* A28 50c blk, *emerald* 2.50 1.00
*232* A28 $1 red & blk, *bl* 3.25 1.65
*233* A28 $2 rose red & gray grn 13.00 11.00
*234* A28 $5 grn & red, *grn* ('37) 30.00 16.00
*Nos. 217-234 (15)* 58.85 33.67

**Coronation Issue**

Common Design Type

**1937, May 12** **Engr.** ***Perf. 13½x14***

*235* CD302 4c dp org 7 7
*236* CD302 8c gray blk 24 14
*237* CD302 12c brt ultra 26 26

Two Dies

Die I. Printed in two operations. Lines of background touch outside of central oval. Foliage of palms touches outer frame line. Lowest palm leaf forked at tip.

Die II. Printed from a single plate. Lines of background separated from central oval by a white line. Foliage of palms does not touch outer frame line. Lowest palm leaf pointed at tip.

**1937-41** **Typo.** ***Perf. 14***

*238* A29 1c blk (I) 14 5
*239* A29 2c grn (I) 8 5
*c.* Die II ('38) 1.40 14
*239A* A29 2c brn org ('41) (II) 22 22
*239B* A29 3c grn ('41) (II) 28 28
*240* A29 4c brn org (I) 55 6
*a.* Die II ('38) 3.50 8
*241* A29 5c brn (I) 55 12
*a.* Die II ('39) 1.10 7
*242* A29 6c rose red ('38) (I) 32 6
*243* A29 8c gray ('38) (I) 5.50 6
*244* A29 10c dl vio (I) 70 5
*245* A29 12c ultra ('38) (I) 70 7
*245A* A29 15c ultra ('41) (II) 1.65 1.65
*246* A29 25c rose red & vio (I) 5.00 22
*247* A29 30c org & vio (I) 5.00 42
*248* A29 40c dk vio & rose red (I) 5.50 55
*249* A29 50c blk, *emer* ('38) (I) 1.00 28
*250* A29 $1 red & blk, *bl* ('38) (I) 1.65 28
*251* A29 $2 rose red & gray grn ('38) (I) 11.00 1.40
*252* A29 $5 grn & red, *grn* ('38) (I) 11.00 2.75
*Nos. 238-252 (18)* 50.84 8.57

Stamps and Type of 1937-41 Overprinted in Red or Black

**B M A**
**MALAYA**

**1945-48**

*256* A29 1c blk (R) 5 5
*257* A29 2c brn org (II) 5 5
*a.* Die I ('46) 60 60
*258* A29 3c green 5 5
*259* A29 5c brown 5 5
*260* A29 6c gray 5 5
*261* A29 8c rose red 5 5
*262* A29 10c dl vio (I) 9 5
*a.* 10c cl (II) ('48) 9 7
*263* A29 12c ultra 18 18
*264* A29 15c ultra (Bk) 1.25 1.50
*265* A29 15c ultra (R) 9 5
*266* A29 25c rose red & vio 12 5
*a.* Double overprint
*267* A29 50c blk, *emer* (R) 24 5
*268* A29 $1 rose red & blk 60 7
*269* A29 $2 rose red & gray grn 90 18
*270* A29 $5 grn & red, *grn* 27.50 24.00
*271* A29 $5 brn org & vio 2.75 40
*Nos. 256-271 (16)* 34.02 26.83

The letters "B M A" are initials of "British Military Administration".

An 8c gray with BMA overprint was prepared but not issued. Value $5.

The 6c gray, 8c rose red and $5 brown orange & violet exist without BMA overprint, but were issued only with it.

No. 262a does not exist without overprint. No. 262 exists in at least three shades.

## SEMI-POSTAL STAMPS

Nos. 152-153 Surcharged

**RED CROSS**
**2c.**

**1917** **Wmk. 3** ***Perf. 14***

*B1* A22 3c + 2c scarlet 75 *2.00*
*a.* No period after "C" 55.00
*B2* A23 4c + 2c gray violet 75 *2.00*
*a.* No period after "C" 77.50

## POSTAGE DUE STAMPS

D1

**1924-26** **Typo.** **Wmk. 4** ***Perf. 14.***

*J1* D1 1c violet 4.00 2.25
*J2* D1 2c black 4.00 30
*J3* D1 4c grn ('26) 2.50 *7.50*
*J4* D1 8c red 4.50 38
*J5* D1 10c orange 4.50 1.10
*J6* D1 12c ultra 7.50 75
*Nos. J1-J6 (6)* 27.00 12.28

## OCCUPATION STAMPS

**Issued Under Japanese Occupation**

Straits Settlements Nos. 238, 239A, 239B, 243 and 245A Handstamped in Red

**1942, Mar. 16** **Wmk. 4** ***Perf. 14***

*N1* A29 1c black 7.50 7.50
*N2* A29 2c brn org 10.00 10.00
*N3* A29 3c green 25.00 *37.50*
*N4* A29 8c gray 12.50 12.50
*N5* A29 15c ultra 12.50 12.50

Other denominations with this handstamp are believed to be proofs.

The handstamp reads: "Seal of Post Office of Malayan Military Department".

Stamps of Straits Settlements, 1937-41, Handstamped in Red, Black, Violet or Brown

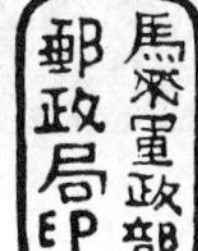

**1942, Apr. 3**

*N6* A29 1c black 2.50 2.50
*N6A* A29 2c grn (V) 500.00 500.00
*N7* A29 2c brn org 3.00 3.00
*N8* A29 3c green 3.00 3.00
*N9* A29 5c brown 12.50 12.50
*N10* A29 8c gray 2.50 2.50
*N11* A29 10c dl vio 17.50 17.50
*N12* A29 12c ultra 37.50 37.50
*N13* A29 15c ultra 3.75 3.00
*N14* A29 30c org & vio 350.00 350.00
*N15* A29 40c dk vio & rose red 37.50 45.00
*N16* A29 50c blk, *emerald* 37.50 37.50
*N17* A29 $1 red & blk, *bl* 50.00 50.00
*N18* A29 $2 rose red & gray grn 62.50 75.00
*N19* A29 $5 grn & red, *grn* 100.00 125.00

Nos. N6-N7, N9, N11-N12, N15-N19 with red handstamp were used in Sumatra. The 2c green with red handstamp was not regularly issued.

Straits Settlements Nos. 239A, 239B, 243 and 245A Overprinted in Black

**DAI NIPPON**
**2602**
**MALAYA**

**1942**

*N20* A29 2c brn org 50 50
*a.* Inverted overprint 7.00 5.00
*b.* Dbl. ovpt., one invtd. 25.00
*N21* A29 3c green 37.50 37.50
*N22* A29 8c gray 1.75 1.65
*a.* Inverted overprint 10.00
*N23* A29 15c ultra 4.00 3.25

Straits Settlements Nos. 239A and 243 Overprinted in Black

**SELANGOR**
**EXHIBITION**
**DAI NIPPON**
**2602**
**MALAYA**

**1942, Nov. 3**

*N24* A29 2c brn org 7.50 *12.50*
*a.* Inverted overprint 225.00 225.00
*N25* A29 8c gray 5.00 *10.00*
*a.* Inverted overprint 225.00 225.00

Agricultural-Horticultural Exhibition held at Kuala Lumpur, Selangor, Nov. 1-2, 1942. Sold only at a temporary post office at the exhibition.

Straits Settlements Nos. 243, 245 and 248 Overprinted in Black or Red

**大日本郵便**

**1943**

*N26* A29 8c gray (Bk) 50 50
*a.* Invtd. overprint 19.00
*N27* A29 8c gray (R) 50 50
*N28* A29 12c ultramarine 75 50
*N29* A29 40c dk vio & rose red 1.00 1.25

The Japanese characters read: "Japanese Postal Service."

Common Design Types pictured in section before Great Britain.

# SUDAN

LOCATION — In northeastern Africa, south of Egypt.
GOVT. — Republic.
AREA — 967,500 sq. mi.
POP. — 20,564,364 (1983).
CAPITAL — Khartoum.

10 Milliemes = 1 Piastre
100 Piastres = 1 Egyptian Pound

**Catalogue values for unused stamps in this country are for Never Hinged items, beginning with Scott 79 in the regular postage section, Scott C35 in the air post section, Scott CO1 in the air post official section, Scott J12 in the postage due section, and Scott O28 in the officials section.**

Egyptian Stamps of 1884-93 Overprinted in Black

**السودان**
**SOUDAN**

**1897, Mar. 1** **Wmk. 119** ***Perf. 14***

*1* A18 1m brown 1.25 *1.40*
*a* Inverted overprint 350.00

*2* A19 2m green 1.40 1.40
*3* A21 3m orange 1.75 1.75
*4* A20 5m car rose 3.00 3.00
a Inverted overprint 400.00
*5* A14 1pi ultra 6.50 6.00
*6* A15 2pi org brn 22.50 21.00
*7* A16 5pi gray 27.50 30.00
a Double ovpt.
*8* A22 10pi violet 22.50 22.50
*Nos. 1-8 (8)* 86.40 87.05

Counterfeits of Nos. 1-8 are plentiful.

Camel Post — A1

Wmk. 71- Rosette

**1898, Mar. 1 Typo. Wmk. 71**

*9* A1 1m rose & brn 25 20
*10* A1 2m brn & grn 60 55
*11* A1 3m grn & vio 65 60
*12* A1 5m blk & rose 25 25
*13* A1 1pi yel brn & ultra 85 75
*14* A1 2pi ultra & blk 4.25 1.10
*15* A1 5pi grn & org brn 7.50 2.75
*16* A1 10pi dp vio & blk 8.50 3.00
*Nos. 9-16 (8)* 22.85 9.20

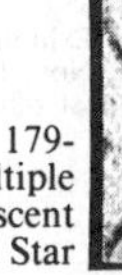

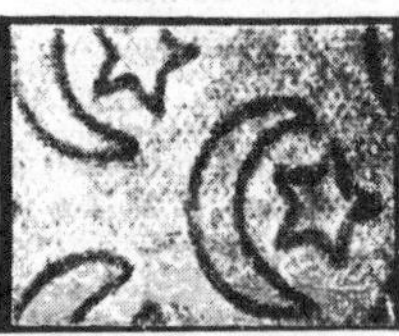

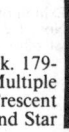

Wmk. 179- Multiple Crescent and Star

**1902-21 Wmk. 179**

*17* A1 1m car rose & brn ('05) 16 12
*18* A1 2m brn & grn 16 16
*19* A1 3m grn & vio ('03) 30 28

*20* A1 4m ol brn & bl ('07) 40 1.00
*21* A1 4m brn & red ('07) 1.10 85
*22* A1 5m blk & rose red ('03) 1.10 10
*23* A1 1pi brn & ultra ('03) 1.40 16
*24* A1 2pi ultra & blk ('08) 8.00 1.40
*25* A1 2pi org & vio brn ('21) 2.00 1.75
*26* A1 5pi grn & org brn ('08) 3.00 42
*27* A1 10pi dp vio & blk ('11) 12.50 85
*Nos. 17-27 (11)* 30.12 7.09

No. 15 Surcharged in Black **5 Milliemes**

**1903, Sept. Wmk. 71**

*28* A1 5m on 5pi grn & org brn 4.00 4.00
a Inverted surch. 375.00 *375.00*

A2

**1921-22 Typo. Wmk. 179**

*29* A2 1m org & blk ('22) 65 55
*30* A2 2m dk brn & org ('22) 3.25 2.00
*31* A2 3m grn & vio ('22) 1.00 1.00
*32* A2 4m brn & grn ('22) 1.25 1.25
*33* A2 5m blk & ol brn ('22) 1.65 25
*34* A2 10m blk & car ('22) 2.25 40
*35* A2 15m org brn & ultra 2.50 90
*Nos. 29-35 (7)* 12.55 6.35

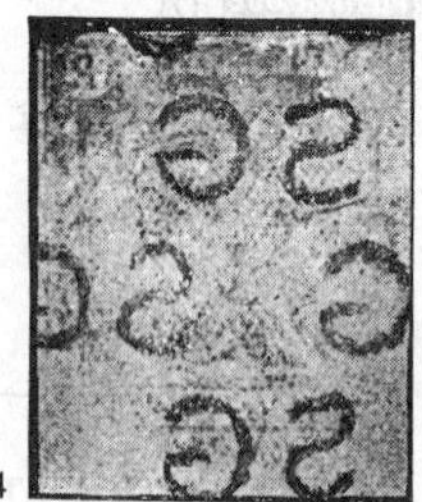

Wmk.214

**1927-40 Wmk. Multiple S G (214)**

*36* A2 1m org yel & blk 5 5
*37* A2 2m dk brn & org 5 5
*38* A2 3m grn & vio 9 6
*39* A2 4m brn & grn 9 6
*40* A2 5m blk & ol brn 9 5
a Booklet pane of 4
*41* A2 10m blk & car 18 6
*42* A2 15m org brn & ultra 18 7
*43* A1 2pi org & vio brn 22 7
*44* A1 3pi dk bl & red brn ('40) 42 15
*45* A1 4pi blk & ultra ('36) 42 15
*46* A1 5pi dk grn & org brn 48 15
*47* A1 6pi blk & pale bl ('36) 90 22
*48* A1 8pi blk & pck grn ('36) 90 30
*49* A1 10pi dp vio & blk 1.50 22
*50* A1 20pi bl & lt bl ('35) 2.25 50
*Nos. 36-50 (15)* 7.82 2.16

Charles George Gordon — A3

Gordon Memorial College A4

Memorial Service at Khartoum — A5

**1935, Jan. 1 Engr. *Perf. 13½x14***

*51* A3 5m dp grn 40 40
*52* A3 10m brown 42 42
*53* A3 13m ultra 1.75 2.75
*54* A3 15m carmine 1.00 1.00
*55* A4 2pi dp bl 1.00 1.00
*56* A4 5pi orange 1.40 1.40
*57* A4 10pi dl vio 3.50 3.50
*58* A5 20pi black 25.00 27.50
*59* A5 50pi red brn 65.00 67.50
*Nos. 51-59 (9)* 99.47 105.47

50th anniv. of the death of Gen. Charles George ("Chinese") Gordon (1833-85).

No. 41 Surcharged in Black **5 Mills.** ٥ مليم

**Wmk. Multiple S. G. (214)**

**1940, Feb. 25 Typo. *Perf. 14***

*60* A2 5m on 10m blk & car 10 20

Nos. 40 and 48 Surcharged in Black

**4½ PIASTRES** a

**4½ Piastres** ٤ ١/٢ قرش b

**1940-41**

*61* A2 (a) 4½pi on 5m blk & ol brn ('41) 15.00 12.00
*62* A1 (b) 4½pi on 8pi blk & pck grn 10.00 8.00

Sudan Landscape — A6

***Perf. 13½, 14x13½***

**1941 Litho. Unwmk.**

**Size: 21½x17½mm**

*63* A6 1m org & sl bl 22 22
*64* A6 2m choc & org 40 40
*65* A6 3m grn & rose vio 22 22
*66* A6 4m choc & bl grn 20 30
*67* A6 5m ind & ol bis 20 12
*68* A6 10m ind & rose pink 3.50 2.75
*69* A6 15m chnt & ultra 35 14

**Size: 29x25mm**

*71* A6 2pi org & cl 2.75 1.75
*72* A6 3pi dk bl & fawn 38 20
*73* A6 4pi blk & brt ultra 50 35
*74* A6 5pi dk grn & brn org 2.25 2.25
*75* A6 6pi ind & turq bl 4.00 3.75
*76* A6 8pi blk & grn 5.00 4.25
*77* A6 10pi rose vio & gray 19.00 10.00
*78* A6 20pi dk bl & lt bl 27.50 22.50
*Nos. 63-78 (15)* 66.47 49.20

**Catalogue values for unused stamps in this section, from this point to the end of the section, are for Never Hinged items.**

Types of 1898-1940 with Changed Arabic Wording Below Camel.

A7

A8

**Wmk. 214**

**1948, Jan. 1 Typo. *Perf. 14***

*79* A7 1m dk org & blk 8 5
*80* A7 2m choc & org 8 5
*81* A7 3m grn & rose lil 60 60
*82* A7 4m choc & sl grn 9 9
*83* A7 5m blk & ol brn 9 6
*84* A7 10m blk & car 15 5
*85* A7 15m org brn & ultra 22 14
*86* A8 2pi org yel & vio brn 25 15
*87* A8 3pi dk bl & red brn 30 15
*88* A8 4pi blk & ultra 32 16
*89* A8 5pi dk grn & org 55 30
*90* A8 6pi blk & pale bl 65 35
*91* A8 8pi blk & pck grn 80 50
*92* A8 10pi dp rose lil & blk 1.25 70
a Center inverted
*93* A8 20pi dk bl & bl 3.75 1.25
a Perf. 13 19.00 *37.50*
*94* A8 50pi ultra & car 5.25 2.00
*Nos. 79-94 (16)* 14.43 6.60

Arabic inscription, types A7 and A8: "Berid es-Sudan"; types A1 and A2; "Postai-Sudaniye."

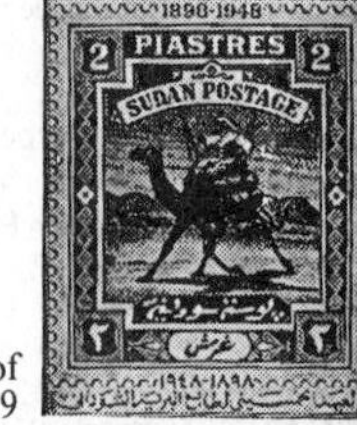

Stamp of 1898 — A9

**1948, Oct. 1 *Perf. 12½x13***

*95* A9 2pi dl bl & gray blk 35 30

50th anniv. of Sudan's 1st postage stamp.

A10

**1948, Dec. 19 *Perf. 13***

*96* A10 10m blk & car 20 8
*97* A10 5pi dk grn & org 50 30

Legislative Assembly opening, Dec., 1948.

Nubian Ibex — A11

Cotton Picking — A12

Camel Post — A13

Designs: 2m, Shoebill. 3m, Giraffe. 4m, Baggara girl. 5m, Shilluk warrior. 10m, Hadendowa. 15m, Sudan policeman. 3pi, Ambatch canoe. 3½pi, Nuba wrestlers. 4pi, Weaving. 5pi, Saluka farming. 6pi, Gum tapping. 8pi, Darfur chief. 10pi, Stack laboratory. 20pi, Nile lechwe.

**1951, Sept. 1 Typo. *Perf. 14***
**Center in Black (#98-104)**

*98* A11 1m orange 5 5
*99* A11 2m ultra 10 7
*100* A11 3m dk grn 65 65
*101* A11 4m emerald 10 10
*102* A11 5m plum 7 6
*103* A11 10m lt bl 10 6
*104* A11 15m dp org brn 18 6

***Perf. 13***

*105* A12 2pi lt bl & dk bl 18 7
*106* A12 3pi vio bl & brn 25 12
*107* A12 3½pi brn & bl grn 32 15
*108* A12 4pi blk & dp bl 32 15

*109* A12 5pi emer & org brn 38 15
*110* A12 6pi blk & bl 42 18
*111* A12 8pi brn & dp bl 55 25
*112* A12 10pi grn & blk 75 32
*113* A12 20pi blk & bl grn 1.50 50
*114* A13 50pi blk & car 4.00 1.25
*Nos. 98-114 (17)* 9.92 4.19

Camel Post — A14

**1954, Jan. 9** ***Perf. 12½x13***
*115* A14 15m emer & brn org 14 10
*116* A14 3pi blk & bl 22 20
*117* A14 5pi red vio & blk 40 35

Self-government in the Sudan.

A quantity of these sets inscribed "1953" was sold in London. They were not valid for postage. Value for set, $15.

### Independent Republic

Map of Sudan and Sun — A15

Rhinoceros Carrying Globe — A16

**Wmk. 214**
**1956, Sept. 15** **Engr.** ***Perf. 14***
*118* A15 15m rose lil & org 14 10
*119* A15 3pi dk bl & org 20 16
*120* A15 5pi grn & org 30 28

Independence Day, Jan. 1, 1956.

**1958, Aug. 2**
**Center in Orange**
*121* A16 15m plum 14 10
*122* A16 3pi blue 22 20
*123* A16 5pi green 35 30

APU Cong., Khartoum, Aug. 2, 1958.

Soldier, Farmer and Map of Nile — A17

Uprooted Oak Emblem, Refugee Man and Child — A18

**Lithographed and Engraved**
**1959, Nov. 17** **Unwmk.** ***Perf. 14***
*124* A17 15m brn, yel & ultra 14 10
*125* A17 3pi multi 20 16
*126* A17 55m multi 35 30

Issued to commemorate the first anniversary of the Sudanese army revolution.

### Arab League Center Issue

Type of Jordan, 1960

***Perf. 13x13½***
**1960, Mar. 22** **Photo.** **Wmk. 328**
*127* A28 15m dl grn & blk 10 8

Opening of the Arab League Center and the Arab Postal Museum in Cairo.

**Wmk. 214**
**1960, Apr. 7** **Litho.** ***Perf. 14***
*128* A18 15m blk, buff & ultra 14 10
*129* A18 55m blk, beige & org 35 35

Issued to publicize World Refugee Year, July 1, 1959-June 30, 1960.

Soccer Player — A19

Forest — A20

**1960, Aug. 25** **Wmk. 214** ***Perf. 14***
*130* A19 15m ultra, blk & yel 14 10
*131* A19 3pi yel, blk & grn 22 20
*132* A19 55m emer, blk & yel 38 35

Issued to commemorate the 17th Olympic Games, Rome, Aug. 25-Sept. 11.

**1960, Sept. 6**
*133* A20 15m multi 10 8
*134* A20 3pi multi 16 16
*135* A20 55m multi 30 28

5th World Forestry Cong., Seattle, WA, Aug. 29-Sept. 10.

King Tirhaqah, 689-663 B.C. — A21

Girl with Book — A22

**Unwmk.**
**1961, March 1** **Engr.** ***Perf. 14***
*136* A21 15m yel grn & brn 10 10
*137* A21 3pi sal & vio 16 16
*138* A21 55m lt bl & red brn 30 28

Save historic monuments in Nubia.

An imperf. souvenir sheet exists, not sold at post offices, containing one each of Nos. 136-138 with yellow green marginal inscription. Size: 154x97mm. The sheet was not issued for postal purposes and cancellation requests are declined.

**1961, Nov. 17** **Litho.** **Wmk. 214**
*139* A22 15m vio, cl & pink 10 8
*140* A22 3pi org, blk & bl 16 14
*141* A22 55m gray grn, blk & ocher 30 28

50 years of girls' education in the Sudan.

Malaria Eradication Emblem — A23

Arab League Building, Cairo — A24

**1962, Apr. 7** **Unwmk.** ***Perf. 14***
*142* A23 15m blk, pur & bl 7 7
*143* A23 55m dk brn & grn 30 30

WHO drive to eradicate malaria.

**1962, April 22** **Photo.** ***Perf. 13½x13***
*144* A24 15m dp org 7 6
*145* A24 55m bl grn 28 22

Arab League Week, Mar. 22-28.

Type of 1951 and

Palace of the Republic, Khartoum A25

Cotton Picker A26

Wmk. 345- Rhinoceros

Designs: 15m, Straw cover. 35m, 4pi, Wild animals. 55m, 6pi, Cattle. 8pi, Date palms. 10pi, Sailboat. 20pi, Bohein Temple, 1500 B.C. 50pi, Sennar Dam. £1, Camel Post (A13 redrawn).

***Perf. 14½x14, 14x14½***
**1962, Oct. 1** **Litho.** **Wmk. 345**
**Size: 23x19mm, 19x23mm**
*146* A25 5m blue 5 5
*a.* Unwmkd. ('76) 5 5
*147* A26 10m bl & lil 5 5
*a.* Unwmkd. ('76) 5 5
*148* A25 15m multi 5 5
*149* A25 2pi lt pur 6 5
*150* A26 3pi bl grn, red brn & brn 9 5
*a.* Unwmkd. ('76) 9 5
*151* A26 35m yel grn, brn & org brn 12 5
*a.* Unwmkd. ('75) 12 5
*152* A26 4pi red, lt bl & lil 12 5
*153* A25 55m gray & yel ol 20 8
*a.* Unwmkd. ('79) 20 8
*154* A25 6pi brn & lt bl 20 8
*155* A25 8pi green 28 9
*a.* Unwmkd. ('77) 28 9

***Perf. 14x14½, 13x13½, 14x13½, 13½x14***
**Size: 24½x30mm, 30x24½mm**
*156* A26 10pi lt bl, red brn & blk 35 10
*a.* Unwmkd. ('75) 35 10
*157* A25 20pi gray ol & yel grn 80 30
*158* A25 50pi dk gray, ol & bl 2.00 50

**Engr.**
*159* A13 £1 grn & brn org 4.00 3.00
*Nos. 146-159 (14)* 8.37 4.50

The frame of No. 159 has been altered with Arabic inscription on top and English at bottom.

Corn and Millet — A27

Centenary Emblem and Medals — A28

**1963, Mar. 21** **Litho.** **Wmk. 345**
*160* A27 15m, emer, gray & brn 9 8
*161* A27 55m vio, lt & dk bl 30 25

"Freedom from Hunger" campaign of the FAO.

**1963, Oct. 1** ***Perf. 14***
*162* A28 15m blk, red, gray & gold 9 8
*163* A28 55m grn, gray, red & gold 30 25

Centenary of the International Red Cross.

The Catalogue editors cannot undertake to appraise, identify or judge the genuineness or condition of stamps.

Melchior A29

Khashm El Girba Dam A30

Designs: 30m, St. Joseph seated, with cross and manuscript (horiz.). 55m, Archangel with cross. Designs from frescoes in excavated Faras Church.

**1964, Mar. 8** **Litho.** ***Perf. 14***
*164* A29 15m multi 15 12
*165* A29 30m red brn, blk & brn 35 30
*166* A29 55m red brn, blk & brn 60 55

UNESCO world campaign to save historic monuments in Nubia.

***Perf. 14x14½, 14½x14***
**1964, Apr. 22** **Wmk. 345**

Designs: 3pi, N.Y. World's Fair pavilion. 55m, Illustrated map of Sudan (vert.).

*167* A30 15m lt vio bl & vio brn 12 6
*168* A30 3pi multi 18 12
*169* A30 55m multi 35 25

New York World's Fair, 1964-65.

Eleanor Roosevelt and People Breaking Chains — A31

Arab Postal Union Emblem — A32

**1964, Dec. 10** ***Perf. 14***
*170* A31 15m grnsh bl & blk 12 6
*171* A31 3pi vio & blk 16 14
*172* A31 55m org brn & blk 35 25

Issued in memory of Eleanor Roosevelt (1884-1962), on the 16th anniversary of the Universal Declaration of Human Rights.

**1964, Dec. 30** **Litho.**
*173* A32 15m brick red, blk & gold 12 6
*174* A32 3pi gray grn, blk & gold 18 14
*175* A32 55m vio, blk & gold 35 25

Issued to commemorate the 10th anniversary of the Permanent Office of the Arab Postal Union.

ITU Emblem, Old and New Communication Equipment A33

**1965, May 17** **Wmk. 345** ***Perf. 13½***
*176* A33 15m brn & gold 12 6
*177* A33 3pi blk & gold 18 14
*178* A33 55m grn & gold 35 25

Cent. of the ITU.

"Gurashi" and Revolutionists — A34

**1965, Nov. 10 Litho. *Perf. 12***
*179* A34 15m dp ocher & blk 9 6
*180* A34 3pi brt red & blk 18 14
*181* A34 55m dk gray & blk 30 25

Issued to commemorate the first anniversary of the October 21st Revolution and to honor "Gurashi," one of its heroes.

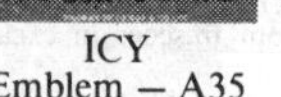

ICY Emblem — A35

El Siddig el Mahdi — A36

***Perf. 14½x14***
**1965, Dec. 10 Litho. Wmk. 345**
*182* A35 15m vio & blk 9 6
*183* A35 3pi yel grn & blk 15 14
*184* A35 55m ver & blk 30 25

International Cooperation Year, 1965.

**1966, Jan. 1 *Perf. 13***
*185* A36 15m lt bl & vio bl 9 6
*186* A36 3pi org & brn 15 12
*187* A36 55m gray & red brn 30 22

El Siddig el Mahdi (1911-61), imam of Ansar region and political leader.

Mubarak Zaroug A37

**1966, Jan. 1 Litho.**
*188* A37 15m pink & lt ol grn 9 6
*189* A37 3pi brt yel grn & dk grn 18 12
*190* A37 55m org brn & dk brn 30 22

Issued in memory of Mubarak Zaroug (1917-65), lawyer and political leader.

WHO Headquarters, Geneva — A38

**1966, June 11 Photo. *Perf. 11½x11***
*191* A38 15m blue 8 6
*192* A38 3pi magenta 15 12
*193* A38 55m brown 30 22

Inauguration of WHO Headquarters, Geneva.

Map of Sudan and Crests of Upper Nile, Blue Nile and Kassala Provinces — A39

Designs: 3pi, Map of Sudan and crests of Equatoria, Kordofan and Khartoum Provinces. 55m, Map of Sudan and crests of Bahr El Gazal, Darfur and Northern Provinces.

**1967, Apr. 1 Litho. *Perf. 14***
*194* A39 15m org, pur & lt bl grn 8 6
*195* A39 3pi dp org, vio & lt bl 15 12
*196* A39 55m yel, dp cl & yel grn 25 22

Month of the South.

Giraffe and ITY Emblem A40

Clasped Hands and Arab League Emblem A41

***Perf. 12½x13***
**1967, Aug. 15 Litho. Wmk. 345**
*197* A40 15m multi 25 9
*198* A40 3pi multi 15 12
*199* A40 55m multi 75 35

Issued for International Tourist Year 1967.

***Perf. 11x11½***
**1967, Aug. 29 Photo. Unwmk.**
*200* A41 15m org & ultra 8 6
*201* A41 3pi brn org & emer 15 12
*202* A41 55m lem & vio 25 22

Arab League Summit Conference.

Emblem of Palestine Liberation Organization — A42

**1967, Aug. 29 *Perf. 11½x11***
*203* A42 15m ol, car & yel 8 6
*204* A42 3pi grn, car & yel 22 22
*205* A42 55m brt grn, car & yel 38 30

Palestine Liberation Organization.

Abdullahi el Fadil el Mahdi A43

***Perf. 11½x11***
**1968, Feb. 15 Photo. Unwmk.**
*206* A43 15m ultra & brt pur 8 6
*207* A43 3pi dp ultra & brt grn 15 9
*208* A43 55m org & grn 25 18

Issued in memory of Abdullahi el Fadil el Mahdi (1892-1966), political leader.

Mohammed Nur el Din — A44

**1968, Feb. 15**
*209* A44 15m sl bl & ap grn 8 6
*210* A44 3pi bl & ol 15 9
*211* A44 55m bl & vio bl 25 18

Issued in memory of Mohammed Nur el Din (1898-1964), political leader.

Ahmed Yousif Hashim A45

***Perf. 11½x11***
**1968, Mar. 5 Photo. Unwmk.**
*212* A45 15m grn & brn 8 6
*213* A45 3pi brt bl & sep 15 9
*214* A45 55m ind & vio 25 18

Issued in memory of Ahmed Yousif Hashim (1906-1958), journalist.

Mohammed Ahmed el Mardi — A46

***Perf. 11x11½***
**1968, Mar. 5 Photo. Unwmk.**
*215* A46 15m Prus bl & vio bl 30 8
*216* A46 3pi ultra, ocher & dl rose 50 15
*217* A46 55m dk bl & brn 65 22

Issued in memory of Mohammed Ahmed el Mardi (1905-1966), political leader.

DC-3 A47

20th anniv. of Sudan Airways: 2p, De Havilland Dove. 3p, Fokker Friendship. 55m, De Havilland Comet 4C.

**1968, Dec. 15 Litho. *Perf. 13½x13***
*218* A47 15m multi 12 9
*219* A47 2p multi 15 12
*220* A47 3p multi 22 18
*221* A47 55m multi 35 30

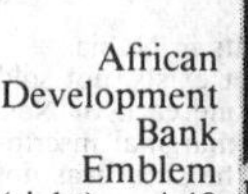

African Development Bank Emblem (right) — A48

**Wmk. Rectangles (334)**
**1969, Dec. 20 Photo. *Perf. 13***
*222* A48 2p blk, gray & gold 10 8
*223* A48 4p dk red & gold 20 15
*224* A48 65m grn & gold 35 22

Issued to commemorate the 5th anniversary of the African Development Bank.

ILO Emblem — A49

**Unwmk.**
**1969, Dec. 27 Litho. *Perf. 14***
*225* A49 2p bl, blk & pink 12 8
*226* A49 4p yel, blk & sil 20 15
*227* A49 65m grn, blk & lil 35 22

50th anniv. of the ILO.

Citizens A50

**1970, May 25 *Perf. 11½x11***
*228* A50 2p brn org, ol & bl

First anniv. of May 25th Revolution.

No. 228 was withdrawn on day of issue; 4p and 65m stamps in same design were prepared but not issued. Nos. 229-231 were issued instead.

Citizens A51

**1970, Oct. 21 Photo. *Perf. 11½x11***
*229* A51 2p brn, ol & red 12 8
*230* A51 4p lt bl, ol & red 20 15
*231* A51 65m ol, dk bl & red 35 22

1st anniv. of the May 25th Revolution.

Map and Flags of UAR, Libya, Sudan A52

**1971, Jan. 2 Unwmk. *Perf. 11½***
*232* A52 2p lt grn, car & blk 12 8

Signing of the Charter of Tripoli affirming the unity of United Arab Republic, Libya and the Sudan, Dec. 27, 1970.

Education Year Emblem A53

Emblem A54

**1971, May 2 Photo. *Perf. 11x11½***
*233* A53 2p bl, blk & brn 12 8
*234* A53 4p car, blk & brn 20 15
*235* A53 65m vio brn, blk & brn 35 22

International Education Year.

**1971, Nov. 10 *Perf. 11x11½***
*236* A54 2p yel, grn & blk 14 10
*237* A54 4p bl, grn & blk 35 30
*238* A54 10½p gray, grn & blk 90 75

2nd anniversary of May 25th Revolution.

Arab League and Sudanese Emblems A55

U.N. Emblem A56

**1972, Feb. 10 Photo. *Perf. 11x11½***
*239* A55 2p yel, grn & blk 12 8
*240* A55 4p org, bl & blk 25 22
*241* A55 10½p org, brn & blk 70 60

25th anniv. (in 1971) of the Arab League.

**1972, Mar. 12 Photo. *Perf. 11x11½***

*242* A56 2p emer, rose red & org 12 8

*243* A56 4p ultra, rose red & org 25 22

*244* A56 10½p blk, rose red & org 70 60

25th anniv. (in 1970) of the UN.

Emblems and Measure A57

**1972, Apr. 22 Photo. *Perf. 11½x11***

*245* A57 2p multi 12 8

*246* A57 4p lt bl & multi 25 22

*247* A57 10½p pink & multi 70 60

World Standards Day, Oct. 14, 1970.

Pres. Nimeiry and Arms of Sudan A58

**1972, May 2 Litho. *Perf. 13x13½***

*248* A58 2p vio bl, blk & gold 12 8

*249* A58 4p dp org, blk & gold 25 22

*250* A58 10½p ol grn, blk & gold 70 60

Election of Gaafar al-Nimeiry as President, Oct. 1971.

Arms of Sudan and Congress Emblem A59

**1972, Oct. 15 Photo. *Perf. 11½x11***

*251* A59 2p bl & multi 12 8

*252* A59 4p multi 25 22

*253* A59 10½p lt ol & multi 70 60

Founding Congress of the Sudanese Socialist Union.

Letter and African Postal Union Emblem A60

**1972, Dec. 16**

*254* A60 2p yel & multi 12 8

*255* A60 4p multi 25 22

*256* A60 10½p bl & multi 70 60

10th anniv. (in 1971) of the APU.

Emblems of Sudanese Provinces A61

Designs: 4p, Governing Council of Sudan. 10½p, Heraldic eagle and Unity emblem (vert.).

**1973, Jan. 1 Litho. *Perf. 13***

*257* A61 2p gold & multi 12 8

*258* A61 4p dk red brn & blk 25 22

*259* A61 10½p sil, org & grn 70 55

National Unity Day, March 3, 1972.

Emperor Haile Selassie — A62

**1973, June 25 Unwmk. *Perf. 13***

*260* A62 2p tan & multi 12 8

*261* A62 4p sil & multi 25 22

*262* A62 10½p gold & multi 70 55

80th birthday of Haile Selassie, Emperor of Ethiopia.

Nasser and Crowd A63

**1973, July 15 Photo. *Perf. 11½x11***

*263* A63 2p black 12 8

*264* A63 4p pale grn & blk 25 22

*265* A63 10½p lil & blk 70 55

Gamal Abdel Nasser (1918-70), President of Egypt.

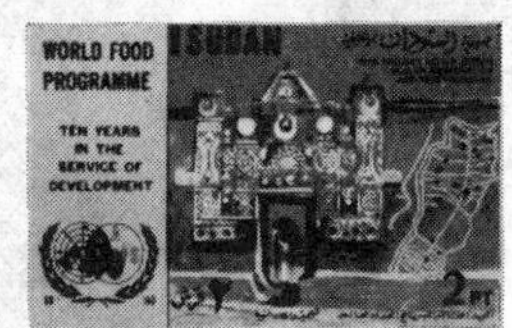


U.N. and FAO Emblems, Portal and Map of Resettlement Project — A64

**1973, Dec. 30 Litho. *Perf. 13***

*266* A64 2p multi 12 8

*267* A64 4p multi 25 22

*268* A64 10½p multi 70 60

World Food Program, 10th anniversary.

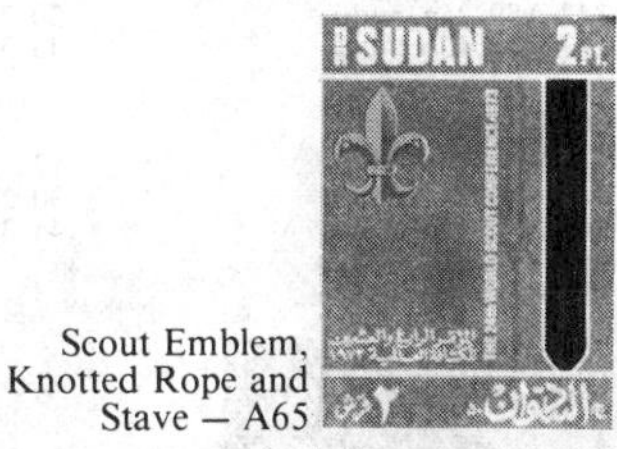


Scout Emblem, Knotted Rope and Stave — A65

**1974, Jan. 15**

*269* A65 2p multi 16 8

*270* A65 4p multi 38 15

*271* A65 10½p multi 75 38

24th World Boy Scout Conference.

INTERPOL Emblem A66

**1974, Feb. 16 Litho. *Perf. 13x13½***

*272* A66 2p org & multi 12 8

*273* A66 4p gray & multi 20 15

*274* A66 10½p lt bl & multi 50 38

50th anniv. of Intl. Criminal Police Organ.

K.S.M. Building A67

**1974, July 1 Litho. *Perf. 13x13½***

*275* A67 2p lil rose & multi 18 8

*276* A67 4p lt grn & multi 38 15

*277* A67 10½p ver & multi 90 38

50th anniversary of the Faculty of Medicine, University of Khartoum.

African Postal Union and UPU Emblems — A68

Designs: 4p, Letters, UPU and Arab Postal Union emblems. 10½p, Letters, UPU and African Postal Union emblems.

**1974, Sept. 9 Litho. *Perf. 13½***

*278* A68 2p multi 12 8

*279* A68 4p lt bl & multi 20 15

*280* A68 10½p lil & multi 50 38

Centenary of Universal Postal Union.

Ali Abdel Latif, Abdel Fadil Elmaz, Revolutionary Flag and Nile — A69

**1975, July 26 Litho. *Perf. 14x13½***

*281* A69 2½p grn & vio bl 22 9

*282* A69 4p rose & vio bl 50 15

*283* A69 10½p sep & vio bl 90 38

50th anniversary of 1924 revolution. Portraits show political and military leaders of the revolution.

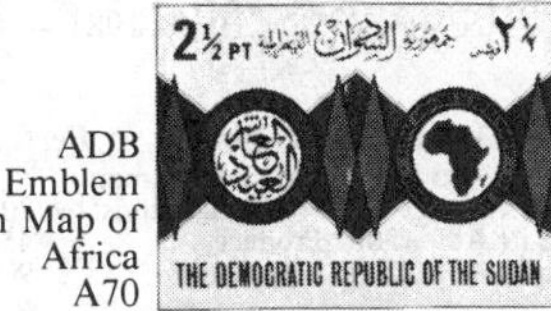


ADB Emblem with Map of Africa A70

**1975, July 26**

*284* A70 2½p multi 22 9

*285* A70 4p multi 45 15

*286* A70 10½p multi 90 38

African Development Bank, 10th anniv.

Radar Station and Camel Rider — A71

**1976, Feb. 2 Litho. *Perf. 13½x14***

*287* A71 2½p lt grn & multi 14 02

*288* A71 4p lil & multi 20 15

*289* A71 10½p vio bl & multi 50 38

Umm Haraz Satellite Station.

IWY Emblem, Flag and Woman A72

**1976, May 10 Litho. *Perf. 14x13½***

*290* A72 2½p multi 14 9

*291* A72 4p multi 22 15

*292* A72 10½p dk bl & multi 50 38

International Women's Year 1975.

Arms of Sudan, Olympic Rings, Track — A73

**1976, July 17 Litho. *Perf. 13½x14***

*293* A73 2½p grn & multi 22 15

*294* A73 4p grn & multi 50 30

*295* A73 10½p grn & multi 90 55

21st Olympic Games, Montreal, Canada, July 17-Aug. 1.

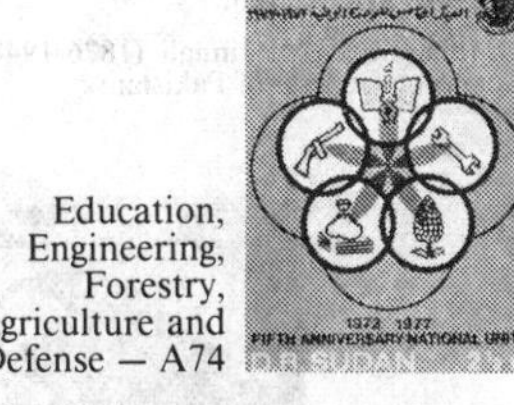


Education, Engineering, Forestry, Agriculture and Defense — A74

**1977, July 20 Litho. *Perf. 13½x14***

*296* A74 2½p multi 14 9

*297* A74 4p multi 20 15

*298* A74 10½p multi 50 38

5th anniversary of national unity.

Archbishop Capucci — A75

**1977, Oct. 22 Photo. *Perf. 11x11½***

*299* A75 2½p black 55 22

*300* A75 4p blk & grn 90 55

*301* A75 10½p blk & red 1.40 75

Palestinian Archbishop Hilarion Capucci, Jailed by Israel in 1974.

Fair Emblem, Sudanese Flag — A76

The indexes in each volume of the Scott Catalogue contain many listings which help to identify stamps.

*Perf. 11½x 11*

**1978, Jan. 19 Photo. Wmk. 342**

| | | | | |
|---|---|---|---|---|
| *302* A76 | 3p multi | 15 | 12 |
| *303* A76 | 4p multi | 20 | 15 |
| *304* A76 | 10½p multi | 50 | 38 |

International Khartoum Fair, Jan. 19-27.

APU Emblem A77

**1978, Mar. 8 Litho. *Perf. 14x13½***

| | | | |
|---|---|---|---|
| *305* A77 | 3p blk, car & sil | 22 | 12 |
| *306* A77 | 4p dk grn, blk & sil | 30 | 15 |
| *307* A77 | 10½p ultra, blk & sil | 75 | 38 |

APU, 25th anniv. (in 1977).

Jinnah and Sudanese Flag — A78

**1978, May 6 Litho. *Perf. 13***

| | | | |
|---|---|---|---|
| *308* A78 | 3p multi | 15 | 12 |
| *309* A78 | 4p multi | 30 | 15 |
| *310* A78 | 10½p multi | 50 | 38 |

Mohammed Ali Jinnah (1876-1948), first Governor General of Pakistan.

Desert A79

**1978, May 6 *Perf. 14x13½***

| | | | |
|---|---|---|---|
| *311* A79 | 3p multi | 15 | 12 |
| *312* A79 | 4p multi | 20 | 15 |
| *313* A79 | 10½p multi | 50 | 38 |

U.N. Desertification Conference.

Lion God Apedemek, African Unity Emblems — A80

**1978, July 18 Litho. *Perf. 13½x14***

| | | | |
|---|---|---|---|
| *314* A80 | 3p multi | 15 | 12 |
| *315* A80 | 4p multi | 20 | 15 |
| *316* A80 | 10½p multi | 40 | 38 |

15th African Summit Conference, Khartoum, July 18-21.

May Revolution, 10th Anniversary — A81

**1979, Oct. 1 Litho. *Perf. 13½x14***

| | | | |
|---|---|---|---|
| *317* A81 | 3½p multi | 12 | 10 |
| *318* A81 | 6p multi | 20 | 15 |
| *319* A81 | 13p multi | 40 | 38 |

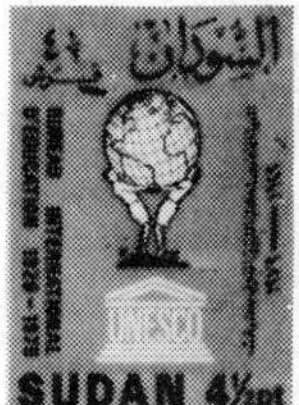


UNESCO Emblem, Children Holding Globe — A82

**1980, Jan. 19 Litho. *Perf. 13½x14***

| | | | |
|---|---|---|---|
| *320* A82 | 4½p org & blk | 15 | 14 |
| *321* A82 | 8p ol grn & blk | 25 | 22 |
| *322* A82 | 15½p bl & blk | 50 | 45 |

IYC Emblem, Hands Protecting Child A83

**1980, Mar. 15 *Perf. 14x13½***

| | | | |
|---|---|---|---|
| *323* A83 | 4½p multi | 15 | 14 |
| *324* A83 | 8p multi | 25 | 22 |
| *325* A83 | 15½p multi | 50 | 45 |

International Year of the Child (1979).

25th Anniv. of Independence — A84

**1982, Mar. 4 Photo. *Perf. 11½***

| | | | |
|---|---|---|---|
| *326* A84 | 60m multi | 20 | 15 |
| *327* A84 | 120m multi | 45 | 30 |
| *328* A84 | 250m multi | 90 | 75 |

World Food Day, Oct. 16, 1981 — A85

**1983, Jan. 15 Photo. *Perf. 11½***

| | | | |
|---|---|---|---|
| *329* A85 | 60m Emblem on map, reaching hands | 20 | 15 |
| *330* A85 | 120m Produce | 45 | 30 |
| *331* A85 | 250m Map, grain | 90 | 75 |

25th Anniv. of Economic Commission for Africa (1983) — A86

**1984, Feb. 20 Litho. *Perf. 13½***

| | | | |
|---|---|---|---|
| *332* A86 | 10p pink & sil | 12 | 8 |
| *333* A86 | 25p lt bl & sil | 30 | 22 |
| *334* A86 | 40p grn & sil | 40 | 38 |

Centenary of Shaykan Battle, Kordofan (1983) — A87

**1984, June 16 Litho. *Perf. 14***

| | | | |
|---|---|---|---|
| *335* A87 | 10p multi | 12 | 8 |
| *336* A87 | 25p multi | 30 | 22 |
| *337* A87 | 40p multi | 45 | 38 |

Olympic Week A88

**1984, Dec. 1 Litho. *Perf. 14***

| | | | |
|---|---|---|---|
| *338* A88 | 10p multi | 12 | 8 |
| *339* A88 | 25p multi | 30 | 22 |
| *340* A88 | 40p multi | 45 | 38 |

Sudan-Egypt Integration Charter, 2nd Anniv. A89

Bakht Erruda, Teacher Training Institute A90

**1985, Mar. 16 Photo. *Perf. 13½x13***

| | | | |
|---|---|---|---|
| *341* A89 | 10p multi | 12 | 8 |
| *342* A89 | 25p multi | 30 | 22 |
| *343* A89 | 40p multi | 45 | 38 |

**1985, Apr. 1**

| | | | |
|---|---|---|---|
| *344* A90 | 10p multi | 12 | 8 |
| *345* A90 | 25p multi | 30 | 22 |
| *346* A90 | 40p multi | 45 | 38 |

April 6 Uprising, 1st Anniv. A91

**1986, Apr. 1 Litho. *Perf. 14***

| | | | |
|---|---|---|---|
| *347* A91 | 5p multi | 6 | 5 |
| *348* A91 | 25p multi | 30 | 22 |
| *349* A91 | 40p multi | 45 | 38 |

World Food Day 1986 — A92

***Perf. 13x13½, 13½x13 (30p), 14 (50p)***

**1988, Jan. 1 Litho.**

| | | | |
|---|---|---|---|
| *350* A92 | 25p Net fishermen | 12 | 8 |
| *351* A92 | 30p Two fish, vert. | 14 | 10 |
| *352* A92 | 50p Globe | 22 | 15 |
| *353* A92 | 75p Stylized fish on wave | 35 | 24 |
| *354* A92 | 300p Fish in sea | 1.40 | 95 |
| | *Nos. 350-354 (5)* | 2.23 | 1.52 |

**Souvenir Sheet**

***Imperf***

| | | | |
|---|---|---|---|
| *354A* A92 | 75p like 25p | 70 | 70 |

No. 354A has buff and black inscribed decorative margin. Size: 100x70mm.

Child Survival A93

***Perf. 14, Imperf. (No. 357)***

**1988, Mar. 15 Litho.**

| | | | |
|---|---|---|---|
| *355* A93 | 50p Breast-feeding, vert. | 24 | 16 |
| *356* A93 | 75p Oral rehydration | 35 | 24 |
| *357* A93 | 75p like 50p, vert. | 35 | 24 |
| *358* A93 | 100p Oral vaccine | 45 | 30 |
| *359* A93 | 150p Growth monitoring | 68 | 45 |
| | *Nos. 355-359 (5)* | 2.07 | 1.39 |

No. 357 issued without gum. Size: 63x84mm.

Red Crescent in Sudan, 30th Anniv. (in 1987) — A94

World Food Day, Oct. 16, 1987, and the Small Farmer — A95

Designs: 100f, Crescent, candle. 150f, Crescent, stylized figure of a man.

**1988, Oct. 31 Litho. *Perf. 14***

| | | | |
|---|---|---|---|
| *360* A94 | 40p org yel, blk & dark red | 18 | 14 |
| *361* A94 | 100p blk, blue grn & dark red | 45 | 30 |
| *362* A94 | 150p blk, brt blue & dark red | 68 | 45 |

Nos. 361-362 horiz.

***Perf. 13x13½, 13½x13***

**1988, Oct. 31**

FAO emblem and: 40p, Early farming tools, horiz. 100p, Ox-drawn plow. 150p, Crude public water supply.

| | | | |
|---|---|---|---|
| *363* A95 | 40p multi | 18 | 14 |
| *364* A95 | 100p shown | 45 | 30 |
| *365* A95 | 150p multi | 68 | 45 |

Khartoum Bank, 75th Anniv. A96

Designs: 40p, Anniv. emblem. 100p, Spheres, emblem, medallion on ribbon. 150p, Text, emblem.

**1988, Oct. 31 *Perf. 14***

| | | | |
|---|---|---|---|
| *366* A96 | 40p multi | 18 | 14 |
| *367* A96 | 100p multi | 45 | 30 |
| *368* A96 | 150p multi | 68 | 45 |

## AIR POST STAMPS

Nos. 40-41, 43 Overprinted in Black

**AIR MAIL** — Nos. C1-C2

**AIR MAIL** — No. C3

**Wmk. Multiple S. G. (214)**

**1931** *Perf. 11 1/2x12 1/2, 14*

*C1* A2 5m blk & ol brn 60 *1.00*
*C2* A2 10m blk & car 60 *2.00*
*C3* A1 2pi org & vio brn 80 *2.75*

Statue of Gen. C. G. Gordon AP3

**1931-35** **Engr.** *Perf. 14*

*C4* AP3 3m dk brn & grn ('33) 2.00 *3.50*
*C5* AP3 5m grn & blk 75 75
*C6* AP3 10m car rose & blk 1.10 1.10
*C7* AP3 15m dk brn & brn 50 35
*C8* AP3 2pi org & blk 50 40
*C9* AP3 2 1/2pi bl & red vio ('33) 1.10 1.10
*C10* AP3 3pi gray & blk 65 65
*C11* AP3 3 1/2pi dl vio & blk 1.10 1.10
*C12* AP3 4 1/2pi gray & brn 4.25 5.00
*C13* AP3 5pi ultra & blk 1.50 1.40
*C14* AP3 7 1/2pi pck grn & dk grn ('35) 4.00 3.75
*C15* AP3 10pi pck bl & sep ('35) 7.00 2.50
*Nos. C4-C15 (12)* 24.45 21.60

See Nos. C23-C30.

2½ 2½

No. 43 Surcharged in Black **AIR MAIL**

٢½ ٢½

**1932, July 18** **Typo.**

*C16* A1 2 1/2pi on 2pi org & vio brn 9.00 9.00

Nos. C6, C4-C5, C12 Surcharged **7½ PIASTRES** ٧½ قروش

**1935** **Engr.** *Perf. 14*

*C17* AP3 15m on 10m car rose & blk 85 85
*a.* Double surcharge 650.00 *700.00*
*b.* Arabic characters omitted 650.00
*C18* AP3 2 1/2pi on 3m dk brn & grn 2.00 2.00
*a.* "½" 2¼mm high instead of 3mm 8.25 8.25
*b.* Second Arabic character of surcharge omitted 140.00 140.00
*C19* AP3 2 1/2pi on 5m grn & blk 1.00 1.00
*a.* "½" 2¼mm high instead of 3mm 8.00 8.00
*b.* Second Arabic character of surcharge omitted 80.00 80.00
*c.* Inverted surcharge 825.00 825.00
*d.* As "b." inverted *2,100.*
*C20* AP3 3pi on 4 1/2pi gray & brn 3.75 *5.00*
*C21* AP3 7 1/2pi on 4 1/2pi gray & brn 7.50 *10.00*
*a.* "7½" instead of "7½" 
*C22* AP3 10pi on 4 1/2pi gray & brn 7.00 *8.00*
*Nos. C17-C22 (6)* 22.10 *26.85*

Type of 1931-35

**1936-37** *Perf. 11 1/2x12 1/2*

*C23* AP3 15m dk brn & brn ('37) 90 50
*C24* AP3 2pi org & blk ('37) 4.25 4.25
*C25* AP3 2 1/2pi bl & red vio 50 50
*C26* AP3 3pi gray & blk ('37) 1.50 1.10
*C27* AP3 3 1/2pi dl vio & blk ('37) 3.50 3.50
*C28* AP3 5pi ultra & blk ('37) 1.25 90
*C29* AP3 7 1/2pi pck grn & dk grn ('37) 2.00 2.00
*C30* AP3 10pi pck bl & sep ('37) 3.25 3.25
*Nos. C23-C30 (8)* 17.15 16.00

Nos. C25, C11, C14 and C15 Surcharged as in 1935

**Wmk. Multiple S. G. (214)**

**1938** *Perf. 11 1/2x12 1/2, 14*

*C31* AP3 5m on 2 1/2pi bl & red vio 25 25
*C32* AP3 3pi on 3 1/2pi dl vio & blk 4.00 4.00
*a.* On No. C27 375.00 *425.00*
*C33* AP3 3pi on 7 1/2pi pck grn & dk grn 90 90
*a.* On No. C29 375.00 *425.00*
*C34* AP3 5pi on 10pi pck bl & sep 1.10 1.10
*a.* On No. C30 450.00 *500.00*

**Catalogue values for unused stamps in this section, from this point to the end of the section, are for Never Hinged items.**

Bridge Over Blue Nile, Khartoum AP4

Designs: 2 1/2pi, Kassala Jebel. 3pi, Water wheel. 3 1/2pi, Port Sudan. 4pi, Gordon Memorial College. 4 1/2pi, Nile post boat. 6pi, Suakin. 20pi, General Post Office, Khartoum.

**1950, July 1** **Engr.** *Perf. 12*

*C35* AP4 2pi dk bl grn & blk 50 35
*C36* AP4 2 1/2pi red org & bl 60 60
*C37* AP4 3pi dp bl & plum 75 75
*C38* AP4 3 1/2pi chnt & choc 75 75
*C39* AP4 4pi bl & brn 1.20 1.20
*C40* AP4 4 1/2pi ultra & blk 1.25 1.25
*C41* AP4 6pi car & blk 1.25 1.25
*C42* AP4 20pi plum & blk 5.50 4.00
*Nos. C35-C42 (8)* 11.80 10.15

## AIR POST OFFICIAL

**Catalogue values for unused stamps in this section, from this point to the end of the section, are for Never Hinged items.**

Nos. C35 to C42 Overprinted in Carmine or Black **S.G.**

**1950, July 1** **Wmk. 214** *Perf. 12*

*CO1* AP4 2pi dk bl grn & blk (C) 90 60
*CO2* AP4 2 1/2pi red org & bl 90 90
*CO3* AP4 3pi dp bl & plum 90 90
*CO4* AP4 3 1/2pi chnt & choc 1.20 1.20
*CO5* AP4 4pi bl & brn 1.25 1.25
*CO6* AP4 4 1/2pi ultra & blk (C) 2.00 1.75
*CO7* AP4 6pi car & blk (C) 1.60 1.60
*CO8* AP4 20pi plum & blk (C) 1.00 1.00
*Nos. CO1-CO8 (8)* 9.75 9.20

## POSTAGE DUE STAMPS

Postage Due Stamps of Egypt, 1889, Overprinted in Black السودان SOUDAN

**1897** **Wmk. 119** *Perf. 14*

*J1* D3 2m green 2.25 1.75
*J2* D3 4m maroon 2.25 2.00
*J3* D3 1pi ultra 5.00 3.50
*J4* D3 2pi orange 10.50 9.00

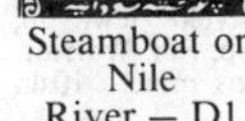

Steamboat on Nile River — D1

Bottom inscription altered — D2

**1901** **Typo.** **Wmk. 179**

*J5* D1 2m org brn & blk 70 50
*J6* D1 4m bl grn & brn 1.00 60
*J7* D1 10m bl vio & bl grn 1.50 75
*J8* D1 20m car rose & ultra 4.50 3.25

**1927-30** **Wmk. Multiple S G (214)**

*J9* D1 2m org brn & blk ('30) 60 60
*J10* D1 4m bl grn & brn 1.25 1.25
*J11* D1 10m vio & bl grn 1.50 1.50

**Catalogue values for unused stamps in this section, from this point to the end of the section, are for Never Hinged items.**

Redrawn

**1948, Jan. 1**

*J12* D2 2m dp org & blk 1.20 1.20
*J13* D2 4m bl grn & choc 1.20 1.20
*J14* D2 10m rose lil & bl grn 4.00 4.00
*a.* Wmk. 345 ('73)
*J15* D2 20m brt car rose & ultra 5.00 5.00
*a.* Wmk. 345 ('73)

## ARMY OFFICIAL

Regular Issues of 1898 and 1902-08 Overprinted in Black:

ARMY OFFICIAL — Nos. MO1, MO3
ARMY OFFICIAL — Nos. MO2, MO4

**1905** **Wmk. 71** *Perf. 14*

*MO1* A1 1m rose & brn 100.00 85.00
*a.* "OFF!CIAL" 1,750.
*MO2* A1 1m rose & brn 1,600. *2,000.*

**Wmk. 179**

*MO3* A1 1m car rose & brn 2.00 1.25
*a.* "OFF!CIAL" 22.50 12.00
*b.* Inverted overprint 35.00 35.00
*c.* Horizontal overprint 300.00
*MO4* A1 1m car rose & brn 16.00 6.50
*a.* Inverted overprint 350.00 375.00

Regular Issues of 1902-11 Overprinted in Black **Army Service**

**1906-11**

*MO5* A1 1m car rose & brn 1.10 20
*a.* "Army" and "Service" 14mm apart 160.00 140.00
*b.* Invt. overprint 400.00 400.00
*c.* Pair, one without overprint 3,750.
*d.* Double overprint 600.00
*e.* "Service" omitted 3,500.
*MO6* A1 2m brn & grn 5.00 35
*a.* Pair, one without overprint 1,800.
*b.* "Army" omitted 2,000.
*MO7* A1 3m grn & vio 9.00 28
*a.* Inverted ovpt. 2,000.
*MO8* A1 5m blk & rose red 1.40 10
*a.* Inverted overprint 200.00
*b.* Double overprint 300.00 300.00
*c.* Double overprint, one inverted 65.00 350.00
*MO9* A1 1pi yel brn & ultra 6.00 16
*a.* "Army" omitted 2,000. 2,000.
*MO10* A1 2pi ultra & blk ('09) 10.00 6.50
*MO11* A1 5pi grn & org brn ('08) 70.00 22.50
*MO12* A1 10pi dp vio & blk ('11) 625.00 650.00
*Nos. MO5-MO12 (8)* 727.50 680.09

**Same Overprint On Regular Issue of 1898**

**Wmk. Rosette. (71)**

*MO13* A1 2pi ultra & blk 20.00 6.50
*a.* Inverted overprint
*MO14* A1 5pi grn & org brn 65.00 *70.00*
*MO15* A1 10pi dp vio & blk 130.00 150.00

There are two types of this overprint which may be distinguished by the size and shape of the "y".

## OFFICIAL STAMPS

Regular Issue of 1898 Overprinted in Black **O.S.G.S.**

**1902-06** **Wmk. 71** *Perf. 14*

*O1* A1 1m rose & brn 2.75 2.75
*a* Invt. overprint 700.00
*b* Round periods 10.00 10.00
*c* Double overprint 850.00
*d* Oval "O" in overprint 165.00
*e* As "d." invtd. overprint 5,000.
*O2* A1 10pi dp vio & blk ('06) 8.50 6.00

Same Ovpt. on Stamps of 1902-11

**1903-12** **Wmk. 179**

*O3* A1 1m car rose & brn ('04) 45 38
*a* Double ovpt.
*O4* A1 3m grn & vio ('04) 60 45
*a* Double ovpt.
*O5* A1 5m blk & rose red 1.25 20
*O6* A1 1pi yel brn & ultra 3.00 28
*O7* A1 2pi ultra & blk 5.50 40
*O8* A1 5pi grn & org brn 2.00 90
*O9* A1 10pi dp vio & blk 3.00 11.00
*Nos. O3-O9 (7)* 15.80 13.61

Regular Issue of 1927-40 Overprinted in Black **S.G.**

*Perf. 14, 13 1/2x 14*

**1936-46** **Wmk. 214**

*O10* A2 1m dk org & int blk ('46) 28 16
*O11* A2 2m dk brn & dk org ('45) 12 8
*O12* A2 3m grn & vio ('37) 10 10
*O13* A2 4m brn & grn 10 10
*O14* A2 5m blk & ol brn ('40) 10 10
*O15* A2 10m blk & car ('46) 50 6
*O16* A2 15m org brn & ultra ('37) 16 14

**S.G.**

*O17* A1 2pi org & vio brn ('37) 20 20
*O18* A1 3pi dk bl & red brn ('46) 80 60
*O19* A1 4pi blk & ultra ('46) 65 50
*O20* A1 5pi dk grn & org brn 40 40
*O21* A1 6pi blk & pale bl ('46) 2.00 1.20
*O22* A1 8pi blk & pck grn ('46) 1.40 1.20
*O23* A1 10pi dp vio & blk ('37) 1.40 1.20
*O24* A1 20pi bl & lt bl ('46) 3.50 2.75
*Nos. O10-O24 (15)* 11.71 8.79

**Catalogue values for unused stamps in this section, from this point to the end of the section, are for Never Hinged items.**

Nos. 79-85 Overprinted Like Nos. O10-O16

**1948, Jan. 1**

*O28* A7 1m dk org & blk 10 10
*O29* A7 2m choc & org 10 10
*O30* A7 3m grn & rose lil 10 10
*O31* A7 4m choc & sl grn 20 10
*O32* A7 5m blk & ol brn 10 10
*O33* A7 10m blk & car 20 9
*O34* A7 15m org brn & ultra 25 18

**Nos. 86-94 Overprinted Like Nos. O17-O24**

*O35* A8 2pi org yel & vio brn 32 18
*O36* A8 3pi dk bl & red brn 45 20
*O37* A8 4pi blk & ultra 65 25
*a* Perf. 13 14.00 14.00
*O38* A8 5pi dk grn & org 80 40
*O39* A8 6pi blk & pale bl 1.10 70
*O40* A8 8pi blk & pck grn 1.40 65
*O41* A8 10pi dp rose lil & blk 1.90 1.00
*O42* A8 20pi dk bl & bl 3.25 1.50
*a* Perf. 13
*O43* A8 50pi ultra & car 10.00 6.00
*Nos. O28-O43 (16)* 20.92 11.65

Nos. 98-104 Overprinted Liked Nos. O10-O16 in Red

**1951, Sept. 1 Wmk. 214 *Perf. 14***

**Center in Black**

| | | | | |
|---|---|---|---|---|
| *O44* A11 | 1m orange | | 5 | 5 |
| *O45* A11 | 2m ultra | | 5 | 5 |
| *O46* A11 | 3m dk grn | | 30 | 30 |
| *O47* A11 | 4m emerald | | 5 | 5 |
| *O48* A11 | 5m plum | | 5 | 5 |
| *O49* A11 | 10m lt bl | | 7 | 5 |
| *O50* A11 | 15m dp org brn | | 15 | 5 |

**Nos. 105-114 Overprinted Like Nos. O17-O24 in Black or Red**

***Perf. 13***

| | | | |
|---|---|---|---|
| *O51* A12 | 2pi lt bl & dk bl | 15 | 10 |
| *a* | Inverted ovpt. | 800.00 | |
| *O52* A12 | 3pi vio bl & brn | 30 | 12 |
| *O53* A12 | 3½pi brn & bl grn | 38 | 20 |
| *O54* A12 | 4pi blk & dp bl | 38 | 15 |
| *O55* A12 | 5pi emer & org brn | 42 | 15 |
| *O56* A12 | 6pi blk & bl | 55 | 18 |
| *O57* A12 | 8pi brn & dp bl | 70 | 22 |
| *O58* A12 | 10pi grn & blk (R) | 90 | 22 |
| *O59* A12 | 20pi blk & bl grn | 1.40 | 60 |
| *a* | Inverted ovpt. | | 700.00 |
| *O60* A13 | 50pi blk & car | 4.50 | 1.90 |
| | *Nos. O44-O60 (17)* | 10.40 | 4.44 |

No. 112 Overprinted Like Nos.O17-O24 in Black

**1958**

| | | | |
|---|---|---|---|
| *O61* A12 | 10pi green & black | 65 | 18 |

Nos. 146-159 Overprinted ح.س.

***Perf. 14½x14, 14x14½***

**1962, Oct. 1 Litho. Wmk. 345**

**Size: 23x19mm, 19x23mm**

| | | | |
|---|---|---|---|
| *O62* A25 | 5m blue | 5 | 5 |
| *O63* A26 | 10m bl & lil | 10 | 5 |
| *a.* | Unwmkd. ('76) | 10 | 5 |
| *O64* A25 | 15m yel, vio, org & brn | 18 | 5 |
| *a.* | Unwmkd. ('75) | 18 | 5 |
| *O65* A25 | 2pi lt pur | 22 | 10 |
| *O66* A26 | 3pi bl grn, red brn & brn | 35 | 15 |
| *O67* A26 | 35m yel grn, brn & org brn | 40 | 22 |
| *O68* A26 | 4pi red, lt bl & lil | 45 | 25 |
| *O69* A25 | 55m gray & yel ol | 75 | 45 |
| *O70* A25 | 6pi brn & lt bl | 85 | 45 |
| *a.* | Unwmkd. ('76) | 85 | 45 |
| *O71* A25 | 8pi green | 1.10 | 55 |

**Size: 24½x30mm, 30x24½mm**

| | | | |
|---|---|---|---|
| *O72* A26 | 10pi lt bl, red brn & blk | 1.50 | 65 |
| *O73* A25 | 20pi gray ol & yel grn | 3.00 | 1.40 |
| *a.* | Perf. 13½x12½ | 2.75 | 1.10 |
| *O74* A25 | 50pi dk gray, ol & bl | 7.50 | 3.50 |
| *a.* | Perf. 13½x14 | 6.50 | 3.25 |

**Engr.**

| | | | |
|---|---|---|---|
| *O75* A13 | £1 grn & brn org | 19.00 | 15.00 |
| *a.* | Unwmkd. ('79) | 19.00 | 15.00 |
| | *Nos. O62-O75 (14)* | 35.45 | 22.87 |

The overprint measures 12x4½mm on Nos. O62-O71; 16x6mm on Nos. O72-O75.

# SWAZILAND

LOCATION — In southeast Africa bordered by the Transvaal and Zululand in South Africa and by Mozambique.

GOVT. — Constitutional monarchy.

AREA — 6,705 sq. mi.

POP. — 626,000 (est. 1984).

CAPITAL — Mbabane.

An independent state in the 19th century, Swaziland was administered by Transvaal from 1894 to 1906, when the administration was transferred to the British High Commissioner for South Africa. In 1934 Swaziland and Bechuanaland Protectorate came under the administration of the British High Commissioner for Basutoland. The issuing of individual postage stamps had been resumed in 1933. Internal self-government was introduced in 1967. Independence was proclaimed September 6, 1968.

12 Pence = 1 Shilling
20 Shillings = 1 Pound
100 Cents = 1 Rand (1961)
100 Cents = 1 Emalangeni (1975)

**Catalogue values for unused stamps in this country are for Never Hinged items, beginning with Scott 38 in the regular postage section and Scott J1 in the postage due section.**

Coat of Arms
A1

George V
A2

Black Overprint

**1889 Unwmk. *Perf. 12½, 12½x12***

| | | | |
|---|---|---|---|
| *1* A1 | ½p gray | 7.50 | 7.50 |
| *a* | Inverted overprint | 450.00 | 500.00 |
| *b* | "Swazielan" | 900.00 | 800.00 |
| *c* | As "b", invtd. overprint | | 2,750. |
| *2* A1 | 1p rose | 12.00 | 12.00 |
| *a* | Inverted overprint | 240.00 | 240.00 |
| *3* A1 | 2p ol bis | 6.00 | 6.00 |
| *a* | Invtd. ovpt. | 240.00 | 240.00 |
| *b* | "Swazielan" | 475.00 | 475.00 |
| *c* | Perf. 12½x12 | 75.00 | 21.00 |
| *4* A1 | 6p gray bl | 14.00 | 25.00 |
| *5* A1 | 1sh green | 7.50 | 10.00 |
| *a* | Inverted overprint | 475.00 | 475.00 |
| *6* A1 | 2sh6p yellow | 70.00 | 92.50 |
| *7* A1 | 5sh slate | 100.00 | 100.00 |
| *a* | Invtd. overprint | 2,750. | 2,750. |
| *b* | "Swazielan" | 6,000. | |
| *c* | As "b", invtd. overprint | | |
| *8* A1 | 10sh lt brn | 4,000. | 3,000. |

**1892 Red Overprint**

| | | | |
|---|---|---|---|
| *9* A1 | ½p gray | 4.50 | 5.75 |
| *a* | Inverted ovpt. | 475.00 | |
| *b* | Double overprint | 300.00 | 300.00 |

*Reprints have a period after "Swazieland."*

Stamps of Swaziland were replaced by those of Transvaal in 1895. Swaziland issues were resumed in 1933.

**Wmk. 4**

**1933, Jan. 2 Engr. *Perf. 14***

| | | | |
|---|---|---|---|
| *10* A2 | ½p green | 16 | 30 |
| *11* A2 | 1p carmine | 24 | 20 |
| *12* A2 | 2p lt brn | 28 | 35 |
| *13* A2 | 3p ultra | 30 | 42 |
| *14* A2 | 4p orange | 60 | 80 |
| *15* A2 | 6p rose vio | 80 | 1.10 |
| *16* A2 | 1sh ol grn | 1.40 | 3.00 |
| *17* A2 | 2sh6p violet | 8.00 | 12.50 |
| *18* A2 | 5sh gray | 30.00 | 45.00 |
| *19* A2 | 10sh blk brn | 80.00 | 125.00 |
| | *Nos. 10-19 (10)* | 121.78 | 188.67 |

**Silver Jubilee Issue**

Common Design Type

**1935, May 4 *Perf. 11x12***

| | | | |
|---|---|---|---|
| *20* CD301 | 1p car & bl | 28 | 24 |
| *21* CD301 | 2p blk & ultra | 48 | 50 |
| *22* CD301 | 3p ultra & brn | 1.10 | 1.25 |
| *23* CD301 | 6p brn, vio & ind | 1.40 | 1.50 |

**Coronation Issue**

Common Design Type

**1937, May 12 *Perf. 11x11½***

| | | | |
|---|---|---|---|
| *24* CD302 | 1p dk car | 20 | 20 |
| *25* CD302 | 2p brown | 25 | 25 |
| *26* CD302 | 3p dp ultra | 35 | 35 |

George VI — A3

**1938, Apr. 1 *Perf. 13, 13x13½***

| | | | |
|---|---|---|---|
| *27* A3 | ½p green | 5 | 5 |
| *28* A3 | 1p rose car | 8 | 8 |
| *29* A3 | 1½p lt bl | 10 | 10 |
| *a* | Perf. 14 ('42) | 20 | 20 |
| *30* A3 | 2p brown | 10 | 10 |
| *31* A3 | 3p ultra | 16 | 16 |
| *32* A3 | 4p red org | 24 | 24 |
| *33* A3 | 6p rose vio | 32 | 32 |
| *34* A3 | 1sh ol grn | 48 | 48 |
| *35* A3 | 2sh6p dk vio | 80 | 80 |
| *36* A3 | 5sh gray | 2.25 | 2.25 |
| *37* A3 | 10sh blk brn | 3.00 | 3.00 |
| | *Nos. 27-37 (11)* | 7.58 | 7.58 |

**Catalogue values for unused stamps in this section, from this point to the end of the section, are for Never Hinged items.**

**Peace Issue**

South Africa, Nos. 100-102 Overprinted **Swaziland**

Basic stamps inscribed alternately in English and Afrikaans.

**1945, Dec. 3 Wmk. 201 *Perf. 14***

| | | | |
|---|---|---|---|
| *38* A42 | 1p rose pink & choc | 8 | 8 |
| *a* | Pair | 16 | 16 |
| *39* A43 | 2p vio & sl bl | 10 | 10 |
| *a* | Pair | 20 | 20 |
| *40* A43 | 3p ultra & dp ultra | 15 | 15 |
| *a* | Pair | 30 | 30 |

World War II victory of the Allies.

**Royal Visit Issue**

Type of Basutoland, 1947

***Perf. 12½***

**1947, Feb. 17 Wmk. 4 Engr.**

| | | | |
|---|---|---|---|
| *44* A3 | 1p red | 8 | 8 |
| *45* A4 | 2p green | 8 | 8 |
| *46* A5 | 3p ultra | 10 | 10 |
| *47* A6 | 1sh dk vio | 20 | 20 |

Issued to commemorate the visit of the British Royal Family, March 25, 1947.

**Silver Wedding Issue**

Common Design Types

**1948, Dec. 1 Photo. *Perf. 14x14½***

| | | | |
|---|---|---|---|
| *48* CD304 | 1½p brt ultra | 20 | 20 |

**Engraved; Name Typographed**

***Perf. 11½x11***

| | | | |
|---|---|---|---|
| *49* CD305 | 10sh vio brn | 17.50 | 27.50 |

**UPU Issue**

Common Design Types

**Engr.; Name Typo. on 3p, 6p**

***Perf. 13½, 11x11½***

**1949, Oct. 10 Wmk. 4**

| | | | |
|---|---|---|---|
| *50* CD306 | 1½p blue | 15 | 15 |
| *51* CD307 | 3p indigo | 35 | 35 |
| *52* CD308 | 6p red lil | 42 | 42 |
| *53* CD309 | 1sh olive | 85 | 85 |

**Coronation Issue**

Common Design Type

**1953, June 3 Engr. *Perf. 13½x13***

| | | | |
|---|---|---|---|
| *54* CD312 | 2p yel brn & blk | 25 | 25 |

Asbestos Mine — A4

Married Woman — A5

Designs: 1p, 2sh 6p, Highveld view. 3p, 1sh 3p, Courting couple. 4½p, 5sh, Warrior. 6p, £1, Kudu. 1sh, Asbestos mine. 10sh, Married woman.

***Perf. 13x13½, 13½x13***

**1956, July 2 Engr. Wmk. 4**

**Center in Black, except Nos. 63-64.**

| | | | |
|---|---|---|---|
| *55* A4 | ½p orange | 8 | 5 |
| *56* A4 | 1p emerald | 9 | 6 |
| *57* A5 | 2p redsh brn | 12 | 9 |
| *58* A5 | 3p rose red | 16 | 12 |
| *59* A5 | 4½p ultra | 35 | 25 |
| *60* A5 | 6p magenta | 35 | 25 |
| *61* A4 | 1sh gray ol | 75 | 50 |
| *62* A5 | 1sh3p brown | 85 | 60 |
| *63* A4 | 2sh6p car & brt grn | 1.25 | 1.10 |
| *64* A5 | 5sh bl gray & vio | 3.00 | 2.25 |
| *65* A5 | 10sh dl vio | 6.75 | 4.75 |
| *66* A5 | £1 turquoise | 12.50 | 10.50 |
| | *Nos. 55-66 (12)* | 26.25 | 20.52 |

Nos. 55-61 and 63-66 Surcharged with New Value

| 2½c | 2½c | 4c | 4c | |
|---|---|---|---|---|
| I | II | I | II | |
| 5c | 5c | 25c | 25c | |
| I | II | I | II | |
| 50c | 50c | 50c | | |
| I | II | III | | |
| R1 | R1 | R1 | R2 | R2 |
| I | II | III | I | II |

**1961**

**Center in Black Except Nos. 76-77**

| | | | |
|---|---|---|---|
| *67* A4 | ½c on ½p org | 1.25 | 1.25 |
| *a* | Invtd. surch. | 200.00 | |
| *68* A4 | 1c on 1p emer | 12 | 12 |
| *a* | "1c" at center | 27.50 | |
| *b* | Dble. surch. | 150.00 | |
| *69* A5 | 2c on 2p redsh brn | 22 | 22 |
| *70* A5 | 2½p on 2p redsh brn | 22 | 22 |
| *71* A5 | 2½c on 3p rose red (I) | 50 | 50 |
| *a* | Type II | 1.10 | 1.10 |
| *72* A5 | 3½c on 2p redsh brn | 10 | 10 |
| *73* A5 | 4c on 4½p ultra (II) | 22 | 22 |
| *a* | Type I | 30 | 30 |
| *74* A5 | 5c on 6p mag (II) | 22 | 22 |
| *a* | Type I | 25 | 25 |
| *75* A4 | 10c on 1sh gray ol | 5.50 | 5.50 |
| *a* | Double surch. | 250.00 | |
| *76* A4 | 25c on 2sh6p car & brt grn (I) | 1.25 | 1.25 |
| *a* | Type II, "25c" centered | 1.25 | 1.25 |
| *b* | Type II, "25c" at lower left | 100.00 | 125.00 |
| *77* A5 | 50c on 5sh bl gray & vio (I) | 1.15 | 1.25 |
| *a* | Type II | 6.25 | 6.25 |
| *b* | Type III | 250.00 | 275.00 |
| *78* A5 | 1r on 10sh dl vio (I) | 2.50 | 2.50 |
| *a* | Type II | 6.25 | 6.25 |
| *b* | Type III | 30.00 | 35.00 |
| *79* A5 | 2r on £1 turq (II, "R2" at middle left) | 4.75 | 4.75 |
| *a* | Type I | 12.00 | 12.00 |
| *b* | Type II, "R2" at center bottom | 24.00 | 24.00 |
| | *Nos. 67-79 (13)* | 18.00 | 18.10 |

The type II "25c" surcharge is nearly centered in the sky on No. 76a, and is at lower left touching the value tablet on No. 76b.

Surcharge types are numbered chronologically.

Types of 1956

Designs: ½c, 10c, Asbestos mine. 1c, 25c, Highveld view. 2c, 1r, Married woman. 2½c, 12½c, Courting couple. 4c, 50c, Warrior. 5c, 2r, Kudu.

***Perf. 13x13½, 13½x13***

**1961 Engr. Wmk. 4**

**Center in Black, except Nos. 88-89**

| | | | |
|---|---|---|---|
| *80* A4 | ½c orange | 6 | 6 |
| *81* A4 | 1c emerald | 8 | 8 |
| *82* A5 | 2c redsh brn | 18 | 18 |
| *83* A5 | 2½c rose red | 28 | 28 |
| *84* A5 | 4c ultra | 45 | 45 |
| *85* A5 | 5c magenta | 45 | 45 |
| *86* A4 | 10c gray ol | 65 | 65 |
| *87* A5 | 12½c brown | 90 | 90 |
| *88* A4 | 25c car & brt grn | 1.25 | 1.25 |
| *89* A5 | 50c bl gray & vio | 2.75 | 2.75 |
| *90* A5 | 1r dl vio | 5.25 | 5.25 |
| *91* A5 | 2r turquoise | 11.50 | 11.50 |
| | *Nos. 80-91 (12)* | 23.80 | 23.80 |

A particular stamp may be scarce, but if few collectors want it, its market value may remain relatively low.

Swazi Shields — A6

Train and Railroad Map — A7

Designs: 1c, Battle axe. 2c, Forestry. 2½c, Ceremonial headdress. 3½c, Musical instrument. 4c, Irrigation. 5c, Widow bird. 7½c, Rock paintings. 10c, Secretary bird. 12½c, Pink arum lily. 15c, Married woman. 20c, Malaria control. 25c, Swazi warrior. 50c, Ground hornbill (horiz.). 1r, Aloes. 2r, Msinsi (flame tree) (horiz.).

*Perf. 12½x14, 14x12½*

**1962, Apr. 24 Photo. Wmk. 314**

92 A6 ½c ocher, blk & brn 6 6
93 A6 1c gray & org 6 6
94 A6 2c lt yel grn, dk grn & blk 10 10
95 A6 2½c ver & blk 10 8
96 A6 3½c gray & emer 18 18
97 A6 4c aqua & blk 18 18
98 A6 5c org red & blk 22 22
99 A6 7½c dl ocher & brn 28 28
100 A6 10c lt bl & blk 35 35
101 A6 12½c lt ol & dp car 50 50
102 A6 15c red lil & blk 55 55
103 A6 20c emer & blk 60 60
104 A6 25c ultra & blk 80 80
105 A6 50c rose red & dk brn 1.50 1.50
106 A6 1r bis & emer 3.00 3.00
107 A6 2r ultra & scar 6.00 6.00
*Nos. 92-107 (16)* 14.48 14.46

**Freedom from Hunger Issue**
Common Design Type

**1963, June 4** *Perf. 14x14½*

108 CD314 15c lilac 70 70

**Red Cross Centenary Issue**
Common Design Type

**1963, Sept. 2 Litho.** *Perf. 13*

109 CD315 2½c blk & red 20 20
110 CD315 15c ultra & red 1.00 1.00

*Perf. 11½x12*

**1964, Nov. 5 Engr. Wmk. 314**

111 A7 2½c pur & brt grn 12 12
112 A7 3½c dk ol & bl 20 20
113 A7 15c dk brn & org 48 48
114 A7 25c dk bl & yel 80 80

Opening of the Swaziland Railroad linking Ka Dake with Lourenco Marques.

**ITU Issue**
Common Design Type
*Perf. 11x11½*

**1965, May 17 Litho. Wmk. 314**

115 CD317 2½c bl & bis 12 12
116 CD317 15c red lil & rose red 60 60

**Intl. Cooperation Year Issue**
Common Design Type

**1965, Oct. 25** *Perf. 14½*

117 CD318 ½c bl grn & cl 8 8
118 CD318 15c lt vio & grn 60 60

**Churchill Memorial Issue**
Common Design Type

**1966, Jan. 24 Photo.** *Perf. 14*
**Design in Black, Gold and Carmine Rose**

119 CD319 ½c brt bl 8 5
120 CD319 2½c green 16 12
121 CD319 15c brown 80 52
122 CD319 25c violet 1.40 1.00

**UNESCO Anniversary Issue**
Common Design Type

**1966, Dec. 1 Litho.** *Perf. 14*

123 CD323 2½c "Education" 8 8
124 CD323 7½c "Science" 30 30
125 CD323 15c "Culture" 65 65

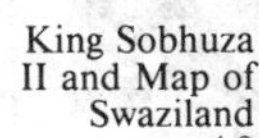

King Sobhuza II and Map of Swaziland A8

Design: 7½c, 25c, King Sobhuza II (vert.).

*Perf. 14½x14, 14x14½*

**1967, Apr. 25 Photo. Wmk. 314**

126 A8 2½c multi 6 6
127 A8 7½c multi 14 14
128 A8 15c multi 28 28
129 A8 25c multi 45 45

Attainment of internal self-government.

**Common Design Types**
pictured in section before Great Britain.

King Sobhuza II, University Buildings and Graduates — A9

*Perf. 14x14½*

**1967, Sept. 1 Photo. Unwmk.**

130 A9 2½c yel, sep & dp bl 6 6
131 A9 7½c bl, sep & dp bl 14 14
132 A9 15c dl rose, sep & dp bl 28 28
133 A9 25c lt vio, sep & dp bl 45 45

1st conferment of degrees by the University of Botswana, Lesotho and Swaziland at Roma, Lesotho.

Swazi Reed Dance (Umhlanga) — A10

Designs: 3c, 15c, Feast of the First Fruits, Incwala (bull, sun and king) (horiz.).

*Perf. 14½x14, 14x14½*

**1968, Jan. 5 Photo. Wmk. 314**

134 A10 3c red, blk & sil 7 7
135 A10 10c brn, blk, org & sil 24 24
136 A10 15c red, blk & gold 35 35
137 A10 25c brn, blk, org & gold 60 60

No. 98 Surcharged with New Value

**1968, May 1** *Perf. 12½x14*

138 A6 3c on 5c org red & blk 15 15

**Independent Kingdom**

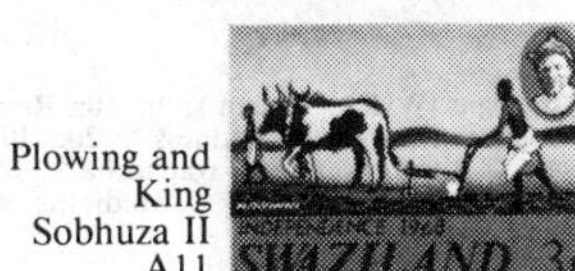

Plowing and King Sobhuza II A11

Designs: 4½c, Cable lift carrying asbestos. 17½c, Worker cutting sugar cane. 25c, Iron ore mining and map showing Swaziland railroad.

*Perf. 14x12½*

**1968, Sept. 6 Photo. Wmk. 314**

139 A11 3c gold & multi 5 5
140 A11 4½c gold & multi 8 8
141 A11 17½c gold & multi 22 22
142 A11 25c sl & gold 1.50 1.50
a Strip of 4 3.25 3.25

Swaziland's independence.

Nos. 139-142 printed in sheets of 50. No. 142a contains one each of Nos. 139-142 printed se-tenant in sheets of 20 (4x5).

Nos. 92-107 Overprinted; No. 96 also Surcharged with New Value

**INDEPENDENCE 1968**

**1968, Sept. 6** *Perf. 12½x14, 14x12½*

143 A6 ½c ocher, blk & brn 5 5
144 A6 1c gray & org 8 6
145 A6 2c multi 10 10
146 A6 2½c ver & blk 12 10
147 A6 3c on 2½c ver & blk 15 15
148 A6 3½c gray & emer 15 15
149 A6 4c aqua & blk 20 20
150 A6 5c org red & blk 25 25
151 A6 7½c dl ocher & brn 35 35
152 A6 10c lt bl & blk 50 50
153 A6 12½c lt ol & dp car 60 60
154 A6 15c red lil & blk 75 75
155 A6 20c emer & blk 80 80
156 A6 25c ultra & blk 1.00 1.00
157 A6 50c rose red & dk brn 1.75 1.75
a Wmk. sideways 1.65 1.65
158 A6 1r bis & emer 3.50 3.50
159 A6 2r ultra & scar 8.00 8.00
a Wmk. sideways 6.75 6.75
*Nos. 143-159 (17)* 18.35 18.31

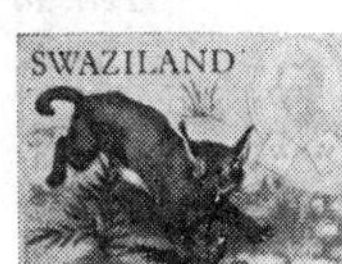

Caracal (African Lynx) A12

Waterbuck A12a

Designs (Sobhuza II and): 1c, Cape porcupine. 2c, Crocodile. 3c, Lion. 3½c, African elephants. 5c, Bush pig. 7½c, Impalas. 10c, Chacma baboon. 12½c, Ratel (honey badger). 15c, Leopard. 20c, Blue wildebeest (brindled gnu). 25c, White (square-lipped) rhinoceros. 50c, Burchell's zebra. 2r, Giraffe.

*Perf. 13x12½, 12½x13*

**1969, Aug. 1 Litho. Wmk. 314**
**Size: 30½x21½mm**

160 A12 ½c multi 5 5
161 A12 1c multi 8 5
162 A12 2c multi 15 12

**Size: 35x25mm**

163 A12 3c multi 22 18
a Wmk. upright ('75) 65 50
164 A12 3½c multi 22 18

**Size: 30½x21½mm, 21½x30½mm**

165 A12 5c multi 30 25
166 A12 7½c multi 40 35
167 A12 10c multi 60 50
168 A12 12½c multi 70 60
169 A12 15c multi 75 70
170 A12 20c multi 85 70
171 A12 25c multi 1.10 85
172 A12 50c multi 2.00 1.65
173 A12a 1r multi 4.75 3.50
174 A12a 2r multi 10.50 6.75
*Nos. 160-174 (15)* 22.67 16.43

See Nos. 228-229.

King Sobhuza II and Flags — A13

Designs: 7½c, 25c, UN emblem, UN Headquarters, NY, and King Sobhuza II.

**1969, Sept. 24 Litho.** *Perf. 13½*

175 A13 3c dp bl & multi 9 9
176 A13 7½c pink & multi 20 20
177 A13 12½c yel & multi 35 35
178 A13 25c lt bl & multi 75 75

Issued to commemorate the first anniversary of Swaziland's admission to the U.N.

Walking Racer, Shield and King — A14

Bauhinia Galpinii and King — A15

Designs: 7½c, Runner. 12½c, Hurdler. 25c, Parade of Swaziland team with flag bearer.

*Perf. 14x14½*

**1970, July 16 Litho. Wmk. 314**

179 A14 3c red org & multi 12 12
180 A14 7½c yel & multi 24 24
181 A14 12½c lt bl & multi 45 45
182 A14 25c multi 90 90

Issued to publicize the 9th Commonwealth Games, Edinburgh, July 16-25.

*Perf. 14x14½*

**1971, Feb. 1 Litho. Wmk. 314**

Flowers of Swaziland: 10c, Crocosmia aurea. 15c, Gloriosa superba. 25c, Watsonia densiflora.

183 A15 3c bis & multi 15 12
184 A15 10c pale sal & multi 50 40
185 A15 15c pale grn & multi 85 60
186 A15 25c multi 1.25 1.00

King Sobhuza II — A16

Designs (King Sobhuza II): 3½c, In 1971. 7½c, In tribal costume at gathering of chiefs (Incwala). 25c, Opening Swazi parliament.

**1971, Dec. 22**

187 A16 3c bl & multi 10 10
188 A16 3½c gold, blk, bl & brn 12 12
189 A16 7½c gold & multi 22 22
190 A16 25c lil & multi 85 85

50th anniv. of the reign of Sobhuza II.

UNICEF Emblem, King Sobhuza II — A17

**1972, Apr. 17** *Perf. 14½x14*

191 A17 15c vio & blk 60 60
192 A17 25c ol & blk 1.00 1.00

25th anniv. (in 1971) of UNICEF.

Traditional Reed Dancers — A18

*Perf. 13½x14*

**1972, Sept. 11 Wmk. 314**

*193* A18 3½c *shown* 12 12
*194* A18 7½c *Swazi beehive hut* 28 28
*195* A18 15c *Ezulwini Valley* 55 55
*196* A18 25c *Usutu River fishing* 90 90

Tourist publicity.

Mosquito Control A19

**1973, May 21 Litho. *Perf. 14½***

*197* A19 3½c *shown* 15 15
*198* A19 7½c *Anti-malaria vaccination* 35 35

25th anniv. of WHO.

Mpaka Coal Mines A20

Designs: 7½c, Oxen pulling plow. 15c, Weir over Komati River. 25c, Experimental rice plantation.

*Perf. 13½x14*

**1973, June 21 Wmk. 314**

*199* A20 3½c multi 10 10
*200* A20 7½c multi 20 20
*201* A20 15c multi 45 45
*202* A20 25c multi 75 75

Development of natural resources.

Swaziland Coat of Arms A21

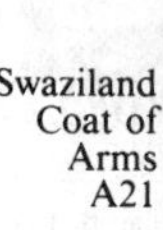

Designs: 10c, King Sobhuza II in dress uniform. 15c, Parliament. 25c, National Somhlolo Stadium.

**1973, Sept. 7 Litho. *Perf. 14***

*203* A21 3c brick red & blk 12 12
*204* A21 10c dl org & multi 38 38
*205* A21 15c bl & multi 55 55
*206* A21 25c yel & multi 95 95

5th anniversary of independence.

Botswana, Lesotho, Swaziland Flags and Cap — A22

Designs: 12½c, Kwaluseni Campus. 15c, Map of Africa and location of Botswana, Lesotho and Swaziland. 25c, Shield of University.

**1974, Mar. 29 Litho. *Perf. 14***

*207* A22 7½c org & multi 22 22
*208* A22 12½c emer & multi 35 35
*209* A22 15c yel & multi 45 45
*210* A22 25c ultra & multi 65 65

10th anniversary of the University of Botswana, Lesotho and Swaziland.

Sobhuza as Student at Lovedale College, South Africa — A23

**1974, July 22 Litho. *Perf. 13x11***

*211* A23 3c *shown* 10 10
*212* A23 9c *Sobhuza as middle-aged man* 32 32
*213* A23 50c *As old man* 1.75 1.75

75th birthday of King Sobhuza II.

Mail Carried by Overhead Cable A24

**1974, Oct. 9 *Perf. 14***

*214* A24 4c *Post Office, Lobamba* 9 9
*215* A24 10c *Mbabane temporary P.O., 1902* 24 24
*216* A24 15c *shown* 35 35
*217* A24 25c *Mule-drawn mail coach* 75 75

Centenary of Universal Postal Union.

Animal Type of 1969
"E" instead of "R"

Designs as before.

**1975, Jan. 2 Litho. *Perf. 12½x13***

*228* A12a 1e multi 4.25 4.25
*229* A12a 2e multi 8.75 8.75

Girl's Umcwasho Ceremony — A26

Swazi youth: 10c, Butimba, hunting ceremony. 15c, Lusekwane, ceremony of preparation (horiz.). 25c, Gcina Regiment marching with flags.

**1975, Mar. 20 Wmk. 314 *Perf. 14***

*232* A26 3c lt grn & multi 8 8
*233* A26 10c lt vio & multi 28 28
*234* A26 15c brn org & multi 42 42
*235* A26 25c yel & multi 70 70

Matsapa Airport Control Tower A27

Designs: 5c, Fire brigade car and staff. 15c, Douglas C-47 Dakota. 25c, Hawker Siddeley 748.

**1975, Aug. 18 Litho. *Perf. 14½***

*236* A27 4c multi 25 25
*237* A27 5c multi 30 30
*238* A27 15c multi 1.00 1.00
*239* A27 25c multi 1.75 1.75

10th anniversary of internal air service.

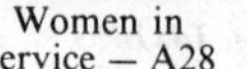

Women in Service — A28

Green Pigeon — A29

Designs: 4c, Elephant with IWY emblem (horiz.). 5c, Queen Labotsibeni, grandmother of King Sobhuza II (horiz.). 15c, Handicrafts women.

**Wmk. 373**

**1975, Dec. 22 Litho. *Perf. 14***

*240* A28 4c ultra, blk & gray 12 12
*241* A28 5c bis & multi 16 16
*242* A28 15c multi 48 48
*243* A28 25c multi 80 80

International Women's Year 1975.

**1976, Jan. 2 Wmk. 373 *Perf. 14***

Birds: 1c, Black-headed oriole (horiz.). 3c, Melba finch (horiz.). 4c, Plum-colored starling. 5c, Black-headed heron. 6c, Stonechat. 7c, Chorister robin. 10c, Gorgeous bush shrike. 15c, Black-collared barbet. 20c, Gray heron. 25c, Giant kingfisher. 30c, Black eagle. 50c, Red bishop. 1e, Pin-tailed whydah. 2e, Lilacbreasted roller (horiz.).

*244* A29 1c org & multi 5 5
*245* A29 2c lil & multi 8 8
*246* A29 3c yel grn & multi 10 10
*247* A29 4c gray bl & multi 12 12
*248* A29 5c org & multi 15 15
*249* A29 6c org & multi 16 16
*250* A29 7c org & multi 22 22
*251* A29 10c sl & multi 30 30
*252* A29 15c lt grn & multi 45 45
*253* A29 20c ocher & multi 60 60
*254* A29 25c org & multi 75 75
*255* A29 30c org & multi 95 95
*256* A29 50c sep & multi 1.50 1.50
*257* A29 1e ver & multi 3.25 3.25
*258* A29 2e lt bl & multi 6.25 6.25
*Nos. 244-258 (15)* 14.93 14.93

Nos. 166 and 168 Surcharged in Ultramarine or Brown

3c

**1976 Wmk. 314 *Perf. 13x12½***

*259* A12 3c on 7½c multi (U) 50 50
*260* A12 6c on 12½c multi (B) 1.25 1.25

Denomination at lower left on No. 260.

Blindness from Malnutrition — A30

Designs (WHO Emblem and): 10c, Retina: "Operation prevents blindness." 20c, Blind eye: "Blindness from trachoma." 25c, Medicine and syringe: "Medicine and rehabilitation."

**Wmk. 373**

**1976, June 15 Litho. *Perf. 14***

*261* A30 5c multi 12 12
*262* A30 10c multi 24 24
*263* A30 20c multi 48 48
*264* A30 25c multi 60 60

World Health Day: Foresight prevents blindness.

Marathon Runner — A31

Soccer — A32

Designs (Olympic Rings and): 6c, Boxing. 20c, Soccer. 25c, Olympic torch and flame.

**1976, July 17 Litho. Wmk. 373**

*265* A31 5c lt bl & multi 12 12
*266* A31 6c ol & multi 15 15
*267* A31 20c lt vio & multi 52 52
*268* A31 25c dl org & multi 65 65

21st Olympic Games, Montreal, Canada, July 17-Aug. 1.

**1976, Sept. 13 Litho. *Perf. 14½***

Designs: 5c, Player heading ball. 20c, Goalkeeper catching ball. 25c, Player kicking ball.

*269* A32 4c bl & multi 10 10
*270* A32 5c ol & multi 14 14
*271* A32 20c red & multi 55 55
*272* A32 25c multi 70 70

FIFA membership for Swaziland in 1976 (Federation Internationale de Football Associations).

A. G. Bell and 1976 Telephone — A33

Designs (A. G. Bell and Telephone): 5c, 1895. 10c, 1876. 15c, 1877. 20c, 1905.

**1976, Nov. 22 *Perf. 14***

*273* A33 4c multi 12 12
*274* A33 5c multi 16 16
*275* A33 10c multi 32 32
*276* A33 15c multi 50 50
*277* A33 20c multi 70 70
*Nos. 273-277 (5)* 1.80 1.80

Centenary of first telephone call by Alexander Graham Bell, Mar. 10, 1876.

Elizabeth II and Sobhuza II — A34

Designs: 25c, Queen's coach at Admiralty Arch. 50c, Queen seated in coach.

**1977, Feb. 7 *Perf. 13½***

*278* A34 20c sil & multi 35 35
*279* A34 25c sil & multi 45 45
*280* A34 50c sil & multi 90 90

25th anniv. of the reign of Elizabeth II.

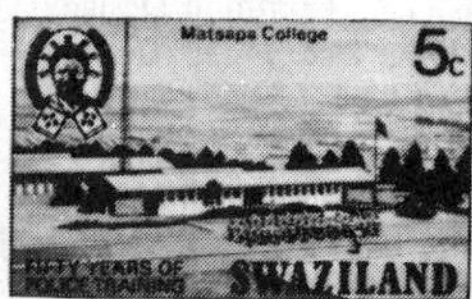


Matsapa College A35

Designs: 10c, Men's and Women's uniforms and jeep. 20c, Police badge (vert.). 25c, Dog handler and dog.

**1977, May 2 Litho. *Perf. 14***

| | | | | |
|---|---|---|---|---|
| *281* | A35 | 5c multi | 12 | 12 |
| *282* | A35 | 10c multi | 25 | 25 |
| *283* | A35 | 20c multi | 50 | 50 |
| *284* | A35 | 25c multi | 60 | 60 |

50 years of police training in Swaziland.

Various Animals A36

Rock Paintings: 10c, 20c, Groups of men. 15c, Cattle and herdsman.

***Perf. 14x14½***

**1977, Aug. 8 Wmk. 373**

| | | | | |
|---|---|---|---|---|
| *285* | A36 | 5c multi | 18 | 18 |
| *286* | A36 | 10c multi | 35 | 35 |
| *287* | A36 | 15c multi | 55 | 55 |
| *288* | A36 | 20c multi | 75 | 75 |
| *a* | | Souvenir sheet of 4 | 2.00 | 2.00 |

Rock paintings from Highveld area, c. 1700-1850. No. 288a contains one each of Nos. 285-288; multicolored margin with description of rock paintings. Size: 114x124mm.

Evergreens, Timber, Map of Highveld — A37

Designs: 10c, Pineapple and map of Middleveld. 15c, Map of Lowveld, orange and lemon. 20c, Map of Lubombo and grazing cattle. No. 293, Map of Swaziland and produce (vert.): UL, Evergreens; UR, Orange and lemon; LL, Pineapple; LR, Cattle.

**1977, Oct. 17 Litho. *Perf. 13½***

| | | | | |
|---|---|---|---|---|
| *289* | A37 | 5c multi | 24 | 24 |
| *290* | A37 | 10c multi | 45 | 45 |
| *291* | A37 | 15c multi | 70 | 70 |
| *292* | A37 | 20c multi | 1.00 | 1.00 |

**Souvenir Sheet**

| | | | | |
|---|---|---|---|---|
| *293* | A37 | Sheet of 4, multi | 2.75 | 2.75 |
| *a-d* | | 25c, single stamp | 65 | 65 |

No. 293 contains 4 vertical stamps; orange and yellow margin with black inscription. Size: 86x130mm.

Cussonia Spicata Thunb. — A38

Trees: 10c, Sclerocarya birrea. 20c, Pterocarpus angolensis. 25c, Erythrina lysistemon.

**1978, Jan. 12 Litho. Wmk. 373**

| | | | | |
|---|---|---|---|---|
| *294* | A38 | 5c multi | 12 | 12 |
| *295* | A38 | 10c multi | 24 | 24 |
| *296* | A38 | 20c multi | 48 | 48 |
| *297* | A38 | 25c multi | 60 | 60 |

Rural Electrification, Lobamba — A39

Hydroelectric Power: 10c, Edwaleni Power Station. 20c, Switchgear, Maguduza Power Station. 25c, Hydroturbine hall, Edwaleni.

**1978, Mar. 6 Litho. *Perf. 13½***

| | | | | |
|---|---|---|---|---|
| *298* | A39 | 5c blk & ocher | 10 | 10 |
| *299* | A39 | 10c blk & yel grn | 20 | 20 |
| *300* | A39 | 20c blk & bl | 40 | 40 |
| *301* | A39 | 25c blk & rose mag | 52 | 52 |

**Elizabeth II Coronation Anniversary Issue**

Souvenir Sheet

Common Design Types

**1978, Apr. 21 Unwmk. *Perf. 15***

| | | | | |
|---|---|---|---|---|
| *302* | | Sheet of 6 | 2.75 | 2.75 |
| *a* | | CD326 25c *Queen's lion* | 45 | 45 |
| *b* | | CD327 25c *Elizabeth II* | 45 | 45 |
| *c* | | CD328 25c *African Elephant* | 45 | 45 |

No. 302 contains 2 se-tenant strips of Nos. 302a-302c, separated by horizontal gutter with commemorative and descriptive inscriptions and showing central part of coronation procession with coach. Size: 100x135mm.

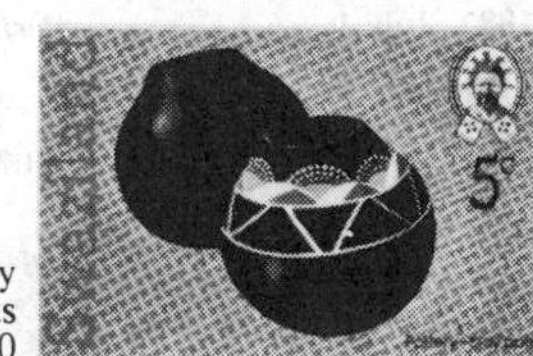


Clay Pots A40

Handicrafts: 10c, Basketwork. 20c, Wooden utensils. 30c, Wooden pot with lid.

**Wmk. 373**

**1978, June 26 Litho. *Perf. 13½***

| | | | | |
|---|---|---|---|---|
| *303* | A40 | 5c multi | 9 | 9 |
| *304* | A40 | 10c multi | 18 | 18 |
| *305* | A40 | 20c multi | 35 | 35 |
| *306* | A40 | 30c multi | 55 | 55 |

See Nos. 317-320.

Defense Force A41

Designs: 6c, King's Regiment. 10c, Tinkabi tractor and ox-drawn plow. 15c, Laying water pipe. 25c, Adult literacy class. 50c, Fire engine and ambulance.

**1978, Sept. 6 Litho. *Perf. 14***

| | | | | |
|---|---|---|---|---|
| *307* | A41 | 4c multi | 8 | 8 |
| *308* | A41 | 6c multi | 10 | 10 |
| *309* | A41 | 10c multi | 18 | 18 |
| *310* | A41 | 15c multi | 28 | 28 |
| *311* | A41 | 25c multi | 45 | 45 |
| *312* | A41 | 50c multi | 90 | 90 |
| | | *Nos. 307-312 (6)* | 1.99 | 1.99 |

10th anniversary of independence.

Angel Appearing to the Shepherds — A42

Christmas: 10c, Adoration of the Kings. 15c, Angel warning Joseph in a dream. 25c, Flight into Egypt.

**1978, Dec. 12 Litho. *Perf. 14***

| | | | | |
|---|---|---|---|---|
| *313* | A42 | 5c multi | 52 | 52 |
| *314* | A42 | 10c multi | 20 | 20 |
| *315* | A42 | 15c multi | 30 | 30 |
| *316* | A42 | 25c multi | 52 | 52 |

Handicrafts Type of 1978

**1979, Jan. 10 *Perf. 13½***

| | | | | |
|---|---|---|---|---|
| *317* | A40 | 5c Sisal bowls | 9 | 9 |
| *318* | A40 | 15c Clay pots | 28 | 28 |
| *319* | A40 | 20c Basketwork | 35 | 35 |
| *320* | A40 | 30c Hide shield | 55 | 55 |

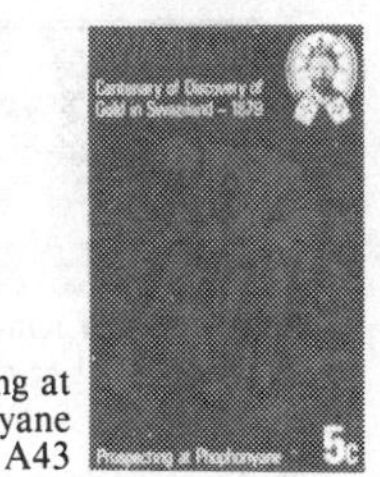


Prospecting at Phophonyane A43

Designs: 15c, Early 3-stamp battery mill. 25c, Cyanide tanks at Piggs Peak. 50c, Pouring off molten gold.

**Wmk. 373**

**1979, Mar. 27 Litho. *Perf. 14***

| | | | | |
|---|---|---|---|---|
| *321* | A43 | 5c vio brn & gold | 12 | 12 |
| *322* | A43 | 15c vio brn & gold | 35 | 35 |
| *323* | A43 | 25c vio brn & gold | 60 | 60 |
| *324* | A43 | 50c vio brn & gold | 1.25 | 1.25 |

Centenary of discovery of gold in Swaziland.

Girls at Piano, 1892, by Renoir A44

Paintings by Renoir: 15c, Madame Charpentier and her Children, 1878. 25c, Girls Picking Flowers, 1889. 50c, Girl with Watering Can, 1876.

**1979, May 8 *Perf. 13½***

| | | | | |
|---|---|---|---|---|
| *325* | A44 | 5c multi | 10 | 10 |
| *326* | A44 | 15c multi | 30 | 30 |
| *327* | A44 | 25c multi | 50 | 50 |
| *328* | A44 | 50c multi | 1.00 | 1.00 |
| *a* | | Souvenir sheet of 4 | 2.00 | 2.00 |

International Year of the Child. No. 328a contains Nos. 325-328; multicolored margin shows boys. Size: 123x136mm.

Swaziland No. 40 and Rowland Hill — A45

Designs (Rowland Hill and): 20c, Swaziland No. 18. 25c, Swaziland No. 142. 50c, Swaziland No. 105.

**1979, July 17 Litho. *Perf. 14½***

| | | | | |
|---|---|---|---|---|
| *329* | A45 | 10c multi | 12 | 12 |
| *330* | A45 | 20c multi | 40 | 40 |
| *331* | A45 | 25c multi | 50 | 50 |

**Souvenir Sheet**

| | | | | |
|---|---|---|---|---|
| *332* | A45 | 50c multi | 1.10 | 1.10 |

Sir Rowland Hill (1795-1879), originator of penny postage. No. 332 has multicolored margin. Size: 115x90mm.

5c Cupro-Nickel Coin — A46

Coins: 10c, King Sobhuza II and sorghum. 20c, King and elephant head. 50c, Coat of arms. 1e, Mother and son.

***Perf. 13½x14***

**1979, Sept. 6 Litho. Wmk. 373**

| | | | | |
|---|---|---|---|---|
| *333* | A46 | 5c multi | 8 | 8 |
| *334* | A46 | 10c multi | 15 | 15 |
| *335* | A46 | 20c multi | 30 | 30 |
| *336* | A46 | 50c multi | 75 | 75 |
| *337* | A46 | 1e multi | 1.50 | 1.50 |
| | | *Nos. 333-337 (5)* | 2.78 | 2.78 |

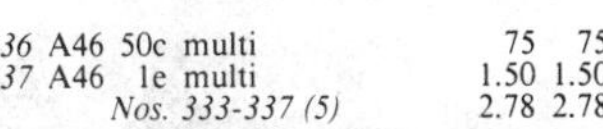

Big Bend Post Office A47

Designs: 15c, Mount Ntondozi microwave station (vert.). 20c, Swaziland No. 53. 50c, Swaziland No. 217.

**1979, Nov. 22**

| | | | | |
|---|---|---|---|---|
| *338* | A47 | 5c multi | 9 | 9 |
| *339* | A47 | 15c multi | 28 | 28 |
| *340* | A47 | 20c multi | 35 | 35 |
| *341* | A47 | 50c multi | 90 | 90 |

25th anniv. of Post and Telecommunications service (5c, 15c); 10th anniv. of UPU membership (20c, 50c).

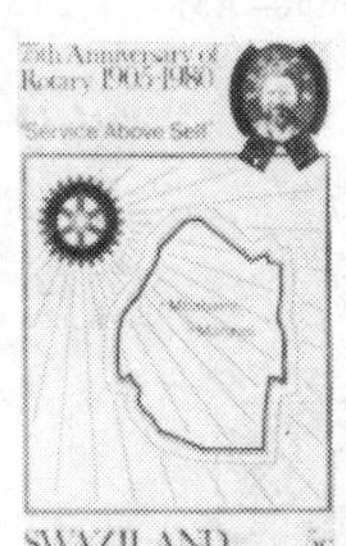


Rotary International, 75th Anniversary A48

**Wmk. 373**

**1980, Feb. 23 Litho. *Perf. 14***

| | | | | |
|---|---|---|---|---|
| *342* | A48 | 5c *shown* | 10 | 10 |
| *343* | A48 | 15c *Hospital equipment* | 30 | 30 |
| *344* | A48 | 50c *Rotary principles* | 1.00 | 1.00 |
| *345* | A48 | 1e *Headquarters, Evanston, Ill.* | 2.00 | 2.00 |

Eucomis Autumnalis — A49

Flowers: 1c, Brunsvigia radulosa. 2c, Aloe suprafoliata. 3c, Haemanthus magificus. 4c, Aloe marlothii. 5c, Dicoma zeyheri. 6c, Aloe kniphofioides. 7c, Cyrtanthus bicolor. 15c, Leucospermum gerrardii. 20c, Haemanthus multiflorus. 30c, Acridocarpus natalitius. 50c, Adenium swazicum. 1e, Protea simplex. 2e, Calodendrum capense. 5e, Gladiolus ecklonii. All vert. except. 15c, 20c, 30c, 50c.

**1980, Apr. 28 Litho. *Perf. 13½***

| | | | | |
|---|---|---|---|---|
| *346* | A49 | 1c multi | 5 | 5 |
| *a* | | Perf. 12 | 5 | 5 |
| *347* | A49 | 2c multi | 6 | 6 |
| *a* | | Perf. 12 | 6 | 6 |
| *348* | A49 | 3c multi | 9 | 9 |
| *349* | A49 | 4c multi | 9 | 9 |
| *a* | | Perf. 12 | 9 | 9 |
| *350* | A49 | 5c multi | 12 | 12 |
| *351* | A49 | 6c multi | 14 | 14 |
| *a* | | Perf. 12 | 14 | 14 |
| *352* | A49 | 7c multi | 15 | 15 |
| *353* | A49 | 10c multi | 22 | 22 |
| *a* | | Perf. 12 | 22 | 22 |
| *354* | A49 | 15c multi | 35 | 35 |
| *355* | A49 | 20c multi | 45 | 45 |
| *a* | | Perf. 12 | 45 | 45 |
| *356* | A49 | 30c multi | 65 | 65 |
| *357* | A49 | 50c multi | 80 | 80 |

**Size: 22x37½mm.**

| | | | | |
|---|---|---|---|---|
| *358* | A49 | 1e multi | 1.65 | 1.65 |
| *359* | A49 | 2e multi | 3.50 | 3.50 |
| *360* | A49 | 5e multi | 8.25 | 8.25 |
| | | *Nos. 346-360 (15)* | 16.57 | 16.57 |

Perf. 12 stamps inscribed 1983.

Mail Runner, London 1980 Emblem A50

**1980, May 6 Wmk. 373 Perf. 14**

| | | | |
|---|---|---|---|
| 361 A50 10c *shown* | 18 | 18 |
| 362 A50 20c *Mail truck* | 35 | 35 |
| 363 A50 25c *Mail sorting* | 40 | 40 |
| 364 A50 50c *Mail ropeway* | 80 | 80 |

London 80 Intl. Stamp Exhib., May 6-14.

Yellow Fish — A51

**1980, Aug. 25 Litho. Perf. 14**

| | | |
|---|---|---|
| 365 A51 5c *shown* | 12 | 12 |
| 366 A51 10c *Silver barbel* | 24 | 24 |
| 367 A51 15c *Tigerfish* | 35 | 35 |
| 368 A51 30c *Squeaker fish* | 65 | 65 |
| 369 A51 1e *Bream* | 2.25 | 2.25 |
| *Nos. 365-369 (5)* | 3.61 | 3.61 |

Oribi Antelope A52

**1980, Oct. 1 Litho. Perf. 14**

| | | |
|---|---|---|
| 370 A52 5c *shown* | 12 | 12 |
| 371 A52 10c *Nile crocodile*, vert. | 20 | 20 |
| 372 A52 50c *Pangolin* | 1.00 | 1.00 |
| 373 A52 1e *Leopard*, vert. | 2.00 | 2.00 |

Bus A53

**1981, Jan. 5 Litho. Perf. 14½**

| | | |
|---|---|---|
| 374 A53 5c *shown* | 10 | 10 |
| 375 A53 25c *Jet* | 50 | 50 |
| 376 A53 30c *Truck* | 60 | 60 |
| 377 A53 1e *Train* | 2.00 | 2.00 |

Mantenga Falls A54

**1981, Apr. 16 Litho. Perf. 14**

| | | |
|---|---|---|
| 378 A54 5c shown | 10 | 10 |
| 379 A54 15c Mananga Yacht Club | 30 | 30 |
| 380 A54 30c White rhinoceri, Mlilwane Game Sanctuary | 60 | 60 |
| 381 A54 1e Gambling | 2.00 | 2.00 |

**Royal Wedding Issue**
Common Design Type
**Wmk. 373**

**1981, July 21 Litho. Perf. 14**

| | | |
|---|---|---|
| 382 CD331 10c Bouquet | 18 | 18 |
| 383 CD331 25c Charles | 45 | 45 |
| 384 CD331 1e Couple | 1.75 | 1.75 |

Demand, as well as supply, determines a stamp's market value. One is as important as the other.

Installation of King Sobhuza II, 1921 — A55

60th Anniv. of King Sobhuza II's Reign (King and): 10c, Visit of Royal Family, 1947. 15c, Coronation of Queen Elizabeth II, 1953. 25c, Independence ceremony, 1968. 30c, Early portrait. 1e, Parliament buildings.

**Wmk. 373**

**1981, Aug. 24 Litho. Perf. 14½**

| | | |
|---|---|---|
| 385 A55 5c multi | 10 | 10 |
| 386 A55 10c multi | 20 | 20 |
| 387 A55 15c multi | 30 | 30 |
| 388 A55 25c multi | 50 | 50 |
| 389 A55 30c multi | 60 | 60 |
| 390 A55 1e multi | 2.00 | 2.00 |
| *Nos. 385-390 (6)* | 3.70 | 3.70 |

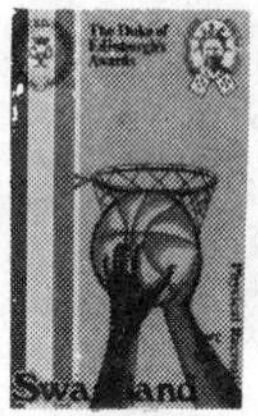

Duke of Edinburgh's Awards, 25th Anniv. — A56

Intl. Year of the Disabled — A57

**1981, Nov. 5 Litho. Perf. 14**

| | | |
|---|---|---|
| 391 A56 5c Basketball | 9 | 9 |
| 392 A56 30c Compass reading | 35 | 35 |
| 393 A56 50c Square | 90 | 90 |
| 394 A56 1e Duke of Edinburgh | 1.75 | 1.75 |

**1981, Dec. 7 Perf. 14x14½, 14½x14**

| | | |
|---|---|---|
| 395 A57 5c Men learning carpentry, horiz. | 12 | 12 |
| 396 A57 15c Boy learning Braille | 30 | 30 |
| 397 A57 25c Carpentry, diff. | 52 | 52 |
| 398 A57 1e Driving, horiz. | 2.00 | 2.00 |

Papilio Demodocus — A58

**1982, Jan. 6 Litho. Perf. 14**

| | | |
|---|---|---|
| 399 A58 5c shown | 12 | 12 |
| 400 A58 10c Charaxes candiope | 25 | 25 |
| 401 A58 50c Papilio nireus | 1.25 | 1.25 |
| 402 A58 1e Eurema desjardinsii | 2.50 | 2.50 |

First Intl. Conference on Smoking and Health, Apr. 25-29 — A59

**1982, Apr. 27 Litho. Perf. 14**

| | | |
|---|---|---|
| 403 A59 5c Non-smoker, flowers | 12 | 12 |
| 404 A59 10c Smoker, non-smoker | 25 | 25 |

Female Fishing Owl — A60

Designs: b. Pair. c. Owl in nest, egg. d. Adult and young owls. e. Male.

**Perf. 13½x13**

**1982, June 16 Litho. Wmk. 373**

| | | |
|---|---|---|
| 405 Strip of 5, multi | 4.75 | 4.75 |
| *a.-e.* A60 35c, any single | 95 | 95 |

**Princess Diana Issue**
Common Design Type

**1982, July 1 Perf. 14½**

| | | |
|---|---|---|
| 406 CD333 5c Arms | 9 | 9 |
| 407 CD333 20c Diana | 35 | 35 |
| 408 CD333 50c Wedding | 90 | 90 |
| 409 CD333 1e Portrait | 1.75 | 1.75 |

Sugar Industry A61

**1982, Sept. 1 Litho.**

| | | |
|---|---|---|
| 410 A61 5c Planting sugar cane | 12 | 12 |
| 411 A61 20c Harvesting cane | 45 | 45 |
| 412 A61 30c Mhlume Mills | 65 | 65 |
| 413 A61 1e Rail transport | 2.25 | 2.25 |

Baphalali Red Cross Society A62

**1982, Nov. 9 Perf. 14**

| | | |
|---|---|---|
| 414 A62 5c Immunization | 9 | 9 |
| 415 A62 20c Red Cross Juniors | 35 | 35 |
| 416 A62 50c Disaster relief | 90 | 90 |
| 417 A62 1e Red Cross founder Henry Dunant | 1.75 | 1.75 |

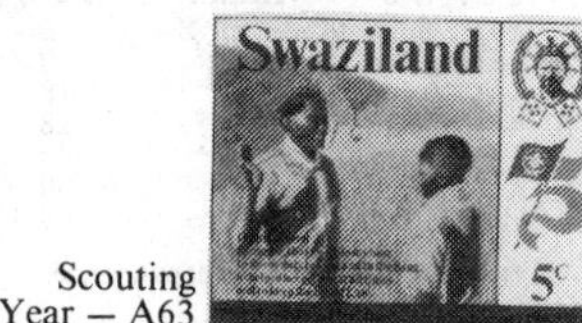

Scouting Year — A63

**Perf. 14½x14**

**1982, Dec. 6 Litho. Wmk. 373**

| | | |
|---|---|---|
| 418 A63 5c Reciting promise | 12 | 12 |
| 419 A63 10c Hiking | 25 | 25 |
| 420 A60 25c Community development | 60 | 60 |
| 421 A63 75c Baden-Powell | 1.90 | 1.90 |

**Souvenir Sheet**

| | | |
|---|---|---|
| 422 A63 1e Emblem | 3.00 | 3.00 |

**Commonwealth Day**
Common Design Type

**1983, Mar. 14 Litho. Perf. 14**

| | | |
|---|---|---|
| 423 CD334 6c Satellite view, vert. | 12 | 12 |
| 424 CD334 10c King Sobhuza II, flag, vert. | 20 | 20 |
| 425 CD334 50c Beehive huts | 1.00 | 1.00 |
| 426 CD334 1e Spraying sugar crop | 2.00 | 2.00 |

Beaded Vulture — A65

Designs: a. Male. b. Pair. c. Nest, egg. d. Female at nest. e. Adult, fledgeling.

**Perf. 13½x13**

**1983, May 16 Litho. Wmk. 373**

| | | |
|---|---|---|
| 427 Strip of 5 | 4.00 | 4.00 |
| *a.-e.* A65 35c, any single | 75 | 75 |

**Souvenir Sheets**

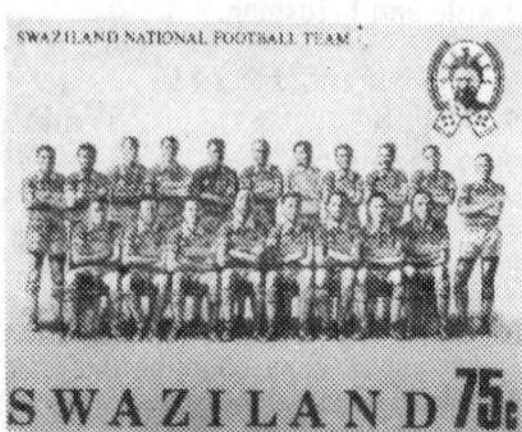

Soccer Tour of Swaziland 1983 — A66

**1983, Aug. 20 Litho. Perf. 14x13½**

| | | |
|---|---|---|
| 428 A66 75c Natl. team | 1.40 | 1.40 |
| 429 A66 75c Tottenham Hotspur | 1.40 | 1.40 |
| 430 A66 75c Manchester United | 1.40 | 1.40 |

Souv. sheets Nos. 428-430 each contain one stamp. Sheet size: 103x73mm.

Manned Flight Bicentenary — A67

**1983, Sept. 22 Litho. Perf. 14**

| | | |
|---|---|---|
| 431 A67 5c Montgolfiere, 1783, vert. | 10 | 10 |
| 432 A67 10c Wright brothers' plane | 20 | 20 |
| 433 A67 25c Royal Swazi Fokker Fellowship | 50 | 50 |
| 434 A67 50c Bell X-1 jet | 1.00 | 1.00 |

**Souvenir Sheet**

| | | |
|---|---|---|
| 435 A67 1e Columbia space shuttle take-off, vert. | 2.00 | 2.00 |

Alfred Nobel, 100th Birth Anniv. A68

**1983, Oct. 21**

| | | |
|---|---|---|
| 436 A68 6c Albert Schweitzer | 12 | 12 |
| 437 A68 10c Dag Hammarskjold | 32 | 20 |
| 438 A68 50c Albert Einstein | 1.00 | 1.00 |
| 439 A68 1e shown | 2.00 | 2.00 |

World Food Program A69

**1983, Nov. 29**

| | | |
|---|---|---|
| 440 A69 6c Maize | 12 | 12 |
| 441 A69 10c Rice | 32 | 20 |
| 442 A69 50c Cattle | 1.00 | 1.00 |
| 443 A69 1e Tractor | 2.00 | 2.00 |

Women's College A70

**Wmk. 373**

**1984, Mar. 12 Litho. *Perf. 14***
*444* A70 5c shown 9 9
*445* A70 15c Technical training school 28 28
*446* A70 50c University 90 90
*447* A70 1e Primary school 1.75 1.75

Bald Ibis — A71

Designs: a. Male. b. Male, female. c. Nest, egg. d. Female at nest. e. Adult, fledgeling.

**1984, May 18 Litho. *Perf. 13½x13***
*448* Strip of 5 3.25 3.25
*a.-e.* A71 35c, any single 60 60

1984 UPU Congress A72

Mail Coaches.

**1984, June 15 Litho. *Perf. 14½***
*449* A72 7c Mule-drawn coach 14 14
*450* A72 15c Oxen-drawn post wagon 28 28
*451* A72 50c Mule-drawn, diff. 90 90
*452* A72 1e Bristol-London 1.75 1.75

1984 Summer Olympics A73

**1984, July 28 *Perf. 14***
*453* A73 7c Running 14 14
*454* A73 10c Swimming 20 20
*455* A73 50c Shooting 1.00 1.00
*456* A73 1e Boxing 2.00 2.00
*a* Souv. sheet of 4, #453-456 3.50 3.50

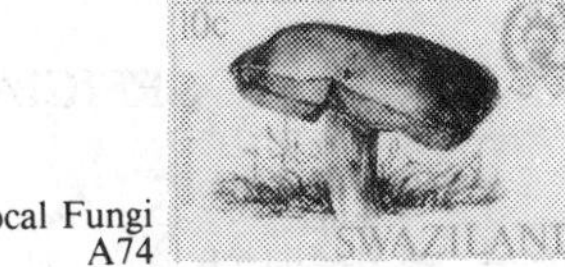

Local Fungi A74

**1984, Sept. 19 Litho. *Perf. 14***
*457* A74 10c Suillus bovinus 18 18
*458* A74 15c Langermannia gigantea, vert. 28 28
*459* A74 50c Coriolus versicolor, vert. 90 90
*460* A74 1e Boletus edulis 1.75 1.75

20th Anniv. of Swazi Railways A75

**1984, Nov. 5 Litho. Wmk. 373**
*461* A75 10c Opening ceremony 20 20
*462* A75 25c Type 15A locomotive, Siweni Exchange Yard 50 50
*463* A75 30c Container loading, Matsapha Station 60 60
*464* A75 1e No. 268, Alto Tunnel 2.00 2.00
*a* Souvenir sheet of 4 3.25 3.25

No. 464a contains Nos. 461-464; multicolored margin shows map.

Nos. 346-349, 351-352 Surcharged

**1984, Dec. 15 Litho. *Perf. 13½***
*465* A49 10c on 4c #349 8 8
*466* A49 15c on 7c #352 12 12
*467* A49 20c on 3c #348 16 16
*468* A49 25c on 6c #351 20 20
*469* A49 30c on 1c #346 24 24
*470* A49 30c on 2c #347 24 24
*Nos. 465-470 (6)* 1.04 1.04

Rotary Intl., 80th Anniv. A76

**1985, Feb. 23 Wmk. 373 *Perf. 14***
*471* A76 10c Rotary emblem, world map 8 8
*472* A76 15c Training scholarships 18 18
*473* A76 50c Two children 60 60
*474* A76 1e Nurse, children 1.25 1.25

Life Cycle of the Ground Hornbill — A77

Audubon birth bicentenary.

**1985, May 15 Wmk. 373**
*475* Strip of 5 1.40 1.40
*a.-e.* A77 25c, Any single 25 25

**Queen Mother 85th Birthday**
Common Design Type

***Perf. 14½x14***

**1985, June 7 Litho. Wmk. 384**
*476* CD336 10c Visit to South Africa, 1947 8 8
*477* CD336 15c With Elizabeth II and Margaret 16 16
*478* CD336 50c 75th birthday celebration 52 52
*479* CD336 1e Holding Prince Henry 1.10 1.10

**Souvenir Sheet**

*480* CD336 2e Greeting Prince Andrew 2.00 2.00

No. 480 has multicolored margin continuing design, showing jet aircraft. Size: 92x74mm.

Classic Automobiles — A78

**Wmk. 373**

**1985, Sept. 16 Litho. *Perf. 14***
*481* A78 10c Buick Tourer 10 10
*482* A78 15c Four-cylinder Rover 14 14
*483* A78 50c De Dion Bouton 45 45
*484* A78 1e Ford Model-T 88 88

Intl. Youth Year A79

**1985, Dec. 2**
*485* A79 10c Bridge-building 10 10
*486* A79 20c Girl Guides camping 18 18
*487* A79 50c Recreation 45 45
*488* A79 1e Guides collecting branches 88 88

Girl Guide Movement, 20c, 1e. IYY, 10c, 50c.

Halley's Comet A80

**1986, Feb. 27 Wmk. 384 *Perf. 14½***
*489* A80 1.50e multi 1.50 1.50

**Queen Elizabeth II 60th Birthday**
Common Design Type

Designs: 10c Princess Anne's christening, 1950. 30c, Wedding of Prince Charles and Lady Diana, 1981. 45c, With George VI, the Dutchess of York and Sobhuza II at Nhlangano, 1947. 1e, At Windsor Polo Ground, 1984. 2e, Visiting Crown Agents' offices, 1983.

**1986, Apr. 21 *Perf. 14x14½***
*490* CD337 10c scar, blk & sil 10 10
*491* CD337 30c ultra & multi 35 35
*492* CD337 45c grn, blk & sil 52 52
*493* CD337 1e vio & multi 1.10 1.10
*494* CD337 2e rose vio & multi 2.25 2.25
*Nos. 490-494 (5)* 4.32 4.32

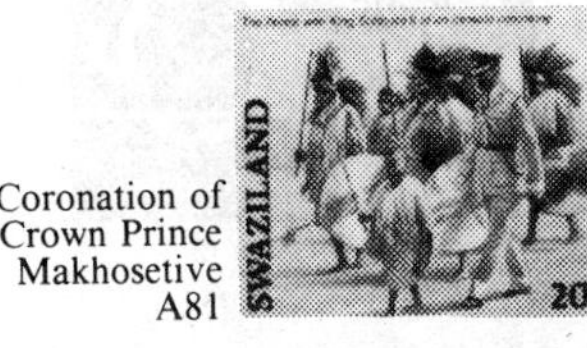

Coronation of Crown Prince Makhosetive A81

Designs: 10c, Portrait, vert. 20c, Prince and King Sobhuza II at an Incwala ceremony. 25c, Prince at primary school. 30c, At school in England. 40c, Escorted from Matsapha Airport by Guard of Honor. 2e, Dancing the Simemo.

**1986, Apr. 25 *Perf. 14½***
*495* A81 10c multi 10 10
*496* A81 20c multi 22 22
*497* A81 25c multi 28 28
*498* A81 30c multi 35 35
*499* A81 40c multi 45 45
*500* A81 2e multi 2.25 2.25
*Nos. 495-500 (6)* 3.65 3.65

Assoc. of Round Tables in Central Africa, 50th Anniv. — A82

Club emblems.

**Wmk. 384**

**1986, Oct. 4 Litho. *Perf. 14***
*501* A82 15c Orbis 14 14
*502* A82 25c Ehlanzeni 51 22 22
*503* A82 55c Mbabane 30 48 48
*504* A82 70c Bulembu 54 62 62
*505* A82 2e Manzini 44 1.75 1.75
*Nos. 501-505 (5)* 3.21 3.21

Butterflies — A83

**Unwmk.**

**1987, Mar. 17 Litho. *Perf. 14***
*506* A83 10c Yellow pansy 10 10
*507* A83 15c Guineafowl 14 14
*508* A83 20c Red forest charaxes 18 18
*509* A83 25c Paradise skipper 22 22
*510* A83 30c Broad-bordered acraea 28 28
*511* A83 35c Veined swallowtail 32 32
*512* A83 45c Large striped swordtail 40 40
*513* A83 50c Eyed pansy 45 45
*514* A83 55c Zebra white 48 48
*515* A83 70c Gaudy commodore 62 62
*516* A83 1e Common dotted border 88 88
*517* A83 5e Queen purple tip 4.25 4.25
*518* A83 10e Natal barred blue 8.50 8.50
*Nos. 506-518 (13)* 16.82 16.82

White Rhinoceros — A84

**1987, July 1 Wmk. 384 *Perf. 14½***
*519* A84 15c Two adults 14 14
*520* A84 25c Adult, calf 22 22
*521* A84 45c Adult walking 40 40
*522* A84 70c Adult in mud 62 62

World Wildlife Fund.

Flowers — A85

**1987, Oct. 19 Litho. *Perf. 14½***
*523* A85 15c Blue moon 15 15
*524* A85 35c Danse de feu 35 35
*525* A85 55c Odin 55 55
*526* A85 2e Lilium davidii 2.00 2.00

Nos. 491-494 Ovptd. "40TH WEDDING ANNIVERSARY" in Silver

***Perf. 14x14½***

**1987, Dec. 9 Litho. Wmk. 384**
*527* CD337 30c ultra & multi 30 30
*528* CD337 45c grn, blk & sil 45 45
*529* CD337 1e vio & multi 1.00 1.00
*530* CD337 2e rose vio & multi 2.00 2.00

Insects A86

**Wmk. 384**

**1988, Mar. 14 Litho. *Perf. 14***
*531* A86 15c Zabalius aridus 16 16
*532* A86 55c Callidea bohemani 58 58
*533* A86 1e Phymateus viridipes 1.05 1.05
*534* A86 2e Nomadacris septemfasciata 2.05 2.05

1988 Summer Olympics, Seoul
A87

**1988, Aug. 22 Litho. Wmk. 384**
*535* A87 15c Flag-bearer, stadium 16 16
*536* A87 35c Tae kwon do 38 38
*537* A87 1e Boxing 1.05 1.05
*538* A87 2e Tennis 2.00 2.00

Intl. Tennis Federation, 75th anniv. (2e).

### POSTAGE DUE STAMPS

**Catalogue values for unused stamps in this section, from this point to the end of the section, are for Never Hinged items.**

D1

D2

**1933 Typo. Wmk. 4 *Perf. 14***
*J1* D1 1p car rose 35 *2.00*
*a.* Wmk 41 (error) 100.00
*J2* D1 2p violet 2.50 *8.50*

No. 57 Surcharged

**Postage Due**
**1c**
I

**Postage Due**
**1c**
II

**1961 Engr. *Perf. 13½x13***
*J3* A5 (2d) on 2p, type I 10.00 *12.00*
*a.* Type II 1.25
*J4* A5 1c on 3p, type I 2.00 *3.25*
*a.* Type II 1.25 1.25
*J5* A5 2c on 2p, type I 2.00 *3.25*
*a.* Type II 80 80
*J6* A5 5c on 2p, type I 2.00 *3.25*
*a.* Type II 1.50 1.50

No. J3a was surcharged after decimal currency was introduced.

Type of 1933

**1961 Typo. *Perf. 14***
*J7* D1 1c car rose 15 15
*J8* D1 2c violet 30 30
*J9* D1 5c green 75 1.00

**Wmk. 314**

**1971, Feb. 1 Litho. *Perf. 11½***
*J10* D2 1c carmine rose 28 32
*J11* D2 2c dull purple 40 48
*J12* D2 5c green 70 80

**1977, Jan. 17 Wmk. 373**
*J10a* D2 1c car rose 5 5
*J11a* D2 2c dl pur 8 8
*J12a* D2 5c green 14 14

## TANGANYIKA

LOCATION — In southeastern Africa bordering on the Indian Ocean.
GOVT. — Republic within British Commonwealth.
AREA — 362,688 sq. mi.
POP. — 9,404,000 (est. 1961).
CAPITAL — Dar es Salaam.

Before World War I, this area formed part of German East Africa It was mandated to Britain after World War I and (in 1946) became a trust territory under the United Nations. In 1935, stamps of the mandate were replaced by those used jointly by Kenya, Uganda and Tanganyika (see Kenya, Uganda and Tanzania). On Dec. 9, 1961, Tanganyika became independent. On Dec. 9, 1962, it became a republic. On April 26, 1964, it joined Zanzibar to form the United Republic of Tanganyika and Zanzibar (later renamed Tanzania). See Tanzania.

100 Cents = 1 Rupee
100 Cents = 1 Shilling (1922)
20 Shillings = 1 Pound

**Catalogue values for unused stamps in this country are for Never Hinged items, beginning with Scott 45 in the regular postage section and Scott O1 in the officials section.**

Stamps of Kenya, Uganda & Tanganyika Overprinted **G.E.A.**

**1921 Wmk. 4 *Perf. 14***
*1* A1 12c gray 3.50 *6.50*
*2* A1 15c ultra 75 *2.75*
*3* A1 50c dl vio & blk 10.00 *22.50*

Overprinted **G. E. A.**

*4* A2 2r blk & red, *bl* 40.00 *85.00*
*5* A2 3r gray grn & vio 45.00 *100.00*
*7* A2 5r dl vio & ultra 55.00 *110.00*

Overprinted in Red or Black **G.E.A.**

**1922**
*8* A1 1c blk (R) 10 *1.40*
*9* A1 10c org (Bk) 40 *3.50*

Giraffe
A3 A4

***Perf. 14½x14***
**1922-25 Engr. Wmk. 4**
*10* A3 5c dk vio & blk 40 9
*a.* Booklet pane of 6
*11* A3 5c grn & blk ('25) 42 15
*12* A3 10c grn & blk 40 9
*a.* Booklet pane of 6
*13* A3 10c yel & blk ('25) 1.10 25
*a.* Booklet pane of 6
*14* A3 15c car & blk 32 6
*a.* Booklet pane of 6
*15* A3 20c org & blk 50 8
*a.* Booklet pane of 6
*16* A3 25c black 2.25 3.00
*17* A3 25c bl & blk ('25) 3.00 3.50
*18* A3 30c bl & blk 85 55
*19* A3 30c dl vio & blk ('25) 1.00 1.90
*20* A3 40c brn & blk 1.25 1.50
*21* A3 50c gray blk 1.10 85
*22* A3 75c bis & blk 3.00 4.50

***Perf. 14***
*23* A4 1sh grn & blk 1.25 1.10
*a.* Wmk. sideways 1.50 1.90
*24* A4 2sh brn vio & blk 2.50 3.25
*a.* Wmk. sideways 3.25 3.75
*25* A4 3sh blk (Wmk.) sideways) 4.75 *9.00*
*26* A4 5sh red & blk 6.00 *10.00*
*a.* Wmk. sideways 6.00 *11.25*
*27* A4 10sh dp bl & blk 20.00 22.50
*a.* Wmk. sideways 21.00 27.50
*28* A4 £1 org & blk 50.00 55.00
*a.* Wmk. sideways 62.50 75.00
*Nos. 10-28 (19)* 100.09 117.37

On No. 28 the words of value are in a curve between the circle and "POSTAGE & REVENUE".

King George V
A5 A6

**1927-31 Typo.**
*29* A5 5c grn & blk 12 6
*a.* Booklet pane of 6
*b.* Booklet pane of 10
*30* A5 10c yel & blk 20 6
*a.* Booklet pane of 6
*b.* Booklet pane of 10
*31* A5 15c red & blk 20 6
*a.* Booklet pane of 6
*b.* Booklet pane of 10
*32* A5 20c org & blk 20 6
*33* A5 25c ultra & blk 25 20
*34* A5 30c dl vio & blk 50 40
*35* A5 30c ultra & blk ('31) 17.50 32
*36* A5 40c brn & blk 55 75
*36* A5 50c gray & blk 30 15
*38* A5 75c ol grn & blk 1.10 1.65
*39* A6 1sh grn & blk 1.00 50
*40* A6 2sh vio brn & blk 3.25 2.00
*41* A6 3sh black 4.25 *9.00*
*42* A6 5sh scar & blk 4.25 3.50
*43* A6 10sh ultra & blk 17.50 *26.00*
*44* A6 £1 brn org & blk 55.00 *62.50*
*Nos. 29-44 (16)* 106.17 *107.21*

For issues of 1935-61, see Kenya and Uganda.

**Catalogue values for unused stamps in this section, from this point to the end of the section, are for Never Hinged items.**

**Independent State**

Nurse and Infant
A7


Torch above Mt. Kilimanjaro
A8

Designs: 5c, Teacher instructing villagers (horiz.). 15c, Coffee picker. 20c, Harvesting corn. 30c, Flag (horiz.). 50c, Serengeti lions. 1sh, Nurse showing infant to mother and hospital. 2sh, Dar es Salaam harbor. 5sh, Tractor and field workers. 10sh, Diamond mine and rose diamond. 1sh, 2sh, 5sh, 10sh, horiz.

***Perf. 14x14½, 14½x14***
**1961, Dec. 9 Photo. Unwmk.**
*45* A7 5c sep & yel grn 5 5
*46* A7 10c Prus grn 5 5
*a.* Bklt pane of 4 12
*47* A7 15c sep & bl 5 5
*a.* Bklt. pane of 4 15
*b.* bl omitted 200.00
*48* A7 20c org brn 5 5
*a.* Bklt. pane of 4 20
*49* A7 30c dp grn blk & yel 6 6
*a.* Bklt. pane of 4 25
*50* A7 50c sep & yel 8 5
*a.* Bklt. pane of 4 40

***Perf. 14½***
*51* A8 1sh cit brn & gray bl 15 6
*52* A8 1sh30c multi 30 10
*53* A8 2sh multi 42 17
*54* A8 5sh Prus grn & dp org 1.00 35
*55* A8 10sh blk, bl & rose 1.75 75
*a.* rose (diamond) omitted 75.00
*56* A8 20sh multi 4.50 1.50
*Nos. 45-56 (12)* 8.46 3.24

Tanganyika's independence, Dec. 9, 1961.

Pres. Julius Nyerere with Pickax — A9

Designs: 50c, Flag hoisting on Mt. Kilimanjaro. 1sh30c, Presidential emblem. 2sh50c, Independence monument, Mnazi Moja.

**1962, Dec. 9 *Perf. 14½x14***
*57* A9 30c brt grn 8 8
*58* A9 50c multi 12 12
*59* A9 1sh30c multi 25 25
*60* A9 2sh50c dk bl, blk & red 50 50

Issued to commemorate the establishment of the Republic of Tanganyika, Dec. 9, 1962.

### OFFICIAL STAMPS

**Catalogue values for unused stamps in this section, from this point to the end of the section, are for Never Hinged items.**

**Issued for use by the Tanganyika Government.**

Stamps of Kenya and Uganda, 1954-59, Overprinted

**OFFICIAL**

***Perf. 12½x13, 13x12½***
**1959 Engr. Wmk. 4**
*O1* A19 5c choc & blk 5 5
*O2* A19 10c carmine 5 5
*O3* A20 15c lt bl & blk (on No. 106) 7 5
*O4* A19 20c org & blk 12 7
*a.* Double ovpt. 350.00
*O5* A19 30c ultra & blk 18 15
*O6* A19 50c dp red lil 25 18
*O7* A19 1sh dp mag & blk 30 25
*O8* A20 1sh30c pur & red org 42 35
*O9* A20 2sh dp grn & gray 60 60
*O10* A20 5sh blk & org 1.50 1.50
*O11* A20 10sh ultra & blk 3.25 3.25
*O12* A21 £1 blk & ver 6.50 6.25
*Nos. O1-O12 (12)* 13.29 12.75

Stamps of Kenya and Uganda, 1960, Overprinted **OFFICIAL**

***Perf. 14½x14***
**1960, Oct. 1 Photo. Wmk. 314**
*O13* A23 5c dl bl 5 5
*O14* A23 10c lt ol grn 5 5
*O15* A23 15c dl pur 5 5
*O16* A23 20c brt lil rose 7 7
*O17* A23 30c brt ver 10 8
*O18* A23 50c dl vio 16 14

Overprinted **OFFICIAL**

**Engr. *Perf. 14***
*O19* A24 1sh vio & lil red 40 25
*O20* A24 5sh rose red & lil 1.75 1.50
*Nos. O13-O20 (8)* 2.63 2.19

Nos. 45-51 and 54 Overprinted "OFFICIAL" in Sans-serif Type of Various Sizes

***Perf. 14x14½, 14½x14***
**1961, Dec. 9 Unwmk.**
*O21* A7 5c sep & yel grn 5 5
*O22* A7 10c Prus grn 5 5
*O23* A7 15c sep & bl 6 6
*O24* A7 20c org brn 10 6
*O25* A7 30c dp grn blk & yel 12 10
*O26* A7 50c sep & yel 20 15
*O27* A8 1sh cit brn & gray bl 40 25
*O28* A8 5sh Prus grn & dp org 1.50 1.10
*Nos. O21-O28 (8)* 2.48 1.82

# TANZANIA

## (Tanganyika and Zanzibar)

LOCATION — In southeastern Africa bordering on the Indian Ocean, and a group of islands about 20 miles off the coast.
GOVT. — United republic in British Commonwealth.
AREA — 364,886 sq. mi.
POP. — 19,730,000 (est. 1983).
CAPITAL — Dodoma.

Tanganyika joined Zanzibar on April 26, 1964, to form the United Republic of Tanganyika and Zanzibar. In October 1965 the name was changed to United Republic of Tanzania.

Zanzibar stamps include two (Nos. 331, 334) inscribed "Tanzania."

100 Cents = 1 Shilling

**Catalogue values for all unused stamps in this country are for Never Hinged items.**

Map — A1

Design: 30c, 1sh30c, Emblem (hands holding torch and spear).

*Perf. 14x14½*

**1964, July 7 Photo. Unwmk.**

| | | | | |
|---|---|---|---|---|
| *1* | A1 | 20c bl & emer | 8 | 8 |
| *2* | A1 | 30c brn dk & lt bl | 10 | 10 |
| *3* | A1 | 1.30sh ultra blk & org | 30 | 30 |
| *4* | A1 | 2.50sh ultra & pur | 60 | 60 |

Union of Tanganyika and Zanzibar. Not sold in Zanzibar, nor valid there.

Flag
A2

Native Handicraft
A3

Designs: 5c, Hale hydroelectric plant. 15c, Army squad. 20c, Road building. 40c, Giraffes. 50c, Zebras. 65c, Mt. Kilimanjaro. 1sh, Dar es Salaam harbor. 1.30sh, Zinjanthropus skull and Olduvai Gorge excavation. 2.50sh, Sailfish, dhow and map of Mafia Island. 5sh, Sisal industry. 10sh, State House, Dar es Salaam. 20sh, Tanzania coat of arms.

*Perf. 14x14½, 14½x14*

**1965, Dec. 9 Photo. Unwmk.**

**Size: 21x17½mm, 17½x21mm**

| | | | | |
|---|---|---|---|---|
| *5* | A2 | 5c org & ultra | 5 | 5 |
| *6* | A2 | 10c ultra, grn, yel & blk | 5 | 5 |
| *7* | A3 | 15c grn, bl, brn & buff | 5 | 5 |
| *a* | | Bklt. pane of 4 | 22 | |
| *8* | A2 | 20c bl & brn | 6 | 5 |
| *9* | A3 | 30c blk & red brn | 8 | 5 |
| *a* | | Bklt. pane of 4 | 35 | |
| *10* | A3 | 40c bl, yel grn & brn | 10 | 6 |
| *11* | A2 | 50c yel grn & bl | 12 | 6 |
| *a* | | Bklt. pane of 4 | 50 | |
| *12* | A2 | 65c ultra, grn & red brn | 25 | 25 |

*Perf. 14½*

**Size: 41½x25, 25x41½mm**

| | | | | |
|---|---|---|---|---|
| *13* | A2 | 1sh bl, grn, yel & brn | 30 | 8 |
| *14* | A2 | 1.30sh multi | 45 | 12 |
| *15* | A2 | 2.50sh bl & red brn | 65 | 30 |
| *16* | A2 | 5sh bl, brt grn & red brn | 1.40 | 45 |
| *17* | A2 | 10sh bl & yel | 2.75 | 1.25 |
| *18* | A3 | 20sh gray & multi | 5.50 | 2.75 |
| | | *Nos. 5-18 (14)* | 11.81 | 5.57 |

Turkeyfish — A4

Fish: 5c, Cardinalfish. 10c, Mudskipper. 15c, Toby puffer. 20c, Two sea horses. 30c, Batfish. 40c, Sweetlips. 50c, Birdfish. 65c, Butterflyfish. 70c, Grouper. 1.30sh, Surgeonfish. 1.50sh, Caesio xanthonotus. 2.50sh, Emperor snapper. 5sh, Moorish idol. 10sh, Striped triggerfish. 20sh, Squirrelfish.

**1967-71 Photo.** ***Perf. 14x14½***

**Size: 21x17½mm**

**Fish in Natural Colors**

| | | | | |
|---|---|---|---|---|
| *19* | A4 | 5c blk & cit | 5 | 5 |
| *20* | A4 | 10c brn & ol | 5 | 5 |
| *a* | | Booklet pane of 4 | 12 | |
| *21* | A4 | 15c brn & bl | 5 | 5 |
| *a* | | Booklet pane of 4 | 30 | |
| *22* | A4 | 20c brn & dk bl grn | 6 | 5 |
| *a* | | Booklet pane of 4 | 30 | |
| *23* | A4 | 30c blk & yel grn | 8 | 6 |
| *a* | | Booklet pane of 4 | 40 | |
| *24* | A4 | 40c brn & emer | 12 | 10 |
| *a* | | Booklet pane of 4 ('71) | 50 | |
| *25* | A4 | 50c blk & dl bl grn | 15 | 12 |
| *a* | | Booklet pane of 4 | 70 | |
| *26* | A4 | 65c blk & gray grn | 60 | 60 |
| *27* | A4 | 70c blk & ol ('69) | 50 | 50 |
| *a* | | Booklet pane of 4 ('71) | 2.10 | |

*Perf. 14½*

**Size: 41x25mm**

| | | | | |
|---|---|---|---|---|
| *28* | A4 | 1sh brn & multi | 40 | *5* |
| *29* | A4 | 1.30sh blk & ol | 60 | *5* |
| *30* | A4 | 1.50sh blk & ol ('69) | 70 | 20 |
| *31* | A4 | 2.50sh brn yel & grn | 1.25 | *8* |
| *32* | A4 | 5sh blk & bl grn | 2.00 | *20* |
| *33* | A4 | 10sh brn & gray grn | 4.50 | *60* |
| *34* | A4 | 20sh blk & gray ol | 10.00 | *1.40* |
| | | *Nos. 19-34 (16)* | 21.11 | 4.16 |

Issue dates: Nos. 27, 30, Sept. 15, 1969. Others, Dec. 9, 1967.

Values of Nos. 28-34 are for canceled-to-order stamps with printed cancellations. Postally used copies sell for higher prices.

Papilio Hornimani
A5

Euphaedra Neophron
A6

Butterflies: 10c, Colotis ione. 15c, Amauris makuyuensis. 20c, Libythea laius. 30c, Danaus chrysippus. 40c, Sallya rosa. 50c, Axiocerses styx. 60c, Eurema hecabe. 70c, Acraea insignis. 1.50sh, Precis octavia. 2.50sh, Charaxes eupale. 5sh, Charaxes pollux. 10sh, Salamis parhassus. 20sh, Papilio ophidicephalus.

**1973, Dec. 3 Photo.** ***Perf. 14½x14***

| | | | | |
|---|---|---|---|---|
| *35* | A5 | 5c yel grn & multi | 5 | 5 |
| *a* | | Booklet pane of 4 | 12 | |
| *36* | A5 | 10c lt brn & multi | 5 | 5 |
| *a* | | Booklet pane of 4 | 12 | |
| *37* | A5 | 15c ultra & multi | 5 | 5 |
| *38* | A5 | 20c fawn & multi | 5 | 5 |
| *a* | | Booklet pane of 4 | 20 | |
| *39* | A5 | 30c yel & multi | 8 | 6 |
| *a* | | Booklet pane of 4 | 32 | |
| *40* | A5 | 40c multi | 10 | 8 |
| *a* | | Booklet pane of 4 | 40 | |
| *41* | A5 | 50c cit & multi | 13 | 10 |
| *a* | | Booklet pane of 4 | 52 | |
| *42* | A5 | 60c multi | 15 | 13 |
| *43* | A5 | 70c brt grn & multi | 18 | 14 |
| *a* | | Booklet pane of 4 | 72 | |

*Perf. 14½*

| | | | | |
|---|---|---|---|---|
| *44* | A6 | 1sh grn & multi | 30 | 24 |
| *45* | A6 | 1.50sh org & multi | 45 | 35 |
| *46* | A6 | 2.50sh multi | 75 | 60 |
| *47* | A6 | 5sh multi | 1.50 | 1.20 |
| *48* | A6 | 10sh lt grn & multi | 3.00 | 2.40 |
| *49* | A6 | 20sh bl & multi | 6.00 | 4.80 |
| | | *Nos. 35-49 (15)* | 12.84 | 10.30 |

### Nos. 42, 45-46, 49 Surcharged with New Value and 2 Bars

*Perf. 14½x14, 14½*

**1975, Nov. 17 Photo.**

| | | | | |
|---|---|---|---|---|
| *50* | A5 | 80c on 60c multi | 50 | 50 |
| *51* | A6 | 2sh on 1.50sh multi | 1.25 | 1.25 |
| *52* | A6 | 3sh on 2.50sh multi | *10.00* | *10.00* |
| *53* | A6 | 40sh on 20sh multi | *12.50* | *12.50* |

### Communication Type of Kenya 1976

Designs: 50c, Microwave tower. 1sh, Cordless switchboard and operators (horiz.). 2sh, Telephones of 1880, 1930 and 1976. 3sh, Message switching center (horiz.).

**1976, Apr. 15 Litho.** ***Perf. 14½***

| | | | | |
|---|---|---|---|---|
| *54* | A5 | 50c bl & multi | 12 | 10 |
| *55* | A5 | 1sh red & multi | 25 | 20 |
| *56* | A5 | 2sh yel & multi | 48 | 40 |
| *57* | A5 | 3sh multi | 72 | 60 |
| *a* | | Souvenir sheet of 4 | 2.50 | 2.50 |

Telecommunications development in East Africa. No. 57a contains 4 stamps similar to Nos. 54-57 with simulated perforations; dark carmine rose margin with black inscription and white telephones. Size: 120x120mm.

### Olympics Type of Kenya 1976

Designs: 50c, Akii Bua, Ugandan hurdler. 1sh, Filbert Bayi, Tanzanian runner. 2sh, Steve Muchoki, Kenyan boxer. 3sh, Olympic torch, flags of Kenya, Tanzania and Uganda.

**1976, July 5 Litho.** ***Perf. 14½***

| | | | | |
|---|---|---|---|---|
| *58* | A6 | 50c bl & multi | 12 | 10 |
| *59* | A6 | 1sh red & multi | 25 | 20 |
| *60* | A6 | 2sh yel & multi | 48 | 40 |
| *61* | A6 | 3sh bl & multi | 72 | 60 |
| *a* | | Souvenir sheet of 4 | *9.25* | *9.25* |

21st Olympic Games, Montreal, Canada, July 17-Aug. 1. No. 61a contains one each of Nos. 58-61, perf. 13; orange and multicolored margin. Size: 130x154mm.

### Railway Type of Kenya 1976

Designs: 50c, Tanzania-Zambia Railway. 1sh, Nile Bridge, Uganda. 2sh, Nakuru Station, Kenya. 3sh, Class A locomotive, 1896.

**1976, Oct. 4 Litho.** ***Perf. 14½***

| | | | | |
|---|---|---|---|---|
| *62* | A7 | 50c lil & multi | 20 | 12 |
| *63* | A7 | 1sh emer & multi | 35 | 24 |
| *64* | A7 | 2sh brt rose & multi | 85 | 48 |
| *65* | A7 | 3sh yel & multi | 1.25 | 72 |
| *a* | | Souvenir sheet of 4 | 4.00 | 3.00 |

Rail transport in East Africa. No. 65a contains one each of Nos. 62-65, perf. 13; yellow and multicolored margin showing African scenes with animals and birds. Size: 154x104mm.

### Fish Type of Kenya 1977

**1977, Jan. 10 Litho.** ***Perf. 14½***

| | | | | |
|---|---|---|---|---|
| *66* | A8 | 50c Nile perch | 16 | 15 |
| *67* | A8 | 1sh Tilapia | 30 | 28 |
| *68* | A8 | 3sh Sailfish | 90 | 75 |
| *69* | A8 | 5sh Black marlin | 1.60 | 1.50 |
| *a* | | Souv. sheet of 4, Nos. 66-69 | 3.25 | 3.25 |

Game fish. No. 69a has multicolored margin shows fishing vessel and sea floor. Size: 153x129mm.

### African Festival Type of Kenya 1977

Designs (Festival Emblem and): 50c, Masai tribesmen bleeding cow. 1sh, Dancers from Uganda. 2sh, Makonde sculpture. 3sh, Tribesmen skinning hippopotamus.

**1977, Jan. 15** ***Perf. 13½x14***

| | | | | |
|---|---|---|---|---|
| *70* | A9 | 50c multi | 15 | 10 |
| *71* | A9 | 1sh multi | 28 | 16 |
| *72* | A9 | 2sh multi | 50 | 32 |
| *73* | A9 | 3sh multi | 85 | 48 |
| *a* | | Souvenir sheet of 4 | 3.00 | 3.00 |

2nd World Black and African Festival, Lagos, Nigeria, Jan. 15-Feb. 12. No. 73a contains one each of Nos. 70-73; bright green margin with black inscription and decoration. Size: 132x98mm.

### Rally Type of Kenya 1977

Designs (Safari Rally Emblem and): 50c, Automobile passing through village. 1sh, Winner at finish line. 2sh, Car going through washout. 5sh, Car, elephants and Mt. Kenya.

**1977, Apr. 5 Litho.** ***Perf. 14***

| | | | | |
|---|---|---|---|---|
| *74* | A10 | 50c multi | 15 | 12 |
| *75* | A10 | 1sh multi | 30 | 24 |
| *76* | A10 | 2sh multi | 80 | 48 |
| *77* | A10 | 5sh multi | 2.00 | 1.25 |
| *a* | | Souvenir sheet of 4 | 3.50 | 3.50 |

25th Safari rally, Apr. 7-11. No. 77a contains one each of Nos. 74-77; blue and multicolored margin showing automobiles and antelopes. Size: 126x93mm.

### Church Type of Kenya 1977

Designs: 50c, Rev. Canon Apolo Kivebulaya. 1sh, Uganda Cathedral. 2sh, Early grass-topped Cathedral. 5sh, Early tent congregation, Kigezi.

**1977, June 20 Litho.** ***Perf. 14***

| | | | | |
|---|---|---|---|---|
| *78* | A11 | 50c multi | 15 | 10 |
| *79* | A11 | 1sh multi | 25 | 20 |
| *80* | A11 | 2sh multi | 50 | 32 |
| *81* | A11 | 5sh multi | 1.50 | 1.00 |
| *a* | | Souvenir sheet of 4 | 3.00 | 3.00 |

Church of Uganda, centenary. No. 81a contains one each of Nos. 78-81; ocher and black margin. Size: 125x89mm.

### Wildlife Type of Kenya 1977

Designs (Wildlife Fund Emblem and): 50c, Pancake tortoise. 1sh, Nile crocodile. 2sh, Hunter's hartebeest. 3sh, Red Colobus monkey. 5sh, Dugong.

**1977, Sept. 26 Litho.** ***Perf. 14x13½***

| | | | | |
|---|---|---|---|---|
| *82* | A13 | 50c multi | 20 | 18 |
| *83* | A13 | 1sh multi | 25 | 22 |
| *84* | A13 | 2sh multi | 85 | 45 |
| *85* | A13 | 3sh multi | 1.25 | 70 |
| *86* | A13 | 5sh multi | 2.00 | 1.10 |
| *a* | | Souvenir sheet of 4 | 4.75 | 4.75 |
| | | *Nos. 82-86 (5)* | 4.55 | 2.65 |

Endangered species. No. 86a contains one each of Nos. 83-86; multicolored margin shows storks in flight and marsh. Size: 128x102mm.

Prince Philip and Julius Nyerere, 1961
A7

Designs: 5sh, Queen Elizabeth II, Prince Philip, Prime Minister Nyerere in London, 1975. 10sh, Royal crown, flags of Tanzania and Commonwealth nations. 20sh, Coronation.

**1977, Nov. 23 Litho.** ***Perf. 14x13½***

| | | | | |
|---|---|---|---|---|
| *87* | A7 | 50c multi | 12 | 10 |
| *88* | A7 | 5sh multi | 1.10 | 1.00 |
| *89* | A7 | 10sh multi | 2.25 | 2.25 |
| *90* | A7 | 20sh multi | 4.50 | 4.50 |
| *a* | | Souvenir sheet of 4 | 8.50 | 8.50 |

25th anniversary of reign of Queen Elizabeth II. No. 90a contains one each of Nos. 87-90; multicolored margin shows flags and crown. Size: 128x102mm.

Women Fetching Water from Stream and Tap — A8

Designs: 1sh, Flag raising. 3sh, Health care, laboratory and hospital. 5sh, Pres. Julius Nyerere.

**1978, Feb. 5 Litho.** ***Perf. 13½x14***

| | | | | |
|---|---|---|---|---|
| *91* | A8 | 50c multi | 12 | 10 |
| *92* | A8 | 1sh multi | 25 | 20 |
| *93* | A8 | 3sh multi | 72 | 60 |
| *94* | A8 | 5sh multi | 1.25 | 1.10 |
| *a* | | Souvenir sheet of 4 | 2.50 | 2.50 |

First anniversary of the New Revolutionary Party (Chama cha Mapinduzi). No. 94a contains one each of Nos. 91-94; black and green margin. Size: 143x105mm.

### Soccer Type of Kenya

Designs (Soccer Cup and): 50c, Soccer scene and Joe Kadenge. 1sh, Mohammed Chuma receiving trophy, and his portrait. 2sh, Shot on goal and Omari S. Kidevu. 3sh, Backfield defense and Polly Ouma.

**1978, Apr. 17 Litho. *Perf. 14x13½***

| | | | | |
|---|---|---|---|---|
| *95* | A17 | 50c grn & multi | 12 | 10 |
| *96* | A17 | 1sh lt brn & multi | 25 | 22 |
| *97* | A17 | 2sh lil & multi | 50 | 40 |
| *98* | A17 | 3sh dk bl & multi | 75 | 60 |
| *a* | | Souvenir sheet of 4 | 1.75 | 1.75 |

World Soccer Cup Championships, Argentina, 78, June 1-25. No. 98a contains one each of Nos. 95-98; yellow green and dark green margin. Size: 136x82mm.

**Nos. 87-90a Overprinted: "25th ANNIVERSARY / CORONATION / 2nd JUNE 1953"**

**1978, June 2**

| | | | | |
|---|---|---|---|---|
| *99* | A7 | 50c multi | 15 | 12 |
| *100* | A7 | 5sh multi | 1.50 | 1.50 |
| *101* | A7 | 10sh multi | 3.00 | 3.00 |
| *102* | A7 | 20sh multi | 6.00 | 6.00 |
| *a* | | Souvenir sheet of 4 | 7.50 | 7.50 |

25th anniversary of coronation of Queen Elizabeth II. No. 102a contains Nos. 99-102. Size: 128x102mm.

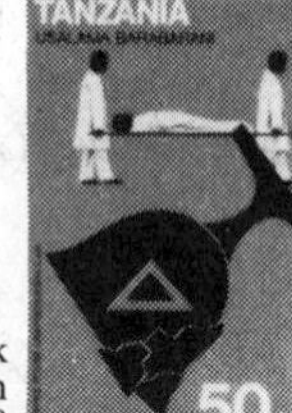


"Do not Drink when Driving" — A9

Designs: 1sh, "Courtesy to the young, old and handicapped." 3sh, "Observe highway code." 5sh, "Do not drive faulty vehicle."

**1978, July 1 Litho. *Perf. 13½x13***

| | | | | |
|---|---|---|---|---|
| *103* | A9 | 50c multi | 15 | 10 |
| *104* | A9 | 1sh multi | 25 | 25 |
| *105* | A9 | 3sh multi | 65 | 60 |
| *106* | A9 | 5sh multi | 1.40 | 1.10 |
| *a* | | Souvenir sheet of 4 | 3.00 | 3.00 |

Road Safety Campaign. No. 106a contains Nos. 103-106, perf. 14; olive green, red and black margin. Size: 92x129mm.

Lake Manyara Hotel — A10

Designs: 1sh, Lobo Wildlife Lodge. 3sh, Ngorongoro Crater Lodge. 5sh, Ngorongoro Wildlife Lodge. 10sh, Mafia Island Lodge. 20sh, Mikumi Wildlife Lodge.

**1978, Sept. 11 Litho. *Perf. 13½***

| | | | | |
|---|---|---|---|---|
| *107* | A10 | 50c multi | 12 | 12 |
| *108* | A10 | 1sh multi | 25 | 25 |
| *109* | A10 | 3sh multi | 60 | 60 |
| *110* | A10 | 5sh multi | 1.10 | 1.10 |
| *111* | A10 | 10sh multi | 2.25 | 2.25 |
| *112* | A10 | 20sh multi | 4.50 | 4.50 |
| *a* | | Souvenir sheet of 6 | 9.25 | 9.25 |
| | | *Nos. 107-112 (6)* | 8.82 | 8.82 |

Game Lodges of Tanzania. No. 112a contains Nos. 107-112; multicolored margin shows landscape and giraffe. Size: 117x112mm.

Chained African — A11

Designs (Anti-Apartheid Year Emblem and): 1sh, Division of races (black and white heads). 2.50sh, Racial harmony (black and white handshake and heads). 5sh, End of suppression and rise of freedom (hands breaking loose from chains).

**1978, Oct. 24 Litho. *Perf. 14½x14***

| | | | | |
|---|---|---|---|---|
| *113* | A11 | 50c multi | 12 | 12 |
| *114* | A11 | 1sh multi | 25 | 25 |
| *115* | A11 | 2.50sh multi | 60 | 60 |
| *116* | A11 | 5sh multi | 1.25 | 1.25 |
| *a* | | Souvenir sheet of 4 | 2.25 | 2.25 |

Anti-Apartheid Year. No. 116a contains Nos. 113-116; black marginal inscription and black and white handshakes. Size: 125x132mm.

Fokker Friendship at Dar Es Salaam Airport — A12

Designs: 1sh, Single-engine Dragon, 1930, Zanzibar. 2sh, British Airways Concorde. 5sh, Wright Brothers' Flyer 1, 1903.

**1978, Dec. 28 Litho. *Perf. 13½***

| | | | | |
|---|---|---|---|---|
| *117* | A12 | 50c multi | 12 | 12 |
| *118* | A12 | 1sh multi | 25 | 25 |
| *119* | A12 | 2sh multi | 50 | 50 |
| *120* | A12 | 5sh multi | 1.25 | 1.25 |
| *a* | | Souvenir sheet of 4 | 2.25 | 2.25 |

75th anniversary of 1st powered flight. No. 120a contains Nos. 117-120; multicolored margin. Size: 133x97mm.

Emblem A13

Design: 5sh, Headquarters buildings.

**1979, Feb. 3 Litho. *Perf. 14½x14***

| | | | | |
|---|---|---|---|---|
| *121* | A13 | 50c multi | 10 | 10 |
| *122* | A13 | 5sh multi | 1.10 | 1.10 |
| *a* | | Souvenir sheet of 2 | 1.25 | 1.25 |

Tanzania Post and Telecommunications Corporation, 1st anniversary. No. 122a contains Nos. 121-122; multicolored margin with means of communications. Size: 82x96mm.

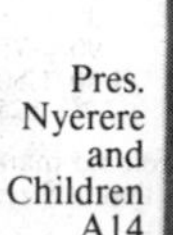

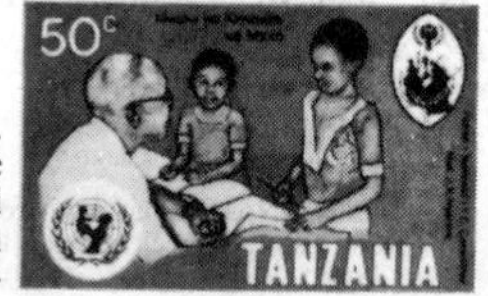


Pres. Nyerere and Children A14

Designs (UNICEF and Tanzanian IYC Emblems and): 1sh, Kindergarten. 2sh, Vaccination of infant. 5sh, Emblems.

**1979, June 25 Litho. *Perf. 14½***

| | | | | |
|---|---|---|---|---|
| *123* | A14 | 50c multi | 12 | 12 |
| *124* | A14 | 1sh multi | 25 | 25 |
| *125* | A14 | 2sh multi | 50 | 50 |
| *126* | A14 | 5sh multi | 1.25 | 1.25 |
| *a* | | Souvenir sheet of 4 | 2.00 | 2.00 |

International Year of the Child. No. 126a contains Nos. 123-126; multicolored margin shows children. Size: 127x92mm.

Tree Planting — A15

Forest Preservation and Expansion: 1sh, Seedling. 2sh, Rainfall. 5sh, Forest fire.

**1979, Sept. 29 Litho. *Perf. 14½***

| | | | | |
|---|---|---|---|---|
| *127* | A15 | 50c multi | 12 | 12 |
| *128* | A15 | 1sh multi | 25 | 25 |
| *129* | A15 | 2sh multi | 50 | 50 |
| *130* | A15 | 5sh multi | 1.25 | 1.25 |

Mwenge Satellite Earth Station Opening A16

**1979, Dec. 3 Litho. *Perf. 13½***

| | | | | |
|---|---|---|---|---|
| *131* | A16 | 10c multi | 5 | 5 |
| *132* | A16 | 40c multi | 12 | 10 |
| *133* | A16 | 50c multi | 12 | 10 |
| *134* | A16 | 1sh multi | 25 | 20 |

**Nos. 36, 43 Surcharged**

**1979 Litho. *Perf. 14½x14***

| | | | | |
|---|---|---|---|---|
| *135* | A5 | 40c (10 + 30) multi | 15 | 15 |
| *136* | A5 | 50c on 70c multi | 20 | 20 |

Tabata Dispensary, Dar-es-Salaam, Rotary Emblem — A17

**1980, Mar. 1 Litho. *Perf. 13x13½***

| | | | | |
|---|---|---|---|---|
| *137* | A17 | 50c shown | 10 | 10 |
| *138* | A17 | 1sh *Ngomvu water project* | 20 | 20 |
| *139* | A17 | 5sh *Flying doctor service* | 1.10 | 1.10 |
| *140* | A17 | 20sh *Torch, anniversary emblem* | 4.50 | 4.50 |
| *a* | | Souvenir sheet of 4 | 6.00 | 6.00 |

Rotary International, 75th anniversary. No. 140a contains Nos. 137-140; multicolored margin shows Rotary emblems. Size: 131x102mm.

Zanzibar Nos. 49 and 309, "Stamp History" Cancel A18

Cancel and: 50c, Tanganyika No. 58, postal worker (vert.). 10sh, Tanganyika Nos. 16 and 52. 20sh, Penny Black, Rowland Hill (vert.).

**1980, Apr. *Perf. 14***

| | | | | |
|---|---|---|---|---|
| *141* | A18 | 40c multi | 10 | 10 |
| *142* | A18 | 50c multi | 12 | 12 |
| *143* | A18 | 10sh multi | 2.50 | 2.50 |
| *144* | A18 | 20sh multi | 5.00 | 5.00 |
| *a* | | Souvenir sheet of 4 | 7.25 | 7.25 |

Sir Rowland Hill (1795-1879), originator of penny postage; Tanzanian stamp history. No. 144a contains Nos. 141-144; multicolored margin shows flag of Tanzania and "stamp history" cancel. Size: 156x111½mm.

**Overprinted: "LONDON 1980" / PHILATELIC EXHIBITION**

**1980, May 6 Litho. *Perf. 14***

| | | | | |
|---|---|---|---|---|
| *145* | A18 | 40c multi | 8 | 8 |
| *146* | A18 | 50c multi | 10 | 10 |
| *147* | A18 | 10sh multi | 2.25 | 2.25 |
| *148* | A18 | 20sh multi | 4.50 | 4.50 |
| *a* | | Souvenir sheet of 4 | 7.25 | 7.25 |

London 80 Intl. Stamp Exhib., May 6-14.

**Nos. 137-140a with Additional Inscription on 1 or 2 Lines: "District 920-55th Annual / Conference, Arusha, Tanzania"**

**1980, June 23 Litho. *Perf. 13x13½***

| | | | | |
|---|---|---|---|---|
| *149* | A17 | 50c multi | 12 | 12 |
| *150* | A17 | 1sh multi | 25 | 25 |
| *151* | A17 | 5sh multi | 1.25 | 1.25 |
| *152* | A17 | 20sh multi | 5.00 | 5.00 |
| *a* | | Souvenir sheet of 4 | 6.50 | 6.50 |

District 920 Rotary Club, 55th Annual Conference, Arusha.

Pan African Postal Union and U.P.U. Emblems A19

**1980, July 1 *Perf. 13x13½***

| | | | | |
|---|---|---|---|---|
| *153* | A19 | 50c pur & blk | 12 | 12 |
| *154* | A19 | 1sh ultra & blk | 25 | 25 |
| *155* | A19 | 5sh red org & blk | 1.25 | 1.25 |
| *156* | A19 | 10sh grn & blk | 2.50 | 2.50 |

Pan African Postal Union Plenipotentiary Conference, Arusha, Jan. 8-18.

Gidamis Shahanga, Marathon A20

Tanzanian Olympic Team: 1sh, Nzael Kyomo and sprinters. 10sh, Zakayo Malekwa and javelin. 20sh, William Lyimo and boxers.

**1980, Aug. 18 Litho. *Perf. 13x13½***

| | | | | |
|---|---|---|---|---|
| *157* | A20 | 50c multi | 12 | 12 |
| *158* | A20 | 1sh multi | 25 | 25 |
| *159* | A20 | 10sh multi | 2.50 | 2.50 |
| *160* | A20 | 20sh multi | 5.00 | 5.00 |
| *a* | | Souvenir sheet of 4 | 7.75 | 7.75 |

22nd Summer Olympic Games, Moscow, July 19-Aug. 3. No. 160a contains Nos. 157-160. Multicolored margin shows Moscow '80 emblem and victorious athlete. Size 172x108mm.

Issued also in sheets of 20 (5 of each value).

Spring Hare — A21

**1980, Oct. 1 Litho. *Perf. 14***

| | | | | |
|---|---|---|---|---|
| *161* | A21 | 10c *shown* | 5 | 5 |
| *162* | A21 | 20c *Genet* | 5 | 5 |
| *163* | A21 | 40c *Mongoose* | 8 | 8 |
| *164* | A21 | 50c *Ratel* | 10 | 10 |
| *165* | A21 | 75c *Rock hyrax* | 15 | 15 |
| *166* | A21 | 80c *Leopard* | 16 | 16 |

***Perf. 14½***

**Size: 40x24mm**

| | | | | |
|---|---|---|---|---|
| *167* | A21 | 1sh *Impalas* | 20 | 20 |
| *168* | A21 | 1.50sh *Giraffes* | 30 | 30 |
| *169* | A21 | 2sh *Zebras* | 40 | 40 |
| *170* | A21 | 3sh *Buffalo* | 60 | 60 |
| *171* | A21 | 5sh *Lions* | 1.00 | 1.00 |
| *172* | A21 | 10sh *Rhinoceros* | 2.00 | 2.00 |
| *173* | A21 | 20sh *Elephants* | 4.00 | 4.00 |
| *174* | A21 | 40sh *Cheetahs* | 8.00 | 8.00 |
| | | *Nos. 161-174 (14)* | 17.09 | 17.09 |

National Parks Emblem A22

**1981, Jan. 26 Litho. *Perf. 13x13½***

| | | | | |
|---|---|---|---|---|
| *175* | A22 | 50c Ngorongoro Park | 12 | 12 |
| *176* | A22 | 1sh shown | 25 | 25 |
| *177* | A22 | 5sh Friends of Serengeti | 1.25 | 1.25 |
| *178* | A22 | 20sh Friends of Ngorongoro | 5.00 | 5.00 |

Ngorongoro and Serengeti Parks, 60th anniversary.

Nos. 89-90 Overprinted: "ROYAL WEDDING/ H.R.H. PRINCE CHARLES/ 29th JULY 1981"

**1981, July 29 Litho. *Perf. 14x13½***

*179* A7 10sh multi 2.25 2.25
*180* A7 20sh multi 4.50 4.50
*a* Souvenir sheet of 2 17.50 17.50

Royal wedding. No. 180a contains Nos. 179-180 multicolored margin shows crown, flag of Tanzania. Size: 87x97mm.

Mail Runner A23

**1981, Oct. 23 Litho. *Perf. 12½x12***

*181* A23 50c shown 12 12
*182* A23 1sh Letter sorting 25 25
*183* A23 5sh Post horn, carrier pigeon 1.10 1.10
*184* A23 10sh Commonwealth members' flags 2.25 2.25
*a* Souvenir sheet of 4 3.75 3.75

Commonwealth Postal Administrations Conference, Arusha, June 29-July 10. No. 184a contains Nos. 181-184; multicolored decorative margin. Size: 131x101mm.

Intl. Year of the Disabled A24

**1981, Nov. 30 Litho. *Perf. 14***

*185* A24 50c Morris Nyunyusa, blind drummer 12 12
*186* A24 1sh Sewing 25 25
*187* A24 5sh Prostheses 1.10 1.10
*188* A24 10sh Children 2.25 2.25

20th Anniv. of Independence — A25

**1982, Jan. 13 Litho. *Perf. 13x13½***

*189* A25 50c Pres. Nyerere, flag 12 12
*190* A25 1sh Zanzibar Electricity Plant 25 25
*191* A25 3sh Sisal plant, weaver 75 75
*192* A25 10sh Pupils 2.50 2.50
*a* Souvenir sheet of 4 3.75 3.75

No. 192a contains Nos. 189-192; multicolored margin. Size: 120x85mm.

Ostrich — A26

**1982, Jan. 25 Litho. *Perf. 13½***

*193* A26 50c shown 12 12
*194* A26 1sh Secretary bird 25 25
*195* A26 5sh Kori bustard 1.25 1.25
*196* A26 10sh Saddle-bill stork 2.50 2.50

1982 World Cup — A27

**1982, June 2 Litho. *Perf. 14***

*197* A27 50c Jella Mtagwa 10 10
*198* A27 1sh Stadium 22 22
*199* A27 10sh Diego Armando Maradona 2.00 2.00
*200* A27 20sh Globe 4.25 4.25
*a* Souvenir sheet of 4 6.75 6.75

No. 200a contains Nos. 197-200; multicolored margin shows mascot. Size: 131x100mm.

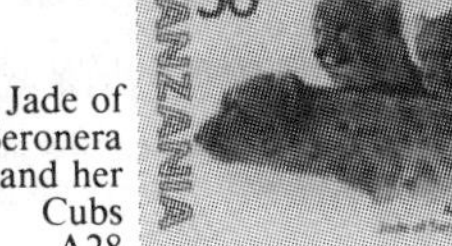


Jade of Seronera and her Cubs A28

Animals Appearing in Movies or TV Shows: 1sh, Wild dog and puppies, Havoc. 5sh, Fifi and sons, Gombe. 10sh, Bahati and twins Rashidi and Ramadhani, Lake Manyara.

**1982, July 15 Litho. *Perf. 14***

*201* A28 50c multi 12 12
*202* A28 1sh multi 25 25
*203* A28 5sh multi 1.25 1.25
*204* A28 10sh multi 2.50 2.50
*a* Souvenir sheet of 4 5.00 5.00

No. 204a contains Nos. 201-204 (perf. 14½); multicolored margin shows animal heads. Size: 121x90mm.

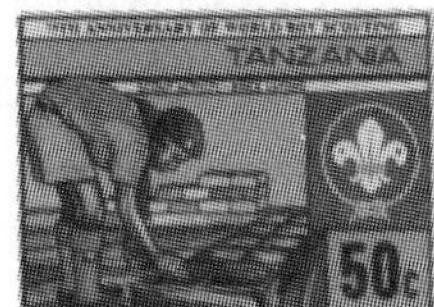


Scouting Year A29

**1982, Aug. 25**

*205* A29 50c Brick laying 8 8
*206* A29 1sh Camping 15 15
*207* A29 10sh Tracing marks 1.75 1.75
*208* A29 20sh Baden-Powell 3.50 3.50
*a* Souvenir sheet of 4 5.50 5.50

No. 208a contains Nos. 205-208; gray and yellow margin shows knots. Size: 130x100mm.

World Food Day — A30

**1982, Oct. 16 Litho. *Perf. 14***

*209* A30 50c Plowing 10 10
*210* A30 1sh Dairy cows 20 20
*211* A30 5sh Corn harvest 1.00 1.00
*212* A30 10sh Grain storage 2.00 2.00
*a* Souvenir sheet of 4 3.50 3.50

No. 212a contains Nos. 209-212. Size: 130x100mm.

TB Bacillus Centenary A31

**1982, Dec. 5 *Perf. 12½x12***

*213* A31 50c Child immunization 10 10
*214* A31 1sh Koch 20 20
*215* A31 5sh TB emblem 1.00 1.00
*216* A31 10sh WHO emblem 2.00 2.00

**Commonwealth Day**
Common Design Type

**1983, Mar. 14 Litho. *Perf. 14***

*217* CD334 50c Pres. Nyerere 10 10
*218* CD334 1sh Running, boxing 20 20
*219* CD334 5sh Flags 1.00 1.00
*220* CD334 10sh Pres. Nyerere, Royal Family 2.00 2.00
*a* Souvenir sheet of 4 3.50 3.50

No. 220a contains Nos. 217-220. Size: 122x100mm.

5th Anniv. of Posts and Telecommunications Dept. — A32

**1983, Feb. 3 Litho. *Perf. 12½x12***

*221* A32 50c Letter post 10 10
*222* A32 1sh Training Institute 20 20
*223* A32 5sh Satellite communications 1.00 1.00
*224* A32 10sh Emblems 2.00 2.00
*a* Souvenir sheet of 4 3.50 3.50

No. 224a contains Nos. 221-224. Size: 127x96mm.

25th Anniv. of Economic Commission for Africa — A33

**1983, Sept. 12 Litho. *Perf. 12½x12***

*225* A33 50c Eastern & Southern African Management Institute, Arusha 10 10
*226* A33 1sh Emblems 20 20
*227* A33 5sh Mineral collections 1.00 1.00
*228* A33 10sh Emblems, diff. 2.00 2.00
*a* Souvenir sheet of 4 3.25 3.25

No. 228a contains Nos. 225-228. Size: 132x100mm.

World Communications Year — A34

**1983, Oct. 17 Litho. *Perf. 14***

*229* A34 50c Rural telephone service 10 10
*230* A34 1sh Emblems 20 20
*231* A34 5sh Post Office 1.00 1.00
*232* A34 10sh Microwave tower 2.00 2.00
*a* Souvenir sheet of 4 3.50 3.50

No. 232a contains Nos. 229-232. Size: 102x92mm.

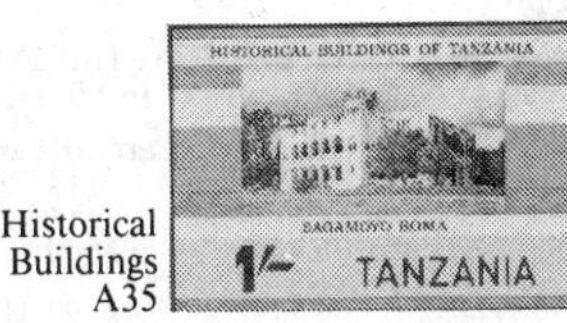


Historical Buildings A35

**1983, Dec. 12 Litho. *Perf. 12½x12***

*233* A35 1sh Bagamoyo Boma 20 20
*234* A35 1.50sh Beit-El-Ajaib 30 30
*235* A35 5sh Anglican Church 90 90
*236* A35 10sh State House, old and new 1.75 1.75
*a* Souvenir sheet of 4 3.50 3.50

No. 236a contains Nos. 233-236; black border. Size: 131x100mm.

20th Anniv. of Revolution A36

**1984, June 18 Litho. *Perf. 14***

*237* A36 1sh Muasisi Kwanza 20 20
*238* A36 1.50sh Clove farming 32 32
*239* A36 5sh Industrial development 1.00 1.00
*240* A36 10sh Housing developments 2.00 2.00

**Souvenir Sheet**

*241* A36 15sh Map, ship 3.25 3.25

No. 241 has multicolored margin showing scenes. Size: 130x100mm.

1984 Summer Olympics A37

**1984, Aug. 6 *Perf. 12½x12***

*242* A37 1sh Boxing 15 15
*243* A37 1.50sh Running 20 20
*244* A37 5sh Basketball 75 75
*245* A37 20sh Soccer 2.50 2.50
*a* Souvenir sheet of 4 3.50 3.50

No. 245a contains Nos. 242-245. Size: 130x101mm.

Intl. Civil Aviation Org. 40th Anniv. A38

**1984, Nov. 15 Litho. *Perf. 13***

*246* A38 1sh Icarus 15 15
*247* A38 1.50sh Air Tanzania jets, traffic controller 20 20
*248* A38 5sh Aircraft maintenance 75 75
*249* A38 10sh ICAO emblem 1.25 1.25
*a* Souvenir sheet of 4, #246-249 2.25 2.25

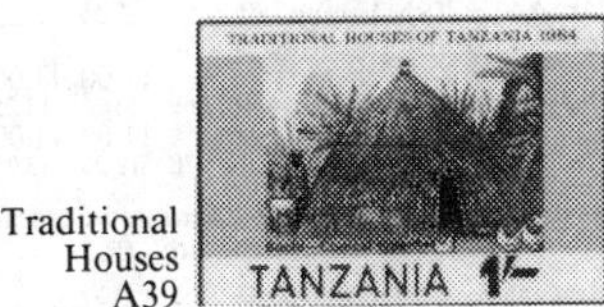


Traditional Houses A39

**1984, Dec. 20 *Perf. 12½x12***

*250* A39 1sh Sochi 12 12
*251* A39 1.50sh Isyenga 20 20
*252* A39 5sh Tembe 65 65
*253* A39 10sh Banda 1.25 1.25
*a* Souvenir sheet of 4, #250-253 2.25 2.25

Textile Industry A40

5th anniversary of the Southern Africa Development Coordination Conference.

**1985, Apr. 1 *Perf. 14***

*254* A40 1.50sh shown 15 15
*255* A40 4sh Mining 45 45
*256* A40 5sh Transportation and communications 55 55
*257* A40 20sh Flags of member nations 2.25 2.25
*a* Souvenir sheet of 4, #254-257 3.25 3.25

Rare Species of Zanzibar A41

***Perf. 13½x13, 13x13½***

**1985, May 8** **Litho.**

*258* A41 1sh Tortoise 12 12
*259* A41 4sh Leopard 45 45
*260* A41 10sh Civet cat 1.10 1.10
*261* A41 17.50sh Red colobus, vert. 2.00 2.00

**Souvenir Sheet**

*262* Sheet of 2 3.75 3.75
*a* A41 15sh Black rhinoceros 1.60 1.60
*b* A41 20sh Giant ground pangolin 2.15 2.15

No. 262 has multicolored margin picturing habitat. Size: 111x94mm.

Automobile Centenary — A42

Classic autos manufactured by Rolls-Royce.

**1985, May 14** ***Perf. 14½x14***

*263* A42 1.50sh 1936 20/25 16 16
*264* A42 5sh 1933 Phantom II 55 55
*265* A42 10sh 1926 Phantom I 1.10 1.10
*266* A42 30sh 1907 Silver Ghost 3.25 3.25
*a* Souvenir sheet of 4, #263-266 5.25 5.25

No. 266a has gray and black decorative margin. Size: 125x92mm.

Queen Mother, 85th Birthday — A43

**1985, Sept. 30**

*267* A43 20sh Waving 2.25 2.25
*268* A43 20sh Facing left 2.25 2.25
*269* A43 100sh Wearing green hat 11.00 11.00
*a* Souvenir sheet of 2, #267, 269 13.25 13.25
*270* A43 100sh Facing right 11.00 11.00
*a* Souvenir sheet of 2, #268, 270 13.25 13.25

Nos. 269a, 270a have multicolored decorative margins. Sizes: 125x62mm.

Tanzania Railways Locomotives — A44

**1985, Oct. 7** **Litho.** ***Perf. 14½x14***

*271* A44 5sh No. 3022 55 55
*272* A44 10sh No. 3107 1.10 1.10
*273* A44 20sh No. 6004 2.15 2.15
*274* A44 30sh No. 3129 3.25 3.25
*a* Souvenir sheet of 4, #271-274 7.05 7.05

No. 274a has multicolored decorative margin. Size: 125x93mm.

Nos. 242-245 Ovptd. with Winners and "GOLD MEDAL" in 2 or 3 Lines.

**1985, Oct. 22** ***Perf. 12½x12***

*275* A37 1sh Henry Tillman, USA 12 12
*276* A37 1.50sh USA 18 18
*277* A37 5sh USA 55 55
*278* A37 20sh France 2.15 2.15
*a* Souvenir sheet of 4, #275-278 3.00 3.00

Pottery A45

**1985, Nov. 4**

*279* A45 1.50sh Water and cooking pots 18 18
*280* A45 2sh Frying pot and caldron 22 22
*281* A45 5sh Woman selling pots 55 55
*282* A45 40sh Beer pot 4.25 4.25

**Souvenir Sheet**

*283* A45 30sh Water pot 3.25 3.25

No. 283 has decorative margin picturing water pots. Size: 130x98mm.

Locomotives — A46

**1985, Nov. 25**

*284* A46 1.50sh Class 64 18 18
*285* A46 2sh Class 36 22 22
*286* A46 5sh Shunting DFH1013 55 55
*287* A46 10sh Diesel Electric DE1001 1.10 1.10
*288* A46 30sh Zanzibar, 1906 3.25 3.25
*Nos. 284-288 (5)* 5.30 5.30

**Souvenir Sheet**

*289* Sheet of 2 3.80 3.80
*a* A46 15sh Class 30 steam 1.65 1.65
*b* A46 20sh Class 11 steam 2.15 2.15

No. 289 has multicolored margin picturing prairie. Size: 130x100mm.

Intl. Youth Year — A47

**1986, Jan. 20** ***Perf. 14***

*290* A47 1.50sh Young Pioneers 18 18
*291* A47 4sh Health care 45 45
*292* A47 10sh Uhuru torch race 1.10 1.10
*293* A47 20sh World map 2.15 2.15

**Souvenir Sheet**

*294* A47 30sh Agriculture 3.25 3.25

No. 294 has bright yellow and black margin picturing emblem. Size: 130x100mm.

Nos. 267-270 Ovptd. "CARIBBEAN/ ROYAL VISIT/ 1985" in Silver.

**1986, Feb. 10** ***Perf. 14½x14***

*295* A43 20sh on #267 2.15 2.15
*296* A43 20sh on #268 2.15 2.15
*297* A43 100sh on #269 11.00 11.00
*a* Souvenir sheet of 2, #295, 297
*298* A43 100sh on #270 11.00 11.00
*a* Souvenir sheet of 2, #296, 298

Nos. 175-178, 208a Ovptd. "75th ANNIVERSARY GIRL GUIDES/ 1910-1985" in Silver or Black.

**1986, Feb.** **Litho.** ***Perf. 13x13½, 14***

*299* A22 50c multi (S)
*300* A22 1sh multi
*301* A22 5sh multi
*302* A22 20sh multi

**Souvenir Sheet**

*303* Sheet of 4
*a* A29 50c multi
*b* A29 1sh multi
*c* A29 10sh multi
*d* A29 20sh multi

Rotary Intl., World Chess Championships — A48

**1986, Mar. 17** ***Perf. 14***

*304* A48 20sh shown 2.40 2.40
*305* A48 100sh Chess board 12.00 12.00
*a* Souvenir sheet of 2, #304-305 14.50 14.50

No. 305a has multicolored decorative margin. Size: 125x64mm.

Audubon Birth Bicent. — A49

Illustrations of American bird species by Audubon.

**1986, May 22**

*306* A49 5sh Mallard 60 60
*307* A49 10sh American eider 1.20 1.20
*308* A49 20sh Scarlet ibis 2.40 2.40
*309* A49 30sh Roseate spoonbill 3.60 3.60
*a* Souvenir sheet of 4, #306-309 7.80 7.80

No. 309a has blue and yellow orange inscribed margin. Size: 120x91mm.

Gemstones A50

**1986, May 22**

*310* A50 1.50sh Pearls 18 18
*311* A50 2sh Sapphires 24 24
*312* A50 5sh Tanzanite 60 60
*313* A50 40sh Diamonds 4.80 4.80

**Souvenir Sheet**

*314* A50 30sh Rubies 3.60 3.60

No. 314 has multicolored margin picturing faceted stones. Size: 130x100mm.

Indigenous Flowers — A51

**1986, June 2**

*315* A51 1.50sh Hibiscus calyphyllus 5 5
*316* A51 5sh Aloe graminicola 35 35
*317* A51 10sh Nersium oleander 70 70
*318* A51 30sh Nymphaea caerulea 2.10 2.10
*a* Souvenir Sheet of 4, #315-318 3.25 3.25

No. 318a has violet and brown orange decorative margin. Size: 89x120mm.

The only foreign revenue stamps listed in this Catalogue are those authorized for prepayment of postage.

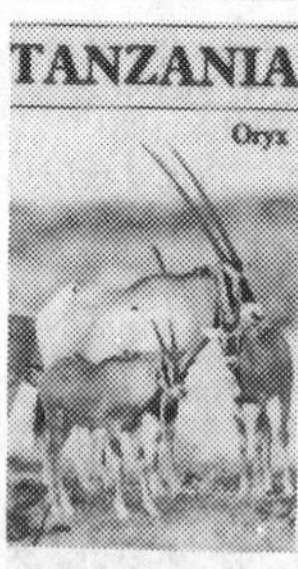


Endangered Wildlife — A52

**1986, June 30** **Litho.** ***Perf. 14x14½***

*319* A52 5sh Oryx 35 35
*320* A52 10sh Giraffe 70 70
*321* A52 20sh Rhinoceros 1.40 1.40
*322* A52 30sh Cheetah 2.10 2.10
*a* Miniature sheet of 4, #319-322 4.55 4.55

No. 322a has rose magenta and light blue decorative margin. Size: 91x121mm.

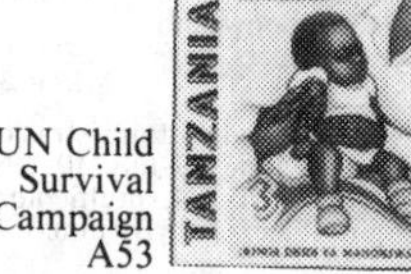


UN Child Survival Campaign A53

**1986, July 29** ***Perf. 12½x12***

*323* A53 1.50sh Immunization 5 5
*324* A53 2sh Growth monitoring 8 8
*325* A53 5sh Oral rehydration therapy 20 20
*326* A53 40sh Breast feeding 1.65 1.65

**Souvenir Sheet**

*327* A53 30sh Healthy child 1.25 1.25

No. 327 has dark ultramarine, yellow bister and black inscribed margin. Size: 111x102mm.

Marine Life — A54

**1986, Aug. 20**

*328* A54 1.50sh Butterflyfish 5 5
*329* A54 4sh Parrotfish 16 16
*330* A54 10sh Sea turtle 40 40
*331* A54 20sh Octopus 85 85

**Souvenir Sheet**

*332* A54 30sh Coral 1.25 1.25

No. 332 has multicolored margin picturing painting of coral. Size: 131x101mm.

Queen Elizabeth II, 60th Birthday — A55

Photographs: 5sh, Royal family, Buckingham Palace balcony. 10sh, With princes in open carriage. 40sh, Elizabeth II. 60sh, Greeting crowd.

**1987, Mar. 24** **Litho.** ***Perf. 14***

*333* A55 5sh multi
*334* A55 10sh multi
*335* A55 40sh multi
*336* A55 60sh multi
*a* Souv. sheet of 4, Nos. 333-336

No. 336a has multicolored decorative margin. Size: 125x91mm.

1986 World Cup Soccer Championships, Mexico — A57

Designs: 1.50sh, Map, team captains, officials. 2sh, Foul. 10sh, Goal. 20sh, Goalie save. 30sh, Argentine natl. team.

**1986, Oct. 30** **Litho.** ***Perf. 14***

| | | | | |
|---|---|---|---|---|
| *341* | A57 | 1.50sh multi | 8 | 8 |
| *342* | A57 | 2sh multi | 10 | 10 |
| *343* | A57 | 10sh multi | 50 | 50 |
| *344* | A57 | 20sh multi | 1.00 | 1.00 |

**Souvenir Sheet**

| | | | | |
|---|---|---|---|---|
| *345* | A57 | 30sh multi | 1.50 | 1.50 |

No. 345 has multicolored margin picturing players and emblem. Size: 95x72mm.

Hair Styles — A58

**1987, Mar. 16** ***Perf. 14½***

| | | | | |
|---|---|---|---|---|
| *346* | A58 | 1.50sh Nungu Nungu | 8 | 8 |
| *347* | A58 | 2sh Upanga wa Jogoo | 10 | 10 |
| *348* | A58 | 10sh Morani | 50 | 50 |
| *349* | A58 | 20sh Twende Kilioni | 1.00 | 1.00 |

**Souvenir Sheet**

| | | | | |
|---|---|---|---|---|
| *350* | A58 | 30sh Kusuka Nywele | 1.50 | 1.50 |

No. 350 has multicolored decorative margin. Size: 109x100mm.

Intl. Peace Year A59

Designs: 1.50sh, Julius K. Nyerere, Beyond War Award winner. 2sh, Peace among nations. 10sh, Peaceful use of outer space. 20sh, Emblem, UN building. 30sh, Emblem, handshake.

**1986, Dec. 22** **Litho.** ***Perf. 14½***

| | | | | |
|---|---|---|---|---|
| *351* | A59 | 1.50sh multi | 8 | 8 |
| *352* | A59 | 2sh multi | 10 | 10 |
| *353* | A59 | 10sh multi | 50 | 50 |
| *354* | A59 | 20sh multi | 1.00 | 1.00 |

**Souvenir Sheet**

| | | | | |
|---|---|---|---|---|
| *355* | A59 | 30sh multi | 1.50 | 1.50 |

No. 355 has decorative multicolored margin. Size: 110x85mm.

Natl. Bank of Commerce, 20th Anniv. — A60

**1987, Feb. 6** **Litho.** ***Perf. 14***

| | | | | |
|---|---|---|---|---|
| *356* | A60 | 1.50sh Mobile bank | 8 | 8 |
| *357* | A60 | 2sh Headquarters | 10 | 10 |
| *358* | A60 | 5sh Pres. Mwinyi laying foundation stone | 25 | 25 |
| *359* | A60 | 20sh Cotton harvest | 1.00 | 1.00 |

New Revolutionary Party (CCM), 10th Anniv. — A61

**1987, Apr. 10** ***Perf. 14½x14***

| | | | | |
|---|---|---|---|---|
| *360* | A61 | 2sh Soldiers in formation | 8 | 8 |
| *361* | A61 | 3sh Woman picking coffee beans | 12 | 12 |
| *362* | A61 | 10sh Speaker at podium | 40 | 40 |
| *363* | A61 | 30sh Nyerere, Mwinyi | 1.25 | 1.25 |

Arush Declaration, 20th anniv.

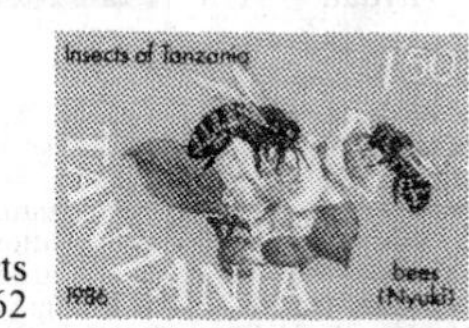

Insects A62

**1987, Apr. 22** ***Perf. 12½x12***

| | | | | |
|---|---|---|---|---|
| *364* | A62 | 1.50sh Bees | 6 | 6 |
| *365* | A62 | 2sh Greater grain borer | 8 | 8 |
| *366* | A62 | 10sh Tse-tse fly | 40 | 40 |
| *367* | A62 | 20sh Wasp | 80 | 80 |

**Souvenir Sheet**

| | | | | |
|---|---|---|---|---|
| *368* | A62 | 30sh Mosquito | 1.25 | 1.25 |

No. 368 has multicolored margin picturing insects, larvae. Size: 112x102mm.

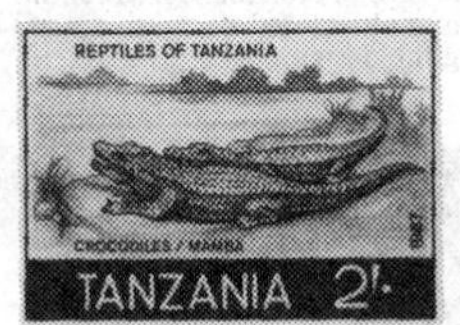

Reptiles A63

**1987, July 2**

| | | | | |
|---|---|---|---|---|
| *369* | A63 | 2sh Crocodiles | 8 | 8 |
| *370* | A63 | 3sh Black-striped grass snake | 12 | 12 |
| *371* | A63 | 10sh Adder | 40 | 40 |
| *372* | A63 | 20sh Green mamba | 80 | 80 |

**Souvenir Sheet**

| | | | | |
|---|---|---|---|---|
| *373* | A63 | 30sh Tortoise | 1.25 | 1.25 |

No. 373 has decorative inscribed margin picturing reptiles. Size: 102x101mm.

Posts and Telecommunications, Railways Emblems — A64

**1987, July 27** ***Perf. 14***

| | | | | |
|---|---|---|---|---|
| *374* | A64 | 2sh shown | 10 | 10 |
| *375* | A64 | 8sh Air Tanzania, Port Authority | 40 | 40 |

**Souvenir Sheet**

| | | | | |
|---|---|---|---|---|
| *376* | A64 | 20sh Modes of communication and transportation | 1.00 | 1.00 |

No. 376 has inscribed multicolored margin. Size: 100x67mm.

Traditional Crafts A65

**1987, Dec. 15** **Litho.** ***Perf. 12½x12***

| | | | | |
|---|---|---|---|---|
| *377* | A65 | 2sh Baskets | 6 | 6 |
| *378* | A65 | 3sh Gourds | 10 | 10 |
| *379* | A65 | 10sh Stools | 30 | 30 |
| *380* | A65 | 20sh Makonde carvings | 60 | 60 |

**Souvenir Sheet**

| | | | | |
|---|---|---|---|---|
| *381* | A65 | 40sh Makonde carver at work | 1.20 | 1.20 |

No. 381 has black inscribed decorative margin. Size: 89x89mm.

Plateosaurus — A66

**1988, Apr. 22** ***Perf. 12½***

| | | | | |
|---|---|---|---|---|
| *382* | A66 | 2sh shown | 6 | 6 |
| *383* | A66 | 3sh Pteranodon | 10 | 10 |
| *384* | A66 | 5sh Brontosaurus | 15 | 15 |
| *385* | A66 | 7sh Lions | 22 | 22 |
| *386* | A66 | 8sh Tiger | 25 | 25 |
| *387* | A66 | 12sh Orangutans | 35 | 35 |
| *388* | A66 | 20sh Elephants | 60 | 60 |
| *389* | A66 | 100sh Stegosaurus | 3.00 | 3.00 |
| | | *Nos. 382-389 (8)* | 4.73 | 4.73 |

Traditional Games A67

**1988, Feb. 15** **Litho.** ***Perf. 12½x12***

| | | | | |
|---|---|---|---|---|
| *390* | A67 | 2sh Mdako (marbles) | 6 | 6 |
| *391* | A67 | 3sh Mieleka (wrestling) | 10 | 10 |
| *392* | A67 | 8sh Bull fight | 25 | 25 |
| *393* | A67 | 20sh Bao (African chess) | 60 | 60 |

**Souvenir Sheet**

| | | | | |
|---|---|---|---|---|
| *394* | A67 | 30sh Kulenga shabaha (archery) | 90 | 90 |

Dated 1987. No. 394 has decorative margin. Size: 101x91mm.

### Miniature Sheets

Statue of Liberty, Cent. (in 1986) — A68

No. 395: 1sh, Re-opening gala (evening), 1986. 2sh, Musicians performing. 3sh, Cheerleaders. 15sh, Statue holding tablet. 30sh, Tablet inscription. 40sh, Liberty Island. 50sh, Re-opening gala (afternoon), 1986. 60sh, Blimps over Liberty Island.

No. 396: 4sh, Statue, blimp. 5sh, Torch. 6sh, Torch and crown obeservatories lit at night, scaffolding. 7sh, Worker gilding torch. 8sh, Statue shrouded in scaffolding. 10sh, Two workers, torch. 12sh, Head, scaffolding. 18sh, Celebrant at re-opening (evening). 20sh, Goodyear blimp, skirt of Statue. 25sh, Boys' choir, statue. 35sh, Torch held aloft, full moon. 45sh, Worker cleaning tablet.

**1988, June 15** **Litho.** ***Perf. 14***

| | | | |
|---|---|---|---|
| *395* | Sheet of 8 + label | 6.00 | 6.00 |
| ***a.*** | A68 1sh multi | 5 | 5 |
| ***b.*** | A68 2sh multi | 5 | 5 |
| ***c.*** | A68 3sh multi | 10 | 10 |
| ***d.*** | A68 15sh multi | 45 | 45 |
| ***e.*** | A68 30sh multi | 90 | 90 |
| ***f.*** | A68 40sh multi | 1.20 | 1.20 |
| ***g.*** | A68 50sh multi | 1.50 | 1.50 |
| ***h.*** | A68 60sh multi | 1.75 | 1.75 |
| *396* | Sheet of 12 | 5.85 | 5.85 |
| ***a.*** | A68 4sh multi | 12 | 12 |
| ***b.*** | A68 5sh multi | 15 | 15 |
| ***c.*** | A68 6sh multi | 18 | 18 |
| ***d.*** | A68 7sh multi | 20 | 20 |
| ***e.*** | A68 8sh multi | 24 | 24 |
| ***f.*** | A68 10sh multi | 30 | 30 |
| ***g.*** | A68 12sh multi | 35 | 35 |
| ***h.*** | A68 18sh multi | 55 | 55 |
| ***i.*** | A68 20sh multi | 60 | 60 |
| ***j.*** | A68 25sh multi | 75 | 75 |
| ***k.*** | A68 35sh multi | 1.05 | 1.05 |
| ***l.*** | A68 45sh multi | 1.35 | 1.35 |

No. 395 contains a center label inscribed "THE STATUE / OF LIBERTY / 100th ANNIVERSARY." Sizes: 172x122mm, 123x214mm.

Natl. Monuments — A69

**1988, June 15** **Litho.**

| | | | | |
|---|---|---|---|---|
| *397* | A69 | 5sh Independence Torch | 15 | 15 |
| *398* | A69 | 12sh Arusha Declaration | 35 | 35 |
| *399* | A69 | 30sh Askari | 85 | 85 |
| *400* | A69 | 60sh Independence | 1.75 | 1.75 |

**Souvenir Sheet**

| | | | | |
|---|---|---|---|---|
| *401* | A69 | 100sh Soldier (Askari detail) | 3.00 | 3.00 |

No. 401 has multicolored margin picturing the Independence Monument. Size: 100x89mm.

3rd Natl. Census, Aug. 28 — A70

**1988, Aug. 8**

| | | | | |
|---|---|---|---|---|
| *402* | A70 | 2sh shown | 6 | 6 |
| *403* | A70 | 3sh Enumeration | 8 | 8 |
| *404* | A70 | 10sh Health care | 28 | 28 |
| *405* | A70 | 20sh Population figures | 58 | 58 |

**Souvenir Sheet**

| | | | | |
|---|---|---|---|---|
| *405A* | A70 | 40sh Segments of economy and society | 1.20 | 1.20 |

No. 405A has multicolored inscribed margin picturing outline map and natl. colors. Size: 97x91mm.

Stamps of 1983-86 Ovptd:
*a.* "125TH ANNIVERSARY / INTERNATIONAL RED CROSS / AND RED CRESCENT"
*b.* "40TH WEDDING ANNIVERSARY / H.M. QUEEN ELIZABETH II / H.R.H. THE DUKE OF EDINBURGH"
*c.* "63RD ANNIVERSARY / ROTARY INTERNATIONAL / IN AFRICA"

***Perfs. as before***

**1988, Aug. 15** **Litho.**

| | | | | |
|---|---|---|---|---|
| *406* | A53(a) | 5sh on No. 325 | 15 | 15 |
| *407* | CD334(b) | 10sh on No. 220 | 30 | 30 |
| ***a.*** | | Souv. sheet of 4, Nos. 218-220, 407 | 50 | 50 |
| *408* | A41(c) | 10sh on No. 260 | 30 | 30 |
| *409* | A41(c) | 17.50sh on No. 261 | 55 | 55 |
| *410* | A53(a) | 40sh on No. 326 | 1.20 | 1.20 |
| | | *Nos. 406-410 (5)* | 2.50 | 2.50 |

**Souvenir Sheets**

| | | | | |
|---|---|---|---|---|
| *411* | | Sheet of 2 | 1.05 | 1.05 |
| ***a.*** | A41(c) | 15sh on No. 262a | 45 | 45 |
| ***b.*** | A41(c) | 20sh on No. 262b | 60 | 60 |
| *412* | A53(a) | 30sh on No. 327 | 90 | 90 |

1988 Olympics, Seoul and Calgary — A71

**1988, Aug. 29** ***Perf. 14***

*414* A71 5sh Biathlon 15 15
*415* A71 10sh Soccer 30 30
*416* A71 20sh Cycling 58 58
*417* A71 25sh Pairs figuring skating 72 72
*418* A71 50sh Fencing 1.45 1.45
*419* A71 50sh Downhill skiing 1.45 1.45
*420* A71 70sh Volleyball 2.00 2.00
*421* A71 75sh Bobsled 2.15 2.15
*Nos. 414-421 (8)* 8.80 8.80

**Souvenir Sheets**

*422* A71 100sh Flags, hockey sticks 3.00 3.00
*423* A71 100sh Gymnastics 3.00 3.00

Nos. 422-423 have multicolored decorative margins picturing Olympic medal. Sizes: 77x92mm.

Disney Characters, Special Occasions — A72

**1988, Sept. 9** ***Perf.***

*424* A72 4sh Love You, Dad 12 12
*425* A72 5sh Happy Birthday 15 15
*426* A72 10sh Trick or Treat 30 30
*427* A72 12sh Be Kind to Animals 38 38
*428* A72 15sh Love 45 45
*429* A72 20sh Let's Celebrate 60 60
*430* A72 30sh Keep In Touch 90 90
*431* A72 50sh Love You, Mom 1.50 1.50
*Nos. 424-431 (8)* 4.40 4.40

**Souvenir Sheet**

*432* A72 150sh Let's Work Together 4.50 4.50
*433* A72 150sh Have a Super Sunday 4.50 4.50

Mickey Mouse, 60th anniv. Nos. 432-433 have multicolored margins continuing the designs. Sizes: 127x102mm.

Domestic Animals A73

**1988, Sept. 9** ***Perf.***

*434* A73 4sh Goat, vert. 12 12
*435* A73 5sh Rabbit 15 15
*436* A73 8sh Cows 24 24
*437* A73 10sh Cat 30 30
*438* A73 12sh Horse, vert. 38 38
*439* A73 20sh Dog, vert. 60 60
*Nos. 434-439 (6)* 1.79 1.79

**Souvenir Sheet**

*440* A73 100sh Chicken 3.00 3.00

No. 440 has multicolored inscribed margin picturing a lamb and chick. Size: 103x73mm.

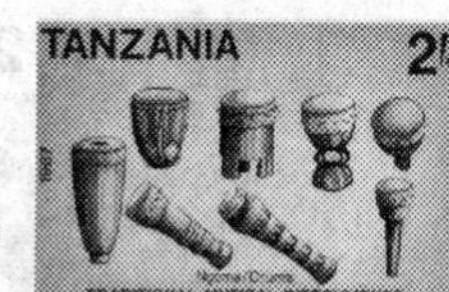


Traditional Musical Instruments — A74

**1988, Sept. 30 Litho.** ***Perf. 14***

*441* A74 2sh Drums 6 6
*442* A74 3sh Xylophones 10 10
*443* A74 10sh Thumb pianos 30 30
*444* A74 20sh Fiddles 60 60

**Souvenir Sheet**

*445* A74 40sh Violins with calabash resonators 1.20 1.20

Dated 1987. No. 445 has multicolored decorative margin picturing two perspectives of additional instruments. Size: 90x80mm.

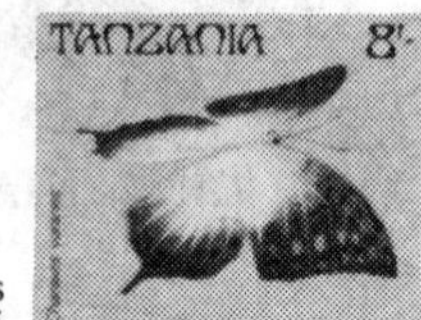


Butterflies A75

**1988, Oct. 17** ***Perf. 14½***

*446* A75 8sh Charaxes varanes 24 24
*447* A75 30sh Neptis melicerta 90 90
*448* A75 40sh Mylothris chloris 1.20 1.20
*449* A75 50sh Charaxes bohemani 1.50 1.50
*450* A75 60sh Myrina ficedula 1.80 1.80
*451* A75 75sh Papilio phorcas 2.25 2.25
*452* A75 90sh Cyrestis camillus 2.70 2.70
*453* A75 100sh Salamis temora 3.00 3.00
*Nos. 446-453 (8)* 13.59 13.59

**Souvenir Sheets**

*454* A75 200sh Asterope rosa 6.00 6.00
*455* A75 250sh Kallima rumia 7.50 7.50

Nos. 454-455 have multicolored margins continuing the designs. Sizes: 79x50mm.

Intl. Lions Club at Dar es Salaam, 25th Anniv. A76

**1988, Nov. 30 Litho.** ***Perf. 14½***

*456* A76 2sh Eye operation 6 6
*457* A76 3sh Shallow water well 10 10
*458* A76 7sh Map, rhinoceros 22 22
*459* A76 12sh Donating school desks 35 35

**Souvenir Sheet**

*460* A76 40sh Emblem 1.20 1.20

Community services: Matibabu Ya Macho Eye Camp (2sh); sanitary water supply in Dar es Salaam (3sh); wildlife conservation (7sh); aid to local schools (12sh).

No. 460 has multicolored margin picturing emblems and inscribed "We Serve" and "Embrace Lionism with Pride & Dignity." Size: 100x65mm.

Intl. Red Cross and Red Crescent Organizations, 125th Annivs. — A77

Design: 2sh, Assisting the wounded and sick. 3sh, Postnatal care clinic. 7sh, Red Cross flag. 12sh, Jean-Henry Dunant, founder. 40sh, Dunant, Thomas Maunier, Louis Appia, Gustave Moynier and Gen. Guillaume Henri Dufour, members of intl. committee that sponsored the conference in 1863 where the Red Cross was founded.

**1988, Dec. 30 Litho.** ***Perf. 12½x12***

*461* A77 2sh multi 5 5
*462* A77 3sh multi 6 6
*463* A77 7sh multi 15 15
*464* A77 12sh multi 25 25

**Souvenir Sheet**

*465* A77 40sh multi 80 80

**Miniature Sheet**

Paradise Whydah — A78

Birds: a, Paradise whydah. b, Black-collared barbet. c, Bataleur eagle. d, Openbill storks, lilac-breasted roller. e, Scarlet-tufted malachite sunbird. f, Dark chanting goshawk. g, White-fronted bee-eater, little bee-eater, carmine bee-eater. h, Marabou stork, Narina's trocon. i, African gray parrot. j, Hoopoe. k, Yellow-collared lovebird. l, Yellow-billed hornbill. m, Hammerkop. n, Flamingos, violet-crested turaco. o, Malachite kingfisher. p, Greater flamingo. q, Yellow-billed stork. r, Shoebill stork. s, Saddle-billed stork, blacksmith plover. t, Crowned crane.

**1989, Jan. 10** ***Perf. 14***

*466* Sheet of 20 8.00 8.00
*a.-t.* A78 20sh any single 40 40

**Souvenir Sheet**

*467* A78 350sh Helmeted guineafowl 7.00 7.00

Nos. 466a-466t printed se-tenant in a continuous design. Size of No. 466: 182x182mm.

No. 467 has multicolored decorative margin continuing the design.

Endangered Species
A79 A80

World Wildlife Fund: Various bushbabies, *Galago zanzibaricus*. 350sh, African palm civet.

**1989, Jan. 24** ***Perf. 14***

*468* A79 5sh shown 10 10
*469* A79 10sh multi, horiz. 20 20
*470* A79 20sh multi, diff. 40 40
*471* A79 45sh multi, diff., horiz. 90 90

**Souvenir Sheet**

*472* A79 350sh multi, horiz. 7.00 7.00

No. 472 has multicolored margin continuing the design.

**1989, Jan. 24** ***Perf.***

Designs: 30sh, Black cobra, umbrella acacia. 70sh, Red-tailed tropic bird, tree fern. 100sh, African tree frog, cocoa tree. 150sh, African black-necked heron, Egyptian papyrus. 350sh, Pink-backed pelicans, baobab tree.

*473* A80 30sh shown 60 60
*474* A80 70sh multi 1.40 1.40
*475* A80 100sh multi 2.00 2.00
*476* A80 150sh multi 3.00 3.00

**Souvenir Sheet**

*477* A80 350sh multi 7.00 7.00

No. 477 has multicolored margin continuing the design.

## SEMI-POSTAL STAMPS

Natl. Solidarity Walk — SP1

**1988, July 1 Litho.** ***Perf.***

*B1* SP1 2sh +1sh Flag, crowd 10 10
*B2* SP1 3sh +1sh Map, Pres. Mwinyi 12 12

**Souvenir Sheet**

*B3* SP1 50sh+1sh Flag, Pres. Mwinyi 1.55 1.55

Surtax for Chama Cha Mapinduzi party activities. No. B3 has multicolored inscribed margin. Size:

## POSTAGE DUE STAMPS

Type of Kenya, 1967

***Perf. 14x13½, 14x15, 15, 14x14½***

**1967, Jan. 3 Litho. Unwmk.**

*J1* D1 5c red 5 5
*J2* D1 10c green 5 5
*J3* D1 20c dk bl 8 8
*J4* D1 30c redsh brn 10 10
*J5* D1 40c brt rose lil 12 12
*J6* D1 1sh orange 30 30
*Nos. J1-J6 (6)* 70 70

Nos. J1-J6 were reissued in 1969-71 with perf. 14x15; in 1973 with perf. 15, and in 1978 with perf. 14x14½.

## OFFICIAL STAMPS

Nos. 5-9, 11, 13 and 16 Overprinted: "OFFICIAL"

***Perf. 14x14½, 14½x14***

**1965, Dec. 9 Photo. Unwmk.**

**Size: 21x17½mm, 17½x21mm**

*O1* A2 5c org & ultra 5 5
*O2* A2 10c multi 5 5
*O3* A3 15c grn bl brn & buff 6 6
*O4* A2 20c bl & brn 8 5
*O5* A3 30c blk & red brn 10 6
*O6* A2 50c yel grn & blk 15 8

***Perf. 14½***

**Size: 41½x25**

*O7* A2 1sh multi 30 15
*O8* A2 5sh bl, brt grn & red brn 1.50 1.00
*Nos. O1-O8 (8)* 2.29 1.50

Overprint size: 17mm on 5c, 10c, 20c, 50c. 14mm on 15c, 30c. 29x3½mm on 1sh, 5sh.

The overprint was also applied in 1967 in Dar es Salaam to 50c, 1sh and 5sh. Size: 29x3mm.

Nos. 19-23, 25, 27 and 30 Overprinted: "OFFICIAL"

**1967, Dec. 9 Photo.** ***Perf. 14x14½***

**Fish in Natural Colors**

**Size: 21x17½mm**

**Overprint Litho., 17mm Wide**

*O9* A4 5c blk & cit 5 5
*O10* A4 10c brn & ol 5 5
*O11* A4 15c brn & bl 5 5
*O12* A4 20c brn & dk bl grn 6 5
*O13* A4 30c blk & yel grn 10 5
*O14* A4 50c blk & dl bl grn 20 10

***Perf. 14½***

**Size: 41x25mm**

**Overprint 29mm Wide**

*O15* A4 1sh brn & multi 40 15
*O16* A4 5sh blk & bl grn 1.75 1.25
*Nos. O9-O16 (8)* 2.66 1.75

**1970-73**

**Overprint Typo., 17½mm Wide**

*O9a* A4 5c blk & cit 6 5
*O10a* A4 10c brn & ol 10 5
*O12a* A4 20c brn & dk bl grn 15 12

*O13a* A4 30c blk & yel grn 30 22
*O13B* A4 40c multi ('73)

The overprint was also applied in 1973 to 15c, 50c, 1sh (28mm wide), and 5sh.

Nos. 35-36, 38, 40-41, 43-47 Overprinted

**OFFICIAL** a　**OFFICIAL** b

**1973, Dec. 10 Photo. *Perf. 14½x14***

*O17* A5(a) 5c multi 5 5
*O18* A5(a) 10c multi 5 5
*O19* A5(a) 20c multi 5 5
*O20* A5(a) 40c multi 8 8
*O21* A5(a) 50c multi 10 10
*O22* A5(a) 70c multi 15 15

***Perf. 14½***

*O23* A6(b) 1sh multi 18 18
*O24* A6(b) 1.50sh multi 30 30
*O25* A6(b) 2.50sh multi 50 50
*O26* A6(b) 5sh multi 1.00 1.00
*Nos. O17-O26 (10)* 2.46 2.46

A larger overprint (17½mm wide instead of 14½mm) was applied locally to 10c, 20c, 40c, and 50c.

Nos. 161-167, 169-171 Overprinted: OFFICIAL

**1980, Oct. 1 *Perf. 14***

*O27* A21 10c multi 5 5
*O28* A21 20c multi 5 5
*O29* A21 40c multi 8 8
*O30* A21 50c multi 10 10
*O31* A21 75c multi 15 15
*O32* A21 80c multi 18 18

***Perf. 14½***

*O33* A21 1sh multi 20 20
*O34* A21 2sh multi 40 40
*O35* A21 3sh multi 60 60
*O36* A21 5sh multi 1.00 1.00
*Nos. O27-O36 (10)* 2.81 2.81

Overprint measures 13mm on Nos. O33-O36; reads up or down.

## TASMANIA

LOCATION — An island off the southeastern coast of Australia.
GOVT. — A former British Colony.
AREA — 26,215 sq. mi.
POP. — 172,475 (1901).
CAPITAL — Hobart.

Tasmania was one of the six British colonies that united in 1901 to form the Commonwealth of Australia. The island was originally named Van Diemen's Land by its discoverer, Abel Tasman, the present name having been adopted in 1853. Stamps of Australia are now used.

12 Pence = 1 Shilling
20 Shillings = 1 Pound

Values of early Tasmania stamps vary according to condition. Quotations for Nos. 1-16 are for fine copies. Very fine to superb specimens sell at much higher prices, and inferior or poor copies sell at reduced prices, depending on the condition of the individual specimen.

Queen Victoria
A1　A2

**Unwmk.**

**1853, Nov. 1 Engr. *Imperf.***

*1* A1 1p blue 3,250. 450.00
*2* A2 4p red orange 2,150. 200.00
**a.** 4p yellow orange 2.250. 200.00
Cut to shape 1.75

Twentyfour varieties of each.

*The reprints are made from defaced plates and show marks across the face of each stamp. They are on thin and thick, unwatermarked paper and thin cardboard; only the first are perforated. Nearly all the reprints of Tasmania may be found with and without the overprint "REPRINT".*

*Nos. 1-47A with pen or revenue cancellations sell for a small fraction of the price of postally used specimens. Copies are found with pen cancellation removed.*

Queen Victoria — A3

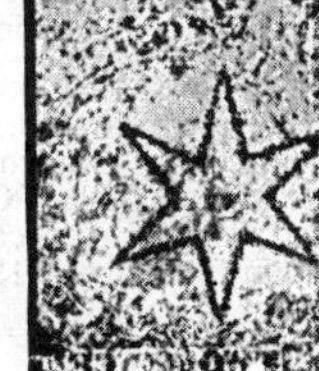

Wmk. 6- Large Star

**1855 Wmk. 6 Wove Paper**

*4* A3 1p dk carmine 6,000. 825.00
*5* A3 2p deep green 1,800. 350.00
*6* A3 4p deep blue 1,250. 52.50

**1856-57 Unwmk.**

*7* A3 1p pale red 6,000. 400.00
*8* A3 2p emerald ('57) 7,200. 900.00
*9* A3 4p blue ('57) 750.00 55.00

**1856 Pelure Paper**

*10* A3 1p brown red 2,400. 400.00

Wmk. 49- Double-lined Numeral

Wmk. 75- Double-lined Numeral

**1857 Wmk. 49, 75**

*11* A3 1p carmine 70.00 10.00
**a.** 1p orange red 85.00 10.00
**b.** 1p brown red 400.00 21.00
**c.** Double impression 165.00
*12* A3 2p green 175.00 30.00
**a.** 2p yellow green 250.00 40.00
**b.** 2p sage green 130.00 35.00
*13* A3 4p blue 130.00 12.00
**b.** Printed on both sides

A4

A4a

**1858**

*14* A4 6p gray lilac 100.00 20.00
**a.** 6p red violet 600.00 125.00
**b.** Double impression 75.00
*15* A4 6p blue gray 125.00 32.50
*16* A4a 1sh vermilion 325.00 40.00

No. 15 watermarked large star was not regularly issued.

**1864 *Rouletted***

*17* A3 1p carmine 375.00 125.00
**a.** 1p brick red 180.00
*18* A3 2p yellow grn 275.00
*19* A3 4p blue 180.00
*21* A4 6p gray lilac 225.00
*22* A4a 1sh vermilion 625.00

**1864-69 *Perf. 10***

*23* A3 1p brick red 45.00 12.50
**a.** 1p carmine 45.00 12.50
**b.** 1p orange red 45.00 12.50
*24* A3 2p yellow grn 275.00 55.00
**a.** 2p sage green 375.00 150.00
*25* A3 4p blue 125.00 9.00
**a.** Double impression 125.00
*26* A4 6p lilac 125.00 10.50
**a.** 6p red lilac 375.00 55.00
*27* A4 6p slate blue 160.00 12.50
*28* A4a 1sh vermilion 100.00 10.50
**a.** Imperf. vertically

**1864-69 *Perf. 11½, 12, 12½, 13***

*29* A3 1p carmine 20.00 6.00
**a.** 1p orange red 30.00 14.00
**b.** 1p brick red 42.50 40.00
**c.** Double impression 82.50
**d.** Wmkd. "2" 650.00
As "d", pen cancel 165.00
*30* A3 2p yellow grn 130.00 35.00
**a.** 2p dark green 100.00 35.00
**b.** 2p sage green 250.00 115.00
*31* A3 4p blue 65.00 6.00
*32* A4 6p red lilac 45.00 13.00
**a.** 6p purple 60.00 16.00
**b.** 6p violet 65.00 16.00
**d.** Horiz. pair, imperf. vert.
**e.** Double impression 100.00
*33* A4 6p slate blue 180.00 20.00
*34* A4a 1sh vermilion 100.00 12.50
**a.** Double impression 120.00
**b.** Horiz. pair, imperf. vert.

*The reprints are on unwatermarked paper, perforated 11½, and on thin cardboard, imperforate and perforated.*

***Pin-perf. 5½ to 9½, 13½ to 14½***

**1867**

*35* A3 1p carmine 350.00 76.50
*36* A3 2p yellow grn 275.00
*37* A3 4p blue 165.00
*38* A4 6p gray 150.00
*38A* A4 6p red lilac 450.00
*38B* A4a 1sh vermilion 650.00

***Oblique Roulette***

*39* A3 1p carmine 165.00
*40* A3 2p yellow grn 410.00
*41* A3 4p blue 325.00
*42* A4 6p gray 550.00
*43* A4 6p red lilac 350.00
*44* A4a 1sh vermilion 750.00

**1868 *Serrate Perf. 19***

*45* A3 1p carmine 225.00 90.00
*46* A3 2p yellow grn 175.00
*47* A3 4p blue 650.00 82.500
*47A* A3 6p purple 500.00

Queen Victoria — A5

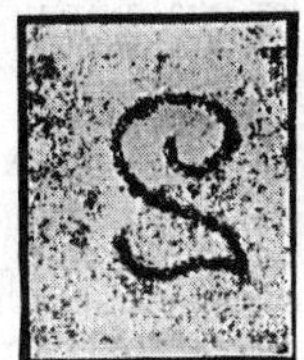

Wmk. 50- Single-lined "2"

**1870-71 Typo. Wmk. 50 *Perf. 12***

*48* A5 2p green 65.00 6.50
**a.** Imperf.
**b.** Perf. 11½ 50.00 5.00
**c.** Double impression

Wmk. 51- Single-lined "4"

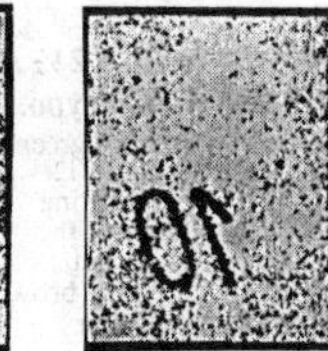

Wmk. 52- Single-lined "10"

**Wmk. 51**

*49* A5 1p rose ('71) 52.50 20.00
**a.** Imperf., pair 600.00 215.00
*50* A5 4p blue 725.00 300.00

**Wmk. 52**

*51* A5 1p rose 40.00 9.00
**a.** Imperf. pair 265.00 250.00
**c.** Perf. 11½ 1.000.
*52* A5 10p black 11.50 6.00
**a.** Imperf. pair 120.00
**b.** Perf. 11½ 21.00 20.00

*The reprints are on unwatermarked paper. The 4 pence has also been reprinted on thin cardboard, imperforate and perforated.*

Wmk. 76- TAS

Wmk. 77- TAS

**1871-76 Wmk. 76 *Perf. 11½***

*53* A5 1p rose 4.00 60
**a.** Imperf.
**c.** Perf. 12 60.00 9.00
*53B* A5 1p ver ('73) 210.00 75.00
*54* A5 2p deep grn ('72) 12.00 60
**a.** 2p yellow green 120.00 1.25
**b.** 2p blue green 45.00 60
**c.** Imperf. pair 120.00
**d.** 2p green, perf. 12 450.00 135.00
**e.** Double impression
*55* A5 3p brown 27.50 4.50
**a.** 3p purple brown 30.00 4.50
**b.** As "a," imperf. pair 325.00
*56* A5 3p red brn ('71) 30.00 4.50
**a.** 3p indian red 35.00 4.50
**b.** Imperf. pair 120.00
**c.** Vert. pair, imperf. horiz.
**d.** Perf. 12 75.00 21.00
*57* A5 4p dull yel ('76) 30.00 7.50
**a.** Perf. 12 225.00 15.00
*58* A5 9p blue 15.00 7.50
**a.** Imperf. pair 120.00
**b.** Perf. 12 30.00 30.00
*59* A5 5sh bright vio 105.00 25.00
**a.** Imperf.
**b.** Horiz. pair, imperf. vert.
**c.** Perf. 12 175.00 150.00
Pen cancel 30

*The reprints are on unwatermarked paper, the 5 shillings has also been reprinted on thin cardboard; all are perforated.*

**1878 Wmk. 77 *Perf. 14***

*60* A5 1p rose 4.50 60
*61* A5 2p deep green 4.50 60
*62* A5 8p violet brn 10.50 4.50

*The 8 pence has been reprinted on thin unwatermarked paper, perforated 11½.*

**1880-83 *Perf. 12, 11½***

*63* A5 3p indian red, perf. 12 4.75 2.00
**a.** Imperf. pair 85.00
**b.** Horiz. pair, imperf. between 600.00
**c.** Perf. 11½ 10.50 3.00
*64* A5 4p lem, perf. 11½ ('83) 30.00 7.50
**a.** 4p olive yel, perf. 11½ 85.00 21.00
**b.** Printed on both sides 210.00
**c.** Imperf.
**d.** 4p deep yel, perf. 12 60.00 22.50

Type of 1871 Surcharged in Black **Halfpenny**

**1889 *Perf. 14***

*65* A5 ½p on 1p car 2.25 1.75
**a.** "al" sideways in surcharge 825.00 *500.00*

*No. 65 has been reprinted on thin cardboard, perforated 12, with the surcharge "Half penny" 19mm. long.*

**1889-96 *Perf. 11½***

*66* A5 ½p red orange 2.00 65
**a.** ½p yellow orange 2.00 65
**b.** Perf. 12 2.00 85
*67* A5 1p dull red 8.25 2.00
**a.** 1p vermilion 5.00 2.00
*68* A5 1p car, perf. 12 8.25 3.25
**a.** 1p pink, perf. 12 27.50 5.00
**b.** 1p salmon rose, perf. 12 8.25 3.25
**c.** Imperf. pair 92.50 92.50

***Perf. 12***

*69* A5 4p bister ('96) 14.00 8.25
*70* A5 9p chlky bl ('96) 8.25 3.25

**1891 Wmk. 76 *Perf. 11½***

*71* A5 ½p orange 16.00 8.25
**a.** ½p brown orange 16.00 8.25
**b.** Imperf. pair 82.50
**c.** Perf. 12 18.00 9.25
*72* A5 1p salmon rose 20.00 11.50
**a.** 1p carmine, perf. 12 40.00 20.00
*73* A5 4p ol bis, perf. 12 13.00 6.50

See Nos. 98, 108-109.

Surcharged in Black **d. 2½**

*Tasmania stamps can be mounted in Scott's Australia and Dependencies Album.*

**1891** **Wmk. 77** ***Perf. 11½***

**Surcharge 14mm. High**

*74* A5 2½p on 9p lt bl 4.25 4.50
**a.** Dbl. surcharge, one invtd. 210.00 200.00
**b.** Imperf. pair 135.00

***Perf. 12***

**Surcharge 15mm. High**

*75* A5 2½p on 9p lt bl 3.25 3.25
**a.** Surcharged in blue

*No. 74 has been reprinted on thin unwatermarked paper, imperforate. There is also a reprint on thin cardboard, in deep ultramarine, with surcharge 16½mm. high, and perforated 12.*

A8

A9

**1892-99** **Typo.** ***Perf. 14***

*76* A8 ½p org & vio 75 38
*77* A9 2½p magenta 2.25 75
*78* A8 5p pale bl & brn 3.00 1.50
*79* A8 6p bl vio & blk 1.90 1.65
*80* A8 10p red brn & green ('99) 5.75 4.75
*81* A8 1sh rose & green 4.00 1.50
*82* A8 2sh6p brown & bl 15.00 7.50
*83* A8 5sh brn vio & red 20.00 18.00
*84* A8 10sh brt vio & brn 67.50 37.50
*85* A8 £1 green & yel 550.00 300.00
*Nos. 76-85 (10)* 670.15 373.53

No. 80 shows the numeral on white tablet. See Nos. 99, 110-111.

Lake Marion A10

Mt. Wellington A11

Tasman's Arch — A13

View of Hobart — A12

Spring River, Port Davey — A14

Russell Falls — A15

Mt. Gould and Lake St. Clair — A16

Dilston Falls — A17

*Tobago stamps can be mounted in Scott's British East Caribbean Album.*

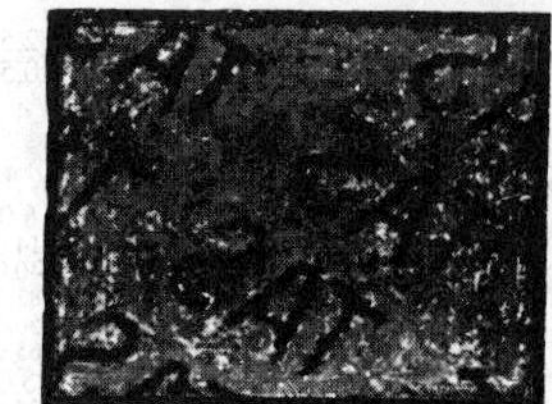
Wmk. 78- Multiple TAS

**1899-1900** **Engr.** **Wmk. 78** ***Perf. 14***

*86* A10 ½p dark green 75 35
*87* A11 1p carmine 75 28
*88* A12 2p violet 1.50 10
*89* A13 2½p dark blue 6.00 3.25
*90* A14 3p dark brown 6.00 1.00
*91* A15 4p ocher 12.00 1.40
*92* A16 5p ultramarine 13.00 3.75
*93* A17 6p lake 17.50 3.50
*Nos. 86-93 (8)* 57.50 13.63

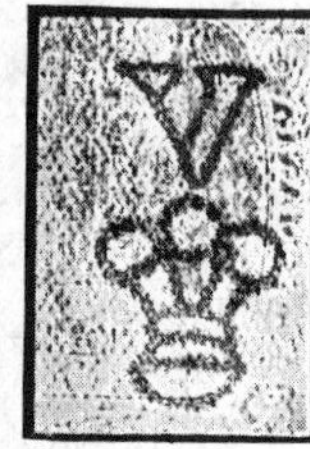
Wmk. 70- V and Crown

Wmk. 13- Crown & Double-lined A

***Perf. 11, 12½, 11x12½***

**1902-03** **Litho., Typo.** **Wmk. 70**

*94* A10 ½p green 1.25 30
*95* A11 1p carmine 1.65 12
*96* A11 1p dull red 1.75 20
*97* A12 2p violet 1.10 10
*98* A5 9p blue 6.25 3.00
**a.** 9p ultramarine 225.00
**b.** 9p indigo 90.00
**c.** Perf. 11 7.25 3.50
*99* A8 1sh rose & grn 8.50 5.00
**a.** Perf. 11 27.50 27.50
*Nos. 94-99 (6)* 20.50 8.72

Nos. 94 and 97 are lithographed, Nos. 96, 98-99 typographed. No. 95 was printed both ways.

No. 78 Surcharged in Black **1½d.**

**1904** **Wmk. 77** ***Perf. 14***

*100* A8 1½p on 5p bl & brn 1.50 1.25

***Perf. 11, 12, 12½ and Compound***

**1905-08** **Typo.** **Wmk. 13**

*102* A10 ½p dull green 65 10
**a.** Booklet pane of 12
*103* A11 1p carmine 65 5
**a.** Booklet pane of 18
*104* A12 2p violet 1.25 5
*105* A14 3p dark brown 3.80 75
*106* A15 4p ocher 6.25 1.25
*107* A17 6p lake 10.00 3.00
*108* A5 8p violet brown 6.25 2.50
*109* A5 9p blue 4.00 2.00
*110* A8 1sh rose & green 5.00 1.75
*111* A8 10sh brt vio & brn 87.50 62.50
**a.** Perf. 11 175.00
*Nos. 102-111 (10)* 125.35 73.95

Lithograph printings were also made of Nos. 104 to 107.

**1911** **Redrawn**

*114* A12 2p bright vio 1.50 15
*115* A15 4p dl yellow 11.50 2.00
*116* A17 6p lake 13.00 4.00

The redrawn 2p measures 33½x25mm. instead of 32½x24½mm. There are many slight changes in the clouds and other parts of the design.

The 4p is much lighter, especially the waterfall and trees above it. This appears to be a new or cleaned plate rather than a redrawn one.

In the redrawn 6p there are more colored lines in the waterfall and the river and more white dots in the trees.

No. 114 Surcharged in Red ***ONE PENNY***

**1912**

*117* A12 1p on 2p brt vio 85 50

## TOBAGO

LOCATION — An island in the West Indies lying off the Venezuelan coast north of Trinidad.
GOVT. — A former British Colony
AREA — 116 sq. mi.
POP. — 25,358.
CAPITAL — Scarborough (Port Louis).

In 1889 Tobago, then an independent colony, was united with Trinidad under the name of Colony of Trinidad and Tobago. It became a ward of that colony January 1, 1899.

12 Pence = 1 Shilling
20 Shillings = 1 Pound

Queen Victoria
A1 A2

**Wmk. Crown and C. C. (1)**

**1879** **Typo.** ***Perf. 14***

*1* A1 1p rose 20.00 16.00
*2* A1 3p blue 24.00 20.00
*3* A1 6p orange 17.50 16.00
*4* A1 1sh green 250.00 40.00
**a.** Half used as 6p on cover
*5* A1 5sh slate 450.00 600.00
*6* A1 £1 violet *3,250.*

Stamps of the above set with revenue cancellations sell for a small fraction of the price of postally used copies.

Stamps of Type A1, watermarked Crown and C. A., are revenue stamps.

**1880**

**Manuscript Surcharge**

*7* A1 1p on half of 6p org *6,250.* 800.00

**1880**

*8* A2 ½p brn violet 13.50 20.00
*9* A2 1p red brown 32.50 16.00
**a.** Half used as ½p on cover *1,650.*
*10* A2 4p yellow grn 150.00 22.50
**a.** Half used as 2p on cover *1,650.*
*11* A2 6p bister brn 180.00 82.50
*12* A2 1sh bister 32.50 18.00
**a.** Imperf.

No. 11 Surcharged in Black **2½ PENCE**

**1883**

*13* A2 2½p on 6p bis brn 10.00 7.50
**a.** Double surch. 3,000. 1,350.

**1882-96** **Wmk. Crown and C. A. (2)**

*14* A2 ½p brn vio ('83) 1.90 *9.75*
*15* A2 ½p dl grn ('86) 22 28
*16* A2 1p red brn ('82) 2.00 1.90
**a.** Diagonal half used as ½p on cover
*17* A2 1p rose ('86) 28 28
*18* A2 2½p ultra ('83) 1.10 80
*19* A2 4p yel grn ('84) 135.00 55.00
*20* A2 4p gray ('85) 55 80
**a.** Imperf., pair 1,800.
*21* A2 6p bis brn ('84) 425.00 275.00
**a.** Imperf.
*22* A2 6p brn org ('86) 1.10 2.25
*23* A2 1sh ol bis ('94) 2.00 3.75
*24* A2 1sh brn org ('96) 7.50

Stamps of 1882-96 Surcharged in Black:

**½ PENNY** Nos. 25-29

**2½ PENCE** No. 30

**1886-92**

*25* A2 ½p on 2½p ultra 1.40 *4.25*
**a.** Inverted surch.
**b.** Pair, one without surcharge 8,000.
**c.** Space between "½" and "PENNY" 3mm 12.00 *14.00*
**d.** Dbl. surch. 1,250. 875.00
*26* A2 ½p on 4p gray 9.50 *14.00*
**a.** Space between "½" and "PENNY" 3mm
**b.** Double surcharge 1,650.
*27* A2 ½p on 6p bis brn 1.50 *3.50*
**a.** Inverted surcharge 1,250.
**b.** Space between "½" and "PENNY" 3mm 22.50 *30.00*
**c.** Double surcharge 1,250.
*28* A2 ½p on 6p brn org 45.00 55.00
**a.** Space between "½" and "PENNY" 3mm 200.00 *250.00*
**b.** Double surcharge 1,750.
*29* A2 1p on 2½ ultra 7.50 5.50
**a.** Space between "1" and "PENNY" 4mm 60.00 *60.00*
**b.** Half used as ½p on cover *1,650.*
*30* A2 2½p on 4p gray 4.50 *5.00*
**a.** Double surcharge 1,650.

Revenue Stamp Type A1 Surcharged in Black **½d POSTAGE**

**1896**

*31* A1 ½p on 4p lil & rose 8.75 12.50
**a.** Space between "½" and "d" 1½ to 2½mm 15.00 17.50

Tobago stamps were replaced by those of Trinidad or Trinidad and Tobago

## TOGO

LOCATION — In Western Africa bordering on the Gulf of Guinea.
GOVT. — Former mandate of Great Britain and France.
AREA — 13,041 sq. mi.
POP. — 294,000. (estimated 1915).
CAPITAL — Lome.

The German protectorate of Togo was occupied by Great Britain and France in World War I, and later mandated to them. The British area became part of Ghana. The French area was granted internal authonomy in 1956 and achieved independence in 1958. See "Togo" in Vol. IV for German, French and Republic issues.

100 Pfennig = 1 Mark
12 Pence = 1 Shilling

Kaiser's Yacht, the "Hohenzollern"
A3 A4

Wmk. 125- Lozenges

Stamps of German Togo Overprinted or Surcharged

**TOGO**
**Anglo-French**
**Occupation**

First (Wide) Setting. 3mm between Lines. 2mm between "Anglo" and "French"

**Wmk. 125 (5pf, 10pf); Unwmkd.**

**1914, Oct. 1** ***Perf. 14, 14½***

*33* A ½p on 3pf brn 240.00 210.00
**a.** Thin "y" in "penny" *900.00* *525.00*
*34* A3 1p on 5pf grn *240.00* *210.00*
**a.** Thin "y" in "penny" *900.00* *525.00*
*35* A3 3pf brown *85.00* *42.50*
*36* A3 5pf green *85.00* *42.50*
*37* A3 10pf carmine *85.00* *42.50*
**a.** Inverted ovpt. *10,000.* *5,500.*
**b.** Unwmk. *5,500.*

38 A3 20pf ultra 22.00 15.00
39 A3 25pf org & blk, *yel* 22.00 15.00
40 A3 30pf org & blk, *sal* 22.00 15.00
41 A3 40pf lake & blk 150.00 100.00
42 A3 50pf pur & blk, *sal* 10,000. 7,500.
43 A3 80pf lake & blk, *rose* 175.00 130.00
44 A4 1m carmine 4,500. 2,250.
45 A4 2m blue 9,250. 7,500.
*a.* Invtd. ovpt. 10,000.
*b.* "Occupation" double 10,000. 10,000.

On Nos. 33-34, the surcharge line ("Half penny" or "One penny") was printed separately and its position varies in relation to the 3-line overprint. On Nos. 46-47, the surcharge and overprint lines were printed simultaneously.

**TOGO**
**Anglo-French**
**Occupation**
**Half penny**

Second (Narrow) Setting. 2mm between Lines. 2mm between "Anglo" and "French"

**1914, Oct.**
46 A3 ½p on 3pf brn 25.00 19.00
*a.* Thin "y" in "penny" 50.00 25.00
*b.* "TOG" 425.00 165.00
47 A3 1p on 5pf grn 4.00 3.00
*a.* Thin "y" in "penny" 13.00 13.00
*b.* "TOG" 125.00
48 A3 3pf brown 1,500. 1,100.
*a.* "Occupation" omitted
49 A3 5pf green 1,500. 1,100.
50 A3 10pf carmine 3,750. 2,750.
51 A3 20pf ultra 13.00 7.50
*a.* "TOG" 5,500. 5,500.
*b.* Vert. pair, #51 & #38
52 A3 25pf org & blk, *yel* 19.00 12.50
*a.* "TOG" 10,000.
53 A3 30pf org & blk, *sal* 19.00 12.50
54 A3 40pf lake & blk 1,100. 1,100.
55 A3 50pf pur & blk, *sal* 5,500.
56 A3 80pf lake & blk, *rose* 1,100. 1,100.
57 A4 1m carmine 7,500. 4,500.
58 A4 2m blue 9,250.
59 A4 3m blk vio
60 A4 5m sl & car

Third Setting. 1¼mm between "Anglo" and "French". 2mm between Lines. "Anglo-French" 15mm Wide

**1915, Jan. 7**
61 A3 3pf brown 6,250. 3,250.
62 A3 5pf green 150.00 100.00
63 A3 10pf carmine 150.00 100.00
64 A3 20pf ultra 2,750. 825.00
64A A3 40pf lake & blk 7,500.
65 A3 50pf pur & blk, *sal* 10,000. 7,500.

Stamps of Gold Coast Overprinted Locally **TOGO ANGLO-FRENCH OCCUPATION**

**1915, May Wmk. 3 *Perf. 14***
66 A7 ½p green 12 12
*a.* Double overprint 90.00 125.00
67 A8 1p scarlet 12 12
*a.* Double ovpt. 90.00 100.00
*b.* Inverted ovpt. 60.00 65.00
*c.* As "b," "Togo" omitted
68 A7 2p gray 20 30
69 A7 2½p ultra 30 45

**Chalky Paper**
70 A7 3p vio, *yel* 45 60
71 A7 6p dl vio & red vio 60 90
72 A7 1sh blk, *grn* 1.25 1.50
*a.* Double overprint 150.00
73 A7 2sh vio & bl, *bl* 4.25 6.00
74 A7 2sh6p blk & red, *bl* 4.00 5.00
75 A7 10sh grn & red, *grn* 24.00 30.00
76 A7 20sh vio & blk, *red* 60.00 80.00

**Surfaced-Colored Paper**
77 A7 3p vio, *yel* 3.50 7.25
78 A7 5sh grn & red, *yel* 9.00 18.00
*Nos. 66-78 (13)* 107.79 150.24

Nos. 66 to 78 exist with small "F" in "French" and thin "G" in "Togo". Several values are known without the hyphen between "Anglo-French" and all but No. 77 without the first "O" in "Occupation".

Stamps of Gold Coast Overprinted in London **TOGO ANGLO-FRENCH OCCUPATION**

**1916, Apr.**

**Ordinary Paper**
80 A7 ½p green 12 20
81 A8 1p scarlet 12 20
*a.* Inverted overprint
82 A7 2p gray 28 40
83 A7 2½p ultra 40 55

**Chalky Paper**
84 A7 3p vio, *yel* 55 1.10
85 A7 6p dl vio & red vio 55 1.10
86 A7 1sh blk, *grn* 1.10 1.65
*a.* 1sh blk, *emer* 55.00 200.00
*b.* 1sh blk, *bl grn*, ol back 3.25 3.75
87 A7 2sh vio & ultra, *bl* 2.50 3.25
88 A7 2sh6p blk & red, *bl* 2.50 3.25
89 A7 5sh grn & red, *yel* 5.00 6.75
90 A7 10sh grn & red, *bl grn*, ol back 7.50 12.50
*a.* 10sh grn & red, *grn* 14.00 16.00
91 A7 20sh vio & blk, *red* 55.00 67.50
*Nos. 80-91 (12)* 75.62 98.45

The overprint on Nos. 80 to 91 is in heavier letters than on Nos. 66 to 78 and the 2nd and 3rd lines are each ½mm longer. The letter "O" on Nos. 80 to 91 is narrower and more oval.

# TOKELAU

## (Union Islands)

LOCATION — In the Pacific Ocean 300 miles north of Apia, Western Samoa.
GOVT. — A dependency of New Zealand.
AREA — 4 sq. mi.
POP. — 1,572 (est. 1981).

The Tokelau islands consist of three atolls: Atafu, Nukunono and Fakaofo, which span 100 miles of ocean.

12 Pence = 1 Shilling
100 Cents = 1 Dollar (1967)

**Catalogue values for all unused stamps in this country are for Never Hinged items.**

Map and Scene on Atafu — A1

Nukunono Dwelling and Map — A2

Fakaofo Shore Line and Map — A3

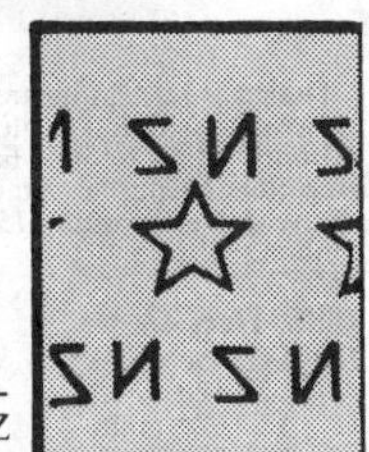
Wmk. 253-Multiple NZ and Star

***Perf. 13½x13***
**1948, June 22 Wmk. 253 Engr.**
1 A1 ½p red brn & rose lil 18 18
2 A2 1p dp grn & org brn 30 30
3 A3 2p dp ultra & grn 55 55

**Coronation Issue**
Type of New Zealand
**1953, May 25 Photo. *Perf. 14x14½***
4 A113 3p brown 6.00 8.00

No. 1 Surcharged in Black:

**ONE SHILLING**

***Perf. 13½x13***
**1956, Mar. 27 Engr. Wmk. 253**
5 A1 1sh on ½p 4.00 5.50

Postal-Fiscal Type of New Zealand, 1950, Surcharged **6D TOKELAU ISLANDS**

**Wmk. 253**
**1966, Nov. Typo. *Perf. 14***
6 A109 6p lt bl 2.00 1.00
7 A109 8p lt grn 3.50 2.00
8 A109 2sh pink 6.75 4.75

Nos. 1-3 Surcharged with New Value and Dots Obliterating Old Denomination

**1967, July 10 Engr. *Perf. 13½x13***
9 A2 1c on 1p 50 50
10 A3 2c on 2p 1.25 1.25
11 A1 10c on ½p 4.00 4.00

The 1c and 2c surcharges include two dots, the 10c surcharge has only one.

Postal Fiscal Type of New Zealand, 1950, Surcharged **5c TOKELAU ISLANDS**

**1967, July 10 Typo. *Perf. 14***
12 A109 3c light lilac 65 65
13 A109 5c light blue 1.25 1.25
14 A109 7c light green 2.00 2.00
15 A109 20c pink 5.00 5.00

1877, British Protectorate — A4

History of Tokelau: 10c, 1916, part of Gilbert and Ellice Islands Colony. 15c, 1925, administration transferred to New Zealand. 20c, 1948, New Zealand Territory.

***Perf. 13x12½***
**1969, Aug. 8 Litho. Wmk. 253**
16 A4 5c ultra yel & blk 90 90
17 A4 10c rose red, yel & blk 1.75 1.75
18 A4 15c dl grn, yel & blk 2.75 2.75
19 A4 20c brn, yel & blk 3.50 3.50

**Christmas Issues**
Type of New Zealand
**1969, Oct. 1 Photo. *Perf. 13½x14***
20 A168 2c multi 60 60

Type of New Zealand
***Perf. 12½***
**1970, Oct. 1 Unwmk. Litho.**
21 A180 2c multi 60 60

"Dolphin," 1765, Map of Atafu — A5

Fan — A6

Designs: 10c, "Pandora," 1791, and map of Nukunono. 25c, "General Jackson," 1835, and map of Fakaofo (horiz.).

**1970, Dec. 9 Unwmk. *Perf. 13½***
22 A5 5c yel & multi 1.75 1.50
23 A5 10c multi 3.50 3.00
24 A5 25c pink & multi 9.00 7.50

Discovery of Tokelau Islands.

**1971, Oct. 20 Litho. *Perf. 14***

Native Handicrafts: 2c, Round vessel. 3c, Hexagonal box. 5c, Shoulder bag. 10c, Handbag. 15c, Jewelry box with beads. 20c, Outrigger canoe model. 25c, Fish hooks.

25 A6 1c ol & multi 22 15
26 A6 2c red & multi 30 18
27 A6 3c dk vio & multi 45 30
28 A6 5c dl bl & multi 75 45
29 A6 10c dp org & multi 1.50 90
30 A6 15c emer & multi 2.25 1.50
31 A6 20c multi 3.00 2.00
32 A6 25c vio bl & multi 3.75 2.50
*Nos. 25-32 (8)* 12.22 7.98

Windmill Pump, Map of Atafu — A7

Horny Coral — A8

Designs (South Pacific Commission Emblem and): 10c, Community well, map of Fakaofo. 15c, Eradication of rhinoceros beetle, map of Nukunono. 20c, members.

**1972, Sept. 6 Litho. *Perf. 14x13½***
33 A7 5c lt bl grn & multi 85 60
34 A7 10c grnsh bl & multi 1.75 1.10
35 A7 15c lil & multi 2.75 1.50
36 A7 20c vio bl & multi 3.50 2.25

South Pacific Commission, 25th anniversary. On 15c, "PACIFIC" reads "PACFIC."

**1973, Sept. 12 Litho. *Perf. 13x13½***
37 A8 3c *shown* 1.00 65
38 A8 5c *Soft coral* 1.60 1.00
39 A8 15c *Mushroom coral* 5.00 3.25
40 A8 25c *Staghorn coral* 8.00 5.00

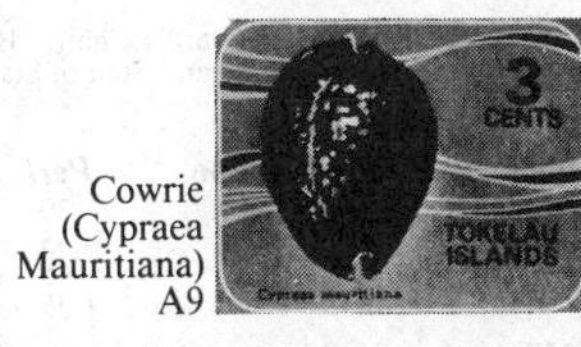

Cowrie (Cypraea Mauritiana) A9

Cowrie shells: 5c, Cypraea tigris. 15c, Cypraea talpa. 25c, Cypraea argus.

**1974, Nov. 13 Litho. *Perf. 14***
41 A9 3c ap grn & multi 1.00 50
42 A9 5c dk bl & multi 1.60 80
43 A9 15c bl & multi 5.00 2.50
44 A9 25c grn & multi 8.00 4.00

Moorish Idol — A10

Fish: 10c, Long-nosed butterflyfish. 15c, Lined butterflyfish. 25c, Red firefish.

**1975, Nov. 19 Litho. *Perf. 14***
45 A10 5c bl & multi 1.00 75
46 A10 10c brn & multi 2.25 1.40
47 A10 15c lil & multi 3.75 2.25
48 A10 25c multi 6.00 4.00

Canoe Making
A11

Designs: 2c, Reef fishing. 3c, Woman preparing pandanus leaves for weaving. 5c, Communal kitchen (umu). 9c, Wood carving. 20c, Husking coconuts. 50c, Wash day. $1, Meal time. 9c, 20c, 50c, $1, vertical.

**1976, Oct. 27 Litho. *Perf. 14***

*49* A11 1c pink & multi 5 5
*a.* Perf. 15 ('81) 5 5
*50* A11 2c multi 5 5
*51* A11 3c lt bl & multi 6 6
*a.* Perf. 15 ('81) 5 5
*52* A11 5c yel & multi 10 10
*a.* Perf. 15 ('81) 6 6
*53* A11 9c bis & multi 18 18
*a.* Perf. 15 ('81) 18 18
*54* A11 20c multi 40 40
*a.* Perf. 15 ('81) 40 40
*55* A11 50c tan & multi 80 80
*a.* Perf. 15 ('81) 80 80
*56* A11 $1 multi 1.50 1.50
*a.* Perf. 15 ('81) 1.50 1.50
*Nos. 49-56 (8)* 3.14 3.14
*Nos. 49a-56a (7)* 3.04 3.04

White Tern — A12

Birds of Tokelau: 10c, Turnstone. 15c, White-capped noddy. 30c, Brown noddy.

**1977, Nov. 16 Litho. *Perf. 14½x15***

*57* A12 8c multi 55 45
*58* A12 10c multi 75 55
*59* A12 15c multi 1.10 95
*60* A12 30c multi 2.25 2.00

Westminster Abbey — A13

Designs: 10c, King Edward's Chair. 15c, Scepter, Crown, Orb, Bible and Staff of State. 30c, Elizabeth II.

**1978, June 28 Litho. *Perf. 14***

*61* A13 8c multi 30 30
*62* A13 10c multi 45 45
*63* A13 15c multi 65 65
*64* A13 30c multi 1.25 1.25

25th anniv. of coronation of Elizabeth II.

Canoe Racing
A14

Designs: Various canoe races.

**1978, Nov. 8 Litho. *Perf. 13½x14***

*65* A14 8c multi 55 22
*66* A14 12c multi 70 35
*67* A14 15c multi 80 42
*68* A14 30c multi 1.25 80

**1979, Nov. 7 Photo. *Perf. 14***

*69* A14 10c Rugby 28 20
*70* A14 15c Cricket 45 30
*71* A14 20c Rugby, diff. 55 45
*72* A14 30c Cricket, diff. 1.10 60

*Tokelau stamps can be mounted in Scott's annual New Zealand Dependencies Supplement.*

**1980, Nov. 5 Litho. *Perf. 13½***

*73* A14 10c Surfing 18 18
*74* A14 20c Surfing, diff. 35 35
*75* A14 30c Swimming 50 50
*76* A14 50c Swimming, diff. 90 90

**1981, Nov. 4 Photo. *Perf. 14***

*77* A14 10c High jump, vert. 18 18
*78* A14 20c Volleyball, vert. 35 35
*79* A14 30c Running, vert. 50 50
*80* A14 50c Volleyball, vert., diff. 90 90
*Nos. 65-80 (16)* 9.54 7.20

Wood Carving — A15

**1982, May 5 Litho. *Perf. 13½x13***

*81* A15 10s shown 12 12
*82* A15 22s Bow-drilling sea shells 25 25
*83* A15 34s Bowl finishing 42 42
*84* A15 60s Basket weaving 85 85

Octopus Lure Fishing — A16

Designs: Fishing Methods.

**1982, Nov. 3 Litho. *Perf. 14***

*85* A16 5s shown 7 7
*86* A16 18s Multiple-hook 20 20
*87* A16 23s Ruvettus 28 28
*88* A16 34s Netting flying fish 40 40
*89* A16 63s Noose 65 65
*90* A16 75s Bonito 80 80
*Nos. 85-90 (6)* 2.40 2.40

Outrigger Canoe — A17

**1983, May 4 Litho. *Perf. 13½x14***

*91* A17 5s shown 8 8
*92* A17 18s Whale boat 25 25
*93* A17 23s Aluminium whale boat 35 35
*94* A17 34s Alia fishing boat 50 50
*95* A17 63s Cargo ship 80 80
*96* A17 75s Seaplane 1.00 1.00
*Nos. 91-96 (6)* 2.98 2.98

Traditional Games — A18

**1983, Nov. 2 Litho. *Perf. 14***

*97* A18 5s Javelin throwing 8 8
*98* A18 18s Tifaga string game 25 25
*99* A18 23s Fire making 35 35
*100* A18 34s Shell throwing 50 50
*101* A18 63s Handball 80 80
*102* A18 75s Mass wrestling 1.00 1.00
*Nos. 97-102 (6)* 2.98 2.98

Planting, Harvesting Copra — A19

Copra Industry: b. Husking, splitting. c. Drying, cutting. d. Bagging, weighing. c. Shipping. Continuous design.

**1984, May 2 Litho. *Perf. 13½x13***

*103* Strip of 5 3.00 3.00
*a.-e.* A19 48s, any single 60 60

Local Fish — A20

**1984, Dec. 5 Litho. *Perf. 14½x14***

*104* A20 1c Manini 5 5
*105* A20 2c Hahave 5 5
*106* A20 5c Uloulo 7 7
*107* A20 9c Ume Ihu 12 12
*108* A20 23c Lifilafi 30 30
*109* A20 34c Fagamea 35 35
*110* A20 50c Kakahi 48 48
*111* A20 75c Palu Po 70 70
*112* A20 $1 Mokoha 90 90
*113* A20 $2 Hakula 1.75 1.75
*Nos. 104-113 (10)* 4.77 4.77

Trees, Fruits and Herbs — A21

**1985, June 26 Litho. *Perf. 13½***

*114* A21 5c Mati 5 5
*115* A21 18c Nonu 25 25
*116* A21 32c Ulu 40 40
*117* A21 48c Fala 65 65
*118* A21 60c Kanava 80 80
*119* A21 75c Niu 1.00 1.00
*Nos. 114-119 (6)* 3.15 3.15

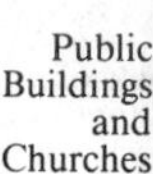

Public Buildings and Churches A22

Designs: 5c, Administration Center, Atafu. 18c, Administration Center, Nukunonu. 32c, Administration Center, Fakaofo. 48c, Congregational Church, Atafu. 60c, Catholic Church, Nukunonu. 75c, Congregational Church, Fakaofo.

**1985, Dec. 4**

*120* A22 5c multi 6 6
*121* A22 18c multi 22 22
*122* A22 32c multi 38 38
*123* A22 48c multi 60 60
*124* A22 60c multi 70 70
*125* A22 75c multi 90 90
*Nos. 120-125 (6)* 2.86 2.86

Hospitals and Schools A23

Designs: 5c, Atafu Hospital. 18c, St. Joseph's Hospital, Nukunonu. 32c, Fenuafala Hospital, Fakaofo. 48c, Matauala School, Atafu. 60c, Matiti School, Nukunonu. 75c, Fenuafala School, Fakaofo.

**1986, May 7 *Perf. 13½***

*126* A23 5c multi 6 6
*127* A23 18c multi 20 20
*128* A23 32c multi 35 35
*129* A23 48c multi 55 55
*130* A23 60c multi 68 68
*131* A23 75c multi 85 85
*Nos. 126-131 (6)* 2.69 2.69

Fauna A24

**1986, Dec. 3 Litho. *Perf. 14***

*132* A24 5c Coconut crab 7 7
*133* A24 18c Pigs 25 25
*134* A24 32c Chickens 45 45
*135* A24 48c Turtles 65 65
*136* A24 60c Goats 85 85
*137* A24 75c Ducks 1.00 1.00
*Nos. 132-137 (6)* 3.27 3.27

Flora — A25

**1987, May 6**

*138* A25 5c Gahu 6 6
*139* A25 18c Puka 22 22
*140* A25 32c Higano 38 38
*141* A25 48c Tialetiale 58 58
*142* A25 60c Gagie 72 72
*143* A25 75c Puapua 90 90
*Nos. 138-143 (6)* 2.86 2.86

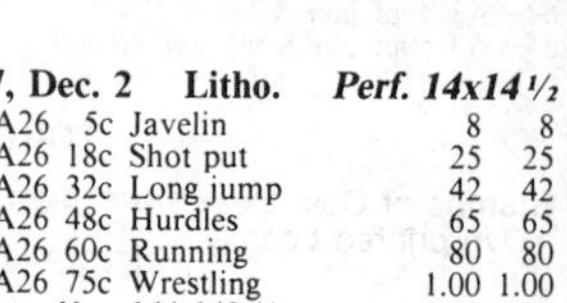

Olympic Sports A26

**1987, Dec. 2 Litho. *Perf. 14x14½***

*144* A26 5c Javelin 8 8
*145* A26 18c Shot put 25 25
*146* A26 32c Long jump 42 42
*147* A26 48c Hurdles 65 65
*148* A26 60c Running 80 80
*149* A26 75c Wrestling 1.00 1.00
*Nos. 144-149 (6)* 3.20 3.20

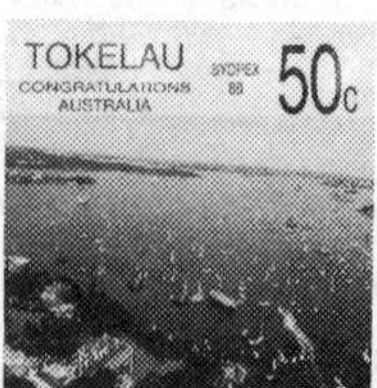

Australia Bicentennial, SYDPEX '88 — A27

Re-enactment of the arrival of the First Fleet in Sydney Harbor, Jan. 26, 1988 (in a continuous design): a. Ships in harbor, building (LL). b. Ships in harbor, tall ship (LR). c. Ships in harbor, Sydney Opera House. d. Bridge. e. North Sydney.

**1988, July 30 Litho. *Perf. 13½x13***

*150* Strip of 5 3.60 3.60
*a.-e.* A27 50c any single 72 72

Political Development — A28

Designs: 5c, Transfer of administration from the New Zealand Department of Maori and Island Affairs to the Ministry of Foreign Affairs, 1975. 18c, The General Fono empowered as the decision-making body of Tokelau, 1977. 32c, 1st Visit of New Zealand's prime minister, 1985. 48c, 1st Visit of UN representatives, 1976. 60c, 1st Tokelau delegation to go to the UN, 1987. 75c, 1st Tokelau appointed to the office of Official Secretary, 1987.

**1988, Aug. 10** — *Perf. 14½*

*151* A28 5c multi 8 8
*152* A28 18c multi 28 28
*153* A28 32c multi 48 48
*154* A28 48c multi 70 70
*155* A28 60c multi 88 88
*156* A28 75c multi 1.10 1.10
*Nos. 151-156 (6)* 3.52 3.52

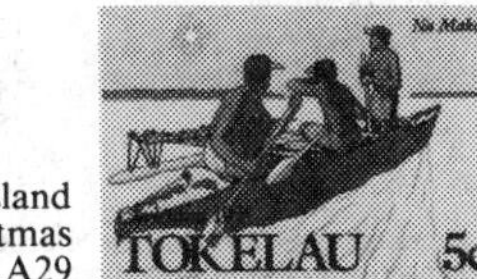

Island Christmas A29

Designs: 5c, Three Wise Men *(Na Makoi)*. 20c, Holy family *(He Tala)*. 40c, Escape into Egypt *(Fakagagalo ki Aikupito)*. 60c, Christmas presents *(Meaalofa Kilihimahi)*. 70c, Christ child *(Pepe ko Iesu)*. $1, Christmas parade *(Holo Tamilo)*.

**1988, Dec. 7 Litho.** — *Perf. 13½*

*157* A29 5c multi 8 8
*158* A29 20c multi 28 28
*159* A29 40c multi 55 55
*160* A29 60c multi 80 80
*161* A29 70c multi 95 95
*162* A29 $1 multi 1.35 1.35
*Nos. 157-162 (6)* 4.01 4.01

## TONGA

LOCATION — A group of islands in the south Pacific Ocean, south of Samoa.
GOVT. — Kingdom in British Commonwealth.
AREA — 289 sq. mi.
POP. — 98,750 (est. 1983).
CAPITAL — Nuku'alofa.

This group, also known as the Friendly Islands, became a British Protectorate in 1900 under the Anglo-German Agreement of 1899. On June 4, 1970, the United Kingdom ceased to have any responsibility for the external relations of Tonga.

12 Pence = 1 Shilling
20 Shillings = 1 Pound
100 Seniti = 1 Pa'anga (1967)

**Catalogue values for unused stamps in this country are for Never Hinged items, beginning with Scott 87 in the regular postage section, Scott B1 in the semi-postal section, Scott C1 in the air post section Scott CO1 in the air post official section, and Scott O11 in the officials section.**

King George I — A1

Wmk. 62- NZ and Small Star Wide Apart

*Perf. 12x11½*

**1886-92 Typo. Wmk. 62**

*1* A1 1p car rose ('87) 12.00 6.00
*a* Perf. 12½ 75.00 15.00
*b* Perf. 12½x10
*2* A1 2p vio ('87) 15.00 12.00
*a* Perf. 12½ 16.00 12.00
*3* A1 6p ultra ('88) 16.00 5.00
*a* Perf. 12½ 15.00 5.00
*4* A1 6p org yel ('92) 14.00 *30.00*
*5* A1 1sh bl grn ('88) 20.00 6.75
*a* Perf. 12½ 35.00 6.75
*b* Half used as 6p on cover
*Nos. 1-5 (5)* 77.00 59.75

Nos. 1 and 2 Surcharged or Overprinted in Black:

**FOUR PENCE** a — ✱ b

**1891, Nov. 10** — *Perf. 12x11½*

*6* A1(a) 4p on 1p car rose 4.50 7.50
*a* No period after "PENCE" 42.50 *50.00*
*7* A1(a) 8p on 2p vio 40.00 45.00

**1891, Nov. 23** — *Perf. 12½*

Two types of overprint:
I. Solid stars, rays pointed and short.
II. Open-center stars, rays blunt and long.

*8* A1(b) 1p car rose (I) 32.50 32.50
*a* Overprinted with 3 stars (I) 150.00
*b* Overprinted with 4 stars (I) 200.00
*c* Overprinted with 5 stars (I) 375.00
*d* Type II 27.50 27.50
*e* Perf. 12x11½ (I or II) 100.00 90.00
*9* A1(b) 2p vio (I) 50.00 *55.00*
*a* Type II 50.00 *55.00*
*b* Perf. 12x11½ (I or II) 100.00

Coat of Arms A4

King George I A5

**1892, Nov. 10 Typo.** — *Perf. 12x11½*

*10* A4 1p rose 11.00 12.50
*a* Diagonal half used as ½p on cover 500.00
*11* A5 2p ol gray 10.00 *12.00*
*12* A4 4p red brn 22.50 25.00
*13* A5 8p violet 50.00 55.00
*14* A5 1sh brown 47.50 50.00
*Nos. 10-14 (5)* 141.00 154.50

Types A4 and A5 Surcharged in Carmine or Black:

**½d.** c — **2½d.** d — **7½d.** f

**FIVE PENCE.**

**1893**

*15* A4 ½p on 1p ultra (C) 20.00 21.00
*a* Surcharge omitted
*16* A4 ½p on 1p ultra (Bk) 40.00 42.50
*17* A5 2½p on 2p bl grn (C) 22.50 20.00
*18* A5 2½p on 2p bl grn (Bk) 20.00 20.00
*a* Dbl. surch. 675.00
*19* A4 5p on 4p org yel (C) 12.50 14.00
*20* A5 7½p on 8p rose (C) 30.00 35.00

Stamps of 1886-92 Surcharged in Blue or Black:

SURCHARGE. HALF-PENNY g — SURCHARGE. 2½d. h

**1894**

*21* A4 ½p on 4p red brn (Bl) 3.50 *5.00*
*a* "SURCHARCE" 6.00 *10.00*
*b* Pair, one without surcharge
*c* "HALF PENNY" omitted
*22* A5 ½p on 1sh brn (Bk) 4.00 *7.50*
*a* Dbl. surch. 150.00
*b* "SURCHARCE" 11.00 11.50
*c* As "b," double surch. 750.00
*23* A5 2½p on 8p vio (Bk) 6.50 *7.50*
*a* No period after "SURCHARGE" 20.00 25.00
*24* A1 2½p on 1sh bl grn (Bk) 21.00 22.50
*a* No period after "SURCHARGE" 50.00
*b* Perf. 12x11½ 12.50 17.50

Type A5 with Same Surcharges in Carmine

**1895 Unwmk.**

*25* A5(g) 1p on 2p lt bl 22.50 15.00
*26* A5(h) 1½p on 2p lt bl perf. 12x11 24.00 25.00
*a* Perf. 12 25.00 25.00
*27* A5(h) 2½p on 2p lt bl 40.00 40.00
*b* Without period 200.00 200.00
*28* A5(h) 7½p on 2p lt bl perf. 12x11 52.50 60.00
*a* Perf. 12 140.00

King George II — A13

**1895, Aug. 16** — *Perf. 12*

*29* A13 1p gray grn 20.00 12.50
*a* Diagonal half used as ½p on cover *425.00*
*b* Horiz. pair, imperf. btwn. *750.00* *5,000.*
*30* A13 2½p dl rose 18.00 12.50
*31* A13 5p brt bl, perf. 12x11 14.00 15.00
*a* Perf. 12 14.00 15.00
*b* Perf. 11 300.00
*32* A13 7½p yellow 15.00 *20.00*

**Type A13 Redrawn and Surcharged "g" or "h" in Black**

*33* A13(g) ½p on 2½p red 40.00 *42.50*
*a* "SURCHARCE" 60.00
*b* Period after "Postage" 80.00
*34* A13(g) 1p on 2½p red 27.50 *30.00*
*a* Period after "Postage" 75.00
*35* A13(h) 7½p on 2½p red 50.00 50.00
*a* Period after "Postage" 85.00

Nos. 26 and 28 with Additional Surcharge in Violet and Black: *Half Penny-* VAEUA-OE-PENI.

**1896, May** — *Perf. 12x11*

*36* A5 ½p on 1½p on 2p lt bl 175.00
*a* Tongan surcharge reading upwards 190.00
*b* Perf. 12 175.00 *200.00*
*c* As "a", perf. 12 180.00 *225.00*
*d* "Haalf" 600.00
*37* A5 ½p on 7½p on 2p lt bl 27.50 *40.00*
*a* "Half penny" inverted 900.00
*b* "Half penny" double
*c* Tongan surcharge reading upwards 27.50 *40.00*
*d* Tongan surcharge as "c" and double
*e* "Hafl Penny" 450.00 *600.00*
*f* "Hafl" only 600.00
*g* "Hwlf"
*h* Periods instead of hyphens after words 225.00
*i* Perf. 12 275.00

Coat of Arms — A17

Breadfruit Tree — A18

George II — A19

Prehistoric Trilithon, Tongatabu — A20

Breadfruit A21

Coral Formations A22

View of Haabai A23

Red-breasted Musk Parrot — A24

View of Vavau — A25

Wmk. 79- Turtles

Two types of 2p:
I. Top of sword hilt shows above "2."
II. No hilt shows.

**1897-1934 Engr. Wmk. 79** — *Perf. 14*

*38* A17 ½p dk bl 30 30
*39* A17 ½p grn ('34) 50 15
*40* A18 1p dp red & blk 35 30
*41* A19 2p bis & blk (I) 1.50 1.50
*a* 2p bis & blk (II) 1.25 1.25
*42* A19 2½p lt bl & blk 90 90
*a* "½" without fraction bar 55.00 55.00
*43* A20 3p ol grn & blk 65 *1.00*
*44* A21 4p dl vio & grn 3.00 3.00
*45* A19 5p org & blk 2.50 2.75
*46* A22 6p red 1.90 2.00
*47* A19 7½p grn & blk 3.00 3.50
*a* Center invtd. 3,500.
*48* A19 10p car & blk 8.75 8.75
*49* A19 1sh red brn & blk 5.00 5.00
*50* A23 2sh dk ultra & blk 12.50 15.00
*51* A24 2sh6p dk vio 20.00 17.50
*52* A25 5sh dl red & blk 15.00 16.25
*Nos. 38-52 (15)* 75.85 77.90

See Nos. 73-81.

**T - L**

Stamp of 1897
Overprinted in Black

*1 June, 1899.*

**1899, June 1**

*53* A18 1p red & blk 30.00 30.00
*a* "1889" instead of "1899" 200.00 200.00
*b* Comma omitted after June
*c* Double ovpt.

Issued in commemoration of the marriage of King George II to Lavinia, June 1, 1899. The letters "T L" are the initials of Taufa'ahau, the King's family name, and Lavinia.

Queen Salote — A26

Dies of 2p:
Die I. Ball of "2" smaller.
Die II. Ball of "2" larger. "U" has spur at left.

**1920-35** **Engr.**

*54* A26 1½p gray blk ('35) 20 *65*
*55* A26 2p vio & sep 4.50 4.75
*56* A26 2p dl vio & blk (I) ('24) 1.40 1.10
*a* Die II 2.00 1.75
*57* A26 2½p bl & blk 2.25 *6.50*
*58* A26 2½p ultra ('34) 1.10 1.40
*59* A26 5p red org & blk 2.75 4.00
*60* A26 7½p grn & blk 1.10 1.40
*61* A26 10p car & blk 2.75 *4.00*
*62* A26 1sh red brn & blk 2.25 3.00
*Nos. 54-62 (9)* 18.30 26.80

Stamps of 1897 Surcharged in Dark Blue or Red

TWO PENCE

PENI-E-UA

**1923**

*63* A19 2p on 5p org & blk 85 1.00
*64* A19 2p on 7½p grn & blk 16.00 20.00
*65* A19 2p on 10p car & blk 12.50 *16.00*
*66* A19 2p on 1sh red brn & blk 25.00 25.00
*67* A23 2p on 2sh ultra & blk (R) 5.50 *10.00*
*68* A24 2p on 2sh 6p dk vio (R) 6.50 8.25
*69* A25 2p on 5sh dl red & blk (R) 4.00 5.00
*Nos. 63-69 (7)* 70.35 85.25

Queen Salote — A27

Inscribed "1918-1938"

**1938, Oct. 12** ***Perf. 14***

*70* A27 1p car & blk 25 50
*71* A27 2p vio & blk 2.50 1.50
*72* A27 2½p ultra & blk 2.50 1.50

20th anniv. of the accession of Queen Salote Tupou.

See Nos. 82-86.

Types of 1897-1920

**1942** **Engr.** **Wmk. 4**

Die III of 2p:
Foot of "2" longer than in Die II, extending beyond curve of loop.

*73* A17 ½p green 6 6
*74* A18 1p scar & blk 20 20
*75* A26 2p dl vio & blk (II) 12 12
*a* Die III 3.75 3.75
*76* A26 2½p ultra 16 16
*77* A20 3p grn & blk 22 22
*78* A22 6p org red 45 45
*79* A26 1sh red brn & gray blk 40 40
*80* A24 2sh 6p dk vio 4.25 5.75
*81* A25 5sh dl red & brn blk 5.50 6.50
*Nos. 73-81 (9)* 11.36 13.86

Type of 1938, Inscribed "1918-1943"

**1944, Jan. 28**

*82* A27 1p rose car & blk 7 10
*83* A27 2p pur & blk 10 12
*84* A27 3p dk yel grn & blk 16 22
*85* A27 6p red org & blk 28 35
*86* A27 1sh dk red brn & blk 42 50
*Nos. 82-86 (5)* 1.03 1.29

25th anniv. of the accession of Queen Salote.

**Catalogue values for unused stamps in this section, from this point to the end of the section, are for Never Hinged items.**

**UPU Issue**
Common Design Types
**Engr.; Name Typo. on 3p, 6p**
***Perf. 13½, 11x11½***

**1949, Oct. 10** **Wmk. 4**

*87* CD306 2½p ultra 15 20
*88* CD307 3p dp ol 25 30
*89* CD308 6p dp car 35 40
*90* CD309 1sh red brn 75 80

A28

A29

Queen Salote — A30

**1950, Nov. 1** **Photo.** ***Perf. 12½***

*91* A28 1p cerise 16 16
*92* A29 5p green 40 40
*93* A30 1sh violet 50 50

50th anniv. of the birth of Queen Salote.

Map and Island Scene — A31

Badges and Royal Palace A32

Designs: 2½p, Queen Salote and coastal scene. 3p, Queen Salote and ship "Bellona." 5p, Flag of Tonga, island view. 1sh, Arms of Tonga and Great Britain.

***Perf. 13x13½ (1p), 13½x13, 12½ (3p)***

**1951, July 2** **Engr.** **Wmk. 4**

*94* A31 ½p dp grn 16 16
*95* A32 1p car & blk 22 22
*96* A32 2½p choc & dp grn 50 50
*97* A31 3p ultra & org yel 65 65
*98* A32 5p dp grn & car 85 85
*99* A32 1sh pur & org 1.40 1.40
*Nos. 94-99 (6)* 3.78 3.78

50th anniv. of the treaty of friendship between Tonga and Great Britain.

Royal Palace, Nukualofa A33

Swallows' Cave, Vavau — A34

Designs: 1½p, Fisherman. 2p, Canoe and schooners. 3½p, Map of Tongatabu. 4p, Vavau harbor. 5p, Post Office, Nukualofa. 6p, Fuaamotu airport. 8p, Wharf, Nukualofa. 1sh, Map of Tonga Islands. 2sh, Beach at Lifuka, Haapai. 5sh, Mutiny on the Bounty. 10sh, Queen Salote. £1, Arms of Tonga.

***Perf. 11½x11, 11x11½***

**1953, July 1** **Wmk. 79**

*100* A33 1p choc & blk 9 5
*101* A33 1½p emer & ultra 12 9
*102* A33 2p blk & aqua 12 9
*103* A34 3p dk grn & ultra 15 12
*104* A33 3½p car & yel 18 15
*105* A33 4p rose car & yel 18 15
*106* A33 5p choc & ultra 20 18
*107* A33 6p blk & dp ultra 25 22
*108* A33 8p pur & emer 30 25
*109* A34 1sh blk & ultra 45 38
*110* A33 2sh choc & ol grn 1.00 90
*111* A33 5sh pur & yel 2.50 2.50
*112* A34 10sh blk & yel 5.50 5.25
*113* A34 £1 ultra, car & yel 11.00 10.50
*Nos. 100-113 (14)* 22.04 20.83

Whaling Ship and Longboat A35

Designs: 1p, Stamp of 1886. 4p, Post Office, Customs and Treasury Building and Queen Salote. 5p, Diesel-driven ship Aoniu. 1sh, Plane over Tongatabu.

**1961, Dec. 1** **Photo.** ***Perf. 14½x13½***

*114* A35 1p brn org & car rose 16 16
*115* A35 2p ultra 16 16
*116* A35 4p brt grn 20 20
*117* A35 5p purple 28 28
*118* A35 1sh red brn 60 60
*Nos. 114-118 (5)* 1.40 1.40

75th anniversary of postal service.

Stamps of 1953 and 1961 Overprinted in Red: "1862 / TAU'ATAINA / EMANCIPATION / 1962"

***Perf. 11½x11, 11x11½, 14½x13***
**Engr.; Photo. (4p)**

**1962, Feb. 7** **Wmk. 79**

*119* A33 1p choc & blk 20 20
*120* A35 4p brt grn 35 35
*121* A33 5p choc & ultra 35 35
*122* A33 6p blk & dp ultra 50 50
*123* A33 8p pur & emer 55 55
*124* A34 1sh blk & ultra 65 65
*125* A34 2sh on 3p dk grn & ultra 1.10 1.10
*126* A33 5sh pur & yel 2.75 2.75
*Nos. 119-126 (8)* 6.45 6.45

Centenary of emancipation. See Nos. CO1-CO6.

**Freedom from Hunger Issue**
Common Design Type with Portrait of Queen Salote
***Perf. 14x14½***

**1963, June 4** **Wmk. 79** **Photo.**

*127* CD314 11p ultra 45 45

Coat of Arms, ¼ Koula Coin, Reverse A36

Designs: 2p, 9p, 2sh, Queen Salote (head), ¼-koula coin, obverse.

**Litho.; Embossed on Gilt Foil**
**1963, July 15** **Unwmk.** ***Imperf.***
**Diameter: 40mm**

*128* A36 1p dp car 8 8
*129* A36 2p vio bl 12 12
*130* A36 6p dp grn 30 30
*131* A36 9p magenta 35 35
*132* A36 1sh6p violet 75 75
*133* A36 2sh emerald 80 80
*Nos. 128-133,C1-C6,CO7 (13)* 13.50 13.50

1st gold coinage of Polynesia. Backed with paper inscribed in salmon-colored alternating rows: "TONGA" and "THE FRIENDLY ISLANDS" in multiple.

**Red Cross Centenary Issue**
Common Design Type with Portrait of Queen Salote
**Wmk. 79**

**1963, Sept. 2** **Litho.** ***Perf. 13***

*134* CD315 2p blk & red 10 10
*135* CD315 11p ultra & red 50 50

Queen Salote on ¼-Koula Coin A37

**Litho.; Embossed on Gilt Foil**
**1964, Oct. 19** **Unwmk.** ***Imperf.***

*136* A37 3p pink 5 5
*137* A37 9p lt bl 15 15
*138* A37 2sh yel grn 38 38
*139* A37 5sh pale lil 90 90
*Nos. 136-139,C7-C10 (8)* 3.61 3.61

Pan-Pacific and Southeast Asia Women's Association Conf., Nukualofa, Aug. 1964. See note on paper backing after No. 133.

Nos. 128-133 Surcharged in Red, White or Black

**1965, Mar. 18**

*140* A36 1sh3p on 1sh6p vio (R) 16 16
*141* A36 1sh9p on 9p mag (W) 22 22
*142* A36 2sh6p on 6p dp grn (R) 40 40
*143* A36 5sh on 1p dp car (B) 14.00 14.00
*144* A36 5sh on 2p vio bl (B) 2.25 2.25
*145* A36 5sh on 2sh emer (B) 1.00 1.00
*Nos. 140-145,C11-C15,CO8 (12)* 66.05 66.05

Nos. 114-115 Overprinted and Surcharged in Purple or Red

**1866-1966**
**TUPOU COLLEGE**
**& SECONDARY**
**EDUCATION**

**3d XX**

*Perf. 14½x13½*

**1966, June 18 Photo. Wmk. 79**

| | | | | |
|---|---|---|---|---|
| *146* | A35 | 1p brn org & car rose (P) | 5 | 5 |
| *147* | A35 | 3p on 1p brn org & car rose (P) | 6 | 6 |
| *148* | A35 | 6p on 2p ultra (R) | 8 | 8 |
| *149* | A35 | 1sh2p on 2p ultra (R) | 22 | 22 |
| *150* | A35 | 2sh on 2p ultra (R) | 40 | 40 |
| *151* | A35 | 3sh on 2p ultra (R) | 60 | 60 |
| | | *Nos. 146-151,C16-C21,CO9-CO10 (14)* | 8.55 | 8.55 |

Issued to commemorate the centenary of Tupou College and of Secondary Education.

Nos. 136-137 Overprinted and Surcharged in Silver on Black or Ultramarine

reduced

**Litho.; Embossed on Gilt Foil**

**1966, Dec. 16 Unwmk. *Imperf.***

| | | | | |
|---|---|---|---|---|
| *152* | A37 | 3p pink (U) | 6 | 6 |
| *153* | A37 | 5p on 9p lt bl | 7 | 7 |
| *154* | A37 | 9p lt bl | 14 | 14 |
| *155* | A37 | 1sh7p on 3p pink (U) | 30 | 30 |
| *156* | A37 | 3sh6p on 9p lt bl | 60 | 60 |
| *157* | A37 | 6sh6p on 3p pink (U) | 1.10 | 1.10 |
| | | *Nos. 152-157,C22-C26 (11)* | 5.57 | 5.57 |

In memory of Queen Salote (1900-65).

Nos. 100-110, 147 and 151 Surcharged in Black or Red

**4 SENITI 4**

***Perf. 11½x11, 11x11½, 14½x13½***

**1967, Mar. 25 Wmk. 79**

| | | | | |
|---|---|---|---|---|
| *158* | A33 | 1s on 1p choc & blk | 5 | 5 |
| *159* | A33 | 2s on 4p rose car & yel | 6 | 6 |
| *160* | A33 | 3s on 5p choc & ultra | 9 | 9 |
| *161* | A33 | 4s on 5p choc & ultra | 10 | 10 |
| *162* | A33 | 5s on 3½p car & yel | 12 | 12 |
| *163* | A33 | 6s on 8p pur & emer | 15 | 15 |
| *164* | A33 | 7s on 1½p emer & ultra | 16 | 16 |
| *165* | A33 | 8s on 6p blk & dp ultra | 20 | 20 |
| *166* | A34 | 9s on 3p dk grn & ultra | 22 | 22 |
| *167* | A34 | 10s on 1sh blk & ultra | 25 | 25 |
| *168* | A35 | 11s on 3p on 1p brn org & car rose | 32 | 32 |
| *169* | A35 | 21s on 3sh on 2p ultra | 55 | 55 |
| *170* | A33 | 23s on 1p choc & blk | 60 | 60 |
| *171* | A33 | 30s on 2sh choc & ol grn (R) (1-line surch.) | 1.20 | 1.20 |
| *172* | A33 | 30s on 2sh choc & ol grn (R) (3-line surch.) | 1.40 | 1.40 |
| *173* | A33 | 50s on 6p blk & dp ultra (R) | 1.60 | 1.60 |
| *174* | A33 | 60s on 2p blk & aqua (R) | 2.00 | 2.00 |
| | | *Nos. 158-174,CO11 (18)* | 12.07 | 12.07 |

The size, typeface and arrangement of surcharge vary on the different denominations.

King Taufa'ahau IV — A38

Designs: 1s, 4s, 28s, 1pa, Coat of Arms, reverse of new palladium coins.

**Litho.; Embossed on Palladium Foil**

**1967, July 4 Unwmk. *Imperf.***

Diameter: 1s, 44mm.; 2s, 50s, 52mm.; 4s, 59mm.; 15s, 68mm.; 28s, 40mm.; 1pa, 74mm.

| | | | | |
|---|---|---|---|---|
| *175* | A38 | 1s org & brt bl | 5 | 5 |
| *176* | A38 | 2s brt bl & dp mag | 5 | 5 |
| *177* | A38 | 4s emer & mag | 12 | 12 |
| *178* | A38 | 15s bl grn & vio | 35 | 35 |
| *179* | A38 | 28s blk & brt red lil | 68 | 68 |
| *180* | A38 | 50s red & vio bl | 1.20 | 1.20 |
| *181* | A38 | 1pa ultra & brt rose | 2.50 | 2.50 |
| | | *Nos. 175-181,C27-C33 (14)* | 12.28 | 12.28 |

Issued to commemorate the coronation of King Taufa'ahau IV, July 4, 1967. Backed with paper incribed in yellow alternating rows: "Tonga The Friendly Islands" and "Historically The First Palladium Coinage."

Types of Regular Issue, 1953, Surcharged

The Friendly Islands welcome the United States Peace Corps 8

**Wmk. 79**

**1967, Dec. 15 Engr. *Imperf.***

| | | | | |
|---|---|---|---|---|
| *182* | A33 | 1s on 1p yel & blk | 5 | 5 |
| *183* | A33 | 2s on 2p car & ultra | 14 | 14 |
| *184* | A34 | 3s on 3p brn org & yel | 16 | 16 |
| *185* | A33 | 4s on 4p pur & yel | 20 | 20 |
| *186* | A33 | 5s on 5p grn & yel | 25 | 25 |
| *187* | A34 | 10s on 10p rose red & yel | 50 | 50 |
| *188* | A33 | 20s on 2sh car & ultra | 1.00 | 1.00 |
| *189* | A33 | 50s on 5sh sep & yel | 2.50 | 2.50 |
| *190* | A34 | 1pa on 10sh org yel | 5.00 | 5.00 |
| | | *Nos. 182-190 (9)* | 9.80 | 9.80 |

Arrival of U.S. Peace Corps.

Nos. 100-111 Surcharged in Red, Black or Ultramarine

**1 SENITI 1**

***Perf. 11½x11, 11x11½***

**1968, Apr. 6 Engr. Wmk. 79**

| | | | | |
|---|---|---|---|---|
| *191* | A33 | 1s on 1p choc & blk (R) | 5 | 5 |
| *192* | A33 | 2s on 4p rose car & yel | 8 | 8 |
| *193* | A34 | 3s on 3p dk grn & ultra (U) | 10 | 10 |
| *194* | A33 | 4s on 5p choc & ultra (R) | 12 | 12 |
| *195* | A33 | 5s on 2p blk & aqua (R) | 15 | 15 |
| *196* | A33 | 6s on 6p blk & dp ultra (R) | 20 | 20 |
| *197* | A33 | 7s on 1½p emer & ultra (R) | 20 | 20 |
| *198* | A33 | 8s on 8p pur & emer (R) | 25 | 25 |
| *199* | A33 | 9s on 3½p car & yel | 25 | 25 |
| *200* | A34 | 10s on 1sh blk & ultra (R) | 30 | 30 |
| *201* | A33 | 20s on 5sh pur & yel (R) | 60 | 60 |
| *202* | A33 | 2pa on 2sh choc & ol grn (R) | 6.00 | 6.00 |
| | | *Nos. 191-202,C37-C39,CO15-CO18 (19)* | 21.85 | 21.85 |

Surcharge on 3s and 10s is vertical.

Nos. 175-181 Overprinted: "H.M'S BIRTHDAY / 4 July 1968" in Gold on Red Panel on 1s, 4s, 28s and 1pa. "HIS MAJESTY'S 50th BIRTHDAY" in Silver on Blue Panel on 2s, 15s and 50s.

**Litho.; Embossed on Palladium Foil**

**1968, July 4 Unwmk. *Imperf.***

| | | | | |
|---|---|---|---|---|
| *203* | A38 | 1s org & brt bl | 5 | 5 |
| *204* | A38 | 2s brt bl & dp mag | 5 | 5 |
| *205* | A38 | 4s emer & mag | 12 | 12 |
| *206* | A38 | 15s bl grn & vio | 55 | 55 |
| *207* | A38 | 28s blk & brt red lil | 1.00 | 1.00 |
| *208* | A38 | 50s red & vio bl | 1.60 | 1.60 |
| *209* | A38 | 1pa ultra & brt rose | 3.25 | 3.25 |
| | | *Nos. 203-209,C40-C46,CO21-CO24 (18)* | 34.24 | 34.24 |

Types of 1953 Surcharged in Red, Black or Green: "Friendly Islands / Field & Track Trials / South Pacific Games / Port Moresby 1969"

Designs as Before.

**Wmk. 79**

**1968, Dec. 19 Engr. *Imperf.***

| | | | | |
|---|---|---|---|---|
| *210* | A33 | 5s on 5p grn & yel (R) | 10 | 10 |
| *211* | A34 | 10s on 1sh cer & buff | 20 | 20 |
| *212* | A33 | 15s on 2sh rose car & bl | 30 | 30 |
| *213* | A33 | 25s on 2p rose car & bl | 50 | 50 |
| *214* | A33 | 50s on 1p yel & blk | 1.00 | 1.00 |
| *215* | A34 | 75s on 10sh org (G) | 1.50 | 1.50 |
| | | *Nos. 210-215,C47-C54,CO19-CO20 (16)* | 9.62 | 9.62 |

Issued to publicize the field and track trials for the third South Pacific Games, Port Moresby, 1969. The overprint is in 5 lines on the horizontal stamps, in 7 lines on vertical stamps. On the vertical stamps "Trial" is printed on the line ahead of "Field & Track". On No. 215 the denomination is spelled out.

Nos. 149-150 and Types of 1953 Surcharged

***Perf. 14½x13½***

**1968 Photo. Wmk. 79**

| | | | | |
|---|---|---|---|---|
| *216* | A35 | 1s on 1sh2p on 2p ultra | 45 | 45 |
| *217* | A35 | 1s on 2sh on 2p ultra | 45 | 45 |

**Engr. *Imperf.***

| | | | | |
|---|---|---|---|---|
| *218* | A33 | 1s on 6p yel & blk | 12 | 12 |
| *219* | A33 | 2s on 3½p dk bl | 15 | 15 |
| *220* | A33 | 3s on 1½p lt grn | 22 | 25 |
| *221* | A33 | 4s on 8p blk & pale grn | 30 | 30 |
| | | *Nos. 216-221,C55-C57 (9)* | 3.04 | 3.07 |

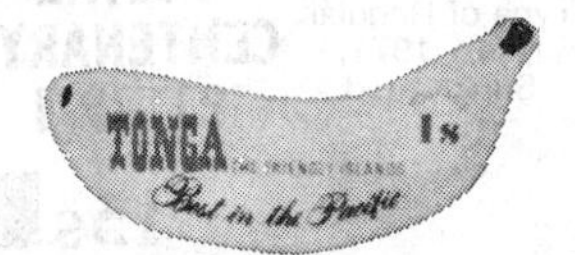


Banana — A39

**Unwmk.**

**1969, Apr. 21 Typo. *Imperf.***

**Self-adhesive**

| | | | | |
|---|---|---|---|---|
| *222* | A39 | 1s yel, blk & red | 15 | 10 |
| *223* | A39 | 2s yel, blk & emer | 20 | 15 |
| *224* | A39 | 3s yel, blk & lil | 35 | 25 |
| *225* | A39 | 4s yel, blk & ultra | 50 | 40 |
| *226* | A39 | 5s yel, blk & ol grn | 60 | 50 |
| | | *Nos. 222-226 (5)* | 1.80 | 1.40 |

Packed in boxes of 200. See Nos. 248-252, 297-301.

Peelable Backing Inscribed

Starting in 1969, self-adhesive stamps are attached to peelable paper backing printed with "TONGA where time begins" in multiple rows and various colors, unless otherwise stated.

Shot-putter — A40

**1969, Aug. 13 Litho. *Imperf.***

**Self-adhesive**

| | | | | |
|---|---|---|---|---|
| *227* | A40 | 1s bis, red & blk | 5 | 5 |
| *228* | A40 | 3s bis, red & emer | 12 | 12 |
| *229* | A40 | 6s bis, red & bl | 25 | 25 |
| *230* | A40 | 10s bis, red & pur | 38 | 38 |
| *231* | A40 | 30s bis, red & bl | 1.10 | 1.10 |
| | | *Nos. 227-231,C58-C62,CO25-CO26 (12)* | 15.45 | 15.45 |

3rd Pacific Games, Port Moresby, Papua and New Guinea, Aug. 13-23.

Oil Derrick and Map of Tonga Islands — A41

**1969, Dec. 23 Litho. *Imperf.***

**Self-adhesive**

| | | | | |
|---|---|---|---|---|
| *232* | A41 | 3s brn & multi | 10 | 10 |
| *233* | A41 | 7s brt bl & multi | 20 | 20 |
| *234* | A41 | 20s multi | 60 | 60 |
| *235* | A41 | 25s org & multi | 90 | 90 |
| *236* | A41 | 35s hn brn & multi | 1.20 | 1.20 |

Type of Regular Issue, 1953, Surcharged in Red: "1969 / OIL / SEARCH / T$1.10" and Oil Derrick Obliterating Old Denomination.

**Wmk. 79 *Imperf.***

| | | | | |
|---|---|---|---|---|
| *237* | A34 | 1.10pa on £1 grn & multi | 4.00 | 4.00 |
| | | *Nos. 232-237,C63-C67,CO27 (12)* | 13.95 | 13.95 |

First scientific search for oil in Tonga.

British and Tongan Royal Families — A42

**Litho.; Gold Embossed**

**1970, Mar. 7 Self-adhesive *Imperf.***

| | | | | |
|---|---|---|---|---|
| *238* | A42 | 3s bl, vio bl & dk brn | 10 | 10 |
| *239* | A42 | 5s emer, vio bl & dk brn | 20 | 20 |
| *240* | A42 | 10s org, blk & dk brn | 40 | 40 |
| *241* | A42 | 25s red lil, blk & dk brn | 90 | 90 |
| *242* | A42 | 50s red, blk & dk brn | 2.00 | 2.00 |
| | | *Nos. 238-242,C68-C72,CO28-CO30 (13)* | 19.75 | 19.75 |

Visit of Elizabeth II, Prince Philip and Princess Anne, Mar. 1970.

An enhanced introduction to the Scott Catalogue begins on Page V. A thorough understanding of the material presented there will greatly aid your use of the catalogue itself.

Open Book, George Tupou I and II, Salote Tupou III, Taufa'ahau Tupou IV and Tonga Flag — A43

**Litho.; Gold Embossed**

**1970, June 4** *Imperf.*

**Self-adhesive**

*243*A43 3s multi 12 12
*244*A43 7s multi 28 28
*245*A4315s multi 60 60
*246*A4325s multi 1.00 1.00
*247*A4350s multi 2.25 2.25
*Nos. 243-247,C73-C77,CO31-CO33 (13)* 21.20 21.20

Tonga's independence and entry into the British Commonwealth of Nations.

Banana Type of 1969 redrawn and

Coconut — A44

**1970, June 9** **Typo.**

**Self-adhesive**

*248* A39 1s yel, blk & mag 5 5
*249* A39 2s yel, blk & bl 8 8
*250* A39 3s yel, blk & brn 12 12
*251* A39 4s yel, blk & grn 18 18
*252* A39 5s yel, blk & org 20 20

**Typo.; Embossed on Gilt Foil**

**Coconut Brown**

*253* A44 6s bl, grn & mag 25 25
*254* A44 7s pur & grn 30 30
*255* A44 8s gold, grn & vio bl 35 35
*256* A44 9s car & grn 40 40
*257* A44 10s gold, grn & org 45 45
*Nos. 248-257,O11-O20 (20)* 4.76 4.76

Nos. 248-252 have no white shading in upper part of the banana, Nos. 222-226 have white shading. Nos. 253-256 have self-adhesive control numbers in lower left corner of paper backing. Paper backing is green on Nos. 253-257.

See Nos. 302-306, O26-O30.

Red Cross and Arms of Tonga A45

**1970, Oct. 17** **Litho.** *Imperf.*

**Self-adhesive**

*258* A45 3s red, blk & grn 12 12
*259* A45 7s red, blk & vio bl 25 25
*260* A45 15s red, blk & red lil 55 55
*261* A45 25s red, blk & brt grn 90 90
*262* A45 75s red, blk & brn 3.00 3.00
*Nos. 258-262,C78-C82,CO34-CO36 (13)* 22.52 22.52

Centenary of the British Red Cross.

Nos. 153, 152 Surcharged

**Litho.; Embossed on Gilt Foil**

**1971, Jan. 31** *Imperf.*

*263* A37 2s on 9p lt bl 7 5
*264* A37 3s on 9p lt bl 15 12
*265* A37 5s on 3p pink 25 12
*266* A37 15s on 9p lt bl 75 62
*267* A37 25s on 3p pink 1.10 95
*268* A37 50s on 3p pink 2.50 90
*Nos. 263-268,C83-C86,CO37-CO40 (14)* 24.82 17.94

In memory of Queen Salote (1900-65). The "In Memoriam" inscription is in silver on black panel on the 2s, 3s and 15s; in silver on ultramarine panel on the 5s, 25s and 50s. The dates and denominations are all on black panels in silver and metallic red, green, bronze, magenta or gold respectively.

Type of Regular Issue, 1953, Surcharged in Red and Black

3s

PHILATOKYO '71

**1971** **Engr.** **Wmk. 79** *Imperf.*

*269* A33 3s on 8p blk & pale grn 18 12
*270* A33 7s on 4p pur & yel 30 25
*271* A33 25s on 1p yel & blk 1.10 95
*272* A33 75s on 2sh car & ultra 3.75 3.25
*Nos. 269-272,C87-C89,CO41-CO43 (10)* 18.73 14.58

Philatokyo 71, Philatelic Exposition, Tokyo, Apr. 19-29.

Type of Regular Issue, 1971, Surcharged

HONOURING
JAPANESE
POSTAL
CENTENARY
1871-1971
15s

**1971**

*273* A34 15s on 1sh car & buff 30 30

Centenary of Japanese postal service. See Nos. C90-C91.

Self-adhesive & Imperf.
Starting with Nos. 274-278, all issues are self-adhesive and imperforate, unless otherwise stated.

Pole Vault A46

Gold Medal of Merit A47

**1971, July** **Litho.** **Unwmk.**

*274* A46 3s grn, blk & brn 12 12
*275* A46 7s red, blk & brn 30 30
*276* A46 15s grn, blk & brn 62 62
*277* A46 25s rose lil, blk & brn 95 95
*278* A46 50s dk bl, blk & brn 1.90 1.90
*Nos. 274-278,C92-C96,CO44-CO46 (13)* 15.89 15.89

4th South Pacific Games, Papeete, French Polynesia, Sept. 8-19.

**1971, Oct. 30** **Litho; Embossed**

Designs: 24s, Silver Medal of Merit. 38s, Bronze Medal of Merit, obverse (King Taufa'ahau IV).

*279* A47 3s gold & multi 12 12
*280* A47 24s sil & multi 95 95
*281* A47 38s brnz & multi 1.50 1.50
*Nos. 279-281,C99-C101,CO49-CO51 (9)* 18.95 18.95

First investiture of Tongan Medal of Merit.

Juggler, UNICEF Emblem A48

**1971, Dec.** **Litho.**

*282* A48 2s vio & multi 7 7
*283* A48 4s multi 15 15
*284* A48 8s bl & multi 32 32
*285* A48 16s emer & multi 70 70
*286* A48 30s lil rose & multi 1.25 1.25
*Nos. 282-286,C102-C106,CO52-CO54 (13)* 19.52 19.52

25th anniv. of UNICEF.

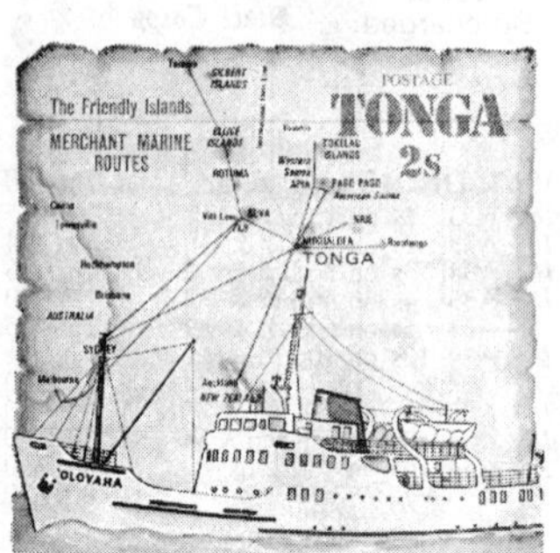


Merchant Marine Routes from Tonga and "Olovaha" — A49

**1972, Apr. 14**

*287* A49 2s bl & multi 5 5
*288* A49 10s mag & multi 30 30
*289* A49 17s brn & multi 50 50
*290* A49 21s dk grn & multi 75 75
*291* A49 60s multi 2.00 2.00
*Nos. 287-291,C107-C111,CO55-CO57 (13)* 17.10 17.10

Tongan Merchant Marine publicity.

King Taufa'ahau IV Coronation Coin, ¼ Hau — A50

**Litho.; Embossed on Metallic Foil**

**1972, July 15**

*292* A50 5s sil & multi 25 25
*293* A50 7s sil & multi 32 32
*294* A50 10s sil & multi 40 40
*295* A50 17s sil & multi 75 75
*296* A50 60s sil & multi 2.75 2.75
*Nos. 292-296,C112-C116,CO58-CO60 (13)* 22.54 22.54

Coronation of King Taufa'ahau IV, 5th anniv.

Coconut Type of 1970 and

Banana A51

Watermelon — A52

**1972, Sept. 30** **Typo.**

*297* A51 1s brt yel, red & blk 5 5
*298* A51 2s brt yel, bl & blk 8 8
*299* A51 3s brt yel, emer & blk 12 12
*300* A51 4s brt yel & blk 15 15
*301* A51 5s brt yel & brn blk 16 16
*302* A44 6s brn, org & grn 18 18
*303* A44 7s brn, ultra & grn 20 20
*304* A44 8s brn, mag & grn 25 25
*305* A44 9s brn, red & grn 30 30
*306* A44 10s brn, bl & grn 35 35
*307* A52 15s grn, org brn & ultra 55 55
*308* A52 20s grn, bl & red 70 70
*309* A52 25s grn, red & brn 85 85
*310* A52 40s grn, bl & org 1.40 1.40
*311* A52 50s grn, dk bl & yel 1.50 1.50
*Nos. 297-311,O21-O35 (30)* 13.53 13.53

Paper backing is brown on Nos. 302-311. Nos. 302-306 have self-adhesive control number in lower left corner of paper backing.

Flag Raising, Minerva Reef — A53

**1972, Dec. 9** **Litho.**

*312* A53 5s blk & multi 15 15
*313* A53 7s grn & multi 20 20
*314* A53 10s pur & multi 35 35
*315* A53 15s org & multi 50 50
*316* A53 40s ultra & multi 1.25 1.25
*Nos. 312-316,C119-C123,CO63-CO65 (13)* 15.40 15.40

Tonga's proclamation of sovereignty over the Minerva Reefs, June 1972.

Tongan Coins and Bank Building — A54

**1973, Mar. 30** **Litho.**

*317* A54 5s sil & multi 18 18
*318* A54 7s sil & multi 25 25
*319* A54 10s sil & multi 38 38

*320* A54 20s sil & multi 75 75
*321* A54 30s sil & multi 1.10 1.10
*Nos. 317-321 (5)* 2.66 2.66

Establishment of Bank of Tonga.

Handshake, Outrigger Canoe — A55

**1973, June 29**

*322* A55 5s sil & multi 48 48
*323* A55 7s sil & multi 72 72
*324* A55 15s sil & multi 1.80 1.80
*325* A55 21s sil & multi 2.50 2.50
*326* A55 50s sil & multi 6.25 6.25
*Nos. 322-326 (5)* 11.75 11.75

25th anniversary of Tongan Boy Scout Movement.

Capt. of Cook's Report and Tongan Rulers — A56

**Litho.; Embossed on Gilt Foil**

**1973, Oct. 2**

*327* A56 6s multi 38 38
*328* A56 8s multi 50 50
*329* A56 11s multi 62 62
*330* A56 35s multi 1.50 1.50
*331* A56 40s multi 1.90 1.90
*Nos. 327-331 (5)* 4.90 4.90

Bicentenary of Capt. Cook's arrival. Design is from the manuscript in British Museum.

Nos. 278, 281, C100-C101 and 280 Surcharged and Overprinted in Silver or Gold on Red (12s, 14s) or Black Panels (5s, 20s, 50s): "Commonwealth Games Christchurch 1974"

**1973, Dec. 19** **Litho.**

*332* A46 5s on 50s multi (G) 25 25

**Litho.; Embossed**

*333* A47 12s on 38s brnz (S) 55 55
*334* A47 14s on 75s sil (G) 65 65
*335* A47 20s on 1pa brnz & multi (G) 1.00 1.00
*336* A47 50s on 24s sil & multi (S) 2.50 2.50
*Nos. 332-336 (5)* 4.95 4.95

10th British Commonwealth Games, Christchurch, N.Z., Jan. 24-Feb. 2, 1974.

Letter Addressed to Tonga, Names of UPU Members — A57

**1974, June 20** **Typo.**

*337* A57 5s tan & multi 22 22
*338* A57 10s tan & multi 50 50
*339* A57 15s tan & multi 1.00 1.00
*340* A57 20s tan & multi 60 60
*341* A57 50s tan & multi 1.50 1.50
*Nos. 337-341 (5)* 3.82 3.82

Centenary of Universal Postal Union.

Girl Guide Badges — A58

**1974, Sept. 11** **Litho.**

*342* A58 5s multi 28 28
*343* A58 10s multi 52 52
*344* A58 20s multi 1.10 1.10
*345* A58 40s multi 2.25 2.25
*346* A58 60s multi 3.00 3.00
*Nos. 342-346 (5)* 7.15 7.15

Girl Guides of Tonga.

Sailing Ship and Anchors A59

**1974, Dec. 11**

*347* A59 5s bl & multi 20 15
*348* A59 10s bl & multi 40 40
*349* A59 25s bl & multi 90 75
*350* A59 50s bl & multi 1.80 1.50
*351* A59 75s bl & multi 2.75 2.25
*Nos. 347-351 (5)* 6.05 5.05

Establishment of Royal Marine Institute.

Dateline Hotel, Nukualofa — A60

**1975, Mar. 11**

*352* A60 5s bl & multi 20 20
*353* A60 10s grn & multi 40 40
*354* A60 15s scar & multi 60 60
*355* A60 30s pur & multi 1.10 1.10
*356* A60 1pa org & multi 4.00 4.00
*Nos. 352-356 (5)* 6.30 6.30

First meeting of South Pacific area Prime Ministers. See note after No. 226.

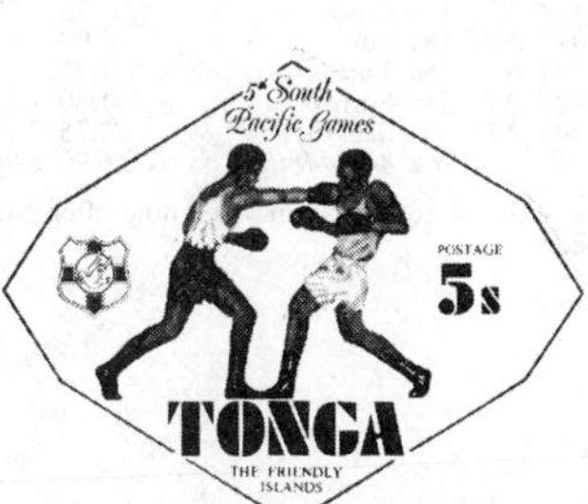


Boxing and Games' Emblem — A61

**1975, June 11** **Litho.**

*357* A61 5s blk & multi 25 25
*358* A61 10s grn & multi 32 32
*359* A61 20s brn & multi 65 65
*360* A61 25s org & multi 1.50 1.50
*361* A61 65s vio & multi 2.75 2.75
*Nos. 357-361 (5)* 5.47 5.47

5th South Pacific Games, Guam, Aug. 1-10. See note after No. 226.

King Taufa'ahau IV Coin — A62

Designs (FAO Coins): 5s, Chicken. 20s, like 1pa, (small coin, 27mm.). 50s, School of fish. 2pa, Animals and plants on reverse, King on obverse (large coin, 42mm.).

**1975, Sept. 3**

*362* A62 5s red, sil & blk 22 22
*363* A62 20s ultra, grn, sil & blk 65 65
*364* A62 50s bl, sil & blk 1.50 1.50
*365* A62 1pa sil & blk 3.25 3.25
*366* A62 2pa sil & blk 7.50 7.50
*Nos. 362-366 (5)* 13.12 13.12

Coinage issued for the benefit of the U.N. Food and Agriculture Organization. Size of paper backing of 2pa: 82x50mm.; others 45x45mm. See note after No. 226.

Coat of Arms, 5pa Coin, Reverse — A63

George Tupou I Coin, Reverse and Obverse — A64

Coins: 20s, King Taufa'ahau IV. 50s, King George Tupou II, 50pa obverse and reverse. 75s, 20pa reverse.

**Litho.; Embossed on Gilt Foil**

**1975, Nov. 4**

**Pink Background**

*367* A63 5s blk, sil & vio bl 15 15
*368* A64 10s gold, blk & red 25 25
*369* A63 20s blk, sil & grn 50 50
*370* A64 50s gold, blk & vio 90 90
*371* A63 75s blk, sil & red lil 1.40 1.40
*Nos. 367-371 (5)* 3.20 3.20

Centenary of Constitution of Tonga. Size of paper backing of Nos. 367 and 369: 65x60mm; of No. 371, 87x78mm. See note after No. 226.

Montreal Olympic Games Emblem — A65

**1976, Feb. 24** **Litho.**

*372* A65 5s red, ultra & blk 20 15
*373* A65 10s red, grn & blk 40 30
*374* A65 25s red, lt brn & blk 90 75
*375* A65 35s red, lil & blk 1.25 1.00
*376* A65 70s red, bis & blk 2.50 2.00
*Nos. 372-376 (5)* 5.25 4.20

21st Olympic Games, Montreal, Canada, July 17-Aug. 1. See note after No. 226.

William Hooper, William Floyd, John Penn, Francis Lightfoot Lee — A66

Signers of Declaration of Independence, Flags of U.S. and Tonga: 10s, Benjamin Franklin, Thomas Nelson, Jr., Benjamin Harrison, William Ellery. 15s, Oliver Wolcott, Lyman Hall, William Whipple, Carter Braxton. 25s, George Taylor, Thomas Stone, Arthur Middleton, Richard Stockton. 75s, Stephen Hopkins, Eldridge Gerry, James Wilson, Francis Hopkinson.

**1976, May 26** **Litho.**

*377* A66 9s buff & multi 50 38
*378* A66 10s buff & multi 50 38
*379* A66 15s buff & multi 75 55
*380* A66 25s buff & multi 1.10 90
*381* A66 75s buff & multi 6.25 5.50
*Nos. 377-381 (5)* 9.10 7.71

American Bicentennial. Printed on peelable buff paper backing, inscribed in carmine with facsimile of Declaration of Independence.

Nathaniel Turner and John Thomas — A67

**1976, Aug. 25**

*382* A67 5s yel & multi 15 15
*383* A67 10s multi 25 25
*384* A67 20s multi 50 50
*385* A67 25s multi 55 55
*386* A67 85s multi 1.50 1.50
*Nos. 382-386 (5)* 2.95 2.95

Sesquicentennial of the arrival of Methodist missionaries and establishment of Christianity in Tonga. Printed on peelable paper backing inscribed in manuscript with segments of John Thomas's Tonga diary.

Wilhelm I and George Tupou I — A68

**1976, Nov. 1**

| | | | | |
|---|---|---|---|---|
| *387* | A68 | 9s yel & multi | 30 | 30 |
| *388* | A68 | 15s yel & multi | 50 | 50 |
| *389* | A68 | 22s yel & multi | 70 | 70 |
| *390* | A68 | 50s yel & multi | 1.20 | 1.20 |
| *391* | A68 | 73s yel & multi | 1.75 | 1.75 |
| | | *Nos. 387-391 (5)* | 4.45 | 4.45 |

Tonga-Germany Friendship Treaty, centenary. Printed on peelable paper backing showing reproduction of original treaty.

Queen Salote in Coronation Procession, 1953 — A69

**1977, Feb. 7** **Litho.**

| | | | | |
|---|---|---|---|---|
| *392* | A69 | 11s bl & multi | 1.40 | 1.40 |
| *393* | A69 | 20s grn & multi | 1.65 | 1.65 |
| *394* | A69 | 30s vio bl & multi | 1.00 | 1.00 |
| *395* | A69 | 50s lt grn & multi | 1.50 | 1.50 |
| *396* | A69 | 75s vio & multi | 2.50 | 2.50 |
| | | *Nos. 392-396 (5)* | 8.05 | 8.05 |

25th anniv. of the reign of Elizabeth II. Printed on peelable paper backing showing replica of handwritten Proclamation of Accession.

Various Coins — A70

**1977, July 4**

| | | | | |
|---|---|---|---|---|
| *397* | A70 | 10s multi | 35 | 30 |
| *398* | A70 | 15s multi | 48 | 45 |
| *399* | A70 | 25s multi | 85 | 75 |
| *400* | A70 | 50s multi | 1.75 | 1.50 |
| *401* | A70 | 75s multi | 2.75 | 2.25 |
| | | *Nos. 397-401 (5)* | 6.18 | 5.25 |

10th anniversary of coronation of King Taufa'ahau IV. Printed on peelable paper backing showing multicolored replicas of Tongan stamps.



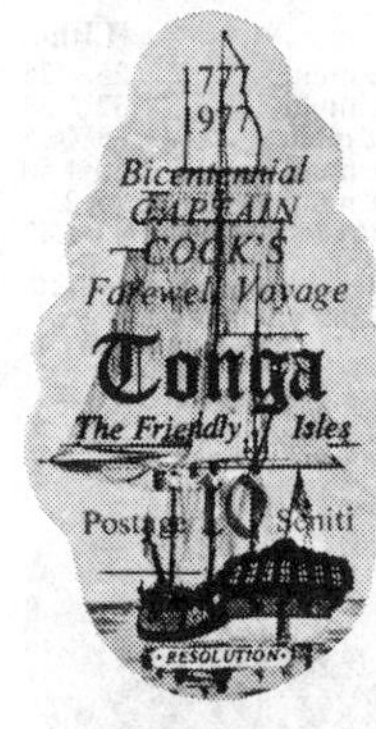


Capt. Cook's Resolution A71

**1977, Sept. 27** **Litho.**

| | | | | |
|---|---|---|---|---|
| *402* | A71 | 10s multi | 65 | 50 |
| *403* | A71 | 17s multi | 1.75 | 1.25 |
| *404* | A71 | 25s multi | 1.20 | 90 |
| *405* | A71 | 30s multi | 2.00 | 1.50 |
| *406* | A71 | 40s multi | 2.00 | 1.50 |
| | | *Nos. 402-406 (5)* | 7.60 | 5.65 |

Bicentenary of Capt. Cook's farewell voyage.

Humpback Whale — A72

**1977, Dec. 16**

| | | | | |
|---|---|---|---|---|
| *407* | A72 | 15s ultra & blk | 35 | 25 |
| *408* | A72 | 22s grn & blk | 50 | 35 |
| *409* | A72 | 31s org & blk | 75 | 50 |
| *410* | A72 | 38s lil & blk | 1.00 | 60 |
| *411* | A72 | 64s red & blk | 1.10 | 1.00 |
| | | *Nos. 407-411 (5)* | 3.70 | 2.70 |

Whale protection.

Stamps of 1975-77 Surcharged in Black, Green, Brown or Black on Silver

**1978**

| | | | | |
|---|---|---|---|---|
| *412* | A61 | 15s on 20s (#359;B) | 75 | 75 |
| *413* | A62 | 15s on 5s (#362;B) | 75 | 75 |
| *414* | A65 | 15s on 10s (#373;G) | 75 | 75 |
| *415* | A67 | 15s on 5s (#382;Br) | 75 | 75 |
| *416* | A67 | 15s on 10s (#383;B) | 75 | 75 |
| *417* | A69 | 15s on 11s (#392;B on S) | *3.75* | *3.75* |
| *418* | OA11 | 15s on 38s (#CO99;B) | 75 | 75 |
| | | *Nos. 412-416,418 (6)* | 4.50 | 4.50 |

The surcharge on No. 413 is only the "1," and on No. 418 includes "postage."

Flags of Canada and Tonga A73

**1978, May 5** **Litho.**

| | | | | |
|---|---|---|---|---|
| *419* | A73 | 10s red & multi | 30 | 30 |
| *420* | A73 | 15s red & multi | 42 | 42 |
| *421* | A73 | 20s red & multi | 60 | 60 |
| *422* | A73 | 25s red & multi | 75 | 75 |
| *423* | A73 | 45s red & multi | 1.25 | 1.25 |
| | | *Nos. 419-423 (5)* | 3.32 | 3.32 |

11th Commonwealth Games, Edmonton, Canada, Aug. 3-12. See note after No. 226.

King Taufa'ahau IV — A74

**1978, July 4**

| | | | | |
|---|---|---|---|---|
| *424* | A74 | 2s multi | 5 | 5 |
| *425* | A74 | 5s multi | 14 | 14 |
| *426* | A74 | 10s multi | 30 | 30 |
| *427* | A74 | 25s multi | 75 | 75 |
| *428* | A74 | 75s multi | 2.25 | 2.25 |
| | | *Nos. 424-428 (5)* | 3.49 | 3.49 |

60th birthday of King Taufa'ahau IV. See note after No. 226.

Two Bananas A75

Coconut A76

Designs: 1s to 5s, Bananas. 6s to 10s, Coconuts. 15s to 1pa, Pineapples.

**1978, Sept. 29** **Typo.**

| | | | | |
|---|---|---|---|---|
| *429* | A75 | 1s yel & blk | 5 | 5 |
| *430* | A75 | 2s yel & dk bl | 5 | 5 |
| *431* | A75 | 3s multi | 8 | 8 |
| *432* | A75 | 4s multi | 10 | 10 |
| *433* | A75 | 5s multi | 12 | 12 |
| *434* | A76 | 6s multi | 15 | 15 |
| *435* | A76 | 7s multi | 18 | 18 |
| *436* | A76 | 8s multi | 20 | 20 |
| *437* | A76 | 9s multi | 22 | 22 |
| *438* | A76 | 10s brn & grn | 24 | 24 |
| *439* | A76 | 15s grn & lt brn | 35 | 35 |
| *440* | A76 | 20s multi | 48 | 48 |
| *441* | A76 | 30s multi | 70 | 70 |
| *442* | A76 | 50s multi | 1.20 | 1.20 |
| *443* | A76 | 1pa multi | 2.40 | 2.40 |
| | | *Nos. 429-443 (15)* | 6.52 | 6.52 |

Nos. 429-443 issued in coils; self-adhesive control numbers on paper backing, except on 1s and 5s. See note after No. 226.

See No. 529.

Whale A77

**1978, Dec. 15** **Litho. & Typo.**

| | | | | |
|---|---|---|---|---|
| *444* | A77 | 15s shown | 70 | 70 |
| *445* | A77 | 18s Bat | 90 | 90 |
| *446* | A77 | 25s Turtle | 1.25 | 1.25 |
| *447* | A77 | 28s Parrot | 1.30 | 1.30 |
| *448* | A77 | 60s like 15s | 2.75 | 2.75 |
| | | *Nos. 444-448 (5)* | 6.90 | 6.90 |

Wildlife conservation. See note after No. 226.

Introduction of Metric System — A78

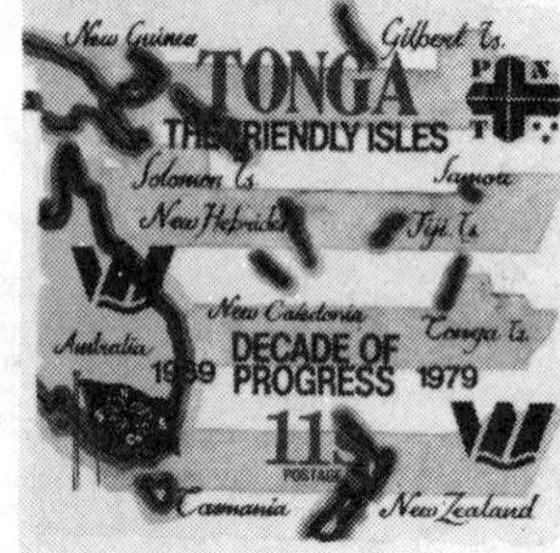


Shipping Routes, South Pacific Map — A79

Peace Corps — A80

Designs: 22s, New church buildings. 50s, Air routes to Auckland, Suva, Apia and Pago Pago.

**1979, Feb. 16** **Litho.**

| | | | | |
|---|---|---|---|---|
| *449* | A78 | 5s multi | 18 | 18 |
| *450* | A79 | 11s multi | 38 | 38 |
| *451* | A80 | 18s multi | 70 | 70 |
| *452* | A79 | 22s multi | 75 | 75 |
| *453* | A79 | 50s multi | 1.75 | 1.75 |
| | | *Nos. 449-453 (5)* | 3.76 | 3.76 |

Decade of Progress. Paper backing shows map of Tonga.

Tongan First Day Covers — A81

**1979, June 1**

| | | | | |
|---|---|---|---|---|
| *454* | A81 | 5s multi | 12 | 12 |
| *455* | A81 | 10s multi | 24 | 24 |
| *456* | A81 | 25s multi | 60 | 60 |
| *457* | A81 | 50s multi | 1.20 | 1.20 |
| *458* | A81 | 1pa multi | 1.80 | 1.80 |
| | | *Nos. 454-458 (5)* | 3.96 | 3.96 |

10th anniversary of introduction of self-adhesive stamps and for Bernard Mechanick, inventor of self-adhesive, free-form stamps; death centenary of Sir Rowland Hill.

Printed on peelable paper backing showing advertisement.

Eua Island through Camera Lens — A82

**1979, Nov. 23** **Litho.**

| | | | |
|---|---|---|---|
| *459* | A82 10s multi | 24 | 24 |
| *460* | A82 18s multi | 45 | 45 |
| *461* | A82 31s multi | 75 | 75 |
| *462* | A82 50s multi | 1.20 | 1.20 |
| *463* | A82 60s multi | 1.45 | 1.45 |
| | *Nos. 459-463 (5)* | 4.09 | 4.09 |

Printed on peelable paper backing showing film and camera.

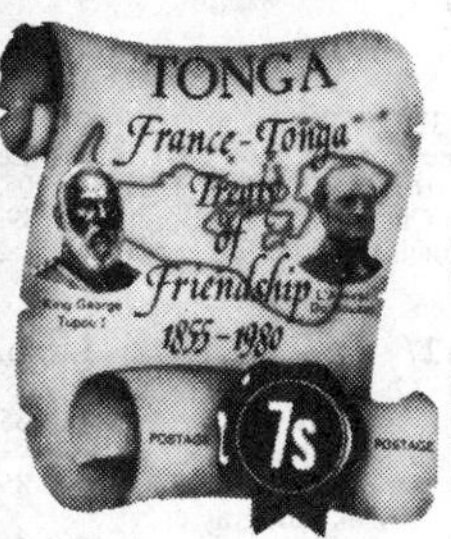


King George Tupou I, Admiral du Bouzet, Map of Tonga A83

**1980, Jan. 9** **Litho.**

| | | | |
|---|---|---|---|
| *464* | A83 7s multi | 16 | 16 |
| *465* | A83 10s multi | 24 | 24 |
| *466* | A83 14s multi | 35 | 35 |
| *467* | A83 50s multi | 1.20 | 1.20 |
| *468* | A83 75s multi | 1.80 | 1.80 |
| | *Nos. 464-468 (5)* | 3.75 | 3.75 |

Tongan-French Friendship Treaty, 125th anniversary. Printed on peelable paper; multicolored backing shows map of Tonga.

Nos. 454-458 Surcharged and Overprinted in Black on Silver: "1980 OLYMPIC GAMES," Moscow '80 and Bear Emblems.

**1980, Apr. 30** **Litho.**

| | | | |
|---|---|---|---|
| *469* | A81 13s on 5s multi | 32 | 32 |
| *470* | A81 20s on 10s multi | 48 | 48 |
| *471* | A81 25s multi | 60 | 60 |
| *472* | A81 33s on 50s multi | 80 | 80 |
| *473* | A81 1pa multi | 2.40 | 2.40 |
| | *Nos. 469-473 (5)* | 4.60 | 4.60 |

Boy Scout Cooking over Campfire — A84

**1980, Sept. 30** **Litho.**

| | | | |
|---|---|---|---|
| *474* | A84 9s multi | 30 | 30 |
| *475* | A84 13s multi | 45 | 45 |
| *476* | A84 15s multi | 50 | 50 |
| *477* | A84 30s multi | 1.00 | 1.00 |

Boy Scout Jamboree; Rotary Intl., 75th anniv. Peelable backing shows map of Tonga.

Nos. 361, 375, 380, 384-385 Surcharged

**1980, Dec. 3** **Litho.**

| | | | |
|---|---|---|---|
| *478* | A65 9s on 35s multi | 22 | 22 |
| *479* | A67 13s on 20s multi | 32 | 32 |
| *480* | A67 13s on 25s multi | 32 | 32 |
| *481* | A66 19s on 25s multi | 45 | 45 |
| *482* | A61 1pa on 65s multi | 2.40 | 2.40 |
| | *Nos. 478-482 (5)* | 3.71 | 3.71 |

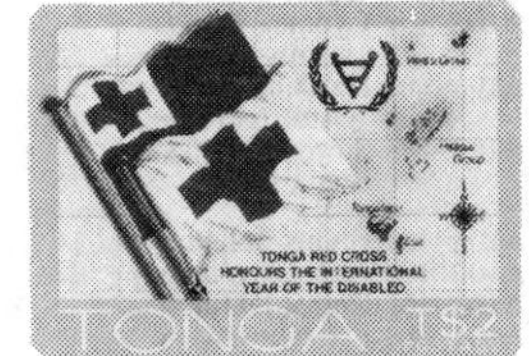


Intl. Year of the Disabled — A85

**1981, Sept. 9** **Litho.**

| | | | |
|---|---|---|---|
| *483* | A85 2pa multi | 6.00 | 6.00 |
| *484* | A85 3pa multi | 9.00 | 9.00 |

Prince Charles and Lady Diana — A86

Designs: 13s, Charles, King Taufa'ahau. 47s, 1.50pa, Couple (diff.).

**1981, Oct. 21** **Litho.**

| | | | |
|---|---|---|---|
| *485* | A86 13s multi | 32 | 32 |
| *486* | A86 47s multi | 1.00 | 1.00 |
| *487* | A86 1.50pa multi | 3.60 | 3.60 |
| *488* | A86 3pa multi | 7.25 | 7.25 |

Royal Wedding and Gt. Britain-Tonga Friendship Treaty centenary. Issued in sheets of 20 (2x10) and 5 labels in vert. center row.

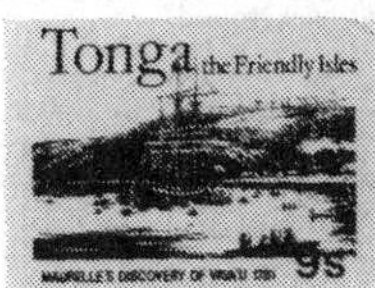


Bicentenary of Discovery of Vavau by Francisco Maurelle A87

Designs: 18th century Spanish engravings and maps.

**1981, Nov. 25** **Litho.**

| | | | |
|---|---|---|---|
| *489* | A87 9s multi | 20 | 20 |
| *490* | A87 13s multi | 32 | 32 |
| *491* | A87 47s multi | 1.00 | 1.00 |
| *492* | A87 1pa multi | 2.40 | 2.40 |
| *a.* | Souvenir sheet | 3.50 | 3.50 |

No. 492a contains No. 492 (32x25mm., imperf.); multicolored margin continues design. Size: 100x78mm.

Bible Class, 1830 Print A88

**1981, Nov. 25**

| | | | |
|---|---|---|---|
| *493* | A88 9s Open book | 20 | 20 |
| *494* | A88 13s Book, diff. | 32 | 32 |
| *495* | A88 32s Type | 80 | 80 |
| *496* | A88 47s shown | 1.00 | 1.00 |

Christmas 1981 and sesquicentennial of books printed in Tonga.

175th Anniv. of Capture of The Port-au-Prince — A89

**1981, Dec. 16** **Litho.**

| | | | |
|---|---|---|---|
| *497* | A89 29s Battle | 70 | 70 |
| *498* | A89 32s Battle, diff. | 80 | 80 |
| *499* | A89 47s Map | 1.10 | 1.10 |
| *500* | A89 47s Sinking ship | 1.10 | 1.10 |
| *501* | A89 1pa Ship | 2.40 | 2.40 |
| | *Nos. 497-501 (5)* | 6.10 | 6.10 |

Nos. 499-500 se-tenant.

Nos. CO179-CO180 Surcharged

**1982, Jan. 4** **Litho.**

| | | | |
|---|---|---|---|
| *502* | OA19 5pa on 25s multi | 10.00 | 10.00 |
| *503* | OA19 5pa on 2pa multi | 10.00 | 10.00 |

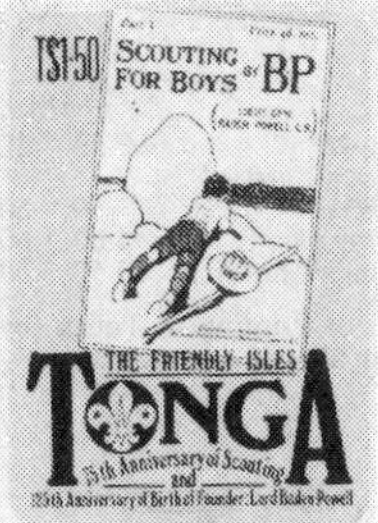


Scouting Year — A90

**1982, Feb. 22** **Litho.**

| | | | |
|---|---|---|---|
| *504* | A90 29s Brownsea Isld. Camp, 1907 | 55 | 55 |
| *505* | A90 32s Baden-Powell, horse | 60 | 60 |
| *506* | A90 47s Imperial Jamboree, 1924 | 90 | 90 |
| *507* | A90 1.50pa "Scouting for Boys" | 2.75 | 2.75 |
| *508* | A90 2.50pa Mafeking stamp | 4.50 | 4.50 |
| | *Nos. 504-508 (5)* | 9.30 | 9.30 |

1982 World Cup — A91

Designs: Various soccer players, map showing match sites.

**1982, July 7** **Litho.**

| | | | |
|---|---|---|---|
| *509* | A91 32s multi | 60 | 60 |
| *510* | A91 47s multi | 90 | 90 |
| *511* | A91 75s multi | 1.40 | 1.40 |
| *512* | A91 1.50pa multi | 2.75 | 2.75 |

Inter-island Transport A92

Designs: 92, 13s, Ferry Olovaha. 47s, 1pa SPIA Twin Otter (Niuatoputapu Airport opening).

**1982, Aug. 11**

| | | | |
|---|---|---|---|
| *513* | A92 9s multi | 15 | 15 |
| *514* | A92 13s multi | 25 | 25 |
| *515* | A92 47s multi | 90 | 90 |
| *516* | A92 1pa multi | 1.75 | 1.75 |

Tin Can Mail Centenary A93

Designs: 13s, 32s, 47s, Collecting mail. 2pa, Map. Nos. 517-519 form continuous design.

**1982, Sept. 29** **Litho.**

| | | | |
|---|---|---|---|
| *517* | A93 13s multi | 25 | 25 |
| *518* | A93 32s multi | 55 | 55 |
| *519* | A93 47s multi | 90 | 90 |
| *a.* | Souv. sheet of 3 (13s, 32s, 47s) | 1.75 | 1.75 |
| *520* | A93 2pa multi | 4.00 | 4.00 |
| *a.* | Souvenir sheet | 4.00 | 4.00 |

No. 519a has multicolored margin continuing design. Size: 135x90mm. No. 520a has multicolored margin showing cover. Size: 135x90mm.

Tonga College Centenary — A94

**1982, Oct. 25** **Size: 42x30mm (5s)**

| | | | |
|---|---|---|---|
| *521* | A94 5s Students | 16 | 16 |
| *522* | A94 29s King George Tupou I | 1.00 | 1.00 |
| *523* | A94 29s Monument | 1.00 | 1.00 |

Nos. 522-523 se-tenant; Nos. 521-523 inscribed in English or Tongan.

12th Commonwealth Games, Brisbane, Australia, Sept. 30-Oct. 9 — A95

**1982, Oct. 25**

| | | | |
|---|---|---|---|
| *524* | A95 32s Decathlon, vert. | 50 | 50 |
| *525* | A95 1.50pa Opening ceremony | 2.25 | 2.25 |

Nos. 517-519 Overprinted in Red or Silver in 1 or 2 Lines: "Christmas / Greetings / 1982"

**1982, Nov. 17**

| | | | |
|---|---|---|---|
| *526* | A93 13s multi | 32 | 32 |
| *527* | A93 32s multi | 80 | 80 |
| *528* | A93 47s multi | 1.10 | 1.10 |

Common Design Types are pictured in section before Great Britain.

Pineapple Type of 1978 and

Fruit — A96

**1982, Nov. 17**

*529* A76 13s multi 25 25
*530* A96 2pa multi 4.00 4.00
*531* A96 3pa multi 6.00 6.00

Capt. Cook's Resolution, 1777 and Canberra, 1983 A96a

Designs: 32s, like 29s. 47s, 1.50pa, Montgolfier Bros. balloon, 1783, Concorde. 2.50pa, Concorde, Canberra. 29s se-tenant with label showing Resolution.

**1983, Feb. 22** **Litho.**

*532* A96a 29s multi 50 50
*533* A96a 32s multi 60 60
*534* A96a 47s multi 90 90
*535* A96a 1.50pa multi 2.50 2.50

**Souvenir Sheet**

*536* A96a 2.50pa multi 4.50 4.50

Pacific Forum of Sea and Air Transport (29s, 32s, 2.50pa); manned flight bicentenary (47s, 1.50pa). Size of No. 536; 120x65mm.

**Commonwealth Day**
Common Design Type

**1983, Mar. 14**

*537* CD334 29s Map 1.40 1.40
*538* CD334 32s Dancers 1.60 1.60
*539* CD334 47s Fishermen 2.25 2.25
*540* CD334 1.50pa King Taufa'ahau IV, flag 7.00 7.00

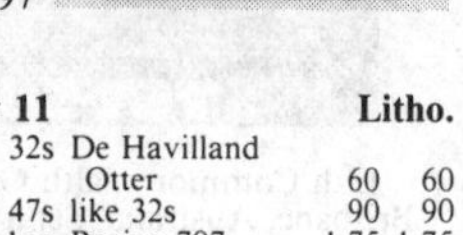

Niuafo'ou Airport Opening A97

**1983, May 11** **Litho.**

*541* A97 32s De Havilland Otter 60 60
*542* A97 47s like 32s 90 90
*543* A97 1pa Boeing 707 1.75 1.75
*544* A97 1.50pa like 1pa 2.75 2.75

World Communications Year — A98

**1983, June 22** **Litho.**

*545* A98 29s Intelsat IV 70 70
*546* A98 32s Intelsat IV-A 80 80
*547* A98 75s Intelsat V 1.80 1.80

**Size: 45x32mm**

*548* A98 2pa Apollo 15 Moon post cover 4.80 4.80

10th Anniv. of Bank of Tonga A99

Various banknotes.

**1983, Aug. 3** **Litho.**

*549* A99 1pa multi 1.75 1.75
*550* A99 2pa multi 3.50 3.50

Printing Press, 1830 — A100

**1983, Sept. 22** **Litho.**

*551* A100 13s shown 22 22
*552* A100 32s Woon's arrival, 1831 60 60
*553* A100 1pa Print 1.60 1.60
*554* A100 2pa Tonga Chronicle 3.50 3.50

Sesquicentennial of Printing in Tonga (by Missionary William Woon)

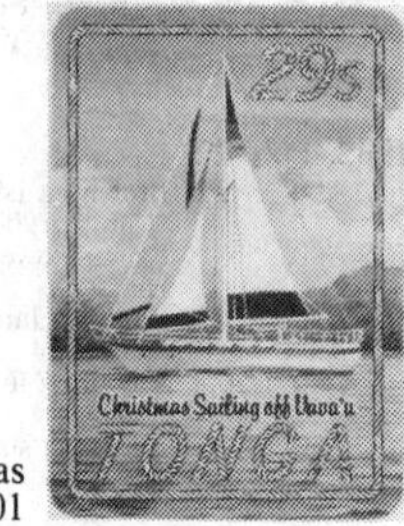


Christmas 1983 — A101

Designs: Various sailboats off Vava'u.

**1983, Nov. 17** **Litho.**

*555* A101 29s multi 50 50
*556* A101 32s multi 60 60
*557* A101 1.50pa multi 2.50 2.50
*558* A101 2.50pa multi 4.50 4.50

Abel Tasman, Discoverer of Tonga, and his Zeehan A102

Navigators and Explorers of the Pacific and their Ships.

**1984, Mar. 12** **Litho.**

*559* A102 32s shown 70 70
*560* A102 47s Samuel Wallis, Dolphin 90 90
*561* A102 90s William Bligh, Bounty 1.75 1.75
*562* A102 1.50pa James Cook, Resolution 3.00 3.00

Swainsonia Casta — A103

Shells, fish.

**1984-85** **Litho.**

*563* A103 1s shown 5 5
*564* A103 2s Porites (coral) 5 5
*565* A103 3s Holocentrus ruber 6 6
*566* A103 5s Cypraea mappa viridis 8 8
*567* A103 6s Dardanus megistos (crab) 12 12
*568* A103 9s Stegostoma fasciatum 15 15
*a* Perf. 14½ ('85) 15 15
*569* A103 10s Conus bullatus 16 16
*570* A103 13s Pterois volitans 22 22
*571* A103 15s Conus textile 25 25
*572* A103 20s Dascyllus aruanus 32 32
*573* A103 29s Conus aulicus 50 50
*574* A103 32s Acanthurus leucosternon 50 50
*575* A103 47s Lambis truncata 80 80

**Size: 39x25mm**

*576* A103 1pa Millepora dichotama (coral) 1.60 1.60
*577* A103 2pa Birgus latro (crab) 3.25 3.25
*578* A103 3pa Chicoreus palma-rosae 5.00 5.00
*579* A103 5pa Thunnus albacares 8.25 8.25
*Nos. 563-579 (17)* 21.36 21.36

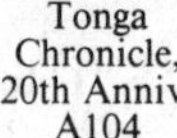

Tonga Chronicle, 20th Anniv. A104

1984 Summer Olympics A105

**1984, June 26**

*580* A104 3s multi 6 6
*581* A104 32s multi 60 60

Nos. 580-581 issued in sheets of 12; sheet backgrounds show pages of Chronicle, giving each stamp different background.

**1984, July 23**

*582* A105 29s Running 55 55
*583* A105 47s Javelin 90 90
*584* A105 1.50pa Shot put 2.75 2.75
*585* A105 3pa Torch 5.50 5.50

Intl. Dateline Centenary A106

**1984, Aug. 20**

*586* A106 47s George Airy, Greenwich Meridian pioneer 75 75
*587* A106 2pa Sandford Fleming, time zone pioneer 3.25 3.25

Ausipex '84 — A107

**1984, Sept. 17**

*588* A107 32s Australia No. 18 50 50
*589* A107 1.50pa Tonga No. 51 2.50 2.50
*a* Souvenir sheet of 2 3.00 3.00

No. 589a contains Nos. 588-589 (gold embossing, no emblem); multicolored margin shows Royal Exhibition Building, Melbourne. Size: 90x100mm.

Nos. 588-589 each printed se-tenant with label showing exhibition emblem.

Christmas 1984 — A108

Christmas Carols in local settings.

**1984, Nov. 12** **Litho.**

*590* A108 32s Silent Night 50 50
*591* A108 47s Away in a Manger 75 75
*592* A108 1pa I Saw Three Ships 1.60 1.60

Famous Mariners A109

Designs: 32s, Willem Schouten (c. 1580-1625), The Eendracht, 1616. 47s, Jakob Le Maire (1585-1616), The Hoorn, 1615. 90s, Lt. Fletcher Christian, The Bounty, 1789. 1.50 pa, Francisco Maurelle, La Princessa, 1781.

**1985, Feb. 27** **Litho.**

*593* A109 32s dl grnsh bl, gray & blk 55 55
*594* A109 47s dl bluish grn, gray & blk 85 85
*595* A109 90s dk red, gray & blk 1.50 1.50
*596* A109 1.50pa yel bis, gray & blk 2.75 2.75

Nos. 593-596 printed se-tenant with self-adhesive label picturing anchor.

Geological Survey of Tonga Trench for Oil A110

Designs: 29s, Tonga Trench and islands. 32s, Marine exploration, seismic surveying. 47s, Search for oil off Tongatapu, vert. No. 600, Exploration of sea bed, vert. No. 601, Angler fish.

**1985, Apr. 10**

*597* A110 29s multi 42 42
*598* A110 32s multi 45 45
*599* A110 47s multi 68 68
*600* A110 1.50pa multi 2.15 2.15

**Souvenir Sheet**

*601* A110 1.50pa multi 2.50 2.50

Nos. 597-600 printed in sheets of 40, 2 panes of 20 separated by labels inscribed "Proof 1," etc. No. 601 has multicolored margin continuing design picturing marine habitat. Size: 100x100mm.

Adventures of Will Mariner — A111

Designs: 29s, Readying Port au Prince for sail, Gravesend, 1805. 32s, Captured and set afire, 1806. 47s, Mariner taken prisoner by Chief Finow, Tonga. 1.50pa, Passage to China aboard brig Favourite. 2.50pa, Returning to England aboard East Indiaman Cuffnells, 1810.

**1985, June 18**

*602* A111 29s multi 42 42
*603* A111 32s multi 45 45
*604* A111 47s multi 68 68

*605* A111 1.50pa multi 2.15 2.15
*606* A111 2.50pa multi 3.50 3.50
*Nos. 602-606 (5)* 7.20 7.20

Mutiny on the Bounty, Film 50th Anniv.
A112

Designs: a, Byron Russell (Quintal), Stanley Fields (Muspratt) and Charles Laughton (Capt. Bligh). b, Laughton, Donald Crisp (Burkitt), Eddie Quillon (Ellison) and David Thursby (Maxwell). c, Clark Gable (Fletcher Christian). d, Russell, Alec Craig (McCoy), Laughton and Fields. e, Laughton and Franchot Tone (Roger Byam).

**1985, July 16** ***Perf. 14***
*607* Strip of 5 3.40 3.40
*a.-e.* A112 47s, any single 68 68

Sheets consist of four strips of 5 and a central strip of labels showing film credits.

Queen Mother, 85th Birthday
A113

Designs: 32s, Age 10. 47s, At Hadfield Girl Guides rally, 1931. 1.50pa, In Guide uniform. 2.50pa, Portrait by Norman Parkinson, 1985.

**1985, Aug. 20** ***Imperf.***
*608* A113 32s multi 45 45
*a.* Perf. 14 45 45
*609* A113 47s multi 68 68
*a.* Perf. 14 68 68
*610* A113 1.50pa multi 2.15 2.15
*a.* Perf. 14 2.15 2.15
*611* A113 2.50pa multi 3.50 3.50
*a.* Perf. 14 3.50 3.50

Girl Guides movement, 75th anniv.

Christmas — A114

**1985, Nov. 12**
*612* A114 32s No room at the inn 45 45
*613* A114 42s Shepherds follow star 60 60
*614* A114 1.50pa The three kings 2.15 2.15
*615* A114 2.50pa Holy family 3.50 3.50

Self-adhesive Discontinued
In 1986, imperforate self-adhesive stamps attached to peelable paper backing were no longer issued, unless otherwise stated.

Halley's Comet
A115

Designs: Nos. 616a, 617a, Comet. Nos. 616b, 617b, Edmond Halley. Nos. 616c, 617c, Solar system. Nos. 616d, 617d, Telescope. Nos. 616e, 617e, Giotto space probe.

**1986, Mar. 26** ***Perf. 14***
*616* Strip of 5 3.00 3.00
*a.-e.* A115 42s, any single 60 60
*617* Strip of 5 4.00 4.00
*a.-e.* A115 57s, any single 80 80

Nos. 564, 570, 565, 568, 567, 572, 577 and 579 Surcharged.

**1986, Apr. 16** **Litho.** ***Imperf.***
**Self-adhesive**
*618* A103 4s on 2s, No. 564 6 6
*619* A103 4s on 13s, No. 570 6 6
*620* A103 42s on 3s, No. 565 60 60
*621* A103 42s on 9s, No. 568 60 60
*622* A103 57s on 6s, No. 567 82 82
*623* A103 57s on 20s, No. 572 82 82
*624* A103 2.50pa on 2pa, No. 577 3.50 3.50
*625* A103 2.50pa on 5pa, No. 579 3.50 3.50
*Nos. 618-625 (8)* 9.96 9.96

Royal Links with the United Kingdom
A116

**1986, May 22** ***Perf. 14***
*626* A116 57s Taufa'ahau IV 80 80
*627* A116 57s Elizabeth II 80 80
**Size: 40x40mm**
*628* A116 2.50pa King and queen 3.50 3.50

Queen Elizabeth II, 60th birthday. One label printed between se-tenant pairs of Nos. 626-627. No. 628 printed in sheets of 5 plus one label.

AMERIPEX '86, Chicago, May 22-June 1 — A117

Peace Corps activities: No. 629, Health care. No. 630, Education.

**1986, May 22**
*629* A117 57s multi 80 80
*630* A117 1.50pa multi 2.15 2.15
*a.* Souvenir sheet of 2, #629, 630 imperf. 3.00 3.00

Peace Corps in Tonga, 20th anniv. Nos. 629-630 printed se-tenant. No. 630a has multicolored margin picturing quadrille album page, tongs and magnifying glass. Size: 90x90mm.

Intl. Sporting Events — A118

Designs: 42s, 1986 Field Hockey World Cup, London. 57s, Women's basketball, 13th Commonwealth Games, Scotland. 1pa, Boxing, Commonwealth Games. 2.50pa, 1986 World Cup Soccer Championships, Mexico.

**1986, July 23** **Litho.** ***Perf. 14***
*631* A118 42s multi 60 60
*632* A118 57s multi 82 82
*633* A118 1pa multi 1.40 1.40
*634* A118 2.50pa multi 3.50 3.50

Postage Stamp Cent.
A119

Stamps on stamps: No. 635, #1. No. 636, #47a. No. 637, #91. No. 638, #628. No. 639a, #40, UL portion of #C29. No. 639b, UR portion of #C29, left side #245. No. 639c, Center of #245, Type AP10. No. 639d, Left side #245, #C148. No. 639e, LL portion of #C29, #429, #440. No. 639f, LR portion of #C29, #C135. No. 639g, #507. No. 639h, #514. Nos. 639a-639h, vert.

**1986, Aug. 27**
*635* A119 32s multi 45 45
*636* A119 42s multi 60 60
*637* A119 57s multi 82 82
*638* A119 2.50pa multi 3.50 3.50
**Souvenir Sheet**
*639* Sheet of 8 5.60 5.60
*a.-h.* A119 50s, any single 70 70

No. 639 has inscribed decorative margin. Size: 132x104mm.

Christmas
A120

Designs: 32s, Girls wearing shell jewelry. 42s, Boy, totem poles, vert. 57s, Folk dancers, vert. 2pa, outrigger canoe.

**1986, Nov. 12** **Litho.** ***Perf. 14***
*640* A120 32s multi 45 45
*641* A120 42s multi 60 60
*642* A120 57s multi 82 82
*643* A120 2pa multi 2.85 2.85

Nos. 642-643 Ovptd. with Jamboree Emblem and "BOY SCOUT / JAMBOREE / 5th-10th DEC '86" in Silver

**1986, Dec. 2** **Litho.** ***Perf. 14***
*644* A120 42s multi 60 60
*645* A120 57s multi 82 82

Dumont d'Urville's Second Voyage — A121

Designs: 32s, D'Urville and ship Astrolabe. 42s, Four Tongan girls, detail fron D'Urville's engraving, Voyage au Pole et dans l'Oceanie. 1pa, Map of voyage. 2.50pa, Wreck of the Astrolabe.

**1987, Feb. 24**
*646* A121 32s multi 45 45
*647* A121 42s multi 60 60
*648* A121 1pa multi 1.40 1.40
*649* A121 2.50pa multi 3.50 3.50

Dumont d'Urville (1790-1842), explorer and admiral.

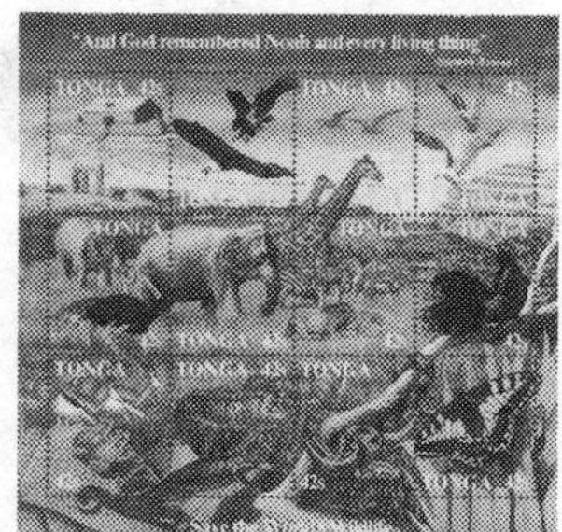


Wildlife Conservation — A122

Fauna: a, Noah's Ark. b, Eagles. c, Giraffes, birds. d, Seagulls. e, Elephants, ostriches. f, Elephant. g, Lions, zebras, antelopes. h, Chimpanzees. i, Antelope, frogs. j, Tigers, lizard. k, Tiger, snake. l, Butterfly.

**1987, May 6** ***Perf. 13½***
*650* Sheet of 12 7.25 7.25
*a.-l.* A122 42s any single 60 60

Size of No. 650: 115x110mm.

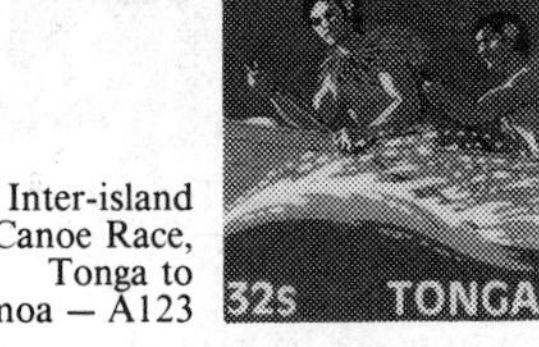


1st Inter-island Canoe Race, Tonga to Samoa — A123

**1987, July 1** ***Perf. 14***
*651* A123 32s Two paddlers 45 45
*652* A123 42s Five paddlers 60 60
*653* A123 57s Three paddlers 80 80
*654* A123 1.50pa Two, diff. 2.15 2.15
*a.* Souv. sheet of 4, Nos. 651-654 4.00 4.00

No. 654a has inscribed margin; stamps printed in a continuous design. Size: 154x58mm.

Coronation of King Taufa'ahau IV, 20th Anniv. — A124

**Booklet Stamps**
**1987, July 1** ***Imperf.***
**Self-Adhesive**
*655* A124 1s grn & yel grn 5 5
*656* A124 5s blk & brt pink 8 8
*a.* Bklt. pane of 12 (6 5s plus 1 5s, 2 10s, 3 15s with gutter between) 1.60
*657* A124 10s blk & bluish lil 14 14
*658* A124 15s brn blk & org ver 22 22
*659* A124 32s Prus blk & aqua 45 45
*a.* Bklt. pane of 12 (4 32s, 2 15s plus 4 10s, 2 1s with gutter between) 2.95
*Nos. 655-659 (5)* 94 94

Parliament, 125th Anniv. — A125

**1987, Sept. 2** **Litho.** ***Perf. 14½***
*660* A125 32s multi 50 50
*661* A125 42s multi 65 65
*662* A125 75s multi 1.15 1.15
*663* A125 2pa multi 3.00 3.00

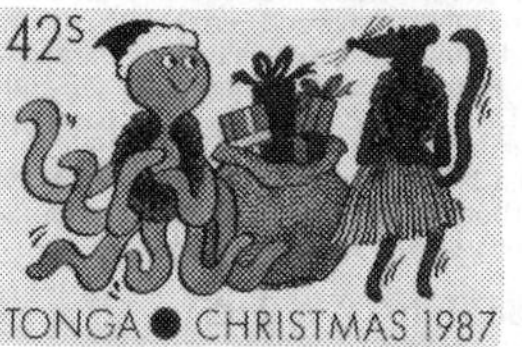


Christmas 1987 — A126

Cartoons featuring Octopus as Santa Claus and mouse as his helper.

**1987, Nov. 18** **Litho.** ***Perf. 14***
*664* A126 42s Sack of gifts 68 68
*665* A126 57s Delivering them by canoe 92 92
*666* A126 1pa By automobile 1.60 1.60
*667* A126 3pa Sipping tropical drinks 4.85 4.85

King Taufa'ahau Tupou IV, 70th Birthday — A127

Portrait and: 32s, M.V. *Olovaha* inter-island ship, athlete pole vaulting and offshore oil derrick. 42s, Banknote and coins, Ha'Amonga Trilithon and traditional craftsman. 57s, Rowing, Red Cross nurse and communications satellite. $2.50, Tonga Scouts emblem, No. 506 and Friendly Islands Airways passenger plane.

**1988, July 4 Litho. *Perf. 11½***
*668* A127 32s multi 48 48
*669* A127 42s multi 60 60
*670* A127 57s multi 82 82
*671* A127 $2.50 multi 3.60 3.60

Souvenir Sheet

Australia Bicentennial — A128

Designs: a. Cook and his journal. b. List of stores shipped aboard the *Lady Juliana*, the ship, Arthur Philip, 1st gov. of New South Wales, 1788, and left half of the list of sentences of all the prisoners tried at Glo'ster Assizes. c. Right half of list of sentences, Australia Type A59 redrawn and aerial view of an early settlement. d. Robert O'Hara Burke (1820-61) and W.J. Wills (1834-61), the 1st explorers to cross Australia from south to north. e. Emu pictured on a Player's cigarette card, U.R. Stuart's (gold) prospecting license and opals. f. Australian Commonwealth Military Forces emblem, WW I recruit on cigarette card, and war poster. g. Souv. card commemorating 1st overland mail delivery by transcontinental railway, and Australia Type A4 on cover. h. Hand-canceled cover commemorating the 1st England-Australia transcontinental airmail flight, Nov. 12-Dec.10, 1919, aviator Capt. Ross Smith (1892-1922) and Great Britain No. 588. i. Don Bradman and Harold Larwood, cricket champions of the 1930s, on cigarette cards, and era newspaper frontispiece. j. Frontispiece of Hulton's natl. weekly *Picture Post* Victory Special issue, and WW II campaign medals. k. Australia No. 676 and a sheep station. l. Sydney Harbor Bridge, Opera House and theater tickets to *The Bartered Bride*.

**1988, July 11 Litho. *Perf. 13½***
*672* A128 Souv. sheet of 12 7.25 7.25
*a.-l.* 42s any single 60 60

No. 672 has multicolored inscribed margin continuing the design. Size: 115x110mm.

1988 Summer Olympics, Seoul — A129

**1988, Aug. 11 *Perf. 14***
*673* A129 57s Running 82 82
*674* A129 75s Yachting 1.05 1.05
*675* A129 $2 Cycling 2.85 2.85
*676* A129 $3 Women's tennis 4.25 4.25

Music of Tonga A130

**1988, Sept. 9 Litho. *Perf. 14***
*677* A130 32s shown 45 45
*678* A130 42s Choir 60 60
*679* A130 57s Tonga Police Band 82 82
*680* A130 $2.50 The Jets 3.50 3.50

Souvenir Sheet

*681* Sheet of 2 1.65 1.65
*a.* A130 57s like $2.50 82 82
*b.* A130 57s Olympic eternal flame 82 82

SPORT AID '88. No. 681 has multicolored inscribed margin. Size: 105x75mm.

## SEMI-POSTAL STAMP

**Catalogue values for unused stamps in this section are for Never Hinged items.**

No. 488 Surcharged in Silver for Cyclone Relief

**1982, Apr. 14 Litho.**
*B1* A86 3pa + 50s multi 8.50 8.50

## AIR POST STAMPS

**Catalogue values for unused stamps in this section, from this point to the end of the section, are for Never Hinged items.**

Type of Regular Gold Coin Issue

Designs: 10p, 1sh1p, Queen Salote standing, ½-koula coin, obverse. 11p, Coat of arms, ½-koula coin, reverse. 2sh1p, 2sh9p, Queen Salote standing, 1-koula coin, obverse. 2sh4p, Coat of arms, 1-koula coin, reverse.

**Litho.; Embossed on Gilt Foil**
**1963, July 15 Unwmk. *Imperf.***
**Diameter: 54mm**
*C1* A36 10p dp car 40 40
*C2* A36 11p green 60 60
*C3* A36 1sh6p vio bl 60 60
**Diameter: 80mm**
*C4* A36 2sh1p magenta 1.00 1.00
*C5* A36 2sh4p emerald 1.00 1.00
*C6* A36 2sh9p violet 1.50 1.50
*Nos. C1-C6 (6)* 5.10 5.10

See note after No. 133.

Map of Tongatabu and ¼-Koula Coin — AP1

**Litho.; Embossed on Gilt Foil**
**1964, Oct. 19**
*C7* AP1 10p dp grn 15 15
*C8* AP1 1sh2p black 18 18
*C9* AP1 3sh6p carmine 60 60
*C10* AP1 6sh6p purple 1.20 1.20

Pan-Pacific and Southeast Asia Women's Association Conf., Nukualofa, Aug. 1964. See note after No. 133.

Nos. C1-C2, C4-C6 Surcharged like Regular Issue, 1965, in Black, White or Red

**1965, Mar. 18**
*C11* A36 2sh3p on 10p dp car (B) 42 42
*C12* A36 2sh9p on 11p grn (W) 60 60
*C13* A36 4sh6p on 2sh1p mag 14.00 14.00
*C14* A36 4sh6p on 2sh4p emer 14.00 14.00
*C15* A36 4sh6p on 2sh9p vio 14.00 14.00
*Nos. C11-C15 (5)* 43.02 43.02

Nos. 114-115, 117-118 Overprinted and Surcharged

AIRMAIL
1866 CENTENARY 1966
TUPOU COLLEGE
&
SECONDARY EDUCATION
10d XX

***Perf. 14½x13½***
**1966, June 18 Wmk. 79**
*C16* A35 5p purple 7 7
*C17* A35 10p on 1p brn org & car rose 8 8
*C18* A35 1sh red brn 14 14
*C19* A35 2sh9p on 2p ultra 40 40
*C20* A35 3sh6p on 5p pur 55 55
*C21* A35 4sh6p on 1sh red brn 65 65
*Nos. C16-C21 (6)* 1.89 1.89

Centenary of Tupou College and secondary education. The overprint or surcharge is spaced differently on other values.

Nos. C7-C8 Overprinted and Surcharged in Silver or Gold on Black, or in Black on Gold

4/-

**Litho.; Embossed on Gilt Foil**
**1966, Dec. 16 Unwmk. *Imperf.***
*C22* AP1 10p dp grn (S on B) 10 10
*C23* AP1 1sh2p blk (B on G) 20 20
*C24* AP1 4sh on 10p dp grn (S on B) 65 65
*C25* AP1 5sh6p on 1sh2p blk (B on G) 85 85
*C26* AP1 10sh6p on 1sh2p blk (G on B) 1.50 1.50
*Nos. C22-C26 (5)* 3.30 3.30

In memory of Queen Salote (1900-65).

King Taufa'ahau Type of Regular Issue, 1967

Designs: 7s, 11s, 23s, 2pa, Taufa'ahau IV, obverse of new palladium coins. 9s, 21s, 29s, Coat of Arms, reverse.

**Litho.; Embossed on Palladium Foil**
**1967, July 4**

Diameter: 7s, 44mm.; 9s, 29s, 52mm.; 11s, 59mm.; 21s, 68mm.; 23s, 40mm.; 2pa, 74mm.

*C27* A38 7s red & blk 16 16
*C28* A38 9s mar & emer 25 25
*C29* A38 11s brt bl & org 32 32
*C30* A38 21s blk & emer 55 55
*C31* A38 23s mag & emer 60 60
*C32* A38 29s vio bl & emer 70 70
*C33* A38 2pa mag & org 4.75 4.75
*Nos. C27-C33 (7)* 7.33 7.33

See note after No. 181.

Type of Regular Issue, 1953 Surcharged in Red or Black

The
Friendly Islands
welcome the
United States
Peace Corps

AIRMAIL
21s

**Wmk. 79**
**1967, Dec. 15 Engr. *Imperf.***
*C34* A33 11s on 3½p ultra (R) 60 60
*C35* A33 21s on 1½p emer 1.00 1.00
*C36* A33 23s on 3½p ultra (R) 1.25 1.25

Arrival of the United States Peace Corps.

No. 112 Surcharged in Red

AIRMAIL
11
SENITI
11

**1968, Apr. 6 Engr. *Perf. 11x11½***
*C37* A34 11s on 10sh blk & yel 40 40
*C38* A34 21s on 10sh blk & yel 75 75
*C39* A34 23s on 10sh blk & yel 90 90

Nos. C27-C33 Overprinted: "HIS MAJESTY'S 50th BIRTHDAY" in Silver on Blue Panel on 7s, 11s, 23s and 2pa. "H.M.'s BIRTHDAY / 4 . JULY . 1968" in Gold on Red Panel on 9s, 21s and 29s.

**Litho.; Embossed on Palladium Foil**
**1968, July 4 Unwmk. *Imperf.***
*C40* A38 7s red & blk 25 25
*C41* A38 9s mar & emer 32 32
*C42* A38 11s brt bl & org 40 40
*C43* A38 21s blk & emer 85 85
*C44* A38 23s mag & emer 1.00 1.00
*C45* A38 29s vio bl & emer 1.40 1.40
*C46* A38 2pa mag & org 8.00 8.00
*Nos. C40-C46 (7)* 12.22 12.22

50th birthday of King Taufa'ahau IV.

Types of 1953 Surcharged: "Friendly Islands / Field & Track Trials / South Pacific Games / Port Moresby 1969 / AIRMAIL"

Designs as Before.

**1968, Dec. 19 Engr. Wmk. 79**
*C47* A33 6s on 6p yel & blk 10 10
*C48* A33 7s on 4p pur & yel 12 12
*C49* A33 8s on 8p blk & lt grn 14 14
*C50* A33 9s on 1½p emer 16 16
*C51* A34 11s on 3p brn org & yel 20 20
*C52* A33 21s on 3½p dk bl 40 40
*C53* A33 38s on 5sh sep & yel 80 80
*C54* A34 1pa on 10sh org yel 2.00 2.00
*Nos. C47-C54 (8)* 3.92 3.92

Issued to publicize the field and track trials for the third South Pacific Games, Port Moresby, 1969. The overprint is in 5 lines on the horizontal stamps, in 7 lines on the vertical stamps. On the vertical stamps "Trial" is printed on the line ahead of "Field & Track". On No. C54 the denomination is spelled out.

Nos. C19-C21 Surcharged

***Perf. 14½x13½***
**1968 Photo. Wmk. 79**
*C55* A35 1s on 2sh9p on 2p ultra 45 45
*C56* A35 1s on 3sh6p on 5p pur 45 45
*C57* A35 1s on 4sh6p on 1sh red brn 45 45

Pacific Games Type of Regular Issue

Design: Boxer.

**1969, Aug. 13 Litho. *Imperf.***
**Self-adhesive**
*C58* A40 9s org, blk & pur 38 38
*C59* A40 11s org, blk & dk bl 42 42
*C60* A40 20s org, blk & yel grn 75 75
*C61* A40 60s org, blk & scar 2.25 2.25
*C62* A40 1pa org, blk & grn 3.75 3.75
*Nos. C58-C62 (5)* 7.55 7.55

See note after No. 231.

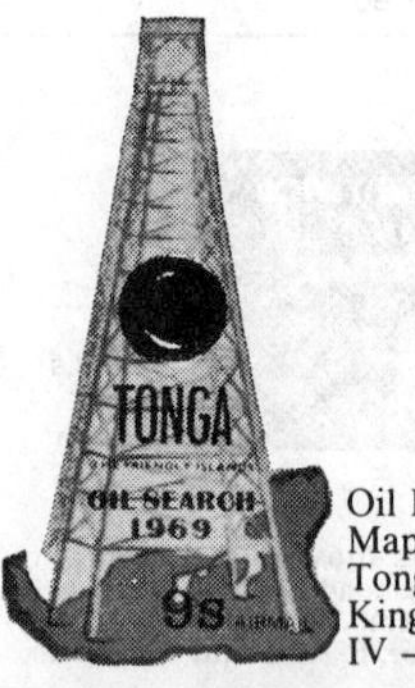


Oil Derrick on Map of Tongatabu and King Taufa'ahau IV — AP2

**Litho.; Gold Embossed**

**1969, Dec. 23** **Self-adhesive**

| | | | |
|---|---|---|---|
| *C63* AP2 | 9s multi | 30 | 30 |
| *C64* AP2 | 10s multi | 30 | 30 |
| *C65* AP2 | 24s multi | 75 | 75 |
| *C66* AP2 | 29s multi | 90 | 90 |
| *C67* AP2 | 38s multi | 1.20 | 1.20 |
| | *Nos. C63-C67 (5)* | 3.45 | 3.45 |

1st scientific search for oil in Tonga.

King Taufa'ahau IV and Queen Elizabeth II — AP3

**Litho.; Gold Embossed**

**1970, Mar. 7** **Self-adhesive**

| | | | |
|---|---|---|---|
| *C68* AP3 | 7s multi | 30 | 30 |
| *C69* AP3 | 9s multi | 35 | 35 |
| *C70* AP3 | 24s multi | 90 | 90 |
| *C71* AP3 | 29s multi | 1.10 | 1.10 |
| *C72* AP3 | 38s multi | 1.50 | 1.50 |
| | *Nos. C68-C72 (5)* | 4.15 | 4.15 |

See note after No. 242.

King Taufa'ahau Tupou IV Medal — AP4

**Litho.; Gold Embossed**

**1970, June 4** **Self-adhesive**

| | | | |
|---|---|---|---|
| *C73* AP4 | 9s grnsh bl, ver & gold | 40 | 40 |
| *C74* AP4 | 10s lil, bl & gold | 40 | 40 |
| *C75* AP4 | 24s yel, grn & gold | 1.00 | 1.00 |
| *C76* AP4 | 29s ultra, org & gold | 1.40 | 1.40 |
| *C77* AP4 | 38s ocher, emer & gold | 2.25 | 2.25 |
| | *Nos. C73-C77 (5)* | 5.45 | 5.45 |

See note after No. 247.

Red Cross Type of Regular Issue Without Coat of Arms

**1970, Oct. 17** **Litho.** ***Imperf.***

**Self-adhesive**

| | | | |
|---|---|---|---|
| *C78* A45 | 9s red & sil | 35 | 35 |
| *C79* A45 | 10s red & mag | 35 | 35 |
| *C80* A45 | 18s red & brt grn | 75 | 75 |
| *C81* A45 | 38s red & brt bl | 1.50 | 1.50 |
| *C82* A45 | 1pa red & grn | 4.50 | 4.50 |
| | *Nos. C78-C82 (5)* | 7.45 | 7.45 |

Centenary of the British Red Cross.

Nos. C22-C24 Surcharged

**Lithographed; Embossed on Gilt Foil**

**1971, Jan. 31** ***Imperf.***

| | | | |
|---|---|---|---|
| *C83* AP1 | 9s on #C22 (S on B) | 50 | 38 |
| *C84* AP1 | 24s on #C24 (G on B) | 1.10 | 95 |
| *C85* AP1 | 29s on #C23 (R on B) | 1.50 | 1.10 |
| *C86* AP1 | 38s on #C23 (G on B) | 2.50 | 1.50 |

In memory of Queen Salote (1900-1965).

Type of Regular Issue, 1953, Surcharged in Red and Black

**1971** **Engr.** **Wmk. 79** ***Imperf.***

| | | | |
|---|---|---|---|
| *C87* A33 | 9s on 1½p grn | 50 | 38 |
| *C88* A33 | 10s on 4p pur & yel | 50 | 38 |
| *C89* A33 | 38s on 1p yel & blk | 2.25 | 1.50 |

See note after No. 272.

Types of Regular Issue Surcharged in Purple or Black: "AIRMAIL," New Denomination and "HONOURING JAPANESE POSTAL CENTENARY 1871-1971"

**1971**

| | | | |
|---|---|---|---|
| *C90* A34 | 18s on 1sh car & buff (P) | 40 | 40 |
| *C91* A33 | 1pa on 2sh car & ultra | 2.25 | 2.25 |

Surcharge on No. C90 in 6 lines, on No. C91 in 4.

---

Self-adhesive & Imperf.

Starting with Nos. C92-C96, all airmail issues are self-adhesive and imperforate, unless otherwise stated.

---

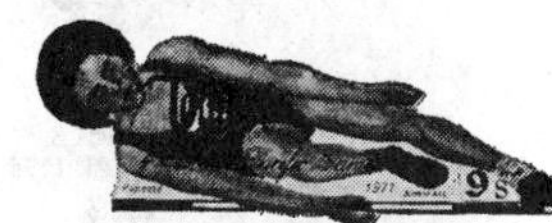

High Jump — AP5

**1971, July** **Litho.** **Unwmk.**

| | | | |
|---|---|---|---|
| *C92* AP5 | 9s brn, mag & blk | 25 | 25 |
| *C93* AP5 | 10s brn, bl & blk | 30 | 30 |
| *C94* AP5 | 24s brn, dk grn & blk | 60 | 60 |
| *C95* AP5 | 29s brn, vio & blk | 90 | 90 |
| *C96* AP5 | 38s brn, red & blk | 1.20 | 1.20 |
| | *Nos. C92-C96 (5)* | 3.25 | 3.25 |

4th South Pacific Games, Papeete, French Polynesia, Sept. 8-19.

Prehistoric Trilithon, King's Watch and Portrait AP6

**Litho. and Embossed**

**1971, July 20**

| | | | |
|---|---|---|---|
| *C97* AP6 | 14s dk brn & multi | 65 | 65 |
| *C98* AP6 | 21s ocher & multi | 90 | 90 |

2nd anniversary of man's first landing on the moon and the placement of a Bulova Accutron there. See Nos. C117-118, CO47-CO48, CO61-CO62. Advertisement on peelable paper backing.

Medal Type of Regular Issue

Designs: 10s, Gold Medal of Merit, obverse (King Taufa'ahau IV). 75s, Silver Medal of Merit, obverse (King Taufa'ahau IV). 1pa, Bronze Medal of Merit, reverse.

**1971, Oct. 30** **Litho. & Embossed**

| | | | |
|---|---|---|---|
| *C99* A47 | 10s gold & multi | 38 | 38 |
| *C100* A47 | 75s sil & multi | 2.75 | 2.75 |
| *C101* A47 | 1pa brnz & multi | 3.75 | 3.75 |

Girl with Blocks and UNICEF Emblem — AP7

**1971, Dec.** **Litho.**

| | | | |
|---|---|---|---|
| *C102* AP7 | 10s multi | 38 | 38 |
| *C103* AP7 | 15s multi | 55 | 55 |
| *C104* AP7 | 25s multi | 95 | 95 |
| *C105* AP7 | 50s multi | 1.90 | 1.90 |
| *C106* AP7 | 1pa multi | 3.75 | 3.75 |
| | *Nos. C102-C106 (5)* | 7.53 | 7.53 |

25th anniversary of UNICEF.

Ship Type of Regular Issue

Design: Map of Merchant Marine routes from Tonga and cargo ship "Niuvakai."

**1972, Apr. 14**

| | | | |
|---|---|---|---|
| *C107* A49 | 9s ver & multi | 25 | 25 |
| *C108* A49 | 12s multi | 35 | 35 |
| *C109* A49 | 14s dk pur & multi | 40 | 40 |
| *C110* A49 | 75s ol & multi | 2.50 | 2.50 |
| *C111* A49 | 90s blk & multi | 3.00 | 3.00 |
| | *Nos. C107-C111 (5)* | 6.50 | 6.50 |

Coin Type of Regular Issue

Design: Coins on top; panel at bottom inscribed "5th anniversary world's first palladium coinage."

**Litho.; Embossed on Metallic Foil**

**1972, July 15**

| | | | |
|---|---|---|---|
| *C112* A50 | 9s sil & multi | 40 | 40 |
| *C113* A50 | 12s sil & multi | 52 | 52 |
| *C114* A50 | 14s sil & multi | 65 | 65 |
| *C115* A50 | 21s sil & multi | 1.00 | 1.00 |
| *C116* A50 | 75s sil & multi | 3.25 | 3.25 |
| | *Nos. C112-C116 (5)* | 5.82 | 5.82 |

Watch Type of 1971

**Litho. and Embossed**

**1972, July 20**

| | | | |
|---|---|---|---|
| *C117* AP6 | 17s multi | 75 | 75 |
| *C118* AP6 | 38s multi | 1.50 | 1.50 |

Advertisement on peelable paper backing.

Proclamation of Sovereignty — AP8

**1972, Dec. 9** **Litho.**

| | | | |
|---|---|---|---|
| *C119* AP8 | 9s ultra & multi | 30 | 30 |
| *C120* AP8 | 12s red brn & multi | 40 | 40 |
| *C121* AP8 | 14s mag & multi | 50 | 50 |
| *C122* AP8 | 38s brn org & multi | 1.25 | 1.25 |
| *C123* AP8 | 1pa ol & multi | 3.00 | 3.00 |
| | *Nos. C119-C123 (5)* | 5.45 | 5.45 |

Tonga's proclamation of sovereignty over the Minerva Reefs, June 1972.

No. C107 Surcharged

NOVEMBER 1972
INAUGURAL
Internal Airmail
Nuku'alofa — Vava'u

**1972, Nov.** **Litho.**

| | | | |
|---|---|---|---|
| *C124* A49 | 7s on 9s multi | 1.50 | 1.50 |

Inauguration of internal airmail service Nukualofa-Vavau, Nov. 1972.

Tongan Bank Notes and Bank Building — AP9

**1973, Mar. 30** **Litho.**

| | | | |
|---|---|---|---|
| *C125* AP9 | 9s multi | 32 | 32 |
| *C126* AP9 | 12s ultra & multi | 45 | 45 |
| *C127* AP9 | 17s dp car & multi | 62 | 62 |
| *C128* AP9 | 50s lt bl & multi | 2.25 | 2.25 |
| *C129* AP9 | 90s multi | 3.75 | 3.75 |
| | *Nos. C125-C129 (5)* | 7.39 | 7.39 |

Establishment of Bank of Tonga.

Boy Scout Emblem — AP10

**1973, June 29** **Litho.**

| | | | |
|---|---|---|---|
| *C130* AP10 | 9s sil & multi | 90 | 90 |
| *C131* AP10 | 12s sil & multi | 1.50 | 1.50 |
| *C132* AP10 | 14s sil & multi | 1.80 | 1.80 |
| *C133* AP10 | 17s sil & multi | 2.00 | 2.00 |
| *C134* AP10 | 1pa sil & multi | 21.00 | 21.00 |
| | *Nos. C130-C134 (5)* | 27.20 | 27.20 |

See note after No. 326.

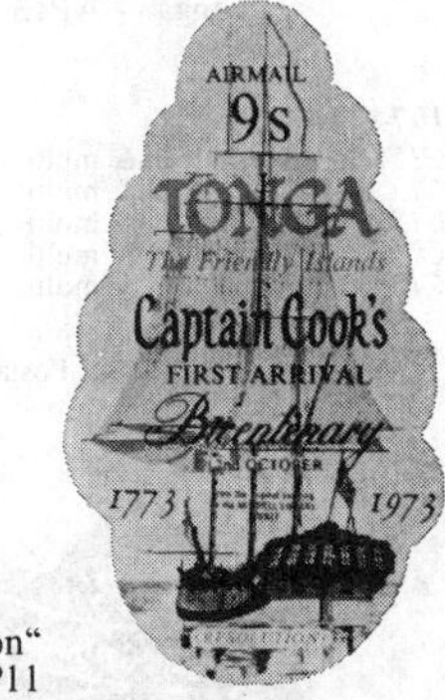


"Resolution" AP11

**1973, Oct. 2** **Litho.**

| | | | |
|---|---|---|---|
| *C135* AP11 | 9s multi | 1.10 | 1.10 |
| *C136* AP11 | 14s multi | 1.90 | 1.90 |
| *C137* AP11 | 29s multi | 5.50 | 5.50 |
| *C138* AP11 | 38s multi | 9.00 | 9.00 |
| *C139* AP11 | 75s multi | 5.00 | 5.00 |
| | *Nos. C135-C139 (5)* | 22.50 | 22.50 |

Bicentenary of Capt. Cook's arrival.

The first price column gives the catalogue value of an unused stamp, the second that of a used stamp.

Nos. 277, C96, C94, C130 and C132 Surcharged in Silver, Violet or Black: "Commonwealth Games Christchurch 1974"

**1973, Dec. 19**

| | | | |
|---|---|---|---|
| *C140* | A46 7s on 25s multi (S) | 32 | 32 |
| *C141* | AP5 9s on 38s multi (V) | 40 | 40 |
| *C142* | AP5 24s multi (B) | 1.25 | 1.25 |
| *C143* | AP10 29s on 9s multi (V) | 1.50 | 1.50 |
| *C144* | AP10 40s on 14s multi (B) | 2.00 | 2.00 |
| | *Nos. C140-C144 (5)* | 5.47 | 5.47 |

10th British Commonwealth Games, Christchurch, New Zealand, Jan. 24-Feb. 2, 1974. No. C140 is overprinted "AIRMAIL" in black; the silver surcharge and overprint are on black panels.

Parrot of Eua – AP12

**1974, Mar. 20** **Litho.**

| | | | |
|---|---|---|---|
| *C145* | AP12 7s multi | 25 | 25 |
| *C146* | AP12 9s multi | 30 | 30 |
| *C147* | AP12 12s multi | 30 | 30 |
| *C148* | AP12 14s multi | 45 | 45 |
| *C149* | AP12 17s multi | 50 | 50 |
| *C150* | AP12 29s multi | 90 | 90 |
| *C151* | AP12 38s multi | 1.20 | 1.20 |
| *C152* | AP12 50s multi | 1.50 | 1.50 |
| *C153* | AP12 75s multi | 2.25 | 2.25 |
| | *Nos. C145-C153 (9)* | 7.65 | 7.65 |

Printed in rolls of 500. Self-adhesive rose red control number in upper left corner.

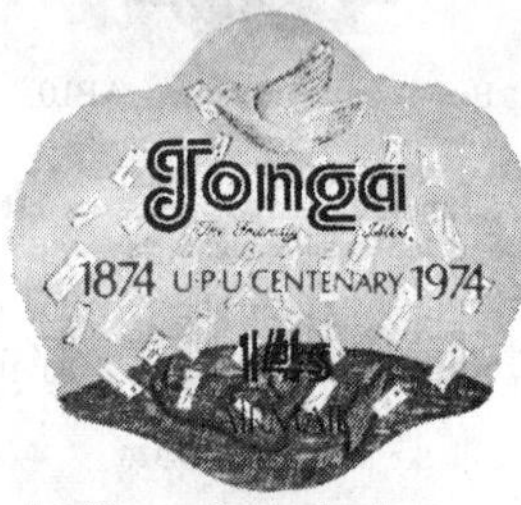


Carrier Pigeon Scattering Letters over Tonga – AP13

**1974, June 20** **Typo.**

| | | | |
|---|---|---|---|
| *C154* | AP13 14s lt bl & multi | 65 | 65 |
| *C155* | AP13 21s lt bl & multi | 85 | 85 |
| *C156* | AP13 60s lt bl & multi | 1.60 | 1.60 |
| *C157* | AP13 75s lt bl & multi | 2.25 | 2.25 |
| *C158* | AP13 1pa lt bl & multi | 5.50 | 5.50 |
| | *Nos. C154-C158 (5)* | 10.85 | 10.85 |

Centenary of Universal Postal Union.

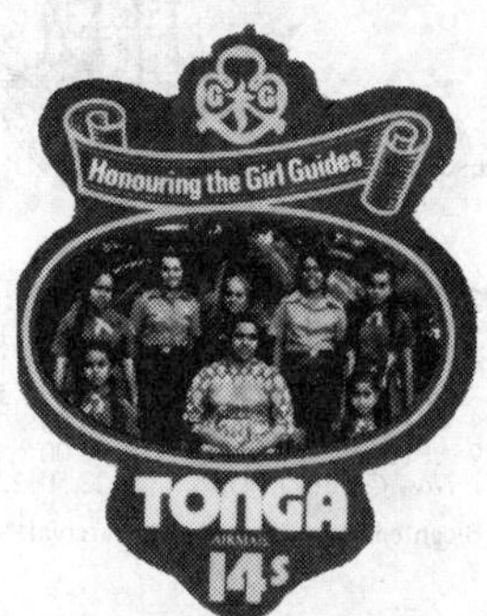


Girl Guide Leaders – AP14

**1974, Sept. 11** **Litho.**

| | | | |
|---|---|---|---|
| *C159* | AP14 14s bl & multi | 48 | 48 |
| *C160* | AP14 16s bl & multi | 75 | 75 |
| *C161* | AP14 29s bl & multi | 1.50 | 1.50 |
| *C162* | AP14 31s bl & multi | 1.90 | 1.90 |
| *C163* | AP14 75s bl & multi | 4.00 | 4.00 |
| | *Nos. C159-C163 (5)* | 8.63 | 8.63 |

Girl Guides of Tonga.

Freighter "James Cook" and List of Tongan Merchantmen – AP15

**1974, Dec. 11**

| | | | |
|---|---|---|---|
| *C164* | AP15 9s bl & multi | 40 | 30 |
| *C165* | AP15 14s bl & multi | 60 | 45 |
| *C166* | AP15 17s bl & multi | 70 | 55 |
| *C167* | AP15 60s bl & multi | 2.50 | 2.00 |
| *C168* | AP15 90s bl & multi | 4.00 | 3.00 |
| | *Nos. C164-C168 (5)* | 8.20 | 6.30 |

Establishment of Royal Marine Institute.

Beach AP16

Designs: 12s, 14s, like 9s. 17s, 38s, Surf.

**1975, Mar. 11** **Litho.**

| | | | |
|---|---|---|---|
| *C169* | AP16 9s gold & multi | 40 | 40 |
| *C170* | AP16 12s gold & multi | 48 | 48 |
| *C171* | AP16 14s gold & multi | 60 | 60 |
| *C172* | AP16 17s gold & multi | 65 | 65 |
| *C173* | AP16 38s gold & multi | 1.50 | 1.50 |
| | *Nos. C169-C173 (5)* | 3.63 | 3.63 |

First meeting of South Pacific area Prime Ministers. See note after No. 226.

Women's Discus and Games' Emblem AP17

**1975, June 11**

| | | | |
|---|---|---|---|
| *C174* | AP17 9s multi | 40 | 40 |
| *C175* | AP17 12s multi | 48 | 48 |
| *C176* | AP17 14s multi | 50 | 50 |
| *C177* | AP17 17s blk & multi | 75 | 75 |
| *C178* | AP17 90s ol & multi | 3.00 | 3.00 |
| | *Nos. C174-C178 (5)* | 5.13 | 5.13 |

5th South Pacific Games, Guam, Aug. 1-10. See note after No. 226.

FAO Type of 1975

Designs (FAO Coins): 12s, Coins showing cattle, corn and pig. 14s, Cornucopias; coins showing king, family planning emblem and melons. 25s, Bananas and treasure chest. 50s, King Taufa'ahau. 1pa, Palms.

**1975, Sept. 3**

| | | | |
|---|---|---|---|
| *C179* | A62 12s multi | 38 | 38 |
| *C180* | A62 14s bl & multi | 45 | 45 |
| *C181* | A62 25s sil, blk & org | 80 | 80 |
| *C182* | A62 50s car, sil & blk | 1.50 | 1.50 |
| *C183* | A62 1pa sil & blk | 3.25 | 3.25 |
| | *Nos. C179-C183 (5)* | 6.38 | 6.38 |

Size of paper backing of 14s: 82x50mm; others 45x45mm. See note after No. 226.

Coin Type of 1975

Coins: 9s, King Taufa'ahau IV, obverse. 12s, Queen Salote III, 75pa reverse and obverse. 14s, 10pa reverse. 38s, King Taufa'ahau IV, 10pa reverse and observe. 1pa, Heads of four constitutional monarchs.

**1975, Nov. 5**

**Light Blue Background**

| | | | |
|---|---|---|---|
| *C184* | A63 9s blk, sil & red | 22 | 22 |
| *C185* | A63 12s gold, blk & grn | 30 | 30 |
| *C186* | A63 14s blk, sil & ol | 35 | 35 |
| *C187* | A63 38s gold, blk & org | 90 | 90 |
| *C188* | A63 1pa blk, sil & bl | 2.25 | 2.25 |
| | *Nos. C184-C188 (5)* | 4.02 | 4.02 |

Size of paper backing of 1pa: 87x78mm, others 65x60mm. See note after No. 226.

Nos. 344-345, C160, C163 Surcharged and Overprinted in Carmine on Silver, Green or Gold

a

b

**1976, Feb. 24** **Litho.**

| | | | |
|---|---|---|---|
| *C189* | A58 (a) 12s on 20s (S) | 50 | 35 |
| *C190* | AP14 (b) 14s on 16s (Gr) | 60 | 45 |
| *C191* | AP14 (b) 16s (G) | 65 | 50 |
| *C192* | A58 (a) 38s on 40s (G) | 1.50 | 1.25 |
| *C193* | AP14 (b) 75s (S) | 3.00 | 2.50 |
| | *Nos. C189-193 (5)* | 6.25 | 5.05 |

21st Olympic Games, Montreal, Canada, July 17-Aug. 1. See note after No. 226.

Bicentennial Type of 1976

Signers of Declaration of Independence, Flags of U.S. and Tonga: 12s, Abraham Clark, George Ross, Thomas Lynch, Jr., Charles Carroll, Roger Sherman (no flags). 14s, Robert Treat Paine, Thomas Jefferson, Thomas McKean, John Adams. 17s, Button Gwinnett, Lewis Morris, Caesar Rodney, Richard Henry Lee. 38s, John Hart, Samuel Huntington, Philip Livingstone, John Morton. 1pa, John Hancock, Joseph Hewes, Josiah Bartlett, John Witherspoon.

**1976, May 26**

| | | | |
|---|---|---|---|
| *C194* | A66 12s buff & multi | 75 | 55 |
| *C195* | A66 14s buff & multi | 80 | 62 |
| *C196* | A66 17s buff & multi | 90 | 80 |
| *C197* | A66 38s buff & multi | 3.75 | 3.25 |
| *C198* | A66 1pa buff & multi | 6.25 | 5.00 |
| | *Nos. C194-C198 (5)* | 12.45 | 10.22 |

See note after No. 381.

Missionary Ship "Triton" – AP18

**1976, Aug. 25** **Litho.**

| | | | |
|---|---|---|---|
| *C199* | AP18 9s pink & multi | 22 | 22 |
| *C200* | AP18 12s multi | 30 | 30 |
| *C201* | AP18 14s multi | 35 | 35 |
| *C202* | AP18 17s buff & multi | 42 | 42 |
| *C203* | AP18 38s multi | 75 | 75 |
| | *Nos. C199-C203 (5)* | 2.04 | 2.04 |

See note after No. 386.

Treaty Signing Ceremony, Nukualofa – AP19

**1976, Nov. 1**

| | | | |
|---|---|---|---|
| *C204* | AP19 11s multi | 40 | 40 |
| *C205* | AP19 17s multi | 55 | 55 |
| *C206* | AP19 18s multi | 60 | 60 |
| *C207* | AP19 31s multi | 1.00 | 1.00 |
| *C208* | AP19 39s multi | 1.25 | 1.25 |
| | *Nos. C204-C208 (5)* | 3.80 | 3.80 |

See note after No. 391.

Elizabeth II and Taufa'ahau IV – AP20

**1977, Feb. 7**

| | | | |
|---|---|---|---|
| *C209* | AP20 15s gray & multi | 65 | 65 |
| *C210* | AP20 17s gray & multi | 1.00 | 1.00 |
| *C211* | AP20 22s gray & multi | *32.50* | *6.50* |
| *C212* | AP20 31s gray & multi | 1.65 | 1.65 |
| *C213* | AP20 39s gray & multi | 1.65 | 1.65 |
| | *Nos. C209-C213 (5)* | *37.45* | *11.45* |

See note after No. 396.

Coronation Coin — AP21

**1977, July 4** **Litho.**
*C214* AP21 11s multi 35 30
*C215* AP21 17s multi 65 55
*C216* AP21 18s multi 75 60
*C217* AP21 39s multi 1.50 1.25
*C218* AP21 1pa multi 3.50 3.00
*Nos. C214-C218 (5)* 6.75 5.70

See note after No. 401.

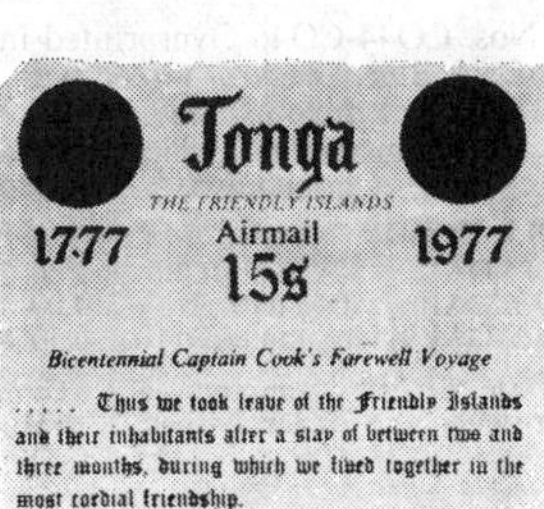


Capt. Cook Medal and Journal Quotation — AP22

**1977, Sept. 27**
*C219* AP22 15s multi 55 45
*C220* AP22 22s multi 90 60
*C221* AP22 31s multi 2.00 1.25
*C222* AP22 50s multi 6.00 3.00
*C223* AP22 1pa multi 12.00 6.00
*Nos. C219-C223 (5)* 21.45 11.30

Bicentenary of Capt. Cook's farewell voyage.

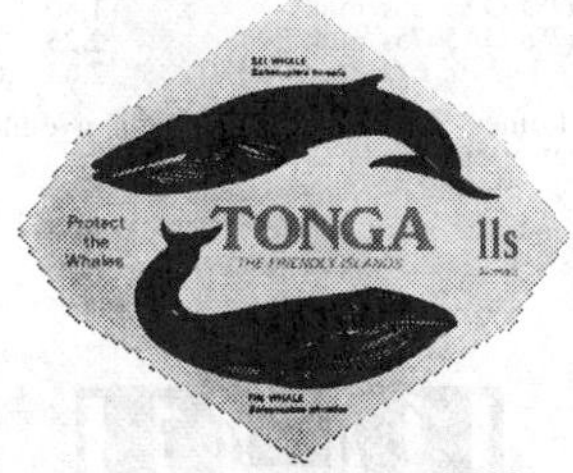


Sei and Fin Whales — AP23

**1977, Dec. 16**
*C224* AP23 11s blk, vio & bl 25 18
*C225* AP23 17s blk, red & bl 1.10 85
*C226* AP23 18s blk, grn & bl 50 30
*C227* AP23 39s blk, brn & bl 1.80 65
*C228* AP23 50s blk, mag & bl 1.10 80
*Nos. C224-C228 (5)* 4.75 2.78

Whale protection.

Stamps of 1975-77 Surcharged in Various Colors

**1978**
*C229* AP16 17s on 38s (#C173;Gr) 90 90
*C230* AP17 17s on 9s (#C174:B) 90 90
*C231* AP17 17s on 12s (#C175:DBl) 90 90
*C232* A63 17s on 38s (#C187:B) 90 90
*C233* A66 17s on 12s (#C194: R on G) 90 90
*C234* AP18 17s on 9s (#C199: B) 90 90
*C235* AP19 17s on 18s (#C206: G on Bl) 90 90
*C236* A66 1pa on 75s (#381: Gr on S) *9.00 9.00*
*C237* A66 1pa on 38s (#C197; DBl on G) *9.00 9.00*
*C238* OA15 1pa on 1.10pa (#CO119; S on DBl) *52.00 52.00*

Edmonton Games Type of 1978

Design: Canadian Maple leaf and Tongan coat of arms.

**1978, May 5** **Litho.**
*C239* A73 17s red & multi 55 55
*C240* A73 35s red & multi 1.10 1.10
*C241* A73 38s red & multi 1.20 1.20
*C242* A73 40s red & multi 1.25 1.25
*C243* A73 65s red & multi 1.90 1.90
*Nos. C239-C243 (5)* 6.00 6.00

See note after No. 423.

King Type of 1978

Design: Head of King Taufa'ahau IV within 6-pointed star.

**1978, July 4**
*C244* A74 11s multi 30 30
*C245* A74 15s multi 45 45
*C246* A74 17s multi 55 55
*C247* A74 39s multi 1.20 1.20
*C248* A74 1pa multi 3.00 3.00
*Nos. C244-C248 (5)* 5.50 5.50

See note after No. 226.

Wildlife Type of 1978

**1978, Dec. 15** **Litho. & Typo.**
*C249* A77 17s Whale 90 90
*C250* A77 22s Bat 1.00 1.00
*C251* A77 31s Turtle 1.50 1.50
*C252* A77 39s Parrot 2.00 2.00
*C253* A77 45s like 17s 2.25 2.25
*Nos. C249-C253 (5)* 7.65 7.65

Wildlife conservation. See note after No. 226.

Types of 1979

Designs: 15s, like No. 453. 17s, like No. 450. 31s, Rotary emblem. 39s, Ministry and tourism buildings, Bank of Tonga, GPO. 1pa, Dish antenna and map of Tonga.

**1979, Feb. 16** **Litho.**
*C254* A79 15s multi 50 50
*C255* A79 17s multi 70 70
*C256* A78 31s vio bl & gold 1.10 1.10
*C257* A79 39s multi 1.50 1.50
*C258* A79 1pa multi 3.50 3.50
*Nos. C254-C258 (5)* 7.30 7.30

Decade of Progress. Paper backing shows map of Tonga.

Type of 1979

Design: Tongan self-adhesive, free-form stamps.

**1979, June 1**
*C259* A81 15s multi 35 35
*C260* A81 17s multi 45 45
*C261* A81 18s multi 48 48
*C262* A81 31s multi 75 75
*C263* A81 39s multi 95 95
*Nos. C259-C263 (5)* 2.98 2.98

See note after No. 458.

Jet — AP24

**1979, Aug. 17**
*C264* AP24 5s multi 12 12
*C265* AP24 11s multi 25 25
*C266* AP24 14s multi 34 34
*C267* AP24 15s multi 35 35
*C268* AP24 17s multi 45 45
*C269* AP24 18s multi 48 48
*C270* AP24 22s multi 52 52
*C271* AP24 31s multi 75 75
*C272* AP24 39s multi 95 95
*C273* AP24 75s multi 1.75 1.75
*C274* AP24 1pa multi 2.40 2.40
*Nos. C264-C274 (11)* 8.36 8.36

Nos. C264-C274 issued in coils; self-adhesive control number in lower left corner of paper backing except on 14s, 18s, 22s, 75s. See note after No. 226.
See Nos. C303-C305.

View Type of 1979

Design: Kao Island. See note after No. 463.

**1979, Nov. 23**
*C275* A82 5s multi 12 12
*C276* A82 15s multi 35 35
*C277* A82 17s multi 45 45
*C278* A82 39s multi 95 95
*C279* A82 75s multi 1.75 1.75

Friendship Treaty Type of 1980

Design: George Tupou I, Admiral du Bouzet, Adventure. See notes over No. 464 and after No. 468.

**1980, Jan. 9** **Litho.**
*C280* A83 15s multi 35 35
*C281* A83 17s multi 45 45
*C282* A83 22s multi 52 52
*C283* A83 31s multi 75 75
*C284* A83 39s multi 95 95

Nos. C259-C263 Surcharged and Overprinted in Black on Silver: "1980 OLYMPIC GAMES," Moscow '80 and Bear Emblems.

**1980, Apr. 30** **Litho.**
*C285* A81 9s on 15s multi 22 22
*C286* A81 16s on 17s multi 38 38
*C287* A81 29s on 18s multi 70 70
*C288* A81 32s on 31s multi 78 78
*C289* A81 47s on 39s multi 1.15 1.15

22nd Summer Olympic Games, Moscow, July 19-Aug. 3.

Scouting Activities in Rotary Emblem — AP25

**1980, Sept. 30** **Litho.**
*C290* AP25 29s multi 1.00 1.00
*C291* AP25 32s multi 1.10 1.10
*C292* AP25 47s multi 1.50 1.50
*C293* AP25 1pa multi 3.25 3.25

Boy Scout Jamboree; Rotary International, 75th anniversary. Peelable backing shows map of Tonga.

Nos. C170, C185, C195, C200-C201, C208 Surcharged

**1980, Dec. 3** **Litho.**
*C294* AP18 29s on 14s multi 70 70
*C295* AP19 29s on 39s multi 70 70
*C296* A63 32s on 12s multi 78 78
*C297* A66 32s on 14s multi 78 78
*C298* AP16 47s on 12s multi 1.15 1.15
*C299* AP18 47s on 12s multi 1.15 1.15

IYD Type of 1981

**1981, Sept. 9** **Litho.**
**Size: 25x32mm.**
*C300* A85 29s multi 85 85
*C301* A85 32s multi 1.00 1.00
*C302* A85 47s multi 1.50 1.50

Jet Type of 1979

**1982, Nov. 17** **Litho.**
*C303* AP24 29s pink & blk 85 85
*C304* AP24 32s pale yel & blk 1.00 1.00
*C305* AP24 47s lt brn & blk 1.50 1.50

## AIR POST OFFICIAL

**Catalogue values for unused stamps in this section, from this point to the end of the section, are for Never Hinged items.**

Nos. 115, 117-118, 111-113 Overprinted "OFFICIAL AIR MAIL / 1862 / TAU'ATAINA / EMANCIPATION / 1962" in Red.

**Engr.; Photo. (A35)**

**1962, Feb. 7** **Wmk. 79**
*CO1* A35 2p ultra 17.50
*CO2* A35 5p purple 17.50
*CO3* A35 1sh red brn 12.50
*CO4* A33 5sh pur & yel 100.00
*CO5* A34 10sh blk & yel 45.00
*CO6* A34 £1 ultra, car & yel 55.00

Centenary of emancipation.

Type of Regular Gold Coin Issue

Design: 15sh, Queen Salote standing, 1-koula coin, obverse.

**Litho.; Embossed on Gilt Foil**
**1963, July 15** **Unwmk.** ***Imperf.***
**Diameter: 80mm.**
*CO7* A36 15sh black 6.00 6.00

Note after No. 133 also applies to No. CO7.

No. CO7 Surcharged like Regular Issue of 1965 in Black

**1965, Mar. 18**
*CO8* A36 30sh on 15sh blk 5.00 5.00

No. 116 Surcharged in Italic Letters Similarly to Nos. C16-C21

***Perf. 14½x13½***
**1966, June 18** **Wmk. 79**
*CO9* A35 10sh on 4p brt grn 1.75 1.75
*CO10* A35 20sh on 4p brt grn 3.50 3.50

Centenary of Tupou College and secondary education.

No. 111 Surcharged in Red: "OFFICIAL / AIRMAIL / ONE PA'ANGA"

**1967, Mar. 25** **Engr.** ***Perf. 11½x11***
*CO11* A33 1p on 5sh pur & yel 3.00 3.00

Type of Regular Issue Surcharged

The Friendly Islands
welcome the
United States
Peace Corps Official Airmail
30s

**1967, Dec. 15** **Wmk. 79** ***Imperf.***
*CO12* A34 30s on £1 multi 1.50 1.50
*CO13* A34 70s on £1 multi 3.50 3.50
*CO14* A34 1.50pa on £1 multi 7.50 7.50

Arrival of U.S. Peace Corps.

No. 113 Surcharged with New Value and "OFFICIAL/AIRMAIL"

**1968, Apr. 6** **Engr.** ***Perf. 11x11½***
*CO15* A34 40s on £1 multi 1.00 1.00
*CO16* A34 60s on £1 multi 1.50 1.50
*CO17* A34 1pa on £1 multi 3.00 3.00
*CO18* A34 2pa on £1 multi 6.00 6.00

Type of 1953 Surcharged: "Friendly Islands / Trials / Field & Track / South Pacific / Games / Port Moresby / 1969 / OFFICIAL AIRMAIL"

**Wmk. 79**
**1968, Dec. 19** **Engr.** ***Imperf.***
*CO19* A34 20s on £1 grn & multi 35 35
*CO20* A34 1pa on £1 grn & multi 1.75 1.75

No. 176 Overprinted and Surcharged in Gold on Colored Panels (Green, Emerald, Violet or Lilac) like Nos. 203-209.

**Litho.; Embossed on Palladium Foil**
**1968** **Unwmk.**
*CO21* A38 40s on 2s (G) 1.40 1.40
*CO22* A38 60s on 2s (E) 2.00 2.00
*CO23* A38 1pa on 2s (V) 4.00 4.00
*CO24* A38 2pa on 2s (L) 8.00 8.00

50th birthday of King Taufa'ahau IV.

Pacific Games Type of Regular Issue

Design: Boxer.

**1969, Aug. 13** **Litho.** ***Imperf.***
**Self-adhesive**
*CO25* A40 70s gray, red & grn 2.75 2.75
*CO26* A40 80s gray, red & org 3.25 3.25

See note after No. 231.

Type of Regular Issue, 1953, Surcharged: "OFFICIAL AIRMAIL / 1969 OIL / SEARCH / 90s" and Oil Derrick Obliterating Old Denomination.

**1969, Dec. 23** ***Imperf.***
*CO27* A34 90s on £1 grn & multi 3.50 3.50

First scientific search for oil in Tonga.

Type of Regular Issue, 1953, Surcharged: "Royal Visit / MARCH / 1970 / OFFICIAL / AIRMAIL" in Black, Violet Blue or Emerald

**1970, Mar. 7** **Engr.** **Wmk. 79**
*CO28* A34 75s on 1sh car & buff 3.00 3.00
*CO29* A34 1pa on 1sh car & buff (VBl) 4.00 4.00
*CO30* A34 1.25pa on 1sh car & buff (E) 5.00 5.00

See note after No. 242.

Type of Regular Issue Surcharged in Black, Red or Emerald

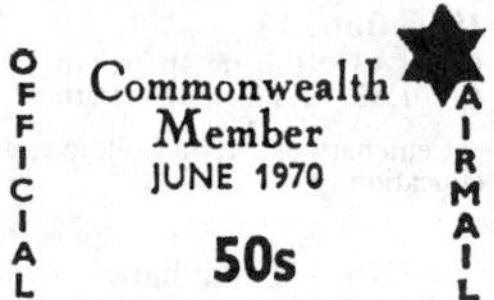


**1970, June 4** **Wmk. 79** ***Imperf.***
*CO31* A33 50s on 5sh brn & yel (B) 2.00 2.00
*CO32* A33 90s on 5sh brn & yel (R) 3.50 3.50
*CO33* A33 1.50pa on 5sh brn & yel (E) 6.00 6.00

See note after No. 247.

Type of Regular Issue, 1953, Surcharged in Red and Purple or Black:

**1970, Oct. 17** **Engr.** ***Imperf.***
*CO34* A33 30s on 1½p grn (B & R) 1.50 1.50
*CO35* A33 80s on 5sh pur & yel (P & R) 4.00 4.00
*CO36* A33 90s on 5sh pur & yel (P & R) 4.75 4.75

Centenary of the British Red Cross.

Type of Regular Issue, 1953, Surcharged in Black, Purple, Blue or Green

1965 IN MEMORIAM 1970

**1971, Jan. 31** **Engr.** ***Imperf.***
*CO37* A34 20s on 10sh org (Bk) 90 75
*CO38* A34 30s on 10sh org (P) 1.50 1.10
*CO39* A34 50s on 10sh org (Bl) 2.50 1.90
*CO40* A34 2pa on 10sh org (G) 9.50 7.50

In memory of Queen Salote (1900-1965).

Type of Regular Issue, 1953, Surcharged in Red and Blue, Black or Purple

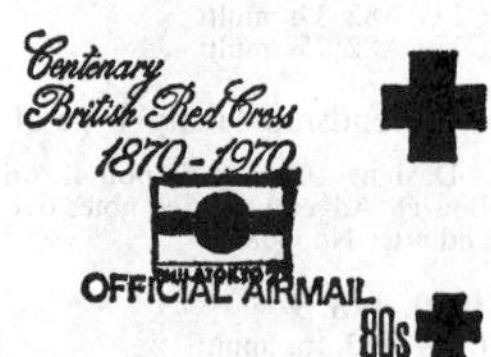


**1971** **Engr.** **Wmk. 79** ***Imperf.***
*CO41* A33 30s on 5p grn & yel (R & Bl) 1.90 1.25
*CO42* A33 80s on 5p grn & yel (R & Bk) 3.75 3.25
*CO43* A33 90s on 5p grn & yel (R & P) 4.50 3.25

See note after No. 272.

Self-adhesive & Imperf.
Starting with Nos. CO44-CO46, all airmail official issues are self-adhesive and imperforate, unless otherwise stated.

Soccer Ball — OA1

**1971, July** **Litho.** **Unwmk.**
*CO44* OA1 50s brn, red & blk 1.50 1.50
*CO45* OA1 90s brn, red & blk 2.75 2.75
*CO46* OA1 1.50pa brn, red & blk 4.50 4.50

4th South Pacific Games, Papeete, French Polynesia, Sept. 8-19.

Watch Type of Air Post Issues
**Litho. and Embossed**
**1971, July 20**
*CO47* AP6 14s brn & multi 65 65
*CO48* AP6 21s brn red & multi 90 90

Advertisement on peelable paper backing.

Nos. 243-244, 246 Surcharged

INVESTITURE 1971
OFFICIAL 60s AIRMAIL

Reduced illustration.

**Litho.; Gold Embossed**
**1971, Oct. 30**
*CO49* A43 60s on 3s multi 2.25 2.25
*CO50* A43 80s on 25s multi 3.25 3.25
*CO51* A43 1.10pa on 7s multi 4.00 4.00

First investiture of Tongan Medal of Honor.

"UNICEF" — OA2

**1971, Dec.** **Litho.**
*CO52* OA2 70s blk & multi 2.75 2.75
*CO53* OA2 80s multi 3.25 3.25
*CO54* OA2 90s multi 3.50 3.50

25th anniversary of UNICEF.

Ship Type of Regular Issue

Design: Map of Merchant Marine routes from Tonga and tanker "Aoniu."

**1972, Apr. 14**
*CO55* A49 20s multi 75 75
*CO56* A49 50s multi 1.75 1.75
*CO57* A49 1.20pa multi 4.50 4.50

Coin Type of Regular Issue

Design: Coins in center, inscription panel above, date below coins.

**Litho.; Embossed on Metallic Foil**
**1972, July 15**
*CO58* A50 50s sil & multi 2.50 2.50
*CO59* A50 70s sil & multi 3.25 3.25
*CO60* A50 1.50pa sil & multi 6.50 6.50

Watch Type of Air Post Issue
**1972, July 20** **Litho.; Embossed**
*CO61* AP6 17s multi 60 60
*CO62* AP6 38s ocher & multi 1.25 1.25

Advertisement on peelable paper backing.

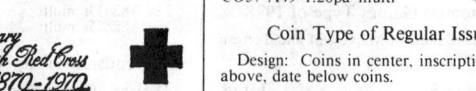

Flags and Map of Tonga Islands — OA3

**1972, Dec. 9** **Litho.**
*CO63* OA3 25s blk & multi 75 75
*CO64* OA3 75s multi 2.25 2.25
*CO65* OA3 1.50pa multi 4.50 4.50

Tonga's proclamation of sovereignty over the Minerva Reefs, June 1972.

No. 290 Surcharged in Black, Ultramarine or Green

1973
ESTABLISHMENT
BANK OF TONGA
40s
OFFICIAL AIRMAIL

**1973, Mar. 30** **Litho.**
*CO66* A49 40s on 21s (B) 1.90 1.90
*CO67* A49 85s on 21s (U) 3.75 3.75
*CO68* A49 1.25pa on 21s (G) 5.00 5.00

Establishment of Bank of Tonga.

Nos. CO55, CO53 and 247 Overprinted or Surcharged in Silver:
No. CO69: New value, 4 wavy lines, fleur-de-lis and "SILVER JUBILEE/ TONGAN SCOUTING / 1948-1973"
No. CO70: "SILVER / JUBILEE" (vertically), fleur-de-lis and "1948 1973"
No. CO71: Silver surcharge and overprint on dark blue panels "OFFICIAL AIRMAIL / T$1.40," "1948-1973" "SILVER / JUBILEE/ TONGAN / SCOUTING," "1948-1973" in dark blue.

**1973, June 29**
*CO69* A49 30s on 20s 12.00 12.00
*CO70* OA2 80s multi 42.50 30.00
*CO71* A43 1.40pa on 50s 90.00 60.00

25th anniv. of Tongan Boy Scout movement.

For unused stamps, more recent issues are valued as never hinged, with the beginning point determined on a country-by-country basis. Notes to show the beginning points are prominently placed in the text.

Tanker James Cook and Cook Medal — OA4

**1973, Oct. 2** **Litho.**
*CO72* OA4 25s multi 1.25 1.25
*CO73* OA4 80s multi 4.00 4.00
*CO74* OA4 1.30pa multi 6.25 6.25

Bicentenary of Capt. Cook's arrival.

Nos. CO44-CO46 Overprinted in Dark Blue, Black or Green with Games' Emblems and: "1974 / Commonwealth / Games / Christchurch"

**1973, Dec. 19**
*CO75* OA1 50s multi (DBl) 2.00 2.00
*CO76* OA1 90s multi (B) 4.00 4.00
*CO77* OA1 1.50pa multi (G) 6.50 6.50

10th British Commonwealth Games, Christchurch, N.Z., Jan. 24-Feb. 2, 1974.

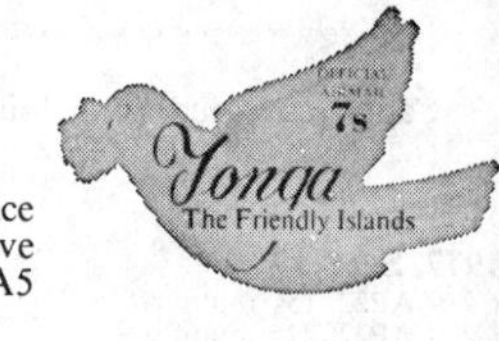


Peace Dove OA5

**1974, Mar. 20** **Litho.**
*CO78* OA5 7s multi 25 25
*CO79* OA5 9s multi 30 30
*CO80* OA5 12s multi 30 30
*CO81* OA5 14s multi 45 45
*CO82* OA5 17s multi 50 50
*CO83* OA5 29s multi 90 90
*CO84* OA5 38s multi 1.20 1.20
*CO85* OA5 50s multi 1.50 1.50
*CO86* OA5 75s multi 2.25 2.25
*Nos. CO78-CO86 (9)* 7.65 7.65

Printed in rolls of 500. Self-adhesive lilac control number in upper left corner.

"UPU Centenary" — OA6

**1974, June 20** **Typo.**
*CO87* OA6 25s red, grn & blk 1.40 1.40
*CO88* OA6 35s yel, red lil & blk 1.40 1.40
*CO89* OA6 70s dp org, bl & blk 2.75 2.75

Centenary of Universal Postal Union.

Lady Baden-Powell — OA7

**1974, Sept. 11** **Litho.**

*CO90* OA7 45s emer & multi 2.50 2.50
*CO91* OA7 55s emer & multi 3.50 3.50
*CO92* OA7 1pa emer & multi 5.00 5.00

Girl Guides of Tonga.

Handshake and Institute's Emblem — OA8

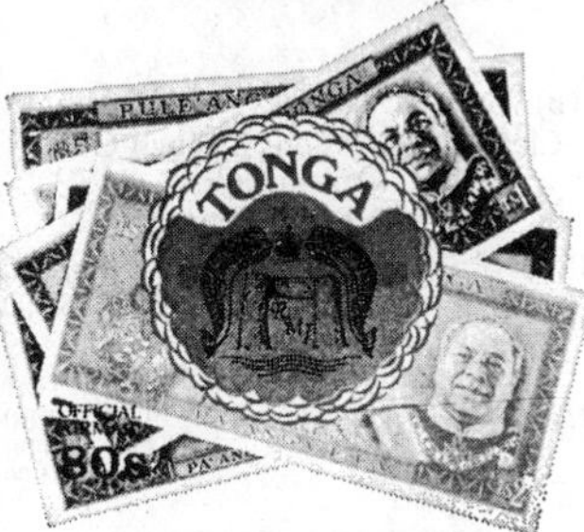


Institute's Emblem and Banknotes — OA9

**1974, Dec. 11**

*CO93* OA8 30s multi 1.50 1.00
*CO94* OA8 35s multi 1.75 1.25
*CO95* OA9 80s red & multi 4.00 3.00

Establishment of Royal Marine Institute.

Arch and Palms — OA10

Designs: 75s, 1.25pa, Dawn over lagoon.

**1975, Mar. 11** **Litho.**

*CO96* OA10 50s multi 1.65 1.65
*CO97* OA10 75s multi 2.50 2.50
*CO98* OA10 1.25pa multi 4.25 4.25

First meeting of South Pacific area Prime Ministers. See note after No. 226.

Track and Games' Emblem — OA11

**1975, June 11**

*CO99* OA11 38s multi 1.25 1.25
*CO100* OA11 75s multi 2.50 2.50
*CO101* OA11 1.20pa multi 4.00 4.00

5th South Pacific Games, Guam, Aug. 1-10. See note after No. 226.

Four Constitutional Monarchs — OA12

**Litho.; Embossed on Gilt Foil**

**1975, Nov. 4**

**Buff Background**

*CO102* OA12 17s gold, org brn & blk 40 40
*CO103* OA12 60s gold, bl & blk 1.10 1.10
*CO104* OA12 90s gold, lil & blk 1.75 1.75

Centenary of Constitution of Tonga.

No. CO90-CO92 Overprinted in Carmine on Blue, Silver or Gold

**1976, Feb. 24** **Litho.**

*CO105* OA7 45s multi (B) 1.50 1.25
*CO106* OA7 55s multi (S) 1.75 1.50
*CO107* OA7 1pa multi (G) 4.00 3.00

21st Olympic Games, Montreal, Canada, July 17-Aug. 1. See note after No. 226.

Bicentennial Type of 1976

Signers of Declaration of Independence: 20s, William Paca, Francis Lewis, George Read, Edward Rutledge, Thomas Heyward, Jr. 50s, George Walton, Matthew Thornton, Robert Morris, William Williams, James Smith. 1.15pa, Benjamin Rush, Samuel Adams, Samuel Chase, George Wythe, George Clymer.

**1976, May 26**

*CO108* A66 20s buff & multi 1.10 90
*CO109* A66 50s buff & multi 3.25 2.75
*CO110* A66 1.15pa buff & multi 7.50 6.25

See note after No. 381.

Inside View of Lifuka Chapel — OA13

**1976, Aug. 25** **Litho.**

*CO111* OA13 65s multi 1.50 1.50
*CO112* OA13 85s multi 1.60 1.60
*CO113* OA13 1.15pa multi 2.25 2.25

See note after No. 386.

OA14

**1976, Nov. 1**

*CO114* OA14 30s sil & multi 72 72
*CO115* OA14 60s sil & multi 1.45 1.45
*CO116* OA14 1.25pa sil & multi 3.00 3.00

See note after No. 391.

Flags and Arms of Great Britain and Tonga — OA15

**1977, Feb. 7** **Litho.**

*CO117* OA15 35s sil & multi 12.50 3.25
*CO118* OA15 45s sil & multi 1.65 1.65
*CO119* OA15 1.10pa sil & multi 4.00 4.00

See note after No. 396.

Coin Type of Air Post Stamps 1977

Design: Coronation coin, inscriptions in round upper panel.

**1977, July 4**

*CO120* AP21 20s multi 72 60
*CO121* AP21 40s multi 1.50 1.20
*CO122* AP21 80s multi 3.00 2.50

See note after No. 401.

Capt. Cook Type of Air Post Stamps 1977

Design: Inscription and flying dove.

**1977, Sept. 27**

*CO123* AP22 20s gold & multi 90 60
*CO124* AP22 55s on 20s multi 5.50 3.00
*CO125* AP22 85s on 20s multi 12.00 6.00

Printed on peelable paper backing showing dark brown replica of entry in Capt. Cook's diary.

Whale Type of Air Post Stamps 1977

Design: Blue whale.

**1977, Dec. 16**

*CO126* AP23 45s multi 1.00 75
*CO127* AP23 65s multi 1.10 90
*CO128* AP23 85s multi 2.00 1.50

Whale protection.

Games' Emblem and Athletes OA16

**1978, May 5** **Litho.**

*CO129* OA16 30s red & multi 90 90
*CO130* OA16 60s red & multi 1.75 1.75
*CO131* OA16 1pa red & multi 3.00 3.00

See note after No. 423.

King Type of 1978

Design: Head of King Taufa'ahau IV on medal.

**1978, July 4**

*CO132* A74 26s multi 75 75
*CO133* A74 85s multi 2.50 2.50
*CO134* A74 90s multi 2.75 2.75

See note after No. 226.

Wildlife Type of 1978

**1978, Dec. 15** **Litho. & Typo.**

*CO150* A77 40s Whale 2.00 2.00
*CO151* A77 50s Bat 2.50 2.50
*CO152* A77 1.10pa Turtle 5.00 5.00

Wildlife conservation. See note after No. 226.

Types of 1979

Designs: 38s, Red Cross and star. 74s, like No. 451. 80s, like No. 450.

**1979, Feb. 16** **Litho.**

*CO153* A78 38s multi 1.40 1.40
*CO154* A80 74s multi 2.75 2.75
*CO155* A79 80s multi 3.00 3.00

Decade of Progress. Paper backing shows map of Tonga.

Hands Peeling off No. CO118 — OA17

**1979, June 1**

*CO156* OA17 45s multi 1.10 1.10
*CO157* OA17 65s multi 1.50 1.50
*CO158* OA17 80s multi 1.90 1.90

See note after No. 458.

Parrot — OA18

**1979, Aug. 1**

*CO159* OA18 5s multi 12 12
*CO160* OA18 11s multi 25 25
*CO161* OA18 14s multi 34 34
*CO162* OA18 15s multi 35 35
*CO163* OA18 17s multi 45 45
*CO164* OA18 18s multi 48 48
*CO165* OA18 22s multi 52 52
*CO166* OA18 31s multi 75 75
*CO167* OA18 39s multi 95 95
*CO168* OA18 75s multi 1.75 1.75
*CO169* OA18 1pa multi 2.40 2.40
*Nos. CO159-CO169 (11)* 8.36 8.36

Nos. CO159-CO169 issued in coils. See note after No. 226.

View Type of 1979

Design: Niuatoputapu and Tafahi Islands. See note after No. 463.

**1979, Nov. 23** **Litho.**

*CO170* A82 35s multi 85 85
*CO171* A82 45s multi 1.10 1.10
*CO172* A82 1pa multi 2.40 2.40

Friendship Treaty Type of 1980

Design: Church. See note after No. 468.

**1980, Jan. 9** **Litho.**

*CO173* A83 40s multi 95 95
*CO174* A83 55s multi 1.30 1.30
*CO175* A83 1.25pa multi 3.00 3.00

Nos. CO156-CO158 Surcharged and Overprinted in Black on Silver: "1980 OLYMPIC GAMES," Moscow '80 and Bear Emblems.

**1980, Apr. 30** **Litho.**

*CO176* OA17 26s on 45s 65 65
*CO177* OA17 40s on 65s 95 95
*CO178* OA17 1.10pa on 80s 2.65 2.65

22nd Summer Olympic Games, Moscow, July 19-Aug. 3.

Tents and Rotary Emblem — OA19

**1980, Sept. 30** **Litho.**

*CO179* OA19 25s multi 80 80
*CO180* OA19 2pa multi 6.50 6.50

Boy Scout Jamboree; Rotary International, 75th anniversary. Peelable backing shows map of Tonga.

No. CO111 Surcharged

**1980, Dec. 3** **Litho.**

*CO181* OA13 2pa on 65s multi 4.80 4.80

## OFFICIAL STAMPS

Types of Postage Issue of 1892 Overprinted in Carmine

**G.F.B.**

***Perf. 12x11½***

**1893, Feb. 13** **Wmk. 62**

*O1* A4 1p ultra 9.00 *25.00*
  **a.** Half used as ½p on cover
*O2* A5 2p ultra 15.00 *30.00*
*O3* A5 4p ultra 32.50 *62.50*
*O4* A5 8p ultra 80.00 *175.00*
*O5* A5 1sh ultra 87.50 *200.00*

Values are for copies of good color. Faded and discolored copies sell for much less.

The overprinted initials stand for "Gaue Faka Buleaga" (On Government Service).

Nos. O1 to O5 with Additional Surcharge Handstamped in Black

**1893**

*O6* A4 ½p on 1p ultra 12.50 *25.00*
*O7* A5 2½p on 2p ultra 12.50 *25.00*
*O8* A4 5p on 4p ultra 12.50 *25.00*
*O9* A5 7½p on 8p ultra 17.50 *30.00*
*O10* A5 10p on 1sh ultra 17.50 *37.50*

**Catalogue values for unused stamps in this section, from this point to the end of the section, are for Never Hinged items.**

Redrawn Banana and Coconut Types of Regular Issue, 1970, Inscribed "Official Post"

**1970, June 9** **Typo.** ***Imperf.***

**Self-adhesive**

*O11* A39 1s yel, blk & dp car 5 5
*O12* A39 2s yel, blk & bl 8 8
*O13* A39 3s yel, blk & brn 12 12
*O14* A39 4s yel, blk & emer 18 18
*O15* A39 5s yel, blk & org 20 20

**Litho.; Embossed on Gilt Foil**

*O16* A44 6s brn & multi 25 25
*O17* A44 7s brn & multi 30 30
*O18* A44 8s brn & multi 35 35
*O19* A44 9s brn & multi 40 40
*O20* A44 10s brn & multi 45 45
*Nos. O11-O20 (10)* 2.38 2.38

Nos. O13, O17-O18 and O20 have self-adhesive control numbers in lower left corner of paper backing.

Types of Regular Issue 1970-72

**1972, Sept. 30** **Typo.**

**Self-adhesive**

*O21* A51 1s yel, red & brn 5 5
*O22* A51 2s yel, grn & brn 8 8
*O23* A51 3s yel, emer & brn 12 12
*O24* A51 4s yel, blk & brn 15 15
*O25* A44 5s yel & brn 16 16
*O26* A44 6s brn & grn 18 18
*O27* A44 7s brn & grn 20 20
*O28* A44 8s brn & grn 25 25
*O29* A44 9s brn & grn 30 30
*O30* A44 10s brn & grn 35 35
*O31* A52 15s grn & ultra 55 55
*O32* A52 20s grn & ver 70 70
*O33* A52 25s grn & dk brn 85 85
*O34* A52 40s grn & org 1.25 1.25
*O35* A52 50s grn & vio bl 1.50 1.50
*Nos. O21-O35 (15)* 6.69 6.69

Paper backing is brown on Nos. O26-O35. Nos. O30-O35 have self-adhesive control number in lower left corner. Nos. O21-O29 lower right corner.

Types of Regular Issue 1978

Designs: 1s to 5s, Bananas. 6s to 10s, Coconuts. 15s to 1pa, Pineapples.

**1978, Sept. 29** **Typo.**

*O36* A75 1s yel & lil 5 5
*O37* A75 2s yel & brn 5 5
*O38* A75 3s multi 7 7
*O39* A75 4s multi 8 8
*O40* A75 5s multi 10 10
*O41* A76 6s multi 12 12
*O42* A76 7s multi 15 15
*O43* A76 8s multi 16 16
*O44* A76 9s multi 18 18
*O45* A76 10s multi 20 20
*O46* A76 15s multi 28 28
*O47* A76 20s multi 40 40
*O48* A76 30s multi 55 55
*O49* A76 50s multi 1.00 1.00
*O50* A76 1pa multi 2.00 2.00
*Nos. O36-O50 (15)* 5.39 5.39

Nos. O36-O50 issued in coils; self-adhesive control numbers on paper backing except on 1s. See note after No. 226.

Type of 1984 Overprinted "OFFICIAL"

**1984-85** **Litho.** ***Imperf.***

*O52* A103 1s multi 5 5
*O53* A103 2s multi 5 5
*O54* A103 3s multi 5 5
*O55* A103 5s multi 7 7
*O56* A103 6s multi 9 9
*O57* A103 9s multi 12 12
  **a.** Perf. 14½ ('85) 12 12
*O58* A103 10s multi 15 15
*O59* A103 13s multi 18 18
*O60* A103 15s multi 20 20
*O61* A103 20s multi 25 25
*O62* A103 29s multi 40 40
*O63* A103 32s multi 45 45
*O64* A103 47s multi 65 65
*O65* A103 1pa multi 1.25 1.25
*O66* A103 2pa multi 2.75 2.75
*O67* A103 5pa multi ('85) 7.50 7.50

Nos. 532-534 Ovptd. "OFFICIAL."

**1983, Feb. 22** **Litho.** ***Imperf.***

*O68* A96a 29s multi *2.50 2.50*
*O69* A96a 32s multi *2.50 2.50*
*O70* A96a 47s multi *2.50 2.50*

O68-O70 handstamped.

Nos. 564-565, 567-568, 570, 572 and 577 Surcharged "OFFICIAL."

**1986, Apr. 16** **Litho.** ***Imperf.***

**Self-adhesive**

*O71* A103 4s on 2s, No. 564 6 6
*O72* A103 4s on 13s, No. 570 6 6
*O73* A103 42s on 3s, No. 565 60 60
*O74* A103 42s on 9s, No. 568 60 60
*O75* A103 57s on 6s, No. 567 82 82
*O76* A103 57s on 20s, No. 572 82 82
*O77* A103 2.50pa on 2pa, No. 577 3.50 3.50
*Nos. O71-O77 (7)* 6.46 6.46

# TRANSVAAL

## (South African Republic)

LOCATION — Southern Africa.
GOVT. — A former British Colony.
AREA — 110,450 sq. mi.
POP. — 1,261,736 (1904).
CAPITAL — Pretoria.

Transvaal was known as the South African Republic until 1877 when it was occupied by the British. The republic was restored in 1884 and continued until 1900 when it was annexed to Great Britain and named "The Transvaal."

Although issued by an independent state, the stamps of the South African Republic are included in this section in accord with established philatelic practice.

12 Pence = 1 Shilling
20 Shillings = 1 Pound

Values of Transvaal Nos. 1-96 vary according to condition. Quotations are for fine copies. Very fine to superb specimens sell at much higher prices, and inferior or poor copies sell at reduced prices, depending on the condition of the individual specimen.

**First Republic.**

Coat of Arms
A1 A2

**Mecklenburg Printings.**
By Adolph Otto, Gustrow.
Fine Impressions.
Thin Paper.

**1869** **Unwmk.** ***Imperf.***

*1* A1 1p brn lake 375.00
  **a.** 1p red 425.00
*2* A1 6p ultra 120.00 *150.00*
*3* A1 1sh dk grn 350.00
  **a.** Tete beche pair *10,000.*

***Rouletted 15½, 16***

*4* A1 1p red 60.00
  **a.** 1p brn lake 65.00
*5* A1 6p ultra 55.00
*6* A1 1sh bl grn 65.00 *125.00*
  **a.** 1sh yel grn 65.00
  **b.** 1sh dp grn 80.00

Nos. 1-6 were printed from 2 sets of plates, differing in the spacing between the stamps.

**1871-74**

*7* A2 3p lilac 50.00 37.50
  **a.** 3p vio 50.00 37.50
*8* A2 6p brt ultra ('74) 40.00 37.50
  **a.** Half used as 3p on cover

So-called reprints and trial impressions of the stamps in types A1 and A2 are counterfeits. This applies to Nos. 1 through 96. All copies in other than the issued colors are known to be forgeries. Many forgeries exist in colors duller or lighter than he genuine stamps.

In forgeries of type A1, all values, the "D" of "EENDRAGT" is not noticeably larger than the other letters and does not touch the top of the ribbon. In type A1 genuine stamps, the "D" is large and touches the ribbon top. The eagle's eye is a dot and its face white on the genuine stamps; the eye is a loop or blob attached to the beak, and the beak is strongly hooked, on the forgeries. Many forgeries of the 1sh have the top line of the ribbon broken above "EENDRAGT".

Forgeries of type A2 usually can be detected only by color.

A sharply struck cancellation of a numeral in three rings is found on many of these forgeries. The similar genuine cancellation is always roughly or heavily struck.

Tete beche pairs of the 6p and 1sh are known both genuine and counterfeit.

**Local Printings.**
(A) By M. J. Viljoen, Pretoria.
Poor Impressions,
Overinked and Spotted.
Thin Soft Paper.

**1870** ***Imperf.***

*9* A1 1p carmine 65.00
  **a.** 1p rose red 72.50
  **b.** 1p pink 72.50
*10* A1 6p dl ultra 400.00 400.00
  **a.** Tete beche pair *6,500.*

***Rouletted 15½, 16.***

*11* A1 1p carmine 500.00 225.00
  **a.** Rouletted 6½ 1,100.
*12* A1 6p dl ultra 200.00 125.00

**Hard Paper, Thick to Medium.**

***Imperf***

*13* A1 1p carmine 65.00 65.00
*14* A1 6p ultra
*15* A1 1sh gray grn 100.00 90.00
  **a.** 1sh dk grn *650.00 300.00*
  **b.** Tete beche pair *8,250. 6,500.*
  **c.** Half used as 6p on cover

***Rouletted 15½, 16.***

*16* A1 1p carmine 40.00 40.00
  **a.** 1p lt car 40.00 40.00
*17* A1 6p ultra 47.50 47.50
  **a.** Tete beche pair *6,500. 4,750.*
*18* A1 1sh dk grn 80.00 50.00
  **a.** 1sh gray grn 300.00 165.00

Copies of Nos. 16 to 18 are sometimes so heavily inked as to be little more than blots of color.

(B) By J. P. Borrius, Potchefstroom.
Clearer Impressions Though Often Overinked.
Thick Porous Paper.

**1870** ***Imperf.***

*19* A1 1p black 80.00 80.00
*20* A1 6p indigo 250.00

***Rouletted 15½, 16***

*21* A1 1p black 9.00 11.00
*22* A1 6p gray bl 55.00 20.00
  **a.** 6p ind 90.00 35.00
  **b.** 6p brt ultra

**Thin Transparent Paper.**

*23* A1 1p black 120.00 *325.00*
*24* A1 1p brt car 90.00 24.00
  **a.** 1p dp car 90.00 24.00
*25* A2 3p gray lil 45.00 24.00
*26* A1 6p ultra 35.00 19.00
*27* A1 1sh yel grn 35.00 19.00
  **a.** 1sh dp grn 35.00 14.00
  **b.** Half used as 6p on cover

**Thick Soft Paper.**

*28* A1 1p dl rose 275.00 40.00
  **a.** 1p brn rose 350.00 67.50
  **b.** Printed on both sides
*29* A1 6p dl bl 50.00 27.50
  **a.** 6p brt bl 125.00 27.50
  **b.** 6p ultra 135.00 37.50
  **c.** Rouletted 6½
*30* A1 1sh yel grn 675.00 550.00

The paper of Nos. 28 to 30 varies considerably in thickness.

(C) By P. Davis & Son, Natal.
Thin to Medium Paper.

**1874** ***Perf. 12½***

*31* A1 1p red 45.00 22.50
  **a.** 1p brnsh red 50.00 24.00
*32* A1 6p dp bl 75.00 25.00
  **a.** 6p bl 75.00 25.00
  **b.** Horiz. pair, imperf. between

(D) By the Stamp Commission, Pretoria.
Pelure Paper.

**1875-76** ***Imperf.***

*33* A1 1p pale red 35.00 12.50
  **a.** 1p org red 35.00 12.50
  **b.** 1p brn red 40.00 15.00
  **c.** Pin-Perf. 500.00 225.00
*34* A2 3p gray lil 42.50 25.00
  **a.** 3p dl vio 50.00 27.50
  **b.** Pin-Perf. 200.00
*35* A1 6p blue 27.50 14.00
  **a.** 6p pale bl 27.50 14.00
  **b.** 6p dk bl 27.50 14.00
  **c.** Tete beche pr. *7,500. 6,000.*
  **d.** Pin-Perf. 180.00

***Rouletted 15½, 16***

*36* A1 1p org red 240.00 67.50
  **a.** Rouletted 6½. 650.00 100.00
*37* A2 3p dl vio 300.00 95.00
  **a.** Rouletted 6½ 180.00
*38* A1 6p blue 165.00 60.00
  **a.** Rouletted 6½ 725.00 75.00

The paper of this group varies slightly in thickness and is sometimes divided into pelure and semipelure. We believe there was only one lot of the paper and that the separation is not warranted.

**Thick Hard Paper.**

***Imperf***

*39* A1 1p org red ('76) 18.00 11.00
*40* A2 3p lilac
*41* A1 6p dp bl 60.00 11.00
  **a.** 6p bl 65.00 12.50
  **b.** Tete beche pair *5,500.*

***Rouletted 15½, 16***

*42* A1 1p org red ('76) 350.00 100.00
  **a.** Rouletted 6½ ('75) 450.00 100.00
*42B* A2 3p lilac 240.00
*43* A1 6p dp bl *600.00* 85.00
  **a.** 6p bl *600.00* 120.00

b. Rouletted 6½ ('75) 650.00 135.00

**Soft Porous Paper**

44 A1 1p org red 75.00 27.50
45 A1 6p dp bl 120.00 25.00
a. 6p dl bl 275.00 65.00
46 A1 1sh yel grn 105.00 50.00

**Rouletted 15½, 16.**

47 A1 1p org red 200.00
a. Rouletted 6½ 200.00
48 A1 6p dp bl 37.50
a. Rouletted 6½
49 A1 1sh yel grn 575.00 150.00
a. Rouletted 6½
b. Rouletted 15½-16x16½ 500.00 325.00

### First British Occupation

Stamps and Types of 1875 Overprinted

V. R.
TRANSVAAL.

**Red Overprint**
**Pelure Paper**

**1877 Unwmk. Imperf.**

50 A2 3p lilac 1,300. 100.00
a. Overprinted on back 3,000.
b. Double overprint, red and blk 7,500.

**Rouletted 15½, 16**

51 A2 3p lilac 8,000. 1,700.
a. Rouletted 6½ 8,000. 1,700.

**Thin Hard Paper.**
**Imperf**

52 A2 3p lilac 1,400. 125.00

**Soft Porous Paper.**

53 A1 6p blue 1,500. 200.00
a. 6p dp bl 225.00
b. Inverted overprint 5,750.
c. Double overprint 4,900.
54 A1 1sh yel grn 425.00 75.00
a. Inverted overprint 3,750.
b. Half used as 6p on cover 1,900.

**Rouletted 15½, 16**

55 A1 6p blue 6,000. 1,700.
a. Rouletted 6½ 7,000. 1,700.
56 A1 1sh yel grn 1,500. 600.00
a. Rouletted 6½ 2,250. 900.00

**Black Overprint.**
**Pelure Paper.**
**Imperf**

57 A1 1p red 175.00 100.00

**Rouletted 15½, 16**

58 A1 1p red 5,500. 1,500.

**Thick Hard Paper.**
**Imperf**

59 A1 1p red 18.00 15.00
a. Inverted overprint 500.00 375.00

**Rouletted 15½, 16**

60 A1 1p red 150.00 45.00
a. Rouletted 6½ 650.00 275.00
b. Inverted ovpt.
c. Double ovpt.

**Soft Porous Paper.**
**Imperf**

61 A1 1p red 16.00 12.00
a. Double overprint 1,500.
62 A2 3p lilac 50.00 19.00
a. 3p dp lil 125.00 50.00
b. Inverted ovpt. 3,500.
63 A1 6p dl bl 75.00 15.00
a. 6p brt bl 125.00 15.00
b. 6p dk bl 125.00 15.00
c. Tete beche pair 5,000.
d. Inverted ovpt. 2,000. 400.00
e. Double ovpt. 5,000.
64 A1 6p bl, *rose* 40.00 20.00
a. Tete beche pair 3,750.
b. Inverted ovpt. 45.00 20.00
c. Ovpt. omitted 4,000.
d. Half used as 3p on cover
65 A1 1sh yel grn 60.00 25.00
a. Tete beche pair 5,000.
b. Inverted ovpt. 1,400. 250.00
c. Half used as 6p on cover 1,650.

**Rouletted 15½, 16**

66 A1 1p red 47.50 40.00
a. Rouletted 6½ 750.00 185.00
67 A2 3p lilac 45.00 35.00
a. Rouletted 6½ 700.00
68 A1 6p dl bl 150.00 42.50
a. Inverted ovpt. 5,000. 600.00
b. Rouletted 6½ 5,000. 600.00
c. As "a." rouletted 6½
69 A1 6p bl, *rose* 135.00 32.50
a. Inverted ovpt. 500.00 70.00
b. Rouletted 6½
c. Tete beche pair
d. Ovpt. omitted
e. As "a." rouletted 6½
f. As "d." rouletted 6½
70 A1 1sh yel grn 150.00 60.00
a. Inverted ovpt. 1,000. 575.00
b. Rouletted 6½ 500.00 180.00
c. As "a." rouletted 6½ 1,700. 550.00

In this issue the space between "V. R." and "TRANSVAAL" is normally 8½mm but occasionally it is 12mm. In this and the following issues there are numerous minor varieties of the overprint, missing periods, etc.

Types A1 and A2 Overprinted

V. R.
Transvaal

**1877-79 Imperf.**

71 A1 1p red, *bl* 30.00 15.00
a. "Transvral" 6,000. 3,000.
b. Inverted ovpt. 900.00 575.00
c. Double overprint 5,000.
d. Ovpt. omitted
72 A1 1p red, *org* ('78) 12.00 10.00
a. Printed on both sides
b. Pin perf.
73 A2 3p lil, *buff* 13.00 12.50
a. Inverted overprint 850.00
b. Pin perf.
74 A2 3p lil, *grn* ('79) 90.00 17.50
a. Inverted overprint 2,000.
b. Double ovpt.
c. Pin perf.
75 A1 6p bl, *grn* 55.00 17.50
a. Tete beche pair 4,750.
b. Inverted ovpt. 5,000. 1,100.
c. Half used as 3p on cover
d. Pin perf.
76 A1 6p bl, *bl* ('78) 35.00 14.00
a. Tete beche pair 8,000.
b. Ovpt. omitted 7,000. 2,500.
c. Inverted overprint 1,100.
d. Half used as 3p on cover 1,100.
e. Double overprint 5,000. 3,250.
f. Pin perf.

**Rouletted 15½, 16**

77 A1 1p red, *bl* 55.00 24.00
a. "Transvral" 4,000.
b. Inverted overprint
c. Double overprint
78 A1 1p red, *org* ('78) 21.00 17.50
a. Imperf. vertically
b. Rouletted 6½ 325.00 125.00
79 A2 3p lil, *buff* 75.00 15.00
a. Invtd. overprint 5,500. 4,750.
b. Imperf. horiz., pair
c. Rouletted 6½ 160.00
80 A2 3p lil, *grn* ('79) 350.00 100.00
a. Inverted overprint
b. Rouletted 6½ 400.00
81 A1 6p bl, *grn* 55.00 14.00
a. Inverted overprint 675.00
b. Ovpt. omitted 4,500.
c. Tete beche pair
d. Half used at 3p on cover 850.00
e. Rouletted 6½ 5,750. 1,200.
82 A1 6p bl, *bl* ('78) 175.00 32.50
a. Invtd. overprint 4,250. 1,500.
b. Ovpt. omitted 8,000. 3,000.
c. Tete beche pair
d. Imperf. vert., pair
e. Half used as 3p on cover 850.00
f. Double overprint
g. Rouletted 6½ 300.00
h. As "a." rouletted 6½

Types A1 and A2 Overprinted

V. R.
Transvaal

**Imperf.**

83 A1 1p red, *org* ('78) 30.00 15.00
84 A2 3p lil, *buff* ('78) 30.00 15.00
a. Pin perf.
85 A2 3p lil, *grn* ('79) 75.00 16.00
a. Inverted overprint 2,000.
b. Ovpt. omitted 2,600.
c. Printed on both sides
86 A1 6p bl, *bl* ('78) 600.00 16.00
a. Tete beche pair 14,000.
b. Inverted overprint 450.00

**Rouletted 15½, 16**

87 A1 1p red, *org* ('78) 87.50
a. Rouletted 6½ 375.00
88 A2 3p lil, *buff* ('78) 150.00 65.00
a. Imperf. horiz., pair
b. Rouletted 6½ 400.00
89 A2 3p lil, *grn* ('79) 425.00 110.00
a. Inverted overprint
b. Ovpt. omitted
c. Rouletted 6½ ('97) 300.00
90 A1 6p bl, *bl* ('78) 75.00
a. Tete beche pair
b. Inverted ovpt. 6,500. 1,200.
d. Rouletted 6½ 425.00
e. As "b." rouletted 6½

Types A1 and A2 Overprinted

V. R.
Transvaal

**1879 Imperf.**

91 A1 1p red, *org* 30.00 30.00
a. 1p red, *yel* 32.50 27.50
b. Small capital "T" 200.00 165.00
92 A2 3p lil, *grn* 30.00 18.00
a. Small capital "T" 225.00 165.00
93 A2 3p lil, *bl* 30.00 18.00
a. Small capital "T" 165.00 75.00

**Rouletted 15½, 16**

94 A1 1p red, *yel* 200.00
a. 1p red, *org* 325.00
b. Small capital "T" 775.00 265.00
c. Rouletted 6½ 650.00
d. Pin perf. 500.00
95 A2 3p lil, *grn* 825.00 200.00
a. Small capital "T"
b. Rouletted 6½
96 A2 3p lil, *bl* 115.00
a. Small capital "T" 800.00
b. Rouletted 6½
c. Pin perf.

Queen Victoria — A3

**1878-80 Engr. Perf. 14, 14½**

97 A3 ½p ver ('80) 15.00 15.00
98 A3 1p red brn 3.50 2.00
99 A3 3p claret 4.50 2.00
100 A3 4p ol grn 7.50 5.50
101 A3 6p slate 4.50 2.75
a. Half used as 3p on cover
102 A3 1sh green 45.00 30.00
103 A3 2sh blue 60.00 30.00
*Nos. 97-103 (7)* 140.00 87.25

No. 101 Surcharged in Red or Black:

(a) Surcharged **1 PENNY**

**1879**

104 A3 1p on 6p sl (R) 82.50 47.50
105 A3 1p on 6p sl (Bk) 35.00 22.50

(b) Surcharged **1 Penny**

106 A3 1p on 6p sl (R) 350.00 165.00
107 A3 1p on 6p sl (Bk) 165.00 50.00

(c) Surcharged **1 Penny**

108 A3 1p on 6p sl (R) 200.00 115.00
109 A3 1p on 6p sl (Bk) 65.00 32.50

(d) Surcharged **1 Penny**

110 A3 1p on 6p sl (R) 165.00 100.00
111 A3 1p on 6p sl (Bk) 55.00 42.50
a. Pair, one without surcharge

(e) Surcharged ***1 Penny***

112 A3 1p on 6p sl (R) 350.00 130.00
113 A3 1p on 6p sl (Bk) 145.00 65.00

(f) Surcharged **1 Penny**

114 A3 1p on 6p sl (R) 325.00 145.00
115 A3 1p on 6p sl (Bk) 115.00 42.50

(g) Surcharged **1 Penny**

116 A3 1p on 6p sl (R) 1,500.
117 A3 1p on 6p sl (Bk) 550.00 145.00

Surcharge distinctions: a. "PENNY" in gothic capitals. b. "1" has heavy serif at base; "P", thin serif at base. c. No serif at base of "1". d. Heavy serifs at base of "1" and "p". e. Italics. f. "1" has long, sloping serif at top, thin serif at base. g. Tail of "y" missing.

### Second Republic

No. 100 Surcharged **EEN PENNY**

**1882 Unwmk. Perf. 14, 14½**

118 A3 1p on 4p ol grn 2.75 2.75
a. Inverted surcharge 300.00 300.00

**1883 Perf. 12.**

119 A1 1p black 1.50 1.10
a. Imperf.
b. Imperf. horiz., pair
c. Imperf. vert., pair
120 A2 3p red 2.50 1.10
a. Imperf. vert., pair
b. Half used as 1p on cover
121 A2 3p blk, *rose* 4.75 3.50
a. Half used as 1p on cover 750.00
122 A1 1sh green 7.75 1.75
a. Tete beche pair 500.00 115.00
b. Half used as 6p on cover 400.00

The so-called reprints of this issue are forgeries. They were made from the counterfeit plates described in the note following No. 8, plus a new false plate for the 3p. The false 3p plate has many small flaws and defects.

Forgeries of No. 120 are in dull orange red, clearly printed on whitish paper, and those of No. 121 in brownish or grayish black on bright rose. Genuine copies of No. 120 lack the orange tint and the paper is yellowish; genuine copies of No. 121 are in black without gray or brown shade, on dull lilac rose paper.

A 6p in slate on white, apparently of this issue, is a late print from the counterfeit plate.

A4

**Perf. 13½, 11½x12, 12½, 12½x12.**

**1885-93 Typo.**

123 A4 ½p gray 5 5
124 A4 1p rose 8 5
125 A4 2p brown 10 8
126 A4 2p ol bis ('87) 10 5
127 A4 2½p pur ('93) 12 10
128 A4 3p violet 15 12
129 A4 4p brnz grn 38 15
130 A4 6p blue 15 12
a. Imperf.
131 A4 1sh green 25 15
132 A4 2sh6p yellow 85 32
133 A4 5sh stl bl 1.25 42
134 A4 10sh pale brn 1.50 45
135 A4 £5 dk grn ('92)
*Nos. 123-134 (12)* 4.98 2.06

*Reprints of Nos. 123-137, 140-163, 166-174 closely resemble the originals. Paper is whiter; perf. 12½, large holes.*

Excellent counterfeits of No. 135 exist.

A5

A7

Black Surcharge

**1885 Perf. 12**

136 A5 ½p on 3p red 1.00 1.00
a. Surcharge reading down 1.00 1.00
137 A5 ½p on 1sh grn 3.25 3.25
a. Surcharge reading down 3.25 3.25
b. Tete beche pair 250.00 250.00

No. 101 Surcharged in Red

HALVE PENNY
Z. A. R.

**Perf. 14**

138 A3 ½p on 6p slate 10.50 10.50
139 A3 2p on 6p slate 1.25 1.25
a. Imperf. vertically

**Perf. 11½x12, 12½x12**

140 A7 ½p on 3p vio 1.00 1.00
a. "PRNNY" 50.00
b. Second "N" of "PENNY" inverted 125.00

A8

A9

**1887**

*141* A8 2p on 3p violet 30 30
*a.* Double surch. 250.00
*142* A9 2p on 3p violet 1.25 1.25
*a.* Double surch. 160.00

A10

A11

A12

Red Surcharge

**1893**

*143* A10 ½p on 2p ol bis 30 30
*a.* Inverted surcharge 2.25 2.25
*b.* Bars 14mm apart 1.30 1.30
*c.* As "b." inverted 6.50 6.50

**Black Surcharge**

*144* A10 ½p on 2p ol bis 30 30
*a.* Inverted surcharge 4.25 4.25
*b.* Bars 14mm apart 1.30 1.30
*c.* As "b." inverted 13.00 11.00
*145* A11 1p on 6p bl 12 12
*a.* Inverted surcharge 1.30 1.30
*b.* Double surcharge 50.00 50.00
*c.* Pair, one without surcharge 150.00
*d.* Bars 14mm apart 55 55
*e.* As "d." inverted 5.50 5.50
*f.* As "d." double 90.00
*146* A11 2½p on 1sh grn 30 30
*a.* Inverted surcharge 2.40 2.40
*b.* Fraction line misplaced "2/½" 27.50 27.50
*c.* As "b." invtd. 240.00
*d.* Bars 14mm apart 1.50 1.50
*e.* As "d." inverted 7.25 7.25
*147* A12 2½p on 1sh grn 1.00 1.00
*a.* Inverted surcharge 6.50 6.50
*b.* Bars 14mm apart 4.25 4.25
*c.* As "b." invtd. 32.50
*d.* Double surcharge 47.50 47.50

A13

Wagon with Two Shafts

**1894** **Typo.** ***Perf. 12½***

*148* A13 ½p gray 10 10
*149* A13 1p rose 10 10
*150* A13 2p ol bis 10 10
*151* A13 6p blue 40 40
*152* A13 1sh yel grn 1.75 1.75
*Nos. 148-152 (5)* 2.45 2.45

Counterfeits of Nos. 148 to 152 are plentiful.

**1895-96** **Wagon with Pole**

*153* A13 ½p gray 5 5
*154* A13 1p rose 5 5
*155* A13 2p ol bis 8 5
*156* A13 3p violet 8 8
*157* A13 4p slate 15 10
*158* A13 6p blue 12 8
*159* A13 1sh green 40 25
*160* A13 5sh sl bl ('96) 1.65 1.50
*161* A13 10sh red brn ('96) 2.10 80
*Nos. 153-161 (9)* 4.68 2.96

Most of the unused specimens of Nos. 153 to 161 now on the market are reprints.

A14

A15

**1895** **Red or Green Surcharge**

*162* A14 ½p on 1sh grn (R) 6 6
*a.* Inverted surcharge 5.25 5.25
*b.* "Pennij" instead of "Penny" 60.00 60.00
*c.* Double surcharge 60.00 60.00
*163* A15 1p on 2½p pur (G) 6 6
*a.* Inverted surch. 27.50 27.50
*b.* Surcharge sideways
*c.* Surcharge on back
*d.* Space between "1" and "d" 1.30 1.30

A16

**1895** ***Perf. 11½***

*164* A16 6p rose (G) 65 65
*a.* Vertical pair, imperf. between

Counterfeits of No. 164 are on the 6p dark red revenue stamp of 1898, and have a shiny green ink for the overprint. The false overprint is also found on other revenue denominations, though only the 6p rose was converted to postal use.

Coat of Arms, Wheat Field and Railroad Train — A17

**1895, Sept. 6** **Litho.**

*165* A17 1p red 20 20
*a.* Imperf.
*b.* Vertical pair, imperf. between 25.00 25.00

Penny Postage in Transvaal.

**With Pole**

**1896** **Typo.** ***Perf. 12½.***

*166* A13 ½p green 5 5
*167* A13 1p rose & grn 5 5
*168* A13 2p brn & grn 5 5
*169* A13 2½p ultra & grn 5 5
*170* A13 3p red vio & grn 5 5
*171* A13 4p ol & grn 5 5
*172* A13 6p vio & grn 8 8
*173* A13 1sh bis & grn 8 8
*174* A13 2sh6p hel & grn 15 15
*Nos. 166-174 (9)* 61 61

**Pietersburg Issue**

Date large; "P" in Postzegel large — A18

Date small; "P" in Postzegel large — A19

Date small; "P" in Postzegel small — A20

**1901** **Typeset** ***Imperf.***

*175* A18 ½p *green* 35.00
*a.* Initials omitted 125.00
*b.* Initials in blk 45.00
*176* A19 ½p *green* 45.00
*a.* Initials omitted 125.00
*b.* Initials in blk 45.00
*177* A20 ½p *green* 45.00
*a.* Initials omitted 125.00
*b.* Initials in blk 45.00
*178* A18 1p *rose* 9.00
*179* A19 1p *rose* 12.00
*180* A20 1p *rose* 15.00
*181* A18 2p *orange* 13.00
*182* A19 2p *orange* 18.00
*183* A20 2p *orange* 21.00
*184* A18 4p *dl bl* 22.50
*185* A19 4p *dl bl* 27.50
*186* A20 4p *dl bl* 35.00
*187* A18 6p *green* 30.00
*188* A19 6p *green* 45.00
*189* A20 6p *green* 60.00
*190* A18 1sh *yellow* 35.00
*191* A19 1sh *yellow* 50.00
*192* A20 1sh *yellow* 75.00

***Perf. 11½.***

*193* A18 ½p *green* 12.00
*194* A19 ½p *green* 13.00
*195* A20 ½p *green* 18.00
*196* A18 1p *rose* 9.00
*a.* Horiz. pair, imperf. vert. 125.00
*197* A19 1p *rose* 12.00
*a.* Horiz. pair, imperf. vert. 150.00
*198* A20 1p *rose* 12.00
*a.* Horiz. pair, imperf. vert. 150.00
*199* A18 2p *orange* 13.00
*200* A19 2p *orange* 15.00
*201* A20 2p *orange* 15.00

Nos. 193 to 201 inclusive are always imperforate on one side.

The setting consisted of 12 stamps of type A18, 6 of type A19, and 6 of type A20. The first printings, for all values, were without errors; but many errors found their way into the later printings of the ½p, 1p, 2p and 4p stamps. The perforated stamps are from the first printing and were put into use first. Part of the ½p stamps of late printings were initialled in black instead of the red normally used for this value. The other values were initialled in black. Used copies are not valued as all seen show evidence of having been canceled to order.

**Second British Occupation**
**Issued under Military Authority**

A21

Black Overprint ("V.R.I.")

**1900** **Unwmk.** ***Perf. 12½***

*202* A21 ½p green 5 5
*a.* "V.I.R." 650.00
*203* A21 1p rose & grn 5 5
*204* A21 2p brn & grn 5 5
*a.* "V.I.R." 650.00
*205* A21 2½p ultra & grn 5 5
*206* A21 3p red vio & grn 5 5
*207* A21 4p ol & grn 8 8
*a.* "V.I.R." 650.00
*208* A21 6p vio & grn 10 10
*209* A21 1sh bis & grn 18 18
*210* A21 2sh6p hel & grn 28 28
*211* A21 5sh sl bl 1.25 1.25
*212* A21 10sh red brn 1.40 1.40
*213* A4 £5 dk grn
*Nos. 202-212 (11)* 3.54 3.54

Nos. 202 to 213 have been extensively counterfeited. The overprint on the forgeries is clear and clean, with small periods and letters showing completely. In the genuine, letters are worn and lack many or all serifs; the periods are large and oval.

The genuine overprint exists inverted; double; with period missing after "V," after "R," after "I," etc.

**Issued in Lydenburg**

Overprinted in Black **V.R.I.**

**1900**

*214* A13 ½p green 150.00 150.00
*215* A13 1p rose & grn 110.00 110.00
*216* A13 2p brn & grn 1,000. 800.00
*217* A13 2½p ultra & grn 900.00
*218* A13 4p ol & grn 1,800. 650.00
*219* A13 6p vio & grn 1,800. 575.00
*220* A13 1sh bis & grn 3,000.

A22

*221* A22 3p on 1p rose & grn 45.00 45.00

**Issued in Rustenburg**

A23

Violet Handstamped Overprint

**1900** ***Perf. 12½***

*223* A23 ½p green 150.00 150.00
*224* A23 1p rose & grn 95.00 95.00
*225* A23 2p brn & grn 300.00 300.00
*226* A23 2½p ultra & grn 120.00 120.00
*227* A23 3p red vio & grn 250.00 180.00
*229* A23 6p vio & grn 700.00 700.00
*230* A23 1sh bis & grn 1,500. 1,000.
*231* A23 2sh 6p hel & grn *4,250.*

**Issued in Schweizer Reneke**

Nos. 166-168 and 172 Handstamped "BESIEGED" in Black

**1900** **Typo.** ***Perf. 12½***

*232* A13 ½p green 175.00
*233* A13 1p rose & grn 175.00
*234* A13 2p brn & grn 350.00
*235* A13 6p vio & grn 1,300.

**Same Overprint on Cape of Good Hope No. 59 and Type of 1893**

***Perf. 14***

*236* A15 ½p green 775.00
*236A* A15 1p carmine 450.00

In 1902 five revenue stamps overprinted "V.R.I." are said to have been used postally in Volksrust. There seems to be some doubt that this issue was properly authorized for postal use.

**Issued in Wolmaransstad**

A24

Blue or Rose Handstamped Overprint

**1900**

*237* A24 ½p green 175.00
*238* A24 1p rose & grn 150.00 *175.00*
*239* A24 2p brn & grn 1,100. *1,100.*
*240* A24 2½p ultra & grn (R) 1,100. *1,100.*
*241* A24 3p red vio & grn 2,000.
*242* A24 4p ol & grn 2,500. *3,250.*
*243* A24 6p vio & grn 2,250. *2,750.*
*244* A24 1sh bis & grn

No. 165 Overprinted in Blue **Cancelled V-R-I.**

*245* A17 1p red 110.00 *150.00*

**Regular Issues.**

A25

A26

Black Surcharge or Overprint

**1901-02**

*246* A25 ½p on 2p brn & grn 5 5
*247* A26 ½p green 5 5
*248* A26 1p rose & grn 5 5
*a.* "E" (ovpt.) omitted 65.00
*249* A26 3p red vio & grn 25 25
*250* A26 4p ol & grn 32 32
*251* A26 2sh6p hel & grn 3.50 3.50
*Nos. 246-251 (6)* 4.22 4.22

Excellent counterfeits of Nos. 246 to 251 are plentiful. See note after No. 213 for the recognition marks of the counterfeits.

Edward VII — A27

Nos. 260, 262 to 267 and 275 to 280 have "POSTAGE" at each side; the other stamps of type A27 have "REVENUE" at the right.

**Wmk. Crown and C. A. (2)**

**1902-03 Typo. *Perf. 14.***

*252* A27 ½p gray grn & blk 8 6
*253* A27 1p rose & blk 8 8
*254* A27 2p vio & blk 15 10
*255* A27 2½p ultra & blk 25 20
*256* A27 3p ol grn & blk ('03) 42 25
*257* A27 4p choc & blk ('03) 60 45
*258* A27 6p brn org & blk 32 22
*259* A27 1sh ol grn & blk 65 60
*260* A27 1sh red brn & blk ('03) 60 35
*261* A27 2sh brn & blk 3.25 2.50
*262* A27 2sh yel & blk ('03) 14.00 *9.25*
*263* A27 2sh6p blk & vio 1.40 1.10
*264* A27 5sh vio & blk, *yel* 4.25 3.25
*265* A27 10sh vio & blk, *red* 14.00 10.00
*266* A27 £1 vio & grn ('03) 65.00 47.50
*267* A27 £5 vio & org ('03) 1,400. 525.00
*Nos. 252-266 (15)* 105.05 75.91

**1904-09 Wmk. 3**

*268* A27 ½p gray grn & blk 85 12
*269* A27 1p rose & blk 65 8
*270* A27 2p vio & blk ('06) 1.10 12
*271* A27 2½p ultra & blk ('05) 42 15
*272* A27 3p ol grn & blk ('06) 22 12
*273* A27 4p choc & blk ('06) 45 10
*274* A27 6p brn org & blk ('05) 50 10
*275* A27 1sh red brn & blk ('05) 45 10
*276* A27 2sh yel & blk ('06) 1.75 1.25
*277* A27 2sh6p blk & red vio ('09) 4.00 85
*278* A27 5sh vio & blk, *yel* 6.50 65
*279* A27 10sh vio & blk, *red*('07) 18.00 1.00
*280* A27 £1 vio & grn ('08) 65.00 10.00
*Nos. 268-280 (13)* 99.89 14.64

The 2p and 3p are on chalky paper, the 2½p, 4p, 6p and £1 on both chalky and ordinary, and the other values on ordinary paper only.

**1905-10**

*281* A27 ½p green 10 6
*a.* Booklet pane of 6
*282* A27 1p carmine 8 5
*a.* Wmkd. Anchor (16). (error). ('07) 450.00
*b.* Booklet pane of 6
*283* A27 2p dl vio ('10) 42 8
*284* A27 2½p ultra ('10) 3.25 65

Some of the above stamps are found with the overprint "C. S. A. R." for use by the Central South African Railway, the control mark being applied after the stamps had left the post office.

## POSTAGE DUE STAMPS.

D1

**Wmk. Multiple Crown and C. A. (3)**

**1907 Typo. *Perf. 14.***

*J1* D1 ½p grn & blk 35 35
*J2* D1 1p car & blk 35 22
*J3* D1 2p brn & org 38 22
*J4* D1 3p bl & blk 1.65 40
*J5* D1 5p vio & blk 1.00 80
*J6* D1 6p red brn & blk 2.25 90
*J7* D1 1sh blk & car 2.25 1.75
*Nos. J1-J7 (7)* 8.23 4.64

Most canceled copies of Nos. J1 to J7 were used outside the Transvaal under the Union of South Africa administration in 1910 to 1916.

The stamps of Transvaal were replaced by those of South Africa.

# TRINIDAD

LOCATION — In the West Indies lying off the Venezuelan coast.
GOVT. — A British Colony which became part of the Colony of Trinidad and Tobago in 1889.
AREA — 1,864 sq. mi.
POP. — 387,000.
CAPITAL — Port of Spain.

12 Pence = 1 Shilling
20 Shillings = 1 Pound

In 1847 David Bryce, owner of the "Lady McLeod," issued a blue, lithographed, imperf. stamp to prepay his 5-cent rate for carrying letters on his sail-equipped steamer between Port of Spain and San Fernando, another Trinidad port. The stamp pictures the "Lady McLeod" above the monogram "LMcL," expressing no denomination. Value, used (pen canceled), $10,000.

"Britannia"
A1 A2

**1851-53 Unwmk. Engr. *Imperf.***

**Blued Paper**

*1* A1 (1p) brick red ('53) 140.00 45.00
*a.* (1p) brn red ('53) 300.00 40.00
*2* A1 (1p) pur brn 6.00 *30.00*
*3* A1 (1p) blue 6.00 *30.00*
*a.* (1p) dp bl 10.00 *30.00*
*4* A1 (1p) gray 25.00 25.00
*a.* (1p) gray brn 13.00 *18.00*

**1854-57**

**White Paper**

*6* A1 (1p) brn red ('57) 1,500. 40.00
*7* A1 (1p) gray 15.00 *30.00*
*8* A1 (1p) blk vio 9.00 *20.00*

**1852 Litho.**

**Yellowish Paper**

*9* A2 (1p) blue *11,500.* 2,500.
*a.* (1p) dp bl *11,500.* 2,500.
*b.* white paper 1,600.

**1853**

**Bluish Paper**

*10* A2 (1p) blue *8,000.* 2,400.

Same, Lines of Background More or Less Worn

**1855-60**

**Thin Paper**

*11* A2 (1p) sl bl *5,500.* 400.00
*12* A2 (1p) blue 275.00
*a.* (1p) grnsh bl 400.00
*13* A2 (1p) rose 11.00 *450.00*
*a.* (1p) dl red 11.00 *450.00*

A3

**1859 Engr. *Imperf.***

**White Paper**

*14* A1 (1p) dl rose 600.00 50.00
*15* A3 4p gray lil 30.00 *110.00*
*a.* 4p dl lil *425.00*
*16* A3 6p green 275.00
*17* A3 1sh sl bl 40.00 *175.00*

***Pin-perf. 12½***

*18* A1 (1p) dl rose red 750.00 35.00
*a.* (1p) lake 750.00 35.00
*19* A3 4p brn lil *10,000.* 1,350.
*20* A3 6p dp grn 2,250. 200.00
*21* A3 1sh blk vio *5,000.* 400.00

***Pin-perf. 14***

*22* A1 (1p) rose red 95.00 21.00
*a.* (1p) car 210.00 21.00
*23* A3 4p brn lil 85.00 *100.00*
*a.* 4p vio 110.00
*b.* 4p dl vio 900.00 110.00
*24* A3 6p dp grn 350.00 75.00
*25* A3 6p yel grn 65.00 65.00
*a.* Vert. pair, imperf. between *4,250.*
*26* A3 1sh blk vio *12,000.* *500.00*

Nos. 18-26 with full perforations on all sides sell at higher prices.

**1860 *Clean-cut Perf. 14 to 15½***

*27* A1 (1p) dl rose 100.00 30.00
*a.* (1p) lake 100.00 30.00
*b.* Imperf. vertically, pair *3,000.*
*29* A3 4p vio brn 100.00 45.00
*a.* 4p dl vio 300.00
*30* A3 6p dp grn 225.00 160.00
*31* A3 6p yel grn 175.00 110.00
*32* A3 1sh blk vio

**1861 *Rough Perf. 14 to 16½***

*33* A1 (1p) dl rose 82.50 11.00
*34* A3 4p gray lil 550.00 27.50
*35* A3 4p brn lil 175.00 27.50
*a.* 4p dl vio 575.00 27.50
*36* A3 6p green 350.00 35.00
*a.* 6p bl grn 700.00 35.00
*37* A3 1sh indigo 1,000. 130.00
*a.* 1sh pur bl 1,250. 200.00

**1863 *Perf. 11½ to 12***

**Thick Paper**

*39* A1 (1p) carmine 50.00 11.00
*a.* Perf. 11½-12x11 *500.00*
*40* A3 4p dl vio 65.00 20.00
*41* A3 6p dp bl grn *900.00* 20.00
*a.* Perf. 11½-12x11 *12,500.*
*42* A3 1sh indigo 1,000. 70.00

***Perf. 12½***

*43* A1 (1p) lake 16.00 11.00

***Perf. 13***

*45* A1 (1p) lake 22.00 11.00
*46* A3 6p emerald 400.00 32.50
*47* A3 1sh brt vio 4,000. 225.00

**1864-72 Wmk. 1 *Perf. 12½***

*48* A1 (1p) red 11.00 1.10
*a.* (1p) lake 17.00 1.90
*b.* (1p) rose 2.00 1.10
*c.* (1p) car 17.00 1.10
*d.* Imperf., pair *800.00* *800.00*
*49* A3 4p brt vio 45.00 5.50
*a.* 4p pale vio 90.00 6.00
*b.* Imperf. *600.00*
*50* A3 4p lilac 25.00 5.50
*a.* 4p gray lil
*51* A3 4p gray ('72) 60.00 2.75
*52* A3 6p bl grn 50.00 3.00
*a.* 6p emer 35.00 8.25
*53* A3 6p yel grn 35.00 2.25
*a.* 6p dp grn 350.00 8.25
*b.* Imperf., pair *800.00*
*54* A3 1sh purple 40.00 3.75
*a.* 1sh lil 40.00 3.75
*b.* 1sh vio 90.00 3.75
*c.* 1sh red lil 125.00 3.75
*d.* Imperf *750.00*
*55* A3 1sh org yel ('72) 75.00 1.65

Queen Victoria
A4 A7

**1869-94 Typo. *Perf. 12½***

*56* A4 5sh dl lake 55.00 37.50
*a.* Imperf. pair *1,250.*

***Perf. 14***

*57* A4 5sh cl ('94) 12.00 20.00

**1876 Engr. *Perf. 14***

*58* A1 (1p) carmine 3.00 55
*a.* (1p) red 30.00 70
*b.* (1p) lake 3.00 55
*c.* Half used as ½p on cover 600.00
*59* A3 4p gray 35.00 1.65
*60* A3 6p yel grn 35.00 1.10
*a.* 6p dp grn 35.00 1.10
*61* A3 1sh org yel 32.50 2.75

***Perf. 14 x 12½***

*61A* A3 6p yel grn *7,000.*

Type A1 Surcharged in Black **HALFPENNY**

**1879 Wmk. 1 *Perf. 14***

*62* A1 ½p lilac 3.00 3.00

Same Surcharge

**1882 Wmk. Crown and C. A. (2)**

*63* A1 ½p lilac *250.00* 42.50
*64* A1 1p carmine 7.00 50
*a.* Half used as ½p on cover 400.00

Type of 1859

**1882 Wmk. 2**

*65* A3 4p gray 75.00 3.00

No. 60 Surcharged by pen and ink in Black or Red

**1882 Wmk. 1**

*67* A3 1p on 6p grn (R) 3.00 1.50
*a.* Half used as ½p on cover 400.00
*b.* Black surcharge *2,000.*

Counterfeits of No. 67b are plentiful. Various handwriting exists on both 60 and 60a.

**1883-84 Typo. Wmk. 2**

*68* A7 ½p green 30 15
*69* A7 1p rose 1.00 15
*a.* Half used as ½p on cover 200.00
*70* A7 2½p ultra 2.00 15
*a.* 2½p bl 2.00 25
*71* A7 4p slate 2.50 40
*72* A7 6p ol brn ('84) 1.40 1.10
*73* A7 1sh org brn ('84) 4.00 1.75
*Nos. 68-73 (6)* 11.20 3.70

A8 A9

ONE PENNY:
Type I. Round "O" in "ONE".
Type II. Oval "O" in "ONE".

**1896-1904 *Perf. 14***

*74* A8 ½p lil & grn 14 8
*75* A8 ½p gray grn ('02) 14 14
*76* A8 1p lil & car, type I 45 8
*77* A8 1p lil & car, type II ('00) 225.00 2.75
*78* A8 1p blk, *red*, type II('01) 22 14
*a.* Value omitted *12,000.*
*79* A8 2½p lil & ultra 75 30
*80* A8 2½p vio & bl, *bl* ('02) 3.25 75
*81* A8 4p lil & org 1.50 1.50
*82* A8 4p grn & ultra, *buff* ('02) 1.25 1.25
*83* A8 5p lil & vio 2.50 2.50
*84* A8 6p lil & blk 2.50 2.25
*85* A8 1sh grn & org brn 3.75 4.00
*86* A8 1sh blk & bl, *yel* ('04) 3.75 3.00

**Wmk. C A over Crown (46)**

*87* A9 5sh grn & org 22.50 25.00
*88* A9 5sh lil & red vio ('02) 18.00 22.50
*89* A9 10sh grn & ultra 110.00 130.00
*90* A9 £1 grn & car 95.00 110.00
*Nos. 74-90 (17)* 490.70 306.24

No. 82 also exists on chalky paper. Nos. 88 and 90 exist on both ordinary and chalky paper.

Circular "Registrar General" cancels are revenue usage and of minimal value.

Landing of Columbus — A10

**1898** **Engr.** **Wmk. 1**
*91* A10 2p gray vio & yel brn 1.25 60

400th anniv. of the discovery of the island of Trinidad by Columbus, July 31, 1498.

**1904-09** **Wmk. 3**

**Chalky Paper**

*92* A8 ½p gray grn 35 22
*93* A8 1p blk, *red*, type II 35 14
*94* A8 2½p vio & bl, *bl* 12.50 75
*95* A8 4p blk & car, *yel* ('06) 65 95
*96* A8 6p lil & blk ('05) 3.75 3.00
*97* A8 6p vio & dp vio ('06) 1.40 1.40
*98* A8 1sh blk & bl, *yel* 3.25 2.00
*99* A8 1sh vio & bl, *yel* 2.75 3.25
*100* A8 1sh *grn* ('06) 95 65
*101* A9 5sh lil & red vio ('07) 27.50 37.50
*102* A9 £1 grn & car ('07) 125.00 165.00
*Nos. 92-102 (11)* 178.45 214.86

The ½p and 1p also exist on ordinary paper.

**1906-07**
*103* A8 1p car ('07) 65 9
*104* A8 2½p ultra 42 15

A11

A12

**1909**

**Ordinary Paper**

*105* A11 ½p gray grn 15 9
*106* A12 1p carmine 10 5
*107* A11 2½p ultra 1.50 1.00

---

## POSTAGE DUE STAMPS

D1

**Wmk. Crown and C. A. (2)**
**1885, Jan. 1** **Typo.** ***Perf. 14***
*J1* D1 ½p black 24.00 10.00
*J2* D1 1p black 1.25 9
*J3* D1 2p black 7.50 22
*J4* D1 3p black 15.00 25
*J5* D1 4p black 12.00 3.75
*J6* D1 5p black 14.00 50
*J7* D1 6p black 22.50 4.25
*J8* D1 8p black 24.00 5.00
*J9* D1 1sh black 30.00 8.00
*Nos. J1-J9 (9)* 150.25 32.06

**1906-07** **Wmk. 3**
*J10* D1 1p black 2.00 15
*J11* D1 2p black 2.50 15
*J12* D1 3p black 2.75 20
*J13* D1 4p black 3.75 3.25
*J14* D1 5p black 4.50 3.75
*J15* D1 6p black 7.00 6.25
*J16* D1 8p black 10.50 11.00
*J17* D1 1sh black 17.50 15.00
*Nos. J10-J17 (8)* 50.50 39.75

See Trinidad and Tobago Nos. J1-J16.

---

*Trinidad stamps can be mounted in Scott's British East Caribbean Album.*

## OFFICIAL STAMPS.

Postage Stamps of 1869-84 Overprinted in Black  

**1893-94** **Wmk. 2** ***Perf. 14***
*O1* A7 ½p green 22.50 *30.00*
*O2* A7 1p rose 32.50 *40.00*
*O3* A7 2½p ultra 32.50 *40.00*
*O4* A7 4p slate 35.00 *42.50*
*O5* A7 6p ol brn 40.00 *47.50*
*O6* A7 1sh org brn 50.00 *55.00*

**Wmk. Crown and C. C. (1)**
***Perf. 12½***
*O7* A4 5sh dl lake 82.50 *165.00*
*Nos. O1-O7 (7)* 295.00 420.00

Nos. 92 and 103 Overprinted **OFFICIAL**

**1909-10** **Wmk. 3** ***Perf. 14***
*O8* A8 ½p gray grn 60 85
*O9* A8 1p carmine 20 32
*a.* Dbl. overprint 315.00
*b.* Invtd. overprint 165.00
*c.* Vertical overprint 50.00

Same Overprint on No. 105

**1910**
*O10* A11 ½p gray grn 20 25

Stamps of Trinidad have been superseded by those inscribed "Trinidad and Tobago."

---

# TRINIDAD AND TOBAGO

LOCATION — In the West Indies off the coast of Venezuela.
GOVT. — Republic.
AREA — 1,980 sq. mi.
POP. — 1,160,000 (est. 1984).
CAPITAL — Port-of-Spain.

The two British colonies of Trinidad and Tobago were united from 1889 until 1899, when Tobago became a ward of the united colony. From 1899 until 1913 postage stamps of Trinidad were used. The two islands became a state in August 1962, and the independent Republic of Trinidad and Tobago on August 1, 1976.

12 Pence = 1 Shilling
20 Shillings = 1 Pound
100 Cents = 1 Dollar (1935)

**Catalogue values for unused stamps in this country are for Never Hinged items, beginning with Scott 62 in the regular postage section and Scott J9 in the postage due section.**

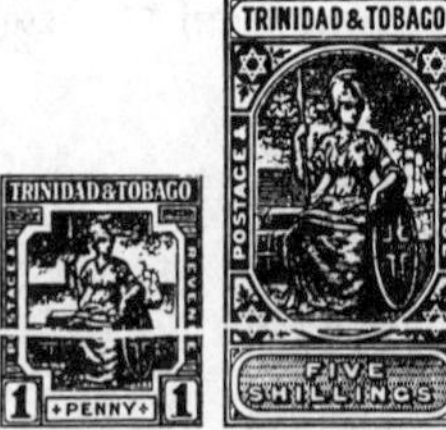

"Britannia"
A1 A2

**1913** **Typo.** **Wmk. 3** ***Perf. 14***

**Ordinary Paper**

*1* A1 ½p green 12 5
*2* A1 1p scarlet 35 14
*a* 1p car 10 5
*4* A1 2½p ultra 1.65 28

**Chalky Paper**

*5* A1 4p scar & blk, *yel* 1.00 85
*6* A1 6p red vio & dl vio 2.25 1.75
*7* A1 1sh blk, *green* 1.75 1.75
*a* 1sh blk, *emer* 1.40 1.40
*b* 1sh blk, *bl grn*, ol back 1.65 1.65
*Nos. 1-2,4-7 (6)* 7.12 4.82

**1914**

**Surface-colored Paper**

*8* A1 4p scar & blk, *yel* 3.50 *5.50*
*9* A1 1sh blk, *green* 1.10 1.65

**Chalky Paper**

*10* A2 5sh dl vio & red vio 21.00 *35.00*
*11* A2 £1 grn & car 110.00 *165.00*

**1921-22** **Wmk. 4**

**Ordinary Paper**

*12* A1 ½p green 48 5
*13* A1 1p scarlet 12 9
*14* A1 1p brn ('22) 18 8
*15* A1 2p gray ('22) 1.90 38
*16* A1 2½p ultra 52 80
*17* A1 3p ultra ('22) 1.50 1.40

**Chalky Paper**

*18* A1 6p red vio & dl vio 1.10 95
*19* A2 5sh dl vio & red vio 25.00 *37.50*
*20* A2 £1 grn & car 80.00 *140.00*
*Nos. 12-20 (9)* 110.80 *181.25*

"Britannia" and King George V — A3

**1922-28**

**Ordinary Paper**

*21* A3 ½p green 9 6
*22* A3 1p brown 12 5
*23* A3 1½p rose red 18 12
*24* A3 2p gray 22 18
*25* A3 3p ultra 75 32

**Chalky Paper**

*26* A3 4p red & blk, *yel* ('28) 2.50 65
*27* A3 6p red vio & dl vio 5.00 *10.00*
*28* A3 6p red & grn, *emer* ('24) 1.25 75
*29* A3 1sh blk, *emer* ('25) 1.25 1.00
*30* A3 5sh vio & dl vio 18.00 *25.00*
*31* A3 £1 rose & grn 90.00 *140.00*

**Wmk. Multiple Crown and C. A. (3)**

**Chalky Paper**

*32* A3 4p red & blk, *yel* 60 60
*33* A3 1sh blk, *emerald* 3.00 3.25
*Nos. 21-33 (13)* 122.96 *181.98*

First Boca — A4

Designs: 2c, Agricultural College. 3c, Mt. Irvine Bay, Tobago. 6c, Discovery of Lake Asphalt. 8c, Queen's Park, Savannah. 12c, Town Hall, San Fernando. 24c, Government House. 48c, Memorial Park. 72c, Blue Basin.

**1935-37** **Engr.** **Wmk. 4** ***Perf. 12***
*34* A4 1c emer & bl, perf. 12½ ('36) 8 5
*a* Perf. 12 50 5
*35* A4 2c lt brn & ultra, perf. 12½ ('36) 18 9
*a* Perf. 12 70 9
*36* A4 3c red & blk 14 12
*a* Perf. 12½ ('36) 18 12
*37* A4 6c bl & brn, perf. 12½ ('37) 32 20
*a* Perf. 12 35 20
*38* A4 8c red org & yel grn 52 60
*39* A4 12c dk vio & blk 52 35
*a* Perf. 12½ ('37) 95 75
*40* A4 24c ol grn & blk 1.00 55
*a* Perf. 12½ ('37) 1.75 1.50
*41* A4 48c sl grn 5.25 4.50
*42* A4 72c mag & sl grn 12.50 13.00
*Nos. 34-42 (9)* 20.51 19.46

**Silver Jubilee Issue**
Common Design Type
**1935, May 6** ***Perf. 11x12***
*43* CD301 2c blk & ultra 10 10
*44* CD301 3c car & bl 20 20
*45* CD301 6c ultra & brn 42 42
*46* CD301 24c brn vio & ind 1.75 1.75

**Coronation Issue**
Common Design Type
**1937, May 12** ***Perf. 13½x14***
*47* CD302 1c dp grn 8 8
*48* CD302 2c yel brn 14 14
*49* CD302 8c dp org 24 24

First Boca — A13

Agricultural College A14

Mt. Irvine Bay, Tobago A15

Memorial Park — A16

General Post Office and Treasury A17

Discovery of Lake Asphalt A18

Queen's Park, Savannah A19

Town Hall, San Fernando A20

Government House A21

Blue Basin A22
George VI A23

***Perf. 11½x11***
**1938-41** **Wmk. 4** **Engr.**
*50* A13 1c emer & bl 5 5
*51* A14 2c lt brn & ultra 6 5
*52* A15 3c dk car & blk 4.50 30
*52A* A15 3c vio brn & bl grn ('41) 8 5
*53* A16 4c brown 2.50 85
*53A* A16 4c red ('41) 20 9
*54* A17 5c mag ('41) 9 5
*55* A18 6c brt bl & sep 15 8
*56* A19 8c red org & yel grn 15 12
*57* A20 12c dk vio & blk 45 15
*58* A21 24c dk ol grn & blk 30 15

59 A22 60c mag & sl grn 75 42

*Perf. 12.*

60 A23 $1.20 dk grn ('40) 1.75 60
61 A23 $4.80 rose pink ('40) 11.00 4.50
*Nos. 50-61 (14)* 22.03 7.46

Watermark sideways on Nos. 50-59.

**Catalogue values for unused stamps in this section, from this point to the end of the section, are for Never Hinged items.**

**Peace Issue**
Common Design Type
*Perf. 13½x14*

**1946, Oct. 1 Engr. Wmk. 4**
62 CD303 3c brown 18 18
63 CD303 6c dp bl 25 25

**Silver Wedding Issue**
Common Design Types

**1948, Nov. 22 Photo. *Perf. 14x14½***
64 CD304 3c red brown 20 20

**Engr. *Perf. 11½x11***
65 CD305 $4.80 rose car 18.00 *27.50*

**UPU Issue**
Common Design Types
**Engr.; Name Typo. on 6c, 12c**
*Perf. 13½, 11x11½*

**1949, Oct. 10 Wmk. 4**
66 CD306 5c red vio 16 16
67 CD307 6c indigo 26 20
68 CD308 12c rose vio 55 45
69 CD309 24c olive 1.00 80

**University Issue**
Common Design Types
Inscribed: "Trinidad"

**1951, Feb. 16 Engr. *Perf. 14x14½***
70 CD310 3c choc & grn 25 18
71 CD311 12c pur & blk 70 55

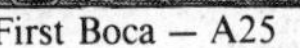
First Boca — A25

Elizabeth II — A26

Designs: 2c, Agricultural College. 3c, Mt. Irvin Bay, Tobago. 4c, Memorial Park. 5c, General Post Office and Treasury. 6c, Discovery of Lake Asphalt. 8c, Queens Park, Savannah. 12c, Town Hall, San Fernando. 24c, Government House. 60c, Blue Basin.

**1953, Apr. 20 *Perf. 11½x11***
72 A25 1c yel grn & dp bl 6 5
73 A25 2c org brn & sl bl 6 5
74 A25 3c vio brn & bl grn 6 5
75 A25 4c red 7 6
76 A25 5c magenta 9 5
77 A25 6c bl & brn 20 9
78 A25 8c red org & dp grn 20 10
79 A25 12c dk vio & blk 25 14
80 A25 24c dk ol grn & blk 52 18
81 A25 60c rose car & grnsh blk 90 35

*Perf. 11½*

82 A26 $1.20 dk grn 2.25 1.50
a. Perf. 12 2.25 1.50
83 A26 $4.80 rose pink 9.25 6.25
a. Perf. 12 9.25 6.25
*Nos. 72-83 (12)* 13.91 8.87

Common Design Types pictured in section before Great Britain.

**Coronation Issue**
Common Design Type

**1953, June 3 *Perf. 13½x13***
84 CD312 3c dk grn & blk 15 12

No. 73 Surcharged "ONE CENT"
*Perf. 11½x11*

**1956, Dec. 20 Wmk. 4**
85 A25 1c on 2c org brn & sl bl 90 90

**West Indies Federation**
Common Design Type
*Perf. 11½x11*

**1958, Apr. 22 Engr. Wmk. 314**
86 CD313 5c green 12 5
87 CD313 6c blue 14 8
88 CD313 12c car rose 28 28

Cipriani Memorial, Port-of-Spain A27

Queen's Hall, Port-of-Spain A28

Designs: 5c, Whitehall. 6c, Treasury Building. 8c, Governor General's House. 10c, General Hospital, San Fernando. 12c, Oil refinery. 15c, Crest of colony. 25c, Scarlet ibis. 35c, Lake Asphalt (Pitch). 50c, Jinnah Memorial Mosque. 60c, Anthurium lilies. $1.20, Copper-rumped hummingbird and hibiscus. $4.80, Map.

*Perf. 13½x14, 14x13½*

**1960, Sept. 24 Photo. Wmk. 314**
**Size: 22½x25mm, 25x22½mm**
89 A27 1c dk gray & buff 8 5
a. Wmkd. sideways ('66) 6 5
90 A28 2c ultra 6 5
91 A28 5c dk bl 8 5
92 A28 6c lt red brn 9 8
93 A28 8c yel grn 12 9
94 A28 10c lt pur 14 8
95 A28 12c brt red 16 8
96 A28 15c orange 48 18
97 A28 25c dk bl & crim 38 14
98 A28 35c grn & blk 55 18
99 A28 50c bl, yel & ol 65 24
100 A27 60c multi 85 32
a. Perf. 14 ('65) 160.00 24.00

**Size: 48x25mm**
101 A28 $1.20 multi 2.75 1.00
102 A28 $4.80 lt bl & lt yel grn 6.00 4.00
*Nos. 89-102 (14)* 12.39 6.54

See No. 116.

Scouts and Map of Trinidad and Tobago — A29

**1961, Apr. 4 *Perf. 13½x14***
103 A29 8c multi 20 20
104 A29 25c multi 42 42

2nd Caribbean Scout Jamboree, Valsayn Park, Trinidad, Apr. 4-14.

**Independent State**

Underwater Scene from Painting by Carlisle Chang — A30

Designs: 8c, Elizabeth II and new Terminal Building, Piarco Airport. 25c, Elizabeth II and Hilton Hotel. 35c, Map and greater bird of paradise. 60c, Map and scarlet ibis.

**1962, Aug. 31 Photo. *Perf. 14½***
105 A30 5c bl grn 9 9
106 A30 8c slate 12 12
107 A30 25c purple 24 24
108 A30 35c emer, yel, brn & blk 28 28
109 A30 60c multi, blk & ver 45 45
*Nos. 105-109 (5)* 1.18 1.18

Issued to mark Trinidad and Tobago's independence, Aug. 31, 1962.

**Freedom from Hunger Issue**

Protein Food — A31

**1963, June 1 *Perf. 14x13½***
110 A31 5c hn brn 10 8
111 A31 8c citron 12 12
112 A31 25c vio bl 40 40

See note in Common Design section.

Girl Guide Emblem A32

*Perf. 14½x14*

**1964, Sept. 15 Wmk. 314**
113 A32 6c red, dk bl & yel 8 8
114 A32 25c brt bl, dk bl & yel 30 30
115 A32 35c lt grn, dk bl & yel 45 45

50th anniv. of the Trinidad and Tobago Girl Guide Association.

Arms of Independent State — A33

**1964, Sept. 15 *Perf. 14x13½***
116 A33 15c orange 60 40

ICY Emblem A34

**Unwmk.**
**1965, Nov. 15 Litho. *Perf. 12***
**Granite Paper**
117 A34 35c dl yel, red brn & grn 35 35

International Cooperation Year, 1965.

Eleanor Roosevelt — A35

*Perf. 13½x14*

**1965, Dec. 10 Wmk. 314**
118 A35 25c vio bl, red & blk 22 22

Issued to honor Eleanor Roosevelt and to publicize the Eleanor Roosevelt Memorial Foundation.

"Redhouse," Parliament Building — A36

Designs: 8c, Map of Trinidad and Tobago, royal yacht "Britannia" and arms of State. 25c, Flag and map. 35c, Flag, Trinity Hills, General Post Office, sugar cane, coconut palms and derricks.

*Perf. 13½x14*

**1966, Feb. 8 Photo. Wmk. 314**
119 A36 5c ultra, red, blk & grn 16 16
120 A36 8c ultra, sil, blk & yel brn 24 24
121 A36 25c red, blk emer 70 70
122 A36 35c ultra, red, blk & grn 1.00 1.00

Visit of Elizabeth II and Prince Philip.

Nos. 93, 94, 116 and 100 Overprinted: "FIFTH YEAR OF / INDEPENDENCE / 31st AUGUST 1967"

*Perf. 14x13½, 13½x14*

**1967, Aug. 31 Photo. Wmk. 314**
123 A28 8c yel grn 8 8
124 A28 10c lt pur 9 9
125 A33 15c orange 20 20
126 A27 60c multi 80 80

On 60c, the overprint is arranged in 5 lines.

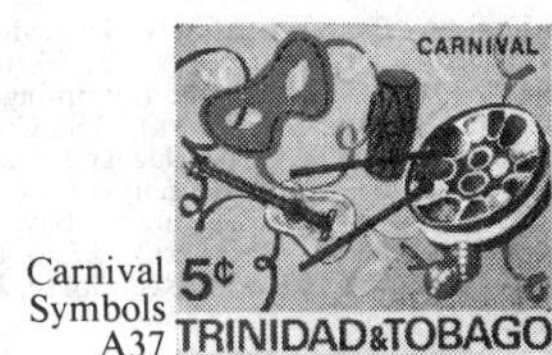

Carnival Symbols A37

Designs: 10c, Calypso King (vert.). 15c, Steel band. 25c, Chinese masks. 35c, Carnival King (vert.). 60c, Carnival Queen (vert.).

**Unwmk.**
**1968, Feb. 16 Litho. *Perf. 12***
127 A37 5c pink & multi 5 5
128 A37 10c vio bl & multi 7 7
129 A37 15c multi 9 9
130 A37 25c multi 12 12
131 A37 35c dk pur & multi 18 18
132 A37 60c brn ol & multi 35 35
*Nos. 127-132 (6)* 86 86

Issued to publicize the Trinidad Carnival.

WHO Emblem and Eye Examination A38

Dancing Children and Human Rights Flame A39

**Wmk. 314**
**1968, May 7 Photo. *Perf. 14***
133 A38 5c rose red, gold & blk 6 5
134 A38 25c org, gold & blk 32 32
135 A38 35c brt bl, gold & blk 40 40

**1968, Aug. 5 *Perf. 14***
136 A39 5c car, yel & blk 8 8
137 A39 10c brt bl yel, & blk 12 12
138 A39 25c yel grn, yel & blk 26 26

International Human Rights Year.

Bicycling and Map A40

Designs (Olympic Rings, Map of Trinidad and Tobago and): 15c, Weight lifting. 25c, Relay race. 35c, Running. $1.20, Map of Mexico and flags of Mexico and Trinidad and Tobago.

**Photo.; Gold Impressed (except $1.20)**

**1968, Oct. 12** ***Perf. 14***

| No. | Type | Description | Unused | Used |
|---|---|---|---|---|
| *139* | A40 | 5c vio, gold & multi | 5 | 5 |
| *140* | A40 | 15c red, gold & multi | 14 | 12 |
| *141* | A40 | 25c org, gold & multi | 15 | 12 |
| *142* | A40 | 35c brt grn, gold & multi | 26 | 18 |
| *143* | A40 | $1.20 bl, gold & multi | 1.00 | 1.00 |
| | | *Nos. 139-143 (5)* | 1.60 | 1.47 |

Issued to commemorate the 19th Olympic Games, Mexico City, Oct. 12-27.

Cacao A41

Designs: 3c, Sugar refinery. 5c, Redtailed chachalaca. 6c, Oil refinery. 8c, Fertilizer plant. 10c, Green hermit (hummingbird; vert.). 12c, Citrus fruit (vert.). 15c, Coat of arms (vert.). 20c, 25c, Flag and map of islands (vert.). 30c, Wild poinsettia (vert.). 40c, Scarlet ibis. 50c, Maracas Bay. $1, Blooming tabebuia (tree; vert.). $2.50, Fishermen hauling in net. $5, Red House, Port-of-Spain.

**Photo.; Silver or Gold Impressed**

**1969, Apr. 1** **Wmk. 314** ***Perf. 14***

| No. | Type | Description | Unused | Used |
|---|---|---|---|---|
| *144* | A41 | 1c sil & multi | 5 | 5 |
| *145* | A41 | 3c gold & multi | 5 | 5 |
| *a.* | | Wmk. upright ('74) | 50 | 50 |
| *146* | A41 | 5c gold & multi | 5 | 5 |
| *a.* | | Wmk. upright ('73) | 7.50 | 4.00 |
| *147* | A41 | 6c gold & multi | 6 | 5 |
| *a.* | | Wmk. upright ('74) | 30 | 25 |
| *148* | A41 | 8c sil & multi | 8 | 7 |
| *149* | A41 | 10c gold & multi | 10 | 8 |
| *b.* | | Wmk. 373 ('76) | 30 | 25 |
| *150* | A41 | 12c sil & multi | 12 | 8 |
| *151* | A41 | 15c sil & multi | 15 | 12 |
| *152* | A41 | 20c gold & multi | 20 | 12 |
| *153* | A41 | 25c sil & multi | 25 | 15 |
| *154* | A41 | 30c sil & multi | 30 | 18 |
| *155* | A41 | 40c gold & multi | 40 | 25 |
| *156* | A41 | 50c sil & multi | 50 | 30 |
| *157* | A41 | $1 gold & multi | 1.00 | 75 |
| *158* | A41 | $2.50 gold & multi | 3.00 | 2.50 |
| *159* | A41 | $5 gold & multi | 6.00 | 5.00 |
| | | *Nos. 144-159 (16)* | 12.31 | 9.80 |

Capt. A. A. Cipriani, ILO Emblem and Gate — A42

Design: 15c, Industrial Court's and ILO emblems, and Woodford Square gate.

**Unwmk.**

**1969, May 1** **Photo.** ***Perf. 12***

| No. | Type | Description | Unused | Used |
|---|---|---|---|---|
| *160* | A42 | 6c dp car, gold & blk | 8 | 8 |
| *161* | A42 | 15c brt bl, gold & blk | 20 | 20 |

ILO, 50th anniv.

Union Jack and Flags of CARIFTA Members A43

Designs: 6c, Cornucopia (vert.). 30c, Map of Caribbean (vert.). 40c, Jet plane and "Strength through Unity" emblem.

**1969, Aug. 1** ***Perf. 14x13½, 13½x14***

| No. | Type | Description | Unused | Used |
|---|---|---|---|---|
| *162* | A43 | 6c lil, gold & multi | 6 | 6 |
| *163* | A43 | 10c multi | 12 | 12 |
| *164* | A43 | 30c red, emer, blk & gold | 40 | 40 |
| *165* | A43 | 40c bl, blk, grn & gold | 52 | 52 |

Caribbean Free Trade Area (CARIFTA).

*Trinidad and Tobago stamps can be mounted in Scott's annually supplemented British East Caribbean Album.*

Moon Landing and Earth — A44

Designs: 40c, Lunar landing module and astronauts on moon (vert.). $1, Astronauts Aldrin at control panel, and Armstrong collecting rocks.

**1969, Sept. 1** **Litho.** ***Perf. 14***

| No. | Type | Description | Unused | Used |
|---|---|---|---|---|
| *166* | A44 | 6c multi | 6 | 6 |
| *167* | A44 | 40c multi | 50 | 50 |
| *168* | A44 | $1 multi | 1.25 | 1.25 |

See note after U.S. No. C76.

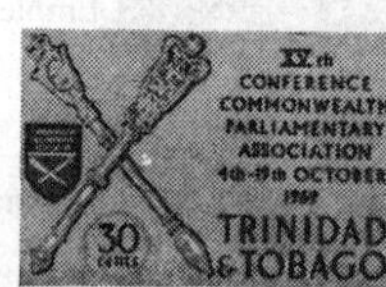


Maces of Senate and House of Representatives — A45

Designs: 10c, Chamber of Parliament. 15c, View of Kennedy Complex, University of the West Indies at St. Augustine. 40c, Cannon and view of Scarborough from Fort King George.

***Perf. 14x13½***

**1969, Oct. 23** **Photo.** **Wmk. 314**

| No. | Type | Description | Unused | Used |
|---|---|---|---|---|
| *169* | A45 | 10c multi | 12 | 12 |
| *170* | A45 | 15c multi | 20 | 20 |
| *171* | A45 | 30c lt bl & multi | 38 | 38 |
| *172* | A45 | 40c multi | 50 | 50 |

15th Conf. of the Commonwealth Parliamentary Assoc., Port-of-Spain, Oct. 4-19.

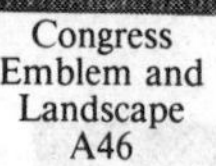

Congress Emblem and Landscape A46

Carnival King as "Man in the Moon" A47

Designs: 6c, Congress emblem (steel drum and bird). 30c, Palms, landscape and emblem (horiz.).

***Perf. 14x13½, 13½x14***

**1969, Nov. 2** **Litho.** **Unwmk.**

| No. | Type | Description | Unused | Used |
|---|---|---|---|---|
| *173* | A46 | 6c red, blk & gold | 7 | 7 |
| *174* | A46 | 30c lt bl, plum & gold | 35 | 35 |
| *175* | A46 | 40c ultra, blk & gold | 45 | 45 |

24th Cong. of the Intl. Junior Chamber of Commerce.

**1970, Feb. 2** **Wmk. 314** ***Perf. 14***

Designs: 6c, Carnival Queen as "City Beneath the Sea." 15c, Bambara god (antelope) from the Band of the Year. 30c, Pheasant Queen (Chanticleer) of Malaya. 40c, Steel Band of the Year with 1969 Calypso and Road March Kings (horiz.).

| No. | Type | Description | Unused | Used |
|---|---|---|---|---|
| *176* | A47 | 5c dk brn & multi | 5 | 5 |
| *177* | A47 | 6c dk bl & multi | 6 | 6 |
| *178* | A47 | 15c vio bl & multi | 14 | 14 |
| *179* | A47 | 30c dk grn & multi | 28 | 28 |
| *180* | A47 | 40c grn & multi | 38 | 38 |
| | | *Nos. 176-180 (5)* | 91 | 91 |

Issued to publicize the Trinidad Carnival.

Mahatma Gandhi and Indian Flag — A48

Design: 10c, Gandhi monument (vert.).

**Unwmk.**

**1970, Mar. 2** **Photo.** ***Perf. 12***

| No. | Type | Description | Unused | Used |
|---|---|---|---|---|
| *181* | A48 | 10c ultra & multi | 32 | 22 |
| *182* | A48 | 30c crim & multi | 90 | 70 |

Mohandas K. Gandhi (1869-1948), leader in India's fight for independence.

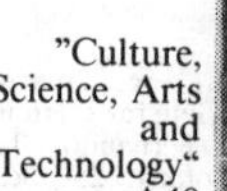

"Culture, Science, Arts and Technology" A49

Designs: 10c, Children of various races, map of Trinidad and Tobago and "UNICEF." 20c, Noah's ark, rainbow, dove and U.N. emblem.

**1970, June 26** **Photo.** ***Perf. 13½***

| No. | Type | Description | Unused | Used |
|---|---|---|---|---|
| *183* | A49 | 5c multi | 7 | 7 |
| *184* | A49 | 10c multi | 15 | 15 |
| *185* | A49 | 20c multi | 30 | 30 |

25th anniversary of the United Nations.

UPU Headquarters, Bern — A50

**1970, June 26** **Unwmk.** ***Perf. 12***

| No. | Type | Description | Unused | Used |
|---|---|---|---|---|
| *186* | A50 | 30c ultra & multi | 38 | 38 |

Opening of new UPU Headquarters in Bern.

No. 146 Overprinted: "NATIONAL / COMMERCIAL / BANK / ESTABLISHED / 1.7.70"

**Photo.; Gold Embossed**

**1970, July 1** **Wmk. 314** ***Perf. 14***

| No. | Type | Description | Unused | Used |
|---|---|---|---|---|
| *187* | A41 | 5c gold & multi | 15 | 15 |

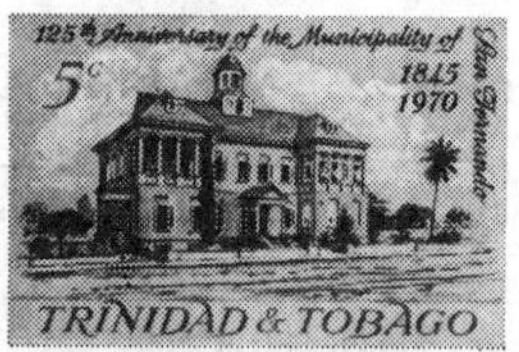


San Fernando Town Hall — A51

Designs: 3c, East Indian Immigrants, 1820, after painting by Cazabon (vert.). 40c, Ships in San Fernando Harbor, 1860, after painting by Michel J. Cazabon.

***Perf. 14x13½, 13½x14***

**1970, Nov.** **Litho.** **Wmk. 314**

| No. | Type | Description | Unused | Used |
|---|---|---|---|---|
| *188* | A51 | 3c bis & multi | 6 | 5 |
| *189* | A51 | 5c lem & multi | 9 | 7 |
| *190* | A51 | 40c lem & multi | 60 | 50 |

Issued to commemorate the 125th anniversary of the municipality of San Fernando.

Madonna and Child, by Titian — A52

Paintings: 3c, Adoration of the Shepherds, School of Saville. 30c, Adoration of the Shepherds, by Louis Le Nain. 40c, Virgin and Child with St. John and Angel, by Morando. $1, Adoration of the Magi, by Paolo Veronese.

***Perf. 13½***

**1970, Dec. 8** **Unwmk.** **Litho.**

| No. | Type | Description | Unused | Used |
|---|---|---|---|---|
| *191* | A52 | 3c dl org & multi | 5 | 5 |
| *a.* | | Booklet pane of 2 | 15 | |
| *192* | A52 | 5c brt pink & multi | 5 | 5 |
| *a.* | | Booklet pane of 2 | 22 | |
| *193* | A52 | 30c lt utra & multi | 28 | 28 |
| *a.* | | Booklet pane of 2 | 70 | |
| *194* | A52 | 40c yel grn & multi | 40 | 40 |
| *a.* | | Booklet pane of 2 | 90 | |
| *b.* | | Souvenir sheet of 4 | 2.00 | 2.00 |
| *195* | A52 | $1 pale lil & multi | 1.00 | 1.00 |
| | | *Nos. 191-195 (5)* | 1.78 | 1.78 |

No. 194b contains one each of Nos. 191-194. Multicolored margin with inscription. Size: 115½x153mm.

Brocket Deer — A53

***Perf. 14x13½***

**1971, Aug. 9** **Litho.** **Wmk. 314**

| No. | Type | Description | Unused | Used |
|---|---|---|---|---|
| *196* | A53 | 3c shown | 18 | 5 |
| *197* | A53 | 5c Collared peccary | 25 | 8 |
| *198* | A53 | 6c Paca | 35 | 22 |
| *199* | A53 | 30c Agouti | 1.75 | 1.10 |
| *200* | A53 | 40c Ocelot | 2.25 | 1.40 |
| | | *Nos. 196-200 (5)* | 4.78 | 2.85 |

Capt. A. A. Cipriani A54

Virgin and Child with St. John, by Bartolommeo A55

Design: 30c, Chaconia medal (for distinction in social field).

**1971, Aug. 31** ***Perf. 14***

| No. | Type | Description | Unused | Used |
|---|---|---|---|---|
| *201* | A54 | 5c multi | 8 | 5 |
| *202* | A54 | 30c multi | 38 | 38 |

9th anniversary of independence. Capt. Arthur Andrew Cipriani (died 1945) was mayor of Port of Spain and member of First Executive Council.

**1971, Oct. 25** **Litho.** ***Perf. 14x14½***

Christmas: 5c, Local creche. 10c, Virgin and Child with Sts. Jerome and Dominic, by Filippino Lippi. 15c, Virgin and Child with St. Anne, by Gerolamo dai Libri.

| No. | Type | Description | Unused | Used |
|---|---|---|---|---|
| *203* | A55 | 3c yel & multi | 7 | 5 |
| *204* | A55 | 5c dl bl & multi | 10 | 10 |
| *205* | A55 | 10c red & multi | 26 | 26 |
| *206* | A55 | 15c org & multi | 42 | 42 |

Satellite Earth Station, Matura
A56

Dish Antenna
A57

Design: 40c, Satellite over earth (Africa).

**1971, Nov. 18** *Perf. 14*

| No. | Type | Description | Unused | Used |
|---|---|---|---|---|
| *207* | A56 | 10c ultra & multi | 12 | 12 |
| *208* | A57 | 30c grn & multi | 42 | 42 |
| *209* | A57 | 40c blk & multi | 55 | 55 |
| *a* | | Souvenir sheet of 3 | 1.65 | 1.65 |

Opening of Satellite Earth Station at Matura. No. 209a contains 3 imperf. stamps with simulated perforations similar to Nos. 207-209. Green decorative margin with black inscription. Size: 139x76mm.

Morpho Hybrid
A58

Butterflies: 5c, Purple mort bleu. 6c, Jaune d'abricot. 10c, Purple king shoemaker. 20c, Southern white pape. 30c, Little jaune.

**1972, Feb. 18** **Photo.** **Wmk. 314**

| No. | Type | Description | Unused | Used |
|---|---|---|---|---|
| *210* | A58 | 3c ol & multi | 18 | 10 |
| *211* | A58 | 5c ocher & multi | 24 | 18 |
| *212* | A58 | 6c yel & multi | 30 | 22 |
| *213* | A58 | 10c yel grn & multi | 60 | 35 |
| *214* | A58 | 20c lil & multi | 1.25 | 75 |
| *215* | A58 | 30c dl grn & multi | 1.90 | 1.10 |
| | | *Nos. 210-215 (6)* | 4.47 | 2.70 |

S.S. Lady McLeod and Stamp
A59

Designs (Lady McLeod Stamp and): 10c, Map of Trinidad and Tobago. 30c, Commemorative inscription.

**1972, Apr. 12** **Litho.** *Perf. 14½x14*

| No. | Type | Description | Unused | Used |
|---|---|---|---|---|
| *216* | A59 | 5c bl & multi | 9 | 9 |
| *217* | A59 | 10c bl & multi | 18 | 18 |
| *218* | A59 | 30c bl & multi | 55 | 55 |
| *a* | | Souvenir sheet of 3 | 1.65 | 1.65 |

125th anniv. of the Lady McLeod stamp. No. 218a contains one each of Nos. 216-218. Violet blue margin with white inscription. Size: 83x140mm.

Trinity Cross — A60

Medals: 10c, Chaconia medal. 20c, Hummingbird medal. 30c, Medal of Merit.

**1972, Aug. 28** **Photo.** *Perf. 13½x13*

| No. | Type | Description | Unused | Used |
|---|---|---|---|---|
| *219* | A60 | 5c bl & multi | 7 | 7 |
| *220* | A60 | 10c multi | 15 | 15 |
| *221* | A60 | 20c yel grn & multi | 28 | 28 |
| *222* | A60 | 30c brt rose & multi | 42 | 42 |
| *a* | | Souvenir sheet of 4 | 1.40 | 1.40 |

10th anniversary of independence. No. 222a contains one each of Nos. 219-222. Black and red margin and black inscription. Size: 92½x121mm.

See Nos. 235-238.

Olympic Rings, Relay Race Medal, 1964
A61

Designs (Olympic Rings and): 20c, Bronze medal, 200-meters, 1964. 30c, Bronze medals, weight lifting, 1952. 40c, Silver medal, 400-meters, 1964. 50c, Silver medal, weight lifting, 1948.

**1972, Sept. 7** **Litho.** *Perf. 14*

| No. | Type | Description | Unused | Used |
|---|---|---|---|---|
| *223* | A61 | 10c yel & multi | 15 | 15 |
| *224* | A61 | 20c multi | 30 | 30 |
| *225* | A61 | 30c lil & multi | 40 | 40 |
| *226* | A61 | 40c lt bl & multi | 52 | 52 |
| *227* | A61 | 50c org & multi | 60 | 60 |
| *a* | | Souvenir sheet of 5 | 2.00 | 2.00 |
| | | *Nos. 223-227 (5)* | 1.97 | 1.97 |

20th Olympic Games, Munich, Aug. 26-Sept. 11. No. 227a contains one each of Nos. 223-227 and label with Olympic rings. Red and black margin and black inscription. Size: 153x81mm.

Holy Family, by Titian
A62

Designs: 3c, Adoration of the Kings, by Dosso Dossi. 30c, Like 5c.

**1972, Nov. 9** **Photo.** **Wmk. 314**

| No. | Type | Description | Unused | Used |
|---|---|---|---|---|
| *228* | A62 | 3c bl & multi | 8 | 6 |
| *229* | A62 | 5c rose lil & multi | 12 | 12 |
| *230* | A62 | 30c lt grn & multi | 62 | 62 |
| *a* | | Souvenir sheet of 3 | 1.50 | 1.50 |

Christmas 1972. No. 230a contains one each of Nos. 228-230. Claret, green and black margin. Size: 72x98½mm.

ECLA Headquarters, Santiago, Chile — A63

Designs: 20c, INTERPOL emblem. 30c, WHO emblem. 40c, University of West Indies Administration Building.

**1973, Aug. 15** **Litho.** **Wmk. 314**

| No. | Type | Description | Unused | Used |
|---|---|---|---|---|
| *231* | A63 | 10c org & multi | 12 | 12 |
| *232* | A63 | 20c multi | 24 | 24 |
| *233* | A63 | 30c ultra & multi | 40 | 40 |
| *234* | A63 | 40c lil & multi | 52 | 52 |
| *a* | | Souvenir sheet of 4 | 1.50 | 1.50 |

Economic Commission for Latin America, 25th anniv. (10c); Intl. Criminal Police Organization, 50th anniv. (20c); Intl. Meteorological cooperation, cent. (30c); Admission of 1st students to the University of West Indies, 25th anniv. (40c).

No. 234a contains one each of Nos. 231-234, blue margin, black inscription. Size: 155x91mm.

### Medal Type of 1972 Redrawn

Medals: 10c, Trinity Cross. 20c, Medal of Merit. 30c, Chaconia medal. 40c, Hummingbird medal.

**1973, Aug. 30** **Photo.** *Perf. 14½x14*

| No. | Type | Description | Unused | Used |
|---|---|---|---|---|
| *235* | A60 | 10c dk grn & multi | 12 | 12 |
| *236* | A60 | 20c dk brn & multi | 25 | 25 |
| *237* | A60 | 30c dk bl & multi | 42 | 42 |
| *238* | A60 | 40c dp vio & multi | 52 | 52 |
| *a* | | Souvenir sheet of 4 | 1.65 | 1.65 |

11th anniversary of independence. No. 238a contains one each of Nos. 235-238, perf. 14. Deep rose and multicolored margin with commemorative inscription. Size: 75x127mm. "Trinidad and Tobago" in one line on Nos. 235-238.

General Post Office, Port of Spain
A64

Design: 40c, Conference Hall and flags, Chagaramas.

**1973, Oct. 8** **Photo.** *Perf. 14*

| No. | Type | Description | Unused | Used |
|---|---|---|---|---|
| *239* | A64 | 30c multi | 40 | 40 |
| *240* | A64 | 40c multi | 52 | 52 |
| *a* | | Souvenir sheet of 2 | 1.10 | 1.10 |

2nd Commonwealth Conference of Postal Administrations, Trinidad, Oct. 8-20. No. 240a contains one each of Nos. 239-240. Yellow margin with black inscription and map showing British Commonwealth of Nations. Perforations extend through margin and divide map. Size: 115x115mm.

Virgin and Child, by Murillo — A65

**1973, Oct. 22** *Perf. 14½x14*

| No. | Type | Description | Unused | Used |
|---|---|---|---|---|
| *241* | A65 | 5c pink & multi | 8 | 8 |
| *242* | A65 | $1 lt bl & multi | 1.25 | 1.25 |
| *a* | | Souvenir sheet of 2 | 1.65 | 1.65 |

Christmas 1973. No. 242a contains one each of Nos. 241-242 perf. 14. Blue margin with red inscription. Size: 93x87mm.

Post Office and UPU Emblem — A66

Design: 50c, Map of Islands, UPU emblem, means of transportation.

**1974, Nov. 18** **Photo.** *Perf. 13½x14*

| No. | Type | Description | Unused | Used |
|---|---|---|---|---|
| *243* | A66 | 40c brt pur & multi | 50 | 50 |
| *244* | A66 | 50c bl gray & multi | 65 | 65 |
| *a* | | Souvenir sheet of 2 | 22.50 | 22.50 |

Cent. of the UPU. No. 244a contains one each of Nos. 243-244. Size: 117x104mm.

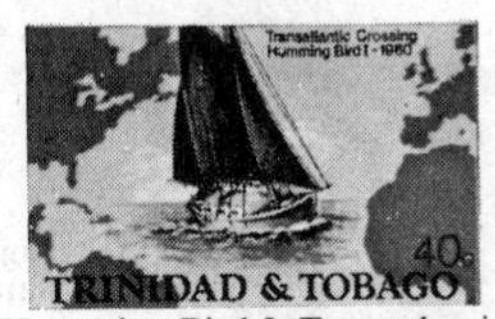


Humming Bird I, Transatlantic Crossing, 1960 — A67

Design: 50c, Globe, Humming Bird II, Harold and Kwailan La Borde.

**1974, Dec. 2** *Perf. 14½*

| No. | Type | Description | Unused | Used |
|---|---|---|---|---|
| *245* | A67 | 40c multi | 52 | 52 |
| *246* | A67 | 50c multi | 70 | 70 |
| *a* | | Souvenir sheet of 2 | 3.00 | 3.00 |

First anniversary of the voyage around the world by Harold and Kwailan La Borde aboard Humming Bird II, 1969-1973. No. 246a contains one each of Nos. 245-246, multicolored margin. Size: 108x83mm.

"Equality" and IWY Emblem — A68

**1975, June 23** **Litho.** **Wmk. 314**

| No. | Type | Description | Unused | Used |
|---|---|---|---|---|
| *247* | A68 | 15c multi | 28 | 28 |
| *248* | A68 | 30c multi | 55 | 55 |

International Women's Year 1975.

Dr. Pawan and Laboratory Equipment — A69

Design: 25c, Vampire bat, microscope, syringe, bat's head.

*Perf. 14x14½*

**1975, Sept. 23** **Photo.** **Wmk. 373**

| No. | Type | Description | Unused | Used |
|---|---|---|---|---|
| *249* | A69 | 25c yel & multi | 40 | 40 |
| *250* | A69 | 30c lt bl & multi | 48 | 48 |

Isolation of rabies virus by Dr. Joseph Lennox Pawan (1887-1957).

Boeing 707, BWIA Emblem, Air Routes
A70

Designs: 30c, Boeing 707 on ground. 40c, Boeing 707 in the air.

**Wmk. 373**

**1975, Nov. 27** **Litho.** *Perf. 14½*

| No. | Type | Description | Unused | Used |
|---|---|---|---|---|
| *251* | A70 | 20c dk bl & multi | 25 | 25 |
| *252* | A70 | 30c dp ultra & multi | 35 | 35 |
| *253* | A70 | 40c dl grn & multi | 50 | 50 |
| *a* | | Souvenir sheet of 3 | 1.25 | 1.25 |

35th anniversary of British West Indian Airways. No. 253a contains one each of Nos. 251-253; multicolored margin with BWIA emblem. Size: 118x109mm.

Land of the Hummingbird Costume — A71

Design: $1, Carib Prince riding pink ibis. Designs show prize-winning costumes from 1974 carnival.

**1976, Jan. 12** **Photo.** *Perf. 14½*

| No. | Type | Description | Unused | Used |
|---|---|---|---|---|
| [illegible] | | [illegible] multi | 25 | 25 |
| [illegible] | | [illegible] multi | 80 | 80 |
| *a* | | Souvenir sheet of 2 | 1.10 | 1.10 |

Carnival 1976. No. 255a contains one each of Nos. 254-255, multicolored margin with carnival scene. Size: 82x108mm.

Angostura Building, Port of Spain
A72

Designs (Exposition Medals, obverse and reverse): 35c, New Orleans, 1885-86. 45c, Sydney, 1879. 50c, Brussels, 1897.

**1976, July 14 Litho. *Perf. 13***

*256* A72 5c bis & multi 5 5
*257* A72 35c yel grn & multi 35 35
*258* A72 45c bl & multi 42 42
*259* A72 50c vio & multi 52 52
*a* Souvenir sheet of 4 1.50 1.50

Sesquicentennial of the manufacture of Angostura Bitters. No. 259a contains one each of Nos. 256-259, perf. 14; black and red margin. Size: 128½x112mm.

**Cricket Cup Issue**

Types of Barbados, 1976

**1976, Oct. 4 Unwmk. *Perf. 14***

*260* A63 35c lt bl & multi 55 55
*261* A64 45c lil rose & blk 75 75
*a* Souvenir sheet of 2 2.00 2.00

World Cricket Cup, won by West Indies Team, 1975. No. 261a contains one each of Nos. 260-261; decorative gray and black margin. Size: 94½x92mm.

Columbus Sailing through the Bocas, by A. Camps-Campins — A73

Paintings: 10c, View, by Jean Michael Cazabon. 20c, Landscape, by Cazabon. 35c, Los Gallos Point, by Cazabon. 45c, Corbeaux Town, by Cazabon.

**1976, Nov. 1 Litho. Wmk. 373**

*262* A73 5c ocher & multi 5 5
*263* A73 10c lil & multi 6 6
*264* A73 20c grn & multi 12 12
*265* A73 35c red org & multi 20 20
*266* A73 45c bl & multi 25 25
*a* Souvenir sheet of 5 80 80
*Nos. 262-266 (5)* 68 68

No. 266a contains one each of Nos. 262-266; decorative ocher and green margin. Size: 165x99mm.

Hasely Crawford and Gold Medal
A74

**1977, Jan. 4 Litho. *Perf. 12½***

*267* A74 25c multi 52 45
*a* Souvenir sheet 60 50

Hasely Crawford, winner of 100-meter dash at Montreal Olympic Games. No. 267a contains one stamp, multicolored margin with Olympic torches. Size: 97x74mm.

Sikorsky S-38 (Lindbergh's Plane) — A75

Designs: 35c, Charles Lindbergh delivering first airmail to Port of Spain, 1927. 45c, Boeing 707, British West Indies Airways. 50c, Boeing 747, British Airways.

**1977, Apr. Wmk. 373 *Perf. 13***

*268* A75 20c lt bl & multi 30 30
*269* A75 35c lt bl & multi 48 48
*270* A75 45c lt bl & multi 60 60
*271* A75 50c lt bl & multi 1.10 75
*a* Souvenir sheet of 4 3.00 3.00

50th anniversary of airmail to Trinidad and Tobago. No. 271a contains one each of Nos. 268-271, perf. 14; blue and red margin showing plane and inscription. Size: 128x100mm.

Trinidad and Tobago Flag
A76

White Poinsettia
A77

Designs: 35c, Coat of arms. 45c, Government House.

**1977, July 26 Litho. *Perf. 13½x13***

*272* A76 20c yel & multi 22 22
*273* A76 35c red & multi 38 38
*274* A76 45c L & multi 45 45
*a* Souvenir sheet of 3 1.25 1.25

Inauguration of the Republic, Aug. 1, 1976. No. 274a contains one each of Nos. 272-274, perf. 14; red and black decorative margin. Size: 116x84mm.

**1977, Oct. 11 Litho. *Perf. 14½***

Designs: 35c, like 10c. 45c, 50c, Red poinsettia.

*275* A77 10c multi 9 9
*276* A77 35c multi 30 30
*277* A77 45c multi 40 40
*278* A77 50c multi 42 42
*a* Souvenir sheet of 4 1.40 1.40

Christmas 1977. No. 278a contains Nos. 275-278; decorative multicolored margin. Size: 112½x147mm.

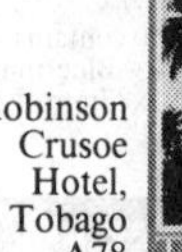

Robinson Crusoe Hotel, Tobago
A78

Designs: 15c, Turtle Beach Hotel, Tobago. 25c, Mount Irvine Hotel, Tobago. 70c, Mount Irvine beach, Tobago. $5, Holiday Inn, Trinidad.

**Wmk. 373**

**1978, Jan. 17 Litho. *Perf. 14***

*279* A78 6c multi 5 5
*280* A78 15c multi 10 10
*281* A78 25c multi 16 16
*282* A78 70c multi 45 45
*283* A78 $5 multi 3.25 3.25
*a* Souvenir sheet of 5 4.50 4.50
*Nos. 279-283 (5)* 4.01 4.01

No. 283a contains one each of Nos. 279-283; dark blue and red decorative margin. Size: 170x86mm.

Paphinia Cristata
A79

Orchids: 30c, Caularthron bicornutum. 40c, Miltassia. 50c, Oncidium ampiliatum. $2.50, Oncidium papilio.

**1978, June 7 Wmk. 373 *Perf. 14***

*284* A79 12c multi 10 10
*285* A79 30c multi 24 24
*286* A79 40c multi 32 32
*287* A79 50c multi 40 40
*288* A79 $2.50 multi 2.00 2.00
*a* Souvenir sheet of 5 3.50 3.50
*Nos. 284-288 (5)* 3.06 3.06

No. 288a contains Nos. 284-288; orange and blue decorative margin. Size: 171x91mm.

Miss Universe and Trophy — A80

Designs: 35c, Portrait with crown. 45c, Miss Universe in evening dress.

**1978, Aug. 2 Litho. *Perf. 14½***

*289* A80 10c multi 9 9
*290* A80 35c multi 30 30
*291* A80 45c multi 35 35
*a* Souvenir sheet of 3 1.00 1.00

Janelle (Penny) Commissiong, Miss Universe, 1977. No. 291a contains Nos. 289-291; multicolored margin shows island landscape. Size: 186x120mm.

Tayra
A81

**1978, Nov. 7 *Perf. 13½x14***

*292* A81 15c shown 18 14
*293* A81 25c Ocelot 28 24
*294* A81 40c Porcupine 45 38
*295* A81 70c Yellow anteater 95 65
*a* Souvenir sheet of 4 2.00 2.00

No. 295a contains Nos. 292-295; multicolored decorative margin. Size: 128x101mm.

"Burst of Beauty" — A82

Costumes: 10c, Rain worshipper. 35c, Zodiac. 45c, Praying mantis. 50c, Eye of the hurricane. $1, Steel orchestra.

**1979, Feb. 1 Litho. *Perf. 13½***

*296* A82 5c multi 5 5
*297* A82 10c multi 6 6
*298* A82 35c multi 24 24
*299* A82 45c multi 30 30
*300* A82 50c multi 35 35
*301* A82 $1 multi 65 65
*Nos. 296-301 (6)* 1.65 1.65

Day Care Center — A83

IYC Emblem and: 10c, School lunch program. 35c, Dental care. 45c, Nursery school. 50c, Free school bus. $1, Medical care.

**Unwmk.**

**1979, June 5 Litho. *Perf. 13***

*302* A83 5c multi 5 5
*303* A83 10c multi 6 6
*304* A83 35c multi 22 22
*305* A83 45c multi 28 28
*306* A83 50c multi 32 32
*307* A83 $1 multi 65 65
*a* Souvenir sheet of 6 1.90 1.90
*Nos. 302-307 (6)* 1.58 1.58

International Year of the Child. No. 307a contains Nos. 302-307; fawn and brown margin with IYC emblems. Size: 114x132½mm.

Geothermal Exploration
A84

Designs: 35c, Hydrogeology. 45c, Petroleum exploration. 70c, Preservation of the environment.

**1979, July 3 Wmk. 373**

*308* A84 10c multi 8 8
*309* A84 35c multi 28 28
*310* A84 45c multi 35 35
*311* A84 70c multi 55 55
*a* Souvenir sheet of 4 1.50 1.50

4th Latin American Geological Congress, July 7-15. No. 311a contains Nos. 308-311; multicolored margin.

Map of Tobago and Tobago No. 1 — A85

Designs: 15c, Tobago Nos. 2 & 7. 35c, Tobago Nos. 28 & 11. 45c, Tobago Nos. 25 & 4. 70c, Great Britain No. 28 used in Scarborough and Tobago No. 5. $1, General Post Office, Scarborough and Tobago No. 6.

***Perf. 13½x14***

**1979, Aug. 1 Litho. Wmk. 373**

*312* A85 10c multi 6 6
*313* A85 15c multi 10 10
*314* A85 35c multi 22 22
*315* A85 45c multi 28 28
*316* A85 70c multi 45 45
*317* A85 $1 multi 65 65
*a* Souvenir sheet of 6 1.90 1.90
*Nos. 312-317 (6)* 1.76 1.76

Centenary of Tobago's postage stamps. No. 317a contains Nos. 312-317; multicolored margin shows map of Tobago and sailing ships. Size: 166x155mm.

Rowland Hill, Trinidad and Tobago No. 109 — A86

Rowland Hill and: 45c, Trinidad and Tobago No. 273. $1, Trinidad No. 62, Tobago No. 10.

**1979, Oct. 4 *Perf. 13***

*318* A86 25c multi 15 15
*319* A86 45c multi 28 28
*320* A86 $1 multi 60 60
*a* Souvenir sheet of 3 1.25 1.25

Sir Rowland Hill (1795-1879), originator of penny postage. No. 320a contains Nos. 318-320; multicolored margin shows Lady McLeod stamp.

Poui Tree A87

Designs: 10c, Court House. 50c, Royal Train locomotive. $1.50, Bacchante freighter.

**Wmk. 373**

**1980, Jan. 21 Litho. *Perf. 14½***
*321* A87 5c multi 5 5
*322* A87 10c multi 9 9
*323* A87 50c multi 45 45
*324* A87 $1.50 multi 1.40 1.40
*a* Souvenir sheet of 4 2.00 2.00

Princes Town centenary. No. 324a contains Nos. 321-324; town history in margin. Size: 177x103mm.

**Nos. 262, 279, 263 Overprinted in 3 or 5 Lines: "1844-1980 POPULATION CENSUS 12th MAY 1980"**

**1980, Apr. 8 Litho. *Perf. 14***
*325* A73 5c multi 5 5
*326* A78 6c multi 6 6
*327* A73 10c multi 10 10

Scarlet Ibis Hen and Nest — A88

Scarlet Ibis: b. Nest and eggs. c. Chick in nest. d. Male. e. Male and female.

**Wmk. 373**

**1980, May 6 Litho. *Perf. 14½***
*328* Strip of 5, multi 2.50 2.50
*a.-e.* A88 single stamp 50 50

Bronze and Silver Medals, 1948, 1952 A89

**Wmk. 373**

**1980, July 22 Litho. *Perf. 14***
*329* A89 10c *shown* 9 9
*330* A89 15c *Hasely Crawford, 1976 gold medal* 14 14
*331* A89 70c *1964 silver, bronze medals* 65 65

**Souvenir Sheet**

*332* A89 $2.50 *Moscow '80 emblem*, vert. 1.65 1.65

22nd Summer Olympic Games, Moscow, July 19-Aug. 3. No. 332 has red and black margin showing map of Olympia, Greece. Size: 110x148½mm.

Charcoal Production — A90

**Wmk. 373**

**1980, Sept. 8 Litho. *Perf. 14***
*333* A90 10c *shown* 6 6
*334* A90 55c *Logging* 32 32
*335* A90 70c *Teak plantation* 40 40
*336* A90 $2.50 *Watershed management* 1.50 1.50
*a* Souvenir sheet of 4 3.00 3.00

11th Commonwealth Forestry Conference. No. 336a contains Nos. 333-336, multicolored margin with Congress emblem. Size: 135x87mm.

Elizabeth Bourne, Judiciary and Isabella Tesbier, Government — A91

Decade for Women: No. 338, Beryl McBurnie, dance and culture; Audrey Jeffers, social work. No. 339, Dr. Stella Abidh, public health; Louise Horne, nutrition.

**1980, Sept. 29**
*337* A91 $1 multi 70 70
*338* A91 $1 multi 70 70
*339* A91 $1 multi 70 70

Stadium and Netball League Emblem — A92

**1980, Oct. 21**
*340* A92 70c multi 55 55

1979 World Netball Tournament, Port-of-Spain.

Athlete, Man in Wheelchair, IYD Emblem — A93

**Wmk. 373**

**1981, Apr. 6 Litho. *Perf. 14½***
*341* A93 10c shown 6 6
*342* A93 70c Amputee with crutch 38 38
*343* A93 $1.50 Blind people 85 85
*344* A93 $2 IYD emblem 1.10 1.10

International Year of the Disabled.

Marine Preservation — A94

**1981, July 7 Litho. *Perf. 13x13½***
*345* A94 10c Land 8 8
*346* A94 55c shown 42 42
*347* A94 $3 Sky 2.50 2.50
*a* Souvenir sheet of 3 3.00 3.00

No. 347a contains Nos. 345-347; multicolored margin shows birds, sea and land. Size: 142x89mm.

World Food Day — A95

**1981, Oct. 16 Litho. *Perf. 14½x14***
*348* A95 10c Produce 7 7
*349* A95 15c Rice threshing, mill 10 10
*350* A95 45c Bigeye 30 30
*351* A95 55c Cow, pig, goats 38 38
*352* A95 $1.50 Poultry 1.00 1.00
*353* A95 $2 Smallmouth grunt 1.40 1.40
*a* Souvenir sheet of 6 3.50 3.50
*Nos. 348-353 (6)* 3.25 3.25

No. 353a contains Nos. 348-353.

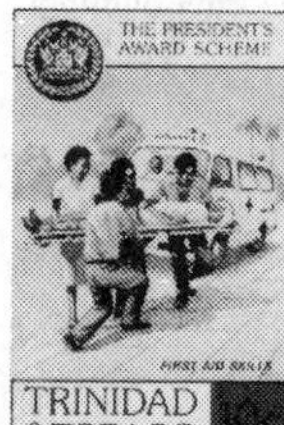
President Awards — A96

**1981, Nov. 30 *Perf. 14***
*354* A96 10c First aid 7 7
*355* A96 70c Motor mechanics 50 50
*356* A96 $1 Hiking 70 70
*357* A96 $2 President giving award 1.40 1.40

Commonwealth Pharmaceutical Conference — A97

**1982, Feb. 12 Litho. *Perf. 14½x14***
*358* A97 10c Pharmacist 8 8
*359* A97 $1 Pluchea symphitfolia 1.85 85
*360* A97 $2 Nopalea cochenilifera 1.65 1.65

Scouting Year — A98

**1982, June 28 Litho. *Perf. 14***
*361* A98 15c Production 12 12
*362* A98 55c Tolerance 45 45
*363* A98 $5 Discipline 4.00 4.00

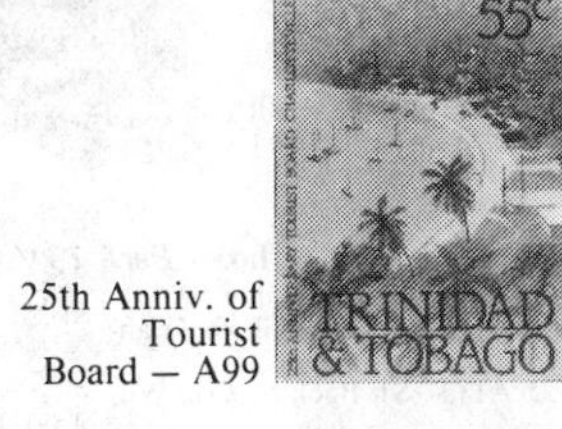
25th Anniv. of Tourist Board — A99

***Perf. 13½x14***

**1982, Oct. 18 Litho. Wmk. 373**
*364* A99 55c Charlotteville 45 45
*365* A99 $1 Boating 85 85
*366* A99 $3 Fort George 2.50 2.50

Pa Pa Bois — A100

Designs: Various folklore characters.

**1982, Nov. 8**
*367* A100 10c multi 8 8
*368* A100 15c multi 12 12
*369* A100 65c multi 55 55
*370* A100 $5 multi 4.25 4.25
*a* Souvenir sheet of 4 5.50 5.50

No. 370a contains Nos. 367-370; margin shows scenes from folktales.

Canefarmers' Centenary — A101

**1982, Dec. 13 Litho. *Perf. 14***
*371* A101 30c Harvest 42 42
*372* A101 70c Loading bullock cart 95 95
*373* A101 $1.50 Field 2.00 2.00
*a* Souvenir sheet of 3 5.50 5.50

No. 373a contains Nos. 371-373 (perf. 14½). Size: 73x118mm.

20th Anniv. of Independence — A102

**1982, Dec. 28 *Perf. 13½x14***
*374* A102 10c Natl. Stadium 8 8
*375* A102 35c Caroni Arena Water Treatment Plant 26 26
*376* A102 50c Mount Hope Maternity Hospital 38 38
*377* A102 $2 Natl. Insurance Board Mall, Tobago 1.50 1.50

Commonwealth Day — A103

**1983, Mar. 14 *Perf. 14***
*378* A103 10c Flags 8 8
*379* A103 55c Satellite view 42 42
*380* A103 $1 Oil industry, vert. 75 75
*381* A103 $2 Maps, vert. 1.50 1.50

10th Anniv. of CARICOM — A104

**1983, July 11 Litho. *Perf. 14***
*382* A104 35c Jet, map 65 65

World Communications Year — A105

**1983, Aug. 5 *Perf. 14½***
*383* A105 15c Operator 12 12
*384* A105 55c Scarborough PO, Tobago 45 45

*385* A105 $1 Textel Building 80 80
*386* A105 $3 Morne Bleu Receiving Station 2.50 2.50

Commonwealth Finance Ministers Conference — A106

**Wmk. 373**

**1983, Sept. 19 Litho. *Perf. 14***
*387* A106 $2 multi 1.75 1.75

World Food Day — A107

**1983, Oct. 17 *Perf. 14x13½***
*388* A107 10c Kingfish 7 7
*389* A107 55c Flying fish 40 40
*390* A107 70c Queen conch 52 52
*391* A107 $4 Red shrimp 3.00 3.00

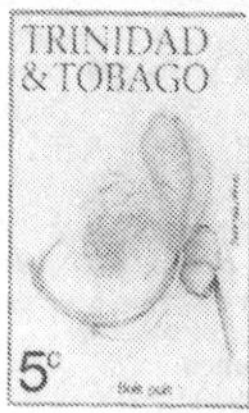


Flowers — A108

**1983, Dec. 14 Litho. *Perf. 14***
*392* A108 5c Bois pois 5 5
*a.* Wmk. 384 ('85) 5 5
*393* A108 10c Maraval Lily 7 7
*a.* Wmk. 384 ('85) 8 8
*394* A108 15c Star grass 10 10
*395* A108 20c Bois caco 14 14
*396* A108 25c Strangling fig 18 18
*397* A108 30c Cassia moschata 20 20
*a.* Wmk. 384 ('87) 20 20
*398* A108 50c Chalice flower 35 35
*399* A108 65c Black stick 45 45
*a.* Wmk. 384 ('87) 45 45
*400* A108 80c Columnea scandens 55 55
*a.* Wmk. 384 ('87) 55 55
*401* A108 95c Cats Claws 65 65
*a.* Wmk. 384 ('85) 80 80
*402* A108 $1 Bois l'agli 70 70
*a.* Wmk. 384 ('85) 85 85
*403* A108 $1.50 Eustoma exeltatum 1.00 1.00
*a.* Wmk. 384 ('87) 1.00 1.00
*404* A108 $2 Chaconia, horiz. 1.40 1.40
*a.* Wmk. 384 ('87) 1.40 1.40
*405* A108 $2.50 Chysothemis pulchella, horiz. 1.75 1.75
*406* A108 $5 Centratherum punctatum, horiz. 3.50 3.50
*a.* Wmk. 384 ('85) 4.15 4.15
*407* A108 $10 Savanna flower, horiz. 6.75 6.75
*a.* Wmk. 384 ('85) 8.30 8.30
*Nos. 392-407 (16)* 17.84 17.84
*Nos. 392a-407a (11)* 19.48 19.48

"1985" imprint: Nos. 392a, 393a, 401a, 402a, 406a, 407a. "1987", Nos. 393a, 397a, 399a, 400a, 403a, 404a. "1988", 406a, 407a.

Canceled-to-order stamps are often from remainders. Most collectors of canceled stamps prefer postally used specimens.

Castles on Chess Board A109

1984 Summer Olympics A110

World Chess Fedn., 60th Anniv.: Various chess pieces.

**Wmk. 373**

**1984, Sept. 12 Litho. *Perf. 14***
*408* A109 50c multi 35 35
*409* A109 70c multi 48 48
*410* A109 $1.50 multi 1.00 1.00
*411* A109 $2 multi 1.40 1.40

**1984, Sept. 21 *Perf. 14x14½***
*412* A110 15c Swimming 12 12
*413* A110 55c Running 42 42
*414* A110 $1.50 Yachting 1.10 1.10
*415* A110 $4 Bicycling 3.00 3.00
*a* Souv. sheet of 4, Nos. 412-415 5.00 5.00

St. Mary's Children's Home, 125th Anniv. A111

**1984, Nov. 13 Litho. *Perf. 13½***
*416* A111 10c Children's band 10 10
*417* A111 70c St. Mary's Home 65 65
*418* A111 $3 Group scene 3.00 3.00

Christmas 1984 — A112

**1984, Nov. Litho. *Perf. 14***
*419* A112 10c Parang Band 8 8
*420* A112 30c Musical notes, Poinsettia 25 25
*421* A112 $1 Bandola, Cuatro, Bandolin 85 85
*422* A112 $3 Fiddle, Guitar, Double Bass 2.50 2.50

Emancipation, 150th Anniv. — A113

**1984, Oct. 22 Litho. *Perf. 13½x13***
*423* A113 35c Slave ship 35 35
*424* A113 55c Map, Slave Triangle 55 55
*425* A113 $1 Book by Eric Williams 1.00 1.00
*426* A113 $2 Toussaint L'Ouverture 2.00 2.00
*a* Souvenir sheet of 4 4.00 4.00

Nos. 426a contains Nos. 423-426; margin shows drawing of slave ship's hold. Size: 95x100mm.

Labor Day — A114

Labor leaders: No. 427, A.A. Cipriani and T.U.B. Butler. No. 428, A. Cola Rienzi and C.T.W.E. Worrell. No. 429, C.P. Alexander and Q. O'Connor.

**Wmk. 373**

**1985, June 17 Litho. *Perf. 14***
*427* A114 55c dull rose & blk 50 50
*428* A114 55c brt grn & blk 50 50
*429* A114 55c lt org & blk 50 50

Ships — A115

**Wmk. 373**

**1985, Aug 20 Litho. *Perf. 14½***
*430* A115 30c Lady Nelson 22 22
*431* A115 95c Lady Drake 75 75
*432* A115 $1.50 Federal Palm 1.10 1.10
*433* A115 $2 Federal Maple 1.50 1.50

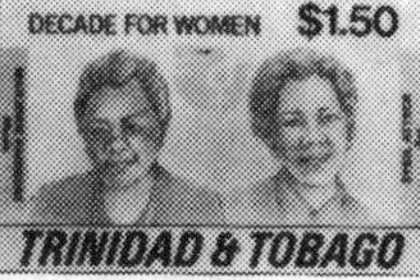


UN Decade for Women A116

Women in the arts, public service and education: No. 434, Sybill Atteck, Marjorie Padmore. No. 435, May Cherrie, Evelyn Tracey. No. 436, Jessica Smith-Phillips, Irene Omilta McShine.

**1985, Oct. 30 Wmk. 384 *Perf. 14***
*434* A116 $1.50 multi 1.10 1.10
*435* A116 $1.50 multi 1.10 1.10
*436* A116 $1.50 multi 1.10 1.10

Intl. Youth Year — A117

Anniversaries and events: 10c, Natl. Cadet Force, 75th anniv. 65c, Girl Guides, 75th anniv.

**1985, Nov. 27 *Perf. 14x14½***
*437* A117 10c Cadet emblem 8 8
*438* A117 65c Badges, anniv. emblem 48 48
*439* A117 95c shown 70 70

Sisters of St. Joseph de Cluny in Trinidad, 150th Anniv. — A118

Designs: 10c, Sister Anne-Marie Javouhey, founder. 65c, St. Joseph's Convent, Port-of-Spain. 95c, Statue of Sr. Anne-Marie.

***Perf. 14x14½***

**1986, Mar. 19 Litho. Wmk. 384**
*440* A118 10c multi 6 6
*441* A118 65c multi 45 45
*442* A118 95c multi 70 70

Queen Elizabeth II, 60th Birthday — A119

**Wmk. 384**

**1986, Apr. 21 Litho. *Perf. 14½***
*443* A119 10c At the Cenotaph 6 6
*444* A119 15c Aboard HMY Britannia 8 8
*445* A119 30c With Pres. Clarke 14 14
*446* A119 $5 Receiving bouquet 2.50 2.50

Locomotives, AMERIPEX '86 — A120

***Perf. 14½x14***

**1986, May 26 Wmk. 373**
*447* A120 65c Arma tank locomotive 32 32
*448* A120 95c Canadian-built No. 22 55 55
*449* A120 $1.10 Tender engine 60 60
*450* A120 $1.50 Saddle tank 85 85
*a* Souv. sheet of 4, #447-450 2.50 2.50

No. 450a has multicolored decorative margin picturing rail yard and exhibition logo. Size: 105x80mm.

Boy Scouts, 75th Anniv. A121

**1986, July 21 Wmk. 384 *Perf. 14***
*451* A121 $1.70 Campsite 1.00 1.00
*452* A121 $2 Uniforms, 1911, 1986 1.20 1.20

Dr. Eric Williams (1911-1981), First Prime Minister — A122

**Wmk. 373**

**1986, Sept. 25 Litho. *Perf. 14***
*453* A122 10c Graduating college, 1935 6 6
*454* A122 30c Wearing red tie 18 18
*a* Black tie 18 18
*455* A122 95c Pro-Chancellor of UWI 58 58
*456* A122 $5 Williams, prime minister's residence 3.00 3.00
*a* Souv. sheet of 4, Nos. 453-456 4.00 4.00

Nos. 453-454 vert. No. 456a has bright blue inscribed margin. Size: 106x101mm.

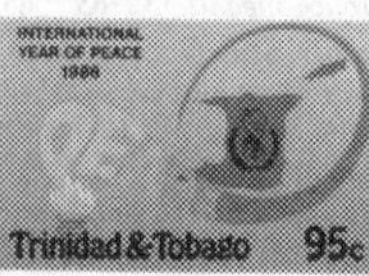


Intl. Peace Year A123

**1986, Oct. 30 Wmk. 384**
*457* A123 95c shown 58 58
*458* A123 $3 Dove 2.40 2.40

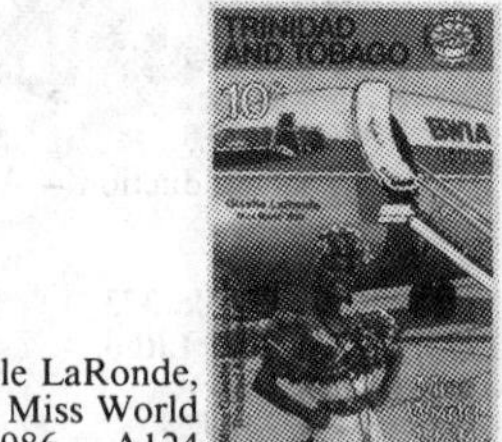


Giselle LaRonde, Miss World 1986 — A124

**Wmk. 384**

**1987, July 27 Litho. *Perf. 14***

| | | | | |
|---|---|---|---|---|
| *459* A124 | 10c | Wearing folk costume | 5 | 5 |
| *460* A124 | 30c | Bathing suit | 16 | 16 |
| *461* A124 | 95c | Crown | 50 | 50 |
| *462* A124 | $1.65 | Crown and sash | 85 | 85 |

Republic Bank, 150th Anniv. A125

Designs: 10c, Colonial Bank, Port of Spain. 65c, Cocoa plantation. 95c, Oil fields. $1.10, Tramcar, Belmont Tramway Co.

**Wmk. 373**

**1987, Dec. 21 Litho. *Perf. 14***

| | | | | |
|---|---|---|---|---|
| *463* A125 | 10c | buff, red brn & blk | 5 | 5 |
| *464* A125 | 65c | buff, red brn & blk | 32 | 32 |
| *465* A125 | 95c | buff, red brn & blk | 50 | 50 |
| *466* A125 | $1.10 | buff, red brn & blk | 58 | 58 |

Defense Force, 25th Anniv. — A126

Various army, coast guard and navy uniforms.

**Wmk. 384**

**1988, Feb. 29 Litho. *Perf. 14***

| | | | | |
|---|---|---|---|---|
| *467* A126 | 10c | Army | 6 | 6 |
| *468* A126 | 30c | Army (women) | 18 | 18 |
| *469* A126 | $1.10 | Navy, army, coast guard | 60 | 60 |
| *470* A126 | $1.50 | Navy | 82 | 82 |

Cricket A127

Bat, wicket posts, ball, 18th cent. belt buckle and batters: 30c, George John. 65c, Learie Constantine. 95c, Sonny Ramadhin. $1.50, Gerry Gomez. $2.50, Jeffrey Stollmeyer.

**Wmk. 373**

**1988, June 6 Litho. *Perf. 14***

| | | | | |
|---|---|---|---|---|
| *471* A127 | 30c | multi | 16 | 16 |
| *472* A127 | 65c | multi | 35 | 35 |
| *473* A127 | 95c | multi | 52 | 52 |
| *474* A127 | $1.50 | multi | 85 | 85 |
| *475* A127 | $2.50 | multi | 1.40 | 1.40 |
| | | *Nos. 471-475 (5)* | 3.28 | 3.28 |

Oilfield Workers' Trade Union, 50th Anniv. — A128

50, Star, oil well and: 10c, Uriah Buzz Butler, labor leader. 30c, Adrian C. Rienzi, pres. from 1937-42. 65c, John Rojas, pres. from 1943-62. $5, George Weekes, pres. from 1962-87.

**Wmk. 384**

**1988, July 11 Litho. *Perf. 14½***

| | | | | |
|---|---|---|---|---|
| *476* A128 | 10c | dark car, deep org & gold | 6 | 6 |
| *477* A128 | 30c | multi | 18 | 18 |
| *478* A128 | 65c | deep green, deep org & gold | 38 | 38 |
| *479* A128 | $5 | brt ultra, deep org & gold | 2.75 | 2.75 |

Borough of Arima, Cent. A129

Designs: 20c, Mary Werges, Santa Rosa Church. 30c, Gov. W. Robinson, royal charter. $1.10, Mayor C.P. Lopez greeting Gov. Robinson at train station. $1.50, Mayor J.F. Wallen, centennial emblem.

**Wmk. 384**

**1988, Aug. 22 Litho. *Perf. 14½***

| | | | | |
|---|---|---|---|---|
| *480* A129 | 20c | multi | 12 | 12 |
| *481* A129 | 30c | multi | 18 | 18 |
| *482* A129 | $1.10 | multi | 62 | 62 |
| *483* A129 | $1.50 | multi | 85 | 85 |

**Lloyds of London, 300th Anniv.**

Common Design Type

Designs: 30c, Queen Mother at the "Topping Out" ceremony of new Lloyds's building, 1984. $1.10, BWIA Tristar 500, horiz. $1.55, ISCOTT iron and steel mill, horiz. $2, *Atlantic Empress* on fire off Tobago.

**1988, Nov. 21 Litho. *Perf. 14***

| | | | | |
|---|---|---|---|---|
| *484* CD341 | 30c | multi | 14 | 14 |
| *485* CD341 | $1.10 | multi | 52 | 52 |
| *486* CD341 | $1.55 | multi | 75 | 75 |
| *487* CD341 | $2 | multi | 95 | 95 |

## SEMI-POSTAL STAMPS.

Emblem of Red Cross — SP1

***Perf. 11, 12***

**1914, Sept. 18 Typo. Unwmk.**

*B1* SP1 ½p red (on cover) 325.00

This seal was allowed to pay ½p postage on one day, Sept. 18, 1914. Value unused, $12.50.

No. 2 Overprinted in Red (Cross) and Black (Date):

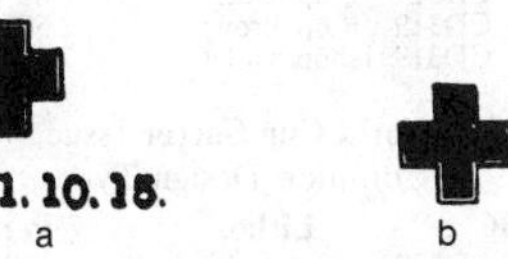


a b

**1915, Oct. 21 Wmk. 3 *Perf. 14***

*B2* A1(a) 1p scarlet 25 25

**1916, Oct. 19**

*B3* A1 (b) 1p scarlet 12 12
 *a.* Date omitted

## POSTAGE DUE STAMPS

Type of Trinidad, 1885, inscribed "Trinidad."

**1923-45 Typo. Wmk. 4 *Perf. 14***

| | | | | |
|---|---|---|---|---|
| *J1* D1 | 1p | black | 38 | 48 |
| *J2* D1 | 2p | black | 60 | 60 |
| *J3* D1 | 3p | blk ('25) | 75 | 65 |
| *J4* D1 | 4p | blk ('29) | 2.25 | 2.25 |
| *J5* D1 | 5p | blk ('45) | 14.00 | 1.90 |
| *J6* D1 | 6p | blk ('45) | 19.00 | 19.00 |
| *J7* D1 | 8p | blk ('45) | 24.00 | 24.00 |
| *J8* D1 | 1sh | blk ('45) | 47.50 | 47.50 |
| | | *Nos. J1-J8 (8)* | 108.48 | 96.38 |

**Catalogue values for unused stamps in this section, from this point to the end of the section, are for Never Hinged items.**

Denominations in Cents

**1947, Sept. 1**

| | | | | |
|---|---|---|---|---|
| *J9* D1 | 2c | black | 22 | 22 |
| | *a.* | Wmk. 4a (error) | 35.00 | |
| *J10* D1 | 4c | black | 60 | 60 |
| *J11* D1 | 6c | black | 1.10 | 1.10 |
| | *a.* | Wmk. 4a (error) | 60.00 | |
| *J12* D1 | 8c | black | 1.50 | *1.65* |
| *J13* D1 | 10c | black | 1.50 | *1.65* |
| *J14* D1 | 12c | black | 1.65 | *2.75* |
| | *a.* | Wmk. 4a (error) | 87.50 | |
| *J15* D1 | 16c | black | 1.65 | *3.25* |
| *J16* D1 | 24c | black | 3.75 | *8.50* |
| | | *Nos. J9-J16 (8)* | 11.97 | *19.72* |

Nos. J9-J16 also exist on chalky paper.

D2

**1970 Unwmk. Litho. *Perf. 14x13½***

**Size: 18x23mm**

| | | | | |
|---|---|---|---|---|
| *J17* D2 | 2c | green | 5 | 5 |
| *J18* D2 | 4c | car rose | 20 | 20 |
| *J19* D2 | 6c | brown | 6 | 6 |
| *J20* D2 | 8c | lt vio | 8 | 8 |
| *J21* D2 | 10c | brick red | 10 | 10 |
| *J22* D2 | 12c | dl org | 40 | 40 |
| *J23* D2 | 16c | brt yel grn | 16 | 16 |
| *J24* D2 | 24c | gray | 24 | 24 |
| *J25* D2 | 50c | blue | 50 | 50 |
| *J26* D2 | 60c | ol grn | 60 | 60 |
| | | *Nos. J17-J26 (10)* | 2.39 | 2.39 |

**1976, Apr. 1 *Perf. 13½x14***

**Size: 17x21mm**

| | | | | |
|---|---|---|---|---|
| *J27* D2 | 4c | lil rose | 7 | 7 |
| *J28* D2 | 12c | ocher | 15 | 15 |

## WAR TAX STAMPS

Regular Issue of 1913 Overprinted WAR TAX

**1917 Wmk. 3 *Perf. 14***

*MR1* A1 1p scarlet 18 18
 *a.* Invtd. overprint 200.00 *200.00*

Overprinted WAR TAX

| | | | | |
|---|---|---|---|---|
| *MR2* A1 | ½p | green | 10 | 10 |
| | *a.* | Overprinted on face and back | 350.00 | |
| | *b.* | Pair, one without overprint | 250.00 | |
| *MR3* A1 | 1p | scarlet | 14 | 14 |
| | *a.* | Pair, one without overprint | 250.00 | |
| | *b.* | Double overprint | 125.00 | |

Overprinted WAR TAX

| | | | | |
|---|---|---|---|---|
| *MR4* A1 | ½p | green | 22 | 22 |
| *MR5* A1 | 1p | scarlet | 14 | 14 |

Overprinted WAR TAX

| | | | | |
|---|---|---|---|---|
| *MR6* A1 | ½p | green | 10 | 10 |
| *MR7* A1 | 1p | scarlet | 14 | 14 |

Overprinted WAR TAX

| | | | | |
|---|---|---|---|---|
| *MR8* A1 | ½p | green | 14 | 14 |
| *MR9* A1 | 1p | scarlet | 17.50 | 21.00 |

Overprinted WAR TAX

| | | | | |
|---|---|---|---|---|
| *MR10* A1 | 1p | scarlet | 14 | 14 |
| | *a.* | Inverted overprint | 100.00 | *100.00* |

Overprinted WAR TAX

| | | | | |
|---|---|---|---|---|
| *MR11* A1 | 1p | scarlet | 14 | 14 |
| | *a.* | Double overprint | 200.00 | *200.00* |
| | *b.* | Inverted overprint | 125.00 | *125.00* |

Overprinted War Tax

**1918**

| | | | | |
|---|---|---|---|---|
| *MR12* A1 | ½p | green | 10 | 10 |
| *MR13* A1 | 1p | scarlet | 10 | 10 |
| | *a.* | Double overprint | 140.00 | *140.00* |

The War Tax Stamps show considerable variations in the colors, thickness of the paper, distinctness of the watermark, and the gum. Counterfeits exist of the errors of Nos. MR1-MR13.

## OFFICIAL STAMPS

Regular Issue of 1913 Overprinted OFFICIAL

**1913 Wmk. 3 *Perf. 14***

*O1* A1 ½p green 32 40

Same Overprinted OFFICIAL

**1914**

*O2* A1 ½p green 2.75 3.00

Same Overprinted OFFICIAL.

**1916**

*O3* A1 ½p green 1.00 1.00
 *a.* Double overprint 22.50

Same Overprint without Period.

**1917**

*O4* A1 ½p green 60 60

Same Overprinted OFFICIAL

**1917, Aug. 22**

*O5* A1 ½p green 20 20

The official stamps are found in several shades of green and on paper of varying thickness.

# TRISTAN DA CUNHA

LOCATION — A group of islands in the south Atlantic Ocean midway between the Cape of Good Hope and South America.

GOVT. — A dependency of St. Helena.

AREA — 40 sq. mi.

POP. — 325 (1982).

12 Pence = 1 Shilling
100 Cents = 1 Rand (1961)
12 Pence = 1 Shilling (1963)
20 Shillings = 1 Pound
100 Pence = 1 Pound (1971)

**Catalogue values for all unused stamps in this country are for Never Hinged items.**

Stamps of St. Helena, 1938-49, Overprinted in Black **TRISTAN DA CUNHA**

**1952, Jan. 1 Wmk. 4 *Perf. 12½***
1 A24 ½p purple 38 22
2 A24 1p bl grn & blk 50 32
3 A24 1½p car rose & blk 60 40
4 A24 2p car & blk 90 55
5 A24 3p gray 1.25 1.70
6 A24 4p ultra 1.65 90
7 A24 6p gray bl 2.25 1.25
8 A24 8p olive 2.75 1.65
9 A24 1sh sepia 3.00 3.25
10 A24 2sh6p dp cl 11.50 10.00
11 A24 5sh brown 30.00 22.50
12 A24 10sh violet 67.50 52.50
*Nos. 1-12 (12)* 122.28 95.24

**Coronation Issue**
Common Design Type

**1953, June 2 Engr. *Perf. 13½x13***
13 CD312 3p dk grn & blk 1.50 2.00

Tristan Crayfish — A1

Carting Flax — A2

Designs: 1½p, Rockhopper penguin. 2p, Factory. 2½p, Mollymauk. 3p, Island boat. 4p, View of Tristan. 5p, Potato patches. 6p, Inaccessible Island. 9p, Nightingale Island. 1sh, St. Mary's Church. 2sh 6p, Elephant seal. 5sh, Flightless rail. 10sh, Island spinning wheel.

**1954-58 *Perf. 12½***
14 A1 ½p choc & red 30 20
a. Bklt. pane 4 ('58) 2.50
15 A2 1p grn & choc 50 25
a. Bklt. pane 4 ('58) 4.00
16 A1 1½p dp plum & blk 55 28
a. Bklt. pane 4 ('58) 6.00
17 A2 2p org & vio bl 65 32
18 A2 2½p car & blk 65 32
19 A1 3p ol grn & ultra 70 35
a. Bklt. pane 4 ('58) 9.00
20 A2 4p dp bl & aqua 80 40
a. Bklt. pane 4 ('58) 11.00
21 A2 5p gray & bl grn 1.10 55
22 A2 6p vio & dk ol grn 1.40 65
23 A2 9p hn brn & rose lil 2.25 1.10
24 A2 1sh choc & ol grn 2.75 1.40
25 A2 2sh6p bl & choc 13.00 6.75
26 A2 5sh red org & blk 30.00 15.00
27 A2 10sh red vio & org 60.00 30.00
*Nos. 14-27 (14)* 114.65 57.57

Starfish — A3

Fish: 1p, Concha. 1½p, Klipfish. 2p, Heron fish (saury). 2½p, Snipefish ("swordfish"). 3d, Tristan crawfish. 4p, Soldier fish. 5p, Five finger fish. 6p, Mackeral scad. 9p, Stumpnose. 1sh, Bluefish. 2sh6p, Snoek (snake mackerel). 5sh, Shark. 10sh, Atlantic right whale.

***Perf. 12½x13***

**1960, Feb. 1 Engr. Wmk. 314**
28 A3 ½p org & blk 28 20
a. Booklet pane of 4 1.75
29 A3 1p rose lil & blk 40 22
a. Booklet pane of 4 3.00
30 A3 1½p grnsh bl & blk 55 32
a. Booklet pane of 4 3.50
31 A3 2p grn & blk 65 35
32 A3 2½p brn & blk 70 38
33 A3 3p rose red & blk 80 45
a. Booklet pane of 4 4.75
34 A3 4p gray ol & blk 1.00 55
a. Booklet pane of 4 5.25
35 A3 5p org yel & blk 1.25 65
36 A3 6p bl & blk 1.40 80
37 A3 9p rose car & blk 2.50 1.10
38 A3 1sh brn org & blk 3.00 1.40
39 A3 2sh6p vio bl & blk 8.00 4.50
40 A3 5sh emer & blk 27.50 13.00
41 A3 10sh vio & blk 57.50 30.00
*Nos. 28-41 (14)* 105.53 53.92

**1961, Apr. 15 *Perf. 12½x13***

Fish: ½c, Starfish. 1c, Concha. 1½c, Klipfish. 2c, Snipefish. 2½c, Tristan crawfish. 3c, Soldier fish. 4c, Five finger fish. 5c, Mackerel scad. 7½c, Stumpnose. 10c, Bluefish. 25c, Snoek. 50c, Shark. 1r, Atlantic right whale.

42 A3 ½c org & blk 12 7
43 A3 1c rose lil & blk 15 9
44 A3 1½c grnsh bl & blk 22 14
45 A3 2c brn & blk 30 18
46 A3 2½c rose red & blk 40 22
47 A3 3c gray ol & blk 52 32
48 A3 4c org yel & blk 65 40
49 A3 5c bl & blk 95 55
50 A3 7½c rose car & blk 1.50 90
51 A3 10c brn org & blk 2.25 1.40
52 A3 25c vio bl & blk 11.00 6.75
53 A3 50c emer & blk 24.00 15.00
54 A3 1r vio & blk 60.00 35.00
*Nos. 42-54 (13)* 102.06 61.02

Nos. 46, 49-51 surcharged for "Tristan Relief" are listed as St. Helena Nos. B1-B4.

Types of St. Helena, 1961 Overprinted **TRISTAN DA CUNHA RESETTLEMENT 1963**

***Perf. 11½x12, 12x11½***

**1963, Apr. 12 Photo. Wmk. 4**
55 A29 1p rose, ultra, yel & grn 5 5
56 A29 1½p bis sep, yel & grn 6 6
57 A29 2p gray & red 8 6
58 A30 3p dk bl, rose & grnsh bl 9 6
a. Double ovpt.
59 A29 4½p sl, brn & grn 15 10
60 A29 6p cit, brn & dp car 24 16
61 A29 7p vio, blk & red brn 30 20
62 A29 10p bl & dp cl 40 25
63 A29 1sh red brn, grn & yel 75 50
64 A29 1sh6p gray bl & blk 1.25 80
65 A29 2sh6p grnsh bl, yel & red 2.75 1.75
66 A29 5sh grn, brn & yel 5.50 3.75
67 A29 10sh gray bl, blk & sal 12.00 8.00
*Nos. 55-67 (13)* 23.62 15.74

**Freedom from Hunger Issue**
Common Design Type
***Perf. 14x14½***

**1963, Oct. 2 Photo. Wmk. 314**
68 CD314 1sh6p rose car 2.50 1.40

**Red Cross Centenary Issue**
Common Design Type

**1964, Jan. 2 Litho. *Perf. 13***
69 CD315 3p blk & red 32 22
70 CD315 1sh6p ultra & red 2.75 1.75

Flagship of Tristao da Cunha, 1506 — A4

Queen Elizabeth II — A5

Designs: ½p, Map of South Atlantic Ocean. 1½p, Dutch ship Heemstede, first landing, 1643. 2p, New England whaler. 3p, Confederate ship Shenandoah. 4½p, H.M.S. Galatea, 1867. 6p, H.M.S. Cilicia, 1942. 7p, H.M. Royal Yacht Britannia, 1957. 10p, H.M.S. Leopard, Evacuation, 1961. 1sh, Dutch ship Tjisadane, 1961. 1sh6p, M.V. Tristania. 2sh6p, M.V. Boissevain, returning islanders, 1963. 5sh, M.S. Bornholm, returning islanders, 1963.

***Perf. 11x11½***

**1965, Feb. 17 Engr. Wmk. 314**
71 A4 ½p blk & dk bl 8 5
a. Bklt. pane of 4 32
72 A4 1p blk & emer 15 9
a. Bklt. pane of 4 60
73 A4 1½p blk & ultra 22 12
a. Bklt. pane of 4 90
74 A4 2p blk & lil 25 15
75 A4 3p blk & grnsh bl 38 22
a. Bklt. pane of 4 1.50
76 A4 4½p blk & brn 75 45
77 A4 6p blk & grn 60 38
a. Bklt. pane of 4 2.50
78 A4 7p blk & ver 85 50
79 A4 10p blk & dk brn 1.10 62
80 A4 1sh blk & lil rose 1.25 75
81 A4 1sh6p blk & ol 2.50 1.50
82 A4 2sh6p blk & brn org 4.25 2.50
83 A4 5sh blk & vio 8.50 5.00

***Perf. 11½x11***
84 A5 10sh lil rose & dk bl 10.50 6.25
*Nos. 71-84 (14)* 31.38 18.58

See Nos. 113-115.

**ITU Issue**
Common Design Type

**1965, May 11 Litho. *Perf. 11x11½***
85 CD317 3p ver & gray 1.10 52
86 CD317 6p pur & org 2.00 1.10

**Intl. Cooperation Year Issue**
Common Design Type

**1965, Oct. 25 Wmk. 314 *Perf. 14½***
87 CD318 1p bl grn & cl 45 20
88 CD318 6p lt vio & grn 2.75 1.40

Common Design Types pictured in section before Great Britain.

**Churchill Memorial Issue**
Common Design Type
**Wmk. 314**

**1966, Jan. 24 Photo. *Perf. 14***
**Design in Black, Gold and Carmine Rose**
89 CD319 1p brt bl 15 6
90 CD319 3p green 60 25
91 CD319 6p brown 2.50 1.10
92 CD319 1sh6p violet 7.50 3.50

**World Cup Soccer Issue**
Common Design Type

**1966 Litho. *Perf. 14***
93 CD320 3p multi 40 20
94 CD321 2sh6p multi 2.25 1.25

Nos. 93-94 were issued Oct. 1 in Tristan da Cunha, but on July 1 in St. Helena.

Light Dragoon of 19th Century and Sailing Ship — A6

**Wmk. 314**

**1966, Aug. 15 Litho. *Perf. 14½***
95 A6 3p pale grn & multi 15 7
96 A6 6p tan & multi 38 18
97 A6 1sh6p gray & multi 1.00 60
98 A6 2sh6p multi 1.65 95

150th anniv. of the establishment of a garrison on Tristan da Cunha.

**WHO Headquarters Issue**
Common Design Type

**1966, Oct. 1 Litho. *Perf. 14***
99 CD322 6p multi 60 35
100 CD322 5sh multi 3.00 1.75

**UNESCO Anniversary Issue**
Common Design Type

**1966, Dec. 1 Litho. *Perf. 14***
101 CD323 10p "Education" 60 32
102 CD323 1sh6p "Science" 1.40 70
103 CD323 2sh6p "Culture" 2.50 1.40

Calshot Harbor A7

***Perf. 14x14½***

**1967, Jan. 2 Litho. Unwmk.**
104 A7 6p dl grn & multi 10 9
105 A7 10p brn & multi 18 14
106 A7 1sh6p dl bl & multi 35 28
107 A7 2sh6p org brn & multi 60 48

Opening of the artificial Calshot Harbor.

No. 76 Surcharged with New Value and Three Bars
***Perf. 11x11½***

**1967, May 10 Engr. Wmk. 314**
108 A4 4p on 4½p blk & brn 32 32

Tristan da Cunha, Prince Alfred, Queen Elizabeth II and Prince Philip — A8

**1967, July 10 Litho. *Perf. 14x14½***
109 A8 3p bl grn, dk grn & blk 8 7
110 A8 6p dk car & blk 14 12
111 A8 1sh6p brt grn, gray grn & blk 30 25
112 A8 2sh6p dl ultra, sep & blk 50 45

Cent. of the visit of Prince Alfred, First Duke of Edinburgh, to Tristan da Cunha.

Types of 1965

Designs: 4p, H.M.S. Challenger, 1870. 10sh, South African research vessel, R.S.A. £1, Queen Elizabeth II.

***Perf. 11x11½***

**1967, Sept. 1 Engr. Wmk. 314**
113 A4 4p blk & org 1.50 60
114 A4 10sh blk & dl grn 27.50 15.00

***Perf. 11½x11***
115 A5 £1 brn org & dk bl 24.00 15.00

Wandering Albatross Nest — A9

Birds: 1sh, Big-billed buntings. 1sh6p, Tristan thrushes. 2sh6p, Great shearwaters.

*Perf. 14x14½*

**1968, May 15 Photo. Wmk. 314**

| | | | | |
|---|---|---|---|---|
| *116* | A9 | 4p multi | 18 | 10 |
| *117* | A9 | 1sh multi | 60 | 35 |
| *118* | A9 | 1sh6p multi | 1.10 | 60 |
| *119* | A9 | 2sh6p multi | 1.75 | 1.00 |

Union Jack and St. Helena Flag — A10

Design: 9p, 2sh6p, Map showing locations of St. Helena and Tristan da Cunha.

**1968, Nov. 1 Litho. Wmk. 314**

| | | | | |
|---|---|---|---|---|
| *120* | A10 | 6p vio & multi | 16 | 12 |
| *121* | A10 | 9p brn, bl grn & vio bl | 30 | 22 |
| *122* | A10 | 1sh6p grn & multi | 55 | 45 |
| *123* | A10 | 2sh6p dp car, bl grn & vio bl | 1.00 | 80 |

30th anniv. of Tristan da Cunha as a Dependency of St. Helena.

Frigate A11

Designs: 1sh, Cape Horner. 1sh6p, Barque. 2sh6p, Tea Clipper.

*Perf. 11x11½*

**1969, June 1 Engr. Wmk. 314**

| | | | | |
|---|---|---|---|---|
| *124* | A11 | 4p brt bl | 24 | 14 |
| *125* | A11 | 1sh rose car | 50 | 45 |
| *126* | A11 | 1sh6p green | 70 | 60 |
| *127* | A11 | 2sh6p sepia | 1.25 | 1.00 |

Islanders Going to First Religious Service, 1851 — A12

Designs: 4p, Tristan da Cunha, birds and ship. 1sh6p, Landing at the beach. 2sh6p, St. Mary's Church, 1969, and procession.

*Perf. 14½x14*

**1969, Nov. 1 Litho. Wmk. 314**

| | | | | |
|---|---|---|---|---|
| *128* | A12 | 4p multi | 18 | 10 |
| *129* | A12 | 9p multi | 38 | 25 |
| *130* | A12 | 1sh6p multi | 75 | 50 |
| *131* | A12 | 2sh6p multi | 1.50 | 95 |

Issued to honor the work of the United Society for the Propagation of the Faith.

No. 77 Overprinted in Deep Orange: "NATIONAL / SAVINGS"

*Perf. 11x11½*

**1970, May 15 Engr. Wmk. 314**

| | | | | |
|---|---|---|---|---|
| *132* | A4 | 6p blk & grn | 35 | 35 |

Issued to promote national savings. No. 132 also used as savings stamp.

In 1971, No. 132 was locally surcharged "2½p" and 3 short bars by means of a rubber handstamp.

Globe and Red Cross A13

Design: 1sh9p, 2sh6p, British and Red Cross flags (vert.).

*Perf. 13½x13, 13x13½*

**1970, June 1 Litho.**

| | | | | |
|---|---|---|---|---|
| *133* | A13 | 4p emer, red & grnsh bl | 18 | 10 |
| *134* | A13 | 9p bis, red & grnsh bl | 45 | 25 |
| *135* | A13 | 1sh9p gray, vio bl & red | 1.25 | 70 |
| *136* | A13 | 2sh6p rose cl, vio bl & red | 1.90 | 1.10 |

Centenary of the British Red Cross Society.

Rock Lobster and Lobster Men Placing Trap — A14

Designs: 10p, 2sh6p, Workers in processing plant and side view of rock lobster (jasus tristani).

*Perf. 12½x13*

**1970, Nov. 1 Litho. Wmk. 314**

| | | | | |
|---|---|---|---|---|
| *137* | A14 | 4p lil rose & multi | 20 | 10 |
| *138* | A14 | 10p dl yel & multi | 52 | 25 |
| *139* | A14 | 1sh6p brn org & multi | 1.40 | 70 |
| *140* | A14 | 2sh6p ol & multi | 2.25 | 1.10 |

Issued to publicize the Tristan da Cunha rock lobster (crawfish) industry.

Nos. 72-74, 77-83, 113-114 Surcharged with New Value and Three Bars

*Perf. 11x11½*

**1971, Feb. 15 Engr. Wmk. 314**

| | | | | |
|---|---|---|---|---|
| *141* | A4 | ½p on 1p blk & emer | 5 | 5 |
| *142* | A4 | 1p on 2p blk & lil | 8 | 6 |
| *143* | A4 | 1½p on 4p blk & org | 16 | 12 |
| *144* | A4 | 2½p on 6p blk & grn | 24 | 18 |
| *145* | A4 | 3p on 7p blk & ver | 35 | 25 |
| *146* | A4 | 4p on 10p blk & dk brn | 48 | 32 |
| *147* | A4 | 5p on 1sh blk & lil rose | 60 | 40 |
| *148* | A4 | 7½p on 1sh6p blk & ol | 1.00 | 70 |
| *149* | A4 | 12½p on 2sh6p blk & brn org | 2.00 | 1.40 |
| *150* | A4 | 15p on 1½p blk & ultra | 3.00 | 2.00 |
| *151* | A4 | 25p on 5sh blk & vio | 4.00 | 2.75 |
| *152* | A4 | 50p on 10sh blk & dl grn | 12.00 | 8.25 |
| | | *Nos. 141-152 (12)* | 23.96 | 16.48 |

"Quest" — A15

Designs: 4p, Presentation of Scout Troop flag in front of Tristan school. 7½p, Great Britain No. 167a with Tristan da Cunha cancellation. 12½c, Sir Ernest Henry Shackleton, boat and expedition cancellations.

*Perf. 13½x14*

**1971, June 1 Litho. Wmk. 314**

| | | | | |
|---|---|---|---|---|
| *153* | A15 | 1½p lt bl & multi | 28 | 14 |
| *154* | A15 | 4p buff, yel grn & blk | 80 | 38 |
| *155* | A15 | 7½p pale grn, rose lil & blk | 2.00 | 1.00 |
| *156* | A15 | 12½p buff & multi | 3.25 | 1.70 |

50th anniversary of the Shackleton-Rowett South Atlantic expedition.

"Victory" at Trafalgar and Thomas Swain Catching Nelson — A16

Ships and Island Families: 2½p, "Emily of Stonington" and inscribed P. W. Green, 1836. 4p, "Italia" and inscribed Gaetano Lavarello, 1892, and Andrea Repetto. 7½p, "Falmouth" and Corp. William Glass, 1816. 12½p, American Whaler and inscribed 1836 Joshua Rogers, 1849, Capt. Andrew Hangan.

**1971, Nov. 1**

| | | | | |
|---|---|---|---|---|
| *157* | A16 | 1½p bis & multi | 28 | 30 |
| *158* | A16 | 2p multi | 55 | 62 |
| *159* | A16 | 4p gray & multi | 1.10 | 1.25 |
| *160* | A16 | 7½p multi | 1.75 | 2.00 |
| *161* | A16 | 12½p bl & multi | 2.75 | 3.00 |
| | | *Nos. 157-161 (5)* | 6.43 | 7.17 |

Cow Pudding — A17

Native Flora: 1p, Peak berry and crater lake. 1½p, Sand flower (horiz.). 2½p, New Zealand flax (horiz.). 3p, Island tree. 4p, Bog fern and snow-capped mountain. 5p, Dog catcher and albatrosses. 7½p, Celery and terns. 12½p, Pepper tree and waterfall. 25p, Foul berry (horiz.). 50p, Tussock and penguins. £1, Tussac and islands (horiz.).

*Perf. 13½x13, 13x13½*

**1972, Feb. 26 Wmk. 314**

| | | | | |
|---|---|---|---|---|
| *162* | A17 | ½p gray & multi | 10 | 8 |
| *163* | A17 | 1p sal & multi | 12 | 14 |
| *164* | A17 | 1½p grn & multi | 16 | 15 |
| *165* | A17 | 2½p multi | 25 | 25 |
| *166* | A17 | 3p multi | 30 | 30 |
| *167* | A17 | 4p lem & multi | 35 | 35 |
| *168* | A17 | 5p yel grn & multi | 45 | 40 |
| *169* | A17 | 7½p dl yel & multi | 60 | 60 |
| *170* | A17 | 12½p multi | 1.00 | 1.00 |
| *171* | A17 | 25p gray & multi | 2.00 | 2.00 |

**Litho. and Engr.**

| | | | | |
|---|---|---|---|---|
| *172* | A17 | 50p multi | 5.00 | 4.50 |
| *173* | A17 | £1 lt bl & multi | 8.75 | 9.00 |
| | | *Nos. 162-173 (12)* | 19.08 | 18.77 |

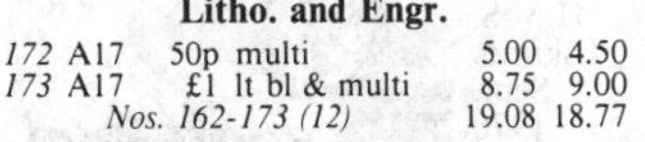

Coxswain — A18

Designs: 2½p, Launching longboat (horiz.). 4p, Men rowing longboat (horiz.). 12½p, Longboat under sail.

**1972, June 1 Litho. *Perf. 14***

| | | | | |
|---|---|---|---|---|
| *174* | A18 | 2½p multi | 30 | 20 |
| *175* | A18 | 4p multi | 45 | 35 |
| *176* | A18 | 7½p multi | 90 | 70 |
| *177* | A18 | 12½p multi | 1.50 | 1.10 |

**Silver Wedding Issue, 1972**

Common Design Type

Design: Queen Elizabeth II, Prince Philip, thrush and wandering albatrosses.

*Perf. 14x14½*

**1972, Nov. 20 Photo. Wmk. 314**

| | | | | |
|---|---|---|---|---|
| *178* | CD324 | 2½p multi | 45 | 40 |
| *179* | CD324 | 7½p ultra & multi | 1.10 | 1.00 |

Altar, St. Mary's Church — A19

**1973, July 8 Litho. *Perf. 13½***

| | | | | |
|---|---|---|---|---|
| *180* | A19 | 25p dk bl & multi | 2.50 | 2.50 |

50th anniversary of St. Mary's Church, Tristan da Cunha.

"Challenger" off Tristan, Steil's Sounding Instrument — A20

Designs: 4p, Challenger's laboratory. 7½p, Challenger off Nightingale Island. 12½p, Map of Challenger's voyage. Each stamp shows an instrument for deep sea soundings.

*Perf. 13½x14*

**1973, Oct. 15 Wmk. 314**

| | | | | |
|---|---|---|---|---|
| *181* | A20 | 4p multi | 30 | 30 |
| *182* | A20 | 5p multi | 50 | 50 |
| *183* | A20 | 7½p multi | 80 | 80 |
| *184* | A20 | 12½p multi | 1.50 | 1.50 |
| *a.* | | Souvenir sheet of 4 | 5.25 | 5.50 |

Centenary of "Challenger's" visit to Tristan da Cunha during oceanographic exploration world trip, 1872-76.

No. 184a contains one each of Nos. 181-184, perf. 13½. Multicolored marginal design with birds and sailing ship. Size: 144x95mm.

View of English Port from Shipboard — A21

Designs: 5p, Inspectors at volcano rim. 7½p, Islanders disembarking from "Bornholm." 12½p, Islanders on board ship approaching Tristan da Cunha.

**1973, Nov. 10 *Perf. 14½***

| | | | | |
|---|---|---|---|---|
| *185* | A21 | 4p yel, blk & gold | 48 | 35 |
| *186* | A21 | 5p multi | 60 | 45 |
| *187* | A21 | 7½p multi | 90 | 65 |
| *188* | A21 | 12½p multi | 1.25 | 90 |

10th anniversary of return of islanders to Tristan da Cunha.

**Princess Anne's Wedding Issue**

Common Design Type

**1973, Nov. 14 Wmk. 314 *Perf. 14***

| | | | | |
|---|---|---|---|---|
| *189* | CD325 | 7½p multi | 28 | 28 |
| *190* | CD325 | 12½p bl grn & multi | 45 | 45 |

Rockhopper Penguin — A22

Designs: Rockhopper penguins.

**1974, May 1 Litho.**

| | | | | |
|---|---|---|---|---|
| *191* | A22 | 2½p *shown* | 2.75 | 1.25 |
| *192* | A22 | 5p *Colony* | 3.25 | 1.65 |
| *193* | A22 | 7½p *Penguins fishing* | 3.75 | 2.00 |
| *194* | A22 | 25p *Penguin and fledgling* | 8.75 | 5.00 |

**Souvenir Sheet**

Map of Tristan da Cunha, Penguin and Sea Gull — A23

**1974, Oct. 1 Wmk. 314 *Perf. 13½***
*195* A23 35p multi 4.50 3.00

No. 195 contains one stamp, and has multicolored margin. Size: 152x102mm.

Blenheim Palace A24

Design: 25p, Churchill and Queen Elizabeth II.

**Wmk. 373**

**1974, Nov. 30 Litho. *Perf. 14***
*196* A24 7½p blk & yel 38 35
*197* A24 25p blk & brn 95 90
*a.* Souvenir sheet of 2 1.75 1.50

Sir Winston Churchill (1874-1965), birth centenary. No. 197a contains one each of Nos. 196-197, gray blue margin showing Churchill aboard ship. Size: 92x92mm.

Plocamium Fuscorubrum — A25

Aquatic Plants: 5p, Ulva lactuca. 10p, Epymenia flabellata. 20p, Macrocystis pyrifera.

***Perf. 13x14***

**1975, Apr. 16 Wmk. 314**
*198* A25 4p lil & multi 30 25
*199* A25 5p ultra & multi 40 32
*200* A25 10p yel & multi 75 62
*201* A25 20p lt grn & multi 1.50 1.25

Killer Whales A26

**Wmk. 314**

**1975, Nov. 1 Litho. *Perf. 13½***
*202* A26 2p *shown* 32 18
*203* A26 3p *Rough-toothed dolphins* 50 25
*204* A26 5p *Atlantic right whale* 1.40 70
*205* A26 20p *Finback whales* 3.25 1.65

Tristan da Cunha No. 1 — A27

Designs: 9p, Tristan da Cunha No. 13 (vert.). 25p, Freighter Tristania II.

***Perf. 13½x14, 14x13½***

**1976, May 4 Litho. Wmk. 373**
*206* A27 5p lil, vio & blk 28 28
*207* A27 9p bluish gray, grn & blk 45 45
*208* A27 25p multi 1.50 1.50

Festival of Stamps 1976. For souvenir sheet containing No. 208 see Ascension No. 214a.

The Patches A28

Views, by Roland Svensson: 3p, Tristan house (vert.). 10p, Tristan Settlement and Cliffs. 20p, Huts at Nightingale (vert.).

**1976, Oct. 4 Litho. *Perf. 14***
*209* A28 3p multi 22 16
*210* A28 5p multi 32 24
*211* A28 10p multi 65 50
*212* A28 20p multi 1.40 1.00
*a.* Souvenir sheet of 4 3.50 2.50

An artist's view of Tristan da Cunha. No. 212a contains one each of Nos. 209-212; seagull and dark blue inscription in margin. Size: 127x114mm.
See Nos. 234-237.

Royal Yacht Britannia — A29

Designs: 15p, Royal standard. 25p, Royal family.

**1977, Feb. 7 Wmk. 373 *Perf. 13***
*213* A29 10p multi 75 60
*214* A29 15p multi 60 50
*215* A29 25p multi 1.00 80

25th anniv. of the reign of Elizabeth II.

H.M.S. Eskimo, Sept. 1970 A30

Royal Naval Ships and Arms: 10p, Naiad, Nov. 1968. 15p, Jaguar, March 1964. 20p, London, Dec. 1964. Dates of visits to island.

**1977, Oct. 1 Litho. *Perf. 14½***
*216* A30 5p multi 25 20
*217* A30 10p multi 50 40
*218* A30 15p multi 75 60
*219* A30 20p multi 1.00 80
*a.* Souvenir sheet of 4 3.50 3.00

No. 219a contains one each of Nos. 216-219; blue and black margin shows arms of Juno and description of ships. Size: 155x149mm.

**Nos. 214-215 Surcharged with New Value and Bar**

**1977, Oct. 13 Wmk. 373 *Perf. 13***
*220* A29 4p on 15p multi 11.00 10.00
*221* A29 7½p on 25p multi 11.00 10.00

Prices of premium quality never hinged stamps will be in excess of catalogue price.

Giant Fulmars — A31

Birds: 1p, Gray-faced petrel (horiz.). 2p, White-faced storm petrel (horiz.). 4p, Soft-plumed petrel. 5p, Wandering albatross. 10p, Kerguelen petrel. 15p, Antarctic terns. 20p, Greater shearwater. 25p, Broad-billed prion. 50p, Great skuas. £1, Common diving petrels. £2, Yellownosed albatross.

***Perf. 13½x14, 14x13½***

**1977, Dec. 1 Litho.**
*222* A31 1p multi 5 5
*223* A31 2p multi 8 6
*224* A31 3p multi 10 6
*225* A31 4p multi 14 8
*226* A31 5p multi 18 10
*227* A31 10p multi 35 20
*228* A31 15p multi 55 30
*229* A31 20p multi 70 40
*230* A31 25p multi 90 50
*231* A31 50p multi 1.75 1.00
*232* A31 £1 multi 2.75 1.50
*233* A31 £2 multi 6.25 3.50
*Nos. 222-233 (12)* 13.80 7.75

Painting Type of 1976

Views by Roland Svensson: 5p, St. Mary's Church. 10p, Longboats. 15p, A Tristan home. 20p, Harbor, 1970.

**Wmk. 373**

**1978, Mar. 1 Litho. *Perf. 14½***
*234* A28 5p multi 30 18
*235* A28 10p multi 60 35
*236* A28 15p multi 95 52
*237* A28 20p multi 1.40 75
*a.* Souvenir sheet of 4 3.50 3.00

An artist's view of Tristan da Cunha. No. 237a contains one each of Nos. 234-237; view of fishing factory at Tristan. Size: 115x128mm.

**Elizabeth II Coronation Anniversary Issue**

Common Design Types

**Souvenir Sheet**

**1978, Apr. 21 Unwmk. *Perf. 15***
*238* Sheet of 6 3.75 4.00
*a.* CD326 25p *King's Bull* 70 70
*b.* CD327 25p *Elizabeth II* 70 70
*c.* CD328 25p *Tristan crawfish* 70 70

No. 238 contains 2 se-tenant strips of Nos. 238a-238c, separated by horizontal gutter with commemorative and descriptive inscriptions and showing central part of coronation procession with coach. Size: 100x135mm.

Sodalite — A32

Local Minerals: 5p, Aragonite. 10p, Sulphur. 20p, Lava containing pyroxene crystal.

***Perf. 13½x14***

**1978, June 9 Litho. Wmk. 373**
*239* A32 3p multi 20 12
*240* A32 5p multi 32 20
*241* A32 10p multi 65 40
*242* A32 20p multi 1.25 80

Fish A33

**1978, Sept. 29 Litho. *Perf. 14***
*243* A33 5p Klipfish 24 16
*244* A33 10p Fivefinger 48 32
*245* A33 15p Concha 75 50
*246* A33 20p Soldier 95 60

Orangeleaf and Navy Flag — A34

Royal Fleet Auxiliary Vessels: 10p, Tarbatness. 20p, Tidereach. 25p, Reliant.

**1978, Nov. 24 Litho. *Perf. 12½***
*247* A34 5p multi 20 14
*248* A34 10p multi 42 28
*249* A34 20p multi 85 55
*250* A34 25p multi 1.10 70
*a.* Souvenir sheet of 4 3.75 3.75

No. 250a contains Nos. 247-250. Multicolored margin with naval flags and vessel descriptions. Size: 134x137mm.

Fur Seals — A35

Wildlife conservation: 5p, Elephant seal. 15p, Tristan thrush. 20p, Tristan buntings.

**Wmk. 373**

**1979, Jan. 3 Litho. *Perf. 14***
*251* A35 5p multi 20 18
*252* A35 10p multi 42 35
*253* A35 15p multi 60 52
*254* A35 20p multi 85 70

Tristan Longboat — A36

Ships: 10p, Queen Mary. 15p, Queen Elizabeth. 20p, Q.E.II. 25p, Q.E.II, longboat, view of Tristan.

**1979, Feb. 8 *Perf. 14½***
*255* A36 5p multi 34 30
*256* A36 10p multi 45 40
*257* A36 15p multi 65 60
*258* A36 20p multi 90 80

**Souvenir Sheet**

*259* A36 25p multi *7.50 5.25*

Visit of cruise ship Q.E.II, Feb. 8.
No. 259 has multicolored margin showing longboats and coat of arms. Size: 148x96mm.

Tristan da Cunha No. 12 A37

Tristan da Cunha Stamps: 10p, No. 26. 25p, No. 58 (vert.). 50p, 1p-local "potatoe" stamp.

***Perf. 14½x14, 14x14½***

**1979, Aug. 27 Litho. Wmk. 373**
*260* A37 5p multi 18 18
*261* A37 10p multi 32 32
*262* A37 25p multi 80 80

### Souvenir Sheet

*263* A37 50p multi 1.75 1.75

Sir Rowland Hill (1795-1879), originator of penny postage. No. 263 has multicolored margin showing portrait of Rowland Hill. Size: 83x102mm.

The Padre's House, IYC Emblem A38

IYC Emblem, Children's Drawings: 10p, "Houses in the Village." 15p, "St. Mary's Church." 20p, "Rockhopper Penguins."

**1979, Nov. 26** **Litho.** ***Perf. 14***

*264* A38 5p multi 12 12
*265* A38 10p multi 25 25
*266* A38 15p multi 40 40
*267* A38 20p multi 52 52

International Year of the Child.

Stoltenhoff Island — A39

Views (Sketches by Roland Svensson): 10p, Nightingale from the East. 15p, The Administrator's abode (vert.). 20p, "Ridge where the goat jumped off" (vert.).

**1980, Feb.** **Litho.** ***Perf. 14***

*268* A39 5p multi 16 12
*269* A39 10p multi 35 22
*270* A39 15p multi 50 32
*271* A39 20p multi 70 45
*a.* Souvenir sheet of 4 1.75 1.75

No. 271a contains Nos. 268-271; multicolored margin shows Stoltenhoff Island. Size: 127x109mm.

Mail Pickup Boat, London 1980 Emblem — A40

**1980, May 6** **Litho.** ***Perf. 14***

*272* A40 5p *shown* 12 10
*273* A40 10p *Unloading mail* 24 20
*274* A40 15p *Truck transport* 35 30
*275* A40 20p *Delivery bell* 48 40
*276* A40 25p *Distribution* 60 50
*Nos. 272-276 (5)* 1.79 1.50

London 80 Intl. Stamp Exhib., May 6-14.

### Queen Mother Elizabeth Birthday Issue

Common Design Type

**1980, Aug. 11** **Litho.** ***Perf. 14***

*277* CD330 14p multi 42 42

Golden Hinde — A41

**1980, Sept. 6** ***Perf. 14½***

*278* A41 5p *shown* 16 12
*279* A41 10p *Drake's route* 35 22
*280* A41 20p *Sir Francis Drake* 65 45
*281* A41 25p *Queen Elizabeth I* 80 55

Sir Francis Drake's circumnavigation, 400th anniversary.

Humpty Dumpty A42

**Wmk. 373**

**1980, Oct. 31** **Litho.** ***Perf. 13½***

*282* Sheet of 9 4.00 2.50
*a.* A42 15p *shown* 42 25
*b.* A42 15p *Mary had a Little Lamb* 42 25
*c.* A42 15p *Little Jack Horner* 42 25
*d.* A42 15p *Hey Diddle Diddle* 42 25
*e.* A42 15p *London Bridge* 42 25
*f.* A42 15p *Old King Cole* 42 25
*g.* A42 15p *Sing a Song of Sixpence* 42 25
*h.* A42 15p *Tom Tom the Piper's Son* 42 25
*i.* A42 25p *The Owl and the Pussy Cat* 42 25

Christmas 1980. No. 282 has black decorative margin. Size: 154x112mm.

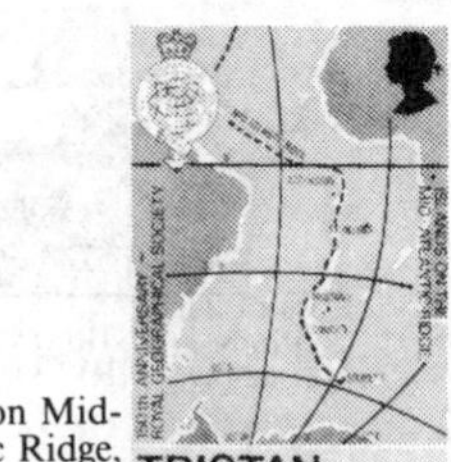

Islands on Mid-Atlantic Ridge, Society Emblem — A43

150th Anniversary of Royal Geographical Society (Maps and Expeditions): 10p, Tristan da Cunha, Francis Beaufort, 1806. 15p, Tristan Island, Norwegian expedition, 1937-1938. 20p, Gough Island, scientific survey, 1955-1956.

**1980, Dec. 15**

*283* A43 5p multi 16 14
*284* A43 10p multi 32 28
*285* A43 15p multi 48 45
*286* A43 20p multi 65 55

Rev. Edwin Dodgson A44

**Wmk. 373**

**1981, Mar. 23** **Litho.** ***Perf. 14***

*287* A44 10p portrait, vert. 32 22
*288* A44 20p shown 65 45
*289* A44 30p Dodgson preaching, vert. 1.00 70
*a.* Souvenir sheet of 3 2.00 1.65

Centenary of arrival of Rev. Edwin H. Dodgson, who saved population from starvation. No. 289a contains Nos. 287-289; brown and black margin shows Dodgson family (identified on back). Size: 141x133½mm.

Map of Tristan da Cunha showing L'heure du Berger Route, 1767 (Dalrymple's Map, 1781) — A45

Early Maps and Charts By: 5p, 21p, Capt. Denham, 1853 (diff.). 35p, Ivan Keulen, 1700.

**1981, May 22**

*290* A45 5p multi 15 20
*291* A45 14p multi 55 40
*292* A45 21p multi 65 85

### Souvenir Sheet

*293* A45 35p multi 1.10 80

No. 293 has multicolored margin showing entire map. Size: 110½x70mm.

### Royal Wedding Issue

Common Design Type

**Wmk. 373**

**1981, July 22** **Litho.** ***Perf. 14***

*294* CD331 5p Bouquet 12 10
*295* CD331 20p Charles 52 45
*296* CD331 50p Couple 1.25 1.10

Hiking — A46

**1981, Sept. 14**

*297* A46 5p shown 16 12
*298* A46 10p Camping 35 22
*299* A46 20p Map reading 70 45
*300* A46 25p Prince Philip 85 55

Duke of Edinburgh's Awards, 25th anniv.

Inaccessible Island Rail — A47

**1981, Nov. 1** **Litho.** ***Perf. 13½x14***

*301* Strip of 4 1.40 1.10
*a.* A47 10p Nest 35 25
*b.* A47 10p Eggs 35 25
*c.* A47 10p Chicks 35 25
*d.* A47 10p Adult rail 35 25

Six-gilled Shark A48

**1982, Feb. 8** **Litho.** ***Perf. 13½x14***

*302* A48 5p shown 16 12
*303* A48 14p Porbeagle shark 45 30
*304* A48 21p Blue shark 70 48
*305* A48 35p Hammerhead shark 1.10 75

Marcella — A49

**1982, Apr. 5** **Litho.** ***Perf. 14***

*306* A49 5p shown 12 10
*307* A49 15p Eliza Adams 40 32
*308* A49 30p Corinthian 85 70
*309* A49 50p Samuel & Thomas 1.25 1.10

See Nos. 324-327.

### Princess Diana Issue

Common Design Type

***Perf. 14½x14***

**1982, July 1** **Litho.** **Wmk. 373**

*310* CD333 5p Arms 12 10
*311* CD333 15p Diana 40 30
*312* CD333 30p Wedding 85 60
*313* CD333 50p Portrait 1.25 1.00

Scouting Year — A50

***Perf. 13½x13, 13x13½***

**1982, Aug. 23** **Litho.**

*314* A50 5p Baden-Powell, vert. 16 12
*315* A50 20p Brownsea Isld. camp, 1907, vert. 65 52
*316* A50 50p Saluting 1.50 1.25

### Souvenir Sheet

***Perf. 14***

*317* A50 50p Tree illustration, vert. 1.45 1.25

No. 317 has multicolored margin showing Moral of the Acorn and the Oak. Size: 89x115mm.

Nos. 226, 230 Overprinted: "1st PARTICIPATION / COMMONWEALTH / GAMES 1982"

***Perf. 13½x14***

**1982, Sept. 28** **Litho.** **Wmk. 373**

*318* A31 5p multi 15 12
*319* A31 25p multi 75 65

12th Commonwealth Games, Brisbane, Australia, Sept. 30-Oct. 9.

Formation of Volcanic Island — A51

**1982, Nov. 1** ***Perf. 14x14½***

*320* A51 5p shown 12 10
*321* A51 15p Surface cinder cones 40 32
*322* A51 25p Eruption 65 55
*323* A51 35p 1961 eruption 90 75

Ship Type of 1982

**1983, Feb. 1** **Litho.** ***Perf. 14***

*324* A49 5p Islander, vert. 12 12
*325* A49 20p Roscoe 52 52
*326* A49 35p Columbia 90 75
*327* A49 50p Emeline, vert. 1.25 1.10

Tractor Pulling Trailer A52

**1983, May 2** **Litho.** ***Perf. 14***

*328* A52 5p shown 14 10
*329* A52 15p Pack mules 45 32
*330* A52 30p Oxen pulling cart 90 70
*331* A52 50p Jeep 1.40 1.10

Map of South Atlantic A53

Island History.

**Wmk. 373**

**1983, Aug. 1 Litho. *Perf. 14***

*332* A53 1p shown 5 5
*333* A53 3p Tristao d'Acunha's flagship 9 7
*334* A53 4p Landing, 1643 10 9
*335* A53 5p 17th cent. views 14 12
*336* A53 10p Landing party, 1815 28 22
*337* A53 15p Settlement 40 35
*338* A53 18p Governor Glass's house 50 40
*339* A53 20p Rev. W.F. Taylor, Peter Green 55 45
*340* A53 25p Three-master John and Elizabeth 65 55
*341* A53 50p Dependency declaration of St. Helena, 1938 1.40 1.10
*342* A53 £1 Commissioning ceremony 2.75 2.25
*343* A53 £2 Evacuation, 1961 5.50 4.50
*Nos. 332-343 (12)* 12.41 10.15

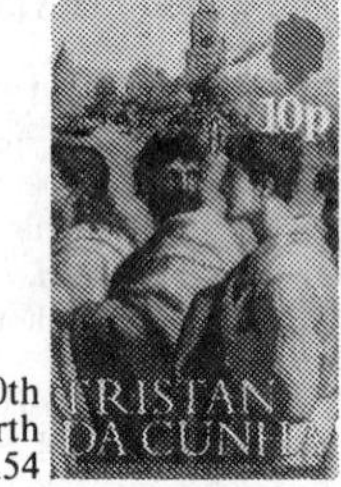


Raphael, 500th Birth Anniv. — A54

**1983, Oct. 27 Litho. *Perf. 14½***

*344* A54 10p multi 30 24
*345* A54 25p multi 75 60
*346* A54 40p multi 1.20 1.00

**Souvenir Sheet**

*347* A54 50p multi, horiz. 1.50 1.25

Details from Christ's Charge to St. Peter. Multicolored margin continues design. Size: 115x90mm.

St. Helena Colony Sesquicentenary — A55

**Wmk. 373**

**1984, Jan. 3 Litho. *Perf. 14***

*348* A55 10p No. 7 25 20
*349* A55 15p No. 9 40 30
*350* A55 25p No. 10 65 50
*351* A55 60p No. 12 1.65 1.25

Local Fungi A56

**Wmk. 373**

**1984, Mar. 26 Litho. *Perf. 14***

*352* A56 10p Agrocybe praecox, vert. 25 20
*353* A56 20p Laccaria tetraspora, vert. 52 40
*354* A45 30p Agrocybe cylindracea 80 60
*355* A56 50p Sarcoscypha coccinea 1.25 1.00

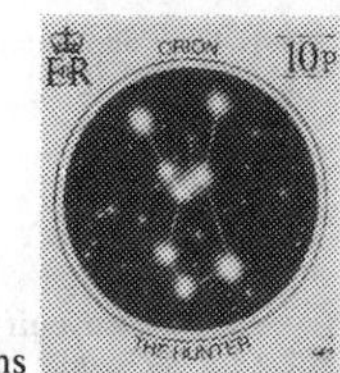


Constellations A57

**Wmk. 373**

**1984, July 30 Litho. *Perf. 14½***

*356* A57 10p Orion 25 22
*357* A57 20p Scorpius 52 45
*358* A57 25p Canis Major 65 55
*359* A57 50p Crux 1.25 1.10

Sheep Shearing — A58

**1984, Oct. 1 Litho. Wmk. 373**

*360* A58 9p shown 24 20
*361* A58 17p Carding wool 45 38
*362* A58 29p Spinning 75 65
*363* A58 45p Knitting 1.25 1.00
*a.* Souvenir Sheet of 4, Nos. 360-363 2.75 2.25

Christmas 1984 A59

**Wmk. 373**

**1984, Dec. 3 Litho. *Perf. 14***

*364* A59 10p Three angels, Christmas dinner 25 24
*365* A59 20p Two angels, cart 50 48
*366* A59 30p Candles, sailboat 80 70
*367* A59 50p Trees, Nativity 1.25 1.10

Shipwrecks — A60

***Perf. 14x13½, 13½x14***

**1985, Feb. 4 Litho. Wmk. 373**

*368* A60 10p HMS Julia, 1817, vert. 32 25
*369* A60 25p Bell from Mabel Clark, 1878, vert. 80 65
*370* A60 35p Barque Glenhuntley, 1898 1.10 85

**Souvenir Sheet**

*371* A60 60p Map of shipwreck sites 2.00 1.65

No. 371 contains one stamp (48x32mm); multicolored margin shows map legend. Size: 142x102mm.

See Nos. 393-396, 412-415.

**Queen Mother 85th Birthday**

Common Design Type

***Perf. 14½x14***

**1985, June 7 Litho. Wmk. 384**

*372* CD336 10p With Prince Charles, 1954 30 30
*373* CD336 20p With Margaret at Ascot 60 60
*374* CD336 30p Queen Mother 90 90
*375* CD336 50p Holding Prince Henry 1.10 1.10

**Souvenir Sheet**

*376* CD336 80p With Anne 2.75 2.75

No. 376 has multicolored margin continuing design. Size: 92x74mm.

Flags A61

Designs: 10p, Jonathan Lambert and flag of 1811, Isles of Refreshment. 15p, Cannon and flag of 21st Light Dragoons, 1816-17, Fort Malcolm. 25p, HMS Falmouth, 1816, and flag of HMS Atlantic Isle, HMS JOB 9, 1942-46. 60p, View of Tristan and Union Jack, 1816 to date.

**Wmk. 373**

**1985, Sept. 30 Litho. *Perf. 14***

*377* A61 10p multi 28 28
*378* A61 15p multi 42 42
*379* A61 25p multi 72 72
*380* A61 60p multi 1.75 1.75

Nos. 378-380 vert.

Loss of The Lifeboat, Cent. — A62

**1985, Nov. 28**

*381* A62 10p Lifeboat, barque West Riding 30 30
*382* A62 30p Map 90 90
*383* A62 50p Death toll 1.50 1.50

Halley's Comet A63

**1986, Mar. 3 Wmk. 384**

*384* A63 10p Bayeux Tapestry, c. 1092 28 28
*385* A63 20p Trajectory around Earth 55 55
*386* A63 30p Comet over Inaccessible Is. 80 80
*387* A63 50p Ship Paramour 1.40 1.40

**Queen Elizabeth II 60th Birthday**

Common Design Type

Designs: 10p, With Prince Charles, 1950. 15p, Birthday Parade, wearing uniform of Scots Guards, 1976. 25p, At Westminster Abbey, London, 1972, wearing mantle and robes of the Most Noble Order of Bath. 45p, Silver Jubilee Tour, Canada, 1977. 65p, Visiting Crown Agents' offices, 1983.

**1986, Apr. 21 *Perf. 14½***

*388* CD337 10p scar, blk & sil 28 28
*389* CD337 15p ultra & multi 40 40
*390* CD337 25p grn & multi 65 65
*391* CD337 45p vio & multi 1.25 1.25
*392* CD337 65p rose vio & multi 1.65 1.65
*Nos. 388-392 (5)* 4.23 4.23

Shipwrecks Type of 1985

**1986, June 2 *Perf. 13½***

*393* A60 9p SV Allanshaw, 1893 35 35
*394* A60 20p Church font from Edward Vittery, 1881 80 80
*395* A60 40p Figurehead, 1940 1.65 1.65

***Perf. 13½x13***

**Souvenir Sheet**

*396* A60 65p Barque Italia, 1892 2.50 2.50

Nos. 394-395 vert. No. 396 has pale yellow green and black inscribed margin picturing verse from well-known hymn.

**Royal Wedding Issue, 1986**

Common Design Type

Designs: 10p, Informal portrait. 40p, Andrew operating helicopter.

**Wmk. 384**

**1986, July 23 Litho. *Perf. 14***

*397* CD338 10p multi 25 25
*398* CD338 40p multi 1.10 1.10

Flora & Fauna of Inaccessible Island — A64

**Wmk. 384**

**1986, Sept. 30 Litho. *Perf. 14***

*399* A64 5p Wandering albatross 12 12
*400* A64 10p Daisy 25 25
*401* A64 20p Vanessa butterfly 50 50
*402* A64 25p Wilkins's bunting 60 60
*403* A64 50p Ring-eye 1.25 1.25
*Nos. 399-403 (5)* 2.72 2.72

Indigenous Flightless Species and Habitats — A65

Designs: 10p, Flightless moth, Edinburgh Settlement. 25p, Strap-winged fly, Crater Lake. 35p, Flightless rail, Inaccessible Island. 50p, Gough Island moorhen, Gough Island.

**Wmk. 384**

**1987, Jan. 23 Litho. *Perf. 14½***

*404* A65 10p multi 30 30
*405* A65 25p multi 75 75
*406* A65 35p multi 1.05 1.05
*407* A65 50p multi 1.50 1.50

Rockhopper Penguins — A66

**1987, June 22**

*408* A66 10p Swimming 30 30
*409* A66 20p Nesting 60 60
*410* A66 30p Adult and young 90 90
*411* A66 50p Adult's head 1.50 1.50

Shipwrecks Type of 1985

Designs: 11p, Castaways attacking sea elephant, vert. 17p, Henry A. Paull, 1879, Sandy Point. 45p, Gustav Stoltenhoff, Stoltenhoff Is., vert. 70p, Map of wrecks off Inaccessible Is.

**1987, Apr. 2 *Perf. 14***

*412* A60 11p olive gray & blk 32 32
*413* A60 17p dark vio & blk 50 50
*414* A60 45p myrtle grn & blk 1.35 1.35

**Souvenir Sheet**

415 A60 70p lt blue, royal blue & apple grn 2.10 2.10

No. 415 has multicolored inscribed margin picturing music from a hymn by C. Wesley. Size: 131x70mm.

Norwegian Scientific Expedition, 50th Anniv. — A67

Designs: 10p, Microscope and textbooks symbolic of expedition results. 20p, Scientists tagging a mollymawk. 30p, Expedition headquarters on the island. 50p, S.S. Thorshammer.

**Wmk. 384**

**1987, Dec. 7 Litho. *Perf. 14***

*416* A67 10p multi 38 38
*417* A67 20p multi 75 75

**Wmk. 373**

*418* A67 30p multi 1.15 1.15
*419* A67 50p multi 1.90 1.90

Fauna of Nightingale Island — A68

**Wmk. 384**

**1988, Mar. 21 Litho. *Perf. 14***

*420* A68 5p Tristan bunting 20 20
*421* A68 10p Tristan thrush 38 38
*422* A68 20p Yellow-nosed albatross 75 75
*423* A68 25p Great shearwater 92 92
*424* A68 50p Elephant seal 1.85 1.85
*Nos. 420-424 (5)* 4.10 4.10

Handicrafts A69

**1988, May 30 *Perf. 14½***

*425* A69 10p Painted penguin eggs 38 38
*426* A69 15p Moccasins 55 55
*427* A69 35p Woolen clothing 1.30 1.30
*428* A69 50p Model canvas boats 1.85 1.85

Nos. 388-392 Ovptd. "40TH WEDDING ANNIVERSARY" in Silver.

**Wmk. 384**

**1988, Mar. 9 Litho. *Perf. 14½***

*429* CD337 10p scar, blk & sil 38 38
*430* CD337 15p ultra & multi 55 55
*431* CD337 25p grn & multi 92 92
*432* CD337 45p vio & multi 1.65 1.65
*433* CD337 65p rose vio & multi 2.35 2.35
*Nos. 429-433 (5)* 5.85 5.85

19th Cent. Whaling A70

**1988, Oct. 6 Litho. Wmk. 384 *Perf.***

*434* A70 10p "Trying out" blubber 38 38
*435* A70 20p Harpoon guns 75 75
*436* A70 30p Scrimshaw 1.15 1.15
*437* A70 50p Ships 1.90 1.90

**Souvenir Sheet**

*438* A70 £1 Right whale 3.50 3.50

No. 438 has black and gray decorative margin picturing 19th cent. whaling ships, whalers in longboats and artifacts. Size: 76x55mm.

**Lloyds of London, 300th Anniv.**

Common Design Type

Designs: 10p, Lloyds's new building, 1988. 25p, Cargo ship *Tristania II*, horiz. 35p, Supply ship *St. Helena*, horiz. 50p, Square-rigger *Kobenhavn*, lost at sea.

**Wmk. 384**

**1988, Nov. 7 Litho. *Perf. 14***

*439* CD341 10p multi 35 35
*440* CD341 25p multi 85 85
*441* CD341 35p multi 1.20 1.20
*442* CD341 50p multi 1.70 1.70

Paintings of the Island, 1824, by Augustus Earle (1793-1838) — A71

Designs: 1p, *Government House*. 3p, *Squall off Tristan*. 4p, *Rafting Blubber*. 5p, *Tristan*. 10p, *Man Killing an Albatross*. 15p, *View on the Summit*. 20p, *Nightingale Island*. 25p, *Tristan*, diff. 35p, *"Solitude," Watching the Horizon*. 50p, *North Eastern*. £1, *Tristan*, diff. £2, *Governor Glass and His Companions*.

**1988, Dec. 10**

*443* A71 1p multi 5 5
*444* A71 3p multi 10 10
*445* A71 4p multi 14 14
*446* A71 5p multi 18 18
*447* A71 10p multi 35 35
*448* A71 15p multi 50 50
*449* A71 20p multi 68 68
*450* A71 25p multi 85 85
*451* A71 35p multi 1.20 1.20
*452* A71 50p multi 1.70 1.70
*453* A71 £1 multi 3.40 3.40
*454* A71 £2 multi 6.75 6.75
*Nos. 443-454 (12)* 15.90 15.90

Gough Is. Fauna — A72

**1989, Feb. 6 Litho. Wmk. 384**

*455* A72 5p Giant petrel 18 18
*456* A72 10p Gough moorhen 35 35
*457* A72 20p Gough bunting 75 75
*458* A72 25p Sooty albatross 90 90
*459* A72 50p Amsterdam fur seal 1.80 1.80
*Nos. 455-459 (5)* 3.98 3.98

## POSTAGE DUE STAMPS

Type of Barbados 1934-47

**Wmk. 4**

**1957, Feb. 1 Typo. *Perf. 14***

**Chalky Paper**

*J1* D1 1p rose red 3.50 *5.75*
*J2* D1 2p org yel 4.50 *7.50*
*J3* D1 3p green 5.00 *9.25*
*J4* D1 4p ultra 6.00 *11.00*
*J5* D1 5p dp cl 7.50 *13.00*
*Nos. J1-J5 (5)* 26.50 *46.50*

Numeral — D2

***Perf. 13½x14***

**1976, Sept. 3 Litho. Wmk. 373**

*J6* D2 1p lil rose 52 40
*J7* D2 2p grysh grn 65 65
*J8* D2 4p violet 70 85
*J9* D2 5p lt bl 1.00 1.50
*J10* D2 10p brown 2.75 3.25
*Nos. J6-J10 (5)* 5.62 6.65

**1976, May 31 Wmk. 314**

*J6a* D2 1p lil rose 25 25
*J7a* D2 2p grysh grn 50 50
*J8a* D2 4p violet 1.00 1.00
*J9a* D2 5p lt bl 1.25 1.25
*J10a* D2 10p brown 3.25 3.25
*Nos. J6a-J10a (5)* 6.25 6.25

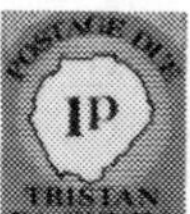

Outline Map of Tristan da Cunha — D3

***Perf. 15x14***

**1986, Nov. 20 Litho. Wmk. 384**

*J11* D3 1p pale yel brn & brn 5 5
*J12* D3 2p org & brn 6 6
*J13* D3 5p crim rose & brn 15 15
*J14* D3 7p lt lil & blk 22 22
*J15* D3 10p pale ultra & blk 30 30
*J16* D3 25p lt grn & blk 75 75
*Nos. J11-J16 (6)* 1.53 1.53

## TRUCIAL STATES

LOCATION — Qatar Peninsula, Persian Gulf.

GOVT. — Sheikdoms under British Protection.

AREA — 32,300 sq. mi.

POP. — 86,000.

CAPITAL — Dubai.

The Trucial States are: Abu Dhabi, Ajman, Dubai, Fujeira, Ras al Khaima, Sharjah and Kalba, and Umm al Qiwain.

Stamps inscribed "Trucial States" were issued and used only in Dubai. Beginning Aug. 1972 all Trucial States used the stamps of United Arab Emirates.

100 Naye Paise = 1 Rupee

**Catalogue values for all unused stamps in this country are for Never Hinged items.**

7 Palm Trees — A1

Dhow — A2

***Perf. 14½x14***

**1961, Jan. 7 Photo. Unwmk.**

*1* A1 5np emerald 7 14
*2* A1 15np red brn 14 12
*3* A1 20np ultra 16 14
*4* A1 30np orange 22 20
*5* A1 40np purple 30 28
*6* A1 50np brn ol 38 38
*7* A1 75np gray 60 50

**Engr. *Perf. 13x12½***

*8* A2 1r emerald 90 70
*9* A2 2r black 1.75 1.75
*10* A2 5r rose red 5.00 5.00
*11* A2 10r vio bl 11.00 11.00
*Nos. 1-11 (11)* 20.52 20.21

Stamps inscribed "Trucial States" were withdrawn in June, 1963, when the individual states began issuing their own stamps.

*Turks Islands stamps can be mounted in Scott's British North and West Caribbean Album.*

## TURKS ISLANDS

LOCATION — In the West Indies, at the southern extremity of the Bahamas.

GOVT. — Former dependency of Jamaica.

AREA — 616 sq. mi.

POP. — 2,000 (approx.).

CAPITAL — Grand Turk.

In 1848 the Turks Islands together with the Caicos group, lying to the northwest, were made a British colony. In 1873 the Colony became a dependency under the government of Jamaica although separate stamp issues were continued. Postage stamps inscribed Turks and Caicos Islands have been used since 1900.

12 Pence = 1 Shilling

Queen Victoria — A1

Wmk. 5- Small Star

***Perf. 11½ to 13***

**1867 Unwmk. Engr.**

*1* A1 1p rose 22.50 30.00
*2* A1 6p gray black 32.50 32.50
*3* A1 1sh slate blue 32.50 32.50

***Perf. 11 to 13x14 to 15***

**1873-79 Wmk. 5**

*4* A1 1p dull red 20.00 20.00
**a.** Horiz. pair, imperf. btwn. *7,500.*
**b.** Perf. 11-12 *1,500.*
*5* A1 1p rose red ('79) 30.00 30.00
*6* A1 1sh violet *7,250.* *3,000.*

Stamps offered as No. 6 are often copies from which the surcharge has been removed.

Stamps of 1867-79 Surcharged in Black:

$\frac{1}{2}$ $\frac{1}{2}$ $\frac{1}{2}$ $\frac{1}{2}$ $\frac{1}{2}$

*a b c d e*

Twelve settings of the ½p, nine of 2½p, and six of 4p.

**1881 Unwmk. *Perf. 11 to 13***

*7* (a) ½p on 6p gray blk 40.00 40.00
*7A* (b) ½p on 6p gray blk 27.50
*8* (b) ½p on 1sh sl bl 35.00 42.50
**a.** Double surcharge *3,000.*
*8B* (c) ½p on 1sh sl bl *12,500.*
**c.** Without fraction bar

***Perf. 11 to 13x14 to 15***

**Wmk. 5**

*9* (a) ½p on 1p dl red 21.00 21.00
**a.** Double surcharge
*10* (b) ½p on 1p dl red 27.50 27.50
*11* (c) ½p on 1p dl red 18.00 18.00
**a.** Double surcharge *2,750.*
*12* (d) ½p on 1p dl red 90.00
**a.** Without fraction bar 1,100.
**b.** Double surcharge
*13* (e) ½p on 1p dl red 525.00
*14* (a) ½p on 1sh vio 100.00 100.00
**a.** Double surcharge 850.00
*15* (b) ½p on 1sh vio 175.00 175.00
**a.** Without fraction bar 500.00
*16* (c) ½p on 1sh vio 80.00 80.00

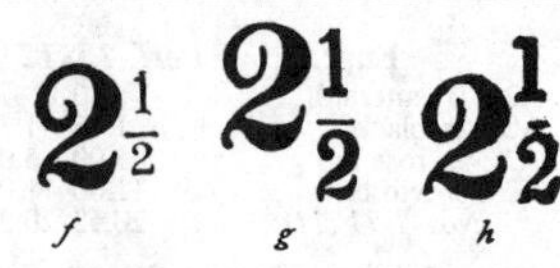
f g h

*Perf. 11 to 13*

**Unwmk.**

| No. | Type | Description | Unused | Used |
|---|---|---|---|---|
| 17 | (f) | 2½p on 6p gray blk | 6,000. | |
| 18 | (g) | 2½p on 6p gray blk | 350.00 | 350.00 |
| a. | | Horiz. pair, imperf. between | | |
| b. | | Double surcharge | 4,500. | |
| 19 | (h) | 2½p on 6p gray blk | 150.00 | 150.00 |

i

j

*Perf. 11 to 13x14 to 15*

**Wmk. 5**

| No. | Type | Description | Unused | Used |
|---|---|---|---|---|
| 20 | (i) | 2½p on 1sh vio | 1,400. | |
| 21 | (h) | 2½p on 1sh vio | 650.00 | 650.00 |
| 22 | (j) | 2½p on 1sh vio | 6,000. | |

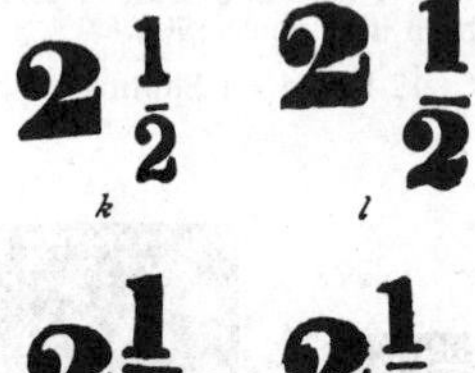
k l m n

*Perf. 11 to 13*

**Unwmk.**

| No. | Type | Description | Unused | Used |
|---|---|---|---|---|
| 24 | (k) | 2½p on 6p gray blk | 11,000. | |
| 25 | (k) | 2½p on 1sh sl bl | 11,000. | |
| 26 | (l) | 2½p on 1sh sl bl | 1,000. | |
| 27 | (m) | 2½p on 1sh sl bl | 1,500. | |
| a. | | Without fraction bar | 7,000. | |
| 28 | (n) | 2½p on 1sh sl bl | 10,000. | |

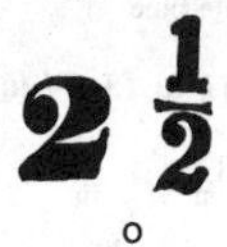
o

*Perf. 11 to 13x14 to 15*

**Wmk. 5**

| No. | Type | Description | Unused | Used |
|---|---|---|---|---|
| 29 | (l) | 2½p on 1p dl red | 300.00 | |
| 30 | (o) | 2½p on 1p dl red | 500.00 | |
| 31 | (l) | 2½p on 1sh vio | 500.00 | |
| a. | | Double surcharge of "½" | 3,500. | |
| 32 | (o) | 2½p on 1sh vio | 1,250. | |
| b. | | Double surcharge of "½" | 5,750. | |

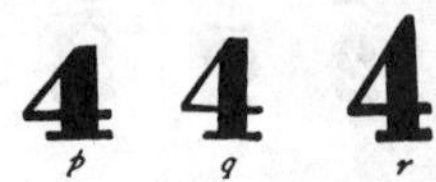
p q r

*Perf. 11 to 13*

**Unwmk.**

| No. | Type | Description | Unused | Used |
|---|---|---|---|---|
| 33 | (p) | 4p on 6p gray blk | 45.00 | 45.00 |
| 34 | (q) | 4p on 6p gray blk | 350.00 | 350.00 |
| 35 | (r) | 4p on 6p gray blk | 275.00 | 275.00 |

Copies of No. 33 with top of "4" painted in are sometimes offered as No. 35.

*Perf. 11 to 13x14 to 15*

**Wmk. 5**

| No. | Type | Description | Unused | Used |
|---|---|---|---|---|
| 36 | (r) | 4p on 1p dl red | 375.00 | 375.00 |
| a. | | Inverted surch. | 3,000. | |
| 37 | (p) | 4p on 1p dl red | 400.00 | 400.00 |
| a. | | Inverted surcharge | | |
| 38 | (p) | 4p on 1sh vio | 225.00 | 225.00 |
| 39 | (q) | 4p on 1sh vio | 3,000. | |

**Wmk. Crown and C. C. (1)**

**1881** **Engr.** ***Perf. 14***

| No. | Type | Description | Unused | Used |
|---|---|---|---|---|
| 40 | A1 | 1p brn red | 16.00 | 16.00 |
| a. | | Diagonal half used as ½p on cover | | |
| 41 | A1 | 6p ol brn | 57.50 | 45.00 |
| 42 | A1 | 1sh sl grn | 75.00 | 62.50 |

A2

A5

**1881** **Typo.**

| No. | Type | Description | Unused | Used |
|---|---|---|---|---|
| 43 | A2 | 4p ultra | 45.00 | 22.50 |

**1882-95** **Engr.** **Wmk. 2**

| No. | Type | Description | Unused | Used |
|---|---|---|---|---|
| 44 | A1 | 1p org brn ('83) | 10.50 | 12.00 |
| a. | | Half used as ½p on cover | | 1,500. |
| 45 | A1 | 1p car lake ('89) | 60 | 85 |
| 46 | A1 | 6p yel brn ('87) | 2.00 | 3.00 |
| 47 | A1 | 1sh blk brn ('87) | 1.50 | 3.00 |
| a. | | 1sh dp brn | 1.75 | 4.00 |

**Typo.**

**Die A**

| No. | Type | Description | Unused | Used |
|---|---|---|---|---|
| 48 | A2 | ½p dl grn ('84) | 2.00 | 3.50 |
| a. | | ½p bl grn ('82) | 5.50 | 6.00 |
| 49 | A2 | 2½p red brn ('82) | 7.25 | 8.00 |
| 50 | A2 | 4p gray ('84) | 4.00 | 2.25 |
| a. | | Half used as 2p on cover | | 1,200. |

**Die B**

| No. | Type | Description | Unused | Used |
|---|---|---|---|---|
| 51 | A2 | ½p gray grn ('94) | 30 | 30 |
| 52 | A2 | 2½p ultra ('93) | 70 | 70 |
| 53 | A2 | 4p dk vio & bl ('95) | 1.25 | 3.75 |

For explanation of dies A and B see back of this volume.

**1887** **Engr.** ***Perf. 12***

| No. | Type | Description | Unused | Used |
|---|---|---|---|---|
| 54 | A1 | 1p car lake | 5.00 | 5.00 |

No. 49 Surcharged in Black **One Penny**

**1889**

| No. | Type | Description | Unused | Used |
|---|---|---|---|---|
| 55 | A2 | 1p on 2½p red brn | 3.50 | 4.00 |
| a. | | Double surcharge | | |
| b. | | Double surcharge, one inverted | | |

No. 50 Surcharged in Black

Two types of surcharge:
I. Upper bar continuous across sheet.
II. Upper bar breaks between stamps.

**1893**

| No. | Type | Description | Unused | Used |
|---|---|---|---|---|
| 56 | A2 | ½p on 4p gray (I) | 90.00 | 90.00 |
| a. | | Type II | 180.00 | 105.00 |

This surcharge exists in five settings.

**1894** **Typo.**

| No. | Type | Description | Unused | Used |
|---|---|---|---|---|
| 57 | A5 | 5p ol grn & car | 1.50 | 3.75 |
| a. | | Diagonal half used as 2½p on cover | | 3,000. |

# TURKS AND CAICOS ISLANDS

LOCATION — A group of islands in the West Indies, at the southern extremity of the Bahamas.
GOVT. — British colony; a dependency of Jamaica until 1959.
AREA — 192 sq. mi.
POP. — 7,436 (1980).
CAPITAL — Grand Turk.

12 Pence = 1 Shilling
20 Shillings = 1 Pound
100 Cents = 1 U.S. Dollar (1969)

**Catalogue values for unused stamps in this country are for Never Hinged items, beginning with Scott 90.**

Dependency's Badge
A6 A7

**Wmk. Crown and C. A. (2)**

**1900** **Engr.** ***Perf. 14***

| No. | Type | Description | Unused | Used |
|---|---|---|---|---|
| 1 | A6 | ½p green | 1.65 | 2.00 |
| 2 | A6 | 1p rose | 1.50 | 1.65 |
| 3 | A6 | 2p blk brn | 45 | 60 |
| 4 | A6 | 2½p gray bl | 65 | 70 |
| a | | 2½p bl | 6.50 | 7.00 |
| 5 | A6 | 4p orange | 85 | 1.50 |
| 6 | A6 | 6p violet | 1.50 | 3.00 |
| 7 | A6 | 1sh pur brn | 1.50 | 3.00 |

**Wmk. Crown and C. C. (1)**

| No. | Type | Description | Unused | Used |
|---|---|---|---|---|
| 8 | A7 | 2sh violet | 40.00 | 60.00 |
| 9 | A7 | 3sh brn lake | 45.00 | 65.00 |
| | | *Nos. 1-9 (9)* | 93.10 | 137.45 |

**Wmk. Multiple Crown and C. A. (3)**

**1905-08**

| No. | Type | Description | Unused | Used |
|---|---|---|---|---|
| 10 | A6 | ½p green | 42 | 42 |
| 11 | A6 | 1p carmine | 7.25 | 1.65 |
| 12 | A6 | 3p vio, *yel* ('08) | 2.50 | 5.00 |

King Edward VII — A8

**1909** ***Perf. 14***

| No. | Type | Description | Unused | Used |
|---|---|---|---|---|
| 13 | A8 | ½p yel grn | 15 | 15 |
| 14 | A8 | 1p carmine | 18 | 20 |
| 15 | A8 | 2p gray | 2.50 | 3.50 |
| 16 | A8 | 2½p ultra | 1.40 | 2.00 |
| 17 | A8 | 3p vio, *yel* | 60 | 1.50 |
| 18 | A8 | 4p red, *yel* | 3.50 | 5.25 |
| 19 | A8 | 6p violet | 4.50 | 6.00 |
| 20 | A8 | 1sh *green* | 3.75 | 6.50 |
| 21 | A8 | 2sh red, *grn* | 17.50 | 32.50 |
| 22 | A8 | 3sh *red* | 19.00 | 35.00 |
| | | *Nos. 13-22 (10)* | 53.08 | 92.60 |

Turk's-Head Cactus
A9

George V
A10

**1910-11** **Wmk. 3**

| No. | Type | Description | Unused | Used |
|---|---|---|---|---|
| 23 | A9 | ¼p claret | 9 | 12 |
| 24 | A9 | ¼p red ('11) | 7 | 10 |

**1913-16**

| No. | Type | Description | Unused | Used |
|---|---|---|---|---|
| 25 | A10 | ½p yel grn | 32 | 45 |
| 26 | A10 | 1p carmine | 42 | 45 |
| 27 | A10 | 2p gray | 95 | 1.25 |
| 28 | A10 | 2½p ultra | 1.40 | 1.10 |
| 29 | A10 | 3p vio, *yel* | 60 | 1.25 |
| 30 | A10 | 4p scar, *yel* | 1.25 | 2.00 |
| 31 | A10 | 5p ol grn ('16) | 2.75 | 4.00 |
| 32 | A10 | 6p dl vio | 2.00 | 2.75 |
| 33 | A10 | 1sh orange | 1.40 | 2.75 |
| 34 | A10 | 2sh red, *bl grn* | 5.50 | 8.00 |
| a | | 2sh red, *grnsh white* | 17.50 | 32.50 |
| b | | 2sh red, *emer* | 6.25 | 8.50 |
| 35 | A10 | 3sh *red* | 11.00 | 16.00 |
| | | *Nos. 25-35 (11)* | 27.59 | 40.00 |

**1921, Apr. 23** **Wmk. 4**

| No. | Type | Description | Unused | Used |
|---|---|---|---|---|
| 36 | A9 | ¼p red | 30 | 55 |
| 37 | A10 | ½p green | 42 | 50 |
| 38 | A10 | 1p scarlet | 42 | 50 |
| 39 | A10 | 2p gray | 60 | 1.00 |
| 40 | A10 | 2½p ultra | 1.50 | 1.10 |
| 41 | A10 | 5p ol grn | 2.75 | 5.75 |
| 42 | A10 | 6p dl vio | 4.25 | 8.25 |
| 43 | A10 | 1sh brn org | 8.50 | 16.00 |
| | | *Nos. 36-43 (8)* | 18.74 | 33.65 |

A11

A12

Inscribed "Postage"

**1923-26**

| No. | Type | Description | Unused | Used |
|---|---|---|---|---|
| 44 | A9 | ¼p gray blk ('26) | 8 | 12 |
| 45 | A11 | ½p green | 20 | 25 |
| 46 | A11 | 1p brown | 75 | 90 |
| 47 | A11 | 1½p rose red ('25) | 75 | 90 |
| 48 | A11 | 2p gray | 60 | 85 |
| 49 | A11 | 2½p vio, *yel* | 30 | 35 |
| 50 | A11 | 3p ultra | 75 | 1.00 |
| 51 | A11 | 4p red, *yel* | 1.25 | 1.65 |
| 52 | A11 | 5p yel grn | 1.25 | 1.65 |
| 53 | A11 | 6p dl vio | 1.65 | 2.00 |
| 54 | A11 | 1sh orange | 1.75 | 2.25 |
| 55 | A11 | 2sh red, *grn* ('25) | 4.25 | 5.75 |

**Wmk. 3**

| No. | Type | Description | Unused | Used |
|---|---|---|---|---|
| 56 | A11 | 2sh red, *green* | 7.50 | 11.50 |
| 57 | A11 | 3sh black, *red* | 4.25 | 6.50 |
| | | *Nos. 44-57 (14)* | 25.33 | 35.67 |

Inscribed "Postage and Revenue"

**1928** **Wmk. 4**

| No. | Type | Description | Unused | Used |
|---|---|---|---|---|
| 60 | A12 | ½p green | 12 | 12 |
| 61 | A12 | 1p brown | 12 | 12 |
| 62 | A12 | 1½p red | 38 | 22 |
| 63 | A12 | 2p dk gray | 95 | 22 |
| 64 | A12 | 2½p vio, *yel* | 40 | 55 |
| 65 | A12 | 3p ultra | 48 | 85 |
| 66 | A12 | 6p brn vio | 1.25 | 2.00 |
| 67 | A12 | 1sh brn org | 1.65 | 3.00 |
| 68 | A12 | 2sh red, *grn* | 5.25 | 11.50 |
| 69 | A12 | 5sh grn, *yel* | 15.00 | 40.00 |
| 70 | A12 | 10sh vio, *bl* | 37.50 | 65.00 |
| | | *Nos. 60-70 (11)* | 63.10 | 123.58 |

**Silver Jubilee Issue**

Common Design Type

**1935, May 6** ***Perf. 11x12***

| No. | Type | Description | Unused | Used |
|---|---|---|---|---|
| 71 | CD301 | ½p grn & blk | 35 | 30 |
| 72 | CD301 | 3p ultra & brn | 85 | 65 |
| 73 | CD301 | 6p ol grn & lt bl | 1.50 | 1.25 |
| 74 | CD301 | 1sh brn vio & ind | 4.00 | 3.75 |

**Coronation Issue**

Common Design Type

**1937, May 12** ***Perf. 13½x14***

| No. | Type | Description | Unused | Used |
|---|---|---|---|---|
| 75 | CD302 | ½p dp grn | 8 | 8 |
| 76 | CD302 | 2p gray | 12 | 12 |
| 77 | CD302 | 3p brt ultra | 20 | 20 |

Raking Salt
A13

Salt Industry
A14

**1938-45** **Wmk. 4** ***Perf. 12½***

| No. | Type | Description | Unused | Used |
|---|---|---|---|---|
| 78 | A13 | ¼p black | 6 | 6 |
| 79 | A13 | ½p green | 6 | 6 |
| 80 | A13 | 1p brown | 6 | 6 |
| 81 | A13 | 1½p carmine | 8 | 6 |
| 82 | A13 | 2p gray | 10 | 10 |
| 83 | A13 | 2½p orange | 14 | 12 |
| 84 | A13 | 3p ultra | 14 | 12 |
| 85 | A13 | 6p rose vio | 1.65 | 1.25 |
| 85A | A13 | 6p blk brn ('45) | 22 | 25 |
| 86 | A13 | 1sh bister | 80 | 1.00 |
| 86A | A13 | 1sh dk ol grn ('45) | 45 | 52 |
| 87 | A14 | 2sh rose car | 80 | 1.00 |
| 88 | A14 | 5sh green | 2.50 | 3.00 |
| 89 | A14 | 10sh dp vio | 3.50 | 3.75 |
| | | *Nos. 78-89 (14)* | 10.56 | 11.35 |

**Catalogue values for unused stamps in this section, from this point to the end of the section, are for Never Hinged items.**

**Peace Issue**

Common Design Type

**1946, Nov. 4** **Engr.** ***Perf. 13½x14***

| No. | Type | Description | Unused | Used |
|---|---|---|---|---|
| 90 | CD303 | 2p gray blk | 18 | 10 |
| 91 | CD303 | 3p dp bl | 25 | 15 |

**Silver Wedding Issue**

Common Design Types

**1948, Sept. 13** **Photo.** ***Perf. 14x14½***

| No. | Type | Description | Unused | Used |
|---|---|---|---|---|
| 92 | CD304 | 1p red brn | 16 | 15 |

**Engr.; Name Typo.**

***Perf. 11½x11***

| No. | Type | Description | Unused | Used |
|---|---|---|---|---|
| 93 | CD305 | 10sh purple | 8.25 | 11.00 |

Dependency's Badge — A17

Flag and Merchant Ship — A18

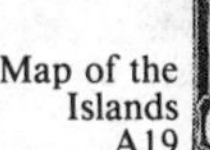

Map of the Islands A19

Victoria and George VI A20

**1948, Dec. 14 Engr. *Perf. 12½***
*94* A17 ½p green 15 16
*95* A17 2p carmine 25 28
*96* A18 3p dp bl 45 50
*97* A19 6p violet 75 85
*98* A20 2sh ultra & blk 1.25 *1.50*
*99* A20 5sh bl grn & blk 3.00 *5.25*
*100* A20 10sh choc & blk 4.50 *7.50*
*Nos. 94-100 (7)* 10.35 *16.04*

Cent. of political separation from the Bahamas.

**UPU Issue**
Common Design Types
**Engr.; Name Typo. on 3p, 6p**
***Perf. 13½, 11x11½***
**1949, Oct. 10 Wmk. 4**
*101* CD306 2½p red org 15 15
*102* CD307 3p indigo 25 25
*103* CD308 6p chocolate 50 50
*104* CD309 1sh olive 1.00 1.00

Common Design Types pictured in section before Great Britain.

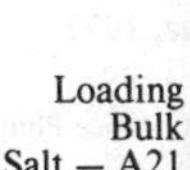
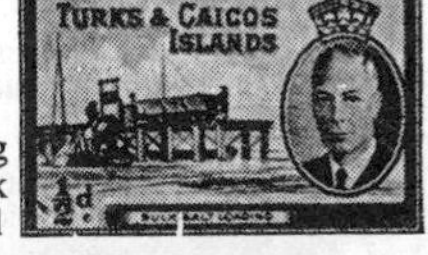
Loading Bulk Salt — A21

Dependency's Badge — A22

Designs: 1p, Salt Cay. 1½p, Caicos mail. 2p, Grand Turk. 2½p, Sponge diving. 3p, South Creek. 4p, Map. 6p, Grand Turk Light. 1sh, Government House. 1sh6p, Cockburn Harbor. 2sh, Government offices. 5sh, Salt Loading.

**1950, Aug. 2 Engr. *Perf. 12½***
*105* A21 ½p dp grn 30 10
*106* A21 1p chocolate 40 14
*107* A21 1½p carmine 50 16
*108* A21 2p red org 50 16
*109* A21 2½p ol grn 70 24
*110* A21 3p ultra 70 24
*111* A21 4p rose car & blk 1.00 35
*112* A21 6p ultra & blk 1.10 38
*113* A21 1sh bl gray & blk 1.25 45
*114* A21 1sh6p red & blk 2.50 90
*115* A21 2sh ultra & emer 3.25 1.10
*116* A21 5sh blk & ultra 5.50 2.75
*117* A22 10sh pur & blk 17.00 *7.75*
*Nos. 105-117 (13)* 34.70 *14.72*

**Coronation Issue**
Common Design Type
**1953, June 2 *Perf. 13½x13***
*118* CD312 2p red org & blk 45 35

M. S. Kirksons A23

Design: 8p, Flamingos in flight.

**1955, Feb. 1 Wmk. 4 *Perf. 12½***
*119* A23 5p emer & blk 65 52
*120* A23 8p yel brn & blk 90 70

Queen Elizabeth II — A24

Bonefish A25

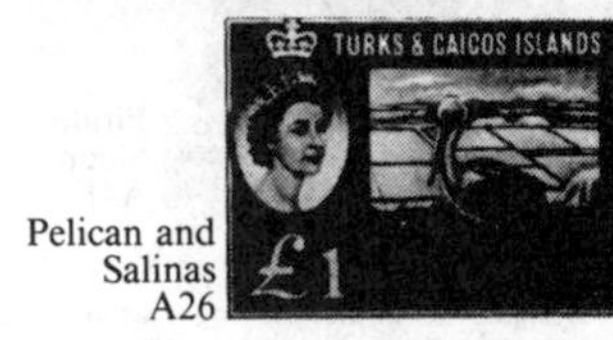
Pelican and Salinas A26

Designs: 2p, Red grouper. 2½p, Spiny lobster. 3p, Albacore. 4p, Muttonfish snapper. 5p, Permit. 6p, Conch. 8p, Flamingos. 1sh, Spanish mackerel. 1sh6p, Salt Cay. 2sh, Caicos sloop. 5sh, Cable office. 10sh, Dependency's badge.

***Perf. 13½x14 (1p), 13½x13***
**1957-60 Engr. Wmk. 314**
*121* A24 1p lil rose & dk bl 8 8
*122* A25 1½p org & sl 10 10
*123* A25 2p ol & brn red 10 10
*124* A25 2½p brt grn & car 12 12
*125* A25 3p pur & bl 14 14
*126* A25 4p blk & dp rose 18 18
*127* A25 5p brn & grn 22 22
*128* A25 6p ultra & car 30 30
*129* A25 8p blk & ver 42 42
*130* A25 1sh blk & dk bl 60 60
*131* A25 1sh6p vio bl & dk brn 1.25 1.25
*132* A25 2sh lt brn & vio bl 1.75 1.75
*133* A25 5sh brt car & blk 3.25 3.25

***Perf. 14***
*134* A26 10sh pur & blk 7.50 7.50

***Perf. 14x14½* Photo.**
*135* A26 £1 dk red & brn ('60) 20.00 20.00
*Nos. 121-135 (15)* 36.01 36.01

Map of Islands A27

***Perf. 13½x14***
**1959, July 4 Wmk. 4 Photo.**
*136* A27 6p ol grn & sal 40 45
*137* A27 8p vio & sal 50 55

Granting of a new constitution.

**Freedom from Hunger Issue**
Common Design Type
***Perf. 14x14½***
**1963, June 4 Wmk. 314**
*138* CD314 8p car rose 75 75

**Red Cross Centenary Issue**
Common Design Type
**1963, Sept. 2 Litho. *Perf. 13***
*139* CD315 2p blk & red 15 15
*140* CD315 8p ultra & red 1.00 1.00

**Shakespeare Issue**
Common Design Type
**1964, Apr. 23 Photo. *Perf. 14x14½***
*141* CD316 8p green 75 75

**ITU Issue**
Common Design Type
***Perf. 11x11½***
**1965, May 17 Litho. Wmk. 314**
*142* CD317 1p ver & brn 15 15
*143* CD317 2sh emer & lt bl 1.10 1.10

**Intl. Cooperation Year Issue**
Common Design Type
**1965, Oct. 25 Wmk. 314 *Perf. 14½***
*144* CD318 1p bl grn & cl 8 8
*145* CD318 8p lt vio & grn 75 75

**Churchill Memorial Issue**
Common Design Type
**1966, Jan. 24 Photo. *Perf. 14***
**Design in Black, Gold and Carmine Rose**
*146* CD319 1p brt bl 6 6
*147* CD319 2p green 10 10
*148* CD319 8p brown 55 55
*a* Gold impression double *200.00*
*149* CD319 1sh6p violet 1.25 1.25

**Royal Visit Issue**
Common Design Type
**1966, Feb. 4 Litho. *Perf. 11x12***
**Portraits in Black**
*150* CD320 8p vio bl 70 70
*151* CD320 1sh6p dk car rose 1.40 1.40

Andrew Symmers Landing with Union Jack A28

Designs: 8p, Andrew Symmers, his signature, Royal Warrant and Union Jack. 1sh6p, New coat of arms, Royal Cypher and St. Edward's crown.

***Perf. 13½***
**1966, Oct. 1 Unwmk. Photo.**
*152* A28 1p dk bl & dp org 6 6
*153* A28 8p dk bl, dl yel & car 30 35
*154* A28 1sh6p multi 55 65

200th anniv. of the landing of Andrew Symmers, British agent, establishing the ties with Great Britain.

**UNESCO Anniversary Issue**
Common Design Type
**Wmk. 314**
**1966, Dec. 1 Litho. *Perf. 14***
*155* CD323 1p "Education" 8 8
*156* CD323 8p "Science" 38 38
*157* CD323 1sh6p "Culture" 75 75

Turk's-head Cactus — A29

Boat Building A30

Designs: 2p, Donkey cart. 3p, Sisal industry. 4p, Conch industry. 6p, Salt industry. 8p, Skin diving. 1sh, Fishing. 1sh6p, Water skiing. 2sh, Crawfish industry. 3sh, Map of Islands. 5sh, Fishing industry. 10sh, Coat of arms. £1, Queen Elizabeth II.

***Perf. 14½x14, 14x14½***
**1967, Feb. 1 Photo. Wmk. 314**
*158* A29 1p vio, red & yel 5 5
*159* A30 1½p choc & org yel 6 6
*160* A29 2p gray, yel & sl 6 6
*161* A29 3p grn & dk brn 6 6
*162* A30 4p grnsh bl, blk & pink 8 8
*163* A29 6p bl & dk brn 12 12
*164* A29 8p aqua, dk bl & yel 20 20
*165* A30 1sh grnsh bl & red brn 35 35
*166* A29 1sh6p brt grnsh bl, yel & brn 52 52
*167* A30 2sh multi 70 70
*168* A30 3sh grnsh bl & mar 1.00 1.00
*169* A30 5sh sky bl, dk bl & yel 1.75 1.75
*170* A30 10sh multi 3.50 3.50
*171* A29 £1 dk car rose, sil & dk bl 7.00 7.00
*Nos. 158-171 (14)* 15.45 15.45

See Nos. 181, 217-230.

Turks Islands No. 1 A31

Designs: 6p, Turks Islands No. 2 and portrait of Queen Elizabeth on simulated stamp. 1sh, Turks Islands No. 3 (like 1p).

**Wmk. 314**
**1967, May 1 Photo. *Perf. 14½***
*172* A31 1p lil rose & blk 8 8
*173* A31 6p gray & blk 25 25
*174* A31 1sh Prus bl & blk 48 48

Centenary of Turks Islands stamps.

Human Rights Flame A32

**1968, Apr. 1 *Perf. 14x14½***
*175* A32 1p lt grn & multi 8 8
*176* A32 8p lt bl & multi 25 25
*177* A32 1sh6p multi 48 48

International Human Rights Year.

Martin Luther King, Jr. and Protest March of 1968 A33

**1968, Oct. 1 Photo. Wmk. 314**
*178* A33 2p dk bl, dk & lt brn 8 8
*179* A33 8p dk car rose, dk & lt brn 22 22
*180* A33 1sh6p dp vio, dk & lt brn 45 45

Martin Luther King, Jr. (1929-68), American civil rights leader.

Nos. 158-171 Surcharged

4c

Designs as before and: ¼c, Coat of arms like 10sh.

***Perf. 14x14½, 14½x14***
**1969, Sept. 8 Photo. Wmk. 314**
*181* A30 ¼c lt gray & multi 5 5
*182* A29 1c on 1p multi 5 5
*183* A29 2c on 2p multi 5 5
*184* A29 3c on 3p multi 7 7
*185* A30 4c on 4p multi 7 7
*186* A29 5c on 6p multi 10 10
*187* A29 7c on 8p multi 14 14

*188* A30 8c on 1½p multi 16 16
*189* A30 10c on 1sh multi 24 24
*190* A29 15c on 1sh6p multi 38 38
*191* A30 20c on 2sh multi 52 52
*192* A30 30c on 3sh multi 60 60
*193* A30 50c on 5sh multi 1.00 1.00
*194* A30 $1 on 10sh multi 2.50 2.50
*195* A29 $2 on £1 multi 10.50 10.50
*Nos. 181-195 (15)* 16.43 16.43

The surcharge is differently arranged on each denomination to fit the design; the old denomination is obliterated with a rectangle on the 8c and 15c.

See Nos. 217-230.

**1969 Wmk. 314 Sideways**

*182a* A29 1c on 1p 5 5
*183a* A29 2c on 2p 7 7
*184a* A29 3c on 3p 10 10
*186a* A29 5c on 6p 18 18
*187a* A29 7c on 8p 27 27
*190a* A29 15c on 1sh6p 70 70
*195a* A29 $2 on £1 7.25 7.25
*Nos. 182a-195a (7)* 8.62 8.62

Nativity with John the Baptist — A34

Designs from the Book of Hours of Eleanora, Duchess of Tuscany: 3c, 30c, Flight into Egypt.

*Perf. 13x12½*

**1969, Oct. 20 Litho. Wmk. 314**

*196* A34 1c plum & multi 5 5
*197* A34 3c dk bl & multi 6 6
*198* A34 15c ol & multi 30 30
*199* A34 30c yel brn & multi 55 55

Christmas 1969.

Coat of Arms — A35

*Perf. 13x12½*

**1970, Feb. 2 Litho. Wmk. 314**

*200* A35 7c brn & multi 15 15
*201* A35 35c vio bl & multi 75 75

Issued to commemorate the new Constitution, inaugurated June 16, 1969.

Christ Bearing the Cross, by Dürer — A36

Albrecht Dürer Engravings: 7c, Christ on the Cross. 50c, The Lamentation for Christ.

*Perf. 13½x14*

**1970, Mar. 17 Engr. Wmk. 314**

*202* A36 5c dp bl & blk 16 16
*203* A36 7c ver & blk 24 24
*204* A36 50c dk brn & multi 1.50 1.50

Easter 1970.

Dickens and "Oliver Twist" Scene A37

Designs (Charles Dickens and Scene from): 3c, "A Christmas Carol." 15c, "Pickwick Papers." 30c, "The Old Curiosity Shop."

**Litho. & Engr.**

*Perf. 13½x13*

**1970, June 17 Wmk. 314**

*205* A37 1c yel, red brn & blk 5 5
*206* A37 3c sal pink, sl & blk 9 9
*207* A37 15c sal, bl & blk 40 40
*208* A37 30c lt bl, ol & blk 85 85

Charles Dickens (1812-70), English novelist.

Red Cross Ambulance, 1870 — A38

Design: 5c, 30c, Red Cross ambulance, 1970.

**1970, Aug. 4 Litho. *Perf. 13½x14***

*209* A38 1c org & multi 5 5
*210* A38 5c ocher & multi 16 10
*211* A38 15c brt pink & multi 52 32
*212* A38 30c multi 1.00 60

Centenary of British Red Cross Society.

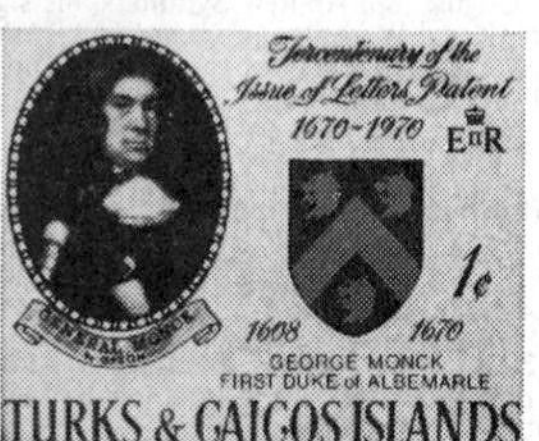

Gen. George Monck, Duke of Albemarle, and his Coat of Arms — A39

Designs: 8c, 35c, Coats of arms of Charles II and Queen Elizabeth II.

**1970, Dec. 1 Litho. *Perf. 12½x13½***

*213* A39 1c multi 6 8
*214* A39 8c multi 32 28
*215* A39 10c multi 40 35
*216* A39 35c multi 1.40 1.10

Tercentenary of the issue of Letters Patent to the Six Lords Proprietors.

Types of 1967 Values in Cents and Dollars

Designs: 1c, Turk's-head cactus. 2c, Donkey cart. 3c, Sisal industry. 4c, Conch industry. 5c, Salt industry. 7c, Skin diving. 8c, Boat building. 10c, Fishing. 15c, Water skiing. 20c, Crawfish industry. 30c, Map of Islands. 50c, Fishing industry. $1, Arms of Colony. $2, Queen Elizabeth II.

*Perf. 14x14½, 14½x14*

**1971, Feb. 2 Photo. Wmk. 314**

*217* A29 1c vio, red & yel 5 5
*218* A29 2c gray, yel & sl 6 6
*219* A29 3c grn & dk brn 9 9
*220* A30 4c grnsh bl, blk & pink 12 12
*221* A29 5c bl & dk brn 15 15
*222* A29 7c aqua, dk bl & yel 20 20
*223* A30 8c choc & org yel 25 25
*224* A30 10c grnsh bl & red brn 30 30
*225* A29 15c brt grnsh bl, yel & brn 50 50
*226* A30 20c multi 75 75
*227* A30 30c grnsh bl & mar 1.10 1.10
*228* A30 50c sky bl, dk bl & yel 1.65 1.65
*229* A30 $1 bl & multi 3.50 3.50
*230* A29 $2 dk car rose, sil & dk bl 6.75 6.75
*Nos. 217-230 (14)* 15.47 15.47

The ¼c, released with this set is a shade of No. 181, the background being a greenish, slightly darker gray.

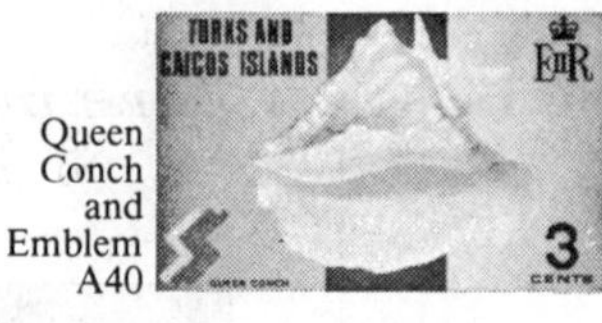

Queen Conch and Emblem A40

Tourist publicity (Sun, Sea and Sand Emblem and): 1c, Seahorse (vert.). 15c, American oyster catcher. 30c, Blue Marlin.

*Perf. 14½x14, 14x14½*

**1971, May 2 Litho. Wmk. 314**

*232* A40 1c multi 5 5
*233* A40 3c multi 10 10
*234* A40 15c multi 52 52
*235* A40 30c multi 1.00 1.00

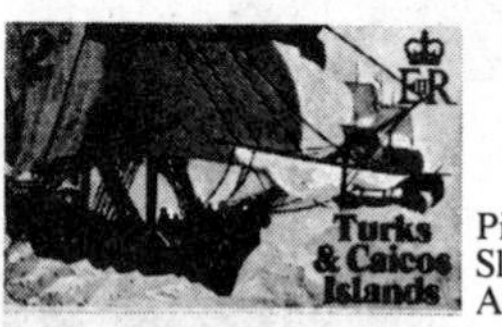

Pirate Sloop A41

Designs: 3c, Pirates burying treasure. 15c, Marooned pirate. 30c, Buccaneers.

**1971, July 17 *Perf. 14½x14***

*236* A41 2c multi 8 8
*237* A41 3c multi 12 12
*238* A41 15c multi 65 1.65
*239* A41 30c multi 1.25 1.25

Adoration of the Virgin and Child, from Wilton Diptych, French School, c. 1395
A42 A43

**1971, Oct. 12 Litho. *Perf. 14x13½***

*240* A42 2c dl brn & multi 7 6
*241* A43 2c dl brn & multi 7 6
*242* A42 8c grn & multi 22 24
*243* A43 8c grn & multi 25 24
*244* A42 15c dk bl gray & multi 50 45
*245* A43 15c dk bl gray & multi 50 45
*Nos. 240-245 (6)* 1.61 1.50

Christmas 1971.

Rocket Launch, Cape Canaveral — A44

Designs: 10c, Space capsule in orbit around earth. 15c, Map of Turks and Caicos Islands and splashdown. 20c, Distinguished Service Medal (vert.).

**1972, Feb. 21 *Perf. 13½***

*246* A44 5c lt bl & blk 16 14
*247* A44 10c multi 35 30
*248* A44 15c lt grn & multi 52 45
*249* A44 20c bl & multi 70 60

First orbital flight by U.S. astronaut Lt. Col. John H. Glenn, Jr., and splashdown off Turks and Caicos Islands, 10th anniversary.

The Three Crosses, by Rembrandt — A45

Details from Etchings by Rembrandt: 2c, Christ Before Pilate (vert.). 30c, Descent from the Cross (vert.).

*Perf. 14x13½, 13½x14*

**1972, Mar. 17**

*250* A45 2c lil & blk 6 6
*251* A45 15c pink & blk 40 40
*252* A45 30c yel & blk 85 85

Easter 1972.

Richard Grenville and "Revenge" — A46

Designs: ¼c, Christopher Columbus, Nina, Pinta and Santa Maria (vert.). 10c, Capt. John Smith and three-master (vert.). 30c, Juan Ponce de Leon and three-master.

**1972, July 4**

*253* A46 ¼c multi 5 5
*254* A46 8c multi 75 25
*255* A46 10c multi 95 32
*256* A46 30c multi 2.75 95

Discoverers and explorers of the Americas.

**Silver Wedding Issue, 1972**

Common Design Type

Design: Queen Elizabeth II, Prince Philip, turk's-head cactus and spiny lobster.

*Perf. 14x14½*

**1972, Nov. 20 Photo. Wmk. 314**

*257* CD324 10c ultra & multi 35 35
*258* CD324 20c multi 65 65

Treasure Hunting, c. 1700 — A47

Designs: 5c, Replica of silver bank medallion, 1687, obverse. 10c, Same, reverse. 30c, Scuba diver, 1973.

*Perf. 14x14½*

**1973, Jan. 18 Litho. Wmk. 314**

*259* A47 3c Prus bl & multi 12 12
*260* A47 5c plum, sil & blk 20 20
*261* A47 10c brt rose, sil & blk 40 40
*262* A47 30c vio bl & multi 1.25 1.25
*a* Souvenir sheet of 4 2.75 2.75

Treasure hunting. No. 262a contains one each of Nos. 259-262. Black inscription and drawing of ship in margin. Size: 126x107mm.

Arms of Jamaica, Turks and Caicos Islands — A48

**1973, Apr. 16 Litho. *Perf. 13½x14***

*263* A48 15c buff & multi 52 48
*264* A48 35c lt grn & multi 1.10 1.10

Centenary of annexation to Jamaica.

Sooty Tern — A49

Birds: 1c, Magnificent frigate bird. 2c, Noddy tern. 3c, Blue gray gnatcatcher. 4c, Little blue heron. 5c, Catbird. 7c, Black-whiskered vireo. 8c, Osprey. 10c, Flamingo. 15c, Brown pelican. 20c, Parula warbler. 30c, Northern mockingbird. 50c, Ruby-throated hummingbird. $1, Bahama bananaquit. $2, Cedar waxwing. $5, Painted bunting.

**Wmk. 314 Sideways**

**1973, Aug. 1 Litho. *Perf. 14***

*265* A49 ¼c yel & multi 5 5
*266* A49 1c pink & multi 9 9
*267* A49 2c org & multi 15 15
*268* A49 3c lil rose & multi 30 30
*269* A49 4c lt bl & multi 15 15
*270* A49 5c lt grn & multi 22 24
*271* A49 7c sal & multi 25 25
*272* A49 8c bl & multi 30 30
*273* A49 10c brt bl & multi 38 38
*274* A49 15c tan & multi 55 55
*275* A49 20c brt yel & multi 1.50 1.50
*276* A49 30c yel & multi 1.25 1.25
*277* A49 50c yel & multi 2.00 2.00
*278* A49 $1 bl & multi 4.25 4.25
*279* A49 $2 gray & multi 8.50 8.50
*Nos. 265-279 (15)* 19.94 19.96

**1974-75 Wmk. 314 Upright**

*266a* A49 1c pink & multi ('75) 25 25
*267a* A49 2c org & multi 50 50
*268a* A49 3c lil rose & multi ('75) 75 75
*275a* A49 20c brt yel & multi ('75) 2.50 2.50

**1976-77 Wmk. 373**

*265a* A49 ¼c yel & multi ('77) 5 5
*266b* A49 1c pink & multi ('77) 5 5
*267b* A49 2c org & multi ('77) 6 6
*268b* A49 3c lil rose & multi 7 7
*269a* A49 4c lt bl & multi ('77) 9 9
*270a* A49 5c lt grn & multi ('77) 10 10
*273a* A49 10c brt bl & multi ('77) 22 22
*274a* A49 15c tan & multi ('77) 35 35
*275b* A49 20c brt yel & multi 45 45
*276a* A49 30c yel & multi ('77) 65 65
*277a* A49 50c yel & multi ('77) 1.10 1.10
*278a* A49 $1 bl & multi ('77) 2.25 2.25
*279b* A49 $2 gray & multi ('77) 4.50 4.50
*279A* A49 $5 yel grn & multi 11.50 11.50
*Nos. 265a-279A (14)* 21.44 21.44

Bermuda Sloop — A50

Old Sailing Ships: 5c, HMS Blanche. 8c, US privateer Grand Turk and packet Hinchinbrooke. 10c, HMS Endymion. 15c, RMS Medina. 20c, HMS Daring.

**1973, July 19 Litho. *Perf. 13½***

*280* A50 2c multi 8 8
*281* A50 5c multi 24 24
*282* A50 8c multi 40 40
*283* A50 10c multi 52 52
*284* A50 15c multi 75 75
*285* A50 20c multi 1.10 1.10
*a* Souvenir sheet of 6 3.50 3.50
*Nos. 280-285 (6)* 3.09 3.09

No. 285a contains one each of Nos. 280-285. Black pen drawing of ships and birds in margin. Size: 196x101mm.

**Princess Anne's Wedding Issue**

Common Design Type

**1973, Nov. 14 Wmk. 314 *Perf. 14***

*286* CD325 12c bl grn & multi 35 35
*287* CD325 18c sl & multi 52 52

Lucayan Stool A51

Designs: Lucayan artifacts.

**1974, July 17 Litho. *Perf. 14½***

**Black & Multicolored**

*288* A51 6c *shown* 15 10
*289* A51 10c *Broken wood bowl* 24 18
*290* A51 12c *Greenstone exe* 30 22
*291* A51 18c *Wood bowl* 45 34
*292* A51 35c *Animal head, fragment of stool* 90 65
*a* Souvenir sheet of 5 3.75 4.25
*Nos. 288-292 (5)* 2.04 1.49

Carvings made by Lucayan Indians, first inhabitants of the islands. No. 292a contains one each of Nos. 288-292, black and ocher margin with white inscription. Size: 237x87mm.

Grand Turk G.P.O. A52

Designs (UPU Emblem and): 12c, Map of Turks and Caicos Islands and local mail sloop. 18c, "United Service" (globe and "UPU"). 55c, Design symbolic of the Islands joining the UPU in 1881.

**1974, Oct. 9 Wmk. 314 *Perf. 14***

*293* A52 4c yel & multi 10 8
*294* A52 12c bl & multi 28 25
*295* A52 18c vio & multi 40 38
*296* A52 55c lt bl & multi 1.25 1.10

Centenary of Universal Postal Union.

"His Finest Hour" A53

Design: 12c, Churchill and Franklin D. Roosevelt.

**1974, Nov. 30 Wmk. 373**

*297* A53 12c multi 42 50
*298* A53 18c multi 60 75
*a* Souvenir sheet of 2 1.10 1.50

Sir Winston Churchill (1874-1965), birth centenary. No. 298a contains one each of Nos. 297-298, blue, black and red margin. Size: 85x85mm.

*Turks and Caicos Islands stamps can be mounted in Scott's annually supplemented British North and West Caribbean Album.*

Spanish Captain, c. 1492 — A54

Old Windmill, Salt Cay — A55

Uniforms: 20c, Officer, Royal Artillery, 1783. 25c, Officer, 67th Foot, 1798. 35c, Private, First West India Regiment, 1833.

**1975, Mar. 26 Wmk. 314 *Perf. 14½***

*299* A54 5c bl & multi 15 15
*300* A54 20c bl & multi 65 60
*301* A54 25c bl & multi 75 70
*302* A54 35c bl & multi 1.10 1.00
*a* Souvenir sheet of 4 4.00 5.00

No. 302a contains one each of Nos. 299-302; black marginal inscription and blue ornaments. Size: 145x88mm.

**1975, Oct. 16 Litho. Wmk. 373**

Salt industry: 10c, Pink salt pans (horiz.). 20c, Salt raking at Salt Cay (horiz.). 25c, Unprocessed salt ready for shipment.

*303* A55 6c vio & multi 20 15
*304* A55 10c lt brn & multi 35 25
*305* A55 20c red & multi 70 50
*306* A55 25c mag & multi 90 60

Star Coral A56

**1975, Dec. 4 Litho. Wmk. 373**

*307* A56 6c *shown* 20 15
*308* A56 10c *Elkhorn coral* 32 25
*309* A56 20c *Brain coral* 65 50
*310* A56 25c *Staghorn coral* 85 60

Schooner — A57

Designs: 20c, Ship of the line. 25c, Frigate Grand Turk. 55c, Ketch.

**1976, May 28 *Perf. 14x13½***

*311* A57 6c org & multi 38 10
*312* A57 20c vio bl & multi 1.10 35
*313* A57 25c brn & multi 1.25 45
*314* A57 55c multi 2.25 1.00
*a* Souvenir sheet of 4 6.00 7.50

American Bicentennial. No. 314a contains one each of Nos. 311-314; multicolored margin shows American flags, Great Seal of the U.S. Size: 95x150mm.

Turks and Caicos Islands No. 151 A58

Design: 25c, Turks and Caicos Islands No. 150.

**Wmk. 373**

**1976, July 14 Litho. *Perf. 14½***

*315* A58 20c car & multi 70 55
*316* A58 25c vio bl & multi 85 70

Visit of Queen Elizabeth II and Prince Philip to the Caribbean, 10th anniversary.

Virgin and Child, by Carlo Dolci — A59

Christmas: 10c, Virgin and Child with St. John, by Botticelli. 20c, Adoration of the Kings, from Retable by the Master of Paradise. 25c, Adoration of the Kings, illuminated page, French, 15th century.

***Perf. 14x13½***

**1976, Nov. 10 Litho. Wmk. 373**

*317* A59 6c multi 10 10
*318* A59 10c org & multi 22 22
*319* A59 20c red lil & multi 45 45
*320* A59 25c multi 55 55

Queen with Regalia — A60

Designs: 6c, Queen presenting Order of British Empire to E. T. Wood, Grand Turk, 1966. 55c, Royal family on balcony of Buckingham Palace. $5, Portrait of Queen from photograph taken during her 1966 visit to Grand Turk.

**1977 Litho. *Perf. 14x13½***

*321* A60 6c multi 14 15
*322* A60 25c multi 50 55
*323* A60 55c multi 1.10 1.10

**Souvenir Sheet**

***Perf. 14***

*324* A60 $5 multi 9.00 7.50

25th anniv. of the reign of Elizabeth II.

No. 324 has green & multicolored margin showing map of islands, coat of arms and crowns. Size: 120x96mm.

Nos. 322 and 323 were also issued in booklet panes of 2.

Issue dates: Nos. 321-323, Feb. 7. No. 324, Dec. 6.

Friendship 7 Capsule — A61

Designs: 3c, Lunar rover (vert.). 6c, Tracking Station on Grand Turk. 20c, Moon landing craft (vert.). 25c, Col. Glenn's rocket leaving launching pad (vert.). 50c, Telstar 1 satellite.

**Wmk. 373**

**1977, June 20 Litho. *Perf. 13½***

*325* A61 1c multi 5 5
*326* A61 3c multi 6 6
*327* A61 6c multi 14 12
*328* A61 20c multi 45 40

*329* A61 25c multi 55 50
*330* A61 50c multi 1.10 1.00
*Nos. 325-330 (6)* 2.35 2.13

U.S. Tracking Station on Grand Turk, 25th anniversary.

Adoration of the Kings, 1634 by Rubens — A63

Rubens Paintings: ¼c, Flight into Egypt. 1c, Adoration of the Kings, 1624. 6c, Madonna with Garland. 20c, $1, Virgin and Child Adored by Angels. $2, Adoration of the Kings, 1618.

**1977, Dec. 23**

*331* A63 ¼c multi 5 5
*332* A63 ½c multi 5 5
*333* A63 1c multi 5 5
*334* A63 6c multi 12 9
*335* A63 20c multi 35 28
*336* A63 $2 multi 3.50 3.50
*Nos. 331-336 (6)* 4.12 4.02

**Souvenir Sheet**

*337* A63 $1 multi 1.90 1.90

Christmas 1977 and 400th birth anniversary of Peter Paul Rubens (1577-1640). No. 337 contains one stamp. Salmon and brown margin shows Rubens drawings. Size: 100x80mm.

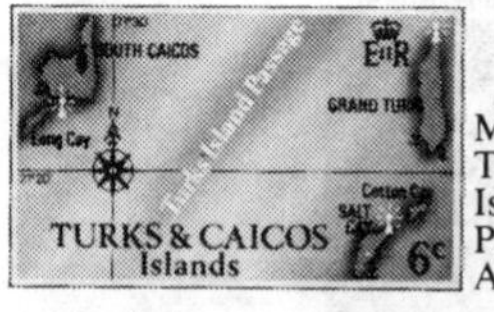


Map of Turks Island Passage A64

Designs: 20c, Grand Turk lighthouse and sailboat (LUG cargo vessel). 25c, Deepsea fishing yacht. 55c, S.S. Jamaica Planter.

**Wmk. 373**

**1978, Feb. 2 Litho. *Perf. 13½***

*338* A64 6c multi 12 12
*339* A64 20c multi 40 35
*340* A64 25c multi 50 45
*341* A64 55c multi 1.10 1.10
*a* Souvenir sheet of 4, unwmkd. 2.75 3.50

Turks Island Passage, a major Caribbean shipping route.

No. 341a contains one each of Nos. 338-341. Multicolored margin shows map of area and merchantmen. Size: 135x88mm. Exists watermarked.

Queen Victoria in Coronation Regalia — A65

British Monarchs in Coronation Regalia: 10c, Edward VII. 25c, George V. $2, George VI. $2.50, Elizabeth II.

**1978, June 2 Litho. *Perf. 14***

*342* A65 6c multi 10 8
*343* A65 10c multi 15 12
*344* A65 25c multi 40 30
*345* A65 $2 multi 3.25 2.50

**Souvenir Sheet**

*346* A65 $2.50 multi 4.25 3.25

25th anniversary of coronation of Queen Elizabeth II. No. 346 has multicolored margin showing heraldic flowers and Queen's monogram. Size: 161x103½mm.

Nos. 342-345 were also issued in sheets of 3 plus label showing ruler's portrait. Perf. 12, multicolored margin. Size: 157x128mm.

Wilbur Wright and Flyer 3 A66

Designs: 6c, Cessna 337 and Wright brothers. 10c, Southeast Airlines' Electra and Orville Wright. 15c, C47 cargo plane on South Caicos runway. 35c, Norman-Britten Islander at Grand Turk airport. $1, Orville Wright and Flyer, 1902. $2, Wilbur Wright and Flyer.

**1978, June 29 Litho. *Perf. 14½***

*347* A66 1c multi 5 5
*348* A66 6c multi 10 9
*349* A66 10c multi 18 15
*350* A66 15c multi 30 24
*351* A66 35c multi 1.75 60
*352* A66 $2 multi 3.75 3.00
*Nos. 347-352 (6)* 6.13 4.13

**Souvenir Sheet**

*353* A66 $1 multi 2.00 1.50

Aviation progress. No. 353 has multicolored margin showing air routes to Turks and Caicos Islands. Size: 112x84mm.

Queen Elizabeth II A67

Designs: 15c, Ampulla and anointing spoon. 25c, St. Edward's crown.

**1978, July 24 Litho. *Imperf.***

**Self-adhesive**

*354* Souvenir booklet 7.00
*a* A67 Bklt. pane of 3 (15c, 25c, $2) 4.25 4.25
*b* A67 Bklt. pane of 6 (3 each, 15c, 25c) 2.50 2.50

25th anniversary of coronation of Queen Elizabeth II. No. 354 contains Nos. 354a-354b printed on peelable paper backing with music and text of hymns. Size of panes: 154x93mm.

Hurdling A68

**1978, Aug. 3 Litho. *Perf. 15***

*355* A68 6c shown 10 8
*356* A68 20c Weight lifting 32 28
*357* A68 55c Boxing 90 75
*358* A68 $2 Bicycling 3.25 2.75

**Souvenir Sheet**

*359* A68 $1 Sprinting 2.75 2.50

11th Commonwealth Games, Edmonton, Canada, Aug. 3-12. No. 359 has multicolored margin showing runners. Size: 106x80mm.

Fish A69

**1978-79 Litho. *Perf. 14***

*360* A69 1c Indigo hamlet 5 5
*a* Perf. 12½x12 ('81) 5 5
*361* A69 2c Tobacco fish 5 5
*362* A69 3c Passing Jack 6 6
*363* A69 4c Porkfish 6 6
*364* A69 5c Spanish grunt 9 9
*a* Perf. 12½x12 ('81) 9 9
*365* A69 7c Yellowtail snapper 12 12
*366* A69 8c Foureye butterflyfish 14 14
*367* A69 10c Yellow fin grouper 16 16
*a* Perf. 12½x12 ('81) 16 16
*368* A69 15c Beau Gregory 25 25
*369* A69 20c Queen angelfish 35 35
*a* Perf. 12½x12 ('81) 35 35
*370* A69 30c Hogfish 50 50
*371* A69 50c Fairy Basslet 85 85
*a* Perf. 12½x12 ('81) 85 85
*372* A69 $1 Clown wrasse 1.65 1.65
*a* Perf. 12½x12 ('81) 1.65 1.65
*373* A69 $2 Stoplight parrotfish 3.50 3.50
*a* Perf. 12½x12 ('81) 3.50 3.50
*374* A69 $5 Queen triggerfish 8.50 8.50
*a* Perf. 12½x12 ('81) 8.50 8.50
*Nos. 360-374 (15)* 16.33 16.33
*Nos. 360a-374a (8)* 15.15 15.15

Issue dates: 1c, 3c, 5c, 10c, 15c, 20c, Nov. 17, 1978; others Feb. 6, 1979.

Virgin with the Goldfinch, by Dürer — A70

Dürer Paintings: 20c, Virgin and Child with St. Anne. 35c, Nativity (horiz.). $1, Adoration of the Kings (horiz.). $2, Praying Hands.

**1978, Dec. 11 Litho. *Perf. 14***

*375* A70 6c multi 8 7
*376* A70 20c multi 28 24
*377* A70 35c multi 50 42
*378* A70 $2 multi 2.75 2.50

**Souvenir Sheet**

*379* A70 $1 multi 1.50 1.50

Christmas 1978 and 450th death anniversary of Albrecht Dürer (1471-1528), German painter.

No. 379 has multicolored margin showing beach scene. Size: 136x122mm.

Ospreys A71

Endangered Species: 20c, Green turtle. 25c, Queen conch. 55c, Rough-toothed dolphin. $1, Humpback whale. $2, Iguana.

**1979, May 17 Litho. *Perf. 14***

*380* A71 6c multi 10 8
*381* A71 20c multi 35 24
*382* A71 25c multi 42 30
*383* A71 55c multi 95 65
*384* A71 $1 multi 1.65 1.25
*Nos. 380-384 (5)* 3.47 2.52

**Souvenir Sheet**

*385* A71 $2 multi 3.75 2.50

No. 385 has multicolored margin showing beach scene. Size: 118x85mm.

The Beloved, by Dante Gabriel Rossetti A72

Paintings and IYC Emblem: 25c, Tahitian Girl, by Paul Gauguin. 55c, Calmady Children, by Sir Thomas Lawrence. $1, Mother and Daughter (detail), by Gauguin. $2, Marchesa Elena Grimaldi, by Van Dyck.

**1979, July 2 Litho. *Perf. 14***

*386* A72 6c multi 10 8
*387* A72 25c multi 42 30
*388* A72 55c multi 95 65
*389* A72 $1 multi 1.65 1.75

**Souvenir Sheet**

*390* A72 $2 multi 3.50 3.00

International Year of the Child. No. 390 has multicolored margin with IYC emblem and cassia flowers. Size: 113x86mm.

Stampless Cover and "Medina" A73

Designs: 20c, Map of Islands and Rowland Hill. 45c, Stamped envelope and "Orinoco." 75c, Paddlewheeler "Shannon" and letter. $1, Royal Packet "Trent," map of Islands. $2, New and old seals.

***Perf. 14, 12 ($2)***

**1979, Aug. 27 Litho.**

*391* A73 6c multi 10 8
*392* A73 20c multi 35 24
*393* A73 45c multi 75 55
*394* A73 75c multi 1.25 90
*395* A73 $1 multi 1.65 1.25
*396* A73 $2 multi ('80) 3.50 3.50
*a* Souv. sheet of 1, perf. 14 ('79) 3.50 3.50
*Nos. 391-396 (6)* 7.60 6.52

Nos. 391-395 were issued in sheets of 40, and in sheets of 5 stamps and label, in changed colors, perf. 12. Multicolored sheet margins show Penny Black and Hill.

No. 396 issued May 6, 1980 in sheet of 5 plus label picturing signal flags and map.

No. 396a overprinted: "BRASILIANA 79"

**Souvenir Sheet**

**1979, Sept. 10 Litho. *Perf. 14***

*397* A73 $2 multi 3.75 3.75

Brasiliana 79, Comprising 1st Interamerican Exhibition of Classical Philately and 3rd World Topical Exhibition, Rio de Janeiro, Sept. 15-23. Size 170x113½mm.

Cuneiform Script — A74

Designs: 5c, Egyptian papyrus; Chinese writing. 15c, Greek runner; Roman post horse; Roman ship. 25c, Pigeon post; railway post; steamship postal packet. 40c, Balloon post; first airmail plane; supersonic airmail jet. $1, Original stamp press (3 designs each of 5c, 15c, 25c, 40).

***Imperf. x Roulette 9***

**1979, Sept. 27 Litho.**

**Self-adhesive**

*398* Souvenir booklet *6.60*
*a* A74 Booklet pane of 1 ($1)
*b* A74 Booklet pane of 6 (5cx3, 15cx3)
*c* A74 Booklet pane of 6 (25cx3, 40cx3)

Sir Rowland Hill (1795-1879), originator of penny postage. No. 398 contains 3 booklet panes printed on peelable paper backing with descriptions of stamp designs. No. 398a has light and dark brown margin with Hill statue. Size of pane: 148½x92mm.

International Year of the Child A74a

Designs: Aquatic scenes.

**1979, Nov. 2 Litho. *Perf. 11***

399 A74a 1/4c *Pluto and starfish* 5 5
400 A74a 1/2c *Minnie Mouse* 5 5
401 A74a 1c *Mickey Mouse skin-diving* 5 5
402 A74a 2c *Goofy riding turtle* 5 5
403 A74a 3c *Donald and dolphin* 6 5
404 A74a 4c *Mickey Mouse and fish* 8 5
405 A74a 5c *Goofy surfing* 12 5
406 A74a 25c *Pluto and lobster* 60 25
407 A74a $1 *Daisy Duck waterskiing* 2.50 1.00
*Nos. 399-407 (9)* 3.56 1.60

**Souvenir Sheet**

***Perf. 13 1/2x14***

408 A74a $1.50 *Goofy* 3.25 1.50

No. 408 has multicolored margin showing waterskis and ocean. Size: 126 1/2x96 1/2mm.

St. Nicholas, Icon, 17th Century — A75

Icons or Illuminations: 3c, Emperor Otto II, 10th century. 6c, St. John, Book of Lindisfarne. 15c, Christ and angels. 20c, Christ attended by angels, Book of Kells, 9th century. 25c, St. John the Evangelist. 65c, Christ enthroned, 17th century. $1, St. John, 8th century. $2, St. Matthew, Book of Lindisfarne.

**1979, Nov. 26**

409 A75 1c multi 5 5
410 A75 3c multi 6 6
411 A75 6c multi 10 8
412 A75 15c multi 25 20
413 A75 20c multi 35 25
414 A75 25c multi 42 32
415 A75 65c multi 1.10 85
416 A75 $1 multi 1.65 1.25
*Nos. 409-416 (8)* 3.98 3.06

**Souvenir Sheet**

417 A75 $2 multi 3.50 2.50

Christmas 1979. No. 417 has multicolored margin showing illumination border. Size: 116x133mm.

Christina's World, by Andrew Wyeth — A76

Art Treasures: 10c, Ivory leopards, Benin, 19th century. 20c, The Kiss, by Gustav Klimt (vert.). 25c, Portrait of a Lady, by Rogier van der Weyden (vert.). 80c, Sumerian bull's head harp, 2600 B.C. (vert.). $1, The Wave, by Hokusai. $2, Holy Family, by Rembrandt (vert.).

**1979, Dec. 19 Litho. *Perf. 13 1/2***

418 A76 6c multi 10 8
419 A76 10c multi 16 12
420 A76 20c multi 35 25
421 A76 25c multi 42 32
422 A76 80c multi 1.40 1.10
423 A76 $1 multi 1.65 1.25
*Nos. 418-423 (6)* 4.08 3.12

**Souvenir Sheet**

424 A76 $2 multi 3.50 2.50

No. 424 has multicolored margin showing entire painting. Size: 111x139 1/2mm.

Pied-billed Grebe — A77

**1980, Feb. 20 Litho. *Perf. 14***

425 A77 20c *shown* 35 25
426 A77 25c *Ovenbirds* 45 32
427 A77 35c *Marsh hawks* 65 45
428 A77 55c *Yellow-bellied sapsucker* 1.00 65
429 A77 $1 *Blue-winged teals* 1.75 1.25
*Nos. 425-429 (5)* 4.20 2.92

**Souvenir Sheet**

430 A77 $2 *Glossy ibis* 4.75 4.00

No. 430 has multicolored margin showing birds. Size: 106 1/2x81mm.

Stamp Under Magnifier, Perforation Gauge, London 1980 Emblem A78

**1980, May 6 Litho. *Perf. 14x14 1/2***

431 A78 25c *shown* 42 42
432 A78 40c *Stamp in tongs, gauge* 70 70

**Souvenir Sheet**

433 A78 $2 *Exhibition Hall* 3.50 2.50

London 1980 International Stamp Exhibition, May 6-14. No. 433 has multicolored margin showing London landmarks, flags, London 1980 emblem. Size: 76x97 1/2mm.

Trumpet Triton A79

**1980, June 26 Litho. *Perf. 14***

434 A79 15c *shown* 25 25
435 A79 20c *Measled cowry* 35 35
436 A79 30c *True tulip* 50 50
437 A79 45c *Lion's paw* 75 75
438 A79 55c *Sunrise tellin* 95 95
439 A79 70c *Grown cone* 1.25 1.25
*Nos. 434-439 (6)* 4.05 4.05

Queen Mother Elizabeth, 80th Birthday — A80

**1980, Aug. 4 Litho. *Perf. 14***

440 A80 80c multi 2.25 2.50

**Souvenir Sheet**

***Perf. 12***

441 A80 $1.50 multi 2.50 2.50

No. 441 has blue and black decorative margin. Size: 57x80mm.

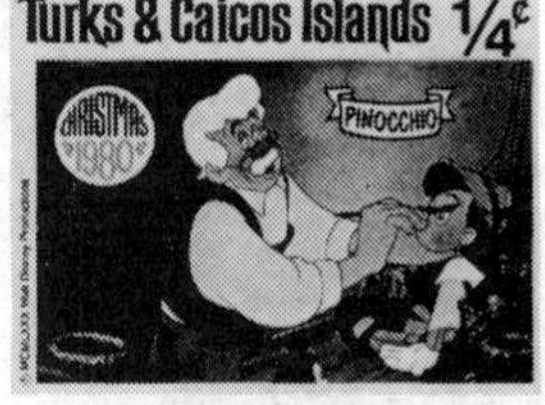


Pinocchio — A81

Designs: Scenes from Walt Disney's Pinocchio.

**1980, Sept. 25 *Perf. 11***

442 A81 1/4c multi 5 5
443 A81 1/2c multi 5 5
444 A81 1c multi 5 5
445 A81 2c multi 5 5
446 A81 3c multi 6 6
447 A81 4c multi 8 8
448 A81 5c multi 10 10
449 A81 75c multi 1.50 1.50
450 A81 $1 multi 2.00 2.00
*Nos. 442-450 (9)* 3.94 3.94

**Souvenir Sheet**

451 A81 $2 multi, vert. 4.00 4.00

Christmas 1980. No. 451 has multicolored margin showing Geppetto dancing. Size: 127x102mm.

Medical Examination, Lions — A82

**1980, Oct. 8 Litho. *Perf. 14***

452 A82 10c *shown* 16 16
453 A82 15c *Scholarships, Kiwanis* 25 25
454 A82 45c *Education, Soroptimists* 75 75
455 A82 $1 *Lobster boat, Rotary* 1.65 1.65

**Souvenir Sheet**

456 A82 $2 *Funds for schools, Rotary* 4.00 4.00

Lions, Rotary, Kiwanis and Soroptimists service organizations; 75th anniversary of Rotary International. No. 456 has multicolored margin showing school and service organization emblems. Size: 101x75mm.

Martin Luther King, Jr. (1929-68) — A83

Human Rights Leaders: 30c, John F. Kennedy. 45c, Roberto Clemente (1934-72), baseball player. 70c, Frank Worrel (1927-67), cricket player. $1, Harriet Tubman (1823-1913), born slave, helped others escape to freedom. $2, Marcus Garvey (1887-1940), Jamaican black nationalist leader.

**1980, Dec. 22 Litho. *Perf. 14***

457 A83 20c multi 35 35
458 A83 30c multi 50 50
459 A83 45c multi 75 75
460 A83 70c multi 1.25 1.25
461 A83 $1 multi 1.65 1.65
*Nos. 457-461 (5)* 4.50 4.50

**Souvenir Sheet**

462 A83 $2 multi 3.75 3.75

No. 462 has multicolored margin showing loading dock. Size: 104x79mm.

Racing Yachts A84

Designs: Racing yachts.

**1981, Jan. 29 Litho. *Perf. 14***

463 A84 6c multi 10 10
464 A84 15c multi 25 25
465 A84 35c multi 60 60
466 A84 $1 multi 1.65 1.65

**Souvenir Sheet**

467 A84 $2 multi 4.00 4.00

South Caicos Regatta. No. 467 contains one stamp (28x42mm.); multicolored margin shows map of Turks and Caicos islands, Prince Philip. Size: 114x85mm.

Pluto Listening to Sea Shell — A85

**1981, Feb. 16 *Perf. 13 1/2x14***

468 A85 10c shown 25 25
469 A85 75c Pluto on raft, dolphin 1.90 1.90

**Souvenir Sheet**

470 A85 $1.50 Pluto 3.00 3.00

50th anniversary of Walt Disney's Pluto. No. 470 has multicolored margin showing scene from Simple Things, 1953. Size: 127x102mm.

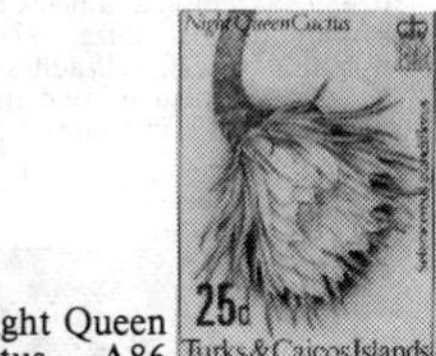


Night Queen Cactus — A86

**1981, Feb. 10 *Perf. 14***

471 A86 25c shown 45 45
472 A86 35c Ripsaw cactus 65 65
473 A86 55c Royal strawberry cactus 1.00 1.00
474 A86 80c Caicos cactus 1.50 1.50

**Souvenir Sheet**

475 A86 $2 Turks head cactus 4.00 4.00

No. 475 has multicolored margin showing flowering cactus. Size: 72x87mm.

Donald Duck and Louie with Easter Egg — A87

Easter 1981: Various Disney characters with Easter eggs.

**1981, Mar. 20 Litho. *Perf. 11***

476 A87 10c multi 25 25
477 A87 25c multi 65 65
478 A87 60c multi 1.65 1.65
479 A87 80c multi 2.00 2.00

**Souvenir Sheet**

*480* A87 $4 multi 8.00 8.00

No. 480 has multicolored margin showing Chip and Dale in floating basket of eggs. Size: 127x102mm.

Woman with Fan, 1909 — A88

**1981, May 28 Litho. *Perf. 14***

*481* A88 20c shown 35 35
*482* A88 45c Woman with Pears, 1909 80 80
*483* A88 80c The Accordionist, 1911 1.50 1.50
*484* A88 $1 The Aficionado, 1912 1.50 1.50

**Souvenir Sheet**

*485* A88 $2 Girl with a Mandolin, 1910 4.00 4.00

Pablo Picasso (1881-1973). No. 485 has multicolored margin showing violin and Sheet Music. Size: 102½x128mm.

**Royal Wedding Issue**
Common Design Type

**1981, June 23 Litho. *Perf. 14***

*486* CD331 35c Couple 60 60
*487* CD331 65c Kensington Palace 1.10 1.10
*488* CD331 90c Charles 1.50 1.50

**Souvenir Sheet**

*489* CD331 $2 Glass coach 3.50 3.50

**Booklet**

*490* CD331 14.00
*a* Pane of 6 (3x20c, Lady Diana, 3x$1, Charles) 9.00
*b* Pane of 1, $2, Couple 5.00

No. 489 has lemon and black margin showing heraldic designs. Size: 97x83mm. No. 490 contains imperf., self-adhesive stamps.
Nos. 486-488 also printed in sheets of 5 plus label, perf. 12, in changed colors.

Underwater Marine Biology Observation — A89

**1981, Aug. 21 Litho. *Perf. 14***

*491* A89 15c shown 28 28
*492* A89 40c Underwater photography 70 70
*493* A89 75c Diving for wreckage 1.40 1.40
*494* A89 $1 Diver, dolphins 1.75 1.75

**Souvenir Sheet**

*495* A89 $2 Diving flag 4.00 4.00

No. 495 has multicolored margin showing coral. Size: 91x76mm.

Brer Rabbit Barricading his Door — A90

Christmas 1981: Scenes from Walt Disney's Uncle Remus.

**1981, Nov. 2 Litho. *Perf. 14x13½***

*496* A90 ¼c multi 5 5
*497* A90 ½c multi 5 5
*498* A90 1c multi 5 5
*499* A90 2c multi 5 5
*500* A90 3c multi 6 6
*501* A90 4c multi 8 8
*502* A90 5c multi 10 10
*503* A90 75c multi 1.50 1.50
*504* A90 $1 multi 2.00 2.00
*Nos. 496-504 (9)* 3.94 3.94

**Souvenir Sheet**

*505* A90 $2 multi 5.00 5.00

No. 505 has multicolored margin continuing design. Size: 129x103mm.

Flags of Turks and Caicos Islands A91

Maps of Various Islands: a. Grand Turk. b. Salt Cay. c. South Caicos. d. East Caicos. e. Middle Caicos. f. North Caicos. g. Caicos Cays. h. Providenciales. i. West Caicos.

**1981, Dec. 1 *Perf. 14***

*506* Strip of 10 3.50 3.50
*a.-j.* A91 20c, any single 35 35

Caribbean Buckeyes A92

Scouting Year A93

**1982, Jan. 21 Litho. *Perf. 14***

*507* A92 20c shown 40 40
*508* A92 35c Clench's hairstreaks 70 70
*509* A92 65c Gulf fritillarys 1.30 1.30
*510* A92 $1 Bush sulphurs 2.00 2.00

**Souvenir Sheet**

*511* A92 $2 Turk Isld. leaf butterfly 4.00 4.00

No. 511 has multicolored margin showing butterflies on branches. Size: 72x56mm.

**1982, Feb. 17 Litho. *Perf. 14***

*512* A93 40c Flag ceremony 65 65
*513* A93 50c Building raft 80 80
*514* A93 75c Cricket match 1.25 1.25
*515* A93 $1 Nature study 1.50 1.50

**Souvenir Sheet**

*516* A93 $2 Baden-Powell, salute 3.50 3.50

No. 516 has multicolored margin showing activities. Size: 100x70mm.

1982 World Cup Soccer — A94

Designs: Various soccer players.

**1982, Apr. 30 Litho. *Perf. 14***

*517* A94 10c multi 18 18
*518* A94 25c multi 45 45
*519* A94 45c multi 80 80
*520* A94 $1 multi 1.75 1.75

**Souvenir Sheet**

*521* A94 $2 multi, horiz. 3.50 3.50

Nos. 517-520 issued in sheets of 5 plus label. No. 521 has multicolored margin continuing design. Size: 118x83mm.

Phillis Wheatley (1753-1784), Poet, and Washington Crossing Delaware — A95

Washington's 250th Birth Anniv. and F.D. Roosevelt's Birth Centenary: 35c, Washington, Benjamin Banneker (1731-1806), astronomer and mathematician, map. 65c, FDR, George Washington Carver (1864-1943). 80c, FDR with stamp collection. $2, FDR examining Washington stamp.

**1982, May 3 Litho. *Perf. 14***

*522* A95 20c multi 40 40
*523* A95 35c multi 70 70
*524* A95 65c multi 1.30 1.30
*525* A95 80c multi 1.60 1.60

**Souvenir Sheet**

*526* A95 $2 multi 4.00 4.00

No. 526 has multicolored margin continuing design. Size: 102x72mm.

Second Thoughts, by Norman Rockwell — A96

**1982, June 23 Litho. *Perf. 14x13½***

*527* A96 8c shown 14 14
*528* A96 15c The Proper Gratuity 28 28
*529* A96 20c Before the Shot 35 35
*530* A96 25c The Three Umpires 45 45

**Princess Diana Issue**
Common Design Type

**1982 Litho. *Perf. 14½x14***

*530A* CD332 8c Sandringham 12 12
*530B* CD332 35c Wedding 55 55
*530C* CD332 $1.10 Diana 1.75 1.75

**1982, July 1 *Perf. 14½x14***

*531* CD332 55c Sandringham 1.00 1.00
*532* CD332 70c Wedding 1.00 1.00
*533* CD332 $1 Diana 1.75 1.75

Also issued in sheetlets of 5 + label.

**Souvenir Sheet**

*534* CD332 $2 Diana, diff. 4.00 4.00

No. 534 has multicolored margin showing family tree, Winston Churchill. Size: 103x77mm.

Skymaster over Caicos Cays — A97

**1982, Aug. 26 Litho. *Perf. 14***

*535* A97 8c shown 14 14
*536* A97 15c Jetstar, Grand Turk 28 28
*537* A97 65c Helicopter, South Caicos 1.10 1.10
*538* A97 $1.10 Seaplane, Providenciales 2.00 2.00

**Souvenir Sheet**

*539* A97 $2 Boeing 727 4.00 4.00

No. 539 has multicolored margin continuing design. Size: 100x69mm.

Christmas 1982 — A98

Designs: Scenes from Walt Disney's Mickey's Christmas Carol.

**1982, Dec. 1 Litho. *Perf. 13½***

*540* A98 1c multi 5 5
*541* A98 1c multi 5 5
*542* A98 2c multi 5 5
*543* A98 2c multi 5 5
*544* A98 3c multi 6 6
*545* A98 3c multi 6 6
*546* A98 4c multi 8 8
*547* A98 65c multi 2.00 2.00
*548* A98 $1.10 multi 3.50 3.50
*Nos. 540-548 (9)* 5.90 5.90

**Souvenir Sheet**

*549* A98 $2 multi 4.50 4.50

Trams and Locomotives — A99

**1983, Jan. 18 Litho. *Perf. 14***

*550* A99 15c West Caicos trolley tram 25 25
*551* A99 55c West Caicos steam locomotive 95 95
*552* A99 90c Mule-drawn tram, East Caicos 1.50 1.50
*553* A99 $1.60 Sisal locomotive, East Caicos 2.75 2.75

**Souvenir Sheet**

*554* A99 $2.50 Steam engine 4.50 4.50

No. 554 has multicolored margin continuing design. Size: 100x70mm.

**Commonwealth Day**
Common Design Type

**1983, Mar. 14**

*555* CD334 1c Woman crossing guard 5 5
*556* CD334 8c Wind and solar energy sources 14 14
*557* CD334 65c Sailing 1.10 1.10
*558* CD334 $1 Cricket game 1.75 1.75

Nos. 555-558 se-tenant.

Easter 1983 — A100

Crucifixion, by Raphael. $2.50 shows entire painting.

**1983, Apr. 7 Litho. *Perf. 14***

*559* A100 35c Mary Magdalene, St. John 60 60
*560* A100 50c Mary 90 90
*561* A100 95c Angel looking to heaven 1.65 1.65
*562* A100 $1.10 Angel looking to earth 2.00 2.00

**Souvenir Sheet**

*563* A100 $2.50 multi 5.00 5.00

Size of No. 563: 100x130mm.

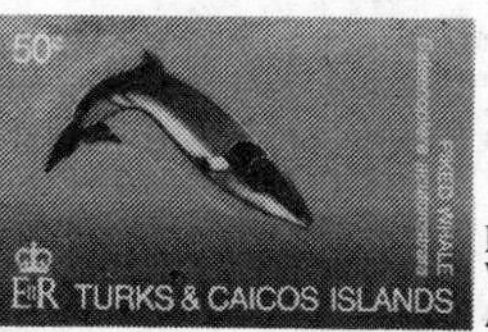

Piked Whale
A101

**1983 Litho. *Perf. 14***

*564* A101 50c shown 1.00 1.00
*565* A101 65c Right whale 1.30 1.30
*566* A101 70c Killer whale 1.40 1.40
*567* A101 95c Sperm whale 1.90 1.90
*568* A101 $1.10 Gooseback whale 2.20 2.20
*569* A101 $2 Blue whale 4.00 4.00
*570* A101 $2.20 Humpback whale 4.40 4.40
*571* A101 $3 Longfin pilot whale 6.00 6.00
*Nos. 564-571 (8)* 22.20 22.20

**Souvenir Sheet**

*572* A101 $3 Fin whale 6.00 6.00

Issue dates: 50c, $2.20, No. 571, May 16; 70c, 95c, $2, June 13; others July 11. Size of No. 572: 113x82mm.

Manned Flight Bicentenary — A102

**1983, Aug. 30 Litho. *Perf. 14***

*573* A102 25c 1st hydrogen balloon, 1783 50 50
*574* A102 35c Friendship 7, 1962 70 70
*575* A102 70c Montgolfiere, 1783 1.40 1.40
*576* A102 95c Columbia space shuttle 1.90 1.90

**Souvenir Sheet**

*577* A102 $2 Montgolfiere, Columbia 4.00 4.00

Size of No. 577: 102x76mm.

A103

**1983 Litho.**

*578* A103 4c Dug-out canoe 8 8
*579* A103 5c Santa Maria 10 10
*a* Perf. 12½x12 ('85) 14 14
*580* A103 8c Spanish treasure galleons 16 16
*581* A103 10c Bermuda sloop 20 20
*582* A103 20c Privateer Grand Turk 40 40
*a* Perf. 12½x12 ('85) 52 52
*583* A103 25c Nelson's Frigate Boreas 50 50
*a* Perf. 12½x12 ('85) 65 65
*584* A103 30c Warship Endymion 60 60
*585* A103 35c Bark Cesear 70 70
*a* Perf. 12½x12 ('85) 90 90
*586* A103 50c Schooner Grapeshot 1.00 1.00
*a* Perf. 12½x12 ('85) 1.40 1.40
*587* A103 65c Invincible 1.30 1.30
*588* A103 95c Magicienne 1.90 1.90
*a* Perf. 12½x12 ('85) 2.50 2.50
*589* A103 $1.10 Durban 2.20 2.20
*590* A103 $2 Sentinel 4.00 4.00
*a* Perf. 12½x12 ('85) 5.25 5.25
*591* A103 $3 Minerva 6.00 6.00
*a* Perf. 12½x12 ('85) 8.00 8.00
*592* A103 $5 Caicos sloop 10.00 10.00
*Nos. 578-592 (15)* 29.14 29.14
*Nos. 579a-591a (8)* 19.36 19.36

Christmas 1983 — A104

Designs: Scenes from Walt Disney's Oh Christmas Tree.

**1983, Nov. *Perf. 11***

*593* A104 1c Fifer Pig 5 5
*594* A104 1c Fiddler Pig 5 5
*595* A104 2c Practical Pig 5 5
*596* A104 2c Pluto 5 5
*597* A104 3c Goofy 6 6
*598* A104 3c Mickey Mouse 6 6
*599* A104 35c Gyro Gearloose 70 70
*600* A104 50c Ludwig Von Drake 1.00 1.00
*601* A104 $1.10 Huey, Dewey and Louie 2.20 2.20
*Nos. 593-601 (9)* 4.22 4.22

**Souvenir Sheet**

***Perf. 13½***

*602* A104 $2.50 Around the tree 5.50 5.50

Multicolored margin continues design.

John F. Kennedy (1917-1963), 20th Death Anniv. — A105

**1983, Dec. 22 Litho. *Perf. 14***

*603* A105 20c multi 40 40
*604* A105 $1 multi 2.00 2.00

Classic Cars
A106

**1984, Mar. 15 Litho. *Perf. 14***

*605* A106 4c Cadillac V-16, 1933 8 8
*606* A106 8c Rolls Royce Phantom III, 1937 20 20
*607* A106 10c Saab 99, 1969 24 24
*608* A106 25c Maserati Bora, 1973 60 60
*609* A106 40c Datsun 260Z, 1970 95 95
*610* A106 55c Porsche 917, 1971 1.40 1.40
*611* A106 80c Lincoln Continental, 1939 2.00 2.00
*612* A106 $1 Triumph TR3A, 1957 2.50 2.50
*Nos. 605-612 (8)* 7.97 7.97

**Souvenir Sheet**

*613* A106 $2 Daimler, 1886 4.00 4.00

125th anniv. of first commercially productive oil well, Drak's Rig, Titusville, Pa. Nos. 605-612 se-tenant with labels showing flags and auto museum names. No. 613 for 150th birth anniv. of Gotlieb Daimler, inventer of high-speed internal combustion engine.

Easter 1984 — A107

450th Death Anniv. of Antonio Allegri Correggio (Various cameo portraits of Correggio, paintings): 15c, Rest on the Flight to Egypt with St. Francis. 40c, St. Luke and St. Ambrose. 60c, Diana and her Chariot. 95c, Deposition of Christ. $2, Nativity with St. Elizabeth and the Infant St. John.

**1984, Apr. 9**

*614* A107 15c multi 30 30
*615* A107 40c multi 80 80
*616* A107 60c multi 1.20 1.20
*617* A107 95c multi 1.90 1.90

**Souvenir Sheet**

*618* A107 $2 multi, horiz. 4.00 4.00

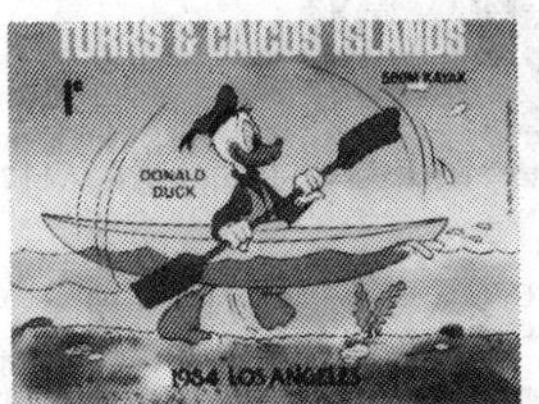

1984 Los Angeles Olympics — A108

Various Disney characters participating in Olympic sports.

**1984, Feb. Litho. *Perf. 14***

*619* A108 1c 500-meter 5 5
*a* Perf. 12½x12 5 5
*620* A108 1c Diving 5 5
*a* Perf. 12½x12 5 5
*621* A108 2c Single kayak 5 5
*a* Perf. 12½x12 5 5
*622* A108 2c 1000-meter kayak 5 5
*a* Perf. 12½x12 5 5
*623* A108 3c Highboard diving 6 6
*a* Perf. 12½x12 6 6
*624* A108 3c Kayak slalom 6 6
*a* Perf. 12½x12 6 6
*625* A108 25c Freestyle swimming 50 50
*a* Perf. 12½x12 50 50
*626* A108 75c Water polo 1.50 1.50
*a* Perf. 12½x12 1.50 1.50
*627* A108 $1 Yachting 2.00 2.00
*a* Perf. 12½x12 2.00 2.00
*Nos. 619-627 (9)* 4.32 4.32
*Nos. 619a-627a (9)* 4.32 4.32

**Souvenir Sheet**

*628* A108 $2 Platform diving 4.00 4.00
*a* Olympic rings emblem inscribed 4.00 4.00

No. 628 has multicolored margin continuing design. Size: 117x92mm. Nos. 619a-627a inscribed with Olympic rings emblem. Printed in sheets of 5.

Sir Arthur Conan Doyle (1859-1930) — A109

Scenes from the Adventures of Sherlock Holmes.

**1984, July 16 Litho. *Perf. 14***

*629* A109 25c Second Stain 50 50
*630* A109 45c Final Problem 90 90
*631* A109 70c Empty House 1.40 1.40
*632* A109 85c Greek Interpreter 1.75 1.75

**Souvenir Sheet**

*633* A109 $2 Doyle, vert. 4.00 4.00

No. 633 has light green and black margin showing characters, text. Size: 100x70mm.

**Nos. 567-568, 572 Overprinted with UPU Emblem and: "19TH UPU CONGRESS / HAMBURG, WEST GERMANY./ 1874-1984"**

**1984 Litho. *Perf. 14***

*637* A101 95c multi 1.90 1.90
*638* A101 $1.10 multi 2.20 2.20

**Souvenir Sheet**

*639* A101 $3 multi 5.50 5.50

Scott's editorial staff cannot undertake to identify, authenticate or appraise stamps and postal markings.

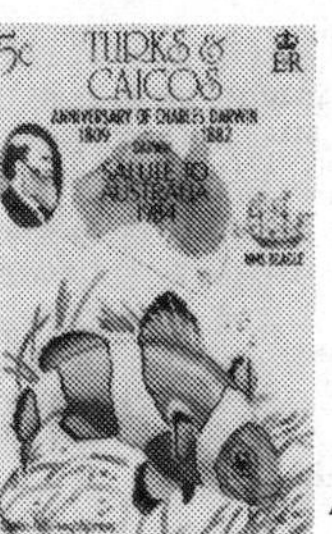

AUSIPEX '84
A110

Darwin, Ship, Map of Australia, Fauna.

**1984, Aug. 22 *Perf. 14x13½***

*640* A110 5c Clown fish 10 10
*641* A110 35c Monitor lizard 70 70
*642* A110 50c Rainbow lorikeets 1.00 1.00
*643* A110 $1.10 Koalas 2.25 2.25

**Souvenir Sheet**

*644* A110 $2 Grey kangaroo 4.00 4.00

No. 644 has multicolored margin continuing design. Size: 100x70mm.

Christmas 1984 — A111

Scenes from Walt Disney's The Toy Tinkers.

**1984, Nov. Litho. *Perf. 14***

*645* A111 20c multi 45 45
*646* A111 35c multi 75 75
*647* A111 50c multi 1.10 1.10
*648* A111 75c multi 1.65 1.65
*649* A111 $1.10 multi 2.50 2.50
*Nos. 645-649 (5)* 6.45 6.45

**Souvenir Sheet**

*650* A111 $2 multi 4.50 4.50

No. 650 has multicolored margin continuing design.

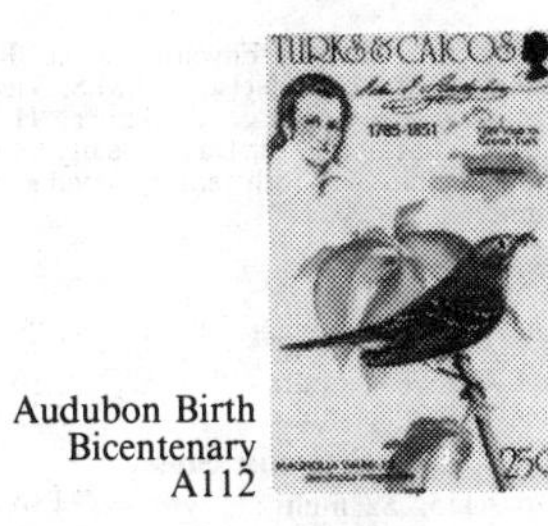

Audubon Birth Bicentenary
A112

Cameo portrait of Audubon, signature and illustrations from Birds of North America.

**1985, Jan. 28 Litho. *Perf. 14***

*651* A112 25c Dendroica magnoliae 45 45
*652* A112 45c Asio flammeus 80 80
*653* A112 70c Zenaida macroura 1.25 1.25
*654* A112 85c Progne subis 1.50 1.50

**Souvenir Sheet**

*655* A112 $2 Haematopus ostralegus 4.00 4.00

No. 655 has multicolored margin continuing the design and picturing a map of Audubon's early travels. Size: 100x70mm.

Intl. Civil Aviation Org., 40th Anniv.
A113

Pioneers & inventions: 8c, Leonardo da Vinci, 15th century glider wing. 25c, Sir Alliott Verdon Roe, 1949 C. 102 Jet. 65c, Robert H. Goddard, first liquid fuel rocket launch, 1926. $1, Igor Sikorsky, 1939 Sikorsky VS300. $2, Aviator Amelia Earhart, 1937 Lockheed 10E Electra.

**1985, Feb. 21**

| | | | | |
|---|---|---|---|---|
| *656* | A113 | 8c multi | 16 | 16 |
| *657* | A113 | 25c multi | 50 | 50 |
| *658* | A113 | 65c multi | 1.30 | 1.30 |
| *659* | A113 | $1 multi | 2.00 | 2.00 |

**Souvenir Sheet**

*660* A113 $2 multi 4.00 4.00

No. 660 has multicolored margin continuing the design and picturing Amelia Earhart. Size: 100x70mm.

Arrival of the Statue of Liberty in New York, USA, Cent. A114

Designs: 20c, Flags of U.S., France, Benjamin Franklin, Marquis de Lafayette. 30c, Designer Frederic A. Bartholdi, engineer Gustave Eiffel, Statue, Eiffel Tower. 65c, Isere, arriving in New York with Statue, 1885. $1.10, Fund raisers Louis Agassiz, H.W. Longfellow, Charles Sumner, Joseph Pulitzer. $2, Dedication day, Oct. 28, 1886.

**1985, Mar. 28**

| | | | | |
|---|---|---|---|---|
| *661* | A114 | 20c multi | 45 | 45 |
| *662* | A114 | 30c multi | 67 | 70 |
| *663* | A114 | 65c multi | 1.50 | 1.50 |
| *664* | A114 | $1.10 multi | 2.50 | 2.50 |

**Souvenir Sheet**

*665* A114 $2 multi 4.50 4.50

No. 665 has multicolored margin continuing the design and picturing Pres. Grover Cleveland; inscribed with first lines of sonnet, The New Colossus, by Emma Lazarus. Size: 100x70mm.

Royal Navy A115

Designs: 20c, Sir Edward Hawke, Royal George. 30c, Lord Nelson, H.M.S. Victory. 65c, Adm. Sir George Cockburn, H.M.S. Albion. 95c, Adm. Sir David Beatty, H.M.S. Indefatigable. $2, 18th century naval gunner, cannons.

**1985, Apr. 17**

| | | | | |
|---|---|---|---|---|
| *666* | A115 | 20c multi | 45 | 45 |
| *667* | A115 | 30c multi | 70 | 70 |
| *668* | A115 | 65c multi | 1.50 | 1.50 |
| *669* | A115 | 95c multi | 2.25 | 2.25 |

**Souvenir Sheet**

*670* A115 $2 multi 4.50 4.50

No. 670 has buff and black margin picturing ships hull, cannons in position on various decks. Size: 101x71mm.

Intl. Youth Year A116

Anniversaries: 25c, Return of Halley's Comet, 1986. 35c, Mark Twain (1835-1910), Mississippi river boat. 50c, Jakob Grimm (1785-1863), Hansel & Gretel, vert. 95c, Grimm, Rumpelstiltskin, vert. $2, Twain, Grimm, portraits.

**1985, May 17**

| | | | | |
|---|---|---|---|---|
| *671* | A116 | 25c multi | 55 | 55 |
| *672* | A116 | 35c multi | 75 | 75 |
| *673* | A116 | 50c multi | 1.10 | 1.10 |
| *674* | A116 | 95c multi | 2.25 | 2.25 |

**Souvenir Sheet**

*675* A116 $2 multi 4.50 4.50

No. 675 has multicolored margin picturing scenes from Twain's and Grimm's best known children's tales. Size: 99x69mm.

Queen Mother, 85th Birthday — A117

Designs: 30c, Queen Mother outside Clarence House, vert. 50c, Visiting Biggin Hill Airfield by helicopter. $1.10, 80th birthday portrait, vert. $2, With Prince Charles at the 1968 Garter Ceremony, Windsor Castle, vert.

**1985, July 15**

| | | | | |
|---|---|---|---|---|
| *676* | A117 | 30c multi | 80 | 80 |
| *677* | A117 | 50c multi | 1.25 | 1.25 |
| *678* | A117 | $1.10 multi | 2.75 | 2.75 |

**Souvenir Sheet**

*679* A117 $2 multi 4.00 4.00

No. 679 has multicolored margin picturing flowers. Size: 57x84mm.

George Frideric Handel (1685-1759) A118

Johann Sebastian Bach (1685-1750) A119

Handel or Bach and: 4c, King George II, Zadok the Priest music, 1727. 10c, Queen Caroline, Funeral Anthem, 1737. 15c, Bassoon, Invention No. 3 in D Major. 40c, Natural horn, Invention No. 3 in D Major. 50c, King George I, Water Music, 1714. 60c, Viola d'amore, Invention No. 3 . . . 95c, Clavichord, Invention No. 3 . . . $1.10, Queen Anne, Or la Tromba from Rinaldo. No. 688, Handel, portrait. No. 689, Bach, portrait.

**1985, July 17** *Perf. 15*

| | | | | |
|---|---|---|---|---|
| *680* | A118 | 4c multi | 8 | 8 |
| *681* | A118 | 10c multi | 22 | 22 |
| *682* | A119 | 15c multi | 32 | 32 |
| *683* | A119 | 40c multi | 90 | 90 |
| *684* | A118 | 50c multi | 1.10 | 1.10 |
| *685* | A119 | 60c multi | 1.40 | 1.40 |
| *686* | A119 | 95c multi | 2.00 | 2.00 |
| *687* | A118 | $1.10 multi | 2.50 | 2.50 |
| | | *Nos. 680-687 (8)* | 8.52 | 8.52 |

**Souvenir Sheets**

| | | | | |
|---|---|---|---|---|
| *688* | A118 | $2 multi | 4.50 | 4.50 |
| *689* | A119 | $2 multi | 4.50 | 4.50 |

Nos. 688-689 have multicolored margins continuing designs and picture Music from the Messiah, 1742, and the Fishamble Street Music Hall, Dublin, Bach's lineage. Sizes: 102x77mm.

Motorcycle Centenary A120

Flag of U.S., U.K., Fed. Rep. of Germany or Japan and: 8c, 1915 dual cylinder Harley-Davidson. 25c, 1950 Thunderbird Triumph. 55c, 1985 BMW K100RS. $1.20, 1985 Honda 1100 Shadow. $2, 1885 Daimler Single Track, vert.

**1985, Sept. 4** *Perf. 14*

| | | | | |
|---|---|---|---|---|
| *690* | A120 | 8c multi | 18 | 18 |
| *691* | A120 | 25c multi | 58 | 58 |
| *692* | A120 | 55c multi | 1.25 | 1.25 |
| *693* | A120 | $1.20 multi | 2.75 | 2.75 |

**Souvenir Sheet**

*694* A120 $2 multi 4.50 4.50

No. 694 has multicolored margin picturing various motorcycles. Size: 107x77mm.

Pirates of the Caribbean — A121

Designs: No. 695, Fate of Capt. Kidd. No. 696, Pirates imprisoned. No. 697, Bartholomew Roberts, church-going pirate. No. 698, Buccaneers in battle. No. 699, Bride auction. No. 700, Plunder. No. 701, Singing pirates. No. 702, Blackbeard. No. 703, Henry Morgan. No. 704, Mary Read, Anne Bonney.

**1985, Oct. 4** **Litho.** *Perf. 14*

| | | | | |
|---|---|---|---|---|
| *695* | A121 | 1c multi | 5 | 5 |
| *696* | A121 | 1c multi | 5 | 5 |
| *697* | A121 | 2c multi | 5 | 5 |
| *698* | A121 | 2c multi | 5 | 5 |
| *699* | A121 | 3c multi | 6 | 6 |
| *700* | A121 | 3c multi | 6 | 6 |
| *701* | A121 | 35c multi | 70 | 70 |
| *702* | A121 | 75c multi | 1.50 | 1.50 |
| *703* | A121 | $1.10 multi | 2.20 | 2.20 |
| | | *Nos. 695-703 (9)* | 4.72 | 4.72 |

**Souvenir Sheet**

*704* A121 $2.50 multi 5.00 5.00

Disneyland, 30th anniv. No. 704 has multicolored margin continuing the design, picturing Calico Jack Rackham and crew after plundering the Bella Christina. Size: 124x86mm.

Girl Guides, 75th Anniv. A122

Uniforms of Turks and Caicos and: 10c, Papua New Guinea and China brownies. 40c, Surinam and Korea brownies. 70c, Australia and Canada girl guides. 80c, West Germany and Israel girl guides.

**1985, Nov. 4**

| | | | | |
|---|---|---|---|---|
| *705* | A122 | 10c multi | 20 | 20 |
| *706* | A122 | 40c multi | 80 | 80 |
| *707* | A122 | 70c multi | 1.40 | 1.40 |
| *708* | A122 | 80c multi | 1.60 | 1.60 |

**Souvenir Sheet**

*709* A122 $2 Anniv. emblem 4.00 4.00

Grand Turk Chapter, 35th anniv. No. 709 has multicolored margin picturing guides of different nations. Size: 107x77mm.

World Wildlife Fund A123

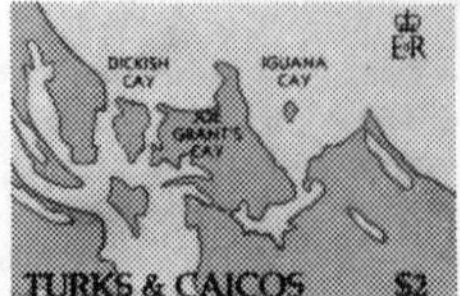


Map of the Islands A124

Turks & Caicos ground iguanas.

**1986, Nov. 20** *Perf. 14*

| | | | | |
|---|---|---|---|---|
| *710* | A123 | 8c multi | 16 | 16 |
| *711* | A123 | 10c multi | 20 | 20 |
| *712* | A123 | 20c multi | 40 | 40 |
| *713* | A123 | 35c multi | 70 | 70 |

**Souvenir Sheet**

*714* A124 $2 multi 4.00 4.00

No. 714 has multicolored inscribed margin continuing the design and picturing ground iguana. Size: 105x76mm.

Wedding of Prince Andrew and Sarah Ferguson — A125

Wedding pictures.

**1986, Dec. 19** **Litho.** *Perf. 14*

| | | | | |
|---|---|---|---|---|
| *715* | A125 | 35c Couple | 70 | 70 |
| *716* | A125 | 65c Sarah in coach | 1.30 | 1.30 |
| *717* | A125 | $1.10 Couple, close-up | 2.20 | 2.20 |

**Souvenir Sheet**

*718* A125 $2 In Westminster Abbey 4.00 4.00

No. 718 has inscribed multicolored margin continuing the design, picturing congregation. Size: 85x85mm.

Christmas — A126

Illuminations by miniaturist Giorgio Giulio Clovio (1498-1578) from the Farnese Book of Hours: 35c, Prophecy of the Birth of Christ to King Achaz. 50c, The Annunciation. 65c, The Circumcision. 95c, Adoration of the Kings. $2, The Nativty.

**1987, Dec. 9** **Litho.** *Perf. 14*

| | | | | |
|---|---|---|---|---|
| *719* | A126 | 35c multi | 70 | 70 |
| *720* | A126 | 50c multi | 1.00 | 1.00 |
| *721* | A126 | 65c multi | 1.30 | 1.30 |
| *722* | A126 | 95c multi | 1.90 | 1.90 |

**Souvenir Sheet**

*723* A126 $2 multi 4.00 4.00

No. 723 has multicolored margin continuing the illumination. Size: 77x106mm.

Accession of Queen Victoria to the Throne of England, 150th Anniv. A127

Ships and memorials: 8c, HMS Victoria, Victoria Cross. 35c, SS Victoria, coin. 55c, Victoria & Albert I, Great Britain No. 1. 95c, Victoria & Albert II, Victoria Public Library, Turks & Caicos. $2, Bark Victoria.

**1987, Dec. 24**

| | | | | |
|---|---|---|---|---|
| *724* | A127 | 8c multi | 16 | 16 |
| *725* | A127 | 35c multi | 70 | 70 |
| *726* | A127 | 55c multi | 1.10 | 1.10 |
| *727* | A127 | 95c multi | 1.90 | 1.90 |

**Souvenir Sheet**

*728* A127 $2 multi 4.00 4.00

No. 728 has multicolored inscribed margin picturing library, Great Britain No. 2 and 1887 silver crown. Size: 130x76mm.

U.S. Constitution Bicentennial
A128

Designs: 10c, New Jersey state flag. 35c, Freedom of Worship, vert. 65c, U.S. Supreme Court, vert. 80c, John Adams, vert. $2, George Mason, vert.

**1987, Dec. 31**

*729* A128 10c multi 8 8
*730* A128 35c multi 50 50
*731* A128 65c multi 1.40 1.40
*732* A128 80c multi 2.00 2.00

**Souvenir Sheet**

*733* A128 $2 multi 4.00 4.00

No. 733 has multicolored inscribed margin picturing "We the People," frontispiece of the Federal Edifice and colonial architecture. Size: 105x76mm.

Discovery of America, 500th Anniv. (in 1992)
A129

Emblem and: 4c, Caravel, first sighting of land, Oct. 12, 1492. 25c, Columbus meets with Indians, Oct. 14. 70c, Fleet anchored in harbor, Oct. 15. $1, Landing, Oct. 16. $2, Nina, Pinta and Santa Maria.

**1988, Jan. 20**

*734* A129 4c multi 8 8
*735* A129 25c multi 50 50
*736* A129 70c multi 1.40 1.40
*737* A129 $1 multi 2.00 2.00

**Souvenir Sheet**

*738* A129 $2 multi 4.00 4.00

No. 738 has multicolored decorative margin picturing map and portraits of Columbus, Martin Alonzo Pinzon and Vicente Yanez Pinzon. Size: 105x76mm.

Sea Scouts Salute Jamboree and Australia
A130

Designs: 8c, Arawak artifact, scouts exploring cave on Middle Caicos, vert. 35c, Santa Maria, scouts rowing to Hawks Nest. 65c, Scouts diving to explore a sunken Spanish galleon, vert. 95c, Plantation worker cutting sisal, scouts exploring plantation ruins. $2, Splashdown of Friendship 7, piloted by John Glenn, Feb. 20, 1962, vert.

**1988, Feb. 12 Litho. *Perf. 14***

*739* A130 8c multi 16 16
*740* A130 35c shown 70 70
*741* A130 65c multi 1.30 1.30
*742* A130 95c multi 1.90 1.90

**Souvenir Sheet**

*743* A130 $2 multi 4.00 4.00

Australia Bicentennial. No. 743 has multicolored inscribed margin like 35c. Size: 118x82mm.

Nos. 581, 583 and 590 Ovptd. "40th WEDDING ANNIVERSARY / H.M. QUEEN ELIZABETH II / H.R.H. THE DUKE OF EDINBURGH."

**1988, Mar. 14 Litho. *Perf. 14***

*744* A103 10c multi 20 20
*745* A103 25c multi 50 50
*746* A103 $2 multi 4.00 4.00

1988 Summer Olympics, Seoul — A131

**1988, Aug. 29 Litho.**

*747* A131 8c Soccer 16 16
*748* A131 30c Yachting 60 60
*749* A131 70c Cycling 1.40 1.40
*750* A131 $1 Running 2.00 2.00

**Souvenir Sheet**

*751* A131 $2 Swimming 4.00 4.00

No. 751 has multicolored inscribed margin continuing the design. Size: 102x71mm.

Billfish Tournament
A132

Designs: 8c, Passenger jet, fishing boat and fisherman reeling-in giant swordfish. 10c, Photographing prize catch. 70c, Fishing boat, lighthouse. $1, Blue marlin. $2, Sailfish.

**1988, Sept. 5 Litho.**

*752* A132 8c multi 16 16
*753* A132 10c multi 20 20
*754* A132 70c multi 1.40 1.40
*755* A132 $1 multi 2.00 2.00

**Souvenir Sheet**

*756* A132 $2 multi 4.00 4.00

No. 756 has multicolored decorative margin picturing sailfish and a blue marlin. Size: 119x86mm.

Christmas
A133

Paintings by Titian: 15c, *Madonna and Child with St. Catherine and the Infant John the Baptist*, c. 1530. 25c, *Madonna with a Rabbit*, c. 1526. 35c, *Virgin and Child with Sts. Stephen, Jerome and Mauritius*, c. 1520. 40c, *The Gypsy Madonna*, c. 1510. 50c, *The Holy Family and a Shepherd*, c. 1510. 65c, *Madonna and Child*, c. 1510. $3, *Madonna and Child with St. John the Baptist and St. Catherine*, c. 1530. No. 764, *Adoration of the Magi*, c. 1560. No. 765, *The Annunciation*, c. 1560.

**1988, Oct. 24 Litho.**

*757* A133 15c multi 30 30
*758* A133 25c multi 50 50
*759* A133 35c multi 70 70
*760* A133 40c multi 80 80
*761* A133 50c multi 1.00 1.00
*762* A133 65c multi 1.30 1.30
*763* A133 $3 multi 6.00 6.00
*Nos. 757-763 (7)* 10.60 10.60

**Souvenir Sheets**

*764* A133 $2 multi 4.00 4.00
*765* A133 $2 multi 4.00 4.00

Nos. 764-765 have multicolored inscribed margins continuing the paintings. Sizes: 110x95mm.

Visit of Princess Alexandra, 1st Cousin of Queen Elizabeth II — A134

Various portraits and: 70c, Government House. $1.40, Map. $2, Flora, vert.

**1988, Nov. 14 Litho. *Perf. 14***

*766* A134 70c multi 1.40 1.40
*767* A134 $1.40 multi 2.80 2.80

**Souvenir Sheet**

*768* A134 $2 multi 4.00 4.00

No. 768 has multicolored inscribed margin picturing coat of arms and the Treasury. Size: 92x71mm.

---

## WAR TAX STAMPS.

Regular Issue of 1913-16 Overprinted **WAR TAX**

**1917 Wmk. 3 *Perf. 14***
**Black Overprint at Bottom of Stamp**

*MR1* A10 1p carmine 18 30
*a.* Dbl. overprint 150.00
*b.* "TAX" omitted
*c.* Pair, one without ovpt.
*MR2* A10 3p vio, *yel* 32 38
*a.* Double overprint 75.00

Black Overprint at Top or Middle of Stamp

**1917**

*MR3* A10 1p carmine 12 12
*a.* Inverted overprint 25.00
*b.* Double overprint 27.50 16.00
*c.* Pair, one without overprint 200.00
*MR4* A10 3p vio, *yel* 60 85
*a.* Double overprint 17.50
*b.* Double overprint, one inverted 37.50

Same Overprint in Violet or Red

**1918-19**

*MR5* A10 1p car (V) ('19) 25 25
*a.* Double overprint 12.50
*b.* "WAR" omitted 100.00
*MR6* A10 3p vio, *yel* (R) 3.50 3.50
*a.* Double overprint 50.00

Regular Issue of 1913-16 Overprinted in Black **WAR TAX**

**1918**

*MR7* A10 1p carmine 20 20
*MR8* A10 3p vio, *yel* 50 50

Same Overprint in Red

**1919**

*MR9* A10 3p vio, *yel* 25 25

Regular Issue of 1913-16 Overprinted in Black **WAR TAX**

*MR10* A10 1p carmine 10 10
*a.* Double ovpt. 100.00 100.00
*MR11* A10 3p vio, *yel* 32 32

Regular Issue of 1913-16 Overprinted **WAR TAX**

*MR12* A10 1p carmine 12 12
*a.* Double ovpt. *100.00*
*MR13* A10 3p vio, *yel* 38 38

---

# TUVALU

LOCATION — A group of islands in the Pacific Ocean northeast of Australia.
GOVT. — Independent state in the British Commonwealth
AREA — 9½ sq. mi.
POP. — 7,349 (1979)
CAPITAL — Funafuti

Tuvalu, formerly Ellice Islands, consists of nine islands.

**Catalogue values for all unused stamps in this country are for Never Hinged items.**

Gilbert and Ellice Islands Types of 1971 Overprinted "TUVALU" and Bar in Violet Blue or Silver (35c).

**Wmk. 373**

**1976, Jan. 1 Litho. *Perf. 14***

*1* A18 1c multi 8 8
*2* A19 2c multi 18 18
*a* Wmk. 314 sideways 165.00 55.00
*b* Wmk. 314 upright 725.00 140.00
*3* A19 3c multi, wmk. 314 18 18
*a* Wmk. 373 18 18
*4* A19 4c multi 22 22
*5* A19 5c multi, wmk. 314 28 28
*6* A18 6c multi 40 40
*7* A18 8c multi, wmk. 314 50 50
*8* A18 10c multi, wmk. 314 60 60
*9* A18 15c multi 60 60
*10* A19 20c multi 80 80
*11* A19 25c multi, wmk. 314 1.25 1.25
*a* Wmk. 373 1.25 1.25
*12* A19 35c multi 2.00 1.65
*13* A18 50c multi 4.75 3.75
*a* Wmk. 314 30.00 16.00
*14* A18 $1 multi 13.00 11.00
*a* Wmk. 314 67.50 60.00
*15* A18 $2 multi 30.00 24.00
*Nos. 1-15 (15)* 54.84 45.49

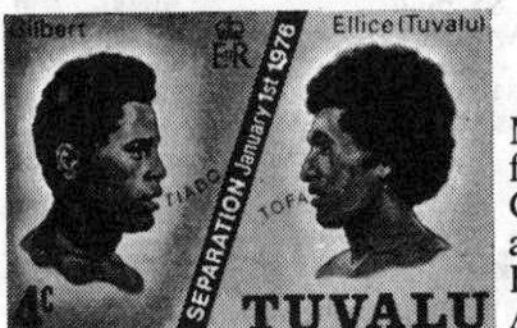


Men from Gilbert and Ellice
A1

Designs: 10c, Map of Gilbert and Ellice Islands (vert.). 35c, Gilbert and Ellice canoes.

**1976, Jan. 1 Wmk. 373**

*16* A1 4c multi 80 52
*17* A1 10c multi 1.65 1.25
*18* A1 35c multi 4.25 3.25

Separation of the Gilbert and Ellice Islands.

50c Coin and Octopus — A2

New coinage: 10c, 10c-coin and red-dyed crab. 15c, 20c-coin and flyingfish. 35c, $1-coin and green turtle.

**Wmk. 373**

**1976, Apr. 21 Litho. *Perf. 14***

*19* A2 5c bis & multi 52 40
*20* A2 10c ultra & multi 1.40 1.00
*21* A2 15c bl & multi 2.00 1.50
*22* A2 35c lt grn & multi 3.25 3.00

Map of Niulakita, Leathery Turtle — A3

Te Ano Game A4

Designs: 2c, Map of Nukulaelae and sleeping mat. 4c, Map of Nui and talo vegetable. 5c, Map of Nanumanga and grass dancing skirt. 6c, Map of Nukufetau and coconut crab. 8c, Map of Funafuti and banana tree. 10c, Map of Tuvalu Islands. 15c, Map of Niutao and flyingfish. 20c, Map of Vaitupu and maneapa (house). 25c, Map of Nanumea and palu fish hook. 50c, Canoe pole fishing. $1, Reef fishing by flare. $2, House. $5, Colony Ship M.V. Nivanga.

**1976 Wmk. 373 Litho. *Perf. 13½***

| | | | | |
|---|---|---|---|---|
| *23* | A3 | 1c multi | 30 | 26 |
| *24* | A3 | 2c multi | 22 | 18 |
| *25* | A3 | 4c multi | 28 | 22 |
| *26* | A3 | 5c multi | 55 | 42 |
| *27* | A3 | 6c multi | 30 | 26 |
| *28* | A3 | 8c multi | 45 | 32 |
| *29* | A3 | 10c multi | 55 | 42 |
| *30* | A3 | 15c multi | 45 | 32 |
| *31* | A3 | 20c multi | 55 | 42 |
| *32* | A3 | 25c multi | 5.75 | 3.00 |
| *33* | A4 | 35c multi | 85 | 70 |
| *34* | A4 | 50c multi | 1.40 | 1.25 |
| *35* | A4 | $1 multi | 3.50 | 2.75 |
| *36* | A4 | $2 multi | 7.25 | 5.75 |
| *37* | A4 | $5 multi | 70.00 | 27.50 |
| | | *Nos. 23-37 (15)* | 92.40 | 43.77 |

Issue dates: $5, Sept. 1, others July 1.
See Nos. 58-72.

New Testament A5

Designs: 20c, Lotolelei Church, Nanumea. 25c, Kelupi Church, Nui. 30c, Mataloa o Tuvalu Church, Vaitupu. 35c, Palataiso o Keliso Church, Nanumanga.

***Perf. 14x14½***

**1976, Oct. 6 Litho. Wmk. 373**

| | | | | |
|---|---|---|---|---|
| *38* | A5 | 5c multi | 55 | 32 |
| *39* | A5 | 20c multi | 2.00 | 1.40 |
| *40* | A5 | 25c multi | 2.50 | 1.75 |
| *41* | A5 | 30c multi | 3.25 | 2.00 |
| *42* | A5 | 35c multi | 4.25 | 3.25 |
| | | *Nos. 38-42 (5)* | 12.55 | 8.72 |

Christmas 1976. Printed in sheets of 10 stamps and 2 labels.

Prince Philip Carried Ashore at Vaitupu — A6

Designs: 15c, Queen and Prince Philip on Buckingham Palace balcony. 50c, Queen Leaving Buckingham Palace for coronation.

**1977, Feb. 9 Litho. *Perf. 13½x14***

| | | | | |
|---|---|---|---|---|
| *43* | A6 | 15c multi | 4.00 | 3.00 |
| *44* | A6 | 35c multi | 5.00 | 3.25 |
| *45* | A6 | 50c multi | 5.50 | 4.00 |
| *a* | | Souvenir sheet of 3 | 15.00 | 12.50 |

25th anniversary of the reign of Queen Elizabeth II. No. 45a contains one each of Nos. 43-45, perf. 15; multicolored margin shows various crowns. Size: 98x144mm.

Health (Microscope) — A7

Designs: 20c, Education (blackboard). 30c, Fruit growing (palm). 35c, Map of South Pacific Territory.

**1977, May 4 Litho. *Perf. 13½x14***

| | | | | |
|---|---|---|---|---|
| *46* | A7 | 5c lil & multi | 65 | 45 |
| *47* | A7 | 20c org & multi | 1.25 | 1.00 |
| *48* | A7 | 30c yel grn & multi | 1.40 | 1.25 |
| *49* | A7 | 35c lt bl & multi | 1.50 | 1.65 |

South Pacific Commission, 30th anniv.

Swearing-in Ceremony and Scout Emblem — A8

Designs (Scout Emblem and): 20c, Scouts in outrigger canoe. 30c, Scouts under sun shelter. 35c, Lord Baden-Powell.

***Perf. 13½x14***

**1977, Aug. 10 Litho. Wmk. 373**

| | | | | |
|---|---|---|---|---|
| *50* | A8 | 5c multi | 65 | 48 |
| *51* | A8 | 20c multi | 1.25 | 95 |
| *52* | A8 | 30c multi | 1.65 | 1.40 |
| *53* | A8 | 35c multi | 1.65 | 1.75 |

50th anniversary of Scouting in Tuvalu (Ellice Islands).

Hurricane Beach and Coral — A9

Designs: 20c, Boring apparatus on "Porpoise" (vert.). 30c, Map of islands showing line of dredgings to prove Darwin's theory (vert.). 35c, Charles Darwin and "Beagle."

***Perf. 13½***

**1977, Nov. 2 Unwmk. Litho.**

| | | | | |
|---|---|---|---|---|
| *54* | A9 | 5c multi | 32 | 28 |
| *55* | A9 | 20c multi | 1.00 | 80 |
| *56* | A9 | 30c multi | 1.40 | 1.25 |
| *57* | A9 | 35c multi | 1.65 | 1.50 |

1896-97 Royal Soc. of London Expeditions to explore coral reefs by dredging and boring.

Types of 1976

Designs: 30c, Fatele, local dance. 40c, Screw pine. Others as before.

**1977-78 Unwmk. *Perf. 13½***

| | | | | |
|---|---|---|---|---|
| *58* | A3 | 1c multi | 5 | 5 |
| *59* | A3 | 2c multi | 9 | 9 |
| *60* | A3 | 4c multi | 20 | 20 |
| *61* | A3 | 5c multi | 26 | 26 |
| *62* | A3 | 6c multi | 26 | 26 |
| *63* | A3 | 8c multi | 35 | 30 |
| *64* | A3 | 10c multi | 45 | 38 |
| *66* | A3 | 20c multi | 10.00 | 9.00 |
| *67* | A3 | 25c multi | 75 | 65 |
| *68* | A4 | 30c multi | 85 | 75 |
| *69* | A4 | 40c multi | 95 | 85 |
| *72* | A4 | $5 multi | 11.00 | 10.00 |
| | | *Nos. 58-72 (12)* | 25.21 | 22.79 |

Issue dates: Nos. 58, 61, 67 and 72, 1977. Others, 1978.

Pacific Pigeon — A10

Wild Birds of Tuvalu: 20c, Reef heron. 30c, Fairy tern. 40c, Lesser frigate bird.

***Perf. 14x13½***

**1978, Jan. 25 Litho. Unwmk.**

| | | | | |
|---|---|---|---|---|
| *73* | A10 | 8c lil & multi | 1.65 | 65 |
| *74* | A10 | 20c ocher & multi | 2.75 | 1.65 |
| *75* | A10 | 30c dl grn & multi | 3.25 | 2.50 |
| *76* | A10 | 40c brt grn & multi | 4.00 | 3.25 |

Lawedua — A11

Ships: 20c, Tug Wallacia. 30c, Freighter Cenpac Rounder. 40c, Pacific Explorer.

**1978 Unwmk. *Perf. 13½x14***

| | | | | |
|---|---|---|---|---|
| *77* | A11 | 8c multi | 26 | 22 |
| *78* | A11 | 20c multi | 65 | 55 |
| *79* | A11 | 30c multi | 95 | 80 |
| *80* | A11 | 40c multi | 1.25 | 1.10 |

Canterbury Cathedral — A12

Designs: 30c, Salisbury Cathedral. 40c, Wells Cathedral. $1, Hereford Cathedral.

**1978, June 2 Litho. *Perf. 13½x14***

| | | | | |
|---|---|---|---|---|
| *81* | A12 | 8c multi | 20 | 20 |
| *82* | A12 | 30c multi | 35 | 35 |
| *83* | A12 | 40c multi | 45 | 45 |
| *84* | A12 | $1 multi | 1.10 | 1.10 |
| *a* | | Souvenir sheet of 4 | 2.10 | 2.10 |

25th anniversary of coronation of Queen Elizabeth II. No. 84a contains Nos. 81-84, perf. 15; lilac and brown margin. Size: 136x107½mm.

Nos. 81-84 were also issued in booklet panes of 2.

Types of 1976 Overprinted: "INDEPENDENCE 1ST OCTOBER 1978"

**1978, Oct. 1 Litho. *Perf. 13½***
**Wmk. 373, Unwmk.**

| | | | | |
|---|---|---|---|---|
| *85* | A3 | 8c multi | 10 | 10 |
| *86* | A3 | 10c multi | 14 | 14 |
| *87* | A3 | 15c multi | 22 | 22 |
| *88* | A3 | 20c multi | 28 | 28 |
| *89* | A4 | 30c multi | 42 | 42 |
| *90* | A4 | 35c multi | 48 | 48 |
| *91* | A4 | 40c multi | 55 | 55 |
| | | *Nos. 85-91 (7)* | 2.19 | 2.19 |

Independence, Oct. 1, 1978. Overprint in 3 lines on vertical stamps, one line on horizontal.

White Frangipani — A13

Wild Flowers: 20c, Zephyrantes rosea. 30c, Gardenia taitensis. 40c, Clerodendron inerme.

**1978, Oct. 4 Unwmk. *Perf. 14***

| | | | | |
|---|---|---|---|---|
| *92* | A13 | 8c multi | 18 | 14 |
| *93* | A13 | 20c multi | 42 | 38 |
| *94* | A13 | 30c multi | 70 | 60 |
| *95* | A13 | 40c multi | 1.00 | 85 |

Squirrelfish A14

Fish: 2c, Yellow-banded goatfish. 4c, Imperial angelfish. 5c, Rainbow butterfly. 6c, Blue angelfish. 8c, Blue striped snapper. 10c, Orange clownfish. 15c, Chevroned coralfish. 20c, Fairy cod. 25c, Clown triggerfish. 30c, Long-nosed butterfly. 35c, Yellowfin tuna. 40c, Spotted eagle ray. 45c, Black-tipped rock cod. 50c, Hammerhead shark. 70c, Lionfish (vert.). $1, White-barred triggerfish (vert.). $2, Beaked coralfish (vert.). $5, Tiger shark (vert.).

**1979, Jan. 24 Litho. *Perf. 14***

| | | | | |
|---|---|---|---|---|
| *96* | A14 | 1c multi | 5 | 5 |
| *97* | A14 | 2c multi | 5 | 5 |
| *98* | A14 | 4c multi | 6 | 6 |
| *99* | A14 | 5c multi | 7 | 7 |
| *100* | A14 | 6c multi | 8 | 8 |
| *101* | A14 | 8c multi | 12 | 12 |
| *102* | A14 | 10c multi | 14 | 14 |
| *103* | A14 | 15c multi | 22 | 22 |
| *104* | A14 | 20c multi | 25 | 25 |
| *105* | A14 | 25c multi | 28 | 28 |
| *106* | A14 | 30c multi | 32 | 32 |
| *107* | A14 | 35c multi | 42 | 42 |
| *108* | A14 | 40c multi | 48 | 48 |
| *108A* | A14 | 45c multi ('81) | 55 | 55 |
| *109* | A14 | 50c multi | 60 | 60 |
| *110* | A14 | 70c multi | 85 | 85 |
| *111* | A14 | $1 multi | 1.10 | 1.10 |
| *112* | A14 | $2 multi | 2.50 | 2.50 |
| *113* | A14 | $5 multi | 6.25 | 6.25 |
| | | *Nos. 96-113 (19)* | 14.39 | 14.39 |

No. 108A issued June 16, 1981.

Capt. Cook A15

Designs: 30c, Flag raising on new island. 40c, Observation of transit of Venus. $1, Death of Capt. Cook.

**1979, Feb. 14 *Perf. 14x14½***

| | | | | |
|---|---|---|---|---|
| *114* | A15 | 8c multi | 12 | 10 |
| *115* | A15 | 30c multi | 48 | 38 |
| *116* | A15 | 40 multi | 65 | 52 |
| *117* | A15 | $1 multi | 1.65 | 1.25 |

Bicentenary of death of Capt. James Cook (1728-1779). Nos. 114-117 printed se-tenant horizontally in sheets of 12 (4x3) with gutters between horizontal rows.

Grumman Goose over Nukulaelae — A16

Grumman Goose over: 20c, Vaitupu. 30c, Nui. 40c, Funafuti.

**1979, May 16 Litho. *Perf. 14x13½***

| No. | Type | Description | Unused | Used |
|---|---|---|---|---|
| *118* | A16 | 8c multi | 12 | 12 |
| *119* | A16 | 20c multi | 22 | 22 |
| *120* | A16 | 30c multi | 55 | 55 |
| *121* | A16 | 40c multi | 70 | 70 |

Inauguration of internal air service.

Hill, Tuvalu No. 16, Letterbox, London, 1855 — A17

Hill, Stamps of Tuvalu and: 40c, No. 17, Penny Black. $1, No. 18, mail coach.

**1979, Aug. 20 Litho. *Perf. 13½x14***

| No. | Type | Description | Unused | Used |
|---|---|---|---|---|
| *122* | A17 | 30c multi | 32 | 32 |
| *123* | A17 | 40c multi | 45 | 45 |
| *124* | A17 | $1 multi | 1.10 | 1.10 |
| *a* | | Souvenir sheet of 3 | 2.00 | 2.00 |

Sir Rowland Hill (1795-1879), originator of penny postage. No. 124a contains Nos. 122-124; multicolored margin shows Hill statue and Exhibition Hall. Size: 147x141mm.

Boy — A18

Designs: Children of Tuvalu.

**1979, Oct. 20 Litho. *Perf. 14***

| No. | Type | Description | Unused | Used |
|---|---|---|---|---|
| *125* | A18 | 8c multi | 15 | 15 |
| *126* | A18 | 20c multi | 28 | 28 |
| *127* | A18 | 30c multi | 40 | 40 |
| *128* | A18 | 40c multi | 55 | 55 |

International Year of the Child.

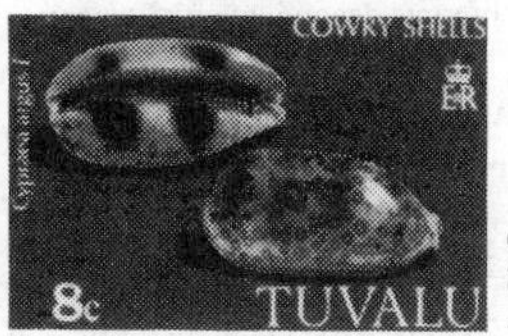
Cowry Shells A19

**1980, Feb. Litho. *Perf. 14***

| No. | Type | Description | Unused | Used |
|---|---|---|---|---|
| *129* | A19 | 8c *Cypraea Argus* | 12 | 12 |
| *130* | A19 | 20c *Cypraea scurra* | 28 | 28 |
| *131* | A19 | 30c *Cypraea carneola* | 42 | 42 |
| *132* | A19 | 40c *Cypraea aurantium* | 55 | 55 |

Foreign postal stationery (stamped envelopes, postal cards and air letter sheets) lies beyond the scope of this Catalogue, which is limited to adhesive postage stamps.

Philatelic Bureau, Funafuti, Tuvalu No. 28, Arms, London 1980 Emblem — A20

Coat of Arms, London 1980 Emblem and: 20c, Gilbert and Ellice No. 41, Nukulaelae cancel, Tuvalu No. 24. 30c, U.S. airmail cover. $1, Map of Tuvalu.

**1980, Apr. 30 Litho. *Perf. 13½x14***

| No. | Type | Description | Unused | Used |
|---|---|---|---|---|
| *133* | A20 | 10c multi | 16 | 16 |
| *134* | A20 | 20c multi | 20 | 20 |
| *135* | A20 | 30c multi | 32 | 32 |
| *136* | A20 | $1 multi | 1.00 | 1.00 |
| *a* | | Souvenir sheet of 4 | 2.00 | 2.00 |

London 1980 International Stamp Exhibition, May 6-14. No. 136a contains Nos. 133-136; multicolored margin shows Mulready envelope, London 1980 emblem, Earl's Court exhibition hall. Size: 160x136½mm.

Queen Mother Elizabeth, 80th Birthday — A21

**1980, Aug. 14 Litho. *Perf. 14***

| No. | Type | Description | Unused | Used |
|---|---|---|---|---|
| *137* | A21 | 50c multi | 80 | 55 |

Issued in sheets of 10 plus 2 labels.

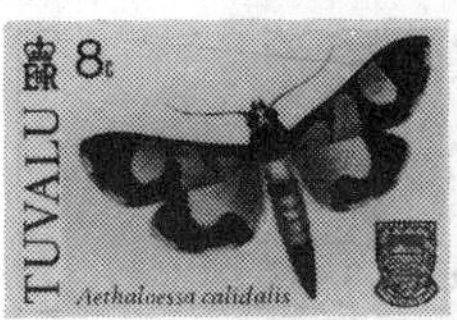
Aethaloessa Calidalis — A22

**1980, Aug. 20 Litho. *Perf. 14***

| No. | Type | Description | Unused | Used |
|---|---|---|---|---|
| *138* | A22 | 8c *shown* | 12 | 12 |
| *139* | A22 | 20c *Parotis suralis* | 28 | 28 |
| *140* | A22 | 30c *Dudua aprobola* | 42 | 42 |
| *141* | A22 | 40c *Decadarchis simulans* | 55 | 55 |

Air Pacific Heron (First Regular Air Service to Tuvalu, 1964) A23

Aviation Anniversaries: 20c, Hawker Siddeley 748 (air service to Tuvalu). 30c, Sunderland Flying Boat (War time service to Funafuti, 1945. 40c, Orville Wright and Flyer (Wright brothers' first flight, 1903).

**1980, Nov. 5 Litho. *Perf. 14***

| No. | Type | Description | Unused | Used |
|---|---|---|---|---|
| *142* | A23 | 8c multi | 12 | 12 |
| *143* | A23 | 20c multi | 28 | 28 |
| *144* | A23 | 30c multi | 42 | 42 |
| *145* | A23 | 40c multi | 55 | 55 |

Hypolimnas Bolina Elliciana A24

**1981, Feb. 3 Litho. *Perf. 14½***

| No. | Type | Description | Unused | Used |
|---|---|---|---|---|
| *146* | A24 | 8c shown | 12 | 12 |
| *147* | A24 | 20c Hypolimnas, diff. | 28 | 28 |
| *148* | A24 | 30c Hypolimnas, diff. | 42 | 42 |
| *149* | A24 | 40c Junonia vallida | 55 | 55 |

No. 109 Surcharged

**1981, Feb. 24 Litho. *Perf. 14***

| No. | Type | Description | Unused | Used |
|---|---|---|---|---|
| *150* | A14 | 45c on 50c multi | 60 | 60 |

Elizabeth, 1809 A25

**Wmk. 373**

**1981, May 13 Litho. *Perf. 14***

| No. | Type | Description | Unused | Used |
|---|---|---|---|---|
| *151* | A25 | 10c shown | 15 | 15 |
| *152* | A25 | 25c Rebecca, 1819 | 40 | 40 |
| *153* | A25 | 35c Independence II, 1821 | 55 | 55 |
| *154* | A25 | 40c Basilisk, 1872 | 60 | 60 |
| *155* | A25 | 45c Royalist, 1890 | 70 | 70 |
| *156* | A25 | 50c Olivebank, 1920 | 75 | 75 |
| | | *Nos. 151-156 (6)* | 3.15 | 3.15 |

See Nos. 216-221, 353-356, 410-413.

Royal Wedding Type of Montserrat

**Wmk. 380**

**1981, July 10 Litho. *Perf. 14***

| No. | Type | Description | Unused | Used |
|---|---|---|---|---|
| *157* | A66 | 10c Couple, Carolina | 15 | 15 |
| *a* | | Bklt pane of 4, perf. 12, unwmkd. | 60 | |
| *158* | A67 | 10c Couple | 15 | 15 |
| *159* | A66 | 45c Victoria and Albert III | 70 | 70 |
| *160* | A67 | 45c like #158 | 70 | 70 |
| *a* | | Bklt pane of 2, perf. 12, unwmkd. | 1.40 | |
| *161* | A66 | $2 Britannia | 3.00 | 3.00 |
| *162* | A67 | $2 like #158 | 3.00 | 3.00 |
| | | *Nos. 157-162 (6)* | 7.70 | 7.70 |

Issued in sheets of 7 (6 type A66; 1 type A67).

**Souvenir Sheet**

**1981, Dec. Litho. *Perf. 12***

| No. | Type | Description | Unused | Used |
|---|---|---|---|---|
| *163* | A67 | $1.50 Couple | 2.50 | 2.50 |

No. 163 has green decorative margin. Size: 120x109mm.

Admission to UPU — A26

**Wmk. Harrison's, London**

**1981, Nov. 19 Engr. *Perf. 14½x14***

| No. | Type | Description | Unused | Used |
|---|---|---|---|---|
| *164* | A26 | 70c dk bl | 95 | 95 |
| *165* | A26 | $1 dk red brn | 1.40 | 1.40 |
| *a* | | Souvenir sheet of 2, unwmkd. | 2.50 | 2.50 |

No. 165a contains Nos. 164-165; gray margin. Size: 87x71mm.

Amatuku Maritime School — A27

**1982, Feb. 17 Litho. *Perf. 13½x14***

| No. | Type | Description | Unused | Used |
|---|---|---|---|---|
| *166* | A27 | 10c Map | 16 | 16 |
| *167* | A27 | 25c Motorboat | 35 | 35 |
| *168* | A27 | 35c School, dock | 48 | 48 |
| *169* | A27 | 45c Flag, ship | 65 | 65 |

Princess Diana Type of Kiribati.

**Wmk. 380**

**1982, May 19 Litho. *Perf. 14***

| No. | Type | Description | Unused | Used |
|---|---|---|---|---|
| *170* | A64 | 10c Caroline of Brandenburg-Ansbach, 1714 | 15 | 15 |
| *171* | A64 | 45c Brandenburg-Ansbach arms | 60 | 60 |
| *172* | A64 | $1.50 Diana | 2.25 | 2.25 |

Nos. 170-172 Overprinted: "ROYAL BABY"

**1982, July 14 Litho. *Perf. 14***

| No. | Type | Description | Unused | Used |
|---|---|---|---|---|
| *173* | A64 | 10c multi | 16 | 16 |
| *174* | A64 | 45c multi | 65 | 65 |
| *175* | A64 | $1.50 multi | 2.25 | 2.25 |

Birth of Prince William of Wales, June 21.

Scouting Year — A28

**1982, Aug. 18**

| No. | Type | Description | Unused | Used |
|---|---|---|---|---|
| *176* | A28 | 10c Emblems | 18 | 18 |
| *177* | A28 | 25c Campfire | 48 | 48 |
| *178* | A28 | 35c Parade | 65 | 65 |
| *179* | A28 | 45c Scout | 85 | 85 |

Visit of Queen Elizabeth II and Prince Philip — A29

**1982, Oct. 26 Litho. *Perf. 14***

| No. | Type | Description | Unused | Used |
|---|---|---|---|---|
| *180* | A29 | 25c Arms, Duke of Edinburgh's Personal Standard | 42 | 42 |
| *181* | A29 | 45c Flags | 70 | 70 |
| *182* | A29 | 50c Queen Elizabeth II, maps | 85 | 85 |
| *a* | | Souvenir sheet of 3 | 2.00 | 2.00 |

No. 182a contains Nos. 180-182; multicolored margin. Size: 104x86mm.

Handicrafts A30

**1983, Mar. 14 Litho. *Perf. 14***

| No. | Type | Description | Unused | Used |
|---|---|---|---|---|
| *183* | A30 | 1c Fisherman's hat, lures, hooks | 5 | 5 |
| *184* | A30 | 2c Cowrie shell handbags | 5 | 5 |
| *185* | A30 | 5c Wedding and baby food baskets | 10 | 10 |
| *186* | A30 | 10c Canoe model | 22 | 22 |
| *186A* | A30 | 15c Women's sun hats ('84) | 25 | 25 |
| *187* | A30 | 20c Climbing rope | 30 | 30 |
| *188* | A30 | 25c Pandanus baskets | 35 | 35 |
| *188A* | A30 | 30c Tray, coconut stands | 32 | 32 |
| *189* | A30 | 35c Pandanus pillows, shell necklaces | 55 | 55 |
| *190* | A30 | 40c Round baskets, fans | 60 | 60 |
| *191* | A30 | 45c Reef sandals, fish trap | 70 | 70 |
| *192* | A30 | 50c Rat trap, vert. | 75 | 75 |
| *192A* | A30 | 60c Waterproof boxes | 65 | 65 |
| *193* | A30 | $1 Pump drill, adze, vert. | 1.50 | 1.50 |
| *194* | A30 | $2 Fisherman's hat, canoe bailers, vert. | 3.00 | 3.00 |
| *195* | A30 | $5 Fishing rod, lures, scoop nets, vert. | 7.50 | 7.50 |
| | | *Nos. 183-195 (16)* | 16.89 | 16.89 |

Commonwealth Day — A31

**Wmk. 373**

**1983, Mar. 14 Litho. *Perf. 14***

*196* A31 20c Fishing industry 32 32
*197* A31 35c Traditional dancing 55 55
*198* A31 45c Satellite view 70 70
*199* A31 50c First container ship 75 75

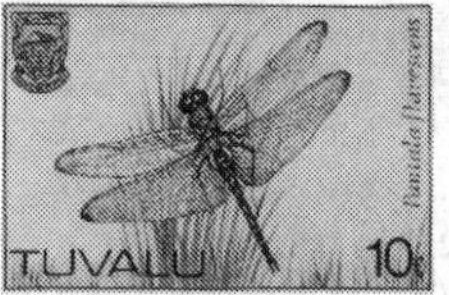


Dragonflies — A32

**Wmk. 380**

**1983, May 25 Litho. *Perf. 14***

*200* A32 10c Pantala flavescens 16 16
*201* A32 35c Anax guttatus 60 60
*202* A32 40c Tholymis tillarga 65 65
*203* A32 50c Diplacodes bipunctata 85 85

Boys Brigade Centenary — A33

**Wmk. 373**

**1983, Aug. 10 Litho. *Perf. 14***

*204* A33 10c Running, emblem 20 20
*205* A33 35c Canoeing 55 55
*206* A33 $1 Officer, boys 1.50 1.50

No. 193 Surcharged in Black

**Wmk. 380**

**1983, Aug. 26 Litho. *Perf. 14***

*207* A30 60c on $1 multi 1.10 1.10

First Manned Flight Bicentenary — A34

**Wmk. 373**

**1983, Sept. 21 Litho. *Perf. 14***

*208* A34 25c Montgolfier balloon, vert. 42 42
*209* A34 35c McKinnon Turbo Goose 60 60
*210* A34 45c Beechcraft Super King Air 200 75 75
*211* A34 50c Double Eagle II Balloon, vert. 80 80
*a* Souvenir sheet of 4 2.60 2.60

No. 211a contains Nos. 208-211. Multicolored margin depicts balloons in flight. Size: 104x145mm.

World Communications Year — A35

**Wmk. 380**

**1983, Nov. 18 Litho. *Perf. 14***

*212* A35 25c Conch Shell Trumpet, vert. 40 40
*213* A35 35c Radio Operator, vert. 60 60
*214* A35 45c Teleprinter 70 70
*215* A35 50c Transmitting station 80 80

Ship Type of 1981

**Wmk. 380**

**1984, Feb. 16 Litho. *Perf. 14***

*216* A25 10c Titus, 1897 14 14
*217* A25 20c Malaita, 1905 28 28
*218* A25 25c Aymeric, 1906 35 35
*219* A25 35c Anshun, 1965 48 48
*220* A25 45c Beaverbank, 1970 60 60
*221* A25 50c Benjamin Bowring, 1981 70 70
*Nos. 216-221 (6)* 2.55 2.55

Historic Locomotives — A36

A37

Locomotives from side view (A36) and on tracks (A37). Stamps of same denomination se-tenant.

***Perf. 12½x13***

**1984, Feb. 29 Unwmk.**

*222* A36 1c Class GS-4, U.S., 1941 5 5
*223* A37 1c GS-4 5 5
*224* A36 15c AD-60, Australia, 1952 25 25
*225* A37 15c AD-60 25 25
*226* A36 40c C38, Australia, 1943 65 65
*227* A37 40c C38 65 65
*228* A36 60c Achilles England, 1892 95 95
*229* A37 60c Achilles 95 95
*Nos. 222-229 (8)* 3.80 3.80

See Nos. 235-258, 291-298, 320-327.

No. 191 Surcharged.

**Wmk. 380**

**1984, Feb. 1 Litho. *Perf. 14***

*230* A30 30c on 45c multi 55 55

Beach Flowers A38

**1984, May 30**

*231* A38 25c Ipomoea pes-caprae 35 35
*232* A38 45c Ipomoea macrantha 60 60
*233* A38 50c Triumfetta procumbens 70 70
*234* A38 60c Portulaca quadrifida 85 85

Train Type of 1984

**1984 Litho. *Perf. 12½x13***

*235* A36 1c Class 9700, Japan, 1897 5 5
*236* A36 1c 9700 5 5
*237* A36 10c Casey Jones, U.S., 1896 12 12
*238* A36 10c Jones 12 12
*239* A36 15c Class 2310K, France, 1909 18 18
*240* A36 15c 231CK 18 18
*241* A36 15c Triplex, U.S., 1914 18 18
*242* A36 15c Triplex 18 18
*243* A36 20c Class 370, Gt. Britain, 1981 24 24
*244* A36 20c 370 24 24
*245* A36 25c Class 4F, Gt. Britain, 1924 28 28
*246* A36 25c 4F 28 28
*247* A36 30c Glass 640, Italy, 1907 35 35
*248* A36 30c 640 35 35
*249* A36 40c Tornado, Gt. Britain, 1888 45 45
*250* A36 40c Tornado 45 45
*251* A36 50c Broadlands, Gt. Britain, 1967 60 60
*252* A36 50c Broadlands 60 60
*253* A36 60c Locomotion, Gt. Britain, 1825 75 75
*254* A36 60c Locomotion 75 75
*255* A36 $1 C57, Japan, 1937 1.10 1.10
*256* A36 $1 C57 1.10 1.10
*257* A36 $1 Class 4500, France, 1906 1.10 1.10
*258* A36 $1 4500 1.10 1.10
*Nos. 235-258 (24)* 10.80 10.80

Issue dates: Nos. 235-236, 239-240, 247-248, 257-258, Oct. 4; others, June 27.

15th South Pacific Forum A38a

**1984, Aug. 21 Litho. *Perf. 14***

*258A* A38a 60c National flag 70 70
*258B* A38a 60c Tuvalu crest 70 70

Ausipex '84 A38b

**1984, Aug. 21 *Perf. 14***

*258C* A38b 60c Exhibition emblem 70 70
*258D* A38b 60c Royal Exhibition Building 70 70

A. Shrewsbury Playing Cricket — A39

Cricket players in action or portrait. Stamps of same denomination se-tenant.

**1984, Nov. 5 Litho. *Perf. 12½***

*259* A39 5c shown 7 7
*260* A39 5c Portrait 7 7
*261* A39 30c H. Verity 38 38
*262* A39 30c Portrait 38 38
*263* A39 50c E.H. Hendren 60 60
*264* A39 50c Portrait 60 60
*265* A39 60c J. Briggs 80 80
*266* A39 60c Portrait 80 80
*Nos. 259-266 (8)* 3.70 3.70

Drawings, Christmas 1984 — A40

**1984, Nov. 14 Litho. *Perf. 14½x14***

*267* A40 15c By Eli Faalata 22 22
*268* A40 40c By Toakai Niutao 55 55
*269* A40 50c By Falesa Teuila 70 70
*270* A40 60c By Piuani Talie 90 90

Classic Automobiles A41

Stamps of same denomination se-tenant. Sketch listed first followed by angled view.

**1984, Dec. 7 Litho. *Perf. 12½x13***

*271* A41 1c Morris Minor, 1949 5 5
*272* A41 1c multi 5 5
*273* A41 15c Studebaker Avanti, 1963 20 20
*274* A41 15c multi 20 20
*275* A41 50c Chevrolet International Six, 1929 65 65
*276* A41 50c multi 65 65
*277* A41 $1 Allard J2, 1950 1.25 1.25
*278* A41 $1 multi 1.25 1.25
*Nos. 271-278 (8)* 4.30 4.30

See Nos. 299-306, 332-347, 396-396J, 414-437.

John J. Audubon — A42

**1985, Feb. 12 Litho. *Perf. 12½***

*279* A42 1c Common flicker 5 5
*280* A42 1c Say's phoebe 5 5
*281* A42 25c Townsend's warbler 35 35
*282* A42 25c Bohemian waxwing 35 35
*283* A42 50c Prothonotary warbler 65 65
*284* A42 50c Worm-eating warbler 65 65
*285* A42 70c Broad-winged hawk 90 90
*286* A42 70c Northern harrier 90 90
*Nos. 279-286 (8)* 3.90 3.90

Stamps of the same denomination se-tenant.

Birds and Eggs A43

**1985, Feb. 27 *Perf. 14***

*287* A43 15c Black-naped tern 24 24
*288* A43 40c Black noddy 60 60
*289* A43 50c White-tailed tropicbird 75 75
*290* A43 60c Sooty tern 95 95

Train Type of 1984

**1985, Mar. 19 *Perf. 12½***

*291* A36 5c Churchward, U.K. 10 10
*292* A37 5c Churchward 10 10
*293* A36 10c Class K.F., China 18 18
*294* A37 10c Class K.F. 18 18
*295* A36 30c Class 99.77, East Germany 56 56
*296* A37 30c Class 99.77 56 56
*297* A36 $1 Pearson, U.K. 1.80 1.80
*298* A37 $1 Pearson 1.80 1.80
*Nos. 291-298 (8)* 5.28 5.28

Stamps of same denomination se-tenant.

Automobile Type of 1984

**1985, Apr. 3**

*299* A41 1c Rickenbacker, 1923 5 5
*300* A41 1c Like No. 299 5 5
*301* A41 20c Detroit-Electric, 1914 36 36
*302* A41 20c Like No. 301 36 36
*303* A41 50c Packard Clipper, 1941 90 90
*304* A41 50c Like No. 303 90 90
*305* A41 70c Audi Quattro, 1982 1.25 1.25
*306* A41 70c Like No. 305 1.25 1.25
*Nos. 299-306 (8)* 5.12 5.12

Stamps of the same denomination se-tenant.

World War II Aircraft A44

**1985, May 29 Litho. *Perf. 14***
*307* A44 15c Curtiss P-40N 20 20
*308* A44 40c Consolidated B-24D Liberator 55 55
*309* A44 50c Lockheed PV-1 Ventura 70 70
*310* A44 60c Douglas C-54 Skymaster 85 85
*a* Souvenir sheet of 4, #307-310 2.50 2.50

No. 310a has multicolored margin picturing U.S. fighter planes ready for take-off on tropical beach. Size: 111x109mm.

Queen Mother, 85th Birthday — A45

Photographs.

**1985, July 4 Litho. *Perf. 12½***
*311* A45 5c Facing right 8 8
*312* A45 5c Facing left 8 8
*313* A45 30c Facing right, diff. 42 42
*314* A45 30c Facing front 42 42
*315* A45 60c Waving to crowd 85 85
*316* A45 60c Facing front, diff. 85 85
*317* A45 $1 Facing front, diff. 1.40 1.40
*318* A45 $1 Facing left, diff. 1.40 1.40
*Nos. 311-318 (8)* 5.50 5.50

**Souvenir Sheets**
*319* Sheet of 2 3.50 3.50
*a.-b* A45 $1.20. Any single 1.75 1.75
*319C* Sheet of 2 ('86) 5.50 5.50
*e* A45 $2 like #315 2.75 2.75
*f* A45 $2 like #316 2.75 2.75
*319D* Sheet of 2 ('86) 8.50 8.50
*g* A45 $3 like #313 4.25 4.25
*h* A45 $3 like #314 4.25 4.25

No. 319 contains 2 se-tenant stamps picturing classic black & white photographs of the Queen Mother as a young woman and as Queen Consort. Multicolored margin pictures Windsor Castle. Size: 86x115mm. Stamps of same denomination se-tenant.

Nos. 319C-319D, issued June 10, 1986, have multicolored decorative margins picturing the Concorde jet; flora and fauna. Sizes: 141x109mm.

Train Type of 1984

**1985, Sept. 18**
*320* A36 10c 1936 Green Arrow, U.K. 16 16
*321* A37 10c Green Arrow, diff. 16 16
*322* A36 40c 1982 G.M. (EMD) SD-50, USA 55 55
*323* A37 40c SD-50, diff. 55 55
*324* A36 65c 1932 DRG Flying Hamburger, Germany 85 85
*325* A37 65c Flying Hamburger, diff. 85 85
*326* A36 $1 1908 JNR Class 1070, Japan 1.40 1.40
*327* A37 $1 Class 1070, diff. 1.40 1.40
*Nos. 320-327 (8)* 5.92 5.92

Girl Guides, 75th Anniv. — A46

**1985, Aug. 28 Litho. *Perf. 15***
*328* A46 15c Playing guitar 22 22
*329* A46 40c Camping 58 58
*330* A46 50c Flag bearer 72 72
*331* A46 60c Guides' salute 88 88
*a.* Souv. sheet of 4, Nos. 328-331 2.40 2.40

No. 331a has multicolored inscribed margin. Size: 141x77mm.

Car Type of 1984

**1985, Oct. 8 *Perf. 12½***
*332* A41 5c 1929 Cord L-29, US 8 8
*333* A41 5c Cord, diff. 8 8
*334* A41 10c 1932 Horch 670 V-12, Germany 15 15
*335* A41 10c Horch, diff. 15 15
*336* A41 15c 1901 Lanchester, UK 22 22
*337* A41 15c Lanchester, diff. 22 22
*338* A41 35c 1950 Citroen 2 CV, France 52 52
*339* A41 35c Citroen, diff. 52 52
*340* A41 40c 1957 MGA, UK 58 58
*341* A41 40c MGA, diff. 58 58
*342* A41 55c 1962 Ferrari 250-GTO, Italy 80 80
*343* A41 55c Ferrari, diff. 80 80
*344* A41 $1 1932 Ford V-8, US 1.50 1.50
*345* A41 $1 Ford V-8, diff. 1.50 1.50
*346* A41 $1.50 1977 Aston Martin-Lagonda, UK 2.25 2.25
*347* A41 $1.50 Aston Martin 2.25 2.25
*Nos. 332-347 (16)* 12.20 12.20

Stamps of same denomination printed se-tenant.

Crabs A47

**1986, Jan. 7 *Perf. 15***
*348* A47 15c Stalk-eyed ghost 22 22
*349* A47 40c Red and white painted 55 55
*350* A47 50c Red-spotted 70 70
*351* A47 60c Red hermit 85 85

**Souvenir Sheet**

Events — A48

Designs: No. 352a, American and Soviet flags, chess board and knight. No. 352b, Rotary Intl. emblem.

**1986, Mar. 19 Litho. *Perf. 13x12½***
*352* Sheet of 2 8.00 8.00
*a.-b.* A48 $3 any single 4.00 4.00

Fischer and Karpov, world chess champions; Rotary Intl., 80th anniv. No. 352 has black on pale green inscribed margin picturing Scouting trefoil and 15th World Jamboree emblem. Size: 148x127mm.

Ship Type of 1981

**1986, Apr. 14 *Perf. 15***
*353* A25 15c Messenger of Peace 22 22
*354* A25 40c John Wesley 60 60
*355* A25 50c Duff 75 75
*356* A25 60c Triton 85 85

Queen Elizabeth II, 60th Birthday — A49

Various portraits.

**1986, Apr. 21 *Perf. 12½***
*357* A49 10c multi 15 15
*358* A49 90c multi 1.35 1.35
*359* A49 $1.50 multi 2.25 2.25
*360* A49 $3 multi 4.50 4.50

**Souvenir Sheet**
*361* A49 $4 multi 6.00 6.00

No. 360 vert. No. 361 has multicolored margin picturing portrait enlargement. Size: 85x115mm.

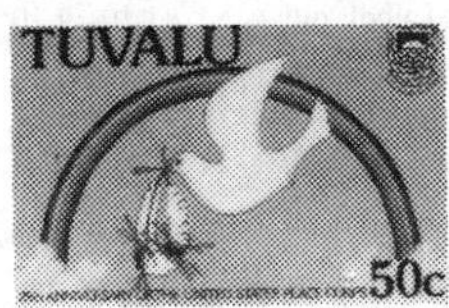

Peace Corps, 25th Anniv. A50

**1986, May 22 *Perf. 14***
*362* A50 50c multi 75 75

AMERIPEX '86 — A51

**1986, May 22 *Perf. 14x13½***
*363* A51 60c multi 90 90

1986 World Cup Soccer Championships A52

Players and teams.

**1986, June 30 Litho. *Perf. 15***
*364* A52 1c So. Korea 5 5
*365* A52 5c France 6 6
*366* A52 10c W. Germany, 1974 14 14
*367* A52 40c Italy 55 55

**Size: 60x40mm**
***Perf. 13x12½***
*368* A52 60c W. Germany vs. Holland, 1974 80 80
*369* A52 $1 Canada 1.35 1.35
*370* A52 $2 No. Ireland 2.70 2.70
*371* A52 $3 England 4.00 4.00
*Nos. 364-371 (8)* 9.65 9.65

**Souvenir Sheets**
*372* A52 $1.50 like #369 2.00 2.00
*373* A52 $2.50 like #370 3.35 3.35

Nos. 366 and 368 picture emblem; others picture character trademark. Nos. 372-373 have multicolored margins picturing match scenes and soccer cup. Sizes: 85x114mm.

No. 362 Ovptd. with STAMPEX '86 Emblem

**1986, Aug. 4 Litho. *Perf. 14***
*374* A50 50c multi 75 75

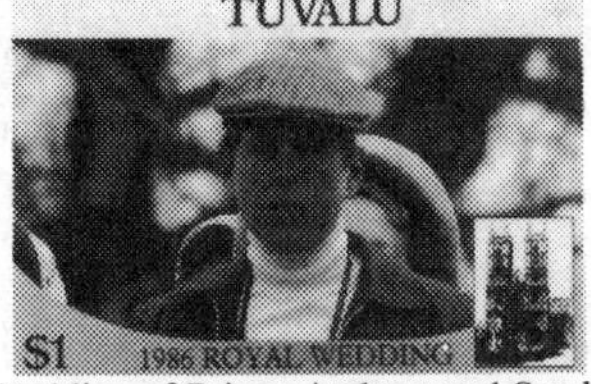

Wedding of Prince Andrew and Sarah Ferguson — A53

***Perf. 12½***
**1986, July 18 Litho. Unwmk.**
*382* A53 60c Andrew, vert. 80 80
*383* A53 60c Couple, vert. 80 80
*384* A53 $1 Andrew, diff. 1.35 1.35
*385* A53 $1 Princess Diana, Sarah 1.35 1.35

Stamps of the same denomination printed se-tenant. No. 384 pictures Westminster Abbey in LR.

Geckos A54

**1986, July 30 Litho. *Perf. 14***
*386* A54 15c Mourning gecko 18 18
*387* A54 40c Oceanic stump-toed 48 48
*388* A54 50c Azure-tailed skink 60 60
*389* A54 60c Moth skink 85 85

Souvenir Sheet

South Pacific Forum, 15th Anniv. A55

Flags and maps: a, Australia. b, Cook Islands. c, Micronesia. d, Fiji. e, Kiribati. f, Nauru. g, New Zealand. h, Niue. i, Papua New Guinea. j, Solomon Islands. k, Tonga. l, Tuvalu. m, Vanuatu. n, Western Samoa.

**Wmk. 380**
**1986, Aug. 4 Litho. *Perf. 15***
*390* Sheet of 14 + label 7.00 7.00
*a.-n* A55 40c, any single 50 50

No. 390 has center label picturing Executive Committee headquarters, Suva, Fiji. Size: 235x140mm.

Souvenir Sheet

Wedding of Prince Andrew and Sarah Ferguson — A56

**1986 Litho. *Perf. 13x12½***
*391* A56 $6 Newlyweds 8.00 8.00

No. 391 has inscribed multicolored margin continuing the design picturing the Duke and Duchess of York greeting crowd after the ceremony. Size: 85x115mm.

Nos. 382-385 Ovptd. "Congratulations to T.R.H. The Duke & Duchess of York" in Silver

**1986 Unwmk. *Perf. 12½***
*392* A53 60c No. 382 80 80
*393* A53 60c No. 383 80 80
*394* A53 $1 No. 384 1.35 1.35
*395* A53 $1 No. 385 1.35 1.35

Stamps of the same denomination exist printed tete-beche and se-tenant.

Car Type of 1984

**1986, Oct. Litho. *Perf. 12½***
*396* A41 15c 1953 Cooper, UK 22 22
*396A* A41 15c Cooper, diff. 22 22
*396B* A41 40c 1964 Rover 2000, UK 58 58
*396C* A41 40c Rover, diff. 58 58
*396D* A41 50c 1930 Ruxton, US 72 72
*396E* A41 50c Ruxton, diff. 72 72
*396F* A41 60c 1950 Jowett Jupiter, UK 88 88
*396G* A41 60c Jupiter, diff. 88 88

*396H* A41 90c 1964 Cobra Daytona Coupe, US 1.30 1.30
*396I* A41 90c Daytona, diff. 1.30 1.30
*396J* A41 $1.50 1903 Packard Model F "Old Pacific," US 2.20 2.20
*396K* A41 $1.50 "Old Pacific," diff. 2.20 2.20
*Nos. 396-396K (12)* 11.80 11.80

Stamps of the same denomination printed se-tenant.

Marine Life — A57

**1986, Nov. 5 Unwmk. *Perf. 14***
*397* A57 15c Sea star 20 20
*398* A57 40c Pencil urchin 55 55
*399* A57 50c Fragile coral 68 68
*400* A57 60c Pink coral 80 80

See Nos. 465-468.

Souvenir Sheets

Statue of Liberty, Cent. — A58

Various views of the statue.

**1986, Nov. 24**
*401* A58 $1.25 multi 1.65 1.65
*402* A58 $1.50 multi 2.00 2.00
*403* A58 $1.80 multi 2.40 2.40
*404* A58 $2 multi 2.65 2.65
*405* A58 $2.25 multi 3.00 3.00
*406* A58 $2.50 multi 3.35 3.35
*407* A58 $3 multi 4.00 4.00
*408* A58 $3.25 multi 4.35 4.35
*409* A58 $3.50 multi 4.65 4.65

Nos. 401-409 have multicolored margins picturing views of the statue and American presidents James Monroe, John Quincy Adams, James K. Polk, Zachary Taylor, Andrew Johnson, Ulysses S. Grant, Rutherford B. Hayes, Theodore Roosevelt and Franklin D. Roosevelt. Sizes: 85x115mm.

Ships Type of 1981

**1987, Feb. 4 Unwmk. *Perf. 14***
*410* A25 15c Southern Cross IV 20 20
*411* A25 40c John Williams VI 55 55
*412* A25 50c John Williams IV 68 68
*413* A25 60c M.S. Southern Cross 80 80

Car Type of 1984

***Perf. 12½***

**1987, May 7 Litho. Unwmk.**
*414* A41 1c 1938 Talbot-Lago, France 5 5
*415* A41 1c Talbot-Lago, diff. 5 5
*416* A41 2c 1930 Dupont Model G, U.S. 5 5
*417* A41 2c Model G, diff. 5 5
*418* A41 5c 1950 Riley RM, U.K. 8 8
*419* A41 5c RM, diff. 8 8
*420* A41 10c 1915 Chevrolet Baby Grand, U.S. 15 15
*421* A41 10c Baby Grand, diff. 15 15
*422* A41 20c 1968 Shelby Mustang GT 500 KR, U.S. 30 30
*423* A41 20c Shelby, diff. 30 30
*424* A41 30c 1952 Ferrari 212 Export Barchetta, Italy 42 42
*425* A41 30c Ferrari, diff. 42 42
*426* A41 40c 1912 Peerless Model 48-Six, U.S. 58 58
*427* A41 40c Peerless, diff. 58 58
*428* A41 50c 1954 Sunbeam Alpine, U.K. 72 72
*429* A41 50c Sunbeam, diff. 72 72
*430* A41 60c 1969 Matra-Ford MS80, France 88 88
*431* A41 60c MS80, diff. 88 88
*432* A41 70c 1934 Squire 1-Litre, U.K. 1.00 1.00
*433* A41 70c Squire, diff. 1.00 1.00
*434* A41 75c 1931 Talbot 105, U.K. 1.10 1.10
*435* A41 75c Talbot, diff. 1.10 1.10
*436* A41 $1 1928 Plymouth Model Q, U.S. 1.45 1.45
*437* A41 $1 Model Q, diff. 1.45 1.45
*a* Souv. sheet of 2, Nos. 436-437 3.00 3.00
*Nos. 414-437 (24)* 13.56 13.56

No. 437a has multicolored margin picturing New York City, buildings, street; issued June 8. Size: 101x86mm. Stamps of the same denomination printed se-tenant.

Ferns — A59

**1987, July 7 Wmk. 380 *Perf. 14***
*438* A59 15c Nephrolepis saligna 22 22
*439* A59 40c Asplenium nidus 58 58
*440* A59 50c Microsorum scolopendria 72 72
*441* A59 60c Pteris tripartita 88 88

**Souvenir Sheet**

*442* A59 $1.50 Psilotum nudum 2.25 2.25

No. 442 has multicolored margin picturing ferns growing at base of coconut palm. Size: 62x62mm.

Flowers and Women Wearing Fous — A60

**1987, Aug. 12 Wmk. 380**
*443* A60 15c Flowers 22 22
*444* A60 15c Woman wearing fou 22 22
*445* A60 40c Woman wearing fou, diff. 58 58
*446* A60 40c Flowers, diff. 58 58
*447* A60 50c Flowers, diff. 72 72
*448* A60 50c Woman wearing fou, diff. 72 72
*449* A60 60c Woman wearing fou, diff. 88 88
*450* A60 60c Flowers, diff. 88 88
*Nos. 443-450 (8)* 4.80 4.80

Crayfish and Coconut Crabs A61

**Wmk. 380**

**1987, Nov. 11 Litho. *Perf. 14***
*451* A61 40c Coconut crabs 60 60
*452* A61 50c Painted crayfish 75 75
*453* A61 60c Ocean crayfish 88 88

Photograph of Queen Victoria, 1897, by Downey — A62

Designs: 60c, Elizabeth and Philip on their wedding day, 1947. 80c, Elizabeth, Charles, Philip, c. 1950. $1, Elizabeth, Anne, 1950. $2, Elizabeth, 1970. $3, Elizabeth, children, 1950.

**1987, Nov. 20 Unwmk. *Perf. 15***
*454* A62 40c olive grn & blk 60 60
*455* A62 60c dull blue grn & blk 88 88
*456* A62 80c dark blue & blk 1.20 1.20
*457* A62 $1 rose mag & blk 1.50 1.50
*458* A62 $2 multi 2.95 2.95
*Nos. 454-458 (5)* 7.13 7.13

**Souvenir Sheet**

*459* A62 $3 red org & blk 4.40 4.40

Accession of Queen Victoria to the throne of England, sesquicentennial; wedding of Queen Elizabeth II and Prince Philip, 40th anniv. No. 459 has inscribed decorative margin picturing royal family. Size: 86x101mm.

16th World Scout Jamboree, Australia, 1987-88 — A63

Jamboree and Australia bicentennial emblems plus: 40c, Aborigine, Ayer's Rock. 60c, Capt. Cook, by Dance, and HMS Endeavor. $1, Scout and Scout Park Arch. $1.50, Koala and kangaroo. $2.50, Lord and Lady Baden-Powell.

***Perf. 13x12½***

**1987, Dec. 2 Litho. Unwmk.**
*460* A63 40c multi 60 60
*461* A63 60c multi 88 88
*462* A63 $1 multi 1.50 1.50
*463* A63 $1.50 multi 2.20 2.20

**Souvenir Sheet**

*464* A63 $2.50 multi 3.70 3.70

No. 464 has multicolored decorative margin picturing Scouts of different nationalities. Size: 115x85mm

Marine Life Type of 1986

**Unwmk.**

**1988, Feb. 29 Litho. *Perf. 15***
*465* A57 15c Spanish dancer 22 22
*466* A57 40c Hard corals 60 60
*467* A57 50c Feather stars 75 75
*468* A57 60c Staghorn corals 90 90

Birds A64

**1988, Mar. 2 *Perf. 15***
*469* A64 5c Jungle fowl 8 8
*470* A64 10c White tern 15 15
*471* A64 15c Brown noddy 22 22
*472* A64 20c Phoenix petrel 30 30
*473* A64 25c Pacific golden plover 38 38
*474* A64 30c Crested tern 45 45
*475* A64 35c Sooty tern 52 52
*476* A64 40c Bristle-thighed curlew 60 60
*477* A64 45c Eastern bar-tailed godwit 68 68
*478* A64 50c Reef heron 75 75
*479* A64 55c Greater frigatebird 82 82
*480* A64 60c Red-footed booby 90 90
*481* A64 70c Red-necked stint 1.05 1.05
*482* A64 $1 New Zealand long-tailed cuckoo 1.50 1.50
*483* A64 $2 Red-tailed tropicbird 3.00 3.00
*484* A64 $5 Banded rail 7.50 7.50
*Nos. 469-484 (16)* 18.90 18.90

Intl. Red Cross and Red Crescent Organizations, 125th Annivs. — A65

***Perf. 12½***

**1988, May 9 Litho. Unwmk.**
*485* A65 15c Jean-Henri Dunant 22 22
*486* A65 40c Junior Red Cross 60 60
*487* A65 50c Care for the handicapped 75 75
*488* A65 60c First aid training 90 90

**Souvenir Sheet**

*489* A65 $1.50 Lecture 2.25 2.25

No. 489 has vermilion and green inscribed margin picturing Red Cross headquarters on Funafuti. Size: 97x66mm.

A66

Voyages of Capt. Cook — A67

Designs: 20c, HMS *Endeavour* (starboard side). 40c, *Endeavour* (stern). 50c, Landing, Tahiti, 1769, vert. 60c, Maori chief, vert. 80c, *Resolution* and native Hawaiian sail ship. $1, Cook, by Sir Nathaniel Dance-Holland (1735-1811), vert. $2.50, Antarctic icebergs surrounding the *Resolution*.

**1988, June 15 Litho. *Perf. 12½***
*490* A66 20c shown 35 35
*491* A66 40c multi 68 68
*492* A66 50c multi 82 82
*493* A66 60c multi 1.00 1.00
*494* A66 80c multi 1.30 1.30
*495* A66 $1 multi 1.65 1.65
*Nos. 490-495 (6)* 5.80 5.80

**Souvenir Sheet**

*496* A67 $2.50 shown 4.25 4.25

No. 496 has multicolored margin continuing the design. Size: 116x86mm.

Fungi — A68

**1988, July 25 Litho. *Perf. 15***
*497* A68 40c Ganoderma applanatum 65 65
*498* A68 50c Rigidoepicoccum cocos 82 82
*499* A68 60c Rigidoporus zonalis 1.00 1.00
*500* A68 90c Rigidoporus microporus 1.50 1.50

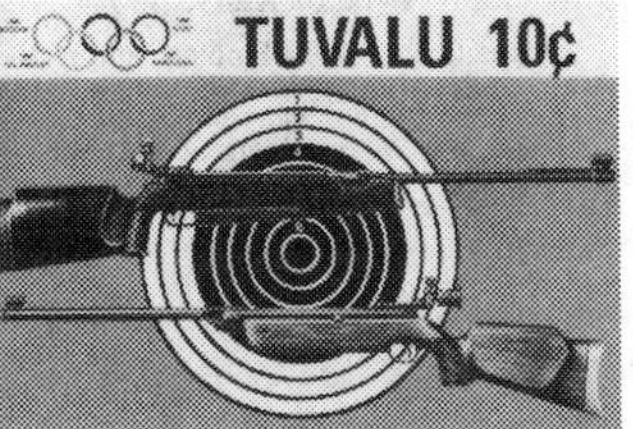


1988 Summer Olympics, Seoul — A69

***Perf. 12½***
**1988, Aug. 19 Litho. Unwmk.**
*501* A69 10c Rifles, target 16 16
*502* A69 20c Judo 32 32
*503* A69 40c One-man kayak 65 65
*504* A69 60c Swimming 1.00 1.00
*505* A69 80c Yachting 1.30 1.30
*506* A69 $1 Balance beam 1.65 1.65
*Nos. 501-506 (6)* 5.08 5.08

Natl. Independence, 10th Anniv. — A70

**Wmk. 380**
**1988, Sept. 28 Litho. *Perf. 14***
*507* A70 60c Queen Elizabeth in boat 1.00 1.00
*a.* Souv. sheet of one 1.00 1.00
*508* A70 90c In sedan chair 1.45 1.45
*a.* Souv. sheet of one 1.45 1.45
*509* A70 $1 shown 1.60 1.60
*a.* Souv. sheet of one 1.60 1.60
*510* A70 $1.20 Seated at dais 1.95 1.95
*a.* Souv. sheet of one 1.95 1.95

Nos. 507-508 and 510 vert. Nos. 507a-510a have mutlicolored inscribed margins continuing the designs. Sizes: 85x86mm.

## SEMI-POSTAL STAMPS

Nos. 159-160 Surcharged and Overprinted: "TONGA CYCLONE / RELIEF / 1982" in 1 or 3 Lines.

**Wmk. 380**
**1982, May 20 Litho. *Perf. 14***
*B1* A66 45c + 20c multi 1.25 1.25
*B2* A67 45c + 20c multi 1.25 1.25

## POSTAGE DUE STAMPS

Arms of Tuvalu — D1

**1981, May 13 Litho. *Perf. 14***
*J1* D1 1c brt rose lil & blk 5 5
*J2* D1 2c grnsh bl & blk 5 5
*J3* D1 5c yel brn & blk 12 12
*J4* D1 10c bl grn & blk 20 20
*J5* D1 20c choc & blk 25 25
*J6* D1 30c org & blk 38 38
*J7* D1 40c ultra & blk 50 50
*J8* D1 50c yel grn & blk 65 65
*J9* D1 $1 brt lil & blk 1.25 1.25
*Nos. J1-J9 (9)* 3.45 3.45

Nos. J1-J5 reissued inscribed 1982.

## OFFICIAL STAMPS

Nos. 96-113 Overprinted: "OFFICIAL"

**1981 Litho. Unwmk. *Perf. 14***
*O1* A14 1c multi 5 5
*O2* A14 2c multi 5 5
*O3* A14 4c multi 6 6
*O4* A14 5c multi 7 7
*O5* A14 6c multi 9 9
*O6* A14 8c multi 12 12
*O7* A14 10c multi 14 14
*O8* A14 15c multi 22 22
*O9* A14 20c multi 30 30
*O10* A14 25c multi 35 35
*O11* A14 30c multi 45 45
*O12* A14 35c multi 52 52
*O13* A14 40c multi 60 60
*O14* A14 45c multi 70 70
*O15* A14 50c multi 75 75
*O16* A14 70c multi 1.00 1.00
*O17* A14 $1 multi 1.50 1.50
*O18* A14 $2 multi 3.00 3.00
*O19* A14 $5 multi 7.25 7.25
*Nos. O1-O19 (19)* 17.22 17.22

No. 193 Surcharged and Overprinted "OFFICIAL"

**Wmk. 380**
**1983, Aug. Litho. *Perf. 14***
*O20* A30 60c on $1 multi 1.00 1.00

Nos. 185-186A, 188, 230, 188A-195 Overprinted: "OFFICIAL"

**1984 Litho. Wmk. 380 *Perf. 14***
*O21* A30 5c multi 6 6
*O22* A30 10c multi 12 12
*O23* A30 15c multi 20 20
*O24* A30 25c multi 32 32
*O25* A30 30c on 45c multi 40 40
*O25A* A30 30c multi 40 40
*O26* A30 35c multi 45 45
*O27* A30 40c multi 50 50
*O28* A30 45c multi 55 55
*O29* A30 50c multi 65 65
*O29A* A30 60c multi 80 80
*O30* A30 $1 multi 1.25 1.25
*O31* A30 $2 multi 2.50 2.50
*O32* A30 $5 multi 6.25 6.25
*Nos. O21-O32 (14)* 14.45 14.45

Issue dates: Nos. O23, O29A Apr. 30; others Feb. 1.

# UGANDA

LOCATION — In East Africa, at the Equator and separated from the Indian Ocean by Kenya and Tanzania.
GOVT. — Independent state
AREA — 91,343 sq. mi.
POP. — 13,990,000 (est. 1983)
CAPITAL — Kampala

Stamps of 1898-1902 were replaced by those issued for Kenya, Tanganyika and Uganda. Uganda became independent October 9, 1962.

Cowries (50 = 4 Pence)
16 Annas = 1 Rupee (1896)
100 Cents = 1 Shilling (1962)

**Catalogue values for unused stamps in this country are for Never Hinged items, beginning with Scott 79 in the regular postage section and Scott J1 in the postage due section.**

Unused values for Nos. 1-68 are for copies without gum.

A1 A2

**1895 Unwmk. *Imperf.***
**Without Gum**
**Wide Letters**
**Typewritten on Thin Laid Paper**
**Stamps 20 to 26mm wide**

Nos. 1-53 were produced with a typewriter by Rev. Ernest Millar of the Church Missionary Society. They were 20-26mm wide, with nine stamps in a horizontal row. Later two more were added to each row, and the stamps became narrower, 16-18mm.

Mr. Millar got a new typewriter in 1895, and the stamps he typed on it have a different appearance. A violet ribbon in the machine, inserted late in 1895, resulted in Nos. 35-53.

*1* A1 5 (c) black
*2* A1 10 (c) black *2,500.*
*3* A1 15 (c) black
*4* A1 20 (c) black *3,500. 3,000.*
*5* A1 25 (c) black
*6* A1 30 (c) black *2,500. 2,500.*
*7* A1 40 (c) black *3,000.*
*8* A1 50 (c) black *1,000. 1,000.*
*9* A1 60 (c) black *3,000.*

Nos. 1-53 are on thin, tough, white paper, laid horizontally with traces of a few vertical lines.

**Surcharged with New Value in Black, Pen-written**
*10* A1 10 on 50 (c) blk
*11* A1 15 on 10 (c) blk
*12* A1 15 on 20 (c) blk
*13* A1 15 on 40 (c) blk
*14* A1 15 on 50 (c) blk
*15* A1 25 on 50 (c) blk
*16* A1 50 on 60 (c) blk

Forgeries of Nos. 1-43 are known.

**Stamps 16 to 18mm wide**
*17* A1 5 (c) black *1,750. 1,750.*
*18* A1 10 (c) black *1,350. 1,350.*
*19* A1 15 (c) black *1,350. 1,350.*
*20* A1 20 (c) black *1,350. 1,350.*
*21* A1 25 (c) black *1,350. 1,350.*
*22* A1 30 (c) black *2,500. 2,500.*
*23* A1 40 (c) black *6,000. 6,000.*
*24* A1 50 (c) black *1,750. 1,750.*
*25* A1 60 (c) black *3,500. 3,500.*

**Narrow Letters**
**Stamps 16 to 18mm wide**
*26* A2 5 (c) black *650.00*
*27* A2 10 (c) black *650.00*
*28* A2 15 (c) black *1,000.*
*29* A2 20 (c) black *550.00*
*30* A2 25 (c) black *650.00*
*31* A2 30 (c) black *800.00*
*32* A2 40 (c) black *650.00*
*33* A2 50 (c) black *650.00*
*34* A2 60 (c) black *1,100.*
*35* A2 5 (c) violet *450.00 450.00*
*36* A2 10 (c) violet *450.00 450.00*
*37* A2 15 (c) violet *450.00 450.00*
*38* A2 20 (c) violet *450.00 450.00*
*39* A2 25 (c) violet *750.00 750.00*
*40* A2 30 (c) violet *1,100. 900.00*
*41* A2 40 (c) violet *1,000. 900.00*
*42* A2 50 (c) violet *1,000.*
*43* A2 100(c) violet *3,500.*

As a favor to a philatelist, 35c and 45c denominations were made in black and violet. They were not intended for postal use and no rate called for those denominations.

A3 A4

**1896**
*44* A3 5 (c) violet *500.00 450.00*
*45* A3 10 (c) violet *500.00 450.00*
*46* A3 15 (c) violet *500.00 450.00*
*47* A3 20 (c) violet *500.00 450.00*
*48* A3 25 (c) violet *650.00*
*49* A3 30 (c) violet *650.00*
*50* A3 40 (c) violet *650.00*
*51* A3 50 (c) violet *650.00*
*52* A3 60 (c) violet *1,500.*
*53* A3 100 (c) violet *2,500.*

Overprinted "L" in Black

**1896 Typeset White Paper**
*54* A4 1a blk (thin "1") 32.50 50.00
*a* Small "O" in "POSTAGE" 500.00
*55* A4 2a black 32.50 55.00
*a* Small "O" in "POSTAGE" 115.00 *125.00*
*56* A4 3a black 50.00 *65.00*
*a* Small "O" in "POSTAGE" 625.00
*57* A4 4a black 50.00 *65.00*
*a* Small "O" in "POSTAGE" 115.00

**Yellowish Paper**
*58* A4 8a black 100.00 *165.00*
*a* Small "O" in "POSTAGE" 375.00
*59* A4 1r black 145.00 *165.00*
*a* Small "O" in "POSTAGE" 575.00
*60* A4 5r black

Without Overprint

**White Paper**
*61* A4 1a blk (thin "1") 32.50 40.00
*a* Small "O" in "POSTAGE" 125.00 145.00
*62* A4 1a blk (thick "1") 11.50 11.50
*a* Small "O" in "POSTAGE" 32.50 32.50
*63* A4 2a black 13.00 13.00
*a* Small "O" in "POSTAGE" 32.50 32.50
*64* A4 3a black 13.00 13.00
*a* Small "O" in "POSTAGE" 32.50 32.50
*65* A4 4a black 13.00 13.00
*a* Small "O" in "POSTAGE" 32.50 32.50

**Yellowish Paper**
*66* A4 8a black 20.00 20.00
*a* Small "O" in "POSTAGE" 70.00 *82.50*
*67* A4 1r black 40.00 40.00
*a* Small "O" in "POSTAGE" 200.00 *215.00*
*68* A4 5r black 125.00 *165.00*
*a* Small "O" in "POSTAGE" 425.00 425.00

Queen Victoria
A5 A6

**Wmk. Crown and C. A. (2)**
**1898-1902 Engr. *Perf. 14***
*69* A5 1a red 32 32
*70* A5 1a car rose ('02) 42 42
*71* A5 2a brown 38 42
*72* A5 3a gray 85 1.00
*73* A5 4a dk grn 85 1.00
*74* A5 8a ol gray 1.75 *3.00*

**Wmk. Crown and C. C. (1)**
*75* A6 1r ultra 8.25 8.25
*76* A6 5r brown 40.00 *55.00*
*Nos. 69-76 (8)* 52.82 *69.41*

A7

**1902 Wmk. 2 Black Overprint**
*77* A7 ½a yel grn 50 50
*a* Inverted overprint 550.00
*b* Double overprint 1,000.
*c* Pair, one without overprint 1,250.

**Red Overprint**
*78* A7 2½a dk bl 60 60
*a* Double overprint 1,000.

**Catalogue values for unused stamps in this section, from this point to the end of the section, are for Never Hinged items.**

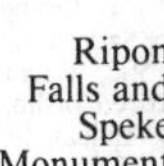

Ripon Falls and Speke Monument
A8

**Wmk. 314**
**1962, July 28 Engr. *Perf. 14***
*79* A8 30c ver & blk 12 12
*80* A8 50c vio & blk 15 15
*81* A8 1.30sh grn & blk 24 24
*82* A8 2.50sh ultra & blk 60 60

Cent. of the discovery of the source of the Nile by John Hanning Speke.

**Independent State**

Murchison Falls — A9

Mulago Hospital, X-Ray Service A10

Designs: 10c, Tobacco growing. 15c, Coffee growing. 20c, Ankole cattle. 30c, Cotton growing. 50c, Mountains of the Moon. 1.30sh, Rubaga and Namirembe Cathedrals and Kibuli Mosque. 2sh, Makerere College and students. 5sh, Copper mining. 10sh, Cement factory. 20sh, Parliament.

***Perf. 14½x14, 14x14½***

**1962, Oct. 9 Photo. Unwmk.**

*83* A9 5c Prus grn 8 5
*84* A9 10c red brn 8 5
*85* A9 15c grn, blk & car 8 5
*86* A9 20c bis & pur 8 5
*87* A9 30c brt bl 12 5
*88* A9 50c bluish grn & blk 16 8
*89* A10 1sh bl grn, sep & red 24 12
*90* A10 1.30sh pur & ocher 35 14
*91* A10 2sh grnsh bl, blk & dk car 50 28
*92* A10 5sh dk grn & red 1.25 60
*93* A10 10sh red brn & sl 2.50 1.25
*94* A10 20sh bl & pale brn 7.00 3.50
*Nos. 83-94 (12)* 12.44 6.22

Uganda's independence, Oct. 9, 1962.

Crowned Crane — A11

**1965, Feb. 20 Photo. *Perf. 14½***

*95* A11 30c bl grn, blk, yel & red 25 15
*96* A11 1sh30c ultra, blk, yel & red 75 50

Intl. Trade Fair at Lugogo Stadium, Kampala, Feb. 20-28.

Black Bee-eater — A12

African Jacana — A13

Arms of Uganda and Birds: 15c, Orange weaver. 20c, Narina trogon. 30c, Sacred ibis. 40c, Blue-breasted kingfisher. 50c, Whale-headed stork. 65c, Black-winged red bishop. 1sh, Ruwenzori turaco. 1.30sh, African fish eagle. 2.50sh, Great blue turaco. 5sh, Lilac-breasted roller. 10sh, Black-collared lovebird. 20sh, Crowned crane.

***Perf. 14½x14, 14x14½***

**1965, Oct. 9 Photo. Unwmk.**

**Birds in Natural Colors**

**Size: 17x21mm, 21x17mm**

*97* A12 5c lt vio bl & blk 5 5
*98* A13 10c dl bl & red 8 5
*99* A12 15c dk brn & org 10 5
*100* A12 20c bis & brt grn 12 6
*101* A13 30c hn brn & blk 15 6
*102* A12 40c lt yel grn & red 30 8
*103* A12 50c dp pur & gray 35 10
*104* A13 65c gray & brick red 1.00 75

***Perf. 14½***

**Size: 41x25mm, 25x41mm**

*105* A13 1sh lt bl & blk 65 15
*106* A12 1.30sh yel & red brn 2.00 20
*107* A13 2.50sh brt yel grn & blk 3.00 50
*108* A12 5sh lil gray & vio bl 5.00 90
*109* A13 10sh lt brn & blk 8.00 2.25
*110* A13 20sh ol grn & blk 15.00 4.75
*Nos. 97-110 (14)* 35.80 9.95

Parliament Building — A14

Designs: 30c, Animal carvings from entrance hall of Uganda Parliament. 50c, Arms of Uganda. 2.50sh, Parliament Chamber.

**1967, Oct. 26 Photo. *Perf. 14½***

*111* A14 30c multi 8 8
*112* A14 50c multi 16 10
*113* A14 1.30sh multi 35 32
*114* A14 2.50sh multi 70 60

13th Commonwealth Parliamentary Assoc. Conf.

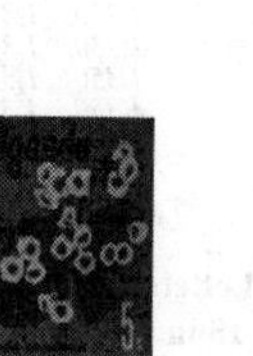

Cordia Abyssinica A15

Black-galled Acacia A16

Flowers: 10c, Grewia similis. 15c, Cassia didymobotrya. 20c, Coleus barbatus. 30c, Ochna ovata. 40c, Ipomoea spathulata (morning glory). 50c, Spathodea nilotica (flame tree). 60c, Oncoba spinosa. 70c, Carissa edulis. 1.50sh, Clerodendrum myricoides (blue butterfly bush). 2.50sh, Acanthus arboreus. 5sh, Kigelia aethiopium (sausage tree). 10sh, Erythrina abyssinica (Uganda coral). 20sh, Monodora myristica.

***Perf. 14½x14***

**1969, Oct. 9 Photo. Unwmk.**

*115* A15 5c multi 5 5
*116* A15 10c multi 5 5
*117* A15 15c multi 8 5
*118* A15 20c multi 8 5
*119* A15 30c multi 10 6
*120* A15 40c gray & multi 12 7
*121* A15 50c tan & multi 15 8
*122* A15 60c multi 18 10
*123* A15 70c multi 22 10

***Perf. 14***

*124* A16 1sh multi 38 *5*
*125* A16 1.50sh multi 55 *5*
*126* A16 2.50sh multi 70 *10*
*127* A16 5sh multi 1.25 *18*
*128* A16 10sh multi 3.00 *55*
*129* A16 20sh tan & multi 7.75 *1.25*
*Nos. 115-129 (15)* 14.66 *2.79*

Values of Nos. 124-129 are for canceled-to-order stamps. Cancellations were printed on Nos. 128-129. Postally used copies sell for higher prices.

Nos. 125-126, 129 Surcharged

**1975, Sept. 29 Photo. *Perf. 14***

*130* A16 2sh on 1.50sh multi 1.10 1.10
*131* A16 3sh on 2.50sh multi 22.50 22.50
*132* A16 40sh on 20sh multi 9.00 9.00

Millet — A17

Designs (Ugandan Crops): 20c, Sugar cane. 30c, Tobacco. 40c, Onions. 50c, Tomatoes. 70c, Tea. 80c, Bananas. 1sh, Corn. 2sh, Pineapple. 3sh, Coffee. 5sh, Oranges. 10sh, Peanuts. 20sh, Cotton. 40sh, Beans.

**1975, Oct. 9 Photo. *Perf. 14x14½***

**Size: 21x17mm**

**Multicolored, Name Panel as follows**

*133* A17 10c lt brn 5 5
*134* A17 20c blue 6 5
*135* A17 30c vermilion 9 6
*136* A17 40c lilac 10 7
*137* A17 50c olive 12 8
*138* A17 70c brt grn 18 10
*139* A17 80c purple 22 12

***Perf. 14½***

**Size: 41x25mm**

*140* A17 1sh ocher 25 12
*141* A17 2sh slate 50 28
*142* A17 3sh blue 75 40
*143* A17 5sh yel grn 1.00 55
*144* A17 10sh brn red 2.00 1.10
*145* A17 20sh rose lil 4.00 2.25
*146* A17 40sh orange 8.00 4.25
*Nos. 133-146 (14)* 17.32 9.48

See Nos. 195-198.

Communications Type of Kenya 1976

Designs: 50c, Microwave tower. 1sh, Cordless switchboard and operators (horiz.). 2sh, Telephones of 1880, 1930 and 1976. 3sh, Message switching center (horiz.).

**1976, Apr. 15 Litho. *Perf. 14½***

*147* A5 50c bl & multi 12 10
*148* A5 1sh red & multi 25 22
*149* A5 2sh yel & multi 50 40
*150* A5 3sh multi 75 60
*a* Souvenir sheet of 4 2.25 2.25

Telecommunications development in East Africa. No. 150a contains 4 stamps similar to Nos. 147-150 with simulated perforations; dark carmine rose margin with black inscription and white telephone. Size: 120x120mm.

Olympics Type of Kenya 1976

Designs: 50c, Akii Bua, Ugandan hurdler. 1sh, Filbert Bayi, Tanzanian runner. 2sh, Steve Muchoki, Kenyan boxer. 3sh, Olympic torch, flags of Kenya, Tanzania and Uganda.

**1976, July 5 Litho. *Perf. 14½***

*151* A6 50c bl & multi 15 12
*152* A6 1sh red & multi 28 20
*153* A6 2sh yel & multi 52 45
*154* A6 3sh bl & multi 80 65
*a* Souvenir sheet of 4 7.50 5.25

21st Olympic Games, Montreal, Canada, July 17-Aug. 1. No. 154a contains one each of Nos. 151-154, perf. 13; orange and multicolored margin. Size: 130x154mm.

Railway Type of Kenya 1976

Designs: 50c, Tanzania-Zambia Railway. 1sh, Nile Bridge, Uganda. 2sh, Nakuru Station, Kenya. 3sh, Class A locomotive, 1896.

**1976, Oct. 4 Litho. *Perf. 14***

*155* A7 50c lil & multi 20 12
*156* A7 1sh emer & multi 40 20
*157* A7 2sh brt rose & multi 80 45
*158* A7 3sh yel & multi 1.25 65
*a* Souvenir sheet of 4 4.25 4.25

Rail transport in East Africa. No. 158a contains one each of Nos. 155-158, perf. 13; yellow and multicolored margin showing African scenes with animals and birds. Size: 154x104mm.

Fish Type of Kenya 1977

**1977, Jan. 10 Litho. *Perf. 14½***

*159* A8 50c Nile perch 12 10
*160* A8 1sh Tilapia 32 15
*161* A8 3sh Sailfish 85 60
*162* A8 5sh Black marlin 1.25 1.00
*a* Souvenir sheet of 4 3.25 2.75

No. 162a contains one each of Nos. 159-162; multicolored margin shows fishing vessel and sea floor. Size: 153x129mm.

Festival Type of Kenya 1977

Designs (Festival Emblem and): 50c, Masai tribesmen bleeding cow. 1sh, Dancers from Uganda. 2sh, Makonde sculpture, Tanzania. 3sh, Tribesmen skinning hippopotamus.

**1977, Jan. 15 *Perf. 13½x14***

*163* A9 50c multi 14 12
*164* A9 1sh multi 28 20
*165* A9 2sh multi 52 45
*166* A9 3sh multi 80 70
*a* Souvenir sheet of 4 2.25 2.25

2nd World Black and African Festival, Lagos, Nigeria, Jan. 15-Feb. 12. No. 166a contains one each of Nos. 163-166; ocher margin with black inscription and decoration. Size: 132x98mm.

Rally Type of Kenya 1977

Designs (Safari Rally Emblem and): 50c, Automobile passing through village. 1sh, Winner at finish line. 2sh, Car passing though washout. 5sh, Car, elephants and Mt. Kenya.

**1977, Apr. 5 Litho. *Perf. 14***

*167* A10 50c multi 12 8
*168* A10 1sh multi 25 15
*169* A10 2sh multi 50 30
*170* A10 5sh multi 1.25 85
*a* Souvenir sheet of 4 2.75 2.75

25th Safari Rally, Apr. 7-11. No. 170a contains one each of Nos. 167-170; blue and multicolored margin showing automobiles and antelopes. Size: 126x93mm.

Church Type of Kenya 1977

Designs: 50c, Rev. Canon Apolo Kivebulaya. 1sh, Uganda Cathedral. 2sh, Early grass-topped Cathedral. 5sh, Early tent congregation, Kigezi.

**1977, June 30 Litho. *Perf. 14***

*171* A11 50c multi 12 9
*172* A11 1sh multi 24 15
*173* A11 2sh multi 45 30
*174* A11 5sh multi 1.25 75
*a* Souvenir sheet of 4 2.25 2.25

Church of Uganda, centenary. No. 174a contains one each of Nos. 171-174; ocher and black margin. Size: 125x89mm.

Type of 1975 Surcharged with New Value and 2 Bars

Design: 80c on 60c, Bananas.

**1977, Aug. 22 Photo. *Perf. 14x14½***

*175* A17 80c on 60c multi 24 20

No. 175 was not issued without surcharge.

Wildlife Type of Kenya 1977

Designs (Wildlife Fund Emblem and): 50c, Pancake tortoise. 1sh, Nile crocodile. 2sh, Hunter's hartebeest. 3sh, Red colobus monkey. 5sh, Dugong.

**1977, Sept. 26 Litho. *Perf. 14x13½***

*176* A13 50c multi 12 8
*177* A13 1sh multi 25 15
*178* A13 2sh multi 75 30
*179* A13 3sh multi 1.00 48
*180* A13 5sh multi 1.65 75
*a* Souvenir sheet of 4 4.00 3.25
*Nos. 176-180 (5)* 3.77 1.76

Endangered species. No. 180a contains one each of Nos. 177-180; multicolored margin shows storks in flight and marsh. Size: 128x102mm.

Soccer Type of Kenya

Designs (Soccer Cup and): 50c, Soccer scene and Joe Kadenge. 1sh, Mohammed Chuma receiving trophy, and his portrait. 2sh, Shot on goal and Omari S. Kidevu. 5sh, Backfield defense and Polly Ouma.

**1978, May 3 Litho. *Perf. 14x13½***

*181* A17 50c grn & multi 12 9
*182* A17 1sh lt brn & multi 24 15
*183* A17 2sh lil & multi 45 30
*184* A17 5sh dk bl & multi 1.25 75
*a* Souvenir sheet of 4 2.50 2.50

World Soccer Cup Championships, Argentina, 78, June 1-25. No. 184a contains one each of Nos. 181-184; yellow green and dark green margin. Size: 135½x82mm.

Crop Type of 1975

Designs as before

**1978, June Litho. *Perf. 14½***

**Size: 41x25mm**

**Multicolored, Name Panel as follows**

*195* A17 5sh blue 1.00 52
*196* A17 10sh rose lil 1.90 1.00
*197* A17 20sh brown 3.75 2.00
*198* A17 40sh dp org 7.75 4.25

Shot Put — A18

**1978, July 10** **Litho.** ***Perf. 14***

*199* A18 50c shown 22 16
*200* A18 1sh Broad jump 35 30
*201* A18 2sh Running 70 55
*202* A18 5sh Boxing 1.65 1.25
*a* Souvenir sheet of 4 3.75 3.75

Commonwealth Games, Edmonton, Canada, Aug. 3-12. No. 202a contains Nos. 199-202, perf. 12; multicolored margin with sport scenes. Size: 114x85mm.

Soccer Type of 1978 Inscribed: "WORLD CUP 1978"

Designs: 50c, Backfield defense and Polly Ouma. 2sh, Shot on goal and Omari S. Kidevu. 5sh, Soccer scene and Joe Kadenge. 10sh, Mohammed Chuma receiving trophy, and his portrait.

**1978, Sept. 11** ***Perf. 14x13½***

*203* A17 50c dk bl & multi 10 8
*204* A17 2sh lil & multi 45 35
*205* A17 5sh grn & multi 1.00 90
*206* A17 10sh lt brn & multi 2.00 1.75
*a* Souvenir sheet of 4 4.00 4.00

World Cup Soccer Championship winners. No. 206a contains Nos. 203-206, perf. 12; yellow green and dark green margin. Size: 141x87mm.

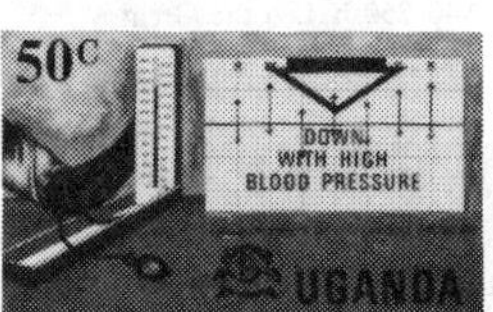


Blood Pressure Gauge and Chart — A19

**1978, Sept. 25** **Litho.** ***Perf. 14***

*207* A19 50c shown 12 9
*208* A19 1sh Heart 22 18
*209* A19 2sh Retina 45 38
*210* A19 5sh Kidneys 1.10 95
*a* Souvenir sheet of 4 2.00 2.00

World Health Day and Hypertension Month. No. 210a contains Nos. 207-210; multicolored margin. Size: 180x128mm.

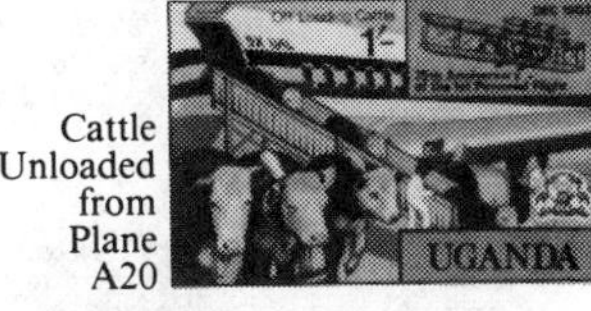


Cattle Unloaded from Plane A20

Designs (Flyer 1 and): 1.50sh, "Islander" on runway, Kampala. 2.70sh, Coffee loaded on transport jet. 10sh, Concorde.

**1978, Dec. 16**

*211* A20 1sh multi 22 18
*212* A20 1.50sh multi 32 28
*213* A20 2.70sh multi 55 50
*214* A20 10sh multi 2.25 1.75
*a* Souvenir sheet of 4 3.50 3.50

75th anniversary of 1st powered flight. No. 214a contains Nos. 211-214; ocher and black margin shows portraits of Orville and Wilbur Wright. Size: 166x111mm.

Elizabeth II Leaving Owen Falls Dam — A21

Designs: 1.50sh, Coronation regalia. 2.70sh, Coronation ceremony. 10sh, Royal family on balcony of Buckingham Palace.

**1979, Feb. 15** **Litho.** ***Perf. 12½x12***

*215* A21 1sh multi 20 15
*216* A21 1.50sh multi 30 24
*217* A21 2.70sh multi 50 45
*218* A21 10sh multi 2.00 1.65
*a* Souvenir sheet of 4 3.50 3.50

25th anniversary of coronation of Queen Elizabeth II. No. 218a contains Nos. 215-218; multicolored margin shows Idi Amin. Size: 151x102mm.

Bishop Joseph Kiwanuka A22

Designs: 1.50sh, Lubaga Cathedral. 2.70sh, Ugandan pilgrims and St. Peter's, Rome. 10sh, Friar Lourdel-Mapeera, missionary.

**1979, Feb. 15** ***Perf. 14***

*219* A22 1sh multi 20 15
*220* A22 1.50sh multi 30 24
*221* A22 2.70sh multi 50 45
*222* A22 10sh multi 2.00 1.65
*a* Souvenir sheet of 4 3.50 3.50

Ugandan Catholic Church, centenary. No. 222a contains Nos. 219-222; multicolored decorative margin. Size: 128x91½mm.

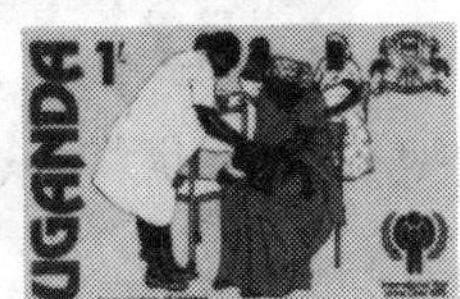


Child Receiving Vaccination — A23

IYC Emblem and: 1.50sh, Handicapped children playing. 2.70sh, Ugandan IYC emblem. 10sh, Teacher and pupils.

**1979, June 28** **Litho.** ***Perf. 14***

*223* A23 1sh multi 22 18
*224* A24 1.50sh multi 32 28
*225* A24 2.70sh multi 55 50
*226* A24 10sh multi 2.25 1.75
*a* Souvenir sheet of 4 3.50 3.50

International Year of the Child. No. 226a contains Nos. 223-226; multicolored margin shows IYC and Ugandan IYC emblems. Size: 136x113mm.

Nos. 133-146, 195-198, 215-218 Overprinted: "UGANDA / LIBERATED / 1979"

**1979, July 12** **Photo.** ***Perf. 14x14½***

**Size: 21x17mm.**

*227* A17 10c multi 5 5
*228* A17 20c multi 6 5
*229* A17 30c multi 9 6
*230* A17 40c multi 10 8
*231* A17 50c multi 12 10
*232* A17 70c multi 15 14
*233* A17 80c multi 18 15

***Perf. 14½***

**Size: 41x25mm**

*234* A17 1sh multi 22 18
*235* A17 2sh multi 45 38
*236* A17 3sh multi 65 55
*237* A17 5sh multi 95 80
*238* A17 10sh multi 1.90 1.50
*239* A17 20sh multi 3.75 3.25
*240* A17 40sh multi 7.75 6.50
*Nos. 227-240 (14)* 16.42 13.79

**1979** **Litho.** ***Perf. 14½***

**Multicolored, name panel as follows**

*241* A17 5sh blue 1.25 1.00
*242* A17 10sh rose lil 2.50 2.00
*243* A17 20sh brown 4.75 4.00
*244* A17 40sh dp org 9.50 8.00

**1979, July 12** **Litho.** ***Perf. 12½x12***

*245* A21 1sh multi 22 18
*246* A21 1.50sh multi 32 30
*247* A21 2.70sh multi 50 60
*248* A21 15sh on 10sh multi 3.25 2.25
*a* Souvenir sheet of 4 4.25

No. 248a contains Nos. 245-247 and a 15sh in design of No. 218; multicolored margin shows flags of Uganda and Great Britain (replacing Idi Amin). Size: 152x103mm. Issued Aug. 1.

Nos. 199-202; 203, 204-206; 211-214; 219-222, 223-226 Overprinted: "UGANDA LIBERATED 1979"

**1979, Aug. 1** **Litho.** ***Perf. 14***

*249* A18 50c multi 12 10
*250* A18 1sh multi 20 16
*251* A18 2sh multi 45 35
*252* A18 5sh multi 1.10 95

Type A17 of Kenya

**1979, Aug. 1** ***Perf. 14x13½***

*253* A17 50c multi 12 10
*255* A17 2sh multi (#204) 48 40
*256* A17 5sh multi 1.25 1.00
*257* A17 10sh multi 2.50 2.00

Overprint exists on No. 183.

**1979, Aug. 1** ***Perf. 14***

*258* A20 1sh multi 25 22
*259* A20 1.50sh multi 38 32
*260* A20 2.70sh multi 70 60
*261* A20 10sh multi 2.50 2.00

**1979, Aug. 1**

*262* A22 1sh multi 20 16
*263* A22 1.50sh multi 30 25
*264* A22 2.70sh multi 55 48
*265* A22 10sh multi 2.00 1.75

**1979, Aug. 16**

*266* A23 1sh multi 20 16
*267* A23 1.50sh multi 30 25
*268* A23 2.70sh multi 55 48
*269* A23 10sh multi 2.00 1.75
*a* Souvenir sheet of 4 3.25 3.25

No. 269a contains Nos. 266-269. Size: 136½x111mm.

ITU Emblem, Radio Waves A24

**1979, Sept. 11**

*270* A24 1sh lt gray & multi 20 16
*271* A24 1.50sh org & multi 30 25
*272* A24 2.70sh yel & multi 55 48
*273* A24 10sh bl & multi 2.00 1.75

50th anniversary of International Radio Consultative Committee (CCIR) of the International Telecommunications Union.

No. 222a Redrawn and Inscribed: FREEDOM OF WORSHIP DECLARED

**Souvenir Sheet**

**1979, Sept.** ***Perf. 12***

*274* A22 Sheet of 4 3.25 3.25
*a* 1sh No. 219 20 16
*b* 1.50sh No. 220 30 25
*c* 2.70sh No. 221 55 48
*d* 10sh No. 222 2.00 1.75

In top panel of margin scrolls and coat of arms have been replaced by inscription.

A25

**1979, Nov. 12** **Litho.** ***Perf. 14***

*275* A25 1sh #110 20 16
*276* A25 1.50sh #112 30 25
*277* A25 2.70sh #94 55 48
*278* A25 10sh #69 2.00 1.75
*a* Souvenir sheet of 4 3.50 3.50

Sir Rowland Hill (1795-1879), originator of penny postage. No. 278a contains Nos. 275-278; multicolored margin shows Maltese cross postmarks. Size: 115x98mm.

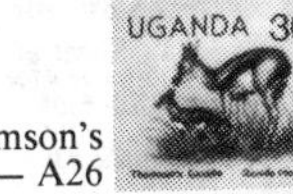


Thomson's Gazelle — A26

Designs: 10c, Impalas. 20c, Large-spotted genet. 50c, Bush babies. 80c, Wild hunting dogs. 1sh, Lions. 1.50sh, Mountain gorillas. 2sh, Zebras. 2.70sh, Leopards. 3.50sh, Black rhinoceroses. 5sh, Defassa waterbucks. 10sh, African black buffaloes. 20sh, Hippopotami. 40sh, African elephants.

**1979, Dec. 3** **Litho.** ***Perf. 14***

**Size: 21x17mm**

*279* A26 10c multi 5 5
*280* A26 20c multi 6 5
*281* A26 30c multi 6 5
*282* A26 50c multi 15 12
*283* A26 80c multi 25 20

**Size: 39x25mm**

*284* A26 1sh multi 30 25
*285* A26 1.50sh multi 35 30
*286* A26 2sh multi 45 35
*287* A26 2.70sh multi 55 50
*288* A26 3.50sh multi 70 60
*289* A26 5sh multi 1.00 90
*290* A26 10sh multi 2.00 1.75
*291* A26 20sh multi 4.25 3.50
*292* A26 40sh multi 8.50 7.00
*Nos. 279-292 (14)* 18.67 15.62

No. 284, 286, 289 reissued inscribed 1982. See Nos. 400-406

Nos. 275-278a Overprinted: "LONDON 1980"

**1980, May 6** **Litho.** ***Perf. 14***

*293* A25 1sh multi 20 16
*294* A25 1.50sh multi 30 25
*295* A25 2.70sh multi 55 48
*296* A25 10sh multi 2.00 2.00
*a* Souvenir sheet of 4 3.50 3.50

London 80 Intl. Stamp Exhib., May 6-14.

Paul Harris Wheeling Rotary Cart A27

**1980, Aug.** **Litho.** ***Perf. 14***

*297* A27 1sh *Rotary emblem, vert.* 20 15
*298* A27 20sh *shown* 4.00 3.25
*a* Souvenir sheet of 2 4.25

Rotary International, 75th anniversary. No. 298a contains Nos. 297-298; light violet and black margin shows Rotary emblem. Size: 100x77mm.

Soccer, Flags of Olympic Participants, Flame — A28

**1980, Dec. 29** **Litho.** ***Perf. 14***

*299* A28 1sh *shown* 20 15
*300* A28 2sh *Relay race* 40 32
*301* A28 10sh *Hurdles* 2.00 2.00
*302* A28 20sh *Boxing* 4.00 4.00

**Souvenir Sheet**

*303* Sheet of 4 7.75 7.75
*a* A28 2.70sh *like #299* 55 50
*b* A28 3sh *like #300* 60 52
*c* A28 5sh *like #301* 1.00 90
*d* A28 25sh *like 302* 5.25 4.50

22nd Summer Olympic Games, Moscow, July 19-Aug. 3. No. 303 has multicolored decorative margin. Size: 119½x90½mm.

Nos. 299-303 Overprinted with Sport, Winner and Country

**1980, Dec. 29**

*304* A28 1sh multi 20 15
*305* A28 2sh multi 40 32
*306* A28 10sh multi 2.00 1.65
*307* A28 20sh multi 4.00 3.25

**Souvenir Sheet**

308 Sheet of 4 7.75 7.75
a A28 2.70sh *like #304* 55 50
b A28 3sh *like #305* 60 52
c A28 5sh *like #306* 1.00 90
d A28 25sh *like #307* 5.25 4.50

Souvenir Sheet

Christ in the Storm on the Sea of Galilee, by Rembrandt — A29

**1980, Dec. 31** *Imperf.*
*309* A29 25sh multi 5.50 4.50

Christmas 1980. Size: 79½x101½mm.

Heinrich von Stephan and UPU Emblem A30

**1981, June 2** **Litho.** *Perf. 14*
*310* A30 1sh shown 22 18
*311* A30 2sh UPU headquarters 45 38
*312* A30 2.70sh Mail plane, 1935 60 52
*313* A30 10sh Mail train, 1927 2.25 1.90
a Souvenir sheet of 4 3.75 3.75

Heinrich von Stephan (1831-1897), founder of Universal Postal Union, birth sesquicentennial. No. 313a contains Nos. 310-313; multicolored margin shows UPU emblem. Size: 112x95mm.

**Royal Wedding Issue**

Common Design Type

**1981** **Litho.** *Perf. 14*
*314* CD331 10sh Couple 22 18
a 10sh on 1sh 22 18
*315* CD331 50sh Tower of London 1.10 95
a 50sh on 5sh 1.10 95
*316* CD331 200sh Prince Charles 4.50 3.75
a 200sh on 20sh 4.50 3.75

**Souvenir Sheet**

*317* CD331 250sh Royal mews 5.00 4.00
a 250sh on 25sh, lt org 5.00 4.00

Royal wedding. No. 317 has tan and black margin showing heraldic designs. Size: 96x82mm. Issue dates: surcharges, July 13; others, July 29. Nos. 314-316 also issued in sheets of 5 plus label, perf. 12, in changed colors.

Sleeping Woman Before Green Shutters, by Picasso — A31

Picasso Birth Centenary: 20sh, Bullfight. 30sh, Nude Asleep on a Landscape. 200sh, Interior with a Girl Drawing. 250sh, Minotaur.

**1981, Sept. 21** **Litho.** *Perf. 14*
*318* A31 10sh multi 22 18
*319* A31 20sh multi 45 38
*320* A31 30sh multi 65 55
*321* A31 200sh multi 4.50 3.75

**Size: 120x146mm**

***Imperf***

*322* A31 250sh multi 6.00 5.00
*Nos. 318-322 (5)* 11.82 9.86

Intl. Year of the Disabled A32

**1981, Dec.** *Perf. 15*
*323* A32 1sh Sign language 5 5
*324* A32 10sh Teacher in wheelchair 22 18
*325* A32 50sh Retarded children 1.10 95
*326* A32 200sh Blind man 4.50 3.75
a Souvenir sheet of 4 6.25 5.50

No. 326a contains Nos. 323-326; multicolored margin shows emblem. Size: 122x93mm.

1982 World Cup Soccer A33

Designs: Various soccer players.

**1982, Jan. 11** **Litho.** *Perf. 14*
*327* A33 1sh multi 5 5
*328* A33 10sh multi 22 18
*329* A33 50sh multi 1.10 95
*330* A33 200sh multi 4.50 3.75

**Souvenir Sheet**

*331* A33 250sh World Cup 6.00 6.00

No. 331 has multicolored margin showing winners' flags. Size: 116x77mm.

TB Bacillus Centenary — A34

**1982, June 14** **Litho.**
*332* A34 1sh Koch 5 5
*333* A34 10sh Microscope 22 18
*334* A34 50sh Inoculation 1.10 95
*335* A34 100sh Virus under microscope 2.25 1.90

**Souvenir Sheet**

*336* A34 150sh Medical School 3.75 3.00

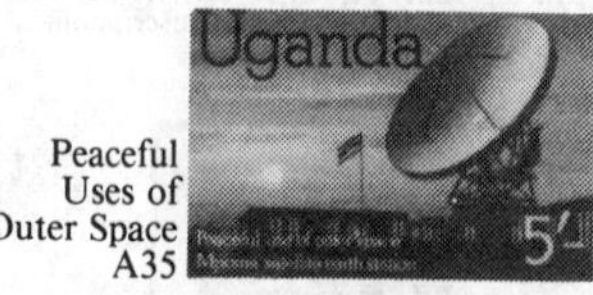


Peaceful Uses of Outer Space A35

**1982, May 17** **Litho.** *Perf. 15*
*337* A35 5sh Mpoma Satellite Earth Station 10 8
*338* A35 10sh Pioneer II 20 15
*339* A35 50sh Columbia space shuttle 1.00 85
*340* A35 100sh Voyager II, Saturn 2.00 1.65

**Souvenir Sheet**

*341* A35 150sh Columbia shuttle 3.50 3.00

No. 341 has multicolored margin continuing design. Size: 118x89mm.

Nos. 314-316 Overprinted: "21st BIRTHDAY / HRH Princess of Wales / JULY 1 1982"

**1982, July 7** *Perf. 14*
*342* CD331 10sh multi 20 15
*343* CD331 50sh multi 1.00 85
*344* CD331 200sh multi 4.00 3.25

**Souvenir Sheet**

*345* CD331 250sh multi 5.25 4.50

Issued in sheets of 5 + label in changed colors, perf. 12 x 12½.

Hornbill — A36

**1982, July 12**
*346* A36 1sh shown 5 5
*347* A36 20sh Superb starling 45 35
*348* A36 50sh Bateleur eagle 1.00 90
*349* A36 100sh Saddle-bill stork 2.00 1.75

**Souvenir Sheet**

*350* A36 200sh Laughing dove 4.25 3.50

Scouting Year A37

**1982, Aug. 23**
*351* A37 5sh Scouts 12 9
*352* A37 20sh Trophy presentation 45 38
*353* A37 50sh Helping disabled 1.10 95
*354* A37 100sh First aid instruction 2.25 1.90

**Souvenir Sheet**

*355* A37 150sh Baden-Powell 3.50 3.00

No. 355 has multicolored margin showing camp, flags. Size: 113x85mm.

Franklin D. Roosevelt (1882-1945) — A38

Franklin D. Roosevelt and George Washington (1732-1799): 50sh, 200sh, Inaugurations. No. 358, Mount Vernon. No. 359, Hyde Park.

**1982, Sept.** **Litho.**
*356* A38 50sh multi 90 75
*357* A38 200sh multi 3.50 3.00

**Souvenir Sheets**

*358* A38 150sh multi 3.00 2.75
*359* A38 150sh multi 3.00 2.75

Nos. 358-359 have multicolored margins continuing design. Size: 100x70mm.

Italy's Victory in 1982 World Cup A39

**1982, Oct.** **Litho.** *Perf. 14½*
*359A* A39 10sh Players 20 20
*359B* A39 200sh Team 4.25 4.25

**Souvenir Sheet**

*359C* A39 250sh Globe 4.75 4.75

Size: 98x118mm.

**Commonwealth Day**

Common Design Type

**1983, Mar. 14** **Litho.** *Perf. 14*
*360* CD334 5sh Dancers 9 9
*361* CD334 20sh Traditional currency 35 35
*362* CD334 50sh Village 90 90
*363* CD334 100sh Drums 1.75 1.75

St. George and the Dragon, by Raphael A40

**1983, Apr.**
*364* A40 5sh shown 9 9
*365* A40 20sh St. George and the Dragon, 1505 35 35
*366* A40 50sh Moses Parts the Red Sea 90 90
*367* A40 200sh Expulsion of Heliodorus 3.50 3.50

**Souvenir Sheet**

*368* A40 250sh Leo the Great and Attila, 1513 4.25 4.25

A41

7th Non-aligned Summit Conference — A42

**1983, Aug. 15** **Litho.** *Perf. 14½*
*369* A41 5sh multi 6 6
*370* A42 200sh multi 2.50 2.50

African Elephants and World Wildlife Emblem A43

5sh, 10sh, 30sh, 70sh Various African elephants. 300sh, Zebras (vert.).

**1983, Aug. 22** *Perf. 15*
*371* A43 5sh multi 6 6
*372* A43 10sh multi 12 12
*373* A43 30sh multi 35 35
*374* A43 70sh multi 85 85

**Souvenir Sheet**

*375* A43 300sh multi 3.25 3.25

No. 375 has multicolored margin continuing design. Size: 88x64mm.

Nos. 351-355 Overprinted or Surcharged: "BOYS BRIGADE CENTENARY 1883-1983"

**1983, Sept. 19** **Litho.** *Perf. 14*
*376* A37 5sh multi 6 6
*377* A37 20sh multi 22 22
*378* A37 50sh multi 55 55
*379* A37 400sh on 100sh multi 4.50 4.50

**Souvenir Sheet**

*380* A37 150sh multi 1.75 1.75

Size: 113x85mm.

World Communications Year — A44

Designs: 20sh, Mpoma Satellite Earth Station. 50sh, Railroad, Computer Operator. 70sh, Filming Lions. 100sh, Pilots, Radio Communications. 300sh, Communications Satellite.

**1983, Oct. 3 Litho. *Perf. 15***

*381* A44 20sh multi 12 12
*382* A44 50sh multi 60 60
*383* A44 70sh multi 85 85
*384* A44 100sh multi 1.25 1.25

**Souvenir Sheet**

*385* A44 300sh multi 3.50 3.50

Nos. 279, 281-285, 289 Surcharged.

**1983, Nov. 7 Litho. *Perf. 14***

*386* A26 100sh on 10c multi
*387* A26 135sh on 1sh multi
*388* A26 175sh on 30c multi
*389* A26 200sh on 50c multi
*390* A26 400sh on 80c multi
*391* A26 700sh on 5sh multi
*392* A26 1000sh on 1.50sh
*Nos. 386-392 (7)* 15.00 15.00

World Food Day — A45

**1984, Jan. 12 Litho. *Perf. 14***

*393* A45 10sh Plowing 10 10
*394* A45 200sh Banana crop 2.25 2.25

Christmas 1983 — A46

**1983, Dec. 12 Litho. *Perf. 14***

*395* A46 10sh Navitity 8 8
*396* A46 50sh Sheperds and Angel 38 38
*397* A46 175sh Flight into Egypt 1.25 1.25
*398* A46 400sh Angels Blowing Trumpets 3.00 3.00

**Souvenir Sheet**

*399* A46 300sh Three Kings 2.25 2.25

Multicolored margin shows holly and bells. Size: 85x57mm.

Animal Type of 1979

**1983, Dec. 19**

*400* A26 100sh like No. 284 60 60
*401* A26 135sh like No. 285 75 75
*402* A26 175sh like No. 286 1.00 1.00
*403* A26 200sh like No. 287 1.25 1.25
*404* A26 400sh like No. 288 2.50 2.50
*405* A26 700sh like No. 292 4.25 4.25
*406* A26 1000sh like No. 291 6.00 6.00
*Nos. 400-406 (7)* 16.35 16.35

1984 Summer Olympics A48

**1983 *Perf. 14½***

*417* A48 5sh Ruth Kyalisiima 5 5
*418* A48 115sh Javelin 65 65
*419* A48 155sh Wrestling 80 80
*420* A48 175sh Rowing 1.10 1.10

**Souvenir Sheet**

*421* A48 500sh Akii-Bua 3.00 3.00

Intl. Civil Aviation Org., 40th Anniv. A49

**1984, Sept.**

*422* A49 5sh Passenger service 5 5
*423* A49 115sh Cargo service 65 65
*424* A49 155sh Police airwing 80 80
*425* A49 175sh Soroti Flying School plane 1.10 1.10

**Souvenir Sheet**

*426* A49 250sh Hot air balloon 1.50 1.50

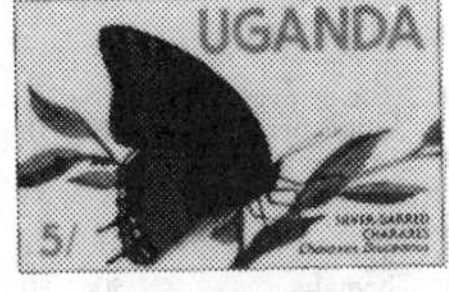


Butterflies A50

**1984, Oct. Litho. *Perf. 14½***

*427* A50 5sh Silver-barred Charaxes 5 5
*428* A50 115sh Western Emperor Swallowtail 65 65
*429* A50 155sh African Giant Swallowtail 90 90
*430* A50 175sh Blue Salamis 1.10 1.10

**Souvenir Sheet**

*431* A50 250sh Veinted Yellow 1.40 1.40

Margin continues design. Size: 128x90mm.

Freshwater Fish — A51

**1985 Litho. *Perf. 15***

*432* A51 5sh Nothobranchius taeniopygus 5 5
*433* A51 10sh Bagrus dogmac 5 5
*434* A51 50sh Polypterus senegalus 18 18
*435* A51 100sh Clarias 35 35
*436* A51 135sh Mormyrus kannume 48 48
*437* A51 175sh Synodontis victoriae 60 60
*438* A51 205sh Haplochromis brownae 70 70
*439* A51 400sh Lates niloticus 1.40 1.40
*440* A51 700sh Protopterus aethiopicus 2.25 2.25
*441* A51 1000sh Barbus radcliffii 3.75 3.75
*442* A51 2500sh Malapterus electricus 8.50 8.50
*Nos. 432-442 (11)* 18.31 18.31

Issue dates: Nos. 432-435, 437-441, Apr. 1. Nos. 436, 442, June 10.

Easter 1985 — A52

**1985, May 13 Litho. *Perf. 14***

*443* A52 5sh The Last Supper 5 5
*444* A52 115sh Jesus confronts doubting Thomas 42 42
*445* A52 155sh Crucifixion 60 60
*446* A52 175sh Pentecost 65 65

**Souvenir Sheet**

*447* A52 250sh Last prayer in garden 90 90

No. 447 has multicolored margin continuing the design. Size: 100x70mm.

U.N. Child Survival Campaign A53

**1985, July 1**

*448* A53 5sh Mother breastfeeding 5 5
*449* A53 115sh Growth monitorization 42 42
*450* A53 155sh Immunization 60 60
*451* A53 175sh Oral rehydration therapy 65 65

**Souvenir Sheet**

*452* A53 500sh Expectant Mother, food 1.90 1.90

No. 452 has multicolored decorative margin picturing prepared and raw foods. Size: 75x55mm.

Audubon Birth Bicentenary — A54

**1985, July**

*453* A54 115sh Acrocephalus schoenobaenus 35 35
*454* A54 155sh Ardeola ibis 50 50
*455* A54 175sh Galerida gristata 55 55
*456* A54 500sh Aythya fuligula 1.50 1.50

**Souvenir Sheet**

*457* A54 1000sh Strix aluco 3.25 3.25

No. 457 has multicolored decorative margin picturing a tawny owl in flight. Size: 100x70mm. See Nos. 469-473.

Nos. 417-421 Ovptd. or Surcharged with Winners Names, Medals and Countries in Gold.

Gold medalists: 5sh, Benita Brown-Fitzgerald, USA, 100-meter hurdles. 115sh, Arto Haerkoenen, Finland, javelin. 155sh, Atsuji Miyahara, Japan, 115-pound Greco-Roman wrestling. 100sh, West Germany, quadruple sculls. 1200sh, Edwin Moses, USA, 400-meter hurdles.

**1985, July *Perf. 15***

*458* A48 5sh multi 5 5
*459* A48 115sh multi 28 28
*460* A48 155sh multi 38 38
*461* A48 1000sh on 175sh multi 2.40 2.40

**Souvenir Sheet**

*462* A48 1200sh on 500sh multi 4.00 4.00

UN Decade for Women — A56

Designs: 5sh, Natl. Women's Day, Mar. 8. 115sh, Girl Guides 75th anniv., horiz. 155sh, Mother Theresa, 1979 Nobel Peace Prize laureate. No. 468, like 115sh, horiz.

**1985 Litho. *Perf. 14***

*463* A56 5sh multi 5 5
*464* A56 115sh multi 35 35
*465* A56 155sh multi 48 48
*466* A56 1000sh Queen Mother 3.25 3.25
*467* A56 1500sh Inspecting troops 5.00 5.00

**Souvenir Sheet**

*468* A56 1500sh multi 5.00 5.00

No. 467 has multicolored margin continuing the design. No. 468 has margin picturing Acanthus arboreus and Clerodendron myricoides. Sizes: 56x82mm, 85x59mm (No. 468)

Issue dates: Nos. 466-467, Aug. 21. Others Nov. 1.

Audubon Type of 1985

**1985, Dec. 23 *Perf. 12½x12***

*469* A54 5sh Rock ptarmigan 5 5
*470* A54 155sh Sage grouse 55 55
*471* A54 175sh Lesser yellowlegs 60 60
*472* A54 500sh Brown-headed cowbird 1.75 1.75

**Souvenir Sheet**

***Perf. 14***

*473* A54 1000sh Whooping crane 3.75 3.75

No. 473 has multicolored margin continuing the design. Size: 73x102mm.

UN, 40th Anniv. A57

Designs: 10sh, Forest resources, vert. 180sh, UN Peace-keeping Force. 200sh, Emblem, UN Development Project. 250sh, Intl. Peace Year. 2000sh, Natl., UN flags, vert. 2500sh, Flags, UN Building, New York, vert.

**1986, Feb. *Perf. 15***

*474* A57 10sh multi 5 5
*475* A57 180sh multi 28 28
*476* A57 200sh multi 32 32
*477* A57 250sh multi 40 40
*478* A57 2000sh multi 3.25 3.25
*Nos. 474-478 (5)* 4.30 4.30

**Souvenir Sheet**

*479* A57 2500sh multi 4.00 4.00

No. 479 has multicolored margin continuing the design. Size: 69x69mm.

1986 World Cup Soccer Championships, Mexico — A58

Various soccer plays.

**1986, Mar. *Perf. 14***

*480* A58 10sh multi 5 5
*481* A58 180sh multi 28 28
*482* A58 250sh multi 40 40
*483* A58 2500sh multi 4.00 4.00

**Souvenir Sheet**

*484* A58 3000sh multi 4.75 4.75

No. 484 contains vert. stamp; multicolored margin continues the design. Size: 87x66mm.

A59

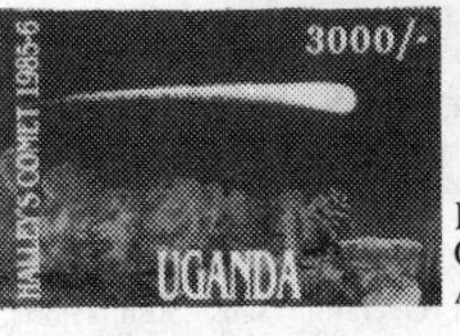


Halley's Comet A60

Designs: 50sh, Arecibo radio telescope, Puerto Rico, and Tycho Brahe (1546-1601), Danish astronomer. 100sh, Recovery of Astronaut John Glenn, US space capsule, Caribbean, 1962. 140sh, Adoration of the Magi, 1301, by Giotto (1276-1337). 2500sh, Sighting, 1835, Davy Crockett at The Alamo.

**1986, Mar. Litho. *Perf. 14***

*485* A59 50sh multi 8 8
*486* A59 100sh multi 15 15
*487* A59 140sh multi 22 22
*488* A59 2500sh multi 3.75 3.75

**Souvenir Sheet**

*489* A60 3000sh multi 4.75 4.75

No. 489 has multicolored margin picturing Murchison Falls and Edmond Halley. Size: 102x70mm.

Nos. 437, 440-442 and 468 Ovptd. "NRA LIBERATION / 1986" in Silver or Black.

**1986, Apr. *Perf. 15***

*490* A51 175sh multi 28 28
*491* A51 700sh multi 1.10 1.10
*492* A51 1000sh multi 1.50 1.50
*493* A51 2500sh multi 3.75 3.75

**Souvenir Sheet**

***Perf. 14***

*494* A56 1500sh multi 5.00 5.00

No. 494 has multicolored margin ovptd. in one line.

Queen Elizabeth II, 60th Birthday
Common Design Type

**1986, Apr. 21 *Perf. 14***

*495* CD339 100sh At London Zoo, c. 1938 15 15
*496* CD339 140sh At the races, 1970 22 22
*497* CD339 2500sh Sandringham, 1982 3.75 3.75

**Souvenir Sheet**

*498* CD339 3000sh Engagement, 1947 4.75 4.75

No. 498 has beige and gray inscribed margin. Size: 120x85mm.

AMERIPEX '86 — A61

**1986, May 22 *Perf. 15***

*499* A61 50sh Niagara Falls 8 8
*500* A61 100sh Jefferson Memorial 14 14
*501* A61 250sh Liberty Bell 35 35
*502* A61 1000sh The Alamo 1.35 1.35
*503* A61 2500sh George Washington Bridge 3.50 3.50
*Nos. 499-503 (5)* 5.42 5.42

**Souvenir Sheet**

*504* A61 3000sh Grand Canyon 4.10 4.10

Statue of Liberty, cent. No. 504 has multicolored margin continuing the design. Size: 87x64mm.

A62

Statue of Liberty, Cent. — A63

Tall ships, Operation Sail: 50sh, Gloria, Colombia, vert. 100sh, Mircea, Romania, vert. 140sh, Sagres II, Portugal. 2500sh, Gazela Primero, US.

**1986, July *Perf. 14***

*505* A62 50sh multi 8 8
*506* A62 100sh multi 14 14
*507* A62 140sh multi 20 20
*508* A62 2500sh multi 3.50 3.50

**Souvenir Sheet**

*509* A63 3000sh multi 4.10 4.10

No. 513 has multicolored margin continuing the design, picturing Liberty Island, tall ship and smaller ships in New York Harbor. Size: 114x82mm.

Royal Wedding Issue, 1986
Common Design Type

Designs: 50sh, Prince Andrew and Sarah Ferguson. 140sh, Andrew and Princess Anne. 2500sh, At formal affair. 3000sh, Couple diff. Nos. 510-512 horiz.

**1986, July 23**

*510* CD340 50sh multi 8 8
*511* CD340 140sh multi 20 20
*512* CD340 2500sh multi 3.50 3.50

**Souvenir Sheet**

*513* CD340 3000sh multi 4.10 4.10

No. 513 has multicolored margin picturing Andrew at helicopter controls. Size: 88x88mm.

Nos. 480-484 Ovptd. or Surcharged "WINNERS Argentina 3 W. Germany 2" in Gold in 2 or 3 Lines.

**1986, Sept. 15 Litho. *Perf. 14***

*514* A58 50sh on 10sh multi 8 8
*515* A58 180sh multi 25 25
*516* A58 250sh multi 35 35
*517* A58 2500sh multi 3.50 3.50

**Souvenir Sheet**

*518* A58 3000sh multi 3.75 4.25

Nos. 485-489 Ovptd. with Halley's Comet Emblem

**1986, Oct. 15 Litho. *Perf. 14***

*519* A59 50sh multi 8 8
*520* A59 100sh multi 14 14
*521* A59 140sh multi 20 20
*522* A59 2500sh multi 3.50 3.50

**Souvenir Sheet**

*523* A59 3000sh multi 4.00 4.00

Christian Martyrs A64

Designs: 50sh, St. Kizito. 150sh, St. Kizito educating Ganda converts. 200sh, Execution of Bishop James Hannington. 1000sh, Mwanga's execution of converts, cent. 1500sh, King Mwanga sentencing Christians to death.

**1986, Oct. 15**

*524* A64 50sh multi 8 8
*525* A64 150sh multi 22 22
*526* A64 200sh multi 30 30
*527* A64 1000sh multi 1.50 1.50

**Souvenir Sheet**

*528* A64 1500sh multi 2.25 2.25

No. 528 has multicolored inscribed margin. Size: 89x59mm.

A65

Christmas — A66

Paintings by Albrecht Durer and Titian: 50sh, Madonna of the Cherries. 150sh, Madonna and Child, vert. 200sh, Assumption of the Virgin, vert. 2500sh, Praying Hands, vert. No. 533, Adoration of the Magi. No. 534, Presentation of the Virgin in the Temple.

**1986, Nov. 26 Litho. *Perf. 14***

*529* A65 50sh multi 8 8
*530* A65 150sh multi 24 24
*531* A65 200sh multi 32 32
*532* A65 2500sh multi 3.50 3.50

**Souvenir Sheets**

*533* A66 3000sh multi 4.00 4.00
*534* A66 3000sh multi 4.00 4.00

Nos. 533-534 have inscribed multicolored margins continuing the paintings. Sizes: 102x76mm.

Birds and Animals A67

**1987 *Perf. 15***

*535* A67 2sh Red-billed firefinch 6 6
*536* A67 5sh African pygmy kingfisher 18 18
*537* A67 10sh Scarlet-chested sunbird 32 32
*538* A67 25sh White rhinoceros 85 85
*539* A67 35sh Lion 1.25 1.25
*540* A67 45sh Cheetahs 1.50 1.50
*541* A67 50sh Cordon bleu 1.65 1.65
*542* A67 100sh Giant eland 3.25 3.25

**Souvenir Sheets**

*543* A67 150sh Carmine bee-eaters 5.00 5.00
*544* A67 150sh Cattle egret, zebra 5.00 5.00

Issue dates: Nos. 535-537, 541, 543, Nov. 2; Nos. 538-540, 542-544, July 22. Nos. 543-544 have multicolored margins continuing the designs. Sizes: 99x68mm.

Transportation Innovations — A68

**1987, Aug. 14**

*545* A68 2sh Eagle, 1987 8 8
*546* A68 3sh Bremen, 1928 10 10
*547* A68 5sh Winnie Mae, 1933 16 16
*548* A68 10sh Voyager, 1986 32 32
*549* A68 15sh Chanute biplane glider, 1896 48 48
*550* A68 25sh Norge, 1926 80 80
*551* A68 35sh Curtis biplane, USS Pennsylvania, 1911 1.10 1.10
*552* A68 45sh Freedom 7, 1961 1.40 1.40
*553* A68 100sh Concorde, 1976 3.25 3.25
*Nos. 545-553 (9)* 7.69 7.69

1988 Summer Olympics, Seoul A69

Flags and athletes.

**1987, Oct. 5 *Perf. 14½x14***

*554* A69 5sh Torch bearer 18 18
*555* A69 10sh Swimming 32 32
*556* A69 50sh Cycling 1.65 1.65
*557* A69 100sh Gymnastic rings 3.35 3.35

**Souvenir Sheet**

*558* A69 150sh Boxing 5.00 5.00

No. 558 has multicolored inscribed margin continuing the design. Size: 101x75mm.

A70

Natl. Independence, 25th Anniv. — A71

**1987, Oct. 8**

*559* A70 5sh shown 18 18
*560* A70 10sh Mulago Hospital 35 35
*561* A70 25sh Independence Monument 82 82
*562* A70 50sh High Court 1.65 1.65

**Souvenir Sheet**

*563* A71 100sh shown 3.50 3.50

No. 563 has black, yellow and red inscribed margin. Size: 90x71mm.

A72

Science and Space — A73

Designs: 5sh, Hippocrates, father of modern medicine, caduceus and surgeons. 25sh, Albert Einstein and Theory of Relativity equation. 35sh, Sir Isaac Newton and Optics Theory. 45sh, Karl Benz (1844-1929), German engineer, automobile pioneer, and the Velocipede, Mercedes-Benz sports coupe and manufacturers' emblems.

**1987, Nov. 2 *Perf. 14½x14***

*564* A72 5sh multi 18 18
*565* A72 25sh multi 85 85
*566* A72 35sh multi 1.20 1.20
*567* A72 45sh multi 1.50 1.50

**Souvenir Sheet**

***Perf. 14x14½***

*568* A73 150sh shown 5.00 5.00

No. 568 has multicolored margin picturing the crew of the space shuttle *Challenger*. Size: 98x70mm.

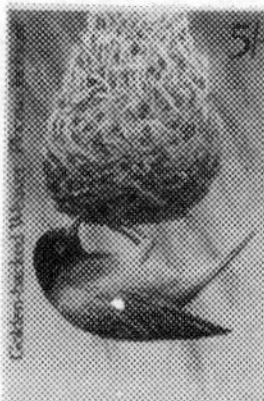

Birds — A74

**1987, Nov. 2 Litho. *Perf. 14***

*569* A74 5sh Golden-backed weaver 18 18
*570* A74 10sh Hoopoe 35 35
*571* A74 15sh Red-throated bee-eater 50 50
*572* A74 25sh Lilac-breasted roller 85 85
*573* A74 35sh Pygmy goose 1.20 1.20

*574* A74 45sh Scarlet-chested sunbird 1.50 1.50
*575* A74 50sh Crowned crane 1.70 1.70
*576* A74 100sh Long-tailed fiscal shrike 3.35 3.35
*Nos. 569-576 (8)* 9.63 9.63

**Souvenir Sheets**

*577* A74 150sh African barn owl, horiz. 5.00 5.00
*578* A74 150sh African fish-eagle, horiz. 5.00 5.00

Nos. 577-578 have multicolored margins continuing the designs and respectively picturing frontier at dusk and river on an overcast day. Sizes: 80x62mm (No. 577); 80x60mm (No. 578).

14th World Boy Scout Jamboree, Australia, 1987-88
A75

Activities: 5sh, Stamp collecting, Uganda Nos. 84 and 116. 25sh, Planting trees, Natl. flag. 35sh, Canoeing on Lake Victoria. 45sh, Hiking and camping. 150sh, Logo of 1987 jamboree and natl. Boy Scout organization emblem.

**1987, Nov. 20**

*579* A75 5sh multi 18 18
*580* A75 25sh multi 85 85
*581* A75 35sh multi 1.20 1.20
*582* A75 45sh multi 1.50 1.50

**Souvenir Sheet**

*583* A75 150sh multi 5.00 5.00

No. 583 has multicolored inscribed margin picturing the national boy scout emblems of Panama, Ireland, Ghana, Colombia, Israel, Greece, the world crest, Peru, Japan, Uganda, India, Dominican Republic, Luxembourg and Pakistan. Size: 95x66mm.

Christmas 1987
A76

The life of Christ and the Virgin pictured on bas-reliefs, c. 1250, and a tapestry from France: 5sh, The Annunciation. 10sh, The Nativity. 50sh, Flight into Egypt. 100sh, The Adoration of the Magi. 150sh, The Mystic Wine Tapestry.

**1987, Dec. 18**

*584* A76 5sh multi 18 18
*585* A76 10sh multi 35 35
*586* A76 50sh multi 1.70 1.70
*587* A76 100sh multi 3.35 3.35

**Souvenir Sheet**

*588* A76 150sh multi 5.00 5.00

No. 588 has multicolored margin continuing the tapestry. Size: 176x106mm.

Locomotives — A77

Designs: 5sh, Class 12 2-6-2T light shunter. 10sh, Class 92 1Co-Co1 diesel electric. 15sh, Class 2-8-2. 25sh, Class 2-6-2T light shunter. 35sh, Class 4-8-0. 45sh, Class 4-8-2. 50sh, Class 4-8-4+4-8-4 Garratt. 100sh, Class 87 1Co-Co1 diesel electric. No. 597, Class 59 4-8-2+2-8-4 Garratt. No. 598, Class 31 2-8-4.

**1988, Jan. 18**

*589* A77 5sh multi 18 18
*590* A77 10sh multi 35 35
*591* A77 15sh multi 55 55
*592* A77 25sh multi 82 82
*593* A77 35sh multi 1.20 1.20
*594* A77 45sh multi 1.50 1.50
*595* A77 50sh multi 1.65 1.65
*596* A77 100sh multi 3.50 3.50
*Nos. 589-596 (8)* 9.75 9.75

**Souvenir Sheets**

*597* A77 150sh multi 5.00 5.00
*598* A77 150sh multi 5.00 5.00

Nos. 597-598 have multicolored margins continuing the designs and respectively picturing zebras and elephants in the wild. Sizes: 100x74mm.

Minerals — A78

**1988, Jan. 18**

*599* A78 1sh Columbite-tantalite 5 5
*600* A78 2sh Galena 8 8
*601* A78 5sh Malachite 18 18
*602* A78 10sh Cassiterite 35 35
*603* A78 35sh Ferberite 1.20 1.20
*604* A78 50sh Emerald 1.70 1.70
*605* A78 100sh Monazite 3.35 3.35
*606* A78 150sh Microcline 5.00 5.00
*Nos. 599-606 (8)* 11.91 11.91

1988 Summer Olympics, Seoul
A79

**1988, May 16 Litho. *Perf. 14***

*607* A79 5sh Hurdles 18 18
*608* A79 25sh High jump 85 85
*609* A79 35sh Javelin 1.20 1.20
*610* A79 45sh Long jump 1.50 1.50

**Souvenir Sheet**

*611* A79 150sh Medals, five-ring emblem 5.00 5.00

No. 611 has multicolored decorative margin picturing eternal flame, ribbon and medal. Size: 85x114mm.

Flowers
A80

**1988, July 28 Litho. *Perf. 15***

*612* A80 5sh Spathodea campanulata 16 16
*613* A80 10sh Gloriosa simplex 32 32
*614* A80 20sh Thevetica peruviana, vert. 65 65
*615* A80 25sh Hibiscus schizopetalus 82 82
*616* A80 35sh Aframomum sceptrum 1.15 1.15
*617* A80 45sh Adenium obesum 1.50 1.50
*618* A80 50sh Kigelia africana, vert. 1.65 1.65
*619* A80 100sh Clappertonia ficifolia 3.30 3.30
*Nos. 612-619 (8)* 9.55 9.55

**Souvenir Sheets**

*620* A80 150sh Costus spectabiis 5.00 5.00
*621* A80 150sh Canarina abyssinica, vert. 5.00 5.00

Nos. 620-621 have multicolored inscribed margins continuing the designs. Sizes: 110x79mm.

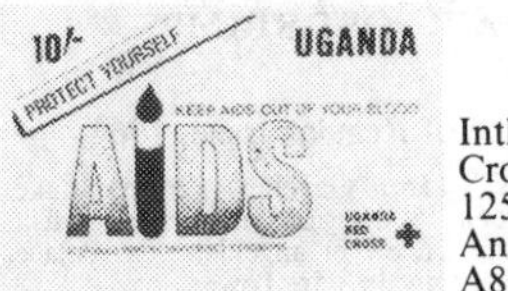


Intl. Red Cross, 125th Anniv.
A81

**1988, Oct. 28 Litho. *Perf. 14***

*622* A81 10sh "AIDS" 25 25
*623* A81 40sh Immunize children 1.00 1.00
*624* A81 70sh Relief distribution 1.75 1.75
*625* A81 90sh First aid 2.25 2.25

**Souvenir Sheet**

*626* A81 150sh Jean-Henri Dunant, vert. 5.00 5.00

No. 626 has multicolored margin picturing Clara Barton (1821-1912), founder of the American Red Cross, scholar Romain Rolland (1866-1944), Jean Courvoisier, Herbert Beckh and Andre Rochat. Size: 110x78mm.

Paintings by Titian — A82

Designs: 10sh, *Portrait of a Lady*, c. 1508. 20sh, *Portrait of a Man*, 1507. 40sh, *Portrait of Isabella d'Este*, c. 1534. 50sh, *Portrait of Vincenzo Mosti*, 1520. 70sh, *Pope Paul III Farnese*, c. 1545. 90sh, *Violante*, 1515. 100sh, *Lavinia, Titian's Daughter*, c. 1565. 250sh, *Portrait of Dr. Parma*, c. 1515. No. 635, *The Speech of Alfonso D'Avalos*, c. 1540. No. 636, *Cain and Abel*.

**1988, Oct. 31 *Perf. 14***

*627* A82 10sh multi 14 14
*628* A82 20sh multi 18 18
*629* A82 40sh multi 55 55
*630* A82 50sh multi 68 68
*631* A82 70sh multi 95 95
*632* A82 90sh multi 1.20 1.20
*633* A82 100sh multi 1.35 1.35
*634* A82 250sh multi 3.40 3.40
*Nos. 627-634 (8)* 8.45 8.45

**Souvenir Sheets**

*635* A82 150sh multi 3.00 3.00
*636* A82 350sh multi 4.75 4.75

Nos. 635-636 have multicolored inscribed margins continuing the paintings. Sizes: 110x95mm.

Game Preserves — A83

Designs: 10sh, Giraffes, Kidepo Valley Natl. Park. 25sh, Zebras, Lake Mburo Natl. Park. 100sh, African buffalo, Murchison Falls Natl. Park. 250sh, Pelicans, Queen Elizabeth Natl. Park. 350sh, Roan antelopes, Lake Mburo Natl. Park.

**1988, Nov. 18 Litho. *Perf. 14***

*637* A83 10sh multi 14 14
*638* A83 25sh multi 32 32
*639* A83 100sh multi 1.35 1.35
*640* A83 250sh multi 3.35 3.35

**Souvenir Sheet**

*641* A83 350sh multi 4.75 4.75

No. 641 has multicolored inscribed margin picturing map of Uganda with location of natl. parks highlighted. Size: 97x68mm.

The lack of a price for a listed item does not necessarily indicate rarity.

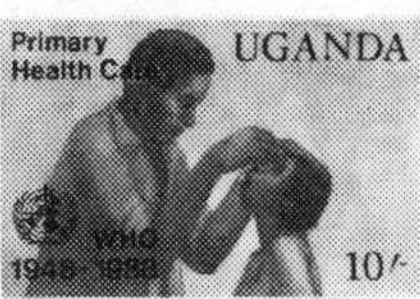


WHO 40th Anniv., Alma Ata Declaration 10th Anniv. — A84

**1988, Dec. 1**

*642* A84 10sh Primary health care 14 14
*643* A84 25sh Mental health 35 35
*644* A84 45sh Rural health care 60 60
*645* A84 100sh Dental care 1.35 1.35
*646* A84 200sh Postnatal care 2.70 2.70
*Nos. 642-646 (5)* 5.14 5.14

**Souvenir Sheet**

*647* A84 350sh Conference Hall, Alma-Ata, Russia 4.75 4.75

No. 647 has multicolored margin continuing the design. Size: 107x78mm.

Miniature Sheet

Christmas, Mickey Mouse 60th Birthday — A85

Walt Disney characters: No. 648a, Santa Claus. No. 648b, Goofy. No. 648c, Mickey Mouse. No. 648d, Huey at conveyor belt. No. 648e, Dewey packing building blocks. No. 648f, Donald Duck. No. 648g, Chip-n-Dale. No. 648h, Louie at conveyor belt controls. No. 649, Preparing reindeer for Christmas eve flight. No. 650, Mickey loading sleigh with toys, horiz.

**1988, Dec. 2 *Perf. 13½x14, 14x13½***

*648* Sheet of 8 5.50 5.50
***a.-h.*** A85 50sh any single 68 68

**Souvenir Sheets**

*649* A85 350sh multi 4.75 4.75
*650* A85 350sh multi 4.75 4.75

Nos. 649-650 have multicolored inscribed margins continuing the designs. Sizes: 177x139mm (No. 648); 127x102mm (Nos. 649-650).

---

## POSTAGE DUE STAMPS

**Catalogue values for unused stamps in this section, from this point to the end of the section, are for Never Hinged items.**

Type of Kenya, 1967

***Perf. 14x13½, 14x15, 15***

**1967, Jan. 3 Litho. Unwmk.**

*J1* D1 5c red 8 8
*J2* D1 10c green 8 8
*J3* D1 20c dk bl 22 22
*J4* D1 30c redsh brn 30 30
*J5* D1 40c red lil 50 50
*J6* D1 1sh orange 1.25 1.25
*Nos. J1-J6 (6)* 2.43 2.43

Nos. J1-J5 were reissued Mar. 31, 1970, with perf. 14x15; Nos. J1-J6 in 1973 with perf. 15.

Nos. J1-J6 Overprinted in Black: "LIBERATED / 1979"

**1979, Dec. Litho. *Perf. 14***

*J7* D1 5c red 5 5
*J8* D1 10c green 5 5
*J9* D1 20c vio bl 6 5
*J10* D1 30c redsh brn 15 6

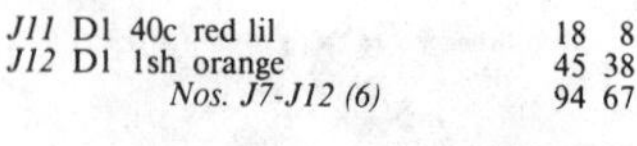

| | | | | |
|---|---|---|---|---|
| *J11* | D1 | 40c red lil | 18 | 8 |
| *J12* | D1 | 1sh orange | 45 | 38 |
| | | *Nos. J7-J12 (6)* | 94 | 67 |

Wildlife — D2

**1985, Mar. 11 Litho. *Perf. 15x14***

| | | | | |
|---|---|---|---|---|
| *J13* | D2 | 5sh Lion | 5 | 5 |
| *J14* | D2 | 10sh African buffalo | 5 | 5 |
| *J15* | D2 | 20sh Kob antelope | 5 | 5 |
| *J16* | D2 | 40sh Elephant | 12 | 12 |
| *J17* | D2 | 50sh Zebra | 15 | 15 |
| *J18* | D2 | 100sh Rhinoceros | 28 | 28 |
| | | *Nos. J13-J18 (6)* | 70 | 70 |

## UMM AL QIWAIN

LOCATION — Oman Peninsula, Arabia, on Arabian Gulf.
GOVT. — Sheikdom under British protection
AREA — 300 sq. mi.
POP. — 5,700

Umm al Qiwain is one of six Persian Gulf sheikdoms to join the United Arab Emirates which proclaimed independence Dec. 2, 1971. See United Arab Emirates.

100 Naye Paise = 1 Rupee
100 Dirham = 1 Riyal (1967)

**Catalogue values for all unused stamps in this country are for Never Hinged items.**

Sheik Ahmed bin Rashid al Mulla and Gazelles A1

Designs (Sheik and): 2np, 50np, Snake. 3np, 70np, Hyena. 4np, 1r, Conspicuous triggerfish. 5np, 1.50r, Fish. 10np, 2r, Silver angelfish. 15np, 3r, Palace. 20np, 5r, Umm al Qiwain. 30np, 10r, Tower.

**Photogravure and Lithographed**
**1964, June 29 Unwmk. *Perf. 14***
**Size: 35x22mm**

| | | | | |
|---|---|---|---|---|
| *1* | A1 | 1np gold & multi | 5 | 5 |
| *2* | A1 | 2np gold & multi | 5 | 5 |
| *3* | A1 | 3np gold & multi | 5 | 5 |
| *4* | A1 | 4np gold & multi | 5 | 5 |
| *5* | A1 | 5np gold & multi | 5 | 5 |
| *6* | A1 | 10np gold & multi | 5 | 5 |
| *7* | A1 | 15np gold & multi | 5 | 5 |
| *8* | A1 | 20np gold & multi | 5 | 5 |
| *9* | A1 | 30np gold & multi | 6 | 5 |

**Size: 42x26mm**

| | | | | |
|---|---|---|---|---|
| *10* | A1 | 40np gold & multi | 9 | 5 |
| *11* | A1 | 50np gold & multi | 10 | 5 |
| *12* | A1 | 70np gold & multi | 14 | 5 |
| *13* | A1 | 1r gold & multi | 20 | 6 |
| *14* | A1 | 1.50r gold & multi | 30 | 8 |
| *15* | A1 | 2r gold & multi | 40 | 10 |

**Size: 52x33mm**

| | | | | |
|---|---|---|---|---|
| *16* | A1 | 3r gold & multi | 60 | 20 |
| *17* | A1 | 5r gold & multi | 1.00 | 25 |
| *18* | A1 | 10r gold & multi | 2.00 | 50 |
| | | *Nos. 1-18 (18)* | 5.29 | 1.79 |

National Stadium, Tokyo, and Discobolus — A2

Designs: 1r, 2r, National Stadium, Tokyo. 1.50r, Indoor swimming arena. 3r, Komazawa Gymnasium. 4r, Stadium entrance. 5r, like 50np.

**1964, Nov. 25 Photo. *Perf. 14***

| | | | | |
|---|---|---|---|---|
| *19* | A2 | 50np multi | 10 | 5 |
| *20* | A2 | 1r multi | 20 | 5 |
| *21* | A2 | 1.50r multi | 30 | 8 |
| *22* | A2 | 2r multi | 40 | 10 |
| *23* | A2 | 3r multi | 60 | 15 |
| *24* | A2 | 4r multi | 80 | 20 |
| *25* | A2 | 5r multi | 1.00 | 25 |
| | | *Nos. 19-25 (7)* | 3.40 | 88 |

Issued to commemorate the 18th Olympic Games, Tokyo, Oct. 10-25, 1964. Perf. and imperf. souvenir sheets contain four stamps similar to Nos. 22-25 in changed colors. Dark red marginal inscription. Size: 145x115mm.

Pres. Kennedy's Funeral Cortege Leaving White House — A3

Designs: 15np, Mrs. Kennedy with children, and Robert Kennedy following coffin. 50np, Horse-drawn caisson. 1r, Presidents Truman and Eisenhower, and Margaret Truman Daniels. 2r, Pres. Charles de Gaulle, Emperor Haile Selassie, Chancellor Ludwig Erhart, Sir Alec Douglas-Home and King Frederick IX. 3r, Kennedy family on steps of St. Matthew's Cathedral. 5r, Honor guard at tomb. 7.50r, Portrait of Pres. John F. Kennedy.

***Perf. 14½***
**1965, Jan. 20 Unwmk. Photo.**
**Black Design with Gold Inscriptions**
**Size: 29x44mm**

| | | | | |
|---|---|---|---|---|
| *26* | A3 | 10np pale bl | 5 | 5 |
| *27* | A3 | 15np pale yel | 5 | 5 |
| *28* | A3 | 50np pale grn | 10 | 5 |
| *29* | A3 | 1r pale pink | 20 | 8 |
| *30* | A3 | 2r pale grn | 40 | 10 |

**Size: 33x51mm**

| | | | | |
|---|---|---|---|---|
| *31* | A3 | 3r pale gray | 60 | 20 |
| *32* | A3 | 5r pale bl | 1.00 | 30 |
| *33* | A3 | 7.50r pale yel | 1.50 | 50 |
| | | *Nos. 26-33 (8)* | 3.90 | 1.33 |

Issued in memory of Pres. John F. Kennedy (1917-63). A souvenir sheet contains 2 stamps similar to Nos. 32-33 with pale green (5r) and pale salmon (7.50r) backgrounds, size: 29x44mm. Gold and black marginal design includes portrait of Sheik Ahmad. Size of sheet: 114x70mm.

Astronaut on Moon — A4

Designs: 20d, Landing module approaching moon. 30d, Apollo XII on launching pad. 50d, Commanders Charles Conrad, Jr., Alan L. Bean, Richard F. Gordon, Jr., earth and moon (horiz.). 75d, Earth and Apollo XII (horiz.). 1r, Sheik Ahmed, rocket and lunar landing module (horiz.).

**1969, Nov. 19 Litho. *Perf. 14½***

| | | | | |
|---|---|---|---|---|
| *34* | A4 | 10d multi | 5 | |
| *35* | A4 | 20d multi | 8 | |
| *36* | A4 | 30d multi | 12 | |
| *37* | A4 | 50d emer & multi | 20 | |
| *38* | A4 | 75d pur & multi | 30 | |
| *39* | A4 | 1r dk bl & multi | 40 | |
| | | *Nos. 34-39 (6)* | 1.15 | |

Issued to commemorate the U.S. Apollo XII moon landing mission, Nov. 14-24, 1969.

Two imperf. souvenir sheets of 3 exist, containing stamps similar to Nos. 34-36 and Nos. 37-39.

Capt. James A. Lovell — A5

Designs: 30d, Fred W. Haise, Jr. 50d, John L. Swigert, Jr.

**1970, May 29 Litho. *Perf. 14***

| | | | | |
|---|---|---|---|---|
| *40* | A5 | 10d multi | 5 | |
| *41* | A5 | 30d multi | 12 | |
| *42* | A5 | 50d multi | 20 | |
| ***a.*** | | Souvenir sheet of 3 | 40 | |

Issued to commemorate the safe return of the crew of Apollo 13. No. 42a contains one each of Nos. 40-42, multicolored margin showing trajectory of flight. Size: 121x98mm.

EXPO '70 Emblem — A6

Designs: 10d, 20d, Japanese Pavilion.

**1970, Aug. 14 Litho. *Perf. 13½x14***

| | | | | |
|---|---|---|---|---|
| *43* | A6 | 5d yel & multi | 5 | |
| *44* | A6 | 10d bl & multi | 5 | |
| *45* | A6 | 20d red & multi | 5 | |
| *48* | A6 | 1.25r red & multi | 25 | |

EXPO '70 Intl. Exhib., Osaka, Japan, Mar. 15-Sept. 13, 1970.

A 40d and 1r, showing the Emperor and Empress of Japan, and a souvenir sheet containing these and Nos. 43-45, 48 were prepared, but not issued.

Private, North Lancashire Regiment — A7

Uniforms: 20d, Royal Navy seaman. 30d, Officer, North Lancashire (Loyal) Regiment. 50d, Private, York and Lancaster Regiment. 75d, Royal Navy officer. 1r, Officer, York and Lancaster Regiment.

**1970, Oct. 12 Litho. *Perf. 14½x14***

| | | | | |
|---|---|---|---|---|
| *49* | A7 | 10d multi | 8 | |
| *50* | A7 | 20d multi | 14 | |
| *51* | A7 | 30d multi | 20 | |
| ***a.*** | | Souv. sheet of 3, #49-51 | 50 | |
| *52* | A7 | 50d buff & multi | 35 | |
| *53* | A7 | 75d multi | 50 | |
| *54* | A7 | 1r buff & multi | 75 | |
| ***a.*** | | Souv. sheet of 3, #52-54 | 1.75 | |
| | | *Nos. 49-54 (6)* | 2.02 | |

150th anniv. of the British landings on the Trucial Coast. Nos. 51a and 54a have pale green decorative margins with commemorative inscriptions. Size: 113x91mm.

Stamps of Umm al Qiwain were replaced in 1972 by those of United Arab Emirates.

### AIR POST STAMPS

Type of Regular Issue, 1964

Designs: 15np, Gazelles. 25np, Snake. 35np, Hyena. 50np, Conspicuous triggerfish. 75np, Fish. 1r, Silver angelfish. 2r, Palace. 3r, Umm al Qiwain. 5r, Tower.

**Photogravure and Lithographed**
**1965 Unwmk. *Perf. 14***
**Size: 42x26mm.**

| | | | | |
|---|---|---|---|---|
| *C1* | A1 | 15np sil & multi | 5 | 5 |
| *C2* | A1 | 25np sil & multi | 5 | 5 |
| *C3* | A1 | 35np sil & multi | 8 | 5 |
| *C4* | A1 | 50np sil & multi | 10 | 5 |
| *C5* | A1 | 75np sil & multi | 15 | 5 |
| *C6* | A1 | 1r sil & multi | 20 | 8 |

**Size: 52x33mm.**

| | | | | |
|---|---|---|---|---|
| *C7* | A1 | 2r sil & multi | 40 | 12 |
| *C8* | A1 | 3r sil & multi | 60 | 20 |
| *C9* | A1 | 5r sil & multi | 1.00 | 32 |
| | | *Nos. C1-C9 (9)* | 2.63 | 97 |

Nos. C1-C6 were issued Oct. 18; Nos. C7-C9, Nov. 6.

### AIR POST OFFICIAL STAMPS

Type of Regular Issue, 1964

Designs: 75np, Silver angelfish. 2r, Palace. 3r, Buildings. 5r Tower.

**Photogravure and Lithographed**
**1965, Dec. 22 Unwmk. *Perf. 14***
**Size: 42x26mm.**

| | | | | |
|---|---|---|---|---|
| *CO1* | A1 | 75np gold & multi | 15 | 5 |

**Size: 52x33mm.**

| | | | | |
|---|---|---|---|---|
| *CO2* | A1 | 2r gold & multi | 40 | 12 |
| *CO3* | A1 | 3r gold & multi | 60 | 20 |
| *CO4* | A1 | 5r gold & multi | 1.00 | 32 |

### OFFICIAL STAMPS

Type of Regular Issue, 1964

Designs: 25np, Gazelles. 40np, Snake. 50np, Hyena. 75np, Conspicuous triggerfish. 1r, Fish.

**Photogravure and Lithograped**
**1965, Dec. 22 Unwmk. *Perf. 14***
**Size: 42x26mm.**

| | | | | |
|---|---|---|---|---|
| *O1* | A1 | 25np gold & multi | 5 | 5 |
| *O2* | A1 | 40np gold & multi | 9 | 5 |
| *O3* | A1 | 50np gold & multi | 10 | 5 |
| *O4* | A1 | 75np gold & multi | 15 | 5 |
| *O5* | A1 | 1r gold & multi | 20 | 5 |
| | | *Nos. O1-O5 (5)* | 59 | 25 |

## UNITED ARAB EMIRATES

LOCATION — Arabia, on Arabian Gulf
GOVT. — Federation of sheikdoms
AREA — 32,300 sq. mi.
POP. — 1,175,000 (est. 1982)
CAPITAL — Abu Dhabi

The U.A.E. was formed December 2, 1971, by the union of Abu Dhabi, Ajman, Dubai, Fujeira, Sharjah and Umm al Qiwain. Ras al Khaima joined in February 1972.

1,000 Fils = 1 Dinar
100 Fils = 1 Dirham (1973)

**Catalogue values for all unused stamps in this country are for Never Hinged items.**

Abu Dhabi Nos. 56-67 Overprinted.

دولة الامارات العربية المتحدة

a

**UAE**

دولة الامارات العربية المتحدة

b

**UAE**

دولة الامارات العربية المتحدة

c

**UAE**

**1972, Aug. Litho. Unwmk. *Perf. 14***

| No. | Type | Description | Unused | Used |
|---|---|---|---|---|
| *1* | A10 (a) | 5f lt grn & multi | | |
| *2* | A10 (a) | 10f bis & multi | | |
| *3* | A10 (a) | 25f lil & multi | | |
| *4* | A10 (a) | 35f vio & multi | | |
| *5* | A10 (a) | 50f sep & multi | | |
| *6* | A10 (a) | 60f vio & multi | | |
| *7* | A10 (a) | 70f multi | | |
| *8* | A10 (a) | 90f multi | | |
| *9* | A11 (b) | 125f multi | | |
| *10* | A11 (b) | 150f multi | | |
| *11* | A11 (b) | 500f multi | | |
| *12* | A11 (c) | 1d multi | | |
| | | *Nos. 1-12 (12)* | 250.00 | |

The overprint on 5f, 25f, 60f and 90f is without bars.

Nos. 1-12 were used in Abu Dhabi. Nos. 2-3 were placed on sale later in Dubai and Sharjah.

Map and Flag of UAE A1

Almagta Bridge, Abu Dhabi — A2

Designs: 10f, Like 5f. 15f, 35f, Coat of arms of UAE (eagle). 75f, Khor Fakkan, Sharjah. 1d, Steel Clock Tower, Dubai. 1.25d, Buthnah Fort, Fujeira. 2d, Alfalaj Fort, Umm al Qiwain. 3d, Khor Khwair, Ras al Khaima. 5d, Palace of Sheik Rashid bin Humaid al Nuaimi, Ajman. 10d, Sheik Zaid bin Sultan al Nahayyan, Abu Dhabi.

***Perf. 14½***

**1973, Jan. 1 Litho. Unwmk.**

**Size: 41x25mm**

| No. | Type | Description | Unused | Used |
|---|---|---|---|---|
| *13* | A1 | 5f multi | 5 | 5 |
| *14* | A1 | 10f multi | 10 | 10 |
| *15* | A1 | 15f bl & multi | 15 | 15 |
| *16* | A1 | 35f ol & multi | 35 | 35 |

***Perf. 14x15***

**Size: 45x29½mm**

| No. | Type | Description | Unused | Used |
|---|---|---|---|---|
| *17* | A2 | 65f multi | 65 | 65 |
| *18* | A2 | 75f multi | 75 | 75 |
| *19* | A2 | 1d multi | 1.00 | 1.00 |
| *20* | A2 | 1.25d multi | 1.75 | 2.50 |
| *21* | A2 | 2d multi | 20.00 | 5.00 |
| *22* | A2 | 3d multi | 3.00 | 3.00 |
| *23* | A2 | 5d multi | 5.00 | 5.00 |
| *24* | A2 | 10d multi | 10.00 | 10.00 |
| | | *Nos. 13-24 (12)* | 42.80 | 28.55 |

Festival Emblem — A3

Design: 1.25d, Trophy.

**1973, Mar. 27 Litho. *Perf. 13½x14***

| No. | Type | Description | Unused | Used |
|---|---|---|---|---|
| *25* | A3 | 10f pur & multi | 2.25 | 10 |
| *26* | A3 | 1.25d bl & multi | 5.50 | 3.75 |

National Youth Festival, Mar. 27.

Pedestrian Crossing in Dubai — A4

Designs: 35f, Traffic light and school crossing sign (vert.). 1.25d, Traffic policemen with car and radio (vert.).

**1973, Apr. 1 *Perf. 13½x14, 14x13½***

| No. | Type | Description | Unused | Used |
|---|---|---|---|---|
| *27* | A4 | 35f grn & multi | 1.50 | 70 |
| *28* | A4 | 75f bl & multi | 2.75 | 1.40 |
| *29* | A4 | 1.25d vio & multi | 4.50 | 2.00 |

Traffic Week, Apr. 1-7.

Human Rights Flame and People — A5

**1973, Dec. 10 Litho. *Perf. 14½x14***

| No. | Type | Description | Unused | Used |
|---|---|---|---|---|
| *30* | A5 | 35f bl, blk & org | 1.10 | 40 |
| *31* | A5 | 65f red, blk & org | 1.75 | 75 |
| *32* | A5 | 1.25d ol, blk & org | 3.00 | 1.50 |

25th anniversary of the Universal Declaration of Human Rights.

UPU and Arab Postal Union Emblems — A6

**1974, Aug. 5 Litho. *Perf. 14x14½***

| No. | Type | Description | Unused | Used |
|---|---|---|---|---|
| *33* | A6 | 25f multi | 75 | 40 |
| *34* | A6 | 60f emer & multi | 1.50 | 75 |
| *35* | A6 | 1.25d lt brn & multi | 3.00 | 1.75 |

Centenary of Universal Postal Union.

Health Care — A7

Education — A8

Designs: 65f, Construction. 1.25d, UAE flag, UN and Arab League emblems.

**1974, Dec. 2 Litho. *Perf. 13½***

| No. | Type | Description | Unused | Used |
|---|---|---|---|---|
| *36* | A7 | 10f multi | 55 | 6 |
| *37* | A8 | 35f multi | 1.10 | 45 |
| *38* | A8 | 65f bl & brn | 1.60 | 90 |
| *39* | A8 | 1.25d multi | 3.00 | 2.00 |

Third National Day.

Arab Man and Woman Holding Candle over Book — A9

Man and Woman Reading Book — A10

***Perf. 14x14½, 14½x14***

**1974, Dec. 27**

| No. | Type | Description | Unused | Used |
|---|---|---|---|---|
| *40* | A9 | 35f dp ultra & multi | 50 | 20 |
| *41* | A10 | 65f org brn & multi | 75 | 40 |
| *42* | A10 | 1.25d gray & multi | 1.40 | 80 |

World Literacy Day.

Oil De-gassing Station — A11

Designs: 50f, Off-shore drilling platform. 100f, Underwater storage tank. 125f, Oil production platform.

**1975, Mar. 10 Litho. *Perf. 13x13½***

| No. | Type | Description | Unused | Used |
|---|---|---|---|---|
| *43* | A11 | 25f multi | 75 | 25 |
| *44* | A11 | 50f multi | 1.00 | 50 |
| *45* | A11 | 100f multi | 2.00 | 1.10 |
| *46* | A11 | 125f multi | 2.75 | 1.25 |
| *a* | | Souvenir sheet of 4 | 6.50 | 4.50 |

9th Arab Petroleum Conference. No. 46a contains one each of Nos. 43-46; pink margin with black inscription. Size: 168x121mm.

Three stamps to commemorate the 2nd Gulf Long Distance Swimming Championship were prepared in June, 1975, but not issued.

Jabal Ali Earth Station — A12

Jabal Ali Earth Station: 35f, 65f, Communications satellite over globe.

**1975, Nov. 8 Litho. *Perf. 13***

| No. | Type | Description | Unused | Used |
|---|---|---|---|---|
| *47* | A12 | 15f multi | 45 | 12 |
| *48* | A12 | 35f multi | 75 | 32 |
| *49* | A12 | 65f multi | 1.10 | 55 |
| *50* | A12 | 2d multi | 2.75 | 1.60 |

Various Scenes — A13

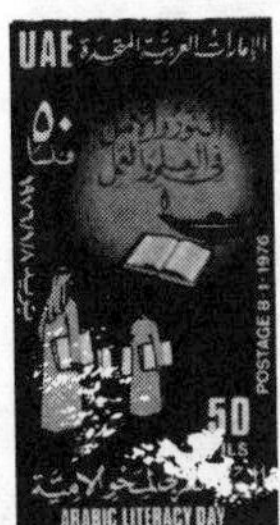


Sheik Hamad, Fujeira Ruler — A14

Supreme Council Members (Sheikdom rulers): 60f, Sheik Rashid bin Humaid al Naimi, Ajman. 80f, Sheik Ahmed bin Rashid al Mulla, Umm al Qiwain. 90f, Sheik Sultan bin Mohammed al Qasimi, Sharjah. 1d, Sheik Saqr bin Mohammed al Qasimi, Ras al Khaima. 140f, Sheik Rashid bin Said al Maktum, Dubai. 5d, Sheik Zaid bin Sultan al Nahayan, Abu Dhabi.

**1975, Dec. 2 Litho. *Perf. 14***

| No. | Type | Description | Unused | Used |
|---|---|---|---|---|
| *51* | A13 | 10f multi | 22 | 18 |
| *52* | A14 | 35f multi | 90 | 75 |
| *53* | A14 | 60f multi | 1.50 | 1.25 |
| *54* | A14 | 80f multi | 2.00 | 1.65 |
| *55* | A14 | 90f multi | 2.25 | 1.75 |
| *56* | A14 | 1d multi | 2.50 | 2.00 |
| *57* | A14 | 140f multi | 3.50 | 2.75 |
| *58* | A14 | 5d multi | 14.00 | 10.50 |
| | | *Nos. 51-58 (8)* | 26.87 | 20.83 |

Fourth National Day.

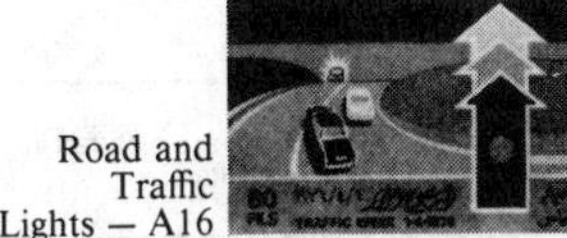


Students and Lamp of Learning — A15

Arab Literacy Day: 15f, Lamp of learning. 3d, like 50f.

**1976, Feb. 8 Litho. *Perf. 14***

| No. | Type | Description | Unused | Used |
|---|---|---|---|---|
| *59* | A15 | 15f org & multi | 30 | 10 |
| *60* | A15 | 50f ultra & multi | 50 | 35 |
| *61* | A15 | 3d multi | 3.00 | 2.00 |

Road and Traffic Lights — A16

Traffic Week: 15f, Traffic lights and signals (vert.). 140f, Children crossing street.

***Perf. 14½x14, 14x14½***

**1976, Apr. 1** **Litho.**

| No. | Type | Description | Unused | Used |
|---|---|---|---|---|
| *62* | A16 | 15f brt bl & multi | 40 | 40 |
| *63* | A16 | 80f bl & multi | 2.00 | 2.00 |
| *64* | A16 | 140f ocher & multi | 3.50 | 3.50 |

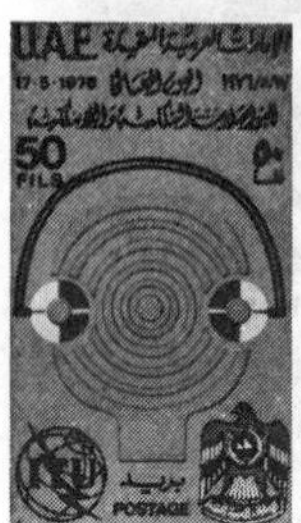


Waves and Ear Phones, ITU Emblem, Coat of Arms — A17

**1976, May 17** **Litho.** ***Perf. 14***

| No. | Type | Description | Unused | Used |
|---|---|---|---|---|
| *65* | A17 | 50f gray grn & multi | 65 | 28 |
| *66* | A17 | 80f pink & multi | 1.20 | 45 |
| *67* | A17 | 2d tan & multi | 2.50 | 1.12 |

International Telecommunications Day.

No. 18 Surcharged

50 ٥٠

**1976** **Litho.** ***Perf. 14x15***

| No. | Type | Description | Unused | Used |
|---|---|---|---|---|
| *68* | A2 | 50f on 75f multi | *20.00* | 1.50 |

Coat of Arms — A18

**1976, Aug. 15** **Litho.** ***Perf. 11½***

| No. | Type | Description | Unused | Used |
|---|---|---|---|---|
| *69* | A18 | 5f dl rose | 6 | 6 |
| *70* | A18 | 10f gldn brn | 14 | 12 |
| *71* | A18 | 15f orange | 20 | 18 |
| *72* | A18 | 35f dl red brn | 38 | 35 |
| *73* | A18 | 50f brt lil | 50 | 45 |
| *74* | A18 | 60f bister | 55 | 50 |
| *75* | A18 | 80f yel grn | 75 | 70 |
| *76* | A18 | 90f ultra | 85 | 80 |
| *77* | A18 | 1d blue | 1.10 | 1.00 |
| *78* | A18 | 140f ol grn | 1.40 | 1.25 |
| *79* | A18 | 150f rose vio | 1.50 | 1.40 |
| *80* | A18 | 2d slate | 1.90 | 1.75 |
| *81* | A18 | 5d bl grn | 5.00 | 4.50 |
| *82* | A18 | 10d lil rose | 10.00 | 9.00 |
| | | *Nos. 69-82 (14)* | 24.33 | 22.06 |

See Nos. 91-104.

Sheik Zaid — A19

**1976, Dec. 12** **Litho.** ***Perf. 13***

| No. | Type | Description | Unused | Used |
|---|---|---|---|---|
| *83* | A19 | 15f rose & multi | 90 | 15 |
| *84* | A19 | 140f bl & multi | 2.25 | 1.50 |

5th National Day.

Common Design Types are pictured in section before Great Britain.

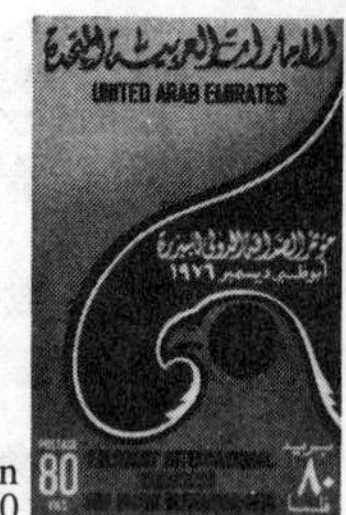


Symbolic Falcon and Globe — A20

**1976, Dec. 15** ***Perf. 14x13½***

| No. | Type | Description | Unused | Used |
|---|---|---|---|---|
| *85* | A20 | 80f yel & multi | 1.10 | 52 |
| *86* | A20 | 2d red & multi | 2.75 | 1.50 |

International Falconry Congress, Abu Dhabi, Dec. 1976.

Mohammed Ali Jinnah — A21

**1976, Dec. 30** **Litho.** ***Perf. 13***

| No. | Type | Description | Unused | Used |
|---|---|---|---|---|
| *87* | A21 | 50f multi | 1.40 | 70 |
| *88* | A21 | 80f multi | 2.00 | 1.10 |

Mohammed Ali Jinnah (1876-1948), 1st Governor General of Pakistan.

APU Emblem, Members' Flags — A22

**1977, Apr. 12** **Litho.** ***Perf. 13½x14***

| No. | Type | Description | Unused | Used |
|---|---|---|---|---|
| *89* | A22 | 50f multi | 1.25 | 65 |
| *90* | A22 | 80f multi | 1.75 | 90 |

Arab Postal Union, 25th anniversary.

Arms Type of 1976

**1977, July 25** **Litho.** ***Perf. 11½***

| No. | Type | Description | Unused | Used |
|---|---|---|---|---|
| *91* | A18 | 5f dl rose & blk | 8 | 6 |
| *92* | A18 | 10f gldn brn & blk | 8 | 6 |
| *93* | A18 | 15f dl org & blk | 12 | 10 |
| *94* | A18 | 35f lt brn & blk | 65 | 50 |
| *95* | A18 | 50f brt lil & blk | 45 | 35 |
| *96* | A18 | 60f bis & blk | 1.00 | 75 |
| *97* | A18 | 80f yel grn & blk | 65 | 50 |
| *98* | A18 | 90f ultra & blk | 80 | 60 |
| *99* | A18 | 1d bl & blk | 1.00 | 70 |
| *100* | A18 | 140f ol grn & blk | 1.60 | 1.25 |
| *101* | A18 | 150f rose vio & blk | 1.60 | 1.25 |
| *102* | A18 | 2d sl & blk | 2.00 | 1.50 |
| *103* | A18 | 5d bl grn & blk | 4.50 | 3.50 |
| *104* | A18 | 10d lil rose & bl | 9.50 | 7.00 |
| | | *Nos. 91-104 (14)* | 24.03 | 18.12 |

Man Reading Book, UAE Arms, UN Emblem A23

**1977, Sept. 8** **Litho.** ***Perf. 14x13½***

| No. | Type | Description | Unused | Used |
|---|---|---|---|---|
| *105* | A23 | 50f grn, brn & gold | 65 | 28 |
| *106* | A23 | 3d bl & multi | 2.75 | 1.68 |

International Literacy Day.

A set of three stamps for the 6th Natl. Day was withdrawn from sale on the day of issue, Dec. 2, 1977.

Post Horn and Sails — A24

**1979, Apr. 14** **Photo.** ***Perf. 12x11½***

| No. | Type | Description | Unused | Used |
|---|---|---|---|---|
| *107* | A24 | 50f multi | 45 | 28 |
| *108* | A24 | 5d multi | 4.50 | 2.80 |

Gulf Postal Organization, 2nd Conference, Dubai.

Arab Achievements — A25

**1980, Mar. 22** **Litho.** ***Perf. 14x14½***

| No. | Type | Description | Unused | Used |
|---|---|---|---|---|
| *109* | A25 | 50f multi | 28 | 28 |
| *110* | A25 | 140f multi | 80 | 80 |
| *111* | A25 | 3d multi | 1.70 | 1.70 |

9th National Day — A26

**1980, Dec. 2** **Litho.** ***Perf. 13½***

| No. | Type | Description | Unused | Used |
|---|---|---|---|---|
| *112* | A26 | 15f multi | 25 | 10 |
| *113* | A26 | 50f multi | 60 | 28 |
| *114* | A26 | 80f multi | 90 | 45 |
| *115* | A26 | 150f multi | 1.25 | 85 |

Souvenir Sheet

***Perf. 13½x14***

| No. | Type | Description | Unused | Used |
|---|---|---|---|---|
| *116* | A26 | 3d multi | 6.00 | 3.50 |

No. 116 has multicolored margin showing flag of UAE. Size: 120x85mm.

Family on Graph — A27

Hegira (Pilgrimage Year) — A28

**1980, Dec. 15**

| No. | Type | Description | Unused | Used |
|---|---|---|---|---|
| *117* | A27 | 15f shown | 22 | 12 |
| *118* | A27 | 80f Symbols | 90 | 50 |
| *119* | A27 | 90f like #118 | 1.10 | 60 |
| *120* | A27 | 2d like #117 | 2.25 | 1.25 |

1980 population census.

**1980, Dec. 18** ***Perf. 14x13½***

| No. | Type | Description | Unused | Used |
|---|---|---|---|---|
| *121* | A28 | 15f multi | 25 | 12 |
| *122* | A28 | 80f multi | 1.00 | 50 |
| *123* | A28 | 90f multi | 1.25 | 60 |
| *124* | A28 | 140f multi | 1.75 | 90 |

**Souvenir Sheet**

| No. | Type | Description | Unused | Used |
|---|---|---|---|---|
| *125* | A28 | 2d multi | 4.25 | 2.50 |

No. 125 contains one stamp (36x57mm.); gold decorative margin. Size: 90x121mm.

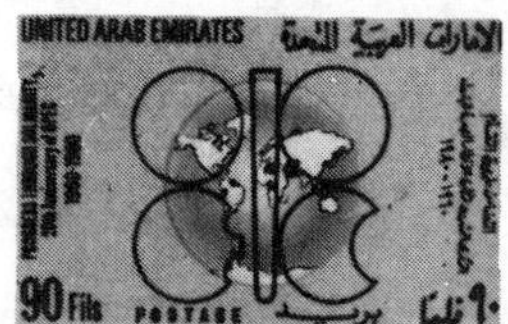


OPEC Emblem — A29

**1980, Dec. 21** ***Perf. 14***

| No. | Type | Description | Unused | Used |
|---|---|---|---|---|
| *126* | A29 | 50f Men holding OPEC emblem, vert. | 45 | 35 |
| *127* | A29 | 80f like #126 | 75 | 60 |
| *128* | A29 | 90f shown | 80 | 65 |
| *129* | A29 | 140f like #128 | 1.25 | 1.00 |

**Souvenir Sheet**

| No. | Type | Description | Unused | Used |
|---|---|---|---|---|
| *130* | A29 | 3d like #128 | 6.00 | 3.50 |

Traffic Week — A30

Designs: 15f, 80f, Crossing guard, students, traffic light. 50f, 5d, Crossing guard, traffic light and signs.

**1981, Mar. 26** **Litho.** ***Perf. 14½***

| No. | Type | Description | Unused | Used |
|---|---|---|---|---|
| *131* | A30 | 15f multi | 25 | 25 |
| *132* | A30 | 50f multi | 50 | 50 |
| *133* | A30 | 80f multi | 1.00 | 1.00 |
| *134* | A30 | 5d multi | 4.00 | 4.00 |

Size of Nos. 131 and 133: 25½x35mm.

10th Natl. Day — A31

**1981, Dec. 2** **Litho.** ***Perf. 15x14***

| No. | Type | Description | Unused | Used |
|---|---|---|---|---|
| *135* | A31 | 25f Cogwheel | 25 | 16 |
| *136* | A31 | 150f Soldiers | 1.65 | 1.00 |
| *137* | A31 | 2d UN emblem | 2.00 | 1.35 |

Intl. Year of the Disabled — A32

***Perf. 14½x14, 14x14½***

**1981, Dec. 26** **Litho.**

| No. | Type | Description | Unused | Used |
|---|---|---|---|---|
| *138* | A32 | 25f Couple | 30 | 20 |
| *139* | A32 | 45f Man in wheelchair, vert. | 50 | 35 |
| *140* | A32 | 150f like #139 | 1.75 | 1.25 |
| *141* | A32 | 2d like #138 | 2.50 | 1.75 |

Natl. Arms — A33

**1982, Mar. 7**

| No. | Type | Description | Unused | Used |
|---|---|---|---|---|
| *142* | A33 | 5f multi | 5 | 5 |
| *143* | A33 | 10f multi | 8 | 8 |
| *144* | A33 | 15f multi | 10 | 10 |
| *145* | A33 | 25f multi | 18 | 18 |
| *145A* | A33 | 35f multi ('84) | 20 | 20 |
| *146* | A33 | 50f multi | 36 | 36 |
| *147* | A33 | 75f multi | 55 | 55 |
| *148* | A33 | 100f multi | 75 | 75 |
| *149* | A33 | 110f multi | 85 | 85 |
| *150* | A33 | 125f multi | 95 | 95 |
| *151* | A33 | 150f multi | 1.10 | 1.10 |
| *151A* | A33 | 175f multi ('84) | 95 | 95 |

**Size: 23x27mm**
***Perf. 13***

*152* A33 2d multi 1.35 1.35
*152A* A33 250f multi ('84) 1.40 1.40
*153* A33 3d multi 2.00 2.00
*154* A33 5d multi 3.35 3.35
*155* A33 10d multi 6.75 6.75
*156* A33 20d multi 13.50 13.50
*157* A33 50d multi ('86) 27.00 27.00
*Nos. 142-157 (19)* 61.47 61.47

Issue dates: Nos. 145A-152A, Dec. 15, 1984. No. 157, Feb. 6, 1986.

6th Arab Gulf Soccer Championships — A34

**1982, Apr. 4 Litho.** ***Perf. 14***
*167* A34 25f Emblem, flags 22 22
*168* A34 75f Eagle, soccer ball, stadium, vert. 62 62
*169* A34 125f Players, vert. 1.05 1.05
*170* A34 3d like 75f, vert. 2.50 2.50

2nd Disarmament Meeting — A35

**1982, Oct. 24 Litho.** ***Perf. 13x13½***
*171* A35 25f multi 25 20
*172* A35 75f multi 80 65
*173* A35 125f multi 1.40 1.10
*174* A35 150f multi 1.50 1.25

11th Natl. Day — A36

Designs: 25f, 150f, Skyscraper, communications tower, natl. crest, castle turret, open book, flag. 75f, 125f, Sun, bird, vert.

**1982, Dec. 2 Litho.** ***Perf. 14½***
*175* A36 25f multi 28 22
*176* A36 75f multi 80 62
*177* A36 125f multi 1.40 1.05
*178* A36 150f multi 1.60 1.25

World Communications Year — A37

**1983, Dec. 20 Litho.** ***Perf. 14x14½***
*179* A37 25f multi 18 18
*180* A37 150f multi 1.10 1.10
*181* A37 2d multi 1.35 1.35
*182* A37 3d multi 2.00 2.00

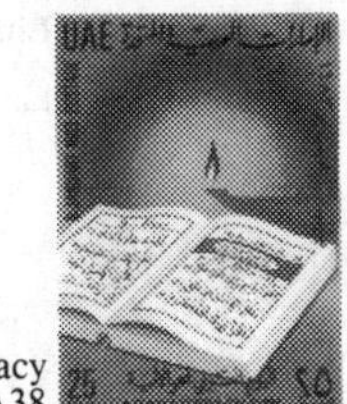

Arab Literacy Day — A38

Designs: 25f, 75f, Oil lamp, open Koran. 35f, 3d, Scribe.

**1983, Jan. 8 Litho.** ***Perf. 14½***
*183* A38 25f multi *10.00*
*184* A38 35f multi 28 28
*185* A38 75f multi *15.00*
*186* A38 3d multi 2.00 2.00

Nos. 183 and 185 withdrawn from sale on day of issue because of an error in Koranic inscription.

INTELSAT, 20th Anniv. — A39

**1984, Nov. 24 Litho.** ***Perf. 14½***
*187* A39 2d multi 2.00 2.00
*188* A39 2.50d multi 2.50 2.50

13th Natl. Day — A40

Flag, portrait of an Emir and building or view from each capital.

**1984, Dec. 2** ***Perf. 14½x13½***
*189* A40 1d Building, pavilion 1.00 1.00
*190* A40 1d Fortress, cannon 1.00 1.00
*191* A40 1d Port, boats 1.00 1.00
*192* A40 1d Fortress 1.00 1.00
*193* A40 1d Oil refinery 1.00 1.00
*194* A40 1d Building, garden 1.00 1.00
*195* A40 1d Oil well, palace 1.00 1.00
*Nos. 189-195 (7)* 7.00 7.00

Tidy Week — A41

**1985, Mar. 15** ***Perf. 12½***
*196* A41 5d multi 4.75 3.35

World Junior Chess Championships, Sharjah, Sept. 10-27 — A42

**1985, Sept. 10** ***Perf. 13½x14½***
*197* A42 2d multi 1.40 1.10
*198* A42 250f multi 1.75 1.35

14th Natl. Day — A43

**1985, Dec. 2** ***Perf. 14x13½***
*199* A43 50f multi 50 28
*200* A43 3d multi 3.00 1.65

Population Census — A44

**1985, Dec. 16**
*201* A44 50f multi 50 28
*202* A44 1d multi 1.00 55
*203* A44 3d multi 3.00 1.65

Intl. Youth Year A45

**1985, Dec. 23** ***Perf. 14½***
*204* A45 50f Silhouettes, sapling, vert. 50 28
*205* A45 175f Globe, open book 1.50 95
*206* A45 2d Youth carrying world, vert. 1.75 1.10

Women and Family Day — A46

**1986, Mar. 21** ***Perf. 13½***
*207* A46 1d multi 75 55
*208* A46 3d multi 2.25 1.65

General Postal Authority, 1st Anniv. A47

Designs: 50f, 250f, Posthorn, map, natl. flag, globe. 1d, 2d, Emblem, globe, vert.

**1986, Apr. 1**
*209* A47 50f multi 35 28
*210* A47 1d multi 75 55
*211* A47 2d multi 1.40 1.10
*212* A47 250f multi 1.75 1.35

United Arab Shipping Co., 10th Anniv. A48

**1986, Aug. 20** ***Perf. 13x13½***
*213* A48 2d shown 1.75 1.10
*214* A48 3d Ship's bow, vert. 2.50 1.65

Emirates Telecommunications Corp., Ltd., 10th Anniv. — A49

**1986, Sept. 1** ***Perf. 13½x13***
*215* A49 250f multi 2.00 1.35
*216* A49 3d multi 2.50 1.65

Hawk — A50

**1986, Sept. 9 Photo.** ***Perf. 15x14***
**Background Color**
*217* A50 50f pale grn 50 50
*218* A50 75f pink 75 75
*219* A50 125f gray 1.25 1.25
*a* Bklt. pane of 4 (2 50f, 75f, 125f) 3.00

Nos. 217-219 issued in booklets only.

Emirates Airlines, 1st Anniv. — A51

**1986, Oct. 25** ***Perf. 13½***
*220* A51 50f Jet, camel 50 50
*221* A51 175f Jet 1.75 1.75

State Crests, GCC Emblem A52

**1986, Nov. 2** ***Perf. 13***
*222* A52 50f shown 50 50
*222A* A52 175f like no. 223 1.75 1.75
*223* A52 3d Tree, emblem 3.00 3.00

Gulf Cooperation Council supreme council 7th session, Abu Dhabi, Nov. 1986. No. 222A incorrectly inscribed "1.75f."

15th Natl. Day — A53

**1986, Dec. 2 Litho.** ***Perf. 13½***
*224* A53 50f shown 50 50
*225* A53 1d like 50f 1.00 1.00
*226* A53 175f Flag, emblem 1.75 1.75
*227* A53 2d like 175f 2.00 2.00

27th Chess Olympiad, Dubai — A54

**1986, Nov. 14** *Perf. 12½*
228 A54 50f Skyscraper, vert. 50 50
229 A54 2d shown 2.00 2.00
230 A54 250f Tapestry, diff. 2.50 2.50
*a* Souvenir sheet of 3, Nos. 228-230, perf. 13 5.00 5.00

No. 230a has pink inscribed margin. Exists imper. Size: 155x90mm.

Arab Police Day — A55

**1986, Dec. 18** *Perf. 13½*
231 A55 50f multi 50 50
232 A55 1d multi 1.00 1.00

Municipalities and Environment Week — A56

**1987, Mar. 15**
233 A56 50f multi 50 50
234 A56 1d multi 1.00 1.00

UAE Flight Information Region, 1st Anniv. — A57

**1987, Apr. 10**
235 A57 200f multi 2.00 2.00
236 A57 250f multi 2.50 2.50

Conservation A58

**1987, May 25**
237 A58 50f Water 50 50
238 A58 2d Solar energy, oil well 2.00 2.00

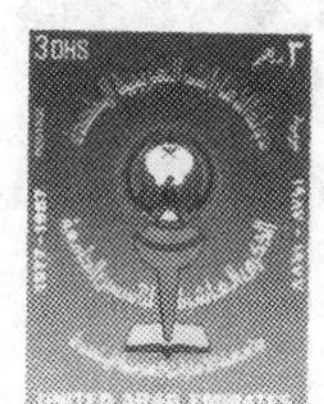


United Arab Emirates University, 10th Anniv. — A59

**1987, June 23**
239 A59 1d multi 1.00 1.00
240 A59 3d multi 3.00 3.00

1st Shipment of Crude Oil from Abu Dhabi, 25th Anniv. — A60

**1987, July 4** *Perf. 13*
241 A60 50f Oil rig 50 50
242 A60 1d Drilling well, vert. 1.00 1.00
243 A60 175f Crew, drill 1.75 1.75
244 A60 2d Oil tanker 2.00 2.00

Arab Palm Tree and Date Day — A61

**1987, Sept. 15** Litho. *Perf. 14x15*
245 A61 50f shown 50 50
246 A61 1d Tree, fruit, diff. 1.00 1.00

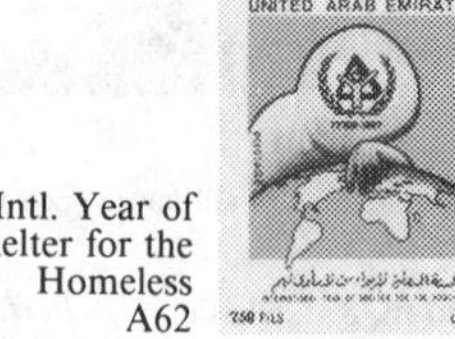


Intl. Year of Shelter for the Homeless A62

**1987, Nov. 21** Litho. *Perf.*
247 A62 2d multi 2.00 2.00
248 A62 250f multi 2.50 2.50

Salim Bin Ali Al-Owais (b. 1887), Poet — A63

**1987, Dec. 15** *Perf. 13½*
249 A63 1d multi 1.00 1.00
250 A63 2d multi 2.00 2.00

U.N. Child Survival Campaign A64

Abu Dhabi Intl. Airport, 6th Anniv. A65

**1987, Oct. 25** Litho. *Perf. 13*
251 A64 50f Growth monitoring 35 35
252 A64 1d Immunization 68 68
253 A64 175f Oral rehydration therapy 1.20 1.20
254 A64 2d Breast feeding, horiz. 1.35 1.35

**1988, Jan. 2**
255 A65 50f Control tower 35 35
256 A65 50f Terminal interior 35 35
257 A65 100f Aircraft over airport 70 70
258 A65 100f Aircraft at gates 70 70

Natl. Arts Festival A66

**1988, Mar. 21** Litho. *Perf. 13½*
259 A66 50f multi 28 28
260 A66 250f multi 1.40 1.40

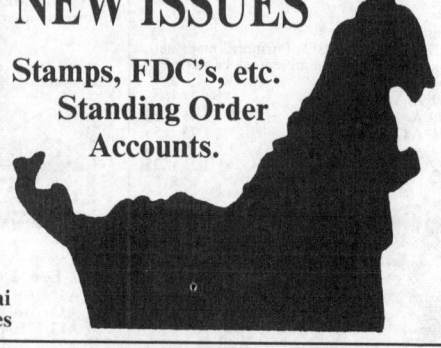

Youth Cultural Festival A67

Winning children's drawings of a design contest sponsored by the Ministry of Education and the Sharjah Cultural and Information Department.

*Perf. 13x13½, 13½x13*

**1988, May 25** **Litho.**
261 A67 50f Net fisherman 28 28
262 A67 1d Woman 58 58
263 A67 1.75d Youth as flower 98 98
264 A67 2d Recreation 1.15 1.15

Palestinian Uprising — A68

**1988, June 28** Litho. *Perf. 13½*
265 A68 2d multi 1.35 1.35
266 A68 250f multi 1.70 1.70

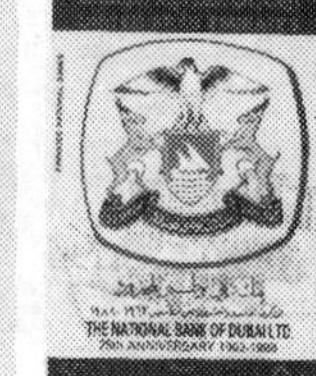


Banks
A69 A70

**1988, July 16** Litho. *Perf. 13½*
267 A69 50f multi 28 28
268 A70 50f multi 28 28

Abu Dhabi Natl. Bank, Ltd., 20th anniv. (No. 267); Natl. Bank of Dubai, Ltd., 25th anniv. (No. 268).

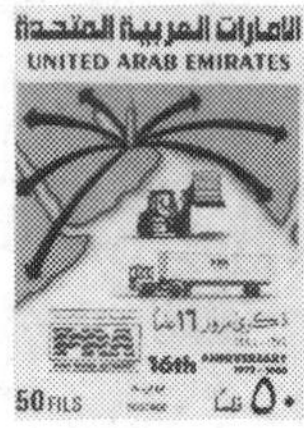


Port Rashid, Dubai, 16th Anniv. — A71

**1988, Aug. 31** Litho. *Perf. 13½*
269 A71 50f Ground transportation 28 28
270 A71 1d Piers 58 58
271 A71 175f Ship at dock 1.00 1.00
272 A71 2d Ship, unloading cranes 1.15 1.15

1988 Summer Olympics, Seoul
A72 A73

**1988, Sept. 17** *Perf. 15x14½*
273 A72 2d Swimming 1.15 1.15
274 A73 250f Cycling 1.45 1.45

## VANUATU

LOCATION — Island group in south Pacific Ocean northeast of New Caledonia.
GOVT. — Republic
AREA — 5,700 sq. mi.
POP. — 117,000 (est. 1980)
CAPITAL — Vila

The Anglo-French condominium of New Hebrides (Vol. 1 and Vol. 3) became the independent state of Vanuatu July 30, 1980.

Hebrides franc
Vatu (1981)

**Catalogue values for all unused stamps in this country are for Never Hinged items.**

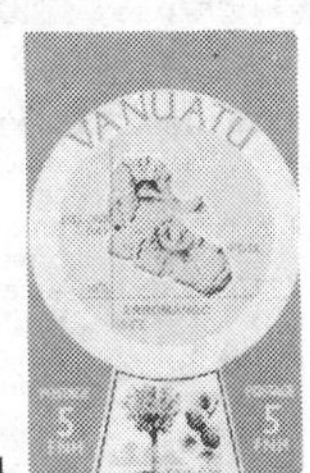

A44

Designs: 10fr, Archipelago and man making copra. 15fr, Espiritu Santo Island and cattle. 20fr, Efate Island and Post Office, Vila. 25fr, Malakula Island and headdresses. 30fr, Aoba and Maewo Islands and pig tusks. 35fr, Pentecost Island and land diving. 40fr, Tanna Island and Prophet John Frum's Red Cross. 50fr, Shepherd Island and canoe with sail. 70fr, Banks Island and dancers. 100fr, Ambrym Island and carvings. 200fr, Aneityum Island and decorated baskets. 500fr, Torres Islands and fishing with bow and arrow.

**Wmk. 373**

**1980, July 30 Litho. *Perf. 14***

| | | | | |
|---|---|---|---|---|
| *280* | A44 | 5fr multi | 12 | 12 |
| *281* | A44 | 10fr multi | 16 | 16 |
| *282* | A44 | 15fr multi | 20 | 20 |
| *283* | A44 | 20fr multi | 28 | 28 |
| *284* | A44 | 25fr multi | 35 | 35 |
| *285* | A44 | 30fr multi | 45 | 45 |
| *286* | A44 | 35fr multi | 48 | 48 |
| *287* | A44 | 40fr multi | 55 | 55 |
| *288* | A44 | 50fr multi | 75 | 75 |
| *289* | A44 | 70fr multi | 1.00 | 1.00 |
| *290* | A44 | 100fr multi | 1.40 | 1.40 |
| *291* | A44 | 200fr multi | 2.75 | 2.75 |
| *292* | A44 | 500fr multi | 7.50 | 7.50 |
| | | *Nos. 280-292 (13)* | 15.99 | 15.99 |

**Inscribed in French**

**Unwmk**

| | | | | |
|---|---|---|---|---|
| *280a* | A44 | 5fr multi | 10 | 10 |
| *281a* | A44 | 10fr multi | 15 | 15 |
| *282a* | A44 | 15fr multi | 18 | 18 |
| *283a* | A44 | 20fr multi | 25 | 25 |
| *284a* | A44 | 25fr multi | 35 | 35 |
| *285a* | A44 | 30fr multi | 40 | 40 |
| *286a* | A44 | 35fr multi | 45 | 45 |
| *287a* | A44 | 40fr multi | 55 | 55 |
| *288a* | A44 | 50fr multi | 70 | 70 |
| *289a* | A44 | 70fr multi | 90 | 90 |
| *290a* | A44 | 100fr multi | 1.25 | 1.25 |
| *291a* | A44 | 200fr multi | 2.50 | 2.50 |
| *292a* | A44 | 500fr multi | 7.00 | 7.00 |
| | | *Nos. 280a-292a (13)* | 14.78 | 14.78 |

Rotary Emblem — A52

Kiwanis Emblem — A53

**1980, Sept. 16 Wmk. 373**

| | | | | |
|---|---|---|---|---|
| *293* | A52 | 10fr Emblem, horiz. | 18 | 18 |
| *294* | A52 | 40fr shown | 75 | 75 |

**Inscribed in French**

| | | | | |
|---|---|---|---|---|
| *293a* | A52 | 10fr multi | 20 | 20 |
| *294a* | A52 | 40fr multi | 85 | 85 |

75th anniv. of Rotary Intl. and 8th anniv. of Port Vila Rotary Club (40fr).

**1980, Sept. 16**

| | | | | |
|---|---|---|---|---|
| *295* | A53 | 10fr shown | 20 | 20 |
| *296* | A53 | 40fr Emblem, horiz. | 85 | 85 |

**Inscribed in French**

| | | | | |
|---|---|---|---|---|
| *295a* | A53 | 10fr multi | 20 | 20 |
| *296a* | A53 | 40fr multi | 85 | 85 |

New Zealand District Kiwanis Convention, Port Vila, Sept. 16-18.

Christmas 1980 — A54

Blue-faced Parrott Finches — A55

Paintings: 10fr, Virgin and Child, by Michael Pacher. 15fr, Virgin and Child, by Hans Memling. 30fr, Rest on the Flight to Egypt, by Adriaen van der Werff.

**1980, Nov. 12 Wmk. 373**

| | | | | |
|---|---|---|---|---|
| *297* | A54 | 10fr multi | 20 | 20 |
| *298* | A54 | 15fr multi | 30 | 30 |
| *299* | A54 | 30fr multi | 60 | 60 |

**1981, Feb. 18**

| | | | | |
|---|---|---|---|---|
| *300* | A55 | 10fr shown | 25 | 20 |
| *301* | A55 | 20fr Emerald doves | 45 | 40 |
| *302* | A55 | 30fr Golden whistler | 70 | 65 |
| *303* | A55 | 40fr Tanna Isld. fruit doves | 85 | 85 |

Duke of Edinburgh's 60th Birthday — A56

**1981, June 10 *Perf. 14x14½***

| | | | | |
|---|---|---|---|---|
| *304* | A56 | 15v Tribesman, portrait | 25 | 25 |
| *305* | A56 | 25v Portrait | 45 | 45 |
| *306* | A56 | 35v Family | 65 | 65 |
| *307* | A56 | 45v shown | 85 | 85 |

**Royal Wedding Issue**

Common Design Type

**1981, July 29**

| | | | | |
|---|---|---|---|---|
| *308* | CD331 | 15v Bouquet | 32 | 32 |
| *309* | CD331 | 45v Charles | 70 | 70 |
| *310* | CD331 | 75v Couple | 1.10 | 1.10 |

First Anniv. of Independence — A57

**1981, July 19**

| | | | | |
|---|---|---|---|---|
| *311* | A57 | 15v Map, flag, vert. | 30 | 30 |
| *312* | A57 | 25v Emblem | 40 | 40 |
| *313* | A57 | 45v Anthem | 75 | 75 |
| *314* | A57 | 75v Arms, vert. | 1.10 | 1.10 |

Christmas 1981 A58

Designs: Children's drawings.

**Wmk. 373**

**1981, Nov. 11 Litho. *Perf. 14***

| | | | | |
|---|---|---|---|---|
| *315* | A58 | 15v Three kings | 30 | 30 |
| *316* | A58 | 25v Girl holding lamb, vert. | 45 | 45 |
| *317* | A58 | 35v Butterfly-angel | 65 | 65 |
| *318* | A58 | 45v Gift bearer, vert. | 90 | 90 |
| *a* | | Souv. sheet, #315-318 | 2.25 | 2.25 |

Broadbills — A59

Orchids — A60

**1982, Feb. 8 *Perf. 14½x14***

| | | | | |
|---|---|---|---|---|
| *319* | A59 | 15v shown | 42 | 42 |
| *320* | A59 | 20v Rainbow lorries | 55 | 55 |
| *321* | A59 | 25v Buff-bellied fly-catchers | 70 | 70 |
| *322* | A59 | 45v Fantails | 1.25 | 1.25 |

***Perf. 14x13½, 13½x14***

**1982, June 15**

| | | | | |
|---|---|---|---|---|
| *323* | A60 | 1v Flickengeria comata | 5 | 5 |
| *324* | A60 | 2v Calanthe triplicata | 6 | 6 |
| *325* | A60 | 10v Dendrobium sladei | 28 | 28 |
| *326* | A60 | 15v Dendrobium mohlianum | 30 | 30 |
| *327* | A60 | 20v Dendrobium macrophyllum | 35 | 35 |
| *328* | A60 | 25v Dendrobium purpureum | 45 | 45 |
| *329* | A60 | 30v Robiquetia mimus | 55 | 55 |
| *330* | A60 | 35v Dendrobium mooreanum | 65 | 65 |
| *331* | A60 | 45v Spathoglottis plicata | 85 | 85 |
| *332* | A60 | 50v Dendrobium seemannii | 90 | 90 |
| *333* | A60 | 75v Dendrobium conanthum | 1.25 | 1.25 |
| *334* | A60 | 100v Dendrobium Macranthum | 1.75 | 1.75 |
| *335* | A60 | 200v Coelogyne lamellata | 3.50 | 3.50 |
| *336* | A60 | 500v Bulbophyllum longiscapum | 9.25 | 9.25 |
| | | *Nos. 323-336 (14)* | 20.19 | 20.19 |

Nos. 330-333, 336 horiz.

Scouting Year A61

**Wmk. 373**

**1982, Sept. 1 Litho. *Perf. 14***

| | | | | |
|---|---|---|---|---|
| *337* | A61 | 15v Around campfire | 30 | 30 |
| *338* | A61 | 20v First aid | 35 | 35 |
| *339* | A61 | 25v Signal tower | 45 | 45 |
| *340* | A61 | 45v Building raft | 85 | 85 |
| *341* | A61 | 75v Scout sign | 1.25 | 1.25 |
| | | *Nos. 337-341 (5)* | 3.20 | 3.20 |

Christmas 1982 A62

Designs: Details from Nativity painting. 35v, 45v horiz.

**1982, Nov. 16**

| | | | | |
|---|---|---|---|---|
| *342* | A62 | 15v multi | 30 | 30 |
| *343* | A62 | 25v multi | 45 | 45 |
| *344* | A62 | 35v multi | 65 | 65 |
| *345* | A62 | 45v multi | 85 | 85 |
| *a* | | Souvenir sheet of 4 | 2.25 | 2.25 |

No. 345a contains Nos. 342-345; multicolored margin shows entire painting. Size: 134x95mm.

Hypolimnas Octocula A63

**1983, Jan. 17 *Perf. 14½***

| | | | | |
|---|---|---|---|---|
| *346* | | Pair | 60 | 60 |
| *a* | | A63 15v shown | 30 | 30 |
| *b* | | A63 15v cuploea sylvester | 30 | 30 |
| *347* | | Pair | 75 | 75 |
| *a* | | A63 20v Polyura sacco | 35 | 35 |
| *b* | | A63 20v Papilio canopus | 35 | 35 |
| *348* | | Pair | 1.00 | 1.00 |
| *a* | | A63 25v Parantica pumila | 50 | 50 |
| *b* | | A63 25v Luthrodes cleotas | 50 | 50 |

**Commonwealth Day**

Common Design Type

**1983, Mar. 14 *Perf. 13½x14***

| | | | | |
|---|---|---|---|---|
| *349* | CD334 | 15v Pres. Sokomanu | 30 | 30 |
| *350* | CD334 | 20v Fisherman | 40 | 40 |
| *351* | CD334 | 25v Herdsman, cattle | 45 | 45 |
| *352* | CD334 | 75v Flags, map | 1.40 | 1.40 |

20v, 75v inscribed in French.

Economic Zone — A65

Designs: a. Thunnus albacares. b. Map. c. Matthew Isld. d. Hunter Isld. e. Epinephelus morrhua, etelis carbunculus. f. Katsuwonus pelamis.

***Perf. 14x13½***

**1983, May 23 Litho. Wmk. 373**

| | | | | |
|---|---|---|---|---|
| *353* | | Sheet of 6 | 3.25 | 3.25 |
| *a.-f* | | A65 25v multi | 52 | 52 |

Size: 121x121mm.

Manned Flight Bicentenary — A66

Balloons or Airships: 15v, Montgolfiere, 1783. 20v, J.A.C. Charles first hydrogen balloon, 1783. 25v, Blanchard and Jeffries first English Channel crossing, 1785. 35v, H. Giffard's first mechanically powered airship, 1852. 40v, Renard and Krebs' airship, 1884. 45v, Graf Zeppelin's first transworld flight, 1929. 15v, 20v, 25v vert.

**Wmk. 373**

**1983, Aug. 4 Litho. *Perf. 14***

| | | | | |
|---|---|---|---|---|
| *354* | A66 | 15v multi | 35 | 35 |
| *355* | A66 | 20v multi | 40 | 40 |
| *356* | A66 | 25v multi | 52 | 52 |
| *357* | A66 | 35v multi | 65 | 65 |
| *358* | A66 | 40v multi | 80 | 80 |
| *359* | A66 | 45v multi | 95 | 95 |
| | | *Nos. 354-359 (6)* | 3.67 | 3.67 |

The Catalogue editors cannot undertake to appraise, identify or judge the genuineness or condition of stamps.

World Communications Year — A67

**1983, Oct. 10 Litho. Wmk. 373**

*360* A67 15v Mail transport, Bauerfield Airport 42 42
*361* A67 20v Switchboard operator 55 55
*362* A67 25v Telex operator 70 70
*363* A67 45v Satellite earth station 1.25 1.25
*a* Souvenir sheet of 4 2.50 2.50

No. 363a contains Nos. 360-363; marginal inscription in English and French.

Local Fungi A68

**Wmk. 373**

**1984, Jan. 9 Litho. *Perf. 14***

*364* A68 15v Cymatoderma elegans, vert. 35 35
*365* A68 25v Lignosus rhinoceros, vert. 60 60
*366* A68 35v Stereum ostrea 85 85
*367* A68 45v Ganoderma boninenze, vert. 1.10 1.10

**Lloyd's List Issue**

Common Design Type

**1984, Apr. 30 Litho. *Perf. 14½x14***

*368* CD335 15v Port Vila 35 35
*369* CD335 20v Induna 45 45
*370* CD335 25v Air Vanuatu jet 60 60
*371* CD335 45v Brahman Express 1.10 1.10

No. 359 Overprinted "UPU CONGRESS / HAMBURG"

**Wmk. 373**

**1984, June 11 Litho. *Perf. 14***

*372* A66 45v multi 90 90

Cattle A69

**Wmk. 373**

**1984, July 3 Litho. *Perf. 14***

*373* A69 15v Charolais 30 30
*374* A69 25v Charolais-Afrikaner 50 50
*375* A69 45v Friesian 90 90
*376* A69 75v Charolais-Brahman 1.50 1.50

Ausipex '84 — A70

Ships.

**1984, Sept. 7**

*377* A70 25v Makambo 50 50
*378* A70 45v Rockton 90 90
*379* A70 100v Waroonga 2.00 2.00
*a* Souvenir sheet of 3 3.50 3.50

Christmas 1984 A71

**1984, Nov. 19 Litho. Wmk. 373**

*380* A71 25v Father Christmas, child in hospital 50 50
*381* A71 45v Nativity 90 90
*382* A71 75v Father Christmas, children 1.50 1.50

No. 323 Surcharged with 2 Black Bars

**1985, Jan. 22 Litho. *Perf. 14x13½***

*383* A60 5v on 1v 10 10

Ceremonial Dance Costumes — A71a

**1985, Jan. 22 *Perf. 14***

*384* A71a 20v Ambrym Island 40 40
*385* A71a 25v Pentecost Island 50 50
*386* A71a 45v Women's Grade Ceremony, S.W. Malakula 90 90
*387* A71a 75v Same, men's 1.50 1.50

Audubon Birth Bicentenary — A72

Peregrine falcons.

**Wmk. 373**

**1985, Mar. 26 Litho. *Perf. 14***

*388* A72 20v multi 40 40
*389* A72 35v multi 70 70
*390* A72 45v multi 90 90
*391* A72 100v multi 2.00 2.00

**Queen Mother 85th Birthday**

Common Design Type

***Perf. 14½x14***

**1985, June 7 Litho. Wmk. 384**

*392* CD336 5v Wedding photo 10 10
*393* CD336 20v 80th birthday celebration 40 40
*394* CD336 35v At Ancona, Italy 70 70
*395* CD336 55v Holding Prince Henry 1.10 1.10

**Souvenir Sheet**

*396* CD336 100v At Covent Garden Opera 2.00 2.00

No. 396 has multicolored margin continuing design. Size: 92x74mm.

EXPO '85, Tsukuba A73

Designs: 35v, Mala naval patrol boat. 45v, Japanese fishing fleet, Port Vila. 55v, Mobile Force Band. 100v, Prime Minister Walter H. Lini.

**Wmk. 373**

**1985, July 26 Litho. *Perf. 14***

*397* A73 35v multi 70 70
*398* A73 45v multi 90 90
*399* A73 55v multi 1.10 1.10
*400* A73 100v multi 2.00 2.00
*a* Souvenir sheet of 4, #397-400 4.75 4.75

Natl. independence, 5th anniv. No. 400a has multicolored margin picturing Air Melanesia monoplane and beach-front resort. Size: 116x102mm.

Intl. Youth Year A74

Children's drawings.

**1985, Sept. 16 Wmk. 373 *Perf. 14***

*401* A74 20v Alain Lagaliu 40 40
*402* A74 30v Peter Obed 60 60
*403* A74 50v Mary Estelle 1.00 1.00
*404* A74 100v Abel M rani 2.00 2.00

Natl. and UN Flags, Map A75

**1985, Sept. 24 Litho. *Perf. 14***

*405* A75 45v multi 90 90

Admission of Vanuatu to UN, 4th anniv.

Sea Slugs — A76

Scuba Diving — A77

**1985, Nov. 11 Wmk. 373 *Perf. 14½***

*406* A76 20v Chromodoris elisabethina 40 40
*407* A76 35v Halgerda aurantiomaculata 70 70
*408* A76 55v Chromodoris kuniei 1.10 1.10
*409* A76 100v Notodoris minor 2.00 2.00

Nos. 407-408 horiz. See Nos. 497-500.

**1986, Jan. 22 Wmk. 384 *Perf. 14***

*410* A77 30v shown 60 60
*411* A77 35v Volcanic eruption 70 70
*412* A77 55v Land diving 1.10 1.10
*413* A77 100v Wind surfing 2.00 2.00

See No. 479.

Queen Elizabeth II 60th Birthday

Common Design Type

Designs: 20v, With Prince Charles and Princess Anne, 1951. 35v, At christening of Prince William, the Music Room, Buckhingham Palace, 1982. 45v, State visit, 1985. 55v, State visit to Mexico, 1974. 100v, Visiting Crown Agents' offices, 1983.

***Perf. 14x14½***

**1986, Apr. 21 Litho. Wmk. 384**

*414* CD337 20v scar, blk & sil 40 40
*415* CD337 35v ultra & multi 70 70
*416* CD337 45v grn & multi 90 90
*417* CD337 55v vio & multi 1.10 1.10
*418* CD337 100v multi 2.00 2.00
*Nos. 414-418 (5)* 5.10 5.10

AMERIPEX '86 — A78

**Wmk. 373**

**1986, May 19 Litho. *Perf. 14***

*419* A78 45v SS President Coolidge 90 90
*420* A78 55v As troop ship, 1942 1.10 1.10
*421* A78 135v Site of sinking, 1942 2.70 2.70
*a* Souvenir sheet of 3, #419-421 4.70 4.70

No. 421a has multicolored decorative margin picturing Statue of Liberty and statue of deity. Size: 80x105mm.

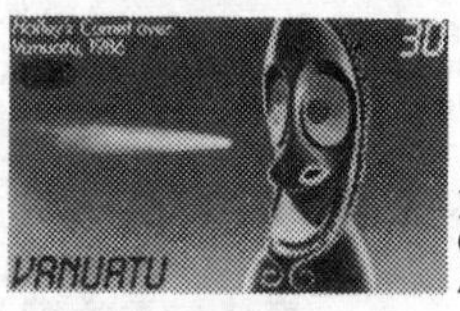

Halley's Comet A79

**1986, June 23 Wmk. 384 *Perf. 14½***

*422* A79 30v Comet, deity statue 60 60
*423* A79 45v Family sighting comet 90 90
*424* A79 55v Comet over SW Pacific 1.10 1.10
*425* A79 100v Edmond Halley, manuscript 2.00 2.00

Coral A80

**Wmk. 373**

**1986, Oct. 27 Litho. *Perf. 14***

*426* A80 20v Daisy 40 40
*427* A80 45v Organ pipe 90 90
*428* A80 55v Sea fan 1.10 1.10
*429* A80 135v Soft 2.75 2.75

Intl. Peace Year A81

**Wmk. 373**

**1986, Nov. 3 Litho. *Perf. 14***

*430* A81 30v Children of the world 60 60
*431* A81 45v Child praying 90 90
*432* A81 55v UN building, negotiators 1.10 1.10
*433* A81 135v Peoples working in harmony 2.70 2.70

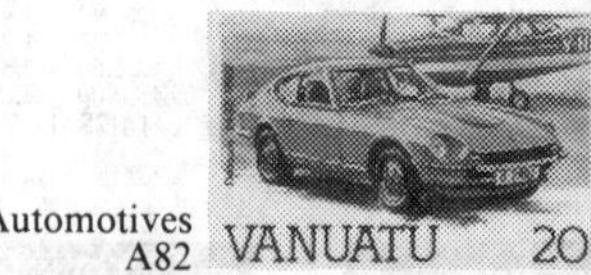

Automotives A82

**1987, Jan. 22**

*434* A82 20v Datsun 240Z, 1969 40 40
*435* A82 45v Model A Ford, 1927 90 90
*436* A82 55v Unic, 1924-25 1.00 1.00
*437* A82 135v Citroen DS19, 1975 2.50 2.50

IRHO Coconut Research Station, 25th Anniv. A83

**1987, May 13 *Perf. 14½x14***

*438* A83 35v Nursery 70 70
*439* A83 45v Cocos nucifera tree 90 90
*440* A83 100v Cocos nucifera fruit 2.00 2.00
*441* A83 135v Station 2.75 2.75

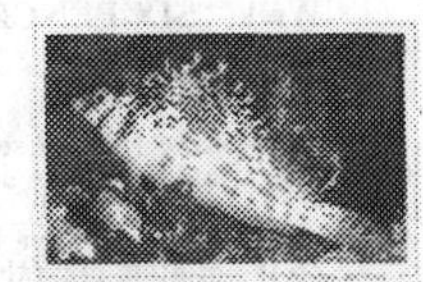


Fish — A84

*Perf. 14x14½*

**1987, July 15 — Wmk. 384**

| No. | Type | Value | Description | Unused | Used |
|---|---|---|---|---|---|
| *442* | A84 | 1v | Cirrhitichthys aprinus | 5 | 5 |
| *443* | A84 | 5v | Zanclus cornutus | 10 | 10 |
| *444* | A84 | 10v | Canthigaster cinctus | 20 | 20 |
| *445* | A84 | 15v | Amphiprion rubrocinctus | 30 | 30 |
| *446* | A84 | 20v | Acanthurus lineatus | 40 | 40 |
| *447* | A84 | 30v | Thalassoma hardwicki | 60 | 60 |
| *448* | A84 | 35v | Anthias tuka | 70 | 70 |
| *449* | A84 | 40v | Adioryx microstomus | 80 | 80 |
| *450* | A84 | 45v | Balistoides conspicillum | 90 | 90 |
| *451* | A84 | 50v | Xyrichtys taeniouris | 1.00 | 1.00 |
| *452* | A84 | 55v | Hemitaurichthys polyepis | 1.10 | 1.10 |
| *453* | A84 | 65v | Pterois volitans | 1.30 | 1.30 |
| *454* | A84 | 100v | Paracirrhites forsteri | 2.00 | 2.00 |
| *455* | A84 | 300v | Balistapus undulatus | 6.00 | 6.00 |
| *456* | A84 | 500v | Chaetodon ephippium | 10.00 | 10.00 |
| | | | *Nos. 442-456 (15)* | 25.45 | 25.45 |

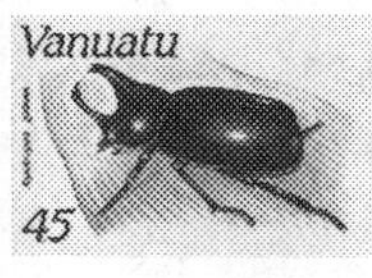


Insects — A85

**1987, Sept. 22 — Wmk. 373 — *Perf. 14***

| No. | Type | Value | Description | Unused | Used |
|---|---|---|---|---|---|
| *457* | A85 | 45v | Xylotrupes gideon | 90 | 90 |
| *458* | A85 | 55v | Phyllodes imperialis | 1.10 | 1.10 |
| *459* | A85 | 65v | Cyphogaster | 1.30 | 1.30 |
| *460* | A85 | 100v | Othreis fullonia | 2.00 | 2.00 |

Christmas Carols — A86

**1987, Nov. 10 — *Perf. 13½x14***

| No. | Type | Value | Description | Unused | Used |
|---|---|---|---|---|---|
| *461* | A86 | 20v | Away in a Manger | 40 | 40 |
| *462* | A86 | 45v | Once in Royal David's City | 90 | 90 |
| *463* | A86 | 55v | While Shepherds Watched Their Flocks | 1.10 | 1.10 |
| *464* | A86 | 65v | We Three Kings of Orient Are | 1.30 | 1.30 |

Nos. 414-418 Ovptd. "40TH WEDDING ANNIVERSARY" in Silver.

*Perf. 14x14½*

**1987, Dec. 9 — Litho. — Wmk. 384**

| No. | Type | Value | Description | Unused | Used |
|---|---|---|---|---|---|
| *465* | CD337 | 20v | scar, blk & sil | 38 | 38 |
| *466* | CD337 | 35v | ultra & multi | 68 | 68 |
| *467* | CD337 | 45v | grn & multi | 90 | 90 |
| *468* | CD337 | 55v | vio & multi | 1.05 | 1.05 |
| *469* | CD337 | 100v | rose vio & multi | 1.90 | 1.90 |
| | | | *Nos. 465-469 (5)* | 4.91 | 4.91 |

World Wildlife Fund — A87

Dugongs.

**1988, Feb. 29 — *Perf. 13x13½***

| No. | Type | Value | Description | Unused | Used |
|---|---|---|---|---|---|
| *470* | A87 | 5v | Mother, calf | 10 | 10 |
| *471* | A87 | 10v | Adult | 20 | 20 |
| *472* | A87 | 20v | Two adults | 40 | 40 |
| *473* | A87 | 45v | Herd | 88 | 88 |

Australia Bicentennial — A88

Burns Philip emblem, bicent. emblem and steamships.

**Wmk. 373**

**1988, May 18 — Litho. — *Perf. 12***

| No. | Type | Value | Description | Unused | Used |
|---|---|---|---|---|---|
| *474* | A88 | 20v | S.S. *Tambo* | 40 | 40 |
| *475* | A88 | 45v | S.S. *Induna* | 88 | 88 |
| *476* | A88 | 55v | S.S. *Morinda* | 1.05 | 1.05 |
| *477* | A88 | 65v | S.S. *Marsina* | 1.25 | 1.25 |

Capt. James Cook (1728-1779), Explorer — A89

***Perf. 14 on 2 or 3 Sides.***

**1988, July 29 — Litho. — Wmk. 384**

| No. | Type | Value | Description | Unused | Used |
|---|---|---|---|---|---|
| *478* | A89 | 45v | blk & red | 90 | 90 |

SYDPEX '88. No. 478 printed in panes of 10 plus 5 center labels picturing a map of Vanuatu, HMS *Resolution*, exhibition emblem, HMS *Endeavour* or a map of Australia.

Tourism Type of 1986

**Wmk. 373**

**1988, Aug. 24 — Litho. — *Perf. 14***

| No. | Description | Unused | Used |
|---|---|---|---|
| *479* | Souv. sheet of 2 | 3.10 | 3.10 |
| *a.* | A77 55v like No. 412 | 1.10 | 1.10 |
| *b.* | A77 100v like No. 413 | 2.00 | 2.00 |

EXPO '88. Nos. 479a-479b differ from Nos. 412-413. Nos. 479a-479b are dated 1988 and "Vanuatu" is inscribed in violet blue. No. 479 has multicolored margin picturing map of Australia, EXPO '88 emblem and flag of Vanuatu. Size: 100x80mm.

1988 Summer Olympics, Seoul — A90

**1988, Sept. 19 — *Perf. 13½x14***

| No. | Type | Value | Description | Unused | Used |
|---|---|---|---|---|---|
| *480* | A90 | 20v | Boxing | 40 | 40 |
| *481* | A90 | 45v | Track events | 90 | 90 |
| *482* | A90 | 55v | Signing Olympic agreement | 1.10 | 1.10 |
| *483* | A90 | 65v | Soccer | 1.25 | 1.25 |

**Souvenir Sheet**

| No. | Type | Value | Description | Unused | Used |
|---|---|---|---|---|---|
| *484* | A90 | 150v | Tennis | 3.00 | 3.00 |

Intl. Tennis Federation, 75th anniv. (150v). No. 484 has multicolored margin picturing athletes. Size: 54x65mm.

**Lloyds of London, 300th Anniv.**

Common Design Type

Designs: 20v, Lloyds new building, 1988. 55v, Cargo ship *Shirrabank*, horiz. 65v, *Adela*, horiz. 145v, Excursion steamer *General Slocum* on fire in New York Harbor, 1904.

**Wmk. 384**

**1988, Oct. 25 — Litho. — *Perf. 14***

| No. | Type | Value | Description | Unused | Used |
|---|---|---|---|---|---|
| *485* | CD341 | 20v | multi | 40 | 40 |
| *486* | CD341 | 55v | multi | 1.10 | 1.10 |
| *487* | CD341 | 65v | multi | 1.25 | 1.25 |
| *488* | CD341 | 145v | multi | 2.75 | 2.75 |

FAO — A91

***Perf. 14½x14, 14x14½***

**1988, Nov. 14 — Litho. — Wmk. 384**

| No. | Type | Value | Description | Unused | Used |
|---|---|---|---|---|---|
| *489* | A91 | 45v | Tending crops | 85 | 85 |
| *490* | A91 | 55v | Fishing, vert. | 1.05 | 1.05 |
| *491* | A91 | 65v | Animal husbandry, vert. | 1.20 | 1.20 |
| *492* | A91 | 120v | Produce market | 2.25 | 2.25 |

Christmas — A92

Carols: 20v, *Silent Night, Holy Night*. 45v, *Angels From the Realms of Glory*. 65v, *O Come All Ye Faithful*. 155v, *In That Poor Stable How Charming Jesus Lies*.

**1988, Dec. 1 — Litho. — *Perf. 14½x14***

| No. | Type | Value | Description | Unused | Used |
|---|---|---|---|---|---|
| *493* | A92 | 20v | multi | 38 | 38 |
| *494* | A92 | 45v | multi | 85 | 85 |
| *495* | A92 | 65v | multi | 1.20 | 1.20 |
| *496* | A92 | 155v | multi | 2.90 | 2.90 |

Marine Life Type of 1985

Shrimp.

**1989, Feb. 1 — *Perf. 14***

| No. | Type | Value | Description | Unused | Used |
|---|---|---|---|---|---|
| *497* | A76 | 20v | Periclimenes brevicarpalis | 38 | 38 |
| *498* | A76 | 45v | Lysmata grabhami | 85 | 85 |
| *499* | A76 | 65v | Rhynchocinetes | 1.20 | 1.20 |
| *500* | A76 | 150v | Stenopus hispidus | 2.85 | 2.85 |

## VICTORIA

LOCATION — In the extreme south-eastern part of Australia.
GOVT. — A former British Colony
AREA — 87,884 sq. mi.
POP. — 1,201,341 (1901)
CAPITAL — Melbourne

Victoria was one of the six former British colonies which united on Jan. 1, 1901, to form the Commonwealth of Australia.

12 Pence = 1 Shilling
20 Shillings = 1 Pound

> Values of Victoria Nos. 1-26 vary according to condition. Quotations are for fine copies. Very fine to superb specimens sell at much higher prices, and inferior or poor copies sell at reduced prices, depending on the condition of the individual specimen.

Queen Victoria — A1

Victoria on Throne — A2

**1850 — Litho. — Unwmk. — *Imperf.***

| No. | Type | Description | Unused | Used |
|---|---|---|---|---|
| *1* | A1 | 1p dl red | 875.00. | 60.00 |
| *a.* | | 1p ver | 600.00 | 90.00 |
| *2* | A1 | 1p rose | 375.00 | 26.00 |
| *a.* | | 1p pink | 410.00 | 26.00 |
| *3* | A1 | 3p blue | 600.00 | 26.00 |
| *a.* | | 3p lt bl | 550.00 | 27.50 |
| *4* | A1 | 3p indigo | 625.00 | 27.50 |

Nos. 1-4 exist with and without frame line.

THREE TYPES OF 2p:
I. Border, two sets of nine wavy lines criss-crossing. Background, 22 groups of wavy triple lines below "VICTORIA".
II. Border, same. Background, 15 groups of wavy triple lines below "VICTORIA".
III. Border, two sets of five wavy lines crisscrossing. Background, same as type II.

| No. | Type | Description | Unused | Used |
|---|---|---|---|---|
| *5* | A1 | 2p lil, I | *3,000.* | 215.00 |
| *a.* | | 2p brn lil, I | *3,750.* | 325.00 |
| *6* | A1 | 2p brn lil, II | 875.00 | 75.00 |
| *a.* | | 2p gray lil, II | 925.00 | 75.00 |
| *7* | A1 | 2p brn lil, III | 875.00 | 60.00 |
| *a.* | | 2p gray lil, III | 875.00 | 70.00 |
| *b.* | | Value omitted, III | | 2,500. |
| *8* | A1 | 2p yel brn, III | 650.00 | 40.00 |

***Rouletted 7***

| No. | Type | Description | Unused | Used |
|---|---|---|---|---|
| *9* | A1 | 1p vermilion | | *1,250.* |
| *10* | A1 | 3p blue | | 140.00 |
| *a.* | | 3p dp bl | 1,600. | 190.00 |

***Perf. 12***

| No. | Type | Description | Unused | Used |
|---|---|---|---|---|
| *12* | A1 | 3p blue | *2,000.* | 125.00 |
| *a.* | | 3p dp bl | *2,000.* | 125.00 |

**1852 — Engr. — *Imperf.***

| No. | Type | Description | Unused | Used |
|---|---|---|---|---|
| *14* | A2 | 2p redsh brn | 160.00 | 16.00 |

No. 14 was reprinted on paper with watermark 70, imperf. and perf. 12½, overprinted "REPRINT."

**1854 — Litho.**

| No. | Type | Description | Unused | Used |
|---|---|---|---|---|
| *15* | A2 | 2p gray brn | 220.00 | 14.00 |
| *16* | A2 | 2p brn lil | 200.00 | 12.50 |
| *a.* | | 2p red lil | 250.00 | 14.00 |

Fifty varieties.

A3

A4

**1854-58 — Typo.**

| No. | Type | Description | Unused | Used |
|---|---|---|---|---|
| *17* | A3 | 6p orange | 150.00 | 11.50 |
| *a.* | | 6p red org | 180.00 | 12.00 |

**Lithographed**

| No. | Type | Description | Unused | Used |
|---|---|---|---|---|
| *18* | A4 | 1sh blue | 240.00 | 15.00 |

**Typographed**
*19* A3 2sh green 1,100. 125.00

**1857-58** ***Rouletted 7, 9½***
*20* A3 6p orange 525.00 40.00

**Lithographed**
*21* A4 1sh blue 1,500. 120.00

**Typographed**
*22* A3 2sh grn ('58) *4,000.* 215.00

***Small Serrate Perf. 19***
*23* A3 6p orange *1,200.* 65.00

***Large Serpentine Perf. 10½***
*24* A3 6p orange 800.00 55.00

***Serrate x Serpentine Perf.***
*24A* A3 6p orange 125.00

**1859** **Litho.** ***Perf. 12***
*25* A4 1sh blue 180.00 7.50

**Typographed**
*26* A3 2sh green 260.00 20.00

Wmk. 80

Wmk. 50

**1861** **Wmk. "SIX PENCE" (80)**
*27* A3 6p black 260.00 30.00

**Wmk. Single-lined "2" (50)**
**1864** ***Perf. 12, 13.***
*28* A3 2sh blue, *green* 175.00 4.50

A5

Wmk. 6

**Wmk. Large Star. (6)**
**1856, Oct.** **Engr.** ***Imperf.***
*29* A5 1p green 50.00 10.00

**1858** ***Rouletted 5½-6½***
*30* A5 6p blue 80.00 7.00

Nos. 29 and 30 have been reprinted on paper watermarked V and Crown. They are imperforate and overprinted "REPRINT."

A6

A7

**1857-61** **Typo.** ***Imperf.***
*31* A6 1p yel grn 45.00 9.00
*a.* Printed on both sides *1,200.*
*32* A6 4p vermilion 325.00 5.50
*a.* Printed on both sides *900.00*
*33* A6 4p rose 260.00 6.25

***Rouletted 7 to 9½***
*34* A6 1p yel grn 400.00 80.00
*35* A6 4p rose 525.00 25.00

***Perf. 12***
*36* A6 1p yel grn 600.00 365.00

**Unwmk.** ***Imperf.***
*37* A6 1p bl grn 400.00 10.00
*38* A6 2p lilac 240.00 7.50
*39* A6 4p rose *500.00* 20.00

Copies of No. 39 printed in dull carmine on thin paper are regarded as printer's waste and of little value. They are also found printed on both sides.

***Rouletted 7 to 9½***
*40* A6 1p bl grn 300.00 10.00
*a.* 1p yel grn 400.00 15.00
*b.* Horiz. pair, imperf. btwn. *1,000.*
*41* A6 2p lilac 1,200. 32.50
*42* A6 4p rose 400.00 4.50
*a.* Horiz. pair, imperf. btwn. *1,000.*

***Perf. 12***
*43* A6 1p bl grn 160.00 7.25
*a.* 1p yel grn 200.00 7.00
*b.* Horiz. pair, imperf. btwn. *650.00*
*44* A6 2p lilac 90.00
*45* A6 4p rose 180.00 2.75
*b.* Vert. pair, imperf. btwn.

***Serrate Perf. 19***
*45A* A6 2p lilac 600.00 125.00

**Laid Paper.**
***Imperf***
*46* A6 4p rose 600.00 15.00

***Rouletted 5 to 7***
*47* A6 2p dk lil 200.00 5.00
*a.* 2p brn lil 150.00 4.50
*b.* 2p vio 150.00 4.50
*48* A6 4p rose 160.00 2.50

***Perf. 12***
*49* A6 1p green 240.00 7.50
*50* A6 4p rose 150.00 3.75

**Wove Paper**
**1860** **Wmk. Value in Words (80)**
*51* A6 1p yel grn 60.00 4.75
*a.* Wmk. "FOUR PENCE" (error) *2,000.*
*52* A6 2p gray lil 140.00 3.75
*a.* 2p brn lil 400.00 24.00

**Wmk. "THREE PENCE" (80)**
*53* A6 2p gray lil 240.00 10.00

**Single-lined "2" (50)**
*54* A6 2p lilac 160.00 10.00
*a.* 2p gray lil 160.00 10.00
*b.* 2p brn lil 160.00 10.00
*c.* As "b" wmkd. single-lined "6" *4,500.*

**1860** **Unwmk.** **Laid Paper**
*56* A7 3p dp bl 360.00 26.00

**Wmk. Value in Words (80)**
***Perf. 11½ to 12***
**1860-62** **Wove Paper**
*57* A7 3p blue 125.00 5.75
*58* A7 3p claret 150.00 25.00
*a.* Perf. 13 190.00 30.00
*59* A7 4p rose 140.00 2.00
*60* A7 6p orange *3,000.* 250.00
*61* A7 6p black 250.00 5.00

**Wmk. "FIVE SHILLINGS" (80)**
*62* A7 4p rose 1,500. 27.50

Wmk. 80a

Wmk. 139

**Wmk. Single-lined "4" (80a)**
**1863** ***Imperf.***
*63* A7 4p rose *1,200.* 135.00

***Rouletted***
*64* A7 4p rose *2,400.* 200.00

***Perf. 11½ to 12***
*65* A7 4p rose 100.00 3.00

**1863** **Unwmk.** ***Perf. 12***
*66* A7 4p rose 450.00 6.25

A8

A9

**1861-63** **Wmk. 80** ***Perf. 11½ to 12***
*67* A8 1p green 90.00 6.00
*68* A9 6p black 150.00 3.50

**Wmk. Double-lined "1" (139)**
*69* A8 1p green 200.00 10.50

**Wmk. Single-lined Figures (50)**
*70* A8 1p green 45.00 4.00
*71* A9 6p black 150.00 2.25

The 1p and 6p of 1861-63 are known on paper without watermark but were probably impressions on the margins of watermarked sheets.

A10

A11

A12

A13

Wmk. 81

**Wmk. Single-lined Figures. (50, 80a, 81)**
**1863-67** ***Perf. 11½ to 13.***
*74* A10 1p green 30.00 2.75
*a.* Dlb. impression 900.00
*75* A10 2p gray lil 62.50 1.65
*a.* 2p vio 50.00 1.65
*76* A10 4p rose 110.00 1.25
*a.* Dbl. impression 900.00
*77* A11 6p blue 87.50 1.10
*78* A10 8p orange 225.00 50.00
*79* A12 10p brn, *rose* 150.00 2.25
*80* A13 1sh blue, *blue* 150.00 2.00

A14

**Wmk. Double-lined "1" (139)**
*81* A10 1p green 32.50 3.00
*82* A10 2p gray lil 200.00 4.25
*83* A14 3p lilac 300.00 55.00
*84* A11 6p blue 125.00 3.75

Wmk. 49

Wmk. 75

**Wmk. Double-lined "2" (49)**
*85* A11 6p blue *1,500.*

**Wmk. Single-lined "4" (80a)**
*86* A10 1p green 100.00 11.00
*87* A10 2p gray lil 175.00 4.50
*88* A11 6p blue *1,500.*

**Wmk. Double-lined "4" (75)**
*89* A10 1p green 1,300. 135.00
*90* A10 2p gray lil 175.00 1.75
*91* A10 4p rose 190.00 3.75
*92* A11 6p blue 325.00 18.00

**Wmk. Single-lined "6" (50)**
*93* A10 1p green 225.00 15.00
*94* A10 2p gray lil 250.00 5.75

**Wmk. Single-lined "8" (50)**
*95* A10 1p green 200.00 11.50
*96* A10 2p gray lil 225.00 2.75
*97* A14 3p lilac 175.00 21.00
*99* A12 10p slate 350.00 45.00

**Wmk. "SIX PENCE" (80)**
*100* A10 1p green 750.00 21.00
*101* A11 6p blue 350.00 15.00

All values of the 1864-67 series except the 3p and 8p are known on unwatermarked paper. They are probably varieties from watermarked sheets which have been so placed on the printing press that some of the stamps escaped the watermark.

One copy of the 2p gray lilac, type A10, is reported to exist with only "PENCE" of watermark 80 showing. Some believe this is part of the "SIX PENCE" watermark.

**Wmk. "THREE PENCE" (80)**
**1870**
*108* A11 6p blue 225.00 6.25

**Wmk. "FOUR PENCE" (80)**
*109* A11 6p blue 500.00 40.00

A15

Wmk. 70

**Wmk. V and Crown. (70)**
**1867-78** ***Perf. 11½ to 13***
*110* A10 1p green 30.00 1.40
*111* A10 2p lilac 75.00 65
*a.* 2p gray lil 62.50 65
*112* A10 2p lil, *lil* 75.00 5.75
*113* A14 3p red lil 300.00 18.00
*a.* 3p lil 350.00 20.00
*114* A14 3p orange 22.50 1.50
*a.* 3p yel 62.50 1.90
*115* A10 4p rose 62.50 2.75
*116* A11 6p blue 25.00 45
*117* A11 6p ultra 27.50 55
*a.* 6p lil bl 62.50 2.25
*118* A10 8p brn, *rose* 100.00 3.75
*119* A13 1sh bl, *bl* 250.00 6.75
*120* A15 5sh bl, *yel* 1,250. 200.00
*121* A15 5sh bl & rose 125.00 7.75
*a.* Without bl line under crown 140.00 7.75
*122* A15 5sh ultra & rose 175.00 7.75

See Nos. 126, 144, 188, 191.

A16

A19

**1870** ***Perf. 13***
*123* A16 2p lilac 22.50 28
*a.* Perf. 12 32.50 40

No. 110 Surcharged in Red ½ **HALF** ½

**1873, July 19** ***Perf. 13, 12***
*124* A10 ½p on 1p green 25.00 3.50

No. 79 Surcharged in Blue 9 **NINEPENCE** 9

**1871** **Wmk. Single-lined "10." (81)**
*125* A12 9p on 10p brn, *rose* 350.00 6.75
*a.* Double surcharge *1,200.*

**1873-78** **Typo.**
*126* A10 8p brn, *rose* ('78) 125.00 4.00
*127* A19 9p brn, *rose* 90.00 3.50

**1875** **Wmk. V and Crown. (70)**
*128* A19 9p brn, *rose* 140.00 6.75

8d 8d

No. 128 Surcharged in Black

EIGHTPENCE

**1876**

| | | | | |
|---|---|---|---|---|
| *129* | A19 | 8p on 9p brn, *rose* | 175.00 | 9.00 |

A21 A22 A23

A24 A25

**1873-81** ***Perf. 13, 12***

| | | | | |
|---|---|---|---|---|
| *130* | A21 | ½p rose ('74) | 5.50 | 28 |
| *131* | A21 | ½p rose, *rose* ('78) | 14.00 | 4.50 |
| *132* | A22 | 1p grn ('75) | 12.50 | 20 |
| *133* | A22 | 1p grn, *gray* ('78) | 82.50 | 30.00 |
| *134* | A22 | 1p grn, *yel* ('78) | 40.00 | 7.75 |
| *135* | A23 | 2p violet | 12.50 | 18 |
| *136* | A23 | 2p vio, *grnsh* ('78) | 125.00 | 3.50 |
| *137* | A23 | 2p vio, *buff* ('78) | 125.00 | 3.75 |
| *137A* | A23 | 2p vio, *lil* ('78) | | 340.00 |
| *138* | A24 | 1sh bl, *bl* ('76) | 55.00 | 1.40 |
| *139* | A25 | 2sh bl, *grn* ('81) | 165.00 | 10.50 |

**1878**

**Double-lined Outer Oval**

| | | | | |
|---|---|---|---|---|
| *140* | A23 | 2p violet | 17.50 | 18 |
| *a.* | | Imperf., pair | | 400.00 |

A26 A27

A28

**1881-83** ***Perf. 12½***

| | | | | |
|---|---|---|---|---|
| *141* | A26 | 1p grn ('83) | 12.00 | 28 |
| *142* | A27 | 2p brown | 27.50 | 8 |
| *143* | A27 | 2p lilac | 12.00 | 14 |
| *144* | A10 | 4p car rose | 200.00 | 2.75 |
| *145* | A28 | 4p car rose | 30.00 | 1.50 |

A29 A30

A31 A32

A33

A34

**1884-86**

| | | | | |
|---|---|---|---|---|
| *146* | A29 | ½p rose | 4.00 | 30 |
| *147* | A30 | 1p green | 4.00 | 14 |
| *148* | A31 | 2p violet | 4.75 | 14 |
| *a.* | | 2p lil rose | 10.50 | 16 |
| *149* | A30 | 3p bister | 6.50 | 14 |
| *a.* | | 3p ocher | 6.50 | 14 |
| *150* | A32 | 4p magenta | 32.50 | 2.25 |
| *a.* | | 4p vio (error) | *4,000.* | 400.00 |
| *151* | A30 | 6p gray bl | 35.00 | 1.40 |
| *a.* | | 6p ultra | 35.00 | 1.40 |
| *152* | A33 | 8p rose, *rose* | 16.00 | 4.50 |
| *153* | A34 | 1sh bl, *yel* | 47.50 | 3.25 |
| *154* | A33 | 2sh ol, *grn* | 18.00 | 2.00 |

Nos. 114, 145, 138-139 Overprinted "STAMP / DUTY" Vertically in Blue or Black

**1885**

| | | | | |
|---|---|---|---|---|
| *155* | A14 | 3p org (Bl) | 42.50 | 11.00 |
| *156* | A28 | 4p car rose (Bl) | 50.00 | 12.50 |
| *156A* | A24 | 1sh bl, *bl* (Bl) | | 1,250. |
| *157* | A24 | 1sh bl, *bl* (Bk) | 87.50 | 20.00 |
| *158* | A25 | 2sh bl, *grn* (Bk) | 72.50 | 12.50 |

Reprints of 4p and 1sh have brighter colors than originals. They lack the overprint "REPRINT".

A35 A36

A37 A38

A39 A40

**1886-87** ***Perf. 12½***

| | | | | |
|---|---|---|---|---|
| *159* | A35 | ½p lilac | 9.75 | 2.00 |
| *160* | A35 | ½p rose | 3.50 | 9 |
| *160A* | A35 | ½p scarlet | 2.75 | 8 |
| *161* | A36 | 1p green | 3.50 | 8 |
| *162* | A37 | 2p violet | 2.00 | 6 |
| *a.* | | 2p red lil | 2.00 | 6 |
| *b.* | | Imperf. | | |
| *163* | A38 | 4p red | 4.00 | 38 |
| *164* | A39 | 6p blue | 4.50 | 20 |
| *165* | A39 | 6p ultra | 4.50 | 10 |
| *166* | A40 | 1sh lil brn | 19.00 | 1.25 |

A41 A42

**1889**

| | | | | |
|---|---|---|---|---|
| *167* | A41 | 1sh6p blue | 87.50 | 62.50 |
| *168* | A41 | 1sh6p orange | 11.00 | 3.75 |

Southern Cross A43

Queen Victoria A44

**1890-95** ***Perf. 12½***

| | | | | |
|---|---|---|---|---|
| *169* | A42 | 1p org brn | 1.00 | 8 |
| *a.* | | 1p chocolate brn | 2.75 | 8 |
| *170* | A42 | 1p yel brn | 2.00 | 6 |
| *171* | A42 | 1p brn org, *pink* ('91) | 1.40 | 50 |
| *172* | A43 | 2½p brn red, *yel* | 3.50 | 22 |
| *173* | A44 | 5p choc ('91) | 5.25 | 28 |
| *174* | A19 | 9p grn ('92) | 15.00 | 5.00 |
| *175* | A19 | 9p rose red | 7.25 | 1.50 |
| *a.* | | 9p rose ('95) | 7.25 | 1.50 |
| *176* | A40 | 1sh dp cl | 13.00 | 30 |
| *a.* | | 1sh red brn | 13.00 | 38 |
| *b.* | | 1sh maroon | 20.00 | 1.00 |
| *177* | A33 | 2sh yel grn | 20.00 | 10.00 |
| *178* | A33 | 2sh emerald | 16.00 | 4.50 |

In 1891 many stamps of the early issues were reprinted. They are on paper watermarked V and Crown, perforated 12, 12½, and overprinted "REPRINT."

A45

**1897**

| | | | | |
|---|---|---|---|---|
| *179* | A45 | 1½p yel grn | 2.50 | 1.75 |

**1899**

| | | | | |
|---|---|---|---|---|
| *180* | A35 | ½p emerald | 1.65 | 8 |
| *181* | A42 | 1p brt rose | 2.00 | 8 |
| *182* | A45 | 1½p red, *yel* | 2.75 | 1.50 |
| *183* | A43 | 2½p dk bl | 3.50 | 1.25 |

**1901, February**

| | | | | |
|---|---|---|---|---|
| *184* | A21 | ½p bl grn | 1.65 | 15 |
| *a.* | | "VICTCRIA" | 65.00 | 25.00 |
| *185* | A27 | 2p violet | 2.75 | 9 |
| *186* | A14 | 3p brn org | 7.75 | 1.50 |
| *187* | A28 | 4p bister | 16.00 | 5.00 |
| *188* | A11 | 6p emerald | 6.50 | 2.50 |
| *189* | A24 | 1sh org yel | 11.50 | 3.00 |
| *190* | A25 | 2sh bl, *rose* | 27.50 | 11.00 |
| *191* | A15 | 5sh rose red & bl | 55.00 | 20.00 |
| | | *Nos. 184-191 (8)* | 128.65 | 43.24 |

**1901, May**

| | | | | |
|---|---|---|---|---|
| *192* | A42 | 1p ol grn | 6.50 | 6.50 |
| *192A* | A30 | 3p sage grn | 15.00 | 12.00 |

Nos. 192-192A were available for postal use until June 30, 1901, and thereafter restricted to revenue use.

A46 A47

A48 A49

A50 A51

A52 A53

A54 A55

A56 A57

A58

***Perf. 11, 12½ and Compound***

**1901, June**

| | | | | |
|---|---|---|---|---|
| *193* | A46 | ½p bl grn | 1.50 | 6 |
| *194* | A47 | 1p rose red | 1.25 | 6 |
| *a.* | | 1p rose | 1.25 | 5 |
| *195* | A48 | 1½p red, *yel* | 2.25 | 9 |
| *a.* | | Perf. 11 | 50.00 | 32.50 |
| *196* | A49 | 2p violet | 2.75 | 6 |
| *197* | A50 | 2½p blue | 3.25 | 8 |
| *198* | A51 | 3p brn org | 6.00 | 8 |
| *199* | A52 | 4p bister | 6.00 | 15 |
| *200* | A53 | 5p chocolate | 5.25 | 25 |
| *201* | A54 | 6p emerald | 6.00 | 32 |
| *202* | A55 | 9p rose | 10.00 | 75 |
| *203* | A56 | 1sh org yel | 11.50 | 75 |
| *204* | A57 | 2sh bl, *rose* | 21.00 | 2.25 |
| *205* | A58 | 5sh rose red & bl | 65.00 | 12.50 |
| *a.* | | 5sh carmine & blue | 65.00 | 12.50 |
| | | *Nos. 193-205 (13)* | 141.75 | 17.40 |

King Edward VII

A59 A60

**1901-05**

| | | | | |
|---|---|---|---|---|
| *206* | A59 | £1 dp rose | 210.00 | 100.00 |
| *a.* | | Perf. 11 ('05) | 250.00 | 140.00 |
| *208* | A60 | £2 dk bl ('02) | 900.00 | 240.00 |
| *a.* | | Perf. 11 ('05) | 1,000. | 600.00 |

**1903** **Redrawn**

| | | | | |
|---|---|---|---|---|
| *209* | A56 | 1sh yellow | 13.00 | 1.40 |
| *a.* | | 1sh org | 13.00 | 1.40 |

No. 209 has the network lighter than No. 203. In the latter the "P" and "E" of "POSTAGE" are in a position more nearly horizontal than on No. 209.

Wmk. 13- Crown and Double-lined A

***Perf. 11, 12x12½, 12½, 12½x11***

**1905-10** **Wmk. 13**

| | | | | |
|---|---|---|---|---|
| *218* | A46 | ½p bl grn | 1.25 | 58 |
| *219* | A47 | 1p rose red | 1.00 | 5 |
| *a.* | | 1p car rose | 2.00 | 5 |
| *220* | A49 | 2p violet | 3.25 | 6 |
| *a.* | | 2p pur | 3.25 | 6 |

| | | | | |
|---|---|---|---|---|
| *221* | A50 | 2½p blue | 3.50 | 25 |
| *222* | A51 | 3p brn org | 4.50 | 30 |
| *a.* | | 3p dl yel | 5.25 | 25 |
| *223* | A52 | 4p bister | 5.25 | 30 |
| *224* | A53 | 5p chocolate | 6.00 | 30 |
| *225* | A54 | 6p emerald | 8.25 | 25 |
| *226* | A55 | 9p brn rose | 10.00 | 1.10 |
| *a.* | | 9p org brn | 10.00 | 1.10 |
| *227* | A55 | 9p car rose | 10.00 | 1.10 |
| *228* | A56 | 1sh yel ('08) | 10.00 | 50 |
| *229* | A58 | 5sh rose red & ultra | 62.50 | 12.50 |
| *a.* | | 5sh org red & ultra | 62.50 | 12.50 |
| *230* | A59 | £1 pale red ('07) | 285.00 | 110.00 |
| *a.* | | £1 rose ('10) | 275.00 | 100.00 |
| *231* | A60 | £2 dl bl | 600.00 | 300.00 |
| | | *Nos. 218-229 (12)* | 125.50 | 17.29 |

No. 220 Surcharged in Red **ONE PENNY**

**1912, July 1**

| | | | | |
|---|---|---|---|---|
| *232* | A49 | 1p on 2p violet | 30 | 20 |

## POSTAL-FISCAL STAMPS

On January 1, 1884, all postage and fiscal stamps were made available for either purpose. Therefore all stamps inscribed "Stamp Duty" on hand at that date or issued thereafter can be considered as postage stamps.

Values for used are for postally canceled.

Coat of Arms — PF5

PF6

PF7

PF8

PF9

PF10

PF11

**Wmk. V and Crown. (70)**

**1884-96 Typo. *Perf. 12½***

| | | | | |
|---|---|---|---|---|
| *AR1* | PF5 | 1sh6p rose | 150.00 | 12.00 |
| *AR2* | PF6 | 2sh bl, *grn* | 150.00 | 12.00 |
| *AR3* | PF7 | 2sh6p orange | 150.00 | 30.00 |
| *AR4* | PF8 | 3sh bister | 82.50 | 10.50 |
| | | **Lithographed** | | |
| *AR5* | PF8 | 3sh vio, *bl* | 275.00 | 30.00 |
| *AR6* | PF9 | 4sh orange | 77.50 | 5.75 |
| *a.* | | 4sh ver | 77.50 | 5.75 |
| | | **Typographed** | | |
| *AR7* | PF10 | 5sh claret, *yel* | 70.00 | 3.50 |
| *AR8* | PF10 | 5sh car rose ('96) | 110.00 | 6.75 |
| *AR9* | PF11 | 6sh yel grn | 275.00 | 22.50 |

PF12

PF13

PF14

PF15

PF16

PF17

PF18

PF19

| | | | | |
|---|---|---|---|---|
| *AR10* | PF12 | 10sh brown | 350.00 | 100.00 |
| *AR11* | PF12 | 10sh gray grn | 240.00 | 17.50 |
| | | **Lithographed** | | |
| *AR12* | PF13 | 15sh lilac | | 250.00 |
| | | **Typographed** | | |
| *AR13* | PF13 | 15sh pale brn | 500.00 | 150.00 |
| | | **Lithographed** | | |
| *AR14* | PF14 | £1 org, *yel* | 350.00 | 27.50 |
| *AR15* | PF15 | £1 5sh pink | *1,350.* | 90.00 |
| *AR16* | PF16 | £1 10sh ol grn | 1,000. | 22.50 |
| *AR17* | PF17 | 35sh violet | | |
| | | Revenue cancellation | | 250.00 |
| | | **Typographed** | | |
| *AR18* | PF18 | £2 blue | 1,200. | 47.50 |
| *AR19* | PF19 | 45sh gray lil | *1,650.* | 250.00 |

PF20

PF21

**Litho.**

| | | | | |
|---|---|---|---|---|
| *AR20* | PF20 | £5 rose | | 225.00 |
| | | **Typographed** | | |
| *AR21* | PF21 | £5 cl & ultra | *1,200.* | 60.00 |

## SEMI-POSTAL STAMPS

SP1

Queen Victoria and Figure of Charity — SP2

**Wmk. V and Crown. (70)**

**1897, Oct. Typo. *Perf. 12½***

| | | | | |
|---|---|---|---|---|
| *B1* | SP1 | 1p dp bl | 5.00 | 5.00 |
| *B2* | SP2 | 2½p red brn | 75.00 | 75.00 |

These stamps were sold at 1 shilling and 2 shillings 6 pence respectively. The difference between the face value and selling price was given to a charitable institution.

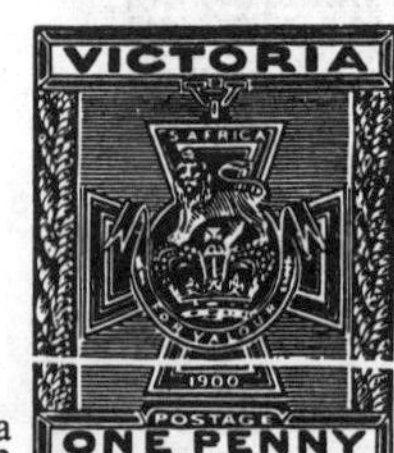

Victoria Cross — SP3

Scout Reporting SP4

**1900**

| | | | | |
|---|---|---|---|---|
| *B3* | SP3 | 1p brn ol | 52.50 | 52.50 |
| *B4* | SP4 | 2p emerald | 100.00 | 100.00 |

These stamps were sold at 1 and 2 shillings respectively. The difference between the face value and selling price was given to a patriotic fund in connection with the South African War.

## REGISTRATION STAMPS

R1

**Unwmk.**

**1854, Dec. 1 Typo. *Imperf.***

| | | | | |
|---|---|---|---|---|
| *F1* | R1 | 1sh rose & blue | 1,000. | 75.00 |

**1857 *Rouletted 7***

| | | | | |
|---|---|---|---|---|
| *F2* | R1 | 1sh rose & blue | 5,000. | 150.00 |

## LATE FEE STAMP

LF1

**Unwmk.**

**1855, Jan. 1 Typo. *Imperf.***

| | | | | |
|---|---|---|---|---|
| *I1* | LF1 | 6p lilac & green | 650.00 | 165.00 |

## POSTAGE DUE STAMPS

D1

**Wmk. V and Crown (70)**

**1890 Typo. *Perf. 12½***

| | | | | |
|---|---|---|---|---|
| *J1* | D1 | ½p cl & bl | 1.75 | 1.65 |
| *J2* | D1 | 1p cl & bl | 2.00 | 1.25 |
| *J3* | D1 | 2p cl & bl | 3.75 | 1.50 |
| *J4* | D1 | 4p cl & bl | 3.00 | 1.75 |
| *J5* | D1 | 5p cl & bl | 3.00 | 1.65 |
| *J6* | D1 | 6p cl & bl | 2.75 | 1.50 |
| *J7* | D1 | 10p cl & bl | 50.00 | 32.50 |
| *J8* | D1 | 1sh cl & bl | 10.00 | 5.00 |
| *J9* | D1 | 2sh cl & bl | 100.00 | 42.50 |
| *J10* | D1 | 5sh cl & bl | 150.00 | 100.00 |
| | | *Nos. J1-J10 (10)* | 326.25 | 189.30 |

**1891**

| | | | | |
|---|---|---|---|---|
| *J11* | D1 | ½p lake & bl | 70 | 52 |
| *J12* | D1 | 1p brn red & bl | 1.00 | 42 |
| *J13* | D1 | 2p brn red & bl | 2.75 | 60 |
| *J14* | D1 | 4p lake & bl | 4.50 | 2.25 |

**1894**

| | | | | |
|---|---|---|---|---|
| *J15* | D1 | ½p bl grn & rose | 1.00 | 60 |
| *J16* | D1 | 1p bl grn & rose | 50 | 32 |
| *J17* | D1 | 2p bl grn & rose | 70 | 32 |
| *J18* | D1 | 4p bl grn & rose | 1.25 | 70 |
| *J19* | D1 | 5p bl grn & rose | 3.00 | 2.25 |
| *J20* | D1 | 6p bl grn & rose | 1.65 | 85 |
| *J21* | D1 | 10p bl grn & rose | 4.50 | 3.75 |
| *J22* | D1 | 1sh bl grn & rose | 4.50 | 2.75 |
| *J23* | D1 | 2sh grn & rose | 32.50 | 16.00 |
| *J24* | D1 | 5sh grn & rose | 82.50 | 30.00 |
| | | *Nos. J15-J24 (10)* | 132.10 | 57.54 |

**1906 Wmk. 13**

| | | | | |
|---|---|---|---|---|
| *J25* | D1 | ½p yel grn & rose | 1.65 | 1.65 |
| *J26* | D1 | 1p yel grn & rose | 3.00 | 65 |
| *J27* | D1 | 2p yel grn & rose | 6.50 | 1.50 |
| *J28* | D1 | 4p yel grn & rose | 13.00 | 10.00 |

# VIRGIN ISLANDS

LOCATION — In the West Indies, southeast of Puerto Rico.
GOVT. — British colony
AREA — 59 sq. mi.
POP. — 12,034 (1980)
CAPITAL — Road Town

The British Virgin Islands constituted one of the presidencies of the former Leeward Islands colony until it became a colony itself in 1956. For many years stamps of Leeward Islands were used concurrently.

The Virgin Islands group is divided between Great Britain and the United States. See Danish West Indies.

12 Pence = 1 Shilling
20 Shillings = 1 Pound
100 Cents = 1 Dollar (1951)
100 Cents = 1 U.S. Dollar (1962)

**Catalogue values for unused stamps in this country are for Never Hinged items, beginning with Scott 88 in the regular postage section and Scott O1 in the officials section.**

Virgin and Lamps — A1

St. Ursula — A2

A3

A4

**1866 Litho. Unwmk. *Perf. 12***

**Toned or White Paper**

| | | | |
|---|---|---|---|
| 1 | A1 1p green | 30.00 | 35.00 |
| a | Toned paper | 30.00 | 35.00 |
| c | Perf. 15x12, toned paper | 5,500. | 10,000. |
| 2 | A3 6p rose | 47.50 | 67.50 |
| a | Large "V" in "VIRGIN" | 575.00 | 650.00 |
| b | White paper | 65.00 | 80.00 |
| c | As "a," white paper | 600.00 | 675.00 |

**1867-70 *Perf. 15***

| | | | |
|---|---|---|---|
| 3 | A1 1p bl grn ('70) | 50.00 | 57.50 |
| 4 | A1 1p yel grn ('68) | 62.50 | 67.50 |
| a | Toned paper | 80.00 | 65.00 |
| 5 | A2 4p lake, *buff* | 27.50 | 45.00 |
| a | 4p lake, *rose* | 27.50 | 45.00 |
| 6 | A3 6p rose | 600.00 | 600.00 |
| a | Toned paper ('68) | 325.00 | 375.00 |
| 7 | A4 1sh rose & blk | 140.00 | 175.00 |
| a | Toned paper | 140.00 | 200.00 |
| b | Double lined frame | 140.00 | 175.00 |
| c | As "b," bluish paper | 165.00 | 200.00 |

**Colored Margins**

| | | | |
|---|---|---|---|
| 8 | A4 1sh rose & blk | 30.00 | 30.00 |
| a | White paper | 30.00 | 30.00 |
| b | Bluish paper | 825.00 | 1,000. |
| c | Central figure omitted | 100,000. | |

**1878 Wmk. 1 *Perf. 14***

| | | | |
|---|---|---|---|
| 9 | A1 1p green | 55.00 | 60.00 |

Queen Victoria — A5

**1880 Typo.**

| | | | |
|---|---|---|---|
| 10 | A5 1p green | 27.50 | 37.50 |
| 11 | A5 2½p red brn | 45.00 | 55.00 |

**1883-84 Wmk. Crown and C. A. (2)**

| | | | |
|---|---|---|---|
| 12 | A5 ½p yellow | 55.00 | 67.50 |
| 13 | A5 ½p green | 2.25 | 5.75 |
| a | Imperf., pair | 1,750. | |
| 14 | A5 1p rose | 9.25 | 11.00 |
| 15 | A5 2½p ultra ('84) | 2.75 | 4.25 |

**1887 Litho.**

| | | | |
|---|---|---|---|
| 16 | A2 4p brick red | 26.00 | 30.00 |
| a | 4p brn red | 32.50 | 30.00 |
| 17 | A3 6p violet | 13.00 | 22.50 |

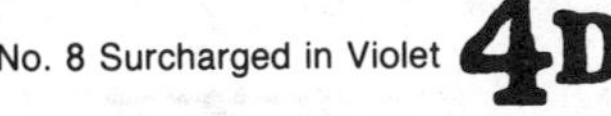
No. 8 Surcharged in Violet 4D

**1888 Unwmk. *Perf. 15***

| | | | |
|---|---|---|---|
| 18 | A4 4p on 1sh dp rose & blk | 77.50 | 80.00 |
| a | Double surch. | 10,000. | |
| b | Inverted surcharge | 45,000. | |

**1889 Wmk. 2 *Perf. 14***

| | | | |
|---|---|---|---|
| 19 | A1 1p carmine | 1.40 | 1.65 |
| 20 | A4 1sh brown | 42.50 | 57.50 |
| a | 1sh blk brn | 55.00 | 70.00 |

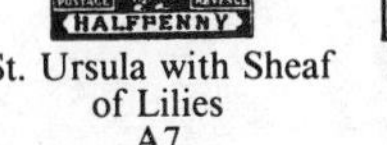
St. Ursula with Sheaf of Lilies A7

Edward VII A8

**1899 Engr.**

| | | | |
|---|---|---|---|
| 21 | A7 ½p yel grn | 55 | 32 |
| a | "PFNNY" | 65.00 | 75.00 |
| b | "F" without cross bar | 65.00 | 82.50 |
| c | Horiz. pair, imperf. between | 10,000. | |
| d | Imperf. pair | | |
| 22 | A7 1p red | 1.50 | 1.25 |
| 23 | A7 2½p ultra | 8.00 | 6.50 |
| 24 | A7 4p chocolate | 6.00 | 8.50 |
| a | "PENCF" | 1,750. | 1,750. |
| 25 | A7 6p dk vio | 3.50 | 4.00 |
| 26 | A7 7p sl grn | 5.50 | 8.00 |
| 27 | A7 1sh ocher | 13.00 | 16.00 |
| 28 | A7 5sh dk bl | 42.50 | 55.00 |
| | *Nos. 21-28 (8)* | 80.55 | 99.57 |

**1904 Typo. Wmk. 3**

| | | | |
|---|---|---|---|
| 29 | A8 ½p vio & bl grn | 42 | 55 |
| 30 | A8 1p vio & scar | 65 | 95 |
| 31 | A8 2p vio & bis | 5.50 | 4.25 |
| 32 | A8 2½p vio & ultra | 1.50 | 2.50 |
| 33 | A8 3p vio & blk | 2.00 | 3.50 |
| 34 | A8 6p vio & brn | 3.75 | 5.50 |
| 35 | A8 1sh grn & scar | 4.00 | 7.00 |
| 36 | A8 2sh 6p grn & blk | 20.00 | 35.00 |
| 37 | A8 5sh grn & ultra | 32.50 | 55.00 |
| | *Nos. 29-37 (9)* | 70.32 | 114.25 |

Numerals of 2p, 3p, 1sh and 2sh6p of type A8 are in color on plain tablet.

George V A9

Colony Seal A10

**Die I**

For description of dies I and II see back of this volume.

**1913**

**Ordinary Paper**

| | | | |
|---|---|---|---|
| 38 | A9 ½p green | 40 | 50 |
| 39 | A9 1p scarlet | 1.65 | 1.65 |
| a | 1p car | 3.50 | 4.25 |
| 40 | A9 2p gray | 1.50 | 1.90 |
| 41 | A9 2½p ultra | 1.90 | 2.25 |

**Chalky Paper**

| | | | |
|---|---|---|---|
| 42 | A9 3p vio, *yel* | 1.25 | 1.50 |
| 43 | A9 6p dl vio & red vio | 1.90 | 2.00 |
| 44 | A9 1sh blk, *green* | 2.75 | 4.25 |
| 45 | A9 2sh6p blk & red, *bl* | 18.00 | 22.50 |
| 46 | A9 5sh grn & red, *yel* | 30.00 | 42.50 |
| | *Nos. 38-46 (9)* | 59.35 | 79.05 |

Numerals of 2p, 3p, 1sh and 2sh6p of type A9 are in color on plain tablet.

**Wmk. Multiple Crown and Script CA (4)**

**1921**

**Die II**

| | | | |
|---|---|---|---|
| 47 | A9 ½p green | 60 | 65 |
| 48 | A9 1p carmine | 1.10 | 1.20 |

**1922 Wmk. 3**

| | | | |
|---|---|---|---|
| 49 | A10 3p vio, *yel* | 90 | 1.00 |
| 50 | A10 1sh blk, *emerald* | 65 | 1.00 |
| 51 | A10 2sh6p blk & red, *bl* | 3.50 | 4.50 |
| 52 | A10 5sh grn & red, *yel* | 20.00 | 27.50 |

**1922-28 Wmk. 4**

| | | | |
|---|---|---|---|
| 53 | A10 ½p green | 16 | 24 |
| 54 | A10 1p rose red | 24 | 35 |
| 55 | A10 1p vio ('27) | 50 | 1.10 |
| 56 | A10 1½p rose red ('27) | 90 | 1.10 |
| 57 | A10 1½p fawn ('28) | 1.90 | 2.00 |
| 58 | A10 2p gray | 55 | 1.40 |
| 59 | A10 2½p ultra | 1.10 | 2.25 |
| 60 | A10 2½p org ('23) | 2.50 | 2.75 |
| 61 | A10 3p dl vio, *yel* ('28) | 90 | 1.90 |
| 62 | A10 5p dl lil & ol grn | 5.75 | 11.00 |
| 63 | A10 6p dl vio & red vio | 75 | 1.50 |
| a | 6p brn lil & red vio | 75 | 1.10 |
| 64 | A10 1sh *emer* ('28) | 1.90 | 2.75 |
| 65 | A10 2sh6p blk & red, *bl* ('28) | 12.50 | 14.00 |
| 66 | A10 5sh grn & red, *yel* ('23) | 14.00 | 20.00 |
| | *Nos. 53-66 (14)* | 43.65 | 62.34 |

The ½, 1, 2 and 2½p are on ordinary paper, the others on chalky.

**Silver Jubilee Issue**

Common Design Type

**1935, May 6 Engr. *Perf. 11x12***

| | | | |
|---|---|---|---|
| 69 | CD301 1p car & dk bl | 16 | 20 |
| 70 | CD301 1½p blk & ultra | 20 | 28 |
| 71 | CD301 2½p ultra & brn | 55 | 70 |
| 72 | CD301 1sh brn vio & ind | 2.75 | 3.25 |

**Coronation Issue**

Common Design Type

**1937, May 12 *Perf. 11x11½***

| | | | |
|---|---|---|---|
| 73 | CD302 1p dk car | 10 | 10 |
| 74 | CD302 1½p brown | 14 | 14 |
| 75 | CD302 2½p dp ultra | 35 | 35 |

King George VI and Seal of the Colony — A11

**1938-47 Photo. *Perf. 14***

| | | | |
|---|---|---|---|
| 76 | A11 ½p green | 8 | 8 |
| 77 | A11 1p scarlet | 8 | 8 |
| 78 | A11 1½p red brn | 8 | 8 |
| 79 | A11 2p gray | 10 | 10 |
| 80 | A11 2½p ultra | 14 | 10 |
| 81 | A11 3p orange | 16 | 16 |
| 82 | A11 6p dp vio | 30 | 30 |
| 83 | A11 1sh ol bis | 45 | 45 |
| 84 | A11 2sh6p sepia | 2.25 | 3.50 |
| 85 | A11 5sh rose lake | 3.50 | 4.50 |
| 86 | A11 10sh brt bl ('47) | 7.00 | 9.75 |
| 87 | A11 £1 gray blk ('47) | 11.00 | 16.00 |
| | *Nos. 76-87 (12)* | 25.14 | 35.10 |

**Catalogue values for unused stamps in this section, from this point to the end of the section, are for Never Hinged items.**

**Peace Issue**

Common Design Type

***Perf. 13½x14***

**1946, Nov. 1 Engr. Wmk. 4**

| | | | |
|---|---|---|---|
| 88 | CD303 1½p red brn | 10 | 10 |
| 89 | CD303 3p orange | 16 | 16 |

**Silver Wedding Issue**

Common Design Types

**1949, Jan. 3 Photo. *Perf. 14x14½***

| | | | |
|---|---|---|---|
| 90 | CD304 2½p brt ultra | 38 | 38 |

**Engr.; Name Typo.**

***Perf. 11½x11***

| | | | |
|---|---|---|---|
| 91 | CD305 £1 gray blk | 14.00 | 14.00 |

**UPU Issue**

Common Design Types

**Engr.; Name Typo. on Nos. 93 & 94**

**1949, Oct. 10 *Perf. 13½, 11x11½***

| | | | |
|---|---|---|---|
| 92 | CD306 2½p ultra | 50 | 50 |
| 93 | CD307 3p dp org | 60 | 60 |
| 94 | CD308 6p red lil | 1.10 | 1.00 |
| 95 | CD309 1sh olive | 3.00 | 2.00 |

**University Issue**

Common Design Types

**1951 Engr. *Perf. 14x14½***

| | | | |
|---|---|---|---|
| 96 | CD310 3c red brn & gray blk | 25 | 25 |
| 97 | CD311 12c pur & blk | 85 | 85 |

Map of the Islands A12

**1951, Apr. 2 Wmk. 4 *Perf. 14½x14***

| | | | |
|---|---|---|---|
| 98 | A12 6c red org | 30 | 30 |
| 99 | A12 12c purple | 40 | 40 |
| 100 | A12 24c ol grn | 65 | 65 |
| 101 | A12 $1.20 carmine | 2.75 | 2.75 |

Restoration of the Legislative Council, 1950.

Sombrero Lighthouse A13

Map of Jost van Dyke A14

Designs: 3c, Sheep. 4c, Map, Anegada. 5c, Cattle. 8c, Map, Virgin Gorda. 12c, Map, Tortola. 24c, Badge of the Presidency. 60c, Dead Man's Chest. $1.20, Sir Francis Drake Channel. $2.40, Road Town. $4.80, Map, Virgin Islands.

***Perf. 12½x13, 13x12½***

**1952, Apr. 15**

| | | | |
|---|---|---|---|
| 102 | A13 1c gray blk | 24 | 24 |
| 103 | A14 2c dp grn | 60 | 40 |
| 104 | A14 3c choc & gray blk | 30 | 30 |
| 105 | A14 4c red | 50 | 50 |
| 106 | A14 5c gray blk & rose lake | 1.00 | 90 |
| 107 | A14 8c ultra | 60 | 60 |
| 108 | A14 12c purple | 1.10 | 1.10 |
| 109 | A13 24c dk brn | 1.25 | 1.25 |
| 110 | A14 60c bl & ol grn | 2.00 | 2.00 |
| 111 | A14 $1.20 ultra & blk | 4.50 | 4.50 |
| 112 | A14 $2.40 hn brn & dk grn | 8.00 | 8.00 |
| 113 | A14 $4.80 rose car & bl | 16.00 | 16.00 |
| | *Nos. 102-113 (12)* | 36.09 | 35.79 |

**Coronation Issue**

Common Design Type

**1953, June 2 *Perf. 13½x14***

| | | | |
|---|---|---|---|
| 114 | CD312 2c dk grn & blk | 25 | 25 |

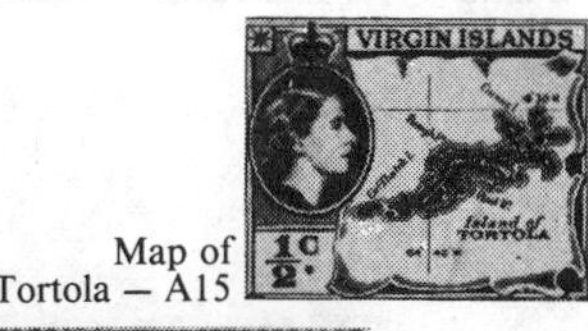
Map of Tortola — A15

Brown Pelican A16

Designs: 1c, Virgin Islands sloop. 2c, Nelthrop Red Poll bull. 3c, Road Harbor. 4c, Mountain travel. 5c, St. Ursula. 8c, Beach scene. 12c, Boat launching. 24c, White Cedar tree. 60c, Skipjack tuna. $1.20, Treasury Square. $4.80, Magnificent frigatebird.

***Perf. 13x12½***

**1956, Nov. 1 Engr. Wmk. 4**

| | | | |
|---|---|---|---|
| 115 | A15 ½c claret & blk | 15 | 15 |
| 116 | A15 1c dk bl & grnsh bl | 12 | 12 |
| 117 | A15 2c blk & ver | 15 | 15 |
| 118 | A15 3c ol & brt bl | 15 | 15 |
| 119 | A15 4c bl grn & brn | 15 | 15 |
| 120 | A15 5c gray | 18 | 18 |
| 121 | A15 8c dp ultra & org | 25 | 25 |
| 122 | A15 12c car & brt ultra | 35 | 35 |
| 123 | A15 24c dl red & grn | 75 | 75 |
| 124 | A15 60c yel org & dk bl | 2.50 | 2.50 |
| 125 | A15 $1.20 car & yel grn | 3.50 | 3.50 |

***Perf. 12x11½***

| | | | |
|---|---|---|---|
| 126 | A16 $2.40 vio brn & dl yel | 11.00 | 11.00 |
| 127 | A16 $4.80 grnsh bl & dk brn | 24.00 | 24.00 |
| | *Nos. 115-127 (13)* | 43.25 | 43.25 |

Types of 1956 Surcharged ≡ 2¢

***Perf. 13x12½, 12x11½***

**1962, Dec. 10 Engr. Wmk. 314**

| | | | |
|---|---|---|---|
| 128 | A15 1c on ½c cl & blk | 6 | 6 |
| 129 | A15 2c on 1c dk bl & grnsh bl | 8 | 8 |
| 130 | A15 3c on 2c blk & ver | 9 | 9 |
| 131 | A15 4c on 3c ol & brt bl | 12 | 12 |
| 132 | A15 5c on 4c bl grn & brn | 15 | 15 |

*133* A15 8c on 8c dp ultra & org 22 22
*134* A15 10c on 12c car & brt ultra 30 30
*135* A15 12c on 24c dl red & grn 38 38
*136* A15 25c on 60c yel org & dk bl 80 80
*137* A15 70c on $1.20 car & yel grn 2.00 2.00
*138* A16 $1.40 on $2.40 vio brn & dl yel 4.75 4.75
*139* A16 $2.80 on $4.80 grnsh bl & dk brn 9.25 9.25
*Nos. 128-139 (12)* 18.20 18.20

### Freedom from Hunger Issue
Common Design Type

**1963, June 4 Photo. *Perf. 14x14½***
*140* CD314 25c lilac 52 52

### Red Cross Centenary Issue
Common Design Type

**Wmk. 314**

**1963, Sept. 2 Litho. *Perf. 13***
*141* CD315 2c blk & red 15 15
*142* CD315 25c ultra & red 1.00 1.00

### Shakespeare Issue
Common Design Type

**1964, Apr. 23 Photo. *Perf. 14x14½***
*143* CD316 10c ultra 24 24

Bonito — A17

Map of Tortola Island — A18

Designs: 2c, Seaplane at Soper's Hole. 3c, Brown pelican. 4c, Dead Man's Chest (mountain). 5c, Road Harbor. 6c, Fallen Jerusalem Island. 8c, The Baths, Virgin Gorda. 10c, Map of Virgin Islands. 12c, Ferry service, Tortola—St. Thomas. 15c, The Towers. 25c, Plane at Beef Island Airfield. $1, Virgin Gorda Island. $1.40, Yachts, Tortola. $2.80, Badge.

***Perf. 13x12½***

**1964, Nov. 2 Engr. Wmk. 314**
*144* A17 1c gray ol & dk bl 5 5
*145* A17 2c rose red & ol 6 6
*146* A17 3c grnsh bl & sep 8 8
*147* A17 4c car & blk 14 14
*148* A17 5c grn & blk 18 18
*149* A17 6c org & blk 22 22
*150* A17 8c pink & blk 32 32
*151* A17 10c lt vio & mar 38 38
*152* A17 12c vio bl & Prus grn 45 45
*153* A17 15c gray & yel grn 55 55
*154* A17 25c pur & yel grn 85 85

***Perf. 13x13½***

**Size: 27x30½mm**
*155* A18 70c bis brn & blk 2.75 2.75
*156* A18 $1 red brn & yel grn 3.75 3.75
*157* A18 $1.40 pink & bl 5.25 5.25

***Perf. 11½x12***

**Size: 27x37mm**
*158* A18 $2.80 rose lil & blk 10.00 10.00
*Nos. 144-158 (15)* 25.03 25.03

### ITU Issue
Common Design Type

***Perf. 11x11½***

**1965, May 17 Litho. Wmk. 314**
*159* CD317 4c yel & bl grn 12 12
*160* CD317 25c bl & org yel 80 80

### Intl. Cooperation Year Issue
Common Design Type

**1965, Oct. 25 Wmk. 314 *Perf. 14½***
*161* CD318 1c bl grn & cl 8 8
*162* CD318 25c lt vio & grn 70 70

### Churchill Memorial Issue
Common Design Type

**1966, Jan. 24 Photo. *Perf. 14***

**Design in Black, Gold and Carmine Rose**
*163* CD319 1c brt bl 8 8
*164* CD319 2c green 9 9
*165* CD319 10c brown 40 40
*166* CD319 25c violet 1.00 1.00

### Royal Visit Issue
Common Design Type

**1966, Feb. 22 Litho. *Perf. 11x12***
*167* CD320 4c vio bl 12 12
*168* CD320 70c dk car rose 1.40 1.40

Stamps of 1866 — A19

Designs: 5c, R.M.S. Atrato, 1866. 25c, Beechcraft mail plane on Beef Island Airfield and 6p stamp (No. 2). 60c, Landing mail at Road Town, 1866, and 1p stamp (No. 1).

***Perf. 12½x13***

**1966, Apr. 25 Litho. Wmk. 314**
*169* A19 5c grn, yel, red & blk 10 10
*170* A19 10c yel, grn, red, blk & rose 20 20
*171* A19 25c lt grn, bl, red, blk & rose 50 50
*172* A19 60c bl, red, blk, & grn 1.00 1.00

Centenary of Virgin Islands postage stamps.

### Nos. 155, 157-158 Surcharged with New Value and Two Bars

***Perf. 13x12½, 11½x12***

**1966, Sept. 15 Engr. Wmk. 314**
*173* A18 50c on 70c bis brn & blk 2.50 2.50
*174* A18 $1.50 on $1.40 pink & bl 5.75 5.75
*175* A18 $3 on $2.80 rose lil & blk 11.50 11.50

### UNESCO Anniversary Issue
Common Design Type

**1966, Dec. 1 Litho. *Perf. 14***
*176* CD323 2c "Education" 7 7
*177* CD323 12c "Science" 32 32
*178* CD323 60c "Culture" 1.25 1.25

Common Design Types pictured in section before Great Britain.

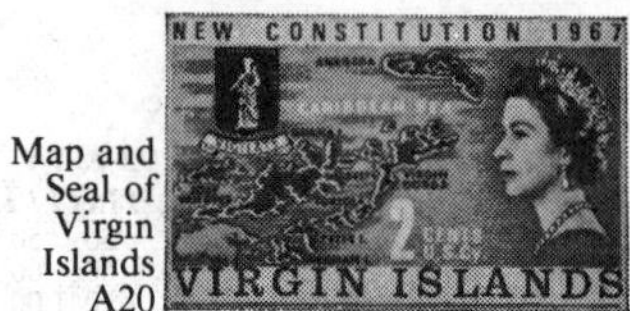

Map and Seal of Virgin Islands A20

**Wmk. 314**

**1967, Apr. 18 Photo. *Perf. 14½***
*179* A20 2c gold, grn & org 8 8
*180* A20 10c gold, rose red, grn & org 15 15
*181* A20 25c gold, red brn, grn & org 40 40
*182* A20 $1 gold, bl, grn & org 1.50 1.50

Introduction of new constitution.

Map of Virgin Islands, Bermuda and C.S. Mercury A21

Designs: 10c, Communications center, Chalwell, Virgin Islands. 50c, Cable ship Mercury.

**1967, Sept. 14 Wmk. 314 *Perf. 14½***
*183* A21 4c grn & multi 12 12
*184* A21 10c dp plum & multi 15 15
*185* A21 50c bis & multi 80 80

Completion of the Bermuda-Tortola, Virgin Islands, telephone link.

Blue Marlin A22

Designs: 10c, Sergeant fish (cobia). 25c, Peto fish (Wahoo). 40c, Fishing boat, map of Virgin Islands and fishing records.

***Perf. 12½x12***

**1968, Jan. 2 Photo. Wmk. 314**
*186* A22 2c multi 8 8
*187* A22 10c multi 25 25
*188* A22 25c multi 48 48
*189* A22 40c multi 80 80

Game fishing in Virgin Islands waters.

### Nos. 151 and 154 Overprinted: "1968 / INTERNATIONAL / YEAR FOR / HUMAN RIGHTS"

**1968, July 1 Engr. *Perf. 13x12½***
*190* A17 10c lt vio & mar 20 20
*191* A17 25c pur & grn 52 52

Martin Luther King, Bible and Sword A23

**1968, Oct. 15 Litho. *Perf. 14***
*192* A23 4c dl org, vio & blk 8 8
*193* A23 25c dl org, gray grn & blk 50 50

Martin Luther King, Jr. (1929-68), American civil rights leader.

DHC-6 Twin Otter A24

Designs: 10c, Hawker Siddeley 748. 25c, Hawker Siddeley Heron. $1, Badge from cap of Royal Engineers.

**Unwmk.**

**1968, Dec. 16 Litho. *Perf. 14***
*194* A24 2c brn red & multi 8 8
*195* A24 10c grnsh bl, blk & red 20 20
*196* A24 25c ultra, lt bl, org & blk 52 52
*197* A24 $1 grn & multi 2.00 2.00

Opening of enlarged Beef Island Airport.

Long John Silver and Jim Hawkins — A25

Tourist and Rock Grouper — A26

Scenes from Treasure Island: 10c, Jim's escape from the pirates (horiz.). 40c, The fight with Israel Hands. $1, Treasure trove (horiz.).

***Perf. 13½x13, 13x13½***

**1969, Mar. 18 Photo. Wmk. 314**
*198* A25 4c dp car & multi 10 10
*199* A25 10c multi 22 22
*200* A25 40c ultra & multi 65 65
*201* A25 $1 blk & multi 2.00 2.00

Robert Louis Stevenson (1850-94). The Virgin Islands were used as the setting for "Treasure Island."

**1969, Oct. 20 Litho. *Perf. 12½***

Designs: 10c, Yachts in Road Harbor, Tortola (horiz.). 20c, Tourists on beach in Virgin Gorda National Park (horiz.). $1, Pipe organ cactus and woman tourist.

*202* A26 2c multi 7 7
*203* A26 10c multi 20 20
*204* A26 20c multi 38 38
*205* A26 $1 multi 2.00 2.00

Tourist publicity.

Carib Canoe A27

Ships: 1c, Santa Maria. 2c, H.M.S. Elizabeth Bonaventure. 3c, Dutch buccaneer, 1660. 4c, Thetis (1827 merchant ship). 5c, Henry Morgan's ship. 6c, Frigate Boreas. 8c, Schooner L'Eclair, 1804. 10c, H.M.S. Formidable. 12c, H.M.S. Nymph burning. 15c, Packet Windsor Castle fighting French privateer. 25c, Frigate Astrea, 1808. 50c, H.M.S. Rhone. $1, Tortola sloop. $2, H.M.S. Frobisher. $3, Booker Line Viking (cargo ship). $5, Hydrofoil Sun Arrow.

**Wmk. 314 Sideways**

**1970, Feb. 16 *Perf. 14½***
*206* A27 ½c brn & ocher 5 5
*207* A27 1c bl, lt grn & vio 5 5
*208* A27 2c red brn, org & gray 8 8
*209* A27 3c ver, bl & brn 10 10
*210* A27 4c brn, bl & vio bl 12 12
*211* A27 5c grn, pink & blk 14 14
*212* A27 6c lil, grn & blk 16 16
*213* A27 8c lt ol, yel & brn 24 24
*214* A27 10c ocher, bl & brn 28 28
*215* A27 12c sep, yel & dp cl 35 35
*216* A27 15c org, grnsh bl & brn 42 42
*217* A27 25c bl, grnsh gray & pur 60 60
*218* A27 50c rose car, lt grn & brn 1.25 1.25
*219* A27 $1 brn, sal pink & dk grn 2.50 2.50
*220* A27 $2 gray & yel 5.00 5.00
*221* A27 $3 brn, ol bis & dk bl 7.75 7.75
*222* A27 $5 lil & gray 12.50 12.50
*Nos. 206-222 (17)* 31.59 31.59

**1973, Oct. 17 Wmk. 314 Upright**
*206a* A27 ½c brn & ocher 8 8
*209a* A27 3c ver, bl & brn 45 45
*210a* A27 4c brn, bl & vio bl 75 75
*211a* A27 5c grn, pink & blk 75 75
*214a* A27 10c ocher, bl & brn 1.50 1.50
*215a* A27 12c sep, yel & dp cl 1.75 1.75
*Nos. 206a-215a (6)* 5.28 5.28

"A Tale of Two Cities," by Dickens A28

Charles Dickens: 10c, "Oliver Twist." 25c, "Great Expectations."

**1970, May 4 Litho. *Perf. 14½***
*223* A28 5c blk, gray & pink 15 15
*224* A28 10c blk, pale yel grn & bl 40 40
*225* A28 25c blk, yel & lt yel grn 1.00 1.00

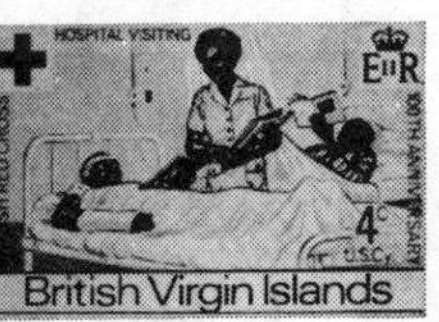

Hospital Visitor A29

Designs: 10c, Girl Scouts receiving first aid training at lake side. 25c, Red Cross and Virgin Islands coat of arms.

**Wmk. 314**

**1970, Aug. 10 Litho. *Perf. 14***

*226* A29 4c multi 12 12
*227* A29 10c multi 30 30
*228* A29 25c multi 75 75

Centenary of British Red Cross.

Mary Read — A30

Pirates: 10c, George Lowther. 30c, Edward Teach (Blackbeard). 60c, Henry Morgan.

**1970, Nov. 16 Wmk. 314 *Perf. 14***

*229* A30 ½c dp rose & multi 5 5
*230* A30 10c bl grn & multi 32 32
*231* A30 30c ultra & multi 1.00 1.00
*232* A30 60c multi 2.00 2.00

Children Spelling out "UNICEF" A31

**1971, Dec. 13**

*233* A31 15c tan & multi 50 50
*234* A31 30c lt bl & multi 1.00 1.00

25th anniv. of UNICEF.

**Nos. 210 and 217 Dated "1972" and Overprinted: "VISIT OF / H.R.H. / THE / PRINCESS MARGARET"**

**1972, Mar. 7 *Perf. 14½***

*235* A27 4c multi 14 14
*236* A27 25c multi 70 70

Seaman, 1800 — A32

Designs: 10c, Boatswain, 1787-1807. 30c, Captain, 1795-1812. 60c, Admiral in full dress uniform, 1787-1795.

**1972, Mar. 17 *Perf. 14x13½***

*237* A32 ½c yel & multi 5 5
*238* A32 10c brt pink & multi 45 45
*239* A32 30c org & multi 1.35 1.35
*240* A32 60c bl & multi 2.75 2.75

INTERPEX, 14th Intl. Stamp Exhib., NYC, Mar. 17-19.

**Silver Wedding Issue, 1972**
Common Design Type

Design: Queen Elizabeth II, Prince Philip, sailfish and "Sir Winston Churchill" yacht.

**1972, Nov. 24 Photo. *Perf. 14x14½***

*241* CD324 15c ultra & multi 40 40
*242* CD324 25c Prus bl & multi 60 60

Allison Tuna A33

**1972, Dec. 12 Litho. *Perf. 13½x14***

*243* A33 ½c *Wahoo* 5 5
*244* A33 ½c *Blue marlin* 5 5
*245* A33 15c *shown* 60 60
*246* A33 25c *White marlin* 95 95
*247* A33 50c *Sailfish* 1.75 1.75
*248* A33 $1 *Dolphin* 3.75 3.75
*a* Souvenir sheet of 6 8.00 8.00
*Nos. 243-248 (6)* 7.15 7.15

Game fish. Nos. 243-244 printed checkerwise in sheets of 25. No. 248a contains one each of Nos. 243-248. Blue black and red margin with data of Virgin Islands fishing records. Size: 192x159mm.

Lettsom House and Medal — A34

Designs (Themes from Quaker History): ½c, Dr. John Coakley Lettsom (vert.). 15c, Dr. William Thornton (vert.). 30c, U.S. Capitol, Washington, D.C., and Dr. Thornton who designed it. $1, Library Hall, Philadelphia, and William Penn.

**1973, Mar. 9 Litho. *Perf. 13½***

*249* A34 ½c rose & multi 5 5
*250* A34 10c multi 20 20
*251* A34 15c multi 30 30
*252* A34 30c ultra & multi 60 60
*253* A34 $1 multi 1.90 1.90
*Nos. 249-253 (5)* 3.05 3.05

INTERPEX, 15th Intl. Phil. Exhib., NYC, Mar. 9-11.

Hummingbirds on 1c Coin — A35

Coins and Beach Scenes: 5c, Zenaida doves. 10c, Kingfisher. 25c, Mangrove cuckoos. 50c, Brown pelicans. $1, Magnificent frigate birds.

**1973, June 30 Wmk. 314 *Perf. 14½***

*254* A35 1c org & multi 5 5
*255* A35 5c lt bl & multi 10 10
*256* A35 10c pale ultra & multi 18 18
*257* A35 25c yel & multi 40 40
*258* A35 50c lt vio & multi 75 75
*259* A35 $1 ultra & multi 1.65 1.65
*Nos. 254-259 (6)* 3.13 3.13

New Virgin Islands coinage.

**Princess Anne's Wedding Issue**
Common Design Type

**1973, Nov. 16 Wmk. 314 *Perf. 14***

*260* CD325 5c cit & multi 9 9
*261* CD325 50c bl grn & multi 90 90

Virgin and Child, by Bernardino Pintoricchio A36

Arms of French Minesweeper Canopus A37

Paintings of the Virgin and Child by: 3c, Lorenzo Credi. 25c, Carlo Crivelli. 50c, Bernardino Luini.

**1973, Dec. 7 *Perf. 14x14½***

*262* A36 ½c lt grn & multi 5 5
*263* A36 3c rose & multi 6 6
*264* A36 25c ocher & multi 55 55
*265* A36 50c lt bl & multi 1.10 1.10

Christmas 1973.

**Wmk. 314**

**1974, Mar. 22 Litho. *Perf. 14***

*266* A37 5c *shown* 9 9
*267* A37 18c *USS Saginaw* 38 38
*268* A37 25c *HMS Rothesay* 50 50
*269* A37 50c *HMCS Ottawa* 1.00 1.00
*a* Souvenir sheet of 4 3.00 3.00

INTERPEX Phil. Exhib., NYC, Mar. 22-24. No. 269a contains one each of Nos. 266-269; multicolored margin, inscription and map of Virgin Islands. Size: 195x127½mm.

Christopher Columbus — A38

**1974, Aug. 19 *Perf. 14½***

*270* A38 5c *shown* 12 12
*271* A38 10c *Sir Walter Raleigh* 25 25
*272* A38 25c *Sir Martin Frobisher* 65 65
*273* A38 40c *Sir Francis Drake* 1.10 1.10
*a* Souvenir sheet of 4 2.25 2.25

Famous explorers. No. 273a contains one each of Nos. 270-273, brown margin and inscription. Size: 78x119mm.

Trumpet Triton — A39

**1974, Sept. 30 *Perf. 13x13½***

*274* A39 5c *shown* 24 24
*275* A39 18c *West Indian murex* 80 80
*276* A39 25c *Bleeding tooth* 1.10 1.10
*277* A39 75c *Virgin Island latirus* 3.50 3.50
*a* Souvenir sheet of 4 7.50 7.50

Sea shells. No. 277a contains one each of Nos. 274-277. Multicolored margin, black inscription. Size: 145x95mm.

St. Mary, Aldermanbury, London, — A40

Design: 50c, St. Mary, Fulton, Missouri.

**1974, Nov. 30 Wmk. 373 *Perf. 14***

*278* A40 10c multi 20 20
*279* A40 50c multi 1.00 1.00
*a* Souvenir sheet of 2 1.40 1.40

Sir Winston Churchill (1874-1965), birth centenary. No. 279a contains one each of Nos. 278-279, gray and black margin showing U.S. and British flags. Size: 140x108mm.

Figurehead from "Boreas" — A41

Figureheads: 18c, The Golden Hind. 40c, Crowned lion from the "Superb." 85c, Warrior, from the "Formidable."

***Perf. 13½x13***

**1975, Mar. 14 Wmk. 314**

*280* A41 5c multi 14 14
*281* A41 18c multi 45 45
*282* A41 40c multi 95 95
*283* A41 85c multi 1.90 1.90
*a* Souvenir sheet of 4 4.50 4.50

INTERPEX, 17th Phil. Exhib., NYC, Mar. 14-16. No. 283a contains one each of Nos. 280-283, perf. 14. Multicolored margin shows battle scene between British and French sailing ships. Size: 190x126mm.

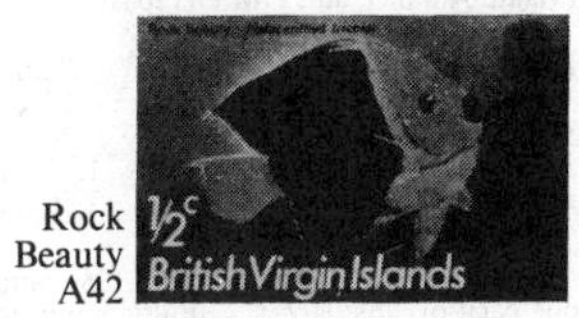

Rock Beauty A42

Designs: Fish.

**1975 Wmk. 373 *Perf. 14***

*284* A42 ½c *shown* 5 5
*285* A42 1c *Squirrelfish* 5 5
*286* A42 3c *Queen triggerfish* 8 8
*287* A42 5c *Blue angelfish* 10 10
*288* A42 8c *Stoplight parrotfish* 16 16
*289* A42 10c *Queen angelfish* 22 22
*290* A42 12c *Nassau grouper* 25 25
*291* A42 13c *Blue tang* 25 25
*292* A42 15c *Sergeant major* 30 30
*293* A42 18c *Jewfish* 38 38
*294* A42 20c *Bluehead wrasse* 42 42
*295* A42 25c *Gray angelfish* 55 55
*296* A42 60c *Glasseye snapper* 1.25 1.25
*297* A42 $1 *Blue chromis* 2.00 2.00
*298* A42 $2.50 *French angelfish* 5.25 5.25
*299* A42 $3 *Queen parrotfish* 6.25 6.25
*300* A42 $5 *Four-eye butterflyfish* 10.50 10.50
*Nos. 284-300 (17)* 28.06 28.06

Issue dates: Nos. 284-299, June 16, No. 300, Aug. 15.

In 1977 eight denominations (½c, 5c, 8c, 10c, 12c, 13c, 15c, 20c) were reissued with "1977" below design instead of "1975."

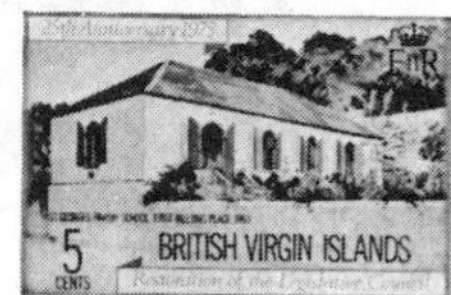


St. Georges Parish School
A43

Designs: 25c, Legislative Council Building. 40c, Mace and gavel of Legislative Council. 75c, Scroll with dates of historical events.

**1975, Nov. 27 Litho. Wmk. 373**

| | | | | |
|---|---|---|---|---|
| *301* | A43 | 5c ultra & multi | 12 | 12 |
| *302* | A43 | 25c grn & multi | 55 | 55 |
| *303* | A43 | 40c ocher & multi | 90 | 90 |
| *304* | A43 | 75c ultra & multi | 1.65 | 1.65 |

Restoration of Legislative Council, 25th anniversary.

Copper Mine Point
A44

Historic Sites: 18c, Dr. Thornton's Ruin, Pleasant Valley. 50c, Callwood distillery. 75c, The Dungeon.

**1976, Mar. 12 Litho. *Perf. 14½***

| | | | | |
|---|---|---|---|---|
| *305* | A44 | 5c red & multi | 12 | 12 |
| *306* | A44 | 18c red & multi | 40 | 40 |
| *307* | A44 | 50c red & multi | 1.10 | 1.10 |
| *308* | A44 | 75c red & multi | 1.65 | 1.65 |

Massachusetts Brig Hazard — A45

Designs: 22c, American Privateer Spy. 40c, Continental Navy Frigate Raleigh. 75c, Frigate Alliance and HMS Trepasy.

**1976, May 29 Wmk. 373 *Perf. 14***

| | | | | |
|---|---|---|---|---|
| *309* | A45 | 8c multi | 28 | 20 |
| *310* | A45 | 22c multi | 70 | 52 |
| *311* | A45 | 40c multi | 1.40 | 1.00 |
| *312* | A45 | 75c multi | 2.50 | 1.75 |
| *a.* | | Souvenir sheet of 4 | 7.00 | 7.00 |

American Bicentennial. No. 312a contains one each of Nos. 309-312, multicolored margin. Size: 117x92½mm.

Government House, Tortola — A46

Designs: 15c, Government House, St. Croix (vert.). 30c, Flags of U.S. and British Virgin Islands (vert.). 75c, Arms of British and U.S. Virgin Islands.

**1976, Oct. 29 Litho. *Perf. 14***

| | | | | |
|---|---|---|---|---|
| *313* | A46 | 8c grn & multi | 22 | 22 |
| *314* | A46 | 15c grn & multi | 38 | 38 |
| *315* | A46 | 30c grn & multi | 75 | 75 |
| *316* | A46 | 75c grn & multi | 1.90 | 1.90 |

U.S. and British Virgin Islands Friendship Day, 5th anniversary.

The indexes in each volume of the Scott Catalogue contain many listings which help to identify stamps.

Holy Bible — A47

Designs: 8c, Queen visiting Agricultural Station, Tortola, 1966. 60c, Presentation of Holy Bible.

**1977, Feb. 7 *Perf. 14x13½***

| | | | | |
|---|---|---|---|---|
| *317* | A47 | 8c sil & multi | 20 | 20 |
| *318* | A47 | 30c sil & multi | 80 | 80 |
| *319* | A47 | 60c sil & multi | 1.50 | 1.50 |

25th anniv. of the reign of Elizabeth II.

Virgin Islands Chart, 1739 — A48

18th Century Maps of Virgin Islands: 22c, 1758. 30c, 1775. 75c, 1779.

**Wmk. 373**

**1977, June 12 Litho. *Perf. 13½***

| | | | | |
|---|---|---|---|---|
| *320* | A48 | 8c multi | 22 | 20 |
| *321* | A48 | 22c multi | 55 | 48 |
| *322* | A48 | 30c multi | 70 | 60 |
| *323* | A48 | 75c multi | 1.65 | 1.50 |

Type of 1977 Inscribed: "ROYAL VISIT"

Designs: 5c, Queen visiting Agricultural Station, Tortola, 1966. 25c, Holy Bible. 50c, Presentation of Holy Bible.

**1977, Oct. 26 Litho. *Perf. 14x13½***

| | | | | |
|---|---|---|---|---|
| *324* | A47 | 5c yel brn & multi | 9 | 9 |
| *325* | A47 | 25c dk bl & multi | 45 | 45 |
| *326* | A47 | 50c pur & multi | 90 | 90 |

Caribbean visit of Queen Elizabeth II.

Divers Checking Equipment — A49

Tourist publicity: 5c, Cup coral inside bow of "Rhone." 8c, Sponge growing on superstructure of "Rhone." 22c, Sponge and cup coral. 30c, Scuba diver searching for sponges in cave. 75c, Marine life.

**Wmk. 373**

**1977, Dec. 15 Litho. *Perf. 13½***

| | | | | |
|---|---|---|---|---|
| *327* | A49 | ½c multi | 5 | 5 |
| *328* | A49 | 5c multi | 12 | 12 |
| *329* | A49 | 8c multi | 20 | 20 |
| *330* | A49 | 22c multi | 52 | 52 |
| *331* | A49 | 30c multi | 70 | 70 |
| *332* | A49 | 75c multi | 1.75 | 1.75 |
| | | *Nos. 327-332 (6)* | 3.34 | 3.34 |

Corals
A50

**1978, Feb. 10 *Perf. 14***

| | | | | |
|---|---|---|---|---|
| *333* | A50 | 8c Fire | 25 | 25 |
| *334* | A50 | 15c Staghorn | 45 | 45 |
| *335* | A50 | 40c Brain | 1.10 | 1.10 |
| *336* | A50 | 75c Elkhorn | 2.00 | 2.00 |

**Elizabeth II Coronation Anniversary Issue**

Common Design Types

**Souvenir Sheet**

**1978, June 2 Unwmk. *Perf. 15***

| | | | | |
|---|---|---|---|---|
| *337* | | Sheet of 6 | 4.75 | 4.75 |
| *a.* | | CD326 50c *Falcon of the Plantagenets* | 75 | 75 |
| *b.* | | CD327 50c *Elizabeth II* | 75 | 75 |
| *c.* | | CD328 50c *Iguana* | 75 | 75 |

No. 337 contains 2 se-tenant strips of Nos. 337a-337c, separated by horizontal gutter with commemorative and descriptive inscriptions and showing central part of coronation procession with coach. Size: 100x135mm.

Lignum Vitae
A51

Flowering Trees: 22c, Ginger thomas. 40c, Dog almond. 75c, White cedar.

**1978, Sept. 4 Litho. *Perf. 13x13½***

| | | | | |
|---|---|---|---|---|
| *338* | A51 | 8c multi | 20 | 20 |
| *339* | A51 | 22c multi | 52 | 52 |
| *340* | A51 | 40c multi | 90 | 90 |
| *341* | A51 | 75c multi | 1.50 | 1.50 |
| *a.* | | Souvenir sheet of 4 | 3.25 | 3.25 |

No. 314a contains one each of Nos. 338-341; multicolored decorative margin. Size: 130x95mm.

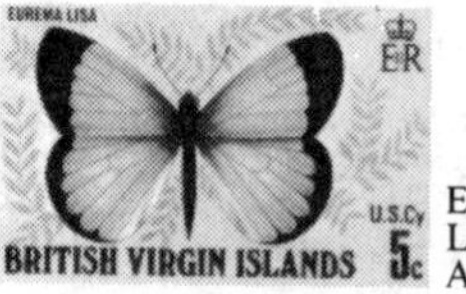


Eurema Lisa
A52

Butterflies: 22c, Dione vanillae. 30c, Heliconius charitonius. 75c, Hemiargus hanno.

**1978, Dec. 4 Wmk. 373 *Perf. 14***

| | | | | |
|---|---|---|---|---|
| *342* | A52 | 5c multi | 22 | 18 |
| *343* | A52 | 22c multi | 80 | 65 |
| *a.* | | Sheet of 9 | 4.50 | 4.50 |
| *344* | A52 | 30c multi | 1.00 | 90 |
| *345* | A52 | 75c multi | 2.25 | 2.25 |

No. 343a contains 6 No. 342 and 3 No. 343. Blue decorative margin. Size: 158x113mm.

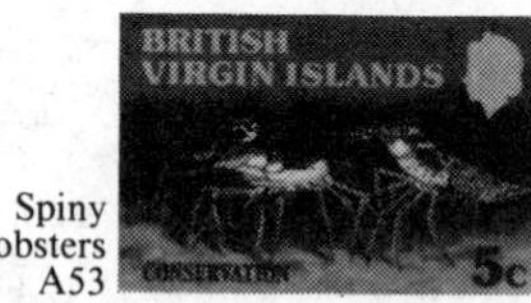


Spiny Lobsters
A53

Designs: 15c, Iguana (vert.). 22c, Hawksbill turtle. 75c, Black coral (vert.).

**1979, Feb. 10 Litho.**

| | | | | |
|---|---|---|---|---|
| *346* | A53 | 5c multi | 15 | 12 |
| *347* | A53 | 15c multi | 50 | 35 |
| *348* | A53 | 22c multi | 70 | 55 |
| *349* | A53 | 75c multi | 2.00 | 1.75 |
| *a.* | | Souvenir sheet of 4 | 3.50 | 3.50 |

Conservation. No. 349a contains Nos. 346-349; multicolored margin shows beach. Size: 130x154mm.

Strawberry Cactus — A54

West Indies Girl and Church — A55

Native Cacti: 5c, Snowy cactus. 13c, Barrel cactus. 22c, Tree cactus. 30c, Prickly pear. 75c, Dildo cactus.

**Wmk. 373**

**1979, May 7 Litho. *Perf. 14***

| | | | | |
|---|---|---|---|---|
| *350* | A54 | 1½c multi | 5 | 5 |
| *351* | A54 | 5c multi | 10 | 10 |
| *352* | A54 | 13c multi | 28 | 28 |
| *353* | A54 | 22c multi | 50 | 50 |
| *354* | A54 | 30c multi | 65 | 65 |
| *355* | A54 | 75c multi | 1.65 | 1.65 |
| | | *Nos. 350-355 (6)* | 3.23 | 3.23 |

***Perf. 14x14½***

**1979, July 9 Litho. Wmk. 373**

Children and IYC Emblem: 10c, African boy and dancers. 13c, Asian girl and children playing. $1, European girl and bicycle.

| | | | | |
|---|---|---|---|---|
| *356* | A55 | 5c multi | 7 | 7 |
| *357* | A55 | 10c multi | 16 | 16 |
| *258* | A55 | 13c multi | 20 | 20 |
| *359* | A55 | $1 multi | 1.50 | 1.50 |
| *a.* | | Souvenir sheet of 4 | 2.25 | 2.25 |

International Year of the Child. No. 359a contains Nos. 356-359. Black and yellow margin shows children from various countries. Size: 93x115mm.

No. 118 — A56

Rowland Hill's Signature and: 13c, Virgin Islands No. 11 (horiz.). 75c, Unissued Great Britain 2sh stamp, 1910 (horiz.). $1, Virgin Islands No. 8c.

**1979, Oct. 1 Photo. *Perf. 13½***

| | | | | |
|---|---|---|---|---|
| *360* | A56 | 5c multi | 10 | 10 |
| *361* | A56 | 13c multi | 24 | 24 |
| *362* | A56 | 75c multi | 1.40 | 1.40 |

**Souvenir Sheet**

| | | | | |
|---|---|---|---|---|
| *363* | A56 | $1 multi | 1.75 | 1.75 |

Sir Rowland Hill (1795-1879), originator of penny postage. Multicolored margin of No. 363 shows Mulready envelope. Size: 137x91mm.

Pencil Urchin — A57

**1979-80 Litho. *Perf. 14***

| | | | | |
|---|---|---|---|---|
| *364* | A57 | ½c *Calcified algae* | 5 | 5 |
| *365* | A57 | 1c *Purple-tipped sea anemone* | 5 | 5 |
| *366* | A57 | 3c *Starfish* | 6 | 6 |
| *367* | A57 | 5c *shown* | 10 | 10 |
| *368* | A57 | 8c *Triton's trumpet* | 14 | 14 |
| *369* | A57 | 10c *Christmas tree worms* | 18 | 18 |

370 A57 13c *Flamingo tongue snails* 22 22
371 A57 15c *Spider crab* 28 28
372 A57 18c *Sea squirts* 32 32
373 A57 20c *Tree tulip* 35 35
374 A57 25c *Rooster tail conch* 45 45
375 A57 30c *Fighting conch* 55 55
376 A57 60c *Mangrove crab* 1.10 1.10
377 A57 $1 *Coral polyps* 1.75 1.75
378 A57 $2.50 *Peppermint shrimp* 4.50 4.50
379 A57 $3 *West Indian murex* 5.25 5.25
380 A57 $5 *Carpet anemone* 9.00 9.00
*Nos. 364-380 (17)* 24.35 24.35

Issue dates: 5c, 8c, 10c, 15c, 20c, 25c, $2.50, $3, Dec. 17, 1979. Others, April 1, 1980.

Nos. 367-368, 370-371, 373, 375 reissued inscribed 1982.

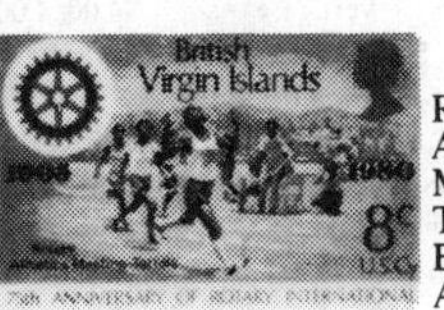

Rotary Athletic Meet, Tortola, Emblem A58

**1980, Mar. 3 Litho. *Perf. 13½x14***
381 A58 8c *shown* 12 12
382 A58 22c *Paul P. Harris* 35 35
383 A58 60c *Mount Sage National Park* 1.00 1.00
384 A58 $1 *Anniversary emblem* 1.50 1.50
*a* Souvenir sheet of 4 3.25 3.25

Rotary Intl., 75th anniv. No. 384 contains Nos. 381-384; multicolored margin shows Rotary creed and emblem. Size: 150x148mm.

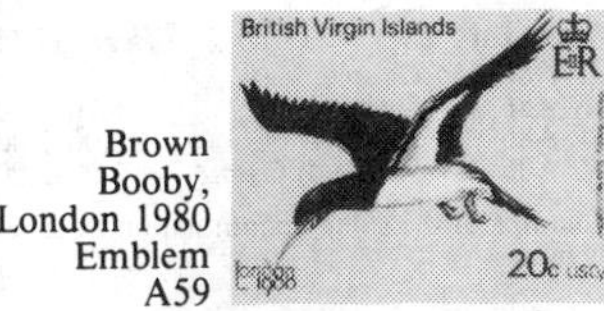

Brown Booby, London 1980 Emblem A59

**Wmk. 373**

**1980, May 6 Litho. *Perf. 14***
385 A59 20c *shown* 35 35
386 A59 25c *Magnificent frigatebird* 45 45
387 A59 50c *White-tailed tropic bird* 90 90
388 A59 75c *Brown pelican* 1.40 1.40
*a* Souvenir sheet of 4 3.50 3.50

London 80 Intl. Stamp Exhib., May 6-14. No. 388a contains Nos. 385-388; multicolored margin shows map of Virgin Islands, London 1980 emblem. Size: 152x130mm.

Nos. 361-362 Overprinted: "CARIBBEAN COMMONWEALTH PARLIAMENTARY ASSOCIATION MEETING TORTOLA 11-19 JULY 1980"

**1980, July 7 Photo. *Perf. 13½***
389 A56 13c multi 24 24
390 A56 75c multi 1.40 1.40

Sir Francis Drake — A60

**1980, Sept. 26 Litho. *Perf. 14½***
391 A60 8c *shown* 12 12
392 A60 15c *Queen Elizabeth I* 24 24
393 A60 30c *Drake knighted* 48 48
394 A60 75c *Golden Hinde* 1.25 1.25
*a* Souvenir sheet of 4 2.25 2.25

400th anniversary of circumnavigation of the world. No. 394a contains Nos. 391-394, multicolored margin shows globes and ships in continuous design. Size: 173x123mm.

Jost Van Dyke A61

**Wmk. 373**

**1980, Dec. 1 Litho. *Perf. 14***
395 A61 2c *shown* 5 5
396 A61 5c *Peter Island* 9 9
397 A61 13c *Virgin Gorda* 22 22
398 A61 22c *Anegada* 38 38
399 A61 30c *Norman Island* 50 50
400 A61 $1 *Tortola* 1.65 1.65
*a* Souvenir sheet 2.00 2.00
*Nos. 395-400 (6)* 2.89 2.89

No. 400a contains No. 400; multicolored margin shows islands. Size: 95x87mm.

Dancing Lady — A62

**Wmk. 373**

**1981, Mar. 3 Litho. *Perf. 11***
401 A62 5c shown 9 9
402 A62 20c Love in the mist 35 35
403 A62 22c Red pineapple 38 38
404 A62 75c Dutchman's pipe 1.25 1.25
405 A62 $1 Maiden apple 1.65 1.65
*Nos. 401-405 (5)* 3.72 3.72

Royal Wedding Issue
Common Design Type

**Wmk. 373**

**1981, July 22 Litho. *Perf. 14***
406 CD331 10c Bouquet 16 16
407 CD331 35c Charles, Queen Mother 60 60
408 CD331 $1.25 Couple 2.00 2.00

Nos. 406-408 each se-tenant with decorative label.

Duke of Edinburgh's Awards, 25th Anniv. — A63

**Wmk. 373**

**1981, Sept. 16 Litho. *Perf. 14***
409 A63 10c Stamp collecting 16 16
410 A63 15c Running 25 25
411 A63 50c Camping 85 85
412 A63 $1 Duke of Edinburgh 1.65 1.65

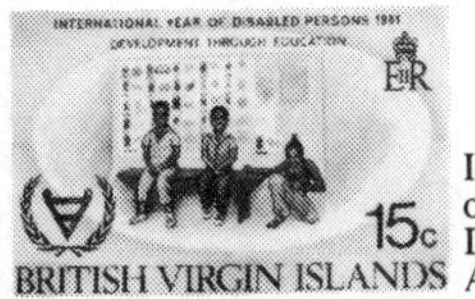

Intl. Year of the Disabled A64

**Wmk. 373**

**1981, Oct. 19 Litho. *Perf. 14***
413 A64 15c Children 30 30
414 A64 20c Fort Charlotte Children's Center 40 40
415 A64 30c Playing music 60 60
416 A64 $1 Center, diff. 2.00 2.00

Virgin and Child — A65

Christmas 1981: Details from Adoration of the Shepherds, by Rubens. 50c, horiz.

**Wmk. 373**

**1981, Nov. 30 Litho. *Perf. 14***
417 A65 5c multi 8 8
418 A65 15c multi 24 24
419 A65 30c multi 48 48
420 A65 $1 multi 1.50 1.50

**Souvenir Sheet**

421 A65 50c multi 1.00 1.00

No. 421 has multicolored margin showing entire painting. Size: 116x91mm.

Hummingbirds on Local Flora — A66

**1982, Apr. 15 Litho. *Perf. 14x14½***
422 A66 15c Green-throated carib, erythrina 35 35
423 A66 30c Same, bougainvillea 70 70
424 A66 35c Antillean crested hummingbird, granadilla passiflora 80 80
425 A66 $1.25 Same, hibiscus 2.75 2.75

10th Anniv. of Lions Club of Tortola — A67

**1982, May 3 *Perf. 13½x14***
426 A67 10c Helping disabled 18 18
427 A67 20c Headquarters 35 35
428 A67 30c Map 50 50
429 A67 $1.50 Emblem 2.50 2.50
*a* Souvenir sheet of 4 3.75 3.75

No. 429a contains Nos. 426-429; multicolored margin shows emblem. Size: 124x102mm.

**Princess Diana Issue**
Common Design Type

**1982, July 1 Litho. *Perf. 14***
430 CD333 10c Arms 16 16
431 CD333 35c Diana 55 55
432 CD333 50c Wedding 80 80
433 CD333 $1.50 Portrait 2.50 2.50

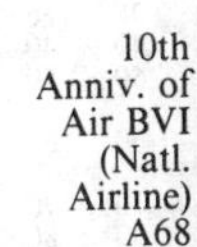

10th Anniv. of Air BVI (Natl. Airline) A68

**Wmk. 373**

**1982, Sept. 10 Litho. *Perf. 14***
434 A68 10c Douglas DC-3 20 20
435 A68 15c Britten-Norman Islander 30 30
436 A68 60c Hawker-Siddeley 1.20 1.20
437 A68 75c Planes 1.50 1.50

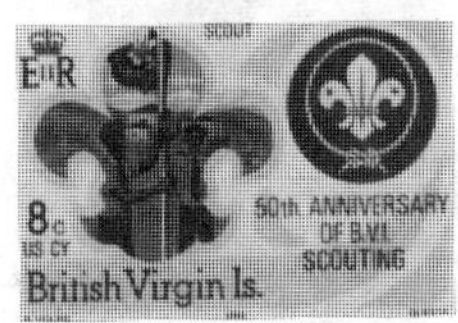

Scouting Year A69

**1982, Nov. 18**
438 A69 8c Emblem, Flag raising 16 16
439 A69 20c Cub scout, nature study 40 40
440 A69 50c Kayak, sea scout 1.00 1.00
441 A69 $1 Camp Brownsea Isld., Baden-Powell 2.00 2.00

Commonwealth Day — A70

**1983, Mar. 14 *Perf. 13½x14***
442 A70 10c Legislature in session 18 18
443 A70 30c Wind surfing 55 55
444 A70 35c Globe 65 65
445 A70 75c Flags 1.40 1.40

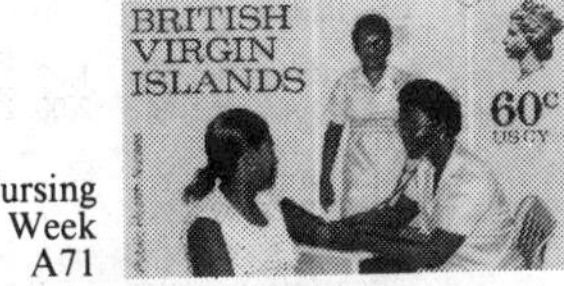

Nursing Week A71

**1983, May 9 Litho. *Perf. 14½***
446 A71 10c Florence Nightingale (1820-1910), vert. 20 20
447 A71 30c Nurse, assistant, vert. 60 60
448 A71 60c Public health 1.20 1.20
449 A71 75c Peebles Hospital 1.50 1.50

Boat Building A72

**1983, July 25 *Perf. 14***
450 A72 15c First stage 30 30
451 A72 25c 2nd stage 50 50
452 A72 50c Launching 1.00 1.00
453 A72 $1 First voyage 2.00 2.00
*a* Souvenir sheet of 4 (#450-453) 4.75 4.75

Manned Flight Bicentenary — A73

**Wmk. 373**

**1983, Sept. 15 Litho. *Perf. 14***
454 A73 10c Grumman Goose 20 20
455 A73 30c De Havilland Heron 60 60
456 A73 60c EMB Bandeirante 1.20 1.20
457 A73 $1.25 Hawker-Siddeley 748 2.50 2.50

Christmas 1983 — A74

Raphael Paintings.

**1983, Nov. 7 Litho. *Perf. 14½***

*458* A74 8c Madonna & Child with Infant Baptist 16 16
*459* A74 15c La Belle Jardiniere 30 30
*460* A74 50c Madonna del Granduca 1.00 1.00
*461* A74 $1 Terranuova Madonna 2.00 2.00
*a* Souv. sheet of 4, #458-461 3.50

World Chess Federation, 60th Anniv. A75

**1984, Feb. 20 Litho. *Perf. 14***

*462* A75 10c Local tournament 20 20
*463* A75 35c Chess pieces, vert. 70 70
*464* A75 75c 1980 Olympiad, Winning board, vert. 1.50 1.50
*465* A75 $1 Gold medal 2.00 2.00

**Lloyd's List Issue**

Common Design Type

**1984, Apr. 16 Litho. *Perf. 14½x14***

*466* CD335 15c Port Purcell, Tortola 30 30
*467* CD335 25c Boeing 747 50 50
*468* CD335 50c Shipwreck of RMS Rhone 1.00 1.00
*469* CD335 $1 Booker Viking 2.00 2.00

**Souvenir Sheet**

UPU Congress A76

**Wmk. 373**

**1984, May 16 Litho. *Perf. 14***

*470* A76 $1 Emblem, jet, mailboat 2.00 2.00

Size: 91x71mm.

1984 Summer Olympics A77

**1984, July 3**

*471* A77 15c Runners 35 35
*472* A77 15c Runner 35 35
*473* A77 20c Wind surfers 48 48
*474* A77 20c Wind surfer 48 48
*475* A77 30c Yachts 70 70
*476* A77 30c Yacht 70 70
*Nos. 471-476 (6)* 3.06 3.06

**Souvenir Sheet**

*477* A77 $1 Torch bearer, vert. 2.25 2.25

Stamps of same demonimation se-tenant. No. 477 has multicolored margin showing maps. Size: 97x69mm.

The Scott Catalogue value is a retail price, what you could expect to pay for the stamp in a grade of Fine-Very Fine. The value listed is a reference which reflects recent actual dealer selling price.

Festival (Slavery Abolition Sesquicentennial) A78

Designs: No. 478: a. Steel band. b. Calypso dancers. c. Dancers (men). d. Woman in traditional dress. e. Parade float. No. 479 (Sail color of boat(s) in foreground): a. Green & white. b. Red & white, white, purple & white. c. white, yellow & white, blue & white. d. Yellow, red & white. e. Purple & white, white. Nos. 478 and 479 each in continuous design.

***Perf. 13½x14***

**1984, Aug. 14 Litho. Wmk. 373**

*478* Strip of 5, Parade 1.00 1.00
*a.-e.* A78 10c, any single 20 20
*479* Strip of 5, Regatta 3.00 3.00
*a.-e.* A78 30c, any single 60 60

Local Boats A79

**Wmk. 373**

**1984, Nov. 15 Litho. *Perf. 13***

*480* A79 10c Sloop 20 20
*481* A79 35c Fishing boat 70 70
*482* A79 60c Schooner 1.20 1.20
*483* A79 75c Cargo boat 1.50 1.50
*a* Souv. sheet of 4, #480-483 3.75 3.75

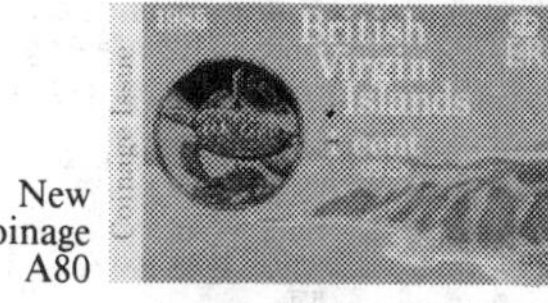


New Coinage A80

**1985, Jan. 15 Litho. *Perf. 14½***

*484* A80 1c Hawksbill Turtle 5 5
*485* A80 5c Bonito 10 10
*486* A80 10c Great Barricuda 20 20
*487* A80 25c Blue Marlin 50 50
*488* A80 50c Dolphin 1.00 1.00
*489* A80 $1 Spotfin Butterfly Fish 2.00 2.00
*a* Miniature sheet 4.00 4.00
*Nos. 484-489 (6)* 3.85 3.85

No. 489a contains Nos. 484-489; light green margin.

Birds — A81

**1985, July 3 Litho. *Perf. 14***

*490* A81 1c Red-billed tropic-bird 5 5
*491* A81 2c Yellow-crowned night heron 5 5
*492* A81 5c Mangrove cuckoo 10 10
*493* A81 8c Northern mock-ingbird 16 16
*494* A81 10c Gray kingbird 20 20
*495* A81 12c Red-necked pig-eon 24 24
*496* A81 15c Least bittern 30 30
*497* A81 18c Smooth-billed ani 36 36
*498* A81 20c Clapper rail 40 40
*499* A81 25c American kestrel 50 50
*500* A81 30c Pearly-eyed thrasher 60 60
*501* A81 35c Bridled quail dove 70 70
*502* A81 40c Green heron 80 80
*503* A81 50c Common ground dove 1.00 1.00
*504* A81 60c Little blue heron 1.20 1.20
*505* A81 $1 Audubon's shear-water 2.00 2.00
*506* A81 $2 Masked booby 4.00 4.00
*507* A81 $3 Cattle egret 6.00 6.00
*508* A81 $5 Zenaida dove 10.00 10.00
*Nos. 490-508 (19)* 28.66 28.66

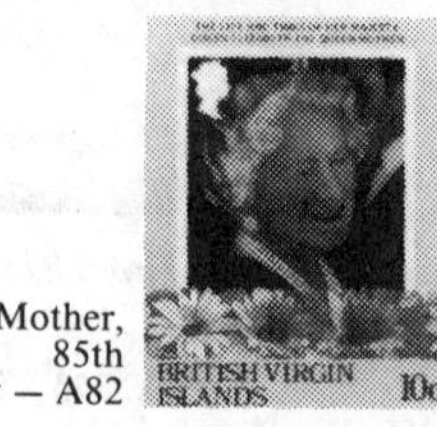


Queen Mother, 85th Birthday — A82

Portraits.

**1985, Aug. 26 Litho. *Perf. 12½***

*509* A82 10c Facing right 22 22
*510* A82 10c Facing left 22 22
*511* A82 25c Facing right 55 55
*512* A82 25c Facing left 55 55
*513* A82 50c Facing right 1.10 1.10
*514* A82 50c Facing forward 1.10 1.10
*515* A82 75c Facing right 1.65 1.65
*516* A82 75c Facing forward 1.65 1.65
*Nos. 509-516 (8)* 7.04 7.04

**Souvenir Sheets**

**1985-86 Litho. *Perf. 13x12½***

*517* Sheet of 2 4.00 4.00
*a.-b.* A82 $1 dl grn & multi 2.00 2.00
*518* Sheet of 2 4.00 4.00
*a.-b.* A82 $1 org & multi 2.00 2.00
*519* Sheet of 2 10.00 10.00
*a.-b.* A82 $2.50 dl yel & multi 5.00 5.00

Issue dates: No. 517, Dec. 18. Nos. 518-519, Feb. 18, 1986. Nos. 517-519 have multicolored margins picturing Buckingham Palace or flora, fauna and the Concorde.

Audubon Birth Bicent. — A83

**1985, Dec. 17 *Perf. 15***

*520* A83 5c Seaside sparrow 10 10
*521* A83 30c Passenger pigeon 60 60
*522* A83 50c Yellow-breasted chat 1.00 1.00
*523* A83 $1 American kestrel 2.00 2.00

Cruise Ships A84

**1986, Jan. 27**

*524* A84 35c Flying Cloud 70 70
*525* A84 50c Newport Clipper 1.00 1.00
*526* A84 75c Cunard Countess 1.50 1.50
*527* A84 $1 Sea Goddess 2.00 2.00

Nos. 511-512, 515-516 Ovptd. "MIAMI/ B.V.I./ INAUGURAL FLIGHT."

**1986, Apr. 17 Litho. *Perf. 12½***

*528* A82 25c on #511 50 50
*529* A82 25c on #512 50 50
*530* A82 75c on #515 1.50 1.50
*531* A82 75c on #516 1.50 1.50

Queen Elizabeth II, 60th Birthday — A85

***Perf. 13x12½, 12½x13***

**1986, Apr. 21 Litho.**

*532* A85 12c Portrait, 1958 24 24
*533* A85 35c Maundy service 70 70
*534* A85 $1.50 Contemporary photograph 3.00 3.00
*535* A85 $2 Canberra, 1982, vert. 4.00 4.00

**Souvenir Sheet**

*536* A85 $3 Contemporary photograph, diff. 6.00 6.00

No. 536 has multicolored margin picturing portrait enlargement.

Wedding of Prince Andrew and Sarah Ferguson — A86

**1986, July 23 *Perf. 12½***

*537* A86 35c Couple, vert. 70 70
*538* A86 35c Sarah, vert. 70 70
*539* A86 $1 Andrew 2.00 2.00
*540* A86 $1 Sarah, diff. 2.00 2.00

Stamps of the same denomination exist se-tenant.

Traditional Rum Production — A87

**1986, July 30 *Perf. 14***

*541* A87 12c Harvesting sugar cane 24 24
*542* A87 40c Grinding 80 80
*543* A87 60c Distillery 1.20 1.20
*544* A87 $1 Transport 2.00 2.00

**Souvenir Sheet**

*545* A87 $2 Up Spirits ceremony, 19th cent. 4.00 4.00

No. 545 has multicolored margin picturing flag signal, Trafalgar, tall ship and bottles of British Navy Pusser's Rum. Size: 115x85mm.

**Souvenir Sheet**

Wedding of Prince Andrew and Sarah Ferguson — A88

**1986, Oct. 15 Litho. *Perf. 13x12½***

*546* A88 $4 Newlyweds in open coach 8.00 8.00

No. 546 has inscribed multicolored margin continuing the design. Size: 105x85mm.

Cable-Laying Ships — A89

**Wmk. 380**

**1986, Oct. 15 Litho. *Perf. 12½***

*547* A89 35c Sentinel 70 70
*548* A89 35c Retriever 70 70
*549* A89 60c Cable Enterprise 1.20 1.20
*550* A89 60c Mercury 1.20 1.20
*551* A89 75c Recorder 1.50 1.50
*552* A89 75c Pacific Guardian 1.50 1.50
*553* A89 $1 Great Eastern 2.00 2.00
*554* A89 $1 Cable Venture 2.00 2.00
*Nos. 547-554 (8)* 10.80 10.80

**Souvenir Sheets**

*555* Sheet of 2 1.60 1.60
***a.-b*** A89 40c. like #547-548 80 80
*556* Sheet of 2 2.00 2.00
***a.-b*** A89 50c. like #549-550 1.00 1.00
*557* Sheet of 2 3.25 3.25
***a.-b*** A89 80c. like #551-552 1.60 1.60
*558* Sheet of 2 6.00 6.00
***a.-b*** A89 $1.50. like #553-554 3.00 3.00

Cable and wireless in the islands, 20th anniv. Stamps of the same denomination printed se-tenant. Nos. 555-556 and 557-558 have inscribed multicolored margins picturing detailed maps of cable routes.

**Souvenir Sheets**

Statue of Liberty, Cent. — A90

Various views of the statue.

**1986, Dec. 15 Litho. *Perf. 14***

*559* A90 50c multi 1.00 1.00
*560* A90 75c multi 1.50 1.50
*561* A90 90c multi 1.80 1.80
*562* A90 $1 multi 2.00 2.00
*563* A90 $1.25 multi 2.50 2.50
*564* A90 $1.50 multi 3.00 3.00
*565* A90 $1.75 multi 3.50 3.50
*566* A90 $2 multi 4.00 4.00
*567* A90 $2.50 multi 5.00 5.00

Nos. 559-567 have inscribed multicolored margins picturing views of the statue and US presidents Garfield, Taft, Truman, Arthur, Wilson, Eisenhower, Cleveland, Harding and Kennedy.

Nos. 537-540 Overprinted "Congratulations to T.R.H. The Duke & Duchess of York"

***Perf. 12½x13, 13x12½***

**1986, Oct. 15 Litho.**

*568* A86 35c No. 537 70 70
*569* A86 35c No. 538 70 70
*570* A86 $1 No. 539 2.00 2.00
*571* A86 $1 No. 540 2.00 2.00

Stamps of the same denomination exist printed se-tenant and tete-beche.

A91

Shipwrecks — A92

**1987, Apr. 15 *Perf. 14***

*572* A91 12c Spanish galleon, 18th cent. 24 24
*573* A91 35c HMS Astrea, 1808 70 70
*574* A91 75c RMS Rhone, 1867 1.50 1.50
*575* A91 $1.50 SS Rocus, 1929 3.00 3.00

**Souvenir Sheet**

*576* A92 $2.50 Brig Volvart, 1918 5.00 5.00

No. 576 has inscribed multicolored margin continuing the design. Size: 86x66mm.

Natl. Flags, Outline Maps — A93

**1987, May 28**

*577* A93 10c Montserrat 20 20
*578* A93 15c Grenada 30 30
*579* A93 20c Dominica 40 40
*580* A93 25c St. Kitts-Nevis 50 50
*581* A93 35c St. Vincent and Grenadines 70 70
*582* A93 50c Virgin Isls. 1.00 1.00
*583* A93 75c Antigua & Barbuda 1.50 1.50
*584* A93 $1 St. Lucia 2.00 2.00
*Nos. 577-584 (8)* 6.60 6.60

11th Meeting of the Organization of Eastern Caribbean States.

Botanical Gardens — A94

**1987, Aug. 12 Wmk. 384**

*585* A94 12c Spider lily 24 24
*586* A94 35c Barrel cactus 70 70
*587* A94 $1 Wild plantain 2.00 2.00
*588* A94 $1.50 Little butterfly orchid 3.00 3.00

**Souvenir Sheet**

*589* A94 $2.50 White cedar 5.00 5.00

No. 589 has multicolored margin picturing trellis in garden. Size: 139x103mm.

Postal Service Bicent. A95

Designs: 10c, 18th Cent. packet, No. 7 canceled "A13." 20c, Map of the islands, No. 22 canceled "A91." 35c, Tortola Post Office and Customs House, and No. 5 canceled "Tortola De 20 61." $1.50, Mail plane and No. 154 canceled "Road town No 2 64 Tortola W.I." $2.50, Late 19th cent. steam packet and No. 10 canceled "A Tortola Ap 12 70."

**Wmk. 384**

**1987, Dec. 17 Litho. *Perf. 14½***

*590* A95 10c multi 20 20
*591* A95 20c multi 40 40
*592* A95 35c multi 70 70
*593* A95 $1.50 multi 3.00 3.00

**Souvenir Sheet**

*594* A95 $2.50 multi 5.00 5.00

No. 594 has multicolored margin picturing various postmarks, registrations and postal markings. Size: 70x60mm.

Paintings by Titian — A96

Designs: 10c, *Salome,* 1512. 12c, *Man with the Glove,* c. 1520-1522. 20c, *Fabrizio Salvaresio,* 1558. 25c, *Daughter of Roberto Strozzi,* 1542. 40c, *Pope Julius II.*50c, *Bishop Ludovico Beccadelli,* 1552. 60c, *Philip II.*$1, *Empress Isabella of Portugal,* 1548. No. 603, *Emperor Charles V at Muhlberg,* 1548. No. 604, *Pope Paul III and His Grandsons,* 1546.

***Perf. 13½x14***

**1988, Aug. 11 Litho. Unwmk.**

*595* A96 10c multi 20 20
*596* A96 12c multi 24 24
*597* A96 20c multi 40 40
*598* A96 25c multi 50 50
*599* A96 40c multi 80 80
*600* A96 50c multi 1.00 1.00
*601* A96 60c multi 1.20 1.20
*602* A96 $1 multi 2.00 2.00
*Nos. 595-602 (8)* 6.34 6.34

**Souvenir Sheet**

*603* A96 $2 multi 4.00 4.00
*604* A96 $2 multi 4.00 4.00

Nos. 603-604 have multicolored margins continuing the paintings. Sizes: 110x95mm.

1st Annual Open Chess Tournament — A97

Designs: 35c, Pawn and Transporter aircraft over Sir Francis Drake Channel. $1, King and Jose Raul Capablanca (1888-1942), Cuban chess master and world champion from 1921 to 1927. $2, Match scene.

**Unwmk.**

**1988, Aug. 25 Litho. *Perf. 14***

*605* A97 35c multi 70 70
*606* A97 $1 multi 2.00 2.00

**Souvenir Sheet**

*607* A97 $2 multi 4.00 4.00

No. 607 has multicolored margin picturing board and chessmen: India, 19th cent., Persia, 11th cent., China, 18th cent., and Europe 12th cent. Size: 112x81mm.

1988 Summer Olympics, Seoul A98

**1988, Sept. 8**

*608* A98 12c Hurdling 24 24
*609* A98 20c Windsurfing 40 40
*610* A98 75c Basketball 1.50 1.50
*611* A98 $1 Tennis 2.00 2.00

**Souvenir Sheet**

*612* A98 $2 Running 4.00 4.00

No. 612 has multicolored margin continuing the design and picturing medalist. Size: 72x102mm.

Intl. Red Cross, 125th Anniv. A99

Safety warnings and steps in administering cardiopulmonary resuscitation (CPR): 12c, "Don't swim alone." 30c, "No swimming during electrical storms." 60c, "Don't eat before swimming." $1, "Proper equipment for boating." No. 617a, Turn victim on back. No. 617b, Position victim's chin so breathing passages are not blocked. No. 617c, Mouth-to-mouth resuscitation. No. 617d, Chest compressions. Nos. 617a-617d vert.

**1988, Sept. 26**

*613* A99 12c multi 24 24
*614* A99 30c multi 60 60
*615* A99 60c multi 1.20 1.20
*616* A99 $1 multi 2.00 2.00

**Souvenir Sheet**

*617* Sheet of 4 4.00 4.00
***a.-d.*** A99 50c any single 1.00 1.00

Nos. 617a-617d printed se-tenant in a continuous design. No. 617 has red and white margin in shape of a cross. Size: 68x96mm.

Visit of Princess Alexandra A100

World Wildlife Fund A101

Various photographs of the princess.

**1988, Nov. 9 Litho. *Perf. 14***

*618* A100 40c shown 80 80
*619* A100 $1.50 multi, diff. 3.00 3.00

**Souvenir Sheet**

*620* A100 $2 multi, diff. 4.00 4.00

No. 620 has multicolored margin picturing aircraft flying over the islands. Size: 102x98mm.

**1988, Nov. 15**

Brown pelicans, *Pelecanus occidentalis.*

*621* A101 10c Pelican in flight 20 20
*622* A101 12c Perched 24 24
*623* A101 15c Close-up of head 30 30
*624* A101 35c Swallowing fish 70 70

Reptiles, Marine Mammals and Birds A102

Designs: 20c, Anegada rock iguana. 40c, Virgin gorda dwarf gecko. 60c, Hawksbill turtle. $1, Humpback whale. No. 629, Northern shoveler, American wigeon and ring-necked ducks. No. 630, Trunk turtle.

**1988, Nov. 15**

*625* A102 20c multi 40 40
*626* A102 40c multi 80 80
*627* A102 60c multi 1.20 1.20
*628* A102 $1 multi 2.00 2.00

**Souvenir Sheets**

*629* A102 $2 multi 4.00 4.00
*630* A102 $2 multi 4.00 4.00

Nos. 629-630 have multicolored margins continuing the designs. Size: 107x76mm.

---

## WAR TAX STAMPS

Regular Issue of 1913 Overprinted **WAR STAMP**

**1916-17** **Wmk. 3** ***Perf. 14***
**Die I**

*MR1* A9 1p scarlet 25 25
*a.* 1p carmine 1.00 1.00
*MR2* A9 3p violet, *yellow* 1.00 1.00

---

## OFFICIAL STAMPS

**Catalogue values for unused stamps in this section, from this point to the end of the section, are for Never Hinged items.**

Nos. 365-368, 370-380 Overprinted "OFFICIAL" in Silver.

**1985, July** **Litho.** ***Perf. 14***

*O1* A57 1c Purple-tipped sea anemone 5 5
*O2* A57 3c Starfish 6 6
*O3* A57 5c Pencil urchin 10 10
*O4* A57 8c Triton's trumpet 16 16
*O5* A57 13c Flamingo tongue snail 25 25
*O6* A57 15c Spider crab 30 30
*O7* A57 18c Sea squirts 35 35
*O8* A57 20c True tulip 40 40
*O9* A57 25c Rooster tail conch 50 50
*O10* A57 30c Fighting conch 60 60
*O11* A57 60c Mangrove crab 1.20 1.20
*O12* A57 $1 Coral polyps 2.00 2.00
*O13* A57 $2.50 Peppermint shrimp 5.00 5.00
*O14* A57 $3 West Indian Murex 6.00 6.00
*O15* A57 $5 Carpet anemone 10.00 10.00
*Nos. O1-O15 (15)* 26.97 26.97

Nos. 490-508 Ovptd. "OFFICIAL."

**1986** **Litho.** ***Perf. 14***

*O16* A81 1c multi 5 5
*O17* A81 2c multi 5 5
*O18* A81 5c multi 10 10
*O19* A81 8c multi 16 16
*O20* A81 10c multi 20 20
*O21* A81 12c multi 24 24
*O22* A81 15c multi 30 30
*O23* A81 18c multi 36 36
*O24* A81 20c multi 40 40
*O25* A81 25c multi 50 50
*O26* A81 30c multi 60 60
*O27* A81 35c multi 70 70
*O28* A81 40c multi 80 80
*O29* A81 50c multi 1.00 1.00
*O30* A81 60c multi 1.20 1.20
*O31* A81 $1 multi 2.00 2.00
*O32* A81 $2 multi 4.00 4.00
*O33* A81 $3 multi 6.00 6.00
*O34* A81 $5 multi 10.00 10.00
*Nos. O16-O34 (19)* 28.66 28.66

Issue dates: 1c, 5c, 10c, 15c, 20c, 25c, 30c, 35c and $5, July 3. Others, Jan. 28.

---

# WESTERN AUSTRALIA

LOCATION — In the western part of Australia, occupying about a third of that continent.
GOVT. — A former British Colony
AREA — 975,920 sq. mi.
POP. — 184,124 (1901)
CAPITAL — Perth

Western Australia was one of the six British colonies that united on January 1, 1901, to form the Commonwealth of Australia.

12 Pence = 1 Shilling
20 Shillings = 1 Pound

Values of early Western Australia stamps vary according to condition. Quotations for Nos. 1-19 are for fine copies. Very fine to superb specimens sell at much higher prices, and inferior or poor copies sell at reduced prices, depending on the condition of the individual specimen.

Swan
A1 A2

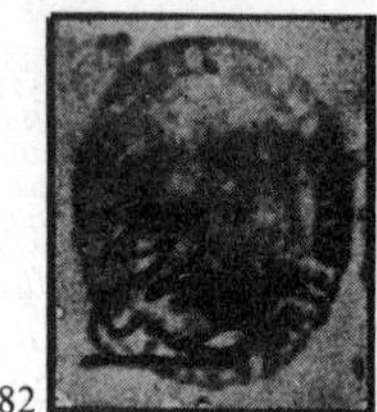

Wmk. 82

**Wmk. Swan. (82)**

**1854-57** **Engr.** ***Imperf.***

*1* A1 1p black 750.00 125.00

**Litho.**

*2* A2 2p brn, *red* ('57) 1,150. 350.00
*a.* 2p brn, *dp red* ('57) 1,300. 400.00
*b.* Printed on both sides 1,200. 800.00

See Nos. 4, 6-7, 9, 14-39, 44-52, 54, 59-61.

A3

A4

*3* A3 4p blue 300.00 125.00
*a.* Frame inverted 60,000.
As "a", cut to shape 6,000.
*b.* 4p sl bl 1,050. 475.00
*4* A2 6p brnz ('57) 3,000. 400.00
*5* A4 1sh pale brn 475.00 175.00
*a.* 1sh dk brn 600.00 375.00
*b.* 1sh dk red brn 900.00 550.00
*c.* 1sh pale red brn 1,800.

**Engraved**
***Rouletted***

*6* A1 1p black 1,750. 500.00

**Lithographed**

*7* A2 2p brn, *red* ('57) 3,250. 1,200.
*a.* Printed on both sides
*8* A3 4p blue 1,600. 600.00
*9* A2 6p brnz ('57) 3,500. 1,000.
*10* A4 1sh brown 2,250. 825.00

The 2p, 4p and 6p are known with pin-perforation but this is believed to be unofficial.

**1860** **Engr.** ***Imperf.***

*14* A1 2p vermilion 100.00 87.50
*a.* 2p pale org 95.00 60.00
*15* A1 4p blue 185.00 750.00
*16* A1 6p dl grn 1,200. 400.00

***Rouletted***

*17* A1 2p vermilion 600.00 180.00
*a.* 2p pale org 900.00 180.00
*18* A1 4p dp bl 2,500.
*19* A1 6p dl grn 400.00

**1861** ***Clean-Cut Perf. 14 to 16***

*20* A1 1p rose 330.00 75.00
*a.* Imperf.
*21* A1 2p blue 65.00 22.50
*a.* Imperf., pair
*b.* Imperf. vert., pair
*22* A1 4p vermilion 265.00 140.00
*a.* Imperf.
*23* A1 6p pur brn 145.00 35.00
*a.* Imperf.
*24* A1 1sh green 250.00 40.00
*a.* Imperf.

***Rough Perf. 14 to 16***

*24B* A1 1p rose 280.00 25.00
*24C* A1 6p pur brn, *bluish* 750.00 50.00
*24D* A1 1sh dp grn 1,350. 200.00

***Perf. 14***

*25* A1 1p rose 125.00 32.50
*25A* A1 2p blue 65.00 30.00
*25B* A1 4p vermilion 165.00 125.00

**Unwmk.** ***Perf. 13***

*26* A1 1p lake 32.50 5.50
*28* A1 6p violet 82.50 25.00

**1865-79** **Wmk. 1** ***Perf. 12½***

*29* A1 1p bister 37.50 1.40
*30* A1 1p yel ocher 67.50 4.00
*31* A1 2p yellow 37.50 60
*a.* 2p lil (error) ('79) 7,500. 3,750.
*32* A1 4p carmine 42.50 5.50
*a.* Double impression 7,500.
*33* A1 6p violet 62.50 6.00
*a.* 6p lil 130.00 6.00
*b.* 6p red lil 120.00 6.00
*c.* Double impression
*34* A1 1sh brt grn 65.00 10.50
*a.* 1sh sage grn 120.00 18.00

**1872-78** ***Perf. 14***

*35* A1 1p bister 42.50 2.00
*36* A1 1p yel ocher 40.00 48
*37* A1 2p yellow 40.00 40
*38* A1 4p carmine 180.00 47.50
*39* A1 6p lilac 90.00 3.25

A5 A8

**1872** **Typo.**

*40* A5 3p red brn 20.00 3.75
*a.* 3p brown 20.00 3.75

See Nos. 53, 92.

No. 31 Surcharged in Green ONE PENNY

**1875** **Engr.** ***Perf. 12½***

*41* A1 1p on 2p yel 250.00 32.50
*a.* Pair, one without surcharge
*b.* "O" of "ONE" omitted
*c.* Triple surcharge

Forged surcharges exist.

**Wmk. Crown and C. A. (2)**

**1882** **Engr.** ***Perf. 12***

*44* A1 1p ocher yel 70.00 1.65
*46* A1 2p yellow 82.50 1.10
*47* A1 4p carmine 145.00 27.50
*48* A1 6p pale vio 215.00 27.50

**1882** ***Perf. 14***

*49* A1 1p ocher yel 11.50 20
*50* A1 2p yellow 13.00 20
*51* A1 4p carmine 13.00 11.50
*52* A1 6p pale vio 47.50 2.00
*a.* 6p violet 47.50 2.00

**Typographed**

*53* A5 3p red brn 6.50 45
*a.* 3p brown 10.00 45

**1883** **Engr.** ***Perf. 12x14***

*54* A1 1p ocher yellow 1,650. 200.00

Nos. 44 and 49 Surcharged in Red $\frac{1}{2}$

**1884** ***Perf. 12***

*55* A1 ½p on 1p ocher yel 6.00 4.00

***Perf. 14***

*56* A1 ½p on 1p ocher yel 11.50 8.00

No. 40 Surcharged in Green **1d.**

**1885** **Typo.** **Wmk. 1**

*57* A5 1p on 3p red brn 11.50 5.00
*a.* 1p on 3p brown 11.50 5.00
*b.* "1" with straight top 27.50 11.00

**Wmk. Crown and C. A. (2)**

**1885** **Typo.** ***Perf. 14***

*58* A8 ½p green 75 10

See No. 89.

**1888** **Engr.**

*59* A1 1p rose 13.00 70
*60* A1 2p slate 17.50 2.00
*61* A1 4p red brn 82.50 15.00

A9 A10

A11 A12

**1890-93** **Typo.**

*62* A9 1p car rose 3.25 10
*63* A10 2p slate 3.25 10
*64* A11 2½p blue 6.00 50
*65* A12 4p org brn 6.00 50
*66* A12 5p bister 8.25 65
*67* A12 6p violet 10.00 50
*68* A12 1sh ol grn 11.50 65
*Nos. 62-68 (7)* 48.25 3.00

See Nos. 73-74, 76, 80, 90, 94.

Nos. 40 and 53a Surcharged in Green **ONE PENNY**

**1893** **Wmk. Crown and C. C. (1)**

*69* A5 1p on 3p red brn 8.00 6.75
*a.* 1p on 3p brown 8.00 6.75
*b.* Double surcharge 725.00

**Wmkd. Crown and C. A. (2)**

*70* A5 1p on 3p brown 40.00 9.00

Nos. 40a and 53a Surcharged in Green **Half-penny**

**1895** **Wmk. Crown and C. C. (1)**

*71* A5 ½p on 3p brn 2.50 2.75
*a.* Double surcharge 700.00

**Green and Red Surcharge**

*72* A5 ½p on 3p brn 125.00

**Wmk. Crown and C. A. (2)**

*72A* A5 ½p on 3p brn 70.00

After the supply of paper watermarked Crown and C C was exhausted, No. 72A was printed. Ostensibly this was to provide samples for Postal Union distribution, but a supply for philatelic demands was also made.

Types of 1890-93 and

A15

Wmk. 83- Crown and W A

**1899-1901** **Typo.** **Wmk. 83**

*73* A9 1p car rose 3.00 10
*74* A10 2p yellow 5.00 15
*75* A15 2½p blue ('01) 5.00 18

A16

A17

*Western Australia stamps can be mounted in Scott's Australia and Dependencies Album.*

A18 A19

A20 A21

A22 Southern Cross — A23

Queen Victoria
A24 A25

Wmk. 70- V and Crown

Wmk. 13- Crown and Double-lined A

***Perf. 12½, 12x12½***

**1902-05** **Wmk. 70**

*76* A9 1p car rose 1.10 8
**a.** 1p salmon
**b.** Perf. 11 100.00 5.00
**c.** Perf. 12½x11 180.00
*77* A16 2p yellow 1.65 20
**a.** Perf. 11 125.00 5.50
**b.** Perf. 12½x11 220.00
*79* A17 4p org brn 4.00 80
**a.** Perf. 11 365.00 110.00
*80* A12 5p ol bis ('05) 72.50 19.00
**a.** Perf. 11 72.50 19.00
*81* A18 8p pale yel grn 14.00 2.75
*82* A19 9p orange 16.00 4.00
**b.** Perf. 11 60.00 40.00
*83* A20 10p red 32.50 5.50
*84* A21 2sh red, *yel* 42.50 8.25
**a.** Perf. 11 125.00 55.00
*85* A22 2sh6p dk bl, *rose* 37.50 8.25
*86* A23 5sh bl grn 75.00 19.00
*87* A24 10sh violet 180.00 67.50
*88* A25 £1 brn org 600.00 150.00
*Nos. 76-88 (12)* 1,076. 285.33

***Perf. 12½, 12x12½***

**1905-12** **Wmk. 13**

*89* A8 ½p dp grn ('10) 1.25 28
*90* A9 1p rose 2.00 10
**e.** Perf. 11 6.50 70
**f.** Perf. 12½x11 200.00 82.50
*91* A16 2p yellow 1.25 10
**a.** Perf. 11 10.00 2.25
**b.** Perf. 12½x11 230.00 95.00
*92* A5 3p brown 4.00 40
**a.** Perf. 11 8.25 2.75
**b.** Perf. 12½x11 265.00 82.50
*93* A17 4p org brn 5.00 32
**a.** 4p bis brn 6.50 32
**b.** Perf. 11 465.00 90.00
*94* A12 5p ol bis 6.00 70
**a.** Perf. 11 16.00 1.65
*95* A18 8p pale yel grn ('12) 11.50 5.50
*96* A19 9p orange 8.25 1.65
**b.** Perf. 11 65.00 55.00
*97* A20 10p red org 13.00 4.75
*98* A23 5s bl grn 140.00 32.50
*Nos. 89-98 (10)* 192.25 46.30

A26

A27

**1906-07** **Wmk. 83** ***Perf. 14***

*99* A26 6p bright vio 11.50 70
*100* A27 1sh olive green 25.00 6.00

Wmk.74

**Wmk. Crown and Single-lined A (74)**

**1912** ***Perf. 11½x12***

*101* A26 6p brt vio 11.00 3.00
*102* A27 1sh gray grn 18.00 4.00
**a.** Perf. 12½

No. 91 Surcharged **ONE PENNY**

**1912** **Wmk. 13** ***Perf. 12½***

*103* A16 1p on 2p yellow 75 38

Stamps of Western Australia were replaced by those of Australia.

---

## ZAMBIA

LOCATION — Southern Africa
GOVT. — Republic
AREA — 290,586 sq. mi.
POP. — 6,242,000 (est. 1982)
CAPITAL — Lusaka

The former British protectorate of Northern Rhodesia became an independent republic October 24, 1964, taking the name Zambia. See Northern Rhodesia; see Rhodesia and Nyasaland.

12 Pence = 1 Shilling
20 Shillings = 1 Pound
100 Ngwee = 1 Kwacha (1968)

**Catalogue values for all unused stamps in this country are for Never Hinged items.**

Pres. Kenneth D. Kaunda, Victoria Falls — A1

College of Further Education, Lusaka — A2

Design: 1sh3p, Barotse dancer.

***Perf. 14½x14, 14x14½***

**1964, Oct. 24** **Photo.** **Unwmk.**

*1* A1 3p bl, brn & grn 8 8
*2* A2 6p dk vio & yel 15 15
*3* A1 1sh3p org, blk & red 30 30

Zambia's independence, Oct. 24, 1964.

Farmer and Silo
A3

X-Ray Technician
A4

Designs: 2p, Chinyau dancer. 3p, Woman picking cotton. 4p, Angoni bull. 6p, Communications by drum and teletype. 9p, Redwood blossoms and factory. 1sh, Night fishing on Lake Tanganyika. 1sh3p, Woman tobacco worker. 2sh, Tonga basket maker and child. 2sh6p, Elephants in Luangwa Valley Game Reserve. 5sh, Child and school. 10sh, Copper mining. £1, Makishi dancer.

**1964, Oct. 24** **Photo.** ***Perf. 14½***
**Size: 23x19mm, 19x23mm**

*4* A3 ½p emer, blk & red 5 5
*5* A4 1p ultra, blk & brn 5 5
*6* A4 2p org, brn & red 6 6
*7* A4 3p red & blk 8 5
*8* A3 4p org & blk 8 8

***Perf. 13½x14½, 14½x13½***
**Size: 32x23mm, 23x32mm**

*9* A3 6p Prus grn, brn & org 12 18
*10* A3 9p ultra, brn & dk car rose 16 12
*11* A3 1sh bl, bis & blk 24 14
*12* A4 1sh3p dk bl, ver, blk & yel 28 14
*13* A4 2sh org, blk, brn & ultra 50 35
*14* A3 2sh6p org yel & blk 55 42
*15* A3 5sh emer, blk & yel 1.25 70
*16* A3 10sh org & blk 2.50 1.90
*17* A4 £1 red, blk, brn & yel 5.00 3.25
*Nos. 4-17 (14)* 10.92 7.49

ITU Emblem, Old and New Communication Equipment — A5

**1965, July 26** **Photo.** ***Perf. 14***

*18* A5 6p brt lil & gold 20 16
*19* A5 2sh6p gray & gold 70 55

Cent. of the ITU.

ICY Emblem
A6

**1965, July 26** ***Perf. 14***

*20* A6 3p grnsh bl & gold 20 15
*21* A6 1sh3p ultra & gold 50 45

International Cooperation Year, 1965.

Pres. Kaunda and State House, Lusaka
A7

Clematopsis
A8

Designs: 6p, Fireworks over Independence Stadium. 2sh6p, Tithonia diversifolia.

***Perf. 13½x14½***

**1965, Oct. 18** **Photo.** **Unwmk.**

*22* A7 3p multi 8 8
*23* A7 6p ind, yel & brt pink 12 12

***Perf. 14***

*24* A8 1sh3p pink, yel & brn 28 28
*25* A8 2sh6p brt grn, dp org & brn 55 55

1st anniv. of independence, Oct. 24.

WHO Headquarters, Geneva — A9

**1966, May 18** ***Perf. 14***

*26* A9 3p rose brn, brt bl & gold 10 10
*27* A9 1sh3p vio bl, brt bl & gold 50 50

Inauguration of the WHO Headquarters, Geneva.

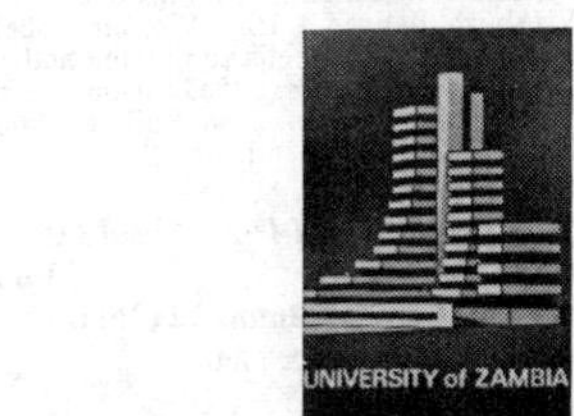

University of Zambia — A10

**1966, July 12** **Photo.** ***Perf. 14***

*28* A10 3p brt grn & gold 10 10
*29* A10 1sh3p brt pur & gold 50 50

Issued to commemorate the opening of the University of Zambia, March 17, 1966.

National Assembly Building
A11

**1967, May 2** **Unwmk.** ***Perf. 14***

*30* A11 3p sl & brnz 10 10
*31* A11 6p yel grn & brnz 35 35

Completion of National Assembly Building.

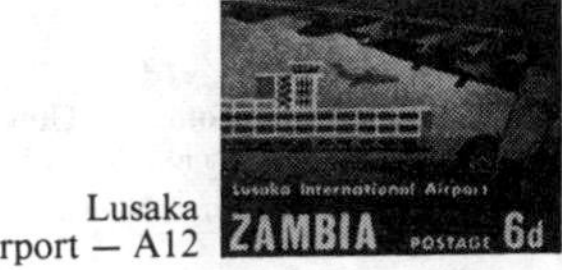

Lusaka Airport — A12

**1967, Oct. 2** **Photo.** ***Perf. 13½x14½***

*32* A12 6p vio bl & brnz 15 15
*33* A12 2sh6p brn & brnz 70 70

Opening of Lusaka International Airport.

Symbols of Agriculture
A13

Radio, Telephone and Television
A14

Designs: 4p, Emblem of Zambia Youth Service. 1sh, Map showing locations of Zambia coalfields. 1sh6p, Map showing Zambia-Tanzania Road.

***Perf. 14½x13½, 13½x14½***

**1967, Oct. 23**

| | | | | |
|---|---|---|---|---|
| *34* | A14 | 4p gray, red & gold | 8 | 8 |
| *35* | A13 | 6p lt vio bl, gold & blk | 12 | 12 |
| *36* | A14 | 9p dl bl, sil & blk | 16 | 16 |
| *37* | A14 | 1sh gold, red, blk & vio bl | 20 | 20 |
| *38* | A13 | 1sh6p bl grn, ultra, gold & blk | 35 | 35 |
| | | *Nos. 34-38 (5)* | 91 | 91 |

Issued to publicize National Development.

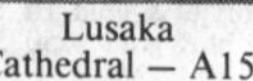


Lusaka Cathedral — A15

Baobab Tree — A16

Designs: 3n, Zambia Airways plane. 5n, National Museum, Livingstone. 8n, Vimbuza dancer. 10n, Woman tobacco picker. 15n, Nudaurelia zambesina butterfly. 20n, Crowned cranes. 25n, Angoni warrior. 50n, Chokwe dancer. 1k, Railroad bridge, Kafue River. 2k, Eland.

***Perf. 13½x14½, 14½x13½***

**1968, Jan. 16** **Photo.**

**Size: 26x22mm, 22x26mm**

| | | | | |
|---|---|---|---|---|
| *39* | A15 | 1n brnz & multi | 5 | 5 |
| *a* | | Booklet pane of 6 | 20 | |
| *b* | | Booklet pane of 4 | 15 | |
| *40* | A16 | 2n brnz & multi | 6 | 5 |
| *41* | A15 | 3n brnz & multi | 9 | 5 |
| *a* | | Booklet pane of 6 | 60 | |
| *b* | | Booklet pane of 4 | 40 | |
| *42* | A16 | 5n sep & brnz | 10 | 6 |
| *43* | A16 | 8n brnz & multi | 20 | 12 |
| *44* | A16 | 10n brnz & multi | 24 | 10 |

**Size: 32x26mm, 26x32mm**

| | | | | |
|---|---|---|---|---|
| *45* | A15 | 15n brnz & multi | 35 | 16 |
| *46* | A16 | 20n brnz & multi | 50 | 28 |
| *47* | A16 | 25n brnz & multi | 55 | 35 |
| *48* | A16 | 50n brnz, org & blk | 1.25 | *35* |
| *49* | A15 | 1k dk bl & brnz | 2.00 | *90* |
| *50* | A15 | 2k cop & blk | 5.00 | *2.00* |
| | | *Nos. 39-50 (12)* | 10.39 | *4.47* |

Used values of Nos. 48-50 are for canceled-to-order stamps. Postally used copies sell for higher prices.

Map of Zambia, Arrow Pointing to Ndola — A17

***Perf. 14½x14***

**1968, June 29** **Photo.** **Unwmk.**

| | | | | |
|---|---|---|---|---|
| *51* | A17 | 15n brt grn & gold | 38 | 38 |

Zambia Trade Fair at Ndola.

Children and Human Rights Flame — A18

WHO Emblem — A19

Children A20

**Photogravure; Gold Impressed**

**1968, Oct. 23** ***Perf. 14½x14***

| | | | | |
|---|---|---|---|---|
| *52* | A18 | 3n ultra, dk bl & gold | 10 | 10 |
| *53* | A19 | 10n brt vio & gold | 28 | 28 |
| *54* | A20 | 25n brt bl, blk & gold | 70 | 70 |

Intl. Human Rights Year; 20th anniv. of WHO; 21st anniv. of UNICEF (25n).

Copper Miner — A21

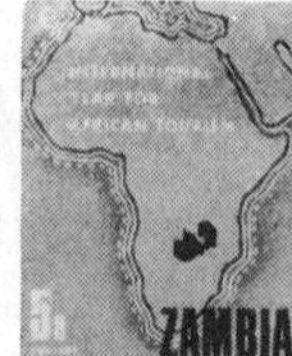


Map of Africa with Zambia — A22

Design: 25n, Worker poling furnace (horiz.).

***Perf. 14½x13½***

**1969, June 18** **Photo.**

| | | | | |
|---|---|---|---|---|
| *55* | A21 | 3n dp vio & cop | 8 | 8 |
| *56* | A21 | 25n yel, blk & cop | 75 | 75 |

50th anniv. of the ILO.

***Perf. 13½x14, 14x13½***

**1969, Oct. 23** **Photo.**

Designs: 10n, Waterbucks, Kafue National Park (horiz.). 15n, Golden perch, Kasaba Bay (horiz.). 25n, Carmine bee-eater, Luangwa Valley.

| | | | | |
|---|---|---|---|---|
| *57* | A22 | 5n ultra, yel & cop | 18 | 18 |
| *58* | A22 | 10n cop & multi | 35 | 35 |
| *59* | A22 | 15n cop & multi | 55 | 55 |
| *60* | A22 | 25n cop & multi | 90 | 90 |

International Year of African Tourism.

Nimbus III Weather Satellite — A23

**1970, Mar. 23** **Litho.** ***Perf. 13x11***

| | | | | |
|---|---|---|---|---|
| *61* | A23 | 15n multi | 55 | 55 |

Issued for World Meteorological Day.

"Clean Water" — A24

Designs: 15n, "Nutrition" (infant on scale). 25n, Children's immunization and Edward Jenner, M.D.

**1970, July 4** **Litho.** ***Perf. 13x12½***

| | | | | |
|---|---|---|---|---|
| *62* | A24 | 3n multi | 12 | 12 |
| *63* | A24 | 15n multi | 55 | 55 |
| *64* | A24 | 25n multi | 95 | 95 |

Issued to publicize preventive medicine and the "Under Five" children's clinics.

Mural by Gabriel Ellison A25

**1970, Sept. 8** **Litho.** ***Perf. 14x14½***

| | | | | |
|---|---|---|---|---|
| *65* | A25 | 15n multi | 40 | 40 |

Opening of the Conf. of Non-Aligned Nations in Mulungushi Hall (decorated with murals by Mrs. Ellison) in Zambia.

Ceremonial Axe — A26

Traditional Crafts: 5n, Clay pipe bowl with antelope head. 15n, Makishi mask (vert.). 25n, The Kuomboka Ceremony (dancers and ceremonial boat).

**1970, Nov. 30** **Litho.** ***Perf. 14x14½***

**Size: 34x25mm**

| | | | | |
|---|---|---|---|---|
| *66* | A26 | 3n dp lil rose & multi | 8 | 8 |
| *67* | A26 | 5n dp org, blk & sep | 15 | 15 |

***Perf. 13x13½***

**Size: 30x45½mm**

| | | | | |
|---|---|---|---|---|
| *68* | A26 | 15n dp lil rose & multi | 45 | 45 |

***Perf. 12½***

**Size: 71½x23½mm**

| | | | | |
|---|---|---|---|---|
| *69* | A26 | 25n vio, bl & multi | 75 | 75 |
| *a* | | Souvenir sheet of 4 | 6.00 | 6.00 |

No. 69a contains one each of Nos. 66-69, inscribed in margin "Zambia Traditional Crafts." Size: 132½x82mm.

Dag Hammarskjold and U.N. General Assembly — A27

Designs (Hammarskjold and): 10n, Downed plane. 15n, Dove with olive branch. 25n, Plaque and flowers.

**1971, Sept. 18** ***Perf. 13½***

| | | | | |
|---|---|---|---|---|
| *70* | A27 | 4n brn & multi | 9 | 9 |
| *71* | A27 | 10n yel grn & multi | 24 | 24 |
| *72* | A27 | 15n bl & multi | 35 | 35 |
| *73* | A27 | 25n plum & multi | 60 | 60 |

10th anniv. of the death of Dag Hammarskjold, (1905-61) Secretary-General of the UN, near Ndola, Zambia.

Red-Breasted Bream — A28

**1971, Dec. 10**

| | | | | |
|---|---|---|---|---|
| *74* | A28 | 4n *Red-breasted bream* | 20 | 18 |
| *75* | A28 | 10n *Green-headed bream* | 60 | 50 |
| *76* | A28 | 15n *Tigerfish* | 1.25 | 75 |

Christmas 1971.

Cheetah — A29

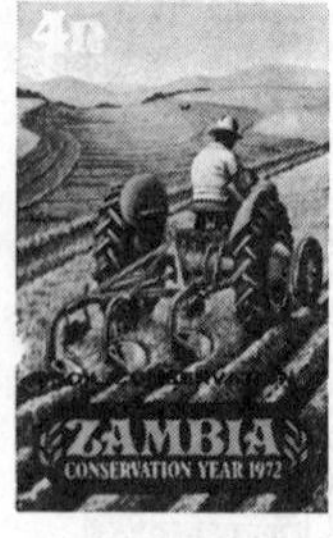


Soil Conservation A30

**1972, Mar. 15** ***Perf. 13½x14***

| | | | | |
|---|---|---|---|---|
| *77* | A29 | 4n *Cheetah* | 30 | 20 |
| *78* | A29 | 10n *Lechue* | 75 | 60 |

***Perf. 14x13½***

| | | | | |
|---|---|---|---|---|
| *79* | A30 | 15n *Cape porcupine* | 1.25 | 90 |
| *80* | A30 | 25n *Elephant* | 3.00 | 1.50 |

Conservation Year 1972.

**1972, June 30** **Litho.** ***Perf. 14x13½***

**Size: 18½x45mm**

| | | | | |
|---|---|---|---|---|
| *81* | A30 | 4n *shown* | 25 | 25 |
| *82* | A30 | 10n *Forest conservation* | 75 | 75 |

***Perf. 13½x14***

| | | | | |
|---|---|---|---|---|
| *83* | A29 | 15n *Water conservation (river view)* | 1.10 | 1.10 |
| *84* | A29 | 25n *Woman in corn field* | 1.90 | 1.90 |

**Souvenir Sheet**

| | | | | |
|---|---|---|---|---|
| *85* | | Sheet of 4 | 7.25 | 7.25 |
| *a* | A30 | 10n *Giraffe and zebra* | 1.40 | |
| *b* | A30 | 10n *Rhinoceros* | 1.40 | |
| *c* | A30 | 10n *Hippopotamus and deer* | 1.40 | |
| *d* | A30 | 10n *Lion* | 1.40 | |

Conservation Year 1972. Nos. 85a-85d printed se-tenant with map of Zambia in background. Multicolored border. Stamp size: 27x50mm.; sheet size: 114x139mm.

**1972, Sept. 22** ***Perf. 13½x14***

Designs: All horizontal.

**Size: 48x35mm**

| | | | | |
|---|---|---|---|---|
| *86* | A30 | 4n *Zambian flowers* | 90 | 60 |
| *87* | A30 | 10n *Citrus swallowtails and roses* | 1.90 | 1.50 |
| *88* | A30 | 15n *Bee* | 3.50 | 2.50 |
| *89* | A30 | 25n *Locusts in corn field* | 5.25 | 3.50 |

Conservation Year 1972.

Mary and Joseph Going to Bethlehem A31

**1972, Dec. 1** **Litho.** ***Perf. 14***

| | | | | |
|---|---|---|---|---|
| *90* | A31 | 4n *shown* | 10 | 10 |
| *91* | A31 | 9n *Holy Family* | 30 | 30 |
| *92* | A31 | 15n *Adoration of the shepherds* | 50 | 50 |
| *93* | A31 | 25n *Kings following the star* | 85 | 85 |

Christmas 1972.

Broken Hill Man — A32

Designs: 4n, Oudenodon and rubidgea (artist's conception; vert.). 10n, Zambia-saurus. 15n, Skull of Luangwa Drysdalli. 25n, Glossoptoris (seed).

*Perf. 14x13½, 14*

**1973, Feb. 1** **Litho.**

**Size: 29x45mm**

| | | | | |
|---|---|---|---|---|
| *94* | A32 | 4n org ver & multi | 65 | 32 |

**Size: 37½x21mm**

| | | | | |
|---|---|---|---|---|
| *95* | A32 | 9n org ver & multi | 1.00 | 65 |
| *96* | A32 | 10n ap grn & multi | 1.10 | 85 |
| *97* | A32 | 15n lil & multi | 1.50 | 1.10 |
| *98* | A32 | 25n org brn & multi | 2.75 | 2.75 |
| | | *Nos. 94-98 (5)* | 7.00 | 5.67 |

Fossils from Luangwa area (except 9n), over 200 million years old.

Meeting of Stanley and Livingstone at Ujiji — A33

Designs: 4n, Livingstone, the missionary. 9n, Livingstone at Victoria Falls. 10n, Livingstone stopping slave traders. 15n, Livingstone, the physician. 25n, Portrait and tree in Chitumbu, marking burial place of heart.

**1973, May 1** *Perf. 13x13½*

| | | | | |
|---|---|---|---|---|
| *99* | A33 | 3n multi | 28 | 28 |
| *100* | A33 | 4n multi | 42 | 42 |
| *101* | A33 | 9n multi | 85 | 85 |
| *102* | A33 | 10n multi | 1.00 | 1.00 |
| *103* | A33 | 15n multi | 1.50 | 1.50 |
| *104* | A33 | 25n multi | 2.50 | 2.50 |
| | | *Nos. 99-104 (6)* | 6.55 | 6.55 |

Dr. David Livingstone (1813-73), medical missionary and explorer.

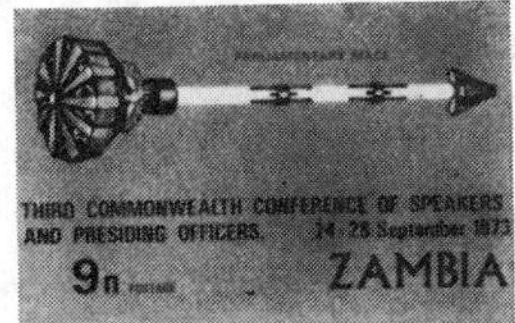


Parliamentary Mace — A34

**1973, Sept. 24** **Litho.** *Perf. 13½x14*

| | | | | |
|---|---|---|---|---|
| *105* | A34 | 9n tan & multi | 80 | 80 |
| *106* | A34 | 15n gray & multi | 1.50 | 1.50 |
| *107* | A34 | 25n brt grn & multi | 2.00 | 2.00 |

Third Commonwealth Conference of Speakers and Presiding Officers, Lusaka.

Vaccination — A35

Designs (WHO Emblem and): 4n, Mother washing infant (vert.). 9n, Nurse weighing infant (vert.). 15n, Child eating cereal and fruit.

**1973, Oct. 16** **Litho.** *Perf. 14*

| | | | | |
|---|---|---|---|---|
| *108* | A35 | 4n bl & multi | *90.00* | *30.00* |
| *109* | A35 | 9n org & multi | 35 | 35 |
| *110* | A35 | 10n brt grn & multi | 45 | 45 |
| *111* | A35 | 15n vio & multi | 60 | 60 |

WHO, 25th anniv.

UNIP Flag — A36

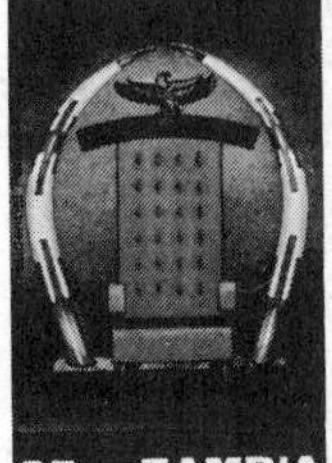


President's Parliamentary Chair — A37

Designs: 9n, United National Independence Party Headquarters, Lusaka. 10n, Army band. 15n, Women dancing and singing.

**1973, Dec. 13** **Litho.** *Perf. 14x13½*

| | | | | |
|---|---|---|---|---|
| *112* | A36 | 4n multi | *25.00* | *5.00* |
| *113* | A36 | 9n multi | 22 | 22 |
| *114* | A36 | 10n multi | 30 | 30 |
| *115* | A36 | 15n multi | 45 | 45 |
| *116* | A37 | 25n multi | 75 | 75 |
| | | *Nos. 112-116 (5)* | *26.72* | *6.72* |

Birth of the Second Republic.

Pres. Kaunda and his Home During Struggle for Independence — A38

Designs: 4n, Pres. Kaunda at Mulungushi (vert.). 15n, Pres. Kaunda holding torch of freedom.

**1974, Apr. 28** **Litho.** *Perf. 14½x14*

| | | | | |
|---|---|---|---|---|
| *117* | A38 | 4n multi | 85 | 85 |
| *118* | A38 | 9n multi | 1.10 | 1.10 |
| *119* | A38 | 15n multi | 1.65 | 1.65 |

50th birthday of Pres. Kenneth Kaunda.

Nakambla Sugar Estate — A39

Designs: 4n, Local market. 9n, Kapiri glass factory. 10n, Kafue hydroelectric plant. 15n, Kafue Bridge. 25n, Conference of Non-aligned Nations, Lusaka, 1970.

**1974, Oct. 24** **Litho.** *Perf. 13½x14*

| | | | | |
|---|---|---|---|---|
| *120* | A39 | 3n multi | 14 | 14 |
| *121* | A39 | 4n multi | 20 | 20 |
| *122* | A39 | 9n multi | 45 | 45 |
| *123* | A39 | 10n multi | 50 | 50 |
| *124* | A39 | 15n multi | 75 | 75 |
| *125* | A39 | 25n multi | 1.25 | 1.25 |
| | | *Nos. 120-125 (6)* | 3.29 | 3.29 |

**Souvenir Sheet**

| | | | | |
|---|---|---|---|---|
| *126* | | Sheet of 4 | 7.00 | 7.00 |
| **a** | A39 | 15n *Academic education* | 1.50 | |
| **b** | A39 | 15n *Teacher Training College* | 1.50 | |
| **c** | A39 | 15n *Technical education* | 1.50 | |
| **d** | A39 | 15n *University of Zambia* | 1.50 | |

10th anniversary of indepencence. No. 126 has multicolored margin with black inscription. Size: 140x105mm.

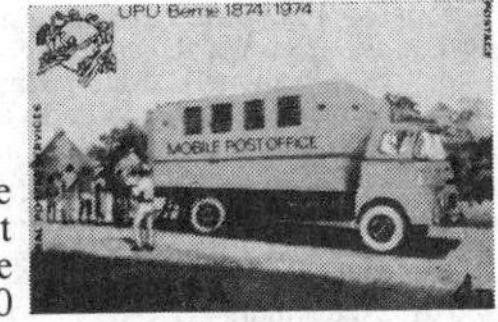


Mobile Post Office A40

Designs (UPU Emblem and): 9n, Rural mail service by Zambia Airways. 10n, Modern Post Office, Chipata. 15n, Ndola Postal Training Center.

**1974, Nov. 15**

| | | | | |
|---|---|---|---|---|
| *127* | A40 | 4n multi | 15 | 10 |
| *128* | A40 | 9n multi | 35 | 22 |
| *129* | A40 | 10n multi | 38 | 25 |
| *130* | A40 | 15n multi | 65 | 38 |

Centenary of Universal Postal Union.

Radar by Day A41

Designs: 9n, Radar by night. 15n, Radar at dawn. 25n, Radar Station.

**1974, Dec. 16**

| | | | | |
|---|---|---|---|---|
| *131* | A41 | 4n multi | 24 | 16 |
| *132* | A41 | 9n multi | 52 | 40 |
| *133* | A41 | 15n multi | 1.00 | 70 |
| *134* | A41 | 25n multi | 1.75 | 1.25 |

Inauguration of Mwembeshi Earth Station, Oct. 21, 1974.

Rhinoceros and Calf — A42

Peanut Harvest A43

**1975, Jan. 3** **Litho.** *Perf. 13½x14*

| | | | | |
|---|---|---|---|---|
| *135* | A42 | 1n *shown* | 5 | 5 |
| *136* | A42 | 2n *Guinea fowl* | 6 | 5 |
| *137* | A42 | 3n *Zambian dancers* | 8 | 5 |
| *138* | A42 | 4n *Fish eagle* | 8 | 5 |
| *139* | A42 | 5n *Bridge, Victoria Falls* | 8 | 6 |
| *140* | A42 | 8n *Sitatunga* | 14 | 8 |
| *141* | A42 | 9n *Elephant, Kasaba Bay Resort* | 15 | 8 |
| *142* | A42 | 10n *Giant pangolin* | 18 | 9 |

*Perf. 13*

| | | | | |
|---|---|---|---|---|
| *143* | A43 | 15n *Zambezi River source, Monument* | 28 | 14 |
| *144* | A43 | 20n *shown* | 38 | 22 |
| *145* | A43 | 25n *Tobacco field* | 45 | 32 |
| *146* | A43 | 50n *Flying doctor service* | 90 | 65 |
| *147* | A43 | 1k *Lady Ross's touraco* | 1.75 | 1.25 |
| *148* | A43 | 2k *Village scene* | 3.50 | 2.50 |
| | | *Nos. 135-148 (14)* | 8.08 | 5.59 |

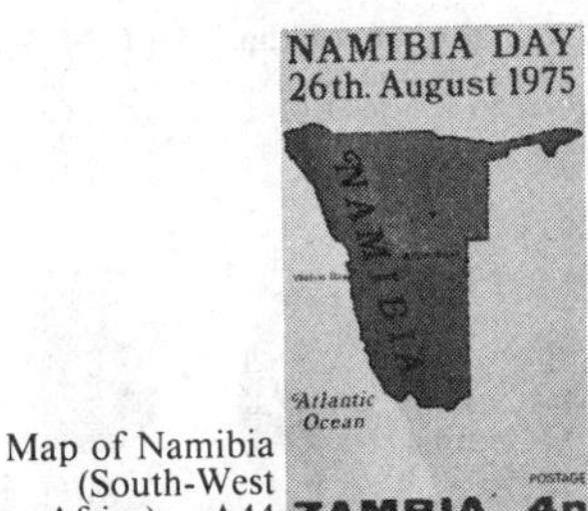


Map of Namibia (South-West Africa) — A44

**1975, Aug. 26** **Litho.** *Perf. 14x13½*

| | | | | |
|---|---|---|---|---|
| *149* | A44 | 4n grn & dk grn | 12 | 12 |
| *150* | A44 | 9n dk bl & gray bl | 24 | 24 |
| *151* | A44 | 15n yel & org | 42 | 42 |
| *152* | A44 | 25n org & dp org | 70 | 70 |

Namibia Day.

Sprinkler Irrigation — A45

Designs: 9n, Sprinkler irrigation over rows of vegetables. 15n, Furrow irrigation.

**1975, Dec. 16** **Litho.** *Perf. 13*

| | | | | |
|---|---|---|---|---|
| *153* | A45 | 4n multi | 28 | 28 |
| *154* | A45 | 9p multi | 65 | 65 |
| *155* | A45 | 15n multi | 1.00 | 1.00 |

International Commission on Irrigation and Drainage, 25th anniversary.

Julbernardia Paniculata — A46

Trees of Zambia: 4n, Sycamore fig. 9n, Baikiaea plurijuga. 10n, Colophospermum. 15n, Uapaca kirkiana. 25n, Pterocarpus angolensis.

**1976, Mar. 22** **Litho.** *Perf. 13*

| | | | | |
|---|---|---|---|---|
| *156* | A46 | 3n multi | 10 | 10 |
| *157* | A46 | 4n multi | 12 | 12 |
| *158* | A46 | 9n multi | 24 | 24 |
| *159* | A46 | 10n multi | 28 | 28 |
| *160* | A46 | 15n multi | 42 | 42 |
| *161* | A46 | 25n multi | 70 | 70 |
| | | *Nos. 156-161 (6)* | 1.86 | 1.86 |

World Forestry Day, Mar. 21.

TAZARA Passenger Train — A47

Designs: 9n, Train carrying copper. 10n, Clearing the bush. No. 164, Train carrying heavy machinery. No. 166b, Track laying. 20n, Reinforcing railroad track. No. 165, Train carrying various goods. No. 166d, Completed tracks.

**1976, Dec. 10** **Litho.** *Perf. 13*

| | | | | |
|---|---|---|---|---|
| *162* | A47 | 4n multi | 20 | 20 |
| *163* | A47 | 9n multi | 45 | 45 |
| *164* | A47 | 15n multi | 80 | 80 |
| *165* | A47 | 25n multi | 1.40 | 1.40 |

*Perf. 13½x14*

**Souvenir Sheet**

| | | | | |
|---|---|---|---|---|
| *166* | | Sheet of 4 | 4.00 | 4.00 |
| **a** | A47 | 10n multi | 40 | 28 |
| **b** | A47 | 15n multi | 60 | 45 |
| **c** | A47 | 20n multi | 70 | 50 |
| **d** | A47 | 25n multi | 1.00 | 65 |

Completion of Tanzania-Zambia Railroad. No. 166 has black marginal inscription. Size: 140x107mm.

A particular stamp may be scarce, but if few collectors want it, its market value may remain relatively low.

Kayowe Dance — A48

**1977, Jan. 18 Litho. *Perf. 13½x14***

*167* A48 4n *shown* 12 10
*168* A48 9n *Lilombola dance* 32 22
*169* A48 15n *Initiation ceremony* 60 54
*170* A48 25n *Munkhwele dance* 1.00 65

2nd World Black and African Festival, Lagos, Nigeria, Jan. 15-Feb. 12.

Grimwood's Longclaw — A49

Birds of Zambia: 9n, Shelley's sunbird. 10n, Black-cheeked lovebird. 15n, Locust finch. 20n, White-chested tinkerbird. 25n, Chaplin's barbet.

**1977, July 1 Litho. *Perf. 14½***

*171* A49 4n multi 35 18
*172* A49 9n multi 60 42
*173* A49 10n multi 70 48
*174* A49 15n multi 95 70
*175* A49 20n multi 1.50 95
*176* A49 25n multi 1.90 1.25
*Nos. 171-176 (6)* 6.00 3.98

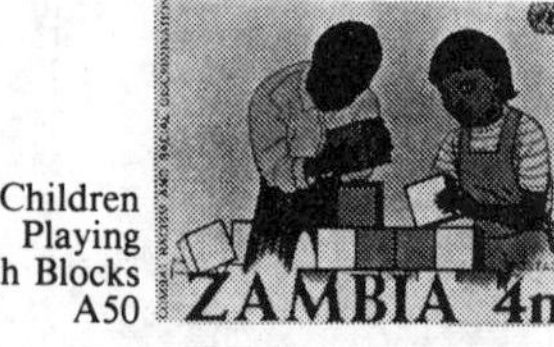

Children Playing with Blocks A50

Designs: 9n, Women of various races dancing in circle. 15n, Black and white girls with young bird.

**1977, Oct. 20 Litho. *Perf. 14x14½***

*177* A50 4n multi 12 12
*178* A50 9n multi 22 22
*179* A50 15n multi 38 38

Combat racism and racial discrimination.

"Glory to God in the Highest" A51

Christmas: 9n, Nativity. 10n, Three Kings and camel. 15n, Presentation at the Temple.

**1977, Dec. 20 Litho. *Perf. 14***

*180* A51 4n multi 12 12
*181* A51 9n multi 24 24
*182* A51 10n multi 24 24
*183* A51 15n multi 35 35

Christmas 1977.

Elephant and Road Check A52

Designs: 18n, Waterbuck and Kafue River boat patrol. 28n, Warthog and helicopter surveillance of National Parks. 32n, Cheetah and armed wildlife guards in Parks and Game Management Areas.

**1978, Aug. 1 Litho. *Perf. 14x14½***

*184* A52 8n multi 24 24
*185* A52 18n multi 55 55
*186* A52 28n multi 90 90
*187* A52 32n multi 1.00 1.00

Anti-poaching Campaign of Zambia Wildlife Conservation Society, Aug. 1978.

Nos. 141, 137, 145 and 143 Surcharged with New Value and 2 Bars.

**1979, Mar. 15 *Perf. 13½x14, 13***

*188* A42 8n on 9n multi 18 18
*189* A42 10n on 3n multi 20 20
*190* A43 18n on 25n multi 38 38
*191* A43 28n on 15n multi 60 60

Kayowe Dance A53

Designs: 32n, Kutambala dance. 42n, Chitwansombo drummers. 58n, Lilombola dance.

**1979, Aug. 1**

*192* A53 18n multi 40 40
*193* A53 32n multi 70 70
*194* A53 42n multi 90 90
*195* A53 58n multi 1.25 1.25

Commonwealth Summit Conf., Lusaka, Aug. 1-9.

"Why the Zebra is Hornless" — A54

Children's Stories: 18n, Kalulu and the Tug of War. 42n, How the Tortoise got his Shell. 58n, Kalulu and the Lion.

**1979, Sept. 21 Litho. *Perf. 14***

*196* A54 18n multi 38 38
*197* A54 32n multi 65 65
*198* A54 42n multi 80 80
*199* A54 58n multi 1.10 1.10
*a* Souvenir sheet of 4 3.25 3.25

International Year of the Child. No. 199a contains Nos. 196-199; multicolored margin. Size: 90½x119mm.

Girls of Different Races Holding Emblem A55

Anti-Apartheid Year (1978): 32n, Boys and toy car. 42n, Infants and butterfly. 58n, Children and microscope.

**1979, Nov. 16 Litho. *Perf. 14½x15***

*200* A55 18n multi 38 38
*201* A55 32n multi 65 65
*202* A55 42n multi 80 80
*203* A55 58n multi 1.10 1.10

Hill, Zambia No. 13 A56

Hill and: 32n, Mailman and bicycle. 42n, Northern Rhodesia No. 75. 58n, Mailman and oxcart.

**1979, Dec. 20 Litho. *Perf. 14½***

*204* A56 18n multi 38 38
*205* A56 32n multi 65 65
*206* A56 42n multi 80 80
*207* A56 58n multi 1.10 1.10
*a* Souvenir sheet of 4 3.25 3.25

Sir Rowland Hill (1795-1879), originator of penny postage. No. 207a contains Nos. 204-207; multicolored margin. Size: 112x88½mm.

Nos. 204-207a Overprinted "LONDON 1980"

**1980, Mar 6 Litho. *Perf. 15***

*208* A56 18n multi 38 38
*209* A56 32n multi 65 65
*210* A56 42n multi 80 80
*211* A56 58n multi 1.10 1.10
*a* Souvenir sheet of 4 3.25 3.25

London 80 Intl. Stamp Exhib., May 6-14.

Anniverary Emblem on Map of Zambia A57

**1980, June 18 Litho. *Perf. 14***

*212* A57 8n multi 16 16
*213* A57 32n multi 65 65
*214* A57 42n multi 80 80
*215* A57 58n multi 1.10 1.10
*a* Souvenir sheet of 4 3.00 3.00

Rotary International, 75th anniversary. No. 215a contains Nos. 212-215; blue and orange decorative margin. Size: 115x90mm.

Running A58

**1980, July 19 Litho. *Perf. 13***

*216* A58 18n *shown* 40 40
*217* A58 32n *Boxing* 70 70
*218* A58 42n *Soccer* 90 90
*219* A58 58n *Swimming* 1.25 1.25
*a* Souvenir sheet of 4 3.50 3.50

22nd Summer Olympic Games, Moscow, July 19-Aug. 3. No. 219a contains Nos. 216-219; blue and black margin shows Olympic rings. Size: 142x114mm.

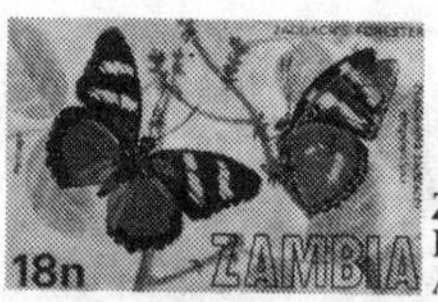

Zaddach's Forester A59

**1980, Sept. 22**

*220* A59 18n *shown* 45 45
*221* A59 32n *Northern highflier* 80 80
*222* A59 42n *Zambezi skipper* 1.00 1.00
*223* A59 58n *Modest blue* 1.50 1.50
*a* Souvenir sheet of 4 3.75 3.75

No. 223a contains Nos. 220-223. Multicolored margin shows butterflies in meadow. Size: 114½x86mm.

Coat of Arms — A60

**1980, Sept. 27 Litho. *Perf. 14½***

*224* A60 18n multi 40 40
*225* A60 32n multi 70 70
*226* A60 42n multi 95 95
*227* A60 58n multi 1.25 1.25

26th Commonwealth Parliamentary Association Conference, Lusaka.

Nativity and St. Francis of Assisi (Stained Glass Window), Ndola Church — A61

**1980, Oct. Litho. *Perf. 14***

*228* A61 8n multi 18 18
*229* A61 28n multi 60 60
*230* A61 32n multi 70 70
*231* A61 42n multi 95 95

Christmas and 50th anniv. of Catholic Church in Copperbelt (central Zambia).

Trichilia Emetica Seed Pods, Musikili A62

Designs: Seed Pods.

**1981, Mar. 21 Litho. *Perf. 14***

*232* A62 8n shown 18 18
*233* A62 18n Afzelia quanzensis, Mupapa 40 40
*234* A62 28n Erythrina abyssinica, Mulunguti 60 60
*235* A62 32n Combretum collinum, Mulama 70 70

World Forestry Day.

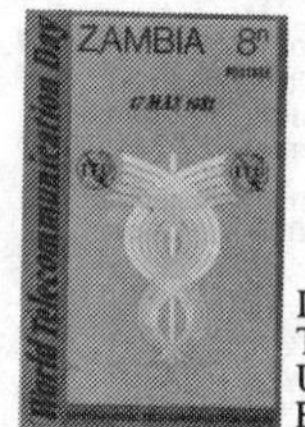

International Telecommunications Union Emblem — A63

Designs: 18n, 32n, WHO emblem.

**1981, May 15 Litho. *Perf. 14½***

*236* A63 8n multi 16 16
*237* A63 18n multi 38 38
*238* A63 28n multi 55 55
*239* A63 32n multi 65 65

13th World Telecommunications Day (8n, 28n).

Mask Maker — A64

**1981-83**

*240* A64 1n shown 5 5
*241* A64 2n Blacksmiths 5 5
*242* A64 5n Potter 7 7
*243* A64 8n Straw basket fishing 12 12
*244* A64 10n Roof thatching 20 20
*244A* A64 12n Picking mushrooms ('83) 18 18
*245* A64 18n Millet grinding 28 28
*246* A64 28n Royal Barge paddler 45 45

*247* A64 30n Makishi tightrope dancer 48 48
*248* A64 35n Tonga-ila granary, house 52 52
*249* A64 42n Cattle herding 65 65

***Perf. 14***

**Size: 37x25mm**

*250* A64 50n Traditional healer 75 75
*251* A64 75n Carrying water jugs ('83) 1.10 1.10
*252* A64 1k Grinding corn ('83) 1.50 1.50
*253* A64 2k Woman smoking pipe 3.50 3.50
*Nos. 240-253 (15)* 9.90 9.90

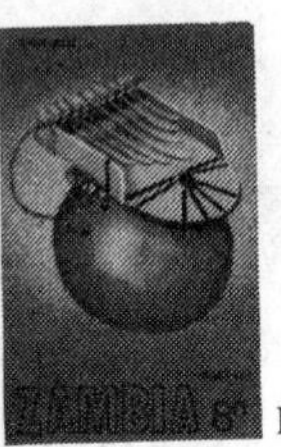

Kankobele — A65

Designs: Traditional musical instruments.

**1981, Sept. 30 Litho.** ***Perf. 14½***

*254* A65 8n shown 14 14
*255* A65 18n Inshingili 32 32
*256* A65 28n Ilimba 55 55
*257* A65 32n Bango 60 60

Banded Ironstone — A66

**1982, Jan. 5 Litho.** ***Perf. 14***

*258* A66 8n shown 15 15
*259* A66 18n Cobaltocalcite 35 35
*260* A66 28n Amazonite 55 55
*261* A66 32n Tourmaline 60 60
*262* A66 42n Uranium ore 80 80
*Nos. 258-262 (5)* 2.45 2.45

**1982, July 1 Litho.** ***Perf. 14***

*263* A66 8n Bornite 15 15
*264* A66 18n Chalcopyrite 35 35
*265* A66 28n Malachite 55 55
*266* A66 32n Azurite 60 60
*267* A66 42n Vanadinite 80 80
*Nos. 263-267 (5)* 2.45 2.45

Scouting Year A67

**1982, Mar. 30 Litho.** ***Perf. 14***

*268* A67 8n Scouts, flag 14 14
*269* A67 18n Baden-Powell 32 32
*270* A67 28n Horned buffalo, patrol pennat 55 55
*271* A67 1k Eagle, conservation badge 1.75 1.75
*a* Souvenir sheet of 4 3.25 3.25

No. 271a contains Nos. 268-271; multicolored decorative margin. Size: 105x78mm.

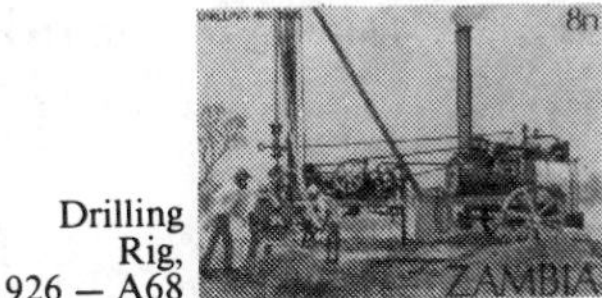

Drilling Rig, 1926 — A68

Steam locomotives.

**1983, Jan. 26** ***Perf. 14x14½***

*272* A68 8n shown 22 22
*273* A68 18n Class B6, 1910 50 50
*274* A68 28n Borsig engine, 1925 85 85
*275* A68 32n 7th class, 1900 90 90

Commonwealth Day — CD334

**1983, Mar. 10 Litho.** ***Perf. 14***

*276* CD334 12n Cotton picking 20 20
*277* CD334 18n Miners 30 30
*278* CD334 28n Ritual pot, dancers 50 50
*279* CD334 1k Victoria Falls, purple-crested lorie 1.65 1.65

Local Flowers — A69

**1983, May 26 Litho.** ***Perf. 14***

*280* A69 12n Eulophia cucullata 20 20
*281* A69 28n Kigelia africana 50 50
*282* A69 35n Protea gaguedi 60 60
*283* A69 50n Leonotis nepotifolia 85 85
*a* Souv. sheet of 4 2.25 2.25

No. 283a contains Nos. 280-283 (perf. 12x12½). Size: 142x72mm.

Thornicroft's Giraffes — A70

**1983, July 21 Litho.** ***Perf. 14***

*284* A70 12n shown 16 16
*285* A70 28n Cookson's wildebeest 45 45
*286* A70 35n Black lechwe 52 52
*287* A70 1k Yellow-backed duiker 1.50 1.50

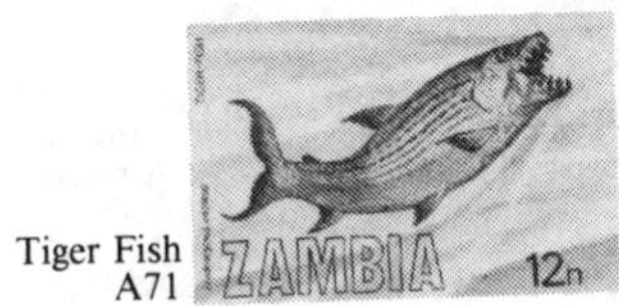

Tiger Fish A71

**1983, Sept. 29 Litho.** ***Perf. 14***

*288* A71 12n shown 16 16
*289* A71 28n Silver Barbel 45 45
*290* A71 35n Spotted Squeaker 52 52
*291* A71 38n Red Breasted Bream 55 55

Christmas 1983 — A72

**1983, Dec. 12 Litho.** ***Perf. 14x14½***

*292* A72 12n Annunciation 16 16
*293* A72 28n Shepherds 45 45
*294* A72 35n Three Kings 52 52
*295* A72 38n Flight into Egypt 55 55

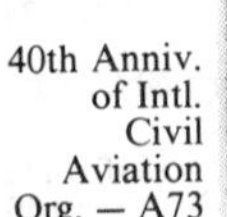

40th Anniv. of Intl. Civil Aviation Org. — A73

**1984, Jan. 26 Litho.** ***Perf. 14***

*296* A73 12n Boeing 737, 1983 16 16
*297* A73 28n Beaver, 1954 35 35
*298* A73 35n Short Solent Flying Boat, 1948 45 45
*299* A73 1k DH-66, 1931 1.25 1.25

60th Birthday of Pres. Kaunda A74

***Perf. 14½x14, 14x14½***

**1984, Apr. 28 Litho.**

*300* A74 12n Receiving greetings 12 12
*301* A74 28n Swearing in, 1983, vert. 32 32
*302* A74 60n Planting cherry tree 65 65
*303* A74 1k Opening Natl. Assembly, vert. 1.10 1.10

1984 Summer Olympics — A75

**1984, July 18 Litho.** ***Perf. 14***

*304* A75 12n Soccer 18 18
*305* A75 28n Running 45 45
*306* A75 35n Hurdles 55 55
*307* A75 50n Boxing 80 80

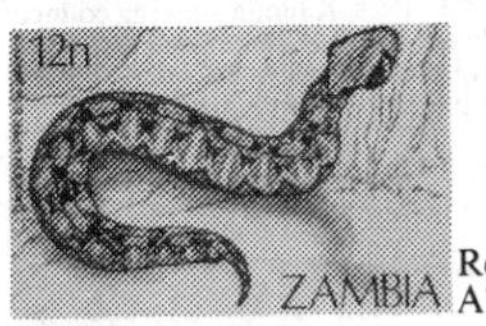

Reptiles A76

**1984, Sept. 5 Litho.** ***Perf. 14***

*308* A76 12n Gabon viper 15 15
*309* A76 28n Chameleon 35 35
*310* A76 35n Nile crocodile 45 45
*311* A76 1k Blue-headed agama 1.25 1.25
*a* Souvenir sheet of 4 2.25 2.25

No. 311a contains Nos. 308-311; multicolored margin shows turtle. Size: 121x102mm.

20th Anniv. of Independence — A77

**1984, Oct. 22 Litho.** ***Perf. 14***

*312* A77 12n Pres. Kaunda, Mulungushi Rock 15 15
*313* A77 28n Freedom Statue 35 35
*314* A77 1k Produce 1.25 1.25

Local Mushrooms A78

**1984, Dec. 12 Litho.** ***Perf. 14x14½***

*315* A78 12n Amanita Flammeola 16 16
*316* A78 28n Amanita Zambiana 32 32
*317* A78 32n Termitomyces Letestui 38 38
*318* A78 75n Cantharellus Miniatescens 85 85

No. 146 Surcharged with New Value and Two Bars

**1985, Mar. 5 Litho.** ***Perf. 13½***

*319* A43 5k on 50n multi 4.25 4.25

Primates A79

**1985, Apr. 25 Litho.** ***Perf. 14***

*320* A79 12n Chacma baboon 12 12
*321* A79 20n Moloney's monkey 18 18
*322* A79 45n Blue monkey 40 40
*323* A79 1k Vervet monkey 90 90

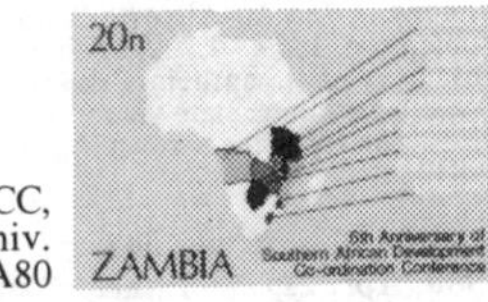

SADCC, 5th Anniv. A80

**1985, July 9 Litho.** ***Perf. 14***

*324* A80 20n Map 18 18
*325* A80 45n Mining 38 38
*326* A80 1k Mulungushi Hall 90 90

Southern African Development Coordination Conference.

Queen Mother, 85th Birthday A81

Designs: 25n, Portrait in blue, age 80, vert. 45n, Queen Consort at Clarence House, 1963, vert. 55n, With Elizabeth II and Princess Margaret. 5k, With royal family, christening of Prince Henry, 1984.

**1985, Aug. 2**

*327* A81 25n multi 20 20
*328* A81 45n multi 38 38
*329* A81 55n multi 50 50
*330* A81 5k multi 4.25 4.25

Postal and Telecommunications Corp., 10th Anniv. — A82

**1985, Dec. 12** ***Perf. 13½x13***

*331* A82 20n Lusaka P.O., 1958 7 7
*332* A82 45n Livingstone P.O., 1950 15 15
*333* A82 55n Kalomo P.O., 1902 18 18
*334* A82 5k Transcontinental Telegraph, 1900 1.75 1.75

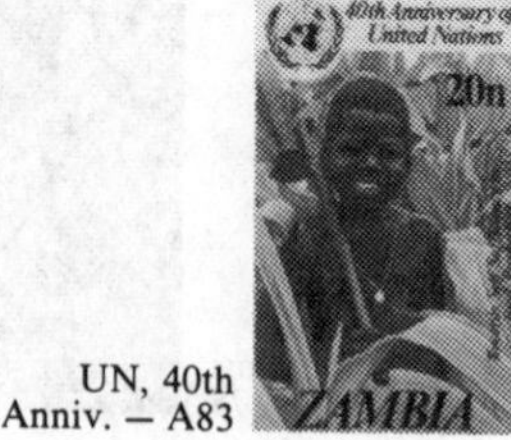


UN, 40th Anniv. — A83

**1985, Dec. 19** *Perf. 14*

*335* A83 20n Boy in cornfield 7 7
*336* A83 45n Emblem 15 15
*337* A83 1k Pres. Kaunda, 1970 35 35
*338* A83 2k Charter signing, 1945 70 70

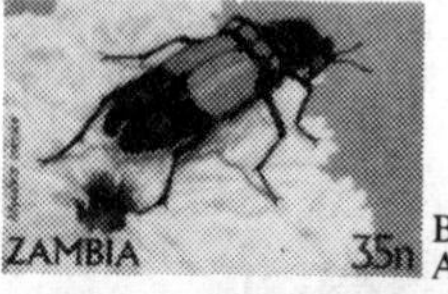


Beetles A84

**1986, Mar. 20**

*339* A84 35n Mylabris tricolor 10 10
*340* A84 1k Phasgonocnema melanianthe 30 30
*341* A84 1.70k Amaurodes passerinii 50 50
*342* A84 5k Ranzania petersiana 1.50 1.50

**Queen Elizabeth II 60th Birthday**
Common Design Type

Designs: 35n, At the Flower Ball, Savoy Hotel, London, 1951. 1.25k, With Prince Andrew at Lusaka Airport, Commonwealth Conference, 1979. 1.70k, With Dr. Kaunda observing natl. anthem. 1.95k, Wearing Queen Mary tiara, state visit to Luxembourg, 1976. 5k, Visiting Crown Agents' offices, 1983.

**Wmk. 384**

**1986, Apr. 21 Litho.** *Perf. 14*

*343* CD337 35n scar, blk & sil 12 12
*344* CD337 1.25k ultra & multi 40 40
*345* CD337 1.70k grn, blk & sil 55 55
*346* CD337 1.95k vio & multi 62 62
*347* CD337 5k rose vio & multi 1.60 1.60
*Nos. 343-347 (5)* 3.29 3.29

**Royal Wedding Issue, 1986**
Common Design Type

Designs: 1.70k, Sarah Ferguson kissing Prince Andrew. 5k, Andrew in informal dress.

**Wmk. 384**

**1986, July 23 Litho.** *Perf. 14*

*348* CD338 1.70k multi 55 55
*349* CD338 5k multi 1.60 1.60

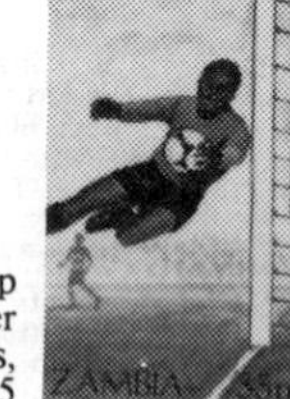


1986 World Cup Soccer Championships, Mexico — A85

Various soccer plays.

**1986, June 27 Litho.** *Perf. 14½*

*350* A85 35n multi 10 10
*351* A85 1.25k multi 32 32
*352* A85 1.70k multi 45 45
*353* A85 5k multi 1.25 1.25

Halley's Comet A86

Designs: 1.25k, Edmond Halley (1656-1742), by Henry Pegram. 1.70k, Giotto space probe approaching comet. 2k, Youth, astronomer. 5k, Halley's map of the southern constellations.

**1986, July 4**

*354* A86 1.25k multi 32 32
*355* A86 1.70k multi 45 45
*356* A86 2k multi 52 52
*357* A86 5k multi 1.25 1.25

No. 244A Surcharged in Light Red Brown

**1986, July Litho.** *Perf. 14½*

*358* A64 20n on 12n multi 10 10

Christmas A87

Children's drawings.

**1986, Dec. 15 Litho.** *Perf. 14*

*359* A87 35n Nativity 8 8
*360* A87 1.25k Magi 22 22
*361* A87 1.60k Nativity 28 28
*362* A87 5k Angel, house, tree 90 90

Tazara Railroad, 10th Anniv. A88

Locomotive traveling various railway lines.

**1986, Dec. 22**

*363* A88 35n Overpass, Kasama 6 6
*364* A88 1.25k Tunnel 21 vicinity 20 20
*365* A88 1.70k Tunnels 6-7 28 28
*366* A88 5k Mpika Station grade separation 80 80

University of Zambia A89

Designs: 35n, Pres. Kaunda shaking council member's hand. 1.25k, University crest, vert. 1.60k, University statue. 5k, Kaunda laying university building cornerstone, vert.

**1987, Jan. 27 Litho.** *Perf. 14*

*367* A89 35n multi 8 8
*368* A89 1.25k multi 22 22
*369* A89 1.60k multi 28 28
*370* A89 5k multi 90 90

No. 137 Surcharged

**1987** *Perf. 13½x14*

*371* A42 10n on 3n Zambian dancers 5 5

No. 243 Surcharged in Blue

**1987** *Perf. 14½*

*372* A64 25n on 8n Basket fishing 10 10

Municipal Arms — A90

Birds — A91

**1987, Mar. 26** *Perf. 14*

*373* A90 35n Kitwe 6 6
*374* A90 1.25k Ndola 20 20
*375* A90 1.70k Lusaka 25 25
*376* A90 20k Livingstone 3.00 3.00

**1987-88** *Perf. 11x13*

*377* A91 25n Long-toed fluff tail 6 6
*378* A91 30n Miombo pied barbet 8 8
*379* A91 35n Black-and-rufous swallow 10 10

**Size: 25x38½mm**
*Perf. 14*

*380* A91 50n Slaty egret 14 14
*381* A91 1k Bradfield's hornbill 25 25
*382* A91 1.25k Margaret's batis 32 32
*383* A91 1.60k Red-and-blue sunbird 40 40
*384* A91 1.70k Boehm's bee-eater 45 45
*385* A91 1.95k Gorgeous bush shrike 50 50
*386* A91 2k Shoebill 52 52
*387* A91 5k Taita falcon 1.25 1.25

**Surcharged**

**K1.65**
**=**

**Size: 20x25½mm**
*Perf. 11x13*

*388* A91 20n on 1n Yellow swamp warbler 5 5
*389* A91 75n on 2n Olive-flanked robin 20 20
*390* A91 1.65k on 30n #378 42 42

**Size: 25x38½mm**
*Perf. 14*

*391* A91 10k on 50n #380 2.50 2.50
*392* A91 20k on 2k #386 5.00 5.00
*Nos. 377-392 (16)* 12.24 12.24

Issue dates: Nos. 377, 379, 381-385 and 387, Sept. 14, 1987. Nos. 391-392, Mar. 10, 1988. Others Oct. 8, 1987.

Nos. 388-389 not issued without overprint. See Nos. 433-435.

Look-out Tree, Livingstone — A92

**1987, June 30** *Perf. 14*

*393* A92 35n shown 5 5
*394* A92 1.25k Rafting, Zambezi River 16 16
*395* A92 1.70k Walking safari, Luangwa Valley 22 22
*396* A92 10k White pelicans 1.25 1.25

Zambia Airways, 20th Anniv. A93

**1987, Sept. 21**

*397* A93 35n De Havilland Beaver 8 8
*398* A93 1.70k DC-10 42 42
*399* A93 5k DC-3 1.20 1.20
*400* A93 10k Boeing 707 2.45 2.45

Issues of 1985-86 Surcharged in Gold or Black

**1987, Sept. 14** *Perfs. as before*

*401* A81 3k on 25n #327 (G) 75 75
*402* CD337 3k on 35n #343 75 75
*403* A85 3k on 35n #350 75 75
*404* A86 3k on 1.25k #354 (G) 75 75
*405* CD337 4k on 1.25k #344 1.00 1.00
*406* A81 6k on 45n #328 1.50 1.50
*407* CD337 6k on 1.70k #345 1.50 1.50
*408* A85 6k on 1.25k #351 1.50 1.50
*409* A86 6k on 1.70k #355 (G) 1.50 1.50
*410* A81 10k on 55n #329 (G) 2.50 2.50
*411* CD337 10k on 1.95k #346 2.50 2.50
*412* A85 10k on 1.70k #352 2.50 2.50
*413* A86 10k on 2k #356 (G) 2.50 2.50
*414* A81 20k on 5k #330 (G) 5.00 5.00
*415* CD337 20k on 5k #347 5.00 5.00
*416* A85 20k on 5k #353 5.00 5.00
*417* A86 20k on 5k #357 (G) 5.00 5.00
*Nos. 401-417 (17)* 40.00 40.00

World Food Day — A94

Cattle.

**1987, Oct. 1** *Perf. 14½x15*

*418* A94 35n Friesian-Holstein 8 8
*419* A94 1.25k Simmental 32 32
*420* A94 1.70k Sussex 42 42
*421* A94 20k Brahma 5.00 5.00

Traditional Heritage — A95

Zambian people.

**1987, Oct. 20** *Perf. 13x12½*

*422* A95 35n Mpoloto Ne Mikobango 8 8
*423* A95 1.25k Zintaka 32 32
*424* A95 1.70k Mufuluhi 42 42
*425* A95 10k Ntebwe 2.50 2.50
*426* A95 20k Kubangwa Aa Mbulunga 5.00 5.00
*Nos. 422-426 (5)* 8.32 8.32

World Wildlife Fund — A96

Wildcats — A97

**1987, Dec. 21 Litho.** *Perf. 14*

*427* A96 50n Black lechwe drinking water 12 12
*428* A96 2k Adults and young, horiz. 50 50
*429* A96 2.50k Running, horiz. 62 62
*430* A96 10k Male, diff. 2.50 2.50

**Souvenir Sheets**

*431* A97 20k Cheetah 5.00 5.00
*432* A97 20k Caracal 5.00 5.00

Nos. 431-432 have multicolored margins continuing the designs. Sizes: 105x75mm.

Bird Type of 1987

**1987 Litho.** *Perf. 11x13*

*433* A91 5n Black-tailed cisticola 5 5
*434* A91 10n White-winged starling 5 5
*435* A91 40n Wattled crane 12 12

Intl. Fund for Agricultural Development (IFAD), 10th Anniv. — A98

**1988, Apr. 2** *Perf. 14*

| | | | | | |
|---|---|---|---|---|---|
| *436* | A98 | 50n | Cassava crop | 14 | 14 |
| *437* | A98 | 2.50k | Net fishing | 65 | 65 |
| *438* | A98 | 2.85k | Cattle breeding | 75 | 75 |
| *439* | A98 | 10k | Coffee picking | 2.60 | 2.60 |

U.N. Child Survival Campaign — A99

**1988, Sept. 12 Litho.** *Perf. 12½*

| | | | | | |
|---|---|---|---|---|---|
| *440* | A99 | 50n | Breast-feeding | 14 | 14 |
| *441* | A99 | 2k | Growth monitoring | 52 | 52 |
| *442* | A99 | 2.85k | Immunization | 75 | 75 |
| *443* | A99 | 10k | Oral rehydration | 2.60 | 2.60 |

Preferential Trade Area Fair — A100

**1988, Oct. 10 Litho.** *Perf. 12½x13*

| | | | | | |
|---|---|---|---|---|---|
| *444* | A100 | 50n | Asbestos cement | 12 | 12 |
| *445* | A100 | 2.35k | Textiles | 60 | 60 |
| *446* | A100 | 2.50k | Tea | 65 | 65 |
| *447* | A100 | 10k | Poultry | 2.60 | 2.60 |

Intl. Red Cross and Red Crescent Organizations, 125th Annivs. — A101

**1988, Oct. 20** *Perf. 14*

| | | | | | |
|---|---|---|---|---|---|
| *448* | A101 | 50n | Famine relief | 12 | 12 |
| *449* | A101 | 2.50k | Giving first aid | 62 | 62 |
| *450* | A101 | 2.85k | Teaching first aid | 72 | 72 |
| *451* | A101 | 10k | Jean-Henri Dunant | 2.60 | 2.60 |

Endangered Species — A102

**1988, Dec. 5 Litho.** *Perf. 14*

| | | | | | |
|---|---|---|---|---|---|
| *452* | A102 | 50n | Aardvark | 14 | 14 |
| *453* | A102 | 2k | Pangolin | 52 | 52 |
| *454* | A102 | 2.85k | Wild dog | 75 | 75 |
| *455* | A102 | 20k | Black rhinoceros | 5.25 | 5.25 |

## POSTAGE DUE STAMPS

Type of Northern Rhodesia

*Perf. 12½*

**1964, Oct. 24 Litho. Unwmk.**

| | | | | | |
|---|---|---|---|---|---|
| *J1* | D1 | 1p | orange | 15 | 15 |
| *J2* | D1 | 2p | dk bl | 25 | 25 |
| *J3* | D1 | 3p | rose cl | 35 | 35 |
| *J4* | D1 | 4p | vio bl | 45 | 45 |
| *J5* | D1 | 6p | purple | 65 | 65 |
| *J6* | D1 | 1sh | emerald | 2.00 | 2.00 |
| | | | *Nos. J1-J6 (6)* | 3.85 | 3.85 |

# ZANZIBAR

LOCATION — A group of islands about twenty miles off the coast of Tanganyika in East Africa.
GOVT. — Republic
AREA — 1,044 sq. mi. (approx.)
POP. — 354,360 (est. 1967)
CAPITAL — Zanzibar

Before 1895, unoverprinted stamps of India were used in Zanzibar.

Zanzibar was a British protectorate until Dec. 10, 1963, when it became independent. After a revolt in January, 1964, a republic was established. Zanzibar joined Tanganyika Apr. 26, 1964, to form the United Republic of Tanganyika and Zanzibar (later renamed Tanzania). See Tanzania.

12 Pies = 1 Anna
16 Annas = 1 Rupee
100 Cents = 1 Rupee (1908)
100 Cents = 1 Shilling (1935)

**Catalogue values for unused stamps in this country are for Never Hinged items, beginning with Scott 201 in the regular postage section and Scott J18 in the postage due section.**

Stamps of British India Overprinted

**Zanzibar**

On Stamps of 1882-95

**1895 Wmk. Star (39)** *Perf. 14*

**Blue Overprint**

| | | | | |
|---|---|---|---|---|
| *1* | A17 | ½a green | *3,750.* | *1,000.* |
| *2* | A19 | 1a violet brown | 650.00 | 350.00 |
| *a.* | | "Zanzidar" | | *4,250.* |

**1895-96**

**Black Overprint**

| | | | | |
|---|---|---|---|---|
| *3* | A17 | ½a green | 1.75 | 1.25 |
| *a.* | | "Zanzidar" | 275.00 | 210.00 |
| *b.* | | "Zanibar" | 350.00 | 240.00 |
| *c.* | | "Zapzibar" | | |
| *4* | A19 | 1a vio brn | 1.75 | 1.40 |
| *a.* | | "Zanzidar" | 360.00 | 240.00 |
| *b.* | | "Zanibar" | 350.00 | 240.00 |
| *5* | A20 | 1a6p bis brn | 1.65 | 1.40 |
| *a.* | | "Zanzidar" | 425.00 | 300.00 |
| *b.* | | "Zanizbar" | 750.00 | |
| *c.* | | "Zanibar" | 350.00 | 275.00 |
| *d.* | | "Zapzibar" | | |
| *6* | A21 | 2a ultra | 1.75 | 1.75 |
| *a.* | | "Zanzidar" | 575.00 | 500.00 |
| *b.* | | "Zanibar" | 450.00 | 350.00 |
| *c.* | | "Zapzibar" | | |
| *d.* | | Double overprint | 175.00 | |
| *7* | A28 | 2a6p green | 2.25 | 1.75 |
| *a.* | | "Zanzidar" | 425.00 | 240.00 |
| *b.* | | "Zanibar" | 195.00 | 195.00 |
| *c.* | | "Zapzibar" | | |
| *d.* | | "Zanzipar" | 500.00 | |
| *8* | A22 | 3a orange | 3.25 | 3.25 |
| *a.* | | "Zanzidar" | 240.00 | 275.00 |
| *b.* | | "Zanizbar" | 900.00 | *900.00* |
| *9* | A23 | 4a ol grn | 4.50 | 4.50 |
| *a.* | | "Zanzidar" | 750.00 | 600.00 |
| *10* | A25 | 8a red vio | 6.50 | 6.50 |
| *a.* | | "Zanzidar" | 900.00 | 900.00 |
| *11* | A26 | 12a vio, *red* | 6.50 | 6.50 |
| *a.* | | "Zanzidar" | 900.00 | 900.00 |
| *12* | A27 | 1r gray | 90.00 | 67.50 |
| *a.* | | "Zanzidar" | 1,650. | 1,650. |
| *13* | A29 | 1r car rose & grn | 6.50 | 7.25 |
| *a.* | | Vertical overprint | 210.00 | |
| *14* | A30 | 2r brn & rose | 21.00 | 27.50 |
| *a.* | | "Zanziba" | 1,500. | |
| *b.* | | Inverted "r" | 600.00 | 600.00 |
| *c.* | | Pair, one without overprint | | |
| *15* | A30 | 3r grn & brn | 9.00 | 9.00 |
| *a.* | | "Zanziba" | 1,500. | |
| *b.* | | Inverted "r" | 600.00 | 600.00 |
| *16* | A30 | 5r vio & bl | 10.50 | 10.50 |
| *a.* | | "Zanziba" | 1,500. | |
| *b.* | | Inverted "r" | 600.00 | 600.00 |
| *c.* | | Dbl. ovpt., one invtd. | 350.00 | |

On Stamp of 1873-76

**Wmk. Elephant's Head. (38)**

| | | | | |
|---|---|---|---|---|
| *17* | A14 | 6a bister | 2.25 | 2.25 |
| *a.* | | "Zanzidar" | 550.00 | 550.00 |
| *b.* | | "Zanzibarr" | *750.00* | *750.00* |
| *c.* | | "Zanibar" | 315.00 | 315.00 |
| *d.* | | "Zapzibar" | | |
| *e.* | | Double overprint | | |
| | | *Nos. 3-17 (15)* | 169.15 | 152.30 |

Nos. 4-6 Surcharged:

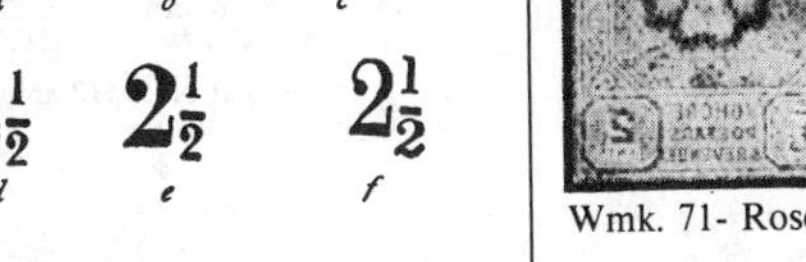


**1896 Wmk. Star (39)**

**Black Surcharge**

| | | | | |
|---|---|---|---|---|
| *18* | (a) | 2½a on 1a vio brn | 45.00 | 45.00 |
| *19* | (b) | 2½a on 1a vio brn | 135.00 | *195.00* |
| *20* | (c) | 2½a on 1a vio brn | 40.00 | 40.00 |

**Red Surcharge**

| | | | | |
|---|---|---|---|---|
| *21* | (a) | 2½a on 1a vio brn | 80.00 | 135.00 |
| *22* | (b) | 2½a on 1a vio brn | 110.00 | 110.00 |
| *23* | (c) | 2½a on 1a vio brn | 135.00 | 165.00 |
| *24* | (a) | 2½a on 1a6p bis brn | 20.00 | 20.00 |
| *a.* | | "Zanzidar" | 450.00 | 450.00 |
| *b.* | | "Zanizbar" | 500.00 | 500.00 |
| *24C* | (b) | 2½a on 1a6p bis brn | 60.00 | *67.50* |
| *25* | (c) | 2½a on 1a6p bis brn | 80.00 | 97.50 |
| *26* | (d) | 2½a on 1a6p bis brn | 60.00 | 67.50 |
| *27* | (e) | 2½a on 1a6p bis brn | 165.00 | 165.00 |
| *27A* | (f) | 2½a on 1a6p bis brn | *2,250.* | *2,250.* |
| *28* | (a) | 2½a on 2a ultra | 40.00 | 47.50 |
| *28A* | (b) | 2½a on 2a ultra | 80.00 | *110.00* |
| *29* | (c) | 2½a on 2a ultra | 35.00 | 40.00 |
| *30* | (d) | 2½a on 2a ultra | 25.00 | 25.00 |
| *31* | (e) | 2½a on 2a ultra | 80.00 | 47.50 |
| *31A* | (f) | 2½a on 2a ultra | *825.00* | *825.00* |

Certain type varieties are found in the word "Zanzibar" on Nos. 1 to 31A viz: Inverted "q" for "b", broken "p" for "n", "i" without dot, small second "z" and tall second "z". These varieties are found on all values from ½a to 1r inclusive and the tall "z" is also found on the 2r, 3r and 5r.

Stamps of British East Africa, 1896, Overprinted in Black or Red **Zanzibar**

**1896 Wmk. Crown and C. A. (2)**

| | | | | |
|---|---|---|---|---|
| *32* | A8 | ½a yel grn | 14.00 | 11.00 |
| *33* | A8 | 1a carmine | 15.00 | 12.50 |
| *a.* | | Dbl. overprint | 165.00 | 150.00 |
| *34* | A8 | 2½a dk bl (R) | 55.00 | 27.50 |
| *35* | A8 | 4½a orange | 11.00 | 11.00 |
| *36* | A8 | 5a dk ocher | 14.00 | 14.00 |
| *37* | A8 | 7½a lilac | 16.00 | 16.00 |
| | | *Nos. 32-37 (6)* | 125.00 | 92.00 |

Sultan Seyyid Hamed-bin-Thwain
A2 A3

Wmk. 71- Rosette

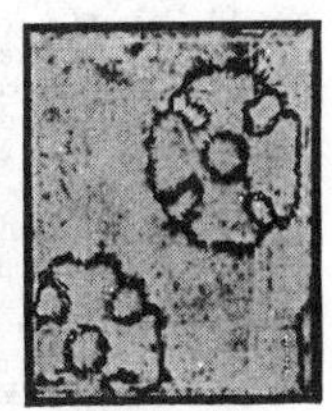

Wmk. 47- Multiple Rosette

**1896, Sept. 20 Engr. Wmk. 71**

| | | | | | |
|---|---|---|---|---|---|
| *38* | A2 | ½a | yel grn & red | 25 | 30 |
| *39* | A2 | 1a | ind & red | 1.10 | 1.10 |
| *40* | A2 | 2a | red brn & red | 60 | 42 |
| *41* | A2 | 2½a | ultra & red | 85 | 35 |
| *42* | A2 | 3a | sl & red | 1.90 | 1.90 |
| *43* | A2 | 4a | dk grn & red | 95 | 95 |
| *44* | A2 | 4½a | org & red | 2.75 | 2.75 |
| *45* | A2 | 5a | bis & red | 1.65 | 1.25 |
| *a.* | | | Half used as 2½a on cover | | *1,000.* |
| *46* | A2 | 7½a | lil & red | 1.65 | 1.40 |
| *47* | A2 | 8a | ol gray & red | 1.90 | 2.25 |
| *48* | A3 | 1r | ultra & red | 5.50 | 4.25 |
| *49* | A3 | 2r | grn & red | 5.50 | 4.25 |
| *50* | A3 | 3r | vio & red | 11.00 | 7.00 |
| *51* | A3 | 4r | lake & red | 13.50 | 8.50 |
| *52* | A3 | 5r | blk brn & red | 19.00 | 11.00 |
| | | | *Nos. 38-52 (15)* | 68.10 | 47.67 |

No. 43 Surcharged in Red

**1897**

| | | | | |
|---|---|---|---|---|
| *53* | A2 (a) | 2½a on 4a | 32.50 | *40.00* |
| *54* | A2 (b) | 2½a on 4a | 75.00 | *45.00* |
| *55* | A2 (c) | 2½a on 4a | 32.50 | *40.00* |

**1898 Engr. Wmk. 47**

| | | | | | |
|---|---|---|---|---|---|
| *56* | A2 | ½a | yel grn & red | 15 | 20 |
| *57* | A2 | 1a | ind & red | 22 | 20 |
| *58* | A2 | 2a | red brn & red | 2.25 | 32 |
| *58A* | A2 | 2½a | ultra & red | 32 | 22 |
| *59* | A2 | 3a | sl & red | 55 | 55 |
| *60* | A2 | 4a | dk grn & red | 60 | 65 |
| *60A* | A2 | 4½a | org red | 1.00 | 60 |
| *61* | A2 | 5a | bis & red | 1.25 | 1.00 |
| *61A* | A2 | 7½a | lil & red | 4.00 | 4.00 |
| *61B* | A2 | 8a | ol gray & red | 5.00 | 4.00 |
| | | | *Nos. 56-61B (10)* | 15.34 | 11.74 |

Sultan Seyyid Hamoud-bin-Mahommed-bin-Said
A4 A5

**1899-1901**

| | | | | | |
|---|---|---|---|---|---|
| *62* | A4 | ½a | yel grn & red | 16 | 16 |
| *63* | A4 | 1a | ind & red | 20 | 20 |
| *64* | A4 | 1a | car & red ('01) | 35 | 14 |
| *65* | A4 | 2a | red brn & red | 45 | 24 |
| *66* | A4 | 2½a | ultra & red | 80 | 28 |
| *67* | A4 | 3a | sl & red | 65 | 60 |
| *68* | A4 | 4a | dk grn & red | 1.00 | 60 |

69 A4 4½a org & red 90 90
70 A4 4½a ind & red ('01) 5.25 3.50
71 A4 5a bis & red 80 65
72 A4 7½a lil & red 80 1.00
73 A4 8a ol gray & red 1.00 1.00

**Wmk. 71**

74 A5 1r ultra & red 14.50 5.25
75 A5 2r grn & red 10.50 9.25
76 A5 3r vio & red 12.50 16.00
77 A5 4r lil rose & red 16.00 27.50
78 A5 5r gray brn & red 27.50 *40.00*
*Nos. 62-78 (17)* 93.36 107.27

Monogram of Sultan Ali bin Hamoud
A6 A7

**1904, June 8 Typo. Wmk. 47**

79 A6 ½a emerald 22 12
80 A6 1a rose red 35 15
81 A6 2a bis brn 70 60
82 A6 2½a ultra 70 35
83 A6 3a gray 55 55
84 A6 4a bl grn 1.10 95
85 A6 4½a black 1.10 1.10
86 A6 5a ocher 1.10 1.10
87 A6 7½a violet 1.90 1.50
88 A6 8a ol grn 2.75 1.40
89 A7 1r ultra & red 7.25 3.00
90 A7 2r grn & red 13.00 13.00
91 A7 3r vio & red 30.00 32.50
92 A7 4r mag & red 32.50 *40.00*
93 A7 5r ol & red 40.00 *47.50*
*Nos. 79-93 (15)* 133.22 *143.82*

Nos. 69-70, 72-73 Surcharged in Black or Lake:

One *g* Two *h* Two & Half *i*

**1904**

94 A4 (g) 1a on 4½a (Bk) 1.25 *2.50*
95 A4 (g) 1a on 4½a (L) 4.75 *7.75*
96 A4 (h) 2a on 4a (L) 9.25 7.75
97 A4 (i) 2½a on 7½a (Bk) 9.25 6.25
*a.* "Hlaf" *1,000.*
98 A4 (i) 2½a on 8a (Bk) 11.00 11.00
*a.* "Hlaf" *1,000.*

Sultan Ali bin Hamoud
A8 A9

A10

Palace of the Sultan — A11

**1908-09 Engr. Wmk. 47**

99 A8 1c gray ('09) 14 14
100 A8 3c yel grn 28 24
101 A8 6c carmine 1.10 24
102 A8 10c org brn ('09) 1.10 2.00
103 A8 12c violet 1.10 50
104 A9 15c ultra 1.50 70
105 A9 25c brown 1.75 80
106 A9 50c dp grn 2.75 2.75
107 A9 75c sl ('09) 4.75 5.75
108 A10 1r yel grn 5.75 2.50
109 A10 2r violet 10.00 6.25
110 A10 3r yel brn 24.00 24.00
111 A10 4r red 27.50 35.00
112 A10 5r blue 35.00 37.50
113 A11 10r brn & dk grn 75.00 80.00
114 A11 20r yel grn & blk 87.50 95.00
115 A11 30r dk brn & blk 150.00 150.00
116 A11 40r org brn & blk 300.00
117 A11 50r lil & blk 325.00
118 A11 100r bl & blk 450.00
119 A11 200r blk & brn 1,200.
*Nos. 99-112 (14)* 116.72 118.37

It is probable that Nos. 118 and 119 were used only for fiscal purposes.

Sultan Khalifa bin Harub — A12

Dhow — A13

Dhow — A14

**1913 Perf. 14**

120 A12 1c gray 10 10
121 A12 3c yel grn 20 12
122 A12 6c carmine 25 15
123 A12 10c brown 60 90
124 A12 12c violet 55 20
125 A12 15c ultra 75 35
126 A12 25c blk brn 70 45
127 A12 50c dk grn 2.00 65
128 A12 75c dk gray 65 50
129 A13 1r yel grn 1.50 75
130 A13 2r dk vio 4.00 3.00
131 A13 3r orange 10.00 12.50
132 A13 4r red 15.00 17.50
133 A13 5r blue 17.50 17.50
134 A14 10r brn & grn 42.50 42.50
135 A14 20r yel grn & blk 75.00 75.00
136 A14 30r dk brn & blk 82.50 *82.50*
137 A14 40r org & blk 125.00 *125.00*
138 A14 50r dl vio & blk 275.00 *275.00*
139 A14 100r bl & blk 350.00 *350.00*
140 A14 200r blk & grn 600.00 *600.00*
*Nos. 120-134 (15)* 96.30 97.17

**1914-22 Wmk. 3**

141 A12 1c gray 12 16
142 A12 3c yel grn 48 12
143 A12 6c carmine 28 10
144 A12 8c vio, *yel* ('22) 65 *1.25*
145 A12 10c dk grn, *yel* ('22) 52 *80*
146 A12 15c ultra 48 *80*
148 A12 50c dk grn 2.75 *5.25*
149 A12 75c dp gray 2.50 *4.00*
150 A13 1r yel grn 2.75 80
151 A13 2r dk vio 3.25 *1.75*
152 A13 3r brn org 4.75 *6.50*
153 A13 4r red 10.50 *13.00*
154 A13 5r blue 13.00 *16.00*
155 A14 10r brn & grn 52.50 *80.00*
*Nos. 141-155 (14)* 94.53 *130.53*

**1921-29 Wmk. 4**

156 A12 1c gray 12 12
157 A12 3c yel grn 18 25
158 A12 3c org ('22) 20 15
159 A12 4c grn ('22) 40 40
160 A12 6c carmine 30 40
161 A12 6c vio, *bl* ('22) 50 15
162 A12 10c lt brn 70 1.25
163 A12 12c violet 50 35
164 A12 12c car ('22) 50 50
165 A12 15c ultra 70 1.00
166 A12 20c dk bl ('22) 75 70
167 A12 25c blk brn 85 1.25
168 A12 50c bl grn 75 1.50
169 A12 75c dk gray 2.00 5.00
170 A13 1r yel grn 65 1.00
171 A13 2r dk vio 2.00 3.50
172 A13 3r ocher 2.50 5.00
173 A13 4r red 5.00 12.50
174 A13 5r blue 8.75 17.50
175 A14 10r brn & grn 25.00 37.50
176 A14 20r grn & blk 75.00 *150.00*
177 A14 30r dk brn & blk ('29) 85.00 *175.00*
*Nos. 156-175 (20)* 52.35 90.02

Sultan Khalifa bin Harub ("CENTS" with Serifs) — A15

**1926-27**

184 A15 1c brown 8 8
185 A15 3c yel org 22 10
186 A15 4c dp grn 25 25
187 A15 6c dk vio 35 12
188 A15 8c slate 75 1.65
189 A15 10c ol grn 60 25
190 A15 12c dp red 70 16
191 A15 20c ultra 60 16
192 A15 25c vio, *yel* 85 60
193 A15 50c claret 1.25 1.10
194 A15 75c ol brn 1.50 3.75
*Nos. 184-194 (11)* 7.15 8.22

**Catalogue values for unused stamps in this section, from this point to the end of the section, are for Never Hinged items.**

"CENTS" without Serifs — A16

Dhow — A17

Dhow — A18

**1936 Perf. 14**

201 A16 5c dp grn 8 8
202 A16 10c black 14 12
203 A16 15c carmine 18 18
204 A16 20c brn org 24 18
205 A16 25c vio, *yel* 35 30
206 A16 30c ultra 42 35
207 A16 40c blk brn 42 42
208 A16 50c claret 60 60
209 A17 1sh yel grn 75 65
210 A17 2sh dk vio 1.40 95
211 A17 5sh red 4.50 4.50
212 A17 7.50sh blue 5.75 9.00
213 A18 10sh brn & grn 7.25 7.25
*Nos. 201-213 (13)* 22.08 24.58

Sultan Khalifa bin Harub — A19

**1936, Dec. 9**

214 A19 10c ol grn & blk 50 50
215 A19 20c red vio & blk 55 55
216 A19 30c dp ultra & blk 55 55
217 A19 50c red org & blk 85 85

25th anniv. of the reign of Sultan Khalifa bin Harub.

Dhow and Map Showing Zanzibar and Muscat — A20

**Wmk. 4**

**1944, Nov. 20 Engr. Perf. 14**

218 A20 10c vio bl 12 12
219 A20 20c brn org 18 18
220 A20 50c Prus grn 25 25
221 A20 1sh dl pur 45 45

200th anniv. of the Al Busaid Dynasty.

Nos. 202 and 206 Overprinted in Red

VICTORY ISSUE
8TH JUNE 1946

**1946, Nov. 11**

222 A16 10c black 12 12
223 A16 30c ultra 30 30

Victory of the Allied Nations in WW II.

**Silver Wedding Issue**
Common Design Types

**1949, Jan. 10 Photo. Perf. 14x14½**

224 CD304 20c orange 30 30

**Engraved; Name Typographed**
***Perf. 11½x11***

225 CD305 10sh lt brn 8.50 8.50

**UPU Issue**
Common Design Types
**Engr.; Name Typo. on 30c, 50c**
***Perf. 13½, 11x11½***

**1949, Oct. 10 Wmk. 4**

226 CD306 20c red org 20 15
227 CD307 30c indigo 25 20
228 CD308 50c red lil 50 40
229 CD309 1sh bl grn 75 65

Sultan Khalifa bin Harub — A21

Seyyid Khalifa Schools
A22

***Perf. 12x12½, 13x12½***

**1952, Aug. 26 Engr.**

230 A21 5c black 6 5
231 A21 10c red org 8 6
232 A21 15c green 14 8
233 A21 20c carmine 18 12
234 A21 25c plum 22 18
235 A21 30c bl grn 22 18
236 A21 35c ultra 25 24
237 A21 40c chocolate 42 35
238 A21 50c purple 42 30
239 A22 1sh choc & bl grn 48 42
240 A22 2sh cl & ultra 1.10 90
241 A22 5sh car & blk 1.90 1.75
242 A22 7.50sh emer & gray 6.00 9.00
243 A22 10sh gray blk & rose red 4.25 3.75
*Nos. 230-243 (14)* 15.72 17.38

Sultan Khalifa bin Harub — A23

**1954, Aug. 26 *Perf. 12½x12***

244 A23 15c green 18 18
245 A23 20c scarlet 22 22
246 A23 30c ultra 25 25
247 A23 50c purple 38 38
248 A23 1.25sh brn org 95 95
*Nos. 244-248 (5)* 1.98 1.98

The frames differ on Nos. 245 and 247. Issued to commemorate the 75th anniversary of the birth of Sultan Khalifa bin Harub.

Cloves — A24

Dhows
A25

Sultan's Barge
A26

Malindi Minaret Mosque
A27

Kibweni Palace — A28

Sultan Khalifa bin Harub and: 25c, 35c, and 50c Map showing location of Zanzibar. 1sh, 2sh, Dimbani Mosque.

***Perf. 11½ (A24), 11x11½ (A25), 14x13½ (A26), 13½x14 (A27), 13x13½ (A28)***

| **1957, Aug. 26** | | **Engr.** | **Wmk. 314** | |
|---|---|---|---|---|
| *249* | A24 | 5c dl grn & org | 6 | 5 |
| *250* | A24 | 10c rose car & brt grn | 8 | 5 |
| *251* | A25 | 15c dk brn & grn | 8 | 6 |
| *252* | A26 | 20c ultra | 10 | 6 |
| *253* | A26 | 25c blk & brn org | 10 | 6 |
| *254* | A25 | 30c int blk & rose car | 14 | 12 |
| *255* | A26 | 35c brt grn & ind | 15 | 15 |
| *256* | A27 | 40c int blk & redsh brn | 20 | 18 |
| *257* | A26 | 50c dl grn & bl | 30 | 22 |
| *258* | A27 | 1sh int blk & brt car | 38 | 30 |
| *259* | A25 | 1.25sh rose car & dk grn | 55 | 45 |
| *260* | A27 | 2sh dl grn & org | 75 | 65 |
| *261* | A28 | 5sh ultra | 1.65 | 1.25 |
| *262* | A28 | 7.50sh green | 2.75 | 5.75 |
| *263* | A28 | 10sh rose car | 3.75 | 3.25 |
| | | *Nos. 249-263 (15)* | 11.04 | 12.60 |

Sultan Seyyid Abdulla bin Khalifa — A29

Designs as before with portrait of Sultan Seyyid Abdulla bin Khalifa.

***Perf. 11½ (A29), 11x11½ (A25), 14x13½ (A26), 13½x14 (A27), 13x13½ (A28)***

| **1961, Oct. 17** | | **Engr.** | **Wmk. 314** | |
|---|---|---|---|---|
| *264* | A29 | 5c dl grn & org | 6 | 6 |
| *265* | A29 | 10c rose car & brt grn | 8 | 6 |
| *266* | A25 | 15c dk brn & grn | 8 | 8 |
| *267* | A26 | 20c ultra | 8 | 8 |
| *268* | A26 | 25c blk & brn org | 10 | 10 |
| *269* | A25 | 30c int blk & rose car | 10 | 10 |
| *270* | A26 | 35c brt grn & ind | 12 | 12 |
| *271* | A27 | 40c int blk & redsh brn | 15 | 15 |
| *272* | A26 | 50c dl grn & bl | 20 | 20 |
| *273* | A27 | 1sh int blk & brt car | 30 | 25 |
| *274* | A25 | 1.25sh rose car & dk grn | 60 | 50 |
| *275* | A27 | 2sh dl grn & org | 65 | 65 |
| *276* | A28 | 5sh ultra | 1.25 | 1.10 |
| *277* | A28 | 7.50sh green | 2.75 | 2.75 |
| *278* | A28 | 10sh rose car | 3.25 | 3.25 |
| *279* | A28 | 20sh dk brn | 8.00 | 8.00 |
| | | *Nos. 264-279 (16)* | 17.77 | 17.45 |

### Freedom from Hunger Issue

Common Design Type with Portrait of Sultan Seyyid Abdulla bin Khalifa

| **1963, June 4** | | **Photo.** | ***Perf. 14x14½*** | |
|---|---|---|---|---|
| *280* | CD314 | 1.30sh sepia | 55 | 55 |

### Independent State

Sultan Seyyid Jamshid bin Abdulla and Zanzibar Clove — A30

Designs: 50c, "To Prosperity," arch and sun. 1.30sh, "Religious Tolerance," composite view of churches and mosques (horiz.). 2.50sh, "Towards the Light," Mangapwani Cave.

***Perf. 12½***

| **1963, Dec. 10** | | **Photo.** | **Unwmk.** | |
|---|---|---|---|---|
| *281* | A30 | 30c multi | 15 | 15 |
| *282* | A30 | 50c multi | 28 | 28 |
| *283* | A30 | 1.30sh multi | 42 | 42 |
| *284* | A30 | 2.50sh multi | 65 | 65 |

Zanzibar's independence, Dec. 10, 1963.

### Republic

Nos. 264-279 Overprinted **JAMHURI 1964**

***Perf. 11½, 11x11½, 14x13½, 13½x14, 13x13½***

| **1964, Feb. 28** | | **Engr.** | **Wmk. 314** | |
|---|---|---|---|---|
| *285* | A29 | 5c dl grn & org | 5 | 5 |
| *286* | A29 | 10c rose car & brt grn | 6 | 6 |
| *287* | A25 | 15c dk brn & grn | 8 | 8 |
| *288* | A26 | 20c ultra | 8 | 8 |
| *289* | A26 | 25c blk & brn org | 8 | 8 |
| *290* | A25 | 30c int blk & rose car | 10 | 10 |
| *291* | A26 | 35c brt grn & ind | 10 | 10 |
| *292* | A27 | 40c int blk & redsh brn | 12 | 12 |
| *293* | A26 | 50c dl grn & bl | 12 | 12 |
| *294* | A27 | 1sh int blk & brt car | 24 | 24 |
| *295* | A25 | 1.25sh rose car & dk grn | 28 | 28 |
| *296* | A27 | 2sh dl grn & org | 48 | 48 |
| *297* | A28 | 5sh ultra | 1.25 | 1.25 |
| *298* | A28 | 7.50sh green | 2.00 | 2.00 |
| *299* | A28 | 10sh rose car | 2.50 | 2.50 |
| *300* | A28 | 20sh dk brn | 4.75 | 4.75 |
| | | *Nos. 285-300 (16)* | 12.29 | 12.29 |

The overprint was applied in England. It is in two lines on 40c, 1sh, 2sh, 5sh, 7.50sh, 10sh and 20sh. Nos. 264-279 also exist with a similar one-line handstamped overprint applied locally. The local overprints are found diagonal, vertical, horizontal, double and inverted. "Jamhuri" means "republic."

Nos. 281-284 Overprinted **JAMHURI 1964**

***Perf. 12½***

| **1964, Feb. 28** | | **Photo.** | **Unwmk.** | |
|---|---|---|---|---|
| *301* | A30 | 30c multi | 20 | 20 |
| *302* | A30 | 50c multi | 30 | 30 |
| *303* | A30 | 1.30sh multi | 45 | 45 |
| *304* | A30 | 2.50sh multi | 75 | 75 |
| *a.* | | Green omitted | 60.00 | |

One-line overprint on 1.30sh. Similar one-line handstamped overprint was applied locally to Nos. 281-284.

Moorish Arch, Ax, Sword and Spear — A31

Designs: 10c, 20c, Arch and arrow piercing chain. 25c, 40c, Man with rifle. 30c, 50c, Man breaking chain. 1sh, Man, flag and sun. 1.30sh, Hands breaking chain and cloves (horiz.). 2sh, Hands waving flag (horiz.). 5sh, Map of Zanzibar and Pemba and flag (horiz.). 10sh, Flag and map of Zanzibar and Pemba. 20sh, Flag of Zanzibar (horiz.)

***Perf. 13x13½, 13½x13***

| **1964, June 21** | | **Litho.** | **Unwmk.** | |
|---|---|---|---|---|
| *305* | A31 | 5c multi | 5 | 5 |
| *306* | A31 | 10c multi | 5 | 5 |
| *307* | A31 | 15c multi | 6 | 6 |
| *308* | A31 | 20c multi | 8 | 8 |
| *309* | A31 | 25c multi | 10 | 10 |
| *310* | A31 | 30c multi | 12 | 8 |
| *311* | A31 | 40c multi | 16 | 12 |
| *312* | A31 | 50c multi | 20 | 16 |
| *313* | A31 | 1sh multi | 24 | 24 |
| *314* | A31 | 1.30sh multi | 28 | 28 |
| *315* | A31 | 2sh multi | 45 | 45 |
| *316* | A31 | 5sh multi | 1.10 | 1.10 |
| *317* | A31 | 10sh multi | 2.00 | 2.00 |
| *318* | A31 | 20sh multi | 4.25 | 4.25 |
| | | *Nos. 305-318 (14)* | 9.14 | 9.02 |

Soldier and Maps of Zanzibar and Pemba — A32

Reconstruction A33

***Perf. 13½x13, 13x13½***

| **1965, Jan. 12** | | | **Unwmk.** | |
|---|---|---|---|---|
| *319* | A32 | 20c grn & yel grn | 8 | 8 |
| *320* | A33 | 30c dk brn & ocher | 8 | 8 |
| *321* | A32 | 1.30sh vio bl & bl | 30 | 30 |
| *322* | A33 | 2.50sh pur & rose | 55 | 55 |

First anniversary of the revolution.

### Zanzibar and Tanzania

Rice Planting A34

Design: 3c, 1.30sh, Hands holding rice.

***Perf. 13x12½***

| **1965, Oct. 17** | | **Litho.** | **Unwmk.** | |
|---|---|---|---|---|
| *323* | A34 | 2c bl & blk brn | 8 | 8 |
| *324* | A34 | 3c brt pink & blk brn | 8 | 8 |
| *325* | A34 | 1.30sh org & blk brn | 30 | 30 |
| *326* | A34 | 2.50sh emer & blk brn | 60 | 60 |

Issued to publicize agricultural development.

Symbols of Trade, Agriculture, Industry and Education A35

Pres. Abeid Amani Karume and Vice-Pres. Abdulla Kassim Hanga A36

Designs: 50c, 2.50sh, Soldier and sunburst.

| **1966, Jan. 12** | | **Litho.** | ***Perf. 12½x13*** | |
|---|---|---|---|---|
| *327* | A35 | 20c ultra, red & gray | 8 | 8 |
| *328* | A35 | 50c blk & yel | 14 | 14 |
| *329* | A35 | 1.30sh multi | 35 | 35 |
| *330* | A35 | 2.50sh blk & org | 55 | 55 |

2nd anniv. of the revolution of Jan. 12, 1964.

| **1966, Apr. 26** | | **Photo.** | ***Perf. 13½x13*** | |
|---|---|---|---|---|

Design: 50c, 1.30sh, Flag, laurel and hands holding Flame of the Union (inscribed: Jamhuri Tanzania Zanzibar).

| No. | Type | Denomination | Unused | Used |
|---|---|---|---|---|
| *331* | A36 | 30c multi | 8 | 8 |
| *332* | A36 | 50c multi | 14 | 14 |
| *333* | A36 | 1.30sh multi | 30 | 30 |
| *334* | A36 | 2.50sh multi | 55 | 55 |

2nd anniv. of the Union of Tanganyika and Zanzibar.

Logging A37

Designs: 10c, 1sh, Clove trees and man. 15c, 40c, Cabinetmaker. 20c, 5sh, Lumumba College and book. 25c, 1.30sh, Farmer and tractor. 30c, 2sh, Volunteer farm workers. 50c, 10sh, Street scene (vert.).

***Perf. 13x12½, 12½x13***

| **1966, June 5** | | | **Litho.** | |
|---|---|---|---|---|
| *335* | A37 | 5c lem & vio brn | 5 | 5 |
| *336* | A37 | 10c brt grn & vio brn | 5 | 5 |
| *337* | A37 | 15c vio brn & bl | 5 | 5 |
| *338* | A37 | 20c vio bl & org | 5 | 5 |
| *339* | A37 | 25c vio brn & yel | 8 | 8 |
| *340* | A37 | 30c vio brn & dl yel | 9 | 9 |
| *341* | A37 | 40c vio brn & rose | 10 | 10 |
| *342* | A37 | 50c grn & yel | 12 | 12 |
| *343* | A37 | 1sh ultra & vio brn | 24 | 24 |
| *344* | A37 | 1.30sh lt bl grn & vio brn | 35 | 35 |
| *345* | A37 | 2sh brt grn & vio brn | 50 | 50 |
| *346* | A37 | 5sh ver & gray | 1.25 | 1.25 |
| *347* | A37 | 10sh red brn & yel | 2.50 | 2.50 |
| *348* | A37 | 20sh brt pink & vio brn | 5.00 | 5.00 |
| | | *Nos. 335-348 (14)* | 10.43 | 10.43 |

Symbols of Education — A38

| **1966, Sept. 25** | | | ***Perf. 13½x13*** | |
|---|---|---|---|---|
| *349* | A38 | 50c bl, blk & org | 15 | 15 |
| *350* | A38 | 1.30sh bl, blk & yel grn | 30 | 30 |
| *351* | A38 | 2.50sh bl, blk & pink | 55 | 55 |

Introduction of free education.

People and Flag A39

Design: 50c, 1.30sh, Vice-President Abdulla Kassim Hanga, flag and crowd (vertical).

***Perf. 14x14½, 14½x14***

| **1967, Feb. 5** | | **Litho.** | **Unwmk.** | |
|---|---|---|---|---|
| *352* | A39 | 30c multi | 9 | 9 |
| *353* | A39 | 50c multi | 15 | 15 |
| *354* | A39 | 1.30sh multi | 30 | 30 |
| *355* | A39 | 2.50sh multi | 55 | 55 |

10th anniversary of Afro-Shirazi Party.

Volunteer Workers A40

*Perf. 12½x12*

| **1967, Aug. 20** | **Photo.** | **Unwmk.** | |
|---|---|---|---|
| *356* A40 1.30sh multi | | 30 | 30 |
| *357* A40 2.50sh multi | | 55 | 55 |

Volunteer (Young) Workers Brigade.
All Zanzibar stamps were withdrawn July 1, 1968, and replaced with current Kenya, Uganda and Tanzania stamps.

## POSTAGE DUE STAMPS

Insufficiently prepaid. Postage due.
1 cent.
D1

*Rouletted 10*
**1931 Typeset Unwmk.**
**Thin Paper**
**Without Gum**

| | | | | |
|---|---|---|---|---|
| *J1* | D1 | 1c *orange* | 1.90 | |
| *J2* | D1 | 2c *orange* | 1.40 | |
| *J3* | D1 | 3c *orange* | 1.90 | |
| *J3A* | D1 | 6c *orange* | | |
| *J4* | D1 | 9c *orange* | 1.65 | |
| *J4A* | D1 | 12c *orange* | | |
| *J4B* | D1 | 12c *green* | *500.00* | *350.00* |
| *J5* | D1 | 15c *orange* | 1.65 | *6.50* |
| *J6* | D1 | 18c *orange* | 6.75 | |
| *a.* | | 18c *salmon* | 3.25 | |
| *J7* | D1 | 20c *orange* | 3.25 | |
| *J8* | D1 | 21c *orange* | 1.90 | |
| *J8A* | D1 | 25c *orange* | | |
| *J8B* | D1 | 25c *magenta* | *1,500.* | *1,000.* |
| *J9* | D1 | 31c *orange* | 6.75 | |
| *J10* | D1 | 50c *orange* | 16.00 | |
| *J11* | D1 | 75c *orange* | 40.00 | |

The variety "cent.s" occurs once on each sheet of Nos. J3 to J11 inclusive.

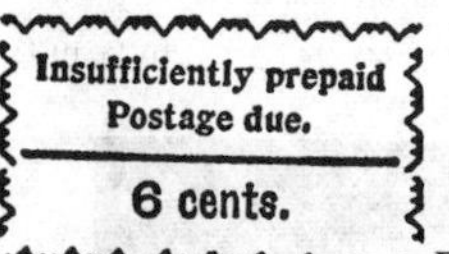

D2

**1931-33** *Rouletted 5*
**Thick Paper**

| | | | |
|---|---|---|---|
| *J12* | D2 | 2c *salmon* | 1.90 |
| *J13* | D2 | 3c *rose* | 2.25 |
| *J14* | D2 | 6c *yellow* | 2.50 |
| *J15* | D2 | 12c *blue* | 4.00 |
| *J16* | D2 | 25c *pink* | 8.25 |
| *J17* | D2 | 25c *dull violet* | 5.50 |
| | | *Nos. J12-J17 (6)* | 24.40 |

**Catalogue values for unused stamps in this section, from this point to the end of the section, are for Never Hinged items.**

D3

| **1936** | **Typo.** | **Wmk. 4** | ***Perf. 14*** | |
|---|---|---|---|---|
| *J18* D3 | 5c violet | | 15 | 15 |
| *J19* D3 | 10c carmine | | 30 | 30 |
| *J20* D3 | 20c green | | 45 | 45 |
| *J21* D3 | 30c brown | | 75 | 75 |
| *J22* D3 | 40c ultra | | 90 | 90 |
| *J23* D3 | 1sh gray | | 2.25 | 2.25 |
| | *Nos. J18-J23 (6)* | | 4.80 | 4.80 |

Chalky paper was introduced in 1956 for the 5c, 30c, 40c, and 1sh, and in 1962 for the 10c and 20c.

# ZIMBABWE

LOCATION — Southeastern Africa, bordered by Zambia, Mozambique, South Africa, and Botswana.
GOVT. — Republic
AREA — 150,699 sq. mi.
POP. — 7,532,000 (1982)
CAPITAL — Harare

Rhodesia became Zimbabwe December 31, 1978. The Republic of Zimbabwe was established April 18, 1980.

100 Cents = 1 Dollar

**Catalogue values for all unused stamps in this country are for Never Hinged items.**

Morganite A69

Black Rhinoceros A70

Odzani Falls — A71

*Perf. 14½, 14½x14 (A70)*

| **1980** | | | **Litho.** | |
|---|---|---|---|---|
| *414* | A69 | 1c *shown* | 5 | 5 |
| *415* | A69 | 3c *Amethyst* | 7 | 7 |
| *416* | A69 | 4c *Garnet* | 8 | 8 |
| *417* | A69 | 5c *Citrine* | 10 | 10 |
| *418* | A69 | 7c *Blue topaz* | 15 | 15 |
| *419* | A70 | 9c *shown* | 18 | 18 |
| *420* | A70 | 11c *Lion* | 22 | 22 |
| *421* | A70 | 13c *Warthog* | 25 | 25 |
| *422* | A70 | 15c *Giraffe* | 30 | 30 |
| *423* | A70 | 17c *Zebra* | 32 | 32 |
| *424* | A71 | 21c *shown* | 40 | 40 |
| *425* | A71 | 25c *Goba Falls* | 45 | 45 |
| *426* | A71 | 30c *Inyangombe Falls* | 55 | 55 |
| *426A* | A71 | 40c *Bundi Falls* | 65 | 65 |
| *427* | A71 | $1 *Bridal Veil Falls* | 1.75 | 1.75 |
| *428* | A71 | $2 *Victoria Falls* | 3.25 | 3.25 |
| | | *Nos. 414-428 (16)* | 8.77 | 8.77 |

Rotary International, 75th Anniversary — A72

| **1980, June 18** | | ***Perf. 14½*** | |
|---|---|---|---|
| *429* A72 | 4c multi | 8 | 8 |
| *430* A72 | 13c multi | 25 | 25 |
| *431* A72 | 21c multi | 40 | 40 |
| *432* A72 | 25c multi | 50 | 50 |
| *a* | Souvenir sheet of 4 | 1.50 | 1.50 |

No. 432a contains Nos. 429-432; black marginal inscription. Size: 140x84½mm.

Olympic Rings A73

| **1980, July 19** | | |
|---|---|---|
| *433* A73 17c multi | 35 | 35 |

22nd Summer Olympic Games, Moscow, July 19-Aug. 3.

Gatooma Post Office, 1912 A74

Post Offices: 7c, Salisbury, 1912. 9c, Umtali, 1901. 17c, Bulawayo, 1895.

| **1980** | **Litho.** | ***Perf. 14½*** | |
|---|---|---|---|
| *434* A74 | 5c multi | 12 | 12 |
| *435* A74 | 7c multi | 18 | 18 |
| *436* A74 | 9c multi | 25 | 25 |
| *437* A74 | 17c multi | 40 | 40 |
| *a* | Souvenir sheet of 4 | 1.00 | 1.00 |

Post Office Savings Bank, 75th anniv. No. 437a contains Nos. 434-437; black marginal inscription. Size: 127x84mm.

Intl. Year of the Disabled — A75

Natl. Tree Day — A76

Designs: Various disabilities. Nos. 438-441 form a continuous design.

| **1981, Sept. 23** | **Litho.** | ***Perf. 14½*** | |
|---|---|---|---|
| *438* A75 | 5c multi | 12 | 12 |
| *439* A75 | 7c multi | 18 | 18 |
| *440* A75 | 11c multi | 28 | 28 |
| *441* A75 | 17c multi | 40 | 40 |

| **1981, Dec. 4** | | | |
|---|---|---|---|
| *442* A76 | 5c Msasa | 10 | 10 |
| *443* A76 | 7c Mopane | 15 | 15 |
| *444* A76 | 21c Flat-crowned acacia | 50 | 50 |
| *445* A76 | 30c Pod mahogany | 60 | 60 |

Rock Paintings A77

| **1982, Mar. 17** | **Litho.** | ***Perf. 14½*** | |
|---|---|---|---|
| *446* A77 | 9c Khoisan figures, Gwamgwadza Cave | 18 | 18 |
| *447* A77 | 11c Kudus, human figures, Epworth Mission | 22 | 22 |
| *448* A77 | 17c Diana's Vow, Rusape | 32 | 32 |
| *449* A77 | 21c Giraffes, Gwamgwadza Cave | 45 | 45 |
| *450* A77 | 25c Warthog, Mucheka Cave | 50 | 50 |
| *451* A77 | 30c Hunters, Shinzwini Shelter | 60 | 60 |
| | *Nos. 446-451 (6)* | 2.27 | 2.27 |

Scouting Year — A78

| **1982, July 21** | | | |
|---|---|---|---|
| *452* A78 | 9c Emblem | 18 | 18 |
| *453* A78 | 11c Campfire | 20 | 20 |
| *454* A78 | 21c Map reading | 40 | 40 |
| *455* A78 | 30c Baden Powell | 55 | 55 |

TB Bacillus Centenary A79

| **1982, Nov. 17** | | ***Perf. 14½*** | |
|---|---|---|---|
| *456* A79 | 11c Koch | 25 | 25 |
| *457* A79 | 30c Scientist examining slide | 60 | 60 |

Commonwealth Day — A80

Sculptures: 9c, Wing Woman, by Henry Mudzengerere (vert.). 11c, Telling Secrets, by Joseph Ndandarika. 30c, Hornbill Man, by John Takawira. $1, The Chief, by Nicholas Mukomberanwa (vert.).

| **1983, Mar. 14** | | ***Perf. 14½*** | |
|---|---|---|---|
| *458* A80 | 9c multi | 16 | 16 |
| *459* A80 | 11c multi | 18 | 18 |
| *460* A80 | 30c multi | 55 | 55 |
| *461* A80 | $1 multi | 1.75 | 1.75 |

World Plowing Contest, May A81

Various plowing scenes. Stamps of same denomination in continuous design.

| **1983, May 13** | **Litho.** | ***Perf. 14½*** | |
|---|---|---|---|
| *462* | Pair | 85 | 85 |
| *a.-b* | A81 21c, any single | 42 | 42 |
| *463* | Pair | 1.10 | 1.10 |
| *a.-b* | A81 30c, any single | 55 | 55 |

World Communications Year — A82

Means of communication and transportation. Nos. 464-467 vert.

| **1983, Oct. 12** | **Litho.** | ***Perf. 14½*** | |
|---|---|---|---|
| *464* A82 | 9c Mailman | 12 | 12 |
| *465* A82 | 11c Signaling airplane | 15 | 15 |
| *466* A82 | 15c Telephone operators | 20 | 20 |
| *467* A82 | 17c Reading newspapers | 25 | 25 |
| *468* A82 | 21c Truck on highway | 30 | 30 |
| *469* A82 | 30c Train | 45 | 45 |
| | *Nos. 464-469 (6)* | 1.47 | 1.47 |

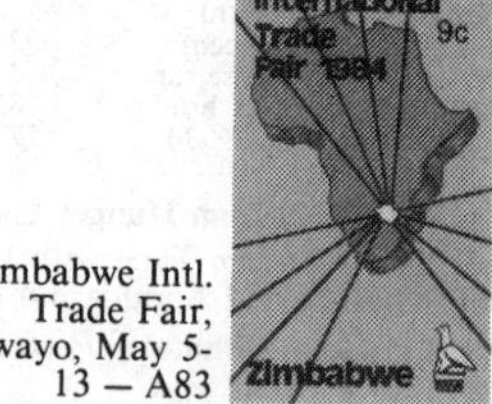

Zimbabwe Intl. Trade Fair, Bulawayo, May 5-13 — A83

**1984, Apr. 11 Litho. Perf. 14½**
*470* A83 9c Map of Africa showing Zimbabwe 18 18
*471* A83 11c Globe 22 22
*472* A83 30c Emblem 60 60

1984 Summer Olympics A84

Children's Drawings.

**1984, July 18 Litho. Perf. 14½**
*473* A84 11c Bicycling 15 15
*474* A84 21c Swimming 25 25
*475* A84 30c Running 40 40
*476* A84 40c Hurdles 55 55

Heroes' Day — A85

**1984, Aug. 8 Litho. Perf. 14½**
*477* A85 9c Heroes 14 14
*478* A85 11c Monument, vert. 16 16
*479* A85 17c Statue, vert. 25 25
*480* A85 30c Bas-relief 45 45

Fish Eagle — A86

**1984, Oct. 10 Litho. Perf. 14½**
*481* A86 9c shown 15 15
*482* A86 11c Long crested eagle 16 16
*483* A86 13c Bateleur 20 20
*484* A86 17c Black eagle 28 28
*485* A86 21c Martial eagle 35 35
*486* A86 30c African hawk eagle 35 48
*Nos. 481-486 (6)* 1.62 1.62

Superheat Engine No. 86, Mashonaland Railways, 1918 — A87

Steam locomotives: 11c, Engine No. 190, North British Locomotive Co., 1926. 17c, Engine No. 424, Beyer Peacock & Co., 1950. Engine No. 726, Beyer Peacock & Co., 1957.

**1985, May 15 Litho.**
*487* A87 9c multi 15 15
*488* A87 11c multi 16 16
*489* A87 17c multi 28 28
*490* A87 30c multi 48 48

INTELSAT V A88

Design: 57c, Mazowe Earth Satellite Station.

**Perf. 14½x14, 14½**

**1985, July 8 Litho.**
*491* A88 26c multi 32 32

**Size: 62x23mm**
*492* A88 57c multi 72 72

Zimbabwe Bird and Tobacco — A89

Agriculture and industry.

**1985, Aug. 21 Litho. Perf. 15**
*493* A89 1c shown 5 5
*494* A89 3c Corn 5 5
*495* A89 4c Cotton 5 5
*496* A89 5c Tea 6 6
*497* A89 10c Cattle 12 12
*498* A89 11c Birchenough Bridge 14 14
*499* A89 12c Stamp mill 16 16
*500* A89 13c Gold production 18 18
*501* A89 15c Coal mining 20 20
*502* A89 17c Amethyst mining 22 22
*503* A89 18c Electric train 24 24
*504* A89 20c Kariba Dam 26 26
*505* A89 23c Elephants 30 30
*506* A89 25c Zambezi River sunset 32 32
*507* A89 26c Baobab tree 35 35
*508* A89 30c Great Zimbabwe ruins 40 40
*509* A89 35c Folk dancing 45 45
*510* A89 45c Crushing corn 60 60
*511* A89 57c Wood carving 75 75
*512* A89 $1 Mbira drum 1.30 1.30
*513* A89 $2 Mule-drawn scotch cart 2.60 2.60
*514* A89 $5 Natl. coat of arms 6.50 6.50
*Nos. 493-514 (22)* 15.30 15.30

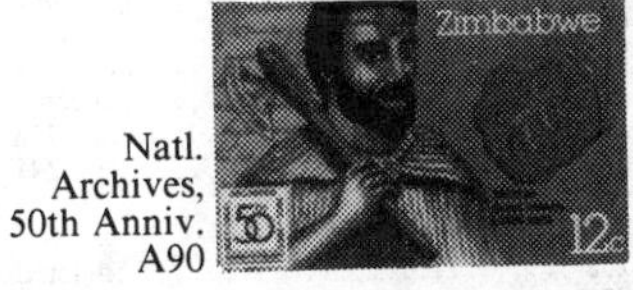

Natl. Archives, 50th Anniv. A90

Designs: 12c, Gatsi Rusere (c. 1589-1623), ruler of Mashonaland and Zambezi area; mutapa, 17th cent. 18c, Lobengula, ruler of Ndebele State (1870-94), sketch by E. A. Maund, 1889; 1888 Moffat Treaty and elephant seal. 26c, Archives exhibition hall. 35c, Archives building.

**1985, Sept. 18 Perf. 14½**
*515* A90 12c multi 15 15
*516* A90 18c multi 22 22
*517* A90 26c multi 32 32
*518* A90 35c multi 45 45

UN Decade for Women A91

**1985, Nov. 13**
*519* A91 10c Computer operator 12 12
*520* A91 17c Nurse, child 22 22
*521* A91 26c Engineer 34 34

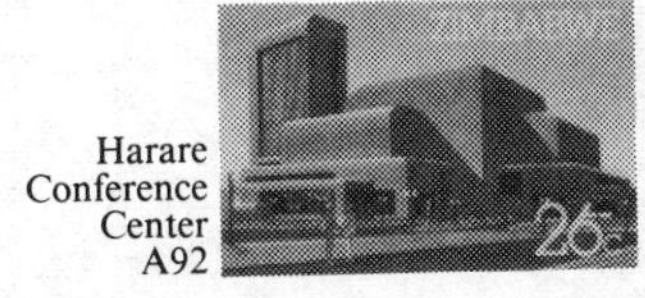

Harare Conference Center A92

**1986, Jan. 29 Litho. Perf. 14½**
*523* A92 26c Facade 35 35
*524* A92 35c Interior 45 45

Southern African Development Coordination Conference — A93

**1986, Apr. 1 Perf. 14½**
*525* A93 12c Grain elevators 15 15
*526* A93 18c Rhinoceros 22 22
*527* A93 26c Map, jet 32 32
*528* A93 35c Map, flags 45 45

Moths — A94

**1986, June 18 Litho. Perf. 14½x14**
*529* A94 12c Jackson's emperor 15 15
*530* A94 18c Oleander hawk 22 22
*531* A94 26c Zaddach's emperor 32 32
*532* A94 35c Southern marbled emperor 45 45

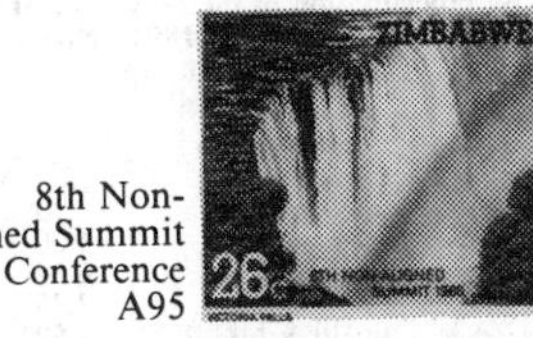

8th Non-aligned Summit Conference A95

**1986, Aug. 28 Litho. Perf. 14½x14**
*533* A95 26c Victoria Falls 32 32

**Size: 66x26mm**

**Perf. 14½**
*534* A95 $1 Great Zimbabwe Enclosure 1.25 1.25

Motoring Cent. A96

**1986, Oct. 8 Perf. 14½**
*535* A96 10c Sopwith, 1921 12 12
*536* A96 12c Gladiator, 1902 15 15
*537* A96 17c Douglas, 1920 22 22
*538* A96 26c Ford Model-A, 1930 32 32
*539* A96 35c Schacht, 1909 45 45
*540* A96 40c Benz Velocipede, 1886 50 50
*Nos. 535-540 (6)* 1.76 1.76

UN Child Survival Campaign — A97

Designs: a, Growth monitoring. b, Breast-feeding. c, Oral rehydration. d, Immunization.

**1987, Feb. 11 Litho. Perf. 14x14½**
*541* Block of 4 60 60
***a.-d.*** A97 12c any single 15 15

Demand, as well as supply, determines a stamp's market value. One is as important as the other.

Indigenous Owls — A98

**1987, Apr. 15 Perf. 14½**
*542* A98 12c Barred 15 15
*543* A98 18c Pearl-spotted 22 22
*544* A98 26c White-faced 32 32
*545* A98 35c Scops 45 45

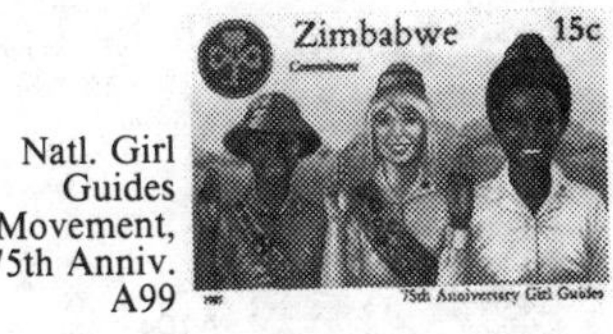

Natl. Girl Guides Movement, 75th Anniv. A99

**1987, June 24**
*546* A99 15c Commitment 20 20
*547* A99 23c Adventure 30 30
*548* A99 35c Service 45 45
*549* A99 $1 Intl. friendship 1.25 1.25

Duikers and Population Maps — A100

**1987, Oct. 7 Perf. 14½x14**
*550* A100 15c Common gray 20 20
*551* A100 23c Zebra 28 28
*552* A100 25c Yellow-backed 32 32
*553* A100 30c Blue 38 38
*554* A100 35c Jentink's 45 45
*555* A100 38c Red 48 48
*Nos. 550-555 (6)* 2.11 2.11

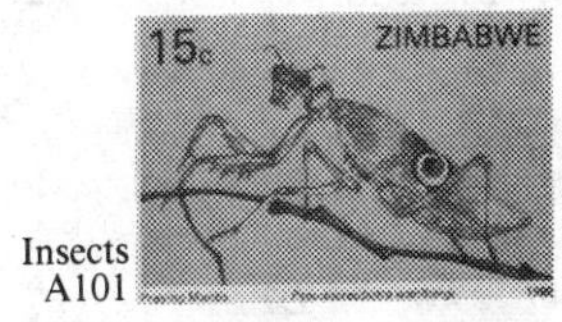

Insects A101

**1988, Jan. 12 Litho. Perf. 14½**
*556* A101 15c Praying mantis 20 20
*557* A101 23c Scarab beetle 28 28
*558* A101 35c Short-horned grasshopper 45 45
*559* A101 45c Giant shield bug 58 58

Natl. Gallery of Art, 30th Anniv. A102

Aloes and Succulents A103

Sculpture and paintings: 15c, *Cockerel*, by Arthur Azevedo. 23c, *Changeling*, by Bernard Matemera. 30c, *Spirit Python*, by Henry Munyaradzi. 35c, *Spirit Bird Carrying People*, by Thomas Mukarobgwa, horiz. 38c, *The Song of the Shepherd Boy*, by George Nene, horiz. 45c, *War Victim*, by Joseph Muzondo, horiz.

*Perf. 14x14½, 14½x14*

**1988, Apr. 14** **Litho.**

| | | | | |
|---|---|---|---|---|
| *560* | A102 | 15c multi | 20 | 20 |
| *561* | A102 | 23c multi | 28 | 28 |
| *562* | A102 | 30c multi | 38 | 38 |
| *563* | A102 | 35c multi | 45 | 45 |
| *564* | A102 | 38c multi | 48 | 48 |
| *565* | A102 | 45c multi | 58 | 58 |
| | | *Nos. 560-565 (6)* | 2.37 | 2.37 |

**1988, July 14** ***Perf. 14½***

| | | | | |
|---|---|---|---|---|
| *566* | A103 | 15c Aloe cameronii bondana | 20 | 20 |
| *567* | A103 | 23c Orbeopsis caudata | 28 | 28 |
| *568* | A103 | 25c Euphorbia wildii | 32 | 32 |
| *569* | A103 | 30c Euphorbia fortissima | 38 | 38 |
| *570* | A103 | 35c Aloe aculeata | 45 | 45 |
| *571* | A103 | 38c Huernia zebrina | 48 | 48 |
| | | *Nos. 566-571 (6)* | 2.11 | 2.11 |

A104

**1988, Oct. 6** **Litho.** ***Perf. 14½x14***

| | | | | |
|---|---|---|---|---|
| *572* | A104 | 15c White-faced duck | 16 | 16 |
| *573* | A104 | 23c Pygmy goose | 25 | 25 |
| *574* | A104 | 30c Hottentot teal | 32 | 32 |
| *575* | A104 | 35c Knob-billed duck | 38 | 38 |
| *576* | A104 | 38c White-backed duck | 40 | 40 |
| *577* | A104 | 45c Maccoa | 48 | 48 |
| | | *Nos. 572-577 (6)* | 1.99 | 1.99 |

## POSTAGE DUE

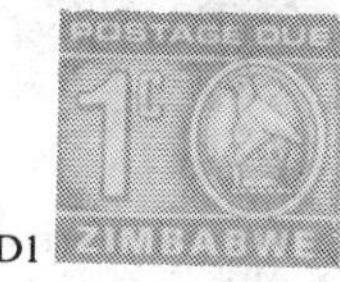


D1

**1981** **Litho.** ***Perf. 14½***

| | | | | |
|---|---|---|---|---|
| *J20* | D1 | 1c emerald | 5 | 5 |
| *J21* | D1 | 2c ultramarine | 5 | 5 |
| *J22* | D1 | 5c lilac | 10 | 10 |
| *J23* | D1 | 6c yellow | 18 | 18 |
| *J24* | D1 | 10c red | 45 | 45 |
| | | *Nos. 20-24 (5)* | 83 | 83 |

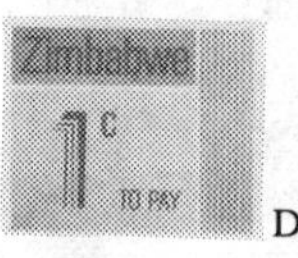


D2

**1985, Aug. 21** **Litho.** ***Perf. 14½***

| | | | | |
|---|---|---|---|---|
| *J25* | D2 | 1c pale orange | 5 | 5 |
| *J26* | D2 | 2c lilac rose | 5 | 5 |
| *J27* | D2 | 6c light green | 8 | 8 |
| *J28* | D2 | 10c tan | 14 | 14 |
| *J29* | D2 | 13c bright blue | 18 | 18 |
| | | *Nos. J25-J29 (5)* | 50 | 50 |

# ZULULAND

LOCATION — Northeastern part of Natal, South Africa.
GOVT. — British Colony, 1887-1897
AREA — 10,427 sq. mi.
POP. — 230,000 (estimated 1900)
CAPITAL — Eshowe

12 Pence = 1 Shilling
20 Shillings = 1 Pound

Stamps of Great Britain Overprinted **ZULULAND**

**1888-93** **Wmk. 30, 31 (5sh)** ***Perf. 14***

| | | | | |
|---|---|---|---|---|
| *1* | A54 | ½p vermilion | 2.75 | 2.75 |
| *2* | A40 | 1p violet | 8.50 | 1.65 |
| *3* | A56 | 2p grn & red | 8.50 | 11.00 |
| *4* | A57 | 2½p vio, *bl* ('91) | 14.00 | 9.25 |
| *5* | A58 | 3p vio, *yel* | 8.50 | 9.25 |
| *6* | A59 | 4p grn & brn | 18.00 | 18.00 |
| *7* | A61 | 5p lil & bl ('93) | 42.50 | 50.00 |
| *8* | A62 | 6p vio, *rose* | 17.00 | 18.00 |
| *9* | A63 | 9p bl & lil ('92) | 50.00 | 50.00 |
| *10* | A65 | 1sh green ('92) | 95.00 | 105.00 |
| *11* | A51 | 5sh rose ('92) | 625.00 | 800.00 |
| | | *Nos. 1-10 (10)* | 264.75 | 274.90 |

Natal No. 66 Overprinted **ZULULAND.**

**1888-94** **Wmk. 2**

| | | | | |
|---|---|---|---|---|
| *12* | A14 | ½p green | 11.00 | 14.00 |
| *a.* | | Without period after "Zululand" | 60.00 | 60.00 |
| *b.* | | Double overprint | 1,500. | |
| *c.* | | Inverted overprint | 1,750. | |
| *d.* | | Pair, one without ovpt. | *4,500.* | *4,500.* |

**Natal No. 71 Ovptd. Like Nos. 1-11**

| | | | | |
|---|---|---|---|---|
| *13* | A11 | 6p vio ('94) | 40.00 | 40.00 |

A1

A2

**1891**

| | | | | |
|---|---|---|---|---|
| *14* | A1 | 1p lilac | 1.90 | 1.65 |

By proclamation of the Governor of Zululand, dated June 27th, 1891, No. 14 was declared to be a postage stamp.

**1894-96** **Typo.**

| | | | | |
|---|---|---|---|---|
| *15* | A2 | ½p lil & grn | 90 | 1.40 |
| *16* | A2 | 1p lil & rose | 4.00 | 90 |
| *17* | A2 | 2½p lil & blue | 6.50 | 4.00 |
| *18* | A2 | 3p lil & brn | 7.25 | 4.00 |
| *19* | A2 | 6p lil & blk | 8.50 | 8.50 |
| *20* | A2 | 1sh green | 18.00 | 20.00 |
| *21* | A2 | 2sh6p grn & blk ('96) | 65.00 | *75.00* |
| *22* | A2 | 4sh grn & car rose | 90.00 | *175.00* |
| *23* | A2 | £1 vio, *red* | 475.00 | 550.00 |
| *24* | A2 | £5 vio & blk, *red* | 4,500. | *1,500.* |
| | | *Nos. 15-22 (8)* | 200.15 | 288.80 |

Numerals of Nos. 19-24 are in color on plain tablet.

Zululand was annexed to Natal in Dec. 1897 and separate stamps discontinued June 30th, 1898.

# Number Changes (Vol. 1)

| No. in 1989 Cat. | No. in 1990 Cat. |
|---|---|
| **United States** | |
| 25a | deleted |
| 1338c | deleted |
| 1384a | delettered |
| 1889b | deleted |
| 2395a | combined with 2396a |
| 2397a | combined with 2398a |
| **Palau** | |
| C18-C21 | 121B-121E |
| C21a | 121f |
| **Great Britain** | |
| 623d perf 15x14 | deleted |
| 978a perf 15x14 | deleted |
| 1079 22p | 1078 |
| 1079A 23p | 1079 |
| 1082A 32p | 1083 |
| 1083 34p | 1084 |
| 1084 35p | 1085 |
| **Bahamas** | |
| 616c | 616a |
| **Basutoland** | |
| J1 | J1a |
| J1a | J1 |
| **Bermuda** | |
| 109a, 112a | deleted |
| 118b, 119b, 120c, 121b | deleted |
| **British Guiana** | |
| 66 | 66a |
| 66a | 66 |
| 88 | 85a |
| 101b, 101c | deleted |
| 241 | 241a |
| 241a | 241 |
| **British Honduras** | |
| 25a | deleted |
| 93a | deleted |
| **Bushire** | |
| N30 | deleted |
| **Cameroons** | |
| 55d, 55e | deleted |
| **Canada** | |
| 938 | 937 |
| 938A | 938 |
| 941B | 942 |
| 941A | 943 |
| 942 | 944 |
| 1181, 1184 | deleted |
| **Ceylon** | |
| 120A | deleted |
| **Christmas Island** | |
| 209a | 211a |
| **Cook Islands** | |
| 63a | deleted |
| 1102-1106 | 1002-1006 |
| **Falkland Islands** | |
| 19a, 19b, 19c, 19h | deleted |

| No. in 1989 Cat. | No. in 1990 Cat. |
|---|---|
| **Fiji** | |
| 476a, 476b | deleted |
| **Guyana** | |
| 624D | E4 |
| **India** Nabha | |
| 6a | deleted |
| **India** Patiala | |
| O4b, O7a | deleted |
| **Labuan** | |
| 10A | deleted |
| **Lesotho** | |
| 577A | 612 |
| **Malaya** Negri Sembilan | |
| 19c | deleted |
| **Malaya** Selangor | |
| 12B | deleted |
| **Norfolk Island** | |
| 405-416A | 404-416 |
| **North Borneo** | |
| 59b, 60a, 63a | deleted |
| J39a | deleted |
| **Papua New Guinea** | |
| 268a, 269a | deleted |
| 341a | deleted |
| 359a | deleted |
| 674 | 663 |
| 663 | 664 |
| 675 | 665 |
| 668-670 | 666-668 |
| 676 | 669 |
| 664 | 670 |
| 665 | 672 |
| 672 | 673 |
| 666 | 674 |
| 673 | 675 |
| 667 | 676 |
| **Qatar** | |
| 520a | 520e |
| **Sabah** | |
| 42a, 43a | 35a, 36a |
| **St. Helena** | |
| 1a, 2a | deleted |
| **Seychelles** | |
| 22c, 23c, 25a, 26a, 22e | deleted |
| 443A-443H | 403A-403H |
| **South Australia** | |
| 71c | deleted |
| **Tasmania** | |
| 2b | deleted |
| **Transvaal** | |
| 222, 222A | deleted |

# Dies of British Colonial Stamps Referred to in the Catalogue

DIE A.

DIE B.

DIE I.

DIE II.

**DIE A:**

**1.** The lines in the groundwork vary in thickness and are not uniformly straight.

**2.** The seventh and eighth lines from the top, in the groundwork, converge where they meet the head.

**3.** There is a small dash in the upper part of the second jewel in the band of the crown.

**4.** The vertical color line in front of the throat stops at the sixth line of shading on the neck.

**DIE B:**

**1.** The lines in the groundwork are all thin and straight.

**2.** All the lines of the background are parallel.

**3.** There is no dash in the upper part of the second jewel in the band of the crown.

**4.** The vertical color line in front of the throat stops at the eighth line of shading on the neck.

**DIE I:**

**1.** The base of the crown is well below the level of the inner white line around the vignette.

**2.** The labels inscribed "POSTAGE" and "REVENUE" are cut square at the top.

**3.** There is a white "bud" on the outer side of the main stem of the curved ornaments in each lower corner.

**4.** The second (thick) line below the country name has the ends next to the crown cut diagonally.

DIE Ia.
1 as die II.
2 and 3 as die I.

DIE Ib.
1 and 3 as die II.
2 as die I.

**DIE II:**

**1.** The base of the crown is aligned with the underside of the white line around the vignette.

**2.** The labels curve inward at the top inner corners.

**3.** The "bud" has been removed from the outer curve of the ornaments in each corner.

**4.** The second line below the country name has the ends next to the crown cut vertically.

Wmk. 1
Crown and C C

Wmk. 2
Crown and C A

Wmk. 3
Multiple Crown
and C A

Wmk. 4
Multiple Crown
and Script C A

Wmk. 4a

Wmk. 314
St. Edward's Crown
and C A Multiple

Wmk. 373

Wmk. 384

# British Colonial and Crown Agents Watermarks

Watermarks 1 to 4, 314, 373, and 384, common to many British territories, are illustrated here to avoid duplication.

The letters "CC" of Wmk. 1 identify the paper as having been made for the use of the Crown Colonies, while the letters "CA" of the others stand for "Crown Agents." Both Wmks. 1 and 2 were used on stamps printed by De La Rue & Co.

Wmk. 3 was adopted in 1904; Wmk. 4 in 1921; Wmk. 314 in 1957; Wmk. 373 in 1974; and Wmk. 384 in 1985.

In Wmk. 4a, a non-matching crown of the general St. Edwards type (bulging on both sides at top) was substituted for one of the Wmk. 4 crowns which fell off the dandy roll. The non-matching crown occurs in 1950-52 printings in a horizontal row of crowns on certain regular stamps of Johore and Seychelles, and on various postage due stamps of Barbados, Basutoland, British Guiana, Gold Coast, Grenada, Northern Rhodesia, St. Lucia, Swaziland and Trinidad and Tobago. A variation of Wmk. 4a, with the non-matching crown in a horizontal row of crown-CA-crown, occurs on regular stamps of Bahamas, St. Kitts-Nevis and Singapore.

Wmk. 314 was intentionally used sideways, starting in 1966. When a stamp was issued with Wmk. 314 both upright and sideways, the sideways varieties usually are listed also — with minor numbers. In many of the later issues, Wmk. 314 is slightly visible.

Wmk. 373 is usually only faintly visible.

# Index and Identifier

# Addenda

## GAMBIA

Tribute to John F. Kennedy
A126

| **1988, Sept. 1** | | **Litho.** | ***Perf.*** | |
|---|---|---|---|---|
| *763* A126 | 75b | Sailing | 22 | 22 |
| *764* A126 | 1d | Peace Corps enactment | 30 | 30 |
| *765* A126 | 1.25d | Public address, vert. | 38 | 38 |
| *766* A126 | 12d | Grave, Arlington Natl. Cemetery | 3.60 | 3.60 |

**Souvenir Sheet**

| | | | | |
|---|---|---|---|---|
| *767* A126 | 15d | Kennedy, vert. | 4.50 | 4.50 |

No. 767 has multicolored margin continuing the design and picturing the Mercury space capsule in orbit. Size:

# For the Record

The items recorded here appeared on the stamp market in the 1960's and '70s, and have not been listed in the *Scott Standard Postage Stamp Catalogue.* They are arranged chronologically and briefly described. Completeness is not claimed.

## Contents



### ADEN

All Aden issues without overprint exist perf. and imperf.

**Kathiri State of Seiyun**
**1,000 Fils = 1 Dinar (1966)**

**1966**

**Issues of 1954-64 Surcharged "SOUTH ARABIA" and New Values**

**Narrow Space between "South Arabia" and New Value.** *Apr. 1.* 5f on 5c, 5f on 10c, 10f on 15c, 15f on 25c, 20f on 35c, 25f on 50c, 35f on 70c, 50f on 1sh, 65f on 1sh25c, 75f on 1sh50c, 100f on 2sh, 250f on 5sh, 500f on 10sh (13v).

**Wide Space between "South Arabia" and New Value.** *Aug. 13.* Same denominations on same basic stamps (13v).

**Olympics, Past and Future (1932-68).** Inscriptions and Olympic rings overprinted on South Arabia surcharges. 10, 20, 35, 50, 65, 75, 100, 250, 500f (9v).

**World Cup Soccer Championships.** "CHAMPION: ENGLAND" and "FOOTBALL 1966" overprinted on South Arabia surcharges. *July 30.* 10, 20, 35, 50, 100, 250, 500f (7v).

**International Telecommunication Union.** *Oct. 25.* 5, 10, 15, 25, 35, 50, 65f (7v). Souv. sheet of 2 (25, 35f.) (Telstar, Relay, Ranger).

**Churchill paintings.** *Dec. 5.* 10, 15, 20, 25, 35, 60, 65, (8v). Souv. sheet, 65f.

**1967**

**"WORLD PEACE"** and famous names overprinted on South Arbia surcharges. 10, 20, 35, 50, 65, 75, 100, 250, 500f (9v) (Nehru, Churchill, Hammarskjold, J.F. Kennedy, Ludwig Ehrhard, L.B. Johnson, Eleanor Roosevelt).

**American Astronauts'** names overprinted on South Arabia surcharges. 10, 20, 35, 50, 100, 250f (6v) (Shepard, Grissom, Glenn, Carpenter, Schirra, Cooper).

**Paintings.** 5, 10, 15, 20, 25, 35, 50, 65, 75f (9v). 2 Souv. sheets. 65f and 75f (Reynolds, Degas, Manet, Bellows, Goya, Van Dyck, Gainsborough, Gauguin, da Vinci).

**Churchill Coin.** 75f. Souv. sheet, 75f.

**Gazelle.** 20f.

**Renoir paintings.** 10, 35, 50, 65, 75f; airmail, 100, 200, 250f (8v). Souv. sheet, 250f.

**10th Winter Olympics,** Grenoble. *June.* 10, 25, 35, 50, 75f; airmail, 100, 250f (7v). Souv. sheet, 250f.

**12th Boy Scout Jamboree,** Idaho. *Aug.* Airmail, 150f. Souv. sheet, 150f.

**Toulouse-Lautrec paintings.** 10, 35, 50, 65, 75f; airmail, 100, 200, 250f (8v). Souv. sheet, 250f.

**Spanish Riding Academy,** Vienna. 10, 25, 35, 50, 75f; airmail, 100, 250f (7v). Souv. sheet, 250f.

**Vermeer paintings.** 25f; airmail, 150, 500f. Souv. sheet, 500f.

**Japanese prints.** 25f; airmail, 150, 500f. Souv. sheet, 500f.

**19th Summer Olympics,** Mexico City. Airmail, 500f. Souv. Sheet. 500f.

**Qu'aiti State in Hadhramaut**

**1966**

**Aden Nos. 41-52 Surcharged** "SOUTH ARABIA" and New Values **Wide Space between Bar and "South Arabia."** *Apr. 1.* 5f on 5c, 5f on 10c, 10f on 15c, 15f on 25c, 20f on 35c, 25f on 50c, 35f on 70c, 50f on 1sh, 65f on 1sh 25c, 100f on 2sh, 250f on 5sh, 500f on 10sh (12v).

**Same. Overprinted "1874-1965 WINSTON CHURCHIL."** *Apr. 1.* 5f on 10c, 10f on 15c, 15f on 25c.

**Same. Overprinted "1917-1963 JOHN F. KENNEDY."** *Apr. 1.* 20f on 35c, 25f on 50c, 35f on 70c.

**World Cup Soccer Championships.** *Aug. 11.* 5, 10, 15, 20, 25, 35, 50, 65f (6v). Souv. sheet of 2: 50, 65f.

**Pre-Olympics,** Mexico. *Oct. 25.* 75f. Souv. sheet, 75f.

**International Cooperation Year.** *Oct. 6.* 5, 10, 15, 20, 25, 35, 50, 65f (9v). Souv. shet of 2: 5, 25f.

**1967**

**Stampex, London.** 5, 10, 15, 20, 25f; airmail, 50, 65f (7v). Souv. sheet, 65f.

**Pre-Olympics,** Mexico. 75f. Souv. sheet, 75f.

**Moon Exploration.** 10, 25, 35, 50, 75f; airmail, 100, 250f (7v). Souv. sheet of 2: 100, 250f.

**Famous paintings.** 5, 10, 15, 20, 25f; airmail, 50, 65f (7v). Souv. sheet of 2: 50, 65f.

**12th Boy Scout Jamboree,** Idaho. Airmail 35f. Souv. sheet, 35f.

**10th Winter Olympics,** Grenoble. 5, 10, 15, 20, 25f; airmail, 35, 50, 65f (8v). Souv. sheet of 2: 50, 65f.

**Amphilex,** Amsterdam. Airmail, 75f. Souv. sheet, 75f.

**American Astronauts' Memorial.** Airmail, 500f. Souv. sheet, 500f.

**Expo '67,** Montreal. Airmail, 150f. Souv. sheet, 150f.

**36th Monte Carlo Rally.** Airmail, 75f. Souv. sheet, 75f.

**Manet paintings.** 10, 35, 50, 65, 75f; airmail, 200, 250f (7v). Souv. sheet, 250f, perf., imperf.

**Kennedy and Space Projects.** 10, 25, 35, 50, 75f; airmail, 100, 250f (7v). Souv. sheet of 2: 100, 250f.

**1968**

**Lucas Cranach paintings.** 25, 50f; airmail, 100, 150f, se-tenant (2 each) (8v). Souv. sheet, 500f.

**Cave Men and Creatures.** 5, 10, 35, 50, 65, 75f; airmail, 200f triangles (2 each) (14v).

**Renoir paintings.** 25f; airmail. 100, 150, 500f (4v). Souvenir sheet, 500f.

**Wolf Hunt, by Rubens.** Airmail 75f. Souvenir sheet, 75f.

**Horse paintings.** 10, 35, 50, 65, 75f; airmail, 200, 250f (7v) (Clouet, Uccello, Renoir, El Greco, Gericault, Del Cossa).

**Mahra State**

**1967**

**Flag.** 5, 10, 15, 20, 25, 35, 50, 65, 100, 250, 500f (11v).

**Kennedy.** 10, 15, 25, 50, 75, 100, 150f; airmail, 250, 500f (9v). Souvenir sheet, 500f.

**12th Boy Scout Jamboree,** Idaho. 15, 75, 100, 150f (4v).

**19th Summer Olympics, Mexico City 1968,** 10, 25, 50f; airmail, 250, 500f (5v). Souvenir sheet, 500f.

**Arab miniatures.** 10, 15, 25, 50, 75, 100, 150f; airmail, 250, 500f (9v). Souvenir sheet of 2: 250, 500f.

**Paintings,** 10, 15, 25, 50, 75, 100, 150f; airmail, 250, 500f (9v) (Hals, Gauguin, Fragonard, van Orley, Botticelli, Velazquez, Van Dyck, Caravaggio, David). Souvenir sheet, 500f.

**Space Exploration.** 10, 15, 25, 50, 75, 100, 150f; airmail, 250, 500f (9v). Souvenir sheet of 2: 250, 500f.

**10th Winter Olympics,** Grenoble, 10, 15, 25, 50, 75, 100, 150f; airmail, 250, 500f (9v). Souvenir sheet of 2: 250, 500f.

**BANGLADESH**
**1974**
**Universal Postal Union,** centenary. *Oct. 9.* Perf. 25p, 1.25, 1.75, 5t (4v). Souvenir sheet of 4, imperf.

**BARBUDA** 100 Cents = 1 Dollar
**1968**
**Map of Barbuda.** *Nov. 19.* ½, 1, 2, 3, 4, 5, 6, 10, 15c (9v).
**19th Summer Olympics,** Mexico. *Dec. 20.* 25, 35, 75c (3v). Souvenir sheet, $1.

**1969**
**Fish.** *Feb. 5, Mar. 6.* 25, 35, 50, 75c, $1, 2.50, 5 (7v).
**Easter.** *Mar. 24.* 25, 35, 75c (3v).
**3rd Caribbean Scout Jamboree.** *Aug. 7.* 25, 35, 75c (3v).
**Christmas** (Sistine Madonna). *Oct. 20.* ½, 25, 35, 75c (4v).

**1970**
**Provisional.** *Feb. 26.* 20c on ½c of 1968 map issue.
**Easter** (Italian paintings). *Mar. 16.* 25, 35, 75c, triptych (3v).
**Monarchs of England.** *1970-71.* 35cx37 (37v). William I-Victoria).
**Dickens,** death centenary. *July 10.* 20, 75c.
**Great barracuda.** *July 22.* 20c.
**Christmas paintings.** *Oct. 15.* 20, 50, 75c (3v). (Bellini, detail from Wilton diptych, della Francesca).
**British Red Cross** centenary. *Dec. 21.* 20, 35, 75c (3v).

**1971**
**Easter** (Raphael paintings). *Apr. 7.* 35, 50, 75c, triptych (3v).
**Tourism** (tower, boats, hotel, Mystery stone). *May 10.* 20, 25, 50c, 75c (4v).
**Christmas paintings.** *Oct. 4.* ½, 35, 50, 75c (4v). (Raphael, Botticelli, Bellini).
**Durer,** 500th birth anniversary. *Dec. 7.* 20, 35, 50, 75c (4v). (Crab, beetle, young hare, knight on horseback).

**Stamps of Antigua Overprinted "Barbuda"**
**1973**
**Princess Anne's Wedding.** *Nov. 14.* 35c, $2.
**Carnival.** *Nov. 26.* 20, 35, 75c (3v). Souvenir sheet of 4 (5, 20, 35, 75c).
**British Military Uniforms.** *Nov. 26.* ½, 20 (2 types), 75c (3v). Souvenir sheet of 5 (½, 10, 20, 35, 75c).
**Definitives.** *Nov. 26, Dec. 11.* ½, 1, 2, 3, 4, 5, 6, 10, 15, 20, 25, 35, 50, 75c, $1, 5 (16v).
**Christmas paintings.** *Dec. 11.* 3, 5, 20, 35c, $1 (5v) (David, Stomer, Raphael, Battista, Murillo). Souvenir sheet of 5.
**Royal Visit** (on Wedding issue). *Dec. 16.* 35c, $2. Souvenir sheet of 2: 35c, $2.

**1974**
**Definitives.** *Feb. 18.* $2.50, both upright and sideways watermarks.
**University of West Indies,** 25th anniversary. *Feb. 18.* 5, 20, 35, 75c (4v).
**British Military Uniforms.** *May 1.* ½, 10, 20, 35, 75c (5v).
**UPU Centenary.** *July 15.* Se-tenant stamps overprinted in red alternating: "Barbuda / 15 Sept. / 1874 G.P.U." and "Barbuda / 13 July 1922." ½cx2, 1cx2, 2cx2, 5cx2, 20cx2, 35cx2, $1x2 (14v). Souvenir sheet of 7 plus label (½, 1, 2, 5, 20, 35c, $1).
*Sept. 30.* 35c, $1.20, $2.50 (3v). Souvenir sheet of 3.*
**Carnival** (steel bands). *Aug. 14.* 5, 20, 35, 75c (4v). Souvenir sheet of 4.
**World Cup Soccer Championships,** Munich. *Sept. 2.* 35c, $1.20, $2.50. Souvenir sheet of 3 (35c, $1.20, $2.50).*
*Sept. 23.* 5, 35, 75c, $1 (4v). Souvenir sheet of 4.
**Christmas.** *Oct. 15.* ½, 1, 2, 3, 5, 20, 35, 75c (8v). Souvenir sheet of 4.
**Churchill,** birth centenary (first issue, Antigua A70). *Oct. 20.* 5, 35, 75c, $1 (4v). Souvenir sheet of 4.
**Churchill,** birth centenary (second issue). *Nov. 20.* 5, 35, 75c, $1 (4v). Souvenir sheet of 4.*
**Definitives.** *Oct. 15.* 4, 5, 6, 10, 15, 20, 25, 35, 75c (9v). (Fish, buildings, plane).*

**1975**
**Definitives.** *Jan. 6.* ½, 1, 2, 3, 50c, $1, 2.50, 5 (8v). (Flowers, building, fauna).*
**Nelson's Dockyard.** *Mar. 17.* 5, 15, 35, 50c, $1 (5v). Souvenir sheet of 5 and label.
**Sea Battles of the West Indies.** *May 30.* 35, 50, 75c, 95c (4v).*
**Apollo-Soyuz Space Project.** $5 (1975 type, perf. 14x14½) ovptd. "Apollo" and "Soyuz", se-tenant in sheets of 25 (last vertical row without ovpt.)*
**Definitive.** *Sept. 19.* $10 (Hibiscus).*
**Military Uniforms.** *Sept. 17.* 35, 50, 75, 95c (4v).*
**U.N. 30th Anniversary,** Churchill second issue ovpt. *Oct. 24.* 5, 35, 75c, $1 (4v). Souvenir sheet of 4.*
**Christmas paintings.** *Nov. 17.* ½, 1, 2, 3, 5, 10, 35c, $2 (8v). Souvenir sheet of 4 (Correggio, El Greco, Durer, Antonello, Bellini).
**World Cricket Cup Winners.** *Dec. 15.* 5, 35c, $2 (3v).

**1976**
**U.S. Bicentennial.** *Mar. 8.* 15, 35c, $1, 2 in se-tenant horizontal strips of 3 forming composite design depicting revolutionary scenes (12v). Sheets of 18 including 5 strips of 3 and one strip of 3 symbolic labels. 2 souvenir sheets of 6 with marginal stars and stripes (15cx3, 35cx3; $1x3, $2x3).*
**Birds.** *June 30.* 35, 50, 75, 95c, $1.25, 2 (6v).*
**Royal Visit to U.S.A.** *Aug. 26.* Overprinted on Bicentennial issue "H.M. Queen Elizabeth/Royal Visit 6th July 1976/H.R.H. Duke of Edinburgh." Se-tenant strip of 3 of each value imperf. between, 15, 35c, $1, 2. 2 souvenir sheets (15cx3, 35cx3; $1x3, $2x3).*
**Christmas,** paintings. *Dec. 2.* 8, 10, 15, 50c, $1 (5v).
**Summer Olympics,** Montreal. *Dec. 20.* ½, 1, 2, 15, 30c, $1, 2 (7v). Souvenir sheet of 4 (15, 30c, $1, 2).
**Special Events 1976,** UNPA, Nobel, Viking, Cricket, Telephone, Operation Sail. *Dec. 28.* ½, 1, 10, 50c, $1, 2 (6v). Souvenir sheet of 4 (10, 50c, $1, 2).

**1977**
**Telephone Centennial.** *Jan. 31.* 75c, $1.25, 2 (3v). Souvenir sheet of 3.*
**Silver Jubilee, QEII.** *Feb. 7.* 75c, $1.25 in se-tenant strips of 3 (6v). Printed in sheets of 15 with 3 strips and 2 strips of 3 labels. Souvenir sheet of 6 (75cx3, $1.25x3).*
**Definitives,** flora, fauna, buildings. *Apr. 4.* ½, 1, 2, 3, 4, 5, 6, 10, 15, 20, 25, 35, 50, 75c, $1, 2.50, 5, 10 (18v).
**Silver Jubilee QEII.** *Apr. 4.* 10, 30, 50, 90c, $2.50 (5v). Souvenir sheet, $5. Booklet containing 2 self-adhesive panes; 50cx6 and Souvenir sheet, $5.
**Caribbean Scout Jamboree.** *June 13.* ½, 1, 2, 10, 30, 50c, $2 (7v). Souvenir sheet of 3 (30, 50c, $2).*
**Carnival,** 21st anniversary. *Aug. 12.* 10, 30, 50, 90c, $1 (5v). Souvenir sheet of 4 (30, 50, 90c, $1).
**Christmas,** paintings. ½, 1, 2, 8, 10, 25c, $2 (7v) (Tura, Crivelli, Pontarino, Lotto). Souvenir sheet of 4 (8, 10, 25c, $2).
**Royal Visit.** *Oct. 28.* 50c, $1.50, 2.50 (3v). Souvenir sheet of 3.*
Jubilee issue ovpt. "Royal Visit/28th October 1977." 10, 30, 50, 90c, $2.50 (5v). Souvenir sheet, $5.
**Special Events.** *Dec. 29.* 75cx4 (75th anniv. Navigable Airships); 95cx4 (20th anniv. Russian Space); $1.25x4 (50th anniv. Lindbergh); $2x4 (QEII Jubilee); $5x4 (400th anniv. Rubens) (20v). Souvenir sheet of 20 with 4 designs of each value printed in setenant blocks of 4 plus label.

**1978**
**Statehood,** 10th anniversary. *Feb. 15.* 10, 15, 50, 90c, $2 (5v). Souvenir sheet of 4 (15, 50, 90c, $2).
**Easter,** Michelangelo paintings, sculptures. *Mar. 23.* 75, 90c, $1.25, 2 (4v). Souvenir sheet of 4.
**First Powered Flight,** 75th anniversary. *Mar. 23.* ½, 1, 2, 10, 50, 90c, $2 (7v). Souvenir sheet, $2.50 (Flyer A).
**Sailing Week.** *May 22.* 10, 50, 90c, $2 (4v). Souvenir sheet, $2.50.
**Coronation,** 25th anniversary. *June 2.* 75cx2, $1.50x2, $2.50x2 (6v). Each value printed in strip with 2 stamps + label in sheet of 4. Souvenir sheet of 6, 10, 30, 50, 90c, $2.50 (5v). Souvenir sheet, $5. Also printed in sheets of 3 with backgrounds in different colors.
**Coronation,** 25th anniversary. Royal Stagecoaches. *June.* Booklet containing 2 self-adhesive panes: 25cx3 plus 50cx3; souvenir sheet, $5.
**World Cup Soccer,** Argentina. *Sept. 12.* 10, 15c, $3 (3v). Souvenir sheet of 4 (25, 30, 50c, $2).
**Flowers.** *Nov. 20.* 25, 50, 90c, $2 (4v). Souvenir sheet, $2.50.
**Christmas,** Rubens paintings. *Nov. 20.* 8, 25c, $2 (3v). Souvenir sheet, $4.
**Flora and Fauns.** *Nov. 20.* 25, 50, 75, 95c, $1.25 (5v).*
**Special Events.** *Dec. 29.* 75c (World Cup Soccer, Argentina). 95c (75th anniv. Powered Flight), $1.25 (1st Atlantic Balloon Crossing), $2 (25th anniv. Coronation) (4v). Souvenir sheet of 4 (75, 95c, $1.25).*
*Issues with original design, not overprinted on those of Antigua.

**1979**
**Sir Rowland Hill** (1795-1879), originator of Penny Postage. *Apr. 4.* 75, 95c, $1.25, 2 (4v). Souvenir sheet of 4 (75, 95c, $1.25, 2). 25, 50c, $1, 2 (4v). Souvenir sheet, $2.50.
**Easter,** works by Albrecht Durer. *Apr. 29.* 10, 50c, $4 (3v). Souvenir sheet, $2.50.
**International Civil Aviation Organization,** 30th anniverary. *May 24.* 75, 95c, $1.25 (3v). Exist in se-tenant block of 4 with label.
**International Year of the Child.** *May 24.* 25, 50, 90c, $2 (4v). Souvenir sheet, $5.
**Sport Fish.** *Aug. 1.* 30, 50, 90c, $3 (4v). Souvenir sheet, $2.50.
**Capt. James Cook.** 200th death anniversary. *Aug. 1.* 25, 50, 90c, $3 (4v). Souvenir sheet, $2.50.
**International Year of the Child,** Paintings by Albrecht Durer. *Sept. 24.* 25, 50, 75c, $1.25 (4v). Souvenir sheet of 4 (25, 50, 75c, $1.25).
**Christmas,** simulated stained-glass window. *Nov. 21.* 8, 25, 50c, $4 (4v). Souvenir sheet, $3.

**1980**
**Summer Olympic Games.** Moscow. *Feb. 10.* 25c, $1, 2, (4v). Souvenir sheet, $3.
**"London 1980".** *May 6.* (Antigua overprinted Barbuda). 25, 50, $1, 2 (4v).
**First Moon Landing,** 10th anniv. *May 21.* 75, 95, $1.25, 2 (4v). Souvenir sheet of 4, contains stamps of same design.
**Birds.** *June 16.* 1, 2, 4, 6, 10, 15, 20, 25, 35, 50, 75, $1, 1.50, 2, 2,50, 5, 7.50, 10 (18v).
**Famous Art Masterpieces.** *July 29.* 10, 30, 50, 90, $1, 4 (6v). (Donatello, Botticelli, Cerveteri, Bosch, van der Goes, Bronzino, Rembrandt). Souvenir sheet, $5.
**Rotary Intl.,** 75th anniv. *Sept. 8.* 30, 50, 90, $3 (4v). Souvenir sheet, $5.
**Queen Mother Elizabeth.** 80th birthday. *Oct. 6.* (Antigua overprinted Barbuda). 10, $2.50. Souvenir sheet $3.
**Birds.** *Dec. 8.* (Antigua overprinted Barbuda). 10, 30, $1, 2 (4v). Souvenir sheet, $2.50.

**1981**
**Locomotives,** Sugar-Cane Railway. *Jan. 26.* (Antigua overprinted Barbuda). 25, 50, 90, $3 (4v).Souvenir sheet, $2.50.
**Famous Women.** *March 9.* 50, 90, $1, 4 (4v). (Nightingale, Curie, Johnson, Roosevelt).
**Walt Disney,** various scenes from "Chips Ahoy." *May 15.* 10, 20, 25, 30, 35, 40, 75, $1, 2 (9v). Souvenir sheet. $2.50.
**Picasso, 100th birth anniv. Paintings.** *June 9.* (Antigua overprinted Barbuda). 10, 50, 90, $4 (4v). Souvenir sheet, $5.
**Royal Wedding,** Prince Charles and Lady Diana. *Aug. 14.* (Antigua overprinted Barbuda). 25, 50, $4.
**Royal Wedding.** Self Adhesive Booklet of 7. *Oct. 12.* (Antigua overprinted Barbuda). 2 panes: (2) 25, (2) $1, (2) $2, (1) $5.
**Girl Guides,** 50th anniv. *Dec. 14.* (Antigua overprinted Barbuda). 10, 50, 90, $2.50 (4v). Souvenir sheet, $5.
**Intl. Year for Disabled People,** *Dec. 14.* (Antigua overprinted Barbuda). 10, 50, 90, $2 (4v). Souvenir sheet, $5.
**Independence,** *Nov. 1.* 6c, 10c, 20c, 25c, 35c, 50c, 75c, $1, $2.50, $5, $10 (11v).
**Christmas,** *Dec. 22.* (Antigua overprinted Barbuda). 8c, 30c, $1, $3 (4v). Souvenir sheet $5.
**Royal Wedding. Buildings.** *July 27.* Pairs: $1, $1.50, $4 (6v).

**1983**
**Commonwealth Day.** *Mar. 14.* (Antigua overprinted Barbuda). 25c, 45c, 60c, $3 (4v).
**1981 Royal Wedding Buildings surcharged.** *Oct. 21.* Pairs: 45c on $1, 50c on $1.50, 60c on $4 (6v).

**BIAFRA**
**1968**
**Independence,** first anniversary. *Feb. 5.* 2p, 4p, 1sh (3v).
**Definitives.** Nigeria Nos. 184-187, 189-197 overprinted "Sovereign Biafra" and arms. *Apr.* ½, 1, 1½, 2, 4, 6, 9p, 1sh, 1sh3p, 2sh6p, 5sh, 10sh, £1 (13v).
**Biafra-France, Friendship.** Nigeria Nos. 184, 185 surcharged ½d+5sh, 1d+£1.
**Independence,** 2nd issue. *May 30.* 4p, 1sh, 2sh6p, 5sh, 10sh (5v). Same, overprinted "Help Biafran Children." 4p+2p, 1sh+6p, 2sh6p+1sh, 5sh+2sh6p, 10sh+2sh6p (5v).
**Butterflies and Flowers.** *Sept. 2.* 4p, 1sh6p, 2sh6p, 5sh (4v).
**19th Summer Olympics,** Mexico. Butterfly issue overprinted with Olympic rings and "Mexico Olympics/1968." *Oct.* 4p, 1sh6p, 2sh6p, 5sh (4v).

**1969**
**Independence,** 2nd anniversary. *May 30.* 2, 4p, 1sh, 2sh6p (4v). Souvenir sheet, 10sh. perf., imperf.
**Pope's Visit to Africa** (Paul VI). *Sept. 25.* 4, 6, 9p, 3sh (4v). Souvenir sheet, 10sh, perf., imperf.
**Christmas.** Papal Visit issue overprinted "Peace on Earth/and Good Will/To All Men." *Dec. 17.* 4, 6, 9p, 3sh (4v). Souvenir sheet, 10sh.

**1970**
**Save Biafra.** *Feb. 25.* Independence issue of 1969 overprinted in red "Save Biafra / 9th Jan. / 1970". 2p+8p, 4p+1sh4p, 1sh+4sh, 2sh6p+10sh (4v). Souvenir sheet. 10sh+£1, perf., imperf.

**BOPHUTHATSWANA**
**1977**
**Independence,** arms and flag. *Dec. 6.* 4, 10, 15, 20c (4v). Souvenir sheet of 4, imperf.
**Definitives,** fauna. *Dec. 6.* 1, 2, 3, 4, 5, 6, 7, 8, 9, 10, 15, 20, 25, 30, 50c. 1r, 2 (17v).

**1978**
**High Blood Pressure.** *Apr. 7.* 4, 10, 15c.
**Road Safety.** *July 12.* 4, 10, 15, 20c (4v).
**Precious Stones and Marble Industry.** *Oct. 3.* 4, 10, 15, 20c (4v).
**First Powered Flight,** 75th anniversary. *Dec. 1.* 10, 15c.
**Independence Anniversary.** *Dec. 6.* 4, 15c.

**1979**
**Beer Industry.** *Jan. 4.* 15, 20, 25c (4v)
**Knoetze-Tate Boxing Match.** *June 2.* 15cx2 in setenant pair.
**International Year of the Child,** local fables. *June 7.* 4, 15, 20, 25c (4v).
**Platinum Industry.** *Aug. 15.* 4, 15, 20, 25c (4v).

**1980**
**Anti-smoking Campaign.** *Mar. 5.* 5c.
**Edible wild fruit.** *June 4.* 5, 10, 15, 20c (4v).
**Birds.** *Sept. 10.* 5, 10, 15, 20c (4v).
**Tourism.** *Dec. 5.* 5, 10, 15, 20c (4v).

**1981**
**Intl. Year of the Disabled.** *Jan. 30.* 5, 15, 20, 25c (4v).
**Easter.** *April 1.* 5, 15, 20, 25c (4v).
**History of the Telephone.** *July 31.* 5, 15, 20, 25c (4v).
**Indigenous Grasses.** *Nov. 25.* 5, 15, 20, 25c (4v).

**1982**
**Scouting,** *Jan. 29.* 5c, 15c, 20c, 25c (4v).
**Communications,** *Sept. 3.* 8c, 15c, 20c, 25c (4v).

**CISKEI**
**1981**
**Independence.** *Dec. 4.* 5c, 15c, 20c, 25c (4v).
**Birds.** *Dec. 4.* 1c, 2c, 3c, 4c, 5c, 6c, 7c, 8c, 9c, 10c, 15c, 20c, 25c, 30c, 50c, 1r, 2r (17v).

**1982**
**Pineapple Industry.** *Aug. 20.* 8c, 15c, 20c, 30c (4v).

**CYPRUS Turkish Cypriot Mail**
**1973**
**Turkish Republic,** 50th anniversary. *Oct. 19.* 3, 5, 10, 15, 20, 50, 70m (7v).

**1975**
**Federation Issue.** *Mar. 3.* Local issue of 1973-1974 surcharged KIBRIS / TURK / FEDERE / DEVLETI / 13.2.75. 30m on 20m, 100m on 10m (2v).
**Cyprus Scenes.** *Apr. 21.* 3, 10, 15, 20, 25, 30, 50, 100, 250, 500m (10v).
**Peace in Cyprus.** *July 20.* 30, 50, 150m (3v).
**Europa, paintings.** *Dec. 29.* 90, 100m (2v). (I. Guney, F. Direkoglu).

**1976**
**Provisionals.** *Apr. 29.* 1975 definitives surcharged 10m on 50m, 30m on 100m (2v).
**Europa,** ceramic statuettes. *May 5.* 60, 120m (2v).
**Export Products,** fruits. *June 28.* 10, 25, 40, 60, 80m (5v).
**Summer Olympics,** Montreal. *July 17.* 60, 100m (2v).
**Tourist Series,** various scenes. *Aug. 2.* 5, 15, 20m (3v).
**Liberation Monument.** *Nov. 1.* 30, 150m (2v).

**1977**
**Europa.** *May 2.* 80, 100m (2v).
**Handicrafts.** *June 27.* 15, 30, 125M (3v).
**Namik Kemal,** poet. 30, 140m (2v).
**Tourist Series,** edifices. 20, 40, 70, 80m (4v).

**1978**
**Social Security.** *Apr. 17.* 150, 275, 375k.
**Europa 1978.** *May 2.* 225, 450k.
**Transport,** land, sea, air. *July 10.* 75, 100, 650k.
**National Oath.** *Sept. 13.* 150, 225, 775k.
**Ataturk Memorial.** *Nov. 10.* 75, 450, 650k.

**1979**
**Provisional Surcharges** (on Export Product issue). *June 4.* 50k on 25m, ITL on 40m, 3TL on 60m, 5TL on 80m (4v).
**Turkish Peace Operation in Cyprus,** 5th anniversary. *July 20.* Souvenir sheet, 15TL.
**Europa (CEPT).** *Aug. 20.* 2, 3, 8TL. (3v).
**International Telecommunications Union** (U.T.I.), 50th anniversary. *Sept. 24.* 2, 5, 6TL (3v).
**International Year of the Child.** *Oct. 29.* 1.50, 4.50, 6TL (3v).

**1980**
**Islamic Conference.** *Mar.* 2.50TL, conference in Cyprus: 10TL, 8th World Muslim conference; 20TL, Hejira, 1500th anniverary (3v).
**Europa (CEPT),** portraits. *May 23.* 5, 30TL.
**Historical Monuments.** *June 25.* 2½, 3½, 5, 10, 20TL. (5v).
**Cyprus Stamp Centenary.** *Aug. 16.* 7½, 15, 50TL.
**Dome of the Rock,** Palestinian Solidarity, *Oct. 16.* 15, 35TL.

**1981**
**Day of Islamic Solidarity** with the T.F.S.K. *March 24.* 1, 35TL.
**ATATURK,** Stamp Exhibition. *May 19.* 20TL and label.
**Europa (CEPT),** folk dances. *June 29.* 10, 30TL.
**Ataturk,** birth centenary. *July 23.* Souvenir sheet, 150TL.
**Wild Flowers,** *Sept. 28.* 1, 10, 25, 150TL (4v).
**Intl. Year of the Disabled,** Campaign Against Discrimination. World Food Day. *Oct. 16.* 7½, 10, 20TL (3v).
**Solidarity with the People of Palestine.** *Nov. 29.* 10TL.
**Royal Wedding.** Prince Charles and Lady Diana. *Nov. 30.* 50TL.

**1982**
**Wildflowers,** *Jan. 22.* 5, 30, 50, 100TL (4v).

**GRENADA Grenadines of Grenada**
**1973**
**Princess Anne's Wedding** (overprinted on Grenada issue). *Dec. 24.* 25c, $2. Souvenir sheet of 2 (75c, $1).

**1974**
**Definitives** (overprinted on Grenada issue). *May 29.* 1, 2, 3, 5, 8, 10, 12, 25c, $1, 2, 3, 5 (12v).
**World Cup Soccer Championships,** Munich. (Grenada type A81). *Sept. 17.* ½, 1, 2, 10, 25, 50, 75c, $1 (8v). Souvenir sheet, $2.
**Churchill,** birth centenary (Grenada type A83). *Nov. 11.* 35c, $2. Souvenir sheet of 2 (75c, $1).
**UPU Centenary** (Grenada type A82). *Oct. 15.* 8, 25, 35c, $1 (4v). Souvenir sheet of 2 ($1, 2).
**Christmas paintings** (Grenada type A84). *Nov. 27.* ½, 1, 2, 3, 10, 25, 50c, $1 (8v). (Botticelli, di Pietro, van der Weyden, Bastiani, Giovanni, Mantegna). Souvenir sheet, $2.

**1975**
**Big Game Fishing** (Grenada type A86). *Feb. 17.* ½, 1, 2, 10, 25, 50, 70c, $1 (8v). Souvenir sheet, $2.
**Flowers** (Grenada type A87). *Mar. 11.* ½, 1, 2, 3, 10, 25, 50c, $1 (8v). Souvenir sheet, $2.
**Easter, paintings.** *June 24.* ½, 1, 2, 3, 35, 75c, $2 (7v). Souvenir sheet, $1. (Titian, Giotto, Tintoretto, Cranach. Caravaggio, Tiepolo, Velazquez).
**Michelangelo,** 500th birth anniversary. *July 16.* ½, 1, 2, 40, 50, 75c, 2 (7v). Souvenir sheet. $1.
**Butterflies.** *Aug. 12.* ½, 1, 2, 35, 45, 75c, $2 (7v). Souvenir sheet, $1.
**14th World Boy Scout Jamboree, Norway.** *Aug.* ½, 1, 2, 35, 45, 75c, $2 (7v). Souvenir sheet, $1.
**U.S. Bicentennial,** Scenes and events. *Oct.* ½, 1, 2, 3, 5, 45, 75c, $2 (8v). 2 souvenir sheets (Washington, White House) $2. Also in sheets of 5 with decorative border and label.

**Pan-American Games, Mexico City.** *Nov.* ½, 1, 2, 35, 45, 75c $2 (7v). Souvenir sheet, $1.
**Definitives.** *Nov. 6.* ½, 1, 2, 3, 5, 6, 8, 10, 12, 15, 20, 25, 35, 50, 75c, $1, 2, 3, 5, (19v). (Boats, plants, scenes).
**Christmas, paintings.** *Dec. 17.* ½, 1, 2, 40, 50, 75c, $2 (7v). Souvenir sheet, $1. (Durer, Correggio, Botticelli, Niccolo da Cremona, Bellini).
**Shells,** *Dec.* ½, 1, 2, 3, 25, 50, 75c (7v). Souvenir sheet, $2.

**1976**
**Flora and Fauna.** *Jan.* ½, 1, 2, 35, 50, 75c, $1 (7v). Souvenir sheet, $2.
**U.S. Bicentennial.** $2x2.
**Definitive.** $10.
**Tourism.** *Feb. 17.* ½, 1, 2, 18, 22, 75c, $1 (7v). Souvenir sheet, $2 (Boats and water sports).
**Girl Guides,** 50th anniversary. *Mar. 17.* ½, 1, 2, 50c, $1 (5v). Souvenir sheet, $2.
**Easter,** paintings. *Apr.* ½, 1, 2, 3, 35c, $3 (6v). (Bosch, da Messina, Durer, van der Weyden, Raphael). Souvenir sheet, $2 (Bellini).
**U.S. Bicentennial,** Ships of the Revolution. *May.* ½, 1, 2, 35, 50c, $1, 2 (7v). Souvenir sheet, $3.
**Air Transport,** various planes. *June 10.* ½, 1, 2, 40, 50c, $2 (6v). Souvenir sheet, $3.
**Summer Olympics,** Montreal. *July 1.* ½, 1, 2, 35, 45, 75c, $2 (7v). Souvenir sheet, $3.
**Christmas,** Old master paintings. *Oct. 19.* ½, 1, 2, 35, 50, 75c, $2 (7v) (Cima, Romanino, Brueghel, Girolamo, Giorgione, Angelico). Souvenir sheet, $3 (Garofalo).

**1977**
**Telephone Centennial,** various phones, 1876-1976. *Jan.* ½, 1, 2, 35, 75c, $1, 2 (7v). Souvenir sheet, $3.
**Silver Jubilee, QEII.** *Feb. 8.* 35c, $2, 4 (3v). Souvenir sheet, $5.
**Easter,** paintings. *May.* ½, 1, 2, 18, 35, 50c, $2 (7v) (Fra Angelico, da Messina, Giottino, El Greco). Souvenir sheet, $3 (Fra Angelico).
**Silver Jubilee, QEII,** self-adhesive booklet. *June.* Contains pane of 6x35c and Souvenir sheet of 3 (50c, $2, 5).
**Royal Visit,** ovptd. on QEII Silver Jubilee set. *Oct.* 35c, $2, 4. (3v) se-tenant with silver foil labels depicting Imperial crowns. Souvenir sheet, $5.
**Christmas,** paintings. *Nov.* ½, 1, 2, 18, 35, 50c, $2 (7v) (Correggio, Giorgione, Morales, Raphael, Anthony Van Dyck, Filippo Lippi). Souvenir sheet, $3 (Ghirlandaio).
**Caribbean Boy Scout Jamboree.** *Nov.* ½, 1, 2, 22, 35, 75c, $3 (7v). Souvenir sheet, $2.
**Space Shuttle,** aspects of system. *Ded.* ½, 1, 2, 22, 50c, $3 (6v). Souvenir sheet, $2.

**1978**
**Nobel Prize Awards.** *Jan.* ½, 1, 2, 22, 75c, $3 (6v). Souvenir sheet, $2.
**Lindbergh, Zeppelin,** anniversaries. *Mar.* 5, 15, 25, 35, 50c, $3 (6v). Souvenir sheet of 2 (75c, $2).
**Coronation QEII,** 25th anniversary. *Apr. 12.* Booklet containing 2 self-adhesive panes: 18cx3 plus 50cx3; souvenir sheet, $5.
*June 2.* 50c, $2, 2.50 (3v). Souvenir sheet, $5. Also printed in sheets of 3 with label, backgrounds in different colors.
**Peter Paul Rubens,** 400th birth anniversary. *May 18.* 5, 15, 18, 22, 35c, $3 (6v). Souvenir sheet, $2 (self-portrait).
**Birds.** *June.* 5, 10, 18, 22, 40c, $1, 2 (7v). Souvenir sheet, $5.
**First Powered Flight.** 75th anniversary. *Aug. 10.* 5, 15, 18, 25, 35, 75c, $3 (7v). Souvenir sheet, $2.
**World Cup Soccer,** Argentina. *Sept.* 15, 35, 50c, $3 (4v). Souvenir sheet, $2.
**Capt. James Cook,** 250th birth anniversary. *Nov.* 18, 22, 50c, $3 (4v). Souvenir sheet, $4.
**Christmas, Durer paintings.** *Dec. 18.* 40, 60, 90c, $2 (4v). Souvenir sheet, $4.

**1979**
**Flowers.** *Jan. 22.* 40c, $1, 3 (4v). Souvenir sheet, $2.
**International Year of the Child.** *Mar.* 18, 50c, $1, 3 (4v). Souvenir sheet, $5.
**Jules Verne,** 150th birth anniversary. *Apr.* 18, 38, 75c, $2 (4v). Souvenir sheet, $3.
**Sir Rowland Hill** (1795-1879). Originator of Penny Postage,. *Apr.* 15c, $1, 2, 3, (4v). Souvenir sheet, $4.
*Aug. 10.* Sheetlets of 5 plus label in different colors.
**Marine Wildlife.** *Oct.* 40, 45, 50, 60, 70, 75, 90c, $1 (8v). Souvenir sheet, $2.50.
**Christmas,** sculptures. *Oct. 24.* 6, 25, 30, 40, 90c, $1, 2 (7v). Souvenir sheet, $4.
**International Year of the Child,** Disney characters. *Dec. 10.* ½, 1, 2, 3, 4, 5, 10, $2, 2.50 (9v). Souvenir sheet, $3.

**1980**
**Rotary International,** 75th anniversary. *Feb. 6.* 30, 60c, $3 (4v). Souvenir sheet, $3.
**Revolution, First anniversary,** ovptd. "People's Revolution/13 March 1979" on 1975-76 definitives. *Mar.* 6, 12, 15, 20, 25, 35, 50, 75c, $1, 2, 3, 5, 10 (13v).
**Indigenous Birds.** *April 14.* 25, 40, 90, $2 (4v). *Souvenir sheet, $4.*
**Summer Olympics.** Moscow. *April 21.* 30, 40, 90, $2 (4v). Souvenir sheet, $4.
**"London 1980",** overprint on Rowland Hill. *May 6.* Sheetlets. 15, $1, 2, 3 (4v).
**Caribbean Fish.** *Aug. 6.* ½, 1, 2, 4, 5, 6, 10, 12, 15, 20, 25, 30, 40, 50, 90, $1, 3, 5, 10 (19v).
**Christmas,** Walt Disney's "Bambi". *Oct. 7.* ½, 1, 2, 3, 4, 5, 10, $2.50, 3 (9v).

**1981**
**Walt Disney's Pluto,** 50th birthday. *Jan. 2.* Souvenir sheet, $4.
**Famous Art Masterpieces.** *Feb. 6.* 10, 25, 90, $2, 3 (6v). (Turner, Seurat, Eakins, El Greco, Stuart, Durer). Souvenir sheet, $4.
**Easter,** Walt Disney. *April.* 35, 40, $2, 2.50 (4v). Souvenir sheet, $4.
**Picasso,** 100th birth. anniv. Paintings. *April 6.* 40, 90, $4 (4v). Souvenir sheet, $5.
**Royal Wedding,** Prince Charles and Lady Diana. *July.* 40, $2, 4, Souvenir sheet, $5.
**Space Shuttle.** *Nov. 10.* 40c, $1.10, 3 (4v). Souvenir sheet, $5.
**World Football Cup.** *Nov. 30.* 20, 40c, $1, 2 (4v). Souvenir sheet, $4.
**Christmas,** Walt Disney's "Lady and the Tramp." *Nov.* ½, 1, 2, 3, 4, 5, 10c, $2.50, 3 (9v). Souvenir sheet, $5.
**U.P.U. Membership,** 100th anniv. *Dec. 10.* 30, 40c, $2.50, 4 (4v).

**1982**
**Boy Scouts,** *Feb. 19.* 6c, 90c, $1.10, $3 (4v). Souvenir Sheet $5.

**1984**
**Ships.** July 16. 30c, 60c, $1, $4, Souvenir sheet $5. (5v).

**JORDAN**
**1964**
**Astronauts.** *Mar. 25.* Perf., imperf. 20fx10, se-tenant triangles, (10v). 2 souvenir sheets, 100f, imperf.

**1965**
**Dead Sea Scrolls.** *Sept. 23.* 35fx4, se-tenant (4v).
**Gemini 4 Space Mission.** *Sept. 25.* Nos. C29-C34 overprinted "James McDivitt/Edward White/2-6-65" in English and Arabic. 10, 15, 20, 30, 40, 60f (6v). Souvenir sheet, 100f, imperf.

**King Hussein's Visit to U.S. and France.** *Oct. 5.* Perf., imperf. 5, 10, 20, 50f (4v). Souvenir sheet, 50f, imperf.
**International Cooperation year.** *Oct. 24.* 5, 10, 45f (3v).
**Arab Postal Union.** *Nov. 5.* 15, 25f (2v).
**Dome of the Rock.** *Nov. 20.* 15, 25f (2v).

**1966**
**Voskhod II.** *Jan. 15.* Nos. 491-496 overprinted "Alex Leonov/Pavel Belyaev/18-3-65" in English and Arabic, 40fx6 (6v). 2 souvenir sheets, 100f, imperf.
**Pope Paul VI Visit to U.N.** *Apr. 27.* Nos. 471-475 overprinted "Papa Paulus VI, World Peace Visit to United Nations 1965" in English and Arabic, 10, 15, 25, 50, 80f (5v). Souvenir sheet of 5 (10, 15, 50, 80f), imperf.
**Anti-Tuberculosis Campaign.** *May 17.* Perf., imperf. Overprinted on un-issued Freedom from Hunger set. 15fx2, 35fx2, 50fx2 (6v). 2 souvenir sheets of 3 (each 15, 35, 50f), imperf.
**Stations of the Cross.** *Sept. 14.* Perf., imperf., 1, 2, 3, 4, 5, 6, 7, 8, 9, 10, 11, 12, 13, 14f (14v). Souvenir sheet, 100f, imperf.
**U.S. Space Missions.** *Nov. 15.* Perf., imperf. 1, 2, 3, 4, 30, 60f (6v). Souvenir sheet, 100f, imperf.
**Christmas.** *Dec. 21.* Perf., imperf. 5, 10, 35f (3v). Souvenir sheet, 50f. imperf.

**1967**
**Builders of World Peace.** *Jan. 5.* Perf., imperf. 5fx2, 10fx2, 35fx2, 50fx2, 100fx2 (10v). 2 souvenir sheets, 100f, imperf.
**King Hussein.** *Feb.* 5, 10, 50, 100, 200f (5v). embossed gold foil coins.
**Crown Prince Hassan.** *Feb.* 5, 10, 50, 100, 200f (5v), embossed gold foil coins.
**Kennedy, John F.** *Feb.* 5, 10, 50, 100, 200f (5v), embossed gold foil coins.
**Pre-Olympics.** Mexico, 1968. *Mar.* Perf., imperf. 1, 2, 3, 4, 30, 60f (6v). Souvenir sheet, 100f, imperf.

**1969**
**Tragedy in Holy Land.** *Dec. 10.* 1, 2, 3, 4, 5, 6, 7, 8, 9, 10, 11, 12, 13, 14, 15, 16, 17, 18, 19, 20, 21, 22, 23, 24, 25, 26, 27, 28, 29, 30f se-tenant strips of 5 (30v).
**Tragedy and Plight of Refugees.** *Dec. 10.* 1, 2, 3, 4, 5, 6, 7, 8, 9, 10, 11, 12, 13, 14, 15, 16, 17, 18, 19, 20, 21, 22, 23, 24, 25, 26, 27, 28, 29, 30f se-tenant strips of 5 (30v).
**Tragedy in Holy Land** surcharged. *Aug.* 25f on 1-10f; 40f on 11-15f; 50f on 16-20f, 75f on 21-25f; 125f on 26-30f, se-tenant strips of 5 (30v).
**Tragedy and Plight of Refugees** surcharged. *Aug.* 25f on 1-10f; 40f on 11-15f; 50f on 16-20f; 75f on 21-25f; 125f on 26-30f, se-tenant strips of 5 (30v).

**QATAR**
**1966**
**Sheik Ahmad bin Ali al-Thani.** *Feb. 24.* Imperf. 1, 3, 4, 5, 10, 40, 70, 80np, 1, 2, 5, 10r (12v), embossed gold and silver foil coins (3 sizes).
**United Nations,** 20th anniversary. *Mar. 8.* Perf., imperf. sheet of Nos. 99-102 with 5 additional 5np stamps printed in gutter, with various overprints (9v). Souvenir sheet of 4 (40npx4), imperf. Same with new currency.
**Kennedy, John F.** *July 18.* Perf., imperf. 10, 30, 50, 70, 80np, 1r, se-tenant strips of 3 (6v). Souvenir sheet, 50np imperf. Same with new currency.
**1980 Summer Olympics, Mexico, 1968.** *July 20.* Perf., imperf. 1, 4, 5, 70, 80, 90np (6v), se-tenant strips of 3. Souvenir sheet, 50np, imperf. Same with new currency.
**Astronauts,** *Aug. 20.* Perf., imperf. 5, 10, 15np (se-tenant), 20, 30, 40, 50, 60np (se-tenant) (8v). (Lovell, Stafford, Shepard, Glenn, Carpenter, Schirra, Grissom, Cooper). Souvenir sheet, 50np, imperf. Same with new currency.
**World Cup Soccer Championships,** London, *Nov. 27.* Perf., imperf. 60, 70, 80, 90np; airmail, 1, 2, 3, 4np (8v). Sheets of 36, se-tenant, 4 souvenir sheets of 1 with 2 labels, 25np.
**Education Day** (Library, school buildings). *Oct. 10.* 2, 3, 5np, 1, 2, 5r (6v). Same with new currency (6v).
**Buildings** (palace, mosque, etc.). *Nov. 10.* 2, 3, 10, 15, 20, 30, 40, 50, 60, 70, 90np, 1, 2r (14v).

**1967**
**100 Dirhams = 1 Riyal**
**Currency Changes.** Nos. 26-36, 37-41, 42-46, 47-52, 53-60, 61-68, 69-85, 86-90, 91-98, 99-102 with new currency.
**Apollo Project.** *May 1.* 5, 10, 20, 30, 40, 70, 80d, 1, 1.20, 2r (10v). Souvenir sheet, 2r imperf.

**ST. VINCENT Grenadines of St. Vincent**
**1973**
**Princess Anne's Wedding** (Omnibus design). *Nov. 14.* 25c, $1.

**1974**
**Definitives** (overprinted on St. Vincent issue). *Apr. 24.* 1, 2, 3, 4, 5, 6, 8, 10, 12, 20, 25, 50c, $1, 2.50, 5 (15v).
**Map of Grenadines .** *May 9.* 5, 15, 20, 30, 40c, $1 (6v).
**Definitives.** *June 7.* (St. Vincent's 1973 issue with wmk. sideways), 3c.
**UPU Centenary** (St. Vincent type A56). *July 25.* 2, 15, 40c, $1 (4v).
**Bequia Island.** *Sept. 26.* 5, 30, 35c, $1 (4v). Same, 5c (Wmk. 373).
**Shells and mollusks** (definitives). *Nov.* 1, 2, 3, 4, 5, 6, 8, 10, 12, 15, 20, 25, 35, 45, 50c, $1, 2.50, 5 (18v). 9 values reissued with 1976 imprint and 7 with 1977 imprint.
**Churchill,** birth centenary (St. Vincent type A56). *Nov. 28.* 5, 40, 50c, $1 (4v).

**1975**
**Mustique Island,** views. *Feb. 27.* 5, 35, 45, $1 (4v).
**Butterflies.** *May 15.* 3, 5, 35, 45, $1 (5v).
**Petit St. Vincent,** views. *July 24.* 5, 35, 45, $1 (4v).
**Christmas,** churches. *Nov. 20.* 5, 25, 50, $1 (4v).
**Union Island,** views. *Feb. 26.* 5, 35, 45c, $1 (4v).
**Coral.** *May 13.* 5, 35, 45c, $1 (4v).
**Definitive,** cowrie. *July 12.* $10.
**U.S. Bicentennial,** three current U.S. Bicentennial coins. *July 15.* 25, 50c, $1 (3v).
**Maps of the Islands.** *Sept. 23.* 7 booklets inscribed Bequia, Canouan, Mayreau, Mustique, Petit St. Vincent, Prune or Union. Each booklet contains 4 panes of 3 plus label. (5, 5, 10c; 5, 10, 45c; 35, 35, 45c; 10, 10, 35c) (28v, 28 booklet panes).
**Mayreau Island,** views. *Dec. 2.* 5, 35, 45c, $1 (4v).

**1977**
**Silver Jubilee, QEII.** *March.* 25, 50c, $1 (3v).
**Crabs and Lobster.** *May 19.* 5, 35, 50c, $1.25 (4v).
**Prune Island,** views. *Aug. 25.* 5, 35, 45c, $1 (4v).
**Mustique, Royal Visit,** ovpt. on map stamps. *Oct. 31.* 40c, $2 (2v).
**Christmas,** hymn verses. *Nov. 5.* 10, 15, 25, 50c, $1.25 (6v). Souvenir sheet of 6.
**Canouan Island,** views. *Dec.* 5, 35, 45c, $1 (4v).

**1978**
**Birds and their Eggs.** *May 11.* 1, 2, 3, 4, 5, 6, 8, 10, 12, 15, 20, 25, 40, 50, 80c, $1, 2, 3, 5, 10 (20v).
**Coronation QEII,** 25th anniversary. *June 2.* 5, 40c, $1, 3 (4v). Souvenir sheet of 4 (5, 40c, $1, 3). Each value also in booklet pane of 2.

**Turtles.** *July 20.* 5, 40, 50c, $1.25 (4v).
**Christmas,** "We Three Kings of Orient Are." *Nov. 2.* 5, 10, 25, 50c, $2 (5v). Souvenir sheet of 5 plus label.

**1979**
**National Regatta.** *Jan. 25.* 5, 40, 50c, $2 (4v).
**Wildlife of the Grenadines.** *Mar. 8.* 20, 40c, $2 (3v).
**Sir Rowland Hill** (1795-1879). Originator of Penny Postage. *May 31.* 80c, $1, 2 (3v). Souvenir sheet of 6 (London 80), 80c, $1, 2 se-tenant with 80c, $1, 2 of Birds and their Eggs issue (1978). Booklet of 6 values in se-tenant pairs of each denomination.
**International Year of the Child.** *Oct. 24.* 6, 40c, $1, 3 (4v).
**Independence.** *Oct. 27.* 5, 40c, $1 (3v) se-tenant checkerwise with label denoting Independence.

**1980**
**Whales and Dolphins.** *Jan. 31.* 10, 50, 90, $2 (4v).
**"London 1980",** Intl. Stamp Exhibition. *April 24.* 40, 50, $3. Souvenir sheet of 6 (London 1980), 40, 50, $3, se-tenant with 40, 50, $3 of Birds and their Eggs Issue (1978).
**"Sports for All".** *Aug. 7.* 25, 50, $1, 2 (4v).
**"Sports for All",** overprinted "Hurricane Relief" and surcharged. *Aug. 7.* 25+50, 50+50, $1+50, $2+50 (4v).
**Christmas.** *Nov. 13.* 5, 50, 60, $1, 2 (5v). Souvenir sheet contains 5 of same design plus label.

**1981**
**Island Scenes.** *Feb. 19.* 50c, 60c, $1.50. $2 (4v).
**Early Maps.** *Apr. 2.* 50c, 50c, 60c, 60c, $2, $2 (6v) printed se-tenant.
**Agriculture.** *May 21.* 10, 50c, $1, 2 (4v).
**Royal Wedding.** Prince Charles and Lady Diana. July 17. Sheetlets of 7, 50c, $3, 3.50, Booklet of 10. 3 panes: (8) 50c, (2) $3. Souvenir sheet, $5.
**Fish.** *Oct. 9.* 10c, 50c, 60c, $2 (4v).

**1982**
**Ships,** *Jan. 28.* 1c, 3c, 5c, 6c, 10c, 15c, 20c, 25c, 30c, 50c, 60c, 75c, $1, $2, $3, $5, $10 (17).
**Plants.** *Apr. 5.* 10c, 50c, $1, $2 (4v).
**21st Birthday of Princess Diana of Wales.** *July 1.* 50c, 60c, $6 (3v).
**Birth of Prince William of Wales.** *July 19.* 21st Birthday overprinted with names of Islands. 50c, 60c, $6 (3v).

**1983**
**Commonwealth Day.** *Mar. 14.* 45c, 60c, $1.50, $2 (4v).

**1984**
**Coins.** *Dec. 1.* 20c, 45c, 75c, $3 (4v).

**Bequia**
**1984**
**Ships.** *August 23.* (St. Vincent Grenadines overprinted Bequia). 1c, 3c, 5c, 6c, 10c, 15c, 20c, 25c, 30c, 50c, 60c, 75c, $1, $2, $5, $10 (16v).

**Union Island**
**1984**
**Ships.** *August 23.* (St. Vincent Grenadines overprinted Union Island). 1c, 3c, 5c, 6c, 10c, 15c, 20c, 30c, 50c, 60c, 75c,$1, $2, $3, $5, $10 (17v).

**TRANSKEI**
**1976**
**Definitives,** scenes. *Oct. 26.* 1, 2, 3, 4, 5, 6, 7, 8, 9, 10, 15, 20, 25, 30, 50c, R1, 2 (17v).
**Independence,** flag and arms. *Oct. 26.* 4, 10, 15, 20c, (4v).

**1977**
**Airmail, Umtata-Johannesburg.** *Feb. 11.* 4, 15c (2v).
**Medicinal Plants.** 4, 10, 15, 20c (4v).
**Radio Transkei.** *Oct. 26.* 4, 15c (2v).
**Help to the Blind.** *Nov. 18.* 4, 15, 20c (3v).

**1978**
**Pipes,** various. *Mar. 1.* 4, 10, 15, 20c (4v).
**Weaving Industry.** *June 9.* 4, 10, 15, 20c (4v).
**Edible Wild Fruits.** *Sept. 25.* 4, 10, 15, 20c (4v).
**Care for Cripples.** *Nov. 30.* 4, 10, 15c.

**1979**
**Initiation Ceremonies,** Abakwetha. *Jan. 30.* 4, 10, 15, 20c (4v).
**President Matanzina Inauguration.** *Feb. 20.* 4, 15c (2v).
**Water Resources,** various scenes. *Mar. 13.* 4, 10, 15, 20c (4v).
**Waterfalls.** *Sept. 4.* 4, 10, 15, 20c (4v).
**Agriculture.** *Oct. 25.* 5, 15, 20, 25c (4v).
**Child Health.** *Dec. 3.* 5, 15, 20 (3v).

**1980**
**Fishing Files.** *Jan. 15.* 5cx25 in se-tenant sheet of 25.
**Rotary International.** *Feb. 22.* 15c.
**Cycads.** *April 30.* 5, 10, 15, 20 (4v).
**Birds.** *July 30.* 5, 10, 15, 20 (4v).
**Tourism.** *Oct. 29.* 5, 10, 15, 20 (4v).

**1981**
**Fishing-Files.** *Jan. 15.* 10cx25 in se-tenant sheet of 25.
**Medicinal Plants.** *April 15.* 5c, 15c, 20c, 25cc (4v).
**Headdress.** *Aug. 15.* 5, 10, 15, 20 (4v). Souvenir sheet of 4, (5, 15, 20, 25c).
**Independence,** 5th anniv. *Oct. 26.* 5, 15c.

**1982**
**Fishing flies,** *Jan. 6.* 10cx25 in se-tenant sheet of 25.

**VENDA**
**1979**
**Independence,** flag and arms. *Sept. 13.* 4, 15, 20, 25c (4v).
**Flowers,** various. *Sept. 13.* 1, 2, 3, 4, 5, 6, 7, 8, 9, 10, 15, 20, 25, 30, 50c, 1R, 2 (17v).

**1980**
**Wood Carvings.** *Feb. 13.* 5, 10, 15, 20c (4v).
**Tea Cultivation.** *May 14.* 5, 10, 15, 20 (4v).
**Banana Industry.** *Aug. 13.* 5, 10, 15, 20 (4v).
**Butterflies.** *Nov. 13.* 5, 10, 15, 20 (4v).

**1981**
**Orchids.** *Sept. 11.* 5, 15, 20, 25 (4v). Souvenir sheet of 4 (5, 15, 20, 25).
**Musical Instruments.** *Nov. 13.* 5, 15, 20, 25 (4v).
**Sunbirds,** *Feb. 16.* 5c, 15c, 20c, 25c (4v).
**Lakes and Waterfalls.** *June 5.* 5c, 15c, 20c, 25c (4v).

**1982**
**Sisal Industry,** *Feb. 26.* 5c, 10c, 20c, 25c (4v).

**ZIL ELWAGNE SESEL**
**1980**
**Fish.** *June 20.* 5, 10, 15, 20, 25, 40, 50, 75c, 1, 1, 1, 1, 5, 10, 20r (16v).
**Traveling Post Office.** *Oct. 24.* 1, 2, 5r (3v).
**Fish.** *Nov. 28.* 1, 2, 5r (3v).

**1981**
**Royal Wedding.** *June 23.* 40, 40c, 5, 5, 10, 10r (6v).
**Wildlife.** *Dec. 11.* 1, 2, 5r (3v).

**1982**
**Island Development.** *Mar. 11.* 1, 2, 5r (3v).

# INDEX TO ADVERTISERS - 1990 VOLUME 1



# READER SERVICE CARD ADVERTISER'S INDEX

The following is a listing of the advertisers in this Volume 1 who offer Scott readers the convenience of using the Reader Service Card to request information on the products or services shown below. The Reader Service Card, along with instructions on completion and mailing, is located in the back of this catalogue. If the card is missing, write numbers on a postcard or letter, include your name, address, city, state and zip and mail to: Scott Publishing Co., Reader Service Dept. 90-1, P.O. Box 828, Sidney, OH 45365 U.S.A.

**Reader Service Number**

**70 B. ALAN LTD.**
184 Portland Road
London SE25 4QB ENGLAND
INFORMATION ON BRITISH ERRORS.
*(see our advertisement on page 174)*

**45 EASTERN AUCTIONS LTD.**
P.O. Box 250, Bathurst, N.B.
Canada E2A 3Z2
FREE AUCTION CATALOGUE.
*(see our advertisement on page 332 & 761)*

**12 ARON R. HALBERSTAM PHILATELISTS, LTD.**
P.O. Box 150168, Van Brunt Station
Brooklyn, NY 11215-0003
ELUSIVE BRITISH COMMONWEALTH — FREE LIST.
*(see our advertisement on page 158, 240, 422, 774)*

**14 IAN KIMMERLY STAMPS**
90 Sparks Street — Store No. 1
Ottawa, Canada K1P 5B4.
FREE COPY - MONTHLY SPECIAL OFFERS LIST.
*(see our advertisement on page 334)*

**Reader Service Number**

**75 PETER SINGER**
Post Office Box 25249
Portland, Oregon 97225.
FREE PRICE LIST.
*(see our advertisement on page 297, 336, 421, 509, 657, 676, 762, 817, 851, 887)*

**83 SAM HOUSTON PHILATELICS**
P.O. Box 820087
Houston, Texas 77282.
FREE PRICE LIST.
*(see our advertisement on page 96)*

**99 SCOTT STAMP MONTHLY MAGAZINE**
P.O. Box 828, Sidney, OH 45365.
Circle #99 and we will bill you $18 for a 1-year (12 issues) subscription (U.S. only).

**100 SCOTT MOUNTS**
P.O. Box 828
Sidney, OH 45365.
FREE Sample Package.

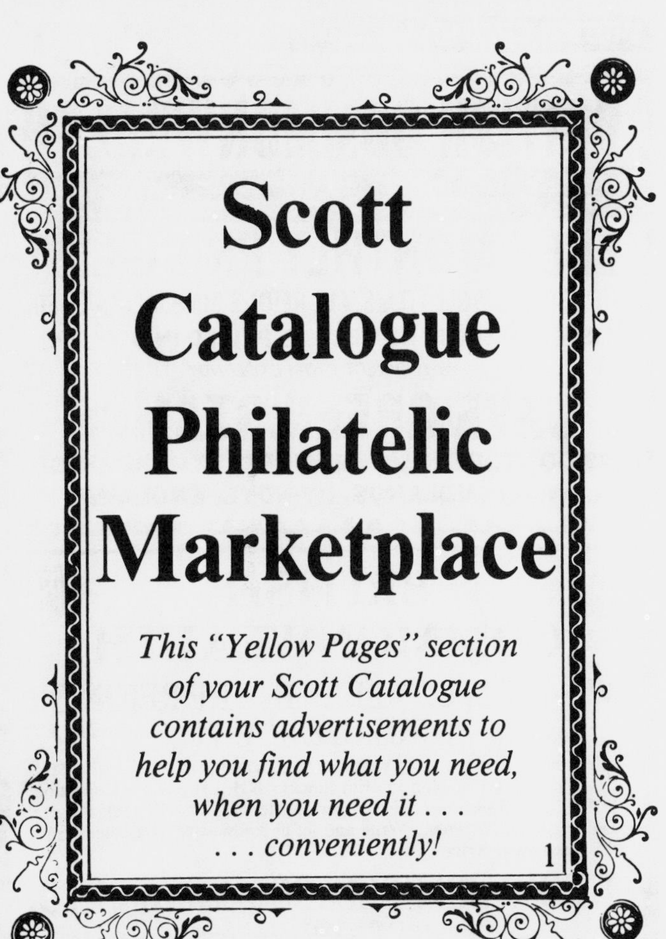
Scott
Catalogue
Philatelic
Marketplace
This "Yellow Pages" section
of your Scott Catalogue
contains advertisements to
help you find what you need,
when you need it . . .
. . . conveniently!
1

For information about membership in America's national philatelic society send attached card or contact

**American Philatelic Society**
**P.O. Box 8000, Dept. Z**
**State College, PA 16803**
**(814) 237-3803**

# AMERICAN PHILATELIC SOCIETY

***Founded 1886: In our 2nd century of service to collectors***

Find out about the benefits of membership in America's national stamp society. Send this postpaid card for a descriptive brochure of the many APS services.

Z-90

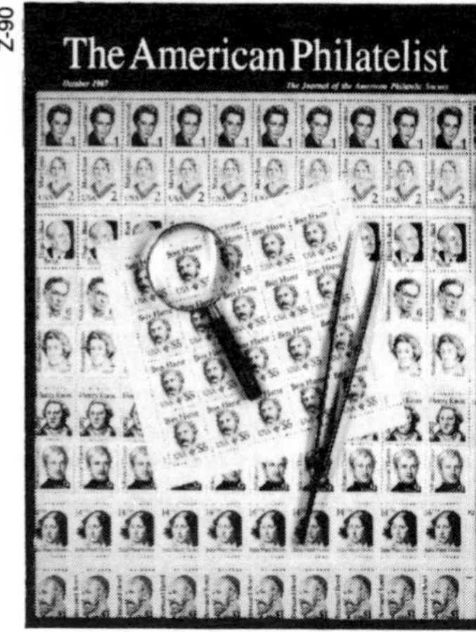


- ***Monthly Magazine** ***Sales Circuits**
- ***Philatelic Library** ***Stamp Insurance**
- ***Correspondence Courses** ***Seminars**
- ***Expertizing Service** ***And Much More**

**PLEASE PRINT:**

Name: ______________________

Address: ______________________

______________________

***Send $1.00 with this card to receive a sample copy of The American Philatelist***

CLASSIC STAMPS
CLASSIC SERVICE

*The Classic Collector*

**P.O. Box 6277, Station "J"**
**Ottawa, Ontario, Canada K2A 1T4**

Mail this card stating your approval preferences.

If the card has been used, print your name, address and collecting interests on a postcard or letter and mail it to the above address.

See our full page advertisement on page 153 of this catalogue.

# HOW TO ACQUIRE THE STAMPS YOU NEED FOR YOUR COLLECTION

***Please send a selection of approvals from the choices I have checked below:***

| | | | |
|---|---|---|---|
| ☐ THE WORLD | ☐ WESTERN EUROPE | ☐ BRITISH AMERICA | ☐ MINT ☐ USED |
| ☐ UNITED STATES | ☐ FRANCE | ☐ BRITISH AFRICA | ☐ MINT BLOCKS |
| ☐ CANADA | ☐ SPAIN | ☐ BRITISH ASIA | ☐ PROOFS & SPECIMENS |
| ☐ GREAT BRITAIN | ☐ JAPAN | ☐ BRITISH OCEANIA | ☐ CLASSICS |

☐ Specific countries ______________ Year/period ______________

If you have specialized interests drop us a line today. Approximate amount desired per shipment $ ______

INCLUDE PHILATELIC REFERENCES OR SEND A REASONABLE DEPOSIT, CHECK OR MONEY ORDER, NOT CASH ______________

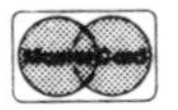

*As a convenience to our customers, we offer Charge Card Services.*

Name ______________ Phone ______________

Address ______________

City ______________ State ______________ Zip ______________

**SCOTT**

**Stamp Monthly**

**Subscribe Now And Save *At Least***

**50%**

**Off The Cover Price!**

**2 YEARS 24 issues for $32**
**(55% OFF the cover price.)**
**1 YEAR 12 issues for $18**
**(50% OFF the cover price.)**
If card has been used send your name and address to
**Scott Publishing Company**
**P.O. Box 828, Sidney, OH 45365**
Indicate 1 or 2 years. Send no money now - WE WILL BILL YOU LATER. In Canada add $8 per year for postage. Outside U.S./Canada add $23 per year for postage. Please allow 6 to 8 weeks for delivery of first issue.

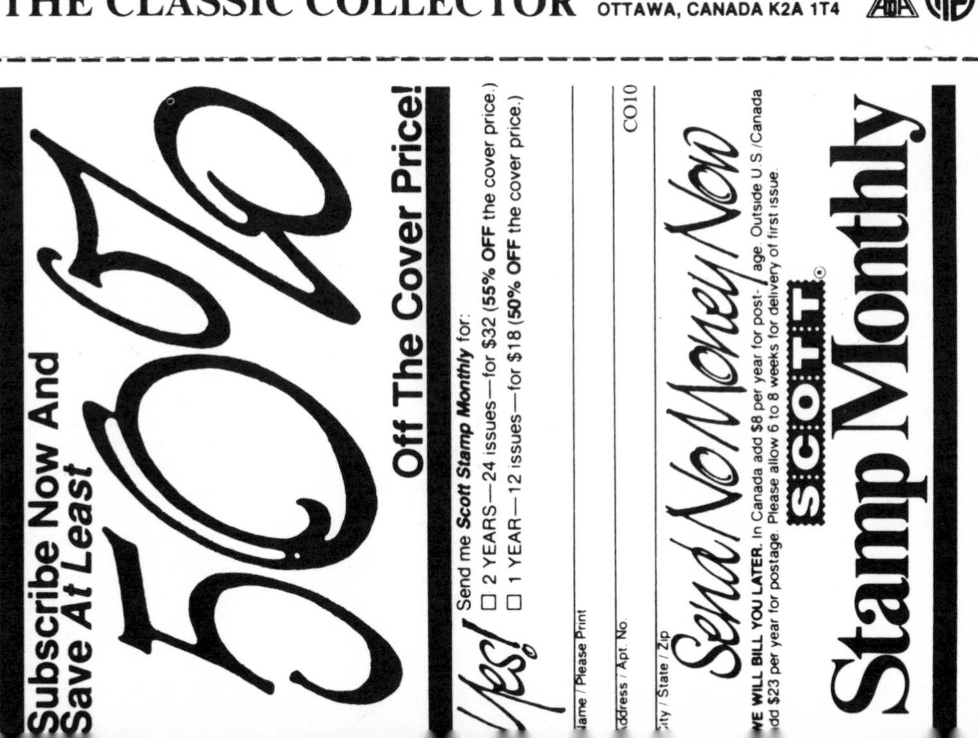

NO POSTAGE
NECESSARY
IF MAILED
IN THE
UNITED STATES

**BUSINESS REPLY MAIL**

FIRST CLASS PERMIT NO. 68 STATE COLLEGE, PA 16801

**Postage Will be Paid by Addressee**

**American Philatelic Society**
**P.O. Box 8000**
**State College, PA 16803-9983**

*From*

**Place Stamp Here**

# THE CLASSIC COLLECTOR

**P.O. Box 6277, Station "J"**
**Ottawa, Ontario**
**Canada K2A 1T4**

NO POSTAGE
NECESSARY
IF MAILED
IN THE
UNITED STATES

BUSINESS REPLY MAIL

FIRST CLASS PERMIT NO. 131 SIDNEY, OH

POSTAGE WILL BE PAID BY ADDRESSEE

**SCOTT**®

Scott Publishing Co.
911 Vandemark Road
P.O. Box 828
Sidney, OH 45365-9906

NO POSTAGE
NECESSARY
IF MAILED
IN THE
UNITED STATES

## BUSINESS REPLY MAIL

FIRST CLASS PERMIT NO. 131 SIDNEY, OH

POSTAGE WILL BE PAID BY ADDRESSEE

SCOTT®

Scott Publishing Co.
911 Vandemark Road
P.O. Box 828
Sidney, OH 45365-9906

NO POSTAGE
NECESSARY
IF MAILED
IN THE
UNITED STATES

## BUSINESS REPLY MAIL

FIRST CLASS PERMIT NO. 131 SIDNEY, OH

POSTAGE WILL BE PAID BY ADDRESSEE

SCOTT®

Scott Publishing Co.
911 Vandemark Road
P.O. Box 828
Sidney, OH 45365-9906

NO POSTAGE
NECESSARY
IF MAILED
IN THE
UNITED STATES

## BUSINESS REPLY MAIL

FIRST CLASS MAIL PERMIT NO. 131 SIDNEY, OH

POSTAGE WILL BE PAID BY ADDRESSEE

911 Vandemark Rd.
P.O. Box 29
Sidney, OH 45365-9977